VOX
Modern
SPANISH
and
ENGLISH
Dictionary

VOX

Modern

SPANISH

and

ENGLISH

Dictionary

English-Spanish/Spanish-English

Dictionary Compiled by
the Editors of Biblograf, S. A.

North American Edition Prepared by
the Editors of National Textbook Company

Printed on recyclable paper

NTC *Publishing Group*
Lincolnwood, Illinois USA

In Spanish, the best, by definition

1995 Printing

Library of Congress Catalog Number: 86-61160
ISBN 0-8442-7990-0 (Hardcover Edition)
ISBN 0-8442-7988-9 (Vinyl-Cover Edition)

5 6 7 8 9 0 AG 9 8

CONTENTS

PREFACE

For educators, students, business people, tourists, and the general public, a dictionary provides answers to all kinds of questions about language. The *VOX Modern Spanish and English Dictionary* has been designed as a reference tool that offers a bridge of understanding between the two languages, as well as between the two cultures. Far more than a mere lexicon, this dictionary presents broad lexical, grammatical, and cultural information in a concise and practical form that will assure its extensive, daily use.

All of the sections of the *VOX Modern* dictionary help the reader derive the most benefit from one single reference source without having to consult countless grammar books, almanacs, or other reference works. The entries contain many examples of current word usage so that the reader may select the precise word or expression. There are other labor-saving features, as well. Irregular verbs are generally conjugated as part of the main verb entry, rather than being marked with an asterisk and requiring the reader to look elsewhere for the models of irregular verbs. Also among the entries is terminology from business, science, the arts, and culture.

Preceding the English-Spanish section and the Spanish-English section is a summary of grammar that gives the reader a quick reference that clarifies the most frequently confused rules. To this end also, a pronunciation guide is offered for each language.

The dictionary also contains a section of more than 3,500 idioms and expressions in English and Spanish and appendices with tables of weights and measures, monetary units, and temperatures; six detailed maps; and common abbreviations in the two languages. There is a section with examples of appropriate phrases in each language to aid in translating or writing business correspondence and, to assure that the reader chooses the exact word, there is a bilingual list of false cognates.

Without a doubt, the North American edition of the *VOX Modern Spanish and English Dictionary* offers a practical and up-to-date tool that is easy to use and completely reliable.

PRÓLOGO

Para educadores, alumnos, comerciantes, turistas y la pública en general, un diccionario provee las respuestas a todas clases de preguntas linguísticas. El *VOX Modern Spanish and English Dictionary* ha sido concebido como un instrumento de trabajo y de consulta que ofrece un puente de entendimiento tanto entre las dos lenguas como entre las dos culturas. Mucho más que un simple léxico, este diccionario ofrece amplios datos léxicos, gramaticales y culturales en una forma concisa y práctica que asegurará su uso extensivo diario.

Todas las secciones del diccionario *VOX Modern* ayudan al lector a sacar mayor provecho de una sola obra sin tener que buscar en una infinidad de libros gramaticales, almanaques u otras obras de consulta. Los artículos contienen muchos ejemplos del uso actual de las palabras para que el lector escoja la palabra o expresión exacta. Hay también otras economías de trabajo. Las irregularidades de los verbos figuran como parte del mismo artículo en vez de indicarse con asterisco para que el lector tenga que buscar en otra parte los modelos de verbos irregulares. Además, entre los artículos se encuentra la terminología del comercio, la ciencia, las artes y la cultura.

Antes de la sección inglés-español y la español-inglés, se encuentra un resumen gramatical que da al lector un medio rápido de consulta sobre los casos de dificultad más frecuentes. A este fin también se ofrece una lista que provee ejemplos de la pronunciación de cada idioma.

El diccionario contiene también una sección de más de 3.500 modismos y expresiones en inglés y español. Y en los apéndices, ofrece al lector tablas de pesas y medidas, unidades monetarias, temperaturas, seis mapas detallados y abreviaturas comunes en los dos idiomas. Hay una sección de ejemplos de correspondencia comercial con frases apropiadas en cada idioma, y para asegurar que el lector escoja la palabra exacta, hay una lista bilingüe de cognados falsos.

Sin duda, la edición norteamericana del *VOX Modern Spanish and English Dictionary* tiene la seguridad de ofrecer un instrumento práctico y al día, de fácil manejo y digno de toda confianza.

INGLÉS-ESPAÑOL
ENGLISH-SPANISH

OBSERVACIONES

Al consultar este Diccionario, el lector ha de tener en cuenta que:

- Dentro de cada artículo, la palabra o el grupo de palabras correspondiente a cada una de las acepciones del vocablo inglés constituyen una entidad separada y numerada.

- Los ejemplos, frases y modos no se dan, como es corriente en esta clase de Diccionarios, al final del artículo, sino que van agregados a la acepción a que corresponden, con lo cual ilustran mejor el sentido de ésta.

- En general, los ejemplos, frases y modos, se dan, dentro de cada acepción, en el siguiente orden: grupos de nombre y adjetivo o compuestos formados por palabras separadas; oraciones con verbo expreso, y modos adverbiales, conjuntivos, etc.

- Las frases y modos no atribuibles a ninguna acepción determinada tienen lugar independiente y numerado dentro del artículo.

- Los compuestos formados por palabras separadas se encuentran en el artículo correspondiente a su primer elemento. Los compuestos cuyos elementos van unidos por un guión o formando una sola palabra se hallarán como artículos independientes.

- Los sinónimos y aclaraciones encerradas entre corchetes sirven para determinar el sentido en que han de tomarse las palabras que se dan como traducción.

- A este fin se usan también abreviaturas de materia, uso, etc., cuya interpretación se da en la lista correspondiente. (V. Abreviaturas usadas en este diccionario.)

Para completar las indicaciones de naturaleza gramatical que se dan en los artículos del Diccionario, se incluye una sección gramatical referente a temas concretos. No se trata de dar con ella, ni siquiera en resumen, toda la doctrina gramatical del inglés, sino de ofrecer al lector (especialmente de habla española) un medio rápido de consulta sobre los casos de dificultad más frecuentes.

- Un asterisco en el cuerpo de un artículo indica que la palabra española que precede sólo tiene uso en América.

El lector encontrará en este Diccionario secciones de referencia que facilitarán su aprendizaje y uso del idioma. Por ejemplo, en el centro del Diccionario se encuentra una lista de más de tres mil idiomas y expresiones: Español-Inglés e Inglés-Español.

Además se incluyen en los apéndices:

- False Cognates and "Part-Time" Cognates
- Monetary Units / Unidades monetarias
- Weights and Measures / Pesas y medidas
- Numbers / Numerales
- Temperature / La temperatura
- Abreviaturas más usadas en inglés
- Abbreviations Most Commonly Used in Spanish
- Business Correspondence in Spanish / La carta comercial en español
- Maps/Mapas

ABREVIATURAS USADAS EN ESTE DICCIONARIO

abrev.	abreviatura
adj., adj.	adjetivo
adv., adv.	adverbio
AER.	aerostación
AGR.	agricultura
AJED.	ajedrez
ÁLG.	álgebra
ANAT.	anatomía
ant.	antiguamente; anticuado
ARIT.	aritmética
ARM.	armaduras; armas
ARQ.	arquitectura
ARQUEOL.	arqueología
art.	artículo
ARTILL.	artillería
ASTR.	astronomía; astrología
AUTO.	automóvil; automovilismo
aux.	verbo auxiliar
AVIA.	aviación
BACT.	bacteriología
B. ART.	bellas artes
BIB.	Biblia
BIOL.	biología
BIOQUÍM.	bioquímica
BOT.	botánica
CARN.	carnicería
CARP.	carpintería
CERÁM.	cerámica
CINEM.	cinematografía
CIR.	cirugía
COC.	cocina
COM.	comercio
compar.	comparativo
Cond.	Condicional
conj.	conjunción
CONJUG.	Conjugación
CONSTR.	construcción
contr.	contracción
CORR.	Correos
COST.	costura
CRISTAL.	cristalografía
CRON.	cronología
def.	definido; defectivo
DEP.	deportes
DER.	derecho; forense
desp.	despectivo
desus.	desusado

dial.	dialectal
DIB.	dibujo
dim.	diminutivo
ECLES.	eclesiástico; iglesia
ECON.	economía
E. U.	Estados Unidos
ELECT.	electricidad
ENTOM.	entomología
EQUIT.	equitación
ESC.	escultura
ESGR.	esgrima
esp.	especialmente
f.	femenino; nombre femenino
fam.	familiar
FERROC.	ferrocarriles
fig.	figurado
FIL.	filosofía
FÍS.	física
FISIOL.	fisiología
FORT.	fortificación
FOT.	fotografía
gal.	galicismo
GEOGR.	geografía
GEOL.	geología
GEOM.	geometría
ger., GER.	gerundio
gralte.	generalmente
GRAM.	gramática
HIST.	historia
ICT.	ictiología
impers.	verbo impersonal
IMPR.	imprenta
IND.	industria
indef.	indefinido
INDIC., indic.	indicativo
INF., inf.	infinitivo
ING.	ingeniería
Ingl.	Inglaterra
interj.	interjección
interr., *interrog.*	interrogativo
intr.	verbo intransitivo
irón.	irónico
irreg.	irregular
JOY.	joyería
lat.	latín

LIT.	literatura	S.	sur
LITURG.	liturgia	s.	nombre substantivo
loc.	locución	simplte.	simplemente
LÓG.	lógica	SUBJ.	Subjuntivo
		superl.	superlativo
m.	masculino; nombre masculino	TEAT.	teatro
MAR.	marina; marítimo	TÉCN.	técnica
MAT.	matemáticas	TELEF.	telefonía
may.	mayúscula	TELEGR.	telegrafía
MEC.	mecánica	TELEV.	televisión
MED.	medicina	TEOL.	teología
METAL.	metalurgia	TOP.	topografía
METEOR.	meteorología	tr., tr.	verbo transitivo
MÉTR.	métrica	TRIG.	trigonometría
MIL.	militar; milicia		
MIN.	minería	us.	usado
min.	minúscula		
MINER.	mineralogía	V.	Véase
MIT.	mitología	vulg.	vulgarismo
MÚS.	música	VET.	veterinaria
n. pr.	nombre propio	ZOOL.	zoología
num.	numeral		
ORNIT.	ornitología		
PART. PAS.	Participio pasivo		
pers.	persona(s); personal		
pl.	plural		
poc. us.	poco usado		
poét.	poético		
POL.	política		
pop.	popular		
por ext.	por extensión		
pos.	posesivo		
p. p., p. p.	participio pasivo		
pref.	prefijo		
prep.	preposición		
Pres., pres.	presente		
Pret., pret.	pretérito		
pron.	pronombre		
pron. rel.	pronombre relativo		
QUÍM.	química		
RADIO.	radiotelefonía; radiotelegrafía		
ref.	verbo reflexivo		
REL.	religión		

PRONUNCIACIÓN FIGURADA DE LA LENGUA INGLESA

Normas para su interpretación*

Signos	Sonidos
a	Sonido parecido al de la a de mano.
a	Sonido más obscuro y cerrado que la a de seda.
æ	Sonido intermedio entre el de la a de mano y el de la e de seda.
ai	Sonido del diptongo ai de aire.
au	Sonido del diptongo au de lauro.
e	Sonido parecido al de la e de seda.
ei	Sonido del diptongo ei de veis.
ø	En sílaba tónica, sonido parecido al de la oe francesa de *coeur*. En sílaba átona, sonido más obscuro, como el de la e francesa de *le*.
i	Sonido intermedio entre la i de ánimo y la e de dicen.
ı	Sonido parecido al de la i de pila, pero más cerrado y más largo.
iu	Sonido del diptongo iu de triunfo.
o	Sonido parecido al de la o de volar.
o	Sonido parecido al de la o española de soy, pero más largo y cerrado.
ou	Sonido parecido al del diptongo ou de bou.
u	Sonido parecido al de la u de mulo.
b	Sonido parecido al de la b de barón, pero algo más explosivo.
ch	Sonido de la ch de mucho.
d	Sonido de la d de dar.
đ	Sonido parecido al de la d de seda.
f	Sonido parecido al de la f de fe.
g	Sonido de la g de garra.
j	Sonido aspirado, parecido a la j de juerga, pero más breve y suave.
dȳ	Sonido parecido al de la g y la j de las palabras francesas *général* y *jambe*.
ȳ	Sonido parecido al anterior, pero más suave.
k	Sonido de la c de casa.
l	Sonido parecido al de la l de lana.
m	Sonido de la m de mano.
n	Sonido de la n de nadie.
ng	Sonido parecido al de la n de tan, pero seguido de un leve sonido velar.

* Hemos querido dar la mayor sencillez posible a la pronunciación figurada que ofrecemos entre paréntesis al principio de cada artículo porque estimamos que su objeto sólo puede ser orientar a los lectores que ya posean un conocimiento general de la pronunciación inglesa. Ésta debe aprenderse de viva voz. Su exposición requeriría prolijas explicaciones o el empleo del alfabeto fonético, cuya interpretación no se halla al alcance de los profanos.

Signos	Sonidos
ñ	Sonido de la ñ de cañón.
p	Sonido de la p de pan.
r	Sonido semivocal que se articula con la punta de la lengua hacia atrás y sin hacerla vibrar.
ᵣ	Sonido parecido al anterior, pero mucho más débil, que en algunos casos llega a perderse. Cuando va precedido de una vocal tónica, ésta queda alargada. Después de una vocal átona, muchos no lo pronuncian.
s	Sonido parecido al de la s de sal.
s̄	Sonido de la s francesa de *rose* y la catalana de *casa*.
sh	Sonido parecido al de la ch francesa de *machine* y al de la x catalana de *xàfec*.
t	Sonido parecido al de la t de tan, pero pronunciado con la punta de la lengua más próxima a los alvéolos.
v	Sonido labiodental de la v de valle.
w	Sonido parecido al de la u de hueso.
y	Sonido de la y de yugo.
z	Sonido parecido al de la z de zorro, pero más suave.
(·)	El punto volado (·) indica que sobre la vocal o diptongo que lo precede recae el acento tónico de la palabra.

RESUMEN DE GRAMÁTICA INGLESA

ARTÍCULO / ARTICLES

El inglés tiene dos clases de artículo: el definido y el indefinido.

- Artículo definido: **the**. Es invariable y corresponde a *el, la, los, las* y (en ciertos casos) *lo*.

- Artículo indefinido: **a** o **an**. Se usa para el singular en todos los géneros.
  —La forma **a** se usa: a) delante de consonantes (incluyendo entre ellas la **h** aspirada, la **w** y la **y**); b) delante de **u, eu** y **ew**, cuando suenan como en **use, European** y **ewe**, y delante de **o**, cuando suena como en **one**.
  —El plural español *unos* y *unas* se traduce al inglés por el adjetivo **some**: he had some papers in his hand, tenía unos papeles en la mano.

NOTA: El uso que hace el español del artículo determinado en expresiones como: me lavo *las* manos, ponte *el* sombrero, él se ha roto *el* brazo, no existe en inglés. Estas expresiones se traducen por: I wash **my** hands, put on **your** hat, he has broken **his** arm.

GÉNERO / GENDER

Por regla general, en inglés, son
- **Masculinos.** Los nombres que significan varón o animal macho: **man** (hombre); **knight** (caballero); **bull** (toro).

- **Femeninos.** Los que significan mujer o animal hembra: **woman** (mujer); **spinster** (solterona); **lady** (dama); **cow** (vaca).

- **Comunes.** Como en español, los de persona de una sola terminación para los dos géneros: **friend** (amigo, -ga); **neighbor** (vecino, -na); **companion** (compañero, -ra).

- **Neutros.** Los nombres de cosa concretos o abstractos; los de animales cuando no se especifica su sexo; los que significan niño [niño o niña indiferentemente] o niño de pecho como **child** o **baby**.

Excepciones:
- Los nombres de países, barcos y máquinas son generalmente del género femenino: **Poland** has lost **her** independence, Polonia ha perdido su independencia; **she** was a fine **ship**, era un hermoso barco.

Indicación del género
Hay cierto número de nombres que tienen palabras distintas para cada género: **man** (hombre); **woman** (mujer); **father** (padre); **mother** (madre); **widow** (viuda); **widower** (viudo); **bull** (toro); **cow** (vaca); **rooster** (gallo); **hen** (gallina), etc.
En los demás casos, el género se infiere del contexto (**she is an orphan**, ella es huérfana), o se distingue:
- Por medio de las terminaciones femeninas **-ess, -ix** o **-ine**: actor, **actress** (actor, actriz); duke, **duchess** (duque, duquesa); testator, **testatrix** (testador, testadora); hero, **heroine** (héroe, heroína).

- Por medio de **male, female, woman**, etc., en función de adjetivo o de los pronombres **he-**, **she-** como prefijos: **female fish** (pez hembra); **woman lawyer** (abogada, licenciada); **he-goat** (macho cabrío); **she-ass** (asna, jumenta).

- Por medio de palabras compuestas en que uno de los elementos expresa el género: **man-servant** (criado); **maidservant** (criada); **bull-elephant** (elefante), **doe-hare** (liebre hembra), **cock-sparrow** (gorrión).

PLURAL (Sustantivos) / THE PLURAL OF NOUNS
Regla general

En inglés la desinencia del plural es una s que se añade a la forma propia del singular: bale, bales; chair, chairs.

Observ.: Los nombres terminados en se, ce, ge y ze ganan una sílaba en el plural al tomar la s, ya que la e muda se pronuncia como [i]: fence [fens], valla; pl. fences ['fensiz], vallas.

Excepciones y casos particulares

*   Toman es en el plural:

    —Los nombres terminados en o precedida de consonante: virago, viragoes; potato, potatoes.

    Sin embargo, los nombres de formación moderna o de origen extranjero hacen el plural en s: auto, autos; contralto, contraltos; dynamo, dynamos; memento, mementos; piano, pianos.

    —Los nombres terminados en s, sh, ch (con sonido de *ch*), x y z: brass, brasses; bush, bushes; wrench, wrenches; box, boxes; chintz, chintzes.

    Observ.: Los terminados en ex hacen el plural en exes o ices; los terminados en ix lo hacen en ixes o ices: vortex, vortexes o vortices; appendix, appendixes o appendices.

*   Los nombres terminados en f o fe hacen el plural en ves: half, halves; knife, knives; wolf, wolves.

    —Se exceptúan: dwarf, gulf, safe, still-life, strife y los terminados en ff, ief y oof, que hacen el plural en s: dwarf, dwarfs; cliff, cliffs; belief, beliefs; roof, roofs. Sin embargo, *thief* hace thieves.

    —Algunos tienen plural doble en fs y en ves, como: beef, beefs y beeves; hoof, hoofs y hooves; scarf, scarfs y scarves; wharf, wharfs y wharves.

*   Los nombres terminados en quy o en y precedida de consonante hacen el plural cambiando la y en ies: colloquy, colloquies; cry, cries; oddity, oddities.

    —Sin embargo, los nombres propios terminados en y, con muy raras excepciones, hacen el plural en s: Henry, Henrys.

*   Algunos nombres son invariables: sheep (carnero, carneros); swine (cerdo, cerdos). Otros tienen formas propias para el singular y para el plural: child, children; die, dice; foot, feet; man, men; mouse, mice; woman, women; tooth, teeth.

GENITIVO / THE GENITIVE CASE

En ciertos casos, el inglés expresa el genitivo añadiendo una s apostrofada ('s) al nombre del poseedor y poniendo sin artículo el nombre de lo poseído (John's father, el padre de Juan). Es lo que se llama *caso genitivo o genitivo sajón.*

Se omite la s (nunca el apóstrofe):

*   Después de un nombre en plural terminado en s: the birds' nests, los nidos de los pájaros.

*   Después de un nombre en singular cuya última sílaba empiece con s: Moses' law, la ley de Moisés.

*   Después de un nombre propio latino, griego o extranjero terminado en s, es o x: Cassius' dagger, el puñal de Casio; Achilles' heel, el talón de Aquiles. Nótese, sin embargo: Venus's beauty, la hermosura de Venus.

*   Después de un nombre terminado en s o ce, cuando va seguido de sake: for goodness' sake!, ¡por Dios!; for conscience' sake, por conciencia.

Casos especiales

*   Puede usarse con elipsis del nombre de la cosa poseída cuando éste significa *iglesia, hospital, casa, tienda:* St. Paul's, la catedral de San Pablo; at my aunt's, en casa de mi tía; I am going to the grocer's, voy a la tienda de comestibles. También se usa con elipsis en casos como: this car is my father's, este coche es de mi padre; Is this your hat? No, it is Mr. Brown's; Este sombrero es el suyo? No, es el del señor Brown.

*   Si hay más de dos nombres propios de poseedor, el signo del genitivo se pone detrás del último: Mary and Robert's brother, el hermano de María y Roberto.

ADJETIVO / ADJECTIVES

El adjetivo inglés es invariable. Una misma forma sirve para todos los géneros en singular y en plural: an old man, un hombre viejo; an old house, una casa vieja; these trees are old, estos árboles son viejos.

Lugar del adjetivo

Por regla general, el adjetivo (cuando no tiene función de predicado) precede al sustantivo que califica o determina: a clever man, un hombre inteligente; a long journey, un largo viaje.

El adjetivo va pospuesto:

- Cuando lleva un complemento: a man worthy of esteem, un hombre digno de aprecio.
- Cuando completa el sentido del verbo: he found the plot absurd, halló absurdo el argumento.
- Cuando equivale a una oración subordinada: the garden proper is not very large, el jardín propiamente dicho no es muy grande.
- Cuando significa de alto, de ancho, de edad, etc.: the tree is twenty feet high, el árbol tiene veinte pies de alto.
- Cuando califica un pronombre terminado en -thing o -body: there is nothing strange about that, eso no tiene nada de extraño.
- En algunas denominaciones de cargo, empleo, etc. y en ciertas expresiones procedentes del francés: accountant general, jefe de contabilidad; court martial, consejo de guerra.
- Los adjetivos worth, ill, left (que queda), missing y los compuestos con el prefijo a- suelen usarse sólo como predicados. Si alguno de ellos se aplica directamente al sustantivo, debe ir detrás de éste: a life worth preserving, una vida que merece ser conservada; he has only three dollars left, sólo le quedan tres dólares.
- La palabra alone va siempre detrás del nombre o el pronombre: leave him alone, déjalo solo.

El sustantivo usado como adjetivo

En inglés puede usarse un sustantivo para calificar a otro sustantivo. En este caso el primero va inmediatamente antes del segundo: coal ship, barco carbonero; pocket knife, navaja.

El comparativo y el superlativo

Al comparativo español *tan...como,* corresponde el inglés as...as para la afirmación, y so...as para la negación: my house is as beautiful as yours, mi casa es tan hermosa como la de usted; my house is not so beautiful as yours, mi casa no es tan hermosa como la de usted.

Al comparativo *más* (o *menos)...que,* corresponde el inglés more (o less)...than: my house is more (o less) beautiful than yours, mi casa es más (o menos) hermosa que la de usted.

El inglés no lleva desinencia propia para el superlativo absoluto. Este superlativo se forma anteponiendo al adjetivo los adverbios very, most, etc.: very high, altísimo; most excellent, excelentísimo.

Al superlativo relativo *el más* (o *el menos)... de,* corresponde el inglés the most (o the least)... in [delante de un nombre de lugar] u of [delante de los demás nombres]: the most populous quarter in town, el barrio más populoso de la ciudad; the least brave man of the regiment, el hombre menos valiente del regimiento.

Sin embargo, el comparativo correspondiente a *más...* y el superlativo correspondiente a *el más...* suelen formarse, cuando se trata de adjetivos monosílabos y de algunos bisílabos, añadiendo -er y -est respectivamente a la forma del positivo. Así, de short (corto) se hace shorter (más corto) y shortest (el más corto).

Al agregar -er y -est a la forma del positivo, la terminación de éste queda modificada en los casos siguientes:

- Adjetivos terminados en -e. Pierden la -e: nice, nicer, nicest; large, larger, largest.
- Adjetivos terminados en -y precedida de consonante. Cambian la -y en -i: burly, burlier, burliest.
- Adjetivos monosílabos terminados en consonante precedida de vocal breve. Doblan la consonante: big, bigger, biggest; fat, fatter, fattest.

Observaciones:

No se pueden usar las formas en -er y -est con adjetivos compuestos con el prefijo a-, ni con los terminados en -al, -ed, -ful, -ic, -ile, -ive, -ose y -ous: alive, mortal, aged, rustic, fragile, massive, verbose, famous.

NUMERALES / NUMERALS

Algunas particularidades

Cardinales

- Los números compuestos de decenas y unidades (a partir de *veinte*) se expresan poniendo las unidades a continuación de las decenas, separadas por un guión: **twenty-one** (21); **forty-six (46).**

- Los números de cien, ciento, mil, un millón, etc., se expresan así: **a** o **one hundred; a** o **one thousand; a** o **one million.** Generalmente se usa **a** para los números redondos y **one** con los demás: **a hundred** men, cien hombres; **one hundred sixty** dollars, ciento sesenta dólares.

  A doscientos, trescientos, dos mil, tres mil, etc., corresponden **two hundred, three hundred, two thousand, three thousand,** etc.

Ordinales

- Los ordinales (excepto los tres primeros: **first, second, third**) se forman añadiendo **th** a la forma del cardinal: four (cuatro), **fourth** (cuarto); seven (siete), **seventh** (séptimo).

  Al recibir la desinencia del ordinal, el cardinal queda modificado en los casos siguientes:
  —**five** y **twelve** cambian la **v** en **f: fifth, twelfth.**
  —**eight** pierde la **t: eighth.**
  —**nine** pierde la **e: ninth.**
  —**twenty, thirty,** etc., cambian la **y** en **ie: twentieth, thirtieth,** etc.
  En los números compuestos, sólo toma la forma de ordinal él último elemento: **thirty-first, twenty-second, forty-third, fifty-eighth.**

- Cuando el ordinal se aplica al nombre de un soberano se escribe con mayúscula y se le antepone el artículo: Henry **the Fourth,** Enrique cuarto; Pius **the Twelfth,** Pío doce.

PRONOMBRE PERSONAL / PERSONAL PRONOUNS

Formas del pronombre personal

Personas	Oficio	Singular		Plural	
1.ª	sujeto complemento reflexivo	I me myself	} masc. y fem.	we us ourselves	} masc. y fem.
2.ª	sujeto complemento reflexivo	thou, you thee, you thyself, yourself	} masc. y fem.	ye, you you yourselves	} masc. y fem.
3.ª	sujeto complemento reflexivo	he she it him her it himself herself itself	(masc.) (fem.) (neut.) (masc.) (fem.) (neut.) (masc.) (fem.) (neut.)	they them themselves	todos los géneros

Observaciones

- El pronombre complemento indirecto lleva la preposición to: she promised it **to me**, ella me la prometió.

  Sin embargo, con ciertos verbos, se puede omitir el **to** a condición de poner el complemento indirecto delante del directo: my father gave **me** this book, mi padre me dio este libro.

  Con **to tell** y **to answer**, se usa siempre esta última forma: he told **me** what had happened, me contó lo que había ocurrido.

- Después de los verbos seguidos de una partícula, el pronombre personal complemento directo se coloca entre el verbo y la partícula. Así a *he took off his coat* (se quitó el abrigo), corresponderá *he took it off*, se lo quitó.

- **All**, con un pronombre personal, se coloca después de éste; **all of**, delante: they **all, all of** them, todos, todos ellos o ellas.

- Después de las preposiciones **about, around, behind, with** y de las que indican movimiento, el inglés emplea el pronombre personal no reflexivo en vez del reflexivo: she brought her workbasket **with her**, ella trajo consigo su neceser de costura; he looked **behind him**, miró detrás de sí.

- El pronombre personal usado como antecedente de un relativo forma las expresiones **he who** o **that, she who** o **that**, etc., equivalentes a las españolas *el que, aquel que, la que*, etc.

  Sin embargo, en el lenguaje moderno no se dice they **who** o **that**, sino **those who** o **that**, los que, aquellos que.

- **They** puede ser sujeto de una oración impersonal, como: **they say that**, dicen que, se dice que.

- Las formas reflexivas del pronombre personal se usan también para reforzar el pronombre sujeto: I saw it **myself**, yo mismo lo vi.

POSESIVO (Adjetivo y pronombre) / POSSESSIVE ADJECTIVES AND PRONOUNS

Los adjetivos y pronombres posesivos ingleses son invariables por lo que se refiere a la cosa poseída. Sólo concuerdan con el nombre del posesor.

Adjetivos

Singular

1.ª persona:	**my**	mi, mis
2.ª persona:	**thy, your**	tu, tus*
3.ª persona:	**his**	su, sus [de él]
	her	su, sus [de ella]
	its	su, sus [de ello; de un animal o cosa en género neutro]

Plural

1.ª persona:	**our**	nuestro, nuestra, nuestros, nuestras
2.ª persona:	**your**	tu, tus; vuestro, vuestra; vuestros, vuestras; su, sus [de usted o ustedes]
3.ª persona:	**their**	su, sus [de ellos, de ellas, tanto para el masc. y el fem. como para el neutro]

Observaciones:

- Cuando el adjetivo posesivo se refiere a dos o más nombres de género diferente se pone en masculino: all the pupils, **boys and girls**, were there, **each carrying his** little present, todos los alumnos, niños y niñas, estaban allí llevando cada uno su pequeño regalo.

- Cuando no hay idea de posesión, suele sustituirse el adjetivo posesivo por el genitivo con **of**: the remembrance **of it**, su recuerdo; the directions for the use **of them**, las instrucciones para su uso.

Pronombres

Singular

1.ª persona:	mine	el mío, la mía, los míos, las mías
2.ª persona:	thine, yours	el tuyo, la tuya, los tuyos, las tuyas*
3.ª persona:	his	el suyo, la suya, los suyos, las suyas [de él]
	hers	el suyo, la suya, los suyos, las suyas [de ella]
	its own	el suyo, la suya, los suyos, las suyas [de un animal o cosa en género neutro]

Plural

1.ª persona:	ours	el nuestro, la nuestra, los nuestros, las nuestras
2.ª persona:	yours	el tuyo, la tuya, los tuyos, las tuyas; el vuestro, la vuestra, los vuestros, las vuestras; el suyo, la suya, los suyos, las suyas [de usted o de ustedes]
3.ª persona:	theirs	el suyo, la suya, los suyos, las suyas [de ellos, de ellas, tanto para el masc. y el fem. como para el neutro]

Observaciones:
- Cuando el pronombre posesivo va después del verbo **to be** puede traducirse también por el posesivo español sin artículo: this hat is **mine**, este sombrero es mío (o es el mío).
- El pronombre posesivo precedido de **of** equivale al adjetivo español *mío, tuyo,* etc., o *a uno de mis, de tus,* etc.: a friend **of mine**, un amigo mío, uno de mis amigos.

---

*El adjetivo posesivo **thy** y el pronombre **thine** sólo se usan en poesía, en la Biblia y en las oraciones. En el lenguaje corriente se usa **your** y **yours** para la segunda persona del singular, lo mismo que para la del plural.

CONJUGACIÓN DE VERBOS / CONJUGATION OF VERBS

La conjugación regular de un verbo inglés comprende un número de formas muy reducido. En todos los tiempos personales se usa la misma forma para todas las personas del singular y del plural, con excepción de la tercera persona del singular del presente de indicativo y de la segunda del singular del presente y el pretérito de indicativo.

Observación: La segunda persona del singular (que se forma añadiendo **st** a la forma propia del tiempo) sólo se emplea en poesía, en la oración y en la Biblia. En el lenguaje corriente se emplea la forma del plural, lo mismo para éste que para el singular. Así, **you dance** equivale, según los casos, a *tú bailas, usted baila, vosotros bailáis* o *ustedes bailan.*

Presente de indicativo

Tiene la forma del infinitivo sin **to** para la primera persona del singular y todas las del plural: I, we, you, they **dance.**

La tercera persona del singular

Se forma añadiendo **es** o **s** a la forma del infinitivo.

Toma **es:**
- En los verbos cuyo infinitivo termina en **ch, sh, ss, x** o **z:** reaches, brushes, passes, boxes, buzzes.
- En los verbos **to do** y **to go:** does, goes.

Toma **s:**
- En los verbos cuyo infinitivo termina en una **e** muda, una vocal o un diptongo: dances, lives, baas, sees, draws, knows.
- En aquellos cuyo infinitivo termina en una consonante que *no* es **ch, sh, ss, x** o **z:** sobs, packs, rings, kills, hears, bleats.

Observaciones:

- Los verbos terminados en y precedida de consonante cambian la y en ie: cry, cries; fly, flies. Los terminados en y precedida de vocal no cambian la y: buy, buys; play, plays.

- Los verbos terminados en ce, se o ge y los terminados en ch, sh, ss, x o z, ganan fonéticamente una sílaba al tomar la desinencia de la tercera persona del singular: dance, danc·es; buzz, buzz·es; brush, brush·es.

Pretérito de indicativo

La forma del pretérito de indicativo distingue, una de otra, dos clases de verbos:

Verbos débiles

Forman el pretérito y el participio pasivo añadiendo ed, d o t a la forma del infinitivo: walk, walked; live, lived. Algunos acortan (no cambian) la vocal de la raíz y añaden t: keep, kept; sweep, swept.

Observaciones:

- Los verbos débiles terminados en y precedida de consonante cambian la y en ie al tomar la desinencia del pretérito y del participio pasivo: cry, cried; spy, spied. Los terminados en y precedida de vocal no cambian la y: cloy, cloyed; play, played. Por excepción, to lay y to pay hacen el pretérito y el participio pasivo en aid: laid y paid.

- Los verbos que terminan en una consonante dental ganan fonéticamente una sílaba al tomar la desinencia del pretérito y el participio pasivo: blind, blind·ed; wait, wait·ed.

- Los verbos monosílabos y los polisílabos acentuados en la última sílaba, cuando terminan en una vocal breve seguida de una sola consonante, doblan ésta en el pretérito, el participio pasivo y el gerundio: fit, fitted, fitting; bar, barred, barring; compel, compelled, compelling.
  Cuando la consonante final es l precedida de una sola vocal, pueden doblar la l aunque no estén acentuados en la última sílaba: travel, traveled o travelled.

Verbos fuertes

Forman el pretérito y el participio pasivo cambiando la vocal de la raíz y añadiendo o no e, en, n o ne. Generalmente tienen el pretérito diferente del participio pasivo: break, broke, broken; bear (llevar), born, borne.

Advertencia: Los pretéritos, participios pasivos y gerundios de los verbos fuertes, así como los de otros que ofrezcan particularidades de forma u ortografía, se encontrarán en el cuerpo de este Diccionario al final del artículo correspondiente a cada verbo.

Futuro de indicativo

Se forma anteponiendo shall o will al infinitivo sin to (véase lo referente al uso de shall y will en los respectivos artículos de este Diccionario): I shall come, yo vendré; we will come, nosotros vendremos; you will come, tú vendrás, usted vendrá, vosotros vendréis, ustedes vendrán; he will come, él vendrá; they will come, ellos vendrán.

Potencial

Se forma anteponiendo should y would al infinitivo sin to (véase lo referente al uso de should y would en los respectivos artículos de este Diccionario): I should come, yo vendría; we would come, nosotras vendríamos; you would come, tú vendrías, usted vendría, vosotros vendríais, ustedes vendrían; he would come, él vendría; they would come, ellos vendrían.

Imperativo

El imperativo inglés sólo tiene una forma propia que es la del infinitivo sin to y sólo se usa para las segundas personas: come, ven, venga usted, venid, vengan ustedes.

Para las personas 1.ª y 3.ª hay que recurrir a una oración formada con el verbo to let: let us see, veamos.

Tiempos compuestos

Se forman, como en español, con el verbo auxiliar **to have** (haber) y el participio pasivo.
Ejemplos:
I have played, yo he jugado; **he has played**, él ha jugado (pretérito perfecto).
I had played, yo había jugado o hube jugado (pretérito pluscuamperfecto o pretérito anterior).
I shall have played, yo habré jugado; **he will have played**, él habrá jugado (futuro perfecto).
I should have played, yo habría jugado; **he would have played**, él habría jugado (potencial compuesto o perfecto).

Conjugación continua

Además de esta forma de conjugación, el inglés tiene otra llamada *continua* que se forma con el auxiliar **to be** y el gerundio del verbo: **I am coming, I was coming.** Esta forma se usa para indicar una acción en curso de realización, o sea no terminada.

En el presente, corresponde a un presente español del verbo en cuestión o de una oración del verbo *estar:* **I am writing** a letter, escribo una carta o estoy escribiendo una carta.

En el pretérito simple corresponde a un imperfecto español: **he was writing** a letter, él escribía una carta o estaba escribiendo una carta.

Observación: La forma continua no puede usarse para expresar una acción instantánea o definitiva, como tampoco una acción habitual o permanente. Así no se dirá: **I am forgiving** him, **the sun is setting** every day, **he is being** her father, sino: **I forgive** him, **the sun sets** every day, **he is** her father.

INFINITIVO / THE INFINITIVE

Por regla general, el infinitivo va precedido de la partícula **to**, que en muchos casos equivale a las preposiciones *a* o *para.*

Infinitivo sin to
El infinitivo se usa sin **to:**

- Después de los auxiliares defectivos **shall, will, can, may** y **must:** **I shall write** to him, le escribiré; **you cannot speak** French, usted no sabe hablar francés; **we must be** quiet, hemos de callar.
  —Nótese que después de **ought** se usa el infinitivo con **to: you ought to know** it, usted debería saberlo.
- Después de **to dare** y **to need** usados como auxiliares: **he dared not speak** to him, él no se atrevió a hablarle; **they need not fear,** no tienen por qué temer.
- Después de los verbos que expresan sensación o percepción, como **to hear, to see, to feel, to behold, to observe, to watch,** etc.: **I hear** him **speak** in the hall, le oigo hablar en el vestíbulo; **I felt** the child **tremble** in my arms, sentí al niño temblar en mis brazos.
- Después de los verbos **to let** (dejar, permitir), **to bid** (ordenar, mandar) y **to make** (hacer que se ejecute una acción): **let me read** this letter, déjeme leer esta carta; **he bade her open** the door, le mandó abrir la puerta.
  —Sin embargo, en la voz pasiva, estos verbos van seguidos del infinitivo con **to: I was let to read** the letter, se me dejó leer la carta.
- Después de **and, or, than** y **but** en oraciones como: they decided **to stop** there **and wait** for him, decidieron detenerse allí y esperarle; he was told **to be** quiet **or go,** se le dijo que se callara o que se fuera; she did nothing other **than laugh,** ella no hizo más que reír.
- En ciertas oraciones interrogativas o exclamatorias: a father not **love** his son!, ¡un padre no querer a su hijo!
- Después de las locuciones **had better, had rather, would rather,** etc.: you **had better wait,** vale más que espere.

Infinitivo traducido por el subjuntivo o el indicativo
El infinitivo inglés se traduce algunas veces por un subjuntivo y, aun, por un indicativo español.

Ejemplos: he asked me **to pay** the bill, me pidió que pagase la cuenta; the captain ordered the soldiers **to bring** the prisoner, el capitán ordenó a los soldados que trajesen el prisionero; I want him **to do** this, quiero que él haga esto; they expect him **to go** soon, esperan que se irá pronto.

GERUNDIO / THE GERUND

El gerundio inglés, o sea la forma verbal terminada en -ing, puede hacer varios oficios y generalmente se traduce, según los casos:

Como gerundio
Por el gerundio español: he was **waiting** for me, él me estaba esperando.

Como participio—adjetivo
- Por un participio activo: **cutting** tool, instrumento cortante; in a **surprising** manner, de un modo sorprendente.

- Por un participio pasivo: an **amusing** book, un libro entretenido; **lying** on a sofa, echado en un sofá.

- Por un adjetivo, o por una expresión equivalente a éste: a **calculating** person, una persona calculadora, interesada; **hunting** season, temporada de caza; **sewing** machine, máquina de coser.
  Observación: Por su naturaleza verbal puede tener un complemento directo. En este caso se traduce por *que* y un verbo en tiempo personal: a package **containing** six pairs of gloves, un paquete *que* contiene seis pares de guantes.

Como infinitivo o nombre verbal
- Por un infinitivo nominal: before **speaking**, antes de hablar; an organization for **helping** the poor, una organización para socorrer a los pobres.

- Por *que* y un verbo en tiempo personal (generalmente en subjuntivo): this door needs **painting**, esta puerta necesita que la pinten.

- Por un sustantivo: he was engaged in the **reading** of that book, estaba ocupado en la lectura de aquel libro.

Observaciones:
—*On*, delante de la forma verbal en -ing, se traduce generalmente por *al* seguido de un infinitivo: **on** arriving, *al* llegar.
—Cuando un nombre va delante de la forma en -ing, debe ponerse en genitivo si es de los que lo admiten: my father was annoyed at Peter's **coming** so late, mi padre estaba enojado de que Pedro viniese tan tarde (o porque Pedro venía tan tarde).
—Si en lugar del nombre hay un pronombre, éste debe tomar la forma del posesivo: would you mind **my opening** the window?, ¿le molestaría que yo abriese la ventana?

NEGACIÓN / EXPRESSING NEGATION

Construcción de la oración negativa
- Cuando el verbo es to be o to have; to dare o to need (como auxiliares), o alguno de los defectivos shall, will, can, may, must o ought, la negación se expresa poniendo **not** inmediatamente después del verbo: they **are not** here, no están aquí; he **dared not** come, no se atrevía a venir; John **will not** win the prize, Juan no ganará el premio; if I **may not** go, si no puedo ir.
  Observ.: El presente **can not** se escribe en una sola palabra: **cannot**.

- Cuando el verbo es otro cualquiera en tiempo simple, la negación se expresa por medio del auxiliar to do seguido de not; el verbo toma la forma invariable del infinitivo sin to: I **do not** see it, no lo veo; he **does not** play, él no juega; her father **did not** come, su padre no vino.
  En los tiempos compuestos no se usa do, does, did y se pone not inmediatamente después del auxiliar: he **has not seen** it, él no lo ha visto.
  Observ.: Con dare la negación puede expresarse también así, pero el verbo regido lleva to: they **did not dare to** come, no se atrevieron a venir.

- En las oraciones interrogativas, not se pone después del sujeto si éste es un pronombre y antes de él si es un nombre: do you **not** see it?, ¿no lo ve usted?; **did not** (o **didn't**) your brother win the prize?, ¿no ganó el premio su hermano?

- En el infinitivo y en el gerundio se antepone not al verbo: not to understand, no entender; not understanding, no entendiendo.

- En el imperativo se antepone do not al verbo: do not (o don't) laugh, no rías (ría usted, rían ustedes, riáis); do not (o don't) let them come, que no vengan.

- En el lenguaje corriente not se contrae frecuentemente con do o con otros verbos: don't (do not); didn't (did not); aren't (are not); can't (cannot); isn't (is not); won't (will not); etc.

- Cuando el carácter negativo de la oración está determinado por palabras como never, no, nobody, nothing, nowhere, by no means, no se usa not ni el auxiliar to do: it is never too late, nunca es tarde; I have no time, no tengo tiempo.

INTERROGACIÓN / INTERROGATIVES

Construcción de la oración interrogativa

- Cuando el verbo es to be o to have; to dare o to need (como auxiliares) o algún defectivo como shall, will, can, may, must o ought, el sujeto va inmediatamente después del verbo: are they here?, ¿están aquí?; have you any money?, ¿tiene usted dinero?; dare you go there?, ¿se atreve usted a ir allí?; need he do it?, ¿necesita hacerlo?; can this boy write?, ¿sabe escribir este niño?

- Cuando el verbo es otro cualquiera en tiempo simple, la oración se construye con el auxiliar to do, que va delante del sujeto; el verbo toma la forma invariable del infinitivo sin to: do you see this tree?, ¿ve usted este árbol?; did your brother win the race?, ¿ganó la carrera su hermano?
  —En los tiempos compuestos no se usa do, does, did y el sujeto va inmediatamente después del auxiliar: have you seen the house?, ¿ha visto usted la casa?

- Cuando la oración empieza con un pronombre interrogativo sujeto del verbo o con un adjetivo interrogativo que acompaña al sujeto, no se usa do, did y no hay inversión del sujeto: who wins the prize?, ¿quién gana el premio?; what happened to him?, ¿qué le pasó?; which pillars support the arch?, ¿qué pilares sostienen el arco?

- Después de un adverbio interrogativo la oración se construye como se ha indicado: how long will they remain here?, ¿cuánto tiempo permanecerán aquí?

CONJUGACIÓN DE TO HAVE (TENER), HAD (TENÍA, TUVE), HAD (TENIDO)

INDICATIVO

	Afirmación	Negación	Interrogación (Negación)
Presente	*yo tengo* I have he, she, it has we, you, they have	*yo no tengo* I have not he, she, it has not we, you, they have not	*¿(no) tengo yo?* have I (not)? has he, she, it (not)? have we, you, they (not)?
Pretérito (Past)	*yo tenía, tuve* I had you had, etc.	*yo no tenía, tuve* I had not you had not, etc.	*¿(no) tenía, tuve yo?* had I (not)? had you (not)?, etc.
Futuro simple	*yo tendré* I, we shall have you, he, they will have	*yo no tendré* I, we shall not have you, he, they will not have	*¿(no) tendré yo?* shall I, we (not) have? will you, he, they (not) have?

	Afirmación	Negación	Interrogación (Negación)
Condicional simple	*yo tendría* I, we should have you, he, they would have	*yo no tendría* I, we should not have you, he, they would not have	*¿(no) tendría yo?* should I, we (not) have? would you, he, they (not) have?
Pretérito perfecto	*yo he tenido* I, we, you, they have had he has had	*yo no he tenido* I, we, you, they have not had he has not had	*¿(no) he tenido yo?* have I, we, you, they (not) had? has he (not) had?
Pretérito plusc.	*yo había tenido* I, you...had had	*yo no había tenido* I, you...had not had	*¿(no) había tenido yo?* had I, you...(not) had?
Futuro perfecto	*yo habré tenido* I, we shall have had you, he, they will have had	*yo no habré tenido* I, we shall not have had you, he, they will not have had	*¿(no) habré yo tenido?* shall I, we (not) have had? will he, you, they (not) have had?
Condicional compuesto	*yo habría tenido* I, we should have had you, he, they would have had	*yo no habría tenido* I, we should not have had you, he, they would not have had	*¿(no) habría yo tenido?* should I, we (not) have had? would you, he, they (not) have had?

IMPERATIVO

	Afirmación	Negación
	tenga yo	*no tenga yo*
	let me have	don't let me have
	have	don't have, etc.
	let him (her, it) have	
	let us have	
	have	
	let them have	

PARTICIPIO PRES. GERUNDIO	}	having *teniendo*
PARTICIPIO PAS.		had *tenido*
INFINITIVO SIMPLE		(not) to have *(no) tener*
INFINITIVO COMP.		to have had *haber tenido*

CONJUGACIÓN DE TO BE (SER, ESTAR), WAS (ERA, FUI), BEEN (SIDO)

INDICATIVO

		Afirmación	Negación	Interrogación (Negación)
Presente		*yo soy* I am he, she, it is we, you, they are	*yo no soy* I am not he, she, it is not we, you, they are not	*¿(no) soy yo?* am I (not)? is he, she, it (not)? are we, you, they (not)?
Pretérito (Past)		*yo era, fui* I, he was we, you, they were	*yo no era, fui* I, he was not we, you, they were not	*¿(no) era, fui yo?* was I, he (not)? were we, you, they (not)?
Futuro simple		*yo seré* I, we shall be he, you, they will be	*yo no seré* I, we shall not be he, you, they will not be	*¿(no) seré yo?* shall I, we (not) be? will you, he, they (not) be?
Condicional simple		*yo sería* I, we should be he, you, they would be	*yo no sería* I, we should not be he, you, they would not be	*¿(no) sería yo?* should I, we (not) be? would you, he, they (not) be?
Pretérito perfecto		*yo he sido* I, we, you, they have been he has been	*yo no he sido* I, we, you, they have not been he has not been	*¿(no) he sido yo?* have I, we, you, they (not) been? has he (not) been?
Pretérito plusc.		*yo había sido* I, you...had been	*yo no había sido* I, you...had not been	*¿(no) había sido yo?* had I, you...(not) been?
Futuro perfecto		*yo habré sido* I, we shall have been you, he, they will have been	*yo no habré sido* I, we shall not have been you, he, they will not have been	*¿(no) habré yo sido?* shall I, we (not) have been? will you, he, they (not) have been?
Condicional compuesto		*yo habría sido* I, we should have been you, he, they would have been	*yo no habría sido* I, we should not have been you, he, they would not have been	*¿(no) habría yo sido?* should I, we (not) have been? would you, he, they (not) have been?

IMPERATIVO

Afirmación	Negación
sea yo let me be be let him (her, it) be let us be be let them be	*no sea yo* don't let me be don't be, etc.

PARTICIPIO PRES. GERUNDIO	}	being *siendo*
PARTICIPIO PAS.		been *sido*
INFINITIVO SIMPLE		(not) to be *(no) ser*
INFINITIVO COMP.		to have been *haber sido*

CONJUGACIÓN DE UN VERBO REGULAR

to look (mirar), **looked** (miraba, miré), **looked** (mirado)

INDICATIVO

		Afirmación	Negación	Interrogación (Negación)
Presente		*yo miro* I look you look he, she, it looks we, you, they look	*yo no miro* I do not look you do not look he, she, it does not look we, you, they do not look	*¿ (no) miro yo?* do I (not) look? do you (not) look? does he, she, it (not) look? do we, you, they (not) look?
Pretérito (Past)		*yo miré, miraba* I looked you looked he looked, etc.	*yo no miré, miraba* I did not look you did not look he did not look, etc.	*¿ (no) miré, miraba yo?* did I (not) look? did you (not) look? did he (not) look?, etc.
Futuro simple		*yo miraré* I, we shall look you, he, they will look	*yo no miraré* I, we shall not look you, he, they will not look	*¿ (no) miraré yo?* shall I, we (not) look? will you, he, they (not) look?
Condicional simple		*yo miraría* I, we should look you, he, they would look	*yo no miraría* I, we should not look you, he, they would not look	*¿ (no) miraría yo?* should I, we (not) look? would you, he, they (not) look?
Pretérito perfecto		*yo he mirado* I, we, you, they have looked he has looked	*yo no he mirado* I, we, you, they have not looked he has not looked	*¿ (no) he mirado yo?* have I, we, you, they (not) looked? has he (not) looked?
Pretérito plusc.		*yo había mirado* I, you...had looked	*yo no había mirado* I, you...had not looked	*¿ (no) había mirado yo?* had I, you...(not) looked?
Futuro perfecto		*yo habré mirado* I, we shall have looked you, he, they will have looked	*yo no habré mirado* I, we shall not have looked you, he, they will not have looked	*¿ (no) habré yo mirado?* shall I, we (not) have looked? will you, he, they (not) have looked?
Condicional compuesto		*yo habría mirado* I, we should have looked you, he, they would have looked	*yo no habría mirado* I, we should not have looked you, he, they would not have looked	*¿ (no) habría yo mirado?* should I, we (not) have looked? would you, he, they (not) have looked?

IMPERATIVO

Afirmación	Negación
mire yo	*no mire yo*
let me look	don't let me look
look	don't look, etc.
let him (her, it) look	
let us look	
look	
let them look	

PARTICIPIO PRES. GERUNDIO	looking *mirando*
PARTICIPIO PAS.	looked *mirado*
INFINITIVO SIMPLE	(not) to look *(no) mirar*
INFINITIVO COMP.	to have looked *haber mirado*

CONJUGACIÓN DE UN VERBO IRREGULAR

to go (ir), **went** (iba, fui), **gone** (ido)

INDICATIVO

		Afirmación	Negación	Interrogación (Negación)
Presente		*yo voy*	*yo no voy*	*¿ (no) voy yo?*
		I go	I do not go	do I (not) go?
		you go	you do not go	do you (not) go?
		he, she, it goes	he, she, it does not go	does he, she, it (not) go?
		we, you, they go	we, you, they do not go	do we, you, they (not) go?
Pretérito (Past)		*yo iba, fui*	*yo no iba, fui*	*¿ (no) fui, iba yo?*
		I went	I did not go	did I (not) go?
		you went	you did not go	did you (not) go?
		he went, etc.	he did not go, etc.	did he (not) go?, etc.
Futuro simple		*yo iré*	*yo no iré*	*¿ (no) iré yo?*
		I, we shall go	I, we shall not go	shall I, we (not) go?
		you, he, they will go	you, he, they will not go	will you, he, they (not) go?
Condicional simple		*yo iría*	*yo no iría*	*¿ (no) iría yo?*
		I, we should go	I, we should not go	should I, we (not) go?
		you, he, they would go	you, he, they would not go	would you, he, they (not) go?

	Afirmación	Negación	Interrogación (Negación)
Pretérito perfecto	*yo he ido* I, we, you, they have gone he has gone	*yo no he ido* I, we, you, they have not gone he has not gone	*¿(no) he ido yo?* have I, we, you, they (not) gone? has he (not) gone?
Pretérito plusc.	*yo había ido* I, you...had gone	*yo no había ido* I, you...had not gone	*¿(no) había ido yo?* had I, you...(not) gone?
Futuro perfecto	*yo habré ido* I, we shall have gone you, he, they will have gone	*yo no habré ido* I, we shall not have gone you, he, they will not have gone	*¿(no) habré yo ido?* shall I, we (not) have gone? will you, he, they (not) have gone?
Condicional compuesto	*yo habría ido* I, we should have gone you, he, they would have gone	*yo no habría ido* I, we should not have gone you, he, they would not have gone	*¿(no) habría yo ido?* should I, we (not) have gone? would you, he, they (not) have gone?

IMPERATIVO

Afirmación	Negación
vaya yo let me go go let him (her, it) go let us go go let them go	*no vaya yo* don't let me go don't go, etc.

PARTICIPIO PRES. GERUNDIO	}	going *yendo*
PARTICIPIO PAS.		gone *ido*
INFINITIVO SIMPLE		(not) to go *(no) ir*
INFINITIVO COMP.		to have gone *haber ido*

SUBJUNTIVO / THE SUBJUNCTIVE MOOD

El inglés no tiene formas propias para el subjuntivo, excepto en el verbo **to be,** cuyo presente de subjuntivo es **be** y cuyo pretérito de subjuntivo es **were** para todas las personas del singular y del plural: whoever he **be,** quienquiera que sea; if I **were** in his place, si yo estuviese en su lugar.

En todo otro caso, el inglés expresa el subjuntivo mediante: a) el infinitivo; b) una forma de indicativo; c) una forma compuesta con los auxiliares **may** o **might** y **should.**

Por regla general:
- Cuando la acción expresada por el subjuntivo es pensada como cierta, se usa el infinitivo o el indicativo: tell him **to go away,** dígale que se vaya; as you **please,** como usted quiera o guste; wait till he **comes,** aguarde hasta que él venga.
- Cuando la acción es pensada como incierta, dudosa o simplemente deseada, se usa una forma compuesta con **may, might** o **should.**

    May, might se usan:
    —Para expresar la idea del verbo *poder:* however strong he **might** be, por fuerte que fuese.
    —Para expresar un deseo, una orden: **may** he live long, que viva muchos años.
    —En oraciones finales después de **that, in order that, so that** (para que, a fin de que): he went away **that** they **might** not find him in the house, se fue para que no le encontrasen en la casa.

    Se usa **should:**
    —Después de **that** (conjunción *que*): he seemed to expect **that** I **should** assent to this, parecía esperar que yo asintiese a esto; **that** I **should** be so unfortunate!, ¡que sea yo tan desgraciado!
    —Después de conjunciones condicionales o concesivas, como **if, though, even though,** etc.: if he **should** come, si él viniese; **though** he **should** come, aunque él viniese.
    —Después de **lest:** I shall keep your book **lest** you **should** lose it, guardaré tu libro para que no lo pierdas.

Observaciones:
- **If** puede omitirse en ciertos casos a condición de poner el sujeto detrás de **should, had** o **were:** should he know it, si él lo supiese; had I known it, si yo lo hubiese sabido; were I in his place, si yo estuviese en su lugar.
- Después de **for fear that** se usa **should** en el presente y **should** o **might** en el pretérito: he is running away **for fear that** his father **should** punish him, huye por miedo de que su padre le castigue; he ran away **for fear that** his father **should** (o **might**) punish him, huyó por miedo de que su padre lo castigase.

ADVERBIO / ADVERBS

El inglés tiene muchos adverbios derivados de adjetivo, análogos a los españoles terminados en *-mente.* Se forman añadiendo **-ly** al adjetivo. Así de **bad,** se forma **badly;** de **bright, brightly,** etc.

Esta forma de derivación tiene las siguientes alteraciones:
- Los adjetivos terminados en **-le** pierden esta terminación: possible, **possibly;** tolerable, **tolerably.**
- Los terminados en **-ue** pierden la e: due, **duly;** true, **truly.**
- Los terminados en **-ll** sólo añaden la y: dull, **dully;** full, **fully.**
- Los terminados en **-y** cambian esta letra en i: guilty, **guiltily;** showy, **showily.**

Lugar del adverbio

Cuando modifica una palabra que no es el verbo:
- Por regla general, va delante de la palabra que modifica: **seriously** ill, gravemente enfermo; **very** well, muy bien; **long** before, mucho antes.
    —Se exceptúan **enough,** que siempre va detrás de la palabra que modifica: good **enough** for me, suficientemente bueno para mí; y **ago,** que siempre va detrás de las palabras que expresan el período de tiempo: two years **ago,** hace dos años.

Cuando modifica al verbo:

- Si el verbo es transitivo, el adverbio no puede separar el verbo del complemento directo: va delante del verbo o después del complemento. En los tiempos compuestos, puede ir también después del verbo auxiliar: he **easily** defeated his opponent, he defeated his opponent **easily**, ha derrotado fácilmente a su adversario.

    —Sin embargo, cuando el complemento directo consta de muchas palabras o está complementado por una oración, el adverbio puede ir entre el verbo y el complemento directo: he rewarded **liberally** all those who had served his father, recompensó liberalmente a todos los que habían servido a su padre.

- Si el verbo es intransitivo, el adverbio va después del verbo, tanto en los tiempos simples como en los compuestos: she has sung **wonderfully**, ha cantado maravillosamente.

    —Sin embargo, algunos adverbios, como **suddenly, promptly,** etc., pueden ir después del auxiliar de los tiempos compuestos: the wind has **suddenly** risen, el viento ha soplado de pronto.

- Si el verbo es **to be,** el adverbio suele ir después del verbo o después del auxiliar de los tiempos compuestos: he is **always** silent, siempre está callado.

- Como en español, el adverbio va al principio de la oración cuando modifica la oración entera o cuando se quiere dar mayor fuerza a la expresión: **meanwhile,** I was writing the letter, entretanto yo escribía la carta.

Casos particulares

No yendo con el verbo **to be,** los adverbios **also, even, first, once** y **quite,** los de tiempo indefinido y los seminegativos como **almost, nearly, hardly, only** y **scarcely,** van siempre entre el sujeto y el verbo o después del auxiliar de los tiempos compuestos: he **never** spoke about it, él nunca ha hablado de ello.

En cambio, los adverbios de tiempo **early, late, today, tonight** y los polisílabos como **yesterday, presently,** etc.; los de lugar; los de cantidad, y los de modo **very well, badly** y **worse,** van al final de la oración: they arrived **late,** ellos llegaron tarde.

El comparativo y el superlativo

El comparativo y el superlativo de los adverbios se forman como los del adjetivo. Algunos tienen formas propias que se encontrarán en los artículos correspondientes de este Diccionario.

PREPOSICIÓN / PREPOSITIONS

Traslado de la preposición

La preposición mediante la cual el verbo rige a un complemento se puede trasladar al final de la oración:

- En las oraciones interrogativas: whom are you speaking **to?** (o sea: **to** whom are you speaking?), ¿a quién habla usted?

- En las subordinadas que empiezan por un pronombre relativo: I did not know the man whom I was speaking **with** (o the man **with** whom I was speaking), yo no conocía al hombre con quien estaba hablando.

Esta construcción es obligatoria cuando el pronombre relativo es **that,** ya sea expreso o elíptico: he has the book **(that)** you are looking for, él tiene el libro que usted busca.

Omisión de la preposición

En algunas frases adverbiales o prepositivas y en ciertas expresiones, se omiten las preposiciones:

at: (at) every moment, en todo momento; (at) full speed, a toda velocidad; (at) that hour, entonces; (at) the next moment, un momento después; he looked (at) me in the face, me miró a la cara.

of: on board (of) the ship, a bordo del buque; (of) what use is this to me?, ¿de qué me sirve esto?

with: (with) tooth and nail, con dientes y uñas, encarnizadamente, desesperadamente.

COMPLEMENTOS DIRECTO E INDIRECTO / DIRECT AND INDIRECT OBJECTS

En inglés, el complemento directo se construye siempre sin preposición. El complemento indirecto suele llevar preposición.

En la construcción regular, el complemento directo va inmediatamente después del verbo y el complemento indirecto, después del directo: John has explained **his conduct**, Juan ha explicado su conducta; John has explained his conduct **to Peter**, Juan ha explicado su conducta a Pedro.

Cambios de lugar del complemento

Con ciertos verbos, como to allow, to answer, to bring, to do, to get, to give, to lend, to owe, to send, to show, to take, to teach, to tell, to write, etc., el complemento indirecto puede ir delante del directo. En este caso no lleva preposición: he gave **his son** a book, dio un libro a su hijo.

Pero cuando estos dos complementos son pronombres, el acusativo precede siempre al dativo: John gave **it** to him, Juan se lo dio.

El complemento directo va delante del verbo:

- Para dar mayor realce al complemento: he had two fine horses: **the black one** he gave to his son, **the white one** to his daughter, tenía dos hermosos caballos: el negro lo dio a su hijo; el blanco, a su hija.

- Cuando el complemento es un pronombre relativo o interrogativo: the man **that** (o **whom**) we saw, el hombre que vimos; **what** do you see?, ¿qué ve usted?

- Cuando va precedido de un adjetivo interrogativo: **which road** must I take?, ¿qué camino he de tomar?

- En las oraciones exclamativas precedidas de **what**: **what nonsense** you talk!, ¡qué tonterías dice usted!; **what a beautiful book** he has written!, ¡qué hermoso libro ha escrito!

Omisión del complemento directo

El complemento directo se omite frecuentemente cuando es un pronombre relativo: the man (**that** o **whom**) we were looking for, el hombre que buscábamos.

MAYÚSCULAS / CAPITAL LETTERS

Se escriben con mayúscula:

- Las mismas palabras que llevan mayúscula en español.
- Las derivadas de nombres propios: **Aristotelian, Aristotelianism, Christian, Christianity, Victorian.**
- Los nombres de pueblos, razas, naciones, tribus y lenguas con sus compuestos y derivados: **Angles, Anglo-Norman, Anglican, Chinaman, Chinese, French, Hispanic, Hispanophile, Inca, Incan.**
- Los de credos o confesiones, de religiones o sectas y de las órdenes religiosas, con sus derivados: **Apostles' Creed, Augsburg Confession, Catholic, Catholicism, Protestant, Protestantism.**
- Los de instituciones, congresos, exposiciones, cuerpos legisladores, organizaciones, partidos políticos, etc.: **Congress of Vienna, Columbian Exposition, House of Representatives, Spanish Army.**
- Los de tratados, batallas, acontecimientos históricos, períodos, épocas, eras: **Treaty of Westphalia, Battle of Verdun, Revolutionary War, Middle Ages, Jurassic, Christian Era, Before Christ.**
- Los de los días de la semana, de los meses del año y de las fiestas: **Monday, June, Good Friday, Mother's Day.**
- Los de calle, plaza, etc.: **Madison Avenue, Trafalgar Square, Central Park.**
- Los de las estaciones del año y los de ciertas ideas abstractas cuando se quieren personificar: **Spring, Winter, Autumn.**
- Los de los tipos, clases, órdenes, familias, etc., de plantas y animales: **Monocotyledones, Platanaceae, Mammalia, Ursidae.**
- Las palabras que constituyen el saludo de las cartas, comunicaciones, etc.: **Dear Father.**
- Las palabras State, Territory, Dominion, Province, Department, etc., cuando forman parte del nombre de una división determinada: **the State of Texas, the Dominion of Canada.**
- La palabra Church cuando se aplica a una iglesia determinada: **Roman Catholic Church, St. Peter's Church.**
- **I** (pronombre, *yo*) y **O** (interjeccion).

A

A, a (ei) *s.* A, a [vocal]. *2* MÚS. la.
a *art. indef.* un, una. V. ARTÍCULO (cuadro gramatical). *2* un tal, cierto: ~ *Mr. Brown,* un tal (o cierto) señor Brown. *3* el, la, al, a la, por, cada [con valor distributivo]: *two dollars* ~ *yard,* dos dólares la (o cada) yarda. *4 what* ~...!, ¡qué...! *5 such* ~..., tal..., tan...
Aaron (e·ørøn) *n. pr.* Aarón.
abaca (abaka·) *s.* abacá.
aback (abæk·k) *adv.* atrás, hacia atrás. *2* MAR. en facha. *3* fig. *to take* ~, sorprender, desconcertar.
abacus (æ·bakøs) *s.* ábaco.
abaft (abæ·ft) *adv.* MAR. a popa, hacia popa.
abandon (abæ·ndøn) *s.* abandono, naturalidad, desenvoltura. *2* desenfreno.
abandon (to) *tr.* abandonar. *2 ref.* abandonarse, entregarse.
abandoned (-d) *adj* abandonado. *2* vicioso, depravado.
abandonment (-mønt) *s.* abandono, dejación; entrega de sí mismo. *2* abandono, desamparo. *3* desenfreno.
abase (to) (abei·s) *tr.* humillar. *2* rebajar, envilecer.
abasement (-mønt) *s.* humillación. *2* degradación, envilecimiento.
abash (to) (abæ·sh) *tr.* correr, avergonzar, confundir, desconcertar.
abashment (-mønt) *s.* vergüenza, confusión.
abate (to) (abei·t) *tr.* rebajar, reducir, disminuir, moderar. *2* deducir, quitar. *3* DER. suprimir, anular. *4 intr.* menguar, disminuir, amainar, calmarse, ceder, remitir.
abatement (-mønt) *s.* disminución. *2* mitigación, moderación. *3* rebaja, deducción. *4* DER. supresión, anulación.
abatis (æ·batis) *s.* FORT. tala.
abattoir (æbætua·ʳ) *s.* matadero.
abbacy (æ·basi) *s.* abadía, abadiado, abiadato.
abbatial (æbei·shal) *adj.* abacial, abadengo.
abbess (æ·bis) *f.* abadesa.
abbey (æ·bi) *s.* abadía, monasterio.
abbot (æ·bøt) *m.* abad.
abbotship (-ship) *s.* ABBACY.
abbreviate (to) (abri·vieit) *tr.* abreviar.
abbreviation (-ei·shøn) *s.* abreviación. *2* abreviatura.
abbreviature (-viachuʳ) *s.* compendio, resumen.

abdicate (to) (æ·bdikeit) *intr.* abdicar.
abdication (-kei·shøn) *s.* abdicación.
abdomen (æ·bdømen) *s.* abdomen.
abdominal (æbda·minɑl) *adj.* abdominal.
abdominous (-nøs) *adj.* panzudo.
abducent (æbdiu·sønt) *adj.* FISIOL. abductor.
abduct (to) (æbdø·kt) *tr.* raptar, secuestrar. *2* FISIOL. producir la abducción de.
abduction (æbdø·kshøn) *s.* rapto, robo, secuestro. *2* FISIOL. abducción.
abductor (æbdø·ktøʳ) *s.* raptor, secuestrador. *2* ANAT. abductor.
abeam (abɪ·m) *adv.* MAR. por el través.
abed (abe·d) *adv.* en cama, acostado.
abelmosk (ei·bølmask) *s.* BOT. abelmosco.
aberrance, -cy (æbe·rans, -si) *s.* error, extravío. *2* H. NAT. anormalidad.
aberrant (æbe·rant) *s.* aberrante, extraviado.
aberration (æbørei·shøn) *s.* aberración.
abet (to) (abe·t) *tr.* alentar, consentir, ayudar [delito o delincuente]. ¶ Pret. y p. p.: *abetted;* ger.: *-tting.*
abetment (-mønt) *s.* ayuda, complicidad.
abetter, abettor (abe·tør) *s.* fautor, instigador, cómplice.
abhor (to) (æbjo·ʳ) *tr.* aborrecer, detestar, repugnar.
abhorrence (æbjo·røns) *s.* aborrecimiento, detestación.
abhorrent (-rønt) *adj.* aborrecible, detestable. *2* opuesto, incompatible. *3* que aborrece.
abidance (abai·dans) *s.* estancia, permanencia. *2* observancia [de leyes, reglas, etc.].
abide (to) (abai·d) *intr.* morar, habitar. *2* quedarse, permanecer. *3* mantenerse, continuar [en un estado o condición]. *4 to* ~ *by,* apoyar, estar con o por; mantener [lo dicho, una opinión, etc.]; cumplir, observar; conformarse con, atenerse a. *5 tr.* esperar, aguardar. *6* sufrir, tolerar, aguantar. ¶ Pret. y p. p.: *abode* o *abided.*
abiding (abai·ding) *adj.* permanente, durable. *2* observante. *3* ~ *place,* domicilio, morada.
Abietineae (æbieti·nii) *s. pl.* BOT. abietáceas.
abigail (æ·bigeil) *s.* fig. doncella, camarera.
ability (abi·liti) *s.* habilidad, capacidad, talento, aptitud, ingenio. *2* poder, facultad; posibilidades.
abintestate (æbinte·steit) *adj.* abintestato.

abject (æ·bdẏekt) *adj.* abyecto.
abjection (æbdẏe·kshøn), abjectness (-tnis) *s.* abyección.
abjuration (æbdẏurei·shøn) *s.* abjuración.
abjure (to) (æbdẏū·ʳ) *tr.* abjurar.
ablation (æblei·shøn) *s.* ablación.
ablative (æ·blativ) *adj.-s.* ablativo.
ablaze (ablei·ŝ) *adv.* y *adj.* ardiendo, en llamas. *2 adj.* resplandeciente. *3* fig. encendido.
able (ei·bøl) *adj.* que puede: *to be ~,* poder. *2* hábil, diestro, capaz, competente. *3* DER. capaz.
able-bodied *adj.* sano, robusto, válido.
abloom (ablu·m) *adj.* y *adv.* en flor; floreciente.
ablush (ablø·sh) *adj.* y *adv.* ruborizado.
ablution (æblu·shøn) *s.* ablución.
ably (ei·bli) *adv.* hábilmente, inteligentemente.
abnegate (to) (æ·bnigeit) *tr.* renunciar, negarse [algo] a sí mismo. *2* abjurar.
abnegation (-gei·shøn) *s.* renuncia, abnegación.
abnormal (æbno·ʳmal) *adj.* anormal.
abnormality (-mæ·liti) *s.* anormalidad.
abnormity (-miti) *s.* anomalía; monstruosidad.
aboard (abo·ʳd) *adv.* a bordo. *2* en un tren, etc.: *all ~!,* ¡viajeros al tren! *3* MAR. junto a: *to keep the land ~,* costear.
abode (abou·d) *pret.* y *p. p.* de TO ABIDE. *2 s.* morada, domicilio. *3* estancia [en un lugar].
abolish (to) (aba·lish) *tr.* abolir, suprimir.
abolishment (-mønt), abolition (æboli·shøn) *s.* abolición, supresión.
abolitionist (-ist) *s.* abolicionista.
A-bomb (ei·bam) *s.* bomba atómica.
abominable (aba·minabøl) *adj.* abominable.
abominate (to) (aba·mineit) *tr.* abominar, abominar de.
abomination (-nei·shøn) *s.* abominación.
aboriginal (æbori·dẏinal) *adj.-s.* aborigen.
aborigines (-dẏinis) *s. pl.* aborígenes.
abort (to) (abo·t) *intr.* abortar.
abortion (abo·ʳshøn) *s.* aborto. *2* fracaso.
abortive (abo·ʳtiv) *adj.-s.* abortivo. *2 adj.* abortado, malogrado.
abound (to) (aba·nd) *intr.* abundar.
about (abau·t) *prep.* cerca de, junto a, alrededor, en torno de. *2* por, en [un espacio, lugar, etc.]: *to play ~ the garden,* jugar en el jardín. *3* encima, consigo, en [una pers. o cosa]: *have you much money ~ you?,* ¿lleva usted mucho dinero [encima]? *4* tocante a, con respecto a, sobre, acerca de, de, en: *to speak ~,* hablar de; *to think ~,* pensar en. *5* poco más o menos, sobre, cosa de, unos, unas. *6* hacia, a eso de: *~ three o'clock,* a eso de las tres. *7* ocupado en, cuidando de. *8 to be ~ to* [con un inf.], estar a punto de, estar para, ir a. *9 adv.* alrededor, en torno, por todas partes, aquí y allí, circularmente, en contorno: *all ~,* por todas partes. *10* casi, aproximadamente. *11* en sentido o posición opuesta: *to face ~,* volverse, dar media vuelta.
about-face *s.* media vuelta.
above (abø·v) *prep.* sobre, encima de, por encima de; superior a, fuera de: *~ zero,* sobre cero; *~ my strength,* superior a mis fuerzas; *~ my reach,* fuera de mi alcance; *~ mean actions,* incapaz de acciones mezquinas. *2* arriba de, más de o más que. *3 ~ all,* sobre todo, principalmente.
4 adv. arriba, en lo alto. *5* antes, anteriormente, más arriba [en un escrito].
6 adj. antedicho, arriba expresado; anterior, precedente. *7 s.* lo antedicho, lo dicho o mencionado más arriba.

aboveboard (-boʳd) *adv.* abiertamente, francamente. *2 adj.* franco, sincero.
abracadabra (æbrakadæ·bra) *s.* abracadabra.
abrade (to) (æbrei·d) *tr.* desgastar.
Abraham (ei·brajæm) *n. pr.* Abrahán.
abrasion (æbrei·ẏøn) *s.* abrasión.
abrasive (æbrei·siv) *adj.-s.* abrasivo.
abreast (abre·st) *adv.* de frente [uno al lado de otro]: *four ~,* a cuatro de frente. *2 to keep ~ of the times,* estar al día. *3* MAR. por el través.
abridge (to) (abri·dẏy) *tr.* abreviar, acortar. *2* resumir, compendiar. *3* privar, despojar.
abridg(e)ment (-mønt) *s.* abreviación, acortamiento. *2* compendio. *3* privación, merma.
abroad (abro·d) *adv.* fuera de casa; en el extranjero, al extranjero. *2* sobre un gran espacio, hasta lejos. *3* suelto, en libertad; en circulación por todas partes: *to set ~,* divulgar, propalar; *there is a rumor ~,* corre la voz. *4 to be all ~,* estar equivocado.
abrogate (to) (æ·brogeit) *tr.* abrogar.
abrupt (abrø·pt) *adj.* abrupto, escarpado. *2* brusco. *3* precipitado, súbito. *4* inconexo [estilo].
abruption (-shøn) *s.* rotura, desgajamiento.
abruptness (-nis) *s.* escabrosidad [de un terreno]. *2* brusquedad. *3* precipitación.
abscess (æ·bses) *s.* MED. absceso.
abscissa (æbsi·sa) *s.* GEOM. abscisa.
abscission (-shøn) *s.* CIR. abscisión.
abscond (to) (æbsca·nd) *intr.* esconderse. *2* huir, substraerse a la justicia.
absence (æ·bsøns) *s.* ausencia: *leave of ~,* permiso [a un militar o funcionario]. *2* falta de asistencia. *3* falta, carencia. *4 ~ of mind,* distracción, abstracción.
absent (æ·bsønt) *adj.* ausente. *2* distraído.
absent oneself (to) (æbse·nt) *ref.* ausentarse.
absentee (æbsøntı·) *s.* ausente. *2* absentista.
absenteeism (-iŝm) *s.* absentismo. *2* costumbre de faltar al trabajo.
absent-minded *adj.* distraído, abstraído.
absinth, absinthe (æ·bsinz) *s.* ajenjo.
absolute (æ·bsoliut) *adj.* absoluto. *2* categórico. *3* autoritario, perentorio. *4 s.* lo absoluto.
absolutely (-li) *adv.* absolutamente. *2* categóricamente, terminantemente.
absolution (æ·bsoliu·shøn) *s.* absolución.
absolutism (æ·bsoliutiŝm) *s.* absolutismo.
absolutist (-ist) *adj.-s.* absolutista.
absolve (to) (æbsa·lv) *tr.* absolver. *2* perdonar, remitir.
absorb (to) (æbsoʳb) *tr.* absorber. *2 ref.* abstraerse, enfrascarse.
absorbed (-d) *adj.* absorbido. *2* embebido, absorto.
absorbent (-ønt) *adj.-s.* absorbente: *~ cotton,* algodón hidrófilo.
absorber (-øʳ) *s.* absorbente. *2* MEC. amortiguador.
absorbing (-ing) *adj.* absorbente [que interesa o preocupa].
absorption (æbso·ʳoshøn) *s.* absorción. *2* embebecimiento, enfrascamiento.
abstain (to) (æbstei·n) *intr.* abstenerse.
abstainer (-øʳ) *s.* abstemio.
abstemious (æbstı·miøs) *adj.* abstemio. *2* sobrio, templado. *3* de abstinencia [día].
abstention (æbste·nshøn) *s.* abstención.
abstergent (æbstø·ʳdẏønt) *adj.-s.* abstergente.
abstersion (-shøn) *s.* abtersión.
abstinence, abstinency (æ·bstinøns, -i) *s.* abstinencia. *2* sobriedad, templanza.
abstinent (æ·bstinønt) *adj.* abstinente.

abstract (æ·bstrækt) *adj.* abstracto: *in the* ~, en abstracto. *2 s.* extracto, resumen, compendio.
abstract (to) (æbstræ·kt) *tr.* abstraer. *2* sustraer, robar. *3* distraer [apartar la atención de uno]. *4* resumir, compendiar.
abstracted (æbstræ·ktid) *adj.* abstraído. *2* distraído.
abstraction (æbstræ·kshøn) *s.* abstracción. *2* distracción, ensimismamiento. *3* sustracción, hurto. *4* retiro, recogimiento.
abstractive (æbstræ·ktiv) *adj.* abstractivo.
abstruse (æbstru·s) *adj.* abstruso.
absurd (æbsø·ʳd) *adj.* absurdo.
absurdity (-iti) *s.* absurdidad, absurdo.
abulia (æbiu·lia) *s.* abulia.
abundance (abø·ndans) *s.* abundancia.
abundant (abø·ndant) *adj.* abundante: ~ *in* o *with*, abundante en, lleno de.
abuse (abiu·š) *s.* abuso. *2* corruptela. *3* maltrato, insultos, denuestos.
abuse (to) *tr.* abusar de. *2* maltratar, denostar, denigrar, hablar mal de.
abusive (abiu·siv) *adj.* abusivo. *2* injurioso, insultante.
abut (to) (abø·t) *intr. to* ~ *on, upon* o *against*, terminar en; lindar, confinar con; empalmar con; estribar en. ¶ Pret. y p. p.: *abutted;* ger.: *-tting.*
abutment (-mønt) *s.* punto donde estriba algo; estribo, contrafuerte. *2* contigüidad [de terrenos]; linde. *3* CARP. empalme.
abysm (abi·šm) *s.* ABYSS.
abysmal (-al) *adj.* ABYSSAL.
abyss (abi·s) *s.* abismo.
abyssal (abi·sal) *adj.* abismal, abisal. *2* insondable.
Abyssinia (æbisi·nia) *n. pr.* Abisinia.
Abyssinian (-n) *adj.-s.* abisinio.
acacia (akei·sha) *s.* BOT. acacia.
academic (ækade·mik) *adj.-s.* académico. *2 s.* universitario.
academical (-al) *adj.* académico. *2* teórico.
academicals (-s) *s. pl.* traje o distintivos usados en ciertas universidades.
academician (ækade·mishan) *s.* académico.
academy (akæ·dømi) *s.* academia. *2* colegio, escuela. *3* (con may.) Academia [de Platón].
acalephan (ækøle·fan) *adj.-s.* acalefo.
acanthaceous (ækænze·shøs) *adj.* acantáceo.
acanthopterygian (ækænzaptøri-ỹian) *adj.-s.* ICT. acantopterigio.
acanthus (ækæ·nzøs) *s.* BOT., ARQ. acanto.
acarid (æ·kørid) *s.* acárido.
acarus (æ·karøs), *pl.* **-ri** (-ri o -rai) *s.* ácaro.
acaulescent (ækole·sønt) *adj.* BOT. acaule.
accede (to) (æksi·d) *intr.* acceder, asentir. *2* ascender, subir [a un cargo o dignidad].
accelerate (to) (ækse·løreit) *tr* acelerar, apresurar. *2 intr.* acelerarse, apresurarse.
acceleration (-ei·shøn) *s.* aceleración.
accelerative (-tiv) *adj.* acelerador, -triz.
accelerator (-tør) *s.* acelerador.
accent (æ·ksent) *s.* acento. *2* dejo, tonillo.
accent (to) (ækse·nt) *tr.* acentuar.
accentuate (to) (ækse·nchueit) *tr.* acentuar. *2* intensificar.
accentuation (-ei·shøn) *s.* acentuación.
accept (to) (ækse·pt) *tr.* aceptar. *2* admitir [como cierto], creer. *3* entender, interpretar.
acceptable (-abøl) *adj.* aceptable, admisible. *2* acepto, grato, bien recibido.
acceptance (-ans) *s.* aceptación, admisión. *2* aceptación, buena acogida. *3* COM. aceptación.

acceptation (ei·shøn) *s.* acepción, sentido.
acceptor (-tøʳ) *s.* aceptador, aceptante.
acces (æ·kses) *s.* acceso [en todos sus sentidos]. *2* aumento, añadidura.
accessible (ækse·sibøl) *adj.* accesible. *2* asequible.
accession (-shøn) *s.* asentimiento. *2* entrada [en un grupo, etc.]. *3* advenimiento, subida [a un cargo o dignidad]. *4* aumento, agregación. *5* MED., DER. accesión.
accessit (-sit) *s.* accésit.
accessory (-sori) *adj.* accesorio, adicional. *2* que contribuye o tiene complicidad. *3 s.* accesorio. *4* cómplice, encubridor, inductor: ~ *after the fact,* encubridor; ~ *before the fact,* cómplice, inductor.
accidence (æ·ksidøns) *s.* GRAM. los accidentes.
accident (æ·ksidønt) *s.* accidente. *2* casualidad. *3* percance.
accidental (ækside·ntal) *adj.* accidental. *2* casual, imprevisto. *3 m.* accidente [lo no esencial]. *4* MÚS. accidental, accidente.
acclaim (æklei·m) *s.* aclamación [grito].
acclaim (to) *tr.-intr.* aclamar. *2* proclamar.
acclamation (ækl;amei·shøn) *s.* aclamación.
acclimate (to) (æklai·mit) *tr.-intr.* ACCLIMATIZE.
acclimation (æklimei·shøn), **acclimatization** (æklaimatišei·shøn) *s.* aclimatación.
acclimatize (to) (æklai·mataiš) *tr.* aclimatar. *2 intr.* aclimatarse.
acclivity (ækli·viti) *s.* cuesta, pendiente.
accolade (ækolei·d) *s.* acolada, espaldarazo. *2* MÚS. corchete, barra.
accommodate (to) (aka·modeit) *tr.* acomodar, ajustar, amoldar. *2* arreglar, reconciliar. *3* acomodar, proveer [de]; servir, hacer un favor [a]. *4* hospedar, alojar. *5 intr.* conformarse, avenirse. *6* tener cabida [para].
accommodating (-ing) *adj.* servicial, complaciente, amable.
accommodation (-ei·shøn) *s.* acomodación, adaptación. *2* acomodamiento, arreglo, conciliación. *3* complacencia, carácter servicial. *4* servicio, favor: ~ *bill,* o simplte. *accommodation,* letra de favor. *5* cabida, sitio; alojamiento [en un hotel]. *6* FISIOL. acomodación. *7 pl.* facilidades, comodidades.
accompaniment (akø·mpanimønt) *s.* acompañamiento.
accompanist (-nist) *s.* MÚS. acompañante.
accompany (to) (akø·mpani) *tr.* acompañar. ¶ Pret. y p. p.: *accompanied.*
accomplice (aka·mplis) *s.* cómplice.
accomplish (to) (aka·mplish) *tr.* hacer, ejecutar, acabar, llevar a cabo, cumplir. *2* lograr. *3* dotar, adornar [física o moralmente].
accomplished (-t) *adj.* cumplido, perfecto, consumado. *2* culto, instruido; distinguido.
accomplishment (-mønt) *s.* realización, ejecución, cumplimiento. *2* logro. *3 pl.* talentos, habilidades.
accord (aka·ʳd) *s.* acuerdo, concierto, armonía: *with one* ~, unánimemente, de consuno. *2* acuerdo, convenio. *3* MÚS. concordancia, acorde. *4 of one's own* ~, espontáneamente.
accord (to) *tr.* concordar, poner de acuerdo. *2* conciliar. *3* otorgar, conceder. *4 intr.* convenir, estar de acuerdo; concordar.
accordance (-ans) *s.* acuerdo, conformidad: *in* ~ *with,* de acuerdo con.
accordant (-ant) *adj.* acorde. *2* conforme, consonante, correspondiente.

according (-ing) *adj.* acorde, conforme, armónico. 2 ACCORDINGLY: ~ *to*, según, conforme a; ~ *to him*, según él.

accordingly (-li) *adv.* de conformidad, de acuerdo [con]. 2 en consecuencia, por lo tanto.

accordion (aka·ʳdiøn) *s.* acordeón.

accordionist (-ist) *s.* acordeonista.

accost (to) (aka·st) *tr.* abordar, hablar, dirigirse [a uno].

account (akau·nt) *s.* cuenta [cálculo, cómputo; estado de cantidades o partidas]: ~ *current*, cuenta corriente; *to settle accounts*, ajustar cuentas; *on* ~, a cuenta. 2 cuenta [que se da o pide]: *to call to* ~, pedir cuentas. 3 causa, razón, motivo: *on* ~ *of*, a causa de, en atención a; *on no* ~, de ningún modo. 4 explicación. 5 relación, informe, relato, descripción. 6 cuenta, interés: *for* ~ *of*, por cuenta de; *to turn to* ~, sacar provecho de, hacer útil. 7 importancia: *of no* ~, sin importancia, despreciable. 8 *to take into* ~, tener en cuenta.

account (to) *tr.* tener por, estimar, considerar, juzgar. 2 intr. *to* ~ *for*, responder de; dar cuenta de; explicar, justificar.

accountability (-abi·liti) *s.* responsabilidad.

accountable (-abøl) *adj.* responsable. 2 explicable.

accountant (-ant) *s.* contador, perito mercantil, tenedor de libros.

accounting (-ing) *s.* contabilidad. 2 estado de cuentas. 3 explicación, justificación.

accouter, accoutre (to) (aku·tøʳ) *tr.* vestir, ataviar, equipar.

accouterment, accoutrement (aku·tøʳmønt) *s.* vestido, atavíos. 2 equipo [del soldado].

accredit (to) (ækre·dit) *tr.* acreditar. | No tiene el sentido de abonar en cuenta. 2 creer, dar crédito. 3 atribuir, imputar.

accredited (-id) *adj.* acreditado. 2 creído, aceptado.

accrescent (ækre·sønt) *adj.* BOT. acrescente.

accretion (ækri·shøn) *s.* acrecimiento. 2 MINER. acreción. 3 DER. accesión.

accrual (ækru·øl) *s.* incremento, acumulación.

accrue (to) (ækru·) *intr.* aumentar, crecer, acumularse. 2 provenir, resultar.

accumulate (to) (akiu·miuleit) *tr.* acumular; atesorar. 2 intr. aumentar, acumularse.

accumulation (-lei·shøn) *s.* acumulación, amontonamiento. 2 pl. ahorros.

accumulative (-iv) *adj.* acumulativo. 2 acumulado.

accumulator (-øʳ) *s.* acumulador, amontonador. 2 ELECT. acumulador.

accuracy (æ·kiurøsi) *s.* exactitud, corrección, precisión. 2 cuidado, esmero.

accurate (æ·kiurit) *adj.* exacto, correcto, fiel. 2 preciso, de precisión. 3 cuidadoso, esmerado.

accurateness (-nis) *s.* ACCURACY.

accursed, accurst (akø·ʳst) *adj.* maldito, maldecido. 2 execrable. 3 afligido, perseguido [por una enfermedad, la desgracia]. 4 infausto.

accusal (akiu·šal) *s.* ACCUSATION.

accusation (akiušei·shøn) *s.* acusación. 2 denuncia. 3 imputación, cargo.

accusative (akiu·šativ) *adj.-s.* GRAM. *1* acusativo.

accusatory (-tori) *adj.* acusatorio.

accuse (to) (akiu·š) *tr.* acusar, denunciar. 2 culpar, tachar, tildar [de].

accused (-d) *s.* acusado.

accuser (-øʳ) *s.* acusador.

accustom (to) (akø·støm) *tr.* acostumbrar.

accustomed (-d) *adj.* acostumbrado, avezado; que acostumbra. 2 acostumbrado, usual.

ace (eis) *s.* as. 2 punto, tanto. 3 *within an* ~ *of*, a punto de, a dos dedos de.

acephalous (eise·faløs) *adj.* acéfalo.

acerb (asø·ʳb) *adj.* acerbo.

acerbate (to) (æ·sø·ʳbeit) *tr.* agriar. 2 exasperar.

acerbity (æsø·ʳbiti) *s.* acerbidad, aspereza, rigor.

acescent (æse·sønt) *adj.* acescente.

acetabulum (æsitæ·biuløm) *s.* acetábulo.

acetate (æ·siteit) *s.* acetato.

acetic (æsı·tic) *adj.* acético.

acetone (æ·sitoun) *s.* QUÍM. acetona.

acetose (æsi·tous), **acetous** (-tøs) *adj.* acetoso.

acetylene (æse·tilin) *s.* acetileno.

Achaea (akı·a) *n. pr.* Acaya.

Achaean (akı·an) *adj.-s.* aqueo.

ache (eich) *s.* nombre de la letra *h*.

ache (eik) *s.* dolor [continuo]; achaque, mal.

ache (to) *intr.* doler [dar dolor]: *my head aches*, me duele la cabeza. 2 sentir pena, sufrir. 3 *to* ~ *to*, desear, anhelar.

achene (akı·n) *s.* BOT. aquenio.

achieve (to) *tr.* acabar, llevar a cabo, realizar. 2 lograr, conseguir. 3 intr. triunfar.

achievement (-mønt) *s.* realización, ejecución. 2 logro. 3 proeza, hazaña.

Achilles (akı·lıš) *n. pr.* Aquiles.

aching (ei·ng) *adj.* dolorido, doliente. 2 deseoso, anheloso. 3 *s.* dolencia. 4 dolor, pena. 5 anhelo.

achromatism (ækrou·matišm) *s.* acromatismo.

acicular (æsi·kiular) *adj.* acicular.

acid (æ·sid) *adj.-s.* ácido. 2 *adj.* acre, mordaz.

acidity (æsi·diti), **acidness** (æ·sidnis) *s.* acidez. 2 acritud.

acidulate (to) (æsi·diuleit) *tr.* acidular.

acidulous (-løs) *adj.* acídulo.

acierate (to) (æ·siøreit) *tr.* acerar.

acknowledge (to) (ækna·lidẙ) *tr.* reconocer, confesar. 2 agradecer. 3 *to* ~ *receipt*, acusar recibo. 4 der. autenticar.

acknowledgement (-mønt) *s.* reconocimiento, confesión. 2 expresión de gratitud. 3 acuse de recibo. 4 der. autenticación.

ıcme (æ·mi) *s.* pináculo, punto culminante, apogeo. 2 MED. acmé.

acne (æ·kni) *s.* MED. acné, barros.

acolyte (æ·kolait) *s.* acólito.

acolythate (æka·lizeit) *s.* acolitado.

aconite (æ·konait) *s.* acónito.

acorn (ei·koʳn) *s.* bellota.

acotyledonous (eikatili·dønøs) *adj.* acotiledóneo.

acoustic (aku·stic) *adj.* acústico.

acoustics (-s) *s.* acústica.

acquaint (to) (akuei·nt) *tr.* enterar, informar, familiarizar, hacer saber o conocer: *to be acquainted with*, saber, estar enterado de; conocer, tener trato con.

acquaintance (-ans) *s.* conocimiento [de una cosa]. 2 trato, relación. 3 conocido [pers.].

acquaintanceship (-ship) *s.* conocimiento, trato, relaciones.

acquiesce (to) (ækuie·s) *intr.* asentir, consentir, conformarse, allanarse.

acquiescence (-øns) *s.* aquiescencia, conformidad.

acquiescent (-ønt) *adj.* anuente, conforme.

acquire (to) (akuai·ʳ) *tr.* adquirir. 2 contraer [hábitos, etc.].

acquirement (-mønt) *s.* adquisición. 2 pl. saber, conocimientos.

acquisition (ækuiši·shøn) *s.* adquisición.

acquisitive (ækui·šitiv) *adj.* adquisitivo. 2 codicioso, ahorrativo.

acquit (to) (*akui·t*) *tr.* descargar [de una deuda, etc.]. 2 absolver [declarar inocente]. 3 pagar, satisfacer. 4 *ref.* desempeñar [un cometido], cumplir, portarse: *to ~ oneself well,* portarse bien; quedar bien, lucirse. ¶ Pret. y p. p.: *acquitted;* ger.: *-tting.*

acquittal (*-al*) *s.* descargo [de deuda]. 2 recibo, quitanza, finiquito.

acre (ei·køʳ) *s.* acre [40.47 a.].

acreage (ei·køridẏ) *s.* extensión en acres.

acrid (æ·krid) *adj.* acre.

acridity (ækri·diti) *s.* acritud, acrimonia.

acrimonious (ækrimou·niøs) *adj.* acre. 2 áspero, mordaz, sarcástico.

acrimoniousness (-nis), **acrimony** (æ·krimouni) *s.* acritud, acrimonia. 2 aspereza, mordacidad.

acritude (æ·kritiud) *s.* acritud.

acrobat (æ·krobæt) *s.* acróbata.

acrobatic (æ·krobæ·tic) *adj.* acrobático.

acrobatics (-s), **acrobatism** (æ·krobatišm) *s.* acrobacia, acrobatismo.

acromion (ækrou·mian) *s.* ANAT. acromio(n.

acropolis (ækra·polis) *s.* acrópolis.

across (akro·s) *prep.* a través, por, sobre, de una parte a otra de: *~ country,* a campo traviesa. 2 al otro lado de: *~ the way,* enfrente, en la acera de enfrente. 3 atravesado, cruzando. 4 *to come* o *to run ~,* tropezar, topar con. 5 *adv.* de través, al través, al otro lado, cruzado, en cruz. 6 ELECT. en paralelo.

acrostic (akro·stic) *adj.-s.* acróstico.

acroterium (ækrotı·triøm) *s.* ARQ. acrotera.

acrylic (akri·lik) *adj.* QUÍM. acrílico.

act (ækt) *s.* acto, hecho, acción: *~ of God,* fuerza mayor, caso fortuito; *in the (very) ~,* in fraganti. 2 TEAT. acto. 3 ley, decreto. 4 *pl.* actos [de los apóstoles].

act (to) *intr.* obrar, actuar, conducirse, portarse: *to ~ as,* hacer de; *to ~ for,* representar [a uno]. 2 funcionar [un órgano]. 3 obrar, influir. 4 TEAT. representar. 5 fingir. 6 *tr.* interpretar, desempeñar [un papel]; fingirse. 7 fingir, simular. 8 interinar.

acting (æ·kting) *adj.* que obra. 2 interino, suplente. 3 que finge. 4 *s.* acción, efecto. 5 TEAT. desempeño. 6 fingimiento.

actinia (ækti·nia) *s.* actinia.

actinic (ækti·nic) *adj.* actínico.

actinism (æ·ktinišm) *s.* actinismo.

actinium (ækti·niøm) *s.* QUÍM. actinio.

action (æ·kshøn) *s.* acción: *to take ~,* tomar medidas; DER. proceder [contra]. | No tiene el sentido de acción de una compañía anónima. 2 mecanismo [de un piano, órgano, etc.]. 3 cierre [de fusil].

actionable (-abøl) *adj.* DER. perseguible.

activate (to) (æ·ktiveit) *tr.* QUÍM., BIOL. activar.

active (æ·ktiv) *adj.* activo. 2 vivo, ligero. 3 vigoroso, enérgico. 4 en actividad. 5 vigente.

actively (-li) *adv.* activamente. 2 acuciosamente.

activity (ækti·viti) *s.* actividad, agilidad, vivacidad, vigor. 2 *pl.* actividades.

actor (æ·ktøʳ) *s.* actor [en un suceso]. 2 TEAT., DER. actor.

actress (æ·ktris) *s.* actriz.

actual (æ·kchual) *adj.* real, efectivo, de hecho; propiamente dicho. 2 actual.

actuality (ækchuæ·liti) *s.* realidad.

actually (æ·kchuali) *adv.* realmente, efectivamente, de hecho.

actuary (æ·kchueri) *s.* escribano. 2 actuario de seguros.

actuate (to) (æ·kchueit) *tr.* actuar, poner en acción; mover, impulsar.

acuity (akiu·iti) *s.* acuidad, agudeza.

acumen (akiu·min) *s.* cacumen, perspicacia.

acuminate (-eit) *adj.* BOT. acuminado.

acute (akiu·t) *adj.* agudo.

acute-angled *adj.* GEOM. acutángulo.

acuteness (akiu·tnis) *s.* agudeza [intensidad; sutileza; perspicacia].

ad (æd) *s.* fam. anuncio [en los periódicos].

adage (æ·didẏ) *s.* adagio, refrán.

adagio (ada·dẏou) *s.* MÚS. adagio.

Adam (æ·dam) *n. pr.* Adán: *Adam's apple,* fam. nuez [de la garganta].

adamant (æ·damænt) *s.* adamante. 2 *adj.* adamantino. 3 inexorable.

adamantine (ædamæ·ntin) *adj.* adamantino.

adapt (to) (adæ·pt) *tr.* adaptar.

adaptable (adæ·ptabøl) *adj.* adaptable. 2 aplicable.

adaptation (ædæptei·shøn) *s.* adaptación.

adapter (adæ·ptøʳ) *s.* adaptador. 2 QUÍM. alargadera.

add (to) (æd) *tr.* añadir, agregar. 2 *tr.-intr.* sumar: *to ~ up,* sumar, totalizar. 3 *to ~ to,* aumentar, acrecentar.

addendum (æde·ndøm), *pl.* **-da** (-dæ) *s.* adición, aditamento. 2 *pl.* addenda.

adder (æ·døʳ) *s.* ZOOL. víbora. 2 culebra.

addict (æ·dikt) *s.* persona aficionada al uso de [un narcótico, etc.].

addict (to) (adi·kt) *tr.* dedicar, aplicar, consagrar. 2 *ref.* dedicarse, entregarse, darse (a).

addicted (-id) *adj.* aficionado, dado, entregado (a). 2 apasionado (por), partidario [de].

addiction (adi·kshøn) *s.* afición, apego.

addition (ædi·shøn) *s.* adición, añadidura; aditamento: *in ~ to,* además de. 3 ARIT. adición, suma.

additional (-al) *adj.* adicional. 2 *s.* aditamento.

addle (æ·døl) *adj.* huero, podrido, vacío, vano.

addle (to) *tr.* enhuerar. 2 hacer estéril. 3 embrollar, confundir.

addle-brained, addle-pated *adj.* mentecato.

address (æ·dres o adre·s) *s.* discurso, plática, alocución. 2 dedicatoria. 3 acción o manera de hablar a otro; palabra: *form of ~,* tratamiento. 4 dirección, sobrescrito. 5 destreza, habilidad. 6 garbo, donaire. 7 *pl.* corte, galanteo.

address (to) *tr.* dirigir [la palabra, un ruego, etc.]. 2 dirigir la palabra, arengar, hacer una petición a [uno o unos]. 3 dirigir, enviar. 4 COM. consignar. 5 cortejar, galantear. 6 *ref.* dirigirse [a una pers.]; dedicarse, aplicarse.

addressee (adre·si) *s.* destinatario.

adduce (to) (ædiu·s) *tr.* aducir.

adduction (ædø·kshøn) *s.* aducción.

adductor (ædø·ktøʳ) *s.* ANAT. músculo aductor.

Adele (æde·l) *n. pr.* Adela.

adenoid (æ·dønoid) *adj.* adenoideo. 2 *s. pl.* vegetaciones adenoideas.

adept (ade·pt) *adj.* y *s.* adepto, iniciado. 2 experto, perito.

adequacy (æ·dikuøsi) *s.* calidad de adecuado. 2 suficiencia.

adequate (æ·dikuit) *adj.* adecuado, proporcionado, suficiente.

adhere (to) (ædjɪ·ʳ) *intr.* adherir, adherirse. *2* tener apego.
adherence (-øns) *s.* adhesión, apego.
adherent (-ønt) *adj.* adherente. *2* adhesivo. *3 s.* adherido, adicto, partidario, seguidor.
adherer (-øʳ) *s.* ADHERENT.
adhesion (ædjɪ·ȳøn) *s.* adherencia. *2* adhesión.
adhesive (ædjɪ·siv) *adj.-s.* adhesivo.
adieu (adiu·) *interj.* ¡adiós! *2 s.* adiós, despedida: *to bid* ~, despedirse.
adipose (æ·dipous) *adj.* adiposo.
adit (æ·dit) *s.* MIN. socavón. *2* entrada, acceso.
adjacent (ædȳei·sønt) *adj.* adyacente.
adjectival (ædjektai·val) *adj.* adjetival, adjetivo.
adjective (æ·djektiv) *adj.-s.* adjetivo.
adjoin (to) (adȳoi·n) *tr.* unir, anexar. *2* asociar. *3* lindar con. *4 intr.* lindar, colindar, estar contiguo.
adjoining (-ing) *adj.* contiguo, inmediato.
adjourn (to) (adȳø·ʳn) *tr.* aplazar, trasladar, suspender. *2 intr.* levantar la sesión. *3* levantarse, suspenderse [la sesión]; terminar sus sesiones [una asamblea]. *4* trasladarse.
adjournment (-mønt) *s.* aplazamiento, suspensión, clausura. *2* DER. espera.
adjudge (to) (adȳø·dȳ) *tr.* adjudicar. *2* juzgar [un asunto]; decidir, sentenciar. *3 intr.* fallar, dictar sentencia.
adjudgement (-mønt) *s.* adjudicación. *2* decisión, fallo.
adjudicate (to) (adȳu·dikeit) *tr.* declarar judicialmente. *2* juzgar [un asunto]. *3 intr.* juzgar, actuar como juez.
adjudication (adȳudikei·shøn) *s.* juicio, fallo.
adjunct (æ·dȳønkt) *adj.* adjunto, accesorio. *2 s.* aditamento, cosa accesoria. *3* adjunto, ayudante. *4* GRAM. modificativo.
adjunction (ædȳø·nkshøn) *s.* adjunción, agregación.
adjuration (ædȳurei·shøn) *s.* conjuro, ruego encarecido, orden solemne.
adjure (to) (adȳu·ʳ) *tr.* conjurar, rogar encarecidamente, ordenar solemnemente.
adjust (to) (adȳø·st) *tr.* ajustar, areglar [diferencias, cuentas, etc.]. *2* ajustar, acomodar, adaptar. *3* reglar, graduar, enfocar, ajustar [un instrumento]. *4 intr.* ajustarse, acomodarse.
adjuster (-øʳ) *s.* ajustador. *2* mediador. *3* comisario de averías. *4* MEC. mecanismo regulador.
adjustment (-mønt) *s.* arreglo, composición. *2* liquidación (de cuentas). *3* acomodación, adaptación. *4* regulación, corrección (de un instrumento).
adjutancy (æ·dȳutansi) *s.* ayudantía.
adjutant (æ·dȳutant) *s.* ayudante. *2* ORN. marabú de la India.
adjuvant (ædȳu·vant) *adj.* adyuvante.
adminicle (ædmi·nikøl) *s.* adminículo, ayuda.
administer (to) (ædmi·nistøʳ) *tr.-intr.* administrar. *2 tr.* dar, propinar. *3* dirigir [los negocios públicos]; ejercer [un cargo]; aplicar [las leyes]. *4 to* ~ *an oath*, tomar juramento. *5* intr. *to* ~ *to*, contribuir a.
administration (ædministrei·shøn) *s.* administración [acción]. *2* dirección, gobierno. *3* gobierno, ministerio; tiempo que dura el mando de un gobierno, un ministro, etc.
administrative (ædmi·nistreitiv) *adj.* administrativo. *2* gubernativo.
administrator (-treitøʳ) *s.* administrador; gobernante, director. *2* DER. curador.

admirable (æ·dmirabøl) *adj.* admirable.
admiral (æ·dmiral) *s.* almirante. *2* capitana [nave].
admiralty (æ·dmiralti) *s.* almirantazgo. *2* ministerio de marina. *3 Court of* ~, tribunal marítimo; ~ *law*, derecho marítimo, código marítimo.
Admiralty Islands *s. pl.* GEOGR. Islas Almirantes.
admiration (ædmirei·shøn) *s.* admiración.
admire (to) (ædmai·ʳ) *tr.* admirar. *2 intr.* admirarse.
admirer (-øʳ) *s.* admirador. *2* apasionado, gran aficionado.
admiring (-ing) *adj.* admirativo. *2* admirado [que admira]. *3* enamorado.
admissible (ædmi·sibøl) *adj.* admisible, concesible. *2* lícito, permitido.
admission (ædmi·shøn) *s.* admisión, entrada, acceso. *2* precio de la entrada. *3* ingreso, entrada [en una escuela, etc.]. *4* reconocimiento [de la certeza de una cosa], concesión.
admit (to) (ædmi·t) *tr.* admitir, dar entrada a. *2* reconocer, confesar, conceder. *3 intr. to* ~ *of*, admitir, permitir, sufrir. ¶ Pret. y p. p.: *admitted;* ger.: *admitting.*
admittance (-ans) *s.* admisión, entrada: *no* ~, se prohíbe la entrada.
admittedly (-itly) *adv.* reconocidamente.
admix (to) (æ·dmiks) *tr.* mezclar.
admixtion (-shøn), **admixture** (-chu·ʳ) *s.* mixtura, mezcla. *2* ingrediente.
admonish (to) (ædma·nish) *tr.* advertir, prevenir. *2* amonestar, exhortar.
admonishment (-mønt), **admonition** (-i·shøn) *s.* advertencia, admonición. *2* amonestación, exhortación.
admonitive (ædma·nitiv), **admonitory** (-tori) *adj.* exhortatorio.
adnate (æ·dneit) *s.* adnato.
ado (adu·) *s.* ruido, alboroto, ajetreo; trabajo, dificultad.
adobe (dou·bi) *s.* (E.U.) adobe.
adolescence, -cy (ædole·søns, -i) *s.* adolescencia.
Adolph (æ·dalf) *n. pr.* Adolfo.
adonic (ada·nik) *adj.* y *s.* adónico.
Adonis (ada·nis) *n. pr.* y *s.* Adonis.
adopt (to) (ada·pt) *tr.* adoptar. *2* aprobar [una proposición].
adoption (ada·pshøn) *s.* adopción. *2* aprobación [de una proposición].
adoptive (ada·ptiv) *adj.* adoptivo.
adorable (ado·rabøl) *adj.* adorable.
adoration (ædorei·shøn) *s.* adoración. *2* culto, veneración.
adore (to) (ado·ʳ) *tr.* adorar.
adorer (ado·røʳ) *s.* adorador.
adorn (to) (ado·ʳn) *tr.* adornar, ornar.
adornment (-mønt) *s.* adorno, ornamento.
adrenalin (ædre·nalin) *s.* adrenalina.
Adrian (ei·drian) *n. pr.* Adrián. *2* Adriano.
Adriatic (eidriæ·tic) *adj.* y *s.* Adriático.
adrift (adri·ft) *adv.* y *adj.* MAR. a la deriva, al garete. *2* fig. sin rumbo; divagando.
adroit (adroi·t) *adj.* diestro, hábil.
adroitness (-nis) *s.* destreza, habilidad.
adulate (to) (æ·diuleit) *tr.* adular.
adulation (-ei·shøn) *s.* adulación.
adulator (æ·diuleitøʳ) *s.* adulador.
adulatress (-tris) *s.* aduladora.
adult (adø·lt) *adj.* y *s.* adulto.

adulterate (adø·ltøreit) *adj.* adúltero, adulterino. *2* falso, contrahecho.
adulterate (to) *tr.* adulterar, sofisticar.
adulteration (-ei·shøn) *s.* adulteración.
adulterer (-ø^r) *s.* adúltero.
adulteress (-is) *s.* adúltera.
adulterine (-in) *adj.* adulterino.
adulterize (to) (-aiš) *intr.* adulterar [cometer adulterio].
adulterous (-øs) *adj.* adúltero.
adultery (-i) *s.* adulterio.
adultness (adø·ltnis) *s.* edad adulta.
adumbrate (to) (ædø·mbreit) *tr.* bosquejar. *2* anunciar, presagiar. *3* sombrear.
adumbration (-brei·shøn) *s.* bosquejo. *2* anuncio, presagio. *3* sombra.
adust (adø·st) *adj.* adusto, abrasado, tostado.
advance (ædvæ·ns) *s.* avance. *2* adelanto. *3* progreso, mejora, ascenso. *3* anticipo. *4* alza, aumento [de precio o valor]. *5 in* ~, al frente, adelante; de antemano, por adelantado. *6 pl.* primeros pasos para entablar un asunto, una conversación, etc.; insinuaciones, proposiciones. *7 adj.* ~ *guard*, MIL. avanzada; ~ *payment*, adelanto, anticipo.
advance (to) *tr.* adelantar, avanzar. *2* ascender, promover [a uno]. *3* acrecentar, mejorar, fomentar. *4* apresurar. *5* adelantar, anticipar [dinero]. *6* proponer, insinuar, alegar, enunciar. *7* subir [el precio]. *8 intr.* adelantarse, avanzar. *9* adelantar, progresar; medrar. *10* subir [de precio].
advanced (ædvæ·nst) *adj.* avanzado. *2* superior [no elemental]: ~ *algebra*, álgebra superior. *3* ~ *in years*, entrado en años.
advancement (ædvæ·nsmønt) *s.* adelantamiento, fomento. *2* ascenso, promoción, elevación. *3* adelanto, progreso. *4* anticipo [de dinero].
advantage (ædvæ·ntiđy) *s.* ventaja [superioridad, condición favorable]; conveniencia, comodidad: *to hare the* ~ *of one*, llevar ventaja a uno; *to show to* ~, lucir, hacer brillar; *to take of*, aprovecharse de.
advantage (to) *tr.* adelantar, promover, favorecer, beneficiar.
advantageous (ædvantei·đyøs) *adj.* ventajoso, conveniente, provechoso, útil.
advent (æ·dvent) *s.* advenimiento. *2* adviento.
adventitious (ædventi·shøs) *adj.* adventicio.
adventive (ædven·tiv) *adj.* BOT. advenedizo.
adventure (ædven·chø^r) *s.* aventura. *2* especulación comercial.
adventure (to) *tr.* aventurar, arriesgar. *2 ref.* arriesgarse; atreverse, osar.
adventurer (-ø^r) *s.* aventurero.
adventuresome (-søm) *adj.* ADVENTUROUS.
adventuress (-is) *s.* aventurera.
adventurous (-øs) *adj.* aventurero, emprendedor, arrojado. *2* aventurado, arriesgado.
adverb (æ·dvø^rb) *s.* adverbio.
adverbial (ædvø·^rbial) *adj.* adverbial.
adversary (æ·dvø^rseri) *s.* adversario. *2 the Adversary*, el enemigo, Satanás.
adversative (ædvø·^rsativ) *adj.* adversativo.
adverse (æ·dvø^rs) *adj.* adverso.
adversity (ædvø·^rsiti) *s.* adversidad.
advert (to) (ædvø·^rt) *intr. to* ~ *to*, referirse, aludir a: hacer notar.
advertence, -cy (-øns, -i) *s.* advertencia, atención, cuidado.
advertent (-ønt) *adj.* atento, cuidadoso.

advertise o **-tize (to)** (ædvø·^rtaiš) *tr.* avisar, informar. *2 tr.-intr.* COM. anunciar.
advertisement (ædvø·^rtišmønt) *s.* aviso. *2* COM. anuncio.
advertiser o **-tizer** (ædvø·^rtai·šø^r) *s.* avisador. *2* anunciador, anunciante.
advertising (-ing) *s.* publicidad, propaganda.
advice (ædvai·s) *s.* consejo, dictamen, parecer. *2* COM. aviso, noticia.
advice-boat *s.* MAR. aviso [embarcación].
advisable (-šabøl) *adj.* aconsejable, prudente.
advise (to) (ædvai·š) *tr.* aconsejar. *2* avisar, advertir. *3 intr.* aconsejarse, consultar.
advised (-d) *adj.* avisado, aconsejado. *2* deliberado, premeditado.
advisedly (-li) *adv.* deliberadamente.
advisement (ædvai·šmønt) *s.* consideración, estudio.
adviser (-ø^r) *s.* aconsejador, consejero, asesor.
advisory (-ori) *adj.* asesor, consultivo.
advocacy (æ·dvocasi) *s.* abogacía, defensa. *2* intercesión.
advocate (æ·dvokeit) *s.* abogado, defensor, intercesor. *2* partidario.
advocate (to) *tr.* abogar por, en favor de; defender, propugnar.
adz, adze (adš) *s.* azuela.
ædile (ı·dail) *s.* edil.
Aegean (ıđÿı·an) *adj.* Egeo: ~ *Sea*, Mar Egeo.
ægis (ı·dÿis) *s.* égida, escudo.
Aeneas (ını·as) *n. pr.* Eneas.
Aeolian (ıou·lian) *adj.* eolio, eólico. *2* [con min.] *æolian harp*, arpa eólica.
Aeolus (ıou·løs) *n. pr.* MIT. Eolo.
aeon (ı·øn) *s.* eón. *2* evo.
aerate (to) (ei·øreit) *tr.* someter a la aeración.
aeration (eiørei·shøn) *s.* aeración.
aerial (ei·rial) *adj.* aéreo. *2* atmosférico. *3* etéreo. *4 s.* RADIO. antena.
aerie (e·ri) *s.* EYRIE.
aeriform (ei·rørifo^rm) *adj.* aeriforme.
aerobe (ei·øroub) *s.* aerobio.
aerodrome (ei·ørodroum) *s.* aeródromo.
aerodynamic (eiørodainæ·mik) *adj.* aerodinámico.
aerodynamics (-s) *s.* aerodinámica.
aerolite (ei·ørolait) *s.* aerolito.
aeromancy (ei·øromænsi) *s.* aeromancia.
aerometer (eiøra·mitø^r) *s.* aerómetro.
aeronaut (ei·øronot) *s.* aeronauta.
aeronautic (eiørono·tik) *adj.* aeronáutico.
aeronautics (-s) *s.* aeronáutica.
aeroplane (ei·øroplein) *s.* aeroplano.
aeroscope (ei·øroskoup) *s.* aeroscopio.
aerostat (ei·ørostæt) *s.* aerostato.
aerostatic (-stæ·tik) *adj.* aerostático.
aerostatics (-s) *s.* aerostática.
aerostation (-tei·shøn) *s.* aerostación.
aeroview (ei·øroviu) *s.* fotografía aérea.
Aesculapius (eskiulei·piøs) *n. pr.* Esculapio.
Aesop (ı·sap) *n. pr.* Esopo.
aesthete (e·szit) *s.* esteta.
aesthetic (esze·tik) *adj.* estético.
aesthetics (-s) *s.* estética.
aesthetician (-tishan) *s.* estético.
aestival (e·stival) *adj.* estival.
aether (ı·zø^r) *s.* éter.
aetherial (ıziri·al) *adj.* etéreo.
Aetna (e·tna) *n. pr.* Etna.
afar (afa·^r) *adv.* lejos, a lo lejos: ~ *off*, muy distante; *a lo lejos*.
affability (æfabi·liti) *s.* afabilidad.

affable (æ·fabøl) *adj.* afable.
affair (æfe·ʳ) *s.* asunto, negocio, cuestión, lance; amorío, aventura. *2* MIL. acción, encuentro. *3* objeto, cosa.
affect (to) (afe·kt) *tr.* tener afición a, gustar de. *2* frecuentar. *3* tomar [cierta forma, disposición, etc.]. *4* afectar, fingir. *5* afectar, alterar, influir en. *6* afectar, conmover.
affectation (æfektei·shøn) *s.* afectación.
affected (afe·ktid) *adj.* afectado. *2* dado a la afectación. *3* inclinado, afecto.
affecting (afe·kting) *adj.* conmovedor, patético. *2* concerniente a.
affection (afe·kshøn) *s.* afecto, cariño. *2* inclinación, propensión. *3* afección, impresión. *4* afecto [del alma]. *5* MED. afección. *6* cualidad, propiedad.
affectionate (-it) *adj.* afectuoso, cariñoso, tierno.
affective (afe·ktiv) *adj.* afectivo. *2* emotivo.
afferent (æ·førønt) *adj.* aferente.
affiance (afai·ans) *s.* confianza. *2* palabra de casamiento, esponsales.
affiance (to) *tr.-ref.* prometer en matrimonio.
affidavit (æfidei·vit) *s.* declaración jurada; afidávit.
affiliate (afi·lieit) *adj.-s.* afiliado.
affiliate (to) *tr.* afiliar, asociar. *2* adoptar, prohijar. *3* establecer o atribuir la paternidad de; referir a un origen. *4* intr. to ~ with, afiliarse a.
affiliation (-ei·shøn) *s.* afiliación. *2* prohijamiento. *3* atribución de la paternidad u origen.
affined (afai·nd) *adj.* afín.
affinity (afi·niti) *s.* afinidad.
affirm (to) (afø·ʳm) *tr.* afirmar, aseverar. *2* DER. confirmar, ratificar [un fallo, etc.].
affirmation (æfø·ʳmei·shøn) *s.* afirmación, aserción. *2* DER. confirmación, ratificación.
affirmative (afø·ʳmativ) *adj.* afirmativo. *2 s.* afirmativa.
affix (æ·fiks) *s.* añadidura. *2* afijo.
affix (to) *tr.* pegar, añadir. *2* poner [una firma, un sello, etc.]. *3* atribuir, aplicar. *4* afijar.
afflatus (æflei·tøs) *s.* aflato, inspiración.
afflict (to) (afli·kt) *tr.* afligir. *2* aquejar: to be afflicted with, padecer de.
afflicting (-ing) *adj.* aflictivo, penoso.
affliction (afli·kshøn) *a.* aflicción. *2* desgracia, calamidad. *3* achaque, mal.
affluence (æfluøns) *s.* afluencia, aflujo. *2* afluencia, abundancia. *3* riqueza, opulencia.
affluent (æ·fluønt) *adj.* abundante. *2* rico, opulento. *3 s.* GEOGR. afluente.
afflux (æ·føks) *s.* aflujo.
afford (to) (afo·ʳd) *tr.* producir, dar, deparar, proporcionar, ofrecer. *2* soportar, permitirse [un gasto, el lujo de, etc.]; poder, tener medios o recursos para. | Gralte. con can, could, might, etc.
afforest (to) (afa·rist) *tr.* convertir en bosque.
affranchise (afræ·nchaiš) *tr.* ENFRANCHISE.
affray (afrei·) *s.* riña, pendencia.
affreight (to) (afrei·t) *tr.* fletar.
affreightment (-mønt) *s.* fletamiento.
affright (afrai·t) *s.* terror, espanto.
affright (to) *tr.* asustar, aterrar.
affront (afrø·nt) *s.* afrenta, insulto, desaire.
affront (to) *tr.* afrentar. *2* afrontar, arrostrar.
affusion (afiu·yøn) *s.* afusión.
Afghan (æ·fgan) *adj.-s.* afgano.
afield (afi·ld) *adv.* al campo, en el campo; fuera, lejos.

afire (afai·ʳ) *adv.* ardiendo.
aflame (aflei·m) *adj.-adv.* en llamas; inflamado.
afloat (aflou·t) *adj.-adv.* flotante, a flote. *2* en circulación. *3* sin rumbo. *4* inundado.
afoot (afu·t) *adv.* a pie. *2* en marcha; en preparación.
afore (afo·øʳ) *adv.* delante. *2* MAR. a proa.
aforegoing (-gouing) *adj.* anterior, precedente.
aforementioned (-menshønd), **aforesaid** (-sed) *adj.* mencionado, antedicho, susodicho.
aforethought (-zot) *adj.* premeditado. *2 s.* premeditación.
aforetime (-taim) *adj.* antiguamente.
afoul (afau·l) *adj.* y *adv.* MAR. en colisión; enredado.
afraid (afrei·d) *adj.* asustado, temeroso, que teme: to be ~, tener miedo.
afresh (afre·sh) *adv.* de nuevo, otra vez.
Africa (æ·frika) *n. pr.* GEOGR. África.
African (-n) *adj.-s.* africano.
aft (æft) *adv.* MAR. a popa, en popa.
after (æ·ftøʳ) *prep.* después de, detrás de, tras, en seguimiento de, en busca de, por: the day ~ tomorrow, pasado mañana; to inquire ~ a friend, preguntar por un amigo; ~ all, después de todo. *2* en imitación de, en conformidad con, según, a la [manera de]. *3 adv.* después, luego: soon ~, poco después. *4 adj.* posterior, ulterior, siguiente, subsiguiente. *5* MAR. de popa. *6 conj.* después que, o de que.
afterdamp (-dæmp) *s.* MIN. gases de explosión.
afterdeck (-dek) *s.* MAR. cubierta de popa.
after-dinner (-dinøʳ) *adj.* de sobremesa.
afterglow (-glou) *s.* resplandor crepuscular.
after-hours (-auʳs) *s. pl.* horas extraordinarias.
aftermath (-mæz) *s.* segunda siega, renadío. *2* consecuencias, resultados.
aftermost (-moust) *adj.* posterior, último.
afternoon (-nu·n) *s.* la tarde.
afterpiece (-pis) *s.* sainete, entremés.
aftertaste (-teist) *s.* resabio, dejo, gustillo.
afterthought (-zot) *s.* idea que se ocurre a uno después de un acto, etc.
afterward (-wøʳd), **afterwards** (-wøʳdš) *adv.* después, luego.
again (agei·n) *adv.* de nuevo, otra vez, segunda vez, aún: come ~, vuelva usted; again and ~, muchas veces; as much ~, otro tanto más; now and ~, de vez en cuando; never ~, nunca más. *2* por otra parte, además, asimismo.
against (age·nst) *prep.* contra: ~ time, contra el reloj. *2* enfrente de. *3* junto a, cerca de. *4* en contraste con, comparado con.
agalloch (æ·gælok) *s.* agáloco.
agami (æ·gami) *s.* ORN. agamí.
agape (agei·p) *s.* HIST. ágape.
agape (agei·p) *adj.* y *adv.* boquiabierto.
agaric (æ·garik) *s.* agárico.
agate (æ·git) *s.* MINER. ágata.
Agatha (æ·gaza) *n. pr.* Águeda.
agave (ægei·vi) *s.* agave, pita.
age (ei·dy) *s.* edad: full ~, mayoría de edad; of ~, mayor de edad; under ~, menor de edad. *2* vejez, senectud. *3* siglo, centuria. *4* generación [de hombres]. *5 pl.* mucho tiempo, una eternidad.
age (to) *intr.-tr.* envejecer. *2 tr.* añejar.
aged (ei·dyid) *adj.* viejo, anciano; envejecido. *2* de [tantos años de] edad: ~ twelve, de doce años.
ageing (ei·dying) *s.* AGING.
ageless (ei·dylis) *adj.* eternamente joven.
agency (ei·dyønsi) *s.* acción, operación, obra: free ~, libre albedrío. *2* mediación, intervención;

medio, influencia. *3* COM. agencia, factoría, representación.

agenda (adẏ·nda) *s.* agenda. *2* orden del día.

agent (ei·dẏønt) *adj.* agente. *2 s.* agente [lo que produce un efecto]. *3* agente, factor, representante.

agglomerate (ægla·møreit) *adj.-s.* aglomerado.

agglomerate (to) *tr.* aglomerar. *2 intr.* aglomerarse.

agglomeration (-ei·shøn) *s.* aglomeración.

agglutinant (aglu·tinant) *adj.-s.* aglutinante.

agglutinate (-nit) *adj.* aglutinado.

agglutinate (to) (-neit) *tr.* aglutinar.

agglutination (-nei·shøn) *s.* aglutinación.

agglutinative (-neitiv) *adj.* aglutinante.

aggrandize (to) (æ·grændaiš) *tr.* agrandar. *2* engrandecer, elevar.

aggrandizement (agrændi·šmønt) *s.* agrandamiento. *2* engrandecimiento.

aggravate (to) (æ·graveit) *tr.* agravar. *2* irritar, exasperar.

aggravating (-ing) *adj.* agravante. *2* irritante, exasperante.

aggravation (-i·shøn) *s.* agravamiento. *2* agravante. *3* irritación, exasperación.

aggregate (æ·grigeit) *adj.* agregado, reunido, conjunto, total. *2 s.* agregado, conjunto, totalidad: *in the* ~, en conjunto, en total.

aggregate (to) *tr.* agregar, juntar. *2* sumar, ascender a [un total].

aggregately (-li) *adv.* colectivamente, en junto.

aggregation (-ei·shøn) *s.* agregación. *2* agregado, colección, conjunto, total.

aggression (agre·shøn) *s.* agresión.

aggressive (-siv) *adj.* agresivo.

aggressor (-sø⁰) *s.* agresor.

aggrieve (agrɪ·v) *tr.* afligir, apenar. *2* vejar, oprimir.

aghast (agæ·st) *adj.* espantado, horrorizado. *2* estupefacto.

agile (æ·dẏil) *adj.* ágil, vivo, pronto.

agility (adẏi·liti) *s.* agilidad, expedición, prontitud.

aging (ei·dẏing) *s.* envejecimiento. *2* añejamiento.

agio (æ·dẏiou) *s.* agio.

agiotage (-tidẏ) *s.* agiotaje.

agitate (to) (æ·dẏiteit) *tr.* agitar. *2* conmover. *3* debatir, discutir. *4* maquinar, discurrir. *5 intr.* agitar la opinión pública.

agitation (-ei·shøn) *s.* agitación. *2* examen, discusión.

agitator (-tø⁰) *s.* agitador.

agleam (aglɪ·m) *adj.* y *adv.* brillante, centelleante.

aglet (æ·glit) *s.* herrete. *2 pl.* MIL. cordones.

aglow (aglou·) *adj.* y *adv.* encendido, ardiente.

agnail (æ·gneil) *s.* panadizo, uñero.

agnate (æ·gneit) *adj.-s.* agnado.

agnation (ægnei·shøn) *s.* agnación.

Agnes (æ·gnis) *n. pr.* Inés.

agnostic (ægna·stik) *adj.-s.* agnóstico.

agnosticism (-tisišm) *s.* agnosticismo.

Agnus Dei (æ·gnøs dei·i) *s.* agnusdéi.

ago (agou·) *adv.* atrás, hace, ha: *two years* ~, dos años atrás, hace dos años.

agog (aga·g) *adv.* ansiosamente, con viva curiosidad. *2 adj.* anhelante, excitado, curioso.

agoing (agou·ing) *adv.* en acción, en movimiento.

agonist (æ·gonist) *s.* agonista, luchador.

agonistic (ægoni·stic) *adj.* agonístico.

agonize (to) (æ·gonaiš) *intr.* agonizar, sufrir angustiosamente, retorcerse de dolor. *2* hacer grandes esfuerzos. *3 tr.* atormentar.

agony (æ·goni), *pl.* **-nies** (-niš) *s.* agonía. *2* angustia, aflicción extrema. *3* paroxismo.

agora (æ·gøra), *pl.* **-ræ** (-ri) *s.* ágora.

agouti (agu·ti) *s.* ZOOL. agutí.

agraffe (agræ·f) *s.* broche.

agrarian (agrei·rian) *adj.-s.* agrario.

agree (to) (agrɪ·) *intr.* asentir, consentir. *2* concordar, cuadrar, conformarse. *3* avenirse, estar o ponerse de acuerdo, convenir. *4* venir bien, sentar bien. *5* GRAM. concordar.

agreeable (agrɪ·abøl) *adj.* agradable. *2* conforme, conveniente. *3* fam. que quiere, que consiente, que acepta.

agreeably (-bli) *adv.* agradablemente. *2* de acuerdo [con], conformemente [a].

agreement (agrɪ·mønt) *s.* acuerdo, convenio, pacto, avenencia. *2* armonía, unión. *3* acuerdo, conformidad, concordancia.

agricultural (ægrico·lchøral) *adj.* agrícola.

agriculturalist (-ist) *s.* AGRICULTURIST.

agriculture (æ·grikølchø⁰) *s.* agricultura.

agriculturist (ægriko·lchørist) *s.* agricultor.

agrimony (æ·grimoni) *s.* BOT. agrimonia.

agronomic(al (ægrona·mik(al) *adj.* agronómico.

agronomics (-s), **agronomy** (agra·nømi) *s.* agronomía.

aground (agrau·nd) *adv.* MAR. encallado, varado: *to run* ~, encallar, varar.

ague (ei·giu) *s.* fiebre intermitente. *2* escalofrío.

ah! (a) *interj.* ¡ah!, ¡ay!

ahead (aje·d) *adv.* delante, al frente, a la cabeza; más allá de, adelante: *to be* ~, ir delante; llevar la delantera; *to go* ~, avanzar; ~ *of time*, adelantado, antes de tiempo. *2* MAR. por la proa, avante.

ahem! (aje·m) *interj.* ¡eh!, ¡ejem!

ahoy! (ajoi·) *inter.* MAR. ¡ah!: *ship* ~*!*, ¡ah del barco!

aid (eid) *s.* ayuda, auxilio, socorro: *first* ~, primeros auxilios. *2* ayudante, auxiliar.

aid (to) *tr.* ayudar, auxiliar, socorrer. *2* apoyar, coadyuvar.

aide-de-camp (ei·døkæ·mp) *s.* MIL. edecán.

aigret, aigrette (ei·gret) *s.* ORN. garzota. *2* gargota, penacho, airón.

ail (to) (eil) *tr.* afligir, molestar, aquejar. *2 intr.* sufrir, estar indispuesto.

ailanthus (eila·nzos) *s.* BOT. ailanto.

aileron (ei·løran) *s.* AVIA. alerón.

ailing (ei·ling) *adj.-s.* enfermo, achacoso.

ailment (ei·lmønt) *s.* dolencia, padecimiento, achaque.

aim (eim) *s.* puntería, encaro, acción de asestar, de dirigir [un arma, un golpe, etc.]. *2* blanco [al que se tira]; *to miss one's* ~, errar el tiro. *3* mira, designio, fin.

aim (to) *intr.* apuntar [con un arma]; dirigir un golpe, la intención, el propósito [a]; poner la mira [en]; tratar [de]. *2 tr.* apuntar, asestar, encarar, dirigir [un arma, un golpe, etc.].

aimless (ei·mlis) *adj.* sin objeto, sin designio.

ain't (eint) *contr. vulg.* de *am not, is not, are not, have not* y *has not.*

air (e·ø⁰) *s.* aire [fluido, atmósfera, viento]: *open* ~, aire libre; *in the* ~, en el aire, en el ambiente; indeciso, incierto; *on the* ~, RADIO. transmitiendo. *2* céfiro, aura. *3* ambiente. *4* aire, semblante, actitud, continente, aspecto. *5* afectación, tono: *to put on airs*, darse tono. *6* manifestación, divulgación: *to give it* ~; decirlo, manifestarlo; *to take* ~, ser conocido, divulgarse. *7* MÚS. aire, tonada. *8 adj.* de aire, neumático; aéreo, aeronáutico; de aviación: ~ *base*, base aérea; ~ *castle*, castillo en el aire; ~ *force*, fuerzas aéreas; ~ *gun*, escopeta de aire comprimido; ~ *hostess*, AVIA. azafata; ~ *mail*, correo aéreo; ~ *pump*, máquina neumática, bomba de aire; ~ *raid*, ataque aéreo.

air (to) *tr.* airear, orear. *2* ventilar. *3* secar [al aire o al calor]. *4* exhibir, ostentar. *5* emitir, divulgar. *6 intr.* tomar el aire.

airbrush (-brøsh) *s.* PINT. pistola.

air-conditioned *adj.* con aire acondicionado.

aircraft (-kraft) *s.* aeronave o avión: ~ *carrier*, portaaviones.

airdrome (-droum) *s.* aeródromo.

airfoil (-foil) *s.* AVIA. superficie de sustentación.

airfled (-ifaid) *adj.* hecho a la ligera, sin fundamento. *2* presumido, entonado.

airiness (-inis) *s.* viveza, vivacidad. *2* ligereza, superficialidad.

airing (-ing) *s.* paseo, excursión [para tomar el aire]. *2* oreo.

airlift (-lift) *s.* puente aéreo.

airline (-lain) *s.* línea aérea.

airman (-mæn) *s.* aviador.

airplane (-plein) *s.* aeroplano.

airport (-po^{r}t) *s.* aeropuerto.

airship (-ship) *s.* aeronave.

airsick (-sik) *adj.* mareado en el aire.

airsickness (-nis) *s.* mareo en avión.

airstrip (-strip) *s.* AVIA. pista.

airtight (-tait) *adj.* hermético, herméticamente cerrado.

airway (-wei) *s.* línea aérea, vía aérea. *2* MIN. pozo o galería de ventilación.

airy (-i) *adj.* airoso, oreado. *2* etéreo, sutil, vaporoso. *3* ágil, ligero. *4* alegre, vivo. *5* delicado, gracioso. *6* vano, sin fundamento. *7* ligero, superficial.

aisle (ail) *s.* pasillo [en un teatro, etc.]. *2* ARQ. nave lateral. *3* calle de árboles.

Aix-la-Chapelle (e·la-chapel) *n. pr.* Aquisgrán.

ajar (adÿa·^{r}) *adj.* entreabierto, entornado. *2* en pugna, en desacuerdo.

akimbo (aki·mbou) *adj.* en jarras.

akin (aki·n) *adj.* pariente. *2* semejante.

alabaster (æ·labæstø^r) *s.* alabastro.

alabastrine (ælabæ·strin) *adj.* alabastrino.

alacrity (ælæ·criti) *s.* alacridad, presteza.

Aladdin (ælæ·din) *n. pr.* Aladino.

Alans (a·lanš) *s.* HIST. alanos.

alar (ei·la^r) *adj.* alado. *2* BOT. axilar.

alarm (ala·^{r}m) *s.* alarma. *2* mecanismo despertador; timbre de alarma: ~ *clock*, despertador.

alarm (to) *tr.* alarmar. *2* alertar.

alarming (-ing) *adj.* alarmante.

alarmist (-ist) *s.* alarmista.

alarum clock (alæ·røm) *s.* ant. (Ingl.) despertador.

alas (alæ·s) *interj.* ¡ay!, ¡guay!

alate(d (ei·leit(id) *adj.* alado.

alatern (alatø·^{r}n) *s.* BOT. aladierna.

alb (ælb) *s.* LITURG. alba.

albacore (æ·lbacou^r) *s.* ICT. albacora.

Albanian (ælbei·nian) *adj.-s.* albanés.

albatros (æ·lbatrøs) *s.* albatros.

albeit (olbi·it) *conj.* aunque, bien que.

Albert (æ·lbø^{r}t) *n. pr.* Alberto.

albinism (æ·lbinišm) *s.* albinismo.

albino (ælbai·nou), *pl.* **-nos** *s.* albino.

Albion (æ·lbiøn) *n. pr.* Albión.

albugo (ælbiu·gou) *s.* MED. albugo.

album (æ·lbøm) *s.* álbum.

albumen (ælbiu·møn) *s.* albumen. *2* albúmina.

albumin (ælbiu·min) *s.* albúmina.

albuminoid (-oid) *adj.* albuminoideo. *2 s.* albuminoide.

albuminous (-øs) *adj.* albuminoso.

albuminuria (-iu·ria) *s.* albuminuria.

alburnum (ælbø·^{r}nøm) *s.* BOT. alburno.

alchemist (æ·lkemist) *s.* alquimista.

alchemy (æ·lkemi) *s.* alquimia.

alcohol (æ·lcojol) *s.* QUÍM. alcohol.

alcoholic (ælcojo·lic) *adj.* alcohólico. *2 s. pl.* líquidos espirituosos.

alcoholism (æ·lcojolišm) *s.* alcoholismo.

alcoholize (to) (-aiš) *tr.* alcoholizar.

alcoholometer (-a·mitø^r) *s.* alcoholímetro.

Alcoran (ælcora·n) *s.* alcorán.

alcove (æ·lcouv) *s.* hueco o nicho [en una habitación]; alcoba. *2* cenador, glorieta.

aldehyde (æ·ldijaid) *s.* aldehído.

alder (o·ldø^r) *s.* aliso. *2* ~ *buckthorn*, arraclán.

alderman (-mæn) *s.* teniente de alcalde.

Aldine (o·ldin) *adj.* aldino.

ale (eil) *s.* cerveza inglesa muy fuerte.

aleatory (ei·liatori) *adj.* aleatorio.

alee (ali·) *adv.* MAR. a sotavento.

alehouse (ei·ljaus) *s.* cervecería, taberna.

alembic (ale·mbik) *s.* alambique.

Aleppo (æle·pou) *n. pr.* Alepo: *Aleppo pine*, pincarrasco.

alert (alø^{r}t) *adj.* alerta, vigilante. *2* vivo, dispuesto. *3 s.* MIL. alarma: *on the* ~, alerta, sobre aviso.

alert (to) *tr.* alertar.

alertness (-nis) *s.* vigilancia. *2* viveza, presteza.

alette (æle·t) *s.* ARQ. aleta.

alewife (ei·luaif) *s.* cervecera, tabernera.

Alexander (æligšæ·ndø^r) *n. pr.* Alejandro.

Alexandrie (-ndria) *n. pr.* GEOGR. Alejandría.

Alexandrine (-drin) *s.* verso alejandrino.

alfalfa (ælfæ·lfa) *s.* (E.U.) alfalfa.

alfaqui (a·lfaki) *s.* alfaquí.

alga (æ·lga), *pl.* **algae** (æ·ldÿi) *s.* alga.

algebra (æ·ldÿebra) *s.* álgebra.

algebraic(al (ældÿebrei·ik(al) *adj.* algebraico, algébrico.

algebraist (æ·ldÿebreist) *s.* MAT. algebrista.

Algeria (ældÿi·ria) *n. pr.* GEOGR. Argelia.

Algerian (-n), **Algerine** (ældÿeri·n) *adj.-s.* argelino.

algid (æ·ldÿid) *adj.* álgido.

algidity (ældÿi·diti) *s.* algidez.

Algiers (ældÿi·^{r}s) *n. pr.* GEOGR. Argel.

algorism (æ·lgorišm) *s.* algoritmia.

algous (æ·lgøs) *adj.* algoso.

alias (ei·lias) *adv.-s.* alias.

alibi (æ·libai) *s.* coartada.

Alice (æ·lis) *n. pr.* Alicia.

alidade (æ·lideid) *s.* alidada.

alien (ei·liøn) *adj.* ajeno, extraño. *2 adj.-s.* forastero, extranjero.

alien (to) *tr.* ALIENATE.

alienable (abøl) *adj.* alienable, enajenable.

alienate (to) (-eit) *tr.* alienar, enajenar.

alienation (-ei·shøn) *s.* alienación, enajenación. *2* alejamiento, desvío, desapego.

alienism (-išm) *s.* extranjería. *2* frenopatía.

alienist (-ist) *s.* alienista.

aliferous (æli·førøs) *adj.* alífero, alígero.

alight (alai·t) *adj. y adv.* encendido, iluminado; ardiendo.

alight (to) *intr.* bajar, apearse. *2* caer, ir a caer, posarse. *3* dar, topar [con].

align (to) (alai·n) *tr.* alinear. *2 intr.* alinearse.

alignment (-mønt) *s*. alineación.
alike (alai·k) *adj*. igual, semejante. *2 adv*. igualmente, del mismo modo.
aliment (æ·limønt) *s*. alimento.
alimental (ælime·ntal) *adj*. nutritivo.
alimentary (-tari) *adj*. alimentario. *2* alimenticio. *3* ~ *canal*, tubo digestivo.
alimentation (-ei·shøn) *s*. alimentación.
alimony (æ·limoni) *s*. DER. alimentos.
aline (to) *tr.-intr.* TO ALIGN.
alinement *s*. ALIGNMENT.
aliped (æ·liped) *adj*. alípedo.
aliquant (æ·likuant) *adj*. alicuanta.
aliquot (æ·likuat) *adj*. alícuota.
alive (alai·v) *adj*. vivo, viviente. *2* vivo, en actividad, no extinguido. *3* vivo, activo: *to look* ~, menearse, darse prisa. *4* ~ *with*, lleno de [cosas que abundan u hormiguean]. *5* ~ *to*, sensible a, despierto para.
alkalescent (ælkæle·sønt) *adj*. alcalescente.
alkali (ælkali) *s*. álcali.
alkalimetry (-li·metri) *s*. alcalimetría.
alkaline (-lain) *adj*. alcalino.
alkaline-earth *adj*. QUÍM. alcalino-térreo.
alkalinity (-li·niti) *s*. alcalinidad.
alkaloid (-loid) *s*. alcaloide.
alkaloidal (loidal) *adj*. alcaloideo.
alkanet (æ·lkanet) *s*. BOT. orcaneta, onoquiles. *2* ancusa.
all (ol) *adj*. todo, toda, todos, todas: ~ *of us*, todos nosotros. *2 pron*. todo, conjunto, totalidad: *after* ~, después de todo, al fin y al cabo; *at* ~, en absoluto, del todo; siquiera; *not at* ~, de ninguna manera; no hay de qué; *for* ~, a pesar de; *for* ~ *I know*, que yo sepa, quizás, posiblemente. *3* todos, todo el mundo: ~ *and singular*, ~ *and sundry*, todos y cada uno. *4 adv*. del todo, completamente, muy: ~ *but*, casi; por poco; ~ *in*, agotado, rendido de fatiga; ~ *of sudden*, de pronto, de repente; ~ *out*, fam. agotado, rendido; equivocado, confundido; con energía; ~ *right*, sano y salvo, bien de salud; bueno, buena persona, competente, satisfactorio; bien; ~ *right!*, ¡bueno!, ¡está bien!, ¡conformes!; ~ *round*, por todas partes; ~ *the better*, tanto mejor; ~ *the same*, sin embargo, a pesar de todo; ~ *there*, listo, despierto; cuerdo.
Allah (æ·la) *n. pr.* Alá.
allantois (ælæ·ntois) *s*. BIOL. alantoides.
allay (to) (alei·) *tr*. aliviar, mitigar, calmar. *2* aquietar, apaciguar.
allayment (-mønt) *s*. alivio.
allegation (æligei·shøn) *s*. alegación. *2* DER. alegato.
allege (to) (æle·dý) *tr*. alegar, afirmar, sostener.
alleged (-d) *adj*. alegado, supuesto.
allegiance (æli·dýans) *s*. obediencia, fidelidad [a un soberano, etc.]. *2* homenaje, pleito homenaje.
allegoric(al (æligo·rik(al) *adj*. alegórico.
allegorize (to) (æ·ligoraiš) *tr.-intr.* alegorizar.
allegory (æ·ligori) *s*. alegoría.
allegretto (æløgre·tou) *s*. MÚS. alegreto.
allegro (æle·grou) *s*. MÚS. alegro.
alleluia (ælilu·ýa) *s*. e *interj*. aleluya.
allergic (alo·ʳdýik) *adj*. alérgico.
allergy (æ·løʳdýi) *s*. alergia.
alleviate (to) (alɪ·vieit) *tr*. aliviar, mitigar.
alleviation (-ei·shøn) *s*. alivio, mitigación.
alley (æ·li) *s*. calleja, callejón. *2* calle de árboles; camino entre setos. *3* bolera.

All Fools' Day *s*. primero de abril, especie de día de los Inocentes.
all fours (on) *adv*. a cuatro patas, a gatas.
Allhallows (oljæ·louš) *s*. día de Todos los Santos.
alliance (ala·ians) *s*. alianza.
allied (alai·d) *adj*. aliado. *2* afin. *3* emparentado.
allies (alai·š) *s. pl.* [de ALLY] aliados.
alligator (æligei·tøʳ) *s*. ZOOL. caimán. *2* BOT. ~ *pear*, aguacate.
alliteration (alitørei·shøn) *s*. aliteración.
alliterative (-rei·tiv) *adj*. aliterado.
allocate (to) (æ·lokeit) *tr*. señalar, asignar. *2* colocar, situar.
allocation (-kei·shøn) *s*. asignación, distribución.
allocution (ælokiu·shøn) *s*. alocución.
allodium (ælou·diøm) *s*. alodio.
allopathist (ala·pazist) *s*. alópata.
allopathy (ala·pazi) *s*. alopatía.
allot (to) (ala·t) *tr*. repartir, distribuir, asignar, adjudicar. ¶ Pret. y p. p.: *allotted;* ger.: -*tting*.
allotment (-mønt) *s*. reparto, asignación. *2* parte, porción, lote.
allotropism (æla·tropišm), **allotropy** (-tropi) *s*. alotropía.
allow (to) (alau·) *tr*. conceder, dar, asignar. *2* dejar, permitir, consentir. *3* conceder, reconocer [como cierto]. *4* COM. descontar, rebajar. *5* intr. *to* ~ *of*, permitir, admitir. *6 to* ~ *for*, tener en cuenta; dejar [espacio, etc.] para.
allowable (-abøl) *adj*. aceptable, permisible, lícito.
allowance (-ans) *s*. concesión, asignación [acción]. *2* permiso, autorización. *3* asignación, pensión, subsidio: *family* ~, subsidio familiar. *4* ración. *5* COM. descuento, bonificación, tara. *6* TÉCN. tolerancia. *7 to make* ~ *for*, tener en cuenta; ser indulgente con.
alloy (æloi·) *s*. liga, aleación. *2* fig. mezcla, impureza.
alloy (to) *tr*. ligar, alear [metales]. *2* fig. adulterar, desvirtuar.
alloyage (-idý) *s*. aleación [operación].
all-powerful *adj*. omnipotente, todopoderoso.
all-round *adj*. apto o que sirve para muchas cosas. *2* general, comprensivo.
All Saints' day *s*. día de Todos los Santos.
All Souls' day *s*. día de Difuntos.
allspice (o·lspais) *s*. pimienta inglesa.
allude (to) (aliu·d) *intr*. aludir, referirse.
allure (to) (aliu·øʳ) *tr*. atraer, tentar, seducir; inducir [con cebo o halago].
allurement (-mønt) *s*. tentación, seducción. *2* atractivo, encanto. *3* incentivo, cebo.
alluring (-ing) *adj*. seductor, tentador, halagüeño.
allusion (aliu·ýøn) *s*. alusión.
allusive (aliu·siv) *adj*. alusivo.
alluvial (aliu·vial) *adj*. aluvial.
alluvion (-viøn) *s*. aluvión.
alluvium (-viøm) *s*. GEOL. aluvión.
all-wave *adj*. RADIO. de toda onda.
ally (alai·), *pl*. **allies** (-š) *s*. aliado.
ally (to) *tr*. aliar. *2* unir, relacionar. *3 intr*. aliarse. ¶ Pret. y p. p.: *allied*.
almagest (æ·lmadýest) *s*. almagesto.
almanac (o·lmanæk) *s*. almanaque.
alme(h (æ·lmi) *s*. alma.
almighty (olmai·ti) *adj*. omnipotente, todopoderoso: *the Almighty*, el Todopoderoso [Dios]. *2* fam. grande, terrible.
almond (a·mønd) *s*. almendra: ~ *brittle*, crocante. *2* amígdala.
almoner (æ·lmønøʳ) *s*. limosnero.

almonry (æ·lmønri) *s.* lugar donde se distribuyen limosnas.
almost (o·lmoust) *adv.* casi; por poco.
alms (amš) *s.* limosna, caridad: ~ *box*, cepillo para las limosnas.
almshouse (a·mšjaus) *s.* hospicio, casa de caridad.
almucantar (ælmiukæ·nta^r) *s.* almicantarat.
aloe (æ·lou) *s.* bot. áloe [planta].
aloes (æ·lous) *s.* áloe, acíbar [jugo]. *2* bot. ~ *wood*, agáloco, palo áloe.
aloft (alo·ft) *adv.* arriba, en alto.
alone (alou·n) *adj.* solo. *2* solitario. *3* único, exclusivo. *4 adv.* sólo, exclusivamente.
along (alo·ng) *adv.* a lo largo, por lo largo. *2* con uno o unos: *come* ~, ven o venid conmigo o con nosotros; ~ *with*, con, junto con. *3* adelante. *4* pop. ~ *of*, por o a causa de. *5 all* ~, todo el tiempo, desde el principio. *6 prep.* a lo largo de.
alongshore (-sho·^r) *adv.* a lo largo de la costa, de la orilla.
alongside (-said) *adv.* y *prep.* a lo largo de, al costado de; lado a lado: ~ *of*, junto a.
aloof (alu·f) *adv.* a distancia. *2 adj.* apartado, distante, frío, reservado: *to keep* o *stand* ~, mantenerse apartado, no mezclarse, retraerse.
aloofness (-nis) *s.* alejamiento, retraimiento, reserva, frialdad.
alopecia (ælopɪ·sia) *s.* alopecia.
aloud (alau·d) *adv.* alto, en voz alta.
alpaca (ælpæ·ka) *s.* alpaca.
alpenstock (æ·lpinstak) *s.* bastón de alpinista.
alpha (æ·lfa) *s.* alfa.
alphabet (æ·lfabet) *s.* alfabeto.
alphabetic(al (ælfabe·tik(al) *adj.* alfabético.
Alphonso (ælfa·nsou) *n. pr.* Alfonso.
alpine (æ·lpain) *adj.* alpino, alpestre.
alpinism (æ·lpinišm) *s.* alpinismo.
alpinist (-nist) *s.* alpinista.
alpist (æ·lpist) *s.* alpiste.
Alps (ælps) *n. pr.* Alpes.
already (olre·di) *adv.* ya.
Alsace (æ·lsæs) *n. pr.* Alsacia.
Alsatian (ælsei·shan) *adj.-s.* alsaciano.
also (o·lsou) *adv.* también, asimismo, además.
Altaic (æltei·k) *adj.* altaico.
altar (o·lta^r) *s.* altar: ~ *boy*, monaguillo; ~ *cloth*, sabanilla, mantel de altar.
altar-piece *s.* retablo.
alter (to) (o·ltø^r) *tr.* alterar, cambiar, modificar. *2 intr.* alterarse, modificarse.
alterable (-abøl) *adj.* alterable.
alteration (-ei·shøn) *s.* alteración, cambio, modificación.
altercate (to) (æ·ltø^rkeit) *intr.* altercar.
altercation (-ei·shøn) *s.* altercado, disputa.
alternant (oltø·^rnant) *adj.* alternating. *2 s.* mat. alternante.
alternate (o·ltø^rnit) *adj.* alternado, alternativo, alterno. *2* alternante. *3 s.* suplente.
alternate (to) (o·ltø^rneit) *tr.* alternar. *2 intr.* alternar, turnar.
alternating (-ing) *adj.* elect., mat. alterna [corriente, función].
alternation (-ei·shøn) *s.* alternación, alternancia, turno.
alternative (oltø·^rnativ) *adj.* alternativo. *2* gram., lóg. disyuntivo. *3 s.* alternativa [opción].
alternator (o·ltø^rneitø^r) *s.* elect. alternador.
althea (ælzi·a) *s.* altea. *2* rosa de Siria.
although (olðou·) *conj.* aunque, aun cuando, si bien, bien que, a pesar de que.

altimetry (ælti·mitri) *s.* altimetría.
altisonant (-sonant), **altisonous** (-sonøs) *adj.* altisonante, retumbante.
altitude (æ·ltitiud) *s.* altitud, altura, elevación. *2* astr., geom. altura.
alto (æ·ltou) *adj.-s.* mús. contralto. *2 s.* viola.
altogether (oltuge·ðø^r) *adv.* enteramente, del todo. *2* en conjunto. *3 s.* conjunto, totalidad.
alto-relievo (æltorilɪ·vou) *s.* alto relieve.
altruism (æ·ltruišm) *s.* altruismo.
altruist (-ist) *s.* altruista.
altruistic (-i·stic) *adj.* altruista.
alum (æ·løm) *s.* alumbre.
alumina (æliu·mina) *s.* quím. alúmina.
aluminite (-ait) *s.* miner. aluminita.
aluminium (æliumi·niøm) *s.* aluminum.
aluminum (-øm) *s.* quím. aluminio.
alumna (alæ·mna) *s.* alumna o ex alumna.
alumnus (-nøs) *s.* alumno o ex alumno.
alunite (æliu·nait) *s.* alunita.
alveolar (ælvɪ·ola^r) *adj.* alveolar.
alveolus (-oløs) *s.* alvéolo. *2* celdilla.
alvine (æ·lvin o -vain) *adj.* alvino.
always (o·lweiš) *adv.* siempre.
am (æm) *1.ª pers. del pres. de ind.* de to be.
amadou (æ·madu) *s.* yesca.
amain (amei·n) *adv.* vehementemente, vigorosamente. *2* a toda prisa.
amalgam (amæ·lgam) *s.* amalgama.
amalgamate (to) (-eit) *tr.* amalgamar. *2* reunir, fusionar [sociedades, etc.].
amanita (amanai·ta) *s.* bot. amanita.
amanuensis (amæniue·nsis) *s.* amanuense.
amaranth (æ·marænz) *s.* bot. amaranto.
amaranthine (æmaræ·nzin) *adj.* de amaranto. *2* purpúreo. *3* inmarcesible, imperecedero.
Amaryllidaceae (æmarilidei·sii) *s. pl.* amarilidáceas.
amass (to) (amæ·s) *tr.* juntar, amontonar, acumular.
amateur (æmatø·^r) *adj.-s.* aficionado.
amateurish (-ish) *adj.* propio de un aficionado, defectuoso, chapucero.
amative (æ·mativ) *adj.* amativo.
amatorial (æma·to·rial), **amatory** (æ·matori) *adj.* amatorio.
amaurosis (æmorou·sis) *s.* med. amaurosis.
amaze (to) (amei·š) *tr.* asombrar, pasmar.
amazed (-d) *adj.* asombrado, pasmado, atónito.
amazing (-ing) *adj.* asombroso, pasmoso.
Amazon (æ·mazan) *s.* mit. Amazona. *2* [con min.] marimacho. *3 n. pr.* Amazonas [río].
ambages (æ·mbidýis) *s. pl.* ambages.
ambagious (æmbei·dýøs) *adj.* ambagioso.
ambassador (æmbæ·sadø^r) *m.* embajador.
ambassadorship (-ship) *s.* embajada [cargo].
ambassadress (-dris) *s.* embajadora.
amber (æ·mbø^r) *s.* ámbar, succino. *2* bot. corazoncillo. *3 adj.* ambarino, de ámbar.
amber (to) *tr.* ambarar. *2* dar color de ámbar.
ambergris (æ·mbø^rgris) *s.* ámbar gris.
ambidexter (æmbide·kstø^r) *adj.-s.* ambidextro. *2* fig. doble, falso, de dos caras.
ambidexterity (-te·riti) *s.* calidad de ambidextro. *2* fig. doblez, falsedad.
ambidextrous (æmbide·kstrøs) *adj.* ambidexter.
ambient (æ·mbient) *adj.* ambiente.
ambiuity (æmbigiui·ti) *s.* ambigüedad.
ambiguous (æmbi·giuøs) *adj.* ambiguo.
ambit (æ·mbit) *s.* ámbito, recinto.
ambition (æmbi·shøn) *s.* ambición.

ambition (to) *tr.* ambicionar.
ambitious (-søs) *adj.* ambicioso. *2* deseoso, ávido.
amble (æ·mbøl) *s.* portante, paso de ambladura.
amble (to) *intr.* amblar.
ambler (æ·mblø^r) *s.* caballo amblador.
ambo (æ·mbou) *s.* ambón.
Ambrose (æ·mbrous) *n. pr.* Ambrosio.
ambrosia (æmbrou·šia) *s.* ambrosía.
ambrosial (-l) *adj.* delicioso, celestial.
ambry (æ·mbri) *s.* armario, alacena; despensa.
ambulacrum (æmbiulei·krøm) *s.* ZOOL. ambulacro.
ambulance (æ·mbiulans) *s.* ambulancia [hospital; vehículo].
ambulant (-ant) *adj.* ambulante.
ambulation (-ei·shøn) *s.* ambulación, paseo.
ambulatory (-tori) *adj.* ambulante, ambulatorio. *2 s.* ARQ. galería.
ambuscade (æ·mbøskeid) *s.* AMBUSH.
ambuscade (to) *tr.-intr.* TO AMBUSH.
ambush (æ·mbush) *s.* emboscada, acecho.
ambush (to) *tr.* emboscar. *2* poner una emboscada a. *3 intr.* estar emboscado, al acecho.
ameer (ami·^{r}) *s.* AMIR.
ameliorate (to) (amı·lioreit) *tr.* mejorar. *2 intr.* mejorar, mejorarse.
amelioration (-ei·shøn) *s.* mejora, mejoramiento.
amen (ame·n) *interj.* amén.
amenability (aminabi·liti) *s.* responsabilidad. *2* docilidad.
amenable (ami·nabøl) *adj.* responsable. *2* sujeto [a]. *3* dócil.
amend (to) (ame·nd) *tr.* enmendar, corregir, mejorar. *2 intr.* enmendarse. *3* restablecerse.
amendment (-mønt) *s.* enmienda, enmendadura; remedio, mejora. *2* enmienda [a un proyecto de ley]. *3* AGR. enmienda.
amends (ame·nds) *s.* satisfacción, reparación, compensación: *to make ~ for,* dar cumplida satisfacción por, reparar, resarcir.
amenity (ame·niti) *s.* amenidad. *2* afabilidad.
amenorrhea (amenørı·a) *s.* amenorrea.
ament (æ·ment) *s.* BOT. amento.
amerce (to) (amø·^{r}s) *tr.* multar; castigar.
amercement (-mønt) *s.* multa.
America (ame·rika) *n. pr.* GEOGR. América.
American (-n) *adj.-s.* americano. *2* norteamericano. *3* BOT. *~ aloe,* pita, magüey.
Americanism (-nišm) *s.* americanismo.
Americanist (-nist) *s.* americanista.
Americanize (to) (-naiš) *tr.* americanizar.
amethyst (æ·mizist) *s.* amatista.
amiability (eimiabi·liti) *s.* amabilidad.
amiable (ei·miabøl) *adj.* amable, afable, bondadoso.
amianthus (æmiæ·nzøs) *s.* amianto.
amicability (æmikabi·liti) *s.* calidad de amistoso.
amicable (æ·mikabøl) *adj.* amigable, amistoso.
amice (æ·mis) *s.* amito.
amid (ami·d) *prep.* en medio de, entre, rodeado por.
amide (æ·mid o æ·mid) *s.* QUÍM. amida.
amidships (ami·dships) *adv.* MAR. en medio del buque.
amidst (ami·dst) *prep.* AMID.
amine (æmı·n) *s.* QUÍM. amina.
amir (ami·^{r}) *s.* emir.
amiss (ami·s) *adv.* erradamente, mal; de más, fuera de lugar o del caso: *to take ~,* llevar a mal; *it is not ~,* no está de más, es conveniente. *2 adj.*

errado, malo, impropio, inoportuno, desarreglado.
amity (æ·miti) *s.* amistad, buena inteligencia.
ammeter (æ·mitø^r) *s.* amperímetro.
ammonia (æmou·nia) *s.* amoníaco [gas]: *~ water,* agua amoniacal.
ammoniac (æmou·niæk) *s.* amoniaco [goma].
ammoniac(al (æmonai·k(al) *adj.* amoniacal.
ammonite (æ·monait) *s.* amonita [fósil]. *2* (con may.) BIB. amonita.
ammonium (æmou·niøm) *s.* amonio.
ammunition (æmiuni·shøn) *s.* MIL. munición, municiones.
ammunition (to) *tr.* municionar.
amnesia (æmnı·šia) *s.* MED. amnesia.
amnesty (æ·mnesti) *s.* amnistía.
amnesty (to) *tr.* amnistiar. ¶ Pret. y p. p.: *amnestied.*
amnicola (æmni·kola) *adj.* amnícola.
amnion (æ·mniøn) *s.* BIOL. amnios.
amock (oma·k) *adv.* AMUCK.
amœba (æmı·ba) *s.* ZOOL. amiba.
amomum (æmou·møn) *s.* amomo.
among(st (ama·ng(st) *prep.* entre, en medio de, en el número de.
amoral (eima·ral) *adj.* amoral.
amorality (eimoræ·liti) *s.* amoralidad.
amorous (æ·mørøs) *adj.* amoroso, tierno. *2* enamoradizo. *3* enamorado.
amorphous (amo·^{r}føs) *adj.* amorfo, informe.
amortization (amo·^{r}tišei·shøn) *s.* amortización.
amortize (to) (amo·^{r}taiš) *tr.* amortizar.
amount (amau·nt) *s.* cantidad, suma. *2* importe. *3* cuantía, valor.
amount (to) *intr. ~ to,* montar, sumar, importar, ascender a; equivaler a.
amour (amu·^{r}) *s.* amores, amorío.
amourette (æmure·t) *s.* amorío.
ampere (æ·mpi^r) *s.* amperio.
amperemeter (-mitø^r) *s.* AMMETER.
ampersand (æ·mpø^{r}sænd) *s.* el signo & [y].
Amphibia (æmfi·bia) *s. pl.* ZOOL. anfibios.
amphibian (-n) *s.* ZOOL. anfibio.
amphibious (-biøs) *adj.* anfibio.
amphibole (æ·mfiboul) *s.* MINER. anfíbol.
amphibological (æmfibola·dyk̄al) *adj.* anfibológico.
amphibology (æmfiba·lody̌i) *s.* anfibología.
amphibrach (æ·mfibræk) *s.* anfíbraco.
amphictyon (æmfi·ktiøn) *s.* anfiction.
amphimacer (æmfi·masø^r) *s.* anfímacro.
amphisbena (æmfisbı·na) *s.* ZOOL. anfisbena.
amphiscii (æmfi·shiai) *s. pl.* anfiscios.
amphitheater, -tre (æ·mfiziatø^r) *s.* anfiteatro.
Amphitryon (æmfi·triøn) *n. pr. y s.* Anfitrión.
amphora (æ·mfora) *s.* ánfora.
ample (æ·mpøl) *adj.* amplio. *2* extenso, capaz, holgado. *3* suficiente, cumplido, abundante.
ampliation (æmpliei·shøn) *s.* ampliación. *2* DER. aplazamiento de fallo.
amplification (-fikei·shøn) *s.* amplificación. *2* ampliación. *3* ÓPT. aumento.
amplifier (æ·mplifaiø^r) *s.* amplificador, ampliador. *2* ELECT. amplificador. *3* RADIO. altavoz.
amplify (to) (æ·mplifai) *tr.* amplificar, ampliar. *2* extender, aumentar, exagerar. *3 intr.* extenderse en los detalles, explayarse. ¶ Pret. y p. p.: *amplified.*
amplitude (-tiud) *s.* amplitud.
amply (æ·mpli) *adv.* ampliamente, latamente, abundantemente.

ampoule (æmpu·l) *s.* ampolla, inyectable.
amputate (to) (æ-mpiuteit) *tr.* amputar.
amputation (-tei·shøn) *s.* amputación.
amuck (amø·k) *adv.* furiosamente: *to run* ~, atacar ciegamente, a todo el mundo.
amulet (æ·miulit) *s.* amuleto.
amuse (to) (amiu·š) *tr.* entretener, divertir, hacer gracia a. *2 ref.* distraerse, divertirse.
amusement (-mønt) *s.* entretenimiento, solaz, diversión, pasatiempo.
amusing (-ing) *adj.* entretenido, divertido, gracioso, humorístico.
amygdala (ami·gdala) *s.* ANAT. amígdala.
Amygdalaceae (-lei·sii) *s. pl.* BOT. amigdaláceas.
amyl (æ·mil) *s.* QUÍ. amilo. *2 adj.* amílico.
amylic (æ·milic) *adj.* amílico.
an (æn) *art. indef.* un, una. V. ARTÍCULO (cuadro gramatical).
ana (ei·na) *s.* colección de dichos o anécdotas.
Anabaptism (ænabæ·ptišm) *s.* anabaptismo.
Anabaptist (-tist) *s.* anabaptista.
anachronic(al (ænakra·nik(al) *adj.* anacrónico.
anachronism (ænæ·kronišm) *s.* anacronismo.
anaconda (ænaka·nda) *s.* ZOOL. anaconda.
Anacreon (anæ·krian) *n. pr.* Anacreonte.
Anacreontic (anækria·ntik) *adj.* anacreóntico. *2 s.* anacreóntica.
anaemia (ænı·mia) *s.* MED. anemia.
anaemic (-ic) *adj.* anémico.
anaerobe (ænei·øroub) *s.* BIOL. anaerobio.
anaesthesia (æneszı·šia) *s.* anestesia.
anaesthetic (-ze·tik) *adj.-s.* anestésico.
anaesthetist (æne·szitist) *s.* anestesiador.
anaesthetize (to) (-taiš) *tr.* anestesiar.
anaglyph (æ·naglif) *s.* anáglifo.
anagoge (ænagou·dŷi) *s.* anagoge.
anagram (æ·nagræm) *s.* anagrama.
anal (ei·nal) *adj.* ANAT. anal.
analecta (ænale·kta), **analects** (æ·nalekts) *s. pl.* analectas.
analgesia (ænældŷı·sia) *s.* analgesia.
analgesic (-šic) *adj.-s.* analgésico.
analogical (ænala·dŷical) *adj.* de analogía; fundado en ella.
analogize (to) (anæ·lodŷaiš) *tr.-intr.* explicar o razonar por analogía.
analogous (anæ·logøs) *adj.* análogo, semejante, correspondiente.
analogue (æ·nalag) *s.* cosa análoga.
analogy (anæ·lodŷi) *s.* analogía, correlación, correspondencia.
analysis (anæ·lisis) *s.* análisis.
analyst (æ·nalist) *s.* analizador, analista.
analytic(al (ænali·tik(al) *adj.* analítico.
analytics (-s) *s.* analítica. *2* geometría analítica.
analyze (to) (æ·nalaiš) *tr.* analizar.
anana(s) (ana·nas) *s.* anana, ananás.
anapaest, anapest (æ·napest) *s.* anapesto.
anaphrodisia (ænæfrodı·šia) *s.* anafrodisia.
anaphylaxis (ænafilæ·ksis) *s.* MED. anafilaxis.
anarchic(al (ana-ᵣkik(al) *adj.* anárquico.
anarchism (æ·naᵣkišm) *s.* anarquismo.
anarchist (-kist) *adj.-s.* anarquista.
anarchistic (-kistik) *adj.* anarquista.
anarchy (æ·naᵣki) *s.* anarquía.
anastigmatic (ænæstigmæ·tik) *adj.* ÓPT. anastigmático.
anastomose (to) (anæ·stomouš) *intr.* anastomizarse.
anastomosis (anestomou·sis) *s.* anastomosis.
anastrophe (ænæ·strofi) *s.* anástrofe.

anathema (ænæ·zima) *s.* anatema. *2* cosa maldita.
anathematize (to) (-taiš) *tr.* anatematizar.
Anatolia (ænatou·lia) *n. pr.* GEOGR. Anatolia.
Anatolian (-n) *adj.-s.* anatolio.
anatomic(al (ænata·mik(al) *adj.* anatómico.
anatomist (anæ·tomist) *s.* anatomista, disector.
anatomize (to) (-maiš) *tr.* anatomizar, disecar.
anatomy (-mi) *s.* anatomía. *2* disección, análisis. *3* fig. esqueleto, persona flaca.
ancestor (æ·nsestøᵣ) *s.* progenitor, antepasado.
ancestral (ænse·stral) *adj.* de los antepasados, hereditario, solariego.
ancestry (æ·nsestri) *s.* linaje, prosapia, abolengo.
anchor (æ·ngkøᵣ) *s.* ancla, áncora. *2* RELOJ. áncora. *3* tirante, riostra; lo que sirve para sujetar, retener o amarar.
anchor (to) (æ·ngkøᵣ) *tr.* sujetar con el ancla. *2* sujetar, asegurar, fijar, empotrar. *3 intr.* anclar, echar el ancla.
anchorage (æ·ngkøridŷ) *s.* anclaje. *2* ancladero. *3* sitio donde puede asegurarse una cosa.
anchoress (-is) *s.* mujer anacoreta.
anchoret (-ret), **anchorite** (-rait) *s.* anacoreta.
anchorless (-lis) *adj.* sin ancla; inseguro; errante.
anchovy (æ·nchouvi) *s.* ICT. anchoa, boquerón.
ancient (ei·nshønt) *adj.* antiguo. *2* anciano. *3 pl.* los antiguos, la antigüedad.
anciently (-li) *adv.* antiguamente.
ancillary (æ·nsileri) *adj.* auxiliar, subordinado.
and (ænd) *conj.* y, e: ~ *so forth*, ~ *so on*, etcétera; y así sucesivament. *2* con: *bread* ~ *butter*, pan con mantequilla. *3* a, de: *to go* ~ *see*, ir a ver; *to try* ~ *teach*, tratar de enseñar.
Andalusia (ændalu·ŷa) *n. pr.* GEOGR. Andalucía.
Andalusian (-n) *adj.-s.* andaluz.
andante (ændæ·nti) *adv.-s.* MÚS. andante.
andantino (-ı·nou) *adv.-s.* MÚS. andantino.
Andean (ændı·an) *adj.* andino.
Andes (æ·ndiš) *n. pr.* GEOGR. Andes.
andirons (æ·ndaiøᵣns) *s. pl.* morillos.
Andrew (æ·ndru) *n. pr.* Andrés.
androecium (ændrı·shiøm) *s.* BOT. androceo.
androgynous (ændra·dŷnøs) *adj.* andrógino.
anecdotal (æ·nikdoutal) *adj.* anecdótico.
anecdote (æ·nikdout) *s.* anécdota.
anecdotic(al (ænikda·tik(al) *adj.* ANECDOTAL.
anemia *s.*, **anemic** *adj.* ANAEMIA, ANAEMIC. .
anemograph (æne·mogræf) *s.* anemógrafo.
anemometer (ænima·mitøᵣ) *s.* anemómetro.
anemone (ane·moni) *s.* BOT. anemone, anemona: *sea* ~, ZOOL. anemone de mar.
anemoscope (æne·moskoup) *s.* anemoscopio.
aneroid (æ·nøroid) *adj.* aneroide.
anesthesia, anesthetic, etc. ANAESTHESIA, ANAESTHETIC, etc.
aneurism (æ·niurišm) *s.* aneurisma.
anew (aniu·) *adv.* nuevamente, de nuevo, otra vez: *to read* ~, volver a leer.
anfractuosity (ænfrækchua·siti) *s.* anfractuosidad; sinuosidad.
anfractuous (ænfræ·kchuøs) *adj.* anfractuoso; sinuoso.
angel (ei·ndŷøl) *s.* ángel. *2* pop. caballo blanco, pagano. *3* ICT. ~ *fish*, peje ángel.
angelic (ændŷe·lik) *adj.* angélico, angelical.
angelica (ændŷe·lika) *s.* BOT. angélica.
angelical (-l) *adj.* ANGELIC.
Angelus (æ·ndŷeløs) *adj.* Ángelus.
anger (æ·ngøᵣ) *s.* cólera, ira, enojo.
anger (to) *tr.* encolerizar, enfurecer, enojar.

angina (ændⱨai·na) *s.* angina: ~ *pectoris*, angina de pecho.
angiology (ændⱨia·lodⱨi) *s.* angiología.
angiospermous (ændⱨiøspø·ʳmøs) *adj.* BOT. angiospermo.
angle (æ·ngøl) *s.* ángulo: *to be at an* ~ *of*, formar un ángulo de. *2* rincón, esquina, codo, recodo. *3* punto de vista, aspecto. *4* anzuelo.
angle (to) *tr.* pescar con caña en [un río, etc.]. *2 intr.* pescar con caña; fig. *to* ~ *for*, tratar de conseguir o conquistar.
Angles (æ·ngøls) *s. pl.* anglos.
angled (æ·ngøld) *adj.* anguloso, esquinado.
angler (æ·ngløʳ) *s.* pescador de caña. *2* pejesapo, rape.
anglesite (æ·ngløsait) *s.* anglesita.
Anglican (æ·nglikan) *adj.-s.* anglicano.
Anglicanism (-išm) *s.* anglicanismo.
Anglicism (æ·nglisišm) *s.* anglicismo.
Anglicize (to) (-aiš) *tr.* inglesar.
angling (æ·ngling) *s.* pesca con caña.
Anglo-Indian (æ·nglo) *adj.-s.* angloindio.
Anglophile (-fail) *adj.-s.* anglófilo.
Anglophobe (-foub) *adj.-s.* anglófobo.
Anglo-Saxon *adj.-s.* anglosajón.
angrily (æ·ngrili) *adj.* coléricamente, airadamente.
angry (æ·ngri) *adj.* colérico, airado, enojado. *2* furioso, embravecido. *3* MED. irritado.
anguish (æ·ngüish) *s.* angustia, congoja, ansia, aflicción, dolor, tormento.
anguish (to) *tr.* angustiar, acongojar, atormentar.
angular (æ·ngiular) *adj.* angular. *2* anguloso. *3* seco, huesudo, tieso.
angularity (-læ·riti) *s.* angulosidad.
anhelation (ænjilei·shøn) *s.* anhélito.
anhydride (ænjai·drid) *s.* anhídrido.
anhydrous (-drøs) *adj.* anhidro.
anil (æ·nil) *s.* BOT. añil, índigo.
anile (æ·nail) *adj.* de vieja que chochea.
anilin(e (æ·nilin) *s.* QUÍM. anilina.
animadversion (ænimæ·dvøʳshøn) *s.* crítica, censura, reproche.
animadvert (to) (-vøʳt) *intr.* censurar, criticar. | Con *on* o *upon*.
animal (æ·nimal) *s.* animal. *2* bestia, bruto. *3 adj.* animal. *4* ~ *spirits*, vivacidad, animación.
animalcule (ænimæ·lkiul) *s.* animálculo.
animality (-liti) *s.* animalidad.
animalize (to) (æ·nimalaiš) *tr.* animalizar.
animate (æ·nimit) *adj.* animado [viviente; que tiene animación].
animate (to) *tr.* animar.
animated (-id) *adj.* animado: ~ *cartoon*, dibujo animado. *2* vivo, vigoroso.
animation (ænimei·shøn) *s.* animación; vida, calor, movimiento.
animism (æ·nimišm) *s.* animismo.
animosity (ænima·siti) *s.* animosidad.
animus (æ·nimøs) *s.* ánimo, intención. *2* animosidad.
anion (æ·naløn) *s.* QUÍM., FÍS. anión.
anise (æ·nis) *s.* anís [planta y semilla].
aniseed (æ·nisɪid) *s.* anís [semilla].
anisette (ænise·t) *s.* anisete.
anisopetalous (ænaisope·taløs) *adj.* anisopétalo.
ankle (æ·ngkøl) *s.* tobillo.
anklet (æ·ngklit) *s.* ajorca [para el tobillo].
ankylose (to) (æ·nkilous) *tr.* anquilosar. *2 intr.* anquilosarse.
ankylosis (-lou·sis) *s.* anquilosis.

Ann, Anne (æ·n), **Anna** (æ·na) *n. pr.* Ana.
annalist (æ·nalist) *s.* analista, cronista.
annals (æ·nals) *s. pl.* anales.
Annamese (ænamɪ·š), *pl.* **-ese** *adj.-s.* anamita.
annato (ænæ·tou) *s.* BOT. achiote, bija.
anneal (to) (anɪ·l) *tr.* templar, recocer. *2* fig. fortalecer.
annelid (æ·nelid) *adj.-s.* anélido.
annex (ane·ks) *s.* anexo, aditamento, apéndice. *2* dependencia, edificio anexo.
annex (to) *tr.* anexar, anexionar. *2* unir, añadir. *3* poner [una firma].
annexation (-ei·shøn) *s.* anexión.
annexed (ane·kst) *adj.* anexo, anejo, adjunto.
annihilate (to) (anai·ileit) *tr.* aniquilar.
annihilation (-ei·shøn) '*s.* aniquilación, aniquilamiento.
anniversary (ænivø·ʳsari) *adj.* aniversario, anual. *2 s.* aniversario.
annotate (to) (æ·noteit) *tr.* anotar, apostillar.
annotation (ænotei·shøn) *s.* anotación [acción]. *2* anotación, acotación, nota.
annotator (-tøʳ) *s.* anotador.
announce (to) (anau·ns) *tr.* anunciar, hacer saber, proclamar, declarar.
announcement (-mønt) *s.* anuncio, notificación, declaración.
announcer (-øʳ) *s.* anunciador, nuncio. *2* locutor [de radio].
annoy (to) (anoi) *tr.* molestar, incomodar, fastidiar.
annoyance (-ans) *s.* molestia, incomodidad, fastidio, aburrimiento. *2* lata, pejiguera.
annoyer (-øʳ) *s.* molestador, persona enfadosa.
annoying (-ing) *adj.* molesto, fastidioso, enfadoso, engorroso.
annual (æ·nyual) *adj.* anual. *2 s.* LITURG. aniversario. *3* anuario.
annuary (æ·nyueri) *s.* anuario.
annuity (æniu·iti) *s.* anualidad, pensión; renta vitalicia.
annul (to) (anø·l) *tr.* anular, invalidar. *2* abolir. *3* borrar, destruir.
annular (æ·nyular) *adj.* anular.
annulate(d (ænyulei·tid) *adj.* anillado.
annulet (æ·nyulit) *s.* anillito. *2* ARQ., ZOOL. anillo.
annulment (anø·lmønt) *s.* anulación.
annunciate (to) (ænø·nshieit) *tr.* TO ANNOUNCE.
annunciation (-ei·shøn) *s.* anuncio, anunciación.
annunciator (-ei·tøʳ) *s.* anunciador. *2* MEC. indicador. *3* ELECT. indicador de llamadas.
anode (æ·nod) *s.* ELECT. ánodo.
anodyne (æ·nodain) *adj.-s.* anodino.
anoint (to) (anoi·nt) *tr.* untar. *2* ungir, consagrar. *3* administrar la Extremaunción.
anointing (-ing), **anointment** (-mønt) *s.* unción, óleo. *2* untadura.
anomalism (ana·mališm) *s.* anomalía.
anomalistic (anamali·stik) *adj.* anomalístico.
anomalous (ana·maløs) *adj.* anómalo.
anomalousness (-nis), **anomaly** (-li) *s.* anomalía.
anon (ana·n) *adv.* pronto, luego, en seguida.
anonym (æ·nonim) *s.* anónimo [pers.]. *2* pseudónimo.
anonymous (ana·nimøs) *adj.* anónimo.
anorexia (ænore·ksia) *s.* MED. anorexia.
anosmia (ana·šmia) *s.* anosmia.
another (anø·ðøʳ) *adj.-pron.* otro, otra.
anserine (æ·nsørain) *adj.* ansarino. *2* fig. tonto, necio.

answer (æ·nsøʳ) s. respuesta, contestación. 2 explicación, solución [de un problema, enigma, etc.].

answer (to) tr.-intr. respónder, contestar, reponer: to ~ back, replicar, ser respondón. 2 responder, corresponder [guardar, conformidad o correspondencia]. 3 tr. responder, refutar. 4 responder [a esperanzas, deseos, necesidades, etc.]; convenir [a un designio]. 5 obedecer [a una acción, una fuerza]. 6 intr. servir, llenar el objeto. 7 to ~ for, responder por o de; ser o hacerse responsable de.

answerable (-abøl) adj. responsable. 2 correspondiente; conforme. 3 discutible, refutable.

ant (ænt) s. ENT. hormiga: ~ bear, oso hormiguero; ~ lion, hormiga león.

anta (æ·nta) s. ARQ. anta.

Antaeus (ænti·øs) n. pr. Anteo.

antagonism (æntæ·gonišm) s. antagonismo.

antagonist (-ist) s. antagonista.

antagonistic (-i·stik) s. antagónico.

antagonize (to) (-aiš) tr. oponerse a, contrarrestar. 2 provocar el antagonismo, la enemistad de.

antaphrodisiac (æntæfrodi·šilaek) adj.-s. antiafrodisíaco.

antarctic (ænta·ʳtik) adj. antártico. 2 s. tierras antárticas.

antarthritic (-zri·tik) adj. antiartrítico.

antecede (to) (æntisı·d) intr. anteceder, preceder.

antecedence, -cy (-ens, -i) s. predecesión.

antecedent (-ønt) adj.-s. antecedente, precedente, anterior. 2 s. antecedente. 3 pl. antepasados.

antecedently (-li) adv. anteriormente.

antecessor (æntise·søʳ) s. antecesor, predecesor.

antechamber (æ·nticheimbøʳ) s. antecámara, antesala.

antechoir (-kuaiøʳ) s. antecoro.

antedate (æ·ntideit) s. antedata.

antedate (to) tr. antedatar. 2 adelantar; retrotraer.

antediluvian (-diliu·vian) adj. antediluviano.

antelope (æ·nteloup) s. antílope.

antemeridian (æntimøri·dian) adj. antemeridiano.

antenatal (æntinei·tal) adj. prenatal.

antenna (ænte·na), pl. -nae (-ni) ZOOL. antena. 2 (pl. -nas) RADIO. antena.

antenuptial (antinø·pshal) adj. antenupcial.

antependium (-pe·ndiøm) s. antipendio.

antepenultimate (-pinø·lt(imit) adj. y s. antepenúltima [sílaba].

anterior (ænti·riøʳ) adj. anterior.

anteriority (æntiria·riti) s. anterioridad.

anteroom (æ·ntirum) s. antesala, vestíbulo.

anthem (æ·nzøm) s. antífona. 2 himno.

anther (æ·nzøʳ) s. antera.

antheridium (ænzøri·diøm) s. anteridio.

anthill (æ·ntjil) s. hormiguero [montículo].

anthological (ænzola·dȳkal) adj. antológico.

anthology (ænza·lodȳi) s. antología.

Anthony (æ·ntoni) n. pr. Antonio.

anthozoan (ænzøsou·an) adj. y s. ZOOL. antozoario, antozoo.

anthracene (æ·nzrasın) s. QUÍM. antraceno.

anthracite (æ·nzrasait) s. antracita.

anthrax (æ·nzræks) s. MED. ántrax. 2 MED. carbunco.

anthropoid (æ·nzropoid) adj.-s. antropoideo.

anthropologic(al (-pola·dȳik(al) adj. antropológico.

anthropologist (-pa·lodȳist) s. antropólogo.

anthropology (-pa·lodȳi) s. antropología.

anthropometric(al (-pome·trik(al) adj. antropométrico.

anthropometry (-pa·metri) s. antropometría.

anthropomorphism (-pomo·ʳfism) s. antropomorfismo.

anthropomorphous (-pomo·ʳføs) adj. antropomorfo.

anthropophagi (-pa·fadȳai) s. pl. antropófagos.

anthropophagite (-fadȳait) s. antropófago.

anthropophagous (-fagøs) adj. antropófago.

anthropophagy (-faȳi) s. antropofagia.

anti- (ænti) pref. anti-.

antiaircraft (æntie·ø·ʳkraft) adj. antiaéreo.

antialcoholic (-ælkojo·lik) adj. antialcohólico.

antiar (æ·tiaʳ) s. antiar [árbol y veneno].

antibiotic (-baia·tik) adj.-s. antibiótico.

antibody (-ba·di) s. anticuerpo.

antic (æ·ntik) adj. grotesco, estrafalario. 2 s. zapateta, cabriola. 3 bufón, payaso. 4 pl. bufonadas, travesuras.

anticatarrhal (æntikata·ral) adj. anticatarral.

Antichrist (æ·ntikraist) s. antecristo.

anticipate (to) (ænti·sipeit) tr. anticipar, adelantar [una acción, un suceso]. 2 anticiparse, adelantarse a. 3 prevenir, impedir. 4 prever, esperar. 5 prometerse [un placer, etc.]; gozar o experimentar de antemano. 6 gastar por adelantado.

anticipation (-pei·shøn) s. anticipación [acción, efecto]. 2 intuición o impresión de lo que va a suceder. 3 expectación, esperanza, goce anticipado.

anticlerical (-kle·rikal) adj. anticlerical.

anticolonialism (-kolou·niališm) s. anticolonialismo.

anticonstitutional (-konstitiu·shønal) adj. anticonstitucional.

anticyclone (-sai·kloun) s. anticiclón.

antidiptheritic (-difzøri·tik) adj. antidiftérico.

antidote (æ·ntidout) s. antídoto.

antiferment (-føʳmønt) s. antifermento.

antifreeze (-fri·š) adj. anticongelante.

antifriction (-frikshøn) adj. MEC. antifricción.

antigen (æ·ntidȳøn) s. antígeno.

antihydrophobic (-jaidrofou·bik) adj. antirrábico.

anti-knock (-nak) adj. antidetonante [gasolina].

Antillean (ænti·lian) adj.-s. antillano.

Antilles (ænti·lıš) n. pr. GEOGR. Antillas.

antilogarithm (-logariðm) s. MAT. antilogaritmo.

antilogy (-lodȳi) s. antilogía.

antimilitarism (-mi·litarišm) s. antimilitarista.

antimonial (-mou·nial) adj. antimonial.

antimony (æ·ntimouni) s. QUÍM. antimonio.

antinomy (ænti·nomi) s. antinomia.

antioch (æ·ntiak) s. GEOGR. Antioquía.

Antiochus (æntai·okøs) n. pr. Antíoco.

antipathetic(al (antipaze·tik(al) adj. antipático. 2 antagónico, opuesto.

antipathy (ænti·pazi) s. antipatía, aversión.

antiphon (æ·ntiføn) s. antífona.

antiphrasis (ænti·frasis) s. antífrasis.

antipodal (-podal) adj. antípoda.

antipode (æn·tipoud) s. lo contrario u opuesto.

antipodean (-tipodi·an) adj. ANTIPODAL.

antipodes (ænti·podiš) s. pl. GEOGR. antípodas.

antipope (-poup) s. antipapa.

antipyretic (antipaire·tik) adj.-s. antipirético.

antipyrin(e (-pai·rin) s. antipirina.

antiquarian (-kue·rian) adj.-s. anticuario.

antiquary (æ·ntikueri) s. anticuario.

antiquate (to) (æ·ntikueit) tr. anticuar.

antiquated (-id) adj. anticuado.

antique (æntı·k) *adj.* antiguo. *2 s.* antigüedad, antigualla.
antiqueness (-nis) *s.* antigüedad [calidad].
antiquity (-kuiti) *s.* antigüedad. *2* ancianidad, vejez. *3 pl.* antigüedades.
antiscians (ænti·shanš), **antiscii** (-shiai) *s. pl.* antiscios.
anti-Semite (-se·mait) *s.* antisemita.
anti-Semitic (-semi·tik) *adj.* antisemita, antisemítico.
antisepsis (-se·psis) *s.* antisepsia.
antiseptic (-se·ptik) *adj.-s.* antiséptico.
antiskid (æ·ntiskid) *adj.* antideslizante.
antisocial (æntisou·shal) *adj.* antisocial.
antispasmodic (-spæšma·dik) *adj.-s.* antiespasmódico.
antistrophe (anti·strof) *s.* antistrofa.
antitank (æntitæ·nk) *adj.* antitanque.
antitetanic (-titænik) *adj.* antitetánico.
antithesis (ænti·zesis) *s.* antítesis.
antithetical (æntize·tikal) *adj.* antitético.
antitoxin (-ta·ksin) *s.* antitoxina.
antitragus (anti·tragøs) *s.* antitrago.
antitrust (æntitrø·st) *adj.* opuesto a los trusts.
antituberculous (-tiubø·ʳkiuløs) *adj.* antituberculoso.
antler (æntløʳ) *s.* asta, cuerna [de venado].
antlered (æ·ntløʳ) *adj.* provisto de cuerdas o adornado con ellas.
antoecians (anti·shans), **antoeci** (æ-sai) *m. pl.* GEOGR. antecos.
Antoinette (æntuane·t) *n. pr.* Antonieta.
antonomasia (æntonomei·ŷia) *s.* antonomasia.
Antony (æ·ntoni) *n. pr.* Antonio.
antonym (æ·ntonim) *s.* antónimo.
Antwerp (æ·ntwøʳp) *n. pr.* GEOGR. Amberes.
anuran (æniu·ram) *adj.-s.* anuro.
anus (ei·nøs) *s.* ANAT. ano.
anvil (æ·nvil) *s.* yunque, bigornia. *2* ANAT. yunque.
anxiety (ængšai·øti) *s.* ansiedad, inquietud, desasosiego. *2* ansia, anhelo, afán.
anxious (æ·nkshøs) *adj.* ansioso, inquieto, desasosegado. *2* ansioso, anheloso, afanoso. *3* angustioso, penoso.
any (-e·ni) *adj.* cualquier, todo, todos los, algún, alguno; [en frases negativas] ningún, ninguno: ~ *place*, cualquier parte, en cualquier parte; *I have not* ~ *book*, no tengo ningún libro; *at* ~ *rate*, de todos modos; sea como sea. *2* tiene sentido partitivo y en este caso suele no traducirse: *have you* ~ *money?*, ¿tiene usted dinero? *3* todo [la mayor cantidad, etc., posible]: *at* ~ *cost*, a toda costa.
  4 pron. alguno, alguna, algunos, alguien; [en frases negativas] ninguno, ninguna, nadie: *if* ~, si lo hay.
  5 adv. en alguna extensión, en algún grado, algo. | A veces no se traduce: ~ *more*, más, más tiempo; *not...* ~ *longer*, ya no.
anybody (e·nibadi) *pron.* alguien, alguno: [en frases negativas] ninguno, nadie. *2* cualquiera, todos, todo el mundo.
anyhow (e·nijau) *adv.* de cualquier modo. *2* de todos modos, sin embargo. *3* en todo caso, como quiera que sea; sea lo que fuere.
anyone (e·niuøn) *pron.* ANYBODY.
anything (e·nizing) *pron.* algo, alguna cosa, cualquier cosa, todo cuanto; [con negación] nada. *2 as* ~, *like* ~, por demás.
anyway (e·niuei) *adv.* de todos modos, en cual-

quier caso. *2* sin embargo. *3* de cualquier modo, sin orden.
anywhere (e·nijueʳ) *adv.* doquiera, en todas partes; en cualquier parte, adondequiera; *not* ~, en ninguna parte, a ninguna parte.
anywise (e·niwaiš) *adv.* de cualquier modo.
aorist (ei·ørist) *s.* aoristo.
aorta (eio·ʳta) *s.* ANAT. aorta.
apace (apei·s) *adv.* aprisa, rápidamente.
Apache (apæ·chi) *adj.-s.* apache.
apanage (æ·panidŷ) *s.* APPANAGE.
apart (apa·ʳt) *adv.* aparte; a un lado. *2* separadamente, de por sí. *3* en piezas: *to take* ~, desarmar, desmontar.
apartment (-mønt) *s.* aposento. *2* cuarto piso, apartamiento.
apathetic (æpaze·tik) *adj.* apático, indiferente.
apathy (æ·pazi) *s.* apatía, indiferencia.
ape (eip) *s.* ZOOL. mono, mico, simio. *2* fig. mona, imitador.
ape (to) *tr.* imitar, remedar.
Apennines (æ·pønainš) *n. pr.* GEOGR. Apeninos.
aperiodic (eipiria·dik) *adj.* aperiódico.
apéritif (æperiti·f) *s.* aperitivo.
aperture (æ·pøʳchøʳ) *s.* abertura [oficio, portillo, etc.].
apery (ei·pøri) *s.* remedo, monada.
apetalous (eipe·taløs) *adj.* apétalo.
apex (ei·peks) *s.* ápice, cúspide, vértice, cumbre.
aphaeresis (æfe·røsis) *s.* aféresis.
aphasia (æfei·ŷia) *s.* afasia.
aphelion (æfi·liøn) *s.* ASTR. afelio.
apheresis (æfe·røsis) *s.* APHAERESIS.
aphid (ei·fid), **aphis** (-fiš) *s.* ENT. áfido.
aphonia (eifou·nia) *s.* afonía.
aphonic (eifa·nik) *adj.* afónico.
aphonous (æ·fonøs) *adj.* áfono.
aphorism (æ·førišm) *s.* aforismo.
aphrodisia (æfrødı·ŷia) *s.* afrodisia.
aphrodisiac (-ı·ŷiak) *adj.-s.* afrodisíaco.
aphta (æ·fza) *s.* MED. afta.
aphtous (æ·fzøs) *adj.* aftoso.
apiary (ei·pieri) *s.* colmenar.
apical (æ·pikal) *adj.* apical.
apiculture (eipikøl·chøʳ) *s.* apicultura.
apiculturist (-ist) *s.* apicultor.
apiece (apı·s) *adv.* cada uno, a cada uno, por barba, por cabeza.
apish (ei·pish) *adj.* simiesco. *2* que imita servilmente. *3* necio.
aplomb (aplo·m) *s.* aplomo, seguridad. *2* aplomo, verticalidad.
apnea, apnoea (æpnı·a) *s.* apnea.
Apocalypse (apa·kalips) *s.* Apocalipsis.
apocopate (to) (apa·kopeit) *tr.* apocopar.
apocope (apa·kopi) *s.* apócope.
Apocrypha (apa·krifa) *s. pl.* libros apócrifos.
apocryphal (-l) *adj.* apócrifo.
apocynaceous (aposinei·shøs) *adj.* apocináceo.
apod (æ·pad) *s.* ápodo.
apodal (æ·padal) *adj.* ápodo.
apodosis (æpa·dosis) *s.* apódosis.
apogee (æ·podŷi) *s.* apogeo.
Apolline (æ·palin) *adj.* APOLLONIAN.
Apolo (æpa·lou) *n. pr.* Apolo.
Apollonian (æpalou·nian) *adj.* apolíneo.
apologetic(al (apalodŷe·tik(al) *adj.* apologético. *2* de excusa.
apologetically (-i) *adv.* apologéticamente. *2* en tono de excusa.
apologetics (-tiks) *s.* apologética.

apologist (apa·lodȳist) *s.* apologista.
apologize (to) (-aiš) *intr.* excusarse, disculparse, presentar excusas.
apologue (æ·polag) *s.* apólogo.
apology (apa·lodȳi) *s.* apología. *2* excusa, disculpa. *3* cosa que suple la falta de otra.
apophthegm (æ·pozem) *s.* APOTHEGM.
apophyge (æpa·fidȳi) *s.* apófige.
apophysis (-sis), *pl.* **-sis** (siš) *se* apófisis.
apoplectic (æpople·ktik) *adj.*-*s.* apoplético.
apoplexy (æpopleksi) *s.* MED. apoplejía.
apostasy (apa·stasi) *s.* apostasía.
apostate (-teit) *s.* apóstata, renegado. *2 adj.* falso, pérfido.
apostatize (to) (-ataiš) *intr.* apostatar.
aposteme (æ·pastem) *s.* apostema.
apostle (apa·søl) *s.* apóstol.
apostleship (-ship), **apostolate** (-leit) *s.* apostolado.
apostolic(al (æpøsta·lik(al) *adj.* apostólico.
apostrophe (apa·strofi) *s.* apóstrofe. *2* apóstrofo.
apostrophize (to) (apa·strofaiš) *tr.* apostrofar. *2* señalar con un apóstrofo.
apothecary (apa·zikeri) *s.* boticario, farmacéutico.
apothegm (æ·pozem) *s.* apotegma.
apothem (æ·pozem) *s.* GEOM. apotema.
apotheosis (æpaziou·sis) *s.* apoteosis.
apotheosize (to) (æpa·ziosaiš) *tr.* deificar.
appa(l (to) (æpo·l) *tr.* espantar, aterrar. *2* desmayar, desanimar. ¶ Pret. y p. p.: *appalled;* ger.: -*lling.*
appalling (-ing) *adj.* espantoso, aterrador.
appanage (æ·panidȳi) *s.* infantazgo. *2* patrimonio, atributo [cosa o cualidad inherente].
apparatus (æparei·tøs) *s.* aparato, dispositivo.
apparel (apæ·rel) *s.* ropa, vestido. *2* MAR. aparejo [de un buque].
apparel (to) *tr.* vestir, trajear. *2* adornar.
apparent (ape·rønt) *adj.* claro, manifiesto, evidente. *2* aparente. *3* sensible [horizonte].
apparently (-li) *adv.* claramente, evidentemente. *2* al parecer, por lo visto.
apparition (æpari·shøn) *s.* aparición.
apparitor (apæ·ritøʳ) *s.* alguacil; bedel.
appeal (apı·l) *s.* apelación. *2* llamamiento; petición, súplica, clamor. *3* recurso [a un medio; a una autoridad o testimonio]. *4* atracción, atractivo, interés.
appeal (to) *intr.* DER. apelar. *2* apelar, recurrir [a una pers. o cosa]; suplicar; hacer llamamiento a. *3* remitirse [a uno], poner por testigo. *4* mover, atraer, interesar.
appealing (apı·ling) *adj.* suplicante. *2* atrayente. *3* que despierta interés o simpatía.
appear (to) (apı·ʳ) *intr.* aparecer, aparecerse, parecer, salir, mostrarse, asomar, brotar, surgir. *2* salir [un periódico]. *3* comparecer, presentarse. *4* parecer, semejar.
appearance (apı·rans) *s.* aparición, aparecimiento; llegada, entrada. *2* DER. comparecencia. *3* apariencia. *4* aspecto, traza, porte. *5* viso, vislumbre. *6 pl.* apariencias.
appease (to) (apı·š) *tr.* aplacar, calmar. *2* sosegar, aquietar, apaciguar. *3* desenojar.
appeasement (-mønt) *s.* alivio, aplacamiento. *2* aquietamiento. *3* apaciguamiento, desenojo.
appeaser (-øʳ) *s.* aplacador, apaciguador.
appellant (ape·lant) *adj.*-*s.* apelante.
appellation (æpelei·shøn) *s.* denominación, nombre, título.

appelative (ape·lativ) *adj.* GRAM. apelativo, común. *2 s.* apelativo, nombre.
appellee (æpelı·) *s.* DER. apelado.
append (to) (ape·ndi) *tr.* atar, colgar, añadir [una cosa a otra].
appendage (-idȳ) *s.* dependencia, accesorio, aditamento, apéndice.
appendant (-ant) *adj.* anexo, accesorio; colgante. *2 s.* cosa o pers. adjunta o dependiente.
appendicitis (-disai·tis) *s.* MED. apendicitis.
appendix (-diks) *s.* apéndice.
apperception (æpø·ʳse·pshøn) *s.* apercepción.
appertain (to) (æpøʳtei·n) *intr.* pertenecer, tocar, atañer. *2* ser relativo [a].
appetence, -cy (æ·pitøns, -si) *s.* apetencia, deseo. *2* FÍS., QUÍM. afinidad.
appetite (æ·pitait) *s.* apetito.
appetitive (-iv) *adj.* apetitivo.
appetizer (æ·pitaišøʳ) *s.* aperitivo.
appetizing (-ing) *adj.* apetitoso. *2* tentador, incitante.
Appian Way (æ·pian) *s.* Vía Apia.
applaud (to) (aplo·d) *tr.*-*intr.* aplaudir. *2 tr.* alabar, encomiar.
applause (aplo·š) *s.* aplauso.
applausive (aplo·siv) *adj.* laudatorio.
apple (æ·pøl) *s.* BOT. manzana, poma; ~ *mint,* mastranzo; ~ *tree,* manzano. *2* ~ *of the eye,* pupila, niña del ojo; fig. niña de los ojos.
applejack (-dȳæk) *s.* aguardiente de manzanas.
apple-pie order *s.* orden perfecto.
appliance (aplai·ans) *s.* instrumento, utensilio, aparato, medio, artificio. *2* aplicación, empleo.
applicable (æ·plikabøl) *adj.* aplicable.
applicant (æ·plikant) *s.* solicitante, peticionario. *2* pretendiente, aspirante.
application (æplikei·shøn) *s.* aplicación. *2* emplasto, untura. *3* petición, solicitud.
applied (aplai·d) *pret.* y *p. p.* de TO APPLY.
appliqué (æplike·) *s.* aplicación [adorno sobrepuesto].
apply (to) (aplai·) *tr.* aplicar. *2 intr.* aplicarse, referirse, ser apropiado [a]. *3 to* ~ *for,* pedir, solicitar; *to* ~ *to,* recurrir a, pedir a. *4 ref.* aplicarse, consagrarse, dedicarse [a]. ¶ Pret. y p. p.: *applied.*
appoggiatura (apadȳatu·ra) *s.* MÚS. apoyatura.
appoint (to) (apoi·nt) *tr.* fijar, señalar, determinar, establecer, prescribir. *2* ordenar, decretar. *3* asignar, destinar. *4* nombrar, designar, comisionar. *5* proveer, amueblar.
appointee (apointı·) *s.* persona nombrada o electa.
appointment (apoi·ntmønt) *s.* señalamiento, fijación. *2* decreto, mandato. *3* cita, hora dada. *4* nombramiento, designación. *5* empleo, puesto. *6 pl.* equipo; mobiliario.
apportion (to) (apo·ʳshøn) *tr.* prorratear, distribuir.
apportionment (-mønt) *s.* prorrateo, prorrata. *2* repartimiento.
appose (to) (æpou·š) *tr.* poner, aplicar. *2* yuxtaponer.
apposite (æ·pošit) *adj.* apropiado, conveniente, oportuno, a propósito.
apposition (æpoši·shøn) *s.* aposición. *2* adición, yuxtaposición.
appraisal (aprei·šal) *s.* apreciación, estimación, valoración, tasación.
appraise (to) (aprei·š) *tr.* apreciar, estimar, valorar, tasar.
appraisement (-mønt) *s.* APPRAISAL.

appraiser (-ø^r) *s.* estimador, tasador.
appreciable (aprɪ·shiabøl) *adj.* apreciable, estimable, sensible, perceptible.
appreciate (to) (-sieit) *tr.* apreciar, estimar, valuar, tasar. *2* estimar, agradecer. *3* aumentar el valor de. *4 intr.* aumentar de valor.
appreciation (-ei·shøn) *s.* apreciación, aprecio. *2* agradecimiento. *3* aumento de valor.
apprehend (to) (æprije·nd) *tr.* aprehender, prender. *2* FIL. aprehender. *3* comprender, percibir. *4* temer, recelar.
apprehension (-shøn) *s.* aprehensión, prisión, captura. *2* FIL. aprehensión. *3* comprensión. *4* temor, recelo.
apprehensive (-siv) *adj.* aprehensivo. *2* inteligente, perspicaz. *3* consciente [de algo]. *4* temeroso, receloso [de]; que teme [por].
apprentice (apre·ntis) *s.* aprendiz.
apprentice (to) *tr.* poner de aprendiz.
apprise, apprize (to) (aprai·ś) *tr.* informar, avisar, enterar. *2 ant.* TO APPRAISE.
approach (aprou·ch) *s.* proximidad, aproximación. *2* acceso, entrada. *3* tentativas, primeros pasos [para una amistad, un negocio, etc.]; acción de abordar [a una pers., un estudio, etc.], de enfocar [un problema, etc.]. *4 pl.* cercanías. *5* FORT. aproches.
approach (to) *intr.* acercarse, aproximarse; avecinarse. *2 tr.* acercar, aproximar. *3* acercarse a. *4* dirigirse [a uno], hablarle de un asunto, hacerle proposiciones. *5* abordar, enfocar [un asunto]; tocar [un tema].
approachable (-abøl) *adj.* accesible, abordable.
approbate (to) (æ·probeit) *tr.* (E. U.) aprobar, sancionar.
approbation (-ei·shøn) *s.* aprobación.
appropriate (aprou·prieit) *adj.* apropiado. *2* propio, peculiar.
appropriate (to) *tr.* destinar [a un uso]; asignar, votar [una cantidad]. *2* apropiarse.
appropriation (-ei·shøn) *s.* apropiación. *2* (E. U.) crédito, asignación [votados].
approval (apru·val) *s.* aprobación. *2* COM.*on* ~, a prueba.
approve (to) (apru·v) *tr.* aprobar, sancionar; confirmar, ratificar. *2* probar, demostrar; acreditar [de]. *3 intr. to* ~ *of,* aprobar, hallar de su gusto.
approvingly (-ingli) *adv.* con aprobación.
approximate (apra·ksimit) *adj.* próximo, cercano. *2* aproximado.
approximate (to) (-meit) *tr.* aproximar. *2* aproximarse a. *3 intr.* aproximarse, acercarse.
approximately (-li) *adv.* aproximadamente.
approximation (-ei·shøn) *s.* aproximación.
approximative (-ativ) *adj.* aproximado, aproximativo.
appulse (æ·pøls) *s.* ASTR. apulso.
appurtenance (apø·^{r}tønans) *s.* pertenencia, dependencia, accesorio.
apricot (ei·prikat) *s.* BOT. albaricoque: ~ *tree,* albaricoquero.
April (ei·pril) *s.* abril.
April Fool's Day *s.* ALL FOOL'S DAY.
apriorism (eipraiou·rišm) *s.* apriorismo.
apron (ei·prøn) *s.* delantal, mandil: *tied to the* ~ *strings of,* dominado por [la madre, la mujer, etc.]. *2* batiente [de un dique]. *3* MEC. plancha de protección. *4* MAR. albitana.
apropos (æpropou') *adj.* pertinente, oportuno. *2 adv.* a propósito.
apse (æps) *s.* ARQ. ábside.

apsis (æ·psis) *s.* ASTR. ápside.
apt (æpt) *adj.* apto. *2* listo, hábil, pronto. *3* adecuado. *4* propenso, expuesto, capaz.
apterous (æ·ptørøs) *adj.* ZOOL. áptero.
aptitude (æ·ptitiud), **aptness** (æ·ptnis) *s.* aptitud. *2* propensión, disposición, facilidad.
aquafortis (æ·kua*fo*^{r}tis) *s.* B. ART. aguafuerte.
aquafortist (-fo·^{r}tist) *s.* aguafuertista.
aquamarine (-mari·n) *s.* MINER. aguamarina.
aquarelle (ækuare·l) *s.* acuarela.
aquarellist (-ist) *s.* acuarelista.
aquarium (akue·riøm) *s.* acuario.
Aquarius (-riøs) *n. pr.* ASTR. acuario.
aquatic(al (akue·tikal) *adj.* acuático.
aquatint (æ·kuatint) *s.* acuatinta.
aqueduct (æ·kuidøkt) *s.* acueducto.
aqueous (ei·kuiøs) *adj.* ácueo, acuoso.
aquiline (æ·kuilin) *adj.* aquilino, aguileño.
aquose (ei·kuous) *adj.* ACQUEOUS.
Arab (æ·rab) *adj.-s.* árabe. *2 s.* caballo árabe. *3 street* ~, pillete, golfillo.
arabesque (ærabe·sk) *adj.-s.* arabesco.
Arabian (arei·bian) *adj.* arábico, arábigo. *2 the Arabian Nights,* Las mil y una noches. *3 s.* árabe.
Arabic (æ·rabik) *adj.* arábigo. *2 s.* árabe, arábico [idioma].
Arabist (-bist) *s.* arabista.
arable (æ·rabøl) *adj.* labrantío, cultivable.
arachnid(an (æræ·knid(an) *adj.-s.* arácnido.
arachnoid (-noid) *adj.* aracnoideo. *2 adj.-s.* arácnido. *3* ANAT. aracnoides.
Aragonese (ærægoni·ś) *adj.-s.* aragonés.
Aramaic (æramei·ik) *adj.* arameo.
Araucanian (ærokei·nian) *adj.-s.* araucano.
araucaria (æroke·ria) *s.* BOT. araucaria.
arbalest, arbalist (a·^{r}balist) *s.* ballesta [arma]. *2* arbalestrilla.
arbiter (a·^{r}bitø^r) *s.* árbitro, arbitrador.
arbitrage (-tridÿ) *s.* arbitraje.
arbitral (-tral) *adj.* arbitral.
arbitrament (a^r·bi·tramønt) *s.* arbitramento. *2* arbitrio, albedrío.
arbitrary (a·^{r}bitreri) *adj.* arbitrario. *2* discrecional. *3* despótico, autocrático.
arbitrate (to) (-treit) *tr.-intr.* arbitrar, juzgar, decidir.
arbitration (a^{r}bitrei·shøn) *s.* arbitraje, arbitramento.
arbitrator (a·^{r}bitreitø^r) *m.* árbitro. *2* arbitrador, amigable componedor.
arbor (a·^{r}bø^r) *s.* MEC. árbol. *2* ARBOUR.
arboreal (a^{r}bo·rial) *adj.* arbóreo.
arborescent (a^{r}bore·sønt) *adj.* arborescente.
arboretum (a^{r}bori·tøm) *s.* jardín botánico de árboles.
arboriculture (æ·^{r}børikølchø^r) *s.* arboricultura.
arboriculturist (-ist) *s.* arboricultor.
arborist (a·^{r}børist) *s.* arborista.
arbor-vitæ (a·^{r}bø^r vai·ti) *s.* BOT., ANAT. árbol de la vida.
arbour (a·^{r}bø^r) *s.* cenador, glorieta, emparrado.
arbutus (a^{r}biu·tøs) *s.* BOT. madroño [planta].
arc (a·^{r}k) *s.* GEOM., ASTR., ELECT. arco.
arc (to) *tr.* ELECT. formar arco.
arcade (a·^{r}keid) *s.* ARQ. arcada. *2* soportal, galería.
Arcadia (a^{r}kei·dia) *n. pr.* Arcadia.
Arcadian (a^{r}kei·dian) *adj.-s.* arcadio, árcade. *2 adj.* arcádico.
Arcady (a·^{r}keidi) *n. pr.* ARCADIA.
arcane (a·^{r}kei·n) *adj.* arcano.
arcanum (a·^{r}kei·nøm), *pl.* **-na** (-na) *s.* arcano.

arch (aᶜch) *s.* ARQ. arco; bóveda. *2* ANAT. cayado [de la aorta]. *3 adj.* travieso, picaresco. *4* astuto, socarrón. *5* principal, insigne.

arch (to) *tr.* arquear, encarcar. *2* abovedar. *3 intr.* arquearse. *4* formar bóveda.

archaelogic(al (aᶜkiola·dŷik(al) *adj.* arqueológico.

archaelogist (aᶜkia·lodŷist) *s.* arqueólogo.

archaeology (aᶜkia·lodŷi) *s.* arqueología.

archaic (aᶜkei·k) *adj.* arcaico.

archaism (a·ᶜkeišm) *s.* arcaísmo.

archaize (to) (a·ᶜkeiaiš) *intr.* arcaizar.

archangel (a·kei·ndŷøl) *s.* arcángel.

archangelic (aᶜkændŷe·lik) *f.* arcangélico.

archbishop (a·ᶜchbishøp) *s.* arzobispo.

archbishopric (aᶜchdbi·shøprik) *s.* arzobispado.

archdeacon (aᶜchdɪ·køn) *s.* arcediano.

archdeaconry (-ri) *s.* arcedianato.

archdiocese (-dai·søs) *s.* archidiócesis.

archducal (-diu·kal) *adj.* archiducal.

archduchess (-dø·chis) *s.* archiduquesa.

archduchy (-dø·chi) *s.* archiducado.

archduke (-diu·k) *s.* archiduque.

arched (aᶜcht) *adj.* arqueado, abovedado.

archegonium (aᶜkigou·niøm) *s.* BOT. arquegonio.

archeologic(al, etc. ARCHAEOLOGIC(AL, etc.

archer (a·ᶜchøᶜ) *s.* arquero, flechero.

archeress (-is) *s.* arquera.

archery (-i) *s.* tropa de arqueros. *2* tiro de arco.

archetype (a·ᶜkitaip) *s.* arquetipo.

archiepiscopal (aᶜkiipi·skopal) *adj.* arzobispal.

archil (a·ᶜkil) *s.* BOT. urchilla.

archimandrite (-mæ·ndrait) *s.* archimandrita.

Archimedean (aᶜkimɪ·dian) *adj.* de Arquímedes: ~ *screw,* rosca de Arquímedes.

Archimedes (-diš) *n. pr.* Arquímedes.

archipelago (aᶜkipe·lagou) *s.* archipiélago.

architect (a·ᶜkitekt) *s.* arquitecto.

architectonic (aᶜkitekta·nik), **architectural** (aᶜkite·kchøral) *adj.* arquitectónico.

architecture (a·ᶜkitekchøᶜ) *s.* arquitectura.

architrave (a·ᶜkitreiv) *s.* ARQ. arquitrabe.

archives (a·ᶜkaivš) *s. pl.* archivo.

archivist (a·ᶜkivist) *s.* archivero.

archivolt (a·ᶜkivoult) *s.* archivolta.

archly (a·ᶜchli) *adv.* con travesura, con picardía.

archon (a·ᶜkan) *s.* arconte.

archpriest (a·ᶜchprɪst) *s.* gran sacerdote. *2* arcipreste.

archway (a·ᶜchuei) *s.* entrada en forma de arco; pasaje abovedado.

arctic (a·ᶜktik) *adj.* ártico: *Arctic Circle,* círculo polar ártico; ~ *fox,* zorro azul. *2 s.* región ártica.

arcuate (a·ᶜkiueit) *adj.* arqueado.

arcuation (-ei·shøn) *s.* arcuación. *2* ARQ. sistema de arcos.

ardency (a·ᶜdønsi) *s.* ardor.

ardent (a·ᶜdønt) *adj.* ardiente: ~ *spirits,* licores espirituosos. *2* encendido, brillante.

ardo(u)r (a·ᶜdøᶜ) *s.* ardor. *2* celo, entusiasmo, ardimiento.

arduous (a·ᶜdiuøs) *adj.* arduo, difícil. *2* riguroso. *3* enérgico. *4* escarpado, escabroso.

are (aᶜ) *pl. del pres. de indic.* de TO BE.

are (e·øᶜ) *s.* área (medida).

area (e·ria) *s.* área (superficie, espacio). *2* patio bajo que da acceso a la parte delantera de los sótanos.

areca (ari·ka) *s.* BOT. areca. *2* nuez de areca.

arena (arɪ·na) *s.* arena, arenas, liza, redondel, ruedo.

arenaceous (ærinei·shøs), **arenose** (æ·rinous) *adj.* arenáceo, arenoso, arenisco.

areola (ærɪ·ola) *s.* ANAT., MED. aréola.

areometer (æria·mitøᶜ) *s.* areómetro.

Areopagus (æria·pagøs) *s.* areópago.

argent (æ·ᶜdŷønt) *s.* BLAS. argén.

argentiferous (aᶜdŷønti·førøs) *adj.* argentífero.

Argentina (aᶜdŷønt·na) *n. pr.* Argentina.

argentine (a·ᶜdŷøntin) *adj.* argentino. *2 s.* metal blanco.

Argentine, Argentinean (aᶜdŷønti·nian) *adj.-s.* argentino [de la Argentina].

argil (a·ᶜdŷil) *s.* arcilla, alfar.

argilous (aᶜdŷi·løs) *adj.* arcilloso.

argon (a·ᶜgan) *s.* QUÍM. argón.

Argonaut (a·ᶜgønot) *s.* argonauta.

argue (to) (a·ᶜgiu) *intr.* argüir, argumentar. *2 tr.-intr.* discutir. *3 tr.* argüir (probar, indicar). *4 to* ~ *into,* persuadir a; *to* ~ *out of,* disuadir de.

arguer (a·ᶜgiuøᶜ) *s.* arguyente. *2* discutidor.

argument (a·ᶜgiumønt) *s.* argumento. *2* debate, discusión, disputa.

argumentation (-mentei·shøn) *s.* argumentación. *2* debate, discusión.

argumentative (-me·ntativ) *adj.* argumentativo, dialéctico. *2* argumentador, discutidor.

Argus (a·ᶜgøs) *n. pr.* MIT. Argos.

argute (a·ᶜgiu·t) *adj.* astuto, sagaz. *2* estridente.

aria (a·ria) *s.* MÚS. aria.

Arian (e·rian) *adj.-s.* arriano.

Arianism (-išm) *s.* arrianismo.

arid (æ·rid) *adj.* árido.

aridity (ari·diti) *s.* aridez.

Aries (e·riiš) *n. pr.* ASTR. Aries.

aright (arai·t) *adv.* bien, correctamente.

aril (æ·ril) *s.* BOT. arilo.

arise (to) (arai·š) *intr.* subir, elevarse. *2* levantarse. *3* aparecer, surgir. *4* presentarse, suscitarse. *5* originarse. ¶ Pret.: *arose;* p. p.: *arisen.*

Aristarch (ærista·ᶜk) *n. pr. y s.* Aristarco.

aristocracy (ærista·krasi) *s.* aristocracia.

aristocrat (æri·stokræt) *s.* aristócrata.

aristocratic(al (-æ·tik(al) *adj.* aristocrático.

Aristophanes (-ta·fanis) *n. pr.* Aristófanes.

Aristotelian (-totɪ·lian), **Aristotelic** (-toti·lik) *adj.* aristotélico.

Aristotle (-ta·tøl) *n. pr.* Aristóteles.

arithmetic (ari·zmetik) *s.* aritmética.

arithmetical (arizme·tikal) *adj.* aritmético.

arithmetician (arizmeti·shan) *s.* aritmético.

Arius (arai·øs) *n. pr.* Arrio.

ark (aᶜk) *s.* arca [caja]. *2* arca de Noé). *3* ~ *of the covenant,* Arca de la Alianza. *4* (E.U.) chalana.

arm (aᶜm) *s.* ANAT. brazo: ~ *band,* brazal; ~ *in* ~, de bracero, cogidos del brazo. *2* fig. brazo [poder, fuerza, autoridad]. *3* brazo [de animal, de palanca, de mar, de ancla, de sillón, etc.]. *4* rama [de árbol]. *5* arma: *under arms,* sobre las armas; *to arms!,* ¡a las armas!

arm (to) *tr.* armar [con armas]; fortalecer. *2* proveer [de armadura, un imán; de lentes, un telescopio, etc.]. *3 intr.-ref.* armarse.

armada (aᶜma·da) *s.* armada, escuadra: *the Armada,* la Armada Invencible.

armadillo (aᶜmædi·lou) *s.* armadillo.

armament (a·ᶜmamønt) *s.* armamento.

armature (a·ᶜmachøᶜ) *s.* armadura [defensiva]. *2* H. NAT. órganos de defensa. *3* ELECT., MAGNET. armadura. *4* ELECT. inducido.

armchair (a·ᶜmche·ᶜ) *s.* sillón, butaca.

Armenian (aᶜmɪ·nian) *adj.-s.* armenio.

armet (aˑʳmet) s. almete.
armful (aˑʳmful) s. brazado.
armillary (aˑʳmileri) adj. armilar.
armings (aˑʳmmings) s. MAR. empavesada.
armistice (aˑʳmistis) s. armisticio.
armless (aˑʳmlis) adj. inerme. 2 manco.
armlet (aˑʳmlit) s. pequeño brazo de mar. 2 brazal.
armor, armored, armory, etc. ARMOUR, ARMOURED, ARMOURY, etc.
armorial (aʳmoˑrial) adj. heráldico; ~ berings, escudo de armas. 2 s. libro de heráldica.
armour (aˑʳmøʳ) s. armadura [defensiva]. 2 coraza, blindaje.
armoured (-d) adj. armado [cubierto con armadura]. 2 acorazado, blindado. 3 ~ concrete, hormigón armado.
armourer (-øʳ) s. armero [pers.].
armoury (aˑrmøri) s. heráldica. 2 armería, arsenal. 3 (E.U.) fábrica de armas.
armpit (aˑʳmpit) s. sobaco, axila.
army (aˑʳmi) s. ejército: ~ chaplain, capellán castrense; ~ corps, cuerpo de ejército.
arnica (aˑʳnika) s. BOT., FARM. árnica.
aroma (arouˑma) s. aroma, fragancia.
aromatic(al (æromæˑtik(al) adj. aromático.
aromatics (-s) s. pl. aromas, especias.
aromatize (to) (arouˑmataiš) tr. aromatizar.
arose (arouˑš) pret. de to arise.
around (arauˑnd) adv. alrededor, en derredor, en torno, a la redonda, en circuito. 2 por todas partes. 3 en la dirección opuesta. 4 prep. alrededor de. 5 por, de un lado a otro de. 6 al volver, a la vuelta de: ~ the corner, a la vuelta de la esquina.
arousal (arauˑsal) s. despertamiento.
arouse (to) (arauˑš) tr. despertar. 2 mover, excitar.
arpeggio (aʳpeˑyiou) s. arpegio.
arquebus (aˑʳkiubøs) s. HARQUEBUS.
arraign (to) (areiˑn) tr. acusar, hacer cargos a. 2 DER. procesar.
arraignment (-mønt) s. acusación. 2 DER. procesamiento.
arrange (to) (areiˑndȳ) tr. arreglar, poner en orden, disponer, clasificar, ordenar. 2 disponer, preparar. 3 fijar, acordar [un plan, etc.]. 4 MÚS. arreglar, adaptar. 5 intr. convenirse; tomar disposiciones [para].
arrangement (-mønt) s. arreglo, ordenamiento. 2 orden, disposición. 3 arreglo, convenio. 4 MÚS. arreglo.
arrant (æˑrant) adj. acabado, consumado, insigne, de siete suelas.
arras (æˑras) s. tapiz de Arrás.
array (areiˑ) s. orden, formación. 2 pompa, aparato. 3 atavío, gala.
array (to) tr. formar, poner en orden [las tropas]. 2 adornar, ataviar.
arrearge (ariˑøridȳ) s. atraso. 2 pl. ARREARS.
arrears (arıˑøʳs) s. pl. atrasos, caídos.
arrest (areˑst) s. arresto, detención, prisión. 2 paro, detención. 3 MEC. tope.
arrest (to) tr. arrestar, detener, prender. 2 atraer, fijar [la atención, la mirada]. 3 parar, detener, contener.
arresting (-ing) adj. notable, sorprendente.
arris (æˑris) s. ARQ. arista.
arrival (araiˑval) s. llegada, arribo. 2 llegado [pers.].
arrive (to) (araiˑv) intr. llegar. 2 tener éxito, triunfar.
arrogance, -cy (æˑrogans, -si) s. arrogancia, soberbia, altanería.

arrogant (æˑrogant) adj. arrogant, altanero.
arrogate (to) (æˑrogeit) tr. atribuir indebidamente. 2 to ~ oneself, arrogarse.
arrow (æˑrou) s. flecha, saeta.
arrowhead (-jed) s. punta de flecha. BOT. sagitaria.
arrowroot (-rut) s. BOT. arrurruz.
arrowy (æˑroui) adj. aflechado. 2 fig. veloz, cortante, penetrante.
arsenal (aˑʳsinal) s. MIL. arsenal.
arsenic (aˑʳsinik) s. QUÍM. arsénico.
arsenic(al (aʳseˑnik(al) adj. arsenical.
arson (aˑʳsøn) s. incendio provocado.
art (aˑʳt) ant. 2.ª pers. del sing. del pres. de ind. de TO BE.
art s. arte: arts and crafts, artes y oficios.
arterial (aˑʳtiˑrial) adj. arterial.
arterialize (-aiš) tr. arterializar.
arteriole (-riol) s. ANAT. arteriola.
arteriosclerosis (-osclirouˑsis) s. MED. arteriosclerosis.
artery (aˑʳtøri) s. ANAT. arteria.
Artesian (aʳtiˑsian) adj. artesiano.
artful (aˑʳtful) adj. artero, ladino, astuto, artificioso. 2 diestro, ingenioso.
artfully (-i) adv. arteramente, ladinamente. 2 diestramente, con arte.
arthritis (aʳzraiˑtis) s. artritis.
arthritism (aˑʳzritišm) s. artritismo.
arthropod (aˑʳzropad) s. ZOOL. artrópodo.
Arthur (aˑʳzøʳ) n. pr. Arturo.
artichoke (aˑʳtichouk) s. BOT. alcachofa.
article (aˑʳtikøl) s. artículo. 2 cláusula, estipulación: articles of marriage, capítulos matrimoniales; articles of war, código militar. 3 punto, detalle, particular. 4 objeto, cosa. 5 ZOOL. artejo, segmento articulado.
article (to) tr. formular en artículos. 2 escriturar, contratar. 3 poner [a uno] de aprendiz bajo contrato. 4 acusar, hacer cargos.
articular (aʳtiˑkiulaʳ) adj. articular.
articulate (aʳtiˑkiulit) adj. articulado. 2 claro, distinto. 3 s. ZOOL. articulado.
articulate (to) (aʳtiˑkiuleit) tr. articular. 2 enunciar. 3 intr. articularse.
articulation (aʳtikiuleiˑshøn) s. articulación.
artifice (aˑʳtifis) s. artificio. 2 ardid, treta.
artificer (aʳtiˑfisøʳ) s. artífice. 2 inventor, autor. 3 MIL. artificiero.
artificial (aʳtifiˑshal) adj. artificial. 2 afectado, fingido. 3 DER. jurídica [persona].
artificiality (-fishiæˑliti), **artificialness** (-fiˑshalnis) s. calidad de artificial. 2 afectación, falta de naturalidad.
artillerist (aˑʳtiˑlørist) s. artillero.
artillery (aʳtiˑløri) s. artillería.
artilleryman (-mæn) s. artillero.
artiodactyl (aʳtiodæˑktil) adj.-s. artiodáctilo.
artisan (aˑʳtizan) s. artesano.
artist (aˑʳtist) s. artista.
artistic (aʳtiˑstik) adj. artístico.
artistically (-ali) adv. artísticamente.
artistry (aˑʳtiˑstri) s. talento artístico, arte.
artless (aˑʳtlis) adj. natural, sencillo, ingenuo. 2 torpe, sin arte.
arum (eˑrøm) s. BOT. aro, yaro.
aruspex (arøˑspeks), **aruspice** (aræˑspis) s. arúspice.
Aryan (eˑrian) adj. ario.
as (æs) s. [ave; moneda].
as (æs) adv. como, tal como, cual [de la manera que]: ~ you please, como usted guste. 2 como

[igual que; en calidad de; según, conforme]: ~ *a friend*, como, o en calidad de, amigo; ~ *if*, ~ *though*, como si; ~ *it were*, como si dijéramos; ~ *usual*, como de costumbre. *3* así como. *4* tan, como [comparativos]: ~ *slippery* ~ *an eel*, (tan) escurridizo como una anguila. *5 conj.* mientras, cuando, según, a medida que. *6* como, ya que, puesto que. *7* a pesar de: *young* ~ *he is*, a pesar de ser joven. *8* que: *the same* ~, el mismo que. *9* Otros usos: ~ *far* ~, hasta, hasta donde; ~ *good* ~, como si fuera, prácticamente; ~ *for*, ~ *to*, en cuanto a, respecto a; ~ *long* ~, mientras, con tal que; ~ *much*, otro tanto, eso, eso mismo, lo mismo; ~ *per*, según; ~ *well*, también, además; ~ *yet*, aún, todavía, hasta ahora.
asafetida, asafoetida (æsafe·tida) *s.* BOT. asafétida.
asarabacca (æsarabæ·ka) *s.* BOT. ásaro.
asbestos (æsbe·støs) *s.* asbesto.
ascarid (æ·skarid) *s.* ascáride.
ascend (ase·nd) *intr.* ascender, subir, elevarse. *2 tr.* subir [una cuesta, etc.]; subir a.
ascendance, -cy (-ans, -ansi) *s.* ascendiente [dominio moral, influencia].
ascendant (-ant) *adj.* ascendente. *2* superior, predominante. *3 s.* ascendiente [padre, abuelo]. *4* supremacía, poder, influencia.
ascendence, -cy (-øns, -ønsi) *s.* ASCENDANCE, -CY.
ascendent (-ønt) *adj.-s.* ASCENDANT.
ascending (-ing) *adj.* ascendente.
ascension (ase·nshøn) *s.* ascensión. *2* (con may.) Ascensión [de N. S.].
ascensional (-al) *adj.* ascensional.
ascent (ase·nt) *s.* ascensión, subida, elevación. *2* ascenso, promoción. *3* cuesta, pendiente.
ascertain (to) (æsø^rtei·n) *tr.* averiguar, hallar, determinar, cerciorarse de.
ascertainment (-mønt) *s.* averiguación.
ascetic (ase·tik) *adj.* ascético. *2 s.* asceta.
asceticism (-tisišm) *s.* ascetismo.
ascians (æ·shianš) *s. pl.* ascios.
ascidian (asi·dian) *s.* ZOOL. ascidia.
ascomycete (æskomaisi·t) *s.* BOT. ascomiceto.
ascon (æ·skøn) *s.* BOT. ascón.
ascus (æ·skøs) *s.* BOT. asca.
ascribe (to) (askrai·b) *tr.* atribuir, imputar.
ascription (askri·pshøn) *s.* atribución, imputación.
asepsis (ase·psis) *s.* asepsia.
aseptic (ase·ptik) *adj.* aséptico.
asexual (eise·kshual) *adj.* asexual.
ash (æsh), *pl.* **ashes** *s.* ceniza: ~ *tray*, cenicero [de fumador]. *2* BOT. fresno. *3 pl.* ceniza, cenizas. *4* restos mortales.
Ash Wednesday *s.* miércoles de ceniza.
ashamed (ashei·md) *adj.* avergonzado: *to be* ~, avergonzarse.
ashen (æ·shøn) *adj.* fresnal. *2* ceniciento.
ashlar (æ·shla^r) *s.* sillar, piedra de talla.
ashore (asho·^r) *adv.* MAR. en tierra, a tierra: *to go* ~, desembarcar; *to run* ~, encallar.
ashpan (æ·shpæn) *s.* cenicero [de estufa, hogar, etc.].
ashy (æ·shi) *adj.* ceniciento: ~ *pale*, pálido, lívido.
Asia (ei·sha) *n. pr.* GEOGR. Asia.
Asian (-n), **Asiatic** (eishiæ·tik) *adj.-s.* asiático.
aside (asai·d) *adv.* al lado, a un lado, aparte: ~ *from this*, esto aparte, fuera de esto. *2 s.* TEAT. aparte.
asinine (æ·sinain) *adj.* asinino, asnal.
ask (to) (æsk) *tr.* preguntar [una cosa]; preguntar [a uno]. *2* pedir, solicitar, rogar que. *3* requerir,

exigir [hacer necesario]. *4* invitar, convidar. | A veces con *out*. *5 fam.* amonestar [publicar las amonestaciones de]. *6 intr. to* ~ *after, for* o *about*, preguntar por. *7 to* ~ *for*, pedir [una cosa].
askance (askæ·ns), **askant** (-nt) *adv.* al sesgo, de soslayo, de reojo, de refilón. *2* con desdén, con recelo.
askew (askiu·) *adv.* al sesgo, oblicuamente. *2 adj.* sesgado, oblicuo.
asking (æ·sking) *s.* acción de pedir; ruego, petición. *2 fam.* publicación de amonestaciones.
aslant (aslæ·nt) *adv.* oblicuamente, en posición inclinada. *2 adj.* inclinado. *3 prep.* al través de.
asleep (asli·p) *adj.-adv.* dormido, durmiendo. *2* adormecido, entumecido.
aslope (aslou·p) *adv.-adj.* en declive.
asp (æsp) *s.* ZOOL. áspid. *2* BOT. tiemblo.
asparagus (æspæ·ragøs) *s.* BOT. espárrago. *2* COC. espárragos.
aspect (æ·spekt) *s.* aspecto. *2* aire, semblante.
aspen (æ·spøn) *s.* tiemblo, álamo temblón. *2 adj.* tembloroso.
aspergillum (-ÿi·løm) *s.* hisopo, asperges.
asperity (æspe·riti) *s.* aspereza.
asperse (to) (æspø·^rs) *tr.* difamar, calumniar. *2* asperjar.
aspersion (-shøn) *s.* difamación, calumnia. *2* aspersión.
asphalt (æ·sfalt) *s.* asfalto.
asphalt (to) *tr.* asfaltar.
asphaltic (æsfo·ltik) *adj.* asfáltico.
asphodel (æ·sfødel) *s.* BOT. asfódelo, gamón.
asphyxia (æsfi·ksia) *s.* asfixia.
asphyxiate (to) (-sieit) *tr.* asfixiar.
asphyxiation (-sie·shøn) *s.* asfixia.
aspic (æ·spik) *s.* ZOOL. áspid. *2* espliego. *3* gelatina con carne picada, jugo de tomate, etc.
aspirant (aspai·rant) *s.* aspirante, pretendiente.
aspirate (æ·spireit) *adj.-s.* aspirado [sonido].
aspirate (to) (æ·spireit) *tr.* GRAM., FONÉT. aspirar. *2* aspirar, sorber.
aspiration (-ei·shøn) *s.* aspiración. *2* anhelo.
aspirator (æspirei·tø^r) *s.* aspirador.
aspire (to) (aspai·^r) *intr.* aspirar a, ambicionar. | Gralte. con *to* o *after*. *2* elevarse [como una llama, etc.].
aspirin (æ·spirin) *s.* aspirina.
aspiring (aspai·ring) *adj.* ambicioso, con aspiraciones.
asquint (askui·nt) *adv.* de través, de soslayo.
ass (æs) *s.* ZOOL. asno, burro, jumento. *2 fig.* asno, majadero.
assagai (æ·sagai) *s.* azagaya.
assail (to) (asei·l) *tr.* asaltar, atacar, acometer. *2* asediar, acosar.
assailant (-ant) *adj.-s.* atacante, agresor. *2* atracador.
assassin (asæ·sin) *s.* asesino.
assassinate (to) (-eit) *tr.* asesinar.
assassination (-ei·shøn) *s.* asesinato.
assault (asolt) *s.* MIL., ESGR. asalto. *2* ataque, acometida. *3* agresión; atraco. *4* DER. ~ *and battery*, injurias y golpes.
assault (to) *tr.* asaltar. *2* atacar, acometer. *3* saltear, atracar.
assay (æ·sei) *s.* ensaye; contraste. *2* QUÍM. ensayo. *3* ESSAY¹.
assay (to) *tr.* ensayar, aquilatar, contrastar [metales]. *2* QUÍM. ensayar. *3* analizar, experimentar. *4* tentar, intentar.

assayer (*asei·ø^r*) *s.* ensayador [de metales]; contraste.

assemblage (*ase'mblidӯ*) *s.* reunión [acción]. *2* reunión, agregado, conjunto, multitud, concurso. *3* MEC., CARP. montaje.

assemble (to) (*-bøl*) *tr.* congregar, reunir, juntar, agrupar. *2* MEC., CARP. montar, armar. *3* intr. reunirse.

assembly (*-bli*) *s.* asamblea, junta. *2* reunión, fiesta [de sociedad]. *3* concurrencia, concurso. *4* MEC., CARP. montaje, armazón. *5* MEC. grupo, juego, unidad.

assent (*ase·nt*) *s.* asenso, asentimiento, aquiescencia, beneplácito.

assent (to) *intr.* asentir, consentir.

assentient (*ase·nshiønt*) *adj.-s.* que asiente.

assert (to) (*asø^{r}t*) *tr.* aseverar, afirmar. *2* mantener, defender, hacer valer. *3* to ~ *oneself*, imponerse, hacer valer sus derechos; hacerse sentir.

assertion (*-shøn*) *s.* aserción, aserto. *2* mantenimiento, reivindicación.

assertive (*asø^{r}tiv*) *adj.* asertivo; dogmático.

assess (to) (*ase·s*) *tr.* ámillarar; evaluar [para la aplicación de impuestos]. *2* fijar [una indemnización, impuesto, etc.]. *3* imponer una contribución a.

assessment (*-mønt*) *s.* amillaramiento, avalúo. *2* imposición, repartimiento [de contribuciones]. *3* tasa de tributación. *4* dividendo pasivo.

assessor (*-ø^r*) *s.* DER. asesor. *2* tasador de la propiedad para efectos fiscales.

asset (*æ·set*) *s.* COM. partida del activo. *2* fig. recurso, medio, etc., con que se cuenta. *3* pl. COM. activo. *4* haber, capital, fondos, créditos.

asseverate (to) (*ase·vøreit*) *tr.* aseverar.

asseveration (*-rei·shøn*) *s.* aseveración.

assiduity (*æsidiu·iti*) *s.* asiduidad.

assiduous (*æsi·diuøs*) *adj.* asiduo. *2* constante, laborioso.

assign (to) (*asai·n*) *tr.* asignar. *2* destinar, designar. *3* adscribir, atribuir. *4* DER. ceder, transferir, consignar.

assignation (*æsignei·shøn*) *s.* asignación; designación, destinación, atribución. *2* DER. cesión. *3* cita [para encontrarse]. | Tómase gralte. en mala parte.

assignment (*asai·nmønt*) *s.* ASSIGNATION 1 y 2. *2* DER. escritura de cesión.

assimilable (*asi·milabøl*) *adj.* asimilable. *2* semejante.

assimilate (to) (*asi·mileit*) *tr.* asimilar. *2* intr. FISIOL. asimilarse.

assimilation (*-le·shøn*) *s.* asimilación.

Assisi (*asi·ši*) *n. pr.* GEOGR. Asís.

assist (to) (*asi·st*) *tr.* asistir, ayudar. *2* intr. asistir, estar presente.

assistance (*-ans*) *s.* asistencia, ayuda, socorro. *2* asistencia (presencia). *3* concurrencia [pers. presentes].

assistant (*-ant*) *s.* ayudante, auxiliar, adjunto; acólito. *2* adj. auxiliar, segundo, sub-: ~ *manager*, subdirector.

assize (*asai·š*) *s.* tasa, tipo. *2* pl. sesiones de un tribunal.

associate (*asou·shieit*) *adj.* asociado; adjunto. *2* s. asociado, socio, consocio. *3* compinche; cómplice.

associate (to) *tr.* asociar. *2* intr. asociarse. *3* juntarse, acompañarse.

association (*-ei·shøn*) *s.* asociación. *2* ~ *football*, fútbol, balompié.

assonance (*æ·sønans*) *s.* asonancia.

assonant (*-ant*) *adj.-s.* asonante.

assonate (to) (*-eit*) *intr.* asonar, asonantar.

assort (to) (*aso·^{r}t*) *tr.* ordenar, clasificar, agrupar con. *2* surtir [de cosas varias]. *3* intr. cuadrar, convenir. *4* juntarse, asociarse.

assorted (*-id*) *adj.* surtido, variado. *2* apareado.

assortment (*-mønt*) *s.* ordenación, clasificación. *2* surtido, variedad.

assuage (to) (*asuei·dӯ*) *tr.* suavizar, mitigar, aliviar, calmar. *2* apaciguar, ablandar.

assuagement (*-mønt*) *s.* mitigación, alivio.

assuassive (*asuei·siv*) *adj.* mitigativo, calmante.

assume (to) (*asiu·m*) *tr.* aşumir. *2* arrogarse, usurpar. *3* tomar, adoptar [una forma, actitud, etc.]. *4* simular. *5* suponer, dar por sentado. *6* intr. ser arrogante o presuntuoso.

assumed (*-d*) *adj.* supuesto, dado por sentado. *2* supuesto, falso, fingido.

assuming (*-ing*) *adj.* arrogante, altivo; presuntuoso.

assumption (*asø·mpshøn*) *s.* asunción. *2* arrogación. *3* adopción [de una actitud, etc.]. *4* suposición, supuesto. *5* (con may.) Asunción [de la Virgen].

assumptive (*-tiv*) *adj.* supositivo; supuesto. *2* arrogante, presuntuoso.

assurance (*ashu·rans*) *s.* seguridad [que se tiene o que se da], certidumbre, convicción. *2* seguridad, confianza en sí mismo. *3* aplomo, descaro. *4* COM. seguro; aseguramiento.

assure (to) (*ashu·^{r}*) *tr.* asegurar, afirmar, certificar. *2* infundir confianza. *3* asegurar [hacer cierto o seguro]. *4* COM. asegurar.

assured (*-d*) *adj.* seguro, cierto. *2* confiado, atrevido, audaz. *3* COM. asegurado.

assurer (*ashu·rø^r*) *s.* asegurador.

Assyria (*asi·ria*) *n. pr.* HIST. Asiria.

Assyrian (*asi·rian*) *adj.-s.* Asirio.

astatic (*eistæ·tik*) *adj.* astático.

asterisk (*æ·størisk*) *s.* asterisco.

astern (*astø·^{r}n*) *adv.* MAR. a popa, por la popa.

asteroid (*æ·støroid*) *s.* ASTR. asteroide.

asthenia (*æszı·nia*) *s.* MED. astenia.

asthenic (*æsze·nik*) *adj.-s.* asténico.

asthma (*æ·šma*) *s.* asma.

asthmatic (*æšmæ·tik*) *adj.-s.* asmático.

astigmatic (*æstigmæ·tik*) *adj.* ÓPT. astigmático.

astigmatism (*æsti·gmatišm*) *s.* astigmatismo.

astir (*astø·r*) *adv.* en movimiento, en actividad. *2* levantado (de la cama).

astonish (to) (*asta·nish*) *tr.* asombrar, pasmar, sorprender.

astonished (*-t*) *adj.* atónito, asombrado, pasmado.

astonishing (*-ing*) *adj.* asombroso, pasmo, sorpresa.

astonishment (*-mønt*) *s.* asombro, pasmo, sorpresa.

astound (to) (*astau·nd*) *tr.* pasmar, sorprender. *2* aturdir, aterrar.

astounding (*-ing*) *adj.* asombroso, pasmoso.

astraddle (*astra·døl*) *adv.* a horcajadas.

astragal (*æ·stragal*) *s.* ARQ., ARTILL. astrágalo.

astragalus (*æstræ·galøs*) *s.* ANAT., BOT. astrágalo.

astrak(h)an (*æ·strakan*) *s.* astracán [piel].

astral (*æ·stral*) *adj.* astral.

astrand (*astræ·nd*) *adv.* MAR. encallado, varado.

astray (*astrei·*) *adv.-adj.* descaminado, extraviado, errado: *to go* ~, descarriarse, extraviarse.

astriction (*æstri·kshøn*) *s.* astricción.

astride (astrai·d) *adv.* a horcajadas. *2 prep.* a caballo de; a horcajadas en.
astringe (to) (astri·ndȳ) *tr.* astreñir, astringir, constreñir.
astringency (-ønsi) *s.* astringencia. *2* severidad, austeridad.
astringent (-ønt) *adj.-s.* astringente. *2 adj.* severo, austero.
astrochemistry (æstroke·mistri) *s.* astroquímica.
astrolabe (æ'stroleib) *s.* astrolabio.
astrologer (æstra·lodȳøʳ) *s.* astrólogo.
astrologic(al (æstrola·dȳik(al) *adj.* astrológico.
astrology (æstra·lodȳi) *s.* astrología.
astronaut (æ·stronot) *s.* astronauta.
astronautics (æ·strono·tiks) *s.* astronáutica.
astronomer (æstra·nomøʳ) *s.* astrónomo.
astromic(al (æstrona·mik(al) *adj.* astronómico.
astronomy (æstra·nomi) *s.* astronomía.
astrophysics (æstrofi·šiks) *s.* astrofísica.
astrut (astrø·t) *adj.* hinchado [de orgullo]; que anda con orgullo.
Asturian (æstiu·rian) *adj.-s.* asturiano.
astute (æstiu·t) *adj.* astuto, sagaz.
asunder (asø·ndøʳ) *adj.* separado. *2 adv.* en dos, en pedazos: *to cut* ~, partir en dos, en pedazos.
asylum (asai·løm) *s.* asilo, refugio. *2* acogida, sagrado. *3* casa de beneficencia; manicomio.
asymmetric(al (eisime·trik(al) *adj.* asimétrico.
asymmetry (eisi·mitri) *s.* asimetría.
asymptote (æ·simtout) *s.* asíntota.
asystole (eisi·stoli) *s.* MED. asistolia.
at (æt) *prep.* en, a, de, con, cerca de, delante de con significaciones varias. | A veces no se traduce: *look* ~ *him*, miradle. *2* Con ciertos nombres, equivale a un gerundio: ~ *work*, trabajando.
atavism (æ·tavišm) *s.* atavismo.
atavistic (ætavi·stik) *adj.* atávico.
ate (eit) *pret.* de TO EAT.
atelier (æ·tøliei) *s.* taller, estudio.
atheism (ei·ziišm) *s.* ateísmo.
atheist (ei·ziist) *s.* ateo.
atheistic(al (eizii·stik(al) *adj.* ateo, ateísta.
atheneum (æzini·øm) *s.* ateneo.
Athenian (æzi·nian) *adj.-s.* ateniense.
Athens (æ·zins) *n. pr.* Atenas.
athirst (azø·ʳst) *adj.* sediento.
athlete (æ·zlit) *s.* atleta.
athletic (æzle·tik) *adj.* atlético.
athletics (-s) *s.* atletismo.
at-home *s.* horas en que se reciben visitas.
athwart (azwo·ʳt) *adv.-prep.* al través o por el través [de]; atravesado [en]. *2* contrariamente [a], contra.
atilt (ati·lt) *adv.* en posición inclinada. *2* lanza en ristre.
atlantes (ætlæ·ntiš) *s. pl.* ARQ. atlantes.
Atlantic (-tik) *adj.* atlántico. *2 n. pr.* GEOGR. Atlántico.
Atlantis (-tis) *n. pr.* Atlántida.
atlas (æ·tlas) *s.* atlas. *2* ARQ. atlante. *3* (con may.) MIT. Atlante; GEOGR. Atlas.
atmosphere (ætmøsfi·ʳ) *s.* atmósfera.
atmospheric(al (-fe·rik(al) *adj.* atmosférico.
atmospherics (-fe·riks) *s. pl.* RADIO. parásitos atmosféricos.
atoll (æta·l) *s.* atolón.
atom (æ·tøm) *s.* átomo.
atomic(al (æta·mik(al) *adj.* atómico.
atomize (to) (æ·tømaiš) *tr.* atomizar, pulverizar.
atomizer (-øʳ) *s.* pulverizador.

atone (to) (atou·n) *intr.-tr.* reparar, dar satisfacción, compensar, expiar. | Gralte. con *for*.
atonement (-mønt) *s.* reparación, compensación, expiación.
atonic (æta·nik) *adj.* GRAM. átono. *2* MED. atónico.
atony (æ·tøni) *s.* atonía.
atop (ata·p) *prep.-adv.* encima.
atrabiliary (æ·trabilieri), **atrabilious** (ætrabiliøs) *adj.* atrabiliario, melancólico.
atrium (ei·triøm) *s.* atrio.
atrocious (atrou·shøs) *s.* atroz. *2* abominable.
atrocity (atra·siti) *s.* atrocidad.
atrophy (æ·trofi) *s.* atrofia.
atrophy (to) *tr.* producir atrofia. *2 intr.* atrofiarse.
attach (to) (atæ·ch) *tr.* atar, ligar, vincular; pegar, adherir, unir, sujetar, enganchar, prender. *2* granjearse el afecto de. *3* agregar, adscribir. *4* dar, atribuir [valor, importancia, etc.]. *5* DER. embargar, secuestrar. *6 intr.* acompañar, ser inherente. *7 ref.* unirse, adherirse. *8* cobrar afecto.
attaché (atachei·) *s.* agregado [diplomático].
attachment (atæ·chmønt) *s.* atadura, unión, enlace, conexión, fijación. *2* accesorio. *3* apego, afecto, adhesión. *4* DER. embargo, incautación, secuestro.
attack (ætæ·k) *s.* ataque, embestida, agresión. *2* MED. ataque.
attack (to) *tr.* atacar [acometer, embestir: combatir], agredir. *2* MÚS., QUÍM., MED. atacar.
attain (atei·n) *tr.* lograr, obtener. *2 tr.* e *intr.* alcanzar llegar [a una edad, un punto, etc.].
attainable (atei·nabøl) *adj.* asequible, obtenible, realizable.
attainder (atei·ndøʳ) *s.* DER. proscripción, muerte civil.
attainment (-mønt) *s.* logro, consecución, adquisición. *2 pl.* dotes, prendas, saber.
attaint (to) (atei·nt) *s.* DER. proscribir. *2* manchar, deshonrar. *3* viciar, corromper.
attar (æ·taʳ) *s.* esencia [esp. de rosas].
attemper (to) (ate·mpøʳ) *tr.* temperar, moderar. *2* atemperar, acomodar.
attempt (ate·mpt) *s.* intento, prueba, esfuerzo, tentativa. *2* atentado [contra la vida].
attempt (to) *tr.* intentar, procurar, probar a. *2* atacar, atentar contra.
attend (to) (ate·nd) *tr.* atender a, cuidar de. *2* asistir [a un enfermo]. *3* acompañar, servir, escoltar. *4* asistir, concurrir a. *5* acompañar, seguir [como efecto o consecuencia], ser inherente a. *6* esperar [a que suceda algo]. *7 intr. to* ~ *to*, atender a, hacer caso de, ocuparse de. *8 to* ~ *on* o *upon*, servir a.
attendance (-ans) *s.* asistencia, servicio. *2* cuidado, vigilancia. *3* asistencia, presencia. *4* concurrencia, concurso. *5* séquito, acompañamiento. *6* espera.
atendant (-ant) *adj.* acompañante. *2 s.* servidor. *3* acompañante, seguidor. *4* asistente, concurrente. *5 pl.* séquito, acompañamiento.
attention (ate·nshøn) *s.* atención. *2* MIL. *to stand to* ~, cuadrarse; *attention!*, ¡firmes! *3 pl.* atenciones, obsequios.
attentive (ate·ntiv) *adj.* atento [que pone atención]. *2* atento, obsequioso.
attenuate (ate·niueit) *adj.* atenuado, disminuido, diluido. *2* delgado.
attenuate (to) *tr.* atenuar, disminuir, diluir, debilitar. *2* adelgazar.
attenuation (ateniuei·shøn) *s.* atenuación, dismi-

nución, debilitación, extenuación. 2 dilución. 3 adelgazamiento.

attest (to) (ate·st) *tr.-intr.* atestar, testificar, atestiguar, certificar. 2 *tr.* autenticar.

attestation (ætestei·shøn) *s.* atestación, testimonio, prueba. 2 autenticación. 3 certificación.

Attic (æ·tik) *adj.* ático: ~ *salt*, sal ática.

attic *s.* ARQ. ático, buhardilla.

atticism (æ·tisišm) *s.* aticismo.

Attila (æ·tila) *n. pr.* Atila.

attire (atai·ʳ) *s.* traje, vestido, atavío.

attire (to) *tr.* vestir, ataviar. 2 engalanar.

attitude (æ·titiud) *s.* actitud. 2 AVIA. posición.

attitudinize (ætitiu·dinaiš) *intr.* obrar con afectación.

attorney (atø·ʳni) *s.* apoderado, poderhabiente, procurador, agente: ~ *at law*, procurador judicial; abogado; *private* ~, apoderado, representante; *by* ~, por poder. 2 ~ *general*, fiscal de la Corona o de la República. 3 (E.U.) *district* ~ fiscal de distrito.

attract (to) (atræ·ct) *tr.* atraer. 2 llamar [la atención].

attraction (atræ·kshøn) *s.* atracción. 2 atractivo.

attractive (atræ·ktiv) *adj.* atractivo, atrayente. 2 agradable, simpático.

attractiveness (-nis) *s.* fuerza atractiva. 2 atractivo, simpatía.

attribute (æ·tribiut) *s.* atributo.

attribute (to) *tr.* atribuir.

attribution (ætribiu·shøn) *s.* atribución.

attributive (ætri·biutiv) *adj.* atributivo. 2 *adj.-s.* GRAM. calificativo.

attrite (atrai·t) *adj.* atrito.

attrition (ætri·shøn) *s.* atrición. 2 roce, fricción, desgaste.

attune (to) (atiu·n) *tr.* armonizar, acordar. 2 MÚS. afinar.

aubade (ou·bæd) *s.* MÚS. alborada.

auburn (o·bø·ʳn) *adj.* castaño rojizo.

auction (o·kshøn) *s.* subasta, almoneda, remate. 2 ~ *bridge*, bridge subastado.

auction (to) *tr.* subastar, almonedar.

auctionneer (okshønɪ·ʳ) *s.* subastador.

auctionneer (to) *tr.* TO AUCTION.

audacious (odei·shøs) *adj.* audaz, osado. 2 atrevido, descarado.

audaciousness (-nis), **audacity** (odæ·siti) *s.* audacia, osadía. 2 atrevimiento, descaro.

audibility (odibi·liti) *s.* calidad de audible.

audible (o·dibøl) *adj.* audible.

audience (o·diøns) *s.* acción de escuchar. 2 auditorio, público. 3 audiencia (entrevista).

audio-frequency (o·diou) *s.* RAD. audiofrecuencia.

audit (o·dit) *s.* intervención, revisión, ajuste [de cuentas].

audit (to) *tr.* intervenir, revisar [cuentas].

audition (odi·shøn) *s.* audición.

auditive (o·ditiv) *adj.* auditivo.

auditor (o·ditøʳ) *s.* interventor, revisor de cuentas. 2 ordenador de pagos. 3 oyente. 4 auditor.

auditorium (odito·riøm) *s.* sala de conferencias, de conciertos, etc.; paraninfo.

auditory (o·ditori) *s.* auditorio, concurrencia. 2 AUDITORIUM. 3 *adj.* auditorio.

auger (o·gøʳ) *s.* barrena, taladro, berbiquí.

aught (ot) *pron.* ant. algo, alguna cosa. 2 (con negación) nada.

augment (to) (ogme·nt) *tr.* aumentar. 2 abultar, engrosar. 3 *intr.* aumentar, crecer.

augmentation (-ei·shøn) *s.* aumento, acrecentamiento, añadidura.

augmentative (-ativ) *adj.-s.* aumentativo.

augur (o·gøʳ) *s.* augur. 2 agorero, adivino.

augur (to) *tr.-intr.* augurar, pronosticar, presagiar.

augury (o·giuri) *s.* augurio, pronóstico. 2 auguración.

August (o·gøst) *s.* agosto.

august (ogø·st) *adj.* augusto.

Augustine (o·gøstin) *n. pr.* Agustín.

Augustinian (ogøsti·nian) *adj.-s.* agustino, agustiniano.

augustness (ogø·stnis) *s.* majestad, grandeza.

Augustus (ogø·støs) *n. pr.* Augusto.

auk (ok) *s.* ORN. alca.

aulic (o·lic) *adj.* áulico.

aunt (ænt o ant) *s.* tía.

auntie, aunty (æ·nti) *s.* tiíta.

aura (o·ra) *s.* aura, céfiro. 2 efluvio, emanación. 3 MED., ORN. aura.

aural (o·ral) *adj.* del oído.

aureola (orɪ·ola), **aureole** (o·rioul) *s.* aureola.

aureole (to) *tr.* aureolar.

aureomycin (oriomai·sin) *s.* FARM. aureomicina.

aureous (o·riøs) *adj.* áureo.

auricle (o·rikøl) *s.* aurícula.

auricula (ori·kiula) *s.* ZOOL. apéndice en forma de oreja. 2 BOT. oreja de oso.

auricular (ori·kiulaʳ) *adj.* auricular.

auriferous (ori·førøs) *adj.* aurífero.

auriga (orai·ga) *s.* auriga.

aurist (o·rist) *s.* otólogo.

aurochs (o·raks) *s.* ZOOL. uro.

aurora (oro·ra) *s.* aurora: ~ *australis*, aurora austral; ~ *borealis*, aurora boreal.

auscultate (to) (o·skølteit) *tr.* MED. auscultar.

auscultation (oskøltei·shøn) *s.* auscultación.

auspicate (to) (o·spikeit) *tr.* augurar. 2 dar buen principio a.

auspice (o·spis) *s.* auspicio.

auspicious (ospi·shøs) *adj.* próspero, feliz, favorable, propicio.

austere (ostɪ·ʳ) *adj.* austero. 2 sencillo, sin adornos. 3 grave, serio.

austereness (-nis), **austerity** (oste·riti) *s.* austeridad. 2 gravedad, seriedad.

Austin (o·stin) *n. pr.* Agustín.

austral (ostral) *adj.* austral.

Australia (ostrei·lia) *n. pr.* GEOGR. Australia.

Australian (-n) *adj.-s.* australiano.

Austria (o·stria) *n. pr.* GEOGR. Austria.

Austrian (-n) *adj.-s.* austríaco.

autarchy o **-ky** (o·taʳki) *s.* autarquía.

authentic(al (oze·ntik(al) *adj.* auténtico. 2 fiel, fidedigno.

authenticate (to) (-tikeit) *tr.* autenticar, autorizar, legalizar.

authenticity (-ti·siti) *s.* autenticidad.

author (o·zøʳ) *s.* autor; escritor.

authoress (-ris) *s.* autora; escritora.

authoritarian (ozarite·rian) *adj.-s.* autoritario.

authoritative (oza·riteitiv) *adj.* autorizado, que tiene autoridad. 2 autoritario. 3 imperativo, terminante.

authority (oza·riti) *s.* autoridad: *on the best* ~, de buena tinta. 2 autorización, licencia. 3 *pl.* autoridades. 4 consejeros, junta directiva.

authorization (ozørišei·shøn) *s.* autorización.

authorize (to) (o·zøraiš) *tr.* autorizar, facultar, dar autoridad o poder. 2 justificar. 3 autorizar, sancionar.

authorship (*o·zø*^rship) *s.* calidad o profesión de autor o escritor. *2* paternidad literaria.
auto (*o·*tou) *s.* fam. auto, automóvil.
autobiography (otobaia·grafi) *s.* autobiografía.
autobus (*o·*tobøs) *s.* autobús.
autocar (-ka^r) *s.* autocar. *2* automóvil.
autochthon (ota·kzøn) *s.* autóctono.
autochthonous (-øs) *adj.* autóctono.
autoclave (*o·*tokleiv) *s.* autoclave.
autocracy (ota·krasi) *s.* autocracia.
autocraft (*o·*tokræt) *s.* autócrata.
auto-da-fe (otodafei·) *s.* auto de fe.
autodrome (*o·*todroum) *s.* autódromo.
autogenous (ota·dȳinøs) *adj.* autógeno.
autogiro o **-gyro** (otodȳai·rou) *s.* autogiro.
autograph (otogræf) *adj.-s.* autógrafo. *2 s.* copia autográfica.
autography (ota·grafi) *s.* autografía.
autoist (*o'*toist) *s. fam.* automovilista.
automat (*o·*tomæt) *s.* (E.U.) bar o restaurante de servicio automático.
automatic (otomæ·tic) *adj.* automático.
automation (-ei·shøn) *s.* automación.
automatization (otomætišei·shøn) *s.* automatización.
automaton (ota·matan) *s.* autómata.
automobile (otomou·bil) *s.* automóvil.
automobilism (-išm) *s.* automovilismo.
automobilist (-ist) *adj.-s.* automovilista.
automotive (-tiv) *adj.* automotor, triz.
autonomic (otona·mik) *adj.* autonómico.
autonomous (ota·nomøs) *adj.* autónomo.
autonomy (-mi) *s.* autonomía.
autopsy (*o·*tapsi) *s.* autopsia.
autosuggestion (otosødtye·schøn) *s.* autosugestión.
autumn (ota·m) *s.* otoño.
autumnal (-nal) *adj.* otoñal.
auxiliary (ogši·liari) *adj.* auxiliar.
avail (avei·l) *s.* provecho, utilidad, eficacia.
avail (to) *intr.* servir, ser útil, llenar el objeto. *2 tr.* aprovechar, servir, valer [a uno]. *3 ref. to ~ oneself of*, aprovechar, valerse de.
availability (aveilabi·liti) *s.* disponibilidad. *2* utilidad, eficacia. *3* validez.
available (avei·labøl) *adj.* aprovechable, disponible. *2* obtenible.
avalanche (æ·valænch) *s.* salud.
avarice (æ·varis) *s.* avaricia, codicia.
avaricious (ævari·shøs) *adj.* avaro, avariento.
avariciousness (-nis) *s.* AVARICE.
avatar (ævata·^r) *s.* avatar.
avaunt (avo·nt) *interj.* ant. ¡fuera!, ¡atrás!
Ave Maria (a·vi mari·a) *s.* avemaría.
avenge (to) (ave·ndȳ) *tr.* vengar.
avenger (-ø^r) *s.* vengador.
avengress (-øris) *f.* vengadora.
avenue (æ·viniu) *s.* avenida, paseo, alameda. *2* vía, entrada, pasadizo.
aver (to) (avo·^r) *tr.* afirmar, asegurar, declarar. ¶ Pret. y p. p.: *averred;* ger.; *-rring.*
average (æ·vøridȳ) *s.* promedio, término medio: *on an ~*, por término medio. *2* prorrata. *3* lo corriente, lo común. *4* MAR. avería. *5 adj.* medio, de promedio. *6* ordinario, corriente.
average (to) *intr.* hacer un promedio de. *2 tr.* determinar el promedio de. *3* prorratear.
averment (avø·^rmønt) *s.* aseveración.
Avernus (avø·^rnøs) *s.* Averno.
averse (avø·^rs) *adj.* contrario, opuesto, renuente.

aversion (avo·^rshøn) *s.* aversión. *2* repugnancia. *3* cosa aborrecida.
avert (to) (av·^rt) *tr.* apartar, desviar. *2* impedir, evitar, conjurar.
aviary (ei·vieri) *s.* pajarera.
aviate (to) (-eit) *intr.* ant. volar [en avión].
aviation (-ei·shøn) *s.* ant. aviación.
aviator (ei·vieitø^r) *s.* ant. aviador.
aviculture (ei·vikølchø^r) *s.* avicultura.
avid (æ·vid) *adj.* ávido.
avidity (avi·diti) *s.* avidez, codicia.
avocado (ævoka·dou) *s.* BOT. aguacate.
avocation (ævokei·shøn) *s.* distracción, pasatiempo, afición. *2* ocupación, negocio.
avocet (æ·voset) *s.* ORN. avoceta.
avoid (to) (avoi·d) *tr.* evitar, eludir, rehuir. *2* anular, invalidar.
avoidance (-ans) *s.* evitación. *2* DER. anulación.
avoirdupois (ævø^røpoi·š) *s.* sistema de pesos cuya unidad es la libra de 16 onzas.
avouch (to) (avau·ch) *tr.* afirmar; decir. *2* probar, garantizar. *3* reconocer, confesar.
avow (to) (avau·) *tr.* confesar, reconocer.
avowal (-al) *s.* confesión, reconocimiento.
avowed (avau·d) *adj.* confesado, declarado, manifiesto.
avuncular (avø·nkiula^r) *adj.* de tío.
await (to) (auei·t) *tr.-intr.* aguardar, esperar.
awake (auei·k) *adj.* despierto. *2* atento, vigilante. *3 ~ to*, consciente de.
awake (to) *tr.* despertar. *2 intr.* despertar, despertarse. ¶ Pret.: *awoke;* p. p.: *awaked, awaken* o *awoke.*
awaken (-øn) *tr.* e *intr.* TO AWAKE.
awakening (-øning) *s.* despertamiento, despertar.
award (auo·^rd) *s.* sentencia, decisión; laudo. *2* concesión, adjudicación. *3* premio, galardón.
award (to) *tr.* DER. adjudicar. *2* dar, conceder, otorgar, conferir. *3* tributar [elogios].
aware (aue·^r) *adj.* sabedor, enterado, consciente de: *to be ~ of*, saber, darse cuenta de.
awareness (-nis) *s.* conocimiento, conciencia [de un hecho].
awash (aua·sh) *adj.-adv.* MAR. a flor de agua.
away (auei·) *adv.* lejos, a distancia, fuera, afuera, alejándose: *to be ~*, estar fuera, ausente; *to go ~*, irse, ausentarse. | Indica libertad o continuidad en la acción: *talk ~*, hable usted; diga usted lo que quiera; *he was firing ~*, iba disparando. *2 interj.* ¡fuera de ahi!
awe (*o*) *s.* temor. *2* temor reverencial. *3* asombro, sobrecogimiento.
awe (to) *tr.* atemorizar, sobrecoger.
awesome (*o·*søm) *adj.* impotente.
awestricken (ostrikøn), **awestruck** (*o·*strøk) *adj.* atemorizado, sobrecogido.
awful (*o·*ful) *adj.* atroz, horrible. *2* tremendo, espantoso, imponente. *3* fam. enorme, muy malo, muy feo.
awfully (-i) *adv.* atrozmente, terriblemente. *2* fam. muy, mucho, enormemente.
awhile (ajuai·l) *adv.* un rato, algún tiempo.
awkward (*o·*kua^rd) *adj.* torpe, encogido, desmañado, desgarbado. *2* embarazoso, delicado, difícil. *3* de mal manejar.
awkwardness (-nis) *s.* torpeza, desmaña. *2* encogimiento, cortedad.
awl (*o*l) *s.* lezna, punzón. *2* MEC. lengüeta.
awn (*o*n) *s.* BOT. arista, raspa.
awning (*o·*ning) *s.* toldo, tendal, entalamadura. *2* marquesina. *3* MAR. toldo, toldilla.

awoke (auou·k) *pret.* y *p. p.* de TO AWAKE.
awry (arai·) *adv.* de través. *2* erradamente, desca-
minadamente. *3 adj.* torcido, ladeado. *4* errado,
descaminado.
ax, axe (aks) *s.* hacha, destral, segur.
ax, axe (to) *tr.* hachear.
axial (æ·ksial) *adj.* axil, axial.
axil (æ·ksil) *s.* BOT. axila.
axilla (æksi·la) *s.* BOT., ZOOL. axila.
axillar (a·ksila^r), **axillary** (-leri) *s.* axilar.
axiom (æ·ksiøm) *s.* axioma.
axiomatic (æksiømæ·tik) *adj.* axiomático.
axis (æ·ksis) *s.* eje. *2* ANAT. axis.
axle (æ·ksøl) *s.* eje [de rueda]; árbol [de máquina].
2 bolo [de escalera].

axletree (-trɪ) *s.* eje [de carruaje].
axoloti (æ·ksolatøl) *s.* ZOOL. ajolote.
axon(e (æ·ksøn) ANAT. cilindroeje.
ay (ai) *adv.* sí.
aye (ei) *adv.* siempre.
aye-aye (ai·ai) *s.* ZOOL. ayeaye.
azalea (aše·lia) *s.* BOT. azalea.
azarole (æ·šaroul) *s.* BOT. acerola.
azedarach (aše·daræk) *s.* BOT. acederaque.
azimuth (æ·šimøz) *s.* ASTR. acimut.
azoic (ašou·ik) *adj.* azoico.
azote (æ·šout) *s.* QUÍM. ázoe.
Aztec (æ·štek) *adj.-s.* azteca.
azure (æ·ȳø^r) *adj.-s.* azul celeste. *2 s.* azur.
azurite (æ·ȳorait) *s.* MINER. azurita.
azymous (æ·šimøs) *adj.* ázimo.

B

B, b (bi) *s.* B, b, segunda letra del alfabeto inglés. *2* MÚS. si.

baa (ba) *s.* be [balido].

baa (to) *intr.* balar.

Babbit metal (bæ·bit) *s.* metal antifricción.

babble (bæ·bøl) *s.* charla, cháchara. *2* balbuceo. *3* murmullo [de una corriente].

babble (to) *intr.* charlar. *2* balbucear. *3* murmurar [una corriente]. *4 tr.* decir [lo que debería callarse].

babbler (bæ·blø^r) *s.* charlatán, hablador.

babbling (bæ·bling) *s.* charla, garrulería.

babe (beib) *s.* BABY.

Babel, babel (bei·bøl) *s.* babel, confusión, algarabía.

babiroussa (bæbiru·sa) *s.* ZOOL. babirusa.

baboon (bæbu·n) *s.* ZOOL. babuino, mandril.

babouche (bæbu·sh) *s.* babucha.

baby (bei·bi) *s.* criatura, rorro, bebé, nene, niño. *2* benjamín. *3 adj.* de niño; infantil; pequeño. *4 ~ sitter*, niñera por horas, canguro.

baby (to) *tr.* tratar como niño, mimar. ¶ Pret. y p. p.: *babied.*

babyish (-ish) *adj.* pueril, infantil.

Babylon (bæ·bilan) *n. pr.* HIST. Babilonia.

Babylonian (bæbila·nian) *adj.-s.* babilonio. *2 adj.* babilónico, de Babilonia.

baccalaureate (bækalo·rit) *s.* bachillerato.

baccarat (bækara) *s.* bacará [juego].

bacchanal (bæ·kanal), **bacchanalian** (bækanelian) *adj.* bacanal. *2* ebrio. *3 s.* discípulo de Baco; borracho, calavera.

Bacchanalia (-ne·lia) *s. pl.* bacanales. *2* [ús. en sing.] bacanal, orgía.

Bacchanals (bæ·kanels) *s. pl.* bacanales.

bacchante (bæka·nti) *s.* bacante.

Bacchic (bæ·kik) *adj.* báquico.

Bacchus (bæ·køs) *n. pr.* MIT. Baco.

bachelor (bæ·chølø^r) *m.* soltero, célibe; *old ~*, solterón. *2* bachiller.

bachelorhood (-jud) *s.* soltería [del hombre].

bachelor's button *s.* nombre del azulejo, la centaurea y otras plantas.

bacillus (bæsi·løs) *s.* bacilo.

back (bæk) *s.* espalda [del hombre]; lomo, cerro [de un animal]; espinazo; *to turn one's ~ on* o *upon*, abandonar, desertar; volver la espalda a; *behind one's ~*, a espaldas de uno; *on one's ~*, a

cuestas; de espaldas, boca arriba. *2* espalda, dorso, envés, revés [de una cosa]; trasera, fondo, parte de atrás. *3* espaldar [de coraza]. *4* respaldo [de silla, etc.]. *5* lomo [de libro]. *6* canto, lomo, recazo [de cuchillo]. *7* parte convexa [de una cosa arqueada]. *8* FÚTBOL defensa. *9* TEAT. foro.

10 adj. posterior, dorsal, trasero, que está atrás; interior, apartado: *~ door*, puerta trasera o excusada. *11* atrasado [renta, número de un periódico]. *12* que vuelve, que va hacia atrás, dirigido hacia atrás. *13 adv.* atrás, hacia atrás, en situación apartada: *to go ~*, retroceder. *14* de vuelta, de regreso, en reciprocidad, en pago: *to come ~*, volver, regresar; *to give ~*, devolver. *15* en ocultación o retención: *to keep ~*, callar; retener.

16 interj. ¡atrás!

back (to) *tr.* apoyar, sostener, respaldar, secundar. *2* apostar por o a. *3* empujar o tirar hacia atrás, hacer recular. *4* formar, estar en o resguardar la espalda, el dorso, el envés o el lomo de. *5* respaldar [un escrito]. *6* MAR. engalgar. *7* montar [un caballo]. *8* pop. llevar a cuestas. *9 to ~ up*, sostener, apoyar. *10 to ~ water*, MAR. ciar. *11 intr.* recular, retroceder. *12 to ~ down, to ~ out*, volverse atrás.

backbite (to) (bæ·kbait) *intr.-tr.* murmurar [de]; criticar, calumniar [a uno]. ¶ Pret.: *backbit*; p. p.: *backbit* o *-bitten*; ger.: *backbitting.*

backbiter (-ø^r) *s.* murmurador, calumniador.

backbone (bæ·kboun) *s.* espinazo, columna vertebral. *2 fig.* firmeza, nervio, resistencia.

backdoor (bæ·kdoø^r) *adj.* clandestino, secreto.

backdown (-daun) *s.* fam. retractación, palinodia.

backer (bæ·kø^r) *s.* apoyador, respaldador, financiador, partidario. *2* el que apuesta.

backfire (bæ·kfai^r) *s.* AUTO. petardeo.

backfire (to) *intr.* AUTO. petardear.

backgammon (-gæmøn) *s.* chaquete.

background (-graund) *s.* fondo, último término, lontananza. *2* fondo [de un dibujo, etc.].

backhand(ed (bækjæ·nd(id) *adj.* de revés, dado con la mano vuelta. *2* inclinada a la izquierda [escritura]. *3* insincero, irónico. *4* desmañado.

backing (bæ·king) *s.* apoyo, sostén. *2* garantía. *3* lo que sostiene o refuerza por detrás, forro. *4* azogado [de un espejo]. *5* retroceso.

backpiece (-pɪs) *s.* espaldar [de armadura].
backset (-set) *s.* contratiempo, contrariedad. *2* remanso, contracorriente.
backshop (-shap) *s.* trastienda; rebotica.
backside (-said) *s.* espalda, parte de atrás. *2* trasero, tafanario.
backslide (-slaid) *intr.* deslizarse hacia atrás. *2* recaer, reincidir, volver a un estado de culpa o atraso.
backspacer (-peisøʳ) *s.* tecla de retroceso.
backstairs (bakste·ʳs) *adj.* de intriga, secreto, clandestino.
backstitch (bæ·kstitch) *s.* pespunte.
backstitch (to) *tr.* pespunt(e)ar.
backward (-woʳd) *adj.* dirigido hacia atrás, retrógrado, retrospectivo. *2* que retrocede. *3* dicho o hecho al revés. *4* atrasado; tardío. *5* lento, tardo. *6* lerdo, torpe. *7* corto, tímido. *8* renuente.
backward(s (-woʳd(s) *adv.* hacia atrás, atrás. *2* al revés. *3* de espaldas. *4* a reculones.
backwardation (-ei·shøn) *s.* doble [en Bolsa].
backwater (-uøtøʳ) *s.* remanso.
backwoods (-wuds) *s. pl.* (E.U.) región de bosques alejada de los centros de población.
bacon (bei·køn) *s.* tocino [esp. el entreverado].
bacteria (bæktɪ·ria) *pl.* de BACTERIUM.
bacteriology (-a·lodŷi) *s.* bacteriología.
bacterium (bæktɪ·riøm) *s.* bacteria.
bad (bæd) *adj.* malo, mal: ~ *form*, mala educación. *2* malo, enfermo. *3* podrido [huevo]. *4* incobrable [deuda]. *5* falsa [moneda]. *6 adv.* mal: ~ *looking*, de mal aspecto. *7 s.* mal, lo malo: *to go to the* ~, perderse, arruinarse; *from* ~ *to worse*, de mal en peor.
bade *pret.* de TO BID.
badge (bæ·dŷi) *s.* insignia, distintivo, placa, condecoración. *2* divisa, símbolo.
badger (-øʳ) *s.* ZOOL. tejón.
badger (to) *tr.* molestar, atormentar.
badinage (bæ·dinidŷ) *s.* broma, burla, chanza.
badly (bæ·dli) *adv.* mal, malamente: ~ *off*, en mal estado o situación; maltrecho. *2* muy mucho. *3* gravemente.
badminton (bæ·dmintøn) *s.* volante [juego].
badness (bæ·dnis) *s.* maldad [calidad de malo]; mala calidad.
baffle (bæ·føl) *s.* confusión, desconcierto [de uno]. *2* MEC. pantalla; deflector.
baffle (to) *tr.* confundir, desconcertar, chasquear. *2* burlar, frustrar. *3* desviar, detener.
bag (bæg) *s.* saco, bolsa, talega. *2* cartera, valija; maletín, saco de mano; bolso, monedero. *3* zurrón, morral. *4* ANAT. bolsa, saco. *5* bolsa [en la piel o en la ropa].
bag (to) *tr.* embolsar, ensacar, meter en el zurrón. *2* cazar, pescar, atrapar, coger. *3* abolsarse, hacer bolsa. *4* hincharse, abotagarse. ¶ Pret. y p. p.: *bagged;* ger.: *bagging*.
bagasse (bagæ·s) *s.* bagazo.
bagatelle (bægate·l) *s.* bagatela.
baggage (bæ·gidŷ) *s.* (E.U. y Can.) equipaje [de viaje]. *2* MIL. bagaje. *3* pelandusca. *4* fam. picaruela.
baggy (bæ·gi) *adj.* holgado, flojo, que hace bolsas.
bagnio (bæ·nou) *s.* baño [prisión de esclavos]. *2* lupanar.
bagpipe (bæ·gpaip) *s.* MÚS. gaita, cornamusa.
bagpiper (-ø·) *s.* gaitero.
bah (ba) *interj.* ¡bah!
bail (beil) *s.* DER. fianza. *2* DER. fiador. *3* asa [de

cubo o caldero]. *4* arco [que sostiene un toldo]. *5* achicador. *6* aro, cerco, zuncho.
bail (to) *tr.* DER. dar fianza por [uno]. *2* poner en libertad bajo fianza. *3* achicar [sacar agua]. *4* zunchar, asegurar con aros. *5 intr.* AVIA. *to* ~ *out*, tirarse con paracaídas.
bailey (bei·li) *s.* muralla o patio de un castillo o fortaleza.
bailiff (bei·lif) *s.* baile [ant. magistrado]. *2* administrador, mayordomo. *3* alguacil, corchete.
bailiwick (bei·liuik) *s.* bailía. *2* mayordomía. *3* alguacilazgo.
bairn (beʳn) *s.* [Esc.] niño, niña.
bait (beit) *s.* cebo, carnada. *2* fig. cebo, señuelo, anzuelo: *to take the* ~, tragar el anzuelo. *3* pienso.
bait (to) *tr.* cebar [poner cebo; atraer con cebo]. *2* dar un pienso a. *3* atormentar, acosar, hostigar.
baize (beiš) *s.* bayeta.
bake (beik) *s.* cocción al horno. *2* cosa cocida al horno.
bake (to) *tr.* cocer, asar, etc., al horno. *2* secar, endurecer [por la acción del calor]; calcinar. *3 intr.* hornear. *4* cocerse [en el horno]. *5* secarse, endurecerse [al sol, etc.].
bakelite (bei·kølait) *s.* baquelita.
baker (bei·køʳ) *s.* hornero, panadero: *baker's dozen,* docena de fraile.
bakery (-i) *s.* horno, panadería, tahona.
baking (bei·king) *s.* cochura, cocción [al horno]; ~ *powder*, levadura química. *2* hornada.
balance (bæ·lans) *s.* balanza [instrumento]. *2* ASTR. Libra. *3* contrapeso. *4* equilibrio. *5* comparación, estimación. *6* COM. balance. *7* COM. saldo, alcance. *8* volante [de reloj]. *9* MEC. ~ *wheel*, volante. *10* ~ *of trade*, balanza comercial.
balance (to) *tr.* pesar [en la balanza]. *2* estimar, comparar. *3* equilibrar; nivelar. *4* balancear, contrapesar. *5* COM. saldar, finiquitar. *6 intr.* estar en equilibrio. *7* equilibrarse, compensarse. *8* balancear[se; vacilar.
balancer (-øʳ) *s.* pesador. *2* equilibrista. *3* ELECT. estabilizador. *4* ENT. balancín [de díptero].
balas (bæ·las) *s.* balaje [rubí].
balcony (bæ·lkøni) *s.* balcón; galería exterior. *2* TEAT. galería, anfiteatro.
bald (bold) *adj.* calvo. *2* desnudo, pelado. *3* escueto. *4* pobre [estilo].
baldachin (bæ·ldakin) *s.* baldaquín.
balderdash (bo·ldøʳdæsh) *s.* vaciedades, tonterías, monserga.
bald-faced *adj.* cariblanco, careto.
baldly (-li) *adv.* desnudamente, escuetamente. *2* pobremente.
baldness (-nis) *s.* calvicie. *2* desnudez [falta de pelo, plumas, adornos, etc.].
baldric (bol·arik) *s.* tahalí.
bale (beil) *s.* bala, fardo. *2* poét. mal, dolor.
bale (to) *tr.* embalar, enfardar, empacar. *2* MAR. achicar.
Balearic (bæliæ·rik) *adj.* balear, baleárico.
balefire (bei·lfaiʳ) *s.* almenara, hoguera.
baleful (bei·lful) *adj.* funesto, pernicioso.
balk (bok) *s.* AGR. caballón. *2* yerro, desliz. *3* fracaso, contrariedad. *4* impedimento. *5* viga. *6* BILLAR. cabaña, casa; cuadro.
balk (to) *tr.* evitar. *2* burlar, desbaratar, contrariar. *3* malograr, perder. *4 intr.* plantarse, resistirse. *5* repropiarse.
Balkan (bo·lkan) *adj.* balcánico.
ball (bol) *s.* bola, globo, esfera. *2* pelota. *3* bala

[proyectil redondo]. *4* ovillo; burujo. *5* yema [del pulgar o del dedo]. *6* AGR. cepellón. *7* baile [fiesta].

ball (to) *tr.* ovillar. *2* apelotonar, convertir en bola. *3* intr. *to* ~ *up*, apelotonarse.

ballad (bæ·lad) *s.* balada. *2* canción, copla.

ballast (bæ·last) *s.* lastre. *2* grava, balasto.

ballast (to) *tr.* lastrar. *2* balastar; afirmar.

ballet (bæ·lei) *s.* baile de espectáculo.

ballista (bali·sta) *s.* balista.

ballistic (bali·stik) *adj.* balístico.

ballistics (-s) *s.* balística.

balloon (balu·n) *s.* globo [aerostático; juguete]. *2* QUÍM. balón.

balloon (to) *intr.* ir en globo. *2* hincharse.

ballot (bæ·lot) *s.* balota; papeleta de voto, candidatura. *2* votación, sufragio.

ballot (to) *intr.* y *tr.* votar. *2* insacular.

ball-point pen *s.* bolígrafo.

ballroom (bo·lrum) *s.* salón de baile.

balm (bam) *s.* bálsamo. *2* aroma, perfume. *3* BOT. melisa, cidronela, toronjil.

balmy (ba·mi) *adj.* balsámico, calmante, reparador. *2* suave [clima, tiempo]. *3* fam. chiflado, idiota.

balsam (bo·lsam) *s.* bálsamo. *2* BOT. balsamina [de jardín]. *3* ~ *apple*, balsamina [cucurbitácea].

balsamic (bolsæ·mik) *adj.* balsámico.

Balthasar (balza·saᵗ) *n. pr.* Baltasar.

Baltic (bo·ltik) *adj.* báltico.

baluster (bæ·løstøᵗ) *s.* balaustre.

balustrade (bæløstrei·d) *s.* balaustrada.

bamboo (bambu·) *s.* BOT. bambú.

bamboozle (-sløl) *s.* engaño, embeleco.

bamboozle (to) *tr.* engañar, embaucar, burlar.

bamboozler (-sløᵗ) *s.* ~ engañador, embaucador.

ban (bæn) *s.* proclama, edicto. *2* proscripción. *3* excomunión, entredicho. *4 pl.* BANNS.

ban (to) *tr.* proscribir, desterrar. *2* excomulgar, anatematizar. *3* prohibir.

banal (bæ·nal) *adj.* trivial, común, trillado.

banality (-iti) *s.* trivialidad, vulgaridad.

banana (banæ·na) *s.* BOT. plátano, banana.

band (bænd) *s.* faja, venda, fleje, cinta, tira [para atar]; vencejo, vilorta; sortija de cigarro. *2* abrazadera, zuncho. *3* faja, cenefa, cinta, lista, zona. *4* ARQ. filete, listón. *5* RADIO. banda [de ondas]. *6* MEC. correa. *7* MÚS. banda, música. *8* banda, cuadrilla, partida.

band (to) *tr.* atar, fajar, vendar, precintar. *2* acuadrillar, juntar. *3* intr. *to* ~ *together*, acuadrillarse, juntarse.

bandage (bæ·ndidў) *s.* venda, vendaje.

bandanna (bændæ·na) *s.* pañuelo de hierbas.

bandbox (bæ·ndbaks) *s.* sombrerera [caja].

banderol(e (bæ·ndøroul) *s.* banderola.

bandit (bæn·dit) *s.* bandido, bandolero.

banditry (bæ·nditri) *s.* bandidaje, bandolerismo.

bandog (bæ·ndog) *s.* mastín, perro de presa.

bandoleer, bandolier (bændolɪ·ᵗ) *s.* bandolera.

bandore (bæ·ndøᵗ) *s.* bandurria.

band-saw *s.* sierra sin fin.

bandy (bæ·ndi) *adj.* arqueado, torcido hacia afuera.

bandy (to)) *tr.* lanzar, tirar de un lado a otro. *2* cambiar [palabras, golpes, etc.]. *3* intr. discutir, contender.

bandy-legged *adj.* estevado.

bane (bein) *s.* muerte, ruina, daño, perdición. *2* veneno.

baneful (bei·nful) *adj.* letal, funesto, pernicioso, venenoso.

banewort (-uøᵗt) *s.* planta venenosa.

bang (bæng) *s.* golpe, porrazo [que resuena], portazo, detonación. *2* flequillo [de cabello]. *3* adv. con estrépito, con golpe. *4* de repente, impetuosamente.

bang (to) *tr.* golpear [haciendo ruido]: *to* ~ *the door*, dar un portazo. *2* aporrear, apalear, maltratar. *3* sobrepujar. *4* cortar el cabello en flequillo. *5* intr. hacer estrépito.

banian (bæ·nian) *s.* baniano.

banish (to) (bæ·nish) *tr.* desterrar, proscribir. *2* expulsar. *3* ahuyentar, desechar.

banishment (-mønt) *s.* destierro, proscripción, expulsión.

banister (bæ·nistøᵗ) *s.* balaustre. *2 pl.* balaustrada, barandilla.

banjo (bæ·ndўou) *s.* banjo.

bank (bank) *s.* ribazo, talud. *2* lomo [de tierra]. *3* margen, orilla [de río o lago]. *4* peralte [de carretera]. *5* banco [de arena]. *6* masa [de nubes]. *7* hilera, batería [de remos, teclas, lámparas, etc.]. *8* banda [del billar]. *9* COM. banco: ~ *note*, ~ *bill*, billete de banco; ~ *vault*, cámara acorazada. *10* hucha, alcancía. *11* banca [en el juego].

bank (to) *tr.* amontonar [formando dique o talud]; aporcar, cubrir. | Gralte. con *up*. *2* proteger, represar [con dique o reparo]. *3* juntar en serie o batería. *4* depositar en un banco. *5* intr. hacer negocios de banca. *6* tener dinero en un banco. *7* *to* ~ *up*, elevarse formando lomo o talud; AVIA. inclinarse al virar. *8* *to* ~ *on*, contar con.

banker (-øᵗ) *s.* banquero.

banking (bæ·nking) *s.* banca [negocio]. *2* adj. bancario de banca: ~ *house*, casa de banca.

bankrupt (bæ·nkrøpt) *adj.-s.* insolvente, quebrado, falldo, arruinado.

bankrupt (to) *tr.* hacer quebrar; arruinar.

bankruptcy (-si) *s.* quiebra, bancarrota.

banner (bæ·nøᵗ) *s.* bandera, estandarte, pendón.

banneret (-et) *s.* caballero con bandera.

banns (bæns) *s.* amonestaciones.

banquet (bæ·nkuit) *s.* banquete, festín.

banquet (to) *tr.-intr.* banquetear.

bantam (bæ·ntam) *s.* ORN. gallina enana.

bantam-weight *s.* BOX. peso gallo.

banter (bæ·ntøᵗ) *s.* burla, chanza, vaya.

banter (to) *tr.* embromar, dar vaya. *2* intr. bromear, chancearse.

bantling (bæ·ntling) *s.* pequeñuelo, pequeñuela.

banyan (bæ·nian) *s.* BANIAN.

baobab (bei·oubæb) *s.* BOT. baobab.

baptism (bæ·ptism) *s.* bautismo. *2* bautizo.

baptismal (bæpti·śmal) *s.* bautismal; ~ *name*, nombre de pila.

Baptist (bæ·ptist) *s.* bautista. *2* baptista.

baptistery (bæ·ptistøri) *s.* baptisterio.

baptize (to) (bæ·ptaiš) *tr.* bautizar.

baptizer (-øᵗ) *s.* bautista, bautizante.

bar (baᵗ) *s.* barra, barrote, varilla. *2* barra [de plata, oro, etc.]. *3* GEOGR. barra, alfaque. *4* tranca [de puerta]. *5* raya, faja, lista. *6* barrera, valla, reja. *7* barra [de un tribunal o asamblea]. *8* DER. estrados. *9* abogacía, foro; colegio de abogados. *10* mostrador [de taberna o restaurante]; sala donde está; bar. *11* MÚS. barra, compás. *12* FÍS. bar. *13* prep. excepto, salvo.

bar (to) *tr.* atrancar [una puerta]. *2* barrear. *3* listar, rayar. *4* MÚS. dividir en compases. *5* obs-

truir; obstar, impedir, prohibir. ¶ Pret. y p. p.: *barred;* ger.: *barring.*
Barabbas (baræ·bas) *n. pr.* Barrabás.
barb (ba^rb) *s.* púa, lengüeta [de flecha, anzuelo, etc.]. *2* barbilla [de pez]. *3* caballo árabe. *4 pl.* barbas [de pluma].
barb (to) *tr.* armar con púas o lengüetas.
barbarian (barbe·rian) *adj.-s.* bárbaro [de los pueblos bárbaros; no civilizado].
barbaric (ba^rbæ·rik) *s.* bárbaro, barbárico.
barbarism (ba·^rbarišm) *s.* barbarismo. *2* barbarie.
barbarity (ba·bæ·riti) *s.* barbarie, crueldad.
barbarize (to) (ba·^rbaraiš) *tr.-intr.* barbarizar. *2* volver o volverse bárbaro.
barbarous (ba·^rbarøs) *adj.* bárbaro.
Barbary (ba·^rbikiu) *n. pr.* GEOGR. Berbería.
barbecue (ba·^rbikiu) *s.* barbacoa [parrilla; carne].
barbecue (to) *tr.* asar un animal entero; churrasquear.
barbed (ba·^rbd) *adj.* armado con púas o lengüetas: ~ *wire,* alambre con púas, espino artificial.
barbel (ba·^rbøl) *s.* barbilla [de pez]. *2* barbo.
bar-bell *s.* GIMN. barra con pesas.
barber (ba·^rbø^r) *s.* barbero: *barber's shop,* barbería.
barberry (ba·^rbøri) *s.* bérbero, agracejo.
barbet (ba·^rbet) *s.* perro de aguas.
barbican (ba·^rbikan) *s.* FORT. barbacana.
barcarol (ba·^rkaroul) *s.* barcarola.
bard (ba^rd) *s.* bardo; vate. *2* barda [del caballo]. *3* COC. albardilla.
bard (to) *tr.* COC. albardillar, embozorrar.
bare (be^r) *adj.* desnudo; descubierto: *to lay* ~, desnudar, descubrir. *2* pelado, raso. *3* raído. *4* desprovisto de. *5* mero, puro, solo. *6* liso, sencillo.
bare (to) *tr.* desnudar, despojar, descubrir.
barebone (-boun) *s.* esqueleto [persona flaca].
barefaced (-feist) *adj.* descarado, desfachatado, insolente, atrevido.
barefoot (-fut), **barefooted** (-id) *adj.* descalzo.
bareheaded (-jedid) *adj.* descubierto, destocado.
barelegged (-legid) *adj.* en pernetas.
barely (-li) *adv.* desnudamente. *2* apenas, escasamente. *3* insuficientemente.
barenecked (-nekt) *adj.* descotado.
bareness (-nis) *s.* desnudez. *2* desabrigo. *3* miseria, escasez.
bargain (ba·^rgin) *s.* trato, convenio, ajuste, negocio: *into the* ~, de más, por añadidura. *2* ganga, buen negocio: *at a* ~, muy barato.
bargain (to) *intr.* negociar, ajustar un trato; regatear: *I did not* ~ *for it,* fig. no esperaba yo esto. *2 tr.* vender, negociar, trocar.
bargaining (-ing) *s.* trato, regateo.
barge (ba^rdÿ) *s.* barcaza, gabarra. *2* chalupa. *3* HOUSEBOAT.
barge (to) *intr.* moverse, meterse, entrometerse.
bargeman (-mæn) *s.* barquero, gabarrero.
barilla (bari·la) *s.* barrilla, sosa.
baritone (bæ·ritoun) *s.* QUÍM. bario.
barium (be·riøm) *s.* QUÍM. bario.
bark (ba^rk) *s.* corteza [de árbol]; casca. *2* ladrido. *3* fam. tos. *4* MAR. bricbarca, barca.
bark (to) *tr.* curtir [con casca]. *2* descortezar. *3* rozar, desollar. *4* cubrir con corteza. *5 intr.* ladrar.
barker (-ø^r) *s.* descortezador. *2* animal ladrador. *3* voceador.
barkentine (ba·^rkøntin) *s.* barca goleta.
barking (-ing) *s.* ladrido. *2 adj.* ladrador.
barley (ba·^rli) *s.* BOT. cebada; alcacer.

barm (ba^rm) *s.* levadura [esp. de cerveza].
barmaid (ba·^rmeid) *s.* camarera, moza de taberna.
barman (ba·^rmæn) *s.* mozo de taberna, barman.
barmy (ba·^rmi) *adj.* espumoso. *2* fig. chiflado.
barn (ba^rn) *s.* granero, pajar; cobertizo.
barnacle (ba·^rnakøl) *s.* acial. *2* ORN. barnacla. *3* bellota de mar, percebe. *4 pl.* gafas.
barn-owl *s.* ORN. lechuza.
barnyard (-ya^rd) *s.* corral [de granja]: ~ *fowl,* ave de corral.
barometer (bara·mitø^r) *s.* barómetro.
baron (bæ·røni) *s.* barón. *2* magnate.
baronage (-idÿ) *s.* baronía [dignidad].
baroness (-is) *s.* baronesa.
baronet (-et) *s.* baronet.
baronetage (-idÿ), **baronetcy** (-si) *s.* título o dignidad de baronet.
baronial (barou·nial) *adj.* del barón o la baronía.
barony (bæ·røni) *s.* baronía.
baroque (barou·k) *adj.* barroco.
barouche (baru·sh) *s.* birlocho.
barque (ba^rk) *s.* especie de bricbarca.
barrack (to) (bæ·rak) *tr.* acuartelar, poner en cuarteles. *2* DEP. abuchear. *3 intr.* alojarse en cuarteles.
barracks (bæ·raks) *s. pl.* cuartel [edificio].
barracuda (baraku·da) *s.* ICT. picuda.
barrage (bara·dÿ) *s.* barrera. *2* presa [en un río, etc.].
barratry (bæ·ratri) *s.* MAR. baratería.
barrel (bæ·røl) *s.* barril, tonel. *2* cañón, cilindro. *3* cañón [de un arma; de la pluma de ave]. *4* cuerpo [de bomba]. *5* MEC. cilindro, tambor. *6* cubo [de reloj]. *7* tronco [de un cuadrúpedo].
barrel (to) *tr.* embarrilar, entonelar. ¶ Pret. y p. p.: *barreled* o *-lled;* ger.: *barreling* o *-lling.*
barren (bæ·røn) *adj.* estéril, infecundo, infructuoso. *2* árido, yermo. *3* falto, desprovisto de. *4 s.* yermo, erial.
barricade (bærikei·d) *s.* barricada.
barricade (to) *tr.* fortificar u obstruir con barricada.
barrier (bæ·riø^r) *s.* barrera, valla, empalizada. *2* barrera, obstáculo.
barring (ba·ring) *prep.* excepto, salvo, quitando.
barrister (bæ·ristø^r) *s.* abogado.
barroom (ba·^rrum) *s.* cantina, bar.
barrow (bæ·rou) *s.* angarillas, parihuela. *2* carrito de mano, carretilla. *3* túmulo [montículo]. *4* cerdo castrado.
bartender (ba·^rtendø^r) *s.* BARMAN.
barter (ba·^rø^r) *s.* trueque, cambio, cambalache.
barter (to) *tr.-intr.* trocar, cambiar, permutar, cambalachear.
Bartholomew (barza·lømiu) *n. pr.* Bartolomé.
baryta (bærai·ta) *s.* QUÍM. barita.
barytone (bæ·ritoun) *s.* BARITONE.
basal (bei·sal) *s.* basal. *2* básico.
basalt (bæsolt) *s.* basalto.
basaltic (-ik) *adj.* basáltico.
basan (bæ·san) *s.* badana.
bascule (bæ·skiul) *s.* báscula [aparato para levantar un puente].
base (beis) *adj.* inferior, de baja calidad, de poco valer. *2* bajo, de baja ley [metal, moneda]. *3* bajo, ruin, vil. *4* MÚS. bajo, grave. *5* base, que sirve de base. *6 s.* base. *7* basa, basamento, pie, zócalo.
base (to) *tr.* basar, fundar, fundamentar. *2 intr.* basarse, estar basado.
baseball (-bol) *s.* béisbol.

baseboard (-bo^{r}d) *s.* zócalo [en una pared]. *2* rodapié. *3* tablero que sirve de base.
baseless (-lis) *adj.* sin base; infundado.
basement (-mønt) *s.* basamento. *2* sótano, cuarto bajo.
bash (to) (bæsh) *tr.* quebrar o aplastar a golpes.
bashful (-ful) *adj.* vergonzoso, tímido, encogido, modesto, ruboroso.
basic (bei·sik) *adj.* básico.
basidium (basi·diøm) *s.* BOT. basidio.
Basil (bei·sil) *n. pr.* Basilio.
basil (bæ·sil) *s.* BOT. albahaca. *2* badana.
basilar (-a^r) *adj.* basilar.
basilic(a (bæ·silik(a) *s.* basílica.
basilisk (bæ·silisk) *s.* basilisco.
basin (bei·sin) *s.* jofaina, palangana, bacía, cubeta, lebrillo. *2* taza, pilón [de fuente]. *3* dársena. *4* GEOGR. cuenca, valle, hoya. *5* estanque.
basinet (bæ·sinet) *s.* bacinete.
basis (bei·sis) *s.* base, fundamento. *2* ARQ., ZOOL., BOT. base.
bask (to) (bæks) *intr.* calentarse, estarse expuesto [al sol, a un calor agradable]. *2 tr.* calentar, asolear.
basket (bæ·skit) *s.* cesto, cesta, canasta, cuévano. *2* barquilla [de globo].
basketball (-bol) *s.* baloncesto.
basket-handle *adj.* ARQ. carpanel [arco].
basket-work *s.* cestería; obra de cestería o que la imita.
basketry (bæ·skøtri) *s.* cestería.
Balse (bal) *n. pr.* GEOGR. Basilea.
Basque (bask) *adj.-s.* vasco. *2 s.* vascuence.
bas-relief (ba-rilıf) *s.* bajo relieve.
bass (bæs) *s.* ICT. róbalo, lobina. *2* ICT. perca. *3* BOT. liber. *4* fibra de ciertas plantas.
bass (beis) *adj.* MÚS. bajo, grave: ~ *viol*, violón. *2 s.* MÚS. bajo.
basset (bæ·sit) *s.* perro de patas muy cortas.
bassinet (-sinet) *s.* cuna de mimbres. *2* BASINET.
basso (bæ·sou) *s.* MÚS. bajo.
bassoon (bæsu·n) *s.* MÚS. bajón, piporro; fagot.
basswood (bæ·swud) *s.* BOT. tilo americano.
bast (bæst) *s.* liber, fibra.
bastard (bæ·sta^{r}d) *adj.-s.* bastardo. *2 adj.* degenerado. *3* IMPR. ~ *title*, anteportada.
bastardize (to) (-aiš) *tr.* declarar bastardo. *2 intr.* bastardear, degenerar.
bastardy (-i) *s.* bastardía.
baste (to) (beist) *tr.* hilvanar, embastar. *2* fam. apalear. *3* COC. lardear, lardar.
bastinado (bæstinei·dou) *s.* bastonazo. *2* paliza.
bastinado (to) *tr.* apalear.
bastings (bæ·stings) *s. pl.* hilvanes.
bastion (bæ·schøn) *s.* bastión, baluarte.
bat (bæt) *s.* ZOOL. murciélago. *2* palo, bate, raqueta [para ciertos juegos]. *3* pedazo de ladrillo, tejoleta.
bat (to) *tr.* golpear con el bate. *2* mover: *to ~ the eyelashes*, parpadear.
batch (bæch) *s.* hornada, cochura. *2* cantidad de cosas que se producen, se emplean, se necesitan, etc., de una vez. *3* fam. soltero.
bate (to) (beit) *tr.* rebajar, disminuir. *2* cortar, contener: *with bated breath*, con aliento entrecortado. *3 intr.* disminuir.
bath (bæz) *s.* baño. *2* bañera [recipiente]. *3 pl.* baños [edificio; balneario].
bathe (to) (beið) *tr.* bañar. *2 intr.* bañarse.
bather (-ø^r) *s.* bañista [que se baña].

bathhouse (bæ·zjaus) *s.* casa de baños. *2* caseta de baño.
bathrobe (-roub) *s.* albornoz, bata.
bathroom (-rum) *s.* cuarto de baño.
bathtub (-tøb) *s.* bañera, baño.
bathymetry (bæzi·metri) *s.* batimetría.
bating (bei·ting) *prep.* excepto, exceptuando.
batiste (bætı·st) *s.* batista.
batman (bæ·tmæn) *s.* MIL. asistente, ordenanza.
baton (bæ·toøn) *s.* bastón [de mando]. *2* MÚS. batuta.
baton (to) *tr.* bastonear.
batrachian (bætrei·kian) *adj.-s.* batracio.
batsman (bæ·tsmæn) *s.* jugador de pelota con bate.
battalion (bætæ·liøn) *s.* batallón.
batten (bæ·tøn) *s.* tabla [para entarimar]; lata, listón. *3* batán [del telar].
batten (to) *tr.* reforzar o asegurar con listones. *2* cebar, engordar. *3 intr.* engordar, medrar.
batter (bæ·tø^r) *s.* COC. pasta, batido. *2* pasta de yeso. *3* talud, releje [de un muro].
batter (to) *tr.* batir, golpear. *2* MIL. batir, cañonear. *3* romper, abollar, estropear: *to ~ down*, demoler. *4* ataludar [un muro]. *5 intr.* tener talud [un muro].
battered (-d) *adj.* hecho una pasta. *2* derruido, estropeado, abollado.
battering (-in) *adj.* MIL. de batir: ~ *ram*, ariete.
battery (-i) *s.* batería. *2* DER. agresión.
battle (bæ·tøl) *s.* batalla, combate, lucha: ~ *front*, frente de combate.
battle (to) *intr.* batallar, luchar.
battled (bæ·tøld) *adj.* almenado.
battledore (-do^r) *s.* raqueta [para jugar al volante]. *2* pala [de lavandera].
battlefield (-fild) *s.* campo de batalla.
battlement (-mønt) *s.* almenaje, muro almenado.
battleship (-ship) *s.* acorazado.
bauble (bo·bøl) *s.* chuchería, fruslería; perifollo. *2* cetro de bufón.
baulk (to) (bok) *intr.* TO BALK.
Bavaria (bave·ria) *n. pr.* GEOGR. Baviera.
Bavarian (-n) *adj.-s.* bávaro.
bawd (bod) *s.* alcahuete, ta.
bawd (to) *intr.* alcahuetear.
bawdiness (bo·di[nis) *adj.* obscenidad.
bawdy (bo·di) *adj.* obsceno, verde.
bawl (to) (bol) *intr.-tr.* gritar, vociferar; berrear.
bawler (bo·lø^r) *s.* voceador, vocinglero, gritador, gritón.
bay (bei) *adj.-s.* bayo [caballo]. *2 s.* bahía, ensenada, abra. *3* entrada de un llano en una cordillera. *4* ARQ. intercolumnio, vano, entrepaño. *5* ojo [de puente]. *6* ventana salediza: ~ *window*, mirador, cierro de cristales. *7* compartimiento [de cuadra; de granero o henil]. *8* ladrido [esp. del perro que persigue]. *9* acorralamiento: *at* ~, acorralado, acosado; haciendo frente a los que le acosan. *10* laurel.
bay (to) *intr.* ladrar. *2 tr.* ladrar a. *3* acorralar.
bayadere (baiadi·ø^r) *s.* bayadera.
bayberry (bei·beri) *s.* BOT. arrayán brabántico; su fruto. *2* fruto del laurel.
bayonet (bei·ønit) *s.* bayoneta.
bayonet (to) *tr.* herir con bayoneta. *2* cargar a la bayoneta.
baza(a)r (baša·^{r}) *s.* bazar. *2* feria o tómbola benéfica.
bazooka (bašu·ka) *s.* cañón lanzacohetes.
be (to) (bı) *intr.* ser: *so ~ it*, así sea. *2* existir, vivir.

3 celebrarse, efectuarse. *4* tener [una edad]: *he is fifty o fifty years old*, tiene cincuenta años. *5* estar, hallarse, encontrarse; verse: *he is ill*, está enfermo; *I am obliged to do it*, me veo obligado a hacerlo. *6* llevar [tiempo] en un sitio. *7* Precedido de *there* se traduce por haber [impers.]: *there is something*, hay algo. *8* En ciertos casos, la oración se traduce por una del verbo tener: *to ~ hungry*, tener hambre, tener apetito; *to ~ right*, tener razón. *9* Otros sentidos: *to ~ at [a thing]*, estar ocupado en, estar haciendo [una cosa]; *it is not for me to say*, no soy yo quien ha de decir; *it is to ~ regretted*, es de lamentar. *10 impers.* hacer, haber: *it is cold*, hace frío; *it is foggy*, hay niebla; *it is now a year*, hace un año. *11 aux.* Forma la voz pasiva: *she is loved*, ella es amada. *12* Forma los tiempos compuestos de ciertos verbos intransitivos: *he is gone*, se ha ido. *13* Con un gerundio denota acción que se está realizando o que se va a realizar: *I am coming*, vengo; *he was going to speak*, él iba a hablar. *14* Con un infinitivo equivale a haber de, tener que: *I am to go out*, he de salir; *what are we to do?*, ¿qué hemos de hacer? ¶ CONJUG. INDIC. Pres.: *am, art, is; are.* | Pret.: *was, was, was; were.* | SUBJ. Pres. *be.* | Pret.: *were.* PART. PAS.: . | GER.: *being.*

beach (bɪ·ch) *s.* playa. *2* guijo.

beach (to) *intr.-tr.* MAR. encallar, varar [en la playa].

beachy (-i) *adj.* playado. *2* cubierto de guijo.

beacon (bɪ·kən) *s.* almenara. *2* atalaya [torre, eminencia]. *3* faro, farola, fanal. *4* baliza, señal. *5* radiofaro.

beacon (to) *tr.* iluminar, guiar. *2* guarnecer de faros, señales, etc. *3 intr.* brillar [como un faro].

bead (bɪd) *s.* cuenta [de rosario]. *2* cuenta, abalorio, agallón. *3* glóbulo, grano, gota, burbuja. *4* ARQ., QUÍM. perla. *5* pallón. *6* punto [de un arma de fuego]. *7* moldura convexa; junquillo, astrágalo. *8* reborde redondeado. *9 pl.* sarta de cuentas; rosario.

bead (to) *tr.* adornar con cuentas o abalorios. *2 intr.* burbujear, ser espumoso.

beading (-ing) *s.* cuentas, abalorios. *2* BEAD. *3* espuma [en un licor].

beadle (bɪ·dəl) *s.* alguacil, macero. *2* pertiguero. *3* bedel.

beady (bɪ·di) *adj.* parecido a un abalorio: *~ eyes*, ojos pequeños, redondos y brillantes. *2* espumoso [licor].

beagle (bɪ·gəl) *s.* sabueso.

beak (bik) *s.* pico [de ave, de vasija, de un objeto]. *2* pitorro. *3* fig. nariz. *4* promontorio. *5* mechero [de gas]. *6* MAR., BOT. espolón. *7* MÚS. boquilla. *8* pop. juez, magistrado.

beaker (-øʳ) *s.* copa o vaso de boca ancha. *2* QUÍM. vaso de precipitados.

beaky (-i) *adj.* picudo, narigudo.

beam (bɪm) *s.* viga, madero. *2* astil [de balanza o romana]. *3* enjulio; plegador [de telar]. *4* MEC. balancín. *5* lanza [de coche]. *6* bao. *7* manga [de un buque]: *on the ~*, por el través. *8* rayo, haz de rayos [de luz, calor, etc.].

beam (to) *tr.* emitir [luz, calor, etc.]. *2 intr.* destellar, brillar. *2* sonreír.

beaming (-ing) *adj.* brillante, resplandeciente. *2* radiante, sonriente.

beamy (-i) *adj.* BEAMING. *2* macizo como una viga.

bean (bin) *s.* BOT. haba; alubia, habichuela, judía.

2 grano, semilla [de café o cacao]. *3* fam. cabeza, chola.

bear (beʳ) *s.* oso, osa. *2* fig. bajista [en Bolsa]. *3* ASTR. *Great Bear*, Osa Mayor; *Little Bear*, Osa Menor.

bear (to) *tr.* llevar [una carga; una inscripción, una señal, una fecha; un nombre; espada, arma; una insignia, etc.]. *2* dar, producir, rendir. *3* dar [hijos]; dar a luz. *4* sostener, soportar. *5* sufrir, padecer; tolerar, aguantar, resistir. *6* tener [un aspecto, una cualidad; responsabilidad, parte, etc.]. *7* tener, profesar [amor, etc.]; guardar [rencor]. *8* tener, guardar [relación, analogía, etc.]. *9* hacer bajar [los valores]. *10* Otros sentidos: *to ~ a hand*, ayudar; *to ~ company*, hacer compañía; *to ~ in mind*, tener presente; *to ~ oneself*, portarse, conducirse; *to ~ witness*, dar testimonio.

11 intr. tener aguante, resistir. *12* ser paciente. *13* inclinarse, dirigirse o estar situado hacia. *14 to ~ on o upon*, referirse, aplicarse a; versar sobre; apuntar a [hablando de un arma]; pesar, tener efecto sobre. *15 to ~ up*, tener valor, mantenerse firme. ¶ Pret.: *bore*; p. p.: *borne*.

beard (bɪ·ʳd) *s.* barba [pelo]. *2* barbilla [de pez]. *3* lengüeta [de flecha]. *4* raspas [de la espiga].

beard (to) *tr.* mesar, arrancar las barbas. *2* desafiar, retar.

bearded (-id) *adj.* barbado, barbudo. *2* aristado. *3* barbato [cometa].

beardless (-lis) *adj.* imberbe, carilampiño. *2* desraspado, mocho [trigo].

bearer (be·røʳ) *s.* portador. *2* dador [de una carta]. *3* camillero. *4* andero. *5* ARQ., MEC. soporte, caballete, asiento. *6* árbol fructífero.

bearing (be·ring) *s.* porte, conducción. *2* presión, acción sobre. *3* producción [de frutos, flores, etc.]. *4* conducta, porte, aire, continente. *5* paciencia, aguante. *6* ARQ., MEC. apoyo, sostén. *7* MEC. cojinete. *8* MAR. orientación, situación, marcación, demora. *9* relación, conexión. *10* intención, fuerza; sentido [de lo que se dice]. *11 pl.* armas, blasones. *12 adj.* de apoyo, de contacto. *13* productivo, que lleva: *fruit ~*, fructífero.

bearish (-ish) *adj.* rudo, brusco; osuno.

bear's-ear *s.* BOT. oreja de oso.

bearskin (be·øʳskin) *s.* piel de oso. *2* birretina.

beast (bist) *s.* bestia, animal. *2* hombre brutal.

beastly (-li) *s.* bestial, brutal; horrible.

beat (bɪt) *s.* golpe; latido, pulsación; son repetido. *2* toque [en el tambor]. *3* tictac [del reloj]. *4* MÚS. tiempo [del compás]. *5* ronda, recorrido [de un guardia, un vigilante, etc.].

beat (to) *tr.* pegar, apalizar. *2* golpear, aporrear, azotar. *3* moler, sacudir [golpeando], machacar. *4* tocar [el tambor o en el tambor]. *5* batir [metales; huevos]. *6* hollar [un camino]. *7* batir, vencer, derrotar. *8* ganar, aventajar, sobrepujar. *9* marcar con golpes o movimientos: *to ~ time*, llevar el compás. *10* MONT. batir [el monte, etc.]. *11 to ~ a retreat*, emprender la retirada. *12 intr.* batir, golpear [en]; llamar [a la puerta]; ludir. *13* latir, palpitar, vibrar. *14* MAR. voltejear. *15 to ~ about the bush*, fig. andar con rodeos. ¶ Pret.: *beat*; p. p.: *beaten*.

beaten (-n) *adj.* batido. *2* trillado [camino]. *3* vencido; cansado, agotado.

beater (-øʳ) *s.* batidor, golpeador, apaleador. *2* vencedor. *3* MONT. batidor.

beatific(al (bɪati·fik(al) *f.* beatífico.

beatification (biætifikei·shøn) *s.* beatificación.
beatify (to) (biæ·tifai) *tr.* beatificar.
beating (bı·ting) *s.* paliza. 2 golpeo. 3 latido, pulsación. 4 ojeo. 5 MAR. voltejeo.
beatitude (biæ·titiud) *s.* beatitud. 2 *the Beatitudes*, las bienaventuranzas.
beau (bou), *pl.* **beaux** o **beaus** *s.* elegante, lechuguino. 2 galán, cortejo.
beauteous (biu·tiøs) *adj.* BEAUTIFUL.
beautiful (biu·tiful) *adj.* hermoso, bello. 2 lindo, precioso.
beautify (to) (biu·tifai) *tr.* hermosear, embellecer, adornar, acicalar. 2 *intr.* hermosearse, embellecerse. ¶ Pret. y p. p.: *beautified.*
beauty (biu·ti) *s.* belleza, hermosura, perfección: ~ *spot*, lunar, postizo. 2 belleza, beldad [mujer].
beaver (bı·vøʳ) *s.* castor [animal, piel, pelo, fieltro, tela]. 2 sombrero de copa. 3 ARM. babera. 4 ARM. visera.
becalm (to) (bika·m) *tr.* calmar, sosegar, serenar. 2 detener [a un buque] la falta de viento.
became (bikei·s) *pret.* de TO BECOME.
because (biko·s) *conj.* porque. 2 ~ *of*, a causa de, por causa de.
beccafico (bekafı·kou) *s.* ORN. papafigo.
bechance (to) (bichæ·ns) *tr.* e *intr.* ocurrir, suceder, acontecer.
beck (bek) *s.* seña [con la cabeza o la mano]; *at one's* ~ *and call*, a la disposición de uno. 2 riachuelo.
beck (to) *tr.-intr.* TO BECKON.
beckon (be·køn) *s.* BECK.
beckon (to) *tr.* llamar, indicar algo [a uno] por señas. 2 *intr.* hacer señas.
becloud (to) (biklau·d) *tr.* obscurecer, anublar.
become (to) (bikø·m) *tr.* convenir, cuadrar, sentar, caer o ir bien; ser propio o decoroso. 2 *intr.* volverse, hacerse, convertirse en, llegar a ser; ponerse: *to* ~ *angry*, ponerse furioso, enojarse; *to* ~ *old*, hacerse viejo, envejecer. 3 *to* ~ *of*, ser de, parar en, hacerse: *what has become of Peter?*, ¿qué ha sido, o se ha hecho de Pedro? ¶ Pret.: *became*; p. p.: *become.*
becoming (-ing) *adj.* que sienta, va o está bien. 2 adecuado, conveniente, propio, decoroso. 3 apuesto.
bed (bed) *s.* cama, lecho, yacija: *to go to* ~, acostarse. 2 GEOGR. lecho, álveo, cauce, madre. 3 solera [de acequia]. 4 macizo, cuadro, tabla [de jardín o huerto]. 5 asiento, base, cimiento. 6 MAR. basada. 7 ALBAÑ. lecho. 8 lecho, capa, estrato, yacimiento.
bed (to) *tr.* acostar. 2 dar cama. 3 asentar, dar asiento o base. 4 plantar, sembrar [en cuadros o tablas]. 5 disponer en cama. 6 *intr.* acostarse; yacer. ¶ Pret. y p. p.: *bedded*; ger.: *bedding.*
bedabble (to) (bidæ·bøl) *tr.* mojar, rociar.
bedaub (to) (bido·b) *tr.* embadurnar. 2 TO BEDIZEN.
bedazzle (to) (bidæ·søl) *tr.* deslumbrar.
bedbug (be·dbug) *s.* ENT.. chinche.
bedchamber (-cheimbøʳ) *s.* alcoba, dormitorio.
bedclothes (-clouðs) *s. pl.* ropas de cama.
bedcover (-køvøʳ) *s.* cubrecama.
bedding (-ing) *s.* colchones y ropa de cama. 2 cama [para el ganado]. 3 ALBAÑ., MEC. asiento. 4 empotramiento. 5 estratificación.
bedeck (to) (bide·k) *tr.* adornar, engalanar, ataviar.
bedevil (to) (bide·vøl) *tr.* endemoniar. 2 hechizar. 3 enredar. 4 enloquecer.
bedew (to) (bidiu·) *tr.* rociar, regar.
bedim (to) (bidi·m) *tr.* oscurecer, ofuscar.

bedizen (bidai·søn) *tr.* emperejilar.
bedlam (be·dlam) *s.* casa de orates, manicomio. 2 belén, confusión, desbarajuste.
bedlamite (-ait) *s.* loco, orate.
Bedouin (be·duin) *adj.-s.* beduino. 2 nómada.
bedpan (be·dpæn) *s.* chata, silleta. 2 calentador de cama.
bedplate (-pleit) *s.* MEC. bancada, platina.
bedraggle (bidræ·gøl) *s.* ensuciar arrastrando por el suelo, el lodo, etc.
bedrid(en (be·drid(øn) *adj.* postrado en cama.
bedrock (-rak) *s.* lecho de roca, roca firme. 2 *fig.* fondo, base, fundamento.
bedroom (-rum) *s.* alcoba, dormitorio.
bedside (-said) *s.* lado de la cama, cabecera.
bedsore (-soʳ) *s.* encentadura, úlcera de decúbito.
bedspread (-spred) *s.* cobertor, cubrecama.
bedspring (-spring) *s.* colchón de muelles, somier.
bedstead (-sted) *s.* armadura de la cama.
bestraw (-stro) *s.* BOT. cuajaleche.
bedtime (be·dtaim) *s.* hora de acostarse.
bee (bı) *s.* ENT. abeja; ~ *eater*, ORN. abejaruco. 2 reunión, tertulia.
beech (bıch) *s.* BOT. haya.
beechen (-øn) *adj.* de haya.
beechnut (-nøt) *s.* fabuco, hayuco.
beef (bıf) *s.* carne de vaca, buey o toro. 2 res vacuna de matadero. 3 *fam.* músculo, fuerza muscular.
beefeater (-itøʳ) *s.* alabardero.
beefsteak (-stek) *s.* biftec, bisté.
beehive (bı·jaiv) *s.* colmena.
beekeeper (bıkı·pøʳ) *s.* colmenero.
bee-line *s.* línea recta, derechura: *to make a* ~ *for*, ir en línea recta hacia.
Beelzebub (bie·lssibøb) *n. pr.* Belcebú.
been (lbin) *p. p.* de TO BE.
beer (bı·ʳ) *s.* cerveza.
beerhouse (-jaus) *s.* cervecería.
beeswax (bı·ṡuæks) *s.* cera de abejas.
beet (bıt) *s.* remolacha.
beetle (bı·tøl) *s.* ENT. escarabajo. 2 ENT. cucaracha. 3 pisón, aplanadera. 4 mazo; mano, majadero. 5 TEJ. batán. 6 *adj.* saliente.
beetle (to) *tr.* apisonar; majar. 2 batanar. 3 *intr.* salir, sobresalir.
beetrave (bı·treiv), **beetrot** (-rut) *s.* BEET.
beeves (bıvṡ) *s. pl.* reses vacunas.
befall (to) (bifo·l) *intr.-tr.* ocurrir, acontecer, sobrevenir. ¶ Pret.: *befell*; p. p.: *befallen.*
befit (to) (bifi·t) *intr.* convenir, cuadrar, sentar bien; ser propio o digno de. ¶ Pret. y p. p.: *befitted*; ger.: *befitting.*
befitting (-ing) *adj.* conveniente, adecuado, digno de. 2 propio, decoroso.
befog (to) (bifo·g) *tr.* envolver en niebla. 2 *fig.* confundir, obscurecer. ¶ Pret. y p. p.: *befogged*; ger.: *befogging.*
befool (to) (bifu·l) *tr.* engañar. 2 entontecer.
before (bifo·ʳ) *adv.* antes, anteriormente, primero. 2 delante, al frente, enfrente. 3 *prep.* antes de o que. 4 delante de, enfrente de; ante, en presencia de.
beforehand (-jænd) *adv.* de antemano, con antelación: *to be* ~ *with*, anticiparse a. 2 *adj.* hecho de antemano.
befoul (to) (bifau·l) *tr.* ensuciar, emporcar.
befriend (to) (bifre·nd) *tr.* tratar como amigo; favorecer, amparar, proteger.
befuddle (to) (bifu·døl) *tr.* turbar los sentidos.
beg (to) (beg) *tr.* pedir, mendigar, solicitar; rogar.

2 Ús. por cortesía: *I ~ to inform you that*, he de comunicarle que. *3 to ~ the question*, cometer petición de principio. *4 intr.* pedir limosna. ¶ Pret. y p. p.: *begged;* ger.: *begging.*
began (bigæ·n) *pret.* de TO BEGIN.
beget (to) (bige·t) *tr.* engendrar [procrear, originar]. ¶ Pret.: *begot;* p. p.: *begotten* o -*got.*
begettal (-al) *s.* engendramiento.
beggar (be·gaʳ) *s.* mendigo, pordiosero. *2* pobre, miserable. *3* pícaro, bribón.
beggar (to) *tr.* empobrecer, arruinar. *2* agotar, apurar.
beggarly (-li) *adj.* pobre, miserable; mezquino. *2 adv.* pobremente.
begging (be·ging) *adj.* mendicante. *2 s.* acción de pedir; mendicación, pordioseo.
begin (to) (bigi·n) *tr.* e *intr.* empezar, comenzar, principiar. *2 tr.* iniciar. *3 intr.* nacer [tomar principio]. ¶ Pret.: *began;* p. p.: *begun;* ger.: *beginning.*
beginner (-øʳ) *s.* principiante, novicio, novato. *2* iniciador, originador.
beginning (-ing) *s.* principio, comienzo, iniciación; albores. *2* principio, causa, origen.
begird (to) (bigø·ʳd) *tr.* ceñir, rodear.
begone! (bigo·n) *interj.* ¡fuera!, ¡vete!
begonia (bigou·nia) *s.* begonia.
begot (biga·t) *pret.* y *p. p.* de TO BEGET.
begotten (-øn) *p. p.* de TO BEGET.
begrime (to) (bigrai·m) *tr.* tiznar, ensuciar.
begrudge (to) (bigrø·dy̆) *tr.* TO GRUDGE.
beguile (to) (bigai·l) *tr.* engañar, seducir: *to ~ of*, estafar, defraudar. *2* entretener [el ocio], pasar [el tiempo].
beguiler (-øʳ) *s.* engañador.
begun (bigø·n) *p. p.* de TO BEGIN.
behalf (bijæ·f) *s.* nombre, cuenta, interés, defensa: *in ~ of*, en interés de, en defensa de; *on ~ of*, en nombre de; por cuenta de.
behave (to) (bijei·v) *intr.-ref.* obrar, proceder, conducirse, portarse. *2* portarse bien.
behavio(u)r (-iøʳ) *s.* proceder, conducta, comportamiento. *2* BIOL., MEC. comportamiento.
behead (to) (bije·d) *tr.* decapitar, descabezar.
beheading (-ing) *s.* decapitación.
beheld (bije·ld) *pret.* y *p. p.* de TO BEHOLD.
behind (bijai·nd) *adv.* detrás. *2* a la zaga, en zaga. *3* atrás, hacia atrás. *4 prep.* detrás de; después de: *~ time*, tarde, con retraso.
behindhand (-jænd) *adv.* con retraso, con atraso. *2* en déficit. *3 adj.* atrasado, retrasado.
behold (to) (bijou·ld) *tr.* ver, mirar, contemplar, observar. ¶ Pret. y p. p.: *beheld.*
beholden (-øn) *s.* obligado [por gratitud]; deudor [de beneficios].
beholder (-øʳ) *s.* espectador, observador.
behoof (biju·f) *s.* provecho, utilidad, interés.
behoove (to) (biju·v), **behove (to)** (bijou·v) *intr.* tocar, atañer, corresponder, incumbir. *2* importar, ser necesario.
being (bı·ing) *ger.* de TO BE: siendo, estando; que es o está. *2 s.* ser, existencia. *3* estado, condición. *4* ser, ente, criatura, esencia, substancia.
bejewel (to) (biy̆u·l) *tr.* enjoyar.
belabo(u)r (to) (bilei·bøʳ) *tr.* pegar, apalear, maltratar. *2* trabajar [una materia].
belated (-tid) *adj.* retardado, tardío. *2* sorprendido por la noche.
belaying pin (bile·ing) *s.* MAR. cabilla.
belch (belch) *s.* eructo.

belch (to) *intr.* eructar. *2 tr.* vomitar [llamas, injurias, etc.].
beldam (bel·dam) *s.* vieja, bruja, arpía.
beleaguer (to) (bilı·gøʳ) *tr.* sitiar, cercar, rodear.
beleaguerer (-øʳ) *s.* sitiador.
belfry (be·lfri) *s.* campanario, torre.
Belgian (be·ldy̆ian) *adj.-s.* belga.
Belgium (be·ldy̆iøm) *n. pr.* GEOGR. Bélgica.
Belgrade (belgrei·d) *n. pr.* Belgrado.
belie (to) (bilai·) *tr.* desmentir, contradecir. *2* disfrazar, falsear. *3* calumniar. *4* defraudar [una esperanza].
belief (bilı·f) *s.* creencia. *2* credo, religión, opinión, convicción. *3* REL. fe. *4* fe, confianza.
believe (to) (bilı·v) *tr.-intr.* creer. *2* pensar, opinar [bien, mal, etc., de].
believer (-øʳ) *s.* creyente, fiel.
believing (-ing) *adj.* creyente.
belittle (to) (bili·tøl) *tr.* empequeñecer. *2* rebajar, hablar con desprecio de.
bell (bel) *s.* campana; campanilla; timbre: *~ boy*, botones; *~ glass*, *~ jar*, campana de vidrio; *~ ringer*, campanero. *2* cencerro, esquila, cascabel. *3* tañido de campanas, campanada: *passing ~*, doble [por los difuntos]. *4* BOT. carola acampanada. *5* pabellón [de trompeta, etc.]. *6* MÚS. *~ tree*, chinesco.
bell (to) *tr.* poner campanilla, etc.: *to ~ the cat*, poner el cascabel al gato. *2* acampanar. *3 intr.* crecer en forma de campana. *4* bramar [el ciervo].
belladonna (belada·na) *s.* belladona.
belle (bel) *f.* bella, beldad.
bellflower (be·lflauøʳ) *s.* BOT. campánula, farolillo.
bellicose (be·likous) *adj.* belicoso.
bellied (be·lid) *adj.* ventrudo, panzudo.
belligerence, -cy (bili·dy̆ørøns, -i) *s.* beligerancia.
belligerent (bili·dy̆ørønt) *adj.-s.* beligerante. *2 adj.* belicoso, guerrero.
bellman (be·lmæn) *s.* campanillero, pregonero.
bellow (be·lou) *s.* bramido, mugido, berrido, rugido.
bellow (to) *intr.* bramar, mugir, berrear, rugir. *2* vociferar.
bellows (be·lous) *s. sing.* y *pl.* fuelle.
belly (be·li) *s.* vientre, panza, barriga. *2* estómago.
belly (to) *tr.* hinchar, combar, abultar. *2 intr.* pandear. *3* hincharse [las velas].
bellyful (-ful) *s.* panzada, hartazgo.
belong (to) (bilo·ng) *intr.* pertenecer. *2* tocar, corresponder, incumbir; ser propio [de]. *3* ser [de un lugar].
belongings (-ings) *s. pl.* pertenencias. *2* efectos, bártulos.
beloved (bilø·v(i)d) *adj.* querido, amado, dilecto. *2 s.* persona amada.
below (bilou·) *adv.* abajo, debajo. *2* en el infierno. *3* más abajo [en un escrito]. *4 prep.* bajo, debajo de, por debajo de; *~ zero*, bajo cero. *5* indigno de.
belt (belt) *s.* cinturón, cinto, faja, ceñidor; *to hit below the ~*, dar un golpe bajo. *2* [lo que rodea], faja. *3* ARQ. cinta, faja. *4* ASTR., GEOGR. zona. *5* correa de transmisión. *6 ~ conveyor*, correa o banda transportadora.
belt (to) *tr.* ceñir, rodear, fajar. *2* poner correa [a una máquina]. *3* fam. dar correazos.
belting (-ing) *s.* cinturones, correas.
belvedere (belvidı·ʳ) *s.* belvedere. *2* cenador.

bemire (bimai·ʳ) *tr.* arrastrar por el fango, enlodar, manchar.

bemoan (to) (bimou·n) *tr.* llorar, lamentar, deplorar.

bemuse (to) (bimiu·š) *tr.* aturdir, atontar.

bench (bench) *s.* banco, escaño; banqueta [asiento]. *2* consejo, tribunal. *3* asiento de los jueces. *4* judicatura. *5* MAR., MIN. bancada. *6* banco [de artesano]. *7* ~ *show*, exposición canina.

bench (to) *tr.* proveer de bancos. *2* sentar en un banco. *3* poner en un tribunal. *4* exhibir [perros]. *5* *intr.* ocupar un banco.

bend (bend) *s.* inclinación. *2* curvatura, curva, recodo, meandro. *3* codo, ángulo. *4* MAR. nudo, gaza. *5* BLAS. barra.

bend (to) *tr.* encorvar, enarcar, combar, doblar, torcer, acodillar: *to ~ the knee,* doblar la rodilla. *2* poner en tensión; armar [el arco]. *3* inclinar. *4* dirigir, volver, encaminar: *to ~ one's efforts,* dirigir sus esfuerzos. *5* doblegar, someter. *6* MAR. atar, entalingar, envergar. *7* *intr.* encorvarse, combarse, doblegarse, torcerse. *8* desviarse, torcer. *9* inclinarse. *10* dirigirse, tender. *11* aplicarse. ¶ Pret. y p. p.: *bent.*

bending (be·nding) *s.* acción de torcer, doblar, etc.; flexión; cimbreo. *2* recodo, revuelta.

beneath (binɪ·z) *adv.* abajo, debajo. *2* *prep.* bajo, debajo de. *3* por debajo [en rango, dignidad, etc.]. *4* indigno de.

benedicte (benidi·siti) *s.* benedícite.

Benedict (be·nidikt) *n. pr.* Benito, Benedicto.

Benedictine (benidi·ktin) *adj.-s.* benedictino.

benediction (-di·kshøn) *s.* bendición.

benefaction (-æ·kshøn) *s.* beneficio, merced, gracia, donación.

benefactor (-fæ·ktøʳ) *s.* bienhechor. *2* donador, fundador.

benefactress (-fæ·ktris) *s.* bienhechora. *2* donadora, fundadora.

benefice (be·nifis) *s.* beneficio [feudal o eclesiástico].

beneficence (bine·fisøns) *s.* beneficencia, bondad, caridad.

beneficent (-ønt) *adj.* benéfico, bondadoso, caritativo.

beneficial (benifi·shal) *adj.* beneficioso, provechoso.

beneficiary (benifi·shari) *adj.* beneficial. *2 s.* ECLES. beneficiado. *3* beneficiario.

benefit (be·nifit) *s.* beneficio, favor. *2* beneficio, bien, utilidad, provecho; disfrute. *3* TEAT. beneficio.

benefit (to) *tr.* beneficiar, aprovechar [a uno]. *2* *intr.* beneficiarse.

benevolence (bine·voløns) *s.* benevolencia, caridad, humanidad. *2* gracia, merced.

benevolent (-ønt) *adj.* benévolo, bondadoso, caritativo.

Bengal (bengol) *n. pr.* GEÓGR. Bengala.

Bengalese (bengali·š), **Bengali** (bengo·li) *adj.-s.* bengalí.

benighted (binai·tid) *adj.* sorprendido por la noche. *2* rodeado de tinieblas. *3* ignorante.

benign (binai·n) *adj.* benigno, afable. *2* propicio. *3* benigno [clima, enfermedad].

benignancy (bini·gnansi) *s.* benignidad, afabilidad.

benignant (-nant) *adj.* benigno, afable, bondadoso. *2* favorable, beneficioso.

benignity (bini·gniti) *s.* benignidad. *2* favor, merced.

Benjamin (be·ndỹømin) *n. pr.* Benjamín. *2 s.* [con min.] benjuí.

bent (bent) *pret.* y *p. p.* de TO BEND. *2* *adj.* torcido, encorvado, doblado. *3* ~ *on* o *upon,* empeñado en, resuelto a. *4 s.* encorvamiento, curvatura. *5* inclinación, propensión, tendencia, afición. *6* declive. *7* capacidad de resistencia. *8* BOT. nombre de varias plantas.

benthos (be·nzøs) *s.* BIOL. bentos.

benumb (to) (binø·m) *tr.* entumecer, aterir. *2* entorpecer, embotar.

benzene (be·nšin o benši·n) *s.* benceno.

benzine (be·nšin) *s.* bencina [del petróleo].

benzoin (be·nšoin) *s.* benzoina. *2* benjuí.

bequeath (to) (bikui·ð o -kui·z) *tr.* legar, dejar.

bequether (-øʳ) *s.* testador, el que lega.

bequest (bikue·st) *s.* legado, manda.

berate (to) (birei·t) *tr.* reñir, reprender.

Berber (bø·ʳbeʳ) *adj.-s.* bereber.

bereave (to) (birɪ·v) *tr.* privar, desposeer de. *2* desolar, desconsolar; dejar [la muerte] sin un ser querido. ¶ Pret. y p. p.: *bereaved* o *bereft.*

bereavement (-mønt) *s.* privación, despojo. *2* soledad, desamparo, duelo; pérdida de un ser querido.

bereft (bire·ft) *pret.* y *p. p.* de TO BEREAVE.

beret (be·rei) *s.* boina.

berg (bø·ʳg) *s.* ICEBERG.

bergamot (bø·ʳgamat) *s.* BOT. bergamoto. *2* bergamota. *3* sándalo de jardín.

Berlin (bø·ʳli·n) *n. pr.* GEOGR. Berlín. *2 s.* [con min.] berlina [coche, auto].

Bern (bø·ʳn o be·ʳn) *n. pr.* GEOGR. Berna.

Bernard (bø·ʳna·ʳd) *n. pr.* Bernardo.

berry (be·ri) *s.* baya. *2* nombre de otros frutos como la mora, la fresa, etc.

berth (bø·ʳz) *s.* MAR. espacio para maniobrar: *to give a wide ~ to,* evitar, apartarse de. *2* anclaje, amarradero. *3* dársena. *4* camarote, litera. *5* fam. empleo, destino.

berth (to) *tr.* MAR. amarrar. *2* dar litera o empleo.

Bertha (bø·ʳza) *n. pr.* Berta.

beryl (beri·l) *s.* MINER. berilo.

beseech (to) (bisɪ·ch) *tr.* pedir, implorar; suplicar, rogar. ¶ Pret. y p. p.: *besought* o *beseeched.*

beseecher (-øʳ) *s.* rogador, suplicante.

beseem (to) (bisɪ·m) *tr.-intr.* cuadrar, estar bien. *2* ser propio o decoroso.

beset (to) (bise·t) *tr.* asediar, estrechar, acosar. *2* cercar, rodear. *3* adornar, tachonar. ¶ Pret. y p. p.: *beset;* ger.: *besetting.*

besetting (-ing) *adj.* constante, dominante: ~ *sin,* flaco, vicio dominante.

beside (bisai·d) *adv.* cerca, al lado. *2* además. *3* *prep.* al lado de, cerca de, junto a. *4* en comparación de. *5* fuera de: ~ *oneself,* fuera de sí; ~ *the point,* que no viene al caso.

besides (-š) *adv.* además, por otra parte, asimismo. *2* *prep.* además de. *3* excepto, fuera de.

besiege (to) (bisɪ·ỹ) *tr.* sitiar. *2* asediar, acosar.

besieger (-øʳ) *s.* sitiador; asediador.

besmear (to) (bismɪ·ʳ) *tr.* embadurnar, untar.

bismirch (to) (bismø·ʳch) *tr.* manchar, ensuciar. *2* mancillar.

besom (bɪ·šøm) *s.* escoba. *2* retama.

besot (to) (bisa·t) *tr.* entontecer, embrutecer. *2* enamorar tontamente. ¶ Pret. y p. p.: *besotted;* ger.: *besotting.*

besought (biso·t) *pret.* y *p. p.* de TO BESEECH.

bespangle (to) (bispæ·ngøl) *tr.* adornar con lentejuelas o cosas brillantes.

bespatter (bispæ·tø^r) *tr.* salpicar, manchar.
bespeak (to) (bispɪ·k) *tr.* apalabrar, encargar, hacer reservar. *2* indicar, denotar, pronosticar. *3* poét. hablar [a uno]. ¶ Pret.: *bespoke;* p. p.: *bespoken* o *-spoke.*
bespread (to) (bispre·d) *tr.* cubrir [esparciendo]. *2* esparcir, tender. ¶ Pret. y p. p.: *bespread.*
besprinkle (to) (bispri·ngkøl) *tr.* rociar, salpicar, espolvorear, sembrar.
best (best) *adj. superl.* de GOOD; mejor, óptimo, superior: ~ *girl,* novia, amiga preferida; ~ *man,* padrino de boda; ~ *seller,* éxito de librería, libro de mayor venta; *it is* ~, es mejor. *2* mayor [en extensión]: *the* ~ *part of,* la mayor parte de. *3 adv.* super. de WELL: mejor; mucho; más: *the* ~ *known,* el más conocido. *4 s.* lo mejor, lo más: *to do one's* ~, esmerarse; *to get the* ~ *of,* llevar la ventaja a; vencer; *to make the* ~ *of,* sacar el mejor partido de; *at* ~, *at the* ~, en el mejor de los casos; a lo más; *for the* ~, con la mejor intención; conducente al bien, a lo mejor. *5 pron. the* ~, el mejor, el que más.
bestead (biste·d) *adj.* situado. *2* rodeado de peligros, etc.
bestead (to) *tr.* servir, aprovechar, ayudar.
bestial (be·stial) *adj.* bestial, brutal, abrutado.
bestiality (bestiæ·liti) *s.* bestialidad.
bestialize (to) (be·stialaiš) *tr.* embrutecer.
bestiary (be·stieri) *s.* bestiario.
bestir (to) (bistø·^r) *tr.* mover, animar, incitar: *to* ~ *oneself,* menearse, afanarse.
bestow (to) (bistou·) *tr.* dar, conceder, otorgar, dispensar, conferir. *2* gastar, emplear.
bestowal (-al) *s.* concesión, dádiva, don. *2* empleo, dedicación [de tiempo, etc.].
bestower (-ø^r) *s.* donador, dispensador.
bestrew (to) (bistru·) *tr.* cubrir, sembrar [de]. *2* cubrir, estar esparcido sobre. ¶ Pret.: *bestrewed;* p. p.: *bestrewn* o *-trewed.*
bestride (to) (bistrai·d) *tr.* montar [a horcajadas]. *2* estar [sobre algo] a horcajadas. *3* cruzar [de un tranco]. ¶ Pret.: *bestrode;* p. p.: *bestridden* o *bestrid.*
bet (bet) *s.* apuesta.
bet (to) *tr.-intr.* apostar [dinero, etc.]; *to* ~ *on,* apostar a o por. ¶ Pret. y p. p.: *bet* o *betted;* ger.: *betting.*
beta (bei·ta) *s.* beta [letra griega].
betake (to) (bitei·k) *ref.* recurrir, acudir. *2* ir, trasladarse. *3* aplicarse, darse. ¶ Pret.: *betook;* p. p.: *betaken.*
betel (bɪtel) *s.* BOT. betel.
bethink (to) (bizi·nk) *tr.-ref.* hacer memoria de, acordarse de, caer en la cuenta de, pensar, considerar. ¶ Pret. y p. p.: *bethought.*
Bethlehem (be·zlijem) *n. pr.* GEOGR. Belén.
bethought (bizo·t) *pret.* y *p. p.* de TO BETHINK.
betide (to) (bitai·d) *tr.-intr.* ocurrir, acaecer, suceder. *2 tr.* presagiar, indicar.
betime(s (bitai·m(s) *adv.* con tiempo, a tiempo. *2* pronto, temprano.
betoken (to) (bitou·køn) *tr.* presagiar, anunciar. *2* indicar, denotar, dar muestras de.
betony (be·tøni) *s.* BOT. betónica.
betook (bitu·k) *pret.* de TO BETAKE.
betray (to) (bitrei·) *tr.* traicionar, vender, entregar, hacer traición. *2* inducir, llevar [a error, a un peligro, etc.]. *3* revelar, descubrir; mostrar, dejar ver.

betrayal (-al) *s.* traición. *2* revelación [de un secreto, un sentimiento, etc.].
betroth (to) (bitro·z) *tr.-intr.* desposar, prometer: *to be* o *become betrothed,* desposarse, prometerse.
betrothal (-al) *s.* desposorio; noviazgo.
betrothed (-t) *adj.-s.* prometido, novio, futuro.
better (be·tø^r) *adj.* compar. de GOOD: mejor: ~ *half,* fig. costilla, cara, mitad; *to get* ~, mejorarse. *2* mayor, más: *the* ~ *part,* la mayor parte.
3 adv. comp. de WELL; mejor: ~ *off,* en mejor posición; mejor librado.
4 s. lo mejor; ventaja, superioridad: *to change for the* ~, mejorar, mejorarse; *to get the* ~ *of,* aventajar, llevar ventaja, vencer; *all the* ~, so *much the* ~, mejor, tanto mejor. *5* apostante. *6 pl.* superiores, mayores, los que son más [que uno].
better (to) *tr.* mejorar, adelantar, favorecer. *2* aventajar, sobrepujar. *3 intr.* mejorar, mejorarse.
betterment (-mønt) *s.* mejora, mejoramiento, adelanto.
bettor (-ø^r) *s.* apostante.
Betty (-i) *n. pr. dim.* de ELIZABETH.
between (bitʊ·n) *adv.* entremedias, en medio. *2 prep.* entre [una pers. o cosa y otra u otras]: ~ *whiles,* a intervalos.
betwixt (bitʊi·kst) *adv.-prep.* BETWEEN.
bevel (be·vøl) *s.* ángulo oblicuo, bisel, chaflán. *2* baivel, falsa regla. *3 adj.* oblicuo, biselado, achaflanado. *4* MEC. cónico.
bevel (to) *tr.* biselar, chaflanar. *2* ARQ. falsear. ¶ Pret. y p. p.: *beveled* o *-lled;* ger.: *beveling* o *-lling.*
beverage (be·vøridỳ) *s.* bebida, brebaje.
bevy (be·vi) *s.* bandada. *2* grupo [de mujeres].
bewail (to) (biuei·l) *tr.* llorar, lamentar, deplorar. *2 intr.* lamentarse, plañir.
beware (to) (biue·^r) *tr.* guardarse, recelarse de, tener cuidado con: *beware!,* ¡cuidado [con]!. ¶ Sólo se usa en INFIN. e IMPER.
bewilder (to) (biui·ldø^r) *tr.* desconcertar, desorientar, aturdir, confundir, turbar.
bewilderment (-mønt) *s.* desconcierto, desorientación, aturdimiento, confusión, perplejidad.
bewitch (to) (biui·ch) *tr.* embrujar, hechizar, encantar, fascinar.
bewitcher (-ø^r) *s.* hechicero, encantador.
bewitchment (-mønt) *s.* hechizo, embrujamiento. *2* encanto, fascinación.
bey (bei) *s.* bey.
beyond (biya·nd) *adv.* más allá, al otro lado, allende, a lo lejos. *2 prep.* detrás de, al lado de, más allá de, allende. *3* fuera de, excepto, salvo. *4* fuera de o excediendo los límites o posibilidades de: ~ *doubt,* fuera de duda; ~ *measure,* sobremanera; ~ *oneself,* fuera de sí. *5 s.* el otro mundo, el más allá.
bezant (be·šant) *s.* besante.
bezel (be·šøl) *s.* bisel. *2* JOY. faceta. *3* JOY. engaste. *4* sello [de una sortija].
bezel (to) *tr.* biselar, achaflanar.
bezique (beši·k) *s.* juego de naipes.
bias (bai·as) *s.* sesgo, oblicuidad. *2* tendencia, predisposición; parcialidad, prejuicio. *3* RADIO. tensión de rejilla. *4 adj.* sesgado.
bias (to) *tr.* torcer, inclinar, influir, predisponer. ¶ Pret. y p. p.: *biased* o *-ssed;* ger.: *biasing* o *-ssing.*
bib (bib) *s.* barbero, pechero. *2* pechera [de delantal].

bib (to) *tr.-intr.* beber, empinar el codo. ¶ Pret. y p. p.: *bibbed;* ger.: *-bbing.*
bibasic (baibei·sik) *adj.* bibásico.
bibber (bi·bø^r) *s.* bebedor.
Bible (bai·bøl) *s.* Biblia.
biblical (bi·blikøl) *adj.* bíblico.
bibliography (biblia·grafi) *s.* bibliografía.
bibliophile (bi·bliofail o -fil) *s.* bibliófilo.
bibulous (bi·biuløs) *adj.* esponjoso, absorbente. 2 bebedor, borrachín.
bicameral (baikæ·møral) *adj.* bicameral.
bicarbonate (baika·^rbønit) *s.* bicarbonato.
bice (bais) *s.* azul o verde pálidos.
bicephalous (baisep·faløs) *adj.* bicéfalo.
biceps (bai·seps) *adj.-s.* ANAT. bíceps.
bicker (bi·kø^r) *s.* disputa, quisquilla.
bicker (to) *intr.* disputar, altercar. 2 murmurar [un arroyo, etc.]. 3 temblar, destellar, chisporrotear [una luz, etc.].
bickering (-ing) *s.* disputa, altercado.
biconcave (baika·nkeiv) *adj.* bicóncavo.
biconvex (baika·nveks) *adj.* biconvexo.
bicuspid (baikø·spid) *adj.* bicúspide.
bicycle (bai·sikøl) *s.* bicicleta.
bicycle (to) *intr.* ir en bicicleta.
bicyclist (-siklist) *s.* biciclista.
bid (bid) *s.* licitación, oferta, puja. 2 declaración [en el bridge].
bid (to) *tr.* anunciar, expresar, ofrecer: *to ~ good bye,* decir adiós; *to defiance,* desafiar, retar. 2 ofrecer [un precio], pujar, licitar. 3 ordenar, mandar, pedir. 4 invitar. 5 declarar [en el bridge]. 6 *intr.* hacer una oferta, licitar. 7 *to ~ fair to,* prometer, dar indicios de. ¶ Pret.: *bade;* p. p.: *bidden;* ger.: *bidding.* | En las acepciones 2 y 5, pret. y p. p.: *bid.*
bidder (-ø^r) *s.* licitador, postor. 2 declarante [en el bridge].
bidding (-ing) *s.* licitación, postura. 2 mandato, ruego; invitación.
bide (to) (baid) *tr.-intr.* ABIDE: *to ~ one's time,* esperar la ocasión, la oportunidad. ¶ Pret.: *bode, bade* o *bided;* p. p.: *bided.*
bident (bai·dent) *s.* bidente.
bidet (bide·t) *s.* bidé. 2 caballito, jaca.
biding (bai·ding) *s.* espera. 2 residencia, permanencia.
biennial (baie·nial) *adj.* bienal.
biennium (-niøm) *s.* bienio.
bier (bı·^r) *s.* andas, féretro.
biffid (bai·fid) *adj.* bífido.
bifocal (baifou·kal) *adj.* bifocal.
bifurcate (bai·fø^rkeit) *adj.* bifurcado.
bifurcate (to) *tr.* dividir en dos puntas o ramales. 2 *intr.* bifurcarse.
bifurcation (-kei·shøn) *s.* bifurcación.
big (big) *adj.* grande, importante: *~ game,* caza mayor; *~ bug,* fig. fam. personaje. 2 corpulento, voluminoso, hinchado. 3 imponente. 4 fuerte [voz]. 5 jactancioso, pomposo, amenazador. 6 preñado, lleno. 7 *adv.* mucho. 8 pomposamente, jactanciosamente: *to talk ~,* echar bravatas.
bigamist (bi·gamist) *s.* bígamo.
bigamous (-møs) *adj.* bígamo.
bigamy (-mi) *s.* bigamia.
bigger (bi·gø^r) *adj. compar.* de BIG.
biggest (bi·gist) *adj. superl. de* BIG.
biggish (bi·gish) *adj.* grandote.
big-headed *adj.* cabezón. 2 engreído.
big-hearted *adj.* magnánimo, valeroso.

bight (bait) *s.* MAR. seno de un cabo, gaza. 2 meandro, recodo. 3 ensenada, cala.
bigmouthed (bi·gmauzt) *adj.* bocudo. 2 hablador. 3 gritón.
bigot (bi·gøt) *s.* fanático, intolerante.
bigoted (-id) *adj.* fanático, intolerante.
bigotry (-ri) *s.* fanatismo, intolerancia.
bigwig (bi·gwig) *s.* fam. personaje.
bilabial (bailæbial) *adj.* FONÉT. bilabial.
bilander (bi·landø^r) *s.* balandra.
bilateral (bailæ·tøral) *adj.* bilateral.
bilberry (bi·lberi) *s.* BOT. arándano.
bile (bail) *s.* bilis, hiel. 2 fig. cólera, mal humor.
bilge (bildÿ) *s.* barriga [de tonel]. 2 MAR. pantoque, sentina.
bilge (to) *intr.* MAR. sufrir una vía de agua, hacer agua. 2 hacer barriga, abultar.
biliary (bi·liari) *adj.* biliar.
bilingual (baili·ngual) *adj.* bilingüe.
bilious (bi·liøs) *adj.* bilioso.
bilk (bilk) *s.* estafa, trampa. 2 estafador, tramposo.
bilk (to) *s.* estafar, defraudar.
Bill (bil) *n. pr.* dim. de WILLIAM.
bill *s.* pico [de ave]. 2 mandíbulas [de tortuga]. 3 MAR. punta de la uña [del ancla]; extremo [de verga]. 4 pica, alabarda. 5 hocino, podón. 6 cuenta, nota, factura, relación, estado, lista: *~ of fare,* minuta, lista de platos; *~ of lading,* conocimiento de embarque. 7 billete, cédula, documento, letra, pagaré: *~ of exchange,* letra de cambio. 8 patente, certificado. 9 cartel, programa [de teatro], prospecto, hoja. 10 DER. escrito. 11 proyecto de ley; ley.
bill (to) *tr.* cargar en cuenta. 2 facturar. 3 anunciar por carteles; poner carteles en. 4 *intr.* juntar los picos [las palomas]: *to ~ and coo,* fig. besarse, arrullarse.
billboard (bi·lbo^rd) *s.* cartelera.
billet (bi·lit) *s.* billete, esquela. 2 MIL. boleta. 3 MIL. alojamiento. 4 puesto, colocación, destino. 5 trozo de leña. 6 barra [de oro o hierro].
billet (to) *tr.* MIL. alojar. 2 aposentar, colocar.
billhead (bi·ljed) *s.* impreso para facturas. 2 encabezamiento de factura.
billhook (-juk) *s.* podón.
billiard (bi·lia^rd) *adj.* de billar. 2 *s.* (E.U.) carambola.
billiards (-s) *s.* billar.
billingsgate (bi·lingsgeit) *s.* lenguaje soez.
billion (bi·liøn) *s.* (Ingl.) billón. 2 (E.U.) mil millones.
billow (bi·lou) *s.* oleada, golpe de mar. 2 ola, ondulación.
billow (to) *intr.* undular. 2 levantarse como una ola.
billowy (-i) *adj.* ondeante, agitado. 2 ondulado. 3 hinchado como una ola.
Billy (bi·li) *n. pr.* dim. de WILLIAM. 2 *s.* [con min.] cachiporra. 3 *~ goat,* macho cabrío.
bimane (bai·mein) *s.* bímano.
bimanous (bi·manøs) *adj.* bímano.
bimetallism (baime·tališm) *s.* bimetalismo.
bimonthly (baimø·nzli) *adj.* bimestral. 2 quincenal. 3 *s.* publicación bimestral o quincenal. 4 *adv.* bimestralmente. 5 quincenalmente.
bin (bin) *s.* caja, arca, arcón, depósito, recipiente.
binary (bai·neri) *adj.* binario.
bind (baind) *s.* lazo, ligadura. 2 MÚS. ligado.
bind (to) *tr.* ligar, liar, envolver, ceñir, atar, amarrar, sujetar, unir. 2 vendar. 3 ribetear, guar-

necer. *4* trabar, dar consistencia. *5* encuadernar. *6* FISIOL. estreñir, restriñir. *7* obligar, compeler, comprometer. *8* escriturar, contratar [a uno]. *9* *intr.* trabarse, endurecerse, pegarse. *10* obligar. ¶ *Pret.* y p. p.: *bound.*

binder (-ø^r) *s.* atador. agavilladora [máquina]. *3* ribeteador. *4* encuadernador. *5* carpeta, cubierta [para papeles]. *6* aglutinante, cemento. *7* riostra.

bindery (-øri) *s.* encuadernación [taller].

binding (-ing) *s.* atadura, ligamiento. *2* venda, tira, faja, ligadura. *3* COST. ribeteado; ribete, guarnición. *4* encuadernación: *full ~*, pasta entera; *half ~*, media pasta. *5* trabadura; lo que traba o espesa. *6* *adj.* que ata, une, traba, etc. *7* obligatorio, valedero. *8* MED. estíptico.

bindweed (-uid) *s.* BOT. enredadera; correhuela.

binnacle (bi·nakøl) *s.* bitácora.

binocle (bi·nøkøl) *s.* binóculo, gemelos.

binocular (baina·kiula^r) *adj.* binocular. *2 s. pl.* ÓPT. gemelos.

binomial (bainou·mial) *s.* binomio.

biochemistry (baioke·mistri) *s.* bioquímica.

biogeny (-ȳ·ni) *s.* biogenia.

biographer (baia·grafø^r) *s.* biógrafo.

biography (-grɑfi) *s.* biografía.

biologic(al (baiola·dȳk(al) *adj.* biológico.

biologist (baia·lodȳist) *s.* biólogo.

biology (-lodȳi) *s.* biología.

biophysics (baiofi·siks) *s.* biofísica.

bipartite (baipa·^rtait) *adj.* bipartido.

biped (bai·ped) *adj.-s.* bípedo.

bipedal (-al) *adj.* bipede; bípedo.

biplane (bai·plein) *adj.-s.* biplano.

bipolar (baipou·la^r) *adj.* bipolar.

birch (bø^rc) *s.* BOT. abedul. *2* vara de abedul.

birch (to) *tr.* azotar, castigar.

birchen (-øn) *adj.* de abedul.

bird (bø^rd) *s.* ave, pájaro: *~ of paradise*, ave del Paraíso; *~ of passage*, ave de paso; *~ of prey*, ave de rapiña; *birds of a feather*, gente de una misma calaña.

bird (to) *intr.* pajarear, cazar pájaros.

birdcall (-kol) *s.* reclamo; añagaza.

birdcatcher (-kæchø^r) *m.* pajarero, parancero.

birding (-ing) *s.* caza de pájaros.

birdlime (-laim) *s.* liga, ajonje.

bird's-eye view *s.* lo que se ve a vista de pájaro; ojeada general.

bird's-nest (to) *intr.* coger nidos.

birefringent (bairifri·nȳønt) *adj.* birrefringente.

bireme (bai·rim) *s.* birreme.

biretta (bire·ta) *s.* bonete [de eclesiástico].

birth (bø^rz) *s.* nacimiento: *~ rate*, natalidad; *by ~*, de nacimiento. *2* cuna, origen. *3* linaje, alcurnia. *4* parto.

birthday (-dei) *s.* natalicio, cumpleaños.

birthmark (-ma^rk) *s.* antojo, lunar.

birthplace (-pleis) *s.* lugar de nacimiento; pueblo natal.

birthright (-rait) *s.* derecho de nacimiento. *2* primogenitura.

bis (bis) *adv.* MÚS. bis.

Biscay (bi·skei) *n. pr.* Vizcaya.

biscuit (bi·skit) *s.* galleta, bizcocho. *2* CERÁM. bizcocho.

bisect (to) (baise·kt) *tr.* bisecar.

bisector (-ø^r) *s.* bisectriz.

bishop (bi·shøp) *s.* ECLES. obispo. *2* AJED. alfil.

bishopric (-rik) *s.* obispado. *2* diócesis. *3* episcopado [dignidad].

bisk (bisk) *s.* sopa sustanciosa.

bismuth (bi·šmøz) *s.* QUÍM. bismuto.

bison (bai·søn) *s.* ZOOL. bisonte.

bissextile (bise·kstil) *adj.* bisiesto.

bister, bistre (bi·stø^r) *s.* bistre.

bistort (bi·sto^rt) *s.* BOT. bistorta.

bistoury (bi·sturi) *s.* bisturí.

bisulcate (baisø·lkeit) *adj.* bisulco.

bit (bit) *s.* pedazo, trozo, pedacito; migaja, pizca, un poco, un momento: *not a ~*, ni pizca. *2* bocado [de comida]. *3* bocado [del freno]. *4* paletón [de llave]. *5* broca, taladro. *6* boca, corte [de herramienta].

bit (to) *tr.* enfrenar [el caballo]. *2* refrenar. ¶ *Pret.* y p. p.: *bitted;* ger.: *bitting.*

bitch (bich) *s.* ZOOL. perra; loba; zorra. *2* fam. ramera.

bite (bait) *s.* mordedura. *2* mordisco. *3* bocado, tentempié. *4* picadura [de insecto, etc.]. *5* resquemo [en el paladar]. *6* sensación cortante [del aire, del frío].

bite (to) *tr.-intr.* morder, mordiscar, dentellar. *2* picar [un insecto, etc.]. *3* resquemar, escocer [la pimienta, etc.]. *4* cortar [el frío, el aire]. *5* morder, atacar [un ácido, etc.]. *6* MEC. morder, agarrar. *7* *tr.* tascar [el freno]. *8* engañar, pegarla. *9* *intr.* picar, morder el anzuelo. ¶ *Pret.: bit;* p. p.: *bit* o *bitten.*

biter (-ø^r) *s.* mordedor. *2* engañador.

biting (-ing) *adj.* punzante, penetrante. *2* mordaz, sarcástico. *3* picante [al gusto]. *4* mordedor.

bitt (bit) *s.* bita.

bitten (-øn) *p. p.* de TO BITE.

bitter (bi·tø^r) *adj.* amargo. *2* áspero, agrio, duro, cruel, agudo, intenso. *3* mordaz, sarcástico. *4* enconado, encarnizado. *5 s.* amargor, amargura. *6 pl.* amargo [licor].

bittern (-n) *s.* ORN. avetoro.

bitterness (-nis) *s.* amargor, amargura. *2* acritud. *3* dureza, crueldad. *4* rencor. *5 s.* encono.

bittersweet (-suit) *adj.* agridulce. *2 s.* lo agridulce. *3* BOT. dulcamara.

bitterwort (-wo^rt) *s.* BOT. genciana.

bitumen (bitiu·møn) *s.* MINER. betún.

bituminous (-minøs) *adj.* bituminoso.

bivalent (baivei·lønt) *adj.* bivalente.

bivalve (bai·vælv) *adj.* bivalvo.

bivouac (bi·vuæk) *s.* vivac, vivaque.

bivouac (to) *intr.* vivaquear.

biweekly (baiur·kli) *adj.* bisemanal.

bizarre (biša·^r) *adj.* raro, original, extravagante.

blab (blæb) *s.* hablador. *2* chismoso. *3* charla, habladuría, chisme.

blab (to) *tr.* revelar, divulgar. *2* *intr.* chismear. ¶ *Pret.* y p. p.: *blabbed;* ger.: *blagging.*

blabber (-ø^r) *s.* hablador, chismoso; soplón.

black (blæk) *adj.* negro: *~ art*, nigromancia; *~ beetle*, cucaracha; *~ currant* BOT. casis, grosella negra; *~ friar*, dominico; *~ lead*, grafito, lápiz plomo; *~ monk*, benedictino; *Black Sea*, Mar Negro; *~ sheep*, fig. garbanzo negro; *in ~ and white*, por escrito. *2* moreno, atezado. *3* puro [café]. *4* hosco, ceñudo, terrible, amenazador. *5* *~ and blue*, lívido, amoratado. *6 adv.* amenazadoramente. *7 s.* negro. *8* luto. *9* moreno, mulato. *10 pl.* traje negro. *11* colgaduras de luto.

black (to) *tr.* ennegrecer. *2* embetunar, lustrar, dar bola. *3* *intr.* ennegrecerse, negrear. *4 to ~ out*, apagar las luces [como precaución]; desmayarse, perder el sentido.

blackamoor (-amu^r) *s.* negro [esp. africano].

black-and-blue *adj.* acardenalado.
blackball (-bol) *s.* bola negra. *2* betún, bola.
blackball (to) *tr.* dar bola negra. *2* embetunar.
blackberry (-beri) *s.* BOT. zarza. *2* zarzamora.
blackbird (-bøᵣd) *s.* ORN. mirlo.
blackboard (-boᵣd) *s.* pizarra, encerado.
blackdam (-dæmp) *s.* MIN. mofeta.
blacken (-øn) *tr.* dar o teñir de negro; embetunar. *2* ennegrecer, oscurecer. *3* denigrar, infamar. *4 intr.* ennegrecerse, oscurecerse.
blackface (-feis) *s.* IMPR. letra negrilla.
blackguard (blæ·gaᵣd) *s.* pillo, bribón, sinvergüenza.
blackhead (blæ·kjed) *s.* espinilla, comedón. *2* ORN. pato marino.
blacking (-ing) *s.* ennegrecimiento. *2* betún, bola, lustre.
blackish (-ish) *adj.* negruzco, oscuro.
black jack *s.* bandera negra [de pirata]. *2* rompecabezas, porra.
blackleg (-leg) *s.* estafador, tramposo. *2* obrero no sindicado; esquirol.
blackmail (-meil) *s.* chantaje.
blackmail (to) *tr.* hacer un chantaje a.
blackmailer (-øᵣ) *s.* chantajista.
blackness (-nis) *s.* negrura, oscuridad.
black-out *s.* apagón. *2* desmayo; vértigo de los aviadores.
blacksmith (-miz) *s.* herrero, forjador.
blackthorn (-zoᵣn) *s.* BOT. endrino.
bladder (blæ·døᵣ) *s.* ANAT., ZOOL. vejiga. *2* vejiga, ampolla. *3* BOT. ~ *senna*, espantalobos.
blade (bleid) *s.* hoja [de arma, de herramienta]. *2* fig. espada [arma; esgrimidor]. *3* persona lista, decidida, calavera; valentón. *4* pala [de remo]; paleta [de hélice, etc.]. *5* ANAT. parte ancha y plana de un órgano. *6* lámina [de ballena]. *7* limbo [de hoja]. *8* hoja, brizna [de hierba o cereal]. *9* ELECT. cuchilla [de interruptor].
bladebone (-boun) *s.* omóplato, paletilla.
bladesmith (-miz) *s.* espadero, cuchillero.
blain (blein) *s.* ampolla, pústula.
blamable (blei·mabøl) *adj.* reprensible, censurable, culpable.
blame (bleim) *s.* reprobación, censura, reproche, tacha. *2* culpa, responsabilidad.
blame (to) *tr.* reprobar, censurar, reprochar, culpar: *to be to ~*, tener la culpa, merecer reproche.
blameful (-ful) *adj.* de reproche, de censura. *2* culpable, reprochable.
blameless (-lis) *adj.* irreprochable, intachable, sin culpa.
blamer (-øᵣ) *s.* censurador, reprochador.
blameworthy (-uøᵣdi) *adj.* reprensible, censurable, culpable.
blanch (to) (blænch o blanch) *tr.* blanquear, blanquecer. *2* hacer palidecer. *3* COC. escaldar; pelar. *4 intr.* palidecer; ponerse blanco.
Blanche (blænch) *n. pr.* Blanca.
blancher (-øᵣ) *s.* blanqueador. *2* blanquecedor.
blanc-mange (blama·nÿ) *s.* manjar blanco.
bland (blænd) *adj.* blando, suave, dulce, melifluo.
blandish (to) (blæ·ndish) *tr.* halagar, lisonjear, acariciar, engatusar.
blandishment (-mønt) *s.* halago, lisonja, caricia, zalamería.
blank (blænk) *adj.* pálido, descolorido. *2* en blanco: ~ *check*, cheque en blanco; fig. carta blanca. *3* vacío, desierto; desnudo; sin interés; sin afectos, sin esperanzas, infructuoso. *4* sin bala [cartucho]. *5* desconcertado, confuso. *6* vago, inexpresivo [mirada, etc.]. *7* blanco, suelto [verso]. *8 s.* blanco, espacio, hueco. *9* ARQ. vano. *10* hoja, formulario. *11* diana [de un blanco]. *12* cospel.

blanket (blæ·nkit) *s.* manta [de cama o de abrigo], frazada. *2* capa, manto [de nieve, etc.]. *3 adj.* general, comprensivo.
blanket (to) *tr.* cubrir, tapar. *2* mantear.
blankly (blæ·nkli) *adv.* inexpresivamente, desconcertadamente. *2* directamente, a quema ropa. *3* completamente.
blare (bleᵣ) *s.* sonido [de la trompeta]; rugido, fragor.
blare (to) *intr.* sonar [la trompeta o como la trompeta]. *2 tr.* gritar.
blarney (bla·ᵣni) *s.* lisonja, zalamería.
blaspheme (to) (blæsfi·m) *intr.* blasfemar. *2 tr.* blasfemar contra.
blasphemer (-øᵣ) *s.* blasfemo.
blasphemous (-møs) *adj.* blasfemo.
blasphemy (blæ·sfimi) *s.* blasfemia.
blast (blæst) *s.* ráfaga, bocanada, golpe [de viento]. *2* soplo [de un fuelle]; corriente, chorro [de aire, vapor, etc.]. *3* añublo, agostamiento. *4* hálito pernicioso. *5* sonido fuerte [de trompeta, bocina, silbato, etc.]. *6* explosión, voladura. *7* carga [de un barreno].
blast (to) *tr.* añublar, agostar, marchitar, destruir, arruinar. *2* maldecir, infamar. *4* volar [con explosivos].
blasting (blæ·esting) *s.* marchitamiento, agostamiento, añublo. *2* destrucción. *3* voladura.
blastuta (blæ·schula) *s.* BIOL. blástula.
blatant (blei·tant) *adj.* vocinglero, ruidoso. *2* vulgar, llamativo.
blather (blæ·døᵣ) *s.* charlatán. *2* charla.
blather (to) *intr.-tr.* charlar, decir tonterías.
blatherer (-øᵣ) *s.* charlatán, hablador.
blaze (bleiš) *s.* llama, llamarada. *2* hoguera, incendio. *3* luz brillante, ardor [del sol, etc.]. *4* brillo, resplandor, esplendor. *5* explosión, arrebato, estallido. *6* mancha blanca [en la cara de un animal].
blaze (to) *intr.* arder, llamear. *2* brillar, resplandecer. *3 to ~ away*, disparar o ir disparando [con un arma de fuego]. *4 tr.* encender, inflamar. *5* publicar, proclamar.
blazer (-øᵣ) *s.* chaqueta de deporte de colores vivos.
blazing (-ing) *adj.* llameante, resplandeciente. *2* patente, evidente.
blazon (blei·šøn) *s.* blasón. *2* ostentación, divulgación, publicación.
blazon (to) *tr.* BLAS. blasonar. *2* mostrar, publicar, proclamar. *3* adornar.
blazoner (blei·šnøᵣ) *s.* blasonista.
blazonry (blei·šønri) *s.* blasón. *2* esplendor, decoración brillante.
bleach (to) (blɪch) *tr.* blanquear [tejidos]; emblanquecer, descolorar. *2* poner pálido. *3 intr.* ponerse blanco, descolorirse. *4* palidecer.
bleacher (-øᵣ) *s.* blanqueador.
bleachery (-i) *s.* taller de blanqueo.
bleaching (-ing) *s.* blanqueo.
bleak (blɪk) *adj.* desierto, yermo, desolado, frío, helado, triste.
blear (blɪᵣ) *adj.* empañado, legañoso [ojo]. *2* confuso, borroso.
blear (to) *tr.* empañar, hacer legañoso. *2* nublar [la vista]. *3* ofuscar.
bleared (-d) *adj.* BLEAR.

blear-eyed *adj.* legañoso.

bleat (blit) *s.* balido.

bleat (to) *intr.* balar.

bleating (-ing) *s.* balido. 2 *adj.* balador.

bleb (bleb) *s.* ampolla, vejiga. 2 burbuja.

bled (bled) *pret. y p. p.* de TO BLEED.

bleed (to) (blid) *intr.* sangrar; verter su sangre. 2 exudar savia. 3 manar [como de una herida]. 4 *tr.* sangrar [a un enfermo, un árbol, etc.]. 5 sacar dinero [a uno]. ¶ Pret. y p. p.: *bled*.

bleeder (bli·dø^r) *s.* sangrador.

bleeding (-ing) *adj.* sangrante.

blemish (ble·mish) *s.* tacha, defecto, imperfección. 2 mancha, desdoro, borrón.

blemish (to) *tr.* manchar, afear, empañar.

blemishless (-lis) *adj.* inmaculado, intachable.

blench (to) (blench) *intr.* cejar, retroceder, acobardarse. 2 *tr.-intr.* TO BLANCH.

blend (blend) *s.* mezcla, combinación. 2 PINT. gradación.

blend (to) *tr.* mezclar, combinar, fundir. 2 PINT. matizar, armonizar. 3 *intr.* mezclarse, combinarse. 4 pasar insensiblemente de un matiz, etc., a otro. ¶ Pret. y p. p.: *blended* o *blent*.

blende (blend) *s.* blenda.

blent (blent) *pret. y p. p.* de TO BLEND.

bless (to) (bles) *tr.* bendecir. 2 agraciar, favorecer, dotar. 3 guardar, proteger; ~ *me!*, ¡válgame Dios! 4 santiguar, persignar. ¶ Pret. y p. p.: *blessed* o *blest*.

blessed (ble·sid) *adj.* bendito; santo, bienaventurado, feliz, dichoso. 2 Santísimo. 3 beato, beatificado.

blessedness (-nis) *s.* santidad, beatitud, bienaventuranza, felicidad.

blessing (ble·sing) *s.* bendición. 2 don, beneficio, gracia. 3 culto, adoración.

blest (blest) *p. p.* de TO BLESS.

blet (blet) *s.* podredumbre incipiente de la fruta.

blet (to) *intr.* pasarse [la fruta].

blew (blu) *pret.* de TO BLOW.

blight (blait) *s.* lo que daña las plantas; añublo, tizón, roya, pulgón, etc.

blight (to) *tr.* añublar, secar, agostar, marchitar. 2 frustrar, malograr.

blind (blaind) *adj.* ciego. 2 de ciego, para ciegos, hecho a ciegas. 3 oculto, secreto. 4 oscuro, tenebroso. 5 ~ *alley*, callejón sin salida. 6 *s.* pantalla, mampara, persiana, transparente, cortinilla. 7 pantalla [pers.]; engaño, disfraz, fachada, pretexto, subterfugio. 8 anteojera [del caballo]. 9 CAZA. tollo. 10 FORT. blinda.

blind (to) *tr.* cegar [quitar la vista]. 2 deslumbrar, ofuscar, obcecar. 3 vendar [los ojos].

blindage (-idӯ) *s.* MIL. blindaje, blinda.

blinders (-ø^{r}s) *s. pl.* anteojeras [de caballo].

blindfold (-fould) *adj.* vendado [de ojos]. 2 ciego, ofuscado. 3 hecho a ciegas. 4 *s.* ardid, engaño.

blindfold (to) *tr.* vendar los ojos. 2 poner una venda en los ojos, ofuscar; despistar.

blindman's-buff (-mans bøf) *s.* gallina ciega [juego].

blindness (-nis) *s.* ceguedad, ceguera. 2 ofuscación, obcecación.

blink (blindk) *s.* pestañeo, guiño, guiñada. 2 destello, reflejo, ardentía.

blink (to) *intr.* parpadear, pestañear. 2 oscilar [una luz]. 3 *intr.-tr.* mirar con los ojos entornados; fig. hacer la vista gorda.

blinkard (bli·nka^{r}d) *s.* cegarrita.

blinker (-ø^r) *s.* pop. ojo. 2 luz intermitente. 3 *pl.* BLINDERS.

bliss (blis) *s.* bienaventuranza, gloria, felicidad. 2 arrobamiento, embeleso.

blissful (bli·sful) *adj.* bienaventurado, dichoso.

blissfulness (-nis) *s.* suprema felicidad.

blister (bli·stø^r) *s.* vejiga, ampolla. 2 vejigatorio. 3 burbuja [en el vidrio].

blister (to) *intr.* ampollarse. 2 *tr.* ampollar, levantar ampollas en.

blite (blait) *s.* BOT. bledo.

blithe (blaiz), **blitheful** (-ful), **blithesome** (-søm) *adj.* alegre, gozoso, jocundo, jovial.

blizzard (bli·ša^{r}d) *s.* ventisca, tempestad. 2 descarga [de tiros].

bloat (to) (blout) *tr.* hinchar. 2 curar arenques. 3 *intr.* hincharse; abotagarse; engreírse.

bloated (blou·tid) *adj.* hinchado, abotagado. 2 engreído.

bloater (-ø^r) *s.* arenque ahumado.

blobber (bla·bø^r) *adj.* blubber.

block (blak) *s.* bloque. 2 trozo grande, toza, tarugo, adoquín. 3 tajo [de madera]. 4 fam. cabeza, chola. 5 fig. zoquete [pers.]. 6 motón, polea de aparejo. 7 MEC. dado, cubo. 8 zapata [de freno]. 9 cepo [de yunque]. 10 horma [de sombrero]. 11 CARP. calzo, alza, coda. 12 manzana, *cuadra [de casas]. 13 paquete [de acciones]; lote, partida. 14 bloc [de papel]. 15 obstáculo. 16 MEC. tope. 17 DEP. parada. 18 FERROC. tramo. 19 cuadrito [de sellos de correo]. 20 MED. bloqueo.

block (to) *tr.* obstruir, cerrar, bloquear, atascar. 2 ALBAÑ. tapiar, condenar. 3 parar [la pelota]. 4 encerrar [un peón]. 5 calzar [una rueda].

blockade (blakei·d) *s.* MIL. bloqueo, asedio. 2 obstrucción.

blockade (to) *tr.* MIL. bloquear. 2 obstruir.

blockhead (bla·kjed) *s.* tonto, bolonio, zopenco.

block-house *s.* MIL. blocao.

blockish (bla·kish) *adj.* tonto, estúpido.

blond, blonde (bland) *adj. y s.* rubio, blondo.

blood (blød) *s.* sangre: ~ *pressure*, presión arterial; *to make one's ~ run cold*, helar la sangre; *in cold ~*, a sangre fría. 2 asesinato, efusión de sangre. 3 ira, cólera. 4 temperamento, vida. 5 alcurnia, prosapia. 6 hombre animoso. 7 petimetre, calavera. 8 raza, animal de pura raza.

blood-curdling *adj.* horripilante, que hiela la sangre.

bloodguilty (-gilti) *adj.* culpable de homicidio o asesinato.

bloodhound (-jaund) *s.* sabueso.

bloodless (-lis) *adj.* pálido, exangüe. 2 incruento. 3 flojo, sin espíritu. 4 frío, insensible.

bloodletter (-letø^r) *s.* sangrador.

bloodletting (-leting) *s.* sangría, flebotomía.

bloodshed (-shed) *s.* derramamiento o efusión de sangre; matanza.

bloodshot (-shat) *adj.* inyectado en sangre [ojo].

bloodstone (-stoun) *s.* MINER. hematíes. 2 MINER. heliotropo.

bloodsucker (-søkø^r) *s.* ZOOL. y fig. sanguijuela.

bloodthirsty (-zø^{r}sti) *adj.* sanguinario.

bloody (-i) *adj.* sangriento, cruento. 2 ensangrentado, sanguinolento. 3 encarnizado, sanguinario. 4 vulg. maldito.

bloody (to) *tr.* ensangrentar. ¶ Pret. y p. p.: *bloodied*.

bloom (blum) *s.* BOT. flor, flores [colectivamente]. 2 floración, florecimiento: *in ~*, florido, en flor.

3 frescura, lozanía. *4* color rosado [de las mejillas]. *5* flor, polvillo [de ciertas frutas y hojas]. *6* tocho, lingote.
bloom (to) *intr.* florecer, estar en flor. *2* lozanear, aparecer con toda su frescura, belleza o esplendor. *3* *tr.* hacer florecer. *4* dar frescura o lozanía.
bloomers (blu·mø^rs) *s. pl.* ant. pantalones femeninos de deporte.
blooming (-ing) *adj.* florido, en flor. *2* floreciente. *3* fresco, lozano. *4* vulg. maldito.
bloomy (-i) *adj.* florido. *2* lozano.
blossom (bla·søm) *s.* flor [que da fruto]; flores [de un árbol frutal]. *2* flor [de la vida, de la juventud]; lozanía, perfección.
blossom (to) *intr.* florecer, florar. *2* abrirse [las flores]. *3* florecer, prosperar.
blot (blat) *s.* borrón, mancha.
blot (to) *tr.* emborronar, manchar. *2* mancillar, empañar; afear. *3* secar [lo escrito]. *4* oscurecer, eclipsar. *5* *to* ~ *out,* tachar, borrar. *6* *intr.* correrse [la tinta], pasarse [el papel]. ¶ Pret. y p. p.: *blotted;* ger.: *-tting.*
blotch (bla·ch) *s.* mancha, borrón. *2* pústula, roncha.
blotch (to) *tr.* emborronar. *2* cubrir de pústulas.
blotter (bla·tø^r) *s.* papel secante, teleta. *2* borrador, libro de apuntes.
blotting paper (bla·ting) *s.* papel secante.
blotting pad *s.* secafirmas.
blouse (blaus) *s.* blusa.
blow (blou) *s.* golpe, porrazo: ~ *with a hammer,* martillazo; *to*'*come to blows,* venir a las manos, pegarse. *2* golpe, revés, desgracia, desastre. *3* soplido; trompetazo; ~ *of a horn,* bocinazo. *4* resoplido. *5* acción de sonarse las narices. *6* soplo [de aire]. *7* bot. florescenncia. *8* pop. fanfarrón.
blow (to) *tr.* soplar. *2* tocar [la trompeta, el silbato, etc.]: *to* ~ *one's own trumpet,* alabarse. *3* divulgar. *4* impeler, abrir, etc.[una cosa el aire]. *5* hinchar, inflar. *6* cansar, fatigar. *7* volar, hacer estallar. *8* bot. echar [flores]. *9* *to* ~ *off steam,* dejar salir el vapor; fig. desahogarse. *10* *to* ~ *one's nose,* sonarse las narices. *11* *to* ~ *out,* apagar; elect. fundir; volar: *to* ~ *one's brains out,* levantarse la tapa de los sesos. *12* impers. hacer viento. *13* intr. soplar. *14* resoplar, jadear. *15* sonar [la trompeta, etc.]. *16* hincharse, inflarse. *17* abrirse [las flores]. *18* *to* ~ *hot an cold,* estar entre sí y no, vacilar. *19* *to* ~ *out,* estallar; apagarse; elect. fundirse. ¶ Pret. y p. p.: *blew;* p. p.: *blown.*
blower (-ø^r) *s.* soplador. *2* mec. ventilador. *3* sopladero. *4* pop. fanfarrón.
blowfly (-flai) *s.* ent. moscarda.
blowgun (-gøn) *s.* cerbatana, bodoquera.
blown (-n) *p. p.* de to blow. *2* jadeante, rendido.
blowoff (-of) *s.* escape, salida [de vapor, etc.].
blowout (-aut) *s.* reventón, ruptura [por presión interior]. *2* quema [de un fusible]. *3* pop. banquete.
blowpipe (-paip) *s.* soplete. *2* cerbatana.
blowtorch (-to^rch) *s.* lámpara de soldar.
blowy (-i) *adj.* ventoso. *2* ligero.
blowzy (blau·ši) *adj.* coloradote. *2* desaliñado.
blubber (blø·bø^r) *s.* lloro, llanto. *2* ortiga de mar. *3* grasa de ballena. *4* *adj.* abultado, hinchado.
blubber (to) *intr.* llorar, sollozar. *2* *tr.* decir llorando.
blubber-lipped *adj.* bezudo, jetudo.
bludgeon (blø·dÿøn) *s.* porra, cachiporra.

bludgeon (to) *tr.* apalear. *2* amedrentar, intimidar.
blue (blu) *adj.* azul: ~ *devils,* hipocondría; alucinaciones del delirium tremens; ~ *streak,* relámpago, rayo; fig. cosa rápida. *2* lívido, amoratado. *3* rígido, puritano. *4* triste. *5* *s.* azul [color]. *6* *the* ~, el cielo, el mar. *7* *pl. the blues,* tristeza, murria, melancolía. *8* baile de origen negro.
blue (to) *tr.* azular. *2* dar azulete. *3* pavonear.
Bluebeard (-bi^rd) *s.* Barba azul.
blueberry (-beri) *s.* arándano.
bluebotte (-batøl) *s.* ent. moscón. *2* bot. aciano, azulejo.
blueing (-ing) *s.* bluing.
blueprint (-print) *s.* cianotipia. *2* cianotipo.
bluestocking (-staking) *s.* mujer literata. *2* marisabidilla.
bluet (blu·it) *s.* bot. aciano, azulejo.
bluff (bløf) *adj.* mar. ancha, abultada [amura, proa]. *2* escarpado, enhiesto. *3* rudo, francote. *4* *s.* escarpa, risco, farallón. *5* farol, envite falso. *6* falso alarde de fuerzas, recursos, etc.; baladronada.
bluff (to) *intr.* hacer un farol [en el juego]. *2* intr.-tr.* tratar de intimidar o disuadir con un falso alarde de fuerzas, recursos, etc.
bluffness (-nis) *s.* rudeza, franqueza, brusquedad.
bluing (blu·ing) *s.* pavonado. *2* azulete.
bluish (bu·ish) *adj.* azulado, azulino.
blunder (blø·ndø^r) *s.* disparate, equivocación, yerro, pifia, plancha.
blunder (to) *intr.* equivocarse, hacer disparates, pifias, planchas. *2* moverse torpemente, tropezar. *3* *tr.* estropear [un negocio]. *4* decir con torpeza o indiscreción.
blunderbuss (-bøs) *s.* trabuco.
blunderer (-ø^r) *s.* torpe, chapucero.
blunderhead (-jed) *s.*torpe, estúpido.
blunt (blønt) *adj.* embotado, despuntado, romo. *2* embotado, insensible; torpe, obtuso. *3* franco, brusco, descortés.
blunt (to) *tr.* embotar. *2* despuntar, poner romo. *3* adormecer, mitigar. *4* intr.* embotarse.
bluntly (-li) *adv.* claramente, bruscamente.
bluntness (-nis) *s.* embotamiento. *2* brusquedad, aspereza.
blur (blø^r) *s.* borrón, mancha. *2* cosa borrosa.
blur (to) *tr.* manchar, empañar. *2* hacer borroso o confuso. *3* nublar, oscurecer [la vista, el entendimiento]. *4* intr.* oscurecerse, ponerse borroso. ¶ Pret. y p. p.: *blurred;* ger.: *blurring.*
blurt (to) (blø^rt) *s.* decir o soltar bruscamente o indiscretamente.
blush (bløsh) *s.* rubor, sonrojo. *2* color encendido.
blush (to) *intr.* ruborizarse, sonrojarse. *2* tomar un color encendido.
blushful (-ful) *s.* ruboroso, modesto. *2* encendido, róseo.
blushing (-ing) *adj.* ruborizado; encendido. *2* *s.* rubor, sonrojo.
blushless (-lis) *adj.* desvergonzado.
bluster (blø·stø^r) *s.* borrasca ruidosa. *2* ruido, tumulto; violencia, furor. *3* sonido fuerte. *4* fanfarria, gritos, amenazas.
bluster (to) *intr.* soplar recio [el viento]; ser ventoso [el tiempo]. *2* tempestear, fanfarrear, bravear. *3* *tr.* intimidar con gritos y amenazas.
blusterer (-ø^r) *s.* fanfarrón, perdonavidas.
blustering (-ing), **blustery** (-i) *adj.* violento [viento]. *2* ventoso. *3* tempestuoso, ruidoso, tumultuoso. *4* fanfarrón, jactancioso.

boa (bou·a) *s.* boa.

boar (bo^r) *s.* verraco. *2* jabalí.

board (bo^{r}d) *s.* tabla, tablero [de madera]. *2* anaquel. *3* tablilla [de anuncios]. *4* ELECT. cuadro. *5* mesa puesta, comida, pensión, pupilaje. *6* mesa [para una junta o consejo]; junta, consejo: *Board of Admiralty,* Consejo superior de Marina; ~ *of directors,* consejo de administración; junta directiva; *Board of Education,* Consejo de Instrucción Pública. *7* cartón. *8* MAR. bordo: *free on* ~, franco a bordo. *9* canto, borde, orilla. *10* MAR. borda. *11* MAR. bordada. *12* pl. tablazón. *13* TEAT. escenario, tablas.

board (to) *tr.* entarimar, enmaderar. *2* tomar o poner a pupilaje. *3* abordar. *4* subir a un tren, a un buque. *5* intr. estar de pupilo.

boarder (-ø^r) *s.* abordador. *2* huésped, pupilo, pensionista.

boarding (-ing) *s.* tablazón. *2* entablado. *3* tabique de tablas. *4* MAR. abordaje. *5* pensión, hospedaje: ~ *house,* casa de huéspedes; ~ *school,* internado.

boast (boust) *s.* jactancia, ostentación, vanagloria, alarde, baladronada.

boast (to) *intr.* jactarse, alardear, blasonar, vanagloriarse. *2* tr. ponderar, decantar. *3* ostentar, tener.

boastful (-ful) *adj.* jactancioso.

boastless (-lis) *adj.* sencillo, sin ostentación.

boat (bout) *s.* bote, barca, lancha; barco, buque, nave, embarcación: ~ *hook,* bichero. *2* LITURG. naveta. *3* salsera.

boat (to) *tr.* poner o llevar en un bote, barco, etc. *2* intr. ir en bote, lancha, etc.

boathouse (-jaus) *s.* cobertizo para botes.

boating (-ing) *s.* paseo en lancha o bote. *2* transporte en barca. *3* manejo de un bote.

boatman (-mæn) *s.* botero, barquero.

boatswain (bou·søn o bou·tswen) *s.* MAR. contramaestre.

Bob (bab) *n. pr. dim.* de ROBERT.

bob *s.* lenteja [de péndulo]. *2* pilón [de romana]. *3* plomo [de plomada]. *4* corcho [en la pesca con anzuelo]. *5* cierto cebo para pescar. *6* cola cortada [de un caballo]. *7* pelo [esp. de mujer o de niño] cortado a la altura del cogote. *8* meneo, sacudida, movimiento de lo que sube y baja; saludo, reverencia. *9* adorno colgante. *10* peluquín. *11* fam. chelín.

bob (to) *tr.* cortar [la cola]. *2* cortar [el pelo] a la altura del cogote. *3* menear, sacudir, hacer subir y bajar. *4* intr. menearse [con sacudidas]. ¶ Pret. y p. p.: *bobbed;* ger.: *bobbing.*

bobbin (ba·bin) *s.* bolillo, majaderillo. *2* carrete, bobina; canilla, broca.

bobby (ba·bi) *s.* fam. [Ingl.] policía [agente].

bobsled (ba·bsled), **bobsleigh** (-slei) *s.* trineo pequeño.

bobtail (-teil) *adj.* rabón. *2* s. rabo mocho. *3* animal rabón.

bobtail (to) *tr.* cortar la cola a.

bobwig (-uig) *s.* peluquín.

boce (bous) *s.* ICT. boga.

bode (boud) *pret.* y *p. p.* de TO BIDE.

bode (to) *tr.-intr.* anunciar, presagiar: *to* ~ *ill* o *well,* ser un mal o un buen presagio. *2* pronosticar, prever.

bodice (ba·dis) *s.* jubón, corpiño, cuerpo [de vestido].

bodiless (ba·dilis) *adj.* sin cuerpo. *2* incorpóreo.

bodily (-li) *adj.* corporal. *2 adv.* en persona. *3* todos juntos, en peso.

bodkin (ba·dkin) *s.* COST. punzón. *2* pasacintas. *3* espadilla [para el pelo]. *4* ant. puñal.

body (ba·di) *s.* FÍS., QUÍM., GEOM., METAF. cuerpo. *2* cuerpo [de una pers., un animal, un vestido, un escrito, etc.]. *3* persona, individuo. *4* nave [de iglesia]. *5* caja, carrocería [de un coche, etc.]. *6* MÚ. caja, tubo [de instrumento]. *7* cuerpo [grueso, consistencia, etc.]. *8* masa, extensión: ~ *of water,* extensión de agua. *9* grupo, conjunto, cuerpo, gremio, clase: *in a* ~, en masa.

body (to) *tr.* dar forma a. *2* materializar, representar. ¶ Pret. y p. p.: *bodied.*

bodyguard (-ga^{r}d) *s.* guardia personal. *2* séquito.

Boer (bou·^{r}) *adj.-s.* bóer.

bog (bag) *s.* pantano, marjal, cenagal, tremedal. *2* turbera.

bog (to) *tr.-intr.* hundir o hundirse en un pantano; atollar, atollarse. ¶ Pret. y p. p.: *bogged;* ger.: *bogging.*

bogey (bou·gi) *s.* duende, coco.

boggle (-gøl) *s.* espantada [del caballo]. *2* vacilación, indecisión. *3* chapucería, disparate.

boggle (to) *intr.* retroceder asustado. *2* vacilar, titubear. *3* hacer disparates.

boggy (ba·gi) *adj.* pantanoso, turboso.

bogie (bou·gi) *s.* carretilla; vagoneta de carga. *2* FERROC. bogui. *3* BOGEY.

bogle (bou·gøl) *s.* duende, coco. *2* aversión.

bogus (bou·gøs) *adj.* (E.U) falso, ficticio.

bogy (-gil) *s.* BOGEY.

Bohemian (bouji·mian) *adj.-s.* bohemio.

boil (boil) *s.* hervor, ebullición. *2* divieso.

boil (to) *intr.* hervir, bullir: *to* ~ *over,* salirse [un líquido al hervir]; fig. estar excitado, fuera de sí. *2* cocerse [en un líquido]. *3* tr. hacer hervir, cocer, herventar: *to* ~ *down,* reducir por cocción; condensar, abreviar.

boiler (-ø^r) *s.* marmita, olla, caldero. *2* caldera. *3* cocedor.

boilermaker (-meikø^r) *s.* calderero.

boiling (-ing) *s.* hervor, ebullición; cocción: ~ *point,* punto de ebullición.

boisterous (boi·størøs) *adj.* estrepitoso, ruidoso, bullicioso, tumultuoso. *3* violento, tempestuoso.

boisterousness (-nis) *s.* turbulencia, tumulto, ruido, vocinglería.

bold (bould) *adj.* intrépido, valiente. *2* atrevido, audaz. *3* descarado. *4* escarpado, acantilado. *5* claro, destacado, bien definido.

bold-faced (-feist) *adj.* descarado. *2* IMPR. negra [letra].

boldness (-nis) *s.* intrepidez. *2* audacia. *3* atrevimiento, descaro.

bole (boul) *s.* tronco [de árbol]. *2* bol [arménico].

bolero (bole·rou) *s.* bolero.

bolide (bou·laid) *s.* bólido.

boll (boul) *s.* cápsula [del lino, del algodón].

bollard (ba·la^{r}d) *s.* MAR. bolardo.

Bolshevik (ba·lshevik) *s.* bolchevique.

Bolshevism (-višm) *s.* bolchevismo.

Bolshevist (-vist) *adj.-s.* bolchevista.

bolster (bou·lstø^r) *s.* cabezal, travesaño [de cama]. *2* cojín, almohadón, almohadilla. *3* ARQ. zapata. *4* refuerzo, sostén, soporte.

bolster (to) *tr.* apoyar con almohadón. *2* apoyar, sostener. *3* apuntalar.

bolstering (-ing) *s.* apoyadero, apoyo.

bolsterwork (-uø^{r}k) *s.* ARQ. almohadillado.

bolt (boult) *s.* saeta, virote. *2* rayo, centella: ~ *from the blue*, suceso inopinado. *3* suceso o acción repentinos; salto rápido, fuga. *4* perno, tornillo, clavija. *5* cerrojo, pasador, pestillo, falleba. *6* cerrojo [del fusil]. *7* tamiz [para harina]. *8* rollo [de paño o papel pintado]. *9* *adv.* de repente, como una flecha; rígidamente: ~ *upright*, derecho, tieso.

bolt (to) *tr.* echar el cerrojo a, acerrojar. *2* empernar. *3* arrojar, expeler. *4* engullir sin masticar. *5* cerner, tamizar. *6* *intr.* salir, entrar, etc., de repente; echar a correr, huir. *7* desbocarse [el caballo].

bolter (-ø^r) *s.* cedazo, tamiz.

bolthead (-jed) *s.* matraz.

boltrope (-roup) *s.* relinga [de vela].

bolus (bou·løs) *s.* FARM. bolo. *2* bolo alimenticio.

bomb (bam) *s.* bomba [proyectil]; artefacto explosivo: ~ *shelter*, refugio antiaéreo.

bomb (to) *tr.-intr.* bombardear.

bombard (bamba·^rd) *s.* bombarda.

bombard (to) *tr.* bombardear.

bombardier (bamba^rdɪ·^r) *s.* bombardero.

bombardment (-a·^rdmønt) *s.* bombardeo.

bombardon (ba·mba^rdøn) *s.* MÚS. bombardón.

bombast (ba·mbæst) *s.* ampulosidad.

bombastic (-bæ·stik) *adj.* ampuloso, campanudo, altisonante.

bomber (ba·mø^r) *s.* bombardero. *2* avión de bombardeo.

bombshell (-shel) *s.* bomba, granada.

bonbon (ba·nbàn) *s.* bombón.

bond (band) *s.* atadura, amarra, traba. *2* lazo, vínculo, nexo. *3* trabazón. *4* pacto, compromiso. *5* ARQ. aparejo. *6* QUÍM. enlace. *7* fiador [pers.]. *8* depósito [de mercancías] hasta el pago de derechos. *9* COM. bono, obligación. *10* *pl.* cadenas, cautiverio. *11* *adj.* sujeto, esclavizado.

bond (to) *tr.* unir, ligar, vincular. *2* hipotecar. *3* poner como garantía; dar fianza. *4* depositar [mercancías] hasta el pago de derechos.

bondage (-idȳ) *s.* esclavitud, servidumbre, sujeción.

bondholder (-jouldø^r) *s.* tenedor de bonos, obligacionista.

bondman (-mæn) *s.* esclavo, siervo.

bondsman (-smæn) *s.* fiador, garante. *2* BONDMAN.

bondstone (-stoun) *s.* perpiaño.

bone (boun) *s.* hueso: ~ *of contention*, materia de desavenencia; *to have a ~ to pick with someone*, tener algo que discutir con uno; *to make no bones*, no tener empacho [en]. *2* cuesco [de fruta]. *3* espina [de pescado]. *4* ballena [de corsé, etc.]. *5* ficha [de dominó]. *6* *pl.* esqueleto, armazón. *7* dados. *8* especie de castañuelas.

bone (to) *tr.* deshuesar. *2* quitar la espina [a un pescado]. *3* emballenar.

bonebreaker (-breikø^r) *s.* ORN. quebrantahuesos.

boneless (-lis) *adj.* sin huesos; mollar.

bonesetter (-setø^r) *s.* algebrista, ensalmador.

bonfire (ba·nfai^r) *s.* hoguera, fogata.

bonhomie (ba·nomi) *s.* afabilidad.

Boniface (ba·nifeis) *n. pr.* Bonifacio. *2* *s.* hostelero, mesonero.

bonito (boni·tous) *s.* ICT. bonito.

bonnet (ba·nit) *s.* capota, sombrero [de mujer]. *2* gorro. *3* boina escocesa. *4* tocado de plumas [de los pieles rojas]. *5* MEC. sombrerete, casquete. *6* AUTO. capó, cubierta. *7* FORT., ZOOL. bonete. *8* MAR. boneta.

bonnet (to) *tr.-ref.* cubrir [la cabeza].

bonny (ba·ni) *adj.* hermoso, lindo; bueno.

bonus (bou·nøs) *s.* prima, gratificación, plus. *2* dividendo extraordinario.

bony (bou·ni) *adj.* óseo; oseoso. *2* huesudo.

bonze (banŝ) *s.* bonzo.

boo (bu) *s.* grita. *2* *interj.* ¡fuera!, ¡bu!

boo (to) *tr.-intr.* abuchear, silbar.

booby (bu·bi) *s.* bobo. *2* torpe, desmañado.

book (buk) *s.* libro: *the Book*, la Biblia; *to bring to* ~, llamar a capítulo. *2* libreta, cuaderno. *3* libreto.

book (to) *tr.* anotar, inscribir [en un libro o registro]. *2* tomar, sacar, hacerse reservar [pasaje, localidades, etc.]. *3* contratar [a un artista].

bookbinder (-baindø^r) *m.* encuadernador.

bookbinding (-bainding) *s.* encuadernación.

bookcase (-keis) *s.* armario o estante para libros, librería.

bookie (bu·ki) *s.* BOOKMAKER 2.

booking (-ing) *s.* registro, asiento. *2* reserva, venta, compra [de pasajes, localidades, etc.]: ~ *office*, despacho de pasajes o localidades.

bookish (-ish) *adj.* estudioso. *2* libresco.

bookkeeper (-kɪpø^r) *s.* tenedor de libros.

bookkeeping (-kɪping) *s.* teneduría de libros.

booklet (-lit) *s.* librito, folleto, opúsculo.

bookmaker (-meikø^r) *s.* el que hace los libros. *2* corredor de apuestas [en las carreras].

bookmark (-ma^rk) *s.* registro [señal en un libro].

bookseller (-se·lø^r) *s.* librero.

bookshop (-shap) *s.* librería [tienda].

bookstall (-tol) *s.* puesto o quiosco de librería.

bookstore (-sto^r) *s.* BOOKSHOP.

bookworm (-uø^rm) *s.* polilla de los libros. *2* fig. ratón de biblioteca.

boom (bum) *s.* estampido, retumbo. *2* fig. auge, popularidad o prosperidad rápida y creciente; crecimiento rápido [de una ciudad, etc.]; alza rápida [de un artículo]. *3* MAR. botalón, botavara. *4* cadena [de puerto o río]. *5* aguilón [de grúa].

boom (to) *intr.* retumbar, tronar. *2* estar en auge, en prosperidad rápida y creciente; estar en alza sostenida [un artículo]. *3* *tr.* fomentar, hacer prosperar rápidamente. *4* lanzar, anunciar con gran propaganda.

boomerang (bu·møræng) *s.* bomerang.

boon (bun) *s.* don, dádiva; merced. *2* bendición, dicha. *3* *adj.* alegre, jovial.

boor (bu^r) *s.* patán. *2* grosero, mal educado.

boorish (-ish) *adj.* rústico, rudo, grosero.

boost (bust) *s.* (E.U.) empujón, ayuda. *2* alza [de los precios, el voltaje, etc.].

boost (to) *tr.* (E.U) empujar, ayudar. *2* hacer subir [los precios, el voltaje, etc.].

boot (but) *s.* bota, botina: ~ *hook*, tirabotas; ~ *tree*, horma para el calzado; *to give one the* ~, fig. despedir a uno. *2* borceguí [de tormento]. *3* provecho, ganancia: *to* ~, además, por añadidura.

boot (to) *tr.* calzar las botas. *2* dar un puntapié. *3* *to* ~ *it*, ir a pie. *4* *intr.* calzarse las botas. *4* servir, aprovechar.

bootblack (-blæk) *m.* limpiabotas.

booth (buz) *s.* casilla, quiosco; puesto. *2* cabina [telefónica, etc.].

bootjack (bu·tjæk) *s.* sacabotas.

bootlace (-leis) *s.* cordón para los zapatos.

bootleg (to) *tr.-intr.* (E.U) contrabandear [en bebidas alcohólicas]. ¶ Pret. y p. p.: *bootlegged*; ger.: *-gging*.

bootlegger (-ø^r) s. (E.U) contrabandista de bebidas alcohólicas.
boots (buts) s. limpiabotas de hotel.
booty (bu·ti) s. botín, presa. 2 ganancia, premio. 3 saqueo.
booze (buš) s. fam. bebida; borrachera.
booze (to) intr. empinar el codo.
borage (bo·eidÿ) s. borraja.
borate (bo·reit) s. borato.
borax (bo·ræks) s. bórax.
border (bo·^rdø^r) s. borde, orilla, margen. 2 frontera, límite, confín; (E.U) fronteras de la civilización. 3 orla, ribete. 4 repulgo, dobladillo. 5 arriate [de jardín]. 6 pl. TEAT. bambalinas.
border (to) tr. orlar. 2 orillar, ribetear. 3 estar en el borde de. 4 intr. to ~ on o upon, confinar o lindar con; rayar en.
borderland (-laænd) s. zona fronteriza.
borderline (-lain) s. frontera, límite.
bore (bo^r) pret. de TO BEAR.
bore s. taladro, barreno [agujero]. 2 ánima, alma [hueco interior]. 3 calibre [de un tubo]; luz [de un pozo]. 4 lata [cosa fastidiosa]. 5 latoso, pelmazo, posma.
bore (to) tr. horadar, taladrar, perforar. 2 abrir [un agujero, un pozo, etc.]. 3 aburrir, fastidiar, dar la lata a.
boreal (borial) adj. boreal.
Boreas (-rias) s. MIT., METEOR. bóreas.
boredom (bo·^rdøm) s. fastidio, aburrimiento, tedio.
borer (bo·rø^r) s. perforador. 2 barrena, taladro, broca. 3 MIN. sonda. 4 latoso, pelmazo.
boric (bo·rik) adj. bórico.
born (bo^rn) p. p. de TO BEAR; nacido. 2 de nacimiento, nato.
borne p. p. de TO BEAR.
boron (bo·ran) s. boro.
borough (bø·rou) s. villa; burgo. 2 distrito municipal.
borrow (to) (ba·rou) tr. tomar o pedir prestado. 2 apropiarse [una idea, etc.].
borrowed (ba·roud) adj. prestado.
boscage (ba·skidÿ) s. boscaje.
bosh (bash) s. palabrería, tonterías.
bosky (ba·ski) adj. nemoroso, arbolado.
bosom (bu·šøm) s. pecho, seno [parte exterior del pecho]. 2 pecho, corazón [sede de los afectos, etc.]. 3 COST. pechera. 4 seno [parte interna, cavidad]. 5 adj. querido, íntimo; ~ friend, amigo íntimo.
bosom (to) tr. guardar en el pecho. 2 ocultar.
Bosporus (ba·spørøs) n. pr. GEOGR. Bósforo.
boss (bos) s. protuberancia; bollo, bollón; giba. 2 cazoleta [de broquel]. 3 ARQ. clave en relieve. 4 fam. amo, patrón, jefe; (E.U) cacique.
boss (to) tr. repujar, trabajar de relieve. 2 tr.-intr. mandar, dominar.
bossage (bo·sidÿ) s. ARQ. almohadillado.
bossism (-iøm) s. caciquismo.
bossy (-i) adj. mandón, autoritario.
bot (bat) s. ENT. rezno.
botanic(al (botæ·nik(al) adj. botánico.
botanist (ba·tanist) s. botánico.
bonatize (-aiš) intr. herborizar.
botany (-i) s. botánica.
botch (bach) s. remiendo, chapucería, chafallo.
botch (to) tr. remendar chapuceramente, chafallar.
botchy (-i) adj. remendado. 2 chapucero.
botfly (ba·tflai) s. ENT. moscardón.

both (bouz) adj. y pron. ambos, entrambos, el uno y el otro, los dos: ~ of them, los dos; ~ his friends, sus dos amigos. 2 conj. al mismo tiempo, a la vez; tanto ...como: ~ good and cheap, bueno y barato a la vez; ~ A and B, tanto A como B.
bother (ba·ðø^r) s. preocupación. 2 fastidio, molestia; persona o cosa molesta. 3 inconveniente.
bother (to) tr. preocupar, fastidiar, molestar. 2 intr. preocuparse, molestarse: to ~ about, preocuparse de; to ~ to, molestarse en.
botheration (-ei·shøn) s. fastidio, molestia. 2 interj. ¡demonio!
bothersome (-søm) adj. molesto, fastidioso.
bottle (ba·tøl) s. botella, frasco, pomo. 2 zaque, bota. 3 haz [de heno].
bottle (to) tr. embotellar: to ~ up, embotellar [naves]; contener [la ira, etc.].
bottleflower (-flauø^r) s. aciano.
bottleneck (-nek) s. gollete [de botella]. 2 estrechura, camino estrecho. 3 obstáculo.
bottling (ba·tling) s. embotellado.
bottom (ba·tøm) s. fondo [de una cosa, del mar, de un río]: at ~, en el fondo, en realidad. 2 base, fundamento. 3 asiento [de silla o vasija]. 4 pie [parte inferior]; lo último, lo más bajo. 5 fondo [de buque]; casco, nave. 6 fam. trasero. 7 pl. heces, poso. 8 hondonada. 9 adj. fundamental. 10 del fondo, del pie, más bajo, último.
bottom (to) tr. poner fondo o asiento a. 2 fundar, basar. 3 profundizar. 4 intr. basarse.
bottomless (-lis) adj. sin fondo; insondable.
boudoir (budua·^r) s. gabinete [de señora].
bouffe (buf) adj. MÚS. bufo.
bough (bau) s. rama [de árbol].
bought (bot) pret. y p. p. de TO BUY.
bougie (bu·dÿi) s. CIR. sonda, candelilla.
bouillon (bu·lian) s. COC. caldo.
boulder (bou·ldø^r) s. pedrejón, canto rodado.
boulevard (bu·lva^r) s. bulevar.
boulter (bou·ltø^r) s. palangre.
bounce (bauns) s. golpazo. 2 salto, brinco, bote, rebote. 3 bravata, fanfarronada. 4 mentira. 5 fam. (E.U) despido.
bounce (to) tr. hacer botar. 2 fam. (E.U) echar, despedir [a uno]. 3 intr. lanzarse, saltar. 4 botar, rebotar. 5 fanfarronear.
bouncer (-ø^r) s. guapo, fanfarrón. 2 embustero. 3 embuste. 4 cosa grande.
bouncing (-ing) adj. fuerte, robusto. 2 exagerado.
bound (baund) pret. y p. p. de TO BIND. 2 adj. obligado. 3 encuadernado. 4 estreñido. 5 destinado a, que ha de o tiene que: ~ to fail, destinado a fracasar. 6 ~ for, con destino a, rumbo a.
bound s. límite, término, confín. 2 salto, brinco, bote.
bound (to) tr. limitar, circunscribir, encerrar. 2 intr. saltar, brincar, botar. 3 to ~ on o with, limitar, confinar con.
boundary (-ari) s. límite, linde, confín, término frontera: ~ stone, hito, mojón.
bounden (-øn) adj. obligado. 2 obligatorio, forzoso.
boundless (-lis) adj. ilimitado, infinito, vasto.
bounteous (bau·ntiøs), **bountiful** (bau·ntiful) adj. dadivoso, liberal, generoso. 2 amplio, abundante, copioso.
bounty (-i) s. liberalidad, generosidad, munificencia. 2 don, merced. 3 prima, subvención.
bouquet (bukei·) s. ramillete. 2 aroma [del vino].
bourdon (bu·^rdøn) s. bordón [bastón; registro del órgano].

bourgeois (buʳȳ̄ua·) *adj.-s.* burgués.
bourgeoisie (-si·) *s.* burguesía.
bourgeon (bøˑʳȳøn) *s.* BOT. yema, brote.
bourgeon (to) *intr.* brotar, retoñar.
bourn(e (bouʳn) *s.* riachuelo. *2* linde. *3* meta.
bourse (buʳs) *s.* bolsa, lonja.
bout (baut) *s.* rato [de hacer o de dedicarse a algo]; mano [de un juego]; asalto [de esgrima]; combate, encuentro. *2* probatura. *3* ataque [de una enfermedad].
bovine (bouˑvain) *adj.* bovino, vacuno.
bow (bau) *s.* inclinación, reverencia, saludo. *2* MAR. proa; amura.
bow (bou) *s.* arco [arma]. *2* arco, curva. *3* MÚS. arco. *4* ojo [de la llave, de las tijeras]. *5* lazo, lazada: ~ *tie*, corbata de lazo. *6* arzón delantero. *7* ~ *compass*, bigotera.
bow (to) (bau) *intr.* arquear, doblar. *2* MÚS. tocar con arco. *3* *intr.* arquearse, doblarse.
bowel (bauˑuøl) *s.* intestino. *2 pl.* intestinos, vientre. *3* fig. entrañas [lo más oculto].
bowel (to) *tr.* destripar, sacar las tripas.
bower (bauˑøʳ) *s.* glorieta, cenador, emparrado, enramada. *2* casita rústica. *3* gabinete, retrete. *4* MAR. ancla de leva.
bower (bouˑøʳ) *s.* músico de arco.
bowery (bauˑøri) *adj.* frondoso, emparrado, sombreado.
bowie-knife (bouˑi) *s.* cuchillo de monte.
bowl (boul) *s.* cuenco, escudilla, bol; copa. *2* palangana, jofaina. *3* hueco, concavidad. *4* taza [de fuente]. *5* platillo [de balanza]. *6* palita [de cuchara]. *7* cazoleta [de pipa]. *8* bola, bocha. *9 pl.* juego de bochas.
bowl (to) *tr.* hacer rodar. *2* tirar [la bola]; tumbar con una bola. *3* *intr.* jugar a bochas o a los bolos.
bowlegged (bouˑlegd) *adj.* estevado.
bowler (bouˑløʳ) *s.* jugador de bochas o de bolos. *2* [Ingl.] sombrero hongo.
bowline (bouˑlin) *s.* MAR. bolina.
bowling (-ing) *s.* juego de bochas o de bolos.
bowman (-mæn) *s.* arquero. *2* (bau mæn) MAR. remero de proa.
bowsprit (-sprit) *s.* bauprés.
bowstring (-tring) *s.* cuerda de arco.
bow-window *s.* ARQ. mirador de planta curva.
bowwow (bauˑuau) *s.* guau, ladrido.
bowwow (to) *intr.* ladrar. *2* gruñir, regañar.
box (baks) *s.* caja, cajita, estuche. *2* cajón, cofre, arca, baúl. *3* hucha. *4* MEC. buje, cubo, caja, manguito, cojinete. *5* apartado [de correos]. *6* pescante [de carruaje]. *7* casilla, garita. *8* compartimiento, departamento. *9* TEAT. palco. *10* bofetón, puñetazo. *11* BOT. boj. *12* ~ *calf*, cuero de becerro curtido al cromo. *13* TEAT. ~ *office*, taquilla.
box (to) *tr.* meter en caja, embalar. *2* apuñear, abofetear. *3* *intr.* boxear.
boxer (-søʳ) *s.* boxeador. *2* embalador.
boxing (-ing) *s.* boxeo. *2* embalaje.
boxthorn (-zøʳn) *s.* arto, cambronera.
boxwood (-wud) *s.* boj.
boy (boi) *s.* niño, muchacho: ~ *scout*, muchacho explorador. *2* muchacho, chico [hombre joven; término cariñoso o familiar]. *3* mozo, criado.
boyar (boˑȳaʳ) *s.* boyardo.
boycott (-cat) *s.* boicot; boicoteo.
boycott (to) *tr.* boicotear.
boyhood (-jud) *s.* muchachez. *2* los muchachos.
boyish (-ish) *adj.* de muchacho. *2* amuchachado.
bra (bra) *s.* BRASSIÈRE.

braccate (bræˑkeit) *adj.* ORN. calzado.
brace (breis) *s.* abrazadera, grapa, refuerzo, sostén. *2* MEC. riostra, tirante, viento, puntal. *3* berbiquí. *4* MAR. braza. *5* par [de pistolas, etc.]. *6* IMPR. corchete. *7* CIR. braguero. *8 pl.* tirantes [del pantalón].
brace (to) *tr.* atar, trabar, arriostrar, apuntar, ensamblar, asegurar. *2* atesar, atirantar. *3* MAR. bracear. *4* IMPR. abrazar con corchete. *5* cercar, ceñir. *6* vigorizar. *7* dar ánimo. *8* *intr.* animarse, cobrar ánimo.
bracelet (breiˑslit) *s.* brazalete, ajorca, pulsera.
bracer (breˑsøʳ) *s.* ARN. brazal. *2* abrazadera, laña. *3* cinto, venda. *4* MED. tónico.
brachial (bræˑkial) *adj.* ANAT. braquial.
brachycephalic (brakisøfæˑlik) *adj.* braquicéfalo.
bracing (breiˑsing) *adj.* tónico, vigorizante.
bracken (bræˑkøn) *s.* helecho. *2* helechal.
bracket (bræˑkit) *s.* cartela, ménsula, repisa, palomilla. *2* brazo de lámpara fijo en una pared o columna. *3* anaquel, rinconera. *4* IMPR. corchete. *5* IMPR. paréntesis rectangular. *6* clase, categoría.
brackish (bræˑkish) *adj.* salobre.
bract (brækt) *s.* BOT. bráctea.
bractlet (-lit) *s.* BOT. bractéola.
brad (bræd) *s.* clavito, estaquilla, saetín.
brag (bræg) *s.* jactancia, fanfarronada, alarde. *2* fanfarrón, farolero. *3* juego de naipes.
brag (to) *intr.* jactarse, alardear, fanfarronear. ¶ Pret. y p. p.: *bragged;* ger.: *bragging.*
braggadocio (brægadouˑshiou) *s.* fanfarrón. *2* fanfarria.
braggart (bræˑgaʳt) *adj.-s.* jactancioso, baladrón.
bragger (bræˑgøʳ) *s.* jaque, fanfarrón.
Brahman (braˑmæn) *s.* brahman, brahmín.
Brahmanism (-išm) *s.* brahmanismo.
Brahmin (bra·min) *s.* brahmín, brahmán.
braid (breid) *s.* trenza. *2* trencilla, galón, cordoncillo, alamar.
braid (to) *tr.* trenzar. *2* atar [el cabello]. *3* galonear, trencillar, guarnecer.
brail (breil) *s.* MAR. candaliza.
brail (to) *tr.* MAR. cargar [las velas].
brain (brein) *s.* ANAT. cerebro, seso: ~ *fever*, fiebre cerebral. *2* esp. *pl.* cabeza, inteligencia, seso.
brain (to) *tr.* romper la cabeza.
brainless (-lis) *adj.* sin seso, mentecato.
brainsick (-sik) *adj.* loco. *2* de loco.
brainy (-i) *adj.* inteligente, talentudo.
braise (to) (breiˑš) *tr.* rehogar [la carne].
braize *s.* ICT. pagro.
brake (breiˑk) *s.* freno [de máquina o vehículo]. *2* guimbalete. *3* agramadera. *4* amasadora mecánica [de panadero]. *5* AGR. grada, rastra. *6* break [coche]. *7* BOT. helecho. *8* matorral, mato, jaral.
brake (to) *tr.* frenar. *2* amasar [pan]. *3* agramar. *4* AGR. gradar.
brakeman (-mæn) *s.* guardafrenos.
bramble (bræˑmbøl) *s.* zarza. *2 pl.* zarzal.
brambly (bræˑmbli) *adj.* zarzoso.
brambling (-ing) *s.* ORN. pinzón reàl.
bran (bræn) *s.* salvado, afrecho.
branch (branch) *s.* rama [de árbol, de familia, etc.]. *2* ramo [de una ciencia, arte, etc.]. *3* ramal [vía férrea, camino, conducto, etc.]. *4* sección, departamento. *5* COM. sucursal. *6* brazo [de río, de candelero, etc.]. *7* candil [de cuerna]. *8* pierna [de compás]. *9 adj.* filial, sucursal.
branch (to) *intr.* echar ramas. *2* ramificarse, bifurcarse; partir de un punto [una rama, un ramal].

| Gralte. con *off* o *out*. *3 to* ~ *out*, extender sus actividades. *4 tr.* dividir en ramas, bifurcar.

branchia (bræ·nkiɑ) *s.* ZOOL.. branquia.

branchial (-l) *adj.* branquial.

branchy (bra·nchi) *adj.* ramoso.

brand (brænd) *s.* tizón, tea. *2 poét.* antorcha. *3 poét.* espada. *4* hierro [para marcar; marca]. *5* baldón, estigma. *6* marca de fábrica; clase.

brand (to) *tr.* marcar [con hierro o marca de fábrica]. *2* grabar [en la mente]. *3* estigmatizar.

brandish (-ish) *s.* ESGR. floreo, molinete.

brandish (to) *tr.* blandir, blandear.

brand-new *adj.* completamente nuevo, nuevecito, flamante.

brandy (-i) *s.* aguardiente, coñac.

bran-new *adj.* BRAND-NEW.

brant (brænt) *s.* ganso silvestre.

brash (brash) *s.* escombros, broza. *3* MED. acedia.

brasier (brei·ẙøʳ) *s.* BRAZIER.

brass (bræs) *s.* latón, azófar, metal; bronce. *2* MÚS. metal [instrumentos]: ~ *band*, charanga. *3* descaro, desfachatez.

brass (to) *tr.* revestir de latón, de metal.

brassart (bræ·saʳt) *s.* brazal.

brassière (braȘɪ·ʳ) *s.* sostén [prenda femenina].

brassy (bræ·si) *adj.* de latón. *2* bronco, metálico. *3* descarado, desvergonzado.

brat (bræt) *s.* desp. niño, mocoso.

bravado (brɑvɑ·dou) *s.* baladronada; cosa que uno hace para demostrar su valentía.

brave (brei·v) *adj.* bravo, valiente. *2 poét.* airoso, elegante. *3* honrado. *4 s.* valiente.

brave (to) *tr.* arrostrar, desafiar, retar.

bravery (-øri) *s.* bravura, intrepidez. *2* esplendor, ornato; galas.

bravo (brɑ·vous) *s.* asesino a sueldo. *2 interj.* ¡bravo!

brawl (brɔl) *s.* reyerta, alboroto, tumulto. *2* ruido, fragor [de un torrente, etc.].

brawl (to) *intr.* reñir, alborotar, vociferar. *2* hacer ruido o fragor [un torrente, etc.].

brawler (-øʳ) *s.* camorrista, alborotador.

brawn (brɔn) *s.* músculo, carne dura. *2* carne de cerdo adobada.

brawny (-i) *adj.* musculoso, fornido.

bray (brei) *s.* rebuzno. *2* sonido bronco.

bray (to) *intr.* rebuznar. *2* hacer un sonido bronco. *3 tr.* moler, triturar.

braze (to) (breiš) *tr.* soldar con latón. *2* broncear.

brazen (brei·šn) *adj.* de latón. *2* broncíneo; bronceado. *3* descarado, desvergonzado.

brazen (to) *tr.* dar atrevimiento o descaro. *2 to* ~ *it out*, sostener o llevar a cabo con decisión o descaro.

brazen-faced *adj.* descarado, desvergonzado.

brazier (brei·ẙøʳ) *s.* latonero. *2* brasero [para calentarse].

Brazil (braȘi·l) *n. pr.* GEOGR. Brasil. *2 s.* (con min.) palo brasil.

braziletto (braȘile·tou) *s.* brasilete.

Brazilian (braȘilian) *adj.* y *s.* brasileño.

breach (brɪch) *s.* brecha, portillo, abertura. *2* rotura, fractura. *3* hernia. *4* ruptura, desavenencia. *5* infracción, quebrantamiento, violación: ~ *of the peace*, alteración del orden público; ~ *of promise*, incumplimiento de la palabra de matrimonio.

breach (to) *tr.* abrir brecha o boquete en.

bread (bred) *s.* pan [de harina, etc.; sustento diario]: ~ *crumb*, miga de pan; pan rallado; *to*

know on which side one's ~ *is buttered*, saber uno donde le aprieta el zapato.

bread (to) *tr.* COC. empanar.

breadth (bredȥ) *s.* anchura, ancho. *2* envergadura. *3* extensión, latitud, holgura. *4* amplitud [de juicio, de ideas].

breadthwise (-uaiš) *adv.* a lo ancho.

break (breik) *s.* break [coche]. *2* rotura, ruptura, rompimiento. *3* comienzo: ~ *of the day*, amanecer. *4* abertura, grieta. *5* interrupción, pausa, hueco, claro. *6* clara [en el tiempo]. *7* fuga, evasión. *8* ELECT. corte [en un circuito]. *9* GEOL. falla. *10* BILLAR tacada. *11* MÚS. gallo. *12* fig. (E.U) plancha. *13* (E.U) suerte, oportunidad.

break (to) *tr.* romper, quebrar, fracturar, hender, partir, quebrantar. *2* deshacer, descomponer. *3* agramar. *4* romper [filas]. *5* forzar [una puerta]. *6* abrir [un camino, etc.]. *7* templar, amortiguar. *8* parar [un golpe]. *9* penetrar, atravesar. *10* interrumpir, hacer cesar. *11* quebrantar, infringir. *12* hacer fracasar. *13* someter, dominar; domar. *14* causar la quiebra de, arruinar. *15* MIL. degradar. *16* abrumar. *17* comunicar, divulgar; dar [una noticia]. *18* PINT. templar [los colores]. *19 to* ~ *cover*, salir del escondite. *20* ~ *down*, demoler; anonadar; descomponer, analizar. *21 to* ~ *ground*, romper la tierra; comenzar una empresa. *22 to* ~ *in*, forzar la entrada; domar [un caballo]. *23 to* ~ *someone of a bad habit*, quitar un vicio a uno. *24 to* ~ *the record*, batir la marca. *25 to* ~ *up*, desmenuzar; romper; forzar; disolver [una reunión]; levantar [la casa, el campo]. *26 to* ~ *wind*, ventosear.

27 intr. romperse, abrirse, partirse. *28* quebrantarse [la salud]. *29* salir [un grito]; estallar [la tormenta]. *30* prorrumpir. *31* irrumpir. *32* abrirse, reventarse. *33* disolverse, disiparse. *34* romper [con uno]. *35* fallar, cascarse [la voz]. *36* estropearse. *37* debilitarse, perder la salud. *38* aparecer, salir, nacer, brotar, apuntar, comenzar. *39* divulgarse. *40 to* ~ *away*, soltarse; escapar. *41 to* ~ *down*, parar por avería; irse abajo; abatirse; perder la salud; prorrumpir en llanto. *42 to* ~ *forth*, brotar; estallar; prorrumpir. *43 to* ~ *out*, estallar, desatarse, empezar. *44 to* ~ *up*, disolverse, disgregarse; levantarse [una sesión].

¶ Pret.: *broke*; p. p.: *broken*.

breakage (-i·dẙ) *s.* rotura. *2* indemnización por cosas rotas [en el transporte, etc.].

breakdown (-daun) *s.* caída, vuelco, derrumbamiento. *2* fracaso. *3* paro, interrupción, avería. *4* MED. colapso; agotamiento.

breaker (-øʳ) *s.* rompedor. *2* quebrantador. *3* roturador. *4* ELECT. disyuntor. *5* ola que rompe, cachón.

breakfast (-fast) *s.* desayuno, almuerzo.

breakfast (to) *intr.* desayunar, almorzar.

breakneck (-nek) *s.* despeñadero, precipicio. *2 adj.* precipitado, rápido.

breakup (-øp) *s.* disolución, disgregación. *2* separación, dispersión.

breakwater (-uotøʳ) *s.* rompeolas.

bream (brɪm) *s.* ICT. brema; sargo.

breast (brest) *s.* pecho, seno [del cuerpo humano]. *2* pecho, seno, mama, teta [de mujer]; tetilla [de hombre]. *3* pecho [de animal]; pechuga [de ave]. *4* pechera [de una prenda]. *5* parte frontal [de una cosa]. *6* fig. pecho, corazón [interior del hombre].

breast (to) *tr.* arrostrar, luchar con.

breastbone (-boun) s. ANAT. esternón. 2 ORN. quilla.
breastpin (-pin) s. alfiler de pecho, broche.
breastplate (-pleit) s. peto [de armadura]. 2 petral.
3 pectoral, racional [de los judíos].
breastwork (-wøᵏk) s. FORT. parapeto. 2 MAR. propao.
breath (brez) s. hálito, aliento, respiración, resuello: *out of* ~, sin aliento, sofocado; *under one's* ~, en voz baja. 2 fig. vida. 3 hálito, soplo [de aire]. 4 soplo, instante. 5 respiro, descanso. 6 susurro.
breathable (brɪ·ðabøl) *adj.* respirable.
breathe (to) (brɪð) *intr.* alentar, respirar, resollar. 2 respirar, descansar. 3 soplar [un aire suave]. 4 *tr.* respirar [el aire]. 5 exhalar: *to ~ one's last*, dar el último suspiro. 6 dar un descanso. 7 susurrar, decir, revelar. 8 infundir.
breather (-øʳ) s. respirador. 2 viviente. 3 inspirador. 4 respiro, descanso.
breathing (-ing) s. respiración. 2 hálito. 3 inspiración, sugestión. 4 descanso, pausa. 5 momento.
breathless (-lis) *adj.* muerto. 2 jadeante, sin aliento. 3 intenso, expectante.
bred (bred) *pret. y p. p.* de TO BREED.
breech (brɪch) s. trasero, posaderas. 2 recámara, culata [de un arma].
breech (to) *tr.* poner calzones. 2 azotar, zurrar.
breeches (brɪ·chiš) s. pl. calzones, bragas, pantalón corto; fam. pantalones: *to wear the* ~, llevar los pantalones [la mujer].
breeching (-ching) s. retranca, cejadero.
breed (brɪd) s. casta, raza, progenie. 2 clase, especie.
breed (to) *tr.* engendrar. 2 criar [animales]; dar, producir [flores, frutos, etc.]. 3 criar, educar. 4 *intr.* criarse. 5 producirse, originarse. ¶ Pret. y p. p.: *bred*.
breeder (-øʳ) s. criador; productor. 2 animal reproductor.
breeding (-ing) s. cría, crianza; producción. 2 crianza, educación. 3 urbanidad, modales.
breeze (brɪš) s. brisa, airecillo. 2 fam. excitación, enojo. 3 fam. rumor, murmuración.
breezy (-i) *adj.* oreado. 2 airoso, vivo, animado. 3 vivaracho, desenvuelto.
brethren (bre·ðrin) s. pl. hermanos, cofrades.
Breton (bre·tøn) *adj.-s.* bretón.
breve (briv) s. MÚS. breve.
brevet (brøve·t) s. título, despacho. 2 MIL. graduación honoraria; grado.
brevet (to) *tr.* MIL. graduar.
breviary (brɪ·vieri) s. breviario.
brevity (bre·viti) s. brevedad; concisión.
brew (bru) s. bebida preparada, mezcla, infusión.
brew (to) *tr.* hacer [cerveza]. 2 preparar [el té, un ponche, etc.]. 3 urdir, tramar. 4 *intr.* hacer cerveza. 5 prepararse, amenazar [una tempestad, etc.].
brewage (-dỹ) s. BREW.
brewer (-øʳ) s. cervecero [que hace cerveza].
brewry (-øri), **brewhouse** (-jaus) s. cervecería, fábrica de cerveza.
briar (brai·øʳ) s. BRIER.
bribe (braib) s. soborno, cohecho [dinero, etc.]. 2 cebo, incentivo.
bribe (to) *tr.* sobornar, cohechar.
bribery (-øri) s. soborno, cohecho [acción].
bric-a-brac (bri·kabræk) s. artículos de arte, antigüedades.
brick (brik) s. ladrillo; ladrillos. 2 fam. persona excelente, simpática.

brick (to) *tr.* enladrillar.
brickbat (-bæt) s. pedazo de ladrillo.
bricklayer (-leiøʳ) s. albañil.
brickmaker (-meikøʳ) s. ladrillero.
brickyard (-iaʳd) s. ladrillar.
bridal (brai·dal) *adj.* nupcial. 2 de la novia. 3 s. boda.
bride (braid) s. novia, desposada.
bridegroom (-grum) s. novio, desposado.
bridesmaid (-šmeid) s. dama de honor [en una boda].
bridesman (-šmæn) s. padrino de boda.
bridge (bridỹ) s. puente [para pasar un río, etc.]. 2 caballete [de la nariz]. 3 MÚS., ODON., QUÍM. puente. 4 MAR. puente de mando. 5 BILL. violín. 6 bridge [juego]. 7 ELECT. conexión en paralelo.
bridge (to) *tr.* pontear. 2 salvar, cubrir [un espacio].
bridgehead (-jed) s. MIL. cabeza de puente.
bridle (brai·døl) s. EQUIT. brida: ~ *path*, camino de herradura. 2 freno, sujeción. 3 ANAT. frenillo. 4 MAR. boya.
bridle (to) *tr.* embridar. 2 refrenar, dominar. 3 erguir la cabeza, engallarse.
bridoon (brindu·n) s. bridón, filete.
brief (brif) *adj.* breve, corto, conciso, lacónico, seco. 2 fugaz, pasajero. 3 s. breve [apostólico]. 4 resumen, compendio. 5 DER. informe, escrito: ~ *bag*, cartera [para documentos].
briefless (-lis) *adj.* sin pleitos [abogado].
brier (brai·øʳ) s. BOT. escaramujo. 2 BOT. zarza. 3 BOT. brezo. 4 pipa de brezo.
briery (-i) *adj.* zarzoso.
brig (brig) s. MAR. bergantín; bricbarca.
brigade (brigei·d) s. brigada.
brigade (to) *tr.* reunir en brigada.
brigadier (brigadɪ·øʳ) s. brigadier.
brigand (bri·gand) s. bandido, bandolero.
brigandage (-idỹ) s. bandolerismo.
brigantine (bri·gantin) s. bergantín, goleta.
bright (brait) *adj.* brillante. 2 lustroso. 3 luminoso, resplandeciente. 4 límpido. 5 vibrante [sonido]. 6 vivo [color]. 7 claro, ilustre. 8 alegre. 9 inteligente, perspicaz. 10 vivo, animado.
brighten (to) (-øn) *tr.* abrillantar. 2 avivar, animar, alegrar. 3 realzar. 4 *intr.* cobrar brillo. 5 avivarse, alegrarse. 6 aclararse.
brightness (-nis) s. brillo, brillantez. 2 claridad, luz. 3 alegría, viveza. 4 agudeza de ingenio.
brill (bril) s. ICT. rodaballo.
brilliance, -cy (bri·lians, -si) s. brillantez, brillo, resplandor. 2 esplendor, lustre.
brilliant (bri·liant) *adj.* brillante. 2 s. brillante [piedra].
brilliantine (-in) s. brillantina.
brim (brim) s. borde, orilla. 2 borde [de una vasija]. 3 ala [de sombrero].
brim (to) *tr.* llenar hasta el borde. 2 *intr.* rebosar. 3 asomar [las lágrimas]. ¶ Pret. y p. p.: *brimmed*; ger.: *brimming*.
brimful (-ful) *adj.* lleno hasta el borde.
brimless (-lis) *adj.* sin borde o ala.
brimmer (-øʳ) s. copa o vaso lleno.
brimstone (-stoun) s. azufre.
brindled (bri·ndøld) *adj.* leonado, rayado [animal].
brine (brain) s. salmuera; agua salada. 2 fig. mar. 3 poét. lágrimas.
brine (to) *tr.* poner en salmuera.
bring (to) (bring) *tr.* traer, llevar [en varios sentidos]. 2 acarrear, producir, causar. 3 poner [en

un estado, condición, etc.]. *4* inducir [persuadir].' *5* DER. intentar [una acción]. *6* aportar, aducir. *7* rentar. *8 to ~ about,* efectuar, realizar; traer, ocasionar. *9 to ~ down,* bajar, hacer caer, derribar; abatir, humillar; reducir. *10 to ~ forth,* dar [fruto]; dar a luz; poner de manifiesto; aducir. *11 to ~ forward,* presentar; aducir; COM. llevar a otra cuenta. *12 to ~ in,* entrar, introducir; producir, rentar; presentar [un proyecto, etc.]; dar [un fallo]. *13 to ~ out,* sacar; publicar; presentar. *14 to ~ round,* ganar, persuadir; devolver la salud. *15 to ~ to,* hacer volver en sí. *16 to ~ to bear,* aplicar; apuntar, asestar. *17 to ~ up,* subir; criar, educar; traer, presentar, llevar [ante]; parar, detener; *to ~ up by hand,* criar con biberón; *to ~ up the rear,* cerrar la marcha. ¶ Pret. y p. p.: *brought.*

bringing-up *s.* crianza, educación [de un niño].

brink (brink) *s.* borde, orilla, extremidad; *on the ~ of,* al borde, a punto de.

briny (bri·ni) *adj.* salobre, salado.

briquette (brike·t) *s.* aglomerado.

brisk (brisk) *adj.* vivo, activo, animado. *2* ágil, ligero, rápido. *3* fresco [viento]. *4* espumoso [licor].

brisk up (to) *tr.* avivar, activar, apresurar. *2 intr.* animarse; apresurarse.

brisket (bri·skit) *s.* pecho [de una res].

briskness (bris·knis) *s.* viveza, actividad, vivacidad.

bristle (bri·søl) *s.* cerda, porcipelo.

bristle (to) *tr.* erizar. *2 intr.* erizarse, erizar [el pelo, etc.]; encresparse. *3 to ~ with,* estar erizado de.

bristly (bri·sli) *adj.* cerdoso, hirsuto.

Bristol board (bri·støl) *s.* cartulina.

Britain [Great] (bri·tøn) *n. pr.* GEOGR. Gran Bretaña.

Britannia (britæ·nia) *n. pr.* Britania, la Gran Bretaña, el Imperio Británico.

British (bri·tish) *adj.* británico, inglés. *2 s.* britano, inglés.

Briton (bri·tøn) *s.* brítano.

Brittany (bri·tani) *n. pr.* GEOGR. Bretaña.

brittle (bri·tøl) *adj.* quebradizo, friable. *2* vidrioso, irritable.

broach (brouch) *s.* espetón, asador. *2* lezna, punzón. *3* CARP. broca, mecha. *4* aguja, chapitel. *5* broche, prendedor.

broach (to) *tr.* espetar, ensartar. *2* espitar. *3* empezar, decentar. *4* hacer público; mencionar por primera vez.

broad (brod) *adj.* ancho. *2* anchuroso. *3* amplio, extenso, lato. *4* claro, obvio. *5* tolerante, comprensivo. *6* esencial, general. *7* vulgar, grosero, libre, atrevido. *8* cerrado, dialectal. *9 in ~ day,* en pleno día.

broadcast (-kæst) *s.* esparcimiento; siembra al voleo. *2* emisión ðe radio.

broadcast (to) *tr.* esparcir, difundir. *2* sembrar al voleo. *3* radiar, emitir por radio. ¶ Pret. y p. p.: *broadcast,* y también, refiriéndose a la radio; *broadcasted.*

broadcasting (-ing) *s.* radiodifusión; *~ station,* emisora de radio.

boadcloth (-kloz) *s.* paño fino.

broaden (to) (-øn) *tr.* ensanchar. *2 intr.* ensancharse.

broad-minded *adj.* liberal, tolerante, despreocupado.

broadside (-said) *s.* MAR. costado [de un buque], andana. *2* MAR. andanada. *3* IMPR. hoja suelta,

grande. *3* CINEM. lámpara o batería que ilumina fuertemente.

broadsword (so·rd) *s.* espadón, montante.

broadwise (-wuaiš) *adv.* a lo ancho, por lo ancho.

brocade (brokei·d) *s.* brocado.

brocaded (-id) *adj.* brochado; recamado.

broccoli (bra·koli) *s.* BOT. brécol, bróculi.

brochure (broshu·ø·r) *s.* folleto.

brock (bra·k) *s.* ZOOL. tejón.

brocket (-it) *s.* gamo de dos años.

brogue (brou·g) *s.* abarca. *2* acento irlandés.

broil (broil) *s.* asado a la parrilla. *2* calor intenso. *3* riña, alboroto, tumulto.

broil (to) *tr.* asar a la parrilla. *2* achicharrar. *3 intr.* asarse; achicharrarse.

broiler (-ø·r) *s.* COC. parrilla. *2* pollo asadero. *3* camorrista.

broiling (-ing) *adj.* ardiente, achicharrador.

brocke (brouk) *pret.* de TO BREAK. *2 adj.* pop. arruinado.

broken (brou·køn) *p. p.* de TO BREAK. *2 adj.* roto, cascado. *3* roturado. *4* quebrada [linea]. *5* accidentado [suelo]. *6* suelto, disgregado. *7* interrumpido, entrecortado. *8* fragmentario. *9* quebrantado, debilitado. *10* arruinado.

broken-down *adj.* abatido. *2* deshecho, descompuesto. *3* quebrantado. *4* arruinado.

brokenly (-li) *adv.* interrumpidamente, a ratos. *2* entrecortadamente.

broker (brou·kø·r) *s.* COM. corredor, agente. *2* bolsista. *3* (Ingl.) chamarilero; tasador y vendedor de objetos embargados.

brokerage (-dÿ) *s.* corretaje, correduría.

bromatology (broumata·lodÿi) *s.* bromatología.

bromide (brou·mid) *s.* QUÍM. bromuro.

bromine (brou·min) *s.* QUÍM. bromo.

bronchi (bra·nkai) *s. pl.* bronquios.

bronchial (-kial) *adj.* bronquial.

bronchitis (-kaitiš) *s.* bronquitis.

bronchopneumonia (brankoniumou·nia) *s.* bronconeumonía.

bronchus (bra·nkøs) *s.* bronquio.

bronco (bra·nkou) *s.* caballo pequeño y medio salvaje de Norteamérica.

bronze (branš) *s.* bronce.

bronze (to) *tr.* broncear. *2 intr.* broncearse.

brooch (brouch) *s.* broche; alfiler de pecho.

brood (brud) *s.* cría, pollada, nidada, lechigada. *2* progenie. *3* casta.

brood (to) *tr.* empollar, incubar. *2* cobijar. *3* tramar, fraguar. *4 intr.* encobar. *5* meditar, cavilar. | Gralte. con on o over.

brooder (-ø·r) *s.* clueca. *2* incubadora. *3* rumión, caviloso.

broody (-i) *adj.* clueca. *2* caviloso, melancólico.

brook (bruk) *s.* arroyo, riachuelo.

brook (to) *tr.* sufrir, aguantar, tolerar.

brooklet (-lit) *s.* arroyuelo.

broom (brum) *s.* escoba. *2* BOT. escoba; retama de escobas.

broomstick (-stik) *s.* palo de escoba.

broth (broz) *s.* COC. caldo.

brothel (bra·ðøl) *s.* burdel.

brother (brø·ðø·r) *s.* hermano. *2* cofrade, colega.

brotherhood (-jud) *s.* hermandad, hermanazgo. *2* hermandad, cofradía.

brother-in-law *s.* cuñado, hermano político.

brotherly (-li) *adj.* fraterno; fraternal. *2 adv.* fraternalmente.

brougham (bru·am) *s.* berlina [coche].

brought (brot) *pret.* y *p. p.* de TO BRING.

brow (brau) *s.* ANAT. ceja. *2* frente, entrecejo. *3* semblante. *4* cresta, cima, cumbre.

browbeat (to) (-bıt) *tr.* intimidar, aturrullar [con miradas o palabras]. ¶ Pret. *browbeat;* p. p.: *browbeaten.*

brown (braun) *adj.* pardo, moreno, castaño, bazo: ~ *paper,* papel de estraza o de embalar; ~ *race,* raza cobriza; *in a* ~ *study,* absorto en sus pensamientos. *2 s.* pardo, moreno, castaño [color].

brown (to) *tr.* poner moreno; broncear. *2* COC. tostar, dorar. *3 intr.* tostarse.

browning (-ing) *s.* pistola automática.

brownstone (-stoun) *s.* arenisca de color obscuro.

browse (brauš) *s.* pimpollos, hojas tiernas [que roza el ganado]. *2* roza, ramoneo.

browse (to) *tr.* rozar, ramonear; pacer.

bruise (bruš) *s.* magulladura, cardenal, contusión. *2* maca [en la fruta]. *3* abolladura.

bruise (to) *tr.* magullar, contundir. *2* machucar, abollar. *3* majar, machacar.

bruiser (-ø^r) *s.* boxeador. *2* majador.

bruit (to) (brut) *tr.* esparcir, publicar, divulgar. *2* dar fama.

brume (bru·m) *s.* bruma, neblina.

brumous (-øs) *adj.* brumoso.

brunette (-meikø^r) *adj.-s.* morena, trigueña.

brunt (brønt) *s.* choque, embate; lo más recio [de una lucha, etc.].

brush (brøsh) *s.* cepillo, bruza; escobilla. *2* brocha, pincel. *3* hopo [rabo peludo]. *4* cepilladura. *5* roce. *6* ramojo, broza. *7* matorral, maleza. *8* escaramuza.

brush (to) *tr.* cepillar, frotar, restregar; pasar la brocha, el pincel. *2* rozar, rasar, empujar [al pasar]: *to* ~ *aside,* apartar; desechar.

brushmaker (-meikø^r) *s.* brucero.

brushwood (-wud) *s.* ramojo, broza. *2* matorral, zarzal.

brushy (brø·shi) *adj.* matoso. *2* hirsuto.

brusque (brøsk) *adj.* brusco, rudo.

brusque (to) *tr.* tratar con rudeza.

brusqueness (-nis) *s.* brusquedad.

Brussels (brø·sølš) *n. pr.* GEOGR. Bruselas. *2 s.* ~ *sprouts,* coles de Bruselas.

brutal (bru·tal) *adj.* brutal, bestial, cruel.

brutality (bruta·liti) *s.* brutalidad, crueldad.

brutalize (bru·talaiš) *tr.* volver brutal. *2* tratar brutalmente. *3 intr.* bestializarse.

brute (brut) *s.* bruto [animal; pers. brutal]. *2 adj.* brutal, bruto.

brutify (to) (bru·tifai) *tr.* embrutecer. *2 intr.* embrutecerse. ¶ Pret. y p. p.: *brutified.*

brutish (bru·tish) *adj.* abrutado, brutal, bestial. *2* estúpido. *3* sensual, grosero.

bryology (braia·lodÿi) *s.* briología.

bryony (brai·øni) *s.* brionia, nueza.

bubal (biu·bal) *s.* búbalo.

bubble (bø·bøl) *s.* burbuja, ampolla, pompa. *2* borbolleo. *3* quimera, ilusión. *4* ~ *gum,* chicle hinchable.

bubble (to) *intr.* burbujear, borbollar, hervir. *2* murmurar [un río, etc.]. *3* *to* ~ *over,* rebosar.

bubbly (bø·bli) *adj.* burbujeante, espumoso.

bubo (biu·bou) *s.* MED. bubón.

bubonic (biuba·nik) *adj.* bubónico.

buccal (bø·kal) *adj.* bucal.

buccaneer (bøkanı·^r) *s.* bucanero.

bucentaur (biuse·nto^r) *s.* bucentauro.

buck (bøk) *s.* ZOOL. macho cabrío: gamo; macho de otros animales. *2* petimetre. *3* lejía, colada. *4* salto de carnero. *5* fam. dólar.

buck (to) *tr.* colar [ropa]. *2* tirar [al jinete] el caballo. *3* romper [mineral]. *4* embestir; oponerse, resistir. *5 intr.* dar un salto de carnero. *6 tr.-intr.* animar, animarse.

bucket (bo·kit) *s.* cubo, herrada, balde. *2* cangilón [de noria]; paleta [de rueda hidráulica]; cuchara [de excavadora, etc.].

buckle (bø·kol) *s.* hebilla. *2* alabeo.

buckle (to) *tr.* abrochar, enhebillar. *2* alabear. *3 intr.* alabearse. *4 to* ~ *for,* prepararse para; *to* ~ *to,* aplicarse a.

buckler (bø·klø^r) *s.* broquel, rodela, escudo.

buckram (-kram) *s.* zangala. *2* tiesura.

buckshot (-shat) *s.* posta [perdigón].

buckskin (-skin) *s.* ante [piel].

buckthorn (-zo^rn) *s.* BOT. espino cerval. *2* BOT. aladierna.

buckwheat (-juıt) *s.* BOT. alforfón.

bucolic (biuka·lik) *adj.* bucólico. *2 s.* bucólica [poema].

bud (bød) *s.* yema, botón, brote, pimpollo, capullo: *in the* ~, fig. en su principio.

bud (to) *intr.* brotar, pimpollecer, florecer. *2* empezar a desarrollarse. *3 tr.* injertar de escudete. ¶ Pret. y p. p.: *budded;* ger.: *budding.*

Buddha (bu·da) *n. pr.* Buda.

Buddhism (bu·dišm) *s.* budismo.

budding (bø·ding) *adj.* en capullo, en ciernes.

budge (bødÿ) *s.* piel de cordero [en peletería]. *2 adj.* grave, solemne, pomposo.

budge (to) *tr.* mover. *2 intr.* moverse, menearse.

budget (bø·dÿit) *s.* presupuesto. *2* saco [de noticias, etc.].

budget (to) *tr.-intr.* presuponer, presupuestar.

buff (bøf) *adj.* de ante, anteado. *2 s.* ante [piel].

buff (to) *tr.* pulir con ante. *2* parar [un golpe]; amortiguar [un choque].

buffalo (bø·falou) *s.* ZOOL. búfalo; su piel.

buffer (bø·fø^r) *s.* MEC. amortiguador [de choques]. *2* FERROC. tope.

buffet (bø·fit) *s.* bofetada, puñada. *2* embate. *3* aparador [mueble]. *4* ambigú. *5* bar [de estación, etc.]. *6* caja [de órgano].

buffet (to) (bø·fit) *tr.* abofetear, pegar. *2* batir, combatir, aporrear. *3 intr.* luchar [con].

buffing block *s.* FERROC. tope.

buffoon (bøfu·n) *s.* bufón, payaso. *2 adj.* bufón.

buffoonery (-øri) *s.* bufonada.

buffy (bø·fi) *adj.* anteado.

bug (bøg) *s.* insecto, bicho. *2* [Ingl.] chinche.

bugaboo (-abu), **bugbear** (-be^r) *s.* coco, bu, espantajo.

buggy (-i) *adj.* lleno de bichos. *2* pop. chiflado. *3 s.* especie de calesa.

bugle (biu·gøl) *s.* MIL. clarín, corneta. *2* MÚS. bugle. *3* BOT. consuelda menor. *4* cañutillo [abalorio]. *5* MÚS. ~ *horn,* cuerno de caza.

bugler (biu·glø^r) *s.* clarín, corneta, etc. [pers.].

bugloss (biu·glas) *s.* BOT. buglosa.

buhl (bul), **buhlwork** (-uø^rk) *s.* taracea, marquetería. *2* ~ *saw,* segueta.

build (bild) *s.* estructura. *2* forma, figura, talle.

build (to) *tr.* construir, edificar, labrar, erigir. *2* fabricar, crear. *3* fundar, cimentar. *4 intr. to* ~ *on,* o *upon,* contar con. ¶ Pret. y p. p.: *built.*

builder (-ø^r) *s.* constructor, edificador. *2* maestro de obras.

building (-ing) *s.* construcción, edificación. *2* edificio, casa, fábrica, obra.

built (bilt) *pret.* y *p. p.* de TO BUILD.

bulb (bølb) *s.* BOT., ZOOL. bulbo. *2* ELECT. bombilla.

3 bola o depósito [de termómetro o barómetro]. *4* pera de goma.

bulbous (-øs) *adj.* bulboso.

Bulgarian (bølgue·rian) *adj.-s.* búlgaro.

bulge (bø·ldÿ) *s.* protuberancia, pandeo, panza. *2* BILDE.

bulge (to) *intr.* hacer bulto; pandearse.

bulgy (-i) *adj.* abultado, prominente, pandeado.

bulk (bølk) *s.* bulto, volumen, tamaño, corpulencia. *2* mole, balumba. *3* la mayor parte, el grueso. *4* cabida [de un buque]. *5* COM. *in* ~, a granel, suelto.

bulk (to) *intr.* abultar, hacer bulto. *2* tener importancia.

bulkhead (-jed) *s.* mamparo.

bulky (-i) *adj.* abultado, voluminoso, macizo, pesado.

bull (bul) *s.* ZOOL. toro; ~ *ring*, plaza de toros. *2* ASTR. Tauro. *3* macho de algunos animales. *4* COM. alcista. *5* bula [pontificia]. *6* despropósito.

bull (to) *tr.* COM. *to* ~ *the market*, hacer subir la Bolsa.

bulla (bu·la) *s.* bula [sello].

bulbaiting (bu·lbeiting) *s.* lucha de perros y toros.

bulldog (-dog) *s.* perro dogo. *2* revólver de gran calibre.

bulldozer (bu·ldousø^r) *s.* valentón. *2* excavadora, buldozer.

bullet (bu·lit) *s.* bala [de fusil o pistola]. *2* plomo [de la caña de pescar].

bulletin (bu·løtin) *s.* boletín. *2* comunicado.

bullfight (bu·lfait) *s.* corrida de toros.

bullfighter (-ø^r) *s.* torero.

bullfighting (-ing) *s.* tauromaquia, toreo, toros.

bullfinch (bul·finch) *s.* ORN. pinzón real.

bullhead (-jed) *s.* ORN. chorlito. *2* fam. tonto, cabezota. *3* nombre de varios peces.

bullion (bu·liøn) *s.* oro o plata en barras. *2* pasamanería de oro o plata. *3* COM. metálico.

bullish (bu·lish) *adj.* disparatado. *2* en alza, alcista.

bullock (bu·løk) *s.* buey.

bull-roarer *s.* bramadera [juguete].

bull's-eye *s.* ARQ., MAR. ojo de buey. *2* diana [de un blanco]. *3* linterna sorda.

bully (bu·li) *s.* matón, valentón; el que maltrata a los débiles. *2* *adj.* fam. (E. U.) magnífico, excelente.

bully (to) *tr.* intimidar con gritos o amenazas; maltratar [a los débiles]. *2* *intr.* fanfarronear. ¶ Pret. y p. p.: *bullied*.

bulrush (bu·lrøsh) *s.* BOT. anea; junco.

bulwark (-ua^rk) *s.* baluarte. *2* rompeolas. *3* MAR. amurada.

bulwark (to) *tr.* abaluartar.

bum (bøm) *s.* (E. U.) juerga; jira. *2* (E. U.) vago, gorrón. *3* vulg. trasero.

bumbailif (bømbei·lif) *s.* alguacil.

bumblebee (bø·mbølbɪ) *s.* ENT. abejarrón, abejorro.

bump (bømp) *s.* choque, encontrón, coscorrón, porrazo, batacazo. *2* chichón. *3* protuberancia. *4* sacudida [del avión].

bump (to) *tr.-intr.* golpear; chocar [con], dar [contra].

bumper (-ø^r) *s.* lo que golpea. *2* parachoques. *3* FERROC. tope. *4* copa o vaso lleno.

bumpkin (-kin) *adj.* presuntuoso.

bumpy (bø·mpi) *adj.* abollado. *2* lleno de baches. *3* AVIA. agitado [aire].

bun (bøn) *s.* bollo [panecillo]. *2* moño, castaña. *3* rato [de conejo o liebre].

bunch (bønch) *s.* manojo, haz, mazo, ristra. *2* racimo. *3* macolla. *4* grupo, hato. *5* giba.

bunch (to) *tr.* juntar, amanojar, arracimar. *2* *intr.* juntarse, arracimarse.

buncombe (bø·ncøm) *s.* faramalla.

bundle (bø·ndøl) *s.* atado, manojo, mazo, haz. *2* bulto, envoltorio, paquete, lío, fajo.

bundle (to) *tr.* liar, atar, empaquetar, envolver: *to* ~ *up*, arropar. *2* tr.-intr. *to* ~ *off* o *out*, enviar, despedir precipitadamente; salir precipitadamente.

bung (bøng) *s.* tapón de tonel.

bung (to) *tr.* tapar [un tonel]. *2* tapar, obstruir.

bungalow (-alou) *s.* casita de una sola planta con veranda.

bungle (-øl) *s.* chapucería; torpeza.

bungle (to) *tr.* chafallar, estropear; hacer torpemente. *2* *intr.* obrar con torpeza.

bungler (-lø^r) *s.* chapucero.

bunion (bø·niøn) *s.* juanete [del pie].

bunk (bønk) *s.* tarima, litera [para dormir].

bunk (to) *tr.* dormir en litera. *2* acostarse.

bunker (bø·nkø^r) *s.* arcón. *2* MAR. carbonera. *3* GOLF hoyo de arena.

bunny (bø·ni) *s.* fam. conejito, ardilla.

bunt (bønt) *s.* MAR. bolsa [de red]; seno [de vela]. *2* empellón; topetazo. *3* (Ingl.) cola de conejo o liebre. *4* añubio, tizón.

bunt (to) *tr.* empellar; topetar.

bunting (-ing) *s.* lanilla [para banderas]. *2* empavesado. *3* nombre del hortelano y otros pájaros.

buntline (-lain) *s.* briol.

buoy (boi) *s.* boya, baliza.

buoy (to) *tr.* mantener a flote. *2* sostener, animar. *3* aboyar.

buoyancy (-ansi) *s.* propiedad de flotar. *2* fuerza ascensional. *3* elasticidad [del ánimo]; alegría, animación. *4* tendencia [de los precios, valores, etc.] a subir de nuevo.

buoyant (-ant) *adj.-s.* que flota o sostiene a flote. *2* elástico, ligero, alegre, animado, vivaz.

bur (bø^r) *s.* erizo [de castaña]. *2* carda [de cardencha]. *3* BOT. bardana, cadillo. *4* TEJ. mota, nudillo. *5* arandela [de lanza].

bur (to)) *tr.* TEJ. desmotar. ¶ Pret. y p. p.: *burred*; ger.: *-rring*.

burbot (bø·^rbøt) *s.* ICT. lota.

burden (bø·^rdøn) *s.* carga [que se transporta]. *2* fig. carga, peso, gravamen. *3* MAR. porte, tonelaje. *4* poét. estribillo. *5* tema, idea principal.

burden (to) *tr.* cargar, agobiar, gravar.

burdensome (-søm) *adj.* gravoso, pesado, agobiador.

burdock (bø·^rdak) *s.* BOT. bardana; cadillo.

bureau (biu·rou) *s.* escritorio [mesa]. *2* despacho, oficina; negociado, departamento.

bureaucracy (biura·krasi) *s.* burocracia.

bureaucrat (-kræt) *s.* burócrata.

burette (biure·t) *s.* bureta.

burg (bø^rg) *s.* BOROUGH.

burgeon (bø·^rÿøn) *s.* BOURGEON.

bourgeon (to) *intr.* TO BOURGEON.

burgess (bø·^rdÿis) *s.* burgués, ciudadano libre.

burgh (bø·^rg) *s.* municipio escocés.

burglar (bø·^rgla^r) *s.* ladrón [que roba con escalo].

burglary (-i) *s.* robo con escalo.

burgle (to) (bø·^rgøl) *intr.* robar con escalo.

burgomaster (bø·^rgomæstø^r) *s.* burgomaestre.

burgonet (bø·^rgonet) *s.* borgoñota.

Burgundy (bø·ʳgøndi) *n. pr.* Borgoña.
burial (bø·rial) *s.* entierro, sepelio.
burin (biu·rin) *s.* buril, cincel.
burl (bøʳl) *s.* TEJ. mota, nudillo. 2 CARP. nudo.
burl (to) *tr.* desmotar, despinzar.
burlap (bø·ʳlæp) *s.* harpillera.
burlesque (bø·ʳlesk) *adj.* burlesco.
burlesque (to) *tr.* parodiar, ridiculizar.
burly (bø·ʳli) *adj.* corpulento, fornido. 2 nudoso.
Burma (bø·ʳmæ) *n. pr.* GEOGR. Birmania.
Burmese (-ɪ·š) *adj.-s.* birmano.
burn (bøʳn) *s.* quemadura. 2 quema. 3 cocción [de ladrillos]. 4 (Esc.) riachuelo.
burn (to) *tr.* quemar, abrasar, incendiar, inflamar: *to ~ up,* quemar, consumir del todo: *to ~ the midnight oil,* quemarse las cejas. 2 quemar, abrasar [la lengua, el paladar, etc.]. 3 AGR. ahornagar. 4 cocer [ladrillos, etc.]. 5 calcinar. 6 hacer [quemando]. 7 cauterizar. 8 tostar, atezar. 9 *intr.* arder, quemarse, abrasarse. 10 encenderse, inflamarse. 11 *to ~ out,* pasarse [el fuego], quemarse [un fusible, motor, etc.]; fundirse [una bombilla]. ¶ Pret. y p. p.: *burned* o *burnt.*
burner (-øʳ) *s.* quemador. 2 mechero, piquera. 3 punta de soplete.
burnet (-ɪt) *s.* BOT. sanguisorba.
burning (-ing) *adj.* ardiente, encendido, abrasador. 2 ustorio. 3 vehemente. 4 urente.
burnish (bø·ʳnish) *s.* bruñido, pulimento.
burnish (to) *tr.* bruñir, pulir. 2 FOT. satinar.
burnisher (-øʳ) *s.* bruñidor, pulidor. 2 FOT. satinador.
burnous (bø·ʳnøs) *s.* albornoz.
burnt (bø·ʳnt) *prep.* y *p. p.* de *to* BURN.
burr (bøʳ) *s.* BUR. 2 piedra amoladera. 3 METEOR. halo. 4 DENT. buril. 5 METAL. rebaba. 6 zumbido, chirrido [de insecto]. 8 pronunciación gutural de la *r.*
burr (to) *tr.-intr.* pronunciar la *r* con sonido gutural.
burrow (bø·rou) *s.* madriguera, conejera. 2 galería, excavación.
burrow (to) *intr.-tr.* minar [como los conejos]. 2 *intr.* amadrigarse. 3 buscar, investigar.
burrstone (bø·ʳstoun) *s.* piedra de molino.
bursar (bø·ʳsaʳ) *s.* tesorero. 2 becario.
bursary (-i) *s.* tesorería. 2 beca.
burse (bøʳs) *s.* bolsa. 2 bolsa de corporales.
burst (bøʳst) *s.* explosión, estallido, reventón. 2 esfuerzo supremo. 3 ráfaga [de tiros].
burst (to) *intr.* reventar, estallar, volar, hacer explosión; romperse, abrirse. 2 aparecer, entrar, salir, etc., súbitamente o con violencia. 3 prorrumpir. 4 rebosar. 5 *tr.* reventar, romper, hacer estallar. ¶ Pret. y p. p.: *burst.*
bury (to) (be·ri) *tr.* enterrar. 2 sepultar. 3 soterrar; esconder, ocultar. ¶ Pret. y p. p.: *buried.*
burying (-ing) *s.* entierro.
bus (bøs) *s.* fam. ómnibus, autobús.
busby (bø·sbai) *s.* birretina.
bush (bush) *s.* arbusto, mata. 2 matorral, maleza. 3 ramo [de taberna]. 4 hopo [de zorra]. 5 BUSHING.
bush (to) *tr.* sostener o cubrir con matas. 2 MEC. guarnecer de buje, forro, etc. 3 *intr.* crecer espeso.
bushel (bu·shøl) *s.* medida para áridos.
bushhammer (-jæmøʳ) *s.* escoda.
bushing (-ing) *s.* MEC. buje, boquilla, casquillo, forro [de metal].
Bushman (-mæn) *s.* bosquimano.

bushy (-i) *adj.* matoso. 2 espeso, peludo.
busily (bi·šili) *adv.* activamente. 2 atareadamente.
business (bi·šnis) *s.* oficio, ocupación, quehacer, trabajo, asunto: *to mean ~,* obrar o hablar en serio; *mind your own ~,* no se meta en lo que no le importa. 2 negocio, comercio, tráfico. 3 negocio, casa, establecimiento, empresa.
businesslike (-laik) *adj.* metódico, ordenado. 2 práctico, expeditivo. 3 formal, directo.
busk (bøsk) *s.* ballena o hierro [de corsé].
buskin (bø·skin) *s.* borceguí. 2 coturno.
busman (bø·smæn) *s.* conductor de autobús.
buss (bøs) *s.* beso, beso sonoro.
bust (bøst) *s.* busto. 2 pop. fracaso. 3 pop. borrachera.
bust (to) *tr.* pop. reventar, romper. 2 *tr.-intr.* (E.U.) arruinar, arruinarse.
bustard (bø·staʳd) *s.* ORN. avutarda; sisón.
bustle (bø·søl) *s.* movimiento, agitación, bullicio; diligencia oficiosa. 2 polisón.
bustle (to) *tr.-intr.* bullir, menearse, no parar.
bustler (bø·stløʳ) *s.* bullebulle.
busy (bi·ši) *adj.* ocupado, atareado. 2 activo, diligente. 3 bullicioso, entrometido.
busy (to) *tr.* ocupar, emplear; atarear. 2 *ref.* ocuparse, atarearse. ¶ Pret. y p. p.: *busied.*
busybody (-badi) *s.* entremetido, fisgón, chismoso.
but (bøt) *prep.-conj.* excepto, fuera de, menos, sino: *last ~ one,* el penúltimo; *no one ~ you,* nadie sino usted. 2 *conj.* pero, empero, mas. 3 que no, sin que, que. 4 *I cannot ~,* no puedo menos de, no puedo dejar de. 5 *adv.* sólo, no más que. 6 *all ~,* casi, por poco. 7 *~ for,* a no ser por. 8 *s.* pero [objeción, dificultad].
butane (biu·tein) *s.* butano.
butcher (bu·chøʳ) *s.* carnicero. 2 matarife. 3 hombre sanguinario.
butcher (to) *tr.-intr.* matar, sacrificar [reses]. 2 fig. matar cruelmente, asesinar.
butcherly (-li) *adj.* de carnicero. 2 sanguinario, salvaje.
butchery (-i) *s.* matadero. 2 oficio de carnicero. 3 matanza, carnicería.
butler (bø·tløʳ) *s.* mayordomo; despensero.
butlery (-i) *s.* despensa.
butt (but) *s.* extremo o cabo grueso; culata, mocho, mango. 2 cepa; tocón [de árbol]. 3 colilla [de cigarro]. 4 terrero, blanco [de tiro]. 5 pipa, tonel. 6 ESGR. estocada. 7 topetada. 8 límite, término.
butt (to) *tr.-intr.* topetar, acornear; topar. 2 *tr.* apoyar [en]. 3 MEC. juntar a tope. 4 *intr. to ~ in* o *into,* entrometerse; *to ~ out,* salir, sobresalir.
butte (but) *s.* mota, colina aislada.
butter (bø·tøʳ) *s.* manteca [de leche o vegetal]. 2 pasta, mermelada.
butter (to) *tr.* untar con manteca o mantequilla. 2 fam. adular.
buttercup (-køp) *s.* BOT. botón de oro.
butterfly (-flai) *s.* ENT. mariposa.
butterine (-in) *s.* margarina.
buttery (bø·tøri) *s.* despensa. 2 *adj.* mantecoso. 3 fam. adulador, zalamero.
buttock (bo·tøk) *s.* nalga. 2 *pl.* trasero, posaderas.
button (bø·tøn) *s.* botón [de vestido, de florete]. 2 botón, tirador, pulsador. 3 BOT. botón, capullo. 4 ARTILL. cascabel. 5 *pl.* botones [criadito].
button (to) *tr.* abotonar. 2 ESGR. dar un botonazo a. 3 *intr.* abotonarse.
buttonhole (-jout) *s.* ojal, presilla.

buttonhole (to) *tr.* ojalar. *2* asir por la solapa [para obligar a escuchar].

buttonhook (-juk) *s.* abotonador.

buttress (bø·tris) *s.* ARQ. contrafuerte, estribo, machón, arbotante. *2* fig. apoyo, sostén.

buttress (to) *tr.* estribar, sostener.

butyric (biuti·ric) *adj.* butírico.

buxom (bø·ksøm) *adj.* lozana, garrida.

buy (to) (bai) *tr.* comprar, mercar: *to ~ off,* librarse de [con dinero]; comprar [a uno]; *to ~ out,* comprar la parte de un socio o el negocio de un competidor. *2* comprar, sobornar. *3 intr.* comprar, hacer compras. ¶ Pret. y p. p.: *bought.*

buyer (-ø^r) *s.* comprador.

buzz (bøš) *s.* zumbido, susurro, murmullo.

buzz (to) *intr.* zumbar, susurrar, murmurar. *2* circular [un rumor]. *3* moverse, andar.

buzzard (bø·ša^rd) *s.* ORN. alfaneque; dardabasi.

buzzer (bø·šø^r) *s.* zumbador.

by (bai) *prep.* junto a, cerca de, al lado de, cabe. *2* por [indicando lugar del movimiento o de la acción; agente, causa; modo, medio]. *3* de [hecho de; nacido de]. *4* a, con, de, en, por, etc. [expresando relaciones varias]: *~ day,* de día; *~ degrees,* por grados; *~ dint of,* a fuerza de; *~ far,* con mucho; *~ the dozen,* por docenas; *~ train,* en tren, por tren; *~ oneself,* solo, sin ayuda; *~ itself,* de por sí; *one ~ one,* de uno en uno. *5 ~*

and ~, pronto, luego. *6 ~ the bye, ~ the way,* de paso, entre paréntesis, a propósito. *7 adj.* lateral, apartado; secundario. *8 adv.* cerca, al lado, por el lado. *9* aparte; *to put ~,* guardar, ahorrar.

by-blow (-blou) *s.* golpe indirecto; accidente imprevisto.

bye *s.* cosa secundaria. *2 adj.* BY 7.

by-election *s.* elección parcial.

bygone (bai·gon) *adj.* pasado. *2 s.* lo pasado; *let bygones be bygones,* olvidemos lo pasado.

by-lane *s.* sendero o camino apartado.

by-law (-lo) *s.* reglamento, ordenanzas, estatutos.

by-name (-neim) *s.* sobrenombre, apodo.

bypass (-pæs) *s.* camino o canal de derivación; desvío. *2* MEC. Y ELECT. derivación.

bypath (-pæz) *s.* vereda, atajo.

byplay (-plei) *s.* TEAT. escena muda; juego escénico.

by-product *adj.* subproducto, derivado.

bystander (-stændø^r) *s.* espectador, el que está presente. *2 pl.* circunstantes.

by-street *s.* callejuela, travesía.

byway (-uei) *s.* camino desviado.

byword (-uø^r) *s.* objeto de burla u oprobio. *2* apodo. *3* dicho, refrán.

Byzantine (bizæ·ntin) *adj.-s.* bizantino.

Byzantium (baišæ·nshiøn) *n. pr.* Bizancio.

C

C, c (sɪ) *s.* C, c, tercera letra del alfabeto inglés. *2* MÚS. do.

cab (kæb) *s.* cabriolé. *2* coche de punto; taxi. *3* cabina [de maquinista de tren o de conductor de camión].

cabal (kabæ·l) *s.* cábala, intriga. *2* camarilla.

cabal (to) *intr.* intrigar, maquinar. ¶ Pret. y p. p.: *caballed;* ger.: *-lling.*

cabala (kæ·bala) *s.* cábala [de los judíos].

cabalistic(al (kæbali·stik(al) *adj.* cabalístico.

caballer (kabæ·lǿ^r) *s.* maquinador.

cabaret (kæbarei·) *s.* cabaret, café o restaurante con atracciones. *2* taberna.

cabbage (kæ·bidȳ) *s.* BOT. col, berza, repollo. *2* COC. coles.

cabbage (to) *intr.* repollar.

cabby (kæ·bi) *s.* CABMAN.

cabin (kæ·bin) *s.* cabaña, choza. *2* MAR. cámara, camarote: ~ *boy,* grumete; camarero. *3* cabina [de avión].

cabin (to) *intr.* vivir en cabaña o choza. *2* tr. encerrar en cabaña o parte estrecha.

cabinet (kæ·binit) *s.* gabinete [ministerio; colección; aposento]. *2* bargueño, armario, vitrina, escaparate. *3* mueble [de un aparato de radio]. *4* IMPR. chibalete. *5 adj.* ministerial. *6* de gabinete. *7* privado, confidencial.

cabinetmaker (-meikǿ^r) *s.* ebanista.

cabinetmaking (-meiking), **cabinetwork** (-uǿ^rk) *s.* ebanistería.

cable (kei·bǿl) *s.* cable, maroma. *2* TELEGR. cable; cablegrama: ~ *address,* dirección cablegráfica. *3 cable's length,* cable [medida].

cable (to) *tr.* cablegrafiar.

cablegram (-græm) *s.* cablegrama.

cabman (kæ·bmæn) *s.* cochero de punto; taxista.

caboodle (kabu·dǿl) *s.* (E.U.) *the whole* ~, todo el hato.

caboose (kabu·s) *s.* MAR. fogón, cocina. *2* FERROC. (E.U.) furgón de cola.

cabotage (kæ·bǿtidȳ) *s.* MAR. cabotaje.

cabriolet (kæbriolei·) *s.* cabriolé.

cacao (kaka·ou) *s.* cacao [árbol, semilla].

cachalot (kæ·shalat) *s.* ZOOL. cachalote.

cache (kæsh) *s.* escondite, escondrijo.

cache (to) *tr.* esconder.

cachet (kæshei·) *s.* FARM. sello.

cachexia (kæke·ksia) *s.* caquexia.

cachinnation (kækinei·shøn) *s.* risotada.

cacique (kasɪ·k) *s.* cacique [indio].

cackle (kæ·kǿl) *s.* cacareo, cloqueo. *2* risa parecida a un cloqueo. *3* cháchara.

cackle (to) *intr.* cacarear, cloquear. *2* reirse. *3* chacharear.

cackler (kæ·klǿ^r) *s.* cacareador. *2* chismoso; parlanchín.

cackling (-ing) *s.* CACKLE. *2* graznido.

cacodyl (kæ·kodil) *s.* QUÍM. cacodilo.

cacodylate (-eit) *s.* QUÍM. cacodilato.

cacomistle (kæ·kǿmisøl) *s.* ZOOL. cacomiztle, basáride.

cacophony (kæka·føni) *s.* cacofonía.

cactaceous (kæktei·shøs) *adj.* BOT. cactáceo.

cactus (kæ·ktøs) *s.* cacto.

cad (kæd) *s.* canalla, grosero, malcriado.

cadastre, -ter (kadæ·stǿ^r) *s.* catastro.

cadaver (kadæ·vø^r) *s.* cadáver.

cadaveric (kadave·rik), **cadaverous** (kadæ·vørøs) *adj.* cadavérico.

caddie (kæ·di) *s.* hombre o muchacho que lleva las mazas de los jugadores de golf.

caddis (-dis) *s.* jerguilla.

caddish (-dish) *adj.* grosero, mal criado.

caddy (-di) *s.* lata o cajita para el té. *2* CADDIE.

cade (keid) *adj.* manso, favorito [animal]. *2 s.* BOT. enebro.

cadence (kei·døns) *s.* cadencia. *2* ritmo. *3* modulación.

cadenced (-t) *adj.* cadencioso, rítmico.

cadent (kei·dønt) *adj.* caliente. *2* cadencioso.

cadenza (kade·nša) *s.* MÚS. cadencia.

cadet (kade·t) *s.* hijo o hermano menor. *2* cadete.

cadge (to) (kædȳ) *tr.-intr.* mendigar, gorronear.

cadi (ka·di o kei·di) *s.* cadí.

cadmium (kæ·dmiøm) *s.* QUÍM. cadmio.

cadre (ka·dǿ^r) *s.* armazón. *2* cuadro [de oficiales].

caduceus (kadiu·siøs) *s.* caduceo.

caducity (kadiu·siti) *s.* caducidad. *2* caduquez.

caducous (kadiu·køs) *adj.* caduco.

caecal (sɪ·kal) *adj.* cecal.

caecum (sɪ·køm) *s.* intestino ciego.

Caesar (sɪ·šø^r) *n. pr.* César.

Caesarean (-še·rian) *adj.* cesáreo.

Caesarism (sɪ·šørišm) *s.* cesarismo.

caesium (sɪ·šiøm) *s.* QUÍM. cesio.

caesura (siȳu·ra) *s.* cesura.

cafe (kæfei·) *s*. café [establecimiento].
cafeteria (kæføti·ria) *s*. restaurante o café de autoservicio.
caffein(e (kæ·fiin) *s*. QUÍM. cafeína.
caftan (kæ·ftan) *s*. caftán.
cage (keiŷ) *s*. jaula. *2* camarín [de ascensor].
cage (to) *tr*. enjaular.
cageling (·ling) *s*. ave enjaulada.
Caiaphas (kai·afas) *n. pr*. Caifás.
caique (kar·k) *s*. caique.
cagey (kei·dŷi) *adj*. ladino, zorro.
cairn (keʳn) *s*. montón de piedras que sirve de señal.
caisson (kei·søn) *s*. cajón de municiones. *2* ARTILL. armón, furgón. *3* ING. cajón hidráulico. *4* MAR. camello. *5* ARQ. artesón.
caitiff (kei·tif) *adj*. ruin, cobarde. *2 s*. miserable, canalla.
cajole (to) (kadŷou·l) *tr*. engatusar, enlabiar, persuadir con halagos.
cajoler (·øʳ) *s*. engatusador, zalamero.
cajolery (·i) *s*. engatusamiento. *2* halago, zalamerías.
cake (keik) *s*. galleta, bizcocho, torta, pastel, bollo. *2* pastilla, pan [de jabón, cera, etc.].
cake (to) *intr*. hacerse una pasta, una masa dura, una costra.
cakewalk (·wøk) *s*. cake-walk.
calaba (kæ·laba) *s*. calambuco.
calabash (kæ·labæsh) *s*. BOT. calabaza vinatera, güira. *2* vasija hecha de calabaza.
Calabrian (kælei·brian) *adj.-s*. calabrés.
calamary (kæ·lameri) *s*. ZOOL. calamar.
calamine (kæ·lamain) *s*. calamina.
calamint (kæ·lamint) *s*. BOT. calaminta.
calamitous (kalæ·mitøs) *adj*. calamitoso.
calamity (·miti) *s*. calamidad. *2* desgracia, infortunio.
calamus (kæ·lamøs) *s*. BOT. ácoro.
calander (kalæ·ndøʳ) *s*. ORN. calandria.
calash (kalæ·sh) *s*. calesa, carretela. *2* capota [de coche, de señora].
calcaneum (kalkei·niøm) *s*. ANAT. calcáneo.
calcareous (kælke·riøs) *adj*. calcáreo.
calceate (kæ·lsieit), calced (kælst) *adj*. calzado [religioso].
calceolaria (kælsiøle·ria) *s*. calceolaria.
calcic (kæ·lsik) *adj*. cálcico.
calcify (to) (kæ·lsifai) *tr*. calcificar. *2 intr*. calcificarse. ¶ Pret. y p. p.: *calcified*.
calcination (·shøn) *s*. calcinación.
calcine (to) (kæ·lsin) *tr*. calcinar. *2 intr*. calcinarse.
calcium (kæ·lsiøm) *s*. calcio.
calculable (kæ·lkiulabøl) *adj*. calculable.
calculate (to) (·leit) *tr*. calcular. *2* [esp. en p. p.] adaptar a un fin. *3 intr*. hacer cálculos. *4* contar [con]; confiar [en o que].
calculating (·ing) *adj*. calculador.
calculation (·ei·shøn) *s*. calculación, cálculo.
calculator (·tøʳ) *s*. calculador, calculista. *2* máquina calculadora.
calculose (kæ·lkiulous) *adj*. calculoso.
calculus (·løs) *s*. MAT., MED. cálculo.
caldron (ko·ldrøn) *s*. caldera, caldero, paila.
calendar (kæ·lindaʳ) *s*. calendario, almanaque. *2* lista de asuntos. *3* santoral.
calendar (to) *tr*. poner en el calendario. *2* poner en lista [para ser juzgado, discutido, etc.].
calender (kæ·lindøʳ) *s*. calandria [máquina]. *2* derviche mendicante.
calender (to) *tr*. calandrar.

calends (kæ·lindš) *s. pl*. calendas.
calf (kaf), calves (kavš) *s*. ZOOL. becerro, ternero, becerra, ternera. *2* fam. bobo. *3* pantorrilla.
calfskin (ka·fskin) *s*. becerro [piel].
caliber (kæ·libøʳ) *s*. CALIBRE.
calibrate (to) (·breit) *tr*. calibrar, graduar.
calibration (·brei·shøn) *s*. calibración, graduación.
calibre (kæ·libøʳ) *s*. calibre. *2* capacidad, aptitud.
calicie (kæ·likøl) *s*. calículo.
calico (kæ·licou) *s*. calicó, indiana.
calif, califate, CALIPH, CALIPHATE.
Californian (kalifoʳnian) *adj.-s*. californiano, californico, calofornio.
caliga (kæ·liga) *s*. cáliga.
caliginous (kæli·dŷinøs) *adj*. caliginoso.
caliper (kæ·lipøʳ) o *pl*. calipers *s*. compás de calibres o de espesores. *2* pie de rey.
caliph (kei·lif) *s*. califa.
caliphate (kæ·lifeit) *s*. califato.
calisthenics (kælisze·niks) *s*. calistenia.
calix *s*. CALYX.
calk (kok) *s*. ramplón [de herradura]. *2* hierro [para zapatos].
calk (to) *tr*. proveer de ramplones. *2* herrar [zapatos]. *3* calcar [un dibujo]. *4* TO CAULK.
call (kol) *s*. llamada, llamamiento. *2* citación, convocación. *3* toque, grito, etc., de señal o llamada. *4* CAZA reclamo, chilla. *5* llamada o conversación telefónica. *6* grito [de ave o animal]. *7* demanda, exigencia. *8* obligación, derecho, motivo. *9* visita [que se hace]; escala [de un buque]. *10* declaración [en el bridge]. *11 adj*. de llamada, que llama: ~ *boy*, botones; TEAT. avisador.
call (to) *tr*. llamar [dar voces a, hacer venir, atraer, etc.]. *2* convocar. *3* anunciar, proclamar, pregonar. *4* invocar, apelar a. *5* llamar [al que duerme]. *6* pasar lista. *7* llamar, apellidar, denominar, tratar de. *8 to* ~ *attention to*, llamar la atención sobre. *9 to* ~ *down*, hacer bajar; fam. censurar, reprender. *10 to* ~ *forth*, hacer salir; poner de manifiesto o en acción. *11 to* ~ *names*, insultar de palabra. *12 to* ~ *off*, llamar a otra parte; aplazar, suspender. *13 to* ~ *out*, llamar [desde afuera]; desafiar; evocar. *14 to* ~ *to account*, pedir cuentas; reprender. *15 to* ~ *to order*, llamar al orden; abrir la sesión. *16 to* ~ *up*, hacer subir, hacer surgir; evocar, recordar; poner a debate; llamar por teléfono.
17 intr. gritar, dar voces. *18* hacer una visita; detenerse [en]; MAR. hacer escala [en]. *19 to* ~ *for*, pedir, exigir, requerir, necesitar.
calla (kæ·la) *s*. cala, lirio de agua.
caller (ko·løʳ) *s*. llamador [pers.]. *2* visita, visitante.
calligrapher (kæli·graføʳ) *s*. calígrafo.
calligraphy (kæli·grafi) *s*. caligrafía.
calling (ko·ling) *s*. profesión, oficio, ministerio. *2* visita, visiteo. *3* llamamiento.
Calliope (kælai·api) *s*. MIT. Calíope.
calliper (kæ·lipøʳ) *s*. CALIPER.
callisthenics (kælisze·niks) *s*. calistenia.
callosity (kæla·siti) *s*. callosidad, callo.
callous (kæ·løs) *adj*. calloso. *2* fig. duro, insensible.
callousness (·nis) *s*. CALLOSITY. *2* fig. dureza, insensibilidad.
callow (kæ·lou) *adj*. implume. *2* joven, inexperto.
callus (kæ·løs) *s*. callo, dureza.
calm (kam) *s*. calma, sosiego. *2* serenidad, sangre

fría. *3* MAR. calma. *4 adj.* en calma, sosegado; tranquilo, sereno.
calm (to) *tr.* calmar, sosegar, tranquilizar, apaciguar. *2 intr.* calmar[se, sosegarse, abonanzar. | Gralte. con *down.*
calmative (-ativ) *adj.*-*s.* calmante.
calmness (-nis) *s.* CALM.
calmy (-i) *adj.* poét. tranquilo, apacible.
calomel (kæ·lomel) *s.* calomelanos.
caloric (kalo·rik) *adj.*-*s.* calórico.
calorie (kæ·lori) *s.* caloría.
calorific (kæløri·fik) *adj.* calorífico.
calory (kæ·løri) *s.* caloría.
calotte (kæla·t) *s.* casquete, gorro. *2* solideo.
caltrop (kæ·ltrøp) *s.* BOT., MIL. abrojo.
calumet (kæ·liumet) *s.* pipa de los indios de Norteamérica.
calumniate (to) (kalømnieit) *tr.* calumniar.
calumniatio (-ei·shon) *s.* calumnia.
calumniator (kalømnietø͏ʳ) *s.* calumniador.
calumnious (-mniøs) *adj.* calumnioso.
calumny (kæ·lømni) *s.* calumnia.
Calvary (kæ·lvari) *n. pr.* Calvario.
calve (to) (kæv) *intr.* parir [la vaca].
Calvinism (kæ·lvinišm) *s.* calvinismo.
Calvinist (-ist) *s.* calvinista.
calvities (kælvɪ·shiis) *s.* calvicie.
calycle (kæ·likøl) *s.* calículo.
calyx (kei·liks) *s.* BOT. cáliz. *2* ANAT. pelvis [del riñón].
cam (kæm) *s.* MEC. cama, leva, levador.
camail (kamei·l) *s.* almófar.
camaraderie (kamara·døri) *s.* camaradería.
camber (kæ·mbøʳ) *s.* comba, curvatura, bombeo.
camber (to) *tr.* combar, arquear. *2 intr.* combarse, arquearse.
cambist (kæ·mbist) *s.* cambista.
cambium (kæ·mbiom) *s.* BOT. cambium.
cambric (kei·mbrik) *s.* cambray, batista.
came (keim) *pret.* de TO COME.
camel (kæ·møl) *s.* ZOOL., MAR. camello.
camellia (kamɪ·lia) *s.* camelia.
cameo (kæ·miou) *s.* camafeo.
camera (kæ·møra) *s.* despacho particular del juez. *2* cámara apostólica. *3* ANAT. cámara. *4* máquina fotográfica. *5* ~ *lucida,* cámara clara o lúcida; ~ *obscura,* cámara oscura.
cameraman (-mæn) *s.* operador de tomavistas, operador cinematográfico.
Cameroons (kæ·møruninš) *n. pr.* GEOGR. Camerún.
Camillus (kami·løs) *n. pr.* Camilo.
camion (kæ·miøn) *s.* camión, carro bajo y fuerte.
camisado (kæmisei·dou) *s.* MIL. encamisada.
camisole (kæ·misoul) *s.* camiseta, cubrecorsé.
camlet (kæ·mlit) *s.* camelote [tela].
camomile (kæ·momail) *s.* BOT. camomila, manzanilla.
camouflage (kæ·møflaỹ) *s.* camuflaje.
camouflage (to) *tr.* camuflar.
camp (kæmp) *s.* campamento. *2* ranchería. *3* MIL. campo. *4* servicio o vida militar. *5 adj.* ~ *bed,* lecho de campaña; ~ *chair,* silla de tijera.
camp (to) *tr.*-*intr.* acampar.
campaign (kæmpei·n) *s.* campaña [militar, política, etc.].
campaign (to) *intr.* salir a campaña. *2* hacer campaña o propaganda.
campaigner (-ø͏ʳ) *s.* veterano. *2* propagandista.
campanile (kæmpanɪ·li) *s.* campanil, campanario.
campanula (-pæ·niula) *s.* BOT. campánula.
campanulaceous (-ei·shøs) *adj.* campanuláceo.

campeachy-wood (kæmpɪ·chi) *s.* palo campeche.
camper (kæ·mpøʳ) *s.* acampador.
campfire (-faiʳ) *s.* fuego u hoguera de campamento.
camphor (kæ·mføʳ) *s.* alcanfor; ~ *tree,* alcanforero.
camphor, camphorate (to) (-eit) *tr.* alcanforar.
camping (kæ·mping) *s.* campamento.
campus (kæ·mpøs) *s.* (E.U) patio, jardín, recinto [de una universidad].
camshaft (kæ·mshæft) *s.* MEC. árbol de levas.
can (kæn) *s.* vaso, jarro, bote, lata [de metal]: ~ *opener,* abrelatas.
can *aux.* poder o saber [hacer una cosa]. ¶ Pret. y cond.: *could.* | Sólo se usa con las formas *can* y *could* en el presente y pretérito del indicativo o subjuntivo y en el condicional.
can (to) *tr.* enlatar, conservar en latas. ¶ Pret. y p. p.: *canned;* ger.: -*nning.*
Canaanite (kei·nanait) *adj.*-*s.* cananeo.
Canadian (kanei·dian) *adj.*-*s.* canadiense.
canal (kanæ·l) *s.* canal; acequia. *2* ANAT. canal, conducto, tubo. *3* ARQ. canal, estría.
canalization (kanæliši·shøn) *s.* canalización.
canalize (to) (kanæ·laiš) *tr.* canalizar.
canapé (kanapei) *s.* canapé [de caviar, etc.].
canary (kane·ri) *s.* ORN. canario. *2* color de canario. *3* vino de Canarias.
Canary Islands *n. pr.* Islas Canarias.
canasta (kænæ·sta) *s.* canasta [juego].
cancel (kæ·nsøl) *s.* cancelación. *2* IMPR. supresión. *3* MÚS. becuadro.
cancel (to) *tr.* cancelar. *2* rescindir. *3* neutralizar. *4* borrar, tachar. *5* inutilizar [un sello]. *6* MÚS. poner becuadro. *7* IMPR. suprimir. *8* MAT. eliminar. ¶ Pret. y p. p.: *canceled* o -*lled;* ger.: *canceling* o -*lling.*
cancellate (-lit) *adj.* BIOL. reticular.
cancer (kæ·nsør) *s.* MED. cáncer. *2* [con may.] ASTR. Cáncer.
cancerate (to) (-eit) *intr.* cancerarse.
cancerous (-øs) *adj.* canceroso.
cancroid (kæ·nkroid) *adj.* cancroideo. *2 s.* cancroide.
candelabrum (kændølei·brøm) *s.* candelabro.
candent (kæ·ndønt), **candescent** (kænde·sønt) *adj.* candente.
candid (kæ·ndid) *adj.* franco, sincero. *2* imparcial. *3* cándido, ingenuo.
candidate (-eit) *s.* candidato. *2* aspirante, pretendiente. *3* graduando.
candidature (-dachoøʳ), **candidacy** (-si) *s.* candidatura [aspiración, propuesta].
candidness (kæ·ndidnis) *s.* sinceridad, franqueza. *2* candor, ingenuidad.
candied (kæ·ndid) *pret.* y *p. p.* de TO CANDY. *2* confitado, escarchado, garapiñado.
candle (kæ·ndøl) *s.* vela, bujía; candela. *2* Fís. bujía.
candleholder (-jouldøʳ) *s.* candelero.
candlelight (-lait) *s.* luz de vela; luz artificial.
Candlemas (-mas) *s.* Candelaria [fiesta].
candlestick (-stik) *s.* candelero; palmatoria.
candlewick (-wik) *s.* pábilo.
cando(u)r (kæ·ndøʳ) *s.* candor, sinceridad, franqueza. *2* imparcialidad.
candy (kæ·ndi) *s.* azúcar cande. *2* dulce, bombón, confite, caramelo.
candy (to) *tr.* confitar, escarchar, garapiñar. *2* endulzar. *3 intr.* cubrirse de azúcar cristalizado. ¶ Pret. y p. p.: *candied.*
cane (kein) *s.* BOT. caña, rota, junco [de Indias];

bejuco; caña de azúcar. *2* bastón; ~ *stand*, bastonera.
cane (to) *tr.* bastonear. *2* poner asiento de rejilla a.
canephorus (kæne·forøs) *s.* canéfora.
Canicula (kani·kiula) *n. pr.* ASTR. Canícula, Sirio.
canicular (-ʳ) *adj.* canicular.
canid (kæ·nid) *s.* ZOOL. cánido.
canine (kæ·nain) *adj.-s.* canino.
canister (kæ·nistøʳ) *s.* bote, lata [para té, tabaco, etc.].
canker (kæ·nkøʳ) *s.* úlcera maligna. *2* BOT. cancro. *3* fig. cáncer [lo que corroe].
canker (to) *tr.* ulcerar, gangrenar. *2* cancerar, corromper. *3 intr.* cancerarse, corromperse. *4* agriarse [el carácter, etc.].
cankerous (-øs) *adj.* maligno, gangrenoso, corrosivo.
canna (kæ·na) *s.* BOT. cañacoro.
cannaceous (canei·shøs) *adj.* canáceo.
canned (kænd) *adj.* en conserva, en lata.
cannery (kæ·nøri) *s.* fábrica de conservas.
cannibal (kæ·nibal) *adj.-s.* caníbal.
cannibalism (-išm) *s.* canibalismo.
cannikin (kæ·nikin) *s.* vaso de metal. *2* cubo, balde.
cannon (kæ·non) *s.* ARTILL. cañón; cañones, artillería: ~ *fodder*, carne de cañón. *2* MEC. manguito. *3* caña [de cuadrúpedo]. *4* BILLAR carambola.
cannonade (-ei·d) *s.* cañoneo.
cannonade (to) *tr.* cañonear.
cannoneer (-iøʳ) *s.* artillero.
cannot (kæ·nat) forma compuesta de *can* y *not.*
cannula (kæ·niula) *s.* cánula.
canny (kæ·ni) *adj.* sagaz, prudente, cuerdo. *2* cómodo. *3* agradable. *4* apuesto.
canoe (kanu·) *s.* canoa; piragua.
canon (kæ·nøn) *s.* canónigo. *2* canon, regla. *3* ECLES., LITURG., MÚS. canon. *4* IMPR. canon. *5* ~ *law*, derecho canónico.
canoness (-is) *s.* canonesa.
canonic (kana·nik) *adj.* canónico.
canonical (-al) *adj.* canónico. *2* canonical. *3* aceptado, establecido.
canonicals (-als) *s. pl.* vestiduras sacerdotales.
canonicate (-eit) *s.* canonicado, canonjía.
canonist (kæ·nønist) *s.* canonista.
canonization (-iøei·shøn) *s.* canonización.
canonize (to) (-aiš) *tr.* canonizar.
canonry (-ri) *s.* CANONICATE.
canopy (kæ·nøpi) *s.* dosel, baldaquino, palio, pabellón. *2* doselete. *3* bóveda [del cielo].
canopy (to) *tr.* endoselar. ¶ Pret. y p. p.: *canopied.*
canorous (kanou·røs) *adj.* canoro.
can't (kænt) contr. de *can* y *not.*
cant (kænt) *s.* canto, esquina, sesgo. *3* bisel. *4* tumbo, vaivén. *5* jerga, jerigonza. *6* lenguaje gazmoño, hipocresía. *7 adj.* inclinado, sesgado. *8* de una jerga. *9* gazmoño, hipócrita.
cant (to) *tr.* inclinar, ladear; volcar. *2* arrojar, lanzar. *3 intr.* inclinarse, volcarse. *4* hablar en jerga o con gazmoñería.
cantankerous (kæntæ·nkørøs) *adj.* avinagrado, intratable,quisquilloso.
cantata (kænta·ta) *s.* cantata.
canteen (kænti·n) *s.* cantimplora [frasco]. *2* cantina, taberna.
canter (kæ·ntøʳ) *s.* medio galope.
canter (to) *intr.* ir a medio galope.
Canterbury (kæntøʳbe·ri) *n. pr.* GEOGR. Cantórbery. *2* BOT. ~ *bell*, farolillo.
cantharides (kænzæ·ridiš) *s.* cantáridas.

canticle (kæ·ntikøl) *s.* cántico.
cantilever (kæantile·vøʳ) *s.* ARQ. modillón, cónsola. *2* ~ *bridge*, puente de contrapeso.
cantle (kæ·ntøl) *s.* pedazo, porción. *2* borrén o arzón trasero.
canton (kæ·ntøn) *s.* cantón, distrito. *2* BLAS. cantón.
canton (to) *tr.* acantonar, acuartelar.
cantonal (-al) *adj.* cantonal.
cantonment (-mønt) *s.* acantonamiento; cuartel, campamento.
cantor (kæ·ntøʳ) *s.* chantre.
canvas (kæ·nvas) *s.* lona. *2* cañamazo. *3* vela, velamen. *4* PINT. lienzo.
canvass *s.* recorrido en busca de votos, pedidos, etc. *2* examen, discusión.
canvass (to) *tr.-intr.* recorrer una población o distrito en busca de votos, pedidos, etc. *2 tr.* examinar, discutir.
canvasser (-øʳ) *s.* el que solicita votos, pedidos, etc.; agente electoral; corredor.
canyon (kæ·niøn) *s.* GEOGR. (E.U.) cañón, hondonada.
canzonet (kænšøne·t) *s.* cancioncilla.
caoutchouc (kau·chuk) *s.* caucho.
cap (kæp) *s.* gorra; gorro; cofia; birrete; bonete; capelo: *to set one's* ~ *at*, querer conquistar para novio. *2* cima, cumbre. *3* MEC. casquete, casquillo, sombrerete. *4* tapa [de ciertas cosas]. *5* cápsula [de botella o para fulminante]. *6* caballete [de chimenea]. *7* chapa [de brújula]. *8* GEOM. casquete. *9* sombrero [de seta].
cap (to) *tr.* cubrir [la cabeza]. *2* poner tapa, casquillo, cápsula, etc., a. *3* cubrir, coronar, acabar. *4* sobrepujar. *5 tr.-intr.* saludar descubriéndose. ¶ Pret. y p. p.: *capped;* ger.: *capping.*
capability (keipabi·liti) *s.* capacidad, aptitud.
capable (kei·pabøl) *s.* capaz [de hacer algo]. *2* susceptible [de]. *3* capaz, apto, competente.
capacious (kapei·shøs) *adj.* capaz, espacioso.
capaciousness (-nis) *s.* espaciosidad, anchura.
capacitate (to) (kapæ·siteit) *tr.* capacitar.
capacity (-iti) *s.* capacidad. *2* facultad, poder, posibilidad. *3* calidad, condición: *in the* ~ *of*, en calidad de. *4* DER. competencia.
cap-a-pie (kæpapɪ·) *adv.* de pies a cabeza; de punta en blanco.
caparison (kapæ·rišøn) *s.* caparazón, gualdrapa.
caparison (to) *tr.* engualdrapar, enjaezar. *2* vestir ricamente.
cape (keip) *s.* capotillo, capa corta. *2* esclavina, manteleta. *3* cabo, promontorio. *4* *n. pr. Cape Town*, Ciudad del Cabo.
capelin (kæ·pølin) *s.* ICT. capelán.
capeline *s.* ARM., CIR. capellina.
caper (kei·pøʳ) *s.* cabriola, zapateta; travesura. *2* BOT. alcaparro; alcaparra.
caper (to) *intr.* cabriolar, triscar, retozar.
capercailye (kæpøʳkei·li) *s.* urogallo.
Capetown (kei·ptaum) *n. pr.* GEOGR. Ciudad del Cabo.
capillarity (kæpilæ·riti) *s.* capilaridad.
capillary (kæ·pileri) *adj.* capilar. *2 s.* vaso capilar.
capital (kæ·pital) *adj.* capital. *2* primordial, vital, importante. *3* excelente. *4 adj.-s.* mayúscula, versal [letra]. *5 s.* COM. capital, principal. *6* capital [en oposición a trabajo]. *7* capital [población]. *8* ARQ. capitel.
capitalism (-išm) *s.* capitalismo.
capitalist (-ist) *adj.-s.* capitalista.

capitalize (to) (-aiš) *tr.* capitalizar. *2* escribir con mayúscula.
capitation (kapitei·shøn) *s.* capitación.
Capitol (kæ·pitøl) *s.* Capitolio.
capitular (kapi·chøla*ʳ*) *adj.-s.* capitular.
capitulary (-leri) *adj.* capitular. *2 s.* capitulario.
capitulate (to) (-leit) *intr.* capitular.
capitulation (-lei·shøn) *s.* capitulación [pacto; rendición].
capon (kei·pøn) *s.* capón [pollo, etc.].
capotasto (kapota·stou) *s.* MÚS. cejuela.
capote (kapou·t) *s.* capote [prenda]. *2* capota.
Cappadocian (kapadou·shan) *adj.-s.* capadocio.
capped (kæpt) *pret.* y *p. p.* de TO CAP.
caprice (kaprı·s) *s.* capricho, antojo.
capricious (-shøs) *adj.* caprichoso, antojadizo.
Capricorn (kæ·prico·*ʳ*n) *s.* ASTR. Capricornio.
caprifig (kæ·prifig) *s.* BOT. cabrahigo.
caprine (kæ·prain) *adj.* caprino.
capriole (kæ·prioul) *s.* cabriola. *2* corveta.
capriole (to) *intr.* cabriolar, corvetear.
capsize (to) (kæ·psaiš) *tr.-intr.* volcar, dar vuelta. *2* MAR. volver o volverse quilla arriba; zozobrar.
capstan (-stan) *s.* cabrestante.
capstone (-toun) *s.* ARQ. coronamiento.
capsular (-siula*ʳ*) *adj.* capsular.
capsule (-siul) *s.* cápsula.
captain (-tin) *s.* capitán.
captain (to) *tr.* capitanear.
captaincy (-si), **captainship** (-ship) *s.* capitanía.
caption (-shøn) *s.* captura, prisión. *2* título, encabezamiento. *3* texto [de un grabado, etc.]. *4* CINEM. subtítulo.
captious (-shøs) *adj.* capcioso. *2* reparón, quisquilloso.
captivate (to) (-tiveit) *tr.* cautivar.
captivating (-ing) *adj.* cautivador, encantador, seductor.
captive (kæ·tiv) *adj.-s.* cautivo. *2 adj.* de cautiverio.
captivity (-ti·viti) *s.* cautividad, cautiverio.
captor (kæ·ptø*ʳ*) *s.* aprehensor; apresador.
capture (-chø*ʳ*) *s.* captura. *2* apresamiento. *3* presa, botín, prisionero. *4* MIL. toma.
capture (to) *tr.* capturar, prender. *2* apresar. *3* MIL. tomar.
capuchin (kæ·piuchin) *s.* capilla, capucho; capuchón [de dama]. *2* mono capuchino. *3* paloma de toca. *4* [con may.] capuchino [fraile].
capucine (kæ·piusin) *s.* BOT. capuchina. *2* color anaranjado.
capybara (kæpiba·ra) *s.* ZOOL. capiguara, carpincho.
car (ka*ʳ*) *s.* carruaje, carro, carreta. *2* coche, automóvil. *3* tranvía. *4* FERROC. (E.U.) vagón. *5* caja [de acensor]. *6* barquilla [de globo].
carabao (karaba·ou) *s.* ZOOL.
carabineer (kæ·rabinı*ʳ*) *s.* carabinero [soldado].
caracal (ka·rakal) *s.* ZOOL. caracal.
caracole (kæ·rakoul) *s.* EQUIT. caracol, caracoleo.
caracole (to) *intr.* caracolear.
carafe (kæ·raf) *s.* garrafa.
carambole (kæ·ramboul) *s.* carambola por tablas.
caramel (kæ·ramøl) *s.* caramelo. *2* azúcar quemado.
caramelize (to) *tr.* caramelizar.
carapace (kæ·rapeis) *s.* ZOOL. carapacho, caparazón.
carat (kæ·rat) *s.* quilate.
caravan (kæ·ravæn) *s.* caravana. *2* (Ingl.) coche habitación.

caravansary (kæravæ·nsari), **caravanserai** (-rai) *s.* caravanera, caravanseray.
caravel (kæ·ravel) *s.* MAR. carabela.
caraway (-uei) *s.* BOT. alcaravea.
carbide (ka·ʳbaid) *s.* carburo.
carbon (ka·ʳbøn) *s.* QUÍM. carbono. *2* ELECT., FOT. carbón. *3* ~ *paper*, papel carbón.
carbonaceous (-ei·shøs) *adj.* carbonoso.
Carbonarism (ka·ʳbønarišm) *s.* carbonarismo.
carbonate (-eit) *s.* carbonato.
carbonate (to) *tr.* carbonatar.
carbonic (ka·ʳba·nik) *adj.* carbónico.
carboniferous (ka·ʳbøni·førøs) *adj.* carbonífero.
carbonization (ka·ʳbønišei·shøn) *s.* carbonización.
carbonize (to) (ka·ʳbønaiš) *tr.* carbonizar.
carborundum (ka·ʳbørø·ndøm) *s.* carborundo.
carboy (ka·ʳboi) *s.* bombona, garrafón.
carbuncle (ka·ʳbø·nkøl) *s.* carbunclo, carbúnculo. *2* MED. carbunco.
carburet (ka·ʳbiuret) *s.* carburo.
carburet (to) *tr.* carburar ¶ Pret. y p. p.: *carbureted*, o -*tted*; ger.: *carbureting* o -*tting*.
carburetant (-ant) *adj.-s.* carburante.
carburet(t)or (-ø*ʳ*) *s.* carburador.
carcanet (ka·ʳkanet) *s.* gargantilla, collar.
carcase, carcass (ka·ʳkas) *s.* CARN. res muerta. *2* cadáver, carroña. *3* cuerpo, corpachón. *4* armazón, esqueleto. *5* carcasa. *6* MAR. casco.
carcinoma (ka·ʳsinou·ma) *s.* carcinoma.
card (ka·ʳd) *s.* carta, naipe: ~ *sharper*, tramposo, fullero. *2* fam. tipo, sujeto. *3* tarjeta; participación, invitación; felicitación; cédula, ficha. *4* minuta; lista de vinos. *5* carnet, programa. *6* carda, cardencha. *7* almohaza.
cardamon (ka·ʳdamøn) *s.* BOT. cardamomo.
cardan (ka·ʳdan) *adj.* MEC. cardán.
cardboard (ka·ʳbo·ʳd) *s.* cartón, cartulina.
cardcase (ks·ʳkeis) *s.* tarjetero.
carder (ka·ʳdø*ʳ*) *s.* cardador [pers.]. *2* máquina de cardar.
cardia (ka·ʳdia) *s.* ANAT. cardias.
cardiac (ka·ʳdiæk) *adj.-s.* cardíaco.
cardigan (ka·ʳdigan) *s.* chaqueta de punto.
cardinal (ka·ʳdinal) *adj.* cardinal. *2* cardenalicio: ~ *hat*, capelo. *3 s.* ECLES. cardenal. *4* ORN. ~ *bird*, cardenal.
cardinalate (-eit) *s.* cardenalato.
cardiogram (ka·ʳdiogræm) *s.* cardiograma.
cardiography (ka·ʳdia·grafi) *s.* cardiografía.
cardiology (-lodÿi) *s.* cardiología.
cardiologist (-ist) *s.* cardiólogo.
cardoon (ka·ʳdu·n) *s.* BOT. cardo comestible.
cardsharp (ka·ʳdsha·ʳp) *s.* fullero.
care (ke*ʳ*) *s.* preocupación, inquietud. *2* cuidado, solicitud, esmero, atención, cautela: *take ~!*, ¡cuidado! *3* cuidado, cargo, custodia.
care (to) *intr.* [gralte. con *about* o *for*] preocuparse, inquietarse, cuidar de; importarle a uno; apreciar, querer, hacer caso, gustarle a uno; *he cares for me*, él me quiere; *I don't ~*, me tiene sin cuidado. *2* desear, tener ganas de.
careen (karı·n) *s.* MAR. carena, carenadura.
careen (to) *tr.* MAR. dar a la banda; carenar. *2* inclinar, volcar. *3 intr.* MAR. escorar; dar bandazos.
careenage (-idÿ) *s.* carenadura. *2* carenero.
career (kare·*ʳ*) *s.* carrera [paso rápido; curso; progreso que hace uno; profesión].
career (to) *intr.* galopar, correr.
careful (ke·ʳful) *adj.* cuidadoso, preocupado,

atento, solícito. *2* detenido, esmerado. *3* cauteloso, providente.
carefully (-i) *adv.* cuidadosamente, etc.
careless (-lis) *adj.* descuidado, negligente. *2* que no tiene en cuenta, que no considera. *3* desatento. *4* indiferente. *5* despreocupado. *6* irreflexivo, atolondrado. *7* libre de cuidados. *8* hecho o dicho sin atención o advertencia.
caress (kareˑs) *s.* caricia, halago, mimo.
caress (to) *tr.* acariciar, halagar, mimar.
caretaker (keˑʳteikøʳ) *s.* cuidador, custodio, guardián, vigilante; el que cuida de una casa y vive en ella.
careworn (-uøʳn) *adj.* agobiado por los cuidados, devorado por la inquietud. *2* trasojado.
cargo (kaˑʳgou) *s.* MAR. carga, cargamento. *2* barco de carga.
Carib (kæˑrib), **Caribbean** (kæribɪˑan) *adj.-s.* caribe.
caribou (kæribuˑ) *s.* ZOOL. caribú.
caricature (kæˑrikachøʳ) *s.* caricatura.
caricature (to) *tr.* caricaturizar.
caricaturist (-ist) *s.* caricaturista.
caries (keiˑriš) *s.* caries.
carillon (kæˑrilan) *s.* carillon. *2* toque de carillón.
carillon (to) *intr.* tocar el carillón. ¶ Pret. y p. p.: *carillonned;* ger.: *-nning.*
carious (keiˑriøs) *adj.* cariado.
carking (kaˑʳking) *adj.* molesto, inquietante.
carline thistle (kaˑʳlin) *s.* BOT. ajonjera, carlina.
Carlism (kaˑʳlišm) *s.* carlismo.
Carlist (-list) *s.* carlista.
carload (-loud) *s.* carretada. *2* carga de un vagón.
Carlovingian (kaʳløviˑndȳian) *adj.* Carlovingio.
carman (kaˑʳmæn) *s.* carretero. *2* conductor [de tranvía].
Carmelite (kaˑqmølait) *adj.-s.* carmelita.
carmine (kaˑʳmin) *s.* carmín. *2 adj.* carmíneo.
carnage (kaˑʳnidȳ) *s.* carnicería, matanza.
carnal (-nal) *adj.* carnal [de la carne, sensual, terrenal].
carnality (kaʳnæˑliti) *s.* carnalidad.
carnation (-neiˑshøn) *adj.-s.* encarnado [color de carne]. *2 s.* clavel, clavel doble.
carnelian (-nɪˑlian) *s.* CORNELIAN.
carnival (-nival) *s.* carnaval. *2* orgía.
Carnivora (kaʳniˑvøra) *s. pl.* carnívoros.
carnivorous (-vørøs) *adj.* carnívoro.
carnose (kaˑʳnous) *adj.* carnoso.
carnosity (kaʳnaˑsiti) *s.* carnosidad.
carob (kæˑrøb) *s.* BOT. algarrobo; ~ *bean*, algarroba.
carol (kæˑrøl) *s.* canto alegre, villancico.
carol (to) *intr.* cantar villancicos; cantar alegremente. ¶ Pret. y p. p.: *caroled* o *-lled;* ger.: *caroling* o *-lling.*
Caroline (kæˑrølain) *n. pr.* Carolina. *2* ~ *Islands*, Islas Carolinas.
Carolingian (kærøliˑndȳian) *adj.-s.* carolingio.
carom (kæˑrøm) *s.* BILLAR. carambola.
carom (to) *intr.* hacer carambola.
carotid (karaˑtid) *adj.-s.* carótida.
carousal (karauˑsal) *s.* orgía, juerga.
carouse (to) *intr.* hacer una juerga, emborracharse.
carp (kaˑʳp) *s.* ICT. carpa.
carp (to) *intr.* criticar, censurar.
carpal (kaˑʳpal) *adj.-s.* ANAT. carpiano.
Carpathian (kaʳpeiˑzian) *adj.* Cárpato.
carpel (kaˑʳpøl) *s.* carpelo.
carpenter (kaˑʳpøntøʳ) *s.* carpintero.

carpentry (-tri) *s.* carpintería [arte, oficio]. *2* maderamen.
carper (kaˑʳpøʳ) *s.* criticón, reparón.
carpet (kaˑʳpøt) *s.* alfombra, tapiz. *2* tapete.
carpet (to) *tr.* alfombrar, entapizar.
carpetbag (-bæg) *s.* maleta, saco de noche.
carping (kaˑʳping) *adj.* criticón, reparón.
carpus (kaˑʳpøs) *s.* ANAT. carpo.
carrack (kæˑrak) *s.* carraca [galeón].
carriage (kæˑridȳ) *s.* carruaje, coche; ~ *and four*, coche de cuatro caballos. *2* FERROC. (Ing.) vagón, coche. *3* ARTILL. cureña. *4* MEC. carro [de una máquina]. *5* porte, transporte, acarreo. *6* aire, porte, continente [de una pers.].
Carrie (kæˑri) *n. pr. dim.* de CAROLINE.
carrier (kæˑriøʳ) *s.* portador. *2* porteador, empresa de transportes. *3* mandadero; ordinario, cosario. *4* recipiente, etc., donde se lleva algo. *5* RADIO. onda portadora. *6* ~ *pigeon*, paloma mensajera.
carrion (kæˑriøn) *s.* carroña. *2 adj.* carroño, inmundo.
carronade (kæˑrøneid) *s.* carronada.
carrot (kæˑrøt) *s.* zanahoria.
carroty (-i) *adj.* bermejo [pelo]. *2* pelirrojo.
carry (kæˑri) *s.* transporte en hombros. *2* alcance [de un arma].
carry (to) *tr.* llevar, traer, acarrear, conducir, portear, transportar. *2* llevar [encima, consigo, en sí]. *3* entrañar, incluir. *4* sostener, soportar. *5* dirigir, impulsar. *6* entusiasmar, convencer. *7* arrebatar, tomar, conquistar, lograr, ganar. *8* dar, producir [frutos]. *9* hacer aprobar [una moción, etc.]. *10* ARIT. llevar. *11 to* ~ *away*, quitar, llevarse; arrebatar, entusiasmar. *12 to* ~ *forward, to* ~ *over*, COM. llevar a otra página, columna, etc. *13 to* ~ *off*, llevarse; ganar; hacer pasar; arrostrar. *14 to* ~ *on*, continuar; practicar, ejercer. *15 to* ~ *oneself*, portarse, conducirse. *16 to* ~ *one's point*, salirse con la suya. *17 to* ~ *out*, llevar a cabo. *18 to* ~ *the day*, quedar victorioso. *19 to* ~ *through*, llevar a término; tramitar. *20 to* ~ *weight*, pesar, influir.
   21 intr. portear. *22* alcanzar, llegar [la voz, un tiro, etc.]. ¶ Pret. y p. p.: *carried.*
carry-over *s.* sobrante, reserva. *2* COM. suma anterior.
cart (kaˑʳt) *s.* carro, carromato, carreta. *2* especie de tilburí. *3* carro de mano. *4* ~ *wheel*, rueda de carro; GIMN. vuelta que se da de lado sobre manos y pies.
cart (to) *tr.* carretear, acarrear.
cartage (-idȳ) *s.* carretaje, acarreo, transporte.
carte (kaˑʳt) *s.* ESGR. cuarta. *2* carta, lista [de platos]. *3* ~ *blanche*, carta blanca.
cartel (kaˑʳteˑl o kaˑʳtøl) *s.* cartel [de desafío]. *2* ECON., POL. cartel.
carter (kaˑʳtøʳ) *s.* carretero; acarreador.
Cartesian (kaˑʳtɪˑšan) *adj.-s.* cartesiano.
Carthage (kaˑʳzidȳ) *n. pr.* Cartago.
Carthaginian (kaʳzadȳiˑnian) *adj.-s.* cartaginés.
Carthusian (kaʳziuˑȳan) *adj.-s.* cartujo.
cartilage (kaˑʳtilidȳ) *s.* cartílago.
cartilaginous (-aˑdȳinøs) *adj.* cartilaginoso.
cartload (kaˑʳtloud) *s.* carretada.
cartman (-mæn) *s.* carretero, carrero.
cartographer (kaʳtaˑgraføʳ) *s.* cartógrafo.
cartography (-fi) *s.* cartografía.
cartomancy (kaˑʳtømænsi) *s.* cartomancia.
carton (kaˑʳtøn) *s.* caja de cartón. *2* diana [de un blanco].

cartoon (ka^rtu·n) *s.* PINT. cartón. *2* caricatura. *3* película de dibujos animados.

cartoonist (-ist) *s.* caricaturista.

cartouche (ka·^rtush) *s.* ARQ. cartela. *2* orla [de mapa, etc.]. *3* MIL. cartucho [de papel].

cartridge (-tridӯ) *s.* cartucho [de arma]; ~ *belt,* canana.

cartway (-tuei) *s.* camino carretero.

cartwright (-rait) *s.* carretero [que hace carros].

caruncle (kæ·rønkøl) *s.* caruncula.

carve (to) (ka^rv) *tr.* tallar, esculpir, cincelar, grabar. *2* cortar, trinchar [carne].

carvel (ka^r·vøl) *s.* carabela.

carven (-vøn) *adj.* grabado, esculpido.

carver (-vø^r) *s.* tallista, escultor. *2* trinchante [pers.]. *3* cuchillo de trinchar.

carving (-ing) *s.* entalladura, talla, escultura. *2* arte cisoria.

caryatid (kæriæ·tid) *s.* cariátide.

caryophyllaceous (kæriofilei·shøs) *adj.* cariofiláceo.

caryopsis (karia·psis) *s.* BOT. cariópside.

cascade (kæ·skeid) *s.* cascada.

cascade (to) *intr.* caer en forma de cascada.

cascarilla (kæskarı·la) *s.* BOT., FARM. cascarilla.

case (keis) *s.* caso [suceso, ejemplo, coyuntura, etc.]: *in any* ~, en todo caso; *in* ~, en caso de que. *2* GRAM., MED., DER. caso. *3* estado, situación. *4* argumentos o pruebas [en pro o en contra de algo]; lo que uno sostiene. *5* DER. acción, pleito, causa. *6* caja, estuche, vaina, funda, cubierta, carpeta, neceser. *7* MEC. camisa, forro. *8* cápsula [de cartucho]. *9* marco, arco, bastidor [de puerta, ventana, etc.]. *10* IMPR. caja.

case (to) *tr.* embalar, encajonar, enfundar, cubrir, borrar.

casein (kei·siin) *s.* caseína.

casemate (kei·smeit) *s.* FORT. casamata.

casement (-mønt) *s.* ventana de bisagras [hoja]. *2* capa, cubierta.

caseous (kei·siøs) *adj.* caseoso.

cash (kæsh) *s.* numerario, efectivo, dinero contante: ~ *register,* caja registradora; ~ *down,* a toca teja; ~ *on delivery,* contra reembolso. *2* COM. caja. *3* pago al contado. *4* *adj.-adv.* al contado.

cash (to) *tr.* cobrar, hacer efectivo [un cheque, etc.].

cashbook *s.* libro de caja.

cashbox *s.* caja [para el dinero].

cashew (kashu·) *s.* BOT. anacardo.

cashier (kæshi·ø^r) *s.* cajero, contador.

cashier (to) *tr.* destituir. *2* MIL. degradar.

cashmere (kæ·shmiø^r) *s.* cachemir, casimir.

Casimir (kæ·simi^r) *n. pr.* Casimiro.

casing (kei·sing) *s.* cubierta, envoltura, camisa, forro, revestimiento. *2* cubierta [de neumático]. *3* COST. jareta.

casino (kasi·nou) *s.* casino.

cask (kæsk) *s.* casco, tonel, cuba, barrica, barril.

cask (to) *tr.* entonelar, embarrilar.

casket (ka·skit) *s.* arqueta, cofrecito.

Caspian Sea (kæ·spiɑn) *n. pr.* Mar Caspio.

casque (kæsk) *s.* casco, yelmo, almete.

cassation (kæsei·shøn) *s.* casación.

cassava (kæsa·va) *s.* mandioca.

casserole (kæ·søroul) *s.* cacerola.

cassia (kæ·sha) *s.* casia.

cassimere (kæ·simı^r) *s.* casimir.

cassino (kasi·nou) *s.* cierto juego de naipes.

cassis (kasi·s) *s.* BOT. casis.

cassock (kæ·søk) *s.* sotana. *2* casacón.

cassowary (kæ·søueri) *s.* casuario.

cast (kæst) *s.* echada, lanzamiento, tirada. *2* tiro, alcance [de una piedra, etc.]. *3* fundición, vaciado; pieza fundida o vaciada. *4* molde [que se saca]; mascarilla; impronta. *5* IMPR. plancha. *6* aspecto; disposición, tendencia. *7* matiz, tono. *8* TEAT. reparto; cuadro de actores. *9* *to have a* ~ *in one eye,* ser bizco de un ojo. *10* p. p. de TO CAST. *11* *adj.* lanzado, vaciado, fundido, etc.: ~ *iron,* hierro colado, fundición.

cast (to) *tr.* echar, lanzar, tirar, arrojar. *2* verter, derramar. *3* despedir, desechar. *4* perder [una herradura, las hojas, etc.]; soltar, mudar [la pluma, la piel]. *5* arrojar [luz]; proyectar [sombra]. *6* derribar, tumbar. *7* tornar, disponer, arreglar. *8* fundir, vaciar, moldear. *9* volver, poner [los ojos, el pensamiento, etc.]. *10* hacer [cuentas]. *11* TEAT. repartir [los papeles]. *12* dar, depositar [un voto]. *13* *to* ~ *anchor,* echar anclas. *14* *to* ~ *aside,* desechar. *15* *to* ~ *lots,* echar suertes. *16* *intr.* echar el anzuelo. *17* sumar, hacer cálculos. *18* alabearse, deformarse. *19* *to* ~ *about,* buscar, discurrir, hacer planes. ¶ Pret. y p. p.: *cast.*

Castalides (-æ·lids) *s. pl.* MIT. Castálidas.

castanets (kæ·stanets) *s. pl.* castañuelas.

castaway (ka·stauei) *s.* desechado, abandonado. *2* MAR. perdido. *3* *s.* náufrago. *4* fig. réprobo, proscrito.

caste (kast) *s.* casta, clase [social].

castellan (ka·stølan) *s.* castellano, alcaide [de un castillo].

castellated (-eitid) *adj.* encastillado, fortificado.

caster (ka·stø^r) *s.* echador. *2* el que hace sumas, cálculos o pronósticos. *3* vaciador, fundidor. *4* vinagrera. *5* ruedecilla [de muebles]. *6* *pl.* vinagreras.

castigate (to) (kæ·stigeit) *tr.* castigar, corregir.

castigation (-ei·shøn) *s.* castigo; corrección.

Castile (kæsti·l) *n. pr.* Castilla.

Castilian (-ian) *adj.-s.* castellano [de Castilla].

casting (kæ·sting) *s.* echada. *2* fundición, vaciado. *3* alabeo. *4* distribución, arreglo, plan, modelo. *5* *adj.* ~ *vote,* voto decisivo, de calidad.

cast-iron *adj.* de hierro colado. *2* fuerte, duro.

castle (kæ·søl) *s.* castillo, alcázar: ~ *in Spain,* ~ *in the air,* fig. castillo en el aire. *2* AJED. torre.

castle (to) *intr.* AJED. enrocar.

cast off *adj.* abandonado, desechado. *2* de desecho.

castor (ka·stø^r) *s.* castóreo. *2* sombrero de castor. *3* CASTER *4* y *5.* *4* ~ *oil,* aceite de ricino.

castoreum (kastou·riøm) *s.* castóreo.

castrate (to) (kæ·streit) *tr.* castrar, capar.

castration (-ei·shon) *s.* castración, capadura.

castrator (-tø^r) *s.* castrador.

casual (kæ·ʃiual) *adj.* casual, fortuito. *2* ocasional. *3* transeúnte, volandero. *4* hecho o dicho como al descuido.

casually (-i) *adv.* por accidente; ocasionalmente. *2* como al descuido, sin darle importancia.

casualty (-uti) *s.* accidente, desgracia, siniestro. *2* MIL. baja, pérdida. *3* víctima [de un accidente].

casuist (kæ·ʃiuist) *s.* casuista.

casuistic(al (kæʃiui·stik(al) *adj.* casuístico.

casuistry (-tri) *s.* casuística.

cat (kæt) *s.* ZOOL. gato, gata: *cat's cradle,* cunas [juego de niños]; *cat's paw,* intrumento, persona de quien se sirve otra. *2* ZOOL. felino. *3* MAR. aparejo de gata. *4* tala, toña [palito].

cataclysm (kæ·taclišm) *s.* cataclismo.

catacomb (-koum) *s.* catacumba.

catafalque (-fælk) s. catafalco.
Catalan (-lan) adj.-s. catalán.
catalectic (kætale·ktik) adj. cataléctico.
catalepsy (-le·psi) s. catalepsia.
cataleptic (-le·ptik) adj. cataléptico.
catalogue (kæ·talag) s. catálogo.
catalogue (to) tr. catalogar.
Catalonia (kætalou·nia) n. pr. Cataluña.
catalpa (kætæ·lpa) s. BOT. catalpa.
catalysis (kætæ·lisis) s. catálisis.
catalyst (kæ·talist), catalyzer (-laišøʳ) s. catalizador.
catamaran (kætamaræ·n) s. MAR. especie de balsa. 2 mujer pendenciera.
catamount (kæ·tamaunt), catamountain (-ing) s. ZOOL. gato montés; lince; leopardo.
cataplasm (kæ·taplæšm) s. POULTICE.
catapult (kæ·tapølt) s. catapulta. 2 tirador [para lanzar piedrecitas, etc.].
catapult (to) tr. catapultar.
cataract (kæ·tarækt) s. GEOGR., MED. catarata.
catarrh (kata·ʳ) s. catarro.
catarrhal (-ral) adj. catarral.
catastrophe (kætæ·strofi) s. catástrofe. 2 GEOL. cataclismo.
catbird (kæ·tbøʳd) s. pájaro americano.
catboat (kæ·tbout) s. MAR. laúd.
catcall (kæ·tkɔl) s. silbido, silba, abucheo.
catcall (to) tr. silbar, abuchear.
catch (kæch) s. cogedura, asimiento, captura. 2 botín, pesca, redada. 3 pregunta insidiosa, trampa. 4 lo que detiene o sujeta: gancho, trinquete, tope, cerradero, pestillo, pasador, etc. 5 interrupción brusca. 6 trocito, rato. 7 atractivo, buen partido. 8 adj. atractivo, insidioso, que sujeta, etc.: ~ question, pregunta insidiosa; ~ bolt, picaporte.
catch (to) tr. coger, asir, agarrar, retener, sujetar. 2 coger, pescar, cazar, atrapar. 3 coger, pillar [una enfermedad]; contagiarse de. 4 coger, sorprender. 5 comprender, penetrar. 6 engranar, endentar. 7 recoger [en un recipiente]. 8 atraer [la atención,. la mirada]. 9 fam. atizar [un golpe]. 10 to ~ fire, encenderse, inflamarse. 11 to ~ hold of, agarrarse a; apoderarse de. 12 to ~ one's breath, contener bruscamente el aliento. 13 intr. enredarse, engancharse, trabarse. 14 prender el fuego, etc. 15 contagiarse, ser pegadizo. 16 to ~ at, tratar de coger. 17 to ~ up, ponerse al día.
¶ Pret. y p. p.: caught.
catcher (kæ·tchøʳ) s. el o lo que coge, sujeta, etc. 2 DEP. cátcher.
catching (-ing) adj. contagioso, pegadizo. 2 atractivo.
catchpenny (kæ·chpeni) s. baratija, sacadineros. 2 adj. de pacotilla.
catchpole, catchpoll (-poul) s. alguacil.
catchup (-øp) s. salsa hecha con jugo de setas, tomates, etc.
catchword (-wøʳd) s. IMPR. reclamo. 2 TEAT. pie. 3 lema [de un partido, etc.].
catchy (kæ·chi) adj. CATCHING. 2 intermitente.
catechesis (kætøki·sis) s. catequesis, catequismo.
catechetic(al (katøke·tik(al) adj. catequístico.
catechism (kæ·tøkišm) s. catecismo.
catechist (-ist) s. catequista.
catechize (to) (-kaiš) tr. catequizar. 2 interrogar.
catechu (kæ·tøchu) s. catecú, cato.
catechumen (kætikiu·møn) s. catecúmeno.
categoric(al (kætiga·rik(al) adj. categórico.

category (kæ·tigøri) s. categoría.
catenary (kæ·tineri) adj.-s. catenaria.
catenate (to) (kæ·tineit) tr. encadenar, concadenar.
catenation (-ei·shøn) s. encadenamiento, concadenación.
cater (to) (kei·tøʳ) intr. abastecer, proveer.
caterer (-tørøʳ) s. abastecedor, proveedor.
caterpillar (kæ·tøʳpilaʳ) s. ENT. oruga.
caterwaul (-uol) s. maullido.
caterwaul (to) intr. maullar.
catfish (cæ·tfish) s. ICT. siluro; barbo.
catgut (-gøt) s. catgut. 2 cuerda de tripa.
cathartic (kaza·ʳtik) adj.-s. catártico, purgante.
cathead (kæ·tjed) s. serviola.
cathedra (kæzi·dra) s. cátedra [asiento del maestro; dignidad pontificia o episcopal].
cathedral (kæzi·dral) s. catedral. 2 adj. catedral, catedralicio. 3 episcopal.
Catherine (kæ·zørin) n. pr. Catalina: ~ wheel, rueda de fuegos artificiales; ARQ. rosa, rosetón.
catheter (kæ·zøtøʳ) s. catéter.
cathode (kæ·zoud) s. cátodo.
cathodic (-ik) adj. catódico.
catholic (kæ·zølik) adj. católico, universal. 2 [con may.] adj.-s. REL. católico.
catholicism (kaza·lisišm) s. catolicismo.
catholicity (kæzøli·siti) s. catolicidad.
cation (kæ·taiøn) s. QUÍ., FÍS. catión.
catkin (kæ·tkin) s. BOT. amento, candelilla.
catlike (-laik) adj. gatuno, gatesgo.
catmint (-mint) s. BOT. hierba gatera.
Cato (kei·tou) n. pr. Catón.
Catonian (keitou·nian) adj. catoniano.
cat-o'-nine-tails s. azote con nueve ramales.
catoptrics (kata·ptriks) s. catóptrica.
cat's-eye s. MINER. ojo de gato.
catsup (kæ·tsøp) s. CATCHUP.
cattail (-teil) s. BOT. espadaña; anea.
cattish (-tish) adj. gatuno, gatesco.
cattle (kæ·tøl) s. ganado, reses; ganado vacuno; cabeza de ganado: ~ bell, esquila. 2 desp. gentuza.
cattleman (-mæn) s. ganadero.
Caucasian (kokei·shan) adj.-s. caucásico.
Caucasus (ko·kasøs) n. pr. GEOGR. Cáucaso.
caucus (ko·køs) s. junta política.
caudal (ko·dal) adj. ZOOL. caudal.
caudate (ko·deit) adj. caudado, cauato.
caudle (ko·døl) s. bebida confortante.
caul (kol) s. redaño. 2 membrana que envuelve al feto.
cauldron (ko·ldrøn) s. caldero, caldera.
cauliflower (ko·liflauøʳ) s. BOT. coliflor.
caulk (to) (kok) tr. MAR. calafatear. 2 tapar las rendijas de.
caulker (ko·køʳ) s. calafate.
causal (ko·šal) adj. causal.
causality (kosæ·liti) s. causalidad.
causate (to) (ko·šeit) tr. causar, originar.
causative (ko·šativ) adj. causativo.
cause (koš) s. causa [de un efecto; motivo, autor]. 2 causa [en que se toma interés o partido]: common ~, causa común. 3 DER. causa, pleito.
cause (to) tr. causar. 2 hacer [con un inf.]; hacer que, inducir a, impeler a.
causeless (ko·šlis) adj. inmotivado, infundado.
causer (ko·šøʳ) s. causante, causador.
causeway (ko·šwei), causey (-i) s. paso firme que cruza un pantano, etc.; calzada, arrecife.
causidical (koši·dikal) adj.-s. causídico.
caustic (ko·stik) adj.-s. cáustico.

causticity (kosti·siti) *s.* causticidad.
cauter (ko·tøʳ) *s.* cauterio [instrumento].
cauterize (to) (ko·tørais̆) *tr.* cauterizar.
cautery (ko·tøri) *s.* cauterio.
caution (ko·shøn) *s.* caución, cautela, precaución. 2 aviso, amonestación, advertencia.
caution (to) *tr.* cautelar, advertir, avisar; amonestar.
cautious (ko·shøs) *adj.* cauto, precavido, prudente, circunspecto.
cautiousness (-nis) *s.* cautela, precaución, prudencia.
cavalcade (kæ·valkeid) *s.* cabalgata.
cavalier (kæ·valiøʳ) *s.* caballero [noble]. 2 jinete. 3 caballero, galán [de una dama]. 4 *adj.* alegre, desenvuelto. 5 altivo, brusco.
cavaliery (-li) *adv.* caballerescamente. 2 altivamente, bruscamente.
cavalry (kæ·valri) *s.* MIL. caballería.
cave (kiev) *s.* cueva, caverna; antro: ~ *dweller*, cavernícola.
cave (to) *tr.* excavar, hundir. 2 *intr. to* ~ *in*, hundirse [el suelo, etc.]; fam. ceder, rendirse.
cavern (kæ·vøʳn) *s.* caverna, antro.
cavernous (-øs) *adj.* cavernoso.
cavesson (kæ·vøsøn) *s.* cabezón de serreta.
caviar (kæ·viaʳ) *s.* cavial, caviar.
cavicorn (kæ·vikøʳn) *adj.-s.* ZOOL. cavicornio.
cavil (kæ·vil) *s.* quisquilla, objeción frívola, sutileza, argucia.
cavil (to) *intr.* buscar quisquillas; poner tachas o reparos nimios. ¶ Pret. y p. p.: *caviled* o *-lled;* ger.: *caviling* o *-lling.*
caviller (-øʳ) *s.* reparón.
cavity (kæ·viti) *s.* cavidad.
cavy (kei·vi) *s.* nombre que se da al cobayo, al carpincho, al agutí, etc.
caw (ko) *s.* graznido.
caw (to) *intr.* graznar.
cay (kei) *s.* cayo, isleta.
Cayenne (kaie·n) *n. pr.* Cayena.
cayenne pepper *s.* pimentón.
cayman (kei·man) *s.* ZOOL. caimán.
cease (sis) *s.* cesación: *without* ~, sin cesar.
cease (to) *intr.* cesar [no continuar]. 2 *tr.* poner fin a, parar, acabar, dejar de.
ceaseless (si·slis) *adj.* incesante, continuo.
Cecil (si·sil o se·sil) *n. pr.* Cecilio.
Cecilia (sisi·lia) *n. pr.* Cecilia.
cecity (se·siti) *s.* ceguera.
cecum *s.* CAECUM. .
cedar (si·daʳ) *s.* BOT. cedro.
cedarn (si·daʳn) *adj.* poét. cedrino.
cede (to) (sid) *tr.* ceder, traspasar.
cedilla (sidi·la) *s.* cedilla.
cedrine (si·drin) *adj.* cedrino.
ceil (to) (sil) *tr.* poner cielo raso.
ceiling (si·ling) *s.* techo, cielo raso. 2 AVIA. techo, altura máxima.
celadon (se·ladøn) *s.* verdeceledón.
celandine (se·landain) *s.* BOT. celidonia.
celebrant (se·løbrant) *s.* celebrante.
celebrate (se·løbreit) *tr.* celebrar, solemnizar. 2 celebrar, alabar. 3 *intr.* celebrar [decir misa]. 4 divertirse.
celebrated (se·løbreitid) *adj.* célebre, famoso.
celebration (-ei·shøn) *s.* celebración. 2 fiesta.
celebrity (søle·briti) *s.* celebridad.
celerity (-riti) *s.* celeridad.
celery (se·løri) *s.* BOT. apio.
celestial (søle·schal) *adj.* celestial, celeste, célico:

Celestial Empire, Imperio Celeste, China. 2 *s.* chino. 3 morador del cielo.
celiac (si·liæk) *adj.* COELIAC.
celibacy (se·libasi) *s.* celibato, soltería.
celibate (se·libeit) *adj.-s.* célibe.
cell (sel) *s.* celda. 2 célula. 3 celdilla, hueco, nicho, cavidad, alvéolo. 4 ELECT. par, elemento [de pila]; pila simple.
cellar (se·laʳ) *s.* sótano, cueva. 2 bodega [para vinos].
cellaret (selare·t) *s.* frasquera; licorera.
cellist (che·list) *s.* violoncelista.
cello (che·lou) *s.* violoncelo.
cellophane (se·lofein) *s.* celofana.
cellular (se·liulaʳ) *adj.* celular, celuloso.
cellule (-liul) *s.* celdilla, celulilla.
celluloid (-oid) *s.* celuloide.
cellulose (-ous) *adj.* celuloso. 2 *s.* celulosa.
Celt (selt) *s.* celta.
Celtiberian (-ibi·rian) *adj.* celtibérico. 2 *adj.-s.* celtíbero.
Celtic (se·ltik) *adj.* céltico.
cement (søme·nt) *s.* cemento; mortero, argamasa; masilla. 2 ANAT., GEOL., METAL. cemento. 3 lazo de unión, vínculo.
cement (to) *tr.* unir o cubrir con cemento, etc. 2 afianzar, consolidar. 3 METAL. cementar. 4 *intr.* unirse, consolidarse.
cementation (-ei·shøn) *s.* unión, consolidación. 2 METAL. cementación.
cemetery (se·møteri) *s.* cementerio.
cenacle (se·nakøl) *s.* cenáculo.
cenobite (se·nobait) *s.* cenobita.
cenobium (senou·biøm), **cenoby** (se·nobi) *s.* cenobio.
cenotaph (se·notæf) *s.* cenotafio.
cense (to) (sens) *tr.* incensar, turificar.
censer (-øʳ) *s.* incensario.
censor (se·nsøʳ) *s.* censor.
censor (to) *tr.* censurar [libros, etc.].
censorial (senso·rial) *adj.* censorio.
censorious (-riøs) *adj.* censurador, severo, rígido. 2 crítico, de censura.
censorship (se·nsøʳship) *s.* censura [oficio].
censual (se·nshual) *adj.* censual.
censure (se·nshøʳ) *s.* censura, crítica, reprobación. 2 censura [pena].
censure (to) *tr.* censurar, criticar, reprobar.
census (se·nsøs) *s.* censo, padrón. 2 DER. censo.
cent (sent) *s.* centavo [moneda]. 2 ciento, en frases como: *per* ~, por ciento.
centaur (se·ntoʳ) *s.* MIT. centauro.
centaury (-i) *s.* BOT. centaura, centaurea.
centenarian (sentine·rian) *adj.-s.* centenario [pers.].
centenary (se·ntineri) *adj.* centenario, secular. 2 *s.* centenario [cien años, conmemoración].
centennial (sente·nial) *adj.* centenario, secular. 2 *s.* centenario [conmemoración].
center, to center, etc. = CENTRE, TO CENTRE, etc.
centesimal (sente·simal) *adj.* centesimal.
centiare (se·ntieøʳ) *s.* centiárea.
centigrade (-greid) *adj.* centígrado.
centigram[me (-græm) *s.* centigramo.
centilitre o **-liter** (-litoʳ) *s.* centilitro.
centime (santi·m) *s.* céntimo.
centimetre, o **-meter** (se·ntimitøʳ) *s.* centímetro.
centipede (se·ntipid) *s.* ZOOL. ciempiés.
cento (se·ntou) *s.* centón.
central (se·ntral) *adj.* central; céntrico. 2 *s.* central [telefónica]. 3 telefonista.
centralism (-iš̌m) *s.* centralismo.

centralize (to) (-aiš) *tr.* centralizar.
centre (se·ntø^r) *s.* centro. *2* fuente [de energía]. *3* ARQ. cimbra.
centre (to) *tr.* centrar. *2* concentrar [en]. *3* ÓPT. ajustar, enfocar. *4* ARQ. cimbrar. *5 intr.* estar centrado [en]: *to ~ round*, girar en torno de.
centreboard (-bo^rd) *s.* orza de quilla.
centrepiece (-pis) *s.* centro de mesa. *2* rosetón [de techo].
centric(al (se·ntrik(al) *adj.* céntrico, central.
centrifugal (sentri·fiugal), **centrifuge** (se·ntri-fiudỹ) *adj.* centrífugo. *2 s.* centrifugadora.
centrifuge (to) *tr.* centrifugar.
centripetal (sentri·petal) *adj.* centrípeto.
centrosome (se·ntrosoum) *s.* BIOL. centrosoma.
centrosphere (se·ntrosfi^r) *s.* GEOL., BIOL. centroesfera.
centumvir (sentø·mvi^r) *s.* centunviro.
centuple (se·ntiupøl) *adj.* céntuplo.
centuple (to) *tr.* centuplicar.
centuplicate (sentiu·plikeit) *adj.* centuplicado.
centuplicate (to) *tr.* centuplicar.
centurion (sentiu·riøn) *s.* centurión.
century (se·nchøri) *s.* centuria. *2* siglo.
cephalic (sefæ·lik) *adj.* cefálico.
cephalopod (se·falopad) *adj.-s.* ZOOL. cefalópodo.
cephalothorax (-zou·ræks) *s.* ZOOL. cefalotórax.
Cepheus (si·fiøs) *n. pr.* MIT., ASTR. Cefeo.
ceramic (siræ·mik) *adj.* cerámico.
ceramics (-s) *s.* cerámica.
ceramist (se·ræmist) *s.* ceramista.
cerastes (seræ·stiš) *s.* ZOOL. cerasta.
cerate (si·reit) *s.* cerato.
cerated (-id) *adj.* encerado.
Cerberus (sø·^rbørøs) *n. pr.-s.* Cancerbero.
cere (si^r) *s.* ORN. cera.
cereal (si·rial) *adj.-s.* cereal.
cerebellum (seribe·løm) *s.* ANAT. cerebelo.
cerebral (se·røbral) *adj.* cerebral.
cerebrum (se·ribrøm) *s.* ANAT. cerebro. *2* encéfalo.
cerecloth (si·ø^rcloz) *s.* encerado, hule.
ceremonial (serimou·nial) *adj.-s.* ceremonial.
ceremonious (serimou·niøs) *adj.* ceremonioso. *2* ceremonial.
ceremony (se·rimøni) *s.* ceremonia. *2* cumplido, formalidad, etiqueta.
cereous (si·riøs) *adj.* céreo.
Ceres (si·riš) *n. pr.* Ceres.
cerium (si·riøm) *s.* QUÍM. cerio.
certain (sø·^rtøn) *adj.* fijo, determinado. *2* cierto, seguro, indudable, infalible, inevitable, positivo. *3* cierto, seguro, convencido [de algo]. *4 a ~*, cierto [en sentido indeterminado]; un tal. *5 s. for ~*, de fijo, con toda seguridad.
certainly (-li) *adv.* ciertamente, indudablemente, por cierto. *2* seguramente, sin falta.
certainty (-ti) *s.* certeza, certidumbre, seguridad. *2* cosa cierta, segura.
certifiable (sø·^rtifaiabøl) *adj.* certificable. *2* loco.
certificate (sø^rti·fikit) *s.* certificado, partida. *2* acta [notarial]. *3* título [para ejercer ciertas profesiones]. *4* COM. *~ of stock*, título, acción.
certificate (to) (-eit) *tr.* certificar. *2* proveer de título o certificado.
certifier (sø·^rtifaiø^r) *s.* certificador.
certify (to) (sø·^rtifai) *tr.* certificar, afirmar, asegurar. *2* MED. declarar loco. ¶ P. p.: *certified*.
certitude (sø·^rtitiud) *s.* certeza, certidumbre.
cerulean (søru·lian), **-leous** (-liøs) *adj.* cerúleo.
cerumen (søru·møn) *s.* cerumen.
ceruse (si·rus) *s.* cerusa, albayalde.

cervical (sø·^rvikal) *adj.* cervical.
Cervidae (sø^rvidi) *s. pl.* ZOOL. cérvidos.
cervine (sø·^rvin) *adj.* cervino.
cervix (sø·^rviks) *s.* cerviz.
cesium (si·šiøm) *s.* QUÍM. cesio.
cespitose (si·spitous) *adj.* cespitoso.
cessation (sesei·shøn) *s.* cesación, paro, suspensión.
cession (se·shøn) *s.* cesión.
cessionary (se·shøneri) *adj.-s.* cesionario.
cesspool (se·spul) *s.* pozo negro, sumidero.
cesura *s.* CAESURA.
cetacean (sitei·shan) *adj.* y *s.* ZOOL. cetáceo.
cetaceous (-shøs) *adj.* cetáceo.
Ceylon (si·lan) *n. pr.* Ceilán.
Ceylonese (silani·š) *adj.-s.* cingalés.
chafe (cheif) *s.* roce; rozadura, excoriación, sahorno. *2* irritación, impaciencia.
chafe (to) *tr.* calentar frotando. *2* rozar, excoriar. *3* enojar, irritar. *4 intr.* rozar [con]. *5* rozarse, sahornarse. *6* rabiar, impacientarse.
chafer (-ø^r) *s.* calentador [vasija]. *2* lo que roza. *3* COCKCHAFER.
chafery (-i) *s.* fragua, forja.
chaff (chaf) *s.* ahechaduras, barcia, granzas, paja menuda; broza. *2* broma, vaya.
chaff (to) *tr.* embromar, dar vaya.
chaffer (chæ·fø^r) *s.* regateo.
chaffer (to) *tr.* regatear. *2 to ~ away*, gastar, pasar [el tiempo, etc.].
chafferer (-ø^r) *s.* regatón [que regatea].
chaffinch (chæ·finš) *s.* ORN. pinzón.
chafing-dish (chei·fing) *s.* escalfador [braserillo].
chagrin (shagri·n) *s.* mortificación, desazón, disgusto.
chagrin (to) *tr.* mortificar, disgustar.
chain (chein) *s.* cadena [serie de eslabones, de cosas o de sucesos]; *~ gang*, cadena de presidarios; *~ stitch*, punto de cadeneta. *2* cadena de agrimensor. *3* cadenilla. *4* WARP 1. *5 pl.* cadenas, esclavitud.
chain (to) *tr.* encadenar. *2* esclavizar. *3* enlazar, unir.
chainwork (-uø^rk) *s.* labor de cadeneta.
chair (che^r) *s.* silla, sillón, sitial. *2* asiento de juez; cátedra; presidencia: *to take the ~*, presidir. *3* silla de manos. *4* FERROC. cojinete.
chairman *s.* presidente. *2* silletero.
chairwoman *s.* presidenta.
chaise (cheiš) *s.* coche, silla, volante, calesín. *2* silla de posta.
chalcedony (kælse·døni) *s.* calcedonia.
chalcography (kæ·lkagrafi) *s.* calcografía.
Chaldaic (kældei·k) *adj.* caldaico.
Chaldea (kældi·a) *n. pr.* HIST. Caldea.
Chaldean (-n) *adj.-s.* caldeo.
chalet (sha·lei) *s.* chalet.
chalice (chæ·lis) *s.* cáliz.
chalk (chok) *s.* cresta; marga. *2* tiza, yeso; clarión.
chalk (to) *tr.* enyesar, mezclar con yeso. *2* margar. *3* dibujar o marcar con tiza. *4* entizar.
chalky (cho·ki) *adj.* yesoso. *2* blanquecino, pálido. *3* FOT. duro.
challenge (chæ·lindỹ) *s.* desafío, reto. *2* DEP. disputa [de un título]. *3* discusión, impugnación. *4* DER. recusación. *5* MIL. quién vive.
challenge (to) *tr.* desafiar, retar. *2* reclamar, merecer [atención, respeto, etc.]. *3* disputar, discutir, impugnar, poner en duda. *4* DER. recusar. *5* MIL. dar el quién vive.

challenger (-ø^r) *s.* desafiador, retador. *2* DEP. aspirante a un título.

chamade (shæma·d) *s.* MIL. llamada.

chamber (chei-mbø^r) *s.* cámara, aposento: ~ *pot*, vaso de noche. *2* cámara [legislativa, de comercio, etc.]; sala [de tribunal]. *3* cámara, compartimiento, cavidad. *4* ARTILL. recámara.

chamberlain (-lin) *s.* chambelán, camarlengo.

chambermaid (-meid) *s.* camarera, sirvienta.

chameleon (kamɪ·liøn) *s.* camaleón.

chamfer (chæ·mfø^r) *s.* chaflán, bisel. *2* canal, estria.

chamfer (to) *tr.* achaflanar, biselar. *2* acanalar.

chamois (shæ·mua) *s.* ZOOL. gamuza. *2* gamuza [piel].

chamomile (kæ·mømail) *s.* BOT. manzanilla, camomila.

champ (to) (chæmp) *tr.* mordiscar, mascar; tascar: *to ~ the bit*, tascar el freno.

champagne (shæ·mpein) *s.* champán, champaña.

champaign *s.* campiña. *2 adj.* abierto, llano, raso.

champion (chæ·mpiøn) *s.* campeón, paladín, defensor. *2* DEP. campeón.

champion (to) *tr.* defender, abogar por.

championess (-is) *f.* campeona; defensora.

championship (-ship) *s.* campeonato.

chance (chans) *s.* ventura, suerte. *2* azar, albur, accidente, casualidad: *by ~*, por casualidad, por ventura. *3* oportunidad, coyuntura. *4* riesgo, peligro. *5* probabilidad, posibilidad. *6 adj.* casual, fortuito, accidental.

chance (to) *intr.* acaecer, suceder, encontrarse [por acaso], acertar a.

chancel (chæ·nsøl) *s.* presbiterio [de iglesia].

chancellery (-øri) *s.* cancillería.

chancellor (-ø^r) *s.* canciller. *2* magistrado presidente. *3 Chancellor of the Exchequer*, (Ingl.) Ministro de Hacienda.

chancery (chæ·nsøri) *s.* nombre de ciertos tribunales.

chancre (shæ·nkø^r) *s.* chancro.

chancy (chæ·nsi) *adj.* arriesgado.

chandelier (shændøli·ø^r) *s.* lámpara, araña.

chandler (shæ·ndlø^r) *s.* cerero, velero. *2* tendero. *3* abastecedor de buques.

change (chei·ndŷ) *s.* cambio, alteración, variación, mudanza, transformación, mutación. *2* cambio, trueque, sustitución. *3* muda [de ropa]. *4* cambio [de un billete]; vuelta [de un pago]. *5* suelto, moneda suelta. *6* novedad, variedad: *for a ~*, para variar, para cambiar de aire. *7* lonja, Bolsa.

change (to) *tr.* cambiar, alterar, variar, mudar, transformar, convertir, trocar. *2* cambiar de, mudar de: *to ~ colour*, demudarse, ruborizarse. *3* mudar las ropas de. *4 intr.* cambiar, variar, transformarse. *5* corregirse.

changeable (-ɑbøl) *adj.* cambiable. *2* mudable, variable, voluble, inconstante. *3* cambiante, tornasolado.

changeful (-ful) *adj.* cambiante. *2* mudable, variable, inconstante.

changeless (-lis) *adj.* inmutable, constante.

changeling (-ling) *s.* niño cambiado por otro. *2* idiota.

changer (-ø^r) *s.* cambiador, cambista.

channel (chæ·nøl) *s.* cauce, lecho, álveo. *2* canal [porción de mar], canalizo: *English Channel*, Canal de la Mancha. *3* zanja, reguera. *4* conducto, vía. *5* ranura, canal, estría.

channel (to) *tr.* acanalar, estriar. *2* encauzar, conducir. ¶ Pret. y p. p.: *channeled* o *-lled;* ger.: *channeling* o *-lling.*

chant (chant) *s.* canción, canto. *2* canto llano, salmodia. *3* sonsonete.

chant (to) *tr.* cantar, entonar; salmodiar. *2* celebrar cantando.

chanter (-ø^r) *s.* cantor. *2* chantre.

chantey (-i) *s.* MAR. saloma.

chanticleer (chæntikli·ø^r) *s.* gallo [ave].

chantress (cha·ntris) *s.* cantora.

chantry (cha·ntri) *s.* ECLES. capilla.

chaos (kei·øs) *s.* caos.

chaotic (keia·tik) *adj.* caótico.

chap (chæp) *s.* fam. muchacho. *2* fam. sujeto. *3* grieta, raja. *4* carrillo, quijada. *5 pl.* (E.U.) chaparreras.

chap (to) *tr.* resquebrajar, agrietar. *2 intr.* resquebrajarse, agrietarse. ¶ Pret. y p. p.: *chapped;* ger.: *-pping.*

chape (cheip) *s.* boquilla o contera [de vaina]. *2* patilla [de hebilla].

chapel (chæ·pøl) *s.* capilla [para el culto]. *2* capilla [de música]. *3* personal [de una imprenta].

chaperon (shæ·pøroun) *s.* caperuza. *2* persona mayor que acompaña y protege a una joven; carabina.

chaperon (to) *tr.* acompañar y proteger a una joven, servirle de carabina.

chapfallen (chæ·pfoløn) *adj.* alicaído, cariacontecido.

chaplain (chæ·plin) *s.* capellán.

chaplaincy (-si), **chaplainship** (-ship) *s.* capellanía.

chaplet (chæ·plit) *s.* guirnalda. *2* sarta, rosario. *3* collar, gargantilla. *4* ARQ. moldura de cuentas.

chapman (-mæn) *s.* buhonero.

chappy (chæ·pi) *adj.* rajado, agrietado.

chapter (chæ·ptø^r) *s.* capítulo [de un libro]. *2* ECLES. capítulo, cabildo. *3* LITURG. capítula.

char (cha^r) *s.* trabajo a jornal o por horas. *2* especie de trucha.

char (to) *tr.* carbonizar; socarrar. *2 intr.* trabajar a jornal o por horas. ¶ Pret. y p. p.: *charred;* ger.: *charring.*

charabanc (charabæ·ng) *s.* charabán.

character (kæ·raktø^r) *s.* carácter [en todos sus sentidos]. *2* calidad, condición. *3* letra [de una pers.]. *4* fama, reputación. *5* referencias, certificado de conducta. *6* descripción. *7* HIST., LIT. personaje. *8* TEAT. papel. *9* sujeto, tipo.

character (to) *tr.* grabar, inscribir.

characteristic (-ɪ·stik) *s.* característica.

characteristic(al (-ɪ·stik(al) *adj.* característico, distintivo.

characterization (-išei·shøn) *s.* caracterización. *2* representación, descripción.

characterize (to) (-aiš) *tr.* caracterizar. *2* representar, describir.

characterless (-lis) *adj.* sin carácter.

charade (shɑrɑ·d) *s.* charada.

charbon (sha·^rban) *s.* MED. carbunco.

charcoal (cha·^rkoul) *s.* carbón de leña; carbón animal. *2* DIB. carboncillo.

chard (cha^rd) *s.* BOT. acelga. *2* penca de alcachofa.

chare *s.*, **to chare** *intr.* CHAR 1; TO CHAR 2.

charge (cha·^rdŷ) *s.* carga [de un arma, un horno, etc.]. *2* peso [moral]. *3* cargo, obligación, custodia, cuidado. *4* encargo, cometido. *5* persona o cosa de que uno está encargado. *6* orden, mandato. *7* carga, gravamen. *8* precio, costa. *9* COM. cargo [en cuenta]. *10* cargo, acusación. *11* MIL. carga, ataque. *12* BLAS. blasón.

charge (to) *tr.* cargar [un arma, un horno, etc.; saturar, llenar]. *2* confiar, encargar, cometer. *3* mandar, exhortar. *4* cargar, gravar, imponer. *5* cobrar, pedir, llevar [un precio]. *6* COM. adeudar, cargar. *7* poner como blasón [en el escudo]. *8 to ~ with*, acusar, tachar de. *9 tr.-intr.* cargar, embestir. *10* cobrar [caro, barato, etc.].

charger (cha·ʳdŷøʳ) *s.* corcel; caballo de guerra. *2* cargador. *3* ant. fuente [plato].

charily (che·rili) *adv.* con cuidado. *2* parcamente.

chariot (chæ·riøt) *s.* carro [de guerra]. *2* carroza ligera.

charioteer (chariøti·øʳ) *s.* auriga.

charism (kæ·rišm) *s.* carisma.

charitable (chæ·ritabøl) *adj.* caritativo.

charity (chæ·riti) *s.* caridad [virtud]. *2* caridad, limosna. *3* beneficencia; institución benéfica.

charivari (shariva·ri) *s.* cencerrada.

charlatan (sha·ʳlatan) *s.* charlatán, curandero.

charlatanism (-išm) *s.* charlatanismo.

Charles (chaʳlš) *n. pr.* Carlos.

Charle's Waim (cha·rlšiš uein) *s.* Osa Mayor.

Charlotte (cha·ʳløt) *n. pr.* Carlota.

charm (chaʳm) *s.* encantamiento. *2* amuleto. *3* encanto, embeleso, hechizo, atractivo, gracia. *4* dije.

charm (to) *tr.* encantar, hechizar. *2* embelesar, cautivar, prendar.

charmer (-øʳ) *s.* encantador, hechicero.

charming (-ing) *s.* encantador, hechicero, embelesador.

charnel (cha·ʳnøl) *adj.* sepulcral: ~ *house*, osario, carnero.

Charon (kei·røn) *n. pr.* MIT. Carón.

chart (cha·ʳt) *s.* carta de marear. *2* mapa, plano. *2* cuadro, gráfica.

chart (to) *tr.* trazar [un mapa, rumbo, etc.].

charter (cha·ʳtøʳ) *s.* carta constitucional o de privilegio. *2* patente, título; escritura. *3* COM. *charter* o ~ *party*, fletamento.

charter (to) *tr.* estatuir. *2* conceder privilegio o patente. *3* fletar [un buque]; alquilar [un vehículo].

chartographer, chartography = CARTOGRAPHER, CARTOGRAPHY.

Chartreuse (chaʳtrø·š) *s.* Cartuja. *2* (con min.) chartreuse [licor].

charwoman (cha·ʳwumæn) *s.* asistencia, mujer empleada en los trabajos domésticos.

chary (che·ri) *adj.* cuidadoso [de]. *2* circunspecto; receloso [de]. *3* económico, frugal, parco.

chase (cheis) *s.* caza, persecución. *2* montería. *3* partida de cazadores. *4* res, etc., que se persigue. *5* muesca, ranura, encaje. *6* ARTILL. caña. *7* IMPR. rama.

chase (to) *tr.* cazar, dar caza a, perseguir. *2* ahuyentar. *3* cincelar. *4* JOY. engastar, montar.

chaser (-øʳ) *s.* cazador, perseguidor. *2* cincelador. *3* engastador. *4* avión de caza.

chasm (kæšm) *s.* quiebra, grieta, abismo, sima. *2* hueco, laguna, vacío.

chasseur (shasø·ʳ) *s.* MIL. cazador. *2* botones [criado].

chassis (shæsi·) *s.* chasis.

chaste (cheist) *adj.* casto. *2* puro, castizo, neto. *3* BOT. ~ *tree*, agnocasto, sauzgatillo.

chasten (to) (chei·søn) *tr.* castigar, corregir. *2* depurar [el estilo, etc.]. *3* moderar, templar.

chasteness (chei·stnis) *s.* CHASTITY.

chastise (to) (chæ·staiš) *tr.* castigar, corregir.

chastisement (chæ·stišmønt) *s.* castigo, corrección.

chastity (chæ·stiti) *s.* castidad. *2* LIT., B. ART. pureza, corrección, simplicidad.

chasuble (chæ·siubøl) *s.* casulla.

chat (chæt) *s.* charla, plática, conversación. *2* ORN. nombre de algunos pájaros.

chat (to) *intr.* charlar, platicar.

chatelaine (sha·tølein) *s.* castellana. *2* cadena con dijes.

chattels (chæ·tølš) *s.* enseres, bienes muebles.

chatter (chæ·tøʳ) *s.* charla, parloteo. *2* chirrido [de aves]. *3* castañeteo [de dientes]. *4* MEC. vibración, traqueteo.

chatter (to) *intr.* charlar, parlotear. *2* chirriar [las aves]. *3* castañetear [los dientes]. *4* MEC. vibrar, traquetear.

chatterbox (-baks) *s.* parlanchín, tarabilla.

chatty (chæ·ti) *adj.* hablador, parlero. *2* de conversación.

chauffeur (shoufø·ʳ) *s.* chófer.

chauvinism (shou·vinišm) *s.* patriotería.

cheap (chip) *adj.-adv.* barato. *2* adj. ordinario, de pacotilla, de mal gusto; despreciable.

cheapen (to) (-øn) *tr.* abaratar. *2* depreciar. *3* intr. abaratarse.

cheat (chit) *s.* timo, estafa, fraude, trampa. *2* timador, tramposo, fullero.

cheat (to) *tr.* engañar, estafar, defraudar, timar. *2* burlar, frustrar. *3* intr. hacer trampas.

cheater (chi·tøʳ) *s.* timador, estafador, tramposo, fullero.

cheatery (-i), **cheating** (chi·ting) *s.* timo, estafa, trampa, fullería.

check (chek) *s.* detención, interrupción. *2* rechazo. *3* restricción, represión, refrenamiento, freno. *4* obstáculo, impedimento. *5* MEC. tope. *6* contratiempo. *7* comprobación, verificación, repaso. *8* señal, visto bueno. *9* talón, contraseña [de equipajes, de guardarropa, etc.]. *10* COM. cheque, talón. *11* cuenta [de restaurante]. *12* cuadro, jaquel, escaque; dibujo o tela a cuadros. *13* AJED. jaque. *14* resquebrajadura.

check (to) *tr.* parar, detener, contener, reprimir, poner coto a, moderar. *2* comprobar, verificar, repasar. | A veces con *up*. *3* marcar [con una señal]. *4* facturar [equipajes]. *5* hacer cuadros en. *6* AJED. dar jaque. *7* intr. detenerse. *8* corresponder punto por punto. *9* resquebrajarse.

checkbook (-buk) *s.* talonario de cheques.

checker (-øʳ) *s.* refrenador. *2* comprobador, revisor. *3* dibujo a cuadros. *4* (E.U.) peón [del juego de damas]. *5 pl.* (E.U.) damas [juego].

checker (to) *tr.* formar escaques o cuadros en. *2* abigarrar, dar variedad.

checkered (-d) *adj.* ajedrezado, a cuadros. *2* fig. variado, accidentado.

checking account (-ing) *s.* cuenta corriente [en un banco].

checkmate (-meit) *s.* jaque mate.

checkmate (to) *tr.* AJED. dar mate. *2* desbaratar, frustrar. *3* derrotar.

checkroom (che·krum) *s.* (E.U.) vestuario, guardarropa [de restaurante, etc.]; depósito de equipajes.

checkup (-øp) *s.* comprobación. *2* MED. reconocimiento general.

cheek (chik) *s.* mejilla; carrillo. *2* fig. descaro, tupé. *3* lado [de un objeto]. *4* larguero, montante, jamba. *5* MEC. quijada.

cheekbone (-boun) *s.* pómulo.

cheeky (-i) *s.* descarado.
cheep (chɪp) *s.* pío, chirrido [de ave].
cheep (to) *intr.* piar, chirriar.
cheer (chɪ·ʳ) *s.* alegría, ánimo; estado de ánimo: *be of good* ~, alegraos, tened ánimo. *2* viandas, comida. *3* viva, vítor.
cheer (to) *tr.* alegrar, animar, alentar, consolar. *2* vitorear, aclamar, aplaudir.
cheerful (-ful) *adj.* alegre, animado, jovial, placentero.
cheerio (chɪ·riou) *interj.* ¡hola!, ¡adiós! [como saludo jovial].
cheerlees (chɪ·ʳlis) *adj.* triste, sombrío.
cheery (chɪ·ri) *adj.* CHEERFULL.
cheese (chɪ·š) *s.* queso: ~ *cake*, quesadilla, ~ *rennet*, BOT. cuajaleche.
cheesy (chɪ·ši) *adj.* cáseo, caseoso.
chef (shef) *s.* cocinero.
chelicera (kili·søra) *s.* quelícero.
chelonian (kilou·nian) *s.* ZOOL. quelonio.
chemical (ke·mikal) *adj.* químico. *2 s.* substancia química.
chemise (shømɪ·š) *s.* camisa [de mujer]. *2* FORT. camisa.
chemisette (shømiše·t) *s.* camiseta [de mujer].
chemist (ke·mist) *s.* químico. *2* farmacéutico.
chemistry (-si) *s.* química.
chenille (shønɪ·l) *s.* felpilla.
cheque (chek) *s.* CHECK 10.
chequer *s.* CHECKER 3, 4 y 5.
cherish (to) (che·rish) *tr.* acariciar. *2* apreciar, querer. *3* cuidar, criar, cultivar, fomentar. *4* alimentar, abrigar [un sentimiento].
cherry (che·ri) *s.* BOT. cereza; cerezo. *2* ~ *laurel*, lauroceraso.
cherub (che·røb) *s.* querube, querubín.
cherubic(al (chøru·bik(al) *adj.* angélico.
chervil (chø·ʳvil) *s.* BOT. perifollo.
chess (ches) *s.* ajedrez.
chessboard (-boʳd) *s.* tablero de ajedrez.
chessman (-mæn) *s.* trebejo, pieza de ajedrez.
chest (chest) *s.* cofre, arca, baúl: ~ *of drawers*, cómoda. *2* MEC. caja, receptáculo. *3* pecho, tórax.
chested (-id) *adj.* de pecho: *broad-chested*, de pecho ancho.
chestnut (-nøt) *s.* BOT. castaña. *2* castaño [árbol; madera; color]. *3* caballo castaño. *4* fam. cuento o chiste gastados.
cheval-de-frise (chø·vældøfriš) *s.* MIL. caballo de Frisa.
cheval-glass (chø·val) *s.* espejo de vestir.
chevalier (shevali·øʳ) *s.* caballero [de una orden].
cheviot (che·viøt) *s.* TEJ. cheviot.
chevron (she·vrøn) *s.* cheurón. *3* MIL. galón en figura de cheurón.
chew (chu) *s.* mascadura. *2* mascada.
chew (to) *tr.* mascar, masticar. *2 tr.-intr.* rumiar, meditar.
chewing gum (-ing) *s.* goma de mascar.
chiaroscuro (kiaroskiu·rou) *s.* claroscuro.
chibouk (chibu·k) *s.* chibuquí.
chicane (shi·kein) *s.* triquiñuela, argucia.
chicane (to) *intr.* trapacear, andar con triquiñuelas. *2 tr.* embrollar, enredar.
chicanery (shikei·nøri) *s.* triquiñuela, argucia, enredo legal.
chick (chick), **chicken** (chi·køn) *s.* pollo, polluelo [de ave de corral]. *2* fig. jovencito, niño.
chicken-hearted *adj.* tímido; cobarde.
chicken-pox *s.* viruelas locas.

chickpea (chi·kpɪ) *s.* BOT. garbanzo.
chickweed (chi·kwɪd) *s.* BOT. álsine.
chicle (chi·køl) *s.* chicle.
chicory (chi·køri) *s.* BOT. achicoria.
chide (to) (chaid) *tr.* reñir, reprender; reprobar. *2* gruñir, refunfuñar. ¶ Pret.: *child* o *chided;* p. p.: *chidden* o *chided*.
chiding (-ing) *s.* reprensión, reprimenda.
chief (chɪ·f) *adj.* principal, mayor, supremo; primero, en jefe. *2 s.* jefe, cabeza, caudillo: *in* ~, en jefe. *3* BLAS. jefe.
chiefless (-lis) *adj.* sin jefe.
chiefly (-li) *adv.* principalmente, mayormente, sobre todo.
chieftain (-tin) *s.* jefe, capitán, caudillo.
chiffon (shi·fan) *s.* gasa, soplillo [tela].
chiffonier (shiføni·ʳ) *s.* cómoda alta con espejo.
chignon (shi·ñan) *s.* moño, castaña.
chigoe (chi·gou) *s.* ENT. nigua.
chiblain (chi·lblein) *s.* sabañón.
child (chai·ld), *pl.* **children** (chi·ldrøn) *s.* niño, niña; criatura: *with* ~, encinta. *2* hijo, hija.
childbirth (-bøʳz) *s.* parto, alumbramiento.
childhood (-jud) *s.* infancia, niñez.
childish (-ish) *adj.* infantil, pueril. *2* aniñado.
childishness (-nis) *s.* puerilidad.
childless (-lis) *adj.* sin hijos.
childlike (-laik) *adj.* infantil, pueril, de niño. *2* aniñado.
children (chi·ldrøn) *s. pl.* de CHILD.
Chilean (chi·lian) *adj.-s.* chileno.
chili (chi·li) *s.* pimiento, chile, *ají.
chill (chil) *s.* frío [sensación]. *2* escalofrío, estremecimiento. *3* frialdad. *4* enfriamiento [del entusiasmo, etc.], desaliento. *5* resfriado. *6 adj.* frío, desapacible; glacial.
chill (to) *tr.* enfriar, helar; resfriar. *2* desalentar. *3 intr.* enfriarse, calofriarse.
chilly (chi·li) *adj.* que siente frío, calofriado. *2* friolento. *3* frío, glacial.
chimaera *s.* CHIMERA.
chime (chaim) *s.* juego de campanas. *2* campaneo, repique. *3* ritmo, armonía. *4* concordancia, conformidad.
chime (to) *tr.* tocar, tañer [campanas]. *2* dar [la hora]. *3 intr.* sonar [las campanas]. *4* sonar con armonía. *5* armonizar, concordar.
chimera (kaimi·ra) *s.* MIT. quimera. *2* quimera, ilusión.
chimerical (kaime·rikal) *adj.* quimérico.
chimney (chi·mni) *s.* chimenea: ~ *sweeper*, deshollinador. *2* hogar, chimenea francesa: ~ *piece*, delantero de chimenea. *3* tubo de lámpara.
chimpanzee (chimpænšr·) *s.* chimpancé.
chin (chin) *s.* barba, barbilla, mentón: ~ *strap*, carrillera, barboquejo.
China (chai·na) *n. pr.* China.
china *s.* china, porcelana, loza.
Chinaman (-mæn) *s.* chino.
chinaware (-ue·ʳ) *s.* porcelana, loza.
chinchilla (chinchi·la) *s.* ZOOL. chinchilla.
chine (chain) *s.* espinazo, lomo. *2* solomo.
chine (to) *tr.* deslomar.
Chinese (chain·š) *adj.* chino, chinesco, sínico. *2 s.* chino [pers.; idioma].
chink (chink) *s.* grieta, raja; rendija, resquicio. *2* tintineo. *3* pop. dinero.
chink (to) *tr.* agrietar, hender, rajar. *2 intr.-tr.* tintinar, hacer tintinar.
chinky (chi·nki) *adj.* hendido, rajado. *2* resquebradizo.

chintz (chintš) *s.* zaraza, indiana.
chip (chip) *s.* astilla, lasca, desportilladura, viruta, brizna, pedacito. *2* ficha [en el juego]. *3 pl.* patatas a la inglesa.
chip (to) *tr.* cortar, picar. *2* astillar, descantillar, desportillar. *3 intr.* romperse, desportillarrse, desconcharse. *4* chillar, piar [ciertos pájaros]. ¶ Pret. y p. p.: *chipped;* ger.: *-pping.*
chipmunk (-mønk) *s.* zool. ardilla listada.
chirk (chørk) *s.* fam. (E.U.) animado, de buen humor.
chirograph (kai·rogræf) *s.* quirógrafo.
chiromancer (kai·romænsør) *s.* quiromántico.
chiromancy (kai·romænsør) *s.* quiromántico.
chiromancy (-mænsi) *s.* quiromancia.
chiropodist (kaira·podist) *s.* quirópodo.
chiropteran (kaira·ptøran) *s.* quiróptero.
chirp (chørp) *s.* chirrido, pío, gorjeo. *2* canto o voz alegre.
chirp (to) *intr.* chirriar, piar, gorjear. *2* cantar o hablar alegremente.
chirping (-ing), **chirpy** (-pi) *adj.* parlero. *2* alegre, animado.
chirrup (chi·røp) *s.* chirrido, gorjeo; voz que lo imita.
chirrup (to) *intr.* chirriar, gorjear; silbar.
chisel (chi·šøl) *s.* cincel. *2* escoplo, formón. *3* cortafrío.
chisel (to) *tr.* cincelar. *2* escoplear. ¶ Pret. y p. p.: *chiseled* o *-lled;* ger.: *chiseling* o *-lling.*
chit (chit) *s.* desp. chiquillo, chiquilla. *2* bot. brote, grillo.
chit (to) *tr.* quitar los brotés.
chitchat (chi·tchæt) *s.* charla, palique.
chitin (kai·tin) *s.* quitina.
chitterlings (chi·tørlingš) *s. pl.* mondongo de cerdo frito o asado.
chivalric (shi·valrik) *adj.* caballeresco.
chivalrous (shi·valrøs) *adj.* caballeroso.
chivalry (shi·valri) *s.* caballería [institución; empresa o dignidad de caballero]. *2* caballerosidad.
chive (chaiv) *s.* bot. cebollino.
chlamys (klei·mis) *s.* clámide.
chloral (klo·ral) *s.* quím. cloral.
chlorate (-reit) *s.* quím. clorato.
chloride (-raid) *s.* quím. cloruro.
chlorine (-rin) *s.* quím. cloro.
chloroform (to) *tr.* cloroformizar.
chlorophyll (klorou·sis) *s.* clorofila.
chlorosis (klorou·sis) *s.* clororis.
chlorotic (klora·tik) *adj.* clorótico.
choana (kouæ·na) *s.* anat. coana.
chock (chok) *s.* calzo, cuña. *2* mar. taco. *3 adv.* completamente.
chock (to) *tr.* calzar, acuñar, afianzar. *2* tapar [un hueco]; llenar, atestar.
chock-full *adj.* colmado, repleto, atestado.
chocolate (cho·kølit) *s.* chocolate: ~ *cup,* jícara; ~ *pot,* chocolatera.
choice (cho·is) *s.* escogimiento, selección, elección, preferencia. *2* opción, alternativa. *3* cosa escogida. *4* la flor, lo más escogido. *5 adj.* escogido, selecto, exquisito.
choiceness (-nis) *s.* excelencia, exquisitez. *2* discernimiento, delicadeza.
choir (kuai·ør) *s.* coro.
choke (chouk) *s.* ahogo, estrangulación. *2* mec. obturador. *3* elect. ~ *coil,* bobina de reacción.
choke (to) *tr.* ahogar, sofocar. *2* estrangular. *3* aga-

rrotar. *4* reprimir. *5* obstruir, atorar. *6 intr.* ahogarse, atragantarse. *7* atorarse.
chokedamp (-dæ·mp) *s.* anhídrido carbónico de las minas de carbón.
choker (-ør) *s.* ahogador. *2* tapaboca. *3* corbatín. *4* mec. obturador [del carburador]. *5* elect. bobina de reacción.
choler (ka·lør) *s.* cólera, enojo. *2* bilis.
cholera (-a) *s.* med. cólera.
choleric (-ik) *s.* colérico, iracundo. *2* med. colérico.
cholesterin (køle·størin) *s.* colesterina.
chondriome (ka·ndrioum) *s.* condrioma.
choose (to) (chuš) *tr.* escoger, elegir. *2* preferir, optar por; decidir, querer [hacer algo]. *3 intr.* escoger, querer. ¶ Pret.: *chose;* p. p.: *chosen.*
chooser (-ør) *s.* escogedor.
choosey, choosy (chu·ši) *adj.* (E.U.) delicado, melindroso.
chop (chap) *s.* corte, tajo. *2* tajada; chuleta. *3* grieta, raja. *4* mec. quijada. *5* cambio, trueque. *6 pl.* fauces; boca, entrada. *7* cosa desmenuzada.
chop (to) *tr.* cortar, tajar; picar [carne, etc.]: *to* ~ *off,* cortar [separar]. *2* hender, rajar. *3* desbastar. *4* trocar. *5 intr.* dar golpes de hacha, cuchillo, etc. *6* saltar [el viento]; variar, cambiar. ¶ Pret. y p. p.: *chopped;* ger.: *chopping.*
chophouse (-jaus) *s.* figón.
chopper (-ør) *s.* hacha, hacheta. *2* cuchilla de carnicero.
chopping (-ing) *s.* tajadura, picadura; ~ *block,* tajo, tajadero; ~ *knife,* tajadera [cuchilla]. *2 adj.* choppy.
choppy (-i) *adj.* picado [mar]. *2* variable [viento]. *3* mudable. *4* cortado, incoherente. *5* agrietado.
chopsticks (-stiks) *s.* palillos chinos [para comer].
choral (ko·ral) *adj.-s.* mús. coral.
chord (ko·rd) *s.* mús., geom. cuerda. *2* fig. cuerda sensible. *3* mús. acorde. *4* anat. cuerda, cordón.
chore (cho·ͬ) *s.* (E.U.) quehacer, faena.
chorea (kor·a) *s.* med. corea.
choree (kor·) *s.* coreo.
choreography (koria·grafi) *s.* coreografía.
choriamb (ko·riæmb) *s.* coriambo.
chorion (ko·riøn) *s.* anat. corión.
chorist (ko·rist), **chorister** (-ør) *s.* corista.
chorography (kora·grafi) *s.* corografía.
choroid (ko·roid) *adj.-s.* anat. coroides.
chorus (ko·røs) *s.* mús. coro: *in* ~, a coro. *2* teat. coro, conjunto. *3* estribillo [de canción].
chorus (to) *tr.-intr.* cantar o hablar a coro. *2 tr.* hacer coro a.
chose (chouš) *pret.* de to choose.
chosen (-øn) *p. p.* de to choose.
chough (chøf) *s.* orn. chova.
chouse (chaus) *s.* fam. engaño, estafa.
chouse (to) *tr.* fam. engañar, estafar.
chow (chau) *s.* perro chino.
chow-chow *s.* mezcla de encurtidos o de frutas en conserva.
chrematistic (kremati·stik) *adj.* crematístico.
chrism (kri·šm) *s.* liturg. crisma.
chrismatory (-atori) *s.* crismera.
Christ (kraist) *n. pr.* Cristo.
christen (to) (kri·søn) *tr.* bautizar, cristianar.
Christendom (-d) *s.* cristiandad.
christening (-ing) *s.* bautizo, bautismo. *2 adj.* bautismal.
Christian (kri·schan) *adj.-s.* cristiano: ~ *name,* nombre de pila.
Christianism (-išm) *s.* cristianismo.

Christianity (krischiæ·niti) s. cristianidad. 2 cristianismo.
Christianize (kri·schanaiš) tr. cristianizar.
Christine (kristɪ·n) n. pr. Cristina.
Christmas (kri·smas) s. Navidad; pascuas de Navidad: ~ carol, villancico; ~ Eve, nochebuena.
Christopher (kri·støfø^r) n. pr. Cristóbal.
chromatic (kroumæ·tik) adjt. cromático.
chromatics (-tiks) s. cromática.
chrome (kroum), **chromiun** (-iøm) s. QUÍM. cromo.
chromium plate (to) tr. cromar.
chromo (krou·mo), **chromolitograph** (-li·zogræf) s. cromo, cromolitografía.
chromosome (krou·mosoum) s. BIOL. cromosoma.
chronic (kra·nik) adj. crónico, inveterado.
chronicle (kra·nikøl) s. crónica.
chronicle (to) tr. narrar en una crónica. 2 intr. escribir crónicas.
chronicler (kra·niclø^r) s. cronista.
chronograph (kra·nogræf) s. cronógrafo.
chronologic(al (kranola·dȳik(al) adj. cronológico.
chronology (krona·lodȳi) s. cronología.
chronometer (-mitø^r) s. cronómetro.
chronometry (-metri) s. cronometría.
chrysalid (kri·salid), **chrysalis** (-lis) s. crisálida.
chrysanthemum (krisæ·nzimøm) s. BOT. crisantemo.
chrysoberyl (kri·souberil) s. MINER. crisoberilo.
chub (chøb) s. ICT. coto.
chubby (chø·bi) adj. regordete, gordinflón.
chuck (chøk) s. mamola, golpecito debajo de la barba. 2 cloqueo. 3 echada. 4 MEC. calzo, cuña; nuez o mandril de torno; portaherraminta.
chuck (to) intr. cloquear. 2 tr. hacer la mamola, dar un golpecito debajo de la barba. 3 echar, tirar, arrojar.
chuckle (cho·køl) s. risita, risa ahogada. 2 cloqueo.
chuckle (to) intr. reír entre dientes, con risa ahogada. 2 cloquear.
chuckle head s. tonto, zoquete.
chufa (chu·fa) s. BOT. chufa.
chum (chøm) s. fam. camarada. 2 condiscípulo.
chum (to) intr. fam. ser camarada. ¶ Pret. y p. p.: chummed; ger.: chumming.
chummy (-i) adj. íntimo [amigo]. 2 sociable.
chump (chømp) s. zoquete, tarugo. 2 lomo [de carnero]. 3 fam. chola. 4 fam. tonto.
chunk (chønk) s. pedazo corto y grueso. 2 persona o caballo rechonchos.
chunky (-i) adj. rechoncho.
church (chø^rch) s. iglesia: Church of England, Iglesia Anglicana; Roman Catholic Church, Iglesia Católica.
church (to) tr. llevar a la iglesia [para bautizar, etc.].
churchman (-mæn) s. eclesiástico, clérigo. 2 miembro de una iglesia.
churchwarden (-wo·^rdøn) s. obrero, fabriquero.
churchyard (-ia^rd) s. cementerio.
churl (chø·^rl) s. patán, palurdo. 2 grosero. 3 tacaño.
churlish (-ish) adj. rústico, rudo, grosero, intratable. 2 ruin, avaro.
churn (chø·^rn) s. mantequera [para hacer manteca].
churn (to) tr. batir [en una mantequera], mazar. 2 agitar, revolver.
chute (shut) s. cascada, rabión. 2 conducto o canal por donde se hace bajar algo.
chyle (kail) s. FISIOL. quilo.
chylification (kailifikei·shøn) s. quilificación.

chyme (kaim) s. FISIOL. quimo.
chymification (kaimifikei·shøn) s. quimificación.
cibol (si·bøl) s. BOT. cebolleta. 2 BOT. chalote.
ciborium (sibou·riøm) s. ciborio. 2 copón.
cicada (sikei·da) s. ENT. cigarra, chicharra.
cicatrice (si·katris) s. cicatriz.
cicatricle (sikatri·køl), **cicatricula** (-kula) s. galladura.
cicatrix s. CICATRICE.
cicatrization (-šei·shøn) s. cicatrización.
cicatrize (to) (si·katraiš) tr. cicatrizar. 2 intr. cicatrizarse.
cicely (si·søli) s. BOT. perifollo oloroso.
Cicero (si·sørou) n. pr. Cicerón.
cicerone (chichørou·ni) s. cicerone.
cicuta (sikiu·ta) s. cicuta.
cider (sai·dø^r) s. sidra.
cigar (siga·^r) s. cigarro puro, tabaco: ~ case, cigarrera, petaca; ~ holder, boquilla.
cigarette (sigare·t) s. cigarrillo, pitillo: ~ case, pitillera; ~ paper, papel de fumar.
ciliary (si·lieri) adj. ciliar.
ciliate (si·lieit) adj. H. NAT. ciliado.
cilice (si·lis) s. cilicio.
Cimbrian (si·mbrian) adj.-s. cimbro.
cinch (sinch) s. (E.U.) cincha. 2 fam. (E.U.) ganga; cosa fácil o segura.
cinch (to) tr. (E.U.) cinchar. 2 apretar, ceñir.
cinchona (sinkou·na) s. BOT. quino: ~ bark, quina.
cincture (si·nkchø^r) s. cinto, cincho, cingudo. 2 cerca, cercado.
cincture (to) tr. ceñir, cercar, rodear.
cinder (si·ndø^r) s. brasa; carbonilla. 2 pol. cenizas, pavesas, rescoldo.
Cinderella (sindøre·la) s. Cenicienta.
cinema (si·nima) s. (esp. Ingl.) cine, cinema.
cinematograph (sinimæ·tográef) s. cinematógrafo.
cinematography (-mata·grafi) s. cinematografía.
cineraria (sinøre·ria) s. BOT. cineraria.
cinerary (si·nøreri) adj. cinerario.
cineration (-rei·shøn) s. incineración.
cinereous (sini·riøs) adj. cinéreo, ceniciento.
Cingalese (singæli·š) adj.-s. cingalés.
cingulum (si·ngiuløm) s. cíngulo.
cinnabar (si·naba^r) s. cinabrio.
cinnamon (si·namøn) s. canela: ~ tree, canelo.
cinquefoil (si·ngkfoil) s. BOT. cincoenrama. 2 ventana de cinco lóbulos.
cipher (sai·fø^r) s. cero: a mere ~, un cero a la izquierda. 2 cifra [número; escritura secreta; monograma].
cipher (to) tr. cifrar [escribir en cifra]. 2 expresar con cifras; calcular.
Circassian (sø^rkæ·shan) adj.-s. circasiano.
circensian (sø·^rse·nshan) adj. circense.
circle (sø·^rkøl) s. círculo, circunferencia. 2 anillo, redondel, corro, ruedo. 3 ASTR. órbita. 4 círculo, ámbito, esfera, grupo. 5 TEAT. gradería. 6 círculo vicioso. 7 ciclo, serie.
circle (to) tr. circuir, rodear, circundar. 2 intr. girar; dar vueltas.
circlet (sø·^rklit) s. circulito, anillo. 2 brazalete, diadema.
circuit (sø·^rkit) s. circuito: ~ breaker, ELECT. corta-circuitos. 2 ámbito, radio. 3 rodeo; vuelta, recorrido. 4 ASTR. revolución.
circuitous (sø^rkiui·tøs) adj. tortuoso, indirecto.
circular (sø·^rkula^r) adj. circular, redondo. 2 s. circular [carta].
circulate (to) (sø·^rkiuleit) intr. circular. 2 poner en circulación; propalar, esparcir.

circulating (-ing) *adj.* circulante. *2* MAT. periódica [fracción].
circulation (-ei·shøn) *s.* circulación.
circulatory (sø·ʳkiulɑtori) *adj.* circulatorio.
circumambient (sø·ʳkømæ·mbiønt) *adj.* circumambiente.
circumcise (to) (sø·ʳkømsaiš) *tr.* circuncidar.
circumcised (-d) *adj.* circunciso.
circumcision (-si·y̆øn) *s.* circuncisión.
circumference (sø·ʳkø·mførøns) *s.* circunferencia.
circumflex (sø·ʳkømfleks) *adj.* circunflejo. *2* que lleva acento circunflejo. *3* ANAT. encorvado. *4 s.* acento circunflejo.
circumfuse (to) (-fiuš) *tr.* verter o difundir alrededor.
circumjacent (-dy̆ei·søn) *adj.* circunvecino.
circumlocution (sø·ʳkømloukiu·shøn) *s.* circunlocución, circunloquio.
circumnavigate (to) (næ·vigeit) *tr.* circumnavegar.
circumpolar (-pou·lɑʳ) *adj.* circumpolar.
circumscribe (-skrai·b) *tr.* circunscribir.
circumscription (-skrip·shøn) *s.* circunscripción.
circumspect (sø·ʳkømspekt) *adj.* circunspecto, prudente.
circumspection (sø·ʳkømspe·kshøn) *s.* circunspección, prudencia.
circumstance (sø·ʳkømstæns) *s.* circunstancia. *2* detalle, pormenor. *3* ceremonia, formalidad. *4 pl.* medios, posición económica.
circumstantial (sø·ʳkømstæ·nshal) *adj.* circunstancial. *2* circunstanciado. *3* DER. ~ *evidence*, prueba iniciaria, indicios vehementes.
circumstantially (-li) *adv.* circunstancialmente. *2* detalladamente.
circumstantitate (to) (-shieit) *tr.* detallar, referir circunstanciadamente.
circumvallate (to) (-væ·leit) *tr.* circunvalar.
circumvent (to) (-vent) *tr.* engañar, embaucar; entrampar. *2* rodear, evitar.
circumvolution (-vølu·shøn) *s.* circunvolución. *2* rodeo, circunloquio.
circus (sø·ʳkøs) *s.* circo [romano]. *2* circo, circo ecuestre. *3* plaza redonda, glorieta. *4* GEOL. circo.
cirque (sø·ʳk) *s.* CIRCO 1, 2 y 4. *2* círculo, anillo.
cirrhosis (sirou·sis) *s.* cirrosis.
cirrhotic (sirou·tik) *adj.* cirrótico.
cirriped (si·riped) *adj.-s.* ZOOL. cirrípedo; cirrópodo.
cirrus (si·røs) *s.* BOT., ZOOL., METEOR. cirro.
cisalpine (sisæ·lpain) *adj.* cisalpino.
cissoid (si·soid) *s.* GEOM. cisoide.
cist (sist) *s.* ARQUEOL. arquilla.
cistaceous (sistei·shøs) *adj.* BOT. cistáceo.
Cistercian (sistø·ʳshan) *adj.-s.* cisterciense.
cistern (si·stø·ʳn) *s.* cisterna.
cistus (si·støs) *s.* BOT. jara.
citadel (si·tɑdøl) *s.* ciudadela.
citation (saitei·shøn) *s.* cita, citación, mención. *2* DER., MIL. citación.
cite (to) (sait) *tr.* citar, llamar. *2* citar, aducir, mencionar.
cithara (si·zɑrɑ) *s.* MÚS. cítara.
cithern (si·zø·ʳn) *s.* MÚS. especie de laúd.
citizen (si·tišøn) *s.* ciudadano. *2* habitante, vecino.
citizenship (-ship) *s.* ciudadanía.
citrate (si·treit) *s.* QUÍM. citrato.
citric (-trik) *adj.* QUÍM. cítrico.
citrine (-trin) *adj.* citrino.
citron (-trøn) *s.* cidra: ~ *tree*, cidro. *2* acitrón.
citrus fruits *s. pl.* agrios.

city (si·ti) *s.* ciudad. *2 the City*, barrio comercial y bancario de Londres. *3 adj.* municipal, de la ciudad, urbano.
civet (si·vit) *s.* civeto, algalia: ~ *cat*, civeta.
civic (si·vik) *adj.* cívico. *2* ciudadano.
civil (si·vil) *adj.* civil: ~ *servant*, funcionario público. *2* cortés, urbano.
civilian (sivi·lian) *adj.* de paisano. *2 s.* paisano [no militar]. *3* jurisperito.
civility (-liti) *s.* civilidad, cortesía, urbanidad. *2* amabilidad, atención [acto].
civilization (-šei·shøn) *s.* civilización.
civilize (to) (si·vilaiš) *tr.* civilizar.
civilized (-d) *adj.* civilizado.
civilly (si·vili) *adv.* civilmente, cortésmente.
civism (si·višm) *s.* civismo, patriotismo.
clack (klæk) *s.* charla, parloteo. *2* cítola. *3* golpe seco, golpeteo. *4* ~ *valve*, chapaleta.
clack (to) *intr.* charlar. *2* golpetear, tabletear.
clad (klæd) *adj.* vestido, cubierto. *2* investido.
claim (kleim) *s.* demanda, reclamación, reivindicación. *2* derecho, título, pretensión. *3* MIN. pertenencia.
claim (to) *tr.* reclamar, exigir, pedir, tener derecho. *2* reivindicar. *3* denunciar [una mina]. *4* afirmar, declarar.
claimant (-ɑnt) *s.* reclamante, demandante. *2* persona que reivindica un título, derecho, etc.; pretendiente [a un trono]. *3* MIN. denunciante.
clairvoyance (kleʳvo·ians) *s.* clarividencia.
clairvoyant (-iant) *s.* clarividente. *2* vidente.
clam (klæm) *s.* almeja, tellina.
clam (to) *intr.* pescar almejas. *2* ser pegajoso. ¶ Pret. y p. p.: *clammed*; ger.: *clamming*.
clamant (-ɑnt) *adj.* clamoroso; apremiante.
clamber (to) (klæ·mbøʳ) *intr.* trepar, encaramarse, gatear.
clamminess (klæ·minis) *s.* viscosidad.
clammy (klæ·mi) *adj.* viscoso, pegajoso; frío y húmedo.
clamor, to clamor = CLAMOUR, TO CLAMOUR.
clamorous (klæ·mørøs) *adj.* clamoroso, ruidoso, tumultuoso.
clamour (klæ·mø·ʳ) *s.* clamor, clamoreo, griterío, estruendo.
clamour (to) *intr.-tr.* clamar, clamorear, gritar.
clamp (klæmp) *s.* CARP. cárcel. *2* MEC. pieza o instrumento para apretar o sujetar; tornillo de banco o de sujeción, mordaza, abrazadera, etc. *3* ELECT. borne. *4* pisada fuerte.
clamp (to) *tr.* sujetar, unir [con tornillo, abrazadera, etc.]. *2 intr.* pisar recio.
clan (klæn) *s.* clan.
clandestine (klænde·stin) *adj.* clandestino.
clang (klæng) *s.* sonido metálico, resonante.
clang (to) *intr.* sonar, resonar. *2 tr.* golpear haciendo resonar.
clango(u)r (klæ·ngøʳ) *s.* clangor, estruendo.
clank (klænk) *s.* sonido metálico de golpe o choque.
clank (to) *intr.* sonar, resonar al chocar. *2 tr.* hacer sonar [cadenas, etc.].
clannish (klæ·nish) *adj.* de clan; cerrado, exclusivo.
clap (klæp) *s.* ruido o golpe seco: ~ *of thunder*, trueno. *2* palmada. *3* aplauso.
clap (to) *tr.* batir, golpear: *to* ~ *the hands*, palmotear, aplaudir. *2* dar una palmada. *3* cerrar dando golpe. *4* aplicar, poner. *5 intr.* sonar con golpe seco. *6* guachapear. ¶ Pret. y p. p.: *clapped* o *clapt*; ger.: *clapping*.

clapboard (-bo^rd) *s.* tabla de chilla.
clapper (-ø^r) *s.* palmoteador. *2* TEAT. alabardero. *3* cítola. *4* tableta, tejoleta. *5* badajo. *6* fig. la lengua. *7* carraca [instrumento]. *8* chapaleta.
claptrap (-træp) *s.* faramalla. *2 adj.* de faramalla, insincero; de relumbrón.
Clare (kle·^r) *n. pr.* Clara.
clarence (klæ·røns) *s.* clarens [coche].
claret (klæ·ret) *s.* clarete [vino].
clarification (klærifikei·shøn) *s.* clarificación.
clarify (to) (klæ·rifai) *tr.* clarificar, purificar. *2* aclarar, esclarecer. *3 intr.* clarificarse, aclararse.
clarinet (klærine·t) *s.* clarinete [instrumento].
clarinettist (-ist) *s.* clarinete [músico].
clarion (klæ·riøn) *s.* clarín.
clarionet (klæriøne·t) *s.* CLARINETE.
clarity (klæ·riti) *s.* claridad.
clary (kle·ri) *s.* BOT. amaro, esclarea.
clash (klæsh) *s.* ruido, estruendo [de choque, caída, etc.]. *2* choque, encuentro. *3* oposición, conflicto.
clash (to) *intr.* sonar [al chocar]. *2* chocar, entrechocarse. *3* estar en oposición, en conflicto. *4 tr.* hacer chocar, golpear.
clasp (klæsp) *s.* broche, cierre, manecilla, pieza que se cierra o sujeta: ~ *knife,* navaja. *2* abrazo, apretón.
clasp (to) *tr.* abrochar, cerrar, sujetar [con broche, cierre, etc.]. *2* asir, agarrar. *3* abrazar, estrechar.
class (klas) *s.* clase [grupo, categoría, etc.]. *2* clase [en la eneñanza]. *3* fam. distinción, elegancia. *4* MIL. promoción, reemplazo.
class (to) *tr.* clasificar.
classic (klæ·sik) *adj.-s.* clásico.
classical (-al) *adj.* clásico.
clascicism (klæ·sisišm) *s.* clasicismo.
classicist (-sist) *s.* clasicista.
classification (klæsifikei·shøn) *s.* clasificación.
classify (to) (klæ·sifai) *tr.* clasificar. ¶ Pret. y p. p.: *classified.*
classmate (kla·smeit) *s.* condiscípulo.
classroom (-rum) *s.* clase, aula.
classy (kla·si) *adj.* fam. elegante, de categoría.
clastic (klæ·stik) *adj.* clástico.
clatter (klæ·tø^r) *s.* martilleo, guachapeo; ruido repetido como el de pasos o golpes. *2* alboroto, gresca. *3* charla.
clatter (to) *intr.* hacer un ruido repetido como el de pasos o golpes; resonar, guachapear. *2* charlar. *3 tr.* hacer sonar.
Claude (klod), **Claudius** (klo·diøs) *n. pr.* Claudio.
clause (klo·s) *s.* GRAM. oración breve, subordinada. *2* cláusula, estipulación.
claustral (klo·stral) *adj.* claustral.
claustrophobia (klostrofou·bia) *s.* claustrofobia.
clavate(d (klei·veit(id) *adj.* BOT., ZOOL. en forma de clava.
clavichord (klæ·vikø^rd) *s.* clavicordio.
clavicle (klæ·vikøl) *s.* clavícula.
claw (klo) *s.* ZOOL. garfa, garra, presa. *2* uña [de insecto; de pétalo]; pinza [de crustáceo]. *3* MEC. uña, garfio; orejas: ~ *hammer,* martillo de orejas; fam. frac.
claw (to) *tr.-intr.* arañar, arpar, rasgar, desgarrar. *2 tr.* agarrar.
clay (klei) *s.* arcilla, tierra, barro, greda: ~ *pit,* barrera; gredal. *2* tiza.
clay (to) *tr.* embarrar; arcillar; engredar.
clayey (klei·i), **clayish** (-ish) *adj.* arcilloso.

claymore (klei·mo^r) *s.* espada escocesa.
clean (klīn) *adj.* limpio: *to make* ~, limpiar. *2* puro, honesto. *3* libre, despejado. *4* neto, distinto. *5* completo. *6* bien formado, bien proporcionado. *7 adv.* limpiamente. *8* completamente, enteramente.
clean (to) *tr.* limpiar. *2* asear; desempolvar; quitar las manchas de; desengrasar. *3* lavar [la vajilla]. *4* mondar. *5* descombrar. *6* depurar, purificar.
clean-cut *adj.* bien cortado; claro, preciso, definido.
clenaer (-ø^r) *s.* limpiador. *2* detergente. *3* quitamanchas.
cleaning (ing) *s.* limpia, limpieza. *2* monda. *3 pl.* limpiaduras, mondaduras.
cleanlily (-lili) *adv.* CLEANLY.
cleanlines (-linis) *s.* limpieza, aseo, pulidez.
cleanly (-li) *adj.* limpio, curioso, aseado. *2 adv.* limpiamente.
cleanness (-nis) *s.* limpieza [calidad, estado]. *2* pureza, inocencia. *3* elegancia [de estilo].
cleanse (to) (klenš) *tr.* limpiar, lavar. *2* purificar, depurar, purgar. *3* absterger.
cleanser (-ø^r) *s.* limpiador, lavador, purificador. *2* purgante.
clean-shaven *adj.* bien afeitado.
clear (kli·ø^r) *adj.* claro. | No tiene los sentidos de ralo, poco espeso y poco subido [color]. *2* limpio, puro. *3* sereno, despejado. *4* brillante [metal]. *5* terso, fresco [cutis, etc.]. *6* liso, raso, abierto. *7* libre [de culpa, de estorbos, de deudas, etc.], desembarazado, despejado, desenredado, expedito. *8* líquido, neto. *9* apartado, alejado: *to keep* ~ *of,* no acercarse a. *10* preciso, definido. *11* seguro [de una cosa]. *12 s.* claro, espacio. *13* PINT. luz, claros. *14 adv.* claramente. *15* enteramente, absolutamente.
clear (to) *tr.* aclarar [clarificar; disipar; hacer inteligible]. *2* aclarar [el semblante, la voz]. *3* limpiar [de impurezas, etc.]; librar [de estorbos]; despejar, desocupar: *to* ~ *the table,* levantar la mesa. *4* justificar, absolver. *5* desenredar, desembrollar. *6* saltar, salvar [un espacio]. *7* pagar, liquidar. *8* cancelar [una hipoteca]. *9* desempeñar; librar de cargas u obligaciones. *10* despachar [un buque] en la aduana. *11* sacar [un beneficio]. *12* AGR. desmontar, rozar. *13* mondar [un árbol]. *14 to* ~ *up,* desembarazar, limpiar, dilucidar.
15 intr. aclararse, serenarse. *16* desembarazarse, desenredarse. *17* COM. liquidar cuentas. *18 to* ~ *up,* serenarse, desencapotarse; arreglarse [una situación].
clearage (-idÿ) *s.* despejo; descombro, desmonte.
clearance (-ans) *s.* despejo. *2* MEC. huelgo, juego, espacio libre o muerto. *3* despacho [de aduana]. *4* compensación [de cheques, etc.]. *5* COM. ~ *sale,* liquidación de existencias.
clear-cut *adj.* bien perfilado, bien definido.
clear-headed *adj.* inteligente.
clearing (-ing) *s.* aclaramiento, aclaración. *2* AGR. desmonte. *4* claro, raso; terreno desarbolado. *5* COM. liquidación, compensación: ~ *house,* cámara de compensación.
clearly (-li) *adv.* claramente.
clearness (-nis) *s.* claridad.
clear-sighted *adj.* clarividente, perspicaz.
cleat (klīt) *s.* listón, soporte. *2* tojino. *3* MAR. cornamusa. *4* ELECT. aislador.

cleavage (klɪ·vidȳ) *s.* hendidura, división. *2* MINER. crucero.

1) cleave (to) (klɪv) *tr.-intr.* pegarse, adherirse. *2* apegarse. ¶ Pret. y p. p.: *cleaved.*

2) cleave (to) *tr.* hender, rajar, cortar, dividir. *2 intr.* henderse, partirse. *3* abrirse. ¶ Pret.: *cleft, cleaved* o *clove;* p. p.: *cleft, cleaved* o *cloven.*

cleavers (-ø‍ʳš) *s.* BOT. amor de hortelano.

clef (klef) *s.* MÚS. clave, llave.

cleft (kleft) *adj.* hendido, partido. *2 s.* hendidura, raja, grieta, rendija.

clematis (kle·matis) *s.* BOT. clemátide.

clemency (kle·mønsi) *s.* clemencia. *2* benignidad [del tiempo].

clement (kle·mønt) *adj.* clemente. *2* suave [tiempo].

clench (klench) *s.* agarro, presión.

clench (to) *tr.* fijar, asegurar. *2* remachar, roblar. *3* apretar [los puños, los dientes]. *4* agarrar, empuñar.

clencher (-ø‍ʳ) *s.* CLINCHER.

clepsydra (kle·psidra) *s.* clepsidra.

cleptomania (kleptomei·nia) *s.* cleptomanía.

clerestory (cli·ʳstori) *s.* claraboya lateral [de una iglesia, estación, etc.].

clergy (klø·ʳdȳi) *s.* clero; clerecía.

clergyman (-mæn) *s.* clérigo, eclesiástico, sacerdote, pastor.

cleric (kle·rik) *s.* clérigo.

clerical (-al) *adj.* clerical; eclesiástico. *2* de oficinista.

clerk (klø‍ʳk) *s.* empleado, dependiente, pasante, escribiente, secretario, actuario. *2* sacristán. *3* clérigo. *4* ant. docto, erudito.

clever (kle·vø‍ʳ) *adj.* diestro, hábil, mañoso. *2* listo, avisado, capaz, inteligente. *3* (E.U) complaciente.

cleverness (-nis) *s.* destreza, habilidad, maña. *2* talento.

clew (klu) *s.* ovillo. *2* MAR. puño de escota; su anillo. *3* pista, indicio.

clew (to) *tr.* MAR. cargar los puños de [una vela].

click (klik) *s.* golpecito seco; su sonido. *2* seguro, fiador, trinquete.

click (to) *intr.-tr.* sonar o hacer sonar con uno o más golpecitos secos. *2 intr.* hacer tictac.

client (klai·ønt) *s.* cliente.

clientele (kklaiønte·l) *s.* clientela.

cliff (klif) *s.* risco, precipicio, escarpa, farallón, acantilado.

cliffy (-i), **clifty** (-ti) *adj.* escarpado, acantilado; riscoso.

climacteric (klaimækte·rik) *adj.* climatérico. *2 s.* período climatérico.

climate (klai·mit) *s.* clima.

climatic(al (klaimæ·tik[al] *adj.* climático.

climatology (klaimata·lodȳi) *s.* climatología.

climax (klai·mæks) *s.* RET. climax. *2* punto culminante o crítico; cenit, colmo.

climb (klaim) *s.* trepa, subida, ascenso.

climb (to) *tr.* trepar, subir, escalar. *2 intr.* trepar, subir, elevarse, encaramarse: *to ~ down,* bajar; desistir.

climber (-ø‍ʳ) *s.* trepador, escalador. *2* BOT. enredadera. *3* ORN. trepadora.

clime (klaim) *s.* clima, región.

clinch (klinch) *s.* remache, robladura. *2* argumento irrebatible. *3* agarro; lucha cuerpo a cuerpo.

clinch (to) *tr.* TO CLENCH. *2* MAR. entalingar. *3* cerrar

[un trato]. *4 intr.* agarrarse, abrazarse estrechamente.

clincher (-ø‍ʳ) *s.* remachador. *2* roblón, laña. *3* argumento decisivo.

cling (to) (kling) *intr.* asirse, aferrarse, adherirse, pegarse. *2* persistir. ¶ Pret. y p. p.: *clung.*

clinging (-ing) *adj.* adhesivo. *2* adherido, colgante.

clingy (-i) *adj.* adhesivo, tenaz.

clinic (kli·nik) *adj.* clínico. *2 s.* clínica [enseñanza]. *3* clínica, dispensario [de hospital].

clinical (-al) *adj.* clínico.

clinician (klini·šan) *s.* clínico.

clink (klink) *s.* tintín.

clink (to) *tr.* hacer tintinear. *2 intr.* tintinear.

clinker (-ø‍ʳ) *s.* ladrillo muy duro. *2* pedazo de escoria. *3 ~ work,* obra de tingladillo.

Clio (klai·ou) *n. pr.* MIT. Clío.

clip (klip) *s.* grapa, pinza, sujetapapeles, clip. *2* cargador [de pistola, etc.]. *3* tijeretazo, corte. *4* recorte. *5* cercenadura. *6* esquileo. *7* fam. golpe.

clip (to) *tr.* abrazar, sujetar. *2* cortar, recortar, cercenar, acortar. *3* esquilar, trasquilar. *4* fam. arrear [un golpe]. *5 intr.* correr, moverse con rapidez. ¶ Pret. y p. p.: *clipped;* ger.: *clipping.*

clipper (-ø‍ʳ) *s.* recortador, cercenador, esquilador. *2* cizalla. *3* MAR., AVIA. clíper.

clipping (-ing) *s.* recorte, cercenadura. *2* recorte, retal; recorte de prensa. *3 adj.* que recorta, etc. *4* fam. rápido. *5* fam. estupendo.

clique (klik) *s.* pandilla, camarilla.

cloaca (klouei·ka) *s.* cloaca.

cloak (klouk) *s.* capa, manto. *2* fig. capa, excusa, pretexto.

cloak (to) *tr.* encapar, cubrir. *2* encubrir, embozar, disimular.

cloakroom (-rum) *s.* guardarropa [en un teatro, etc.].

clock (klak) *s.* reloj [de mesa o pared]: *what o'clock is it?,* ¿qué hora es? *2* cuadrado [de las medias].

clock (to) *tr.* cronometrar.

clockmaker (-meikø‍ʳ) *s.* relojero.

clockwise (-waiš) *adv.-adj.* en el sentido de las saetas del reloj.

clockwork (-wø‍ʳk) *s.* mecanismo de relojería. *2 adj.* regular, automático.

clod (klad) *s.* terrón, gleba. *2* tierra, suelo, césped. *3* gaznápiro, zoquete.

clod (to) *intr.* aterronarse. *2 tr.* tirar terrones. ¶ Pret. y p. p.: *clodded;* ger.: *-dding.*

clodhopper (-japø‍ʳ) *s.* patán, destripaterrones.

clog (klag) *s.* traba, embarazo, obstáculo, estorbo. *2* zueco, chanclo, chapín.

clog (to) *tr.* cargar, embarazar, estorbar, entorpecer. *2* obstruir. *3 intr.* apiñarse, aterronarse. *4* obstruirse. ¶ Pret. y p. p.: *clogged;* ger.: *clogging.*

cloggy (kla·gi) *adj.* aterronado. *2* pegajoso. *3* embarazoso, entorpecedor.

cloister (kloi·stø‍ʳ) *s.* ARQ., REL. claustro.

cloister (to) *tr.* enclaustrar. *2* proveer de claustro.

cloisterer (-ø‍ʳ) *m.* monje, religioso.

cloistral (kloi·stral) *adj.* claustral.

1) close (klouš) *s.* fin, conclusión. *2* cierre, clausura. *3* lucha cuerpo a cuerpo. *4* MÚS. cadencia.

2) close (klous) *adj.* cerrado. *2* cercado, encerrado, acotado. *3* apretado, ajustado. *4* secreto. *5* reservado [pers.]. *6* mal ventilado. *7* cubierto, pesado, sofocante [tiempo]. *8* agarrado, mezquino. *9* espeso, tupido, compacto. *10* próximo, contiguo, inmediato. *11* reñido, muy igualado. *12* COM. retraído [dinero]. *13* exacto, fiel. *14* estrecho, riguroso, cuidadoso, detenido, concienzudo. *15* estrecho, íntimo [amistad, etc.]. *16* breve, conciso. *17* limitado, restringido. *18* ~ *quarters*, contacto inmediato. *19* ~ *season*, veda. *20 adv.* cerca. *21* de cerca, estrechamente, apretadamente. *22* a raíz. *23* ~ *by*, muy cerca. *24 s.* cercado, recinto.

close (to) (klouš) *tr.* cerrar. *2* tapar, obstruir. *3* apretar, tupir. *4* cercar, rodear. *5* concluir, ultimar. *6* clausurar. *7 to* ~ *in*, encerrar. *8 intr.* cerrarse. *9* acercarse. *10* luchar, agarrarse: *to* ~ *with*, cerrar contra. *11* terminar, acabarse. *12* ponerse de acuerdo. *13 to* ~ *in*, acercarse rodeando; cerrar [la noche].

closed (-d) *adj.* cerrado, concluido, etc. *2* ~ *season*, veda.

closefisted (klou·sfistid) *adj.* tacaño.

closely (klou·sli) *adv.* estrechamente, etc.

closeness (klou·snis) *s.* encierro, estrechez. *2* densidad, apretamiento. *3* proximidad. *4* intimidad. *5* unión, dependencia. *6* mala ventilación. *7* reserva, cautela. *8* tacañería. *9* fidelidad, exactitud.

closet (kla·šit) *s.* gabinete, camarín. *2* retrete, excusado. *3* armario, alacena.

closet (to) *tr.* encerrar en un aposento [para una entrevista reservada].

close-up *s.* fotografía tomada de cerca.

closure (klou·ȳǿʳ) *s.* cierre. *2* fin, conclusión. *3* POL. guillotina parlamentaria.

clot (klat) *s.* grumo, coágulo, cuajarón.

clot (to) *intr.* agrumarse, coagularse, cuajarse. ¶ Pret. y p. p.: *clotted;* ger.: *clotting.*

cloth (kloz) *s.* paño, tela. *2* trapo, paño [para limpiar]. *3* mantel. *4* vestido clerical; clero. *5* MAR. lona.

clothbound (-baund) *adj.* encuadernado en tela.

clothe (to) (klou·ð) *tr.* vestir. *2* revestir, investir. ¶ Pret. y p. p.: *clothed* o *clad.*

clothes (klouš o klou·ðš) *s. pl.* vestido, vestuario, ropa: ~ *hanger*, ~ *tree*, colgador, percha.

clothesline (-lain) *s.* cuerda para tender la ropa.

clothesman (clou·šmæn) *s.* prendero, ropavejero.

clothier (klou·ðiǿʳ) *s.* pañero, ropero.

clothing (-ðing) *s.* ropa, vestidos. *2* MAR. velas. *3* revestimiento.

Clotilda (klouti·lda) *n. pr.* Clotilde.

clotted (kla·tid), **clotty** (-ti) *adj.* grumoso, coagulado.

cloud (klaud) *s.* nube; nublado: *under a* ~, bajo sospecha; en desgracia.

cloud (to) *tr.* nublar, anublar. *2* oscurecer, empeñar, manchar. *3 intr.* anublarse.

cloudburst (klau·dbøʳst) *s.* aguacero, chaparrón.

cloudily (-ili) *adv.* nebulosamente.

cloudless (-lis) *adj.* sereno, sin nubes.

cloudy (-i) *adj.* nuboso; nublado. *2* nebuloso. *3* vaporoso. *4* oscuro, sombrío. *5* turbo. *6* nubarrado.

clough (kløf) *s.* quebrada, cañada.

clout (klaut) *s.* cíbica, cibicón. *2* rodilla, trapo. *3* pañal, metedor. *4* remiendo. *5* fam. bofetada. *6* ~ *nail*, clavo de zapato.

clout (to) *tr.* cubrir, vendar. *2* remendar toscamente. *3* fam. abofetear.

clove (klouv) *s.* clavo [de especia]. *2* diente [de ajo]. *3 pret.* de TO CLEAVE.

cloven (klou·vøn) *p. p.* de TO CLEAVE. *2 adj.* partido, hendido: ~ *foot*, ~ *hoof*, pata hendida.

clover (klou·vøʳ) *s.* trébol: *in* ~, regaladamente, en la abundancia.

Clovis (klou·vis) *n. pr.* Clodoveo.

clown (klaun) *s.* payaso, clown. *2* rústico, patán.

clownish (-ish) *adj.* de payaso. *2* rústico, zafio; grosero.

cloy (to) (kloi) *tr.* hartar, hastiar, empalagar.

cloying (-ing), **cloysome** (-søm) *adj.* hastioso, empalagoso.

club (kløb) *s.* clava, porra, garrote. *2* maza [de gimnasia]. *3* DEP. bate; palo [de golf]. *4* basto, trébol [de la baraja]. *5* club, círculo, sociedad. *6* ~ *moss*, licopodio.

club (to) *tr.* apalear. *2* unir, juntar. *3 intr.* apiñarse. *4* unirse [para un fin], pagar cada uno su escote. ¶ Pret. y p. p.: *clubbed;* ger.: *clubbing.*

clubbed (-d) *adj.* en forma de clava.

clubfooted (-futid) *adj.* zopo del pie.

clubman (-mæn) *s.* socio de un club.

cluck (kløk) *s.* cloqueo.

cluck (to)) *intr.* cloquear.

clue (klu) *s.* indicio, pista, guía, clave.

clump (klømp) *s.* grupo [de árboles]. *2* masa, terrón, zoquete. *3* suela gruesa. *4* pisada fuerte.

clump (to) *tr.* agrupar. *2 intr.* agruparse. *2* andar pesadamente.

clumsiness (klø·mšinis) *s.* torpeza, desmaña. *2* tosquedad, pesadez.

clumsy (klø·mši) *adj.* torpe, desmañado, chapucero. *2* tosco, pesado.

clung (kløng) *pret.* y *p. p.* de TO CLING.

cluster (klø·støʳ) *s.* racimo, macolla, piña, ramo. *2* grupo, hato, agregado. *3* enjambre.

cluster (to) *intr.* arracimarse, agruparse. *2 tr.* apiñar, agrupar.

clustery (-i) *adj.* arracimado, apiñado, agrupado.

clutch (kløch) *s.* uña, garra. *2* agarro, presa, dominio, poder. *3* MEC. embrague: *to push in the* ~, embragar. *4* nidada.

clutch (to) *tr.* asir, agarrar, empuñar, apretar. *2 intr. to* ~ *at*, tratar de coger, asir con avidez.

clutter (klø·tøʳ) *s.* desorden, confusión. *2* barahúnda.

clutter (to) *tr.* desordenar. *2 intr.* alborotar; atropellarse.

clyster (kli·støʳ) *s.* clíster, enema.

coach (kouch) *s.* coche, carroza, diligencia. *2* vagón de pasajeros. *3* profesor particular. *4* DEP. preparador.

coach (to) *tr.* llevar en coche. *2* preparar [para exámenes, etc.]; dar lecciones a, adiestrar. *3 intr.* ir en coche. *4 to* ~ *with*, tomar lecciones de [un profesor].

coaching (-ing) *s.* lecciones particulares. *2* preparación, adiestramiento.

coachmaker (-meikøʳ) *s.* carrocero.

coachman (-mæn) *s.* cochero.

coaction (koækshøn) *s.* coacción.

coadjutor (kouæ·dȳøtøʳ) *s.* coadjutor, ayudante.

coadunate (to) (-diuneit) *tr.* coadunar.

coagulant (-giulønt) *adj.-s.* coagulante.

coagulate (to) (-leit) *tr.* coagular, cuajar. *2 intr.* coagularse, cuajarse.

coagulation (-ei·shøn) *s.* coagulación.

coagulum (kouæ·giuløm) *s.* coágulo.

coal (koul) *s.* carbón [materia]: ~ *basin*, cuenca hullera; ~ *oil*, petróleo, aceite mineral; ~ *tar*, alquitrán de hulla. *2* ascua, brasa: *to haul*, o *drag, over the coals*, reñir, poner como un trapo. *3* ORN. ~ *titmouse*, azabache.

coal (to) *tr.* carbonear; carbonizar. *2* proveer de carbón. *3 intr.* proveerse de carbón.

coalbox (-baks), **coalbin** (-bin) *s.* carbonera.

coalesce (to) (kouale·s) *intr.* unirse, incorporarse, fundirse.

coalescence (-øns) *s.* unión, fusión.

coalition (-li·shøn) *s.* unión, fusión. *2* coalición.

coalmouse (kou·lmaus) *s.* ORN. azabache.

coalpit (kou·lpit) *s.* mina de carbón.

coaly (-i) *adj.* carbonoso.

coalyard (-ya^rd) *s.* carbonería, almacén de carbón.

coaming (kou·ming) *s.* MAR. brazola.

coarse (ko·^rs) *adj.* tosco, grosero, ordinario, basto. *2* vulgar, chabacano, soez. *3* áspero, grueso.

coarsen (to) (-øn) *tr.-intr.* volver o volverse tosco, burdo, grueso o grosero.

coarsenes (-nis) *s.* tosquedad, basteza. *2* ordinariez, vulgaridad, grosería.

coast (koust) *s.* costa; litoral. *2* (E.U. y Can.) pendiente, deslizadero.

coast (to) *intr.* navegar cerca de la costa, perlongar. *2* (E.U. y Can.) deslizarse cuesta abajo [en trineo, bicicleta, etc.]. *3 tr.* MAR. COSTEAR.

coastal (kou·stal) *adj.* costanero.

coaster (-tø^r) *s.* práctico de costa. *2* buque de cabotaje. *3* (E.U. y Can.) deslizadero, tobogán.

coasting (-ing) *s.* cabotaje.

coastline (-lain) *s.* litoral, línea de la costa.

coat (kout) *s.* chaqueta, *saco; casaca; abrigo: *to turn one's* ~, volver casaca. *2* capa, mano [de pintura, etc.]. *3* MEC. cubierta, revestimiento. *4* ANAT. tegumento, túnica. *5* ZOOL. capa, pelaje, plumaje. *6* cota [de malla]. *7* ~ *of arms*, escudo de armas.

coat (to) *tr.* cubrir, revestir. *2* dar una capa o mano a; azogar.

coati (koa·ti) *s.* coatí.

coating (kou·ting) *s.* capa, mano, revestimiento.

coax (to) (kouks) *tr.* halagar, engatusar. *2* obtener con halagos.

coaxer (-ø^r) *s.* engatusador.

coaxial (kouæ·ksial) *adj.* coaxial.

cob (kab) *s.* pedazo redondo. *2* carozo, zuro [de maíz]. *3* jaca. *4* cisne macho. *5* variedad de gaviota. *6* ZOOL. araña. *7* duro [español].

cobalt (kou·bolt) *s.* cobalto.

cobble (ka·bøl) *s.* guijarro.

cobble (to) *tr.* empedrar con guijarros [calles]. *2 tr.-intr.* componer [zapatos]; chapucear.

cobbler (ka·blø^r) *s.* zapatero remendón. *2* chapucero.

cobblestone (ka·bølstoun) *s.* guijarro.

cobnut (ka·bnøt) *s.* avellana grande.

cobra (kou·bra) *s.* ZOOL. cobra.

cobweb (ka·bweb) *s.* telaraña.

cobwebbed (-d) *adj.* telarañoso.

coca (kou·ka) *s.* BOT. coca, *hayo.

cocain[e (koukei·n) *s.* cocaína.

cocculus (ka·kiuløs) *s.* BOT. coca de Levante.

coccus (ka·køs) *s.* coco [bacteria].

coccyx (ka·ksiks) *s.* ANAT. cóccix.

cochineal (ka·chini) *s.* cochinilla, grana: ~ *insect*, cochinilla [insecto].

cock (kak) *s.* gallo [ave]. *2* macho de un ave. *3* fig. gallo, amo; campeón. *4* veleta. *5* llave, espita, grifo. *6* gatillo, can [de escopeta]. *7* estilo, gnomon. *8* montón [de heno]. *9* inclinación hacia arriba; ladeo.

cock (to) *intr.* gallear, darse tono. *2 tr.* amartillar [un arma de fuego]. *3* levantar, dar una inclinación airosa o provocativa a. *4* amontonar heno, etc.

cockade (kakei·d) *s.* escarapela, cucarda.

cock-a-doodle-do (ka·kadudøldu) *s.* quiquiriquí.

cockatoo (kakatu) *s.* ORN. cacatúa.

cockatrice (ka·katris) *s.* basilisco.

cockboat (ka·kbout) *s.* bote, barquilla.

cockchafer (ka·kcheifø^r) *s.* abejorro [coleóptero].

cocked hat (kakt) *s.* sombrero de tres picos.

cocker (ka·kø^r) *s.* sabueso pequeño.

cocker (to) *tr.* acariciar, mimar.

cockerel (ka·kørel) *s.* pollo, gallito.

cock-fight(ing *s.* riña de gallos.

cock-horse *s.* caballito mecedor.

cockle (ka·køl) *s.* berberecho. *2* barquichuelo. *3* cúpula de horno. *4* BOT. cizaña; ballico.

cockle (to) *tr.* arrugar. *2 intr.* arrugarse.

cocklebur (-bø^r) *s.* bardana, cadillo.

cockleshell (-shel) *s.* concha de berberecho. *2* fig. cascarón de nuez [barco].

cockloft (ka·kloft) *s.* desván.

cockney (ka·kni) *s.* londinense de la clase popular.

cockpit (ka·kpit) *s.* gallera [reñidero de gallos]. *2* TEAT. cazuela. *3* AVIA. cabina del piloto.

cockroach (-rouch) *s.* ENT. cucaracha.

cockscomb (-scoum) *s.* cresta de gallo. *2* COXCOMB.

cockspur (-pu^r) *s.* espolón de gallo.

cocksure (-shu^r) *adj.* segurísimo. *2* muy seguro de sí mismo.

cocktail (-teil) *s.* combinado, cóctel: ~ *shaker*, coctelera.

coco(a (kou·kou) *s.* BOT. coco; cocotero.

cocoa *s.* cacao [árbol, polvo y bebida].

cocoanut, coconut (-nøt) *s.* coco [fruto].

cocoon (køku·n) *s.* ENT. capullo.

cocoonery (-nøri) *s.* criadero de gusanos de seda.

coction (ka·kshøn) *s.* cocción.

cod (kad) *s.* bacalao, abadejo. *2* copo [de red]. *3* escroto.

cod (to) *tr.* fam. engañar.

coda (kou·dæ) *s.* MÚS. coda.

coddle (to) *tr.* consentir, mimar.

code (koud) *s.* código. *2* cifra, clave.

codein (koudi·in) *s.* codeína.

codex (kou·deks) *s.* códice.

codfish (ka·dfish) *s.* bacalao, abadejo.

codger (ka·dýø^r) *s.* fam. tipo; chiflado.

codicil (ka·disil) *s.* codicilo.

codification (kadifikei·shøn) *s.* codificación.

codify (to) (ka·difai) *s.* codificar. ¶ Pret. y p. p.: *codified*.

codling (ka·dling) *s.* bacalao pequeño. *2* variedad de manzana.

coeducation (kouedýukei·shøn) *s.* coeducación.

coefficient (-efi·shønt) *adj.-s.* coeficiente.

cœlenterate (sile·ntøreit) *adj.-s.* celentéreo.

cœliac (si·liæk) *adj.* celíaco.

cœlom (si·lom) *s.* ZOOL. celoma.

coerce (to) (kouø·^rs) *tr.* coercer. *2* forzar, obligar.

coercion (-shøn) *s.* coerción. *2* coacción, compulsión.

coercive (-siv) *adj.* coercitivo. *2* coactivo.

coetaneous (kouitei·niøs) *adj.* coetáneo.

coeval (kou·val) *adj.-s.* coevo.

coexist (to) (koui·gšist) *intr.* coexistir.

coexistence (-ši·støns) *s.* coexistencia.

cofee (ko·fi) *s.* café [grano; bebida; planta]: ~ *tree*, cafeto.

coffeehouse (-jaus) *s.* café [establecimiento].

coffeepot (-pat) *s.* cafetera [utensilio].

coffeeroom (-rum) *s.* café, bar [de hotel].

coffer (ko·fø^r) *s.* cofre, arca. *2* ARQ. artesón.

cofferdam (-dæm) *s.* ataguía, caja dique.

coffin (ko·fin) *s.* ataúd, féretro, caja. 2 casco [de caballería]: ~ *bone*, VET. bolillo.
cog (cag) *s.* diente [de engranaje]. 2 CARP. espiga, lengüeta. 3 botequín. 4 engaño.
cog (to) *tr.* dentar [una rueda]. 2 CARP. ensamblar. 3 hacer trampas con [los dados]. 4 engañar. ¶ Pret. y p. p.: *cogged;* ger.: *-gging.*
cogency (kou·dȳønsi) *s.* fuerza [lógica o moral].
cogent (-ønt) *adj.* poderoso, convincente.
cogged (kæ·gd) *adj.* MEC. dentado. 2 cargado [dado].
cogitate (to) (ka·dȳiteit) *intr.* meditar, reflexionar.
cogitation (-tei·shøn) *s.* cogitación.
cognac (kou·ñæk) *s.* coñac.
cognate (ka·gneit) *adj.-s.* cognado. 2 *adj.* afín; análogo.
cognation (-nei·shøn) *s.* cognación.
cognition (kagni·shøn) *s.* cognición.
cognitive (ka·gnitiv) *adj.* cognoscitivo.
cognizable (-šabøl) *adj.* cognoscible. 2 DER. de la competencia de.
cognizance (-šans) *s.* conocimiento, noticia. 2 divisa, distintivo. 3 DER. competencia.
cognizant (-šant) *adj.* sabedor, enterado.
cognize (to) (ka·gnaiš) *tr.* conocer, reconocer.
cognomen (kagnou·møn) *s.* cognomento.
cognoscible (kagna·sibøl) *adj.* cognoscible, conocible.
cognoscitive (-tiv) *adj.* cognoscitivo.
cogwheel (ka·gjuıl) *s.* rueda dentada.
cohabit (to) (koujæ·bit) *intr.* cohabitar.
coheir (koue·ø^r) *s.* coheredero.
coheiress (-ris) *s.* coheredera.
cohere (to) (kouji·ø^r) *intr.* adherirse, pegarse, unirse. 2 adaptarse.
coherence (-øns), **coherency** (-ønsi) *s.* coherencia.
coherent (-ønt) *adj.* coherente.
coherer (-ø^r) *s.* cohesor.
cohesion (kouji·ȳøn) *s.* cohesión.
cohesive (-siv) *adj.* cohesivo.
cohort (kou·jo^rt) *s.* cohorte.
coif (koif) *s.* cofia, gorra, papalina. 2 birrete.
coif (to) *tr.* cubrir la cabeza.
coiffure (kua·fiu^r) *s.* tocado, peinado.
coign (coin) *s.* esquina, ángulo.
coil (koil) *s.* rollo [de cuerda, etc.]; rosca, espiral, vuelta, aduja. 2 ELECT. carrete, bobina. 3 serpentín [de alambique]. 4 rizo [de cabello].
coil (to) *tr.* arrollar, enrollar, adujar. 2 *intr.* enrollarse, enroscarse.
coin (koin) *s.* moneda. 2 dinero. 3 cuña.
coin (to) *tr.* acuñar, batir; amonedar. 2 forjar, inventar.
coinage (koi·nidȳ) *s.* acuñación. 2 sistema monetario. 3 forja, invención.
coincide (kouinsai·d) *intr.* coincidir.
coincidence (koui·nsidøns) *s.* coincidencia.
coincident (-ønt) *adj.* coincidente.
coiner (koi·nø^r) *s.* acuñador. 2 monedero falso. 3 forjador, inventor.
coinsurance (-shu·rans) *s.* coaseguro.
coir (koi^r) *s.* bonote, fibra de coco.
coition (koui·shøn) *s.* coito, cópula.
coke (kouk) *s.* cok, coque.
cola (kou·la) *s.* FARM. cola.
colander (kø·landø^r) *s.* colador, pasador [utensilio].
colchicum (ka·lkikøm) *s.* BOT. cólquico.
cold (kould) *adj.* frío: ~ *chisel*, cortafrío: ~ *cream*, colcrén; ~ *meat*, fiambre; *to be* ~, estar frío; tener frío; *it is* ~, hace frío; *in* ~ *blood*, a sangre

fría. 2 desalentador; desalentado. 3 débil, perdido [rastro, pista]. 4 desnudo [sin adornos o comentarios]: *the* ~ *fact*, los hechos desnudos. 5 *s.* frío. 6 catarro, resfriado: *to take* ~, resfriarse.
cold-blooded *adj.* de sangre fría. 2 friolento. 3 atroz, despiadado, cruel.
coldly (-li) *adv.* fríamente.
coldness (-nis) *s.* frialdad.
cold-storage *adj.* frigorífico.
cole (koul) *s.* col. 2 colza.
Coleoptera (koulia·ptøra) *s. pl.* ENT. coleópteros.
colewort (kou·lwø^rt) *s.* COLE.
colic (ka·lik) *adj.-s.* cólico.
Coliseum (kalisı·øm) *s.* coliseo.
colitis (kolai·tis) *s.* MED. colitis.
collaborate (to) (kølæ·børeit) *intr.* colaborar.
collaboration (-rei·shøn) *s.* colaboración.
collaborator (-rei·tø^r) *s.* colaborador.
collapse (kølæps) *s.* derrumbamiento, hundimiento, desplome. 2 fracaso, ruina. 3 MED. colapso.
collapse (to) *intr.* derrumbarse, hundirse, desplomarse. 2 fracasar. 3 sufrir colapso. 4 plegarse, doblarse.
collapsible (-ibøl) *adj.* plegable, desmontable.
collar (ka·la^r) *s.* cuello [de una prenda]. 2 cuello postizo, valona, golilla, etc. 3 collar. 4 MEC. collar, manguito, aro. 5 collera. 6 ARQ. collarino.
collar (to) *tr.* poner collar o collera. 2 coger por el cuello de la chaqueta; prender.
collarbone (-boun) *s.* clavícula.
collaret[te (kalare·t) *s.* cuello de encaje o piel.
collate (kølei·t) *tr.* colacionar, cotejar. 2 ECLES. colacionar, colar. 3 DER. colacionar.
collateral (kølæ·tøral) *adj.* colateral. 2 paralelo. 3 accesorio, indirecto, subordinado. 4 COM. subsidiario. 5 *m.* COM. garantía subsidiaria.
collation (kølei·shøn) *s.* colación, cotejo. 2 colación, refacción. 3 DER., ECLES. colación.
colleague (ka·lıg) *s.* colega.
colleague (to) (kølı·g) *intr.* coligarse.
collect (ka·lekt) *s.* LITURG. colecta.
collect (to) (køle·kt) *tr.* congregar. 2 juntar, recoger, coleccionar. 3 colegir, inferir. 4 recaudar, cobrar: ~ *on delivery*, contra reembolso. 5 *to* ~ *oneself*, serenarse, reponerse. 6 *intr.* congregarse, acumularse.
collectable (-abøl) *adj.* cobrable.
collected (-id) *adj.* reunido, juntado. 2 sereno, sosegado, dueño de sí mismo.
collectedness (-nis) *s.* calma, serenidad.
collectible (-ibøl) *adj.* cobrable, cobradero.
collection (køle·kshøn) *s.* reunión [acción]. 2 recogida. 3 cobro, recaudación. 4 colecta, cuestación. 5 colección. 6 recopilación.
collective (køle·ktiv) *adj.* colectivo. 2 formado por unión o agregación.
collectivism (-išm) *s.* colectivismo.
collectivity (-ti·viti) *s.* colectividad.
collectivize (to) (køle·ktivaiš) *tr.* colectivizar.
collector (køle·ktø·) *s.* colector, coleccionista. 2 compilador. 3 recaudador; cobrador. 4 ELECT. colector.
college (ka·lidȳ) *s.* colegio [corporación]. 2 colegio [donde se cursan estudios superiores].
collegial (kølı·dȳial) *adj.* colegial.
collegian (-dȳian) *s.* individuo o estudiante de un colegio.
collegiate (-dȳieit) *adj.* colegiado. 2 colegial [iglesia].
collet (kæ·lit) *s.* MEC. collar. 2 JOY. engaste.

collide (to) (kølai·d) *tr.* chocar, topar. *2* estar en conflicto, oponerse.
collie (ka·li) *s.* (Esc.) perro de pastor.
collier (ka·liø') *s.* minero [de carbón]. *2* barco carbonero. *3* tratante en carbón.
colliery (-i) *s.* mina o comercio de carbón.
colligate (to) (ka·ligeit) *tr.* enlazar, relacionar.
collimation (kølimei·shøn) *s.* colimación.
collimator (-tø') *s.* colimador.
collision (køli·ȳøn) *s.* colisión, choque. *2* oposición, conflicto.
collocate (to) (ka·lokeit) *tr.* colocar, disponer.
collocation (-ei·shøn) *s.* colocación, disposición.
colloid (ka·loid) *adj.-s.* FÍS., QUÍM. coloide.
colloidal (køloi·dal) *adj.* coloidal.
collop (ka·løp') *s.* tajada; pedacito.
colloquial (kølou·kuial) *adj.* familiar [lenguaje, acepción, etc.].
colloquialism (-ism) *s.* estilo o expresión familiar.
colloquy (ka·lokui) *s.* coloquio, conversación.
collude (to) (kølu·d) *intr.* coludir.
collusion (kølu·ȳøn) *s.* colusión, confabulación.
collusive (-siv) *adj.* colusorio.
collyrium (kali·riøm) *s.* colirio.
colocynth (ka·losinz) *s.* BOT. coloquíntida.
Cologne (kølou·n) *n. pr.* GEOGR. Colonia. *2 s.* agua de colonia.
Colombian (kølø·mbian) *adj.-s.* colombiano.
colon (kou·løn) *s.* ANAT. colon. *2* ORT. dos puntos.
colonel (kø·'nøl) *s.* MIL. coronel.
colonelcy (-si), **colonelship** (-ship) *s.* coronelía.
colonial (kolou·nial) *adj.* colonial: ~ *period*, [Am.] coloniaje.
colonialism (-išm) *s.* colonialismo.
colonist (ka·lonist) *s.* colono [de una colonia].
colonize (ka·lonaiš) *tr.* colonizar. *2 intr.* establecerse en una colonia.
colonizer (-ø') *s.* colonizador.
colonnade (kalønei·d) *s.* columnata.
colony (ka·loni) *s.* colonia.
colophon (ka·løføn) *s.* colofón.
colophony (kølo·føni) *s.* colofonía.
color, coloration, etc. COLOUR, COLOURATON, etc.
colorific (kløri·fik) *adj.* colorativo.
colorimeter (-mitø') *s.* colorímetro.
colorimetry (-metri) *s.* colorimetría.
colossal (køla·sal), **colossean** (kaløsi·an) *adj.* colosal.
Colosseum (kaløsi·øm) *s.* COLISEUM.
colossus (kola·søs) *s.* coloso.
colostrum (kola·strøm) *s.* calostro.
colour (kø·lø') *s.* color: *off* ~, pálido, indispuesto; (E.U.) verde, escabroso; *to lose* ~, palidecer. *2* colorido. *3* tinte, matiz. *4* apariencia, visos; excusa, pretexto: *under* ~ *of,* so color de, bajo pretexto de. *5* palo [en los naipes]. *6* [esp. en *pl.*] bandera, pabellón, enseña.
colour (to) *tr.* colorar, colorear, pintar, teñir, iluminar. *2* colorear, paliar, disfrazar. *3 intr.* colorearse. *4* enrojecer.
colourable (-abøl) *adj.* especioso.
colouration (-ei·shøn) *s.* coloración, colorido.
colour-blind *adj.-s.* daltoniano [pers.].
coloured (-d) *adj.* coloreado, pintado, teñido. *2* de color [negro, mulato, etc.]. *3* especioso, adornado, exagerado.
colourful (-ful) *adj.* lleno de colorido. *2* vívido, pintoresco, variado.
colouring (-ing) *s.* color, colorido. *2* colorante. *3* apariencia especiosa.
colourist (-ist) *s.* colorista.

colourless (-lis) *adj.* incoloro; descolorido.
colporteur (ka·lpo'tø') *s.* distribuidor de libros o folletos religiosos.
colt (koult) *s.* ZOOL. potro. *2* joven sin juicio. *3* azote con nudo. *4* (con may.) revólver Colt.
colter (-ø') *s.* cuchilla [del arado].
coltish (-ish) *adj.* juguetón, retozón.
coltsfoot (-sfut) *s.* BOT. tusílago.
columbary (ka·lømbari) *s.* columbario. *2* palomar.
Columbian (kolø·mbian) *adj.* colombino.
columbine (ka·lømbain) *adj.* columbino. *2 s.* BOT. aguileña. *3* [con may.] *n. pr.* Colombina.
Columbus (kølø·mbøs) *n. pr.* Colón.
column (ka·løm) *s.* columna. *2* sección [de un periódico].
columned (-d) *adj.* con columnas.
columniation (-niei·shøn) *s.* columnata.
colure (koliu·') *s.* ASTR., GEOGR. coluro.
colza (kou·lša) *s.* BOT. colza.
coma (kou·ma) *s.* MED. coma. *2* ASTR. cabellera. *3* BOT. vilano.
comatose (kou·matous) *adj.* comatoso.
comb (koum) *s.* peine [para el pelo]. *2* peineta. *3* peine, carda, rastrillo. *4* almohaza. *5* cresta [de ave, de animal, de ola]. *6* API. panal.
comb (to) *tr.* peinar, carmenar. *2* cardar, rastrillar. *3* registrar [en busca de algo]. *4 intr.* romper, encresparse [las olas].
combat (ka·mbæt) *s.* combate, lucha.
combat (to) *tr.-intr.* combatir.
combatant (ka·mbatant) *adj.* luchador, combativo. *2 s.* combatiente.
combative (kømbæ·tiv) *adj.* combativo, belicoso.
comber (kou·mø') *s.* peinador, cardador. *2* peinadora [máquina]. *3* ola con cresta.
combination (kambinei·shøn) *s.* combinación; mezcla. *2* unión, liga. *3* combinación [prenda femenina].
combine (ka·mbain) *s.* monipodio, confabulación. *2* AGR. cosechadora.
combine (to) (kømbai·n) *tr.* combinar. *2 intr.* combinarse. *3* confabularse; maquinar, conspirar.
combing (kou·ming) *s.* peinadura; rastrillaje. *2 pl.* peinaduras.
combustibility (kømbøstibi·liti) *s.* combustibilidad.
combustible (-bø·stibøl) *adj.-s.* combustible.
combustion (-shøn) *s.* combustión. *2* agitación, tumulto.
comby (kou·mi) *adj.* apanalado.
come (to) (køm) *intr.* venir, llegar, acercarse. *2* venir, provenir. *3* avanzar, aparecer, salir. *4* pasar, suceder. *5* entrar [en acción, en contacto, etc.]. *6* ascender [a un total], ser lo mismo [que]. *7 to* ~ *about,* ocurrir; MAR. virar. *8 to* ~ *across,* topar con. *9 to* ~ *apart* o *asunder,* dividirse, desunirse. *10 to* ~ *back,* volver, retroceder. *11 to* ~ *by,* pasar; obtener. *12 to* ~ *down,* bajar, descender; caer; *to* ~ *down with,* pagar [dinero]. *13 to* ~ *forth,* salir, aparecer. *14 to* ~ *forward,* avanzar, presentarse. *15 to* ~ *in,* entrar. *16 to* ~ *near,* acercarse. *17 to* ~ *of age,* llegar a la mayoría de edad. *18 to* ~ *off,* efectuarse; salir [bien, mal, etc.]; despegarse, desprenderse. *19 to* ~ *on,* avanzar; proseguir; entrar; medrar; ~ *on!,* ¡venga!, ¡vamos! *20 to* ~ *out,* salir; debutar; ponerse de largo; *to* ~ *out with,* decir, revelar. *21 to* ~ *round,* llegar, volver; reponerse; ceder; asentir. *22 to* ~ *to,* volver en sí; consentir, ceder; MAR. anclar; orzar. *23 to* ~ *to terms,* ceder, aceptar condiciones. *24 to* ~ *together,* juntarse. *25 to*

~ *true*, realizarse. *26 to* ~ *up*, subir; aparecer; acercarse [a], estar a la altura [de]. *27 to* ~ *upon*, caer sobre; dar con. ¶ Pret.: *came*; p. p.: *come*.

comedian (kømɪ·dian) *s.* cómico, comediante. *2* comediógrafo.

comedienne (kømidie·n) *s.* cómica, comedianta.

comedist (ka·mødist) *s.* comediógrafo.

comedown (kø·mdaun) *s.* caída, revés de fortuna.

comedy (ka·mødi) *s.* comedia.

comeliness (kø·mlinis) *s.* gentileza, apostura. *2* propiedad, decoro.

comely (kø·mli) *adj.* gentil, apuesto, bien parecido. *2* decente.

come-off *s.* fam. excusa, escapatoria.

comer (kø·møʳ) *s.* viniente, llegado.

comestible (køme·stibøl) *adj.-s.* comestible.

comet (ka·mit) *s.* ASTR. cometa.

comfit (kø·mfit) *s.* confitura seca.

comfort (kø·mfoʳt) *s.* consuelo, alivio, confortación. *2* solaz. *3* comodidad, bienestar, regalo.

comfort (to) *tr.* confortar, fortificar. *2* aliviar, consolar. *3* alentar, animar, alegrar.

comfortable (-abøl) *adj.* confortable. *2* cómodo. *3* desahogada [posición]; regular, suficiente. *4* consolador. *5 s.* (E.U) colcha, edredón.

comforter (-øʳ) *s.* confortador, consolador: *the Comforter*, el Espíritu Santo. *2* bufanda. *3* (E.U) COMFORTABLE *5.*

comfortless (-lis) *adj.* triste, desolado. *2* desconsolado. *3* incómodo.

comfrey (kø·mfri) *s.* BOT. CONSUELDA.

comic (ka·mik) *adj.* cómico, bufo, burlesco; gracioso. *2 s. pl.* historieta cómica ilustrada.

comical (-al) *adj.* cómico.

comicalness (-nis) *s.* comicidad, gracia.

coming (kø·ming) *adj.* próximo, venidero. *2 s.* venida, llegada. *3* ~ *out*, salida; puesta de largo.

comitia (komi·shia) *s. pl.* comicios.

comity (ka·miti) *s.* urbanidad, cortesía.

comma (ka·ma) *s.* GRAM., MÚS. coma. *2 inverted commas*, comillas.

command (kømæ·nd) *s.* orden, mandato. *2* mando, dirección; poder, dominio; disposición. *3* dominio, conocimiento [de una lengua, etc.]. *4* vista, perspectiva. *5* MIL. comandancia.

command (to) *tr.* mandar, ordenar. *2* mandar, comandar, dirigir. *3* dominar. *4* disponer de. *5* imponer, merecer [respeto, etc.]. *6 intr.* mandar, imperar.

commandant (kamandæ·nt) *s.* comandante [el que manda].

commander (kømæ·ndøʳ) *s.* comandante, jefe, caudillo. *2* comendador.

commandery (-ri) *s.* comandancia. *2* encomienda.

commanding (-ing) *adj.* que manda. *2* imperativo, autoritario; imponente. *3* dominante.

commandment (-mønt) *s.* mando, comando. *2* mandato, orden: *the Ten Commandments*, los mandamientos de la ley de Dios.

commando (kømæ·ndou) *s.* MIL. comando [grupo de soldados].

commeasurable (køme·ȳurabøl) *s.* conmensurable.

commemorable (-morabøl) *adj.* memorable.

commemorate (to) (-møreit) *tr.* conmemorar.

commemoration (-ei·shøn) *s.* conmemoración.

commence (to) (køme·ns) *tr.* comenzar, empezar, iniciar, entablar. *2 intr.* comenzar, principiar.

commencement (-mønt) *s.* comienzo, principio.

commend (to) (køme·nd) *tr.* encomendar. *2* recomendar, alabar.

commendable (-abøl) *adj.* recomendable, loable.

commendation (-ei·shøn) *s.* encomio, alabanza.

commendatory (køme·ndatori) *adj.* comendatorio, laudatorio.

commender (køme·ndøʳ) *s.* alabador.

commensal (køme·nsal) *adj.-s.* comensal.

commensurable (køme·nshurabøl) *adj.* conmensurable. *2* proporcionado.

commensurate (-reit) *adj.* proporcionado, correspondiente.

commensurate (to) *tr.* conmensurar; proporcionar.

comment (ka·ment) *s.* comento, comentario.

comment (to) *intr.* comentar. | Gralte. con *in* o *upon*.

commentary (ka·mønteri) *s.* comentario, glosa.

commentator (-ei·tøʳ), **commenter** (-øʳ) *s.* comentador, comentarista.

commerce (ka·møʳs) *s.* comercio, tráfico. *2* comercio [trato, comunicación].

commercial (kømø·ʳshal) *adj.* comercial, mercantil.

commination (køminei·shøn) *s.* conminación, amenaza.

commingle (to) (kømi·ngøl) *tr.* mezclar. *2 intr.* mezclarse, unirse, barajarse.

comminute (to) (ka·miniut) *tr.* quebrantar, triturar.

comminution (-iu·shøn) *s.* trituración. *2* CIR. fractura conminuta.

commiserate (to) (kømi·søreit) *tr.* compadecer.

commiseration (-ei·shøn) *s.* conmiseración.

commissariat (kamise·riat) *s.* administración militar. *2* comisariado.

commissary (ka·miseri) *s.* comisario, delegado. *2* intendente militar. *3* economato [almacén].

commission (kømi·shøn) *s.* comisión, perpetración. *2* comisión, misión, encargo, cometido. *3* COM. comisión. *4* comisión, junta. *5* MIL. despacho, nombramiento. *6 to put into* ~, poner [un buque] en servicio.

commission (to) *tr.* comisionar, encargar, facultar, delegar, nombrar.

commissioned (-d) *adj.* comisionado. *2* MIL. ~ *officer*, oficial [desde alférez para arriba]; *non* ~ *officer*, sargento, cabo, clase.

comissioner (-øʳ) *s.* comisionado. *2* apoderado, factor. *3* comisario.

commissure (ka·mishuʳ) *s.* comisura.

commit (to) (kømi·t) *tr.* cometer, perpetrar. *2* cometer, encargar. *3* confiar, depositar, entregar. *4* encarcelar. *5* comprometer: *to* ~ *oneself*, comprometerse, soltar prendas. ¶ Pret. y p. p.: *committed*; ger.: *committing*.

commitment (-mønt), **committal** (-al) *s.* comisión, perpetración. *2* acción de confiar, de entregar; auto de prisión; encarcelamiento. *3* compromiso, promesa.

committee (kømi·ti) *s.* comisión, comité, junta, delegación.

commix (kømi·ks) *tr.* mezclar. *2 intr.* mezclarse.

commixtion (kømi·kshøn), **commixture** (-chøʳ) *s.* conmixtión, mezcla.

commode (kømou·d) *s.* cómoda. *2* lavabo cubierto. *3* sillico.

commodious (kømou·diøs) *adj.* cómodo, conveniente. *2* espacioso, holgado.

commodiousness (-nis) *s.* comodidad, espaciosidad, holgura.

commodity (kømɑ·diti) s. artículo [de consumo], género, producto. 2 comodidad, conveniencia.

commodore (ka·mǿdøʳ) s. MAR. comodoro.

common (ka·møn) adj. común [de varios, de la mayoría]: ~ crier, pregonero; ~ sense, sentido común. 2 común, vulgar, corriente, ordinario. 3 raso [soldado]. 4 adocenado, trivial. 5 regular, usual. 6 GRAM., MAT. común. 7 s. lo común. 8 pl. pueblo, estado llano. 9 tierras comunales. 10 the Commons, the House of Commons, la Cámara de los Comunes.

commonable (-abøl) adj. comunal.

commonalty (-ɑlti) s. común, comunidad.

commoner (-øʳ) s. plebeyo. 2 miembro de la Cámara de los Comunes.

commonplace (-pleis) adj. común, vulgar, trivial. 2 s. lugar común, trivialidad. 3 apunte, nota.

commonweal (-uıl) s. bien público.

commonwealth (-uelz) s. nación, república, cosa pública. 2 comunidad de naciones.

commotion (kømou·shøn) s. conmoción, agitación. 2 levantamiento, alboroto, tumulto; revuelo.

commove (to) (kømu·v) tr. conmover, alterar, agitar.

communal (ka·miunɑl) adj. comunal.

commune (ka·miun) s. comunicación, comunión, trato.

commune (to) intr. conversar, estar en comunión o trato íntimo. 2 (E.U) comulgar.

communicable (kømiu·nikɑbøl) adj. comunicable, transmisible. 2 comunicativo.

communicant (kɑnt) adj.-s. comunicante. 2 s. comulgante.

communicate (to) (-keit) tr. comunicar, participar. 2 comunicar, transmitir. 3 tr.-intr. comulgar [dar o recibir la comunión]. 4 intr. comunicarse. 5 consultar, conferenciar.

communication (-ei·shøn) s. comunicación [acción de comunicar o comunicarse], trato, correspondencia. 2 transmisión [de calor, movimiento, etc.]. 3 noticia, mensaje. 4 acceso, paso. 5 pl. comunicaciones.

communicative (kømiu·nikeitiv) adj. comunicativo, expansivo.

communicatory (-kɑtori) adj. comunicatorio.

communion (kømiu·niøn) s. comunión. 2 Holy Communion, la Sagrada Comunión.

communism (ka·miunišm) s. comunismo.

communist (-ist) adj. comunista.

communistic (-i·stik) adj. comunista.

community (kømiu·niti) s. comunidad [calidad de común]. 2 comunidad, común, público, sociedad. 3 comunidad [religiosa, etc.]. 4 vecindario, municipio, barrio.

commutable (-tɑbøl) adj. conmutable.

commutate (ka·miuteit) tr. ELECT. CONMUTAR.

commutation (-ei·shøn) s. conmutación, cambio, trueque. 2 FERROC. (E.U) ~ ticket, abono.

commutator (-øʳ) s. ELECT. conmutador. 2 ELECT. colector.

commute (kømiu·t) tr. conmutar, cambiar, substituir. 2 cambiar una forma de pago por otra; igualar, tomar abono para. 3 ELECT. conmutar. 4 intr. FERROC. (E.U) abonarse.

compact (ka·mpɑkt) s. pacto, convenio, trato. 2 polvera de bolsillo.

compact (kømpæ·ct) adj. compacto, denso, apretado, comprimido. 2 breve, conciso. 3 ~ of, compuesto de.

compact (to) tr. apretar, comprimir, condensar, hacer compacto. 2 hacer o componer [de].

compactness (-nis) s. compacidad, densidad, tamaño reducido. 2 firmeza, solidez.

companion (kømpæ·niøn) s. compañero, ra; camarada. 2 acompañante. 3 caballero [de ciertas órdenes]. 4 MAR. carroza, chupeta: ~ way, escalera de cámara.

companionable (-abøl) adj. sociable, afable.

companionship (-ship) s. compañerismo, camaradería. 2 unión, compañía.

company (ka·mpani) s. compañía [efecto de acompañar; personas que acompañan]. 2 compañía, gremio, sociedad. 3 grupo, banda. 4 COM., TEAT. compañía. 5 MAR. tripulación. 6 banda [de música]. 7 visitas, invitados; vida de sociedad.

comparable (ka·mpɑrabøl) adj. comparable.

comparative (kømpæ·rativ) adj. comparativo. 2 relativo [no absoluto]. 3 comparado [filológia, etc.].

comparatively (-li) adv. comparativamente. 2 relativamente.

compare (kømpe·øʳ) s. comparación: beyond ~, sin comparación.

compare (to) tr. comparar. 2 cotejar, confrontar. 3 parangonar, equiparar. 4 intr. poderse comparar.

comparison (kømpæ·rišøn) s. comparación [acción y efecto]. 2 RET. comparación, símil.

compartment (kømpa·ʳtmønt) s. compartimiento, departamento, división; cajoncito, gaveta. 2 BLAS. cuartel.

compass (kø·mpɑs) s. área, ámbito, recinto, circunferencia. 2 alcance, esfera, círculo [de acción, etc.]. 3 límites, moderación. 4 (a veces en pl.) compás [instrumento]. 5 brújula: ~ card, rosa náutica. 6 MÚS. extensión [de la voz o de un instrumento].

compass (to) tr. idear, planear. 2 conseguir. 3 comprender, entender. 4 circuir, cercar. 5 rodear, contornear.

compassable (-abøl) adj. asequible.

compassion (kømpæ·shøn) s. compasión.

compassionable (-abøl) adj. compasible, lastimoso.

compassionate (-it) adj. compasivo.

compassionate (to) (-eit) tr. compadecer.

compatibility (kømpætibi·liti) s. compatibilidad.

compatible (-pæ·tibøl) adj. compatible.

compatriot (kømpei·triøt) adj.-s. compatriota. 2 compatricio, paisano.

compeer (kømpi·øʳ) s. igual, par. 2 compañero.

compel (to) (kømpe·l) tr. compeler, constreñir, obligar, forzar. 2 imponer [respeto, silencio, etc.]. ¶ Pret. y p. p.: compelled; ger.: -lling.

compellent (-ønt) adj. compulsivo.

compend (ka·mpend) s. compendio.

compendious (kømpe·ndiøs) adj. compendioso, breve, sucinto, sumario.

compendium (-diøm) s. compendio, resumen, epitome, sumario.

compensate (to) (ka·mpenseit) tr. compensar, contrapesar. 2 resarcir, indemnizar. 3 recompensar. 4 intr. to ~ for, compensar.

compensation (-ei·shøn) s. compensación.

compensator (ka·mpenseitøʳ) s. compensador.

compete (to) (kømpi·t) intr. competir, contender, rivalizar.

competence (ka·mpitøns), **competency** (-si) s. competencia, aptitud. 2 medios de vida, buen pasar. *3* cantidad suficiente. *4* DER. competencia.

competent (-ønt) *adj.* competente, capaz. *2* suficiente, adecuado, idóneo. *3* DER. competente.

competition (kømpiti·shøn) *s.* competición, competencia, rivalidad. *2* certamen, concurso, oposición. *3* COM. competencia.

competitive (kømpe·titiv) *adj.* de competición, de competencia.

competitor (-tø^r) *s.* competidor, rival, contrincante. *2* opositor.

compilation (kampilei·shøn) *s.* compilación, recopilación.

compile (to) (kømpai·l) *tr.* compilar, recopilar.

compiler (-ø^r) *s.* compilador, recopilador.

complacence (kømplei·søns), **complacency** (-si) *s.* complacencia, contento. *2* satisfacción de sí mismo.

complacent (-ønt) *adj.* satisfecho de sí mismo. *2* complaciente.

complain (to) (kømplei·n) *intr.* quejarse, lamentarse. *2* DER. querellarse, demandar.

complainant (-ant) *s.* querellante, demandante.

complainer (-ø^r) *s.* el que se queja.

complaint (-t) *s.* queja, lamento. *2* queja, agravio. *3* DER. demanda; reclamación. *4* mal, enfermedad.

complaisance (kømplei·šans) *s.* condescendencia, amabilidad, cortesía.

complaisant (-ant) *adj.* complaciente, amable, atento, cortés.

complement (ka·mplimønt) *s.* complemento. *2* cantidad o número total [asignados]. *3* MAR. dotación.

complement (to) *tr.* complementar, completar.

complemental (-me·ntal) *adj.* completivo.

complementary (-tari) *adj.* complementario.

complete (kømplı·t) *adj.* completo. *2* concluido. *3* acabado, consumado. *4* pleno, absoluto.

complete (to) *tr.* completar. *2* acabar, concluir, consumar. *3* efectuar.

completion (kømplı·shøn) *f.* complemento, perfección, acabamiento. *2* realización.

completive (-tiv) *adj.* completivo.

complex (ka·mpleks) *adj.* complejo, complexo. *2* complicado, intrincado. *3* *s.* complejo.

complexion (kømple·kshøn) *s.* cutis, tez, color. *2* temperamento, carácter. *3* aspecto, cariz.

complexional (-al) *adj.* temperamental.

complexioned (-d) *adj.* de tal o cual tez, cutis o temperamento.

complexity (kømple·ksiti), **complexness** (-nis) *s.* complejidad.

compliance (kømplai·ans) *s.* condescendencia, docilidad, sumisión, obediencia. *2* anuencia, consentimiento: *3 in* ~ *with*, conforme a.

compliant (-ant) *adj.* complaciente, condescendiente. *2* dócil, obediente, sumiso.

complicacy (ka·mplikasi) *s.* complicación; complejidad.

complicate (-keit) *adj.* complicado.

complicated (-id) *adj.* complicado, intrincado.

complication (-ei·shøn) *s.* complicación.

complicity (kømpli·siti) *s.* complicidad. *2* complejidad, complicación.

compliment (ka·mplimønt) *s.* cumplimiento, cumplido, lisonja, galantería, requiebro. *2* atención, fineza; regalo, obsequio. *3 pl.* saludos, respetos.

compliment (to) *tr.* cumplimentar, felicitar, obsequiar. *2* lisonjear, alabar, requebrar.

complimentary (-me·ntari) *adj.* obsequioso, galante, lisonjero. *2* de alabanza, de felicitación. *3* de regalo; gratuito.

complin[e (ka·mplin) *s.* LITURG. completas.

complot (ka·mplat) *s.* complot, conspiración.

complot (to) (kampla·t) *tr.* tramar. *2 intr.* conspirar. ¶ Pret. y p. p.: *complotted;* ger.: *complotting.*

comply (to) (kømplai·) *intr.* (gralte. con *with*) condescender, acceder. *2* complacer, obedecer, cumplir, llenar, conformarse. ¶ Pret. y p. p.: *complied.*

component (kømpou·nent) *adj.-s.* componente.

comport (to) (kømpo^{r}t) *intr.* concordar, convenir. *2 ref.* comportarse, conducirse.

comportment (-mønt) *s.* comportamiento.

compose (to) (kømpou·š) *tr.* componer [formar, integrar]. *2* IMPR., LIT., MÚS., PINT. componer. *3* redactar, escribir. *4* concertar, arreglar, ordenar, disponer. *5* calmar, serenar.

composed (-d) *adj.* compuesto [de]. *2* sosegado, tranquilo, sereno.

composedness (kømpou·šidnis) *s.* compostura, sosiego, serenidad, mesura.

composer (kømpou·sø^r) *s.* autor, escritor. *2* compositor. *3* cajista. *4* apaciguador.

composite (kømpa·šit) *adj.* compuesto [no simple]. *2* mixto. *3* ARQ., BOT. compuesto. *4 s.* compuesto; mixtura. *5* BOT. flor compuesta.

composition (kampoši·shøn) *s.* composición. *2* tema, redacción [escolar]. *3* arreglo, transacción. *4* compuesto; mixtura.

compositor (kømpa·šitø^r) *s.* IMPR. cajista.

compost (ka·mpoust) *s.* AGR. abono, estiércol.

compost (to) *tr.* abonar, estercolar.

composure (kømpou·ŷø^r) *s.* calma, serenidad, sangre fría.

compote (ka·mpout) *s.* compota.

compound (ka·mpaund) *adj.* compuesto [formado por unión o combinación]. *2* ARIT. complejo. *3* COM. compuesto [interés]. *4* MEC. compound. *5 s.* compuesto; mezcla. *6* recinto, empalizada.

compound (to) (kampau·nd) *tr.* componer, confeccionar; combinar, mezclar. *2* arreglar, transigir. *3 intr.* pactar, avenirse, transigir.

compounder (-ø^r) *s.* mezclador, preparador. *2* el que pacta o transige.

comprehend (to) (kamprije·nd) *tr.* comprender, entender. *2* comprender, contener, incluir.

comprehensible (-sibøl) *adj.* comprensible.

comprehension (-shøn) *s.* comprensión.

comprehensive (-siv) *adj.* comprensivo. *2* amplio, extenso.

comprehensiveness (-nis) *s.* comprensión, inteligencia. *2* amplitud, extensión.

compress (ka·mpres) *s.* compresa.

compress (to) (kømpre·s) *tr.* comprimir. *2* apretar, condensar, reducir.

compressibility (-ibi·liti) *s.* comprensibilidad.

compression (kømpre·shøn) *s.* comprensión. *2* reducción, condensación.

compressor (-sø^r) *s.* compresor.

comprise (to) (kømprai·š) *tr.* comprender, incluir, abrazar, constar de.

compromise (ka·mprømaiš) *s.* transacción, arreglo, componenda. *2* término medio. *3* DER. compromiso.

compromise (to) *tr.* componer, arreglar [por vía de transacción]. *2* comprometer [poner en peligro, etc.]. *3 intr.* transigir, hacer concesiones.

comptroller (køntrou·lø^r) *s.* interventor.

compulsion (kømpø·lshøn) *s.* compulsión, constreñimiento, coacción.

compulsory (-sori) *adj.* compulsivo. *2* obligatorio.

compunction (kømpø·nkshøn) *s.* compunción, remordimiento, escrúpulo.

compunctious (-søs) *adj.* compungido, contrito.

compurgation (kampø^rgei·shøn) *s.* compurgación.

computation (kampiutei·shøn) *s.* computación, cómputo, cuenta, cálculo.

compute (to) (kømpiu·t) *tr.* computar, calcular, estimar.

computer (-ø^r) *s.* calculador. *2* máquina calculadora.

comrade (ka·mræd) *s.* compañero, camarada.

con (kan) *adv.-s.* contra. **V. PRO.**

con (to) *tr.* estudiar, aprender. *2* gobernar [un buque]. ¶ Pret. y p. p.: *conned;* ger.: *conning.*

concatenate (kankæ·tineit) *adj.* concadenado.

concatenate (to) *tr.* concadenar.

concatenation (-ei·shøn) *s.* concatenación.

concave (ka·nkeiv) *adj.* cóncavo. *2 s.* concavidad, bóveda.

concaveness (-nis), **concavity** (-kæ·viti) *s.* concavidad.

conceal (to) (kønsı·l) *tr.* ocultar, esconder, disimular, tapar, encubrir.

concealment (-mønt) *s.* ocultación, encubrimiento, disimulación. *2* escondite, escondrijo.

concede (to) (kønsı·d) *tr.* conceder, reconocer. *2* conceder, otorgar. *3 intr.* hacer concesiones.

conceit (kønsı·t) *s.* vanidad, presunción, orgullo, engreimiento. *2* concepto, opinión. *3* concepto, expresión ingeniosa o afectada. *4* capricho, fantasía.

conceited (-id) *adj.* engreído, presumido, pagado de sí mismo.

conceivable (kønsı·vabøl) *adj.* concebible, imaginable.

conceive (to) (kønsı·v) *tr.* concebir [en todas sus acepciones]. *2* comprender. *3* creer, suponer. *4* expresar, formular. *5 intr.* concebir [la hembra].

concenter (to) *tr.* TO CONCENTRE.

concentrate (ka·nsøntreit) *adj.* concentrado.

concentrate (to) *tr.* concentrar, reconcentrar. *2* enfocar. *3 intr.* concentrarse, reconcentrarse.

concentration (-ei·shøn) *s.* concentración. *2* reconcentración.

concentre (to) (kønse·ntø^r) *tr.* concentrar, reunir en un centro común. *2 intr.* concentrarse; tener un centro común.

concentric(al (-trik(al) *adj.* concéntrico.

concentus (kønse·tøs) *s.* concento.

concept (kæ·nsept) *s.* concepto, noción, idea.

conception (kønse·pshøn) *s.* concepción. *2* concepto, idea; noción, comprensión.

conceptual (-chual) *adj.* conceptual.

concern (kønsø^rn) *s.* interés, afecto. *2* preocupación, inquietud, ansiedad. *3* interés, parte. *4* concernencia, incumbencia. *5* lo que importa; importancia. *6* asunto. *7* negocio, empresa, establecimiento.

concern (to) *tr.* concernir, atañer. *2* importar, interesar, afectar. *3* preocupar, inquietar. *4 ref.* interesarse, preocuparse.

concerned (-t) *adj.* interesado, comprometido. *2* preocupado, inquieto.

concerning (-ing) *prep.* tocante a, acerca de.

concernment (-mønt) *s.* concernencia. *2* interés, importancia. *3* interés, parte. *4* asunto. *5* preocupación, inquietud.

concert (ka·nsø^rt) *s.* concierto, acuerdo: *in* ~, de concierto. *2* MUS. concierto.

concert (to) (kønsø·^rt) *tr.* concertar, convenir. *2* planear, disponer. *3 intr.* concertarse.

concertina (kansø^rtı·na) *s.* concertina.

concertmaster (ka·nsø^rtmæstø^r) *s.* MÚS. concertino.

concerto (kønche·^rtou) *s.* MÚS. concierto [composición].

concession (kønse·shøn) *s.* concesión.

concessionary (-eri) *s.* concesionario. *2 adj.* otorgado por concesión.

concessive (kønse·siv) *adj.* concesivo.

conch (kank o kanch) *s.* caracol marino; caracola. *2* ARQ. concha.

conchiferous (kanki·førøs) *adj.* conchífero.

conchoid (ka·nkoid) *s.* concoide.

conchoidal (kankoi·dal) *adj.* concoide, concoideo.

conchology (kanka·lodÿi) *s.* conquiliología.

conciliar (kønsı·lia^r) *adj.* conciliar.

conciliate (to) (kønsı·lieit) *tr.* conciliar [ganar, atraerse], propiciar, apaciguar. *2* conciliar [doctrinas, etc.].

conciliation (-ei·shøn) *s.* conciliación.

conciliatory (-nsı·liatori) *adj.* conciliatorio.

concise (kønsai·s) *adj.* conciso, breve.

conciseness (-nis) *s.* concisión.

concision (kønsi·ÿøn) *s.* concisión. *2* corte, cortadura.

conclave (ka·nkleiv) *s.* cónclave.

conclude (to) (kønklu·d) *tr.* concluir, dar fin a. *2* concluir, hacer [un tratado, etc.]. *3* concluir, inferis. *4* decidir, determinar. *5 intr.* concluir, finalizar. *6* formar un juicio definitivo.

conclusion (kønclu·ÿøn) *s.* conclusión [en todas sus acepciones]. *2* decisión final, resultado. *3* final, despedida [de una carta].

conclusive (-siv) *adj.* conclusivo. *2* concluyente.

concoct (to) (kønka·kt) *tr.* mezclar, preparar, confeccionar. *2* urdir, tramar, forjar, inventar.

concoction (-shøn) *s.* mezcla, preparado. *2* trama, maquinación, invención.

concomitance, -cy (kønka·mitans, -si) *s.* concomitancia.

concomitant (-nt) *adj.-s.* concomitante.

concord (ka·ko^rd) *s.* concordia, armonía. *2* acuerdo, convenio. *3* GRAM., MÚS. concordia.

concordance (kanko·^rdans) *s.* concordancia, armonía, conformidad. *2* concordancias [índice].

concordant (-ønt) *adj.* concordante, concorde, conforme.

concordat (kanko·^rdat) *s.* concordato.

concourse (ka·nko^rs) *s.* concurso, concurrencia [de cosas]. *2* concurso, concurrencia, gentío.

concrescence (kønkre·søns) *s.* concrescencia.

concrete (ka·nkrit) *adj.* concreto [no abstracto; concrecionado]. *2* de hormigón. *3 s.* lo concreto. *4* hormigón.

concrete (to) (kønkrı·t) *tr.* concrecionar, solidificar. *2* cubrir con hormigón. *3 intr.* concrecionarse, cuajarse.

concretion (kønkrı·shøn) *s.* concreción. *2* solidificación, coagulación.

concubinage (kankiu·binidÿ) *s.* concubinato.

concubine (ka·nkiubain) *f.* concubina.

concupiscence (kankiu·pisøns) *s.* concupiscencia.

concupiscent (-sønt) *adj.* concupiscente.

concur (to) (kønkø·^r) *intr.* concurrir, coincidir. *2* cooperar. *3* concurrir, convenir, hallarse de acuerdo. ¶ Pret. y p. p.: *concurred;* ger.: *concurring.*

concurrence (-røns), **concurrency** (-si) *s.* concurrencia, coincidencia, conjunción. *2* acuerdo, consenso. *3* cooperación, ayuda. *4* competencia, rivalidad.
concurrent (-rønt) *adj.* concurrente, coincidente, coexistente. *2 s.* contribuidor. *3* rival, competidor.
concuss (kønkø·s) *tr.* sacudir, agitar. *2* coaccionar.
concussion (kønkø·shøn) *s.* concusión, sacudida, golpe. *2* MED. conmoción.
condemn (to) (kønde·m) *tr.* condenar. *2* desahuciar [a un enfermo]. *3* confiscar, expropiar.
condemnation (kandemnei·shøn) *s.* condenación.
condemnatory (kande·mnatori) *adj.* condenatorio.
condensate (kønde·nseit) *s.* producto de una condensación.
condensation (-ei·shøn) *s.* condensación.
condense (to) (kønde·ns) *tr.* condensar. *2* reducir, abreviar. *3 intr.* condensarse. *4* expresarse con concisión.
condenser (-ø^r) *s.* condensador.
condensing (-ing) *adj.* condensador.
condescend (to) (kandise·nd) *intr.* dignarse, acomodarse a un inferior; tomar un aire de protección o de superioridad.
condescendence (-øns), **condescension** (-se·nshøn) *s.* dignación, actitud afable de protección o superioridad.
condign (køndai·n) *adj.* condigno.
condiment (ka·ndimønt) *s.* condimento.
condisciple (køndi·sipøl) *s.* condiscípulo.
condition (køndi·shøn) *s.* condición, requisito. *2* condición, estado, circunstancia [de las cosas]. *3* condición [social]; estado [de las personas]. *4* estado físico [de los cuerpos].
condition (to) *tr.* condicionar. *2* estipular, convenir. *3* acondicionar [el aire, etc.].
conditional (-al) *adj.* condicional. *2 adj.-s.* GRAM. potencial [modo].
conditioned (-d) *adj.* condicionado. *2* acondicionado.
condole (to) (køndou·l) *intr.* condolerse, dar el pésame. | Gralte. con *with*.
condolement (-mønt), **condolence** (-øus) *s.* condolencia, lástima, pésame.
condominium (kandomi·niøm) *s.* condominio.
condonation (køndounei·shøn) *s.* perdón, olvido [de agravio o culpa].
condone (to) (køndou·n) *tr.* perdonar, olvidar [un agravio o culpa].
condor (ka·ndø^r) *s.* cóndor [ave; moneda].
conduce (to) (køndiu·s) *tr.* conducir, tender, contribuir.
conducive (-iv) *adj.* conducente.
conduct (ka·ndøkt) *s.* conducta, comportamiento. *2* conducta, gobierno, manejo. *3* MIL. escolta.
conduct (to) (køndø·kt) *tr.* conducir, guiar, llevar, escoltar, acompañar. *2* conducir, dirigir, mandar. *3* FÍS. conducir [el calor, etc.]. *4* MÚS. dirigir.
conductibility (-ibi·liti) *s.* conductibilidad.
conduction (køndø·kshøn) *s.* conducción [de un líquido, del calor, de la electricidad]; traída.
conductive (-tiv) *adj.* conductivo. *2* FÍS. conductor.
conductivity (-iti) *s.* conductividad; conductibilidad.
conductor (-tø^r) *s.* conductor, guía. *2* MÚS. director. *3* cobrador [de tranvía]; (E.U) revisor [de tren]. *4* FÍS. conductor.
conductress (-tris) *s.* conductora, directora.
conduit (ka·ndit) *s.* conducto. *2* caño, encañado, tubería, canalización.

condyle (ka·ndil) *s.* ANAT. cóndilo.
cone (koun) *s.* GEOM., BOT. cono. *2* cucurucho. *3* piñón [de azúcar].
coney (kou·ni) *s.* conejo, gazapo.
confabulate (to) (kønfæ·biuleit) *intr.* confabular, platicar, departir.
confabulation (-ei·shøn) *s.* confabulación, plática.
confection (kønfe·kshøn) *s.* confección, preparación. *2* confitura, dulce. *3* confección [ropa hecha].
confection (to) *tr.* preparar, confitar.
confectionary (-ari) *adj.* confitado, de confitería.
confectioner (-ø^r) *s.* confitero, repostero.
confectionery (-eri) *s.* confitería, repostería. *2* dulces, confituras.
confederacy (kønfe·dørasi) *s.* confederación, coalición, liga. *2* asociación [para un acto delictivo], complicidad.
confederate (to) (-eit) *adj.-s.* confederado, aliado. *2* socio, compinche, cómplice.
confederate (to) *tr.* confederar, unir. *2 intr.* confederarse, unirse.
confederation (ei·shøn) *s.* confederación.
confer (to) (kønfø·^r) *tr.* conferir, dar, otorgar. *2* dar, comunicar [una cualidad, etc., a una cosa]. *3* conferir, comparar. *4 intr.* conferir, conferenciar. ¶ Pret. y p. p.: *conferred*; ger.: *conferring*.
conference (ka·nførøns) *s.* conferencia, junta, entrevista.
conferment (kønfø·^rmønt) *s.* acción de conferir o dar.
conferrer (kønfø·rø^r) *s.* el que confiere o da.
confess (to) (kønfe·s) *tr.* confesar [pecados, etc.]. *2* confesar, reconocer. *3* confesar [oír en confesión]. *4 intr.* confesarse.
confessed (-t) *adj.* confesado, declarado, reconocido.
confession (kønfe·shøn) *s.* confesión. *2* religión, credo. *3* profesión [de fe].
confessional (-al), **confessionary** (-eri) *adj.* confesional. *2 s.* confesonario.
confessor (kønfe·sø^r) *s.* confesor. *2* confesante.
confetti (kønfe·ti) *s.* confeti.
confidant *m.*, **confidante** (kanfidæ·nt) *f.* confidente [de una persona].
confide (to) (kønfai·d) *intr.* confiar [poner la fe o confianza en]. *2 tr.* confiar [un secreto, un objeto, etc.].
confidence (ka·nfidøns) *s.* confianza, fe, seguridad. *2* confianza, presunción, atrevimiento. *3* confidencia.
confident (-ønt) *adj.* seguro, que tiene fe o confianza. *2* confiado, presuntuoso, atrevido. *3* confidente [pers.].
confidential (kanfide·nshal) *adj.* confidencial, reservado. *2* de confianza.
confiding (kønfai·ding) *adj.* confiado, crédulo.
configurate (to) (kønfi·giureit) *tr.* configurar.
configuration (-ei·shøn) *s.* configuración.
configure (-giu^r) *tr.* configurar.
confine (ka·nfain) *s.* confín, límite, término.
confine (to) *tr.* confinar, lindar. *2 tr.* limitar, restringir. *3* encerrar, recluir: *to be confined*, estar de parto; *to be confined to bed*, guardar cama.
confineless (-lis) *adj.* ilimitado.
confinement (-mønt) *s.* encierro, reclusión, cautiverio. *2* alumbramiento; sobreparto. *3* restricción, limitación.
confirm (to) (kønfø·^rm) *tr.* confirmar, corroborar, revalidar, ratificar. *2* confirmar, fortalecer. *3* ECLES. confirmar.

confirmation (-ei·shøn) s. confirmación, corroboración. 2 ECLES. confirmación.

confirmed (kønfø·ʳmd) adj. confirmado. 2 inveterado.

confiscate (to) (ka·nfiskeit) tr. confiscar; decomisar.

confiscation (ei·shøn) s. confiscación; decomiso.

confiteor (ka·nfitiø·ʳ) s. confiteor.

confiture (ka·nfichø·ʳ) s. confitura, dulce.

conflagration (kanfkagrei·shøn) s. conflagración, incendio.

conflict (ka·nflikt) s. conflicto, lucha, choque, pugna, antagonismo.

conflict (to) intr. chocar, estar en conflicto, en pugna.

confluence (ka·nfluøns) s. confluencia. 2 concurso [de gentes].

confluent (-ønt) adj. confluente. 2 s. confluencia, confluente. 3 río confluente.

conflux (ka·nfløks) s. CONFLUENCE.

conform (to) (kønfo·ʳm) tr. conformar, acomodar, ajustar. 2 intr. conformarse, acomodarse, cumplir, obedecer.

conformable (-abøl) adj. conforme, acorde, consonante, proporcionado. 2 sumiso, obediente.

conformation (-ei·shøn) s. conformación, forma, estructura. 2 adaptación.

conformist (kønfo·ʳmist) s. conformista.

conformity (-iti) s. conformidad, concordancia, consonancia. 2 obediencia.

confound (to) (kønfau·nd) tr. confundir [mezclar, desordenar, embrollar]. 2 CONFUSE 2. 3 confundir, equivocar. 4 desbaratar, frustrar. 5 interj. ~ it!, ¡maldito sea!

confounded (-id) adj. confuso. 2 vulg. maldito, condenado, dichoso.

confraternity (kanfratø·ʳniti) s. confraternidad. 2 cofradía, hermandad, sociedad.

confront (to) (kønfrø·nt) tr. confrontar, enfrentar, carear. 2 confrontar, cotejar. 3 arrostrar, hacer frente a.

confrontation (-ei·shøn), **confrontment** (kønfrø·ntmønt) s. confrontación, careo.

Confucianism (kønfiu·shaniŝm) s. confucianismo.

Confucius (-shøs) n. pr. Confucio.

confuse (to) (kønfiu·š) tr. confundir [mezclar, embrollar], oscurecer. 2 confundir, turbar, avergonzar; desconcertar, desorientar. 3 confundir, equivocar.

confused (-d) adj. confuso. 2 perplejo, desconcertado.

confusion (kønfiu·ȳøn) s. confusión.

confutation (kanfiutei·shøn) s. confutación.

confute (to) (kønfiu·t) tr. confutar. 2 confundir [en la disputa].

congé (ka·nȳei) s. despedida; despido.

congeal (to) (køndȳɪ·l) tr. congelar, helar. 2 cuajar, coagular. 3 intr. congelarse, helarse, cuajarse.

congealment (-mønt) s. congelación.

congee (ka·nȳi) s. CONGÉ.

congelation (-ei·shøn) s. congelación. 2 solidificación.

congener (ka·ndȳinø·ʳ) s. congénere.

congeneric (kandȳøne·rik) adj. congénere.

congenial (ka·ndȳɪ·nial) adj. congenial. 2 afín, análogo, concordante. 3 que conviene al gusto o a la naturaleza de uno; simpático.

congeniality (-iti), **congenialness** (-nis) s. conformidad, afinidad; simpatía. 2 calidad de lo que conviene al gusto o a la naturaleza de uno.

congenital (køndȳe·nital) adj. congénito.

conger (ca·ngø·ʳ), **conger eel** s. ICT. congrio.

congeries (køndȳi·riiŝ) s. congerie.

congest (to) (køndȳe·st) tr. congestionar. 2 intr. congestionarse.

congested (-id) adj. congestionado. 2 BOT. apiñado.

congestion (køndȳe·schøn) s. congestión.

conglobate (kønglou·beit) adj. conglobado.

conglobate (to) tr. conglobar.

conglomerate (køngla·mørit) adj.-s. conglomerado. 2 adj. apiñado, denso.

conglomerate (to) (-reit) tr. conglomerar. 2 intr. conglomerarse.

conglutinate (kønglu·tineit) adj. conglutinado.

conglutinate (to) tr. conglutinar. 2 intr. conglutinarse.

Congo (ka·ngou) n. pr. GEOGR. Congo. 2 adj.-s. congoleño.

congo(l)ese (kangou[l]ɪ·š) adj.-s. congoleño.

congratulate (køngræ·chuleit) tr. congratular, felicitar, dar el parabién.

congratulation (-ei·shøn) s. congratulación, felicitación, enhorabuena.

congratulatory (køngræ·chulatori) adj. congratulatorio.

congregate (to) (ka·ngrigeit) tr. congregar, juntar, reunir. 2 intr. congregarse, juntarse.

congregation (-ei·shøn) s. congregación. 2 reunión, agregado. 3 concurso, auditorio. 4 grey; feligresía.

congregational (-al) adj. de congregación; colectivo. 2 perteneciente a una grey o feligresía.

congress (ka·ngris) s. congreso, asamblea, reunión. 2 (con may.) Congreso [cámara legislativa]. 4 (E.U) conjunto de las dos Cámaras legislativas.

congressman (-mæn), **congresswoman** (-wumæn) f. congresista. 2 diputado. 3 (E.U) miembro del Congreso.

congruence, congruency (ka·ngruøns, -i) s. congruencia, consonancia, conformidad. 2 MAT., TEOL. congruencia.

congruent (ka·ngruønt) adj. congruente, congruo, consonante, conforme. 2 MAT. congruente.

congruity (køngru·iti) s. CONGRUENCE.

congruous (ka·ngruøs) adj. CONGRUENT.

conic (ka·nik) adj. cónico, coniforme. 2 s. GEOM. sección cónica.

conical (-al) adj. cónico.

conicalness (-nis) s. conicidad.

conifer (kou·nifø·ʳ) s. BOT. conífera.

coniferous (-røs) adj. conífero.

coniform (kounifo·ʳm) adj. coniforme.

conirostral (kounira·stral) adj. ORN. conirrostro.

conjectural (køndȳe·kchøral) adj. conjetural.

conjecture (-kchø·ʳ) s. conjetura, presunción.

conjecture (to) tr. conjeturar, presumir.

conjoin (to) (køndȳoi·n) tr. unir, juntar, asociar. 2 intr. unirse, juntarse, asociarse.

conjoint (-t) adj. unido. 2 aunado. 3 s. asociado, aliado.

conjointly (-li) adv. conjuntamente, mancomunadamente.

conjugal (ka·ndȳugal) adj. conyugal.

conjugate (ka·ndȳugeit) adj. conjugado. 2 GRAM. de la misma derivación. 3 s. BOT. conjugada [alga].

conjugate (to) tr. unir, enlazar. 2 BIOL., GRAM. conjugar. 3 intr. BIOL. conjugarse.

conjugation (-ei·shøn) s. unión, conjunción. 2 BIOL., GRAM. conjugación.

conjunct (køndȳø·nkt) adj. unido, conjunto, asociado.

conjunction (køndÿø·nshøn) s. conjunción, unión. 2 ASTR., GRAM. conjunción.
conjunctiva (køndÿønktai·va) s. ANAT. conjuntiva.
conjunctive (køndÿø·nktiv) adj. conjuntivo. 2 conjunto.
conjunctivitis (-tivai·tis) s. MED. conjuntivitis.
conjunctly (køndÿø·nktli) adv. conjuntamente.
conjuncture (-chøʳ) s. coyuntura, circunstancias. 2 ASTR. conjunción.
conjuration (kandÿurei·shøn) s. conjuro [ruego]. 2 conjuro, sortilegio. 3 prestidigitación.
conjure (køndÿu·øʳ) tr. conjurar, rogar, implorar. 2 evocar [a un espíritu, etc.]; conjurar, exorcizar. 3 producir, enviar, hacer aparecer o desaparecer, etc., por [o como por] arte mágica. 4 to ~ up, evocar; traer a la memoria o a la imaginación. 6 intr. practicar las artes mágicas. 7 hacer juegos de manos.
conjurement (køndÿu·øʳmønt) s. conjuro, exorcismo. 2 adjuración.
conjurer, conjuror (ka·ndÿørøʳ) s. hechicero, mago. 2 prestidigitador, ilusionista.
connate (kanei·t) adj. innato. 2 afín. 3 connato.
connatural (kanæ·chøral) adj. connatural. 2 de igual naturaleza.
connect (to) (køne·kt) tr. unir, enlazar, coordinar. 2 conectar. 3 relacionar, asociar. 4 poner en comunicación. 5 intr. unirse, enlazarse, tener conexión. 6 FERROC. enlazar, empalmar.
connected (-id) adj. unido, enlazado, conexo. 2 relacionado. 3 emparentado. 4 coherente, que tiene ilación.
connectedly (-li) adv. con coherencia.
connecting (-ing) adj. de unión o conexión: ~ link, eslabón; ~ rod, MEC. biela.
connection (køne·kshøn) s. conexión, unión, enlace. 2 coherencia, ilación. 3 relación, analogía, respecto. 4 relación [de amistad, comercial, etc.], parentesco. 5 pariente, deudo. 6 clientela. 7 secta. 8 medio de comunicación. 9 FERROC. empalme.
connective (-tiv) adj. conectivo, conjuntivo. 2 s. GRAM. palabra que enlaza.
connexion s. CONNECTION.
connivance (kønai·vans) s. connivencia, consentimiento.
connive (to) (køvai·v) intr. disimular o tolerar culpablemente. 2 BOT. ser connivente.
connivent (-ønt) adj. BOT. ser connivente.
conniver (-øʳ) s. consentidor, cómplice.
connoisseur (kanisø·ʳ) s. perito, conocedor.
connotation (kanotei·shøn) s. connotación.
connote (to) (kønou·t) tr. connotar. 2 suponer [traer consigo].
connubial (køniu·bial) adj. connubial.
conoid (kou·noid) s. conoide.
conoidal (konoi·dal) adj. conoide, conoidal.
conquer (ka·nkøʳ) tr. conquistar. 2 vencer, dominar. 3 vencer, superar. 4 intr. triunfar.
conquerable (-abøl) adj. conquistable. 2 domable. 3 vencible, superable.
conqueror (-øʳ) s. conquistador. 2 vencedor, sojuzgador.
conquest (ka·nkuest) s. conquista.
Conrad (ka·nræd) n. pr. Conrado.
consaguineous (kansængüi·niøs) adj. consanguíneo.
consanguinity (-niti) s. consanguinidad.
conscience (ka·nshøns) s. conciencia [esp. en sentido moral]: in (all) ~, en conciencia; en verdad.

conscienceless (-lis) adj. sin conciencia, desalmado.
conscientious (kanshie·nshøs) adj. concienzudo, escrupuloso, detenido. 2 de conciencia.
conscientiousness (-nis) s. conciencia, rectitud, escrupulosidad.
conscious (ka·nshøs) adj. consciente. 2 que se da cuenta, que se percata.
consciousness (-nis) s. FIL., PSIC. conciencia. 2 conciencia [de una cosa]. 3 conocimiento, sentimiento, sentido, estado consciente.
conscript (ka·nskript) adj. conscripto. 2 reclutado. 3 s. recluta, quinto.
conscript (to) (kønskri·pt) tr. MIL. alistar, reclutar.
conscription (-kri·pshøn) s. alistamiento, reclutamiento [forzoso].
consecrate (ka·nsikreit) adj. consagrado.
consecrate (to) tr. consagrar. 2 intr. LITURG. consagrar.
consecration (-ei·shøn) s. consagración. 2 dedicación.
consecrator (-øʳ) s. consagrante.
consecution (kansikiu·shøn) s. ilación. 2 sucesión, serie.
consecutive (kønse·kiutiv) adj. consecutivo. 2 sucesivo.
consensual (kønse·nshual) adj. consensual.
consensus (-søs) s. consenso, acuerdo general.
consent (kønse·nt) s. consentimiento, asentimiento, aquiescencia, aprobación, permiso: all with one ~, unánimemente.
consent (to) intr. consentir, acceder, estar de acuerdo.
consentaneous (kønsentei·niøs) adj. unánime. 2 conforme [a], consonante [con].
consentient (kønse·nshiønt) adj. anuente. 2 acorde, unánime.
consequence (ka·nsikuøns) s. consecuencia, resultado: in ~ of, de resultas de, a consecuencia de. 2 consecuencia, deducción. 3 importancia, entidad.
consequent (-kuønt) adj. consecuente, consiguiente. 2 lógico. 3 s. consecuencia, resultado. 4 LÓG., MAT. consecuente.
consequential (-kue·nshal) adj. consiguiente. 2 importante [pers.]. 3 pomposo, engreído.
consequently (kønse·kuøntli) adv. por consiguiente, por ende, en consecuencia.
conservancy (kønsø·ʳvansi) s. conservación, cuidado.
conservant (-vant) adj. conservador, preservador.
conservation (-ei·shøn) s. conservación.
conservatism (kønsø·ʳvatiśm) s. conservadurismo.
conservative (-tiv) adj. conservativo, conservador. 2 adj.-s. POL. conservador.
conservatoire (kansøʳvatua·ʳ) s. conservatorio.
conservator (ka·nsøʳveitøʳ) s. conservador, protector.
conservatory (kønsø·ʳvatori) adj.-s. conservatorio. 2 s. invernáculo, invernadero.
conserve (kønsø·ʳv) s. conserva, confitura.
conserve (to) tr. conservar, mantener. 2 confitar.
conserver (-øʳ) s. conservador. 2 confitero.
consider (to) (lønsi·døʳ) tr. considerar, pensar, tener en cuenta. 2 examinar, estudiar. 3 considerar, juzgar, tener por. 4 considerar [tratar con respeto o bondad].
considerable (-abøl) adj. considerable. 2 notable, importante [pers.].

considerate (-it) *adj.* considerado [para con los demás]. *2* reflexivo, circunspecto, mirado.
considerateness (-itnis) *s.* consideración [para con los demás]. *2* prudencia, circunspección, moderación.
consideration (-ei·shøn) *s.* consideración [acción de considerar]; examen, estudio. *2* motivo, razón. *3* consideración, respeto, benevolencia. *4* importancia. *5* retribución, precio.
considering (kønsi·døring) *prep.* considerando [que], en atención a.
consideringly (-li) *adv.* con reflexión, seriamente.
consign (to) (kønsai·n) *tr.* COM. consignar. *2* consignar, confiar, depositar, entregar, relegar.
consignation (-ei·shøn) *s.* COM. consignación. *2* consignación, entrega.
consignee (konsaini·) *s.* consignatario.
consigner *s.* CONSIGNOR.
consignment (konsai·nmønt) *s.* COM. consignación; remesa, envío; partida.
consignor (kønsai·nø^r) *s.* consignador.
consist (to) (kønsi'st) *intr.* consistir. *2* componerse, constar [de]. *3* concordar, ser compatible [con].
consistence, -cy (-øns) *s.* consistencia. *2* congruencia, consonancia, compatibilidad. *3* consecuencia [en la conducta].
consistent (-ønt) *adj.* consistente, sólido, estable. *2* congruente, consonante, compatible. *3* consecuente [en la conducta].
consistory (kønsi·stori) *s.* consistorio.
consolable (kønsou·labøl) *adj.* consolable.
consolation (kansolei·shøn) *s.* consolación, consuelo, alivio.
consolatory (kønsou·latori) *adj.* consolatorio.
console (ka·nsoul) *s.* cónsola. *2* ARQ. cartela; repisa.
console (to) (kønsou·l) *tr.* consolar, confortar.
consolidate (kønsa·lideit) *tr.* consolidar, solidar. *2* unir, fusionar. *3* *intr.* consolidarse, solidarse. *4* unirse, fusionarse.
consolidation (-eishøn) *s.* consolidación. *2* COM. fusión, unión [de entidades].
consols (ka·nsoulš) *s. pl.* (Ingl.) títulos de la deuda consolidada.
consommé (kansømei·) *s.* consumado, caldo.
consonance, -cy (ka·nsønans, -si) *s.* consonancia, conformidad. *2* MÚS. consonancia.
consonant (-ant) *adj.* consonante, cónsono, conforme. *2 adj.-s.* GRAM. consonante.
consonous (-nøs) *adj.* cónsono, armonioso.
consort (ka·nso^{r}t) *s.* consorte, cónyuge. *2* compañero. *3* MAR. buque que acompaña a otro.
consort (to) (kønso·^{r}t) *intr.* juntarse, acompañarse. *2* concordar, armonizar. *3 tr.* casar, asociar.
consortium (-shiøm) *s.* consorcio.
conspectus (kønspe·ktøs) *s.* ojeada general, sumario, compendio.
conspicuity (kønspikiu·iti) *s.* visibilidad, claridad. *2* nombradía.
conspicuous (kønspi·kiuøs) *adj.* conspicuo, eminente. *2* notable. *3* visible, manifiesto.
conspiracy (-pi·rasi) *s.* conspiración, complot.
conspirator (-ratø^r) *s.* conspirador.
conspire (to) (kønspai·^{r}) *intr.* conspirar, conjurarse. *2 tr.* planear, tramar.
conspirer (-rø^r) *s.* conspirador.
constable (ka·nstabøl) *s.* condestable. *2* alguacil. *3* policía [uniformado].
constableship (-ship) *s.* condestablía.
constabulary (kønstæ·biuleri) *s.* policía uniformada.

Constance (ka·nstans) *n. pr.* Constancia. *2 n. pr.* Constancio.
constancy (-i) *s.* constancia [firmeza, perseverancia]. *2* fidelidad. *3* persistencia.
constant (ka·nstant) *adj.* constante [firme, perseverante; durable]. *2* leal. *3* continuo, prsistente. *4 s.* MAT. constante.
Constantine (-tin o -tain) *n. pr.* Constantino.
Constantinople (kanstæntinou·pøl) *n. pr.* GEOGR. Constantinopla.
constellation (kanstelei·shøn) *s.* constelación.
consternate (to) (ka·nstø^{r}neit) *tr.* consternar.
consternation (-ei·shøn) *s.* consternación; terror, espanto.
constipate (to) (ka·nstipeit) *tr.* estreñir.
constipation (-ei·shøn) *s.* MED. estreñimiento.
constituency (kønsti·chuønsi) *s.* distrito electoral; electores de un distrito. *2* grupo de comitentes.
constituent (-ønt) *adj.* constitutivo, componente. *2* POL. constituyente. *3* elector, electoral. *4 s.* componente. *5* comitente, poderdante, mandante. *6* elector [de un diputado].
constitute (to) (ka·nstitiut) *tr.* constituir. *2* nombrar, hacer. *3* establecer, instituir. *4 ref.* constituirse en o por.
connectedly (-li) *adv.* con coherencia.
constitution (kanstitiu·shøn) *s.* constitución. *2* complexión; temperamento.
constitutional (-al) *adj.* constitucional. *2 s.* fam. paseíto.
constitutionality (-æ·liti) *s.* constitucionalidad.
constitutive (ka·nstitiutiv) *adj.-s.* constitutivo. *2 adj.* legislativo.
constrain (kønstrei·n) *adj.-s.* constitutivo. *2 adj.* legislativo.
constrain (to) (kønstrei·n) *tr.* constreñir, obligar. *2* estrechar, apretar. *3* restringir, reprimir, contener.
constrained (-d) *adj.* constreñido. *2* forzado, violento; encogido, embarazado; ~ *smile*, sonrisa forzada.
constraint (-t) *s.* constreñimiento, coacción, fuerza, apremio. *2* represión, contención. *3* embarazo, violencia.
constrict (to) (kønstri·kt) *tr.* constreñir, apretar, estrechar. *2* atar, ligar.
constriction (-kshøn) *s.* constricción, encogimiento.
constrictor (-tø^r) *s.* constrictor. *2* ZOOL. boa.
constringe (to) (kønstri·ndÿ) *tr.* constreñir, apretar, contraer.
construct (to) (kønstrø·kt) *tr.* construir, fabricar, hacer. *2* idear, componer. *3* GRAM. construir.
constructer (-ø^r) *s.* constructor.
construction (-kshøn) *s.* construcción [acción de construir]. *2* construcción, edificio, artefacto. *3* interpretación, sentido que se atribuye. *4* GRAM. construcción.
constructive (-tiv) *adj.* constructivo. *2* implícito, inferido, sobrentendido.
constructor (-tø^r) *s.* constructor.
construe (to) (kønstru·) *tr.* GRAM. construir. *2* traducir. *3* interpretar, explicar.
consubstantial (kønsøbstæ·nshal) *adj.* consubstancial.
consubstantiation (-shiei·shøn) *s.* consubstanciación.
consuetude (ka·nsuitiud) *s.* uso, costumbre.
consuetudinary (-tiu·dineri) *adj.* consuetudinario, de costumbre.
consul (ka·nsøl) *s.* cónsul.

consular (ka·nsiula^r) *adj.* consular.
consulate (-lit) *s.* consulado.
consulship (ka·nsølship) *s.* consulado [dignidad o cargo].
consult (to) (kønsø·lt) *tr.-intr.* consultar. *2 tr.* tener en cuenta. *3 intr.* deliberar, conferenciar.
consultation (kansøltei·shøn) *s.* consultación, consulta. *2* junta, deliberación.
consultative (kansø·ltativ) *adj.* consultivo.
consulter (-tø^r) *s.* consultor, consultante.
consulting (-ting) *adj.* consultante. *2* consultor, llamado a consulta. *3* de consulta: ~ *office,* consultorio.
consume (to) (kønsiu·m) *tr.* consumir. *2* gastar, disipar. *3 consumed with,* absorbido por, muerto de. *4 intr.* consumirse, deshacerrse.
consumedly (-idli) *adv.* extremadamente.
consumer (-ø^r) *s.* consumidor.
consummate (kansø·mit) *adj.* consumado. *2* completo, extremado.
consummate (to) (ka·nsømeit) *tr.* consumar.
consummation (kansømei·shøn) *s.* consumación. *2* complemento, perfección.
consumption (-shøn) *s.* consunción, consumimiento, consumición. *2* gasto, consumo. *3* MED. consunción; tisis.
consumptive (-tiv) *adj.* consuntivo. *2 adj.-s.* MED. tísico.
contact (ka·ntækt) *s.* contacto: ~ *breaker,* ELECT. interruptor. *3 pl.* contactos, relaciones.
contact (to) *tr.* ponerse o estar en contacto con.
contagion (køntei·dÿøn) *s.* contagio.
contagious (-dÿøs) *adj.* contagioso, pegadizo.
contain (to) (kønte·in) *tr.* contener, encerrar, incluir; tener cabida para. *2* MAT. ser múltiplo de. *3* contener, reprimir.
container (-ø^r) *s.* continente, recipiente, caja, vasija, envase.
contaminate (to) (køntæ·mineit) *tr.* contaminar. *2* impurificar, adulterar.
contamination (-nei·shøn) *s.* contaminación. *2* impurificación.
contemn (kønte·m) *tr.* despreciar, menospreciar.
contemner (-nø^r) *tr.* despreciador.
contemplate (to) (ka·ntempleit) *tr.* contemplar [con los ojos o la mente]. *2* proponerse, proyectar; tener intención de. *3 intr.* meditar, reflexionar.
contemplation (-ei·shøn) *s.* contemplación [con los ojos o la mente]. *2* espera, consideración [de algo] como probable. *3* intención, propósito [de].
contemplative (kønte·mplativ) *adj.* contemplativo.
contemporaneous (-rei·niøs) *adj.* contemporáneo.
contemporary (kønte·mpøreri) *adj.-s.* contemporáneo, coetáneo. *2 s.* colega [dicho de periódicos].
contempt (kønte·mpt) *s.* desprecio, menosprecio, desdén. *2* DER. ~ *pf court,* desacato a un juez o tribunal.
contemptible (-ibøl) *adj.* despreciable. *2* desdeñable.
contemptuous (kønte·mpchuøs) *adj.* despreciativo, despectivo, desdeñoso.
contemptuousness (-nis) *s.* desprecio, desdén.
contend (to) (kønte·nd) *intr.* contender. *2* competir, oponerse. *3* luchar, esforzarse, bregar. *4 tr.* sostener, afirmar.
contendent (-ønt) *adj.* contendiente.

contender (-ø^r) *s.* contendedor, contendiente. *2* competidor. *3* sostenedor, mantenedor.
content (ka·ntent) *s.* contenido, capacidad, cabida, extensión, volumen. *2 pl.* contenido [de un recipiente o de un libro]: *table of contents,* tabla de materias, índice general.
content (kønte·nt) *adj.* contento, satisfecho. *2 s.* contento, contentamiento, satisfacción.
content (to) (tr. contentar, satisfacer.
contented (-id) *adj.* contento, satisfecho; tranquilo, resignado.
contention (kønte·nshøn) *s.* contención, contienda, disputa. *2* afirmación, lo que uno sostiene. *3* tema u objeto de disputa.
contentious (-shøs) *adj.* contencioso, disputador. *2* contencioso, litigioso.
contentment (kønte·ntmønt) *s.* contentamiento, contento.
conterminal (kantø·^rminal), **conterminous (-nøs)** *adj.* contérmino, limítrofe.
contest (ka·ntest) *s.* contienda, lucha, lid. *2* disputa, litigio. *3* torneo, competición, concurso, certamen.
contest (to) (kønte·st) *tr.* disputar, luchar por. *2* negar, discutir, controvertir, impugnar. *3 intr.* contender, competir, litigar.
contestable (-abøl) *adj.* contestable, discutible.
contestant (-ønt) *s.* contendiente. *2* impugnador, oponente.
contestation (kantestei·shøn) *s.* altercación, contestación.
context (ka·ntekst) *s.* contexto.
contexture (kønte·kschø^r) *s.* contextura. *2* tejido, enlazamiento.
contiguity (kantigiu·iti) *s.* contigüidad, inmediación. *2* continuidad.
contiguous (kønti·giuøs) *adj.* contiguo, inmediato, próximo.
continence, continency (ka·ntinøns, -i) *s.* continencia, templanza, castidad.
continent (ka·ntinønt) *adj.* continente, templado, casto. *2 s.* GEOGR. continente.
continental (kantine·ntal) *adj.* continente, templado, casto. *2 s.* GEOGR. continente.
continental (kantine·ntal) *adj.* continental. *2 s.* habitante de la Europa continental.
contingence (kønti·ndÿøns) *s.* contacto, tangencia.
contingency (-i) *s.* contingencia. *2* eventualidad.
contingent (-ønt) *adj.* contingente, eventual, accidental. *2 s.* contingente, contingencia. *3* contingente, cuota.
continual (kønti·niual) *adj.* continuo, incesante.
continuance (-ans) *s.* continuación, persistencia. *2* duración. *3* DER. aplazamiento.
continuate (-eit) *adj.* continuo, ininterrumpido.
continuation (-ei·shøn) *s.* continuación. *2* prolongación, extensión.
continuative (-eitiv) *adj.* continuativo.
continue (to) (kønti·niu) *tr.* continuar. *2* prolongar. *3* persistir en. *4* mantener, perpetuar. *5* prorrogar, aplazar. *6 intr.* continuar, seguir, proseguir, durar.
continued (-d) *adj.* continuado, continuo, prolongado, seguido. *2* MAT. continua [fracción].
continuity (kantiniu·iti) *s.* continuidad. *2* continuo. *3* CINEM. guión.
continuous (kønti·niuøs) *adj.* continuo.
continuum (-niuøm) *s.* continuo, todo.
contort (to) (kønto·^rt) *tr.* torcer, retorcer.
contortion (-to·^rshøn) *s.* contorsión.
contortionist (-ist) *s.* contorsionista.

contour (kaˑntuʳ) s. contorno, perfil. 2 perímetro. 3 TOP. curva de nivel.

contour (to) tr. contornear, perfilar.

contraband (kaˑntrabænd) s. contrabando. 2 adj. de contrabando, ilegal.

contrabandist (-ist) s. contrabandista.

contrabass (kaˑntrabeis) s. MÚS. contrabajo.

contraceptive (-seˑptiv) adj. anticoncepcional.

contract (kaˑntrækt) s. contrato. 2 contrata. 3 DER. escritura. 4 esponsales. 5 GRAM. forma contraída.

contract (to) (køntræˑkt) tr. contraer, reducir, encoger, estrechar, fruncir, arrugar. 2 GRAM. contraer, acortar [una palabra]. 3 contratar, pactar. 4 contraer [matrimonio, una enfermedad, etc.]. 5 intr. contraerse, reducirse, encogerse. 6 contratar.

contracted (-id) adj. contraído, fruncido. 2 abreviado. 3 estrecho, mezquino. 4 escaso. 5 contratado, pactado.

contractile (køntræˑktil) adj. contráctil.

contractility (-tiˑliti) s. contractilidad.

contracting (køntræˑkting) adj. contractivo. 2 contratante. 3 contrayente.

contraction (-shøn) s. contracción. 2 reducción, encogimiento. 3 estrechez [de miras]. 4 reducción [de créditos, etc.].

contractor (-tøʳ) s. contratante. 2 contratista.

contractual (-chual) adj. contractual.

contradict (to) (kantradiˑkt) tr. contradecir. 2 desmentir, negar.

contradicter (-øʳ) s. contradictor.

contradiction (-diˑkshøn) s. contradicción. 2 lo que envuelve contradicción en sí.

contradictory (-diˑktori) adj. contradictorio. 2 contrario, opuesto. 3 s. LÓG. contradictoria.

contradistinction (-distiˑnkshøn) s. distinción por oposición o contraste: *in ~ to*, por oposición a.

contraindicate (to) (-iˑndikeit) tr. MED. contraindicar.

contraindication (-keiˑshøn) s. MED. contraindicación.

contralto (køntræˑltou) s. MÚS. contralto.

contraposition (kantrapouˑshøn) s. contraposición.

contraption (køntræˑpshøn) s. desp. artefacto, artilugio.

contrariety (kantraraiˑiti) s. contrariedad, oposición. 2 cosa contraria u opuesta.

contrariness (kaˑntrerinis) s. contrariedad, oposición. 2 terquedad.

contrariwise (-uaiš) adv. al contrario, inversamente, al revés. 2 tercamente.

contrary (kaˑntreri) adj. contrario. 2 adverso. 3 dado a la oposición, díscolo, terco. 4 adv. ~ *to*, contrariamente a; contra, en contra de; al contrario de. 5 s. cada una de dos cosas contrarias. 6 lo contrario: *on the ~*, al contrario; *to the ~*, en contrario, en contra.

contrast (kaˑntræst) s. contraste; contraposición.

contrast (to) (køntræˑst) tr. hacer contrastar. 2 intr. contrastar.

contravene (to) (kantraviˑn) tr. contravenir. 2 contradecir, discutir.

contravener (-øʳ) s. contraventor, infractor.

contravention (-veˑnshøn) s. contravención, infracción.

contribute (to) (køntriˑbiut) tr. contribuir con, aportar, donar. 2 colaborar con [un artículo] en un periódico. 3 intr. contribuir [a].

contribution (kantribiuˑshøn) s. contribución [ac-

ción de contribuir]. 2 contribución, aportación, cuota, donativo. 3 colaboración [en un periódico]. 4 contribución [de guerra].

contributor (køntriˑbiutøʳ) s. contribuidor. 2 colaborador [de un periódico].

contrite (kaˑntrait) adj. contrito.

contrition (køntriˑshøn) s. contrición.

contrivance (køntraiˑvans) s. inventiva. 2 traza, artificio, invención, medio, arbitrio. 3 utensilio, aparato, artefacto, mecanismo. 4 plan, idea.

contrive (to) (køntraiˑv) tr. idear, inventar, discurrir. 2 maquinar, tramar. 3 procurar, lograr. 4 intr. hacer planes, darse maña.

contriver (-øʳ) s. autor, inventor, causante. 2 maquinador. 3 arbitrista.

control (køntrouˑl) s. mando, poder, dominio, autoridad. 2 sujeción, freno. 3 gobierno, dirección. 4 inspección, intervención, fiscalización. 5 verificación, comprobación. 6 MEC. mando, control, regulación: ~ *board*, cuadro de control; ~ *lever*, palanca de mando.

control (to) tr. dominar, sujetar, reprimir. 2 gobernar, dirigir, controlar. 3 inspeccionar, revisar, fiscalizar, intervenir, regular. ¶ Pret. y p. p.: *controlled*; ger.: *-lling*.

controller (-øʳ) s. director, interventor, inspector, superintendente. 2 MEC., ELECT. regulador; aparato de manejo. 3 MAR. estopor.

controversial (kantrovøˑʳshal) adj. de controversia, polémico.

controversialist (-ist) s. controversista.

controversy (kaˑntrovøʳsi) s. controversia, polémica disputa.

controvert (to) (kantrovøˑʳt) tr.-intr. controvertir. 2 tr. negar, contradecir.

contumacious (kantiumeiˑshøs) adj. contumaz, rebelde.

contumacy (kaˑntiumasi) s. contumacia, rebeldía. 2 desobediencia, desacato [a la autoridad].

contumelious (kantiumiˑliøs) adj. contumelioso, injurioso.

contumely (kaˑntiumili) s. contumelia.

contuse (to) (køntiuˑš) tr. contundir, magullar.

contusion (køntiuˑyøn) s. contusión.

contusive (-šiv) adj. contundente.

conundrum (kønøˑndrøm) s. acertijo, rompecabezas.

convalesce (to) (kanvaleˑs) intr. convalecer.

convalescence (-øns) s. convalecencia.

convalescent (-ønt) adj. convaleciente.

convection (kønveˑkshøn) s. conducción, transmisión. 2 FÍS. convección.

convene (kønviˑn) tr. reunir, convocar. 2 citar, emplazar. 3 intr. reunirse.

convenience, -cy (-iøns, -si) s. conveniencia, utilidad, comodidad, oportunidad: *at your ~*, cuando buenamente pueda. 2 retrete. 3 pl. comodidades.

convenient (-iønt) adj. conveniente, oportuno. 2 a propósito. 3 cómodo. 4 próximo, a mano.

convent (kaˑnvønt) s. convento.

conventicle (kønveˑntikøl) s. conventículo.

convention (kønveˑnshøn) s. convocación. 2 asamblea, convención. 3 convención, convenio. 4 costumbre o regla comúnmente aceptada, convencionalismo.

conventional (-al) adj. convencional. 2 convenido, pactado. 3 corriente, tradicional, clásico. 4 s. convencional.

conventionalism (-išm) s. convencionalismo.

conventionality (kønvenshønæˑliti) s. calidad de

convencional. *2* regla o práctica establecida por el uso.
conventual (kønve·nchual) *adj.* conventual.
converge (to) (kønvø^r·dỹ) *intr.* converger. *2 tr.* hacer converger.
convergence, -cy (-øns, -i) *s.* convergencia.
convergent (-ønt) *adj.* convergente.
conversable (kønvø·^rsabøl) *adj.* conversable. *2* propio para la conversación.
conversance, -cy (ka·nvø^rsans, -i) *s.* familiaridad, conocimiento.
conversant (-ant) *adj.* ~ *with,* que tiene trato con; versado, entendido en.
conversation (kanvø^rsei·shøn) *s.* conversación. *2* familiaridad, conocimiento.
conversationalist (-alist) *s.* conversador.
converse (ka·nvø^rs) *adj.* inverso, opuesto. *2 s.* lo inverso, lo opuesto. *3* conversación; trato.
converse (to) (kønvø·^rs) *intr.* conversar. *2* tener trato.
conversely (-li) *adv.* a la inversa, recíprocamente.
conversion (kønvø·^rshøn) *s.* conversión [en todos sus sentidos]. *2* inversión, transposición.
conversive (kønvø·^rsiv) *adj.* conversivo.
convert (ka·nvø^rt) *s.* convertido, converso.
convert (to) (kønvø·^rs) *intr.* conversar. *2* tener trato.
conversely (-li) *adv.* a la inversa, recíprocamente.
conversion (kønvø·^rshøn) *s.* conversión [en todos sus sentidos]. *2* inversión, transposición.
conversive (kønvø·^rsiv) *adj.* conversivo.
convert (ka·nvø^rt) *s.* convertido, converso.
convert (to) (kønvø·^rt) *tr.* convertir [en todos sus sentidos]. *2* invertir, transponer. *3 intr.* convertirse.
converter (-ø^r) *s.* convertidor.
convertible (-ibøl) *adj.* convertible. *2* AUTO. descapotable.
convex (ka·nveks) *adj.* convexo. *2 s.* convexidad.
convexity (kønve·ksiti) *s.* convexidad.
convey (to) (kønvei·) *tr.* llevar, transportar. *2* conducir, transmitir, comunicar, enviar. *3* dar [idea, información, etc.]. *4* ceder, transferir [bienes].
conveyance (-ans) *s.* transporte, conducción. *2* comunicación, transmisión. *3* medio de transporte, vehículo. *4* DER. cesión, traspaso. *5* DER. escritura de traspaso.
conveyer, -yor (-ø^r) *s.* portador, llevador. *2* DER. cedente. *2 adj.-s.* MEC. transportador.
convict (kønvi·kt) *s.* reo convicto; condenado. *2* penado, presidiario.
convict (to) *tr.* DER. declarar culpable; probar la culpabilidad de. *2* convencer [de error].
conviction (kønvi·kshøn) *s.* DER. prueba o declaración de culpabilidad. *3* convicción, convencimiento.
convince (to) (kønvi·ns) *tr.* convencer.
convincing (-ing) *adj.* convincente.
convivial (kønvi·vial) *adj.* convival. *2* sociable, jovial.
conviviality (-æ·liti) *s.* jovialidad, buen humor.
convocation (kanvokei·shøn) *s.* convocación, llamamiento. *2* asamblea.
convoke (to) (kønvou·k) *s.* convocar, reunir.
convolute (ka·nvoliut) *adj.* convoluto, enroscado.
convolution (-liu·shøn) *s.* convolución, circunvolución.
convolve (to) (kønva·lv) *tr.* enrollar, retorcer. *2 intr.* enroscarse, retorcerse.

convolvulaceous (-viulei·shøs) *adj.* BOT. convolvuláceo.
convolvulus (-viuløs) *s.* BOT. convólvulo.
convoy (ka·nvoi) *s.* convoy.
convoy (to) (kønvoi·) *tr.* convoyar.
convulse (to) (konvø·ls) *tr.* convulsionar; crispar. *2 intr.* sufrir convulsión; crisparse: *to be convulsed with laughter,* desternillarse de risa.
convulsion (kønvø·lshøn) *s.* convulsión. *2 pl.* ataque de risa.
convulsive (kønvø·lsiv) *adj.* convulsivo.
coo (ku) *s.* arrullo.
coo (to) *intr.* arrullar; arrullarse.
cooing (-ing) *adj.* arrullador. *2* enamorado. *3 s.* arrullo.
cook (kuk) *s.* cocinero, cocinera.
cook (to) *tr.-intr.* cocer, guisar, cocinar. *2 tr.* echar a perder, hacer fracasar. *3 to* ~ *up,* urdir; amañar, falsear.
cooker (ku·kø^r) *s.* cocedor. *2* hornilla, fogón.
cookery (-i) *s.* cocina [arte; lugar].
cookie (ku·ki) *s.* bizcochito, galletita.
cooking (-ng) *s.* cocina [arte]. *2* acción de guisar, cocción. *3 adj.* de cocina; para cocer.
cookshop (-shap) *s.* casa de comidas.
cooky (-i) *s.* fam. cocinera. *2* COOKIE.
cool (kul) *adj.* fresco [algo frío]. *2* frío, tibio, indiferente. *3* frío [hecho con frialdad]. *4* sereno, osado. *5 s.* fresco, frescor, frescura.
cool (to) *tr.* refrescar, enfriar, entibiar: *to* ~ *one's heels,* estar esperando. *2* orear. *3* templar, calmar. *4 intr.* refrescarse, enfriarse, entibiarse. *5* calmarse.
cooler (-ø^r) *s.* enfriador. *2* enfriadera. *3* refrigerador.
coolie (ku·li) *s.* peón chino o indio.
cooling (ku·ling) *adj.* refrescante. *2* refrigerador. *3* atemperador.
coolish (-lish) *adj.* fresquito.
coolness (ku·lnis) *s.* fresco, frescura, frescor. *2* frialdad. *3* serenidad.
coomb, coombe (kum) *s.* vallecito estrecho.
coop (kup) *s.* caponera, gallinero. *2* fam. cárcel. *3* cuba, barril.
coop (to) *tr.* encerrar, enjaular.
cooper (ku·pø^r) *s.* cubero, tonelero.
cooper (to) *tr.-intr.* hacer toneles.
cooperage (-idỹ) *s.* tonelería.
co-operate (to) (koua·pøreit) *intr.* cooperar, coadyuvar.
co-operation (-rei·shøn) *s.* cooperación.
co-operative (-rativ) *adj.* cooperativo. *2 s.* cooperativa [sociedad].
co-ordinate (kouo·^rdinit) *adj.* coordinado; del mismo orden, clase, etc. *2* MAT. coordinado, de las coordenadas. *3 s.* MAT. coordenada.
co-ordinate (to) (-neit) *tr.* coordinar. *2 intr.* coordinarse.
coot (kut) *s.* ORN. foja.
cop (kap) *s.* fam. policía, polizonte. *2* TEJ. enrollamiento cónico.
copaiba (koupei·ba) *s.* copaiba.
copal (kou·pal) *s.* copal.
copartner (koupa·^rtnø^r) *s.* socio. *2* copartícipe.
cope (koup) *s.* capa pluvial. *2* COPING. *3* lo que cubre; bóveda, cúpula.
cope (to) *tr.* cubrir. *2 intr. to* ~ *with,* contender, rivalizar con; habérselas o poder con; hacer frente a.
copeck (kou·pek) *s.* copeck.

Copenhaguen (kapønje·gøn) *n. pr.* GEOGR. Copenhague.
copestone (kou·pstoun) *s.* ALBAÑ. piedra de albardilla. *2* fig. fin, coronamiento.
copier (ka·piøʳ) *s.* copiador, imitador. *2* copista.
coping (kou·ping) *s.* ALBAÑ. albardilla.
copious (kou·piøs) *adj.* copioso, abundante. *2* profuso, exuberante, rico.
copper (ka·pøʳ) *s.* QUÍM. cobre. *2* moneda de cobre. *3* caldera. *4* pop. policía, polizonte. *5* grabado en cobre. *6 adj.* de cobre, cobrizo.
copper (to) *tr.* forrar de cobre, encobrar.
copperas (-as) *s.* caparrosa verde, aceche.
copperish (-ish) *adj.* cobrizo, cobreño.
copperplate (-pleit) *s.* lámina de cobre; grabado en cobre.
coppersmith (-smiz) *s.* calderero.
coppery (-i) *adj.* cobrizo, cobreño.
coppice (ka·pis), **coppice woods** *s.* bosquecillo, soto. *2* tallar. *3* maleza.
copra (ka·pra) *s.* copra.
copse (kaps) *s.* COPPICE. *2* matorral.
Copt (kapt) *s.* copto.
Coptic (ka·ptic) *adj.* cóptico, copto.
copula (ka·piula) *s.* GRAM., LÓG. cópula. *2* ANAT. ligamento.
copulate (to) (ka·piuleit) *tr.* unir. *2 intr.* copularse.
copulation (-lei·shøn) *s.* unión. *2* cópula, ayuntamiento.
copulative (-lativ) *adj.* copulativo.
copy (ka·pi) *s.* copia, reproducción, imitación. *2* ejemplar [de un libro]; número [de un periódico]. *3* muestra, modelo [para copiar]. *4* IMPR. original, manuscrito. *5 rough* ~, borrador.
copy (to) *tr.* copiar. *2* imitar, remedar.
copybook (-buk) *s.* cuaderno de escritura. *2 adj.* común, trillado.
copying (-ing) *adj.* de copiar. *2 s.* copia, imitación [acción].
copyist (-ist) *s.* COPIER.
copyright (-rait) *s.* [derechos de] propiedad literaria: ~ *by*, es propiedad de.
copyright (to) *tr.* registrar la propiedad literaria de.
coquet (to) (kake·t) *intr.* coquetear. ¶ Pret. y p. p.: *coquetted;* ger.: *coquetting.*
coquetry (kou·ketri) *s.* coquetería. *2* coqueteo.
coquette (koke·t) *s.* coqueta [mujer].
coquettish (-ish) *adj.* coqueta. *2* de coqueta, de coquetería.
coracoid (ka·rakid) *adj.-s.* ANAT. coracoides.
coral (ka·ral) *s.* coral. *2* chupador; sonajero. *3 adj.* de coral, coralino.
coralline (-in) *adj.* coralino. *2 s.* BOT., ZOOL. coralina.
corbel (ko·ʳbøl) *s.* ARQ. ménsula, repisa, modillón; voladizo. *2* ARQ. zapata.
corbel (to) *tr.* ARQ. sostener con ménsulas, etc.; disponer en voladizo. *2 intr.* ARQ. sobresalir, volar.
corbie (ko·ʳbi) *s.* BLAS. cuervo.
cord (ko·ʳd) *s.* cordón, cordel, bramante. *2* cuerda, dogal. *3* TEJ. . cordoncillo. *4* TEJ. pana. *5* ELECT. flexible. *6* ANAT. cuerda, cordón, tendón. *7 pl.* pantalones de pana.
cord (to) *tr.* encordelar. *2* guarnecer con cordón.
cordage (-idẙ) *s.* cordaje, cordería.
cordate (-eit) *adj.* BOT. acorazonado.
corded (-id) *adj.* encordelado. *2* de cuerda. *3* TEJ. que forma cordoncillo.
cordial (ko·ʳdẙal o -dial) *adj.* cordial. *2 s.* cordial, licor espirituoso.

cordiality (-æ·liti) *s.* cordialidad.
cordially (ko·ʳdẙali) *adv.* cordialmente.
cordite (ko·ʳdait) *s.* cordita.
cordon (-døn) *s.* cordón [para adorno], cíngulo. *2* cordón [de tropa, etc.]. *3* ARQ. cordón.
Cordova (ko·ʳdova) *n. pr.* GEOGR. Córdoba.
Cordovan (-n) *adj.-s.* cordobés. *2 s.* (con min.) cordobán.
corduroy (ko·ʳdiuroi) *s.* TEJ. pana. *2 pl.* pantalones o vestido de pana.
cordwain (ko·ʳduein) *s.* cordobán.
core (ko·ʳ) *s.* corazón, centro, alma, núcleo, parte interior. *2* substancia, esencia, médula, fondo. *3* corazón [de una fruta, de la madera].
core (to) *tr.* quitar el corazón o centro a.
Corean (ka·rian) *adj.-s.* coreano.
coregency (kouri·dẙønsi) *s.* corregencia.
coregent (-dẙønt) *s.* corregente.
corespondent (kourispa·ndønt) *s.* cómplice del demandado en una demanda de divorcio por adulterio.
coriaceous (koriei·shos) *adj.* coriáceo, correoso.
coriander (koriæ·ndøʳ) *s.* BOT. cilantro.
Corinth (kori·nz) *n. pr.* GEOGR. Corinto.
Corinthian (-ian) *adj.-s.* corintio.
cork (ko·ʳk) *s.* corcho. *2* tapón de corcho. *3* BOT. suber. *4* BOT. ~ *oak,* ~ *tree,* alcornoque.
cork (to) *tr.* tapar [con corcho], encorchar. *2* tiznar con corcho quemado.
corking (-ing) *adj.* fam. estupendo, de primera.
corkscrew (-scru) *s.* sacacorchos: ~ *curl,* tirabuzón.
corky (-i) *adj.* de corcho; corchoso.
cormophytic (ko·ʳmøfitik) *adj.* BOT. cormofita.
cormorant (ko·ʳmørant) *s.* ORN. cormorán, cuervo marino. *2* fig. glotón; avaro.
corn (ko·ʳn) *s.* grano, trigo, cereal. *2* (E.U.) maíz. *3* mies [no segada]. *4* callo, ojo de gallo: ~ *doctor,* callista. *5* ORN. ~ *crake,* rey de codornices.
corn (to) *tr.* salar, curar, acecinar. *2* granular.
corncob (-kab) *s.* (E.U.) carozo, zuro [del maíz].
cornea (ko·ʳnia) *s.* ANAT. córnea.
cornel (ko·ʳnel) *s.* BOT. cornejo.
cornelian (ko·ʳni·lian) *s.* MINER. cornalina.
corneous (ko·ʳniøs) *adj.* córneo.
corner (ko·ʳnøʳ) *s.* ángulo, esquina, esconce, recodo. *2* pico [del sombrero, etc.]. *3* rabillo [del ojo]. *4* cantonera. *5* rincón: ~ *bracket,* ~ *shelf,* rinconera. *6* aprieto, apuro. *7* COM. acaparamiento, monopolio. *8* FÚTBOL córner, saque de esquina.
corner (to) *tr.* arrinconar, acorralar, poner en un aprieto. *2* COM. acaparar, monopolizar.
cornered (-d) *adj.* que tiene ángulos o picos. *2* acorralado, en un aprieto. *3* acaparado.
cornerstone (-stoun) *s.* piedra angular. *2* primera piedra.
cornet (ko·ʳne·t) *s.* corneta de llaves, cornetín. *2* cucurucho. *3* toca de las hermanas de la caridad. *4* ant. alférez, portaestandarte. *5* MAR. corneta.
cornet(t)ist (-ist) *s.* cornetín [músico].
cornfield (ko·ʳnfild) *s.* sembrado.
cornflower (ko·ʳnflauøʳ) *s.* BOT. aciano, azulejo.
cornice (ko·ʳnis) *s.* ARQ. cornisa.
cornucopia (ko·ʳniukou·pia) *s.* cornucopia, cuerno de la abundancia.
cornute(d (ko·ʳniu·ti(d) *adj.* cornudo.
Cornwall (ko·ʳnuol) *n. pr.* GEOGR. Cornualles.
corny (ko·ʳni) *adj.* de los callos; con callos [en los pies]. *3* abundante en grano.
corolla (kora·la) *s.* BOT. corola.

corollary (ka·røleri) s. corolario.
corona (kørou·na), pl. -nas o -nae (-ni) s. ANAT., ASTR., METEOR. corona. 2 corona [tonsura; rosario].
coronal (-l) adj. coronal. 2 s. ANAT. coronal. 3 corona, guirnalda.
coronary (ka·roneri) adj. coronario.
coronation (karonei·shøn) s. coronación.
coroner (ka·ronø^r) s. funcionario encargado de investigar, en una especie de juicio, si una muerte ha sido debida a causas naturales o no.
coronet (-ronet) s. corona [de noble]. 2 diadema [adorno]. 3 VET. corona [del casco].
corporal (ko·^{r}pøral) adj. corporal. 2 s. LITURG. corporal. 3 MIL. cabo.
corporality (-æ·liti) s. corporalidad.
corporate (ko·^{r}porit) adj. conjunto, colectivo, social. 2 constituido legalmente en corporación, sociedad o compañía.
corporation (-ræ·shøn) s. corporación, gremio. 2 COM. sociedad, compañía. 3 ayuntamiento, cabildo.
corporative (ko·^{r}poreitiv) adj. corporativo.
corporeal (ko^{r}pou·rial) adj. corpóreo. 2 material, tangible.
corporeity (ko^{r}porr·iti) s. corporeidad.
corposant (ko·^{r}pošænt) s. MAR. fuego de Santelmo.
corps (kou^r) s. cuerpo [agregado de personas].
corpse (ko^{r}ps) s. cadáver.
corpulence, -cy (kø·^{r}piuløns, -i) s. corpulencia.
corpulent (-ønt) adj. corpulento.
corpus (ko·^{r}pøs) s. cuerpo [de escritos, etc.]. 2 ECLES. Corpus Christi, Corpus, Corpus Cristi.
corpuscle (ko·^{r}pøsøl) s. corpúsculo. 2 FISIOL. glóbulo.
corral (køræ·l) s. (E.U.) corral, cercado.
corral (to) tr. (E.U.) acorralar [el ganado].
correct (kore·kt) adj. correcto. 2 exacto, justo.
correct (to) tr. corregir.
correction (køre·kshøn) s. CORRECN, enmienda. 2 corrección, castigo.
correctional (-al) adj. correccional, penal. 2 s. reformatorio.
correctitude (køre·ktitiud) s. corrección [en la conducta].
corrective (-tive) adj.-s. correctivo.
correctness (-nis) s. corrección [calidad de correcto]; exactitud.
corrector (-ø^r) s. corrector, enmendador.
correlate (to) (ka·røleit) tr. poner en correlación. 2 intr. tener correlación.
correlation (karølei·shøn) s. correlación.
correlative (køre·lativ) adj.-s. correlativo [que tiene correlación].
correspond (to) (karispa·nd) intr. corresponder, corresponderse, responder [tener proporción o analogía, convenir]. 2 corresponderse [escribirse].
correspondence (-øns) s. correspondencia [proporción, analogía, conveniencia]. 2 correspondencia [por escrito].
correspondency (-i) s. CORRESPONDENCE 1.
correspondent (-ønt) adj. correspondiente [análogo, conforme, conveniente]. 2 s. correspondiente; corresponsal.
corresponding (-ing) adj. CORRESPONDENT 1. 2 correspondiente [que corresponde por escrito].
corridor (ka·ridø^r) s. corredor, pasillo.
corrigible (ka·ridŷibøl) adj. corregible.
corroborant (køra·børant) adj.-s. corroborante.
corroborate (to) (-eit) tr. corroborar, confirmar.

corroboration (-ei·shøn) s. corroboración.
corroborative (køra·børativ) adj. corroborativo. 2 adj.-s. corroborante, tónico.
corrode (to) (kørou·d) tr. corroer; roer. 2 intr. corroerse.
corrodent (-ønt) adj.-s. CORROSIVE.
corrosion (kørou·ỹøn) s. corrosión.
corrosive (-siv) adj.-s. corrosivo.
corrugate (to) (ka·rugeit) tr. arrugar, contraer. 2 plegar, ondular.
corrugate(d (-id) adj. arrugado; ondulado.
corrupt (køra·pt) adj. corrupto. 2 corrompido. 3 adulterado [texto].
corrupt (to) tr. corromper. 2 adulterar, falsear. 3 intr. corromperse.
corrupter (-ø^r) s. corruptor, corrompedor.
corruptible (-ibøl) adj. corruptible.
corruption (køra·pshøn) s. corrupción.
corruptless (køra·ptlis) adj. incorruptible.
corruptress (-ris) s. corruptora.
corsage (ko·^{r}sidŷ) s. cuerpo [de vestido], corpiño.
corsair (-e^r) s. corsario. 2 buque corsario.
corselet (ko·^{r}slit) s. coselete. 2 especie de corsé ligero.
corset (-sit) s. corés: ~ cover, cubrecorsé.
corset (to) tr. encorsetar.
Corsica (-sika) n. pr. GEOGR. Córcega.
Corsican (-n) adj.-s. corso [de Córcega].
corslet (ko·^{r}slit) s. CORSELET 1.
cortege (-teỹ) s. comitiva, cortejo, séquito.
cortical (-tikal) adj. cortical.
cortisone (-šon) s. cortisona.
corundum (korø·ndøm) s. MINER. corindón.
coruscate (to) (ko·røskeit) intr. coruscar, brillar.
corvette (ko^{r}ve·t) s. MAR. corbeta.
corvine (ko·^{r}vain) adj. ZOOL. córvido.
corybant (ko·ribant) s. coribante.
corymb (ko·rim) s. BOT. corimbo.
coryphaeus (korifi·øs) s. corifeo.
coryphée (korifei·) s. primera bailarina.
coryza (kørai·ša) s. MED. coriza.
cosecant (kousr·kant) s. TRIG. cosecante.
cosher (··shø^r) tr. mimar, regalar.
cosily (-šili) adv. cómodamente, confortablemente.
cosine (kou·sain) s. TRIG. coseno.
cosmetic (kašme·tik) adj.-s. cosmético.
cosmic(al (ka·šmik(al) adj. cósmico. 2 vasto, grandioso. 3 ordenado, armónico.
cosmogony (ka·smo·goni) s. cosmogonía.
cosmographer (-grafø^r) s. cosmógrafo.
cosmography (-grafi) s. cosmografía.
cosmology (-lodŷi) s. cosmología.
cosmonaut (ka·šmønot) s. cosmonauta.
cosmopolitan (-møpa·litan) adj.-s. cosmopolita.
cosmopolitanism, cosmopolitism (-išm) s. cosmopolitismo.
cosmopolite (-ma·pølait) adj.-s. COSMOPOLITAN.
cosmos (ka·smøs) s. cosmos.
Cossack (ka·sæk) adj.-s. cosaco.
cosset (ka·sit) s. cordero favorito.
cosset (to) tr. acariciar, mimar.
cost (køst) s. coste, costo, costa, precio, expensas: at all costs, at any ~, a toda costa. 2 DER. costas.
cost (to) intr. costar, valer.
costal (ka·stal) adj. ANAT. costal.
costard (ka·sta^{r}d) s. variedad de manzana. 2 fam. chola.
coster (monger (kastø^r(møngø^r) s. vendedor ambulante de frutas, pescado, etc.
costive (ka·stiv) adj. estreñido. 2 fig. agarrado.

costiveness (-nis) *s.* estreñimiento.
costliness (kostlinis) *s.* suntuosidad.
costly (ko·stli) *adj.* costoso, caro. 2 suntuoso.
costmary (ka·stmeri) *s.* BOT. atanasia.
costume (ka·stium) *s.* traje, vestido. 2 traje de época, disfraz: ~ *ball*, baile de trajes. *3 pl.* TEAT. vestuario.
costume (to) *tr.* vestir; disfrazar.
costumer (-øʳ), **-mier** (ɪ·øʳ) *s.* sastre de teatro.
cosy (kou·ši) *adj.* cómodo, agradable. 2 contento, satisfecho. 3 (Ingl.) hablador, sociable.
cot (kat) *s.* choza. 2 catre, coy, camita. 3 sitio para animales domésticos.
cotangent (koutæ·ndȳønt) *s.* TRIG. cotangente.
cote (kout) *s.* corral, aprisco. 2 COT 3.
coterie (kou·tøri) *s.* tertulia, corrillo.
cothurnus (kozø·ʳnøs) *s.* coturno.
cotill(i)on (koti·liøn) *s.* cotillón.
cotise (ka·tis) *s.* BLAS. cotiza.
cottage (ka·tidȳ) *s.* cabaña, casita. 2 hotelito; casita de campo. *3* ~ *cheese*, requesón.
cottager (-øʳ) *s.* el que vive en un COTTAGE. 2 campesino, labrador.
cotter (ka·tøʳ) *s.* MEC. chaveta, pasador.
cotton *s.* algodón: ~ *powder*, algodón pólvora; ~ *wool*, algodón en rama. 2 BOT. algodonero. 3 BOT. pelusa. 4 BOT. ~ *thistle*, cardo borriquero. 5 BOT. ~ *trez*, chopo; ceiba. *6 pl.* géneros de algodón.
cotton (to) *tr.* algodonar. 2 mimar. *3 intr.* avenirse, hacer buenas migas. 4 tomar cariño.
cottonwood (-wud) *s.* BOT. chopo americano.
cottony (-i) *adj.* algodonoso.
cotyledon (katɪ·døn) *s.* BOT. cotiledón.
couch (kauch) *s.* cama, lecho, yacija. 2 canapé, meridiana. 3 capa, tonga. 4 madriguera. 5 BOT. ~ *grass*, grama del Norte.
couch (to) *tr.* acostar, tender. 2 poner en capas. 3 incrustar, bordar. 4 expresar [con palabras]. 5 bajar, agachar. 6 calar, enristrar [una pica, lanza, etc.]. 7 MED. batir [las cataratas]. *8 intr.* acostarse, tenderse. 9 agacharse. 10 esconderse, estar al acecho.
couchant (-ant) *adj.* BLAS. acostado.
cougar (ku·gaʳ) *s.* ZOOL. puma, jaguar.
cough (kof) *s.* tos. 2 carraspeo.
cough (to) *intr.* toser. 2 carraspear. 3 expectorar.
coughing (-ing) *s.* tos, tosidura.
could (cud) *pret.* del *aux.* CAN.
coulisse (kulɪ·s) *s.* corredera [ranura]. 2 TEAT. bastidor; entre bastidores.
coulomb (kula·m) *s.* ELECT. culombio.
coulter (kou·ltøʳ) *s.* COLTER.
council (kau·nsil) *s.* concilio. 2 consejo, junta. 3 ayuntamiento, concejo.
councilman (-mæn) *s.* concejal.
council(l)or (-øʳ) *s.* consejero [de un consejo]. 2 concejal.
counsel (kau·nsøl) *s.* consejo, parecer; deliberación, consulta. 2 designio, pensamiento: *to keep one's own* ~, callar lo que uno piensa o se propone. 3 asesor; abogado; abogados que asesoran o defienden a uno.
counsel (to) *tr.* aconsejar; asesorar.
counsel(l)or (-øʳ) *s.* consejero. 2 consiliario. 3 abogado.
count (kaunt) *s.* cuenta, cuento, cálculo, cómputo. 2 contaje. 3 suma, total. 4 conde [no inglés].
count (to) *tr.* contar, numerar, computar. 2 considerar, tener por. *3 intr.* contar [formar cuentas]. 4 ser tenido en cuenta, valer. *5 to* ~ *on*, contar con, confiar en.

countenance (kau·ntønans) *s.* cara, rostro, semblante, expresión del rostro; serenidad: *to change (one's)* ~, demudarse; *to keep one's* ~, no alterarse, no inmutarse, no reírse; *to put out of* ~, turbar, desconcertar. 2 favor, apoyo, aprobación: *to give* ~ *to*, TO COUNTENANCE.
countenance (to) *tr.* favorecer, apoyar, aprobar, alentar.
counter (kau·ntøʳ) *s.* ficha, tanto. 2 contador, computador. 3 contador, mostrador [mesa]. 4 MAR. bovedilla. 5 ZAP. contrafuerte. 6 ESGR. contra. 7 ˈlo opuesto. *8 adv.* contrariamente, contra.
counter (to) *tr.* oponerse a. *2 intr.* devolver un golpe; responder [a una pregunta, etc.] con otra.
counteract (-æ·ct) *tr.* contrarrestar, neutralizar.
counterattack (- atæ·k) *s.* contraataque.
counterattack (to) *tr.-intr.* contraatacar.
counterbalance (-bæ·lans) *s.* contrabalanza, contrapeso; compensación.
counterbalance (to) *tr.* contrabalancear, contrapesar; compensar.
countercheck (-che·k) *s.* oposición, rechazo. 2 segunda comprobación.
countercheck (to) *tr.* resistir, contrarrestar. 2 comprobar por segunda vez.
countercurrent (-cørønt) *s.* contracorriente.
counterdie (-dai) *s.* contramatriz, punzón.
counterdike (-daik) *s.* contradique.
counterespionage (-e·spiønidȳ) *s.* contraespionaje.
counterfeit (-fit) *adj.* falso, contrahecho. 2 fingido. *3 s.* falsificación, imitación; moneda falsa.
counterfeit (to) *tr.* falsificar, contrahacer. 2 fingir, simular.
counterfeiter (-øʳ) *s.* falsario, falsificador. 2 simulador.
counterfoil (-foil) *s.* matriz [de un cheque, etc.].
counterfort (-foʳt) *s.* ARQ. contrafuerte.
counterfugue (-fiu·g) *s.* MÚS. contrafuga.
counterindication (-indikei·shøn) *s.* MED. contraindicación.
counterlight (-lait) *s.* contraluz.
countermand (-mænd) *s.* contraorden.
countermand (to) *tr.* contramandar.
countermarch (-maʳch) *s.* contramarcha.
countermarch (to) *intr.* contramarchar.
countermark (-maʳk) *s.* contramarca.
countermark (to) *tr.* contramarcar.
countermine (-main) *s.* contramina.
countermine (to) *tr.* contraminar.
counteroffensive (-ofe·nsiv) *s.* contraofensiva.
counteroffer (-oføʳ) *s.* contraoferta.
counterpane (-pein) *s.* colcha, cobertor.
counterpart (-paʳt) *s.* duplicado, trasunto, imagen. 2 parte que corresponde a otra. 3 MÚS. contrapaso.
counterpoint (-point) *s.* MÚS. contrapunto.
counterpoise (-poiš) *s.* contrapeso. 2 equilibrio.
counterpoise (to) *tr.* contrapesar, equilibrar.
counterpunch (-pønch) *s.* contrapunzón.
Counter Reformation *s.* Contrarreforma.
counterrevolution (-røvoliu·shøn) *s.* contrarrevolución.
counterscarp (-skaʳp) *s.* FORT. contraescarpa.
countersign (-sain) *s.* refrendata. 2 MIL. contraseña.
countersign (to) *tr.* refrendar, visar.
countersink (-si·nk) *s.* MEC. avellanador. 2 MEC. avellanado.
countersink (to) *tr.* MFC. avellanar. ¶ Pret. y p.p.: *countersunk.*

countersunk (-sønk) *adj.* MEC. avellanado. *2* MEC. de cabeza embutida.
countervail (to) (-veil) *tr.* contrapesar, equivaler. *2* contrarrestar.
counterweigh (to) (-uel) *tr.* contrapesar.
counterweight (-ueit) *s.* contrapeso, pesa.
counterwork (to) (-uøᵣk) *tr.* contrarrestar.
countess (kau·ntis) *s.* condesa.
countinghouse (kau·ntinjaus) *s.* COM. despacho, escritorio, oficina.
countless (kau·ntlis) *adj.* incontable, innumerable, sin cuento.
countrified (køⁿtrifaid) *adj.* rural, campesino.
country (kø·ntri) *s.* país, nación, región, comarca. *2* tierra, patria. *3* campo, campiña. *4 adj.* del campo, rural, campestre, campesino.
country-dance *s.* contradanza.
countryfolk (-fouk) *s.* gente del campo. *2* lugareños. *3* paisanos, compatricios.
countryman (-mæn) *s.* compatriota, paisano. *2* campesino, aldeano.
countryseat (-sit) *s.* residencia señorial en el campo.
countryside (-said) *s.* campo, campiña. *2* distrito rural.
county (kau·nti) *s.* condado. *2* distrito, provincia.
coup (cu) *s.* golpe maestro.
coupé (kupei·) *s.* cupé.
couple (kø·pøl) *s.* par, pareja. *2* lo que une dos cosas; trailla.
couple (to) *tr.* aparear, emparejar. *2* unir, acoplar, conectar, enganchar. *3 intr.* aparearse.
couplet (kø·plit) *s.* pareado. *2* copla, cuplé.
coupon (ku·pan) *s.* cupón.
courage (kø·ridy) *s.* coraje, valor, ánimo, denuedo.
courageous (kørei·dyøs) *adj.* valeroso, valiente, animoso, denodado.
courier (ku·riøᵣ) *s.* correo, mensajero, expreso.
course (koᵣs) *s.* curso, marcha. *2* camino, trayecto, recorrido. *3* rumbo, derrotero. *4* MAR. rumbo. *5* MAR. punto del compás. *6* serie, curso [de los sucesos]; curso, transcurso [del tiempo]. *7* salida, circulación, expansión. *8* línea [de conducta]. *9* carrera [en la vida]. *10* curso [de estudios], asignatura. *11* DEP. pista, campo. *12* plato, servicio [de una comida]. *13* capa, tongada. *14* ALBAÑ. hilada. *15* MIN. galería. *16* MAR. papahigo. *17 pl.* regla, menstruo. *18 adv. of ~*, naturalmente, desde luego, por supuesto.
course (to) *tr.* correr por. *2* hacer correr. *3* dar caza, perseguir. *4 intr.* correr. *5* corretear.
courser (-øᵣ) *s.* cazador. *2* perro corredor. *3* corcel.
court (koᵣt) *s.* patio; atrio. *2* callejón sin salida; plazuela cerrada. *3* pista [de tenis, etc.]. *4* corte [de un soberano]. *5* corte [que se hace a una pers.]. *6* estrados, sala de justicias. *7* tribunal. *8* consejo superior. *9 ~ card*, figura [de la baraja]. *10 ~ plaster*, tafetán inglés.
court (to) *tr.* cortejar. *2* galantear. *3* solicitar, buscar.
courteous (kø·ᵣtiøs) *adj.* cortés, atento.
courteously (-li) *adv.* cortésmente.
courtesan (kou·ᵣtišan) *s.* cortesana.
courtesy (kø·ᵣtisi) *s.* cortesía, urbanidad. *2* amabilidad, fineza, atención. *3* favor, gracia.
courtier (kø·ᵣtiøᵣ) *s.* cortesano, palaciego.
courtlike (-laik) *adj.* cortesano, elegante.
courtly (-li) *adj.* cortesano. *2* elegante, refinado. *3* obsequioso, adulador. *4 adv.* cortésmente.
court-martial *s.* consejo de guerra.
courtship (-ship) *s.* cortejo, galanteo. *2* noviazgo.

courtyard (-iaᵣd) *s.* patio.
couscous (kusku·s) *s.* alcuzcuz.
cousin (kø·šøn) *s.* primo, prima: *~ german*, primo hermano, prima hermana.
cove (kouv) *s.* abra, ancón, cala, ensenada. *2* ARQ. miembro cóncavo. *3* fam. tipo, individuo.
cove (to) *tr.* ARQ. abovedar.
covenant (kø·vønant) *s.* convenio, pacto; contrato. *2* BIB. alianza, testamento.
covenant (to) *tr.* pactar, estipular. *2 intr.* pactar, convenirse.
covenanter (-øᵣ) *s.* pactante, contratante. *2* presbiteriano escocés.
cover (kø·vøᵣ) *s.* tapa, tapadera, cobertera. *2* cubierta, envoltura, funda, forro. *3* sobre, sobrecarta. *4* ENCUAD. tapa, cubierta. *5* portada [de una revista]. *6* tapete, cobertor. *7* abrigo, refugio, cubierto, techado, albergue. *8* fig. pantalla, velo. *9* capa, pretexto. *10* cubierto [servicio de mesa]. *11* huidero [de la caza], maleza. *12* COM. provisión de fondos. *13 under ~ of*, a favor de [la oscuridad, etc.]; so pretexto de.
cover (to) *tr.* cubrir, tapar. *2* recubrir, revestir, forrar. *3* abrigar, arropar. *4* proteger, resguardar. *5* MIL. cubrir [la retirada]. *6* empollar [huevos]. *7* tapar, ocultar, disimular, encubrir. *8* comprender, abarcar, incluir. *9* recorrer [una distancia]. *10* COM. cubrir [gastos, riesgos, etc.]. *11* ARTILL., FORT. dominar [un espacio]. *12* apuntar [a uno] con un arma. *13* cubrir, fecundar. *14 intr.* cubrirse. *15* COM. hacer provisión de fondos.
coverage (-idy̆) *s.* cantidad o espacio cubiertos. *2* riesgos que cubre una póliza de seguro. *3* cobertura [del papel moneda].
covering (-ing) *s.* acción de cubrir. *2* cubierta, techado. *3* cubierta, envoltura, ropa, abrigo. *4* tegumento.
coverlet (-lit), **coverlid** (-lid) *tr.* tapete. *2* colcha, cobertor.
coversed sine (kou·vøᵣst sain) *s.* MAT. coseno verso.
covert (kø·vøᵣt) *adv.* cubierto, abrigado. *2* escondido, secreto. *3* encubierto, disimulado. *4 s.* abrigo, refugio. *5* ORN. cobija [pluma].
coverture (-chøᵣ) *s.* abrigo, defensa.
covet (to) (kø·vit) *tr.* codiciar, desear, ambicionar.
covetous (-øs) *adj.* codicioso.
covetousness (-nis) *s.* codicia, avidez.
covey (kø·vi) *s.* nidada, pollada. *2* bandada.
cow (kau) *s.* ZOOL. vaca. *2* ZOOL. hembra del alce, la foca, etc.
cow (to) *tr.* acobardar, amilanar.
coward (kau·aᵣd) *adj.-s.* cobarde.
cowardice (-is) *s.* cobardía.
cowardly (-li) *adj.* cobarde, pusilánime. *2 adv.* cobardemente.
cowbell (-bel) *s.* cencerro.
cowboy (-boi) *s.* (E.U.) vaquero, jinete vaquero.
cower (to) (-øᵣ) *intr.* agacharse [por miedo o frío].
cowhide (-jaid) *s.* cuero [de vaca o toro]. *2* zurriago de cuero, rebenque.
cowhide (to) *tr.* azotar, zurriagar.
cowl (kaul) *s.* cogulla. *2* capucha, capucho. *3* sombrerete [de chimenea]. *4* AUTO. bóveda del tablero. *5* AVIA. cubierta del motor.
cowled (-d) *adj.* encapuchado.
cowlick (kau·lik) *s.* remolino [de cabellos].
cowling (-ling) *s.* COWL 5.
cowpox (-paks) *s.* vacuna [de vaca].
cowslip (-slip) *s.* BOT. primavera. *2* BOT. (E.U.) hierba centella.
coxa (ka·ksa) *s.* ANAT. cadera. *2* ENT. COXA.

coxal (-l) *adj.* coxal.
coxcomb (ka·kskoum) *s.* petimetre, presumido, fatuo. *2* gorro de bufón. *3* BOT. moco de pavo.
coxcombry (-ri) *s.* fatuidad, presunción.
coxswain (ka·ksuein) *s.*MAR. nostramo. *2* patrón de un bote de regatas.
coy (koi), **coyish** (-ish) *adj.* recatada, tímida, esquiva; que se hace la tímida o esquiva.
coyness (-nis) *s.* modestia, timidez; afectación de modestia o timidez.
coyote (kaiou·ti) *s.* ZOOL. coyote.
coz (kaš) *s.* fam. primo, prima.
cozen (ka·šøn) *tr.* engañar, estafar.
cozenage (-idÿ) *s.* engaño, estafa.
cozy (kou·ši) *adj.* COSY.
crab (kræb) *s.* ZOOL. cámbaro, cangrejo de mar. *2* ENT. *crab* o ~ *louse*, ladilla. *3* cascarrabias. *4* MEC. molinete; carro de grúa. *5 adj.* agrio, avinagrado. *6* BOT. ~ *apple*, manzana silvestre.
crab (to) *tr.* censurar, agriamente. ¶ Pret. y p. p.: *crabbed;* ger.: *-bbing.*
crabbed (-id) *adj.* gruñón, avinagrado. *2* obscuro, enrevesado. *3* irregular, apretada [letra].
crabby (-i) *adj.* CRABBED 1 y 2.
crack (kræk) *s.* crujido, chasquido, restallido; estampido: *the ~ of doom*, el juicio final. *2* fam. golpe seco. *3* fam. instante. *4* rotura, hendidura, grieta, raja, rendija. *5* bronquedad [de la voz cuando se muda]. *6* tornillo flojo, chifladura. *7 adj.* fam. de primera.
crack (to) *intr.* crujir, restallar. *2* reventar, estallar, rajarse, resquebrajarse, agrietarse, cuartearse: *to ~ up*, fracasar; arruinarse; estrellarse. *3* cascarse, enronquecerse [la voz]. *4* fam. volverse loco. *5 tr.* romper, rajar, hender, resquebrajar. *6* trastornar, enloquecer. *7* hacer restallar. *8* QUÍM. someter a destilación fraccionada. *9* fam. *to ~ a bottle*, beber una botella. *10* fam. *to ~ jokes*, hacer chistes, bromear. *11 to ~ up*, elogiar, bombear; estrellar.
crackbrain (-brein) *s.* chiflado, medio loco.
cracker (-ø^r) *s.* petardo, triquitraque. *2* especie de galleta. *3 pl.* cascanueces.
crackle (-øl) *s.* crujido, chasquido, crepitación. *2* B. ART. superficie finamente agrietada.
crackle (to) *intr.* crujir, chasquear, crepitar.
crackling (-ing) *s.* CRACKLE 1. *2* corteza de tocino asada. *3* chicharrón.
cracknel (-nøl) *s.* galletita crujiente. *2* chicharrón.
crackpot (-pat) *s.* pop. chiflado.
cracksman (-mæn) *s.* pop. BURGLAR.
crack-up (øp) *m.* hundimiento [físico o mental]. *2* AVIA. aterrizaje violento.
cracky (-i) *adj.* rajado. *2* que se raja fácilmente.
Cracow (krei·kou) *s.* GEOGR. Cracovia.
cradle (-døl) *s.* cuna [para niños; niñez,origen]. *2* armazón, soporte, etc., en forma de cuna. *3* TELÉF. horquilla. *4* MAR. cuna, basada. *5* andamio colgante. *6* MIN. artesa oscilante.
cradle (to) *tr.* acunar, mecer. *2* poner o tener en una cuna. *3 intr.* estar en la cuna.
craft (kraft) *s.* arte, destreza. *2* oficio, profesión; gremio. *3* artificio, astucia, artería. *4* treta, maña. *5* embarcación; embarcaciones.
craftiness (-inis) *s.* astucia, artería.
craftsman (-smæn) *s.* artesano. *2* artífice.
craftsmanship (-ship) *s.* arte, habilidad [en un oficio]. *2* artesanía.
crafty (kra·fti) *adj.* astuto, artero, artificioso.
crag (kræg) *s.* risco, despeñadero.

cragged (-id), **craggy** (-i) *adj.* escarpado, riscoso, áspero, fragoso.
crake (kreik) *s.* ORN. rey de codornices. *2* ORN. rascón.
cram (kræm) *s.* apretura; atiborramiento. *2* atracón. *3* preparación [para exámenes]. *4* CRAMMER.
cram (to) *tr.* henchir, atestar, atiborrar. *2* atracar [de comida]. *3* meter apretando o llenando, embutir. *4* fam. preparar [para exámenes]. *5 intr.* atracarse [de comida]. *6* fam. estudiar, empollar [para aprender en poco tiempo]. ¶ Pret. y p. p.: *crammed;* ger.: *cramming.*
crambo (-bou) *s.* juego de hallar consonantes.
crammer (-ø^r) *s.* preparador [para exámenes]. *2* pop. mentira.
cramp (kræmp) *s.* calambre, rampa. *2* laña, grapa. *3* MEC. CLAMP 1 y 2. *4* fig. aprieto, estrechez. *5* fig. sujeción, traba.
cramp (to) *tr.* dar calambres; entumecer. *2* fig. restringir, trabar. *3* apretar, sujetar; engrapar.
cramp-iron *s.* laña, grapa.
crampon (kræmpøn) *s.* BOT. raicilla aérea. *2* gancho para trepar. *3* pieza con puntas para andar sobre el hielo. *4 pl.* tenazas de garfios [para elevar piedras, etc.].
cranberry (kræ·nberi) *s.* BOT. arándano agrio.
crane (krein) *s.* ORN. grulla. *2* MEC. grúa, árgana. *3* MAR. abanico. *4* brazo o pescante giratorio. *5* sifón, cantimplora.
crane (to) *tr.* levantar con grúa. *2* estirar [el cuello]. *3 intr.* estirar el cuello [para ver mejor].
crane-fly *s.* ENT. típula.
crane's-bill *s.* BOT. variedad de geranio.
cranial (krei·nial) *adj.* craneal.
cranium (-niøm) *s.* ANAT. cráneo.
crank (kræŋk) *s.* MEC. cigüeña, manubrio, manivela; codo, palomilla. *2* fantasía, capricho, humorada. *3* maniático, chiflado. *4 adj.* CRANKY.
crank (to) *tr.* doblar, acodar. *2* mover, etc., con manivela.
crankcase (-keis) *s.* MEC. cárter de cigüeñal.
crankle (kræ·nkøl) *s.* recodo, repliegue, vuelta.
crankle (to) *intr.* serpentear, zigzaguear.
crankshaft (-shæft) *s.* MEC. cigüeñal.
cranky (-i) *adj.* chiflado, extrafalario. *2* irritable. *3* caprichoso, raro. *4* inseguro, desvencijado. *5* torcido, sinuoso.
crannied (kræ·ni) *adj.* grietoso.
cranny (kræ·ni) *s.* grieta, hendedura, rendija. *2* rincón, hueco.
crape (kreip) *s.* crespón.
craps (kræps) *s.* juego de dados.
crapulence (kræ·piuløns) *s.* crápula, intemperancia.
crash (kræsh) *s.* estallido, estampido, estrépito [de cosas que chocan o se rompen]. *2* caída, choque, acción de estrellarse. *3* COM. quiebra, bancarrota.
crash (to) *tr.* romper, estrellar. *2* poner, mover, hacer chocar, etc., con estrépito. *3 intr.* estallar, romperse, chocar, estrellarse. *4* COM. quebrar, hacer bancarrota.
crass (kræs) *adj.* espeso, basto, grosero. *2* craso, estúpido.
crassitude (kræ·sitiud), **crassness** (-nis) *s.* grosería, tosquedad; estupidez.
crassulaceous (kræsiulei·shøs) *adj.* BOT. crasuláceo.
Crassus (krøsøs) *n. pr.* Craso.
crate (kreit) *s.* canasta, banasta. *2* cesta o embalaje de listones.

crater (krei·tø^r) *s.* cráter. *2* crátera. *3* (con may.) ASTR. Copa, Cráter.

craunch (to) (kronch) *tr.* TO CRUNCH.

cravat (kravæ·t) *s.* corbata, pañuelo para el cuello.

crave (to) (kreiv) *tr.* pedir, implorar. *2* ansiar, anhelar. *3 intr. to* ~ *after* o *for*, pedir, implorar; ansiar, anhelar.

craven (-vøn) *adj.-s.* cobarde. *2 to cry* ~, rendirse.

craving (-ving) *s.* deseo, anhelo, ansia, sed.

craw (cro) *s.* buche.

crawfish (cro·fish) *s.* ZOOL. langosta [de mar].

crawl (kro·l) *s.* reptación, arrastramiento; marcha lenta. *2* crol [modo de nadar]. *3* criadero de tortugas.

crawl (to) *intr.* reptar, arrastrarse; gatear. *2* fig. arrastrarse servilmente. *3* andar o moverse lentamente. *4* nadar haciendo el crol. *5* sentir hormigueo. *6 to* ~ *with*, estar lleno de [cosas que bullen u hormiguean].

crawler (-ø^r) *s.* reptil. *2* planta rastrera. *3* MEC. tractor de oruga.

crayfish (krei·fish) *s.* CRAWFISH.

crayon (-øn) *s.* DIB. barrita de lápiz, pastel, etc. *2* dibujo al lápiz, pastel, etc. *3* ELECT. carbón.

crayon (to) *tr.* dibujar al lápiz, pastel, etc. *2* fig. esbozar, planear.

craze (kreiš) *s.* manía, antojo, chifladura, moda. *2* locura, demencia. *3* resquebrajadura [de un barniz o esmalte].

craze (to) *tr.* trastornar [el juicio]; enloquecer. *2* resquebrajar finamente el barniz de. *3 intr.* volverse loco. *4* resquebrajarse finamente [un barniz].

crazed (-d) *s.* loco. *2* lleno de pequeñas resquebrajaduras.

crazy (-i) *adj.* agrietado, roto, cascado, desvencijado, ruinoso. *3* loco, insensato. *4* extravagante. *5* fig. loco [por].

creak (to) (krık) *intr.* crujir, rechinar, chirriar.

creaking (-ing) *s.* crujido, rechinamiento, chirrido. *2* adj. CREAKY.

creaky (-i) *adj.* crujiente, rechinante, chirriante.

cream (krım) *s.* crema, nata [de la leche]. *2* fig, flor, flor y nata. *3* crema [cosmético]. *4* COC. crema [sopa]. *5* ~ *of tartar*, crémor tártaro.

cream (to) *intr.* criar nata. *2 tr.* desnatar. *3* preparar con nata.

creamery (-øri) *s.* lechería, mantequería.

creamy (-i) *adj.* cremoso. *2* fig. meloso.

crease (krıs) *s.* pliegue, doblez, arruga. *2* raya [del pantalón].

crease (to) *tr.* plegar, doblar, arrugar. *2* ENC. filetear. *3 intr.* arrugarse.

creasy (-i) *adj.* arrugado, lleno de arrugas.

create (to) (kriei·t) *tr.* crear, criar [producir Dios de la nada]. *2* crear [en los demás sentidos]. *3* producir, causar. *4* hacer [conde, marqués, etc.].

creation (-shøn) *s.* creación [acción; cosa creada]. *2* la creación, el universo. *3* acción de hacer conde, marqués, etc.

creative (-tiv) *adj.* creador.

creativeness (-nis) *s.* facultad creadora, inventiva.

creator (kriei·tø^r) *s.* creador. *2 The Creator*, el Creador, Dios.

creatress (-tris) *s.* creadora.

creature (krı·chø^r) *s.* criatura [cosa creada]. *2* hechura, instrumento [de otro]. *3* ser viviente. *4* individuo, persona [a veces desp.].

crèche (kresh) *s.* nacimiento, belén. *2* casa cuna.

credence (kri·døns) *s.* creencia, crédito, fe. *2* credencia.

credential (kride·nshal) *adj.* credencial. *2 s. pl.* credenciales.

credibility (kredibi·liti) *s.* credibilidad.

credible (kre·dibøl) *adj.* creíble, creedero.

credit (-dit) *s.* crédito, asenso, fe. *2* autoridad [para ser creído]. *3* crédito, buena reputación. *4* influencia, valimiento. *5* honor, honra, lo que honra o enaltece. *6* COM. crédito: *on* ~, a crédito, al fiado. *7* COM. haber. *8* fig. *to give someone* ~ *for*, atribuir a uno [una cualidad, etc.].

credit (to) *tr.* dar crédito a, creer. *2* COM. acreditar, abonar. *3 to* ~ *someone with*, atribuir a uno [una cualidad, etc.].

creditable (-abøl) *adj.* loable, honroso, meritorio.

creditor (-ø^r) *s.* acreedor. *2* COM. haber, partida del haber.

Credo (kri·dou) *s.* LITÚRG., MÚS. credo.

credulity (krediu·liti) *s.* credulidad.

creed (krıd) *s.* credo [símbolo; conjunto de doctrinas]. *2* creencia, religión.

creek (krık) *s.* abra o cala estrecha. *2* (E.U.) ría; riachuelo. *3* rincón, recodo.

creel (krıl) *s.* cesta de pescador. *2* TEJ. fileta.

creep (krıp) *s.* arrastramiento, deslizamiento. *2 pl. the creeps*, hormigueo, escalofrío, horror.

creep (to) *intr.* arrastrarse, serpear, gatear; correr [los insectos]; extenderse, trepar [las plantas rastreras o trepadoras]. *2* deslizarse, insinuarse; penetrar, invadir, acercarse, entrar, salir, etc., lenta, insensible o furtivamente. | Gralte. con *in, out, on* o *upon*. *3* fig. arrastrarse servilmente. *4* sentir hormigueo, escalofrío. *5* MAR. rastrear. ¶ Pret. y p. p.: *crept*.

creeper (-ø^r) *s.* lo que se arrastra, insecto, reptil. *2* BOT. enredadera. *3* ORN. nombre de varios pájaros. *4* garabato, arpeo.

creepy (-i) *adj.* lento. *2* que produce hormigueo o escalofrío; que lo siente.

creese (krıs) *s.* cris [arma].

cremate (to) (krı·meit) *tr.* incinerar.

cremation (krimei·shøn) *s.* cremación, incineración.

crematory (krı·matori) *s.* horno crematorio.

crenate(d (krı·neit(id) *adj.* BOT. festeoneado.

crenel(l)ate(d (kre·nøleit(id) *adj.* almenado. *2* BOT. festeoneado.

creole (krı·oul) *adj.-s.* criollo.

creosote (krı·osout) *s.* QUÍM. creosota.

crepe, crêpe (kreip) *s.* TEJ. crespón.

crepitate (to) (kre·piteit) *intr.* crepitar. *2* chirriar, chisporrotear [al fuego].

crepitation (-ei·shøn) *s.* crepitación. *2* chisporroteo.

crept (krept) *pret.* y *p. p.* de TO CREEP.

crepuscular (krepø·skiula^r) *adj.* crepuscular.

crepuscle (-kiul) *s.* crepúsculo.

crescendo (kre·ndou) *adv.-s.* MÚS. crescendo.

crescent (kre·sønt) *adj.* creciente. *2 s.* media luna. *3* cosa en figura de media luna. *4* creciente [de la luna]; luna creciente.

cress (kres) *s.* BOT. lepidio, mastuerzo.

cresset (kre·sit) *s.* fogaril, tedero. *2* fig. tea, antorcha.

crest (krest) *s.* cresta. *2* penacho, copete. *3* crestón. *4* cimera. *5* BLAS. timbre. *6* cima, cumbre. *7* fig. coraje; orgullo.

crest (to) *tr.* coronar, cubrir. *2* alcanzar la cresta de. *2* BLAS. timbrar. *4 intr.* erguirse. *5* encresparse [las olas].

crested lark (-id) *s*. ORN. cochevís, cogujada.
crestfallen (foløn) *adj*. cabizbajo, abatido, alicaído.
cretaceous (kritei·shøs) *adj*. cretáceo.
Cretan (krı·tan) *adj.-s*. cretense.
cretin (krı·tin) *s*. cretino.
cretinism (-išm) *s*. cretinismo.
cretonne (kre·tan) *s*. TEJ. cretona.
crevasse (krøva·s) *s*. GEOL. grieta.
crevice (kre·vis) *s*. raja, hendedura, rendija.
crew (kru) *s*. MAR., AVIA. tripulación, equipaje. 2 equipo, cuadrilla; banda. 3 Pret. de TO CROW.
crewel (kru·øl) *s*. lana para bordar.
crib (krib) *s*. pesebre. 2 nacimiento, belen. 3 camita [de niño]. 4 casucha, chiribitil. 5 arcón, granero, depósito. 6 emparrillado; refuerzo. 7 HIDR. cajón. 8 hurto; plagio. 9 fam. chuleta [para el que se examina].
crib (to) *tr*. encerrar. 2 hurtar, plagiar. ¶ Pret. y p. p.: *cribbed;* ger.: *cribbing*.
cribbage (kri·bidŷ) *s*. juego de naipes.
cribble (kri·bøl) *s*. criba, harnero.
cribble (to) *tr*. cribar, cerner. 2 GRAB. puntear.
crick (krik) *s*. tortícolis, calambre.
cricket (kri·kit) *s*. ENT. grillo. 2 cricquet [juego]. 3 escabel, taburete.
cricketer (-ø̣ʳ) *s*. jugador de cricquet.
cricoid (krai·koid) *adj.-s*. ANAT. cricoides.
cried (kraid) *pret*. y *p. p*. de TO CRY.
crier (krai·ø̣ʳ) *s*. pregonero. 2 voceador.
crime (kraim) *s*. delito. 2 crimen.
criminal (kri·minal) *adj*. delictivo, delictuoso; criminal. 2 DER. penal. 3 *s*. delincuente; criminal.
criminalist (-ist) *s*. criminalista.
criminate (to) (kri·mineit) *tr*. acriminar, acusar. 2 censurar, reprobar.
criminous (-nøs) *adj*. delictuoso, criminoso.
crimp (krimp) *adj*. rizado. 2 quebradizo, friable. 3 *s*. rizado. 4 rizador.
crimp (to) *tr*. rizar, encrespar. 2 plegar, ondular. 3 amoldar, dar forma.
crimpy (-i) *adj*. rizado. 2 arrugado.
crimson (kri·mšøn) *adj.-s*. carmesí, rojo.
crimson (to) *tr*. teñir de carmesí. 2 *intr*. enrojecerse. 3 sonrojarse.
cringe (krindŷ) *s*. obsequiosidad servil, adulación, bajeza.
cringe (to) *intr*. encogerse [ante un pøligro, dolor, etc.]. 2 arrastrarse [servilmente], ádular.
cringing (-ing) *adj*. bajo, vil, rastrero.
crinite (krai·nait) *adj*. crinito.
crinkle (kri·nkøl) *s*. arruga, rizo, sinuosidad, ondulación.
crinkle (to) *tr*. rizar, arrugar. 2 *intr*. ondularse, rizarse, arrugarse.
crinoid (krai·noid) *adj.-s*. ZOOL. crinoideo.
crinoline (kri·nølin) *s*. tela de crin. 2 miriñaque.
cripple (kri·pøl) *s*. cojo, manco, lisiado, tullido, inválido. 2 MAR. desmantelado, desarbolado.
cripple (to) *tr*. encojar, mancar, lisiar, estropear: 2 MAR. desmantelar, desarbolar. 3 *intr*. lisiarse. 4 cojear.
crippled (-d) *adj*. lisiado, tullido.
crisis (krai·sis) *s*. crisis.
crisp (krisp) *adj*. crespo, rizado. 2 tieso, crujiente. 3 quebradizo, seco, bien tostado. 4 gráfico, expresivo. 5 vivo, chispeante. 6 decidido, resuelto. 7 vigorizante, tónico [aire, frío].
crisp (to) *tr*. encrespar, rizar. 2 hacer quebradizo, tostar bien. 3 hacer crujir. 4 *intr*. encresparse, rizarse.

crispation (krispei·shøn) *s*. encrespadura. 2 crispatura.
crisping iron *s*. encrespador.
crispy (kri·spi) *adj*. crespo, rizado. 2 crujiente, quebradizo. 3 CRISP. 7.
criss-cross (kri·skros) *adj*. cruzado, entrecruzado. 2 *adv*. CROSSWISE.
criterion (kraiti·riøn) *s*. criterio.
critic (kri·tik) *s*. crítico. 2 censurador. 3 crítica.
critical (kri·tikal) *adj*. crítico. 2 exacto, escrupuloso. 3 de censura.
criticism (-tisišm) *s*. crítica [juicio crítico]. 2 crítica, censura.
criticize (to) (-tisaiš) *tr.-intr*. criticar.
critique (kritı·k) *s*. crítica [arte; juicio crítico].
croak (krouk) *s*. graznido [de cuervo]. 2 croar [de rana].
croak (to) *intr*. graznar, crascitar. 2 croar. 3 gruñir, refunfuñar. 4 fam. morir.
Croatia (kroei·sha) *n. pr*. GEOGR. Croacia.
Croatian (-shan) *adj.-s*. croata.
croceous (krou·shøs) *adj*. crocino.
crochet (kroshei·) *s*. ganchillo [labor].
crochet (to) *tr*. hacer [algo] con ganchillo. 2 *intr*. hacer ganchillo.
crock (krak) *s*. vaṣija de barro o loza, cacharro.
crockery (-øri) *s*. cacharros, loza, vidriado.
crocodile (kra·kodail) *s*. ZOOL. cocodrilo.
Croesus (krı·søs) *n. pr*. y fig. Creso.
croft (kroft) *s*. (Ingl.) pejugal; cercado.
cromlech (kra·mlek) *s*. ARQUEOL. crónlech.
crone (kroun) *s*. vieja arrugada.
Cronus (krou·nøs) *n. pr*. MIT. Cronos.
crony (krou·ni) *s*. camarada, compinche.
crook (kruk) *s*. curva, curvatura, cosa encorvada. 2 gancho, garfio. 3 cayado. 4 MÚS. tudel. 5 artificio, trampa. 6 fam. estafador, fullero, bribón.
crook (to) *tr*. torcer, encorvar. 2 *intr*. torcerse, encorvarse.
crookback (-bæk), **crookbacked** (bækt) *adj.-s*. jorobado, corcovado.
crooked (-id) *adj*. corvo, encorvado, ganchudo, torcido, deformado. 2 torcido, avieso, falto de honradez, falso, fraudulento.
crooklegged (-legid) *adj*. patituerto.
croon (to) (krun) *tr.-intr*. canturrear. 2 cantar ciertas canciones exagerando el sentimiento.
crop (krap) *s*. cosecha. 2 cultivo, producción. 3 cabello o barba que crece. 4 acción de cortar corto o al rape; cabello corto o cortado al rape. 5 corte en la oreja [de un animal]. 6 buche [de ave]. 7 mango de látigo, látigo corto. 8 *pl*. campos, mieses, trigos.
crop (to) *tr*. segar, cosechar, coger. 2 cultivar, sembrar [una tierra]. 3 despuntar, cercenar, desmochar; trasquilar, desorejar. 4 *intr*. dar cosechas. 5 pacer. 6 *to* ~ *out* o *forth*, aparecer, salir. 7 MIN. *to* ~ *out* o *up*, aflorar.
crop-eared (-iørd) *adj*. desorejado.
cropper (-ø̣ʳ) *s*. cosechador. 2 aparcero. 3 recortador. 4 ORN. paloma buchona.
croquet (kroukei·) *s*. croquet [juego].
croquette (krouke·t) *s*. COC. croqueta.
crosier (krou·šø̣ʳ) *s*. báculo pastoral.
cross (kros) *s*. cruz [instrumento de suplicio; la de Nuestro Señor; imagen de ella; pena, trabajo; insignia de una orden]. 2 signo de la cruz. 3 cruz [señal o cosa en forma de cruz]. 4 cruce [de líneas, caminos, etc.]. 5 ELECT. cruce. 6 cruzamiento, mezcla [de razas, características, etc.]. 7 oposición, disputa. 8 *adj*. en cruz, atravesado,

transversal: ~ *street*, travesía, calle transversal; ~ *vault*, ARQ. bóveda por arista. *9* contrario, adverso. *10* recíproco: ~ *reference*, referencia, remisión [en un libro]. *11* COM. cruzado [cheque]. *12* malhumorado, enojado, regañón: *to be* ~, enfurruñarse. *13* ~ *grain*, repelo [de la madera].
cross (to) *tr.* signar, santiguar, persignar. *2* tachar, tildar, rayar. | Gralte. con *off* o *out.* *3* marcar con cruces. *4* cruzar, atravesar; fig. *to* ~ *one's mind*, ocurrírsele a uno. *5* cruzar [un cheque]. *6* cruzar, poner en cruz: *to* ~ *swords*, cruzar las espadas, reñir. *7* cruzarse con. *8* cruzar [razas o castas]. *9* estorbar [los planes, etc., de uno]. *10 intr.* estar al través. *11* cruzarse. *12* cortarse, intersecarse. *13 to* ~ *over*, pasar al otro lado.
crossbar (-ba^r) *s.* tranca [de puerta]. *2* travesaño.
cross-bearer *s.* cruciferario.
crossbill (-bill) *s.* ORN. piquituerto.
crossbow (-bou) *s.* ballesta [arma].
crossbowman (mæn) *s.* ballestero.
crossbred (-bred) *adj.-s.* cruzado, híbrido, mestizo.
crossbreed (-brɪd) *s.* casta cruzada. *2* planta o animal cruzado, híbrido, mestizo.
crosbreed (to) *tr.* cruzar [animales o plantas].
cross-country *adj.* que se hace a campo traviesa. *2 s.* carrera a campo traviesa.
crosscut (-køt) *s.* corte transversal. *2* atajo. *3* entrecruzamiento. *4 adj.* cortado al través; para cortar al través.
crossed (-t) *adj.* cruzado. *2* de través, transversal.
cross-examination *s.* DER. repregunta.
cross-examine (to) *tr.* DER. repreguntar.
cross-eyed *adj.* bizco.
cross-fire *s.* MIL. fuego cruzado. *2* tiroteo [de preguntas, etc.].
cross-grained *adj.* de grano o fibra diagonal o irregular. *2* difícil, terco, irritable.
crossing (-ing) *s.* acción de signar o persignar; santiguada. *2* cruce [acción]. *3* cruce, intersección, encrucijada: *level* ~, FERROC. paso a nivel. *4* paso, vado [de un río]. *5* MAR. travesía. *6* cruzamiento [de castas]. *7* estorbo, oposición [a los planes, etc., de uno].
cross-legged *adj.-adv.* con las piernas cruzadas.
crosslet (-lit) *s.* crucecita.
crossly (-li) *adv.* con enojo o mal humor.
crossness (-nis) *s.* enojo, enfado, mal humor.
crosspiece (-pɪs) *s.* travesaño.
cross-purpose *s.* hecho contrario; designio opuesto: *at cross-purposes*, interpretándose mal; contradiciéndose o haciéndose la contra sin querer. *2 pl.* juego de los despropósitos.
cross-question *s.* DER. pregunta. *2* interrogatorio detenido.
cross-question (to) *tr.* DER. repreguntar. *2* estrechar a preguntas.
crossroad (-roud) *s.* travesía [camino]; atajo. *2* cruce, encrucijada. *3 pl.* punto crítico, momento crucial.
cross-section paper *s.* papel cuadriculado.
cross-staff (-tæf) *s.* escuadra de agrimensor. *2* MAR. ballestilla.
cross-stitch *s.* COST. punto cruzado o de cruz.
crosstie (-tai) *s.* FERROC. traviesa.
crosstree (-trɪ) *s.* MAR. cruceta.
crosswalk (-uok) *s.* cruce señalado [en una calle].
crossway (-uei) *s.* CROSSROAD.
crossways (-ueis), **crosswise** (uaiš) *adv.* de través. *2* en cruz. *3* al revés, mal, en contra.
crossword (-uø^rd), **crossword puzzle** *s.* crucigrama.

crotalum (kra·taløm) *s.* MÚS. crótalo.
crotch (krach) *s.* horquilla, horca [para sostener algo]. *2* horcadura, cruz, bifurcación. *3* horcajadura.
crotchet (kra·chit) *s.* ganchito. *2* MÚS. negra. *3* capricho, rareza, excentricidad.
crotchety (-i) *adj.* caprichoso, raro, excéntrico.
crouch (to) (krauch) *intr.* agacharse, agazaparse, acuclillarse. *2* arrastrarse [servilmente].
croup (krup) *s.* anca, grupa. *2* MED. crup, garrotillo.
croupier (kru·piø^r) *s.* crupié.
crow (krou) *s.* ORN. cuervo; grajo; corneja; chova: *to eat* ~, fam. cantar la palinodia; *as the* ~ *flies*, fig. en línea recta. *2* canto [del gallo]. *3* palanca, alzaprima.
crow (to) *intr.* cantar [el gallo]. *2* jactarse, bravear, gallear; cantar victoria. *3* gorjear [el niño]. ¶ Pret.: *crowed* o *crew.*
crowbar (krou·ba^r) *s.* palanca, alzaprima, pie de cabra.
crowd (kraud) *s.* multitud, muchedumbre, tropel [de pers. o cosas], gentío, apretura. *2* turba, masa, populacho, vulgo. *3* fam. grupo, pandilla.
crowd (to) *tr.* apretar, apiñar, amontonar. *2* atestar, llenar. *3 intr.* agolparse, apiñarse, amontonarse.
crowded (-id) *adj.* atestado, abarrotado, de bote en bote.
crowfoot (-fut), *pl.* **foots** *s.* BOT. ranúnculo, botón de oro. *2 (pl. -feet)* MIL. abrojo. *3* MAR. araña.
crown (kraun) *s.* corona [para la cabeza; dignidad real, reino; premio, galardón]: ~ *prince*, príncipe, heredero; ~ *princess*, princesa heredera; esposa del príncipe heredero. *2* ANAT. coronilla; cabeza. *3* cima, cumbre, parte superior. *4* complemento, colmo. *5* copa [de árbol, de sombrero]. *6* ARQ. coronamiento. *7* corona [de diente]. *8* corona [moneda; esp. la inglesa de 5 chelines]. *9* AGR. ~ *grafting*, injerto de corona. *10* ~ *saw*, sierra circular.
crown (to) *tr.* coronar [en todos sus sentidos]: *to* ~ *it all*, para colmo, por remate.
crowning (-ing) *s.* coronación, remate.
crownlet (-lit) *s.* coronita.
crow's-foot (-sifai) *s.* pata de gallo [arrugas]. *2* CROWFOOT.
crozier *s.* CROSIER.
crucial (kru·šʌl) *adj.* crucial.
cruciate (-shiet) *adj.* cruciforme.
crucible (-sibøl) *s.* crisol.
crucifer (-sifø^r) *s.* cruciferario. *2* BOT. crucífero.
cruciferous (krusi·før øs) *adj.* BOT. crucífero.
crucifix (kru·sifiks) *s.* crucifijo.
crucifixion (-krusifi·kshøn) *s.* crucifixión.
cruciform (kru·sifo^rm) *adj.* cruciforme.
crucify (to) (-sifai) *tr.* crucificar. *2* mortificar; atormentar. ¶ Pret. y p. p.: *crucified.*
crude (krud) *adj.* crudo [sin cocer, sin preparar]; imperfecto, mal acabado, no sazonado; bruto [sin refinar]. *2* crudo, desnudo [sin atenuantes]. *3* tosco, basto, rudo. *4* brusco, descortés.
crudity (-iti) *s.* crudeza. *2* imperfección, tosquedad.
cruel (kru·øl) *adj.* cruel. *2* despiadado, atroz.
cruelty (-ti) *s.* crueldad, inhumanidad, atrocidad.
cruet (kru·it) *s.* ampolla, vinagrera. *2* vinajera. *3 cruet* o ~ *stand*, vinagreras.
cruise (kru·š) *s.* MAR., AVIA. crucero [acción de cruzar; viaje].
cruise (to) *tr.* MAR., AVIA. cruzar, navegar, viajar. *2* circular [un taxi] en busca de pasaje.

cruiser (-ø^r) *s.* buque o pers. que realiza un crucero. *2* MAR. crucero [buque].
cruller (krø·lø^r) *s.* (E.U.) buñuelo.
crumb (krøm) *s.* miga [del pan]. *2* pedacito, mendrugo, migaja.
crumb (to) *tr.* migar, desmenuzar, desmigajar. *2* empanar [con pan rallado].
crumble (to) (krø·mbøl) *tr.* desmenuzar, deshacer. *2 intr.* desmenuzarse, deshacerse, desmoronarse, derrumbarse.
crumbly (-bli) *adj.* desmenuzable, friable.
crumby (-bi) *adj.* blando, lleno de migas.
crumpet (-pit) *s.* especie de bollo.
crumple (to) (-pøl) *tr.* arrugar, chafar, ajar, apabullar. *2 intr.* arrugarse, encogerse, aplastarse.
crunch (to) (krønch) *tr.* mascar haciendo crujir; ronzar, tascar. *2* hacer crujir [bajo los pies, etc.]. *3 intr.* crujir [al ser mascado, pisado, etc.].
crupper (krø·pø^r) *s.* baticola, grupera. *2* grupa.
crural (kru·ral) *adj.* ANAT. crural.
crusade (krusei·d) *s.* cruzada.
crusade (to) *intr.* tomar parte en una cruzada.
crusader (-ø^r) *s.* cruzado [pers.].
crush (krøsh) *s.* compresión, presión, aplastamiento, machacamiento, estrujamiento. *2* apretura, apiñamiento, aglomeración.
crush (to) *tr.* aplastar, machacar, quebrantar, moler, triturar. *2* machucar, estrujar, exprimir. *3* aplastar, sojuzgar, oprimir, abrumar. *4* destruir, aniquilar.
crusher (-ø^r) *s.* el o lo que aplasta, machaca, oprime, etc. *2* fam. argumento o respuesta contundente, decisiva.
crust (krøst) *s.* corteza [de pan, queso, etc.]. *2* mendrugo. *3* corteza [terrestre]. *4* costra. *5* MED. postilla. *6* pasta [de un pastel]. *7* ZOOL. carapacho.
crust (to) *tr.* encostrar, incrustar. *2 intr.* encostrarse.
crustacean (krøstei·shian) *adj.-s.* ZOOL. crustáceo.
crustaceous (-shøs) *adj.* crustáceo.
crustation (-shøn) *s.* costra, incrustación.
crusty (krø·sti) *adj.* costroso. *2* rudo, áspero, brusco.
crutch (krøch) *s.* muleta [de cojo]. *2* horquilla, puntal. *3* horcajadura.
crux (krøks) *s.* cosa difícil, enigma. *2* el quid, lo esencial.
cry (krai) *s.* grito. *2* alarido. *3* lamento, lloro, llanto: *to have a good ~*, desahogarse llorando. *4* gritería, clamor: *much ~ and little wool*, es más el ruido que las nueces. *5* pregón. *6* voz pública. *7* jauría, muta, ladridos de la jauría. *8* a *far ~*, una gran distancia o diferencia.
cry (to) *intr.-tr.* gritar. *2* vocear, pregonar. *3 intr.* aullar. *4* llorar, lamentarse. *5 tr.* exclamar. *6* pedir: *to ~ quarter*, pedir cuartel. *7* proclamar, pregonar. *8 to ~ down*, rebajar, desacreditar. *9 to ~ for*, pedir llorando o a gritos; llorar de: *to ~ for help*, pedir socorro; *to ~ for joy*, llorar de alegría. *10 to ~ off*, deshacer [un trato, etc.]. *11 to ~ one's eyes out*, llorar amargamente. *12 to ~ out*, gritar, vociferar. *13 to ~ up*, ensalzar, alabar. ¶ Pret. y p. p.: *cried*.
crying (-ing) *s.* grito, griterío; lloro, llanto. *2 adj.* que grita o llora. *3* patente, notorio. *4* enorme, atroz, odioso.
crypt (kript) *s.* cripta.
cryptic(al (-tik(al) *adj.* secreto, oculto, enigmático.
cryptogam (-togæm) *s.* BOT. criptógama.
cryptogamous (kripta·gamøs) *adj.* criptógamo.
cryptogram (kri·ptogræm) *s.* criptograma.

cryptography (kripta·grafi) *s.* criptografía.
crystal (kri·stal) *s.* cristal. *2* RADIO. galena. *3 adj.* de cristal, cristalino.
crystalline (-in) *adj.* cristalino. *2 s.* ANAT. cristalino [del ojo].
crystallization (-išei·shøn) *s.* cristalización.
crystallize (to) (-aiš) *tr.* cristalizar. *2 intr.* cristalizar(se.
crystallography (-a·grafi) *s.* cristalografía.
cub (køb) *s.* cachorro. *2* ballenato. *3* fig. mocoso, joven mal educado.
cubage (kiu·bidў) *s.* cubicación.
Cuban (-ban) *adj.-s.* cubano.
cube (kiub) *s.* GEOM., MAT. cubo. *2 adj.* MAT. *~ root*, raíz cúbica.
cube (to) *tr.* cubicar.
cubeb (kiu·beb) *s.* BOT. cubeba.
cubic(al (-bik(al) *adj.* cúbico.
cubicle (-bikøl) *s.* cubículo.
cubism (-bišm) *s.* cubismo.
cubist (-bist) *s.* cubista.
cubit (-bit) *s.* codo [medida]. *2* ANAT. cúbito.
cubital (-al) *adj.* cubital. *2* codal.
cuboid (-boid) *adj.-s.* ANAT. cuboides. *2 s.* GEOM. paralelepípedo rectángulo.
cuckold (kø·køld) *s.* cornudo [marido].
cuckold (to) *tr.* encornudar.
cuckoo (ku·ku) *s.* ORN. cuclillo, cuco. *2* cucú [canto]. *3 ~ clock*, reloj de cuco.
cuckoopint (-pint) *s.* BOT. aro, alcatraz.
cucumber (kiu·kømbø^r) *s.* BOT. cohombro; pepino.
cucurbit (kiu·ø^rbit) *s.* cucúrbita. *2* BOT. calabaza.
cucurbitaceous (-ei·shøs) *adj.* BOT. cucurbitáceo.
cud (kød) *s.* lo que rumia un rumiante: *to chew the ~*, fig. rumiar, meditar.
cuddle (to) (kø·døl) *tr.* abrazar, tener en brazos [para acariciar, dar calor, etc.]. *2 intr.* estar abrazado o arrimado a.
cuddy (-di) *s.* MAR. camareta. *2* pequeño aposento. *3* alacena.
cudgel (kø·dўøl) *s.* garrote corto, porra.
cudgel (to) *tr.* apalear, aporrear: *to ~ one's brains*, devanarse los sesos. ¶ Pret. y p. p.: *cudgeled* o *-lled*; ger.: *cudgeling* o *-lling*.
cue (kiu) *s.* señal, indicación [para hacer algo]; indirecta, sugestión. *2* TEAT. pie. *3* BILL. taco. *4* coleta. *5* cola [de personas].
cuff (køf) *s.* puño [de camisa o vestido]: *~ links*, gemelos [de puño]. *2* doblez, vuelta [de pantalón]. *3* bofetada, sopapo, puñetazo. *4* pl. HANDCUFFS.
cuff (to) *tr.* abofetear, apuñear, pegar. *2 intr.* dar puñetazos, boxear.
cuirass (kuira·s) *s.* coraza.
cuirassier (kuirasi·ø^r) *s.* coracero.
cuisine (kuiši·n) *s.* cocina [arte].
culinary (kiu·lineri) *adj.* culinario.
cull (to) (køl) *tr.* escoger, elegir, entresacar. *2* coger [frutos, flores, etc.].
cullender (kø·løndø^r) *s.* COLANDER.
cullion (-liøn) *s.* belitre, bribón.
culm (kølm) *s.* BOT. caña [tallo]. *2* cisco [carbón].
culminant (kø·lminant) *adj.* culminante. *2* dominante, predominante.
culminate (to) (-neit) *tr.* culminar.
culmination (-nei·shøn) *s.* culminación.
culpability (kølpabi·liti) *s.* culpabilidad.
culpable (kø·lpabøl) *adj.* culpable.
culprit (-prit) *s.* culpable, reo, delincuente.
cult (kølt) *s.* culto. *2* secta religiosa.
cultism (-išm) *s.* LIT. culteranismo.

cultist (-ist) *s.* culterano.
cultivable (kø·ltivabøl) *adj.* cultivable.
cultivate (to) (-veit) *tr.* cultivar. 2 civilizar.
cultivated (-id) *adj.* cultivado. 2 culto, ilustrado, instruido.
cultivation (-ei·shøn) *s.* cultivo. 2 cultura, refinamiento.
cultivator (kø·ltiveitøʳ) *s.* cultivador. 2 agricultor. 3 AGR. escarificador.
cultual (kø·lchual) *adj.* cultual.
culture (-chøʳ) *adj.* cultura. 2 cultivo. 3 producción, cría.
culture (to) *tr.* cultivar. 2 educar, refinar.
cultured (-chøʳd) *adj.* culto, ilustrado.
culverin (kø·lvørin) *s.* ARTILL. culebrina.
culvert (kø·lvøʳt) *s.* alcantarilla [en un camino]; atarjea.
cumber (to) (kø·mbøʳ) *tr.* embarazar, estorbar, cargar, molestar, causar engorro.
cumbersome (-søm) *adj.* embarazoso, engorroso, pesado, incómodo, difícil de mover o manejar.
cumbrance (-brans) *s.* ENCUMBRANCE.
cumbrous (-brøs) *adj.* CUMBERSOME.
cum(m)in (kø·min) *s.* BOT. comino [planta].
cuminseed (-sɪd) *s.* BOT. comino [semilla].
cumulate (kiu·miuleit) *tr.* cumular, acumular, amontonar. 2 *intr.* acumularse, amontonarse.
cumulation (-ei·shøn) *s.* acumulación, amontonamiento.
cumulative (-miulativ) *adj.* cumulativo.
cumulus (-miuløs), *pl.* **-li** (-li) *s.* cúmulo, montón. 2 METEOR. cúmulo.
cuneal (-nial), **cuneate(d** (-nieit(id) **cuneiform** (-niiføʳm) *adj.* cuneiforme.
cunning (kø·ning) *adj.* hábil, diestro, ingenioso. 2 sagaz, astuto, taimado. 3 (E.U.) gracioso, mono. 4 *s.* habilidad, destreza, ingenio. 5 astucia, maña, artería. 6 ardid, artificio.
cup (køp) *s.* taza, jícara; copa o hueco en forma de copa: ~ *and ball*, boliche [juguete]. 2 copa, trago: *in one's cups*, bebido, achispado. 3 copa [trofeo]. 4 cáliz [vaso]. 5 BOT. cúpula; cáliz; corola. 6 ANAT. glena. 7 ELECT. campana [aislador]. 8 cubeta [de barómetro]. 9 ASTR. (con may.) Copa.
cup (to) *tr.* poner ventosas a. 2 ahuecar en forma de copa. ¶ Pret. y p. p.: *cupped;* ger.: *-pping.*
cupbearer (køpbe·røʳ) *s.* copero, escanciador.
cupboard (kø·pbøʳd) *s.* aparador, armario, alacena.
cupel (kiu·pøl) *s.* METAL. copela.
cupel (to) *tr.* copelar.
cupful (kø·pful) *s.* copa, taza [contenido].
Cupid (kiu·pid) *n. pr.* MIT. Cupido. 2 *s.* (con min.) amorcillo.
cupidity (-pi·diti) *s.* codicia, avidez, avaricia.
cupola (-pøla) *s.* ARQ., MAR. cúpula. 2 METAL. cubilote.
cupreous (-priøs) *adj.* cobrizo, cobreño.
cupric (-pric) *adj.* QUÍM. cúprico.
cupule (-piul) *s.* BOT. cúpula.
cupuliferous (kiupiuli·førøs) *adj.* BOT. cupulífero.
cur (køʳ) *s.* desp. perro, gozque. 2 canalla, hombre vil.
curable (kiu·rabøl) *adj.* curable.
curaçao (kiurasou·) *s.*
curacy (kiu·rasi) *s.* coadjutoria.
curare (kura·ri) *s.* BOT., QUÍM. curare.
curassow (kiu·rasou) *s.* ORN. guaco.
curate (kiu·reit) *s.* coadjutor, teniente cura.
curative (-rativ) *adj.* curativo.

curator (kiurei·tøʳ) *s.* DER. curador. 2 conservador, guardián, administrador.
curatrix (-triks) *f.* de CURATOR.
curb (køʳb) *s.* barbada [del freno]. 2 fig. sujeción, restricción, freno. 3 bordillo, encintado. 4 brocal [de pozo].
curb (to) *tr.* refrenar, contener, reprimir, sujetar.
curbstone (-stoun) *s.* piedra de encintado. 2 CURB 3 y 4.
curcuma (køʳkiuma) *s.* cúrcuma.
curd (køʳd) *s.* cuajada. 2 requesón.
curd (to) *tr.* cuajar, coagular. 2 *intr.* cuajarse, coagularse.
curdle (to) (køʳdøl) *tr.* cuajar, coagular, espesar; helar [la sangre]. 2 *intr.* cuajarse, coagularse, engrumecerse; helarse.
cure (kiu·øʳ) *s.* cura, curación, remedio. 2 cura [de almas]. 3 feligresía, parroquia. 4 acción de curar pescado, madera, etc.
cure (to) *tr.* curar, remediar. 2 curar [pescado, madera, etc.]; vulcanizar [caucho]. 3 *intr.* curarse.
curfew (køʳfiu) *s.* queda, toque de queda.
curia (kiu·ria) *s.* curia [de los ant. romanos]. 2 curia [papal].
curie (-ri) *s.* FÍS. curie.
curio (-riou) *s.* curiosidad, antigüedad, objeto curioso.
curiosity (kiuria·siti) *s.* curiosidad [deseo de saber o averiguar]. 2 lo curioso [de una cosa]. 3 curiosidad, objeto raro o curioso.
curious (kui·riøs) *adj.* curioso [deseoso de saber o averiguar]. 2 curioso, raro, singular. 3 minucioso. 4 primoroso.
curiousness (-nis) *s.* CURIOSITY 1 y 2. 2 delicadeza, primor.
curl (køʳl) *s.* rizo, bucle, sortija, tirabuzón. 2 espiral [de humo, etc.]. 3 curva, sinuosidad. 4 encorvadura, enroscamiento, abarquillamiento.
curl (to) *tr.* rizar, ensortijar, encrespar. 2 torcer, encorvar, enroscar, abarquillar: *to ~ one's lip*, hacer un gesto de desprecio con los labios. 3 *intr.* rizarse, ensortijarse. 4 encorvarse, enroscarse, abarquillarse.
curlew (køʳliu) *s.* ORN. zarapito.
curling (-ling) *s.* rizado, ensortijamiento, encorvadura. 2 juego en que se hacen correr unas piedras sobre el hielo. 3 *adj.* de rizar: ~ *irons*, ~ *tongs*, rizador, encrespador, tenacillas.
curly (-li) *adj.* rizado, rizoso, ensortijado, crespo, ondulado.
curmudgeon (køʳma·dyøn) *s.* avaro, tacaño.
currant (kø·rant) *s.* uva o pasa de Corinto. 2 grosella. 3 BOT. grosellero.
currency (kø·rønsi) *s.* curso, circulación. 2 valor corriente. 3 moneda corriente, dinero. 4 dinero en circulación.
current (kø·rønt) *adj.* corriente, que corre: ~ *account*, COM. cuenta corriente. 2 corriente [generalmente aceptado]; común, general; en boga, reinante; en circulación. 3 presente, actual. 4 corrida [letra]. 5 *s.* corriente. 6 curso, marcha, progresión.
curricle (kø·rikøl) *s.* carrocín.
curriculum (køri·kiuløm) *s.* plan de estudios.
currier (kø·riøʳ) *s.* curtidor, zurrador.
curriery (-ri) *s.* tenería.
curry (kø·ri) *s.* condimento de origen indio. 2 plato sazonado con él.
curry (to) *tr.* zurrar, adobar [pieles]. 2 almohazar. 3 COC. sazonar con CURRY. 4 fig. *to ~ favour*, adular. ¶ Pret. y p. p.: *curried.*

curry-comb s. almohaza, rascadera.
curse (kø^rs) s. maldición, imprecación, anatema. *2* juramento, voto, reniego. *3* azote, calamidad.
curse (to) tr. maldecir. *2* afligir, azotar [con males, calamidades, etc.]. *3* intr. jurar, renegar, echar votos.
cursed (kø·^rsid) adj. maldito, abominable, execrable.
cursive (-siv) adj.-s. cursiva [letra].
cursor (kø·^rsø^r) s. MEC. cursor.
cursory (-i) adj. superficial, sumario, rápido, hecho sin detención, por encima o de pasada.
curt (kø^rt) adj. corto, breve, conciso. *2* brusco, seco.
curtail (to) (kø^rtei·l) tr. acortar, cercenar, mutilar. *2* abreviar, reducir, restringir, escatimar.
curtailment (-mønt) s. acortamiento, abreviación, reducción.
curtain (kø·rtin) s. cortina [paño colgante; cosa que oculta]: *to draw the ~*, correr la cortina, correr un velo. *2* TEAT. telón [de boca]: *behind the ~*, entre bastidores, en secreto. *3* FORT. cortina.
curtain (to) tr. encortinar. *2* velar, ocultar.
curtation (ko^rtei·shøn) s. ASTR. curtación.
curtesy, curtsy (kø·^rtsi) s. cortesía, reverencia [saludo femenino].
curtesy, curtsy (to) intr. hacer una cortesía o reverencia [la mujer]. ¶ Pret. y p. p.: *curtsied.*
curule (kiu·rul) adj. curul.
curvate(d (kø·^rveit(id) adj. corvo, encorvado.
curvation (-ei·shøn) s. encorvadura.
curvature (kø·^rvachø^r) s. curvatura.
curve (kø·^rv) adj. curvo, encorvado. *2* s. curva.
curve (to) tr. encorvar, torcer, combar. *2* intr. encorvarse, torcerse; describir una curva.
curvet (kø·^rvet o kø^rve·t) s. corveta, corcovo. *2* retozo, brinco.
curvet (to) intr. corvetear, corcovear. *2* retozar, brincar. ¶ Pret. y p. p.: *-ted* o *-tted;* ger.: *-ting* o *-tting.*
curvilinear (kø^rvili·nia^r) adj. curvilíneo.
curvity (kø·^rviti) s. curvidad.
cushion (ku·shøn) . cojín, almohadón, almohadilla. *2* BILL. banda. *3* MEC. amortiguador. *4* ARQ. almohadón. *5* VET. ranilla [del casco].
cushion (to) tr. proveer de cojines. *2* sentar o poner sobre cojín. *3* suavizar, apagar [la voz]. *4* MEC. amortiguar, acojinar. *5* ahogar [quejas, etc.].
cusp (køsp) s. cúspide. *2* cuerno [de la luna].
cuspidor (-ø^r) s. escupidera.
cuss (køs) s. (E.U.) reniego, terno. *2* desp. bicho, individuo.
cussedness (kø·sidnis) s. (E.U.) terquedad; mal genio.
custard (kø·sta^rd) s. flan; natillas.
custard-apple s. BOT. guanábana.
custodian (køstou·dian) s. custodio, guardián.
custody (kø·stødi) s. custodia, guarda. *2* prisión, detención; encarcelamiento: *to take into ~*, detener, prender. *3* custodia [de la orden franciscana].
custom (kø·støm) s. costumbre, hábito, uso, usanza. *2* DER. costumbre. *3* parroquia, clientela; hecho de ser parroquiano o cliente. *4* pl. derechos de aduana: *customs officer*, aduanero, vista de aduanas. *5* adv.-adj. a medida, por encargo; que hace algo a medida o por encargo.
customable (-abøl) adj. sujeto al pago de derechos de aduana.
customary (-eri) adj. acostumbrado, de costumbre, habitual, usual. *2* DER. consuetudinario.

customer (-ø^r) s. parroquiano, cliente. *2* fam. tipo, individuo.
custom-free adj. libre de derechos de aduana.
customhouse (-jaus) s. aduana: *~ broker*, agente de aduanas.
custom-made adj. hecho a medida.
cut (køt) s. corte, cortadura, incisión. *2* tajo, cuchillada. *3* lámina, grabado [esp. en madera]. *4* labra, tallado [de la piedra, etc.]. *5* corte, reducción. *6* corte [en los naipes]. *7* trozo [de carne], tajada. *8* zanja, foso, cortadura. *9* camino directo: *short ~*, atajo. *10* corte, estilo [de un vestido]. *11* hechura, forma, figura. *12* golpe dado con el canto de algo, golpe cortante. *13* palabra o acto que hiere; desaire, ofensa. *14* acto de negar el saludo a uno. *15* falta [a clase]. *16 pret.* y *p. p.* de TO CUT: cortado, tallado, interrumpido, etc.
cut (to) tr. cortar, hender, partir, dividir, separar: *to ~ the throat*, degollar. *2* cortar [un vestido, etc.]. *3* segar. *4* abrir, excavar. *5* cortar, interrumpir, interceptar. *6* cortar [el suministro de agua, gas, etc.]. *7* reducir, acortar. *8* recortar. *9* trinchar. *10* labrar, esculpir, tallar, cincelar, grabar. *11* cortar, cruzar [una línea o superficie a otra]. *12* atravesar, abrirse paso en; surcar [el agua]; hender [el aire]. *13* cortar, alzar [los naipes]. *15* castrar [un animal]. *16* dar un golpe vivo [con un látigo, etc.]. *17* herir [lastimar los sentimientos de]. *18* faltar a [una clase]; dejar [una costumbre, etc.]; desentenderse de. *19* dejar de tratarse con, negar el saludo a. *20* diluir, aguar, adulterar [un licor]. *21* templar [un color]. *22* golpear de cierto modo la pelota. *23* parar [un motor]. *24 to ~ a caper*, hacer una cabriola. *25 to ~ a figure*, hacer papel [en sociedad, etc.]. *26 to ~ down*, derribar [cortando]; rebajar, reducir. *27 to ~ ice*, tener peso o influencia. *28 to ~ in*, mezclar, introducir en; ELECT. conectar, intercalar. *29 to ~ off*, cortar, separar; llevarse, quitar la vida prematuramente; poner fin a; cortar [la comunicación, la retirada, el encendido, etc.]. *30 to ~ out*, cortar [quitar o hacer cortando], dividir; quitar, separar, suprimir; desconectar; preparar, trazar; hacer formar. *31 to ~ short*, interrumpir bruscamente.
32 intr. cortar: *to ~ both ways*, ser arma de dos filos. *33 to ~ in diente*, los dientes]. *34* pasar [con rapidez o por el camino más corto], atajar. *35 to ~ in*, intervenir, meter baza.
¶ CONJUG. pret. y p. p.: *cut;* ger.: *cutting.*
cutaneous (kiutei·niøs) adj. cutáneo.
cutaway coat (kø·tauel) s. chaqué.
cute (kiut) adj. listo, astuto. *2* (E.U.) lindo, mono.
cuticle (kiu·tikøl) s. cutícula.
cutlass (kø·tlas) s. machete; sable de abordaje, sable corto.
cutler (-lø^r) s. cuchillero.
cutlery (-løri) s. cuchillería.
cutlet (-lit) s. COC. chuleta.
cutoff (-of) s. atajo. *2* MEC. cortavapor.
cutout (-aut) s. recortado; figura recortada. *2* ELECT. cortacircuito.
cutpurse (-pø^rs) s. cortabolsas, ratero.
cutter (-ø^r) s. cortador. *2* tallador, grabador. *3* MEC. cuchilla, fresa. *4* MAR. cúter. *5* MAR. escampavía. *6* pequeño trineo.
cutthroat (-zrout) s. asesino.
cutting (-ing) adj. cortante. *2* frío, penetrante. *3* hiriente, incisivo, mordaz. *4* s. corte, cortadura,

incisión. *5* recorte, retazo. *6* alce [de los naipes]. *7* talla [de la piedra, etc.]. *8* AGR. esqueje, estaca.
cuttlebone (kø·tølboun) *s.* jibión.
cuttlefish (-fish) *s.* ZOOL. jibia, sepia. *2 por* ext. calamar, pulpo, etc.
cutwater (kø·tuotø^r) *s.* tajamar.
cuvette (kiuve·t) *s.* FOT. cubeta.
cyanic (saiæ·nic) *adj.* QUÍM. ciánico. *2* BOT. azulado.
cyanide (sai·anaid) *s.* QUÍM. cianuro.
Cybele (si·bøli) *n. pr.* MIT. Cibeles.
cybernetics (saibø^rne·tics) *s.* cibernética.
Cyclades (si·kladiš) *n. pr.* GEOGR. Cícladas.
cyclamen (si·klamin) *s.* BOT. ciclamino, pamporcino.
cycle (sai·cøl) *s.* ciclo. *2* ELECT. período. *3* biciclo, triciclo.
cycle (to) *intr.* ir en bicicleta.
cyclic(al (-klic(al) *adj.* cíclico.
cycling (-kling) *s.* ciclismo. *2* acción de ir en bicicleta.
cyclism (-klišm) *s.* ciclismo.
cyclist (-ist) *s.* ciclista.
cycloid (-kloid) *s.* GEOM. cicloide.
cyclone (-kloun) *s.* METEOR. ciclón.
cyclopa(e)dia (saiklopɪ·dia) *s.* ENCYCLOPAEDIA.
Cyclopean (saiklopɪ·an), **Cyclopic** (-kla·pic) *adj.* ciclópeo, ciclópico, gigantesco.
Cyclops (sai·klaps) *s.* MIT. cíclope.
cyclorama (saiklora·ma) *s.* ciclorama.
cyclostyle (-tail) *s.* ciclostilo.
cyclotron (sai·klotran) *s.* FÍS. ciclotrón.
cygnet (si·gnit) *s.* pollo del cisne.

cylinder (si·lindø^r) *s.* GEOM., MEC. cilindro. *2* cuerpo cilíndrico, rodillo.
cylindric(al (sili·ndrik(al) *adj.* cilíndrico.
cyma (sai·ma), **cymatium** (simei·shiøm) *s.* ARQ. cimacio, gola.
cymbal (si·mbal) *s.* MÚS. címbalo, platillos.
cyme (saim) *s.* BOT. cima.
cymose (-ous) *adj.* BOT. cimoso.
cynegetic (sinidẙe·tik) *adj.* cinegético.
cynic (si·nik) *adj.-s.* FIL. cínico.
cynical (-al) *adj.* FIL. cínico. *2* pesimista.
cynicism (-sišm) *s.* FIL. cinismo. *2* pesimismo.
Cynosure (sai·nøẙu^r) *s.* ASTR. Cinosura. *2* (con min.) blanco de las miradas.
cyperaceous (saipørei·shøs) *adj.* BOT. ciperáceo.
cypher (sai·fø^r) *s.* CIPHER.
cypress (-pres) *s.* BOT. ciprés.
Cyprian (si·prian) *n. pr.* Cipriano. *2 adj.-s.* chipriota.
Cyprus (sai·prøs) *n. pr.* GEOGR. Chipre.
Cyril (si·ril) *n. pr.* Cirilo.
Cyrus (sai·røs) *n. pr.* Ciro.
cyst (sist) *s.* quiste.
cystic (si·stic) *adj.* ANAT. cístico.
cystis (si·stis) *s.* CYST.
cystitis (sistai·tis) *s.* MED. cistitis.
Cytherea (siirɪ·a) *n. pr.* MIT. Citerea.
cytisus (si·tisøs) *s.* BOT. citiso, codeso.
cytoplasm (sai·toplæšm) *s.* BIOL. citoplasma.
czar (ša^r) *s.* zar.
czarevitch (ša·revich) *s.* zarevitz.
czarevna (šare·vna) *s.* zarina.
Czecho-Slovakia (che·kou·slova·kia) *n. pr.* GEOGR. Checoslovaquia.

D

D, d (dɪ) *s.* D, d, cuarta letra del alfabeto inglés. *2* MÚS. re.

dab (dæb) *s.* golpecito, toque ligero, picotazo leve. *2* pincelada, untadura. *3* ICT. platija. *4* fig. hacha [pers. diestra en algo].

dab (to) *tr.* dar golpecitos a, picar, picotear. *2* chapotear [con una esponja, un paño mojado, etc.]. *3* dar brochazos o pinceladas ligeras; aplicar [algo] con ellos. ¶ Pret. y p. p.: *dabbed;* ger.: *dabbing.*

dabble (to) (dæ·bøl) *tr.* rociar, salpicar, mojar, humedecer. *2* dar golpecitos a. *3 intr.* chapotear [en el agua]. *4* hacer algo o meterse en algo en pequeña escala, como aficionado.

dabbler (dæ·bløʳ) *s.* diletante, aficionado.

dabchick (-chik) *s.* ORN. somorgujo.

dabster (dæ·bstøʳ) *s.* DAB 4.

dace (deis) *s.* ICT. albur, dardo, breca.

dachsund (da·ksjunt) *s.* perro de patas muy cortas.

Dacia (dei·sha) *n. pr.* GEOGR. Dacia.

Dacian (dei·shan) *adj.-s.* dacio.

dactyl (dæ·ctil) *s.* MET. dáctilo.

dactylology (dæctila·lodȳi) *s.* dactilología.

dactylography (-grafi) *s.* estudio de las huellas digitales. *2* dactilología.

dactyloscopy (-skopi) *s.* dactiloscopia.

dad (dæd), **daddie, daddy** (-i) *s.* fam. papá, papaíto, taíta.

daddy-longlegs *s.* ENT. típula. *2* ZOOL. segador [arácnido].

dado (dei·dou) *s.* ARQ. dado, neto. *2* rodapié, friso, alizar.

Daedalus (dɪ·deløs) *n. pr.* MIT. Dédalo.

daffodil (dæ·fodil) *s.* BOT. narciso, trompón.

daft (dæft) *adj.* tonto, chiflado, loco.

dagger (dæ·gøʳ) *s.* daga, puñal: *to be at daggers drawn,* fig. estar a matar. *2* IMPR. obelisco.

dago (dei·gou) *s.* (E.U. y Can.) desp. italiano, español o portugués.

daguerrotype (dáge·røtaip) *s.* daguerrotipo.

dahlia (da·lia) *s.* BOT. dalia.

daily (dei·li) *adj.* diario, cotidiano. *2* diurno. *3 s.* periódico diario. *4 adv.* diariamente, cotidianamente, cada día.

daintily (dei·ntili) *adv.* delicadamente, exquisitamente.

dainty (dei·nti) *adj.* delicado, primoroso, exquisito, elegante, refinado. *2* sabroso, delicioso. *3* delicado, exigente. *4 s.* bocado exquisito, golosina.

dairy (de·ri) *s.* lechería. *2* quesería. *3* vaquería: ~ *farm,* granja lechera.

dairymaid (-meid) *s.* lechera [pers.].

dairyman (-mæn) *s.* lechero.

dais (dei·is) *s.* tarima, estrado. *2* (gal.) dosel.

daisy (dei·si) *s.* BOT. margarita, maya, vellorita.

dale (deil) *s.* cañada, hondonada, valle.

dalliance (dæ·lians) *s.* jugueteo, devaneo.

dally (to) (dæ·li) *intr.* jugar, juguetear, coquetear. *2* perder el tiempo. *3* tardar, entretenerse. *4 tr.* *to* ~ *away,* pasar, perder [el tiempo].

Dalmatia (dælmei·shia) *n. pr.* GEOGR. Dalmacia.

Dalmatian (-n) *adj.-s.* dálmata.

dalmatic (dælme·tik) *s.* dalmática.

daltonism (da·ltøniŝm) *s.* MED. daltonismo.

dam (dæm) *s.* dique, presa. *2* embalse, pantano. *3* madre [en ganadería].

dam (to) *tr.* represar, embalsar. *2* cerrar, obstruir. ¶ Pret. y p. p.: *dammed;* ger.: *-mming.*

damage (dæ·midȳ) *s.* daño, perjuicio, detrimento. *2* COM. avería, siniestro. *3 pl.* daños y perjuicios. *4* indemnización.

damage (to) *tr.* dañar, perjudicar, deteriorar. *2 intr.* deteriorarse, averiarse.

damaging (-ing) *adj.* perjudicial, nocivo.

Damascene (dæ·masin) *adj.* y *s.* damasceno. *2* (con min.) *adj.* damasquino.

damascene (to) (dæmasi·n) *tr.* damasquinar.

Damascus (damæ·skøs) *n. pr.* GEOGR. Damasco.

damask (dæ·mask) *s.* damasco [tejido]. *2* damasquinado, ataujía. *3 adj.* damasceno. *4* adamascado. *5* damasquino.

damask (to) *tr.* damasquinar. *2* adamascar.

damaskeen (to) (dæmaski·n) *tr.* TO DAMASCENE.

dame (deim) *s.* dama, señora. *2* fam. mujer.

damn (dæm) *s.* maldición. *2* fig. *I don't care a* ~, me importa un bledo.

damn (to) *tr.* TEOL. condenar. *2* condenar, reprobar. *3* maldecir. *4 intr.* echar ternos.

damnable (-nabøl) *adj.* condenable, detestable, abominable.

damnation (-ei·shøn) *s.* condenación, perdición.

damned (dæ·mnd) *adj.* condenado, réprobo. *2* fig. condenado, maldito, detestable. *3 adv.* sumamente.

damnify (to) (-nifai) *tr.* damnificar.

damp (dæmp) *adj.* húmedo, mojado. *2 s.* humedad. *3* fig. desaliento. *4* MIN. grisú, mofeta.
damp (to) *tr.* humedecer, mojar. *2* ahogar, apagar, amortiguar. *3* enfriar [los ánimos]; desalentar. *4 intr.* humedecerse. *5* desalentarse.
dampen (to) (-øn) *tr.* (esp. E.U.) TO DAMP.
damper (dæ·mpøʳ) *s.* apagador, amortiguador. *2* regulador de tiro [de chimenea]. *3* MÚS. apagador [del piano]; sordina. *4* desalentador.
dampness (-nis) *s.* humedad.
damsel (dæ·mšøl) *s.* damisela.
damson (dæ·mšøn) *s.* ciruela damascena.
Dan (dæn) *n. pr.* BIB. Dan. *2* dim. de Daniel.
dance (dæns) *s.* danza, baile.
dance (to) *intr.* danzar, bailar: *to ~ attendance on*, servir obsequiosamente a. *2* bailar [un baile]. *3* hacer bailar.
dancer (-øʳ) *s.* bailador, ra. *2* bailarín, danzarín, na. *3* pl. parejas de baile.
dancing (-ing) *s.* danza, baile [acción]. *2 adj.* de baile, que baila: *~ girl*, bailarina.
dandelion (dæ·ndilaiøn) *s.* BOT. amargón, diente de león.
dander (dæ·ndøʳ) *s.* fam. ira, enojo.
dandify (to) (dæ·ndifai) *s.* acicalar, componer.
dandle (to) (dæ·ndøl) *tr.* hacer saltar [a un niño] sobre las rodillas. *2* mimar, acariciar.
dandler (-løʳ) *s.* niñero.
dandruff (dæ·ndrøf) *s.* caspa.
dandy (dæ·ndi) *adj. y s.* dandi, elegante, gomoso. *2 adj.* fam. estupendo.
dandyism (-išm) *s.* dandismo.
Dane (dein) *s.* danés, dinamarqués. *2* perro danés.
danewort (-uøʳt) *s.* BOT. cimicaria, yezgo.
danger (dei·ndýøʳ) *s.* peligro, riesgo, escollo.
dangerous (-øs) *adj.* peligroso. *2* de cuidado, grave.
dangerously (-li) *adv.* peligrosamente, gravemente.
dangle (to) (dæ·ngøl) *tr.* hacer balancear [en el aire]. *2 intr.* colgar, pender, bambolearse. *3 to ~ after*, rondar, andar detrás de.
Danish (dei·nish) *adj. y s.* danés, dinamarqués.
dank (dønk) *adj.* liento, húmedo.
danseuse (dansø·š) *s.* bailarina.
Dantesque (dænte·sk) *adj.* dantesco.
Danube (dæ·niub) *n. pr.* GEOGR. Danubio.
Danubian (dæniu·bian) *adj.* danubiano.
Daphne (dæ·fni) *n. pr.* MIT. Dafne. *2 s.* (con min.). BOT. adelfilla.
dapper (dæ·pøʳ) *adj.* vivaracho. *2* atildado, pulcro, elegante.
dapple (dæ·pøl) *adj.* DAPPLED.
dapple (to) *tr.* manchar, salpicar de manchas.
dappled (-d) *adj.* manchado, moteado. *2* rodado [caballo].
dare (deʳ) *s.* fam. reto, desafío.
dare (to) *tr.* atreverse a, osar. *2* arrostrar, desafiar. *3* desafiar, retar [a hacer algo]. ¶ Pret.: *dared* o *durst*; p. p.: *dred*.
daredevil (-de·vøl) *adj. y s.* atrevido, temerario.
daring (dæ·ring) *adj.* atrevido, osado. *2* emprendedor. *3 s.* atrevimiento, osadía.
Darius (dara·iøs) *n. pr.* Darío.
dark (daʳk) *adj.* oscuro: *~ room*, cuarto oscuro; *it grows ~*, oscurece, anochece. *2* moreno negruzco. *3* negro, sombrío, triste, infausto. *4* amenazador, siniestro. *5* negro, perverso, atroz. *6* callado, reservado. *7* secreto, enigmático. *8* ignorante. *9 ~ lantern*, linterna sorda. *10 s.* oscuridad; sombra, noche, tinieblas. *11* ignorancia: *in the ~*, a oscuras, en la ignorancia de una cosa.

darken (to) (-øn) *tr.* oscurecer, ensombrecer. *2* anublar. *3* entristecer. *4* cegar, ofuscar. *5* embrollar, confundir. *6* denigrar, manchar. *7 intr.* obscurecerse, ensombrecerse.
darkle (to) (-øl) *intr.* acechar en la oscuridad. *2* oscurecerse.
darkling (-ling) *adj.* oscuro. *2 adv.* a oscuras.
darkly (-li) *adv.* oscuramente. *2* misteriosamente. *3* secretamente. *4* sombríamente.
darkness (-nis) *s.* oscuridad. *2* tinieblas, lobreguez. *3* tristeza. *4* ignorancia, maldad. *5* reserva, secreto.
darksome (-søm) *s.* poét. oscuro, sombrío.
darky (-i) *s.* fam. negro, mulato.
darling (da·ʳling) *adj.* amado, querido. *2 s.* ser querido: *my ~*, vidita, amor mío.
darn (daʳn) *s.* zurcido.
darn (to) *tr.* zurcir.
darnel (da·ʳnøl) *s.* BOT. cizaña, joyo.
darning (da·ʳning) *s.* zurcidura, zurcido.
dart (daʳt) *s.* dardo, flecha, venablo. *2* rehilete, flechilla. *3* aguijón [de insecto]. *4* ARQ. dardo. *5* movimiento rápido.
dart (to) *tr.* lanzar, tirar, arrojar, despedir. *2 intr.* lanzarse, precipitarse.
Darwinism (da·ʳuinišm) *s.* darvinismo.
Darwinist (-ist) *s.* darvinista.
dash (dæsh) *s.* arremetida. *2* golpe, choque, embate: *at a ~*, de un golpe. *3* chapaleteo. *4* movimiento súbito. *5* DEP. carrera corta y rápida. *6* trazo, plumada, raya, guión largo. *7* TELEGR. raya. *8* un poco, unas gotas, un chorrito. *9* ostentación: *to cut a ~*, hacer gran papel. *10* empuje, energía, brío. *11* DASHBOARD.
dash (to) *tr.* golpear, romper, estrellar. *2* arrojar, lanzar. *3* rociar, salpicar. *4* echar, mezclar. *5* frustrar, destruir. *6* desanimar. *7 to ~ off*, escribir o hacer aprisa. *8 to ~ out*, rayar, tachar. *9 intr.* moverse, arrojarse con ímpetu: *to ~ out*, salir corriendo. *10* chocar, estrellarse, batir. *11* fachendear.
dashboard (-boʳd) *s.* guardafangos. *2* AUTO. salpicadero.
dashing (dæ·shing) *adj.* enérgico, brioso, arrollador. *2* ostentoso, vistoso.
dastard (dæ·staʳd) *adj. y s.* cobarde, vil.
dastardize (to) (-aiš) *tr.* acobardar.
dastardly (-li) *adj.* cobarde, vil.
data (dei·ta) *s.* datos, detalles.
datary (dei·tari) *s.* dataria. *2* datario.
date (deit) *s.* fecha, data. *2* cita [para verse]. *3* época, período. *4* ahora, el presente: *down to ~*, hasta ahora; *out of ~*, anticuado, desusado, pasado de moda; *up to ~*, hasta ahora; al día; a la última. *5* BOT. dátil: *~ palm*, datilera, palmera. *6* ZOOL. *~ shell*, dátil [molusco].
date (to) *tr.* datar, fechar. *2* contar [por años, etc.]. *3* pop. dar cita [a uno]. *4 intr.* anticuarse. *5 to ~ from*, llevar fecha de; datar de.
dated (-id) *adj.* datado, fechado. *2* anticuado.
dateless (-lis) *adj.* sin fecha. *2* inmemorial.
dater (-øʳ) *s.* fechador.
dative (-tiv) *adj. y s.* GRAM. dativo.
datum (-øm) *s.* dato.
daub (dob) *s.* unto, embadurnadura. *2* PINT. pintarrajo.
daub (to) *tr.* untar, embadurnar. *2* pintarrajear.
dauber (-øʳ) *s.* embadurnador. *2* pintamonas. *3* cepillo, etc., para embadurnar.
daubing (-ing) *s.* embadurnamiento. *2* afeite.
dauby (-i) *adj.* untuoso, pegajoso. *2* pintarrajeado.

daughter (do·tø^r) *s.* hija.
daughter-in-law *s.* nuera, hija política.
daughterly (-li) *adj.* filial, de hija.
daunt (to) (dont) *tr.* acobardar, intimidar, asustar, arredrar, desanimar.
dauntless (-lis) *adj.* impávido, intrépido.
dauphin (do·fin) *s.* delfín [de Francia].
dauphiness (-is) *s.* delfina.
davit (dæ·vit) *s.* MAR. pescante; serviola.
Davy (dei·vi) *n. pr.* dim. de DAVID.
daw (do) *s.* ORN. corneja.
dawdle (to) (do·døl) *intr.* haronear, perder el tiempo.
dawdler (do·dlø^r) *s.* ocioso, paseante.
dawn (don) *s.* alba, aurora, amanecer, madrugada. *2* fig. comienzo, albor, albores.
dawn (to) *intr.* amanecer, alborear, clarear, romper el día. *2* apuntar asomar. *3 to ~ on* o *upon,* empezar a ser visto o comprendido por.
dawning (-ing) *s.* alba, amanecer. *2* fig. *first dawnings,* albores.
day (dei) *s.* día: ~ *of doom, Day of Judgment,* día del juicio; ~ *off,* día de asueto, día libre; *day's run,* MAR. singladura; *all ~ long,* todo el día; *by ~,* de día; *by the ~,* por día; ~ *by* o ~ *in,* ~ *out,* día tras día; *from ~ to ~,* de día en día; *some fine ~,* un buen día, el mejor día; *the ~ after tomorrow,* pasado mañana; *the ~ before yesterday,* anteayer; *up to this ~,* hasta hoy. *2* jornada, jornal [horas de trabajo]. *3* luz del día. *4 pl.* días, tiempo, época: *in the days of old,* antaño. *5 adj.* de día, diurno; a jornal, de jornal: ~ *school,* escuela diurna, con internado; ~ *labour,* trabajo a jornal; ~ *labourer,* jornalero.
daybook (-buk) *s.* COM. libro diario.
daybreak (-breik) *s.* alba, amanecer.
daydream (-drɪm) *s.* ensueño, ilusión, quimera, castillo en el aire.
dayfly (-flai) *s.* ENT. cachipolla, efímera.
daylight (-lait) *s.* luz del día, luz natural.
daylong (-long) *adj.* de todo el día. *2 adv.* todo el día.
dayspring (-spring) *s.* alba, albor.
daystar (-sta^r) *s.* lucero del alba.
daytime (-taim) *s.* día [de sol a sol]: *in the ~,* de día.
daywork (-uø^rk) *s.* jornada, jornal.
daze (deiš) *s.* deslumbramiento, aturdimiento: *to be in a ~,* estar aturdido.
daze (to) *tr.* deslumbrar, ofuscar, aturdir.
dazzle (dæ·šøl) *s.* deslumbramiento. *2* brillo.
dazzle (to) *tr.* deslumbrar, ofuscar. *2 intr.* deslumbrarse. *3* brillar.
dazzling (-šling) *adj.* deslumbrador.
deacon (dɪ·køn) *s.* diácono.
deaconess (-is) *s.* diaconisa.
deaconry (-ri), **deaconship** (-ship) *s.* diaconato, diaconado; diaconía.
dead (ded) *adj.* muerto [en todas sus acepciones]: *Dead Sea,* GEOGR. Mar Muerto. *2* difunto, finado. *3* inerte, inanimado. *4* insensible, sordo, indiferente. *5* estéril, inútil. *6* frío, sin fervor, sin energía, gastado. *7* apagado [volcán, brasa, etc.]. *8* sordo [sonido]. *9* mate. *10* uniforme, monótono. *11* despoblado. *12* seguro, cierto, certero: ~ *shot,* tirador certero. *13* absoluto, completo, profundo: ~ *calm,* calma profunda; MAR. calma chicha. *14* imitada, condenada [puerta, ventana]. *15* mortal, terrible. *16* ELECT. inactivo, sin corriente. *17* insípido, desbravado, que ya no fermenta. *18* Otros sentidos: ~ *end,* callejón sin

salida; RADIO. punto muerto; ~ *heat,* DEP. empate [en una carrera]; ~ *reckoning,* MAR. estima; ~ *stop,* parada en seco; paro completo. *19 adv.* absolutamente, completamente, del todo. *20* de pronto. *21* directamente. *22* exactamente.
23 s. lo más callado, muerto, etc., de: *the ~ of night,* el silencio de la noche; *the ~ of winter,* lo más crudo del invierno. *24* usado como plural: *the ~,* los muertos.
deaden (to) (de-døn) *tr.* amortiguar. *2* retardar, frenar. *3* apagar [el sonido, el brillo]. *4* hacer insípido, desbravado. *5 intr.* amortiguarse, apagarse.
deadhead (de·djed) *s.* el que tiene pase [en el teatro, etc.]. *2* MAR. bolardo.
dead-letter office *s.* CORR. departamento de cartas devueltas o no reclamadas.
deadliness (-linis) *s.* calidad de mortífero.
deadlock (-lak) *s.* detención, paro, situación sin salida, punto muerto.
deadly (-li) *adj.* mortal, mortífero, letal. *2* mortal [odio, enemigo, palidez, etc.]. *3* intenso, sumo. *4* capital [pecado]. *5 adv.* mortalmente, sumamente.
dead-nettle *s.* BOT. ortiga muerta.
dead-stick landing *s.* AVIA. aterrizaje con el motor parado.
dead-struck *adj.* aterrado, anonadado.
deaf (def) *adj.* sordo [pers. o animal]: ~ *and dumb,* sordomudo; *to turn a ~ ear,* hacerse el sordo. *2* sordo, apagado [sonido].
deafen (to) (-øn) *tr.* asordar, ensordecer. *2* apagar [un sonido].
deafening (-ing) *adj.* ensordecedor.
deaf-mute *adj.-s.* sordomudo.
deafness (de·fnis) *s.* sordera.
deal (dɪl) *s.* porción, cantidad: *a good ~ [of],* bastante; *a great ~ [of],* mucho. *2* trato, negociación. *3* trato [que se da o recibe]. *4* distribución, reparto. *5* mano [de un juego de naipes]. *6* tabla [de pino o abeto]. *7* política económica.
deal (to) *tr.* distribuir, repartir, dispensar. ~ *Gralte.* con *out.* *2* arrear [un golpe, etc.]. *3* dar [naipes]. *4 intr. to ~ in,* tratar, comerciar, negociar. *5 to ~ by* o *with,* portarse [con uno], tratarlo. *6 to ~ with,* tratar con; tratar de o sobre; ocuparse en o de; intervenir en; habérselas con. ¶ Pret. y p. p.: *dealt.*
dealer (dɪ·lø^r) *s.* comerciante, negociante, tratante. *2* distribuidor. *3 plain ~,* hombre sincero; *double ~,* hombre falso.
dealing (-ling) *s.* proceder, comportamiento: *fair ~,* buena fe; *double ~,* doblez, mala fe. *2 pl.* trato, relaciones. *3* tratos, negocios.
dealt (delt) pret. y p. p. de TO DEAL.
dean (dɪn) *s.* deán. *2* decano.
deanery (-øri), **deanship** (-ship) *s.* deanato, deanazgo. *2* decanato.
dear (di·ø^r) *adj.* querido, caro, amado, estimado, preciado. *2* caro, costoso. *3 Dear Sir, Dears Messrs.,* muy señor mío, muy señores míos [en las cartas]. *4 s.* persona amada, excelente. *6* interj. ~ *me!,* ¡Dios mío! *9 adv.* caro.
dearly (-li) *adv.* amorosamente, tiernamente. *2* caro, caramente.
dearth (dø^rz) *s.* carestía, hambre. *2* escasez, falta.
deary (di·øri) *s.* vidita, amor mío.
death (dez) *s.* muerte: *the Death,* la muerte, la descarnada: *to ~, to the ~,* a muerte, hasta la

muerte; sumamente; ~ *to...!*, ¡muera...! *2* defunción, fallecimiento, óbito. *3 adj.* de muerte, de difuntos, de defunción: ~ *bell,* ~ *knell,* ~ *toll,* toque de difuntos; ~ *certificate,* partida de defunción; ~ *duties,* derechos sucesorios; ~ *mask,* mascarilla [de un difunto]; ~ *penalty,* pena de muerte; ~ *rate,* mortalidad; ~ *rattle,* estertor de la muerte.

deathbed (-bed) *s.* lecho de muerte.
deathblow (-blou) *s.* golpe mortal.
deathful (-ful) *adj.* mortal, letal, mortífero.
deathless (-lis) *adj.* inmortal; imperecedero.
deathlike (-laik) *adj.* DEATHLY 1.
deathly (-li) *adj.* mortal, de muerte, letárgico, cadavérico. *2 adv.* mortalmente; sumamente.
deathtrap (-træp) *s.* lugar peligroso, trampa.
deathwatch (-uøtch) *s.* velatorio. *2* guardia de un reo de muerte.
debacle (dibæ·køl) *s.* deshielo [en un río]; avenida que lo sigue. *2* desastre, ruina.
debar (to) (diba·ʳ) *tr.* excluir [de]. *2* privar, prohibir. ¶ Pret. y p. p.: *debarred;* ger.: *-rring.*
debark (to) (diba·ʳk) *tr.-intr.* desembarcar. *2 tr.* descortezar [un árbol].
debarkation (-ei·shøn) *s.* desembarco, desembarque.
debase (to) (dibei·s) *tr.* rebajar, degradar, envilecer, deshonrar. *2* adulterar, viciar.
debasement (-mønt) *s.* degradación, envilecimiento. *2* adulteración.
debatable (dibei·tabøl) *adj.* discutible.
debate (dibei·t) *s.* debate, discusión.
debate (to) *tr.-intr.* debatir, discutir. *2 intr.* deliberar, reflexionar.
debauch (di·boch) *s.* exceso, orgía, libertinaje.
debauch (to) *tr.* seducir, corromper. *2 intr.* entregarse al libertinaje.
debauchee (di·boshı) *s.* libertino.
debaucher (dibo·shøʳ) *s.* seductor, corruptor.
debauchery (-i) *s.* libertinaje, intemperancia. *2* corrupción. *3 pl.* orgías.
debenture (dibe·nchøʳ) *s.* COM. obligación, bono. *2* abonaré de la aduana.
debilitate (to) (dibi·liteit) *tr.* debilitar, enervar.
debility (dibi·liti) *s.* debilidad.
debit (de·bit) *s.* COM. debe. *2* COM. débito, adeudo, cargo. *3* COM. ~ *balance,* saldo deudor.
debit (to) *tr.* COM. adeudar, cargar [en cuenta].
debonair (debone·øʳ) *adj.* afable, jovial.
Deborah (de·bora) *n. pr. f.* Débora.
debouch (to) (dibu·sh) *intr.* desembocar, salir.
debouchment (-mønt) *s.* desembocadura.
debris (debrı·) *s.* ruinas, escombros, restos. *2* GEOL. deyecciones.
debt (det) *s.* deuda, débito: *National* ~, deuda pública; *to run into* ~, endeudarse.
debtor (de·tøʳ) *s.* deudor.
debut (debiu·) *s.* TEAT. estreno, debut. *2* entrada en sociedad [de una joven].
debutant (-tan) *adj.-s.* debutante.
debutante (-tant) *adj.-s.* debutante. *2* díc. de la joven que hace su entrada en sociedad.
decade (de·keid) *s.* década, decenio.
decadence, -cy (de·kadøns, -si) *s.* decadencia, ocaso.
decadent (-ønt) *adj.-s.* decadente. *2* decadentista.
decagon (de·kagøn) *s.* GEOM. decágono.
decagram, decagramme (de·kagæm) *s.* decagramo.
decahedron (dekaji·drøn) *s.* GEOM. decaedro.
decalcomania (dikákoumei·nia) *s.* calcomanía.

decalitre, decaliter (de·kalitøʳ) *s.* decalitro.
decalogue (-log) *s.* decálogo.
decametre, decameter (-mitøʳ) *s.* decámetro.
decamp (to) (dikæ·mp) *intr.* decampar. *2* largarse, huir.
decanal (de·kanal) *adj.* del deán o del decano.
decant (to) (dikæ·nt) *tr.* decantar. *2* trasegar.
decantation (-ei·shøn) *s.* decantación. *2* trasiego.
decanter (dikæ·ntøʳ) *s.* ampolla, garrafa.
decapitate (to) (dikæ·piteit) *tr.* decapitar.
decapitation (-ei·shøn) *s.* decapitación.
decapod (de·kapad) *adj.-s.* ZOOL. decápodo.
decasyllable (dekasi·labøl) *s.* decasílabo.
decay (dikei·) *s.* decaimiento, decadencia. *2* ruina, desmedro. *3* putrefacción, podredumbre. *4* MED. caries.
decay (to) *intr.* decaer, descaecer, declinar, venir a menos. *2* arruinarse, deteriorarse. *3* pudrirse. *4* pasarse, marchitarse. *5* MED. cariarse. *6* tr. arruinar, echar a perder.
decease (disı·s) *s.* defunción, fallecimiento.
decease (to) *intr.* morir, fallecer.
deceased (-t) *adj.-s.* difunto, finado.
deceit (disı·t) *s.* engaño, dolo, falacia. *2* artificio, superchería.
deceitful (-ful) *adj.* engañoso, doloso, falaz. *2* falso, engañador.
deceivable (disı·vabøl) *adj.* engañadizo.
deceive (to) (disı·v) *tr.* engañar. *2* defraudar, burlar.
deceiver (-øʳ) *s.* engañador.
December (dise·mbøʳ) *s.* diciembre.
decemvir (dise·mvøʳ) *s.* decenviro.
decency (dı·sønsi) *s.* decencia. *2* decoro. *3 pl.* conveniencias sociales.
decennial (dise·nial) *adj.* decenal.
decennium (-niøm) *m.* decenio.
decent (dı·sønt) *adj.* decente. *2* razonable, regular.
decenter (to) (dise·ntøʳ) *tr.* to DECENTRE.
decentralize (to) (dıse·ntralaiś) *tr.* descentralizar.
decentre (to) (dise·ntøʳ) *tr.* descentrar.
deception (dise·pshøn) *s.* decepción, engaño.
deceptive (-tiv) *adj.* engañoso, falaz.
dechristianize (to) (dikri·stianaiś) *tr.* descristianizar.
decide (to) (disai·d) *tr.-intr.* decidir: *to* ~ *to,* decidir o decidirse a [hacer algo].
decided (-id) *adj.* decidido. *2* definido, indudable, categórico.
deciduous (-ŷuøs) *adj.* H. NAT. caedizo, caduco.
decigram(me (de·sigræm) *s.* decigramo.
decilitre, deciliter (-litøʳ) *s.* decilitro.
decimal (-mal) *adj.* decimal.
decimate (to) (-meit) *tr.* diezmar.
decimation (-ei·shøn) *s.* acción de diezmar. *2* estrago, mortandad.
decimetre, decimeter (-mitøʳ) *s.* decímetro.
decipher (to) (disai·føʳ) *tr.* descifrar.
decision (disı·ŷøn) *s.* decisión, resolución, acuerdo. *2* decisión, firmeza.
decisive (disai·siv) *adj.* decisivo. *2* conclusivo. *3* decidido, firme.
deck (dek) *s.* MAR. cubierta, puente: *between decks,* entrepuente. *2* MEC. sección o parte plana. *3* piso [de un autobús, etc.]. *4* techo [de vagón]. *5* baraja. *6* baceta, monte [en los naipes].
deck (to) *tr.* vestir, ataviar, adornar. *2* cubrir, revestir.
deckle o **deckle edge** (de·køl) *s.* barba [del papel].
declaim (to) (diklei·m) *intr.-tr.* declamar. *2 intr.* perorar.

declaimer (-ø^r) *s*. declamador, perorador.
declamation (-ei·shøn) *s*. declamación. *2* perorata.
declamatory (diklæ·matori) *adj*. declamatorio.
declaration (diklarei·shøn) *s*. declaración. *2* aserto. *3* manifiesto.
declarative, -tory (diklæ·rativ, -tori) *adj*. declaratorio. *2* afirmativo, enunciativo.
declare (to) (dikle·ø^r) *tr.-ref*. declarar. *2 tr*. manifestar, afirmar. *3* intr. *to ~ for* o *against*, declararse partidario o enemigo de.
declaredly (-idly) *adv*. declaradamente.
declension (dikle·nshøn) *s*. GRAM., MAGNET. declinación. *2* declive. *3* decadencia, caída.
declination (deklinei·shøn) *s*. ASTR., MAGNET. declinación. *2* desviación, apartamiento. *3* declive. *4* negativa, acción de rehusar.
decline (dikla·in) *s*. declinación, decadencia, ocaso, fin. *2* decaimiento, consunción. *3* mengua, baja. *4* declive.
decline (to) *tr*. inclinar, bajar. *2* desviar. *3* rehusar, negarse a; renunciar. *4* GRAM. declinar. *5* intr. inclinarse, bajar. *6* desviarse. *7* declinar, decaer, venir a menos. *8* menguar, ir de baja.
declivity (-viti) *s*. declividad, declive.
declutch (to) (dıclø·ch) *tr*. MEC. desembragar.
decoction (dika·kshøn) *s*. decocción, cocimiento.
decode (to) (dikou·d) *tr*. descifrar [lo escrito en cifra].
decollate (to) (dika·leit) *tr*. degollar, decapitar.
decollation (-lei·shøn) *s*. degollación.
decolleté (deikaltei·) *adj*. escotado [vestido].
decolorant (dika·lørant) *adj.-s*. decolorante.
decolo(u)rate (dika·løreit), **decolo(u)rize (to)** (-raiš) *tr*. decolorar, descolorar, descolorir.
decompose (to) (dikømpøu·š) *tr*. descomponer [separa los elementos de; pudrir]. *2* intr. descomponerse.
decomposition (dikampoši·shøn) *s*. descomposición.
decompression (dikømpre·shøn) *s*. descompresión.
decontaminate (to) (dikøntæ·mineit) *tr*. desinfectar.
decorate (to) (de·køreit) *tr*. decorar, adornar, embellecer. *2* condecorar.
decoration (-rei·shøn) *s*. decoración, ornamentación; ornamento, adorno. *2* condecoración.
decorative (de·kørativ) *adj*. decorativo, ornamental.
decorator (-reitø^r) *s*. decorador, adornista.
decorous (de·kørøs) *adj*. decoroso, correcto.
decorticate (to) (diko·^rtikeit) *tr*. descortezar, mondar, pelar.
decorum (diko·røm) *s*. decoro.
decoy (dikoi·) *s*. señuelo, reclamo, cimbel. *2* añagaza. *3* entruchón, gancho [pers.].
decoy (to) *tr*. reclamar, atraer con señuelo. *2* atraer a un peligro, emboscada, etc.
decrease (dikrı·s) *s*. decrecimiento, disminución. *2* menguante [de la luna].
decrease (to) *intr*. decrecer, disminuir, menguar. *2 tr*. disminuir, reducir.
decreasing (-ing) *adj*. decreciente.
decree (dikrı·) *s*. decreto, orden, edicto, mandato.
decree (to) *tr*. decretar, ordenar, mandar.
decrement (de·krimønt) *s*. decremento.
decrepit (dikre·pit) *adj*. decrépito, caduco.
decrepitude (-tiud) *s*. decrepitud, caduquez.
decrescent (dikre·sønt) *adj*. decreciente.
decretal (dikrı·tal) *adj.-s*. decretal. *2 s. pl*. decretales.

decrial (dikrai·al) *s*. descrédito, rebaja, censura.
decrier (-ø^r) *s*. censurador, denigrador.
decry (to) (dikrai·) *tr*. desacreditar, rebajar, censurar. *2* desvalorizar.
decubitus (dikiu·bitøs) *s*. decúbito.
decumbent (dikø·mbønt) *adj*. decumbente.
decuple (de·kiupøl) *adj.-s*. décuplo.
decuple (to) *tr*. decuplicar.
decurion (dikiu·riøn) *s*. decurión.
decurrent (dikø·rønt) *adj*. BOT. decurrente.
decussate (dikø·seit) *adj*. decusado.
dedicate (to) (de·dikeit) *tr*. dedicar [un libro, etc.].
dedication (-ei·shøn) *s*. dedicación. *2* dedicatoria. *3* advocación [de una iglesia].
deduce (to) (didiu·s) *tr*. deducir, inferir. *2* hacer derivar.
deducible (-ibøl) *adj*. deducible, inferible.
deduct (to) (didø·kt) *tr*. deducir, rebajar, descontar, restar.
deduction (didø·kshøn) *s*. deducción, rebaja, descuento. *2* deducción, inferencia.
deductive (-tiv) *adj*. deductivo.
deed (dıd) *s*. hecho; acción, obra, acto; realidad: *in ~*, de hecho, en verdad. *2* hazaña, proeza. *3* DER. escritura, instrumento.
deed (to) *tr*. DER. transferir por escritura o instrumento.
deem (to) (dım) *tr.-intr*. juzgar, creer, pensar, estimar, considerar.
deep (dıp) *adj*. hondo, profundo. *2* espeso [nieve, etc.]. *3* alta [hierba]. *4* hundido, sumergido [en]; cubierto [de]. *5* impenetrable, abstruso. *6* penetrante, sagaz. *7* astuto. *8* grave, grande. *9* absorto, embebido, enfrascado, muy metido [en]. *10* agudo, intenso, extremo, cordial. *11* grave [sonido]. *12* oscuro [color]. *13* riguroso [luto]. *14* de profundidad, de espesor; hundido hasta [cierta profundidad].
    15 adv. hondamente, profundamente, muy, mucho. *16* muy adentro: *~ into the night*, muy entrada la noche.
    17 s. profundidad. *18* piélago, abismo, sima. *19* misterio.
-deep, elemento final de compuestos como: *ankle-deep, knee-deep*, metido hasta los tobillos, las rodillas.
deep-chested *adj*. ancho de pecho.
deepen (to) (-øn) *tr*. ahondar, intensificar. *2* oscurecer. *3* hacer más grave [un sonido]. *4* intr. ahondarse, intensificarse, oscurecerse, hacerse más grave.
deep-felt *adj*. hondamente sentido.
deep-laid *adj*. dispuesto con astucia.
deepness (-nis) *s*. profundidad, intensidad. *2* penetración, sagacidad.
deep-rooted *adj*. profundamente arraigado.
deer (di·ø^r) *s*. ZOOL. ciervo, venado: *red ~*, ciervo común; *fallow ~*, gramo.
deerskin (-skin) *s*. piel de venado.
deface (to) (difei·s) *tr*. borrar, desfigurar, mutilar, estropear, afear.
defacement (-mønt) *s*. desfiguración, mutilación, estropeo, afeamiento.
de facto (di·fæ·ctou) *loc*. de hecho.
defalcate (to) (difæ·lkeit) *intr*. desfalcar, cometer desfalcos.
defalcation (-ei·shøn) *s*. desfalco.
defamation (defamei·shøn) *s*. difamación, infamación.
defamatory (difæ·matori) *adj*. difamatorio, infamatorio.

defame (to) (difei·m) *tr.* difamar, infamar.
defamer (-ø^r) *s.* difamador, infamador.
default (difo·lt) *s.* falta, defecto, carencia. 2 descuido, negligencia; incumplimiento; falta de pago. 3 no comparecencia; DER. rebeldía.
default (to) *tr.-intr.* dejar de cumplir, faltar [a un deber, obligación, etc.]; no pagar. 2 *intr.* DEP. no comparecer, estar en rebeldía. 3 *tr.* DER. declarar en rebeldía.
defaulter (-ø^r) *s.* el que falta o no cumple. 2 desfalcador. 3 DER. rebelde.
defeat (difi·t) *s.* derrota, vencimiento. 2 frustración.
defeat (to) *tr.* derrotar, vencer. 2 desbaratar, frustrar. 3 DER. anular.
defeatist (-ist) *adj.-s.* derrotista.
defecate (to) (de·fikeit) *tr.-intr.* defecar.
defecation (-ei·shøn) *s.* defecación.
defect (dife·kt) *s.* defecto.
defection (dife·kshøn) *s.* defección.
defective (dife·ktiv) *adj.* defectivo, defectuoso. 2 GRAM. defectivo. 3 corto, deficiente. 4 *s.* PSIC. deficiente [pers.].
defence (dife·ns) *s.* defensa. 2 *pl.* FORT. defensas.
defenceless (-lis) *adj.* indefenso, inerme.
defend (to) (dife·nd) *tr.-ref.* defender.
defendant (-ant) *adj.* que defiende. 2 *s.* DER. demandado; acusado, procesado.
defender (-ø^r) *s.* defensor. 2 campeón, abogado.
defense, defenseless, etc. = DEFENCE, DEFENCELESS, etc.
defensible (dife·nsibøl) *adj.* defendible.
defensive (-siv) *adj.* defensivo. 2 *s.* defensiva: *on the ~,* a la defensiva.
defer (to) (difø·^{r}) *tr.* diferir, aplazar, retardar. 2 remitir [al juicio, etc. de]. 3 esperar. 4 *to ~ to,* deferir a, ceder a. ¶ Pret. y p. p.: *deferred;* ger.: -*rring.*
deference (de·førøns) *s.* deferencia.
deferent (-ønt) *adj.* deferente, respetuoso. 2 ASTR., ANAT. deferente.
deferential (deføre·nshal) *adj.* DEFERENT 1.
deferment (difø·^{r}mønt) *s.* dilación, aplazamiento.
deferred (difø·rd) *pret.* y *p. p.* de TO DEFER.
defiance (difai·ans) *s.* desafío, reto, provocación: *to bid ~ to, to set at ~,* desafiar; *in ~ of,* a despecho de.
defiant (-ant) *adj.* desafiador, provocativo.
deficiency (difi·shønsi) *s.* deficiencia. 2 falta, insuficiencia. 3 COM. déficit. 4 MED. carencia.
deficient (-shønt) *adj.* deficiente. 2 falto, insuficiente. 3 faltante.
deficit (de·fisit) *s.* déficit. 2 *adj.* deficitario.
defier (difai·ø^r) *s.* desafiador, retador.
defilade (to) (defilei·d) *tr.* MIL. desenfilar.
defile (di·fail) *s.* desfiladero.
defile (to) (difai·l) *tr.* manchar, ensuciar. 2 mancillar, deshonrar, profanar. 3 *intr.* MIL. desfilar.
defilement (-mønt) *s.* ensuciamiento. 2 mancilla, deshonra, profanación.
define (to) (difai·n) *tr.* definir. 2 delimitar, circunscribir. 3 distinguir, caracterizar.
definite (de·finit) *adj.* definido: *~ article,* artículo definido o determinado. 2 claro, preciso, terminante.
definition (defini·shøn) *s.* definición. 2 precisión, claridad [de una imagen, etc.].
definitive (difi·nitiv) *adj.* definitivo. 2 definido. 3 que distingue o define.
definitor (definai·tø^r) *s.* ECLES. definidor.

deflagrate (to) (de·flagreit) *intr.* deflagrar. 2 *tr.* hacer deflagrar.
deflate (to) (diflei·t) *tr.* desinflar, deshinchar. 2 ECON. reducir la inflación. 3 *intr.* deshincharse.
deflation (-ei·shøn) *s.* desinflamiento. 2 ECON. deflación.
deflect (to) (difle·kt) *tr.* desviar, apartar. 2 *intr.* desviarse, apartarse.
deflection (difle·kshøn) *s.* desvío, desviación. 2 MEC. deflexión.
defloration (deflorei·shøn) *s.* desfloración. 2 desflorecimiento. 3 selección.
deflower (to) (diflau·ø^r) *tr.* desflorar [ajar, deslustrar; violar]. 3 despojar de flores.
defoliate (to) (difou·lieit) *tr.* deshojar. 2 *intr.* deshojarse.
deforce (to) (difo·^{r}s) *tr.* DER. detentar.
deforest (to) (difa·rist) *tr.* despoblar de árboles.
deform (to) (difo·^{r}m) *tr.* deformar. 2 desfigurar, afear. 3 degradar, envilecer.
deformed (-d) *adj.* deformado. 3 deforme, feo, monstruoso.
deformity (-iti) *s.* deformidad, fealdad.
defrauder (-ø^r) *s.* defraudador.
defraud (to) (difro·d) *tr.* defraudar, estafar.
defray (to) (difrei·) *tr.* costear, sufragar, pagar.
defrayal (-al) *s.* pago, acción de costear o sufragar.
defreeze (to) (difrı·š) *tr.* descongelar.
deft (deft) *s.* ágil, diestro, hábil, mañoso.
defunct (difø·nkt) *adj.-s.* difunto.
defy (to) (difai·) *tr.* desafiar. 2 retar, provocar. 3 arrostrar. 4 despreciar, contravenir.
degeneracy (didÿe·nørasi) *s.* degeneración. 2 degradación, perversión.
degenerate (-nørit) *adj.-s.* degenerado.
degenerate (to) (-nøreit) *intr.* degenerar.
degeneration (-ei·shøn) *s.* degeneración.
deglutition (digluti·shøn) *s.* deglución.
degradation (degradei·shøn) *s.* degradación. 2 degeneración, disminución, deterioro.
degrade (to) (digrei·d) *tr.* degradar. 2 minorar, rebajar, reducir. 3 *intr.* degradarse.
degrading (-ing) *adj.* degradante.
degrease (to) (digrı·s) *tr.* desgrasar.
degree (digrı·) *s.* grado [en todas sus acepciones, menos en la de voluntad, gusto y en la de grado militar]: *by degrees,* gradualmente; *to a ~,* algo, en cierto modo, hasta cierto punto; sumamente. 2 rango, categoría.
degustation (digøstei·shøn) *f.* degustación.
dehiscence (diji·søns) *s.* BOT. dehiscencia.
dehiscent (-sønt) *adj.* BOT. dehiscente.
dehorn (to) (dijø·^{r}n) *tr.* descornar.
dehumanize (dijiu·manaiš·) *tr.* deshumanizar.
dehydrate (to) (dıjai·dreit) *tr.* deshidratar.
deice (to) (dıaı·s) *tr.* AVIA. descongelar.
deicide (dı·isaid) *s.* deicida. 2 deicidio.
deific(al (dii·fik(al) *adj.* deifico.
deify (to) (dı·ifai) *tr.* deificar, divinizar.
deign (to) (dein) *intr.* dignarse. 2 *tr.* dignarse dar.
deigning (-ing) *s.* dignación.
Deipara (dıi·para) *adj.* deípara.
deism (dı·išm) *s.* deísmo.
deist (dı·ist) *s.* deísta.
deity (dı·iti) *s.* deidad. 2 *the Deity,* Dios.
deject (to) (didÿe·kt) *tr.* abatir, desanimar.
dejected (-id) *adj.* abatido, desanimado.
dejection (didÿe·kshøn) *s.* abatimiento, desánimo. 2 FISIOL. deyección.
delate (to) (dilei·t) *tr.* delatar, denunciar.
delation (-ei·shøn) *s.* delación.

delay (dilei) *s.* dilación, demora, tardanza, retraso.

delay (to) *tr.* dilatar, diferir, aplazar, retardar, demorar. *2 intr.* tardar, retrasarse, entretenerse.

delectable (dile·ktabøl) *adj.* deleitable, deleitoso.

delectation (ei·shøn) *s.* deleite, delectación.

delegacy (de·løgasi) *s.* DELEGATION.

delegate (de·løgeit) *adj.-s.* delegado, comisionado. *2 s.* lugarteniente, comisario.

delegate (to) (tr. delegar, comisionar, diputar.

delegation (-ei·shøn) *s.* delegación, diputación, comisión.

delete (to) (dilı·t) *tr.* borrar, tachar, suprimir.

deleterious (deløti·riøs) *adj.* deletéreo. *2* nocivo, pernicioso.

deletion (dilı·shøn) *s.* tachadura, supresión.

deliberate (dili·børit) *adj.* deliberado, premeditado, hecho de intento. *2* cauto, circunspecto. *3* lento, pausado.

deliberate (to) (-børeit) *tr.* reflexionar, pensar, considerar, premeditar. *2 intr.* deliberar, consultar. *3* vacilar, dudar.

deliberately (-ly) *adv.* deliberadamente. *2* a sabiendas. *3* pausadamente.

deliberation (-ei·shøn) *s.* deliberación, premeditación, reflexión. *2* deliberación [acción de deliberar].

deliberative (dili·børativ) *adj.* deliberativo. *2* deliberante.

delicacy (de·likasi) *s.* delicadeza, delicadez. *2* finura, sensibilidad [de un instrumento, etc.]. *3* exigencia, miramiento. *4* refinamiento, exquisitez, primor. *5* cosa delicada, lujo, golosina.

delicate (de·likit) *adj.* delicado. *2* mirado, considerado. *3* exquisito, primoroso. *4* de gusto exigente.

delicateness (-nis) *adj.* delicadeza, delicadez.

delicatessen (delikate·søn) *s. pl.* fiambre, queso, conservas, etc.; tienda en que se venden.

delicious (dili·shøs) *adj.* delicioso. *2* sabroso.

delight (dilai·t) *s.* deleite, delicia, placer, gozo, encanto.

delight (to) *tr.* deleitar, encantar, dar gusto, recrear. *2 intr.* deleitarse, gozarse, complacerse.

delightful (-ful) *adj.* deleitable, deleitoso, delicioso, ameno, exquisito, encantador.

delightsome (-søm) *adj.* deleitoso, placentero.

Delilah (dilai·la) *n. pr.* Dalila.

delimit(ate) (to) (dili·mit(eit) *tr.* delimitar.

delineament (-niamønt) *s.* DELINEATION.

delineate (to) (-nieit) *tr.* delinear, trazar, bosquejar. *2* pintar, describir.

delineation (-ei·shøn) *s.* delineación, traza, bosquejo. *2* pintura, descripción.

delineator (-nieitøʳ) *s.* delineador, dibujante.

delinquency (dili·nkuønsi) *s.* delincuencia. *2* culpa, falta.

delinquent (-kuønt) *adj.-s.* delincuente, culpable. *2* moroso [deudor].

delisquesce (to) (delikue·s) *intr.* liquidarse lentamente.

deliquescence (-øns) *s.* delicuescencia.

deliquescent (-ønt) *adj.* delicuescente.

delirious (dili·riøs) *adj.* delirante, desvariado.

delirium (-riøm) *s.* delirio, desvarío. *2* MED. ~ *tremens,* delirium tremens.

deliver (to) (dili·vøʳ) *tr.* libertar. *2* librar, salvar. *3* entregar, dar; rendir, resignar. ~ *Gralte.* con *over o up. 4* despachar [un pedido]; repartir [géneros, correspondencia]. *5* descargar [un golpe]; lanzar, tirar. *6* recitar; pronunciar [dis-

cursos]; emitir [conceptos]. *7 to be delivered of a child,* dar a luz un hijo.

deliverance (-ans) *s.* liberación, rescate, salvación. *2* DER. traspaso. *3* dictamen, declaración.

deliverer (-øʳ) *s.* libertador, salvador. *2* entregador. *3* repartidor [de paquetes, etc.].

delivery (-i) *s.* liberación, rescate. *2* entrega, dación. *3* remesa, reparto [de géneros o correspondencia]. *4* lo entregado. *5* pronunciación [de un discurso, etc.], elocuencia, dicción; manera de expresarse o de cantar. *6* DEP. acción o manera de tirar o lanzar. *7* parto, alumbramiento.

dell (del) *s.* hondonada, cañada, vallecito.

delouse (to) (dilou·s) *tr.* despiojar.

Delphian (de·lfian), **Delphic** (-fik) *adj.* délfico.

delta (de·lta) *s.* delta.

deltoid (-oid) *adj.-s.* deltoides.

delude (to) (diliu·d) *tr.* engañar, deludir.

deluding (-ing) *adj.* engañoso, delusorio.

deluge (de·liudỹ) *s.* diluvio. *2* inundación.

deluge (to) *tr.* inundar.

delusion (dilui·ỹøn) *s.* engaño, decepción, error, ilusión.

delusive (-siv), **delusory** (-sori) *adj.* engañoso, delusivo, mentiroso, ilusorio.

delve (to) (delv) *tr.-intr.* cavar, ahondar, inquirir, escudriñar.

demagnetize (to) (dımæ·gnetaiš) *tr.* desimantar.

demagogic (demaga·dŷik) *adj.* demagógico.

demagogue (de·magag) *s.* demagogo.

demagogy (-gadŷi) *s.* demagogia.

demand (dımæ·nd) *s.* demanda, petición, requerimiento; *on ~,* COM. a la presentación. *2* COM., ECON., DER. demanda. *3* pregunta.

demand (to) *tr.* demandar, pedir, requerir, exigir, reclamar. *2* preguntar.

demandant (-ant) *s.* DER. demandante.

demanding (-ing) *adj.* exigente.

demarcate (to) (dima·ʳkeit) *tr.* demarcar, deslindar.

demarcation (-kei·shøn) *s.* demarcación, deslinde.

demarche (dema·ʳsh) *s.* paso, gestión.

demean (to) (dimı·n) *tr.* rebajar, degradar. *2 ref.* portarse, conducirse. *3* rebajarse, degradarse.

demeano(u)r (-øʳ) *s.* conducta, comportamiento. *2* aire, porte.

dement (to) (dime·nt) *tr.* dementar, enloquecer.

demented (-id) *adj.* demente, insano.

dementia (dime·nshia) *s.* demencia, locura.

demerit (dime·rit) *s.* demérito, desmerecimiento.

demesne (dimeı·n o -mın) *s.* heredad. *2* región, territorio. *3* fig. dominio, campo.

demi- (de·mi-) *pref.* semi-.

demigod (-gad) *s.* semidiós.

demijohn (-dỹan) *s.* damajuana, castaña.

demilitarize (to) (dımi·litaraiš) *tr.* desmilitarizar.

demineralization (dıminørališei·shøn) *s.* MED. desmineralización.

demise (dimai·š) *s.* fallecimiento. *2* transmisión de la corona. *2* DER. transmisión de dominio.

demise (to) *tr.* DER. transmitir, transferir.

demi-semi-quaver (-ʳ) *s.* MÚS. fusa.

demission (dimi·shøn) *s.* dimisión, abdicación.

demit (to) (dimi·t) *tr.* dimitir, renunciar.

demiurge (de·miøʳdỹ) *s.* demiurgo.

demobilize (to) (dımou·bilaiš) *tr.* MIL. desmovilizar.

democracy (dima·krasi) *s.* democracia.

democrat (de·møkræt) *s.* demócrata.

democratic (al (-ik(al) *adj.* democrático.

democratize (to) (dima·krataiš) *tr.* democratizar.

demographic (dimogræ·fik) *adj.* demográfico.
demography (dima·grafi) *s.* demografía.
demoiselle (demuaše·l) *s.* ORN. zaida.
demolish (to) (dima·lish) *tr.* demoler. *2* arrasar, derruir, destruir.
demolishment (-mønt), **demolition** (-shøn) *s.* demolición. *2* destrucción.
demon (-dımøn) *m.* demonio.
demonetize (to) (dima·netaiš) *tr.* desmonetizar.
demoniac (dimou·niæk) *adj.* demoníaco. *2 adj.-s.* endemoniado, energúmeno.
demoniacal (dimønai·akal) *adj.* DEMONIAC 1.
demonology (dimøna·lodỹi) *s.* demonología.
demonstrable (dima·nstrabøl) *adj.* demostrable.
demonstrate (to) (de·mønstrei·t) *tr.* demostrar, hacer ver, probar.
demonstration (-ei·shøn) *s.* demostración. *2* COM. exposición, presentación [de un artículo]. *3* manifestación pública.
demonstrative (dima·nstrativ) *adj.* demostrativo.
demonstrator (de·mønstreitø^r) *s.* demostrador. *2* POL. manifestante.
demoralize (to) (dima·ralaiš) *tr.* desmoralizar.
Demosthenes (dima·szønis) *n. pr.* Demóstenes.
demotic (dima·tik) *adj.* demótico.
demount (to) (dımau·nt) *tr.* desmontar, desarmar.
demulcent (dimø·lsønt) *adj.* demulcente.
demur (dimø·^{r}) *s.* irresolución, vacilación. *2* objeción, escrúpulo, reparo.
demur (to) *intr.* objetar, poner dificultades. *2* vacilar, fluctuar. ¶ Pret. y p. p.: *demurred;* ger.: *-rring.*
demure (dimiu·^{r}) *adj.* grave, serio, formal. *2* recatado. *3* gazmoño.
demurrage (dimø·ridỹ) *s.* COM. estadía.
demurrer (dimø·rø^r) *s.* el que objeta o pone reparos. *2* DER. excepción.
den (den) *s.* cubil, guarida. *2* cueva, antro. *3* cochitril. *4* fig. rincón, cuarto de estudio o retiro.
denarius (dine·riøs) *s.* denario.
denationalize (to) (dınæ·shønalaiš) *tr.* desnacionalizar.
denaturalize (to) (-churlaiš) *tr.* desnaturalizar.
denature (to) (dınei·chø^r) *tr.* QUÍM. desnaturalizar.
dendrite (de·ndrait) *s.* dendrita.
dendrology (dendra·lodỹi) *s.*dendrología.
denegation (denigei·shøn) *s.* negación, negativa.
dengue (de·ngei) *s.* MED. dengue.
deniable (dinai·abøl) *adj.* negable.
denial (dinai·al) *s.* negación, negativa, contradicción. *2* denegación, negativa.
denier (dinai·ø^r) *s.* negador, contradictor.
denier (deni·ø^r) *s.* dinero [moneda, medida].
denigrate (to) (de·nigreit) *tr.* denigrar. *2* ennegrecer.
denigration (-ei·shøn) *s.* denigración.
Denis, Denys (de·nis) *n. pr. m.* Dionisio.
denizen (de·nišøn) *s.* ciudadano, vecino, habitante. *2* (Ingl.) extranjero naturalizado.
Denmark (de·nma^{r}k) *n. pr.* GEOGR. Dinamarca.
denominate (to) (dina·mineit) *tr.* denominar, llamar.
denomination (-ei·shøn) *s.* denominación. *2* clase, categoría. *3* secta, comunión.
denominative (-eitiv) *adj.* denominativo.
denominator (-eitø^r) *s.* MAT. denominador.
denote (to) (dinou·t) *tr.* denotar. *2* indicar, señalar.
denouement (deinu·man) *s.* desenlace.
denounce (to) (dinau·ns) *tr.* denunciar. *2* anunciar, presagiar.
denouncement (-mønt) *s.* denunciación, denuncia.

dense (dens) *adj.* denso, espeso, apretado, tupido. *2* crasa [ignorancia]; profunda [estupidez]. *3* estúpido.
denseness (-nis) *s.* densidad, espesor. *2* estupidez.
densimeter (densi·mitø^r) *s.* densímetro.
density (de·nsiti) *s.* densidad. *2* espesor [de un bosque, etc.].
dent (dent) *s.* mella, escotadura, hoyo, abolladura. *2* MEC. diente.
dent (to) *tr.* mellar, abollar.
dental (de·ntal) *adj.* dental, dentario; ~ *surgeon,* dentista. *2 s.* dental [consonante].
dentate (d (de·nteit(id) *adj.* BOT., ZOOL. dentado.
denticle (de·ntikøl) *s.* dentículo.
denticulate (d (denti·kiuleit(id) *adj.* denticulado.
dentifrice (de·ntifris) *adj.-s.* dentífrico.
dentil (-til) *s.* ARQ. dentículo, dentellón.
dentilabial (dentilei·bial) *adj.* FONÉT. labiodental.
dentin(e (de·ntin) *s.* ANAT. dentina.
dentirostral (dentira·stral) *adj.* ORN. dentirrostro.
dentist (de·ntist) *s.* dentista.
dentistry (-ri) *s.* cirugía dental, odontología.
dentition (denti·shøn) *s.* dentición. *2* dentadura.
denture (de·nchø^r) *s.* dentadura [esp. la postiza].
denudation (diniudei·shøn) *s.* denudación.
denude (to) (diniu·d) *tr.* denudar, desnudar, despojar.
denunciate (to) (dinø·nshieit) *tr.* TO DENOUNCE.
denunciation (-ei·shøn) *s.* denuncia, acusación, estigmatización pública. *2* denuncia [de un tratado].
denutrition (dınutri·shøn) *s.* desnutrición.
deny (to) (dinai·) *tr.* negar: *to* ~ *oneself,* negarse a sí mismo; negarse a recibir [a uno].
deodar (dı·oda^r) *s.* BOT. cedro, deodara.
deodorant (diou·dørant) *adj.-s.* desodorante.
deodorize (to) (-raiš) *tr.* desodorar.
deodorizer (-ø^r) *s.* desodorante.
deontology (dianta·lodỹi) *s.* deontología.
deoxidize (to) (dıa·csidaiš) *tr.* QUÍM. desoxidar.
depart (to) (dipa·^{r}t) *intr.* partir, salir, irse, retirarse. *2* morir: *the departed,* los difuntos. *3* apartarse, desviarse, salirse de; desistir: *to* ~ *from life,* morir.
department (-mønt) *s.* departamento, ministerio, ramo, sección, negociado, despacho.
departmental (-tal) *adj.* de un ramo o departamento.
departure (dipa·^{r}chu^r) *s.* partida, marcha, salida. *2* muerte, fallecimiento. *3* apartamiento, desviación, abandono [de una regla, proceder, plan, etc.].
depauperate (to) (dıpo·pørei·t) *tr.* depauperar.
depauperize (to) (dıpo·pøraiš) *tr.* librar de pobres. *2* sacar de la pobreza.
depend (to) (dipe·nd) *intr.* pender, colgar. *2* depender. *3* estar pendiente, sin decidir. *4 to* ~ *on,* o *upon,* depender de, estribar en; confiar en, contar con, estar seguro de.
dependable (-abøl) *adj.* seguro, fidedigno, confiable.
dependant (-ant) *s.* DEPENDENT 4.
dependence (-døns) *s.* dependencia [subordinación; estado de lo condicionado, anexo o que se sigue a una cosa]. *2* dependencia [de otros para cubrir las propias necesidades]. *3* confianza, fe, seguridad. *4* apoyo, sostén; aquello con que se cuenta.
dependency (-si) *s.* DEPENDENCE 2. *2* dependencia [lo que depende]. *3* posesión, protectorado.
dependent (dipe·ndønt) *adj.* dependiente. *2* subor-

dinado, anexo. *3* pendiente, colgante. *4 s.* persona mantenida por otra, carga de familia.
depict (dipi·kt), **depicture (to)** (dipi·kchø^r) *tr.* pintar, representar, retratar, describir.
depilate (to) (de·pileit) *tr.* depilar.
depilation (-ei·shøn) *s.* depilación.
depilatory (dipi·latori) *adj.-s.* depilatorio.
deplete (to) (diplı·t) *tr.* vaciar, agotar, esquilmar.
depletion (diplı·shøn) *s.* vaciamiento, agotamiento.
deplorable (diplo·rbøl) *adj.* deplorable, lamentable, lastimoso.
deplore (to) (diplo·^r) *tr.* deplorar, lamentar, llorar.
deploy (to) (diploi·) *tr.* MIL. desplegar. *2 intr.* MIL. desplegarse.
deployment (-mønt) *s.* MIL. despliegue.
deplume (to) (dıplu·m) *tr.* desplumar.
depolarize (dıpou·laraiš) *tr.* FÍS. despolarizar.
depone (to) (dipou·n) *tr.-intr.* DEPOSE 2.
deponent (-ønt) *adj.* GRAM. deponente. *2 s.* DER. deponente. *3* verbo deponente.
depopulate (to) (dıpa·piuleit) *tr.* despoblar, deshabitar. *2 intr.* despoblarse [de habitantes].
depopulation (-ei·shøn) *s.* despoblación.
deport (to) (dipo·rt) *tr.* deportar, desterrar. *2 to ~ oneself*, portarse, conducirse.
deportation (-ei·shøn) *s.* deportación.
deportment (dipo·^rtmønt) *s.* conducta, proceder, comportamiento, porte, maneras.
deposal (dipou·šal) *s.* DEPOSITION 1.
depose (to) (dipou·š) *tr.* deponer, destronar, destituir. *2 tr.-intr.* deponer, declarar.
deposit (dipa·šit) *s.* depósito [cosa depositada; poso, sedimento]: *on ~*, en depósito. *2* arras, señal. *3* GEOL. yacimiento.
deposit (to)) *tr.* depositar. *2* sedimentar. *3 intr.* depositarse, sedimentarse.
depositary (-eri) *s.* depositario. *2* depósito, almacén.
deposition (depøši·shøn) *s.* deposición, destitución. *2* B. ART. descendimiento. *3* DER. deposición, declaración. *4* depósito [acción].
depositor (dipa·šitø^r) *s.* depositante; cuentacorrentista, imponente.
depository (-tori) *s.* depositaria; depósito [donde se deposita]. *2* depositario.
depot (dı·pou) *s.* depósito, almacén. *2* MIL., FISIOL. depósito. *3* FERROC. (E.U.) estación.
depravation (depravei·shøn) *s.* depravación.
deprave (to) (diprei·v) *tr.* depravař. *2* corromper, viciar.
depravity (dipræ·viti) *s.* depravación. *2* acción depravada.
deprecate (to) (de·prikeit) *tr.* deprecar. *2* desaprobar, censurar.
deprecation (-ei·shøn) *s.* deprecación. *2* desaprobación.
depreciate (diprı·shieit) *tr.* depreciar. *2* despreciar, desestimar, rebajar. *3 intr.* depreciarse.
depreciation (-ei·shøn) *s.* depreciación. *2* desprecio, desestimación.
depredate (to) (de·prideit) *tr.* depredar.
depredation (-ei·shøn) *s.* depredación. *2 pl.* estragos.
depress (to) (dipre·s) *tr.* deprimir. *2* abatir, desanimar. *3* bajar, inclinar. *4* disminuir la actividad, bajar el tono, el precio, de. *5* MAT. reducir el grado de.
depression (dipre·shøn) *s.* depresión. *2* abatimiento, desánimo. *3* crisis [económica].
depressive (-siv) *adj.* depresivo. *2* deprimente.

deprivación (deprivei·shøn) *s.* privación, desposesión. *2* falta, carencia, pérdida.
deprive (to) (diprai·v) *tr.* privar, despojar, desposeer. *2* destituir.
depth (depz) *s.* profundidad, hondura. *2* grueso, espesor. *3* fondo [lo más profundo o alejado], lo hondo. *4* abismo. *5* mitad, corazón: *in the ~ of night*, en mitad de la noche. *6* gravedad [del sonido], intensidad [del color]. *7* sagacidad. *8* MAR. puntal. *9 out of one's ~*, perdiendo pie [en el agua]; metido en algo superior a los alcances de uno.
depurate (to) (de·piureit) *tr.* depurar, purificar.
depurative (-iv) *adj.-s.* MED. depurativo.
deputation (depiutei·shøn) *s.* diputación, delegación, comisión.
depute (to) (dipiu·t) *tr.* diputar, delegar. *2* nombrar [a uno] agente, comisario o lugarteniente.
deputy (de·piuti) *s.* diputado. *2* delegado, agente, comisario, lugarteniente. *3 adj.* segundo, teniente, vice.
derail (to) (direi·l) *tr.* hacer descarrilar. *2 intr.* descarrilar.
derailment (-mønt) *s.* descarrilamiento.
derange (to) (direi·ndỹ) *tr.* desarreglar, descomponer, trastornar. *2* trastornar el juicio a. *3* interrumpir, estorbar.
derangement (-mønt) *s.* desarreglo, desconcierto. *2* perturbación mental.
deratization (dıræ·tišei·shøn) *s.* desratización.
Derby (dø·^rbi) *n. pr.* GEOGR. Derby. *2* carrera anual de caballos que se celebra en Epsom (Inglaterra).
derby *s.* (E.U.) sombrero hongo.
derelict (de·rølikt) *adj.* derrelicto, abandonado. *2* negligente. *3 s.* MAR. derrelicto. *4* persona o cosa abandonada.
dereliction (derøli·kshøn) *s.* abandono, dejación. *2* desamparo. *3* negligencia culpable.
deride (to) (dirai·d) *tr.* burlarse, mofarse de, ridiculizar.
derision (diri·ỹøn) *s.* mofa, escarnio, irrisión.
derisive (dirai·siv) *adj.* de burla, de mofa.
derisory (-sori) *adj.* DERISIVE. *2* irrisorio, ridículo.
derivation (derivei·shøn) *s.* derivación [deducción, descendencia]. *2* GRAM., MAT., MED. derivación. *3* origen, procedencia, derivo.
derivative (diri·vativ) *adj.-s.* derivativo. *2* derivado. *3 s.* MAT. derivada.
derive (to) (dirai·v) *tr.* derivar, sacar, deducir. *2* GRAM., ELECT. derivar. *3 intr.* derivar, derivarse, provenir.
derived (-d) *adj.* derivado. *2* ELECT. en derivación.
derm (dø·^rm), **derma** (dø·^rma) *s.* dermis.
dermal (dø·^rmal) *adj.* DERMIC.
dermatology (dø·^rmata·lødỹi) *s.* dermatología.
dermic (dø·^rmik) *adj.* dérmico, cutáneo.
dermis (dø·^rmis) *s.* DERM.
derogate (to) (de·røgeit) *intr. to ~ from*, restar, mermar, ser en mengua de; obrar de manera que desdice del [rango, posición, etc. de uno].
derogation (-eishøn) *s.* derogación, mengua, menoscabo. *2* acción de desdecir de.
derogative (dira·gativ), **derogatory** (-tori) *adj.* que rebaja o menoscaba, que es en mengua o desprecio de. *2* despectivo.
derrick (de·rik) *s.* grúa, cabria. *2* torre de perforación o extracción [de petróleo, etc.].
dervish (dø·^rvish) *s.* derviche.
descant (de·skænt) *intr.* comentar, disertar [sobre].

descend (to) (dise·nd) *intr.* descender; bajar: *to ~ from*, descender de, derivarse de; *to ~ to*, descender a, rebajarse a. *2* caer [la lluvia, etc.]. *3 to ~ on* o *upon*, caer sobre, invadir, hacer un desembarco en. *4 tr.* bajar [recorrer bajando].

descendant (-ant) *adj.-s.* descendiente. *2 adj.* descendente.

descendent (-ønt) *adj.* descendente. *2* descendiente.

descending (-ing) *adj.* descendente.

descent (-dise·nt) *s.* descenso, bajada, baja; caida. *2* nacimiento, origen, linaje, abolengo. *3* descendencia. *4* grado descendente; generación. *5* pendiente, bajada; escalera. *6* MIL. incursión, desembarco.

describe (to) (diskrai·b) *tr.* describir.

description (diskri·pshøn) *s.* descripción. *2* clase, género, especie, calidad, linaje.

descriptive (-tiv) *adj.* descriptivo.

descry (to) (diskrai·) *tr.* descubrir, avistar, divisar, distinguir, columbrar. ¶ Pret. y p. p.: *descried*.

desecrate (to) (de·sicreit) *tr.* profanar.

desensitize (to) (dise·nsitaiš) *tr.* desensibilizar.

1) desert (dišø·ʳt) *s.* mérito, valía. *2 pl.* merecimiento, merecido, premio o castigo merecido.

2) desert (de·šøʳt) *adj.* desierto. *2 s.* desierto, yermo.

desert (to) (dišø·ʳt) *tr.* abandonar, dejar, desemparar. *2 tr.-intr.* desertar.

deserter (-øʳ) *m.* desertor, tránsfuga.

desertion (dišø·ʳshøn) *s.* abandono, desamparo. *2* deserción.

deserve (to) (dišø·ʳv) *tr.-intr.* merecer.

deservedly (-idli) *adv.* merecidamente.

deserving (dišø·ʳving) *adj.* merecedor, digno de, acreedor a, meritorio. *2 s.* merecimiento.

desiccate (to) (de·sikeit) *tr.* desecar, secar. *2* pasar [higos, etc.]. *3 intr.* desecarse.

desiccative (-keitiv), **desiccatory** (katori) *adj.-s.* desecativo.

desideratum (disidørei·tøm) *s.* desideratum.

design (dišai·n) *s.* plan, proyecto. *2* intención, mira, propósito, designio: *by ~*, de intento; *to have designs on*, proponerse algo contra. *3* dibujo, diseño, plano, modelo. *4* invención artística.

design (to) *tr.* designar, destinar. *2* idear, proyectar, tramar, maquinar. *3* proponerse. *4* trazar, diseñar. *5 intr.* hacer diseños, planes, proyectos.

designate (to) (de·šigneit) *tr.* indicar, señalar. *2* denotar. *3* designar [denominar; destinar].

designation (-ei·shøn) *s.* acción de señalar o indicar. *2* denominación, nombre, título. *3* designación.

designedly (dišai·nidli) *adv.* adrede, de intento.

designer (dišai·nøʳ) *s.* diseñador, dibujante. *2* inventor, planeador. *3* maquinador, intrigante.

designing (-ning) *adj.* artero, insidioso, intrigante.

desinence (de·sinøns) *s.* GRAM. desinencia.

desirable (disai·rabøl) *adj.* deseable, apetecible.

desire (disai·øʳ) *s.* deseo. *2* anhelo, ansia.

desire (to) *tr.* desear, anhelar, ansiar. *2* rogar, pedir.

desirous (-røs) *adj.* deseoso, anheloso, ganoso.

desist (to) (diši·st) *intr.* desistir. *2 tr.* cesar de.

desistance (-ans) *s.* desistimiento, cesación.

desk (desk) *s.* pupitre, escritorio, bufete, buró. *2* (E.U.) púlpito.

desman (de·sman) *s.* ZOOL. desmán.

desolate (de·sølit) *adj.* desolado, desierto, solitario; triste. *2* solo, desconsolado.

desolate (to) (de·soleit) *tr.* desolar, asolar, devastar. *2* afligir, desconsolar.

desolation (-ei·shøn) *s.* desolación. *2* soledad.

despair (dispe·øʳ) *s.* desesperación; desesperanza.

despair (to) *intr.* desesperar; desesperanzarse.

despairing (-ing) *adj.* desesperado, sin esperanza.

despatch (to) = DISPATCH (TO).

desperado (despørei·dou) *s.* facineroso; malhechor peligroso.

desperate (de·spørit) *adj.* desesperado. *2* arriesgado, temerario. *3* grave, terrible, violento. *4* heroico [remedio].

desperation (-ei·shøn) *s.* desesperación.

despicable (de·spikabøl) *adj.* despreciable, bajo, vil.

despisable (dispai·šbøl) *adj.* despreciable.

despise (to) (dispai·š) *tr.* despreciar, menospreciar.

despite (to) (dispai·t) *s.* malquerencia, inquina. *2* despecho. *3 prep. despite* (o ~ *of*, *in ~ of*) a despecho de, a pesar de, pese a.

despiteful (-ful) *adj.* lleno de odio, malévolo, maligno, rencoroso.

despoil (to) (dispoi·l) *tr.* despojar, privar [de]. *2* saquear, robar.

despollation (dispouliei·shøn) *s.* despojo; saqueo.

despond (to) (dispa·nd) *intr.* desalentarse, descorazonarse.

despondence, -cy (-øns, -si) *s.* desaliento, desánimo, abatimiento.

despondent (-ønt), **desponding** (-ing) *adj.* desalentado, desanimado, abatido.

despot (de·spat) *s.* déspota, tirano.

despotic(al (despa·tik(al) *adj.* despótico.

despotism (de·spøtišm) *s.* despotismo.

desquamate (to) (de·skuameit) *intr.* MED. descamarse.

desquamation (-ei·shøn) *s.* MED. descamación.

dessert (dišø·ʳt) *s.* postres.

destination (destinei·shøn) *s.* destinación, destino.

destine (to) (de·stin) *tr.* destinar.

destiny (-i) *s.* destino, sino, suerte; hado.

destitute (de·stitiud) *adj.* destituido, falto, desprovisto. *2* desvalido, menesteroso.

destitute (to) *tr.* destituir, privar.

destitution (destitiu·shøn) *s.* destitución, privación, falta. *2* miseria, indigencia.

destroy (to) (distroi·) *tr.* destruir. *2* demoler. *3* romper, destrozar. *4* aniquilar, exterminar, matar: *to ~ oneself*, suicidarse. *5* minar, consumir.

destroyer (-øʳ) *s.* destructor, destruidor. *2* MAR. destructor.

destruction (distrø·kshøn) *s.* destrucción; ruina; muerte. *2* perdición.

destructive (-tiv) *adj.* destructivo.

desuetude (de·suitiud) *s.* desuso.

desultory (de·sltori) *adj.* intermitente, discontinuo, deshilvanado, inconexo; que salta de un tema a otro.

detach (to) (ditæ·ch) *tr.* desatar, desligar. *2* despegar, desunir, separar. *3* MIL. destacar.

detachable (-abøl) *adj.* separable, desmontable; de quita y pon.

detached (ditæ·cht) *adj.* aislado, suelto, separado. *2* desinteresado. *3* imparcial.

detachment (-mønt) *s.* separación, desprendimiento. *2* despego, alejamiento, indiferencia; desapasionamiento. *3* MIL. destacamento.

detail (ditei·l) *s.* detalle, pormenor: *in ~*, en detalle. *2* MIL. pequeño destacamento.

detail (to) *tr.* detallar, especificar, enumerar. *2* MIL. destacar.

detain (to) (ditei·n) *tr.* detener, parar; entretener, retardar. *2* retener, detentar. *3* contener, represar. *4* tener preso [a uno].

detect (dite·kt) *tr.* descubrir, averiguar, hallar, percibir. *2* RADIO. detectar.

detecter (-ø^r) *s.* DETECTOR.

detection (-shøn) *s.* descubrimiento, averiguación. *2* RADIO. detección.

detective (-tiv) *adj.* que descubre. *2* policíaco: ~ *story*, novela policíaca. *3 s.* detective.

detector (-tø^r) *s.* descubridor. *2* MEC. indicador. *3* RADIO. detector.

detent (dite·nt) *s.* MEC. trinquete, fiador, seguro.

detention (dite·nshøn) *s.* detención [acción]. *2* detención, prisión, encierro. *3* DER. retención, detentación.

deter (to) (ditø·^r) *tr.* detener, disuadir, impedir. ¶ Pret. y p. p.: *deterred;* ger.: *-rring.*

deterge (to) (ditø·^rdÿ) *tr.* deterger.

detergent (-ønt) *adj.-s.* detergente, detersivo.

deteriorate (diti·riøreit) *tr.* deteriorar. *2* empeorar. *3 intr.* deteriorarse, decaer, empeorar.

deterioration (-ei·shøn) *s.* deterioración; empeoramiento.

determent (ditø·^rmønt) *s.* disuasión. *2* estorbo, impedimento.

determinant (ditø·^rminant) *adj.-s.* determinante.

determinate (-nit) *adj.* determinado. *2* definitivo.

determination (-ei·shøn) *s.* determinación [acción y efecto de determinar]. *2* decisión, fallo. *3* determinación, voluntad decidida. *4* H. NAT. clasificación.

determine (to) (ditø·^rmin) *tr.* determinar. *2 intr.* determinarse, decidirse. | Gralte. con *on.*

determined (-d) *adj.* determinado, decidido, resuelto.

determinism (ditø·^rminišm) *s.* FIL. determinismo.

deterrent (ditø·rønt) *adj.* disuasivo. *2 s.* lo que disuade; freno, impedimento.

detersion (ditø·^rshøn) *s.* detersión.

detersive (-iv) *adj.-s.* detersivo.

detest (to) (dite·st) *tr.* detestar, aborrecer.

detestable (-abøl) *adj.* detestable, aborrecible.

detestation (-ei·shøn) *s.* detestación.

dethrone (to) (dizrou·n) *tr.* destronar.

dethronement (-mønt) *s.* destronamiento.

detonate (to) (de·toneit) *intr.* detonar, estallar. *2 tr.* hacer estallar.

detonation (-ei·shøn) *s.* detonación.

detonator (de·toneitø^r) *s.* detonador.

detour (ditu·^r) *s.* desvío; vuelta, rodeo. *2* manera indirecta.

detract (to) (ditra·kt) *tr.* detraer, quitar, restar. *2* detraer, detractar. *3 intr. to ~ from,* menoscabar, rebajar, hacer desmerecer.

detraction (-kshøn) *s.* detracción, calumnia, maledicencia.

detractor (-ktø^r) *s.* detractor, calumniador.

detriment (de·trimønt) *s.* detrimento, perjuicio.

detrimental (-me·ntal) *adj.* perjudicial, nocivo.

detrition (ditri·shøn) *s.* desgaste.

detritus (ditrai·tøs) *s.* detrito.

detune (to) (ditiu·n) *tr.* RADIO. desintonizar.

deuce (dius) *s.* dos [en naipes o dados]. *2* demonios, diantre: *what the ~ ...?,* ¿qué demonios...?

deuced (diu·sid) *adj.* endemoniado, del demonio [malo, extremado].

Deuteronomy (diutøra·nømi) *s.* Deuteronomio.

devaluate (to) (divæ·liueit) *tr.* desvalorizar.

devaluation (-ei·shøn) *s.* devalorización, devaluación.

devastate (de·vasteit) *tr.* devastar, asolar.

devastation (-ei·shøn) *s.* devastación, asolamiento.

develop (to) (dive·løp) *tr.* desenvolver, desarrollar. *2* fomentar, mejorar. *3* explotar [una mina, etc.]; urbanizar, edificar [un terreno], ensanchar [una población]. *4* desplegar, mostrar. *5* echar [pelo, hojas, etc.]. *6* FOT. revelar. *8 intr.* desarrollarse, evolucionar.

developer (-ø^r) *s.* FOT. revelador.

development (-mønt) *s.* desarrollo, desenvolvimiento. *2* crecimiento, progreso. *3* evolución. *4* fomento, explotación, urbanización. *5* caserío nuevo, ensanche. *6* acontecimiento, hecho nuevo. *7* MAT. desarrollo. *8* FOT. revelado.

deviate (to) (dɪ·vieit) *intr.* desviarse, apartarse, divergir.

deviation (-ei·shøn) *s.* desviación. *3* extravío, error.

device (divai·s) *s.* artificio, invención; traza, proyecto. *2* aparato, dispositivo, mecanismo. *3* ardid, recurso, expediente. *4* dibujo [de tela, bordado, etc.]. *5* vidisa, empresa, lema, mote. *6 pl.* voluntad, antojo.

deviceful (-ful) *adj.* inventivo, ingenioso.

devil (de·vøl) *s.* demonio, diablo: *poor ~,* pobre diablo, desgraciado; *between the ~, and the deep sea,* entre la espada y la pared; *the ~!,* ¡demonio!, ¡diantre! *2* aprendiz de impresor. *3* escritor a sueldo. *4* nombre de varias máquinas.

devil (to) *tr.* hacer diabólico. *2* COC. condimentar con mucho picante. ¶ Pret. y p. p.: *deviled* o *-lled;* ger.: *deviling* o *-lling.*

devilish (-ish) *adj.* diabólico. *2* endemoniado, endiablado; extremado.

devilkin (-kin) *s.* diablejo, diablillo.

devilment (-mønt) *s.* diablura, diablería.

devilry (-ri) *s.* diablura, diablería. *2* acción diabólica; maldad, crueldad.

devil's-darning-needle *s.* ENT. libélula, caballito del diablo. *2* BOT. aguja de pastor o de Venus.

deviltry (-tri) *s.* devilry.

devious (dɪ·viøs) *adj.* desviado, apartado, extraviado. *2* tortuoso. *3* indirecto. *4* errante.

devisal (divai·šal) *s.* invención.

devise (to) *tr.* inventar, idear, discurrir. *2* DER. legar. *3 intr.* formar planes.

devisee (diviši·) *s.* DER. legatario.

devitalize (to) (divai·talaiš) *tr.* privar de vitalidad.

devold (divoi·d) *adj.* falto, desprovisto, exento.

devoir (de·vua^r) *s.* deber. *2 pl.* homenaje, respetos.

devolution (devoliu·shøn) *s.* entrega, traspaso. *2* transmisión por sucesión. *3* BIOL. degeneración.

devolve (to) (diva·lv) *tr.* transmitir, traspasar. *2 intr.* pasar [por sucesión]; recaer, tocar, incumbir, corresponder.

Devonian (devou·nian) *adj.-s.* GEOL. devoniano, devónico.

devote (to) (divou·t) *tr.* consagrar, dedicar, aplicar. *2* destinar, condenar.

devoted (-id) *adj.* consagrado, dedicado, aplicado. *2* destinado, condenado. *3* devoto, ferviente, celoso. *4* adicto, fiel, apegado.

devotee (devotiˑ) *s.* devoto, beato. *2* fanático, partidario ardiente.

devotion (divou·shøn) *s.* devoción. *2* fervor, celo. *3* afecto, lealtad. *4 pl.* devociones.

devotional (-al) *adj.* devoto, de devoción.

devour (to) (divau·^r) *tr.* devorar.

devouring (-ing) *adj.* devorador.

devout 110

devout (divau·t) *adj.* devoto, piadoso. 2 fervoroso, sincero, cordial.
dew (diu) *s.* rocío; sereno, relente.
dew (to) *tr.* rociar, refrescar. 2 *intr.* rociar, formarse el rocío.
dewberry (-beri) *s.* BOT. zarzamora.
dewclaw (-klo) *s.* ZOOL. dedo rudimentario [del perro].
dewdrop (-drap) *s.* gota de rocío.
dewlap (-læp) *s.* papada.
dewy (-i) *adj.* cubierto de rocío; parecido al rocío.
dexter (de·kstø') *adj.* derecho, diestro. 2 de buen augurio.
dexterity (-iti) *s.* destreza, habilidad.
dexterous (-tørøs) *adj.* diestro, hábil.
dextral (-tral) *adj.* derecho, diestro.
dextrin(e (-trin) *s.* QUÍM. dextrina.
dextrose (-trous) *s.* QUÍM. dextrosa.
dey (dei) *s.* dey.
diabetes (dáiabɪ·tis) *s.* MED. diabetis.
diabetic (-be·tik) *adj.-s.* diabético.
diablerie, -ry (dia·bløri) *s.* brujería, magia negra. 2 diablura.
diabolic (al (daiaba·lik(al) *adj.* diabólico.
diabolo (diæ·bølou) *s.* diábolo [juguete].
diaconal (daiæ·konal) *adj.* diaconal.
diaconate (-koneit) *s.* diaconato.
diacoustics (daiaku·stiks) *s.* diacústica.
diacritic (-kri·tik) *adj.-s.* diacrítico.
diacritical (-al) *adj.* DIACRITIC.
diadelphous (-de·lføs) *adj.* BOT. diadelfo.
diadem (dai·adem) *s.* diadema.
diaeresis (daie·risis) *s.* diéresis.
diagnose (to) (daiægnou·s) *tr.* diagnosticar.
diagnosis (-is) *s.* diagnosis. 2 diagnóstico.
diagnosticate (to) (-eit) *tr.* diagnosticar.
diagonal (daiæ·gonal) *adj.-s.* diagonal.
diagram (dai·agræm) *s.* diagrama, esquema.
diagram (to) *tr.* hacer el diagrama de; esquematizar.
dial (dai·al) *s.* reloj de sol, cuadrante. 2 esfera [de reloj]. 3 disco [de teléfono]. 4 RADIO. dial.
dial (to) *tr.* TELEF. marcar. 2 RADIO. sintonizar. ¶ Pret. y p. p.: dialed o -lled; ger.: -ling o -lling.
dialect (dai·alekt) *s.* dialecto. 2 *adj.* dialectal.
dialectic (al (daiale·ktik(al) *adj.* dialéctico.
dialectician (-ti·shan) *s.* dialéctico.
dialectics (daiale·ktiks) *s.* dialéctica.
dial(l)ing (-ling) *s.* gnomónica.
dialogic (al (daialo·dy̆ik(al) *adj.* dialogal, dialogístico.
dialogism (daiæ·lody̆iŝm) *s.* dialogismo, diálogo.
dialogist (-dy̆ist) *s.* dialoguista.
dialogistic (al (daialody̆i·stik(al) *adj.* dialogístico.
dialogize (to) (daiæ·lody̆aiš) *intr.* TO DIALOGUE.
dialogue (dai·alag) *s.* diálogo.
dialogue (to) *intr.* dialogar.
dialysis (daiæ·lisis) *s.* QUÍM. diálisis.
dialyze (to) (dai·alaiš) *tr.* QUÍM. dializar.
dialyzer (-ø') *s.* dializador.
diamantiferous (daiamænti·førøs) *adj.* diamantífero.
diamantine (daiamæ·ntin) *adj.* diamantino.
diametral (-metral), diametrical (daiame·trical) *adj.* diametral.
diameter (daiæ·metø') *s.* diámetro.
diamond (dai·amønd) *s.* diamante: ~ cutter, diamantista. 2 GEOM. rombo. 3 rombo [palo de la baraja].
diandrous (dai·ændrøs) *adj.* BOT. diandro.
diapason (daiapei·šøn) *s.* MÚS. diapasón.

diaper (dai·apø') *s.* lienzo adamascado. 2 culero, pañal. 3 labor o adorno de motivos que se repiten indefinidamente.
diaper (to) *tr.* adamascar. 2 labrar o adornar con motivos que se repiten indefinidamente.
diaphaneity (daiafanɪ·iti) *s.* diafanidad.
diaphanous (daiæ·fanøs) *adj.* diáfano.
diaphragm (dai·afræm) *s.* diafragma.
diaphysis (daiæ·fisis) *s.* ANAT. diáfisis.
diapositive (daiapa·šitiv) *s.* FOT. diapositiva.
diarrhea, diarrhoea (daiarɪ·a) *s.* MED. diarrea.
diarthrosis (-a'zrou·sis) *s.* ANAT. diartrosis.
diary (dai·ari) *s.* diario, dietario.
Diaspora (daiæ·spøra) *s.* Diáspora.
diastase (dai·ateis) *s.* QUÍM. diastasa.
diastole (daiæ·støli) *s.* FISIOL. diástole.
diathermia (daiazø·'mia), diathermy (-mi) *s.* MED. diatermia.
diatom (dai·atam) *s.* BOT. diatomea.
diatonic (-ata·nik) *adj.* MÚS. diatónico.
diatribe (-atraib) *s.* diatriba.
dibble (di·bøl) *s.* plantador [instrumento].
dibble (to) *tr.* plantar con plantador. 2 hacer hoyos [en la tierra].
dibs (dibs) *s. pl.* taba [juego]. 2 fam. dinero.
dibstone (-toun) *s.* piedrecita, taba, etc., para jugar.
dice (dais) *s. pl.* dados: ~ box, cubilete. 2 cubitos.
dice (to) *intr.* jugar a los dados. 2 *tr.* cortar en cubitos.
dicer (-ø') *s.* jugador de dados.
dichotomy (dai·katømi) *s.* dicotomía.
dichorism (-ata·nik) *adj.* MÚS. diatónico. [dicer...]
dichorism (dai·kroišm) *s.* FÍS. dicroísmo.
Dick (dik) *n. pr.* Ricardito.
dickens (di·kønš) *s.* fam. demonio, diantre.
dicker (di·kø') *s.* (E.U.) trato, cambalache.
dicker (to) *intr.* (E.U.) tratar, regatear.
dick(e)y (di·ki) *s.* camisolín. 2 delantal, babero. 3 pajarito. 4 AUT. asiento del conductor; trasera [de coche].
dicotyledon (daikatilɪ·døn) *s.* BOT. dicotiledónea.
dicotyledonous (-dønøs) *adj.* BOT. dicotiledóneo.
dictaphone (di·ktafoun) *s.* dictáfono.
dictate (di·kteit) *s.* dictado [inspiración, mandato].
dictate (to) *tr.* dictar. 2 *intr.* mandar.
dictation (-ei·shøn) *s.* dictado [acción de dictar; lo dictado]. 2 mandato, imposición.
dictator (-ei·tø') *s.* dictador.
dictatorial (diktato·rial) *adj.* dictatorial.
dictatorship (diktei·tø'ship), dictature (-shø') *s.* dictadura.
diction (di·kshøn) *s.* dicción, estilo, lenguaje.
dictionary (di·kshøneri) *s.* diccionario, léxico.
dictum (di·ctøm), pl. -ta *s.* sentencia, aforismo.
did (did) pret. de TO DO.
didactic(al (daidæ·ktik(al) *adj.* didáctico.
didactics (-tiks) *s.* didáctica.
diddle (to) (di·døl) *tr.* estafar. 2 perder [el tiempo]. 3 zarandearse.
didn't (di·dønt) contrac. de did y not.
1) die (dai), pl. dice (dais) *s.* dado [para jugar]. 2 cubito.
2) die, pl. dies *s.* ARQ. dado, neto. 3 MEC. troquel, cuño. 4 MEC. cojinete de la terraja.
1) die (to) *intr.* morir, fallecer, acabar, fenecer, extinguirse. 2 agostarse, marchitarse. 3 to ~ of laughing, desternillarse de risa. 4 to be dying for o to, morirse por, desear ardientemente. ¶ Pret. y p. p.: died; ger.: dying.

2) die (to) *tr.* cortar o estampar con troquel. ¶ Pret. y p. p.: *died;* ger.: *dieing.*
die-hard *adj.-s.* POL. intransigente.
dielectric (daiile·ktrik) *adj.-s.* dieléctrico.
dieresis (daie·risis) *s.* DIAERESIS.
diesinker (dai·sinkø^r) *s.* grabador en hueco.
diesis (-esis) *s.* MÚS. diesi.
diestock (-stak) *s.* MEC. terraja.
diet (dai·et) *s.* MED. dieta, régimen alimenticio. *2* dieta [asamblea].
dietetics (daiete·tiks) *s.* dietética.
differ (to) (di·fø^r) *intr.* diferir, diferenciarse, distinguirse; discrepar, disentir. *2* reñir, tener una diferencia.
difference (-øns) *s.* diferencia. *2* disparidad, desigualdad. *3* distinción [que se hace entre pers. o cosas]. *4* cambio, alteración: *it makes no* ~, es igual, lo mismo da. *5* divergencia, discrepancia.
difference (to) *tr.* diferenciar, distinguir.
different (-ønt) *adj.* diferente, distinto. *2* diferente de lo usual; poco corriente.
differential (diføre·nsh*a*l) *adj.* diferencial. *2 s.* MAT., MEC. diferencial.
differentiate (to) (-shieit) *tr.* diferenciar, distinguir. *2 intr.* diferenciarse.
differentiation (-ei·shøn) *s.* diferenciación.
difficult (di·fikølt) *adj.* difícil. *2* dificultoso, trabajoso. *3* apurado, penoso.
difficulty (-i) *s.* dificultad. *2* obstáculo, objeción, reparo, inconveniente. *3* apuro, aprieto.
diffidence (di·fidøns) *s.* falta de confianza en sí mismo; cortedad, timidez, apocamiento.
diffident (-dønt) *adj.* que desconfía de sí mismo; tímido, apocado.
diffluent (di·fluønt) *adj.* difluente.
diffract (to) (difræ·kt) *tr.* FÍS. difractar. *2 intr.* difractarse.
diffraction (difræ·kshøn) *s.* difracción.
diffuse (difiu·s) *adj.* difuso.
diffuse (to) (difiu·ś) *tr.* difundir. *2* esparcir, diseminar. *3 intr.* difundirse.
diffused (-d) *adj.* difundido. *2* difuso, disperso.
difuser (difiu·śø^r) *s.* difusor.
diffusion (-ȳøn) *s.* difusión.
dig (dig) *s.* hurgonazo, metido, codazo o golpe parecido. *2* fam. pulla, sarcasmo.
dig (to) *tr.* cavar, excavar, ahondar, ahoyar. *2* escarbar. *3* extraer, buscar, hacer, abrir, etc., cavando o escarbando: *to* ~ *out* o *up*, extraer, desenterrar. *4* clavar, hundir [las uñas, un cuchillo, etc.]. *5* dar un metido a, hurgar, aguijonear, picar. *6 intr.* cavar. *7* clavarse, entrar, penetrar. *8* fam. trabajar de firme. ¶ Pret. y p. p.: *dug* o *digged;* ger.: *digging.*
digest (dai·dȳest) *s.* compendio, recopilación. *2* DER. digesto.
digest (to) (daidȳe·st) *tr.* digerir. *2* resumir, recopilar. *3 intr.* digerirse.
digester (-ø^r) *s.* digestor. *2* MED. digestivo. *3* compendiador, recopilador.
digestion (daiȳe·stshøn) *s.* digestión.
digestive (-stiv) *adj.* digestivo.
digger (di·gø^r) *s.* cavador. *2* azada. *3* máquina cavadora.
digging (-ing) *s.* cava, excavación. *2 pl.* lo que se saca cavando. *3* mina [esp. de oro o diamantes]. *4* fam. domicilio, alojamiento.
digit (di·dȳit) *s.* ZOOL. dedo. *2* dedo [medida]. *3* número dígito. *4* ASTR. dígito.
digital (-al) *adj.* digital.
digitalin (didȳite·lin) *s.* FARM. digitalina.

digitalis (-tei·lis) *s.* BOT. digital.
digitate(d (di·dȳiteit(id) *adj.* digitado.
digitigrade (di·dȳitigreid) *adj.* ZOOL. digitígrado.
dignified (di·gnifaid) *adj.* dignificado; enaltecido. *2* digno, serio, grave; noble, majestuoso.
dignify (to) (-fai) *tr.* dignificar, enaltecer. ¶ Pret. y p. p.: *dignified.*
dignitary (-teri) *s.* dignatario.
dignity (di·gniti) *s.* dignidad. *2* honor. *3* rango, elevación.
digraph (dai·græf) *s.* dígrafo.
digress (to) (digre·s) *intr.* desviarse del tema, divagar.
digression (-ei·shøn) *s.* digresión.
dihedral (daijɪ·dr*a*l) *adj.* GEOM. diedro.
dike (daik) *s.* dique, malecón, represa. *2* zanja, acequia.
dike (to) *tr.* proteger con dique. *2* avenar [un terreno].
dilacerate (dilæ·søreit) *tr.* romper, desgarrar; dilacerar.
dilapidate (to) (-pideit) *tr.* arruinar, estropear, echar a perder. *2* dilapidar.
dilapidated (-id) *adj.* ruinoso, estropeado, viejo, en mal estado.
dilatability (daileitabi·liti) *s.* dilatabilidad.
dilatation (dilatei·shøn) *s.* dilatación.
dilate (to) (dai·leit) *tr.* dilatar. *2 intr.* dilatarse. *3 to* ~ *in* o *upon*, extenderse, explayarse, sobre.
dilation (dailei·shøn) *s.* DILATATION.
dilative (-tiv) *adj.* dilativo.
dilatory (di·latori) *adj.* dilatorio. *2* tardo, lento, moroso.
dilemma (dile·ma) *s.* dilema. *2* disyuntiva.
dilettante (diløtæ·nti), *pl.* **-tes** o **-ti** (-ti) *s.* diletante, aficionado.
diligence (di·lidȳøns) *s.* diligencia, cuidado, aplicación, asiduidad. *2* diligencia [coche].
diligent (-ønt) *adj.* diligente, aplicado, activo, solícito, cuidadoso.
dill (dil) *s.* BOT. eneldo.
dilly-dally (to) (di·lidæli) *intr.* holgazanear, perder el tiempo.
diluent (di·liuønt) *adj.-s.* diluente.
dilute (to) (di·liut) *tr.* diluir, desleír. *2* aguar. *3 intr.* diluirse; desleírse.
dilution (diliu·shøn) *s.* dilución, desleimiento.
diluvial (-vial) *adj.* diluvial.
diluvian (-vian) *adj.* diluviano.
dim (dim) *adj.* oscuro, opaco. *2* anublado, caliginoso. *3* empañado, deslustrado. *4* vago, confuso. *5* apagado, débil. *6* ciego. *7* obtuso, torpe.
dim (to) *tr.* oscurecer, ofuscar, anublar. *2* empañar, deslustrar. *3* hacer confuso, indistinto. *4* amortiguar [una luz]. *5 intr.* oscurecerse.
dime (daim) *s.* diezmo. *2* (E.U.) diez centavos.
dimension (dime·nshøn) *s.* dimensión.
diminish (to) (dimi·nish) *tr.* disminuir. *2* empequeñecer. *3* abatir, humillar. *4 intr.* disminuir, menguar.
diminution (diminiu·shøn) *s.* disminución.
diminutive (dimi·niutiv) *adj.-s.* diminutivo. *2 adj.* pequeño, diminuto.
dimissory (di·misori) *adj.* dimisorio.
dimity (di·miti) *s.* cotonada.
dimmer (di·mø^r) *s.* amortiguador [de luz]. *2* AUT. luz de cruce.
dimness (di·mnis) *s.* semioscuridad, penumbra. *2* oscuridad, anublamiento.
dimorphism (daimo·^{r}fiśm) *s.* dimorfismo.
dimorphous (-føs) *adj.* dimorfo.

dimple (di·mpøl) *s.* hoyuelo.
dimple (to) *tr.-intr.* formar o formarse hoyuelos [en].
dimpled (-d), **dimply** (-pli) *adj.* que tiene hoyuelos.
din (din) *s.* fragor, estrépito, estruendo, batahola.
din (to) *tr.* golpear con ruido; ensordecer, aturdir. 2 clamorear; repetir con pesadez. 3 *intr.* resonar, hacer estrépito.
dine (to) (dain) *intr.* comer [hacer la comida principal]. 2 *tr.* tener convidado a comer.
diner (-ø^r) *s.* comensal [en una comida]. 2 FERROC. vagón restaurante.
ding-a-ling (di·ngalin) *s.* tintín.
ding-dong (di·ndan) *s.* din don [sonido]. 2 *adj.* disputado, con ventaja alterna [carrera, etc.].
dingey, dinghy (di·ngɪ) *s.* MAR. bote.
dinginess (di·ndÿinis) *s.* suciedad, empañamiento.
dingle (di·ngøl) *s.* cañada, vallecito umbroso.
dingo (di·ngou) *s.* ZOOL. dingo [perro salvaje].
dingy (di·ndÿi) *adj.* oscuro, negruzco, sucio, deslucido; sórdido. 2 *s.* DINGEY.
dining car (dai·nig) *s.* FERROC. vagón restaurante.
dining-room *s.* comedor [pieza].
dinner (di·nø^r) *s.* comida [principal], banquete: ~ *coat*, ~ *jacket*, smoking.
dinosaur (dai·noso^r) *s.* PALEONT. dinosaurio.
dinothere (dai·nozi^r) *s.* PALEONT. dinoterio.
dint (dint) *s.* golpe, abolladura. 2 *adv. by . of*, a puro, a fuerza de.
dint (to) *tr.* abollar.
diocesan (daia·sisan) *adj.-s.* diocesano.
diocese (dai·øsis) *s.* diócesis.
Diocletian (daiokli·shan) *n. pr.* Diocleciano.
dioecions (dair·shøs) *adj.* BOT. dioico.
Dionysius (daioni·shiøs) *n. pr.* Dionisio.
Dioniysos o **-sus** (-shøs) *n. pr.* MIT. Dioniso.
diopter (daia·ptø^r) *s.* dioptra. 2 dioptría.
dioptric (-trik) *adj.* dióptrico. 2 *s.* DIOPTER 2.
dioptrics (-triks) *s.* dióptrica.
diorama (daiora·ma) *s.* diorama.
diorite (dai·orait) *s.* MINER. diorita.
dioxide (daia·ksaid) *s.* QUÍM. bióxido.
dip (dip) *s.* zambullida, inmersión, baño corto. 2 declive, pendiente, depresión, inclinación, grado de inclinación. 3 baño [en que se sumerge una cosa]. 4 GEOL. buzamiento.
dip (to) *tr.* zambullir, sumergir, bañar, mojar. 2 sacar [con cuchara, etc.]; achicar. 3 bajar, inclinar [banderas, etc.]. 4 *intr.* zambullirse, sumergirse; bajar, inclinarse. 5 meter la mano, un cucharón, etc. [en un sitio para sacar algo]. 6 hacer pendiente [un terreno]. 7 GEOL. buzar. 8 descender rápidamente. 9 desaparecer [bajo una superficie o nivel]. 10 investigar, penetrar. 11 meterse [en algo]. ¶ Pret. y P. P.: *dipped*; ger. *dipping*.
diphtheria (difzi·ria) *s.* MED. difteria.
diphtherial (-al), **diphtheritic** (-i·tik) *adj.* diftérico.
diphthong (di·fzong) *s.* diptongo.
diphtong, diphtongize (to) (-gaiš) *tr.* diptongar.
diplodocus (diploda·køs) *s.* PALEONT. diplodoco.
diploma (diplou·ma) *s.* diploma.
diplomacy (-si) *s.* diplomacia.
diplomat (di·plomæt) *s.* diplomático.
diplomate (di·plomit) *adj.* diplomado, titulado.
diplomatic(al (diplomæ·tik(al) *adj.* diplomático.
diplomatics (-tiks) *s.* diplomacia. 2 diplomática.
diplomatist (diplou·matist) *s.* diplomático.
dipper (di·pø^r) *s.* cazo, cacillo, cucharón. 2 MEC. cuchara [de excavadora]. 3 ASTR. *The Dipper*, el Carro.

dipsomania (dipsoumei·nia) *s.* dipsomanía.
dipsomaniac (-niæk) *s.* dipsómano.
dipter (di·ptø^r) *s.* ENT. díptero.
dipteral (-al) *adj.* ARQ., ENT. díptero.
dipteran (-an) *adj.-s.* ENT. díptero.
dipteros (-rous) *adj.* ARQ. díptero.
dipterous (-røs) *adj.* ENT. díptero.
diptych (di·ptik) *s.* díptica. 2 díptico.
dire (dai·ø^r) *adj.* horrible, horrendo. 2 extremo, sumo.
direct (dire·kt) *adj.* directo. 2 recta [línea de descendencia]. 3 inmediato. 4 claro, categórico. 5 franco, sincero. 6 ELECT. continua [corriente]. 7 GRAM. ~ *object*, complemento directo. 8 *adv.* directamente [esp. en compuestos].
direct (to) *tr.* dirigir. 2 encaminar, encauzar. 3 mandar, encargar; decir [a uno lo que ha de hacer], dar instrucciones a. 4 dedicar [una obra a uno]. 5 *intr.* dirigir, servir de guía.
directer (-ø^r) *s.* DIRECTOR.
direction (dire·kshøn) *s.* dirección. 2 consejo de administración, junta directiva. 3 sobrescrito. 4 *pl.* mandato, orden, encargo; instrucciones.
directional (-al) *adj.* de dirección.
directive (dire·ktiv) *adj.* director, directivo. 2 dirigible, gobernable. 3 *s.-pl.* directrices.
directly (dire·ktli) *adv.* directamente. 2 inmediatamente, en seguida. 3 exactamente, completamente. 4 francamente. 5 sinceramente. 6 *conj.* fam. en cuanto, tan pronto como.
directness (-nis) *s.* derechura. 2 franqueza, lealtad, rectitud.
director (-ø^r) *s.* director. 2 caudillo, guía. 3 gerente; consejero [de una compañía], individuo de una junta directiva. 4 *adj.* MAT. director, directriz.
directorate (-ørit) *s.* dirección [cargo]. 2 consejo de administración, junta directiva, directorio.
directory (-ori) *adj.* directorio. 2 *s.* libro de reglas o instrucciones. 3 guía [libro con direcciones]: *telephone* ~, guía telefónica.
directress (dire·ktris) *s.* directora.
directrix (-iks) *s.* GEOM. directriz.
direful (dai·ø^{r}ful) *adj.* horrendo, terrible, espantoso.
dirge (dø^{r}dÿ) *s.* endecha, treno, canto fúnebre.
dirigible (di·ridÿibøl) *adj.-s.* dirigible.
diriment (di·rimønt) *s.* dirimente.
dirk (dø^{r}k) *s.* daga escocesa. 2 puñal.
dirt (dø^{r}t) *s.* tierra, barro, lodo. 2 suciedad, mugre, porquería, inmundicia, basura. 3 bajeza, vileza.
dirt-cheap *adj.* y *adv.* muy barato, baratísimo.
dirty (-i) *adj.* enlodado, manchado, mugriento, sucio. 2 cochino, indecente. 3 bajo, vil, despreciable. 4 malo [tiempo, mar, etc.]. 5 ~ *trick*, perrada, cochinada.
dirty (to) *tr.* ensuciar, manchar, enlodar.
disability (disabi·liti) *s.* impotencia, incapacidad, inhabilidad. 2 inutilidad [para el trabajo].
disable (to) (disei·bøl) *tr.* inutilizar, imposibilitar, incapacitar, inhabilitar. 2 lisiar. 3 MAR. desaparejar, desmantelar.
disablement (-mønt) *s.* incapacitación, inhabilitación. 2 invalidez [física]. 3 MAR. desmantelamiento.
disabuse (to) (disabiu·š) *tr.* desengañar, sacar del error o del engaño.
disaccord (disa·ko^{r}d) *s.* desacuerdo, disensión.
disaccord (to) *intr.* discordar, disentir.
disaccustom (to) (-kø·støm) *tr.* desacostumbrar.
disadjust (to) (-dÿø·st) *tr.* desajustar, desarreglar.

disadvantage (-dvæ·ntidẏ) *s.* desventaja. *2* inconveniente. *3* detrimento.

disadvantage (to) *tr.* perjudicar, dañar.

disadvantageous (-dvæntei·dẏøs) *adj.* desventajoso, perjudicial, inconveniente.

disaffect (to) (disafe·kt) *tr.* indisponer, enemistar.

disaffected (-id) *adj.* desafecto.

disaffection (-fe·kshøn) *s.* desafección, desafecto.

disagregate (disa·grigeit) *tr.* disgregar.

disagree (to) (disagrɪ·) *intr.* desconvenir, disonar. *2* discordar, discrepar, diferir. *3* disentir. *4* desavenirse, estar en pugna. *5 to ~ with*, no estar de acuerdo con; no probar, sentar mal.

disagreeable (-abøl) *adj.* desagradable, ingrato. *2* desabrido, descortés.

disagreement (-grɪ·mønt) *s.* discordancia, discrepancia, desacuerdo, disconformidad. *2* disentimiento. *3* disensión, desavenencia.

disallow (to) (-lau·) *tr.-intr.* desaprobar. *2 tr.* denegar, rechazar.

disappear (to) (-pi·øʳ) *intr.* desaparecer.

disappearance (-ans) *s.* desaparición.

disappoint (-poi·nt) *tr.* privar [de lo que uno espera]; defraudar, burlar, frustrar; chasquear, decepcionar, desilusionar;·contrariar. *2* dejar plantado.

disappointment (-mønt) *s.* desilusión, desengaño, decepción. *2* frustración, chasco, contrariedad.

disapprobation (-probei·shøn), **disapproval** (-pru·val) *s.* desaprobación, censura.

disapprove (to) (-pru·v) *tr.* desaprobar. *2* no aprobar, rechazar [un proyecto, etc.]. *3 intr. to ~ of*, no aprobar, no hallar de su gusto.

disarm (to) (disa·ʳm) *tr.* desarmar [quitar las armas; aplacar, apaciguar]. *2 intr.* desarmarse. *3* MIL. efectuar el desarme.

disarmament (-amønt) *s.* desarme.

disarrange (disarei·ndẏ) *tr.* desarreglar, desordenar, descomponer.

disarray (-rei·) *s.* desorden, confusión. *2* desatavio, desaliño, trapillo.

disarray (to) *tr.* desarreglar, desordenar. *2* derrotar. *3* desaliñar, desnudar.

disarticulate (to) (disaʳti·kiuleit) *tr.* desarticular.

disassemble (to) (disase·mbøl) *tr.* desmontar, desarmar [un artefacto].

disassimilation (dišasimilei·shøn) *s.* desasimilación.

disassociate (to) (-sou·shieit) *tr.* disociar.

disaster (diša·støʳ) *s.* desastre.

disastrous (-trøs) *adj.* desastroso.

disavow (to) (disavau·) *tr.* repudiar, desconocer, negar. *2* desautorizar, desaprobar.

disavowal (-al), **disavowment** (-mønt) *s.* repudiación, desconocimiento. *2* desautorización, desaprobación.

disband (to) (disbæ·nd) *tr.* disolver [una banda, etc.]; despedir, licenciar [huestes]. *2 intr.* dispersarse, desbandarse.

disbar (to) (disba·ʳ) *tr.* expulsar del foro.

disbark (to) (-k) *tr.* descortezar.

disbelief (disbilɪ·f) *s.* incredulidad.

disbelieve (to) (-v) *tr.-intr.* descreer; no creer; no dar fe.

disburden (to) (-bø·ʳdøn) *tr.* descargar, aligerar. *2* descargarse de.

disburse (to) (-bø·ʳs) *tr.* desembolsar. *2* gastar.

disbursement (-mønt) *s.* desembolso. *2* gasto.

disc (disk) *s.* disco.

discalced (-kæ·lst) *adj.* descalzo [religioso].

discard (-ka·ʳd) *s.* descarte. *2* cosa desechada, desecho.

discard (to) *tr.-intr.* NAIPES. descartarse [de]. *2 intr.* descartar, desechar; abandonar, dejar de usar. *3* despedir, destituir.

discern (to) (disø·ʳn) *tr.* discernir, distinguir. *2* ver, distinguir, descubrir, percibir.

discernible (-ibøl) *adj.* discernible. *2* perceptible, visible.

discerning (-ing) *adj.* discernidor. *2* inteligente, sagaz, perspicaz.

discernment (-mønt) *s.* discernimiento. *2* buen criterio, gusto, juicio recto.

discharge (discha·ʳdẏ) *s.* descarga [de un buque, de un arma, etc.]. *2* tiro, disparo. *3* ARQ., ELECT. descarga. *4* salida, derrame [de un líquido]; desagüe. *5* líquido que sale, gasto. *6* supuración. *7* pus, humor [despedidos]. *8* descargo. *9* exoneración, absolución. *10* pago [de una deuda]. *11* cumplimiento, desempeño. *12* recibo, quitanza. *13* liberación [de un preso]. *14* despido, destitución. *15* MIL. licenciamiento, licencia.

discharge (to) *tr.* descargar. *2* dejar [sus pasajeros un tren, etc.]. *3* disparar [un arma, un proyectil]. *4* verter [sus aguas]. *5* despedir, arrojar, echar [fuera de sí]. *6* desembarazar [de]. *7* exonerar, absolver. *8* poner en libertad [un preso]. *9* saldar, pagar. *10* cumplir [un deber], desempeñar [un cometido]. *11* relevar, [de servicio]; despedir, destituir. *12* MIL. licenciar. *13 intr.* descargarse. *14* dispararse [un arma]. *15* salir, desaguar.

disciple (disai·pøl) *s.* discípulo, seguidor, secuaz.

disciplinant (di·siplinant) *s.* disciplinante.

disciplinarian (disipline·rian) *s.* ordenancista, rigorista.

disciplinary (di·siplineri) *adj.* disciplinario.

discipline (di·siplin) *s.* disciplina. *2* enseñanza, doctrina. *3* educación, ejercicio. *4* castigo.

discipline (to) *tr.* disciplinar. *2* enseñar, educar. *3* castigar, corregir.

disclaim (to) (disklei·m) *tr.* negar, desconocer, repudiar. *2* DER. renunciar.

disclose (to) (-klou·s) *tr.* descubrir, destapar. *2* revelar, exponer, divulgar, publicar.

disclosure (-klou·ẏøʳ) *s.* descubrimiento, revelación, declaración.

discobolus (diska·boløs) *s.* discóbolo.

discolo(u)r (to) (-kø·løʳ) *tr.* descolorir, desteñir; alterar el color, manchar. *2 intr.* descolorirse, desteñirse.

discolo(u)ration (-ei·shøn) *s.* descolorimiento. *2* mancha [donde se ha alterado el color].

discomfit (to) (diskø·mfit) *tr.* derrotar. *2* burlar, frustrar, desconcertar.

discomfiture (-mfichøʳ) *s.* derrota. *2* frustración, desconcierto. *3* decepción.

discomfort (-mfø·ʳt) *s.* incomodidad, molestia. *2* malestar.

discomfort (to) *tr.* incomodar, molestar. *2* afligir.

discommend (to) (-køme·nd) *tr.* censurar.

discompose (to) (-kømpou·š) *tr.* turbar, desconcertar, agitar. *2* desarreglar.

discomposure (-pou·ẏøʳ) *s.* turbación, desconcierto, agitación. *2* desorden, desarreglo.

disconcert (to) (-kønsø·ʳt) *tr.* desconcertar, desbaratar. *2* desconcierto, confundir, turbar.

disconnect (to) (-køne·kt) *tr.* desunir, separar, disociar. *2* MEC., ELECT. desacoplar, desconectar, desenchufar.

disconnected (-id) *adj*. desconectado. 2 inconexo, incoherente.
disconnection, disconnexion (-ne·kshøn) *s*. desunión, separación. 2 inconexión, incoherencia.
disconsolate (-ka·nsolit) *adj*. desconsolado.
disconsolateness (-nis) *s*. desconsuelo.
discontent (-kønte·nt) *s*. descontento, disgusto. 2 *adj*. descontento, disgustado.
discontent (to) *tr*. descontentar, disgustar.
discontented (-id) *adj*. descontento, disgustado. 2 descontentadizo.
discontentment (-mønt) *s*. descontento, mal humor.
discontinuance (diskønti·niuans), **discontinuation** (-ei·shøn) *s*. discontinuación, interrupción, intermisión, suspensión, cesación.
discontinue (to) (-niu) *tr*. discontinuar, interrumpir, suspender, hacer cesar. 2 dejar [una suscripción o abono]. 3 *intr*. no continuar, interrumpirse, cesar.
discontinuity (diskantinu·ti) *s*. discontinuidad.
discontinuous (-niuøs) *adj*. discontinuo.
discord (di·sko^rd) *s*. discordia. 2 MÚS. discordancia, disonancia.
discord (to) *intr*. desconvenir, discordar.
discordance, -cy (-ko·^rdans, -si) *s*. discordancia. 2 disonancia.
discordant (-dant) *adj*. discordante, discorde.
discount (-kau·nt) *s*. descuento; rebaja, bonificación.
discount (to) *tr*. descontar, rebajar, reducir. 2 COM. descontar. 3 desestimar, no tener en cuenta.
discountenance (-ønans) *s*. desaprobación, desagrado.
discountenance (to) *tr*. desconcertar, turbar, avergonzar. 2 no alentar o apoyar; desaprobar.
discourage (to) (-kø·ridÿ) *tr*. descorazonar, desalentar. 2 reprimir o impedir desaprobando, disuadir.
discourse (-ko·^rs) *s*. discurso; disertación. 2 plática, conversación.
discourse (to) *intr*. disertar, discurrir, hablar, conversar.
discourteous (-kø·^rtiøs) *adj*. descortés.
discourtesy (-kø·^rtiši) *s*. descortesía.
discover (to) (-kø·vø^r) *tr*. descubrir, hallar. 2 descubrir, revelar, manifestar.
discoverer (-ø^r) *s*. descubridor.
discovery (-i) *s*. descubrimiento, hallazgo.
discredit (-kre·dit) *s*. descrédito; deshonra. 2 desconfianza, duda.
discredit (to) *tr*. desacreditar; deshonrar. 2 no creer, dudar de, desconfiar de.
discreditable (-abøl) *adj*. deshonroso.
discreet (-krı·t) *adj*. discreto [que procede con discreción]; juicioso, cuerdo, prudente.
discreetness (-nis) *s*. discreción, sensatez, cordura, prudencia.
discrepance, -cy (kre·pans, -si) *s*. discrepancia.
discrepant (-pant) *adj*. discrepante.
discrete (-krı·t) *adj*. discontinuo, separado. 2 MAT. discreto. 3 FIL. abstracto.
discretion (-kei·shøn) *s*. discreción [sensatez, reserva]; juicio, discernimiento. 2 discreción, arbitrio: *at the ~ of*, a la discreción de.
discretional (-al), **discretionary** (-eri) *adj*. discrecional.
discretive (di·skritiv) *adj*. disyuntivo. 2 que distingue.
discriminant (diskri·minant) *s*. MAT. discriminante.

discriminate (-minit) *adj*. distinto, diferenciado.
discriminate (to) (-eit) *tr*. discernir, distinguir, diferenciar; discriminar. 2 *intr*. hacer diferencias, distinciones [en favor o en contra].
discriminating (-ing) *adj*. que distingue finamente, agudo. 2 distintivo. 3 que hace diferencias, parcial.
discrimination (-ei·shøn) *s*. discernimiento. 2 diferencia, distinción, discriminación. 3 trato diferente.
discriminative (diskri·mineitiv), **discriminatory** (-atori) *adj*. discernidor. 2 distintivo. 3 que hace diferencias.
discrown (to) (-krau·n) *tr*. deponer, destronar.
discursive (-kø·^rsiv) *adj*. digresivo, descosido; extenso, lato. 2 razonado, no intuitivo.
discus (di·skøs) *s*. DEP. disco.
discuss (to) (diskø·s) *tr.-intr*. discutir. 2 ventilar, dilucidar; hablar de.
discussion (-shøn) *s*. discusión [debate, examen].
disdain (-dei·n) *s*. desdén, menosprecio.
disdain (to) (tr. desdeñar, menospreciar. 2 desdeñarse de.
disdainful (-ful) *adj*. desdeñoso. 2 altanero.
disease (-diš·š) *s*. enfermedad, mal, afección, dolencia.
disease (to) *tr*. enfermar, hacer daño.
diseased (-d) *adj*. enfermo; morboso.
disembark (to) (-emba·^rk) *tr.-intr*. desembarcar.
disembarkation (-ei·shøn), **disembarkment** (-mønt) *s*. desembarque. 2 desembarco.
disembarrass (to) (-embæ·ras) *tr*. desembarazar. 2 despejar. 3 zafar.
disembody (to) (-emba·di) *tr*. desencarnar. 2 licenciar [huestes]. ¶ Pret. y p. p.: *disembodied*.
disembogue (to) (-bou·g) *intr*. desembocar. 2 *tr*. vaciar [sus aguas]. 3 *tr.-intr*. arrojar [lavas, etc.].
disembowel (to) (-bau·øl) *tr*. desentrañar, destripar.
disembroil (to) (-broi·l) *tr*. desembrollar.
disenchant (to) (-encha·nt) *tr*. desencantar.
disencumber (to) (-kø·mbø^r) *tr*. desembarazar, descargar [de lo que embaraza]; descombrar.
disengage (to) (-gei·dÿ) *tr*. desasir, soltar, desenredar, desembarazar, librar. 2 librar, eximir, desligar [de una obligación, etc.]. 3 *intr*. zafarse, desasirse, soltarse, librarse. 4 MIL. despegarse.
disengaged (-d) *adj*. desembarazado, libre. 2 suelto, desasido, despegado. 3 vacante. 4 desocupado, sin empleo.
disentangle (to) (-tæ·ngøl) *tr*. desenredar, desenmarañar, desembrollar; zafar.
disentomb (-tu·m) *tr*. desenterrar, exhumar.
disestablish (to) (disestæ·blish) *tr*. separar [la Iglesia] del Estado.
disesteem (-estı·m) *s*. desestima.
disesteem (to) *tr*. desestimar, no estimar.
disfavour (-fei·vø^r) *s*. disfavor. 2 desagrado, malquerencia. 3 desgracia [pérdida del favor].
disfavour (to) *tr*. desfavorecer, desairar.
disfigure (to) (-fi·giu^r) *tr*. desfigurar, afear.
disfigurement (-mønt) *s*. desfiguración, afeamiento. 2 mancha, borrón, cosa que afea.
disgarnish (to) (-ga·^rnish) *tr*. desguarnecer.
disgorge (to) (-go·^rdÿ) *tr*. arrojar, vomitar, desembuchar. 2 devolver [lo robado].
disgrace (-grei·s) *s*. desgracia [pérdida del favor]. 2 deshonor, deshonra, vergüenza, oprobio. 3 baldón, mancha.
disgrace (to) *tr*. hacer perder el favor. 2 deshonrar, causar oprobio. 3 afear.

disgraceful (-ful) *adj.* deshonroso, vergonzoso, ignominioso.

disgracious (-grei·shøs) *adj.* falto de gracia.

disgregation (-grøgei·shøn) *s.* disgregación.

disgruntle (-grø·ntøl) *tr.* enfadar, disgustar.

disguise (-gaiš) *s.* disfraz. *2* embozo, rebozo, fingimiento.

disguise (to) *tr.* disfrazar. *2* enmascarar, ocultar, encubrir, disimular.

disgust (-gøst) *s.* aversión, hastío, repugnancia, asco.

disgust (to) *tr.* hastiar, repugnar, asquear.

disgusting (-ing) *adj.* repugnante, asqueroso.

dish (dish) *s.* plato, fuente: ~ *rack,* escurreplatos. *2* plato [manjar]. *3* concavidad. *4 pl.* vajilla.

dish (to) *tr.* servir, poner en platos. *2* aderezar, disponer. *3* burlar, frustrar. *4 intr.* hacerse cóncavo.

dishabille (disabı·l) *s.* trapillo, vestido casero.

dishabituate (-jabi·chueit) *tr.* deshabituar.

disharmony (-ja·ʳmoni) *s.* falta de armonía, discordancia.

dishcloth (di·shkloz) *s.* albero.

dishearten (to) (disja·ʳtøn) *tr.* descorazonar.

dished (di·sht) *adj.* cóncavo.

dishevel (to) (dishe·vøl) *tr.* desgreñar, despeinar; desarreglar. ¶ Pret. y p. p.: *disheveled* o *-lled;* ger.: *-ling* o *-lling.*

dishful (dish·ful) *s.* plato, fuente [contenido].

dishonest (disa·nist) *adj.* falto de honradez, ímprobo, falso. *2* poco honrado, ilícito, deshonroso.

dishonesty (-i) *s.* improbidad, falta de honradez.

dishono(u)r (disa·nøʳ) *s.* deshonor, deshonra. *2* afrenta. *3* com. falta de pago o de aceptación de un efecto.

dishono(u)r (to) *tr.* deshonorar. *2* deshonrar, infamar. *3* afrentar. *4* com. no pagar o no aceptar [un efecto].

dishono(u)rable (-abøl) *adj.* deshonroso. *3* poco honrado.

dishpan (di·shpæn) *s.* lebrillo de fregar platos.

dishwasher (-uoshøʳ) *s.* lavaplatos.

disillusion (disilu·ẏøn) *s.* desilusión, desengaño.

disillusion, disillusionize (to) (-aiš) *tr.* desilusionar.

disinclination (-inklinei·shøn) *s.* desafición, aversión.

disincline (-inklai·n) *tr.* desinclinar.

disinfect (to) (-infe·kt) *tr.* desinfectar.

disinfectant (-ænt) *s.* desinfectante.

disinfection (-fe·kshøn) *s.* desinfección.

disingenuous (-indẏe·niuøs) *adj.* falso, insincero.

disinherit (-je·rit) *tr.* desheredar.

disinheritance (-ans) *s.* desheredamiento.

disintegrate (to) (-tigrei·t) *tr.* desintegrar, disgregar, deshacer, desmoronar. *2 intr.* desintegrarse, deshacerse, desmoronarse.

disintegration (-ei·shøn) *s.* desintegración, disgregación.

disinter (to) (disi·ntøʳ) *tr.* desenterrar, exhumar. ¶ Pret. y p. p.: *-rred;* ger.: *-rring.*

disinterest (-tørest) *s.* perjuicio. *2* desinterés. *2* indiferencia.

disinterest (to) *tr.* despojar de interés o de motivos interesados. *2 ref.* desinteresarse.

desinterested (-id) *adj.* desinteresado. *2* que no tiene beneficio en una cosa. *3* imparcial.

disjoin (to) (disẏoi·n) *tr.* desjuntar, desunir, separar. *2 intr.* desunirse, separarse.

disjoint (-t) *tr.* desarticular, descoyuntar, dislocar,

desquiciar, devencijar. *2* desunir, separar. *3 intr.* desarticularse, dislocarse.

disjointed (-id) *adj.* desarticulado, descoyuntado. *2* inconexo, incoherente.

disjunction (-jø·nkshøn) *s.* disyunción. *2* separación.

disjunctive (-tiv) *adj.-s.* disyuntivo. *2 s.* disyuntiva.

disk (disk) *s.* disco [pieza circular]. *2* astr., bot., zool. disco.

dislike (dislai·k) *s.* aversión, antipatía, aborrecimiento.

dislike (to) *tr.* tener aversión o antipatía a, detestar; no encontrar de su gusto.

dislocate (to) (di·slokeit) *tr.* dislocar, descoyuntar. *2* desarreglar.

dislocation (-ei·shøn) *s.* dislocación.

dislodge (to) (disla·dẏ) *tr.* desalojar, echar fuera.

disloyal (-lo·ial) *adj.* desleal.

disloyalty (-ti) *s.* deslealtad.

dismal (di·šmal) *adj.* triste, lúgubre, tétrico. *2* funesto, desgraciado. *3 pl. the dismals,* tristeza, melancolía.

dismantle (to) (dismæ·ntøl) *tr.* desmantelar. *2* desguarnecer, desamoblar. *3* mec. desmontar.

dismast (to) (-mæ·st) *tr.* mar. desarbolar.

dismay (-mei·) *s.* desmayo, desaliento. *2* consternación, espanto.

dismay (to) *tr.* desanimar, espantar, aterrar.

dismember (-me·mbøʳ) *tr.* desmembrar.

dismemberment (-mønt) *s.* desmembración.

dismiss (to) (-mi·s) *tr.* despedir [hacer salir; dar permiso para irse]; disolver [una junta, etc.]. *2* despedir, destituir, separar, licenciar. *3* desechar, alejar del pensamiento; deshacerse [de un asunto].

dismissal (-al), **dismission** (-shøn) *s.* despido [invitación a retirarse]. *2* despido, destitución. *3* acción de desechar.

dismount (to) (-mau·nt) *tr.* desmontar [apear]. *2* desmontar [la artillería, una joya, etc.]. *3 intr.* desmontar, apearse.

disobedience (-obı·diøns) *s.* desobediencia.

disobedient (-diønt) *adj.* desobediente, insumiso, rebelde.

disobey (to) (-obei·) *tr.-intr.* desobedecer.

disoblige (to) (-oblai·dẏ) *tr.* desobligar. *2* no complacer, ser desatento con. *3* molestar, ofender.

disobliging (-ing) *adj.* poco complaciente, desatento. *2* molesto, ofensivo.

disorder (-o·ʳdøʳ) *s.* desorden. *2* trastorno, desarreglo; enfermedad. *3* enajenación mental.

disorder (to) *tr.* desordenar. *2* desarreglar, perturbar, trastornar.

disorderly (-li) *adj.* desordenado, desarreglado. *2* alborotador, escandaloso: ~ *conduct,* faltas contra la moral o el orden público. *3 adv.* desordenadamente.

disorganization (-o·ʳganišei·shøn) *s.* desorganización.

disorganize (to) (-o·ʳganiš) *tr.* desorganizar.

disorientate (to) (-o·rienteit) *tr.* desorientar.

disorientation (-ei·shøn) *s.* desorientación.

disown (to) (-ou·n) *tr.* repudiar; desconocer, negar; renegar de.

disparage (to) (-pæ·ridẏ) *tr.* desacreditar, despreciar, rebajar. *2* desdorar, hacer desmerecer.

disparagement (-mønt) *s.* detracción, menosprecio. *2* desdoro, descrédito.

disparate (di·sparit) *adj.* dispar, disparejo, discorde. *2 s.* una de dos cosas dispares.

disparity (-i) *s.* disparidad.
dispart (to) (-pa·ʳt) *tr.* despartir, dividir. 2 *intr.* dividirse.
dispassionate (-pæ·shønit) *adj.* desapasionado, sereno, frío, imparcial.
dispatch (-pæ·ch) *s.* despacho [acción]. 2 expedición, prontitud. 3 despacho, parte, comunicación. 4 MAR. ~ *boat*, aviso.
dispatch (to) *tr.* despachar [enviar, expedir; matar; comer]. 2 despachar, concluir, apresurar.
dispel (to) (-pe·l) *tr.* dispersar, disipar. 2 *intr.* dispersarse, disiparse. ¶ Pret. y p. p.: *-lled;* ger.: *-lling.*
dispendious (-pe·ndiøs) *adj.* dispendioso.
dispensary (-sari) *s.* dispensario farmacéutico.
dispensation (-ei·shøn) *s.* dispensación, distribución, administración. 2 gobierno. 3 providencia divina. 4 dispensa, exención. 5 ley, religión.
dispensatory (dispe·nsatori) *s.* farmacopea.
dispense (to) (-pe·ns) *tr.* dispensar, distribuir, conceder. 2 administrar [justicia]. 3 despachar [medicamentos]. 4 dispensar, eximir, excusar. ⅋5 *intr. to ~ with*, prescindir de.
dispeople (to) (-pɪ·pøl) *tr.* despoblar.
dispersal (-pø·ʳsal) *s.* dispersión.
disperse (-pø·ʳs) *adj.* disperso.
disperse (to) *tr.* dispersar. 2 disipar, desvanecer. 3 esparcir. 4 *intr.* dispersarse, esparcirse; disiparse.
dispersed (-t) *adj.* dispersado, disperso.
dispersion (-pø·ʳshøn) *s.* dispersión. 2 disipación, desvanecimiento. 3 esparcimiento, difusión.
dispirit (to) (-pɪ·rit) *tr.* desalentar, desanimar.
dispiritedness (-idnis) *s.* desaliento, desánimo.
displace (to) (-plei·s) *tr.* cambiar de sitio, remover, desalojar, quitar el sitio a. 2 MAR. desplazar. 3 destituir, separar.
displacement (-mønt) *s.* remoción, traslado. desalojamiento. 2 destitución, separación. 3 MAR. desplazamiento. 4 GEOL. falla, quiebra.
displant (-plænt) *tr.* desplantar.
display (-plei·) *s.* despliegue, exhibición, manifestación. 2 ostentación, alarde. 3 pompa, fausto.
display (to) *tr.* desplegar, abrir, extender. 2 exponer, poner de manifiesto. 3 exhibir, lucir, ostentar. 4 MAR. enarbolar.
displease (to) (-plɪ·š) *tr.* desplacer, desagradar, descontentar. 2 disgustar, enojar, ofender.
displeasure (-ple·ȳøʳ) *s.* desplacer, desagrado, descontento, enojo. 2 desgracia, disfavor. 3 disgusto, sinsabor.
displume (to) (-plu·m) *tr.* desplumar.
disport (-po·ʳt) *s.* juego, diversión.
disport (to) *tr.* divertir. 2 *intr.* juguetear, divertirse.
disposal (-pou·šal) *s.* disposición, colocación, arreglo [acción]. 2 DISPOSITION 4. 3 acción de deshacerse [de]; donación, venta, enajenación.
dispose (to) (-pou·š) *tr.* disponer, arreglar, ordenar. 2 disponer, establecer, determinar. 3 disponer, inclinar el ánimo de. 4 *intr. to ~ of*, disponer de; deshacerse o despachar, consumir; dar, vender, enajenar.
disposition (-poši·shøn) *s.* disposición, arreglo, ordenación. 2 condición, genio, humor. 3 tendencia, inclinación, propensión. 4 disposición [acción o facultad de disponer]. 5 *pl.* disposiciones [que se toman].
dispositioned (-t) *adj.* de tal o cual condición, genio, humor, etc.

dispossess (to) (-pøse·s) *tr.* desposeer. 2 DER. desahuciar, lanzar.
dispossession (-se·shøn) *s.* desposeimiento. 2 DER. desahucio, lanzamiento.
dispraise (disprei·š) *s.*ʳdesalabanza, censura.
dispraise (to) *tr.* desalabar, censurar.
disproof (-pru·f) *s.* refutación.
disproportion (-propo·ʳshøn) *s.* desproporción.
disproportion (to) *tr.* desproporcionar.
disproportionate (-it) *adj.* desproporcionado.
disproval (-pru·val) *s.* refutación, confutación.
disprove (-pru·v) *tr.* refutar, confutar.
disputable (-piu·tabøl) *adj.* disputable, discutible.
disputant (-tant) *adj.-s.* disputador.
disputation (-ei·shøn) *s.* disputa, debate.
disputatious (-ei·shøs) *adj.* disputador, reparón.
dispute (-piu·t) *s.* disputa, discusión. 2 controversia. 3 litigio, pleito.
dispute (to) *tr.-intr.* disputar, discutir. 2 controvertir. 3 *intr.* impugnar, poner en duda.
disputeless (-lis) *adj.* indiscutible.
disqualification (-kualifikei·shøn) *s.* inhabilitación, incapacidad, impedimento. 2 DEP. descalificación.
disqualify (to) (-kua·lifai) *tr.* inhabilitar, incapacitar. 2 DEP. descalificar.
disquiet (-kuai·øt) *s.* inquietud, desasosiego.
disquiet (to) *tr.* inquietar, intranquilizar, desasosegar, atormentar.
disquietness (-nis), **disquietude** (-iud) *s.* DISQUIET.
disquisition (-kuiši·shøn) *s.* disquisición.
disregard (-riga·ʳd) *s.* desatención, descuido, olvido, desprecio. 2 desconsideración, desaire.
disregard (to) *tr.* desatender, descuidar, olvidar, despreciar, no hacer caso [de]. 2 desconsiderar, desairar.
disregardful (-ful) *adj.* desatento, descuidado, que no hace caso.
disrelish (-re·lish) *s.* repugnancia, aversión.
disreputable (-re·piutabøl) *adj.* desacreditado, de mala fama o aspecto. 2 deshonroso, vergonzoso.
disrepute (-ripiu·t) *s.* descrédito, mala fama, deshonra.
disrespect (-rispe·kt) *s.* falta de respeto, desacato.
disrespect (to) *tr.* faltar al respeto a, desacatar.
disrespectful (-ful) *adj.* irrespetuoso.
disrobe (to) (-rou·b) *tr.* desnudar. 2 *intr.* desnudarse.
disrupt (to) (-rø·pt) *tr.* romper, dividir; desgajar.
disruption (-rø·pshøn) *s.* ruptura; desgajamiento.
disruptive (-rø·ptiv) *adj.* que rompe. 2 ELECT. disruptivo.
dissatisfaction (disætisfæ·kshøn) *s.* descontento, disgusto.
dissatisfactory (-tori) *adj.* poco o nada satisfactorio.
dissatisfy (to) (-sæ·tisfai) *tr.* descontentar, no satisfacer. ¶ Pret. y p. p.: ~ *fied.*
dissect (to) (-se·kt) *tr.* disecar, anatomizar.
dissector (-øʳ) *s.* disector.
dissemble (to) (-se·mbøl) *tr.* disimular, disfrazar, ocultar. 2 fingir, fingirse. 3 *intr.* fingir.
dissembler (-bløʳ) *s.* disimulador, fingidor, simulador, hipócrita.
disseminate (to) (-se·mineit) *tr.* diseminar. 2 difundir, propagar.
dissension (-se·nshøn) *s.* disensión, discordia.
dissent (-se·nt) *s.* disentimiento. 2 disidencia.
dissent (to) *intr.* disentir, diferir. 2 disidir.
dissenter (-øʳ) *s.* discorde [que disiente]. 2 disidente [esp. de la Iglesia anglicana].

dissentient (-se·nshiønt) *adj.* disconforme, opuesto. *2 s.* disidente.
dissert (to) (-sø·ʳt), **dissertate (to)** (-teit) *intr.* disertar.
dissertation (-ei·shøn) *s.* disertación.
disserve (to) (-sø·ʳv) *tr.* deservir, perjudicar.
disservice (-is) *s.* deservicio, perjuicio.
dissever (-e·vøʳ) *tr.* desunir, separar.
dissidence (di·sidøns) *s.* disidencia.
dissident (-ønt) *adj.-s.* disidente.
dissimilar (disi·milaʳ) *adj.* disímil, desemejante.
disimilarity (-similæ·riti) *s.* disimilitud, disparidad.
dissimilation (-ei·shøn) *s.* disimilación.
dissimilitude (-simi·litiud) *s.* disimilitud.
dissimulate (to) (-simiuleit) *tr.-intr.* disimular, fingir.
dissimulation (-ei·shøn) *s.* disimulación, disimulo, hipocresía.
dissipate (to) (di·sipeit) *tr.* dispersar. *2* esparcir. *3* disipar [desvanecer; malgastar]. *4 intr.* disiparse, desvanecerse. *5* entregarse a los placeres.
dissipated (-id) *adj.* disipado, disoluto.
dissipation (-ei·shøn) *s.* dispersión, evaporación. *2* disipación. *3* diversión, devaneo. *4* deroche. *5* disolución, vida relajada.
dissociate (to) (-shieit) *tr.* disociar. *2 intr.* disociarse.
dissolubility (-saliubi·liti) *s.* disolubilidad.
dissoluble (-sa·liubøl) *adj.* disoluble.
dissolute (di·søliut) *adj.* disoluto, relajado.
dissoluteness (-nis) *s.* disolución, relajamiento.
dissolution (-søliu·shøn) *s.* disolución [acción de disolver o disolverse]. *2* muerte. *3* licuación, fusión.
dissolvable (-ša·lvabøl) *adj.* disoluble.
dissolve (-ša·lv) *tr.* disolver. *2 DER.* abrogar. *3 intr.* disolverse. *4* deshacerse. *5* desvanecerse, desaparecer, morir. *6* decaecer.
dissolvent (-ønt) *adj.-s.* disolvente.
dissonance, -cy (di·sønans, -si) *s.* disonancia.
dissonant (-ant) *adj.* disonante, discordante.
dissuade (to) (disuei·d) *tr.* disuadir.
dissuasion (-ei·ȳøn) *s.* disuasión; consejo.
dissuasive (-siv) *adj.* disuasivo.
dissyllabic (-silæ·bik) *adj.* disílabo, bisílabo.
dissyllable (-si·labøl) *s.* disílabo, bisílabo.
dissymetry (-metri) *s.* disimetría.
distaff (di·stæf) *s.* rueca. *2* fig. la mujer.
distal (di·stal) *adj.* BIOL. distal.
distance (-tans) *s.* distancia. *2* alejamiento; lejos, lejanía, lontananza: *in the ~*, a lo lejos. *3* trecho, espacio. *4* reserva en el trato: *to keep at ~*, mantener [a uno] a distancia; no permitirle familiaridades.
distance (to) *tr.* distanciar. *2* alejar. *3* dejar atrás, adelantar. *4* espaciar.
distant (di·stant) *adj.* distante. *2* lejano. *3* diferente. *4* reservado en el trato, esquivo, frío, altivo.
distaste (distei·st) *s.* hastío, disgusto, aversión, repugnancia.
distasteful (-ful) *adj.* desagradable, repugnante.
distemper (-te·mpøʳ) *s.* mal humor. *2* enfermedad. *3* VET. moquillo. *4* tumulto, disturbio. *5* PINT. templa; pintura al temple.
distemper (to) *tr.* perturbar, enfermar. *2* incomodar, irritar. *3* pintar al temple.
distend (to) (-te·nd) *tr.* estirar, ensanchar, dilatar, hinchar. *2* MED. distender.

distension, distention (-te·nshøn) *s.* dilatación. *2* MED. distensión.
distich (di·stik) *s.* dístico.
distil(l (to) (disti·l) *tr.* destilar, alambicar. *2 tr.-intr.* destilar [gota a gota].
distillate (-eit) *s.* destilado.
distillation (-ei·shøn) *s.* destilación. *2* extracto, esencia.
distillery (-ti·løri) *s.* destilería.
distinct (-ti·nkt) *adj.* distinto, claro; preciso, definido. *2* distinto, diferente.
distinction (-nkshøn) *s.* distinción: *in ~ from* o *to*, a distinción de. *2* distingo. *3* diferencia. *4* distintivo, característica.
distinctive (-tiv) *adj.-s.* distintivo.
distinguish (to) (-ti·ngüish) *tr.* distinguir. *2* discernir. *3* dividir, clasificar. *4 ref.* distinguirse.
distinguished (-t) *adj.* distinguido.
distort (to) (-to·ʳt) *tr.* torcer, deformar. *2* desfigurar, falsear, tergiversar.
distorsion (-to·ʳshøn) *s.* torcimiento, distorsión. *2* falseamiento, tergiversación.
distract (to) (-træ·kt) *tr.* distraer [apartar la atención]. *2* perturbar, agitar, enloquecer.
distracted (-id) *adj.* distraído. *2* trastornado, enloquecido; loco, frenético.
distraction (-kshøn) *s.* distracción. *2* perturbación, agitación, enloquecimiento, frenesí, locura. *3* confusión, desorden.
distrain (to) (-trei·n) *tr.* DER. embargar, secuestrar.
distraint (-t) *s.* DER. embargo, secuestro.
distraught (-tro·t) *adj.* DISTRACTED.
distress (-tre·s) *s.* dolor, pena, aflicción. *2* infortunio, desgracia. *3* miseria, escasez. *4* apuro, peligro: *ship in ~*, barco en peligro. *5* DER. embargo.
distress (to) *tr.* afligir, apenar, angustiar. *2* poner en aprieto. *3* DER. embargar.
distressful (-ful) *adj.* doloroso, desdichado, lleno de trabajos o calamidades.
distressing (-ing) *adj.* penoso, aflictivo.
distribute (to) (-tri·biut) *s.* distribuir.
distributive (-iv) *adj.* distributivo.
district (di·strikt) *adj.* distrito. *2* partido, comarca, región, territorio.
distrust (distrø·st) *s.* desconfianza, recelo, suspicacia.
distrust (to) *tr.* desconfiar, sospechar de, no confiar en, recelar.
distrustful (-ful) *adj.* desconfiado, que desconfía, receloso, difidente.
disturb (to) (-tø·ʳb) *tr.* turbar, perturbar, alterar, desordenar. *2* inquietar, desasosegar. *3* distraer, estorbar. *4* molestar, incomodar.
disturbance (-bans) *s.* perturbación, alteración. *2* disturbio, desorden, alboroto. *3* inquietud, malestar.
disunion (-iu·niøn) *s.* desunión.
disunite (to) (-iunai·t) *tr.* desunir. *2 intr.* desunirse.
disuse (-iu·s) *s.* desuso. *2* falta de práctica o ejercicio.
disuse (to) *tr.* desusar. *2* dejar de usar, desechar.
ditch (dich) *s.* caz, reguera, zanja, foso, cuneta. *2* BOT. *~ reed*, carrizo.
ditch (to) *tr.* abrir zanjas en.
dither (di·døʳ) *s.* temblor, agitación.
dither (to) *intr.* temblar, estar agitado.
tithyramb (di·ziræmb) *s.* ditirambo.
ditone (dai·toun) *s.* MÚS. ditono.
dittany (di·tani) *s.* BOT. díctamo, orégano.
ditto (di·tou) *s.-adv.* idem.

ditty (-ti) *s.* canción, cantinela.
diuretic (daiure·tik) *adj.-s.* MED. diurético.
diurnal (daiø·ʳnal) *adj.* diurno. *2* diario, cotidiano.
diuturnal (-iutø·ʳnal) *adj.* diuturno.
diva (dɪ·va) *s.* diva, cantante.
divagate (to) (dai·vageit) *intr.* divagar.
divagation (-ei·shøn) *s.* divagación.
divan (divæ·n) *s.* diván.
divaricate (to) (daivæ·rikeit) *intr.* bifurcarse.
dive (daiv) *s.* zambullida, inmersión. *2* buceo. *3* NAT. salto. *4* AVIA. picado. *5* fam. (E.U.) taberna.
dive (to) *intr.* zambullirse. *2* arrojarse de cabeza. *3* sumergirse. *4* AVIA. picar. *5* bucear, profundizar, penetrar, enfrascarse [en]. *6* tr. zambullir, sumergir. ¶ Pret. y p.p.: *dived* o *dove.*
diver (-ø̱ʳ) *s.* buzo. *2* zambullidor. *3* ORN. somorgujo.
diverge (to) (divø·ʳdȳ) *intr.* divergir.
divergence (-øns) *s.* divergencia.
divergent (-ønt) *adj.* divergente.
divers (daivø·ʳs) *adj.* diversos, varios.
diverse (divø·ʳs) *adj.* diverso, diferente. *2* multiforme, variado.
diversify (to) (-ifai) *tr.* diversificar. *2* matizar, dar variedad a. ¶ Pret. y p. p.: *diversified.*
diversion (-vø·ʳshøn) *s.* diversión.
diversity (-siti) *s.* diversidad.
divert (to) (-vø·ʳt) *tr.* divertir, desviar, apartar. *2* distraer [de un trabajo, etc.]. *3* divertir, recrear.
divertisement (divø·ʳtišmønt) *diversión, entretenimiento. *2* intermedio de baile.
divest (to) (-ve·st) *tr.* desnudar. *2* despojar, desposeer.
divestiture (-ichø̱ʳ) *s.* despojo, desposeimiento.
divide (-vai·d) *s.* divisoria de aguas.
divide (to)) *tr.* dividir, partir, repartir; separar. *2* MAT. dividir. *3* compartir. *4* intr. dividirse. *5* tener una parte, ir a partes.
dividend (di·vidønd) *s.* MAT., COM. dividendo.
divider (divai·dø̱ʳ) *s.* partidor; distribuidor. *2* MAT. divisor. *3* pl. compás divisor.
divi-divi (di·vi·di·vi) *s.* BOT. dividiví.
divination (divinei·shøn) *s.* adivinación.
divinatory (di·vinatori) *adj.* adivinatorio.
divine (divai·n) *adj.* divino. *2* teológico, sagrado. *3 s.* sacerdote; teólogo.
divine (to) *tr.-intr.* adivinar. *2* conjeturar.
diviner (-ø̱ʳ) *s.* adivino. *2* adivinador.
divineress (-øris) *s.* adivina. *2* adivinadora.
diving (dai·ving) *s.* buceo [trabajo del buzo]: ~ *bell*, campana de buzo; ~ *dress* o *suit*, escafandra. *2* NAT. zambullidura, salto. *3* AVIA. picado.
divinity (divi·niti) *s.* vidinidad. *2* deidad. *3* teología.
divinize (to) (di·vinaiš) *tr.* divinizar.
divisibility (divisibi·liti) *s.* divisibilidad.
divisible (-vi·šibøl) *adj.* divisible.
division (-ÿøn) *s.* división [acción de dividir]. *2* división, desunión. *3* tabique, etc., que divide. *4* MAT., MIL., MAR. división. *5* ramo, sección, negociado. *6* compartimento; parte, segmento. *7* FERROC. ramal.
divisional (-al), **divisionary** (-eri) *adj.* divisional, divisionario. *2* divisorio.
divisor (divai·šø̱ʳ) *s.* MAT. divisor.
divorce (divo·ʳs) *s.* divorcio.
divorce (to) *tr.* divorciar. *2* divorciarse de. *3 intr.* divorciarse.
divorcee (divo·ʳsi) *s.* persona divorciada.
divulgation (-vølgei·shøn) *s.* divulgación, publicación.

divulge (to) (-vø·ldȳ) *tr.* divulgar, publicar.
dizen (to) (di·søn) *tr.* ataviar, emperejilar.
dizzines (-šinis) *s.* vértigo, mareo, vahído.
dizzy (-ši) *adj.* vertiginoso, mareador. *2* desvanecido, mareado. *3* aturdido. *4* caprichoso, alocado.
dizzy (to) *tr.* causar vértigo o vahído. *2* aturdir.
do (dou) *s.* MÚS. do.
do (to) (du) *tr.* hacer [en sentido general o indeterminado]: *what are you going to* ~?, ¿qué va usted a hacer? *2* hacer [producir un efecto; infligir, causar]: *that does you credit,* esto le hace honor. *3* hacer [los honores de; justicia, un favor]; rendir, tributar [homenaje]. *4* hacer [efectuar, realizar]; cumplir con: *to* ~ *our duty,* cumplir con nuestro deber. *5* acabar, concluir, terminar, cesar, dejar de [en frases con el part. *done*]: *have done!,* ¡acaba ya! *6* COC. preparar, aderezar, cocer, guisar [convenientemente]: *done to a turn,* en su punto. *7* arreglar, ordenar, limpiar, adornar, disponer: *to* ~ *one's hair,* peinarse. *8* hacer [una distancia, una velocidad]. *9* recorrer, visitar [como turista]. *10* verter, traducir. *11* hacer el papel de. *12* engañar, estafar. *13* hacer, cumplir [un tiempo de servicio, de cárcel, etc.]. *14* servir, bastar [al propósito, al objeto]. *15 to* ~ *away with,* deshacerse de; disipar; suprimir; dar al traste con; matar. *16 to* ~ *for,* acabar, arruinar; matar. *17 to* ~ *over,* rehacer; cubrir, untar. *18 to* ~ *up,* atar, envolver; planchar; limpiar, peinar; arreglar; fatigar, cansar.

19 intr. obrar, conducirse, portarse. *20* estar, hallarse, pasarlo: *how* ~ *you* ~?, ¿cómo está usted? *21* servir, bastar, ser suficiente: *that will* ~, esto servirá o bastará; ¡basta!, ¡está bien!, ¡no diga más! *22 to* ~ *well,* prosperar, medrar, ir bien. *23 to do without,* prescindir de, pasar sin.

25 do se usa además: a) como verbo auxiliar en las frases negativas e interrogativas y después de ciertos adverbios cuando hay inversión; b) en tono imperativo o deprecativo: *be quiet, do!,* ¡vamos, estáte quieto!; c) para dar más energía a frases afirmativas; d) para sustituir un verbo que no se quiere repetir: *I wanted to see him, and I did so,* quería verle, y le vi. ¶ INDIC. Pres. sing.: 1.ª pers., *do;* 2.ª pers., *doest* o *do;* 3.ª pers., *does;* pl., *do.* | Pret.: *did* (2.ª pers. del sing. *didst*). | PART. P: *done.* | GER: *doing.*
doat (to) *intr.* TO DOTE.
dobbin (da·bin) *s.* caballo de labor.
docile (dou·sil) *s.* dócil.
docility (dousi·liti) *s.* docilidad.
dock (dak) *s.* maslo [de la cola]; cola cortada. *2* codón. *3* MAR. dique; dársena. *4* desembarcadero; muelle. *5* banquillo [de los acusados], barra. *6* BOT. romaza.
dock (to) *tr.* cortar, cercenar. *2* descolar, desrabotar. *3* privar [de]. *4* MAR. hacer entrar en el dique. *5 intr.* MAR. fondear, atracar.
dockage (-idȳ) *s.* reducción, rebaja. *2* muellaje. *3* entrada en dique.
docker (-ø̱ʳ) *s.* trabajador del muelle.
docket (da·kit) *s.* minuta, sumario; lista, orden del día. *2* DER. lista de causas pendientes. *3* recibo de la aduana. *4* rótulo, etiqueta.
docket (to) *tr.* etiquetar, rotular. *2* extractar. *3* poner en la lista de causas pendientes o en la orden del día.
dockyard (-yaʳd) *s.* MAR. astillero, arsenal.
doctor (da·ktø̱ʳ) *m.* doctor. *2* médico, facultativo.

doctor (to) *tr.* doctorar. *2* medicinar. *3* reparar, componer. *4* adulterar, amañar. *5 intr.* ejercer la medicina.
doctoral (-al) *adj.* doctoral.
doctorate (-it) *s.* doctorado.
doctoress (-is) *s.* doctora.
doctorship (-ship) *s.* doctorado; borla.
doctrinal (da·ktrinal) *adj.* doctrinal, didáctico.
doctrinarian (daktrine·rian) *adj.-s.* doctrinario.
doctrine (ka·ktrin) *s.* doctrina.
document (-kiumønt) *s.* documento.
document (to) *tr.* documentar.
documental (-me·ntal), **documentary** (-me·ntari) *adj.* documental.
documentation (-ei·shøn) *s.* documentación.
dodder (da·dø^r) *s.* BOT. cúscuta.
dodder (to) *intr.* temblar, temblequear. *2* tambalear.
doddered (-d) *adj.* decrépito.
dodecagon (dode·kagan) *s.* GEOM. dodecaedro.
dodge (-dadӯ) *s.* regate. *2* argucia, artificio, manganilla.
dodge (to) *intr.* hurtar el cuerpo, regatear; escabullirse, dar esquinazo. *2* usar de argucias. *3* evitar, eludir, soslayar, burlar. *4* seguir con disimulo.
dodger (-ø^r) *s.* mañero, tramposo.
dodo (dou·dou) *s.* ORN. dido. *2* fig. persona anticuada.
doe (dou) *s.* ZOOL. gama; coneja; liebre, canguro o antílope hembra.
doer (du·ø^r) *s.* hacedor, autor, agente.
does (døs) *3.ª pers. sing. del Pres. de Ind.* de TO DO.
doeskin (dou·skin) *s.* ante, piel de gama.
doff (to) (daf) *tr.* quitarse [el sombrero, la ropa, etc.].
dog (dog o dag) *s.* ZOOL. perro, perra, can: *the ~ in the manger,* el perro del hortelano: *to go to the dogs,* arruinarse. *2* macho de algunos animales [zorro, lobo, chacal, etc.]. *3* fig. hombre, sujeto: *sly ~,* astuto, marrullero. *4* ASTR. Can. *5* piel de perro. *6* MEC. garra, grapa, barrilete. *7* morillo. *8* *hot ~,* salchicha caliente. *9 adj.* de perro, perruno, canino: *~ days,* canícula; *~ tooth,* colmillo; *~ Latin,* latín macarrónico. *10* BOT. *~ brier, ~ rose,* agavanzo, zarza perruna. *11 adv.* sumamente [esp. en compuestos].
dog (to) *tr.* perseguir, seguir, espiar. ¶ Pret. y p. p.: *dogged;* ger.: *dogging.*
dogaressa (dogare·sa) *s.* dogaresa.
dogbane (dogbei·n) *s.* BOT. acónito.
dogcart (-ka·rt) *s.* coche ligero de dos ruedas.
dog-cheap (adj. muy barato, tirado.
doge (doudӯ) *s.* dux.
dogfight (-fait) *s.* riña de perros.
dogfish (-fish) *s.* ICT. cazón, tollo, lija.
dogged (do·gid) *adj.* terco, obstinado, tenaz.
dogger (do·gø^r) *s.* MAR. dogre.
doggerel (-gørøl) *s.* coplas de ciego, versos malos. *2 adj.* malo, ramplón.
doggy (-i) *s.* perrito. *2 adj.* de perro. *3* aficionado a los perros.
doghouse (dogjau·š) *s.* caseta de perro.
dogma (do·gma) *s.* dogma.
dogmatic(al (-mæ·tik(al) *adj.* dogmático.
dogmatism (do·gmatišm) *s.* dogmatismo.
dogmatize (to) (-mataiš) *intr.* dogmatizar.
dog's-ear *s.* esquina doblada en una hoja de libro.
dogskin (do·gskin) *s.* piel de perro.
dog-tired *adj.* cansadísimo.
dogwood (-wud) *s.* BOT. cornejo, sanguiñuelo.

doily (doi·li) *s.* tapetito.
doing (du·ing) *ger.* de TO DO. *2 s.* acción, obra. *3 pl.* hechos, acciones; acontecimientos.
doldrums (da·ldrømš) *s. pl.* MAR. calmas ecuatoriales. *2* fam. murria; aburrimiento.
dole (doul) *s.* reparto regular, ración, limosna, subsidio. *2 poét.* dolor, aflicción.
dole (to) *tr.* dar, distribuir.
doleful (dou·lful), **dolesome** (-søm) *adj.* dolorido, lastimero, lúgubre, triste.
dolichocephalic (dolikousefæ·lik) *adj.* dolicocéfalo.
Doll (dal) *n. pr. f.* dim. de DOROTHY.
doll *s.* muñeca, muñeco.
dollar (da·la^r) *s.* dólar. *2* peso [moneda].
Dolly (da·li) *n. pr. f.* dim. de DOROTHY.
dolly *s.* muñequita [voz infantil]. *2* MEC., MIN. nombre de varios artefactos. *3* FERROC. locomotora auxiliar.
dolman (da·lman) *s.* dormán.
dolmen (da·lmen) *s.* dolmen.
dolomite (da·lomait) *s.* MINER. dolomita.
dolor (dou·lø^r) *s.* DOLOUR.
dolorous (-øs) *adj.* doloroso, penoso. *2* triste, lastimero.
dolour (dou·lø^r) *s. poét.* dolor, duelo.
dolphin (da·lfin) *s.* ZOOL., ASTR. delfín. *2* MAR. poste de amarre.
dolt (doult) *s.* tonto, zote, zopenco.
doltish (-ish) *adj.* tonto, lerdo, estúpido.
domain (domei·n) *s.* heredad, finca. *2* dominio [territorio]. *3* dominio, campo, esfera.
dome (doum) *s.* ARQ. cúpula, domo, cimborio. *2 poét.* edificio majestuoso. *3* AUTO. techo abovedado.
domesday (du·mšdei) *s.* DOOMSDAY.
domestic (dome·stik) *adj.* doméstico. *2* casero. *3* nacional, interior, del país: *~ commerce,* comercio interior. *4* intestino. *5 s.* doméstico, criado.
domesticate (to) (-eit) *tr.* domesticar. *2* civilizar. *3* naturalizar [costumbres, vocablos, etc.].
domesticity (-tisiti) *s.* domesticidad. *2 pl.* asuntos domésticos.
domicile (da·misil) *s.* domicilio.
domicile (to) *tr.* domiciliar. *2 intr.* domiciliarse, morar.
domiciliary (domisi·lieri) *adj.* domiciliario.
domiciliate (to) (-lieit) *tr.-intr.* TO DOMICILE.
dominant (da·minant) *adj.* dominante. *2 s.* MÚS. dominante.
dominate (to) (-mineit) *tr.-intr.* dominar. *2 intr.* predominar.
domination (-ei·shøn) *s.* dominación. *2* dominio, imperio; tiranía.
domineer (to) (damini·r) *intr.-tr.* dominar, tiranizar.
domineering (-ing) *adj.* dominante, autoritario.
Dominic (da·minik) *n. pr. m.* Domingo.
dominical (domi·nikal) *adj.* dominical [del Señor].
Dominican (-nikan) *adj.-s.* dominicano. *2* dominico.
dominie (da·mini) *s.* dómine.
dominion (domi·niøn) *s.* dominio, dominación, señorío, poder. *2* dominio [territorio].
dominium (-ni·øm) *s.* DER. dominio.
domino (da·minou), *pl.* **-nos** o **noes** (-nøs) *s.* dominó [traje; pieza del juego]. *2 pl.* dominó [juego].
Domitian (dou·mishan) *n. pr.* Domiciano.
Don (dan) *n. pr. m.* dim. de DONALD.
don *s.* don [tratamiento español]. *2* caballero, personaje. *3* profesor de Oxford o Cambridge.

don (to) *tr.* vestirse, ponerse. *2* investirse de. ¶ Pret. y p. p.: *donned;* ger.: *-nning.*
donate (to) (dou·neit) *tr.* donar.
donation (-ei·shøn) *s.* donación. *2* donativo; dádiva, don.
donative (da·nativ) *s.* donativo.
donator (dounei·tø^r) *s.* donador.
done (døn) *p. p.* de TO DO: hecho, acabado, fatigado, cocido, arruinado, perdido, muerto, etc.
donee (dounı·) *s.* donatario.
donjon (dø·ndўøn) *s.* torre del homenaje.
donkey (da·ngki) *s.* asno, burro, borrico, jumento. *2 adj.* MEC. auxiliar.
donor (dou·nø^r) *s.* donador, donante.
do-nothing *adj.-s.* inactivo, perezoso.
don't (dount) *contr.* de DO NOT.
doodle (to) (du·døl) *tr.-intr.* garrapatear.
doom (dum) *s.* sentencia, condena. *2* destino, suerte. *3* ruina, perdición. *4* juicio final.
doom (to) *tr.* condenar, sentenciar. *2* destinar, predestinar [a la ruina, destrucción, etc.].
doomsday (-sdei) *s.* día del juicio final.
door (do·ø^r) *s.* puerta: ~ *bolt,* pasador; ~ *catch,* golpete; ~ *mat,* felpudo; *in* ~, *within doors,* en casa, dentro de la casa; *out of doors, without doors,* fuera de casa, en la calle, al aire libre. *2* portal [de ciudad]. *3* MAR. porta.
doorcase (-keis) *s.* marco de la puerta.
doorhead (-jed) *s.* dintel.
doorkeeper (-kıpø^r) *s.* portero, conserje.
doorknob (-nab) *s.* botón o tirador de puerta.
doorplate (-pleit) *s.* placa de puerta.
doorpost (-post) *s.* jamba [de puerta]; quicial.
doorsill (-sil) *s.* umbral.
doorstep (-step) *s.* escalón delante de la puerta; umbral.
doorway (-wei) *s.* puerta, entrada, portal.
dope (doup) *s.* fam. droga, narcótico, estupefaciente: ~ *fiend,* morfinómano. *2* pop. información confidencial. *3* barniz [para ciertas telas].
dope (to) *tr.* drogar, narcotizar.
dor (do^r) *s.* ENT. escarabajo.
Dorian (do·rian), **Doric** (-rik) *adj.-s.* dorio; dérico.
dormancy (do·^rmansi) *s.* letargo, inactividad, estado latente.
dormant (-mant) *adj.* durmiente, dormido. *2* inactivo, latente, secreto.
dormer (-mø^r) o **dormer window** *s.* buharda.
dormitive (-mitiv) *s.* dormitivo, soporífero.
dormitory (-tori) *s.* dormitorio [de colegio, etc.].
dormouse (-maus) *s.* ZOOL. lirón.
Dorothy (do·rozi) *n. pr. f.* Dorotea.
dorsal (do·^rsal) *adj.* dorsal.
dory (do·ri) *s.* ICT. gallo, ceo. *2* bote de fondo plano.
dosage (dou·sidў) *s.* MED. dosificación.
dose (dous) *s.* dosis, toma. *2* fig. píldora, mal trago.
dose (to) *tr.* medicinar, dar una toma a. *2* dosificar.
dosimetry (dosi·metri) *s.* dosimetría.
dossal (da·sal) *s.* bancal [tapete]. *2* colgadura [detrás de un altar, etc.].
dossier (da·sie^r) *s.* expediente, papeles; historial.
dossil (-sil) *s.* CIR. lechino.
dost (døst) *2.ª* pers. pres. ind. de TO DO.
dot (dat) *s.* punto, señal, pinta. *2* MÚS. puntillo. *3 on the* ~, en punto, a la hora exacta.
dot (to) *tr.* puntear [marcar con puntos]; poner punto [a la i]. *2* salpicar, esparcir. ¶ Pret. y p. p.: *dotted;* ger.: *-tting.*
dotage (dou·tidў) *s.* chochera, chochez.
dotal (-tal) *adj.* dotal.
dotard (-ta^rd) *s.* viejo chocho, imbécil.

dote (to) (dout) *intr.* chochear, estar chocho: *to* ~ *upon,* estar chocho o loco por.
doting (dou·ting) *adj.* chocho.
dotted line (da·tid) *s.* línea de puntos.
dotterel (-tørøl) *s.* ORN. especie de chorlito.
dotty (-ti) *adj.* manchado, punteado.
double (dø·bøl) *adj.* doble, duplo, dúplice: ~ *chin,* papada; ~ *entry,* COM. partida doble; ~ *the amount,* el doble. *2* doble, insincero, ambiguo. *3* BOT. doble [flor]. *4 s.* doble, duplo. *5* duplicado, copia. *6* doble [de una pers.]. *7* sombra [aparición]. *8* doblez, pliegue. *9* artificio, engaño. *10 pl.* dobles [en el tenis]. *11 adv.* doblemente, dos veces, de dos en dos.
double (to) *tr.* doblar [duplicar; valer el doble de]. *2* redoblar, repetir. *3* doblar, plegar. *4* MAR. doblar [un cabo, etc.]. *5* escapar a [volviendo atrás]. *6* CINE., TEAT. sustituir, doblar. *7* forrar. *8 intr.* doblarse. *9* encorvarse, plegarse. *10* escapar volviendo atrás. *11* obrar con doblez.
double-acting *adj.* MEC. de doble efecto.
double-barrel(l)ed *adj.* de dos cañones.
double-breasted *adj.* cruzado [chaqueta, etc.].
double-cross *s.* traición [hecha a un cómplice].
double-cross (to) *tr.* traicionar [a un cómplice].
double-dealing *s.* doblez, falsía.
double-edged *adj.* de dos filos.
double-faced *adj.* de dos caras. *2* doble, hipócrita.
double-hearted *adj.* falso, traicionero.
double-minded *adj.* indeciso. *2* inconsecuente. *3* doble, de dos caras.
doubleness (-nis) *s.* duplicidad.
double-quick *adj.* redoblado [paso].
doublet (dø·blit) *s.* par, pareja. *2* jubón. *3* JOY., FILOL. doblete.
doubloon (døblu·n) *s.* doblón [moneda].
doubt (daut) *s.* duda: *no* ~, *without* ~, sin duda, indudablemente. *2* incertidumbre. *3* objeción, reparo.
doubt (to) *tr.* dudar, dudar de. *2* temer, sospechar. *3 intr.* dudar, vacilar.
doubtful (-ful) *adj.* dudoso. *2* dubitativo. *3* indeciso. *4* incierto, problemático. *5* ambiguo.
doubting (-ing) *adj.* dudoso, que duda.
doubtless (-lis) *adj.* indudable. *2 adv.* indudablemente.
douche (dush) *s.* ducha. *2* MED. irrigación. *3* MED. irrigador.
douche (to) *tr.* duchar. *2 intr.* ducharse.
dough (dou) *s.* masa [del pan]. *2* pasta [masa blanda]. *3* pop. pasta [dinero].
doughnut (dou·nøt) *s.* buñuelo, fruta de sartén.
doughty (dau·ti) *adj.* fuerte, valiente.
doughy (dou·i) *adj.* pastoso, blando, crudo.
Douro (dou·ru) *n. pr.* GEOGR. Duero.
douse (to) (daus) *tr.* rociar, remojar. *2* chapuzar, zambullir. *3* fam. apagar. *4* MAR. recoger, arriar. *5* TO DOFF. *6 intr.* zambullirse.
dove (døv) *s.* paloma, palomo: *the Dove,* el Espíritu Santo. *2* p. p. de TO DIVE.
dovecot (-kat) *s.* palomar.
dovetail (-teil) *s.* CARP. cola de milano o de pato.
dovetail (to) *tr.* ensamblar a cola de milano. *2* unir, enlazar.
Dover (dou·vø^r) *n. pr.* GEOGR. Dóver o Dovres.
dowager (dau·adўø^r) *s.* viuda [con título que procede del marido]: *queen* ~, reina viuda. *2* fam. matrona respetable.
dowdy (dau·di) *adj.* desaliñado, mal vestido.
dowel (dau·øl) *s.* CARP. clavija, tarugo, espiga.
dower (dau·ø^r) *s.* DER. bienes asignados a la viuda.

2 DER. dote [de la mujer]. **3** don, dote, prenda [de una pers.].

dower (to) tr. DER. asignar bienes a la viuda. **2** dotar.

dowery (dau·ri) s. DOWRY.

down (daun) adv.-prep. abajo, hacia abajo, a lo largo de, por: ~ *the river*, río abajo; ~ *the street*, calle abajo, por la calle. **2** pasando de un tiempo, lugar, etc. a otro posterior: ~ *from*, desde; ~ *to*, hasta; ~ *to date*, hasta la fecha. **3** en o por tierra: ~ *on one's knees*, de rodillas. **4** en sujección. **5** completamente. **6** *interj.* ¡abajo!: ~ *with him!*, ¡abajo!, ¡muera! **7** adj. pendiente, que baja, descendente: ~ *train*, tren descendente. **8** de abajo. **9** bajo, caído, decaído, abatido, enfermo: ~ *in the mouth*, cariacontecido. *10 to be* ~ *on*, tratar con severidad. *11* adj. y adv. al contado. *12* s. pulmón, flojel: ~ *bed*, edredón. *13* bozo, vello. *14* pelo suave, pelusa. *15* duna. *16* loma. *17* revés de fortuna, caída. *18 pl.* tierra alta ondulada propia para pastos.

down (to) tr. derribar. **2** vencer, derrotar. **3** tragar. **4** bajar. *5 to* ~ *tools*, declararse en huelga.

downcast (dau·nkæst) adj. inclinado hacia abajo. **2** bajo [ojos, mirada]. **3** abatido, alicaído.

downfall (-fol) s. caída [esp. de agua o nieve], chaparrón, nevada. **2** caída, ruina.

downfallen (-øn) adj. caído, arruinado.

downhaul (dau·njol) s. MAR. cargadera.

downhearted (-je·ᶠtid) adj. abatido, desanimado.

downhill (-jil) adj. pendiente, en declive. **2** adv. hacia abajo, cuesta abajo; de capa caida. **3** s. declive, bajada.

downpour (-poᶠ) s. aguacero; lluvia fuerte y seguida.

downright (-rait) adj. claro, categórico. **2** franco, brusco. **3** absoluto, completo. **4** vertical. **5** adv. francamente. **6** absolutamente, completamente.

downstairs (-te·rš) adj. de abajo, del piso inferior. **2** adv. abajo; en el piso inferior, en la planta baja, en los sótanos o hacia ellos.

downstream (-stri·m) s. aguas abajo.

downstroke (-trouk) s. MEC. carrera descendente.

downtown (-tau·n) adv.-adj. hacia el centro o en el centro de la ciudad.

downward (-uaᶠd) adj. descendente; que se dirige o extiende hacia abajo. **2** adv. DOWNWARDS.

downwards (-š) adv. hacia abajo. **2** hacia una época posterior.

downy (-i) adj. velloso, cotudo, felpudo, plumoso. **2** blando, suave, dulce.

dowry (-i) s. dote.

doze (douš) s. sueño ligero, adormecimiento, sopor.

doze (to) intr. dormitar, estar medio dormido.

dozen (dø·šn) s. docena.

dozy (dou·ši) adj. soñoliento, amodorrado.

drab (dræb) adj. pardusco, pardo amarillento. **2** soso, monótono. **3** s. monotonía. **4** ramera. **5** pazpuerca.

drabble (to) (dræ·bøl) tr. arrastrar, enlodar.

drachma (-kma) s. dracma.

Draconian (dreikou·nian) adj. draconiano.

draff (dræf) s. heces, desperdicios.

draffish (-ish), **draffy**(-i) adj. inútil, despreciable.

draft, draught (dræft) s. acción de sacar; cosa sacada. **2** corriente [de aire]. **3** tiro [de chimenea]. **4** succión, aspiración; inhalación; trago. **5** be-

bida, pócima. **6** atracción; tracción, tiro: *draft horse*, caballo de tiro. **7** estiramiento, estiraje. **8** redada. **9** traza, trazado. *10* diseño, boceto, dibujo. *11* plan, plano, proyecto. *12* borrador, minuta. *13* giro, libramiento, letra de cambio, orden de pago. *14* MIL. leva, reclutamiento. *15* MIL. destacamento. *16* MAR. calado. *17 pl.* (Ingl.) DRAUGHTS, juego de damas.

¶ En las acepciones 2, 3, 10, 12, 13, 14 y 15, úsase de preferencia *draft*; en las acepciones 4, 5 y 8, úsase de preferencia *draught*.

draft, draught (to) tr. aspirar [un líquido, etc.]. **2** hacer el borrador de, redactar. **3** trazar, diseñar, bosquejar. **4** destacar [para un servicio]. **5** MIL. reclutar.

draftsman (dræ·ftsmæn) s. dibujante, delineante.

drafty (-fti) adj. que tiene o produce corrientes de aire.

drag (dræg) s. rastra, grada. **2** carro bajo, narria. **3** gancho, etc. para arrastrar. **4** instrumento para rastrear. **6** entorpecimiento; traba, rémora. **7** AVIA. resistencia al avance. *8* ~ *boat*, draga.

drag (to) tr. arrastrar. **2** rastrear, dragar. **3** AGR. gradar. **4** intr. arrastrar [ir rozando el suelo]. **5** MAR. garrear. **6** avanzar, lentamente. **7** rezagarse. **8** decaer [la acción o el interés]. *9 to* ~ *on* o *out*, alargarse, durar demasiado. ¶ Pret. y p. p.: *dragged*; ger.: *-gging*.

draggle (to) (dræ·gøl) tr.-intr. ensuciar o ensuciarse arrastrando. **2** intr. rezagarse.

dranet (-net) s. red barredera, jábega.

dragoman (dræ·goman) s. dragomán, drogmán.

dragon (-gøn) s. dragón. **2** persona severa o de mal genio. **3** BOT. dragontea. *4* BOT. ~ *tree*, drago.

dragonfly (-flai) s. ENT. libélula.

dragonish (-ish) adj. dragontino.

dragoon (dragu·n) s. MIL. dragón.

dragoon (to) tr. intimidar, acosar, perseguir.

drain (drei·n) s. acción de sacar poco a poco; agotamiento. **2** desagüe. **3** cacera, zanja de derivación. **4** albañal, atarjea, sumidero. **5** CIR. tubo de drenaje. *6 pl.* restos [de un líquido], heces.

drain (to) tr. sacar poco a poco, agotar, apuᵣar; escurrir. **2** vaciar, empobrecer, sangrar. **3** secar, enjugar. **4** desaguar, desecar, avenar [un terreno]. **5** MIN. achicar. **6** MEC. purgar. **7** filtrar. **8** intr. vaciarse, escurrirse. **9** GEOGR. desaguar.

drainage (-idỹ) s. acción de sacar, agotamiento. **2** desagüe. **3** avenamiento. **4** drenaje. *5* ~ *basin*, cuenca [de un río].

drainer (-øᶠ) s. palero. **2** colador, filtro. **3** secadero, escurridero.

drake (dreik) s. dragón [monstruo]. **2** ORN. pato [macho].

dram (dræm) s. dracma [peso]. **2** trago. **3** poquito, miaja.

drama (dra·ma) s. drama.

dramatic (al (dramæ·tik(al) adj. dramático.

dramatics (-s) s. sing. TEAT. representación de aficionados.

dramatism (dræ·matišm) s. dramatismo.

dramatist (-tist) s. dramaturgo.

dramatize (-taiš) tr. dramatizar.

dramaturge, -gist (dræ·matøᶠdỹ, -ỹist) s. dramaturgo.

dramaturgy (-dỹi) s. dramática.

drape (to) (dreip) tr. cubrir con ropajes. **2** colgar, entapizar, adornar. **3** disponer los pliegues de.

draper (-øᶠ) s. pañero.

drapery (-i) *s.* pañería, paños. 2 ropaje, colgaduras, tapicería.
drastic (dræ·stik) *adj.* drástico. 2 enérgico, riguroso.
draught (dræft) *s.* DRAFT.
draught (to) *tr.* TO DRAFT.
draughtboard (-bo^{r}d) *s.* tablero de damas.
draughtsman (-smæn) *s.* peón [del juego de damas]. 2 DRAFTSMAN.
draw (dro·) *s.* arrastre, tracción, tiro. 2 atracción. 3 lo que se dice para hacer hablar a uno. 4 BILL. retroceso. 5 NAIPES robo. 6 tablas, empate. 7 sorteo; premio [en la lotería]. 8 TEJ. carrera, pasada.
draw (to) *tr.* arrastrar, tirar de. 2 atraer. 3 apartar, distraer. 4 persuadir, inducir, impulsar. 5 hacer hablar, sonsacar. 6 subir [un puente levadizo]. 7 sacar, retirar, extraer, arrancar, obtener. 8 sacar, desenvainar [la pistola, la espada]. 9 correr, descorrer [cortinas, etc.]. 10 hacer salir. 11 batir [un bosque, etc.]. 12 dragar, rastrear. 13 chupar. 14 aspirar, respirar, inhalar. 15 cobrar [un sueldo]; devengar [interés]. 16 retirar [fondos]. 17 COM. librar, girar. 18 echar [suertes]; sortear. 19 estirar. 20 tirar [metales]. 21 tender [un arco]. 22 dibujar, bosquejar, delinear, trazar. 23 redactar, extender. 24 sacar, deducir, inferir. 25 hacer [comparaciones, distinciones]. 26 BILL. picar bajo. 27 MAR. calar. 28 to ~ along, arrastrar. 29 to ~ aside, correr, descorrer [una cortina, etc.]. 30 to ~, breath, respirar, tomar aliento. 31 to ~ forth, hacer salir, sacar. 32 to ~ lots, echar suertes. 33 to ~ out, sacar; extender; sonsacar, hacer hablar. 34 to ~ the long bow, exagerar. 35 to ~ oneself up, erguirse, ponerse tieso. 36 intr. tirar [arrastrando]. 37 atraer público. 38 tirar [una chimenea, etc.]. 39 encogerse, contraerse. 40 estirarse, alargarse. 41 dibujar. 42 echar suertes. 43 MAR. tener calado. 44 NAIPES ir al robo. 45 NAIPES arrastrar. 46 empatar. 47 moverse: to ~ along, arrastrarse; to ~ aside, hacerse a un lado; to ~ away, alejarse; to ~ back, retroceder; to ~ near, acercarse. 48 COM. girar [contra]. 49 sacar la pistola, desenvainar la espada. 50 to ~ to a head, madurar, empezar a supurar.
¶ Pret.: *drew;* p. p.: *drawn.*
drawback (-bæk) *s.* inconveniente, desventaja. 2 descuento. 3 reembolso de derechos de aduana.
drawbridge (-bridỹ) *s.* puente levadizo o giratorio.
drawee (-I·) *s.* COM. librado, girado.
drawer (-ø^r) *s.* cajón [de mueble]; gaveta. 2 COM. librador, girador. 3 dibujante. 4 extractor. 5 pl. calzoncillos, pantalones.
drawing (-ing) *s.* dibujo; ~ board, tablero de dibujo. 2 trazado, delineación. 3 tracción, arrastre. 4 tirado [de metales]. 5 TEJ. estiramiento, estiraje. 6 extracción, saca. 7 sorteo. 8 ~ room, sala de recibo, salón, estrado.
drawl (drol) *s.* enunciación lenta y penosa.
drawl (to) *tr.* pronunciar con lentitud. 2 intr. arrastrar las palabras.
drawn (dron) p. p. de TO DRAW. 2 adj. arrastrado, estirado, dibujado, trazado, etc. 3 de aspecto fatigado, ojeroso [facciones, rostro].
dray (drei), **dray-cart** *s.* carretón, carro fuerte, camión.
drayage (drei·idỹ) *s.* carretaje, acarreo.
drayman (-mæn) *s.* carretero, camionero.
dread (dred) *s.* miedo, temor. 2 terror, espanto,

pavor. 3 adj. temible, terrible, espantoso. 2 augusto, venerable.
dread (to) *tr.-intr.* temer [a], tener miedo [de].
dreadful (-ful) adj. terrible, espantoso, horrendo. 2 horrible, desagradable, repugnante.
dreadless (-lis) adj. intrépido.
dreadnought, o **-naught** (not) *s.* MAR. tipo de acorazado grande.
dream (drim) *s.* sueño, ensueño. 2 visión, quimera.
dream (to) *tr.-intr.* soñar: to ~ of, soñar con o en. 2 tr. imaginar, fantasear. ¶ Pret. y p. p.: *dreamed* o *dreamt.*
dreamer (-ø^r) *s.* soñador. 2 visionario, iluso.
dreamily (-ili), **dreamingly** (-ingli) adv. como en sueños; vagamente.
dreamt (dremt) pret. y p. p. de TO DREAM.
dreamy (drɪ·mi) adj. soñador. 2 irreal, fantástico. 3 vago, borroso.
drear (drɪ·ø^r) adj. poét. DREARY.
dreary (-i) adj. triste, lúgubre, sombrío. 2 monótono, aburrido.
dredge (dredỹ) *s.* draga. 2 MAR. aparato para rastrear.
dredge (to) *tr.-intr.* dragar, excavar, limpiar. 2 MAR. rastrear. 3 COC. espolvorear.
dredger (-ø^r) *s.* dragador. 2 draga. 3 COC. vaso para espolvorear.
dredging-machine *s.* draga.
dreggy (dre·gi) adj. turbio, zurraposo.
dregs (dregš) *s. pl.* hez, heces, poso, sedimento. 2 madre [del vino]. 3 hez [lo más vil].
drench (drench) *s.* mojadura, remojón. 2 inundación, diluvio. 3 trago, poción.
drench (to) (tr. mojar, remojar, empapar, calar. 2 llenar, saturar. 3 VET. purgar.
dress (dres) *s.* vestido, vestuario, indumentaria. 2 traje; hábito; vestido de mujer. 3 atavío, tocado, compostura. 4 aderezo [para una tela, etc.]. 5 adj. de vestir, de etiqueta, de gala: ~ ball, baile de etiqueta; ~ circle, TEAT. galería principal; el gran mundo; ~ coat, frac, casaca; ~ suit, traje de etiqueta.
dress (to) *tr.* vestir. 2 vestir de etiqueta o de ceremonia. 3 ataviar, engalanar. 4 peinar, arreglar [el cabello]. 5 almohazar. 6 curar [las heridas]. 7 poner [la mesa]. 8 preparar, disponer, arreglar, aderezar, guisar, aliñar, aprestar, almidonar, engomar. 9 zurrar [pieles]; desbastar [madera]; labrar [piedra]. 10 enlucir, revocar. 11 podar [una planta]. 12 despabilar [una luz]. 13 to ~ down o off, reprender, calentar las orejas.
14 intr. vestirse, ataviarse: to ~ up, vestirse de ceremonia o con lujo. 15 MIL. alinearse.
¶ Pret. y p. p.: *dressed* o *drest.*
dresser (dre·sø^r) *s.* el que viste, adereza, prepara, etc. 2 cómoda con espejo. 3 mesa o aparador de cocina.
dressing (-ing) *s.* acción de vestir o vestirse. 2 preparación, arreglo, adorno, aderezo. 3 CIR. cura; apósito, vendaje. 4 COC. aderezo, condimento, salsa. 5 TEN. adobo. 6 TEJ. aderezo. 7 AGR. abono. 8 AGR. poda. 9 desbaste, labra. 10 dressing o ~ down, rapapelo, castigo. 11 adj. de vestir, para vestir, etc.: ~ case, neceser; ~ gown, bata, peinador; ~ table, tocador [mueble].
dressmaker (-mei·kø^r) *s.* costurera, modista.
dressmaking (-king) *s.* modistería.
dressy (-i) adj. elegante, vistoso, que viste demasiado. 2 demasiado peripuesto.
drew (dru) pret. de TO DRAW.

dribble (dri·bøl) *s.* goteo, chorrillo. 2 llovizna. 3 FÚTBOL. dribling, regate.

dribble (to) *intr.* gotear. 2 babear. 3 *tr.* dejar caer en gotas. 4 FÚTBOL. driblar, regatear.

dribblet (-blit) *s.* gota. 2 pizca.

dried (draid) *pret.* y *p. p.* de TO DRY. 2 *adj.* seco, desecado: ~ *beef*, cecina, tasajo. 3 pasa [fruta].

drier (drai·ø^r) *s.* secador, enjugador.

drier, driest *adj.* comp. y superl. de DRY.

drift (drift) *s.* lo arrastrado, impulsado o amontonado por una corriente, el mar, el viento, etc. 2 corriente [de agua, de aire]; movimiento, fluctuación [de lo impulsado o arrastrado]; masa que va en una dirección. 3 tendencia, rumbo, dirección, giro. 4 impulso, fuerza, móvil. 5 intención, sentido. 6 MAR., AVIA. deriva. 7 ARQ. empuje. 8 MEC. escariador. 9 MIN. galería.

drift (to) *tr.* impeler, llevar, amontonar [como hacen una corriente, el viento, etc.]. 2 MIN. abrir [una galería]. 3 MEC. escariar. 4 *intr.* flotar, ir a la deriva; ir a la ventura, sin rumbo. 5 MAR., AVIA. derivar, devalar. 6 correr, amontonarse [al impulso del viento, etcétera].

driftage (-idẏ) *s.* MAR. deriva. 2 lo llevado por una corriente, el viento, etc.

driftwood (-wud) *s.* madera llevada por el agua.

drill (dril) *s.* taladro, broca, perforador. 2 MIN. sonda. 3 AGR. sembradora mecánica. 4 hilera de semillas sembradas. 5 ZOOL. mandril. 6 dril [tela]. 7 adiestramiento. 8 MIL. instrucción, ejercicio.

drill (to) *tr.* taladrar, barrenar, perforar. 2 abrir, hacer [un agujero]. 3 MIL. instruir, enseñar el ejercicio. 4 *tr.-intr.* AGR. sembrar en surcos o hileras. 5 *intr.* MIL. hacer el ejercicio. 6 ejercitarse, adiestrarse.

drillings (dri·lings) *s. pl.* material extraído por un taladro.

drink (drink) *s.* bebida, poción; bebida alcohólica: *in* ~, borracho. 2 trago: *to take a* ~, echar un trago. 3 bebida [vicio].

drink (to) *tr.* beber; beberse: *to* ~ *someone's health*, brindar por uno. 2 aspirar, inhalar. 3 absorber, chupar. 4 *to* ~ *in*, absorber, embeber, beber [conocimientos], absorber con placer. 5 *intr.* beber, emborracharse. ¶ Pret.: *drank;* p. p.: *drunk*.

drinkable (-abøl) *adj.* bebible, potable. 2 *s. pl.* bebidas.

drinker (-ø^r) *s.* bebedor.

drinking (-ing) *s.* acción de beber. 2 bebida [vicio]. 3 *adj.* bebedor; de beber, para beber: ~ *place*, ~ *trough*, abrevadero.

drip (drip) *s.* goteo, chorreadura; reguero. 2 gotera [del techo]. 3 ARQ. alero, cornisa.

drip (to) *tr.* verter o dejar caer a gotas. 2 *intr.* gotear, chorrear, destilar, caer gota a gota. ¶ Pret. y p. p.: *dripped;* ger.: *-pping*.

dripping (-in) *s.* goteo, chorreo. 2 *pl.* líquido o grasa que gotea o chorrea: *dripping pan*, grasera.

drive (draiv) *s.* paseo en coche. 2 paseo o avenida para coches. 3 urgencia, presión, exigencia. 4 impulso, empuje. 5 campaña vigorosa, esfuerzo. 6 movimiento rápido, ataque, embestida. 7 tendencia, rumbo. 8 manada de reses. 9 MEC. mando, transmisión. 10 conducción [de un vehículo]: *left* ~, conducción a la izquierda. 11 COM. saldo, liquidación [venta].

drive (to) *tr.* impeler, impulsar, mover, llevar. 2 inducir, forzar [a]. 3 guiar, conducir [un vehículo, el ganado]. 4 llevar [en vehículo]. 5 hacer, realizar. 6 hacer trabajar mucho. 7 meter, clavar, hundir. 8 MEC. mover, accionar. 9 MIN. abrir, prolongar [una galería]. 10 DEP. golpear [la pelota]. 11 *to* ~ *away*, ahuyentar, espantar; alejar. 12 *to* ~ *in* o *into*, clavar, hacer entrar. 13 *to* ~ *mad*, volver loco. 14 *to* ~ *out*, echar fuera.

15 *intr.* conducir un vehículo [a]; saber conducir. 16 ir en coche, auto, etc. 17 correr, ser impelido. 18 *to* ~ *at*, batir, golpear, aspirar a, proponerse; insinuar, querer decir. 19 *to* ~ *away*, trabajar con ahinco. 20 *to let* ~, asestar un golpe.

Pret.: *drove*; p. p. *driven*.

drivel (dri·vøl) *s.* baba. 2 tonterías, vaciedades.

drivel (to) *intr.* babear, babosear. 2 chochear, decir tonterías. ¶ Pret.: y p. p.: *diveled* o ~ lled; ger.: ~ *ling* o ~ *lling*.

drivel(l)er (-ø^r) *s.* baboso. 2 simple, tonto, chocho.

driven (dri·vøn) *p. p.* de TO DRIVE.

driver (drai·vø^r) *s.* conductor [de animales o vehículos], carretero, cochero; chófer, mecánico; maquinista [de tren]. 2 MEC. rueda motriz, pieza impulsora. 3 mazo. 4 persona despótica, cabo de vara.

driving (-ing) *s.* acción de impulsar, mover, conducir, etc. 2 impulso. 3 tendencia. 4 *adj.* de conducción o conducir. 5 impetuoso, violento. 6 motor, motriz, impulsor. 7 MEC. de mando, de transmisión.

drizzle (dri·šøl) *s.* llovizna, cernidillo.

drizzle (to) *tr.* rociar, salpicar. 2 *intr.* lloviznar.

drizzly (-šli) *adj.* lloviznoso.

droll (droul) *adj.* cómico, chusco, gracioso, raro, estrambótico. 2 *s.* bufón, chusco.

droll (to) *intr.* bromear, hacer el bufón.

drollery (dou·løri) *s.* comicidad, humor. 2 broma, farsa, bufonada] chascarrillo.

dromedary (dra·møderi) *s.* ZOOL. dromedario.

drone (droun) *s.* ENT. y fig. zángano. 2 zumbido 3 roncón de gaita. 4 ENT. ~ *fly*, moscardón.

drone (to) *intr.* holgazanear, zanganear. 2 zumbar.

droop (drup) *s.* inclinación, caída, caimiento.

droop (to) *tr.* inclinar, bajar. 2 *intr.* inclinarse, caer, colgar, pender. 3 declinar, decaer, consumirse, marchitarse, abatirse.

drooping (-ing) *adj.* bajo, caído: ~ *lashes*, ojos bajos; medio cerrados. 2 BOT. colgante.

drop (drap) *s.* gota [de líquido]. 2 lágrima [adorno]. 3 JOY. pendiente, zarcillo. 4 pastilla, confite. 5 traguito. 6 caída, caimiento. 7 lanzamiento [desde lo alto]. 8 baja, descenso. 9 declive. 10 MAR. caída [de vela]. 11 trampa, escotillón. 12 MEC. pieza que cae. 13 MEC. ~ *hammer*, martinete. 14 MED. ~ *serene*, gota serena.

drop (to) *tr.* dejar caer, soltar, echar, verter: *to* ~ *anchor*, echar anclas; *to* ~ *a hint*, soltar una indirecta. 2 parir [un animal]. 3 dejar, abandonar, desprenderse de, suspender, desistir de. 4 omitir, comerse [una letra o palabra]. 6 tumbar, derribar. 7 bajar [una cortina, los ojos, etc.]. 8 *to* ~ *a line*, poner unas líneas.

9 *intr.* gotear, chorrear. 10 caer, bajar, descender. 11 caer desmayado o muerto. 12 acabarse, cesar, parar. 13 quedarse atrás. 14 *to* ~ *in*, dejarse caer, entrar al pasar. 15 *to* ~ *off*, decaer; quedar dormido, morir. 16 *to* ~ *out*, retirarse, desaparecer.

¶ Pret. y p. p.: *dropped* o dropt; ger.: *dropping*.

droplet (-lit) *s.* gotita.

dropper (-ø^r) *s.* cuentagotas.

dropping (-ing) *s.* caída, goteo, etc. 2 *pl.* excrementos de animales. *4* adj. ~ *bottle*, frasco cuentagotas.

dropsical (dra·psikal), **dropsied** (-sid) *adj.* MED. hidrópico.

dropsy (-si) *s.* MED. hidropesía.

dropwort (-uɵ^rt) *s.* BOT. filipéndula.

dross (dros) *s.* escoria [de los metales]. *2* espuma, horrura, borra, desecho, hez.

drossy (-i) *adj.* que tiene escoria; feculento, impuro. *2* sin valor.

drought (draut) *s.* sequedad, aridez [del suelo]. *2* sequía. *3* fam. sed.

droughty (drau·ti) *adj.* árido, seco. *2* fam. sediento.

drove (drouv) *s. pret.* de TO DRIVE. *2 s.* manada, hato, rebaño, recua. *3* multitud, gentío.

drover (-ɵ^r) *s.* ganadero.

drown (to) (draun) *tr.* ahogar, anegar. *2* inundar, sumergir. *3* ahogar, apagar [el sonido, etc.]. *4 intr.* ahogarse, anegarse.

drowse (draus) *s.* DROWSINESS.

drowse (to) *tr.* adormecer, amodorrar. *2 intr.* adormilarse, adormecerse, amodorrarse.

drowsiness (-inis) *s.* adormecimiento, somnolencia, modorra, sopor.

drowsy (-i) *adj.* soñoliento, adormecido, amodorrado. *2* soporífero.

drub (drɵb) *s.* golpe, palo, puñada.

drub (to) *tr.* abrumar de trabajo. *2 intr.* afanarse, fatigarse, azacanearse.

drudgery (-ɵri) *s.* reventadero, trabajo penoso.

drug (drɵg) *s.* droga, medicamento. *2* estupefaciente. *3* COM. macana, artículo invendible.

drug (to) *tr.* medicinar con exceso. *2* narcotizar. *3* mezclar con drogas. *4 intr.* tomar estupefacientes. ¶ Pret. y p. p.: *drugged;* ger.: *-gging.*

druggist (-gist) *s.* droguero. *2* boticario.

drugstore (-tɵ^r) *s.* (E.U.) farmacia, botica, droguería.

druid (dru·id) *s.* druida.

Druidism (drui·diŝm) *s.* druidismo.

drum (drom) *s.* MÚS. tambor, caja. *2* sonido del tambor. *3* MEC. tambor, cilindro; cuerpo [de caldera, etc.]. *4* COM. bidón, cuñete, barril. *5* ~ *major*, tambor mayor.

drum (to) *intr.* tocar el tambor. *2* tabalear, tamborilear, teclear. *3 tr.* tocar [en el tambor]. *4* meter en la cabeza [una lección, etc.].

drumbeat (-bɪt) *s.* toque de tambor.

drumfire (-fai·ɵ^r) *s.* MIL. fuego graneado.

drumhead (-jed) *s.* parche [del tambor]. *2* ANAT. membrana del tímpano.

drummer (-mɵ^r) *s.* tambor, bombo [músico]. *2* (E.U.) COM. viajante.

drumstick (-stik) *s.* baqueta, palillo [de tambor].

drunk (drɵŋk) *p. p.* de TO DRINK. *2 adj.* bebido, ebrio, borracho. *3 s.* borracho. *4* borrachera.

drunkard (-a^rd) *s.* borrachín.

drunken (-øn) *adj.* ebrio, borracho, beodo. *2* ~ *fit,* borrachera.

drunkenness (-is) *s.* embriaguez, borrachera.

drupe (drup) *s.* BOT. drupa.

dry (drai) *adj.* seco: ~ *beef*, cecina, *charqui; ~ pile,* ELECT. pila seca; ~ *cleaning,* lavado en seco; ~ *goods,* COM. tejidos, lencería, mercería, etc.; ~ *law,* ley seca; ~ *nurse,* ama seca, niñera; ~ *wall,* pared de piedra seca. *2* enjuto. *3* árido. *4* sequeroso. *5* pasa [fruta]. *6* para áridos [medida]. *7* insulso, insubstancial. *8* frío, pobre. *9* satírico, mordaz. *10* B. ART. duro, sin matices.

dry (to) *tr.* secar, desecar, enjugar. *2* pasar [fruta].

3 acecinar. *4* dar sed. *5 intr.* secarse, desecarse, enjugarse. | Gralte. con *up*. ¶ Pret. y p. p.: *dried.*

dryad (drai·æd) *s.* dríada.

dryer (-ɵ^r) *s.* DRIER.

dryness (-nis) *s.* sequedad. *2* aridez.

dry-salt (to) *tr.* salar y secar [carnes, pescado].

drysalter (-sɵltɵ^r) *s.* vendedor de drogas, salazones, etc.

dry-shod *adj.* a pie enjuto.

dual (ditu·al) *adj.* dual, doble.

dualism (-iŝm) *s.* dualismo.

duality (diuæ·liti) *s.* dualidad.

dub (to) (dɵb) *tr.* armar [caballero]. *2* titular, apellidar, apodar. *3* alisar, aparar. *4* engrasar [las pieles]. *5* CINEM. doblar. *6 intr.* sonar como un tambor. ¶ Pret. y p. p.: *dubbed;* ger.: *dubbing.*

dubiety (diubai·eti) *s.* lo dudoso, cosa dudosa, incertidumbre.

dubious (diu·biøs) *adj.* dudoso. *2* ambiguo, equívoco; sospechoso.

dubitable (-bitabøl) *adj.* dubitable, dudable.

dubitative (-bitei·tiv) *adj.* dubitativo.

ducal (diu·kal) *adj.* ducal.

ducat (dɵ·ka) *s.* ducado [moneda].

duchess (-chis) *s.* duquesa.

duchy (dɵ·chi) *s.* ducado [territorio].

duck (dɵk) *s.* ORN. ánade, pato. *2* ORN. pata [hembra]. *3* fam. pichón, pichona, amor mío. *4* acción de agacharse rápidamente, chapuz, zambullida. *5* dril, *loneta. 6 pl.* pantalones de dril. *7 to play ducks and drakes* [*with*], hacer saltar piedras sobre el agua; malgastar, derrochar.

duck (to) *tr.* zambullir. *2* bajar rápidamente [la cabeza, etc.]. *3 intr.* zambullirse, chapuzar. *4* agacharse o bajar la cabeza rápidamente. *5* pop. *to ~ out,* escaparse.

duckbill (dɵ·kbil) *s.* ZOOL. ornitorrinco.

duck-legged *adj.* corto de piernas.

duckling (-ling) *s.* patito, patita.

duct (dɵkt) *s.* conducto, tubo. *2* ANAT. conducto. *3* BOT. vaso.

ductile (-il) *adj.* dúctil.

ductility (dɵkti·liti) *s.* ductilidad.

dud (dɵd) *adj.* flojo, sin energía. *2 s.* granada que no estalla; fracaso, cosa o persona inútil. *3 pl.* trapos, pingajos.

dude (diud) *s.* petimetre, lechuguino.

dudgeon (dɵ·dỹøn) *s.* resentimiento, enojo: *in* ~ , resentido, enojado.

due (diu) *adj.* debido: *in* ~ *time,* a su debido tiempo. *2* vencido, devengado, pagadero: *to become* o *fall* ~, vencer. *3* esperado, que tiene su llegada: *the train is* ~ *at two o'clock,* el tren llega a las dos. *4* propio, justo. *5* legal, regular. *6 s.* deuda, obligación. *7* merecido; lo que se debe a uno. *8 pl.* derechos [que se pagan]. *9 adv.* directamente, exactamente.

duel (diu·øl) *s.* duelo, desafío.

duel (to) *intr.* batirse en duelo.

dueller (-ɵ^r) *s.* el que se desafía.

duellist (-ist) *s.* duelista.

duenna (diue·na) *s.* dueña, señora de compañía.

duet (diue·t) *s.* dúo.

duff (to) (dɵf) *tr.* amañar, falsificar, engañar.

duffel (dɵ·føl) *s.* tela de lana basta. *2* saco o equipo de acampador.

dug (dɵg) *pret.* y p. p. de TO DIG. *2 s.* teta, ubre.

dugong (diu·gan) *s.* ZOOL. vaca marina.

dugout (dɵ·gaut) *s.* canoa, piragua. *2* cueva. *3* MIL. cueva de protección, trinchera cubierta.

duke (diuk) *s.* duque.

dukedom (-døm) s. ducado [título, territorio].
dulcet (dø·lsit) adj. dulce, agradable, armonioso.
dulcify (to) (dø·lsifai) tr. dulcificar, ablandar, apaciguar. ¶ Pret. y p. p.: *dulcified*.
dulcimer (-simø^r) s. MÚS. dulcémele.
dulia (dulai·a) s. REL. dulia.
dull (døl) adj. embotado, obtuso, romo. *2* torpe, lerdo. *3* poco agudo [vista, oído]; que los tiene así: ~ *of hearing*, duro de oído. *4* inservible [cosa]. *5* lento, pesado; soñoliento. *6* débil, mortecino. *7* triste, sombrío. *8* aburrido, insulso, prosaico. *9* apagado, mate, sordo. *10* empañado, deslustrado; obscuro, nebuloso. *11* nublado [tiempo]. *12* COM. encalmado.
dull (to) tr. embotar. *2* entontecer, entorpecer. *3* hacer pesado, monótono. *4* apagar, amortiguar. *5* mitigar. *6* contristar. *7* ofuscar, ensombrecer. *8* empañar, deslustrar. *9* intr. embotarse. *10* entorpecerse. *11* apagarse; mitigarse. *12* empañarse.
dullard (dø·la^rd) adj.-s. estúpido, zoquete.
dull-head s. zote.
dullness (-nis) s. embotamiento, etc.
dull-sighted adj. cegato.
dull-witted adj. tonto, estúpido.
dulness s. DULLNESS.
duly (-i) adv. debidamente. *2* puntualmente, a su tiempo.
dumb (døm) adj. mudo, callado, sin habla: ~ *show*, pantomima: *to strike* ~, dejar sin habla, asombrar.
dumbbell (-bel) s. pesa de gimnasia.
dumbfound (to) (-faund) tr. confundir, dejar atónito, sin habla.
dumbfounded (-id) adj. confuso, atónito, sin habla.
dumbness (-nis) s. mudez, mutismo; silencio.
dumb-waiter s. (Ingl.) estante giratorio para platos, vasos, etc. *2* (E.U.) montaplatos.
dummy (dø·mi) adj. mudo, silencioso. *2* falso, simulado. *3* s. mudo. *4* testaferro. *5* personaje que no habla. *6* objeto simulado. *7* maniquí [para vestidos, pelucas, etc.]. *8* maqueta [de libro]. *9* WHIST, BRIDGE muerto.
dump (dømp) s. baque. *2* vaciadero, vertedero: depósito; vaciamiento: ~ *truck*, camión volquete. *3* ~ *the dumps*, murria, melancolía.
dump (to) tr. vaciar de golpe, descargar, verter [escombros, etc.]. *2* COM. vender al extranjero a precios inferiores a los corrientes.
dumping (døm·ping) s. COM. dumping.
dumpish (-pish) adj. estúpido. *2* murrio.
dumpling (-pling) s. bollito relleno.
dumpy (-pi) adj. corto y grueso; rechoncho.
dun (døn) adj. pardo, castaño. *2* s. acreedor importuno. *3* apremio.
dun (to) tr. perseguir, apremiar [esp. a un deudor].
dunce (døns) s. tonto, zote, ignorante.
dunderhead (døndø^rjed) s. zopenco, badulaque.
dune (diun) s. duna, médano.
dung (døng) s. estiércol, bosta, tullidura. *2* ENT. ~ *beetle*, escarabajo bolero.
dung (to) tr.-intr. estercolar.
dungeon (dø·ndÿøn) s. calabozo, mazmorra. *2* DONJON.
dungeon (to) tr. encalabozar.
dunghill (dø·ngjil) s. muladar, estercolero, basurero. *2* adj. bajo, vil.
dungy (-i) adj. estercolizo.
dunnage (dø·nidÿ) s. MAR. abarrote.
duo (diu·ou) s. MÚS. dúo.

duodecimal (diuode·simal) adj. duodecimal. *2* s. duodécimo.
duodenum (-di·nøm) s. ANAT. duodeno.
dupe (diup) s. víctima [de un engaño], engañado. *2* incauto, primo.
dupe (to) tr. engañar, embaucar.
duple (diu·pøl), **duplex** (-plecs) adj. duplo, doble, dúplice.
duplicate (-plikit) adj. duplicado, doble. *2* s. duplicado.
duplicate (to) (-plikeit) tr. duplicar, doblar. *2* hacer un duplicado de.
duplication (-ei·shøn) s. duplicación.
duplicator (diu·plikeitø^r) s. duplicador, copiador.
duplicity (diupli·siti) s. duplicidad.
durability (diurabi·liti) s. durabilidad, duración; estabilidad, permanencia.
durable (diu·rabøl) adj. durable, duradero. *2* resistente, de duración. *3* estable, permanente.
dura mater (diu·ra mei·tø^r) s. ANAT. duramadre.
durance (diu·rans) s. prisión, encierro, cautividad. *2* TEJ. sempiterna.
duration (-reishøn) s. duración, vida.
duress (diure·s) s. coacción. *2* prisión, encierro.
during (diu·ring) prep. durante. *2* adj. duradero.
durst (dø^rst) pret. irreg. de TO DARE.
dusk (døsk) adj. oscuro, sombrío. *2* s. crepúsculo, anochecida: *at* ~, al anochecer. *3* sombra, penumbra, oscuridad.
dusky (-i) adj. oscuro, moreno, pardo, negruzco. *2* sombrío.
dust (døst) s. polvo: *gold* ~, oro en polvo; pop. dinero; ~ *coat*, guardapolvo [prenda]. *2* tierra, suelo. *3* oro en polvo. *4* cenizas [restos mortales]. *5* polvareda. *6* trapatiesta, riña, alboroto: *to raise a* ~, armar una trapatiesta. *7* basura; barreduras.
dust (to) tr. desempolvar, quitar o sacudir el polvo a: *to* ~ *one's jacket*, sacudir el polvo a uno. *3* empolvar, llenar de polvo. *4* espolvorear. *5* pulverizar.
dustbin (-bin) s. recipiente para barreduras, cenizas, etc.
dustcloth (-kloz) s. trapo para quitar el polvo.
duster (-ø^r) s. el o lo que quita el polvo; paño, plumero, zorros. *2* guardapolvo [prenda]. *3* utensilio para espolvorear.
dustman (-mæn) s. basurero, barrendero.
dustpan (-pæn) s. recogedor [para las barreduras].
dusty (-i) adj. polvoriento. *2* del color del polvo. *3* pulverulento.
Dutch (dø·ch) adj.-s. holandés: ~ *tile*, azulejo.
Dutchman (-mæn) s. holandés [pers.].
duteous (diu·tiøs) adj. obediente, respetuoso, obsequioso.
dutiable (-tiabøl) adj. sujeto al pago de derechos.
dutiful (-tiful) adj. obediente, respetuoso, solícito.
duty (-ti) s. deber, obligación, incumbencia. *2* sumisión, obediencia, respeto. *3* quehaceres; funciones [de un cargo, etc.]. *4* servicio, guardia: *on* ~, de servicio, de guardia. *5* impuesto, derecho [de aduanas, consumos, etc.]. *6* MEC. trabajo mecánico, efecto útil.
duumvir (diuø·mvø^r) s. duunviro.
dwarf (duo^rf) adj. enano, diminuto. *2* s. enano, enana.
dwarf (to) tr. impedir el crecimiento de. *2* empequeñecer, achicar. *3* intr. empequeñecerse, achicarse.
dwarfish (-ish) adj. enano, diminuto.
dwell (to) (duel) intr. habitar, morar, residir, vivir.

2 permanecer. *3 to* ~ *on* o *upon*, entretenerse, detenerse, espaciarse en. ¶ Pret. y p. p.: *dwelt* o *dwelled.*

dweller (due·lø^r) *s.* morador, habitante.

dwelling (-ing) *s.* morada, vivienda, casa, domicilio.

dwindle (to) (dui·ndøl) *intr.* menguar, disminuirse. *2* consumirse. *3* decaer, degenerar.

dye (dai) *s.* tintura, tinte, color.

dye (to) *tr.-intr.* teñir, tinturar, colorar: *to* ~ *in grain, to* ~ *in the wool*, teñir en rama. *2 intr.* teñirse. ¶ Pret. y p.p.: *dyed;* ger.: *dyeing.*

dyeing (-ing) *adj.* colorante, tintóreo. *2 s.* tinte, tintura, tintorería.

dyer (-ø^r) *s.* tintorero.

dyers'-broom *s.* BOT. retama de tintes.

dyestuff (-støf) *s.* materia colorante.

dying (-ing) *ger.* de TO DIE. *2 adj.* moribundo, agonizante. *3* de la muerte. *4* mortal, perecedero.

dynamic (al (dainæ·mik(al) *adj.* dinámico.

dynamics (-miks) *s.* dinámica.

dynamism (-mišm) *s.* dinamismo.

dynamite (dai·namait) *s.* dinamita.

dynamite (to) *tr.* dinamitar.

dynamiter (-ø^r) *s.* dinamitero.

dynamo (-namou) *s.* ELECT. dinamo.

dynamometer (dainama·metø^r) *s.* dinamómetro.

dynast (dai·næst) *s.* dinasta.

dynastic(al (dainæ·stik(al) *adj.* dinástico.

dynasty (dai·nasti) *s.* dinastía.

dyne (dain) *s.* Fís. dina.

dysentery (di·sønteri) *s.* MED. disentería.

dyspepsia, dispepsy (dispe·psia, -si) *s.* MED. dispepsia.

dyspeptic (-ptik) *adj.-s.* dispéptico.

disphasia (-fei·šia) *s.* MED. disfasia.

dyspnea, dyspnœa (dispnɪ·a) *s.* MED. disnea.

dysuria (disiu·rias) *s.* MED. disuria.

E

E, e (ɪ) *s*. E, e, quinta letra del alfabeto inglés. *2* MÚS. mi.
each (ɪch) *adj*. cada, todo. *2 pron*. cada uno, cada cual, todos: ~ *other*, mutuamente, uno a otro, los unos a los otros. *3 adv*. cada uno, por cabeza.
eager (ɪ·gøʳ) *adj*. ávido, ansioso, afanoso, anheloso. *2* ardiente, vehemente. *3* encarnizado [combate, etc.].
eagerness (-nis) *s*. avidez, ansia, afán, anhelo, ahínco. *2* ardor, vehemencia.
eagle (ɪ·gøl) *s*. águila. *2* (E.U.) moneda de oro de diez dólares.
eagless (ɪ·glis) *s*. ORN. águila hembra.
eaglet (-glit) *s*. ORN. aguilucho.
ear (i·øʳ) *s*. ANAT. oreja: ~ *flap*, orejera; ~ *trumpet*, trompetilla acústica; *to set by the ears*, fig. hacer reñir, enemistar; *up to the ears*, fig. hasta los ojos. *2* oído, oídos: *to give* ~ *to*, prestar oído a; *to have one's* ~, ser escuchado por uno, gozar de su favor; *to play by* ~, tocar de oído. *3* orejuela; asa, asidero. *4* ORN. plumas sobre el oído de un ave. *5* BOT. aurícula. *6* BOT. espiga, mazorca [de cereal].
ear (to) *intr*. BOT. espigar, echar espigas.
earache (-eik) *s*. otalgia, dolor de oídos.
eardrop (-drap) *s*. arracada.
eardrum (-drøm) *s*. ANAT. tímpano [del oído].
eared (-d) *adj*. que tiene orejas o espigas.
earl (øʳl) *s*. conde [título inglés].
earlap (i·øʳlæp) *s*. lóbulo de la oreja. *2* orejera [de gorra].
earldom (øʳldøm) *s*. condado.
earless (i·øʳlis) *adj*. desorejado.
earlock (-lak) *s*. aladar.
early (øʳli) *adj*. primitivo, antiguo, remoto. *2* próximo [en el futuro]. *3* perteneciente o relativo al principio de la mañana, de la vida, de una época: ~ *riser*, madrugador; ~ *Victorian* del principio de la época victoriana. *4* precoz, temprano, anticipado: ~ *fruit*, fruto temprano. *5 to be* ~, llegar temprano. *6 adv*. temprano, tempranamente; pronto. *7* al principio: ~ *in the morning*, de madrugada.
earmark (i·øʳmarʳk) *s*. señal en la oreja. *2* señal característica.
earmark (to) marcar [el ganado] en la oreja. *2* destinar, reservar [para un fin determinado].

earn (to) (øʳn) *tr*. ganar, merecer, lograr. *2* devengar.
earnest (o·ʳnist) *adj*. serio, formal. *2* sincero, ardiente, encarecido. *3* celoso, diligente. *4* ansioso. *5 s*. seriedad, buena fe, veras: *in* ~, en serio, de veras. *7* señal, prenda.
earnestness (-nis) *s*. seriedad, buena fe. *2* veras, ahínco, ardor.
earnings (øʳnings) *s. pl*. ganancias; sueldo, salario.
earpiece (i·øʳpis) *s*. TELEF. auricular, receptor.
earring (-ing) *s*. pendiente, zarcillo, arete.
earshot (-shat) *s*. alcance del oído.
earth (øʳz) *s*. tierra, barro, materia térrea. *2* tierra [mundo; país, región; suelo]. *3* mundo, [cosas terrenales]. *4* madriguera. *5* ELECT. tierra.
earth (to) *tr*. AGR. acollar, aporcar. *2* ELECT. conectar con tierra. *3 tr.-intr*. hacer entrar o meterse en la madriguera.
earthboard (-boʳd) *s*. orejera [del arado].
earthen (-øn) *adj*. terrizo, de barro.
earthenware (-ønueʳ) *s*. ollería, vasijas de barro.
earthly (-li) *adj*. terreno, terrestre. *2* mundano, carnal. *4 to be of no* ~ *use*, no servir para nada.
earthnut (-nøt) *s*. BOT. chufa; cacahuete; tubérculo de ciertas plantas.
earthquake (-kueik) *s*. terremoto.
earthworhm (-uøʳm) *s*. lombriz de tierra.
earthy (-zi) *adj*. terroso, térreo. *2* terrenal. *3* basto, grosero.
earwax (i·øʳueks) *s*. cerumen.
earwig (-ig) *s*. ENT. tijereta. *2* ZOOL. ciempiés.
ease (ɪs) *s*. alivio, descanso. *2* tranquilidad. *3* comodidad, holgura, desahogo: *at* ~, con desahogo, a gusto; *ill at* ~, incómodo, violento. *4* facilidad, soltura, desembarazo, naturalidad.
ease (to) *tr*. aliviar, moderar, mitigar. *2* descargar, desembarazar. *3* tranquilizar. *4* aflojar. *5* hacer más fácil. *6* MAR. lascar. *7 intr. to* ~ *off* o *up*, moderarse, disminuir; moderar la marcha.
easel (ɪ·søl) *s*. caballete [de pintor].
easement (ɪ·šmønt) *s*. alivio, aflojamiento. *2* ARQ. descarga. *3* DER. servidumbre.
easiness (-šinis) *s*. comodidad, holgura. *2* facilidad. *3* soltura, desembarazo. *4* tranquilidad. *5* indiferencia. *6* indulgencia, condescendencia. *7* credulidad.

east (ɪst) s. este, oriente, levante. 2 adj. oriental, del este. 3 adv. hacia el este.
Easter (ɪ·støʳ) s. Pascua de Resurrección o florida.
easterly (-li) adj. oriental, del este. 2 adv. al este, hacia el este.
eastern (-n) adj.-s. oriental.
eastward (ɪ·stuaʳd) adj. que va o mira hacia el este. 2 adv. hacia el este.
easy (ɪ·ši) adj. fácil, llano, corriente. 2 sencillo, natural. 3 fluido [estilo]. 4 cómodo, holgado: ~ chair, butaca, sillón. 5 acomodado. 6 sociable, condescendiente. 7 asequible. 8 tranquilo. 9 suelto, desembarazado, desenvuelto. 10 manejable, fácil de engañar. 11 lento, moderado. 12 ligero, suave. 13 adv. fácilmente. 14 con calma; quedo, quedito.
easy-going adj. comodón, indolente.
eat (to) (ɪt) tr. comer, comerse: to ~ one's heart out, fig. sufrir en silencio; to ~ one's words, retractarse. 2 devorar, tragar. 3 corroer. 4 roer, consumir, gastar. 5 intr. comer. ¶ Pret.: ate; p. p.: eaten.
eatable (-abøl) adj. comestible, comedero. 2 s. pl. comestibles, vituallas.
eaten (-øn) p. p. de TO EAT.
eating-house s. bodegón, figón, restaurante.
eaves (ɪ·vš) s. pl. alero, socarrén.
eavesdrop (to) (-drap) intr. escuchar detrás de las puertas, fisgonear.
eavesdropper (-øʳ) s. el que escucha escondido.
ebb (eb) s. MAR. menguante, reflujo: ~ tide, marea menguante. 2 decadencia: ~ of life, vejez.
ebb (to) intr. menguar [la marea]. 2 decaer, bajar, disminuir.
ebbing (e·biŋ) s. reflujo, bajamar.
ebon (e·bøn) adj. de ébano; negro.
ebonite (e·bønait) s. ebonita.
ebony (e·bøni) s. BOT. ébano.
ebullience, -cy (ibø·liøns, -si) s. ebullición, hervor, entusiasmo.
ebullition (ebø·lishøn) s. ebullición. 2 efervescencia. 3 fig. explosión, arranque.
eburnean (ibø·ʳnian) adj. ebúrneo.
écarté (eikaʳtei·) s. ecarté [juego de naipes].
Ecce homo (e·ksijou·mou) s. eccehomo.
eccentric (ikse·ntrik) s. MEC. excéntrica. 2 excéntrico [pers.].
eccentric(al (-al) adj. excéntrico.
eccentricity (iksentri·siti) s. excentricidad.
ecchymosis (ekimou·sis) s. equimosis.
Ecclesiastes (icklisiæ·stiš) s. Eclesiastés.
ecclesiastic (-stik) s. eclesiástico.
ecclesiastic(al (-al) adj. eclesiástico.
ecclesiology (iclisia·lodŷi) s. eclesiología.
echelon (e·shølan) s. MIL. escalón.
echidna (iki·dna) s. ZOOL. equidna.
echinoderm (ikai·nodøʳm) adj.-s. ZOOL. equinodermo.
echinus (ikai·nøs) s. ZOOL. equino, erizo de mar. 2 ARQ. equino. 3 ARQ. gallón.
echo (e·kou) s. eco.
echo (to) tr. devolver [el sonido]. 2 hacer eco a, repetir, imitar. 3 intr. repercutir, resonar.
echoic (ekou·ik) adj. ecoico.
éclat (ekla·) s. brillo, magnificencia. 2 aplauso, aprobación. 3 fama, notoriedad.
eclectic (ikle·ktik) adj.-s. ecléctico.
eclecticism (-tisišm) s. eclecticismo.
eclipse (ikli·ps) s. eclipse.
eclipse (to) tr. eclipsar. 2 intr. poét. eclipsarse.
ecliptic (ikli·ptik) adj. elíptico. 2 s. ASTR. elíptica.

eclogue (e·klag) s. égloga.
economic (ikøna·mik) adj. económico [de la economía]. 2 que compensa, que paga los gastos.
economical (-al) adj. económico.
economics (-s) s. economía [ciencia].
economist (ika·nomist) s. economista.
economize (to) (-nomaiš) tr.-intr. economizar.
economy (-nomi) s. economía [en todas las acepciones].
ecru (e·cru) adj. crudo [sin blanquear].
ecstasy (e·kstasi) s. éxtasis, arrobamiento.
ecstasy (to) tr. extasiar, arrobar.
ecstatic (al (ekstæ·tik(al) adj. extático.
ectasis (e·ktæsis) s. éxtasis. 2 MED. ectasia.
ectoblast (-toblæst) s. BIOL. ectoblasto.
ectoderm (-døʳm) s. BIOL. ectodermo.
ectropion (ektrou·piøn) s. MED. ectropión.
ecumenic (al (ekiume·nik(al) adj. ecuménico.
eczema (e·kšima) s. MED. eczema.
edacious (idei·shøs) adj. voraz, glotón.
edaphology (edafa·lodŷi) s. edafología.
eddy (e·di) s. remanso, regolfo. 2 remolino, torbellino.
eddy (to) tr. arremolinar, remolinear. 2 intr. regolfar, arremolinarse, remolinar.
edelweis (ei·dølvais) s. BOT. edelweis, pie de león.
edema (idɪ·ma) s. MED. edema.
Eden (ɪ·døn) s. Edén.
edentate (ide·nteit) adj.-s. ZOOL. desdentado.
edge (edŷ) s. filo, corte. 2 canto, borde, esquina. 3 extremo, margen, orilla. 4 ribete, pestaña. 5 fuerza, agudeza. 6 DEP. ventaja. 7 to set the teeth on ~, dar dentera. 8 on ~, de canto; fig. impaciente, ansioso, nervioso.
edge (to) tr. afilar, aguzar. 2 ribetear, orlar. 3 limitar, rodear. 4 incitar, aguijonear. 5 mover o empujar poco a poco. 6 intr. avanzar de lado. 7 tr.-intr. to ~ in, introducir, introducirse.
edged (e·dŷid) adj. afilado, cortante.
edgeless (-lis) adj. embotado, romo, sin filo.
edgeways (-ueiš), **edgewise** (-uaiš) adv. de filo, de canto, de lado.
edging (-iŋ) s. orilla, orla, ribete, guarnición.
edible (e·dibøl) adj.-s. comestible.
edict (ɪ·dikt) s. edicto, decreto, orden, bando.
edification (edifikei·shøn) s. edificación [en sentido moral].
edificatory (e·difikatori) s. edificante.
edifice (e·difis) s. edificio.
edify (to) (e·difai) tr. edificar moralmente. ¶ Pret. y p. p.: edified.
edile (ɪ·dail) s. edil.
edit (to) (e·dit) tr. revisar, preparar para la publicación. 2 redactar, dirigir [un periódico].
edition (edi·shøn) s. edición. | No tiene el sentido de acción de editar.
editor (e·ditøʳ) s. director, redactor [de una publicación].
editorial (edito·rial) adj. de la dirección o redacción [de una publicación]: ~ staff, redacción, cuerpo de redactores. 2 s. editorial, artículo de fondo.
educate (to) (e·diukeit) tr. educar, instruir. 3 amaestrar.
educated (-id) adj. educado, instruido, culto.
education (-ei·shøn) s. educación. | No tiene el sentido de urbanidad. 2 instrucción, enseñanza. 3 ilustración, cultura.
educational (-al) adj. educativo. 2 docente. 3 cultural.
educative (e·diukeitiv) adj. educativo.

educator (-tø^r) *s.* educador, pedagogo.
educe (to) (idiu·s) *tr.* educir. *2* desarrollar, hacer aparecer.
edulcorate (to) (idø·lkoreit) *tr.* edulcorar, endulzar.
Edward (e·dua^rd) *n. pr. m.* Eduardo.
eel (il) *s.* ICT. anguila: *electric* ~, gimnoto.
e'en (i·n) *adv.* EVEN.
e'er (e·ø^r) *adv.* EVER.
eerie, eery (i·ri) *adj.* asustadizo [de aparecidos, etc.]. *2* temeroso, misterioso, fantástico, sobrenatural.
efface (to) (efei·s) *tr.* borrar, hacer desaparecer.
effect (ife·kt) *s.* efecto. | No tiene el sentido de efecto mercantil ni del que se da a una pelota o bola: *of no* ~, ineficaz, vano. *2* consecuencia, resultado. *3* cumplimiento; vigencia, vigor: *to take* ~, producir su efecto; tener cumplimiento, ponerse en vigor. *4* realidad: *in* ~, de hecho, en realidad. *5 pl.* efectos, bienes.
effect (to) *tr.* efectuar, realizar, llevar a cabo.
effective (-iv) *adj.* efectivo, real. *2* eficaz. *3* que hace o produce. *4* impresionante, de efecto. *5* vigente. *6 s.* MIL., COM. efectivo.
effectless (-lis) *adj.* ineficaz, sin resultado.
effectual (-chual) *adj.* eficaz. *2* DER. válido.
effectuate (to) (-chueit) *tr.* efectuar, realizar.
effeminacy (efe·minasi) *s.* afeminamiento, molicie.
effeminate (-minit) *adj.* afeminado.
effeminate (to) (-mineit) *tr.* afeminar, enervar. *2 intr.* afeminarse.
efferent (e·førønt) *s.* FISIOL. eferente.
effervesce (to) (efø^rve·s) *intr.* hervir, estar en efervescencia.
effervescence (-øns) *s.* efervescencia, hervor.
effervescent (-ønt) *adj.* efervescente.
effete (efi·t) *adj.* estéril, infructuoso. *2* gastado, agotado.
efficacious (efikei·shøs) *adj.* eficaz.
efficacy (e·fikasi) *s.* eficacia. *2* virtud, poder.
efficiency (efi·shønsi) *s.* eficiencia. *2* fuerza, virtud. *3* rendimiento, efecto útil.
efficient (-shønt) *adj.* eficiente. *2* MEC. de buen rendimiento. *3 s.* causa eficiente.
effigy (e·fidÿi) *s.* efigie.
effloresce (to) (eflore·s) *intr.* QUÍM. eflorescerse. *2* BOT. florecer.
efflorescence (-øns) *s.* BOT. florescencia. *2* QUÍM., MED. eflorescencia.
effluence (e·fluøns) *s.* emanación. *2* efusión, flujo.
effluent (-ønt) *adj.* efluente.
effluvium (eflu·viøm) *s.* efluvio, emanación.
effort (e·fø^rt) *s.* esfuerzo, conato, empeño.
effrontery (efrø·ntøri) *s.* descaro, desfachatez.
effulgence (efø·ldÿøns) *s.* brillantez, resplandor, esplendor, fulgor.
effulgent (-ønt) *adj.* brillante, resplandeciente.
effuse (to) (efiu·š) *tr.* efundir. *2* esparcir. *3 intr.* emanar, fluir.
effusion (efiu·ÿøn) *s.* efusión. *2* expansión, desahogo.
effusive (-siv) *adj.* efusivo, expansivo.
eft (eft) *s.* ZOOL. tritón, salamandra acuática.
egg (eg) *s.* huevo: ~ *laying*, postura.
egg (to) *tr.* cubrir o mezclar con huevo. *2 to* ~ *on*, incitar, instigar.
eggcup (e·gkøp) *s.* huevera [utensilio].
eggnog (-nag) *s.* yema mejida; ponche de huevo.
eggplant (-plænt) *s.* BOT. berenjena.
eggshell (-shel) *s.* cáscara de huevo, cascarón.

egis (i·dÿis) *s.* égida, escudo.
eglantine (e·glantain) *s.* BOT. zarzarrosa.
egoism (i·goušm) *s.* egoísmo.
egoist (-ist) *s.* egoísta.
egoistic (igoui·stik) *adj.* egoísta.
egotism (i·goutišm) *s.* egotismo.
egotize (-taiš) *intr.* hablar mucho de sí mismo.
egregious (igri·dÿøs) *adj.* egregio. *2* insigne, notable [por una mala cualidad].
egress (i·gress) *s.* salida [acción, lugar].
egression (igre·shøn) *s.* salida [acción].
egret (e- o i·gret) *s.* ORN. garceta. *2* ORN. garzota. *3* airón, penacho.
Egypt (i·dÿipt) *n. pr.* GEOGR. Egipto.
Egyptian (idÿi·pshøn) *adj.-s.* egipcio, egipcíaco.
Egyptology (-ta·lodÿi) *s.* egiptología.
eh (e) *interj.* ¿eh?, ¿qué?
eider, eider-duck (ai·dø^r) *s.* ORN. . eider, pato de flojel: ~ *down*, plumón; edredón.
eight (eit) *adj.-s.* ocho: ~ *o'clock*, las ocho.
eighteen (-i·n) *adj.s.* diez y ocho, dieciocho.
eighteenth (-i·nz) *adj.* decimoctavo. *2 adj.-s.* dieciochavo.
eighth (eitz) *adj.-s.* octavo. *2 s.* MÚS. octavo.
eightieth (ei·tiez) *adj.-s.* octogésimo.
eight-sided *adj.* octogonal. *2* ochavado.
eighty (ei·ti) *adj.-s.* ochenta.
either (ai·dø^r) *adj.* uno y otro, ambos, entrambos. *2* uno a otro. *3* cada [de dos]. *4 pron.* uno o cualquiera de los dos; el uno o el otro. *5 conj.* o, ya. *6 adv.* también; [con negación] tampoco.
ejaculate (to) (idÿæ·kiuleit) *tr.* eyacular. *2* exclamar, proferir.
ejaculation (-ei·shøn) *s.* eyaculación. *2* exclamación, jaculatoria.
eject (to) (idÿe·kt) *tr.* arrojar, expeler, vomitar. *2* echar fuera, expulsar. *3* DER. lanzar.
ejection (-shøn) *s.* eyección, evacuación. *2* expulsión [de un sitio]; desahucio.
ejector (-tø^r) *s.* MEC. eyector, expulsor.
eke out (to) (ik) *tr.* reunir [poco a poco]. *2* ganarse [el sustento] con dificultad.
elaborate (ilæ·børit) *adj.* trabajado, primoroso, detallado. *2* complicado, recargado. *3* suntuoso.
elaborate (to) (ilæ·børeit) *tr.* elaborar. *2* laborar, trabajar con primor. *3 intr.* extenderse, detallar.
elaboration (-ei·shøn) *s.* elaboración. *2* obra acabada.
eland (ilæ·nd) *s.* ZOOL. antílope africano.
elapse (to) (ilæ·ps) *intr.* pasar, transcurrir [un tiempo].
elastic (ilæ·stik) *adj.* elástico. *2* cinta o tejido elástico. *3 pl.* ligas.
elasticity (-ti·siti) *s.* elasticidad, resorte.
elate (to) (ilei·t) *tr.* exaltar, alborozar. *2* engreír.
elate (d) (-t(id) *adj.* triunfante, gozoso. *2* engreído.
elation (-ei·shøn) *s.* elación. *2* júbilo, alborozo.
elbow (e·lbou) *s.* ANAT. codo: *at one's* ~, al lado, a mano; *out at elbows*, roto, desharrapado. *2* codo, recodo, ángulo; codillo, tubo acodado. *3* brazo [de sillón].
elbow (to) *tr.* empujar o dar con el codo. *2 to* ~ *one's way*, abrirse paso a codazos. *3* codear. *4* formar ángulo o codo.
elbowpiece (-pis) *s.* codal [de armadura].
elbowroom (-rum) *s.* espacio para moverse. *2* libertad de acción.
elder (e·ldø^r) *adj.* mayor, de más edad, más antiguo, viejo. *2* superior [en categoría, etc.]. *3 s.* mayor [antepasado]; superior; persona mayor

[que uno]. *4* persona de edad. *5* anciano [de una tribu o familia]. *6* BOT. saúco.

elderberry (-beri) *s.* BOT. baya del saúco.

elderly (-li) *adj.* mayor, de alguna edad, anciano.

elderwort (-wø^rt) *s.* BOT. yezgo.

eldest (e·ldist) *adj. superl.* mayor; más antiguo. *2* primogénito.

Eleanor, Elinor (e·linø^r) *n. pr. f.* Leonor.

elecampane (elikømpei·n) *s.* BOT. helenio.

elect (ile·kt) *adj.* elegido, escogido. *2* electo. *3 s.* TEOL. elegido.

elect (to) *tr.* elegir, escoger. *2* elegir [para un cargo].

election (ile·kshøn) *s.* elección.

electioneer (to) (-i·ø^r) *intr.* POL. hacer propaganda o trabajar para una elección.

elective (ile·ktiv) *adj.* electivo. *2* facultativo.

elector (ile·ktø^r) *s.* elector.

electoral (-ral) *adj.* electoral.

electorate (-rit) *s.* electorado.

electric(al (-trik(al) *adj.* eléctrico: ~ *chair*, silla eléctrica; ~ *eel*, ICT. gimnoto: ~ *tape*, cinta aislante; ~ *wave*, onda hertziana. *2* electricista: ~ *engineer*, ingeniero electricista. *3* fig. vivo, fogoso, electrizante.

electrically (-li) *adv.* eléctricamente.

electrician (ilektri·shan) *s.* electricista.

electricity (-tri·siti) *s.* electricidad.

electrification (-trifikei·shøn) *s.* electrización. *2* electrificación.

electrify (to) (-trifai) *tr.* electrizar. *2* electrificar. ¶ Pret. y p. p.: *electrified.*

electrization (-triše·shøn) *s.* electrización.

electrize (to) (ile·ktraiš) *intr.* electrizar.

electroanalysis (ilektroanæ·lisis) *s.* electroanálisis.

electrocardiogram (-ka·^rdiogræm) *s.* MED. electrocardiograma.

electrocardiography (-ka^rdia·grafi) *s.* electrocardiografía.

electrochemistry (-ke·mistri) *s.* electroquímica.

electrocute (to) (ile·ktrokiut) *tr.* electrocutar.

electrocution (-kiu·shøn) *s.* electrocución.

electrode (ile·ktroud) *s.* electrodo.

electrodynamics (ilektrodainæ·miks) *s.* electrodinámica.

electro-encephalogram *s.* MED. electroencefalograma.

electrokinetics (-kine·tiks) *s.* electrocinética.

electrolier (li·ø^r) *s.* araña de lámparas eléctricas.

electrolysis (-tra·lisis) *s.* electrólisis.

electrolyte (ile·ktrolait) *s.* electrólito.

electrolyze (to) (-laiš) *tr.* electrolizar.

electromagnet (-mæ·gnit) *s.* electroimán.

electromagnetism (-mæ·gnetišm) *s.* electromagnetismo.

electromechanical (-mikæ·nikal) *adj.* electromecánico.

electrometer (ilektra·mitø^r) *s.* electrómetro.

electrometry (-metri) *s.* electrometría.

electromotive (ilektromou·tiv) *adj.* electromotor, electromotriz.

electron (ile·ktran) *s.* FÍS., QUÍM. electrón. *2 adj.* electrónico; de vacío, termiónico.

electronic (ilektra·nik) *adj.* electrónico.

electronics (-s) *s.* electrónica.

electrophorus (-tra·førøs) *s.* electróforo.

electroplate (to) (ile·ktropleit) *tr.* galvanizar [recubrir de metal].

electroplating (-ing) *s.* galvanoplastia.

electroscope (ile·ktroskoup) *s.* electroscopio.

electrostatics (ilektrostæ·tiks) *s.* electrostática.

electrotechnics (-te·kniks) *s.* electrotecnia.

electrotherapy (-ze·rapi) *s.* electroterapia.

electrothermancy (-ze·^rmansi), **electrothermics** (-ze·^rmiks) *s.* electrotermia.

electrotype (ile·ktrotaip) *s.* electrotipo. *2* electrotipia [estampa].

electrotype (to) *tr.* electrotipar, reproducir por electrotipia.

electrotypy (-i) *s.* electrotipia.

electrum (ile·ktrøm) *s.* electro. *2* plata alemana.

elegance (e·ligans) *s.* elegancia. *2* refinamiento.

elegant (-ant) *adj.* elegante. *2* refinado, delicado.

elegiac (elidŷai·æk) *adj.* elegíaco.

elegize (to) (e·lidŷaiš) *intr.* escribir una elegía. *2 tr.* llorar o alabar [a uno] en una elegía.

elegy (e·lidŷi) *s.* elegía.

element (e·limønt) *s.* elemento [en todas sus acepciones]: *the four elements*, los cuatro elementos; *to be in one's* ~, estar en su elemento. *2 pl.* elementos [rudimentos; fuerzas naturales]. *3* el pan y el vino en la Eucaristía.

elemental (elime·ntal) *adj.* elemental, esencial. *2* simple [no compuesto]. *3* de los elementos o fuerzas de la naturaleza; comparable a ellos.

elementary (-ari) *adj.* elemental [relativo a los elementos o rudimentos], primario: ~ *school*, escuela elemental o primaria. *2* QUÍM. simple.

elephant (e·lifant) *s.* ZOOL. elefante.

elephantiasis (elifanti·asis) *s.* MED. elefantiasis, elefancía.

elephantine (elifæ·ntin) *adj.* elefantino.

elevate (to) (e·liveit) *tr.* elevar, levantar, alzar. *2* elevar, encumbrar, engrandecer. *3* levantar los ánimos, alegrar, excitar.

elevated (-id) *adj.* elevado: ~ *railroad*, (E.U.) ferrocarril aéreo o elevado. *2* exaltado, encumbrado. *3* animado, gozoso.

elevation (eli·shøn) *s.* elevación [acción, estado]. *2* encumbramiento, exaltación. *3* alteza, altura. *4* GEOGR. altitud. *5* ARQ., DIB. alzado. *6* TOP. cota. *7* LITURG. elevación.

elevator (e·liveitø^r) *s.* elevador [el o lo que eleva]. *2* montacargas. *3* (E.U.) ascensor. *4* (Ingl.) escalera mecánica. *5* edificio para almacenar granos. *6* AVIA. timón de profundidad.

eleven (ile·vøn) *adj.-s.* once: ~ *o'clock*, las once.

eleventh (-z) *adj.* onceno, undécimo. *2 adj.-s.* onceavo.

elf (elf) *s.* elfo, duende. *2* enano. *3* diablillo [niño travieso].

elfish (-ish) *adj.* de elfo o duende. *2* mágico, fantástico. *3* travieso.

elicit (to) (i·lisit) *tr.* sacar, sonsacar, arrancar, producir, despertar.

elide (to) (ilai·d) *tr.* elidir.

eligibility (elidŷibi·liti) *s.* elegibilidad.

eligible (e·lidŷibøl) *adj.* elegible. *2* deseable, conveniente.

Elijah (ilai·dŷa) *n. pr. m.* Elías.

eliminate (to) (ili·mineit) *tr.* eliminar.

elimination (-ei·shøn) *s.* eliminación.

Eliot (e·liøt) *n. pr. m.* Elías.

Elisha (ilai·sha) *n. pr. m.* Elíseo.

elision (ili·ŷøn) *s.* elisión.

elite (eli·t) *s. the* ~, la flor y nata.

elixir (ili·ksø^r) *s.* elixir.

Eliza (ilai·ša) *n. pr. f.* Elisa. *2* Isabel.

Elizabeth (ili·šabez) *n. pr. f.* Isabel.

elk (elk) *s.* ZOOL. anta, alce.

ell (el) *s.* ana [medida].

Ellen (e·løn) *n. pr. f.* Elena.
ellipse (eli·ps) *s.* GEOM. elipse.
ellipsis (-is) *s.* GRAM. elipsis.
ellipsoid (-oid) *s.* GEOM. elipsoide.
elliptic(al (-tik(al) *adj.* elíptico.
elm (elm) *s.* BOT. olmo, negrillo.
elocution (elokiu·shøn) *s.* elocución, declamación.
éloge (e·loudȳ) *s.* elogio, oración fúnebre.
elongate (ila·ngeit) *adj.* alargado.
elongate (to) *tr.* alargar, prolongar. *2 intr.* alargarse, prolongarse.
elongation (-ei·shøn) *s.* alargamiento, prolongación, extensión. *2* ASTR. elongación.
elope (to) (ilou·p) *intr.* fugarse [con un amante]. *2* escapar, huir, evadirse.
elopement (-mønt) *s.* fuga, rapto.
eloquence (e·løkuøns) *s.* elocuencia. *2* retórica. *3* prosa literaria.
eloquent (-ønt) *adj.* elocuente.
else (els) *adj.* más, otro: *nobody* ~, nadie más; *what* ~?, ¿qué más?, ¿qué otra cosa? *2 adv.* de otro modo; en otro tiempo, lugar, dirección, etc.: *how* ~?, ¿de qué otro modo? *3 conj.* si no, de otro modo, en otro caso.
elsewhere (-jue·ǿ^r) *adv.* en o a otra parte.
elucidate (to) (iliu·sideit) *tr.* elucidir, dilucidar, aclarar.
elucidation (-ei·shøn) *s.* elucidación, dilucidación, aclaración.
elude (to) (i·liud) *tr.* eludir, evadir, evitar, esquivar. *2* escapar [a la observación, etc.].
elusion (iliu·ȳøn) *s.* acción de eludir, evasión.
elusive (-siv) *adj.* huidizo; que escapa [esp. al entendimiento], vago, impalpable.
elusory (-sori) *adj.* ELUSIVE.
elves (e·lv̄s) *s. pl.* de ELF.
Elysian (ili·ȳan) *adj.* elisio, elíseo.
Elysium (-ȳøm) *n. pr.* MIT. Elíseo, Elisio.
elytron (e·litrøn) *s.* ENT. élitro.
em (em) *s.* eme [letra]. *2* cosa en forma de M.
'em *pron.* elisión de THEM.
emaciate (to) (imei·shieit) *tr.* enflaquecer, demacrar. *2 intr.* demacrarse.
emaciate(d (-id) *adj.* flaco, demacrado.
emaciation (-ei·shøn) *s.* demacración, emaciación.
emanate (to) (e·maneit) *intr.* emanar, brotar, proceder. *2* radiar [estar radiante].
emanation (-ei·shøn) *s.* emanación. *2* efluvio.
emancipate (to) (imæ·nsipeit) *tr.* emancipar. *2* libertar.
emancipation (-ei·shøn) *s.* emancipación.
emasculate (to) (imæ·skiuleit) *tr.* castrar, capar. *2* afeminar. *3* debilitar.
embalm (to) (emba·m) *tr.* embalsamar [un cadáver]. *2* embalsamar, perfumar.
embalmment (-mønt) *s.* embalsamamiento.
embank (to) (embæ·nk) *tr.* limitar o proteger con dique o terraplén; represar.
embankment (-mønt) *s.* terraplén, dique, malecón, presa.
embargo (emba·^rgou) *s.* embargo o detención [de buques o mercancías, decretado por el gobierno].
embargo (to) *tr.* embargar, prohibir [la entrada o salida de buques o mercancías].
embark (to) (emba·^rk) *tr.* embarcar. *2* invertir [dinero en una empresa]. *3 intr.* embarcarse.
embarkation (-ei·shøn) *s.* embarco, embarque.
embarrass (to) (embæ·ras) *tr.* turbar, confundir, desconcertar. *2* embarazar, estorbar. *3* enredar, embrollar. *4* poner en apuros [de dinero].

embarrassment (-mønt) *s.* turbación, perplejidad, compromiso. *2* embarazo, estorbo. *3* complicación, enredo. *4* apuros, dificultades.
embassador (embæ·sadø^r) *s.* AMBASSADOR.
embassy (e·mbasi) *s.* embajada.
embattle (to) (embæ·tøl) *tr.* MIL. formar en batalla. *2* fortificar, almenar.
embay (to) (embei·) *tr.* abrigar o encerrar [buques] en una bahía. *2* cercar, rodear.
embed (to) (embe·d) *tr.* encajar, empotrar, incrustrar. ¶ Pret. y p. p.: *embedded*; p. a.: *embedding*.
embellish (to) (embe·lish) *tr.* embellecer, hermosear, adornar.
embellishment (-mønt) *s.* embellecimiento. *2* adorno.
ember (e·mbø^r) *s.* ascua, pavesa. *2 pl.* rescoldo, brasas. *3* ECLES. ~ *days*, témporas.
embezzle (to) (embe·šøl) *tr.* desfalcar [apropiarse].
embezzlement (-mønt) *s.* desfalco, peculado.
embitter (to) (embi·tø^r) *tr.* amargar, acibarar; agriar. *2* excitar la animosidad de.
emblazon (to) (emblei·šøn) *tr.* blasonar. *2* adornar o esmaltar con colores brillantes. *3* celebrar, ensalzar.
emblazonry (-ri) *s.* blasón, figuras del blasón.
emblem (emble·m) *s.* emblema. *2* símbolo, signo.
emblem (to) *tr.* simbolizar.
emblematic (al (-æ·tik(al) *adj.* emblemático.
embodiment (emba·dimønt) *s.* encarnación, personificación. *2* incorporación, inclusión.
embody (to) (emba·di) *tr.* encarnar, personificar. *2* dar forma perceptible [a una idea, etc.]. *3* incorporar, incluir, englobar. *4* organizar en cuerpo. ¶ CONJUG. Pret. y p. p.: *embodied*.
embolden (to) (embou·ldøn) *tr.* animar, envalentonar.
embolism (e·mbolišm) *s.* ASTR. embolismo. *2* MED. embolia.
embolus (e·mboløs) *s.* MED. émbolo.
embosom (to) (embu·šøm) *tr.* abrigar o guardar en el seno; abrazar. *2* envolver, encerrar.
emboss (to) (embo·s) *tr.* abollonar, realzar, estampar en relieve.
embossment (-mønt) *s.* abollonadura, realce, figura en relieve.
embowel (embau·øl) *tr.* desentrañar, destripar.
embower (-ǿ^r) *tr.* emparrar, enramar.
embrace (embrei·s) *s.* abrazo.
embrace (to) *tr.* abrazar [en todos sus sentidos]. *2* adoptar, seguir. *3* aceptar [una suerte, etc.]; aprovechar [una oportunidad, etc.]. *4 intr.* abrazarse.
embracing (-ing) *adj.* abrazador, comprensivo [que incluye]. *2 s.* abrazamiento.
embrasure (-ȳǿ^r) *s.* ARQ. alféizar. *2* FORT. cañonera, tronera.
embrocation (embrokei·shøn) *s.* embrocación.
embroider (to) (embroi·dø^r) *tr.* bordar, recamar. *2* adornar, embellecer.
embroidery (-i) *s.* bordado, bordadura; recamado.
embroil (to) (embroi·l) *tr.* embrollar, enredar.
embroilment (-mønt) *s.* embrollo, enredo, confusión. *2* intriga. *3* alboroto.
embryo (e·mbriou) *s.* embrión. *2 adj.* incipiente.
embryology (-bria·lodȳi) *s.* embriología.
embryonic (-nik) *adj.* embrionario.
emend (to) (ime·nd) *tr.* enmendar, corregir.
emendation (-ei·nd) *s.* enmienda, corrección.
emerald (e·mørald) *s.* esmeralda.
emerge (to) (imø·^rdȳ) *intr.* emerger. *2* salir, aparecer, surgir. *3* salir [de una situación, etc.].

emergence (-øns) s. emergencia. 2 salida, aparición. 3 BOT. prominencia.

emergency (-i) s. emergencia, apuro, caso de necesidad; urgencia: ~ *exit*, salida de auxilio; ~ *hospital*, hospital de urgencia; ~ *landing*, aterrizaje forzoso.

emergent (ime·ʳdẏønt) adj. emergente. 2 urgente. 3 súbito.

emeritus (ime·ritøs) adj. emérito.

emersion (ime·ʳshøn) s. emergencia, emersión.

emery (e·møri) s. esmeril.

emery (to) tr. cubrir de esmeril. 2 esmerilar. ¶ Pret. y p. p.: *emeried*.

emetic (eme·tik) adj.-s. emético.

emigrant (e·migrant) adj. emigrante. 2 s. emigrante, emigrado.

emigrate (to) (-greit) intr. emigrar.

emigration (emigrei·shøn) s. emigración.

Emily (e·mili) n. pr. f. Emilia.

eminence (e·minøns) s. eminencia, altura. 2 eminencia, distinción. 3 eminencia [título].

eminent (e·minønt) adj. eminente. 2 relevante; manifiesto; notable.

emir (emi·øʳ) s. emir.

emissary (emi·seri) s. emisario, agente secreto, espía. 2 canal, conducto, orificio de salida.

emission (-shøn) s. emisión. | No tiene el sentido de emisión de radio.

emit (to) (emi·t) tr. emitir. 2 dar [una orden o decreto].

emitter (-øʳ) s. emisor.

Emma (e·ma) n. pr. f. Ema, Manuela.

Emmanuel (imæ·niuøl) n. pr. m. Manuel.

emollient (ima·liønt) adj.-s. emoliente.

emolument (ima·liumønt) s. emolumento.

emotion (imou·shøn) s. emoción. 2 afecto del ánimo. 3 agitación, perturbación.

emotional (-al) adj. emocional. 2 emotivo, impresionable.

empanel (to) (empa·nøl) tr. TO IMPANEL.

emperor (e·mpørøʳ) s. emperador.

emperorship (-ship) s. imperio, dignidad imperial.

emphasis (e·mfasis) s. énfasis. 2 insistencia, intensidad, fuerza, relieve. 3 recancanilla.

emphasize (to) (saiš) tr. dar énfasis a. 2 recalcar, acentuar, subrayar, poner de relieve, hacer hincapié en.

emphatic (al (emfæ·tik) adj. enfático. 2 categórico, enérgico, fuerte, acentuado, marcado.

emphysema (emfisɪ·ma) s. MED. enfisema.

emphyteusis (-tiu·sis) s. DER. enfiteusis.

empire (e·mpair) s.imperio. 2 (E.U.) *Empire State*, estado de Nueva York.

empiric (empi·rik) adj.-s. empírico. 2 s. curandero, charlatán.

empiricism (-risiøm) s. empirismo. 2 curanderismo, charlatanismo.

emplacement (emplei·smønt) s. emplazamiento, situación.

employ (emploi·) s. empleo, puesto, servicio: *to be in one's* ~, estar al servicio de uno.

employ (to) tr. emplear. 2 ocupar [dar trabajo].

employee (emploi·) s. empleado, dependiente.

employer (emploi·ør) s. dueño, patrón, principal, el que emplea.

employment (-mønt) s. empleo. 2 ocupación, trabajo, colocación. 3 profesión, oficio.

empoison (to) (empoi·søn) tr. envenenar, corromper, inficionar.

emporium (empo·riøm) s. emporio. 2 almacén, bazar.

empower (to) (empou·øʳ) tr. autorizar, facultar, comisionar, dar poder, habilitar.

empress (e·mpris) f. emperatriz.

emptiness (e·mptinis) s. vacío, vacuidad. 2 futilidad, vanidad.

empty (e·mpti) adj. vacío. 2 vacante. 3 vacuo, vano. 4 ignorante. 5 frívolo. 6 desprovisto [de]. 7 fam. hambriento.

empty (to) tr. vaciar, evacuar, desocupar. 2 descargar, verter. 3 intr. vaciarse. 4 GEOGR. desaguar.

empty-handed adj. manivacío.

empty-headed (adj. tonto, de cabeza vacía.

empurple (to) (empø·ʳpøl) tr. purpurar.

empyrean (empi·rian) adj.-s. empíreo.

emu (ı·miu) s. ORN. emeu.

emulate (to) (e·miuleit) tr. emular. 2 rivalizar con.

emulation (-ei·shøn) s. emulación. 2 rivalidad.

emulous (e·miuløs) adj. émulo, competidor.

emulsify (to) (imø·lsifai) tr. emulsionar.

emulsion (imø·lshøn) s. emulsión.

en (en) s. ene [letra].

enable (to) (enei·bøl) tr. habilitar, capacitar, facultar. 2 hacer posible, permitir, facilitar.

enact (to) (e·nækt) tr. aprobar y sancionar [una ley]. 2 establecer, estatuir, decretar. 3 TEAT. representar [una escena]; desempeñar [un papel o el papel de].

enactment (-mønt) s. aprobación y sanción [de una ley]. 2 ley, norma, decreto.

enallage (enæ·ladẏi) s. GRAM. enálage.

enamel (-møl) s. esmalte.

enamel (to) tr. esmaltar. 2 charolar [papel, cuero, etc.]. ¶ Pret. y p. p.: *enameled* o *-lled*; ger.: *enameling* o *-lling*.

enamo(u)r (to) (enæ·møʳ) tr. enamorar.

enamo(u)red (-d) adj. enamorado, prendado.

encamp (to) (enkæ·mp) tr.-intr. acampar.

encampment (-mønt) s. acampamento. 2 campamento.

encage (to) (enkei·dẏ) tr. enjaular.

encase (to) (enkei·s) tr. TO INCASE.

encash (to) (enka·sh) tr. (Ingl.) convertir en dinero, hacer efectivo.

encaustic (enko·stik) adj. PINT. encáustico. 2 s. PINT. encauste, encausto.

encave (to) (enkei·v) tr. encovar. 2 embodegar.

enceinte (ansæ·nt) s. ARQ., FORT. recinto. 2 adj. gal. encinta, embarazada [mujer].

encephalic (ensefæ·lik) adj. ANAT. encefálico.

encephalon (ense·falan) s. ANAT. encéfalo.

enchain (to) (enchei·n) tr. encadenar.

enchainment (-mønt) s. encadenamiento.

enchant (to) (encha·nt) tr. encantar, hechizar.

enchanting (-ing) adj. encantador, embelesador.

enchantment (-mønt) s. encantamiento, hechicería. 2 encanto, hechizo, embeleso.

enchantress (-tris) s. encantadora, hechicera.

enchase (to) (enchei·s) tr. engastar, embutir, incrustar.

encircle (to) (ensø·ʳkøl) tr. abrazar, ceñir. 2 rodear; cercar, circundar, circunvalar.

encirclement (-mønt) s. cerco, rodeo, circunvalación.

enclave (e·nkleiv) s. enclavado.

enclitic (enkli·tik) adj.-s. enclítico.

encloister (to) (enklois·tøʳ) tr. enclaustrar.

enclose (to) (enklou·š) tr. encerrar, cercar, rodear. 2 incluir, englobar; acompañar, enviar adjunto.

enclosure (enklou·ẏøʳ) s. cercamiento, encerra-

miento. *2* cerca, vallado, reja. *3* cercado, recinto, coto. *4* documento que acompaña a una carta; anexo.
encomium (enkou·miøn) *s.* encomio, elogio.
encompass (to) (enkø·mpɑs) *tr.* cercar, rodear, ceñir, circundar. *2* abarcar, comprender.
encore (angko·ʳ) *interj.* ¡que se repita! *2 s.* TEAT. repetición [pedida por el público].
encounter (enkau·ntøʳ) *s.* encuentro, choque, combate. *2* encuentro [cara a cara].
encounter (to) *tr.* encontrar, tropezar con. *2* combatir, luchar con. *3 intr.* encontrarse, entrevistarse. *4* luchar.
encourage (to) (enkø·ridȳ) *tr.* alentar, animar, dar alas a. *2* incitar. *3* estimular, fomentar. *4* dar pábulo a.
encouragement (-mønt) *s.* aliento, ánimo. *2* estímulo, fomento, pábulo.
encouraging (-ing) *adj.* alentador.
encroach (to) (enkrou·ch) *intr.* pasar los límites de, usurpar, invadir, intrusarse, abusar. | Gralte. con *on* o *upon*.
encroachment (-mønt) *s.* usurpación, intrusión, abuso, intromisión.
encumber (to) (enkø·mbøʳ) *tr.* embarazar, estorbar: *2* cargar, abrumar, gravar.
encumbrance (-brɑns) *s.* embarazo, estorbo. *2* carga, gravamen.
encyclical (ensi·klikɑl) *s.* encíclica.
encyclopaedia, encyclopedia (ensaiklopi·diɑ) *s.* enciclopedia.
encyst (to) (ensi·st) *tr.* enquistar. *2 intr.* enquistarse.
end (end) *s.* fin, cabo, extremo, punta, cola, remate: *at loose ends*, en desorden, desarreglado; *on* ~, derecho, de pie, de canto; de punta, erizado; seguido, consecutivo. *2* cabo, trozo, retazo, colilla. *3* fin, cabo, término, conclusión, muerte: *to come to an* ~, acabarse, terminarse; *to make an* ~ *of*, acabar con; *at the* ~ *of*, al final, a fines de; *in the* ~, al fin, a la larga; *no* ~ *of*, un sinfín de, la mar de. *4* fin, objeto, mira: *to the* ~ *that*, a fin de que. *5* consecuencia, resultado: *to no* ~, sin efecto, en vano. *6* FÚTBOL extremo.
end (to) *tr.* acabar, terminar, concluir, poner fin a. *2 intr.* acabar, terminar, finalizar: *to* ~ *in*, acabar en. *3* cesar, morir. *4 to* ~ *by*, acabar por.
endanger (to) (endei·ndȳoʳ) *tr.* poner en peligro, comprometer, arriesgar.
endear (to) (endr·øʳ) *tr.* hacer amar, hacer querido o amado.
endearing (-ing) *adj.* cariñoso.
endearment (-mønt) *s.* acción de hacer querer. *2* lo que excita el afecto. *3* fiesta, caricia.
endeavo(u)r (ende·vøʳ) *s.* esfuerzo, empeño, tentativa.
endeavo(u)r (to) *intr.* esforzarse, empeñarse, hacer lo posible, tratar, procurar.
endemic (ende·mic) *adj.* endémico. *2 s.* endemia.
ending (e·nding) *s.* fin, final, parte final; conclusión, desenlace. *2* acabamiento; muerte. *3* GRAM. terminación, desinencia. *4* MÚS. coda.
endive (-iv) *s.* BOT. endibia, escarola.
endless (-lis) *adj.* inacabable, interminable, sin fin. *2* continuo, incesante, perpetuo, eterno. *3* infinito.
endmost (-moust) *adj.* más remoto, extremo.
endocardium (endokɑ·ʳdiøm) *s.* ANAT. endocardio.
endocarp (e·ndokɑʳp) *s.* BOT. endocarpio.
endocrine (-krain) *adj.* FISIOL. endocrino.
endoderm (-døʳm) *s.* BIOL. endodermo.

endogenous (endɑ·dȳinøs) *adj.* H. NAT. endógeno.
endolymph (e·ndolimf) *s.* ANAT. endolinfa.
endorse (to) (endo·ʳs) *tr.* COM. endosar. *2* respaldar [un documento]. *3* aprobar, sancionar.
endorsee (-ɪ) *s.* endosado, endosatario.
endorsement (-mønt) *s.* endoso. *2* aval, garantía, aprobación.
endorser (-øʳ) *s.* endosante.
endosmosis (endosmou·sis) *s.* Fɪs. endósmosis.
endosperm (e·ndospøʳm) *s.* BOT. endospermo.
endow (to) (endau·) *tr.* dotar [una fundación, instituto, etc.]. *2* dotar [de una cualidad, etc.].
endowment (-mønt) *s.* dotación [acción; cantidad con que se dota], fundación. *2* dote, don, prenda personal.
endue (to) (endiu·) *tr.* dotar, proveer [de cualidades, etc.]. *2* investir. *3* vestir.
endurance (-rɑns) *s.* sufrimiento. *2* paciencia, resistencia, aguante: *to be beyond* ~, ser insoportable. *3* duración, continuación.
endure (to) (-øʳ) *tr.* soportar, sufrir, aguantar, resistir. *2 intr.* durar, perdurar.
enduring (-ring) *adj.* paciente, sufrido, resistente. *2* constante. *3* durable, permanente.
endways (e·ndweiš), **endwise** (e·ndwaiš) *adv.* de punta, de pie, derecho. *2* longitudinalmente.
enema (eni·mɑ) *s.* MED. enema.
enemy (e·nømi) *adj.-s.* enemigo.
energetic (al (enøʳdȳe·tik(ɑl) *adj.* enérgico, vigoroso.
energize (to) (e·nøʳdȳaiš) *tr.* dar energía, vigorizar. *2 intr.* obrar con energía.
energumen (enøʳ·giu·men) *s.* energúmeno.
energy (e·nøʳdȳi) *s.* energía.
enervate (e·nøʳveit) *adj.* enervado, debilitado.
enervate (to) *tr.* enervar, debilitar.
enervating (-ting) *adj.* enervante, enervador.
enfeeble (to) (enfɪ·bøl) *tr.* debilitar, enervar.
enfeoff (to) (enfe·f) *tr.* enfeudar, infeudar. *2* investir con un feudo.
enfilade (enfilei·d) *s.* MIL. enfilada.
enfilade (to) *tr.* MIL. enfilar.
enfold (to) (enfou·ld) *tr.* envolver. *2* abrazar.
enforce (to) (enfo·ʳs) *tr.* dar fuerza a. *2* poner en vigor, hacer cumplir [una ley, etc.]. *3* obtener por la fuerza, imponer [obediencia, etc.]. *4* forzar [un paso]. *5* hacer valer [argumentos, razones].
enfranchise (to) (enfræ·nchaiš) *tr.* franquear, manumitir. *2* conceder privilegios o derechos políticos. *3* dar carta de naturaleza.
engage (to) (engei·dȳ) *tr.* comprometer, empeñar. *2* ajustar, tomar, contratar; alistar; alquilar; hacerse reservar [una habitación, etc.]. *3* ocupar, absorber, atraer, cautivar. *4* trabar batalla, conversación, etc.]. *5* MEC., ARQ. endentar, encajar, empotrar. *6 intr.* comprometerse, obligarse. *7* prometerse: *engaged couple*, novios. *8* entrar [en batalla, conversación, etc.]. *9* ocuparse. *10* MEC. engranar, encajar.
engagement (-mønt) *s.* compromiso, obligación; cita. *2* palabra de casamiento; esponsales; noviazgo. *3* ajuste, contrato. *4* TEAT. contrata. *5* colocación, acomodo. *6* MIL. encuentro, combate. *7* MEC. engranaje; acoplamiento.
engaging (-ing) *adj.* atractivo, simpático.
engender (to) (endȳe·ndøʳ) *tr.* engendrar. *2 intr.* engendrarse, formarse.
engine (e·ndȳin) *s.* ingenio, artefacto, mecánico, máquina, motor; locomotora: ~ *driver*, FERROC.

maquinista; ~ *fitter*, montador; ~ *trouble*, ~ *failure*, avería del motor.
engineer (endȳinɪ·ʳ) *s.* ingeniero. *2* maquinista.
engineer (to) *tr.* proyectar, dirigir [como ingeniero]. *2* gestionar, manejar, conducir. *3 intr.* hacer de ingeniero o maquinista. *4* darse maña.
engineering (-ring) *s.* ingeniería. *2* dirección, manejo
enginery (e·ndȳinri) *s.* maquinaria. *2* ingenios o máquinas de guerra. *3* astucias, tretas.
England (i·ngland) *n. pr.* GEOGR. Inglaterra.
Englander (-øʳ) *s.* inglés [natural de Inglaterra].
English (i·nglish) *adj.* y *s.* inglés: ~ *Channel*, GEOGR. Canal de la Mancha. *2 s.* efecto [en el billar].
Englishman (-mæn) *s.* inglés [hombre]. *2* MAR. buque inglés.
Englishwoman (-wumæn) *s.* inglesa.
englut (to) (englø·t) *tr.* engullir.
engorge (to) (engo·ʳdȳ) *tr.* engullir, devorar. *2* atracar [de comida]. *3 intr.* comer con voracidad.
engraft (to) (engræ·ft) *tr.* injertar, enjertar.
engrailed (engrei·id) *adj.* angrelado.
engrain (to) (engrei·n) *tr.* teñir en rama. *2* imbuir, inculcar.
engrave (to) (engrei·v) *tr.* grabar, cincelar. *2* grabar [en la memoria, etc.]. *3* imprimir [un grabado].
engraver (-øʳ) *s.* grabador.
engraving (-ing) *s.* grabado. *2* lámina, estampa.
engross (to) (engrou·s) *tr.* poner en limpio, copiar o transcribir caligráficamente. *2* absorber, acaparar, monopolizar.
engrossing (-ing) *adj.* monopolizador, acaparador, absorbente.
engulf (to) (engø·lf) *tr.* engolfar, sumergir, sumir.
enhance (to) (enja·ns) *tr.* acrecentar, intensificar, engrandecer. *2* realzar, dar mayor valor. *3* exaltar, elevar. *4* ensalzar, encarecer.
enharmonic (enjaʳmo·nik) *adj.* MÚS. enarmónico.
enhearten (to) (enja·ʳtøn) *tr.* alentar, animar.
enigma (ini·gmɑ) *s.* enigma.
enigmatic (al (inigmæ·tik(ɑl) *adj.* enigmático.
enjoin (to) (endȳoi·n) *tr.* mandar, ordenar, prescribir, encargar. *2 to* ~ *from*, prohibir, vedar.
enjoy (to) (endȳoi·) *tr.* gozar o disfrutar de, tener, poseer. *2* gozar con o en; gustar, saborear; gustar de. *3 to* ~ *oneself*, divertirse, deleitarse.
enjoyable (-abøl) *adj.* agradable, deleitable.
enjoyment (-mønt) *s.* goce, disfrute; uso, usufructo. *2* fruición. *3* gusto, placer, solaz.
enkindle (to) (enki·ndøl) *tr.* encender, inflamar.
enlace (to) (enlei·s) *tr.* enlazar, entrelazar. *2* rodear, ceñir.
enlarge (to) (enla·ʳdȳ) *tr.* agrandar. *2* engrosar, aumentar. *3* ensanchar, ampliar, extender. *4* amplificar. *5 intr.* agrandarse, ensancharse, extenderse. *6 to* ~ *upon*, extenderse sobre [un tema, etc.].
enlargement (-mønt) *s.* agrandamiento, ensanchamiento, extensión, etc. *2* FOT. ampliación.
enlarger (-øʳ) *s.* ampliador, amplificador. *2* FOT. ampliadora.
enlighten (to) (enlai·tøn) *tr.* iluminar, alumbrar. *2* ilustrar, instruir. *3* aclarar, esclarecer.
enlightened (-d) *adj.* ilustrado, culto.
enlightenment (-mønt) *s.* ilustración, luces, instrucción, cultura. *2* esclarecimiento. *3 the Enlightenment*, movimiento filosófico del siglo XVIII.
enlist (to) (enli·st) *tr.* alistar, enrolar. *2* enganchar, reclutar. *3 intr.* alistarse, sentar plaza.

enliven (to) (enlai·vøn) *tr.* avivar, vivificar. *2* animar, alegrar, alentar.
enmesh (to) (enme·sh) *tr.* coger, enredar [en mallas o redes]. *2 tr.-intr.* endentar, engranar.
enmity (e·nmiti) *s.* enemistad, hostilidad.
ennoble (to) (enou·bøl) *tr.* ennoblecer.
ennui (anui·) *s.* tedio, fastidio, aburrimiento.
enology (ina·lodȳi) *s.* OENOLOGY.
enormity (ino·ʳmiti) *s.* enormidad, exceso, demasía, atrocidad.
enormous (ino·ʳmøs) *adj.* enorme, descomunal. *2* perverso, atroz.
enough (inø·f) *adj.* bastante, suficiente. *2 s.* lo bastante, lo suficiente. *3 interj.* ¡basta!, ¡bueno! *4 adv.* bastante, suficientemente.
enounce (to) (inau·ns) *tr.* enunciar. *2* presentar, aducir [un argumento, etc.]. *3* pronunciar [palabras]. *4* declarar, anunciar.
enquire (to) = TO INQUIRE.
enrage (to) (enrei·dȳ) *tr.* enfurecer, encolerizar, exasperar, llenar de rabia.
enrapt (enræ·pt) *adj.* arrobado, extasiado.
enrapture (to) (enræ·pchøʳ) *tr.* arrebatar, arrobar, extasiar, transportar, enajenar.
enrich (to) (enri·ch) *tr.* enriquecer. *2* AGR. fertilizar. *3* realzar el gusto, el olor, el color de.
enrobe (to) (enrou·b) *tr.* vestir, adornar.
enrol(l (to) (enrou·l) *tr.* alistar, matricular, empadronar, inscribir, registrar. *2* enrollar, envolver. *3 intr.* alistarse, inscribirse, sentar plaza.
enrol(l)ment (enrou·lmønt) *s.* alistamiento, empadronamiento, inscripción. *2* registro, padrón.
ensanguine (to) (ensæ·ngüin) *tr.* ensangrentar.
ensconce (to) (enska·ns) *tr.* esconder. *2* acomodar, situar, poner en sitio cómodo o seguro.
ensemble (angsa·mbøl) *s.* conjunto, totalidad. *2* conjunto [vestido de mujer].
enshrine (to) (enshrai·n) *tr.* envolver, encerrar, guardar [como una cosa preciosa, sagrada].
enshroud (to) (enshrau·d) *tr.* amortajar. *2* envolver, ocultar.
ensign (e·nsain) *s.* bandera, pabellón, enseña. *2* insignia, divisa. *3* (E.U.) alférez [de marina].
ensign-bearer *s.* abanderado.
ensilage (e·nsilidȳ) *s.* ensilaje.
ensilage (to) *tr.* ensilar.
enslave (to) (enslei·v) *tr.* esclavizar.
enslavement (enslei·vmønt) *s.* avasallamiento. *2* esclavitud, servidumbre.
ensnare (to) (ensne·øʳ) *tr.* entrampar, coger en una trampa. *2* tender un lazo a, atraer, seducir.
ensue (to) (ensiu·) *intr.* seguir, suceder, sobrevenir. *2* seguirse, resultar.
ensuing (ensiu·ing) *adj.* siguiente. *2* resultante.
ensure (to) (enshu·ʳ) *tr.* asegurar, garantizar.
entablature (entæ·blachuʳ) *s.* ARQ. entablamento, cornisamiento.
entail (entei·l) *s.* DER. vinculación, vínculo. *2* bienes vinculados, mayorazgo.
entail (to) *tr.* vincular [bienes]. *2* suponer, traer consigo, ocasionar, acarrear.
entangle (to) (entæ·ngøl) *tr.* enredar, enmarañar, intrincar. *2* enredar [a uno].
entanglement (-mønt) *s.* enredo, maraña, enmarañamiento, complicación.
enter (to) (e·ntøʳ) *tr.* entrar en o por: *to* ~ *a room*, entrar en una habitación. *2* ingresar en, afiliarse a, hacerse socio de. *3* inscribir o inscribirse para. *4* entrar, meter, introducir. *5* asentar, anotar, inscribir, registrar. *6* DER. *to* ~ *an action*, entablar una acción. *7 intr.* entrar. *8 in-*

gresar. *9* penetrar, introducirse. *10* TEAT. salir, entrar en escena. *11 to* ~ *into*, entrar en, formar parte de. *12 to* ~ *on* o *upon*, comenzar, emprender.

enteric (ente·rik) *adj.* ANAT. entérico.

enteritis (entørai·tis o -itis) *s.* MED. enteritis.

enterprise (e·ntø^rpraiš) *s.* empresa, demanda [acción u obra que se emprende]. *2* energía, resolución. *3* carácter emprendedor.

enterprising (-ing) *adj.* emprendedor, atrevido, activo.

entertain (to) (entø^rtei·n) *tr.* entretener, divertir. *2* tener [como huésped o invitado]; hospedar, agasajar. *3* tomar en consideración. *4* tener, acariciar, abrigar,. [ideas, sentimientos]. *5 intr.* recibir huéspedes, dar comidas o fiestas.

entertainer (-ø^r) *s.* anfitrión. *2* entretenedor. *3* actor, músico [esp. de variedades].

entertaining (-ing) *adj.* entretenido, divertido.

entertainment (-mønt) *s.* acogida, hospitalidad; convite, agasajo, fiesta. *2* entretenimiento, diversión; función, espectáculo.

enthrall (to) (enzro·l) *tr.* esclavizar, sojuzgar. *2* hechizar, cautivar.

enthrone (to) (enzrou·n) *tr.* entronizar.

enthronement (-mønt) *s.* entronización.

enthuse (to) (enzu·š) *intr.* fam. entusiasmarse.

enthusiasm (enzu·šiæšm) *s.* entusiasmo.

enthusiastic(al (en·iušsiæ·stik(al) *adj.* entusiástico, entusiasta, caluroso. *2* entusiasmado.

enthymeme (e·nzimɪm) *s.* LÓG. entimema.

entice (to) (entai·s) *tr.* atraer, tentar, incitar.

enticement (-mønt) *s.* tentación, incitación. *2* atractivo, cebo.

entire (entai·ø^r) *adj.* entero, completo, cabal, íntegro, total. *2* VET., BOT. entero.

entirely (-li) *adv.* enteramente, íntegramente, completamente, del todo, por completo.

entirety (-ti) *s.* integridad, entereza, totalidad.

entitle (to) (entai·tøl) *tr.* titular, intitular. *2* dar derecho a; autorizar.

entity (e·ntiti) *s.* FILOS. entidad.

entomb (to) (entu·m) *tr.* enterrar, sepultar. *2* servir de tumba a.

entomology (entoma·lodŷi) *s.* entomología.

entourage (angtura·dŷ) *s.* gal. medio ambiente, gente que rodea a uno.

entr'acte (angtra·kt) *s.* gal. entreacto.

entrails (e·ntreilš) *s. pl.* entrañas, vísceras. *2* entrañas [interior].

entrance (e·ntrans) *s.* entrada, acceso, ingreso: *no* ~, se prohíbe la entrada. *2* entrada [por donde se entra], puerta, zaguán. *3* boca, embocadura. *4* MÚS. entrada.

entrance (to) (entræ·ns) *tr.* extasiar, arrebatar, hechizar.

entranceway (e·ntranswei) *s.* entrada, portal.

entrant (e·ntrant) *adj.* entrante. *2 s.* socio nuevo. *3* principiante. *4* DEP. participante.

entrap (to) (entræ·p) *tr.* entrampar [coger o hacer caer en una trampa], atrapar, engañar. ¶ Pret. y p. p.: *entrapped*; ger.: *entrapping*.

entreat (to) (entrɪ·t) *tr.-intr.* suplicar, rogar, solicitar, instar, implorar, pedir.

entreaty (-i) *s.* súplica, ruego, instancia.

entrechat (antrøcha·) *s.* trenzado [en el baile].

entrée (angtrei·) *s.* gal. entrada [derecho de entrar]. *2* COC. entrada.

entrench (to) (entre·nch) *tr.* atrincherar. *2* intr. *to* ~ *on* o *upon*, invadir, transgredir, infringir.

entrenchment (-mønt) *s.* atrincheramiento.

entrepreneur (antrøprønø·^r) *s.* empresario [esp. de teatro]; contratista.

entresol (a·ntrøsol) *s.* gal. entresuelo.

entrust (to) (entrø·st) *tr.* confiar, dejar al cuidado de. *2 to* ~ *one with*, confiar a uno [una cosa].

entry (e·ntri) *s.* entrada, ingreso. *2* puerta, portal, vestíbulo, zaguán. *4* asiento, anotación. *5* artículo [de diccionario]. *6* COM. partida: *double* ~, partida doble. *7* DEP. lista de participantes. *8* MÚS. entrada.

entwine (to) (entwai·n) *tr.* entrelazar, entretejer. *2* enroscar [alrededor de], enlazar, abrazar.

entwist (to) (entwi·st) *tr.* torcer, retorcer. *2* enroscar [alrededor de].

enucleate (to) (iniu·klieit) *tr.* explicar, aclarar. *2* CIR. enuclear.

enumerate (to) (iniu·møreit) *tr.* enumerar. *2* contar, numerar.

enumeration (-ei·shøn) *s.* enumeración. *2* recuento, censo.

enunciate (to) (inø·nshieit) *tr.* enunciar. *2* articular, pronunciar.

enunciation (-ei·shøn) *s.* enunciación. *2* pronunciación.

envelop (to) (enve·løp) *tr.* envolver, cubrir, forrar.

envelope (e·nvøloup) *s.* envoltura, cubierta. *2* funda, carpeta. *3* sobre, sobrecarta.

envelopment (mønt) *s.* envolvimiento. *2* envoltura, cubierta.

envenom (to) (enve·nøm) *tr.* envenenar, emponzoñar [hacer venenoso]. *2* viciar, corromper.

enviable (e·nviabøl) *adj.* envidiable.

envious (e·nviøs) *adj.* envidioso.

environ (to) (envai·røn) *tr.* rodear, cercar.

environment (-mønt) *s.* ambiente, medio ambiente. *2* alrededores.

environs (envai·rønš) *s. pl.* contornos, alrededores, cercanías, inmediaciones, afueras.

envisage (to) (envi·šidŷ) *tr.* mirar a la cara. *2* encararse con, afrontar. *3* mirar, considerar. *4* representar, imaginarse.

envoy (e·nvoi) *s.* enviado, mensajero. *2* LIT. envío.

envy (e·nvi) *s.* envidia.

envy (to) (e·nvi) *tr.* envidiar. *2* anhelar, codiciar.

enwrap (to) (enræ·p) *tr.* envolver, cubrir, abrigar. *2* absorber, embargar.

enwreathe (to) (enrɪ·d) *tr.* enguirnaldar. *2* envolver, rodear.

enzyme (e·nšaim o -šim) *s.* BIOQUÍM. enzima.

Eocene (i·osin) *adj.-s.* GEOL. eoceno.

Eolian (iou·lian) *adj.-s.* AEOLIAN.

eolithic (ioli·zik) *adj.* PREHIST. eolítico.

eon (i·øn) *s.* eón, evo.

epact (i·pæct) *s.* epacta.

epaulet (e·polet) *s.* MIL. charretera, capona.

ephebe (e·fib) *s.* efebo.

ephemera (efe·møra) *s.* EPHEMERON.

ephemeral (efe·møral) *adj.* efímero.

ephemeris (efe·møris) *s.* efemérides astronómicas.

ephemeron (efe·møran) *s.* ENT. efímera, cachipolla.

Ephesus (e·føsøs) *n. pr.* GEOGR. Éfeso.

ephod (e·fad) *s.* efod.

epic (e·pic) *adj.* épico. *2 s.* epopeya. *3* épica.

epical (e·pikal) *adj.* épico.

epicarp (e·pika^rp) *s.* BOT. epicarpio.

epicedium (episɪ·diøm) *s.* epicedio, elegía.

epicene (e·pisin) *adj.* GRAM. epiceno.

epicentra, epicenter (e·pisentø^r) *s.* GEOL. epicentro.

epicure (e·pikiu^r) *s.* epicúreo, gastrónomo, sibarita.

Epicurean (epikiuɾɪ·an) adj.-s. FIL. epicúreo. 2 (con min.) epicúreo, sibarita.
Epicureanism (-išm) s. epicureismo.
epicycloid (episai·kloid) s. GEOM. epicicloide.
epidemic (epide·mik) adj. epidémico. 2 s. epidemia.
epidermis (-dø·ʳmis) s. epidermis, cutícula.
epigastrium (epigæ·striøm) s. ANAT. epigastrio.
epiglottis (-glo·tis) s. ANAT. epiglotis.
epigram (e·pigræm) s. epigrama.
epigrammatic (al (epigramæ·tik(al) adj. epigramático.
epigraph (e·pigræf) s. epígrafe.
epigraphy (epi·grafi) s. epigrafía.
epilepsy (e·pilepsi) s. MED. epilepsia.
epileptic (epile·ptik) adj.-s. epiléptico.
epilogize (to) (epi·lodÿaiš) tr. poner epílogo a. 2 intr. recitar o pronunciar un epílogo.
epilogue (e·pilog) s. epílogo.
epinicion (-ni·shøn) s. epinicio, himno triunfal.
Epiphany (ipi·fani) n. pr. Epifanía.
epiphonema (epifoni·ma) s. RET. epifonema.
epiphysis (epi·fisis) s. ANAT. epífisis.
epiphyte (e·pifait) s. BOT. epifito.
Epirus (ipai·røs) n. pr. GEOGR. El Epiro.
episcopacy (ipi·skopasi) s. episcopado.
episcopal (ipi·skopal) adj. episcopal.
Episcopalian (ipiskopei·lian) adj.-s. de la iglesia episcopal protestante.
episcopate (ipi·skopeit) s. episcopado.
episode (e·pisoud) s. episodio.
episodic (al (episa·dik(al) adj. episódico. 2 esporádico, ocasional.
epistle (ipi·søl) s. epístola, carta, misiva. 2 (con may.) Epístola [de la misa].
epistolary (ipi·stoleri) adj. epistolar. 2 s. ECLES. epistolario.
epitaph (e·pitæf) s. epitafio.
epithalamium (epizalei·miøm) s. epitalamio.
epithelium (epizi·lium) s. ANAT. epitelio.
epithet (e·pizet) s. epíteto.
epitome (epi·tomi) s. epítome.
epitomize (to) (-aiš) tr. epitomar, compendiar.
epizooty (epišo·ati) s.VET. epizootia.
epoch (e·pok) s. época, edad, período.
epoch-making) adj. trascendental, memorable, que hace época.
epode (e·poud) s. epodo.
eponym (e·ponim) s. personaje o héroe epónimo.
eponymous (epa·nimøs) adj. epónimo.
epopee (e·popɪ) s. epopeya. 2 épica.
Epsom-salt (e·psømsolt) s. QUÍM. sal de la Higuera.
equable (e·kuabøl) adj. igual, uniforme. 2 tranquilo, ecuánime.
equal (ɪ·kual) adj. igual. 2 distribuido o formado con igualdad. 3 justo, equitativo, imparcial. 4 adecuado, suficiente. 5 to be ~ to, servir para, poder con, estar a la altura de. 6 s. igual.
equal (to) tr. igualar, ser igual a, igualarse con, emparejar. 2 corresponder [al afecto, etc.]. ¶ Pret. y p. p.: equaled o -lled; ger.: equaling o -lling.
equalitarian (ikualite·rian) adj.-s. igualitario.
equality (ikua·liti) s. igualdad. 2 paridad. 3 uniformidad, lisura.
equalize (to) (i·kualaiš) tr. igualar. 2 compensar, equilibrar, regularizar.
equalizer (ikualai·šøʳ) s. igualador.
equanimity (ikuani·miti) s. ecuanimidad.
equanimous (ikua·nimøs) adj. ecuánime.
equate (to) (i·kueit) tr. igualar; poner en ecuación.

equation (ikuei·shøn) s. MAT. ecuación.
equator (ikuei·tøʳ) s. GEOM., GEOGR., ASTR. ecuador.
equatorial (ikueito·rial) adj.-s. ecuatorial.
equerry (e·kueri) s. caballerizo.
equestrian (ikue·strian) adj. ecuestre. 2 s. jinete.
equid (e·kuid) s. ZOOL. équido.
equidistant (ikuidi·stant) adj. equidistante.
equilateral (-læ·tøral) adj.-s. GEOM. equilátero.
equilibrate (to) (-lai·breit) tr. equilibrar, compensar. 2 intr. estar en equilibrio.
equilibration (-brei·shøn) s. equilibrio [acción de equilibrar].
equilibrium (-li·briøm) s. equilibrio.
equine (i·kuain) adj. equino, caballar. 2 s. caballo.
equinoctial (ikuina·kshal) adj. equinoccial. 2 s. línea equinoccial. 3 tempestad equinoccial.
equinox (i·kuinoks) s. ASTR. equinoccio.
equip (to) (ikui·p) tr. equipar, pertrechar, proveer, municionar. 2 MAR. armar, aparejar.
equipage (e·kuipidÿ) s. equipo, avíos, pertrechos. 2 tren, séquito, carroza, carruaje.
equipment (ikui·pmønt) s. equipo, aparejamiento, habilitación. 2 equipo, material, avíos, vestuario, armamento. 3 MEC. equipo, tren, juego.
equipoise (i·kuipoiš) s. equilibrio. 2 contrapeso.
equipoise (to) tr. equilibrar, contrapesar.
equiponderate (to) (ikuipo·ndereit) intr. equiponderar. 2 tr. hacer de igual peso. 3 contrapesar.
equisetaceous (equisitei·shøs) adj. BOT. equisetáceo.
equitable (e·kuitabøl) adj. justo, equitativo, imparcial.
equitation (-ei·shøn) s. equitación.
equity (e·kuiti) s. equidad, rectitud, imparcialidad. 2 DER. derecho que se aplica en ciertos tribunales.
equivalence, equivalency (ikui·valøns, -si) s. equivalencia.
equivalent (-valønt) adj. equivalente.
equivocal (-vokal) adj. equívoco, ambiguo. 2 incierto, dudoso, sospechoso.
equivocate (to) (vokeit) tr. hacer equívoco. 2 intr. usar de equívocos, mentir.
equivocation (-vokei·shøn) s. equívoco, anfibología. 2 engaño por medio de frases equívocas.
era (i·ra) s. era [de tiempo].
eradicate (to) (iræ·dikeit) tr. erradicar, desarraigar, extirpar.
erase (to) (irei·š) tr. borrar. 2 tachar, rayar, raspar.
eraser (irei·šøʳ) s. raspador, goma de borrar, borrador, etc.
erasion (irei·ÿøn) s. ERASURE. 2 CIR. raspado.
erasure (irei·ÿøʳ) s. raspadura, borradura, tachón. 2 acción de raspar, de borrar.
ere (e·øʳ) prep. antes de o de que. 2 conj. antes que [indicando preferencia].
erect (ire·kt) adj. derecho, levantado, erguido, enhiesto. 2 vertical. 3 erizado [púa, etc.].
erect (to) tr. erigir [levantar, edificar; instituir]. 2 levantar, elevar. 3 poner derecho, erguir, enhestar, erizar. 4 GEOM. levantar. 5 MEC. montar, instalar.
erectile (-il) adj. eréctil.
erection (ire·kshøn) s. erección. 2 erguimiento, enhestadur. 3 MEC. montaje, instalación.
erector (-tøʳ) s. erector. 2 MEC. montador.
erelong (eøʳlo·ng) adv. antes de mucho, dentro de poco, a no tardar.
eremite (e·rimait) s. eremita, ermitaño.
erenow (eøʳnau·) adv. antes de ahora; hasta aquí.
erg (øʳg) s. FÍS. ergio.
ergot (ø·ʳgøt) s. BOT. cornezuelo del centeno.

ergotism (-išm) *s.* MED., LÓG. ergotismo.
ergotize (to) (-aiš) *intr.* ergotizar. *2 tr.* infestar de cornezuelo.
ericaceous (erikei·shøs) *adj.* BOT. ericáceo.
Erin (e·rin) *n. pr.* poét. Erin, Irlanda.
ermine (ø·ʳmin) *s.* ZOOL., BLAS. armiño. *2* armiño [piel]. *3* fig. toga, judicatura.
ern, erne (øʳn) *s.* ORN. halieto.
Ernest (ø·ʳnist) *n. pr. m.* Ernesto.
erode (to) (irou·d) *tr.* corroer, roer, desgastar. *2* causar erosión. *3 intr.* sufrir erosión.
erosion (irou·ȳon) *s.* corrosión. *2* desgaste, erosión.
erotic (al (era·tik(al) *adj.* erótico.
err (to) (øʳ) *intr.* errar, equivocarse, pecar, descarriarse. *2* errar, vagar.
errable (ø·rabøl) *adj.* falible.
errand (e·rand) *s.* misión, encargo, recado, mandado, diligencia: ~ *boy*, botones.
errant (e·rant) *adj.* errante, errabundo. *2* andante [caballero]. *3* errático. *4* erróneo. *5* falible.
errantry (-ri) *s.* vida errante, aventurera. *2* caballería andante.
errata (irei·tæ) *s. pl.* de ERRATUM. *2* fe de erratas.
erratic (iræ·tic) *adj.* errático. *2* irregular, variable, inconstante. *3* excéntrico, raro.
erratum (irei·tøm) *s.* IMPR. errata.
erroneous (erou·niøs) *adj.* erróneo, falso, equivocado.
error (e·røʳ) *s.* error. *2* yerro, equivocación. *3* pecado.
ersatz (eʳsa·ts) *adj.* sintético, artificial. *2 s.* substitutivo.
Erse (øʳs) *s.* lenguaje gaélico de los escoceses.
erst (øʳst) *adv.* antiguamente, anteriormente. *2 adj.* de otro tiempo.
erstwhile (ø·ʳstjuail) *adj.* antiguamente, antaño, antes, al principio.
erubescence (erube·søns) *s.* erubescencia, rubor.
eruct (to) (irøkt), **eructate (to)** (irø·kteit) *intr.* y *tr.* eructar.
eructation (irøktei·shøn) *s.* eructación, eructo.
erudite (e·rudait) *adj.-s.* erudito.
erudition (erudi·shøn) *s.* erudición, conocimientos.
erupt (to) (irø·pt) *intr.* hacer erupción. *2* salir [las lavas]. *3 tr.* arrojar [lavas, etc.].
eruption (irø·pshøn) *s.* GEOL., MED. erupción. *2* estallido, explosión [de una pasión, de risa, etc.].
eruptive (irø·ptiv) *adj.* eruptivo.
erysipelas (erisi·pelas) *s.* MED. erisipela.
Erythraen (erizri·an) *adj.-s.* eritreo.
escadrille (eskadri·l) *s.* escuadrilla aérea o naval.
escalade (eskalei·d) *s.* MIL. escalada.
escalade (to) *tr.* escalar [una pared, etc.].
escalator (eskæle·tøʳ) *s.* escalera mecánica.
escalop, escallop (eska·lop) *s.* venera, pechina.
escapade (eskapei·d) *s.* evasión, fuga. *2* travesura, correría, aventura.
escape (eskei·p) *s.* escape, evasión, fuga, escapatoria. *2* escape [de un fluido; de un reloj]. *3* desagüadero.
escape (to) *intr.* escapar, escaparse; fugarse, huir. *2* escaparse [un fluido]. *3 tr.* escapar a, evitar, eludir, rehuir.
escapement (-mønt) *s.* escape [de reloj, etc.].
escarp (to) (eska·ʳp) *tr.* MIL. escarpar.
escarpment (-mønts). escarpa, acantilado.
eschalot (e·shalot) *s.* BOT. chalote, escaloña.
eschar (e·skaʳ) *s.* CIR. escara.
eschatology (eskæta·lodȳi) *s.* TEOL. escatología.

escheat (to) (eschı·t) *intr.-tr.* revertir [los bienes] o hacer revertir [bienes] al estado.
eschew (to) (eschu·) *tr.* evitar, rehuir.
escort (e·scoʳt) *s.* escolta, convoy; acompañante.
escort (to) (esco·ʳt) *tr.* escoltar, convoyar, acompañar.
escritoire (escritua·ʳ) *s.* escritorio, escribanía [mueble].
Escurial (eskiu·rial) *n. pr.* Escorial.
escutcheon (escø·chøn) *s.* escudo de armas. *2* escudo [de cerradura]. *3* MAR. espejo de popa.
Eskimo (e·skimou) *adj.-s.* esquimal.
esophagus (isa·fagøs) *s.* ANAT., ZOOL. esófago.
esoteric (esote·rik) *adj.* esotérico.
espalier (espæ·liøʳ) AGR. espaldar, espaldera.
esparto o **esparto grass** (espa·ʳtou) *s.* BOT. esparto.
especial (espe·shal) *adj.* especial, peculiar, particular. *2* notable.
especially (espe·shali) *adv.* especialmente, sobre todo, máxime. *2* especialmente, señaladamente.
Esperanto (espøra·ntou) *s.* esperanto.
espionage (e·spionidȳ) *s.* espionaje. *2* acecho.
esplanade (esplanei·d) *s.* explanada.
espousal (espau·šal) *s.* desposorio, esponsales. *2* adhesión a una causa.
espouse (to) (espau·š) *tr.* desposarse, casarse con. *2* adoptar, abrazar, defender [una idea, causa, etc.].
esprit (esprı·) *s.* ingenio, agudeza, gracejo. *2* ~ *de corps*, compañerismo, espíritu de cuerpo.
espy (to) (espai·) *tr.* divisar, columbrar.
esquire (eskuai·øʳ) *s.* escudero. *2* caballero [de una dama]. *3* título de cortesía que se pospone al apellido, gralte. en la forma abreviada *Esq.* y sin anteponer *Mr.* 4 (Ingl.) hacendado.
essay (e·sei) *s.* tentativa, esfuerzo, probatura. *2* ensayo [literario].
essay (to) (esei·) *tr.* ensayar, probar, examinar. *2* intentar, tentar.
essayist (e·seist) *s.* ensayista.
essence (e·søns) *s.* FIL. esencia. *2* ser, entidad. *3* substancia, médula [de una cosa]. *4* esencia, extracto, perfume.
essential (ese·nshal) *adj.* esencial. *2* substancial, capital, vital, indispensable. *3 s.* esencia, lo esencial.
establish (to) (estæ·blish) *tr.* establecer. *2* afirmar, consolidar. *3* sentar, probar, demostrar. *4* hacer oficial [una iglesia o religión].
establishment (-mønt) *s.* establecimiento. *2* acción de hacer oficial una iglesia o religión. *3* casa [residencia, muebles, criados]. *4* renta vitalicia.
estate (estei·t) *s.* estado [orden, clase de pers.]: *third* ~, estado llano. *2* bienes, propiedades: *personal* ~, bienes muebles; *real* ~, bienes raíces. *3* hacienda, heredad, finca. *4* herencia [bienes].
esteem (estı·m) *s.* estima, estimación, aprecio.
esteem (to) *tr.* estimar, apreciar, tener en mucho. *2* estimar, juzgar, considerar.
ester (e·støʳ) *s.* QUÍM. éster.
Esther *n. pr. f.* Ester.
esthetic (esze·tik) *adj.* estético.
esthetics (-s) *s.* estética.
Esthonia (eszou·nia) *n. pr.* GEOGR. Estonia.
estimable (e·stimabøl) *adj.* estimable, apreciable.
estimate (e·stimeit) *s.* estimación, cálculo, avalúo. *2* opinión. *3* presupuesto [de un trabajo].
estimate (to) *tr.* estimar, apreciar, evaluar, calcular, juzgar. *2* hacer el presupuesto de.

estimation (estimei·šhøn) *s.* estima, estimación, aprecio. *2* estimación, evaluación.

estimator (e·stimeitø^r) *s.* estimador, tasador.

estival (e·stival) *adj.* estival, estivo, veraniego.

estop (to) (esta·p) *tr.* rellenar, tapar. *2* prohibir, impedir.

estrade (estrei·d) *s.* estrado, tarima.

estrange (to) (estrei·ndÿ) *tr.* extrañar, alejar, enajenar, hacer perder la amistad.

estrangement (-mønt) *s.* extrañamiento, alejamiento, desvío, enajenamiento.

estuary (e·schueri) *s.* GEOGR. estuario, ria.

et cetera, &c. (et se·tera) *s.* etcétera, etc.

etch (to) (ech) *tr.* grabar al aguafuerte. *2* atacar con un ácido, etc.

etching (e·ching) *s.* grabado al aguafuerte, aguafuerte.

eternal (itø·^rnal) *adj.* eterno, eternal, sempiterno: ~ *flower*, BOT. perpetua. *2* perpetuo, incesante. *3 s. the Eternal*, al Eterno, Dios.

eternity (-iti) *s.* eternidad.

eternize (to) (itø·^rnaiš) *tr.* eternizar. *2* perpetuar, inmortalizar.

etesian (itï·ÿan) *adj.* METEOR. etesio.

ether (i·zø^r) *s.* éter.

ethereal (izi·rial) *adj.* etéreo. *2* aéreo, vaporoso, sutil.

etherealize (to) (iz·rialais) *tr.* hacer etéreo, aéreo; espiritualizar. *2* QUÍM. convertir en éter.

etherize (to) (i·zøraiš) *tr.* MED. eterizar. *2* QUÍM. convertir en éter.

ethic (al (e·zik(al) *adj.* ético, moral.

ethics (e·ziks) *s.* ética.

Ethiopian (iziou·pian) *adj.* etíope; negro. *2 s.* etíope.

ethmoid (e·zmoid) *adj.-s.* ANAT. etmoides.

ethnic (al (e·znik(al) *adj.* étnico.

ethnography (ezna·grafi) *s.* etnografía.

ethnologist (ezna·lodÿist) *s.* etnólogo.

ethnology (ezna·lodÿi) *s.* etnología.

ethos (i·zos) *s.* carácter, genio, rasgo distintivo [de un pueblo o colectividad].

ethyl (e·zil) *s.* QUÍM. etilo. *2 adj.* etílico.

ethylic (ezi·lik) *adj.* QUÍM. etílico.

etiolate (to) (i·tioleit) *tr.* descolorarse [esp. las plantas] por falta de luz; ahilarse.

etiology (itia·lodÿi) *s.* etiología.

etiquette (e·tiket) *s.* etiqueta, ceremonia. *2* normas de conducta profesional [esp. de abogados y médicos].

Etruscan (etrø·skan) *adj.-s.* etrusco.

etude (etiu·d) *s.* gal. estudio [de música].

etymologist (etima·lodÿist) *s.* etimólogo.

etymology (etima·lodÿi) *s.* etimología.

eucalypt (yu·kalipt), **eucalyptus** (yu·kaliptøs) *s.* BOT. eucalipto. *2 pl.* de eucalipto.

Eucharist (yu·karist) *s.* Eucaristía.

euchology (yuka·lodÿi) *s.* eucologio.

euchre (yu·kø^r) *s.* juego de naipes.

Euclid (yu·klid) *n. pr. m.* Euclides.

eudiometer (yudia·mitø^r) *s.* FÍS. eudiómetro.

Eugene (yu·dÿin) *n. pr. m.* Eugenio.

Eugenia (yudÿi·nia) *n. pr. f.* Eugenia.

eugenics (yudÿe·nics) *s.* eugenesia.

eulogist (yu·lodÿist) *s.* elogiador, panegirista.

eulogistic (-ic) *adj.* laudatorio, panegírico.

eulogium (yu·loudÿiøm) *s.* EULOGY.

eulogize (to) (yu·lodÿais) *tr.* elogiar, loar, alabar.

eulogy (yu·lodÿi) *s.* elogio, panegírico, encomio.

eunuch (yu·nøk) *s.* eunuco.

euphemism (yu·fimišm) *s.* eufemismo.

euphemize (to) (yu·fimaiš) *intr.* usar de eufemismos.

euphonic(al (yufa·nik(al), **euphonious** (yufou·niøs) *adj.* eufónico.

euphony (yu·føni) *s.* eufonía.

Euphorbiaceae (yufø^rbiei·sii) *s. pl.* BOT. euforbiáceas.

euphoria (yufo·ria), **euphory** (yu·fori) *s.* euforia.

euphuism (yu·fiuišm) *s.* eufuismo, culteranismo.

Eurasian (yurei·shan) *adj.-s.* eurasiático.

eureka (yurï·ka) *interj.* ¡eureka!

Europe (yu·rop) *n. pr.* GEOGR. Europa.

European (yuropï·an) *adj.-s.* europeo. *2* ~ *plan* (E.U.), cuarto sin comida [en los hoteles].

Europeanize (to) (yuropï·anaiš) *tr.* europeizar.

eurythmy (yuri·dmi) *s.* euritmia.

Eustace (yu·stis) *n. pr. m.* Eustaquio.

Eustachian tube (yustei·kian) *adj.* ANAT. trompa de Eustaquio.

euthanasia (yuzanei·šia) *s.* eutanasia.

evacuate (to) (ivæ·kiueit) *tr.* evacuar. *2* desocupar, vaciar. *3 intr.* evacuar una ciudad, etc.

evacuation (ivækiuei·shøn) *s.* evacuación.

evacuee (ivækiur·) *s.* gal. evacuado [pers.].

evade (ivei·d) *tr.* evadir, eludir, evitar, rehuir, escapar a. *2 intr.* usar de evasivas. *3* escabullirse.

evaginate (ivæ·dÿineit) *tr.* volver de dentro a fuera.

evaluate (to) (-liueit) *tr.* evaluar, valorar, valuar, tasar.

evaluation (-shøn) *s.* evaluación, valoración, avalúo.

evanesce (to) (evane·s) *intr.* desvanecerse, disiparse, esfumarse, desaparecer, evaporarse.

evanescence (-søns) *s.* desvanecimiento, disipación. *2* fugacidad.

evanescent (-nt) *adj.* evanescente; fugaz.

evangel (ivæ·ndÿøl) *s.* evangelio. *2* buena nueva.

evangelic(al (ivandÿe·lik(al) *adj.* evangélico.

evangelism (evæ·ndÿølišm) *s.* predicación del evangelio.

evangelist (-list) *s.* evangelista. *2* predicador protestante.

evangelize (to) (-laiš) *tr.* evangelizar.

evaporate (to) (ivæ·poreit) *tr.* evaporar; vaporizar. *2* secar, desecar. *3* desvanecer, disipar. *4 intr.* evaporarse. *5* disiparse. *6* exhalar vapor.

evaporation (-ei·shøn) *s.* evaporación, vaporización.

evaporator (ivæ·poreitø^r) *s.* evaporador, desecador.

evasion (ivei·ÿøn) *s.* evasión, evasiva, efugio, subterfugio, escapatoria.

evasive (ivei·siv) *adj.* evasivo, ambiguo.

eve (IV) *s.* víspera, vigilia: *on the* ~ *of*, en vísperas de.

Eve *n. pr. f.* Eva.

even (i·vn) *adj.* igual, llano, liso, nivelado, parejo. *2* uniforme, regular, constante, invariable. *3* ecuánime, sereno. *4* justo, imparcial. *5* igualado, equilibrado. *6* igual [del mismo valor, etc.]. *7* en línea [con]; situado al mismo nivel [que], paralelo, coincidente. *8* exacto. cabal. *9* par [divisible por dos]. *10* en paz, desquitado: *to be* ~ *with*, estar en paz con, haber ajustado cuentas con.

11 adv. aún, hasta, también, incluso: *if,* ~ *though*, aun cuando, aunque: ~ *so*, aun así. *12* siquiera: *not* ~, ni siquiera. *13* de un modo igual, con uniformidad, con suavidad.

even (to) *tr.* igualar, allanar, nivelar, enrasar. *2*

igualar, igualarse con. *3* liquidar [cuentas]; desquitar.

even-handed *adj.* justo, imparcial.

evening (í·vning) *s.* tarde, anochecer: prima noche, noche [hasta que uno se acuesta]; velada: ~ *dress*, traje de noche, traje de etiqueta; ~ *party*, tertulia, velada, sarao; ~ *star*, estrella vespertina. *2* atardecer [de la vida].

evenness (í·vønnis) *s.* igualdad, uniformidad, llanura, lisura. *2* constancia. *3* serenidad. *4* imparcialidad. *5* exactitud.

evensong (-song) *s.* LITURG. vísperas.

event (ive·nt) *s.* caso, hecho, suceso, evento, acontecimiento; consecuencia, resultado: *at all events, in any* ~, en todo caso: *in the* ~ *of*, en caso de.

even-tempered *adj.* ecuánime, sereno, tranquilo.

eventful (-ful) *adj.* lleno de acontecimientos. *2* importante, memorable.

eventide (í·vøntaid) *s.* atardecer, anochecer.

eventual (ive·nchual) *adj.* eventual, contingente, fortuito. *2* final, consiguiente.

eventuality (ivenchuæ·liti) *s.* eventualidad, contingencia. *2* consecuencia, resultado.

eventually (ive·nchuali) *adv.* eventualmente. *2* finalmente, con el tiempo.

eventuate (ive·nchueit) *intr.* acontecer, acaecer, ocurrir. *2* resultar.

ever (e·vø^r) *adv.* siempre: *for* ~, para siempre; *for* ~ *and* ~, para siempre jamás; continuamente. *2* alguna vez: *have you* ~ *heard him sing?*, ¿le ha oído usted cantar alguna vez? *3* nunca, jamás: *hardly* ~, casi nunca; *more than* ~, más que nunca: *the best book* ~ *writen*, el mejor libro que jamás se haya escrito. *4* ~ *after*, ~ *since*, desde entonces, después; desde que. *5* ~ *and anon*, de vez en cuando. *6* ~ *so*, ~ *so much*, muy, mucho, muchísimo. *7* ~ *so little*, muy poco, un poquitín. *8* A veces *ever* no es más que un expletivo que sirve para dar mayor energía a la frase. En este caso no se traduce o se traduce libremente: *where* ~ *did I drop it?*, ¿dónde demonio se habrá caído?; *did you* ~*?*, ¿ha visto, o ha oído usted cosa igual?

everglade (-gleid) *s.* paúl, terreno pantanoso cubierto de yerbas altas.

evergreen (-grin) *adj.* BOT. de hojas persistentes. *2 s.* árbol o planta de hojas persistentes. *3 pl.* ramas que se ponen como adorno.

everlasting (-la·sting) *adj.* eterno, sempiterno, perpetuo, perdurable, perenne. *2* fastidioso, pesado. *3 s.* eternidad. *4* BOT. siempreviva. *5 the Everlasting*, el Eterno, Dios.

evermore (-mø^r) *adv.* eternamente, siempre; *for* ~, para siempre jamás.

every (e·vri) *adj.* cada, todo, todos, todas, todos los, todas las: ~ *day*, cada día, todos los días: ~ *one*, cada uno, cada cual; ~ *one of them*, todos, todos sin excepción; ~ *other day*, cada dos días; *his* ~ *word*, todas sus palabras, cada palabra suya. *2* completo, entero: *I have* ~ *confidence in him*, tengo entera confianza en él. *3* Forma modos adverbiales, como: ~ *bit*, enteramente, en todo: ~ *now and then*, ~ *now and again*, de vez en cuando.

everybody (e·vribadi) *pron.* todos, todo el mundo; cada uno, cada cual.

everyday (evridei·) *adj.* diario, cotidiano, de todos los días, ordinario.

everyone (evriuon) *pron.* todos, todo el mundo; cada uno.

everything (e·vrizing) *pron.* todo, cada cosa.

everywhere (e·vrijue^r) *adv.* por o en todas partes; a todas partes. *2* dondequiera, por dondequiera.

evict (to) (evi·kt) *tr.* DER. desahuciar, expulsar. *2* DER. recobrar por evicción.

eviction (evi·kshøn) *s.* DER. evicción; desahucio.

evidence (e·vidøns) *s.* evidencia. *2* señal, prueba, demostración: *circunstantial* ~, DER. prueba indiciaria. *3* testimonio; deposición, declaración [testifical]: *to give* ~, deponer, declarar.

evidence (to) *tr.* evidenciar, patentizar, revelar.

evident (e·vidønt) *adj.* evidente, claro, patente, manifiesto, visible, notorio.

evidential (evide·nshal) *adj.* indicativo, indicador. *2* basado en testimonios o pruebas, probatorio.

evil (í·vøl) *adj.* malo [no bueno; nocivo; malvado, maligno; desagradable, ofensivo]; aciago, funesto: ~ *eye*, mal de ojo, aojadura: *the Evil One*, el Malo, Satanás. *2 s.* mal. *3 adv.* mal, malignamente.

evildoer (-duø^r) *s.* malhechor; persona que obra mal.

evil-favo (u) red *adj.* feo.

evil-minded *adj.* mal intencionado. *2* malicioso, mal pensado.

evince (to) (ivi·ns) *tr.* demostrar, hacer patente. *2* mostrar, revelar, indicar.

eviscerate (to) (ivi·søreit) *tr.* desentrañar, destripar.

evisceration (-shøn) *s.* destripamiento.

evitable (e·vitabøl) *adj.* evitable.

evocation (evokei·shøn) *s.* evocación. *2* DER. avocación.

evoke (to) (ivou·k) *tr.* evocar, llamar.

evolution (evoliu·shøn) *s.* evolución, desarrollo, crecimiento. *2* MIL., MAR., FIL., BIOL. evolución. *3* MAT. extracción de raíces.

evolutional (-al), **evolutionary** (-eri) *adj.* evolutivo.

evolutionism (-ism) *s.* evolucionismo.

evolve (to) (iva·lv) *tr.* desenvolver, desarrollar, desplegar, producir. *2* convertir, transformar. *3* despedir [gases, etc.]. *4 intr.* evolucionar, desarrollarse, abrirse, desplegarse.

ewe (yu) *f.* ZOOL. oveja: ~ *lamb*, cordera.

ewer (yu·ø^r) *s.* jarro, aguamanil.

ex (eks) *prep.* COM. ex [sin incluir]: ~ *coupon*, ex cupón.

exacerbate (to) (egšæ·sø^rbeit) *tr.* exacerbar. *2* irritar.

exact (egšæ·kt) *adj.* exacto. *2* preciso, estricto, riguroso.

exact (to) *tr.* exigir, imponer [tributos, etc.]; obtener por exacción. *2* exigir, requerir [hacer necesario].

exacting (-ing) *adj.* exigente.

exaction (-shør) *s.* exacción.

exactitude (-itiud) *s.* exactitud. *2* precisión. *3* puntualidad.

exaggerate (to) (egšæ·dÿøreit) *tr.* exagerar. *2* abultar, ponderar.

exaggeration (-ei·shøn) *s.* exageración *2* abultamiento.

exalt (to) (egšo·lt) *tr.* exaltar, ensalzar; elevar, engrandecer. *2* enorgullecer, alegrar. *3* exaltar [la imaginación, etc.].

exaltation (-ei·shøn) *s.* exaltación, ensalzamiento. *2* elevación, engrandecimiento, promoción. *3* contento, alborozo. *4* exaltación [de la imaginación, etc.].

exam (egšæ·m) *s.* fam. examen.

examination (egšæminei·shøn) s. examen. 2 inspección, reconocimiento. 3 DER. interrogatorio.
examine (to) (egšæ·min) tr. examinar. 2 inspeccionar, reconocer, explorar. 3 DER. interrogar.
example (egšæ·mpøl) s. ejemplo: for ~, por ejemplo. 2 modelo, dechado. 3 muestra, ejemplar. 4 escarmiento, lección.
exanimate (egšæ·nimit) adj. exánime, inanimado, muerto. 2 abatido, sin ánimo.
exasperate (to) (egšæ·spøreit) tr. exasperar, irritar, encolerizar. 2 agravar, enconar, encrudecer.
exasperation (-ei·shøn) s. exasperación, irritación, encono.
excavate (to) (e·kskaveit) tr. excavar. 2 extraer cavando.
excavation (-ei·shøn) s. excavación. 2 material extraído por excavación.
excavator (e·kskaveitøʳ) s. excavador. 2 excavadora [máquina].
exceed (to) (eksɪ·d) tr. exceder, sobrepujar. 2 ser superior a [las fuerzas, etc., de]. 3 intr. exceder. 4 descollar.
exceedingly (-ingli) adv. extremamente, sumamente, por demás, muy.
excel (to) (ekse·l) tr. aventajar, sobrepujar, superar. 2 descollar, distinguirse, sobresalir.
excellence, excellency (e·ksøløns, -si) s. excelencia.
excellent (e·ksølønt) adj. excelente. 2 sobresaliente, relevante. 3 primoroso; magnífico.
except (ekse·pt) prep. excepto, salvo, menos, a excepción de, fuera de.
except (to) tr. exceptuar. 2 intr. poner reparos, oponerse, objetar.
excepting (-ing) prep. exceptuando, excepto, salvo, a excepción de.
exception (ekse·pshøn) s. excepción. 2 salvedad. 3 objeción, reparo: to take ~, objetar, desaprobar. 4 DER. excepción.
exceptionable (-abøl) adj. recusable. 2 reprochable, tachable.
exceptional (-al) adj. excepcional.
excerpt (e·ksøʳpt) s. cita, pasaje, fragmento [escogido de un texto]. 2 excerpta.
excerpt (to) (eksø·ʳpt) tr. escoger, sacar, citar [un pasaje o fragmento].
excess (ekse·s) s. exceso, demasía, sobra: in ~ of, más de; to ~, en exceso, con demasía, inmoderadamente. 2 exceso, abuso. 3 superfluidad, abundancia. 4 excelente, sobrante. 5 pl. excesos.
excess (to) tr. (Ingl.) pagar, exigir o cobrar un suplemento por exceso de peso, etc.
excessive (-iv) adj. excesivo, desmedido. 2 sumo, extremo.
excessively (-li) adv. excesivamente. 2 sumamente, extremadamente.
exchange (ekschei·ndỹ) s. cambio, trueque, permuta: in ~ for, a cambio de. 2 cambio [de saludos, cumplidos, golpes, etc.]. 3 canje. 4 COM. bolsa, lonja. 5 COM. cambio; premio del cambio: ~ rate, tipo del cambio. 6 central [de teléfonos].
exchange (to) tr. cambiar, canjear, trocar, permutar, conmutar. 2 cambiar, cambiarse, hacerse, etc. [mutuamente]: to ~ greetings, saludarse, mandarse felicitaciones. 3 intr. cambiar, hacer un cambio.
exchangeable (-abøl) adj. cambiable.
exchequer (eks·chekoʳ) s. (Ingl.) hacienda pública, erario, fisco, tesorería del Estado. 2 bolsa, fondos, recursos pecuniarios.
excise (eksai·š) s. sisa, alcabala, impuesto sobre ciertos artículos de comercio interior.

excise (to) tr. gravar con el impuesto llamado EXCISE. 2 cortar, separar cortando. 3 quitar, borrar.
excisión (eksi·ỹøn) s. excisión. 2 corte [en un texto].
excitable (eksai·tabøl) adj. excitable.
excitant (-tant) adj.-s. excitante.
excitation (eksitei·shøn) s. excitación [acción y efecto de excitar]. 2 FÍS., FISIOL. excitación.
excite (to) (eksai·t) tr. excitar. 2 acalorar, animar.
excitement (-mønt) s. excitación, agitación, acaloramiento. 2 animación, estímulo. 3 interés, emoción. 4 FISIOL. excitación.
exciter (-øʳ) s. excitador.
exciting (-ing) adj. excitante, excitador. 2 estimulante, animador. 3 interesante, emocionante.
exclaim (to) (eksklei·m) tr.-intr. exclamar, clamar: to ~ against, clamar contra.
exclamation (eksklamei·shøn) s. exclamación, grito, clamor. 2 GRAM. ~ point, punto de admiración.
exclude (to) (eksklu·d) tr. excluir. 2 dejar fuera, impedir la entrada.
exclusion (-ỹøn) s. exclusión. 2 acción de impedir la entrada.
exclusive (-siv) adj. exclusivo. 2 privativo. 3 que sólo admite cierta clase de clientes [establecimiento, hotel, etc.], o de personas [grupo, sociedad, etc.]; selecto, distinguido, a la moda. 4 que rehuye el trato social con los que no son de su clase o gusto [pers.]. 5 ~ of, con exclusión de.
exclusiveness (-nis) s. exclusividad. 2 calidad de selecto, único.
excluvivism (-išm) s. exclusivismo. 2 tendencia a excluir.
excogitate (to) (ekska·dỹiteit) tr. excogitar.
excommunicate (to) (ekskømiu·nikeit) tr. excomulgar.
excommunication (-ei·shøn) s. excomunión.
excoriate (to) (eksko·rieit) tr. excoriar, desollar.
excoriation (-ei·shøn) s. excoriación.
excorticate (to) (eksko·ʳtikeit) tr. descortezar.
excrement (e·kskrimønt) s. excremento.
excrescence (ekskre·søns) s. excrecencia.
excrete (to) (ekskrɪ·t) tr. FISIOL. excretar.
excretion (ekskrí·shøn) s. excreción.
excretory (e·kskritori) adj. excretorio. 2 s. FISIOL. emuntorio.
excruciate (to) (ekskru·shieit) tr. atormentar, torturar.
excruciating (-ing) adj. torturador, angustioso. 2 agudísimo, vivísimo, atroz [dolor].
exculpate (to) (ekskø·lpeit) tr. exculpar, justificar, disculpar.
exculpation (-ei·shøn) s. exculpación, justificación, disculpa.
excursion (ekskø·ʳshøn) s. excursión. 2 divagación, digresión.
excursionist (-ist) s. excursionista.
excursive (ekskø·ʳsiv) adj. errante, errático. 2 digresivo; dado a la digresión.
excusable (ekskiu·šabøl) adj. excusable, disculpable.
excuse (ekskiu·š) s. excusa, disculpa. 2 justificación, exculpación. 3 excusa, exención.
excuse (to) tr. excusar, disculpar. 2 justificar, exculpar. 3 perdonar, dispensar: excuse me!, ¡dispense usted! 4 excusar, eximir.
execrable (e·ksikrabøl) adj. execrable, abominable.
execrate (to) (e·ksikreit) tr. execrar, abominar, maldecir.

execration (-eiˈshøn) *s.* execración.

executant (egšeˈkiutant) *s.* MÚS. ejecutante.

execute (to) (eˈksikiut) *tr.* ejecutar, cumplir, realizar, llevar a cabo. *2* TEAT. desempeñar. *3* formalizar, otorgar [un documento]. *4* ejecutar, ajusticiar.

execution (eksikiuˈshøn) *s.* ejecución. *2* DER. embargo; mandamiento judicial. *3* DER. otorgamiento.

executioner (eksikiuˈshønøʳ) *s.* ejecutor de la justicia, verdugo.

executive (ekšeˈkiutiv) *adj.* ejecutivo. *2* que gobierna o dirige. *3 m.* poder ejecutivo. *4* (E.U.) presidente, jefe del Estado; gobernador de un Estado. *5* director, gerente; junta directiva.

executor (egšeˈkiutøʳ) *s.* ejecutor. *2* albacea.

executory (egšeˈkiutori) *adj.* ejecutorio. *2* ejecutivo, administrativo.

exedra (eksiˈdra) *s.* ARQ. exedra.

exegesis (eksidÿɪˈsis) *s.* exégesis.

exemplar (egšeˈmplaʳ) *s.* modelo, dechado, prototipo. *2* ejemplar, espécimen, caso, ejemplo.

exemplary (-mpleri) *adj.* ejemplar. *2* ilustrativo.

exemplification (egšemplifikeiˈshøn) *s.* ejemplificación. *2* DER. copia certificada.

exemplify (to) (egšeˈmplifai) *tr.* ejemplificar. *2* DER. copiar, trasladar. ¶ Pret. y p. p.: *exemplified.*

exempt (egšeˈmpt) *adj.* exento, libre, franco.

exempt (to) *tr.* exentar, eximir, exceptuar, dispensar.

exemption (-mpshøn) *s.* exención.

exequatur (eksekueiˈtøʳ) *s.* exequátur.

exercise (eˈksøʳsaiš) *s.* ejercicio [en todos sus sentidos menos en el de tiempo durante el cual rige una ley de presupuestos]. *2 pl.* ejercicios [de examen, etc.]. *3* MIL. ejercicios.

exercise (to) *tr.* ejercer, practicar. *2* ejercitar, adiestrar. *3* emplear, poner en ejercicio. *4* preocupar, inquietar. *5* fatigar, poner a prueba. *6 intr.-ref.* ejercitarse, practicarse.

exercitation (egsøʳsiteiˈshøn) *s.* ejercicio, ejercitación. *2* discurso, ensayo.

exergue (eksøˈʳg) *s.* exergo.

exert (to) (egšøˈʳt) *tr.* ejercer [influencia]; poner en acción [fuerza, facultades, etc.], esforzar. *2 ref.* esforzarse, empeñarse.

exertion (egšøˈʳshøn) *s.* ejercicio, uso [de una facultad, fuerza, etc.]. *2* esfuerzo, empeño. *3 pl.* esfuerzos, pasos, diligencias.

exfoliate (to) (eksfouˈlieit) *tr.* exfoliar. *2 intr.* exfoliarse.

exfoliation (eiˈshøn) *s.* exfoliación.

exhalation (eksjaleiˈshøn) *s.* exhalación [acción]. *2* exhalación, efluvio, vaho, vapor. *3* explosión [de ira, etc.].

exhale (to) (eksjeiˈl) *tr.* exhalar, despedir. *2* espirar [el aire]. *3* evaporar. *4 intr.* evaporarse, escaparse, disiparse.

exhaust (egšoˈst) *s.* MEC. escape, descarga, salida [de gases, vapor, etc.]: ~ *valve,* válvula de escape o de salida. *2* tubo de escape. *3* FÍS., MEC. vacío, succión, aspiración. *4* aire, vapor, etc., aspirado o de escape.

exhaust (to) *tr.* agotar, apurar, consumir. *2* agotar, fatigar, postrar. *3* FÍS., MEC. practicar el vacío en; dar salida o escape a [gases, vapor]; aspirar [el aire, el polvo]. *4 intr.* escapar, salir [los gases, el vapor].

exhausted (-id) *adj.* exhausto, agotado. *2* agotado, fatigado, rendido.

exhauster (-øʳ) *s.* MEC. bomba; aspirador, ventilador aspirante.

exhausting (-ing) *adj.* agotador.

exhaustion (egšoˈschøn) *s.* agotamiento. *2* FÍS., MEC. aspiración. *3* MEC. vaciamiento, descarga.

exhaustive (egšoˈstiv) *adj.* exhaustivo.

exhibit (egšiˈbit) *s.* objeto (s expuesto (s en una exposición; instalación. *2* exhibición, ostentación.

exhibit (to) *tr.* exhibir. *2* exponer [a la vista, al público]. *3* mostrar, dar muestras de. *4* lucir, ostentar.

exhibiter (-øʳ) *s.* expositor [en una exposición].

exhibition (egšibiˈshøn) *s.* exhibición. *2* exposición [de productos, cuadros, etc.]. *3* (Ingl.) beca, pensión. *4 to make an* ~ *of oneself,* ponerse en ridículo.

exhibitioner (-øʳ) *s.* (Ingl.) estudiante pensionado. *2* expositor.

exhibitionist (-ist) *s.* exhibicionista.

exhibitor (egšiˈbitøʳ) *s.* expositor [en una exposición].

exhilarant (egšiˈlarant) *adj.* alegrador, estimulante.

exhilarate (to) (-reit) *tr.* alegrar, regocijar, animar, estimular, excitar.

exhilaration (-eiˈshøn) *s.* alegría, regocijo, animación, excitación.

exhort (to) (egšoˈʳt) *tr.-intr.* exhortar.

exhortation (-eiˈshøn) *s.* exhortación.

exhumation (eksjiumeiˈshøn) *s.* exhumación.

exhume (to) (eksjiuˈm) *tr.* exhumar, desenterrar.

exigence, exigency (eˈksidÿøns, -si) *s.* exigencia, necesidad, urgencia.

exigent (eˈksidÿønt) *adj.* exigente [que requiere mucho]. *2* apremiante.

exiguity (eksiˈguiti) *f.* exigüidad.

exiguous (-giuøs) *adj.* exiguo.

exile (eˈksail) *s.* destierro, expatriación, exilio. *2* desterrado, expatriado, exilado.

exile (to) *tr.* desterrar, proscribir, extrañar.

exist (to) (egšˈist) *intr.* existir. *2* vivir. *3* subsistir.

existence (-øns) *s.* existencia.

existentialism (egšisteˈnshališm) *s.* existencialismo.

exit (eˈksit) *s.* salida [acción; sitio]. *2* partida, muerte. *3* TEAT. mutis.

exit (to) *intr.* TEAT. irse. | Ús. sólo en el presente: ~ *Joan,* vase Juana.

exodus (eˈksødøs) *s.* éxodo.

exonerate (to) (egšaˈnøreit) *tr.* exonerar, descargar, aliviar. *2* exculpar.

exoneration (-eiˈshøn) *s.* exoneración, descargo; exculpación.

exorbitance, exorbitancy (egšoˈʳbitans, -si) *s.* exorbitancia.

exorbitant (egšoˈʳbitant) *adj.* exorbitante.

exorcise (to) (eˈksoʳsaiš) *tr.* exorcizar.

exorcism (eˈksoʳsišm) *s.* exorcismo, conjuro.

exorcist (eˈksoʳsišt) *s.* exorcista.

exordium (egšoˈʳdiøm) *s.* exordio.

exosmose (eˈksasmous), **exosmosis** (eksasmouˈsis) *s.* FÍS. exósmosis.

exoteric (al (eksoteˈrik(al) *adj.* exotérico.

exotic (al (eksaˈtik(al) *adj.* exótico. *2* extranjero, forastero. *3 s.* planta o palabra exótica.

exoticism (eksaˈtisišm), **exotism** (eksaˈtišm) *s.* exotiquez, exotismo.

expand (ekspæˈnd) *tr.* extender, dilatar, ensanchar, alargar. *2* abrir, desplegar. *3* tender, esparcir. *4* desarrollar [una idea, una ecuación, etc.]. *5 intr.* extenderse, dilatarse. *6* abrirse, desplegarse.

expanding (-ing) *adj.* que extiende o ensancha. *2* que se extiende o ensancha. *3* de expansión, de dilatación.

expanse (ekspæ·ns) *s.* extensión, espacio.

expansion (-shøn) *s.* expansión, dilatación. *2* extensión, ensanchamiento, aumento. *3* expansión [parte ensanchada]. *4* desarrollo [de una idea, ecuación, etc.].

expansive (-iv) *adj.* expansivo. *2* ancho, extenso.

expatiate (to) (ekspei·shieit) *intr.* espaciarse, explayarse, dilatarse [en el discurso, etc.].

expatiation (-ei·shøn) *s.* acción de explayarse, extenderse.

expatiatory (ekspei·shiatori) *adj.* extenso, difuso.

expatriate (to) (ekspæ·trieit) *tr.* expatriar, desterrar. *2 intr.* expatriarse.

expatriation (-ei··shøn) *s.* expatriación.

expect (to) (ekspe·kt) *tr.* esperar [contar con, creer que ha de suceder alguna cosa]: *I ~ to see him,* espero verle. *2* esperar [a uno]: *don't ~ me,* no me esperen. *3* esperar que [uno] hará alguna cosa: *I ~ him to come,* espero que vendrá. *4 fam.* pensar, creer, suponer.

expectable (-abøl) *adj.* esperable.

expectance, expectancy (-ans, -si) *s.* espera, expectación. *2* esperanza, expectativa.

expectant (-ant) *adj.* expectante; que espera. *2* que puede o espera ser, futuro, en perspectiva. *3 s.* candidato o aspirante a un cargo.

expectation (-ei·shøn) *s.* espera, expectación, lo que se espera. *2* expectativa, perspectiva, esperanza, probabilidad: *~ of life,* índice de longevidad. *3 pl.* perspectivas de heredar.

expectorate (to) (ekspe·ctøreit) *tr.-intr.* expectorar, esputar.

expectoration (-ei·shøn) *s.* expectoración. *2* esputo.

expedience, expediency (ekspi·diøns, -si) *s.* conveniencia, oportunidad, utilidad. *2* oportunismo.

expedient (-dient) *adj.* conveniente, propio, oportuno, ventajoso. *2* oportunista. *3 s.* expediente, arbitrio, recurso.

expedite (e·kspidait) *adj.* expedito. *2* rápido, pronto.

expedite (to) *tr.* apresurar; facilitar. *2* despachar, dar curso a.

expedition (ekspidi·shøn) *s.* expedición [militar, científica, etc.]. *2* expedición, prontitud. *3* apresuramiento.

expeditionary (-eri) *adj.* expedicionario.

expeditious (ekspidi·shøs) *adj.* expeditivo, pronto.

expel (to) (ekspe·l) *tr.* expeler. *2* echar, expulsar. ¶ Pret. y p. p.: *expelled;* ger.: *expelling.*

expend (to) (ekspe·nd) *tr.* expender, gastar.

expenditure (-ichø²) *s.* gasto, desembolso.

expense (ekspe·ns) *s.* gasto, desembolso. *2* expensas, costa: *at the ~ of,* a expensas de. *3 pl.* gastos, coste, costo: *to cover expenses,* cubrir gastos.

expensive (-iv) *adj.* costoso, caro, dispendioso.

experience (ekspi·riøns) *s.* experiencia: *by ~,* por experiencia. *2* experimento. *3* paso, lance, aventura, goce, sufrimiento.

experience (to) *tr.* experimentar. *2* probar, pasar, sufrir, vivir. *3* aprender o enseñar por experiencia.

experienced (-d) *adj.* experimentado. *2* experto, práctico. *3* aleccionado. *4* vivido.

experiment (ekspe·rimønt) *s.* experimento, experiencia [prueba, ensayo].

experiment (to) *tr.-intr.* experimentar [probar, ensayar].

experimental (eksperime·ntal) *adj.* experimental.

experimentation (-ei·shøn) *s.* experimentación.

expert (ekspø·²t) *adj.* experimentado, experto, perito, práctico, diestro. *2* pericial, de perito. *3 s.* experto, perito, especialista.

expertise (ekspø²ti·s̄) *s.* pericia. *2* dictamen pericial.

expertness (ekspø·²tnis) *s.* pericia, habilidad.

expiate (to) (e·kspieit) *tr.* expiar, purgar.

expiation (-ei·shøn) *s.* expiación.

expiration (ekspirei·shøn) *s.* expiración, término, vencimiento. *2* FISIOL. espiración. *3* muerte.

expire (to) (ekspai·ø²) *tr.-intr.* FISIOL. espirar. *2 intr.* expirar, vencer, caducar. *3* expirar, morir.

expiry (-ri) *s.* expiración, vencimiento.

explain (to) (eksplei·n) *tr.* explicar, exponer, aclarar: *to ~ oneself,* explicarse. *2 intr.* dar una explicación.

explanation (eksplanei·shøn) *s.* explicación. *2* explanación [de un texto, etc.].

expletive (e·ksplitiv) *adj.* expletivo. *2 s.* voz expletiva. *3* exclamación.

explicate (to) (e·ksplikeit) *tr.* explicar, explanar, interpretar. *2* desarrollar [una idea].

explication (-ei·shøn) *s.* explicación, explanación, exposición. *2* descripción detallada.

explicit (ekspli·sit) *adj.* explícito.

explode (to) (eksplou·d) *tr.* volar, hacer estallar. *2* desacreditar [una moda, etc.]; refutar [una teoría]. *3* expeler por explosión. *4 intr.* estallar, hacer explosión, volar, reventar: fig. *to ~ with laughter,* soltar la carcajada.

exploit (e·ksploit) *s.* hazaña, proeza.

exploit (to) (e·ksploi·t) *tr.* explotar [una mina, etc.]. *2* explotar [aprovecharse de].

exploitation (-eishøn) *s.* explotación.

exploiter (e·ksploitø²) *s.* explotador.

exploration (eksplorei·shøn) *s.* exploración.

explore (eksplo·²) *tr.* explorar. *2* examinar, sondear.

explorer (-ø²) *s.* explorador.

explosion (eksplou·ȳøn) *s.* explosión, estallido. *2* acción de hacer explosión, voladura. *3* refutación [de una teoría]. *4* FONÉT. explosión.

explosive (-siv) *adj.* explosivo. *2* de explosión. *3 s.* explosivo. *4* FONÉT. consonante explosiva.

exponent (ekspou·nønt) *s.* expositor [que interpreta o declara]. *2* exponente [que es representación o ejemplo]. *3* MAT. exponente.

export (e·kspø²t) *s.* exportación. *2 pl.* exportaciones; artículos de exportación.

export (to) (ekspo·²t) *tr.* exportar.

exportation (-ei·shon) *s.* exportación.

exporter (ekspo·²tø²) *s.* exportador.

expose (to) (ekspou·s̄) *tr.* exponer [a la vista, a la intemperie, a un riesgo, a una acción, etc.]. *2* exponer, poner en peligro, comprometer. *3* FOT. exponer. *4* descubrir [poner al descubierto]; revelar. *5* desenmascarar; divulgar las faltas o algo deshonroso de [uno]. *6* abandonar, exponer [a un niño].

exposed (-d) *adj.* expuesto, a la vista. *2* expuesto, en peligro, descubierto, desabrigado.

exposition (ekspoši·shøn) *s.* exposición [acción de exponer, estado de lo expuesto]. *2* exposición, explicación, interpretación. *3* LIT., MÚS. exposición. *4* exposición, situación [de un lugar]. *5* exposición [artística, industrial, etc.].

expository (ekspa·sitori) *adj.* explicativo.

expostulate (to) (ekspa·schuleit) *intr.* hacer reconvenciones, discutir; tratar de disuadir.

expostulation (-ei·shøn) *s.* reconvención, disuasión, protesta, razones.

exposure (ekspou·ȳø^r) *s.* exposición a la intemperie, al peligro, etc.]; desabrigo, falta de protección. *2* exposición, orientación. *3* FOT. exposición. *4* desenmascaramiento; acción de exponer a la vergüenza, al escándalo.

expound (to) (ekspau·nd) *tr.* exponer, explicar, comentar.

express (ekspre·s) *adj.* expreso, claro, explícito. *2* expreso, especial. *3* exacto, parecido. *4* expreso [tren, mensajero]. *5* de transportes rápidos. *6* (Ingl.) ~ *delivery*, correo urgente. *7* *adv.* expresamente, especialmente. *8* de modo expreso. *9* *s.* expreso, mensajero, propio. *10* expreso [tren, autobús, etc.]. *11* (Ingl.) correo urgente.

express (to) *tr.* expresar. *2* describir, designar. *3* exprimir, prensar, estrujar. *4* extraer el juego. *5* *ref.* expresarse, producirse, explicarse.

expression (ekspre·shøn) *s.* expresión. *2* acción de exprimir.

expressionism (-išm) *s.* expresionismo.

expressive (ekspre·siv) *adj.* expresivo. *2* que expresa.

expressiveness (-nis) *s.* expresión, energía, fuerza expresiva.

expressly (ekspre·sli) *adv.* expresamente, especialmente. *2* clara, explícitamente.

expropriate (to) (eksprou·prieit) *tr.* desposeer, expropiar.

expropriation (-ei·shøn) *s.* expropiación.

expugnable (ekspø·gnabøl) *adj.* expugnable.

expulse (to) (e·kspøls) *tr.* expulsar.

expulsion (ekspø·lshøn) *s.* expulsión.

expunge (to) (ekspø·ndȳ) *tr.* borrar, rayar, tachar.

expurgate (to) (e·kspø^{r}gueit) *tr.* expurgar.

expurgation (-ei·shøn) *ts.* expurgación, expurgo; purificación.

exquisite (e·kskuišit) *adj.* exquisitez. *2* delicadeza, refinamiento. *3* intensidad, agudeza.

exquisitness (-nis) *s.* exquisitez. *2* delicadeza, refinamiento. *3* intensidad, agudeza.

exsanguine (eksæ·ngwin) *adj.* exangüe; anémico.

exsiccate (to) (e·ksikeit) *tr.* secar, desecar.

extant (e·kstant) *adj.* existente, en existencia.

extemporaneous (ekstempørei·nïøs) *adj.* improvisado [hecho sin preparación]. *2* improvisado, provisional [hecho para la ocasión].

extemporary (ekste·mpøreri) *adj.* improvisado [discurso, orador, etc.]. *2* repentino, inesperado.

extempore (ekste·mpøri) *adv.* improvisadamente. *2* improvisamente, de improviso. *3* *adj.* improvisado. *4* *s.* improvisación.

extemporize (to) (ekste·mpøraiš) *tr.* improvisar.

extend (to) (ekste·nd) *tr.* extender. *2* explayar, ensanchar, prolongar. *3* alargar [el brazo, la mano]. *4* dar, conceder, ofrecer. *5* MIL. desplegar. *6* aguar, rebajar [un líquido]. *7* prorrogar, dar prórroga. *8* agotar las fuerzas de. *9* *intr.* extenderse. *10* prolongarse. *11* estirarse, dar de sí.

extended (ekste·ndid) *adj.* extendido, estirado. *2* prolongado. *3* diferido.

extensible (ekste·nsibøl) *adj.* extensible, extensivo.

extensile (-sil) *adj.* extensible. *2* extensor.

extension (-shøn) *s.* extensión. *2* prolongación, dilatación, expansión. *3* adición, anexo. *4* MEC. alargadera. *5* prórroga, espera, moratoria.

extensity (-siti) *s.* extensión [calidad de extenso].

extensive (-siv) *adj.* relativo a la extensión. *2* extensivo. *3* extenso, ancho, vasto, dilatado.

extensively (-li) *adv.* extensivamente. *2* extensamente, por extenso: ~ *used*, de uso general o común.

extent (ekste·nt) *s.* extensión [de una cosa]; superficie, anchura, longitud, perímetro; magnitud, grado: *to a certain* ~, hasta cierto punto; *to a great* ~, en grado sumo; *to the full* ~, en toda su extensión, completamente. *2* extensión [de terreno]. *3* GEOM. extensión.

extenuate (to) (ekste·niueit) *tr.* minorar, atenuar, paliar, excusar. *2* extenuar, enflaquecer.

extenuating (-ing) *adj.* atenuante, paliativo.

exterior (eksti·riø^r) *adj.* exterior, externo: ~ *angle*, GEOM. ángulo externo. *2* extrínseco. *3* *s.* exterior. *4* exterioridad, conducta.

exteriority (ekstiria·riti) *s.* exterioridad [calidad].

exteriorize (to) (eksti·riøraiš) *tr.* exteriorizar. *2* dar forma objetiva a.

exterminate (to) (ekstø·^{r}ineit) *tr.* exterminar. *2* desarraigar, extirpar.

extermination (-ei·shøn) *s.* exterminio. *2* extirpación, destrucción.

extern (ekstø·^{r}n) *s.* externo [alumno, médico].

external (-al) *adj.* externo, exterior: ~ *angle*, GEOM. ángulo externo; ~ *remedy*, remedio externo; ~ *trade*, comercio exterior. *2* *s. pl.* exterior, exterioridad, apariencia [de las cosas].

externality (ekstø·^{r}næ·liti) *s.* exterioridad.

externalize (to) (ekstø·^{r}nalaiš) *tr.* exteriorizar. *2* dar forma o cuerpo.

exterritorial (eksterito·rial) *adj.* extraterritorial.

extinct (eksti·nkt) *adj.* extinto, extinguido. *2* apagado [fuego, etc.].

extinction (eksti·nkshøn) *s.* extinción.

extinguish (to) (eksti·ngwish) *tr.* extinguir. *2* apagar. *3* eclipsar, oscurecer.

extinguisher (-ø^r) *s.* el o lo que extingue o apaga. *2* apagador, matacandelas.

extinguishment (-mønt) *s.* extinción.

extirpate (to) (e·cstø^{r}peit) *tr.* extirpar. *2* desarraigar. *3* destruir, exterminar.

extirpation (-ei·shøn) *s.* extirpación. *2* erradicación. *3* exterminio.

extol, extoll (to) (ekstou·l) *tr.* exaltar, ensalzar, alabar. ¶ Pret. y p. p.: *extolled*; ger.: *extolling*.

extort (to) (eksto·^{r}t) *tr.* arrancar, obtener, sacar [algo] por la fuerza, la importunación, etc.

extortion (exto·^{r}shøn) *s.* extorsión. *2* exacción, concusión, violencia.

extortionate (-it) *adj.* opresivo, injusto; excesivo, exorbitante.

extra (e·kstra) *adj.* extra. *2* extraordinario, adicional, suplementario. *3* de repuesto. *4* *s.* extra. *5* pieza de repuesto. *6* *adv.* mucho, muy: *extra-fine*, extrafino.

extract (e·kstrækt) *s.* QUÍM., FARM. extracto. *2* extracto, cita, fragmento [de un libro, etc.].

extract (to) (ekstræ·kt) *tr.* extraer, sacar, obtener. *2* entresacar, seleccionar, citar [fragmentos, pasajes, etc.]. *3* QUÍM. extraer. *4* MAT. extraer [raíces].

extraction (-shøn) *s.* extracción [acción de extraer]. *2* extracto, esencia. *3* extracción, origen, alcurnia.

extractive (-tiv) *adj.* extractivo.

extractor (-tø^r) *s.* extractor [pers., aparato, pieza, mecanismo]. *2* CIR. fórceps.

extradite (to) (e·kstradait) *tr.* conceder o pedir la extradición de.

extradition (ekstradi·shøn) *s.* extradición.

extrados (ekstræ·das) *s.* ARQ. extradós, trasdós.

extrajudicial (ekstradÿudi·shal) *adj.* extrajudicial.

extramural (ekstramiu·ral) *adj.* situado extramuros. *2* fuera del recinto de una institución.

extraneous (ekstrei·niøs) *adj.* extraño, ajeno [a una cosa]: ~ *matter*, materia extraña. *2* extrínseco.

extraordinary (ekstro·ʳdineri) *adj.* extraordinario.

extraterritorial (ekstraterito·rial) *adj.* extraterritorial.

extravagance, -cy (ekstræ·vagans, -si) *s.* prodigalidad, derroche, despilfarro, profusión, exceso. *2* extravagancia, desarreglo, exageración.

extravagant (ekstræ·vagant) *adj.* pródigo, derrochador, despilfarrador. *2* excesivo, exorbitante. *3* extravagante, disparatado. *4 s.* extravagante, excéntrico.

extravaganza (ekstrævagæ·nša) *s.* TEAT. obra extravagante y fantástica.

extravasate (to) (ekstræ·vaseit) *tr.* extravenar. *2 intr.* MED. extravasarse, extravenarse.

extreme (ekstrɪ·m) *adj.* extremo: ~ *unction*, extremaunción. *2* extremado, riguroso. *3 s.* extremo [parte extrema; punto último], extremidad: *to go to extremes*, extremar las cosas; *in the* ~, en extremo, con extremo. *4* LÓG., MAT. extremo.

extremely (-li) *adv.* extremadamente, extremamente, sumamente, con o en extremo.

extremism (-ìšm) *s.* extremismo.

extremity (ekstre·miti) *s.* extremidad, fin. *2* extremo, exceso. *3* situación extrema, necesidad, apuro. *4 pl.* medidas extremas. *5* ANAT. extremidades.

extricate (to) (e·kstrikeit) *tr.* desembarazar, desenredar, desembrollar, zafar, librar, sacar de.

extrication (-ei·shøn) *s.* desembarazo, desembrollo, desenredo.

extrinsic (al (ekstri·nsik(al) *adj.* extrínseco.

extroversion (ekstrovø·ʳshøn) *s.* MED. extroversión. *2* PSIC. extraversión.

extrovert (e·kstrovøʳt) *s.* PSIC. extrovertido.

extrude (to) (ekstru·d) *tr.* empujar fuera, hacer salir.

extrusion (ekstru·ÿøn) *s.* acción de hacer salir; expulsión. *2* operación de hacer pasar [un metal calentado, un plástico, etc.], mediante presión, por los orificios de un molde, hilera, etc.

exuberance (egšiu·børans) *s.* exuberancia. *2* exceso, profusión.

exuberant (egšiu·børant) *adj.* exuberante, lujuriante, profuso. *2* extremado. *3* contento, radiante.

exudate (e·ksiudeit) *s.* exudado.

exudation (eksiudei·shøn) *s.* exudación. *2* exudado.

exude (to) (eksiu·d) *tr.-intr.* exudar, rezumar.

exult (to) (egšø·lt) *intr.* exultar, alegrarse; gozarse en el propio triunfo.

exultant (egšsø·ltant) *adj.* exultante, ufano.

exultation (-ei·shøn) *s.* exultación, alborozo, sentimiento gozoso del propio triunfo.

eyas (a·ias) *s.* halcón niego.

eye (ai) *s.* ojo [órgano de la visión; atención, vigilancia], ojo, vista, mirada: *black* ~, ojo negro, amoratado; *mind your* ~, pop. ¡cuidado!, ¡ojo!; *my eyes!*, exclamación de asombro; *to catch the* ~, llamar la atención, atraer la mirada; *to have a cast in the* ~, ser ligeramente bizco; *to keep an* ~ *on*, vigilar, mirar con sospecha o deseo; *to make eyes at*, poner los ojos tiernos a; *to see* ~ *to* ~, estar completamente de acuerdo; *before one's eyes*, a la vista, en presencia de uno; *in the* ~ *of*, a los ojos de; *up to the eyes*, hasta los ojos; completamente metido o enfrascado; *with an* ~ *to*, con vistas a, con la intención de. *2* ojo [de una aguja, de una herramienta, del pan, del queso, etc.]. *3* COST. cocheta, presilla. *4* ARQ. abertura superior de una cúpula. *5* ocelo [en una pluma]. *6* centro [de una flor]. *7* BOT. yema, grillo.

eye (to) *tr.* mirar, clavar la mirada en. *2* hacer ojos o agujeros en.

eyeball (ai·bol) *s.* ANAT. globo del ojo.

eyebolt (ai·boult) *s.* armella. *2* perno de ojo.

eyebright (ai·brait) *s.* BOT. eufrasia.

eyebrow (ai·brau) *s.* ANAT. ceja.

eyecup (ai·køp) *s.* ojera [para bañar el ojo].

eyed (aid) *adj.* de ojos: *blue-eyed*, de ojos azules.

eyeglass (ai·glæs) *s.* ÓPT. ocular; anteojo. *2 pl.* anteojos, gafas, lentes, quevedos.

eyehole (ai·joul) *s.* COST. ojete. *2* atisbadero.

eyelash (ai·læsh) *s.* ANAT. pestaña.

eyeless (ai·lis) *adj.* ciego. *2* sin ojos.

eyelet (ai·lit) *s.* COST. ojete. *2* MAR. ollao. *3* resquicio, abertura.

eyelet (to) *tr.* ojetear.

eyelid (ai·lid) *s.* ANAT. párpado.

eyepiece (ai·pis) *s.* ÓPT. ocular.

eyeshot (ai·shat) *s.* mirada, vista, alcance de la vista.

eyesight (ai·sait) *s.* vista [sentido]. *2* vista, observación. *3* vista, paisaje.

eyesore (ai·soʳ) *s.* cosa que ofende la vista.

eyestrain (ai·strein) *s.* vista fatigada.

eyetooth (ai·tuz) *s.* colmillo.

eyewash (ai·uash) *s.* colirio. *2* fam. jarabe de pico.

eyewater (ai·uotøʳ) *s.* colirio.

eyewinker (ai·unkøʳ) *s.* ANAT. pestaña.

eyewitness (aiui·tnis) *s.* testigo ocular o presencial.

eyey (ai·i) *adj.* ojoso.

eyrie, eyry (e·øri) *s.* nido de águilas, nido de ave de rapiña.

Ezechias (eši·kias) *n. pr. m.* Ezequías.

Ezekiel (eši·kiøl) *n. pr. m.* Ezequiel.

F

F, f (ef) *s.* F, f, sexta letra del alfabeto inglés. *2* MÚS. fa.

fa (fa) *s.* MÚS. fa.

fabaceous (fabei·shøs) *adj.* BOT. papilionáceo.

Fabian (fæbian) *adj.* fabiano.

fable (fei·bøl) *s.* fábula.

fable (to) *intr.* contar fábulas, fingir, mentir. *2 tr.* inventar, contar falsamente.

fabled (-d) *adj.* legendario, ficticio, fabuloso.

fabric (fæ·brik) *s.* tejido, tela, género. *2* manufactura, textura. *3* fábrica, edificio.

fabricate (to) (fæ·brikeit) *tr.* fabricar, hacer, construir. *2* inventar, forjar.

fabrication (ei·shøn) *s.* fabricación, construcción. *2* invención, fábula, mentira.

fabulist (fæ·biulist) *s.* fabulista, fabulador.

fabulous (fæ·biuløs) *adj.* fabuloso.

façade (fasa·d) *s.* ARQ. fachada, frontispicio. *2* cara, frente [de una cosa].

face (feis) *s.* cara, faz, rostro, gesto, semblante; *to make a wry ~,* torcer el rostro; *to pull a long ~,* poner cara larga; *to save one's ~,* salvar el prestigio; *to set one's ~ against,* oponerse a, ponerse contra; *~ to ~,* cara a cara; *in the ~ of,* ante, en presencia de; luchando contra, a despecho de. *2* valor, osadía, descaro. *3* mueca, gesto: *to make faces,* hacer muecas. *4* aspecto, apariencia: *on the ~ of it,* según las apariencias. *5* cara, faz, haz, superficie [de una cosa]; frente, fachada. *6* CRISTAL., GEOM. cara. *7* IMPR. ojo [de letra]. *8* IMPR. tipo [de letra]. *9* esfera [de reloj]. *10* boca [de herramienta]; cotillo [de martillo]. *11* paramento [de un muro].
12 adj. de cara, etc.: *~ card,* figura [de la baraja]; *~ value,* COM. valor nominal; fig. valor aparente; sentido literal.

face (to) *tr.* volverse o mirar hacia. *2* hacer cara o frente a, enfrentarse con; afrontar, arrostrar: *to ~ the music,* afrontar una situación. *3* dar a, mirar a, estar encarado a. *4* carear con, enfrentar con. *5* cubrir, revestir. *6* forrar, guarnecer [un vestido]. *7* pulir, labrar, etc., la superficie de. *8* *to ~ out,* persistir audazmente en, sostener con descaro. *9 intr.* volver la cara, dar frente [a]. *10* *to ~ about,* volver el rostro, dar media vuelta, cambiar de frente. *11* *to ~ up to,* encararse con.

faced (fei·st) *adj.* de cara: *pale-faced,* de rostro pálido.

facer (fei·sø^r) *s.* el o lo que pule, labra, etc., la superficie de una cosa. *2* fam. puñetazo en la cara. *3* fam. percance, revés.

face-saving *adj.* que salva las apariencias.

facet (fæ·sit) *s.* faceta.

facet (to) *tr.* labrar facetas en; labrar en facetas.

facetious (fasi·shøs) *adj.* jocoso, humorístico. *2* bromista, chancero.

facial (fe·shial) *adj.* facial: *~ eagle,* ángulo facial. *2 s.* fam. masaje facial.

facile (fæ·sil) *adj.* fácil [de hacer u obtener]. *2* complaciente, dócil. *3* listo, diestro, hábil.

facilitate (to) (fasili·liteit) *tr.* facilitar, posibilitar.

facilitation (-shøn) *s.* facilitación.

facility (fasi·liti) *s.* facilidad. *2* destreza. *3* propensión a complacer o a dejarse persuadir.

facing (fei·sing) *s.* paramento, revestimento. *2* COST. vuelta, vistas. *3* encaramiento. *4 pl.* MIL. cuello, puños y franjas [de un uniforme].

facsimile (faksi·mili) *s.* facsímil, facsímile.

fact (fækt) *s.* hecho; verdad, realidad: *the ~ is that,* ello es que; *in ~,* de hecho, en realidad. *2* dato.

faction (fæ·kshøn) *s.* facción, bando, parcialidad. *2* discordia, disensión.

factious (fæ·kshøs) *adj.* faccioso. *2* partidista.

factitious (fæ·ktishøs) *adj.* facticio, artificial.

factitive (fæ·ktitiv) *adj.* GRAM. factitivo.

factor (fæ·ktø^r) *s.* factor [elemento, concausa, lo que contribuye a un resultado]. *2* MAT. factor. *3* COM. factor, agente.

factor (to) *tr.* MAT. descomponer en factores.

factorage (fæ·ktøridý) *s.* factoraje. *2* comisión o sueldo del factor o agente.

factory (fæ·ktøri) *s.* factoría. *2* fábrica, manufactura.

factotum (fæktou·tøm) *s.* factótum.

facture (fæ·ksho^r) *s.* B. ART. factura.

facula (fæ·kiula) *s.* ASTR. fácula.

facultative (fæ·kølteitiv) *adj.* facultativo [de una facultad]. *2* facultativo, potestativo.

faculty (fæ·kølti) *s.* facultad [en todos sus sentidos].

fad (fæd) *s.* novedad, moda. *2* marca, chifladura, afición pasajera.

fade (to) (feid) *intr.* marchitarse; *2* debilitarse, decaer. *3* palidecer, descolorirse; perder [un color]. *4* apagarse, desvanecerse, desaparecer [gradualmente]. *5 tr.* marchitar. *6* debilitar. *7* descolorir; poner pálido.

fade-in *s.* CINEM. fundido.

fading (fei·ding) *s.* marchitamiento. *2* desvanecimiento, pérdida gradual de color, intensidad, etc. *3* RADIO. fading.

fæcal (fe·kal) *adj.* fecal.

fæces (fi·seš) *s. pl.* heces, excrementos. *2* hez, poso.

faerie, faery (fe·øri) *s.* ant. hada, duende. *2* reino de las hadas. *3 adj.* de hadas, maravilloso.

fag (fæg) *s.* (Ingl.) estudiante que sirve a otro mayor. *2* azacán. *3* tarea penosa. *4* fatiga: *brain ~*, fatiga mental. *5* fam. (Ingl.) pitillo. *6 ~ end*, extremo deshilachado; pezolada; cabo, desperdicio, cola, última parte.

fag (to) *tr.* fatigar, reventar, hacer trabajar como un negro. *2 intr.* fatigarse, trabajar como un negro. *3* deshilacharse, destorcerse. ¶ Pret. y p. p.: *fagged;* ger.: *fagging.*

faggot, fagot (fæ·gøt) *s.* haz de leña, fajina. *2* haz de barras de hierro. *3* (Ingl.) vieja, bruja.

faggot, fagot (to) *tr.* atar en haces.

fail (feil) *s.* falta, esp. en *without ~*, sin falta.

fail (to) *intr.* faltar [no existir, ser insuficiente]. *2* menguar, decaer, debilitarse, consumirse, acabarse. *3* faltar, fallar, ceder, inutilizarse. *4* fracasar. *5* salir mal [en un examen]. *6* fallar, frustrarse, malograrse. *7* errar, equivocarse. *8* COM. quebrar. *9 to ~ in*, estar falto o insuficientemente dotado de. *10 to ~ to*, no poder, no lograr, dejar de [hacer algo]. *11 tr.-intr.* faltar [dejar de asistir], abandonar; no cumplir sus compromisos, deberes, etc., con [uno]. *12 tr.* errar, marrar. *13* suspender [en un examen].

failing (fei·ling) *s.* falta, defecto. *2* decadencia. *3* fracaso, malogro. *4 prep.* faltando, a falta de.

failure (fei·liơr) *s.* fracaso, fiasco, malogro. *2* persona que ha fracasado. *3* falta, escasez. *4* falta, no ocurrencia, el no hacer o dejar de hacer [algo]. *5* paro [de un motor, etc.]. *6* COM. quiebra.

fain (fein) *adj.* contento. *2* dispuesto, resignado. *3* obligado. *4 adv.* de buena gana.

faint (feint) *adj.* débil. *2* desfallecido, desmayado. *3* lánguido, abatido. *4* tímido, cobarde. *5* apagado, tenue, leve, imperceptible. *6 s.* FAINTING.

faint (to) *intr.* desmayarse. *2* desfallecer. *3* desalentarse.

faint-hearted *adj.* tímido, cobarde, medroso, pusilánime, apocado.

fainting (fei·inting) *s.* desmayo; desfallecimiento: *~ fit*, desmayo, síncope.

faintly (fei·ntli) *adv.* débilmente. *2* desmayadamente. *3* vagamente, indistintamente.

fair (fe·ør) *adj.* hermoso, bello: *the ~ sex*, el bello sexo. *2* bueno, regular, mediano, bastante grande: *~ chance*, buenas probabilidades; *~ to middling*, fam. mediano, bastante bueno. *3* bueno, favorable, propicio: *to be in a ~ way to*, estar en buen camino de. *4* sereno, despejado [cielo]; bueno, bonancible [tiempo]. *5* limpio, terso, sin defecto, sin tacha: *~ copy*, copia en limpio. *6* justo, recto, honrado, lícito, sincero, leal: *~ and square*, honrado, leal; *~ play*, juego limpio. *7* equitativo, razonable. *8* imparcial; sin ventajas por ninguna parte. *9* afable, franco, cortés. *10* blanco [tez], rubio [cabello, pers.]. *11* legible, bien formada [letra]. *12* suave [línea; curva]. *13* libre, expedito. *14 adv.* favorablemente. *15* bondadosamente, cortésmente. *16* lealmente, imparcialmente: *to*

play ~, jugar limpio. *17* clara, distintamente. *18* exactamente, de lleno.

19 s. mercado, feria, exposición. *20* poét. bella [mujer]. *21 the ~*, el bello sexo.

fair (to) *intr.* aclararse [el tiempo].

fairground (-graund) *s.* (E.U.) cercado al aire libre para una feria.

fairish (-ish) *adv.* bastante bueno o grande, regular.

fairly (-li) *adv.* completamente. *2* bastante, medianamente. *3* favorablemente. *4* razonablemente. *5* justamente, imparcialmente. *6* lealmente, honradamente. *7* claramente, distintamente.

fair-minded *adj.* justo, imparcial.

fairness (-nis) *s.* limpieza, pureza. *2* honradez. *3* imparcialidad, justicia. *4* hermosura. *5* blancura [de la tez]. *6* serenidad [del cielo]. *7* color rubio.

fair-spoken *adj.* cortés, bien hablado.

fairway (-uei) *s.* espacio o camino abierto. *2* parte navegable [de un río, etc.]. *3* canal [de un puerto]. *4* cierta parte del campo de golf.

fairy (-i) *s.* hada, duende: *~ tale*, cuento de hadas.

faith (fei·z) *s.* fe [en todos sus sentidos]: *in good ~*, de buena fe; *upon my ~*, a fe mía. *2* palabra dada: *to break ~ with*, faltar a la palabra dada a. *3 in ~*, a la verdad. *4 interj.* en verdad.

faithful (-ful) *adj.* fiel. *2* leal, creyente. *4* solemne [promesa]. *5 s.* fiel [de una iglesia]. *6* creyente.

faithfully (-i) *adv.* fielmente. *2* firmemente.

faithless (-lis) *adj.* infiel. *2* desleal, pérfido. *3* sin fe.

fake (feik) *s.* MAR. aduja [de cable]. *2* imitación, falsificación, filfa, amaño. *3* impostor. *4 adj.* falso, fingido, amañado.

fake (to) *tr.* MAR. adujar. *2* falsificar, imitar, fingir, falsear, amañar.

fakir (fæ·kiơ) *s.* faquir.

Falange (fei·lændỹ) *s.* POL. Falange.

Falangist (falæ·ndỹist) *adj.-s.* POL. falangista.

falcate(d (fæ·lkit(id) *adj.* falcado.

falchion (fo·lchøn) *s.* cimitarra.

falciform (fæ·lsifoʳm) *adj.* falciforme.

falcon (fo·lcøn) *s.* ORN. halcón. *2* ARTILL. falcón.

falconry (-ri) *s.* halconería, cetrería.

falderal (fæ·ldørəl), **falderol** (fæ·ldørol) *s.* chuchería, fruslería. *2* perendengue.

faldstool (fo·ldstul) *s.* faldistorio. *2* facistol.

fall (fol) *s.* caída: *~ of snow*, nevada; *the Fall*, la caída [del primer hombre]. *2* decadencia, ruina. *3* baja, bajada, descenso. *4* declive, pendiente. *5* cascada, catarata, salto de agua. *6* (E.U.) otoño. *7* corta [de árboles]. *8* desembocadura [de un río]. *9* MÚS. cadencia, disminución del sonido. *10* MAR. beta, tira. *11* velo, cinta, etc., colgante.

fall (to) *intr.* caer. *2* caerse. *3* bajar, descender. *4* menguar, decrecer, disminuir. *5* decaer. *6* calmarse [el mar, el viento]. *7* venirse abajo, desplomarse. *8* desembocar [un río]. *9* ponerse: *to ~ to work*, ponerse a trabajar. *10* tocar, corresponderle [a uno una cosa]; pasar a manos de. *11* MAR. *to ~ aboard*, abordar. *12 to ~ across*, topar con, encontrar. *13 to ~ asleep*, dormirse. *14 to ~ a prey to*, ser presa o víctima de. *15 to ~ away*, enflaquecer, marchitarse; desvanecerse; rebelarse; apostatar. *16 to ~ back*, retroceder; hacerse atrás, no cumplir lo prometido. *17 to ~ back on* o *upon*, recurrir a, echar mano de; MIL. replegarse hacia. *18 to ~ behind*, rezagarse, atrasarse. *19 to ~ down*, caer, caer al suelo, desprenderse; postrarse; hundirse, fracasar. *20 to*

~ *due*, caer, vencer [una letra, etc.]. *21 to* ~ *flat*, caer tendido; no producir efecto, no tener éxito. *22 to* ~ *foul of*, reñir con; atacar; MAR. abordar; enredarse con. *23 to* ~ *in*, desplomarse, hundirse; expirar, caducar; MIL. alinearse. *24 to* ~ *in love*, enamorarse. *25 to* ~ *in with*, encontrarse con; ponerse o estar de acuerdo con, coincidir; armonizar con. *26 to* ~ *into*, trabar [conversación]; adquirir [un hábito]; acceder a. *27 to* ~ *off*, caer, desprenderse; apartarse; desamistarse; rebelarse; disminuir, decaer; MAR. abatir. *28 to* ~ *on*, caer sobre; echarse sobre; encontrarse con; empezar; recurrir a, echar mano de. *29 to* ~ *out*, caerse; reñir, desavenirse; acontecer; resultar. *30 to* ~ *over*, caer por; desertar, pasarse; pop. adular. *31 to* ~ *short*, faltar, escasear; quedar corto, no alcanzar; fracasar. *32 to* ~ *through*, fracasar, malograrse. *33 to* ~ *to*, empezar a; ponerse a comer; reñir, cerrarse [una puerta]. *34 to* ~ *to one's lot*, caber o caerle en suerte a uno, tocarle. *35 to* ~ *upon*, atacar, embestir; recurrir a, echar mano de; tocar, incumbir. ¶ Pret.: *fell;* p. p.: *fallen*.

fallacious (fælei·shøs) *adj.* falaz, engañoso, sofístico.

fallacy (fæ·lasi) *s.* falacia, apariencia engañosa, sofisma. *2* error.

fallen (fo·løn) *p. p.* de TO FALL. *2 s. pl. the fallen*, los caídos [en la lucha].

fallibility (fælibi·liti) *s.* falibilidad.

fallible (fæ·libøl) *adj.* falible.

falling (fo·ling) *adj.* cayente. *2* en baja, que disminuye. *3* decreciente [diptongo]. *4* MED. ~ *sickness*, epilepsia. *5* ASTR. ~ *star*, estrella fugaz. *6 s.* caída, bajada, baja, descenso.

fallow (fæ·lou) *s.* AGR. barbecho [tierra que descansa]. *2 adj.* en barbecho, baldío. *3 adj.-s.* flavo [color]. *4* ZOOL. ~ *deer*, gamo.

false (fols) *adj.* falso: ~ *face*, máscara, careta; ~ *keel*, falsa quilla; ~ *note*, MÚS. nota falsa; ~ *pretences*, dolo, engaño; ~ *rib*, ANAT. costilla falsa; ~ *step*, tropiezo; paso en falso; *to place in a* ~ *light*, poner mal, desacreditar. *2* simulado. *3* postizo: ~ *hair*, cabello postizo. *4* MEC. provisional, de quita y pon. *5* irregular: ~ *imprisonment*, detención ilegal. *6* ~ *bottom*, doble fondo. *7 adv.* falsamente: *to play* ~, engañar.

false-faced *adj.* hipócrita, falso.

false-hearted *adj.* falso, pérfido, traidor.

falsehood (-jud) *s.* falsedad. *2* falsía, perfidia. *3* mentira, inexactitud. *4* mendacidad.

falsely (-li) *adv.* falsamente. *2* erróneamente. *3* mentirosamente. *4* pérfidamente.

falsetto (folse·tou) *s.* MÚS. falsete.

falsification (folsifikei·shøn) *s.* falseamiento, falsificación. *2* confutación.

falsify (fo·lsifai) *tr.* falsear, falsificar. *2* faltar [a la fe o a la palabra dada]. *3* confutar, desmentir. *4 intr.* mentir. ¶ Pret. y p. p.: *falsified*.

falter (fo·ltør) *s.* vacilación, temblor.

falter (to) *intr.* vacilar, titubear. *2* tambalearse, temblar. *34 intr.-tr.* balbucir.

fame (feim) *s.* fama, reputación. *2* renombre.

fame (to) *tr.* afamar, celebrar.

famed (-d) *adj.* afamado.

familiar (fami·lia') *adj.* familiar. | En el sentido de perteneciente a la familia es arcaico. *2* íntimo [amigo, compañero]. *3* ~ *with*, familiarizado con, versado en. *4 s.* amigo íntimo. *5* demonio familiar. *6* ECLES. familiar.

familiarity (familiæ·riti) *s.* familiaridad. *2* intimidad. *3* ~ *with*, conocimiento de.

familiarize (to) (fami·liaraiš) *tr.* familiarizar. *2* acostumbrar, avezar.

family (fæ·mili) *s.* familia. *2* alcurnia, sangre, linaje. *3 adj.* familiar, de familia: ~ *allowance*, subsidio familiar; ~ *circle*, TEAT. galería, ~ *name*, apellido; ~ *tree*, árbol genealógico; *in a* ~ *way*, sin ceremonia; *in the* ~ *way*, encinta, en estado interesante.

famine (fæ·min) *s.* hambre, carestía.

famish (to) (fæ·mish) *tr.-intr.* hambrear; matar o morirse de hambre.

famished (-d) *adj.* hambriento.

famous (fei·møs) *adj.* famoso, afamado, célebre, señalado. *2* fam. excelente, de primera.

fan (fæn) *s.* abanico, ventalle. *2* AGR. aventador. *3* MEC. ventilador. *4* paleta [de hélice]. *5* aficionado [a un deporte], hincha. *6* entusiasta, admirador.

fan (to) *tr.* abanicar. *2* aventar. *3* ventilar. *4* soplar [el fuego, etc.]. *5 tr.-intr. to* ~ *out*, extender o extenderse como un abanico.

fanatic(al (fanæ·tik(al) *adj.* fanático.

fanaticism (fanæ·tisišm) *s.* fanatismo.

fancied (fæ·nsid) *adj.* imaginario. *2* preferido.

fancier (fæ·nsiø') *s.* fantaseador. *2* aficionado. *3* criador de aves y animales.

fanciful (fæ·nsiful) *adj.* imaginativo, quimérico. *2* antojadizo. *3* caprichoso, fantástico.

fancy (fæ·nsi) *s.* fantasía, imaginación. *2* magín. *3* antojo, capricho. *4* imagen, idea, concepción. *5* inclinación, afición, amor. *6* gusto [en materia de vestidos, etc.]. *7* afición [los aficionados]. *8 adj.* fantástico, caprichoso. *9* de capricho, de fantasía: ~ *dress*, disfraz, traje de capricho; ~ *goods*, artículos de fantasía; ~ *skating*, patinaje artístico. *10* de gusto, elegante, precioso.

fancy (to) *tr.* imaginar, fantasear, pensar, figurarse. *2* apetecerle, gustarle a uno [una cosa]; aficionarse a, encapricharse por. *3* criar [animales de raza]. *4 intr.* fantasear. ¶ Pret. y p. p.: *fancied*.

fancy-free *adj.* libre del poder del amor.

fancywork (-uø'k) *s.* labor [de aguja, ganchillo, etc.].

fanfare (fæ·nfeø') *s.* son de trompetas.

fanfaronade (fænfarønei·d) *s.* fanfarronada.

fanfaronade (to) *intr.* fanfarronear.

fang (fæng) *s.* colmillo, navaja [de animal]. *2* diente [de serpiente, venenosa]. *3* raíz [de un diente].

fang (to) *tr.* clavar los dientes o colmillos.

fanion (fæ·niøn) *s.* banderola.

fanlight (fæ·nlait) *s.* ARQ. abanico.

Fanny (fæ·ni) *n. pr. f.* dim. de FRANCES.

fantail (fæ·nteil) *s.* cola en forma de abanico. *2* CARP. cola de milano. *3* ORN. colipava [paloma].

fantasía (fantei·šia) *s.* MÚS. fantasía.

fantast (fæ·ntast) *s.* visionario, soñador.

fantastic(al (fæntæ·stik(al) *adj.* fantástico, grotesco. *2* excéntrico, extravagante, caprichoso. *3* imaginario.

fantasy (fæ·ntasi) *s.* fantasía. *2* ensueño. *3* humor, capricho. *4* dibujo o trabajo fantástico.

far (fa') *adv.* lejos, a lo lejos, a distancia, en lontananza, remotamente: ~ *from*, lejos de; ~ *be it from me*, lejos de mí, no permita Dios; *how* ~, cuán lejos, hasta dónde; *how* ~ *is it?*, ¿cuánto hay de aquí allá?; *to go* ~, ir lejos; alcanzar para mucho, durar mucho; ~ *and near*, ~ *and wide*, por todas partes; *as ~ as*, tan lejos como, hasta, hasta donde; en cuanto, por lo que a mí toca; *as ~ as I know*, que yo sepa; *in so ~ as*, en cuanto, en lo que, hasta donde; *so ~, thus ~*, hasta ahora, hasta aquí; *so ~ so good*, mientras siga así, todo va bien. *2* muy, mucho, en alto grado, en gran parte, con mucho: *~ away*, muy lejos; *~ better*, mucho mejor; *~ into*, hasta muy adentro; hasta muy tarde de [la noche, etc.]; hasta muy avanzado [el invierno, etc.]; *~ off*, remoto, lejano; a gran distancia, a lo lejos; *by ~*, con mucho; *to go ~ to*, o *toward*, contribuir en mucho a.

3 adj. lejano, distante, remoto; hecho a una larga distancia: *the ~ past*, el pasado lejano; *Far East*, el lejano Oriente; *Far West*, el Oeste [de los E.U.]; *it is a ~ cry from*, dista mucho de.

faraway (-auei) *adj.* lejano, alejado. *2* distraído.

farad (fæ·ræd) *s.* ELECT. faradio.

farce (fa^rs) *s.* farsa. *2* comicidad, humor grotesco. *4* COC. relleno; albóndiga.

farce (to) *tr.* henchir o salpimentar [un libro, etc.] con citas o con pasajes graciosos.

farcical (fa·^rsikəl) *adj.* burlesco, bufo.

fare (fe·ø^r) *s.* pasajero, pasaje; precio del pasaje [en un vehículo público]. *2* comida, alimento, mesa, plato.

fare (to) *intr.* pasarlo, irle a uno [bien o mal]: *how did you ~?*, ¿cómo le ha ido? *2* pasar, ocurrir. *3* comer, alimentarse, tratarse. *4 to ~ forth*, ponerse en camino.

farewell (-uel) *interj.* ¡adiós! *2* despedida, adiós: *to bid ~ to*, *to take ~ of*, despedir a, despedirse de.

far-fetched *adj.* rebuscado, forzado, traído por los cabellos.

far-flung (adj.) vasto, extenso.

farina (farı·na) *s.* harina de cereales, raíces, etc. *2* fécula, almidón. *3* BOT. polen.

farinaceous (færinei·shøs) *adj.* farináceo.

farm (fa^rm) *s.* granja, cortijo, hacienda, labranza, estancia, finca agrícola. *2* arrendamiento de rentas o impuestos.

farm (to) *tr.* cultivar, labrar, explotar [la tierra]. *2* arrendar o tomar en arriendo [impuestos, rentas, trabajos].

farmer (-ø^r) *s.* granjero, labrador, hacendado, colono, *estanciero.

farmhand (-jænd) *s.* mozo de labranza, gañán.

farmhouse (-jaus) *s.* granja, alquería, casa de labor.

farming (-ing) *s.* cultivo, labranza. *2* arrendamiento de rentas o impuestos.

farmstead (-sted) *s.* granja, cortijada.

farmyard (-ya^rd) *s.* corral [de una granja].

farness (fa·^rnis) *s.* distancia, lejanía.

faro (fe·rou o fa·rou) *s.* faraón [juego].

farrago (farei·gou) *s.* mezcla, fárrago.

far-reaching *adj.* de mucho alcance o trascendencia.

farrier (fæ·riø^r) *s.* herrador, albéitar.

farriery (fæ·riøri) *s.* albeitería, herrería.

farrow (fe·rou) *s.* lechigada [de cerdos].

farrow (to) *tr.-intr.* parir [la cerda].

farseeing (fa^rsı·ing) *adj.* perspicaz. *2* previsor, precavido.

farsighted (fa^rsai·tid) *adj.* perspicaz. *2* sagaz. *3* présbita.

farther (fa·^rdø^r) *adv.* más lejos, a mayor distancia, más allá. *2* ulteriormente. *3* más, además. *4 adj.* más distante. *5* ulterior. *6* más extenso.

farthermost (-moust) *adj.* [el] más lejano o distante.

farthest (-est) *adj. superl.* [el] más lejano o extremo. *2 adv.* más lejos, a la mayor distancia; más. *4 at (the) ~*, a lo más o lo sumo.

fascicle (fæ·sikøl) *s.* fascículo, hacecillo. *2* BOT. glomérulo. *3* fascículo, entrega [de una obra].

fascinate (to) (fæ·sineit) *tr.* fascinar.

fascination (fæsine·shøn) *s.* fascinación.

fascine (fæsı·n) *s.* FORT. fajina.

Fascism (fæ·sišm) *s.* fascismo.

Fascist (fæ·sist) *adj.-s.* fascista.

fashion (fæ·shøn) *s.* forma, hechura. *2* modo, manera: *in a ~, after a ~*, en cierto modo, hasta cierto punto, así así. *3* clase, suerte. *4* moda, costumbre, uso, estilo: *in ~*, de moda; *out of ~*, pasado de moda, anticuado; *to set the ~*, dictar la moda. *5* elegancia, buen tono, el gran mundo. *6 ~ plate*, figurín.

fashion (to) *tr.* formar, hacer, labrar. *2* amoldar.

fashionable (-əbøl) *adj.* a la moda, de moda, que está en boga. *2* elegante, de buen tono.

fast (fast) *adj.* firme, fuerte, seguro; constante, fiel; sólido, duradero. *2* sujeto, atado, fijo, apretado, estrecho, íntimo: *to make ~*, fijar, amarrar, asegurar, cerrar. *3* atascado. *4* rápido, veloz. *5* adelantado [reloj]. *6* profundo [sueño]. *7* disipado, disoluto. *8* BIOL. resistente: *acid ~*, ácido-resistente.

9 adv. firmemente, fuertemente. *10* estrechamente. *11* duraderamente. *12* rápidamente, aprisa. *13* profundamente [dormido].

14 s. amarra, cable, lo que sujeta. *15* ayuno, abstinencia: *to break one's ~*, desayunarse.

fast (to) *intr.* ayunar. *2* hacer abstinencia.

fasten (to) (fa·søn) *tr.* afirmar, fijar, atar, amarrar, trincar, sujetar. *2* unir, pegar. *3* cerrar [con cerrojo, aldaba, cierre, etc.]. *4* abrochar. *5* fijar [los ojos, el pensamiento, etc.]. *6* atribuir, echar [la culpa]; poner [un mote]. *7* clavar [los dientes, etc.]. *8 intr.* agarrarse, fijarse, pegarse. *9* fraguar [la argamasa, etc.]. *10* cerrarse, abrocharse.

fastener (fa·snø^r) *s.* lo que sirve para sujetar o asegurar; broche, fiador, pasador, falleba, etc.

fastening (-ing) *s.* atadura, amarradura. *2* lo que sirve para sujetar, unir o cerrar; cerradura, cierre, broche, corchete, etc.

faster (fa·stø^r) *s.* ayunador.

fastidious (fæsti·diøs) *adj.* descontentadizo, exigente, delicado, esquilimoso. *2* desdeñoso.

fastigium (fæsti·ÿiøm) *s.* fastigio.

fasting (fa·sting) *s.* ayuno; abstinencia.

fastness (fa·stnis) *s.* firmeza, fijeza, solidez. *2* rapidez. *3* fortaleza, plaza fuerte. *4* disipación, libertinaje. *5 pl.* fragosidades.

fat (fæt) *adj.* gordo, obeso; grueso. *2* lleno, repleto. *3* graso, pingüe. *4* fértil, productivo. *5* lucrativo, provechoso. *6* rico, opulento. *7* grosero, tonto, estúpido. *8 s.* gordura, grasa, manteca. *9* lo mejor, lo más rico o provechoso [de una cosa].

fat (to) *tr.-intr.* engordar. ¶ Pret. y p. p.: *fatted;* ger.: *fatting.*

fatal (fei·tal) *adj.* fatal. *2* mortífero, letal. *3* profético, ominoso. *4 the ~ sisters*, las Parcas.

fatalism (-išm) *s.* fatalismo.

fatality (fatæ·liti) *s.* fatalidad. *2* desgracia, desastre; muerte.

fate (feit) *s.* hado, destino. *2* sino, suerte. *3 pl.* MIT. *the Fates*, las Parcas.

fated (-id) *adj.* predestinado. *2* hadado.

fateful (-ful) *adj.* fatal, funesto. *2* crítico, trascendental. *3* fatídico.

fatheaded (fǽ·tjedid) *adj.* fam. torpe, estúpido.

father (-fa·dǿʳ) *s.* padre. *2* Dios Padre. *3* tío [tratamiento que se da a un hombre de edad].

father (to) *tr.* engendrar, producir, inventar. *2* servir de padre a, tratar como hijo. *3* prohijar, adoptar como suyo. *4* atribuir, achacar.

fatherhood (-jud) *s.* paternidad.

father-in-law *s.* padre político, suegro.

fatherland (-lænd) *s.* patria, madre patria.

fatherliness (-linis) *s.* ternura paternal.

fatherly (-li) *adj.* paternal. *2 adv.* paternalmente.

fathom (fǽ·ðøm) *s.* braza [medida].

fathom (to) *tr.* MAR. sondar. *2* penetrar, profundizar, comprender.

fathomless (fa·ðǿmlis) *adj.* insondable, impenetrable.

fatidical (fati·dikal) *adj.* fatídico.

fatigue (to) *tr.* fatigar, cansar, rendir.

fatigue (fati·g) *s.* fatiga, cansancio. *2* trabajo, ajetreo. *3* MIL. ~ *duty*, mecánica.

fatling (fǽ·tling) *s.* ceboncillo.

fatness (-nis) *s.* gordura, obesidad. *2* crasitud, pinguosidad. *3* fertilidad.

fatten (to) (-øn) *tr.* engordar, cebar. *2* fertilizar, engrasar. *3 intr.* engordar.

fattish (-ish) *adj.* regordete. *2* grasoso.

fatty (-i) *adj.* graso, adiposo: ~ *tissue*, ANAT. tejido adiposo. *2* gordo, gordinflón. *3* grasiento, untuoso. *4* QUÍM. graso.

fatuity (fatiu·iti) *s.* fatuidad, necedad.

fatuous (fǽ·chuøs) *adj.* fatuo, necio. *2* ilusorio.

fauces (fo·siš) *s. pl.* ANAT. fauces.

faucet (fo·sit) *s.* grito, espita, canilla.

fault (folt) *s.* falta, defecto, tacha, imperfección; error, equivocación; culpa, desliz: *it is my* ~, yo tengo la culpa; *to find* ~ *with*, hallar defectos en, censurar, criticar. *2* GEOL., MIN. falla. *3* pérdida del rastro por los perros: *at* ~, perplejo, desorientado; fam. en falta.

fault (to) *tr.* GEOL. producir falla en.

faultfinder (-fai·ndøʳ) *s.* reparón, criticón.

faultfinding (-fai·nding) *adj.* reparón, criticón. *2 s.* crítica; manía de criticar.

faultless (-lis) *adj.* impecable, perfecto, irreprochable, sin defecto, sin tacha, sin culpa.

faulty (-i) *adj.* defectuoso, imperfecto, incorrecto, vicioso, deficiente.

faun (fon) *s.* fauno.

fauna (fo·na) *s.* fauna.

Faust (faust) *n. pr. m.* Fausto.

favo(u)r (fei·vøʳ) *s.* favor [privanza; protección; ayuda, preferencia; beneficio, utilidad]: *to be in* ~ *with*, gozar del favor de; ~ *of*, en pro de; COM. a favor de. *2* favor [merced, beneficio, fineza]: *do me the* ~ *of*, hágame el favor de. *3* permiso: *by your* ~, con su permiso. *4* favor [cinta, etc.]. *5* grata, atenta [carta]. *6 pl.* favores [de una mujer].

favo(u)r (to) *tr.* favorecer. *2* fomentar. *3* agraciar, obsequiar [con]. *4* preferir, apoyar, estar de parte de. *5* apoyar, confirmar [una teoría, etc.]. *6* parecerse, salir a.

favo(u)rable (-abøl) *adj.* favorable, propicio. *2* benévolo, benigno.

favo(u)red (-d) *adj.* favorecido. *2* querido, preferido.

favo(u)rite (-it) *adj.* favorito, predilecto, preferido. *2 s.* favorito, privado, valido, protegido.

favo(u)ritism (-itišm) *s.* favoritismo.

fawn (fon) *s.* ZOOL. cervato. *2* color del cervato.

fawn (to) *tr.-intr.* parir [la cierva]. *2 intr. to* ~ *on* o *upon*, hacer fiestas [el perro]; fig. adular, halagar servilmente.

fay (fei) *s.* hada, duende.

fealty (fı·alti) *s.* homenaje, fe [feudal]. *2* fidelidad, lealtad.

fear (fi·øʳ) *s.* miedo, temor, cuidado. *2* temor, veneración: ~ *of God*, temor de Dios.

fear (to) *tr.* temer, recelar, tener miedo de. *2* temer [tener temor o reverencia a]. *3 intr.* temer, tener miedo.

fearful (-ful) *adj.* temeroso, espantoso, pavoroso. *2* terrible, tremendo, imponente. *3* grande, enorme. *4* temeroso, medroso, que teme. *5* de miedo.

fearless (-lis) *adj.* impávido, intrépido, impertérrito, bravo, osado; que no teme.

fearsome (-søm) *adj.* temeroso, espantoso. *2* temeroso, tímido, miedoso.

feasibility (fišibi·liti) *s.* calidad de factible, posibilidad.

feasible (fı·šibøl) *adj.* factible, hacedero, practicable, posible, viable. *2* a propósito, apropiado.

feast (fıst) *s.* fiesta [día; solemnidad; regocijo]: ~ *day*, día de fiesta. *2* festejo. *3* festín, banquete.

feast (to) *intr.* banquetearse, comer opíparamente. *2* regalarse, deleitarse. *3 tr.* festejar. *4* agasajar, banquetear. *5* recrear, deleitar.

feat (fıt) *s.* hecho, acción. *2* proeza, hazaña. *3* acto de destreza; juego de manos.

feather (fe·døʳ) *s.* pluma [de ave]: *a* ~ *in one's cap*, fig. honor, triunfo para uno; *to show the white* ~, mostrar cobardía, volver las espaldas. *2* penacho, vanidad. *3* estado de espíritu, de salud, etc.; *in high o full* ~, alegre, animado. *4* mechón de pelos. *5* clase, calaña: *birds of a* ~, gente de la misma calaña. *6* MEC. proyección estrecha; nervio, pestaña, aleta. *7* CARP. lengüeta. *8* defecto [en una piedra preciosa]. *9* MAR. espuma que levanta el tajamar: *to cut a* ~, levantar espuma [el buque]; navegar con rapidez; fig. estar hecho un brazo de mar. *10 pl.* plumaje. *11 adj.* de pluma o plumas: ~ *bed*, colchón de plumas; lecho de plumas. *12* leve, suave.

feather (to) *tr.* emplumar. *2* cubrir con plumas: *to* ~ *one's nest*, hacer su agosto, sacar tajada. *3* adelgazar [un borde o filo]. *4* CARP. machihembrar. *5* cortar [el aire] volando. *6* volver [la pala del remo], poniéndola casi horizontal. *7 intr.* emplumecer. *8* tener o tomar aspecto de plumas. *9* correrse [la tinta].

feathered (-d) *adj.* cubierto de plumas, emplumado. *2* de pluma [caza]. *3* fig. alado, ligero, veloz.

featherstitch (-tich) *s.* COST. punto de espina.

featherweight (-ueit) *s.* persona o cosa de poco peso o importancia. *2* BOX. peso pluma.

feathery (-ri) *adj.* plúmeo, plumoso.

feature (fı·chøʳ) *s.* rasgo, facción [del rostro]. *2* forma, figura. *3* característica, rasgo distintivo. *4* lo más notable o principal: ~ *film*, ~ *picture*, película principal, de largo metraje.

feature (to) *tr.* parecerse, asemejarse. *2* destacar, hacer resaltar, dar importancia.

featured (-d) *adj.* formado, cincelado. *2* encarado [bien o mal]. *3* (E.U.) anunciado de un modo destacado.

featureless (-lis) *adj.* sin rasgos distintivos. *2* poco interesante.

febrifuge (fe·brifiudy̆) *adj.-s.* MED. febrífugo.
febrile (fi·bril o fe·bril) *adj.* febril.
February (fe·brueri) *s.* febrero.
fecal (fi·kal) *adj.* fecal.
feces (fi·siš) *s. pl.* heces.
fecula (fe·kiula) *s.* fécula, almidón.
feculent (fe·kiulønt) *adj.* feculento [que contiene heces].
fecund (fe·kønd) *adj.* fecundo.
fecundate (to) (fe·køndeit) *tr.* fecundar, fecundizar.
fecundation (-shøn) *s.* fecundación.
fecundity (fekø·nditi) *s.* fecundidad. *2* fertilidad.
fed (fed) *pret.-p. p.* de TO FEED. *2* ~ up, harto, hastiado, cansado: ~ *up with*, harto de.
federal (fe·døral) *adj.* federal.
federalism (-išm) *s.* federalismo.
federalize (to) (-aiš) *tr.* federar.
federate (to) (fe·døreit) *tr.* federar, confederar. *2* aliar. *3 ref.* federarse, confederarse, aliarse.
federation (fedørei·shøn) *s.* federación, confederación, liga.
fee (fi) *s.* honorarios, derechos; cuota. *2* propina, gratificación. *3* feudo. *4* DER. herencia, propiedad, dominio.
fee (to) *tr.* retribuir, pagar. *2* gratificar.
feeable (fi·abøl) *adj.* retribuible.
feeble (fi·bøl) *adj.* débil. *2* flaco, flojo, endeble. *3* enclenque, enfermizo.
feeble-minded *adj.* imbécil, débil mental. *2* irresoluto, vacilante.
feed (fid) *s.* alimento, comida [esp. de los animales]; forraje, pienso: ~ *bag*, cebadera, morral. *2* MEC. alimentación, dispositivo de alimentación.
feed (to) *tr.* alimentar, mantener. *2* nutrir, sustentar. *3* dar de comer. *4* dar [como comida]. *5* MEC. alimentar, cebar. *6 intr.* comer, alimentarse de. ¶ Pret. y p. p.: *fed*.
feeder (-øʳ) *s.* alimentador. *2* engordador [de ganado]. *3* ELECT. conductor principal. *4* afluente [de un río]. *5* FERROC. ramal. *6* tolva. *7* babero [de niño].
feedback (-bæk) *s.* ELECT. regeneración, realimentación.
feeding (-ing) *s.* alimento [acción de alimentar]. *2* acción de comer o pastar. *3* pasto, forraje.
feel (fil) *s.* tacto [sentido; acción]; palpamiento. *2* sensación, percepción.
feel (to) *tr.* tocar, tentar, palpar, manosear. *2* tomar [el pulso]. *3* examinar, explorar, sondear. *4* sentir, experimentar. *5* creer, pensar. *6 to ~ in one's bones*, presentir, decirle a uno [algo] el corazón. *7 to ~ one's way*, ir a tientas, proceder con tiento. *8 to ~ out*, dar un toque a; tantear, sondear. *9* MAR. *to ~ the helm*, obedecer al timón.
  10 intr. sentirse, estar, tener: *to ~ angry*, estar enojado; *to ~ happy*, sentirse feliz, estar contento; *I ~ cold*, tengo frío. *11* ser suave o áspero al tacto. *12* producir cierta sensación, dolor, etc.: *it feels cold to me*, lo encuentro frío. *13* ser sensible, sentir. *14 to ~ bad*, sentirse mal. *15 to ~ cheap*, avergonzarse, sentirse humillado. *16 to ~ for*, buscar a tientas; dolerse de, compadecer. *17 to ~ like*, tener ganas de, querer. *18 to ~ (like) oneself*, tener la salud, el vigor, el ánimo, etc., acostumbrados. ¶ Pret. y p. p.: *felt*.
feeler (-øʳ) *s.* palpador. *2* el que siente. *3* antena, tentáculo, palpo. *4* lo que se dice para explorar la opinión de los demás. *5* TEJ. pulsador.
feeling (-ing) *s.* tacto [sentido]. *2* tocamiento, tiento, palpadura. *3* sensación, percepción. *4*

sentimiento: *to hurt one's feelings*, herir los sentimientos de uno. *5* calor, pasión, emoción, ternura, compasión. *6* atmósfera [de una cosa]. *7* presentimiento. *8 adj.* sensible, tierno. *9* sentido, conmovedor.
feelingly (-li) *adv.* con sentimiento; vivamente. *2* con compasión. *3* tiernamente.
feet (fit) *s. pl.* de FOOT. pies.
feign (to) (fein) *tr.* fingir, inventar, aparentar, simular. *2 intr.* fingir, disimular.
feigning (-ing) *s.* fingimiento.
feint (feint) *s.* ficción, treta. *2* ESGR. finta.
feldspar (de·ldspaʳ) *s.* MINER. feldespato.
Felicia (feli·shia) *n. pr.* Felisa, Felicia.
felicitate (to) (feli·siteit) *tr.* felicitar.
felicitation (-ei·shøn) *s.* felicitación.
felicitous (feli·sitøs) *adj.* feliz [idea, expresión]. *2* que es feliz en sus expresiones.
felicity (feli·siti) *s.* felicidad. *2* B. ART. acierto, expresión feliz.
Felidæ (fi·lidi) *s. pl.* ZOOL. félidos.
feline (fi·lain) *adj.-s.* felino.
1) fell (fel) *pret.* de TO FALL.
2) fell *s.* cuero, pellejo. *2* páramo elevado. *3* corta [de árboles]. *4* COST. sobrecostura. *5 adj.* fiero, bárbaro, cruel. *6* mortal, destructivo.
fell (to) *tr.* derribar, tumbar. *2* cortar [árboles]. *3* acogotar [reses]. *4* COST. sobrecargar.
felloe (fe·lou) *s.* pina [de rueda].
fellow (fe·lou) *s.* compañero. *2* individuo, sujeto, prójimo, muchacho. *3* igual, pareja. *4* socio, miembro [de una academia o corporación]. *5* el que goza de pensión para ampliar estudios en una universidad.
  6 adj. indica igualdad o asociación en expresiones como: ~ *being*, ~ *creature*, prójimo, semejante; ~ *student*, condiscípulo; ~ *traveller*, compañero de viaje.
fellowship (-ship) *s.* compañerismo, confraternidad. *2* comunión, asociación, mancomunidad, participación. *3* compañía, cuerpo, sociedad. *4* plaza pensionada [para ampliar estudios en una universidad]. *5* ARIT. regla de compañía.
felon (fe·løn) *adj.* fiero, asesino. *2* malvado, traidor. *3 s.* felón, criminal. *4* MED. panadizo.
felonious (felou·niøs) *adj.* malvado, felón, criminal.
felony (fe·løni) *s.* felonía, crimen, delito grave.
felt (felt) *pret.* y *p. p.* de TO FEEL. *2 s.* fieltro.
felt (to) *tr.* enfieltrar. *2* cubrir de fieltro.
felucca (filø·ka) *s.* MAR. falucho.
female (fi·meil) *s.* hembra [mujer, animal o planta]. *2* mujer. *3 adj.* femenino, hembra: ~ *writer*, escritora; ~ *snake*, serpiente hembra.
feminine (fe·minin) *adj.* femenino. *2* mujeril. *3 s.* GRAM. femenino.
femininity (femini·niti) *s.* feminidad, feminidad. *2* las mujeres, el bello sexo.
feminism (fe·minišm) *s.* carácter femenino. *2* POL. feminismo.
feminist (-ist) *adj.-s.* feminista.
femoral (fe·moral) *adj.* ANAT. femoral.
femur (fi·møʳ) *s.* ANAT. fémur.
fen (fen) *s.* marjal, pantano, paúl.
fence (fens) *s.* empalizada, valla, vallado, cerca, cercado, seto, barrera; defensa, reparo: *to sit on the* ~, permanecer neutral, no comprometerse. *2* esgrima. *3 fig.* habilidad en la discusión. *4* MEC. guarda, guía, resguardo. *5* perista. *6* ~ *season*, tiempo de veda.
fence (to) *tr.* cercar, vallar. *2* defender, proteger. *3*

negociar con efectos robados. *4 intr.* esgrimir, luchar. *5* defenderse hábilmente [en una discusión, interrogatorio, etc.]. *6* saltar vallas [el caballo].

fenceless (-lis) *adj.* abierto, no cercado.

fencing (-ing) *s.* esgrima: ~ *bout,* asalto de armas; ~ *foil,* florete. *2* habilidad polemística. *3* material para cercas; valladar.

fend (to) (fend) *tr.* poét. defender. *2 to* ~ *off,* resguardar de; rechazar, parar. *3 intr.* esgrimir, defenderse. *4 to* ~ *for oneself,* ganarse la vida.

fender (-ø^r) *s.* guardafuegos [de chimenea]. *2* guardabarros [de coche, etc.]. *3* salvavidas [de tranvía]. *4* MAR. defensas, pallete.

fenestration (fenestrei·shøn) *adj.* ARQ. ventanaje.

Fenian (fi·nian) *adj.-s.* feniano.

Fenianism (fi·nianism) *s.* fenianismo.

fennel (fe·nøl) *s.* BOT. hinojo. *2* BOT. *giant* ~, cañaheja.

fenny (fe·ni) *adj.* pantanoso, palustre.

fenugreek (fe·niugrik) *s.* BOT. alholva

feoff (fef o fíf) *s.* FIEF.

feracious (førei·shøs) *adj.* feraz.

feracity (føræ·siti) *s.* feracidad.

feral (fi·ral) *adj.* salvaje, silvestre, montaraz. *2* cruel.

Ferdinand (fø·^{r}dinænd) *n. pr. m.* Fernando.

ferine (fi·rain) *adj.* FERAL.

ferment (fø·^{r}ment) *s.* fermento. *2* fermentación, agitación.

ferment (to) (fø^{r}me·nt) *intr.-tr.* fermentar. *2 intr.* bullir, agitarse. *3 tr.* agitar, excitar.

fermentation (-ei·shøn) *s.* fermentación. *3* efervescencia, agitación.

fern (fø^{r}n) *s.* BOT. helecho.

fernery (-øri) *s.* helechal.

ferny (-i) *adj.* de helecho; abundante en helechos.

ferocious (firou·shøs) *adj.* fiero, feroz, terrible.

ferocity (fira·siti) *s.* fiereza, ferocidad.

ferreous (fe·riøs) *adj.* férreo; ferrizo.

ferret (fe·rit) *s.* ZOOL. hurón. *2* fig. hurón, buscador, detective.

ferret (to) *intr.-tr.* cazar con hurón. *2* buscar, huronear. *3 tr.* perseguir, acosar. *4 to* ~ *out,* buscar, averiguar.

ferriage (fe·riidỹ) *s.* barcaje, lo que se paga por pasar un río.

ferric (fe·rik) *adj.* QUÍM. férrico.

ferriferous (feri·førøs) *adj.* ferrífero.

ferroconcrete (feroka·ncrit) *s.* hormigón armado.

ferrotype (fe·rotaip) *s.* FOT. ferrotipo. *2* FOT. ferrotipia.

ferrous (fe·røs) *adj.* QUÍM. ferroso.

ferruginous (feru·dỹinøs) *adj.* ferruginoso. *2* de color de herrumbre.

ferrule (fe·rul) *s.* regatón, contera, virola, zuncho; casquillo.

ferry (fe·ri) *s.* balsadero, lugar donde se cruza un río, canal, etc. *2* barca, balsa, transbordador, para cruzar un río, etc. *3* FERRYBOAT.

ferry (to) *tr.* transportar de una a otra orilla, balsear. *2 tr.-intr.* cruzar [un río, etc.] en barca. ¶ Pret. y p. p.: *ferried.*

ferryage (-idỹ) *s.* FERRIAGE.

ferryboat (-bout) *s.* barca de pasaje. *2* embarcación para transbordar trenes.

ferryman (-mæn) *s.* balsero, barquero; dueño o empleado de un paso de río.

fertile (fø·^{r}til) *adj.* fértil. *2* fecundo.

fertility (fø^{r}ti·liti) *s.* fertilidad. *2* fecundidad.

fertilization (fø^{r}tiliše·shøn) *s.* fertilización. *2* fecundación.

fertilize (to) (fø·^{r}tilaiš) *tr.* fertilizar. *2* fecundar.

fertilizer (fø·^{r}tilaišø^r) *s.* AGR. fertilizante, abono. *2* BOT. agente polinizador.

ferula (fe·rula) *s.* BOT. férula, cañaheja. *2* férula [palmeta].

ferule (fe·rul) *s.* FERULA 2.

fervency (fø·^{r}vønsi) *s.* calor, ardor. *2* fervor.

fervent (fø·^{r}vønt) *adj.* hirviente, ardiente. *2* ferviente, fervoroso, vehemente, ardoroso.

fervid (fø·^{r}vid) *adj.* férvido, ardiente.

fervo (u) r (fø·^{r}vø^r) *s.* ardor, calor, hervor. *2* fervor, celo, devoción.

fescue (fe·skiu) *s.* puntero [para señalar]. *2* BOT. cañuela.

festal (fe·stal) *adj.* festivo, de fiesta.

fester (fe·stø^r) *s.* llaga, úlcera.

fester (to) *intr.* supurar. *2* enconarse, ulcerarse. *3* pudrirse. *4* fig. enconarse. *5 tr.* enconar, emponzoñar.

festival (fe·stival) *adj.* festivo [de fiesta]. *2 s.* fiesta, festividad. *3* festival.

festive (fe·stiv) *adj.* festivo, alegre, convival.

festivity (festi·viti) *s.* alegría, alborozo, animación. *2* fiesta, festividad.

festoon (festu·n) *s.* festón [guirnalda].

festoon (to) (festu·n) *tr.* festonear, adornar con festones y guirnaldas.

fetal (fi·tal) *adj.* fetal.

fetch (fech) *s.* acto de ir a buscar, traer o alcanzar. *2* tirada [distancia], alcance. *3* estratagema, treta, artificio. *4* espectro o fantasma de una persona viva.

fetch (to) *tr.* ir por, ir a buscar, traer. *2* cobrar [la caza]. *3* alcanzar. *4* hacer salir [sangre, etc.]; arrancar [lágrimas]. *5* exhalar [un gemido, un suspiro]. *6* producir. *7* venderse [a un precio]. *8* derivar, sacar. *9* fam. interesar, atraer, conmover, encantar. *10* fam. dar, arrear [un golpe]. *11* cebar [una bomba]. *12 to* ~ *down,* derribar; hacer bajar. *13 to* ~ *in,* rodear, encerrar. *14 to* ~ *out,* hacer resaltar. *15 to* ~ *up,* levantar, elevar; traer [a la memoria]; descubrir, recuperar. *16 intr.* ir, moverse, traer y llevar cosas. *17* MAR. ir, seguir, arribar, virar. *18 to* ~ *and carry,* servir, como un perro, traer y llevar chismes. *19 to* ~ *up,* detenerse, pararse.

fetching (-ing) *adj.* atractivo, encantador.

fete, fête (fet) *s.* fiesta, celebración. *2* ~ *day,* día de fiesta; santo, días [de una pers.].

fete, fête (to) *tr.* festejar.

fetid (fe·tid) *adj.* fétido, hediondo.

fetish (fi·tish) *s.* fetiche.

fetishism (fi·tishišm) *s.* fetichismo.

fetlock (fe·tlak) *s.* cerneja. *2* espolón [del caballo]; ~ *joint,* menudillo.

fetor (fi·tø^r) *s.* hedor.

fetter (fe·tø^r) *s.* grillete, prisión. *2* traba. *3 pl.* grillos, hierros, prisiones.

fetter (to) *tr.* engrillar, encadenar, trabar.

fetterlock (-lak) *s.* traba, maniota.

fettle (fe·tøl) *s.* estado, condición: *in fine* ~, en buen estado; de buen humor; bien preparado.

fetus (fi·tøs) *s.* feto.

feud (fiud) *s.* disputa o enemistad duradera entre familias, grupos o personas. *2* feudo.

feudal (fiu·dal) *adj.* feudal.

feudalism (-išm) *s.* feudalismo.

feudatory (fiu·datori) *adj.-s.* feudatario.

fever (fĭ·vəᵉ) *s.* MED. fiebre, calentura. *2* fiebre, agitación.

fever (to) *tr.* causar o dar fiebre.

feverfew (-fiu) *s.* BOT. matricaria.

feverish (-ish) *adj.* febricitante, calenturiento. *2* febril. *3* infestado con fiebre.

few (fiu) *adj.-pron.* pocos: *a ~*, unos cuantos, algunos; *not a ~*, no pocos; *the ~*, los menos, la minoría.

fewer (-øᵉ) *adj.-pron. compar.* de FEW; menos: *the ~ the better*, cuantos menos, mejor.

fewest (-ist) *adj.-pron. superl.* de FEW.

fey (fei) *adj.* (Esc.) que ha de morir; moribundo.

fez (feš), **fezzes** (fe·šiš) *s.* fez.

fiancé (fiansei·) *s.* novio, prometido.

fiasco (fiæ·skou) *s.* fiasco, fracaso.

fiat (fa·iət) *s.* fiat, orden, mandato, decisión.

fib (fib) *s.* bola, mentirilla, papa, *macana.

fib (to) *intr.* mentir, echar papas. ¶ Pret. y p. p.: *fibbed;* ger.: *fibbing.*

fibber (-øᵉ) *s.* mentiroso, bolero.

fiber, fibre (fai·bøᵉ) *s.* fibra: *~ plant*, planta textil. *2* fig. carácter, índole.

fibril (fai·bril) *s.* fibrilla.

fibrin(e (fai·brin) *s.* fibrina.

fibroma (fibrou·ma) *s.* MED. fibroma.

fibrose (fai·brous), **fibrous** (fai·brøs) *adj.* fibroso.

fibula (fi·biula) *s.* fíbula. *2* ANAT. peroné.

fickle (fi·køl) *adj.* mudable, variable, inconstante, voluble, vleidoso.

fictile (fi·ktil) *adj.* plástico, moldeable.

fiction (fikshøn) *s.* ficción. *2* literatura de imaginación: cuento, novela, fábula. *3* mentira.

fictitious (fikti·shøs) *adj.* ficticio.

fictive (fi·ktiv) *adj.* fingido, imaginario. *2* de la imaginación creadora; creador [arte].

fid (fid) *s.* tarugo, cuña.

fiddle (fi·døl) *s.* MÚS. fam. violín: *fit as a ~*, en buena condición física, animado; *to play second ~*, hacer un papel secundario.

fiddle (to) *intr.* tocar el violín. *2* mover viva o nerviosamente los dedos o las manos; enredar con; ocuparse en tonterías. *3 tr.* tocar [un aire, etc.] con el violín. *4 to ~ away*, malgastar [el tiempo, el dinero, etc.].

fiddle-de-dee (-didɪ·) *s.* fam. disparate, tontería.

fiddle-faddle (-fædøl) *s. fam.* tontería, simpleza. *2* fruslería. *3 interj.* ¡tonterías!

fiddle-faddle (to) *intr.* ocuparse en tonterías.

fiddler (fi·dløᵉ) *s.* fam. violinista. *2* ZOOL. *~ crab*, barrilete [cangrejo].

fiddlestick (fi·dølstic) *s.* arco de violín. *2* tontería, nadería. *3* interj. *fiddlesticks!*, ¡qué tontería!

fiddling (fi·dling) *adj.* fútil, insignificante.

fideicommissum (faidiaikomi·søm) *s.* DER. fideicomiso.

fidelity (fide·liti) *s.* fidelidad.

fidget (fi·džit) *s.* persona agitada, inquieta. *2* agitación, movimiento. *3 pl. the fidgets*, desasosiego, impaciencia, nerviosidad.

fidget (to) *intr.* estar inquieto, agitarse, menearse nerviosamente. *2 to ~ with*, jugar o enredar con, manosear. *3 tr.* molestar, poner nervioso.

fidgety (-ti) *adj.* inquieto, nervioso, impaciente.

fiduciary (fidiu·shieri) *adj.-s.* fiduciario.

fie! (fai) *interj.* ¡uf!, ¡abrenuncio!

fief (fif) *s.* feudo.

field (fild) *s.* campo, sembrado, tierra laborable. *2* campo, campiña. *3* DEP. campo. *4* BÉISBOL porción de campo que queda fuera del cuadro. *5* FÍS., ELECT. campo: *magnetic ~*, campo magnético. *6* BLAS. campo. *7* campo [de una ciencia, ac-

tividad, etc.]. *8* campo [de una lucha]; campo de batalla; la batalla misma: *~ of honour*, campo del honor; *to take the ~*, entrar en campaña, salir a campaña. *9* campaña [campo llano]. *10* extensión de cielo, mar, hielo, nieve, etc.: *~ of ice*, banco de hielo. *11* DEP. jugadores [en un partido]; participantes [en una carrera]. *12 adj.* de campo, de campaña; del campo; *~ artillery*, artillería de campaña; *~ day*, día de campo, día de ejercicios militares o atléticos; *~ glass*, gemelos de campaña; *~ marshal*, mariscal de campo, capitán general; *~ mouse*, ratón de campo; *~ officer*, MIL. jefe. *13* ELECT. conductor: *~ winding*, arrollamiento inductor.

field (to) *tr.* DEP. parar y devolver la pelota. *2 intr.* DEP. actuar como *fielder.*

fielder (fi·ldøᵉ) *s.* en el béisbol o en el cricquet, jugador situado para parar la pelota.

fieldfare (fildfe·øᵉ) *s.* ORN. zorzal.

fiend (fĭnd) *s.* demonio, espíritu malo. *2* persona malvada o cruel.

fiendish (fi·indish) *adj.* diabólico, infernal; malvado, cruel.

fierce (fĭᵉs) *adj.* fiero, feroz, bárbaro, cruel. *2* terrible, espantoso. *3* furioso, violento, impetuoso, vigoroso. *4* vivo, intenso.

fiery (fai·øri) *adj.* ígneo, de fuego. *2* ardiente, abrasador; ardoroso, inflamado, encendido. *3* vehemente, fogoso. *4* violento, irascible, soberbio. *5* furibundo. *6* colorado [tez, etc.]. *7* inflamable.

fife (faif) *s.* MÚS. pífano.

fife (to) *intr.* tocar el pífano.

fifer (fai·føᵉ) *s.* pífano [músico].

fifteen (fiftɪ·n) *adj.-s.* quince.

fifteenth (-z) *adj.* decimoquinto. *2* quince [siglo]. *3 adj.-s.* quinzavo. *4 s.* quince [día].

fifth (fifz) *adj.-s. num.* quinto. *2 s.* MÚS. quinta. *3* cinco [día].

fifthly (fi·fzli) *adv.* en quinto lugar.

fiftieth (fi·ftiez) *adj.-s.* quincuagésimo, cincuenteno, cincuentavo.

fifty (fi·fti) *adj.-s.* cincuenta.

fig (fig) *s.* BOT. higo; higuera: *~ tree*, higuera. *2* fam. higa [signo de desprecio]. *3* fam. ardite, bledo. *4* fam. *in full, ~*, de veinticinco alfileres.

fig (to) *tr.* ataviar, adornar, preparar.

fig-leaf *s.* hoja de higuera. *2* fig. hoja de parra.

fight (fait) *s.* lucha, combate, duelo, riña, pelea, contienda. *2* fuerza o ánimo para lucha: *to show ~*, no acoquinarse, luchar con denuedo.

fight (to) *intr.* luchar, pelear, combatir, contender, lidiar, batirse: *to ~ for*, luchar por; *to ~ shy of*, fig. rehuir, evitar. *2 tr.* luchar con o contra. *3* lidiar [un toro]. *4* librar [una batalla]; sostener [una lucha]: *to ~ another's battles*, tomar la defensa de otro. *5 to ~ one's way*, abrirse paso luchando. *6 to ~ out*, decidir, resolver en una lucha. ¶ Pret. y p. p.: *fought.*

fighter (fai·tøᵉ) *s.* luchador. *2* combatiente, contendiente. *3* de combate o de caza [avión].

fighting (-ing) *adj.* luchador, batallador, combativo. *2* de pelea, de guerra: *~ cock*, gallo de pelea. *3 s.* lucha, pelea, combate, riña.

figment (fi·gmønt) *s.* ficción, invención.

figpecker (fi·gpekøᵉ) *s.* ORN. becafigo.

figuline (fi·giulin) *adj.* figulino.

figurant (fi·giurant) *s.* figurante [de ópera].

figurante (figiura·nt) *s.* figuranta, bailarina del conjunto.

figurate (fi·giureit) *adj.* figurado. *2* MÚS. floreado, adornado.

figuration (-ei·shøn) s. figuración; forma, figura. 2 MÚS. figuración.

figurative (fi·giurativ) adj. figurativo. 2 florido [lenguaje, estilo]. 3 GRAM. figurado, translaticio. 4 plástico, pictórico.

figure (fi·giøʳ) s. figura [forma, hechura; representación; dibujo, estatua, pintura; persona, personaje]. 2 GEOM., GRAM., RET. figura: ~ of speech, tropo. 3 figura, cuerpo, talle, tipo [de una pers.]. 4 dibujo, muestra [de un papel, tejido, etc.]. 5 papel, viso; distinción. 6 figura [en el baile, en el patinaje]: ~ skating, patinaje artístico. 7 horóscopo. 8 ARIT. cifra, guarismo, número: to be good at figures, estar fuerte en aritmética. 9 precio, valor.

figure (to) tr. figurar, delinear, formar, amoldar. 2 representar, simbolizar. 3 adornar con dibujos o figuras. 4 imaginar, figurarse. 5 indicar con números. 6 calcular, computar. 7 to ~ out, resolver, hallar por cálculo; descifrar, entender. 8 to ~ up, sumar. 9 intr. figurar, hacer viso. 10 calcular, planear.

figured (-d) adj. figurado. 2 adornado, labrado, floreado.

figurehead (-jed) s. MAR. mascarón de proa. 2 fig. figura decorativa; testaferro.

figurine (figiuri·n) s. estatuilla, figurita.

figuring (fi·giuring) s. cálculo, computación.

figwort (fi·gwørt) s. BOT. escrofularia.

filament (fi·lamønt) s. filamento.

filamentous (filame·ntøs) adj. filamentoso.

filander (filæ·ndøʳ) s. ZOOL. filandria.

filaria (filei·ria) s. ZOOL. filaria.

filature (fi·lachøʳ) s. hilandería [de seda].

filbert (fi·lbøʳt) s. BOT. avellano. 2 avellana.

filch (to) (filch) tr. hurtar, ratear, birlar.

filcher (fil·chøʳ) s. ratero, garduño.

file (fail) s. lima, escofina. 2 fig. persona astuta. 3 ensartapapeles. 4 carpeta, archivador. 5 legajo o colección de papeles; archivo; ~ case, fichero. 6 fila, cola, hilera.

file (to) tr. limar, pulir [con la lima]. 2 fig. limar, perfeccionar. 3 archivar, guardar; ensartar [en el ensartapapeles]. 4 registrar [un documento]. 5 intr. marchar en fila: to ~ off, MIL. desfilar.

filefish (fai·lfish) s. ICT. lija.

filer (fai·løʳ) s. limador.

filial (fi·lial) adj. filial.

filiation (ffiliei·shøn) s. filiación [lazo de parentesco, procedencia, dependencia].

filibuster (filibø·støʳ) s. filibustero, pirata. 2 (E.U.) POL. obstruccionista.

filibuster (to) s. filibustero, pirata. 2 (E.U.) POL. obstruccionista.

filibuster (to) intr. actuar de filibustero. tr.-intr. POL. (E.U.) obstruccionar.

filibusterism (fi·libøstørišm) s. filibusterismo.

filiform (fi·lifoʳm) adj. filiforme.

filigree (fi·ligrı) s. filigrana [obra, adorno].

filigreed (-d) adj. afiligranado.

filing (fai·ling) s. limadura [acción]. 2 acción de archivar: ~ card, ficha [de fichero]. 3 pl. limaduras, limalla.

fill (fil) s. hartura, hartazgo. 2 henchidura, colmo, abundancia. 3 terraplén.

fill (to) tr. llenar. 2 completar, rellenar, henchir. 3 hinchar. 4 tapar, obstruir. 5 macizar, terraplenar. 6 empastar [un diente]. 7 satisfacer, saciar, hartar. 8 ocupar [un puesto]. 9 proveer [un cargo]. 10 COM. servir, despachar [un pedido]. 11 ELECT. cargar [un acumulador]. 12 envasar.

13 to ~ in, insertar; llenar [un hueco]; rellenar, terraplenar. 14 to ~ out, ensanchar, redondear, completar; llenar [un formulario]. 15 to ~ up, llenar, ocupar; tapar [un agujero].
16 intr. llenarse, henchirse. 17 llenarse de lágrimas [los ojos]. 18 his heart filled, le ahogaba la emoción. 19 to ~ in, llenarse; hacer de suplente. 20 to ~ out, ensancharse, redondearse; ahuecarse, henchirse.

filler (fi·løʳ) s. llenador, envasador. 2 henchidor. 3 embudo. 4 tripa [del cigarro].

fillet (-et) s. cinta [para el cabello]. 2 lista, faja, tira. 3 ARQ., ENCUAD. filete. 4 COC. filete; lonja.

fillet (to) tr. adornar, atar [con cinta]. 2 ARQ. filetear. 3 COC. cortar en lonjas.

filling (-ing) s. relleno. 2 henchimiento. 3 envase [acción]. 4 DENT. empastadura, orificación. 5 llenado.

fillip (-ip) s. capirotazo, papirotazo. 2 estímulo, aguijón.

fillip (to) tr. dar un papirotazo. 2 estimular, aguijar.

filly (fi·li) s. potranca. 2 pop. muchacha retozona.

film (film) s. película. 2 membrana, telilla. 3 tela, nata, flor [en un liquido]. 4 nube [en el ojo]. 5 niebla. 6 CINEM. película, filme, cinta: ~ star, estrella de cine. 7 FOT. película.

film (to) tr. cubrir con película o telilla. 2 cinematografiar, filmar. 3 llevar al cine [una novela, tema, etc.]. 4 intr. cubrirse de una película, tela, etc.

filming (fil·ming) s. filmación.

filmy (-i) adj. membranoso; finísimo, delgadísimo. 2 cubierto de película, empañado, nublado.

filose (fai·lous) adj. filiforme.

filter (fi·ltøʳ) s. filtro [para filtrar líquidos]. 2 ELECT., FOT., ÓPT. filtro.

filter (to) tr. filtrar. 2 purificar, refinar. 3 intr. filtrarse. 5 MIL. infiltrarse.

filth (filz) s. suciedad, inmundicia, porquería, mugre. 2 corrupción, infección, obscenidad.

filthiness (fi·lzinis) s. suciedad, inmundicia, porquería, asquerosidad.

filthy (-i) adj. sucio, inmundo, cochino, asqueroso, mugriento. 2 corrompido, impuro.

filtrate (fi·ltreit) s. líquido filtrado.

filtrate (to) tr. filtrar. 2 intr. filtrarse.

filtration (-ei·shøn) s. filtración.

fin (fin) s. aleta [de pez]. 2 barba [de ballena]. 3 MEC. rebaba, apéndice en forma de aleta. 4 pop. fig. mano, brazo.

final (fa·inal) adj. final. 2 conclusivo. 3 definitivo, decisivo; terminante. 4 s. DEP. final. 5 examen final.

finale (fina·li) s. MÚS. final.

finalist (fai·nalist) s. DEP. finalista.

finality (fainæ·liti) s. calidad de decisivo o terminante. 2 lo que es final o conclusivo.

finally (fai·nali) adv. finalmente, por último, en fin, por fin, al cabo. 2 definitivamente.

finance (finæ·ns) s. ciencia y práctica financiera. 2 pl. finanzas. 3 hacienda, rentas, fondos.

finance (to) tr. financiar. 2 manejar los fondos de. 3 intr. ocuparse en operaciones financieras.

financial (finæ·nshal) adj. financiero, rentístico, bancario. 2 económico [año].

financier (finænsi·ʳ) s. financiero. 2 hacendista.

financier (to) intr.-tr. desp. hacer operaciones financieras. 2 tr. (E.U.) estafar.

finback (fi·nbæk) s. ZOOL. rorcual; yubarta.

finch (finch) *s.* ORN. cualquiera de los pájaros fringílidos; pinzón.

find (faind) *s.* hallazgo, descubrimiento.

find (to) *tr.* encontrar, hallar: *to ~ fault with*, hallar defectos, poner tachas, censurar; *to ~ in one's heart*, estar dispuesto o decidido, decidirse [a]. *2* descubrir; buscar, averiguar. *3* procurar, proveer de; mantener. *4* recobrar el uso de. *5* DER. declarar, pronunciar: *to ~ guilty*, declarar culpable. *6 to ~ out*, hallar; descifrar, adivinar; coger [en falta, etc.]; descubrir [un ladrón, un secreto, el verdadero carácter de]. *7 intr.* DER. pronunciar sentencia. ¶ Pret. y p. p.: *found*.

finder (-ø^r) *s.* hallador, descubridor. *2* ÓPT. buscador. *3* FOT. visor.

finding (fai·nding) *s.* hallazgo, descubrimiento. *2* DER. fallo, decisión.

fine (fain) *s.* multa. *2 adj.* fino [delicado; de buena calidad; puro, precioso; delgado, sutil; no grueso]. *3* de ley [oro, plata]. *4* hermoso, lindo. *5* bueno, excelente, agradable, magnífico. *6* divertido [rato]. *7* guapo, gallardo, distinguido. *8* elegante, primoroso. *9* bueno [tiempo, día]. *10* generoso [vino]. *11 ~ arts*, bellas artes. *12 adv.* fam. finamente. *13* fam. *to feel ~*, sentirse bien de salud.

fine (to) *tr.* multar. *2* afinar. *3* refinar, purificar, clarificar. *4 intr.* refinarse, purificarse. *5* aclararse [el tiempo]. *6* adelgazarse.

fine-drawn *adj.* estirado en hilos muy finos. *2* muy fino o sutil.

fine-grained *adj.* de grano muy fino, compacto.

fineness (-nis) *s.* fineza, finura, delicadeza, primor, excelencia. *2* pureza, perfección. *3* agudeza, sutileza. *4* ley [del metal, la moneda].

finery (fai·nøri) *s.* galas, adornos, atavíos.

finespun (-spøn) *adj.* sutil, alambicado.

finesse (fine·s) *s.* sutileza, astucia, estratagema. *2* tacto, diplomacia.

finesse (to) *intr.* valerse de artificios o subterfugios.

fin-footed *adj.* ORN. palmeado.

finger (fi·ngø^r) *s.* dedo [de la mano o de un guante]: *index ~*, dedo índice; *middle ~*, dedo del corazón; *ring ~*, dedo anular; *little ~*, dedo meñique; *~ board*, MÚS. teclado; diapasón [del violín, etc.]; *~ post*, poste indicador; *~ tip*, punta, yema del dedo; *to have at one's ~ tips*, saber al dedillo. *2* dedo [medida]. *3* aguja indicadora, saetilla, manecilla.

finger (to) *tr.* tocar, manosear. *2* sisar, hurtar. *3* MÚS. tocar, tañer [con los dedos]; pulsar, teclear. *4* hacer [con los dedos].

fingerbreadth (-bredz) *s.* dedo [ancho de un dedo].

fingering (-ing) *s.* manoseo, tecleo. *2* MÚS. digitación, dedeo. *3* lana para medias.

fingernail (-neil) *s.* uña [del dedo].

fingerprint (-print) *s.* huella o impresión digital o dactilar.

fingerstall (-stol) *s.* dedil.

finial (fi·nial) *s.* ARQ. florón de gablete, pináculo, etc.

finical (fi·nikal), **finicking** (-ing), **finicky** (-i) *adj.* melindroso, remilgado, afectado, meticuloso, remirado.

finish (fi·nish) *s.* fin, final, término, remate, conclusión, acabamiento. *2* DEP. línea de llegada. *3* DEP. carrera final. *4* finura de ejecución. *5* última mano, acabado, perfección.

finish (to) *tr.* acabar, terminar, rematar, concluir, consumar. *2* dar la última mano o el acabado a,

retocar, pulir, perfeccionar. *3* completar la educación de. *4* fam. vencer, matar, aniquilar. *5 intr.* acabar, finalizar; fenecer, cesar, morir: *to ~ by*, acabar por; *to ~ with*, terminar, reñir con.

finisher (-ø^r) *s.* acabador. *2* máquina acabadora. *3* golpe que acaba.

finishing (-ing) *s.* acabamiento. *2* perfeccionamiento. *3* acabado. *4 adj.* que acaba, de acabado: *~ blow*, golpe de gracia; *~ touch*, retoque, última mano.

finite (fai·nait) *adj.* finito, limitado. *2* GRAM. personal [forma del verbo].

Finland (fi·nland) *n. pr.* GEOGR. Finlandia.

Finlander (-ø^r) *s.* finlandés.

finless (fi·nlis) *adj.* sin aletas.

Finn (fin) *s.* finés. *2* finlandés.

Finnic (fi·nik) *adj.* finés. *2 s.* lengua finesa.

Finnish (fi·nish) *adj.-s.* finlandés.

finny (fi·ni) *adj.* provisto de aletas. *2* abundante en peces.

fiord (fiø^rd) *s.* GEOGR. fiord, fiordo.

fir (fø^r) *s.* BOT. abeto.

fire (fai·ø^r) *s.* fuego [producido por la combustión; materia que arde], lumbre: *~ clay*, arcilla refractaria; *~ pan*, brasero, chofeta; *to be on ~*, estar ardiendo; *to catch ~*, encenderse, inflamarse; *to set ~ on*, to set on *~*, pegar fuego a, encender, inflamar; *with ~ and sword*, a sangre y fuego. *2* llama. *3* fuego, incendio: *~ alarm*, avisador de incendios; *~ brigade*, *~ company*, cuerpo de bomberos, los bomberos; *~ escape*, escalera de incendios. *4* fuego [disparos con un arma]: *to miss ~*, dar higa; fallar el tiro; fig. fracasar; *under ~*, expuesto al fuego del enemigo. *5* fuego, ardor, pasión, viveza de la imaginación, inspiración. *6* fogosidad. *7* brillo, luminosidad: *~ beetle*, cocuyo. *8* MED. fuego. *9* martirio, aflicción, prueba.

fire (to) *tr.* encender, pegar fuego a. *2* iluminar [dar luz a]. *3* calentar [el horno]; cargar [el hogar]; encender [la caldera]. *4* cocer [ladrillos, el esmalte, etc.]. *5* disparar [un arma de fuego]; lanzar [un torpedo]; hacer estallar [una mina]. *6* inflamar, enardecer. *7* despedir [a un empleado]. *8 intr.* encenderse. *9* enardecerse. *10* disparar, hacer fuego. *11* dar explosiones [un motor]. *12 to ~ away*, empezar, continuar, decir deprisa. *13 to ~ up*, enojarse, encolerizarse.

firearm (-a^rm) *s.* arma de fuego.

fireback (-bæc) *s.* trashoguero.

fireball (-bol) *s.* METEOR. globo de fuego.

firebox (-bacs) *s.* caja de fuegos.

firebrand (-brænd) *s.* tea, tizón. *2* el que enciende la discordia.

firecracker (-krækø^r) *s.* carretilla, petardo.

firedamp (-dæmp) *s.* MIN. grisú, mofeta.

firedog (-dog) *s.* morillo.

fire-eater (-ı·tø^r) *s.* titiritero que finge comer fuego. *2* jaque, matamoros.

firefly (-flai) *s.* ENT. luciérnaga.

firehouse (-jaus) *s.* cuartelillo de bomberos.

firelight (-lait) *s.* luz de un fuego.

firelock (-lak) *s.* fusil de chispa.

fireman (-mæn) *s.* bombero. *2* fogonero.

fireplace (-pleis) *s.* hogar [de chimenea]; chimenea francesa.

fireproof (-pruf) *adj.* incombustible; refractario.

fireside (-said) *s.* sitio junto a la lumbre; fig. hogar, vida doméstica.

firestone (-stoun) *s.* pedernal.

firewater (-uøtø^r) *s.* aguardiente.

firewood (-wud) s. leña [para el fuego].

fireworks (-uøᵏks) s. pl. fuegos artificiales.

firing (fai·ring) s. encendimiento, disparo, etc. V. TO FIRE. 2 encendido [de un motor]. 3 adj. de encender, de disparar, de tiro, etc.: ~ line, MIL. línea de fuego; ~ order, AUTO. orden del encendido: ~ pin, percutor.

firkin (fø·ᵏkin) s. cuñete, barrilillo.

firm (føᵏm) adj. firme. 2 duro, compacto, consistente. 3 fiel, leal. 4 s. firma, razón social.

firmament (fø·rmament) s. firmamento, cielo.

firman (fø·ᵏman) s. firmán.

firmly (fø·ᵏmli) adv. firmemente, fuertemente.

firmness (fø·ᵏmnis) s. firmeza. 2 dureza, consistencia. 3 fidelidad, lealtad.

first (føᵏst) adj. primero: ~ aid, primeros auxilios, cura de urgencia; ~ cousin, primo hermano, prima hermana; ~ floor (Ingl.), primer piso; principal, (E.U.) bajos, planta baja; ~ fruits, primicias; ~ name, nombre de pila; ~ night, TEAT. noche de estreno; ~ person, GRAM. primera persona; ~ quarter, cuarto creciente [de la luna]; at ~ blush o view, a primera vista. 2 pristino, primitivo. 3 anterior, original. 4 temprano.

    5 adv. primero, primeramente: ~ or last, tarde o temprano. 6 antes, al principio. 7 por primera vez. 8 s. primero. 9 principio: at ~, al principio; al pronto; from the ~, desde el principio. 10 AUTO. primera.

first-aid adj. de primeros auxilios: first-aid kit, botiquín.

first-begotten, first-born adj.-s. primogénito.

first-class adj. de primera clase. 2 adv. en primera clase.

first-hand adj.-adv. de primera mano.

firstling (-ling) s. primicias, primer producto, primer nacido.

firstly (-li) adv. primero, primeramente, en primer lugar.

first-rate adj. excelente, de primera.

firth (føᵏth) s. brazo de mar. 2 ría, estuario.

fisc (fisk) s. fisico, erario, hacienda pública.

fiscal (-al) adj. fiscal [del fisco]; rentístico.

fish (fish) s. ICT. pez: ~ bowl, pecera; ~ day, día de vigilia; ~ hawk, halieto; ~ market, pescadería; ~ trap, garlito, nasa; a queer ~, fig. un tipo raro. 2 pescado: to be neither ~ nor fowl, no ser carne ni pescado; to have another, o other, ~ to fry, tener otras cosas que hacer, o en que pensar. 3 MEC. refuerzo. 4 FERROC. eclisa. 5 MAR. jimelga.

fish (to) tr. pescar [peces u otras cosas]. 2 pescar en [un río, etc.]. 3 buscar, coger, sacar. 4 FERROC. empalmar con eclisa. 5 intr. pescar: to ~ in troubled waters, pescar en río revuelto.

fishbone (fi·shboun) s. espina de pez.

fisher (-øᵣ) s. pescador. 2 animal pescador. 3 embarcación de pesca. 4 ZOOL. marta del Canadá.

fisherman (-øᵣmæn) s. pescador. 2 barco pesquero. 3 fig. el Papa.

fishery (-øri) s. pesca [acción]. 2 pesquería.

fishhook (-juk) s. anzuelo.

fishiness (-inis) s. olor o sabor a pescado. 2 calidad de sospechoso o raro.

fishing (-ing) s. pesca [acción]. 2 pesquería. 3 adj. de pesca, pescador, pesquero: ~ fly, mosca artificial; ~ eagle, ORN. halieto; ~ grounds, pesquería, pesquera; ~ rod, caña de pescar; ~ tackle, avíos de pescar.

fishmonger (-mongøᵣ) s. pescadero.

fishplate (-pleit) s. FERROC. eclisa.

fishpond (-pond) s. estanque, vivero.

fishtail (-teil) s. cola de pez o cosa que se le parece. 2 AVIA. coleadura.

fishtail (to) intr. AVIA. colear.

fishwife (-uaif) s. pescadera. 2 fig. verdulera [mujer desvergonzada].

fishy (-i) adj. de pez, o que lo parece. 2 que sabe o huele a pescado. 3 abundante en peces. 4 sospechoso, raro. 5 apagado, sin brillo.

fission (fi·shøn) s. hendimiento. 2 BIOL. escisión. 3 FÍS., QUÍM. fisión.

fissipedal (fisi·pedal) adj. ZOOL. fisípedo.

fissirostral (fi·sirostral) adj. ORN. fisirrostro.

fissure (fi·shøᵣ) s. hendidura, grieta. 2 ANAT., CIR., MINER. fisura.

fissure (to) tr. hender. 2 intr. henderse.

fist (fist) s. puño [mano cerrada]: to shake one's ~ at, amenazar con el puño. 2 fam. mano [del hombre]. 3 fam. letra, escritura.

fist (to) tr. apuñear, dar de puñetazos. 2 empuñar.

fistic (fi·stik) adj. pugilístico.

fisticuff (fi·stikøf) s. puñetazo, puñada. 2 pl. riña a puñetazos.

fistula (fi·schøla) s. caña, tubo. 2 CIR. fístula. 3 BOT. cañaheja.

fistulous (fi·schøløs) adj. fistuloso.

fit (fit) s. ataque, acceso, paroxismo, convulsión. 2 arranque, arrebato. 3 capricho, antojo. 4 rato, intervalo: by fits (and starts), a empujones, intermitentemente. 5 ajuste, encaje. 6 corte, talle [de un traje]. 7 conveniencia, conformidad. 8 preparación. 9 adj. apto, capaz, digno, apropiado, conveniente, a propósito, pintiparado. 10 en buena forma, bien; bien de salud. 11 listo, preparado. 12 to see ~, tener por conveniente.

fit (to) tr.-intr. adaptarse, ajustarse [a], encajar, concordar, corresponder, convenir, cuadrar, compaginarse [con]; ser propio, a propósito, o adecuado [de o para]. 3 caer, ir, venir [bien o mal]. 4 to ~ in with, concordar, armonizar con. 5 tr. ajustar, encajar, acomodar, adaptar, adecuar. 6 entallar [un vestido]. 7 surtir, proveer, equipar, habilitar; tripular, armar. 10 to ~ up, disponer [para un uso]; amueblar; ataviar.

fitch (-ch) s. ZOOL. turón, veso. 2 pincel de pelo de turón.

fitful (-ful) adj. incierto, vacilante, intermitente. 2 caprichoso, impulsivo.

fitness (-nis) s. propiedad, adecuación. 2 conveniencia, pertinencia, oportunidad.

fitter (-øᵣ) s. ajustador. 2 proveedor. 3 MEC. montador. 4 cortador, probador [sastre].

fitting (-ing) adj. propio, adecuado, conveniente, ajustado. 2 s. ajuste, encaje. 3 MEC. montaje. 4 SASTR. prueba, entalladura. 5 pl. accesorios, guarniciones, herrajes; muebles.

five (faiv) adj.-s. cinco: ~ o'clock, las cinco.

livefold (-fould) adj.-s. quíntuplo.

five-year adj. quinquenal.

fix (fiks) s. apuro, aprieto: to be in a ~, hallarse en un aprieto.

fix (to) tr. fijar [un objeto, la atención, la mirada, una fecha, etc.]; poner, establecer. 2 FOT., QUÍM. fijar. 3 grabar [en la mente]. 4 atraer [la atención, la mirada]. 5 arreglar, disponer; componer, reparar. 6 fam. amañar. 7 fam. sobornar; convencer. 8 ajustarse las cuentas [a uno]. 9 to ~ up, componer, arreglar; equipar. 10 intr. fijar su domicilio, establecerse. 11 fijarse, solidificarse. 12 to ~ on, decidirse por, escoger.

fixation (fiksei·shøn) *s.* fijación.
fixative (fi·ksɑtiv) *adj.* que fija. *2 s.* TINT. mordiente. *3* DIB. fijador, fijativo.
fixed (-t) *adj.* fijo, firme, estable, permanente: ~ *idea*, idea fija, obsesión. *2* decidido, determinado. *3* arraigado.
fixer (-ø^r) *s.* FOT. fijador. *2* reparador, componedor.
fixings (-ings) *s. pl.* accesorios, adornos, enseres.
fixity (-iti) *s.* fijeza. *2* cosa fija.
fixture (-chø^r) *s.* fijación. *2* cosa, accesorio, adorno, mueble, fijos en un lugar. *3* persona permanentemente establecida en un lugar o empleo. *4* fecha fija [para ciertos actos]. *5 pl.* instalación [de una tienda; de gas, electricidad, etc.].
fizgig (fi·šgig) *s.* muchacha desenvuelta. *2* buscapiés.
fizz (fiš) *s.* ruido como el de un gas que se escapa. *2* efervescencia. *3 fam.* champaña, bebida gaseosa.
fizz (to) *intr.* hacer un ruido como el de un gas que se escapa.
fizzle (fi·søl) *s.* FIZZ 1 y 2. *2 fam.* fiasco.
fizzle (to) *intr.* TO FIZZ. *2 to* ~ *out*, chisporrotear [al apagarse]; hacer fiasco.
flabbergast (to) (flæ·bø^rgast) *tr.* asombrar, dejar estupefacto.
flabby (flæ·bi) *adj.* fláccido, lacio, flojo.
flabellum (flabe·løm) *s.* flabelo.
flaccid (flæ·ksid) *adj.* fláccido, flojo.
flag (flæg) *s.* bandera, estandarte, banderola. *2* MAR. pabellón, insignia: ~ *officer*, jefe de escuadra; oficial general de la armada. *3* losa, lancha, lastra. *4* BOT. espadaña. *5* BOT. ácoro falso.
flag (to) *tr.* embanderar. *2* marcar, señalar, hacer señal [con una bandera]: *to* ~ *down a train*, hacer señal de parada a un tren. *3* enlosar, pavimentar con lajas. *4 intr.* colgar, pender, estar flojo o lacio. *5* desanimarse. *6* aflojar, flaquear, debilitarse. *7* vacilar. ¶ Pret. y p. p.: *flagged;* ger.: -*gging.*
flagellant (flæ·dy̆elant) *s.* flagelante; disciplinante.
flagellate (-leit) *adj.-s.* BOT., ZOOL. flagelado.
flagellate (to) *intr.* flagelar, azotar.
flagellation (-ei·shøn) *s.* flagelación.
flagellum (flady̆e·løm) *s.* flagelo, azote. *2* BOT., ZOOL. flagelo.
flageolet (flædy̆ole·t) *s.* MÚS. caramillo; chirimía.
flagging (flæ·ging) *adj.* lánguido, flojo, desanimado.
flagitious (flady̆i·shøs) *adj.* malvado, criminal, atroz.
flagman (flæ·gmæn) *s.* el que hace señales con bandera. *2* FERROC. guardavía.
flagon (flæ·gøn) *s.* garrafa, jarra, botella.
flagpole (flæ·gpoul) *s.* asta de bandera. *2* TOP. banderola, jalón.
flagrance, -cy (flei·grans, -si) *s.* notoriedad, escándalo, atrocidad.
flagrant (flei·grant) *adj.* flagrante, ardiente. *2* notorio, escandaloso, insigne, atroz.
flagship (flæ·gship) *s.* MAR. buque insignia.
flagstaff (-staf) *s.* asta de bandera.
flagstone (-stoun) *s.* losa, laja.
flail (fleil) *s.* mayal [para desgranar]. *2* mangual.
flail (to) *tr.* desgranar con mayal. *2* azotar, pegar.
flair (fle·ø^r) *s.* olfato, instinto, penetración.
flake (fleik) *s.* copo [de nieve]. *2* escama, pedacito, hojuela: ~ *of fire*, chispa, centella. *3* BOT. clavel rayado.

flake (to) *tr.* dividir en hojuelas o escamas. *2* cubrir de copos [de nieve]. *3 intr.* formar hojuelas o escamas. *4* descascararse.
flam (flæm) *s.* falsedad, mentira, embuste.
flambeau (flæ·mbou) *s.* hachón, antorcha.
flamboyant (flæmbo·iant) *adj.* flamígero. *2* vistoso, llamativo. *3* resplandeciente.
flame (fleim) *s.* llama. *2* llamarada. *3* fuego, ardor, pasión, amor. *4* ser amado.
flame (to) *intr.* llamear, flamear, arder, encenderse, brillar. *2 fig.* exaltarse, inflamarse. *3 tr.* flamear. *4* encender, inflamar.
flamen (flei·men) *s.* flamen.
flaming (-ming) *adj.* llameante, encendido. *2* inflamado, apasionado. *3* llamativo, fastuoso.
flamingo (flami·ngou) *s.* ORN. flamenco.
flan (flæ·₁ o flan) *s.* cospel. *2* flan; tarta de crema.
Flanders (flæ·ndø^rš) *n. pr.* GEOGR. Flandes.
flange (flæ·ndy̆) *s.* MEC. brida, pestaña, reborde, chapa de cierre.
flange (to) *tr.* hacer o poner brida, pestaña o reborde. *2 intr.* proyectarse, salir, extenderse.
flank (klænk) *s.* ijar, ijada, delgado, vacío. *2* costado, lado. *3* MIL., FORT. flanco.
flank (to) *tr.* flanquear; estar a cada lado de.
flannel (flæ·nøl) *s.* TEJ. franela. *2 pl.* ropa, vestido de franela.
flap (flæp) *s.* SASTR. cartera, golpe, pata; haldeta, faldón. *2* ala flexible [de sombrero]. *3* hoja plegadiza [de mesa]. *4* trampa [tablero]: ~ *door*, trampa [puerta]. *5* oreja [de zapato]. *6* disco [de válvula]: ~ *valve*, chapaleta. *7* CIR. colgajo. *8* mosquedor. *9* revés, cachete. *10* aletazo. *11* gualdrapazo. *12* golpeteo.
flap (to) *tr.* golpear, sacudir [con algo plano]. *2* mosquear. *3* batir, agitar [las alas]. *4 intr.* colgar, pender. *5* gualdrapear; batir. *6* aletear, volar. *7* agitarse. ¶ Pret. y p. p.: *flapped;* ger.: -*pping.*
flapper (flæ·pø^r) *tr.* el o lo que golpea. *2* CAZA patito. *3 fam.* jovencita, tobillera. *4 fam.* mano.
flare (fle·ø^r) *s.* llamarada, destello. *2* señal luminosa, cohete de señales. *3* arrebato [de cólera, etc.]. *4* vuelo [de una falda]. *5* ensanchamiento, abocinamiento.
flare (to) *tr.* señalar con luz o fuego. *2* ostentar. *3* dar forma acampanada, abocinar. *4 intr.* llamear, brillar, fulgurar. *5* tener vuelo [una falda]. *6* tener forma acampanada. *7 to* ~ *up*, encenderse, encolerizarse.
flare-up *s.* llamarada, encendimiento. *2* llamarada, explosión [de cólera, etc.].
flash (flæsh) *s.* llamarada, resplandor, destello; rayo, ráfaga de luz; fogonazo: ~ *of lightning*, relámpago; ~ *in the pan*, fig. esfuerzo súbito y aparatoso que no logra nada. *2* momento, instante: *in a* ~, en un instante. *3* acción rápida. *4* telegrama breve [en un periódico]. *5* descarga [de esclusa]. *6* CINEM. breve proyección explicativa. *7* ostentación, relumbrón; persona ostentosa; cosa de relumbrón. *8* corredor veloz. *9 adj.* vulgar, charro, chillón. *10* ladronesco, de germanía.
flash (to) *tr.* encender, inflamar. *2* hacer brillar. *3* despedir, enviar [luz, destellos]; echar [llamas]. *4* transmitir rápidamente, telegrafiar, radiar. *5* hacer ostentación de. *6 intr.* relampaguear, centellear, llamear, brillar; inflamar. *7* pasar como un relámpago. *8* obrar con ímpetu. *9 pop.* lucir, fachendear. ·
flashback (-bæk) *s.* CINEM. escena retrospectiva.

flashing (-ing) *m.* centelleo, relampagueo, fulguración. *2* vierteaguas, despidiente de agua.

flashlight (-lait) *s.* linterna eléctrica. *2* fanal de destellos; luz intermitente [de un faro]. *3* FOT. luz instantánea [de magnesio, etc.].

flashy (-i) *adj.* relumbrante. *2* llamativo, chillón, ostentoso, de relumbrón; superficial.

flask (flæsk) *s.* frasco, redoma.

flat (flæt) *adj.* plano, llano, liso, raso, arrasado. *2* chato, aplastado. *3* tendido, extendido. *4* positivo, categórico. *5* insulso, insípido. *6* desbravado [champán, cerveza]. *7* apagado, sin brillo; monótono, sin interés. *8* desanimado. *9* MÚS. desentonado. *10* MÚS. bemol. *11* desinflado [neumático].
12 adv. completamente. *13* exactamente; decididamente. *14* desafinadamente.
15 s. llanura, planicie, plano. *16* banco, bajío. *17* parte o cosa plana; palma [de la mano]; pala [de remo]; barca chata; carro de plataforma. *18* piso, apartamento. *19* simple, mentecato.

flat (to) *tr.* aplastar, achatar. *2* hacer insípido. *3* MÚS. abemolar. ¶ Pret. y p. p.: *flatted;* ger.: ~ *tting.*

flatcar (-kaʳ) *s.* FERROC. vagón de plataforma.

flat-footed *adj.* de pies planos. *2* fam. (E.U.) resuelto, determinado; tonto.

flatiron (-aiɵʳn) *s.* plancha [para planchar].

flatland (-lænd) *s.* llano, llanada, llanura.

flat-nosed *adj.* chato [de nariz chata].

flatten (to) (-ø̍n) *tr.* allanar, aplanar, aplastar, achatar. *2* postrar, abatir. *3* desazonar, hacer insípido. *4* to ~ out, extender horizontalmente; enderezar [un avión]. *5 intr.* aplanarse, aplastarse, achatarse. *6* abatirse, desalentarse. *7* perder el sabor. *8* to ~ out, enderezarse [un avión].

flatter (to) (flæ·tɵʳ) *tr.* adular, lisonjear: *to ~ oneself,* lisonjearse, hacerse una ilusión. *2* halagar. *3* favorecer [un retrato].

flatterer (-ɵʳ) *s.* adulador, lisonjero.

flattery (-i) *s.* adulación, lisonja. *2* halago.

flatulence, flatulency (flæ·tiulɵns, -si) *s.* flatulencia. *2* hinchazón, presunción.

flatulent (flæ·tiulønt), **flatuous** (flei·tiuɵs) *adj.* flatulento, flatoso. *2* hinchado, pomposo, vano.

flatus (flei·tøs) *s.* flato. *2* hinchazón.

flatways (flæ·tueiš), **flatwise** (flæ·tuaiš) *adv.* de plano, horizontalmente.

flaunt (flont) *s.* ostentación, alarde.

flaunt (to) *tr.* hacer ondear. *2* lucir, ostentar. *3 intr.* ondear, flotar [al viento]. *4* pavonearse.

flautist (flo·tist) *s.* flautista.

flavo (u) r (flei·vɵʳ) *s.* sabor, gusto. *2* aroma, perfume. *3* COC. sazón, sainete.

flavo (u) r (to) *tr.* saborear, dar sabor. *2* sazonar, condimentar. *3* aromatizar. *4* fig. dar cualidad distintiva [a una cosa]. *5 intr.* saber a, oler a.

flavo (u) ring (-ing) *s.* sainete, condimento.

flaw (flo) *s.* grieta, raja. *2* falla, falta, defecto, imperfección. *3* pelo [en una piedra o metal]. *4* MAR. ráfaga, racha.

flaw (to) *tr.* agrietar, romper. *2* causar defecto, afear, estropear.

flawless (-lis) *adj.* entero, sano. *2* sin defecto, sin tacha.

flax (flæks) *s.* lino [planta, fibra].

flaxen (-øn) *adj.* de lino; parecido al lino.

flaxseed (flæ·ksid) *s.* linaza, semilla del lino.

flay (to) (flei) *tr.* desollar, despellejar. *2* fig. desollar vivo, robar. *3* fig. reprender, fustigar.

flea (fli) *s.* ENT. pulga: *a ~ in one's ear,* fig. reprensión; repulsa.

fleabite (-bait) *s.* picadura de pulga. *2* fig. pequeña molestia.

fleawort (-uɵʳt) *s.* BOT. pulguera, zaragatona.

fleck (flek) *s.* punto, mancha [de color o de luz]; pinta, lunar, peca. *2* copo, vedija.

fleck(er (to) *tr.* manchar, abigarrar.

flection (fle·kshøn) *s.* FLEXIÓN.

fled (fled) *pret.* y *p. p.* de TO FLEE.

fledge (to) (fle·dy̆) *tr.* emplumar. *2* criar plumas en. *3 intr.* emplumecer, pelechar.

fledged (fle·dy̆d) *adj.* plumado, con plumas.

fledg(e)ling (fle·dy̆ling) *adj.-s.* volantón. *2* joven, novel, inexperto.

flee (to) (fli) *tr.* huir de, escapar de, evitar. *2 intr.* huir, escapar, desaparecer. ¶ Pret. y p. p.: *fled.*

fleece (fliˑs) *s.* vellón, vellocino, lana: *the Golden Fleece,* el Vellocino de oro; el Toisón [de oro].

fleece (to) *tr.* esquilar [el ganado]. *2* fig. desplumar, pelar. *3* cubrir de lana o nieve.

fleecy (-i) *adj.* lanudo. *2* blanco y blando. *3* aborregado [cielo].

fleer (fliˑɵʳ) *s.* mueca, burla, risa falsa.

fleer (to) (tr. burlarse, mofarse de. *2 intr.* reirse o sonreirse con burla o desprecio.

fleet (flit) *s.* armada, marina de guerra. *2* MAR., AVIA. flota, escuadra, escuadrilla. *3* conjunto de vehículos pertenecientes a una empresa. *4 adj.* veloz, rápido, ligero.

fleet (to) *tr.* rozar, pasar rápidamente sobre. *2 intr.* pasar velozmente, volar, desvanecerse.

fleeting (-ing) *adj.* fugaz, pasajero, efímero, transitorio.

Fleming (fle·ming) *s.* flamenco [de Flandes].

Flemish (fle·mish) *adj.-s.* flamenco [de Flandes]. *2 s.* flamenco [idioma].

flesh (flesh) *s.* carne [de una pers. o animal vivos; de una fruta; cuerpo; naturaleza humana; sensualidad]: *~ and blood,* carne y hueso; fig. sangre, familia; *in the ~,* vivo; en persona. *2* carne [por oposición a pescado]. *3* género humano. *4* sangre, linaje. *5* piel, cutis.

flesh (to) *tr.* acostumbrar, avezar. *2* cebar, encarnizar. *3* hundir [un arma] en la carne.

fleshings (fle·shingš) *s. pl.* TEAT. mallas de color de carne.

fleshly (-li) *adj.* carnoso. *2* corporal. *3* carnal, sensual, mundano.

fleshy (-li) *adj.* carnoso, pulposo. *2* suculento. *3* gordo, grueso, corpulento.

fleur-de-lis (flɵ·døli·(s) *s.* BLAS., BOT. flor de lis.

flew (flu) *pret.* de TO FLY.

flex (to) (fleks) *tr.* doblar, encorvar. *2 intr.* doblarse.

flexibility (fleksibi·liti) *s.* flexibilidad.

flexible (fle·ksibøl) *adj.* flexible: ~ *cord,* ELECT. flexible. *2* cimbreño, juncal. *3* dócil, manejable.

flexile (-il) *adj.* FLEXIBLE.

flexion (-shøn) *s.* flexión, doblamiento. *2* codo, curvatura. *3* GRAM. flexión.

flexor (-sɵʳ) *s.* ANAT. flexor [músculo].

flexuose (-shuous), **flexuous** (-ɵs) *adj.* flexuoso, tortuoso, sinuoso. *2* vario, inconstante.

flibbertigibbet (flibɵʳtidy̆i·bet) *s.* persona frívola, voluble o chismosa.

flick (flik) *s.* golpecito [con el dedo, el látigo, etc.]. *2* mancha pequeña. *3 pl.* fam. cine.

flick (to) *tr.* dar un golpecito [con el dedo, etc.]. *2* sacudir [la ceniza a un cigarro]. *3* chasquear [un látigo]. *4 intr.* corretear, revolotear.

flicker (-ø^r) *s.* vacilación, titilación, luz trémula. *2* parpadeo. *3* aleteo. *4* estremecimiento. *5* ORN. picamaderos norteamericano.

flicker (to) *intr.* fluctuar, vacilar, temblar. *2* entremorir. *3* aletear.

flier (flai·ø^r) *s.* animal volador. *2* aviador. *3* avión. *4* cosa veloz [coche, tren, caballo, etc.]. *5* IMPR. sacapliegos. *6* fam. empresa u operación arriesgada.

flight (flait) *s.* vuelo [acción, manera de volar; espacio recorrido volando]; volada: *to take* ~, alzar el vuelo; ~ *path*, AVIA. línea de vuelo. *2* viaje aéreo. *3* trayectoria [de un proyectil]. *4* paso rápido [del tiempo]. *5* bandada [de pájaros]. *6* lluvia [de flechas]. *7* escuadrilla [de aviones]. *8* ímpetu, arrebato, exaltación; vuelo [de la fantasía]. *9* fuga, huida, escape, evasión. *10* tramo [de escalera].

flighty (-i) *adj.* fugaz, pasajero. *2* caprichoso, inconstante. *3* alocado. *4* chiflado.

flimflam (fli·mflæm) *s.* necedad, bagatela. *2* soflama, engaño.

flimsy (fli·mši) *adj.* débil, endeble. *2* flaco, fútil, trivial, baladí.

flinch (flinch) *s.* vacilación, titubeo.

flinch (to) *intr.* vacilar, desistir, echarse atrás, retroceder [ante lo peligroso, etc.], arredrarse.

fling (fling) *s.* tiro, echada, echamiento. *2* fam. prueba, tentativa: *to take* o *have a* ~ *at*, probar, ensayar. *3* fam. pulla, sarcasmo, burla. *4* brinco, coz. *5* valor, atrevimiento. *6* baile escocés. *7* *to go on a* ~, echar una cana al aire.

fling (to) *tr.* echar, arrojar, tirar, lanzar; despedir. *2* derribar, echar al suelo. *3* derrotar, vencer. *4* *to* ~ *about*, esparcir. *5* *to* ~ *off*, desechar, sacudirse; despistar [al que persigue]. *6* *to* ~ *open*, abrir de golpe. *7* *to* ~ *out*, arrojar con fuerza; hacer ondear [una bandera]. *8* *intr.* arrojarse, lanzarse, abalanzarse. *9* saltar, brincar. *10* burlarse, mofarse. *11* *to* ~ *out*, lanzarse fuera. ¶ Pret. y p. p.: *flung*.

flint (flint) *s.* pedernal. *2* cosa muy dura. *3* adj. ~ *glass*, cristal [vidrio pesado].

flint-hearted *adj.* empedernido.

flintlock (fli·ntlak) *s.* llave o fusil de chispa.

flinty (-i) *adj.* pedernalino. *2* duro, cruel.

flip (flip) *s.* golpe vivo, capirotazo. *2* especie de ponche.

flip (to) *tr.* arrojar, lanzar al aire. *2* echar [una moneda sobre el mostrador]. *3* tirar con un movimiento del pulgar y otro dedo. *4* dar un golpe vivo. *5* quitar de golpe.

flippancy (-ansi) *s.* ligereza impropia, impertinencia, petulancia.

flippant (-ant) *adj.* ligero, impertinente, petulante.

flipper (-ø^r) *s.* ZOOL. pata [de foca, de tortuga marina, etc.]. *2* pop. mano.

flirt (flø^rt) *s.* flirteador, galanteador. *2* coqueta [mujer]. *3* sacudida, tirón.

flirt (to) *intr.* flirtear, coquetear. *2* juguetear, mariposear. *3* acariciar, dejarse tentar por [una idea, etc.].

flirtation (-ei·shøn) *s.* flirteo, coqueteo, galanteo.

flit (flit) *s.* movimiento rápido y ligero.

flit (to) *intr.* pasar [de un sitio a otro]. *2* moverse rápidamente, volar, revolotear. ¶ Pret. y p. p.: *flitted*; ger.: *flitting*.

flitch (flich) *s.* témpano [de tocino]. *2* lonja [de carne o pescado].

flitter (to) (fli·tø^r) *tr.-intr.* TO FLUTTER.

flittermouse (-ma·us) *s.* ZOOL. murciélago.

flitting (fli·ting) *adj.* fugaz.

float (flout) *s.* flotador; cosa que flota. *2* corcho [de caña de pescar]. *3* boya. *4* salvavidas. *5* balsa; armadía. *6* carromato, carroza, carro alegórico [para procesiones, etc.]. *7* paleta [de rueda].

float (to) *intr.* flotar. *2* sobrenadar, boyar, nadar; hacer la plancha [en la natación]. *3* cernerse. *4* fluctuar. *5* *tr.* hacer flotar, poner o llevar a flote. *6* inundar. *7* COM. emitir, poner en circulación.

floater (flou·tø^r) *s.* flotador. *2* el que cambia frecuentemente de residencia, ocupación, etc.

floating (-ing) *adj.* flotante. *2* boyante, a flote. *3* fluctuante, variable. *4* COM. en circulación.

floculent (fla·kiulønt) *adj.* coposo, lanoso.

flock (flak) *s.* bandada [de aves]; manada; rebaño. *2* grey, congregación. *3* muchedumbre, grupo. *4* hatajo. *5* copo, vedija. *6* borra.

flock (to) *intr.* reunirse, congregarse, atroparse, juntarse. *2* llegar en tropel.

floe (flou) *s.* masa de hielo flotante.

flog (to) (flag) *tr.* azotar, vapulear, fustigar. ‖ Pret. y p. p.: *flogged*; ger.: *flogging*.

flogging (-ing) *s.* azotes, azotamiento.

flood (flød) *s.* riada, avenida, crecida, desbordamiento. *2* diluvio, inundación: *the Flood*, el Diluvio. *3* torrente, abundancia. *4* flujo [del mar]: ~ *tide*, marea montante, pleamar. *5* aguas, mar.

flood (to) *tr.* inundar. *2* sumergir, anegar, diluviar. *3* *intr.* desbordarse; entrar o salir a raudales.

floodgate (-geit) *s.* compuerta; puerta de esclusa.

floodlight (-lait) *s.* reflector, proyector de luz.

floor (flo·ø^r) *s.* suelo, piso, pavimento, entarimado: ~ *tile*, baldosa, baldosín. *2* fondo [del mar, de una piscina, etc.]. *3* plan [de un buque]. *4* piso, alto [de una casa]. *5* hemiciclo [de una asamblea]. *6* *to have the* ~, tener la palabra.

floor (to) *tr.* solar, enlosar, embaldosar, enladrillar, entarimar. *2* derribar, echar al suelo. *3* apabullar, revolcar, vencer [en una discusión].

flooring (-ing) *s.* suelo, piso. *2* embaldosado, entarimado. *3* material para solar.

flop (flap) *s.* fam. sonido como el del choque de un cuerpo blando. *2* fam. fracaso.

flop (to) *tr.* echar, dejar caer con descuido o con ruido. *2* intr. hacer un ruido como el del choque de un cuerpo blando. *3* menearse [una cosa] de un lado a otro. *4* fracasar, hacer fiasco. *5* *to* ~ *down*, dejarse caer, tumbarse. ‖ Pret. y p. p.: *flopped*; ger.: *flopping*.

flora (flo·ra) *s.* BOT. flora. *2* (con may.). MIT. Flora.

floral (-al) *adj.* floral.

Florence (flo·røns) *n. pr. f.* Florencia.

Florentine (flo·røntin) *adj.-s.* florentino.

florescence (flore·søns) *s.* BOT. florescencia.

floret (flo·ret) *s.* BOT. flósculo. *2* florecilla.

floriculture (floricø·lchø^r) *s.* floricultura.

florid (flo·rid) *adj.* florido [estilo]. *2* colorado [rostro]. *3* vigoroso, lozano, fresco. *4* vistoso, llamativo.

floriferous (flo·riforøs) *adj.* florífero.

florin (flo·rin) *s.* florín.

florist (flo·rist) *s.* floricultor. *2* florista.

floscule (flo·skiul) *s.* BOT. flósculo.

floss (flos) *s.* seda floja. *2* cadarzo. *3* fibra sedosa. *4* penacho [del maíz].

flossy (-i) *adj.* ligero, suave. *3* pop. llamativo.

flotation (flotei·shøn) *s.* flotación, flotadura. *2* COM. lanzamiento [de un empréstito, de una empresa].

flotilla (floti·la) *s.* flotilla.

flotsam (flo·tsam) *s.* pecios.
flounce (flauns) *s.* faralá, volante, guarnición. *2* sacudida, movimiento rápido.
flounce (to) *tr.* guarnecer con volantes. *2 intr.* andar o moverse violentamente, mostrando enojo.
flounder (flau·ndøʳ) *s.* forcejeo, esfuerzo torpe. *2* ICT. nombre de la platija, el lenguado, el rodaballo, etc.
flounder (to) *intr.* debatirse, patullar. *2* avanzar o proceder torpemente; equivocarse.
flour (flauʳ) *s.* harina.
flour (to) *tr.* moler, pulverizar. *2* enharinar.
flourish (flø·rish) *s.* molinete o movimiento ostentoso, de saludo, etc., que se hace con un bastón, espada, etc. *2* adorno, rasgo caprichoso. *3* MÚS. adición o preludio improvisado. *5* toque de trompetas. *6* florecimiento, prosperidad, vigor.
flourish (to) *intr.* crecer, florecer, prosperar. *2* MÚS. improvisar un preludio. *3* rasguear, hacer dibujos caprichosos. *4 tr.* ornamentar. *5* blandir, hacer molinetes con; mover con gracia u ostentación.
flourishing (flø·rishing) *adj.* floreciente, próspero.
floury (fla·uri) *adj.* harinoso. *2* enharinado.
flout (flaut) *s.* mofa, escarnio, insulto.
flout (to) *tr.* mofarse de, escarnecer, insultar.
flow (flou) *s.* flujo, corriente. *2* acción de fluir o manar. *3* torrente, chorro, abundancia. *4* afluencia. *5* desagüe. *6* flujo [de la marea]. *7* desbordamiento, inundación. *8* movimiento suave y gradual. *9* FÍS. gasto. *10* ~ *of spirits,* animación habitual.
flow (to) *intr.* fluir, manar, correr. *2* salir, proceder, dimanar. *3* afluir. *4* subir [la marea]. *5* abundar, rebosar. *6* deslizarse, correr fácilmente, ser fluido [el estilo, etc.]. *7* caer en ondas o pliegues; ondear. *8 to* ~ *into,* desaguar en. *9 to* ~ *over,* rebosar. *10 tr.* inundar. *11* derramar.
flower (flau·øʳ) *s.* BOT. flor: ~ *garden,* jardín; ~ *girl,* florista; ~ *vase,* jarrón, florero; ~ *of lice,* flor de lis. *2* flor y nata. *3* adorno, ornamento [esp. del estilo] *4 pl.* QUÍM. flor.
flower (to) *intr.* florecer. *2* florear [adornar con flores].
flowered (-d) *adj.* florido [que tiene flores]. *2* floreado [adornado con flores], espolinado.
floweret (-et) *s.* florecilla, florecita.
flowering (-ing) *adj.* FLOWERY. *2* florido, en flor. *3.* BOT. ~ *rush,* junco florido.
flowerpot (-pat) *s.* maceta, tiesto.
flowery (-i) *adj.* de flores o que lo parece. *2* cubierto de flores. *3* florido, poético [estilo].
flowing (flou·ing) *adj.* fluido, fluente, corriente, manantío. *2* fluido, fácil [estilo]. *3* ondeante.
flown (floun) *p. p.* de TO FLY.
flu (flu) *s.* MED. fam. trancazo, gripe.
fluctuant (fløkchuant) *adj.* fluctuante, fluctuoso.
fluctuate (to) (flø·kchueit) *intr.* fluctuar.
fluctuation (-ei·shøn) *s.* fluctuación. *2* agitación, incertidumbre.
flue (flu) *s.* cañón [de chimenea], humero. *2* conducto o tubo [de ventilación, de humos]. *3* pelusa, tamo. *4* MÚS. *flue* o ~ *pipe,* cañón de planta [del órgano].
fluency (-ønsi) *s.* fluidez. *2* afluencia, facundia, soltura, facilidad [de palabra].
fluent (-ønt) *adj.* fluido, fluente. *2* facundo. *3* fácil, abundante, fluido [lenguaje, estilo].
fluff (fløf) *s.* pelusa, vello, lanilla, tamo. *2* copo [de lana]. *3* masa esponjosa. *4* plumón.
fluff (to) *tr.* mullir, esponjar, ahuecar.

fluffy (-i) *adj.* cubierto de pelusa o plumón. *2* blando, suave, mullido, esponjado, sedoso.
fluid (flu·id) *adj.-s.* fluido.
fluidity (-iti), **fluidness** (-inis) *s.* fluidez.
fluke (fluk) *s.* uña [de ancla, de arpón]; lengüeta [de flecha]. *2* ICT. platija. *3* duela [gusano]. *4* chiripa. *5 pl.* cola [de la ballena].
fluke (to) *tr.* fam. chiripear. *2 intr.* fam. ganar por chiripa. *3* fracasar.
flume (flum) *s.* (E.U.) caz, reguera. *2* canal de madera. *3* garganta por cuyo fondo pasa un torrente.
flummery (flø·møri) *s.* especie de manjar blanco. *2* patarata, pamplina; alabanza insincera.
flung (fløng) *pret. y p. p.* de TO FLING.
flunk (flønk) *s.* (E.U.) fam. fracaso. *2* fam. suspenso [en un examen].
flunk (to) *tr.* (E.U.) fam. fracaso. *2* fam. suspenso [en un examen].
flunk (to) *tr.* (E.U.) suspender [en un examen]. *2 intr.* fam. quedar mal, fracasar [en un examen, etc.].
flunkey, flunky (flø·nki) *s.* lacayo. *2* adulador, persona servil.
fluor (flu·øʳ) *s.* QUÍM. flúor.
fluorescent (fluøre·sønt) *adj.* fluorescente.
flurry (flø·ri) *s.* agitación, excitación, prisa. *2* barullo, conmoción. *3* ráfaga, chubasco.
flurry (to) *tr.* agitar, excitar, turbar, aturrullar.
flush (fløsh) *adj.* lleno, bien provisto, rico. *2* robusto, lleno de vida. *3* rojo, encendido. *4* abundante. *5* pródigo, generoso. *6* próspero. *7* igual, parejo, raso, nivelado, enrasado, al mismo nivel, embutido: ~ *with,* enrasado, ras con ras con. *8* ~ *tank,* depósito de agua para limpia [de inodoros, etc.].
9 s. descarga, flujo rápido y copioso. *10* aumento súbito; floración abundante. *11* vuelo súbito [de un pájaro o bandada]. *12* oleada [de un sentimiento]; emoción, agitación, animación. *13* rubor, encendimiento. *14* flux [de naipes].
flush (to) *intr.* afluir [la sangre, etc.]. *2* salirse, derramarse. *3* llenarse de agua. *4* encenderse; ruborizarse, sonrojarse. *5* echar a volar [las aves]. *6 tr.* animar, excitar. *7* encender, ruborizar. *8* limpiar con un chorro de agua, inundar. *9* igualar, nivelar, emparejar. *10* levantar [las aves de caza].
fluster (flø·stø) *s.* agitación, confusión, aturdimiento.
fluster (to) *tr.* agitar, confundir, aturdir; achispar. *2* encender [el rostro]. *3 intr.* agitarse, aturdirse.
flute (flut) *s.* MÚS. flauta. *2* MÚS. flautado [del órgano]. *3* ARQ. estría. *4* cañón [pliegue].
flute (to) *tr.* estriar, acanalar. *2* alechugar, encañonar. *3 intr.-tr.* tocar la flauta.
fluting (flu·ting) *s.* estría, estriadura, acanaladura.
fluting-iron *s.* hierros o tenacillas de rizar.
flutist (-ist) *s.* flautista.
flutter (flø·tøʳ) *s.* vibración, aleteo, ondulación. *2* vuelco [del corazón]. *3* agitación, confusión, alboroto; actividad sin objeto.
flutter (to) *intr.* temblar, aletear, revolotear, palpitar. *2* tremolar, flamear, ondear. *3* agitarse, alterarse. *4 tr.* batir [las alas]; tremolar, agitar. *5* agitar, turbar.
fluvial (flu·vial) *adj.* fluvial.
fluviatile (flu·viatil) *adj.* fluviatil. *2* fluvial.
flux (fløks) *s.* flujo. *2* derretimiento, fusión. *3* mudanza o alteración continua. *4* METAL. fundente.

flux (to) *tr.* fundir; unir por medio de la fusión. *2* mezclar con fundente. *3 intr.* fluir. *4* fundirse, derretirse.

fluxion (flø·kshøn) *s.* flujo; cambio continuo. *2* fusión. *3* MED. fluxión.

fly (flai) *s.* ENT. mosca: ~ *net*, mosquitero. *2* mosca artificial [para pescar]. *3* calesín. *4* vuelo [de una bandera; de lo que va por el aire]: *on the* ~, al vuelo. *5* bragueta. *6* lona que tapa la puerta [de una tienda de campaña]. *7* MEC. volante. *8 pl.* TEAT. bambalinas.

fly (to) *intr.* volar [moverse en el aire]. *2* huir, escaparse; desaparecer. *3* correr, pasar rápidamente. *4* volar [el tiempo]. *5* lanzarse, precipitarse: *to* ~ *at*, lanzarse sobre. *6* dispararse [un muelle]; saltar, estallar. *7* flotar, ondear [en el aire]. *8 to* ~ *in the face of*, desobedecer abiertamente, desafiar. *9 to* ~ *into a passion, a rage*, montar en clera. *10 to* ~ *off at a tangent*, cambiar de repente, tomar de repente un nuevo rumbo. *11 to* ~ *open, to* ~ *shut*, abrirse o cerrarse de repente.
12 tr. hacer volar. *13* dirigir [un avión]. *14* transportar [en avión]. *15* atravesar [en avión]. *16* desplegar, enarbolar [banderas]. *17* evitar; huir de. ¶ Pret.: *flew;* p. p.: *flown.*

flyaway (-auei) *adj.* suelto, ondeante. *2* inconstante. *3* casquivano.

flyblow (-blou) *s.* huevo de mosca, cresa.

flyblow (to) *tr.* depositar la mosca sus huevos en. *2* fig. contaminar, inficionar.

flyboat (-bout) *s.* MAR. filibote.

flyer (-ø^r) *s.* FLIER.

fly-fishing *s.* pesca con mosca artificial.

flyflap (-flæp) *s.* mosqueador, espantamoscas.

flying (-ing) *s.* vuelo [acción de volar]. *2 adj.* volador, volante, para volar: ~ *bomb*, bomba volante; ~ *field*, campo de aviación; ~ *fortress*, AVIA. fortaleza volante; ~ *gurnard*, ICT. milano; ~ *saucer*, platillo volante; ~ *sickness*, mal de altura. *3* volante [que va de un lado a otro; que vuela o sobresale]: ~ *buttress*, ARQ. botarel, arbotante; ~ *column*, columna volante. *4* fugitivo. *5* rápido, veloz. *6* ondeante, desplegado [bandera, etc.]: *to come off with* ~ *colours*, salir triunfante. *7* MAR. ~ *jib*, petifoque.

flyleaf (-lıf) *s.* ENCUAD. guarda.

flypaper (-peipø^r) *s.* papel atrapamoscas.

flyspeck (-spek) *s.* mancha de mosca.

flytrap (-træp) *s.* atrapamoscas.

flyweight (-ueit) *s.* DEP. peso mosca.

flywheel (-juɪl) *s.* MEC. volante.

foal (foul) *s.* potro, potra; buche [cría de la yegua o de la burra].

foal (to) *tr.-intr.* parir la yegua o la burra.

foam (foum) *s.* espuma.

foam (to) *intr.* espumar, llenarse de espuma. *2* espumajear. *3 tr.* llenar de espuma.

foamy (-i) *adj.* espumante, espumajoso. *2* espumoso.

fob (fab) *s.* bolsillo del reloj. *2* engaño.

fob (to) *tr.* engañar, estafar, pegársela [a uno]. ¶ Pret. y p. p.: *fobbed;* ger.: *fobbing.*

focal (fou·kal) *adj.* focal.

focus (fou·køs) *s.* foco; distancia focal; enfoque: *in* ~, enfocado; *out of* ~, desenfocado.

focus (to) *tr.* enfocar; concentrar [en un foco]. *2 intr.* quedar enfocado. ¶ Pret. y p. p.: *focused o -ssed;* ger.: *focusing o -ssing.*

fodder (fa·dø^r) *s.* forraje, pienso.

fodder (to) *tr.* pensar, dar pienso a.

foe (fou) *s.* enemigo. *2* adversario.

foeman (-mæn) *s.* enemigo [en la guerra].

foetal (fi·tal) *adj.* fetal.

foetus (fi·tøs) *s.* feto.

fog (fog) *s.* niebla, neblina, bruma: ~ *bell*, ~ *whistle*, campana, silbato, de nieblas. *2* confusión, perplejidad. *3* FOT. velo.

fog (to) *tr.* envolver en niebla. *2* empañar; obscurecer. *3* FOT. velar. *4 intr.* ponerse brumoso. *5* hacerse confuso. *6* FOT. velarse. ¶ Pret. y p. p.: *fogged;* ger.: *fogging.*

fogbound (-baund) *adj.* inmovilizado por la niebla.

fogey *s.* FOGY.

foggy (-i) *adj.* de niebla. *2* neblinoso, brumoso. *3* nebuloso, confuso. *4* FOT. velado.

foghorn (-jo^rn) *s.* MAR. bocina, sirena.

fogy (fou·gi) *s.* persona chapada a la antigua, obscurantista.

foible (foi·bøl) *s.* punto flaco, debilidad, flaqueza.

foil (foil) *s.* ESGR. florete. *2* hojuela, laminilla, chapa, pan [de metal]; oropel. *3* azogado [de un espejo]. *4* realce, contraste. *5* ARQ. lóbulo. *6* CAZA rastro.

foil (to) *tr.* anular, frustrar. *2* chasquear, desconcertar. *3* cubrir con laminilla. *4* realzar, hacer contrastar. *5* ARQ. adornar con lóbulos.

foist (to) (foist) *tr.* introducir, encajar, endosar [algo] subrepticiamente o con engaño.

fold (fould) *s.* doblez, pliegue, repliegue, arruga, recogido. *2* hoja [de puerta]. *3* abrazo. *4* IMPR. pliego. *5* envoltorio. *6* redil, aprisco. *7* hato, rebaño. *8* grey. *9* usado como sufijo, veces: *tenfold*, diez veces.

fold (to) *tr.* plegar, doblar. *2* enlazar, abrazar. *3* incluir, envolver. *4* cerrar [una puerta]. *5* cruzar [los brazos]; plegar [las alas]. *6* apriscar, meter en redil. *7 intr.* doblarse, plegarse, cerrarse.

folder (-ø^r) *s.* plegador. *2* plegadera. *3* carpeta. *4* programa, prospecto.

folderol (fa·lderol) *s.* FALDEROL.

folding (fou·lding) *s.* plegado, plegadura. *2 adj.* plegadizo, plegable, que se cierra: ~ *bed*, cama plegable; ~ *chair*, silla plegable o de tijera; ~ *door*, puerta de dos hojas; ~ *screen*, biombo; ~ *seat*, asiento levadizo.

foliaceous (fouliei·shøs) *adj.* foliáceo.

foliage (fou·liidÿ) *s.* follaje.

foliate (fou·lieit) *s.* provisto de hojas, frondoso.

foliate (to) *tr.* foliar. *2* batir, reducir a hojas. *3* azogar [un espejo]. *4* ARQ. adornar con follaje. *5 intr.* BOT. echar hojas.

foliation (-ei·shøn) *s.* foliación. *2* ARQ. follaje.

folio (fou·liou) *s.* folio. *2* IMPR. pliego. *3* infolio. *4* cartera [para papeles]. *5 adj.* en folio.

folio (to) *tr.* foliar.

foliole (-l) *s.* BOT. foliolo.

folk (fouk) *s.* gente, pueblo, nación, tribu. *2 pl.* gente, personas. *3* gente, familia, parientes. *4 adj.* del pueblo, popular: ~ *dance*, baile popular; ~ *music*, música popular.

folklore (fou·klo^r) *s.* folklore.

folkloric (-ik) *s.* folklórico.

folklorist (-ist) *s.* folklorista.

follicle (fa·likøl) *s.* BOT., ANAT. folículo.

follicular (foli·kiula^r) *adj.* folicular.

follow (to) (fa·lou) *tr.* seguir [en todas sus acepciones, menos en la de continuar]. *2* perseguir, tratar de obtener. *3 to* ~ *out*, llevar hasta el fin, llevar a cabo. *4 to* ~ *suit*, servir [en el juego de naipes]; fig. seguir el ejemplo. *5 to ~ up*, perseguir infatigablemente; continuar, hacer algo que completa. *6 intr.* seguir: *as follows*, como sigue. *7 seguirse: it follows*, síguese. *8 to ~ on*, continuar, proseguir.

follower (-ə^r) *s.* seguidor. *2* criado. *3* imitador, discípulo. *4* partidario, secuaz. *5 pl.* séquito, comitiva.

following (-ing) *adj.* siguiente. *2* resultante; consiguiente. *3 s.* séquito, acompañamiento. *4* partidarios, secuaces. *5* profesión, carrera.

folly (fa·li) *s.* tontería, necedad. *2* locura, insensatez, disparate, desatino. *3* falta de juicio.

foment (to) (fome·nt) *tr.* fomentar.

fomentation (ei·shøn) *s.* fomentación, fomento.

fond (fand) *adj.* aficionado [a]; amigo, amante [de], encariñado [con]: *to be ~ of*, querer a [una pers.] tener afición a [una cosa]. *2* afectuoso, tierno. *3* querido, acariciado.

fondle (to) (fa·ndøl) *tr.* tratar con amor; agasajar, mimar, acariciar.

fondling (-ling) *s.* niño mimado. *2* caricia, mimo. *3 adj.* acariciador.

fondness (-nis) *s.* afición. *2* cariño, ternura.

font (fant) *s.* pila bautismal o de agua bendita. *2* fuente, manantial. *3* IMPR. fundición.

fontanel (fantane·l) *s.* ANAT. fontanela.

food (fud) *s.* alimento, nutrimento. *2* comida, sustento. *3* vitualla. *4* fig. materia, pábulo.

foodstuff (fu·dstøf) *s.* comestible, producto alimenticio.

fool (ful) *s.* necio, tonto, simple, bobo: *to play the ~*, hacer el tonto. *2* loco, insensato. *3* bufón. *4* hazmerreír; primo, víctima [de un engaño]: *fool's errand*, empresa tonta o inútil; *to make a ~ of*, poner en ridículo.

fool (to) *tr.* chasquear, engañar; estafar. *2* embromar. *3 to ~ away*, gastar tontamente. *4 intr.* bromear, tontear, pasar el tiempo en tonterías.

foolery (fu·løri) *s.* tontería, locura, absurdidad.

foolhardy (-ja^rdi) *adj.* loco, temerario.

foolish (-ish) *adj.* tonto, simple, necio, bobo. *2* disparatado. *3* imprudente, desatinado. *4* absurdo, ridículo.

foolishness (-nis) *s.* tontería, simpleza, necedad. *2* imprudencia. *3* absurdidad.

foolscap (-skæp) *s.* gorro de bufón. *2* papel de escribir [33 × 43 cm].

fooltrap (-træp) *s.* engañabobos.

foot (fut), *pl.* **feet** (fit) *s.* pie [de pers.]: *to carry someone off is feet*, arrebatar, entusiasmar a uno; *to keep one's feet*, sostenerse, no caer; *to put one's ~ down*, mostrarse firme, proceder con energía; *to set on ~*, poner en marcha, en actividad; iniciar, promover; *on ~*, a pie, en marcha, en actividad; *on one's feet*, de pie, en pie; en buena salud; ganándose la vida; *under ~*, bajo los pies; sujeto. *2* pata, pie [de animal, mueble, objeto]. *3* peal [de media]. *4* pie, parte cercana a la base. *5* pie [medida lineal]: *~ by ~*, palmo a palmo. *6* MÉTR. pie. *7* pierna [de compás]. *8* MAR. pujamen.

9 adj. de pie, del pie o los pies, para el pie o los pies; etc.: *~ bath*, pediluvio; *~ brake*, freno de pedal; *~ race*, carrera a pie; *~ warmer*, calientapiés.

foot (to) *intr.* andar, caminar. *2* bailar, saltar. *3* sumar. *4 tr.* pisar, hollar, recorrer [andando]: *to ~ it*, andar a pie; bailar. *5* poner pie o pies a. *6* sumar [una columna]. *7* pagar [la cuenta].

footage (fu·tidy) *s.* longitud o distancia en pies.

football (-bol) *s.* DEP. fútbol, balompié: *~ player*, futbolista.

footboard (-bo^rd) *s.* estribo [de coche]. *2* tabla en que se apoyan los pies. *3* pie [de cama].

footboy (-boi) *s.* criadito de librea.

footbridge (-bridy) *s.* puente para peatones.

footcloth (-cloz) *s.* alfombrilla. *2* gualdrapa.

footed (fu·tid) *adj.* sumado. *2* de pies o patas: *four-footed*, de cuatro patas.

footfall (-fol) *s.* paso, pisada; ruido de un paso.

footgear (-giø^r) *s.* calzado; medias, calcetines.

foothill (-jil) *s.* colina al pie de una montña.

foothold (-jould) *s.* sitio donde asentar o afirmar el pie. *2* pie firme. *3* posición establecida.

footing (-ing) *s.* pie, base, fundamento. *2* sitio donde asentar el pie; posición segura, estable. *3* paso, marcha; baile. *4* entrada [en una sociedad, etc.]. *5* suma, total [de una columna]. *6* pie, relaciones, términos: *on an equal ~*, en pie de igualdad; *on a friendly ~*, en relaciones amistosas.

footlights (-laits) *s. pl.* TEAT. candilejas. *2* fig. tablas, profesión teatral.

footman (-mæn) *s.* lacayo.

footmark (-ma^rk) *s.* huella, pisada.

footpace (-peis) *s.* paso normal o regular. *2* descansillo [de escalera]. *3* tarima, estrado.

footpad (-pæd) *s.* salteador de caminos.

footpath (-pæz) *s.* senda, camino para peatones.

footprint (-print) *s.* FOOTMARK

foots (-s) *s. pl.* sedimento, heces.

footscraper (-screipø^r) *s.* limpiabarros.

footsore (-so^r) *adj.* despeado.

footstalk (stok) *s.* BOT. pedúnculo, pezón.

footstep (-step) *s.* paso, pisada.

footstool (-stul) *s.* escabel, banqueta.

footwalk (-uoc), **footway** (-uei) *s.* senda, camino para peatones. *2* (Ingl.) acera.

footwear (-ueø^r) *s.* FOOTGEAR.

foozle (fu·søl) *s.* chapucería, chambonada.

foozle (to) *tr.-intr.* chafallar; jugar mal.

fop (fap) *s.* petimetre, pisaverde, lechuguino, currutaco; hombre vano, presumido.

foppish (-ish) *adj.* vanidoso, presumido, currutaco, leghuchino, afectado en el vestir.

for (fo^r) *prep.* por [indicando: a causa de; en favor de; con respecto a; en nombre de; a favor, de parte de, etc.]. *2* para [indicando: destino, uso, aplicación; tiempo; fin, provecho, beneficio]: *what for?* para qué? *3* durante, por espacio de. *4* como: *~ a reward*, como premio. *5* otros empleos: *a cheque ~ 10 £*, un cheque de diez libras; *tall ~ his age*, alto para la edad que tiene; *time ~ dinner*, hora de comer; *it is for you to decide*, usted ha de decidir; *~ all I know*, que yo sepa; *~ the future*, en lo venidero. *6 ~ all that*, no obstante, a pesar de todo. *7 ~ all the world*, por nada del mundo; en todo, exactamente. *8 ~ good*, de fijo, para no volver. *9 ~ short*, para abreviar. *10 conj.* porque, puesto que, pues.

forage (fa·ridy) *s.* forraje, pasto.

forage (to) *tr.* forrajear. *2* dar forraje a. *3* saquear, pillar.

foramen (forei·møn) *s.* foramen.

forasmuch (forašmø·ch) conj. *~ as*, puesto que, ya que, visto que, por cuanto.

foray (fo·rei) *s.* correría, incursión. *2* saqueo.

foray (to) *tr.* saquear, pillar. *2 intr.* hacer correrías.

forbade (fo^rbeid) *pret.* de TO FORBID.

forbear (fo^rbeø^r) *s.* antepasado.

forbear (to) (fo^rbe·ø^r) *tr.* dejar de, abastenerse de.

2 sufrir con paciencia. *3 intr.* tener paciencia. ¶ Pret.: *forbore;* p. p.: *forborne.*

forbearance (foᵗbe·øᵣans) *s.* abstención, contención. *2* paciencia, indulgencia, lenidad.

forbearing (-ing) *adj.* paciente, indulgente.

forbid (to) (foᵗbi·d) *tr.* prohibir, vedar, negar. *2* impedir. ¶ Pret.: *forbad* o *-bade;* p. p.: *forbidden;* ger.: *forbidding.*

forbidden (foᵗbi·døn) *adj.* prohibido, vedado.

forbidding (-ing) *adj.* prohibitivo. *2* repulsivo. *3* inabordable. *4* formidable, adusto.

forbore (foᵗbo·ᵣ) *pret.* de TO FORBEAR.

forborne (foᵗbo·ᵣn) *p. p.* de TO FORBEAR.

force (foᵗs) *s.* fuerza [en todas sus acepciones]: *by* ~, a la fuerza, por fuerza; *by* ~ *of,* a fuerza de; ~ *pump,* FÍS. bomba impelente. *2* fig. brío, fuego, animación. *3* peso, importancia. *4* poder, virtud, eficacia. *5* validez, vigencia. *6 in* ~, en vigor, envigencia; en gran número, en masa. *7* MIL. fuerza, cuerpo: *armed forces,* fuerzas armadas.

force (to) *tr.* forzar. *2* obligar, constreñir: *to* ~ *away,* obligar a alejarse; *to* ~ *back,* obligar a retroceder. *3* esforzar [la voz]. *4* imponer, obligar a aceptar o soportar. *5* obtener, arrancar [por fuerza o violencia]. *6* meter a la fuerza, clavar, encajar. *7* COC. rellenar. *8* AGR. hacer crecer o madurar de prisa. *9* MEC. impulsar. *10 to* ~ *one's way,* abrirse paso. *11 to* ~ *the issue,* hacer que algo se discuta o resuelva pronto.

forced (-t) *adj.* forzado. *2* forzoso.

forceful (-ful) *adj.* fuerte, poderoso, eficaz; violento.

forcemeat (-mɪt) *s.* COC. relleno, picadillo.

forceps (-eps) *s.* CIR. fórceps.

forcible (-ibøl) *adj.* fuerte, potente, enérgico, eficaz. *2* poderoso, concluyente, de mucho peso. *3* violento.

forcibly (-ibli) *adv.* fuertemente, poderosamente. *2* violentamente, a la fuerza.

forcing (-ing) *s.* forzamiento, compulsión. *2* acción de hacer crecer, madurar, etc., de prisa.

ford (foᵗd) *s.* vado. *2* poét. río, riachuelo.

ford (to) *tr.* vadear, esguazar.

fore (fo·øᵣ) *adj.* anterior, delantero. *2* MAR. de proa. *3 adv.* MAR. en la proa o hacia ella. *4 s.* frente, parte delantera: *to the* ~, presente, a la vista. *5* MAR. proa.

fore-and-aft *adj.* MAR. de cuchillo [vela].

forearm (fo·øraᵗm) *s.* antebrazo.

forebode (to) (foøᵗbou·d) *tr.-intr.* pronosticar, presagiar. *2 tr.* prever, presentir.

foreboding (-ing) *s.* presagio, augurio. *2* presentimiento.

forecast (fo·øᵗkæst) *s.* pronóstico, previsión, proyecto, plan.

forecast (to) (foøᵗkæ·st) *tr.* pronosticar, prever, calcular. *2* anunciar [ser signo de]. ¶ Pret. y p. p.: *forecast* o *-ted.*

forecastle (fo·øᵗkæsøl) *s.* MAR. castillo [de proa].

foreclose (to) (foøᵗclou·š) *tr.* excluir. *2* privar, impedir. *3* cerrar de antemano.

foredoom (to) (-du·m) *tr.* destinar, predestinar, condenar de antemano.

forefather (fo·øᵗfadøᵣ) *s.* abuelo, antepasado.

forefinger (-fingøᵣ) *s.* dedo índice.

forefoot (-fut) *s.* pata delantera, mano.

forefront (-frønt) *s.* delantera, primera fila, vanguardia.

forego (to) (gou·) *tr.* preceder, ir delante. *2 tr.-intr.* TO FORGO. ¶ Pret.: *forewent;* p. p.: *foregone.*

foregoing (-ing) *adj.* anterior, precedente.

foregone (-gon) *p. p.* de TO FOREGO. *2 adj.* ~ *conclusion,* prejuicio; resultado seguro, previsible.

foreground (-graund) *s.* PERSP. primer plano o término.

forehand (-jænd) *s.* ventja. *2* cuartos delanteros [del caballo]. *3 adj.* delantero. *4* adelantado, anticipado. *5* dado con la mano vuelta hacia adelante.

forehead (-jed) *s.* ANAT. frente.

foreign (fa·rin) *adj.* extranjero, exterior: ~ *trade,* comercio exterior; *Foreign Office* (Ingl.), ministerio de asuntos exteriores; *Foreign Service* (E.U.), servicio diplomático y consular. *2* forastero, extraño. *3* extraño, ajeno.

foreigner (-øᵣ) *s.* extranjero [pers.].

forejudge (to) (foøᵗdÿø·dÿ) *tr.* prejuzgar.

foreknow (to) (-nou·) *tr.* preconocer, prever.

foreknowledge (-lidÿ) *s.* presciencia.

foreland (fo·øᵗlænd) *s.* GEOGR. cabo, promontorio. *2* tierra de enfrente.

foreleg (-leg) *s.* brazo, pata delantera.

forelock (-lak) *s.* mechón de pelo que cae sobre la frente; copete [del caballo]. *2* MEC. chaveta.

foreman (-mæn) *s.* capataz, encargado, mayoral. *2* IMPR. regente. *3* DER. presidente del jurado.

foremast (-mast) *s.* MAR. trinquete [palo].

foremost (-moust) *adj.* delantero. *2* primero, principal.

forename (-neim) *s.* nombre de pila.

forenoon (-nun) *s.* la mañana.

forensic (fore·nsik) *adj.* forense: ~ *medicine,* medicina legal.

foreordain (to) (foøroᵗdei·n) *tr.* preordinar.

forereach (to) (fo·øriʧ) *tr.* alcanzar, dejar atrás.

forreun (to) (fo·ᵗrø·n) *tr.* preceder. *2* anunciar, presagiar.

forerunner (-øᵣ) *s.* predecesor. *2* precursor. *3* anuncio, presagio. *4* mensajero, heraldo.

foresail (fo·øᵗseil) *s.* MAR. trinquete [vela].

foresee (to) (foøᵗsi·) *tr.* prever, antever.

foreseer (-øᵣ) *s.* previsor.

foreshadow (to) (foøᵗshæ·dou) *tr.* prefigurar, simbolizar.

foreshorten (to) (foøᵗsho·ᵗtøn) *tr.* B. ART. escorzar.

foreshortening (-ning) *s.* B. ART. escorzo.

foresight (fo·øᵗsait) *s.* previsión, presciencia, perspicacia. *2* providencia, prudencia.

foreskin (-kin) *s.* ANAT. prepucio.

forest (fo·rist) *s.* bosque, selva, monte: ~ *ranger* (E.U.), guarda forestal.

forest (to) *tr.* arbolar.

forestal (-al) *adj.* forestal.

forestall (to) (foøᵗsto·l) *tr.* anticiparse a; prevenir; impedir. *2* anticipar.

forester (fo·ristøᵣ) *s.* guardabosque. *2* silvicultor. *3* habitante del bosque [pers. o animal].

forestry (-ri) *s.* silvicultura.

foretaste (foøᵗtei·st) *s.* anticipo, gusto, goce o conocimiento anticipado.

foretaste (to) *tr.* gustar o conocer de antemano.

foretell (to) (-te·l) *tr.* predecir, pronosticar.

foreteller (-øᵣ) *s.* vaticinador, profeta.

forethought (-zot) *s.* providencia, previsión. *2* premeditación.

foretoken (-tou·køn) *s.* presagio; señal anunciadora.

foretoken (to) *tr.* anunciar, prefigurar.

foretop (fo·øᵗtap) *s.* MAR. cofa del trinquete.

forever (fore·vøᵣ) *adv.* siempre, para siempre, por siempre.

forewarn (to) (foøʳuo·ʳn) *tr.* prevenir, advertir, avisar.

forewoman (fo·øʳwumæn) *s.* encargada, primera oficiala.

foreword (-uøʳd) *s.* prefacio, prólogo.

forfeit (fo·ʳfit) *s.* pena, multa, comiso. *2* pérdida legal de una cosa por incumplimiento de un contrato, etc. *3* prenda [en los juegos]: *game of forfeits,* juego de prendas.

forfeit (to) *tr.* perder [algo] como pena o castigo.

forfeiture (fo·ʳfichuʳ) *s.* pérdida de derechos, confiscación, multa.

forgather (foʳgæ·døʳ) *intr.* reunirse.

forge (oʳdỹ) *s.* forja, fragua; herrería.

forge (to) *tr.* forjar, fraguar [metal]. *2* forjar, inventar [mentiras, etc.]. *3* falsificar [documentos, una firma]. *4 intr. to ~ ahead,* avanzar despacio y con esfuerzo.

forger (-øʳ) *s.* forjador. *2* falsificador, falsario.

forgery (-ri) *s.* falsificación.

forget (to) (foʳge·t) *tr.-intr.* olvidar, olvidarse de, olvidársele a uno; descuidar: *~ it,* déjelo, no se preocupe. *2 ref. to ~ oneself,* olvidarse de sí mismo; abstraerse; perder la dignidad, el dominio de sí mismo; desmedirse, propasarse. ¶ Pret.: *forgot;* p. p.: *forgotten.*

forgetful (-ful) *adj.* olvidado [de algo]. *2* olvidadizo.

forgetfulness (-nis) *s.* olvido, descuido.

forget-me-not *s.* BOT. nomeolvides, miosotis.

forgive (to) (foʳgi·v) *tr.* perdonar; dispensar. *2* condonar, remitir, indultar.

forgiveness (-nis) *s.* perdón, remisión. *2* misericordia, clemencia.

forgo (to) (foʳgou·) *tr.* abandonar, renunciar a, privarse de. ¶ Pret.: *forwent;* p.p.: *forgone.*

forgot (foʳga·t) *pret.* de TO FORGET.

forgotten (foʳga·tøn) *p. p.* de TO FORGET.

fork (foʳk) *s.* tenedor [utensilio]. *2* horca, horcón, horqueta, horquilla. *3* bifurcación. *4* confluencia [de ríos]. *5* horcadura.

fork (to) *tr.* ahorquillar. *2 fam. to ~ out* o *over,* entregar, pagar. *3 intr.* ahorquillarse, bifurcarse.

forked (fo·ʳkt) *adj.* ahorquillado, bifurcado.

forlorn (foʳlo·ʳn) *adj.* abandonado, desamparado. *2* triste. *3* desesperado. *4 ~ hope,* empresa desesperada.

form (foʳm) *s.* forma [en sus principales acepciones]: *in due ~,* en debida forma; *to be in ~,* estar en forma. *2* proceder: *bad ~,* mala educación. *3* fórmula, formalidad, etiqueta: *for form's sake,* por pura fórmula. *4* modelo, patrón, horma, molde. *5* formulario, impreso [para llenar]. *6* banco [asiento largo]; sección de una clase [en una escuela].

form (to) *tr.* formar. *2 intr.* formarse. *3* MIL. formar.

formal (-al) *adj.* formal [rel. a la forma]. *2* solemne; de cumplido, de etiqueta: *~ attire,* vestido de etiqueta; *~ call,* visita de cumplido. *3* rígido, metódico. *4* ceremonioso, etiquetero. *5* formulario.

formalism (-išm) *s.* formalismo.

formalist (-ist) *s.* formalista.

formality (-iti) *s.* formalidad, requisito. *2* ceremonia, etiqueta, cumplido. *3* solemnidad; formalismo.

formalize (to) (-aiš) *tr.* formalizar. *2 intr.* mostrarse ceremonioso.

format (fo·ʳmat) *s.* formato, forma [de un libro].

formation (foʳmei·shøn) *s.* formación. *2* disposición, estructura.

former (fo·ʳmøʳ) *adj.* anterior, pasado, precedente. *2* antiguo, que fue, ex: *his ~ teacher,* su antiguo maestro. *3 pron. the ~,* aquél, el primero [de dos]. *4 s.* creador, formador. *5* horma, molde.

formerly (-li) *adv.* anteriormente, antes. *2* antiguamente, en otros tiempos.

formic (fo·ʳmik) *adj.* QUÍM. fórmico.

formication (fo·ʳmikei·shøn) *s.* MED. formicación.

formidable (fo·ʳmidabøl) *adj.* formidable, terrible.

formless (fo·ʳmlis) *adj.* informe caótico.

formula (fo·ʳmiula) *s.* fórmula.

formulary (-eri) *adj.s.* formulario.

formulate (to) (-eit) *tr.* formular.

formulism (-išm) *s.* formulismo.

fornicate (to) (fo·ʳnikeit) *intr.* fornicar.

fornicate(d (fo·ʳnikeit(id) *adj.* ARQ. abovedado.

fornication (fo·ʳnikei·shøn) *s.* fornicación.

forsake (to) (foʳsei·k) *tr.* abandonar, desamparar. *2* apostatar, renegar de. *3* desechar, renunciar, dejar. ¶ Pret.: *forsook;* p. p.: *forsaken.*

forsaken (-øn) *p. p.* de TO FORSAKE.

forsook (foʳsu·k) *pret.* de TO FORSAKE.

forsooth (foʳsu·z) *adv.* ciertamente, en verdad.

forswear (to) (foʳsue·øʳ) *tr.* abjurar, renunciar. *2 to ~ oneself,* perjurarse. ¶ Pret.: *forswore;* p. p.: *forsworn.*

fort (foʳt) *s.* fuerte, fortaleza.

forte (fo·ʳtei) *adj.-s.* MÚS. forte. *? s.* fuerte [aquello en ue sobresale uno].

forth (foʳz) *adv.* delante, adelante. *2* en adelante: *from that day ~,* de aquel día en adelante. *3* fuera, afuera, a la vista: *to go ~,* salir. *4 and so ~,* y así sucesivamente, etcétera.

forthcoming (-kø·ming) *adj.* venidero, próximo, que viene. *2* disponible.

forthwith (-uid) *adv.* inmediatamente.

fortieth (fo·ʳtiøz) *adj.-s.* cuadragésimo. *2* cuarentavo. *3 adj.* cuarenta [ordinal].

fortification (foʳtifikei·shøn). *s.* fortificación, fortalecimiento. *2* MIL. fortificación.

fortify (to) (-fai) *tr.* fortificar. *2* fortalecer. *3* reforzar. *4* confirmar, corroborar. *5 intr.* MIL. hacer fortificaciones. ¶ Pret. y p. p.: *fortified.*

fortitude (-tiud) *s.* fortaleza [de ánimo], firmeza, valor.

fortnight (fo·ʳtnait) *s.* quincena, dos semanas.

fortress (fo·ʳtris) *s.* fortaleza, fuerte, ciudadela.

fortuitous (foʳtiu·itøs) *adj.* fortuito, casual.

fortuity (foʳtiu·iti) *s.* calidad de fortuito. *2* caso fortuito.

fortunate (fo·ʳchunit) *adj.* afortunado, feliz.

fortune (fo·ʳchun) *s.* fortuna, suerte, destino: *to tell one's ~,* decirle a uno la buenaventura. *2* fortuna, caudal: *~ hunter,* cazador de dotes.

fortuneteller (-teløʳ) *s.* adivino.

forty (fo·ʳti) *adj.-s.* cuarenta.

forum (fo·røm) *s.* foro [plaza pública, tribunal].

forward (fo·ʳuøʳd) *adj.* delantero. *2* precoz, adelantado. *3* que se hace hacia adelante. *4* POL. avanzado. *5* dispuesto, ansioso. *6* atrevido, descarado. *7* COM. futuro. *8 adv.* adelante; en adelante; más allá: *from this time ~,* de aquí en adelante. *9* FÚTBOL. *centre ~,* delantero centro.

forward (to) *tr.* enviar, remitir, expedir; reexpedir, hacer seguir. *2* apresurar, activar. *3* adelantar, promover, patrocinar.

forwarder (-døʳ) *s.* COM. agente expedidor.

forwardness (-nis) *s.* adelantamiento, progreso. *2*

prontitud, ansia. *3* precocidad. *4* audacia. *5* descaro, impertinencia.

forwards (-s) *adv.* adelante, hacia adelante.

fossa (fa·ssa) *s.* ANAT. fosa.

fosse (fos) *s.* foso.

fossil (fa·sil) *adj.-s.* fósil. *2* pers. anticuada.

fossilization (-išei·shøn) *s.* fosilización.

fossilize (to) (-aiš) *tr.* convertir en fósil, petrificar. *2 intr.* fosilizarse.

fossorial (foso·rial) *adj.* ZOOL. cavador.

foster (fo·stø*r*) *adj.* de leche; adoptivo, de adopción; ~ *child*, hijo de leche, hijo adoptivo; ~ *home*, hogar de adopción.

foster (to) *tr.* criar, nutrir. *2* alentar, sostener, fomentar.

fosterling (-ling) *s.* hijo de leche, hijo adoptivo.

fought (fot) *pret.* y *p. p.* de TO FIGHT.

foul (faul) *adj.* sucio, asqueroso, inmundo, repugnante. *2* fétido, mal oliente. *3* viciado [aire]. *4* malo [tiempo]. *5* contrario [viento]. *6* malo, injusto, engañoso, obsceno. *7* enredado, atascado, obstruido. *8* sucio, no conforme a las reglas del juego: ~ *play*, juego sucio; fig. dolo, traición. *9* ~ *copy*, borrador. *10* *s.* acción de ensuciar; de chocar o enredarse: *to fall* ~ o *run* ~ *of*, MAR. abordar [un buque a otro]; enredarse en. *11* DEP. falta, juego sucio.

foul (to) *tr.* ensuciar, emporcar, manchar. *2* atascar, obstruir. *3* MAR. abordar, chocar con, enredarse en. *4* DEP. jugar sucio contra. *5* *intr.* ensuciarse. *6* MAR. enredarse; abordarse. *7* DEP. infringir las reglas.

foulard (fula·*r*d) *s.* fular.

foul-mouthed *adj.* malhablado.

found (faund) *pret.* y *p. p.* de TO FIND.

found (to) *tr.* fundar. *2* METAL., VID. fundir.

foundation (-ei·shøn) *s.* fundación [acción; institución]. *2* fundación, base, cimiento: ~ *stone*, primera piedra. *3* MEC. asiento, pie. *4* ING. firme. *5* COST. forro, refuerzo.

founder (fau·ndø*r*) *s.* fundador. *2* fundidor.

founder (to) *tr.* MAR. hundir, echar a pique. *2 intr.* hundirse, desplomarse. *3* MAR. irse a pique. *4* tropezar, caer; despearse [el caballo]. *5* fracasar.

foundling (-ling) *s.* expósito, inclusero.

foundress (-res) *s.* fundadora.

foundry (-ri) *s.* fundición [de metales]. *2* fundición, fundería.

fount (faunt) *s.* fuente, manantial.

fountain (fa·untin) *s.* fuente, manantial. *2* origen, principio. *3* ~ *pen*, estilográfica.

four (fo·ø*r*) *adj.-s.* cuatro; ~ *o'clock*, las cuatro; *on all fours*, a gatas.

four-cycle *adj.* MEC. de cuatro tiempos.

four-flush (to) *intr.* pop. fanfarronear, fachendear.

fourfold (-fould) *adj.* cuádruple, cuádruplo.

four-handed *adj.* cuadrúmano. *2* para cuatro jugadores. *3* MÚS. a cuatro manos.

four-in-hand *s.* carruaje tirado por cuatro caballos.

fouur-motor *adj.* AVIA. cuadrimotor.

four-o'clock *s.* BOT. arrebolera, dondiego de noche.

fourposter (-poustø*r*) *s.* cama imperial.

fourscore (-sko*r*) *adj.* ochenta.

foursome (-søm) *s.* DEP. partida de dos contra dos. *2* DEP. conjunto de cuatro jugadores.

foursquare (-skue*r*) *adj.* cuadrado. *2* franco, sincero. *3* firme, constante.

fourteen (fo*r*tɪ·n) *adj.-s.* catorce.

fourteenth (-z) *adj.* catorceno, decimocuarto, catorce. *2 adj.-s.* catorzavo.

fourth (-fo·*r*z) *adj.-s.* cuarto. *2* cuatro [en las fechas]. *3* MÚS. cuarta.

fourthly (-li) *adv.* en cuarto lugar.

fowl (faul) *s.* gallo, gallina, pollo. *2* ave [en general]. *3* carne de ave.

fowl (to) *intr.* cazar aves.

fowler (fau·lø*r*) *s.* cazador [de aves].

fowling (-ing) *s.* caza de aves: ~ *piece*, escopeta.

fox (faks) *s.* ZOOL. zorro, zorra, raposo, raposa: ~ *terrier*, foxterrier [perro]; ~ *trot*, trote corto; foxtrot [baile]. *2* piel de zorro. *3* zorro, taimado.

fox (to) *intr.* (E.U.) cazar zorras. *2* fingir, raposear. *4* ponerse rojizo, mancharse [el papel]. *5* *tr.* engañar con astucia.

foxglove (-glouv) *s.* BOT. digital, dedalera.

foxhole (-joul) *s.* zorrera. *2* MIL. trinchera individual.

foxhound (-jaund) *s.* perro raposero.

foxiness (-inis) *s.* astucia, zorrería.

foxish (-ish) *adj.* zorruno. *2* astuto.

foxstail (-teil) *s.* BOT. rabo de zorra.

foxy (-i) *adj.* zorruno. *2* del color del zorro. *3* taimado. *4* descolorido, manchado.

foyer (fuaye·) *s.* salón de entrada [de un hotel, etc.]. *2* TEAT. salón de descanso.

fracas (frei·kas) *s.* alboroto, riña, zacapela.

fraction (fræ·kshøn) *s.* fragmento, porción. *2* fam. poquito. *3* LITURG. fracción [del pan]. *4* MAT. fracción, quebrado. *5* QUÍM. fracción.

fraction (to) *tr.* fraccionar.

fractional (-al) *adj.* fraccionario. *2* QUÍM. fraccionado.

fractionate (-neit) *tr.* fraccionar. *2* QUÍM. separar por destilación fraccionada.

fractious (fræ·kshøs) *adj.* quisquilloso, enojado. *2* rebelón.

fracture (fræ·kchø*r*) *s.* fractura, rompimiento. *2* CIR., GEOL. fractura.

fracture (to) *tr.* fracturar. *2 intr.* fracturarse.

fragile (fræ·dyil) *adj.* frágil. *2* quebradizo, delicado.

fragility (fradyi·liti) *s.* fragilidad.

fragment (fræ·gmønt) *s.* fragmento, trozo.

fragment (to) *intr.* fragmentarse.

fragrance, cy (frei·grans, -i) *s.* fragancia.

fragrant (-grant) *adj.* fragante, oloroso.

frail (freil) *adj.* frágil. *2* deleznable, endeble. *3* débil [física o moralmente].

frailty (-ti) *s.* fragilidad. *2* debilidad, flaqueza.

fraise (freš) *s.* FORT. frisa.

frame (freim) *s.* armazón, armadura, esqueleto. *2* cuerpo [del hombre o del animal]. *3* bastidor, marco, cerco, cuadro: ~ *saw*, sierra del bastidor. *4* entramado. *5* bastidor [para bordar]. *6* montura [de unas gafas]. *7* MEC. bancada. *8* MAR. cuaderna. *9* MAR. costillaje. *10* HORT. abrigo encristalado. *11* IMPR. chibalete. *12* MEC., TEJ., HIL. nombre de varias máquinas. *13* constitución, estructura. *14* sistema [de gobierno]. *15* ~ *of mind*, humor, estado de ánimo.

frame (to) *tr.* fabricar, formar, construir. *2* encuadrar, enmarcar. *3* armar, montar. *4* ajustar, adaptar. *5* idear, trazar, forjar, tramar. *6* expresar, formular, redactar. *7* *to* ~ *up*, amañar, preparar fraudulentamente [esp. las pruebas para incriminar a un inocente].

frame-up *s.* cosa preparada fraudulentamente, amaño. *2* arreglo, trama [para incriminar a un inocente].

framework (-uø^{r}k) *s.* armazón, esqueleto. 2 CARP. entramado. 3 sistema [de gobierno, etc.].
franc (frænk) *s.* franco [moneda].
France (fra·ns) *n. pr.* GEOGR. Francia.
Frances (fræ·nsis) *n. pr. f.* Francisca.
franchise (fræ·nchaiš) *s.* franqueza, exención, privilegio. 2 asilo, refugio. 3 derecho político.
Francis (fræ·nsis) *n. pr. m.* Francisco.
Franciscan (fransi·skan) *adj.-s.* franciscano.
francolin (fræ·nkolin) *s.* ORN. francolín.
Francophile (fræ·nkofail) *adj.-s.* francófilo.
Frank (frænk) *s.* franco [del pueblo franco]. 2 *n. pr. dim.* de FRANCIS.
frank *adj.* franco [sincero, claro, no disimulado]. 2 *s.* franquicia postal.
frank (to) *tr.* franquear, exceptuar de pago.
frankfurter (-fø^{r}tø^r) *s.* salchicha de Francfort.
frankincense (-insens) *s.* incienso, olíbano.
frankness (-nis) *adj.* franqueza, sinceridad.
frantic (fræ·ntik) *adj.* frenético, furioso, desesperado.
frappé (fræpei·) *s.* helado de zumo de frutas.
fraternal (fratø·^{r}nal) *adj.* fraternal, fraterno.
fraternity (-iti) *s.* fraternidad. 2 gremio, congregación, hermandad. 3 (E.U.) club de estudiantes.
fraternize (to) (fræ·tø^{r}naiš) *intr.* fraternizar.
fratricidal (frætrisai·dal) *adj.* fratricida.
fratricide (fræ·trisaid) *s.* fratricidio. 2 fratricida.
fraud (frod) *s.* fraude, dolo, engaño. 2 farsante, impostor, timador.
fraudulence, cy (fro·diuløns, -si) *s.* fraudulencia, mala fe.
fraudulent (-ont) *adj.* fraudulento, engañoso.
fraught (frot) *adj.* lleno, cargado, preñado, grávido.
fraxinella (fræksine·la) *s.* BOT. fresnillo.
fray (frei) *s.* riña, pelea. 2 raedura, deshilachado.
fray (to) *tr.* rozar, raer, desgastar. 2 *intr.* deshilacharse.
frayed (-d) *adj.* raído, deshilachado.
freak (frɪk) *s.* capricho, antojo, rareza. 2 fenómeno, monstruosidad; ~ *of nature*, aborto de la naturaleza.
freakish (-ish) *adj.* caprichoso, antojadizo. 2 fantástico, raro, extravagante.
freckle (fre·køl) *s.* peca. 2 mota, pinta.
freckle (to) *tr.* motear. 2 *intr.* llenarse de pecas.
freckled (fre·køld) *adj.* pecoso. 2 moteado.
Fred (fred), **Freddy** (-i) *n. pr. dim.* Federiquito.
Frederica (fre·dørika) *n. pr. f.* Federica.
Frederick (fre·dørik) *n. pr. m.* Federico.
free (frɪ) *adj.* libre; ~ *and easy*, campechano; despreocupado; ~ *hand*, carta blanca; ~ *lance*, condotiero, franco, tirador, hombre independiente; ~ *love*, amor libre; ~ *thought*, librepensamiento; ~ *trade*, librecambio; ~ *will*, libre albedrío; propia voluntad. 2 en libertad. 3 franco, exento: ~ *port*, puerto franco; ~ *on board*, COM. franco a bordo. 4 gratuito, de balde. 5 espontáneo, voluntario, discrecional. 6 permitido. 7 liberal, generoso: *to be* ~ *with*, dar abundantemente. 8 franco, comunicativo. 9 suelto, desembarazado; atrevido, desenvuelto. 10 desocupado, vacante. 11 flojo, suelto, desatado. 12 *adv.* libremente. 13 gratis.
free (to) *tr.* libertar, librar. 2 manumitir. 3 rescatar. 4 eximir. 5 desembarazar; zafar, soltar.
freebooter (-butø^r) *s.* filibustero, pirata.
freedman (-dmæn) *pl. s.* liberto.
freedom (-døm) *s.* libertad; ~ *of the press*, libertad

de imprenta; ~ *of worship*, libertad de cultos. 2 independencia. 3 exención, inmunidad, privilegio. 4 familiaridad atrevida. 5 facilidad, soltura. 6 libertad de usar de una cosa.
freehand (-jænd) *adj.* hecho a pulso [dibujo].
freehanded (-jændid) *adj.* liberal, dadivoso.
freehearted (-ja^{r}tid) *adj.* franco, abierto. 2 generoso.
freehold (-jould) *s.* DER. dominio absoluto.
freely (-li) *adv.* libremente. 2 espontáneamente. 3 profusamente, generosamente.
freeman (-mæn) *s.* hombre libre, ciudadano.
Freemason (-meisøn) *s.* francmasón.
Freemasonry (-meisønri) *s.* francmasonería.
freer (-ø^r) *s.* libertador.
free-spoken *adj.* franco, sin reserva.
freestone (-stoun) *adj.-s.* BOT. abridero [fruto].
freethinker (-zinkø^r) *s.* librepensador.
freeze (frɪ·š) *s.* helada.
freeze (to) *tr.* helar, congelar. 2 aterrar, dejar frío. 3 COM. congelar [créditos, etc.]. 4 *to* ~ *out*, excluir, deshacerse [de uno], tratándole con frialdad, quitándole la clientela, etc. 5 *impers.* helar. 6 *intr.* helarse, congelarse. 7 *fig.* quedarse helado [de susto, etc.]. ¶ Pret.: *froze*; p. p.: *frozen*.
freezer (-ø^r) *s.* helador. 2 heladora, sorbetera; congelador.
freezing (-ing) *adj.* glacial. 2 frigorífico. 3 ~ *point*, punto de congelación.
freight (freit) *s.* COM. carga [que se transporta]; porte; ~ *train*, tren de carga o de mercancías; *by* ~ FERROC. a pequeña velocidad. 2 flete.
freight (to) *tr.* cargar [un buque, etc.]. 2 MAR. fletar. 3 alquilar [para el transporte]. 4 transportar [por buque, tren, etc.].
freightage (-idý) *s.* cargamento. 2 flete. 3 transporte, porte.
freighter (-ø^r) *s.* fletador, cargador. 2 buque de carga.
French (french) *adj.-s.* francés: ~ *bean*, alubia, judía; ~ *horn*, MÚS. trompa; ~ *roof*, mansarda; ~ *window*, puerta vidriera de dos hojas; *to take* ~ *leave*, despedirse a la francesa.
Frenchify (to) (-ifai) *tr.* afrancesar.
Frenchman (-mæn) *s.* francés [hombre].
Frenchwoman (-wumæn) *f.* francesa [mujer].
frenetic (frine·tik) *adj.* frenético.
frenzied (fre·nšid) *adj.* frenético. 2 enloquecido.
frenzy (fre·nši) *s.* frenesí, locura, desvarío.
frequency (frɪ·kuønsi) *s.* frecuencia.
frequent (frɪ·kuønt) *adj.* frecuente. 2 habitual, regular, persistente.
frequent (to) (frikue·nt) *tr.* frecuentar. 2 tratarse, relacionarse con.
frequentation (-ei·shøn) *s.* frecuentación. 2 trato, relación.
fresco (fre·skou) *s.* PINT. fresco.
fresco (to) *tr.* pintar al fresco.
fresh (fre·sh) *adj.* fresco, nuevo, reciente; ~ *from*, recién salido, llegado, etc., de. 2 fresco [flor, fruta, carne, etc.; tez color]. 3 fresco [viento]. 4 fresco [algo frío]. 5 puro [aire]. 6 tierno [pan]. 7 nuevo [otro]. 8 descansado, con nuevas fuerzas. 9 inexperto, bisoño. 10 fresco, descarado. 11 ~ *water*, agua dulce. 12 s. avenida, riada.
freshen (-øn) *tr.* refrescar. 2 *intr.* refrescarse. 3 refrescar [el viento]. 4 adquirir frescura, lozanía.
freshet (-it) *s.* avenida, riada, inundación.
freshman (-mæn) *s.* novato.
freshness (-nis) *s.* frescura, frescor. 2 lozanía, ver-

dor. *3* pureza [del aire]. *4* novedad. *5* frescura, descaro.

fres-water *adj.* de agua dulce.

fret (fret) *s.* roce, rozamiento. *2* raedura, desgaste. *3* impaciencia, irritación, preocupación. *4* greca. *5* B. ART. relieve; calado: ~ *saw*, segueta. *6* MÚS. traste.

fret (to) *tr.* rozar, raer, roer, desgastar. *2* agitar [las aguas]. *3* impacientar, irritar, preocupar. *4* adornar con grecas, relieves o calados. *5 intr.* rozarse, desgastarse. *6* irritarse, impacientarse, lamentarse. *7* agitarse [las aguas]. ¶ Pret. y p. p.: *fretted;* ger.: *fretting.*

fretful (-ful) *adj.* irritable, enojadizo; malhumorado, nervioso, impaciente.

fretwork (-uøʳk) *s.* grecas. *2* entrelazado, calado.

Freudian (froi·dian) *adj.-s.* freudiano.

friable (frai·abøl) *adj.* friable.

friar (frai·øʳ) *s.* fraile, monje.

friary (-i) *s.* convento de frailes. *2 adj.* frailesco.

fribble (-fri·bøl) *adj.* frívolo, vano.

fribble (to) *intr.* tontear, bobear.

fricassee (frikasɪ·) *s.* COC. fricasé.

fricative (fri·kativ) *adj.* FONÉT. fricativo.

friction (fri·kshøn) *s.* fricción, rozamiento, roce, frote. *2* MEC. fricción. *3* fig. rozamiento, desavenencia. *4* ELECT. ~ *tape*, cinta aislante.

Friday (frai·di) *s.* viernes.

fried (fraid) *p. p.* de TO FRY, freído. *2 adj.* frito: ~ *egg*, huevo frito o estrellado.

friend (frend) *s.* amigo, amiga: *to be friends with*, ser amigo de; *to make friends with*, trabar amistad con, hacerse amigo de; reconciliarse. *2* partidario; aliado. *3* allegado. *4* (con may.) cuáquero.

friendless (fre·ndlis) *adj.* desvalido, sin amigos.

friendliness (fre·ndlinis) *s.* amigabilidad, afabilidad, cordialidad; disposición favorable.

friendly (fre·ndli) *adj.* amistoso, amigable. *2* benévolo, favorable, propicio.

friendship (fre·ndship) *s.* amistad.

Friesland (fri·slænd) *n. pr.* GEOGR. Frisia.

frieze (frīš) *s.* TEJ. risa. *2* ARQ. friso.

frieze (to) *tr.* TEJ. frisar.

frigate (fri·git) *s.* MAR. fragata. *2* ORN. ~ *bird*, rabihorcado.

fright (frait) *s.* miedo, terror; susto, espanto. *2* esperpento, adefesio, espantajo.

frighten (to) (frai·tøn) *tr.* asustar, espantar: *to* ~ *away*, ahuyentar. *2 intr.* asustarse.

frightful (frai·tful) *adj.* espantoso, terrible. *2* horroroso, feísimo. *3* fam. tremendo, enorme.

frigid (fri·dÿid) *adj.* frígido, helado, glacial. *2* frío [sin animación, sin vivacidad; sin cordialidad].

frigidity (friÿi·diti) *s.* frigidez, frialdad. *2* fig. frialdad [falta de ardor, de cordialidad].

frigorific (frigori·fik) *adj.* frigorífico.

frill (fril) *s.* COST. adorno alechugado; chorrera, faralá. *2 pl.* fam. arrequives, ringorrangos.

frill (to) *tr.* alechugar. *2* adornar con chorreras, faralaes, etc. *3 intr.* escarolarse.

fringe (frindÿ) *s.* franja, fleco, orla, cairel. *2* flequillo. *3* borde, margen, orilla.

fringe (to) *tr.* orlar, adornar con flecos o franjas; estar en el borde u orilla de.

fringillid (frindÿi·lid) *s.* ORN. fringílido.

frippery (fri·pøri) *s.* perifollos. *2* elegancia afectada, cursilería. *3 adj.* despreciable, frívolo.

frisk (frisk) *s.* retozo, brinco. *2* pop. cacheo.

frisk (to) *intr.* retozar, triscar, cabriolar, brincar. *2 tr.* pop. cachear.

frisky (fri·ski) *adj.* juguetón, alegre, vivaracho.

fritter (fri·tøʳ) *s.* frisuelo, buñuelo.

fritter (to) *tr.* hacer trizas, desmenuzar. *3 to* ~ *away*, malgastar, desperdiciar poco a poco.

frivolity (friva·liti) *s.* frivolidad.

frivolous (fri·vøløs) *adj.* frívolo. *2* vano, baladí.

frizz, frizzle (friš, fri·šøl) *s.* rizo, cosa rizada.

frizz, frizzle (to) *tr.* rizar. *2* encrespar, frisar.

fro (frou) *adv.* hacia atrás: *to and* ~, de un lado a otro; *to go to and* ~, ir y venir.

frock (frak) *s.* hábito [monacal]. *2* blusa [de pintor, etc.]. *3* vestido [de mujer o niño].

frock-coat *s.* levita [prenda].

frog (frag) *s.* ZOOL. rana. *2* ranilla [del caballo]. *3* ~ *in the throat*, ronquera. *4 t.* alarmar.

frolic (fra·lik) *s.* juego, retozo, travesura. *2* holgorio, diversión.

frolic (to) *intr.* juguetear, retozar, travesear; divertirse. ¶ Pret. y p. p.: *frolicked;* ger.: *-king.*

frolicsome (-søm) *adj.* juguetón, travieso, retozón.

from (frøm) *prep.* de, desde: ~ *afar*, de lejos, desde lejos. *2* de [indicando: origen; estado; separación, exclusión, disentimiento; modelo, modo]: *away* ~ *home*, lejos o fuera del hogar; ~ *nature*, del natural; ~ *now on*, de ahora en adelante. *3* de parte de. *4* a contar de. *5* según. *6* por, a causa de: ~ *kindness*, por bondad. *7 a: to take something away* ~, quitar algo a.

frond (frand) *s.* BOT. fronda, fronde.

frondescence (frønde·søns) *s.* BOT. foliación.

front (frønt) *s.* ANAT. frente. *2* rostro, semblante. *3* audacia, descaro. *4* apariencia [de riqueza, etc.]: *to put on a* ~, aparentar, hacer ostentación. *5* frente, fachada. *6* delantera. *7* MIL., POL. frente. *5* pechera [de camisa]. *9* paseo frente al mar. *10* frontalera [de la brida]. *11 in* ~, delante, en frente; de enfrente, frontero.

12 adj. delantero, anterior; frontero, frontal; ~ *door*, puerta principal; ~ *row*, delantera, primera fila.

front (to) *tr.* afrontar, hacer frente a, arrostrar. *2* mirar a, dar a. *3* aparecer delante de. *4* poner fachada a. *5 intr.* estar enfrente de; oponerse. *6 to* ~ *on*, dar a. *7 to* ~ *towards*, mirar hacia.

frontage (-frø·ntidÿ) *s.* terreno que da al mar, un camino, etc.

frontal (-al) *adj.* frontal. *2 s.* ANAT., ECLES. frontal. *3* ARQ. fachada.

frontier (frønti·øʳ) *s.* frontera, raya, confín. *2* fronteras de la civilización. *3 adj.* fronterizo.

frontiersman (frønti·øʳšɱæn) *s.* hombre de la frontera; colonizador, explorador.

frontispiece (frø·ntispɪs) *s.* ARQ. frontispicio, portada [de un libro].

frost (frost) *s.* helamiento. *2* escarcha, helada. *3* fig. indiferencia. *4* fam. fracaso.

frost (to) *tr.* helar, congelar. *2* cubrir de escarcha. *3* quemar [el frío las plantas]. *4* escarchar [frutas], alcorzar [pasteles]. *5* deslustrar [vidrio]. *6 intr.* helarse, cubrirse de escarcha.

frostbite (to) (fro·stbait) *tr.* helar, quemar, dañar [el frío, la helada]. ¶ Pret.: *frostbit;* p. p.: *-bitten.*

frostbitten (-bitøn) *adj.* helado; quemado, dañado [por la helada].

frosted (-id) *adj.* escarchado, alcorzado. *2* deslustrado, mate.

frosty (-i) *adj.* helado, glacial. *2* escarchado [cubierto de escarcha]. *3* canoso.

froth (fro·z) *s.* espuma. *2* espumajo. *3* bambolla.

froth (to) *tr.* producir espuma en. *2* cubrir de espuma. *3 intr.* espumar, espumajear.

frothy (-i) *adj.* espumoso, espumajoso. *2* vano, sin substancia.
froward (frou·waᵣd) *adj.* díscolo, indócil.
frowardness (-nis) *s.* indocilidad.
frown (fraun) *s.* ceño, entrecejo; enojo, rigor.
frown (to) *intr.* fruncir el entrecejo: *to ~ at*, on o *upon*, mirar con ceño, desaprobar.
frowning (-ing) *adj.* ceñudo, torvo, hosco.
frowzy (frau·ši) *adj.* sucio, desaliñado. *2* maloliente.
froze (frouš) *pret.* de TO FREEZE.
frozen (-n) *p. p.* de TO FREEZE.
fructiferous (frøkti·førøs) *adj.* fructífero.
fructification (frøktifikei·shøn) *s.* fructificación.
fructify (to) (frø·ktifai) *intr.* fructificar. *2* hacer fructífero; fertilizar. ¶ Pret. y p. p.: *fructified.*
fructose (frø·ktous) *s.* QUÍM. fructosa.
fructuous (frø·kshiuøs) *adj.* fructuoso.
frugal (fru·gal) *adj.* frugal.
frugality (frugæ·liti) *s.* frugalidad.
frugivorous (frudŷi·vørøs) *adj.* frugívoro.
fruit (frut) *s.* BOT. fruto. *2* fig. fruto [producto, consecuencia, resultado]. *3* fruta, frutas: *~ tree*, árbol frutal; *~ salad*, macedonia de frutas.
fruit (to) *intr.* fructificar, frutar.
fruitage (fru·tidŷ) *s.* fruta. *2* fruto, resultado, efecto.
fruit-bearing *adj.* frutal. *2* fructífero.
fruiter (-øᵣ) *s.* frutal. *2* buque frutero.
fruiterer (-ørøᵣ) *s.* frutero [vendedor].
fruitful (-ful) *adj.* fructífero, fructuoso. *2* prolífico. *3* fértil, abundante.
fruition (frui·shøn) *s.* fruición. *2* goce, posesión.
fruit-piece *s.* PINT. frutaje, frutero.
fruitless (fru·tlis) *adj.* infructuoso, estéril, vano.
frump (frømp) *s.* vieja anticuada, regañona. *2* mujer desaliñada.
frustrate (to) (frø·streit) *tr.* frustrar, desinflar. *2* burlar, hacer fracasar, molestar [a uno].
frustration (-ei·shøn) *s.* frustración, desbaratamiento, desconcierto. *2* fracaso, desenfado.
frustum (frø·støm) *s.* GEOM. tronco [de cono o pirámide].
frutescent (frute·sønt), **fruticose** (fru·tikous) *adj.* FOT. fruticoso.
fry (frai) *s.* freza, morralla, boliche [pececillos, pescado, menudo]: *small ~*, gente menuda.
fry (to) *tr.* COC. freír, saltear. *2* intr. freírse, asarse. *3* fig. estar agitado, hervir.
frying (frai·ing) *s.* freidura: *~ pan*, sartén.
fuchsia (fiu·shia) *s.* BOT. fucsia.
fuddle (to) (fø·døl) *tr.* achispar; confundir, atontar [con la bebida]. *2* intr. achisparse.
fudge (fødŷ) *s.* embuste. *2* dulce de chocolate.
fudge (to) *tr.* arreglar, amañar, inventar. *2* hacer chapuceramente. *3* intr. TO HEDGE 5.
fuel (fiu·øl) *s.* combustible, *~ oil*, acero pesado, fuel oil. *2* pábulo. *3* incentivo.
fugacious (fiugei·shøs) *adj.* fugaz. *2* evanescente.
fugacity (fiugæ·siti) *s.* fugacidad.
fugitive (fiu·dŷitiv) *adj.* fugitivo. *2* errante, vagabundo. *3* fugaz, pasajero; de intenso pasajero. *4 s.* fugitivo. *5* exilado.
fugue (fiug) *s.* MÚS. fuga.
fulcrum (fø·lkrøm) *s.* fulcro.
fulfil(l) (to) (fulfi·l) *tr.* cumplir, realizar, verificar, efectuar. *2* llenar, colmar.
fulfil(l)ment (-mønt) *s.* cumplimiento, desempeño, ejecución, realización. *2* colmo.
fulgent (fø·ldŷent) *adj.* fulgente, fúlguro.
fulgurate (to) (fø·lgiureit) *tr.* fulgurar.

fulgurite (-rait) *s.* fulgurita.
full (ful) *adj.* lleno, colmado, repleto, atascado: *~ house*, lleno [en un espectáculo]: *~ moon*, luna llena; *~ of fun*, chistoso, amigo de bromear. *2* cumplido, pleno, entero, completo, todo: *~ powers*, plenos poderes; *~ stop*, parada completa; GRAM. punto final; *~ time*, jornada completa; *at*, o *in*, *~ blast*, a pelno tiro; en plena actividad; *at ~ speed*, a toda velocidad; *in ~ swing*, en plena operación; *under ~ sail*, a toda vela. *3* plenario. *4* amplio, holgado. *5* absorto, embebido. *6* copioso, abundante. *7* detallado, extenso. *8* carnal [hermano]. *9* bravío [mar]. *10* tendido [galope]. *11* borracho. *12* ~ *age*, mayoría de edad. *13* ~ *dress*, traje de etiqueta, uniforme de gala. *14 adv.* enteramente, del todo, plenamente: *~ nine years*, nueve años cumplidos. *15* detalladamente. *16* de lleno, derechamente. *17 s.* lleno, colmo, plenitud; total, totalidad: *in ~*, por completo, detalladamente, sin abreviar.
full (to) *tr.* TEJ. abatanar, enfurtir.
full-blooded *adj.* de pura raza. *2* pletórico, rubicundo; vigoroso.
full-bodied *adj.* fuerte, espeso, aromático [vino].
fuller (-øᵣ) *s.* batanero: *fuller's earth*, tierra de batán, greda.
fullery (-i) *s.* batán [sitio donde se abatana].
full-faced *adj.* carilleno. *2* de rostro entero [retrato].
full-grown *adj.* crecido, hecho.
full-length *adj.* de cuerpo entero.
fulling (fu·ling) *s.* batanado: *~ mill*, batán.
fullish (-ish) *adj.* llenito, algo lleno.
fullness (-nis) *s.* llenura, plenitud, colmo. *2* copia, abundancia. *3* hartura, saciedad.
full-sized *adj.* de tamaño natural.
fully (-i) *adv.* plenamente, enteramente, completamente. *2* de lleno.
fulminant (-fø·lminant) *adj.* fulminante.
fulminate (-fø·lmineit) *s.* QUÍM. fulminato.
fulminate (to) (tr. fulminar. *2* hacer estallar. *3 intr.* estallar, denotar. *4 to ~ against*, tronar contra.
fulminating (-ing) *adj.* fulminante.
fulmination (-shøn) *s.* fulminación.
fulmine (to) (fø·lmin) *tr.* lanzar, fulminar.
fulsome (fu·lsøm) *adj.* insincero, bajo, vil, empalagoso [adulación, demostraciones de afecto].
fulvous (fø·lvøs) *adj.* leonado, amarillo rojizo.
fumarole (fiu·maroul) *s.* GEOL. fumarola.
fumble (to) (fø·mbøl) *intr.* buscar a tientas, revolver [buscando]. *2 to ~ along*, andar a tientas. *3 intr.-tr.* balbucear. *4 tr.* manosear, enredar con. *5* DEP. dejar caer [la pelota].
fume (fium) *s.* humo [esp. aromático]. *2* vaho, tufo, gas, vapor: *fumes of wine*, vapores del vino. *3* cólera, acaloramiento.
fume (to) *tr.* sahumar. *2* ahumar, fumigar. *3* exhalar [vapor, etc.]. *4 intr.* avahar, vahear, exhalar gases. *5* humear. *6* rabiar, encolerizarse, echar pestes.
fumigate (to) (fiu·migeit) *tr.* fumigar. *2* sahumar.
fumigation (-ei·shøn) *s.* fumigación. *2* sahumerio.
fumitory (fiu·mitori) *s.* BOT. fumaria, palomina.
fun (føn) *s.* broma, chacota, juego, diversión: *for ~*, en broma: *to have ~*, divertirse. *2* chiste, chanza. *3* cosa que divierte: *to be great ~*, ser muy divertido. *4* burla: *to make ~ of, to poke ~ at*, burlarse de, reírse de.
funambulist (fiunæ·mbiulist) *s.* funámbulo, volatinero.
function (føn·kshøn) *s.* función. | No tiene el sen-

tido de función de teatro o de guerra. 2 fiesta, reunión, acto. 3 ocupación, profesión.
function (to) *intr.* funcionar.
functional (-al) *adj.* funcional.
functionary (-eri) *s.* funcionario.
functionate (to) (-eit) *intr.* TO FUNCTION.
fund (fønd) *s.* fondo, caudal, capital. 2 acopio, reserva. 3 *pl.* fondos [dinero].
fund (to) *tr.* consolidar [una deuda].
fundament (fø·ndamønt) *s.* fundamento, base. 2 fam. ano; trasero.
fundamental (føndame·ntal) *adj.* fundamental. 2 *s.* fundamento, principio, parte esencial.
funded (føn·did) *adj.* consolidada [deuda].
funeral (fiu·nøral) *s.* entierro, sepelio; cortejo fúnebre. 2 exequias. 3 *adj.* funeral, fúnebre, mortuorio: ~ *service,* exequias.
funereal (fiuni·rial) *adj.* funerario. 2 fúnebre, triste.
fungi (fø·ndÿai) *pl.* BOT. hongos.
fungosity (fønga·siti) *s.* fungosidad.
fungous (fø·ngøs) *adj.* fungoso.
fungus *s.* BOT. hongo. 2 MED. fungosidad.
funicle (fiu·nikøl) *s.* funículo.
funicular (fiuni·kiula^r) *adj.* funicular.
funk (fønk) *s.* miedo, cobardía. 2 cobarde.
funk (to) *intr.* encogerse, arredrarse. 2 *tr.* asustar, arredrar.
funnel (fø·nøl) *s.* cañón [de chimenea]; chimenea [de vapor]. 2 embudo. 3 FUND. boca de carga.
funnies (the) (fø·nis) *m. pl.* la sección humorística [de un periódico].
funny (fø·ni) *adj.* cómico, gracioso, chistoso, divertido. 2 extraño, raro, curioso. 3 fam. ~ *bone,* punto sensible del codo.
fur (fø^r) *s.* piel [para abrigo o adorno]. 2 pelo espeso de un animal. 3 saburra, sarro. 4 incrustación [en las calderas].
fur (to) *tr.* cubrir, forrar o adornar con pieles. 2 cubrir de saburra. 3 *intr.* cubrirse de saburra. 4 formarse incrustaciones. ¶ Pret. y p. p.: *furred;* ger.: *furring.*
furbelow (-belou) *s.* COST. faralá, volante.
furbish (to) (-bish) *tr.* bruñir, acicalar, limpiar.
furcate (-keit) *adj.* ahorquillado.
furcation (-ei·shøn) *s.* bifurcación.
furious (fiu·riøs) *adj.* furioso, furibundo, airado.
furl (to) (fø^{r}l) *tr.* enrollar, plegar [banderas]. 2 MAR. aferrar [velas].
furlong (-long) *s.* estadio [medida].
furlough (-lou) *s.* MIL. licencia, permiso.
furnace (-nis) *s.* horno, hornillo: *blast* ~, alto horno. 2 hogar [de caldera]; caldera [de calefacción].
furnish (to) (fø·^{r}nish) *tr.* surtir, proveer. 2 equipar, aviar, amueblar. 3 suministrar, proporcionar.
furnished (-t) *adj.* amueblado.
furnisher (-ø^r) *s.* proveedor, suministrador. 2 mueblista, decorador.
furnishing (-ing) *s.* habilitación, equipo, suministro. 2 *pl.* útiles, avíos, adminículos; mobiliario; artículos para caballero.
furniture (fø·^{r}nichø^r) *s.* ajuar, mobiliario, muebles: *piece of* ~, mueble; ~ *van,* carro de mudanzas. 2 equipo, avíos, guarnición; adornos, decoraciones.
furor (fiu·ro^r) *s.* furor, furia. 2 frenesí, locura.
furred (fø·^{r}d) *pret.* y *p. p.* de TO FUR.
furrier (fø·riø^r) *s.* peletero.
furriery (-ri) *s.* peletería.
furrow (fø·rou) *s.* surco. 2 carril, rodada. 3 gárgol, ranura. 4 arruga [en el rostro].

furrow (to) *tr.* surcar. 2 abrir ranuras en. 3 arrugar [el rostro]. 4 AGR. arar.
furry (fø·ri) *adj.* cubierto o vestido de pieles; peludo. 2 saburroso.
further (fø·^{r}dø^r) *adj. compar.* adicional, ulterior, nuevo, otro; más amplio, más: *till* ~ *orders,* hasta nueva orden. 2 más lejano, más distante, más adelantado: *the* ~ *end,* el extremo más lejano. 3 *adv.* más lejos, más allá, en mayor grado, con mayor extensión. 4 además; aún.
further (to) *tr.* adelantar, fomentar, promover, apoyar.
furtherance (-ans) *s.* adelantamiento, fomento, promoción, apoyo.
furtherer (-ø^r) *s.* promotor, fomentador.
furthermore (-mo^r) *adv.* además.
furthermost (-moust) *adj. superl.* más lejano, más remoto.
furthest (fø·^{r}dest) *adj.-adv. superl.* FARTHEST.
furtive (fø·^{r}tiv) *adj.* furtivo, oculto, secreto.
furuncle (fiu·rønkøl) *s.* MED. furúnculo, divieso.
fury (fiu·ri) *s.* furia. 2 entusiasmo, frenesí.
furze (fø·^{r}s) *s.* BOT. aulaga, aliaga; hiniesta.
fuscous (fø·skøs) *adj.* fusco.
fuse (fiuš) *s.* espoleta, cebo, mecha [para dar fuego a una carga]. 2 ELECT. fusible, cortacircuitos: ~ *plug,* tapón fusible.
fuse (to) *tr.* fundir, derretir. 2 mezclar, unir. 3 *intr.* fundirse, derretirse.
fusee (fiuši·) *s.* caracol [de reloj]. 2 FUSE 1. 3 fósforo grande. 4 FERROC. señal luminosa.
fuselage (fiu·šølidÿ) *s.* fuselaje.
fusible (fiu·šibøl) *adj.* fusible.
fusiform (-fo^{r}m) *adj.* fusiforme.
fusil (fiu·šil) *s.* fusil de chispa.
fusileer, fusilier (fiušli·^{r}) *s.* MIL. fusilero.
fusillade (fiu·šilei·d) *s.* descarga cerrada, tiroteo.
fusillade (to) *tr.* tirotear, fusilar.
fusion (fiu·ÿøn) *s.* fusión.
fuss (føs) *s.* alboroto, alharaca; ajetreo o inquietud innecesarios: *to make a* ~, hacer alharacas, alborotarse.
fuss (to) *intr.* enredar, bullir, ajetrearse; preocuparse o alborotarse por cosas de poco momento: *to* ~ *with,* enredar con, manosear. 2 *tr.* encororar, molestar con tonterías.
fussy (-i) *adj.* bullidor, inquieto; minucioso, exigente.
fust (føst) *s.* fuste [de columna].
fustian (fø·schan) *s.* TEJ. fustán. 2 TEJ. pana. 3 hinchazón [del estilo].
fustic (fø·stik) *s.* LOT. fustete.
fustigate (to) (-tigeit) *tr.* fustigar, apalear.
fusty (-ti) *adj.* mohoso, rancio. 2 que huele a cerrado. 3 pasado de moda; anticuado.
futile (fiu·til) *adj.* fútil. 2 frívolo. 3 vano, inútil.
futility (fiuti·liti) *s.* futilidad. 2 frivolidad. 3 inutilidad.
future (fiu·chø^r) *adj.* futuro, venidero. 2 *adj.-s.* GRAM. futuro. 3 *m.* futuro, porvenir: *in the* ~, en el futuro, en lo sucesivo. 4 *pl.* COM. futuros.
futurism (-rišm) *s.* futurismo.
futurity (fiutiu·riti) *s.* futuro, porvenir. 2 lo futuro.
fuzz (føš) *s.* vello, pelusa, borra, tamo.
fuzz (to) *intr.* soltar pelusa o borra.
fuzziness (-inis) *s.* vellosidad.
fuzzy (-i) *adj.* velloso, cubierto de pelusa. 2 indistinto, borroso. 3 crespo, rizado [cabello].
fy! (fai) *interj.* FIE.
fylfot (fi·lføt) *s.* svástica.

G

G, g (dȳi) *s.* G, g, séptima letra del alfabeto inglés. *2* MÚS. sol.

gab (gæb) *s.* MEC. gancho, horquilla. *2* fam. cháchara, locuacidad.

gab (to) *intr.* charlar, parlotear.

gabardine (gæbaᵊdɪ·n) *s.* gabardina [tela].

gabarit (gabari) *s.* gálibo.

gabble (gæ·bøl) *s.* charla, parloteo. *2* cloqueo, graznido.

gabble (to) *tr.* charlar, parlotear. *2* cloquear, graznar. *3* decir o leer precipitadamente.

gabbler (gæ·bløᵊ) *s.* charlatán, picotero.

gaberdine (gæbøᵊdɪ·n) *s.* gabardina [tabardo].

gabion (gei·bjøn) *s.* FORT. gavión, cestón.

gable (gei·bøl) *s.* ARQ. aguilón, hastial: ~ *end*, hastial. *2* ARQ. gablete, frontón [sobre puerta o ventana].

gablet (gei·blit) *s.* ARQ. gablete.

gad (gæd) *s.* aguijada; chuzo. *2* interj. ¡pardiez!

gad (to) *intr.* vagar, callejear, andorrear. ¶ Pret. y p. p.: *gadded;* ger.: *gadding.*

gadabout (-abaut) *adj.* callejero, vagabundo. *2 s.* persona callejera. *3* pindonga.

gadder (-øᵊ) *s.* andorrero, haragán, pindonga.

gadfly (-flai) *s.* ENT. tábano.

gadget (gæ·dȳit) *s.* fam chisme, cosa, mecanismo.

Gael (geil) *s.* escocés, celta.

Gaelic (gei·lik) *adj.-s.* gaélico, céltico.

gaff (gaf) *s.* arpón, garfio. *2* esplón de acero [para un gallo de pelea]. *3* MAR. cangrejo: ~ *sail*, cangreja.

gaff (to) *tr.* enganchar con garfio.

gag (gæg) *s.* mordaza [para la boca; lo que hace callar]. *2* bocado que produce náuseas. *3* burla, engaño. *4* TEAT. morcilla; episodio cómico.

gag (to) *tr.* amordazar. *2* dar náuseas a. *3* TEAT. meter morcillas en. *4* engañar, burlar. *5* MEC. obstruir [una válvula]. ¶ Pret. y p. p.: *gagged;* ger.: *gagging.*

gage (geidȳ) *s.* prenda, caución. *2* guante, reto; gaje. *3* GAUGE. *4* BOT. variedad de ciruela.

gage (to) *tr.* empeñar, dar en prenda. *2* apostar. *3* TO GAUGE.

gagger (gæ·gøᵊ) *s.* el que amordaza. *2* bromista.

gaggle (to) (gæ·gøl) *tr.* graznar.

gaiety (gei·iti) *s.* alegría, jovialidad, algazara, diversión. *2* viveza [de los colores]; lujo [del vestir]; fausto, pompa.

gaily (gei·li) *adv.* alegremente. *2* jovialmente.

gain (gein) *s.* ganancia, beneficio, lucro. *2* aumento, adquisición. *3* CARP. gárgol, ranura.

gain (to) *tr.* ganar [en todas las acepciones, menos en la de vencer o aventajar a uno]: *to* ~ *over,* conquistar; persuadir. *2 intr.* ganar, progresar, mejorarse. *3 to* ~ *on* o *upon,* avanzar, acercarse a, ir alcanzando; ganar ventaja, espacio o terreno a.

gainer (-øᵊ) *s.* ganador [el que sale ganando].

gainful (-ful) *adj.* ganancioso, provechoso, lucrativo.

gainless (-lis) *adj.* improductivo, infructuoso.

gainsaid (geinse·d) *pret.* y *p. p.* de TO GAINSAY.

gainsay (to) (geinsei·) *tr.* contradecir, negar, discutir. *2* oponerse a, contrariar. ¶ Pret y p. p.: *gainsaid* o *-sayed.*

gait (geit) *s.* andar, paso, marcha. *2* porte, continente. *3* (Esc.) viaje, camino.

gaiter (-øᵊ) *s.* polaina, botín. *2* botina.

gala (gei·la) *s.* fiesta, función lucida: ~ *day,* día de gala, de gran fiesta.

galactic (galæ·ktik) *adj.* láctico. *2* ASTR. galáctico.

galactite (galæ·ktait) *s.* MINER. galactita.

galantine (galæ·ntin) *s.* galantina.

Galatian (galei·shian) *adj.-s.* gálata.

Galaxy (gæ·læksi) *s.* ASTR. Galaxia. *2* (con min.) pléyade [de artistas, etc.].

galbanum (gæ·lbanøm) *s.* gálbano.

gale (geil) *s.* viento, ventarrón; temporal. *2* pop. algazara. *3* pago periódico del alquiler.

galea (gei·lia) *s.* gálea.

Galen (gei·len) *n. pr.* Galeno. *2* fig. galeno [médico].

galena (gali·na) *s.* MINER. galena.

Galicia (gæli·sha) *n. pr.* GEOGR. Galicia [de Polonia y de España].

Galician (gæli·shan) *adj.-s.* gallego. *2* galiciano.

Galilean (gælili·an) *s.* galileo.

galiot (gæ·liøt) *s.* MAR. galeota. *2* galeote.

gall (gol) *s.* bilis, hiel: ~ *bladder,* vejiga de la hiel. *2* hiel, amargura, inquina. *3* (E.U.) descaro. *4* rozadura. *5* VET. matadura. *6* BOT. agalla: ~ *oak,* quejigo.

gall (to) *tr.* rozar, desollar. *2* irritar, mortificar, molestar. *3* anhelar. *4 intr.* rozarse, escoriarse.

1) gallant (gæ·lant) *adj.* magnífico, galano. *2* bizarro, gallardo, valiente. *3* caballeroso.

2) **gallant** (gælæ·nt) *adj.* galante [con las damas]. *2* amatorio. *3 s.* galán. *4* cortejador.
gallant (to) *tr.* galantear. *2* escoltar [a una dama].
gallantry (gæ·lantri) *s.* gallardía, bizarría, valor, nobleza. *2* galantería [para con las damas]. *3* galanteo.
galleass (gæ·liæs) *s.* MAR. galeaza.
galleon (gæ·liøn) *s.* MAR. galeón.
gallery (gæ·løri) *s.* ARQ. galería; pórtico, columnata. *2* pasadizo. *3* balcón corrido. *4* galería [de pinturas, etc.]. *5* tribuna [en una iglesia]. *6* FORT., MIN., TEAT. galería. *7* galería [público].
galley (gæ·li) *s.* MAR. galera: ~ *slave*, galeote. *2* MAR. cocina, fogón. *3* (Ingl.) falúa. *4* IMPR. galera.
gallfly (go·lflai) *s.* ENT. cinípedo.
Gallia (gæ·lia) *n. pr.* GEOGR. Galia.
Gallican (gæ·likan) *adj.-s.* galicano.
Gallicanism (-išm) *m.* galicanismo.
Gallicism (gæ·lisišm) *s.* galicismo.
galligaskins (gæligæ·skinš) *s.* fam. calzones.
gallinaceous (galinei·shøs) *adj.* ORN. gallináceo.
galling (go·ling) *adj.* irritante, mortificante.
gallinule (gæ·liniul) *s.* ORN. gallineta.
galliot (gæ·liøt) *s.* GALIOT.
gallipot (gæ·lipat) *s.* orza, bote.
gallium (gæ·liøm) *s.* QUÍM. galio.
gallivant (to) (gælivæ·nt) *intr.* vagar, callejear.
gallnut (go·lnøt) *s.* BOT. agalla.
gallon (gæ·løn) *s.* galón [medida: *Ingl.*, 4.543 l.; E. U., 3785 l.].
galloon (gælu·n) *s.* TEJ. galón, trencilla.
gallop (gæ·løp) *s.* galope.
gallop (to) *intr.* galopar. *2* hacer galopar.
galloping (-ing) *adj.* galopante: ~ *consumption*, tisis galopante.
gallows (gæ·louš) *s.* horca, patíbulo: ~ *bird*, carne de horca. *2* armazón en forma de horca.
gall-stone *s.* MED. cálculo biliar.
gally (fo·li) *adj.* amargo.
galop (gæ·løp) *s.* galop [danza].
galore (galo·ʳ) *adj.* muchísimos. *2 adv.* abundantemente. *3 s.* abundancia.
galosh(e (gala·sh) *s.* chanclo. *2* ant. galocha.
galvanic (gælvæ·nik) *adj.* galvánico.
galvanism (gæ·lvanišm) *s.* galvanismo.
galvanize (to) (gæ·lvanaiš) *tr.* galvanizar. *2* MED. aplicar corrientes eléctricas.
galvanometer (gælvano·meteʳ) *s.* galvanómetro.
galvanoplasty (gæ·lvanoplæsti) *s.* galvanoplastia.
gama grass (ga·ma) *s.* BOT. maicillo.
gambit (gæ·mbit) *s.* gambito.
gamble (gæ·mbøl) *s.* juego [en que se arriesga dinero]. *2* jugada, empresa arriesgada.
gamble (to) *intr.* jugar [por dinero]. *2* especular, aventurarse [en la Bolsa, etc.]. *3 tr.* jugar [dinero]. *4* aventurar, perder [en el juego].
gambler (gæ·mbløʳ) *s.* jugador, tahur.
gambling (gæ·mbling) *s.* juego [por dinero]; ~ *house*, garito.
gambol (gæ·mbøl) *s.* brinco, cabriola, retozo.
gambol (to) *intr.* brincar, cabriolar, retozar, travesar. ¶ Pret. y p. p.: *gamboled* o *-bolled;* ger.: *gamboling* o *-bolling.*
gambrel (gæ·mbrøl) *s.* jarrete, corvejón. *2* gancho, garabato. *3* ARQ. ~ *roof*, techo a la holandesa.
game (geim) *s.* juego, entretenimiento, diversión: ~ *of chance*, juego de azar: *to play the* ~, jugar limpio. *2* partida [de juego]. *3* DEP. partido. *4* juego, manejo, asunto, plan: *the* ~ *is up*, la cosa ha fracasado. *5* burla, broma. *6* caza [animales]: *big* ~, caza mayor. *7* valentía.

8 adj. de juego. *9* de caza: ~ *bag*, zurrón, morral. *10* valiente, animoso, luchador, peleón: *to die* ~, morir peleando. *11* estropeado [brazo, pierna].
game (to) *tr.* jugar [dinero]. *2 intr.* jugar [por dinero].
gamecock (gei·mkak) *s.* gallo de pelea.
gamekeeper (-kıpøʳ) *s.* guardabosque, guarda de coto.
gamesome (-søm) *adj.* alegre, juguetón.
gamester (-støʳ) *s.* jugador, tahur.
gamete (gæ·mit) *s.* BIOL. gameto.
gaming (gei·ming) *s.* GAMBLING.
gamma (gæ·ma) *s.* gamma [letra griega].
gammon (gæ·møn) *s.* jamón curado. *2* partida doble [en el chaquete]. *3* fam. embuste. faramalla.
gammon (to) *tr.* curar [jamón]. *2* ganar partida doble [al chaquete]. *3* fam. enlabiar, embaucar.
gamopetalous (gæmope·taløs) *adj.* BOT. gamopétalo.
gamut (gæ·møt) *s.* escala, gama.
gamy (gei·mi) *adj.* manido. *2* abundante en caza.
gander (gæ·ndøʳ) *s.* ZOOL. ganso.
gang (gæng) *s.* pelotón, cuadrilla, brigada; pandilla, banda. *2* juego [de herramientas, etc.]. *4 adj.* múltiple: ~ *condenser*, RADIO. condensador múltiple.
gang (to) *intr.* juntarse, formar cuadrilla.
ganglion (gæ·ngliøn) *s.* ANAT., MED. ganglio.
ganglionic (gænglia·nik) *adj.* ganglionar.
gangplank (gæ·ngplænk) *s.* plancha, pasarela.
gangrene (gæ·ngrin) *s.* MED. gangrena.
gangrene (to) *tr.* gangrenar. *2 intr.* gangrenarse.
gangrenous (-øs) *adj.* gangrenoso.
gangster (gæ·ngstøʳ) *s.* gangster, pistolero.
gangue (gæng) *s.* MIN. ganga.
gangway (gæ·ngwei) *s.* pasillo. *2* pasarela. *3* MAR. portalón; plancha de atraque.
gannet (gæ·nit) *s.* ORN. planga.
gantlet (ga·ntlit) *s.* GAUNTLET.
gantry (gæ·ntri) *s.* poíno, caballete. *2* puente para grúa corrediza, señales de ferrocarril, etc.
Ganymede (gænimi·d) *n. pr.* Ganimedes.
gaol (dÿeil) *s.* (Ingl.) cárcel.
gaoler (-øʳ) *s.* (Ingl.) carcelero.
gap (gæp) *s.* boquete, portillo, brecha, abertura, resquicio. *2* quebrada, barranca. *4* hueco, claro, espacio, laguna.
gap (to) *tr.* abrir boquete o brecha en.
gape (geip) *s.* bostezo. *2* asombro, embobamiento. *3* abertura, boquete. *4 pl. the gapes*, ganas de bostezar.
gape (to) *intr.* bostezar. *2* abrir la boca: *to* ~ *after*, desear, codiciar. *3* estar o quedar boquiabierto: *to* ~ *at*, mirar embobado. *4* abrirse, estar abierto.
gaper (-øʳ) *s.* bostezador. *2* bobalicón.
gar (gaʳ) *s.* ICT. nombre de la aguja, el sollo, etc.
garage (ga·ÿ) *s.* garaje. *2* AER. hangar.
garage (to) *tr.* dejar o encerrar en el garaje.
garb (gæʳb) *s.* vestido, traje.
garb (to) *tr.* vestir, ataviar.
garbage (ga·ʳbidÿ) *s.* desperdicios, basura.
garble (ga·ʳbøl) *s.* alteración, amaño [de un texto, etc.].
garble (to) *tr.* alterar, amañar [un texto, etc.].
garden (ga·ʳdøn) *s.* jardín [de flores, etc.]: ~ *balm*, BOT. melisa, toronjil; ~ *city*, ciudad jardín; ~ *party*, fiesta en un jardín. *2* huerto: ~ *stuff*, hortalizas.
garden (to) *tr.-intr.* cultivar un huerto o jardín.

gardener (ga·ᶜdnøᶜ) s. jardinero. 2 hortelano.
gardenia (gaᶜdɪ·nɪa) s. BOT. gardenia.
gardening (ga·ᶜdning) s. jardinería; horticultura.
garfish (gaᶜ·fish) s. GAR.
garganey (gæ·ᶜgani) s. ORN. cerceta.
gargle (ga·ᶜgøl) s. gargarismo [licor].
gargle (to) tr.-intr. gargarizar.
gargoyle (ga·ᶜgoil) s. ARQ. gárgola.
garish (ge·rish) adj. deslumbrante, llamativo, charro; ostentoso.
garland (ga·ᶜland) s. guirnalda.
garland (to) tr. enguirnaldar.
garlic (ga·ᶜlik) s. BOT. ajo.
garlicky (-i) adj. aliáceo. 2 que huele o sabe a ajo.
garment (ga·ᶜmønt) s. vestido, prenda.
garner (ga·ᶜnøᶜ) s. granero, hórreo. 2 acopio.
garner (to) tr. entrojar, acopiar, almacenar.
garnet (ga·ᶜnit) s. granate [piedra, color].
garnish (ga·ᶜnish) s. adorno, guarnición. 2 atavío. 3 COC. aderezo.
garnish (to) tr. adornar, guarnecer, ataviar. 2 COC. aderezar [un guiso]. 3 DER. notificar un embargo.
garniture (ga·ᶜnichuᶜ) s. adorno, guarnición.
Garonne (garo·n) n. pr. GEOGR. Garona.
garret (gæ·rit) s. desván, buhardilla, sotabanco.
garrison (gæ·risøn) s. MIL. guarnición, presidio.
garrison (to) tr. MIL. guarnicionar. 2 MIL. guarnecer.
garrot (gæ·røt) s. CIR. torniquete.
garrote (garou·t) s. garrote.
garrot (to) tr. agarrotar, dar garrote.
garrulity (gæ·riuliti) s. garrulidad, locuacidad.
garrulous (gæ·riuløs) adj. gárrulo, locuaz.
garter (ga·ᶜtøᶜ) s. liga, jarretera: *the Garter*, la Orden de la Jarretera.
garter (to) tr. sujetar con ligas. 2 investir con la orden de la Jarretera.
gas (gæs) s. gas: ~ *burner*, mechero de gas; ~ *chamber*, cámara de gases; ~ *generator*, gasógeno; ~ *mask*, careta antigás; ~ *range*, cocina de gas; ~ *works*, fábrica de gas. 2 fam. gasolina: *to cut off the* ~, AUTO. cerrar el carburador. 3 fam. palabrería, jactancia.
gas (to) tr. proveer de gas o gasolina. 2 gasear. 3 intr. despedir gas. 4 fam. charlar, fanfarronear.
Gascon (gæ·skøn) adj.-s. gascón.
gasconade (gæskønei·d) s. fanfarronada.
gasconade (to) intr. jactarse, fanfarronear.
Gascony (gæ·skøni) n. pr. GEOGR. Gascuña.
gaseous (gæ·siøs) adj. gaseoso. 2 vago, sin consistencia.
gash (gæsh) s. cuchillada, herida, incisión.
gash (to) tr. acuchillar, herir, cortar.
gasiform (gæ·sifoᶜm) adj. gaseiforme.
gasify (to) (gæ·sifai) tr. gasificar.
gasket (gæ·skit) s. MAR. tomador. 2 MEC. relleno, empaquetadura.
gaslight (gæ·slait) s. mechero de gas. 2 luz de gas.
gasogen(e (gæ·sodỹin) s. GAZOGENE.
gasoline (gæ·solin) s. gasolina: ~ *pump*, surtidor de gasolina.
gasometer (gæsa·mitøᶜ) s. gasómetro.
gasp (gasp) s. boqueada; respiración entrecortada; grito sofocado.
gasp (to) intr. boquear, abrir la boca [con asombro o jadeando], anhelar: *to* ~ *for breath*, jadear. 2 tr. decir de manera entrecortada.
gassy (gæ·si) adj. gaseoso. 2 fig. ampuloso.
gasteropod (gæ·støropoud) adj.-s. GASTROPOD.
gastralgia (gæstræ·ldỹia) s. gastralgia.

gastric (gæ·strik) adj. gástrico.
gastritis (gæstrai·tis) s. MED. gastritis.
gastronomer (gæstra·nomøᶜ) s. gastrónomo.
gastronomy (gæstra·nomi) s. gastronomía.
gastropod (gæ·stropoud) adj.-s. ZOOL. gasterópodo.
gastrula (gæ·strula) s. BIOL. gástrula.
gate (geit) s. puerta [de entrada; de una ciudad; en un muro], portal, verja, cancilla, portilla, tranquera, barrera. 2 DEP. entrada [dinero]. 3 compuerta [de esclusa, etc.].
gatekeeper (-kɪpøᶜ) s. portero. 2 guardabarrera.
gateway (-wei) s. entrada, puerta. 2 paso [con portillo]; arco [de entrada].
gather (gæ·døᶜ) s. frunce, pliegue, plegado.
gather (to) tr. recoger, juntar, allegar, reunir, amontonar. 2 recolectar, coger, cosechar. 3 congregar, juntar. 4 recaudar. 5 COST. recoger, fruncir. 6 IMPR. alzar. 7 colegir, deducir, inferir. 8 cobrar [fuerzas]. 9 tomar [aliento; color]. 10 cubrirse de [polvo, musgo, etc.]. 11 ganar [terreno]. 12 to ~ *flesh*, criar carnes. 13 to ~ *speed*, ir aumentando su velocidad.
14 intr. amontonarse, acumularse. 15 juntarse, congregarse. 16 concentrarse, aumentar. 17 MED. madurar.
gathering (-ing) s. recolección. 2 acumulación, hacinamiento. 3 reunión [de gente]. 4 recaudación; colecta [caritativa]. 5 IMPR. alzado. 6 contracción, fruncimiento. 7 MED. maduración, supuración; absceso. 8 COST. fruncido.
gauche (goush) adj. torpe, falto de tacto.
gaud (god) s. adorno ostentoso o charro.
gaudery (-øᶜi) s. ostentación, charrería.
gaudiness (-inis) s. pompa, boato, charrería.
gaudish (-ish), **gaudy** (-i) adj. ostentoso, llamativo, chillón, charro.
gauge (geidỹ) s. medida, norma. 2 dimensión, calibre, capacidad. 3 instrumento parar medir ciertas cosas: regla de medir, manómetro, indicador, calibrador, etc. 4 gramil. 5 FERROC. ancho de vía. 6 MAR. calado.
gauge (to) tr. medir, graduar, calibrar, aforar. 2 MAR. arquear. 3 estimar, apreciar, juzgar, calcular.
Gaul (gol) n. pr. GEOGR. Galia. 2 s. galo.
Gaulish (go·lish) adj. galo [de los galos].
gaunt (gont) adj. flaco, desvaído; demacrado. 2 tétrico, desolado.
gauntlet (go·ntlit) s. guantelete, manopla: *to fling down the* ~, arrojar el guante, retar. 2 MIL. baquetas: *ton run the* ~, pasar por las baquetas; pasar entre dos peligros.
gauntry (go·ntri) s. GANTRY.
gauze (goš) s. gasa, cendal.
gauziness (go·šinis) s. ligereza, transparencia.
gauzy (go·ši) adj. ligero, transparente.
gave (geiv) pret. de TO GIVE.
gavel (gæ·vøl) s. martillo o mazo [de presidente]. 2 ALBAÑ. maceta. 3 gavilla.
gavial (gei·vial) s. ZOOL. gavial.
gavot gavotte (gævo·t) s. gavota.
gawk (gøk) s. lerdo, torpe. 2 bobo, papanatas.
gawky (go·ki) adj. torpe, encogido, desmañado. 2 m.-f. torpe, bobo.
gay (gei) adj. alegre, animado, festivo. 2 alegre, vivo, vistoso, elegante. 3 alegre, ligero de cascos, calavera. 4 ~ *science*, gaya ciencia.
gaze (geiš) s. mirada fija, atenta; contemplación.
gaze (to) intr. mirar fijamente; contemplar.
gazelle (gaše·l) s. ZOOL. gacela; gacel.
gazer (gei·šøᶜ) s. contemplador, mirón.

gazette (gaše·t) *s.* gaceta [periódico].
gazette (to) *tr.* anunciar en un periódico oficial.
gazetteer (gæše·tɪ^r) *s.* gacetero. *2* nomenclator o diccionario geográfico.
gazingstock (gei·šingstɑk) *s.* hazmerreír.
gazogene (gæ·sodȳin) *s.* gasógeno.
gear (gɪ·ø^r) *s.* vestidos, atavíos, prendas de uso. *2* guarniciones [del caballo]. *3* equipo, herramientas, utensilios. *4* MAR. aparejo, maniobra. *5* MEC. rueda, engranaje, juego; mecanismo [de transmisión, de gobierno, etc.]: ~ *box*, . caja de engranajes o de velocidades; ~ *shift*, cambio de marcha; *to throw into* ~, engranar, embragar; *to throw out of* ~, desengranar, desembragar; fig. trastornar.
gear (to) *tr.* vestir, ataviar. *2* enjaezar. *3* montar, armar, pertrechar. *4* conectar, hacer engranar. *5 intr.* engranar, estar en juego.
gearing (-ing) *s.* MEC. engranaje; mecanismo o tren de engranaje. *2* MAR. drizas y aparejos.
gearshift (-shift) *s.* AUTO. cambio de marchas.
gearwheel (-juul) *s.* MEC. rueda dentada.
gee (dȳɪ) *interj.* ¡arre!
gee (to) *tr.* arrear hacia la derecha. *2 intr.* torcer hacia la derecha.
geese (gɪs) *s. pl.* de GOOSE.
Gehenna (gije·na) *s.* gehena. *2* infierno.
gel (dȳel) *s.* QUÍM. gel.
gelatine (dȳe·lætin) *s.* gelatina.
gelatinize (to) (dȳilæ·tinais) *tr.-intr.* gelatinar.
gelaitnous (-øs) *adj.* gelatinoso.
gelation (dȳilei·shøn) *s.* congelación.
geld (to) (geld) *tr.* castrar, capar. *2* castrar [la colmena].
gelder (-ør) *s.* castrador, capador.
gelding (-ing) *s.* capón; caballo capado.
gelid (dȳe·lid) *adj.* gélido, helado.
gelidity (dȳeli·diti) *s.* frío o frialdad extremos.
gem (dȳem) *s.* gema, piedra preciosa. *2* fig. perla, joyel, joya.
gem (to) *tr.* adornar con piedras preciosas. ¶ Pret. y p. p.: *gemmed*; ger.: *gemming*.
geminate (dȳe·mineit) *adj.* geminado.
geminate (to) *tr.* geminar.
Gemini (dȳe·minai) *s.* ASTR. Géminis.
gemma (dȳe·ma) *s.* H. NAT. gema, yema,botón.
gemmule (dȳe·miul) *s.* H. NAT. yemecilla.
gender (dȳe·ndø^r) *s.* GRAM. género.
gene (dȳin) *s.* BIOL. gen.
genealogical (dȳeniala·dȳikɑl) *adj.* genealógico.
genealogy (dȳenia·lodȳi) *s.* genealogía.
generable (dȳe·nørɑbøl) *adj.* generable.
general (dȳe·nørɑl) *adj.* general: ~ *delinery*, lista de correos. *2 m.* MIL., ECL. general. *3* lo general: *in* ~, en general, por lo común. *4* el público, el vulgo. *5* MIL. generala [toque].
generalissimo (dȳenørɑli·simou) *s.* generalísimo.
generality (dȳenøræ·liti) *s.* generalidad.
generalization (dȳenørɑlišei·shøn) *s.* generalización.
generalize (to) (dȳe·nørɑlaiš) *tr.* generalizar. *2 intr.* MED. generalizarse.
generally (-i) *adv.* generalmente.
generalship (-ship) *s.* generalato. *2* don de mando.
generate (to) (dȳe·nøreit) *tr.* generar, engendrar, originar. *2* GEOM. generar.
generating (dȳenørei·ting) *adj.* generador: ~ *station*, ELECT. central.
generation (-shøn) *s.* generación.
generative (dȳe·nørativ) *adj.* generativo. *2* generador.

generator (dȳe·nøreitø^r) *s.* generador, engendrador. *2* ELECT., MEC. generador.
generatrix (dȳe·nøratriks) *s.* madre. *2* ELECT. generador, dinamo. *3* GEOM. generatriz.
generic(al (dȳene·rik(ɑl) *adj.* genérico.
generosity (dȳenøra·siti) *s.* generosidad.
generous (dȳe·nørøs) *adj.* generoso. *2* noble, magnánimo. *3* valeroso. *4* abundante, amplio, holgado.
genesial (dȳini·siɑl) *adj.* genésico.
genesis (dȳe·nesis) *s.* génesis. *2* (con may.) Génesis [libro de la Biblia].
genet (dȳe·nit) *s.* ZOOL. jineta. *2* jaca española.
genetic (dȳine·tik) *adj.* genético.
geneticist (dȳine·tisist) *s.* genetista.
genetics (dȳine·tiks) *s.* genética.
Geneva (dȳeni·va) *n. pr.* GEOGR. Ginebra.
Genevan (dȳeni·van) *adj.-s.* ginebrino.
genial (dȳi·niɑl) *adj.* genial. *2* cordial, afable. *3* alegre, jovial. *4* confortante, agradable. *5* ANAT., ZOOL. geniano.
geniality (dȳiniæ·liti) *s.* cordialidad, afabilidad. *2* jovialidad.
genii (dȳi·niai) *s. pl.* de GENIUS 2.
genista (dȳini·stɑ) *s.* BOT. genista, retama.
genital (dȳe·nitɑl) *adj.* genital. *2 s. pl.* partes genitales.
genitive (dȳe·nitiv) *adj.-s.* GRAM. genitivo.
genitor (dȳe·nitø^r) *s.* genitor, progenitor.
1) genius (dȳi·niøs), *pl.* **geniuses** (-iš) *s.* genio [fuerza creadora; pers. que la tiene]. *2* genio, carácter particular [de una nación, época, lugar, etc.].
2) genius (dȳi·niøs), *pl.* **genii** (dȳ·niai) *s.* genio [deidad]; demonio, espíritu elemental.
Genoa (dȳe·noa) *n. pr.* GEOGR. Génova.
genocide (dȳe·nøssaid) *s.* genocidio.
Genoese (dȳenoi·š) *adj.-s.* genovés.
genre (dȳa·n^r) *s.* LIT., B. ART. género, estilo costumbrista.
genteel (dȳentɪ·l) *adj.* urbano, cortés. *2* señoril, elegante, refinado, distinguido. *3* gentil, gallardo.
genteelness (-nis) *s.* urbanidad, cortesía. *2* elegancia, distinción. *3* garbo, gentileza.
gentian (dȳe·nshan) *s.* BOT. genciana.
gentile, Gentile (dȳe·ntail) *adj.-s.* gentil [pagano]. *2 adj.* GRAM. gentilicio.
gentilic (dȳenti·lik) *adj.* gentílico. *2* tribal, nacional, racial. *3* GRAM. gentilicio.
gentilitious (dȳentili·shøs) *adj.* gentilicio.
gentility (dȳenti·liti) *s.* calidad del nacido de buena familia aunque no noble. *2* buena educación, dignidad, valor, gracia, gentileza.
gentle (dȳe·ntøl) *adj.* de buena familia, de clase rica, aunque no noble; distinguido. *2* manso, dócil. *3* afable, apacible, dulce, benigno. *4* suave, ligero, moderado. *5 the* ~ *sex*, el bello sexo.
gentlefolk (-fouk) *s.* señores, gente distinguida.
gentleman (-mæn) *s.* caballero, señor; hombre correcto, bien educado. *2* gentilhombre: ~ *in waiting*, gentilhombre de cámara. *3* ~ *of fortune*, aventurero.
gentlemanly (-mænli) *adj.* caballeroso, civil, urbano, correcto.
gentlemen (-men) *s. pl.* de GENTLEEMAN, señores. *2* muy señores míos o nuestros [en las cartas]. *3* *gentlemen's agreement*, pacto de caballeros, acuerdo verbal entre naciones.
gentleness (-nis) *s.* apacibilidad, mansedumbre. *2*

afabilidad. *3* delicadeza, dulzura, suavidad. *4* distinción, buen tono.

gentlewoman (-wumæn) *f.* señora, dama. *2* dama de honor.

gently (dẏe·ntli) *adv.* mansamente, suavemente, dulcemente. *2* despacio, quedo, con tiento.

gentry (dẏe·ntri) *s.* señorio, gente bien educada, rica, pero no noble. *2* gente, personas.

genuflect (to) (dẏe·niuflekt) *intr.* doblar la rodilla.

genuflection (dẏeniufle·kshøn) *s.* genuflexión.

genuine (dẏe·niuin) *adj.* genuino, auténtico, legítimo, verdadero. *2* franco, sincero.

genuineness (dẏe·niuinnis) *s.* autenticidad, legitimidad, pureza. *2* sinceridad.

genus (dẏi·nøs) *s.* H. NAT., LÓG. género. *2* género, clase, índole.

geocentric (dẏiose·ntrik) *adj.* geocéntrico.

geode (dẏi·oud) *s.* GEOL. geoda.

geodesy (dẏia·døsi) *s.* geodesia.

Geoffrey (dẏe·fri) *n. pr.* Godofredo.

geogeny (dẏia·dẏeni) *s.* GEOL. geogenia.

geognosy (dẏia·gnosi) *s.* GEOL. geognosia.

geographer (dẏia·grafø^r) *s.* geógrafo.

geographic(al (dẏiogræ·fik(al) *adj.* geográfico.

geography (dẏia·grafi) *s.* geografía.

geologic(al (dẏiola·ẏik(al) *adj.* geológico.

geologist (dẏia·lodẏist) *s.* geólogo.

geology (dẏia·lodẏi) *s.* geología.

geometer (dẏia·mitø^r) *s.* geómetra.

geometric(al (dẏiome·trik(al) *adj.* geométrico.

geometrician (dẏiame·trishan) *s.* geómetra.

geometry (dẏia·metri) *s.* geometría.

geophysics (dẏiofi·siks) *s.* geofísica.

geopolitics (dẏiopa·litiks) *s.* geopolítica.

George (dẏo^rdẏ) *n. pr.* Jorge.

georgete (dẏo·^rdẏet) *s.* crespón de seda muy fino.

georgic (dẏo·^rdẏik) *s.* geórgica.

geotropism (dẏia·tropiŝm) *s.* BOT. geotropismo.

geraniaceous (dẏøreiniei·shøs) *adj.* geraniáceo.

geranium (dẏørei·niøm) *s.* BOT. geranio.

Gerald (dẏe·rald) *n. pr. m.* Gerardo.

gerent (dẏe·rønt) *s.* director, gerente.

gerfalcon (dẏe·^rfo·lkøn) *s.* ORN. gerifalte.

germ (dẏø^rm) *s.* germen. *2* BOT. yema. *3* BOT. semilla. *4* pop. microbio.

german (dẏø·^rman) *adj.* carnal [hermano, primo].

German *adj.-s.* alemán: ~ *measles*, MED. rubéola; ~ *silver*, alpaca, metal blanco. *2* germano, tudesco. *3 adj.* germánico.

germander (dẏø^rmæ·ndø^r) *s.* BOT. camedrio; maro.

germane (dẏø^rma·n) *adj.* afín. *2* propio, adecuado, pertinente.

Germanic (dẏø·^rmænik) *adj.* alemán; germánico.

Germanism (dẏø·^rmaniŝm) *s.* germanismo.

germanium (dẏø·^rmei·niøm) *s.* QUÍM. germanio.

Germanophile (dẏø^rmæ·nofail) *adj.-s.* germanófilo.

Germany (dẏø·^rmani) *n. pr.* Alemania.

germicidal (dẏø^rmisi·dal) *adj.* bactericida.

germicide (dẏø·^rmisaid) *s.* bactericida.

germinal (dẏø·^rminal) *adj.* germinal. *2* en embrión.

germinate (to) (dẏø·^rmineit) *intr.* germinar. *2* brotar, desarrollarse. *3 tr.* hacer germinar o brotar.

germination (dẏø^rminei·shøn) *s.* germinación.

gerontology (dẏøranta·lødẏi) *s.* gerontología.

Gertrude (gø·^rtrud) *n. pr. f.* Gertrudis.

gerund (dẏø·rønd) *s.* GRAM. gerundio.

gerundial (dẏirø·ndial) *adj.* GRAM. del gerundio.

Gervas (dẏø·^rvas) *n. pr. m.* Gervasio.

gest, geste (dẏest) *s.* gesta, romance.

gestation (dẏestei·shøn) *s.* gestación. *2* incubación.

gestatorial (dẏestato·rial) *adj.* gestatorio.

gesticulate (to) (dẏesti·kiuleit) *intr.* accionar, manotear, hacer ademanes.

gesticulation (dẏestikiulei·shøn) *s.* acción, manoteo, ademanes.

gesticulator (dẏesti·kiuleitø^r) *s.* el que acciona o hace ademanes.

gesture (dẏe·schø^r) *s.* acción, ademán, signo. *2* cosa dicha o hecha por cortesía o diplomacia.

gesture (to) *intr.* accionar, hacer ademanes.

get (get) *s.* engendro, engendramiento. *2* producto, progenie, casta.

get (to) *tr.* obtener, conseguir, lograr, ganar, sacar, llevarse, recibir, tener. *2* hallar; ir a buscar, traer. *3* coger, capturar, atrapar. *4* vencer, dominar. *5* coger [una enfermedad]. *6* inducir, persuadir; mandar, hacer que: *to ~ one's hair cut*, hacerse cortar el pelo. *7* poner [en un estado, situación, etc.]: *to ~ ready*, preparar; *to ~ going*, poner en marcha; *to ~ together*, juntar, reunir. *8* alcanzar. *9* RADIO. captar, sintonizar con. *10* comunicar con [por teléfono, etc.]. *11* hacer [la comida]; disponer, preparar. *12* proporcionar, suministrar. *13* engendrar, procrear. *14* pop. dar [un puñetazo, etc.]. *15* comprender, entender. *16* aprender [de memoria]. *17* pasar, llevar, hacer llegar o pasar. *18 to ~ air* o *wind*, divulgarse; enterarse, tener noticia [de]. *19 to ~ back*, recobrar. *20 to ~ down*, bajar, descolgar; tragar. *21 to ~ hold of*, asir; apoderarse de. *22 to ~ into*, meter en. *23 to ~ it*, cargársela, recibir un castigo. *24 to ~ off*, quitar, quitarse; librar, hacer salir de. *25 to ~ out*, sacar, quitar; ayudar a salir; publicar. *26 to ~ over*, hacer pasar por encima o más allá de; ganar [a una causa]; acabar. *27 to ~ the better of*, llevar ventaja a, ganar. *28 to ~ the worse*, llevar la peor parte; salir mal parado. *29 to have got*, tener, poseer.

30 intr. ganar dinero, etc. *31* llegar [a un punto, estado, etc.]. *32* estar, hallarse. *33* meterse, introducirse, pasar. *34* hacerse, volverse, ponerse: *to ~ old*, hacerse viejo. *35 to ~ about*, levantarse [un convaleciente]; circular, divulgarse. *36 to ~ abroad*, divulgarse. *37 to ~ along*, marcharse, irse; seguir andando; apresurarse; pasarlo. *38 to ~ along with*, avenirse con. *39 to ~ around*, ir a todas partes; manejar a [una pers.]; eludir [una ley]; TO GET ABOUT. *40 to ~ at*, llegar a, ir a; alcanzar; averiguar, descubrir. *41 to ~ away*, irse, escapar. *42 to ~ away with*, llevarse, escaparse con. *43 to ~ back*, volver. *44 to ~ behind*, quedarse atrás. *45 to ~ better*, mejorar. *46 to ~ down*, bajar, bajarse, descender. *47 to ~ in*, meterse; llegar. *48 to ~ in with*, lograr la amistad o el favor de. *49 to ~ into*, entrar en, meterse en. *50 to ~ near*, acercarse. *51 to ~ off*, partir, marchar; salir de; apearse de; salir bien librado. *52 to ~ on*, montar, subir, ponerse sobre; armonizar; adelantar, medrar. *53 to ~ on one's nerves*, irritar, poner nervioso. *54 to ~ out*, salir; apartarse; divulgarse. *55 to ~ over*, reponerse, recobrarse de; olvidar [un disgusto, etc.]; superar un obstáculo; pasar al otro lado. *56 to ~ through*, pasar por o entre; llegar a su destino; terminar. *57 to ~ under*, ponerse debajo de. *58 to ~ under way*, MAR. zarpar. *59 to ~ up*, levantarse, ponerse en pie; subir. *60 to have got to*, haber de, tener que. *61 ~ out!*, ¡largo de aquí!;

fam. ¡aprieta! [expresando incredulidad].
¶ Pret.: *got;* p. p.: *got* o *gotten;* ger.: *getting.*
getaway (ge·tauei) *s.* partida, escape. *2* DEP. salida [de una carrera]. *3* AUTO. arranque.
Gethsemane (gezse·mani) *n. pr.* BIB. Getsemaní.
get-up (ge·tøp) *s.* fam. arreglo, disposición, presentación. *2* fam. atavío, traje.
gewgaw (giu·go) *s.* chuchería. *2* adorno cursi. *3 adj.* cursi, charro.
geyser (gai·šø⌃) *s.* géiser. *2* calentador de baño.
ghastly (ga·stli) *adj.* horrible, espantoso. *2* espectral, fantasmal. *3* pálido, lívido, cadavérico. *4 adv.* horriblemente. *5* lívidamente.
Ghent (gent) *n. pr.* GEOGR. Gante.
gherkin (gø·⌃kin) *s.* BOT. pepinillo, cohombrillo.
ghetto (ge·tou) *s.* judería, barrio judío.
Ghibelline (gi·bølin) *adj.-s.* gibelino.
ghost (goust) *s.* espíritu, alma: *the Holy Ghost,* el Espíritu Santo: *to give up the ~,* dar el alma a Dios, morir. *2* espectro, fantasma, sombra, alma en pena. *3* fig. sombra, asomo: *not a ~ of,* ni una sombra de. *4* TELEV. fantasma.
ghostly (gou·stli) *adj.* espiritual. *2* espectral, fantasmal. *3* de aparecidos o fantasmas.
ghoul (gul) *s.* demonio, vampiro. *2* ladrón de tumbas. *3* persona que se deleita en cosas horribles.
ghoulish (gu·lish) *adj.* horrible, brutal, asqueroso.
giant (dȳai·ant) *adj* gigante, gigantesco. *2 m.* gigante.
giantness (-is) *s.* giganta.
gib (gib) *s.* chaveta, cuña, contraclavija. *3* aguilón, brazo de grúa.
gibber (gi·bø⌃) *s.* farfulla, charla.
gibber (to)) *intr.* farfullar, charlar.
gibberish (-ish) *s.* charla incoherente. *2* jerga, jerigonza. *3 adj.* incoherente [charla].
gibbet (dȳi·bit) *s.* horca, patíbulo.
gibbet (to) *tr.* ahorcar. *2* fig. poner en la picota.
gibbon (gi·bøn) *s.* ZOOL. mono de Asia.
gibbosity (giba·siti) *s.* gibosidad, giba.
gibbous (gi·bøs) *adj.* giboso. *2* jorobado, corcovado. *3* convexo.
gibe (dȳaib) *s.* burla, mofa, escarnio, pulla.
gibe (to) *tr.* mofarse, escarnecer, ridiculizar. *2 intr.* burlarse, hacer mofa.
giblets (dȳi·blits) *s. pl.* menudillos [de ave, etc.].
gid (gid) *s.* VET. torneo, modorra.
giddiness (gi·dinis) *s.* vértigo, vahído. *2* atolondramiento, aturdimiento, falta de juicio. *3* inconstancia, ligereza.
giddy (gi·di) *adj.* vertiginoso. *2* mareado, aturdido, que sufre vértigo. *3* atolondrado, ligero de cascos. *4* inconstante, veleidoso.
Gideon (gi·diøn) *n. pr. m.* Gedeón.
gift (gift) *s.* donación. *2* donativo, dádiva, don, regalo, obsequio, presente. *3* dación. *4* don, prenda: *~ of tongues,* don de lenguas.
gift (to) *tr.* regalar, hacer don de. *2* dotar, agraciar.
gifted (-id) *adj.* dotado, talentoso, inspirado.
gig (gig) *s.* carruaje ligero de dos ruedas. *2* MAR. bote, lancha, falúa. *3* fisga, arpón.
gig (to) *tr.-intr.* pescar con fisga o arpón.
gigantic (dȳigæ·ntik) *adj.* gigantesco.
giggle (gi·gøl) *s.* risita, risa ahogada.
giggle (to) *intr.* reírse tratando de contener la risa. *2* reír tontamente o con risa afectada.
giggler (gi·glø⌃) *s.* el que ríe tontamente.
Gilbert (gi·lbø⌃t) *n. pr. m.* Gilberto.
gild (gild) *s.* GUILD.
gild (to) *tr.* dorar. ¶ Pret. y p. p.: *gilded* o *gilt.*
gilder (gi·ldø⌃) *s.* dorador.

gilding (-ing) *s.* duradura. *2* dorado.
Giles (dȳails) *n. pr. m.* Giles.
gill (gil) *s.* agalla [de pez]; branquia. *2* barba [de gallo]. *3* papada. *4* torrentera.
gillie (dȳi·li) *s.* (Esc.) servidor, criado.
gillyflower (dȳi·liflauø⌃) *s.* BOT. alhelí.
gilt (gilt) *adj.* dorado; áureo. *2 s.* doradura; dorado. *3* falso brillo, oropel.
gilt-edged *adj.* ENCUAD. de cantos dorados. *2* fig. de lo mejor que hay.
gimcrack (dȳi·mkræk) *s.* chuchería. *2 adj.* de baratillo, de oropel.
gimlet (gi·mlit) *s.* barrena de mano.
gin (dȳin) *s.* ginebra [licor]. *2* trampa, armadijo [para cazar]. *3* cabria, malacate. *4* máquina para alijar el algodón.
gin (to) *tr.* coger con trampa. *2* alijar [el algodón].
¶ Pret. y p. p.: *ginned;* ger.: *ginning.*
ginger (dȳi·ndȳø⌃) *s.* BOT. jengibre: *~ ale,* gaseosa aromatizada con jengibre. *2* color rubio rojizo. *3* fam. viveza, energía.
ginger (to) *tr.* animar; estimular.
gingerbread (-bred) *s.* galleta o bollo de jengibre.
gingerly (-li) *adv.* cautelosamente, con precaución. *2 adj.* cauteloso, escrupuloso.
gingerness (-nis) *s.* cautela; escrupulosidad.
gingham (gi·ngam) *s.* TEJ. guinga.
gipsy (dȳi·psi) *s.* GYPSY.
giraffe (dȳiræ·f) *s.* ZOOL. jirafa.
girandole (dȳi·randoul) *s.* girándula. *2* araña, candelabro. *3* JOY. pendiente, arracada.
gird (gø⌃d) *s.* pulla, sarcasmo, escarnio.
gird (to) *tr.* ceñir, cercar, rodear; ceñir [llevar ceñido]: *to ~ sword,* ceñir espada. *2* investir [de]. *3* mofarse, burlarse. ¶ Pret. y p. p.: *girded* o *girt.*
girder (-ø⌃) *s.* ARQ. viga, jácena. *2* burlón, reparón.
girdle (gø⌃døl) *s.* cinto, faja, ceñidor. *2* circunferencia, cerco, zona. *3* zodíaco.
girdle (to) *tr.* ceñir, circundar, rodear. *2* hacer una incisión circular [en un árbol].
girl (gø⌃l) *s. f.* niña, muchacha, joven: *best ~,* novia. *2* chica, doncella, criada.
girlhood (-ud) *s.* niñez, juventud [en la mujer].
girlish (-ish) *adj.* juvenil; de niña o muchacha.
girt (gø⌃t) *pret.* y *p. p.* de TO GIRD. *2 adj. ~ up,* preparado, animoso.
girt (to) *tr.* ceñir, rodear. *2* sitiar. *3* investir [de].
girth (gø⌃z) *s.* cincha. *2* cinturón, faja. *3* periferia, contorno.
girth (to) *tr.* cinchar. *2* ceñir, rodear.
gist (dȳist) *s.* quid, busilis, punto esencial.
give (giv) *s.* elasticidad.
give (to) *tr.* dar [donar, ofrecer; causar, ocasionar, comunicar]. *2* dar [un golpe, un consejo, etc.]. *3* entregar, confiar. *4* conceder, otorgar. *5* aplicar, dedicar, consagrar. *6* proferir, emitir, lanzar. *7* describir, referir. *8* presentar, exponer. *9* cantar [una canción]; pronunciar [un discurso]; representar [una obra]. *10* brindar por. *11* asignar, atribuir. *12 to ~ away,* dar, regalar; vender regalado; revelar [un secreto]; vender, traicionar. *13 to ~ back,* devolver, restituir. *14 to ~ birth to,* dar a luz; dar origen a. *15 to ~ forth,* publicar, divulgar; producir; despedir [olores, etc.]. *16 to ~ ground,* ceder terreno. *17 to ~ it to one,* dar de palos a uno; regañarle. *18 to ~ off,* despedir [olores, etc.]. *19 to ~ oneself up,* entregarse, rendirse. *20 to ~ oneself up to,* entregarse a; darse a. *21 to ~ out,* publicar, declarar; emitir; repartir. *22 to ~ over,* entregar; desistir de. *23 to ~ rise to,* originar, ocasionar. *24 to ~ the lie to,* dar

glimpse

un mentís, desmentir. *25 to* ~ *the sack*, dar calabazas, despedir. *26 to* ~ *the slip*, dar esquinazo, burlar la vigilancia de. *27 to* ~ *up*, renunciar a, abandonar; entregarse, ceder, rendir; dar por perdido; desahuciar [a un enfermo]; dedicar. *28 to* ~ *way*, ceder; cejar; hundirse; aflojarse, romperse [una cuerda]; ponerse a remar. *29 to* ~ *way to*, ser reemplazado por; ceder a, abandonarse a. *30 intr.* dar, ser dadivoso. *31* aflojarse, ablandarse, dar de sí; ceder, romperse. *32* [hablando de puertas, ventanas, etc.] dar, salir [a]. *33 to* ~ *in*, ceder, consentir; darse por vencido. *34 to* ~ *out*, acabarse, agotarse; no poder más. *35 to* ~ *over*, cesar, discontinuar. *36 to* ~ *up*, desistir, cejar; darse por vencido. ¶ Pret.: *gave*; p. p.: *given*.
giveaway (gi·vauei) *s.* pop. traición, denuncia. *2* revelación involuntaria. *3* ganapierde.
given (gi·vn) *p. p.* de TO GIVE. *2 adj.* dado. *3* MAT. conocido. *4* ~ *name*, nombre de pila. *5 conj.* ~ *that*, suponiendo que.
giver (gi·vøʳ) *s.* dador, donador, donante. *2* distribuidor, dispensador.
guizzard (gi·šaʳd) *s.* molleja [de ave].
glabrous (glei·brøs) *adj.* BOT., ZOOL. glabro.
glacé (glæsei·) *adj.* glaseado. *2* cubierto de una capa de azúcar.
glacial (glei·shial) *adj.* glacial.
glacier (-shiøʳ) *s.* glaciar, helero, ventisquero.
glacis (glæ·sis) *s.* FORT. glacis.
glad (glæd) *adj.* alegre, contento, gozoso: *to be* ~ *of, that, to,* etc., alegrarse de o de que; tener mucho gusto en. *2* alegre, brillante, hermoso.
gladden (to) (glæ·døn) *tr.* alegrar, regocijar, recrear, agradar. *2* animar, hermosear.
gladdon (glæ·don) *s.* BOT. íride. *2* GLADIOLUS.
glade (gleid) *s.* claro herboso [en un bosque].
gladiator (glæ·dieitøʳ) *s.* gladiador.
gladiolus (glædai·oløs) *s.* BOT. gladiolo, estoque.
gladly (glæ·dli) *adv.* alegremente. *2* gustosamente, de buen grado; de buena gana.
gladness (-nis) *s.* alegría, contento.
gladsome (-søm) *adj.* alegre, placentero.
glair (gle·øʳ) *s.* clara de huevo. *2* cualquier substancia viscosa y transparente.
glair (to) *tr.* untar con clara de huevo.
glairy (-i) *adj.* viscoso, pegajoso.
glamorous (glæ·mørøs) *adj.* fascinador.
glamo(u)r (glæ·møʳ) *s.* fascinación, encanto, hechizo.
glance (glæns) *s.* mirada, ojeada, vistazo: *at a* ~, de una ojeada. *2* vislumbre. *3* destello, relámpago. *4* golpe dado oblicuamente; desviación [por choque].
glance (to) *intr.-tr.* dar o lanzar una mirada, dar una ojeada, un vistazo; mirar al soslayo; *to* ~ *over*, hojear [un libro]. *2 intr.* destellar, fulgurar. *3* rebotar y desviarse [una bala, etc.]. *4* aludir o referirse de paso. *5 tr.* dirigir súbitamente u oblicuamente [la mirada, un tiro, etc.].
glancing (-ing) *adj.* oblicuo, de refilón [golpe]. *2* hecho o dicho de paso.
gland (glænd) *s.* ZOOL., BOT. glándula. *2* ANAT. ganglio.
glanders (glæ·ndøʳs) *s.* VET. muermo.
glandula (-ȳula) *s.* glándula.
glandular (-ȳulaʳ) *adj.* glandular.
glandulous (-ȳuløs) *adj.* glanduloso.
glans (glæns) *s.* ANAT. glande. *2* BOT. bellota.
glare (gle·øʳ) *s.* luz intensa, vivo resplandor. *2* re-

sol. *3* viso, destello. *4* aspecto deslumbrante. *5* mirada feroz, penetrante. *6* superficie lisa y brillante.
glare (to) *intr.* brillar, resplandecer, relumbrar, deslumbrar. *2* ser vivo [un color]. *3* mirar con fiereza o enojo.
glaring (-gle·øring) *adj.* brillante, deslumbrador. *2* evidente, notorio, que salta a la vista. *3* de mirada feroz, penetrante [ojos].
glass (glas) *s.* vidrio, cristal [materia]: ~ *blower*, vidriero; ~ *case*, escaparate,vitrina. *2* vaso, copa. *3* cristalería [de mesa]. *4* cristal [de ventana, de reloj, etc.]. *5* espejo. *6* ÓPT. lente; anteojo, catalejo, telescopio, etc. *7* reloj de arena. *8* termómetro o barómetro. *9 pl.* lentes, anteojos, gafas; gemelos.
glassful (-ful) *s.* vaso, copa [contenido].
glasshouse (-jaus) *s.* fábrica de vidrio o cristal. *2* invernáculo. *3* galería de fotógrafo.
glassmaker (-meikøʳ) *s.* vidriero.
glassware (-ueʳ) *s.* cristalería, vajilla de cristal; objetos de vidrio.
glasswork (-uøʳk) *s.* fabricación del vidrio. *2* artículos de vidrio. *3 sing.* o *pl.* fábrica de vidrio o cristal.
glasswort (-uøʳt) *s.* BOT. sosa, barrilla.
glassy (-i) *adj.* cristalino. *2* vítreo; vidrioso.
glaucoma (glokou·ma) *s.* MED. glaucoma.
glaucous (glo·køs) *adj.* glauco.
glaze (gleiš) *s.* vidriado. *2* glaseado, satinado, lustre. *3* velo [de los ojos vidriosos]. *4* capa muy fina de hielo. *5* PINT. veladura.
glaze (to) *tr.* vidriar, barnizar. *2* glasear, satinar, velar [los ojos]. *3* PINT. velar. *4* poner vidrios o cristales a.
glazed (-d) *adj.* vidriado; glaseado, satinado: ~ *tile*, azulejo.
glazing (-ing) *s.* vidriado; satinado, glaseado. *2* lustre, barniz. *3* colocación de cristales. *4* cristalería [de puertas, ventanas, etc.].
gleam (glim) *s.* destello. *2* resplandor, brillo tenue o pasajero. *3* rayo [de luz, de esperanza].
gleam (to) *intr.* destellar, fulgurar, brillar [con luz tenue o pasajera]. *2* aparecer [una luz].
glean (to) (glin) *tr.* espigar, rebuscar.
gleaner (øʳ) *s.* espigador, espigadera.
gleaning (-ing) *s.* espigueo, rebusca.
glebe (glib) *s.* poét. suelo, tierra [laborable]. *2* ECLES. (Ingl.) tierras beneficiales.
glee (gli) *s.* alegría, gozo, júbilo, regocijo. *2* MÚS. canción para voces solas.
gleeful (-ful), **gleesome** (-søm) *adj.* alegre, gozoso, jubiloso.
glen (glen) *s.* cañada, hondonada, valle angosto.
glengarry (glengæ·ri) *s.* gorra escocesa.
glenoid (gli·noid) *adj.* ANAT. glenoideo.
glib (glib) *adj.* locuaz, suelto de lengua.
glibness (-nis) *s.* facundia, labia, locuacidad.
glide (glaid) *s.* deslizamiento, escurrimiento. *2* AVIA. planeo.
glide (to) *intr.* deslizarse, escurrirse, resbalar. *2* correr suavemente. *3* AVIA. planear.
glider (-oʳ) *s.* AVIA. planeador.
glimmer (gli·møʳ) *s.* vislumbre, resplandor, viso, luz débil. *2* MINER. mica.
glimmer (to) *intr.* brillar, lucir [débilmente]; rielar; alborear; titilar.
glimmering (-ing) *s.* luz débil o trémula. *2* vislumbre, atisbo, vaga idea.
glimpse (glimps) *s.* resplandor fugaz; visión rá-

pida, breve; vislumbre: *to catch a ~ of*, vislumbrar, entrever.

glimpse (to) *intr.* echar una ojeada. 2 brillar con luz débil o trémula; destellar. 3 *tr.* vislumbrar, entrever.

glint (glint) *s.* brillo, fulgor, rayo, destello.

glint (to) *intr.* brillar, lucir, destellar. 2 rebotar. 3 *tr.* reflejar [la luz]; hacer brillar.

glisten (gli·søn) *s.* brillo, centelleo.

glisten (to) *intr.* brillar, centellear, relucir.

glitter (gli·tø^r) *s.* luz brillante, resplandor. 2 brillo, resplandor, lustre.

glitter (to) *intr.* brillar, relucir, chispear, rutilar. 2 brillar, resplandecer, ser espléndido.

gloaming (glou·ming) *s.* anochecer, anochecida.

gloat (to) (glout) *intr.* gozarse en; mirar con satisfacción maligna; con avaricia.

globate (d (glou·beit(id) *adj.* esférico, globular.

globe (gloub) *s.* globo, esfera, bola. 2 GEOGR., ASTR.. globo, esfera [terrestre o celeste]. 3 globo [de lámpara]. 4 pecera globular. 5 BOT. ~ *amaranth*, perpetua.

globefish (-fish) *s.* ICT. orbe.

globetrotter (-ratø^r) *s.* trotamundos.

globose (-ous) *adj.* globoso, redondo.

globular (glo·biula^r) *adj.* globular. 2 esférico.

globule (glo·biul) *s.* glóbulo.

globulin (-in) *s.* QUÍM. globulina.

glomerate (glo·mørit) *adj.* aglomerado [en forma de bola], conglobado.

glomerule (glo·mørul) *s.* BOT. glomérulo.

gloom (glum) *s.* oscuridad, lobreguez, tinieblas. 3 tristeza, melancolía.

gloom (to) *tr.* oscurecer, entenebrecer. 2 entristecer. 3 *intr.* oscurecerse, entenebrecerse. 4 aparecer sombrío, destacarse sombríamente. 5 entristecerse.

gloomy (-i) *adj.* oscuro, lóbrego, tenebroso. 2 sombrío, triste, melancólico, tétrico; abatido. 3 adusto, hosco.

Gloria (glo·riæ) *s.* LITURG. Gloria.

glorification (glorifikei·shøn) *s.* glorificación. 2 fam. celebración, fiesta, holgorio.

glorify (to) (glo·rifai) *tr.* glorificar. 2 ensalzar, magnificar. ¶ Pret. y p. p.: *glorified*.

gloriole (glo·rioul) *s.* aureola, halo.

glorious (glo·riøs) *adj.* glorioso. 2 magnífico, espléndido. 3 fam. achispado.

glory (glo·ri) *s.* gloria [bienaventuranza, cielo; fama, celebridad; esplendor, magnificencia]: *to go to ~*, fig. morir. 2 grandeza, brillantez, lustre, belleza radiante. 3 aureola, halo.

glory (to) *intr.* exultar; gloriarse: *to ~ in*, gloriarse de; gloriarse en. ¶ Pret. y p. p.: *gloried*.

gloss (glos) *s.* lustre, brillo, pulimento. 2 falsa apariencia, oropel. 3 colorido, paliativo. 4 glosa.

gloss (to) *tr.* lustrar, glasear, satinar, pulir. 2 colorear, cohonestar, paliar. 3 *tr.-intr.* glosar.

glossarist (gla·sarist) *s.* glosador, escoliasta.

glossary (gla·sari) *s.* glosario.

glossiness (gla·sinis) *s.* lustre, pulimento.

glossy (glo·si) *adj.* lustroso, brillante, glaseado, satinado. 2 especioso, de apariencia plausible.

glottis (gla·tis) *s.* ANAT. glotis.

glove (gløv) *s.* guante: ~ *stretcher*, abridor de guantes.

glove (to) *tr.* enguantar. 2 proveer de guantes.

glover (glø·vø^r) *s.* guantero.

glow (glou) *s.* luz, resplandor [de un ascua, de un cuerpo candente], soflama. 2 resplandor rojo en el cielo, arrebol. 3 viveza de color. 4 color [en

las mejillas, en el cuerpo]. 5 ardor, vehemencia; animación. 6 calor [en el cuerpo].

glow (to) *intr.* dar luz o calor vivos; estar candente, arder sin llama. 2 brillar, resplandecer; estar encendido [el rostro, el cielo, etc.]; mostrar interés, animación. 3 tener colores vivos. 4 arder [de pasión, ira, etc.]. 5 sentir calor.

glower (gla·uø^r) *s.* mirada ceñuda, amenazadora.

glower (to) *intr.* mirar ceñudo.

glowing (glou·ing) *adj.* resplandeciente. 2 ardiente, encendido. 3 brillante [color]. 4 entusiasta.

glowworm (glou·uø^rm) *s.* ENT. luciérnaga; cocuyo.

gloze (to) (glouš) *tr.-intr.* colorear, paliar. 2 adular. 3 abrillantar.

glucemia (glusɪ·mia) *s.* MED. glucemia.

glucinium (glusi·niøm), **glucinum** (glusai·nøm) *s.* QUÍM. glucinio.

glucose (glu·kous) *s.* QUÍM. glucosa.

glue (glu o gliu) *s.* cola [para pegar]; gluten. 2 liga, visco.

glue (to) *tr.* encolar, pegar, conglutinar, unir.

gluepot (glu·pot) *s.* cazo para la cola.

gluey (glu·i) *adj.* viscoso, pegajoso, glutinoso.

glum (gløm) *adj.* malhumorado, hosco, sombrío.

glume (glum) *s.* BOT. gluma.

glut (gløt) *s.* hartura, hartazgo. 2 plétora, exceso, saturación.

glut (to) *tr.* hartar. 2 colmar, saturar; atascar. 3 COM. inundar [el mercado]. 4 *intr.* tragar, atracarse. ¶ Pret. y p. p.: *glutted;* ger.: *glutting.*

gluteal (gluti·al) *adj.* glúteo.

gluten (glu·tøn) *s.* gluten.

gluteus (glu·tiøs) *s.* ANAT. músculo glúteo.

glutinous (glu·tinøs) *adj.* glutinoso.

glutton (gløtøn) *adj.-s.* glotón, tragón. 2 *s.* ZOOL. glotón.

gluttonize (to) (-aiš) *intr.* glotonear.

gluttonous (-øs) *adj.* glotón, tragón.

gluttony (-i) *s.* glotonería, gula.

glycerin (e (gli·serin) *s.* glicerina.

glycine (glai·sin) *s.* BOT., QUÍM. glicina.

glycogen (glaiko·dʸin) *s.* gicógeno.

gliptics (gli·ptiks) *s.* glíptica.

gliptography (glipta·grafi) *s.* gliptografía.

gnarl (na^rl) *s.* nudo [en el árbol o la madera].

gnarl (to) *tr.* torcer, retorcer.

gnarled (-d), **gnarly** (-i) *adj.* nudoso, retorcido. 2 pendenciero, terco.

gnash (to) (næsh) *intr.* hacer rechinar los dientes. 2 rechinar [los dientes]. 3 *tr.* hacer rechinar [los dientes].

gnashing (-ing) *s.* rechinamiento de dientes.

gnat (næt) *s.* ENT. mosquito, cinife.

gnaw (to) (no) *tr.* roer. 2 morder, mordicar.

gnawer (-ø^r) *s.* roedor.

gneiss (nais) *s.* GEOL. gneis.

gnome (noum) *s.* gnomo. 2 máxima, aforismo.

gnomon (nou·møn) *s.* gnomon.

gnomonics (noma·niks) *s.* gnomónica.

Gnostic (na·stik) *adj.-s.* gnóstico.

Gnosticism (-tišism) *s.* gonosticismo.

gnu (nu) *s.* ZOOL. gnu, ñu.

go (gou) *s.* ida, ir. 2 marcha, curso, movimiento. 3 energía, empuje, brío. 4 incidente, situación; *this is a pretty ~*, estamos frescos. 5 tentativa: *to have a ~ at*, probar a, tratar de. 6 breve período. 7 convenio, trato: *is it a ~?*, ¿convenido? 8 moda, boga: *it is all the ~*, es la gran moda. 9 éxito. 10 paso libre [a los automóviles].

go (to) *intr.* ir [en casi todos sus sentidos]. 2 caminar, andar. *3* andar, marchar, funcionar. *4* irse. *5* morir. *6* pasar, desaparecer. *7* acabarse. *8* debilitarse, decaer. *9* dirigirse, acudir, recurrir. *10* correr, circular, tener curso. *11* armonizar, adaptarse. *12* alcanzar, llegar [a un límite, cantidad, etc.]. *13* ponerse, volverse, hacerse: *to ~ mad,* volverse loco. *14* contribuir, conducir, tender. *15* salir, resultar. *16* tener éxito, surtir efecto. *17* gobernarse, guiarse, regularse [por]. *18* ceder, soltarse, romperse. *19* rezar, decir [hablando de un texto, una frase, etc.]. *20* hacer [cierto ruido]: *bang went the door,* la puerta hizo ¡pan! *21* entrar, caber *22 to ~ about,* ir por ahí, ir de un lado a otro; ocuparse en; MAR. virar de bordo. *23 to ~ across,* atravesar, cruzar. *24 to ~ after,* seguir; ir en busca de. *25 to ~ against,* ir en contra, oponerse. *26 to ~ ahead,* avanzar; proseguir; adelantar, progresar. *27 to ~ along,* seguir, continuar. *28 to ~ along with,* acompañar. *29 to ~ around,* ir de un lado a otro; dar vueltas, contornar, rodear; alcanzar para todos. *30 to ~ astray,* extraviarse; descarriarse. *31 to ~ at,* atacar, acometer. *32 to ~ away,* irse, ausentarse; pasar [un dolor, etc.]. *33 to ~ back,* retroceder; volverse atrás; *to ~ back on one's word,* desdecirse, faltar uno a su palabra. *34 to ~ bad,* echarse a perder; ir mal. *35 to ~ between,* interponerse, mediar, terciar. *36 to ~ by,* pasar por, junto a; regirse por, atenerse a; ser conocido por, tener, usar [un nombre o apodo]. *37 to ~ down,* bajar, descender; caer; irse a pique; llegar, continuarse [hasta un punto]; ser anotado o registrado. *38 to ~ far,* ir lejos; durar mucho; servir de mucho; alcanzar para mucho. *39 to ~ for,* ser partidario de; representar; ser tenido por; ir en busca de; embestir. *40 to ~ forth,* salir; divulgarse, publicarse. *41 to ~ in,* entrar, encajar. *42 to ~ in for,* favorecer, apoyar; participar en; competir por [un premio, etc.]; dedicarse a; buscar, perseguir. *43 to ~ into,* entrar en; tomar parte en, emprender, dedicarse a; investigar; discutir, tratar de. *44 to ~ near,* acercarse. *45 to ~ off,* irse, largarse; dispararse, estallar, hacer explosión; dormirse, desmayarse; morir; desaparecer; salir, quedar [bien o mal]; fracasar. *46 to ~ off one's head,* volverse loco. *47 to ~ on,* obrar, portarse; continuar, proseguir; durar; progresar; pasar [a hacer algo]; TEAT. salir a la escena. *48 to ~ out,* salir; apagarse, extinguirse; morir; desafiarse; divulgarse. *49 to ~ out of fashion,* pasar de moda. *50 to ~ out of the way,* apartarse, descarriarse, molestarse [en hacer algo]. *51 to ~ over,* pasar [por encima de], atravesar, salvar; pasarse [a otro partido]; releer, repasar, revisar, examinar. *52 to ~ through,* pasar por; traspasar, hender; recorrer, examinar; sufrir, pasar; llevar a cabo; derrochar. *53 to ~ to sleep,* dormirse. *54 to ~ under,* ser conocido por el nombre, título, etc., de; irse a pique; arruinarse; sucumbir, ser vencido. *55 to ~ up,* subir. *56 to ~ with,* acompañar, ir con; cortejar; armonizar con. *57 to ~ without,* pasar o pasarse sin. *58 to ~ wrong,* salir mal, fracasar; ir por mal camino; darse a la mala vida. *59 tr.* ir o llegar hasta. *60* llevar, seguir [un camino]. *61* soportar, tolerar. *62* apostar [en el juego]. *63 to ~ bail,* salir fiador. *64 to ~ halves,* ir a medias. *65 to ~ it,* obrar, avanzar, etc. impetuosamente; pop. obrar, proceder. *66 to ~ one's way,* seguir uno su camino. *67 to ~ shares,*

ir a la parte.
¶ Pret.: *went;* p. p. *gone;* 3.ª pers. del sing.: *goes.*
goad (goud) *s.* aguijada, focino, pincho, aguijón. *2* acicate [estímulo].
goad (to) *tr.* aguijar, aguijonear, picar.
go-ahead *adj.* emprendedor, activo.
goal (goul) *s.* DEP. meta; puerta, portería. *2* DEP. gol. *3* meta, fin, objeto.
goalkeeper (-kıpøʳ) *s.* DEP. guardameta, portero.
goat (gout) *s.* ZOOL. cabra; *~ buck,* macho cabrío; *wild ~,* cabra montés; *to be the ~,* fig. pagar el pato.
goatee (goutı·) *s.* perilla [barba].
goatherd (-jøʳd) *s.* cabrero, cabrerizo.
goatish (-ish) *adj.* cabruno, hircino. *2* lascivo.
goatskin (-skin) *s.* piel de cabra.
goatsucker (-søkøʳ) *s.* ORN. chotacabras.
gob (gab) *s.* pedazo, masa informe y pequeña.
gobbet (ga·bit) *s.* bocado, pedacito. *2* grumo, pella.
gobble (ga·bøl) *s.* voz del pavo.
gobble (to) *tr.* engullir, tragar. *2 intr.* hacer ruido en la garganta como los pavos.
gobbler (ga·bløʳ) *s.* engullidor, tragón, glotón. *2* ORN. pavo.
go-between *s.* correveidile. *2* alcahuete. *3* intermediario, corredor.
goblet (ga·blit) *s.* copa [para beber].
goblin (ga·blin) *s.* duende, trasgo.
go-by *s.* fam. desaire, esquinazo.
go-cart *s.* carretilla. *2* carruaje ligero. *3* cochecito de niño. *4* andadiño, pollera.
God (gad) *n. pr.* Dios: *act of ~,* fuerza mayor; *~ forbid,* no lo quiera Dios; *~ willing,* Dios mediante; *God's acre,* camposanto. *2 m.* (con min.) dios, deidad [pagana].
godchild (-chaild) *s.* ahijado, ahijada.
goddaughter (-dotøʳ) *s.* ahijada.
goddess (-is) *s.* diosa, deidad, diva.
godfather (-fadøʳ) *s.* padrino [de bautismo].
God-fearing *adj.* temeroso de Dios.
God-forsaken *adj.* abandonado. *2* triste, desierto, desolado.
Godfrey (-fri) *n. pr. m.* Godofredo.
Godhead (-jed) *n. pr.* y *s.* Deidad, Divinidad.
godless (-lis) *adj.* sin Dios, ateo, impío. *2* malvado.
godlike (-laik) *adj.* divino, deiforme.
godliness (-linis) *s.* piedad, devoción, santidad.
godly (-li) *adj.* piadoso, religioso, devoto.
godmother (-mødøʳ) *f.* madrina [de bautismo].
godsend (-send) *s.* merced divina; ganga, suerte inesperada.
godship (-ship) *s.* divinidad.
godson (-søn) *s.* ahijado.
Godspeed (-spıd) *s.-interj.* buena suerte, buen viaje.
godwit (-uit) *s.* ORN. especie de chorlito.
goffer (to) (ga·føʳ) *tr.* plegar, rizar, encrespar. *2* estampar [el cuero].
go-getter *s.* fam. (E.U.) buscavidas, persona emprendedora.
goggle (ga·gøl) *adj.* saltón [ojo]. *2 pl.* gafas ahumadas o protectoras.
goggle (to) *intr.* torcer los ojos o abrirlos desmesuradamente.
goggle-eyed *adj.* de ojos saltones.
going (gou·ing) *p. a. de* TO GO. *2 s.* paso, andar, andadura. *3* ida, marcha, partida. *4* estado del camino. *5 pl.* idas y venidas. *6 goings on,* ocurrencias, sucesos; acciones, conducta.
goiter, goitre (goi·tøʳ) *s.* MED. bocio, papera.

goitrous (goi·trøs) *adj.* que tiene bocio.
gold (gould) *s.* oro [metal]. *2* fig. oro [dinero, riqueza]. *3* color del oro. *4 adj.* de oro; áureo, dorado: *Gold Coast*, GEOGR. Costa de Oro; ~ *lace*, galón o encaje de oro; ~ *leaf*, pan de oro; ~ *standard*, patrón oro.
gold-bearing *adj.* aurífero.
goldbeater (gou·ldbɪtøʳ) *s.* batidor de oro, batihoja.
goldcrest (gou·ldcrest) *s.* ORN. reyezuelo.
golden (-øn) *adj.* de oro, áureo, dorado: ~ *calf*, becerro de oro; ~ *eagle*, águila caudal; *golden Fleece*, MIT. Vellocino de oro, Toisón de oro; ~ *mean*, justo medio, ~ *number*, número áureo; ~ *wedding*, bodas de oro.
goldfinch (-finch) *s.* ORN. jilguero, pintacilgo.
goldfish (-fish) *s.* ICT. carpa dorada. *2* pececillo de color.
gold-laced *adj.* galoneado de oro.
goldsmith (-smiz) *s.* orífice, orfebre.
golf (galf) *s.* DEP. golf: ~ *course*, ~ *links*, campo de golf.
golf (to) *intr.* jugar al golf.
golfer (-øʳ) *s.* jugador de golf.
Golgotha (ga·lgoza) *s.* Gólgota.
Goliath (goulai·az) *n. pr.* BIB. Goliat.
golliwog (ga·liuag) *s.* muñeca grotesca.
gondola (ga·ndola) *s.* góndola. *2* barquilla [de dirigible]. *3* FERROC. batea.
gondolier (gandøli·øʳ) *s.* gondolero.
gone (gon) *p. p.* de TO GO. *2* ido, pasado. *3* muerto. *4* desaparecido. *5* agotado. *6* débil, desfallecido. *7* perdido, arruinado.
gonfalon (ga·nfałøn) *s.* confalón, gonfalón.
gonfalonier (ganfałøni·øʳ) *s.* confalonier, confaloniero.
gong (gong) *s.* gong, batintín.
Gongorism (ga·ngøri̇šm) *s.* gongorismo.
goniometer (gounia·mitøʳ) *s.* goniómetro.
goniometry (gounia·metri) *s.* goniometría.
good (gud) *adj.* bueno; ~ *afternoon*, buenas tardes; ~ *books*, fig. favor, bienquerencia; ~ *cheer*, ánimo, confianza, alegría; festín, buena mesa; ~ *day*, buenos días; ~ *evening*, buenas noches; ~ *for nothing*, inútil; perdido, haragán; ~ *form*, buena educación; *Good Friday*, Viernes Santo; ~ *looks*, buen aspecto; hermosura; ~ *morn*, ~ *morning*, buenos días; ~ *nature*, bondad buen corazón, benevolencia; ~ *night*, buenas noches; ~ *sense*, buen sentido, sensatez; ~ *time*, buen rato, día, etc.; diversión: ~ *turn*, favor, servicio; ~ *will*, buena voluntad; *a* ~ *deal*, bastantes, mucho; *a* ~ *while*, un buen rato, bastante tiempo; *as* ~ *as*, prácticamente, como sí; *as* ~ *as done*, cosa hecha, como si estuviera hecho; *to be as* ~ *as one's word*, ser hombre de palabra; *in* ~ *earnest*, de veras, seriamente; *in* ~ *order*, en buen estado. *2* valiente, animoso. *3* solvente, responsable; que dispone de o responde por [cierta cantidad].
    4 interj. ¡bueno!, ¡bien!, ¡magnífico!
    5 s. bien; beneficio, provecho, ventaja: *to do* ~, hacer el bien; aprovechar; ir bien para la salud; *much* ~ *may it do you*, buen provecho le haga; *what is the* ~ *of it?*, ¿para qué sirve? *6 for* ~, para siempre, definitivamente. *7 for* ~ *and all*, de una vez para siempre. *8 the* ~, el bien; lo bueno; los buenos.
good-by, good-bye (-bai·) *s.* adiós, despedida. *2 interj.* ¡adiós!, ¡hasta la vista!
good-fellowship *s.* compañerismo, camaradería.

good-hearted *adj.* de buen corazón.
good-humoured *adj.* jovial; afable.
goodish (-ish) *adj.* bastante bueno; bastante grande, regular, considerable.
goodlines (-linis) *s.* belleza, hermosura, gracia, elegancia.
good-looking *adj.* guapo, bien parecido.
goodly (-li) *adj.* bello, hermoso, gracioso. *2* guapo, bien parecido. *3* agradable, vistoso. *4* excelente. *5* bueno, bastante grande, considerable.
good-natured *adj.* bonachón, afable.
goodness (-nis) *s.* bondad. *2* virtud. *3* fineza, favor. *4 interj.* ¡válgame Dios!; ~ *gracious!*, ¡Santo Dios!, *for* ~ *sake*, ¡por Dios!
goods (-s) *s. pl.* géneros, mercancías, efectos: ~ *train*, ~ *wagon*, (Ingl.) tren, vagón, de carga o mercancías.
goodwife (-uaif) *s.* ant. ama de casa, señora.
goody (-i) *adj.* bonachón. *2* sensiblero. *3* mojigato. *4 s.* tía, mujer del pueblo. *5* golosina.
goosander (gusæ·ndøʳ) *s.* ORN. mergánsar, mergo.
goose (gus) *pl.* **geese** (gis) *s.* ORN. ganso, ánsar, oca: ~ *flesh*, fig. carne de gallina; ~ *step*, paso de la oca; *to kill the* ~ *that lays the golden eggs*, matar la gallina de los huevos de oro. *2* fig. ganso, bobo.
gooseberry (-beri) *s.* BOT. grosellero silvestre, uva espina o crespa.
foosefoot (-fut) *s.* BOT. quenopodio.
gooseherd (-jøʳd) *s.* ansarero.
gooseneck (-nek) *s.* cuello de cisne. *2* MAR. pescante de bote. *3* barra, tubo, etc., curvos.
Gordian (go·ʳdian) *adj.* gordiano: ~ *knot*, nudo gordiano.
gore (gouʳ) *s.* sangre. *2* sangre espesa o cuajada. *3* COST. cuchillo, nesga. *4* pieza triangular.
gore (to) *tr.* poner cuchillo o nesga a. *2* acornear. *3* herir con los colmillos.
gorge (goʳdỹ) *s.* garganta, gaznate. *2* desfiladero, garganta, barranca. *3* contenido del estómago: *my* ~ *rises at*, me revuelve el estómago. *4* masa que obstruye. *5* FORT. gola.
gorge (to) *tr.* engullir, tragar. *2* hartar, atiborrar. *3* obstruir. *4 intr.* hartarse, atracarse.
gorgeous (go·ʳdỹøs) *adj.* brillante, vistoso, magnífico, suntuoso.
gorget (go·ʳdỹit) *s.* gorguera, gorjal [de la armadura]. *2* MIL. gola. *3* collar, adorno para el cuello.
Gorgon (gø·ʳgøn) *s.* MIT. Gorgona. *2* fam. esperpento; mujer muy fea.
gorilla (gøri·la) *s.* ZOOL. gorila.
gormand (goʳmnd) *s.* glotón, goloso.
gormandize (-aiš) *s.* gastronomía.
gormandize (to) *tr.-intr.* comer con gula.
gormandizer (-aisøʳ) *s.* goloso, glotón.
gorse (goʳs) *s.* BOT. aulaga. *2* BOT. enebro.
gory (gou·ri) *adj.* ensangrentado, sangriento.
goshawk (ga·sjok) *s.* ORN. azor.
gosling (ga·sling) *s.* ORN. ansarino, gansarón.
gospel (ga·spøl) *s.* evangelio: *the* ~ *truth*, la pura verdad, el evangelio.
gospel (to) *intr.* predicar el evangelio.
gossamer (ga·samøʳ) *s.* hilo de araña o telaraña flotante. *2* TEJ. gasa. *3* cosa muy fina o sutil.
gossamer(y (-i) *adj.* sutil, delgado.
gossip (ga·sip) *s.* chismografía, comadreo, murmuración. *2* charla. *3* habladuría, chisme. *4* chismoso, murmurador. *5* compadre, comadre.
gossip (to) *intr.* chismear, murmurar, charlar.
gossipy (-i) *adj.* chismoso, murmurador.
got (gat) *pret. y p. p.* de TO GET.

Goth (goz) s. godo. 2 bárbaro, rudo.
Gothic (-ik) adj. gótico. 2 s. lengua goda.
Gothicism (-isiŝm) s. estilo gótico. 2 (con min.) barbarie, rudeza.
gotten (ga·tøn) (E.U.) p. p. de TO GET.
gouge (gaudŷ) s. gubia, mediacaña. 2 acanaladura, estría. 4 (E.U.) estafa.
gouge (to) tr. estropear, acanalar. 2 to ~ out, sacar [un ojo, esp. con el pulgar]; (E.U.) engañar, estafar.
gourd (gøᵣd o guᵣd) s. BOT. calabaza; calabacera: bottle ~, calabaza vinatera. 2 calabacino.
gourmand (gu·ᵣmand) s. gastrónomo, goloso; glotón.
gourmet (guᵣmei·) s. gastrónomo.
gout (gaut) s. MED. gota.
goutiness (-inis) s. afección gotosa.
gouty (-i) adj. gotoso.
govern (to) (gø·vøᵣn) tr. gobernar, regir, dirigir, manejar, regular. 2 dominar, refrenar. 3 GRAM. regir. 4 MAR. gobernar.
governable (-abøl) adj. dócil, manejable.
governance (-ans) s. gobierno, gobernación.
governess (-is) s. aya, institutriz. 2 ant. gobernadora.
government (-mønt) s. gobierno, gobernación, dirección, manejo, administración; mando, autoridad: for your ~, para su gobierno. 2 gobierno [forma política; ministerio]. 3 GRAM. régimen.
governmental (-mental) adj. gubernamental, gubernativo.
governor (-øᵣ) s. gobernador. 2 director, administrador. 3 ayo, preceptor. 4 pop. padre, tutor; amo, principal. 5 MEC. regulador.
gowan (gau·an) s. DAISY 1.
gown (gaun) s. vestido [de mujer]. 2 bata; túnica; toga, vestido talar: dressing ~, bata.
gownsman (-smæn) s. togado. 2 civil, paisano.
grab (græb) s. agarro, asimiento, presa. 2 arrebatiña. 3 robo, sisa. 4 MEC. garfio, grapa. 5 MEC. ~ bucket, cucharón de quijadas.
grab (to) tr. agarrar, asir, coger, arrebatar. 2 apropiarse indebidamente. 3 intr. to ~ at, tratar de coger, de arrebatar. ¶ Pret. y p. p.: grabbed; ger.: -bbing.
grabble (to) (græ·bøl) intr. ir o hacer a tientas. 2 estar postrado.
Grace (greis) n. pr. f. Gracia.
grace s. gracia [en todos sus sentidos menos en el de chiste y en el de nombre de cada uno]: ~ stroke, golpe de gracia; to be in one's good graces, estar en gracia cerca de uno. 2 dignación, amabilidad. 3 garbo, donaire. 4 disposición, talante: with a bad ~, de mala gana, con aspereza. 5 tratamiento que se da a un duque, un arzobispo, etc. 6 MÚS. adorno: ~ note, nota de adorno. 7 to say ~, dar gracias o bendecir la mesa. 8 pl. MIT. The Graces, las gracias.
grace (to) tr. adornar. 2 agraciar, favorecer. 3 honrar, elevar.
graceful (-ful) adj. gracioso, airoso, agraciado, elegante; fácil, natural.
gracefulness (-fulnis) s. gracia, donosura, garbo, donaire, gentileza, elegancia.
graceless (-lis) adj. desgraciado, falto de gracia, feo, desgarbado. 2 malvado, depravado.
gracile (græ·sil) adj. grácil.
gracious (grei·shøs) adj. gracioso, atractivo. 2 afable, cortés. 3 benigno, bondadoso. 4 de afable superioridad [aire, maneras]. 5 interj. gracious! ¡válgame Dios!

graciously (-i) adv. graciosamente, afablemente, cortesmente, benignamente.
grackle (græ·køl) s. ORN. especie de mirlo.
gradate (to) (grei·deit) intr. ir en gradación. 2 tr. graduar [disponer en grados]. 3 PINT. degradar.
gradation (greidei·shøn) s. gradación; paso gradual. 2 grado [en una serie, etc.]. 3 rango. 4 graduación [disposición en grados]. 5 PINT. degradación.
grade (grei·d) s. grado [que puede tener una cosa]. 2 clase, calidad. 3 MIL. graduación. 4 GEOM. centésima parte del ángulo recto. 5 (E.U.) grado, curso [de una escuela]. 6 ING. pendiente, desnivel; grado de pendiente: down ~, cuesta abajo; up ~, cuesta arriba. 7 (E.U.) ~ crossing, paso a nivel.
grade (to) tr. graduar [disponer por grados]. 2 clasificar [por grados o clases]. 3 matizar [un color, etc.]. 4 ING. nivelar, explanar [un camino, etc.].
grader (-øᵣ) s. el o lo que gradúa, clasifica, etc. 2 ING. nivelador.
gradient (grei·diønt) s. ING. pendiente, inclinación, desnivel. 2 METEOR. gradiente. 3 grado de aumento o disminución de una magnitud variable.
gradin (grei·din) s. grada, escalón. 2 gradilla [de altar]. 3 pl. gradería.
gradine (gra·din) s. GRADIN. 2 gradina [de escultor].
gradual (græ·diual) adj. gradual; graduado. 2 m. LITURG. Gradual.
gradualness (-nis) s. calidad de gradual.
graduate (græ·diuit) adj. graduado [en universidad]. 2 s. el que tiene grado académico. 3 QUÍM. graduador, probeta.
graduate (to) (græ·diueit) tr. graduar [dividir por grados]. 2 aumentar, disminuir, etc., gradualmente. 3 graduar [conferir un grado]. 4 intr. variar gradualmente. 5 graduarse [recibir un grado académico].
graduation (grædiuei·shøn) s. graduación. | No tiene el sentido de categoría de un militar.
graduator (græ·diueitøᵣ) s. graduador.
Gr(a)ecism (gri·siŝm) s. grecismo, helenismo.
graffito (grafi·tou), pl. -ti (tai) s. ARQUEOL. grafito. 2 esgrafiado.
graft (graft) s. AGR., CIR. injerto. 2 fam. (E.U.) ganancia ilícita, malversación, chanchullo.
graft (to) tr. injertar. 2 injerir, inserir, unir. 3 fam. (E.U.) adquirir ilícitamente. 4 intr. hacer injertos. 5 fam. (E.U.) hacer chanchullos.
grafter (-øᵣ) s. injertador. 2 (E.U.) ladrón, chanchullero.
grafting (-ing) s. injerto [acción].
grail (greil) s. grial: the Holy Grail, el Santo Grial.
grain (grein) s. grano [de los cereales, de la uva, etc.; semilla, partícula]: ~ weevil, gorgojo del grano; with a ~ of salt, fig. con cierto escepticismo. 2 plantas que dan grano, cereales. 3 grano [peso]. 4 átomo, pizca, pequeña cantidad. 5 cuenta, perla. 6 grana, quermes, color rojo. 7 grano [de una superficie, de la piedra]; flor [del cuero]; granilla [del paño]; fibra, veta [de la madera]. 8 índole, disposición, inclinación: against the ~, contra la inclinación de uno, cuesta arriba, a contrapelo. 9 to dye in the ~, teñir en rama. 10 BOT. grains of Paradise, granos del Paraíso.
grain (to) intr. formar grano. 2 tr. teñir en rama. 3

granular. *4* granear. *5* granelar [el cuero]. *6* vetear.
grainfield (-fıld) *s.* mies, sembrado.
grainy (-i) *adj.* granular, granoso. *2* lleno de granos.
gram (græm) *s.* GRAMME.
gramercy (gramø·ʳsi) *interj.* ¡gracias! *2* ¡Dios mío!
graminaceous (graminei·shiøs) *adj.* gramináceo.
grammar (græ·maʳ) *s.* gramática. *2* principios, elementos [de una ciencia o arte]. *3* ~ *school*, colegio de segunda enseñanza; (E.U.) escuela elemental.
grammarian (græme·rian) *s.* gramático.
grammatic (al (gr-aemæ·tik(al) *adj.* gramatical, gramático.
grammaticalness (-nis) *s.* corrección gramatical.
gramme (græm) *s.* gramo.
gramophone (græ·mofoun) *s.* gramófono.
grampus (græ·mpøs) *s.* ZOOL. orca, orco.
granadilla (grændi·l) *s.* BOT. granadilla. *2* ~ *tree*, ~ *wood*, granadillo [árbol; madera].
granary (græ·nari) *s.* granero.
grand (grænd) *adj.* grande, gran [en ciertos sentidos]: *Grand Canyon*, Gran Cañón [del Colorado]; ~ *duke*, gran duque; ~ *jury*, DER. jurado que investiga y decide si hay motivo para procesar; ~ *master*, gran maestre; ~ *piano*, piano de cola. *2* grandioso. *3* admirable, magnífico, espléndido, soberbio. *4* solemne, majestuoso. *5* completo, comprensivo.
grandam (-æm) *s.* abuela. *2* anciana.
grandaunt (-ænt) *s.* tía abuela.
grandchild (-chaild) *s.* nieto, nieta.
granddaughter (-dotøʳ) *s.* nieta.
grandee (-ı·) *s.* grande [de un reino]; prócer, magnate.
grandeur (-ŷøʳ) *s.* grandeza, magnificencia.
grandfather (-fadøʳ) *s.* abuelo: *grandfather's clock*, reloj de caja.
grandiloquence (grændi·lokuøns) *s.* grandilocuencia.
grandiloquent (grændi·lokuønt), **grandiloquous** (grændi·lokuøs) *adj.* grandilocuente, grandilocuo.
grandiose (græ·ndiouš) *adj.* grandioso, imponente. *2* pomposo, hinchado, bombástico.
grandma (-ma) *s. fam.* abuela, abuelita.
grandmother (-mødøʳ) *s.* abuela.
grandnephew (-nefiu) *s.* resobrino.
grandness (-nis) *s.* grandeza, grandiosidad, magnificencia.
grandniece (-nıs) *s.* resobrina.
grandpa (-pa) *s. fam.* abuelo, abuelito.
grndparent (-perøn) *s.* abuelo o abuela. *2 pl.* abuelos [el abuelo y la abuela].
grandson (-søn) *s.* nieto.
grandstand (-stænd) *s.* gradería cubierta, tribuna.
granduncle (-ønkøl) *s.* tío abuelo.
grange (greindŷ) *s.* granja, hacienda, cortijo, alquería.
granger (-øʳ) *s.* granjero, cortijero.
granite (græ·nit) *s.* MINER. granito.
granitic(al (græni·tik(al) *adj.* granítico.
granivorous (græni·vørøs) *adj.* granívoro.
granny (græ·ni) *s. fam.* abuela, abuelita.
grant (grant) *s.* concesión, otorgamiento, donación. *2* don, merced, subvención, privilegio; cosa concedida. *3* DER. cesión por escritura. *4* asentimiento, asenso.
grant (to) *tr.* conceder, otorgar, dispensar, dar. *2*

conceder, dar de barato: *to take for granted*, dar por supuesto. *3* DER. ceder, transferir.
grantee (-ı·) *s.* cesionario.
grantor (-øʳ) *s.* otorgador, dispensador, el que concede. *2* cesionista.
granular (græ·niulaʳ), **granulary** (græ·niuleri) *adj.* granular. *2* granuloso, granilloso.
granulate (to) (græ·niuleit) *tr.* granular. *2* granear. *3 intr.* formar gránulos. *4* MED. granular.
granulated (-id) *adj.* granulado, graneado. *2* en grano.
granulation (-ei·shøn) *s.* granulación.
granule (græ·niul) *s.* gránulo.
granulous (-øs) *adj.* granular, granuloso.
grape (greip) *s.* BOT. uva: *sour grapes*, ¡están verdes! *2* BOT. baya de ciertas plantas. *3* vid, parra.
grapefruit (-frut) *s.* BOT. toronja, pomelo.
grapery (-øri) *s.* invernadero o criadero de uvas.
grapeshot (-shat) *s.* ARTILL. metralla.
grapeskin (-kin) *s.* hollejo de uva.
grapestone (-stoun) *s.* semilla de uva.
grapevine (-vain) *s.* vid, parra.
graph (græf) *s.* gráfica, curva, diagrama. *2* GRAM. grafía.
graph (to) *tr.* representar con una gráfica.
graphic (al (-ik(al) *adj.* gráfico.
graphite (græ·fait) *s.* MINER. grafito, plombagina.
graphology (græfa·lodŷi) *s.* grafología.
graphometer (grafa·metøʳ) *s.* grafómetro.
grapnel (græ·pnel) *s.* MAR. rezón, rizón. *2* arpeo, rebañadera, garabato, garfio.
grapple (græ·pøl) *s.* presa, agarro, engarro. *2* lucha cuerpo a cuerpo. *3* GRAPNEL.
grapple (to) *tr.* asir, aferrar, agarrar, sujetar. *2 intr.* agarrarse, cogerse; luchar cuerpo a cuerpo. *3 to* ~ *with*, luchar con; tratar de comprender, resolver, etc.
grappling hook o **iron** (græ·pling) *s.* arpeo, garfio.
grasp (grasp) *s.* asimiento, agarro. *2* apretón de manos. *3* abrazo. *4* dominio, poder, alcance: *within the* ~ *of*, al alcance de. *5* comprensión.
grasp (to) *tr.* asir, coger, empuñar. *2* abrazar, abarcar; apoderarse de. *3* comprender, entender. *4 intr. to* ~ *at*, tratar de asir o coger; aceptar con avidez.
grasping (-ing) *adj.* codicioso, avaro.
grass (græs) *s.* hierba, yerba, herbaje, césped, pasto: *to let the* ~ *grow under one's fett*, perder el tiempo, dormirse en las pajas. *2* BOT. ~ *pink*, clavel coronado.
grass (to) *tr.* apacentar. *2* cubrir de hierba. *3 intr.* pacer.
grass-green *adj.* verde como la hierba.
grass-grown *adj.* cubierto de hierba.
grasshopper (-japøʳ) *s.* ENT. langosta, saltamontes.
grassland (-lænd) *s.* prado, tierra de pasto.
grassplot (-plat) *s.* prado, cuadro de césped.
grassy (-i) *adj.* herboso. *2* herbáceo.
grate (greit) *s.* reja, verja, enrejado. *2* emparrillado. *3* parrilla, rejilla [de hogar].
grate (to) *tr.* COC. rallar. *2* raspar. *3* hacer rechinar. *4* molestar, irritar. *5* enrejar. *6 intr.* rechinar.
grateful (grei·tful) *adj.* agradecido, reconocido. *2* grato, agradable.
grater (grei·tøʳ) *s.* rallador, rallo, raspador.
graticulate (to) (græti·kiuleit) *tr.* DIB. cuadricular.
gratification (grætifikei·shøn) *s.* satisfacción, contento, complacencia, gusto, placer. *2* gratificación, recompensa.
gratify (to) (græ·tifai) *tr.* satisfacer, dar gusto, con-

tentar, complacer, agradar. *2* gratificar. ¶ Pret.
y p. p.: *gratified.*
grating (grei·ting) *adj.* que raspa. *2* rechinante,
chirriante. *3* discordante [sonido]. *4* áspero,
irritante. *5 s.* rechinamiento, chirrido. *6* reja,
rejilla. *7* verja, enrejado. *8* MAR. enjaretado. *9*
ÓPT. retícula. *10 pl.* COC. ralladuras.
gratis (grei·tis) *adv.* gratis, de balde.
gratitude (græ·titiud) *s.* gratitud, reconocimiento.
gratuitous (gratiu·tøs) *adj.* gratuito.
gratuity (gratiu·ti) *s.* don, gratificación, propina.
gratulation (græchulei·shøn) *s.* gratulación.
gratulatory (græ·chulatori) *adj.* gratulatorio.
grave (greiv) *adj.* grave [importante, arduo]. *2*
grave, serio, digno, solemne. *3* serio [color]. *4*
MÚS., GRAM. grave. *6 s.* tumba, sepultura, sepulcro, fosa, hoya. *7* GRAM. acento grave.
grave (to) *tr.* grabar. *2* cincelar, esculpir. ¶ Pret.:
graved; p. p.: *graved* o *graven.*
gravedigger (-digø^r) *s.* sepulturero, enterrador.
gravel (græ·vøl) *s.* arena gruesa, guijo, grava. *2*
MED. cálculos, arenas.
gravel (to) *tr.* enarenar [una superficie], confundir, embarazar. *3* fam. irritar.
graveless (-i·vlis) *adj.* insepulto.
gravelly (græ·vøli) *adj.* arenoso, guijoso.
gravely (grei·vli) *adv.* gravemente.
graven (-n) *p. p.* de TO GRAVE. *2 adj.* grabado, esculpido.
graveness (-nis) *s.* gravedad; seriedad.
graver (-ø^r) *s.* grabador, cincelador, escultor. *2* buril, punzón, cincel.
gravestone (-stoun) *s.* lápida sepulcral.
graveyard (-ia^{r}d) *s.* cementerio, camposanto.
gravid (græ·vid) *adj.* grávido, preñado, fecundo.
gravimeter (grævi·metø^r) *s.* gravímetro.
gravitate (to) (græ·viteit) *intr.* gravitar. *2* gravear.
gravitation (grævitei·shøn) *s.* gravitación.
gravity (græ·viti) *s.* gravedad [importancia; solemnidad, seriedad]. *2* FÍS. gravedad, pesantez.
gravy (grei·vi) *s.* COC. salsa, jugo [de la carne]: ~
boat, salsera.
gray (grei) *adj.* gris, pardo; ~ *matter,* ANAT. substancia gris; ~ *friars,* franciscanos. *2* cano, en-
canecido. *3 adj.-s.* rucio, tordo. *4 s.* color gris o
pardo.
gray (to) *tr.* poner gris o cano. *2 intr.* volverse gris;
encanecer.
gray-haired, gray-headed *adj.* cano, canoso
[pers.].
grayish (-ish) *adj.* grisáceo, agrisado. *2* pardusco.
3 entrecano.
graylag (-læg) *s.* ORN. ánsar, bravo.
grayling (-ling) *s.* ICT. tímalo.
graze (greiš) *s.* rozamiento, roce, rozadura. *2*
pasto, apacentamiento.
graze (to) *tr.* rozar [pasar, herir o desgastar ro-
zando]; arañar, rasguñar; raspar. *2* pacer [la
hierba]. *3* apacentar. *4 intr.* pacer, pastar.
grazier (-ø^r) *s.* ganadero.
grease (gris) *s.* grasa; ~ *cup,* MEC. vaso de engrase;
~ *lift,* AUTO. puente de engrase. *2* manteca, unto,
sebo, pringue. *3* pop. lisonja; soborno.
grease (to) *tr.* engrasar, untar, lubricar, pringar. *2*
fig. untar, sobornar.
greaser (-ø^r) *s.* engrasador.
greasy (-i) *adj.* grasiento, pringoso, aceitoso, mugriento. *2* craso. *3* untuoso.
great (greit) *adj.* grande, gran, magno, mayor: ~
age, edad avanzada; *Great Bear,* ASTR. Osa Mayor; *Great Britain,* la Gran Bretaña; ~ *gun,* ant.

cañón pesado; fig. personaje; *Alexander the
Great,* Alejandro Magno. *2* largo, dilatado. *3* crecido. *4* favorito, preferido. *5* magnífico, estupendo. *6* ASTR. máximo [círculo]. *7* mayúscula
[letra]. *8* fam. *to be* ~ *at,* ser muy hábil o fuerte
en. *9* fam. *to be* ~ *on,* dar mucha importancia a.
10 en nombres de parentesco, indica una generación más, como en *great-grandfather,* bisabuelo. *11 s. the* ~, lo grande, los grandes.
great-aunt *s.* tía abuela.
great-bellied *adj.* barrigudo. *2* preñada.
greatcoat (grei·tkout) *s.* gabán. *2* levitón. *3* capote.
greater (-ø^r) *adj. comp.* de GREAT; mayor, más
grande: *the* ~ *part,* la mayoría. *2 Greater Britain,*
Imperio Británico.
greatest (-ist) *adj. superl.* de GREAT; máximo, sumo,
el mayor; ~ *common divisor,* ART. máximo común divisor.
great-hearted *adj.* animoso, valiente. *2* generoso,
noble, magnánimo.
greatly (-li) *adv.* muy, mucho, grandemente. *2*
grandiosamente. *3* en gran parte.
greatness (-nis) *s.* grandeza. *2* magnitud, amplitud, extensión. *3* pompa, esplendor.
greave (griv) *s.* ARM. greba. *2 pl.* COC. chicharrones.
grebe (grib) *s.* ORN. colimbo.
Grecian (gri·shan) *adj.* griego, greco. *2 s.* griego. *3*
helenista.
Grecianize (to) (-aiš) *tr.-intr.* TO GRECIZE.
Grecism (gri·sišm) *s.* grecismo, helenismo.
Grecize (to) (grisai·š) *tr.-intr.* grecizar, greguizar.
Greco-Latin (gri·kou-) *adj.* grecolatino.
Greco-Roman *adj.* grecorromano.
Greece (gris) *n. pr.* GEOGR. Grecia.
greed (grid), **greediness** (-nis) *s.* ansia, avidez, codicia. *2* avaricia. *3* voracidad, gula.
greedy (gri·di) *adj.* ávido, ansioso, codicioso, hambriento. *2* avaro. *3* voraz, glotón.
Greek (grik) *adj.* griego. *2 s.* griego [persona, lengua griega; lenguaje ininteligible]. *3* (con min.)
fullero.
green (grin) *adj.* verde [de color, de sazón]: ~
barley, alcacer; ~ *cloth,* o *greencloth,* tapete
verde; ~ *fly,* pulgón; ~ *vitriol,* caparrosa verde.
2 lozano, lleno de vigor. *3* crudo [ladrillo, loza,
etc.]. *4* fresco, reciente. *5* bisoño, inexperto: ~
hand, novicio, principiante. *6* verde, lívido, pálido [de miedo, celos, etc.]. *7 s.* verde [color; follaje, hierba]. *8* verdor, verdura. *9* prado, pradera. *10 pl.* verduras, hortalizas.
green (to) *tr.* poner o volver verde; pintar o teñir
de verde. *2 intr.* verdear.
greenback (gri·nbæk) *s.* (E.U.) billete de banco.
greenfinch (-finch) *s.* ORN. verderón.
greengage (-gidŷ) *s.* ciruela verdal.
greengrocer (-grousø^r) *s.* verdulero.
greengrocery (-grousøri) *s.* verdulería.
greenhorn (-jo^{r}n) *s.* pipiolo, novato. *2* palurdo. *3*
bobo, primo, incauto.
greenhouse (-jaus) *s.* invernáculo.
greening (-ing) *s.* BOT. variedad de manzana de color verdoso.
greenish (-ish) *adj.* verdoso, verdusco.
Greenland (-lænd) *n. pr.* GEOGR. Groenlandia.
Greenlander (-lændø^r) *s.* groenlandés.
greenness (-nis) *s.* verdura, verdor. *2* lozanía, vigor, frescura. *3* falta de experiencia. *4* novedad.
greenroom (-rum) *s.* TEAT. sala de espera de los actores.
greensand (-sænd) *s.* GEOL. arenisca verde.
greenstall (-stol) *s.* puesto de verduras.

greensward (-suoᵣd) s. césped.
greenwood (-wud) s. bosque verde. 2 BOT. retama de tintes.
greet (to) (griːt) tr. saludar, acoger, dar la bienvenida. 2 intr. saludarse.
greeter (griːtøᵣ) s. el que saluda.
greeting (-ing) s. saludo, salutación, recibimiento. 2 greetings!, ¡salud!
gregarious (grigeiˑriøs) adj. que vive en grey o compañia, gregal. 2 sociable, que gusta de la compañía.
Gregorian (grigoˑrian) adj. gregoriano.
Gregory (greˑgori) n. pr. m. Gregorio.
gremial (griˑmial) s. ECLES. gremial.
grenade (grineiˑd) s. granada [proyectil].
grenadier (grenadiˑøᵣ) s. MIL. granadero.
grenadine (greˑnadin) s. granadina.
grew (gru) pret. de TO GROW.
grey (grei) adj. GRAY.
greyhound (-jaund) s. ZOOL. galgo.
greyish (-ish) adj. GRAYISH.
grid (grid) s. reja, rejilla, parrilla. 2 RADIO. rejilla. 3 ELECT. red.
griddle (griˑdøl) s. tartera, tortera. 2 plancha [para tapar el hornillo; para asar].
gridiron (griˑdaiøᵣn) s. COC. parrillas. 2 MAR. andamiada. 3 TEAT. telar. 4 red [de vigas, tubos, etc.].
grief (grif) s. dolor, pesar, pesadumbre, duelo, aflicción, congoja. 2 daño, quebranto, fracaso: to come to ~, sufrir algún daño o fracaso; arruinarse.
grievance (griˑvans) s. agravio, ofensa, injusticia, motivo de queja, queja.
grieve (to) (griːv) tr. afligir, apesadumbrar, oprimir. 2 llorar, lamentar. 3 intr. afligirse, dolerse.
grievingly (-ingli) adj. apesaradamente.
grievous (-øs) adj. doloroso, aflictivo, penoso, sensible. 2 lastimoso, lastimero. 3 gravoso, oneroso. 4 fiero, cruel, atroz.
griffin (griˑfin) s. MIT. grifo.
griffon (griˑføn) s. GRIFFIN. 2 perro de cierta raza.
grig (grig) s. ENT. grillo; saltamontes. 2 ICT. anguila pequeña. 3 persona vivaracha.
grill (gril) s. COC. parrillas. 2 asado hecho en parrillas. 3 GRILLROOM.
grill (to) tr. asar en parrillas. 2 fig. atormentar. 3 intr. asarse.
grillade (grileiˑd) s. manjar asado en parrillas.
grillage (griˑlidȳ) s. emparrillado, zampeado.
grille (gril) s. verja, reja.
grillroom (griˑlrum) s. restaurante o comedor de hotel especializado en los asados a la parrilla.
grilse (grils) s. salmón joven.
grim (grim) adj. torvo, ceñudo. 2 feo, horrendo. 3 horrible, siniestro. 4 inflexible, implacable.
grimace (grimeiˑs) s. mueca, mohín, visaje, gesto.
grimace (to) intr. hacer muecas o visajes.
grimalkin (grimæˑlkin) s. gatazo; gata vieja. 2 vieja malévola.
grime (graim) s. tizne, mugre, porquería.
grime (to) tr. tiznar, ensuciar.
grimy (-i) adj. tiznado, sucio, mugriento.
grin (grin) s. mueca de dolor o de cólera. 2 sonrisa burlona, forzada o estúpida.
grin (to) intr. hacer muecas mostrando los dientes. 2 sonreír con toda la boca; con complacencia, burla o sarcasmo.
grind (graind) s. molienda, trituración. 2 fam. trabajo o estudio continuado. 3 fam. empollón.
grind (to) tr. moler, pulverizar, triturar. 2 afilar, amolar. 3 gastar [con el roce]; bruñir, deslus-

trar, esmerilar. 4 hacer rechinar [los dientes]. 5 molestar, oprimir, agobiar. 6 mover [con manubrio]. 7 intr. moler. 8 ser molido o afilado. 9 pulirse [con el roce]. 10 trabajar duramente; estudiar con ahinco. ¶ Pret. y p. p.: ground.
grinder (-øᵣ) s. molendero, moledor. 2 amolador. 3 pulidor, esmerilador. 4 molino, molinillo. 5 muela [de amolar]. 6 torno de pulir. 7 ANAT. muela.
grindstone (-stoun) s. muela, amoladera, piedra de afilar.
gringo (griˑngou) s. desp. gringo.
grip (grip) s. empuñamiento, agarro, presa. 2 capacidad de agarrar y retener; de comprender. 3 poder, dominio. 4 asidero, puño, mango. 5 (E.U.) maletín. 6 MED. gripe. 7 to come to grips, luchar a brazo partido.
grip (to) tr. agarrar, asir, apretar, empuñar, sujetar. 2 intr. agarrarse. 3 absorber la atención. ¶ Pret. y p. p.: gripped o gript; ger.: gripping.
gripe (graip) s. agarro, asimiento. 2 garras, poder, sujeción. 3 mango, puño, manija. 4 MEC. grapa, mordaza. 5 pl. dolor, cólico, retortijones. 6 VET. torozón.
gripe (to) tr. TO GRIP 1. 2 punzar; afligir, oprimir. 3 pop. fastidiar, molestar. 4 dar retortijones. 5 MEC. morder. 6 intr. padecer retortijones. 7 sacar dinero. 8 pop. refunfuñar.
griper (grai-pøᵣ) s. fam. usurero.
grippe (grip) s. MED. gripe.
gripping (gri-ping) adj. muy conmovedor o interesante [drama, novela, etc.].
gripsack (gri-psæk) s. (E.U.) maletín.
gript (gript) p. p. de TO GRIP.
grisly (gri-sli) adj. espantoso, horroroso, terrible. 2 torvo.
grist (grist) s. molienda [cantidad de grano]. 2 provisión [para una ocasión].
gristle (gri-søl) s. cartílago, ternilla.
gristly (gri-sli) s. cartilaginoso.
grit (grit) s. arena, guijo fino. 2 arenisca silícea, asperón. 3 firmeza, entereza, tesón; ánimo, valentía. 4 pl. sémola, farro.
gritty (gri-ti) adj. arenisco. 2 animoso, esforzado.
grizzle (gri-søl) s. color gris. 2 cabellos grises.
grizzle (to) tr.-intr. poner o volverse gris.
grizzled (gri-søld) adj. canoso. 2 tordillo.
grizzly (gri-sli) adj. grisáceo, pardusco: ~ bear, oso pardo.
groan (groun) s. gemido, quejido.
groan (to) intr. gemir, quejarse, ayear.
groaning (-ing) s. GROAN.
groat (grout) s. ant. moneda de cuatro peniques. 2 pl. grano quebrantado; farro, sémola.
grocer (grou-søᵣ) s. especiero, abacero; *pulpero, *bodeguero: grocer's shop, abacería, tienda de comestibles o ultramarinos; *pulpería, *bodega.
grocery (-ri) s. comestibles, ultramarinos; comercio de ellos. 2 (E.U.) abacería, *pulpería.
grog (grag) s. grog. 2 bebida alcohólica.
groggy (gra-gi) adj. calamocano. 2 DEP. vacilante, atontado.
groin (groin) s. ANAT. ingle. 2 ARQ. arista de encuentro. 3 espolón, malecón.
groin (to) tr. ARQ. formar aristas de encuentro.
groined (groind) adj. de arista [arco, etc.].
grommet (gra-mit) s. anillo de cuerda. 2 ojete metálico.
groom (grum) s. novio, desposado. 2 caballerizo, mozo de cuadra, palafrenero; lacayo.

groom (to) *tr.* cuidar, almohazar [caballos]. *2* fam. vestir, componer, asear.

groomsman (-smæn) *s.* padrino de boda.

groove (gruv) *s.* ranura, gárgol, rebajo. *2* estría, surco. *3* carril, rodera. *4* fig. rutina, hábito arraigado.

groove (to) *tr.* acanalar, estriar, hacer ranuras o surcos en.

grooved (gru·vd) *adj.* acanalado, estriado.

grope (to) (group) *tr.-intr.* tentar; andar a tientas: *to ~ for,* buscar a tientas, tentando.

gros (grous) *s.* TEJ. gro.

grosbeak (grou·sbɪk) *s.* nombre de varios pájaros.

grosgrain (grou·grein) *s.* GROS.

gross (grous) *adj.* grueso. *2* denso, espeso. *3* grosero, tosco, basto, vulgar. *4* obsceno. *5* craso, enorme: *~ error,* error craso. *6* lerdo, estúpido. *7* COM. total; bruto [sin deducciones]. *8 ~ ton,* tonelada de 2.240 libras (1.016,06 kg.). *9 s.* gruesa [doce docenas]. *10* grueso [la mayor parte], totalidad, conjunto: *in ~, in the ~,* en grueso, por junto.

grossly (grou·sly) *adv.* en bruto. *2* crasamente; toscamente, groseramente. *3* aproximadamente.

grot (grat) *s.* gruta.

grotesque (grote·sk) *adj.* grotesco, extravagante. *2 adj.-s. B.* ART. grotesco, grutesco.

grotto (gra·tou) *s.* gruta, cueva.

grouch (grauch) *s.* fam. enojo, mal humor. *2* fam. gruñón, cascarrabias.

grouch (to) *intr.* fam. gruñir, refunfuñar.

ground (graund) *s.* tierra, suelo, piso: *to fall to the ~,* caer al suelo; venirse abajo, fracasar. *2* terreno: *to stand,* o *hold one's ground,* mantenerse firme. *3* MAR. tierra, fondo: *to take the ~,* encallar. *4* campo, región, territorio. *5 B.* ART. campo, fondo. *6* PERSP. término. *7* tema, materia, base, fundamento, pie, razón, motivo: *on the ~ of,* con motivo de, por razón de. *8* campo de batalla. *9* ELECT. tierra. *10 pl.* terrenos, recinto [de una finca o edificio]. *11* campo, cancha [de juego]. *12* poso, sedimento.
13 adj. de tierra, del suelo, etc.: *~ floor,* bajos, piso bajo; *~ lead,* ELECT. hilo de tierra; *~ plot,* solar, parcela; *~ rent,* censo; *~ sea,* o *swell,* MAR. mar de fondo. *14* BOT. *~ cherry,* alquequenje; *~ pine,* pinillo. *Pret. y p. p.* de TO GRIND.

ground (to) *tr.* fundamentar, cimentar, establecer, basar, apoyar, vincular. *2* poner en tierra. *3* ELECT. conectar con tierra. *4 intr.* basarse, fundamentarse. *5* descender al suelo. *6* MAR. encallar, varar.

groundless (-lis) *adj.* infundado, inmotivado, gratuito.

groundling (-ling) *s.* persona de poca cultura. *2* planta enana o rastrera.

groundnut (-nøt) *s.* BOT. chufa. *2* BOT. cacahuete.

groundsel (-sel) *s.* BOT. hierba cana, zuzón. *2* GROUNDSILL.

groundwork (-uøʳk) *s.* cimiento, fundamento; base. *2* firme [de carretera].

group (grup) *s.* grupo, agrupación, conjunto.

group (to) *tr.* agrupar. *2 intr.* agruparse.

grouper (gru·pøʳ) *s.* ICT. mero.

grouse (graus) *s.* ORN. nombre de varias gallináceas silvestres, como el urogallo, el lagópodo o perdiz blanca, -la ortega, etc. *2* fam. queja, refunfuño.

grouse (to) *intr.* fam. (Ingl.) quejarse, refunfuñar.

grout (graut) *s.* farro. *2* lechada. *3 pl.* poso, heces.

grove (grouv) *s.* bosquecillo, soto, arboleda.

grovel (to) (grø·vøl) *intr.* arrastrarse. *2* rebajarse servilmente. *3* hundirse [en lo vil o bajo].

grovel (l) er (grø·vløʳ) *s.* persona servil, rastrera.

grovel(l)ing (-ling) *adj.* servil, rastrero.

grow (to) (grou) *intr.* crecer, desarrollarse, formarse, producirse. *2* nacer, salir [el pelo, las plantas, etc.]. *3* nacer, proceder, provenir. *4* aumentar, progresar, extenderse. *5* ponerse, volverse, convertirse en: *to ~ better,* ponerse mejor, mejorar; *to ~ dark,* oscurecer, anochecer; *to ~ fat,* engordar; *to ~ late,* hacerse tarde; *to ~ old,* envejecer. *6 to ~ into fashion,* ponerse de moda; *to ~ out of fashion,* pasar de moda, caer en desuso. *7 to ~ on* o *upon,* hacerse más fuerte en uno [un hábito, pasión, sensación, etc.]. *8 to ~ out of,* nacer de; perder, pasársele a uno [un hábito, un sentimiento, etc.]. *9 to ~ to,* llegar a [amar, odiar, etc.]; arraigarse en.
10 tr. cultivar, criar, producir. *11* salirle a uno o dejarse uno [la barba, el bigote]. ¶ *Pret.: grew;* p. p.: *grown.*

grower (-øʳ) *s.* cultivador, criador.

growing (-ing) *adj.* creciente. *2* que crece, que está en la edad de crecer. *3* de crecimiento. *4 s.* crecimiento, desarrollo. *5* cría, cultivo.

growl (graul) *s.* gruñido. *2* refunfuño. *3* RUMBLE 1.

growl (to) *intr.* gruñir. *2* refunfuñar. *3* TO RUMBLE 1.

growler (-øʳ) *s.* perro gruñidor. *2* gruñón, regañón.

grown (groun) p. p. de TO GROW. *2 adj.* crecido, espigado, desarrollado; adulto. *3* cubierto [de hierba, maleza, etc.].

grown-up *adj.-s.* adulto, mayor [persona].

growth (grouz) *s.* crecimiento, desarrollo. *2* producción, cultivo. *3* vegetación, lo que crece o ha crecido. *4* acrecentamiento, aumento. *5* producto, resultado. *6* tumor, excrecencia. *7* estatura completa.

grub (grøb) *s.* larva, gusano, coco. *2* azacán. *3* persona desaliñada. *4* pop. comida, alimento.

grub (to) *tr.* rozar, desyerbar, desmalezar; cavar. *2* arrancar, descuajar. *3* limpiar de gusanos; descocar. *4* pop. alimentar. *5 intr.* alimentarse. *6* trabajar en oficios bajos. ¶ *Pret. y p. p.: grubbed;* p. a.: *-bbing.*

grubby (-bi) *adj.* gusaniento. *2* sucio, roñoso.

grudge (grødẏ) *s.* resentimiento, rencor, inquina, mala voluntad.

grudge (to) *tr.* regatear, escatimar, dar de mala gana. *2* envidiar [una cosa].

grudgingly (-ingli) *adv.* de mala gana.

gruel (gru·øl) *s.* gachas o puches claros.

gruesome (gru·søm) *adj.* horrible, horripilante. *2* repugnante.

gruff (grøf) *adj.* rudo, brusco, áspero, malhumorado. *2* bronca [voz].

grumble (grø·mbøl) *s.* refunfuño, rezongo, queja. *2* ruido sordo.

grumble (to) *intr.* refunfuñar, rezongar, quejarse. *2* roncar [un animal]. *3* producir un ruido sordo.

grumbler (grø·mbløʳ) *s.* refunfuñón, rezongador, descontento.

grume (grum) *s.* grumo, cuajarón; masa viscosa.

grumous (gru·møs) *adj.* grumoso.

grumpy (grø·mpi) *adj.* gruñón, malhumorado.

grunt (grønt) *s.* gruñido. *2* ICT. nombre de un pez americano.

grunt (to) *intr.* gruñir.

grunter (-øʳ) *s.* gruñón. *2* ZOOL. cerdo.

gruntling (-ling) *s.* lechón, cochinillo.

guaco (gua·kou) *s.* BOT. guaco.

Guadeloupe (guadølu·p) *n. pr.* Guadalupe.

guaiac (gua·iæk), **guaiacum** (-iakøm) *s.* BOT. guacayo, guacayán. *2* resina de guacayo.
guanaco (guana·kou) *s.* ZOOL. guanaco.
guano (gua·nou) *s.* guano.
guarantee (gærantı·) *s.* persona de quien otra sale fiadora. *2* garantía, fianza. *3* garante, fiador.
guarantee (to) *tr.* garantizar, garantir. *2* salir fiador, responder o dar fianza por.
guarantor (gæ·rantø') *s.* garante, fiador.
guaranty (-ti) *s.* garantía [acción]. *2* garantía, fianza, prenda. *3* garante, fiador.
guaranty (to) *tr.* TO GUARANTEE.
guard (ga'd) *s.* guardia [estado de defensa o precaución]: *on ~, on one's ~,* alerta, sobre aviso; en guardia; *off one's ~,* desprevenido. *2* guardia, guardia, vigilancia, custodia, protección. *3* guarda, gurrdián, custodio, vigilante, centinela. *4* guardia [cuerpo; individuo de él]. *5* MIL., ESGR. guardia. *6* guarnición de una espada, un vestido]. *7* arandela [de lanza]. *8* cadena [de reloj]. *9* guardamonte [de fusil]. *10* salvavidas [de tranvía]. *11* FERROC. (Ingl.) revisor; (E.U.) guardafrenos.
guard (to) *tr.* guardar, proteger, defender, resguardar. *2* custodiar, vigilar. *3 intr.* guardarse, estar prevenido.
guarded (-id) *adj.* defendido, protegido. *2* cauteloso, cauto, precavido.
guardedness (-nis) *s.* cautela, precaución, circunspección.
guardian (ga·'dian) *s.* guardián, guarda, custodio. *2* DER. tutor o curador. *3 adj.* ~ *angel,* ángel custodio o de la guarda.
guardianship (-ship) *s.* protección, amparo, guarda, custodia. *2* DER. tutela, curadoría.
guardrail (ga·'dreil) *s.* barandilla. *3* FERROC. contracarril.
guardroom (-rum) *s.* MIL. cuerpo de guardia. *2* MIL. prevención.
guardsman (-šmæn) *s.* militar de uno de los cuerpos llamados guardia.
guava (gua·va) *s.* BOT. guayabo; guayaba.
gubernatorial (giubø'nato·rial) *adj.* gubernativo. *2* del gobernador.
gudgeon (gø·dyøn) *s.* ICT. gobio. *2* bobo, fácil de engañar. *3* ganga, chiripa. *4* MEC. gorrón, muñón, cuello de eje. *6* MAR. hembra del timón.
gudgeon (to) *tr.* engañar, estafar.
Guelf, Guelph (gwelf) *s.* güelfo.
guerdon (gø·'døn) *s.* galardón, premio.
guer (r) illa (gueri·l) *s.* guerrillero. *2* guerrilla, guerra de guerrillas.
guess (ges) *s.* conjetura, suposición; cosa que se piensa o dice tratando de adivinar.
guess (to) *tr.* conjeturar, barruntar, suponer; adivinar o tratar de adivinar. *2* fam. pensar, creer.
guesser (ge·sø') *s.* conjeturador, adivinador.
guesswork (-uø'k) *s.* conjetura: *by ~,* por conjeturas.
guest (gest) *s.* huésped [pers. alojada]; forastero, visita, invitado. *2* pensionista, inquilino. *3* ZOOL. huésped.
guffaw (gøfo) *s.* risotada, carcajada.
guffaw (to) *intr.* reír a carcajadas o groseramente.
Guiana (gaiæø) *n. pr.* GEOGR. Guayana.
guidance (gai·dans) *s.* guía, gobierno, dirección: *for your ~,* para su gobierno.
guide (gaid) *s.* guía [pers. o cosa que guía], norte. *2* guía [libro]. *3* MEC. guía, guiadera. *4* MIL. guía. *5* pauta, patrón.

guide (to) *tr.* guiar. | No tiene el sentido de guiar un coche. *2* dirigir, gobernar. *3* encaminar.
guideboard (gai·dbo'd) *s.* letrero indicador.
guidebook (gai·dbuk) *s.* guía de turismo.
guideless (gai·dlis) *adj.* sin guía. *2* sin gobierno.
guidepost (gai·dpoust) *s.* guía, poste indicador.
guidon (gai·døn) *s.* MIL. banderín.
guild (gild) *s.* gremio, cofradía, asociación.
guilder (gi·ldø') *s.* GULDEN.
guildhall (gi·dljol) *s.* casa de un gremio. *2* casa de Ayuntamiento.
guile (gail) *s.* astucia, artificio, dolo, maña.
guileful (gai·lful) *adj.* artificioso, doloso, engañoso.
guileless (gai·lis) *adj.* sencillo, cándido, sincero.
guillemot (gi·limot) *s.* ORN. pájaro niño.
guillotine (gi·lotin) *s.* guillotina.
guillotine (to) *tr.* guillotinar.
guilt (gilt) *s.* culpa, delito, crimen, pecado. *2* culpabilidad.
guiltless (gi·ltlis) *adj.* inocente, libre de culpa; puro, sin mancha. *2* ignorante [de algo].
guilty (-i) *adj.* culpable, reo; delincuente.
guimpe (gimp) *s.* COST. canesú.
Guinea (gi·ni) *n. pr.* GEOGR. Guinea.
guinea *s.* guinea [moneda]. *2* ORN. ~ *fowl,* ~ *hen,* gallina de Guinea. *3* ZOOL. ~ *pig,* conejillo de Indias, cobayo.
guise (gaiš) *s.* guisa, modo, manera. *2* apariencia, disfraz; capa, pretexto: *under the ~ of,* so capa de.
guitar (gita·') *s.* MÚS. guitarra.
gulch (gølch) *s.* (E.U.) quebrada, barranca.
gulden (gu·ldøn) *s.* guilden.
gules (giulš) *s.* BLAS. gules.
gulf (gølf) *s.* GEOGR. golfo: *Gulf Stream,* corriente del Golfo de Méjico. *2* sima, abismo, vorágine.
gulfweed (-uid) *s.* BOT. sargazo.
gull (gøl) *s.* ORN. gaviota. *2* incauto, primo. *3* engaño, timo.
gull (to) *tr.* engañar, estafar, timar.
gullet (gø·lit) *s.* gaznate. *2* esófago. *3* zanja.
gullibility (gølibi·liti) *s.* tragaderas, credulidad.
gullible (gø·libøl) *adj.* incauto, bobo, crédulo.
gully (gø·li) *s.* cárcava, barranca, hondonada.
gully (to) *tr.* excavar, formar canal.
gulp (gølp) *s.* acción de tragar, contracción de la garganta. *2* trago, engullida.
gulp (to) *tr.* [gralte. con *down*] tragar, engullir. *2* reprimir [las lágrimas], ahogar [un sollozo].
gum (gøm) *s.* ANAT. encía. *2* goma [substancia]: ~ *arabic,* goma arábiga; ~ *elastic,* goma elástica; ~ *resin,* gomorresina. *3* árbol que da goma. *4* (E.U.) chanclo de goma.
gum (to) *tr.* engomar. ¶ Pret. y p. p.: *gummed;* ger.: *gumming.*
gumboil (-boil) *s.* flemón, párulis.
gumdrop (-drap) *s.* pastilla de goma.
gummiferous (gømi·førøs) *adj.* gomífero.
gummous (gø·møs), **gummy** (-i) *adj.* gomoso, viscoso.
gump (gømp) *s.* pop. tonto, majadero.
gumption (gø·mshøn) *s.* fam. perspicacia, sentido común. *2* fam. empuje, iniciativa.
gun (gøn) *s.* ARTILL. cañón: ~ *carriage,* cureña, afuste. *2* fusil, escopeta, carabina, tercerola: ~ *barrel,* cañón de fusil, escopeta, etc. *3* (E.U.) pistola revólver. *4* cañonazo [de salva o señal]. *5* tubo o jeringa. *6* tirador [pers.].
gun (to) *tr.* fam. hacer fuego sobre. *2 intr.* cazar

con escopeta o fusil: *to ~ for*, ir a la caza de. ¶
Pret. y p. p.: *gunned;* ger.: *gunning.*
gunboat (-bout) *s.* cañonero [embarcación].
guncotton (-katøn) *s.* algodón pólvora.
gunlock (-lak) *s.* llave de fusil.
gunman (-mæn) *s.* (E.U.) pistolero.
gunnel (-nøl) *s.* MAR. GUNWALE.
gunner (-ø^r) *s.* artillero. 2 MAR. condestable. 3 cazador.
gunnery (-øri) *s.* artillería.
gunning (-ing) *s.* caza con escopeta.
gunny (-i) *s.* yute; saco de yute.
gunpowder (-paudø^r) *s.* pólvora.
gunshot (-shat) *s.* tiro de fusil, balazo, escopetazo. 2 tiro, alcance del fusil: *within ~*, a tiro de fusil.
gunsmith (-smiz) *s.* armero [pers.].
gunwale (-ueil) *s.* MAR. borda, regala.
gurgitation (gø^rŷite·shøn) *s.* hervor, agitación.
gurgle (gø·^rgøl) *s.* borboteo; gorgoteo. 2 gorjeo [del niño].
gurgle (to) *intr.* borbotar; gorgotear. 2 gorjear [el niño].
gurnard (gø·^rna^rd), **gurnet** (gø·^rnit) *s.* ICT. rubio, escarcho; golondrina: *flying ~*, milano.
gush (gøsh) *s.* chorro, borbollón, borbotón. 2 efusión, extremo.
gush (to) *tr.* echar, derramar a chorros. 2 *intr.* brotar, manar a borbotones. 3 hacer extremos, ser extremoso.
gushing (-ing) *adj.* extremoso.
gusset (gø·sit) *s.* COST. escudete, cuchillo. 2 ARM. gocete. 3 MEC. palomilla de refuerzo.
gust (gøst) *s.* ráfaga, racha. 2 chubasco. 3 explosión, acceso, arrebato.
gustative (-ativ), **gustatory** (gø·statori) *adj.* gustativo.
gusto (-ou) *s.* gusto, placer, afición [con que se hace una cosa].
gusty (-ti) *adj.* borrascoso. 2 impetuoso, explosivo.
gut (gøt) *s.* vulg. intestino, tripa. 2 cuerda de tripa. 3 estrecho, desfiladero. 4 *pl.* pop. tripas, bandullo. 5 pop. valor, agallas.
gut (to) *tr.* destripar, desentrañar.
gutta-percha (gø·ta-pø^rcha) *s.* gutapercha.

gutter (gø·tø^r) *s.* arroyo [de la calle]. 2 albollón. 3 canal, canalón [de un tejado]. 4 surco que hacen las aguas llovedizas. 5 badén, cuneta. 6 zanja. 7 surco, acanaladura.
gutter (to) *tr.* acanalar. 2 poner canalones, etc. 3 *intr.* correr, gotear. 4 correrse [una vela].
guttersnipe (-snaip) *s.* pilluelo, golfillo.
gutiferous (gøti·førøs) *adj.* BOT. gutífero.
guttle (to) (gø·tøl) *tr.-intr.* comer, engullir.
guttural (gø·tøral) *adj.* gutural.
Guy (gai) *n. pr. m.* Guido.
guy *s.* tirante, viento; retenida. 2 desp. tipo, individuo. 3 fam. adefesio, mamarracho.
guy (to) *tr.* sujetar con vientos o retenida. 2 fam. burlarse, hacer mofa de.
guzzle (to) (gø·søl) *tr.-intr.* beber mucho. 2 *intr.* ser muy bebedor.
guzzler (gø·słø^r) *s.* bebedor, borrachín.
gymnasium (dŷimnei·ŷøm) *s.* gimnasio.
gymnast (dŷi·mnæst) *s.* gimnasta.
gymnastic(al (dŷimnæ·stik(al) *adj.* gimnástico.
gymnastics (dŷimnæ·stiks) *s.* gimnasia, gimnástica.
gymnosperm (dŷi·mnospø^rm) *s.* BOT. gimnosperma.
gymnospermous (dŷi·mnospø^rmøs) *adj.* BOT. gimnospermo.
gynaeceum, gynaecium (dŷainisı·øm) *s.* gineceo.
gynaecologist, gynecologist (dŷainika·lodŷist) *s.* ginecólogo.
gynaecology, gynecology (-dŷi) *s.* ginecología.
gypseous (dŷi·psiøs), **gypsine** (-sin) *adj.* yesoso.
gypsum (dŷi·psøm) *s.* yeso, aljez.
gypsy (dŷi·psi) *adj.-s.* gitano, bohemio, cíngaro.
gyrate (to) (dŷai·reit) *intr.* girar [dar vueltas].
gyration (-ei·shøn) *s.* giro, vuelta, rotación, revolución.
gyratory (dŷai·ratori) *s.* giratorio, de rotación.
gyre (dŷai·ø^r) *s.* GYRATION.
gyrfalcon (dŷø·^rfolkøn) *s.* GERFALCON.
gyroscope (dŷai·roskoup) *s.* giroscopio.
gyrostat (dŷai·rostæt) *s.* giróstato.
gyrostatics (dŷairostæ·tiks) *s.* girostática.
gyve (to) (dŷaiv) *tr.* encadenar, apiolar.
gyves (-s) *s. pl.* grillos.

H

H, h (eich) *s.* H, h, octava letra del alfabeto inglés.
ha (ja) *interj.* ¡ah! *2 ha, ha!,* ¡ja, ja!
haberdasher (jæ·bøʳdæshøʳ) *s.* mercero, camisero; comerciante que vende artículos para caballero.
haberdashery (-i) *s.* mercería; camisería; tienda de artículos para caballero.
habergeon (jæ·bøʳdẙøn) *s.* cota de malla.
habiliment (jabi·limønt) *s.* vestido, traje, ropa.
habit (jæ·bit) *s.* hábito, vestido: *riding ~,* traje de amazona. *2* hábito, costumbre, uso, vicio: *to be in the ~ of,* soler, acostumbrar. *4* condición, constitución, complexión. *5* H. NAT. hábito.
habit (to) *tr.* vestir, ataviar.
habitable (-abøl) *adj.* habitable.
habitant (-ant) *s.* habitante, morador.
habitat (jæ·bitat) *s.* H. NAT. habitación.
habitation (-ei·shøn) *s.* habitación, morada.
habitual (jabi·chual) *adj.* habitual; acostumbrado.
habituate (to) (-chueit) *tr.* habituar, acostumbrar.
habitude (jæ·bitiud) *s.* hábito, costumbre. *2* disposición, actitud habitual.
habitué (jabichuei·) *s.* concurrente, habitual.
hack (jæk) *s.* caballo de alquiler. *2* rocín, jamelgo. *3* coche de alquiler, simón. *4* alquilón; escritor o literato a sueldo. *5* azacán, peón. *6* hacha, cuchilla, pico. *7* corte, tajo, muesca. *8* tos seca. *9 adj.* alquiladizo. *10* trillado, gastado. *11* de cortar o picar.
hack (to) *tr.* tajar, cortar, picar. *2* alquilar [un coche, etc.]. *3* toser con tos seca. *4* alquilarse, venderse. *6* escribir artículos, etc., mal pagados. *7* ir a caballo.
hackberry (-beri) *s.* almez. *2* BOT. almeza.
hackle (-øl) *s.* rastrillo [para el lino, etc.]. *2* pluma del cuello de un ave. *3* mosca para pescar.
hackle (to) *tr.* rastrillar [lino, cáñamo]. *2* tajar, cortar, estropear a tajos.
hackman (-mæn) *s.* cochero de punto.
hackney (-ni) *s.* caballo corriente, jaca, cuartago. *2* coche de alquiler. *3* alquilón, azacán. *4 adj.* alquilado, de alquiler: *~ coach,* coche de punto; *~ writer,* escritor a sueldo. *3* común, trillado.
hackney (to) *tr.* gastar, hacer común, trillado.
hackneyed (-nid) *adj.* gastado, trillado, manoseado.
had (jæd) *pret.* y *p. p.* de TO HAVE.
haddock (jæ·døk) *s.* ICT. pez semejante al bacalao.

hade (jeid) *s.* GEOL., MIN. buzamiento.
Hades (jei·diš) *s.* MIT. Hades.
Hadrian (jei·drian) *n. pr. m.* Adriano.
hae-, HE-.
haft (jaft) *s.* mango, puño.
haft (to) *tr.* poner mango o puño a.
hag (jæg) *s.* bruja vieja. *2* bruja, hechicera.
haggard (jæ·gaʳd) *adj.* macilento, ojeroso, trasnochado, demacrado; fatigado, angustiado. *2* arañero [halcón].
haggish (jæ·gish) *adj.* de bruja.
haggle (jæ·gøl) *s.* altercado, disputa. *2* regateo.
haggle (to) *tr.* tajar, cortar toscamente. *2 intr.* altercar, disputar. *3* regatear [discutir un precio].
hagiographer (jædẙia·graføʳ) *s.* hagiógrafo.
hagiography (-grafi) *s.* hagiografía.
hagiolatry (-latri) *s.* culto de los santos.
Hague (The) (jeg) *n. pr.* GEOGR. La Haya.
hah (ja) *interj.* HA.
haik (jeik) *s.* jaique.
hail (jeil) *s.* granizo, pedrisco, piedra. *2* granizada. *3* saludo; grito, llamada: *within ~,* al alcance de la voz; MAR. al habla. *4 interj.* ¡ave!, ¡salve!, ¡salud!: *Hail Mary,* Ave María.
hail (to) *intr.-tr.* granizar. *2 tr.* saludar, aclamar. *3* llamar, vocear. *4 intr. to ~ from,* venir, proceder de.
hail-fellow o **hail fellow** *adj.-s.* amigo, compañero íntimo.
hailstone (-stoun) *s.* piedra de granizo.
hailstorm (-stoʳm) *s.* granizada, pedrisco.
hair (je·øʳ) *s.* cabello, pelo, vello; cabellos, cabellera; ~ *dye,* tintura para el pelo; ~ *net,* redecilla, albanega; ~ *shirt,* cilicio; *head of ~,* cabellera, mata de pelo; *to split hairs,* sutilizar demasiado; *pararse en quisquillas; not to turn a ~,* no inmutarse; quedarse tan fresco; *against the ~,* a contrapelo; *to a ~,* con la mayor exactitud. *2* pelo, hebra, filamento. *3* tejido de pelo. *4* pelo [de un arma de fuego].
hairbreadth (-bredz) grueso de un cabello; casi nada: *to have a ~ escape,* escapar por un pelo, librarse de milagro.
hairbrush (-brøsh) *s.* cepillo para el pelo.
haircloth (-cloz) *s.* tela de crin. *2* cilicio.
haircut (-cøt) *s.* corte de pelo.
hairdo (-du) *s.* peinado, tocado.

hairdresser (-dresøʳ) *s.* peluquero. *2* peluquera, peinadora.
haired (-d) *adj.* cabelludo, peludo. *2* de pelo: *curly-haired*, de pelo rizado o crespo.
hairless (-lis) *adj.* pelón, calvo, lampiño.
hairpin (-pin) *s.* horquilla [para el pelo].
hair-raising *adj.* espeluznante, horripilante.
hairsplitting (-pliting) *adj.* demasiado sutil, que sutiliza demasiado. *2 s.* sutileza excesiva.
hairspring (-spring) *s.* espiral [de un reloj].
hairy (-i) *adj.* cabelludo, peludo, velloso, velludo, hirsuto.
Haiti (jei·ti) *n. pr.* GEOGR. Haití.
Haitian (jei·tian) *adj.-s.* haitiano.
hake (jeik) *s.* ICT. merluza, pescada.
halation (jeilei·shøn) *s.* FOT. halo.
halberd (jælbøʳd) *s.* alabarda.
halberdier (jælbøʳdi·øʳ) *s.* alabardero [soldado].
halcyon (jæl·lsiøn) *adj.* apacible, sereno, tranquilo. *2 s.* ORN. alción, martín pescador.
hale (jeil) *adj.* sano, fuerte, robusto.
hale (to) *tr.* halar, tirar de, arrastrar.
half (jæf o jaf) *s.* mitad: *(the) ~ of*, la mitad de; *by ~*, con mucho; *in ~*, por la mitad. *2* ARIT. medio [quebrado]. *3* DEP. parte [de un partido de fútbol]. *4* V. HALVES.
　　5 adj.-adv. medio, semi, casi; a medias: *a ~*, *~a*, medio; *~ after* o *~ past*, [hablando de horas] y media: *~ after two*, las dos y media; *~ binding*, *~ leather*, ENCUAD. media pasta; *~ brother*, medio hermano; *~ done*, medio hecho; medio cocido; *~ light*, media luz; *~ mesures*, medias tintas, paños calientes; *~ note*, MÚS. blanca; *~ time*, media jornada; media parte [en el fútbol]; *~ tone*, MÚS. semitono; B. ART. media tinta; fotograbado.
half-and-half *adj.* mitad y mitad. *2 adv.* a medias, en partes iguales.
half-back (-bæk) *s.* FÚTBOL. *centre ~*, medio centro.
half-baked *adj.* a medio cocer, asar, hacer, etc. *2* incompleto. *3* poco juicioso, inexperto, tonto.
half-blood *s.* mestizo. *2* medio hermano o media hermana.
half-bound *adj.* encuadernado en pasta.
half-breed *adj.-s.* mestizo.
half-caste *adj.-s.* mestizo.
halfcocked (-kakt) *adj.* amartillado a medias.
half-dead *adj.* medio muerto.
half-full *adj.* mediado, lleno a medias.
half-hearted *adj.* frío, indiferente. *2* sin ánimo.
half-length *adj.* de medio cuerpo [retrato].
half-mast *s.* media asta: *at ~*, a media asta.
half-mast (to) *tr.* poner a media asta.
half-moon *s.* media luna. *2 adj.* en figura de media luna.
half-opened *adj.* entreabierto.
halfpence (-pøns) *s. pl.* medios peniques.
halfpenny (-pøni) *s.* medio penique.
half-seas over *adj.* pop. achispado, entre dos velas.
halftone (-toun) *s.* media tinta. *2* fotograbado. *3 adj.* a media tinta.
half-truth *s.* media verdad, verdad a medias.
halfway (-uei) *adj.* situado a mitad del camino, equidistante. *2* medio, incompleto, parcial. *3 adv.* a medio camino, parcialmente [en parte]: *to meet ~*, partir la diferencia con; hacer o hacerse concesiones.
half-witted *adj.* tonto, simple, imbécil. *2* alocado.
halibut (jæ·libøt) *s.* ICT. especie de lenguado.
hall (jol) *s.* vestíbulo, zaguán, recibimiento, antecámara. *2* pasadizo, corredor. *3* salón, sala [para reuniones, etc.]. *4* paraninfo [de universidad]. *5* edificio público. *6* casa señorial en el campo.
hallelluia, hallelujah (jælilu·ia) *s.* e *interj.* aleluya.
halliard (jæ·liaʳd) *s.* HALYARD.
hallmark (jo·lmaʳk) *s.* marca del contraste.
hallo, halloa (jalou·) *interj.* ¡eh!, ¡hola!, ¡oiga!. *2 s.* grito llamada.
hallo, hallos (to) *intr.* gritar *hallo* o *halloa*.
halloo (jalu) *interj.* voz para llamar la atención. *2* ¡sus!, ¡busca! [para azuzar a los perros].
halloo (to) *tr.* gritar, llamar. *2* perseguir o incitar a gritos, azuzar.
hallooing (-ing) *s.* grita, vocerío.
hallow (to) (jæ·lou) *tr.* santificar, consagrar, reverenciar.
hallowed (-d) *adj.* bendito, santo, sagrado.
Hallowmas (-mas) *s.* día de Todos los Santos.
hallucinate (to) (jæliu·sineit) *tr.* alucinar.
hallucination (-ei·shøn) *s.* alucinación.
hallway (jo·luei) *s.* (E.U.) vestíbulo; corredor.
halo (jei·lou) *s.* METEOR. halo. *2* halo, aureola, nimbo.
halogen (jæ·lodyøn) *s.* QUÍM. halógeno.
haloid (jæ·loid) *adj.* QUÍM. haloideo. *2 s.* QUÍM. sal haloidea.
halt (jolt) *s.* alto, detención, parada. *2* cojera. *3* vacilación. *4 adj.* cojo.
halt (to) *intr.* detenerse, parar, hacer alto. *2* cojear, renquear. *3* vacilar; tartamudear. *4 tr.* detener, mandar hacer alto.
1) halter (-øʳ) *s.* cabestro, ronzal, jáquima. *2* cuerda para ahorcar, dogal. *3* muerte en la horca.
2) halter, halteres *pl.* **-teres** *s.* ENT. balancín [de díptero].
halter (to) *tr.* poner el cabestro, echar el ronzal a.
halting (-ing) *adj.* cojo, renqueante. *2* defectuoso. *3* vacilante.
halve (to) (jav) *tr.* partir en dos. *2* reducir a la mitad. *3* ser la mitad de.
halves (-š) *s. pl.* de HALF. *2 to go halves*, ir a medias.
halyard (jæ·lia·ʳd) *s.* MAR. driza.
ham (jæm) *s.* pernil, jamón. *2* ANAT. corva. *3* fam. (E.U.) aficionado [a la radio, etc.]. *4* fam. (E.U.) comicastro. *5* fam. ANAT. nalgas.
hamadryad (jæ·madraiæd) *s.* MIT. hamadríada.
hamburger (jæ·mbøʳgøʳ) *s.* bocadillo de carne picada y frita.
Hamburg steak *s.* COC. biftec ruso.
hames (jeims) *s. pl.* horcate.
Hamilcar (jami·lkaʳ) *n. pr. m.* Amílcar.
Hamite (jæ·mait) *s.* camita [descendiente de Cam].
hamlet (jæ·mlit) *s.* aldea, caserío.
hammer (jæ·møʳ) *s.* martillo [herramienta]: *wood ~*, mazo. *2* macillo [del piano]. *3* pilón o maza [de martinete]. *4* gatillo, percutor [de arma de fuego]. *5* ANAT. martillo.
hammer (to) *tr.* martillar, golpear, batir. *2* forjar, repujar [metales]. *3* clavar [con martillo]. *4* meter, encajar [a golpes, a martillazos]. *5 to ~ one's brains*, devanarse los sesos. *7 intr.* martillar, dar golpes. *8* fig. trabajar, hacer esfuerzos reiterados; insistir.
hammerhead (-jed) *s.* ICT. pez martillo.
hammering (-ing) *s.* martilleo. *2* repujado.
hammerless (-lis) *adj.* sin martillo. *2* de percutor interior [arma].
hammock (jæ·møk) *s.* hamaca. *2* MAR. coy.
hamper (jæ·mpøʳ) *s.* cesta [con tapa]; cuevano, canasta. *2* traba, impedimento. *3* MAR. aparejo.

hamper (to) *tr.* estorbar, embarazar, enredar. *2* estropear [una cerradura, etc.].

hamstring (jæ·mstring) *s.* tendón de la corva.

hamstring (to) *tr.* desjarretar. *2* fig. debilitar. ¶ Pret. y p. p.: *hamstrung.*

hanaper (jæ·napøʳ) *s.* cestita para documentos, etc.

hand (jænd) *s.* mano [de pers.; posesión, poder, dominio, dirección; pers. que ejecuta una cosa]: *clean hands*, manos limpias, honradez; *to be ~ and glove* o *~ in glove*, ser uña y carne; *to get the upper ~*, llevar ventaja; dominar; *to have in ~*, tener o traer entre manos; *to have one's hands full*, estar muy ocupado; *to keep one's hands off*, no tocar; no intervenir en; *to put* o *set the ~ to* o *into*, meter mano a; principiar, emprender; *at ~, near at ~*, a mano, cerca; próximo a ocurrir, al llegar; *at the ~ of*, a manos de; de manos de [por obra de]; *by ~*, a mano, manualmente; *by the ~*, de la mano; *~ in ~*, asidos de la mano; juntos; *~ over head*, precipitadamente, inconsideradamente; *hands off*, ¡manos quedas!, ¡no tocar!; *hands up!*, ¡manos arriba!; *~ to ~*, cuerpo a cuerpo; *in ~*, contante [dinero]; en mano; *off ~*, sin preparación, en el acto; *on ~*, a mano, disponible; presente; *out of ~*, inmediatamente; terminado; desbocado; incontenible; *to ~*, en poder [de uno]; a la mano; *with a heavy ~*, con mano dura; *with a high ~*, sin miramientos; con arrogancia. *2* mano, parte, participación: *to have a ~ in*, tener mano o parte en. *3* mano, lado, parte: *right ~*, mano derecha, la derecha; *on all hands, on every ~*, por todas partes, por todos lados. *4* mano, habilidad, destreza: *to have a ~ for*, tener mano para. *5* persona hábil o diestra: *to be a good ~ at*, ser hábil o diestro en. *6* mano, auxilio, ayuda: *to bear* o *lend a ~*, echar una mano, dar la mano, ayudar. *7* letra [carácter de letra]. *8* letra, escritura [de una pers.], letra y puño. *9* firma: *under the ~ of*, firmado por. *10* aplauso. *11* mano [origen, fuente]: *at first ~*, de primera mano. *12* ZOOL. mano [de mono]; pinza [de crustáceo]. *13* manecilla, aguja [de reloj]. *14* IMPR. manecilla. *15* palmo menor. *16* NAIPES mano [lance entero]; juego [naipes de un jugador]; jugador; *to show one's ~*, fig. descubrir uno su juego. *17* obrero, peón. *18* MAR. marinero, tripulante: *all hands*, toda la tripulación; todo el mundo.

19 adj. de mano, manual, para la mano, etc.: *~ glass*, espejo de mano; lupa; *~ mill*, molinillo; *~ organ*, organillo, aristón.

hand (to) *tr.* dar, entregar, poner en manos de, pasar. *2* conducir, guiar por la mano. *3 to ~ down*, transmitir; pasar [de arriba abajo]. *4 to ~ in*, entregar, presentar. *5 to ~ out*, distribuir. *6 to ~ over*, entregar, resignar. *7 to ~ up*, pasar [de abajo arriba].

handbag (-bæg) *s.* maletín. *2* bolso [de señora].

handball (-bol) *s.* pelota; juego de pelota a mano.

handbarrow (-bærou) *s.* angarillas, parihuelas. *2* carretilla de mano.

handbill (-bil) *s.* hoja suelta, anuncio [que se entrega a mano].

handbook (-buk) *s.* manual, guía [libro].

handbreadth (-bredz) *s.* palmo menor.

handcart (-kaʳt) *s.* carrito de mano.

handcuff (-køf) *s.* manilla. *2 pl.* manillas, esposas.

handcuff (to) *tr.* esposar, poner manillas a.

handed (-id) *adj.* que tiene mano; de mano, etc.: *left-handed*, zurdo; dado con la izquierda.

handful (-ful) *s.* manojo, puñado.

handhold (-jould) *s.* asidero.

handicap (-ikæp) *s.* DEP. handicap.

handicap (to) *tr.* DEP. handicapar. *2* estorbar, poner trabas a. ¶ Pret. y p. p.: *handicapped;* ger.: *handicapping.*

handicraft (-ikræft) *s.* oficio, arte mecánica. *2* ocupación o habilidad manual.

handicraftsman (-mæn) *s.* artesano, artífice.

handily (-ili) *adv.* diestramente. *2* cómodamente.

handiwork (-uø·k) *s.* obra manual. *2* obra de las manos [de uno]. *3* labor, obra, hechura.

handkerchief (-kø·chif) *s.* pañuelo.

handle (jæ·ndøl) *s.* asa; asidero; astil, mango, manija; manubrio; puño [de bastón, paraguas, etc.]; tirador [de cajón, puerta, etc.]; *~ bar*, manillar, guía [de bicicleta]. *2* tacto [de una cosa].

handle (to) *tr.* tocar, manosear. *2* manejar, manipular, tratar. *3* gobernar, dirigir. *4* tratar, comerciar en. *5* poner mango a. *6 intr.* usar de manos. *7* manejarse, ser manejado [con facilidad, etc.].

handless (-lis) *adj.* manco, sin manos.

handling (-ling) *s.* toque, manoseo. *2* manejo, manipulación, trato. *3* gobierno, dirección.

handmade (jændmei·d) *adj.* hecho a mano.

handmaid (jæ·ndmeid), **handmaiden** (-meidøn) *s.* criada, sirvienta.

hand-me-down *adj.* fam. hecho, de confección; barato; poco elegante [ropa, vestido, etc.].

handrail (jæ·ndreil) *s.* barandal, pasamano.

handsaw (jæ·ndso) *s.* serrucho, sierra de mano.

handsel (jæ·ndsøl) *s.* estreno. *2* aguinaldo. *3* prenda, señal, arras.

handsel (to) *tr.* estrenar. *2* dar aguinaldo. *3* ser el primero en probar o tener conocimiento de [una cosa]. ¶ Pret. y p. p.: *handseled* o *-selled;* ger.: *-seling* o *-selling.*

handset (jæ·ndset) *s.* TELEF. microteléfono.

handshake (jæ·ndsheik) *s.* apretón de manos.

handsome (jæ·nsøm) *adj.* hermoso, elegante, primoroso. *2* guapo, bien parecido. *3* noble, excelente. *4* liberal, generoso. *5* bonito, considerable.

handsomeness (-nis) *s.* hermosura, elegancia, apostura. *2* generosidad.

handspike (jæ·ndspaik) *s.* espeque.

handspring (jæ·ndspring) *s.* voltereta sobre las manos.

hand-to-hand *adj.* cuerpo a cuerpo.

hand-to-mouth *adj.* precario, inseguro.

handwork (jæ·nduø·k) *s.* obra hecha a mano.

handwriting (jæ·ndrai·ting) *s.* carácter de letra, letra, escritura [de una pers.].

handy (jæ·ndi) *adj.* diestro, hábil, mañoso. *2* manual, manuable, fácil de manejar. *3* a la mano, próximo. *4* cómodo, conveniente, útil. *5 ~ man*, mozo para todo.

hang (jæng) *s.* manera que tiene de colgar o inclinarse [una cosa]; caída [de un vestido]. *2* inclinación, declive. *4* sentido, intención [de un discurso, etc.]. *5* modo, manera, tranquilo: *to get the ~ of*, cogerle el tranquillo a. *6* detención, vacilación. *7* fig. nada, un bledo.

hang (to) *tr.* colgar, suspender. *2* colgar, ahorcar. *3* adornar con colgaduras, cuadros, etc., colgar, entapizar, tapizar, empapelar [paredes, habitaciones]; pegar, o fijar en, la pared. *4* tender [la ropa]. *5* bajar [la cabeza]. *6* engoznar [una puerta]. *7 to ~ fire*, fallar [un arma de fuego]; vacilar; alargarse, retardarse [una cosa]. *8 to ~*

out, colgar al exterior. *9 to ~ up*, colgar [el sombrero, el teléfono, etc.]; suspender, dejar en suspenso. *10 ~ it!, ~ it all!,* ¡demonio! *11 intr.* colgar, pender, caer. *12* ser ahorcado. *13* hacer pendiente. *14* estar engoznado. *15* estar adornado con colgaduras. *16* depender, descansar. *17* asirse [a], colgarse [de], abrazarse [a]. *18* adherirse, pegarse. *19* ser inminente, amenazar. *20* estar en suspenso. *21* detenerse, estar [en un sitio]. *22 to ~ around*, rondar, andar holgazaneando; esperar sin hacer nada. *23 to ~ back*, vacilar, titubear; quedarse atrás. *24 to ~ down*, colgar, estar pendiente. *25 to ~ on*, colgar de; abrazarse [al cuello] de; pegarse a [uno]; depender, estar pendiente de; continuar, persistir, insistir. *26 to ~ out*, estar colgado al exterior; asomarse [a una ventana, etc.] sacando fuera el busto; fam. vivir, residir. *27 to ~ over*, amenazar, cernerse sobre; quedar. *28 to ~ up*, TELEF. colgar.
    ¶ Pret. y p. p.: *hung* o *hanged*. | En la acep. *2* se prefiere *hanged*.
hangar (jæ·ngɑ·) *s.* hangar. *2* cobertizo.
hangdog (-dog) *adj.* avergonzado. *2* bajo, rastrero.
hanger (-ø·) *s.* soporte colgante, barra de suspensión. *2* colgadero, percha. *3* el que cuelga o coloca.
hanger-on, *pl.* **hangers-on** *s.* pegote, parásito. *2* el que frecuenta un paraje.
hanging (-ing) *adj.* colgante, pendiente, suspendido. *2* de suspensión. *3* merecedor de la horca. *4 s.* colgamiento. *5* ejecución en la horca. *6 pl.* colgaduras.
hangman (-mæn) *s.* verdugo.
hangnail (-neil) *s.* padrastro, respigón.
hank (jæŋk) *s.* madeja, cadejo. *2* MAR. anillo [de vela].
hank (to) *intr.* hacer madejas. *2* adujar.
hanker (to) (jæ·nko·) *intr.* ansiar, anhelar, apetecer. Gralte. con *for* o *after*.
hankering (jæ·nkøring) *s.* ansia, anhelo, deseo.
Hannah (jæ·na) *n. pr. f.* Ana.
Hannibal (jæ·nibal) *n. pr. m.* Aníbal.
Hanover (jæ·novø·) *n. pr.* GEOGR. Hannover.
Hanse (jæns) Ansa, Hansa.
hanseatic (jænsiæ·tik) *adj.* anseático, hanseático.
hansel (jæ·nsel) *s.* HANDSEL.
hansel (to) *tr.* TO HANDSEL.
hansom o **hansom cab** (jæ·nsøm) *s.* cabriolé con el pescante en la parte alta de la zaga.
hap (jæp) *s.* ant. acaso, ocurrencia; suerte, casualidad.
hap (to) *intr.* ant. acontecer, acaecer.
haphazard (-jæ·ṣa·d) *s.* casualidad, azar. *2 adj.* casual, fortuito, impensado. *3* descuidado, hecho a bulto. *4 adv.* al azar, al buen tuntún.
hapless (-lis) *adj.* desgraciado, desventurado.
haply (-li) *adv.* quizás. *2* acaso, por casualidad.
happen (to) (jæ·pøn) *intr.* acontecer, acaecer, suceder, ocurrir, pasar: *no matter what happens,* pase lo que pase. *2* dar la casualidad de que, ser el caso que, resultar que; acertar a: *it happens that I know it,* el caso es que yo lo sé; *he happened to be there,* él acertaba a estar allí. *3 to ~ in* o *into,* entrar un momento, al pasar. *4 to ~ on,* encontrar, tropezar con.
happening (-øning) *s.* acontecimiento, suceso, sucedido.
happiness (-inis) *s.* felicidad, dicha, ventura. *2* contento.
happy (-i) *adj.* feliz, dichoso, afortunado, fausto. *2*

alegre, contento. *3* hábil, pronto, oportuno. *4 to be ~,* alegrarse de, celebrar, tener gusto en.
happy-go-lucky *adj.-s.* descuidado, impróvido. *2 adv.* a la buena ventura.
harangue (jɑræ·ng) *s.* arenga, perorata.
harangue (to) *tr.* arengar. *2 intr.* discursear.
harass (to) (jæ·rɑs) *tr.* cansar, fatigar, agotar; atormentar; acosar, importunar. *2* MIL. hostigar, hostilizar.
harassment (-mønt) *s.* fatiga. *2* hostigamiento.
harbinger (-jɑ··bindฐø·) *s.* heraldo, nuncio, precursor. *2* anuncio, presagio.
harbinger (to) *tr.* anunciar, presagiar.
harbo (u) r (jɑ··bø·) *s.* puerto [de mar o de río]: *~ master,* capitán de puerto. *2* puerto seguro. *3* asilo, refugio, abrigo.
harbo (u) r (to) *tr.* abrigar, resguardar. *2* acoger, dar asilo. *3* hospedar, albergar. *4* abrigar [ideas, sentimientos]. *5* contener, guardar. *6 intr.* albergarse. *7* refugiarse.
harbo (u) rage (-idฐ) *s.* puerto, refugio, amparo, abrigo. *2* hospedaje, albergue.
hard (jɑ·d) *adj.* duro [en todas sus acepciones]. *2* endurecido. *3* firme, fuerte, enérgico, persistente. *4* arduo, difícil: *~ to please,* descontentadizo, difícil de contentar. *5* inclemente [tiempo]. *6* perverso, incorregible. *7* áspero, agrio [vino, etc.]. *8* cruda, gorda [agua]. *9* COM. sostenido [precio]. *10* apretado [nudo]. *11* FONÉT. gutural, velar. *12 ~ and fast,* rígido, inflexible [regla, etc.]. *~ cash,* dinero efectivo; metálico. *13 ~ facts,* hechos indiscutibles. *14 ~ lines,* apuro, situación angustiosa. *15 ~ of hearing,* duro de oído. *16 ~ usage,* mal trato. *17 to be ~ on,* tratar con dureza; gastar, estropear.
    18 adv. duramente, duro, fuerte, firmemente, de firme, recio, vigorosamente, con ahinco, con violencia. *19* difícilmente. *20 ~ by,* al lado, junto, muy cerca. *21 ~ labour,* trabajos forzados. *22 ~ pressed, pushed* o *run,* acosado; apremiado, apurado. *23 ~ up,* apurado, falto [de dinero, etc.]. *24 to drink ~,* beber fuerte, con exceso.
    25 s. suelo o piso duro.
hard-bitten *adj.* duro, resistente [en la lucha]. *2* terco, tenaz.
hard-boiled *adj.* duro [huevo].
hard-earned *adj.* ganado con dificultad.
harden (to) (jɑ··døn) *tr.* endurecer. *2* encallecer, curtir, hacer insensible. *3* consolidar, solidar. *4* robustecer. *5* fortalecer [en un sentimiento, etc.]. *6 intr.* endurecerse. *7* encallecerse, empedernirse, curtirse. *8* fortalecerse.
hard-favoured, hard-featured *adj.* cariagrio, de facciones duras.
hard-fought *adj.* empeñado, reñido.
hard-headed *adj.* testarudo. *2* astuto, sagaz.
hard-hearted *adj.* duro de corazón, insensible, cruel.
hard-mouthed *adj.* boquiduro [caballo].
hardihood (jɑ··dijud) *s.* valor, intrepidez, resolución. *2* audacia, osadía. *3* descaro.
hardiness (-nis) *s.* vigor, robustez, resistencia. *2* HARDIHOOD.
hardly (jɑ··dli) *adv.* difícilmente. *2* apenas, escasamente. *3* duramente, ásperamente.
hardness (-nis) *s.* dureza. *2* firmeza, solidez. *3* penalidad, trabajo. *4* crueldad, rigor, aspereza.
hardship (-ship) *s.* penalidad, trabajo, privación, estrechez. *2* opresión, injusticia.
hardtack (-tæk) *s.* galleta [de munición].

hardware (-ue^r) *s.* quincalla, ferretería.
hardwood (-wud) *s.* madera dura o noble.
hardy (-i) *adj.* robusto, fuerte. 2 bravo, intrépido. 3 audaz, temerario. 4 BOT. resistente.
hare (je·ø·) *s.* ZOOL., ASTR. liebre: ~ *and hounds*, juego en que se imita la caza de la liebre.
harebell (-bel) *s.* BOT. campanilla.
harebrained (-breind) *adj.* aturdido, casquivano, ligero de cascos.
harefoot (-fut) *s.* BOT. pie de liebre.
harehearted (-ha·tid) *adj.* medroso, tímido.
harehound (-jaund) *s.* lebrel.
harelip (-lip) *s.* labio leporino.
harelipped (-lipt) *adj.* labihendido.
harem (je·røm) *s.* harén, harem, serrallo.
hare's-ear *s.* BOT. perfoliada.
hark (ja^rk) *interj.* ¡eh!, ¡oye!, ¡oigan!, ¡oíd!
hark (to) *tr.-intr.* escuchar, oír con atención, atender.
harken (to) (ja··køn) *tr.* TO HEARKEN.
harl (ja·l) *s.* filamento, hebra.
harlequin (ja··lekuin) *s.* arlequín. 2 *adj.* arlequinesco, abigarrado.
harlequin (to) *tr.-intr.* hacer el bufón, embromar.
harlequinade (ja·lekuinei·d) *s.* arlequinada.
harlot (ja·^rløt) *s.* ramera, prostituta. 2 *adj.* lascivo, soez.
harlotry (-ri) *s.* prostitución.
harm (ja^rm) *s.* mal, daño, detrimento, perjuicio.
harm (to) *tr.* dañar, hacer mal, perjudicar.
harmful (-ful) *adj.* dañoso, dañino, nocivo, perjudicial, pernicioso.
harmless (-lis) *adj.* indemne. 2 inofensivo, inocuo, inocente.
harmonic (ja·ma·nik) *adj.-s.* armónico. 2 *s. pl.* armonía [teoría musical].
harmonica (-a) *s.* MÚS. armónica.
harmonical (-al) *adj.* armónico.
harmonious (ja^rmou·niøs) *adj.* armonioso.
harmonist (ja·^rmonist) *s.* armonista.
harmonium (ja^rmou·niøm) *s.* MÚS. armonio.
harmonize (to) (ja·^rmønaiš) *tr.-intr.* armonizar. 2 *intr.* armonizarse, concordar; congeniar.
harmony (ja·^rmøni) *s.* armonía.
harness (ja·^rnis) *s.* arneses, arreos, guarniciones: ~ *maker*, guarnicionero, talabartero; ~ *room*, guardarnés. 2 ARM. arnés. 3 fig. *in* ~, trabajando, en servicio activo. 4 MEC. equipo. 5 TEJ. montura, lizos.
harness (to) *tr.* poner las guarniciones a; enjaezar, aparejar. 2 armar con arnés. 3 represar [las aguas de un río].
harp (ja·^rp) *s.* MÚS. arpa. 2 ASTR. Lira.
harp (to) *intr.* tocar el arpa. 2 *to* ~ *on* o *upon*, machacar, repetir porfiadamente.
harper (-ø·), **harpist** (-ist) *s.* arpista.
harpoon (ja^rpu·n) *s.* arpón.
harpoon (to) *tr.* arponear.
harpooner (-ø·) *s.* arponero.
harpsichord (ja·^rpsico·d) *s.* MÚS. clavicordio.
harpy (ja·^rpi) *s.* MIT., ORN. arpía. 2 fig. arpía [pers. rapaz y codiciosa].
harquebus (ja·^rkuibøs) *s.* arcabuz.
harquebusier (ja^rkuibøsi·^r) *s.* arcabucero.
harridan (jæ·ridan) *s.* vieja bruja, arpía.
harrier (jæ·riø^r) *s.* lebrel. 2 pillador, asolador. 3 molestador. 4 ORN. nombre de algunas aves falcónidas.
Harriet (jæ·riet) *n. pr. f.* HENRIETTA.
harrow (jæ·rou) *s.* AGR. grada de dientes; escarificador. 2 instrumento de tortura.

harrow (to) *tr.* AGR. gradar, escarificar. 2 desgarrar, atormentar.
harrowing (-ing) *adj.* agudo, desgarrador; horripilante.
Harry (jæ·ri) *n. pr. m. dim.* de HENRY.
harry (to) *tr.* pillar, asolar, devastar. 2 perseguir, acosar, atormentar.
harsh (ja^rsh) *adj.* áspero. 2 rudo, tosco, bronco. 3 discordante, desagradable, chillón. 4 brusco, desabrido, acerbo, duro, riguroso, cruel, injusto.
hart (ja^rt) *s.* ZOOL. ciervo [macho], venado.
hartshorn (-sjo^rn) *s.* cuerna de ciervo. 2 QUÍM. sal amoníaco. 3 BOT. estrellamar.
hart's-tongue (-støng) *s.* BOT. lengua de ciervo.
harum-scarum (je·røm-ske·røm) *adj.-s.* atolondrado, aturdido, tarambana. 2 *adv.* atolondradamente, al tuntún.
haruspex (jarø·speks), **haruspice** (-pis) *s.* arúspice.
harvest (ja·^rvist) *s.* cosecha, recolección, siega, agosto. 2 fig. fruto, premio [de un trabajo, esfuerzo, conducta, etc.]. 3 ENT. ~ *fly*, cigarra.
harvest (to) *tr.* cosechar, recoger, recolectar; segar [la mies]. 2 *intr.* cosechar, segar [hacer la cosecha, la siega].
harvester (-ø^r) *s.* cogedor de frutos, segador, agostero. 2 segadora, máquina de segar.
harvestman (-mæn) *s.* HARVESTER 1. 2 ZOOL. segador.
harvester-thresther *s.* AGR. segadora-trilladora.
has (jæš) 3.ª *pers. pres. ind.* de TO HAVE.
hash (jæsh) *s.* picadillo, jigote. 2 revoltillo, enredo: *to make a* ~ *of*, enredar, estropear [un asunto o trabajo].
hash (to) *tr.* picar, desmenuzar. 2 enredar, estropear.
hasheesh, hashish (jæ·shish) *s.* haxix.
haslet (jæ·slit) *s.* COC. asadura de cerdo.
hasn't (jæ·sønt) contracción de HAS NOT.
hasp (jasp) *s.* manecilla [de libro]; cierre [de baúl].
hasp (to) *tr.* cerrar con broche o cierre.
hassock (jæ·søk) *s.* almohadón, cojín.
hastate (jæ·steit) *adj.* BOT. alabardado.
haste (jeist) *s.* prisa, presteza, celeridad, apresuramiento; precipitación, aturdimiento: *to be in* ~, tener prisa; *to make* ~, darse prisa.
haste (to) *intr.* darse prisa, apresurarse.
hasten (to) (jei·søn) *tr.* acelerar, apresurar, avivar. 2 dar prisa. 3 *intr.* apresurarse, darse prisa.
hasty (jei·sti) *adj.* apresurado. 2 pronto, vivo; de genio vivo; colérico. 3 precipitado, atropellado, inconsiderado, temerario.
hat (jæt) *s.* sombrero: ~ *factory*, ~ *shop*, sombrerería; *to pass round the* ~, hacer una colecta, echar un guante. 2 capelo. 3 MAR. ~ *money*, capa [que percibe el capitán].
hatband (-bænd) *s.* cinta del sombrero.
hatbox (-baks), **hatcase** (-keis) *s.* sombrerera.
hatch (jæch) *s.* compuerta, media puerta. 2 trampa, escotillón. 3 MAR. escotilla. 4 MAR. cuartel [de escotilla]. 5 HIDR. paradera, compuerta. 6 echadura, incubación. 7 salida del cascarón. 8 nidada, pollada. 9 B. ART. línea de sombreado.
hatch (to) *tr.* empollar, incubar. 2 producir, idear, tramar, maquinar. 3 rayar, sombrear con líneas. 4 *intr.* encobar. 5 salir del cascarón. 6 incubarse, formarse.
hatchel (jæ·chøl) *s.* rastrillo [para el lino, etc.].
hatchel (to) *tr.* rastrillar [lino, etc.]. 2 molestar,

inquietar. ¶ Pret. y p. p.: *hatcheled* o *-lled;* p. a.: *-ling* o *-lling*.
hatchery (jæ·chøri) *s.* vivero, criadero [de peces].
hatchet (jæ·chit) *s.* destral. *2* hacha [de los indios]: *to bury the ~,* hacer la paz, olvidar rencores; *to dig up the ~,* hacer la guerra.
hatched-faced *adj.* de facciones enjutas.
hatching (jæ·ching) *s.* B. ART. sombreado, plumeado.
hatchway (jæ·chuei) *s.* MAR. escotilla.
hate (jeit) *s.* odio, aborrecimiento, aversión.
hate (to) *tr.* odiar, aborrecer, detestar.
hateful (-ful) *adj.* odioso, aborrecible. *2* malévolo, rencoroso.
hatefulness (-nis) *s.* odiosidad.
hater (jei·tø^r) *s.* aborrecedor, enemigo.
hath (jæz) ant. *3.*ª *pers. pres. ind.* de TO HAVE.
hatpin (jæ·tpin) *s.* aguja para el sombrero.
hatrack (-ræk) *s:* perchero [para sombreros].
hatred (jei·trid) *s.* odio, aborrecimiento.
hatted (jæ·tid) *adj.* cubierto con sombrero.
hatter (-ø^r) *s.* sombrerero.
Hatty (jæ·ti) *n. pr. f. dim.* de HENRIETTA.
hauberk (jo·bø^rk) *s.* camisote, cota de mallas.
haughtiness (jo·tinis) *s.* orgullo, altivez, altanería.
haughty (jo·ti) *adj.* orgulloso, altivo, altanero.
haul (jol) *s.* tirón, estirón. *2* acción de halar o tirar de, tiro, arrastre. *3* redada.
haul (to) *tr.-intr.* tirar de, arrastrar. *2 tr.* MAR. halar, cazar. *3* acarrear, transportar. *4* sacar [con red]. *5 to ~ down,* arriar. *6 to ~ up,* pedir cuentas a, reprender. *7 intr.* mudarse [el viento]. *8* MAR. virar [la nave]; *to ~ upon the wind,* ceñir el viento.
haulage (-idӯ) *s.* arrastre, acarreo, transporte.
haulm, haum (jom) *s.* paja, rastrojo.
haunch (jonch) *s.* cadera. *2* anca, grupa. *3* COC. pierna [de venado, etc.].
haunt (jo·nt) *s.* lugar que se frecuenta; querencia; guarida. *2* morada.
haunt (to) *tr.* frecuentar, rondar. *2* aparecerse en [hablando de fantasmas]. *3* perseguir, obsesionar [a uno una idea, un recuerdo].
haunting (-ing) *adj.* persistente, obsesionante.
hautboy (jou·boi) *s.* MÚS. óboe.
Havana (javæ·na) *n. pr.* GEOGR. Habana. *2 s.* habano [cigarro].
have (to) (jæv) *aux.* haber: *I ~ worked,* he trabajado; *had he read the letter,* si él hubiera leído la carta; *I had as soon, I had rather,* preferiría, más quisiera; *we had better,* vale más que, es mejor que.
    2 tr. haber, tener, poseer. *3* tener [duda, cuidado, asuntos, un dolor, un niño, etc.]. *4* sufrir [cierto accidente]: *I had my leg broken,* me rompí la pierna. *5* tener, recibir [una carta, una noticia, etc.]. *6* sostener, afirmar, decir: *he will ~ it that,* él sostiene que. *7* conocer, saber: *he has no Latin,* no sabe latín. *8* jugar [una partida]. *9* tomar, comer, beber; aceptar: *~ a cigar,* tome un cigarro. *10* permitir, consentir. *11* desear, querer, mandar, hacer [que se haga una cosa]: *he had his shoes repaired,* se hizo componer los zapatos. *12* coger, atrapar, engañar. *13* obtener, adquirir: *to be had of,* pídase en, de venta en. *14* echar, dar [una mirada]. *15 to ~ a mind to,* tener ganas de, estar tentado de. *16 to ~ at,* atacar, acometer. *17 to ~ at heart,* desear vivamente. *18 to ~ it out,* liquidar un asunto con explicaciones o peleándose. *19 to ~ recourse,* recurrir. *20 to ~ to* o *to ~ got to,* tener que, haber

de, deber. *21 to ~ to do with,* tener que ver con. ¶ *3.*ª pers. pres. ind.: *has;* pret. y p. p.: *had.*
havelock (jæ·vlak) *s.* MIL. cogotera.
haven (jei·vn) *s.* puerto, abra. *2* asilo, abrigo.
haven't (jæ·vønt) contracción de HAVE NOT.
haversack (jæ·vø·sæk) *s.* mochila, barjuleta.
having (jæ·ving) *s.* bienes, hacienda, haber.
havoc (jæ·vøk) *s.* estrago, destrucción, asolamiento: *to play ~,* hacer estragos.
havoc (to) *tr.* asolar, causar estrago en.
haw (jo) *s.* BOT. majuela. *2* especie de tartamudeo. *3* voz para azuzar a una caballería.
haw (to) *3 tr.-intr.* hacer volver o volver [una caballería] a la izquierda. *2 intr.* hacer una especie de tartamudeo.
Hawaiian (jauai·ian) *adj.-s.* hawaiano.
haw-haw *s.* risotada, carcajada.
hawk (jok) *s.* ORN. nombre que se da al halcón, al cernícalo, al gavilán, al azor y a otras aves falcónidas. *2* ORN. *~ owl,* autillo, úlula. *3* fig. ave de presa [pers.].
hawk (to) *tr.* cazar con halcón. *2* pregonar [mercancías, una noticia, un secreto]. *3 intr.* carraspear, gargajear.
hawker (-ø^r) *s.* halconero, cetrero. *2* vendedor ambulante, buhonero.
hawk-eyed *adj.* lince, de mirada perspicaz.
hawking (-ing) *s.* cetrería. *2* buhonería.
hawkweed (-wid) *s.* BOT. vellosilla.
hawse (jo·s) *s.* MAR. frente a los escobenes. *2* MAR. escobén. *3* MAR. longitud de cadenas.
hawsehole (-joul) *s.* MAR. escobén.
hawser (-ø^r) *s.* MAR. guindaleza, estacha.
hawthorn (jo·zo^rn) *s.* BOT. majuelo o espino blanco.
hay (jei) *s.* heno, forraje: *~ fever,* MED. fiebre del heno.
hay (to) *intr.* hacer heno. *2 tr.* dar heno a.
haycock (-kak) *s.* almiar, niara.
hayfield (-fild) *s.* henar.
hayfork (-fo^rk) *s.* AGR. horca, horcón, bieldo.
hayloft (-loft) *s.* henil, pajar.
hayrack (-ræk) *s.* pesebre.
hayrik (-rik), **haystack** (-tæk) *s.* almiar, niara, montón de heno.
hazard (jæ·sa^rd) *s.* azar, suerte, casualidad. *2* albur, riesgo: *at all hazards,* por grande que sea el riesgo. *3* BILLAR. billa. *4* GOLF. obstáculo.
hazard (to) *tr.* arriesgar, aventurar. *2 intr.* correr riesgo.
hazardous (-øs) *adj.* arriesgado, peligroso.
haze (jeiš) *s.* niebla, calina. *2* confusión, vaguedad.
haze (to) *intr.* aneblarse [la atmósfera]. *2 tr.* dar la novatada a.
hazel (jei·šøl) *s.* avellano. *2 adj.* de color de avellana.
hazelnut (-nøt) *s.* BOT. avellana.
hazing (jei·šing) *s.* novatada.
hazy (jei·ši) *adj.* aneblado, nebuloso, brumoso, caliginoso. *2* confuso, vago.
H-bomb *s.* bomba de hidrógeno.
he (ji) *pron. pers.* él. | Se emplea en composición, para designar al macho o varón: *~ bear,* oso [macho]. *2 pron. indef.* el, aquel: *~ who, ~ that,* el que, aquel que, quien.
head (jed) *s.* cabeza [del hombre, del animal, de una cosa; intelecto; talento, capacidad]: *~ of hair,* cabellera, mata de pelo; *to be off one's ~,* delirar, estar loco; *to come into one's ~,* pasarle por la cabeza a uno; *I cannot make ~ or tail of it,* no puedo entenderlo o descifrarlo; *to lose one's ~,* perder la cabeza; *from ~ to foot,* de pies

a cabeza; ~ *on*, de cabeza; *out of one's* ~, de la cabeza de uno, de su cosecha; *over* ~ *and ears*, hasta los ojos; *over one's* ~, por encima de uno; fuera del alcance o comprensión de uno. *2* cabeza, jefe, director, primer puesto, dirección: *at the* ~ *of*, a la cabeza de, al frente de. *3* cabeza [de ganado; pers. unidad]. *4* cima, cumbre. *5* cabecera [de la mesa, de la cama, de un río]. *6* título, encabezamiento. *7* sección [de un escrito]. *8* punto, tema particular, concepto: *on this* ~, sobre este punto, por este concepto. *9* punta, extremo. *10* puño [de bastón]. *11* cuerna [de ciervo]. *12* MAR. proa. *13* tímpano [de tonel]; tapa [de cilindro]; parche [de tambor]; montera [de alambique]. *14* grátil [de vela]. *15* promontorio. *16* BOT. cabezuela. *17* repollo, pella [de col, etc.]. *18* presa, embalse [de molino, etc.]. *19* espuma [de un líquido]. *20* avance, progreso: *to make* ~, avanzar, progresar. *21* punta [de un divieso]. *22* MED. maduración; fig. crisis, punto culminante o decisivo. *23 heads or tails*, cara o cruz.

24 adj. de cabeza, cabecera, proa, etc. *25* principal, primero, jefe: ~ *cook*, primer cocinero.

head (to) *tr.* encabezar. *2* ser el primero de; mandar, acaudillar. *3* poner cabeza, título, etc., a. *4* adelantar [a uno]. *5* conducir [un coche, etc.] en cierta dirección. *5* descabezar; desmochar. *6 to~ off*, cortar el paso a; atajar. *7 intr.* ir, dirigirse. *8* nacer [un río]. *9* repollar [una planta]. *10* supurar [un absceso].

headache (-eik) *s.* dolor de cabeza, jaqueca.

headband (-bænd) *s.* cinta para la cabeza. *2* cabezada [de libro].

headboard (-bord) *s.* cabecera [de cama].

headdress (-dres) *s.* prenda para la cabeza; tocado.

header (-ø^r) *s.* cabecilla, director. *2* descabezador. *3* ARQ. brochal. *4* ALBAÑ. ladrillo puesto a tizón. *5* caída o salto de cabeza; zambullida.

headfirst (-først), **headforemost** (-formoust) *adv.* de cabeza.

headgear (-gir) *s.* prenda para la cabeza. *2* cabezada [de caballería].

heading (je·ding) *s.* título, encabezamiento; membrete. *2* MIN. galería de avance.

headland (-land) *s.* GEOGR. cabo, punta, promontorio.

headless (-lis) *adj.* acéfalo. *2* decapitado. *3* sin seso, estúpido. *4* sin jefe o caudillo.

headlight (-lait) *s.* faro [de locomotora o automóvil]. *2* MAR. farol de tope.

headline (-lain) *s.* titulares [de un periódico]. *2* título de página, titulillo.

headlong (-long) *adj.* precipitado, impetuoso, temerario. *2* de cabeza [zambullida, etc.]. *3 adv.* precipitadamente, temerariamente. *4* de cabeza.

headman (-mæn) *s.* jefe, caudillo.

headmaster (-mæ·sto^r) *s.* director [de un colegio].

headmistress (-mi·stris) *s.* directora [de un colegio].

headmost (je·dmoust) *adj.* más avanzado; delantero, primero, que va en cabeza.

headphone (-foun) *s.* TELÉF. auricular de casco.

headpiece (-pis) *s.* casco, yelmo. *2* IMPR. viñeta, cabecera. *3* fam. chola, mollera.

headquarters (-kuortørs) *s.* MIL. cuartel general. *2* jefatura [de policía]. *3* sede [de una entidad]. *4* dirección, oficina principal.

headrace (-reis) *s.* caz, saetín [de molino].

headrest (-rest) *s.* apoyo para la cabeza.

headsail (-seil) *s.* MAR. vela delantera.

headset (-set) *s.* juego de auriculares con casco.

headsman (-smæn) *s.* verdugo [que decapita].

headstall (-stol) *s.* cabezada [de freno], testera.

headstone (-stoun) *s.* lápida mortuoria. *2* ARQ. piedra angular.

headstream (-strim) *s.* afluente principal [de un río].

headstrong (-strong) *adj.* cabezudo, testarudo, terco, obstinado. *2* ingobernable.

headwaters (-uotø^r s) *s.* fuentes [de un río].

headway (-uei) *s.* marcha [de un buque]. *2* avance, progreso; ímpetu: *to make* ~, avanzar, adelantar, progresar. *3* FERROC. distancia [entre dos trenes en una misma vía].

headwork (-uø^r k) *s.* trabajo intelectual.

heady (-i) *adj.* temerario, arrojado. *2* violento, impetuoso. *3* obstinado. *4* fuerte [vino, licor].

heal (to) (ji·l) *tr.* curar, sanar. *2* remediar, reparar. *3* limpiar [del pecado, etc.]. *4 intr.* curar, curarse, sanar: *to* ~ *up*, cicatrizarse. *5* remediarse.

heald (-d) *s.* TEJ. lizo.

healer (-ø^r) *s.* curador, sanador.

healing (-ing) *s.* cura, curación, cicatrización. *2 adj.* curativo, cicatrizante.

health (jelz) *s.* salud, sanidad: *to be in good (poor* o *bad)* ~, estar bien (mal) de salud; *your* ~*!*, ¡a la salud de usted!; ~ *officer*, inspector de sanidad.

healthful (-ful) *adj.* sano, saludable, salubre.

health-giving *adj.* saludable, que da salud.

healthiness (-inis) *s.* buena salud, sanidad.

healthy (-i) *adj.* sano [en buena salud]. *2* vigoroso, robusto. *3* sano, saludable.

heap (jip) *s.* montón, pila, rimero, cúmulo. *2* fam. [a veces en pl.] gran cantidad, multitud, gentío: *in heaps*, a montones.

heap (to) *tr.* amontonar, apilar, juntar, acumular. *2* cargar, colmar, llenar.

hear (to) (ji·ø^r) *tr.* oír [los sonidos, etc.], escuchar: *to* ~ *it said*, oírlo decir; *to* ~ *someone out*, escuchar a uno hasta el fin. *2* oír decir: *I heard that*, oí decir que. *3* oír [misa]. *4* oír, escuchar, atender [ruegos, etc.]. *5 intr.* oír: *to* ~ *about, from* o *of*, oír hablar de, tener noticias de, enterarse de. ¶ Pret. y p. p.: *heard*.

heard (jø·d) *pret.* y *p. p.* de TO HEAR.

hearer (ji·ørø^r) *s.* oyente.

hearing (-ing) *s.* oído [sentido]; audición [acción de oír]. *2* oportunidad para ser oído, audiencia. *3* DER. examen de testigos. *4* alcance del oído: *within* ~, al alcance del oído.

hearken (to) (ja·^r køn) *intr.* escuchar.

hearsay (ji·ø^r sei) *s.* rumor, voz común: *by* ~, de oídas.

hearse (jø^r s) *s.* coche o carroza fúnebre. *2* tenebrario.

heart (ja·t) *s.* corazón [órgano; parte central; sentimiento interior; ánimo, valor, etc.]: *to be of good* ~, tener ánimo; *to die of broken* ~, morir de pena; *to get to the* ~ *of*, llegar al fondo o al corazón de; *to have at* ~, desear vivamente; *to have one's* ~ *in one's boots*, o *mouth*, estar con el alma en un hilo; estar muerto de miedo; *to take to* ~, tomar en serio; a pecho; *after one's own* ~, a gusto de uno, como uno desea; *at* ~, en el fondo, en realidad; *by* ~, de memoria; ~ *and soul*, en cuerpo y alma; *to one's* ~ *content*, a placer, sin restricción; *with all one's* ~, con toda el alma, de todo corazón. *2* cogollo [de lechuga, etc.]. *3 pl.* copas [de la baraja].

4 adj. del corazón, cardíaco: ~ *failure,* colapso cardíaco; ~ *trouble,* enfermedad del corazón.
heartache (-eik) *s.* dolor de corazón, congoja, pesar, aflicción.
heartbeat (-bɪt) *s.* latido del corazón. *2* emoción profunda.
heartbreak (-breik) *s.* angustia, aflicción grande.
heartbreaking (-ing) *adj.* doloroso, desgarrador.
heartbroken (-broukøn) *adj.* acongojado, transido de dolor.
heartburn (-bø^rn) *s.* acedía.
heartburning (-ning) *s.* envidia, animosidad.
hearten (to) (-øn) *tr.* animar, alentar.
heartfelt (-felt) *adj.* cordial, sincero; sentido.
heartgrief (-grɪf) *s.* congoja, angustia.
hearth (-ja^rz) *s.* hogar; chimenea. *2* hogar [doméstico]. *3* solera, suelo, crisol [de horno].
heartily (ja·^rtili) *adv.* sinceramente, cordialmmente. *2* vigorosamente. *3* copiosamente, con buen apetito.
heartiness (-inis) *s.* sinceridad, cordialidad, calor. *2* ganas, apetito.
heartless (-lis) *adj.* sin corazón, cruel, insensible. *2* tímido, pusilánime, abatido.
heart-rending *adj.* agudo, desgarrador, que parte el corazón.
heartsease o **heart's-ease** (sɪš) *s.* serenidad de ánimo. *2* BOT. pensamiento, trinitaria.
heartseed (-sɪd) *s.* BOT. farolillo.
heartsick (-sik) *adj.* dolorido, desconsolado.
heartstricken (-strikøn) *adj.* afligido, angustiado.
heartstrings (-strings) *s. pl.* fibras del corazón, entretelas.
heart-to-heart *adj.* sincero, franco.
hearty (-i) *adj.* cordial, caluroso, sincero. *2* fuerte, vigoroso. *3* robusto, sano. *4* nutritivo, abundante. *5* que se hace con gusto. *6* ~ *eater,* gran tragón.
heat (jɪt) *s.* calor: ~ *wave,* ola de calor. *2* calórico. *3* calefacción. *4* acaloramiento. *5* ardor, fogosidad. *6* lo más fuerte o recio [de una acción, etc.]. *7* celo [de la hembra]. *8* DEP. carrera [en una serie de ellas], carrera de prueba o eliminatoria.
heat (to) *tr.* calentar, caldear. *2* acalorar, excitar. *3 intr.* calentarse. *4* acalorarse, excitarse.
heater (-ø^r) *s.* calentador. *2* aparato de calefacción.
heath (jɪz) *s.* BOT. brezo, urce. *2* brezal, matorral: ~ *cock,* especie de urogallo.
heathen (jɪ·ðøn) *adj.-s.* pagano, gentil. *2* irreligioso. *3 fig.* salvaje.
heathenism (-išm) *s.* paganismo, gentilidad.
heather (je·ðø^r) *s.* BOT. brezo, urce.
heathery (-i) *adj.* cubierto de brezos, matoso.
heating (jɪ·ting) *s.* calefacción, calentamiento, caldeo, calda. *2 adj.* calefaciente, calorífico; de calefacción: ~ *pad,* almohadilla eléctrica.
heave (jɪv) *s.* esfuerzo para levantar, solevar o levantarse. *2* movimiento de lo que se levanta [como el de una ola]. *3* jadeo. *4* náusea, arcada. *5* lanzamiento, echada.
heave (to) *tr.* levantar, solevar; mover con esfuerzo. *2* lanzar, arrojar, echar. *3* exhalar [un suspiro, etc.]. *4* hinchar [el pecho]. *5* MAR. halar [un cable]. *6* MAR. *to* ~ *to,* poner al pairo o en facha. *7 intr.* levantarse, combarse. *8* levantarse y bajar alternativamente; jadear, agitarse [el pecho]. *9* arquear, basquear. *10* esforzarse. *11 to* ~ *in sight,* aparecer, asomar en el horizonte. ¶ Pret. y p. p.: *heaved* o *hove.*
heaven (je·vøn) *s.* cielo [de los bienaventurados], gloria, paraíso: *for heaven's sake,* ¡por Dios!;

good heavens! ¡válgame Dios! *2* cielo, firmamento.
heavenliness (je·vønlinis) *s.* calidad de celestial.
heavenly (-li) *adj.* celestial, divino. *2* celeste.
heavenward (-uø^rd) *adv.* hacia el cielo.
heaver (jɪ·vø^r) *s.* cargador [obrero]. *2* MAR. tortor.
heaves (jɪvs) *s. pl.* VET. huélfago.
heavily (je·vili) *adv.* pesadamente. *2* lentamente. *3* fuertemente, duramente. *4* sumamente.
heaviness (-nis) *s.* pesadez, pesantez, peso, gravedad. *2* pesadez, torpeza, lentitud. *3* languidez, modorra. *4* peso, importancia. *5* opresión. *6* abatimiento.
heavy (je·vi) *adj.* pesado, ponderoso: ~ *industry,* industria pesada. *2* pesado, opresivo, gravoso, aflictivo, severo. *3* fuerte, grande, serio, grave, recio, violento: ~ *losses,* fuertes pérdidas; ~ *shower,* chaparrón. *4* profundo, intenso. *5* pesado, lento, tardo. *6* amodorrado, soñoliento. *7* pesado [estilo]. *8* cargado, agobiado. *9* oprimido [corazón, etc.]. *10* cansado. *11* grueso, denso, tupido; macizo, tosco. *12* laborioso, difícil. *13* indigesto. *14* fragoroso [cañoneo]. *15* triste, abatido. *16* encapotado, sombrío. *17* malo [camino]; empinada [cuesta]. *18* desanimado [mercado]. *19* ~ *drinker,* gran bebedor. *20 adv.* fuerte, pesadamente.
   21 s. TEAT. personaje solemne o perverso.
heavy-handed *adj.* torpe. *2* de mano dura, opresivo.
heavy-footed *adj.* de andar torpe. *2* despeado.
heavy-eyed *adj.* de ojos soñolientos.
heavy-set *adj.* costilludo, espaldudo.
heavyweight (-ueit) *s.* boxeador o luchador de peso pesado.
hebdomadal (jebda·madal) *adj.* hebdomadario, semanal.
hebetude (je·bitiud) *s.* estupidez, embotamiento.
Hebraic (jibrei·ik) *adj.* hebraico.
Hebraism (ji·briišm) *s.* hebraísmo.
Hebraist (-ist) *s.* hebraísta. *2* hebraizante.
Hebraize (to) (ji·briaiš) *tr.-intr.* hebraizar.
Hebrew (ji·bru) *adj.-s.* hebreo, israelita, judío.
hecatomb (je·katum) *s.* hecatombe.
heckle (to) (je·køl) *tr.* interrumpir [a un orador] con preguntas intencionadas o molestas.
hectare (je·kte^r) *s.* hectárea.
hectic (je·ktik) *adj.-s.* héctico, hético. *2 adj.* fam. febril, excitado, agitado.
hectogram, -gramme (je·ktøgræm) *s.* hectogramo.
hectoliter, -litre (-litø^r) *s.* hectolitro.
hectometer, -metre (-mitø^r) *s.* hectómetro.
hector (je·ktø^r) *s.* matón, fanfarrón.
hector (to) *tr.* atropellar, intimidar, con palabras, amenazas, etc. *2 intr.* bravear, baladronear.
he'd (jid) contracción de HE HAD y de HE WOULD.
heddle (je·døl) *s.* TEJ. lizo, malla.
hedge (jedỹ) *s.* seto vivo; cerca, vallado. *2 fig.* límite, valla.
hedge (to) *tr.* cercar con seto, vallar. *2* defender, circundar. *3* rodear, encerrar. *4 intr.* abrigarse, escudarse. *5* no comprometerse [al hablar].
hedgehog (-jag) *s.* ZOOL. erizo. *2* BOT. ~ *grass,* guizacillo.
hedgehop (to) (-jap) *intr.* AVIA. volar a ras de los árboles o setos.
hedger (-ø^r) *s.* el que hace o cuida setos. *2* el que usa de evasivas.
hedgerow (-rou) *s.* seto vivo.
hedonism (ji·dønišm) *s.* hedonismo.
hedonist (-ist) *adj.-s.* hedonista.

heed (jɪd) *s.* atención, cuidado; caso: *to take* ~, poner atención, ir con cuidado.
heed (to) *tr.* atender, prestar atención a, considerar, hacer caso de. *2* notar, observar, reparar. *3 intr.* poner atención o cuidado.
heedful (-ful) *adj.* atento, cuidadoso, cauto.
heedless (-lis) *adj.* desatento, distraído, descuidado, atolondrado.
heel (jɪl) *s.* talón [de pie, media o zapato]; tacón [de zapato]: *at, on,* o *upon, one's heels,* pisando los talones a uno; *down at (the)* ~, con los tacones gastados; en chancletas; desaliñado; apurado, en mala situación; *heels over head,* patas arriba; precipitadamente, irreflexivamente; *out at the heels,* con las medias rotas, desharrapado. *2* calcañar, zancajo. *3* parte inferior o trasera [de ciertas cosas]. *4* MAR. coz [de mástil]; talón [de quilla]. *5* MÚS. talón [de arco]. *6* cantero, cuscurro [de pan, queso, etc.]. *7* fin, conclusión. *8 pl.* cascos traseros [del caballo].
heel (to) *tr.* poner talón o tacón a. *2* armar con espolones [un gallo de pelea]. *3* seguir de cerca. *4 intr.* taconear [al bailar]. *5* MAR. inclinarse, escorar.
heeltap (-tap) *s.* tapa [de tacón]. *2* escurriduras [de un vaso].
heft (jeft) *s.* fam. peso. *2* fam. influencia. *3* (E.U.) la mayor parte.
heft (to) *tr.* fam. levantar en alto. *2* fam. sopesar.
hefty (-ti) *adj.* pesado. *2* fam. fornido, recio.
Hegelian (jidÿi·lian) *adj.* hegeliano.
hegemony (jedÿi·moni) *s.* hegemonía.
hegira (jidÿai·ra) *s.* hégira, hejira.
heifer (je·føʳ) *s.* novilla, vaquilla.
height (jait) *s.* altura, altitud, elevación. *2* alto, altura [dimensión]; talla, estatura, alzada. *3* alto, altura, elevación [del terreno], cerro, colina, cumbre, punto elevado. *4* extremo, colmo; lo más fuerte de: *at the* ~ *of winter,* en pleno invierno. *5* ARQ. montea [de un arco].
heighten (to) (-øn) *tr.* levantar, elevar [hacer más alto]. *2* exaltar, sublimar. *3* avivar, aumentar, realzar. *4 intr.* elevarse. *5* aumentar.
heinous (jei·nøs) *adj.* odioso, horrible, atroz.
heir (e·øʳ) *s.* heredero.
heirdom (-døm) *s.* condición de heredero.
heiress (-is) *f.* heredera.
heirloom (-lum) *s.* DER. bienes muebles unidos a la herencia. *2* herencia de familia.
held (jeld) *pret.* y *p. p.* de TO HOLD.
Helen (je·løn) *n. pr. f.* Elena.
heliac(al (jilai·ak(al) *adj.* ASTR. helíaco.
helianthus (jilia·nzøs) *s.* BOT. helianto.
helical (je·likal) *adj.* espiral; helicoidal.
helicopter (jelika·ptøʳ) *s.* helicóptero.
heliocentric(al (jiliose·ntrik(al) *adj.* heliocéntrico.
helioengraving (ji·lioengreiving) *s.* heliograbado.
heliograph (-græf) *s.* heliógrafo.
heliostat (-stæt) *s.* helióstato.
heliotherapy (jilioze·rapi) *s.* MED. helioterapia.
heliotrope (ji·liotroup) BOT., MINER. heliotropo.
helium (ji·liøm) *s.* QUÍM. helio.
helix (jɪ·liks) *s.* GEOM., ANAT. hélice. *2* ELECT. arrollamiento en hélice. *3* espira; voluta.
he'll (jɪl) contracción de HE SHALL y de HE WILL.
hell (jel) *s.* infierno [de los condenados; averno; lugar de sufrimiento, etc.]. *2* fig. garito. *3* fig. cajón de sastre.
Hellas (je·las) *s.* Hélade [Grecia].
hellbroth (-broz) *s.* caldo mágico maligno.
hellcat (-kæt) *s.* bruja. *2* arpía, mujer perversa.

hell-doomed *adj.* réprobo, condenado.
hellebore (je·liboʳ) *s.* BOT. eléboro. *2* BOT. vedegambre, veratro.
Hellenic (jele·nik) *adj.* helénico.
Hellenism (je·lønišm) *s.* helenismo.
Hellenist (-ist) *s.* helenista.
Hellenistic (jeløni·stik) *adj.* helenístico.
Hellespont (je·lispønt) *n. pr.* GEOGR. Helesponto.
hellish (-ish) *adj.* infernal, diabólico.
hellishness (-nis) *s.* malicia diabólica.
hello (je·lou) *interj.* ¡hola! *2* ¡ah!, ¡eh! *3* ¡diga! [en el teléfono].
helm (jelm) *s.* MAR. timón; rueda o caña del timón. *2* timón, dirección, gobierno. *3* HELMET 1.
helm (to) *tr.* dirigir, gobernar.
helmet (je·lmit) *s.* yelmo, casco, celada, morrión. *2* casco [de soldado, bombero, etc.].
helmeted (-id) *adj.* cubierto con casco.
helminth (je·lminz) *s.* ZOOL. helminto.
helmless (je·lmlis) *adj.* sin timón.
helmsman (-šmæn) *s.* timonero, timonel.
helot (je·løt) *s.* ilota.
helotism (-išm) *s.* ilotismo.
help (jelp) *s.* ayuda, auxilio, asistencia; socorro, favor, apoyo: *to cry out for* ~, pedir auxilio; *by the* ~ *of,* con ayuda de; *help!,* ¡socorro! *2* remedio, recurso: *there is no* ~ *for it,* no tiene remedio. *3* (E.U.) criado, mozo; criada. *4* fam. HELPING.
help (to) *tr.* ayudar, coadyuvar a, apoyar, secundar, contribuir a, fomentar. *2* ayudar, socorrer, amparar, valer: *so* ~ *me God,* así Dios me valga. *3* remediar, evitar: *I cannot* ~ *it,* no puedo remediarlo; *he cannot* ~ *but,* no puede menos de; no puede dejar de. *4* servir [comida, bebida]: *to* ~ *oneself to,* servirse [algo de comer o beber]. *5 to* ~ *down,* ayudar a caer o a bajar; *to* ~ *forward,* adelantar, activar. *6 to* ~ *out,* ayudar a salir [de una dificultad, etc.]. *7 intr.* ayudar, servir.
helper (-øʳ) *s.* auxiliador. *2* ayudante, peón.
helpful (-lpful) *adj.* que ayuda; útil. *2* saludable.
helping (-ing) porción de comida o bebida que se sirve a uno de una vez.
helpless (-lis) *adj.* desvalido. *2* impotente, imposibilitado, incapaz; inútil. *3* perplejo. *4* irremediable.
helpmate (-meit) *s.* compañero. *2* esposa, mujer.
helter-skelter (je·ltø-ske·ltøʳ) *adv.* atropelladamente, precipitadamente, en confusión, en desorden.
helve (jelv) *s.* ástil, mango [de hacha, etc.].
helve (to) *tr.* poner ástil o mango, enmangar.
Helvetia (jelvi·shia) *n. pr.* GEOGR. Helvecia.
Helvetian (-shan), **Helvetic** (jelve·tik) *adj.-s.* helvético, helvecio.
hem (jem) *s.* COST. dobladillo, bastilla, repulgo. *2* borde, orilla. *3 interj.* ¡ejem!
hem (to) *tr.* COST. dobladillar, bastillar, repulgar. *2 to* ~ *in,* cercar, rodear, encerrar. *3 intr.* fingir tos. *4* vacilar [al hablar].
hemal (jɪ·mal) *s.* de la sangre.
hematin (je·matin) *s.* QUÍM. hematina.
hematite (-tait) *s.* MINER. hematites.
hematoma (-tou·ma) *s.* hematoma.
hematuria (-tiu·ria) *s.* MED. hematuria.
hemelytron (jeme·litran) *s.* hemélitro.
hemi- (je·mi) *pref.* hemi-.
hemicrania (jemikrei·nia) *s.* MED. hemicránea.
hemicycle (je·misaikøl) *s.* hemiciclo.
hemihedral (jemiji·dral) *adj.* CRISTAL. hemiédrico.
hemihedron (-drøn) *s.* CRISTAL. hemiedro.

hemiplegia (jemipli·dÿia), **hemiplegy** (-dÿi) s. MED. hemiplejía.
hemipterous (jimi·ptørøs) adj. ENT. hemíptero.
hemisphere (jemi·sfiø') s. hemisferio.
hemispheric (al (jemisfe·rik(al) adj. hemisférico.
hemistich (je·mistik) s. hemistiquio.
hemlock (je·mlak) s. BOT. cicuta. 2 BOT. abeto del Canadá.
hemoglobin (jimøglou·bin) s. BIOQUÍM. hemoglobina.
hemophilia (jimøfi·lia) s. MED. hemofilia.
hemoptysis (jima·ptisis) s. MED. hemoptisis.
hemorrhage (je·møridÿ) s. MED. hemorragia.
hemorrhoids (je·møroids) s. MED. hemorroides.
hemostatic (jemøstæ·tik) adj. MED. hemostático.
hemp (jemp) s. cáñamo [planta, fibra]. 2 dogal.
hempen (-øn) adj. cañameño.
hempseed (-sid) s. cañamón.
hemstitch (je·mstich) s. COST. vainica.
hemstitch (to) tr. COST. hacer vainica en.
hen (jen) f. ORN. gallina. 2 hembra de ave [esp. de gallinácea]: ~ *turkey*, pava.
henbane (-bein) s. BOT. beleño.
hence (jens) adv. de, o desde, aquí o ahora. 2 de aquí a, dentro de: *two months ~*, de aquí a dos meses. 3 por tanto, por consiguiente, luego, de aquí que. 4 *interj.* ¡largo de aquí!
henceforth (-fo'z), **henceforward** (-fo'uø'd) adv. de aquí en adelante; desde ahora, en lo sucesivo.
henchman (je·nchmæn) s. secuaz, servidor, paniaguado.
hencoop (je·ncup) s. gallinero.
hendecagon (jende·kagan) s. endecágono.
hendecasyllable (jendekasi·labøl) s. endecasílabo.
henhouse (je·njaus) s. gallinero.
henna (je·na) s. BOT. alheña. 2 henné.
hennery (je·nøri) s. gallinero.
henpeck (to) (je·npek) tr. dominar e importunar [la mujer al marido].
henpecked (-t) adj. dominado por la mujer.
Henrietta (jenrie·ta) n. pr. f. Enriqueta.
henroost (je·nrust) s. gallinero.
Henry (je·nri) n. pr. Enrique.
henry (je·nri) s. ELECT. henrio.
hepatic (jipæ·tik) adj. hepático. 2 del color del hígado.
hepatica (jipæ·tika) s. BOT. hepática.
hepatite (je·patait) s. MINER. hepatita.
hepatitis (jepatai·tis) s. MED. hepatitis.
heptachord (je·ptako'd) s. MÚS. heptacordio.
heptad (je·ptad) s. setena.
heptagon (je·ptagon) s. GEOM. heptágono.
heptagonal (jeptæ·gonal) adj. heptagonal.
heptameter (jeptæ·mitø·) s. heptámetro.
heptarchy (je·pta'ki) s. heptarquía.
Heptateuch (je·ptatiuk) s. Heptateuco.
her (jø') pron. pers. f. de 3. pers. sing. (ac. o dat.) la, le. 2 [con prep.] ella: *to ~*, a ella; *for ~*, para ella. 3 adj. pos. f. de 3.ª pers. [indicando una sola poseedora] su, sus [de ella].
herald (je·rald) s. heraldo. 2 nuncio, precursor.
herald (to) tr. anunciar, ser nuncio de.
heraldic (jeræ·ldik) adj. heráldico.
heraldry (je·raldri) s. heráldica, blasón. 2 armas, blasones. 3 pompa heráldica.
herb (ø'b o jø'b) s. BOT. hierba, yerba: ~ *Louisa*, luisa, hierba luisa; ~ *trinity*, trinitaria, pensamiento.
herbaceous (jø'bei·shøs) adj. herbáceo.
herbage (jø·'bidÿ) s. hierba, herbaje.
herbal (jø·'bal) adj. herbario.

herbalist (-ist) s. botánico, herbario. 2 herbolario.
herbarium (jø'be·riøm) s. herbario [colección].
Herbert (jø·'bø't) n. pr. m. Heriberto.
herbivore (jø·'bivo') s. ZOOL. herbívoro.
herbivorous (jø·bi'vørøs) adj. herbívoro.
herborist (jø·'børist) s. HERBALIST.
herborization (jø'børisei·shøn) s. herborización.
herborize (to) (jø·'børaiš) intr. herborizar.
herbose (jø·'bous), **herbous** (-bøs), **herby** (-bi) adj. herboso. 2 herbáceo.
Herculean (jø'kiu·lian) adj. hercúleo.
herd (jø'd) s. rebaño, grey, manada, piara. 2 hato, pandilla. 3 multitud, chusma. 4 pastor [esp. en composición]: *cowherd*, vaquero.
herd (to) intr. ir en manadas o rebaños. 2 juntarse, asociarse. 3 tr. reunir o juntar en rebaño.
herdsman (-smæn) s. pastor, manadero.
here (ji·ø·) adv. aquí, ahí, acá; ahora, en este momento; en este mundo, en esta vida: ~ *goes!*, ¡ahí va!; ~ *it is*, aquí está, helo aquí; ~ *below*, aquí abajo, en la tierra. 2 ~ *is to you*, a la salud de usted.
hereabouts (-abauts) adv. por aquí cerca.
hereafter (-aftø') adv. de aquí en adelante, en lo futuro. 2 s. the ~, el futuro; la otra vida.
hereat (-æt) adv. a esto, en esto, por eso.
hereby (-bai) adv. por este medio, por este acto. 2 por la presente.
hereditary (jire·diteri) adj. hereditario.
heredity (-iti) s. BIOL. herencia.
herefrom (ji·ø'from) adv. de aquí, desde aquí. 2 a causa de esto.
herein (-i·n), **hereinto** (i·ntu) adv. aquí dentro, incluso; en esto.
hereinafter (-ina·ftø') adv. después, más abajo, más adelante [en un libro o escrito].
hereof (jiøra·v) adv. de esto, acerca de esto; de aquí.
hereon (jiøra·n) adv. sobre esto, sobre este punto.
heresiarch (jirt·sia'k) s. heresiarca.
heresy (je·røsi) s. herejía.
heretic (je·retik) s. hereje.
heretic(al (jire·tik(al) adj. herético.
hereto (jiø'tu·) adv. a esto, a este fin.
heretofore (-fo·') adv. hasta aquí, hasta ahora. 2 en el pasado, en otro tiempo. 3 s. the ~, el tiempo pasado, el pasado.
hereunder (-ø·ndø') adv. bajo esto, abajo, al pie. 2 en virtud de esto.
hereunto (-øntu·) adv. a esto, a eso.
hereupon (-øpa·n) adv. a esto. 2 sobre esto, acerca de esto.
herewith (-uiz) adv. con esto, adjunto.
heritage (je·ritidÿ) s. herencia.
hermaphrodite (jø'mæ·frødait) adj.-s. hermafrodita.
hermeneutic(al (jø'miniu·tik(al) adj. hermenéutico.
hermeneutics (-tiks) s. hermenéutica.
hermetic(al (jø'me·tik(al) adj. hermético.
hermit (jø·'mit) s. ermitaño, eremita, anacoreta. 2 ZOOL. ~ *crab*, ermitaño, paguro.
hermitage (-idÿ) s. ermita.
hermitical (jø'mi·tikal) adj. eremítico.
hernia (jø·'nia) s. MED. hernia.
hernial (jø·'nial) adj. herniario.
hero (ji·rou) s. héroe.
Herod (je·rød) n. pr. m. Herodes.
Herodian (jira·dian) adj.-s. herodiano.
heroic(al (jirou·ik(al) adj. heroico. 2 s. poema heroico.

heroicomic (jirouika·mik) *adj.* comicoheroico.
heroics (jirou·iks) *s.* verso heroico. *2* lenguaje rimbombante.
heroin (je·roin) *s.* QUÍM. heroína.
heroine *f.* heroína [mujer].
heroism (je·roišm) *s.* heroísmo.
heron (je·rən) *s.* ORN. garza, airón.
heronry (-ri) *s.* lugar donde anidan las garzas.
heron's-bill *s.* BOT. pico de cigüeña.
herpes (jə·rpiš) *s.* MED. herpe.
herpetic (jəʳpe·tik) *adj.* herpético.
herpetology (jəʳpita·lədẏi) *s.* herpetología.
herring (je·ring) *s.* ICT. arenque.
herringbone (-bou·n) *s.* espinapez. *2* espiga, punto espigado.
hers (jəʳš) *pron. pos. f. de 3.ª pers.* [indicando una sola poseedora] suyo, suya, suyos, suyas; el suyo, la suya, los suyos, las suyas; el, la, lo, las, de ella. *2 a friend of* ~, un amigo suyo [de ella].
herself (jəʳse·lf) *pron. pers. f. de 3.ª pers. sing.* ella, ella misma, se, sí, si misma.
Hertzian (jə·ʳtsian) *adj.* FÍS. hertziano.
he's (jɪš) contracción de HE IS y de HE HAS.
Hesiod (jɪ·siəd) *n. pr. m.* Hesiodo.
hesitancy (je·šitansi) *s.* vacilación, duda.
hesitant (-tənt) *adj.* vacilante, indeciso, irresoluto, titubeante.
hesitate (to) (-eit) *intr.* vacilar, dudar, titubear. *2* tartamudear, balbucear.
hesitation (-ei·shən) *s.* vacilación, duda, titubeo. *2* tartamudeo, balbucencia.
Hesper (je·spəʳ) *s.* véspero, estrella vespertina.
Hesperides (jespe·ridis) *s. pl.* MIT. Hespérides. *2* MIT. jardín de las Hespérides.
hesperidium (jespəri·diəm) *s.* BOT. hesperidio.
hessian (je·shan) *s.* arpillera.
Hester (je·stəʳ) *n. pr. f.* Ester.
heterocercal (je·tørøseʳkal) *adj.* ICT. heterocerca.
heteroclite (-clait) *adj.* heteróclito.
heterodox (-daks) *adj.-s.* heterodoxo.
heterodoxy (-daksi) *s.* heterodoxia.
heterodyne (-dain) *adj.* RADIO. heterodino. *2 s.* RADIO. heterodino [oscilador].
heterogeneity (-dẏna·iti) *s.* heterogeneidad.
heterogeneous (-dẏi·niøs) *adj.* heterogéneo.
heteronomous (jetøra·nomøs) *adj.* heterónomo.
heteroscians (-shans) *adj.-s. pl.* GEOGR. heteroscios.
hew (to) (jiu) *tr.* tajar, cortar, picar, hachear, desbastar; labrar [madera, piedra]. *2* formar, hacer [a golpes de un instrumento cortante]; abrir, esculpir. *3 intr.* dar golpes o hachazos. *4 to* ~ *close to the line,* fig. hilar delgado. ¶ Pret.: *hewed;* p. p.: *hewn.*
hewer (-øʳ) *s.* picapedrero. *2* desbastador.
hewn (-n) *p. p.* de TO HEW.
hexachord (je·ksakoʳd) *s.* MÚS. hexacordo.
hexagon (-gan) *s.* GEOM. hexágono.
hexagonal (jeksæ·gønal) *adj.* hexagonal.
hexahedron (jeksaji·drøn) *s.* GEOM. hexaedro.
hexameter (jeksæ·mitøʳ) *s.* hexámetro.
hexapod (je·ksapad) *adj.-s.* ZOOL. hexápodo.
hexastyle (-stail) *s.* ARQ. hexástilo.
hey (jei) *interj.* ¡eh!, ¡oiga!, ¡digo! *2* ¡ea!
heyday (jei·dei) *s.* apogeo, colmo [de vitalidad, fuerza, etc.]. *2 interj.* ¡hola!
Hezekiah (jesikai·a) *n. pr. m.* Ezequías.
hiatus (jaiei·təs) *s.* blanco, laguna, espacio, vacío, salto. *2* hiato.
hibernal (jaibø·ʳnal) *adj.* ibernal, hiemal.
hibernate (to) (jai·bøʳneit) *intr.* estar en hibernación.

hibernation (-ei·shøn) *s.* hibernación, hiemación.
Hibernian (jaibø·ʳnian) *s.* hibernés.
hibiscus (jaibi·skøs) *s.* BOT. hibisco.
hiccough (ji·kof), **hiccup** (ji·køp) *s.* hipo.
hiccough, hiccup (to) *intr.* hipar [tener hipo].
hickory (ji·køri) *s.* nogal americano.
hickup (ji·køp) *s.* HICCUP.
hid (jid) *pret.* y *p. p.* de TO HIDE.
hidden (-øn) *p. p.* de TO HIDE. *2 adj.* oculto, escondido, recóndito, secreto, latente.
hide (jaid) *s.* cuero, piel, pellejo [de animal]. *2* fig. pellejo [de persona].
hide (to) *tr.* esconder, ocultar, cubrir, tapar, disimular. *2* azotar. *3 intr.* esconderse, ocultarse: *to* ~ *out,* estarse escondido. ¶ Pret.: *hid;* p. p.: *hidden* o *hid.*
hide-and-seek *s.* juego del escondite.
hidebound (-baund) *adj.* de piel pegada a los huesos. *2* fanático, dogmático, de ideas mezquinas.
hideous (ji·diøs) *adj.* horrible, horrendo. *2* feo, horroroso. *3* odioso, repugnante.
hiding (jai·ding) *s.* ocultamiento, escondimiento. *2* retiro. *3* paliza, zurra. *4* ~ *place,* escondite, escondrijo.
hie (to) (jai) *intr.* apresurarse; correr, volar. *2* apresurar, aguijar: ~ *thee,* date prisa.
hierarch (jai·øraʳk) *s.* jerarca.
hierarchical (jaiøra·ʳkikal) *adj.* jerárquico.
hierarchy (jai·øraʳki) *s.* jerarquía.
hieratic(al (jaiøræ·tik(al) *adj.* hierático.
hieroglyph (jaiørøgli·f), **hieroglyphic** (-ik) *s.* jeroglífico, hieroglífico.
hieroglyphic(al (-fik(al) *adj.* jeroglífico, hieroglífico.
Hieronymite (jaiøra·nimait) *adj.-s.* jerónimo [religioso].
hierophant (jai·ørøfant) *s.* hierofanta, hierofante.
high (jai) *adj.* alto [que tiene altura]. *2* de alto: *a wall twelve feet* ~, una pared de doce pies de alto. *3* alto, elevado, encumbrado; noble, ilustre; grande; sublime; superior, principal, sumo: *High Chancellor,* Gran Canciller; ~ *command,* alto mando; ~ *priest,* sumo sacerdote. *4* altivo, altanero. *5* intenso, vivo, fuerte. *6* alborotada, gruesa [mar]. *7* alta [calidad, traición, comedia, frecuencia, presión, tensión]. *8* MÚS. alto, agudo. *9* B. ART. alto [relieve]. *10* subido [precio]; caro: ~ *cost of living,* carestía de la vida. *11* mayor [calle, altar, misa]. *12* remota [antigüedad]. *13* pleno [día, etc.]. *14* pasada, manida [carne]. *15* COC. fuerte, picante. *16* fam. achispado. *17* rico en. *18* Otros sentidos: ~ *and mighty,* fam. orgulloso, altanero; dominador; ~ *colour,* color encendido, rubicundez, rubor; ~ *gear,* AUTO. directa; *High German,* alto alemán; ~ *hand,* despotismo; altanería; ~ *hat,* sombrero de copa, chistera; ~ *life,* alta sociedad, gran mundo; ~ *school,* escuela de segunda enseñanza; ~ *seas,* alta mar, piélago; ~ *spirits,* alegría, buen humor, animación; ~ *tide,* marea alta, pleamar; apogeo; ~ *words,* palabras fuertes, ofensivas; *the Most High,* el Altísimo; *in* ~ *terms,* en términos lisonjeros; *it is* ~ *time to,* ya es hora de o de que.
19 adv. arriba: ~ *and low,* arriba y abajo, por todas partes. *20* alto, a gran altura. *21* altamente. *22* profundamente. *23* en grande. *24* caro.
25 s. lo alto, las alturas, el cielo: *from on* ~, de lo alto. *26* [el] colmo. *27* [el] precio más alto. *28* AUTO. directa; marcha directa.

highborn (-boᵣn) *adj.* noble, linajudo.
highboy (-boi) *s.* especie de cómoda con patas altas.
high-brow *s.* (E.U.) intelectual, sabio; el que se da aires de superioridad intelectual.
high-coloured *adj.* subido de color.
high-duty *adj.* de alto rendimiento [máquina].
higher (-øᵣ) *adj. comp.* de HIGH; más alto; alto, superior: ~ *classes*, clases altas; ~ *mathematics*, matemáticas superiores.
highest (-est) *adj. superl.* de HIGH; el más alto; sumo, supremo, mayor, máximo: ~ *common divisor* o *factor*, ARIT. máximo común divisor.
highfalutin (jaifælu·tin) *adj.* fam. hinchado, ampuloso, retumbante.
high-fidelity *adj.* RADIO. de alta fidelidad.
high-flown (jai·floun) *adj.* de alto vuelo. 2 orgulloso, presuntuoso. 3 hinchado, campanudo.
high-grade *adj.* fino, de calidad superior.
high-handed *adj.* despótico, arbitrario.
high-hearted *adj.* noble, valeroso.
highjack (to) *tr.* TO HIJACK.
high-keyed *adj.* impresionable, sensible. 2 MÚS. agudo.
highland (-land) *s.* montaña, región montañosa. 2 pl. *the Highlands*, región montañosa de Escocia. 3 *adj.* de las tierras altas.
highlander (-øᵣ) *s.* montañés [esp. de Escocia].
highly (-li) *adv.* altamente, sumamente, en sumo grado. 2 elevadamente. 3 a un alto precio. 4 bien, favorablemente.
high-minded *adj.* magnánimo, de nobles o elevados sentimientos; orgulloso, altivo.
highness (-nis) *s.* altura, alteza, elevación, celsitud. 2 alteza [tratamiento].
high-pitched *adj.* MÚS. agudo. 2 chillona [voz]. 3 de mucha pendiente. 4 HIGHSTRUNG 2.
high-priced *adj.* caro, de subido precio.
highroad (-roud) *s.* carretera, camino real.
high-seasoned *adj.* picante, fuerte de especias.
high-sounding *adj.* pomposo, altisonante.
high-spirited *adj.* gallardo, animoso, valiente. 2 fogoso [caballo]. 3 orgulloso.
high-strung *adj.* tenso, vigoroso. 2 en estado de aguda sensibilidad, excitable, nervioso.
high-test *adj.* ~ *fuel*, supercarburante.
high-toned (jai·tound) *adj.* MÚS. agudo. 2 digno, caballeroso. 3 fam. (E. U.) elegante, distinguido.
highty-tighty *adj.* HOITY-TOITY.
high-water mark *s.* nivel más alto a que llega la marea. 2 fig. colmo, apogeo.
highway (-uei) *s.* camino real, carretera.
highwayman (-mæn) *s.* bandolero, salteador [de caminos].
high-wrought *adj.* primorosamente labrado o trabajado. 2 muy excitado.
hijack (to) (jai·dÿæk) *tr.* fam. (E.U.) robar [a un contrabandista de licores].
hike (jaik) *s.* fam. marcha, caminata, viaje a pie.
hike (to) *intr.* fam. hacer una caminata.
hilarious (jaile·riøs) *adj.* alegre, bullicioso.
hilarity (jailæ·riti) *s.* hilaridad, regocijo, bullicioso.
Hilary (ji·lari) *n. pr. m.* Hilario.
hill (jil) *s.* colina, collado, cerro, altozano, cuesta. | A veces se usa por montaña. 2 montón, montículo.
hill (to) *tr.* amontonar. 2 AGR. aporcar. 3 *intr.* amontonarse.
hillock (-øk) *s.* montículo, altillo, altozano.
hillside (-said) *s.* ladera [de una colina].

hilly (-i) *adj.* montuoso. 2 pendiente [en cuesta].
hilt (jilt) *s.* puño, empuñadura [de un arma]: *up to the* ~, hasta el puño, completamente.
him (jim) *pron. pers. m. de 3.ᵃ pers. sing.* [ac. o dat.] lo, le. 2 [con prep. o como atributo] él: *to* ~, a él.
himself (jimse·lf) *pron. pers. m. de 3.ᵃ pers. sing.* él, él mismo, se, sí, sí mismo.
hind (jaind) *adj.* trasero, zaguero, posterior. 2 *s.* ZOOL. cierva. 3 mozo de labranza.
hinder (-øᵣ) *adj.* posterior, trasero.
hinder (to) (ji·ndøᵣ) *tr.* impedir, estorbar, dificultar. 2 *intr.* ser obstáculo, oponerse, obstar.
hindermost (jai·ndø·moust), **hindmost** (hai·ndmoust) *adj.* postrero, último.
Hindoo (ji·ndu) *s.* HINDU.
hindquarter (jai·ndkuøᵣtøᵣ) *s.* cuarto trasero [de res].
hindrance (ji·ndrans) *s.* estorbo, impedimento, embarazo, obstáculo. 2 traba, cortapisa.
Hindu (ji·ndu) *adj.-s.* hindú, indio.
Hinduism (-išm) *s.* hinduismo.
Hindustan (jindusta·n) *n. pr.* GEOGR. Indostán.
Hindustani (-ni) *adj.* indostánico. 2 *s.* indostani, hindustani [lenguaje].
hinge (jindÿ) *s.* gozne, bisagra, pernio, charnela. 2 fig. eje, principio rector, punto capital. 3 ENCUAD. cartivana.
hinge (to) *tr.* engoznar, poner goznes o bisagras a. 2 *intr. to* ~ *on*, girar sobre, depender de.
hinny (ji·ni) *s.* ZOOL. burdégano.
hint (jint) *s.* indicación, insinuación, sugestión, indirecta, alusión.
hint (to) *tr.-intr.* indicar, insinuar, sugerir, aludir vagamente.
hinterland (ji·ntøᵣland) *s.* hinterland.
hip (jip) *s.* ANAT. cadera. 2 ARQ. lima tesa. 3 BOT. *hip* o ~ *rose*, tapaculo, escaramujo. 4 *interj.* voz para llamar o aclamar. 5 *adv.* ~ *and thigh*, duramente, sin piedad.
hip (to) *tr.* descaderar, derrengar. 2 echar sobre la cadera. ¶ Pret. y p. p.: *hipped*; p. a.: *hipping*.
hipbone (ji·pboun) *s.* ANAT. cía, hueso de la cadera.
hipped (jipt) *adj.* renco. 2 melancólico, abatido. 3 obsesionado.
hippocampus (jipokæ·mpøs) *s.* MIT., ICT., ANAT. hipocampo.
hippocras (ji·pokras) *s.* hipocrás.
Hippocrates (jipa·kratiš) *n. pr. m.* Hipócrates.
hippodrome (ji·pødroum) *s.* hipódromo, circo.
hippogriff (ji·pøgrif) *s.* MIT. hipogrifo.
hippopotamus (jipøpa·tamøs) *s.* ZOOL. hipopótamo.
hipshot (ji·pshat) *adj.* renco.
hircine (jøᵣ·sin) *adj.* hircino.
hircocervus (jøᵣcosø·ᵣvøs) *s.* MIT. hircocervo.
hire (jaiᵣ) *s.* alquiler, arrendar. 2 contratar, asoldar, asalariar. 3 *intr.* alquilarse, ajustarse.
hireling (jai·ᵣling) *adj.-s.* asalariado. 2 alquilón, mercenario.
hirer (jai·røᵣ) *s.* alquilador, arrendador.
hirsute (jøᵣ·siut) *adj.* hirsuto, híspido.
his (jiš) *adj. y pron. pos. m. de 3.ᵃ pers.* [indicando un solo poseedor] suyo, suya, suyos, suyas, de él; el suyo, la suya, los suyos, las suyas; el, la, los, las de él. 2 *a friend of* ~, un amigo suyo [de él].
Hispanic (jispæ·nik) *adj.* hispánico, hispano.
Hispanist (ji·spænist) *s.* hispanista.
hispid (ji·spid) *adj.* híspido.

hiss (jis) *s.* siseo. 2 silbido, sonido sibilante, chirrido.

hiss (to) *intr.* silbar, sisear, chirriar. 2 *tr.* silbar, sisear [mostrar desaprobación].

hissing (-ing) *s.* siseo, silba, sonido sibilante.

hist (jist) *interj.* ¡atención!; ¡psit! 2 ¡chitón!

histologist (jista·lødȳist) *s.* histólogo.

histology (jista·lødȳi) *s.* histología.

historian (jisto·rian) *s.* historiador.

historic(al (-rik(al) *adj.* histórico.

historiographer (jistoria·grafø^r) *s.* historiógrafo.

historiography (-grafi) *s.* historiografía.

history (ji·stori) *s.* historia. | No tiene el sentido de chisme, cuento.

histrion (ji·strión) *s.* histrión.

histrionic (al (jistria·nik(al) *adj.* histriónico.

histrionism (ji·strionišm) *s.* histrionismo.

hit (jit) *s.* golpe, choque. 2 golpe de fortuna. 3 golpe certero, acierto, éxito: *to make a ~*, tener gran éxito. 4 agudeza, sarcasmo.

hit (to) *tr.* dar, pegar, golpear, chocar con. 2 dar [un golpe]. 3 afectar, herir [una cosa a uno]. 4 atinar, acertar: *to ~ the nail on the head*, dar en el clavo; *~ or miss*, salga lo que saliere. 5 encontrar, dar con. 6 convenir, adaptarse a. 7 *to ~ it off*, avenirse, congeniar. 8 *to ~ off*, imitar, describir o expresar con acierto. 9 *to ~ the spot*, llenar, satisfacer. 10 *to ~ the trail*, ponerse en camino. 11 *intr.* tocar, chocar. 12 *to ~ on o upon*, dar con; acordarse de; ocurrírsele a uno. ¶ Pret. y p. p.: *hit;* ger.: *hitting.*

hitch (ji·ch) *s.* tirón, sacudida. 2 cojera. 3 obstáculo, impedimento, tropiezo, dificultad. 4 alto, parada. 5 MAR. nombre de varios nudos.

hitch (to) *tr.* mover [a tirones o poquito a poco]. 2 enganchar, unir, atar, sujetar, amarrar. 3 *intr.* moverse [a sacudidas, a saltos]. 4 enredarse, engancharse. 5 avenirse, congeniar.

hitchhike (to) (-jaik) *intr.* hacer autostop.

hitchhiking (-ing) *s.* autostop.

hither (-ji·ðø^r) *adv.* acá, hacia acá: *~ and thither*, acá y acullá. 2 *adj.* citerior, de este lado.

hithermost (-moust) *adj.* más cercano.

hitherto (-tu·) *adv.* hasta aquí, hasta ahora.

Hitlerism (ji·tlørišm) *s.* hitlerismo.

hit-run *adj.* que atropella y se da a la fuga.

Hittite (ji·tait) *adj.-s.* HIST. heteo, hitita.

hive (jaiv) *s.* colmena. 2 enjambre.

hive (to) *tr.* API. enjambrar. 2 *intr.* vivir como en colmena.

hives (-øs) *s.* MED. urticaria.

ho, hoa (jo) *interj.* ¡eh!, ¡ah!; ¡oiga!; ¡alto!

hoar (jo^r) *adj.* blanco, cano, canoso, gris. 2 *s.* blancura, canicie. 4 HOARFROST.

hoard (jø^{r}d) *s.* depósito, acumulamiento, tesoro, repuesto; dinero guardado.

hoard (to) *tr.* acumular, guardar, atesorar.

hoarder (-ø^r) *s.* atesorador.

hoarding (-ing) *s.* amontonamiento, atesoramiento. 2 cerca de construcción. 3 cartelera.

hoarfrost (jo·^{r}frost) *s.* escarcha, helada blanca.

hoarhound (-jaund) *s.* BOT. marrubio.

hoariness (-inis) *s.* blancura, canicie.

hoarse (jo^{r}s) *adj.* ronco, rauco, áspero, bronco.

hoarseness (-nis) *s.* ronquera, bronquedad.

hoary (jo·ri) *adj.* cano, canoso. 2 blanco. 3 venerable, vetusto.

hoax (jouks) *s.* broma, engaño; bulo, pajarota.

hoax (to) *tr.* embromar, engañar.

hob (jab) *s.* repisa, interior del hogar. 2 cubo [de

rueda]. 3 chito, tángano. 4 fam. to play ~ with, trastornar.

hobble (ja·bøl) *s.* cojera. 2 traba, manea, maniota. 3 fam. dificultad, atolladero.

hobble (to) *intr.* cojear. 2 bailar [un pendiente, etc.]. 3 *tr.* manear. 9 hacer cojear.

hobby (ja·bi) *s.* afición [trabajo, estudio, etc., hecho por afición o pasatiempo].

hobbyhorse (-jo^{r}s) *s.* caballito, caballo mecedor [juguete]. 2 fig. manía, tema.

hobgoblin (ja·bgablin) *s.* duende, trasgo.

hobnail (-neil) *s.* clavo de cabeza gruesa para zapatos. 2 rústico, patán.

hobnail (to) *tr.* clavetear [zapatos].

hobnob (to) (-nab) *intr.* beber juntos. 2 codearse, rozarse. ¶ Pret. y p. p.: *hobnobbed;* ger.: *-bbing.*

hobo (jou·bou) *s.* fam. (E. U.) vagabundo.

hock (jak) *s.* corvejón, jarrete. 2 COC. garrón [de cerdo]. 3 vino del Rin.

hock (to) *tr.* desjarretar.

hockey (ja·ki) *s.* hockey [juego de pelota].

hocus (to) (jou·køs) *tr.* burlar, engañar. 2 narcotizar, atontar, con drogas. ¶ Pret. y p. p.: *hocused* o *-ssed;* ger.: *housing* o *-ssing.*

hocus-pocus (-pou·cøs) *s.* fórmula de prestidigitador. 2 pasapasa. 4 treta, engaño.

hod (jad) *s.* ALBAÑ. cuezo. 2 cubo para carbón.

hodgepodge (ja·dȳpadȳ) *s.* almodrote, baturrillo, mezcolanza.

hodman (ja·dmæn) *s.* peón de albañil; bracero.

hoe (jou) *s.* azada, azadón, almocafre, escardillo.

hoe (to) *tr.* cavar, azadonar, sachar.

hog (jog) *s.* cerdo, cochino [animal, persona sucia]. 2 egoísta. 3 glotón. 4 pop. *to go the whole ~*, llegar hasta el último límite. 5 *~ Latin*, latín de cocina.

hog (to) *tr.* recortar [la crin de un caballo]. 2 arquear, combar. 3 *intr.* arquearse, combarse. ¶ Pret. y p. p.: *hogged;* ger.: *hogging.*

hogback (-bæk) *s.* cuchilla, cerro escarpado.

hoggish (-ish) *adj.* puerco. 2 glotón. 3 egoísta.

hogherd (-jø^{r}d) *s.* porquero, porquerizo.

hogshead (-šjed) *s.* pipa, bocoy.

hog's-fennel *s.* BOT. servato.

hogskin (-skin) *s.* piel de cerdo.

hogsty (-stai) *s.* pocilga.

hogwash (-uøsh) *s.* bazofia.

hoiden (joi·døn) *s.* HOYDEN.

hoist (joist) *s.* cabria, grúa, montacargas. 2 lo que se iza o eleva. 3 elevación; enarbolamiento; empujón hacia arriba.

hoist (to) *tr.* izar, subir, elevar. 2 enarbolar.

hoity-toity (joiti-toi·ti) *adj.* frívolo, veleidoso. 2 engreído. 3 *s.* frivolidad, veleidad. 4 engreimiento. 5 *interj.* ¡hombre!, ¡tate!

hokey-pokey (jou·ki-pou·ki) *s.* HOCUS-POCUS.

hold (jould) *s.* presa, agarro, sostenimiento. 2 presa [en la lucha]. 3 asidero, agarradero, sostén. 4 poder, influencia, dominio. 5 custodia, prisión. 6 MAR. bodega, cala. 7 AVIA. cabina de carga. 8 MÚS. calderón. 9 fortaleza, refugio. 10 guarida. 11 receptáculo. 12 *to get, lay* o *take ~ of*, agarrar, agarrarse a; apoderarse de.

hold (to) *tr.* tener, poseer. 2 ocupar [un cargo, etc.]. 3 sujetar, asir, tener asido. 4 aguantar, apoyar, sostener. 5 defender [una posición, etc.]. 6 retener, mantener, tener [en un lugar, situación o estado]. 7 contener, detener, refrenar. 8 tener [en estima, etc.]. 9 juzgar, considerar, tener por. 10 absorber, ocupar [la atención, etc.]. 11 contener; coger, tener cabida para. 12 celebrar

[una reunión]; sostener [una conversación]. *13* guardar, observar. *14* hacer [compañía]. *15* usar [cierto lenguaje]. *16 to* ~ *back,* contener, detener, refrenar. *17 to* ~ *down,* tener sujeto, oprimir; mantenerse en [un cargo]. *18 to* ~ *forth,* presentar; expresar. *19 to* ~ *in,* refrenar. *20 to* ~ *off,* mantener alejado. *21 to* ~ *one's own,* mantenerse firme, resistir. *22 to* ~ *one's peace,* callar. *23 to* ~ *on,* ofrecer, tender; presentar, proponer. *24 to* ~ *over,* aplazar, diferir. *25 to* ~ *up,* levantar, alzar; sostener; mostrar; refrenar; atracar, saltear, detener para robar. *26 to* ~ *up to,* exponer [al desprecio, etc.]. *27 intr.* agarrarse, asirse. *28* pegarse, adherirse. *29* valer, ser válido, estar o seguir en vigor. *30* mantenerse, sostenerse. *31* mantenerse firme o fiel. *32* durar, continuar. *33 to* ~ *back,* detenerse, contenerse; abstenerse; recular. *34 to* ~ *forth,* predicar, perorar. *35 to* ~ *good,* subsistir. *36 to* ~ *in,* contenerse. *37 to* ~ *off,* esperar; mantenerse a distancia; mostrarse frío. *38 to* ~ *on,* agarrarse; aguantar; seguir, continuar; detenerse. *39 to* ~ *out,* mantenerse firme; durar, continuar, resistir. *40 to* ~ *up,* cesar de llover; continuar, durar; no recular.
¶ Pret. y p. p.: *held.*

holdback (-bæk) *s.* restricción, freno. *2* cejadero.
holder (-ǿ^r) *s.* sostenedor, sostén, sustentáculo, agarrador, mango, asa. *2* receptáculo. *3* FOT. chasis. *4* tenedor, poseedor, propietario. *5* arrendatario [de tierras]. *6* COM. tenedor. *7* titular [de un cargo, un pasaporte, etc.].
holdfast (-fast) *s.* grapón, grapa, laña; barrilete. *2* agarradero, sostén. *3* hombre muy avaro.
holding (-ing) *s.* tenencia, pertenencia, posesión. *2* arriendo. *3* tierra arrendada. *4* celebración [de una sesión, reunión, etc.]. *5* opinión, creencia. *6 pl.* COM. valores, títulos. *7 adj.* COM. ~ *company,* compañía tenedora de acciones de otras compañías.
holdup (-ǿp) *s.* fam. atraco, salteamiento.
hole (joul) *s.* agujero, orificio, abertura, boquete. *2* hoyo, hueco, cavidad. *3* ojo [del pan o el queso]. *4* olla, remanso [en un río]. *5* bache. *6* cueva, madriguera. *7* rincón [lugar apartado]. *8* tabuco, cochitril. *9* calabozo. *10* defecto, falla, tacha. *11* aprieto, atolladero. *12* GOLF. hoyo.
hole (to) *tr.* agujerear, horadar. *2* BILLAR entronerar. *3* GOLF meter [la pelota] en el hoyo. *4 intr.* encovarse: *to* ~ *up,* encovarse; buscar un escondrijo o un rincón cómodo.
holiday (ja·lidei) *s.* fiesta, festividad, día festivo. *2* vacación, asueto. *3 pl.* vacaciones. *4 adj.* de fiesta, festivo.
holiness (jou·linis) *s.* santidad, beatitud. *2 His Holiness,* Su Santidad.
Holland (ja·land) *n. pr.* GEOGR. Holanda. *2 s.* holanda [lienzo].
Hollander (-ǿ^r) *s.* holandés.
Hollands (-s) *s.* ginebra holandesa.
hollo, holloa (jǿlou·) *interj.* ¡eh!, ¡hola!; ¡vítor! *2 s.* grito, saludo; grito de triunfo.
hollo, holloa (to) *tr.* decir a gritos. *2 intr.* gritar.
hollow (ja·lou) *adj.* hueco, cóncavo, vacío. *2* hundido [ojos, mejillas]. *3* flaco, hambriento. *4* profundo, cavernoso [sonido, voz]. *5* falso, insincero. *6* vano, sin substancia. *7 s.* hueco. *8* depresión, hondonada, valle.
hollow (to) *tr.* ahuecar, ahondar, acopar, excavar, hundir.
hollow-hearted *adj.* insincero, solapado.

hollowness (-nis) *s.* cavidad, hueco, vacío. *2* doblez, falsía.
holly (ja·li) *s.* BOT. acebo, agrifolio.
hollyhock (-jak) *s.* BOT. malvarrosa, malvaloca.
holm (jou·lm) *s.* mejana, isleta. *2* vega ribereña. *3* BOT. holm o ~ *oak,* encina.
holocaust (ja·lǿkost) *s.* holocausto.
holograph (ja·lǿgræf) *s.* hológrafo, ológrafo.
holographic (jalǿgræ·fik) *adj.* hológrafo, ológrafo.
holohedron (-ji·drǿn) *s.* CRIST. holoedro.
holothurian (-ziu·rian) *s.* ZOOL. holoturia.
holster (jou·lstǿ^r) *s.* pistolera.
holy (jou·li) *adj.* santo: ~ *Cross,* Santa Cruz; *Holy Father,* Santo Padre; ~ *Office,* Santo Oficio; ~ *of holies,* santo de los santos; *Holy See,* Santa Sede; *Holy Week,* semana santa. *2* sacro, sagrado, bendito: *Holy Communion,* sagrada comunión; ~ *water,* agua bendita; *Holy Writ,* Sagradas Escrituras. *3* divino: ~ *lamb,* divino cordero. *4* dedicado a Dios: ~ *day* o *holiday,* día de fiesta; fiesta [de la Iglesia].
homage (ja·midў) *s.* homenaje [feudal]. *2* homenaje, deferencia, respeto.
homard (oma·^r) *s.* ZOOL. bogavante.
home (joum) *s.* hogar, lares, casa, morada, domicilio. *2* asilo, albergue, hospicio. *3* país natal, patria, patria chica. *4* [para los coloniales] Inglaterra. *5* BIOL. habitación. *6* DEP. meta, límite, término. *7 at* ~, en casa; en su país; a gusto, con comodidad: *make yourself at* ~, haga como si estuviera en su casa; póngase cómodo. *8 adj.* doméstico, hogareño, casero. *9* nativo, natal. *10* nacional, del país; del interior: ~ *products,* productos nacionales; *Home office,* (Ingl.) ministerio de la Gobernación. *11* regional: ~ *rule,* autonomía. *12* de regreso [que regresa o acaba de regresar]. *13* eficaz, que da en el clavo. *14 adv.* en, o a casa; en, o al país de uno. *15 to bring,* o *drive* ~, hacer que convenza; *to hit,* o *strike* ~, herir en lo vivo; llegar al alma; dar en el blanco.
home (to) *tr.* mandar a casa. *2* dar morada o domicilio a. *3 intr.* habitar. *4* volver a casa.
homebred (-bred) *adj.* nativo, doméstico, casero; criado en casa. *2* sencillo, inculto, tosco.
homefelt (-felt) *adj.* íntimo, cordial.
homekeeping (-kiping) *adj.* de gustos caseros.
homeless (-lis) *adj.* sin casa ni hogar. *2* inhabitable, inhóspito.
homelike (-laik) *adj.* como de casa; cómodo, acogedor; familiar. *2* sosegado.
homeliness (-linis) *s.* sencillez, simplicidad. *2* falta de elegancia o refinamiento. *3* fealdad.
homely (-li) *adj.* llano, sencillo, casero. *2* feo, vulgar, ordinario. *3* rústico, inculto.
homemade (-meid) *adj.* casero, hecho en casa. *2* fabricado en el país.
homeopath (jou·miopaz), **homeopathist** (-pæ·zist) *s.* homeópata.
homeopathy (joumio·pæzi) *s.* homeopatía.
Homer (jou·mǿ^r) *n. pr. m.* Homero.
homer *s.* fam. paloma mensajera.
Homeric (joume·rik) *adj.* homérico.
homesick (jou·msik) *adj.* nostálgico.
homesickness (-nis) *s.* nostalgia, añoranza.
homespun (-spǿn) *adj.* hilado o hecho en casa. *2* basto, sin elegancia.
homestead (-sted) *s.* casa y tierras adyacentes, heredad. *2* fig. casa, hogar.
homesteader (-stedǿ^r) *s.* dueño de una heredad que habita en ella y la cultiva. *2* (E. U.) colono que ha recibido sus tierras del Gobierno.

homeward (-uaᵗd) *adv.* hacia casa, hacia su país. *2 adj.* de regreso, de vuelta.
homewards (-s) *adv.* HOMEWARD.
homicidal (jamisai·dal) *adj.* homicida.
homicide (ja·misaid) *s.* homicidio. *2* homicida.
homiletics (jamile·tiks) *s.* homilética.
homily (ja·mili) *s.* homilia, sermón.
homing (jou·ming) *adj.* mensajera [paloma].
hominy (ja·mini) *s.* maíz molido o machacado.
homo- (joumo-) *pref.* homo-.
homocerc (al (-sø·ᵗk(al) *adj.* ICT. homocerco.
homogeneity (-dÿi·niiti) *s.* homogeneidad.
homogeneous (-dÿi·niøs) *adj.* homogéneo.
homogenize (to) (-dÿinaiš) *tr.* hacer homogéneo, homogeneizar.
homologate (to) (-logeit) *tr.* homologar.
homologation (-ei·shøn) *s.* homologación.
homologous (jouma·løgøs) *adj.* homólogo.
homolog(ue (ja·møl̥og) *s.* cosa homóloga de otra.
homonym (-nim) *s.* homónimo.
homonymous (jouma·nimøs) *adj.* homónimo.
homophonous (-fønøs) *adj.* homófono.
homophony (-føni) *s.* homofonía.
homopterous (-ptørøs) *adj.* homóptero.
homosexual (joumøse·kshual) *adj.-s.* homosexual.
homunculus (joumø·nkiuløs) *s.* homúnculo.
hone (joun) *s.* piedra de afilar.
hone (to) *tr.* afilar, vaciar, asentar [navajas, etcétera].
honest (a·nist) *adj.* honrado, probo, íntegro. *2* justo, recto. *3* leal, sincero. *4* honesta [mujer]. *5* bien adquirido [dinero].
honesty (-i) *s.* honradez, probidad, rectitud. *2* sinceridad, lealtad. *4* honestidad.
honey (jø·ni) *s.* miel [de abejas]. *2* dulzura, melosidad. *3* fam. cariño, vida mía.
honey (to) *tr.* enmelar. *2* adular, halagar. *3* intr. hablar con melosidad.
honeybee (jø·nibi) *s.* ENT. abeja melífera.
honeycomb (jø·nicoum) *s.* panal de miel. *2* cosa parecida a un panal. *3 adj.* apanalado, de panal, de nido de abeja.
honeycomb (to) *tr.* llenar de hoyos o agujeros.
honeyed (jø·nid) *adj.* enmelado. *2* dulce, meloso, melifluo, adulador.
honeymoon (-mun) *s.* luna de miel.
honeymoon (to) *intr.* pasar la luna de miel.
honeysuckle (-søkøl) *s.* BOT. madreselva.
honeysweet (-suit) *adj.* dulce como la miel.
honk (jonk) *s.* graznido del ganso. *2* bocinazo.
honk (to) *tr.* tocar [la bocina]. *2* intr. graznar [el ganso]. *3* dar bocinazos.
honor, honorability, honorable, etc. HONOUR, HONOURABILITY, HONOURABLE, etc.
honorarium (anøre·riøm) *s.* honorarios.
honorary (a·nørəri) *adj.* honorario, honorífico. *2* de honor.
Honorius (ano·riøs) *n. pr. m.* Honorio.
honour (a·nøᵗ) *s.* honor, honra: *court of* ~, tribunal de honor; *point of* ~, punto de honra; *to do* ~ *to,* hacer honor a, honrar; *on my* ~, por mi honor; ~ *bright,* fam. de veras, a fe de caballero. *2* honradez. *3* prez. *4* lauro, condecoración. *5* *your Honour,* usía, su señoría. *6* pl. honores: *to do the honours of,* hacer los honores de. *7* honras: *funeral honours,* honras fúnebres. *8* nota sobresaliente [en los estudios].
honour (to) *tr.* honrar. *2* reverenciar, respetar. *3* enaltecer. *4* glorificar. *5* laurear, condecorar. *6* COM. hacer honor a [su firma]; aceptar, pagar.

honourable (a·nørabøl) *adj.* honorable. *2* honrado. *3* honroso, meritorio, estimable.
hood (jud) *s.* capucha, capucho, capilla, capirote, caperuza. *2* capirote [de ave]. *3* distintivo que se lleva sobre una toga académica para indicar el grado. *4* cosa que cubre: capota [de coche]; capó [de auto]; campana [de hogar]; sombrerete [de chimenea]. *5* MAR. tambucho.
hood (to) *tr.* encapuchar, encapirotar, cubrir con caperuza, capucho, etc. *2* tapar, ocultar.
hoodlum (-løm) *s.* (E.U.) fam. golfo, matón.
hoodoo (-u) *s.* VOODOO. *2* (E. U.) cenizo; lo que trae mala suerte.
hoodoo (to) *tr.* (E. U.) traer mala suerte a.
hoodwink (to) (-uink) *tr.* vendar los ojos a. *2* engañar, embaucar, burlar.
hoof (juf) *s.* ZOOL. casco, uña [de solípedo]; pesuña, pezuña; pata, pie [de animal ungulado]. *2* pesuño. *3* animal ungulado.
hoof (to) *tr.-intr.* andar, hollar. *2* *to* ~ *it,* andar, ir a pie; bailar.
hoofbeat (-bɪt) *s.* pisada, ruido de la pisada [de un animal ungulado].
hoofed (-t) *adj.* ungulado.
hook (juk) *s.* gancho, garfio, garabato: *to get the* ~, fam. ser despedido; *by* ~ *or by crook,* a tuertas o a derechas. *2* aldabilla. *3* escarpia, alcayata. *4* anzuelo; lazo, trampa. *5* pernio [de gozne]. *6* hoz, hocino. *7* recodo [de camino, etc.]. *8* rasgo [de letra]. *9* MÚS. rabo [de nota]. *10* corchete, gafete: ~ *and eye,* corchete [macho y hembra]. *11* BOXEO golpe de gancho.
hook (to) *tr.* encorvar, dar forma de gancho. *2* engarabatar. *3* enganchar [con gancho]; unir, conectar. *4* pescar, coger, atrapar. *5* cornear, herir con los cuernos. *6* encorchetar, abrochar. *7* birlar, hurtar. *8* fam. *to* ~ *it,* irse, huir. *9* BOXEO dar un golpe de gancho a.
hooked (-t) *adj.* encorvado, corvo, ganchudo. *2* enganchado.
hooknose (-nouš) *s.* nariz aguileña.
hookup (-øp) *s.* RADIO. montaje. *2* RADIO. esquema.
hooky (-i) *adj.* ganchudo. *2* que tiene ganchos. *3* *to play* ~, hacer novillos, fumarse la clase.
hooligan (ju·ligan) *s.* golfo, gamberro.
hoop (jup) *s.* aro, cerco, arco, ceño, fleje, virola: ~ *skirt,* miriñaque. *2* aro [juguete]. *3* anilla, anillo, sortija, argolla.
hoop (to) *tr.* encarcar [un tonel]. *2* zunchar. *3* cercar, ceñir. *4* intr. TO WHOOP.
hooping-cough *s.* WHOOPING-COUGH.
hoopoe (ju·pu) *s.* ORN. abubilla, upupa.
hoot (jut) *s.* grito; grita. *2* silbo [del mochuelo]. *3* pitido [de locomotora, etc.]; bocinazo.
hoot (to) *intr.-tr.* gritar, huchear, abuchear, dar grita. *2* intr. silbar [el mochuelo]. *3* dar pitidos o bocinazos.
hooter (-øᵗ) *s.* bocina, sirena, pito.
hop (jap) *s.* salto, brinco. *2* fam. baile [reunión]. *3* pop. vuelo [en avión]. *4* BOT. lúpulo, hombrecillo. *5* pl. lúpulo [frutos del lúpulo].
hop (to) *intr.* brincar, saltar; andar a saltitos o a la pata coja. *2* fam. bailar. *3* recoger el lúpulo. *4* AVIA. *to* ~ *off,* despegar, alzar el vuelo. *5* tr. cruzar o salvar saltando o volando. *6* aromatizar con lúpulo. ¶ Pret. y p. p.: *hopped;* ger. *-pping.*
hope (joup) *s.* esperanza, confianza.
hope (to) *tr.* esperar [tener esperanza de]. *2* intr. esperar [tener esperanza]; esperar, confiar en. *3* *to* ~ *for,* esperar, desear [una cosa].

hopeful (-ful) *adj.* esperanzado, lleno de esperanzas. *2* risueño, prometedor, que promete.
hopefulness (-nis) *s.* esperanza. *2* buenas perspectivas, aspecto prometedor.
hopeless (-lis) *adj.* desesperado, desesperanzado, sin eperanza. *2* incurable, irremediable; perdido, imposible, inútil.
hoper (-ø^r) *s.* el que espera o tiene esperanza.
hoplite (ja·plaĭt) *s.* hoplita.
hopper (ja·pø^r) *s.* saltador. *2* saltamontes. *3* tolva.
hopple (ja·pøl) *s.* traba, manea, maniota.
hopple (to) *tr.* trabar, manear.
hopscotch (ja·pska·ch) *s.* coxcojita, infernáculo.
Horace (jo·ris), *n. pr. m.* Horacio.
Horatian (jorei·shian) *adj.* horaciano.
horde (jo^{r}d) *s.* horda.
horehound (jo·^{r}jaund) *s.* BOT. marrubio.
horizon (jørai·šøn) *s.* horizonte.
horizontal (jariša·ntal) *adj.* horizontal.
horizontality (-tæ·liti) *s.* horizontalidad.
hormone (jo·^{r}moun) *s.* FISIOL. hormón, hormona.
horn (jo^{r}n) *s.* asta, cuerno [de animal]. *2* cuerno [de caracol, de insecto, de la luna, etc.]. *3* cuerno [materia, vaso]: ~ *of plenty*, cuerno de la abundancia, cornucopia. *4* callosidad, dureza. *5* ZOOL. excrecencia córnea. *6* bocina [de automóvil o fonógrafo]. *7* MÚS. cuerno, trompa, cuerno de caza.
horn (to) *tr.* poner cuernos. *2* acornear. *3 intr.* MÚS. tocar el cuerno.
hornbeam (-bɪm) *s.* BOT. carpe, ojaranzo.
hornbil (-bil) *s.* ORN. cálao.
hornblende (-blend) *s.* MINER. hornablenda.
horned (-d) *adj.* astado, cornudo, cornígero. *2* encornado. *3* en forma de cuerno.
hornet (-it) ENT. avispón: *hornet's nest*, panal el avispón; fig. avispero.
horning (-ing) *s.* cencerrada.
hornish (-ish) *adj.* córneo.
hornless (-lis) *adj.* sin cuernos.
hornpipe (-paip) *s.* baile inglés que ejecuta una sola persona. *2* MÚS. gaita, chirimía.
horn-rimmed *adj.* con montura de concha [gafas].
horny (-ni) *adj.* córneo. *2* de cuerno. *3* calloso.
horologe (ja·røloudỹ) *s.* reloj.
horologer (joura·lodỹø^r), **horologist** (-dỹist) *s.* relojero; el que se dedica a la horología.
horology (-lodỹi) *s.* horología.
horometry (-metri) *s.* medición del tiempo.
horopter (-ptø^r) *s.* ÓPT. horópter, horóptero.
horoscope (ja·røscoup) *s.* horóscopo.
horrendous (jare·ndøs) *adj.* horrendo, espantoso.
horrible (ja·ribøl) *adj.* horrible, horrendo, terrible.
horrid (ja·rid) *adj.* hórrido. *2* muy desagradable.
horrific (ja·rific) *adj.* horrífico.
horrify (to) (-fai) *tr.* horrorizar. ¶ Pret. y p. p.: *horrified.*
horripilation (jaripilei·shøn) *s.* MED. horripilación.
horripilate (to) (jari·pileit) *tr.* horripilar. *2 intr.* horripilarse.
horrisonant (jari·sonant) *adj.* horrísono.
horror (ja·rø^r) *s.* horror. *2* pl. *the horrors*, melancolía, murria; estremecimiento de horror.
horrorous (-øs) *adj.* horroroso.
horse (jo^{r}s) *s.* ZOOL. caballo: *to get on the high* ~, fig. darse tono, tomar una actitud orgullosa; *hold your horses*, fig. pare usted el carro, modérese; *to horse!*, ¡a caballo! *2* bridón, corcel. *3* MIL. caballería, caballos. *4* caballete, asnilla, borriquete. *5* potro [para gimnasia]. *6* fam. manía, chifladura. *7 adj.* de caballo o caballos; para ca-

ballos; montado; hípico: ~ *artillery*, artillería montada; ~ *block*, apeadero, montadero; ~ *doctor*, fam. albéitar; ~ *nail*, clavo de herradura; ~ *pistol*, pistola de arzón; ~ *race*, carrera de caballos; ~ *sense*, sentido práctico, sentido común. *8* grande; ordinario. *9* BOT. ~ *chestnut*, castaño de Indias; su fruto.
horse (to) *tr.* montar [proveer de caballo; poner a caballo]. *2* cargar con, llevar a cuestas. *3* azotar. *4 intr.* montar, cabalgar, andar a caballo.
horseback (-bæk) *s.* lomo de caballo: *on* ~, a caballo, montado. *2 adv.* a caballo.
horsebreaker (-brei·kø^r) *s.* picador, domador de caballos.
horseflesh (-flesh) *s.* carne de caballo. *2* caballos [colectivamente]. *3* variedad de caoba de las Bahamas.
horsefly (-flai) *s.* ENT. tábano. *2* ENT. mosca de burro.
horsehair (-jeø^r) *s.* crin de caballo. *2* tela de crin.
horsekeeper (-kɪpø^r) *s.* establero, mozo de cuadra.
horselaugh (-læf) *s.* risotada, risa grosera.
horseless (-lis) *adj.* sin caballo.
horseman (-mæn) *s.* jinete, caballista. *2* el que guía un caballo.
horsemanship (-ship) *s.* manejo, equitación.
horsemint (-mint) *s.* BOT. hierbabuena rizada.
horseplay (-plei) *s.* payasada, chanza pesada.
horsepower (-pauø^r) *s.* caballo de fuerza o de vapor.
horseradish (-rædish) *s.* BOT. rábano picante.
horseshoe (-shu) *s.* herradura; cosa en forma de herradura: ~ *arch*, ARQ. arco de herradura. *2* ZOOL. cangrejo de las Molucas.
horsetail (-teil) *s.* cola de caballo. *2* BOT. cola de caballo, equiseto.
horseway (-uei) *s.* camino de herradura.
horsewhip (-juip) *s.* látigo.
horsewhip (to) *tr.* azotar, dar latigazos. ¶ Pret. y p. p.: *whipped*; ger.: *-pping.*
horsewoman (-wumæn) *s.* amazona [mujer que monta a caballo].
horsey (jo·^{r}si) *adj.* HORSY.
horsy (-si) *adj.* caballar, caballuno. *2* hípico. *3* aficionado a los caballos.
hortation (jo^{r}tei·shøn) *s.* exhortación.
hortative (jo·^{r}tativ), **hortatory** (jo·^{r}tatori) *adj.* exhortatorio.
hortensial (jo^{r}te·nshal) *adj.* hortense.
horticultural (jo^{r}tɪ·kø·lchural) *adj.* hortícola.
horticulture (jo^{r}tɪkø·lchø·) *s.* horticultura.
horticulturist (jo^{r}tɪkø·lchurist) *s.* horticultor.
hosanna (jošæ·na) *s.-interj.* hosanna.
1) hose (jouš), *pl.* **hose** *s.* calza, media. *2 pl.* calzas, medias calzas,
2) hose, *pl.* **hose** o **hoses** *s.* manga, manguera [de bomba o riego].
Hosea (joši·æ) *n. pr.* Oseas.
hosier (jou·ỹo^r) *s.* mediero, calcetero.
hosiery (-ri) *s.* calcetería, géneros de punto.
hospice (ja·spis) *s.* hospicio; hospedería.
hospitable (ja·spitabøl) *adj.* hospitalario, acogedor.
hospital (ja·spital) *s.* hospital. *2* clínica. *3* asilo [institución].
hospitality (-tæ·liti) *s.* hospitalidad.
hospitalize (to) (jaspi·talaiš) *tr.* hospitalizar.
hospital(l)er (-ø^r) *s.* hospitalero. *2* caballero de una orden hospitalaria. *3* hospiciano.
host (joust) *s.* hospedero, posadero, mesonero, pa-

trón. *2* huésped [que hospeda]; anfitrión. *3* BIOL. huésped. *4* hueste. *5* multitud. *6* hostia.
hostage (ja·stidy̆) *s.* rehén.
hostel (ja·støl) *s.* hostería. *2* residencia para estudiantes.
hostelry (-ri) *s.* posada, hostelería, mesón, parador.
hostess (jou·stis) *s.* posadera, mesonera. *2* huéspeda, señora de la casa. *3* avia. azafata.
hostile (ja·stil) *adj.* hostil.
hostility (jasti·liti) *s.* hostilidad. *2 pl.* hostilidades [actos de guerra].
hostilize (to) (ja·stilaiš) *tr.* hostilizar.
hostler (ja·slø^r) *s.* establero, palafrenero.
hot (jat) *adj.* caliente: ~ *baths,* termas, baños termales; ~ *dog,* salchicha caliente; bocadillo de salchicha caliente; ~ *pad,* almohadilla eléctrica; ~ *springs,* fuentes de aguas termales; ~ *wave,* ola de calor; *it is* ~ *today,* hace calor; *to get* o *grow* ~, calentarse; empezar a hacer calor. *2* cálido, caluroso, tórrido. *3* acalorado, ardoroso. *4* acre, picante, ardiente: ~ *pepper,* pimiento picante. *5* ardiente, fogoso, vehemente, fervoroso. *6* violento, furioso, enérgico, activo: ~ *chase,* ~ *pursuit,* activa persecución. *7* vivo [genio]. *8* ávido, ansioso. *9* fam. incómodo, peligroso: *to make it* ~ *for someone,* perseguir, poner en peligro a uno. *10* empeñado [disputa, etc.]. *11* fresco, reciente [noticia, rastro]. *12* en celo [animal].
  13 adv. HOTLY.
hotbed (-bed) *s.* AGR. almajara cubierta, estufa. *2* fig. foco, plantel.
hot-blooded *adj.* fogoso, irascible, de genio vivo. *2* de pura raza [animal].
hotbox (-baks) *s.* MEC. cojinete recalentado.
hot-brained (-breind) *adj.* impetuoso, exaltado.
hotch-potch (ja·ch-pa·ch) *s.* HODGEPODGE.
hotel (joute·l) *s.* hotel.
hotelkeeper (-kıpø^r) *s.* hotelero.
hotfoot (ja·tfut) *adv.* fam. a toda prisa.
hothead (-jed) *s.* persona impetuosa, exaltada. *2* agitador, alborotador.
hotheaded (-jedid) *adj.* impetuoso, exaltado.
hothouse (-jaus) *s.* invernáculo, estufa [para plantas].
hotly (-li) *adv.* calurosamente. *2* ardientemente, vehementemente.
hotspur (-spø^r) *adj.-s.* temerario, impetuoso.
hottentot (ja·tøntat) *adj.-s.* hotentote.
hough (jak) *s.* corvejón [de cuadrúpedo].
hough (to) *tr.* desjarretar.
hound (jaund) *s.* lebrel, galgo, sabueso, podenco, perro de caza o de busca. *2* fig. canalla, villano. *3 pl.* MAR. cacholas.
hound (to) *tr.* cazar con perros. *2* azuzar. *3* acosar, perseguir, seguir la pista.
hound's-tongue *s.* BOT. cinoglosa, viniebla.
houppelande (ju·plænd) *s.* hopalanda.
hour (au^r) *s.* hora: ~ *circle,* ASTR. círculo horario; ~ *hand,* horario [saetilla]; *small hours,* primeras horas de madrugada; *to keep late hours,* recogerse a deshora, trasnochar; *by the* ~, por horas; *hours on end,* horas enteras; *in evil* ~, en mala hora; *in good* ~, en buena hora. *2* momento, trance. *3 pl.* ECLES. horas [rezo].
hourglass (-glæs) *s.* reloj de arena.
houri (ju·ri) *s.* hurí.
hourly (au·^rli) *adj.* de la hora; de cada hora, continuo. *2 adv.* a cada hora; continuamente.
house (jaus) *s.* casa [habitación; hogar; edificio;

familia, linaje]; ~ *of God,* casa de Dios, iglesia; *to clean* ~, hacer limpieza; *to put* o *set one's* ~ *in order,* fig. arreglar uno sus asuntos. *2* lugar donde se aloja, o guarda, una cosa. *3* cámara legislativa o deliberante: *House of Commons,* Cámara de los Comunes. *4* TEAT. sala, público, entrada: *good* ~, buena entrada; *to bring down the* ~, fig. provocar una tempestad de aplausos. *5* escaque, casilla [de ajedrez]. *6* ~ *of cards,* castillo de naipes.
  7 adj. de casa o casas; casero, doméstico: ~ *agent,* corredor o administrador de fincas; ~ *dove,* paloma doméstica; ~ *painter,* pintor de brocha gorda; ~ *rent,* alquiler de la casa.
house (to) *tr.* albergar, alojar. *2* dar casa o habitación a. *3* entrojar, almacenar o guardar. *4* encajar, empotrar. *5 intr.* alojarse, residir.
houseboat (-bout) *s.* barco vivienda, casa flotante.
housebreaker (-breikø^r) *s.* ladrón que roba con escalo.
housebreaking (-breiking) *s.* robo con escalo.
housefather (-fadø^r) *s.* cabeza de familia.
housefly (-flai) *s.* ENT. mosca común.
household (-hould) *s.* casa, familia [los que viven juntos]. *2 The Household,* la Real Casa. *3 adj.* doméstico, casero: ~ *bread,* pan casero; ~ *furniture,* menaje de casa.
householder (-ø^r) *s.* amo de casa; padre de familia.
housekeeper (-kıpø^r) *s.* guardián de una casa. *2* ama de casa. *3* ama de llaves o de gobierno.
housekeeping (-ing) *s.* gobierno de la casa; quehaceres domésticos. *2 adj.* doméstico, casero.
houseleek (-lik) *s.* BOT. siempreviva mayor.
housemaid (-meid) *s.* criada.
housemother (-modø^r) *s.* mujer encargada de una residencia de estudiantes.
housetop (-tap) *s.* techo, tejado, azotea; *to shout from the housetops,* pregonar a los cuatro vientos.
housewarming (uø^rming) *s.* fiesta para celebrar el estreno de una casa.
housewife (-uaif) *s.* madre de familia, ama de casa. *2* (-sif) agujetero, neceser de costura.
housewifery (-ori) *s.* gobierno de una casa, economía doméstica.
housework (-uø^rk) *s.* quehaceres domésticos.
housing (-ing) *s.* abrigo, albergue. *2* alojamiento, vivienda: ~ *problem,* problema de la vivienda. *3* almacenaje. *4* muesca, encaje. *5* MEC. chumacera. *6* MEC. caja, cárter. *7* ARQ. nicho. *8* mantilla, gualdrapa.
hove (jouv) *pret. y p. p.* de TO HEAVE.
hovel (jø·vøl) *s.* cobertizo. *2* cabaña, choza, tabuco.
hover (to) (jø·vø^r) *tr.* cubrir con las alas. *2 intr.* flotar, cernerse [en el aire], revolotear. *3* rondar, andar alrededor. *4* asomar [una sonrisa, expresión, etc.]. *5* dudar, vacilar.
how (jau) *adv.* cómo, de qué modo, por qué: ~ *do you do?,* ¿cómo está usted? ~ *so?,* ¿cómo es eso?, ¿por qué? *2* a cómo: ~ *do you sell it?,* ¿a cómo lo vende usted? *3* En ciertas locuciones tiene los sentidos de cuán, cuánto, hasta qué punto, qué,lo que, si, etc.: ~ *about it?,* ¿qué le parece?, ¿qué hacemos?; ~ *far?,* ¿a qué distancia? *2* ¿hasta dónde?; ~ *if I could not go?,* ¿y si yo no pudiese ir?; ~ *long?,* ¿cuánto, cuánto tiempo?; ~ *many,* cuántos, cuántas; ~ *much,* cuánto, lo mucho que. *4* qué, cuán [admirativos]: ~ *little!,* ¡qué poco!, ¡cuán poco!
  5 s. como [modo, manera].

howbeit (-bɪ·it) *adv.* sea como fuere; no obstante.

howdah (-da) *s.* castillo [sobre el elefante].

howel (-øl) *s.* argallera.

however (-e·vø^r) *adv.* de cualquier modo que, como quiera que, por muy... que, por mucho que. 2 *conj.* sin embargo, no obstante, con todo.

howitzer (-itšø^r) *s.* ARTILL. obús.

howl (jaul) *s.* aullido. 2 grito, ululato, alarido, chillido. 3 lamento.

howl (to) *intr.* aullar. 2 gritar, dar alaridos; chillar. 3 lamentarse [a gritos]. 4 *tr.* gritar.

howler (-ø^r) *s.* aullador. 2 gritador. 3 ZOOL. mono aullador, araguato. 4 plañidera. 5 fam. adefesio, desacierto, disparate grande.

howling (-ing) *adj.* aullador: ~ *monkey*, HOWLER 2. 2 clamoroso, ruidoso.

howsoever (-soue·vø·) *adv.* como quiera que, de cualquier modo que, por muy... que.

hoyden (joi·døn) *s.* muchacha traviesa, tunantuela.

hub (jøb) *s.* cubo [de rueda]: ~ *cap*, AUTO. tapacubo. 2 fig. centro, eje. 3 centro de actividad.

Hubert (jiu·bø^rt) *n. pr. m.* Huberto.

hubbub (jø·bøb) *s.* griterío, batahola, algazara, barullo, tumulto.

huckleberry (jø·kølberi) *s.* BOT. variedad de gayuba.

hucklebone (-boun) *s.* taba [hueso; juego].

huckster (jø·kstø^r) *s.* buhonero; vendedor ambulante.

huckster (to) *intr.* vender por las calles.

huddle (jø·døl) *s.* montón, tropel, confusión. 2 fam. reunión secreta.

huddle (to) *tr.* amontonar sin orden, confundir. 2 empujar, hacer salir, etc., en tropel. 3 hacer [algo] atropelladamente. 4 *to* ~ *oneself*, acurrucarse. 5 *intr.* amontonarse, apiñarse. 6 acurrucarse. 7 FÚTBOL reunirse para recibir órdenes.

hue (jiu) *s.* color, matiz, tinte. 2 griterío, clamor: ~ *and cry*, alarma, grito para perseguir a un ladrón, etc.; gritos de indignación.

huff (jøf) *s.* enojo, enfado: *in a* ~, enojado, ofendido.

huff (to) *tr.* inflar, hinchar. 2 tratar con arrogancia, maltratar. 3 ofender, enojar. 4 soplar [un peón]. 5 *intr.* enojarse, ofenderse.

huffish (-ish) *adj.* enojadizo, irritable. 2 arrogante, insolente.

huffy (-i) *adj.* HUFFISH.

hug (jøg) *s.* abrazo estrecho; abrazo [de cariño, de luchador].

hug (to) *tr.* abrazar; estrechar contra su pecho. 2 abrazarse a. 3 acariciar. 4 MAR. navegar muy cerca de [la costa]. 5 *to* ~ *oneself*, felicitarse. ¶ Pret. y p. p.: *hugged;* ger.: *hugging.*

huge (jiudȳ) *adj.* grande, enorme, colosal, vasto, inmenso.

hugeness (-nis) *s.* magnitud, enormidad, inmensidad.

Hugh (jiu·) *n. pr. m.* Hugo.

Huguenot (jiu·gønat) *s.* hugonote.

huisache (juisa·chæ) *s.* BOT. aromo.

hulk (jølk) *s.* MAR. casco arrumbado, pontón [que sirve de cárcel], carraca. 2 fig. armatoste.

hulking (-ing) *adj.* tosco, grueso, pesado.

hull (jøl) *s.* cáscara, corteza, hollejo [de fruta]; vaina [de legumbre]. 2 casco [de buque]. 3 armazón [de dirigible]. 4 flotador [de hidroavión].

hull (to) *tr.* pelar, mondar, deshollejar, desvainar.

2 MAR. dar un proyectil en el casco de [un buque].

hullabaloo (jølabalu·) *s.* batahola, barahúnda.

hullo (jølou·) *interj.-s.* HELLO; HOLLO.

hum (jøm) *s.* zumbido; ronroneo [de un motor, etc.]; rumor. 2 canturreo, tarareo.

hum (to) *intr.* zumbar, ronronear; rumorear; fig. *to make things hum*, desplegar actividad. 2 *tr.-intr.* canturrear, tararear.

human (jiu·man) *adj.* humano. 2 *s.* humano, mortal [ser humano].

humane (jiumei·n) *adj.* humano,humanitario, benigno, compasivo.

humanism (jiu·manišm) *s.* humanismo.

humanist (-ist) *s.* humanista.

humanitarian (jiumænite·rian) *adj.* humanitario. 2 *s.* filántropo.

humanity (jiumæ·niti) *s.* humanidad. 2 *pl.* humanidades.

humble (jø·mbøl) *adj.* humilde. 2 modesto, sencillo. 3 *to eat* ~ *pie*, humillarse, dar excusas, pedir perdón.

humble (to) *tr.* humillar. 2 abatir [el poder, el orgullo, etc.]. 3 *ref.* humillarse.

humbleness (-nis) *s.* humildad.

humbug (jø·mbøg) *s.* farsa, engaño, embeleco. 2 charlatanería, charlatanismo. 3 farsante, charlatán, embaucador, embustero.

humbug (to) *tr.* engañar, embaucar, embelecar. 2 timar, sacar [dinero]. ¶ Pret. y p. p.: *humbugged;* ger.: *-gging.*

humbuggery (-ri) *s.* engaño, embeleco.

humdrum (jø·ndrøm) *adj.* monótono, pesado, aburrido, trivial. 2 *s.* lata, cosa aburrida. 3 latoso.

humectate (to) (jøme·kteit) *tr.* humedecer.

humectation (jømektei·shøn) *s.* humectación.

humeral (jiu·møral) *adj.* humeral.

humerus (-øs) *s.* ANAT. húmero.

humid (jiu·mid) *adj.* húmedo.

humidify (to) (jiumi·difai) *tr.* humedecer. ¶ Pret. y p. p.: *humidified.*

humidity (jiumi·diti) *s.* humedad.

humiliate (to) (jiumi·lieit) *tr.* humillar.

humiliation (-ei·shøn) *s.* humillación.

humility (jiumi·liti) *s.* humildad, sumisión.

humming (jø·ming) *adj.* zumbador. 2 muy activo, intenso, grande.

hummingbird (-børd) *s.* ORN. colibrí, pájaro mosca, tominejo.

hummock (jø·mok) *s.* montecillo, mota, colina.

humor, humorous, etc. HUMOUR, HUMOUROUS, etc.

humoresque (jiumøre·sk) *s.* capricho musical.

humorism (jiu·morišm) *s.* MED. humorismo. 2 humor, gracia, ingenio.

humorist (-ist) *s.* humorista. 2 chistoso, chancero [pers.].

humour (jiu·mø^r) *s.* ANAT., MED. humor. 2 humor, disposición del ánimo, inclinación: *to be out of* ~, estar de mal humor; *to be in the* ~ *for*, tener ganas de. 3 genio, temperamento. 4 humor [facultad del humorista]. 5 humorada, capricho. 6 lo cómico [de una situación, etc.].

humour (to) *tr.* complacer, dar gusto. 2 mimar, consentir. 3 adaptarse, acomodarse a.

humourous (-øs) *adj.* cómico, gracioso, humorístico. 2 caprichoso, antojadizo.

hump (jø·mp) *s.* giba, joroba, corcova. 2 pop. murria, mal humor.

hump (to) *tr.* encorvar, hacer jorobado. 2 fam. *to* ~ *it*, hacer un esfuerzo, esforzarse.

humpback (-bæk) *s.* giba, joroba. 2 jorobado.

humpbacked (-bækt) *adj.* jorobado.
humped (-t), humpy (-i) *adj.* giboso, corcovado.
hunch (jø·nch) *s.* joroba, giba. 2 pedazo [de pan, etc.]. *3* fam. corazonada, presentimiento.
hunch (to) *tr.* sacar [formando protuberancia]. *2* encorvar [la espalda]. *3 intr.* encorvarse.
hunchback (-bæk) *s.* HUMPBACK.
hundred (jø·ndrød) *adj.* [precedido de *a* o *one*] cien, ciento. *2 s.* ciento, centena, centenar: *by the ~*, por centenares.
hundred-per-cent (-pø ͬse·nt) *adj.* cien por cien, cabal, perfecto, puro.
hundredth (jø·ndrøz) *adj.* centésimo. *2* centeno. *3* ciento [ordinal]. *4 s.* cento, centena [cifra de las centenas]. *5* centésimo, centésima.
hundredweight (jø·ndrødueit) *s.* quintal: (Ingl.) 112 lbs. (50.8 kg.); (E.U.) 100 lbs. (45.36 kg.).
hung (jøng) *pret.* y *p. p.* de TO HANG.
Hungarian (jønge·rian) *adj.-s.* húngaro.
Hungary (jø·ngari) *n. pr.* GEOGR. Hungría.
hunger (jø·ngø ͬ) *s.* hambre. *2* gana, apetito. *3* ansia, anhelo.
hunger (to) *intr.* tener hambre: *to ~ for*, tener hambre o sed de, anhelar. *2 tr.* hambrear, matar de hambre.
hungry (jø·ngri) *adj.* hambriento: *to be ~, to feel ~*, tener hambre o apetito. *2* famélico. *3* ganoso, deseoso. *4* pobre, estéril [suelo].
hunk (jønk) *s.* fam. trozo, buen pedazo, pedazo grande.
Huns (jøns) *s. pl.* HIST. hunos.
hunt (jønt) *s.* caza [acción]; montería. *2* cacería. *3* conjunto de cazadores. *4* sociedad de cazadores. *5* búsqueda. *6* perseguimiento, acosamiento. *7 on the ~ for*, a caza de.
hunt (to) *tr.* cazar; buscar, perseguir. *2* recorrer buscando, registrar. *3* emplear en la caza [perros, caballos]; cazar y matar, perseguir y destruir; buscar [una cosa]. *4 intr.* cazar, ir de caza: *to ~ for* o *after*, buscar, perseguir, ir tras de. *9* MEC. oscilar.
hunter (-ø ͬ) *s.* cazador. *2* perro o caballo de caza. *3* buscador. *4* saboneta.
hunting (-ing) *s.* caza, ejercicio de la caza, montería: *~ ground*, cazadero; *~ knife*, cuchillo de monte; *~ party*, cacería; partida de caza.
huntress (-ris) *f.* cazadora [mujer].
huntsman (-smæn) *s.* cazador; montero.
hurdle (jø ͬdøl) *s.* zarzo, cañizo. *2* adral. *3* valla [que se salta en las carreras]; fig. obstáculo, dificultad: *~ race*, carrera de saltos o de obstáculos.
hurdle (to) *tr.* cubrir o cercar con zarzos. *2* DEP. saltar [un obstáculo].
hurdy-gurdy (-i-gø ͬdi) *s.* MÚS. zanfonia, organillo.
hurl (jø ͬl) *s.* tiro, lanzamiento.
hurl (to) *tr.* lanzar, tirar, arrojar con fuerza: *to ~ oneself*, lanzarse, arrojarse. *2* derribar. *3* lanzar [gritos, invectivas, etc.].
hurly-burly (-ibø ͬli) *s.* gritería, batahola.
hurra(h (jura·) *interj.* ¡viva!, ¡hurra!
hurra(h (to) *tr.* aclamar, vitorear.
hurricane (jø·rikein) *s.* huracán, ciclón: *~ lamp*, linterna construida a prueba de viento.
hurried (jø·rid) *p. p.* de TO HURRY. *2 adj.* precipitado, apresurado, hecho de prisa.
hurry (jø·ri) *s.* prisa, premura, precipitación; paso o movimiento rápido: *to be in a ~*, tener prisa, ir de prisa; *in a ~*, de prisa.
hurry (to) *tr.* dar prisa, apresurar, acuciar. *2* acelerar, avivar. *3* atropellar, precipitar. *4* llevar

corriendo, con prisa. *5 to ~ on* o *up*, apresurar. *6 intr.* correr, apresurarse, darse prisa, precipitarse. *7 to ~ after*, correr en pos de. *8 to ~ away*, marcharse o salir precipitadamente. *9 to ~ back*, apresurarse a volver. *10 to ~ up*, apresurarse, darse prisa. ¶ Pret. y p. p.: *hurried*.
hurry-scurry (-skø·ri) *s.* precipitación, confusión. *2 adv.* atropelladamente, precipitadamente.
hurt (jø ͬt) *s.* herida, lesión, lastimadura. *2* daño, dolor. *3* daño, perjuicio. *4 adj.* herido, lastimado. *5* ofendido. *6* perjudicado.
hurt (to) *tr.* herir, lastimar: *to ~ one's feelings*, herir los sentimientos de uno, ofenderle. *2* dañar, perjudicar. *3* hacer daño, causar dolor. *4* apenar, afligir. *5 intr.* doler. ¶ Pret. y p. p.: *hurt*.
hurtful (-ful) *adj.* perjudicial, dañino, nocivo, pernicioso.
hurtle (to) (-øl) *tr.* lanzar, arrojar; hacer chocar. *2 intr.* lanzarse, arrojarse. *3* chocar [con]; moverse con estruendo.
hurtless (-lis) *adj.* inofensivo. *2* ileso.
husband (jø·sband) *s.* marido, esposo.
husband (to) *tr.* administrar con prudencia, ahorrar, economizar.
husbandman (-mæn) *s.* agricultor, labrador.
husbandry (-ri) *s.* agricultura, labranza. *2* frugalidad, economía; buen gobierno.
hush (jøsh) *interj.* ¡chitón!, ¡silencio! *2 s.* quietud, silencio.
hush (to) *tr.* callar. *2* acallar, aquietar. *3 to ~ up*, ocultar, echar tierra a. *4 intr.* callar, enmudecer.
husk (jøsk) *s.* cáscara, vaina, cascabillo, bagazo, zurrón o cubierta seca [de fruto]. *2* perfolla [del maíz].
husk (to) *tr.* descascarar, desvainar, desgranar, quitar la cubierta seca de [ciertos frutos].
huskiness (-inis) *s.* calidad de lo que tiene mucha cáscara o cubierta seca. *2* ronquera, bronquedad de la voz. *3* sequedad en la garganta.
husky (-i) *adj.* que tiene perfolla, cáscara, vaina, zurrón o cubierta seca. *2* seco. *3* con la garganta seca. *4* ronco, rauco. *5* fam. robusto, fornido. *6 s.* fam. persona robusta, fornida. *7* perro esquimal.
hussar (jø ͬša·) *s.* húsar.
hussy (jø·si) *s.* pícara, buena pieza. *2* mujer perdida.
hustings (jø·stingš) *s. pl.* tribuna para discursos electorales. *2* elecciones.
hustle (jø·søl) *s.* empujón, sacudida. *2* energía, vigor. *3* apresuramiento, actividad febril.
hustle (to) *tr.* empujar, atropellar; echar a empellones. *2* mezclar, confundir. *3* fam. apresurar. *4 intr.* andar empujando. *5* menearse, apresurarse, bullir, mostrar gran actividad.
hustler (jø·sle ͬ) *s.* trafagón, bullebulle; trabajador enérgico.
hut (jøt) *s.* choza, cabaña. *2* caseta, garita.
hut (to) *tr.-intr.* alojar o vivir en una choza, cabaña, etc.
hutch (jøch) *s.* arca, cofre. *2* conejera. *3* amasadera. *4* MIN. cuba. *5* fam. choza, tugurio.
Hyacinth (jai·asinz) *n. pr.* Jacinto. *2* Jacinta.
hyacinth (s. BOT., MINER. jacinto.
hyaena (jai·ina) *s.* ZOOL. hiena.
hyaline (jai·alin) *adj.* hialino.
hybrid (jai·brid) *adj.-s.* híbrido.
hybridization (jaibridiše·shøn) *s.* hibridación.
hybridize (to) (jai·bridaiš) *tr.-intr.* hacer híbrido, producir o engendrar híbridos.

hydra (jai·dra) *s.* ZOOL., ASTR., MIT. hidra. *2* fig. mal difícil de extirpar.
hydracid (jaidræ·sid) *s.* hidrácido.
hydrangea (-ndÿiæ) *s.* BOT. hortensia.
hydrant (jai·draant) *s.* boca de agua, boca de riego.
hydrate (jai·dreit) *s.* QUÍM. hidrato.
hydrate (to) *tr.* QUÍM. hidratación.
hydraulic (jaidro·lik) *adj.* hidráulico.
hydraulics (-s) *s.* hidráulica.
hydric (jai·drik) *adj.* QUÍM. hídrico.
hydrocarbon (jaidrøka·ʳbøn) *s.* QUÍM. hidrocarburo.
hydrochloric (-clou·rik) *adj.* QUÍM. clorhídrico.
hydrocyanic (-saiæ·nik) *adj.* QUÍM. cianhídrico.
hydrodynamic (-dainæ·mik) *adj.* hidrodinámico.
hydrodynamics (-s) *s.* hidrodinámica.
hydroelectric (-ile·ktrik) *adj.* hidroeléctrico.
hydroelectricity (-ilektri·siti) *s.* hidroelectricidad.
hydrogen (jai·drødÿin) *s.* QUÍM. hidrógeno.
hydrogenate (to) (jaidra·dÿøneit) *tr.* QUÍM. hidrogenar.
hydrography (-grafi) *s.* hidrografía.
hydrology (-lødÿ) *s.* hidrología.
hydrolysis (-lisis) *s.* QUÍM. hidrólisis.
hydrolyze (to) (jai·drølaiš) *tr.* QUÍM. hidrolizar.
hydromel (-mel) *s.* hidromel.
hydrometer (jaidra·metøʳ) *s.* hidrómetro.
hydrometry (-metri) *s.* hidrometría.
hydropathy (-pazi) *s.* hidropatía.
hydrophobe (-foub) *s.* MED. hidrófobo.
hydrophobia (jaidrøfou·bia) *s.* MED. hidrofobia.
hydropic(al (jaidra·pik(al) *adj.* hidrópico.
hydroplane (jai·droplein) *s.* hidroavión.
hydrosphere (-sfiʳ) *s.* hidrosfera.
hydrostat (-stæt) *s.* hidrostato.
hydrostatics (-stæ·tiks) *s.* hidrostática.
hydrosulphide (jaidrøsø·lfaid) *s.* QUÍM. sulfhidrato, hidrosulfuro.
hydrotherapy (-ze·rapi) *s.* hidroterapia.
hydrous (jai·drøs) *adj.* hidratado.
hydroxid(e (jaidra·ksid) *s.* QUÍM. hidróxido.
hydroxyl (jaidra·ksil) *s.* QUÍM. hidroxilo, oxhidrilo.
hyena (jaii·na) *s.* ZOOL. hiena.
hygiene (jai·dÿiin) *s.* higiene, profiláctica.
hygienic (jai·dÿie·nik) *adj.* higiénico.
hygienist (jai·dÿienist) *s.* higienista.
hygrometer (jaigra·metøʳ) *s.* higrómetro.
hygrometry (jaigra·metri) *s.* higrometría.
hygroscope (jai·grøskoup) *s.* higroscopio.
hymen (jai·men) *s.* ANAT. himen. *2* himeneo.
hymeneal (jaimeni·al) *adj.* nupcial. *2 s.* epitalamio.
hymenopter (-a·ptøʳ) *s.* ENT. himenóptero.
hymenopterous (-a·ptørøs) *adj.* ENT. himenóptero.
hymn (jim) *s.* himno.
hymn (to) *tr.* alabar con himnos. *2 intr.* cantar himnos.
hymnal (ji·mnal) *s.* himnario.

hymnology (jimna·lodÿi) *s.* tratado, estudio o composición de himnos. *2* himnos [colect.].
hyoid (jai·oid) *s.* ANAT. hioideo; hioides.
hyperaesthesia (jaipøreszi·šia) *s.* MED. hiperestesia.
hyperbaton (jaipø·ʳbaton) *s.* GRAM. hipérbaton.
hyperbola (-bola) *s.* GEOM. hipérbola.
hyperbole (-boli) *s.* RET. hipérbole.
hyperbolic (al (jaipøʳbø·lik(al) *adj.* hiperbólico.
hyperbolist (jaipø·ʳbolist) *s.* exagerador.
hyperborean (jaipøʳbou·rian) *adj.*-*s.* hiperbóreo.
hyperchlorhydria (-klori·dia) *s.* hiperclorhidria.
hypercritical (-kri·tikal) *adj.* hipercrítico.
hyperdulia (-diulai·a) *s.* TEOL. hiperdulía.
hypericum (jaipø·rikøm) *s.* BOT. hipérico.
hypermetropia (jaipøʳmitrou·pia) *f.* MED. hiper-metropía.
hypersensitive (-se·nsitiv) *adj.* extremadamente sensible. *2* MED. hipersensible.
hypertension (-te·nshøn) *s.* MED. hipertensión.
hipertrophy (-trøfi) *s.* hipertrofia.
hypertrophy (to) *intr.* hipertrofiarse.
hypha (jai·fa) *s.* BOT. hifa.
hyphen (jai·føn) *s.* ORTOG. división, guión.
hyphen, hyphenate (to) (jai·føneit) *tr.* unir con guión. *2* separar con guión.
hypnosis (jipnou·sis) *s.* hipnosis.
hypnotic (jipna·tik) *adj.*-*s.* hipnótico.
hypnotism (ji·pnøtišm) *s.* hipnotismo.
hypnotize (to) (ji·pnøtaiš) *tr.* hipnotizar.
hypo (jai·pou) *s.* FOT. hiposulfito sódico. *2* pop. aguja hipodérmica, inyección hipodérmica.
hypocaust (jai·pøkost) *s.* hipocausto.
hypochlorite (jaipøklo·rait) *s.* QUÍM. hipoclorito.
hypochondria (-ka·ndria) *s.* hipocondria.
hypochondriac (-ndriak) *adj.*-*s.* hipocondríaco.
hypochondrium (-ndriøm) *s.* ANAT. hipocondrio.
hypocrisy (jipa·krisi) *s.* hipocresía.
hypocrite (ji·pøkrit) *s.* hipócrita.
hypocritical (jipøkri·tikal) *adj.* hipócrita.
hypodermic (jaipødø·ʳmik) *adj.* hipodérmico.
hypogastrium (-gæ·striøm) *s.* ANAT. hipogastrio.
hypogeum (-dÿɪ·øm) *s.* ARQ. hipogeo.
hypophysis (jaipa·fisis) ANAT. hipófisis.
hypophosphite (jaipøfa·sfait) *s.* QUÍM. hipofosfito.
hypostasis (jaipa·stasis) *s.* FIL., TEOL. hipóstasis.
hypostatic(al (jaipøstæ·tik(al) *adj.* hipostáticos.
hypotenuse (jaipa·tinius) *s.* GEOM. hipotenusa.
hypothec (-zik) *s.* DER. hipoteca.
hypothecary (-zikeri) *s.* hipotecario.
hypothecate (to) (-zikeit) *tr.* hipotecar.
hypothesis (-zisis) *s.* hipótesis.
hypothetic(al (jaipøze·tik(al) *adj.* hipotético.
hypsometer (jipsa·mitøʳ) *s.* hipsómetro.
hypsometry (-metri) *s.* hipsometría.
hyson (jai·søn) *s.* té verde de China.
hyssop (ji·søp) *s.* BOT. hisopo. *2* hisopo, aspersorio.
hysteresis (jistøri·sis) *s.* FÍS. histérisis.
hysteria (jisti·ria) *s.* histeria, histerismo.
hysterics (jiste·riks) *s.* ataque de nervios, de histerismo.

I

I, I (ai) *s.* I, i, novena letra del alfabeto inglés.
I *pron. pers.* y *s.* yo. | Se escribe siempre con mayúscula.
iamb (ai·æm) *s.* IAMBUS.
iambic (aiæ·mbik) *adj.* yámbico. *2 s.* yambo.
iambus (aiæ·mbøs) *s.* yambo.
Iberia (aibi·ria) *n. pr.* GEOGR. Iberia.
Iberian (aibi·rian) *adj.* ibérico. *2 adj.-s.* ibero.
ibex (ai·beks) *s.* ZOOL. íbice, bicerra.
ibis (ai·bis) *s.* ORN. ibis.
Icarian (aike·rian) *adj.* icario. *2* arriesgado.
ice (ais) *s.* hielo. *2* helado, sorbete, granizado. *3* capa de azúcar, alcorza [en pastelería]. *4 adj.* de hielo, glacial; para el hielo; helado, garapiñado: ~ *age,* GEOL. época glacial; ~ *cream,* helado de crema, mantecado; ~ *drift,* ~ *float,* témpano, banco de hielo; ~ *hockey,* hockey sobre hielo; ~ *plant,* fábrica de hielo.
ice (to) *tr.* helar, congelar, garapiñar. *2* refrigerar, enfriar con hielo. *3* alcorzar, cubrir con capa de azúcar.
iceberg (-bø^rg) *s.* iceberg.
iceboat (-bout) *s.* buque rompehielos. *2* trineo con vela para deslizarse sobre el hielo.
icebound (-baund) *adj.* rodeado de hielo. *2* detenido o aprisionado por el hielo.
icebox (-baks) *s.* nevera.
icebreaker (-breikø^r) *s.* buque rompehielos.
ice-cream *adj.* de helado o mantecado: ~ *freezer,* heladora, sorbetera; ~ *soda,* agua carbónica con helado.
icehouse (-jaus) *s.* depósito de hielo.
Iceland (-lænd) *n. pr.* GEOGR. Islandia.
Icelander (-landø^r) *adj.-s.* islandés.
Icelandic (-lændik) *adj.* islandés. *2 m.* islandés [idioma].
ichneumon (ikniu·møn) *s.* ZOOL., ENT. icneumón.
ichnography (ikna·grafi) *s.* ARQ. icnografía.
ichor (ai·kø^r) *s.* MED. icor.
ichthyol (ikzia·l) *s.* FARM. ictiol.
ichthylogy (-lodγi) *s.* ictiología.
ichthyophagous (-fagøs) *adj.* ictiófago.
ichthyosaurus (ikziøso·røs) *s.* ZOOL. ictiosauro.
icicle (ai·sikøl) *s.* carámbano, candelizo, canelón.
icily (ai·sili) *adv.* fríamente, frígidamente.
icing (ai·sing) *s.* alcorza, capa de azúcar. *2* AVIA. formación de hielo.
icon (ai·kan) *s.* icono. *2* imagen, retrato.

iconoclasm (aika·nøklæšm) *s.* iconoclasia.
iconoclast (-klæst) *s.* iconoclasta.
iconography (aikøna·grafi) *s.* iconografía.
iconology (-lodγ) *s.* iconología.
iconostasis (-stasis) *s.* iconostasio.
icosahedron (aikøsaji·drøn) *s.* GEOM. icosaedro.
icteric (ikte·rik) *adj.-s.* MED. ictérico.
ictus (i·ktøs) *s.* ictus.
icy (ai·si) *adj.* frígido, helado, glacial. *2* cubierto de hielo.
I'd (aid) contracción de *I would, I had* y *I shoud.*
idea (aidɾa) *s.* idea [en todos los sentidos menos en el de ingenio para disponer o inventar].
ideal (aidɾal) *adj.-s.* ideal.
idealism (aidɾališm) *s.* idealismo.
idealist (aidɾalist) *s.* idealista.
idealistic (aidɾali·stik) *adj.* idealista.
idealize (to) (aidɾalaiš) *tr.* idealizar.
ideation (aidiei·shøn) *s.* ideación.
idem (ai·dem) *adj.-pr.* lat. ídem.
identic(al (aide·ntik(al) *adj.* idéntico.
identification (aidentifikei·shøn) *s.* identificación.
identify (to) (aide·ntifai) *tr.* identificar. ¶ Pret. y p. p.: *identified.*
identify (-ti) *s.* identidad.
ideogram (ai·diogræm), **ideograph** (-græf) *s.* ideograma.
ideographic (aidiogræ·fik) *adj.* ideográfico.
ideology (-a·lodγi) *s.* ideología. *2* teorización; especulación visionaria.
ides (aidš) *s.* idus.
idiocy (i·diøsi) *s.* idiotez. *2* necedad, tontería.
idiom (i·diøm) *s.* idioma, habla, lenguaje. *2* genio, índole [de una lengua]. *3* modismo, locución, idiotismo.
idiomatic(al (idiomæ·tik(al) *adj.* idiomático. *2* relativo a las locuciones o idiotismos.
idiosyncrasy (idiosi·nkɾasi) *s.* idiosincrasia. *2* peculiaridad, excentricidad.
idiosyncratic (idiosinkɾæ·tik) *adj.* idiosincrásico.
idiot (i·diat) *s.* idiota. *2* necio, tonto, bobo.
idiotic(al (idia·tik(al) *adj.* idiota, tonto, estúpido.
idle (ai·døl) *adj.* ocioso, desocupado; inactivo. *2* de ocio: ~ *hours,* horas de ocio, ratos perdidos. *3* ocioso, inútil, vano. *4* infundado, futil: ~ *tale,* cuento, patraña. *5* perezoso, holgazán. *6* loca [rueda].
idle (to) *intr.* holgar, estar ocioso. *2* holgazanear.

3 *intr.-tr.* MEC., AUTO. marchar, o hacer marchar [un motor] en vacío, al ralentí. *4 tr.* gastar ociosamente: *to ~ away one's time*, pasar o perder el tiempo.
idleness (-nis) *s.* ocio, ociosidad, inactividad. *2* futilidad, inutilidad. *3* pereza, holgazanería.
idler (ai·dlø^r) *s.* ocioso, holgazán. *2* MEC. rueda loca
idol (ai·døl) *s.* ídolo. *2* LÓG. falsa idea o concepto.
idolater (aida·latø^r) *s.* idólatra.
idolatress (-tris) *f.* idólatra [mujer].
idolatrous (-trøs) *adj.* idolátrico. *2* idólatra.
idolatry (-tri) *s.* idolatría.
idolize (to) (ai·dølaiš) *tr.* convertir en ídolo. *2 tr.-intr.* idolatrar.
idyll, idyl (ai·døl) *s.* LIT. idilio.
idyllic (aidi·lik) *adj.* idílico; pastoral, bucólico.
if (if) *conj.* si; en caso que, con tal que; aunque, aun cuando: *as ~*, como si; *~ only*, si, si al menos [expresando deseo]. *2* Úsase elípticamente en vez de *if it is, if they are*, etc.: *~ so*, si es así; *~ true*, si es verdad. *3 s.* condición, suposición.
igloo (i·glu) *s.* iglú.
Ignatius (ignei·shøs) *n. pr. m.* Ignacio.
igneous (i·gniøs) *adj.* ígneo.
ignifuge (ig·nifiudÿ) *adj.* ignífugo.
ignis fatuus (i·gnis fæ·chøs) *s.* fuego fatuo.
ignite (to) (ignai·t) *tr.* encender, pegar fuego a. *2 intr.* encenderse, inflamarse, arder.
ignition (igni·shøn) *s.* ignición, inflamación. *2* encendido [de un motor]: *~ switch*, interruptor del encendido, contacto.
ignoble (ignou·bøl) *adj.* innoble, indigno, vil. *2* villano, plebeyo.
ignominious (ignømi·niøs) *adj.* ignominioso.
ignominy (i·gnømini) *s.* ignominia.
ignoramus (ignørei·møs) *s.* ignorante; pedante.
ignorance (i·gnørøns) *s.* ignorancia, desconocimiento. *2* ignorancia, falta de cultura.
ignorant (-t) *adj.* ignorante, desconocedor: *to be ~ of*, ignorar [una cosa]. *2* ignorante, ignaro, indocto, inculto.
ignore (to) (igno·^r) *tr.* desconocer, cerrar los ojos a una cosa. *2* hacer caso omiso [de uno]; desairarle. *3* DER. desestimar.
iguana (igua·na) *s.* ZOOL. iguana.
ileum (i·liøm) *s.* ANAT. íleon [intestino].
ileus (i·liøs) *s.* MED. íleo.
ilex (ai·leks) *s.* BOT. encina. *2* BOT. coscoja. *3* BOT. acebo.
iliac (i·liæk) *adj.* ANAT. ilíaco.
Iliad (i·liæd) *s.* Ilíada.
ilium (i·liøm) *s.* ANAT. íleon, ilion [hueso].
ilk (ilk) *s.* fam. raza, clase, especie, jaez:
I'll (ail) *contr.* de I SHALL y I WILL.
ill (il) *adj.* enfermo, malo, doliente: *to fall ~*, caer enfermo. *2* mareado. *3* malo, mal [no bueno, desfavorable; perjudicial; insalubre; infortunado; desagradable; difícil; malévolo, perverso]: *~ breeding*, mala crianza, mala educación, grosería; *~ health*, mala salud; *~ repute*, mala reputación, mala fama; *~ temper*, mal genio, mal humor; *~ will*, mala voluntad, ojeriza; *in ~ part*, en mala parte. *4 s.* mal, desgracia, infortunio. *5 adv.* mal, malamente: *to think ~*, pensar mal; *~ at ease*, molesto; inquieto, intranquilo.
ill-advised *adj.* malaconsejado. *2* desacertado, imprudente.
illation (ilei·shøn) *s.* ilación, inferencia.
illative (i·lativ) *adj.* ilativo.
ill-bred *adj.* malcriado, grosero, descortés.

ill-conditioned *adj.* de mala inclinación; de mal genio. *2* malparado.
illegal (ilı·gal) *adj.* ilegal.
illegality (ilıgæ·liti) *s.* ilegalidad. *2* desaguisado.
illegibility (iledÿibi·liti) *s.* calidad de ilegible.
illegible (ile·dÿibøl) *adj.* ilegible.
illegitimacy (ilidÿi·timasi) *s.* ilegitimidad.
illegitimate (-timit) *adj.* ilegítimo. *2* bastardo. *3* ilógico; erróneo.
illegitimate (to) (-meit) *tr.* ilegitimar.
ill-fated *adj.* malhadado, desgraciado. *2* aciago.
ill-favoured *adj.* mal parecido, feo, repulsivo.
ill-gotten *adj.* mal habido, mal adquirido.
ill-humo (u) red (-jiu·mø^rd) *adj.* malhumorado.
illiberal (ili·børal) *adj.* iliberal. *2* inculto, rústico. *3* mezquino, tacaño. *4* estrecho de miras.
illiberality (ilibøræ·liti) *s.* falta de liberalidad. *2* mezquindad, tacañería. *3* estrechez de miras.
illicit (-sit) *adj.* ilícito.
illicitness (-nis) *s.* ilicitud.
illimitable (-mitabøl) *adj.* ilimitado.
illiquid (-kuid) *adj.* COM. no realizable.
illiteracy (-torasi) *s.* falta de cultura, ignorancia. *2* analfabetismo.
illiterate (-tørit) *adj.* iletrado, analfabeto.
ill-mannered *adj.* mal educado, de malos modales.
illness (i·lnis) *s.* enfermedad, dolencia.
illogical (ila·dÿikal) *adj.* ilógico. *2* que no razona con lógica.
ill-pleased *adj.* descontento.
ill-starred *adj.* desdichado, malaventurado.
ill-suited *adj.* inadecuado; poco a propósito.
ill-timed *adj.* intempestivo, inoportuno.
ill-treat (to) *tr.* maltratar.
illuminant (iliu·minant) *adj.-s.* iluminante.
illuminate (to) (iliu·mineit) *tr.* iluminar, alumbrar. *2* esclarecer, aclarar. *3* hacer resplandeciente. *4* B. ART. iluminar.
illuminati (iliuminei·tai) *s. pl.* iluminados [secta].
illumination (-shøn) *s.* iluminación; alumbrado. *2* esclarecimiento. *3* ilustración, saber. *4* B. ART. iluminación [en colores]. *5 pl.* luminarias.
illumine (to) (iliu·min) *tr.* iluminar.
illusion (iliu·ÿøn) *s.* ilusión; espejismo, engaño. *2* aparición.
illusionist (-ist) *s.* ilusionista.
illusive (iliu·siv) *adj.* ilusivo, ilusorio, irreal.
illusory (-sori) *adj.* ilusorio, engañoso.
illustrate (to) (i·løstreit) *tr.* ilustrar [con explicaciones, dibujos, etc.].
illustration (-ei·shøn) *s.* ilustración. | No tiene el sentido de cultura, luces.
illustrator (-tø^r) *s.* ilustrador.
illustrious (ilø·striøs) *adj.* ilustre, preclaro, famoso.
I'm (aim) contracción de I AM.
image (i·midÿ) *s.* imagen: *in his own ~*, a su imagen. *2* símbolo, representación. *3* retrato, efigie. *4* parecido, semejanza.
image (to) *tr.* figurar, retratar, reproducir, reflejar. *2* concebir, imaginar, representarse. *3* representar, simbolizar.
imagery (-ri) *s.* B. ART. imaginería. *2* imágenes retóricas. *3* fantasías, recuerdos. *4* detalles pintorescos de un paisaje, etc.
imaginary (imæ·dÿineri) *adj.* imaginario.
imagination (imædÿinei·shøn) *s.* imaginación. *2* creación poética o de la imaginación.
imaginative (imæ·dÿineitiv) *adj.* imaginativo.
imagine (to) (imæ·dÿin) *tr.* imaginar, concebir, idear. *2* imaginarse, figurarse.

imago (imei·gou) *s.* ENT. imago.
imam (ima·m) *s.* imán [título mahometano].
imbecile (i·mbisil) *adj.-s.* imbécil, estúpido. 2 débil, sin fuerzas.
imbecility (imbisi·liti) *s.* imbecilidad, tontería, absurdidad.
imbibe (to) (imbai·b) *tr.* embeber, absorber, chupar. 2 fig. empaparse de, asimilar. 3 *intr.* fam. beber, empinar el codo.
imbricate (to) (i·mbrikeit) *tr.* disponer como las tejas de un tejado.
imbrication (-ei·shøn) *s.* imbricación.
imbroglio (imbrou·liou) *s.* enredo, embrollo, lío.
imbrue (to) (imbru·) *tr.* ensangrentar, teñir en sangre, manchar de sangre.
imbue (to) (imbiu·) *tr.* saturar, empapar, impregnar, teñir. 2 imbuir, infundir.
imitable (i·mitabøl) *adj.* imitable.
imitate (to) (i·miteit) *tr.* imitar. 3 contrahacer, remedar.
imitation (-shøn) *s.* imitación. 2 remedo. 3 *adj.* de imitación.
immaculate (imæ·kiulit) *adj.* inmaculado: *Immaculate Conception*, Inmaculada Concepción.
immanence, -cy (i·manøns, -si) *s.* inmanencia.
immanent (i·manønt) *adj.* inmanente.
Immanuel (imæ·niuel) *n. pr.* Emanuel.
Immaterial (imati·rial) *adj.* inmaterial, incorpóreo. 2 indiferente, que no importa, sin importancia: *it is ~*, es indiferente, lo mismo da.
immaterialism (-išm) *s.* FIL. idealismo.
immateriality (imatiriæ·liti) *s.* inmaterialidad, incorporeidad. 2 cualidad de lo que no importa.
immature (imatiu·øʳ) *adj.* inmaturo, sin madurar, joven. 2 inacabado, imperfecto. 3 verde [fruta].
immaturity (-riti) *s.* calidad de inmaturo, falta de madurez, de sazón.
inmmeasurable (ime·ȳurabøl) *adj.* inconmensurable, desmesurado.
immediacy (imi·diasi) *s.* inmediación, proximidad.
immediate (-diit) *adj.* inmediato. 2 directo, intuitivo, intuido, conocido por intuición.
immediately (-li) *adv.* inmediatamente. 2 directamente, intuitivamente. 3 *conj.* tan pronto como, en cuanto.
immemorial (imimo·rial) *adj.* inmemorial, inmemorable.
immense (ime·ns) *adj.* inmenso, infinito, vasto. 2 pop. estupendo, magnífico.
immensity (ime·nsiti) *s.* inmensidad. 2 infinidad, vastedad.
immensurable (ime·nshurabøl) *adj.* inmensurable; inconmensurable.
immerge (to) (imø·ʳdȳ) *tr.* hundir, sumergir. 2 *intr.* hundirse, sumergirse.
immerse (to) (imø·ʳs) *tr.* sumergir, hundir, sumir. 2 bautizar por inmersión. 3 absorber [la atención, el pensamiento, etc.].
immersion (imø·ʳshøn) *s.* inmersión. 2 sumersión. 3 bautismo por inmersión.
immess (to) (ime·sh) *tr.* enredar, enmallar.
immigrant (i·migrant) *adj.-s.* inmigrante.
immigrate (to) (i·migreit) *intr.* inmigrar.
immigration (imigre·shøn) *s.* inmigración.
imminence (i·minøns) *s.* inminencia. 2 cosa inminente, que amenaza.
imminent (-t) *adj.* inminente.
immiscible (imi·sibøl) *adj.* FÍS., QUÍM. inmiscible.
immobile (imou·bil) *adj.* inmóvil, inmoble.
imobility (imoubi·liti) *s.* inmovilidad.

immobilize (to) (imou·bilaiš) *tr.* inmovilizar.
immoderate (ima·dørit) *adj.* inmoderado, desmedido. 2 irrazonable, exagerado.
immoderation (imadørei·shøn) *s.* inmoderación.
immodest (ima·dıst) *adj.* inmodesto. 2 deshonesto, indecente. 3 atrevido, insolente.
immodesty (-i) *s.* inmodestia. 2 indecoro, indecencia. 3 descaro.
immolate (to) (i·moleit) *tr.* inmolar.
immolation (-ei·shøn) *s.* inmolación.
immoral (ima·ral) *adj.* inmoral.
immorality (imøræ·liti) *s.* inmoralidad.
immortal (imo·ʳtal) *adj.* inmortal, imperecedero. 2 *s.* inmortal.
immortality (imoʳtæ·liti) *s.* inmortalidad.
immortalize (to) (imo·ʳtalaiš) *tr.* inmortalizar.
immortelle (imoʳte·l) *s.* BOT. siempreviva.
immovability (inmuvabi·liti) *s.* inamovilidad, inmovilidad, fijeza. 2 inalterabilidad. 3 insensibilidad.
immovable (imu·vabøl) *adj.* inamovible, inmóvil, fijo. 2 inalterable, inflexible. 3 impasible. 4 DER. inmueble. 5 *s. pl.* bienes raíces.
immune (imiu·n) *adj.-s.* inmune.
immunity (imiu·niti) *s.* inmunidad. 2 libertad, privilegio, exención.
immunization (ei·shøn) *s.* inmunización.
immunize (to) (i·miunaiš) *tr.* inmunizar.
immunology (imiuna·lodȳi) *s.* inmunología.
immure (to) (imiu·øʳ) *tr.* emparedar. 2 amurallar.
immutability (imiutabi·liti) *s.* inmutabilidad. 2 constancia, firmeza.
immutable (imiu·tabøl) *adj.* inmutable.
imp (imp) *s.* diablillo, duende. 2 diablillo [niño travieso].
impact (i·mpækt) *s.* golpe, choque, impacto.
impaction (impæ·kshøn) *s.* MED. impacción.
impair (to) (impe·øʳ) *tr.* dañar, perjudicar, estropear, deteriorar, disminuir, debilitar.
impairment (-mønt) *s.* deterioro, menoscabo, mengua, debilitación.
impale (impei·l) *tr.* empalar. 3 empalizar, cercar.
impalpable (impæ·lpabøl) *adj.* impalpable.
impanel (to) (impæ·nøl) *tr.* DER. elegir o designar [un jurado]; incluir en él.
imparity (impæ·riti) *s.* disparidad, desigualdad.
impart (to) (impa·ʳt) *tr.* impartir, dar, comunicar. 2 declarar, dar a conocer.
impartial (impa·ʳshal) *adj.* imparcial.
impartiality (impa·shiæ·liti) *s.* imparcialidad.
impartment (impa·ʳtmønt) *s.* acción de impartir.
impassable (impæ·sabøl) *adj.* impracticable, intransitable.
impasse (impæ·s) *s.* callejón sin salida. 2 atolladero, dificultad insuperable.
impassibility (-sibi·liti) *s.* impasibilidad.
impassible (-ibøl) *adj.* impasible.
impassion (to) (-shøn) *tr.* apasionar, conmover.
impasioned (-d) *adj.* apasionado, vehemente, ardiente. 2 extremoso.
impassive (impæ·siv) *adj.* impasible. 2 insensible, inanimado.
impassiveness (-nis) *s.* impasibilidad.
impaste (to) (impei·st) *tr.* PINT. empastar.
impatience (impei·shøns) *s.* impaciencia.
impatient (impei·shønt) *adj.* impaciente. 2 que no puede sufrir una cosa.
impeach (to) (impı·ch) *tr.* discutir, poner en tela de juicio. 2 acusar [esp. a un funcionario público]; residenciar. 3 acriminar, culpar.
impeachable (-abøl) *adj.* censurable. 2 discutible.

impeachment (-mønt) *s.* acción de poner en tela de juicio. *2* acusación; residencia [acción de residenciar].
impeccability (impekabi·liti) *s.* impecabilidad.
impeccable (impe·kabøl) *adj.* impecable.
impecuniosity (-kiunia·siti) *s.* inopia, pobreza.
impecunious (-kiu·niøs) *adj.* pobre, sin dinero.
impedance (impı·dans) *s.* ELECT. impedancia.
impede (to) (impı·d) *tr.* impedir, estorbar, obstruir.
impediment (impe·dimønt) *s.* impedimento, estorbo, obstáculo, traba. *2 pl.* impedimenta.
impedimenta (impedime·nta) *s. pl.* impedimenta.
impel (to) (impe·l) *tr.* impeler, impulsar. *2* mover, obligar. ¶ Pret. y p. p.: *impelled;* p. a.: *-lling.*
impellent (impe·lønt) *adj.* impelente. *2* impulsor. *3 s.* impulsor, motor, móvil; empuje.
impend (to) (impe·nd) *intr.* pender [sobre]; amenazar, amagar, ser inminente.
impenetrability (impenitrabi·liti) *s.* impenetrabilidad.
impenetrable (impe·nitrabøl) *adj.* impenetrable. *2* duro, inconmovible.
impenitence (impe·nitøns) *s.* impenitencia.
impenitent (impe·nitønt) *adj.-s.* impenitente.
imperative (impe·rativ) *adj.* imperativo, imperioso. *2* perentorio, indispensable. *3 adj.-s.* GRAM. imperativo. *4 s.* imperativo, necesidad imperiosa.
imperceptibility (impø\`septibi·liti) *s.* imperceptibilidad.
imperceptible (impø\`se·ptibøl) *adj.* imperceptible.
imperfect (impø·\`fikt) *adj.* imperfecto, incompleto, defectuoso. *2 s.* GRAM. pretérito imperfecto.
imperfection (impø\`fe·kshøn) *s.* imperfección. *2* falta, defecto.
imperfective (-tiv) *adj.* GRAM. imperfectivo.
imperial (impi·rial) *adj.* imperial. *2 s.* perilla, para [barba]. *3* imperial [de un vehículo].
imperialism (impi·rializhm) *s.* imperialismo.
imperialist (impi·rialist) *s.* imperialista.
imperil (to) (impe·ril) *tr.* poner en peligro. ¶ Pret. y p. p. *-iled* o *-illed;* p. a.: *-iling* o *-illing.*
imperious (impi·riøs) *adj.* imperioso, arrogante, autoritario. *2* imperioso, urgente.
imperiousness (-nis) *s.* autoridad, mando. *2* imperio, arrogancia.
imperishable (impe·rishabøl) *adj.* imperecedero. *2* indestructible.
impermanence (impø·\`manøns) *s.* instabilidad.
impermanent (-nt) *adj.* no permanente, instable.
impermeable (impø·\`miabøl) *adj.* impermeable, impenetrable.
impersonal (impø·\`sønal) *adj.* impersonal.
impersonate (to) (impø·\`søneit) *tr.* personificar. *2* TEAT. representar [a un personaje]. *3* imitar, fingirse, hacerse pasar por [una pers.].
impersonation (-shøn) *s.* personificación. *2* TEAT. representación [de un personaje], papel.
impersonator (-ø\`) *s.* personificador. *2* TEAT. intérprete [de un papel]. *3* TEAT. artista que imita personajes conocidos. *4* el que se hace pasar por otro.
impertinence, -cy (-tinøns, -si) *s.* impertinencia. *2* falta de pertinencia.
impertinent (-tinønt) *adj.* impertinente.
imperturbable (impø\`tø·\`babøl) *adj.* imperturbable.
imperturbed (-tø\`bd) *adj.* tranquilo, sereno.

impervious (impø·\`viøs) *adj.* impenetrable, impermeable. *2* que no atiende a [razones, etc.].
impetigo (impi·taigou) *s.* MED. impétigo.
impetrate (to) (i·mpetreit) *tr.* impetrar.
impetratory (i·mpetratori) *adj.* impetratorio.
impetuosity (impechua·siti) *s.* impetuosidad, impetu, vehemencia.
impetuous (impe·chuøs) *adj.* impetuoso.
impetus (i·mpitøs) *s.* ímpetu. *2* impulso, estímulo.
impiety (impai·øti) *s.* impiedad, irreligiosidad.
impinge (to) (impi·ndÿ) *tr.* dar en o contra, chocar con. *2* intr. *to ~ on* o *upon,* tocar, golpear contra, herir; invadir [derechos, etc.].
impious (i·mpiøs) *adj.* impío, irreverente, profano. *2* malvado.
impiousness (-nis) *s.* impiedad.
impish (i·mpish) *adj.* travieso, endiablado.
implacability (implæcabi·liti) *s.* implacabilidad.
implacable (implæ·cabøl) *adj.* implacable.
implant (to) (implæ·nt) *tr.* implantar, fijar. *2* inculcar. *3* plantar, injerir.
implantation (-ei·shøn) *s.* implantación, fijación. *2* inculcación.
implement (i·mplimønt) *s.* instrumento, herramienta, utensilio. *2 pl.* enseres, avíos.
implement (to) *tr.* llevar a cabo, ejecutar, cumplir.
implicate (to) (i·mplikeit) *tr.* implicar. *2* enredar, entrelazar. *3* complicar, comprometer [a uno].
implication (-ei·shøn) *s.* implicación, enredo. *2* deducción, inferencia. *3* complicación, complicidad.
implicative (i·mplikativ) *adj.* implicatorio.
implicit (impli·sit) *adj.* implícito. *2* virtual, potencial. *3* absoluto, ciego, sin duda ni reserva.
implicitness (-nis) *s.* calidad de implícito.
implied (implai·d) *adj.* implícito, sobreentendido. *2* significado, denotado.
imploration (implorei·shøn) *s.* imploración.
implore (to) (implo·\`) *tr.* implorar.
impluvium (implu·viøm) *s.* impluvio.
imply (to) (implai·) *tr.* implicar, entrañar, argüir, incluir en esencia. *2* dar a entender; significar, denotar. ¶ Pret. y p. p.: *implied.*
impolicy (impa·lisi) *s.* inoportunidad, torpeza, inhabilidad.
impolite (impøla·it) *adj.* impolítico, descortés.
impoliteness (-nis) *s.* impolítica, descortesía.
impolitic (impa·litik) *adj.* impolítico, poco hábil, imprudente.
imponderable (impa·ndørabøl) *adj.-s.* imponderable.
imporous (impo·røs) *adj.* no poroso.
import (i·mpo·\`t) *s.* importancia, peso, entidad. *2* significado, sentido; intención. *3* importación. *4 pl.* géneros importados.
import (to) (impo·\`t) *tr.-intr.* importar [ser de importancia]. *2 tr.* importar, implicar, significar. *3* importar, introducir.
importance (-ans) *s.* importancia. *2* cuantía. *3* vanidad, presunción, engreimiento.
important (-ant) *adj.* importante, considerable. *2* pomposo, presuntuoso, engreído.
importation (-ei·shøn) *s.* importación.
importer (impo·\`tø\`) *s.* importador.
importunacy (impo·\`tiunasi) *s.* importunidad.
importunate (-nit) *adj.* importuno, pesado, insistente.
importune (to) (impo·\`tiun) *tr.-intr.* importunar.
importunity (-tiu·niti) *s.* importunidad, machaquería. *2* importunación.
impose (to) (impou·s) *tr.* imponer [tributos, silen-

cio, las manos, etc.]. 2 hacer aceptar. 3 IMPR. imponer. 4 intr. *to ~ on o upon*, engañar, abusar de la buena fe de.

imposing (-ing) *adj.* imponente, impresionante.

imposition (impøši·shøn) *s.* imposición. 2 carga, tributo, impuesto. 3 engaño, ficción, impostura.

impossibility (impasibi·liti) *s.* imposibilidad. 2 imposible.

impossible (impa·sibøl) *adj.* imposible, irrealizable, impracticable. 2 estrafalario. 3 *s.* imposible.

impost (i·mpoust) *s.* impuesto, tributo, contribución. 2 ARQ. imposta [de un arco].

impostor (impa·stø^r) *s.* impostor, engañador, estafador.

imposture (impa·schø^r) *s.* impostura, engaño.

impotence, -cy (i·mpatøns, -si) *s.* impotencia.

impotent (-tønt) *adj.* impotente. 2 débil [sin fuerzas].

impound (to) (impau'nd) *tr.* encerrar, acorralar. 2 embalsar, represar. 3 DER. depositar.

impoverish (to) (impa·vørish) *tr.* empobrecer, depauperar.

impracticability (impræktikabi·liti) *s.* impracticabilidad.

impracticable (impræ·ktikabøl) *adj.* impracticable. 2 intransitable.

imprecate (to) (i·mprikeit) *tr.* imprecar. 2 *ïntr.* proferir imprecaciones.

imprecation (-ei·shøn) *s.* imprecación.

impregnable (impre·gnabøl) *adj.* inexpugnable.

impregnate (impre·gneit) *adj.* preñado; fecundado. 2 impregnado, empapado, lleno.

impregnate (to) *tr.* empreñar, fecundar. 2 impregnar, empapar, saturar.

impregnation (-ei·shøn) *s.* fecundación. 2 impregnación, empapamiento.

impresario (imprisa·riou) *s.* TEAT. empresario.

imprescriptible (impriskri·ptibøl) *adj.* imprescriptible.

impress (i·mpres) *s.* impresión, señal, marca, huella. 2 sello [carácter distintivo].

impress (to) (impre·s) *tr.* imprimir, estampar, grabar. 2 inculcar. 3 imprimir [un carácter, movimiento, etc.]. 4 impresionar, causar impresión en.

impressible (-ibøl) *adj.* impresionable. 2 imprimible, estampable.

impression (impre·shøn) *s.* impresión [en todos sus sentidos]. 2 estampa, sigilación. 3 marca, señal, huella. 4 edición [ejemplares que se publican de una vez].

impressionable (-abøl) *adj.* impresionable.

impressionism (-iśm) *s.* B. ART. impresionismo.

impressive (impre·siv) *adj.* impresionante, que causa impresión, emocionante, grandioso, solemne.

imprevision (imprevi·ȳøn) *s.* imprevisión.

imprimatur (imprimei·tø^r) *s.* imprimátur. 2 sanción, aprobación.

imprint (i·mprint) *s.* impresión, marca, señal, huella. 2 pie de imprenta.

imprint (to) (impri·nt) *tr.* imprimir, estampar. 2 imprimir, grabar [en el ánimo].

imprison (to) (impri·śøn) *tr.* encarcelar, poner preso, encerrar, aprisionar.

imprisonment (-mønt) *s.* encarcelamiento. 2 encierro, prisión.

improbability (imprababi·liti) *s.* improbabilidad. 2 inverosimilitud.

improbable (impra·babøl) *adj.* improbable. 2 inverosímil.

improbity (improu·biti) *s.* improbidad.

impromptu (impro·mptiu) *adj.* impremeditado, improvisado. 2 *adv.* de repente, en el acto. 3 *s.* improvisación. 4 MÚS. impromptu.

improper (impro·pø^r) *adj.* impropio. 2 incorrecto, inexacto. 3 inconveniente, indecoroso.

impropriety (imprøprai·eti) *s.* impropiedad. 2 inconveniencia, indecoro.

improvable (-abøl) *adj.* mejorable. 2 cultivable. 3 útil.

improve (to) (impru·v) *tr.* mejorar, perfecionar, desarrollar. 2 aprovechar, sacar partido de. 3 beneficiar, explotar, urbanizar. 4 *intr.* mejorar, mejorarse. 5 adelantar, progresar. 6 *to ~ on o upon*, mejorar, perfeccionar.

improvement (-mønt) *s.* mejoramiento, perfeccionamiento. 2 mejora, adelanto, progreso. 3 MED. mejoría. 4 aprovechamiento. 5 explotación, urbanización.

improvidence (impra·vidøns) *s.* imprevisión, descuido.

improvident (-nt) *adj.* impróvido, imprevisor, descuidado.

improvisation (impraviśei·shøn) *s.* improvisación.

improvisator (-tø^r) *s.* improvisador.

improvise (to) (imprøvai·ś) *tr.-intr.* improvisar.

imprudence (impru·døns) *s.* imprudencia.

imprudent (-nt) *adj.* imprudente.

impuberate (impiu·børeit) *adj.* impúber.

impudence (-døns) *s.* aplomo, atrevimiento, impudencia, descaro, desfachatez, insolencia.

impudent (-dønt) *adj.* atrevido, impudente, descarado, insolente.

impudicity (impiudi·siti) *s.* impudicicia, impudicia.

impugn (to) (impiu·n) *tr.* impugnar; poner en tela de juicio.

impugnment (-mønt) *s.* impugnación.

impuissant (impui·sant) *adj.* impotente.

impulse (i·mpøls) *s.* impulso. 2 impulsión; ímpetu.

impulsion (impø·lshøn) *s.* impulsión, impulso.

impulsive (impø·lsiv) *adj.-s.* impulsivo.

impunity (impiu·niti) *s.* impunidad.

impure (impiu·ø^r) *adj.* impuro.

impurity (-riti) *s.* impureza.

imputable (-tabøl) *adj.* adj. imputable, achacable.

impute (to) (impiu·t) *tr.* imputar.

in (in) *prep.* en, con, de, dentro de, durante, mientras, entre, por: ~ *a drawer*, en un cajón; ~ *April*, en abril; *cut ~ two*, partido en dos; ~ *a husky voice*, con voz ronca, *dressed ~ black*, vestido de negro; ~ *an instant*, en un instante, dentro de un instante; ~ *deference to him*, por deferencia hacia él; ~ *the morning*, por la mañana; ~ *the meantime*, mientras, entre tanto; *one ~ a thousand*, uno entre mil. 2 ~ *so far as*, en lo que, hasta donde. 3 ~ *that*, en que; por cuanto. 4 *adj.* interior, entrante; de dentro. 5 encendido [luz, etc.]. 6 *to be ~ with*, tener influencia con.

7 *adv.* dentro, adentro; en casa; en el poder; en su turno: *to be ~*, estar en casa, en la oficina, etc.; ~ *here*, aquí dentro; ~ *there*, allí dentro. 8 *to be ~ for*, estar comprometido, destinado o expuesto a.

9 *s.* rincón, recodo, recoveco: *ins and outs*, recovecos, interioridades, pormenores.

in abreviatura de INCH o INCHES.

inability (inabi·liti) *s.* incapacidad, impotencia. *2* inhabilidad, incompetencia.
inaccessibility (inæksesibi·liti) *s.* inaccesibilidad.
inaccessible (inækse·sibøl) *adj.* inaccesible.
inaccuracy (inæ·kiurasi) *s.* inexactitud, incorrección, error.
inaction (inæ·kshøn) *s.* inacción.
inactive (-tiv) *adj.* inactivo. *2* ocioso. *3* indolente, perezoso.
inactivity (inækti·viti) *s.* inactividad. *2* ociosidad.
inadaptable (inadæ·ptabøl) *adj.* inadaptable.
inadequacy (inæ·dikuisi) *s.* falta de adecuación. *2* desproporción. *3* insuficiencia.
inadequate (-kuit) *adj.* inadecuado. *2* insuficiente.
inadmissible (inædmi·sibøl) *adj.* inadmisible.
inadvertence, -cy (inædvø·^rtøns, -si) *s.* inadvertencia. *2* distracción, falta de atención.
inadvertent (-ønt) *adj.* inadvertido [que no advierte]. *2* distraído, negligente, descuidado. *3* dicho o hecho sin poner atención, al descuido.
inadvisable (inædvai·šabøl) *adj.* poco aconsejable o prudente.
inalienable (inei·liønabøl) *adj.* inalienable.
inalterable (ino·lterabøl) *adj.* inalterable.
inamorata (inæmora·tæ) *s.* enamorada, novia.
inane (inei·n) *adj.* inane. *2* mentecato, sandio. *3 s.* el vacío, el espacio infinito.
inanimate (d (inæ·nimit(id) *adj.* inanimado. *2* exánime.
inanition (inani·shøn) *s.* inanición.
inanity (inæ·niti) *s.* inanidad, vaciedad, sandez.
inappetence (inæ·pitens) *s.* inapetencia.
inapplicable (inæ·plicabøl) *adj.* inaplicable; inadecuado.
inapposite (inæ·pošit) *adj.* inadecuado, poco apropiado.
inappreciable (inæpri·shiabøl) *adj.* inapreciable, inestimable. *2* inapreciable, imperceptible.
inapproachable (inæprou·chabøl) *adj.* inabordable, inaccesible. *2* sin rival, sin par.
inappropriate (inæprou·priit) *adj.* impropio, inadecuado, no apropiado.
inapt (inæ·pt) *s.* no apto. *2* inepto.
inaptitude (-itiud) *s.* ineptitud. *2* insuficiencia.
inarticulate (ina^rti·kiulit) *adj.* inarticulado.
inartistic (ina^rti·stik) *adj.* no artístico. *2* falto de gusto artístico.
inasmuch as (inašmø·ch aš) *loc.* considerando que, visto que, puesto que. *2* tanto como, hasta donde.
inattention (inate·nshøn) *s.* desatención. *2* distracción, inadvertencia.
inattentive (-tiv) *adj.* desatento. *2* distraído, descuidado.
inaudible (ino·dibøl) *adj.* inaudible.
inaugural (ino·giural) *adj.* inaugural.
inaugurate (to) (ino·giureit) *tr.* inaugurar. *2* instalar, dar posesión solemnemente.
inauguration (inogiurei·shøn) *s.* inauguración. *2* toma de posesión solemne.
inauspicious (inospi·shøs) *adj.* poco propicio, desfavorable, siniestro, infeliz.
inborn (i·nbo^rn) *adj.* innato, ingénito, connatural.
inbred (i·nbred) *p. p.* de INBREED. *2 adj.* innato, ingénito. *3* nacido de padres de una misma raza.
inbreed (to) (inbri·d) *tr.* producir, crear [en]. *2* criar o engendrar sin mezcla de razas. ¶ Pret. y p. p.: *inbred.*
Inca (i·nka) *adj.* incaico. *2 s.* inca.
incalculable (inkæ·kiulabøl) *adj.* incalculable. *2* imprevisible. *3* incierto.

incandescence, -cy (inkænde·søns, -si) *s.* incandescencia.
incandescent (-ønt) *adj.* incandescente.
incantation (inkæntei·shøn) *s.* encantamiento, conjuro, sortilegio.
incapability (inkeipabi·liti) *s.* incapacidad.
incapable (inkei·pabøl) *adj.* incapaz. | No tiene el sentido de falto de cabida.
incapacitate (to) (inkapæ·siteit) *tr.* incapacitar, inhabilitar.
incapacitation (-ei·shøn) *s.* incapacitación.
incapacity (-siti) *s.* incapacidad, inhabilidad; simpleza. *2* DER. incapacidad.
incarcerate (to) (inka·^rsøreit) *tr.* encarcelar, encerrar.
incarceration (-ei·shøn) *s.* encarcelamiento, encierro, prisión.
incarnadine (inka·^rnadin) *adj.* encarnado [de color de carne]; encarnadino.
incarnate (inka·^rnit) *adj.* encarnado, personificado: ~ *devil,* demonio encarnado.
incarnate (to) (inca·^rneit) *tr.* tomar la forma o el cuerpo de. *2* encarnar, personificar.
incarnation (-ei·shøn) *s.* encarnación [del Verbo]. *2* encarnación, personificación.
incautious (inco·shøs) *adj.* incauto, imprudente.
incautiousness (-nis) *s.* falta de cautela, descuido, imprudencia.
incendiarism (inse·ndiarišm) *s.* incendio intencionado [delito].
incendiary (inse·ndieri) *s.* incendiario. *2* agitador.
incense (i·nsens) *s.* incienso: ~ *boat,* naveta.
incense (to) (inse·ns) *tr.* incensar. *2* exasperar, irritar, enfurecer, encolerizar.
incensory (-ori) *s.* incensario.
incentive (-tiv) *adj.* incitativo. *2 s.* incentivo, aliciente.
inception (inse·pshøn) *s.* principio, comienzo.
inceptive (-tiv) *adj.* incipiente. *2* incoativo.
incertitude (inse·^rtitiud) *s.* incertidumbre.
incessant (inse·sant) *adj.* incesante, continuo.
incest (i·nsest) *s.* incesto.
incestuous (inse·schuøs) *adj.* incestuoso.
inch (inch) *s.* pulgada [2,54 cm.]; fig. pequeña cantidad: *by inches,* gradualmente; *a poquitos; every ~ a man,* todo un hombre; ~ *by ~,* pulgada por pulgada, palmo a palmo.
inch (to) *intr.* moverse poco a poco: *to ~ ahead,* avanzar poco a poco.
inchmeal (-mıl) *s. adv.* poco a poco.
inchoate (i·nkouit) *adj.* incipiente, en embrión.
inchoate (to) (i·nkoueit) *tr.* incoar, principiar.
inchoative (inkou·ativ) *adj.* incipiente. *2* GRAM. incoativo.
inchworm (i·nchuø^rm) *s.* ENT. geómetra.
incidence (i·nsidøns) *s.* GEOM., FÍS. incidencia. *2* acto o manera de afectar o modificar.
incident (-t) *adj.* incidente. *2* concomitante. *3* incidental, fortuito. *4 s.* incidente. *5* casualidad. *6* suceso, ocurrencia.
incidental (inside·ntal) *adj.* incidental, accidental. *2* casual, contingente. *3* inherente, concomitante. *4 s. pl.* imprevisto.
incinerate (to) (insi·nøreit) *tr.* incinerar.
incineration (-ei·shøn) *s.* incineración.
incipience (insi·piøns) *s.* principio, comienzo.
incipient (-ønt) *adj.* incipiente.
incise (to) (insai·š) *tr.* cortar, hacer incisión; grabar, tallar.
incision (insi·ȳøn) *s.* incisión.

incisive (insai·siv) *adj.* incisivo. 2 agudo, penetrante.
incisor (insai·šøʳ) *adj.-s.* ANAT. incisivo [diente].
incitation (insitei·shøn) *s.* incitación; instigación.
incite (to) (insai·t) *tr.* incitar, aguijonear, estimular.
incitement (-mønt) *s.* incitación, incitamiento. 2 incentivo, estímulo.
incivility (insivi·liti) *s.* incivilidad, descortesía.
inclemency (inkle·mønsi) *s.* inclemencia. 2 intemperie. 3 desgracia.
inclement (-ønt) *adj.* inclemente. 2 tempestuoso. 3 contrario, adverso. 4 severo, cruel.
inclination (inklinei·shøn) *s.* inclinación [en todas sus acepciones]. 2 declive, pendiente. 3 disposición, estado, afecto.
incline (i·nklain) *s.* declive, pendiente, cuesta.
incline (to) (inklai·n) *tr.* inclinar. 2 bajar, doblar [la cabeza, etc.]. 3 *intr.* inclinarse. 4 bajar, hacer pendiente. 5 propender, tender. 6 tirar [a un color].
inclined (-d) *adj.* inclinado. 2 propenso.
inclose (to) (inklou·š) *tr.* ENCLOSE.
inclosure (-ȳøʳ) *s.* ENCLOSURE.
include (to) (inklu·d) *tr.* incluir.
inclusion (-ȳøn) *s.* inclusión. 2 cosa incluida. 3 carta que acompaña a otra.
inclusive (-siv) *adj.* inclusivo, que incluye o contiene. 2 *adv.* inclusive.
incoercible (inkou·ʳsibøl) *adj.* incoercible.
incognito (inka·gnitou) *adj.-s.* incógnito. 2 *adv.* de incógnito.
incognizable (-nišabøl) *adj.* incognoscible; no reconocible.
incoherence, -cy (inkouji·røns, -si) *s.* incoherencia, inconexión, incongruencia.
incoherent (-ønt) *adj.* incoherente, inconexo.
incombustibility (inkømbøstibi·liti) *s.* incombustibilidad.
incombustible (inkømbø·stibøl) *adj.* incombustible.
income (i·nkøm) *s.* entrada, ingreso. 2 ingresos, renta, utilidades: ~ *tax,* impuesto sobre la renta.
incoming (-ing) *adj.* entrante, que está por llegar. 3 que aumenta [beneficio]; que empieza [año, etc.].
incommensurable (inkøme·nshurabøl) *adj.* inconmensurable.
incommensurate (-it) *adj.* inconmensurable. 2 inadecuado, desproporcionado.
incommode (to) (inkømou·d) *tr.* incomodar, molestar, desacomodar.
incommodious (-iøs) *adj.* incómodo, inconveniente, molesto.
incommodity (-iti) *s.* incomodidad, inconveniencia.
incommunicable (inkømiu·nikabøl) *adj.* incomunicable; indecible.
incommunicative (inkømiu·nikativ) *adj.* reservado, poco comunicativo; insociable.
incommutable (inkømiu·tabøl) *adj.* inconmutable.
incomparable (inka·mparabøl) *adj.* incomparable, sin igual, sin par.
incompatibility (inkømpætibi·liti) *s.* incompatibilidad, contrariedad.
incompatible (inkømpæ·tibøl) *adj.* incompatible, contrario.
incompetence, -cy (inka·mpitøns, -si) *s.* incompetencia, inhabilidad. 2 DER. incapacidad.

incompetent (-t) *adj.* incompetente, inhábil, inepto. 2 DER. incapaz.
incomplete (inkømplı·t) *adj.* incompleto.
incomprehensibility (inkamprijensibi·liti) *s.* incomprensibilidad.
incomprehensible (inkamprije·nsibøl) *adj.* incomprensible, impenetrable.
incomprehension (-shøn) *s.* falta de comprensión.
incomprehensive (-siv) *adj.* no comprensivo, limitado, de poco alcance.
incompressible (inkømpre·sibøl) *adj.* incompresible.
inconceivable (inkønsı·vabøl) *adj.* inconcebible. 2 increíble, inimaginable.
inconclusive (inkønklu·siv) *adj.* no concluyente o decisivo; que no convence.
incondite (inkø·ndit) *adj.* tosco, mal acabado.
incongruent (inka·ngruønt) *adj.* incongruente, incongruo. 2 incoherente. 3 inadecuado.
incongruity (inkøngru·iti) *s.* incongruencia, inconexión, incoherencia.
incongruous (inka·ngruøs) *adj.* incongruente, incongruo, inconexo, incoherente. 2 disconforme. 3 impropio, inadecuado.
inconsequence (sikuøns) *s.* inconsecuencia, falta de lógica.
inconsequent (-t) *adj.* inconsecuente, inconsiguiente, ilógico.
inconsequential (inkansikuen·shal) *adj.* inconsiguiente. 2 de poca importancia, sin importancia.
inconsiderable (inkønsi·dørabøl) *adj.* insignificante.
inconsiderate (-it) *adj.* inconsiderado, irreflexivo, precipitado. 2 desconsiderado.
inconsideration (inkønsidøre·shøn) *s.* inconsideración. 2 falta de consideración.
inconsistency (inkønsi·stønsi) *s.* incompatibilidad, contradicción, disconformidad, incoherencia. 2 inconsecuencia. 3 inconsistencia.
inconsistent (-nt) *adj.* incompatible, contradictorio, disconforme, incoherente. 2 inconsecuente. 3 inconsistente.
inconsolable (inkønsou·labøl) *adj.* inconsolable.
inconsonance (inka·nsønans) *s.* discordancia, disconformidad.
inconspicuous (inkønspi·kuøs) *adj.* poco visible o notable.
inconstancy (inka·nstansi) *s.* inconstancia.
inconstant (inka·nstant) *adj.* inconstante.
incontestable (inkønte·stabøl) *adj.* incontestable, inconcuso, indiscutible, incontrovertible.
incontinence (inka·ntinøns) *s.* incontinencia.
incontinent (-t) *adj.* incontinente.
incontrollable (inkøntrou·labøl) *adj.* ingobernable, irrefrenable. 2 incontrolable.
incontrovertible (inkøntrøvø·ʳtibøl) *adj.* incontrovertible, indisputable.
inconvenience (inkønvi·niøns) *s.* inconveniencia; inoportunidad. 2 incomodidad, molestia, engorro, inconveniente.
inconvenience (to) *tr.* incomodar, molestar, estorbar.
inconvenient (-t) *adj.* inconveniente, impropio, inoportuno. 2 incómodo, molesto.
inconvincible (incønvi·nsibøl) *adj.* inconvencible.
incorporate (inkøʳpørit) *adj.* incorporado, unido íntimamente. 2 constituido en cuerpo, corporación o sociedad. 3 incorpóreo.
incorporate (to) (-reit) *tr.* dar cuerpo o forma material. 2 incorporar, unir íntimamente; combi-

nar, reunir en un todo. *3* comprender, incluir. *4* constituir en corporación o sociedad. *5 intr.* incorporarse, unirse, mezclarse. *6* constituirse en corporación o sociedad.

incorporation (inkoᵣpørei·shøn) *s.* incorporación, unión. *2* asociación; formación de un cuerpo, gremio, corporación, etc. *3* acción de dar forma corpórea.

incorporeal (inkoᵣpou·rial) *adj.* incorpóreo.

incorrect (inkøre·kt) *adj.* incorrecto. *2* inexacto.

incorrectness (-nis) *s.* incorrección. *2* inexactitud.

incorrigible (inka·ridÿibøl) *adj.* incorregible.

incorrupt (inkørø·pt) *adj.* incorrupto. *2* honrado, íntegro.

incorruptibility (ibi·liti) *s.* incorruptibilidad.

incorruptible (-ibøl) *adj.* incorruptible.

incorruption (-shøn) *s.* incorrupción.

incrassate (to) (inkra·seit) *tr.* espesar, encrasar.

incrassation (-sei·shøn) *s.* espesamiento.

increase (inkrɪ·s) *s.* aumento, acrecentamiento, incremento: *to be on the* ~, ir en aumento. *2* progenie. *3* productos [de la tierra]. *4* ganancia, interés. *5* creciente [de la luna].

increase (to) *tr.* aumentar, acrecentar, incrementar. *2* abultar, agrandar. *3 intr.* aumentarse, acrecentarse, crecer, multiplicarse.

increasingly (-ingli) *adv.* en aumento, crecientemente.

incredibility (inkredibi·liti) *s.* incredibilidad.

incredible (inkre·dibøl) *adj.* increíble.

indredulity (inkridiu·liti) *s.* incredulidad.

incredulous (inkre·diuløs) *adj.* incrédulo.

increment (i·nkrimøn) *s.* incremento, aumento: *unearned* ~, plusvalía. *2* MAT. incremento.

incriminate (to) (inkri·mineit) *tr.* incriminar, acriminar.

incrimination (-ei·shøn) *s.* incriminación, acriminación.

incrust (to) (inkrø·st) *tr.* incrustar. *2* encostrar.

incrustation (inkrøstei·shøn) *s.* incrustación. *2* encostradura, costra.

incubate (to) (i·nkiubeit) *tr.* incubar. *2* empollar. *3 intr.* estar en incubación.

incubation (-ei·shøn) *s.* incubación.

incubator (i·nkiubeitøᵣ) *s.* incubador. *2* incubadora.

incubus (i·nkiubøs) *s.* incubo. *2* MED. pesadilla.

inculcate (to) (inkø·lkeit) *tr.* inculcar.

inculcation (-ei·shøn) *s.* inculcación.

inculpability (inkølpabi·liti) *s.* inculpabilidad.

inculpable (inkø·lpabøl) *adj.* inculpable, inocente.

inculpate (to) (inkø·lpeit) *tr.* inculpar, acriminar.

inculpation (-ei·shøn) *s.* inculpación.

incult (inkø·lt) *adj.* inculto.

incumbency (inkø·mbønsi) *s.* incumbencia. *2* goce de un empleo o de un beneficio eclesiástico.

incumbent (-ønt) *adj.* extendido o reclinado. *2* que incumbe: *to be* ~ *on* o *upon one,* incumbir a uno. *3 s.* titular de un cargo eclesiástico [párroco, etc.].

incunabula (inkiunæ·biula) *s. pl.* orígenes, cuna. *2* incunables.

incur (to) (inkø·ᵣ) *tr.* incurrir en, atraerse. *2* contraer [una deuda]. ¶ Pret. y p. p.: *incurred;* ger.: *-rring.*

incurable (inkiu·rabøl) *adj.* incurable.

incurious (inkiu·riøs) *adj.* poco curioso, que no se interesa, indiferente. *2* poco interesante.

incursion (inkø·ᵣshøn) *s.* incursión, correría.

incurvate (inkø·ᵣveit) *adj.* encorvado, torcido.

incurvate (to) *tr.* encorvar, torcer.

incus (i·nkøs) *s.* ANAT. yunque [del oído].

incuse (inkiu·s) *adj.* incuso.

indebted (inde·tid) *adj.* endeudado. *2* deudor [de un favor, etc.], obligado, reconocido.

indebtedness (-nis) *s.* deuda; obligación, agradecimiento.

indecency (indi·sønsi) *s.* indecencia. *2* indecoro.

indecent (-nt) *adj.* indecente. *2* indecoroso.

indecipherable (-sai·førabøl) *adj.* indescifrable.

indecision (-si·ÿøn) *s.* indecisión, irresolución.

indecisive (-sai·šiv) *adj.* no decisivo. *2* indeciso, irresoluto. *3* incierto, dudoso.

indeclinable (-klai·nabøl) *adj.* indeclinable.

indecorous (inde·kørøs) *adj.* indecoroso. *2* contrario a la etiqueta, inconveniente.

indecorum (indiko·røm) *s.* indecoro. *2* inconveniencia, mala educación.

indeed (indɪ·d) *adv.* realmente, verdaderamente, de veras, en verdad. *2* sí tal, claro está.

indefatigable (indifæ·tigabøl) *adj.* infatigable, incansable.

indefeasible (-fɪ·sibøl) *adj.* DER. inabrogable, irrevocable.

indefectible (-fe·ktibøl) *adj.* indefectible, indeficiente. *2* sin defecto, sin tacha.

indefensible (-fe·nsibøl) *adj.* indefendible, insostenible.

indefinable (-fai·nabøl) *adj.* indefinible.

indefinite (inde·finit) *adj.* indefinido. *2* indeterminado, impreciso. *3* GRAM. indefinido.

indehiscence (indiji·søns) *s.* BOT. indehiscencia.

indehiscent (-nt) *adj.* BOT. indehiscente.

indeliberate(d (-li·børit(id) *adj.* indeliberado, impremeditado.

indelible (indi·libøl) *adj.* indeleble.

indelicacy (inde·likasi) *s.* falta de delicadeza. *2* indecoro, grosería.

indelicate (-likit) *adj.* indelicado, falta de delicadeza. *2* indecoroso. *3* grosero.

indemnification (indemnifikei·shøn) *s.* indemnización, resarcimiento, reparación.

indemnify (to) (inde·mnifai) *tr.* indemnizar, resarcir, compensar. *2* preservar de pérdida o daño. ¶ Pret. y p. p.: *indemnified.*

indemnity (-ti) *s.* indemnidad, seguridad contra pérdida o daño. *2* indemnización.

indent (inde·nt) *s.* mella, muesca, die ite, entalladura; depresión, surco. *2* IMPR. sangría. *3* COM. pedido del extranjero. *4* INDENTURE.

indent (to) (inde·nt) *tr.* mellar, dentar, hacer muescas en. *2* estampar, hacer depresiones en. IMPR. sangrar.

indentation (indentei·shøn) *s.* mella, muesca, diente, entrada [en el borde de una cosa]. *2* hundimiento, depresión [en una superficie]. *3* IMPR. sangría.

indented (inde·ntid) *adj.* mellado, dentado, etc. *2* BOT. dentado. *3* BLAS. endentado.

indention (-shøn) *s.* mella, muesca, diente, hundimiento, depresión. *2* IMPR. sangría.

indenture (-chøᵣ) *s.* carta partida por a, b, c. *2* escritura, documento [esp. por duplicado]. *3* contrato de aprendizaje.

indenture (to) *tr.* escriturar.

independence (indipe·ndøns) *s.* independencia. *2* estado del que se mantiene a sí mismo. *3* holgura, posición acomodada.

independent (-nt) *adj.* independiente. *2* que se mantiene a sí mismo. *3* altivo. *4* acomodado, que tiene medios suficientes.

indescribable (indiskrai·babøl) *adj.* indescriptible.

indestructibility (indistrøktibi·liti) *s.* indestructibilidad.

indestructible (indistrø·ktibøl) *adj.* indestructible.

indeterminate (inditø·ʳminit) *adj.* indeterminado.

indetermination (inditøʳminei·shøn) *s.* indeterminación. *2* duda, suspensión, indecisión, fluctuación.

index (i·ndeks), *pl.* **indexes** o **indices** *s.* índice [lista; aguja indicadora; relación entre valores]. *2* MAT. índice, exponente. *3* indicio, señal. *4* IMPR. manecilla. *5 adj.-s.* ANAT. índice [dedo].

index (to) *tr.* poner en un índice. *2* proveer de índice [lista].

India (i·ndia) *n. pr.* GEOGR. India. *2* ~ *ink*, tinta china. *3* ~ *rubber*, caucho, goma elástica, goma de borrar.

indiaman (-mæn) *s.* buque que hace el comercio con la India.

Indian (i·ndian) *s.* indio [de Asia o América]. *2 adj.* indio, indiano, índico: ~ *file*, fila india; ~ *Ocean*, Océano Índico; ~ *summer* (E.U.), veranillo de San Martín. *3* ~ *corn*, maíz; ~ *meal*, harina de maíz.

indicant (i·ndikant) *adj.-s.* indicador.

indicate (i·ndikeit) *tr.* indicar.

indication (-ei·shøn) *s.* indicación. *2* indicio, señal.

indicative (indi·kativ) *adj.* indicativo, indicador. *2* GRAM. *adj.-s.* indicativo.

indicator (i·ndikeitøʳ) *s.* indicador, señalador. *2* índice, aguja. *3* QUÍM. indicador.

indicatory (i·ndikatori) *adj.* indicativo, demostrativo.

indicia (indi·šia) *s. pl.* indicios, señales.

indict (to) (indai·t) *tr.* acusar [ante el juez]. *2* procesar, encausar, enjuiciar.

indictable (-abøl) *adj.* procesable, enjuiciable.

indictment (-mønt) *s.* acusación, procesamiento. *2* auto de acusación formulado por el Gran Jurado.

Indies (i·ndiš) *s. pl.* GEOGR. Indias: *West* ~, Indias Occidentales, Antillas.

indifference (indi·førøns) *s.* indiferencia. *2* desinterés, desapego. *3* mediocridad. *4* poca importancia, insignificancia.

indifferent (-nt) *adj.* indiferente. *2* imparcial, neutral. *3* mediocre, ordinario: ni bueno ni malo. *4* sin importancia.

indifferentism (-išm) *s.* indiferentismo.

indigence (i·ndiyøns) *s.* indigencia.

indigenous (indi·ŷinøs) *adj.* indígena. *2* autóctono. *3* innato, nativo, natural.

indigent (i·ndidŷønt) *adj.* indigente.

indigested (indidŷe·stid) *adj.* mal digerido. *2* mal ordenado, confuso.

indigestible (-ibøl) *adj.* indigesto.

indigestion (-chøn) *s.* indigestión.

indignant (indi·gnant) *adj.* indignado.

indignation (indignei·shøn) *s.* indignación.

indignity (indi·gniti) *s.* indignidad. *2* ultraje, afrenta.

indigo (i·ndigou) *adj.* índigo; de añil. *2* añil, índigo [planta y color].

indirect (indire·kt) *adj.* indirecto. *2* oblicuo, torcido. *3* desleal, engañoso.

indirection (-shøn) *s.* rodeo, tortuosidad. *2* medio indirecto. *3* conducta torcida.

indiscernible (indisø·ʳnibøl) *adj.* no discernible, imperceptible.

indiscreet (indiskri·t) *adj.* indiscreto. *2* imprudente, torpe; impolítico, poco hábil u oportuno.

indiscrete (-kri·t) *adj.* compacto, continuo, no dividido o separado.

indiscretion (-kre·shøn) *s.* indiscreción. *2* imprudencia, torpeza.

indiscriminate (kri·minit) *adj.* que no hace distinción, indistinto, confuso; promiscuo.

indiscrimination (-ei·shøn) *s.* indistinción, falta de distinción o separación.

indispensable (-pe·nsabøl) *adj.* indispensable, imprescindible, forzoso.

indispose (to) (-pou·š) *tr.* indisponer. *2* disponer en contra, desinclinar.

indisposition (-pøši·shøn) *s.* indisposición, enfermedad. *2* aversión, repugnancia, falta de inclinación.

indisputable (indi·spiutabøl) *adj.* indisputable, indiscutible, incontestable.

indissolubility (-saliubi·liti) *s.* indisolubilidad. *2* insolubilidad.

indissoluble (-sa·liubøl) *adj.* indisoluble. *2* insoluble; infusible.

indisolvable (-sa·lvabøl) *adj.* indisoluble.

indistinct (indisti·nkt) *adj.* indistinto. *2* confuso, borroso. *3* vago, obscuro.

indistinction (-kshøn) *s.* indistinción. *2* confusión, vaguedad, obscuridad.

indistinguishable (-gwishabøl) *adj.* indistinguible.

indite (to) (indai·t) *tr.* redactar, componer, escribir.

indium (i·ndiøm) *s.* QUÍM. indio.

individual (indivi·dŷual) *adj.* invidiaul, individuo, particular, peculiar. *2 s.* individuo.

individualism (-išm) *s.* individualismo.

individuality (individŷuæ·liti) *s.* individualidad.

individualize (to) (indivi·dŷualaiš) *tr.* individualizar.

individuate (-dŷueit) *adj.* individuado.

individuate (to) *tr.* individuar.

indivisibility (indivišibi·liti) *s.* indivisibilidad.

indivisible (indivi·šibøl) *adj.* indivisible.

indivision (-shøn) *s.* indivisión.

Indo-Chinese (i·ndou-chaini·š) *adj.-s.* indochino.

indocil(e (inda·sil) *adj.* indócil.

indocility (indøsi·liti) *s.* indocilidad.

indoctrinate (to) (inda·ktrineit) *tr.* adoctrinar.

Indo-European *adj.-s.* indoeuropeo.

indolence (i·ndøløns) *s.* indolencia.

indolent (-nt) *adj.* indolente.

indomitable (inda·mitabøl) *adj.* indomable, indómito.

indomitably (-bli) *adv.* indomablemente.

indoor (indo·ʳ) *adj.* interior, interno, de puertas adentro.

indoors (indo·ʳš) *adv.* en, o dentro de, la casa o edificio; en local cerrado.

indorse (to), indorsee, indorsement, indorser ENDORSE (TO), ENDORSEE, ENDORSEMENT, ENDORSER.

indraft, indraught (i·ndraft) *s.* atracción o corriente hacia el interior; absorción, aspiración.

indrawn (i·ndron) *adj.* sorbido, aspirado. *2* abstraido, introspectivo.

indubitable (indiu·bitabøl) *adj.* indubitable, indudable, indiscutible.

induce (to) (indiu·s) *tr.* inducir, instigar. *2* LÓG., ELECT. inducir. *3* producir, causar.

inducement (-mønt) *s.* inducimiento. *2* móvil, incentivo, aliciente.

induct (to) (indø·kt) *tr.* instalar [en un cargo]. *2* introducir. *3* iniciar [en]. *4* MIL. alistar.

inductance (-ans) *s.* ELECT. inductancia.
induction (-shøn) *s.* instalación [en un cargo]. *2* aducción [de pruebas, etc.]. *3* LÓG., ELECT. inducción. *4* MIL. alistamiento.
inductive (-iv) *adj.* inductivo, ilativo. *2* introductor. *3* ELECT. inductivo, inductor.
inductor (-o^r) *s.* ECLES. instalador. *2* ELECT. inductor.
indue (to) (indiu·) *tr.* ponerse, vestirse. *2* vestir, investir, dotar.
indulge (to) (indø·ldỹ) *tr.* satisfacer [pasiones, gustos, etc.]. *2* complacer; dar gusto a; mimar,consentir. *3* COM. dar prórroga a. *4 intr. to ~ in*, entregarse, abandonarse a, permitirse.
indulgence, -cy (-øns, -si) *s.* satisfacción [de las pasiones, gustos, etc.], exceso, intemperancia. *2* indulgencia, lenidad; mimo. *3* COM. prórroga. *4* ECLES. indulgencia.
indulgent (-ønt) *adj.* indulgente.
indult (indø·lt) *s.* ECLES. indulto, dispensa.
indurate (i·ndiurit) *adj.* endurecido. *2* empedernido.
indurate (to) (-reit) *tr.* endurecer. *2* empedernir. *3 intr.* endurecerse, empedernirse.
induration (-ei·shøn) *s.* endurecimiento. *2* dureza de corazón. *3* MED. induración.
Indus (i·ndøs) *n. pr.* GEOGR. Indo.
industrial (indø·strial) *adj.* industrial. *2 s.* industrial; artesano.
industrialism (-išm) *s.* industrialismo.
industrialize (to) (-laiš) *tr.* industrializar.
industrious (-triøs) *adj.* industrioso, hacendoso, laborioso, aplicado.
industry (i·ndøstri) *s.* industria. *2* diligencia, laboriosidad, aplicación.
indwell (to) (indue·l) *tr.* residir, morar en.
inebriate (ini·briit) *adj.* ebrio. *2 s.* borracho, beodo.
inebriate (to) (ini·brieit) *tr.* embriagar, emborrachar.
inedited (ine·ditid) *adj.* inédito.
ineffable (ine·fabøl) *adj.* inefable, indecible.
ineffaceable (inefei·sabøl) *adj.* imborrable, indeleble.
ineffective (inefe·ktiv) *adj.* ineficaz, sin efecto. *2* inútil, incapaz.
ineffectual (-chual) *adj.* ineficaz. *2* inútil, vano, infructuoso.
inefficacious (inefikei·shøs) *adj.* ineficaz.
inefficacy (ine·fikasi) *s.* ineficacia.
inefficiency (inefi·shønsi) *s.* ineficacia. *2* falta de aptitud o capacidad. *3* mal rendimiento.
inefficient (inefi·shøn) *adj.* ineficaz. *2* incapaz. *3* de mal rendimiento.
inelastic (inilæ·stik) *adj.* falto de elasticidad.
inelegance, -cy (ine·ligans, -si) *s.* falta de elegancia.
inelegant (-t) *adj.* inelegante.
ineligible (ine·lidỹibøl) *adj.* inelegible. *2* poco deseable o ventajoso.
ineluctable (inilø·ktabøl) *adj.* ineluctable.
inept (ine·pt) inepto, no apto. *2* inadecuado, impropio. *3* absurdo.
ineptitude (-titiud) *s.* ineptitud, incapacidad. *2* absurdidad.
inequality (inikua·liti) *s.* desigualdad. *2* disparidad, desproporción. *3* insuficiencia.
inequitable (ine·kuitabøl) *adj.* injusto.
ineradicable (iniræ·dikabøl) *adj.* que no se puede desarraigar, indeleble, permanente.
inerrable (ine·rabøl) *adj.* infalible, seguro.
inert (inø·^{r}t) *adj.* inerte.

inertia (inø·^{r}shia) *s.* inercia.
inertness (inø·^{r}tnis) *s.* flojedad, falta de actividad.
inescapable (ineskei·pabøl) *adj.* ineludible.
inestimable (ine·stimabøl) *adj.* inestimable, inapreciable.
inevitable (ine·vitabøl) *adj.* inevitable, ineludible.
inexact (inegšæ·kt) *adj.* inexacto.
inexactitude (-titiud) *s.* inexactitud.
inexcusable (inekskiu·šabøl) *adj.* inexcusable, imperdonable.
inexhausted (inegšo·stid) *adj.* inexhausto.
inexhaustible (inegšo·stibøl) *adj.* inagotable.
inexistence (inegši·støns) *s.* inexistencia.
inexistent (-tønt) *adj.* inexistente.
inexorability (ineksørabi·liti) *s.* inexorabilidad.
inexorable (ine·ksørabøl) *adj.* inexorable; inflexible.
inexpedience, -cy (inekspi·diøns, -si) *s.* inoportunidad, improcedencia, impropiedad.
inexpedient (-iønt) *adj.* inoportuno, improcedente, impropio.
inexpensive (inekspe·nsiv) *adj.* barato, poco costoso.
inexperience (-pi·riøns) *s.* inexperiencia, impericia.
inexperienced (-pi·riønst) *adj.* inexperto.
inexpert (-pø·^{r}t) *adj.* inexperto, imperito.
inexplicable (ine·ksplikabøl) *adj.* inexplicable.
inexplicably (-plikabli) *adv.* inexplicablemente.
inexpressible (inekspre·sibøl) *adj.* inexpresable, indecible.
inexpressibly (-bli) *adv.* indeciblemente.
inexpressive (-iv) *adj.* inexpresivo.
inexpugnable (-pø·gnabøl) *adj.* inexpugnable.
inextensible (-te·nsibøl) *adj.* inextensible.
inextensive (-te·nsiv) *adj.* inextenso.
inextinguishable (-ti·ngwishabøl) *adj.* inextinguible, inapagable.
inextricable (ine·kstrikabøl) *adj.* inextricable.
infallibility (infælibi·liti) *s.* infalibilidad.
infallible (infæ·libøl) *adj.* infalible.
infamous (i·nfamøs) *adj.* infame.
infamy (i·nfami) *s.* infamia, ignominia, deshonor.
infancy (i·nfansi) *s.* infancia, niñez. *2* DER. menor edad.
infant (i·nfant) *s.* infante, criatura, niño. *2 adj.-s.* DER. menor [de edad]. *3 adj.* infantil; pequeño, no desarrollado.
infanta (infa·nta) *s.* infanta [de España o Portugal].
infante (-ei) *s.* infante [de España o Portugal].
infanticidal (infæntisai·dal) *adj.* infanticida.
infanticide (infæ·ntisaid) *s.* infanticidio. *2* infanticida.
infantile (i·nfantil) *adj.* infantil. *2* aniñado, pueril.
infantilism (infa·ntilišm) *s.* infantilismo.
infantine (i·nfantin) *adj.* infantil, pueril.
infantry (-tri) *s.* MIL. infantería.
infarct (infa·^{r}kt) *s.* MED. infarto.
infatuate (to) (infæ·chueit) *tr.* entontecer. *2* enamorar o apasionar locamente.
infatuate(d (-it(id) *adj.* simple, bobo. *2* locamente enamorado o apasionado.
infatuation (-shøn) *s.* tontería, simpleza. *2* enamoramiento, apasionamiento.
infect (to) (infe·kt) *tr.* infectar. *2* inficionar, contaminar. *3* contagiar. *4* comunicar, llenar de [fe, entusiasmo, etc.].
infection (-shøn) *s.* infección. *2* contaminación. *3* contagio.

infectious (-shøs) *adj.* infeccioso. *2* contagioso; pedadizo.
infective (-tiv) *adj.* infectivo, infeccioso.
infelicitous (infili·sitøs) *adj.* desgraciado. *2* poco feliz o acertado; desatinado.
infelicity (-ti) *s.* infelicidad. *2* calidad de poco feliz o acertado; tontería, desatino.
infer (to) (infø·ʳ) *tr.* inferir, deducir, colegir. *2* argüir, probar, indicar. *3 intr.* hacer deducciones. ¶ Pret. y p. p.: *inferred;* ger.: -*rring.*
inference (i·nførøns) *s.* inferencia, ilación, deducción, conclusión.
inferior (infi·riøʳ) *adj.-s.* inferior.
inferiority (infiria·riti) *s.* inferioridad.
infernal (infø·ʳnal) *adj.* infernal.
inferno (infø·ʳnou) *s.* infierno.
infertile (infø·ʳtil) *adj.* infecundo, estéril.
infest (to) (infe·st) *tr.* infestar, plagar.
infestation (-ei·shøn) *s.* infestación.
infeudation (infiudei·shøn) *s.* infeudación.
infidel (i·nfidøl) *adj.-s.* infiel, gentil. *2* descreído.
infidelity (infide·liti) *s.* infidelidad. *2* descreimiento.
infield (i·nfild) *s.* terrenos de una finca rústica más inmediatos a los edificios. *2* BÉISBOL. losange.
infighting (i·nfaiting) *s.* BOX. cuerpo a cuerpo.
infiltrate (to) (infi·ltreit) *tr.* infiltrar. *2* infiltrarse en. *3 intr.* infiltrarse.
infiltration (-ei·shøn) *s.* infiltración.
infinite (i·nfinit) *adj.-s.* infinito: *the Infinite,* el Ser infinito, Dios.
infinitesimal (infinite·simal) *adj.* infinitesimal.
infinitive (infi·nitiv) *adj.-s.* GRAM. infinitivo.
infinitude (-iud) *s.* infinitud.
infinity (-i) *s.* infinidad, sin fin. *2* infinito.
infirm (infø·ʳm) *adj.* débil, vacilante. *3* inseguro, inestable. *4* enfermizo, achacoso.
infirmary (-ri) *s.* enfermería.
infirmity (-iti) *s.* enfermedad, dolencia, achaque. *2* flaqueza, debilidad. *3* defecto, imperfección.
infix (to) (infi·ks) *tr.* clavar, encajar. *2* imprimir, inculcar.
inflame (to) (inflei·m) *tr.* inflamar. *2* encolerizar. *3 intr.* inflamarse. *4* encolerizarse.
inflamed (-d) *adj.* inflamado. *2* encolerizado.
inflammable (inflæ·mabøl) *adj.* inflamable. *2* irascible.
inflammation (inflamei·shøn) *s.* inflamación. *2* irritación, cólera.
inflammatory (inflæ·matori) *adj.* inflamatorio.
inflate (to) (inflei·t) *tr.* inflar, hinchar.
inflated (-id) *adj.* inflado, hinchado, túmido. *2* hinchado [estilo].
inflating (-ing) *adj.* inflativo.
inflation (-ei·shøn) *s.* inflación, hinchazón. *2* ECON. inflación.
inflect (to) (infle·kt) *tr.* torcer, doblar, curvar. *2* modular [la voz]. *3* GRAM. modificar [una palabra] por inflexión.
inflection (-shøn) *s.* inflexión.
inflectional (-al) *adj.* flexional.
inflexibility (infleksibi·liti) *s.* inflexibilidad.
inflexible (infle·ksibøl) *adj.* inflexible.
inflexion *s.* INFLECTION.
inflexional *s.* INFLECTIONAL.
inflict (to) (infli·kt) *tr.* infligir, imponer.
infliction (-shøn) *s.* acción de infligir. *2* pena, castigo, sufrimiento.
inflictive (-tiv) *adj.* que inflige, punitivo.
inflorescence (inflore·søns) *s.* BOT. inflorescencia. *2* BOT. florescencia [época].

inflow (inflou·) *s.* afluencia, flujo; entrada.
inflow (to) *intr.* afluir, entrar.
influence (i·nfluøns) *s.* influencia, influjo. *2* ELECT. inducción.
influence (to) *tr.* influir en o sobre.
influential (influe·nshal) *adj.* influente, influyente.
influenza (influe·nša) *s.* MED. influenza.
influx (i·nfløks) *s.* flujo, entrada, afluencia.
infold (to) (infou·ld) *tr.* envolver, rodear, incluir. *2* abrazar. *3* plegar.
inform (info·ʳm) *adj.* informe.
inform (to) *tr.* informar. *2* participar, comunicar. *3 intr. to ~ against,* delatar, declarar contra [uno].
informal (-al) *adj.* que no se ajusta a formalidades o ceremonias; sin solemnidad, casero, de confianza, familiar.
informality (info·ʳmæ·liti) *s.* calidad o estado de lo que no se ajusta a formalidades o ceremonias; sencillez. *2* acto sencillo o de confianza.
informant (info·ʳmant) *s.* informador.
information (-shøn) *s.* información. *2* informes, noticias, avisos. *3* conocimientos, saber, instrucción. *4* DER. delación.
informative (info·ʳmativ) *adj.* informativo.
informed (info·ʳmd) *adj.* informado. *2* culto, instruido.
informer (info·ʳmøʳ) *s.* informador, informante. *2* DER. delator [esp. el profesional].
infraction (infræ·kshøn) *s.* infracción.
infractor (-toʳ) *s.* infractor.
infrangible (infræ·ndÿibøl) *adj.* infrangible, inquebrantable.
infrared (infrare·d) *adj.* FÍS. infrarrojo.
infrequent (infri·kuønt) *adj.* infrecuente, raro.
infringe (to) (infri·ndÿ) *tr.* infringir. *2 intr. to ~ on* o *upon,* usurpar, invadir [derechos, etc.].
infringement (-mønt) *s.* infracción.
infringer (-øʳ) *s.* infractor.
infuriate (to) (infiu·rieit) *tr.* enfurecer, encolerizar, poner furioso.
infuriated (-id) *adj.* enfurecido, furioso.
infuse (to) (infiu·š) *tr.* infundir. *2 to ~ with,* imbuir de, llenar de.
infusible (infiu·šibøl) *adj.* infusible.
infusion (infiu·ÿøn) *s.* infusión.
infusive (-šiv) *adj.* infusor.
infusory (infiu·sori) *adj.-s.* ZOOL. infusorio.
ingenerate (indÿe·nøreit) *adj.* innato, ingénito.
ingenious (indÿi·niøs) *adj.* ingenioso, hábil, sutil.
ingeniousness (-nis) *s.* ingeniosidad.
ingenuity (indÿiniu·iti) *s.* ingenio, habilidad, inventiva. *2* ingeniosidad, artificio.
ingenuous (indÿe·niuøs) *adj.* ingenuo, sincero, franco.
ingenuousness (-nis) *s.* ingenuidad, sinceridad.
ingest (to) (indÿe·st) *tr.* ingerir, injerir [en el estómago].
ingestion (-chøn) *s.* ingestión.
ingle (i·ngøl) *s.* llama, fuego. *2* chimenea, hogar.
inglenook (-nuk) *s.* rincón de la chimenea.
inglorious (inglo·riøs) *adj.* nada glorioso, obscuro. *2* vergonzoso, ignominioso.
ingoing (i·ngouing) *adj.* entrante, que entra. *2* entrada, ingreso.
ingot (i·ngøt) *s.* lingote.
ingrain (ingrei·n) *adj.* teñido en rama. *2* fijado, inculcado, arraigado profundamente; innato.
ingrain (to) *tr.* teñir con grana. *2* teñir en rama. *3* fijar, arraigar, inculcar.
ingrained (i·ngreind) *adj.* INGRAIN.

ingrate (i·ngreit) *adj.-s.* ingrato.
ingratiate (to) (ingrei·shieit) *tr.* congraciar: *to ~ oneself with*, congraciarse con.
ingratiating (-ing) *adj.* congraciador, obsequioso.
ingratitude (ingræ·titiud) *s.* ingratitud, desagradecimiento.
ingredient (ingrı·diønt) *s.* ingrediente.
ingress (i·ngres) *s.* ingreso, entrada, acceso.
ingression (ingre·shøn) *s.* ingreso, entrada [acción].
ingrowing (i·ngrouing) *adj.* que crece hacia dentro; *~ nail*, uñero.
inguinal (i·ngwinɑl) *adj.* ANAT. inguinal.
ingulf (to) (ingø·lf) *tr.* TO ENGULF.
ingurgitate (to) (ingø·ʳdẏiteit) *tr.* ingurgitar, engullir, tragar.
inhabit (to) (injæ·bit) *tr.* habitar, morar en.
inhabitable (-abøl) *adj.* habitable.
inhabitant (-ant) *s.* habitante, morador, vecino.
inhabited (-id) *adj.* habitado.
inhalation (injɑlei·shøn) *s.* inhalación.
inhale (to) (injei·l) *tr.* inhalar, tragar [el humo].
inharmonic (al (injaʳma·nik(ɑl) *adj.* inarmónico, disonante.
inharmonious (-ou·niøs) *adj.* inarmónico, discordante.
inhere (to) (inji·øʳ) *intr.* ser inherente, pertenecer [como atributo, cualidad, etc.].
inherence, -cy (inji·røns, -si) *s.* inherencia.
inherent (-t) *adj.* inherente. *2* innato.
inherit (to) (inje·rit) *tr.-intr.* heredar.
inheritance (-ans) *s.* herencia.
inheritor (inje·ritøʳ) *s.* heredero.
inheritress, -trix (inje·ritris, -triks) *s.* heredera.
inhesion (inji·ẏon) *s.* inherencia.
inhibit (to) (inji·bit) *tr.* prohibir. *2* detener, suprimir. *3* inhibir [causar inhibición].
inhibition (injibi·shøn) *s.* prohibición, restricción. *2* inhibición.
inhibitive, -tori (inji·bitiv, -tori) *adj.* prohibitivo. *2* inhibitorio.
inhospitable (inja·spitabøl) *adj.* inhospitalario. *2* inhospitable, inhóspito.
inhospitality (injaspitæ·liti) *s.* inhospitalidad.
inhuman (injiu·man) *adj.* inhumano.
inhumane (-mein) *adj.* inhumano, inhumanitario.
inhumanity (injiumæ·niti) *s.* inhumanidad.
inhumate (to) (injiu·meit) *tr.* TO INHUME.
inhumation (-ei·shøn) *s.* inhumación.
inhume (to) (injiu·m) *tr.* inhumar.
inimical (ini·mikal) *adj.* de enemigo, hostil. *2* adverso, enemigo.
inimitable (ini·mitabøl) *adj.* inimitable.
iniquitous (ini·kuitøs) *adj.* inicuo.
iniquity (-ti) *s.* iniquidad.
initial (ini·shal) *adj.* inicial. *2 s.* inicial [letra].
initial (to) *tr.* firmar o marcar con iniciales. ¶ Pret. y p. p.: *initialed* o *-lled*; ger.: *-ling* o *-lling*.
initiate (ini·shieit) *adj.-s.* iniciado.
initiate (to)) *tr.* iniciar [a uno]. *2* iniciar, comenzar.
initiation (-ei·shøn) *s.* iniciación. *2* principio, comienzo.
initiative (ini·shiativ) *adj.* iniciativo, inicial. *2 s.* iniciativa.
initiator (-eitøʳ) *s.* iniciador.
inject (to) (indẏe·kt) *tr.* inyectar. *2* jeringar. *3* introducir.
injectable (-abøl) *adj.* inyectable.
injection (-shøn) *s.* inyección. *2* lavativa.
injector (-tøʳ) *s.* MEC., MED. inyector.

injudicious (indẏudi·shøs) *adj.* torpe, imprudente.
injunction (indẏo·nkshøn) *s.* orden, mandato, requerimiento. *2* DER. entredicho.
injure (to) (i·ndẏøʳ) *tr.* dañar, perjudicar, injuriar. *2* herir, lastimar. *3* ofender, agraviar.
injurious (indẏu·riøs) *adj.* dañoso, perjudicial, nocivo. *2* lesivo. *3* injurioso, ofensivo.
injury (i·ndẏuri) *s.* daño, perjuicio, deterioro, menoscabo. *3* herida, lesión. *4* injuria, ofensa, agravio.
injustice (indẏø·stis) *s.* injusticia.
ink (ink) *s.* tinta [para escribir, etc.]. *2* ZOOL. tinta [del calamar].
ink (to) *tr.* entintar, dar tinta. *2* pasar en tinta.
inkhorn (-joʳn) *s.* tintero de cuerno.
inking (-ing) *s.* entintado.
inkling (-ling) *s.* insinuación. *2* indicio. *3* leve conocimiento o idea, vislumbre, sospecha.
inkstand (-tænd) *s.* tintero; escribaní.
inkwell (-wel) *s.* tintero; frasco de tintero.
inky (-i) *adj.* de tinta; manchado de tinta; negro.
inlaid (inlei·d) *pret.* y *p. p.* de TO INLAY.
inland (i·nland) *adj.* interior, del interior, de tierra adentro, del país. *2 adv.* tierra adentro.
in-law *adj.* político [pariente]: *father in-law*, padre político, suegro.
inlay (inlei·) *s.* embutido, incrustación, taracea.
inlay (to) *tr.* embutir, incrustar. *2* taracear, hacer ataujía o mosaico. ¶ Pret. y p. p.: *inlaid*.
inlet (i·nlet) *s.* abra, caleta, ría pequeña. *2* acceso, entrada. *3* material embutido.
inly (-i) *adj.* interno, interior, íntimo. *2 adv.* interiormente, íntimamente.
inmate (-meit) *s.* asilado, preso, residente, etc. [de un asilo, cárcel, etc.].
inmost (-moust) *adj.* más interior, íntimo, recóndito o profundo.
inn (in) *s.* posada, fonda, mesón.
innate (inei·t) *adj.* innato, ingénito, connatural.
innateness (-nis) *s.* calidad de innato.
inner (i·nøʳ) *adj.* interior, interno, íntimo: *~ tube*, cámara [de neumático].
innermost (-moust) *adj.* INMOST.
innervate (to) (inø·ʳveit) *tr.* FISIOL. inervar.
innervation (-ei·shøn) *s.* FISIOL. inervación.
innings (i·nings) *s.* y *pl.* en béisbol, criquet, etc., turno, entrada.
innkeeper (i·nkıpøʳ) *s.* posadero, fondista.
innocence (i·nøsøns) *s.* inocencia. *2* candor, sencillez. *3* inocuidad.
innocent (-nt) *adj.-s.* inocente. *2 adj.* MED. benigno. *3 fam.* desprovisto [de].
innocuity (ina·kuiti) *s.* inocuidad.
innocuous (-kiuøs) *adj.* inocuo, inofensivo.
innovate (to) (i·noveit) *tr.* innovar. *2* introducir [algo nuevo].
innovation (-ei·shøn) *s.* innovación, novedad.
innoxious (ina·kshøs) *adj.* inocuo.
innuendo (iniue·ndou) *s.* indirecta, insinuación, pulla.
innumerable (iniu·mørabøl) *adj.* innumerable, incontable.
innumerous (-røs) *adj.* innúmero, innumerable.
inobedience (inøbı·diøns) *s.* inobediencia, desobediencia.
inobedient (-nt) *adj.* inobediente, desobediente.
inobservance (inobšø·ʳvans) *s.* inobservancia. *2* inadvertencia.
inoculate (to) (ina·kiuleit) *tr.* inocular.
inoculation (-ei·shøn) *s.* inoculación.
inodorous (inou·dørøs) *adj.* inodoro.

inoffensive (inøfe·nsiv) *adj.* inofensivo. *2* pacífico.
inofficious (inøfi·shøs) *adj.* DER. inoficioso.
inoperable (ina·pørabøl) *adj.* CIR. inoperable.
inoperative (-tiv) *adj.* inoperante, ineficaz.
inopportune (inapø*tiu·n) *adj.* inoportuno.
inordinate (ino·*dinit) *adj.* inmoderado, excesivo.
inorganic (ino*gæ·nik) *adj.* inorgánico.
inosculate (to) (ina·skiuleit) *tr.* unir por anastomosis. *2* fig. unir íntimamente. *3 intr.* anastomizarse.
input (i·nput) *s.* MEC. fuerza consumida, energía absorbida [por una máquina], gasto, consumo.
inquest (i·nkuest) *s.* información o pesquisa judicial con ayuda de un jurado: *coroner's* ~, encuesta judicial que preside el CORONER.
inquietude (inkuai·itiud) *s.* inquietud, desasosiego, descontento.
inquire (to) (inkuai·ø*) *tr.* inquirir, averiguar, investigar. *2* preguntar. *3 intr. to* ~ *about, after* o *for,* preguntar por: *to* ~ *into,* averiguar, investigar, examinar, informarse de.
inquiry (-ri) *s.* indagación, investigación, información, averiguación. *2* pregunta, interrogatorio.
inquisition (inkuiši·shøn) *s.* inquisición, investigación, pesquisa, examen. *2* (con may.) Inquisición.
inquisitive (inkui·šitiv) *adj.* inquisitivo. *2* dado a la investigación. *3* curioso, preguntón.
inquisitor (-ø*) *s.* inquiridor, investigador. *2* inquisidor.
inroad (i·nroud) *s.* incursión, invasión, ataque.
inrush (-røšh) *s.* empuje, corriente hacia dentro; invasión.
insalivate (to) (insæ·liveit) *tr.* insalivar.
insalubrious (insαliu·briøs) *adj.* insalubre, malsano.
insalubrity (-briti) *s.* insalubridad.
insane (insei·n) *adj.* insano, demente, loco, insensato: ~ *asylum,* manicomio, casa de locos.
insanity (insæ·niti) *s.* locura, demencia, insania, enajenación mental.
insatiable (insei·shiabøl) *adj.* insaciable.
insatiate (-shiet) *adj.* no saciado. *2* insaciable.
inscribe (to) (inskrai·b) *tr.* inscribir, grabar. *2* inscribir, apuntar [en un registro, etc.]. *3* GEOM. inscribir. *4* dedicar [un verso, etc.].
inscription (inskri·pshøn) *s.* inscripción. *2* título, epígrafe, rótulo, leyenda. *3* dedicatoria.
inscrutability (inskrutabi·liti) *s.* inescrutabilidad.
inscrutable (inskru·tabøl) *adj.* inescrutable.
insect (i·nsekt) *s.* ZOOL. insecto. *2* bicho [animal pequeño].
insecta (-tæ) *s. pl.* ZOOL. insectos.
insecticide (-isaid) *adj.-s.* insecticida.
insectile (-il) *adj.* insectil.
insection (inse·kshøn) *s.* incisión; segmentación.
insectivorous (insekti·vørøs) *adj.* insectívoro.
insecure (insikiu·ø*) *adj.* inseguro.
insecurity (-riti) *s.* inseguridad. *2* peligro, riesgo.
inseminate (to) (inse·mineit) *tr.* sembrar. *2* inseminar.
insemination (-ei·shøn) *s.* siembra. *2* inseminación.
insensate (inse·nseit) *adj.* insensato. *2* insensible.
insensibility (insensibi·liti) *s.* insensibilidad.
insensible (inse·nsibøl) *adj.* insensible. *2* imperceptible. *3* inanimado. *4* sordo, indiferente.
insensitive (-sitiv) *adj.* insensible, no sensitivo. *2* falto de sensibilidad moral o mental.
insentient (-shønt) *adj.* insensible, inanimado.

inseparable (inse·parabøl) *adj.* inseparable.
insert (i·nsø*t) *s.* cosa inserida, intercalada, etc.; inserción.
insert (to) (insø·*t) *tr.* inserir, insertar, ingerir, introducir, intercalar, encajar.
insertion (insø·*shøn) *s.* inserción, metimiento. *2* COST. entredós. *3* ZOOL., BOT. inserción.
inserviceable (insø·*visabøl) *adj.* inservible, inútil.
inset (i·nset) *s.* intercalación. *2* hoja u hojas encajadas en un libro, folleto, mapa, etc.
inshore (i·nsho*) cercano a la orilla. *2 adv.* cerca de, o hacia la, orilla.
inside (i·nsaid) *s.* interior [de una cosa; del hombre]. *2* forro [de un vestido]. *3* contenido. *4 pl.* entrañas; interioridades. *5 adj.* interior, interno; íntimo, secreto. *6 adv.* dentro, adentro, en el interior: ~ *out,* de dentro afuera, al revés. *7 prep.* dentro de [en el interior de].
insider (-ø*) *s.* persona de dentro [de un grupo, sociedad, etc.]; persona enterada, que está en el secreto.
insidious (insi·diøs) *adj.* insidioso, engañoso, solapado.
insight (i·nsait) *s.* discernimiento, penetración, perspicacia, comprensión, intuición.
insignia (insi·gnia) *s. pl.* insignias, distintivos.
insignificance (insigni·fikans) *s.* insignificancia.
insignificant (-ant) *adj.* insignificante.
insincere (insinsi·ø*) *adj.* insincero, hipócrita.
insincerity (insinse·riti) *s.* insinceridad, hipocresía.
insinuate (to) (insi·niueit) *tr.* insinuar. *2* introducir, deslizar, hacer penetrar, instilar.
insinuation (-shøn) *s.* insinuación, sugestión, indirecta. *2* acción de insinuarse.
insipid (insi·pid) *adj.* insípido, insulso, soso.
insipidity (-iti) *s.* insipidez, insulsez, sosería.
insist (to) (insi·st) *intr.* insistir, persistir, empeñarse en, porfiar; hacer hincapié en.
insistence, -cy (insi·støns, -si) *s.* insistencia, persistencia.
insistent (-nt) *adj.* insistente, persistente.
insobriety (insoubrai·eti) *s.* intemperancia.
insofar as (insoufa·* æš) *adv.* en lo que, hasta donde.
insolate (to) (i·nsouleit) *tr.* insolar.
insolation (-ei·shøn) *s.* MED., METEOR. insolación.
insole (i·nsoul) *s.* plantilla [de zapato].
insolence (i·nsøløns) *s.* insolencia. *2* altanería.
insolent (-nt) *adj.* insolente. *2* altanero.
insolubility (insaliubi·liti) *s.* insolubilidad.
insoluble (insa·liubøl) *adj.* insoluble. *2* impagable [deuda].
insolvable (insa·lvabøl) *adj.* insoluble. *2* indisoluble. *3* que no se puede saldar.
insolvency (insa·lvønsi) *s.* insolvencia.
insolvent (-vønt) *adj.* insolvente.
insomnia (insa·mnia) *s.* insomnio.
insomuch (insomuø·ch) *conj.* de manera, hasta el punto: ~ *that,* de manera que, hasta el punto que. *2* ~ *as,* ya que, puesto que.
insouciance (insu·sians) *s.* despreocupación.
insouciant (-nt) *adj.* despreocupado.
inspect (to) (inspe·kt) *tr.* inspeccionar, examinar, registrar, reconocer.
inspection (-shøn) *s.* inspección, examen, registro, reconocimiento.
inspector (-ø*) *s.* inspector, interventor, controlador.
inspiration (inspirei·shøn) *s.* inspiración.
inspiratory (inspai·ratori) *adj.* inspirador.

inspire (to) (inspai·øʳ) *tr.* inspirar. *2* infundir, comunicar. *3* sugerir. *4 intr.* FISIOL. inspirar.
inspiring (inspai·ring) *adj.* inspirador, animador.
inspirit (to) (inspi·rit) *tr.* animar, vigorizar, alentar, estimular.
inspissate (to) (inspi·seit) *tr.* espesar, condensar, trabar.
instability (instabi·liti) *s.* inestabilidad, mutabilidad, inconstancia.
instable (instei·bøl) *adj.* instable, inestable, mudable, inconstante.
install (to) (insto·l) *tr.* instalar en, dar posesión oficialmente de [un cargo o dignidad]. *2* instalar, colocar [un aparato, etc.].
installation (-ei·shion) *s.* instalación.
installment, instalment (-mønt) *s.* instalación [acción]. *2* plazo [pago o entrega parcial]: *on the ~ plan,* a plazos, con facilidades de pago. *3* entrega, fascículo [de una publicación].
instance (i·nstans) *s.* ejemplo, caso: *for ~,* por ejemplo. *2* vez, ocasión. *3* ruego, petición, instancia. *4* DER. instancia. *5 in the first ~,* en primer lugar, desde el principio.
instance (to) *tr.* poner por caso o por ejemplo, citar.
instancy (i·nstansi) *s.* insistencia, instancia. *2* prontitud, instantaneidad.
instant (i·nstant) *adj.* instante, insistente. *2* inminente, inmediato. *3* apremiante, urgente. *4* presente, corriente, actual: *the 10th ~,* el diez del corriente [mes]. *5 s.* instante, momento.
instantaneous (instantei·niøs) *adj.* instantáneo. *2* inmediato [hecho en seguida].
instanter (instæ·ntøʳ) *adv.* inmediatamente.
instantly (i·nstantli) *adv.* al instante, inmediatamente.
instead (inste·d) *adv.* en cambio, en lugar. *2 ~ of,* en lugar de, en vez de.
instep (i·nstep) *s.* empeine [del pie, del zapato].
instigate (to) (i·nstigeit) *tr.* instigar. *2* promover, fomentar.
instigation (-ei·shøn) *s.* instigación.
instil, instill (to) (insti·l) *tr.* instilar.
instillation (instilei·shøn) *s.* instilación.
1) instinct (i·nstinkt) *s.* instinto.
2) instinct (insti·nkt) *adj.* ~ *with,* animado por; lleno, rebosante de [vida, fuerza, etc.].
instinctive (insti·nktiv) *adj.* instintivo.
institute (i·nstitiut) *s.* instituto, institución. *2* principio, regla, precepto. *3 pl.* instituta, instituciones.
institute (to) *tr.* instituir. *2* abrir, incoar, iniciar.
institution (institu·shøn) *s.* institución [acción de instituir; cosa instituida, organización, fundación]. *2* iniciación, comienzo. *3* costumbre establecida. *4* fig. institución [persona o cosa muy conocida].
instruct (to) (instrø·kt) *tr.* instruir, enseñar. *2* instruir, informar, enterar. *3* ordenar, mandar.
instruction (-shøn) *s.* instrucción, enseñanza. *2* instrucción, saber. *3 pl.* instrucciones, indicaciones.
instructive (-tiv) *adj.* instructivo.
instructor (-tøʳ) *m.* instructor, maestro.
instructress (-tris) *f.* instructora, maestra.
instrument (i·nstrumønt) *s.* instrumento [utensilio, máquina, etc.]. *2* DER., MÚS. instrumento.
instrument (to) *tr.* MÚS. instrumentar.
instrumental (instrume·ntal) *adj.* MÚS. instrumental. *2 to be ~ in,* contribuir a. *3 s.* GRAM. caso instrumental.

instrumentalist (-ist) *s.* MÚS. instrumentista.
instrumentation (-ei·shøn) *s.* MÚS. instrumentación. *2* MÚS. ejecución.
insubordinate (insøbo·ʳdineit) *adj.* insubordinado.
insubordination (-ei·shøn) *s.* insubordinación, indisciplina.
insubstantial (insøbstæ·nshal) *adj.* insubstancial, poco sólido, ligero, tenue, frágil. *2* sin substancia corpórea, irreal.
insufferable (insø·førabøl) *adj.* insufrible.
insufficience, -cy (insøfi·shøns, -si) *s.* insuficiencia. *2* incapacidad, incompetencia.
insufficient (insøfi·shent) *adj.* insuficiente. *2* incapaz, incompetente.
insufflate (to) (insø·fleit) *tr.* insuflar.
insufflation (-ei·shøn) *s.* insuflación, soplo.
insular (i·nsiulaʳ) *adv.* insular, isleño. *2* fig. limitado, de miras estrechas.
insularity (insiulæ·riti) *s.* insularidad. *2* estrechez de miras.
insulate (to) (i·nsiuleit) *tr.* aislar.
insulating (-ing) *adj.* aislador, aislante.
insulation (-ei·shøn) *s.* aislamiento. *2* material aislante.
insulator (i·nsiuleitøʳ) *s.* aislador.
insulin (i·nsiulin) *s.* QUÍM. insulina.
insult (i·nsølt) *s.* insulto, denuesto, ultraje, afrenta.
insult (to) (insø·lt) *tr.* insultar, ultrajar.
insulting (-ing) *adj.* insultante.
insuperable (insiu·pørabøl) *adj.* insuperable, invencible.
insupportable (insøpo·ʳtabøl) *adj.* insoportable, inaguantable, insufrible.
insurance (inshu·rans) *s.* COM. seguro, aseguración: *life ~,* seguro de vida; *~ broker,* corredor de seguros; *~ policy,* póliza de seguro. *2* prima o premio del seguro. *3* garantía, seguridad.
insurant (-ant) *s.* COM. asegurado.
insure (to) (inshu·øʳ) *tr.* COM. asegurar. *2* asegurar, garantizar.
insured (inshu·ʳd) *adj.-s.* COM. asegurado.
insurer (inshu·røʳ) *s.* COM. asegurador.
insurgence, -cy (insø·ʳdÿøns, -si) *s.* insurrección, sublevación.
insurgent (-ønt) *adj.-s.* insurgente, insurrecto.
insurmountable (insøʳmau·ntabøl) *adj.* insuperable, invencible. *2* que no se puede pasar o transponer.
insurrection (insøre·kshøn) *s.* insurrección, rebelión.
insurrectionist (-ist) *s.* insurrecto, rebelde.
insusceptible (insøse·ptibøl) *adj.* no susceptible. *2* insensible.
intact (intæ·kt) *adj.* intacto, íntegro, entero.
intaglio (intæ·liou) *s.* obra de talla, grabado.
intake (i·nteik) *s.* succión, aspiración, toma, entrada. *2* cantidad de aire, etc., que se aspira o que entra de una vez. *3* contracción, estrechamiento. *4* MEC. válvula de admisión, orificio de entrada. *5* acometida [de una conducción]. *6* producto de una finca.
intangibility (intændÿibi·liti) *s.* intangibilidad.
intangible (intæ·ndÿibøl) *adj.* intangible; impalpable.
integer (i·ntidÿøʳ) *s.* número entero. *2* entidad completa.
integral (i·ntigral) *adj.* integrante, esencial. *2* íntegro, entero. *3 adj.-s.* MAT. integral. *4 s.* totalidad.
integrality (intigræ·liti) *s.* integridad.

integrate (to) (i·ntigreit) *tr.* integrar, formar un todo. 2 indicar el total. 3 MAT. integrar.
integration (-ei·shøn) *s.* integración.
integrity (inte·griti) *s.* integridad.
integument (inte-giumønt) *s.* integumento.
intellect (i·ntølekt) *s.* intelecto, inteligencia. 2 persona, o gente, de talento.
intellection (intøle·kshøn) *s.* intelección.
intellectual (-chual) *adj.-s.* intelectual.
intellectuality (intølekchuæ·liti) *s.* intelectualidad.
intelligence (inte·lidÿøns) *s.* inteligencia, entendimiento, penetración, talento. 2 información, conocimiento, noticia: *piece of* ~, informe, noticia, aviso. 3 información secreta: ~ *department* o *service*, servicio de información secreta o de espionaje. 4 inteligencia, armonía [entre personas].
intelligencer (-ø^r) *s.* noticiero. 2 espía.
intelligent (-nt) *adj.* inteligente.
intelligibility (intelidÿibi·liti) *s.* inteligibilidad.
intelligible (inte·lidÿibøl) *adj.* inteligible.
intemperance (inte·mpørans) *s.* intemperancia. 2 inclemencia [del tiempo].
intemperate (-ørit) *adj.* inmoderado, excesivo, extremado. 2 intemperante, desordenado. 3 bebedor.
intend (to) (inte·nd) *tr.* tener la intención de, proponerse, proyectar, pensar, querer. 2 destinar, hacer [para un fin]. 3 entender, querer decir.
intendance (inte·ndans) *s.* intendencia.
intendant (-dant) *s.* intendente.
intended (inte·ndid) *adj.* propuesto, deseado, que se tiene como objeto; hecho [para], destinado [a]. 2 *adj.-s.* fam. prometido, futuro.
intendedly (-li) *adv.* adrede, de intento.
intense (inte·ns) *adj.* intenso. 2 grande, fuerte, vivo, profundo, ardiente. 3 sumo, extremado. 4 que siente profundamente. 5 FOT. duro [negativo].
intensify (to) (-sifai) *tr.* intensificar. 2 FOT. reforzar. 3 *intr.* intensifcarse. ¶ Pret y p. p.: *intensified.*
intension (-shøn) *s.* intensión. 2 intensificación. 3 fuerza, profundidad, ardor, energía.
intensity (-siti) *s.* intensidad.
intensive (-siv) *adj.* intenso. 2 intensivo.
intensively (-li) *adj.* intensamente. 2 intensivamente.
intent (inte·nt) *adj.* profundo, detenido; fijo [pensamiento, mirada]. 2 ~ *on*, atento, dedicado a, absorto, concentrado en; resuelto a, empeñado en. 3 *s.* intento, designio, ánimo, intención, propósito. 4 *to all intents*, en todos los casos o sentidos, prácticamente.
intention (-shøn) *s.* intención.
intentional (-al) *adj.* intencional.
intentness (inte·ntnis) *s.* aplicación asidua, atención, empeño. 2 fijeza [de la mirada, etc.].
inter (to) (intø·^r) *tr.* enterrar, sepultar, inhumar.
interact (to) (intøræ·kt) *tr.* obrar recíprocamente.
interaction (-æ·kshøn) *s.* acción recíproca.
intercalary (intø·^rkaleri) *adj.* intercalar.
intercalation (-ei·shøn) *s.* intercalación.
intercede (to) (intø·^rsı·d) *intr.* interceder; mediar.
intercellular (-se·liula^r) *adj.* BIOL. intercelular.
intercept (to) (-se·pt) *tr.* interceptar.
interception (-shøn) *s.* interceptación.
intercession (-se·shøn) *s.* intercesión.
intercessor (-se·sø^r) *s.* intercesor; medianero.
interchange (i·ntø·^rcheindÿ) *s.* intercambio, cam-

bio, trueque. 2 comercio, tráfico. 3 alternación, sucesión alternada.
interchange (to) (intø·^rchei·ndÿ) *tr.* cambiar, trocar. 2 alternar, variar. 3 *intr.* alternarse.
interchangeable (-abøl) *adj.* intercambiable. 2 de recambio. 3 mutuo, recíproco.
intercollegiate (intø·^rkøli·dÿiit) *adj.* interescolar, interuniversitario.
intercom (i·ntø·^rkam) *s.* teléfono interior.
intercolumniation (intø·^rkølømniei·shøn) *s.* ARQ. intercolumnio.
intercommunicate (to) (-kømiu·nikeit) *intr.* comunicarse con otro.
intercontinental (-kantine·ntal) *adj.* intercontinental.
intercostal (-ka·stal) *adj.* ANAT. intercostal.
intercourse (i·ntø·^rko·^rs) *s.* trato, comunicación; correspondencia, conversación: *sexual* ~, trato carnal, cópula. 2 intercambio, comercio, tráfico.
interdental (-de·ntal) *adj.* interdental.
interdependence (-dipe·ndøns) *s.* interdependencia.
interdict (i·ntø·^rdikt) *s.* interdicto, entredicho.
interdict (to) (intø·^rdi·kt) *tr.* entredecir. 2 interdecir, prohibir, vedar.
interdiction (-shøn) *s.* interdicción. 2 prohibición.
interest (i·ntørest) *s.* interés: *to one's interest*, en interés o provecho de uno; *to put out at* ~, poner a interés, a rédito. 2 participación [en un negocio]. 3 influencia [de una persona]. 4 creces: *with* ~, con creces.
interest (to) *tr.* interesar.
interfere (to) (intø·^rfi·ø^r) *intr.* FÍS. interferir, interferirse. 2 interponerse, meterse, entrometerse, inmiscuirse. 3 oponerse, chocar. 4 VET. tropezarse [los caballos]. 5 *to* ~ *with*, estorbar, dificultar.
interference (-røns) *s.* FÍS., RADIO, interferencia. 2 interposición, intervención, intromisión. 3 estorbo.
interfuse (to) (-fiu·š) *tr.* combinar, mezclar. 2 difundir. 3 penetrar, saturar. 4 *intr.* mezclarse, fundirse.
interfusion (-dÿøn) *s.* combinación, mezcla. 2 difusión. 3 saturación.
interim (i·ntørim) *adj.* interino, provisional. 2 *s.* entretanto, ínterin: *in the* ~, entretanto, en el interín.
interior (inti·riø^r) *adj.* interior, interno. 2 *s.* interior.
interjacent (intø·^rdÿei·šønt) *adj.* interyacente.
interject (to) (intø·^rdÿe·kt) *tr.* interponer, insertar. 2 *intr.* interponerse.
interjection (-shøn) *s.* interposición. 2 GRAM. interjección.
interlace (to) (-lei·s) *tr.* entrelazar. 2 entremezclar.
interlapse (-læ·ps) *s.* intervalo [de tiempo].
interlard (to) (-li·v) *tr.* interfoliar.
interline (to) (-lain) *tr.* interlinear, entrerrenglonar. 2 COST. entretelar.
interlineation (-shøn) *s.* interlineación.
interlink (to) (-li·nk) *tr.* eslabonar.
interlock (i·ntø·^rlak) *s.* traba, trabazón.
interlock (to) (-la·k) *tr.* unir, trabar o entrelazar fuertemente, enclavijar. 2 engranar, engargantar. 3 *intr.* trabarse, enclavijarse.
interlocution (-la·kiutø^r) *s.* interlocutor.
interloper (-lou·pø^r) *s.* entrometido, intruso.
interlude (-lud) *s.* TEATR. intermedio. 2 MÚS. interludio. 3 intervalo.

interlunar (intø'liu·na') *adj.* del interlunio.
intermarriage (-mæ·ridÿ) *s.* casamiento entre personas de distintas tribus, castas, etc. *2* casamiento entre parientes.
intermarry (-mæ·ri) *intr.* unirse por casamientos diferentes familias, tribus, castas, etc.
intermediary (-mɪ·diæri) *adj.* intermedio. *2 s.* medio, conducto.
intermediate (-dieit) *adj.* intermedio. *2 s.* cosa intermedia. *4* intermediario, mediador.
intermediate (to) *intr.* interponerse, intermediar. *2* intervenir, mediar.
intermediation (-shøn) *s.* interposición, intervención, mediación.
interment (intø·'mønt) *s.* entierro, enterramiento.
intermezzo (-me·dšou) *s.* MÚS. intermedio.
interminable (intø·'minabøl) *adj.* interminable.
intermingle (to) (intø'mi·ngøl) *tr.* entremezclar. *2 intr.* entremezclarse.
intermission (intø'mi·shøn) *s.* intermisión, interrupción, tregua. *2* TEAT. intermedio, entreacto.
intermit (to) (-mi·t) *tr.* intermitir. *2 intr.* ser intermitente. ¶ Pret. y p. p.: -*tted;* ger.: -*tting.*
intermittence (-øns) *s.* intermitencia.
intermittent (-ønt) *adj.* intermitente.
intermix (to) (-mi·ks) *tr.* entremezclar. *2 intr.* entremezclarse.
intermixture (-chu') *s.* entremezcladura.
intern (i·ntø'n) *s.* interno [de un hospital]. *2* persona internada.
intern (to) (intø·'n) *tr.* internar.
internal (-nal) *adj.* interior, interno, intestino: *internal-combustion engine,* motor de explosión, de combustión interna.
international (intø'næ·shønal) *adj.* internacional.
internationalism (intø'næ·shønališm) *s.* internacionalismo.
internationalize (to) (-laiš) *tr.* internacionalizar.
internecine (-ni·sin) *adj.* mortífero, sanguinario.
internist (intø·'nist) *s.* MED. internista.
internment (-mønt) *s.* internación.
internode (intø'nou·d) *s.* BOT. entrenudo.
internuncio (intø'nø·nshiou) *s.* internuncio.
interparliamentary (-pa'lime·ntari) *adj.* interparlamentario.
interpellate (to) (-pe·leit) *tr.* interpelar.
interpellation (-ei·shøn) *s.* interpretación.
interpenetrate (to) (-pe·nitreit) *tr.-intr.* penetrar entre, dentro o a través. *2* penetrarse mutuamente.
interphone (i·ntø'foun) *s.* INTERCOM.
interplanetary (intø'plæ·niteri) *adj.* interplanetario.
interpolate (to) (intø·'poleit) *tr.* interpolar.
interpose (to) (intø'pou·š) *tr.* interponer. *2 intr.* interponerse, mediar, intervenir. *3* interrumpir [con una observación, etc.].
interposition (-poši·shøn) *s.* interposición, intervención, mediación.
interpret (to) (intø·'prit) *tr.* interpretar.
interpretation (-ei·shøn) *s.* interpretación.
interpreter (intø·'pritø') *s.* intérprete.
interregnum (intø're·gnøm) *s.* interregno.
interrogate (to) (inte·røgeit) *tr.* interrogar [a un testigo, etc.]. *2 intr.* hacer preguntas.
interrogation (-ei·shøn) *s.* interrogación; pregunta. *2* ORT. ~ *mark* o *point,* interrogante, signo de interrogación.
interrogative (intøra·gativ) *adj.* interrogativo. *2 s.* palabra interrogativa.

interrogator (inte·røgeitø') *s.* interrogante, preguntador.
interrogatory (intøra·gatori) *adj.* interrogativo. *2 s.* interrogatorio.
interrupt (to) (intørø·pt) *tr.-intr.* interrumpir.
interruptedly (-tidli) *adv.* interrumpidamente, de un modo discontinuo.
interruption (-shøn) *s.* interrupción. *2* solución de continuidad. *3* estorbo, obstáculo.
intersect (to) (intø'se·kt) *tr.* cortar, cruzar [una línea, etc., a otra]. *2 intr.* intersecarse, cortarse.
intersection (-shøn) *s.* intersección. *2* cruce [de calles, etc.].
interspace (to) (-pei·s) *tr.* espaciar.
intersperse (to) (-pø·'s) *tr.* esparcir, entremezclar, sembrar, salpicar.
interstate (-teit) *adj.* interestatal.
interstellar (-te·la') *adj.* interestelar.
interstice (intø·'stis) *s.* intersticio. *2* resquicio, hendedura.
intertwine, intertwist (to) (-tuai·n, -tui·st) *tr.* entretejer, entrelazar. *2 intr.* entrelazarse.
interval (i·ntø'val) *s.* intervalo, espacio, claro. *2* intermedio, descanso. *3* MÚS. intervalo.
intervene (to) (intø'vi·n) *intr.* intervenir, mediar. *2* interponerse, atravesarse. *3* sobrevenir, ocurrir [entre dos momentos o hechos].
intervening (intø·vɪ·ning) *adj.* que interviene. *2* intermedio, que media.
intervention (intø've·nshøn) *s.* intervención [acción de tomar parte o mediar]; mediación. *2* interposición.
interview (i·ntø'viu) *s.* entrevista, conferencia. *2* interviev, interviu [periodística].
interview (to) *tr.* entrevistarse con. *2* intervievar.
interweave (to) (intø·'uiv) *tr.* entretejer, entrelazar. *2 intr.* entretejerse, entrelazarse. ¶ Pret.: *interwove* o -*weaved;* p. p.: *interwove, -woven* o -*weaved.*
intestate (inte·steit) *adj.-s.* intestado. *2 adj.* no dejado en testamento.
intestinal (-tinal) *adj.* ANAT., ZOOL. intestinal.
intestine (-tin) *adj.* intestino. *2* interno. *3 s.* ANAT. intestino.
intimacy (i·ntimasi) *s.* intimidad, familiaridad, amistad íntima.
intimate (i·ntimit) *adj.* íntimo. *2* de confianza, casero. *3 s.* amigo íntimo.
intimate (to) (i·ntimeit) *tr.* anunciar, notificar, intimar. *2* indicar, insinuar, dar a entender.
intimation (intimei·shøn) *s.* notificación, intimación. *2* insinuación, indicación.
intimidate (to) (inti·mideit) *tr.* intimidar.
intimidation (-ei·shøn) *s.* intimidación.
into (i·ntu) *prep.* en, dentro, adentro, hacia el interior, a [indicando movimiento o dirección de fuera a dentro; tránsito de un estado a otro; transformación; penetración, inclusión]: *to go ~,* entrar en; *translated ~ many languages,* traducido a muchas lenguas.
intolerable (inta·lørabøl) *adj.* intolerable, insoportable, insufrible.
intolerance (inta·lørans) *s.* intolerancia.
intolerant (-nt) *adj.-s.* intolerante. *2 adj.* que no puede resistir o sufrir.
intonation (intounei·shøn) *s.* entonación.
intone (to) (intou·n) *tr.* entonar [una canción, etc.]. *2* salmear, salmodiar.
intoxicant (inta·ksikant) *adj.* embriagador. *2 s.* bebida alcohólica.

intoxicate (to) (-keit) *tr.* embriagar. *2* MED. intoxicar.

intoxication (-ei·shøn) *s.* MED. intoxicación. *2* embriaguez, borrachera.

intractability (intræktabi·liti) *s.* indocilidad, obstinación.

intractable (intræ·ktabøl) *adj.* indócil, rebelde, obstinado. *2* difícil de trabajar [material].

intrados (intrei·das) *s.* ARQ. intradós.

intranquility (intrænkui·liti) *s.* intranquilidad, desasosiego.

intransigence (intræ·nšidÿøns) *s.* intransigencia.

intransigent (-ønt) *adj.-s.* intransigente.

intransitive (intræ·nsitiv) *adj.* GRAM. intransitivo.

intravenous (intravi·nøs) *adj.* intravenoso.

intrench (to) (intre·nch) *tr.* TO ENTRENCH.

intrepid (intre·pid) *adj.* intrépido, denodado.

intrepidity (intripi·diti) *s.* intrepidez.

intricacy (i·ntrikasi) *s.* intrincación, enredo, complicación.

intricate (i·ntrikit) *adj.* intrincado, complicado, confuso.

intrigue (intri·g) *s.* intriga, conspiración. *2* enredo amoroso, lío. *3* LIT. enredo.

intrigue (to) *intr.* intrigar. *2* tener intrigas amorosas. *3 tr.* intrigar [despertar curiosidad].

intriguer (-øʳ) *s.* intrigante.

intrinsic(al (intri·nsik(al) *adj.* intrínseco.

introduce (to) (intrødiu·s) *tr.* introducir. *2* presentar [un proyecto de ley, etc.; una persona a otra].

introduction (-dø·kshøn) *s.* introducción. *2* presentación.

introductory (-tori) *adj.* introductorio, de introducción, preliminar. *2* de presentación.

introit (introu·it) *s.* LITURG. introito.

introrse (intrø·ʳs) *adj.* BOT. introrso.

introspection (intrøspe·kshøn) *s.* introspección.

introspective (-tiv) *adj.* introspectivo.

introversion (-vø·ʳshøn) *s.* introversión.

introvert (i·ntrøvøʳt) *adj.-s.* introverso, introvertido.

introvert (to) *tr.* volver [el pensamiento, etc.] hacia el propio interior de uno. *2* volver hacia adentro. *3* ZOOL. invaginar.

intrude (to) (intru·d) *tr.* imponer uno [su presencia, sus opiniones, etc.]. *2 intr.* entrometerse, imponer uno su presencia [donde no es llamado]; estorbar. *3* intrusarse.

intruder (-øʳ) *s.* intruso. *2* entremetido.

intrusion (intru·ÿøn) *s.* intrusión, entremetimiento. *2* GEOL. intrusión.

intrusiveness (-sivnis) *s.* tendencia a intrusarse o entremeterse.

intubate (i·ntiubeit) *tr.* MED. intubar.

intuit (i·ntiuit) *tr.-intr.* intuir.

intuition (intiui·shøn) *s.* intuición.

intuitive (intiu·itiv) *adj.* intuitivo.

intumesce (to) (intiume·s) *intr.* hinchar, dilatar.

intumescence, -cy (-øns, -si) *s.* intumescencia; hinchazón.

inunction (inø·nkshøn) *s.* untura, friega.

inundate (to) (-deit) *tr.* inundar, anegar.

inundation (-ei·shøn) *s.* inundación.

inurbane (inøʳbei·n) *adj.* inurbano, descortés.

inure (to) (iniu·øʳ) *tr.* habituar, avezar, hacer, curtir.

inured (-d) *adj.* avezado, hecho [a], curtido [en].

inurement (-mønt) *s.* hábito, práctica, costumbre.

inutility (iniuti·liti) *s.* inutilidad.

invade (to) (invei·d) *tr.* invadir. *2* usurpar, violar [derechos, etc.].

invader (invei·døʳ) *s.* invasor.

invaginate (to) (invæ·dÿineit) *tr.* invaginar.

invagination (invædÿine·shøn) *s.* invaginación.

1) invalid (invæ·lid) *adj.* inválido, irrito, nulo.

2) invalid (i·nvalid) *adj.* inválido, tullido, enfermo, achacoso. *2 s.* inválido. *3* persona achacosa, valetudinario.

invalid (to) (invali·d) *tr.* convertir en un inválido. *2* licenciar como inválido.

invalidate (to) (invæ·lideit) *tr.* invalidar, anular.

invalidation (-shøn) *s.* invalidación.

invalidity (invæli·diti) *s.* invalidez.

invaluable (invæ·liuabøl) *adj.* inestimable, inapreciable, precioso. *2* sin valor.

invariability (inveriabi·liti) *s.* invariabilidad, invariación.

invariable (inve·riabøl) *adj.* invariable.

invasion (invei·ÿøn) *s.* invasión. *2* usurpación, violación [de derechos, etc.].

invective (inve·ktiv) *s.* invectiva.

inveigh (to) (invei·) *intr.* lanzar o decir invectivas [contra].

inveigle (to) (invi·gøl) *tr.* engañar, seducir, engatusar. *2* atraer u obtener con engaño.

invent (to) (inve·nt) *tr.* inventar.

invention (-shøn) *s.* invención. *2* invento. *3* ingenio, mecanismo. *4* inventiva.

inventor (-tøʳ) *s.* inventor. *2* invencionero.

inventory (i·nventori) *s.* inventario.

inventory (to) *tr.* inventariar.

inventress (inve·ntris) *s.* inventora.

inverness (invøʳne·s) *s.* macferlán.

inverse (invø·ʳs) *adj.* inverso. *2 s.* lo inverso.

inversion (-shøn) *s.* inversión.

invert (i·nvøʳt) *s.* COM. invertosa. *3* PSIC. invertido.

invert (to) (invø·ʳt) *tr.* invertir [alterar el orden de; volver de arriba abajo, de fuera a adentro, etc.]. *2* MAT., QUÍM. invertir.

invertebrata (-tøbreita) *s. pl.* ZOOL. invertebrados.

invertebrate (-tøbreit) *s. pl.* ZOOL. invertebrado.

inverted (-tid) *adj.* invertido: ~ *commas,* comillas.

invest (to) (inve·st) *tr.* investir [de una dignidad, etc.]. *2* investir, envolver, cubrir. *3* invertir, emplear [dinero]. *6* MIL. cercar, sitiar.

investigate (to) (inve·stigeit) *tr.* investigar. *2* averiguar, indagar.

investigation (-ei·shøn) *s.* investigación, averiguación, indagación, pesquisa.

investigator (inve·stigeitøʳ) *s.* investigador. *2* averiguador, indagador.

investiture (-ichøʳ) *s.* investidura. *2* vestidura, envoltura.

investment (-mønt) *s.* INVESTITURE. *2* inversión [de dinero]. *3* MIL. cerco, sitio.

investor (-øʳ) *s.* persona que invierte dinero.

inveteracy (inve·tørasi) *s.* calidad de inveterado.

inveterate (inve·tørit) *adj.* inveterado, arraigado. *2* empedernido, pertinaz.

invidious (invi·diøs) *adj.* injusto, irritante, odioso.

invigorate (to) (invi·gøreit) *tr.* vigorizar, fortalecer, animar.

invigoration (invigøre·shøn) *s.* fortalecimiento.

invincibility (invinsibi·liti) *s.* invencibilidad.

invincible (invi·nsibøl) *adj.* invencible.

inviolability (invaiølabi·liti) *s.* inviolabilidad.

inviolable (invai·ølabøl) *adj.* inviolable; sagrado. *2* inquebrantable, infrangible.

invisibility (invišibi·liti) *s.* invisibilidad.

invisible (invi·ŝibøl) *adj.* invisible: ~ *ink*, tinta simpática.
invitation (invitei·shøn) *s.* invitación. *2* llamada, atractivo.
invite (to) (invai·t) *tr.* invitar, convidar. *2* rogar, inducir, tentar.
inviting (invai·ting) *adj.* que invita. *2* atractivo, seductor, tentador, provocativo. *3* apetitoso.
invocation (invøkei·shøn) *s.* invocación. *2* evocación [de los espíritus, etc.].
invoice (i·nvøis) *s.* COM. factura: *as per* ~, según factura.
invoice (to) *tr.-intr.* COM. facturar.
invoke (to) (invou·k) *tr.* invocar. *2* evocar [a los espíritus, etc.].
involucre (invøliu·køʳ) *s.* BOT. involucro.
involuntary (inva·lønteri) *adj.* involuntario.
involute (i·nvøliut) *adj.* intrincado. *2* involuto. *3 s.* GEOM. involuta.
involution (invøliu·shøn) *s.* envolvimiento. *2* complicación, enredo. *3* MAT. potenciación. *4* MAT., BIOL., MED. involución.
involve (to) (inva·lv) *tr.* envolver, enrollar. *2* envolver, complicar, comprometer. *3* enredar, complicar, oscurecer. *4* comprender, incluir.
involved (-d) *adj.* envuelto, enredado; complicado, comprometido. *2* intrincado, obscuro. *3* absorto, engolfado.
involvement (-mønt) *s.* envolvimiento. *2* complicación, intrincación.
invulnerability (invølnørabi·liti) *s.* invulnerabilidad.
invulnerable (invø·lnørabøl) *adj.* invulnerable. *2* inatacable, irrebatible.
inward (i·nuaʳd) *adj.* interior, interno, íntimo. *2* dirigido hacia el centro o el interior. *3 adv.* INWARDS.
inwardness (-nis) *s.* interioridad. *2* interior, fondo, esencia.
inwards (-s) *adv.* hacia el centro, hacia adentro. *2* interiormente, mentalmente.
inweave (to) (inuv·v) *tr.* entretejer, enlazar.
inwrought (inro·t) *adj.* labrado, tejido en; embutido, incrustado.
iodid(e (ai·ødid) . QUÍM. yoduro.
iodin(e (-in) *s.* QUÍM. yodo.
iodize (to) (-aiŝ) *tr.* yodurar.
iodoform (aiou·døfoʳm) *s.* QUÍM. yodoformo.
ion (ai·øn) *s.* FÍS., QUÍM. ion.
ionian (aiou·nian) *adj.-s.* jonio: ~ *Sea*, Mar Jonio.
Ionic (aia·nik) *adj.* jónico.
ionization (aiøniŝei·shøn) *s.* ionización.
ionize (ai·ønaiŝ) *tr.* ionizar. *2* ionizarse.
iota (aiou·ta) *s.* iota [letra griega]. *2* fig. ápice, jota.
I.O.U. (ai ou you) (abreviatura de *I owe you*). pagaré, vale.
Irak (i·rak) *n. pr.* GEOGR. Irak.
Iran (i·ran o ai·ræn) *n. pr.* GEOGR. Irán, Persia.
Iranian (airei·nian) *adj.-s.* iranio, persa.
irascible (airæ·sibøl) *adj.* irascible.
irate (airei·t) *adj.* encolerizado, airado.
ire (ai·øʳ) *s.* ira, iracundia, cólera.
ireful (ai·øʳful) *adj.* iracundo, colérico, airado.
Ireland (ai·ʳland) *n. pr.* GEOGR. Irlanda.
iridaceous (airidei·shiøs) *adj.* BOT. iridáceo.
iridescence (iride·søns) *s.* cambiante, tornasol.
iridescent (iride·sønt) *adj.* iridescente, irisado.
iridium (iri·diøm) *s.* QUÍM. iridio.
iris (ai·ris) *s.* ANAT., ÓPT. iris. *2* arco iris. *3* BOT. lirio.
irisation (-riŝei·shøn) *s.* irisación.

Irish (ai·rish) *adj.* irlandés, de Irlanda. *2 m.* irlandés [idioma]. *3 pl. the Irish*, los irlandeses.
Irishman (ai·rishmæn) *s.* irlandés [hombre].
Irishwoman (ai·rishwumæn) *s.* irlandesa [mujer].
iritis (airai·tis) *s.* MED. iritis.
irk (to) (øʳk) *tr.* fastidiar, cansar, encocorar.
irksome (ø·ʳksøm) *adj.* fastidioso, tedioso, pesado, cargante.
iron (ai·øʳn) *s.* hierro, [metal; arma, instrumento, etc., de hierro]: *to have many irons in the fire*, tener muchos asuntos entre manos; *to strike while the* ~ *is hot*, aprovechar la ocasión. *2* hierro [para marcar]. *3* plancha [para la ropa]. *4 pl.* hierros, cadenas, grilletes. *5 adj.* de hierro, férreo, férrico: *Iron Age*, Edad de Hierro; ~ *curtain*, cortina de hierro; fig. telón de acero; ~ *lung*, MED. pulmón de acero; ~ *scrap*, chatarra; ~ *will*, voluntad de hierro.
iron (to) *tr.* guarnecer de hierro, herrar. *2* aherrojar, poner grilletes a. *3* planchar [la ropa]: *to* ~ *out*, fig. allanar.
iron-bound (-d) *adj.* unido o sujeto con hierro. *2* escabroso, rocoso. *3* férreo, inflexible, duro.
ironclad (-klæd) *adj.* acorazado, blindado. *2* fig. riguroso, severo. *3 s.* MAR. acorazado.
ironic (al (aira·nik(al) *adj.* irónico.
ironing (ai·øʳning) *s.* planchado: ~ *board*, tabla de planchar.
ironmaster (-mæstøʳ) *s.* dueño de una herrería.
ironmonger (-møngøʳ) *s.* ferretero, quincallero.
ironsides (-saidŝ) *s.* hombre fuerte. *2* MAR. acorazado. *3 pl.* caballería de Oliverio Cromwell.
ironware (-ueʳ) *s.* ferretería [artículos].
ironwork (-uøʳk) *s.* herraje.
ironworks (-uoʳks) *s.* fundición de hierro, herrería, ferrería.
ironwort (-uøʳt) *s.* BOT. siderita.
1) irony (-i) *adj.* férreo; ferrugiento.
2) irony (ai·røni) *s.* ironía.
iroquois (i·røkua) *s.* iroqués.
irradiance, -cy (irei·dians, -si) *s.* irradiación. *2* lustre, esplendor.
irradiate (to) (irei·dieit) *tr.* irradiar, esparcir. *2* iluminar. *3* MED., QUÍM. someter a una radiación. *4 intr.* lucir, brillar.
irradiation (-ei·shøn) *s.* irradiación. *2* iluminación. *3* brillo, esplendor.
irrational (iræ·shønal) *adj.* irracional [que carece de razón]. *2* absurdo, ilógico. *3* MAT. irracional.
irrationality (iræshonæ·liti) *s.* irracionalidad.
irreclaimable (iriklei·mabøl) *adj.* incorregible. *2* irredimible.
irreconcilable (irecønsai·labøl) *adj.* irreconciliable. *2* inconciliable, incompatible. *3 s.* POL. intransigente.
irrecoverable (irikø·vørabøl) *adj.* irreparable. *2* irrecuperable. *3* incobrable.
irrecusable (irikiu·ŝabøl) *adj.* irrecusable.
irredeemable (iridı·mabøl) *adj.* irredimible. *2* no convertible en metálico [papel moneda].
irredentism (iride·ntism) *s.* irredentismo.
irreducible (iridiu·sibøl) *adj.* irreducible, irreductible.
irrefragable (ire·fragabøl) *adj.* irrefragable. *2* innegable, incontestable.
irrefutable (irefiu·tabøl) *adj.* irrefutable.
irregular (ire·giulaʳ) *adj.* irregular. *2* anormal, anómalo. *3* desarreglado, desordenado.
irregularity (iregiulæ·riti) *s.* irregularidad. *2* anomalía. *3* desarreglo, desorden.

irrelative (ire·lativ) *adj.* inconexo, que no guarda relación.
irrelevance, -cy (ire·livans, -si) *s.* impertinencia [falta de pertinencia], calidad de lo que no es aplicable o que no viene al caso. *2* cosa que no viene a propósito o al caso.
irrelevant (-nt) *adj.* impertinente [no pertinente], fuera de propósito, que no es aplicable o que no viene al caso, ajeno [a la cuestión].
irreligion (irili·dÿøn) *s.* irreligión, impiedad.
irreligious (-øs) *adj.* irreligioso.
irremediable (irimı·diabøl) *adj.* irremediable, irreparable. *2* incurable.
irremissible (irimi·sibøl) *adj.* irremisible.
irremovable (irimu·vabøl) *adj.* inamovible. *2* que no se puede quitar.
irreparable (ire·parabøl) *adj.* irreparable.
irrepealable (iripı·labøl) *adj.* irrevocable.
irreplaceable (iriplei·sabøl) *adj.* irreemplazable, insustituible.
irreprehensible (ireprije·nsibøl) *adj.* irreprensible.
irrepressible (iripre·sibøl) *adj.* irreprimible, incontenible.
irreproachable (iriprou·chabøl) *adj.* irreprochable.
irresistible (iriši·stibøl) *adj.* irresistible, incontrastable.
irresolute (ire·šøliut) *adj.* irresoluto, indeciso.
irresolution (irešøliu·shøn) *s.* irresolución, indecisión, vacilación.
irresolvable (ireša·lvabøl) *adj.* que no se puede resolver o descomponer.
irrespective (irispe·ktiv) *adj.-adv.* ~ *of*, que no toma en cuenta, que prescinde de, independiente de; prescindiendo de, independientemente de.
irrespirable (irispai·rabøl) *adj.* irrespirable.
irresponsibility (irispansibi·liti) *s.* irresponsabilidad.
irresponsible (irispa·nsibøl) *adj.* irresponsable.
irresponsive (-siv) *adj.* que no responde [a una influencia, acción o afecto].
irretrievable (iritrı·vabøl) *adj.* irreparable, irrevocable. *2* irrecuperable. *3* incobrable.
irreverence (ire·vørøns) *s.* irreverencia; falta de respeto.
irreverent (-nt) *adj.* irreverente, irrespetuoso.
irreversibility (irivø'sibi·liti) *s.* irreversibilidad.
irreversible (irivø'sibøl) *adj.* irreversible.
irrevocability (irevøkabi·liti) *s.* irrevocabilidad.
irrevocable (ire·vøkabøl) *adj.* irrevocable. *2* inalterable, inquebrantable.
irrigable (i·rigabøl) *adj.* irrigable. *2* regadío, regadizo.
irrigate (to) (i·rigeit) *tr.* irrigar, regar. *2* MED. irrigar.
irrigation (-ei·shøn) *s.* irrigación, riego. *2* MED. irrigación.
irritability (iritabi·liti) *s.* irritabilidad.
irritable (i·ritabøl) *adj.* irritable.
irritant (i·ritant) *adj.-s.* irritante. *2* irritador.
irritate (to) (i·riteit) *tr.* irritar. *2* FISIOL. excitar.
irritation (-ei·shøn) *s.* irritación. *2* FISIOL. excitación.
irruption (irø·pshøn) *s.* irrupción.
is (iš) *3.ª pers. sing. pres. ind.* de TO BE.
Isaac (ai·šæk) *n. pr.* Isac.
Isabella (išabe·la) *n. pr.* Isabel.
Isaiah (aišei·æ o aišai·æ) *n. pr.* BIB. Isaías.
Iscariot (iskæ·riøt) *n. pr.* BIB. Iscariote.
ischiatic (iskiæ·tik) *adj.* ANAT. isquiático.

ischium (i·skiøm) *s.* ANAT. isquión.
Ishmael (i·shmiøl) *n. pr.* BIB. Ismael.
Ishmaelite (i·shmiølait) *s.* ismaelita. *2* fig. paria.
Isidore (i·šido') *n. pr.* Isidoro, Isidro.
isinglass (ai·šinglas) *s.* colapez, cola de pescado. *2* MINER. mica.
Islam (i·slæm) *s.* Islam.
Islamism (i·slamišm) *s.* islamismo.
island (ai·land) *s.* isla, ínsula.
islander (-ø') *s.* isleño, insular.
isle (ail) *s.* isla, ínsula. *2* isleta.
islet (ai·let) *s.* isleta, cayo.
ism (išm) *s.* ismo [doctrina, sistema, etc.].
isobar (ai·soba') *s.* METEOR. línea isobárica, isobara.
Isochronous (i·skrønøs) *adj.* isócrono.
isoclinal (aisoclai·nal) *adj.* isoclino. *2 s.* isoclina [línea].
isodactylous (aisodæ·ktiløs) *adj.* isodáctilo.
isogonal (aisa·gonal) *adj.* CRISTAL. isógono.
isogonic (aisoga·njk) *adj.* isogónico.
isolate (to) (ai·søleit) *tr.* aislar. *2* separar, incomunicar.
isolation (-ei·shøn) *s.* aislamiento. *2* soledad, incomunicación.
isolationism (-išm) *s.* aislacionismo.
isomeric (aisome·rik) *adj.* QUÍM. isómero.
isomerous (aisa·mørøs) *adj.* BIOL., QUÍM. isómero.
isomorphic, -phous (aisomo·'fik, -føs) *adj.* isomorfo.
Isopoda (aisa·podæ) *s. pl.* ZOOL. isópodos.
isosceles (aisa·søliz) *adj.* GEOM. isósceles.
isotherm (ai·sozø'm) *s.* isoterma, línea isoterma.
isotope (-toup) *s.* QUÍM. isótopo.
isotropic (aisotra·pik) *adj.* isótropo.
Israel (i·šriøl) *n. pr.* Israel.
israeli (išrai·li) *adj.-s.* israelí.
Israelite (i·šrialait) *s.* israelita.
issuance (i·shuans) *s.* emisión. *2* publicción.
issue (i·shu) *s.* salida, egreso. *2* fuente, principio. *3* conclusión, solución, fin, decisión; consecuencias, resultado. *4* prole, hijos, sucesión. *5* producto, beneficios, rentas. *6* emisión [de valores]; expedición [de una orden, etc.]. *7* punto [que se debate o ha de decidir]: *to join* ~, ponerse a debatir; *to take* ~ *with*, llevar la contraria a, oponerse a; *at* ~, en disputa. *8* edición, tirada, número [de una publicación]. *9* MED. fuente, exutorio.
issue (to) *tr.* arrojar, verter. *2* expedir, dar [una orden, decreto, etc.]. *3* emitir, poner en circulación. *4* publicar, dar a luz. *5 intr.* salir, nacer, manar. *6* provenir, descender. *7* acabar, resolverse. *8* salir, ser publicado o emitido.
Istambul (istanbu·l) *n. pr.* GEOGR. Estambul.
isthmian (i·smian) *adj.-s.* istmeño. *2 adj.* (con may.) ístmico.
isthmus (i·smøs) *s.* GEOGR., ANAT. istmo.
it (it) *pron. neutro* él, ella, ello, eso, lo, la, le. | Se aplica a cosas inanimadas, a niños de teta y a animales cuyo sexo no se determina. *2* Se emplea como sujeto gramatical de los verbos impersonales, como sujeto expletivo o como atributo indeterminado. En todos estos casos no se traduce: ~ *rains*, llueve; ~ *is easy to say*, es fácil decir; *that is* ~, eso es; *who is* ~?, ¿quién es?
Italian (itæ·lian) *adj.-s.* italiano.
Italic (itæ·lik) *adj.* itálico. *2 pl.* IMPR. letra itálica, bastardilla o cursiva.
italicize (to) (itæ·lisaiš) *tr.* poner en bastardilla. *2* subrayar, recalcar.

Italy (i·tali) *n. pr.* GEOGR. Italia.
itch (ich) *s.* MED. sarna. *2* picazón, picor, comezón, prurito. *3* comezón, deseo. *4* ZOOL. ~ *mite*, arador de la sarna.
itch (to) *intr.* sentir picor, picazón, comezón, prurito. *2* tener comezón o deseo [de], rabiar [por]. *3 tr.* picar, producir picazón o comezón.
itching (i·ching) *adj.* que siente o da comezón. *2 s.* ITCH. *2* y *3*.
itchy (i·chi) *adj.* sarnoso. *2* que siente o da comezón.
item (ai·tøm) *adv.* item. *2 s.* partida [de una cuenta] artículo, elemento [de una enumeración]. *3* fam. punto, detalle, particular. *4* noticia, suelto.
itemize (to) (-aiš) *tr.* detallar, especificar, pormenorizar.
iterate (to) (i·tøreit) *tr.* iterar, repetir, reiterar.
iteration (-ei·shøn) *s.* iteración.
iterative (i·tørativ) *adj.* iterativo. *2* GRAM. frecuentativo.

itinerant (aiti·nørant) *adj.* que viaja, ambulante, errante. *2 s.* viandante.
itinerary (-reri) *adj.-s.* itinerario. *2 s.* relación de un viaje. *3* guía [de viajeros].
itinerate (to) (-reit) *intr.* viajar.
its (its) *adj.-pron. pos.* su, sus, suyo, suyos [de él, de ella, de ello, cuando les corresponde estar representados por el pron. neutro IT.].
it's contracción de IT IS.
itself (itse·lf) *pron.* él mismo, ella misma, ello mismo, sí, sí mismo, mismo [aplicado a cosas inanimadas, a niños de teta y a animales cuyo sexo no se determina].
I've (aiv) contracción de I HAVE.
ivied (ai·vid) *adj.* cubierto de hiedra.
ivory (ai·vøri) *s.* marfil. *2* objeto de marfil. *3 pl.* teclas del piano. *4* bolas de billar. *5* dados [para jugar]. *6* fam. dientes. *7 adj.* de marfil, ebúrneo.
ivy (ai·vi) *s.* BOT. hiedra, yedra.
izard (i·šø^rd) *s.* ZOOL. gamuza de los Pirineos.

J

J, j (dȳei) s. J, j, décima letra del alfabeto inglés.
jab (dȳæb) s. pinchazo, hurgonazo.
jab (to) tr. pinchar, picar, hurgonear. ¶ Pret. y p. p.: *jabbed;* ger.: *-bbing.*
jabber (dȳæ·bøʳ) s. cháchara, charla. 2 chapurreo.
jabber (to) intr. charlar, parlotear. 2 tr. farfullar. 3 chapurrear.
jabot (dȳæbo·) s. VEST. chorrera.
jacaranda (dȳækaræ·nda) s. BOT. jacaranda.
jacinth (dȳei·sinz) s. MINER. jacinto, circón.
Jack (dyæk) n. pr. fam. Juan, Juanito.
jack s. hombre; mozo; marinero. 2 sota [naipe]. 3 macho de algunos animales; asno, burro. 4 MEC. gato, cric. 5 boliche [bola pequeña]. 6 torno [de asador]. 7 sacabotas. 8 jaquemar. 9 RADIO., TELEF. clavija de conexión. 10 MAR. bandera de proa. 11 fam. ~ tar, marinero. 12 ~ towel, toalla sin fin colgada de un rodillo. 13 every man ~, todos sin excepción. 14 pl. juego de los cantillos.
jack (to) tr. [con up] alzar [con gato o cric]. 2 subir [precios, salarios, etc.].
jackal (dȳæ·kal) s. ZOOL. chacal.
jackanapes (-aneips) s. mequetrefe.
jackass (-æs) s. ZOOL. y fig. asno, burro.
jackboots (-buts) s. botas altas y fuertes.
jackdaw (-do) s. ORN. chova.
jacket (-it) s. chaqueta; americana; cazadora [prenda]. 2 camisa, cubierta, envoltura. 3 sobrecubierta [de libro].
jacket (to) tr. poner chaqueta, cubierta, etc., a.
jackhammer (-jæmøʳ) s. MEC. martillo perforador.
jack-in-the-box s. muñeco en una caja de resorte.
jackknife (-naif) s. navaja de bolsillc. 2 NAT. salto de carpa.
Jack-of-all-trades s. persona que sirve para muchos oficios.
jack-o'-lantern s. fuego fatuo.
jackscrew (-skru) s. MEC. cric o gato de tornillo.
jackstraw (-stro) s. efigie de paja. 2 pelagatos. 3 pajita [para jugar]. 4 pl. juego de las pajitas.
Jacob (dȳei·køb) n. pr. Jaime, Jacobo. 2 Jacob.
Jacobean (dȳeikøbi·an) adj. de Jacobo I de Inglaterra o de su reinado.
Jacobin (dȳæ·købin) s. jacobino. 2 (con min.) pichón capuchino.
Jacobite (-bait) adj.-s. jacobita.
Jacob's ladder s. BIB. escalera de Jacob. 2 MAR. escala de jarcia.

Jacob's-ladder s. BOT. polemonio. 2 BOT. sello de Salomón.
jaconet (dȳæ·konet) s. chaconá [tela].
jade (dȳeid) s. MINER. jade. 2 rocín, jamelgo. 3 mala pécora; mujerzuela. adj. verde.
jade (to) tr. cansar, agotar. 2 estragar, hastiar. 3 intr. cansarse, desalentarse.
jag (dȳæg) s. diente, punta, mella, corte irregular [esp. en el borde de una cosa]. 2 onda o punta colgante; cuchillada [en un vestido].
jag (to) tr. dentar, mellar, hacer cortes irregulares [esp. en el borde]; 2 hacer cuchilladas [en un vestido]. ¶ Pret. y p. p.: *jagged;* ger.: *-gging.*
jagged (-id) adj. dentado, mellado, cortado irregularmente en el borde.
jaguar (dȳa·guaʳ) s. ZOOL. jaguar.
jail (dȳeil) s. cárcel, prisión, calabozo: *fever,* MED. tifus.
jail (to) tr. encarcelar, meter en la cárcel.
jailbird (-bøʳd) s. fam. preso. 2 delincuente habitual.
jailer (-øʳ) s. carcelero.
jalap (dȳæ·lap) s. BOT., FARM. jalapa.
jalopy (dȳala·pi) s. fam. carraca, fotingo [automóvil o avión viejo].
jalousie (dȳælusi·) s. persiana.
jam (dȳæm) s. compota, confitura, mermelada. 2 apretura, apiñamiento. 3 atasco; obstrucción; embotellamiento [del tráfico]. 4 (E.U.) aprieto, situación difícil.
jam (to) tr. apretar, estrechar, apiñar. 2 estrujar, machucar. 3 atascar, obstruir. 4 meter o introducir apretando, a la fuerza. 5 RADIO. perturbar con interferencias. 6 to ~ on the brakes, frenar de golpe. 7 intr. agolparse, apiñarse. 8 atascarse. ¶ Pret. y p. p.: *jammed;* ger.: *-mming.*
Jamaica (dȳamei·ka) n. pr. GEOGR. Jamaica.
jamb, jambe (dȳæm) s. jamba. 2 ARM. espinillera.
jamboree (dȳæmbøri·) s. pop. jolgorio, fiesta. 2 reunión de muchachos exploradores.
James (dȳeims) n. pr. Jaime.
Jane (dȳein) n. pr. Juana.
jangle (dȳæ·ngøl) s. charla, parloteo. 2 sonido discordante, cencerreo.
jangle (to) intr. charlar, parlotear. 2 altercar, disputar. 3 sonar de un modo discordante, cencerrear.
janitor (dȳæ·nitøʳ) s. portero, conserje.

janizary (dÿæ·nišæri) s. jenízaro.
Jansenism (dÿæ·nsønišm) s. jansenismo.
January (dÿæ·niueri) s. enero.
Janus (dÿæ·nøs) n. pr. MIT. Jano.
Jap (dÿæp) abrev. de JAPAN y JAPANESE.
Japan (dÿapæ·n) n. pr. GEOGR. Japón.
japan s. barniz, laca, charol; laca japonesa.
japan (to) tr. barnizar [esp. con laca]. 2 charolar.
¶ Pret. y p. p.: japanned; ger.: -nning.
Japanese (dÿæpanɪ·š) adj.-s. japonés: ~ lantern, farolillo a la veneciana.
jape (dÿeip) s. broma, burla.
jape (to) tr. embromar, burlar.
Japheth (dÿæ·fez) n. pr. Jafet.
japonica (dÿæpa·nika) s. BOT. camelia japonesa. 2 BOT. membrillo japonés.
jar (dÿaʳ) s. jarra, tarro. 2 sonido áspero, discordante; chirrido. 3 vibración, choque, sacudida. 4 efecto desagradable, irritante. 5 desacuerdo, desavenencia. 6 on the ~, entreabierto, entornado.
jar (to) intr. sonar de un modo áspero o discordante. 2 vibrar, trepidar, chocar [con sonido áspero]. 3 producir un efecto desagradable, irritante. 4 discordar, chocar, no armonizar. 5 reñir, disputar. 6 tr. poner en tarro. 7 hacer sonar de un modo áspero; sacudir, hacer vibrar o trepidar. ¶ Pret. y p. p.: jarred; ger.: rring.
jardiniere (dÿa·dini·øʳ) s. jardinera [para plantas]. 2 jarrón [para flores].
jargon (dÿa·ʳgøn) s. jerga, jerigonza. 2 monserga.
jasmine (dÿæ·smin) s. BOT. jazmín.
Jasper (dÿæ·spøʳ) n. pr. Gaspar.
jasper s. MINER. jaspe.
jaundice (dÿo·ndis) s. MED. ictericia. 2 mal humor, envidia, celos.
jaundice (to) tr. MED. causar ictericia. 2 amargar, predisponer, ofuscar.
jaunt (dÿont) s. paseo, excursión, caminata.
jaunt (to) intr. pasear, hacer una excursión.
jaunty (-i) adj. vivo, garboso, airoso. 2 elegante, vistoso.
javelin (dÿæ·vlin) s. jabalina, venablo.
jaw (dÿo) s. ZOOL. mandíbula, quijada. 2 MEC. quijada, mordaza; horquilla, boca. 3 palabrería; disputa: hold your ~!, ¡cállese ya! 4 pl. boca, entrada [de un valle, desfiladero, etc.]. 5 fig. garras, poder. 6 pop. la boca.
jaw (to) tr. reñir, regañar, sermonear. 2 intr. charlar, dar la lata.
jawbone (-boun) s. quijada, mandíbula.
jawbreaker (-breikøʳ) s. fam. palabra de difícil pronunciación, trabalenguas.
jay (dÿei) s. ORN. arrendajo.
jaywalker (-uokoʳ) s. peatón imprudente que no obedece las reglas de la circulación.
jazz (dÿæš) s. jazz: ~ band, orquesta de jazz. 2 pop. viveza, animación.
jazz (to) tr. transformar en jazz, poner en música de jazz.
jealous (dÿe·løs) adj. celoso [de sus derechos, etc.]. 2 celoso [que tiene celos]; envidioso. 3 receloso.
jealousy (-i) s. celos. 2 envidia. 3 recelo, desconfianza, vigilancia.
Jean (dÿin) n. pr. Juana.
jean (dÿin o dÿen) s. TEJ. dril. 2 pl. pantalones de dril, guardapolvo de dril.
jeep (dÿɪp) s. jip, pequeño automóvil militar.
jeer (dÿi·øʳ) s. burla, pitorreo, mofa, befa.
jeer (to) tr.-intr. burlarse, mofarse de, befar.
Jeff (dÿef) n. pr. abrev. de GEOFFREY.

Jehovah (dÿijou·va) n. pr. Jehová.
jejune (dÿi·dÿun) adj. falto, escaso. 2 seco, árido. 3 insípido, insustancial.
jejunum (dÿidÿu·nøm) s. ANAT. yeyuno.
jellied (dÿe·lid) adj. gelatinoso.
jelly (dÿe·li) s. jalea. 2 gelatina; substancia gelatinosa.
jelly (to) intr. convertirse en jalea o gelatina.
jellyfish (-fish) s. ZOOL. medusa, aguamar.
jennet (dÿe·nit) s. jaca española. 2 burra, jumenta.
Jennie, Jenny (dÿe·ni) n. pr. dim. de JANE.
jenny s. ant. máquina de hilar. 2 MEC. grúa locomóvil. 3 jenny o ~ ass, asna, burra.
jeopardize (to) (dÿe·paʳdaiš) tr. arriesgar, exponer, comprometer, poner en peligro.
jeopardy (-i) s. riesgo, peligro, exposición.
jerboa (dÿøʳbou·a) s. ZOOL. gerbo, jerbo.
jeremiad (dÿerimai·æd) s. jeremiada.
Jeremiah (dÿirimai·a) n. pr. Jeremías.
Jericho (dÿe·rikou) n. pr. GEOGR. HIST. Jericó.
jerk (dÿøʳk) s. tirón, sacudida, movimiento brusco: by jerks, a sacudidas. 2 salto, repullo, respingo. 3 tic, espasmo muscular.
jerk (to) tr. sacudir, traquetear, dar tirones o sacudidas a; mover bruscamente, a tirones o sacudidas. 2 atasajar [la carne]: jerked beef, tasajo, *charqui. 3 intr. moverse a sacudidas; avanzar dando tumbos.
jerkin (-in) s. justillo, jubón.
jerky (-i) adj. accidentado [camino]. 2 desigual [estilo]. 3 que marcha dando sacudidas.
Jerome (dÿirou·m o dÿe·rom) n. pr. m. Jerónimo.
Jerry (dÿe·ri) n. pr. dim de JEREMIAH.
jerry s. fam. vaso de noche.
jerry-build adj. mal construido, hecho con malos materiales.
Jersey (dÿø·ʳsi) n. pr. GEOGR. Jersey. 2 (con min.) estambre fino. 3 jersey.
Jerusalem (dÿiru·salem) n. pr. GEOGR., HIST. Jerusalén. 2 BOT. ~ artichoke, aguaturma, cotufa.
jess (dÿes) s. CETR. pihuela.
jessamine (dÿe·samin) s. BOT. jazmín.
jest (dÿest) s. broma, burla, chanza, chiste: in ~, en broma. 2 cosa de risa.
jest (to) intr. bromear, burlarse, chancearse.
jester (-øʳ) s. bromista. 2 gracioso, bufón.
Jesuit (dÿe·šuit) s. jesuita.
Jesus (dÿi·šøs) n. pr. Jesús. 2 Jesus Christ, Jesucristo.
jet (dÿet) s. MINER. azabache. 2 chorro, vena, surtidor: ~ propulsion, propulsión a chorro; ~ plane, avión de reacción. 3 chorretada. 4 caño, boquilla, mechero: gas ~, mechero de gas.
jet (to) intr. salir, brotar o manar en chorro. 2 tr. lanzar o arrojar en chorro. ¶ Pret. y p. p.: jetted; ger.: -tting.
jet-black adj. negro como el azabache.
jetsam (-sam) s. DER. MAR. echazón. 2 pecio. 3 fig. cosa desechada por inútil.
jettison (to) (dÿe·tisøn) tr. DER. MAR. hacer echazón de. 2 echar, desechar [lo que estorba].
jetton (dÿe·tøn) s. ficha [de juego, etc.].
jetty (dÿe·ti) s. malecón, escollera, rompeolas, dique. 2 muelle, desembarcadero. 3 adj. JETBLACK.
Jew (dÿu) adj.-s. judío, israelita.
jewel (-øl) s. joya, alhaja, joyel. 2 gema, piedra preciosa. 3 rubí [de reloj].
jewel (to) tr. enjoyar. 2 adornar con piedras preciosas. ¶ Pret. y p. p.: jeweled o -lled; p. a.: -ling o -lling.

jewel (l) er (-ø^r) *s.* joyero, platero: *jeweler's shop*, joyería, platería.
jewellery, jewelry (-ri) *s.* joyas, pedrería; aderezo.
Jewess (dẙu·is) *s.* judía, israelita.
Jewish (dẙu·ish) *adj.* judaico, judío. *2* ajudiado.
Jewry (dẙu·ri) *n. pr.* GEOGR. Judea. *2 s.* judería, barrio judío.
Jews'-harp *s.* MÚS. birimbao.
jib (dẙib) *s.* MAR. foque: ~ *boom,* botalón de foque. *2* brazo, aguilón [de grúa].
jib (to) *intr.* MAR. moverse bruscamente una vela de cuchillo cuando se vira. *2* repropiarse [el caballo]. ¶ Pret. y p. p.: *jibbed;* ger.: *-bbing.*
jibe (to) (dẙaib) *tr.-intr.* TO JIB. *2* TO GIBE. *3 intr.* (E.U.) concordar, pegar [dos cosas].
jiffy (dẙi·fi) *s.* fam. instante, periquete, santiamén.
jig (dẙig) *s.* MÚS., DANZA giga, jiga. *2* anzuelo de cuchara. *3* plantilla [para taladrar, etc.]. *4* MIN. criba hidráulica. *5* ~ *saw,* segueta, sierra de vaivén. *6 the* ~ *is up,* se acabó todo, no hay más esperanza.
jig (to) *tr.-intr.* bailar una jiga. *2* mover o moverse de arriba a abajo y de abajo arriba, rítmicamente, con sacudidas. *3* cortar con segueta. *4* pescar con anzuelo de cuchara.
jigger (-ø^r) *s.* bailador de jiga. *2* MEC. cualquier aparato o utensilio con movimiento rápido de vaivén. *3* ELECT. transformador de oscilaciones. *4* anzuelo de cuchara. *5* MAR. contramesana. *6* MAR. pequeña embarcación. *7* ENT. nigua. *8* ZOOL. garrapata. *9* fam. cosa, chisme.
jiggle (dẙi·gøl) *tr.-intr.* mover o moverse a sacudidas o tirones, moverse de un lado a otro.
jigsaw puzzle (dẙi·gso) *s.* rompecabezas.
jilt (to) (dẙilt) *tr.* despedir o dejar plantado [a un novio]. *2 intr.* coquetear.
Jim (dẙim) *n. pr. dim.* de JAMES. *2* ~ *Crow,* fam. y desp. (E.U.) negro.
Jimmy (-i) *n. pr. dim.* de JAMES.
jimmy *s.* palanqueta [de ladrón].
jingle (dẙi·ngøl) *s.* tintineo, cascabeleo, sonido metálico. *2* rima o verso pueril. *3* sonaja [del pandero]; cascabel.
jingle (to) *intr.* tintinear, cascabelear; sonar [las monedas, llaves, etc.]. *2* rimar. *3 tr.* hacer sonar o tintinear.
jingo (dẙi·ngou) *adj.-s.* jingoísta. *3* interj. *by ~!,* ¡caramba!, ¡por Dios!
jingoism (-išm) *s.* jingoísmo, patriotería.
jinnee (dẙini) *s.* genio [en la mitología mahometana].
jitters (dẙi·tø^rš) *s. pl.* fam. (E.U.) agitación, inquietud, nerviosismo: *to give the ~,* poner nervioso, volver loco.
jiujitsu (dẙudẙi·tsu) *s.* JUJITSU.
Joan (dẙou·n o dẙo·an) *n. pr. f.* Juana.
job (dẙab) *s.* obra, trabajo, tarea, quehacer, cometido: *on the ~,* fam. en su puesto, atendiendo a sus obligaciones. *2* empleo, ocupación: *to be out of ~,* estar sin trabajo. *3* asunto, negocio: *bad ~,* mal asunto, mal negocio. *5* destajo: *by the ~,* a destajo. *6* agiotaje. *7* chanchullo. *8* IMPR. remiendo.
job (to) *tr.-intr.* negociar como corredor o intermediario. *2* especular en fondos públicos. *3* hacer o trabajar a destajo. *4* hacer chapuzas. *5* hacer chanchullos. *6 tr.* subarrendar [un trabajo]. *7* pinchar, picar, herir ligeramente. ¶ Pret. y p. p.: *jobbed;* ger.: *-bbing.*
jobber (-bø^r) *s.* COM. intermediario, corredor. *2*

destajista. *3* (Ingl.) agiotista. *4* chanchullero, traficante político.
jobholder (-jouldø^r) *s.* empleado, burócrata.
jobless (-lis) *adj.* desocupado, sin empleo.
Job's-tears *s.* BOT. lágrimas de David o de Job.
jockey (dẙa·ki) *s.* DEP. jockey. *2* (E.U.) chalán. *3* maulero, tramposo, engañador.
jockey (to) *tr.-intr.* engañar, embaucar. *2 intr.* maniobrar [para obtener una ventaja].
jocose (dẙoukou·s) *adj.* jocoso. *2* bromista, chancero.
jocosity (dẙouka·siti) *s.* jocosidad. *2* broma, chanza.
jocular (dẙa·kiula^r) *adj.* jocoso. *2* chancero. *3* alegre, jovial.
jocularity (dẙakiulæ·riti) *s.* jocosidad. *2* jovialidad.
jocund (dẙa·kønd) *adj.* jocundo. *2* animado, jovial.
jocundity (dẙakø·nditi) *s.* jocundidad, jovialidad.
jodhpurs (dẙa·dpø^rs) *s. pl.* pantalón de montar.
Joe (dẙou) *n. pr. dim.* de JOSEPH.
jog (dẙag) *s.* empujoncito, golpecito, sacudida ligera. *2* estímulo [para la memoria]. *3* trote o paso corto.
jog (to) *tr.* empujar. *2* dar un golpecito, tocar con el codo. *3* excitar suavemente; estimular [la memoria]. *4* mover poco a poco. *5* intr. *to ~ on* o *along,* andar despacio o al trote corto. ¶ Pret. y p. p.: *jogged;* ger.: *-gging.*
joggle (dẙa·gøl) *s.* diente, muesca. *2* sacudida.
joggle (to) *tr.* unir o asegurar con diente y muesca. *2* dar una sacudida ligera. *3 intr.* avanzar o moverse a sacudidas, vacilar.
John (dẙan) *n. pr.* Juan. *2* ~ *Bull,* el inglés típico; el pueblo inglés. *3* ~ *Doe,* fulano de tal. *4* ICT. ~ *Dory,* gallo, pez de San Pedro.
Johnny, Johnnie (dẙa·ni) *n. pr. dim.* de JOHN.
join (dẙoin) *s.* punto de unión o de encuentro.
join (to) *tr.* unir, juntar. *2* acoplar, ensamblar. *3* añadir, agregar. *4* asociar. *5* unirse, agregarse, incorporarse a; ingresar en; abrazar [una causa]. *6* aunarse. *7* trabar [batalla]. *8* desaguar en. *9* tocar o lindar con. *10 intr.* unirse, juntarse, asociarse. *11* confluir [dos ríos]. *12 to ~ in,* tomar parte en.
joiner (-ø^r) *s.* el que une o junta. *2* ensamblador, montador. *3* ebanista, carpintero.
joinery (-i) *s.* ebanistería; carpintería de taller.
joint (dẙoint) *s.* ANAT. coyuntura, articulación, nudillo: *out of ~,* dislocado; fig. desbarajustado. *2* junta, juntura, unión, articulación, empalme, ensambladura. *3* ALB. llaga. *4* BOT. nudo, axila; entrenudo. *5* ZOOL. artejo, artículo. *6* CARN. trozo de carne. *7* ENCUD. cartivana. *8* fam. casa, establecimiento.
9 adj. unido, mixto, común, mancomunado, solidario, indiviso: ~ *committee,* comisión mixta; ~ *consent,* común acuerdo; ~ *stock,* capital social; fondo en común. *10* copartícipe, co-: ~ *heir,* coheredero. *11* de articulación, empalme, etc.: ~ *box,* ELECT. caja de empalmes. *12* BOT. ~ *fir,* belcho.
joint (to) *tr.* unir, articular, ajustar, ensamblar. *2* descoyuntar, cortar por las coyunturas. *3* CARN. destazar. *4 intr.* articularse.
jointed (-id) *adj.* articulado [que tiene articulaciones]. *2* nudoso.
jointly (-li) *adv.* juntamente, conjuntamente.
joint-stock company *s.* compañía por acciones, sociedad anónima.
joist (dẙoist) *s.* ARQ. viga, vigueta.

joke (dȳouk) *s.* chiste, chascarrillo; chanza, broma: *to play ~ on*, gastar una broma a; *in ~*, de broma, por chanza.

joke (to) *intr.* bromear, hablar en broma, chancearse. *2 fam.* gastar bromas: *joking aside*, *no joking*, bromas aparte, hablando en serio.

joker (dȳou·køᵣ) *s.* bromista, chancero, guasón. *2* comodín [naipe].

jollity (dȳa·liti) *s.* alegría, animación, regocijo. *2* diversión, fiesta.

jolly (dȳa·li) *adj.* alegre, animado, divertido, jovial. *2 fam.* estupendo; bueno, grande. *3* MAR. *~ boat*, chinchorro. *4 adv.* muy, sumamente.

jolly (to) *tr.* animar, alegrar. *2* candonguear, dar coba a, seguir el humor a.

jolt (dȳoult) *s.* traqueteo, tumbo, sacudida. *2* golpe, choque.

jolt (to) *intr.* dar tumbos o sacudidas. *2 tr.* traquetear, sacudir.

Jonah (ȳou·na) *n. pr.* Jonás. *2 m.* fig. cenizo.

Jonathan (dȳa·nazan) *n. pr.* Jonatán.

jongleur (dȳa·ngløᵣ) *s.* juglar, trovador.

jonquil (dȳa·nkuil) *s.* BOT. junquillo.

Jordan (dȳo·ᵣdan) *n. pr.* GEOGR. Jordán [río]. *2* GEOG. Jordania.

Joseph (dȳou·šef) *n. pr.* José.

Josephine (-šøfin) *n. pr.* Josefina.

josh (to) (dȳash) *tr. fam.* (E.U.) embromar, burlarse de. *2 intr. fam.* (E.U.) chancearse.

Joshua (dȳa·shua) *n. pr.* Josué.

joss (dȳas) *s.* ídolo chino.

jostle (dȳa·søl) *s.* empujones, empellones. *2* choque.

jostle (to) *tr.* empujar, empellar, dar codazos a. *2* meter a empellones. *3* hacer chocar. *4 intr.* empujarse, atropellarse. *5* avanzar a fuerza de empujones o codazos. *6* chocar, encontrarse.

jot (dȳat) *s.* jota, ápice, pizca, tilde.

jot (to) *tr.* escribir de prisa. *2 to ~ down*, apuntar, anotar. ¶ Pret. y p. p.: *jotted*; ger.: *-tting*.

joule (dȳaul o dȳul) *s.* ELECT. julio.

jounce (dȳauns) *s.* sacudida, traqueteo.

jounce (to) *tr.* sacudir, traquetear. *2 intr.* botar, dar tumbos.

journal (dȳø·ᵣnal) *s.* diario, periódico. *2* diario [relación día por día]. *3* COM. diario. *4* MEC. gorrón, espiga.

journalese (dȳøᵣnali·š) *s.* lenguaje periodístico.

journalism (dȳø·ᵣnališm) *s.* periodismo.

journey (dȳø·ᵣni) *s.* viaje; camino, jornada. *2* tránsito, pasaje.

journey (to) *intr.* viajar. *2 tr.* viajar por; recorrer en viaje.

journeyman (-mæn) *s.* jornalero. *2* oficial [de un oficio].

joust (dȳøst o dȳaust) *s.* justa. *2 pl.* torneo.

joust (to) *intr.* justar.

Jove (dȳouv) *n. pr.* MIT. Jove: *by ~!*, ¡por Dios!

jovial (dȳou·vial) *adj.* jovial, alegre, fetivo.

joviality (dȳouviæ·liti) *s.* jovialidad, alegría.

jowl (dȳaul) *s.* carrillo. *2* quijada. *3* papada [de res].

joy (dȳoi) *s.* gozo, júbilo, regocijo, alegría.

joy (to) *tr.* alegrar. *2 intr.* alegrarse, regocijarse.

joyful (-ful) *adj.* jubiloso, gozoso, alegre.

joyless (-lis) *adj.* triste, sin alegría.

joyous (-øs) *adj.* alegre, gozoso.

jubilant (dȳu·bilant) *adj.* jubiloso, alborozado.

jubilate (to) (-eit) *intr.* jubilar, alegrarse.

jubilation (-eišhøn) *s.* jubilación, exultación, exclamación de júbilo.

jubilee (dȳu·bilı) *s.* júbilo. *2* jubileo. *3* aniversario, quincuagésimo aniversario.

Judaic (al (dȳudei·k(al) *adj.* judaico, judío.

Judaism (dȳu·diišm) *s.* judaísmo.

Judaize (to) (dȳu·diaiš) *s.* judaizar.

Judas (dȳu·das) *n. pr.* y fig. Judas; *~ tree*, BOT. ciclamor, árbol de Judas. *2* (con min.). mirilla de puerta.

Judea (dȳudı·a) *n. pr.* GEOGR. HIST. Judea.

judge (dȳødȳ) *s.* juez, magistrado: *~ advocate*, auditor de guerra o de marina. *2* juez, perito, conocedor.

judge (to) *tr.-intr.* DER., FIL. juzgar. *2* juzgar, creer, estimar, deducir, suponer: *judging by*, o *from*, a juzgar por.

judgement, judgment (-mønt) *s.* decisión, fallo, sentencia. *2* juicio, opinión, dictamen. *3* juicio, criterio, discernimiento. *4* castigo de Dios. *5* LÓG., FIL., TEOL. juicio: *the (Last) Judgment*, el juicio final.

judicature (dȳu·dikachuᵣ) *s.* judicatura.

judicial (dȳudi·shal) *adj.* judicial. *2* judiciario. *3* crítico, apto para juzgar.

judiciary (-shiæri) *adj.* judicial. *2 s.* administración de justicia, judicatura.

judicious (-shøs) *adj.* juicioso, de buen sentido, discreto, atinado.

judiciousness (-nis) *s.* juicio, cordura, buen sentido, discernimiento.

Judith (dȳu·diz) *n. pr.* Judit.

jug (dȳøg) *s.* jarro, cántaro. *2* [E.U.] botija. *3* pop. cárcel, chirona.

jug (to) *tr.* COC. estofar. *2 fam.* encarcelar. ¶ Pret. y p. p.: *jugged*; ger.: *-gging*.

juggle (dȳø·gøl) *s.* juego de manos, escamoteo. *2* engaño, trampa.

juggle (to) *intr.* hacer juegos de manos o juegos malabares. *2* hacer trampas, engañar. *3 to ~ away*, escamotear.

juggler (dȳø·gløᵣ) *s.* juglar, prestidigitador, malabarista. *2* tramposo, escamoteador.

jugular (dȳø·giulaᵣ) *adj.-s.* ANAT. yugular.

jugulate (to) (-leit) *tr.* cortar, detener una enfermedad, etc.

juice (dȳu·s) *s.* zumo; jugo. *2 fig.* jugo, substancia. *3 pop.* electricidad, gasolina, etc., como fuerza motriz.

juicy (dȳu·si) *adj.* jugoso, zumoso. *2* picante, divertido.

jujitsu (dȳudȳi·tsu) *s.* jiu-jitsu.

jujube (dȳu·dȳub) *s.* BOT. yuyuba, azufaifa.

juke box (dȳuk) *s.* gramófono, tragaperras.

julep (dȳu·lip) *s.* FARM. julepe. *2 mint ~*, refresco alcohólico con hojas de hierbabuena.

Julian (dȳu·lian) *n. pr.* Julián. *2* Juliano.

julienne (dȳulie·n) *s.* sopa Juliana.

Julius (dȳu·liøs) *n. pr.* Julio.

July (dȳulai·) *s.* julio [mes].

jumble (dȳø·mbøl) *s.* mezcla, revoltillo, confusión. *2* especie de rosquilla [dulce].

jumble (to) *tr.* emburujar, amontonar o mezclar confusamente. *2 intr.* mezclarse, juntarse, moverse de un modo confuso o agitado.

jumbo (dȳø·mbou) *adj.* enorme, grande [en su línea]. *2 s. fam.* elefante.

jump (dȳømp) *s.* salto, brinco. *2* lanzamiento [en paracaídas]. *3* sacudida, movimiento convulsivo. *4* transición brusca, salto, omisión. *5 to be on the ~*, andar de aquí para allá, trafagar.

jump (to) *intr.* saltar, brincar, dar saltos; dar un salto, una sacudida: *to ~ for joy*, brincar de gozo. *2* lanzarse [en paracaídas]. *3* subir repentinamente [los precios]. *4* concordar, coincidir. *5 to ~ at*, apresurarse a aprovechar o aceptar. *6 to ~ on one*, regañar, criticar, poner como nuevo. *7 to ~ to a conclusion*, hacer una deducción precipitada. *8 tr.* saltar [salvar de un salto]. *9* hacer saltar [a un niño, un caballo, etc.]. *10* sobresaltar, hacer dar un salto, un repullo. *11* FERROC. *to ~ the track*, descarrilar.

jumper (-ø^r) *s.* saltador. *2* blusa [de obrero, de marinero]. *3* jersey. *4* ELECT. alambre de cierre. *5 pl.* mono [para niños].

jumpy (dÿø·mpi) *adj.* saltón, que salta. *2* nervioso, excitable en extremo.

junction (dÿø·nkshøn) *s.* unión, reunión. *2* punto de unión o reunión; confluencia. *3* FERROC. empalme. *4* cosa que une.

juncture (dÿø·nkchø^r) *s.* junta, juntura. *2* articulación, conexión. *3* coyuntura, sazón, estado de cosas, momento crítico, ocasión.

June (dÿun) *s.* junio.

jungle (dÿø·ngøl) *s.* selva virgen, manigua. *2* matorral, espesura, maraña.

junior (dÿu·niø^r) *adj.* menor, más joven, menos antiguo, hijo: *X. X. ~*, X. X. hijo; *the ~ partner*, el socio menos antiguo. *2* para jóvenes. *3 s.* joven. *4* junior [religioso].

juniper (dÿu·nipø^r) *s.* BOT. junípero, enebro.

junk (dÿønk) *s.* junco [embarcación]. *2* desechos, desperdicios de vidrio, papel, cuerda, etc.; chatarra. *3* MAR. trozos de viejo para hacer estopa, etc. *4* fig. desecho, borra, basura. *5 ~ room*, trastera, leonera.

junket (dÿø·nkit) *s.* COC. manjar de leche, cuajo y azúcar. *2* banquete, francachela; jira.

junket (to) *intr.* ir de jira o de jolgorio.

junkman (dÿø·nkmæn) *s.* comerciante en desperdicios; chatarrero.

Juno (dÿu·nou) *n. pr.* MIT. Juno.

junto (dÿø·ntou) *s.* camarilla.

Jupiter (dÿu·pitø^r) *n. pr.* MIT., ASTR. Júpiter.

Jurassic (dÿuræ·sik) *adj.-s.* GEOL. jurásico.

jurel (dÿure·l) *s.* ICT. jurel.

juridic(al (dÿuri·dik(al) *adj.* jurídico. *2* judicial.

jurisconsult (dÿuriska·nsølt) *s.* jurisconsulto.

jurisdicción (-di·kshøn) *s.* jurisdicción.

jurisprudence (-pru·døns) *s.* jurisprudencia.

jurisprudent (-prudønt) *s.* jurisperito.

jurist (dÿu·rist) *s.* jurista, legista.

juror (dÿu·rø^r) *s.* jurado [individuo].

jury (dÿu·ri) *s.* DER. jurado [cuerpo e institución]. *2* jurado [de un concurso, etc.].

juryman (-møn) *s.* jurado [individuo].

just (dÿøst) *adj.* justo, recto, honrado. *2* justiciero, imparcial. *3* justo [arreglado a justicia y razón; merecido]. *4* justo, fiel, exacto, preciso. *5* verdadero, bien fundado. *6 adv.* justamente, cabalmente, precisamente: *~ so*, eso mismo. *7* no más que, sólo, nada más; *he is ~ a child*, no es más que un niño. *8* en el mismo instante, poco ha, recién; dentro de un momento; *~ now*, ahora mismo, hace poco; *he has ~ arrived*, acaba de llegar. *9* fam. verdaderamente, muy. *10 ~ about*, casi, bastante, poco más o menos: *11 ~ as*, al tiempo que, en el momento que, cuando, no bien; lo mismo que; semejante a. *12 ~ beyond*, un poco más allá de.

justice (dÿø·stis) *s.* justicia: *to do oneself ~*, hacerlo uno lo mejor que pueda, quedar bien. *2* verdad, exactitud. *3* DER. Juez, magistrado: *~ of the peace*, juez de paz.

justiciary (dÿø·stisheri) *adj.* judicial. *2 s.* juez, magistrado.

justifiable (dÿø·stifaiabøl) *adj.* justificable.

justification (dÿøstifikei·shøn) *s.* justificación. *2* descargo, defensa. *3* razón de ser.

justify (to) (dÿø·stifai) *tr.* justificar. *2* defender, sincerar. *3* demostrar ser justo o exacto. *4 intr.* DER. justificarse. ¶ Pret. y p. p.: *justified*.

justly (dÿø·stli) *adv.* justamente, rectamente. *2* justamente [con justicia o razón; merecidamente]. *3* exactamente, precisamente.

justness (-nis) *s.* justicia, equidad. *2* exactitud, propiedad, precisión, corrección.

jut (dÿøt) *s.* salidizo, proyección, vuelo, resalto.

jut (to) *intr.* [a veces con *out*] salir, sobresalir; proyectarse, extenderse. ¶ Pret. y p. p.: *jutted;* ger.: *-tting*.

jute (dÿut) *s.* yute, cáñamo de Indias.

juvenescence (dÿuvøne·søns) *s.* rejuvenecimiento.

juvenile (dÿu·vønil) *adj.* juvenil, joven. *2* de o para jóvenes o menores. *3 s.* joven, mocito, mocita. *4* TEAT. galancete. *5* libro para niños.

juvenility (dÿuvøni·liti) *s.* juventud, carácter juvenil.

juxtapose (to) (dÿøkstapou·ś) *tr.* yuxtaponer.

juxtaposition (-si·shøn) *s.* yuxtaposición, contigüidad.

K

K, k s. K, k, undécima letra del alfabeto inglés.
Kabyle (kabai·l) s. cabila.
Kaffir, Kafir (kæ·føᵣ) s. cafre [de Cafrería].
kail (keil) s. KALE.
Kaiser (kai·šøᵣ) s. kaiser.
kaki (ka·ki) s. BOT. caqui, níspero del Japón.
kale (keil) s. BOT. col, col rizada.
kaleidoscope (kalai·døskoup) s. calidoscopio.
kaleidoscopic (-ka·pik) adj. calidoscópico.
kalends (kæ·lindš) s. pl. CALENDS.
Kalmuck (kæ·lmøk) adj.-s. calmuco.
Kanaka (kæ·naka) s. canaco.
kangaroo (kængaru·) s. ZOOL. canguro.
Kantian (kæ·ntian) adj. kantiano.
Kantism (kæ·ntišm) s. kantismo.
kaolin (kei·ølin) s. caolín.
kapok (kei·pak) s. capoc, lana de ceiba.
kappa (kæ·pa) s. kappa [letra griega].
karakul (kæ·rakul) s. caracul, astracán [piel].
karat (kæ·rat) s. JOY. quilate.
karyokinesis (kærioukinɪ·sis) s. BIOL. cariocinesis.
Kate (kei·t) n. pr. f. dim. de CATHERINE.
Katherine (kæ·zørin) n. pr. f. CATHERINE.
kation (kæ·taion) s. CATION.
katydid (kei·tidid) s. ENT. especie de saltamontes americano.
kay (kei) s. nombre de la letra k.
kayak (kai·æk) s. canoa de los esquimales.
keck (to) (kek) intr. arquear; vomitar.
kedge (kedÿ) s. MAR. anclote.
keel (kɪl) s. MAR., BOT., ZOOL. quilla.
keel (to) tr. poner quilla. 2 surcar [el mar]. 3 dar de quilla, voltear. 4 intr. to ~ over, volcarse; desplomarse, desmayarse.
keelhaul (to) (kɪ·ljol) tr. MAR. pasar por debajo de la quilla [castigo].
keelson (ke·lsøn) s. MAR. sobrequilla.
keen (kɪn) adj. agudo, afilado. 2 agudo, vivo, intenso, fuerte. 3 agudo, sutil, perspicaz. 4 mordaz, incisivo. 5 vehemente. 6 ansioso, deseoso. 7 muy interesado [por]; entusiasta. 8 (E.U.) lindo, agradable.
keenness (kɪ·nnis) s. agudeza, viveza. 2 sutileza, perspicacia. 3 aspereza. 4 ansia, vehemencia, entusiasmo.
keep (kɪp) s. mantenimiento, subsistencia. 2 fortaleza, torreón. 3 fam. (E.U.) for keeps, para siempre, para quedarse con ello.

keep (to) tr. guardar, tener guardado. 2 tener, mantener [en un lugar, situación o estado]. 3 cuidar, custodiar, guardar. 4 dirigir, tener [un establecimiento, etc.]. 5 llevar [los libros, una cuenta, un diario, etc.]. 6 mantener, conservar, preservar, defender. 7 mantener, sustentar. 8 tener [criados, caballos, huéspedes, etc.]. 9 detener, impedir. 10 retener, guardar [para sí], quedarse con. 11 callar, ocultar. 12 guardar [silencio, etc.]. 13 observar, cumplir, guardar. 14 atenerse a, seguir, no apartarse de. 15 no moverse de, no salir de: to ~ one's bed, guardar cama. 16 celebrar, tener [reunión, sesión, consejo]. 17 hacer [guerra]. 18 to ~ away, tener alejado, no dejar entrar, venir, etc. 19 to ~ back, tener a raya; refrenar, reprimir, impedir; retener, reservar [no divulgar]. 20 to ~ company, acompañar, salir juntos [como novios]. 21 to ~ down, sujetar, oprimir; reprimir. 22 to ~ from, guardar de, impedir, no dejar. 23 to ~ in, no dejar salir; hacer quedar [en la escuela]. 24 to ~ off, mantener a distancia; no dejar entrar o penetrar. 25 to ~ on, conservar puesta [una prenda]. 26 to ~ one's head, no perder la cabeza. 27 to ~ out, no dejar entrar; excluir. 28 to ~ step, llevar el paso. 29 to ~ time, seguir o llevar el compás. 30 to ~ under, tener sujeto, oprimir. 31 to ~ up, mantener, sostener; tener levantado [sin irse a la cama].

32 intr. mantenerse, sostenerse, conservarse. 33 seguir, continuar, permanecer, quedarse. 34 estar, ir, venir [haciendo una cosa]. 35 residir, vivir. 36 to ~ at it, fam. perseverar, persistir. 37 to ~ away, mantenerse apartado, no acercarse. 38 to ~ from, abstenerse de. 39 to ~ off, no acercarse a; no tocar; no andar por, no pisar. 40 to ~ on, ir adelante, proseguir. 41 to ~ out of, evitar, no meterse en. 42 to ~ to, atenerse a; seguir por; llevar [la derecha, la izquierda]. 43 to ~ up, seguir, persistir; seguir, no quedarse atrás.
¶ Pret. y p. p.: kept.
keeper (-øᵣ) s. guardián, guardia, custodio, velador, defensor. 2 alcaide. 3 portero, conserje. 4 carcelero. 5 loquero. 6 guardabosques. 7 el que lleva [una cuenta, registro, etc.]. 8 tenedor [pers.]. 9 propietario o director [de ciertos establecimientos]. 10 armadura [de imán].
keeping (-ing) s. guarda, custodia, cargo, cuidado, conservación, defensa: in safe ~, a buen re-

caudo, en buenas manos. 2 mantenimiento. 3 tenencia, posesión. 4 observancia, cumplimiento. 5 concordancia, armonía. 6 acción de llevar [los libros, una cuenta, un diario, etc.].

keepsake (-seik) s. recuerdo, regalo.

keg (keg) s. cuñete, barril, barrilete.

kelson (ke·lsøn) s. KEELSON.

Kelt (kelt) s. celta.

kelter (-ø^r) s. KILTER.

Keltic (-ik) adj. céltico.

ken (ken) s. (ant. y Esc.) alcance de la vista, de la comprensión.

ken (to) tr. (ant. y Esc.) conocer, comprender, ver, saber. ¶ Pret. y p. p.: kenned; ger.: -nning.

kennel (-øl) s. perrera. 2 jauría. 3 fig. cuchitril. 4 arroyo [de la calle]; reguera.

kennel tr. poner o tener en una perrera. 2 intr. estar en una perrera. ¶ Pret. y p. p.: keneled o -lied; ger.: -ling o -lling.

keno (ki·nou) s. quinterno [en la lotería].

kepi (ke·pi) s. kepis, quepis.

kept (kept) pret. y p. p. de TO KEEP.

keramic (kiræ·mik) adj. CERAMIC.

keramics (-s) s. CERAMICS.

keratin (ke·ratin) s. BIOQUÍM. queratina.

kerb (kø^rb) s. encintado [de las aceras].

kerchief (kø·^rchif) s. pañuelo, pañolón.

kerf (kø^rf) s. corte, muesca, entalladura.

kermes (kø·^miš) s. quermes, alquermes, grana: 2 BOT. kermes o ~ oak, coscoja. 3 ~ berry, coscojo.

kermess (-mes o -mis) s. (E.U.) feria, tómbola, bazar.

kernel (-nøl) s. grano [de trigo o maíz]. 2 almendra, núcleo [de fruto]. 3 fig. corazón [parte esencial].

kerosene (ke·røsin) s. petróleo para lámparas.

kestrel (ke·strøl) s. ORN. cernícalo.

ketch (kech) s. MAR. queche.

ketchup (ke·chøp) s. CATCHUP.

ketone (kı·toun) s. QUÍM. cetona.

kettle (ke·tøl) s. caldero, perol, olla, marmita. 2 tetera, pava. 3 MAR. caja [de brújula].

kettledrum (-drøm) s. MÚS. timbal, atabal.

kettleful (-ful) s. calderada.

key (kı) s. llave [para abrir o cerrar, dar cuerda, etc.]. 2 llave [en sentido figurado]. 3 clave [de un enigma, una traducción, etc.; principio fundamental]. 4 clave, contracifra. 5 llave de tuerca. 6 templador, afinador [instrumento]. 7 MEC. llave, cuña de ajuste; clavija, chaveta. 8 ARQ. clave. 9 MÚS. llave, pistón. 10 TELEG. manipulador. 11 tecla [de piano, etc.]. 12 MÚS. tono: in ~, templado; fig. a tono, en armonía. 13 fig. tono, estilo, tenor. 14 cayo, isleta. 15 BOT. sámara.

key (to) tr. poner a tono, armonizar. 2 MÚS. afinar, templar. 3 cerrar [con llave]; asegurar [con clavijas, chavetas, etc.]. 4 ARQ. poner la clave. 5 to ~ up, elevar el tono, el nivel de; excitar.

keyboard (kı·bø^rd) s. teclado.

keyhole (-joul) s. ojo de la cerradura.

keynote (-nout) s. MÚS. nota tónica. 2 hecho, idea, etc., principal o fundamental.

keystone (-stoun) s. ARQ. clave. 2 base, fundamento principal, piedra angular.

khaki (ka·ki) s. caqui [tela y color]. 2 pl. uniforme caqui.

khan (kan) s. kan, can [título]. 2 caravasar.

khedive (kedı·v) s. jedive.

kibe (kai·b) s. grieta [en la piel]; sabañón ulcerado.

kibed (-d) adj. agrietado, lleno de sabañones.

kiblah (ki·bla) s. alquibla.

kick (kik) s. puntapié, patada, coz: free ~, FÚTBOL golpe franco. 2 coz [de un animal]. 3 coz, retroceso [de un arma]. 4 fam. oposición, protesta, queja. 5 fam. fuerza, efecto estimulante [de una bebida]. 6 fam. placer, gusto. 7 fam. capacidad para reaccionar, elasticidad; vida, animación. 8 fondo entrante [de una botella].

kick (to) tr. dar de puntapiés o un puntapié a, dar patadas o una patada a; acocear; mover o sacudir [los pies]; hacer, echar, etc., de un puntapié o a puntapiés: to ~ down, echar abajo de un puntapié; to ~ one's heels, estar esperando; to ~ out, echar a puntapiés, echar fuera; to ~ the bucket, fam. estirar la pata, morir. 2 to ~ up, levantar, armar, promover. 3 intr. patear, pernear, dar puntapiés, dar coces: to ~ against the pricks, dar coces contra el aguijón. 4 dar coz [un arma]. 5 fam. oponerse, protestar, quejarse. 6 FÚTBOL . poner la pelota en juego.

kicker (ki·kø^r) s. acoceador, pateador. 2 reparón, gruñón.

kickoff (ki·kof) s. FÚTBOL golpe de salida, acción de poner la pelota en juego.

kickshaw (ki·ksho) s. plato de fantasía; golosina. 2 chuchería, fruslería.

kickup (ki·køp) s. pop. riña, alboroto, trapatiesta.

kid (kid) s. ZOOL. cabrito, chivo. 2 cabritilla. 3 fam. niño, niña, chico, chica. 4 pl. guantes o zapatos de cabritilla.

kid (to) intr. parir [la cabra]. 2 tr. embromar, tomar el pelo a. ¶ Pret. y p. p.: kidded; ger.: -dding.

kidder (ki·dø^r) s. fam. bromista, chancero.

kidling (ki·dling) s. choto, cabritillo.

kidnap (to) (ki·dnæp) tr. secuestrar, raptar. ¶ Pret. y p. p.: kidnaped o -pped; ger.: kidnaping o -pping.

kidnapper (ki·dnæpø^r) s. secuestrador, raptor.

kidnapping (ki·dnæping) s. secuestro, rapto.

kidney (ki·dni) s. ANAT. riñón. 2 COC. riñones. 3 fig. temperamento; índole, clase. 4 ~ bean, alubia, judía; judía colorada.

kidney-shaped adj. arriñonado.

kidskin (ki·dskin) s. cabritilla.

kill (kil) s. muerte, matanza [acción]. 2 pieza, caza, cacería [animal o animales muertos]. 3 (E.U.) arroyo, riachuelo.

kill (to) tr. matar [dar muerte a, causar la muerte a; fatigar, alterar la salud de]: to ~ two birds with one stone, matar dos pájaros de un tiro. 2 matar, apagar, destruir, suprimir, neutralizar. 3 matar [el tiempo]. 4 producir una impresión irresistible en.

killdee(r (ki·ldi^r) s. ORN. tildío.

killer (ki·lø^r) s. matador. 2 ZOOL. killer o ~ wale, orca.

killing (ki·ling) s. muerte, matanza [acción]. 2 fam. éxito sensacional; gran ganancia. 3 adj. matador. 4 destructivo. 5 fam. irresistible. 6 muy divertido o ridículo.

kill-joy s. aguafiestas.

kiln (kil o klin) s. horno [para secar, calcinar, etc.].

kilo (ki·lou) s. kilo, quilo, kilogramo.

kilocycle (ki·løsaikøl) s. kilociclo.

kilogram, -gramme (ki·løgræm) s. kilogramo, quilogramo.

kilogrammeter (-ı·tø^r) s. kilográmetro.

kilolitre, -liter (-litø^r) s. kilolitro, quilolitro.

kilometre, -meter (-mıtø^r) s. kilómetro, quilómetro.

kilometric (kiløme·trik) adj. kilométrico, quilométrico.

kilowatt (ki·løuot) s. ELECT. kilovatio.

kilt (kilt) s. falda corta del traje masculino escocés.

kilt (to) tr. (Esc.) arremangar. 2 plegar, hacer pliegues anchos y planos.

kilter (ki·ltør) s. fam. buen estado.

kimono (kimou·nou) s. kimono, quimono.

kin (kin) s. parientes, parentela, familia: of ~, AKIN; near of ~, próximo pariente; the next of ~, el pariente o los parientes más próximos. 2 adj. pariente, allegado.

kind (kaind) adj. bueno, benigno, bondadoso, benévolo. 2 amable. 3 afectuoso, cariñoso. 4 manso, dócil. 5 s. género, especie, clase, naturaleza, linaje, suerte, calaña: a ~ of, una especie de; of a ~, de una misma especie; malo, de poco valor; of the ~, parecido, por el estilo. 6 TEOL., COM. especie: in ~, en especie; fig. en la misma moneda. 7 ~ of, un poco, algo, casi, en cierto modo.

kind-hearted adj. bondadoso, de buen corazón.

kindle (to) (ki·ndøl) tr. encender. 2 inflamar, enardecer. 3 intr. encenderse, arder. 4 inflamarse, enardecerse. 5 prender [el fuego].

kindliness (kai·ndlinis) s. bondad, benevolencia, benignidad. 2 favor, amabilidad.

kindling (ki·ndling) s. encendimiento; ignición. 2 leña menuda, hornija, encendajas.

kindly (kai·ndli) adj. bondadoso, amable, afectuoso. 2 apacible, benigno; favorable. 4 adv. bondadosamente, amablemente, afectuosamente.

kindness (kai·ndnis) s. bondad, benevolencia, benignidad, humanidad, generosidad, amabilidad, afectuosidad. 2 favor, fineza.

kindred (ki·ndrid) adj. pariente. 2 parecido, afín. 3 s. parentesco. 4 parentela, familia.

kine (kain) s. pl. ant. o dial, vacas, ganado.

kinematics (kinimæ·tics) s. FÍS. cinemática.

kinescope (ki·niscoup) s. TELEV. cinescopio.

kinetics (kine·tiks) s. FÍS. cinética.

kinfolk (ki·nfouk) s. KINSFOLK.

king (king) s. rey [monarca; el primero entre los de su clase]: King's speech, discurso de la Corona. 2 rey [pieza del ajedrez]; dama [en el juego de damas]. 3 ZOOL. ~ crab, cangrejo de las Molucas. 4 ARQ. ~ post, pendolón.

kingbird (-bø·d) s. cierto pájaro americano.

kingbolt (-boult) s. perno central o principal.

kingcraft (-kræft) s. arte de reinar o gobernar.

kingcup (-øp) s. BOT. botón de oro.

kingdom (-døm) s. reino.

kingfisher (-fishøʳ) s. ORN. martín pescador.

kinglet (-lit) s. reyezuelo, régulo. 2 ORN. reyezuelo.

king-size adj. de tamaño largo [cigarrillo].

kingly (-li) adj. real, regio. 2 adv. regiamente.

kingship (-ship) s. majestad. 2 realeza. 3 reino, monarquía.

kink (kink) s. anilla, rizo, coca [que forma un hilo, etc., cuando se encarruja]. 2 tortícolis. 3 capricho, chifladura.

kink (to) tr. ensortijar, encarrujar. 2 intr. retorcerse, encarrujarse, formar cocas.

kinky (-i) adj. encarrujado; ensortijado, crespo. 2 fam. excéntrico, chiflado.

kinsfolk (ki·nšfouk) s. parientes, parentela.

kinship (-ship) s. parentesco. 2 afinidad.

kinsman (-šmæn) s. pariente, deudo.

kinswoman (-šwumæn) f. parienta.

kiosk (kia·sk) s. kiosco, quiosco.

kipper (ki·pøʳ) s. salmón o arenque curado. 2 salmón macho en la época de la cría.

kipper (to) tr. curar, salar, ahumar.

kirk (køʳk) s. [Esc. y dial. ingl.] iglesia.

kismet (ki·šmet) s. hado, destino.

kiss (kis) s. beso, ósculo. 2 ligero contacto. 3 dulce, merengue.

kiss (to) tr. besar. 2 to ~ away, borrar, curar, con bèsos [las penas, etc., de otro]. 3 intr. besar. 4 besarse. 5 tocarse ligeramente.

kit (kit) s. equipo, avios; juego, cartera o caja de herramientas, instrumentos, etc. 2 fam. juego, colección, grupo. 3 colodra, cubo. 4 FOT. adaptador. 5 violín pequeño. 6 gatito, gatita.

kit-bag s. mochila.

kitchen (ki·chøn) s. cocina: ~ garden, huerto [de hortalizas]; ~ range, cocina económica; ~ sink, fregadero. 2 fogón portátil.

kitchenette (kichøne·t) s. cocinilla.

kitchenmaid (ki·chønmeid) s. pincha, ayudanta de cocina.

kitchenware (-ueʳ) s. utensilios de cocina.

kite (kait) s. cometa, pájara [juguete]. 2 ORN. milano. 3 fig. bribón, fullero. 4 COM. pelota, letra de favor.

kith and kin (kiz) s. pl. parientes y amigos.

kitten (ki·tøn) s. gatito, minino. 2 conejito.

kitten (to) intr. parir [la gata].

kittenish (-ish) adj. juguetón, retozón. 2 coquetón.

kittiwake (ki·tiueik) s. ORN. especie de gaviota.

Kitty (ki·ti) n. pr. dim. de KATHARINE.

kitty s. gatito minino.

kleptomania (kleptomei·nia) s. cleptomanía.

kleptomaniac (-iæk) adj.-s. cleptómano.

knack (næk) s. maña, don, arte [para hacer una cosa]; tranquillo. 2 hábito, costumbre. 3 artificio, truco.

knag (næg) s. nudo [en la madera].

knaggy (-i) adj. nudoso, rugoso.

knapsack (næ·psæk) s. mochila, morral, barjuleta.

knapweed (-wid) s. BOT. centaura, centaurea.

knave (neiv) s. bribón, granuja, pícaro, bellaco. 2 sota [naipe].

knavery (-øri) s. bribonada, granujada.

knavish (-ish) adj. bribón, bellaco. 2 bribonesco, doloso. 3 travieso.

knead (to) (nid) tr. amasar, heñir, sobar.

kneader (-øʳ) s. amasador, heñidor.

kneading (-ing) s. amasadura, soba: ~ trough, amasadera.

knee (nɪ) s. ANAT. rodilla, hinojo: ~ breeches, calzón corto; to be on the knees of the goods, ser incierto, depender de la voluntad divina; to go down on one's knees, arrodillarse, caer de rodillas. 2 rodilla [en los cuadrúpedos]. 3 MEC. codo, codillo, ángulo, escuadra. 4 MAR. curva.

kneecap (-kæp) s. rótula, choquezuela. 2 rodillera [abrigo de la rodilla].

knee-deep adj.-adv. metido hasta las rodillas.

kneed (nɪd) adj. articulado, acodillado.

knee-high adj. que llega hasta la rodilla.

kneel (to) (nɪl) intr. arrodillarse, hincar o doblar la rodilla. 2 estar de rodillas. ¶ Pret. y p. p.: knelt o kneeled.

kneepad (nɪ·pæd) s. rodillera [abrigo de la rodilla].

kneepan (nɪ·pæn) s. rótula, choquezuela.

knell (nel) s. doble, toque de difuntos: to toll the ~ of, anunciar el fin de.

knell (to) intr. doblar, tocar a muerto; sonar tristemente. *2 tr.* anunciar o llamar a toque de campana.

knew (niu·) *pret.* de TO KNOW.

knickerbockers (ni·kø^rba·kø^rs), **knickers** [ni·kø^rs] *s. pl.* calzón ancho, bragas.

knick-knack (ni·knæk) *s.* chuchería, bujería, chisme.

knife (naif) *s.* cuchillo [para cortar]; cuchilla; navaja: ~ *grinder*, afilador; ~ *switch*, ELECT. interruptor de cuchillo.

knife (to) *tr.* cortar o herir con cuchillo, acuchillar. *2 fig.* perjudicar secretamente.

knight (nait) *s.* caballero [de una orden o de la orden de caballería; dignidad nobiliaria]: ~ *Templar* o *of the Temple*, templario. *2* caballero [de una dama]. *3* caballo [de ajedrez].

knight (to) *tr.* armar caballero.

knight-errant *s.* caballero andante.

knight-errantry *s.* caballería andante.

knighthood (-jud) *s.* caballería [institución; conjunto de caballeros].

knighthood-errant *s.* caballería andante.

knightly (-li) *adj.* caballeresco, caballeroso. *2 adv.* caballerescamente, caballerosamente.

knit (to) (nit) *tr.* hacer, tejer [a punto de aguja o de malla]. *2* unir, trabar, enlazar. *3 to* ~ *one's brow*, fruncir las cejas. *3 intr.* hacer calceta o tejido de punto; hacer malla. *4* unirse, enlazarse, trabarse. *5* contraerse, fruncirse. ¶ Pret. y p. p.: *knit* o *knitted*; ger.; *knitting*.

knit, knitted (-id) *pret.* y *p. p.* de TO KNIT. *2 adj.* de punto: *knit goods*, géneros de punto.

knitting (-ing) *s.* acción de hacer calceta; labor o tejido de punto: ~ *needle*, aguja de hacer media. *2* unión, trabamiento. *3* fruncimiento.

knittle (ni·tøl) *s.* hilo fino para pescar.

knives (nai·vš) *s. pl.* de KNIFE.

knob (nab) *s.* bulto, protuberancia redondeada. *2* perilla, botón, tirador [de puerta, cajón, etc.]. *3* nudo [en la madera]. *4* terrón, pedacito [de azúcar, carbón, etc.]. *5* colina o eminencia redondeada.

knobby (na·bi) *adj.* lleno de protuberancias, nudoso. *2* (E.U.) montuoso.

knock (nak) *s.* golpe, choque, porrazo. *2* golpe, llamada [a una puerta], aldabonazo. *3* pistoneo [del motor]. *4 fam.* (E.U.) censura, crítica.

knock (to) *tr.* golpear, aporrear. *2* hacer chocar o topar. *3* despertar, llamar [golpeando en la puerta]. *4 fam.* asombrar, admirar. *5 fam.* (E.U.) censurar, criticar. *6 to* ~ *down*, derribar, tumbar, hacer sucumbir; atropellar [con un coche, etc.]; desarmar, desmontar; rebajar [los precios]; adjudicar [en una subasta]. *7 to* ~ *off*, quitar, hacer saltar [a golpes]; dejar [el trabajo]; hacer [algo] rápidamente; deducir, rebajar. *8 to* ~ *out*, hacer salir [golpeando]; poner fuera de combate. *9 to* ~ *together*, hacer chocar; juntar o construir precipitadamente.

10 intr. golpear, llamar [a una puerta]. *11* chocar, topar [con], topetar. *12* pistonear [un motor]. *13 to* ~ *about*, viajar, andar de un lado para otro. *14 to* ~ *off*, dejar el trabajo; desistir, morir. *15 to* ~ *under*, sucumbir.

knockabout (-əbaut) *adj.* de vagabundeo. *2* de trabajo, resistente [ropa, vestido]. *3* ruidoso, tumultuoso. *4 s.* MAR. yate pequeño.

knockdown (-daun) *adj.* tremendo, que derriba [golpe]. *2* en piezas; desarmable, desmontable. *3 s.* golpe irresistible; cosa que tumba o derriba. *4* cosa desarmable o desmontable.

knocker (-ø^r) *s.* golpeador. *2* llamador, aldaba, aldabón.

knock-kneed (-nıd) *adj.* zambo, patizambo.

knockout (-aut) *adj.* irresistible, que pone fuera de combate. *2 s.* BOXEO acto de poner fuera de combate.

knoll (noul) *s.* loma, otero. *2* MAR. cima de un bajo.

knot (nat) *s.* nudo, lazo. *2* nudo [de montañas; de la madera; de una cuestión, de una obra dramática, etc.]. *3* BOT., ANAT. nudo. *4* MAR. nudo, milla náutica. *5* grupo, colección, hato.

knot (to) *tr.* anudar; hacer nudo en. *2* atar, unir, enlazar, enredar. *3* fruncir [las cejas]. *4 intr.* anudarse, enredarse. ¶ Pret. y p. p.: *knotted*; ger.: *-tting*.

knotgrass (-græs) *s.* BOT. centinodia, sanguinaria mayor.

knotted (-id) *adj.* anudado. *2* nudoso. *3* enredado, intrincado.

knotty (-ti) *adj.* anudado. *2* difícil, espinoso, intrincado. *3* áspero, rugoso.

knout (naut) *s.* knut [azote ruso].

know (to) (nou) *tr.* conocer: *to* ~ *by sight*, conocer de vista. *2* saber: *to* ~ *a thing*, or *two*, *to* ~ *what is what*, estar enterado; no ser tonto; *to* ~ *how to*, *to* ~ *to* [*do*, etc.], saber [hacer, etc.]; *for all I* ~, a mi ver, a mi juicio. *3* comprender, hacerse cargo, caer en la cuenta, ver. *4* distinguir, discernir.

6 intr. saber: *to* ~ *best*, saber mejor lo que conviene; *to* ~ *better*, saber que no es así; saber uno como debe portarse, lo que debe hacer; *to* ~ *of*, tener noticias o conocimiento de. ¶ Pret.: *knew*; p. p.: *known*.

knowable (-əbøl) *adj.* conocible.

know-how *s.* destreza, habilidad, pericia.

knowing (-ing) *adj.* inteligente; astuto; entendido, enterado. *2* de inteligente. *3* de inteligencia, de complicidad.

knowingly (-li) *adv.* a sabiendas. *2* hábilmente. *3* con aire de inteligencia.

know-it-all *adj.-s.* sabidillo, sabihondo, sábelotodo.

knowledge (na·lidÿ) *s.* conocimiento, cognición, noticia: *to my* ~, a mi conocimiento; que yo sepa. *2* conocimientos, saber: *to the best of my* ~, según mi leal saber y entender.

knowledgeable (-əbøl) *adj. fam.* conocedor, inteligente.

known (noun) *p. p.* de TO KNOW.

know-nothing *s.* ignorante. *2* agnóstico.

knuckle (nø·køl) *s.* ANAT. nudillo. *2* jarrete [de la res]. *3* MEC. *knucke* o ~ *joint*, articulación, junta articulada.

knuckle (to) *intr.* apoyar los nudillos en el suelo [en el juego de las canicas]. *2* someterse, rendirse, ceder. | Gralte. con *down* o *under*. *3 tr.* golpear, apretar, etc., con los nudillos.

knucklebone (-boun) *s.* taba [hueso]. *2 pl.* taba [juego].

knuckled (-d) *adj.* nudoso.

knurl (nø^rl) *s.* protuberancia. *2* botón, asidero. *3* moleteado [de una pieza metálica].

knuried (-d) *adj.* nudoso. *2* MEC. moleteado.

koala (koa·la) *s.* ZOOL. oso marsupial.

kodak (kou·dæk) *s.* FOT. kodak.

kohl (koul) *s.* alcohol [afeite].

kola (kou·la) *s.* COLA.

kopeck (kou·pek) *s.* copec [moneda rusa].

Koran (kora·n) *s.* Alcorán, Corán.

Korea (korı·a) *n. pr.* GEOGR. Corea.

Korean (korɪ·an) *adj.-s.* coreano.
kotow (koutau·), **kowtow** [kau·tau] *s.* saludo chino de reverencia y sumisión.
kotow, kowtow (to) *intr.* hacer el saludo. *2* humillarse servilmente.
kraal (kral) *s.* poblado de hotentotes. *2* (Áfr. del S.) corral, redil.
Krausism (krau·sišm) *s.* FIL. krausismo.

Kuklux, Ku-Klux, Ku-Klux-Klan (kiu-kløks-klæn) *s.* (E.U.), organización secreta que dirige sus actividades contra los negros, los judíos, los católicos y los extranjeros.
kummel (ki·møl) *s.* cúmel [licor].
Kurd (kø^{r}d) *s.* kurdo, curdo.
kurdish (-ish) *adj.* kurdo, curdo.
kyphosis (kaifou·sis) *s.* MED. cifosis.
Kyrie (ki·rɪɪ) *s.* LITURG. kirie: ~ *eleison*, kirieleison.

L

L, l (el) *s.* L, l, duodécima letra del alfabeto inglés.
la (la) *s.* MÚS. la. *2 interj.* para indicar sorpresa.
lab (læb) *s.* fam. laboratorio.
labarum (læ·barøm) *s.* lábaro.
labdanum (læ·bdanøm) *s.* ládano.
label (to) *tr.* rotular, marcar, poner etiqueta; designación, calificación. *2* BLAS. lambel.
label (lei·bøl) *s.* marbete, rótulo, etiqueta; designar, clasificar como. ¶ Pret. y p. p.: *labeled* o *-lled;* ger.: *-ling* o *lling.*
labellum (labe·løm) *s.* BOT., ENT. labelo.
labial (lei·bial) *adj.* labial. *2 s.* letra labial.
labiate(d (lei·bieiti(d) *adj.-s.* BOT. labiado.
labile (lei·bil) *adj.* QUÍM. lábil.
labiodental (leibiode·ntal) *adj.-s.* labiodental.
labium (lei·bøʳ) *s.* ANAT., BOT., ZOOL. labio.
labor (lei·boʳ) *s.* LABOUR. *2* (E.U.) *Labor Day,* fiesta del trabajo.
labor (to) *tr.-intr.* TO LABOUR.
laboratory (læ·boratori) *s.* laboratorio.
labored (-d) *adj.* LABOURED.
laborer (-øʳ) *s.* LABOURER.
laborious (labou·riøs) *adj.* trabajador, laborioso. *2* laborioso, trabajoso, arduo, ímprobo.
labour (lei·bøʳ) *s.* trabajo, labor; pena, fatiga: *lost* ~, trabajo perdido. *2* tarea, faena, quehacer, obra. *3* mano de obra. *4* la clase obrera; trabajo [en oposición a capital]: *Labour Party,* partido laborista. *5* MAR. balanceo, cabeceo. *6* dolores del parto: *to be in* ~, estar de parto.
labour (to) *intr.* trabajar, esforzarse, forcejear. *2* estar de parto. *3* MAR. trabajar [un buque] contra las olas y el viento. *4* moverse, avanzar con dificultad. *5 to* ~ *under,* estar padeciendo [una enfermedad, error, etc.]; estar luchando [con dificultades]. *6 tr.* trabajar; arar, cultivar. *7* pulir, perfilar, exponer en detalle.
laboured (-d) *adj.* trabajado, complicado. *2* forzado, poco natural.
labourer (-øʳ) *s.* trabajador, obrero, jornalero, bracero.
labouring (-ing) *s.* trabajo, esfuerzo. *2 adj.* trabajador, obrero: ~ *classes,* clase obrera.
labourism (-išm) *s.* laborismo, trabajismo.
Labourite (-ait) *s.* (Ingl.) laborista.
labour-saving *adj.* que ahorra trabajo.
laboursome (-øm) *adj.* trabajador, industrioso. *2* arduo, penoso, ímprobo.

labradorite (læ·bradorait) *s.* MINER. labradorita.
labrum (le·brøm) *s.* ENT. labro.
laburnum (labøʳ·nøm) *s.* BOT. laburno.
labyrinth (læ·birinz) *s.* laberinto, dédalo. *2* ANAT. laberinto.
labyrinthine (læbiri·nzin) *adj.* laberíntico.
lac (læk) *s.* laca, goma laca.
lace (leis) *s.* cordón, cinta [de zapatos, corsé, etc.], agujeta. *2* galón [de oro o plata]. *3* encaje, blonda, randa: ~ *pillow,* mundillo [para hacer encaje]. *4* gotas [que se echan al café, etc.].
lace (to) *tr.* atar, ajustar [zapatos, el corsé, etc.] con cordones o cintas; apretar, encorsetar. *2* pasar [un cordón]. *3* galonear. *4* guarnecer con encajes. *5* rayar, adornar con rayas. *6* enlazar, entrelazar. *7* azotar, dar una paliza. *8* aromatizar [con gotas de licor]. *9 intr.* apretarse, encorsetarse. *10 to* ~ *into,* arremeter contra, pegar [a uno].
Lacedaemon (læsidi·møn) *n. pr.* GEOGR., HIST. Lacedemonia.
lacerate (to) (læ·søreit) *tr.* lacerar. *2* rasgar, desgarrar, despedazar.
laceration (-ei·shøn) *s.* laceración, desgarradura.
lace-winged *adj.* de alas membranosas y reticuladas [insecto].
lacewoman (lei·swumæn) *s.* encajera.
lacework (-uøʳk) *s.* obra de encaje.
lachrymal (læ·krimal) *adj.* lacrimal. *2 adj.-s.* ANAT. lagrimal.
lachrymation (-ei·shøn) *s.* secreción de lágrimas. *2* llanto, lloro.
lachrymatory (læ·crimatori) *s.* lacrimatorio.
lachrymose (-mouš) *adj.* lacrimoso.
lacing (lei·sing) *s.* acción de TO LACE. *2* cordones [para zapatos, corsés, etc.], agujetas. *3* borde coloreado [en una flor, pluma, etc.]. *4* zurra, tunda.
lacinia (lasi·nia) *s.* BOT. lacinia.
lack (læk) *s.* falta, carencia. *2* privación, necesidad.
lack (to) *intr.* faltar [no existir]. *2 intr.-tr.* carecer de, faltarle [a uno o algo una cosa]; necesitar.
lackadaisical (lækadei·šikal) *adj.* afectado; afectadamente lánguido o indiferente. *2* sensiblero.
lackey (læ·ki) *s.* lacayo.
lackey (to) *tr.-intr.* servir como lacayo o criado.

lacking (læ·king) *adj.* carente, falto, deficiente: *he is ~ in courage*, le falta valor. *2* faltante.
lacklustre, lackluster (læ·kløstø^r) *adj.* deslustrado.
laconic (laka·nik) *adj.* lacónico.
lacquer (læ·kø^r) *s.* laca, barniz.
lacquer (to) *tr.* barnizar, dar laca, laquear.
lacquering (-ing) *s.* barnizado de laca.
lacrimal, lacrimatory, etc. LACHRYMAL, LACHRYMATORY, etc.
lacrosse (lakro·s) *s.* juego de pelota.
lactase (læ·kteis) *s.* BIOQUÍM. lactasa.
lactate (to) (læ·kteit) *intr.* lactar, amamantar. *2* dar leche.
lactation (-ei·shøn) *s.* segregación de leche. *2* lactación.
lacteal (læ·ktial) *adj.* lácteo. *2* ANAT. quilífero. *3 s.* ANAT. vaso quilífero.
lactescent (lækte·sønt) *adj.* lactescente.
lactic (læ·ktik) *adj.* láctico.
lactiferous (lækti·førøs) *adj.* lactífero. *2* BOT. lechoso, lechal.
lactose (læ·ktous) *s.* QUÍM. lactosa, lactina.
lacuna (lakiu·na) *s.* laguna, blanco, claro, espacio. *2* hoyo, hueco.
lacunar (-na^r) *adj.-s.* ARQ. lagunar.
lacustrine (lakø·strin) *adj.* lacustre.
lacy (lei·si) *adj.* de encaje o parecido a él.
lad (læd) *s.* muchacho, chico, mozo, chaval.
ladder (læ·dø^r) *s.* escalera [hecha de dos banzos y escalones]; escalera de mano, escala. *2* fig. escabel [lo que sirve para subir o medrar]. *3* carrera [en las medias].
laddie (læ·di) *s. dim.* de LAD.
lade (to) (leid) *tr.* cargar [poner o echar carga en o sobre]. *2* cargar, embarcar [mercancías, etc.]. *3* echar o sacar [con cucharón, etc.]. *4 intr.* tomar cargamento. ¶ Pret.: *laded*; p. p.: *laded* o *laden*.
laden (-øn) *p. p. irreg.* de TO LADE. *2 adj.* cargado. *3* abrumado, oprimido.
lading (-ing) *s.* carga, embarque [de mercancías]: *bill of ~*, conocimiento de embarque.
ladle (-øl) *s.* cucharón, cazo, cacillo.
ladle (to) *tr.* servir, verter o sacar con cucharón.
lady (lei·di) *s.* señora, señorita, dama: *ladies and gentlemen*, señoras y caballeros; *~ in waiting*, dama [de una reina o princesa]; *~ of the house*, señora de la casa. *2* señora [esposa]. *3* novia, dulcinea. *4* (con may.) Señora [la Virgen]: *Our Lady*, Nuestra Señora. *5* (Ingl.) título que se antepone al nombre de las señoras de la nobleza.
ladybird (-bø^{r}d), **ladybug** (-bøg) *s.* ENT. mariquita, vaca de san Antón.
ladyfinger (-fingø^r) *s.* melindre, bizcocho.
lady-killer *s.* don Juan Tenorio, hombre irresistible.
ladylike (-laik) *adj.* delicado, elegante. *2* afeminado, amujerado.
ladylove (-løv) *s.* amada, mujer querida.
ladyship (-ship) *s.* señoría [refiriéndose a una señora a quien se da el título de lady].
lady's-mantle *s.* BOT. alquimila, pie de león.
lady's-thumb *s.* BOT. duraznillo, persicaria.
lag (læg) *s.* retardo, retraso. *2* FÍS. retardación.
lag (to) *intr.* andar o moverse lentamente, retrasarse: *to ~ behind*, rezagarse, quedarse atrás. *2* roncear. ¶ Pret. y p. p.: *lagged*; ger.: *-gging*.
lager (la·gø^r) *s.* especie de cerveza.
laggard (læ·gø^{r}d) *adj.-s.* rezagado; perezoso, holgazán.
lagoon (lagu·n) *s.* albufera; laguna junto al mar o en una isla de coral.

laic (lei·ik) *adj.* laico, secular. *2 s.* lego, seglar.
laicism (-isišm) *s.* laicismo.
laicize (-isaiš) *tr.* laicizar, secularizar.
laid (leid) *pret.* y *p. p.* de TO LAY.
lain (lein) *p. p.* de TO LIE [reclinar].
lair (le·ø^r) *s.* yacija. *2* cubil, cueva de fieras.
laird (le·ø^{r}d) *s.* (esp. Esc.) señor; hacendado.
laity (lei·iti) *s.* estado seglar o laico. *2* los laicos, los legos.
lake (leik) *s.* lago, laguna, estanque. *2* laca, carmín [color].
lama (la·ma) *s.* lama [sacerdote]. *2* ZOOL. llama.
Lamaism (-išm) *s.* lamaísmo.
lamasery (-søri) *s.* lamasería.
lamb (læm) *s.* cordero [animal; carne; pers. dócil, inocente]: *Lamb of God*, Divino Cordero. *2* piel de cordero.
lambaste (to) (læmbei·st) *tr.* apalear, dar una paliza a. *2* reprender o criticar duramente.
lambent (læ·mbønt) *adj.* ondulante, lamiente [llama]. *2* suave [luz]. *3* brillante, radiante [cielo, ojos, etc.]. *4* centelleante [ingenio].
lambkin (læ·mkin) *s.* corderito, corderillo.
lambrequin (læ·mbø^{r}kin) *s.* BLAS. lambrequín. *2* guardamalleta, sobrepuerta.
lambskin (læ·mskin) *s.* corderina, corderillo [piel].
lame (leim) *adj.* cojo, renco, lisiado. *2* fig. cojo, defectuoso, imperfecto. *3* fig. pobre, vano, frívolo: *~ excuse*, excusa pobre o frívola.
lame (to) *tr.* encojar, derrengar, lisiar.
lamella (lame·la) *s.* ANAT., ZOOL., BOT. laminilla.
lamellar (læ·mølø^r) *adj.* ANAT., ZOOL., BOT. laminar.
lamellibranch (lame·librænk) *adj.-s.* ZOOL. lamelibranquio.
lamellicorn (-ko^{r}n) *adj.* ENT. lamelicornio.
lameness (lei·mnis) *s.* cojera. *2* imperfección, debilidad, ineficacia.
lament (lame·nt) *s.* lamento, queja. *2* elegía, endecha.
lament (to) *intr.* lamentarse, plañir. *2 tr.* lamentar, llorar, deplorar.
lamentable (-øbøl) *adj.* lamentable, deplorable. *2* lastimoso, lastimero, dolorido.
lamentation (-ei·shøn) *s.* lamentación, lamento.
lamented (lame·ntid) *adj.* lamentado. *2* llorado.
lamia (læ·mia) *s.* MIT., ICT. lamia. *2* bruja.
lamina (læ·mina) *s.* lámina, planchita, hoja.
laminar (-a^r) *adj.* laminar.
laminate (to) (-eit) *tr.* laminar. *2 tr.-intr.* dividir o dividirse en láminas.
lammergeier (læ·mø^{r}gaiø^r) *s.* ORN. quebrantahuesos, águila barbuda.
lamp (læmp) *s.* lámpara, lustro, candil, farol, luz. *2* bombilla eléctrica: *~ holder*, portalámparas. *3* fig. luminar, astro.
lampblack (-blæk) *s.* negro de humo.
lamplight (-lait) *s.* luz artificial.
lamplighter (-laitø^r) *s.* farolero.
lampoon (læmpu·n) *s.* sátira virulenta o grosera, libelo.
lampoon (to) *tr.* satirizar, ridiculizar virulenta o groseramente.
lamp-post *s.* poste o pie de farol [de la calle].
lamprey (læ·mpri) *s.* ICT. lamprea.
lanate (d (lei·neit(id) *adj.* lanoso. *2* lanudo.
lance (læns) *s.* lanza [arma; hombre de armas]. *2* lanceta.
lance (to) *tr.* alancear. *2* CIR. abrir con lanceta.
Lancelot (-ølat) *n. pr.* Lanzarote.
lanceolate (-ioleit) *adj.* lanceolado.

lancer (-ø^r) *s.* lancero. *2 pl.* lanceros [baile].
lancet (-it) *s.* CIR. lanceta. *2* ARQ. ojiva aguda.
lancinate (to) (-ineit) *tr.* lancinar, desgarrar.
land (lænd) *s.* tierra [parte sólida de la superficie del globo]; tierra firme: *to see how the ~ lies,* fig. sondear el terreno; *by ~,* por tierra. *2* terreno, suelo. *3* tierra [cultivada], finca rústica. *4* tierra, país, nación, región; *Land of Promise,* tierra prometida, de promisión; *the ~ of the leal,* la Gloria. *5* reino, dominio. *6 adj.* de tierra; del suelo; de fincas rústicas: *~ forces,* MIL. fuerzas de tierra; *~ gent,* administrador o corredor de fincas rústicas; *~ surveying,* agrimensura, topografía.
land (to) *tr.* desembarcar [a una pers. o cosa]. *2* dejar, echar, hacer llegar, poner [en un punto, situación, estado]. *3 fam.* arrear, atizar [un golpe, etc.]. *4* coger, sacar [un pez]. *5* lograr, conseguir [un empleo, etc.]. *6 intr.* desembarcar. *7* apearse. *8* tomar tierra [un buque]. *9* aterrizar o amarrar [un avión]. *10* ir a parar, llegar, caer: *to ~ on one's feet,* caer de pies.
landau (læ·ndo) *s.* landó.
landed (læ·ndid) *adj.* hacendado. *2* consistente en tierras: *~ property,* propiedad rústica.
landfall (-fol) *s.* herencia de tierras. *2* desprendimiento de tierras. *3* MAR. recalada. *4* AVIA. aterrizaje.
landgrave (-greiv) *s.* landgrave.
landholder (-jouldø^r) *s.* hacendado, terrateniente.
landing (-ing) *s.* desembarco, desembarque. *2* desembarcadero, apeadero. *3* descansillo, meseta, rellano [de escalera]. *4* AVIA. aterrizaje: *~ gear,* tren de aterrizaje.
landlady (-leidi) *s.* propietaria, dueña [de tierras o casas], casera. *2* mesonera, posadera, huéspeda; patrona [de casa de huéspedes].
landlocked (-lakt) *adj.* rodeado de tierra.
landlord (-lo^{r}d) *s.* propietario, dueño [de tierras o casas], casero. *2* mesonero, posadero, huésped; patrón [de casa de huéspedes].
landlubber (-løbø^r) *s. fam.* marinero torpe. *2* marinero de agua dulce.
landmark (-ma^{r}k) *s.* hito, mojón. *2* señal, edificio, etc., que sirve de guía o para reconocer un sitio. *3* MAR. marca. *4* suceso que hace época.
landowner (-ounø^r) *s.* hacendado, terrateniente.
landscape (-skeip) *s.* paisaje, vista. *2* PINT. paisaje: *~ painter,* paisajista.
landscape (to) *tr.* modificar un terreno hermoseándolo.
landscapist (-ist) *s.* PINT. paisajista.
landslide (læ·ndslaid) *s.* derrubamiento o deslizamiento de tierras; argayo. *2* POL. mayoría de votos abrumadora.
landward (-uø^{r}d) *adj.* de hacia la tierra, de la parte de tierra. *2 adv.* hacia la tierra.
landwards (-uø^{r}ds) *adv.* hacia tierra.
lane (lein) *s.* senda, vereda, camino estrecho. *2* faja o división longitudinal [en una carretera, etc.]. *3* callejuela, callejón. *4* ruta [de vapores o aviones].
language (læ·ngwidÿ) *s.* lenguaje, lengua, habla, idioma, vocabulario.
languid (læ·ngwid) *adj.* lánguido. *2* débil, mustio, lacio. *3* flojo, tibio.
languish (to) (-sh) *intr.* languidecer. *2* debilitarse, decaer. *3* consumirse. *4* tomar una expresión lánguida. *5 to ~ for,* penar o suspirar por.
languishing (-ing) *adj.* que languidece. *2* lánguido, tierno. *3* lento, aburrido.

languor (læ·ngø^r) *s.* languidez, desfallecimiento, desaliento. *2* flojedad, indolencia, dejamiento.
languorous (-øs) *adj.* lánguido, flojo.
lank (lænk) *adj.* alto y delgado, enjuto, seco, flaco, cenceño. *2* lacio, colgante [cabello, etc.].
lanky (-i) *adj.* larguirucho, desgarbado.
lanner (læ·nø^r) *s.* ORN. alcotán.
lanolin(e (læ·nolin) *s.* FARM. lanolina.
lansquenet (læ·nskønet) *s.* lansquenete. *2* sacanete.
lantern (læ·ntø^{r}n) *s.* linterna, farol, fanal: *~ slide,* diapositiva, tira de vidrio para la linterna mágica. *2* fanal [de faro]. *3* ARQ., MEC. linterna.
lantern-jawed *adj.* carilargo, carienjuto, chupado de cara.
lanyard (læ·nya^{r}d) *s.* MAR. acollador.
Laoco-on (lei·økouɑn) *n. pr.* MIT. Laoconte.
lap (læp) *s.* falda, faldón, enfaldo. *2* falda, regazo; *~ dog,* perro faldero; *to live in the ~ of luxury,* fig. llevar una vida regalada. *3* parte de una cosa que cae o se extiende sobre otra. *4* traslapo, solapo. *5* DEP. vuelta [en una carrera]. *6* lamedura. *7* chapaleteo [de las olas].
lap (to) *tr.* sobreponer, encaballar, cruzar. *2* traslapar, solapar; juntar a traslapo. *3* plegar, arrollar [sobre algo]. *4* envolver, rodear. *5* tener o reclinar en el regazo. *6* DEP. llevar una o más vueltas de ventaja [a uno]. *7* lamer, besar [dicho de las olas, el agua]. *8 tr.-intr.* lamer, beber lamiendo. *9 intr.* sobresalir, solapar, cruzar. *10* caer, estar doblado o plegado. *11* susurrar [el agua]. ¶ Pret. y p. p.: *lapped;* ger.: *-pping.*
lapel (lape·l) *s.* solapa [de vestido].
lapidary (læ·pideri) *adj.* lapidario. *2* de piedra, grabado en la piedra. *3 s.* lapidario.
lapidate (to) (-eit) *tr.* lapidar.
lapidation (-ei·shøn) *s.* lapidación.
lapidify (to) (lapi·difai) *tr.* lapidificar. *2 intr.* lapidificarse. ¶ Pret. y p. p.: *lapidified.*
lapislazuli (lei·pislašu·li) *s.* MINER. lapislázuli.
Lapland (læ·plønd) *n. pr.* GEOGR. Laponia.
Lapp (læp) *s.* lapón [pers.; idioma].
lappet (læ·pit) *s.* caída, cinta o pliegue colgante [de toca, cofia, vestido, etc.]. *2* pliegue [de una membrana, etc.]. *3* carúnculas [de gallo u otras aves].
lapse (læps) *s.* lapso, error, equivocación, desliz. *2* caída en la herejía, apostasía. *3* caída [en un estado, condición, etc.]. *4* lapso, transcurso [del tiempo]. *5* DER. prescripción, caducidad.
lapse (to) *intr.* deslizarse, pasar, transcurrir. *2* decaer [el interés, etc.]. *3* caer [en un estado o condición]. *4* caer en error, falta o defecto. *6* DER. prescribir, caducar.
lapwing (læ·puing) *s.* ORN. avefría.
lar (la^r) *s.* lar [dios doméstico].
larboard (la·^{r}bo^{r}d) *s.* MAR. ant. babor.
larceny (la·^{r}søni) *s.* robo, hurto, latrocinio: *petty ~,* hurto, ratería; *grand ~,* robo.
larch (la^{r}ch) *s.* BOT. alerce, pino alerce. *2* BOT. pino cascalbo o negral.
lard (la^{r}d) *s.* tocino gordo, lardo. *2* manteca de cerdo.
lard (to) *tr.* COC. mechar. *2* COC. lardear. *3* guarnecer, entreverar.
lardaceous (la·^{r}dei·shøs) *adj.* lardáceo. *2* MED. graso.
larder (la·^{r}dø^r) *s.* despensa.
lardy (-i) *adj.* lardoso, mantecoso.
large (la·^{r}dÿ) *adj.* grande, grueso, cuantioso, copioso: *~ intestine,* ANAT. intestino grueso; *on a*

~ *scale*, en gran escala. *2* amplio, vasto, dilatado: ~ *powers*, amplios poderes. *3* extenso, lato. *4 ant.* generoso, comprensivo. *5* MAR. favorable [viento]. *6 s. at* ~ extensamente, detalladamente; en general; sin limitación; suelto, en libertad.

large-hearted *adj.* magnánimo, desprendido, generoso.

large-minded *adj.* de ideas liberales; comprensivo, de espíritu abierto.

largeness (-nis) *s.* grandor, extensión, amplitud. *2* magnanimidad.

larger (-o^r) *adj. compar.* de LARGE.

largess (-is) *s.* don, dádiva, regalo.

largest (-est) *adj. superl.* de LARGE.

largo (la·^{r}gou) *adj.-s.* MÚS. largo.

lariat (læ·riat) *s.* lazo, mangana; *boleadoras.

lark (la^{r}k) *s.* ORN. alondra, calandria. *2* diversión, retozo, holgorio: *to have a* ~, divertirse, echar una cana al aire.

lark (to) *intr.* bromear, divertirse.

larkspur (-spø^r) *s.* BOT. espuela de caballero.

Larry (la·ri) *n. pr. dim.* de LAWRENCE.

larva (la·^{r}va) *s.* ZOOL. larva.

larvate(d (la·^{r}veit(id) *adj.* MED. larvado.

laryngeal (lari·ndÿial) *adj.* laríngeo.

laryngitis (lærindÿai·tis) *s.* MED. laringitis.

laryngoscope (læri·ngoscoup) *s.* laringoscopio.

larynx (læ·rinks) *s.* ANAT. laringe.

lascivious (læsi·viøs) *adj.* lascivo, torpe.

lasciviousness (-nis) *s.* lascivia.

lash (læsh) *s.* pestaña [del ojo]. *2* trallazo, latigazo, zurriagazo. *3* tralla [del látigo]; látigo, azote. *4* TEJ. tirataco.

lash (to) *tr.* azotar, fustigar, dar latigazos a. *2* romper contra [dicho de las olas]. *3* atar, trincar. *4* fustigar, vituperar. *5* mover vivamente. *6* excitar. *7 intr.* chasquear [el látigo]. *8* caer con fuerza [la lluvia]. *9* relampaguear. *10 to* ~ *out*, cocear; desatarse; desenfrenarse.

lashing (-ing) *s.* zurra, castigo de azotes. *2* fustigación. *3* atadura, cuerda, trinca.

lass (læs) *f.* chica, moza, zagala.

lassie (læ·si) *f.* muchachita.

lassitude (-itiud) *s.* lasitud, dejamiento, flojedad.

lasso (-ou) *s.* lazo, mangana.

lasso (to) *tr.* lazar, echar el lazo a.

last (læst) *adj.* último, postrero, final: ~ *but one*, *next to the* ~, penúltimo; ~ *Judgment*, juicio final; *Last Supper*, Cena [de Jesucristo]; ~ *will and testament*, DER. última voluntad; *the* ~ *straw*, el colmo, lo que faltaba. *2* pasado [más próximo en el pasado]: ~ *night*, anoche; ~ *year*, el año pasado. *3 s.* fin, final, término; lo último: *to see the* ~ *of one*, no volver a ver a uno, librarse de él; *at* ~, al fin, por fin; *to the* ~, hasta el fin. *4* duración, resistencia. *5* horma [de zapato]. *6 adv.* últimamente, finalmente. *7* la última vez, por última vez.

last (to) *intr.* durar. *2* perdurar, permanecer, continuar, conservarse.

lasting (-ing) *adj.* duradero, durable, perdurable. *2* sólido, permanente.

lastly (-li) *adv.* en último lugar, finalmente.

last-minute *adj.* de última hora.

latch (læch) *s.* picaporte, pestillo de golpe.

latch (to) *tr.* cerrar con picaporte o pestillo de golpe.

latchkey (-ki) *s.* llavín, picaporte [llave].

late (leit) *adj.* que llega, ocurre, hace o se hace tarde; retrasado, tardío, avanzado; de fines de:

to be ~, llegar tarde, retrasarse; ~ *fruits*, frutos tardíos; ~ *hour*, hora avanzada. *2* interior, último. *3* difunto: *the Mr. X*, el difunto señor X. *4* reciente. *5 adv.* tarde. *6* hasta una hora avanzada. *7* recientemente. *8 of* ~, últimamente. *9* ~ *in*, hacia fines de.

late-comer *s.* rezagado. *2* recién llegado.

lateen (læti·n) *adj.* MAR. ~ *sail*, vela latina; ~ *yard*, entena.

lately (lei·tli) *adv.* últimamente, recientemente.

latency (-ønsi) *s.* estado latente.

latent (-ønt) *adj.* latente. *2* oculto, disimulado.

later (-ø^r) *adj.-adv. compar.* de LATE: ~ *on*, más adelante.

lateral (læ·tøral) *adj.* lateral, ladero.

Lateran (læ·tøran) *adj.* lateranense. *2 s.* San Juan de Letrán (basílica). *3* palacio de Letrán.

latest (lei·tist) *adj.-adv. superl.* de LATE: *the* ~ *fashion*, la última moda; *at the* ~, a más tardar.

lath (laz) *s.* CARP., ALBAÑ. listón, lata.

lath (to) *tr.* ALBAÑ. listonar, enlatar.

lathe (leid) *s.* MEC. torno [de tornear; de taladrar; de alfarero]. *2* TEJ. batán [del telar].

lathe (to) *tr.* tornear.

lather (læ·ðø^r) *s.* jabonadura, espuma de jabón. *2* espuma de sudor.

lather (to) *tr.* enjabonar, jabonar. *2 fam.* azotar, zurrar. *3 intr.* espumar, hacer espuma. *4* cubrirse de espuma [un caballo, etc.].

lathery (-i) *adj.* espumoso; cubierto de espuma.

lathing (læ·zing) *s.* enlatado, enlistonado.

Latin (læ·tin) *adj.* latino. *2 s.* latín [lengua], latino [pers.].

Latinism (-išm) *s.* latinismo.

Latinist (-ist) *s.* latinista.

Latinity (-iti) *s.* latinidad.

Latinize (to) (-aiš) *tr.* latinizar.

latitude (læ·titiud) *s.* GEOGR., ASTR. latitud. *2* latitud, amplitud, libertad.

Latium (læ·siøm) *n. pr.* GEOGR., HIST. Lacio.

latria (latrai·a) *s.* latria, culto de latría.

latrine (latri·n) *s.* letrina.

latten (læ·tøn) *s.* latón en láminas.

latter (læ·tø^r) *adj.* más reciente, moderno. *2* último. *3 the* ~, éste, esto, el segundo, este último.

latter-day *adj.* de nuestros días, moderno.

Latter-Day Saints (the) *s. pl.* los mormones.

lattice (læ·tis) *s.* celosía, enrejado, rejilla: ~ *window*, ventana con celosía.

lattice (to) (læ·tis) *tr.* enrejar, poner celosías en.

latticework (-wø^{r}k) *s.* enrejado, celosía.

Latvia (læ·tvia) *n. pr.* GEOGR. Letonia.

laud (lod) *s.* alabanza, loor. *2 pl.* LITURG. laudes.

laud (to) *tr.* loar, alabar, encomiar, elogiar.

laudable (-øbøl) *adj.* laudable, loable.

laudanum (-anøm) *s.* láudano.

laudatory (lo·datori) *adj.* laudatorio.

laugh (laf o læf) *s.* risa.

laugh (to) *intr.* reír, reírse: *to* ~ *at*, reírse de, burlarse de; *to* ~ *in one's sleeve*, reír para sus adentros. *2 tr.* expresar riendo. *3 to* ~ *away*, echar a broma; *to* ~ *off*, tomar a risa; hacer desaparecer riendo.

laughable (-øbøl) *adj.* risible, ridículo, divertido.

laughing (-ing) *adj.* riente, risueño, reidor. *2* risible: ~ *matter*, cosa de risa. *3* ~ *gas*, gas hilarante.

laughingstock (la·fing- o læ·fingstak) *s.* hazmerreír.

laughter (-tø^r) *s.* risa, hilaridad.

launch (lonch) *s.* MAR. lanzamiento, botadura. *2* MAR. lancha, chalupa.
launch (to) *tr.* lanzar, arrojar. *2* MAR. lanzar, botar. *3* emprender. *4* lanzar [un producto, una ofensiva]. *5 intr.* lanzarse, arrojarse. *6 to ~ forth* o *out*, salir, ponerse en marcha.
launder (to) (lo·ndø^r) *tr.-intr.* lavar y planchar [la ropa].
laundress (-ris) *s.* lavandera.
laundry (-ri) *s.* lavadero [cuarto]. *2* lavandería. *3* lavado [de la ropa]. *4* ropa lavada o para lavar.
Laura (lo·ra) *n. pr.* Laura.
lauraceous (lorei·shøs) *adj.* BOT. lauráceo.
laureate (lo·rieit o lo·riit) *adj.* laureado. *2* láureo. *3 s.* poeta laureado.
laurel (lo·røl) *s.* BOT. laurel. *2* fig. laurel, lauro.
Laurence (lo·røns) *n. pr.* Lorenzo.
laurustine (lo·røstin) *s.* BOT. durillo.
lava (la·va) *s.* lava [de volcán].
lavabo (lævei·bo) *s.* LITURG. lavabo.
lavaret (la·varet) *s.* ICT. farra.
lavatory (læ·vatori) *s.* lavabo; lavamanos; retrete. *2* LITURG. lavatorio.
lave (to) (lei·v) *tr.* poét. lavar, bañar.
lavement (-mønt) *s.* lavado, baño. *2* lavativa.
lavender (læ·vøndø^r) *s.* BOT. lavándula, espliego, alhucema. *2* color de la flor de lavándula.
lavish (læ·vish) *adj.* pródigo, dadivoso; despilfarrado. *2* abundante, copioso, profuso.
lavish (to) *tr.* prodigar. *2* despilfarrar.
lavishness (-nis) *s.* prodigalidad, profusión, derroche, despilfarro.
law (lo) *s.* ley, regla, precepto, norma: fig. *to lay down the ~,* dictar la ley, hablar dogmáticamente. *2* ley [de Dios, de la natura, de la ciencia]. *3* derecho, jurisprudencia: *to read ~,* estudiar derecho [en el bufete de un abogado]. *4* ley, derecho [conjunto de leyes]; código, legislación; fuero: *commercial ~,* derecho mercantil, código de comercio: *civil ~,* derecho civil; *roman ~,* derecho romano. *5* foro, abogacía: *to enter the ~,* hacerse abogado. *6* justicia, administración de la justicia: *to take the ~ into one's own hands,* tomarse uno la justicia por su mano. *7* BIB. *the ~ of Moses,* la ley de Moisés.
law-abiding *adj.* observante de la ley.
lawbreaker (-breikø^r) *s.* transgresor de la ley.
lawful (-ful) *adj.* legal, legítimo. *2* conforme a la ley, según derecho. *3* justo, válido; lícito. *4* DER. hábil [día]. *5 ~ age,* mayoría de edad.
lawgiver (-givø^r) *s.* legislador.
lawless (-lis) *adj.* sin ley. *2* ilegal, ilícito. *3* desenfrenado, revoltoso, licencioso.
lawmaker (-meikø^r) *s.* legislador.
lawn (lon) *s.* césped [terreno cubierto de], prado: *~ tennis,* lawn tenis, tenis. *3* linón. *3* fig. dignidad de obispo [anglicano].
Lawrence (lo·røns) *n. pr.* Lorenzo.
lawsuit (lo·siut) *s.* DER. proceso, pleito, litigio.
lawyer (lo·yø^r) *s.* letrado, abogado, procurador, hombre de leyes.
lax (læks) *adj.* laxo, relajado, flojo, suelto. *2* flojo, negligente. *3* vago, impreciso.
laxation (-ei·shøn) *s.* laxación, laxamiento.
laxative (læ·ksativ) *adj.-s.* laxativo, laxante.
laxity (-iti) *s.* laxitud, flojedad. *2* relajamiento. *3* negligencia, descuido. *4* imprecisión.
laxly (-li) *adv.* flojamente, sueltamente.
laxness (-nis) *s.* LAXITY.
1) lay (lei) *pret.* de TO LIE [yacer, estar acostado, situado, etc.].

2) lay *adj.* laico, lego, secular, seglar: *~ brother,* converso; *~ sister,* lega. *2* lego, profano, no profesional. *3* MAR. *~ days,* estadía. *4 ~ figure,* maniquí articulado; fig. maniquí, persona manejada por otros. *5 s.* disposición, situación, orientación, caída, inclinación; sesgo, cariz: *~ of the land,* LIE OF THE LAND. *6* grado de torsión de una cuerda o cable. *7* pop. campo de operaciones; género de actividad, ocupación. *8* LIT. lay, balada, canción.
lay (to) *tr.* derribar, tumbar, acostar, tender. *2* poner, depositar, dejar; colocar, instalar. *3* enterrar. *4* poner, dejar [en cierto estado, situación, etc.]. *5* tender [un cable, etc.]. *6* extender, aplicar [sobre]. *7* cubrir, tapizar, adornar. *8* disponer, preparar, trazar, urdir. *9* poner [huevos; la mesa]. *10* imponer [cargas, etc.]. *11* calmar, aquietar, sosegar. *12* hacer huir [a un fantasma o aparecido]. *13* echar [la culpa], atribuir. *14* presentar, exponer. *15* apostar [dinero]; hacer [una apuesta]. *16* situar [la acción de un drama, etc.]. *17* torcer [cabos], hacer [una cuerda]. *18* MAR. alejarse de. *19* apuntar [un cañón]. *20* matar [el polvo]. *21 to ~ aside,* poner a un lado; desechar; guardar, ahorrar. *22 to ~ bare,* desnudar; descubrir, poner al descubierto. *23 to ~ by,* guardar, ahorrar. *24 to ~ claim to,* reclamar, pretender. *25 to ~ down,* acostar, derribar; entregar, rendir; abandonar; dimitir; apostar [dinero]; urdir, tramar, delinear, proyectar; formular, establecer; dictar [la ley]. *26 to ~ hands on,* poner las manos encima a; tomar, coger; ECLES. imponer las manos. *27 to ~ hold of,* asir, tomar, apoderarse de. *28 to ~ in,* hacer provisión de; almacenar; PINT. bosquejar. *29 to ~ low,* derribar, matar. *30 to ~ on,* aplicar, dar [pintura, etc.]; pegar, atacar; distribuir, instalar [gas, agua, electricidad]. *31 to ~ out,* extender, desplegar; disponer, arreglar, trazar, proyectar; amortajar; invertir [dinero]. *32 to ~ siege to,* poner sitio a. *33 to ~ stress on,* insistir, hacer hincapié en. *34* MAR. *to ~ to,* poner al pairo. *35 to ~ to heart,* tomar a pecho. *36 to ~ up,* guardar, amontonar; hacer guardar cama; MAR. desarmar. *37 to ~ waste,* asolar, devastar. *38 intr.* poner [las gallinas]. *39* aplicarse vigorosamente. *40* MAR. situarse. *41 to ~ about,* dar palos en todas direcciones. *42* MAR. *to ~ to,* estar al pairo. ¶ Pret. y p. p.: *laid.*
layer (lei·ø^r) *s.* colocador, instalador. *2* gallina ponedora. *3* capa, lecho, estrato. *4* ALBAÑ. hilada. *5* AGR. acodo.
layer (to) *tr.* AGR. acodar.
layette (leiye·t) *s.* canastilla [de recién nacido].
laying (lei·ing) *s.* colocación, instalación. *2* tendido [de un cable, etc.]. *3* primera capa [de un enlucido]. *4* estiva. *5* postura [de huevos]. *7 ~ on of hands,* imposición de manos.
layman (-mæn) *s.* lego, laico, seglar. *2* lego, profano [en una materia].
layoff (-of) *s.* despido [de obreros].
layout (-aut) *s.* arreglo, disposición, plan, esquema. *2* equipo [de útiles, etc.].
layover (-ouvø^r) *s.* detención [en un viaje].
lazar (læ·ša^r) *s.* apestado. *2* leproso, lazarino.
lazaret (læ·šaret), **lazaretto** (-ou) *s.* lazareto. *2* leprosería. *3* MAR. pañol.
Lazarist (læ·šarist) *s.* lazarista.
Lazarous (læ·šarøs) *n. pr.* Lázaro.
laze (to) (leiš) *intr.* holgazanear, estar ocioso.

laziness (lei·šinis) *s.* pereza, holgazanería, indolencia, ociosidad.
lazuli (læ·šiuli) *s.* lapislázuli.
lazulite (læ·šiulait) *s.* MINER. lazulita.
lazy (lei·ši) *adj.* perezoso, holgazán, indolente, ocioso. *2* lento, pesado.
lea (lı) *s.* pasto, prado.
leach (lıch) *s.* cenizas de lejía. *2* colada [de la ropa]. *3* lixiviación.
leach (to) *tr.* colar [la ropa]. *2* lixiviar.
leachy (lı·chi) *adj.* permeable, poroso.
1) lead (led) *s.* plomo [metal]; objeto de plomo. *2* MAR. plomada, sonda: ~ *line*, sondaleza. *3* IMPR. interlínea, regleta. *4* MINER. grafito, plombagina. *5* mina. *6 pl.* emplomaduras [de las vidrieras].
2) lead (lıd) *s.* primacía, primer lugar. *2* dirección, mando, guía. *3* delantera, ventaja [en una carrera]. *4* ejemplo, indicación, etc. [con que se guía a otro o se le sugiere algo]. *5* salida [en el juego]; palo o ficha con que se sale. *6* MEC., ELECT. avance. *7* ELECT. conductor; hilo de entrada. *8* traílla, correa [de perro]. *9* TEAT. primer papel; primer actor; primera actriz. *10* BOX. primer golpe. *11* MÚS. guía.
1) lead (to) (led) *tr.* emplomar, guarnecer de plomo. *2* IMPR. interlinear, regletear. ¶ Pret. y p. p.: *leaded.*
2) lead (to) (lıd) *tr.* llevar, conducir, guiar; mover, impulsar, inducir; atraer. *2* dirigir, llevar la batuta; acaudillar. *3* hacer pasar [una cuerda, un hilo, etc.]. *4* conducir [agua, vapor, etc.]. *5* llevar [un género de vida]. *6* ir delante o a la cabeza; ser el primero entre. *7* salir [de un palo o ficha]. *8 to* ~ *astray*, descarriar, seducir. *9 to* ~ *off*, iniciar, abrir [el baile, etc.]. *10 to* ~ *out*, sacar a bailar. *11 to* ~ *the way*, ir delante, mostrar el camino. *12 intr.* mandar en jefe, guiar, dirigir. *13* ser el primero. *14* ir delante. *15* ser mano, salir [en el juego]. *16* conducir, llevar [ser camino de]. *17* dar, salir [una puerta, un pasadizo]. *18* BOX. pasar al ataque. *19 to* ~ *up to*, conducir o llevar a; llevar la conversación a. ¶ Pret. y p. p.: *led.*
leaded (le·did) *adj.* emplomado, guarnecido de plomo.
leaden (·øn) *adj.* de plomo. *2* plomizo, plúmbeo. *3* pesado, lento. *4* cargado [de sueño, etc.].
leaden-eyed *adj.* soñoliento, de ojos soñolientos.
leaden-footed *adj.* lento, tardo.
leader (lı·dør) *s.* conductor, guía. *2* jefe, caudillo, adalid, cabecilla. *3* director [de orquesta]. *4* primer violín. *5* el que va delante. *6* guía, caballo delantero. *7* editorial, artículo de fondo. *8* ALBAÑ. condutal. *9* MEC. rueda motriz. *10* MEC., MIN. guía. *11* guía [de un árbol o planta]. *12 pl.* IMPR. línea de puntos para guiar la vista.
leadership (-ship) *s.* dirección, jefatura, caudillaje. *2* dotes de mando.
1) leading (le·ding) *s.* objetos de plomo. *2* IMPR. interlineación.
2) leading (lı·ding) *adj.* que va delante; que guía o conduce; primero, principal, capital: ~ *article*, artículo de fondo; ~ *question*, pregunta que sugiere la respuesta. *2 s.* guía, conducción, dirección.
leadwort (le·duørt) *s.* BOT. belesa.
leady (le·di) *adj.* plomizo.
leaf (lıf) *pl.* **leaves** (-vš) *s.* BOT. hoja; pétalo. *2* hoja [de libro, puerta, etc.]: *to turn a new* ~, mudar

de vida; enmendarse; *over the* ~, a la vuelta. *3* ala [de mesa]. *4* hoja [lámina delgada].
leaf (to) *intr.* BOT. echar hojas. *2 tr.* hojear [un libro].
leafage (-idẏ) *s.* follaje, frondas.
leafed (-t) *adj.* que tiene hojas; de hojas: *broadleafed*, de hojas anchas.
leaflet (-lit) *s.* hojita, hojuela. *2* BOT. folíolo. *3* hoja impresa, papel volante.
leafstalk (-stok) *s.* BOT. pecíolo, rabillo de hoja.
leafy (-i) *adj.* frondoso. *2* hojoso, hojudo.
league (lıg) *s.* liga, unión, alianza, confederación. *2* legua. *3* DEP. liga.
league (to) *tr.* ligar, unir, confederar. *2 intr.* ligarse, unirse, aliarse, confederarse.
leaguer (-ør) *s.* miembro de una liga.
Leah (li·a) *n. pr.* BIB. Lía.
leak (lık) *s.* escape, fuga [de un fluido]; goteo, filtración [de un líquido]. *2 fig.* filtración [de dinero, noticias, etc.]. *3* ELECT. pérdida de corriente. *4* grieta, raja, gotera. *5* MAR. vía de agua.
leak (to) *intr.* salirse, tener escapes o pérdidas [un recipiente, etc.] hacer agua [un buque]. *2* salirse, escapar, perderse [un fluido]. *3* gotear [un techo]. *4* filtrarse [dinero, noticias].
leakage (-idẏ) *s.* goteo, derrame, fuga, escape, filtración. *2* ELECT. pérdida [de corriente]; dispersión. *3* com. pérdida, merma, derrame [avería].
leaky (-i) *adj.* resquebrajado, que se sale, que tiene escapes, que hace agua. *2* llovedizo [techo]. *3 fam.* hablador, indiscreto [persona].
leal (lı·øl) (Esc.) leal, honrado.
lean (lın) *adj.* delgado, flaco, enjuto, cenceño, seco. *2* magro. *3* pobre, escaso; deficiente. *4* estéril, improductivo. *5* de carestía, de escasez. *6 s.* carne magra o mollar. *7* LEANING 2.
lean (to) *intr.* apoyarse; reclinarse, recostarse: *to* ~ *back*, retreparse. *2* inclinarse, ladearse, torcerse. *3* inclinarse [en opinión, deseo, etc.]. *4 tr.* apoyar, recostar, reclinar, descansar.
Leander (lıæ·ndør) *n. pr.* Leandro.
leaning (lı·ning) *s.* inclinación, ladeo. *2* inclinación, propensión, tendencia, preferencia. *3 adj.* inclinado.
leanness (-nis) *s.* delgadez, flacura, magrura. *2* pobreza, escasez, esterilidad.
lean-to (-tu) *s.* alpende, cobertizo.
lean-witted *adj.* necio, tonto.
leap (lıp) *s.* salto, brinco; cabriola, zapateta: *by leaps and bounds*, rápidamente. *2 adj.* ~ *year*, año bisiesto.
leap (to) *intr.* saltar, brincar, dar un salto. *2* saltar [de un tema, etc., a otro]. *3* latir fuertemente. *4 tr.* saltar [salvar de un salto]. *5* hacer saltar. ¶ Pret. y p. p.: *leaped* o *leapt.*
leaper (-ør) *s.* saltador, brincador.
leapfrog (-frag) *s.* fil derecho, salto [juego].
learn (to) (lø⁵n) *tr.-intr.* aprender, instruirse. *2 tr.* enterarse de, tener noticia de, oír decir. ¶ Pret. y p. p.: *learned* o *learnt.*
learned (-id) *adj.* ilustrado, docto, sabio, erudito, versado.
learning (-ing) *s.* instrucción, ilustración, saber, ciencia, erudición. *2* aprendizaje, estudio.
learnt (-t) *pret.* y *p. p.* de TO LEARN.
lease (lıs) *s.* arriendo, arrendamiento.
lease (to) *tr.* arrendar, dar o tomar en arriendo.
leash (lısh) *s.* traílla, correa. *2* pihuela. *3* grupo de tres. *4* TEJ. lizo.
leash (to) *tr.* atraillar, atar.
least (lıst) *adj. superl.* de LITTLE. *2* mínimo, menor,

más pequeño: ~ *common multiple*, mínimo común múltiplo. *3 s. the* ~, lo más pequeño, lo menos; *at* ~, *at the* ~, al menos, a lo menos, por lo menos; *not in the* ~, de ningún modo. *4 adv.* en el menor grado.

leastways (-ueiš), **leastwise** (-uaiš) *adv.* al menos, por lo menos.

leather (-le·ðøʳ) *s.* cuero, piel [curtida]: ~ *dresser*, curtidor; ~ *strap*, correa. *2* fam. pellejo [de persona]. *3* objeto de cuero; suela [de taco].

leather (to) *tr.* forrar o guarnecer de cuero. *2* hacer cuero. *3* fam. pegar, zurrar.

leatherback (-bæk) *s.* ZOOL. laúd [tortuga].

leather-bound *adj.* encuadernado en piel.

leatherette (-e·t) *s.* papel o tela que imita el cuero.

leathern (-n) *adj.* de cuero. *2* coriáceo.

leatheroid (-oid) *s.* cuero artificial.

leathery (-i) *adj.* coriáceo, correoso.

leave (līv) *s.* licencia, permiso, venia: ~ *of absence*, MIL. licencia, permiso; *by your* ~, *with your* ~, con su permiso. *2* despedida: *to take* ~, despedirse.

1) leave (to) *tr.* dejar [no tocar, no ocuparse de, etc.]. *2* dejar [algo tras de sí, hacer que quede algo]; dejar [en un lugar, estado, etc.]: *to* ~ *behind*, dejar atrás; dejar, dejarse olvidado; *to* ~ *in the lurch*, dejar en la estacada; *to* ~ *out*, dejar fuera, omitir; ~ *to word*, dejar dicho, dejar recado. *3* dejar, abandonar, separarse de, salir de. *4* dejar de, cesar de. *5* dejar [al morir]; legar. *6* ARIT. *four from five leaves one*, de cuatro a cinco va uno. *7 to* ~ *off*, dejar de [hacer una cosa]; dejar [el trabajo, un hábito]; dejar de usar [una prenda]. *8 intr.* partir, salir, irse, marcharse. *9* acabar, cesar. ¶ Pret. y p. p.: *left*.

2) leave (to) *intr.* echar hojas [las plantas]. ¶ Pret. y p. p.: *leaved*.

leaved (-d) *adj.* BOT. de hojas: *entire-leaved*, de hojas enteras.

leaven (le·vøn) *s.* levadura, fermento.

leaven (to) *tr.* leudar, hacer fermentar. *2* fig. penetrar, impregnar, imbuir, viciar.

leavening (-ning) *s.* levadura.

leaves (līvš) *s. pl.* de LEAF. *2* ENCUAD. cantos [de un libro]: *gilt* ~, cantos dorados.

leave-taking *s.* despedida.

leavings (lī·vings) *s. pl.* restos, sobras, desperdicios.

Lebanese (le·bøniš) *adj.-s.* libanés.

Lebanon (le·bønøn) *n. pr.* GEOGR. Líbano.

lecher (le·chøʳ) *s.* libertino, disoluto.

lecherous (-øs) *adj.* lujurioso, lascivo, salaz.

lechery (-i) *s.* libertinaje, lujuria.

lecithin (le·sizin) *s.* QUÍM. lecitina.

lectern (le·ktøʳn) *s.* facistol.

lection (-shøn) *s.* LITURG. lección.

lectionary (-eri) *s.* leccionario.

lector (-tøʳ) *s.* ECLES. lector.

lectorate (-it) *s.* ECLES. lectorado.

lecture (-chøʳ) *s.* conferencia, disertación, lección, plática. *2* reprensión, sermón.

lecture (to) *intr.* disertar, dar una conferencia. *2 tr.* enseñar, sermonear, reprender.

lecturer (-øʳ) *s.* disertante, conferenciante. *2* lector.

lectureship (-ship) *s.* lectoría; cátedra.

led (led) *pret.* y *p. p.* de TO LEAD.

ledge (ledž) *s.* anaquel, repisa. *2* saliente o rellano estrecho. *3* arrecife. *4* MIN. vena.

ledger (-øʳ) *s.* COM. mayor [libro]. *2* losa [piedra]. *3* traviesa [de andamio].

lee (lī) *s.* abrigo, socaire. *2* MAR. sotavento.

leeboard (lī·boʳd) *s.* MAR. orza de deriva.

leech (līch) *s.* sanguijuela. *2* MED. ventosa. *3* ant. médico. *4* MAR. caída [de vela].

leech (to) *tr.* poner sanguijuelas a.

leek (līk) *s.* BOT. puerro.

leer (līøʳ) *s.* mirada de soslayo [con expresión maligna, astuta o lujuriosa].

leer (to) *tr.* atraer [con miradas]. *2 intr.* mirar de soslayo [con expresión maligna, astuta o lujuriosa].

leery (-ri) *adj.* fam. astuto, suspicaz, receloso.

lees (līš) *s. pl.* heces, poso.

leeward (līuøʳd o lu·øʳd) *s.* sotavento. *3 adv.* a sotavento, hacia sotavento.

leeway (-uei) *s.* MAR. deriva, abatimiento. *2* margen de tiempo, etc.; plazo, respiro.

left (left) *pret.* y *p. p.* de TO LEAVE: *to be* ~ *over*, ser dejado, quedar, sobrar. *2 adj.* izquierdo, siniestro. *3 s.* izquierda.

left-hand *adj.* izquierdo; de la izquierda; hecho con la izquierda o hacia la izquierda; ~ *drive*, AUTO. conducción a la izquierda.

left-handed *adj.* zurdo. *2* de la mano izquierda. *3* torpe, desmañado. *4* insincero. *5* que gira hacia la izquierda.

leftist (-ist) *adj.-s.* POL. izquierdista.

leftover (-ouvøʳ) *adj.* que queda, sobrante. *2 s.* sobrante, resto. *4 pl.* sobras.

leg (leg) *s.* ANAT. pierna: *to give a* ~ *up*, ayudar a subir; *on one's last legs*, agonizante; en las últimas; sin recursos; *on one's legs*, en pie; restablecido; en próspero estado. *2* pata [de animal]. *3* pie, pata [de un mueble, etc.]. *4* puntal, apoyo: *not to have a* ~ *to stand on*, no tener una razón en que apoyarse. *5* COC. pierna [de cordero, etc.]. *6* pierna [de media, de compás]. *7* pernera, pernil [de pantalón], caña [de bota]. *8* GEOM. cateto. *9* etapa, trecho. *10* MAR. bordada.

leg (to) *tr.* hacer con la pierna; tirar de la pierna; dar en la pierna. *2 to* ~ *it*, andar, correr.

legacy (le·gasi) *s.* legado, manda, herencia.

legal (lī·gal) *adj.* legal: ~ *tender*, curso legal, moneda de curso legal. *2* legítimo, lícito. *3* jurídico.

legalism (lī·gališm) *s.* legalismo.

legality (ligæ·liti) *s.* legalidad; legitimidad.

legalize (to) (lī·galaiš) *tr.* legalizar [dar estado o validez legal]. *2* refrendar, autorizar.

legate (le·git) *s.* legado [pers.].

legate (to) (li·geit) *tr.* DER. legar.

legatee (le·gæti) *s.* legatario.

legateship (le·gitship) *s.* legacía.

legation (ligei·shøn) *s.* legación. *2* misión, embajada.

legend (le·dyønd) *s.* leyenda. *2* legenda.

legendary (-eri) *adj.* legendario.

leger (le·dyøʳ) *adj.* MÚS. suplementario [espacio, línea].

legerdemain (ledyøʳdimei·n) *s.* juego de manos, prestidigitación.

legged (le·gd o le·gid) *adj.* de piernas o patas: *bandy-legged*, estevado.

legging (-ing) *s.* polaina, sobrecalza.

Leghorn (-joʳn) *n. pr.* GEOGR. Liorna.

legibility (ledyibi·liti) *s.* legibilidad.

legible (le·dyibøl) *adj.* legible.

legion (lī·dyøn) *s.* legión.

legionary (-eri) *adj.-s.* legionario.

legislate (to) (le·dyisleit) *intr.* legislar.

legislation (-ei·shøn) *s.* legislación.

legislative (le·dўisleitiv) *adj.* legislativo. *2 s.* poder o cuerpo legislativo.
legislator (-ø^r) *m.* legislador.
legislatress (-ris) *f.* legisladora.
legislature (le·dўislechø^r) *s.* cuerpo o cuerpos legisladores. *2* función legislativa: *term of* ~, legislatura.
legist (lı·dўist) *s.* legista.
legitim (le·dўitim) *s.* DER. legítima.
legitimacy (lidўi·timasi) *adj.* legitimidad.
legitimate (-it) *adj.* legítimo. *2* lógico, razonable. *3 the* ~ *drama*, el teatro serio o clásico.
legitimate (to) (-eit) *tr.* legitimar. *2* justificar, aprobar. *3* dar fuerza legal.
legitimation (-ei·shøn) *s.* legitimación.
legitime (le·dўitim) *s.* LEGITIM.
legitimist (lidўi·timist) *s.* POL. legitimista.
legitimize (to) (-aiš) *tr.* legitimar.
leg-of-mutton *adj.* triangular [vela]; de pernil [manga].
legume (le·gium), **legumen** (legiu·møn) *s.* BOT. legumbre. *2* COC. verdura.
legumin (legiu·min) *s.* QUÍM. legúmina.
leguminous (-øs) *adj.* leguminoso.
leisure (le·ўø^r) *s.* ocio, vagar, desocupación; tiempo libre: ~ *hours*, horas de ocio, ratos perdidos; *at one's* ~, a la conveniencia de uno, cuando uno pueda.
leisurely (-li) *adj.* lento, pausado, sosegado. *2* desocupado. *3 adv.* despacio, sin prisas.
lemma (le·ma) *s.* lema.
lemniscate (le·mniskeit) *s.* GEOM. lemniscata.
lemniscus (le·mniscøs) *s.* lemnisco.
lemon (le·møn) *s.* BOT. limón: ~ *tree*, limonero. *2* BOT. ~ *balm*, toronjil. *3* ~ *verbena*, luisa, hierba luisa.
lemonade (lemønei·d) *s.* limonada.
lemur (lı·mø^r) *s.* ZOOL. lémur, lemúrido.
lemures (le·miuriš) *s. pl.* MIT. lémures.
lend (to) (lend) *tr.* prestar [dar prestado; dar, comunicar, proporcionar]: *to* ~ *oneself*, o *itself*, *to*, entregarse, acomodarse, prestarse a. ¶ Pret. y p. p.: *lent*.
lender (-ø^r) *s.* prestador, prestamista.
lending library (-ing) *s.* biblioteca circulante.
length (lengz) *s.* longitud; largo; extensión, duración: *at full* ~, por extenso; tendido, cuan largo es uno; *at* ~, por extenso; al fin, a la larga. *2* espacio, trecho, trozo. *3* grado, punto, extremo [en una acción, esfuerzo, etc.]: *to go any* ~, hacer uno todo lo posible.
lengthen (to) (-øn) *tr.* alargar, prolongar. *2* aguar, diluir. *3 intr.* alargarse, prolongarse.
lengthways (-ueiš), **lengthwise** (-uaiš) *adv.* longitudinalmente, a la larga.
lengthy (-i) *adj.* largo; difuso, prolijo.
leniency (lı·niønsi) *s.* lenidad, indulgencia; suavidad.
lenient (-ønt) *adj.* indulgente, clemente; suave.
lenify (to) (le·nifai) *tr.* lenificar.
lenitive (-tiv) *adj.-s.* lenitivo.
lenity (-i) *s.* lenidad, blandura, suavidad.
lens (lenš) *s.* ÓPT. lente. *2* ANAT. cristalino.
Lent (lent) *s.* cuaresma, cuadragésima.
lent *pret.* y *p. p.* de TO LEND.
lenten (-øn) *adj.* cuaresmal.
lenticular (lenti·kiula^r) *adj.* lenticular.
lentil (le·ntil) *s.* BOT. lenteja.
lentiscus (lenti·skøs), **lentisk** (le·ntisk) *s.* BOT. lentisco.
Leo (lı·ou) *s.* ASTR. leo, león. *2 n. pr.* León.

Leonard (le·na^rd) *n. pr.* Leonardo.
Leonese (liøni·š), *pl.* -nese (-ši) *adj.-s.* leonés.
leonine (lı·ønain) *adj.* leonino.
Leonora (li·ønora), **Leonore** (li·ønou^r) *n. pr.* Leonor.
leopard (le·pa^rd) *s.* ZOOL. leopardo.
Leopold (lı·øpould) *n. pr.* Leopoldo.
leper (le·pø^r) *s.* leproso.
Lepidoptera (lepida·ptøra) *s. pl.* ENT. lepidópteros.
lepidopteran (-n) *adj.-s.* ENT. lepidóptero.
leporine (le·pørin o le·pørain) *adj.* leporino.
leprosarium (leprøse·riøm) *s.* leprosería.
leprosy (le·prøsi) *s.* MED. lepra.
leprous (le·prøs) *adj.* leproso. *2* HIST. NAT. escamoso.
Lesbian (le·šbian) *adj.-s.* lesbiano, lesbio.
lese-majesty (lı·šmæ·dўesti) *s.* lesa majestad.
lesion (lı·ўøn) *s.* lesión.
less (les) *adj.-adv.-prep.* menos: ~ *and* ~, cada vez menos; *the* ~ ..., *the* ... *(the more)*, cuanto menos..., menos (o más). *2 adj.* menor: *to grow* ~, disminuir.
lessee (lesı·) *adj.* DER. arrendatario.
lessen (to) (le·søn) *tr.* minorar, disminuir, achicar, reducir. *2* rebajar, quitar importancia a. *3 intr.* disminuirse, menguar, decrecer.
lesser (le·sø^r) *adj. compar.* de LITTLE: menor, más pequeño. *2* BOT., ZOOL. menor.
lesson (le·søn) *s.* lección. *2* enseñanza, ejemplo.
lesson (to) *tr.* enseñar; amonestar, reprender.
lessor (le·sø^r) *s.* DER. arrendador.
lest (lest) *conj.* para que no, de miedo de que, por miedo de que, no sea que.
let (let) *s.* estorbo, obstáculo, impedimento.
let (to) *tr.* arrendar, alquilar [dar en arriendo o alquiler]: *to* ~, se alquila, por o para alquilar. *2* dejar, permitir. *3* dejar o hacer entrar, pasar o salir [por una puerta, etc.]. *4* sacar [sangre a un enfermo]. *5* Como auxiliar sirve para formar imperativos y subjuntivos de otros verbos: *let's run*, corramos: ~ *him come*, que venga. *6 to* ~ *alone*, dejar en paz; no tocar; ~ *alone* [usado adverbialmente], por no decir, por no hablar de, y mucho menos. *7 to* ~ *down*, dejar caer, bajar, descolgar; abandonar, traicionar, dejar colgado; chasquear; humillar. *8 to* ~ *go*, dejar ir; soltar, aflojar. *9 to* ~ *in*, dejar o hacer entrar, meter; embutir. *10 to* ~ *know*, hacer saber. *11 to* ~ *loose*, soltar, desatar; desencadenar, aflojar. *12 to* ~ *off*, disparar [un arma]; soltar, dejar salir. *13 to* ~ *out*, dejar o hacer salir; dejar escapar; soltar; aflojar; largar [un cabo]; ensanchar [un vestido]; arrendar, alquilar.

14 intr. arrendarse o alquilarse. *15 to* ~ *up*, cesar, desistir; disminuir, moderarse. ¶ Pret. y p. p.: *let*; ger.: *letting*.
letdown (-daun) *s.* aflojamiento, disminución. *2* chasco, desilusión. *3* humillación.
lethal (lı·zal) *adj.* letal.
lethargic (al (liza·^rdўik(al) *adj.* letárgico.
lethargy (le·za^rdўi) *s.* letargo.
Lethe (le·z) *n. pr.* MIT. Leteo [río]. *2* fig. olvido.
Lethean (lizı·an) *adj.* leteo.
Letitia (leti·shia) *n. pr.* Leticia.
let's (le·ts) *contr.* de LET US.
Lett (let) *s.* letón.
letter (le·tø^r) *s.* letra [del alfabeto]. *2* IMPR. letra, tipo, carácter. *3* letra [sentido literal]: *to the* ~, al pie de la letra. *4* carta, epístola, documento: ~ *of credit*, carta de crédito; *letters patent*, patente, privilegio; ejecutoria [de nobleza]; *letters*

rogatory, DER. exhorto; ~ *book*, copiador [libro]; ~ *box*, buzón [para cartas]; ~ *opener*, plegadera; ~ *press*, prensa de copiar cartas. *5 pl.* letras, literatura.
letter (to) *tr.* rotular, estampar o marcar con letras.
lettered (-d) *adj.* rotulado, marcado con letras. *2* culto, instruido, docto, letrado.
letterhead (-jed) *s.* membrete [de carta]. *2* hoja o pliego de papel con membrete.
lettering (-ing) *s.* inscripción, letrero. *2* acción de poner letras o letreros.
letterless (-lis) *adj.* iletrado.
letterpress (-pres) *s.* IMPR. letra impresa, texto [a distinción de las ilustraciones y grabados].
lettues (le·tis) *s.* BOT. lechuga.
letup (le·tøp) *s.* fam. calma, disminución.
leucocyte (liu·kouseit) *s.* FISIOL. leucocito.
leucoma (liukou·ma) *s.* MED. leucoma.
leukemia (liuki·mia) *s.* MED. leucemia.
Levant (livæ·nt) *n. pr.* Levante [parte oriental del Mediterráneo].
levant (to) *intr.* (Ingl.) marcharse [esp. sin pagar las deudas de juego].
levanter (-ø^r) *s.* viento de levante.
Levantine (-in) *adj.-s.* levantino [del Levante].
1) levee (le·VI o levI·) *s.* besamanos, recepción.
2) levee (le·vi) *s.* (E.U.) dique para contener las aguas. *2* (E.U.) desembarcadero.
level (-øl) *adj.* llano, liso, igualado, nivelado, horizontal: ~ *crossing*, FERROC. paso a nivel. *2* igual, que está al mismo nivel: ~ *with*, al nivel de; igual que. *3* igual, uniforme, poco accidentado. *4* equilibrado; imparcial. *5* juicioso, discreto. *6 to do one's ~ best*, esforzarse, esmerarse. *7 s.* nivel [aparato; grado de elevación; altura, categoría]: *on a ~ with*, al mismo nivel que. *8* plano horizontal, llano, llanura. *9 adv.* a nivel. *10* en línea recta; directamente.
level (to) *tr.* nivelar. *2* enrasar. *3* allanar, igualar. *4* derribar; arrasar. *5* apuntar, asestar [un arma]; dirigir [la mirada, etc.]. *6* poner al nivel o al alcance [de]. *7 to ~ off*, aplanar, nivelar. ¶ Pret. y p. p.: *leveled* o *-lled*; ger.: *leveling* o *-lling*.
level-headed *adj.* juicioso, sensato, de buen sentido.
lever (le·vø^r) *s.* FÍS., MEC. palanca. *2* fig. palanca [medio, influencia].
lever (to) *tr.* apalancar.
leverage (le·vøridŷ) *s.* acción o poder de una palanca. *2* sistema de palancas. *3* fig. medios o influencia para conseguir una cosa.
leveret (le·vøret) *s.* ZOOL. lebrato.
leviathan (livai·azan) *s.* leviatán.
levigate (to) (le·vigeit) *tr.* levigar. *2* pulverizar.
levirate (le·virit) *s.* levirato.
levitation (levitei·shøn) *s.* levitación.
Levite (li·vait) *s.* levita [pers.].
Levitic (al (livi·tik(al) *adj.* levítico.
Leviticus (-øs) *s.* Levítico [libro de la Biblia].
levity (le·viti) *s.* levedad. *2* frivolidad. *3* veleidad.
levulose (le·viulous) *s.* QUÍM. levulosa.
levy (le·vi) *s.* leva, recluta, enganche. *2* exacción, imposición, recaudación [de tributos, etc.]. *3* DER. embargo.
levy (to) *tr.* reclutar, hacer leva de. *2* hacer [guerra]. *3* exigir, recaudar [tributos, etc.]. *4* DER. embargar.
lewd (liu·d) *adj.* lujurioso, lascivo, lúbrico, obsceno. *2* libertino, disoluto.
Lewis (lu·is) *n. pr.* Luis.

lexicographer (leksika·grafø^r) *s.* lexicógrafo.
lexicography (-i) *s.* lexicografía.
lexicon (le·ksikøn) *s.* léxico, diccionario.
Leyden jar (lai·døn) *s.* FÍS. botella de Leiden.
liability (lalabi·liti) *s.* riesgo, exposición, posibilidad de incurrir [en]. *2* responsabilidad, obligación [pecuniaria]. *3 pl.* COM. deudas, obligaciones, pasivo.
liable (la·abøl) *adj.* expuesto, sujeto, propenso. *2* obligado, responsable [pecuniariamente].
liaison (lieŝo·n o liei·ŝøn) *s.* lazo, unión. *2* enlace, coordinación: ~ *officer*, MIL. oficial de enlace. *3* FONÉT. enlace. *4* enredo [relación ilícita].
liana (liæ·na), **liane** (lia·n) *s.* BOT. bejuco, liana.
liar (lai·a^r) *s.* embustero, mentiroso.
Liassic (laiæ·sik) *adj.-s.* GEOL. liásico.
libation (laibei·shøn) *s.* libación.
libel (lai·bøl) *s.* libelo; calumnia, difamación.
libel(l)eus (-øs) *adj.* difamatorio, calumniador.
libellula (laibe·liula) *s.* ENT. libélula.
liber (lai·bø^r) *s.* BOT. líber. *2* libro registro.
liberal (li·børal) *adj.* liberal, generoso. *2* abundante. *3* noble, caballeroso. *4* latitudinario, despreocupado. *5* libre [traducción, etc.]. *6* ~ *arts*, artes liberales. *7 adj.-s.* POL. liberal.
liberalism (-iŝm) *s.* liberalismo.
liberality (libøræ·liti) *s.* liberalidad. *2* don, dádiva.
liberalize (to) (li·børalaiŝ) *tr.* liberalizar.
liberate (to) (li·børeit) *tr.* libertar, liberar.
liberation (libørei·shøn) *s.* liberación. *2* redención [de cautivos].
liberator (libørei·tø^r) *s.* liberador, libertador.
Liberia (laibi·ria) *s.* GEOGR. Liberia.
liberticidal (libø^rtisai·dal) *adj.* liberticida.
libertine (li·bø^rtin) *adj.-s.* libertino; disoluto. *2* librepensador.
libertinism (-iŝm) *s.* libertinaje.
liberty (li·bø^rti) *s.* libertad: ~ *of press*, libertad de imprenta; ~ *cap*, gorro frigio; *to be at ~ to*, ser libre de; tener permiso para [hacer algo]; *to take liberties*, tomarse libertades; *at ~*, en libertad, libre. *2* exención, franqueza, privilegio.
libidinous (libi·dinøs) *adj.* libidinoso.
libido (-ou o libai·dou) *s.* libido.
Libra (lai·bra) *n. pr.* ASTR. Libra.
librarian (laibre·rian) *s.* bibliotecario.
library (lai·breri) *s.* biblioteca. *2* estudio, despacho, gabinete.
libration (laibrei·shøn) *s.* libración.
librettist (libre·tist) *s.* libretista.
libretto (-ou) *s.* libreto.
Libya (li·biæ) *n. pr.* GEOGR. Libia.
Lybyan (-n) *adj.-s.* líbico.
lice (lais) *s. pl.* de LOUSE.
license, licence (lai·søns) *s.* licencia [libertad abusiva], libertinaje. *2* licencia [poética]. *3* libertad de acción. *4* licencia, permiso, venia. *5* autorización, permiso, matrícula, patente, título, concesión: ~ *number*, número de matrícula.
license, licence (to) *tr.* autorizar, dar permiso, título o patente.
licensee (laisensi·) *s.* titular de permiso o concesión.
licentiate (laise·nshiit) *s.* licenciado, persona que tiene título de una facultad.
licentious (-øs) *adj.* licencioso.
licentiousness (-nis) *s.* licencia, libertinaje.
lichen (lai·køn) *s.* BOT., MED. liquen.
lich-gate (lich-geit) *s.* entrada cubierta de un cementerio.
licit (li·sit) *adj.* lícito.

lick (lik) *s.* lamedura, lengüetada. *2* fam. ligera aplicación de algo; pincelada: *to give a ~ and promise to,* fig. hacer de prisa y mal. *3* fam. esfuerzo. *4* pop. paso, velocidad. *5* salegar.
lick (to) *tr.* lamer: *to ~ one's shoes,* fig. adular servilmente; *to ~ the dust,* morder el polvo. *2* fam. pegar, apalizar. *3* fam. vencer, ganar [a uno]. *4* fam. sobrepujar. *5* fam. *that licks me,* no lo entiendo, no puedo entenderlo. *6* fig. *to ~ into shape,* dar forma a, hacer presentable.
licking (-ing) *s.* lengüetada. *2* paliza, tunda; derrota.
lickspittle (-spitøl) *s.* adulón.
licorice (-øris) *s.* BOT. regaliz.
lictor (-tøʳ) *s.* lictor.
lid (lid) *s.* tapa, tapadera. *2* tapa [de un libro]. *3* ANAT. párpado.
lie (lai) *s.* mentira, embuste, falsedad. *2* mentis: *to give the ~ to,* dar un mentis a, desmentir. *3* disposición, situación, orientación: *the ~ of the land,* disposición del terreno; fig. estado de las cosas.
1) **lie (to)** *intr.* mentir. ¶ Pret. y p. p.: *lied;* ger.: *lying.*
2) **lie (to)** *intr.* tenderse, acostarse, recostarse, apoyarse. *2* estar tendido o acostado, yacer. *3* estar, permanecer: *to ~ in wait,* estar al acecho; *to ~ in state,* estar [un difunto] en la capilla ardiente. *4* yacer, estar enterrado. *5* consistir, estribar. *6* estar, hallarse, extenderse. *7* MAR. *to ~ at anchor,* estar anclado. *8 to ~ about,* estar esparcido. *9 to ~ down,* acostarse, echarse. *10 to ~ hard on,* pesar sobre; afligir. *11 to ~ in,* estar de parto. *12 to ~ low,* estar postrado o muerto; agazaparse, estar quieto, escondido. *13 to ~ on,* depender de; pesar, cargar sobre. *14 to ~ over,* aplazarse, quedar aplazado. *15 to ~ to,* MAR. pairar, ponerse en facha. *16 to ~ under,* estar bajo el peso de. *17 to ~ up,* retirarse; irse a la cama. *18 to ~ with,* tocar, incumbir a. ¶ Pret.: *lay;* p. p.: *lain;* ger.: *lying.*
lief (lɪf) *adv.* de buen grado: *I would as ~ go as not,* tanto me da ir como no ir.
liege (lidÿ) *adj.* ligio, feudatario. *2* adj.-s. *liege* o ~ *lord,* señor feudal. *3 s.* vasallo.
Liege (liedÿ) *n. pr.* GEOGR. Lieja.
liegeman (lɪ·dÿmæn) *s.* vasallo. *2* seguidor leal.
lien (lien o lɪn) *s.* DER. embargo preventivo.
lieu (liu·) *s. in ~ of,* en lugar de, en vez de.
lieutenancy (liute·nansi) *s.* lugartenencia. *2* tenencia, tenientazgo.
lieutenant (-nant) *s.* teniente, lugarteniente. *2* MIL. teniente: *~ colonel,* teniente coronel; *~ general,* teniente general. *3* MAR. teniente de navío; *~ commander,* capitán de corbeta.
life (laif), *pl.* **lives** [-vš] *s.* vida: *the other ~,* la otra vida; *~ belt,* cinturón salvavidas; *~ expectancy,* índice de longevidad, promedio vital; *~ preserver,* MAR. salvavidas; (Ingl.) cachiporra flexible; *~ sentence,* cadena perpetua; *to be the ~ and soul of,* ser el alma de; *to come to ~,* volver a la vida, volver en sí; *to have the time of one's ~,* divertirse o gozar como nunca; *to take one's ~ in one's hand,* jugarse la vida; *as big as ~,* de tamaño natural; *for ~,* para toda la vida; *for ~, for one's ~, for dear ~,* desesperadamente, para salvar la vida; *for the ~ of me,* a fe mía; aunque me maten; *to the ~,* al vivo, fielmente. *2* animación, alegría, movimiento. B. ART. natural: *from ~,* del natural.
lifeblood (-blød) *s.* sangre vital. *2* alma, nervio.

lifeboat (-bout) *s.* bote salvavidas.
lifeless (-lis) *adj.* sin vida, muerto, inanimado, inerte. *2* falto de animación. *3* desierto, inhabitado.
lifelike (-laik) *adj.* que parece vivo, natural.
lifelong (-long) *adj.* de toda la vida.
lifesaver (-seivøʳ) *s.* salvador, el que salva la vida. *2* miembro de una estación de salvamento.
lifesaving (-seiving) *adj.* de salvamento: *~ gun,* cañón lanzacabos. *2 m.* acción de salvar vidas. *3* servicio de salvavidas.
life-size *adj.* de tamaño natural.
lifetime (-taim) *s.* vida, curso de la vida. *2* fig. eternidad [largo tiempo]. *3 adj.* perpetuo, vitalicio.
lift (lift) *s.* alzamiento, elevación, levantamiento; esfuerzo para levantar. *2* altura, grado de elevación. *3* fuerza o influencia elevadora; AVIA. fuerza ascensional o de sustentación. *4* ayuda [para levantar]. *5* alza, aumento, ascenso. *6* mecanismo elevador; (Ingl.) ascensor. *7* elevación [del terreno], repecho. *8* tapa [de un tacón de zapato]. *9 to give someone a ~,* llevar uno en su coche a otro; ayudar a uno. *10 adj. ~ force* o *power,* fuerza ascensional o elevadora; *~ pump,* bomba aspirante.
lift (to) *tr.* alzar, levantar, elevar, izar, solevantar. | A veces con *up, off* o *out.* *2* quitar [un peso de encima]. *3* quitarse [el sombrero]. *4* (E.U.) cancelar [una hipoteca]. *5* elevar, exaltar; engreír. | Gralte. con *up.* *6* fam. hurtar, robar; plagiar. *7* levantar [las tiendas]. *8 intr.* levantarse, subir, elevarse. *9* disiparse [las nubes, la niebla, la obscuridad].
lifter (-øʳ) *s.* levantador, alzador, elevador. *2* MEC. leva.
liftman (-mæn) *s.* (Ingl.) ascensorista.
ligament (li·gamønt) *s.* ligadura, atadura. *2* ANAT. ligamento.
ligate (to) (lai·geit) *tr.* CIR. ligar, atar.
ligation (-ei·shøn) *s.* ligación, ligadura.
ligature (li·gæchuʳ) *s.* ligación, ligadura. *2* MÚS. ligado. *3* IMPR. letras unidas [œ, fi, etc.].
light (lait) *s.* luz [agente físico; claridad, resplandor; día; lo que ilumina]: *to bring to ~,* sacar a luz; *to come to ~,* salir a luz; *to see the ~,* ver la luz; ver luz, empezar a comprender; ver la solución; *to throw* o *shed, ~ upon,* arrojar luz sobre; *against the ~,* a contraluz; al trasluz; *in the ~ of,* a la luz de [unos hechos, etc.]. *2* luz, lámpara, vela, etc.; farol, faro; luz, señal [de tráfico]. *3* pop. ojos. *4* fuego, cerilla, etc. [para encender]. *5* lumbrera [pers. notable]. *6* ARQ., PINT. luz. *7* aspecto, punto de vista: *to place in a good ~,* presentar bajo un aspecto favorable. *8 pl.* luces, alumbrado. *9* luces, ilustración; entendimiento: *according to his lights,* según Dios le da a entender. *10* bofes, livianos.
11 adj. de luz; de farol, faro, etc.; luminoso, claro: *~ wave,* onda luminosa; *to be ~,* ser de día. *12* blondo, rubio; blanca [tez]; claro, alegre [color]. *13* ligero, leve, liviano, suave. *14* ligero [comida, sueño]. *15* ligero, ágil, pronto. *16* ligero, inconstante; frívolo, no serio; licencioso. *17* MIL. ligero: *~ horse,* caballería ligera. *18* ligero, libre de penas, confiado. *19* boyante [buque]. *20* flojo [vino, cerveza]. *21* arijo [suelo]. *22 ~ in the head,* atolondrado; mareado; delirante. *23 to make ~ of,* no dar importancia a.
24 adv. ligeramente. *25* fácilmente.
light (to) *tr.* encender [el fuego, el cigarro, una luz, etc.]. *2* alumbrar, iluminar. *3 intr.* encenderse.

4 iluminarse. | Gralte. con *up*. *5* apearse. *6* posarse, descender, caer [en o sobre]. *7 to ~ on* o *upon*, tropezar o topar con, encontrar por casualidad. ¶ Pret. y p. p.: *lighted* o *lit*.

light-complexioned *adj*. de tez blanca.

lighten (to) *tr*. iluminar, alumbrar; hacer brillar o resplandecer. *2* aclarar, avivar [un color]. *3* alegrar. *4* aligerar, aliviar. *5* alijar, descargar [un buque]. *6 intr*. iluminarse. *7* aclararse [hacerse menos obscuro]. *8* relampaguear. *9* aligerarse.

lighter (-ø^r) *adj*. comp. de LIGHT. *2 s*. encendedor [pers.]. *3* encendedor, mechero. *4* MAR. alijador, gabarra.

lighter (to) *tr*. cargar o descargar por medio de alijadores o gabarras.

lighterman (-mæn) *s*. gabarrero.

light-fingered *adj*. ligero de dedos, largo de uñas.

light-footed *adj*. ligero de pies.

light-headed *adj*. ligero de cascos, atolondrado. *2* aturdido, mareado. *3* delirante.

light-hearted *adj*. alegre; libre de cuidados.

lighthouse (lai·tjaus) *s*. MAR. faro, farola.

lighthouseman (-mæn) *s*. torrero [de faro].

lighting (-ing) *s*. iluminación. *2* alumbrado: luz [eléctrica, de gas, etc.]: *~ fixtures*, aparatos de alumbrado. *3* encendido.

lightly (-li) *adv*. ligeramente. *2* alegremente. *3* a la ligera, de ligero. *4* sin seriedad.

light-minded *adj*. voluble, atolondrado.

lightness (-nis) *s*. claridad, luminosidad. *2* lo claro [de un color]. *3* ligereza. *4* delicadeza, suavidad.

lightning (-ning) *s*. METEOR. relámpago, fucilazo; rayo, centella: *~ arrester*, *~ rod*, pararrayos. *2* ENT. *~ bug*, luciérnaga; cocuyo. *3 like ~*, fig. como el rayo.

lightsome (-søm) *adj*. claro, luminoso. *2* alegre, festivo. *3* ligero [ágil; frívolo].

lightweight (-ueit) *adj*. ligero, de poco peso. *2* ligero, de entretiempo [vestido]. *3 s*. DEP. peso ligero [boxeador]. *6* fig. pelele.

light-year *s*. ASTR. año de luz.

ligneous (li·gniøs) *adj*. leñoso.

lignify (to) (-ifai) *tr*. lignificar. *2 intr*. lignificarse. ¶ Pret. y p. p.: *lignified*.

lignin (-in) *s*. BOT., QUÍM. lignina.

lignite (-ait) *s*. MINER. lignito.

lignum-vitæ (-øm-vai·ti) *s*. BOT. guayacán, palo santo.

ligule (li·giul) *s*. BOT. lígula.

Ligurian (ligiu·rian) *adj.-s*. ligur, ligurino.

likable (lai·kabøl) *adj*. agradable, simpático.

like (laik) *adj*. igual, parecido, zemejante, tal, como: *~ father*, *~ son*, de tal palo, tal astilla; *something ~*, algo así como; *to be ~*, parecerse, ser parecido; *what is he ~?*, ¿cómo es él? *2* propio, característico de: *it is just ~ him*, es muy propio de él. *3* probable: *he is ~ to come*, es probable que venga. *4 adv., prep., conj*. como, del mismo modo que: *~ mad*, como un loco; *~ this*, así, de este modo; *nothing ~*, ni con mucho. *4 ~ enough, very ~*, probablemente.

6 s. igual, pers. o cosa igual o semejante: *and the ~*, y cosas así; *the ~ of*, otro igual o que se parezca a. *7 pl*. gustos, simpatías.

like (to) *tr*. querer, tener simpatía a; gustar de, gustarle a uno; querer, desear: *I ~ him*, le quiero, me gusta; *do you ~ tea?*, ¿le gusta el té?; *how do you ~ it?*, ¿qué le parece?, ¿le gusta?; *I should ~ to see it*, quisiera verlo; *as you ~ [it]*, como quiera, como guste; *to ~ better* o *best*, preferir. *2* sentar [una comida o bebida].

likeable (-abøl) *adj*. LIKABLE.

likelihood (-lijud) *s*. probabilidad, posibilidad; verosimilitud.

likely (-li) *adj*. probable: *he is ~ to come*, es probable que venga. *2* verosímil, creíble. *3* apropiado. *4* prometedor. *5 adv*. probablemente.

liken (to) (lai·køn) *tr*. asemejar, comparar.

likeness (-nis) *s*. semejanza, parecido, aire. *2* apariencia, forma. *3* efigie, retrato.

likewise (-uaiŝ) *adv*. igualmente, lo mismo. *2* asimismo, también, además.

liking (-ing) *s*. inclinación, afición, simpatía. *2* agrado, gusto, preferencia.

lilac (lai·lak) *s*. BOT. lilac, lila.

liliaceous (liliei·shøs) *adj*. liliáceo.

lilied (li·lid) *adj*. parecido a un lirio.

Lille (lil) *n. pr*. GEOGR. Lila.

liliputian (lilipiu·shan) *adj.-s*. liliputiense.

lilt (lilt) *s*. canción de movimiento vivo, alegre. *2* ritmo, cadencia.

lilt (to) *tr*. cantar con movimiento vivo, alegre.

lily (li·li) *pl. s*. BOT. lirio; azucena, lis: *~ of the valley*, lirio de los valles, muguete. *2* flor de lis. *3* *water ~*, nenúfar.

lily-livered *adj*. fig. cobarde.

limb (lim) *s*. miembro [del cuerpo del hombre o del animal]. *2* brazo o rama [de una cosa]. *3* rama [de árbol]. *4* limbo, borde graduado. *5* ASTR., BOT. limbo. *6 ~ of the devil*, muchacho travieso.

limb (to) *tr*. lisiar. *2* desmembrar, despedazar.

limber (-bø^r) *adj*. flexible, cimbreño, ágil. *2 s*. ARTILL. armón, avantrén.

limber (to) *tr*. hacer flexible o ágil. *2* ARTILL. enganchar el armón a.

limbo (-bou) *s*. limbo [de las almas]. *2* fig. prisión, encierro; olvido.

lime (laim) *s*. cal: *~ pit*, calera; TEN. encalador. *2* caliza. *3* liga [para cazar pájaros]: *~ twig*, vareta. *4* BOT. tilo. *5* BOT. lima agria; limero agrio.

lime (to) *tr*. encalar. *2* AGR. abonar con cal. *3* untar con liga; cazar con liga.

limekiln (-kiln) *s*. calera [horno de cal].

limelight (-lait) *s*. TEAT. foco, reflector; haz luminoso del reflector. *2* fig.: *to be in the ~*, estar a la vista del público, ser objeto de la curiosidad del público, ser de actualidad, ser notable.

limerick (li·mørik) *s*. quintilla jocosa.

limestone (lai·mstoun) *s*. caliza, piedra caliza.

limit (li·mit) *s*. límite: *without ~*, ilimitado, sin límites. *2* fam. colmo: *to be the ~*, ser el colmo, ser intolerable.

limit (to) *tr*. limitar [poner límite o límites]. *2* DER. fijar, determinar.

limitary (-eri) *adj*. sujeto a restricción, limitado. *2* de límite. *3* limitador, restrictivo.

limitation (ei·shøn) *s*. limitación. *2* restricción.

limited (li·mitid) *adj*. limitado: *~ company*, COM. sociedad limitada. *2* constitucional [monarquía]. *3* (E.U.) expreso, de lujo [tren].

limitless (-lis) *adj*. sin límites, ilimitado.

limitrophe (-traf) *adj*. limítrofe.

limonite (li·monait) *s*. MINER. limonita.

limousine (limuŝi·n) *s*. AUT. limousine.

limp (limp) *s*. cojera, claudicación. *2 adj*. flojo, flexible, flácido, lacio. *3* débil, sin energía.

limp (to) *intr*. cojear. *2* MEC. marchar irregularmente.

limpet (-et) *s*. ZOOL. lapa, lápade [molusco].

limpid (-id) *adj*. límpido, claro, transparente.

limpidity (limpi·diti) *s*. limpidez.

limy (lai·mi) *adj.* viscoso, pegajoso, untado con liga. 2 calizo.

linaceous (lainei·shøs) *adj.* lináceo.

linchpin (li·nchpin) *s.* pezonera [de carruaje].

linden (li·ndøn) *s.* BOT. tilo. 2 madera de tilo.

line (lain) *s.* cuerda, cabo, cable [relativamente delgados], cordel, hilo. 2 sedal [para pescar]. 3 cordel o cinta [para medir o nivelar]. 4 hilo [de la plomada]. 5 línea [en geometría, topografía, etc.]; línea, raya, trazo, rasgo: ~ *of force*, FÍS. línea de fuerza; ~ *of sight*, línea de mira; *the* ~, GEOGR. la línea, el ecuador. 6 línea recta; línea, fila, hilera: *to bring into* ~, alinear; fig. hacer que uno siga una opinión, partido, etc.; *in* ~, alineado; fig. de acuerdo, dispuesto; *out of* ~, desalineado; fig. en desacuerdo. 7 línea, raya, término, límite: *to draw the* ~ *at*, no ir más allá de; *on the* ~, en la línea divisoria. 8 MIL., FORT. línea: ~ *of battle*, línea de combate; *all along the* ~, fig. en toda la línea. 9 línea [aérea, férrea, marítima, telegráfica, etc.]. 10 conducción, cañería, tubería. 11 línea, renglón: *a* ~, fig. unas líneas [breve misiva]. 12 verso [línea]. 13 arruga [en el rostro, etc.], raya [de las manos]. 14 línea [medida]. 15 línea [de parentesco], linaje. 16 línea [de conducta, acción o pensamiento]: ~ *of least resistance*, línea del menor esfuerzo. 17 ramo de negocios, género de actividad, especialidad, estilo. 18 COM. clase de artículos; surtido. 19 *pl.* líneas, contornos, rasgos. 20 verso, versos. 21 TEAT. papel, parte. 22 riendas [del caballo].

line (to) *tr.* linear, rayar, reglar. 2 marcar con rayas. 3 delinear, dibujar. 4 arrugar [el rostro, etc.]. 5 formar fila o hilera a lo largo de. 6 forrar, guarnecer, revestir; llenar. 7 *to* ~ *up*, alinear; MEC. ajustar. 8 *intr.* alinearse. 9 *to* ~ *up*, ponerse en fila.

lineage (li·niidÿ) *s.* linaje, bolengo, prosapia.

lineal (-al) *adj.* lineal. 2 que viene por línea directa; hereditario.

lineament (-amønt) *s.* lineamento. 2 facción [del rostro]. 3 *pl.* facciones; fisonomía.

linear (-ia^r) *adj.* lineal: ~ *drawing*, dibujo lineal; ~ *measure*, medida de longitud. 3 BOT., ZOOL. linear.

lineation (-shøn) *s.* delineación. 2 disposición por líneas.

lined (laind) *adj.* rayado: ~ *paper*, papel rayado. 2 arrugado [rostro, manos]. 3 forrado, revestido.

lineman (-mæn) *s.* FERROC., ELECT., TELEF., TELEGR. operario o empleado que repara la línea.

linen (li·nøn) *s.* hilo de lino. 2 lienzo, lino [tela]. 3 ropa blanca: *bed* ~, ropas de cama; *table* ~, mantelería.

liner (lai·nø^r) *s.* vapor o avión de una línea.

linesman (-šmæn) *s.* LINEMAN. 2 DEP. juez de línea. 3 soldado de línea.

line-up *s.* formación, fila. 2 rueda de presos.

ling (ling) *s.* ICT. bacalao. 2 BOT. brezo.

linger (to) (li·ngø^r) *intr.* demorar, tardarse, ir despacio, quedarse, entretenerse, estar ocioso, vacilar. 2 durar, prolongarse [aunque apagándose, amainando, etc.]; consumirse.

lingerie (læ·nÿøri) *s.* ropa interior [de mujer].

lingering (lı·ngøring) *adj.* lento, prolongado. 2 tardo, moroso. 3 que dura, que subsiste.

lingo (li·ngou) *s.* lenguaje, jerga.

lingua franca (li·ngua fræ·nka) *s.* lengua franca.

lingual (li·ngual) *adj.* lingual.

linguist (-ist) *s.* lingüista. 2 poligloto.

linguistics (lingüi·stiks) *s.* lingüística.

liniment (li·nimønt) *s.* linimento.

lining (lai·ning) *s.* forro, aforro, revestimiento. 2 AUTO. guarnición de freno.

link (link) *s.* eslabón [de cadena]. 2 vínculo, enlace, lo que une o enlaza. 3 gemelo [de puño]. 4 MEC. articulación: varilla de conexión. 4 hacha de viento. 6 *pl.* campo de golf.

link (to) *tr.* eslabonar, unir, enlazar, encadenar, engarzar. 2 *intr.* eslabonarse, unirse, enlazarse.

linkage (-idÿ) *s.* eslabonamiento. 2 MEC. varillaje. 3 QUÍM. enlace. 4 ELECT. acoplamiento inductivo.

linkboy (-boi) *s.* paje de hacha.

linnet (li·nit) *s.* ORN. pardillo. 2 ORN. jilguero.

linoleum (linou·liøm) *s.* linóleo.

linotype (lei·notaip) *s.* IMPR. linotipia. 2 IMPR. linotipo.

linseed (li·nsid) *s.* linaza.

linstock (-tak) *s.* ARTILL. botafuego.

lint (lint) *s.* CIR. hilar. 2 borra de algodón.

lintel (-øl) *s.* ARQ. dintel.

lion (lai·øn) *s.* ZOOL. león: *lion's share*, parte del león. 2 fig. león [hombre valiente]. 3 fig. pers. célebre, muy solicitada en la vida de sociedad. 4 ASTR. Leo. 5 ENT. ~ *ant*, hormiga león.

lioness (-is) *s.* leona.

lion-hearted *adj.* valiente.

lionize (-aiš) *tr.* agasajar mucho [a uno] en la vida de sociedad.

lip (lip) *s.* ANAT. y fig. labio: *stiff upper* ~, fig. firmeza, obstinación; ~ *service*, jarabe de pico; alabanza, apoyo, etc., insinceros. 2 fam. lenguaje insolente. 3 labio [de una herida, una flor, un vaso]; pico [de jarro].

lip (to) *tr.* tocar con los labios; besar. 2 besar, lamer [dicho del agua, etc.]. 3 susurrar, murmurar. ¶ Pret. y p. p.: *lipped*; ger.: *-pping*.

lipoma (lipou·ma) *s.* MED. lipoma.

lipstick (li·pstik) *s.* lápiz para los labios.

liquate (to) (lai·kueit) *tr.* METAL. licuar.

liquefaction (likuifæ·kshøn) *s.* licuación, licuefacción, liquidación.

liquefy (to) (li·kuifai) *tr.* liquidar, licuar, licuefacer. 2 *intr.* liquidarse, licuarse. ¶ Pret. y p. p.: *liquefied*.

liquescent (likue·sønt) *adj.* licuescente.

liqueur (likø·^r) *s.* licor [bebida].

liquid (li·kuid) *adj.* FÍS., FONÉT. líquido. 2 para líquidos [medida o medidas]. 3 claro, cristalino. 4 puro, suave [sonido]. 5 COM. realizable. 6 *s.* líquido. 7 FONÉT. líquida.

liquidambar (li·kuidæmba^r) *s.* liquidámbar.

liquidate (to) (-deit) *tr.* liquidar, saldar [cuentas]. 2 pop. liquidar, acabar con, matar. 3 *intr.* COM. liquidar.

liquidation (-ei·shøn) *s.* COM. liquidación.

liquidity (likui·diti) *s.* liquidez. 2 claridad, transparencia, brillo. 3 pureza [de un sonido].

liquidize (to) (li·kuidaiš) *tr.* liquidar, licuar.

liquor (li·kø^r) *s.* licor, líquido. 2 licor, bebida alcohólica: *in* ~, embriagado.

liquorice (li·køris) *s.* LICORICE.

lira (li·ra) *s.* lira [moneda].

Lisbon (li·šbøn) *n. pr.* GEOGR. Lisboa.

lisp (lisp) *s.* ceceo. 2 balbuceo [de los niños].

lisp (to) *intr.* cecear. 2 balbucir.

lisper (-ø^r) *s.* ceceoso, zopas.

lissome(e (li·søm) *adj.* flexible, elástico. 2 ágil.

list (list) *s.* lista, catálogo, minuta, rol, matrícula. 2 orillo. 3 lista, faja, raya, cenefa. 4 orilla [de una tela]. 5 poét. límite, lindero. 6 ARQ. listel,

filete. *7* CARP. listón. *8* CARP. barandal. *9* MAR. *to have a ~*, irse a la banda, escorar. *10 pl.* liza, palenque.
list (to) *tr.* poner en [una] lista; registrar, catalogar. *2* alistar. *3* COM. cotizar, facturar. *4* guarnecer con cenefa, etc.; listar, rayar. *5* cercar con palenque. *6* MAR. hacer escorar. *7 intr.* alistarse. *8* MAR. escorar.
listel (-øl) *s.* ARQ. lístel.
listen (to) (li·søn) *intr.-tr.* escuchar: *to ~ to*, escuchar, oír, atender, prestar atención a. *2 to ~ in*, escuchar subrepticiamente una conversación telefónica; escuchar por radio.
listener (li·snøʳ) *s.* oyente, escucha, radioyente.
listening post (-ning) *s.* puesto de escucha.
listless (li·stlis) *adj.* distraído, indiferente, que no siente interés, apático, abatido.
lit (lit) *pret. y p. p.* de TO LIGHT.
litany (li·tani) *s.* letanía.
liter (li·tøʳ) *s.* litro.
literacy (li·tørasi) *s.* condición del que sabe leer y escribir.
literal (-al) *adj.* literal. *2* formado o expresado por letras. *3* prosaico, positivista.
literalness (-nis) *s.* exactitud literal. *2* prosaísmo, positivismo.
literary (-eri) *adj.* literario: *~ man*, literato, hombre de letras.
literate (-it) *adj.* instruido; que sabe leer y escribir [pers.].
literati (litørei·tai) *s. pl.* literatos. *2* personas ocultas.
literatim (-tim) *adv.* letra por letra, a la letra, literalmente.
literature (li·tøræchøʳ) *s.* literatura.
lithe (laið), **lithesome** (-søm) *adj.* flexible, elástico, cimbreño, ágil.
lithiasis (lizai·asis) *s.* MED. litiasis.
lithium (li·ziøm) *s.* QUÍM. litio.
lithograph (li·zøgræf) *s.* litografía [impresión].
lithograph (to) *tr.* litografiar.
lithographer (liza·graføʳ) *s.* litógrafo.
lithography (liza·grafi) *s.* litografía [arte].
lithophagous (-fagøs) *adj.* ZOOL. litófago.
Lithuania (li·zyueinia) *n. pr.* GEOGR. Lituania.
Lithuanian (lizyuei·nian) *adj.-s.* lituano.
litigant (li·tigant) *adj.-s.* litigante; contendiente.
litigate (to) (-eit) *tr.-intr.* litigar, contender.
litigation (-ei·shøn) *s.* litigación, litigio, pleito.
litigious (liti·dyøs) *adj.* litigioso.
litmus (li·tmøs) *s.* QUÍM. tornasol.
litre (li·tøʳ) *s.* litro.
litter (li·tøʳ) *s.* litera [vehículo]. *2* camilla, parihuelas. *3* camada, lechigada. *4* cama [de paja para las caballerías]. *5* fig. tendalera; escombros, basura; desorden.
litter (to) *tr.-intr.* parir [un animal]. *2 tr.* esparcir, desordenar. *3* cubrir [de cosas en desorden]; cubrir [el suelo] de paja.
little (-øl) *adj.* pequeño, chico, menudo, menor, parvo: *a ~ one*, un pequeñuelo; *Little Bear*, ASTR. Osa menor; *~ finger*, dedo meñique; *~ hours*, ECLES. horas menores; *~ office*, ECLES. oficio parvo; *Little Red Ridinghood*, caperucita encarnada. Muchas veces se traduce por un diminutivo: *~ house*, casita. *2 adj.-adv.-s.* poco: *~ hope*, poca esperanza; *a ~*, un poco de; algo; *~ more than*, poco más que; *after a ~*, al cabo de un poco; *~ by ~*, poco a poco; *not a ~*, no poco. *3 in ~*, en pequeño, en pequeña escala.

littleness (-nis) *s.* pequeñez, poquedad, cortedad. *2* mezquindad, ruindad.
littoral (li·tøral) *adj.-s.* litoral.
liturgic(al (litø·ʳdyik(al) *adj.* litúrgico.
liturgy (li·tøʳdyi) *s.* liturgia, ritual.
livable (li·vabøl) *adj.* habitable. *2* llevadero. *3* agradable, simpático.
live (laiv) *adj.* vivo [que vive, con vida]. *2 fam.* real, verdadero. *3* ardiente, encendido: *~ coals*, ascuas, carbón encendido. *4* vivo, enérgico, activo. *5* palpitante, de actualidad. *6* viva [peña, roca]. *7* cargado [cartucho, granada]. *8* ELECT. que lleva corriente [conductor]. *9* MEC. vivo. *10* IMPR. útil. *11* BOT. *~ oak*, encina norteamericana.
live (to) (li·v) *intr.* vivir [tener vida, existir; durar; subsistir; conducirse; habitar, morar]: *to ~ and learn*, vivir para ver; *to ~ by one's wits*, vivir de la trampa, ser caballero de industria; *to ~ from hand to mouth*, vivir al día; *to ~ high*, darse buena vida; *to ~ on o upon*, vivir a costa de; vivir o sustentarse de; *to ~ up to*, vivir con arreglo a; cumplir [lo prometido]. *3 tr.* llevar, pasar [tal o cual vida]. *4* vivir, pasar, experimentar, practicar. *5 to ~ down*, olvidar, ver desaparecer [con el tiempo]; borrar uno con su vida [una falta, etc.].
liveable (li·vabøl) *adj.* LIVABLE.
livelihood (lai·vlijud) *s.* vida, medios de vida.
liveliness (-nis) *s.* vida, vivacidad, animación.
livelong (li·vlong) *adj.* todo, largo [que tarda en pasar]: *all the ~ night*, toda la santa noche.
lively (lai·vli) *adj.* vivo, vivaz, vivaracho. *2* animado. *3* vivo, brioso, airoso, rápido. *4* vivo, alegre, brillante. *5* vivo, intenso. *6* vivo, pronto. *7* animador. *8* gráfica [descripción, etc.]. *9 adv.* vivamente. *10* airosamente.
liver (li·vøʳ) *s.* viviente. *2* el que vive de cierto modo. *3* ANAT., ZOOL. hígado.
liveried (-id) *adj.* que lleva librea.
liverwort (-uøʳt) *s.* BOT. hepática.
liverwurst (-uøʳst) *s.* embutido de hígado.
livery (li·vøri) *s.* librea. *2* uniforme [de un gremio, etc.]. *3 fig.* plumaje, ropaje, aspecto característico. *4* pensión o pupilaje de caballos; alquiler de caballos, coches, botes, etc.: *~ horse*, caballo de alquiler; *~ stable*, cuadra o cochería de alquiler.
liveryman (-mæn) *s.* dueño de una cuadra o cochería de alquiler. *2* criado de librea. *3* (Ingl.) individuo de un gremio.
lives (lai·vš) *s. pl.* de LIFE.
livestock (lai·vstak) *s.* ganado, animales que se crían.
livid (li·vid) *adj.* lívido. *2* pálido.
lividity (livi·diti) *s.* lividez.
living (li·ving) *adj.* vivo, viviente. *2* de vivientes. *3* en vivo. *4* vivo, activo. *5* vivaz, animado. *6* donde se está o se vive: *~ room*, cuarto de estar. *7* viva [agua, roca, lengua]. *8* vital [salario]. *9 s.* vida [estado del que vive; modo de vivir]. *10* vida, sustento, medios de vida. *11* (Ingl.) beneficio [eclesiástico]. *12 pl. the living*, los vivientes.
lizard (li·šaʳd) *s.* ZOOL. lagarto: *green ~, wall ~*, lagartija. *2* reptil saurio.
Lizzie (li·ši) *n. pr. dim.* de ELIZABETH.
llama (la·ma) *s.* ZOOL. llama.
lo (lou) *interj.* he aquí, ved aquí, cata; ¡mirad!
loach (louch) *s.* ICT. locha, lobo.
load (loud) *s.* carga [lo que se lleva o soporta]. *2 fig.* carga, peso, agobio. *3* ELECT., MEC. carga. *4*

carga [de un arma]. *5* pl. *loads of*, la mar de, montones de.
load (to) *tr.* cargar [un buque, mercancías, un arma, un dado, etc.]. *2* oprimir, agobiar. *3* cargar, colmar [de honores, etc.]. *4 intr.* cargar; tomar carga.
loader (-ø^r) *s.* cargador, embarcador.
loading (-ing) *s.* carga [acción de cargar]. *2 adj.* que carga, de cargar.
loadstar (-ta^r) *s.* LODESTAR.
loadstone (-stoun) *s.* magnetita; imán.
loaf (louf) *s.* barra de pan, hogaza. *2* pilón [de azúcar]: ~ *sugar*, azúcar de pilón.
loaf (to) *intr.* holgazanear, haraganear; pasearse.
loafer (-ø^r) *s.* holgazán, vago, callejero.
loam (loum) *s.* marga, tierra o suelo margoso. *2* mezcla de arcilla, arena, etc., para hacer ladrillos, moldes, etc.
loam (to) *tr.* tapar o cubrir con barro o arcilla.
loan (loun) *s.* préstamo: *on* ~, a préstamo. *2* empréstito. *3* cosa prestada.
loan (to) *tr.-intr.* prestar [dinero].
loath (louz) *adj.* renuente, poco dispuesto, reacio: *nothing* ~, dispuesto, de buena gana.
loathe (to) (loud) *tr.* aborrecer, abominar, detestar, repugnarle a uno [una cosa].
loathing (-ing) *s.* aborrecimiento, aversión, asco, repugnancia, hastío.
loathsome (-șøm) *adj.* aborrecible, odioso, asqueroso, repugnante, nauseabundo.
loaves (lou·vs) *s. pl.* de LOAF.
lob (lab) *s.* lombriz para cebo. *2* DEP. en el tenis, voleo alto y tendido de la pelota; en el criquet, voleo bajo de la pelota.
lob (to) *tr.* lanzar lenta o pesadamente. *2* DEP. hacer un LOB con la pelota. ¶ Pret. y p. p.: *lobbed*; p. a.: *-bbing*.
lobate(d (lou·beit(id) *adj.* lobulado.
lobby (la·bi) *s.* pasillo [esp. de una Cámara legislativa]; galería, antecámara, vestíbulo. *2* salón de entrada [de un hotel]. *2* (E.U.) camarilla política, grupo de cabilderos.
lobby (to) *intr.* (E.U.) cabildear.
lobbyist (-ist) *s.* cabildero.
lobe (loub) *s.* lóbulo, lobo.
lobed (-d) *adj.* lobulado, lobado.
lobelia (loubɪ·lia) *s.* BOT. lobelia.
lobeliaceous (loubiliei·șøs) *adj.* BOT. lobeliáceo.
loblolly (la·blali) *s.* gachas. *2* MAR. medicina.
lobster (la·bstø^r) *s.* ZOOL. langosta [crustáceo]; bogavante; *spiny* ~, langosta.
lobule (la·biul) *s.* lobulillo.
local (lou·kal) *adj.* local: ~ *anaesthesia*, anestesia local; ~ *call*, TELEF. llamada urbana; ~ *colour*, LIT. PINT. color local. *2* municipal, regional, de un distrito, etc.: ~ *government*, autonomía, descentralización. *3* localizado, no general. *4* FERROC. ~ *train*, tren suburbano. *5 s.* persona de una localidad. *6* sección local [de un sindicato, etc.]. *7* noticias de interés local..
locale (loukæ·l) *s.* sitio, lugar [esp. como escena de ciertos acontecimientos]; ambiente.
localism (lou·kališm) *s.* localismo. *2* costumbre local. *3* limitación de ideas.
locality (loukæ·liti) *s.* situación, lugar [donde se encuentra una cosa]. *2* lugar o escena [de algo]. *3* facultad de recordar y reconocer los lugares.
localization (lou·kališei·șhøn) *s.* localización [limitación a un punto o lugar].
localize (to) (-aiš) *tr.* localizar [limitar a un punto

o lugar]. *2* dar carácter local. *3* descentralizar. *4* concentrar [la atención en].
locate (to) (lou·keit) *tr.* localizar [descubrir la situación de]. *2* establecer, situar, poner, colocar.
location (loukei·șhøn) *s.* localización [acción y efecto de descubrir la situación de]. *2* establecimiento, situación, ubicación. *3* CINEM. lugar fuera del estudio donde se rueda una película o parte de ella.
locative (la·kativ) *adj.* GRAM. locativo.
loch (lak) *s.* (Esc.) lago. *2* (Esc.) ensenada, brazo de mar.
lock (lak) *s.* rizo, bucle, mechón, guedeja. *2* vellón, vedija [de lana]. *3* cerradura, cerraja: *under* ~ *and key*, bajo de llave. *4* llave [de arma de fuego]. *5* esclusa [de canal]. *6* lo que sujeta o traba; acción y resultado de sujetar, trabar o inmovilizar apretando o enlazando unas cosas con otras. *7* presa, llave [en la lucha]; abrazo estrecho. *8* embotellamiento [del tráfico]. *9* pl. cabellos.
lock (to) *tr.* cerrar [con llave o cerradura], echar la llave a, acerrojar; encerrar: *to* ~ *in*, encerrar, poner debajo de llave; *to* ~ *out*, cerrar la puerta [a uno]; *to* ~ *up*, encerrar; encarcelar. *2* apretar [entre los brazos], abrazar. *3* juntar, sujetar, - trabar, inmovilizar [apretando o entrelazando]; enclavijar. *4* hacer pasar [una embarcación] por una esclusa. *5 intr.* cerrarse con llave. *6* unirse, entrelazarse, enclavijarse. *7* pasar por una esclusa.
locker (-ø^r) *s.* el que cierra. *2* cajón, gaveta, cofre, armario [que se cierra con llave].
locket (-it) *s.* guardapelo, medallón, relicario.
lockjaw (-dŷo) *s.* MED. trismo, tétano.
locknut (-nøt) *s.* MEC. fiador, contratuerca.
lockout (-aut) *s.* lockout [cierre de una fábrica, etc., por los patronos].
locksmith (-smiz) *s.* cerrajero.
lockup (-øp) *s.* encierro. *2* cárcel, calabozo.
locomotion (loukømou·șhøn) *s.* locomoción.
locomotive (-tiv) *adj.* locomotor, triz. *2* locomóvil. *3 s.* locomotora.
locomotor (-tø^r) *adj.* locomotor, triz.
loculicidal (lakiulisai·dal) *adj.* BOT. loculicida.
loculus (la·kiuløs) *s.* ARQ., BOT. lóculo.
locust (lou·køst) *s.* ENT. langosta. *2* ENT. (E.U.) cigarra. *3* BOT. *locust* o ~ *tree*, algarrobo; acacia falsa.
locution (lokiu·șhøn) *s.* locución.
locutory (la·kiutori) *s.* locutorio [de convento].
lode (loud) *s.* MIN. vena, veta, filón.·
lodestar (-sta^r) *s.* Estrella del Norte o Polar. *2* fig. norte, guía.
lodestone (-stoun) *s.* LOADSTONE.
lodge (ladŷ) *s.* casita, pabellón [de caza, etc.]. *2* casa del guarda, el portero, etc. [en una finca]; portería. *3* logia [masónica].
lodge (to) *tr.* alojar, hospedar, albergar. *2* alojar, introducir, colocar. *3* depositar, dar a guardar. *4* conferir [poderes]. *5* presentar [una denuncia, etc.]. *6 intr.* alojarse, hospedarse, residir.
lodgement (-mønt) *s.* alojamiento. *2* depósito; acumulación. *3* MIL. ocupación de una posición.
lodger (-ø^r) *s.* huésped, inquilino.
lodging (-ing) *s.* alojamiento, posada, hospedaje [sin manutención]. *2* morada, vivienda. *3* pl. *to take lodgings in*, alojarse, hospedarse en.
lodginghouse (-jaus) *s.* casa de huéspedes.
lodgment (-mønt) *s.* LODGEMENT.
loft (loft) *s.* desván, sobrado. *2* (E.U.) piso alto de

un almacén, etc. *3* GOLF golpe que lanza la pelota en alto.

loft (to) *tr.* GOLF lanzar [la pelota] en alto.

loftiness (-inis) *s.* altura, elevación. *2* excelsitud, sublimidad. *3* altanería, altivez.

lofty (-i) *adj.* alto, elevado [de gran altura]. *2* excelso, sublime, elevado, noble, majestuoso. *3* altanero, altivo, orgulloso.

log (log) *s.* leño, troza, tronco: ~ *cabin,* cabaña de troncos; *like a* ~, como un tronco. *2* MAR. corredera: ~ *chip,* ~ *line,* barquilla, cordel, de la corredera. *3* MAR. cuaderno de bitácora, diario de navegación. *4* AVIA. diario de vuelo.

loganberry (lou·ganberi) *s.* BOT. especie de frambueso; su fruto.

logarithm (lo·gariðm) *s.* MAT. logaritmo.

logbook (lo·gbuk) *s.* LOG 3 y 4.

logger (lo·gøʳ) *s.* hachero, cortador de árboles.

loggerhead (-jed) *s.* cabezota. *2* ZOOL. variedad de tortuga marina. *3 to be at loggerheads,* estar en desacuerdo.

loggia (la·dỹa) *s.* ARQ. pórtico, galería abierta.

logic (la·dỹik) *s.* lógica, dialéctica.

logical (-al) *adj.* lógico.

logician (lodỹi·shan) *s.* lógico, dialéctico.

logistics (-stiks) *s. pl.* MIL. logística.

logogriph (lo·gøgrif) *s.* logogrifo.

logomachy (louga·maki) *s.* logomaquia.

logos (la·gas) *s.* FIL. logos. *2* TEOL. (con may.) El Verbo.

logroll (to) (lo·groul) *tr.* (E.U., Can.) hacer rodar troncos [hasta el agua o dentro del río]. *2* (E.U.) en una Cámara legislativa estorbar o favorecer la aprobación de [un proyecto, etc.] entrando en contubernio individuos de diferentes partidos.

logwood (lo·gwud) *s.* palo de campeche.

loin (loin) *s.* ijada, ijar. *2* CARN. lomo, solomillo. *3 pl.* lomos, riñones: fig. *to gird up one's loins,* apercibirse para la acción.

loincloth (-kloz) *s.* taparrabo, pampanilla.

Loire (lua·ʳ) *n. pr.* GEOGR. Loira.

loiter (to) (loi·tøʳ) *intr.* rezagarse, entretenerse; pasear, holgazanear, vagar. *2 tr. to* ~ *away,* malgastar [un tiempo].

loiterer (-øʳ) *s.* rezagado. *2* callejero, vago.

loll (to) (lal) *intr.* colgar, pender [flojo o lacio]. *2* reclinarse indolentemente; repantigarse. *3 tr.* sacar [la lengua] el animal cansado.

lollypop (la·lipap) *s.* dulce, caramelo.

London (lø·ndøn) *n. pr.* GEOGR. Londres.

Londoner (-øʳ) *s.* londinense.

lone (loun) *adj.* solo, solitario [sin compañía]. *2* solo, único. *3* solitario [lugar].

loneliness (-linis) *s.* soledad. *2* tristeza del que está solo.

lonely (-li) *adj.* solo, solitario [sin compañía]. *2* solitario, desolado, triste [lugar]. *3* solo, soledoso [que siente soledad].

lonesome (-søm) *s.* LONELY 2 y 3.

long (long) *adj.* largo [en sus principales acepciones], luengo, extenso, prolongado, tedioso: ~ *dozen,* docena de fraile; ~ *ton,* tonelada de 2.240 libras inglesas. *2* de largo, de longitud: *a mile* ~, de una milla de largo; ~ *measure,* medida o medidas de longitud. *3* que llega o alcanza lejos. *4* que tarda: *to be* ~ *in coming,* tardar en venir.

5 adv. durante [un tiempo]; mucho, mucho tiempo: *all the day* ~, todo el santo día; *as* ~ *as,* mientras; con tal que, puesto que; *how* ~ *is it since...?,* ¿cuánto hace que...?; *before* ~, dentro de poco; ~ *ago,* hace mucho tiempo; ~ *live!,*

¡viva! *6* lejos, a distancia; *so* ~, hasta la vista. *7 s.* largo, longitud: *the* ~ *and the short of,* la substancia, el resumen de. *8* letra o sílaba larga. *9* MÚS. longa.

long (to) *intr.* [con *for, after* o *to*] ansiar, anhelar; añorar.

longboat (-bout) *s.* lancha, chalupa.

longbow (-bou) *s.* arco [arma]; *to draw the* ~, fig. exagerar, contar cosas increíbles.

long-cut *adj.* en hebra [tabaco].

long-distance *adj.* TELÉF. de larga distancia, interurbano: *long-distance call,* conferencia interurbana. *2* DEP. de fondo [carrera].

longer (-øʳ) *adj.-adv. compar.* de LONG: más largo; más, más tiempo: *no* ~, ya no, no más.

longeron (lo·ndỹørøn) *s.* AVIA. larguero.

longest (lo·ngist) *adj. y superl.* de LONG: *at the* ~, todo lo más, a más tardar.

longevity (londỹe·viti) *s.* longevidad.

longevous (londỹe·vøs) *adj.* longevo.

longhand (lo·ngjænd) *s.* escritura corriente [no taquigráfica].

long-headed *adj.* dolicocéfalo. *2 fam.* listo, sagaz.

longing (-ing) *s.* ansia, anhelo. *2* añoranza, nostalgia. *3 adj.* anhelante, ansioso; nostálgico.

longish (-ish) *adj.* algo largo.

longitude (la·ndỹitiud) *s.* GEOGR., ASTR. longitud.

longitudinal (landỹitiu·dinal) *adj.* longitudinal.

long-legged *adj.* zanquilargo.

long-lived (longlai·vd o -li·vd) *adj.* longevo, de larga vida.

long-necked *adj.* cuellilargo.

long-range *adj.* de largo alcance.

longshoreman (-shoʳmæn) *s.* (E.U.) obrero portuario.

long-sighted *adj.* présbita. *2* perspicaz, sagaz. *3* previsor, precavido.

long-standing *adj.* antiguo, que existe desde hace mucho tiempo.

long-suffering *adj.* sufrido, paciente.

long-term *adj.* COM. a largo plazo.

longways (-weiš) *adv.* a lo largo, longitudinalmente.

long-winded *adj.* de buenos pulmones. *2* pesado, latoso.

loo (lu) *s.* cierto juego de naipes.

look (luk) *s.* mirada, vistazo, ojeada. *2* semblante, cara. *3* aspecto, apariencia, aire, traza, cariz. *4 pl. good looks,* buen parecer, hermosura.

look (to) *intr.* mirar [dirigir la mirada; considerar]. | *Gralte.* con *at,* etc. *2* mirar, dar, caer; estar situado. *3* parecer: *he looked tired,* parecía cansado. *4* parecer, manifestarse. *5* sentar, caer [bien o mal]. *6* buscar, inquirir. | *Gralte.* con *after* o *for.* *7* cuidar, atender. | *Gralte.* con *after.* *8 to* ~ *about,* mirar alrededor, observar. *9 to* ~ *after,* seguir con la vista; buscar; inquirir; cuidar de, atender, mirar por. *10 to* ~ *alike,* parecerse. *11 to* ~ *alive,* darse prisa. *12 to* ~ *back,* volver la vista atrás. *13 to* ~ *down on o upon,* mirar por encima del hombro, despreciar. *14 to* ~ *for,* buscar, esperar. *15 to* ~ *forward to,* esperar con placer. *16 to* ~ *in,* entrar, hacer una corta visita. *17 to* ~ *into,* mirar, examinar, investigar. *18 to* ~ *like,* parecer; parecer que, tener trazas de: *it looks like rain,* parece que va a llover. *19 to* ~ *on o upon,* considerar; tener en aprecio. *20 to* ~ *out,* mirar afuera; asomarse; tener cuidado; ~ *out!,* ¡cuidado! *21 to* ~ *out for,* esperar, vigilar [si llega alguien o algo]; guardarse de; mirar por. *22 to* ~ *sharp,* vigilar, estar ojo avizor. *23 to* ~ *to*, cuidar de, velar por; esperar de [una pers.]. *24 to* ~ *up to*, respetar, tratar con respeto. *25 tr.* mirar [dirigir la vista a; considerar]: ~ *how you behave*, mira como te portas. *26* expresar con la mirada. *27 to* ~ *daggers* [*at*], mirar airadamente o amenazadoramente. *28 to* ~ *one's age*, representar uno los años que tiene. *29 to* ~ *over*, repasar, dar una ojeada; hojear [un libro]. *30 to* ~ *up*, buscar [esp. en un diccionario, guía, etc.]; visitar [a una pers.].

looker, looker-on (-ø^r) *s.* mirón, espectador.

looking (-ing) *adj.* de mirar, para mirar: ~ *glass*, espejo. *2* que tiene cierto aspecto: *good-looking*, guapo, bien parecido.

lockout (-aut) *s.* vigía, atalaya, vigilante. *2* atalaya, miradero. *3* vigilancia, observación, espera: *to be on the* ~ *for*, estar a la mira de. *4* vista, perspectiva. *5* perspectivas. *6* fam. *that is your* ~, allá usted.

loom (lum) *s.* TEJ. telar. *2* guión [del remo]. *3* aparición, presencia [de algo voluminoso, de una sombra o reflejo].

loom (to) *tr.* tejer [en el telar]. *2 intr.* aparecer, asomar [de una manera confusa o impresionante]; destacar, descollar. *5* vislumbrarse, amenazar.

loon (lun) *s.* (Esc. y ant.) bribón; patán; muchacho. *2* ORN. colimbo.

loop (lup) *s.* curva, vuelta muy pronunciada o de algo que cruza sobre sí mismo. *2* gaza, lazo; presilla, alamar. *3* asa, anilla, armella. *4* ELECT. circuito cerrado. *5* AVIA. rizo.

loop (to) *tr.* doblar formando gaza; formar ondas o curvas en. *2* asegurar con presilla, gaza, etc. *3* AVIA. *to* ~ *the loop*, hacer o rizar el rizo. *4 intr.* formar vuelta, gaza o lazo. *5* arrastrarse encorvándose [como ciertas orugas].

loophole (-joul) *s.* aspillera, saetera, tronera; abertura estrecha. *2* fig. salida, escapatoria.

loose (lus) *adj.* suelto, flojo, laxo, desatado, desenredado, desprendido: *to hang* ~, caer suelto, colgar, flotar. *2* flojo [tornillo, diente]. *3* suelto, poco compacto, disgregado. *4* sueltas, sin encuadernar [hojas]. *5* loca [polea]. *6* desgarbado. *7* holgado, ancho [vestido]. *8* suelto, en libertad, no sujeto: *to break* ~, escaparse, soltarse, zafarse; desatarse, desencadenarse. *9* QUÍM. libre. *10* vago, indeterminado; poco exacto, laxo; libre [traducción, interpretación, etc.]. *11* libre, relajado, licencioso, disoluto. *12* ~ *end*, cabo suelto; *at* ~ *end*, sin empleo; *at* ~ *ends*, desarreglado. *13 s.* libertad, soltura: *to give* ~ *to*, dar rienda suelta a.

loose (to) *tr.* soltar, desatar, deshacer, desliar, aflojar, desapretar, desprender. *2* soltar, dejar en libertad. *3* lanzar [flechas, etc.].

loose-leaf *adj.* de hojas sueltas [cuaderno, etc.].

loosen (to) (-øn) *tr.* soltar, desatar, libertar. *2* aflojar, desceñir, desasir. *3* ahuecar, mullir. *4* relajar. *5* soltar [el vientre]. *6* ablandar [la tos]. *7 intr.* aflojarse, relajarse. *8* soltarse, desatarse.

looseness (-nis) *s.* flojedad. *2* holgura [de un vestido]. *3* soltura. *4* relajación, relajamiento. *5* flujo [de vientre]. *6* vaguedad, poca exactitud.

loosestrife (-traif) *s.* BOT. lisimaquia. *2* BOT. salicaria.

loot (lut) *s.* botín, presa. *2* pillaje, saqueo.

loot (to) *tr.-intr.* pillar, saquear, robar.

looting (-ing) *s.* saqueo, saqueamiento.

lop (lap) *s.* chapodo, desmocho. *2 adj.* colgante, gacho [orejas, etc.].

lop (to) *tr.* podar, desmochar, cortar. *2 intr.* colgar, pender flojamente. *3* picarse [el mar].

lope (loup) *s.* medio galope, paso largo.

lope (to) *intr.* ir a medio galope, a paso largo.

lop-eared *adj.* de orejas caídas.

lophobranch (lou·føbrænch) *adj.-s.* lofobranquio.

lopsided (la·psaidid) *adj.* torcido, inclinado, con un lado más bajo o pequeño que otro; asimétrico, desproporcionado. *2* desequilibrado.

loquacious (loukuei·shøs) *adj.* locuaz, gárrulo.

loquacity (-siti) *s.* locuacidad.

lord (lo^{r}d) *s.* señor, dueño, amo. *2* poét. y fam. marido. *3* lord [título]: *Lord Chamberlain*, camarero mayor; *Lord Mayor*, alcalde de Londres, de York, de Dublín, etc.; *the Lords*, la Cámara de los lores. *4 the Lord*, el Señor, Dios: *Our Lord*, Nuestro Señor, Jesucristo; *the Lord's Prayer*, el padrenuestro; *the Lord's Supper*, la Santa Cena, la Eucaristía; *to die in the Lord*, morir en la paz del Señor.

lord (to) *intr.-tr. to* ~ *over* o *to* ~ *it over*, señorear, mandar despóticamente. *2 tr.* hacer lord; dar título de lord.

lordliness (-linis) *s.* señorío, dignidad. *2* altivez, orgullo.

lord(l)ing (-(l)ing) *s.* desp. pequeño señor.

lordly (-li) *adj.* señorial, señoril, noble; espléndido, magnífico. *2* altanero, imperioso.

lordosis (lo^{r}dou·sis) *s.* MED. lordosis.

lordship (lo·^{r}dship) *s.* señoría, dominio. *2 his* ~, *your* ~, su señoría, su excelencia.

lore (lou^r) *s.* saber. *2* ciencia o saber popular.

lorgnette (lo^{r}ñe·t) *s.* impertinentes. *2* gemelos de teatro con mango.

lorica (lorai·ka) *s.* ARM., ZOOL. loriga.

loricate(d (la·rikeit(id) *adj.* ZOOL. loricado.

loriot (la·riat) *s.* ORN. oropéndola.

lorn (lo^{r}n) *adj.* abandonado, solo, sin parientes ni amigos.

Lorrain(e (lore·n) *n. pr.* GEOGR. Lorena.

Lorrainer (lore·nø^r) *s.* lorenés.

lorry (lo·ri) *s.* ORN. especie de loro o perico.

lose (to) (luš) *tr.* perder: *to* ~ *heart*, desalentarse; *to* ~ *one's temper*, perder la calma, encolerizarse; *to* ~ *one's way*, perderse, extraviarse; *to* ~ [*something*] *to*, perder [algo] en beneficio de. *2* hacer perder: *that lost him his place*, eso le hizo perder su empleo. *3 intr.* perder, tener una pérdida. *4 ref.* perderse; extraviarse; engolfarse, ensimismarse. ¶ Pret. y p. p.: *lost*.

loser (-ø^r) *s.* perdedor, el que pierde.

losing (-ing) *s.* pérdida. *2 adj.* perdedor, perdidoso.

loss (los) *s.* pérdida: *to be at a* ~, estar perplejo, no saber qué hacer: *to sell at a* ~, vender con pérdida. *2* perdición. *3* COM. daño, quebranto; siniestro.

lost (lost) *pret. y p. p.* de TO LOSE. *2 adj.* perdido. *3* arruinado. *4* olvidado. *5* extraviado. *6* desorientado, perplejo. *7* ~*in thought*, abstraído, pensativo. *8* ~ *to*, perdido para; insensible a, que ha perdido [el sentimiento] de.

lost-and-found department *s.* oficina de objetos perdidos.

Lot (lat) *n. pr. m.* BIB. Lot.

lot *s.* lote, parte, porción. *2* porción de terreno, solar. *3* suerte [para decidir]: *to draw*, o *cast, lots*, echar suertes; *to fall to one's* ~, caerle a uno en suerte. *4* suerte, sino. *5* colección, hato, partida. *6* fig. sujeto, persona: *a bad* ~, una mala

persona. 7 *a* ~ *of, lots of,* la mar de. *8* adv. *a* ~, mucho.
lot (to) *tr.* dividir en lotes. *2* repartir o asignar echando suertes. ¶ Pret. y p. p.: - *tting.*
loth (louz) *adj.* LOATH.
lotos *s.* LOTUS.
lottery (la·tøri) *s.* lotería, rifa.
lotto (la·tou) *s.* lotería [juego casero].
lotus (lou·tøs) *s.* BOT. loto.
lotus-eater *s.* lotófago.
loud (laud) *adj.* fuerte [sonido]. *2* alta [voz]. *3* recio, clamoroso, ruidoso, estrepitoso. *4* chillón, llamativo. *5* vulgar, ordinario. *6* adv. en voz alta. *7* ruidosamente.
loud-speaker *s.* RADIO. altavoz.
lough (lak) *s.* (Irl.) lago; ría.
Louis (lu·is) *n. pr.* Luis.
Louisa (lui·sa), **Louise** (luis) *n. pr.* Luisa.
lounge (lau·ndȳ) *s.* paseo; acción de pasear o de pasar el rato. *2* salón de descanso, de tertulia. *3* sofá, diván.
lounge (to) *intr.* pasear, callejear, pasar el rato. *2* estar sentado o reclinado indolentemente.
lounger (lau·ndȳøʳ) *s.* ocioso. *2* paseante, azotacalles.
lour (to) (lauʳ) *s.* TO LOWER.
louse (laus), *pl.* **lice** (-lais) *s.* ENT. piojo.
lousewort (-wøʳt) *s.* BOT. estafisagria.
lousiness (-inis) *s.* piojería.
lousy (lau·ši) *adj.* piojoso. *2* astroso, asqueroso.
lout (laut) *s.* patán, rústico, zafio.
loutish (lau·tish) *adj.* rudo, rústico, tosco, zafio.
Louvain (luve·n) *n. pr.* GEOGR. Lovaina.
louver (lu·vøʳ) *s.* ARQ. lumbrera. *2* juego de tablillas a manera de persiana. *3* persiana de automóvil.
lovable (lø·vabøl) *adj.* amable [digno de ser amado].
lovage (lø·vidȳ) *s.* BOT. lingüístico.
love (løv) *s.* amor, cariño afecto, afición: ~ *affair,* amores, amorío; ~ *feast,* ágape; ~ *knot,* lazo, nudo de cinta; *to be in* ~, estar enamorado; *to make* ~ *to,* enamorar, cortejar; *to send one's* ~, mandar afectuosos recuerdos; *for* ~, sin interés, de balde; *not for* ~ *or money,* ni a tiros, por nada del mundo. *2* amor [pers. amada]. *3* fam. preciosidad. *4* B. ART. amorcillo. *5* (con may.) Amor, Cupido. *6* DEP. cero, nada [en el tenis y oros juegos].
love (to) *tr.* amar, querer, adorar; tener cariño a. *2* gustar de, tener afición a. *3* *intr.* amar.
lovebird (-bøʳd) *s.* ORN. periquito.
love-in-a-mist *s.* BOT. ajenuz, arañuela, neguilla.
Lovelace (-leis) *s.* seductor, libertino.
loveless (-lis) *adj.* sin amor. *2* desamado. *3* desamorado.
loveliness (-linis) *s.* amabilidad, encanto, belleza, exquisitez.
lovelock (-lak) *s.* ant. rizo sobre las sienes o la frente.
lovelorn (-loʳn) *adj.* abandonado por su amor; que suspira de amor.
lovely (-li) *adj.* amable, adorable, encantador, hermoso, exquisito. *2* deleitoso, ameno.
love-maker *s.* cortejante, enamorado.
love-making *s.* cortejo, galanteo.
lover (-øʳ) *s.* enamorado. *2* amante, amador, galán. *3* amigo, aficionado.
lovesick (-sik) *adj.* enamorado, enfermo de amor.
lovesickness (-nis) *s.* mal de amor.

loving (-ing) *adj.* amante. *2* amoroso, afectuoso, cariñoso. *3* bondadoso.
low (lou) *adj.* bajo: *Low Countries,* Países Bajos; *Low Latin,* bajo latín; *Low Mass,* misa baja o rezada; ~ *relief,* B. ART. bajo relieve; ~ *shoe,* zapato bajo; ~ *trick,* cochinada, mala pasada; ~ *water,* bajamar, marea baja; estiaje. | Hablando de una pers. de baja estatura, se dice *short.* *2* profunda [inclinación, reverencia]. *3* escotado [vestido]. *4* pobre, humilde. *5* inferior [organismo, mentalidad, etc.]. *6* pobre, escaso, insuficiente. *7* pobre [concepto, opinión]. *8* débil, enfermo; abatido, desalentado: ~ *spirits,* abatimiento, desánimo. *9* muerto. *10* ~ *comedy,* farsa, sainete. *11* AUTO. ~ *gear,* primera. *12* adv. bajo. *13* bajamente. *14* barato, a bajo precio. *15* sumisamente.
  16 *s.* mugido, berrido. *17* lo bajo; punto o lugar bajo, tierra baja. *18* AUTO. primera.
low (to) *intr.* mugir, berrear.
lowbell (-bel) *s.* cencerro.
lowborn (-boʳn) *adj.* de humilde cuna.
lowbred (-bred) *adj.* zafio, grosero.
low-brow *s.* fam. persona inculta.
Low-Church *adj.* perteneciente a la secta anglicana opuesta al ritualismo.
low-down *adj.* fam. bajo, vil. *2* *s.* pop (E. U.) información confidencial o de primera mano.
1) lower (-øʳ) *adj.* y *adv. compar.* de LOW: más bajo, etc.; bajo; ~ *case,* IMPR. caja baja; *Lower Empire,* Bajo Imperio; ~ *floor,* piso bajo; *Lower House,* Cámara baja; *the* ~ *orders* o *classes,* la clase baja, el pueblo.
2) lower (lau·øʳ) *s.* ceño; aspecto amenazador.
1) lower (to) (lou·øʳ) *tr.* bajar [poner más bajo, inclinar hacia abajo]. *2* arriar. *3* agachar. *4* bajar, rebajar, reducir. *5* abatir, humillar. *6* *intr.* bajar, reducirse, disminuir.
2) lower (to) (lau·øʳ) *intr.* mirar ceñudo, fruncir el ceño. *2* amenazar [la tempestad]; encapotarse [el cielo].
lower-case (lou·øʳ) *adj.* IMPR. de caja baja.
lowering (lau·øring) *adj.* ceñudo, amenazador, sombrío. *2* encapotado [cielo].
lowermost (lou·øʳmout), **lowest** (-it) *adj. superl.* de LOW: (el) más bajo.
lowing (-ing) *s.* mugido, berrido.
lowland (-lænd) *s.* tierra baja: *the Lowlands,* las tierras bajas de Escocia.
Lowlander (-øʳ) *s.* natural o habitante de las tierras bajas de Escocia.
lowly (lou·li) *adj.* humilde, modesto, sencillo. *2* bajo [tierras, etc.]. *3* adv. humildemente.
low-necked *adj.* escotado, de cuello bajo [vestido].
low-pitched *adj.* de poca inclinación o pendiente [tejado]. *2* grave [sonido].
low-pressure *adj.* de baja presión.
low-spirited *adj.* abatido, desanimado, triste.
low-tension *adj.* ELECT. de baja tensión.
low-water line o **mark** *s.* línea de nivel mínimo de las aguas. *2* fig. punto más bajo.
loyal (loi·al) *adj.* leal, fiel.
loyalist (loi·alist) *s.* POL. realista. *2* POL. fiel al príncipe o al gobierno establecido, leal.
loyalty (loi·alti) *s.* lealtad, fidelidad.
lozenge (la·šendȳ) *s.* GEOM. rombo. *2* BLAS. losange. *3* pastilla [de menta, etc.].
lozenged (-d) *adj.* rombal.
lubber (lø·bøʳ) *s.* patán, bobalicón. *2* marinero torpe.

lubberly (-li) *adj.* torpe, desmañado. *2 adv.* torpemente, desmañadamente.
lubricant (liu·bricant) *s.* lubrificante.
lubricate (to) (-keit) *tr.* lubrificar.
lubrication (-ei·shøn) *s.* lubrificación.
lubricious (liubri·søs) *adj.* LUBRICOUS.
lubricity (-siti) *s.* lubricidad. *2* inestabilidad.
lubricous (liu·bricøs) *adj.* lúbrico.
luce (lius) *s.* ICT. lucio.
lucent (liu·sønt) *adj.* luciente. *2* claro, transparente.
lucern(e (lusø^rn) *s.* BOT. mielga, alfalfa.
Lucerne *n. pr.* GEOGR. Lucerna.
Lucia (lu·shia) *n. pr. f.* Lucía.
lucid (liu·sid) *adj.* lúcido. *2* luciente.
lucidity (liusi·diti) *s.* lucidez.
lucidly (liu·sidli) *adj.* lúcidamente.
Lucifer (-sifø^r) *n. pr.* Lucifer. *2* ASTR. lucífero.
luciferous (liusi·førøs) *adj.* luminoso, lucífero.
lucifugous (-fiugøs) *adj.* lucífugo.
luck (løk) *s.* suerte, fortuna [buena o mala]; buena suerte: *down on one's* ~, fam. de mala suerte, de malas; *for* ~, para que traiga suerte; *worse* ~, desgraciadamente.
luckily (-ili) *adv.* afortunadamente.
luckiness (-inis) *s.* suerte, buena fortuna, dicha.
luckless (-lis) *adj.* desafortunado. *2* desdichado.
lucky (-i) *adj.* afortunado; de suerte: ~ *hit*, golpe de fortuna; *to be* ~, tener suerte. *2* feliz, oportuno. *3* feliz, dichoso, venturoso.
lucrative (liu·krativ) *adj.* lucrativo.
lucre (liu·kø^r) *s.* lucro.
Lucretia (lukri·shia) *n. pr. f.* Lucrecia.
lucubrate (to) (liu·kiubreit) *tr.-intr.* lucubrar.
lucubration (-ei·shøn) *s.* lucubración.
Lucy (lu·si) *n. pr. f.* Lucía.
ludicrous (liu·dicrøs) *adj.* cómico, ridículo, absurdo.
luff (løf) *s.* MAR. orza, orzada. *2* MAR. caída de proa [de una vela]. *3* MAR. aparejo de bolinear.
luff (to) *tr.* MAR. orzar, ceñir el viento, bolinear.
lug (løg) *s.* oreja, asa, etc., por donde se ase o sujeta una cosa. *2* tirón; tiro, arrastre. *3* lo que se arrastra; peso, carga. *4* MAR. vela al tercio.
lug (to) *tr.* tirar de, halar; arrastrar. *2* introducir forzadamente [una especie] en la conversación. *3 intr.* tirar [de]. ¶ Pret. y p. p.: *lugged;* ger.: *lugging.*
luggage (-idý) *s.* equipaje [de viajero].
lugger (-ø^r) *s.* MAR. lugre.
lugubrious (liugiu·briøs) *adj.* lúgubre, fúnebre.
lugworm (lø·gwø^rm) *s.* lombriz usada como cebo.
Luke (luk) *n. pr.* Lucas.
lukewarm (liu·kwø^rm) *adj.* tibio, templado. *2* fig. tibio.
lukewarmness (-nis) *s.* tibieza.
lull (løl) *s.* momento de calma o de silencio.
lull (to) *tr.* adormecer, arrullar. *2* calmar, aquietar, sosegar. *3 intr.* calmarse, amainar.
lullaby (lø·labai) *s.* arrullo, canción de cuna.
Lullian (lø·lian) *adj.* luliano.
lumbago (lømbei·gou) *s.* MED. lumbago.
lumbar (lø·mba^r) *adj.* ANAT. lumbar.
lumber (lø·mbø^r) *s.* madera [aserrada], madera de construcción. *2* trastos viejos: ~ *room*, trastera. *3* fig. balumba, cosa que estorba.
lumber (to) *tr.* cortar [árboles], aserrar [troncos]. *2* amontonar en; llenar, atestar. *3* moverse pesadamente. *4* avanzar con ruido sordo.
lumbering (-ing) *s.* explotación de bosques made-

rables. *2 adj.* pesado, que se mueve pesadamente.
lumberman (-mæn) *s.* hachero. *2* maderero.
lumberyard (-ya^rd) *s.* almacén de maderas.
lumen (liu·min) *s.* FÍS. lumen.
luminary (liu·mineri) *s.* luminar, astro. *2* fig. luminar, lumbrera.
luminiscence (liumine·søns) *s.* luminescencia.
luminescent (-t) *adj.* luminescente.
luminosity (liumina·siti) *s.* luminosidad.
luminous (liu·minøs) *s.* luminoso.
lummox (lø·maks) *s.* fam. porro [sujeto torpe].
lump (lømp) *s.* trozo, pedazo, terrón, pella, burujo. *2* bulto, protuberancia, chichón. *3* nudo [en la garganta]. *5* TEJ. mota. *6* sujeto torpe. *7* fig. persona rehecha. *9* conjunto, totalidad: *in the* ~, en junto, por junto; ~ *sum*, suma global o total, tanto alzado.
lump (to) *tr.* aburujar. *2* levantar bultos en. *3* tomar en junto, en globo. *4* fam. aguantar, tragar, apechugar con. *5 intr.* aterronarse, aburujarse. *6* abultarse, crecer. *7* moverse pesadamente.
lumpish (-ish) *adj.* parecido a una pella o terrón. *2* pesado, macizo, tosco. *3* torpe, estúpido.
lumpy (lø·mpi) *adj.* lleno de bultos o protuberancias. *2* aterronado, aburujado. *3* agitado [mar].
lunacy (liu·nasi) *s.* locura, demencia.
lunar (-na^r) *adj.* lunar. *2* lunado.
lunate(d (-neit(id) *adj.* lunado.
lunatic (-natik) *adj.-s.* loco, demente: ~ *asylum*, manicomio.
lunation (-ei·shøn) *s.* lunación.
lunch (lønch) *s.* almuerzo, comida ligera: ~ *basket*, fiambrera.
lunch (to) *intr.* almorzar, tomar una comida ligera.
luncheon (-øn) *s.* refacción, tentempié. *2* LUNCH.
luncheon (to) *intr.* tomar un LUNCHEON.
lune (lu·n) *s.* GEOM. lúnula.
lunette (lune·t) *s.* luneta [adorno]. *2* ARQ., FORT. luneta. *3* LITURG. lúnula, viril.
lung (løng) *s.* pulmón.
lunge (løndý) *s.* estocada, hurgonazo. *2* arremetida, embestida. *3* LONGE.
lunge (to) *intr.* ESGR. tirar una estocada. *2* abalanzarse, arremeter.
lungwort (lø·ngwø^r) *s.* BOT. pulmonaria.
lunule (liu·niul) *s.* lúnula, blanco de la uña.
Lupercalia (liu·pø^rkeilia) *s. pl.* lupercales.
lupine (liu·pin) *s.* BOT. altramuz. *2 adj.* lupino.
lupus (-øs) *s.* MED. lupus.
lurch (lø^rch) *s.* sacudida, tumbo, balance brusco. *2* bandazo. *3 to leave in the* ~, dejar en la estacada.
lurch (to) *intr.* andar tambaleándose, dar tumbos, dar un tumbo. *2* MAR. dar bandazos.
lurcher (-ø^r) *s.* acechador. *2* cierto perro de caza.
lure (liu^r) *s.* señuelo, añagaza, reclamo. *2* cebo, atractivo, tentación.
lure (to) *tr.* atraer [con señuelo o engaño]; seducir, inducir, tentar.
lurid (liu·rid) *adj.* rojo, cárdeno, tempestuoso [cielo, nubes, etc.]. *2* fantasmal, pavoroso, espeluznante.
lurk (lø^rk) *s. on the* ~, en acecho.
lurk (to) *intr.* acechar, esconderse; estar escondido, estar latente. *2* moverse furtivamente.
lurking (-ing) *adj.* escondido, en acecho. *2* ~ *place*, escondite; emboscada.
luscious (lø·shøs) *adj.* delicioso, exquisito. *2* dulce, sabroso. *3* meloso, empalagoso.

lush (løsh) *adj.* lujuriante, fresco, lozano. *2* rico, profuso. *3 s.* pop. licor, bebida.
Lusitanian (liusitei·nian) *adj.-s.* lusitano.
lust (løst) *s.* avidez. *2* concupiscencia, lujuria.
lust (to) *intr.* codiciar. *2* desear [con lujuria]. Gralte. con *for* o *after.*
luster (-ø^r) *s.* LUSTRE.
luster (to) *tr.* lustrar, abrillantar.
lustful (-ful) *adj.* sensual, carnal, lujurioso.
lustfulness (-nis) *s.* sensualidad, lujuria.
lustily (-ili) *adv.* fuertemente, vigorosamente.
lustral (lø·stral) *adj.* lustral.
lustration (-ei·shøn) *s.* lustración.
lustre (lø·stø^r) *s.* lustre, brillo. *2* reflejo, viso. *3* lustre, esplendor. *4* araña [lámpara]. *5* lustro.
lustrine (lø·strin) *s.* lustrina.
lustrous (-øs) *adj.* lustroso, brillante.
lustrum (-øm) *s.* lustro.
lusty (lø·sti) *adj.* lozano, fuerte, robusto. *2* vigoroso, enérgico.
lute (liut) *s.* MÚS. laúd. *2* luten; pasta para tapar junturas.
lutecium (liuti·shiøm) *s.* QUÍM. lutecio.
Luther (lu·zø^r) *n. pr.* Lutero.
Lutheran (lu·zøran) *adj.-s.* luterano.
Lutheranism (lu·zøranišm) *s.* luteranismo.
luthier (liutie·^r) *m.* guitarrero.
lux (løks), *pl.* **luces** (liu·siš) *s.* FÍS. lux.
luxate (to) (lø·kseit) *tr.* dislocar, descoyuntar.
luxation (løkse·shøn) *s.* luxación, dislocación.
Luxemburg (lø·ksembø^rg) *n. pr.* GEOGR. Luxemburgo.
luxuriance, -cy (løgshu·rians, -si) *s.* demasía, exuberancia, frondosidad, lozanía.
luxuriant (-riant) *adj.* lujuriante, exuberante, lozano, frondoso.
luxuriate (to) (-rieit) *intr.* crecer con lozanía. *2* vivir con lujo. *3* gozarse, complacerse.

luxurious (-riøs) *adj.* lujoso. *2* dado al lujo. *3* muelle, sibarítico.
luxuriousness (-nis) *s.* lujo, fausto.
luxury (lø·gshuri) *s.* lujo, fausto. *2* regalo, molicie. *3* placer.
lycanthrope (lai·kænzroup) *s.* licántropo.
lyceum (laisi·øm) *s.* liceo, ateneo.
Lycian (li·sian) *adj.-s.* licio.
lycopodium (laicopou·diøm) *s.* BOT. licopodio.
Lycurgus (laicø·^rgøs) *n. pr.* Licurgo.
Lydia (li·dia) *n. pr.* GEOGR. Lidia.
Lydian (li·dian) *adj.-s.* lidio. *2 adj.* blando, voluptuoso.
lye (lai) *s.* lejía. *2* (Ingl.) FERROC. desviadero.
lying (lai·ing) *ger.* de TO LIE. *2 adj.* mentiroso. *3* tendido, echado, yacente: ~ *down*, acostado. *4* sito, situado.
lying-in *s.* parto: ~ *hospital*, clínica maternal.
lymph (limf) *s.* FISIOL. linfa. *2* poét. linfa, agua.
lymphatic (limfæ·tik) *adj.* linfático. *2 s.* ANAT. vaso linfático.
lymphatism (li·mfatišm) *s.* MED. linfatismo.
lymphocyte (li·mfosait) *s.* ANAT. linfocito.
lyncean (li·nsian) *adj.* línceo.
lynch (to) (linch) *tr.* linchar.
lynching (li·nching) *s.* linchamiento.
lynx (links) *s.* ZOOL. lince.
lynx-eyed *adj.* de ojos linces, perspicaz.
Lyon (lai·øn), **Lyons** (lai·ønš) *n. pr.* GEOGR. Lión.
Lyonese (laiøni·š) *adj.-s.* lionés.
lyrate (lai·reit) *adj.* BOT., ORN. lirado.
lyre (lai^r) *s.* MÚS. lira. *2* ASTR. (con may.) Lira.
lyrebird (-bø^rd) *s.* ORN. ave lira.
lyric (li·rik) *adj.* lírico. *2 s.* poema lírico. *3* fam. letra de una canción.
lyrical (-al) *adj.* lírico.
lyricism (li·risišm) *s.* lirismo.
Lysander (laisæ·ndø^r) *n. pr.* Lisandro.
Lysippus (laisi·pøs) *n. pr.* Lisipo.
lysis (lai·sis) *s.* MED. lisis.
lythraceous (litrei·shøs) *adj.* litráceo.

M

M, m (em) *s.* M, m, decimotercera letra del alfabeto inglés.
ma (ma) *s.* fam. madre, mamá.
ma'am (mam o mæm) *s.* contr. de MADAM, señora.
macaber, macabre (maka·bøʳ) *adj.* macabro.
macadam (makæ·dam) *s.* macadam, macadán.
macadamize (to) (-aiš) *tr.* macadamizar.
macaque (maka·k) *s.* ZOOL. macaco.
macaroni (mækarou·ni) *s.* macarrones. *2* pisaverde.
macaronic (mækara·nik) *adj.* macarrónico. *2 s. pl.* macarronea.
macaroon (mækaru·n) *s.* macarrón, mostachón, bollo de almendra, coco, etc.
Macassar (makæ·saʳ) *n. pr.* GEOGR. Macasar.
macaw (maco·) *s.* ORN. ara, guacamayo.
Maccabees (mæ·købɪš) *n. pr.* BIB. Macabeos.
mace (meis) *s.* maza [arma, insignia]: ~ *bearer,* macero. *2* macia, macis [especia].
Macedon (mæ·sidan), **Macedonia** (mæsidou·nia) *n. pr.* GEOGR., HIST. Macedonia.
Macedonian (-*n*) *adj.-s.* macedonio.
macer (mei·søʳ) *s.* macero.
macerate (to) (mæ·søreit) *tr.* macerar.
maceration (mæsørei·shøn) *s.* maceración.
machete (mashe·t o machei·ti) *s.* MATCHET.
Machiavel (Mæ·kiavel) *n. pr.* Maquiavelo.
Machiavel(l)ian (mækiave·lian) *adj.-s.* maquiavelista. *2* maquiavélico.
Machiavellism (mæ·kiavelišm) *s.* maquiavelismo.
machicolation (mæchikole·shøn) *s.* FORT. matacán.
machinate (to) (mæ·kineit) *intr.-tr.* maquinar.
machination (mækinei·shøn) *s.* maquinación.
machinator (mæ·kineitøʳ) *s.* maquinador.
machine (mashi·n) *s.* máquina, ingenio. *2* bicicleta, automóvil, aeroplano, etc. *3* TEAT., LIT. máquina. *4* máquina [política, social, etc.]; (E.U.) camarilla. *5 adj.* ~ *gun,* ametralladora; ~ *tool,* máquina herramienta.
machine (to) *tr.* trabajar a máquina.
machine-gun (to) *tr.* ametrallar.
machinery (-øri) *s.* maquinaria. *2* fig. máquina, organización. *3* LIT. máquina.
machinist (-ist) *s.* maquinista; mecánico. *2* TEAT. tramoyista.
mackerel (mæ·kørøl) *s.* ICT. escombro, caballa. *2* ~ *sky,* cielo aborregado.

mackinaw (mæ·kino) *s.* tela de lana de dos caras para abrigos.
mackintosh (mæ·kintash) *s.* impermeable. *2* tela impermeabilizada.
macle (mæ·køl) *s.* MINER. macla.
macrobian (mækrou·bian) *s.* que vive muchos años.
macrobiotics (mækrøbaia·tiks) *s.* macrobiótica.
macrocephalous (-se·faløs) *adj.* macrocéfalo.
macrocosm (mæ·krøkošm) *s.* macrocosmo.
macrogamete (mækrøgami·t) *s.* BIOL. macrogameto.
macron (me·kran) *s.* IMPR. signo de vocal larga.
Macrura (mækru·ræ) *s. pl.* ZOOL. macruros.
macula (mæ·kiula), *pl.* -**lae** (-li) *s.* ASTR., ANAT., MED. mácula.
maculate (mæ·kiuleit) *adj.* maculado.
maculate (to) *tr.* macular.
maculation (mækiulei·shøn) *s.* mácula, mancha.
mad (mæd) *adj.* loco: *like* ~, como un loco; *to be* ~ *about,* tener una locura por. *2* insensato, desesperado. *3* encolerizado, furioso. *4* disparatado. *5* rabioso [animal].
madam (mæ·dam) *s.* señora [tratamiento de respeto].
madapollam (mædapa·lam) *s.* madapolán.
madcap (mæ·dkæp) *adj.-s.* alocado, alborotado, atolondrado.
madden (to) (mæ·døn) *tr.* enloquecer. *2* exasperar. *3 intr.* enloquecer, volverse loco.
maddening (mæ·dning) *adj.* enloquecedor, exasperante.
madder (mæ·døʳ) *s.* BOT., TINT. rubia, granza.
made (meid) *pret.* y *p. p.* de TO MAKE. *2 adj.* hecho, compuesto, confeccionado, fabricado: ~ *man,* hombre que ha triunfado en la vida.
Madeira (mædi·ra) *s.* vino de Madera.
made-to-order *adj.* hecho de encargo. *2* hecho a la medida.
made-up *adj.* completo, acabado. *2* hecho [vestido, ropa]. *3* maquillado, pintado [rostro]. *4* artificial, ficticio, inventado.
Madge (mæ·dỹ) *n. pr. abrev.* de MARGARET.
madhouse (mæ·djaus) *s.* manicomio, casa de orates.
madly (mæ·dli) *adv.* locamente, furiosamente, desesperadamente, insensatamente.
madman (mæ·dmæn) *s.* loco, orate.

madness (mæ·dnis) s. locura. 2 furia, frenesí.
Madonna (mada·na) s. madona: ~ lily, azucena.
madrepore (mæ·dripøʳ) s. ZOOL. madrépora.
madrigal (mæ·drigal) s. LIT., MÚS. madrigal.
Madrilene (mæ·drilin), Madrilenian (-li·nian) adj.-s. madrileño.
madwort (mæ·duøʳt) s. BOT. raspilla.
Maecenas (misɪ·nas) s. mecenas.
maelstrom (mei·lstrøm) s. remolino, vorágine.
maenad (mɪ·næd) s. ménade.
magazine (mægaŝɪ·n) s. almacén, depósito. 2 polvorín; santabárbara. 3 revista [periódico].
Magdalen (mæ·gdaløn) n. pr. Magdalena. 2 s. (con min.) ramera arrepentida.
Magdalene (mæ·gdalin o -li·ni) n. pr. Magdalena.
Magdalenian (-nian) adj. GEOL. magdaleniense.
Magellan (Strait of) (madŷe·lan) n. pr. GEOGR. Estrecho de Magallanes.
Magellanic (mædŷølæ·nik) adj. magallánico.
magenta (madŷe·nta) s. color magenta.
maggot (mæ·gøt) s. cresa [larva]. 2 capricho, antojo.
maggoty (mæ·gøti) adj. gusaniento. 2 caprichoso.
Magi (mei·dŷai) s. pl. magos o sabios del Oriente.
Magian (mei·dŷian) adj.-s. mago [del Oriente].
magic (mæ·dŷik) s. magia, mágica: as if by ~, como por ensalmo. 2 adj. mágico: ~ lantern, linterna mágica.
magical (-al) adj. mágico; encantado.
magician (madŷi·shan) s. mágico, mago.
magisterial (mædŷisti·rial) adj. de magistrado. 2 magistral, autoritario, dogmático.
magistery (mæ·dŷisteri) s. QUÍM. magisterio.
magistracy (mæ·dŷistrasi) s. magistratura.
magistral (-tral) adj. de maestro o profesores. 2 MAGISTERIAL 2. 3 adj.-s. FARM. magistral.
magistrate (-treit) s. magistrado. 2 juez de paz.
magma (mæ·gma) s. GEOL. magma.
Magna Charta (mæ·gn·ka·ʳta) s. Carta Magna.
magnanimity (mægnani·miti) s. magnanimidad.
magnanimous (mægnæ·nimøs) adj. magnánimo.
magnate (mæ·gneit) s. magnate.
magnesia (mægnɪ·shia) s. magnesia.
magnesian (-an) adj. magnesiano.
magnesic (-sik) adj. magnésico.
magnesite (mæ·gnisait) s. MINER. magnesita.
magnesium (mægnɪ·shiøm) s. QUÍM. magnesio.
magnet (mæ·gnit) s. ELECT. imán. 2 piedra imán. 3 fig. imán [lo que atrae].
magnetic (mægne·tik) adj. magnético: ~ needle, aguja magnética, brújula; ~ recorder, aparato magnetofónico. 2 atrayente, cautivador.
magnetical (mægne·tikal) adj. magnético. 2 atrayente, cautivador.
magnetism (mæ·gnitiŝm) s. magnetismo.
magnetite (-tait) s. MINER. magnetita.
magnetization (-ei·shøn) s. magnetización.
magnetize (to) (mæ·gnitaiŝ) tr. magnetizar. 2 atraer, cautivar, fascinar. 3 intr. imanarse.
magnetizer (-øʳ) s. magnetizador.
magneto (mægni·tou) s. AUTO., ELECT. magneto.
magnetoelectricity (-ile·ctrisiti) s. electromagnetismo.
magnetometer (mægnøta·metøʳ) s. magnetómetro.
magneton (mæ·gnøtan) s. FÍS. magnetón.
Magnificat (mægni·fikat) s. Magnificat [cántico a la Virgen]. 2 canto de alabanza.
magnification (-ei·shøn) s. ÓPT. aumento, amplificación. 2 exageración.
magnificence (mægni·fisøns) s. magnificencia.

magnificent (-t) adj. magnífico, espléndido, suntuoso. 2 noble, elevado.
magnifier (mægnifaiøʳ) s. ÓPT. amplificador, lente de aumento. 2 exagerador.
magnify (to) (mæ·gnifai) tr. agrandar, aumentar, amplificar. 2 abultar, exagerar. ¶ Pret. y p. p.: magnified.
magnifying glass (-ing) s. lente de aumento, lupa.
magniloquence (mægni·løkuøns) s. grandilocuencia.
magniloquent (-t) s. grandílocuo.
magnitude (mæ·gnitiud) s. magnitud.
magnolia (mægnou·lia) s. BOT. magnolia.
magnum (mæ·gnøm) s. botella de dos litros.
magpie (mæ·gpai) s. ORN. urraca, picaza. 2 fig. charlatán, cotorra. 3 fig. regañón.
Magus (mei·gøs), pl., Magi (-dŷai) s. mago [de oriente].
Magyar (mæ·gyaʳ) adj.-s. magiar.
maharaja(h (majara·dŷa) s. maharajá.
Maharanee (majarani·) f. esposa del maharajá.
mahistick (ma·lstik) s. PINT. tiento.
mahogany (maja·gani) s. BOT. caoba, caobo. 2 caoba [madera; color].
Mahomet, Mahometan, etc. MOHAMMED, MOHAMMEDAN, etc.
mahout (mæjau·t) s. cornaca, naire.
maid (meid) s. doncella [soltera, virgen]: ~ of honour, doncella o dama de honor. 2 doncella, criada: ~ of all work, criada para todo.
maiden (-øn) s. doncella, virgen, joven soltera. 2 adj. soltera; de soltera: ~ name, nombre de soltera. 3 virginal. 4 virgen, nuevo. 5 primero, inicial.
maidenhair (-jeʳ) s. BOT. adianto, culantrillo.
maidenhood (-jud) s. f. doncellez.
maidenly (-li) adj. virginal, modesto, candoroso.
maidservant (mei·dsøʳvant) s. criada, doméstica.
mail (meil) s. malla [tejido de anillos, etc., de metal]; cota de malla. 2 correo, correspondencia, saco de la correspondencia, mala, valija. 3 correo, servicio postal [en Ingl., esp. con el extranjero]: ~ boat, buque correo; air ~, correo aéreo. 4 TEJ. malla [de lizo].
mail (to) tr. echar al correo; enviar por correo. 2 armar con malla o cota de malla.
mailbox (-baks) s. buzón; apartado.
mailman (-mæn) s. cartero.
mailplane (-plein) s. avión correo.
maim (meim) s. mutilación, estropeo.
maim (to) tr. mutilar, estropear, mancar, lisiar.
main (mein) adj. primero, principal, esencial, mayor, maestro: ~ body, grueso [del ejército]; ~ office, oficina central, casa matriz; ~ road, carretera principal. 2 grande, fuerte. 3 by ~ force, a pura fuerza, por la fuerza. 4 s. lo principal, lo esencial, la mayor parte: in the ~, en su mayor parte, principalmente. 5 poét. alta mar. 6 línea, tubería, conducto principal [de gas, agua, electricidad, etc.].
mainland (-lønd) s. continente, tierra firme.
mainly (-li) adv. principalmente, en su mayor parte. 2 poderosamente.
mainmast (-mæst) s. MAR. palo mayor.
mainsail (-seil) s. MAR. vela mayor.
mainspring (-spring) s. muelle principal o real. 2 móvil, causa principal.
mainstay (-stei) s. MAR. estay del palo mayor. 2 soporte principal.
maintain (to) (-tei·n) tr. mantener.

maintainer (-tei·nø^r) *s.* mantenedor, defensor, partidario.
maintenance (mei·ntønans) *s.* mantenimiento, sostenimiento. *2* apoyo, sostén. *3* manutención, sustento. *4* IND. mantenimiento, conservación.
maintop (-tap) *s.* MAR. cofa mayor.
main-topgallant *s.* MAR. juanete mayor.
main-topmast *s.* MAR. mastelero mayor.
main-topsail *s.* MAR. gavia [vela].
Mainz (mai·nts) *n. pr.* Maguncia.
maize (meiš) *s.* BOT. maíz.
maizena (meiši·na) *s.* maicena.
majestic (madẙe·stik) *adj.* majestuoso.
majestically (-ali) *adj.* majestuosamente.
majesty (mæ·dẙisti) *s.* majestad; majestuosidad. *2* (con may.) Majestad [tratamiento].
majolica (madẙa·lika) *s.* mayólica.
major (mei·dẙø^r) *adj.* mayor, más grande, principal. *2* MÚS. mayor. *3 s.* DER. mayor de edad. *4* LÓG. mayor. *5* MIL. comandante. *6* MIL. ~ *general*, general de división.
Majorca (madẙo·^rka) *n. pr.* GEOGR. Mallorca.
Majorcan (madẙo·^rkan) *adj.-s.* mallorquín.
major-domo (meidẙø^r-dou·mou) *s.* mayordomo.
majority (madẙa·riti) *s.* mayoría. *2* mayor de edad. *3* MIL. comandancia [empleo de comandante].
majuscule (madẙu·skiul) *s.* PALEOGR. mayúscula.
make (meik) *s.* hechura, forma; estructura; constitución, manera de ser. *2* hechura [acción de hacer], obra, fabricación, producción. *3* marca, modelo.
make (to) *tr.* hacer [crear, confeccionar, elaborar, fabricar; componer, formar; causar, ocasionar, producir, preparar, disponer; efectuar, ejecutar]: *to ~ bread*, hacer pan; *to ~ fun*, hacer burla, burlarse; *to ~ a mistake*, cometer un error, equivocarse; *to ~ a noise*, hacer ruido; *to ~ a stop*, hacer alto, detenerse; *to ~ a will*, hacer u otorgar testamento. *2* hacer [obligar, inducir a]: *he was made to dance*, le hicieron bailar. *3* poner en el estado o dar la cualidad que expresa un adjetivo: *to ~ angry*, enfadar, enojar; *to ~ clear*, hacer claro, aclarar; *to ~ fast*, fijar, amarrar, asegurar; cerrar; *to ~ level*, allanar, nivelar; *to ~ ready*, preparar, disponer; prepararse, disponerse, aprestarse. *4* hacer, convertir en, nombrar. *5* elevar, hacer llegar [a una cifra o cantidad]. *6* tener por, considerar como, creer, suponer. *7* entender, deducir, inferir: *what do you ~ of this?*, ¿qué deduce usted de esto? *8* hacer, ganar: *to ~ money*, hacer dinero; *to ~ a living*, ganarse la vida. *9* recorrer, hacer el trayecto o recorrido de; pasar, cruzar; llegar a, visitar [un lugar]. *10* hacer [tantos nudos, kilómetros, etc., por hora, etc.]. *11* determinar, fijar, calcular. *12* MAR. descubrir, divisar, avistar. *13* ELECT. cerrar [un circuito]; establecer [un contacto]. *14 to ~ a clean breast of it*, desembuchar, confesarlo todo. *15 to ~ a great deal of*, TO ~ MUCH OF. *16 to ~ believe*, hacer creer, fingir. *17 to ~ both ends meet*, pasar o vivir con lo que se tiene o gana. *18 to ~ friends with*, hacerse amigo de, reconciliarse con. *19 to ~ good*, cumplir, llevar a cabo, probar; mantener, defender; justificar [con el éxito o resultado]; compensar, indemnizar. *20 to ~ haste*, apresurarse, darse prisa. *21 to ~ known*, hacer saber, dar a conocer. *22 to ~ much of*, dar mucha importancia a, hacer mucho caso de; apreciar; mimar. *23 to ~ neither head or tail of*, no comprender nada de.

24 to ~ no difference o *no matter*, no importar, ser lo mismo. *25 to ~ one's mark*, firmar con una cruz; distinguirse, señalarse. *26 to ~ one's mouth water*, hacer que se le haga a uno la boca agua. *27 to ~ one's way*, avanzar; abrirse paso. *28 to ~ out*, hacer, escribir, extender [una lista, un documento, etc.]; hacer, componer; comprender, descifrar, descubrir; divisar; probar, justificar; completar; conseguir. *29 to ~ over*, rehacer; ceder, traspasar. *30* MAR. *to ~ sail*, largar velas. *31 to ~ (a) shift*, arreglárselas, componérselas. *32 to ~ the most of*, sacar el mejor partido de. *33 to ~ up*, hacer, componer, formar; envolver, atar; confeccionar, preparar; componer, pintar [el rostro], TEAT. caracterizar, maquillar; completar; sumar; compensar; arreglar, reconciliar; inventar, forjar; IMPR. compaginar. *34 to ~ up one's mind*, decidirse, resolverse, hacer ánimo [de]. *35 to ~ water*, orinar; MAR. hacer aguas.

36 intr. dirigirse, encaminarse a; abalanzarse a. | Con *for, toward* o *at*, *37* contribuir a, servir para, tender a. | Con *for* o *to*. *38* hacerse, crecer, aumentar. *39 to ~ after*, perseguir. *40 to ~ away*, largarse, huir. *41 to ~ away with*, llevarse; derrochar; destruir, matar. *42 to ~ bold to*, atreverse a. *43 to ~ free with*, tomarse libertades con. *44 to ~ merry*, divertirse. *45 to ~ off*, largarse, marcharse, huir. *46 to ~ sure*, cerciorarse, asegurarse. *47 to ~ up*, hacer las paces; componerse, pintarse; TEAT. caracterizarse, maquillarse. *48 to ~ up for*, suplir, compensar. *49 to ~ up to*, tratar de congraciarse con. ¶ Pret. y p. p.: *made*.
make-believe *adj.* fingido, simulado. *2 s.* ficción, simulación, pretexto. *3* simulador.
make-fast *s.* MAR. amarradero.
makepeace (mei·kpis) *s.* PEACEMAKER.
maker (mei·kø^r) *s.* hacedor, autor, artífice: *the Maker*, el Hacedor, Dios. *2* fabricante, confeccionador.
makeshift (-shift) *adj.* provisional, de fortuna. *2 s.* recurso, sustitutivo, sustituto.
make-up (-øp) *s.* composición, constitución, modo de ser. *2* afeite [del rostro]; TEAT. caracterización, maquillaje. *3* IMPR. compaginación.
makeweight (-ueit) *s.* añadidura [para completar el peso]. *2* suplente.
making (-ing) *s.* hechura, confección, fabricación: *in the ~*, haciéndose; sin terminar. *2* causa del éxito o la fortuna de uno. *3* (a veces *pl.*) cualidades [para ser algo]. *4* ganancias.
Malabar (mæ·laba^r) *adj.* malabar, malabárico.
Malacca (malæ·ka) *n. pr.* GEOGR. Malaca: ~ *cane*, malaca, roten.
Malachi (mæ·lakai), **Malachias** (mælaka·ias) *n. pr.* BIB. Malaquías.
malachite (mæ·lakait) *s.* MINER. malaquita.
malacia (malei·shia) *s.* MED. malacia.
malacology (mælaka·lodẙi) *s.* malacología.
malacopterygian (-kaptøri·dẙian) *adj.* ICT. malacopterígio.
malacostracan (-ka·strakan) *adj.-s.* ZOOL. malacostráceo.
maladdress (-dre·s) *s.* torpeza, falta de tacto, descortesía.
maladjusted (-djø·stid) *adj.* de mal ajuste, mal ajustado. *2* inadaptado.
maladministration (-dministrei·shøn) *s.* mal gobierno, desgobierno.
maladroit (-droi·t) *adj.* torpe; falto de tacto.

malady (mæ·ladi) s. enfermedad.
Malagasy (malei·gasi) adj.-s. malgache.
malaise (mælei·š) s. malestar, indisposición.
malapert (mæ·lapøᵣt) adj.-s. descarado, insolente.
malapropos (mælapropou) adj. impropio, inoportuno, fuera de propósito.
malar (mei·laᵣ) adj. ANAT. malar.
malaria (male·ria) s. MED. malaria.
malarial (-l) adj. palúdico.
Malayan (mælei·sha) s. GEOGR. Malasia.
Malaysian (mælei·sha) adj.-s. malasio.
malcontent (mæ·lkøntent) adj.-s. malcontento.
Maldives (mæ·ldaivs) n. pr. pl. GEOGR. Maldivas.
male (meil) adj. ZOOL., BOT., MEC. macho. 2 masculino: ~ *flower*, flor masculina. 3 varón: ~ *child*, hijo varón. 4 varonil, viril. 5 s. varón. 6 animal macho.
malediction (mælidi·kshøn) s. maldición.
malefaction (-fæ·kshøn) s. delito, fechoría.
malefactor (-fæ·ktøᵣ) s. malhechor.
malefic (male·fik) adj. maléfico.
maleficence (-fisøns) s. maleficencia.
maleficent (-fisønt) adj. maléfico.
malevolence (-vøløns) s. malevolencia, malquerencia, mala voluntad.
malevolent (-t) adj. malévolo.
malfeasance (mælfɪ·šans) s. proceder ilegal, desaguisado [esp. de un funcionario].
malformation (mælfoᵣmei·shon) s. malformación.
malic (mei·lik) adj. QUÍM. málico.
malice (mæ·lis) s. mala voluntad, rencor. 2 malicia, malignidad, mala intención.
malicious (mali·shøs) adv. malévolo, rencoroso, maligno. 2 pícaro, travieso. 3 DER. culpable.
maling (malai·n) adj. maligno. 2 dañino, pernicioso.
maling (to) tr. detraer, difamar, calumniar.
malignancy (mali·gnansi) s. malignidad. 2 malevolencia, encono.
malignant (mali·gnant) adj. maligno. 2 maléfico. 3 malévolo.
malignity (-iti) s. malignidad.
malinger (to) (mali·ngøᵣ) intr. hacerse el enfermo, fingirse enfermo.
malingerer (-øᵣ) s. maula, el que se finge enfermo para evitarse un trabajo.
malison (mæ·lišøn) s. poét. maldición.
mall (mol) s. mallo [mazo; juego]. 2 *the Mall*, paseo público.
mallard (mæ·laᵣd) s. ORN. pato silvestre [macho].
malleability (mæliabi·liti) s. maleabilidad.
malleable (mæ·liabøl) adj. maleable.
malleolous (mæli·øløs) s. ANAT. maléolo.
mallet (mæ·lit) s. mazo, mallete.
malleus (mæ·liøs) s. ANAT. martillo.
mallow (mæ·lou) s. BOT. malva.
malmsey (ma·mši) s. malvasía.
malnutrition (mælniutri·shøn) s. desnutrición.
malodour (mælou·døᵣ) s. mal olor, fetidez, hedor.
malpractice (mælpræ·ktis) s. MED., DER. tratamiento o proceder erróneo o ilegal.
malt (molt) s. malta. 2 cerveza.
malt (to) tr. convertir [la cebada] en malta.
Malta (mo·lta) n. pr. GEOGR. Malta.
Maltese (-iš), pl. **-tese** adj.-s. maltés.
Malthusian (mælziu·šian) adj. maltusiano.
malthusianism (-išm) s. maltusianismo.
maltose (mo·ltous) s. QUÍM. maltosa.
maltreat (to) (mæltrɪ·t) s. maltratar.

maltreatment (-mønt) s. maltratamiento, maltrato.
malvaceous (mælvei·shøs) adj. BOT. malvácea.
malversation (-øᵣse·shøn) s. malversación.
malvoise (mæ·lvoiši) s. MALMSEY.
mama (ma·ma o møma) s. mamá, madre.
Mameluke (mæ·meliuk) s. mameluco.
mamma (mæ·ma) s. MAMA. 2 (pl. -mae) mama, teta.
mammal (-al) s. ZOOL. mamífero.
Mammalia (mæmei·lia) s. pl. ZOOL. mamíferos.
mammary (mæ·mari) adj. mamario.
mammee (mamei o mamɪ·) s. BOT. mamey.
mammiferous (mæmi·førøs) adj. mamífero.
mammilla (mami·la), pl. **-lae** (-li) s. ANAT. mamila.
mammiliary (mæ·mileri) adj. mamilar.
mammoth (mæ·møz) s. ZOOL. mamut. 2 adj. gigantesco.
mammy (mæ·mi) s. mamá, mamita. 2 (Ingl.) abuela. 3 (E.U.) negra vieja, ama o criada negra.
man (mæn), pl. **men** (men) s. hombre [pers. humana; varón]: ~ *about town*, hombre desocupado, que hace vida de sociedad; ~ *and wife*, marido y mujer; *Man of Sorrows*, Jesucristo; ~ *of straw*, testaferro; ~ *overboard!*, MAR. ¡hombre al agua!; *the* ~ *in the street*, el hombre corriente; *a* ~, uno, un hombre; *to a* ~, todos sin excepción. 2 hombre, soldado, criado, seguidor, vasallo: *to be one's own* ~, no depender de nadie; ser dueño de sí mismo. 3 [usado sin artículo], el hombre, el género humano. 4 pieza [de ajedrez]; peón [de damas]. 5 [en composición] buque, navío: *merchantman*, buque mercante.
man (to) tr. MAR. tripular, dotar, amarinar. 2 MIL. guarnecer [un fuerte, etc.]. ¶ Pret. y p. p.: *manned;* ger.: *-nning.*
manacle (mæ·nakøl) s. manilla [grillete]. 2 pl. manillas, esposas.
manacle (to) tr. esposar, poner las manillas a.
manage (to) (mæ·nidy̆) tr. manejar. 2 dirigir, regir, gobernar, administrar. 3 tratar con cuidado. 4 adiestrar [el caballo]. 5 tr.-intr. ingeniarse, componérselas; lograr, conseguir.
manageable (-abøl) adj. manejable, dócil.
management (-mønt) s. manejo, dirección, gobierno, gestión, administración. 2 gerencia, consejo de administración. 3 habilidad, trastienda; aptitud para dirigir.
manager (-øᵣ) s. director, administrador, gerente. 2 empresario. 3 buen administrador.
managerial (mænady̆i·rial) adj. directivo, administrativo.
Manasseh (manæ·sø) n. pr. m. BIB. Manasés.
man-at-arms, pl. **men-at-arms** s. hombre de armas.
manatee (mænatɪ·) s. ZOOL. manatí.
manchineel (mænchinɪ·l) s. BOT. manzanillo.
Mancunian (mankiu·nian) adj.-s. manchesteriano.
mandarin (mændari·n) s. mandarín. 2 BOT. mandarina. 3 (con may.) lengua mandarina.
mandatary (mæ·ndateri) s. mandatario.
mandate (mæ·ndeit) s. mandato, orden, precepto. 2 DER., POL. mandato.
mandate (to) tr. asignar o conferir por mandato.
mandator (mændei·tøᵣ) s. mandante.
mandatory (mæ·ndatori) adj. obligatorio. 2 conferido por mandato. 3 s. mandatario.
mandible (mæ·ndibøl) s. ANAT., ZOOL. mandíbula.
mandolin (mæ·ndølin) s. MÚS. mandolina.
mandragora (mændræ·gora), **mandrake** (mæ·ndreik) s. BOT. mandrágora.
mandrel, mandril (mæ·ndrøl) s. MEC. mandril.

mandrill (-dril) *s.* ZOOL. mandril.
mane (mein) *s.* crin [de caballo]; melena [de león, de pers.].
maned (-d) *adj.* crinado, crinito.
manege (mane·ỹ) *s.* EQUIT. picadero. *2* equitación. *3* marcha, aire [del caballo adiestrado].
manes (mei·niš) *s. pl.* manes.
maneuver, to maneuver, maneuverer = MA-NOEUVRE, TO MANOEUVRE, MANOEUVRER.
manful (mæ·nful) *adj.* viril, varonil. *2* bravo, esforzado, noble.
manganate (mænganei·t) *s.* QUÍM. manganato.
manganese (mænganı·s) *s.* QUÍM. manganeso.
mange (meindỹ) *s.* roña, sarna.
manger (mei·ndỹø^r) *s.* pesebre.
mangle (mæ·ngøl) *s.* máquina de planchar, mangle.
mangle (to) *tr.* planchar con máquina. *2* magullar, desgarrar, destrozar, mutilar, estropear.
mango (-gou) *s.* BOT. mango.
mangonel (-gonel) *s.* maganel, almajaneque.
mangosteen (-gøstın) *s.* BOT. mangosto.
mangrove (-grouv) *s.* BOT. mangle.
mangy (mei·ndỹi) *adj.* sarnoso. *2* desastrado, mugriento.
manhole (mæ·njoul) *s.* boca de inspección o acceso a calderas, etc. *2* refugio en un túnel.
manhood (-jud) *s.* condición de hombre. *2* los hombres. *3* virilidad, valor.
mania (mei·nia) *s.* MED. manía. *2* manía, afición.
maniac (-k) *adj.-s.* maníaco, loco furioso.
maniacal (-al) *adj.* MANIAC.
Manichean (mæniki·an) *s.* maniqueo.
Manicheism (-išm) *s.* maniqueísmo.
manichord (mæ·niko^{r}d) *s.* MÚS. manicordio.
manicure (-kiu^r) *s.* manicura [cuidado de las manos]. *2* manicuro, ra [pers.].
manicure (to) *tr.* hacer la manicura a.
manicurist (-kiurist) *s.* manicuro, ra [pers.].
manifest (-fest) *adj.* manifiesto. *2 s.* COM. manifiesto.
manifest (to) *tr.* manifestar; demostrar, revelar. *2 intr.* hacer una manifestación pública, tomar parte en ella.
manifestant (mænife·stant) *s.* manifestador. *2* manifestante.
manifestation (-ei·shøn) *s.* manifestación; demostración, revelación. *2* manifestación [pública].
manifesto (mænife·stou) *s.* manifiesto; proclama.
manifold (-fould) *adj.* múltiple, multíplice, vario, diverso, numeroso. *2 s.* copia [de una carta, etc.]. *3* MEC. tubo de unión múltiple.
manifold (to) *tr.* sacar varias copias a la vez.
manikin (-kin) *s.* enano. *2* maniquí [figura]. *3* hombre clástico.
Manil(l)a (mani·la) *n. pr.* GEOGR. Manila: ~ *hemp*, abacá; ~ *paper*, papel de manila.
manille (mani·l) *s.* mala, malilla [naipe].
manioc (mæ·niak) *s.* BOT. mandioca.
maniple (-pøl) *s.* manípulo.
manipulate (to) (maani·piuleit) *tr.* manipular, manejar.
manipulation (-ei·shøn) *s.* manipulación, manipuleo; manejo.
manipulator (mani·piuleitø^r) *s.* manipulador.
mankind (mænkai·nd) *s.* género humano. *2* [mæ·nkaind] los hombres, el sexo masculino.
manlike (-laik) *adj.* varonil. *2* hombruno. *3* esforzado, noble.
manliness (-linis) *s.* virilidad, hombradía, valor, nobleza.

manly (-li) *adj.* varonil, viril, valeroso, noble.
manna (mæ·na) *s.* BIB., BOT. maná.
mannequin (mæ·nikin) *s.* maniquí [figura]. *2* modelo [de una casa de modas].
manned (mæ·nd) *pret.* y *p. p.* de TO MAN.
manner (mæ·nø^r) *s.* manera, modo: *adverb of* ~, adverbio de modo; *after*, o *in, the* ~ *of*, a la manera de, a la, a lo; *by no* ~ *of means*, de ningún modo; *in a* ~, en cierto modo, hasta cierto punto; *in this* ~, así, de este modo. *2* B. ART., LIT. manera; amaneramiento. *3* hábito, costumbre. *4* clase, género, suerte. *5* aire, porte, conducta. *6 pl.* maneras, modales, educación.
mannerism (-išm) *s.* amaneramiento.
mannerist (-ist) *s.* artista amanerado.
mannerliness (-linis) *s.* cortesía, urbanidad.
mannerly (-li) *adj.* cortés, urbano, atento. *2 adv.* urbanamente.
mannish (mæ·nish) *adj.* varonil, hombruno.
manoeuvre (manu·vø^r) *s.* MIL., MAR. maniobra [evolución]. *2* maniobra, manejo; artificio.
manoeuvre (to) *tr.* hacer maniobrar [las tropas, etc.]. *2* inducir, obligar, etc., con maniobras o manejos.
manoeuvrer (manu·vrø^r) *s.* maniobrero.
man-of-war *pl.*, **men-of-war** *s.* buque de guerra.
manometer (mana·metø^r) *s.* manómetro.
manor (ma·nø^r) *s.* feudo, señorío, hacienda de un señor: ~ *house*, casa señorial en el campo.
manorial (mano·rial) *adj.* señorial.
mansard roof (mæ·nsa^{r}d) *s.* ARQ. mansarda.
manse (mæ·ns) *s.* (Esc.) rectoría.
manservant (mæ·nsø^{r}vant) *s.* criado.
mansion (-shøn) *s.* hotel, palacio, casa grande. *pl.* edificio grande dividido en pisos.
mansion-house *s.* MANOR HOUSE. *2* (con may.) residencia del Lord Mayor de Londres.
manslaughter (-slotø^r) *s.* homicidio.
manslayer (-leiø^r) *s.* homicida.
manteau (-tou) *s.* capa, manto.
mantel (-tøl) *s.* manto [de chimenea]. *2* repisa [de chimenea].
mantelet (-tølet) *s.* capotillo; manteleta. *2* MIL. mantelete.
mantelletta (mæntøle·ta) *s.* ECLES. mantelete.
mantelpiece (-tølpıs) *s.* repisa de chimenea.
mantilla (mænti·la) *s.* mantilla, mantón.
mantis (mæ·ntis) *s.* ENT. campanero.
mantissa (mænti·sa) *s.* MAT. mantisa.
mantle (mæ·ntøl) *s.* manto [prenda]. *2* fig. manto, capa [lo que cubre]. *3* ZOOL. manto. *4* camisa, manguito [de luz de gas].
mantle (to) *tr.* cubrir [con manto], tapar, envolver. *2 intr.* extenderse [como un manto]. *3* cubrirse de espuma, etc. *4* encenderse [el rostro].
mantling (-ling) *s.* BLAS. mantelete.
manual (mæ·niual) *adj.* manual: ~ *arts*, artes mecánicas. *2 s.* manual [libro]. *3* MÚS. teclado de mano. *4* MIL. ejercicio [de armas].
manubrium (maniu·briøm) *s.* ANAT., ZOOL. manubrio.
manufactory (mæniufæ·ktori) *s.* manufactura, fábrica, taller.
manufacture (-chø^r) *s.* manufactura [fabricación; producto fabricado].
manufacture (to) *tr.* manufacturar, fabricar.
manufacturer (-chørø^r) *s.* fabricante.
manufacturing (-chøring) *adj.* manufacturero, industrial, fabril.
manumission (mæniumi·shøn) *s.* manumisión.

manumit (to) (mæniumi·t) *tr.* manumitir. ¶ Pret. y
p. p.: *mitted;* ger.: *-tting.*
manumitter (-tøʳ) *s.* manumisor.
manure (maniu·øʳ) *s.* AGR. abono, estiércol.
manure (to) *tr.* AGR. abonar, estercolar.
manuscript (mæ·niuskript) *adj.-s.* manuscrito.
Manx (mæ·nks) *adj.-s.* de la isla de Man.
many (me·ni) *adj.* muchos, chas: ~ *times,* ~ *a time,*
muchas veces, frecuentemente; *as* ~, otros tantos; *as* ~ *as,* tantos como; hasta [cierto nú-
mero]; *how* ~?, ¿cuántos?; *so* ~, tantos; *too* ~,
demasiados; de más, de sobra; *too* ~ *for* o *one*
too ~ *for,* más listo, más fuerte, etc., que; *twice*
as ~, el doble, dos veces más. *2* [en composi-
ción] multi-, poli-, de muchos: *many-coloured,*
multicolor, policromo. *3 pron.* muchos. *4 s.* número [de]: *a great* ~, un gran número, muchos,
muchísimos.
many-flowered *adj.* multifloro.
manyplies (-plaiš) *s.* ZOOL. libro [de los rumian-
tes].
many-sided *adj.* multilátero; apto para muchas
cosas, de gran curiosidad intelectual.
Maori (ma·ori) *adj.-s.* maorí.
map (mæp) *s.* mapa.
map (to) trazar el mapa de. *2* indicar en el mapa.
3 fig. *to* ~ *out,* planear, trazar el plan de. ¶ Pret.
y p. p.: *mapped;* ger.: *-pping.*
maple (mei·pøl) *s.* BOT. arce,* meple.
mar (to) (maʳ) *tr.* estropear, echar a perder, destruir. ¶ Pret. y p. p.: *marred;* ger.: *-rring.*
marabou (mæ·rabu) *s.* marabú [ave y adorno].
marabout (-t) *s.* morabito.
maraca (mara·ka) *s.* MÚS. maraca.
maraschino (mæraski·nou) *s.* marrasquino.
marasmus (maræ·smøs) *s.* MED. marasmo.
Marathon (mæ·razan) *n. pr.* GEOGR., DEP. Maratón.
maraud (to) (maro·d) *intr.* merodear, pecorear. *2*
tr. saquear, merodear en.
marauder (-øʳ) *s.* merodeador, pecoreador.
marauding (-ing) *s.* merodeo, pillaje.
maravedi (mæravei·di) *s.* maravedí.
marble (ma·ʳbøl) *s.* mármol. *2* canica, pita [bo-
lita]. *3* IMPR. platina. *4* jaspeado. *5 pl.* canicas
[juego].
marble (to) *tr.* jaspear.
marbler (ma·ʳbløʳ) *s.* marmolista. *2* jaspeador.
marbly (-i) *adj.* marmóreo, marmoleño.
marc (maʳk) *s.* orujo.
marcasite (ma·ʳkašait) *s.* MINER. marcasita.
marcel (maʳse·l) o **marcel wave** *s.* ondulación marcel.
marcescent (maʳse·sønt) *adj.* BOT. marcescente.
March (maʳch) *s.* marzo [mes].
march *s.* marcha [acción de caminar, camino;
curso, progreso]. *2* MIL., MÚS. marcha. *3* MIL.
paso. *4* marca [distrito fronterizo].
march (to) *intr.* marchar, andar, caminar. *2* marchar, progresar. *3 to* ~ *with,* limitar, lindar con.
4 tr. hacer marchar [las tropas]; hacer ir [a un
sitio].
marchioness (ma·ʳshønis) *f.* marquesa [título].
marchpane (-pein) *s.* mazapán.
marconigram (markou·nigræm) *s.* marconigrama.
Marcus (mæ·ʳkøs) *n. pr. m.* Marcos.
mare (meʳ) *s.* yegua. *2* mula, asna.
mareograph (mæ·riogræf) *s.* mareógrafo.
mare's-nest *s.* fam. descubrimiento ilusorio.
mare's-tail *s.* BOT. cola de caballo. *2* METEOR. cirro.
Margaret (ma·ʳgarit) *n. pr.* Margarita.

margarine (-in) *s.* margarina.
margarite (-ait) *s.* MINER. margarita.
margay (ma·ʳgei) *s.* ZOOL. maracayá, tigrillo.
marge (ma·ʳdy̆) *s.* poét. margen, orilla.
Margery (-øri) *n. pr.* Margarita.
margin (-in) *s.* margen, borde, orilla. *2* margen [de
una página]. *3* límite [del que una cosa no puede
pasar]. *4* COM., ECON. margen. *5* sobrante, exceso, reserva.
margin (to) *tr.* marginar, margenar, apostillar.
marginal (-al) *s. pl.* notas marginales.
marginate (to) (-eit) *tr.* marginar.
margrave (ma·ʳgreiv) *s.* margrave.
marguerite (ma·ʳgørit) *s.* BOT. margarita.
Marian (mæ·rian o me·rian) *adj.* mariano. *2 n. pr.*
f. Mariana.
Marianne (meriæ·n) *n. pr. f.* Mariana.
Marie (mari·) *n. pr. f.* María.
marigold (mæ·rigould) *s.* BOT. maravilla, caléndula, flamenquilla. *2* BOT. clavelón.
marigraph (-græf) *s.* mareógrafo.
marihuana, marijuana (marijua·na) *s.* BOT. marihuana.
marimba (mari·mba) *s.* MÚS. marimba.
marinade (to) (mærinei·d) *s.* escabeche.
marine (marı·n) *adj.* marino, marítimo. *2* oceánico. *3* náutico, naval, de marina: *Marine Corps*
(E.U.) infantería de marina. *4 s.* soldado de marina. *5* marina [buques]. *6* PINT. marina.
mariner (mæ·rinøʳ) *s.* marinero, marino.
Marion (mæ·riøn) *n. pr. m.* Mariano. *2 n. pr. f.* Mariana.
marionette (mærione·t) *s.* marioneta, títere.
Marist (me·rist) *s.* ECLES. marista.
marital (mæ·rital) *adj.* marital, matrimonial.
maritime (-tim o -taim) *adj.* marítimo.
Marius (me·riøs) *n. pr. m.* Mario.
marjoram (ma·rdy̆øram) *s.* BOT. mejorana.
Mark (maʳk) *n. pr. m.* Marcos.
mark *s.* marca, señal. *2* mancha, pinta. *3* impresión, huella. *4* signo, indicio, prueba. *5* signo,
símbolo. *6* cruz [para firmar]. *7* rótulo, marbete. *8* DEP. línea de salida. *9* importancia, nota,
distinción: *of mark,* de nota [pers.]. *10* tipo, límite, altura, etc., requeridos. *11* punto, nota,
calificación [en exámenes, etc.]. *12* blanco, hito,
fin, propósito: *to miss the* ~, errar el tiro; *beside*
the ~, errado; que no viene al caso. *13* marco
[moneda]. *14* marca [territorio].
mark (to) *tr.* marcar, señalar. *2* indicar [ser señal
o indicio de]. *3* delimitar, señalar los límites de.
4 notar, observar, advertir, fijarse en: ~ *my*
words!, ¡advierte lo que te digo! *5* caracterizar.
6 mostrar, manifestar. *7* puntuar, calificar [en
un examen]. *8* FÚTBOL. marcar [un jugador a
otro]. *9 to* ~ *down,* apuntar, poner por escrito;
rebajar el precio de. *10 to* ~ *out,* indicar, señalar; designar, elegir; separar con un guión o una
raya. *11 to* ~ *time,* MIL. marcar el paso.
markdown (-kdaun) *s.* precio rebajado.
marked (-t) *adj.* marcado, notable. *2* ~ *man,* hombre sospechoso; futura víctima.
marker (-øʳ) *s.* marcador. *2* ficha [de juego]. *3* mojón.
market (-it) *s.* mercado [en todas sus acepciones];
bolsa, mercado de valores; ~ *garden,* huerto [de
hortalizas]; ~ *price,* precio corriente; ~ *town,*
población con mercado, villa.
market (to) *tr.* negociar, comprar o vender [en el
mercado]. *2* llevar al mercado. *3 intr.* hacer la
compra. *4* comerciar.

marketable (-abøl) *adj.* comerciable, vendible.
marketing (-ing) *s.* compra o venta en el mercado.
marksman (-smæn) *s.* tirador [que tiene buena puntería].
marksmanship (-ship) *s.* puntería.
marl (ma^{r}l) *s.* marga.
marl (to) *tr.* AGR. margar. *2* MAR. cubrir o atar con vueltas de cordel.
marlin (-in) *s.* ICT. especie de aguja.
marline *s.* MAR. merlín.
marlpit (-pit) *s.* margal, marguera.
marly (-i) *adj.* margoso.
marmalade (ma^{r}maleid) *s.* mermelada.
marmit (-mit) *s.* marmita.
marmoration (-mørei·shøn) *s.* marmoración.
marmoreal (-mou·rial) *adj.* marmóreo.
marmoset (-mošet) *s.* ZOOL. tití.
marmot (-møt) *s.* ZOOL. marmota.
Maronite (ma·ronait) *s.* maronita.
maroon (maru·n) *adj.* castaño. *2 s.* BOT. castaña. *3* color castaño. *4* cimarrón.
maroon (to) *tr.* dejar abandonado, aislado, en un lugar desierto.
marplot (ma^{r}plat) *s.* entrometido, aguafiestas.
marquee (-ɪ·) *s.* gran tienda de campaña. *2* marquesina.
marquetry (-øtri) *s.* marquetería, taracea.
marquis (-uis) *s.* marqués.
marquisate (-uisit) *s.* marquesado.
marquise (-iš) *s.* marquesa [mujer]. *2* MARQUEE.
marriage (mæ·ridỹ) *s.* matrimonio: ~ *articles*, capitulaciones; ~ *lines*, partida de matrimonio; *by* ~, político [pariente]. *2* casamiento, boda. *3* maridaje.
marriageable (-abøl) *adj.* casadero, núbil.
married (mæ·rid) *adj.* casado; ~ *couple*, matrimonio [marido y mujer]. *2* maridado. *3* matrimonial, conyugal.
marrow (-ou) *s.* ANAT. médula, tuétano. *2* médula, meollo, substancia. *3* BOT. *marrow* o *vegetable* ~, calabacín.
marrowbone (-boun) *s.* canilla, hueso largo. *2 pl.* fam. rodillas.
marrowy (-i) *adj.* medular. *2* meolludo.
marry (to) (mæ·ri) *tr.* casar, desposar. *2* casarse con. *3* unir, juntar, maridar. *4 intr.* casarse.
Mars (ma^{r}s) *s.* MIT., ASTR. Marte.
Marseillais (ma^{r}seye·) *adj.-s.* marsellés.
marseillaise (ma^{r}seye·š) *s.* Marsellesa [himno].
Marseilles (ma^{r}sei·lš) *n. pr.* GEOGR. Marsella.
marsh (ma^{r}sh) *s.* marjal, paúl, pantano, humedal: ~ *harrier*, ORN. arpella; ~ *warbler*, ORN. arandillo.
marshal (ma·^{r}shal) *s.* MIL. mariscal. *2* maestro de ceremonias, bastonero. *3* (E.U.) alguacil; jefe de policía.
marshal (to) *tr.* ordenar, poner en orden. *2* formar [tropas]. *3* conducir con solemnidad o ceremonia. *4* guiar, dirigir, disciplinar. *5 intr.* formar, ponerse en orden. ¶ Pret. y p. p.: *marshaled* o -*lled*; ger.: -*ling* o -*lling*.
marshalship (-ship) *s.* mariscalía, mariscalato.
marshmallow (-mælou) *s.* BOT. malvavisco. *2* pastilla o bombón de malvavisco.
marshy (-i) *adj.* pantanoso. *2* palustre.
marsupial (ma^{r}siu·pial) *adj.-s.* ZOOL. marsupial.
mart (ma^{r}t) *s.* emporio, centro comercial.
marteline (-ølin) *s.* martellina.
marten (-øn) *s.* ZOOL. marta. *2* ZOOL. garduña.
Martha (ma·^{r}za) *n. pr. f.* Marta.
Martial (ma·^{r}shal) *n. pr. m.* Marcial.

martial *adj.* marcial, militar, bélico: ~ *law*, ley marcial, estado de guerra. *2* QUÍM. marcial.
Martian (-ian) *adj.-s.* marciano.
Martin (ma·^{r}tin) *n. pr.* Martín.
martin *s.* ORN. vencejo, avión.
martinet (ma^{r}tine·t) *s.* ordenancista.
martingale (ma·^{r}tingeil) *s.* gamarra. *2* MAR. moco de bauprés.
Martinique (ma^{r}tini·k) *n. pr.* GEOGR. Martinica.
Martinmas (ma·^{r}tinmas) *s.* día de San Martín.
martlet (map^{r}tlet) *s.* MARTIN.
martyr (-ø^r) *s.* mártir.
martyr to *tr.* martirizar.
martyrdom (-døm) *s.* martirio.
martyrize (to) (-aiš) *tr.* hacer mártir.
martyrology (ma^{r}tøra·lodỹi) *s.* martirologio.
marvel (ma·^{r}vøl) *s.* maravilla, prodigio.
marvel (to) *intr.* maravillarse, admirarse. *2* preguntarse.
Marvel-of-Peru *s.* BOT. dondiego [de noche].
marvel(l)ous (-løs) *adj.* maravilloso, prodigioso. *2* asombroso.
Marxian (ma·^{r}ksian) *adj.-s.* marxista.
Marxism (-sišm) *s.* marxismo.
Marxist (-sist) *adj.-s.* marxista.
Mary (me·ri) *n. pr. f.* Máría.
marzipan (ma·^{r}šipæn) *s.* mazapán.
mascot (mæ·skat) *s.* mascota.
masculine (mæ·skiulin) *adj.* masculino, varonil. *2* hombruno. *3 adj.-s.* GRAM. masculino.
masculinity (mæskiuli·niti) *s.* masculinidad.
mash (mæsh) *s.* masa, pasta [de cosas mojadas]. *2* malta remojado. *3* farro [para el ganado]. *4* fig. revoltijo, embrollo.
mash (to) *tr.* majar, machacar, hacer pasta. *2* macerar [el malta].
mashy (-i) *adj.* majado, pastoso.
mask (mæsk) *s.* máscara, antifaz, careta, carátula. *2* máscara [pers.; disfraz; lo que oculta]. *3* mascarilla [vaciado]. *4* FOT. desvanecedor. *5* ARQ. mascarón. *6* mascarada.
mask (to) *tr.* enmascarar. *2 intr.* ponerse careta. *3* disfrazarse, ir disfrazado.
masked ball (-d) *s.* baile de máscaras.
masker (-ø^r) *s.* máscara [pers.].
masochism (mæ·šøkišm) *s.* masoquismo.
masochist (-ist) *s.* masoquista.
masochistic (mæšøki·stik) *adj.* masoquista.
mason (mei·søn) *s.* albañil. *2* masón, francmasón.
masonic (meisa·nik) *adj.* masónico.
masonry (mei·sønri) *s.* albañilería. *2* mazonería. *3* (con may.) masonería.
masque (mæsk) *s.* mascarada; baile de máscaras.
masquerade (mæskørei·d) *s.* mascarada: ~ *ball*, baile de máscaras. *2* máscara [disfraz]. *3* fig. farsa.
masquerade (to) *intr.* tomar parte en una mascarada. *2* disfrazarse.
masquerader (-ø^r) *s.* máscara [pers.].
mass (mæs) *s.* masa [agregado, conjunto], bulto, mole. *2* montón, gran cantidad: ~ *production*, fabricación en serie. *3* FÍS. masa. *4 pl. the masses*, las masas.
Mass o **mass** *s.* LITURG., MÚS. misa.
mass (to) *tr.* amasar, juntar, reunir en masa. *2 intr.* juntarse, reunirse, formar masa.
massacre (to) (mæ·sakør) *tr.* hacer una matanza de. *2* asesinar.
massage (masa·ỹ) *s.* amasamiento, masaje.
massage (to) *tr.* amasar, dar masaje a.
masseter (mæsi·tø^r) *s.* ANAT. masetero.

masseur (mæsø·ᵣ) s. masajista [hombre].
masseuse (-š) s. masajista [mujer].
massicot (mæ·sikat) s. masicote.
massif (masi·f) s. GEOGR. macizo.
massive (mæ·siv) adj. macizo. 2 voluminoso, imponente. 3 pesadas, gruesas [facciones].
massy (mæ·si) adj. macizo, voluminoso, pesado.
mast (mæst) s. MAR. mástil, palo, árbol: *before the* ~, como simple marinero. 2 asta, mástil, poste. 3 RADIO. torre. 4 AGR. bellotas, hayucos, etc. [para los cerdos].
mast (to) tr. MAR. arbolar.
mastaba(h (mæ·staba) s. mastaba.
master (mæ·støᵣ) s. amo, patrón, dueño, señor. 2 señor, señorito [dicho por un criado]. 3 MAR. patrón, capitán. 4 maestro: ~ *of ceremonies*, maestro de ceremonias; *the Master*, el Maestro (Jesucristo). 5 jefe, director, rector. 6 título de ciertos cargos: *Master of the horse*, caballerizo mayor. 7 adj. maestro; magistral, superior, de maestro: ~ *hand*, mano maestra, maestría; ~ *key*, llave maestra.
master (to) tr. dominar, vencer, subyugar, sobreponerse a. 2 dominar [una ciencia, arte, etc.].
masterful (-ful) adj. dominante, autoritario. 2 fuerte, hábil, diestro; de maestro.
masterless (-lis) adj. ingobernable. 2 sin amo.
masterly (-li) adj. magistral, hábil, de maestro. 2 adv. magistralmente.
mastermind (-maind) s. mente directora.
masterpiece (-pis) s. obra maestra.
mastership (-ship) s. dominio, superioridad. 2 magisterio. 3 maestría.
masterwork (-uøᵣk) s. obra maestra.
mastery (-i) s. dominio [poder; conocimiento]. 2 maestría. 3 superioridad, ventaja.
masthead (mæ·stjed) s. MAR. tope. 2 cabecera [de un periódico].
mastic (mæ·stik) s. almáciga, mástique. 2 BOT. almácigo, lentisco. 3 masilla.
masticate (to) (mæ·stikeit) tr. masticar.
mastication (-ei·shøn) s. masticación.
mastiff (mæ·stif) s. mastín.
mastodon (mæ·stødan) s. mastodonte.
masturbate (to) (mæ·støᵣbeit) *intr.* masturbarse.
mat (mæt) s. estera. 2 esterilla, ruedo, felpudo; petate. 3 tapetito. 4 enredijo, greña. 5 MAR. pallete, empalletado. 6 orla de cartón, paspartú. 7 superficie mate. 8 adj. mate, sin lustre.
mat (to) tr. esterar. 2 enredar, enmarañar apelmazar. 3 matar el brillo [un metal]. 4 intr. enredarse, enmarañarse, apelmazarse. ¶ Pret. y p. p.: *matted;* ger.: *-tting*.
matador (mætædo·ᵣ) s. espada, diestro [torero]. 2 matador [naipe].
match (mæch) s. fósforo, cerilla. 2 pajuela, mecha. 3 pareja [cosa que hace juego]; igual [pers. o cosa igual]. 4 contrincante temible, persona capaz de competir o entendérselas con otra: *to meet one's* ~, hallar la horma de su zapato. 5 juego [de dos cosas]. 6 lucha deportiva; partido, partida. 7 casamiento; partido: *good* ~, buen partido.
match (to) tr. casar, hermanar, aparear, emparejar. 2 oponer [a otra una pers. o cosa igual]. 3 igualar a, poder competir con. 4 igualar, proporcionar, adaptar, ajustar. 5 hacer juego con. 6 intr. casarse. 7 casar, hacer juego.
matchbox (-baks) s. fosforera, cerillera.
matchet (-øt) s. machete.
matchless (-lis) adj. sin igual, incomparable.

matchlock (-lak) s. llave de mosquete. 2 mosquete.
matchmaker (mæ·chmeikøᵣ) s. casamentero. 2 organizador de luchas deportivas. 3 fabricante de fósforos.
mate (meit) s. compañero, compañera. 2 consorte, cónyuge. 3 macho [de una hembra]; hembra [de un macho]. 4 MAR. segundo de a bordo, piloto, oficial. 5 ayudante. 6 AJED. mate.
mate (to) tr. casar, desposar. 2 aparear. 3 hermanar. 4 dar jaque mate. 5 fig. contrarrestar, hacer imponente. 6 intr. aparearse. 7 casar, hermanarse. 8 MEC. engranar.
maté (ma·tei) s. BOT. mate, té del Paraguay.
mateless (mei·tlis) adj. solo; desparejado.
mater (ma·tøᵣ) s. fam. madre.
material (mati·rial) adj. material. 2 físico, corpóreo. 3 materialista. 4 importante, esencial. 5 s. material. 6 materia, ingrediente. 7 tela, género. 8 pl. avíos, recado.
materialism (mati·riališm) s. materialismo.
materialist (-ist) m. materialista.
materialistic (matiriali·stik) adj. materialista.
materiality (-æ·liti) s. materialidad. 2 importancia.
materialize (to) (mati·rialaiš) tr. materializar. 2 hacer sensible, perceptible. 3 convertir en realidad. 4 intr. materializarse. 5 hacerse visible o corpóreo, tomar forma, aparecer.
materially (-li) adv. materialmente. 2 esencialmente.
materiel (matirie·l) s. materiales, pertrechos. 2 MIL. material.
maternal (matøᵣnal) adj. maternal. 2 materno.
maternity (-iti) s. maternidad: ~ *hospital*, casa de maternidad, clínica maternal.
maternize (to) (ma·tøᵣnaiš) tr. maternizar.
mathematic(al (mæzimæ·tik(al) adj. matemático.
mathematician (mæzimati·shan) s. matemático.
mathematics (mæzimæ·tiks) s. matemáticas.
Matilda (mati·lda) n. pr. Matilde.
matinal (mæ·tinal) adj. matinal, matutino.
matinée (mæ·tinei·) s. TEAT. matiné.
matins (mæ·tinš) s. pl. LITURG. maitines.
matrass (mæ·tras) s. QUÍM. matraz.
matriarch (mei·triaᵣk) s. matriarca.
matriarchal (meitria·ᵣkal) adj. matriarcal.
matrices (mei·trisiš) s. pl. de MATRIX.
matricidal (meitrisai·dal) adj. matricida.
matricide (mei·trisaid) s. matricida. 2 matricidio.
matriculate (to) (matri·kiuleit) tr. matricular [esp. en una universidad]. 2 intr. matricularse.
matrimonial (mætrimou·nial) adj. matrimonial, conyugal, marital.
matrimony (-i) s. matrimonio [casamiento; sacramento; estado]. 2 juego de naipes.
matrix (mei·triks) s. ANAT., MAT., MINER. matriz. 2 matriz, molde.
matron (mei·trøn) s. matrona [mujer respetable]. 2 ama de llaves [de un hospicio, etc.]. 3 matrona [de un puesto de policía, etc.].
matronly (-li) adj. matronal. 2 de alguna edad. 3 digna, respetable. 4 maternal.
Matt (mæt) n. pr. abrev. de MATTHEW.
matted (mæ·tid) pret. y p. p. de TO MAT.
matter (mæ·tøᵣ) s. materia, substancia. 2 materia, pus. 3 cosa escrita o impresa. 4 materia, asunto, tema, cuestión, cosa: ~ *of course*, cosa lógica, natural, de cajón; ~ *of fact*, hecho cierto o positivo; *as a* ~ *of fact*, de hecho, en realidad; *a decir verdad; for that* ~, en cuanto a eso; *in the* ~, al respecto; *in the* ~ *of*, en materia de. 5 mo-

tivo, ocasión. *6* cosa, obra [cantidad, tiempo, etc., aproximados]: *a ~ of ten years,* cosa de diez años. *7* cosa que ocurre, mal, defecto, inconveniente, etc.: *what is the ~?,* ¿qué ocurre?; *what is the ~ with you?,* ¿qué le pasa a usted?, ¿qué tiene usted? *8* importancia: *no ~,* no importa; *no ~ how,* de cualquier modo [que]; *no ~ how* [*far, much,* etc.], por lejos, mucho, etc., que; *no ~ where,* dondequiera que. *9 pl.* el estado de cosas, las cosas.

matter (to) *intr.* importar, ser de importancia. *2* MED. supurar.

matterless (-lis) *adj.* fútil.

matter-of-fact *adj.* material, positivo. *2* positivista. *3* prosaico.

mattery (-i) *s.* importante. *2* purulento.

Matthew (mæ·ziu) *n. pr.* Mateo.

Mathias (mætza·ias) *n. pr.* Matías.

matting (mæ·ting) *s.* estera; esterado. *2* MAT 5, 6 y 7.

mattock (-øk) *s.* AGR. zapapico, azadón de pico.

mattress (-res) *s.* colchón.

maturate (to) (mæ·chureit) *tr.-intr.* madurar [esp. un tumor].

maturation (-ei·shøn) *s.* maduración.

maturative (mæ·chørativ) *adj.-s.* madurativo.

mature (møtiu·ø^r) *adj.* maduro. *2* adulto; juicioso. *3* perfecto, acabado. *4* COM. vencido, pagadero.

mature (to) *tr.* madurar. *2* llevar a la perfección. *3 intr.* madurar. *4* vencer [una deuda, plazo, etc.].

maturity (matiu·riti) *s.* madurez. *2* perfección. *3* vencimiento [de una deuda, plazo, etc.].

matutinal (-tinal) *adj.* matutinal, matutino.

matweed (mæ·twid) *s.* BOT. esparto, albardín.

maudlin (mo·dlin) *adj.* lacrimoso, sentimental, sensiblero. *2* chisposo y lloroso.

maugre (mo·gø^r) *prep.* ant. a pesar de.

maul (mol) *s.* mazo, machota.

maul (to) *tr.* aporrear, magullar; maltratar.

maulstick (-tik) *s.* tiento [de pintor].

maunder (to) (mo·ndø^r) *intr.-tr.* mascullar, refunfuñar. *2 intr.* obrar o moverse como atontado. *3* divagar.

Maundy (-i) *s.* mandato, lavatorio [del jueves santo]. *2 ~ Thursday,* jueves santo.

Maurice (mo·ris) *n. pr.* Mauricio.

Mauritius (mori·shiøs) *n. pr.* GEOGR. Mauricio [Isla].

Mauser, mauser (mau·šø^r) *s.* máuser.

mausoleum (mosølı·øm) *s.* mausoleo.

mavis (mei·vis) *s.* ORN. malvís. *2* ORN. cagaceite.

maw (mo·) *s.* estómago. *2* cuajar [de los rumiantes]. *3* buche [de las aves]. *4* fauces; tragadero.

mawkish (-kish) *adj.* sensiblero, empalagoso. *2* nauseoso.

maxilla (mæksi·la) *s.* ANAT., ZOOL. hueso maxilar.

maxillar (mæ·ksila^r), **maxillary** (mæ·ksileri) *adj.-s.* maxilar [hueso].

maxim (mæ·ksim) *s.* máxima, sentencia.

maximal (-al) *adj.* máximo.

maximize (to) (-aiš) *tr.* llevar hasta el máximo; abultar, exagerar.

maximum (-øm), *pl.* **-mums** o **-ma** (-ma) *s.* máximum, máximo.

May (mei) *s.* mayo [mes]: *~ Day,* primero de mayo; *~ fly,* ENT. efímera, cachipolla. *2* fig. primavera [de la vida].

1) may *s.* BOT. acerolo, espino albar. *2* BOT. viburno.

2) may *v.* aux. poder [tener facultad, libertad, oportunidad o permiso; ser lícito, permitido, posible o contingente]: *may I go?,* ¿puedo mar-

charme?; *it ~ be, ~ be,* puede ser, acaso. *2* A veces indica deseo vivo y se traduce por «ojalá», «que», etc., o se omite y se pone el verbo en subjuntivo: *~ it be so,* ojalá sea así; *~ you live happily,* viva usted feliz. *3* A veces se usa con elipsis del segundo verbo: *come what ~,* venga lo que viniere. ¶ Pret.: *might.* | Carece de infinitivo, de participios y de gerundio.

Maya (ma·ia), **Mayan** (-n) *adj.-s.* maya [de los mayas].

maybe (mei·bi) *adv.* acaso, quizá, tal vez.

Mayflower (mei·flauø^r) *s.* BOT. (Ingl.) espino blanco; calta, hierba centella. *2* BOT. (E.U.) anémona; epígea rastrera.

mayhap (mei·jæp) *adv.* acaso, quizá, tal vez.

mayonnaise (meiønei·š) *s.* salsa mahonesa.

mayor (mei·iø^r) *s.* alcalde, corregidor.

mayoralty (-alti) *s.* alcaldía, corregimiento.

mayoress (-is) *f.* alcaldesa.

Maypole (mei·poul) *s.* mayo, árbol de mayo.

Maytide (-taid), **Maytime** (mei·taim) *s.* mes de mayo.

mayweed (-uid) *s.* BOT. manzanilla loca.

mazard (mæ·ša^rd) *s.* BOT. cerezo silvestre.

Mazdaism (mæ·šdaišm), **Mazdeism** (-diišm) *s.* mazdeismo.

maze (meiš) *s.* laberinto, dédalo. *2* confusión, perplejidad.

maze (to) *tr.* enredar, intrincar. *2* aturdir, confundir.

mazurka (mašu·^rka) *s.* mazurca.

mazy (mei·ši) *adj.* laberíntico, intrincado.

me (mı) *pron. pers.* me, mí: *with ~,* conmigo.

mead (mıd) *s.* licor de aguamiel.

meadow (me·dou) *s.* prado, pradera.

meadowsweet (-suit) *s.* BOT. ulmaria, reina de los prados.

meadowy (-i) *adj.* pradeño; praderoso.

meager, meagre (mı·gø^r) *adj.* magro, flaco. *2* pobre, estéril, escaso, mezquino. *3* de vigilia.

meal (mıl) *s.* harina [de ciertos granos y semillas]. *2* (E.U.) harina de maíz. *3* comida [que se toma a ciertas horas del día].

mealtime (-taim) *s.* hora de comer.

mealy (-i) *adj.* harinoso, farináceo. *2* polvoriento. *3* meloso [en el hablar].

mean (mın) *s.* bajo, humilde. *2* ordinario, inferior, pobre, mezquino: *no ~,* bueno, excelente. *3* ruin, bajo, vil. *4* mezquino, tacaño, sórdido. *5* (E.U.) avergonzado; indispuesto. *6* medio, mediano, intermedio. *~ term,* LÓG. término medio; *~ time,* ASTR. tiempo medio. *7* medio [punto medio]. *8* MAT. medio [de una proporción], media: *~ proportional,* media proporcional. *9* justo medio, moderación. *10 pl.* [ús. como sing. o pl.] medio, medios [de hacer, obtener, etc.]: *by all means,* de todos modos, a toda costa; sin falta; si, por cierto; *by means of,* por medio de; *by no means,* de ningún modo. *11 pl.* medios, recursos, posibles, bienes de fortuna: *man of means,* hombre rico, de posibles.

mean (to) *tr.* significar, denotar, querer decir. *2* pensar, proponerse, tener intención de: *what do you ~ to do?,* ¿qué piensa usted hacer?; *to ~ business,* ir en serio, estar resuelto a hacer algo. *3* destinar: *his criticism was not meant for me,* su crítica no se dirigía a mí; *clothers are meant for use,* los vestidos se hacen para usarlos. *4 intr.* tener intención [buena o mala]: *he means well,* tiene buena intención. ¶ Pret. y p. p.: *meant.*

mean-born *adj.* de humilde cuna.

meander (miæ·ndøʳ) *s.* meandro. *2* laberinto, camino tortuoso.
meander (to) *intr.* serpentear. *2* errar, vagar.
meandrous (-røs) *adj.* sinuoso.
meaning (mɪ·ning) *s.* significación, significado, sentido, acepción. *2* intención, designio.
meaningful (-ful) *adj.* significante.
meaningless (-lis) *adj.* sin sentido.
meanness (mɪ·nnis) *s.* humildad, pobreza. *2* ordinariez, mala calidad. *3* ruindaz, bajeza. *4* mezquindad, tacañería.
mean-spirited *adj.* bajo, ruin.
meant (ment) *pret.* y *p. p.* de TO MEAN.
meantime (mɪ·ntaim), **meanwhile** (-juail) *adv.* entretanto, mientras tanto. *2 m.* ínterin: *in the meantime*, en el ínterin, mientras tanto.
measles (mɪ·šølš) *s. pl.* MED. sarampión: *German ~*, rubéola. *2* VET. cisticercosis.
measurable (me·ŷørabøl) *adj.* mensurable.
measure (me·ŷøʳ) *s.* medida [de una cosa; lo que sirve para medir; unidad de medida; acción de medir]: *made to ~*, hecho a medida. *2* sistema de medidas. *3* medida; tasa, moderación: *beyond ~*, sobremanera; *without ~*, sin medida, sin tasa. *4* cantidad, grado, extensión: *in some ~*, en cierto grado, en cierto modo. *5* medida, disposición: *to take measures*, tomar las medidas necesarias. *6* ritmo, cadencia. *7* MÚS. compás. *8* fig. baile: *to tread a ~*, bailar. *9* MÉTR. metro, pie.
measure (to) *tr.-intr.* medir: *to ~ one's length*, medir el suelo, caerse a la larga. *2 tr.* ajustar, proporcionar. *3* recorrer [un país, una distancia]. *4 to ~ off*, medir, señalar una medida. *5 to ~ out*, medir, dar o distribuir según medida.
measured (me·ŷøʳd) *adj.* medido. *2* mesurado, lento, rítmico, acompasado. *3* moderado.
measureless (me·ŷøʳlis) *adj.* inconmensurable, ilimitado, infinito.
measurement (me·ŷøʳmønt) *s.* medición. *2* medida.
measuring worm (-ing) *s.* ENT. geómetra [oruga].
meat (mɪt) *s.* carne [como alimento]: *~ ball*, albóndiga; *~ fly*, mosca de la carne; *~ safe*, fresquera. *2* vianda, comida. *3* materia [para reflexión, etc.].
meathook (-uk) *s.* garabato de carnicero.
meatus (miei·tøs) *s.* ANAT. meato.
meaty (mɪ·ti) *adj.* carnoso. *2* jugoso, sustancioso.
mechanic (mikæ·nik) *adj.* mecánico [de los oficios; de las máquinas]. *2 s.* obrero, artesano, mecánico.
mechanical (-al) *adj.* mecánico, de máquinas. *2* maquinal, rutinario. *3* automático.
mechanician (mecani·shan) *s.* mecánico. *2* maquinista [que hace máquinas].
mechanics (mikæ·niks) *s.* mecánica [ciencia, arte]. *2* maquinaria. *3* detalles prácticos, técnica.
mechanism (me·kanišm) *s.* mecanismo. *2* mecanicismo.
mechanist (-st) *s.* mecanicista. *2* mecánico.
mechanistic (-ik) *s.* mecanicista.
mechanization (-ei·shøn) *s.* mecanización. *2* MIL. motorización. *3* maquinismo.
mechanize (to) (me·kanaiš) *tr.* mecanizar. *2* MIL. motorizar.
mechanotherapy (mekanoze·rapi) *s.* mecanoterapia.
Mechlin (me·klin) *n. pr.* GEOGR. Malinas.
meconium (meko·niøm) *s.* meconio, alhorre.
medal (me·dal) *s.* medalla.

medallion (midæ·liøn) *s.* medallón.
medal(l)ist (me·dalist) *s.* numismático. *2* medallista. *3* el que ha ganado una medalla.
meddle (to) (me·døl) *intr.* entrometerse, injerirse, meterse [en]. | Gralte. con *with* o *in*.
meddlesome (me·dølsøm) *adj.* entremetido.
meddling (-ling) *s.* entretenimiento, intromisión.
Mede (mɪd) *adj.-s.* medo.
mediaeval (mɪdi·val) *adj.* medieval. *2* medioeval.
mediaevalism (-išm) *s.* medievalismo.
medial (mɪ·dial) *adj.* medio [que está entre los extremos].
Median (-an) *adj.* meda, médico. *2 s.* meda.
median *adj.* medio [que está en medio; que es el término medio de]. *2 s.* GEOM. mediana.
mediastinum (mɪdiæstai·nøm) *s.* ANAT. mediastino.
mediate (mɪ·dieit) *adj.* mediato. *2* intermedio.
mediate (to) *intr.* mediar, intermediar. *2* mediar, intervenir. *3 tr.* ser el medio o conducto para [algo]; arreglar, procurar, comunicar.
mediation (-ei·shøn) *s.* mediación.
mediatize (to) (mɪ·diætaiš) *tr.* mediatizar.
mediator (mɪ·dieitøš) *s.* mediador, medianero.
mediatrix (-triks) *f.* medidora, medianera.
Medic (mɪ·dik) *adj.* médico, medo [de Media].
medic (me·dik) *s.* BOT. alfalfa, mielga. *2* fam. estudiante de medicina.
medicable (me·dikabøl) *adj.* medicable.
medical (-al) *adj.* médico, de medicina: *~ student*, estudiante de medicina; *~ treatment*, tratamiento médico.
medicament (medi·kamønt) *s.* medicamento.
medicamental (medikame·ntal) *adj.* medicamentoso.
medicaster (me·dikæstøš) *s.* medicastro.
medicate (to) (-eit) *tr.* tratar [a un enfermo]. *2* impregnar con una sustancia medicinal.
medication (-ei·shøn) *s.* medicación. *2* medicamento.
medicinal (medi·sinal) *adj.* medicinal.
medicine (me·disin) *s.* medicina, medicamento: *to take one's ~*, fam. echar el pecho al agua; hacer uno a la fuerza lo que no quisiera hacer. *2* medicina [ciencia y arte].
medieval (mɪdi·val) *adj.* MEDIAEVAL.
medievalism (-išm) *s.* MEDIAEVALISM.
mediocre (mɪ·diøkøš) *adj.* mediocre, mediano.
mediocrity (mɪdia·kriti) *s.* mediocridad, medianía.
meditate (to) (me·diteit) *tr.* proyectar, proponerse. *2 intr.* meditar, reflexionar.
meditation (-ei·shøn) *s.* meditación, reflexión.
meditative (me·diteitiv) *adj.* meditativo, contemplativo. *2* meditabundo.
Mediterranean (meditørei·nian) *adj.-s.* Mediterránea: *~ Sea*, mar Mediterráneo.
medium (mɪ·diøm) *s.* medio, punto o grado medio. *3* medio, conducto. *4* médium [en espiritismo]. *5* BIOL., BACT. medio, elemento. *6 adj.* mediano, medio, intermedio.
medlar (me·dlaš) *s.* BOT. níspero. *2* níspola.
medley (me·dli) *s.* mezcla, mezcolanza, batiburrillo. *2* MÚS. popurrí. *3 adj.* mezclado, confuso.
medulla (medø·la), *pl.* **-lae** (-li) ANAT., BOT. médula.
medullary (me·døleri) *adj.* medular.
medusa (mediu·sa) *s.* ZOOL. medusa. *2* (con may.) MIT. Medusa.
meed (mɪd) *s.* poét. premio, galardón.
meek (mɪk) *adj.* manso, suave, humilde, dócil.

meekness (-nis) *s.* mansedumbre, suavidad, humildad, docilidad.

meerschaum (mi·øšshom) *s.* espuma de mar.

meet (mɪt) *adj.* apropiado, conveniente, idóneo. *2 s.* reunión o concurso deportivo.

meet (to) *tr.* encontrar, hallar, encontrarse con, topar; tropezar, chocar con; enfrentarse con; batirse con. *2* conocer, ser presentado a: *pleased to* ~ *you*, mucho gusto en conocerle. *3* reunirse, entrevistarse con. *4* hacer frente a [gastos, etc.]; satisfacer, llenar [necesidades, requisitos, etc.]; cumplir [obligaciones]; cumplimentar [un pedido]. *5* refutar, responder [a una acusación, una objeción]. *6* enlazar [con otro tren, ómnibus, etc.]. *7 to go to* ~, ir a esperar o recibir a [uno]. *8 to* ~ *half way*, partir la diferencia. *9 intr.* reunirse, juntarse. *10* encontrarse, entrevistarse. *11* chocar, oponerse, pelear. *12* confluir. *13* enlazar [dos trenes, etc.]. *14 to* ~ *with*, encontrar, encontrarse con; tener, sufrir [contrariedades, una desgracia, etc.]. ¶ Pret. y p. p.: *met.*

meeting (mɪ·tiŋ) *s.* reunión, junta, sesión. *2* asamblea, mitin. *3* conferencia, entrevista. *4* encuentro. *5* duelo, desafío. *6* confluencia [de ríos]. *7* cruce, empalme [de caminos, etc.].

meetly (mɪ·tli) *adv.* convenientemente.

Meg (meg) *n. pr. dim.* de MARGARET.

megacycle (me·gasaikøl) *s.* RADIO. megaciclo.

megalith (-liz) *s.* megalito.

megalithic (megali·zik) *adj.* megalítico.

megalomania (megalomei·nia) *s.* megalomanía.

megaphone (me·gafoun) *s.* megáfono, bocina, portavoz.

megatherium (megazi·riøn) *s.* PALEONT. megaterio.

megaton (me·gatøn) *s.* megatón.

megohm (-oum) *s.* megohmio.

megrim (mɪ·grim) *s.* jaqueca, migraña. *2 pl.* malhumor, hipocondría.

melancholia (melankou·lia) *s.* MED. melancolía.

melancholic (-a·lik) *adj.-s.* MED. melancólico.

melancholy (me·lankali) *s.* melancolía, tristeza, hipocondría. *2 adj.* melancólico.

Melanesia (melanɪ·sia) *n. pr.* GEOGR. Melanesia.

mélange (meila·ndỹ) *s.* mezcla.

melanite (me·lanait) *s.* MINER. melanita.

melaphyre (-fai^r) *s.* GEOL. meláfido.

Melchior (me·lkiø^r) *n. pr.* Melchor.

Melchisedec (melki·sedek) *n. pr.* Melquisedec.

melee, mêlée (mei·lei) *s.* refriega, reyerta.

meliaceous (miliei·shøs) *adj.* BOT. meliáceo.

melilot (me·lilat) *s.* BOT. meliloto, trébol oloroso.

melinite (me·linait) *s.* melinita.

meliorate (to) (mɪ·liøreit) *tr.* mejorar [hacer mejor]. *2 intr.* mejorar, mejorarse.

melioration (-ei·shøn) *s.* mejoramiento, mejora.

melissa (møli·sa) *s.* BOT. melisa.

melliferous (meli·førøs) *adj.* melífero.

mellifluence (-fluøns) *s.* melifluidad.

mellifluous (-fluøs) *adj.* melifluo.

mellow (me·lou) *adj.* maduro, sazonado [fruto]. *2* tierno, blando, suave, pastoso, meloso. *3* suave [vino]. *4* AGR. blando, margoso [suelo]. *5* lleno, puro, suave [voz, sonido, color, luz]; melodioso. *6* calamocano.

mellow (to) *tr.* madurar, sazonar. *2* ablandar, suavizar. *3 intr.* madurar, sazonarse. *4* suavizarse.

mellowy (-i) *adj.* MELLOW.

melodic (mela·dik) *adj.* melódico.

melodics (-s) *s.* melódica.

melodious (melou·diøs) *adj.* melodioso.

melodrama (me·lødrama) *s.* melodrama.

melodramatic (melodramæ·tik) *adj.* melodramático.

melody (me·lødi) *s.* melodía.

melomane (me·lømein) *s.* melómano.

melon (me·løn) *s.* BOT. melón. *2* BOT. sandía, melón de agua.

melonry (-ri) *s.* melonar.

melopoeia (melopɪ·ya) *s.* MÚS. melopeya.

Melpomene (melpa·mini) *n. pr.* MIT. Melpómene.

melroze (me·lrouš) *s.* miel rosada.

melt (melt) *s.* fusión, derretimiento. *2* METAL. hornada.

melt (to) *tr.* fundir, derretir. *2* disolver [una sustancia]. *3* dispar, desvanecer. *4* ablandar, aplacar, enternecer. *5* mezclar, confundir. *6 intr.* fundirse, derretirse. *7* deshacerse, disolverse. *8* disiparse, desvanecerse. *9* ablandarse, enternecerse. *10* mezclarse, confundirse. *11 to* ~ *into tears*, deshacerse en lágrimas.

melting point (-ing) *s.* punto de fusión.

melting pot *s.* crisol.

melton (-øn) *s.* TEJ. melton.

member (me·mbø^r) *s.* miembro. *2* socio, individuo. *3* diputado [de una Cámara].

membership (-ship) *s.* calidad de miembro o socio. *2* sociedad, conjunto de socios.

membrane (me·mbrein) *s.* membrana.

membranous (-branøs) *adj.* membranoso.

memento (meme·ntou) *s.* memento. *2* recuerdo, memoria, recordatorio.

memo (me·mou) *s. abrev.* de MEMORANDUM.

memoir (me·muar) *s.* memoria, informe, nota. *2* memoria [disertación, relación]. *3 pl.* memorias [relación escrita].

memorable (me·mørabøl) *adj.* memorable, memorando.

memorandum (memøræ·ndøm), *pl.* dums o da *s.* memorándum. *2* nota, apuntación, apunte.

memorial (mimo·rial) *adj.* conmemorativo: ~ *arch*, arco de triunfo. *2 s.* monumento conmemorativo. *3* recuerdo, memoria. *4* memorial, petición. *5* nota, apuntamiento. *6 pl.* memorias.

memorialize (to) (-aiš) *tr.* dirigir o presentar un memorial a. *2* conmemorar.

memorize (to) (-øraiš) *tr.* aprender de memoria.

memory (-i) *s.* memoria, retentiva [facultad]. *2* memoria, recuerdo, recordación: *within* ~ *of man*, que registra la historia.

Memphis (me·mfis) *n. pr.* GEOGR. Menfis.

men (men) *s. pl.* de MAN: hombres.

menace (me·nis) *s.* amenaza.

menace (to) *tr.-intr.* amenazar.

menad *s.* MAENAD.

menage (me·naỹ) *s.* casa, hogar. *2* economía doméstica, gobierno de la casa.

menagerie (mønæ·dỹøri) *s.* colección de animales; casa de fieras.

mend (mend) *s.* mejoría; reforma. *2* remiendo, reparación.

mend (to) *tr.* componer, reparar, remendar. *2* repasar, zurcir [la ropa]. *3* corregir, enmendar. *4* mejorar. *5 intr.* corregirse, enmendarse. *6* mejorar, mejorarse; restablecerse.

mendacious (mendei·shøs) *adj.* mendaz, mentiroso; falso.

mendacity (mendæ·siti) *s.* mendacidad. *2* mentira, embuste.

mender (me·ndø^r) s. componedor, reparador; enmendador: ~ *of roads*, peón caminero.
mendicant (-ikant) *adj.-s.* mendicante. 2 mendigo.
mendicity (mendi·siti) s. mendicidad.
menfolk (me·nfouk) s. *pl.* hombres.
menhir (-ji^r) s. menhir.
menial (mɪ·nial) *adj.* doméstico, servil. 2 s. criado, lacayo.
meningeal (meni·ndẏial) *adj.* meníngeo.
meninges (-iš) s. *pl.* ANAT. meninges.
meningitis (meninẏai·tis) s. MED. meningitis.
meniscus (meni·skøs) s. ANAT., FÍS., ÓPT. menisco. 2 lúnula.
menisperm (me·nispø^rm) s. BOT. menisperma.
menispermaceous (menispø^rmei·shøs) *adj.* BOT. menispermáceo.
menopause (me·nøupoš) s. FISIOL. menopausia.
menses (me·nsiš) s. *pl.* menstruo, regla.
Menshevik (me·nshøvik) s. menchevique.
menstruate (to) (me·nstrueit) *intr.* menstruar.
menstruation (-ei·shøn) s. menstruación.
menstruum (me·nstruøm) s. QUÍM. menstruo.
mensurability (menshurabi·liti) s. mensurabilidad.
mensurable (me·nshurabøl) *adj.* mensurable.
mensuration (-ei·shøn) s. medición, medida, mensura.
mental (me·ntal) *adj.* mental, intelectual; ~ *reservation*, reserva o restricción mental.
mentality (mentæ·liti) s. mentalidad.
menthol (me·nzal) s. QUÍM. menthol.
mention (me·nshøn) s. mención.
mention (to) *tr.* mencionar, mentar, nombrar; *don't ~ it*, no hay de qué; *not to ~*, sin contar, además de.
mentor (me·ntø^r) s. mentor, guía.
menu (me·niu) s. lista de platos, minuta. 2 comida.
Mentz (ments) *n. pr.* Maguncia.
meow (mi·au) s. maullido, miau.
meow (to) *intr.* maullar.
Mephistopheles (mefista·filis) *n. pr.* Mefistófeles.
Mephistophelian (mefistøfi·lian) *adj.* mefistofélico.
mephitic(al (mifi·tik(al) *adj.* mefítico.
mercantile (mø·^rkantil) *adj.* mercantil, mercante.
mercantilism (mø·^rkantilišm) s. mercantilismo.
Mercedarian (mø·^rsidæ·rian) s. mercedario.
mercenary (mø·^rsøneri) *adj.* mercenario; venal, interesado. 2 s. MIL. mercenario.
mercer (mø·^rsø^r) s. (Ingl.) sedero [comerciante].
mercerize (to) (-aiš) *tr.* mercerizar.
mercery (-i) s. sedería [comercio].
merchandise (mø·^rchandaiš) s. mercadería, mercancía, géneros.
merchandise (to) *intr.-tr.* comerciar, traficar.
merchant (-t) s. mercader, comerciante. 2 tendero. 3 *adj.* mercante, mercantil: ~ *marine*, marina mercante.
merchantable (-abøl) *adj.* comerciable, vendible; corriente.
merchantman (-mæn) s. buque mercante.
merciful (mø·^rsiful) *adj.* misericordioso, clemente, piadoso, compasivo, humano, benigno.
mercifulness (-nis) s. misericordia, clemencia, piedad, compasión.
merciless (mø·^rsilis) *adj.* implacable, despiadado, cruel, inhumano.
mercurial (mø·^rkiu·rial) *adj.* mercurial, mercúrico. 2 activo, vivo, despierto. 3 veleidoso, volátil. 4 s. FARM. preparado mercurial.
mercuric (mø·^rkiu·rik) *adj.* QUÍ. mercúrico.

Mercury (mø·^rkiuri) *n. pr.* ASTR., MIT. Mercurio: *Mercury's wand*, caduceo.
mercury s. QUÍM. mercurio, azogue. 2 BOT. mercurial.
mercy (mø·^rsi) s. misericordia, clemencia, piedad, compasión: *to cry for ~*, pedir misericordia. 2 merced, gracia. 3 merced [voluntad, arbitrio]: *at the ~ of*, a la merced de.
mere (mi·ø^r) *adj.* mero, solo, no más que. 2 s. (Ingl.) lago, estanque.
merely (-li) *adv.* meramente.
meretricious (meritri·shøs) *adj.* meretricio. 2 fig. llamativo, de oropel; de mal gusto.
merganser (mø·^rgæ·nsø^r) s. ORN. mergo, mergánsar.
merge (to) (mø·^rdẏ) *tr.* unir, combinar, fusionar. 2 *intr.* sumergirse, fundirse, unirse, fusionarse. 3 *to ~ into*, convertirse gradualmente en.
merger (-ø^r) s. unión, fusión [esp. de sociedades anónimas].
mericarp (me·rikæ^rp) s. BOT. mericarpio.
meridian (miri·dian) *adj.* ASTR., GEOGR., GEOM. meridiano. 2 fig. culminante, supremo. 3 s. ASTR., GEOGR., GEOM. meridiano. 4 altura meridiana. 5 fig. apogeo.
meridional (miri·diønal) *adj.-s.* meridional.
meringue (meræ·ng) s. merengue.
merino (møri·nou) *adj.-s.* merino [carnero, lana, paño].
meristem (me·ristem) s. BOT. meristemo.
merit (me·rit) s. mérito. 2 merecimiento.
merit (to) *tr.* merecer; ser digno de.
meritorius (merito·riøs) *adj.* meritorio, benemérito.
merle (mø·^rl) s. ORN. poét. mirlo.
merlin (mø·^rlin) s. ORN. esmerejón.
merlon (mø·^rløn) s. FORT. merlón.
mermaid (mø·^rmeid) s. MIT. sirena.
merman (mø·^rmæn) s. MIT. tritón.
Merovingian (merovi·nẏian) *adj.-s.* merovingio.
merrily (me·rili) *adv.* alegremente, regocijadamente, jovialmente.
merriment (-mønt) s. alegría, regocijo. 2 fiesta, diversión.
merry (me·ri) *adj.* alegre, gozoso, regocijado, divertido, jovial, festivo: *to make ~*, divertirse. 2 risueño, placentero.
merry-andrew s. bufón, truán, payaso.
merry-go-round s. tiovivo, caballitos.
merrymaker (-meikø^r) s. persona que se divierte; fiestero, jaranero.
merrymaking (-meiking) s. alegría, diversión, fiesta, holgorio.
merrythought (-zot) s. espoleta [de ave].
mescal (meskæl) s. mezcal.
mesencephalon (mesønse·falan) s. ANAT. mesencéfalo.
mesentery (me·sønteri) s. ANAT. mesenterio.
mesh (mesh) s. malla [de red]. 2 red, tejido de malla. 3 MEC. engranaje [acción]: *in ~*, engranado. 4 *pl.* red, lazos, trampa.
mesh (to) *tr.* coger con red, enredar. 2 *intr.* enredarse, enmallarse. 4 MEC. endentar, engranar.
mesmeric (mešme·rik) *adj.* mesmeriano.
mesmerism (me·smørišm) s. mesmerismo.
mesmerize (to) (-aiš) *tr.* magnetizar, hipnotizar.
mesocarp (me·søka^rp) s. BOT. mesocarpio.
mesothorax (mesøzo·ræks) s. ZOOL. mesotórax.
Mesozoic (-šou·ik) *adj.-s.* GEOL. mesozoico.
mesquite (meskɪ·t) s. BOT. mezquite.
mess (mes) s. plato [cantidad de vianda]. 2 bazo-

fia, comistrajo. *3* enredo, lío, revoltijo; asco, suciedad: *to get into a ~*, meterse en un lío; *to make a ~ of*, desarreglar, enredar, ensuciar, echar a perder. *4* grupo de personas que regularmente comen juntos [esp. en el ejército o en la armada; mesa donde comen; mesa de oficiales].
mess (to) *tr.* desarreglar, enredar, ensuciar, echar a perder. | A veces con *up*. *2 intr.* comer regularmente con. *3 to ~ about in*, meterse en, enredar en.
message (me·sidỹ) *s.* mensaje. *2* recado, mandado, parte, aviso.
Messalina (misælai·na) *n. pr.* Mesalina.
messenger (me·søndỹøʳ) *s.* mensajero. *2* mandadero. *3* heraldo, nuncio.
Messiah (mesai·a) *s.* mesías.
Messianic (mesiæ·nik) *adj.* mesiánico.
Messianism (mesai·anišm) *s.* mesianismo.
messieurs (me·søʳš) *s. pl.* de MISTER, señores.
messmate (me·smeit) *s.* compañero de mesa [esp. en la marina].
messy (me·si) *adj.* desarreglado, enredado; sucio.
mestizo (mesti·šou) *s.* mestizo.
met (met) *pret.* y *p. p.* de TO MEET.
metabolism (metæ·bølišm) *s.* BIOL. metabolismo.
metarcapal (metaka·ʳpal) *adj.* metarcapiano.
metacarpus (-øs) *s.* ANAT. metacarpo.
metal (me·tal) *s.* QUÍM., IMPR., BLAS. metal. *2* metal [aleación]. *3* materia [de que una cosa está hecha]; cualidad esencial; ánimo, temple. *4* vidrio en fusión. *5* material [grava, etc.] para firmes de carretera.
metalepsis (metale·psis) *s.* RET. metalepsis.
metallic (metæ·lik) *adj.* metálico. *2* puro [metal].
metalliferous (metali·førøs) *adj.* metalífero.
metalline (me·talin) *adj.* metálico. *2* que tiene metal en disolución.
metallist (me·talist) *s.* metalario, metalista.
metallize (to) (-aiš) *tr.* metalizar.
metallography (metala·grafi) *s.* metalografía.
metalloid (me·taloid) *adj.-s.* QUÍM. metaloide.
metallurgic(al (metalø·ʳdỹik(al) *adj.* metalúrgico.
metallurgist (me·taløʳdỹist) *s.* metalúrgico.
metallurgy (-i) *s.* metalurgia.
metamere (me·tamiʳ) *s.* ZOOL. metámero.
metamorphic (metamo·ʳfik) *adj.* metamórfico.
metamorphism (-fišm) *s.* GEOL. metamorfismo.
metamorphize (-faiš), **metamorphose (to)** (-fouš) *tr.* metamorfosear.
metamorphosis (-føsis) *s.* metamórfosis.
metaphase (me·tafeiš) *s.* BIOL. metafase.
metaphor (-føʳ) *s.* RET. metáfora.
metaphoric(al (me·taforik(al) *adj.* metafórico.
metaphysic(al (metafi·šik(al) *adj.* metafísico.
metaphysician (metafiši·shan) *s.* metafísico.
metaphysics (metafi·šiks) *s.* metafísica.
metaplasm (me·taplæšm) *s.* GRAM. metaplasmo. *2* BIOL. metaplasma.
metastasis (metæ·stasis) *s.* MED. metástasis.
metatarsus (metata·ʳsøs) *s.* ANAT. metatarso.
metathesis (metæ·zøsis) *s.* GRAM. metátesis.
metazoan (metašou·an) *s.* ZOOL. metazoo.
mete (to) (mıt) *tr.* medir. *2 to ~ out*, distribuir.
metempsychosis (mitempsikou·sis) *s.* metempsicosis.
meteor (mı·tiøʳ) *s.* meteoro. *2* bólido, estrella fugaz.
meteoric (mıtio·rik) *adj.* meteórico.
meteorism (mı·tiørism) *s.* MED. meteorismo.
meteorite (-ait) *s.* meteorito.

meteorological (mıtiørøla·dỹikal) *adj.* meteorológico.
meteorologist (mıtiøra·lødỹist) *adj.* meteorológico.
meteorologist (mıtiøra·lødỹist) *s.* meteorologista.
meteorology (-i) *s.* meteorología.
meteorous (mı·tiørøs) *adj.* meteórico.
meter (mı·tøʳ) *s.* medidor. *2* contador [de agua, gas, etc.]. *3* METRE.
methane (me·zein) *s.* QUÍM. metano.
methinks (mizi·nks) *impers.* poét. me parece, pienso. ¶ Pret.: *methought*.
method (me·zød) *s.* método. *2* técnica.
methodic(al (meza·dik(al) *adj.* metódico.
Methodism (me·zødišm) *s.* metodismo.
Methodist (-t) *s.* metodista.
methodize (to) (-aiš) *tr.* metodizar.
methodology (mezøda·lodỹi) *s.* metodología.
methought (mizo·t) *pret.* de TO METHINKS.
methyl (me·zil) *s.* QUÍM. metilo.
methylene (-in) *s.* QUÍM. metileno.
methylic (mezi·lik) *adj.* metílico.
meticulous (miti·kiuløs) *adj.* meticuloso, minucioso, escrupuloso.
metonymy (mita·nimi) *s.* RET. metonimia.
metope (me·topi) *s.* ARQ. métopa.
metre (mı·tøʳ) *s.* metro [medida de longitud]. *2* metro [del verso]. *3* MÚS. ritmo.
metric (al (me·trik(al) *adj.* métrico.
metrify (to) (me·trifai) *tr.* metrificar, versificar.
metronome (me·tronoum) *s.* metrónomo.
metropolis (mitra·polis) *s.* metrópoli.
metropolitan (metropa·litan) *adj.-s.* metropolitano.
mettle (me·tøl) *s.* temple, brío, ánimo, valor, fuego: *on one's ~*, en estado de hacer todo el esfuerzo posible.
mettlesome (-søm) *adj.* brioso, vivo, fogoso, ardiente.
mew (miu·) *s.* maullido. *2* ORN. gaviota. *3* jaula, muda [para las aves de caza]. *4 pl.* grupo de establos, caballerizas o garajes.
mew (to) *tr.* enjaular, encerrar. *2 intr.* maullar, mayar.
mewl (to) (miul) *intr.* llorar, gimotear [como un niño]. *2* maullar.
Mexican (me·ksikan) *adj.-s.* mejicano.
Mexico (me·ksikou) *n. pr.* GEOGR. Méjico.
mezereon (meze·rion) *s.* BOT. laureola hembra.
mezzanine (me·šanin) *s.* ARQ. entresuelo.
mezzo-rilievo (me·dšou-rilie·vou) *s.* medio relieve.
mezzo-soprano (-sopræ·nou) *s.* MÚS. mezzo soprano.
mi (mi) *s.* MÚS. mi.
miaow (miau·) *s.* miau, maullido.
miaow (to) *intr.* maullar, mayar.
miasm(a (maiæ·šm(a) *s.* miasma.
miasmal (-al), **miasmatic** (maiæšmæ·tik) *adj.* miasmático.
mica (mai·ka) *s.* MINER. mica: *~ schist*, micacita.
mice (mais) *s. pl.* de MOUSE.
Michael (mai·køl) *n. pr.* Miguel.
Michaelmas (mi·kolmas) *s.* día de San Miguel.
mickle (mi·køl) *adj.-adv.* grande, mucho.
microbe (mai·kroub) *s.* microbio.
microbial (maikrou·bial) *adj.-s.* microbicida.
microbiology (maikroubaia·lødỹi) *s.* microbiología.
microcephalic (-sifæ·lik) *adj.* microcéfalo.
micrococcus (-ka·køs) *s.* BACT. micrococo.
microcosm (-kašm) *s.* microcosmo.

microfilm (-film) s. microfilm.
microgamete (-gæ·mit) s. BIOL. microgameto.
micrography (maikra·grafi) s. micrografía.
microgroove (mai·krogruv) s. microsurso.
micrometer (-mitør) s. micrómetro.
micrometric (al (maikroume·trik(al) adj. micrométrico.
micron (mai·kran) s. micra, micrón.
Micronesia (maikrouni·sha) n. pr. GEOGR. Micronesia.
micro-organism s. microorganismo.
microphone (mai·kroufoun) s. micrófono.
microphotograph (maikroufou·tøgræf), **microphotography** (-løta·grafi) s. microfotografía.
micropyle (-pail) s. BOT., ZOOL. micrópilo.
microscope (-skoup) s. microscopio.
microscopic (al (-ska·pik(al) adj. microscópico.
microtome (mai·kroutoum) s. micrótomo.
micturition (miktiuri·shøn) s. micción.
mid (mid) adj. medio, mitad [punto medio]: *in ~ ocean*, en mitad del océano.
midday (mi·ddei) s. mediodía [las doce]. 2 adj. del mediodía.
middle (mi·døl) adj. medio, de en medio, mediano, intermedio: *~ age*, mediana edad; *Middle Ages*, Edad Media; *~ class*, clase media; *~ ear*; ANAT. oído medio; *Middle East*, GEOGR. Oriente medio; *~ finger*, dedo de un medio o del corazón; *~ term*, LÓG. término medio. 2 m. medio, mediados, mitad, centro: *in the ~ of*, en medio de, a medio, a mediados de, a la mitad de. 3 cintura [del cuerpo humano]. 4 promedio.
Middle-Age adj. medieval.
middle-aged adj. de mediana edad.
middle-class adj. de la clase media.
middleman (-mæn) s. intermediario.
middleweight (-ueit) adj. DEP. de peso medio. 2 s. DEP. peso medio.
middling (mi·dling) adj. mediano, regular. 2 adv. fam. medianamente: *fairly ~*, así, así. 3 s. pl. acemite. 4 artículos de calidad o precio mediano.
middy (mi·di) s. (fam.) guardia marina. 2 *~ blouse*, marinera [blusa para mujeres y niños].
midge (midý) s. ENT. cagachín; mosca de agua. 2 enano.
midget (mi·dýit) s. enano, liliputiense.
Midianite (mi·diænait) s. BIBL. madianita.
midland (mi·dland) adj. de tierra adentro, interior. 2 s. interior, corazón [de un país].
midnight (-nait) s. medianoche. 2 adj. de la media noche, oscuro: *~ Mass*, misa del gallo; *~ sun*, sol de medianoche.
midrib (-rib) s. BOT. nervio central.
midriff (-rif) s. ANAT. diafragma.
mid-sea s. alta mar.
midship (-ship) adj. MAR. del medio o en medio del buque.
midshipman (-mæn) s. MAR. alférez alumno, guardia marina.
midships (-s) adv. MAR. en la parte media del buque. 2 s. pl. parte media del buque.
midst (midst) s. centro, medio: *in the ~ of*, en medio de, entre; en lo más recio de.
midstream (-strim) s. el medio de una corriente o río.
midsummer (-sømør) s. canícula, solsticio estival; pleno verano: *Midsummer Day*, día de San Juan.
midway (-wei) s. mitad del camino. 2 avenida central [de una exposición, etc.]. 3 adj. situado a mitad del camino. 4 adv. a mitad del camino.

midweek (-wik) s. mediados de la semana.
midwife (-waif) s. partera, comadrona.
midwife (to) tr.-intr. partear.
midwifery (-waifri) s. partería, obstetricia.
midwinter (-wintør) s. solsticio hiemal; pleno invierno.
mien (min) s. semblante, aire, continente.
miff (mif) s. desavenencia, disgusto, enojo.
miff (to) tr. disgustar, ofender. 2 intr. ofenderse.
might (mait) pretérito de MAY. 2 s. poderío, fuerza, energía: *with ~ and main*, con todas sus fuerzas, a más no poder.
mightily (-ili) adv. poderosamente. 2 muchísimo.
mightiness (-inis) s. poder, poderío. 2 fuerza, potencia. 3 grandeza.
mighty (-i) adj. poderoso. 2 potente, vigoroso. 3 importante, grande, enorme, violento. 5 adv. fam. muy, sumamente.
mignonette (miñøne·t) s. BOT. reseda.
migraine (maigrei·n) s. migraña, jaqueca.
migrant (mai·grant) adj.-s. que efectúa una migración. 2 de paso [ave].
migrate (to) (mai·greit) intr. pasar de un lugar o país a otro; emigrar.
migration (maigre·shøn) s. migración.
migratory (mai·gratori) adj. migratorio.
mihrab (mira·b) s. mihrab.
Mikado (mika·dou) s. micado.
Mike (maik) n. pr. dim. de MICHAEL.
mil (mil) s. milésima de pulgada.
milady (milei·di) s. miladi.
Milanese (milani·ś) n. pr. milanés.
milch (milch) adj. que da leche: *~ cow*, vaca lechera.
mild (maild) adj. apacible, blando, suave. 2 manso, dócil. 3 leve, ligero, moderado, templado. 4 dúctil, maleable.
mildew (mi·ldiu) s. AGR. mildin; añublo. 2 moho [orgánico].
mildew (to) tr.-intr. AGR. atacar o ser atacado de mildiu; añublar (se; enmohecer (se.
mildly (mai·ldli) adv. suavemente, dócilmente. 2 con lenidad. 3 ligeramente, moderadamente.
mildness (mai·ldnis) s. suavidad, benignidad. 2 lenidad, indulgencia. 3 mansedumbre. 4 levedad, moderación. 5 templanza [del clima].
mile (mail) s. milla [1.609 m.]: *~ stone*, piedra miliaria.
mileage (-idý) s. longitud o recorrido en millas. 2 gastos de viaje que se abonan por millas: *~ book*, carnet kilométrico.
Milesian (mili·shian) adj. milesio.
milfoil (mi·lfoil) s. BOT. milenrama, aquilea.
miliary (-ieri) adj. ANAT., MED. miliar.
militancy (-itansi) s. belicosidad, combatividad.
militant (-itant) adj. militante. 2 combativo.
militarism (-itariśm) s. militarismo.
militarist (-t) s. militarista.
militarize (to) (-aiś) tr. militarizar.
military (-iteri) adj. militar. 2 castrense. 3 s. *the ~*, los militares, las tropas.
militate (to) (-iteit) intr. militar: *to ~ against*, militar contra.
militia (mili·sha) s. milicia, guardia nacional.
militiaman (-mæn) s. miliciano.
milk (milk) s. leche: *~ can*, lechera [vasija]; *~ food*, lactinio; *~ sugar*, lactosa; *~ thistle*, cardo lechero; *~ tooth*, diente de leche. 2 lechada [de cal]. 3 BOT. látex. 4 jugo lechoso.
milk (to) tr. ordeñar. 2 fig. chupar, extraer. 3 intr. dar leche.

milk-and-water *adj.* débil [de carácter]. 2 ñoño.
milker (-ø^r) *s.* ordeñador, ordeñadora. 2 animal que da leche.
milking (-ing) *s.* ordeño.
milkmaid (-meid) *s.* lechera; criada de vaquería.
milkman (-mæn) *s.* lechero.
milksop (-sap) *s.* mantecón, marica.
milkwort (-uø^rt) *s.* BOT. polígala.
milky (-i) *adj.* lechoso, lácteo: *Milky Way*, Vía Láctea. 2 fig. tímido, apocado.
mill (mil) *s.* molino: *to go through the ~, to put through the ~*, fig. aprender, hacer aprender por experiencia; entrenarse o entrenar rigurosamente. 2 fábrica, taller. 3 hilandería, fábrica de hilados; fábrica de tejidos. 4 ingenio [de azúcar]. 5 MEC. fresadora. 7 prensa [para estrujar]. 8 volante [para acuñar]. 9 nombre de varias máquinas. 10 pop. pugilato. 11 (E.U.) milésima de dólar.
mill (to) *tr.* moler, triturar. 2 acordonar [monedas]. 3 batanar. 4 aserrar. 5 MEC. fresar. 6 producir, transformar [en fábrica]. 7 batir [hacer espumoso]. 8 pegar, dar una paliza a. 9 *intr.* arremolinarse. 10 dar vueltas en círculo [el ganado]. 11 pop. luchar a puñetazos.
millboard (-bo^rd) *s.* cartón para encuadernar.
millclapper (-klæpø^r) *s.* cítola, tarabilla.
milldam (-dæm) *s.* presa, represa.
millenarian (miløne·rian) *adj.* milenario.
millenary (mi·løneri) *adj.-s.* milenario.
millennial (mile·nial) *adj.* del milenio.
millennium (-iøm) *s.* milenio.
millepede (mi·lipid) *s.* ZOOL. cardador [miriápodo].
miller (mi·lø^r) *s.* molinero. 2 pop. boxeador, púgil. 3 ENT. polilla blanca.
millesimal (mile·simal) *adj.-s.* milésimo, -ma.
millet (mi·lit) *s.* BOT. mijo.
milliard (mi·lia^rd) *s.* mil millones.
milliary (-eri) *adj.* miliar [piedra, columna].
milligram, milligramme (-græm) *s.* miligramo.
milliliter, millilitre (-litø^r) *s.* mililitro.
millimeter, millimetre (-mitø^r) *s.* milímetro.
milliner (-nø^r) *s.* modista de sombreros.
millinery (-neri) *s.* sombreros de señora. 2 ocupación o tienda de la modista de sombreros.
milling (-ing) *s.* molienda, moltura. 2 fabricación. 3 batanado. 4 MEC. fresado. ~ *machine*, fresadora.
million (mi·liøn) *s.* millón.
millionaire (-eø^r) *s.* millonario.
millionth (-z) *adj.-s.* millonésimo.
millipede (-pid) *s.* MILLEPEDE.
millpond (mi·lpand) *s.* alberca o represa de molino.
millrace (-reis) *s.* caz, saetín [de molino].
millstone (-stoun) *s.* muela de molino.
millwork (-uø^rk) *s.* obra de molino, fábrica o taller. 2 carpintería mecánica.
milord (milo·^rd) *s.* milord.
milreis (-reis) *s.* milreis.
milt (milt) *s.* ANAT. bazo. 2 lecha [de los peces].
Miltiades (miltai·ædiš) *n. pr.* Milcíades.
mimbar (mi·mba^r) *s.* mimbar.
mime (maim) *s.* TEAT. mimo. 2 payaso, bufón.
mimesis (mimi·sis) *s.* RET., BIOL. mimesis.
mimetic (al (mime·tik(al) *adj.* mímico, imitativo.
mimetism (mi·mitišm) *s.* BIOL. mimetismo.
mimic (mi·mik) *adj.* mímico. 2 imitativo. 3 *s.* pantomimo; imitador.
mimic (to) *tr.* imitar, parecer. 2 imitar, remedar

[esp. por burla]. ¶ Pret. y p. p.: *mimicked;* ger.: -*cking.*
mimicry (-ri) *s.* imitación, remedo, monería. 2 ZOOL. mimetismo.
mimographer (mima·grafø^r) *s.* mimógrafo.
mimosa (mimou·sa) *s.* BOT. mimosa, sensitiva.
mimosaceous (mimøsei·shøs) *adj.* BOT. mimosáceo.
minacious (minei·shøs) *adj.* amenazador.
minaret (minare·t) *s.* alminar.
minatory (mi·natori) *adj.* amenazador.
mince (mins) *s.* cosa picada o desmenuzada; picadillo: ~ *pie*, pastel de carne picada y frutas. 2 afectación.
mince (to) *tr.* desmenuzar; picar [carne]. 2 medir [las palabras]; andar con rodeos [al hablar de]: *without mincing words*, sin rodeos, sin morderse la lengua. 3 atenuar, suavizar. 4 hacer o decir [algo] remilgadamente. 5 *intr.* andar, hablar, etc., de un modo afectado o remilgado.
mincemeat (-mɪt) *s.* picadillo; carne picada con frutas, etc.
mincing (-ing) *adj.* afectado, remilgado.
mincingly (-i) *adj.* con afectación. 2 a pedacitos, a pasitos.
mind (maind) *s.* mente, espíritu, entendimiento, juicio: *to be in one's right ~*, estar en sus cabales, estar en su juicio; *to go out of one's ~, to lose one's ~*, perder el juicio. 2 mentalidad. 3 espíritu, ánimo, estado de ánimo. 4 intención, propósito, deseo, inclinación, gusto: *to be in two minds*, dudar, vacilar, estar indeciso; *to have a ~*, tener ganas de, estar por [hacer una cosa]; *to know one's ~*, a gusto de uno. 5 pensamiento, mientes, memoria, recuerdo: *to bear*, o *keep*, *in ~*, tener presente, tener en cuenta; *to come to ~*, venir a las mientes; *to pass out of ~*, caer en el olvido; *to put in ~*, recordar [hacer recordar]; *out of ~*, olvidado; inmemorial. 6 pensamiento, opinión, parecer: *to be of one ~*, estar de acuerdo, pensar igual; *to change one's ~*, mudar de opinión, de parecer; *of one ~*, unánimes; *with one ~*, unánimemente.
mind (to) *tr.* notar, observar. 2 considerar, tener en cuenta; mirar, fijarse en. 3 dar importancia a, hacer caso, preocuparse de; tener inconveniente en; molestarle a uno [una cosa]: *do you ~ the smoke?*, ¿le molesta el humo? 4 obedecer, escuchar. 5 cuidar de, atender, ocuparse de: ~ *your own business*, métase en lo que le importa. 6 tener cuidado con: ~ *the step!*, ¡cuidado con el escalón! 7 recordar, acordarse de. 8 *intr. never ~*, no importa, no haga caso, no se preocupe. 9 *mind!*, ¡cuidado!
minded (-id) *adj.* dispuesto, inclinado, intencionado [esp. en composición].
mindful (-ful) *adj.* atento, cuidadoso. 2 ~ *of*, atento a, que tiene presente.
midfulness (-fulnis) *s.* atención, cuidado.
mindless (-lis) *adj.* tonto, necio. 2 descuidado; que no recuerda o no tiene en cuenta.
1) mine (main) *pron. pos.* mío, mía, míos, mías: *this hat is ~*, este sombrero es mío o el mío; *a friend of ~*, un amigo mío. 2 *adj.-pos.* poét. mi, mis, mío, mía, míos, mías.
2) mine *s.* MIN., FORT., MIL. mina. 2 MAR. mina submarina: ~ *sweeper*, dragaminas. 3 fig. mina [de noticias, etc.].
mine (to) *tr.* minar. 2 extraer [mineral]; beneficiar [un filón]. 3 *intr.* hacer minas. 4 dedicarse a la minería.

miner (-ø^r) *s.* minero. *2* minador, zapador. *3* ZOOL. cavador.

mineral (mi·nø*ral*) *adj.* mineral: ~ *kingdom*, reino mineral; ~ *water*, agua mineral. *2 s.* mineral [substancia inorgánica]. *3* MIN. mineral.

mineralize (to) (mi·nøralaiš) *tr.* mineralizar.

mineralogist (minøræ·lodÿist) *s.* mineralogista.

mineralogy (minøræ·lodÿi) *s.* mineralogía.

minever (mi·nivø^r) *s.* MINIVER.

mingle (to) (mi·ngøl) *tr.* mezclar; entremezclar. *2* preparar [mezclando]. *3 intr.* mezclarse, confundirse; juntarse.

Minho (mai·ñou) *n. pr.* GEOGR. Miño.

miniate (to) (mi·nieit) *tr.* pintar con minio, miniar.

miniature (-achø^r) *s.* miniatura: ~ *painter*, miniaturista.

minify (to) (-fai) *tr.* empequeñecer, disminuir.

minim (mi·nim) *m.* cosa o pers. pequeña, insignificante. *2* pizca. *3* MÚS. mínima. *4* (con may.) mínimo [religioso].

minimal (-al) *adj.* mínimo.

minimize (to) (-aiš) *tr.* reducir al mínimo. *2* menospreciar, tener en poco.

minimum (-øm) *s.* mínimo, minimum. *2 adj.* mínimo.

mining (-øm) *s.* minería, mineraje. *2* acción de minar. *3 adj.* minero; de minas.

minion (mi·niøn) *s.* favorito, paniaguado, seguidor servil. *2* esbirro. *3* IMPR. miñona [tipo]. *4 adj.* lindo, delicado.

minister (mi·nistø^r) *s.* ministro [en todas sus acepciones]: ~ *plenipotentiary*, ministro plenipotenciario. *2* pastor protestante.

minister (to) *tr.* dar, suministrar. *2 intr.* oficiar, ministrar. *3* asistir, auxiliar. *4* tender, contribuir.

ministerial (ministi·rial) *adj.* ministerial. *2* sacerdotal. *3* gubernativo. *4* que obra como agente, instrumento o medio.

ministerialism (-ism) *s.* ministerialismo.

ministrant (mini·strant) *s.* ministrante. *2* oficiante.

ministration (-ei·shøn) *s.* suministración. *2* ayuda, agencia, solicitud, cuidado. *3* ECLES. ministerio.

ministry (mi·nistri) *s.* ministerio, oficio, ayuda, intervención. *2* POL. ministerio. *3* ECLES. ministerio. *4* clero, conjunto de ministros.

minium (mi·niøm) *s.* QUÍM. minio.

mink (mink) *s.* ZOOL. visón. *2* piel de visón.

minnow (mi·nou) *s.* cierto pez de agua dulce.

minor (mai·nø^r) *adj.* menor [menos importante, de poca importancia], secundario, inferior: ~ *orders*, órdenes menores. *2* menor de edad. *3* MÚS. menor; ~ *key*, tono menor. *4 adj.-s.* LÓG. menor. *5 s.* menor [de edad]. *6* menor, minorita [religioso]. *7* (E.U.) asignatura de importancia secundaria.

Minorca (mino·^{r}ka) *n. pr.* GEOGR. Menorca.

minority (maina·riti) *s.* minoridad, minoría, menor edad. *2* minoría [los menos]. *3 adj.* minoritario.

minotaur (mi·noto^r) *n. pr.* MIT. Minotauro.

minster (mi·nstø^r) *s.* iglesia de monasterio. *2* basílica, catedral.

minstrel (-trøl) *s.* trovador, juglar, ministril. *2* (E.U.) cantor cómico.

mint (mint) *s.* casa de moneda, ceca. *2* fig. mina, fuente inagotable, gran cantidad: *a* ~ *of money*, un dineral. *3* BOT. menta. *4* pastilla de menta.

mint (to) *tr.* acuñar [moneda]. *2* fig. fabricar, inventar [una palabra, una frase, etc.].

mintage (-idÿ) *s.* acuñación. *2* monedaje. *3* BOT. menta. *4* pastilla de menta.

mint (to) *tr.* acuñar [moneda]. *2* fig. fabricar, inventar [una palabra, una frase, etc.].

mintage (-idÿ) *s.* acuñación. *2* monedaje. *3* moneda acuñada.

minuend (mi·niuend) *s.* ARIT. minuendo.

minuet (miniue·t) *s.* minué, minuete.

minus (mai·nøs) *prep.-adj.* menos: ~ *sign*, signo menos. *2* falto de, sin. *3 adj.* MAT., ELECT. negativo. *4 s.* MAT. signo menos. *5* cantidad negativa.

1) minute (mainiu·t) *adj.* menudo, pequeño, diminuto. *2* nimio, minucioso.

2) minute (mi·nit) *s.* minuto [división de la hora o del grado]: ~ *hand*, minutero; *up to the* ~, al corriente; *de última hora*. *2* momento, instante. *3* minuta, nota, apuntamiento. *4 pl.* acta [de una junta, etc.].

minute (to) *tr.* cronometrar. *2* minutar, anotar; poner en el acta.

minutely (mainiu·tli) *adv.* minuciosamente; detalladamente. *2* (mi·nitli) de minuto en minuto.

minuteman (mi·nitmæn) *s.* (E.U.) HIST. miliciano de la Revolución.

minutiae (miniu·shi) *s. pl.* minucias.

minx (minks) *s.* moza descarada, bribona. *2* ZOOL. marta.

Miocene (mai·øsin) *adj.-s.* GEOL. mioceno.

miracle (mi·rakøl) *s.* milagro: *to a* ~, perfectamente. *2* TEAT. *miracle* o ~ *play* auto [drama religioso].

miraculous (miræ·kiuløs) *adj.* milagroso. *2* maravilloso, prodigioso.

mirage (mira·ø^{r}dÿ) *s.* espejismo, miraje.

mire (mai·ø^r) *s.* cieno, lodo, fango. *2* cenagal.

mire (to) *tr.* enlodar. *2* hundir en el cieno; atascar, atollar.

Miriam (mi·riam) *n. pr.* María.

mirific (miri·fic) *adj.* mirífico.

mirk (mø^{r}k) *s.* MURK.

mirky (-i) *adj.* MURKY.

mirror (mi·rø^r) *s.* espejo.

mirror (to) *tr.* reflejar [una imagen]. *2 intr.* reflejarse, retratarse; mirarse [en un espejo].

mirth (mø^{r}z) *s.* alegría, regocijo, hilaridad.

mirthful (-ful) *adj.* alegre, regocijado, jovial.

mirthless (-lis) *adj.* triste, melancólico.

miry (mai·ri) *adj.* cenagoso, lodoso, fangoso.

misadventure (misadve·nchø^r) *s.* desgracia, percance.

misadvised (-vai·šd) *adj.* mal aconsejado.

misalliance (misalai·ans) *s.* casamiento desigual.

misanthrope (mi·sanzroup) *s.* misántropo.

misanthropic (al (misanzra·pik(al) *adj.* misantrópico.

misanthropy (misæ·nzrøpi) *s.* misantropía.

misapply (to) (misaplai·) *tr.* usar o emplear mal; hacer mal uso de.

misapprehend (to) (-prije·nd) *tr.* entender mal.

misapprehension (-prije·nshøn) *s.* equivocación; mala inteligencia, concepto erróneo.

misappropriate (to) (-prou·prieit) *tr.* malversar. *2* distraer [fondos].

misbecoming (-bikø·ming) *adj.* impropio, indigno; que sienta o cae mal.

misbegot(ten (-bigø·(tøn) *adj.* bastardo.

misbehave (to) (-bijei·v) *intr.* portarse mal.

misbehaved (-d) *adj.* malcriado, descortés.

misbehaviour (-iø^r) *s.* mal comportamiento. *2* descortesía.

misbelief (misbili·f) *s.* error, herejía, falsa creencia.

misbelieve (to) (-v) *intr.* tener creencias erróneas. *2 tr.* no creer, no dar crédito a.

misbeliever (-øʳ) *s.* hereje, infiel. *2* incrédulo.

misbirth (-bøˑʳz) *s.* aborto, parto prematuro.

miscalculate (to) (-kæˑlkiuleit) *tr.* calcular mal.

miscall (to) (-koˑl) *tr.* nombrar impropiamente.

miscarriage (-kæˑridȳ) *s.* aborto. *2* malogro. *3* extravío. *4* desmán.

miscarry (to) (-kæˑri) *intr.* abortar, malparir. *2* malograrse. *3* extraviarse [una carta].

miscellanea (miseleiˑnia) *s. pl.* miscelánea.

miscellaneous (miseleiˑniøs) *adj.* misceláneo.

miscellany (miˑseleini) *s.* miscelánea.

mischance (mischæˑns) *s.* desgracia, mala suerte, fatalidad, percance.

mischarge (to) (-chaˑʳdȳ) *tr.* cargar en cuenta indebidamente.

mischief (-chif) *s.* mal, daño, perjuicio: *to make ~*, enredar, meter cizaña. *2* travesura, diablura. *3* persona molesta; diablillo.

mischief-maker *s.* enredador, cizañero.

mischievous (-vøs) *adj.* malo, dañino. *2* enredador, chismoso. *3* travieso, malicioso, juguetón.

miscible (miˑsibøl) *adj.* miscible.

misconceive (to) (miscønsiˑv) *intr.* entender mal.

misconception (-kønseˑpshøn) *s.* concepto erróneo, mala interpretación.

misconduct (-kaˑndøkt) *s.* mala conducta. *2* dirección o administración.

misconduct (to) (miskøndøˑkt) *tr.* dirigir o administrar mal. *2 to ~ oneself*, conducirse mal.

misconstruction (-kønstrøˑkshøn) *s.* error, mala interpretación.

misconstrue (to) (-kønstruˑ) *tr.* interpretar equivocadamente. *2* torcer el sentido de.

miscount (-kauˑnt) *s.* error de cuenta.

miscreant (miˑskriɑnt) *s.* malandrín, bribón.

miscue (miskiuˑ) *s. fam.* error, desacierto.

miscue (to) *intr.* BILLAR pifiar.

misdate (to) (-deˑt) *tr.* poner fecha equivocada; fechar falsamente.

misdeed (-dɪˑd) *s.* fechoría, mala acción.

misdemeanour (-dimɪˑnøʳ) *s.* mala conducta. *2* fechoría, mala acción. *3* DER. delito menos grave.

misdirect (to) (-direˑkt) *tr.* dirigir erradamente.

misdoer (misduˑøʳ) *s.* malhechor, delincuente, el que obra mal.

misdoing (-duˑing) *s.* yerro. *2* mal obrar; mala acción, delito.

misemploy (to) (-emploˑi) *tr.* emplear mal.

miser (maiˑsøʳ) *adj.-s.* mísero, avaro, roñoso.

miserable (miˑsørabøl) *adj.* miserable, mísero. *2* desdichado, infeliz. *3* que causa molestia o infelicidad. *4* lastimoso.

Miserere (miśørɪˑri) *s.* LITURG. Miserere.

misericorde (-rikoˑʳd) *s.* misericordia [puñal]. *2* misericordia, coma [de silla de coro].

miserly (maiˑsøʳli) *adj.* avaro, tacaño, roñoso.

misery (miˑsøri) *s.* miseria, laceria. *2* desdicha, infelicidad. *3* aflicción, pena, angustia, dolor, sufrimiento.

misfeasance (misfɪˑśans) *s.* abuso de autoridad.

misfire (-faiˑøʳ) *s.* acción de fallar [un arma de fuego, el encendido de un motor, etc.].

misfire (to) *intr.* fallar [un arma de fuego, el encendido de un motor, etc.].

misfit (to) (misfiˑt) *tr.-intr.* no sentar o ajustar bien, no ser propio o a propósito. *2* no encajar.

misfortune (-foˑʳchøn) *s.* infortunio, desdicha, desgracia.

misgive (to) (-giˑv) *tr.* dar dudas o temores [díc. del pensamiento o el corazón]. *2 intr.* recelar, temer.

misgiving (-ing) *s.* presentimiento, recelo, temor.

misgotten (-gaˑtøn) *adj.* mal adquirido.

misgovernment (-gøˑvøʳmøn) *s.* desgobierno, desbarajuste, mala administración.

misguide (to) (-gaiˑd) *tr.* dirigir mal; aconsejar mal, desencaminar, descarriar, engañar.

mishandle (to) (-jæˑndøl) *tr.* manejar mal; maltratar.

mishap (-jæˑp) *s.* mala suerte, desgracia. *2* percance, contratiempo. *3* desliz, tropiezo.

mishear (-jiˑøʳ) *tr.* oír mal, trasoír.

misinform (to) (-infoˑʳm) *intr.* informar o enterar mal.

misinformation (-eiˑshøn) *s.* noticia o informes falsos.

misinterpret (to) (intøˑrprit) *tr.* interpretar mal.

misjudge (to) (-ȳøˑdȳ) *tr.* juzgar mal, erróneamente o injustamente.

mislay (to) (-lei) *tr.* colocar fuera de su sitio; extraviar, perder; traspapelar.

mislead (to) (-lɪd) *tr.* desencaminar, descarriar, despistar. *2* inducir a error, engañar; seducir.

mismanage (to) (mæˑnidȳ) *tr.* manejar o administrar mal.

mismanagement (-møn) *s.* mala administración, desgobierno.

misname (to) (-neiˑm) *tr.* nombrar equivocadamente.

misnomer (-ouˑmøʳ) *s.* nombre equivocado.

misogynist (misa·dȳinist) *s.* misógino.

misogynous (-øs) *adj.* misógino.

misoneism (misonɪˑism) *s.* misoneísmo.

misplace (to) (mispleiˑs) *tr.* poner fuera de su sitio; colocar mal. *2* extraviar, traspapelar.

misprint (-priˑnt) *s.* errata, error de imprenta.

misprint (to) *tr.* imprimir con erratas.

misprize (to) (-praiˑś) *tr.* menospreciar.

mispronounce (to) (-prønauˑns) *tr.* pronunciar mal.

misquotation (-kuoteiˑshøn) *s.* cita falsa o equivocada.

misrate (to) (-reiˑt) *tr.* valuar, tasar mal.

misread (to) (-rɪd) *tr.* leer mal.

misrepresent (to) (-repriśeˑnt) *tr.* desfigurar, tergiversar, falsear.

misrepresentation (-eiˑshøn) *s.* noticia o relación falsa; tergiversación; falsedad.

misrule (-ruˑl) *s.* desgobierno, mal gobierno.

misrule (to) *tr.* desgobernar, gobernar mal.

Miss (mis) *s.* señorita [antepuesto al nombre]. *2* (con min.) señorita, joven.

miss *s.* acción de errar el tiro, el golpe, etc.; errada; fracaso, malogro. *2* falta, pérdida.

miss (to) *tr.* errar [el blanco, la vocación, etc.]. *2* no dar con, no hallar; no coger, no obtener. *3* no ver, no oír, no comprender: *to ~ the point*, no ver la intención. *4* perder [un tren, la ocasión, etc.]. *5* omitir. *6* escapar, evitar: *he barely missed being killed*, por poco se mata o lo matan. *7* echar de menos, sentir o advertir la falta de. *8 to ~ fire*, fallar [un arma]. *9 intr.* errar el blanco. *10* fallar, no surtir efecto.

missal (miˑsal) *s.* LITURG. misal. *2* devocionario.

missel thrush (miˑsøl) *s.* ORN. cagaceite.

misshape (to) (-sheiˑp) *tr.* deformar, afear.

misshapen (-øn) *adj.* deformado, deforme, monstruoso.

missile (mi·sil) *adj.* arrojadizo. 2 *s.* proyectil. 3 arma arrojadiza.

missing (mi·sing) *adj.* extraviado, perdido, que falta: *to be* ~, faltar, estar extraviado o perdido.

mission (mi·shøn) *s.* misión. 2 organización religiosa y benéfica.

missionary (-eri) *adj.* misional. 2 *s.* misionero. 3 misionario.

missis (mi·siš) *s.* fam. señora. 2 ama de casa. 3 esposa.

Mississipi (misisi·pi) *n. pr.* GEOGR. Misisipí.

missive (mi·siv) *adj.* misivo. 2 *s.* carta, misiva.

Missouri (mišu·ri) *n. pr.* GEOGR. Misuri.

misspell (to) (misspe·l) *tr.* deletrear mal. 2 escribir con mala ortografía.

misspend (to) (-spend) *tr.* malgastar.

misstate (to) (-stei·t) *tr.* relatar o afirmar falsamente; desfigurar [un hecho].

misstatement (-mønt) *s.* relación o aserción falsa o equivocada; error.

misstep (-ste·p) *s.* paso en falso; desliz, tropiezo.

missus (mi·søš) *s.* MISSIS.

missy (mi·si) *s.* fam. señorita.

mist (mist) *s.* niebla, vapor, calígine, vaho, llovizna. 2 nube, confusión, obscurecimiento.

mist (to) *intr.* anublarse [el tiempo]; lloviznar. 2 anublarse; empañarse [los ojos]. 3 *tr.* nublar, empañar.

mistake (mistei·k) *s.* equivocación, error, confusión: *to make a* ~, equivocarse; *and no* ~, fam. sin duda alguna; *by* ~, por equivocación, por descuido.

mistake (to) *tr.* equivocar; confundir, tomar [una pers. o cosa] por otra; entender mal. ¶ Pret.: *mistook;* p. p.: *-taken.*

mistaken (-øn) *p. p.* de TO MISTAKE. 2 *adj.* equivocado, errado, engañado. 3 erróneo, incorrecto.

Mister (mi·stør) *s.* Señor [tratamiento de cortesía usado delante del nombre].

mistimed (mistai·md) *adj.* inoportuno; extemporáneo, intempestivo.

mistiness (mi·stinis) *s.* calígine, oscuridad.

mistletoe (mi·søltou) *s.* BOT. muérdago, liga.

mistook (mistu·k) *pret. p. p.* de TO MISTAKE.

mistral (mi·stral) *s.* mistral [viento].

mistreat (to) (mistri·t) *tr.* maltratar.

mistress (mi·stris) *s.* ama, dueña, señora. 2 señora de la casa. 3 directora [de una escuela]. 4 maestra. 5 querida, manceba. 6 cortejo, novia. 7 fam. señora, esposa. 8 (con may.) Señora [tratamiento de cortesía].

mistrust (mistrø·st) *s.* desconfianza, suspicacia.

mistrust (to) *tr.* desconfiar de, recelar.

mistrustful (-ful) *adj.* desconfiado, que desconfía, receloso.

misty (mi·sti) *adj.* brumoso, nublado, caliginoso. 2 empañado. 3 confuso, vago, distinto.

misunderstand (to) (misøndø'stæ·nd) *tr.* entender o interpretar mal.

misunderstanding (-ing) *s.* equivocación, error, mala inteligencia, mala interpretación. 2 desavenencia.

misusage (misiu·sidÿ) *s.* maltrato. 2 MISUSE.

misuse (misyu·s) *s.* mal uso, uso impropio; malversación [de fondos].

misuse (to) (misyu·š) *tr.* maltratar, tratar mal. 2 usar o emplear mal. 3 malversar [fondos].

mite (mait) *s.* ZOOL. ácaro. 2 pizca; pequeñez. 3 criatura, enano. 4 *one's* ~, su óbolo.

miter (-ø') *s.* MITRE.

miter (to) *tr.* TO MITRE.

mitigate (to) (mi·tigeit) *tr.* mitigar, disminuir, atenuar, suavizar, paliar.

mitigation (-ei·shøn) *s.* mitigación.

mitigative (mi·tigeitiv) *adj.-s.* mitigativo, lenitivo, paliativo.

mitosis (mitou·sis) *s.* BIOL. mitosis.

mitral (mai·tral) *adj.* mitral.

mitre (mai·tø') *s.* mitra. 2 CARP. inglete. 3 ~ *sill,* busco [de la esclusa].

mitre (to) *tr.* conferir una mitra a. 2 CARP. ingletear.

mitred (-d) *adj.* mitrado.

mitt (mit) *s.* mitón, confortante. 2 guante sin división para los dedos, excepto para el pulgar. 3 guante de béisbol.

mitten (-øn) *s.* MITT 1 y 2. 2 *to get,* o *give, the* ~, recibir o dar calabazas. 3 *pl.* guantes de boxeo.

mix (miks) *s.* mezcla [de ingredientes]. 2 fam. ~ *up,* lío, embrollo, confusión.

mix (to) *tr.* mezclar, mixturar, barajar. 2 preparar, hacer, amasar [mezclando]. 3 aderezar [ensalada]. 4 *to* ~ *up,* mezclar; confundir; *to be mixed up in* o *with,* tener que ver con [un asunto feo]. 5 *intr.* mezclarse. 6 juntarse, tratarse, alternar. 7 tomar parte. ¶ Pret. y p. p.: *mixed* o *mixt.*

mixed (-t) *adj.* mezclado, barajado. 2 mixto: ~ *number,* número mixto; ~ *train,* tren mixto. 3 misceláneo, variado. 4 formado de gente muy distinta; poco selecto. 5 ~ *up,* confundido, aturdido.

mixer (-ø') *s.* mezclador. 2 fam. (E.U.) persona sociable.

mixtilineal, mixtilinear (mikstili·nial, -nia') *adj.* GEOM. mixtilíneo.

mixture (mi·kschø') *s.* mezcla, mixtura.

mizen, mizzen (mi·šøn) *s.* MAR. mesana.

mizzenmast (-mæst) *s.* MAR. palo de mesana.

mnemonic(al (nima·nık(al) *adj.* mnemotécnico.

mnemonics (-s) *s.* mnemónica, mnemotecnia.

Moabite (mou·abait) *adj.-m.* moabita.

moan (moun) *s.* gemido, quejido, lamento. 2 murmullo [de las olas].

moan (to) *intr.* gemir, quejarse, lamentarse. 2 *tr.* llorar, deplorar.

moanful (-ful) *adj.* plañidero.

moat (mout) *s.* FORT. foso.

moat (to) *tr.* rodear con fosos.

mob (mab) *s.* populacho, chusma; turba, turbamulta. 2 gentío, tropel.

mob (to) *tr.* atacar, rodear tumultuosamente. 2 *intr.* tumultuarse. ¶ Pret. y p. p.: *mobbed;* ger.: -*bbing.*

mobcap (-kæp) *s.* toca o cofia de mujer.

mobile (mou·bil) *adj.* móvil. 2 inconstante, variable.

mobility (moubi·liti) *s.* movilidad. 2 inconstancia.

mobilization (moubilišei·shøn) *s.* movilización.

mobilize (to) (mou·bilaiš) *tr.* movilizar.

moccasin (ma·kasin) *s.* mocasín [calzado, serpiente].

Mocha (mou·ka) *n. pr.* GEOGR. Moca. 2 *s.* (con min.) moca [café].

mock (mak) *adj.* ficticio, falso, imitado. 2 fingido, burlesco. 3 BOT. ~ *cypress,* mirabel; ~ *orange,* jeringuilla. 4 *s.* burla, mofa, irrisión. 5 remedo.

mock (to) *tr.* mofarse de, burlarse de, escarnecer; reírse [de]; engañar. 2 imitar, remedar. 3 *intr. to* ~ *at,* burlarse de.

mockery (-øri) *s.* burla, mofa, escarnio. 2 remedo, imitación.

mock-heroic *adj.* épico-burlesco.

moking (-ing) *adj.* burlón, mofador.
mockingbird (-bø·ʳd) *s.* ORN. sinsonte.
modal (mou·dal) *adj.* modal.
modality (modæ·liti) *s.* modalidad.
mode (moud) *s.* modo, manera. *2* GRAM., LÓG., ME-TAL., MÚS. modo. *3* moda, estilo, uso.
model (ma·døl) *s.* modelo. *2* patrón, plantilla. *3* diseño, muestra. *4* figurín. *5* dechado, ejemplo. *6 adj.* modelo: ~ *school*, escuela modelo.
model (to) *tr.* modelar, formar, moldear. *2 intr.* posar como modelo. ¶ Pret. y p. p.: *model(l)ed;* ger.: *-l(l)ing.*
model(l)er (-øʳ) *s.* modelador. *2* diseñador.
model(l)ing (-ing) *s.* B. ART. modelado.
model(l)ist (-ist) *s.* modelista.
moderate (ma·dørit) *adj.* moderado; templado. *2* morigerado. *3* mesurado. *4* módico. *5* mediano, regular. *6 s.* POL. moderado.
moderate (to) (ma·døreit) *tr.* moderar; templar; reprimir; morigerar. *2 tr.-intr.* presidir [una reunión, etc.]. *3 intr.* moderarse.
moderation (-ei·shøn) *s.* moderación: *in* ~, con moderación. *2* sobriedad, templanza. *3* mesura, comedimiento.
moderator (-eitøʳ) *s.* moderador. *2* concordador, árbitro. *3* MEC. regulador.
modern (ma·døʳn) *adj.* moderno.
modernism (-išm) *s.* modernismo.
modernist (-ist) *s.* modernista.
modernistic (-i·stik) *adj.* modernista.
modernity (mødø·ʳniti) *s.* modernidad.
modernize (to) (ma·døʳnaiš) *tr.* modernizar. *2 intr.* modernizarse.
modest (ma·dist) *adj.* modesto, recatado, decente. *2* modesto, humilde. *3* moderado [no excesivo].
modesty (-i) *s.* modestia. *2* pudor, recato, decencia.
modicum (ma·dikøm) *s.* poco, pequeña cantidad.
modification (madifikei·shøn) *s.* modificación.
modifier (ma·difaiøʳ) *s.* modificador. *2* GRAM. palabra modificativa.
modify (to) (-fai) *tr.* modificar. *2* moderar, templar, suavizar. *3 intr.* modificarse, variar. ¶ Pret. y p. p.: *modified.*
modillion (modi·liøn) *s.* ARQ. modillón.
modish (mou·dish) *adj.* a la moda, hecho a la moda.
modulate (to) (ma·diuleit) *tr.* modular. *2* regular, ajustar. *3 intr.* MÚS. modular.
modulation (madiulei·shøn) *s.* modulación.
modulator (ma·diuleitøʳ) *s.* modulador.
module (ma·dẏul) *s.* ARQ., HIDR., NUM. módulo.
modulus (ma·diuløs) *s.* MAT. módulo.
mof(f)ette (mofe·t) *s.* mofeta [gas].
Mogul (mogø·l) *s.* mogol: *the Great* ~, el Gran Mogol. *2 pl.* naipes de superior calidad.
mohair (mou·jeøʳ) *s.* mohair.
Mohammed (moujæ·mid) *n. pr.* Mahoma.
Mohammedan (moujæ·midan) *s.* mahometano.
Mohammedanism (-išm) *s.* mahometismo.
moiety (mo·ieti) *s.* mitad.
moil (to) (moul) *intr.* afanarse, trabajar sin descanso.
moire, moiré (muaʳ, muarei·) *s.* muaré.
moist (moist) *adj.* húmedo, mojado. *2* guanoso.
moisten (to) (moi·søn) *tr.* humedecer, humectar, mojar ligeramente. *2 intr.* humedecerse.
moisture (moi·schøʳ) *s.* humedad. *2* sudor.
molar (mou·laʳ) *adj.* ANAT., FÍS. molar. *2 s.* molar [diente].
molary (mou·lari) *adj.* molar.

molasses (mølæ·siš) *s.* melaza, melote.
mold, to mold, etc., MOULD, TO MOULD, etc.
Moldavian (maldæ·vian) *adj.-s.* moldavo.
mole (moul) *s.* MED. mola. *2* lunar. *3* rompeolas; dársena. *4* ZOOL. topo. *5* ENT. ~ *cricket*, cortón, grillotalpa.
molecular (møle·kiulaʳ) *adj.* molecular.
molecule (ma·likiul) *s.* molécula.
molehill (mou·ljil) *s.* topera, topinera. *2* (fig.) pequeño obstáculo, dificultad, etc.
moleskin (-skin) *s.* piel de topo. *2* especie de fustán. *3 pl.* pantalón de esta tela.
molest (to) (mole·st) *tr.* molestar, inquietar, vejar. *2* faltar al respeto [a una mujer].
molestation (molestei·shøn) *s.* molestia, vejación.
mollification (malifikei·shøn) *s.* molificación. *2* mitigación. *3* apaciguamiento.
molify (to) (ma·lifai) *tr.* molificar. *2* mitigar. *3* calmar, aplacar, apaciguar. ¶ Pret. y p. p.: *mollified.*
mollusc (ma·løsk) *s.* ZOOL. molusco.
Molly (ma·li) *n. pr. dim.* de MARY, Mariquita.
mollycoddle (-kadøl) *s.* marica, mantecón.
mollycoddle (to) *tr.* consentir, mimar.
Moloch (mou·lak) *n. pr.* MIT. Moloc. *2 s.* (con min.) ZOOL. moloc.
molt, to molt, MOULT, TO MOULT.
molten (mou·ltøn) *p. p. irreg.* de TO MELT. *2 adj.* fundido [metal].
molybdenum (moli·bdønøm) *s.* QUÍM. molibdeno.
moment (mou·mønt) *s.* momento, instante, coyuntura: *at any* ~, de un momento a otro; *for the* ~, de momento, por el momento. *2* momento, importancia. *3* MEC. momento.
momentarily (-erili) *adv.* momentáneamente. *2* instantáneamente.
momentary (-eri) *adj.* momentáneo. *2* que ocurre a cada momento.
momently (mou·møntli) *adv.* a cada momento. *2* por momentos. *3* por un momento.
momentous (moume·ntøs) *adj.* importante, grave, trascendental.
momentum (-øm) *s.* ímpetu, impulso, velocidad adquirida. *2* MEC. cantidad de movimiento.
Momus (mou·møs) *n. pr.* MIT. Momo.
monachal (ma·nakal) *adj.* monacal.
monachism (ma·nakišm) *s.* monaquismo, monacato.
monad (ma·næd) *s.* mónada.
monadelphous (manade·lføs) *adj.* BOT. monadelfo.
monadism (ma·nædišm) *s.* monadismo.
monarch (ma·naʳk) *s.* monarca.
monarchic (al (møna·ʳkik(al) *adj.* monárquico.
monarchism (ma·naʳkišm) *s.* monarquismo.
monarchist (-ist) *s.* monárquico.
monarchy (-i) *s.* monarquía.
monastery (ma·nasteri) *s.* monasterio, convento.
monastic(al (monæ·stik(al) *adj.* monástico.
Monday (mø·ndi) *s.* lunes.
monetary (mø·niteri) *adj.* monetario. *2* pecuniario.
monetize (to) (-aiš) *tr.* monetizar.
money (mø·ni) *s.* moneda, dinero: ~ *of account*, moneda de cuenta; *hard* ~, metálico; *ready* ~, dinero contante; ~ *changing*, cambio de moneda; ~ *order*, giro postal.
moneyage (-idẏ) *s.* monedaje.
moneybag (-bæg) *s.* talega, bolsa. *2 pl.* fam. talegas, riqueza. *3* fam. ricacho.
money-changer *s.* cambista.
moneyed (-d) *adj.* adinerado, acaudalado.

money-lender s. prestamista.
money-making s. lucro, ganancia. 2 prosperidad. 3 adj. lucrativo, provechoso.
monger (møˑngøʳ) s. tratante, traficante.
Mongol (maˑngøl) adj.-s. mogol, mongol.
Mongolia (mangouˑlia) n. pr. GEOGR. Mogolia.
Mongolian (-n) adj.-s. mogol, mongol, mongólico.
mongoose (maˑngus) s. ZOOL. mangosta.
mongrel (mønˑgrøl) adj.-s. mestizo. 2 s. animal o planta cruzados; perro de raza indefinida.
monism (maˑnišm) s. monismo.
monition (mouniˑshøn) s. aviso, consejo, advertencia, amonestación.
monitor (maˑnitoʳ) s. amonestador, admonitor. 2 instructor. 3 MAR., ZOOL. monitor.
monitor (to) tr. amonestar, advertir. 2 RADIO. controlar.
monk (mønk) s. monje, fraile.
monkery (-øri) s. monasterio. 2 vida monástica, frailía. 3 cosa de fraile.
monkey (-i) s. ZOOL. mono, mona, mico, simio. 2 fig. mono, mona [pers.]. 3 to make a ~ of, tomar el pelo a uno. 4 to get one's ~ up, montar en cólera. 5 adj. de mono: ~ trick, monería. 6 MEC. ~ wrench, llave inglesa.
monkey (to) tr. imitar, remedar. 2 intr. to ~ about, hacer payasadas. 3 to ~ with, enredar con.
monkeyshine (-shain) s. fam. (E.U.) monería, payasada.
monkhood (møˑnkjud) s. monacato. 2 los monjes.
monkish (møˑnkish) adj. monacal; frailesco.
monk's-hood s. BOT. acónito, anapelo.
monobasic (manøbeiˑsik) adj. QUÍM. monobásico.
monochord (maˑnøkoʳd) s. MÚS. monocordio.
monochrome (-kroum) adj. monocromo.
monocle (-køl) s. monóculo.
monocled (-køld) adj. con monóculo.
monoclinic (manøkliˑnik) adj. CRISTAL. monoclínico.
monocotyledon (manøkatilˑdøn) s. BOT. monocotiledónea.
monocular (mønaˑkiulaʳ) adj. monóculo. 2 para un solo ojo.
monody (maˑnødi) s. MÚS. monodia. 2 elegía.
monoecious (moniˑshøs) adj. BOT. monoico.
monogamous (mønaˑgamøs) adj. monógamo.
monogamy (-i) s. monogamia.
monogram (maˑnøgræm) s. monograma.
monograph (-f) s. monografía.
monolith (-liz) s. monolito.
monolithic (manøliˑzik) adj. monolítico.
monologist (maˑnolodgist) s. monologador.
monologize (to) (mønaˑlodẏaiš) intr. monologar.
monologue (maˑnølag) s. monólogo; soliloquio.
monomania (manømeiˑnia) s. monomanía.
monometallism (-eˑtališm) s. monometalismo.
monomial (manouˑmial) adj. MAT. de un solo término. 2 s. monomio.
monopetalous (manøpeˑtaløs) adj. BOT. monopétalo.
monophase (maˑnøfeiš) adj. ELECT. monofásico.
monoplane (-plein) s. monoplano.
monopolist (mønaˑpolist) s. monopolista.
monopolize (to) (-aiš) tr. monopolizar.
monopolizer (-šøʳ) s. monopolizador.
monopoly (-i) s. monopolio.
monopteral (-ptøral) adj. ARQ. monóptero.
monorail (maˑnøreil) s. vía de un solo riel.
monosepalous (manøseˑpaløs) adj. BOT. monosépalo.
monospermous (-spøʳmøs) adj. BOT. monospermo.

monosyllable (manøsiˑlabøl) s. monosílabo.
monotheism (maˑnøziišm) s. monoteísmo.
monotheist (-st) s. monoteísta.
monotone (-toun) s. monotonía; unisonancia.
monotone (to) tr. cantar, recitar, etc., en un tono uniforme.
monotonous (mønaˑtønøs) adj. monótono.
monotony (mønaˑtøni) s. monotonía. 2 unisonancia.
monotreme (maˑnøtrim) s. ZOOL. monotrema.
monotype (-taip) s. BIOL. representante único de un género, familia, etc. 2 IMPR. monotipia.
monovalent (-veiˑlønt) adj. QUÍM. monovalente.
monoxide (mønaˑksaid) s. QUÍM. monovalente.
Monseigneur (monseñøˑʳ) s. monseñor.
monsoon (mansuˑn) s. monzón.
monster (maˑnstøʳ) s. monstruo. 2 adj. monstruo, enorme.
monstrance (-trans) s. LITURG. custodia, ostensorio.
monstrosity (manstraˑsiti) s. monstruosidad.
monstrous (maˑnstrøs) adj. monstruoso.
monte (maˑnti) s. monte [juego de naipes].
month (mønz) s. mes.
monthly (-li) adj. mensual: ~ allowance, pay, etc., mensualidad, mesada. 2 menstrual. 3 s. publicación mensual.
monument (maˑniumønt) s. monumento.
monumental (-eˑntal) adj. monumental. 2 conmemorativo.
moo (mu) s. mugido.
moo (to) intr. mugir.
modd (mud) s. genio, talante. 2 humor, disposición: to be in no ~ for o to, no tener ganas de. 3 capricho. 4 GRAM., LÓG., MÚS. modo. 5 pl. mal humor.
moody (-i) adj. malhumorado, mohíno, irritable, triste, caviloso. 2 raro, caprichoso, variable, veleidoso.
moon (mun) s. luna [satélite; lunación]: new ~, luna nueva; full ~, luna llena; once in a blue ~, fig. muy raras veces. 2 luz de la luna. 3 ASTR. satélite.
moon (to) intr. andar absorto y distraído.
moonbeam (-bim) s. rayo de luna.
moon-calf s. bobo, tonto.
moonfish (-fish) s. ICT. pez luna.
moonlight (-lait) s.luz de la luna. 2 escena iluminada por la luna.
moonlit (-lit) adj. iluminado por la luna.
moonrise (-raiš) s. salida de la luna.
moonshine (-shain) s. claridad de la luna. 2 cosa sin substancia; vana fantasía. 3 (E.U.) licor, whisky, destilado clandestinamente.
moonshiner (-øʳ) s. (E.U.) destilador clandestino.
moonstruck (-strøk) adj. lunático.
moony (-i) adj. lunado. 2 alelado, bobo.
moor (muʳ) s. páramo, brezal, marjal: ~ cock, lagópodo.
Moor s. moro. 2 sarraceno.
moor (to) tr. MAR. amarrar, anclar [un buque]. 2 aferrar, arraigar, fijar en un sitio. 3 intr. MAR. anclar, estar amarrado o anclado [un buque].
moorage (muˑridẏ) s. MAR. amarraje.
mooring (muˑring) s. MAR. amarre: ~ berth, amarradero. 2 MAR. amarra. 3 pl. MAR. amarradero, anclaje.
Moorish adj. moro, morisco. 2 ARQ. árabe.
moorland (muˑʳlænd) s. paramera, marjal, brezal.
moose (mus) s. ZOOL. anta, alce americano.

moot (mut) *adj.* discutible, en discusión. *2* que se discute como ejercicio.

moot (to) *tr.* discutir, debatir [esp. como ejercicio].

mop (map) *s.* aljofifa, rodilla. *2* greña, cabello revuelto. *3* mueca.

mop (to) *tr.* aljofifar, fregar. *2* enjugar, limpiar [el sudor, etc.]. *3* MIL. *to ~ up,* limpiar de enemigos. *4 intr.* hacer muecas. ¶ Pret. y p. p.: *mopped;* ger.: *-pping.*

mope (moup) *s.* persona abatida, desanimada, apática. *2 pl.* murria, melancolía, aburrimiento.

mope (to) *intr.* andar abatido y melancólico; aburrirse.

mopish (-ish) *adj.* abatido, melancólico.

mopping-up *s.* MIL. operación de limpieza.

moquete (moke·t) *s.* moqueta.

mora (mou·ra) *s.* morra [juego].

moraine (morei·n) *s.* GEOL. morena.

moral (ma·ral) *adj.* moral: *~ support,* apoyo moral. *2* virtuoso. *3* que tiene sentido moral. *4 s.* moraleja, moralidad, enseñanza. *5 pl.* moral, ética. *6* moral [costumbres, conducta].

morale (moræ·l) *s.* moral [estado de ánimo].

moralist (ma·ralist) *s.* moralista. *2* moralizador. *3* el que lleva una vida moral.

morality (moræ·liti) *s.* moralidad. *2* moraleja. *3* moral [ciencia]. *4* principios éticos [de un hombre, etc.]. *5* TEAT. antiguo drama moral.

moralize (to) (ma·ralaiš) *tr.* moralizar. *2* deducir una moraleja de. *3 intr.* moralizar.

moralizer (-ø^r) *s.* moralizador.

morass (mø̞ra·s) *s.* pantano, cenagal. *2* fig. atolladero.

moratorium (morato·riøm) *s.* moratoria.

moray (mourei·) *s.* ICT. morena.

morbid (mo·^rbid) *adj.* mórbido, morboso. *2* horrible, espantoso.

morbidity (mo^rbi·diti) *s.* morbosidad. *2* morbididad.

mordacious (mo·dei·shøs) *adj.* mordaz, cáustico.

mordacity (mo^rdæ·siti) *s.* mordacidad.

mordant (mo·^rdant) *adj.* mordiente, corrosivo. *2* acre, mordaz. *3 s.* mordente, mordiente.

mordent (-ønt) *s.* MÚS. mordente.

more (mo^r) *adj.-adv.* más: *any ~,* ya no; *~ and ~,* más y más, cada vez más; *~ or less,* (poco) más o menos; *neither,* o *no,* *~ nor less,* ni más ni menos, exactamente; *no ~,* no más; ya no; se acabó; *once ~,* otra vez; *so much the ~,* tanto más; *the ~ ... the better,* cuanto más... mejor; *the ~ the merrier,* cuantos más mejor; *the ~ ...the more,* cuanto más... más.

morel (møre·l) *s.* BOT. colmenilla, cagarria.

moreover (morou·vø^r) *adv.* además, por otra parte, también.

Moresque (more·sk) *adj.* moro, morisco. *2* B. ART. árabe. *3* B. ART. estilo árabe.

morganatic (mø^rganæ·tik) *adj.* morganático.

morgue (mo·^rg) *s.* depósito de cadáveres.

moribund (mo·ribønd) *adj.* moribundo.

morion (mou·riøn) *s.* morrión [casco].

Morisco (møri·skou) *adj.-s.* morisco.

Mormon (mo·^rmøn) *s.* mormón.

morn (mo^rn) *poét.* mañana.

morning (mo·^rning) *s.* mañana [primera parte del día; de la vida]: *good ~,* buenos días; *tomorrow ~,* mañana por la mañana. *2* alba, aurora, albores. *3 adj.* de la mañana, del alba, matinal, matutino: *~ coat,* chaqué; *~ gown,* bata; *~ star,* lucero del alba.

morning-glory *s.* BOT. dondiego de día.

Moroccan (mø̞ra·kan) *adj.-s.* marroquí, marrueco.

morocco (mø̞ra·kou) *s.* marroquí, tafilete.

Morocco *n. pr.* GEOGR. Marruecos.

moron (mou·ran) *s.* atrasado mental.

morose (mørou·s) *adj.* malhumorado, hosco, displicente, arisco. *2* moroso.

morosity (-a·siti) *s.* mal humor, displicencia.

Morpheus (mo·^rfius) *n. pr.* MIT. Morfeo.

morphia (mo·^rfia), **morphine** (mo·^rfin) *s.* morfina.

morphinism (-išm) *s.* MED. morfinismo.

morphology (mo^rfa·lodẏi) *s.* morfología.

Morris (ma·ris) *n. pr.* Mauricio.

morris dance *s.* danza grotesca, mojiganga.

morrow (ma·rou) *s.* mañana, día siguiente: *on the ~,* en el día de mañana, el día siguiente. *2* ant. mañana [primera parte del día].

morse (mo·^rs) *s.* ZOOL. morsa.

Morse code *s.* TELEGR. alfabeto Morse.

morsel (mo·rsøl) *s.* bocado [comida]. *2* pedacito.

mortal (mo·^rtal) *adj.* mortal: *~ sin,* pecado mortal. *2* de la muerte. *3* a muerte. *4* letal, fatal. *5 s.* mortal.

mortality (mo^rtæ·liti) *s.* mortalidad. *2* humanidad, género humano; naturaleza humana.

mortalize (to) (mo·^rtalaiš) *tr.* hacer mortal.

mortar (mo·^rta^r) *s.* mortero, almirez. *2* ARTILL. mortero. *3* PIROT. morterete. *4* mortero, argamasa.

mortarboard (-bo^rd) *s.* ALBAÑ. esparavel. *2* birrete académico cuadrado.

mortgage (mo·^rgidẏ) *s.* hipoteca.

mortgage (to) *tr.* hipotecar.

mortician (mo^rti·shan) *s.* UNDERTAKER 2.

mortiferous (mo^rti·førøs) *adj.* mortífero.

mortification (mo^rtifike·shøn) *s.* mortificación.

mortify (to) (mo·^rtifai) *tr.* mortificar, humillar, herir los sentimientos de. *2* mortificar [el cuerpo]. *3* MED. mortificar. *4 intr.* mortificarse. ¶ Pret. y p. p.: *mortifiea.*

mortise (mo·^rtis) *s.* mortaja, muesca, caja, entalladura.

mortise (to) *tr.* hacer muescas o mortajas en.

mortmain (mo·^rtmein) *s.* DER. manos muertas.

mortuary (mo·^rchuæri) *adj.* mortuorio, funerario. *2 s.* depósito de cadáveres.

Mosaic (mošei·ik) *adj.* mosaico [de Moisés].

mosaic *s.* mosaico [obra taraceada].

mosaicist (mošei·isist) *s.* el que hace o vende mosaicos.

Mosaism (mo·šeiišm) *s.* mosaísmo.

Moscow (ma·skau) *n. pr.* GEOGR. Moscú.

Moses (mou·šiš) *n. pr.* Moisés.

Moslem (ma·slem) *adj.-s.* muslime, musulmán.

mosque (mask) *s.* mezquita.

mosquito (møskı·tou) *s.* ENT. mosquito: *~ net,* mosquitero.

moss (mos) *s.* BOT. musgo, musco; moho, verdín. *2 adj.* musgoso: *~ rose,* BOT. rosa musgosa.

moss-grown *adj.* musgoso [cubierto de musgo].

mossy (-i) *adj.* musgoso, mohoso.

most (moust) *adj.* (*superl.* de MORE, MUCH, MANY). *2* muchos, los más de, la mayoría de. *3* mayor: *for the ~ part,* en su mayor parte. *4* casi: *~ every body,* casi todos. *5 adv.* sumamente, muy; más: *Most Reverend,* reverendísimo; *the ~ courageous men,* los hombres más valientes. *6 s.* lo más, lo sumo: *at the ~,* a lo más, cuando más, a lo sumo.

mostly (-li) *adv.* en su mayor parte, principalmente; generalmente; casi, casi todo o todos.

mote (mout) *s.* mota de polvo: ~ *in another's eye,* fig. paja en el ojo ajeno.

motel (mou·tel) *s.* motel.

motet (mote·t) *s.* MÚS. motete.

moth (moz) *s.* polilla. 2 ENT. pequeña mariposa nocturna.

moth-eaten *adj.* apolillado. 2 *fig.* anticuado.

mother (mø·dø^r) *s.* madre. 2 tía [mujer de edad]. 3 *adj.* madre; materno; natal: ~ *country,* madre patria, país natal; ~ *tongue,* lengua madre; lengua materna. 4 natural, ingénito: ~ *wit,* inteligencia natural; chispa, ingenio.

mother (to) *tr.* servir de madre a. 2 reconocer por hijo. 3 ser causa u origen de.

mother-in-law *s.* madre política, suegra.

motherhood (-jud) *s.* maternidad. 2 madres.

motherless (-lis) *adj.* huérfano de madre.

motherly (-li) *adj.* maternal, materno.

mother-of-pearl *s.* nácar, madreperla.

mothy (mo·zi) *adj.* apolillado.

motif (mouti·f) *s.* MÚS., B. ART. motivo, tema.

motility (mouti·liti) *s.* motilidad.

motion (mou·shøn) *s.* movimiento, moción. 2 impulso: *of his own* ~, de su propio impulso. 3 meneo. 4 seña, signo, ademán. 5 MEC. juego, marcha; mecanismo. 6 MÚS. movimiento. 7 moción, proposición.

motion (to) *intr.-tr.* hacer seña o ademán [a uno].

motionless (-lis) *adj.* inmóvil, inmoble.

motion picture *s.* película [cinematográfica]. 2 *pl.* cine, cinematógrafo.

motivate (to) (mou·tiveit) *tr.* motivar. 2 mover, impulsar.

motive (mou·tiv) *s.* motivo, causa, razón. 2 B. ART., MÚS. motivo. 3 *adj.* motor, motriz: ~ *power,* fuerza motriz.

motley (ma·tli) *adj.* abigarrado. 2 *s.* abigarramiento, mezcolanza. 3 traje de bufón.

motor (mou·tø^r) *s.* motor [lo que mueve]. 2 MEC. motor. 3 automóvil. 4 *adj.* motor, motriz. 5 de motor: automóvil: ~ *oil,* aceite lubricante de motores; ~ *ship,* motonave; ~ *truck,* autocamión.

motor (to) *tr.-intr.* llevar o ir en automóvil.

motorboat (-bout) *s.* canoa, automóvil.

motorcade (-keid) *s.* caravana o desfile de automóviles.

motorcar (-ka^r) *s.* automóvil. 2 autocar. 3 (E.U.) coche motor.

motorcycle (-saikøl) *s.* motocicleta.

motoring (-ing) *s.* automovilismo.

motorist (-ist) *s.* motorista, automovilista.

motorize (to) (-aiš) *tr.* motorizar.

motorman (-mæn) *s.* conductor de tranvía o locomotora eléctrica.

motorway (mou·tø^r uei) *s.* autopista.

mottle (ma·tøl) *s.* pinta, mancha, veta [de color].

mottle (to) *tr.* motear, jaspear, vetear, abigarrar.

motto (ma·tou), *pl.* **-toes** o **-tos** *s.* mote, lema, divisa. 2 máxima.

mouf(f)lon (mu·flan) *s.* ZOOL. musmón.

mould (mould) *s.* moho [orgánico], verdín. 2 tierra vegetal, mantillo, barro. 3 molde, matriz, modelo. 4 forma, hechura. 5 carácter, índole. 6 ARQ. moldura.

mould (to) *tr.* amoldar. 2 moldear. 3 modelar. 4 moldurar. 5 AGR. cubrir con mantillo. 6 *intr.* enmohecerse, florecerse.

mouldboard (-bo^r d) *s.* vertedera [del arado].

moulder (-ø^r) *s.* moldeador.

moulder (to) *tr.* consumir, convertir en polvo. 2 *intr.* consumirse, convertirse en polvo.

moulding (-ing) *s.* CARP., ARQ. moldura. 2 amoldamiento, moldeado. 3 vaciado.

mouldy (-i) *adj.* mohoso, florecido.

moult (moult) *s.* MOULTING.

moult (to) *tr.* mudar [la pluma, la piel, etc.]. 2 *intr.* mudar, hacer la muda [un animal].

moulting (-ing) *s.* muda [de los animales].

mound (maund) *s.* montón de tierra, montículo, túmulo. 2 terraplén, atrincheramiento.

mound (to) *tr.* amontonar. 2 cercar, atrincherar.

mount (maunt) *s.* monte, montaña. 2 manera de montar [a caballo, en bicicleta, etc.]. 3 montura, cabalgadura. 4 MIL. monta [toque]. 5 montura [de un objeto]. 7 varillaje [de abanico]. 8 ~ *of piety,* monte de piedad.

mount (to) *tr.* subir [una cuesta, etc.]. 2 subir, elevarse por. 3 subir, levantar, alzar. 4 montar o montarse en o sobre. 5 montar [poner a caballo, dar caballo]. 6 montar, armar, engastar, engarzar. 7 TEAT. poner en escena. 8 MAR. montar [tantos cañones]. 9 MIL. montar [la guardia]. 10 *intr.* subir, elevarse. 11 remontarse. 12 subir, aumentar. 13 subirse, montarse [en o sobre]. 14 ascender [una cuenta].

mountain (mau·ntin) *s.* montaña, monte. 2 *adj.* montañés, montés, de montaña, montañoso; ~ *ash,* BOT. especie de serbal; ~ *chain,* cadena de montañas; ~ *climber,* montañero; ~ *dew,* whisky de contrabando; ~ *lion,* puma; ~ *range,* cordillera, sierra.

mountaineer (-i·r) *s.* montañés. 2 alpinista, montañero.

mountaineer (to) *intr.* practicar el alpinismo.

mountaineering (-ing) *s.* alpinismo, montañismo.

mountainous (mau·ntinøs) *adj.* montañoso, montuoso. 2 enorme.

mountebank (mou·ntibænk) *s.* charlatán, truhán.

mounted (-id) *adj.* montado.

mounting (-ing) *s.* subida, ascensión. 2 monta [acción]. 3 montaje. 4 montura, engaste, marco.

mourn (to) (mou^r n) *tr.* deplorar, lamentar, llorar. 2 *intr.* lamentarse, dolerse. 3 *to* ~ *for,* llevar luto por; llorar a.

mourner (-ø^r) *s.* afligido, el que llora una pérdida. 2 enlutado. 3 plañidera.

mournful (-ful) *adj.* triste, lúgubre, lastimero, fúnebre. 2 apesadumbrado, dolorido. 3 entristecedor.

mourning (-ing) *s.* aflicción, dolor, pesar, duelo. 2 lamento, llanto. 3 luto; *to be in* ~, estar de luto. 4 *adj.* triste, dolorido, lamentoso. 5 de luto. 6 BOT. ~ *bride,* o *widow,* viuda.

mouse (mous), *pl.* **mice** (mais) *s.* ZOOL. ratón.

mouse (to) *intr.* cazar razones. 2 andar a la caza o al acecho; husmear.

mouse-ear *s.* BOT. miosotis. 2 BOT. vellosilla.

mousehole (-joul) *s.* ratonera [agujero].

mouser (-ø^r) *s.* perro o gato ratonero.

mousetrap (-træp) *s.* ratonera [trampa].

mousse (mus) *s.* COC. especie de crema batida.

moustache (møstæ·sh) *s.* MUSTACHE.

mouth (mauz) *s.* ANAT. boca: ~ *organ,* MÚS. armónica; zampoña; *down in the* ~, alicaído, cariacontecido; *to keep one's* ~ *shut,* guardar silencio. 2 boca [entrada, abertura, orificio]. 3 bocas, desembocadura [de un río].

mouth (to) *tr.* decir, proferir, vocear, declamar. 2 coger con la boca; tomar en la boca. 3 *intr.* ha-

blar [con voz hueca], gritar, declamar. *4* hacer una mueca.
mouther (-ø^r) *s.* declamador.
mouthful (-ful) *s.* bocado [de comida]. *2* pizca.
mouthpiece (-pis) *s.* MÚS. boquilla, embocadura, estrangul, tudel. *2* bocado [del freno]. *3* bocal [de bota]. *4* portavoz, vocero.
mouthwash (-uash) *s.* enjuague, colutorio.
mouthy (-i) *adj.* gritón. *2* ampuloso, pomposo.
movable (mu·vaβøl) *adj.* movible, móvil; locomovible. *2 s. pl.* muebles, mobiliario, efectos.
move (muv) *s.* movimiento [acción de moverse]: *to get a ~ on*, menearse, darse prisa; *on the ~*, en movimiento. *2* cambio de sitio. *3* jugada [de damas, ajedrez, etc.]. *4* paso, diligencia. *5* moción, propuesta.
move (to) *tr.* mover. *2* inducir, persuadir, inclinar. *3* menear. *4* remover, trasladar, mudar. *5* conmover, enternecer. *6* excitar [un sentimiento]. *7* proponer [en una asamblea]. *8* jugar [una pieza, un peón]. *9* exonerar [el vientre]. *10 intr.* moverse; andar: *to ~ about*, moverse, ir de un lado a otro; *to ~ away*, irse, alejarse, apartarse; *to ~ forward*, adelantarse, avanzar; *to ~ round*, dar vueltas. *11* irse, partir, ponerse en marcha. *12* trasladarse, mudarse. *13* marchar, progresar. *14* jugar [hacer una jugada].
movement (-mønt) *s.* movimiento [en todos sus sentidos]. *2* MEC. mecanismo, máquina [de reloj, etc.]. *3* MÚS. tiempo [división de una obra].
mover (-ø^r) *s.* movedor, motor. *2* promovedor. *3* autor de una moción. *4* el que se ocupa del traslado de muebles.
movie (-i) *s.* película [de cine]. *2 pl. the movies*, el cine.
movie-goer *s.* fam. aficionado al cine.
moving (-ing) *s.* movimiento, moción. *2* traslado, mudanza. *3 adj.* móvil, que se mueve: *~ picture*, MOTION PICTURE; *~ staircase* o *stairway*, escalera mecánica. *4* motor, motriz, que mueve: *~ spirit*, alma [de una empresa]. *5* conmovedor. *6* de mudanzas; *~ van*, carro de mudanzas.
mow (mau) *s.* almiar; granero, henil.
mow (to) (mou) *tr.* segar, guadañar, dallar. ¶ P. P.: *mowed* o *mown*.
mower (-ø^r) *s.* segador, guadañador, dallador. *2* segadora o guadañadora mecánica; máquina para cortar el césped.
mown (-n) *p. p. irr.* de TO MOW.
Mozarab (mousæ·rab) *adj.-s.* mozárabe.
mozetta (mošé·ta) *s.* ECLES. muceta.
much (møch) *adj.* mucho, mucha: *~ ado about nothing*, mucho ruido para nada. *2 adv.* muy, mucho: *as ~*, tanto; otro tanto; *as ~ as*, tanto como; *how ~?*, ¿cuánto?; *~ the same*, casi lo mismo; *so ~*, tanto; *so ~ the better*, tanto mejor; *very ~*, muchísimo. *3 s.* mucho, gran cosa: *~ of a [gentleman*, etc.]; todo un [caballero, etc.]; *to make ~ of*, tener en mucho, festejar.
muchness (-nis) *s.* cantidad, demasía.
mucilage (miu·silidȳ) *s.* mucílago.
mucilaginous (miusilæ·dȳinøs) *adj.* mucilaginoso.
muck (møk) *s.* estiércol húmedo. *2* suciedad pegajosa; porquería. *3* desp. dinero.
muck (to) *tr.* AGR. estercolar. *2* fam. *to ~ up*, ensuciar.
muckworm (-uø^{r}m) *s.* gusano de muladar. *2* fig. golfo, pillete. *3* fig. avaro.
mucky (-i) *adj.* sucio, asqueroso.
mucosa (miukou·sa) *pl.* **-sae** *s.* ANAT. mucosa.
mucosity (miuka·siti) *s.* mucosidad, viscosidad.

mucous (miu·køs) *adj.* mucoso: *~ membrane*, membrana mucosa.
mucus (miu·køs) *s.* moco, mucosidad.
mud (mød) *s.* barro, lodo, fango: *~ bath*, baño de lodo; *~ wall*, tapia; *to sling ~ at*, llenar de fango, difamar.
mud (to) *tr.* enlodar, embarrar. *2* enturbiar.
muddle (-øl) *s.* enredo, embrollo, confusión, lío, desorden.
muddle (to) *tr.* enredar, embrollar, confundir. *2* enturbiar. *3* embriagar, entontecer. *4 intr.* hacerse un lío, enredar las cosas: *to ~ through*, hacer algo torpemente, salir del paso a duras penas.
muddle-head *s.* estúpido, atontado.
muddy (-i) *adj.* barroso, fangoso, lodoso. *2* embarrado, enlodado. *3* turbio, empañado. *4* confuso, obscuro.
muddy (to) *tr.* embarrar, enlodar, ensuciar. *2* enturbiar. *3* obscurecer, entontecer, turbar. ¶ Pret. y p. p.: *muddied;* ger.: *-ddying.*
Mudejar (muðei·ja^r) *adj.-s.* mudéjar.
mudguard (mø·dga^{r}d) *s.* guardabarros.
mudhole (mø·djoul) *s.* atolladero.
muezzin (miu·šin) *s.* almuecín, almuédano.
muff (møf) *s.* manguito [de piel]. *2* MEC. manguito. *3* torpeza, fracaso. *4* fam. torpe, tonto.
muff (to) *tr.-intr.* hacer algo torpemente.
muffin (mø·fin) *s.* bollo o panecillo redondo.
muffle (mø·føl) *s.* mufla. *2* MITTEN. *3* apagador de sonido. *4* cuadernal. *5* hocico, morro.
muffle (to) *tr.* envolver, embozar, cubrir, tapar. *2* envolver con ropa la cabeza de [uno] para que no vea, oiga, grite, etc. *3* apagar [un sonido]. *4* *to ~ a drum*, enfundar o destemplar un tambor.
muffler (-lø^r) *s.* bufanda, tapaboca, embozo. *2* MEC. silenciador. *3* MÚS. apagador. *4* guante de boxeo.
mufti (-ti) *s.* muftí. *2* MIL. (Ingl.) traje de paisano.
mug (møg) *s.* jarro [para beber]. *2* pop. cara, jeta. *3* pop. (Ingl.) primo, tonto. *4* fam. (Ingl.) empollón. *5* mueca, visaje.
mug (to) *tr.* fam. fotografiar [esp. a los criminales]. *2 intr.* (Ingl.) empollar [para un examen]. *3 tr.-intr.* hacer muecas.
muggy (-i) *adj.* húmedo, cargado, bochornoso, sofocante [aire, tiempo].
mugwort (-wø^{r}t) *s.* BOT. artemisa.
mulatto (miulæ·tou) *adj.-m.* mulato.
mulattress (miulæ·tris) *adj.-f.* mulata.
mulberry (mø·lberi) *s.* BOT. moral: *white ~*, morera. *2* mora [fruto]. *3* BOT. (Ingl.) zarza, zarzamora.
mulct (mølkt) *s.* multa.
mulct (to) *tr.* multar. *2* privar [de].
mule (miul) *s.* ZOOL. mulo, macho: *she-mule*, mula. *2* fig. mula [pers. terca y necia]. *3* BIOL. planta o animal híbridos. *4* cierta máquina de hilar.
mule-jenny *s.* MULE [máquina de hilar].
muleteer (miuleti·^{r}) *s.* mulero, mulatero.
mull (møl) *s.* muselina clara. *2* fam. confusión, lío; fracaso.
mull (to) *tr.* calentar [vino, etc.] con azúcar y especias. *2* fam. confundir, enredar.
mullein (mø·lin) *s.* BOT. verbasco, gordolobo.
muller (mø·lø^r) *s.* moleta.
mullet (mø·let) *s.* ICT. mújol, múgil. *2* ICT. *red ~*, salmonete.
mulligatawny (møligato·ni) *s.* sopa de arroz y carne sazonada con *curry*.
mullion (mø·liøn) *s.* ARQ. mainel, parteluz.

mullioned (-d) *adj.* ARQ. dividido por maineles o parteluces.

mulse (møls) *s.* vino mulso.

multicoloured (mølticø·lø^rd) *adj.* multicolor.

multifarious (-fe·riøs) *adj.* múltiple, vario, variado, de varias clases.

multiflorous (-flo·røs) *adj.* multifloro.

multifold (mø·ltifould) *adj.* múltiple.

multiform (-fo^rm) *adj.* multiforme.

multimillionaire (-milione·^r) *s.* multimillonario.

multipara (mølti·para) *f.* mujer multípara.

multiparous (-parøs) *adj.* multípara.

multiphase (mø·ltifeis) *adj.* ELECT. polifásico.

multiple (mø·ltipøl) *adj.* múltiple, multíplice. 2 *s.* múltiplo. 3 ELECT. *in* ~, en paralelo.

multiplex (-plex) *adj.* multíplice.

multiplicand (-plikæ·nd) *s.* ARIT. multiplicando.

multiplication (-ei·shøn) *s.* multiplicación: ~ *table*, tabla de multiplicar.

multiply (tc) (-plai) *tr.* multiplicar. 2 *intr.* multiplicarse. ¶ Pret. y p. p.: *multiplied*.

multipolar (-pou·la^r) *adj.* multipolar.

multitude (mø·ltitiud) *s.* multitud, muchedumbre. 2 multitud, vulgo.

multitudinous (møltitiu·dinøs) *adj.* numeroso, numerosos. 2 multitúdinario. 3 de muchos, compuesto o formado por muchos.

multivalent (-vei·lønt) *adj.* QUÍM. polivalente.

multilocular (-la·kiula^r) *adj.* BOT. plurilocular.

mum (møm) *s.* fam. mamá. 2 *adj.* callado: *to keep* ~, callarse; *mum's the word*, punto en boca. 3 *interj.* ¡chitón!, ¡silencio!

mum (to) *intr.* disfrazarse, hacer pantomima.

mumble (to) (-bøl) *tr.-intr.* mascullar, murmurar, musitar, barbotar. 2 mascujar.

Mumbo Jumbo (-bou jø·mbou) *s.* genio tutelar [entre los negros]. 2 fig. (con min.) coco, fetiche. 3 sortilegio ridículo; monserga.

mummer (-ø^r) *s.* máscara [pers.]. 2 bufón, histrión.

mummery (-øri) *s.* momería, mojiganga, mascarada.

mummification (mømifikei·shøn) *s.* momificación.

mummify (to) (mø·mifai) *tr.* momificar. 2 *intr.* momificarse. ¶ Pret. y p. p.: *mummified*.

mummy (-i) *s.* momia. 2 mamá [voz infantil].

mump (to) (mømp) *intr.* estar murrio. 2 mendigar.

mumpish (-ish) *adj.* malhumorado.

mumps (-s) *s.* mal humor. 2 MED. paperas, parótida.

munch (to) (mønch) *tr.* mascar, ronzar.

mundane (mø·ndein) *adj.* mundano. 2 cósmico.

mundanity (miunda·niti) *s.* mundanalidad.

mundify (to) (mø·ndifai) *tr.* mundificar.

municipal (miuni·sipal) *adj.* municipal. 2 que tiene municipio [población].

municipality (miunisipæ·liti) *s.* municipalidad, municipio.

municipalize (to) (miuni·sipalaiš) *tr.* municipalizar.

munificence (miuni·fisøns) *s.* munificencia.

munificient (-t) *adj.* munificiente.

muniment (miu·nimønt) *s.* pl. DER. documentos o títulos que acreditan un derecho.

munition (to) *tr.* municionar, proveer.

munitions (miuni·shøns) *s. pl.* municiones.

mural (miu·ral) *adj.* mural. 2 *s.* pintura mural; decoración mural.

murder (mø·^rdø^r) *s.* asesinato, homicidio.

murder (to) *tr.* asesinar, matar. 2 asesinar, destrozar, estropear [hacer o ejecutar mal].

murderer (-ø^r) *s.* asesino, homicidio, matador.

murderess (-is) *s.* asesina, matadora.

murderous (-øs) *adj.* asesino, homicida. 2 sanguinario, cruel. 3 mortífero, mortal, fatal.

murex (miu·reks), *pl.* **-rexes** o **-rices** (-risiš) *s.* ZOOL. múrice.

murk(y (mø·^rk(i) *adj.* oscuro, lóbrego, sombrío.

murmur (mø·^rmø^r) *s.* murmullo, murmurio, susurro, rumor. 2 queja, descontento.

murmur (to) *intr.-tr.* murmurar, murmullar, susurrar. 2 *intr.* quejarse, murmurar, refunfuñar: *to* ~ *at*, quejarse de.

murmurous (-øs) *adj.* rumoroso. 2 murmurante. 3 quejoso, murmurador.

murrain (mø·rin) *s.* VET. peste, fiebre aftosa.

musaceous (miušei·shøs) *adj.* BOT. musáceo.

muscat (mø·skæt), **muscatel** (møskate·l) *s.* moscatel [vid, uva, vino]. 2 pasa moscatel.

muscid (mø·sid) *adj.-s.* ENT. múscido.

muscle (mø·søl) *s.* ANAT. músculo. 2 fuerza muscular.

muscosity (møska·siti) *s.* calidad de musgoso.

Muscovite (mø·skøvait) *adj.-s.* moscovita.

Muscovy (-vi) *n. pr.* GEOGR. Moscovia.

muscular (mø·skiular) *adj.* muscular. 2 musculoso, vigoroso, fornido.

musculature (møskiu·lachø^r) *s.* ınusculatura.

Muse (miuš) *s.* MIT. Musa. 2 (con min.) musa [que inspira; numen; poesía]. 3 meditación, abstracción.

muse (to) *intr.* meditar, reflexionar, cavilar. 2 estar o mirar absorto, distraído.

museum (miuši·øm) *s.* museo.

mush (møsh) *s.* gacha, masa blanda y espesa. 2 (E.U.) gachas de maíz. 3 sentimentalismo empalagoso. 4 (E.U.) marcha a pie sobre la nieve [esp. con perros]. 5 fam. paraguas.

mushroom (mø·shrum) *s.* BOT. seta, hongo. 2 cosa en forma de hongo.

mushroom (to) *intr.* coger setas. 2 tomar forma de hongo. 3 aparecer y desarrollarse rápidamente.

mushy (-i) *adj.* blando, mollar, pulposo. 2 empalagoso efusivo o sentimental.

music (miu·šik) *s.* música: ~ *cabinet*, musiquero; ~ *hall*, sala de variedades, café concierto; ~ *rack*, atril; *to set to* ~, poner en música. 2 oído musical. 3 MIL. música, banda.

musical (-al) *adj.* musical, músico: ~ *comedy*, comedia musical, opereta. 2 armonioso, melodioso, canoro. 3 aficionado a la música.

musicale (miušika·l) *s.* velada musical.

musician (miuši·shan) *s.* músico.

musicologist (-ka·lodÿist) *s.* musicólogo.

musk (møsk) *s.* almizcle. 2 olor o perfume de almizcle. 3 ZOOL. almizclero. 4 *adj.* almizclero, almizcleño: ~ *deer*, almizclero; ~ *melon*, melón; ~ *rat*, desmán.

musket (-it) *s.* mosquete; fusil.

musketeer (møskiti·^r) *s.* mosquetero; fusilero.

musketry (mø·skitri) *s.* mosquetería, fusilería. 2 tiro con mosquetes o fusiles.

musky (-i) *adj.* almizclado, almizcleño.

Muslim (mø·slim) *s.* MOSLEM.

muslin (mø·šlin) *s.* muselina. 2 percal.

muss (møs) *s.* desorden, confusión.

muss (to) *tr.* desordenar, desarreglar. 2 desgreñar. 3 arrugar, chafar, ensuciar.

mussel (mø·søl) *s.* ZOOL. mejillón.

Mussulman (mø·sølmæn) *s.* musulmán.

must (møst) *s.* mosto. *2* moho [orgánico]; ranciedad.

must (to) *intr.* enmohecerse. *2 aux. def.* [gralte. usado sólo en el presente] deber, haber de, tener que: *I ~ go*, he de irme. *3* deber de: *he ~ be downstairs*, debe de estar abajo. *5* ser preciso, ser necesario, convenir.

mustache (møstæ·šh) *s.* bigote, mostacho.

mustang (mø·stæng) *s.* mustango.

mustard (mø·sta^rd) *s.* BOT., COC. mostaza: *~ seed*, semilla de mostaza; mostacilla [munición]. *2* harina de mostaza: *~ plaster*, sinapismo.

musteline (mø·stilin) *adj.-s.* mustélido.

muster (mø·stø^r) *s.* reunión [esp. para recuento, pasar lista, etc.]. *2* MIL., MAR. lista, revista: *to pass ~*, pasar revista; fig. ser aceptado o aceptable. *3 ~ roll*, rol de la tripulación.

muster (to) *tr.* juntar, reunir. *2* MIL. reunir [para pasar lista, revista, etc.]. *3 to ~ up one's courage*, revestirse de valor, cobrar ánimo. *4 intr.* reunirse, juntarse.

musty (mø·sti) *adj.* mohoso; que huele a cerrado. *2* rancio, trasnochado. *3* mustio, triste.

mutable (miu·tabøl) *adj.* mudable, inconstante.

mutable (to) (miu·teit) *tr.* mudar, alterar. *2 intr.* mudarse, alterarse. *3* BIOL. sufrir mutación.

mutation (-shøn) *s.* mutación, mudanza, variación, cambio. *2* vicisitud.

mute (miut) *adj.* mudo. *2 s.* mudo. *3* MÚS. sordina. *5* FONÉT. letra muda.

mute (to) *tr.* MÚS. poner sordina a. *2 intr.-tr.* arrojar el excremento, tullir [las aves].

mutilate (to) (miu·tileit) *tr.* mutilar.

mutilation (-ei·shøn) *s.* mutilación.

mutineer (miutini·^r) *s.* amotinado. *2* amotinador.

mutinous (miu·tinøs) *adj.* rebelde, indómito. *2* amotinado. *3* subversivo.

mutinously (miu·tinøsli) *adv.* amotinadamente, rebeldemente.

mutiny (-i) *s.* motín, amotinamiento, insubordinación, sedición.

mutiny (to) *intr.* amotinarse, insubordinarse, rebelarse. ¶ Pret. y p. p.: *mutinied*.

mutism (miu·tišm) *s.* mutismo. *2* mudez.

mutter (mø·tø^r) *s.* murmullo.

mutter (to) *tr.-intr.* murmurar, murmujear, barbotar, musitar, refunfuñar.

mutton (mø·tøn) *s.* carnero, carne de carnero: *~ chop*, chuleta de carnero; *~ chops*, fig. chuletas, patillas.

muttonhead (-·jed) *s.* zopenco.

mutual (miu·chual) *adj.* mutual, mutuo; recíproco; respectivo: *~ benefit society*, mutualidad; *by ~ consent*, de común acuerdo.

mutualism (-išm) *s.* mutualismo.

mutuality (miuchuæ·liti) *s.* mutualidad. *2* reciprocidad. *3* interdependencia.

mutualize (to) (miu·chualaiš) *tr.* hacer mutuo.

muzzle (mø·šøl) *s.* hocico, morro, jeta [de animal]. *2* bozal, frenillo [para la boca]. *3* boca [de un arma de fuego]. *4* máscara [para gases, etc.].

muzzle (to) *tr.* abolazar, embozalar. *2* amordazar, imponer silencio.

muzzy (mø·ši) *adj.* abatido, triste. *2* calamocano.

my (mai) *adj. pos.* mi, mis: *~ book*, mi libro; *~ shoes*, mis zapatos. *2* interj. *oh, my!*, ¡Ave María!, ¡caramba!

mycelium (misi·liøm) *s.* BOT. micelio.

Mycenae (maisi·ni) *pr. n.* HIST. Micenas.

mycology (maika·lodÿi) *s.* micología.

myelitis (mailai·tis) *s.* MED. mielitis.

myocardium (maioka·^rdiøm) *s.* ANAT. miocardio.

myology (maia·lodÿi) *s.* miología.

myope (mai·oup) *s.* miope.

myopia (maiou·pia) *s.* miopía.

myopic (maia·pik) *adj.* miope, corto de vista.

myopy (mai·oupi) *s.* miopía.

myosotis (maiø·soutis) *s.* BOT. miositis.

myotic (maia·tik) *adj.* miótico.

myriad (mi·riad) *s.* miríada. *2 adj.* innumerable.

myriagram (mi·riagræm) *s.* miriagramo.

myrialiter, -litre (-litø^r) *s.* mirialitro.

myriameter, -metre (-mitø^r) *s.* miriámetro.

myriapod (-pad) *s.* ZOOL. miriápodo, miriópodo.

myrmidon (mø·^rmidøn) *s.* esbirro.

myrrh (mø^r) *s.* mirra.

myrrhic (-ik) *adj.* mirrino.

myrtaceous (mø^rtei·shøs) *adj.* BOT. mirtáceo.

myrtle (mø·^rtøl) *s.* mirto, arrayán.

myself (maise·lf) *pron.* yo, yo mismo; a mí, a mí mismo, me.

mystagogue (mi·stagag) *s.* mistagogo.

mysterious (misti·riøs) *adj.* misterioso.

mystery (mi·støri) *s.* misterio. *2* arcano, enigma. *3* TEAT. auto, drama religioso.

mystic (mi·stikt) *adj.* místico. *2* enigmático, misterioso. *3* mágico. *4 s.* místico.

mystical (-al) *adj.* místico, simbólico, anagógico. *2* místico [de la mística].

mysticism (mi·stišišm) *s.* misticismo.

mystification (mistifikei·shøn) *s.* confusión, perplejidad. *2* engaño, superchería.

mystify (mi·stifai) *tr.* envolver en misterio, obscurecer. *2* confundir, desconcertar, engañar. ¶ Pret. y p. p.: *mistified*.

myth (miz) *s.* mito. *2* fábula, ficción.

mythical (-al) *adj.* mítico.

mythologist (miza·lodÿist) *s.* mitologista; mitólogo.

mythology (-i) *s.* mitología.

myxomycete (miksomaisi·t) *s.* BOT. mixomiceto.

N

N, n (en) *s.* N, n, decimocuarta letra del alfabeto inglés.

nab (to) (næb) *tr.* prender, agazapar, coger.

nabob (nei·bab) *s.* nabab.

nacarat (næ·kærat) *s.* color nacarado, rosado.

nacelle (næse·l) *s.* AER. barquilla.

nacre (nei·kør) *s.* nácar.

nacreous (nei·kriøs) *adj.* nacarado, nacarino.

nadir (nei·dør) *s.* ASTR. nadir.

nag (næg) *s.* jaca, cuartago. *2* jaco, rocín.

nag (to) *tr.-intr.* encocorar [con reprensiones, críticas, etc.]; regañar, hallarlo todo mal. ¶ Pret. y p. p.: *nagged;* ger.: *-gging.*

naiad (nei·yad) *s.* MIT. náyade.

nail (neil) *s.* ANAT.,ZOOL. uña: ~ *clippers,* cortauñas; ~ *polish,* esmalte para las uñas. *2* clavo, punta; tachón: ~ *puller,* arrancaclavos; *on the* ~, en el acto, a toca teja.

nail (to) *tr.* clavar, enclavar [fijar, asegurar con clavos]; *to* ~ *down, to* ~ *up,* clavar, sujetar con clavos. *2* clavetear, adornar con clavos. *3* fijar, sujetar, agarrar, atrapar. *4 to* ~ *a lie,* acabar con una mentira.

nailbrush (-brøsh) *s.* cepillo para las uñas.

nailer (-ør) *s.* fabricante de clavos. *2* el que clava [con clavos].

nainsook (nei·nsuk) *s.* nansú.

naive, naïve (naɪ·v) *adj.* ingenuo, sencillo, cándido.

naïveté (-tei) *s.* ingenuidad, sencillez, candor.

naked (nei·kid) *adj.* desnudo: *the* ~ *truth,* la verdad desnuda; *with the* ~ *eye,* a simple vista. *2* puro, sin mezcla. *3* descubierto, sin defensa o protección.

nakedness (nei·kidnis) *s.* desnudez.

namby-pamby (næ·mbi-pæ·mbi) *adj.* afectado, insípido, ñoño. *2 s.* melindre, pamplina. *3* persona ñoña o sensiblera.

name (neim) *s.* nombre: *Christian* ~, nombre de pila; *family* ~, apellido; *what is your* ~?, ¿cómo se llama usted?; *by* ~, de nombre; *in the* ~ *of,* en nombre de; ~ *plate,* letrero o placa con el nombre. *2* fama, reputación: *bad* ~, mala reputación. *3* apodo, mote: *to call names,* motejar, insultar.

name (to) *tr.* llamar, denominar, apellidar. *2* nombrar [decir el nombre, hacer mención de]. *2* señalar, indicar, fijar.

nameless (-lis) *adj.* anónimo; no nombrado: *he*

shall be ~, no diremos su nombre. *2* innominado. *3* obscuro, humilde. *4* indescriptible; horrible.

namely (-li) *adv.* a saber, esto es, es decir.

namesake (-seik) *s.* tocayo, homónimo.

Nancy (na·nsi) *n. pr. dim.* de ANN.

nandu (næ·ndu) *s.* ORN. ñandú.

nankeen, nankin (nænkɪ·n) *s.* TEJ. mahón, manquín. *2 pl.* pantalones de nanquín.

nanny (na·ni) *s.* niñera [voz infantil]. *2* ~ *goat,* fam. cabra [animal].

nap (næp) *s.* sueñecito, siesta: *to take a* ~, echar un sueñecito. *2* pelo [de un tejido].

nap (to) *intr.* dormitar, descabezar el sueño: *to catch someone napping,* coger a uno desprevenido. *2 tr.* cardar, perchar [un tejido].

nape (nei·p) *s.* ~ *of the neck,* nuca, cogote.

napery (nei·pøri) *s.* mantelería.

naphtha (næ·fza) *s.* nafta.

Naphtali (-tølai) *n. pr.* Naftalí.

naphthalene (-zalin) *s.* naftalina.

Napierian (neipi·rian) *adj.* neperiano, de Néper.

napkin (næ·pkin) *s.* servilleta: ~ *ring,* servilletero. *2* toalleta.

Naples (nei·pøls) *n. pr.* GEOGR. Nápoles.

napless (næ·plis) *adj.* raído [paño, etc.].

Napoleon (napou·liøn) *n. pr.* Napoleón. *2 s.* (con min.) napoleón [moneda].

napping (næ·ping) *s.* TEJ. perchado.

nappy (-i) *adj.* peludo, velloso. *2* fuerte, con mucha espuma [bebida].

narcissism (na·rsi·sišm) *s.* narcisismo.

narcissus (na·rsi·søs) *s.* BOT. narciso.

narcosis (na·rkou·sis) *s.* MED. narcotismo [sopor].

narcotic (na·rka·tik) *adj.-s.* narcótico.

narcotize (na·rkøtaiš) *tr.* narcotizar.

nard (na·rd) *s.* BOT. espicanardo, nardo. *2* ungüento de nardo.

narghile (na·rgili) *s.* narguile.

narrate (to) (nærei·t) *tr.* narrar.

narration (nærei·shøn) *s.* narración.

narrative (næ·rativ) *adj.* narrativo. *2 s.* narración, relato. *3* narrativa.

narrator (nærei·tør) *s.* narrador.

narrow (næ·rou) *adj.* estrecho, angosto: ~ *gauge,* FERROC. vía estrecha. *2* limitado, reducido, escaso. *3* mezquino, tacaño. *4* iliberal, intolerante. *5* atento, escrupuloso, riguroso. *6* ~ *es-*

cape, escapada difícil, por poco. *7* ~ *circumstances*, pobreza, apuro, estrechez. *8 s. pl.* parte estrecha de un río, estrecho, calle, etc. *9* desfiladero.
narrow (to) *tr.* estrechar, angostar. *2* reducir, limitar, encoger. *3 intr.* estrecharse, reducirse.
narrow-fisted *adj.* agarrado, tacaño.
narrowing (-ing) *s.* estrechamiento. *2* reducción, limitación, mengua, disminución.
narrow-minded *adj.* de miras estrechas; mezquino, liberal, mojigato.
narrow-mindedness *f.* falta de amplitud en las ideas, intolerancia.
narthex (naꞏ‘zeks) *s.* ARQ. nártex.
narwhal (-jual) *s.* ZOOL. narval.
nasal (neiꞏšal) *adj.-s.* nasal: ~ *twang*, gangueo.
nasalize (to) (-aiš) *tr.* nasalizar.
nascent (næꞏsønt) *adj.* naciente.
nastiness (næꞏstinis) *s.* asquerosidad. *2* indecencia. *3* mal genio. *4* mal gusto u olor. *5* condición de malo, peligroso, desagradable, etc.
nasturtium (næstøꞏ‘shøm) *s.* BOT. capuchina.
nasty (næꞏsti) *adj.* sucio, asqueroso, nauseabundo. *2* feo, indecente, grosero. *3* desagradable. *4* repugnante. *5* malo, peligroso: *a* ~ *fall*, una caída peligrosa. *6* avieso, intratable. *7* malo, tempestuoso [tiempo, mar, etc.].
natal (neiꞏtal) *adj.* natal, nativo.
natality (neitæꞏliti) *s.* natalidad.
natant (neiꞏtant) *adj.* BOT. natátil, flotante.
natation (nateiꞏshøn) *s.* natación.
natatory (-tori) *adj.* natatorio.
Nathan (neiꞏzan) *n. pr.* Natán.
Nathaniel (nazæꞏniøl) *n. pr.* Nataniel.
nation (neiꞏshøn) *s.* nación. *2* multitud, hueste.
national (næꞏshønal) *adj.-s.* nacional.
nationalism (-išm) *s.* nacionalismo.
nationality (næshønæꞏliti) *s.* nacionalidad. *2* nación. *3* sentimiento nacional, patriotismo.
nationalization (-išeiꞏshøn) *s.* nacionalización. *2* conversión en nación.
nationalize (to) (næꞏshønalaiš) *tr.* nacionalizar. *2* naturalizar. *3* convertir en nación.
native (neiꞏtiv) *adj.* nativo, natío [metal]. *2* natal, nativo, patrio: ~ *country*, país natal. *3* natural [de un país], indígena, autóctono; vernáculo. *4* originario. *5* natural, sencillo. *6 s.* natural; indígena.
native-born *adj.* natural, indígena.
nativity (neitiꞏviti) *s.* nacimiento, natividad. *2* ASTR. horóscopo. *3* (con may.) Natividad [del Señor, etc.].
natty (næꞏti) *adj.* elegante, pulido. *2* diestro, garboso.
natural (næꞏchøral) *adj.* natural: ~ *history*, ~ *law*, ~ *religion*, ~ *son*, historia, ley, religión, hijo natural. | No tiene el sentido de natural o nativo de un país. *2* innato, nativo. *3* nato, de nacimiento. *4* físico, real. *5* parecido [retrato, etc.]. *6 s.* idiota, simple. *7* MÚS. becuadro; nota natural.
naturalism (-išm) *s.* naturalismo.
naturalist (-ist) *s.* naturalista.
naturalization (næchøraliseiꞏshøn) *s.* naturalización. *2* aclimatación.
naturalize (to) (næꞏchøralaiš) *tr.* naturalizar. *2* aclimatar. *3* habituar.
naturalness (-inis) *s.* naturalidad.
nature (neꞏchø‘) *s.* naturaleza, natura. *2* naturaleza, carácter, especie: *in the* ~ *of*, como, de la naturaleza de. *3* natural, índole, genio. *4* natu-

ralidad, espontaneidad. *5 B.* ‘ART. natural: *from* ~, del natural.
natured (-d) *adj.* de tal o cual natural, genio, etc.: *good-natured*, afable, bondadoso.
naught (not) *s.* cero. *2* nada: *to come to* ~, reducirse a nada, malograrse, frustrarse.
naughtiness (-inis) *s.* desobediencia, travesura.
naughty (-i) *adj.* malo, desobediente, travieso: ~ *boy*, niño malo, picaruelo.
nausea (noꞏshia) *s.* náusea, asco, basca.
nauseate (to) (-ieit) *tr.* dar náuseas. *2* sentir asco. *3 intr.* nausear.
nauseous (-øs) *adj.* nauseoso, nauseabundo, repugnante, asqueroso.
nautic (al (noꞏtik(al) *adj.* náutico, marino.
nautics (-s) *s.* náutica.
nautilus (noꞏtiløs) *s.* ZOOL. nautilo, argonauta.
naval (neiꞏval) *adj.* naval, de marina, de la armada: ~ *base*, base naval; ~ *vessel*, buque de guerra.
Navarre (nævaꞏ‘) *n. pr.* GEOGR. Navarra.
nave (neiv) *s.* ARQ. nave. *2* cubo [de rueda].
navel (-øl) *s.* ombligo. *2* centro, medio. *3* BOT. ~ *orange*, naranja de ombligo.
navicert (næꞏvisø‘t) *s.* MAR. navicert.
navicula (naviꞏkiøla) *s.* BOT. navícula. *2* LITURG. naveta.
navicular (naviꞏkiula‘) *adj.* ANAT., BOT. navicular.
navigability (nævigabiꞏliti) *s.* navegabilidad.
navigable (næꞏvigabøl) *adj.* navegable.
navigate (to) (næꞏvigeit) *intr.-tr.* navegar. *2 tr.* gobernar [un buque o avión].
navigation (nævigeiꞏshøn) *s.* navegación.
navigator (næꞏvigeitø‘) *s.* navegante, mareante.
navvy (næꞏvi) *s.* (Ingl.) peón, bracero. *2* máquina excavadora.
navy (neiꞏvi) *s.* armada, flota, marina de guerra: ~ *blue*, azul marino; ~ *yard*, arsenal, astillero.
nay (nei) *adv.* no: *to say* ~, decir no. *2* es más; y aún. *3 s.* negativa, denegación. *4* voto en contra.
Nazarene (næšariꞏn) *adj.-s.* nazareno.
Nazi (naꞏtsi) *s.* naci.
Nazism (-išm) *s.* nacismo.
neap (nɪp) *s.* marea muerta.
Neapolitan (nɪapaꞏlitan) *adj.-s.* napolitano.
near (nɪø‘) *adj.* cercano, próximo, inmediato: ~ *relation*, pariente cercano; *Near East*, próximo Oriente. *2* íntimo, estrecho. *3* corto, directo [camino]. *4* cicatero, tacaño. *5* fiel, muy aproximada [versión, etc.]. *6* izquierdo [caballo, rueda]. *7 adv.* cerca: ~ *at hand*, cerca, a la mano. *8* casi, a punto de. *9* aproximadamente. *10 prep.* cerca de.
near (to) *tr.-intr.* acercarse [a].
nearby (-bai) *adv.* cerca. *2 adj.* cercano.
nearly (-li) *adv.* cerca, cercanamente. *2* de cerca. *3* íntimamente; estrechamente. *4* casi, aproximadamente.
nearness (-nis) *s.* proximidad. *2* inminencia. *3* intimidad.
nearsighted (-saitid) *adj.* corto de vista, miope.
neat (nɪt) *adj.* aseado, pulcro, ordenado. *2* primoroso. *3* límpido, claro. *4* elegante, de buen gusto, lindo. *5* limpio [ejecutado con limpieza], hábil, diestro. *6* puro, sin mezcla. *7* neto. *8 s.* res vacuna, ganado vacuno.
neatness (-nis) *s.* aseo, pulcritud. *2* elegancia, buen gusto, primor. *3* nitidez. *4* limpieza, precisión, destreza.
neb (neb) *s.* pico [de ave, tortuga, etc.].

Nebuchadnezzar (nebiukødne·šaʳ) *n. pr. m.* Nabucodonosor.
nebula (ne·biula) *s.* ASTR. nebulosa.
nebulosity (nebiula·siti) *s.* nebulosidad.
nebulous (ne·biuløs) *adj.* nebuloso. 2 vago, indeterminado.
necessary (ne·siseri) *adj.* necesario. 2 forzoso, obligado. 3 *s.* cosa necesaria; requisito.
necessitarian (nisesite·rian) *adj.-s.* determinista.
necessitate (to) (nise·siteit) *tr.* hacer necesario, indispensable. 2 reducir a la necesidad de, obligar.
necessitous (-øs) *adj.* necesitado, pobre.
necessity (nise·siti) *s.* necesidad: *of ~*, por necesidad. | No tiene el sentido de evacuación corporal.
neck (nek) *s.* cuello, pescuezo, garganta: *to break one's ~*, desnucarse; fig. matarse [trabajando]; *~ and ~*, lado a lado [en una carrera]; *~ or nothing*, a toda costa. 2 cuello [de una prenda, una vasija, etc.]: *low ~*, escote. 3 gollete [de botella]. 4 GEOGR. istmo; cabo; estrecho; desfiladero. 5 MÚS. mástil.
neck (to) *tr.* MEC. estrechar. 2 pop. besar, acariciar. 3 *intr.* pop. besarse, acariciarse.
neckband (-bænd) *s.* tirilla [de camisa].
neckcloth (-kloz) *s.* pañuelo para el cuello; corbata, corbatín.
neckerchief (-øʳchif) *s.* pañuelo para el cuello. 2 especie de pañoleta. 3 corbata, corbatín.
necklace (-lis), **necklet** (-lit) *s.* collar, gargantilla.
necktie (-tai) *s.* corbata.
neckwear (-ueʳ) *s.* prendas para el cuello.
necrology (nekra·lodÿi) *s.* necrología. 2 obituario.
necromancer (ne·krømænsøʳ) *s.* nigromante.
necromancy (-i) *s.* necromancia, nigromancia.
necropolis (nekra·pølis) *s.* necrópolis.
necrosis (nekrou·sis) *s.* MED. necrosis.
nectar (ne·ktaʳ) *s.* néctar.
nectareous (nekte·riøs) *adj.* nectáreo, nectarino.
nectarine (ne·ktarin) *s.* BOT. griñón, briñón.
nectary (ne·ktari) *s.* BOT. nectario.
Ned (ned) *n. pr.* dim. de EDWARD y EDWIN.
née o **nee** (nei) *adj.* gal. nacida.
need (nıd) *s.* necesidad, carencia, falta; momento de apuro: *if ~ be*, si fuese menester. 2 necesidad, pobreza: *to be in ~*, estar necesitado.
need (to) *tr.* necesitar, haber menester, requerir. 2 *intr.* estar necesitado. 3 *impers.* ser necesario, ser menester, ser preciso.
needful (-ful) *adj.* necesario. 2 necesitado. 3 *s.* lo necesario.
needle (-øl) *s.* aguja [de coser, de media, de gancho, de gramófono, etc.]: *look for a ~ in a haystack*, buscar una aguja en un pajar. 2 aguja [roca puntiaguda]. 3 ARQ. aguja. 4 BOT. hoja acicular. 5 fiel [de balanza]. 6 estilo [de un reloj de sol]. 7 brújula. 8 fig. *the ~*, nerviosismo.
needlecase (-keis) *s.* alfiletero.
needlefish (-fish) *s.* ICT. aguja.
needleful (-ful) *s.* hebra de hilo.
needles (-š) *s.* BOT. aguja de pastor.
needless (nı·dlis) *adj.* innecesario, inútil.
needlewoman (nı·dølwumæn) *f.* costurera.
needlework (-uøʳk) *s.* costura. 2 labor o bordado de aguja.
needn't (nı·dønt) *contr.* de NEED NOT.
needs (nıds) *adv.* necesariamente. | Gralte. con *must*.
needy (nı·di) *adj.* necesitado, menesteroso.
ne'er (ne·øʳ) *adv. contr.* de NEVER.

ne'r-do-well *adj.-s.* haragán, perdido, inútil.
nefarious (nife·riøs) *adj.* nefario, inicuo, atroz.
negate (to) (nigei·t) *tr.* negar. 2 anular, invalidar.
negation (nigei·shøn) *s.* negación.
negative (ne·gativ) *adj.* negativo. 2 *s.* negativa, negación, denegación. 3 GRAM. negación. 4 FOT., ELECT. negativo. 6 MAT. término negativo.
negative (to) *tr.* negar, contradecir. 2 rechazar, no aprobar. 3 contrarrestar. 4 poner el veto a.
negatron (ne·gatran) *s.* QUÍM. negatón.
neglect (nigle·kt) *s.* abandono, descuido, negligencia, olvido. 2 indiferencia, desdén. 3 desuso. 4 inobservancia.
neglect (to) *tr.* abandonar, descuidar, olvidar, omitir. 2 no hacer caso de, desdeñar, arrinconar, preterir.
neglectful (-ful) *adj.* descuidado, negligente, omiso, desaplicado; que desatiende.
négligé, negligee (negliÿei·) *s.* traje de casa; bata de mujer.
negligence (ne·glidÿøns) *s.* negligencia. 2 LIT., B. ART. abandono, naturalidad.
negligent (-ønt) *adj.* negligente, descuidado.
negligible (-ibøl) *adj.* despreciable, insignificante.
negotiable (nigou·shiabøl) *adj.* negociable. 2 que puede ser pasado, salvado, superado.
negotiate (to) (nigou·shieit) *tr.-intr.* negociar. 2 fam. atravesar, saltar, salvar, superar: *to ~ a fence*, saltar una valla.
negotiation (nigoushie·shøn) *s.* negociación. 2 negocio, gestión.
negotiator (nigou·shietøʳ) *m.* negociador.
Negress (nı·gris) *f.* negra [mujer].
Negro (nı·grou) *adj.-s.* negro [pers.]. 2 *adj.* de negro, de los negros.
Negroid (nı·groid) *adj.-s.* negroide.
Negus (nı·gøs) *s.* Negus. 2 (con min.) bebida caliente de vino, agua, azúcar, etc.
neigh (nei) *s.* relincho.
neigh (to) *intr.* relinchar.
neighbo(u)r (nei·bøʳ) *s.* vecino. 2 amigo. 3 prójimo.
neighbo(u)r (to) *tr.-intr.* ser vecino [de]. 2 *intr.* estar en buenas relaciones. 3 vivir o estar situado cerca.
neighbo(u)rhood (-jud) *s.* vecindad. 2 cercanías. 3 vecindario. 4 *in the ~ of*, alrededor de, aproximadamente.
neighbo(u)ring (-ing) *adj.* vecino, adyacente. 2 rayano, cercano.
neighbo(u)rly (-li) *adj.* atento; amistoso; buen vecino.
neither (nai·ðøʳ) *adj.* ninguno de los dos; ni uno ni otro; ninguno, ningún. 2 *conj.* ni: *~ ... nor*, ni ... ni. 3 *adv.* tampoco, ni siquiera. 4 *pron.* ninguno, ni uno ni otro, ni el uno ni el otro: *~ of them*, ninguno de ellos.
nemathelminth (nemazelmi·nz) *s.* ZOOL. nematelminto.
nematode (ne·matoud) *adj.-s.* ZOOL. nematodo.
Nemaean (nimı·an) *adj.* nemeo.
Nemesis (ne·misis) *s.* MIT. Némesis. 2 (con min.) justicia, venganza, justo castigo.
nenuphar (ne·niufaʳ) *s.* BOT. nenúfar.
neoclassic (al (nıoklæ·sik(al) *adj.* neoclásico.
Neo-Latin *adj.* neolatino.
neolithic (nıoli·zik) *adj.* neolítico.
neologism (nıa·lodÿism) *s.* neologismo.
neon (nı·an) *s.* neón: *~ light*, lámpara de neón.
neophyte (nı·ofait) *s.* neófito.
neoplasia (nøplæ·sia) *s.* MED. neoplasia.
Neoplatonic (-pleita·nik) *adj.* neoplatónico.

Neozoic (-šou·ik) *adj.* GEOL. neozoico.
nephew (ne·fiu o ne·viu) *s.* sobrino.
nephridium (nefri·diøm) *s.* ZOOL. nefridio.
nephritic (-tik) *adj.-s.* MED. nefrítico.
nephritis (nefrai·tis) *s.* MED. nefritis.
nepotism (ne·potišm) *s.* nepotismo.
Neptune (ne·ptiun) *s.* MIT., ASTR. Neptuno.
Nereid (ni·riid) *s.* MIT. Nereida.
nerval (nø·ᵛval) *adj.* ANAT. nérveo.
nervation (nøᵛvei·shøn) *s.* BOT. nervadura.
nerve (nøᵛv) *s.* ANAT. nervio: ~ *cell*, célula nerviosa; *to strain every* ~, hacer los mayores esfuerzos. *2* BOT. nervio, vena. *3* nervio, fuerza, vigor. *4* sangre fría, resolución. *5* pop. desfachatez. *6 pl.* nervios, excitabilidad nerviosa: *to get on one's nerves*, crispar los nervios.
nerve (to) *tr.* fortalecer. *2* alentar, dar valor.
nerveless (-lis) *adj.* enervado, débil. *2* acobardado. *3* sin nervios.
nerve-racking (ræ·king) *adj.* irritante, exasperante.
nervosity (-va·siti) *s.* nervosidad.
nervous (-øs) *adj.* nervudo. *2* nervioso: ~ *breakdown*, crisis nerviosa. *3* vigoroso, enérgico. *4* tímido. *5* de nerviosismo.
nervousness (-nis) *s.* nervosidad, nerviosidad. *2* vigor, fuerza.
nervure (-iøᵛ) *s.* ARQ. nervadura. *2* BOT., ENT. nervio.
nervy (-i) *adj.* vigoroso. *2* atrevido, audaz. *3* pop. descarado. *4* (Ingl.) nervioso, excitable.
nescience (ne·shiøns) *s.* nesciencia.
nest (nest) *s.* nido. *2* nidal, ponedero. *3* nidada [de pajaritos]. *4* guarida, manida: ~ *of thieves*, cueva de ladrones. *5* juego de objetos que encajan uno dentro de otro mayor.
nest (to) *intr.* anidar. *2* nidificar. *3* buscar nidos. *4 tr.* poner como en un nido.
nest-egg *s.* nidal [huevo]. *2* gato [dinero]; ahorros.
nestle (to) (ne·søl) *tr.* abrigar, proveer de nido. *2* recostar [una parte del cuerpo] como en un nido. *3* cuidar, mimar. *4 intr.* acurrucarse, recostarse; apretarse [contra]. *5* anidar; establecerse.
nestling (-ling) *s.* pollo que aún no ha abandonado el nido. *2* niño pequeño.
Nestorian (nesto·rian) *adj.* nestoriano.
net (net) *s.* red. *2* malla, redecilla [tejido]. *3* COM. líquido. *4 adj.* puro, sin mezcla. *5* COM. neto, líquido: ~ *profit*, beneficio líquido; ~ *weight*, peso neto.
net (to) *tr.* tejer de malla; hacer malla con. *2* cubrir con red. *3* enredar [coger con red]. *4* COM. producir u obtener [cierto beneficio líquido]. ¶ Pret. y p. p.: *netted*; ger.: *netting*.
netful (-ful) *s.* redada.
nether (ne·ðøᵛ) *adj.* inferior, más bajo, de debajo: ~ *world*, el infierno; el otro mundo.
Netherlander (-lændøᵛ) *s.* holandés.
Netherlands (the) (-lændš) *n. pr.* Países Bajos.
nethermost (-moust) *adj.* [el] más bajo.
netting (ne·ting) *s.* red, obra de malla. *2* alambrado. *3* MAR. jareta.
nettle (-øl) *s.* BOT. ortiga. *2* MED. ~ *rash*, urticaria. *3* BOT. ~ *tree*, almez.
nettle (to) *tr.* picar [como una ortiga]. *2* picar, irritar, provocar.
network (ne·twøᵛk) *s.* red; obra de malla; retículo. *2* FERROC., RADIO., etc. red, cadena.
neume (nium) *s.* MÚS. neuma.
neuralgia (niuræ·ldỹia) *s.* neuralgia.
neurasthenia (niuræszi·nia) *s.* MED. neurastenia.

neuritis (niurai·tis) *s.* MED. neuritis.
neurologist (niura·lødỹist) *s.* neurólogo.
neuron (niu·ran) *s.* ANAT. neurona.
neuropath (niu·røpæz) *s.* MED. neurópata.
neuropathy (niura·pazi) *f.* neuropatía.
neuropteran (-ptøran) *adj.-s.* ENT. neuróptero.
neurosis (niurou·sis) *s.* MED. neurosis.
neurotic (niura·tik) *adj.-s.* MED. neurótico.
neuter (niu·tøᵛ) *adj.* GRAM., BIOL. neutro. *2* neutral.
neutral (niu·tral) *adj.* neutral. *2* BIOL., QUÍM., ELECT., PINT. neutro. *3* gris, indefinido, medio. *4 s.* neutral. *5* AUTO. punto muerto.
neutrality (niutræ·liti) *s.* neutralidad. *2* calidad de neutro.
neutralization (niutrališei·shøn) *s.* neutralización.
neutralize (to) (niu·tralaiš) *tr.* neutralizar.
neutron (niu·tran) *s.* FÍS. neutrón.
never (ne·vøᵛ) *adv.* nunca, jamás: ~ *again*, nunca más. *2* de ningún modo, no, ni... siquiera: ~ *fear*, no hay cuidado; ~ *mind*, no importa.
never-ending *adj.* perpetuo, eterno, continuo.
nevermore (nevøᵛmo·ᵛ) *adv.* nunca más, jamás, más.
nevertheless (nevøᵛðøle·s) *adv.-conj.* no obstante, sin embargo, a pesar de eso.
new (niu) *adj.* nuevo: *a* ~ *man*, un hombre nuevo, otro hombre; ~ *moon*, luna nueva; *New Testament*, Nuevo Testamento; *New World*, Nuevo Mundo; *New Year*, año nuevo; *what is* ~?, ¿qué hay de nuevo? *2* tierno [pan]. *3* moderno. *4* reciente. *5* ~ *arrival*, persona recién llegada. *6 adv.* recientemente; nuevamente.
newborn (niu·boᵛn) *adj.* recién nacido. *2* renacido.
newcomer (-cømøᵛ) *s.* recién venido o llegado.
newel (niu·øl) *s.* ARQ. nabo, bolo [de escalera]. *2* poste, pilar [con que termina la barandilla de una escalera].
New England *n. pr.* GEOGR. Nueva Inglaterra.
newfangled (niufæ·ngøld) *adj.* nuevo, recién inventado, de última moda.
Newfoundland (-fau·ndlænd) *n. pr.* GEOGR. Terranova. *2 s.* perro de Terranova.
New Guinea *n. pr.* GEOGR. Nueva Guinea.
newish (-ish) *adj.* bastante nuevo o reciente.
new-laid *adj.* fresco [huevo].
newness (-nis) *s.* novedad, calidad de nuevo.
New Orleans (-o·ᵛliønš) *n. pr.* GEOGR. Nueva Orleans.
news (niuš) *s.* noticia, noticias: *a piece of* ~, una noticia; *this is* ~ *to me*, esto me coge de nuevas.
| Gralte. se construye en sing.: *what is the* ~?, ¿qué noticias hay? *2* prensa, periódicos: ~ *agency*, agencia informativa; ~ *dealer*, vendedor de periódicos.
newsboy (-boi) *s.* vendedor de periódicos.
newscast (-kæst) *s.* RADIO. noticiario.
newscaster (-kæstøᵛ) *s.* cronista de radio.
newsman (-mæn) *s.* periodista, reportero, noticiero.
newspaper (-peipøᵛ) *s.* diario, periódico: ~ *clipping*, recorte de periódico.
newspaperman (-mæn) *s.* periodista.
newsprint (niu·sprint) *s.* papel de periódico.
newsreel (-ril) *s.* CINEM. noticiario, actualidades.
newstand (-tænd) *s.* quiosco de periódicos.
newt (niut) *s.* ZOOL. tritón.
New York (-yo·ᵛk) *n. pr.* GEOGR. Nueva York.
New Yorker (-yo·ᵛkøᵛ) *s.* neoyorquino.
New Zealand (-zi·land) *n. pr.* GEOGR. Nueva Zelanda.
New Zealander (-zi·landøᵛ) *s.* neozelandés.

next (nekst) *adj.* próximo, inmediato, contiguo; siguiente, sucesivo; futuro, venidero: ~ *door*, la puerta de al lado; ~ *door to*, en la casa de al lado de; rayano en; ~ *month*, el mes que viene; ~ *of kin*, pariente (s más cercano (s; *the* ~ *day*, el día siguiente; *the* ~ *life*, la vida futura. *2 adv.* luego, después, en seguida: ~ *to*, al lado de; después de; casi: ~ *to nothing*, casi nada; *what* ~?, ¿y después qué?, ¿y qué más? *3 prep.* junto a, al lado de; después de.

nexus (ne·ksøs) *s.* nexo, lazo, vínculo.

nib (nib) *s.* ORN. pico. *2* punta, extremo. *3* punto [de la pluma].

nibble (-øl) *s.* mordisco, bocadito.

nibble (to) *tr.-intr.* mordiscar, roer, ramonear, comer a bocaditos. *2* picar [como el pez].

niblick (-lik) *s.* DEP. uno de los palos de golf.

nice (nais) *adj.* fino, sutil; exacto, preciso. *2* concienzudo, escrupuloso, puntilloso. *3* delicado, mirado, exigente. *4* delicado [que exige cuidado, tacto, etc.]. *5* refinado, pulcro, elegante. *6* primoroso. *7* bueno, agradable; delicioso, exquisito. *8* lindo. *9* decoroso, conveniente. *10* bien educado. *11* amable, simpático.

Nice (nɪs) *n. pr.* GEOGR. Niza.

Nicene (nai·sin) *adj.* niceno.

niceness (-nis) *f.* finura. *2* amabilidad, gentileza. *3* lindeza. *4* delicadeza, exactitud, esmero.

nicety (-ti) *s.* finura, sutilidad; sutileza. *2* exactitud, precisión: *to a* ~, con la mayor precisión. *3* delicadeza, cuidado, esmero, primor. *4* refinamiento, atildamiento. *5* amabilidad.

niche (nich) *s.* nicho, hornacina.

Nick (nik) *n. pr. dim.* Nicolás. *2 Old* ~, el diablo.

nick *s.* muesca, entalladura; mella. *2* IMPR. cran. *3 in the* ~ *of time*, en el momento preciso, a tiempo.

nick (to) *tr.* hacer muescas en; cortar; mellar. *2* pop. estafar, robar. *3* acertar; llegar a tiempo.

nickel (ni·køl) *s.* QUÍM. níquel. *2* fam. (E.U.) moneda de cinco centavos.

nickel-plate (to) *tr.* niquelar.

nicknack (ni·knæk) *s.* KNICKNACK.

nickname (-neim) *s.* apodo; nombre familiar.

nickname (to) *tr.* apodar, apellidar.

nicotin(e (ni·køtin) *s.* nicotina.

nictitating (ni·ktiteiting) *adj.* nictitante.

nidification (nidifikei·shøn) *s.* nidificación.

niece (nɪ·s) *f.* sobrina.

niello (nie·lou) *s.* niel; nielado.

niello (to) *tr.* helar.

Niger (nai·dy̆ø') *n. pr.* GEOGR. Niger.

niggard (ni·ga'd) *adj.-s.* tacaño, cicatero, avaro.

niggardly (-li) *adj.* tacaño. *2 adv.* tacañamente.

nigger (ni·gø') *s.* desp. negro, negra [pers.]: ~ *in the woodpile*, fig. gato encerrado.

niggle (to) *intr.* ser meticuloso; pasar el tiempo en minucias.

niggling (ni·gling) *adj.* demasiado minucioso.

nigh (nai·) *adj., adv., prep.* ant NEAR.

night (nait) *s.* noche: *by* ~, por la noche; *good* ~, buenas noches; *last* ~, anoche; *to make a* ~ *of it*, pasar toda la noche en una diversión, etc. *2 adj.* de noche, nocturno: ~ *club*, cabaret, club nocturno; ~ *dew*, sereno, relente; ~ *light*, luz que se deja por la noche; mariposa, lamparilla; ~ *owl*, búho, lechuza; noctámbulo; ~ *shool*, escuela nocturna; ~ *watch*, guardia nocturna; sereno; vigilante de noche.

nightcap (-kæp) *s.* gorro de dormir. *2 fig.* bebida que se toma antes de acostarse.

nightfall (-fol) *s.* anochecer, anochecida, caída de la tarde; *at* ~, al anochecer.

nightgown (-gaun) *s.* camisón, bata de noche.

nighthawk (-jok) *s.* ORN. chotacabras norteamericana.

nightingale (-ingeli) *s.* ORN. ruiseñor.

nightjar (-dy̆ø') *s.* ORN. chotacabras.

nightly (-li) *adj.* nocturno, de noche. *2 adv.* por las noches; todas las noches.

nightmare (-me') *s.* pesadilla.

nightmarish (-merish) *adj.* angustioso [como una pesadilla].

nightshade (-sheid) *s.* BOT. hierba mora. *2* BOT. *deadly* ~, belladona.

nightshirt (-shø't) *s.* camisa de dormir.

nighttime (-taim) *s.* noche: *in the* ~, de noche.

nigtwalker (-uokø') *s.* noctámbulo. *2* sonámbulo. *3* ramera; ladrón nocturno.

night-watchman *s.* sereno; vigilante nocturno.

nightwear (-ue') *s.* camisón, pijama.

nihilism (nai·jilišm) *s.* nihilismo.

nihilist (nai·jilist) *s.* nihilista.

nil (nil) *s.* nada, ninguno.

Nile (nail) *n. pr.* GEOGR. Nilo.

nilgai (ni·lgai) *s.* ZOOL. antílope de la India.

Nilotic (naila·tik) *adj.* nilótico.

nimble (ni·mbøl) *adj.* ágil, ligero, vivo, activo.

nimble-footed *adj.* ligero de pies, veloz.

nimbleness (-nis) *s.* agilidad, ligereza, viveza. *2* expedición, destreza, prontitud.

nimble-witted *adj.* listo, despierto, inteligente.

nimbus (ni·mbøs) *s.* nimbo. *2* aureola.

nincompoop (ninkømpup) *s.* bobo, simple.

nine (nain) *adj.-s.* nueve: ~ *o'clock*, las nueve. *2 The Nine*, las Musas.

ninefold (-fould) *adj.-s.* nónuplo. *2 adv.* nueve veces.

ninepins (-pins) *s.* juego de bolos.

nineteen (tɪ·n) *adj.-s.* diez y nueve.

nineteenth (-tɪnz) *adj.-s.* decimonono. *2* diecinueve [del mes].

ninetieth (-tiez) *adj.-s.* nonagésimo; noventavo.

ninety (-ti) *pl. adj.-s.* noventa.

Nineveh (ni·nivi) *n. pr.* GEOGR. Nínive.

ninny (ni·ni) *s.* bobo, mentecato.

ninth (nainz) *adj.-s.* noveno. *2* nueve [del mes].

niobium (naiou·biøm) *s.* QUÍM. niobio.

nip (nip) *s.* pellizco, mordisco, picotazo. *2* traguito; pedacito. *3* fig. pinchazo, sarcasmo. *4* punzada [del viento frío]. *5* daño del frío [en las plantas].

nip (to) *tr.* pellizcar. *2* mordiscar, picotear. *3* helar, marchitar [el frío]. *4* coger, prender. *5* cortar: *to* ~ *in the bud*, cortar en flor. *6* tr.-intr. beber a tragos. ¶ Pret. y p. p.: *nipped;* ger.: *-pping.*

nipa (nai·pø) *s.* BOT. nipa.

nipper (ni·pø') *s.* boca, pinzas [de crustáceo]. *2 pl.* pinzas, alicates, cortaalambres.

nipple (ni·pøl) *s.* ANAT. pezón, tetilla. *2* pezón de goma. *3* protuberancia.

Nipponese (nipanni·š) *s.* nipón, japonés.

Nirvana, nirvana (ni'va·na) *s.* nirvana.

nit (nit) *s.* liendre.

niter (nai·tø') *s.* nitro, salitre.

nitrate (-treit) *s.* QUÍM. nitrato.

nitre (-tø') *s.* NITER.

nitric (-trik) *adj.* nítrico.

nitrocellulose (naitrøse·liulous) QUÍM. nitrocelulosa.

nitrogen (nai·trødy̆øn) *s.* QUÍM. nitrógeno, ázoe.

nitroglicerin (naitrøgli·sørin) *s.* nitroglicerina.

nitrous (nai·trøs) *adj.* nitroso.
nitty (ni·ti) *adj.* lendroso.
nitwit (ni·twit) *s.* fam. simple, bobo, papanatas.
no (nou) *adv.* no: ~ *longer,* ya no; ~ *more,* no más; *are you going?* —*No,* ¿va usted? —*No. 2 adj.* ningún, ninguna: *by* ~ *means,* de ningún modo; ~ *one,* nadie; ~ *man's land,* tierra de nadie. | En muchos casos, hay que traducir la frase entera: *there is* ~ *wine,* no hay vino; *with* ~ *money,* sin dinero. *3* prohibido, se prohíbe: *no smoking,* prohibido fumar.
Noah (nou·a) *n. pr.* Noé. *2 Noah's ark,* arca de Noé.
nob (nab) *s.* fam. cabeza, chola. *2* pop. persona de viso.
nobby (na·bi) *adj.* pop. elegante.
nobiliary (noubi·lieri) *adj.* nobiliario.
nobility (noubi·liti) *s.* nobleza.
noble (nou·bøl) *adj.-s.* noble. *2 adj.* magnífico, majestuoso.
nobleman (nou·bølmæn) *s.* noble, aristócrata.
nobleness (nou·bølnis) *s.* nobleza [cualidad].
noblewoman (nou·bølwuman) *s.* mujer noble.
nobody (nou·badi) *pron.* nadie, ninguno. *2 s.* nadie [pers. insignificante].
nocturnal (naktø·ʳnal) *adj.* nocturno, nocturnal.
nocturne (na·ktøʳn) *s.* mús. nocturno. *2* pint. escena nocturna.
nod (nad) *s.* inclinación de cabeza [en señal de asentimiento, saludo, etc.]; reverencia. *2* cabeceo, cabezada [del que duerme sentado].
nod (to) *intr.-tr.* inclinar la cabeza [en señal de asentimiento, saludo, etc.]. *2 intr.* cabecear, dar cabezadas, dormitar. *3* estar descuidado. ¶ Pret. y p. p.: *nodded;* ger.: *-dding.*
nodal (nou·dal) *adj.* nodal. *2* anat. nodátil.
noddle (na·døl) *s.* mollera, cabeza.
noddy (na·di) *s.* bobo, simple.
node (noud) *s.* nodo. *2* bulto, protuberancia. *3* bot. nudo. *4* nudo [punto de convergencia].
nodose (-ous) *adj.* nudoso.
nodosity (nøda·siti) *s.* nudosidad.
nodular (na·diulaʳ) *adj.* nodular.
nodule (na·diul) *s.* nódulo.
nodus (na·døs) *s.* nudo, enredo, complicación.
nog (nag) *s.* ~ taco de madera. *2* cierta cerveza fuerte. *3* eggnog.
noggin (-in) *s.* tacita, copa. *2* pequeña cantidad [de un licor].
nohow (nou·jau) *adv.* fam. de ninguna manera.
noise (noiš) *s.* ruido; sonido. *2* ruido, barullo, alboroto, gritería. *3* rumor, fama.
noise (to) *tr.* esparcir, divulgar, rumorear.
noiseless (-lis) *adj.* silencioso, callado, tranquilo.
noisily (-ili) *adv.* ruidosamente.
noisiness (-inis) *s.* ruidosidad. *2* ruido.
noisome (noi·søm) *adj.* nocivo, pernicioso, malsano. *2* fétido, ofensivo, repugnante.
noisy (noi·ši) *adj.* ruidoso, clamoroso, bullicioso.
nolition (noli·shøn) *s.* nolición.
nomad (nou·mæd) *adj.* y *s.* nómada.
nomadism (-išm) *s.* nomadismo.
nomenclature (nou·menkleichøʳ) *s.* nomenclatura.
nominal (na·minal) *adj.* nominal. *2* gram. substantivado, substantivo.
nominalism (-išm) *s.* nominalismo.
nominate (to) (-eit) *tr.* nombrar. *2* proponer [para un cargo], designar como candidato.
nomination (-ei·shøn) *s.* nominación, nombramiento, propuesta.
nominative (na·minativ) *s.* nominativo. *2 adj.* propuesto; de propuesta [para un cargo].

nominator (-eitøʳ) *s.* nominador.
nominee (nmini·) *s.* propuesto, candidato [para un cargo].
non- (nan) partícula negativa que forma compuestos con los sentidos de *no, an, dis, falta de,* etc.
nonacceptance (nanækse·ptans) *s.* falta de aceptación.
nonage (na·nidȳ) *s.* minoridad, menor edad.
nonagenarian (nanadȳine·rian) *adj.-s.* nonagenario.
nonagesimal (-e·simal) *adj.* nonagésimo.
nonagon (na·nagan) *s.* geom. eneágono.
nonaggression (nanagre·shøn) *s.* no agresión.
nonappearance (-pi·rans) *s.* der. incomparecencia.
nonce (nans) *s. for the* ~, por ahora, por el momento. *2 adj.* ~ *word,* palabra para el caso.
nonchalance (na·nshalans) *s.* indiferencia, abandono, indolencia.
non-combatant *adj.-s.* no combatiente.
non-commissioned *adj.* ~ *officer,* cabo, sargento, clase.
non-committal *adj.* reservado, evasivo, que no se compromete.
noncompliance (nankømplai·ans) *s.* incumplimiento, inobediencia.
non-conductor *s.* fís., elect. cuerpo mal conductor; aislador.
non-conformist *adj.-s.* disidente [esp. de la Iglesia Anglicana].
non-delivery *s.* falta de entrega.
nondescript (na·ndiskript) *adj.* indefinible, difícil de clasificar, raro. *2 s.* objeto o persona difícil de clasificar.
none (nøn) *pron.* ninguno; nada: *I have* ~, no tengo ninguno; ~ *of,* ninguno de; nada de. *2* nadie. *3 adv.* no, de ningún modo: ~ *the less,* no menos; no obstante, sin embargo; *he was* ~ *the better* (o *the worse) for it,* no por ello se hallaba mejor (o peor); no ganó (o perdió) nada con ello.
nonentity (nane·ntiti) *s.* nada; no existencia. *2* cosa no existente. *3* nulidad, cero a la izquierda.
nones (nounš) *s. pl.* nonas. *2* liturg. nona.
non-essential *adj.* no esencial.
nonesuch (nø·nsøch) *s.* persona o cosa sin igual.
non-existence *s.* inexistencia.
non-existent *adj.* inexixtente.
non-intervention *s.* no intervención.
nonius (nou·niøs) *s.* nonio.
nonpareil (nanpare·l) *adj.* sin par, sin igual. *2 s.* persona o cosa sin par. *3* impr. nomparell.
nonpartisan (-pa·ʳtišan) *adj.* pol. independiente.
nonpayment (-peimønt) *s.* falta de pago.
nonplus (na·npløs) *s.* perplejidad, confusión, estupefacción.
nonplus (to) *tr.* confundir, dejar perplejo. *2* aplastar, dejar sin palabra.
non-resident *adj.-s.* no residente.
nonsense (-sens) *s.* cosa sin sentido, absurdidad. *2* tontería, necedad, desatino. *3* tonterías, pamplinadas. *4* interj. ¡bah!
nonsensical (nanse·nsikal) *adj.* sin sentido, absurdo, disparatado, desatinado.
non-skid *adj.* antideslizante.
nonstriated (-strai·atid) *adj.* liso [músculo].
non-transferable *adj.* intransferible.
non-union *adj.* no sindicado [obrero].
noodle (nu·døl) *s.* tallarín; fideo. *2* simple, tonto, zote. *3* fam. cabeza.
nook (nuk) *s.* rincón. *2* lugar retirado y apacible.
noon (nun), **noonday** (-dei), **noontide** (-taid) *s.* me-

diodía [hora]: *high noon,* las doce en punto. *2* apogeo, punto culminante.

noose (nus) *s.* lazo, nudo corredizo, gaza. *2* dogal.

noose (to) *tr.* lazar, coger con lazo o trampa. *2* ahorcar. *3* hacer un lazo o nudo corredizo en.

nopal (nou·pal) *s.* BOT. nopal, higuera, chumba.

nor (noʳ) *conj.* ni: *neither you ~ I,* ni usted ni yo. *2* tampoco, y no: *~ I,* yo tampoco; *~ was it all,* y ello no era todo.

Nordic (no·ʳdik) *adj.-s.* nórdico.

norm (noʳm) *s.* norma, pauta, regla, modelo.

normal (no·ʳmal) *adj.* normal. *2 s.* estado normal; lo normal. *3* escuela normal. *4* GEOM. normal.

normalcy (-si), **normality** (-liti) *s.* normalidad.

normalize (to) (-laiš) *tr.* normalizar; regularizar.

Norman (no·ʳman) *adj.-s.* normando.

Normandy (-di) *n. pr.* GEOGR. Normandía.

Norse (noʳs) *adj.-s.* escandinavo.

Norseman (no·ʳsmæn) *s.* NORTHMAN.

north (noʳz) *s.* norte, septentrión. *2* norte [región]. *3 adj.* del norte, septentrional: *North America,* Norteamérica, América del Norte; *North Pole,* polo norte; *North Sea,* mar del norte; *North Star,* estrella del norte. *4 adv.* al norte, hacia el norte.

northeast (-ɪst) *adj.-s.* nordeste.

northeaster (noʳzɪ·støʳ) *s.* viento del norte. *2* norteño.

northerly (-li) *adj.* septentrional, boreal.

northern (-n) *adj.* del norte; septentrional. *2* (E.U.) de los Estados del Norte.

northerner (-nøʳ) *s.* norteño, esp. (E.U.) de los Estados del Norte.

northland (no·ʳzlænd) *s.* tierra del norte. *2* (con may.) región boreal. *3* Península escandinava.

Northman (-mæn) *s.* normando, antiguo escandinavo.

northward (s (-wøʳd (š) *adv.* hacia el norte.

northwest (-we·st) *s.* noroeste, norueste.

Norway (no·ʳwei) *n. pr.* GEOGR. Noruega.

Norwegian (norwɪ·dўian) *adj.-s.* noruego.

nose (nouš) *s.* ANAT., ZOOL. nariz: *to blow one's ~,* sonarse; *to count noses,* contar personas; *to follow one's ~,* seguir en línea recta; *to lead by the ~,* manejar [a uno] a su antojo; *to poke one's ~ into,* meter las narices en; *to turn up one's ~ at,* desdeñar, mirar con desprecio; *before,* o *under, one's ~,* en las barbas de uno. *2* nariz, olfato. *3* morro, hocico; *~ bag,* morral, cebadera. *4* NOOZLE. *5* MAR. proa. *6 adj.* AVIA. *~ dive,* picado.

nose (to) *tr.* oler, olfatear, husmear, rastrear: *2* encararse con. *3* oponerse, hacer frente a. *4* restregar la nariz contra.

noseband (-bænd) *s.* muserola, sobarba.

nosebleed (blɪd) *s.* hemorragia nasal.

nose-dive (to) *intr.* AVIA. picar, descender en picado.

nosegay (-gei) *s.* ramillete [de flores].

nosepiece (-pɪs) *s.* visera [del yelmo]. *2* muserola, sobarba. *3* portaobjetivo [de microscopio].

nosey (nou·ši) *adj.* fam. curioso, entremetido.

nosology (nøsa·lodўi) *s.* nosología.

nostalgia (nastæ·ldўia) *s.* nostalgia.

nostril (na·stril) *s.* ventana de la nariz. *2* ollar.

nostrum (no·strøm) *s.* remedio de curandero; panacea.

not (nat) *adv.* no: *he has ~ come,* no ha venido; *I think ~,* no lo creo, creo que no; *~ at all,* nada, de ningún modo; de nada; *~ that,* no es (decir) que; *~ even,* ni siquiera; *~ yet,* todavía no.

notability (noutabi·liti) *s.* notabilidad. *2* pers. de nota.

notable (nou·tabøl) *adj.* notable. *2* memorable. *3 s.* notable, pers. de nota.

notableness (nou·tabølnis) *s.* notabilidad [calidad].

notably (-bli) *adv.* notablemente.

notarial (noute·rial) *adj.* notarial.

notarize (nou·taraiš) *tr.* autorizar ante notario. *2* dar fe notarial de.

notary (public) (nou·tari) *s.* notario.

notation (notei·shøn) *s.* notación. *2* anotación. *3* acción de notar, observar. *4* sistema de numeración.

notch (na·tch) *s.* muesca, entalladura, mella. *2* fam. grado, escalón. *3* MAR. tojino.

notch (to) *tr.* hacer muescas en, entallar, escoplear. *2* mellar, dentar. *3* tarjar.

note (nout) *s.* nota, marca, señal. *2* mediodía, canción, voz, acento. *3* nota, distinción. *4* nota, apunte, anotación, relación, cuenta. *5* nota [oficial]. *6* billete, esquela: *~ paper,* papel de cartas. *7* billete [de banco]. *8* cédula, vale. *9* MÚS. nota. *10 to take no ~ of,* no hacer caso de.

note (to) *tr.* notar, observar, reparar. *2* distinguir, señalar, hacer notar. *3* notar, anotar. *4* asentar, registrar, apuntar. | Gralte. con *down.*

notebook (-buk) *s.* agenda, memorándum, libro de memoria; libreta.

noted (-id) *adj.* nombrado, conocido, reputado, afamado, prestigioso, célebre, eminente.

noteworthy (-wøʳði) *adj.* notable; digno de ser notado.

nothing (nø·zing) *s.* nada: *~ doing,* imposible, ni por pienso; *~ else,* nada más; *for ~,* inútilmente; por nada, de balde; *to come to ~,* reducirse a nada; fracasar, malograrse; *to make ~ of,* no reparar en; no hacer caso de; no entender, no sacar nada de. *2* ARIT. cero. *3* nadería, insignificancia. *4 adv.* nada, de ningún modo, no: *~ daunted,* sin acobardarse; *~ less,* no menos.

nothingness (nø·zingnis) *s.* [la] nada. *2* nadería.

notice (nou·tis) *s.* informe, aviso, advertencia, anuncio: *on short ~,* con poco tiempo de aviso; *until further ~,* hasta nuevo aviso. *2* conocimiento, observación, atención, caso; mención: *to take ~ of,* notar, observar, hacer caso de; *worthy of ~,* digno de atención, de mención. *3* atención, cortesía. *4* notificación, despido: *to give ~,* dar uno su despido. *6* reseña [literaria, etc.].

notice (to) *tr.* notar, observar, advertir, reparar. *2* hacer mención de; reseñar [un libro]. *3* reconocer, hacer caso de.

noticeable (-abøl) *adj.* notable, visible, perceptible. *2* digno de atención.

notification (-ifikei·shøn) *s.* notificación, aviso.

notify (to) (nou·tifai) *tr.* notificar. *2* informar, avisar. *3* requerir, citar. ¶ Pret. y p. p.: *notified.*

notion (nou·shøn) *s.* noción. *2* idea, concepto, opinión. *3* idea, intención; capricho. *4 pl.* (E.U.) novedades, mercería.

notional (-al) *adj.* nocional. *2* imaginario, ideal. *3* fantaseador. *4* caprichudo.

notoriety (noutørai·iti) *s.* notoriedad [esp. la debida a cosas censurables].

notorious (nouto·riøs) *adj.* notorio, conocido, famoso. | Ús. gralte. en sentido peyorativo.

no-trump (nou·trømp) *adj.-s.* NAIPES. sin triunfo.

notwithstanding (natwidstæ·nding) *adv.* no obstante. *2 prep.* a pesar de. *3 conj.* aunque; por más que.

nougat (nu·gat) *s.* nuégado, guirlache, turrón.

nought (not) *s.* NAUGTH.
noun (noun) *s.* GRAM. nombre.
nourish (to) (nø·rish) *tr.* nutrir, alimentar; sustentar. *2* alimentar, abrigar [sentimientos, etc.].
nourishing (-ing) *adj.* nutritivo, nutricio, alimentoso, substancioso.
nourishment (-mønt) *s.* nutrición, nutrimento. *2* alimento, sustento. *3* pábulo, pasto.
nova (nou·va) *s.* ASTR. nova.
novel (na·vøl) *adj.* nuevo; raro, poco usual. *3 s.* novela; novelística. *4 pl.* DER. novelas.
novelette (navøle·t) *s.* novela corta.
novelist (na·vølist) *s.* novelista.
novelize (to) (-aiš) *tr.* novelar.
novelty (-ti) *s.* novedad. *2* innovación. *3 pl.* COM. novedades.
November (nove·mbø^r) *s.* noviembre.
novena (novi·na) *s.* novena.
novice (na·vis) *s.* novicio, principiante. *2* REL. novicio.
novitiate (novi·shieit) *s.* noviciado.
now (nau) *adv.* ahora; hoy día; actualmente: *from ~ on*, de ahora en adelante; *just ~*, ahora mismo; *~ and again*, *~ and then*, de vez en cuando. *2* entonces. *3 conj.* ahora, ahora bien: *~ then*, ahora bien; pues bien. *4* mas, pero. *5 now ... now*, ora... ora, ya... ya. *6 interj.* ¡vamos!, ¡vaya! *7 adj.* de ahora.
nowadays (-deiš) *adv.* hoy día, hoy en día.
noway (s (nou·wei(š) *adv.* de ningún modo.
nowhere (-jue^r) *adv.* en ninguna parte; a ninguna parte.
nowise (-uaiš) *adv.* de ningún modo, nada.
noxious (na·kshøs) *adj.* nocivo, dañino, pernicioso.
noxiousness (-nis) *s.* nocividad.
nozzle (na·søl) *s.* lanza [de manguera]; punta [de soplete]; pitón [de vasija]. *2* nariz, pico, parte saliente. *3* hocico.
nuance (niu·ans) *s.* matiz.
Nubian (niu·bian) *adj.* nublo.
nubile (niu·bil) *adj.* núbil.
nubility (niubi·liti) *s.* nubilidad.
nuclear (niu·klia^r) *adj.* nuclear, nucleario: *~ fission*, fisión nuclear.
nucleate (to) (-klieit) *tr.-intr.* formar núcleo.
nuclein (-kliin) *s.* BIOQUÍM. nucleína.
nucleus (-kliøs) *s.* núcleo.
nude (niud) *adj.* nudo, desnudo. *2* escueto. *3 s.* B. ART. desnudo.
nudge (nødy̆) *s.* codazo ligero.
nudge (to) *tr.* tocar con el codo [como señal, advertencia, etc.].
nudist (niu·dist) *s.* nudista.
nudity (-diti) *s.* desnudez.
nugatory (-gatori) *adj.* ineficaz, nugatorio. *2* fútil, sin valor.
nugget (nø·git) *s.* MIN. pepita.
nuisance (niu·sans) *s.* daño, molestia, fastidio, lata. *2* pers. o cosa molesta, fastidiosa; chinche.
null (nøl) *adj.* nudo. *2* de ningún valor.
nullification (nølifikei·shøn) *s.* anulación, invalidación.
nullify (to) (nø·lifai) *tr.* anular, invalidar.
nullity (nø·liti) *s.* nulidad. *2* acto o documento nulo.
numb (nøm) *adj.* entumecido, adormecido, envarado, insensible. *2* entorpecido, torpe.
number (nø·mbø^r) *s.* número [en todas sus acepciones]: *back ~*, número atrasado [de un periódico]; *~ one*, fam. uno mismo; *~ plate*, AUTO. placa de matrícula; *a ~ of*, varios, muchos; *out*

of ~, *without ~*, innumerables. *2 pl.* verso, versos. *3* (con may.) Números [libro de la Biblia].
number (to) *tr.* numerar. *2* contar, computar. *3* contar [tener cierto número de años, etc.; incluir en el número de].
numberless (-lis) *adj.* innumerable, innúmero, sinfin de.
numbness (nø·mnis) *s.* entumecimiento, torpor, adormecimiento.
numen (niu·min) *s.* MIT. numen.
numerable (niupmørabøl) *adj.* numerable.
numeral (-al) *adj.* numeral. *2* numérico. *3 s.* número, cifra: *Arabic ~*, número arábigo.
numerary (-eri) *adj.* numerario.
numerate (to) (-eit) *tr.* numerar, contar.
numeration (niumørei·shøn) *s.* numeración.
numerator (niu·møreitø^r) *s.* numerador.
numeric (al (niume·ric(al) *adj.* numérico.
numerous (niu·mørøs) *adj.* numeroso, numerosos, muchos. *2* numeroso, armonioso.
Numidian (niumi·dian) *adj.-s.* númida.
numismatics (niumišmæ·tiks) *s.* numismática.
numismatist (niumi·šmɑtist) *s.* numismático.
numskull (nø·mskøl) *s.* bodoque, zopenco.
nun (nøn) *s.* monja, religiosa.
nunciature (-shiechø^r) *s.* nunciatura.
nuncio (-shiou) *s.* nuncio [apostólico].
nunnery (-øri) *s.* convento [de monjas]. *2* monjío.
nuptial (nø·pshal) *adj.* nupcial. *2 s. pl.* nupcias, boda.
nurse (nø^rs) *s.* ama [de cría], nodriza; niñera: *wet ~*, nodriza. *2* fomentador. *3* enfermero, enfermera.
nurse (to) *tr.* criar, amamantar. *2* alimentar, mantener; abrigar, acariciar; cuidar con esmero; fomentar. *3* cuidar [de un niño, a un enfermo]. *4* curar, cuidar [una enfermedad, una parte enferma]. *5 intr.* amamantarse. *6* ser ama, niñera o enfermera.
nursemaid (-meid) *f.* niñera.
nursery (-øri) *s.* cuarto o aposento destinado a los niños: *~ rhymes*, cuentos en verso para niños. *2* plantel, semillero. *3* criadero, vivero.
nurseryman (nø·^rsørimæn) *s.* dueño o empleado de un plantel o criadero.
nursing (-ing) *s.* crianza, lactancia. *2* cuidado [de un enfermo]: *~ home*, clínica.
nursling (-ling) *s.* niño de teta.
nurture (nø·^rchø^r) *s.* nutrimento, alimentación. *2* crianza, educación. *3* fomento. *4* cuidado, tutela.
nurture (to) *tr.* nutrir, alimentar. *2* criar, educar, cuidar. *3* fomentar.
nut (nøt) *s.* BOT. nuez: *a hard ~ to crack*, fig. hueso duro de roer. *2* pop. cabeza, chola. *4* pop. guillado. *5* petimetre. *6* nuez [del arco del violín]. *7* MÚS. ceja. *8* MEC. tuerca.
nutation (niutei·shøn) *s.* nutación.
nut-brown *adj.* castaño, tostado.
nutcracker (nø·tkrækø^r) *s.* cascanueces.
nutgall (-gol) *s.* BOT. agalla.
nuthatch (-jæch) *s.* ORN. trepatroncos.
nutmeat (-nit) *s.* carne de nuez.
nutmeg (-meg) *s.* BOT. mirística. *2* nuez moscada.
nutria (niu·tria) *s.* ZOOL. coipo. *2* piel de coipo.
nurient (-triønt) *adj.* nutritivo.
nutriment (-trimøn) *s.* nutrimento.
nutrition (niutri·shøn) *s.* nutrición. *2* alimento.
nutritious (-shøs), **nutritive** (niu·tritiv) *adj.* nutritivo, alimenticio.

nutshell (nø·tshel) *s.* cáscara de nuez o avellana: (fig.) *in a* ~, en pocas palabras, en resumidas cuentas.

nutty (-i) *adj.* abundante en nueces. *2* que sabe a nueces. *3* ~ *about*, loco por.

nux-vomica (no·ks-va·mika) *s.* nuez vómica.

nuzzle (to) (nø·zøl) *intr.* husmear; hocicar, hozar. *2* arrimarse cómodamente, acurrucarse.

3 tr. tocar, empujar o restregar con la nariz.

nyctalopy (niktæ·lopi) *s.* nictalopia.

nylon (nai·lan) *s.* nilón. *2 pl.* medias de nilón.

nymph (nimf) *s.* MIT., ZOOL. ninfa. *2 poét.* ninfa.

nympha (ni·mfa) *s.* ZOOL. ninfa, crisálida.

nymphaea (ni·mfia) *s.* BOT. ninfea.

nymphomania (nimfomei·nia) *s.* MED. ninfomanía.

O

O, o (ou) s. O, o, decimoquinta letra del alfabeto inglés.

o' abrev. de OF.

O! *interj.* ¡oh! *2 O that!* ¡ojalá [que]!

oaf (ouf) s. simple, idiota. *2* niño contrahecho.

oafish (ou·fish) *adj.* simple, tonto.

oak (ouk) s. BOT. roble; cualquier árbol o arbusto del gén. *Quercus:* ~ *apple,* ~ *gall,* agalla de roble. *2* roble [madera].

oaken (-øn) *adj.* de roble; roblizo.

oakum (-øm) s. MAR. estopa.

oaky (-i) *adj.* roblizo, duro, fuerte.

oar (oʳ) s. remo [instrumento]: *to lie,* o *rest, on the oars,* cesar de remar; descansar; *to put in one's* ~, meter uno su cucharada. *2* remero.

oar (to) *intr.* remar, bogar. *2 tr.* mover a remo.

oared (-d) *adj.* provisto de remos.

oarlock (-lak) s. MAR. escálamo, tolete, horquilla.

oarsman (-smæn) *m.* remero.

oasis (ouei·sis) s. oasis.

oat (out) s. BOT. avena. *2* pipiritaña. *3 pl.* avena preparada como alimento.

oatcake (-keik) s. torta de avena.

oaten (-øn) *adj.* aveníceo, de avena.

oath (ouz) s. juramento, jura: *to take an* ~, prestar juramento; *on,* o *upon* ~, bajo juramento. *2* juramento, voto, reniego.

oatmeal (ou·tmil) s. harina o puches de avena.

obbligato (abliga·tou) s. MÚS. obligado.

obduracy (a·bdiurasi) s. dureza [de corazón]; obduración, obstinación, impenitencia.

obdurate (a·bdiurit) *adj.* duro, insensible. *2* inexorable, obstinado. *3* impenitente.

obedience (obi·diøns) s. obediencia.

obedient (-t) *adj.* obediente. *2* dócil.

obeisance (obei·sans) s. reverencia, cortesía [saludo]. *2* respeto, homenaje.

obelisk (a·bølisk) s. obelisco.

obese (obi·s) *adj.* obeso, gordo.

obesity (-iti) s. obesidad, gordura.

obey (to) (obei·) *tr.-intr.* obedecer.

obfuscate (to) (abfø·skeit) *tr.* ofuscar, obscurecer. *2* obcecar, cegar.

obituary (obi·chueri) *adj.* necrológico. *2 s.* nota necrológica.

object (a·bdẏekt) s. objeto. *2* espectáculo, cosa que mueve a lástima, risa, etc. *3* GRAM. complemento [directo o indirecto]. *4* BILLAR. ~ *ball,* mingo. *5*

OPT. ~ *glass,* objetivo. *6* ~ *lesson,* lección práctica o de cosas.

object (to) (øbdẏe·kt) *tr.* objetar. *2* reprochar. *3 intr.* oponerse, poner objeción, tener inconveniente, no gustarle a uno.

objectify (to) (-tifai) *tr.* objetivar.

objection (-shøn) s. objeción, reparo, tacha, inconveniente.

objectionable (-shønabøl) *adj.* inaceptable, poco grato. *2* censurable. *3* molesto, inconveniente.

objective (-tiv) *adj.* objetivo. *2* GRAM. ~ *case,* acusativo o dativo. *3 s.* objetivo. *4* objeto, fin, meta, blanco.

objectivity (abdẏekti·viti) s. objetividad.

objector (øbdẏe·ktøʳ) s. objetante.

objurgate (to) (a·bdẏøʳgeit) *tr.* reprender, reconvenir.

objurgation (-eishøn) s. represión, reconvención.

oblate (ablei·t) *adj.-s.* oblato. *2 adj.* GEOM. deprimido en sus polos.

oblation (ablei·shøn) s. oblación. *2* oblata.

obligate (to) (a·bligeit) *tr.* obligar, comprometer.

obligation (-ei·shøn) s. obligación [deber, necesidad, compromiso, etc.]: *of* ~, de precepto. *2* deuda de agradecimiento: *to be under* ~ *to,* deber favores a.

obligatory (øbli·gatori) *adj.* obligatorio; forzoso.

oblige (to) (øblai·dẏ) *tr.* obligar, compeler, constreñir. *2* complacer, servir, hacer un favor; poner en obligación o deuda [por un favor]: *much obliged,* muchas gracias.

obliging (-ing) *adj.* complaciente, servicial, cortés.

oblique (øbli·k) *adj.* oblicuo. *2* indirecto. *3* insincero, evasivo, doloso.

oblique (to) (øblai·k) *intr.* oblicuar. *2* torcerse.

obliquity (øbli·kuiti) s. oblicuidad.

obliterate (to) (øbli·tøreit) *tr.* borrar [tachar; hacer desaparecer]. *2* matar [un sello]. *3* MED. obliterar.

obliteration (-ei·shøn) s. borradura, testadura; extinción.

oblivion (øbli·viøn) s. olvido.

oblivious (-viøs) *adj.* desmemoriado. *2* olvidado [que olvida]. *3* abstraído, sin tener conciencia [de].

oblong (a·blong) *adj.* oblongo. *2 s.* cuadrilongo.

obloquy (a·blokui) s. reprobación, difamación, vilipendio.

obnoxious (øbnaˑkshøs) *adj.* ofensivo, molesto, detestable, odioso.
oboe (ouˑbou) *s.* MÚS. oboe [instrumento].
oboist (-ist) *s.* oboe [músico].
obol (aˑbøl) *s.* óbolo [peso y moneda].
obovate (abouˑveit) *adj.* BOT. trasovado.
obscene (absɪˑn) *adj.* obsceno; indecente.
obscenity (abseˑniti) *s.* obscenidad.
obscurantism (abskiuˑrantišm) *s.* obscurantismo.
obscuration (abskiureiˑshøn) *s.* obscurecimiento.
obscure (øbskiuˑ r) *adj.* oscuro. *2* vago, indistinto.
obscure (to) *tr.* oscurecer. *2* ocultar, disimular.
obscurity (øbskiuˑriti) *s.* oscuridad. *2* confusión, vaguedad.
obsecration (absikreiˑshøn) *s.* obsecración.
obsequies (aˑbsɪkuis) *s. pl.* exequias, funerales.
obsequious (øbsɪˑkuiøs) *adj.* obsequioso, servil, zalamero.
observable (øbšøˑ rvabøl) *adj.* observable, notable.
observance (-vans) *s.* observancia. *2* ceremonia, rito; práctica, uso.
observant (-vant) *adj.* atento, vigilante. *2* observante, obediente. *3* cuidadoso [de].
observation (-eiˑshøn) *s.* observación: *to keep under* ~, tener en observación, vigilar.
observatory (øbšøˑ rvatori) *s.* observatorio. *2* atalaya, mirador, miradero.
observe (to) (øbsøˑ rv) *tr.* observar. *2* guardar [una fiesta]. *3* decir, hacer notar.
observer (-ør) *s.* observador.
obsess (to) (øbseˑs) *tr.* obsesionar; causar obsesión.
obsession (-shøn) *s.* obsesión.
obsidian (absiˑdian) *s.* MINER. obisidiana.
obsidional (absiˑdional) *adj.* que se hace anticuado, que cae en desuso.
obsolescent (aˑbsølit) *adj.* que se hace anticuado, que cae en desuso.
obsolete (aˑbsølit) *adj.* anticuado, desusado, fuera de uso. *2* BIOL. atrofiado, ausente.
obstacle (aˑbstakøl) *s.* obstáculo. *2* embarazo, impedimento, óbice.
obstetrician (øbstetriˑshan) *s.* tocólogo.
obstetrics (øbsteˑtriks) *s.* obstetricia, tocología.
obstinacy (aˑbstinasi) *s.* obstinación. *2* pertinacia, persistencia. *3* MED. rebeldía.
obstinate (-it) *adj.* obstinado. *2* emperrado. *3* persistente. *4* MED. rebelde.
obstreperous (obstreˑpørøs) *adj.* estrepitoso, ruidoso, turbulento.
obstruct (to) (øbstrøˑkt) *tr.* obstruir. *2* atorar, atascar. *3* entorpecer, impedir, estorbar.
obstruction (-shøn) *s.* obstrucción. *2* obstáculo, embarazo, estorbo, impedimento.
obstructionism (-išm) *s.* obstruccionismo.
obstructive (øbstrøˑktiv) *adj.* obstructivo. *2 s.* impedimento, estorbo.
obstructor (-tør) *s.* obstructor.
obstruent (aˑbstruønt) *adj.* MED. opilativo.
obtain (to) (øbteiˑn) *tr.* obtener, alcanzar, conseguir, lograr, adquirir. *2 intr.* ser general, estar en vigor o en boga.
obtainment (-mønt) *s.* obtención, consecución, logro.
obtrude (to) (øbtruˑd) *tr.* imponer o introducir quieras que no. *2 intr.-ref.* entremeterse, intrusarse.
obtruder (-dør) *s.* entremetido, intruso.
obtrusion (-dy̆øn) *s.* entremetimiento, intrusión.
obtrusive (-siv) *adj.* entremetido, intruso, importuno, molesto.
obturate (to) (aˑbtiureit) *tr.* obturar.

obturation (-eiˑshøn) *s.* obturación.
obturator (aˑbtiureitør) *adj.-s.* obturador.
obtuse (øbtiuˑs) *adj.* obtuso [romo; torpe]. *2* embotado [sentido]; sordo [dolor]. *3* GEOM. obtuso.
obtuse-angled *adj.* GEOM. obtusángulo.
obverse (aˑbvøˑrs) *s.* anverso, frente. *2 adj.* del anverso. *3* de base más estrecha que la punta.
obviate (to) (aˑbvieit) *tr.* obviar, prevenir, evitar.
obvious (aˑbviøs) *adj.* obvio, evidente, palmario. *2* sencillo, fácil de descubrir.
obviousness (aˑbviøsnis) *s.* claridad, evidencia.
ocarina (acariˑna) *s.* MÚS. ocarina.
occasion (økeiˑy̆øn) *s.* ocasión, oportunidad, coyuntura, caso, circunstancia: *on* ~, cuando se ofrece, ocasionalmente. *2* causa, motivo, origen, pie: *by* ~ *of*, a consecuencia de. *3* necesidad: *I have no* ~ *for*, no necesito, no me hace falta.
occasion (to) *tr.* ocasionar, causar, motivar.
occasional (-al) *adj.* ocasional. *2* incidental, fortuito. *3* poco frecuente; alguno que otro.
occasionally (-i) *adv.* ocasionalmente, de vez en cuando, a veces.
occident (aˑksidønt) *s.* occidente, ocaso, oeste. *2 n. pr.* (con may.) Occidente [Europa y América].
occidental (aksideˑntal) *adj.-s.* occidental.
occipital (aksiˑpital) *adj.-s.* ANAT. occipital.
occiput (aˑksipøt) *s.* ANAT. occipucio.
occlude (to) (økluˑd) *tr.* ocluir. *2* cerrar, tapar.
occlusion (-y̆øn) *s.* oclusión.
occlusive (-siv) *adj.* oclusivo.
occult (økøˑlt) *adj.* oculto, secreto, esotérico, misterioso: ~ *sciences*, ciencias ocultas.
occultism (økøˑltišm) *s.* ocultismo.
occupancy (øˑkiupansi) *s.* DER. ocupación.
occupant (-nt) *s.* ocupante.
occupation (-eiˑshøn) *s.* ocupación. *2* posesión, tenencia.
occupier (aˑkiupaiør) *s.* ocupante.
occupy (to) (aˑkiupai) *tr.* ocupar. *2* emplear, invertir. ¶ Pret. y p. p.: *occupied*.
occur (to) (økøˑr) *intr.* hallarse. *2* ocurrir, suceder. *3* ocurrirse [venir a la imaginación].
occurrence (-øns) *s.* ocurrencia, incidente, suceso, caso. *2 to be of frequent* ~, suceder a menudo.
ocean (ouˑshan) *s.* océano. *2 pl.* la mar, mares [de].
Oceania (oushiæˑnia) *n. pr.* GEOGR. Oceanía.
oceanic (-nik) *adj.* oceánico.
oceanography (oushænaˑgrafi) *s.* oceanografía.
ocellate(d (ouˑsøleit(id) *adj.* ZOOL. ocelado.
ocellus (ouseˑløs), *pl.* **-lli** (-lai) *s.* ZOOL. ocelo.
ocelot (ouˑselat) *s.* ZOOL. ocelote.
ocher, ochre (ouˑkør) *s.* ocre: *red* ~, almagre.
o'clock (øklaˑk) *loc. contr.* de OF THE CLOCK: *what* ~ *is it?*, ¿qué hora es?; *it is three* ~, son las tres.
octagon (aˑktægøn) *s.* octágono.
octahedron (actajɪˑdrøn) *s.* octaedro.
octane (aˑktein) *s.* QUÍ. octano.
octave (aˑkteiv) *s.* REL., MÚS., LIT. octava.
Octavian (acteiˑvian) *n. pr.* octaviano.
Octavius (-viøs) *n. pr.* Octavio.
octavo (-vou) *adj.* IMPR. en octavo. *2 s.* libro, etc., en octavo.
octet (akteˑt) *s.* MÚS. octeto.
October (aktouˑbør) *s.* octubre.
octogenarian (aktody̆ineˑrian) *adj.-s.* octogenario, ochentón.
octopod (aˑktopad) *adj.-s.* ZOOL. octópodo.
octopus (-øs) *s.* ZOOL. pulpo.
octosyllable (-siˑlabøl) *s.* octosílabo.
octroi (aktuaˑ) *s.* fielato. *2* consumos [impuesto].
octuple (aˑktiupøl) *adj.* óctuplo.

ocular (a·kiula^r) adj. ocular. 2 s. ÓPT. ocular.
oculist (-ist) s. oculista, oftalmólogo.
odalisk, odalisque (ou·dalisk) s. odalisca.
odd (ad) adj. impar, non. 2 suelto, solo, desapareado. 3 ocasional, no regular: ~ job, trabajo ocasional; at ~ times, a ratos perdidos. 4 sobrante, de más; y tanto, y pico: ten pounds ~, diez libras y pico. 5 singular, raro, curioso, extraño.
oddity (-iti) s. singularidad, rareza. 2 ente raro.
oddments (-mønts) s. pl. cosa suelta; pedazos, retales.
odds (adš) s. pl. y sing. desigualdad, disparidad [de condiciones, fuerzas, etc.]; superioridad, exceso [de una cosa sobre otra]: to fight against ~, luchar contra fuerzas superiores. 2 ventaja [en el juego]: to give ~, dar ventaja. 3 probabilidades [en favor o en contra]. 4 desavenencia: to be at ~ with, estar reñido con. 5 ~ and ends, retazos, trozos, cosas sueltas.
ode (oud) s. LIT. oda.
odeum (odi·øm) s. odeón.
odious (ou·diøs) adj. odioso, repugnante.
odium (-øm) s. odio, odiosidad.
odontocete (oda·ntøsit) adj.-s. ZOOL. odontoceto.
odontologist (odanta·lodÿist) s. odontólogo.
odontology (-lodÿi) s. odontología.
odoriferous (oudøri·førøs) adj. odorífero, oloroso.
odorous (ou·dørøs) adj. odorante, oloroso, fragante.
odour (ou·dø^r) s. olor [bueno o malo]. 2 fragancia. 3 olor, fama, estima: to be in bad ~ with, tener mala fama entre.
odourless (-lis) adj. inodoro.
Odyssey (a·disi) s. Odisea; odisea.
œcumenical (ekiume·nikal) adj. ecuménico.
Oedipus (e·dipøs) n. pr. MIT. Edipo.
oenology (ina·lodÿi) s. enología.
o'er (o·ø^r) contr. de OVER.
oesophagus (isa·fagøs) s. ANAT. esófago.
of (av) prep. En muchos casos se traduce por de; en otro, por a, en, con, por, etc.: empty ~, vacío de; to smell ~, oler a; to think ~, pensar en; to dream ~, soñar en o con; ~ an evening, por la noche; he ~ all men, él precisamente; ~ myself, himself, etc., solo; por mí mismo, por sí mismo, etc.; ~ late, últimamente; ~ old, ~ yore, de antaño.
off (of) adv. lejos, fuera; enteramente, del todo; indica alejamiento, ausencia, separación, disminución, privación, cesación: a little way ~, a poca distancia; to be ~, irse, partir, salir; to have the afternoon ~, tener la tarde libre; hands ~!, manos quietas; hats ~!, descúbranse; from ~, de lejos; ~ and on, de vez en cuando, a intervalos.
2 prep. lejos de, fuera de; de o desde: ~ the track, fam. despistado. 3 MAR. frente a, a la altura de.
4 adj. apartado, alejado, ausente. 5 lateral [calle, etc.]. 6 libre, de asueto. 7 suspendido, interrumpido, parado; abandonado: the wedding is ~, se ha deshecho la boda. 8 quitado, sin poner. 9 cerrado, cortado [gas, agua, vapor, etc.]. 10 equivocado. 11 chalado. 12 derecho, de la derecha [caballo, rueda, etc., de un vehículo]. 13 FÚTBOL. ~ side, fuera de juego.
14 interj. ¡fuera!; ¡vamos!
offal (o·fal) s. sing. y pl. despojos de reses muertas; desperdicios, basura.

off-colo(u)r (o·fkølø^r) adj. verde, atrevido, subido de color.
offence (øfe·ns) s. ofensa, agravio: to take ~, ofenderse. 2 ofensa, ataque. 3 pecado. 4 falta, infracción; delito.
offenceless (-lis) adj. inofensivo.
offend (to) (-d) tr. ofender. 2 atacar, acometer. 3 intr. pecar; delinquir.
offender (-dø^r) s. ofensor. 2 pecador, delincuente.
offense s., offenseless adj. OFFENCE, OFFENCELESS.
offensive (-siv) adj. ofensivo. 2 perjudicial. 3 s. ofensiva: to take the ~, tomar la ofensiva.
offer (o·fø^r) s. oferta, ofrecimiento. 2 promesa. 3 envite. 4 proposición, propuesta. 5 COM. oferta: on ~, en venta.
offer (to) tr. ofrecer. 2 brindar. 3 prometer; amenazar. 4 hacer, inferir. 5 intr. ofrecerse.
offering (-ing) s. ofrenda. 2 oblación, sacrificio. 3 ofrecimiento. 4 don, dádiva.
offertory (-tori) s. LITURG. ofertorio. 2 colecta [durante una función religiosa].
offhand (o·fjænd) adv. de improviso, de repente, sin detenerse a pensar; al descuido, bruscamente. 2 adj. dicho o hecho de improviso, al descuido, etc.; brusco.
offhanded (ofjæ·ndid) adj. OFFHAND 2.
office (a·fis) s. oficio, función, ejercicio, ministerio. 2 cargo, empleo [esp. público o de autoridad]: to be in ~, desempeñar un cargo, estar en el poder. 3 oficina, despacho, bufete, agencia, departamento, negociado: ~ boy, meritorio, botones de oficina. 4 oficio [rezo, función de iglesia]. 5 ceremonia, rito. 6 pl. oficios: good offices, buenos oficios, mediación. 7 exequias. 8 cocina y dependencias de servicio.
officeholder (-jouldø^r) s. funcionario.
officer (-ø^r) s. persona que tiene cargo público; funcionario; alto empleado; presidente, secretario, etc., de una sociedad. 2 MIL., MAR. oficial; clase. 3 agente de policía, alguacil, etc.
official (øfi·shal) adj. oficial. 2 autorizado. 3 s. el que tiene un cargo público o de gobierno; funcionario. 4 (Ingl.) provisor o juez eclesiástico.
officially (-shali) adv. oficialmente, de oficio.
officiant (øfi·shant) s. ECLES. oficiante, celebrante.
officiate (to) (-ieit) intr. oficiar. 2 tr. celebrar [un rito, etc.]. 3 suministrar.
officinal (-sinal) adj. oficinal.
officious (-shøs) adj. DIPL. oficioso. 2 oficioso, entrometido.
offing (o·fing) s. mar afuera, alta mar; lejanía: in the ~, mar afuera; en perspectiva.
offish (o·fish) adj. reservado, adusto, esquivo.
offprint (o·fprint) s. IMPR. separata.
offscourings (o·fskauringš) s. pl. hez, desecho, escoria.
offset (o·fset) s. compensación, equivalente. 2 cosa que da realce. 3 AGR. vástago lateral, acodo. 4 ARQ. retallo. 5 ELECT. ramal. 6 GEOGR. estribación. 7 TOP. ordenada. 8 IMPR. offset.
offset (to) tr. compensar, contrapesar, contrabalancear. 2 oponer. 3 ARQ. retallar. 4 imprimir por offset. ¶ Pret. y p. p.: offset; ger.: -setting.
offshoot (-shut) s. vástago, renuevo. 2 ramal, estribación.
offshore (-sho^r) adv. de la costa; a cierta distancia de la costa.
offside (o·fsaid) s. FÚTBOL. fuera de juego.
offspring (-spring) s. vástago, hijo, hijos, prole, descendencia. 2 fig. producto, resultado.
off-stage (-teidÿ) adj. TEAT. de entre bastidores.

oft (oft) *adj.-adv.* poét. y dial. OFTEN.
often (ǫ·føn) *adv.* a menudo, muchas veces, frecuentemente: *as ~ as*, siempre que: *how ~?*, ¿cuántas veces?
ogee (oudȳi·) *s.* ARQ. gola, cimacio.
ogival (odȳai·val) *adj.* ARQ. ojival.
ogive (o·dȳiv) *s.* ARQ. ojiva.
ogle (ou·gøl) *s.* mirada de amor o coquetería; mirada provocativa. *2* pop. ojo.
ogle (to) *tr.-intr.* mirar con amor o coquetería; echar el ojo, comerse con los ojos.
ogre (ou·gøʳ) *s.* ogro.
ogress (-ris) *f.* ogro hembra, ogresa.
oh! (o) *interj.* ¡oh!
ohm (oum) *s.* ELECT. ohm, ohmio.
oidium (oi·diøm) *s.* BOT., AGR. oidio.
oil (oil) *s.* aceite; óleo: *~ of vitriol*, aceite de vitriolo; *to pour ~ on the flame*, fig. echar leña al fuego; *to pour ~ on the (troubled) waters*, fig. calmar el enojo, poner la paz. *2* petróleo. *3 sing.* y *pl.* color o pintura al óleo. *4 adj.* de aceite, oleífero; de petróleo; para aceite o petróleo; *~ beetle*, ENT. carraleja; *~ gauge*, MEC. indicador de nivel de aceite; *~ painting*, pintura o cuadro al óleo; *~ stove*, estufa o fogón de petróleo; *~ tanker*, buque petrolero; *~ well*, pozo de petróleo.
oil (to) *tr.* aceitar. *2* engrasar, lubrificar, untar.
oilbird (-bøʳd) *s.* ORN. guácharo.
oilcan (-kæn) *s.* lata de aceite. *2* alcuza, aceitera.
oilcloth (-kloz) *s.* hule, encerado. *2* linóleo.
oiler (-øʳ) *s.* engrasador. *2* aceitera [para engrasar]. *3* buque petrolero.
oiling (-ing) *s.* aceitado, engrase, lubricación.
oilskin (-skin) *s.* encerado, impermeable.
oilstone (-stoun) *s.* piedra de amolar al aceite.
oily (-i) *adj.* aceitoso, oleaginoso. *2* grasiento; resbaladizo. *3* untuoso. *4* zalamero, hipócrita.
ointment (oi·ntmønt) *s.* unto, untura, ungüento.
O.K., OK., okay (ou·kei) *adj.* bueno, conforme. *2 adv.* bien, está bien. *3 s.* visto bueno, aprobación.
okra (ou·kra) *s.* BOT. quimbombó.
old (ou·ld) *adj.* viejo, anciano, añoso, añejo; antiguo; inveterado: *~ age*, vejez; *~ bachelor*, solterón; *~ boy*, chico, viejo [expresión de afecto; *Old Boy, Old Nick, Old One*, fam. el diablo; *~ fog(e)y*, persona anticuada; *~ hand*, experto, perro viejo; *~ maid*, solterona; la mona [juego de naipes]; *~ man*, viejo; TEAT. barba; *~ salt*, lobo de mar; *Old Testament*, Antiguo Testamento; *~ wive's tale*, cuento de viejas. *2 of ~*, de antaño, antiguamente. *3 how ~ are you?*, ¿qué edad tiene usted?; *the baby is three months ~*, el niño tiene tres meses.
old-clothesman *s.* ropavejero.
olden (ou·ldøn) *adj.* poét. antiguo.
old-fashioned *adj.* anticuado; pasado de moda.
old-fog(e)yish (fou·gish) *adj.* atrasado, anticuado, chapado a la antigua.
oldish (ou·ldish) *adj.* algo viejo.
old-looking *adj.* avejentado.
old-school *adj.* a la antigua; de la vieja escuela.
oldster (-dstøʳ) *s.* fam. viejo, vieja.
old-time *adj.* antiguo, anticuado. *2* de antaño.
old-timer *s.* antiguo residente. *2* antiguo concurrente. *3* veterano [en una profesión]. *4* persona chapada a la antigua.
old-word *adj.* del antiguo mundo.
oleaceous (oliei·shøs) *adj.* BOT. oleáceo.
oleaginous (oliæ·dȳinøs) *adj.* oleaginoso, oleoso.

oleander (-ndøʳ) *s.* BOT. adelfa.
oleaster (-støʳ) *s.* BOT. oleastro, acebuche.
oleic (oli·ik) *adj.* QUÍM. oleico.
oleograph (ou·liøgræf) *s.* oleografía.
olfaction (alfæ·kshøn) *s.* olfacción.
olfactory (-tori) *adj.* olfatorio.
oligarch (a·ligaʳk) *s.* oligarca.
oligarchy (-i) *s.* oligarquía.
Oligocene (a·ligosin) *adj.-s.* GEOL. oligoceno.
olivaceous (alivei·shøs) *adj.* aceitunado.
olive (a·liv) *s.* BOT. olivo: *~ grove*, olivar; *~ branch*, rama de olivo; fig. niño, hijo. *2* oliva, aceituna: *~ oil*, aceite de oliva; *~ tree*, olivo. *3 adj.* aceitunado.
Oliver (a·livøʳ) *n. pr.* Oliverio.
Olympia (oli·mpiæ) *n. pr.* Olimpia.
Olympiad (-iæd) *s.* olimpíada.
Olympian (-ian), **Olympic** (-ik) *adj.* olímpico: *Olimpic games*, juegos olímpicos.
Olympus (-øs) *n. pr.* Olimpo.
omasum (omei·søm) *s.* ZOOL. omaso.
omber, ombre (a·mbøʳ) *s.* tresillo, juego del hombre.
omega (amı·ga) *s.* omega. *2* fig. fin.
omelet, omelette (a·mlit) *s.* tortilla de huevos.
omen (ou·min) *s.* agüero, presagio, pronóstico.
omen (to) *tr.* presagiar, augurar, ominar.
omentum (ome·ntøm) *s.* ANAT. omento.
ominous (a·minøs) *adj.* ominoso. *2* presagioso.
omission (omi·shøn) *s.* omisión. *2* olvido, descuido.
omit (to) (omi·t) *tr.* omitir. *2* dejar de, olvidar.
omnibus (a·mnibøs) *s.* ómnibus. *2 adj.* general, colecticio.
omnifarious (amnifæ·riøs) *adj.* de todo género.
omnimodous (amni·mødøs) *adj.* omnímodo.
omnipotence (-pøtøns) *s.* omnipotencia.
omnipotent (-pøtønt) *adj.* omnipotente. *2 n. pr. Omnipotent*, el Omnipotente, Dios.
omnipresence (amnipre·søns) *s.* omnipresencia.
omnipresent (-t) *adj.* omnipresente, ubicuo.
omniscience (amni·shøns) *s.* omnisciencia.
omniscient (-t) *adj.* omnisciente.
omnium-gatherum (amniømgæ·dørøm) *s.* fam. miscelánea, maremagnum.
omnivorous (amni·vorøs) *adj.* omnívoro.
omoplate (ou·mopleit) *s.* ANAT. omóplato.
on (an) *prep.* en, sobre, a, de, con, contra, por, bajo, so: *bent ~*, empeñado en; *~ the table*, sobre la mesa; *~ horseback*, a caballo; *~ duty*, de servicio; *~ this condition*, con esta condición; *to draw on*, COM. girar contra; *~ all sides*, por todos lados; *~ pain of*, bajo pena de; *~ seeing him*, en viéndole, al verlo. *2* cuando precede a una fecha, no se traduce: *~ the fourth May*, el cuatro de mayo.
3 adv. encima, puesto: *to have one's hat ~*, tener puesto el sombrero. *4* adelante; progresivamente; continuando, sin cesar: *to go ~*, seguir, proseguir, continuar; *farther ~*, más adelante; *later ~*, más tarde; *~ and ~*, sin parar; *and so ~*, y así sucesivamente. *5 to turn the water, steam*, etc., *~*, abrir [la llave de] el agua, el vapor, etc.
6 adj. puesto: *the lid is ~*, la tapa está puesta. *2* que se está verificando, que ha empezado a funciona; abierto; encendido, conectado: *the fight is ~*, la lucha ha empezado; *the light is ~*, la luz está encendida.
onager (a·nadȳoʳ) *s.* ZOOL., MIL. onagro.
onanism (ou·nanišm) *s.* onanismo.
once (uøns) *adv.-s.* vez, una vez: *~ and again*, una

y otra vez; ~ *for all*, de una vez para siempre, definitivamente; ~ *in a while*, de vez en cuando; *all at* ~, de súbito; *at* ~, a la vez, de una vez; en seguida; ~ *upon a time there was*, érase una vez; *this* ~, esta vez. *2* alguna vez. *3* en otro tiempo. *4 adj.* antiguo, que fue. *5 conj.* una vez que, en cuanto.

oncoming (a·ncøming) *adj.* próximo, venidero. *2 s.* proximidad, aproximación, llegada.

ondometer (anda·metø^r) *s.* ELECT. ondómetro.

one (uøn) *adj.* uno, una: ~ *half*, una mitad; ~ *hundred*, ciento. *2* primero [capítulo, etc.]. *3* un solo, solo, único: *his* ~ *chance*, su única oportunidad. *4* uno [no dividido]. *5* uno, unido; idéntico, lo mismo; el mismo, un mismo: *with one accord*, unánimemente; *it is all* ~ *to me*, me da lo mismo; *of* ~ *height*, de una misma talla o altura. *6* un, cierto, un tal: ~ *day*, un día; ~ *Mr. Smith*, un tal señor Smith.
  7 pron. uno, una: *no* ~, nadie; ~ *and all*, todos sin excepción; ~ *another*, el uno al otro, unos a otros; ~ *by* ~, uno a uno; *how is one to know...?*, ¿cómo ha de saber uno...?
  8 s. uno, el número uno. *9* una persona o cosa: | Gralte. no se traduce: *the little ones*, los pequeñuelos; *the* ~ *who*, el que, la que; *the white* ~, el blanco, la blanca; *this* ~, éste, ésta. *10 one o'clock*, la una.

one-act *adj.* TEAT. en un acto.

one-armed *adj.* manco, que sólo tiene un brazo.

one-horse *adj.* de un solo caballo. *2* pop. inferior; de poca importancia.

oneiric (onai·rik) *adj.* onírico.

oneiromancy (-rømænsi) *f.* oniromancía.

oneness (uøn·nis) *s.* unicidad, singularidad. *2* identidad, uniformidad. *3* unión, concordia.

onerous (a·nørøs) *adj.* oneroso, gravoso, molesto.

oneself (uønse·lf) *pron.* se, sí, uno mismo: *with* ~, consigo.

one-sided *adj.* de un solo lado; desigual; unilateral; injusto, parcial.

one's self *pron.* ONESELF.

one-step *s.* cierto baile de salón.

one-track *adj.* FERROC. de una sola vía. *2* fig. estrecha [mentalidad].

one-way *adj.* de dirección única. *2* de ida [billete].

onion (a·nÿøn) *s.* BOT. cebolla. *2* pop. cabeza chola.

onionskin (-skin) *s.* bizna, tela de cebolla. *2* papel cebolla.

onlooker (a·nlukø^r) *s.* espectador, observador.

only (ou·nli) *adj.* solo, único. *2* singular, preeminente. *3 adv.* sólo, solamente, únicamente: *not* ~ *... but also*, no sólo... sino también. *4 if* ~, ojalá; sí, si al menos. *5 conj.* solo que, pero, si no fuera que.

only-begotten *adj.* unigénito.

onomastic (anømæ·stik) *adj.* onomástico.

onomatopœia (-mætøpɪ·a) *s.* onomatopeya.

onomatopœic (-ik) *adj.* onomatopéyico.

onrush (a·nrøsh) *s.* embestida, arremetida, carga, fuerza impetuosa.

onset (-set) *s.* ataque, asalto. *2* principio.

onshore (-sho^r) *adj.-adv.* de tierra; hacia tierra.

onslaught (-slot) *s.* ataque furioso, asalto.

onto (-tu) *prep.* hacia, sobre.

ontogeny (anta·dÿini) *s.* ontogenia.

ontology (-lodÿi) *s.* ontología.

onward (a·nwø^rd) *adj.* que se mueve hacia adelante. *2* avanzado, progresivo.

onward(s (-(š) *adv.* adelante; hacia adelante.

onyx (a·niks) *s.* MINER. ónix, ónice.

oösphere (ou·sfi^r) *s.* BOT. oosfera.

ooze (uš) *s.* fango, légamo, limo, cieno.

ooze (to) *intr.* rezumarse, escurrirse. *2* escaparse, manar, fluir suavemente. *3* llenarse [de sudor]. *4 tr.* exudar, sudar; desprender.

oozy (-i) *adj.* legamoso, limoso, cenagoso.

opacity (opæ·siti) *s.* opacidad. *2* torpeza del entendimiento.

opal (ou·pal) *s.* MINER. ópalo.

opalescence (opale·søns) *s.* opalescencia.

opalescent (opale·sønt) *adj.* opalescente.

opaline (ou·palain) *adj.* opalino.

opaque (opei·k) *adj.* opaco. *2* obscuro, ininteligible. *3* torpe, obtuso.

ope (to) (oup) *tr.-ref.* poét. abrir.

open (ou·pøn) *adj.* abierto: *in the* ~ *air*, a cielo abierto, al aire libre; *with* ~ *arms*, con los brazos abiertos; *to set* o *throw* ~, abrir. *2* raso, descubierto. *3* libre, expedito. *4* descubierto, destapado: ~ *carriage*, coche descubierto. *5* expuesto [a]. *6* visible, manifiesto, público, conocido: ~ *secret*, secreto a voces. *7* franco, sincero. *8* claro, ralo; calado, poroso. *9* pendiente, no resuelto; discutible. *10* accesible [a ideas, ruegos, etc.]. *11* libre de hielos o de heladas [río; tiempo]. *12* MAR. despejado, sin niebla. *13* ~ *season*, temporada de caza o pesca. *14* ~ *water*, mar libre.
  15 s. claro, raso; lugar abierto: *in the* ~, al raso, al aire libre; en alta mar; al descubierto.

open (to) *tr.* abrir. *2* ofrecer a la vista. *3* declarar, descubrir [sus sentimientos, etc.]. *4* iniciar, empezar. *5* MAR. avistar. *6 to* ~ *up*, descubrir [a la vista, al entendimiento]; abrir, hacer accesible. *7 intr.* abrir, abrirse. *8* descubrirse, aparecer. *9* confiarse, abrir su corazón; hablar claro, explicarse. *10* empezar, comenzar. *11* TEAT. estrenarse. *12 to* ~ *into, on, upon, toward*, dar acceso a, salir a, dar a, mirar a. *13 to* ~ *up*, aparecer a la vista, presentarse; perder la reserva, el encogimiento.

open-air *adj.* al aire libre.

opener (ou·pønø^r) *s.* abridor. *2* TEJ. abridora.

open-eyed *adj.* alerta, vigilante. *2* con los ojos abiertos. *3* asombrado.

open-handed *adj.* liberal, generoso, dadivoso.

open-hearted *adj.* franco, sincero; generoso.

opening (ou·pøpning) *s.* abertura, apertura. *2* abertura, entrada, brecha, boquete, portillo. *3* abra, bahía. *4* (E.U.) claro [en un bosque]. *5* comienzo, inauguración. *6* TEAT. estreno: ~ *night*, noche de estreno. *7* AJED. apertura. *8* oportunidad, coyuntura.

openly (-li) *adv.* abiertamente, francamente, públicamente.

open-minded *adj.* de espíritu abierto, razonable.

open-mouthed *adj.* con la boca abierta, boquiabierto. *2* ávido, voraz. *3* clamoroso. *4* ancho de boca.

openness (ou·pønnis) *s.* franqueza, sinceridad.

openwork (ou·pønuø^rk) *s.* calado [obra calada].

opera (a·pøra) *s.* MÚS. ópera: ~ *comique*, ópera cómica, zarzuela; ~ *glasses*, gemelos de teatro; ~ *hat*, clac; ~ *house*, teatro de la ópera.

operate (to) (a·pøreit) *tr.* hacer funcionar, mover, manejar, dirigir, explotar. *2* producir, efectuar. *3 intr.* operar, obrar, producir efecto. *4* COM., MIL. operar. *5* CIR. operar: *to* ~ *upon someone for*, operar a uno de.

operating (-ing) *adj.* operante. *2* de funciona-

miento, de explotación. *3* operatorio, de operación: ~ *room*, quirófano.
operation (apǿrei·shøn) *s.* operación. *2* función, funcionamiento. *3* manejo; explotación. *4* vigor, vigencia.
operative (a·pǿreitiv) *adj.* operativo. *2* CIR. operatorio. *3 s.* operario, obrero, artesano.
operator (a·pǿreitøʳ) *s.* operador, maquinista: *telephone* ~, telefonista. *2* CIR. operador. *3* especulador [en Bolsa], corredor de Bolsa.
operculum (opø·ʳkuløm) *s.* opérculo.
operetta (apøre·ta) *s.* opereta.
ophicleide (a·fiklaid) *s.* MÚS. figle.
ophidian (ofi·dian) *s.* ZOOL. ofidio.
ophiuroidean (afiyuroi·dian) *adj.-s.* ZOOL. ofiuroideo.
opthalmia (afzæ·lmia) *s.* MED. oftalmía.
ophthalmic (-mik) *adj.* oftálmico.
ophthalmology (-ma·lodÿi) *s.* oftalmología.
opiate (ou·pieit) *s.* opiato. *2* narcótico. *3 adj.* opiado. *4* narcótico, adormecedor.
opine (o·pain) *tr.-intr.* opinar.
opinion (øpi·niøn) *s.* opinión: *public* ~, opinión pública. *2* buen concepto: *to have no* ~ *of*, no tener buen concepto de.
opinionable (-abøl) *adj.* opinable.
opinionate(d (-eit(id) *adj.* obstinado, terco.
opinionative (-eitiv) *adj.* doctrinal. *2* pertinaz, porfiado.
opinioned (-d) *adj.* presumido, obstinado.
opium (o·piøm) *s.* opio: ~ *poppy*, BOT. adormidera.
opossum (øpa·søm) *s.* ZOOL. zarigüeya, opósum.
oppilation (apilei·shøn) *s.* opilación.
opponent (øpou·nønt) *s.* oponente, contrario, adversario, antagonista. *2 adj.* opuesto [situado en frente]. *3* contrario, adverso.
opportune (apøʳtiu·n) *adj.* oportuno, conveniente, a propósito.
opportunism (-išm) *s.* oportunismo.
opportunist (-nist) *s.* oportunista.
opportunity (-iti) *s.* oportunidad; sazón, lugar, ocasión.
opposable (øpou·šabøl) *adj.* oponible. *2* resistible.
oppose (to) (øpou·š) *tr.* oponer, contraponer. *2* oponerse a, luchar contra, resistir, contrarrestar.
opposed (-d) *adj.* opuesto, contrario.
opposer (-øʳ) *s.* contrario, el que se opone.
opposite (a·pøšit) *adj.* opuesto: ~ *angles*, ángulos opuestos. *2* frontero. *3* contrario; adverso. *4 s. the* ~, lo opuesto, lo contrario. *5 prep.* frente a, en frente de. *6 adv.* enfrente, en situación opuesta.
opposition (apoši·shøn) *s.* oposición. | No tiene el sentido de concurso de pretendientes. *2* resistencia [acción]. *3* contrariedad, contradicción.
oppositionist (-ist) *s.* oposicionista.
oppress (to) (øpre·s) *tr.* oprimir. *2* tiranizar. *3* agobiar, abrumar, abatir.
oppression (-shøn) *s.* opresión. *2* tiranía. *3* agobio, abatimiento. *4* ahogo, sofocación, pesadez.
oppresive (-siv) *adj.* opresivo, opresor. *2* tiránico. *3* abrumador, agobiador. *4* sofocante.
oppressor (-søʳ) *s.* opresor, tirano.
opprobrious (øprou·briøs) *adj.* oprobioso, infamante. *2* injurioso, ultrajante.
opprobrium (-briøm) *s.* oprobio, deshonra.
oppugn (to) (øpiu·n) *tr.* opugnar, combatir.
opt (to) (apt) *intr.* optar.
optative (a·ptativ) *adj.* optativo.
optic (a·ptic) *adj.* óptico [de la visión, del ojo].
optician (apti·shan) *s.* óptico.

optics (a·ptiks) *s.* óptica [ciencia].
optimist (-ist) *s.* optimista.
optimistic (-istik) *adj.* optimista.
optimum (-øm) *adj.* óptimo, más favorable. *2 s.* cantidad, grado, punto, etc., óptimos.
option (a·pshøn) *s.* opción. *2* alternativa.
optional (-al) *adj.* facultativo, discrecional.
optometer (apta·metøʳ) *s.* ÓPT. optómetro.
opulence (a·piuløns) *s.* opulencia.
opulent (-ønt) *adj.* opulento.
opuscle (øpø·søl), **opuscule** (opø·skiul) *s.* opúsculo.
or (oʳ) *conj.* o, u. *2* si no, de otro modo.
orach (a·ræk) *s.* BOT. armuelle; orgaza.
oracle (a·rakøl) *s.* oráculo.
oracular (oræ·kiula ʳ) *adj.* de oráculo. *2* profético. *3* dogmático, magistral. *4* obscuro, ambiguo.
oral (o·ral) *adj.* oral. *2 s.* examen oral.
orange (a·røndÿ) *s.* BOT. naranja, naranjo; ~ *blossom*, azahar; ~ *grove*, naranjal; ~ *tree*, naranjo. *2* BOT. ~ *jessamine*, boj de China. *3 adj.-s.* anaranjado [color].
orangeade (arøndÿei·d) *s.* naranjada.
orangery (a·røndÿri) *s.* invernadero para naranjos.
orang-outang (orœ·ngutæn) *s.* ZOOL. orangután.
orate (to) (orei·t) *intr.* perorar, discursear.
oration (-shøn) *s.* oración, discurso.
orator (a·ratøʳ) *s.* orador.
oratorical (arato·rikal) *adj.* oratorio; retórico.
oratorio (-riou) *s.* MÚS. oratorio.
oratory (a·ratori) *s.* oratoria. *2* oratorio, capilla.
orb (orb) *s.* orbe, esfera, globo. *2* astro. *3* círculo.
orb (to) *tr.* dar forma de círculo. *2* cercar, rodear, englobar.
orbicular (oʳbi·kiula ʳ) *adj.* orbicular.
orbit (o·ʳbit) *s.* ANAT., ASTR. órbita.
orbital (o·ʳbital) *adj.* orbital. *2* orbitario.
orca (o·ʳka) *s.* ZOOL. orca.
orchard (o·ʳcha ʳd) *s.* huerto [de frutales]; pomar.
orchestra (o·ʳkistra) *s.* orquesta. *2* TEAT. platea.
orchestrate (to) (o·ʳkistreit) *tr.* MÚS. orquestar.
orchestration (o ʳkistre·shøn) *s.* MÚS. orquestación.
orchid (o·ʳkid) *s.* BOT. orquídea.
orchidaceous (o ʳkidei·shøs) *adj.* orquidáceo.
orchis (o·ʳkis) *s.* ORCHID.
ordain (to) (o ʳdei·n) *tr.* ordenar [conferir órdenes]. *2* ordenar, decretar, disponer. *3* destinar, predestinar [Dios, el hado, etc.].
ordainment (-mønt) *s.* decreto [de Dios, el destino, etc.].
ordeal (o·ʳdial) *s.* ordalía. *2* prueba [penosa].
order (o·ʳdøʳ) *s.* orden [disposición o sucesión regular; método, regla; concierto]; condición o estado [de las cosas]; buen estado: ~ *of the day*, orden del día; *in good* ~, en buen estado; *in* ~, en orden; por su orden, en regla; funcionando; *out of* ~, desordenado; descompuesto, estropeado. *2* orden [religiosa, militar, de caballería, etc.]. *3* condecoración o insignia de una orden. *4* orden, clase, grado: *the lower orders*, la clase baja; *in* ~ *of*, del orden de, a modo de. *5* MAT., H. NAT., ARQ. orden. *6* orden [sacramento]: *to take orders*, ordenarse. *7* orden, mandato, precepto: *by* ~ *of*, por orden de. *8* COM. orden; pedido, encargo: *to the* ~ *of*, a la orden de; *to* ~, a la medida, por encargo. *9 in* ~ *to*, para, a fin de; *in* ~ *that*, para que, a fin de que.
order (to) *tr.* ordenar, poner en orden. *2* ordenar, disponer, mandar: *to* ~ *away*, despedir, decir [a uno] que se vaya; *to* ~ *in*, mandar entrar; mandar traer; *to* ~ *out*, mandar salir. *3* pedir, encargar [mercancías, un coche, la comida, etc.];

mandar hacer. 4 ECLES. ordenar. 5 MIL. *Order arms!*, ¡descansen!
orderliness (o·ʳdøʳlinis) *s.* orden, arreglo, método.
orderly (o·ʳdø·ʳli) *adj.* ordenado, arreglado, metódico. 2 obediente, tranquilo. 3 MIL. ~ *officer*, oficial de día. 4 *s.* MIL. ordenanza. 2 practicante [de hospital].
ordinal (o·ʳdinal) *adj.*-*s.* ordinal. 2 *s.* ritual [libro].
ordinance (-ans) *s.* ordenación, arreglo. 2 ordenanza, decreto. 3 ECLES. rito, ceremonia.
ordinarily (-erili) *adv.* ordinariamente.
ordinary (o·ʳdineri) *adj.* ordinario. 2 *s.* ordinario [juez, obispo]. 3 mesa redonda [en una fonda]. 4 ordinario [de la misa]. 5 lo ordinario: *out of the* ~, excepcional, extraordinario. 6 *in* ~, en ejercicio; de cámara.
ordinate (-neit) *s.* GEOM. ordenada.
ordination (-ei·shøn) *s.* ECLES. ordenación.
ordinee (o·ʳdini·) *s.* ordenando.
ordnance (o·ʳdnans) *s.* MIL. artillería, cañones, máquinas de guerra. 2 MIL. pertrechos, suministros.
ordure (o·ʳdiur) *s.* inmundicia, suciedad.
ore (ouʳ) *s.* MIN. mineral, ganga, mena.
oread (ou·riæd) *s.* MIT. oréade.
organ (o·ʳgan) *s.* órgano [de un animal, una planta, un partido, etc.]. 2 MÚS. órgano: *barrel* ~, organillo; ~ *grinder*, organillero.
organdy (o·ʳgandi) *s.* organdí.
organic (o·ʳgæ·nik) *adj.* orgánico; ~ *chemistry*, química orgánica.
organism (o·ʳganišm) *s.* BIOL., FIL. organismo.
organist (o·ʳganist) *s.* organista.
organization (organaise·shøn) *s.* organización.
organize (to) (o·ʳganaiš) *tr.* organizar. 2 *intr.* organizarse.
organography (o·ʳgana·grafi) *s.* organografía.
orgasm (o·ʳgæšm) *s.* orgasmo.
orgeat (o·ʳdÿæt) *s.* horchata; agua de cebada.
orgiastic (o·ʳdÿiæ·stik) *adj.* orgiástico.
orgy (o·ʳdÿi) *s.* orgía.
oriel (ou·riøl) *s.* ARQ. mirador, cierro de cristales.
Orient (ou·riønt) *s.* oriente, levante. 2 [con min.] oriente [de una perla]. 3 *adj.* naciente [sol]. 4 brillante, transparente.
orient (to) *tr.* orientar.
oriental (orie·ntal) *adj.*-*s.* oriental.
orientalist (orie·ntalist) *s.* orientalista.
orientate (to) (ou·rienteit) *tr.* orientar. 2 *intr.* caer o mirar hacia el este.
orientation (orientei·shøn) *s.* orientación.
orifice (a·rifis) *s.* orificio.
oriflame (a·riflæm) *s.* oriflama.
origin (a·ridÿin) *s.* origen. 2 linaje, nacimiento.
original (ori·dÿinal) *adj.* original: ~ *sin*, pecado original. 2 primitivo, prístino, primero. 3 *s.* original. | No tiene sentido de original de imprenta.
originality (oridÿinæ·liti) *s.* originalidad.
originate (to) (ori·dÿineit) *tr.* originar, crear, producir. 2 *intr.* originarse, nacer, dimanar.
origination (-ei·shøn) *s.* origen; creación, producción.
originator (ori·dÿineitøʳ) *s.* originador, creador, inventor, autor; causa primera.
oriole (ou·rioul) *s.* ORN. oropéndola, oriol.
orison (a·risøn) *s.* oración, plegaria.
Orkney Islands (ø·ʳkni) *n. pr.* GEOGR. Orcadas.
orlop (o·ʳlap) *s.* MAR. sollado.
ormolu (o·ʳmolu) *s.* metal dorado, similor. 2 polvo para dorar.

ornament (ø·ʳnamønt) *s.* ornamento, ornato, adorno. 2 honra, gala [pers. que honra]. 3 MÚS. adorno. 4 *pl.* LITURG. ornamentos.
ornament (to) *tr.* ornamentar, adornar, decorar.
ornamental (o·ʳname·ntal) *adj.* ornamental, decorativo.
ornamentation (-ei·shøn) *s.* ornamentación.
ornate (o·ʳnei·t) *adj.* adornado en exceso; recargado. 2 florido [estilo].
ornery (o·ʳnøri) *adj.* (E.U.) fam. malhumorado, difícil.
ornithologist (o·ʳniza·lodÿist) *s.* ornitólogo.
ornithology (o·ʳniza·lodÿ) *s.* ornitología.
orogeny (ora·dÿeni) *s.* orogénesis.
orographic (al (orøgræ·fik(al) *adj.* orográfico.
orography (ora·grafi) *s.* orografía.
orology (ora·lødÿi) *s.* orología.
orotund (ou·rotønd) *adj.* rotundo, sonoro.
orphan (o·ʳfan) *adj.*-*s.* huérfano.
orphan (to) *tr.* dejar huérfano.
orphanage (-idÿ) *s.* orfandad. 2 orfanato.
orphanhood (-jud) *s.* orfandad [estado].
Orpheus (o·ʳfiøs) *n. pr.* MIT. Orfeo.
Orphic (o·ʳfik) *adj.* órfico.
orpiment (o·ʳpimønt) *s.* oropimente.
orrery (o·røri) *s.* planetario.
orris (o·ris) *s.* galón de seda y oro. 2 BOT. lirio de Florencia.
orthodox (o·ʳzødaks) *adj.*-*s.* ortodoxo.
orthodoxy (-i) *s.* ortodoxia.
orthogenesis (-dÿe·nisis) *s.* ortogénesis.
orthogonal (o·ʳza·gønal) *adj.* ortogonal.
orthographic (al (o·ʳzogræ·fik(al) *adj.* ortográfico.
orthography (o·ʳza·grafi) *s.* ortografía.
orthop (a) edy (o·ʳzopidi) *s.* ortopédico.
orthopterous (o·ʳza·ptørøs) *adj.* ortóptero.
ortive (a·ʳtiv) *adj.* ortivo.
ortolan (o·ʳtølan) *s.* ORN. hortelano.
oscillate (to) (a·sileit) *tr.* hacer oscilar. 2 *intr.* oscilar. 3 vibrar. 4 fluctuar.
oscillation (-ei·shøn) *s.* oscilación. 2 vibración. 3 fluctuación.
oscillator (a·sileitøʳ) *s.* oscilador.
oscillatory (asilei·tori) *adj.* oscilatorio.
osculate (to) (a·skiuleit) *tr.* besar. 2 GEOM. tocar por osculación.
osculation (-ei·shøn) *s.* GEOM. osculación.
osier (ou·ÿøʳ) *s.* BOT. mimbrera; sarga. 2 mimbre.
osiery (ou·ÿøri) *s.* mimbreral. 2 objetos de mimbre.
Osmanil (asmæ·nli) *adj.*-*s.* osmanlí.
osmium (a·šmiøm) *s.* QUÍM. osmio.
osmose (a·šmous), **osmosis** (asmou·sis) *s.* ósmosis.
osmotic (asma·tik) *adj.* osmótico.
osprey (a·sprei) *s.* ORN. halieto, osífraga, quebrantahuesos.
osseous (a·siøs) *adj.* óseo.
ossicle (a·sikøl) *s.* huesecillo.
ossification (asifikei·shøn) *s.* osificación.
ossifrage (a·sifridÿ) *s.* OSPREY.
ossify (to) (-fai) *tr.* convertir en hueso. 2 *intr.* osificarse. ¶ Pret. y p. p.: *ossified.*
ossuary (a·siueri) *s.* osario.
Ostend (ste·nd) *n. pr.* GEOGR. Ostende.
ostensible (-sibøl) *adj.* ostensible. 2 aparente.
ostensive (-siv) *adj.* ostensivo. 2 ostensible.
ostensory (aste·nsori) *s.* ostensorio, custodia.
ostentation (astøntei·shøn) *s.* ostentación. 2 boato, pompa. 3 gala, alarde.
ostentatious (-shøs) *adj.* ostentoso, pomposo.
osteologist (astia·lødÿist) *s.* osteólogo.

osteology (-i) *s.* osteología.
osteopath (a·stiøpæz) *s.* osteópata.
osteopathy (astia·pazi) *s.* osteopatía.
ostiary (a·stieri) *s.* ostiario.
ostler (a·sløʳ) *s.* mozo de cuadra, palafrenero.
ostlery (a·sløri) *s.* hostería.
ostracism (a·strasišm) *s.* ostracismo. *2* exclusión del trato social.
ostracize (to) (-saiš) *tr.* condenar al ostracismo. *2* excluir del trato social.
ostrich (a·strich) *s.* ORN. avestruz.
Ostrogoth (a·strogaz) *adj.*-*s.* ostrogodo.
other (ø·ðøʳ) *adj.* otro, otra, otros, otras: *the ~ world*, el otro mundo. *2 pron. (pl.* **others**) otro, otra, otros, otras: *others would do it*, los otros lo harían. *3 adv.* [con *than*], más que, otra cosa que.
otherwise (-uaiš) *adv.* otramente, de otra manera: *~ called*, alias, por otro nombre. *2* en otro caso, por otra parte, fuera de eso. *3 conj.* si no, de otro modo, de lo contrario.
otiose (ou·shious) *adj.* ocioso.
otitis (outai·tis) *s.* MED. otitis.
otocyst (ou·tøsist) *s.* ZOOL. otocisto.
otologist (ota·lodÿist) *s.* otólogo.
otology (-i) *s.* otología.
otoscope (ou·tøskoup) *s.* otoscopio.
otter (o·tøʳ) *s.* ZOOL. nutria. *2* piel de nutria.
Ottoman (a·tomæn) *adj.*-*s.* otomano. *2 s.* [con min.] otomana [mueble]. *3* otomán [tejido].
ouch (auch) *s.* broche, joya. *2 interj.* ¡uy!, ¡ay!
1) ought (ot) *s.*-*adv.* AUGHT.
2) ought *def.* y *aux.*, seguido gralte. de un infinitivo con *to.* Sólo se usa en la forma *ought* que se traduce generalmente por el pres. y el condicional de deber, haber de o haber que: *I ~ to write*, debo escribir o debería escribir.
ounce (auns) *s.* onza [28.35 gr.]. *2* pizca. *3* ZOOL. onza.
our (aur) *adj.* nuestro, nuestra, nuestros, nuestras: *Our Lady*, Nuestra Señora.
ours (-š) *pron. pos.* [el] nuestro, [la] nuestra; [los] nuestros, [las] nuestras: *your room is larger than ~*, vuestro cuarto es mayor que el nuestro; *a friend of ~*, un amigo nuestro.
ourself (aurse·lf) *pron.* nosotros mismos, nos [cuando se usa el plural para una sola pers.].
ourselves (-lvš) *pron.* nosotros mismos. *2* nos, a nosotros mismos.
oust (to) (aust) *tr.* desalojar, desahuciar, echar fuera.
ouster (au·støʳ) *s.* DER. desposeimiento; desahucio.
out (aut) *adv.* fuera, afuera, hacia fuera, en el exterior: *~ of*, fuera de; *to go ~*, partir, salir. *2* en sociedad, en escena, en público. *3* distintamente, claro, sin rodeos: *speak ~*, hable claro, sin rodeos. *4* completamente, enteramente, hasta agotarse, hasta el fin. *5* en partes [para distribuir]: *to pass ~*, distribuir, repartir. *6* por, movido por [un sentimiento, etc.]: *~ of pity*, por compasión. *7* de, con [un recipiente]: *~ of the bottle*, de la botella. *8 adj.* [como predicado o pospuesto al nombre] ausente, fuera de casa. *9* alejado, distante [de un centro, etc.]. *10* fuera de sitio. *11* destituido, cesante. *12* dado, puesto [en arriendo, a préstamo]: *~ at interest*, puesto a interés. *13* expedido, dictado [orden, mandato, etc.]. *14* en huelga. *15* agotado, gastado; acabado; cerrado, apagado; terminado, expirado: *the milk is ~*, se ha acabado la leche; *the lights are ~*, las luces están apagadas; *the time*

is ~, ha pasado la hora; ha expirado el plazo. *16* descubierto, publicado, aparecido: *the book is just ~*, el libro acaba de salir. *17* que ya no está en uso o moda. *18* desavenido, reñido. *19* equivocado.
20 Forma gran número de locuciones, muchas de las cuales se encuentran en otros artículos de este Diccionario: *~ and away*, con mucho; *~ and ~*, completamente; *~ for*, en compaña para, en busca de; en favor de; *~ of favour*, en desgracia; *~ of money*, sin dinero; *~ of this world*, extraordinario, del otro jueves; *~ to win*, decidido a vencer; *three ~ of four*, de cada cuatro, tres.
21 interj. ¡fuera! *22 ~ with it!*, ¡desembuche usted!
23 s. exterior, parte de fuera, esquina, saliente. *24* IMPR. omisión. *25 at outs*, o *on the outs with*, reñido con.
out (to) *tr.* desposeer, echar fuera, expulsar. *2* apagar. *3 intr.* salir. *4* descubrirse, divulgarse.
out-and-out *adj.* acérrimo; consumado. *2* rotundo, categórico.
outbalance (to) (autbæ·lans) *tr.* pesar más que; exceder en peso o efecto, sobrepujar, aventajar.
outbid (autbi·d) *tr.* mejorar, pujar, ofrecer más que [otro] en subasta, etc.
outboard (au·tboʳd) *adv.*-*adj.* MAR. fuera de borda: *~ motor*, motor fuera de borda.
outbound (-baund) *adj.* en viaje de ida, que sale, de salida.
outbrave (to) (-breiv) *tr.* resistir, arrostrar, desafiar. *2* sobrepujar en valentía.
outbreak (-breik) *s.* erupción, brote. *2* arrebato; explosión, estallido. *3* tumulto, motín, insurrección. *4* principio [de una guerra, una epidemia, etc.]: *at the ~ of the war*, al estallar la guerra.
outbreathe (to) (-brez) *tr.* dejar sin aliento, agotar.
outbuilding (-bilding) *s.* dependencia, accesoria, anejo [de un edificio].
outburst (-bøʳst) *s.* arranque, estallido: *~ of laughter*, explosión de risas, risotada.
outcast (-kæst) *adj.*-*s.* desterrado, proscrito; paria, excluido de la sociedad.
outclass (to) (-klæs) *tr.* sobrepujar, ser superior a.
outcome (-køm) *s.* resultado, consecuencia, desenlace.
outcry (-krai) *s.* grito. *2* gritería, clamor, clamoreo, alboroto.
outdare (to) (autde·øʳ) *tr.* ser más atrevido [que otro]. *2* dominar por la osadía; desafiar.
outdate (to) (-dei·t) *tr.* anticuar.
outdistance (to) (-di·stans) *tr.* adelantar, dejar atrás.
outdo (to) (-du) *tr.* exceder, sobrepujar, eclipsar, vencer: *to ~ oneself*, excederse a sí mismo.
outdoor (au·tdoʳ) *adj.* de fuera de casa, al aire libre. *2* externo, a domicilio.
outdoors (autdo·ʳš) *s.* el aire libre, el campo, la calle. *2 adv.* fuera de casa, al aire libre, al raso.
outer (au·tøʳ) *adj.* exterior, externo. *2 s.* círculo exterior de un blanco.
outermost (-moust) *adj.* extremo, más exterior.
outface (to) (autfei·š) *tr.* dominar, intimidar [con la mirada]. *2* arrostrar, desafiar.
outfall (au·tfol) *s.* salida, desembocadura.
outfield (-fild) *s.* campo abierto.
outfit (-fit) *s.* equipo. *2* pertrechos, ajuar, avíos.
outfit (to) *tr.* equipar, aviar, habilitar, armar.
outfitter (-fitøʳ) *s.* abastecedor, proveedor, equipador. *2* vendedor de ropa hecha.

outflank (to) (autflæ·nk) *tr.* MIL. flanquear.

outflow (au·tflou) *s.* efusión, flujo, salida.

outflow (to) *intr.* salir, fluir, manar.

outgeneral (to) (autdȳe·nøral) *tr.* superar en estrategia; ser más listo que.

outgo (-gou·) *s.* salida, gasto, desembolso.

outgo (to) *tr.* aventajar, adelantarse a.

outgoing (-ing) *adj.* saliente, que sale, cesante. *2 s.* salida.

ougrow (to) (autgrou·) *tr.* crecer más que; hacerse demasiado grande para: *to ~ one's clothing,* quedársele a uno corta la ropa. *2* curársele, pasársele a uno [algo] con los años, al crecer.

outgrowth (ou·tgrouz) *s.* excrecencia, nacencia. *2* resultado, consecuencia, producto, efecto.

outhouse (-jaus) *s.* dependencia, anejo [de un edificio]. *2* retrete fuera de la casa.

outing (-ing) *s.* salida, paseo, jira, excursión.

outlander (-lændø͡ʳ) *s.* extranjero, forastero.

outlandish (autlæ·ndish) *adj.* de aspecto extranjero; exótico. *2* extraño, raro. *3* remoto, salvaje.

outlast (to) (-læ·st) *tr.* durar más que.

outlaw (aut·tlo) *s.* bandido, forajido. *2* proscrito.

outlaw (to) *tr.* proscribir. *2* declarar ilegal.

outlawry (-lori) *s.* proscripción, rebeldía.

outlay (-lei) *s.* desembolso, gasto, salida.

outlay (to) *t.* desembolsar, gastar.

outlet (au·tlet) *s.* salida; orificio de salida, desaguadero, desagüe; toma de corriente. *2* corriente que sale [de un río, etc.]. *3* COM. salida, mercado.

outline (au·tlain) *s.* contorno, perfil. *2* bosquejo, esbozo, croquis. *3* plan, idea, esquema. *4* resumen, compendio; líneas generales de.

outline (to) *tr.* perfilar, contornar, delinear. *2* bosquejar, esbozar; trazar las líneas generales de.

outlive (to) (-li·v) *tr.* sobrevivir a; durar más que.

outlook (au·tluk) *s.* atalaya. *2* vista, perspectiva. *3* actitud mental, punto de vista. *4* perspectivas, probabilidades.

outlying (-laiing) *adj.* remoto; alejado del centro, exterior, circundante. *2* extrínseco.

outmatch (to) (autmæ·ch) *tr.* aventajar, mostrarse superior a.

outmeasure (to) (-me·ȳø͡ʳ) *tr.* exceder en medida.

outmoded (-mou·did) *adj.* pasado de moda, anticuado.

outmost (au·tmoust) *adj.* OUTERMOST.

outnumber (to) (autnø·mbø͡ʳ) *tr.* exceder en número, ser más que.

out-of-date *adj.* anticuado, pasado de moda.

out-of-door *adj.* OUTDOOR.

out-of-print *adj.* agotado [libro, edición].

out-of-the-way *adj.* apartado, remoto, desviado, inaccesible. *2* poco usual, poco común.

outpatient (au·tpeishønt) *s.* enfermo ambulatorio.

outpost (-poust) *s.* MIL. avanzada; puesto avanzado. *2* fortín [en las fronteras de la civilización].

outpour (-po͡ʳ), **outpouring** (-ing) *s.* efusión, derramamiento; chorro. *2* fig. efusión, desahogo.

output (-put) *s.* rendimiento, producción. *2* ELECT. salida; circuito de salida. *3* MEC. potencia, capacidad, efecto útil.

outrage (au·treidȳ) *s.* ultraje, desafuero, atropello, daño; atrocidad. *2* violación.

outrage (to) *tr.* ultrajar, atropellar. *2* violar.

outrageous (-rei·dȳøs) *adj.* ultrajante, injurioso. *2* violento, furioso. *2* desaforado, enorme, atroz; desenfrenado.

outreach (to) (au·trich) *tr.* pasar, pasar más allá de, exceder.

outride (to) (-rai·d) *tr.* ganar la delantera [yendo a caballo o en coche]. *2 intr.* cabalgar junto a un coche.

outrider (-ø͡ʳ) *s.* criado a caballo que acompaña a un coche.

outrigger (-ri·gø͡ʳ) *s.* MAR. botalón, tangón, pescante. *2* MAR. outrigger. *3* caballo de refuerzo.

outright (au·trait) *adj.* sincero, franco, directo. *2* completo, absoluto. *3 adv.* completamente. *4* abiertamente, sin reserva. *5* en seguida.

outroot (to) (-ru·t) *tr.* desarraigar.

outrun (to) (-rø·n) *tr.* correr más que; aventajar, dejar atrás.

outsell (to) (-se·l) *tr.* vender más, más caro o más aprisa que.

outset (au·tset) *s.* comienzo, principio, salida.

outshine (to) (-shai·n) *intr.* brillar, resplandecer. *2 tr.* eclipsar, exceder en brillantez.

outside (au·tsaid) *s.* exterior, parte externa; superficie, haz: *on the ~,* por fuera. *2* apariencia. *3* lo más, lo sumo: *at the ~,* a lo más, a lo sumo. *4 adj.* exterior, externo. *5* superficial, aparente. *6* extraño, ajeno. *7* neutral. *8* extremo. *9* extraño a la ocupación normal de uno. *10 adv.* fuera, afuera, por fuera. *11 prep.* fuera de, más allá de; excepto.

outsider (-sai·dø͡ʳ) *s.* forastero. *2* extraño, profano. *3* intruso. *4* DEP. caballo que no figura entre los favoritos.

outskirt (au·tskø͡ʳt) *s.* borde, orilla. *2 pl.* alrededores.

outspoken (-spou·køn) *adj.* claro, franco, abierto; boquifresco.

outspread (-spre·d) *s.* extensión, despliegue, difusión. *2 adj.* extendido; difundido.

outspread (to) *tr.* extender; difundir. *2 intr.* extenderse, difundirse.

outstanding (-stæ·nding) *adj.* saledizo, saliente. *2* destacado, descollante, notable, sobresaliente, principal. *3* pendiente, sin pagar, sin cobrar.

outstay (to) (-stei·) *tr.* quedarse más tiempo que [uno]. *2* quedarse más tiempo de lo que autoriza [la cortesía, el permiso que uno tiene, etc.].

outstretch (to) (-stre·ch) *tr.* extender, alargar.

outstrip (to) (-stre·ch) *tr.* extender, alargar.

outstrip (to) (-stri·p) *tr.* adelantar, dejar atrás.

outtalk (to) (-to·k) *tr.* hablar más o mejor que.

outturn (-tø͡ʳn) *s.* ECON. producción.

outward (au·twø͡ʳd) *adj.* exterior, externo, visible. *2* dirigido hacia fuera; que sale, de ida [tren, cargamento]. *3* aparente, superficial. *4* corporal, carnal. *5 adv.* afuera, hacia fuera. *6* exteriormente. *7* superficialmente. *8* corporalmente.

outwardness (-nis) *s.* exterioridad.

outwards (-s) *adv.* OUTWARD.

outwear (to) (autwe·ʳ) *tr.* gastar; estropear con el uso. *2* durar más que. *3* pasársele a uno [una pena, etc.], con el tiempo.

outweigh (to) (-wei·) *tr.* pesar más que. *2* preponderar sobre. *3* contrapesar.

outwit (to) (-wi·t) *tr.* engañar con astucia; ser más listo que. ¶ Pret. y p. p.: *outwitted;* ger.: *-tting.*

outwork (au·twø͡ʳk) *s.* FORT. obra exterior.

outworn (autwo·ʳn) *adj.* gastado, usado. *2* anticuado.

ouzel (u·søl) *s.* ORN. mirlo.

oval (ou·val) *adj.* oval, ovalado. *2 s.* óvalo.

ovarian (ove·rian) *adj.* ovárico.

ovary (ou·vari) *s.* ANAT., ZOOL., BOT. ovario.
ovate (ou·veit) *adj.* aovado, ovado.
ovation (ovei·shøn) *s.* ovación.
oven (ø·vøn) *s.* horno, hornillo.
over (ou·vø^r) *adv.* arriba, por encima. *2* al otro lado; de una mano a otra: *to go* ~ *to the enemy*, pasarse al enemigo; *to hand* ~, dar, entregar. *3* enfrente. *4* al revés, trastornado. *6* de ancho, a lo ancho; de un extremo a otro. *7* completamente: *all* ~, por todas partes, completamente. *8* más, de más, demasiado. *9* hacia fuera: *to run* ~, salirse, derramarse. *10* en extremo. *11* ~ *again*, de nuevo, otra vez. *12* ~ *and above*, además de; fam. demasiado.
    13 prep. sobre, encima de, por encima de. *14* al otro lado de, allende; a la vuelta de. *15* arriba de, más de: ~ *a million*, más de un millón. *16* durante. *17* por todo, a lo largo de [un espacio, camino, etc.]: *all* ~ *the city*, por toda la ciudad. *18* de, con motivo de, a propósito de.
    19 adj. superior, más alto. *20* que cubre. *21* excesivo, de más. *22* que ha llegado al otro lado. *23* acabado, terminado.
overabundance (-abø·ndans) *s.* sobreabundancia, superabundancia.
overact (-æ·kt) *tr.* exagerar.
over-all *adj.* completo, global, de conjunto.
overalls (ou·vørolš) *s. pl.* pantalones de trabajo, mono. *2* sobrerropa. *3* polainas impermeables.
overarch (to) (ouvøra·^rch) *tr.* abovedar.
overawe (to) (ouvøro·) *tr.* intimidar, atemorizar.
overbalance (to) (-bæ·lans) *tr.* pesar más que, sobrepujar. *2* hacer perder el equilibrio.
overbear (to) (-be·^r) *tr.* agobiar, abrumar, oprimir. *2* dominar, tiranizar, imponerse.
overbearing (ouvø^rbe·ring) *adj.* dominador, despótico, imperioso, altanero.
overblown (ou·vø^rblou) *adj.* que ha florecido demasiado; demasiado abierta, marchita, pasada [flor]. *2* cubierto [de cosas traídas por el viento].
overboard (-bo^rd) *adv.* MAR. por la borda. *2* MAR. al mar, al agua: *man* ~!, ¡hombre al agua!
overbore (-bo·^r) *pret.* de TO OVERBEAR.
overborne (-bo·^rn) *p. p.* de TO OVERBEAR.
overburden (-bø·^døn) *s.* sobrecarga.
overburden (to) *tr.* sobrecargar. *2* abrumar.
overcame (-kei·m) *pret.* de TO OVERCOME.
overcast (ou·vø^rkæst) *adj.* nublado, cubierto, encapotado. *2* sombrío. *3* COST. sobrehilado.
overcast (to) (-kæ·st) *tr.* anublar, obscurecer, entristecer. *2* COST. sobrehilar. *3 intr.* nublarse.
overcharge (ou·vø^rcha^rdy) *s.* sobrescarga. *2* recargo [de precio]; precio exhorbitante.
overcharge (to) (-cha·^rdaỹ) *tr.* sobrecargar, recargar. *2* cobrar demasiado.
overcloud (to) (-klau·d) *tr.* cubrir de nubes, anublar. *2 intr.* anublarse, nublarse.
overcoat (ou·vø^rkout) *s.* sobretodo, gabán, abrigo.
overcome (to) (ouvø^rkø·m) *tr.* vencer, domar, dominar, triunfar de. *2* vencer, superar, allanar [obstáculos, dificultades, etc.]. *3* sobreponerse, hacerse superior a. *4* rendir, agotar, agobiar.
overconfident (-ka·nfidønt) *adj.* presumido; demasiado confiado.
overcrowd (to) (-krau·d) *tr.* apiñar, atestar.
overdevelop (to) (-dive·løp) *tr.* desarrollar excesivamente. *2* FOT. revelar demasiado.
overdid (-di·d) *pret.* de TO OVERDO.
overdo (to) (ouvø^rdu·) *tr.* hacer [algo] demasiado, llevar al exceso; exagerar. *2* cocer demasiado. *3*

fatigar, agotar, agobiar de trabajo. *4 intr.* excederse; hacer o trabajar demasiado.
overdone (-dø·n) *p. p.* de TO OVERDO.
overdose (ou·vø^rdous) *s.* dosis excesiva.
overdraft (-dræft) *s.* COM. sobregiro, giro en descubierto, en exceso.
overdraw (to) (ouvø^rdro·) *intr.-tr.* sobregirar, girar en descubierto.
overdress (to) (-dre·s) *tr.-intr.* vestir, ataviar o ataviarse con exceso.
overdue (-diu·) *adj.* COM. vencido y no pagado. *2* que lleva retraso [buque, etc.].
overestimate (-e·stimeit) *tr.* estimar, tasar, avaluar o presuponer por encima del valor real. *2* atribuir un valor excesivo, exagerar.
overexcite (to) (-ksai·t) *tr.* sobreexcitar.
overexcitement (-mønt) *s.* sobrexcitación.
overexposure (-ekspou·ỹø^r) *s.* FOT. exceso de exposición.
overfeed (to) (-fɪ·d) *tr.* sobrealimentar.
overflow (ou·vø^rflou) *s.* inundación, avenida. *2* desbordamiento, derrame, rebosamiento. *3* superabundancia. *4* rebosadero, descarga.
overflow (to) (-flou·) *tr.* inundar; sobrellenar. *2* salir de [los bordes]. *3 intr.* desbordarse, rebosar.
overflowing (-ing) *adj.* desbordante, rebosante. *2 s.* desbordamiento.
overgrow (to) (-grou·) *tr.* crecer en, cubrir [díc. de plantas, hierbas, etc.]. *2* crecer más que. *3 intr.* crecer, desarrollarse con exceso. *4* cubrirse de plantas, hierbas, etc.
overgrown (-n) *adj.* cubierto de plantas, hierbas. *2* anormalmente crecido o desarrollado.
overgrowth (ou·vø^rgrouz) *s.* crecimiento excesivo. *2* vegetación exuberante, maleza.
overhand (-jænd) *adj.* DEP. voleado por lo alto; palma abajo. *2* COST. sobrehilado.
overhang (-jæng) *s.* proyección, parte que sobresale. *2* ARQ. alero; salidizo; vuelo.
overhang (to) (-jæ·ng) *tr.* hacer saliente, volar, colgar sobre; caer a. *2* estar suspendido sobre; amenazar. *3 intr.* hacer saliente.
overhaul (ou·vø^rjol) *s.* MEC. repaso, recorrido.
overhaul (to) (ouvø^rjo·l) *tr.* repasar, recorrer. *2* revisar. *3* registrar, examinar. *4* alcanzar [al que va delante].
overhead (-je·d) *adv.* sobre la cabeza de uno, arriba, en lo alto. *2 adj.* (ou·vø^rjed) situado en lo alto: ~ *crossing*, cruce o paso superior; ~ *railway*, (Ingl.) ferrocarril aéreo o elevado. *3* ~ *expenses*, COM. gastos generales.
overhear (to) (-ji·^r) *tr.* oír por casualidad o espiando, acertar a oír.
overheat (to) (-ji·t) *tr.* acalorar. *2* sobrecalentar, recalentar.
overindulge (-indø·ldỹ) *tr.* mimar demasiado. *2 intr.* tratarse demasiado bien.
overindulgence (-øns) *s.* indulgencia o mimo excesivo. *2* exceso [en el comer, etc.].
overjoyed (-dỹoi·d) *adj.* alborozado, jubiloso.
overladen (-lei·døn) *adj.* sobrecargado.
overlaid (-lei·d) *pret.* y *p. p.* de TO OVERLAY.
overlain (-lei·n) *p. p.* de TO OVERLIE.
overland (ou·vø^rlæ·nd) *adj.-s.* por tierra, por vía terrestre.
overlap (-læp) *s.* parte que traslapa, cubre o cruza; solapo, traslapo.
overlap (to) (-læ·p) *tr.-intr.* traslapar, solapar, cruzar sobre, cubrir. *2* lamer [las olas].
overlay (ou·vø^rlei) *s.* capa [que recubre]. *2 pret.* de TO OVERLIE.

overlay (to) (-lei·) *tr.* cubrir, recubrir, dar una capa, dorar, platear, chapear. *2* cubrir, obscurecer. *3* oprimir, abrumar.

overleaf (ou·vøʳlıf) *adv.* al dorso, a la vuelta.

overlie (to) (-lai·) *tr.* descansar, estar sobre.

overload (ou·vøʳloud) *s.* carga excesiva, sobrecarga.

overload (to) (-lou·d) *tr.* cargar excesivamente. *2* sobrecargar.

overlook (-luk) *s.* altura, atalaya. *2* ojeada, examen general. *3* descuido, inadvertencia.

overlook (to) (-lu·k) *tr.* mirar desde lo alto. *2* dominar [estar más elevado]. *3* dar a, tener vista a. *4* examinar, inspeccionar, vigilar. *5* repasar, revisar. *6* no notar, dejar de ver. *7* no hacer caso; pasar por alto, descuidar. *8* tolerar, perdonar.

overlord (to) (-lo·ʳd) *tr.* señorear, dominar despóticamente.

overly (ou·vøʳli) *adv.* fam. muy, mucho, demasiado.

overlying (-lai·ng) *ger.* de TO OVERLIE.

overmuch (ou·vøʳmøch) *adj.-adv.* demasiado.

overnice (-nai·s) *adj.* remilgado, dengoso, demasiado escrupuloso o exigente.

overnight (-nai·t) *adv.* en la noche anterior. *2* toda la noche: *to stay ~*, pasar la noche. *3* de la noche a la mañana.

overpass (ou·vøʳpæs) *s.* paso elevado; puente o vía por encima de un ferrocarril, carretera, etc.

overpay (to) (-pei·) *tr.* pagar demasiado.

overpeopled (-pı·pøld) *adj.* excesivamente poblado, superpoblado.

overpopulation (-papiule·shøn) *s.* exceso de población.

overpower (to) (-pau·øʳ) *tr.* predominar, dominar, vencer, subyugar. *2* abrumar, sofocar.

overpowering (-ing) *adj.* dominador, dominante. *2* abrumador, arrollador, irresistible.

overproduction (-prøda·kshøn) *s.* sobreproducción.

overran (-ræ·n) *pret.* de TO OVERRUN.

overrate (to) (-rei·t) *tr.* valorar excesivamente.

overreach (to) (-rı·ch) *tr.* llegar más allá de; exceder, pasar; extenderse sobre. *2* engañar a, ser más listo que. *3 intr.* VET. alcanzarse. *4 intr.-ref.* excederse, querer hacer demasiado, pasarse de listo.

override (to) (-raid) *tr.* pasar sobre o por encima de. *2* atropellar, pisotear. *3* supeditar, vencer. *4* desechar; anular. *5* reventar [a un caballo].

overripe (-rai·p) *adj.* demasiado maduro, papandujo.

overrule (to) (-ru·l) *tr.* dominar, señorear, vencer. *2* gobernar, regir. *3* decidir en contra, revocar. *4* predominar.

overrun (to) (-rø·n) *tr.* cubrir enteramente, inundar, invadir, infestar. *2* recorrer, pasar corriendo. *3* pasar por encima, atropellar. *4* exceder, traspasar los límites de: *to ~ one's time*, quedarse, hablar, etc., más tiempo del debido. *5* IMPR. recorrer. *6 intr.* desbordarse, rebosar.

oversaw (-so·) *pret.* de TO OVERSEE.

overscore (-sko·ʳ) *tr.* poner tilde o raya.

oversea(s (-sı·(s̆) *adv.* ultramar, allende los mares. *2 adj.* de ultramar; (Ingl.) colonial; extranjero.

oversee (to) (-sı·) *tr.* vigilar, superintender, inspeccionar, revisar.

overseer (ou·vøʳsıøʳ) *s.* inspector, superintendente, veedor. *2* sobrestante, capataz.

overset (to) (-ʳse·t) *tr.* volcar, voltear, tumbar, derribar.

overshadow (to) (-shæ·dou) *tr.* sombrear, dar sombra a. *2* oscurecer, eclipsar. *3* fig. cubrir, proteger. *4* dominar [ser más alto].

overshoe (ou·vøʳshu) *s.* (E.U.) chanclo, zapato de goma.

overshoot (to) (-shu·t) *tr.* tirar por encima, más allá de. *2 to ~ oneself, to ~ the mark*, pasar de la raya, excederse; pasarse de listo. *3* pasar rápidamente por encima o más allá de.

overshot (ouvøʳsha·t) *p. p.* de TO OVERSHOOT.

oversight (ou·vøʳsait) *s.* descuido, omisión, inadvertencia. *2* vigilancia, atención, cuidado.

overskirt (-skøʳt) *s.* sobrefalda.

oversleep (to) (-slı·p) *tr.* dormir hasta pasada [cierta hora]. *2 intr.* dormir demasiado.

overspread (to) (-spre·d) *tr.* desparramar, extender. *2* extenderse sobre, cubrir.

overstate (to) (-tei·t) *tr.* exagerar.

overstatement (-mønt) *s.* exageración.

overstep (to) (-ste·p) *tr.* pasar, transgredir.

overstock (ou·vøʳstak) *s.* exceso de existencias.

overstock (to) (-sta·k) *tr.* abarrotar: *to be overstocked with*, tener demasiada existencia de.

overstrung (-strø·ng) *adj.* demasiado tirante. *2* muy sensible, excitable o impresionable. *3* de cuerdas cruzadas [piano].

overt (ou·vøʳt) *adj.* abierto, visible, manifiesto.

overtake (to) (ouvøʳtei·k) *tr.* alcanzar, atrapar. *2* pasar, dejar atrás. *3* sorprender, coger.

overtaken (-øn) *p. p.* de TO OVERTAKE.

overtax (-tæks) *tr.* sobrecargar de impuestos. *2* abrumar, exigir demasiado esfuerzo de.

overthrew (-zru) *pret.* de TO OVERTHROW.

overthrow (-zrou) *s.* vuelco, derribo. *2* derrocamiento. *3* destrucción. *4* trastorno. *5* subversión.

overthrow (to) (-zrou·) *tr.* volcar, tumbar, derribar. *2* derrocar. *3* demoler, destruir. *4* trastornar. *5* subvertir. *6* vencer.

overthrown (-n) *p. p.* de TO OVERTHROW.

overtime (-taim) *s.* tiempo suplementario; horas extraordinarias de trabajo. *2 adj.-adv.* en horas extraordinarias.

overtire (to) (-tai·øʳ) *tr.* fatigar con exceso.

overtly (ou·vøʳtli) *adv.* abiertamente, públicamente.

overtone (-vøʳtoun) *s.* MÚS. armónico.

overtook (-tu·k) *pret.* de TO OVERTAKE.

overtop (to) (-ta·p) *tr.* dominar, descollar sobre; sobresalir entre. *2* rebasar, pasar de. *3* cubrir, pasar por encima de.

overture (ou·vøʳchuʳ) *s.* insinuación, proposición, propuesta [de paz, de amistad, etc.]; declaración [de amor]. *2* MÚS. obertura.

overturn (ou·vøʳtøʳn) *s.* vuelco. *2* derrocamiento. *3* COM. movimiento de mercancías.

overturn (-tøʳn) *tr.* volcar, trabucar. *2* derribar, derrocar. *3* trastornar. *4 intr.* volcar, trabucarse.

overweening (-wı·ning) *adj.* presuntuoso, arrogante.

overweigh (to) (-wei) *tr.* pesar más que, preponderar sobre; prevalecer contra. *2* oprimir, abrumar.

overweight (ou·vøʳueit) *s.* sobrepeso. *2* preponderancia, superioridad.

overwhelm (to) (-jue·lm) *tr.* inundar. *2* aplastar, arrollar, abrumar, oprimir. *3* confundir, anonadar.

overwhelming (-ing) *adj.* aplastante, arrollador, abrumador, irresistible, poderoso.
overwork (ou·vø^ruø^rk) *s.* exceso de trabajo.
overwork (to) (-uø·^rk) *tr.* hacer trabajar con exceso; fatigar el espíritu de, excitar. *2* abrumar de trabajo. *3* trabajar demasiado [un objeto, etc.]. *4 intr.* trabajar demasiado.
overwrought (-ro·t) *adj.* demasiado trabajado; recargado de adornos. *2* rendido por el trabajo. *3* sobrexcitado.
Ovid (a·vid) *n. pr.* Ovidio.
oviduct (ou·vidøkt) *s.* ANAT., ZOOL. oviducto.
ovine (ou·vain) *adj.-s.* ZOOL. ovino.
oviparous (ouvi·parøs) *adj.* ovíparo.
ovipositor (ouvipa·šitø^r) *s.* ENT. oviscapto.
ovoid (ou·void) *adj.* ovoide, aovado.
ovolo (ou·volou) *s.* ARQ. óvolo, cuarto bocel.
ovoviviparous (ouvovaivi·parøs) *adj.* BIOL. ovovivíparo.
ovule (ou·viul) *s.* BOT. óvulo. *2* huevecillo.
owe (to) (ou) *tr.* deber; adeudar. *2 intr.* deber, tener deudas.
owing (-ing) *ger.* de TO OWE. *2 adj.-adv.* ~ *to*, debido a, por causa de.
owl (aul) *s.* ORN. búho, mochuelo, lechuza.
owlet (-it) *s.* polluelo del búho, de la lechuza.
own (oun) *adj.* propio, mismo, de uno. | Acompaña como intensivo a los posesivos: *his* ~ *mother*, su propia madre. *2* carnal, hermano; ~ *cousin*, primo hermano. *3 s. one's* ~, lo suyo, lo de uno; *to hold one's* ~, mantenerse firme; no cejar; *on one's* ~, solo, independientemente, por su cuenta.
own (to) *tr.* poseer, tener. *2* reconocer, confesar. *3 intr. to* ~ *up*, fam. confesar de plano.

owner (-ø^r) *s.* dueño, propietario, poseedor.
ownership (-ship) *s.* propiedad, pertenencia.
ox (aks), *pl.* **oxen** (-øn) *s.* ZOOL. buey.
oxalic (aksæ·lik) *adj.* QUÍM. oxálico.
oxen (a·ksøn) *s. pl.* de OX.
oxeye (-ai) *s.* MAR., BOT. ojo de buey.
oxfly (-flai) *s.* ENT. estro, tábano.
Oxford (-fo^rd) *n. pr.* GEOGR. Oxford. *2* universidad de Oxford.
oxhide (-jaid) *s.* cuero de buey.
oxidation (aksidei·shøn) *s.* oxidación.
oxide (a·ksid) *s.* QUÍM. óxido.
oxidize (to) (-aiš) *tr.* oxidar.
oxidizer (-ø^r) *s.* oxidante.
oxidizing (-ing) *adj.* oxidante.
oxlip (a·kslip) *s.* BOT. planta primulácea.
oxtail (a·ksteil) *s.* cola o rabo de buey.
oxygen (a·ksidỹen) *s.* QUÍM. oxígeno.
oxygenate (to) (-eit) *tr.* oxigenar.
oxygenation (-ei·shøn) *s.* oxigenación.
oxygenize (to) (a·ksidỹenaiš) *tr.* oxigenar.
oxygenous (aksi·dỹenøs) *adj.* de oxígeno, oxigenado.
oxyhydrogen (-jai·drodỹin) *adj.-m.* QUÍM. oxhídrico.
oxymel (a·ksimel) *s.* oximel, o¡imiel.
oxytone (a·ksitoun) *adj.-s.* GRAM. oxítono, agudo.
oyster (oi·stø^r) *s.* ostra; ostión, ostrón; ~ *bed*, ostral, ostrero; ~ *fork*, desbullador; ~ *knife*, cuchillo para abrir ostras.
ozaena (oši·na) *s.* MED. ocena.
ozone (ou·šoun) *s.* QUÍM. ozono. *2* fig. aire puro.
ozonization (-ei·shøn) *s.* ozonización.
ozonize (to) (ou·šonaiš) *tr.* ozonizar.

P

P, p (pi) *s.* P, p, decimosexta letra del alfabeto inglés.

pa (pa) *s.* (fam.) papá.

pabulum (pæ·biuløm) *s.* pábulo.

paca (pæ·ka) *s.* ZOOL. paca.

pace (peis) *s.* paso, marcha, modo de andar: *to keep ~ with*, ir al mismo paso que; *to set the ~*, dar el ejemplo. *2* paso, aire; andadura, portante [del caballo]. *3* paso [medida]. *4* estrado, tarima.

pace (to) *intr.* andar, pasear. *2* amblar. *3 tr.* recorrer o medir a pasos: *to ~ the floor*, pasearse por una habitación. *4* marcar o dirigir el paso de.

pacer (pei·sø^r) *s.* amblador. *2* el que mide a pasos.

pachyderm (pæ·kidø^rm) *s.* ZOOL. paquidermo.

pacific (pasi·fik) *adj.* pacífico. *2* GEOGR. *Pacific Ocean*, océano Pacífico.

pacification (pæsifikei·shøn) *s.* pacificación.

pacifier (pæ·sifaiø^r) *s.* pacificador, apaciguador. *2* chupete [para niños].

pacifism (pæ·sifišm) *s.* pacifismo.

pacifist (pæ·sifist) *adj.-s.* pacifista.

pacify (pæ·sifai) *tr.* pacificar, apaciguar, sosegar, calmar. ¶ Pret. y p. p.: *pacified.*

pack (pæk) *s.* lío, fardo, bala, paca; paquete, mazo. *2* cantidad empaquetada. *3* baraja [de naipes]. *4* hato, hatajo, sarta. *5* cuadrilla, pandilla. *6* manada, bandada. *7* jauría; equipo de perros. *8* carga [de un animal o pers.]; *~ animal*, acémila, bestia de carga. *9* extensión de témpanos flotantes.

pack (to) *tr.-intr.* empacar, empaquetar, embalar; envasar, enlatar. *2 tr.* hacer [el baúl, la maleta]. *3* amontonar, apiñar. *4* llenar, atestar, apretar. *5* cargar [una acémila, etc.]. *6* MEC. empaquetar [una junta]. *7* reunir, juntar [en jauría, baraja, etc.]. *8* preparar, formar, fraudulentamente [una baraja, un jurado, etc.]. *9 to ~ down*, apretar, apisonar. *10 to ~ off*, despedir, enviar. *11 to ~ up*, empaquetar. *12 intr.* reunirse, juntarse. *13* formar masa compacta, endurecerse. *14 to ~* o *to ~ up*, hacer la maleta, el equipaje.

package (pæ·kidў) *s.* paquete, fardo, bulto. *2* cajetilla [de cigarrillos]. *3* empaquetadura, embalaje, envase [acción].

package (to) *tr.* empacar, empaquetar.

packer (pæ·kø^r) *s.* empaquetador, envasador.

packet (pæ·kit) *s.* paquete [fardo pequeño]. *2* MAR. *packet* o *~ boat*, paquete, paquebote.

packing (-ing) *s.* empaque, embalaje; envase: *~ needle*, aguja saquera. *2* MEC. empaquetadura, estopada; guarnición de junta.

packman (pæ·kmæn) *s.* buhonero.

packsack (pæ·ksæk) *s.* barjuleta.

packsaddle (pæ·ksædøl) *s.* albarda, basto.

packthread (pæ·kzred) *s.* bramante.

pact (pækt) *s.* pacto, convenio, acuerdo.

pad (pæd) *s.* cojincillo, almohadilla; postizo, relleno; compresa; hombrera, TONTILLO. *2* secatintas. *3* tampón [para entintar]. *4* ESGR. pleto, plastrón. *5* taco, bloc [de papel]. *6* sillín [de caballería]. *7* pie [de liebre, zorra, etc.]. *8* paso, pisada [ruido]. *9* jaca. *10* pop. camino.

pad (to) *tr.* rellenar, emborrar, acolchar; forrar [de algo blando]. *2* aumentar, hinchar [con elementos superfluos, partidas falsas, etc.]. *3 tr.-intr.* recorrer o andar a pie. ¶ Pret.: *padded;* ger.: *~ -dding.*

padding (-ing) *s.* relleno, acolchado; borra, guata. *2* fig. relleno, paja [en un escrito, etc.].

paddle (pæ·døl) *s.* canalete, zagual [remo]. *2* pala [de lavandera], batidor. *3* paleta [de rueda]: *~ boat*, buque de ruedas; *~ wheel*, rueda de paletas.

paddle (to) *tr.* impulsar con canalete o rueda de paletas. *2* apalear. *3 intr.* remar con canalete o suavemente. *4* chapotear, guachapear.

paddock (pæ·døk) *s.* dehesa, prado [junto a una casa o establo]. *2* cercado adjunto a un hipódromo.

paddy (pæ·di) *s.* arroz; arroz en cáscara. *2* fam. (con may.) irlandés.

padlock (-lak) *s.* candado.

padlock (to) *tr.* cerrar con candado, echar el candado a.

padre (pa·dri) *s.* MIL., MAR. capellán.

paean (pi·in) *s.* canto de júbilo o alabanza.

paederasty (pe·døræsti) *s.* pederastia.

pagan (pei·gan) *adj.-s.* pagano, gentil, infiel.

paganism (-išm) *s.* paganismo.

paganize (to) (-aiš) *tr.-intr.* paganizar.

page (peidў) *s.* paje. *2* botones; criado joven. *3* página; plana, carilla.

page (to) *tr.* buscar [a uno] llamándole [en un hotel, etc.]. *2* paginar, foliar. *3* IMPR. compaginar.

pageant (pæ·dўant) *s.* cabalgata, desfile, espectáculo, etc. [magníficos]. *2* aparato, pompa.

pageantry (-tri) s. pompa, aparato, espectáculo.
pager (pei·dўøʳ) s. IMPR. compaginador, ajustador.
pagination (pædỹinei·shøn) s. paginación.
pagoda (pagou·da) s. pagoda.
paid (peid) pret. y p. p. de TO PAY. 2 adj. pagado, asalariado.
pail (peil) s. herrada, colodra, cubo. 2 MAR. balde.
paillasse (pælia·s) s. jergón.
pain (pein) s. dolor, pena, sufrimiento; aflicción, inquietud. 2 pena [castigo]: on o under ~ of, bajo pena de. 3 trabajo, molestia: to take pains to, esforzarse, esmerarse por. 4 pl. dolores del parto.
pain (to) tr. doler, punzar. 2 causar dolor, afligir.
pained (-d) adj. dolorido, apenado, afligido.
painful (-ful) adj. doloroso. 2 penoso, aflictivo, angustioso. 3 trabajoso, arduo. 4 dolorido.
painstaking (-steiking) adj. afanoso, industrioso, cuidadoso, concienzudo, esmerado.
paint (peint) s. pintura, color. 2 afeite, colorete.
paint (to) tr. pintar. 2 intr. pintar, ser pintor. 3 pintarse el rostro.
paintbox (-baks) s. caja de colores o pinturas.
paintbrush (-brøsh) s. brocha, pincel.
painter (-tøʳ) s. pintor. 2 MAR. boza, amarra.
painting (-ing) s. pintura [acción, arte; color]. 2 pintura, cuadro.
paintress (-tris) f. pintora.
pair (pe·øʳ) s. par, pareja. 2 yunta, mancuerna. 3 grupo, serie [de cosas iguales]. 4 a ~ of scissors, unas tijeras; a ~ of trousers, unos pantalones.
pair (to) tr. aparear, unir en pareja, casar; juntar, asociar; acoplar. 2 parear [poner de dos en dos]. 3 intr. aparearse, formar pareja; unirse, casarse. 4 to ~ off, aparearse.
pajamas (padỹa·mas) s. pl. pijama.
pal (pæl) s. compañero, camarada. 2 compinche.
pal (to) intr. hacerse o ser amigo (s o compañero (s.
palace (pæ·lis) s. palacio.
paladin (pæ·ladin) s. paladín.
palaeography (peilia·grafi) s. paleografía.
palaelogist (-lodỹist) s. paleólogo.
palaeology (-lodỹi) s. paleología.
palaeolithic (peilioli·zik) adj.-s. paleolítico.
palaeontology (peilianta·lodỹi) s. paleontología.
Palaeozoic (-ozou·ik) adj.-s. paleozoico.
palaestra (pale·stra) s. palestra.
palankeen, palanquin (pælankɪ·n) s. palanquín [andas].
palatable (pæ·latabøl) adj. sabroso, apetitoso. 2 agradable, aceptable.
palatal (-tal) adj.-s. palatal. 2 ANAT. palatino.
palate (pæ·lit) s. paladar.
palatial (palei·shal) adj. magnífico, suntuoso.
palatinate (palæ·tinit) s. palatinado.
palatine (pæ·latin) adj. palatino. 2 s. conde palatino.
palaver (palæ·vøʳ) s. conferencia, debate [con los indígenas de África]. 2 fig. conversación, palabrería, embuste.
palaver (to) intr. charlar, discutir.
pale (peil) adj. pálido. 2 descolorido; apagado, sin brillo. 3 s. estaca. 4 estacada, palizada. 5 fig. límites, esfera, gremio, seno. 6 BLAS. palo.
pale (to) intr. palidecer, perder el color. 2 tr. hacer palidecer, descolorir. 3 empalizar, cercar.
paleface (-feis) s. rostro pálido.
paleness (-nis) s. palidez, descolorimiento.
paleography, etc. V. PALAEOGRAPHY, etc.
Palestine (pæ·listain) n. pr. GEOGR. Palestina.

Palestinian (pælisti·nian) adj. palestino.
palestra s. PALAESTRA.
palette (pæ·let) s. PINT. paleta. 2 ~ knife, espátula.
palfrey (po·lfri) s. palafrén.
palimpsest (pæ·limpsest) s. palimpsesto.
paling (pei·ling) s. palenque, estacada.
palingenesis (pælindỹe·nisis) s. palingenesia.
palinode (pæ·linoud) s. palinodia.
palisade (pælisei·d) s. palizada, estacada.
palisade (to) tr. empalizar.
palisander (pælisæ·ndøʳ) s. palisandro.
palish (pei·lish) adj. algo pálido, paliducho.
pall (pol) s. paño mortuorio. 2 fig. capa [lo que cubre u oscurece]. 3 palio [insignia]. 4 LITURG. palia.
pall (to) tr. quitar el sabor a. 2 ahitar, empalagar. 3 intr. perder la fuerza, el sabor: to ~ on o upon, cansar, dejar de gustar.
palladium (pælei·diøm) s. paladión. 2 QUÍM. paladio.
Pallas (pæ·las) n. pr. MIT. Palas.
pallbearer (po·lberøʳ) s. el que lleva o acompaña el féretro.
pallet (pæ·let) s. ALBAÑ., PINT. paleta. 2 pincel plano para dorar. 3 jergón, petate.
palliate (to) (pæ·lieit) tr. paliar. 2 mitigar. 3 excusar, disimular, encubrir.
palliative (pæ·liativ) adj.-s. paliativo.
pallid (pæ·lid) adj. pálido; desvaído.
pallium (pæ·liøm) s. LITURG., HIST., ANAT. palio.
pall-mall (pel·mel) s. mallo [juego].
pallor (pæ·løʳ) s. palidez.
palm (pam) s. palma [de la mano]. 2 palmo menor. 3 MAR. rempujo. 4 BOT. palma, palmera: ~ tree, palmera; Palm Sunday, Domingo de Ramos. 5 fig. palma, victoria.
palm (to) tr. tocar, manosear. 2 esconder en la palma de la mano; escamotear. 3 pop. untar la mano. 4 to ~ something off on someone, encajar, endosar algo a uno.
palmaceous (pælmei·shøs) adj. BOT. palmáceo.
palmar (pæ·lmaʳ) adj. ANAT. palmar.
palmary (pæ·lmari) adj. preeminente, superior.
palmate (d (pæ·lmeit(id) adj. palmado, palmeado.
palmer (pa·møʳ) s. palmero, peregrino.
palmetto (pælme·tou) s. BOT. palmito; palmera enana.
palmiped (pæ·lmiped) adj. ORN. palmípedo. 2 ZOOL. de pies palmeados.
palmist (er (pa·mist(øʳ) s. quiromántico.
palmistry (-tri) s. quiromancía.
palmy (pa·mi) adj. abundante en palmas. 2 próspero, floreciente, glorioso.
palp (pælp) s. ZOOL. palpo.
palpable (pæ·lpabøl) adj. palpable, evidente.
palpably (pæ·lpabli) adv. palpablemente.
palpate (to) (pæ·lpeit) tr. palpar, tentar.
palpebral (pæ·lpibral) adj. palpebral.
palpitate (to) (pæ·lpiteit) intr. palpitar, latir.
palpitation (pælpitei·shøn) s. palpitación.
palsied (po·lšid) adj. paralítico, perlático. 2 vacilante, tembloroso.
palsy (po·lši) s. MED. parálisis, perlesía.
palsy (to) tr. paralizar.
palter (to) (po·ltøʳ) intr. andar con rodeos o subterfugios, engañar. 2 regatear, discutir.
paltriness (po·ltrinis) s. bajeza, mezquindad, pobreza, futilidad.
paltry (po·ltri) adj. vil, ruin, mezquino, despreciable. 2 pobre, fútil, baladí.
paludal (paliu·dal) adj. palustre, palúdico.

paludism (pæ·liudišm) *s.* MED. paludismo.
pampas (pæ·mpaš) *s. pl.* pampa.
pampean (pæmpɪ·an) *adj.-s.* pampero.
pamperer (pæ·mpørø^r) *s.* mimador.
pamphlet (pæ·mfløt) *s.* folleto.
pamphleteer (pæmfløtɪ·^r) *s.* folletista, foliculario.
pan (pæn) *s.* cacerola, cazuela, cazo, caldero; recipiente de poco fondo. *2* MIN. artesa, gamella. *3* platillo [de balanza]. *4* cazoleta [de arma de fuego]: *to flash in the* ~, dar higa [un fusil].
Pan *n. pr.* MIT. Pan: *Pan's pipes,* flauta de Pan.
pan (to) *tr.* cocer, freír. *2* MIN. lavar en artesa. *3* pop. criticar, poner como nuevo. *4 intr. to* ~ *out,* dar oro [la arena], fig. resultar. ¶ Pret. y p. p.: *panned;* ger.: *-nning.*
panacea (pænasɪ·a) *s.* panacea, curalotodo.
panache (pɑnæ·sh) *s.* penacho. *2* fanfarronería.
Panama (pæ·nama o pænama) *n. pr.* GEOGR. Panamá: ~ *hat,* sombrero de jipijapa.
Pan-American *adj.* panamericano.
pancake (pæ·nkeik) *s.* hojuela [fruta de sartén]; torta delgada. *2* AVIA. aterrizaje hecho de plano.
pancratium (pænkrei·shiøm) *s.* pancracio.
pancreas (pæ·nkrias) *s.* ANAT. páncreas.
pancreatic (pænkriæ·tik) *adj.* pancreático.
panda (pæ·nda) *s.* ZOOL. panda.
Pandects (pæ·ndekts) *s. pl.* Pandectas.
pandemic (pænde·mik) *adj.* pandémico. *2 s.* pandemia.
pandemonium (-dimou·niøm) *s.* pandemónium.
pander (pæ·ndø^r) *s.* alcahuete, rufián.
pander (to) *tr.* alcahuetear, rufianear.
panderess (pæ·ndøris) *s.* alcahueta.
Pandora (pændou·ra) *n. pr.* Pandora: *Pandora's box,* caja de Pandora.
pane (pein) *s.* hoja de vidrio o cristal; cristal, vidrio [de ventana o vidriera]. *2* cara, faceta.
panegyric (pænidÿi·rik) *adj.-s.* panegírico.
panegyrist (-ist) *s.* panegirista.
panegyrize (to) (pæ·nidÿiraiš) *tr.* panegirizar.
panel (pæ·nøl) *s.* CARP., ARQ., ING. panel, cuarterón, entrepaño, artesón; compartimiento, sección. *2* PINT. tabla. *3* COST. adorno de tela. *4* recuadro. *5* AUTO., ELECT. tablero, cuadro. *6* lista [de jurados o de pers. designadas para un servicio, etc.]. *7* DER. jurado.
panel (to) *tr.* formar tableros, paneles o artesones; artesonar. *2* TO IMPANEL. ¶ Pret. y p. p.: *panel(l)ed;* ger.: *-l(l)ing.*
paneless (-lis) *adj.* sin cristales [ventana, etc.].
panel(l)ing (pæ·nøling) *s.* entrepaños, cuarterones; revestimiento de madera. *2* artesonado.
panetella (pænøte·la) *s.* panetela [cigarro].
pang (pæng) *s.* punzada, dolor agudo, tormento, ansia, congoja.
pangolin (pængou·lin) *s.* ZOOL. pangolin.
pan-handle *s.* mango de sartén, cacerola, etc.
pan-handle (to) *intr.* mendigar por las calles.
panic (pæ·nik) *adj.-s.* pánico.
panic-grass *s.* BOT. mijo.
panicky (-i) *adj.* pánico. *2* asustadizo.
panicle (pæ·nikøl) *s.* BOT. panícula.
panic-stricken *adj.* aterrorizado, preso de pánico.
paniculate (d (pani·kiuleit(id) *adj.* paniculado.
panification (panifikei·shøn) *s.* panificación.
Pan-Islamism *s.* panislamismo.
panjandrum (pændÿæ·ndrøm) *s.* joc. personaje. *2* joc. ceremonia exagerada.
panniculus (pæni·kiuløs) *s.* BIOL. panículo.
pannier (pæ·niø^r) *s.* cesta grande, cuévano. *2* cestón. *3* tontillo, caderillas.

pannikin (-ikin) *s.* cacillo. *2* vaso de metal.
panoply (-øpli) *s.* panoplia [armadura]. *2* cosa que protege o que envuelve suntuosamente.
panorama (pænøra·ma) *s.* panorama.
panoramic (-mik) *a.* panorámico.
pansy (pæ·nši) *s.* BOT. pensamiento, trinitaria.
pant (pænt) *s.* jadeo, resuello. *2* palpitación.
pant (to) *intr.* jadear, resollar. *2* palpitar. *3 to* ~ *for* o *after,* desear con ansia, suspirar por.
Pantagruelic (pæntagrue·lik) *adj.* pantagruélico.
pantaloon (pæntælu·n) *s.* bufón, gracioso. *2 pl.* pantalones, calzones.
pantheism (pæ·nziišm) *s.* panteísmo.
pantheist (-ist) *s.* panteísta.
Pantheon (-iøn) *s.* panteón.
panther (pæ·nzø^r) *s.* ZOOL. pantera; (E.U.) puma.
panties (-tis) *s. pl.* bragas [de mujer].
pantile (-tail) *s.* teja de sección en S.
panting (-ting) *adj.* jadeante. *2 s.* jadeo; palpitación.
pantograph (-tøgræf) *s.* pantógrafo.
pantomime (-tømaim) *s.* pantomima. *2* pantomimo.
pantomimist (-mai·mist) *s.* pantomimo. *2* autor de pantomimas.
pantry (pæ·ntri) *s.* despensa, repostería.
pants (pæ·nts) *s. fam.* pantalones. *2* (fam.) calzoncillos.
pap (pæp) *s.* papas, gachas, papilla.
papa (pa·pø o pøpa·) *s.* papá.
papacy (pei·pasi) *s.* papado. *2* adhesión al Papa.
papal (-pal) *adj.* papal; pontificio.
papaveraceous (papævørei·shøs) *adj.* papaveráceo.
papaw (papo·) *s.* BOT. asimina. *2* PAPAYA.
papaya (peipa·ia) *s.* BOT. papayo. *2* papaya.
paper (pei·pø^r) *s.* papel [materia; hoja de papel; escrito, documento]: ~ *clip,* sujetapapeles, clip; ~ *currency,* ~ *money,* papel moneda; ~ *cutter,* plegadera; guillotina; ~ *hanger,* empapelador; ~ *knife,* plegadera; ~ *mill,* fábrica de papel. *2* COM. papel [valor negociable]. *3* papel, periódico, diario. *4 pl.* papeles, documentos, apuntes, memorias. *5* papillotes.
paper (to) *tr.* empapelar. *2* envolver en papel.
paperback (-bæk) *s.* libro en rústica.
paper-bound *adj.* ENCUAD. en rústica.
paperweight (-ueit) *s.* pisapapeles.
papery (-i) *adj.* parecido al papel.
papess (pei·pis) *s.* papisa.
papilionaceous (papilionei·shøs) *adj.* papilionáceo.
papilla (papi·la) *s.* ANAT. pezón. *2* ANAT., ZOOL., BOT. papila.
papillary (pæ·pilæri) *adj.* papilar.
papion (pei·pian) *s.* ZOOL. papión, zambo.
papist (pei·pist) *s. desp.* papista, católico.
papistry (-ri) *s. desp.* papismo, catolicismo.
pap(p)oose (pæpu·s) *s.* niño indio [de Norteamérica].
pappus (pæ·pos) *s.* BOT. vilano.
pappy (-i) *s. fam.* papá. *2 adj.* mollar, jugoso.
papule (-iul) *s.* pápula.
papyrus (papai·røs), *pl.* **-ri** (-rai) *s.* papiro.
par (pa^r) *s.* equivalencia, paridad, nivel; COM. par: *at* ~, a la par; *above* ~, con premio, sobre la par; *to be on a* ~ *with,* ser igual a, correr parejas con; ~ *value,* valor nominal.
parable (pæ·røbøl) *s.* parábola [narración].
parabola (paræ·bola) *s.* GEOM. parábola.
parabolic (al (paraba·lik(al) *adj.* parabólico.

paraboloid (paræ·boloid) s. GEOM. paraboloide.
parachute (pæ·rashut) s. paracaídas.
parachutist (-ist) s. paracaidista.
Paraclete (pæ·raclit) n. pr. Paráclito, Paracleto.
parade (parei·d) s. pompa, ostentación; alarde, gala. 2 MIL. parada, revista: ~ ground, plaza de armas. 3 desfile, cabalgata. 4 (Ingl.) paseo público.
parade (to) tr. ostentar, alardear de. 2 tr.-intr. MIL. formar en parada, (hacer) desfilar. 3 intr. exhibirse, pasearse.
paradigm (pæ·radaim) s. paradigma. 2 ejemplo.
paradise (pæ·radais) s. paraíso. 2 ORN. ~ bird, ave del Paraíso.
paradisiacal (pæradisai·akal) adj. paradisíaco.
paradox (pæ·radaks) s. paradoja.
paradoxical (-ikal) adj. paradójico, paradojo.
paraffin(e (pæ·rafin) s. parafina.
paragoge (-gou·dŷi) s. GRAM. paragoge.
paragon (-gan) s. modelo, ejemplar, dechado; tipo de perfección. 2 IMPR. parangona.
paragraph (-græf) s. párrafo, aparte. 2 suelto, artículo corto. 3 IMPR. calderón.
paragraph (to) tr. dividir en párrafos. 2 escribir o comentar en sueltos o artículos cortos.
Paraguay (-gwei) n. pr. GEOGR. Paraguay.
parakeet (-kɪt) s. ORN. periquito.
parallactic (al (-læ·ktik(al) adj. paraláctico.
parallax (pæ·ralæks) s. ASTR. paralaje.
parallel (-el) adj. paralelo: ~ bars, paralelas [de gimnasia]. 2 s. línea o superficie paralela. 3 paralelismo, semejanza. 4 par, igual. 5 paralelo [comparación]. 6 GEOGR., ELECT. paralelo. 7 FORT. paralela.
parallel (to) tr. igualar, parangonar. 2 ser igual a. 3 poner paralelo. 4 ser paralelo a. ¶ Pret. y p. p.: parallel(l)ed; ger.: -l(l)ing.
parallelepiped (-øpai·pid) s. GEOM. paralelepípedo.
parallelism (pæ·raleliŝm) s. paralelismo.
parallelogram (pærale·løgræm) s. GEOM. paralelogramo.
paralysis (paræ·lisis) s. MED. parálisis, perlesía. 2 paralización, estancamiento.
paralytic (pærali·tik) adj.-s. paralítico.
paralyzation (-ŝei·shøn) s. paralización.
paralyze (to) (pæ·ralaiŝ) tr. paralizar.
paralyzed (-d) adj. paralizado. 2 paralítico.
parameter (paræ·metøʳ) s. MAT. parámetro.
paramount (pæ·ramaunt) adj. superior, supremo, máximo, capital, principalísimo.
paramour (-muʳ) s. amante; querido; querida.
paranoia (pærano·ia) s. MED. paranoia.
paranoiac (-iæk) adj.-s. paranoico.
parapet (pæ·rapet) s. parapeto. 2 pretil, baranda, antepecho.
paraph (pæ·raf) s. rúbrica, signo.
paraphernalia (pæraføʳnei·lia) s. pl. avíos, enseres, trastos; atavíos, galas.
paraphrase (pæ·rafreiŝ) s. paráfrasis.
paraphrase (to) tr. parafrasear.
paraselene (pæraseli·ni) s. METEOR. paraselene.
parasite (pæ·rasait) s. parásito. 2 gorrón, gorrero.
parasitic (al (-si·tik(al) adj. parásito, parasitario.
parasiticide (-tisaid) adj.-s. parasiticida.
parasitology (-saita·lodŷi) s. parasitología.
parasol (pæ·rasol) s. sombrilla, parasol, quitasol.
paratrooper (-trupøʳ) s. MIL. paracaidista.
paratroops (-trups) s. pl. MIL. tropas paracaidistas.
paratyphoid (pæratai·foid) adj. MED. paratifoide, paratífico: ~ fever, paratifoidea, paratifus.

parboil (to) (pa·ʳboil) tr. sancochar, cocer a medias.
Parcae (pa·ʳsi) s. pl. MIT. Parcas.
parcel (-søl) s. paquete, bulto, lío, atado: ~ post, servicio de paquetes postales. 2 hatajo, cuadrilla. 3 parcela, solar. 4 COM. lote, partida.
parcel (to) tr. parcelar, dividir: to ~ out, repartir. 2 empaquetar, envolver. ¶ Pret. y p. p.: parcel(l)ed; ger.: -l(l)ing.
parcener (pa·ʳsønøʳ) s. DER. coheredero.
parch (to) (parch) tr. tostar. 2 quemar, abrasar [el calor, el frío, la fiebre, la sed]; resecar; agostar: to be parched with thirst, morirse de sed. 3 intr. tostarse, abrasarse, resecarse.
parchesi (pa·ʳchɪ·ŝi) s. parchís [juego].
parchment (pa·ʳchmønt) s. pergamino; vitela.
pard (pa·ʳd) s. pop. compinche, camarada.
pardon (pa·ʳdøn) s. perdón: I beg your ~, usted perdone. 2 indulto, amnistía.
pardon (to) tr. perdonar. 2 indultar, amnistiar. 3 excusar, dispensar: ~ me, dispense usted.
pardonable (-abøl) adj. perdonable, excusable, dispensable.
pardoner (-øʳ) s. perdonador.
pare (to) (pe·øʳ) tr. móndar, pelar [fruta, patatas, etc.]. 2 cortar, recortar, raer, despalmar: to ~ the nails, cortar las uñas. 3 reducir [gastos, etc.].
parenchyma (pare·nkima) s. ANAT., BOT. parénquima.
parent (pe·rønt) s. padre o madre. 2 autor, causa, origen. 3 pl. padres. 4 adj. de los padres. 5 madre, matriz, principal.
parentage (pe·røntidŷ) s. linaje, nacimiento, origen.
parental (pare·ntal) adj. paternal, maternal.
parenthesis (pare·nzesis) s. paréntesis.
parenthetic (al (pærønze·tik(al) adj. parentético.
paresis (pærsis) s. MED. paresia.
parget (par·dŷit) s. yeso, mortero, enlucido.
parget (to) tr. ALBAÑ. enyesar, enlucir. 2 adornar con molduras de yeso.
parhelion (pa·ʳjɪ·liøn) s. METEOR. parhelio.
pariah (pa·ria o parai·a) s. paria.
parietal (pæ·riøtal) adj. parietal. 2 interno. 3 s. ANAT. parietal [hueso].
parietary (pæ·riøteri) s. BOT. parietaria.
pari-mutuel (peri·miu·chuel) s. apuesta mutua.
paring (pe·ring) s. mondadura, peladura, raedura, corte, despalme: ~ knife, chifla; pujavante. 2 pl. mondaduras, raeduras, recortes.
paripinnate (pæripi·neit) adj. BOT. paripinado.
Paris (pæ·ris) n. pr. MIT. Paris; GEOGR. París.
parish (pæ·rish) s. parroquia, feligresía; pueblo: ~ church, iglesia parroquial; ~ clerk, sacristán.
parishioner (-shønøʳ) s. parroquiano, feligrés.
Parisian (-ŝian) adj.-s. parisiense.
park (pa·ʳk) s. parque.
park (to) tr. encerrar en un parque. 2 aparcar, estacionar. 3 intr. aparcar, estacionarse.
parking (-ing) s. aparcamiento, estacionamiento: no ~, prohibido el estacionamiento.
parkway (pa·ʳkuei) s. gran vía adornada con árboles. 2 (E.U.) autopista.
parlance (pa·ʳlans) s. lenguaje, habla.
parley (pa·ʳli) s. conferencia, discusión. 2 MIL. parlamento.
parley (to) intr. discutir, parlamentar.
Parliament (pa·ʳlimønt) s. parlamento, cortes.
parliamentarian (paʳlimønte·rian) s. parlamentario.

parliamentarism (pa^{r}lime·ntarišm) s. parlamentarismo.
parliamentary (-tari) adj.-s. parlamentario.
parlo (u) r (pa·^{r}lø^r) s. sala de estar o de recibimiento. 2 (E.U.) salón [de peluquería]; sala [de billares, etc.]. 3 locutorio, parlatorio.
parlo (u) rmaid (-meid) s. doncella, camarera.
Parmesan (pa·^{r}mišan) adj.-s. parmesano.
Parnassus (pa^{r}næ·søs) n. pr. GEOGR., MIT., LIT. Parnaso.
parochial (parou·kial) adj. parroquial. 2 fig. limitado, local; mezquino, estrecho.
parodist (pæ·rødist) s. parodista.
parody (pæ·rødi) s. parodia.
parody (to) tr. parodiar.
parole (parou·l) s. palabra de honor [esp. la de un prisionero]. 2 MIL. santo y seña.
parole (to) tr. poner en libertad bajo palabra de honor.
paronomasia (pæranomei·ẏia) s. paronomasia.
paronymy (pæra·nimi) s. paronimia.
paroquet (pæ·roket) s. PARAKEET.
parotid (pæra·tid) adj. parotídeo. 2 s. ANAT. parótida.
paroxysm (pæ·røksišm) s. paroxismo. 2 acceso, arrebato.
paroxytone (pæra·ksitoun) adj.-s. GRAM. paroxitono.
parquet (pa·^{r}keit) s. TEAT. platea. 2 mosaico de madera.
parquetry (pa·^{r}kitri) s. mosaico de madera.
parr (pa^r) s. ICT. esguín, murgón.
parricide (pæ·risaid) s. parricida. 2 parricidio.
parrot (pæ·røt) s. ORN. loro, cotorra, papagayo. 2 ICT. ~ fish, escaro; papagayo.
parrot (to) tr. repetir como un papagayo.
parry (pæ·ri) s. parada, quite.
parry (to) tr.-intr. parar [un golpe, una estocada, etc.]. 2 evitar, eludir. ¶ Pret. y p. p.: parried; ger.: -rrying.
parse (to) (pa^{r}s) tr. GRAM. analizar.
Parsee, Parsi (pa·^{r}si) s. parsi.
parsimonious (parsimou·niøš) adj. parsimonioso, frugal, parco, mezquino, tacaño.
parsimony (pa·^{r}simouni) s. parsimonia, frugalidad, parquedad.
parsing (pa·^{r}sing) s. GRAM. análisis.
parsley (pa·^{r}sli) s. BOT. perejil.
parsnip (pa·^{r}snip) s. BOT. pastinaca, chirivía.
parson (pa·^{r}søn) s. párroco, cura, sacerdote.
parsonage (pa·^{r}sønidẏ) s. rectoría, rectoral.
part (pa^{r}t) s. parte [porción, fracción, división; miembro, elemento; participación]: ~ and parcel, parte esencial o inseparable; ~ of speech, parte de la oración; to take ~ in, tomar parte en; for my ~, por mi parte; in ~, en parte. 2 cuidado, obligación, deber. 3 parte o partido [en una contienda, etc.]: to take in the ~ of, ponerse de parte de. 4 TEAT. parte, papel. 5 MÚS. parte. 6 MEC. pieza. 7 (E.U.) raya [del cabello]. 8 to take in good ~, echar a buena parte. 9 pl. lugares, países. 10 talento, dotes.
    11 adj.-adv. parcial, parcialmente: ~ owner, condueño.
part (to) tr. dividir, partir, separar. 2 repartir. 3 to ~ the hair, hacerse la raya. 4 to ~ company, separarse. 5 intr. partirse, desunirse; separarse, desprenderse. 6 partir, irse, despedirse. 7 fig. morir. 8 to ~ with, desprenderse de, separarse de.
partage (pa·^{r}tidẏ) s. repartimiento. 2 parte, porción.

partake (to) (pa^{r}tei·k) tr. compartir. 2 intr. to ~ in, participar en. 3 to ~ of, participar de, tener algo de; comer, beber.
partaker (-ø^r) s. participante, partícipe.
parterre (pa^{r}te·r) s. parterre, cuadro de jardín.
parthenogenesis (pa^{r}zinodẏe·nesis) s. BIOL. partenogénesis.
Parthenon (pa·^{r}zinan) n. pr. Partenón.
Parthian (pa·^{r}zian) adj.-s. parto [de Partia].
partial (pa·^{r}shal) adj. parcial. 2 afecto, aficionado.
partiality (pa^{r}shæ·liti) s. parcialidad. 2 inclinación, afición.
participant (pa^{r}ti·sipant) adj.-s. participante, partícipe.
participate (to) (-sipeit) intr.-tr. participar [tomar o tener parte].
participation (-ei·shøn) s. participación, parte.
participator (pa^{r}ti·sipeitø^r) adj.-s. partícipe.
participial (pa^{r}tisi·pial) adj. participial.
participle (pa·^{r}tisipøl) s. GRAM. participio.
particle (pa·^{r}tikøl) s. partícula. 2 pizca.
parti-colo (u) red adj. de varios colores, abigarrado.
particular (pa^{r}ti·kiula^r) adj. particular. 2 exacto, minucioso, detallado, esmerado. 3 escrupuloso, delicado, exigente. 4 s. particular, particularidad, pormenor, detalle: to go into particulars, entrar en detalles. 5 in ~, en particular.
particularity (pa^{r}tikiulæ·riti) s. particularidad. 2 minuciosidad.
particularize (to) (pa^{r}ti·kiularaiš) tr. particularizar, detallar, especificar.
parting (pa·^{r}ting) s. separación, división. 2 partida, marcha; separación, despedida. 3 raya, línea divisoria. 4 raya [del pelo]. 5 ~ of ways, bifurcación, cruce de caminos; momento de separarse.
partisan (pa·^{r}tišan) s. partidario. 2 guerrillero. 3 partesana. 4 adj. partidista.
partisanship (-ship) s. partidismo.
partition (pa^{r}ti·shøn) s. partición. 2 división, separación. 3 tabique, barandilla, etc., que divide. 4 parte, porción.
partition (to) tr. dividir, separar. 2 repartir. 3 to ~ off, separar con un tabique.
partitive (pa·^{r}titiv) adj.-s. partitivo.
partizan (pa·^{r}tišan) adj.-s. PARTISAN.
partly (pa·^{r}tli) adv. en parte, en cierto modo.
partner (-nø^r) s. socio [en un negocio]. 2 compañero [en el juego]. 3 pareja [en el baile]. 4 cónyuge. 5 aparcero.
partnership (-ship) s. sociedad, compañía, asociación. 2 aparcería.
partook (pa^{r}tu·k) pret. de to PARTAKE.
partridge (pa·^{r}tridẏ) s. ORN. perdiz.
parturition (pa^{r}tiuri·shøn) s. parto, alumbramiento.
party (pa·^{r}ti) s. partido [político], bando, facción. 2 partido, causa. 3 partida, reunión, convite, fiesta; grupo de personas que viajan, cazan, etc., juntas. 4 MIL. destacamento, pelotón. 5 DER. parte. 6 parte [en contrato, contienda, etc.]. 7 individuo, sujeto. 8 to be a ~ to, tener parte en, contribuir a. 9 adj. de partido; en común; que divide: ~ wall, pared medianera.
parvis (pa·^{r}vis) s. ARQ. atrio.
paschal (pæ·skal) adj. pascual.
pasha (pasha·) s. bajá.
pashalic (-lik) adj. bajalato.
pasqueflower (pæ·skflauø^r) s. BOT. pulsatila.
pasquinade (pæskuinei·d) s. pasquinada; pasquín.

pass (pas) *s.* paso, pasaje; estrecho, desfiladero; desembocadero. *2* paso [acción o permiso de pasar]; pase, permiso, salvoconducto. *3* aprobación [en un examen]. *4* pase [magnético]. *5* ESGR. estocada. *6* trance, situación.

pass (to) *intr.* pasar [en todas sus acepciones]. *2* morir. *3 to ~ along*, pasar de largo; pasar por [una calle, etc.]. *4 to ~ away*, morir; pasar, desaparecer. *5 to ~ by*, pasar de largo, pasar [por el lado o delante de]. *6 to ~ for*, pasar, ser tenido por. *7 to ~ off*, pasar [una enfermedad, tempestad, etc.]. *8 to ~ out*, salir; desmayarse. *9 to ~ over*, pasar al otro lado. *10 to come to ~*, suceder, ocurrir. *11 tr.* pasar [atravesar, cruzar, ir al otro lado de; dejar atrás; trasponer]. *12* pasar por el lado de, cruzarse con. *13* pasar, exceder, pasar de. *14* pasar, sufrir, tolerar. *15* tomar [un acuerdo]; aprobar [a un examinando; un proyecto de ley]. *16* pasar, aprobar [un examen]. *17* pasar, hacer pasar; dar, entregar, transferir. *18* pasar por alto, omitir. *19* no pagar [un dividendo]. *20* emitir [juicios], pronunciar [sentencia]. *21* pasar, colar, cerner. *22 to ~ along* o *around*, pasar de uno a otro, hacer circular. *23 to ~ by*, perdonar, no hacer caso de; omitir. *24 to ~ off*, hacer pasar [moneda falsa, etc.]. *25 to ~ on*, pasar [algo] a otro. *26 to ~ over*, transferir; omitir; postergar; perdonar. ¶ Part. p.: *passed* o *past*.

passable (pæ·sabøl) *adj.* pasadero. *2* transitorio. *3* tolerable, regular, mediano.

passage (pæ·sidȳ) *s.* paso, pasaje, tránsito. *2* paso, entrada, pasadizo. *3* MAR. viaje. *4* pasaje [de un buque]. *5* intercambio [de confidencias, golpes, etc.]; lance, encuentro; ~ *at arms*, asalto combate. *6* incidente, episodio. *7* pasaje [de un libro, etc.].

passageway (-dȳuei) *s.* pasadizo, pasaje.

passant (pæ·sant) *adj.* BLAS. pasante.

passbook (pæ·sbuk) *s.* cartilla o libreta de banco.

passementerie (pæsme·ntri) *s.* pasamanería.

passenger (pæ·sendȳø͏ʳ) *s.* pasajero, viajero.

passer (-by) (pæ·søʳ) *s.* transeúnte, viandante.

passerine (pæ·sørin) *adj.* ORN. del orden de los pájaros.

passible (pæ·sibøl) *adj.* pasible.

passing (pæ·sing) *s.* paso, pasada. *2* transcurso [del tiempo]. *3* tránsito, muerte. *4 adj.* que pasa, de paso. *5* pasajero, transitorio, momentáneo. *6* hecho o dicho de paso.

passion (pæ·shøn) *s.* pasión. *2* cólera, ira: *to fly into a ~*, montar en cólera. *3* (con may.) Pasión [de N. S.].

passionate (-it) *adj.* apasionado. *2* vivo, ardiente. *3* acalorado, colérico, arrebatado.

passionflower (-flauø͏ʳ) *s.* BOT. pasionaria.

passionless (-lis) *adj.* frío, tranquilo, desapasionado.

passive (pæ·siv) *adj.* pasivo. | No tiene el sentido de pasivo [haber] ni el de pasivo [participio]. *2 s.* GRAM. VOZ pasiva.

passivity (pæsi·viti) *s.* pasividad.

passkey (pæ·ski) *s.* llavín, llave maestra.

Passover (-ouvø͏ʳ) *s.* pascua de los hebreos.

passport (-po͏ʳt) *s.* pasaporte. *2* salvoconducto.

password (-uø͏ʳd) *s.* santo y seña, contraseña.

past (pæst o past) *adj.* pasado, pretérito; último, ex, que fue: *for some years ~*, desde hace algunos años. *2* consumado. *3* GRAM. pasivo [participio]; pretérito [tiempo]. *4 s.* pasado. *5* GRAM. preté-

rito: ~ *perfect*, pluscuamperfecto. *6 prep.* pasado, después de, más allá de; fuera de; sin: ~ *two o'clock*, después de las dos, pasadas las dos; ~ *belief*, increíble; ~ *recovery*, incurable, sin remedio. *7 adv.* más allá, por delante.

paste (peist) *s.* pasta, masa. *2* engrudo. *3* imitación de piedra preciosa.

paste (to) *tr.* pegar [con engrudo, etc.] engrudar.

pasteboard (-bo͏ʳd) *s.* cartón.

pastel (pæ·stel) *s.* BOT. hierba pastel. *2* PINT. pastel.

pastel(l)ist (-ist) *s.* PINT. pastelista.

paster (pei·stø͏ʳ) *s.* engrudador. *2* papel engomado.

pastern (pæ·stø͏ʳn) *s.* VET. cuartilla, cerruma.

pasteurize (to) (pæ·størais̆) *tr.* pasterizar.

pastil (pæ·stil), **pastille** (pæsti·l) *s.* pastilla.

pastime (pæ·staim) *s.* pasatiempo, entretenimiento.

pastor (pæ·stø͏ʳ) *s.* pastor [esp. espiritual]; párroco, clérigo. *2* ORN. variedad de estornino.

pastoral (-al) *adj.* pastoril. *2 adj.-s.* pastoral.

pastry (pei·stri) *s.* pastelería, pasteles, pastas, repostería: ~ *cook*, pastelero, repostero; ~ *shop*, pastelería [tienda].

pasturage (pæ·schuridȳ) *s.* pasto, pastura. *2* apacentamiento.

pasture (pæ·schø͏ʳ) *s.* pasto, pastura, dehesa.

pasture (to) *tr.-intr.* pastar, pacer, apacentarse. *2 tr.* pastar, apacentar, pastorear.

pasty (pei·sti) *adj.* pastoso. *2* fofo, pálido, descolorido. *3 s.* (Ingl.) pastel [de carne o pescado].

pat (pæt) *adj.* exacto, conveniente, oportuno. *2* fijo, firme. *3 adv.* oportunamente; a punto; perfectamente, al dedillo. *4 s.* golpecito, palmadita. *5* pastilla [de mantequilla, etc.].

pat (to) *tr.* dar golpecitos o palmaditas a; acariciar: *to ~ on the back*, fig. elogiar, felicitar. ¶ Pret. y p. p.: *patted*; ger.: *-tting*.

Patagonian (pætagou·nian) *adj.-s.* patagón.

patch (pæch) *s.* remiendo; parche. *2* lunar postizo. *3* trozo, retazo. *4* mancha [de color]. *5* pedazo [de terreno]. *6* MED. placa.

patch (to) *tr.* remendar, apedazar, componer. *3* cubrir con manchas de color. *4* chafallar. *5 to ~ up*, componer, arreglar; hacer con retazos.

patchouli (-uli) *s.* pachulí.

patchwork (-uø͏ʳk) *s.* centón, obra de retazos, mezcolanza. *2* chapucería.

patchy (-i) *adj.* lleno de remiendos. *2* fig. manchado, abigarrado.

pate (peit) *s.* fam. cabeza, sesera, coronilla.

paten (pæ·tøn) *s.* LITURG. patena.

patent (pæ·tøn) *adj.* patente, manifiesto. *2* abierto. *3* patentado. *4* ~ *leather*, charol. *5* ~ *medicine*, específico. *6 s.* patente, privilegio exclusivo; diploma, título.

patent (to) *tr.* patentar.

pater (pei·tø͏ʳ) *s.* padrenuestro. *2* pop. padre, papá.

paternal (patø·ʳnal) *adj.* paternal, paterno, patrio.

paternity (patø·ʳniti) *s.* paternidad. *2* linaje, origen [por parte de padre].

paternoster (peitø·ʳna·stø͏ʳ) *s.* padrenuestro, paternóster. *2* rosario.

path (paz) *s.* camino, senda, vereda. *2* ruta, curso, trayectoria. *3* órbita [de un astro].

pathetic (paze·tik) *adj.* patético. *2* lastimoso.

patheticalness (-alnis) *s.* patetismo.

pathless (pa·zlis) *adj.* sin caminos, no transitado.

pathogenic (pæzødȳe·nik) *adj.* patógeno.

pathologic (al (pæzøla·dȳik(al) *adj.* patológico.

pathologist (paza·lodȳist) *s.* patólogo.

pathology (-i) *s.* patología.

pathos (pei·zas) s. patetismo, sentimiento.
pathway (pa·zuei) s. camino, senda.
patience (pei·shøns) s. paciencia: *to have no ~ with*, no poder sufrir. 2 solitario [juego].
patient (-t) adj. paciente. 2 susceptible [de]. 3 s. FIL., GRAM., MED. paciente.
patina (pæ·tina) s. pátina.
patly (pæ·tli) adv. PAT.
patois (pæ·tua) s. jerga, dialecto.
patriarch (pei·tria^rk) s. patriarca.
patriarchal (peitria·^rkal) adj. patriarcal.
patriarchate (pei·tria^rkeit), **patriarchy** (-ki) s. patriarcado.
patrician (pɑtri·shan) adj.-s. patricio.
patriciate (patri·shieit) s. patriciado.
Patrick (pæ·trik) n. pr. Patricio.
patrimony (pæ·trimoni) s. patrimonio.
patriot (pei·triøt) s. patriota.
patriotic (al (peitria·tik(al) adj. patriótico.
patriotism (pei·triøtišm) s. patriotismo.
patristic (patri·stik) adj. patrístico.
patristics (-s) s. patrística.
patrol (patrou·l) s. patrulla; ronda.
patrol (to) intr.-tr. patrullar, rondar. ¶ Pret. y p. p.: *patrolled*; ger.: *patrolling*.
patrolman (patrou·lmæn) s. rondador; vigilante de policía, guardia municipal, etc.
patron (pei·trøn) adj. patrón, tutelar. 2 s. patrón [santo]. 3 patrono, protector. 4 parroquiano, cliente. 5 ECLES. patrono.
patronage (-idŷ) s. protección, patrocinio, amparo. 2 clientela. 3 ECLES. patronato.
patroness (-is) f. protectora, patrocinadora.
patronize (to) (-aiš) tr. proteger, patrocinar, favorecer. 2 ser cliente de. 3 tratar con aire de protección, de superioridad.
patronymic (pætrøni·mik) adj.-s. patronímico.
patten (pæ·tøn) s. galocha, zueco, chanclo.
patter (pæ·tø^r) s. jerga, lenguaje. 2 charla, parlería, ruido de pasitos, de gotas de agua, etc.
patter (to) intr. hacer ruidos ligeros, como los de la lluvia, pasos menudos, etc. 2 rezar de prisa. 3 charlar. 4 hablar en jerga.
pattern (pæ·tø^rn) s. modelo, muestra, dechado; ejemplar,tipo. 2 patron, plantilla. 3 dibujo, diseño, motivo.
pattern (to) tr. servir de ejemplo. 2 *to ~ after, on* o *upon*, hacer, modelar, a imitación de.
patty (pæ·ti) s. pastelillo, empanada.
paucity (po·siti) s. poquedad, exigüidad.
Paul (pol) n. pr. Pablo.
Pauline (po·lin) adj. referente a San Pablo.
paunch (ponch) s. panza, barriga. 2 MAR. pallete.
pauper (po·pø^r) s. pobre [pers.].
pauperism (-išm) s. pauperismo.
pauperize (to) (-aiš) tr. empobrecer.
pause (poš) s. pausa, interrupción, paro, descanso. 2 pausa, cesura. 3 MÚS. calderón, fermata. 4 vacilación. 5 respiro, tregua.
pause (to) intr. pausar, interrumpirse, detenerse. 2 vacilar.
pavan (pæ·van) s. pavana.
pave (to) (peiv) tr. pavimentar, solar, adoquinar, empedrar: *to ~ the way*, preparar el terreno.
pavement (-mønt) s. pavimento, suelo, adoquinado. 2 acera, andén.
pavilion (pavi·liøn) s. pabellón [tienda, dosel]. 2 ANAT., ARQ. pabellón.
paving (pei·ving) s. pavimento, pavimentación.
pavis (pæ·vis) s. pavés.
paw (po) s. garra, zarpa. 2 fig. garra, mano.

paw (to) tr. manosear, sobar. 2 dar manotazos en. 3 tr.-intr. arañar. 4 patear, piafar.
pawl (pol) s. MEC. linguete, trinquete, retén.
pawn (pon) s. peón [de ajedrez]. 2 empeño; garantía, prenda: *~ ticket*, papeleta de empeño; *in ~*, en prenda.
pawn (to) tr. empeñar [dar o dejar en prenda].
pawnbroker (-broukø^r) s. prestamista [sobre prendas].
pawner (-ø^r) s. prendador.
pawnshop (-shap) s. casa de empeños.
pax (pæks) s. LITURG. paz.
pay (pei) s. paga, sueldo, salario: *in the ~ of*, al servicio de. 2 paga, pago [recompensa; acción de pagar]: *~ list* o *roll*, nómina; *good ~, bad ~*, buena paga, mala paga [pers.]. 3 MIN. *~ dirt*, tierra o arena que da buena cantidad de oro.
pay (to) tr.-intr. pagar: *to ~ back*, devolver; *to ~ for*, pagar [lo que se compra]; recompensar; pagar, purgar, expiar; *to ~ off*, pagar y despedir; saldar, pagar todo lo adeudado; vengarse de; *to ~ out*, desembolsar; *to ~ through the nose*, pagar muy caro [comprando]; *to ~ up*, saldar. 2 tr. costear, sufragar. 3 hacer [una visita, la corte]; rendir [homenaje]; ofrecer [sus respetos]; prestar [atención]; dirigir [cumplidos]. 4 MAR. *to ~ out* o *away*, largar, lascar, filar. 5 intr. compensar, ser provechoso. ¶ Pret. y p. p.: *paid*.
payable (pei·abøl) adj. pagable, pagadero.
payday (pei·dei) s. día de pago.
payee (peii·) s. portador, tenedor [de una letra, cheque, etc.].
payer (pei·ø^r) s. pagador.
paying (-ing) s. pago, acción de pagar: *~ teller*, pagador [de un banco].
paymaster (-mæstø^r) s. pagador, contador; habilitado.
payment (-mønt) s. pago, paga: *on the ~ of*, mediante el pago de. 2 pago, recompensa.
pay-office s. pagaduría.
pea (pi) s. BOT. guisante, chicharro: *~ soup*, puré de guisantes; neblina espesa y amarillenta. 2 *~ jacket*, chaquetón de marinero.
peace (pi·s) s. paz: *~ of God*, paz de Dios, tregua de Dios; *~ offering*, sacrificio propiciatorio; prenda de paz; *at ~*, en paz. 2 orden público: *~ officer*, policía, guardia municipal. 3 quietud, tranquilidad, silencio: *to hold one's ~*, guardar silencio, callar. 4 interj. ¡paz!, ¡silencio!
paceable (-abøl) adj. pacífico, tranquilo.
peaceful (-ful) adj. pacífico, tranquilo, sosegado.
peacefulness (-nis) s. paz, tranquilidad, sosiego.
peacemaker (-meikø^r) s. pacificador, conciliador.
peacetime (-taim) s. tiempo o período de paz. 2 adj. de tiempo de paz.
peach (pich) s. BOT. pérsico, melocotón, durazno: *~ tree*, pérsico, melocotonero, duraznero. 2 color de melocotón. 3 pop. persona o cosa excelente.
peach (to) intr. pop. delatar a un cómplice.
peachick (pi·shik) s. ORN. pollo del pavo real.
peachy (pi·chi) adj. amelocotonado. 2 fam. magnífico, estupendo.
peacock (pi·kak) s. ORN. pavón, pavo real. 2 ENT. *~ butterfly*, pavón. 3 ICT. *~ fish*, budión.
pea-gun s. cerbatana.
peahen (pi·jen) s. ORN. pava real.
peak (pik) s. pico, cumbre, cima. 2 cúspide. 3 punto máximo. 4 pico, punta [de una cosa]. 5 cresta [de onda]. 6 adj. máximo o de máximo [precio, actividad, velocidad, etc.].

peak (to) tr. MAR. levantar, poner casi vertical.
peaked (pɪ·kt o pɪ·kit) adj. puntiagudo, picudo, en punta. 2 enjuto, delgado; afilada [nariz].
peaky (-i) adj. puntiagudo. 2 que tiene picos.
peal (pɪl) s. repique [de campanas]. 2 estrépito, estruendo: ~ of thunder, trueno.
peal (to) tr.-intr. repicar [las campanas]. 2 gritar, vocear. 3 sonar, resonar, retronar.
peanut (pɪ·nøt) s. BOT. cacahuete; *maní.
pear (pe·øʳ) s. BOT. pera; peral: ~ tree, peral. 2 perilla [adorno].
pearl (pøʳl) s. perla, margarita: ~ seed, aljófar; to cast pearls before swine, echar margaritas a cerdos. 2 B. ART., FARM., IMPR. perla. 3 adj. ~ barley, cebada perlada.
pearl (to) tr. perlar; aljofarar. 2 dar color de perla. 3 intr. pescar perlas. 4 perlarse.
pearled (-d) adj. perlado, aljofarado.
pearly (-i) adj. perlino, nacarado. 2 aljofarado.
pearmain (pe·ʳmein) s. BOT. pero.
pear-shaped adj. piriforme.
peasant (pe·šant) s. labriego, campesino.
peasantry (-tri) s. paisanaje, gente del campo.
peascod (pɪ·škad) s.vaina de guisante.
peat (pɪt) s. turba [materia]: ~ bog, turbera.
peaty (-i) adj. turboso.
pebble (pe·bøl) s. guija, guijarro, china. 2 cristal de roca.
pebble (to) tr. enguijarrar. 2 granular, abollonar [el cuero, etc.].
pebbly (pe·bli) adj. guijarroso.
pecan (pikæ·n) s. BOT. pacana.
peccadillo (pekadi·lou) s. pecadillo, falta.
peccancy (pe·kansi) s. vicio, defecto. 2 pecado.
peccant (-kant) adj. pecante. 2 incorrecto, defectuoso.
peccary (-kari) s. ZOOL. pécari, báquira.
peck (pek) s. medida de áridos [9 litros]. 2 fam. montón, la mar. 3 picotazo, picotada.
peck (to) tr. picar, picotear. 2 picar, labrar [con algo puntiagudo]. 3 intr. to ~ at, picotear, coger con el pico; comiscar; regañar, censurar.
pecker (-øʳ) s. picoteador. 2 ORN. pico verde.
pectin, pectine (pe·ktin) s.pectina.
pectinate(d (-neit(id) adj. pectinado.
pectoral (pe·ktøral) adj.-s. pectoral. 2 s. ARM. peto.
peculate (to) (pe·kiuleit) tr.-intr. desfalcar, malversar.
peculation (-ei·shøn) s. peculado, desfalco.
peculiar (pikiu·liaʳ) adj. peculiar. 2 particular, especial. 3 raro, singular.
peculiarity (pikiuliæ·riti) s. peculiaridad, particularidad, singularidad. 2 individualidad.
peculiarize (to) (pikiu·liaraiš) tr. particularizar, individualizar.
pecuniary (pikiu·nieri) adj. pecuniario.
pedagogic (al (pedaga·dÿik(al) adj. pedagógico.
pedagogue (pe·dagag) s. pedagogo. 2 pedante.
pedagogy (-goudÿi) s. pedagogía.
pedal (pe·dal) s. pedal. 2 adj. de pie o de pedal: ~ board, teclado de pie.
pedal (to) intr. pedalear. 2 tr. mover con pedal.
pedant (pe·dant) s. pedante.
pedantic (al (pidæ·ntik(al) adj. pedantesco.
pedantry (pe·dantri) s. pedantería.
peddle (to) (pe·døl) tr. vender de puerta en puerta. 2 intr. hacer de buhonero.
peddler (pe·dløʳ) s. buhonero, vendedor ambulante.
pederasty (pe·døræsti) s. pederastia.

pedestal (pe·distal) adj. pedestal; peana, pie. 2 MÚS. cubeta [del arpa].
pedestrian (pide·strian) adj. pedestre. 2 s. peatón, caminante; andarín.
pediatrics (pidiæ·triks) s. pediatría.
pediatrician (pidiatri·shan) s. pediatra.
pedicel (pe·disel) s. BOT., ZOOL. pedicelo.
pedicle (pe·dikøl) s. ANAT. pedículo.
pedicular (pidi·kiulaʳ), **pediculous** (-løs) adj. pedicular.
pedigree (pe·digrɪ) s. genealogía, linaje, árbol genealógico.
pediment (pe·dimønt) s. ARQ. frontón.
pedlar, pedler (pedløʳ) s. PEDDLER.
pedometer (pida·mitøʳ) s. podómetro, cuentapasos.
peduncle (pidø·nkøl) s. ANAT., ZOOL., BOT. pedúnculo.
peek (pɪk) s. atisbo, atisbadura, mirada.
peek (to) intr. atisbar, espiar, mirar con disimulo.
peel (pɪl) s. piel, corteza, cáscara, hollejo, telilla. 2 pala [de horno; de remo].
peel (to) tr. pelar, mondar, descortezar, descascarar. 2 intr. pelarse, descascararse. 3 fam. desnudarse. 4 desprenderse [la piel, la corteza, etc.].
peeling (-ing) s. peladura, mondadura.
peen (pɪn) s. boca o punta [del martillo].
peep (pɪp) s. atisbo, ojeada; mirada a través de una rendija. 2 rendija por donde se mira. 3 asomo: at the ~ of the day, al despuntar el día. 4 pío, piada [de ave]; vocecita.
peep (to) intr. atisbar, fisgar; mirar por una rendija. 2 asomar, mostrarse. 3 piar, pipiar.
peeper (-øʳ) s. atisbador. 2 fam. ojo.
peephole (-joul) s. atisbadero, mirilla.
peer (pɪʳ) s. par, igual, compañero. 2 par [noble].
peer (to) intr. mirar [atentamente, escrutadoramente]. 2 asomar, salir, aparecer.
peerage (-idÿ) s. dignidad de par. 2 cuerpo o catálogo de la nobleza.
peeress (-is) f. paresa.
peerless (-lis) adj. sin par, incomparable.
peevish (pɪ·vish) adj. malhumorado, brusco; displicente, quisquilloso, enojadizo.
peevishness (-nis) s. mal humor, brusquedad, displicencia, quejumbre.
peewit (pɪ·uit) s. PEWIT.
peg (peg) s. clavija, estaquilla, espiga, taco, sobina. 2 percha, colgador. 3 pretexto, razón. 4 grado, escalón: to take down a ~, rebajar o humillar [a uno]. 5 estaca, jalón. 6 (Ingl.) traguito.
peg (to) tr. estaquillar, clavar, atarugar. 2 marcar, jalonar. 3 limitar, fijar, estabilizar [precios, etc.]. 4 lanzar, arrojar. 5 intr. afanarse; andar de prisa. ¶ Pret. y p. p.: pegged; ger.: -gging.
Pegasus (pe·gasøs) n. pr. MIT. Pegaso.
pegbox (pe·gbaks) s. MÚS. clavijero [de violín, etc.].
Peggy (pe·gi) n. pr. dim. de MARGARET.
peg-top s. peonza.
pejorative (pi·dÿøreitiv) adj. peyorativo, despectivo.
Pekin (pikɪ·n) n. pr. GEOGR. Pequín.
Pekinese (pɪ·kinis) adj.-s. pequinés.
pekoe (pɪ·kou) s. té negro de calidad superior.
pelagic (pilæ·dÿik) adj. pelágico.
Pelasgic (pilæ·šdÿik) adj. pelásgico.
pelerine (pe·lørin) s. manteleta, pelerina.
pelf (pelf) s. desp. bienes, dinero.
pelican (pe·likan) s. ORN. pelicano, alcatraz.
pelisse (pøli·s) s. pelliza.

pellagra (pølæ·gra) s. MED. pelagra.
pellet (pe·lit) s. pelotilla, bolita. 2 píldora. 3 bala, perdigón. 4 bodoque.
pellicle (pe·licøl) s. película, telilla.
pellitory (pe·litori) s. BOT. parietaria; pelitre.
pell-mell (pelme·l) adv. revueltamente, atropelladamente. 2 s. confusión, desorden.
pellucid (pøliu·sid) adj. diáfano, transparente.
Peloponnesus (pelopøni·søs) n. pr. GEOGR. Peloponeso.
pelt (pelt) s. pellejo, cuero, zalea. 2 golpe [de algo tirado]; golpear [de la lluvia]. 3 velocidad.
pelt (to) tr. apedrear; tirar, hacer llover [algo] sobre. 2 intr. caer con fuerza [la lluvia, etc.]. 4 apresurarse.
peltry (pe·ltri) s. pellejería, corambre. 2 pellejo.
pelvic (pe·lvik) adj. ANAT. pelviano.
pelvis (pe·lvis) s. ANAT., ZOOL. pelvis.
pemmican (pe·mikan) s. penmicán.
pemphigus (pe·mfigøs) s. MED. pénfigo.
pen (pen) s. pluma [para escribir]: ~ name, seudónimo. 2 corral; departamento [para encerrar ganado o exhibir animales].
pen (to) tr. escribir, pergeñar. 2 encerrar, acorralar. ¶ Pret. y p. p.: penned o pent; ger.: -nning.
penal (pɪ·nal) adj. penal: ~ servitude, presidio, trabajos forzados. 2 penable.
penalize (to) (pɪ·nalaiš) tr. penar, castigar.
penalty (pe·nalty) s. pena, castigo, sanción; multa de. 2 DEP. penalti, castigo.
penance (pe·nans) s. penitencia.
Penates (pinei·tiš) s. pl. MIT. Penates.
pence (pens) s. pl. de PENNY. | Ús. en composición.
penchant (pe·nchant) s. afición, tendencia.
pencil (pe·nsil) s. lápiz; lapicero: ~ sharpener, afilalápices. 2 pincel fino.
pencil (to) tr. dibujar o escribir con lápiz. 2 pintar con pincel fino. ¶ Pret. y p. p.: pencil(l)ed; ger.: -l(l)ing.
pendant (-dant) s. cosa que cuelga; colgante, pendiente, zarcillo; medallón. 2 araña [de luces]. 3 ARQ. pinjante.
pendent (-dønt) adj. pendiente. 2 prep. durante.
pendular (-diula^r) adj. pendular.
pendulous (-iuløs) adj. péndulo, colgante.
pendulum (-diuløm) s. péndulo; péndola.
Penelope (pine·løp) n. pr. Penélope.
penetrable (pe·nitrabøl) adj. penetrable, accesible.
penetrancy (-transi) s. fuerza de penetración.
penetrate (to) (-treit) tr.-intr. penetrar. 2 tr. atravesar, perforar.
penetrating (-treiting) adj. penetrante. 2 perspicaz.
penetration (-ei·shøn) s. penetración.
penguin (pe·ngüin) s. ORN. pingüino.
penholder (pe·njouldø^r) s. portapluma.
penicillin (penisi·lin) s. penicilina.
peninsula (peni·nshiula) s. GEOGR. península.
peninsular (-la^r) adj.-s. peninsular.
penis (pɪ·nis) s. ANAT. pene.
penitence (pe·nitøns) s. penitencia, contricción.
penitent (-ønt) adj.-s. penitente, arrepentido.
penitential (penite·nshal) adj. penitencial.
penitentiary (-shari) adj. penitencial. 2 penitenciario. 3 s. penitenciaría.
penknife (pe·n-naif) s. cortaplumas.
penman (-mæn) s. pendolista. 2 escritor.
pennant (pe·nant) s. flámula, gallardete, banderola. 2 MAR. insignia.
pennies (pe·nis) s. pl. de PENNY.
penniless (pe·nilis) adj. pobre, sin dinero.

pennon (pe·nøn) s. pendón, flámula, banderola.
penninervate (peninø·^rvit) adj. BOT. peninervia.
Pennsylvania (pensilvei·nia) n. pr. GEOGR. Pensilvania.
penny (pe·ni), **pennies** o [en composición] **pence** (pens) s. penique; centavo de dólar: to cost a pretty ~, costar un dineral; to turn an honest ~, ganar algún dinero honradamente.
penny-a-liner s. gacetillero; escritorzuelo.
pennyroyal (peniro·ial) s. BOT. poleo.
penny-wise adj. que sólo es prudente o ahorrativo en cosas sin importancia.
penologist (pina·lodýist) s. penalista.
penology (pina·lodýi) s. ciencia penal.
pensile (pe·nsil) adj. pensil, péndulo, colgante.
pension (pe·nshøn) s. pensión, retiro, jubilación. 2 pensión [pupilaje; casa de huéspedes].
pension (to) tr. pensionar, retirar, jubilar.
pensioner (-ø^r) s. pensionado. 2 retirado, jubilado. 3 MIL. inválido. 4 pensionista.
pensive (pe·nsiv) adj. pensativo; melancólico.
penstock (pe·nstak) s. compuerta [de esclusa, etc.]. 2 paradera [del caz].
pent (pent) adj. encerrado, acorralado. 2 contenido, reprimido. | Gralte. con up o in.
pentacle (pe·ntakøl) s. pentáculo.
pentadactyl(e (pentadæ·ktil) adj. pentadáctilo.
pentagon (pe·ntagan) s. GEOM. pentágono.
pentagonal (pentæ·gonal) adj. pentagonal.
pentahedron (pentaȷi·drøn) s. GEOM. pentaedro.
pentamerous (pentæ·mørøs) adj. H. NAT. pentámero.
pentameter (pentæ·mitø^r) s. MET. pentámetro.
pentane (pe·ntein) s. QUÍM. pentano.
pentapolis (pe·ntapolis) s. pentápolis.
Pentateuch (-atiuk) s. Pentateuco.
Pentecost (pe·nticost) s. Pentecostés.
penthouse (pe·ntjaus) s. cobertizo, alpende. 2 tejadillo, colgadizo. 3 (E.U.) piso en la azotea.
penultimate (pinø·ltimit) adj. penúltimo. 2 s. penúltima sílaba.
penumbra (-mbra) s. ASTR., PINT. penumbra.
penurious (piniu·riøs) adj. pobre. 2 de penuria. 3 cicatero, roñoso.
penury (pe·niuri) s. penuria, estrechez. 2 escasez.
peon (pɪ·an) s. [en la India y Ceilán] peón [soldado]; policía indígena; criado.
peony (pɪ·øni) s. BOT. peonia, saltaojos.
people (pɪ·pøl) s. pueblo, raza, nación, grey. 2 pueblo [de un país, etc.]: the common ~, el pueblo, el vulgo. 3 gente, personas: two ~, dos personas; the young ~, la gente joven; my ~, los míos, mi familia.
people (to) tr. poblar. 2 colonizar.
pep (pep) s. pop. (E.U.) energía, estímulo, brío: to be full of ~, tener mucha energía.
pep (to) tr. animar, estimular, vigorizar.
pepper (pe·pø^r) s. pimienta. 2 pimiento, ají, chile. 3 red ~, pimentón. 4 BOT. ~ cress, masturzo; ~ tree, turbinto.
pepper (to) tr. sazonar con pimiento. 2 salpimentar. 3 esparcir, salpicar. 4 acribillar.
pepperbox (-baks) s. pimentero [vasija].
peppercorn (-ko^rn) s. grano de pimienta.
peppermint (-mint) s. BOT. menta, piperita. 2 pastilla o licor de menta.
peppery (-i) adj. picante. 2 mordaz. 3 colérico, de mal genio.
pepsin(e (pe·psin) s. BIOQUÍM. pepsina.
peptic (-tik) adj. péptico.
peptone (-toun) s. BIOQUÍM. peptona.

per (pǿ^r) *prep.* por: ~ *cent*, por ciento. *2 as per*, según.
peradventure (-adve·nchǿ^r) *adv.* acaso, por ventura. *2 duda: beyond* ~, fuera de duda.
perambulate (to) (pǿræ·mbiuleit) *tr.* recorrer, visitar o inspeccionar andando. *2 intr.* andar, pasear.
perambulator (-ǿ^r) *s.* cochecito de niño.
perborate (pǿ^rbou·reit) *s.* QUÍM. perborato.
percale (pǿ^rkei·l) *s.* percal.
perceivable (pǿ^rsɪ·vabøl) *adj.* perceptible, inteligible.
perceive (to) (pǿrsɪ·v) *tr.* percibir, ver, distinguir, advertir, comprender.
percentage (pǿ^rse·ntidȳ) *s.* porcentaje.
perceptible (pǿ^rse·ptibøl) *adj.* perceptible, sensible, visible.
perception (-shøn) *s.* percepción [con los sentidos, el entendimiento]. *2* DER. perceptivo.
perch (pǿ^rch) *s.* ICT. perca. *2* pértica [medida]. *3* percha, alcándara. *4* pértiga, palo.
perch (to) *tr.* emperchar. *2* encaramar. *3 intr.* encaramarse, posarse [en percha, rama, etc.]; sentarse [en sitio elevado].
perchance (pǿ^rcha·ns) *adv.* acaso, por ventura.
Percheron (pǿ·^rshøran) *adj.-s.* percherón.
percipient (pǿ^rsi·piønt) *adj.-s.* capaz de percepción.
percolate (to) (pǿ·^rkøleit) *tr.* colar, pasar, filtrar. *2 tr.-intr.* trascolarse o filtrarse [por].
percolation (-ei·shøn) *s.* coladura, filtración.
percolator (pǿ·^rkøleitǿ^r) *s.* filtro, colador. *2* cafetera de filtro.
percuss (to) (pǿ^rkø·s) *tr.* percutir.
percussion (-shøn) *s.* percusión: ~ *cap*, pistón, cápsula fulminante; ~ *instrument*, instrumento de percusión.
perdition (pǿ^rdi·shøn) *s.* perdición.
perdurable (pø·^rdiurabøl) *adj.* perdurable.
peregrinate (to) (pe·rigrineit) *intr.* viajar.
peregrination (-ei·shøn) *s.* peregrinación, viaje.
peremptory (pøre·mptori) *adj.* perentorio, terminante, decisivo. *2* autoritario, imperioso.
perennial (pøre·nial) *adj.* perennal, perenne. *2* BOT. perenne, vivaz. *3 s.* planta perenne.
perfect (pǿ·^rfɪkt) *adj.* perfecto. *2* acabado, completo. *3 s.* GRAM. tiempo perfecto.
perfect (to) (pǿ·^rfɪkt) *tr.* perfeccionar, acabar, completar, coronar, redondear.
perfectible (-tibøl) *adj.* perfectible.
perfection (-shøn) *s.* perfección: *to* ~, a la perfección.
perfective (-tiv) *adj.* perfectivo.
perfervid (pǿ^rfø·^rvid) *adj.* muy férvido, ardiente.
perfidious (pǿ^rfi·diøs) *adj.* pérfido.
perfidy (pǿ·^rfidi) *s.* perfidia.
perfoliate (pǿ^rfou·lieit) *adj.* BOT. perfoliada.
perforate (to) (pǿ·^rføreit) *tr.* perforar, horadar. *2* taladrar, trepar.
perforation (-ei·shøn) *s.* perforación. *2* línea de agujeros, calado.
perforator (-tø^r) *s.* perforador. *2* perforadora.
perforce (pǿ^rfo·^rs) *adv.* por fuerza, a la fuerza.
perform (to) (pǿ^rfo·^rm) *tr.* hacer, ejecutar, realizar, cumplir, desempeñar, ejercer. *2 intr.* actuar. *3* desempeñar un papel, tocar un instrumento, etc. *4* funcionar [una máquina].
performance (-ans) *s.* ejecución, cumplimiento, desempeño. *2* obra, acción, hazaña. *3* función, representación, concierto; actuación de un artista, etc.

performer (-ǿ^r) *s.* ejecutante, representante, actor, artista, acróbata.
perfume (pø·^rfium o pø^rfiu·m) *s.* perfume.
perfume (to) *tr.* perfumar, embalsamar.
perfumer (pø^rfiu·mǿ^r) *s.* perfumador. *2* perfumista.
perfumery (-i) *s.* perfumería.
perfunctory (pø^rfø·nktori) *adj.* perfunctorio, hecho sin interés, superficial, formulario.
perfusion (pø^rfiu·dȳøn) *s.* perfusión, baño, aspersión.
pergola (pø·^rgøla) *s.* pérgola.
perhaps (pørjæ·ps) *adv.* quizás, tal vez, acaso.
peri (pɪ·ri) *s.* peri, hada.
perianth(ium (periæ·nz(iøm) *s.* BOT. periantio.
pericardium (-ka·^rdiøm) *s.* ANAT. pericardio.
pericarp (-ka·^rp) *s.* BOT. pericarpo.
perigee (-dȳi) *s.* ASTR. perigeo.
perihelion (-jɪ·liøn) *s.* ASTR. perihelio.
peril (pe·ril) *s.* peligro, riesgo, exposición.
peril (to) *tr.* poner en peligro. *2 intr.* peligrar.
perilous (pe·riløs) *adj.* peligroso; expuesto.
perimeter (peri·mitø^r) *s.* perímetro.
perineum (-nɪ·øm) *s.* ANAT. perineo.
period (pi·riød) *s.* período. *2* hora [de clase]. *3* punto final. *4 pl.* período, menstruación.
periodic (piria·dik) *adj.* periódico.
periodical (-al) *adj.* periódico. *2 s.* publicación periódica, revista.
perioeci (perii·sai) *s. pl.* GEOGR. periecos.
periosteum (-a·shøm) *s.* ANAT. periostio.
peripatetic (-pate·tik) *adj.* ambulante. *2 adj.-s.* (con may.) peripatético.
peripheral (peri·føral) *adj.* periférico.
periphery (-føri) *s.* periferia.
periphrase (to) (pe·rifreiš) *tr.-intr.* RET. perifrasear.
periphrasis (peri·frasis) *s.* RET. perífrasis.
periplus (pe·ripløs) *s.* periplo.
peripteros (peri·ptørøs) *s.* ARQ. períptero.
periscii (-shiai) *s. pl.* GEOGR. periscios.
periscope (pe·riskoup) *s.* periscopio.
perish (to) (pe·rish) *intr.* perecer, fenecer, acabar. *2* pasarse, averiarse.
perishable (-abøl) *adj.* perecedero. *2* deleznable, marchitable. *3* averiable.
perissodactyl(e (pirisødæ·ktil) *s.* ZOOL. perisodáctilo.
perisperm (pe·rispø^rm) *s.* BOT. perispermo.
peristaltic (peristæ·ltik) *adj.* peristáltico.
peristyle (pe·ristail) *s.* ARQ. peristilo.
peritoneum (peritønɪ·øm) *s.* ANAT. peritoneo.
peritonitis (peritønai·tis) *s.* MED. peritonitis.
periwig (pe·riuig) *s.* peluquín.
periwinkle (pe·riuinkøl) *s.* BOT. vincapervinca. *2* ZOOL. litorina.
perjure (to) (pø·^rdȳø^r) *intr.* perjurar. *2 tr. to* ~ *one-self*, perjurarse.
perjurer (-ǿ^r) *s.* perjurador, perjuro.
perjury (-i) *s.* perjurio.
perk (to) (pø·^rk) *tr.* erguir, levantar [la cabeza, las orejas]. *2* ataviar. *3 intr.* asomar; erguirse, darse tono. *4 to* ~ *up*, reponerse, animarse; despejarse.
perky (pø·^rki) *adj.* gallardo, presumido, desenvuelto.
permanence (pø·^rmanøns) *s.* permanencia.
permanent (-nt) *adj.* permanente, estable, fijo, duradero: ~ *wave*, ondulación permanente.
permeable (pø·^rmiabøl) *adj.* permeable, penetrable.

permeate (to) (pøˈᵣmieit) *tr.* penetrar, atravesar, calar; llenar, impregnar.
permeation (-eiˈshøn) *s.* penetración a través de los poros; impregnación.
Permian (pøˈᵣmiɑn) *adj.-s.* GEOL. pérmico.
permissible (pøᵣmiˈsibøl) *adj.* permisible.
permission (-shøn) *s.* permiso, permisión, licencia, venia. 2 MIL. permiso.
permissive (-siv) *adj.* permisivo. 2 permitido, consentido.
permit (pøˈᵣmit) *s.* permiso, licencia, pase, guía.
permit (to) (pøᵣmiˈt) *tr.* permitir. 2 *intr. to ~ of,* admitir, sufrir. ¶ Pret. y p. p.: *permitted;* ger.: *-tting.*
permutation (pøᵣmiuteiˈshøn) *s.* permutación.
permute (to) (pøᵣmiuˈt) *tr.* permutar.
pern (pøᵣn) *s.* ORN. buharro.
pernicious (pøᵣniˈshøs) *adj.* pernicioso. 2 malvado.
pernickety (pøᵣniˈkiti) *adj.* fam. quisquilloso, meticuloso, difícil, delicado.
perorate (to) (peˈrøreit) *intr.* perorar.
peroration (-eiˈshøn) *s.* peroración.
peroxid(e (pøraˈksaid) *s.* QUÍM. peróxido: *~ blonde,* rubia oxigenada.
perpend (pøᵣpeˈnd) *s.* ALBAÑ. perpiaño.
perpendicular (pøᵣpøndiˈkiulɑ̍ᵣ) *adj.-s.* perpendicular. 2 *adj.* vertical. 3 muy pendiente, escarpado.
perpetrate (to) (pøˈᵣpitreit) *tr.* perpetrar.
perpetration (-eiˈshøn) *s.* perpetración.
perpetual (pøᵣpeˈchual) *adj.* perpetuo. 2 continuo, incesante. 3 BOT. perenne.
perpetuate (to) (-chueit) *tr.* perpetuar.
perpetuation (-eiˈshøn) *s.* perpetuación.
perpetuity (pøᵣpitiuˈiti) *s.* perpetuidad.
perplex (to) (pøᵣpleˈks) *tr.* dejar perplejo; confundir. 2 turbar, aturrullar. 3 complicar, enredar.
perplexed (pøᵣpleˈkst) *adj.* perplejo, confuso. 2 turbado, preocupado. 3 complicado, enredado.
perplexity (pøᵣpleˈksiti) *s.* perplejidad, duda, confusión. 2 complicación, enredo.
perquisite (pøˈᵣkuišit) *s.* gaje, obvención, propina.
perron (peˈrøn) *s.* ARQ. escalinata.
perry (peˈri) *s.* sidra de peras.
persecute (to) (pøˈᵣsikiut) *tr.* perseguir, molestar, vejar, oprimir. 2 perseguir, acosar.
persecution (poˈᵣsikiuˈshøn) *s.* persecución.
persecutor (pøˈᵣsikiutøᵣ) *s.* perseguidor.
Perseus (pøˈᵣsiøs) *n. pr.* MIT. Perseo.
perseverance (pøᵣsiviˈrɑns) *s.* perseverancia.
persevere (to) (-øᵣ) *intr.* perseverar.
persevering (-ring) *adj.* perseverante.
Persian (pøˈᵣshɑn) *adj.* persa, pérsico: *~ blinds,* persianas [celosías]; *~ Gulf,* golfo Pérsico. 2 *s.* persa [pers., lengua].
Persic (pøˈᵣsik) *adj.* pérsico.
persicary (pøˈᵣsikeri) *s.* BOT. persicaria, duraznillo.
persiflage (pøˈᵣsifladỹ) *s.* burla, zumba.
persimmon (pøᵣsiˈmøn) *s.* BOT. caqui; su fruto.
persist (to) (pøᵣsiˈst) *intr.* persistir; permanecer; continuar. 2 insistir, porfiar.
persistence, -cy (-øns, -si) *s.* persistencia, constancia. 2 insistencia, porfía.
persistent, -ting- (-ønt, -ting) *adj.* persistente. 2 constante, tenaz. 3 insistente.
person (pøˈᵣsøn) *s.* persona: *first ~,* primera persona; *in ~,* en persona, personalmente.
personable (-abøl) *adj.* bien parecido.
personage (-idỹ) *s.* personaje.
personal (-al) *adj.* personal: *~ pronoun,* pronombre personal. 2 en persona. 3 que incluye personalismo: *to become ~,* hacer alusiones de carácter personal y ofensivo. 4 *~ estate,* bienes muebles. 5 *s.* nota de sociedad; remitido [en un periódico].
personalism (pøˈᵣsønɑlišm) *s.* cualidad, carácter o influencia personal. 2 individualidad. 3 FIL. personalismo.
personality (pøᵣsønæˈliti) *s.* personalidad. 2 individualidad. 3 personalismo, alusión personal.
personalize (to) (pøˈᵣsønalais) *s.* individualizar. 2 personificar. 3 personalizar.
personate (pøˈᵣsøneit) *adj.* BOT. personada.
personate (to) *tr.* TEAT. representar el papel de. 2 fingir, fingirse, hacerse pasar por. 3 personificar.
personation (-eiˈshøn) *s.* representación [de un papel]. 2 DER. usurpación de personalidad.
personator (pøˈᵣsøneitøᵣ) *s.* intérprete [de un papel]. 2 el que se hace pasar por otro.
personification (pøᵣsaˈnifikeiˈshøn) *s.* personificación. 2 RET. prosopopeya.
personify (to) (-nifai) *tr.* personificar. ¶ Pert. y p. p.: *personified.*
personnel (pøᵣsøneˈl) *s.* personal, dependencia.
perspective (pøᵣspeˈktiv) *s.* perspectiva. 2 *adj.* de perspectiva, en perspectiva.
perspicacious (pøᵣspikeiˈshøs) *adj.* perspicaz.
perspicacity (pøᵣspikæˈsiti) *s.* perspicacia, penetración.
perspicuity (pøᵣspikiuˈiti) *s.* perspicuidad.
perspicuous (pøᵣspiˈkiuøs) *adj.* perspicuo.
perspiration (pøᵣspireiˈshøn) *s.* transpiración, sudor.
perspire (to) (pøᵣspaiˈøᵣ) *tr.-intr.* transpirar, sudar, trasudar. 2 *tr.* exudar.
persuade (to) (pøᵣsueiˈd) *tr.* persuadir, inducir, mover. 2 exhortar, tratar de convencer.
persuasible (pøᵣsueiˈsibøl) *adj.* fácil de persuadir.
persuasion (pøᵣsueiˈỹøn) *s.* persuasión. 2 persuasiva. 3 creencia. 4 credo, fe, religión, secta.
persuasive (pøᵣsueiˈsiv) *adj.* persuasivo. 2 *s.* cosa que persuade; incentivo.
pert (pøᵣt) *adj.* petulante, atrevido, descarado. 2 vivo, alegre, desenvuelto.
pertain (to) (pøᵣteiˈn) *intr.* pertenecer; corresponder, tocar, atañer. 2 hacer relación, referirse.
pertinacious (pøᵣtineiˈshøs) *adj.* pertinaz.
pertinacity (pøᵣtinæˈsiti) *s.* pertinacia.
pertinence, -cy (pøˈᵣtinøns, -si) *s.* pertinencia. 2 oportunidad.
pertinent (-nt) *adj.* pertinente, que viene a propósito, oportuno, atinado.
pertness (pøˈᵣtnis) *s.* petulancia, descaro.
perturb (to) (pøᵣtøˈᵣb) *tr.* perturbar, conturbar, agitar.
perturbation (pøᵣtøᵣbeiˈshøn) *s.* perturbación, conturbación, agitación.
perturber (pøᵣtøˈᵣbøᵣ) *s.* perturbador, agitador.
Peru (pøruˈ) *n. pr.* el Perú.
peruke (peruˈk) *s.* peluca, peluquín.
perusal (peruˈšal) *s.* lectura, lectura atenta.
peruse (to) (peruˈš) *tr.* leer, leer con cuidado.
Peruvian (peruˈviɑn) *adj.-s.* peruano.
pervade (to) (pøᵣveiˈd) *tr.* penetrar, llenar, saturar, impregnar, difundirse por.
pervasion (pøᵣveiˈỹøn) *s.* penetración, impregnación, difusión.
perverse (pøᵣvøˈᵣs) *adj.* perverso, avieso. 2 pervertido. 3 terco, indócil, que lleva la contraria.
perverseness (-nis) *s.* perversidad, malicia. 2 terquedad.

perversion (-shøn) s. perversión. 2 pervertimiento. 3 corrupción, alteración.
perversity (-siti) s. PERVERSENESS.
pervert (-t) s. pervertido. 2 apóstata, hereje.
pervert (to) tr. pervertir. 2 corromper, tergiversar, falsear, desnaturalizar.
perverter (-ø^r) s. pervertidor.
pervious (pø·^{r}viøs) adj. penetrable, accesible, permeable: ~ to light, diáfano.
pesade (pisei·d) s. empinada [del caballo].
pesky (pe·ski) adj. fam. (E.U.) molesto, cargante.
pessary (pe·sari) s. CIR. pesario.
pessimism (pe·simišm) s. pesimismo.
pessimist (-ist) s. pesimista.
pessimistic (al (pesimi·stik(al) adj. pesimista.
pest (pest) s. peste; plaga. 2 pers. o cosa molesta. 3 insecto nocivo.
pester (to) (-ø^r) tr. molestar, importunar.
pesthouse (-jaus) s. lazareto.
pestiferous (pesti·førøs) adj. pestífero, pestilente.
pestilence (pe·stiløns) s. peste, pestilencia.
pestilent (-t) adj. pestilente, pernicioso. 2 molesto, cargante, travieso.
pestilential (pestile·nshal) adj. pestilencial.
pestle (pe·søl) s. mano de almirez, majadero.
pestle (to) tr. majar, machacar, pistar, moler.
pet (pet) adj. querido, mimado, favorito. 2 ~ name, apelativo cariñoso. 3 s. animal doméstico. 4 pers. o niño querido, mimado. 5 enojo, despecho, berrinche: to go away in a ~, irse enojado.
pet (to) tr. mimar, regalar, acariciar. ¶ Pret. y p. p.: petted; ger.: -tting.
petal (pe·tal) s. BOT. pétalo.
petalism (-lišm) s. petalismo.
petaloid (-oid) adj. petaloideo.
petard (pita·^{r}d) s. petardo.
Peter (pı·tø^r) n. pr. Pedro: Peter's pence, dinero de San Pedro.
peter (to) intr. disminuir, gastarse, agotarse. | Gralte. con out.
petiolate (pe·tioleit) adj. peciolado.
petiole (pe·tioul) s. BOT. peciolo.
petition (piti·shøn) s. instancia, solicitud, petición, memorial. 2 ruego, súplica.
petition (to) tr. solicitar; suplicar, pedir. 2 dirigir una petición o memorial a.
petitionary (-eri) adj. petitorio.
petitioner (-ø^r) s. solicitante, peticionario.
Petrarch (pi·trark) n. pr. Petrarca.
petrel (pe·trøl) s. ORN. petrel.
petrifaction (petrifæ·kshøn), **petrification** (-fi-kei·shøn) s. petrificación.
petrify (to) (pe·trifai) tr. petrificar. 2 intr. petrificarse, fosilizarse. ¶ Pret. y p. p.: petrified.
petrography (petra·grafi) s. petrografía.
petrol (pe·trøl) s. (Ingl.) gasolina, bencina.
petrol (to) tr. proveer de bencina.
petroleum (pitrou·liøm) s. petróleo.
petroliferous (pitrøli·førøs) adj. petrolífero.
petrology (pitra·lodÿi) s. petrología, petrognosia.
petrous (pe·trøs) adj. pétreo, petroso.
petticoat (pe·tikout) s. enaguas. 2 falda, basquiña, faldellín. 3 fig. faldas, mujer, muchacha. 4 ELECT. campana de aislador. 5 adj. de mujeres, de faldas.
pettifogger (pe·tifagø^r) s. leguleyo, picapleitos.
pettifoggery (-ri) s. triquiñuela, enredo de picapleitos.
pettiness (pe·tinis) s. pequeñez, insignificancia, mezquindad.

pettish (pe·tish) adj. enojadizo, malhumorado, regañón.
pettishness (-nis) s. mal humor, enojo, aspereza.
petty (pe·ti) adj. pequeño, menor, insignificante, mezquino: ~ cash, dinero para gastos menores; ~ jury, jurado [de juicio]; ~ larceny, ratería; ~ prince, principillo. 2 inferior, subalterno.
petulance, -cy (pe·chulans, -si) s. impaciencia, mal humor, mal genio.
petulant (-t) adj. enojadizo, malhumorado, impaciente, áspero. 2 poc. us. petulante.
petunia (pitiu·nia) s. BOT. petunia.
pew (piu) s. banco de iglesia.
pewit (pi·uit) s. ORN. avefría. 2 ORN. laro.
pewter (piu·tø^r) s. peltre. 2 vasijas de peltre.
Phaedra (fı·dræ) s. MIT. Fedra.
Phaeton (fei·tan) n. pr. MIT. Faetón. 2 s. (con min.) faetón.
phagocyte (fæ·gøsait) s. BIOL. fagocito.
phalange (fæ·læ·ndÿ) s. ANAT., ZOOL., POL. falange.
phalanger (falæ·ndÿø^r) s. ZOOL. falangero.
phalanstery (fæ·lansteri) s. falansterio.
phalanx (fæ·lænks), pl. **phalanges** s. MIL., ANAT., ZOOL. falange.
phallus (fæ·løs) s. falo.
phanerogam (fæ·nørøgam) s. BOT. fanerógama.
phanerogamous (fænøra·gamøs) adj. BOT. fanerógamo.
phantasm (fæ·ntæšm) s. fantasma.
phantasmagoria (-ago·ria) s. fantasmagoría.
phantasmal (fæntæ·smal) adj. espectral, fantástico, irreal.
phantasy (fæ·ntasi) s. fantasía, imaginación. 2 fantasía [producto de la imaginación].
phantom (fæ·ntøm) s. fantasma, aparición. 2 ilusión óptica. 3 imaginación engañosa. 4 adj. fantasmal, quimérico; fantasma.
Pharaoh (fe·ørou) s. faraón.
Pharanoic (feria·nik) adj. faraónico.
pharisaic (al (færisei·ik(al) adj. farisaico.
pharisaism (fæ·riseiišm) s. fariseísmo.
Pharisee (fæ·risı) s. fariseo.
pharmaceutic (al (fa·^{r}masiu·tik(al) adj. farmacéutico.
pharmaceutics (-tiks) s. farmacia [ciencia, arte].
pharmacist (fa·^{r}masist) s. farmacéutico, boticario.
pharmacology (fa·^{r}maka·lodÿi) s. farmacología.
pharmacy (fa·^{r}masi) s. farmacia.
pharos (fei·røs) s. MAR. faro.
pharyngeal (færi·ndÿial) adj. ANAT. faríngeo.
pharyngitis (færindÿai·tis) s. MED. faringitis.
pharyngoscope (fari·ngoskoup) s. faringoscopio.
pharynx (fæ·rinks) s. ANAT. faringe.
phase (feiš) s. fase: to be in ~, estar en fase.
pheasant (fe·šant) s. ORN. faisán.
phenic (fe·nik) adj. fénico.
phenix (fı·nix) s. PHOENIX.
phenol (fı·nol) s. QUÍM. fenol.
phenomenal (fina·minal) adj. fenoménico. 2 fenomenal.
phenomenon (-øn), pl. **-na** (-na) s. fenómeno.
phew! (fiu) interj. uf!
phi (fai o fı) s. phi [letra griega].
phial (fai·al) s. redoma, frasco.
Phidias (fı·diæs) n. pr. Fidias.
Philadelphia (filade·lfia) n. pr. GEOGR. Filadelfia.
philander (to) (filæ·ndø^r) intr. galantear, flirtear.
philanderer (-ø^r) s. galanteador, flirteador.
philanthropic (al (filanzra·pik(al) adj. filantrópico.
philanthropist (filæ·nzrøpist) adj. filántropo.

philanthropy (-zrøpi) s. filantropía.
philatelic (al (filate·lik(al) adj. filatélico.
philatelist (filæ·tølist) s. filatelista.
philately (-tøli) s. filatelia.
philharmonic (filjaʳma·nik) adj. filarmónico.
Philip (fi·lip) n. pr. Felipe. 2 Filipo.
philippic (fili·pik) adj. filipica.
Philippine (filipi·n) adj. filipino.
Philippines (-š) n. pr. GEOGR. Filipinas.
Philistine (filisti·n) adj.-s. filisteo. 2 inculto, prosaico. 3 reaccionario.
philologic (al (filøla·dẏik(al) adj. filológico.
philologist (fila·lodẏist) s. filólogo.
philology (-lodẏi) s. filología.
philomel (fi·lømel) s. poét. filomela, ruiseñor.
philosopher (fila·søføʳ) s. filósofo: philosopher's
  stone, piedra filosofal.
philosophic (al (filøsa·fik(al) adj. filosófico.
philosophize (to) (fila·søfaiš) intr. filosofar.
philosophy (-søfi) s. filosofía.
philter, philtre (fi·ltøʳ) s. filtro, bebedizo.
philter o philtre (to) tr. hechizar con filtro.
phimosis (faimou·sis) s. fimosis.
phiz (fiš) s. pop, cara, facha, fisonomía.
phlebitis (flibai·tis) s. MED. flebitis.
phlegm (fle·m) s. flema [mucosidad]. 2 QUÍM.
  flema. 3 flema, calma.
phlegmatic (al (flegmæ·tik(al) adj. flemático.
phlegmon (-man) s. MED. flemón.
phobia (fou·bia) s. fobia.
Phocian (fou·shan) adj.-s. focense.
Phocis (fou·sis) n. pr. GEOGR., HIST. La Fócida.
Phoebe (fi·bi) n. pr. MIT., ASTR. Febe.
Phoebus (fi·bøs) n. pr. MIT., poét. Febo.
Phoenicia (fini·sha) n. pr. GEOGR. Fenicia.
Phoenician (-an) adj.-s. fenicio.
phoenix (fi·niks) s. fénix.
phonation (fonei·shøn) s. fonación.
phone (fou·n) s. fam. teléfono. 2 RADIO. auricular.
phone (to) tr.-intr. fam. telefonear.
phoneme (fou·nim) s. fonema.
phonetic (al (fone·tik(al) adj. fonético.
phonetics (fone·tiks) s. fonética, fonología.
phoney (founi) adj. PHONY.
phonic (fa·nik) adj. fónico.
phonogram (fou·nøgræm) s. fonograma.
phonograph (-græf) s. fonógrafo.
phonographic (al (fonøgræ·fik(al) adj. fonográfico.
phonolite (fou·nølait) s. PETROGR. fonolita.
phonology (fona·lodẏi) s. fonología.
phonoscope (fou·nøskoup) s. FÍS. fonoscopio.
phony (fou·ni) s. fam. (E.U.) farsa, engaño; farsante. 2 adj. fam. (E.U.) falso, imitado.
phosphate (fa·sfeit) s. QUÍM. fosfato.
phosphaturia (fasfatiu·ria) s. MED. fosfaturia.
Phosphor (fa·sføʳ) s. fósforo, lucero del alba.
phosphoresce (to) (fasføre·s) intr. fosforecer.
phosphorescence (-øns) s. fosforescencia.
phosphorescent (-ønt) adj. fosforescente.
phosphoric (fasfo·rik) adj. QUÍM. fosfórico.
phosphorite (fa·sførait) MINER. fosforita.
phosphorous (fa·sførøs) adj. QUÍM. fosforoso.
phosphorus s. QUÍM. fósforo.
phosphuret (fa·sfiurit) adj. QUÍM. fosfuro.
phot (fa·t) s. FÍS. fotio.
photo (fou·tou) s. fam. fotografía, retrato.
photo (to) tr. fam. fotografiar.
photochemical (foutouke·mikal) adj. fotoquímico.
photocopy (fou·toukapi) s. fotocopia.
photoelectric (foutouile·ktrik) adj. fotoeléctrico.
photoengrave (to) (-engrei·v) s. fotograbar.

photoengraving (-ing) s. fotograbado.
photogen (fou·toudẏen) s. BIOL. organismo fotógeno.
photogenic (-dẏe·nik) adj. fotógeno. 2 fotogénico.
photograph (fou·tøgræf) s. fotografía, retrato.
photograph (to) tr.-intr. fotografiar.
photographer (føta·graføʳ) s. fotógrafo.
photography (-fi) s. fotografía [arte].
photogravure (foutougraviu·ʳ) s. fotograbado.
photolithograph (-li·zøgræf) s. fotolitografía [lá-
  mina].
photolithograph (to) tr. fotolitografiar.
photolithography (-liza·grafi) s. fotolitografía
  [arte].
photometry (fouta·metri) s. fotometría.
photomicrography (foutomaikra·grafi) s. microfotografía.
photon (fou·tan) s. FÍS. fotón.
photophobia (foutofou·bia) s. MED. fotofobia.
photoprint (-print) s. fotocalco, fotocopia.
photosphere (-sfiʳ) s. ASTR. fotosfera.
photosynthesis (-si·nzesis) s. BOT. fotosíntesis.
phototropism (fouta·trøpišm) s. BIOL. fototropismo.
phototypography (foutotaipa·grafi) s. fototipografía.
phrase (frei·š) s. frase, expresión, locución, modo,
  modismo. 2 fraseología, estilo. 3 MÚS. frase.
phrase (to) tr. expresar [con palabras]. 2 llamar,
  nombrar. 3 tr.-intr. frasear.
phraseology (freišia·lodẏi) s. fraseología.
phrasing (frei·šing) s. fraseo.
phrenetic (frine·tik) adj. frenético. 2 delirante. 3
  fanático.
phrenic (fre·nik) adj. ANAT., PSIC. frénico.
phrenology (frena·lodẏi) s. frenología.
phrenopathy (-pazi) s. frenopatía.
Phrygia (fri·dẏia) n. pr. GEOGR. Frigia.
Phrygian (fri·dẏian) adj.-s. frigio.
phthisic (al (ti·šik(al) adj. tísico, hético. 2 asmático.
phthisis (zai·sis) s. tisis, hetiquez, consunción.
phylactery (filæ·ktøri) s. filactería.
phyllode (fi·loud) s. BOT. filodio.
phylloxera (filaksi·ra) s. filoxera.
phylum (fai·løm) s. BIOL. tipo.
physic (fi·šik) s. medicina, remedio. 2 purga.
physic (to) tr. medicinar, curar, purgar.
physical (-al) adj. físico: ~ training, educación física.
physician (fiši·shan) s. médico, doctor, facultativo.
physicist (fi·šisist) s. físico [versado en física].
physics (fi·šiks) s. pl. física; filosofía natural.
physicochemistry (fišikoke·mistri) s. fisicoquímica.
physiocracy (ffišia·krasi) s. fisiocracia.
physiocrat (fi·šiokræt) s. fisiócrata.
physiognomic (al (fišiagna·mik(al) adj. fisonómico.
physiognomist (fišia·gnomist) s. fisonomistsa.
physiognomy (-nomi) s. fisonomía.
physiologic (al (fišiola·dẏik(al) adj. fisiológico.
physiologist (fišia·lodẏist) s. fisiólogo.
physiology (-lodẏi) s. fisiología.
physiotherapy (fišioze·rapi) s. fisioterapia.
physique (fiši·k) s. físico, figura, constitución [de
  una pers.].
phytography (faita·grafi) s. fitografía.
phytophagous (faita·fagøs) adj. fitófago.
pi (pai) s. pi [letra griega; signo]. 2 IMPR. pastel.

piaffe (to) (piæ·f) *intr.* EQUIT. piafar.
pia-mater (paiə·mei·tøʳ) *s.* ANAT. pía-mater.
pianissimo (piani·simou) *adv.-adj.* MÚS. pianísimo.
pianist (piæ·nist) *s.* MÚS. pianista.
piano (-nou) *adj.-adv.* MÚS. piano. *2 s.* piano, pianoforte: *grand ~*, piano de cola; *upright ~*, piano vertical.
pianoforte (-noufoʳt) *s.* MÚS. piano, pianoforte.
pianola (piænou·la) *s.* pianola.
plaster, plastre (piæ·støʳ) *s.* piastra.
plazza (piæ·ša) *s.* plaza. *2* pórtico, galería.
pibroch (pi·brak) *s.* música marcial o plañidera tocada con la gaita escocesa.
pica (pai·ka) *s.* MED. pica. *2* IMPR. cícero.
Picard (pi·kaʳd) *adj.-s.* picardo.
Picardy (pi·kaʳdi) *n. pr.* GEOGR. Picardía.
picaresque (pikare·sk) *adj.* picaresco.
picaroon (pikaru·n) *s.* pícaro. *2* ladrón. *3* pirata.
picayune (pikayu·n) *s.* (E.U.) moneda o cosa de poco valor. *2 adj.* mezquino, insignificante.
piccalilli (pi·kalili) *s.* especie de encurtidos.
piccolo (pi·kolou) *s.* MÚS. flautín.
piceous (pi·siøs) *adj.* píceo. *2* inflamable.
pick (pik) *s.* pico [herramienta], zapapico. *2* MÚS. pua, plectro. *3* pinchazo. *4* cosecha. *5* selección; derecho a escoger. *6* flor, lo más escogido.
pick (to) *tr.* picar, agujerear; romper [con pico, punzón, etc.]. *2* hacer [un agujero, etc.]: *to ~ a hole in*, hacer un agujero en; hallar un defecto en. *3* coger [flores, frutos, etc.]; recoger. *4* escoger. *5* limpiar [quitando], mondar, pelar, desplumar: *to ~ a bone*, roer un hueso; ajustar cuentas; *to ~ one's teeth*, mondarse los dientes; *to ~ pockets*, limpiar bolsillos, ser ratero. *6* forzar [una cerradura]. *7* MÚS. puntear [un instrumento]. *8* picar, picotear. *9* comer a bocaditos. *10* hallar [defectos]. *11 to ~ a quarrel*, buscar pendencia. *12 to ~ off*, arrancar, quitar. *13 to ~ out*, escoger; ver, descifrar; quitar. *14 to ~ to pieces*, desmenuzar, analizar. *15 to ~ up*, recoger; coger, adquirir, tomar; captar [una emisión de radio, etc.]; hallar [por casualidad]; aprender [con la práctica]; recobrar [ánimo, vigor, etc.]; entablar conversación con [uno] de un modo casual. *16 to ~ up speed*, ganar velocidad.
17 intr. to ~ at, tirar de; picar de [un manjar]; tomarla con, criticar, regañar. *18 to ~ up*, restablecese; cobrar carnes; ganar velocidad.
pickaback (pi·kabæk) *adv.* fam. a cuestas.
pickaninny (pi·kanini) *s.* negrito, niño negro. *2* muchacho, muchachito.
picax, picaxe (pi·kæks) *s.* piqueta, zapapico.
picker (pi·køʳ) *s.* mondador. *2* escardador. *2* escogedor. *4* recolector. *5* nombre de varios instrumentos.
pickerel (pi·kørøl) *s.* ICT. variedad de lucio.
picket (pi·kit) *s.* estaca, piquete [palo]. *2* MIL. piquete. *3* huelguista puesto de vigilancia cerca de una fábrica, etc.
picket (to) *tr.* cercar con estacas. *2* estacar [un caballo]. *3* MIL. guardar; poner de guardia. *4* vigilar los huelguistas [una fábrica, etc.].
pickings (-ings) *s. pl.* desperdicios, desechos. *2* lo pillado o robado. *3* gajes, ganancias.
pickle (pi·køl) *s.* salmuera, escabeche, vinagre, adobo: *in ~*, en escabeche, en vinagre; fig. en reserva. *2* apuro, aprieto, lío. *3* niño travieso. *4 pl.* encurtidos.
pickle (to) *tr.* encurtir, escabechar, adobar.
picklock (pi·klak) *s.* ganzúa [garfio, ladrón].

pickpocket (-pakit) *s.* ratero, carterista.
pickup (-øp) *s.* recogida. *2* cosa recogida, hallada. *3* AUTO. aceleración. *4* fam. mejoría, recobro. *5* ELECT. fonocaptor, pick-up.
pickwik (-wik) *s.* cigarro barato.
picnic (-nik) *s.* partida de campo, jira, comida al aire libre.
picnic (to) *intr.* ir de jira, comer o merendar en el campo, al aire libre. ¶ Pret. y p. p.: *picnicked*; ger.: *-cking*.
picot (pi·kou) *s.* puntilla [encaje].
picotee (pikotɪ·) *s.* BOT. clavel moteado.
picric (pi·krik) *adj.* QUÍM. pícrico.
Pict (pikt) *s.* picto.
pictography (pikta·grafi) *s.* pictografía.
pictorial (pikto·rial) *adj.* pictórico. *2* gráfico, ilustrado. *3 s.* revista ilustrada.
picture (pi·kchøʳ) *s.* pintura, cuadro: *~ gallery*, galería de pinturas. *2* retrato, fotografía; dibujo, estampa, lámina, grabado: *~ page*, página ilustrada [de un periódico]. *3* cuadro, escena, conjunto. *4* pintura, descripción. *5* imagen, semejanza. *6* ÓPT. imagen. *7* cuadro [clínico]. *8* película cinematográfica: *~ house*, *~ palace*, cinematógrafo [edificio]; *the pictures*, el cinematógrafo, el cine. *9 ~ hat*, especie de pamela.
picture (to) *tr.* pintar, dibujar, retratar. *2* describir. *3 intr.* imaginarse, representarse.
picturesque (pikchøre·sk) *adj.* pintoresco.
piddle (to) (pi·døl) *intr.* malgastar el tiempo. *2* hacer pipí [expr. infantil].
piddling (pi·dling) *adj.* fútil, baladí.
pidgin English (pi·dyin) *s.* inglés chapurrado que sirve como lengua franca en China.
pie (pai) *s.* pastel, empanada. *2* ORN. urraca, marica. *3* IMPR. empastelar.
piebald (-bold) *adj.-s.* pío [caballo]. *2 adj.* mezclado, abigarrado.
piece (pɪs) *s.* pieza, trozo, pedazo, fragmento: *to cut to pieces*, despedazar; destrozar [un ejército]; *to go to pieces*, desvencijarse; fracasar [un negocio]; perder la salud; tener los nervios destrozados; *to take to pieces*, desarmar, desmontar; deshacer. *2* pieza [de tela, de un juego, etc.]; ejemplo, caso, acto: *~ of furniture*, mueble; *~ of advice*, consejo; *~ of news*, noticia; *to give one a ~ of one's mind*, decir las verdades a uno; *of a ~ with*, lo mismo o de la misma clase que. *3* cañón, arma de fuego. *4* moneda. *5* casco, tonel. *6* PINT. cuadro. *7* MÚS., LIT., TEAT. pieza, obra.
piece (to) *tr.* apedazar, remendar. *2* reunir, juntar; formar juntando piezas o partes.
piecemeal (-mil) *adj.* hecho de trozos. *2* hecho por partes. *3 adv.* en pedazos. *4* poco a poco, de trozo en trozo, por partes.
piecework (-wøʳk) *s.* trabajo a destajo.
pied (paid) *adj.* de varios colores, moteado, pinto, abigarrado.
Piedmont (pi·dmant) *n. pr.* GEOGR. Piamonte.
pier (pi·øʳ) *s.* pilar [para sostener]. *2* ARQ. estribo, machón. *3* muelle, embarcadero. *4* malecón, rompeolas. *5* ARQ. entrepaño; *~ glass*, espejo de cuerpo entero; *~ table*, consola.
pierce (to) (pɪʳs) *tr.* atravesar, traspasar; taladrar, perforar, agujerear, punzar. *2* penetrar. *3* conmover. *4* abrir [un agujero, paso, etc.]. *5 intr.* penetrar, internarse.
piercing (-ing) *s.* agudo, penetrante. *2* punzante. *3* terebrante. *4* lastimero, conmovedor.
Pierides (paii·ridiš) *s. pl.* Piérides.
pietism (pai·otišm) *s.* pietismo. *2* mojigatería.

pietist (-øtist) *s.* pietista. *2* mojigato.
piety (-øti) *s.* piedad, devoción.
piezometer (paiiša·mitøʳ) *s.* Fís. piezómetro.
piffle (pi·føl) *s.* tontería, despropósito; palabrería.
piffle (to) *intr.* disparatar, decir tonterías.
pig (pig) *s.* zool. cerdo, puerco, cochino. *2* coc. lechón. *3* fig. cerdo [pers.]. *4* fund. lingote, barra, tejo.
pigeon (pi·dȳøn) *s.* orn. pichón, palomo, paloma: ~ *breast*, med. pecho en quilla; ~ *house*, palomar. *2* fig. primo, incauto.
pigeon-breasted *adj.* med. de pecho en quilla.
pigeonfoot (-fut) *s.* bot. pie de milano.
pigeon-hearted *adj.* tímido, cobarde.
pigeonhole (-joul) *s.* hornilla [de palomar]. *2* casilla [de casillero].
pigeonhole (to) *tr.* encasillar. *2* clasificar y guardar en la memoria. *3* relegar al olvido, archivar, dar carpetazo a.
pigeonry (-ri) *s.* palomar.
pigeon-toed *adj.* de pies torcidos hacia dentro.
pigeon's-blood *s.* miner. granate, piropo.
piggery (pi·gøri) *s.* zahurda.
piggin (pi·gin) *s.* cubeta, balde.
piggish (pi·giš) *adj.* de cerdo. *2* voraz, puerco, cochino.
pig-headed *adj.* terco, testarudo.
pigmean (pigmɪ·an) *adj.-s.* pygmean.
pigment (pi·gmønt) *s.* pigmento. *2* color, pintura, materia colorante.
pigmentary (-teri) *adj.* pigmentario.
pigmentation (-ei·shøn) *f.* pigmentación.
pigmy (pi·gmi) *adj.-s.* pigmy.
pignut (-nøt) *s.* bot. pacanero. *2* bot. pacana. *3* bot. fruto o tubérculo de varias plantas.
pigpen (-pen) *s.* pocilga, zahurda.
pigskin (-skin) *s.* piel de cerdo. *2* fam. silla de montar. *3* fam. balón [de fútbol].
pigsty (-stai) *s.* pocilga, zahurda.
pigtail (-teil) *s.* coleta [de pelo].
pike (paik) *s.* pica [arma]; garrocha; chuzo. *2* camino de barrera. *3* ict. lucio.
pikeman (-mæn) *s.* piquero.
pikestaff (-stæf) *s.* asta de pica; bastón herrado.
pilar (pai·laʳ) *adj.* piloso.
pilaster (pilæ·støʳ) *s.* arq. pilastra.
Pilate (pai·leit) *n. pr.* Pilatos.
pilchard (pi·lchøʳd) ict. sardina.
pile (pail) *s.* pelo, pelusa, lana. *2* pelo [de ciertos tejidos]. *3* pila, montón, rimero. *4* fortuna, caudal. *5* elect. pila, batería. *6* pira. *7* mole, masa de edificios. *8* estaca, pilote. *9* cruz [de una moneda]. *10 pl.* almorranas.
pile (to) *tr.* amontonar, apilar. *2* cubrir, llenar, cargar. *3* sostener con pilotes. *4* tej. formar pelo en. *5 intr.* amontonarse, acumularse.
pileus (pai·liøs) *s.* píleo.
pilework (-uøʳk) *s.* pilotaje [de pilotes].
pilfer (to) (pi·lføʳ) *tr.-intr.* hurtar, ratear, sisar.
pilferage (-idȳ) *s.* ratería, hurto.
pilferer (-øʳ) *s.* ratero, ladrón.
pilfering (-ing) *s.* ratería, hurto.
pilgrim (pi·lgrim) *s.* peregrino, romero; viajero.
pilgrim (to) *intr.* peregrinar.
pilgrimage (-idȳ) *s.* peregrinación, peregrinaje, romería.
piling (pai·ling) *s.* pilework.
pill (pil) *s.* píldora. *2* fig. mal trago. *3* posma, persona cargante. *4 pl.* pop. billar.
pill (to) *tr.* medicinar con píldoras.

pillage (pi·lidȳ) *s.* pillaje, saqueo, extorsión. *2* botín [de un pillaje].
pillage (to) *tr.* pillar, saquear, robar.
pillar (pi·laʳ) *s.* pilar, columna, puntal: *from* ~ *to post*, de Herodes a Pilatos. *2* fig. pilar, sostén.
pillared (pi·laʳd) *adj.* sostenido por columnas.
pillion (pi·lion) *s.* asiento trasero de motocicleta.
pillory (pi·løri) *s.* picota.
pillory (to) *tr.* empicotar, poner en la picota.
pillow (pi·lou) *s.* almohada, cabezal. *2* almohadón, cojín. *3* mundillo [para hacer encaje]. *4* mec. cojín, cojinete, dado: ~ *block*, chumacera.
pillow (to) *tr.* poner sobre una almohada; sostener con almohadas; servir de almohada a.
pillowcase (pi·loukeis) *s.* funda de almohada.
pilose (pai·lous) *adj.* piloso.
pilosity (paila·siti) *s.* vellosidad.
pilot (pai·løt) *m.* mar. piloto, práctico. *2* avia. piloto, aviador. *3* guía, consejero. *4* ferroc. trompa, quitapiedras. *5 adj.* piloto: ~ *lamp*, lámpara piloto.
pilot (to) *t.* pilotar, pilotear. *2* dirigir, gobernar.
pilotage (pai·løtidȳ) *s.* mar. pilotaje, practicaje.
pilous (pai·løs) *adj.* piloso, peludo.
pimento (pime·ntou) *s.* bot. pimienta. *2* bot. pimentero.
pimiento (pimie·ntou) *s.* bot. pimiento.
pimp (pimp) *s.* alcahuete.
pimp (to) *intr.* alcahuetear.
pimpernel (-øʳnel) *s.* bot. murajes. *2* bot. pimpinela.
pimping (-ing) *adj.* pequeño, mezquino. *2* enfermizo.
pimple (-øl) *s.* grano, barro [en la piel].
pimply (-li) *adj.* granujiento, barroso.
pin (pin) *s.* alfiler: *to be on pins and needles*, estar sobre ascuas. *2* prendedor, broche. *3* clavillo, clavija, chaveta, pasador, espiga: *firing* ~, percutor [de un arma]. *4* mec. gorrón; muñón. *5* bolo [para jugar]. *6 pl.* palos [del billar]. *7* fam. piernas.
pin (to) *tr.* prender [con alfileres]: clavar, fijar, sujetar, pegar: *to* ~ *down*, fijar, inmovilizar; hacer dar una respuesta definitiva; *to* ~ *in*, encerrar; *to* ~ *up*, prender y prender con alfileres; fijar [un dibujo, etc.] con alfileres o chinchetas. ¶ Pret. y p. p.: *pinned*; ger.: *pinning*.
pinafore (pi·nafoʳ) *s.* delantal [de niño].
pinaster (pinæ·støʳ) *s.* bot. pinastro, pino rodeno.
pincase (pi·nkeis) *s.* alfiletero.
pince-nez (pæ·nsnei) *s.* lentes [anteojos].
pincers (pi·nsøʳš) *s. pl.* tenazas, mordazas. *2* pinzas, tenacillas. *3* zool. pinza.
pinch (pinch) *s.* aprieto, apuro, necesidad; *at a* ~, en caso de apuro. *2* opresión, punzada, dolor, tormento. *3* pellizco; apretón. *4* pulgarada; polvo de rapé.
pinch (to) *tr.* pellizcar; apretar [con pinzas, etc.]; cogerse [el dedo en la puerta]. *2* apretar, hacer daño [un zapato, etc.]. *3* oprimir, afligir. *4* robar, estafar. *5* contraer, reducir, limitar, escatimar. *6* adelgazar, demacrar. *7* prender, arrestar. *8 intr.* apretar. *9* economizar.
pinchbeck (-bec) *s.* similor.
pinchers (-øʳs) *s. pl.* pincers.
pinchfist (-fist) *s.* avaro, roñoso.
pincushion (pi·nkushøn) *s.* acerico.
Pindar (pi·ndaʳ) *n. pr.* Píndaro.
Pindaric (pindæ·rik) *adj.* pindárico.
pine (pain) *s.* bot. pino: ~ *cone*, piña; ~ *needle*, pinocha; ~ *nut*, piñón.

pine (to) *intr.* desfallecer, languidecer, descaecer, consumirse. | Gralte. con *away*. *2* afligirse, penar. *3 to* ~ *for* o *after*, anhelar.
pineal (pi·nial) *adj.* pineal.
pineapple (pai·næpøl) *s.* BOT. ananás, piña de América.
pinery (-ri) *s.* planación de ananás. *2* pinar.
pinfold (pi·nfould) *s.* corral o depósito donde se recoge el ganado extraviado.
ping-pong (ping-pang) *s.* tenis de salón, pingpong.
pinguid (pi·ngwid) *adj.* pingüe, craso, gordo.
pinhead (pi·njed) *s.* cabeza de alfiler. *2* insignificancia. *3* bobo, tonto.
pinion (pi·niøn) *s.* ORN. ala; extremo del ala. *2* alón. *3* MEC. piñón.
pinion (to) *tr.* cortar las alas a. *2* sujetar los brazos de; atar, maniatar.
pinioned (-d) *adj.* alado. *2* atado, maniatado.
pink (pink) *s.* BOT. clavel; clavellina. *2* color de rosa. *3* modelo, dechado. *4* estado perfecto. *5 adj.* rosado, rojizo.
pinkish (-ish) *adj.* rosáceo, que tira a rosado.
pinky (-i) *adj.* rosado, rosáceo.
pinnace (pi·nis) *s.* MAR. pinaza.
pinnacle (pi·nakøl) *s.* pináculo. *2* cima, cumbre.
pinnate (d (pi·neit(id) *adj.* BOT. pinnado.
pinnatifid (pinæ·tifid) *adj.* BOT. pinatífido.
pinniped (pi·niped) *adj.-s.* ZOOL. pinípedo.
pinnule (pi·nul) *s.* pínula.
pin-oak (pi·nouk) *s.* BOT. carrasca de América.
pinocle (pinø·køl) *s.* pinacle [juego de naipes].
pint (paint) *s.* pinta, cuartillo [medida].
pintail (pi·nteil) *s.* ORN. ánade de cola larga.
pintle (pi·ntøl) *s.* perno [del pernio]. *2* MAR. pinzote.
pinwheel (pi·njuil) *s.* rueda [de fuegos artificiales]. *2* molinete [juguete].
pinworm (-uøᵣm) *s.* ZOOL. lombriz intestinal.
pioneer (pai·øniᵣ) *s.* MIL. zapador, gastador. *2* primer colonizador. *3* precursor; pionero.
pioneer (to) *tr.-intr.* abrir camino; guiar; explorar, colonizar.
pious (pai·øs) *adj.* pío, piadoso.
pip (pip) *s.* pepita [de las aves]. *2* fam. indisposición. *3* BOT. pepita. *4* punto [de naipe, etc.].
pip (to) *intr.* piar. *2 tr.* ORN. romper [el cascarón].
pipe (paip) *s.* tubo, caño, cañería, conducto: ~ *line*, PIPELINE. *2* cañón [de órgano]. *3* caramillo, flauta, zampoña. *4* MAR. silbato [de contramaestre]. *5* pitido, silbo; voz atiplada o aflautada. *6* pipa [para fumar]. *7* tallo [de lila u otras plantas]. *8* pipa, tonel. *9 pl.* tubería. *10* MÚS. gaita.
pipe (to) *tr.* tocar [en el caramillo, etc.]. *2* emitir con voz aguda. *3* conducir por tuberías; proveer de tuberías. *4* MAR. mandar o llamar [con silbato]. *5* COST. adornar con vivos. *6 to* ~ *one's eye*, fam. soltar el trapo, echarse a llorar. *7 intr.* cantar o hablar con voz aguda, chillar. *8* pitar. *9 to* ~ *down*, callar. *10 to* ~ *up*, ponerse a tocar, a cantar, a hablar.
pipeline (-lain) *s.* tubería, oleoducto.
pipeline (to) *tr.* conducir por medio de un oleoducto. *2* proveer de oleoducto.
piper (-øᵣ) *s.* gaitero.
piperaceous (pipørei·shøs) *adj.* BOT. piperáceo.
pipette (pipe·t) *s.* pipeta.
piping (pai·ping) *adj.* agudo, aflautado. *2* adv. ~ *hot*, muy caliente. *3 s.* voz o sonido agudos, aflauados. *4* lloro; gemido. *5* tubería; canalización. *6* COST. vivo.

pipit (pi·pit) *s.* ORN. especie de alondra.
pipkin (pi·pkin) *s.* pucherito, ollita.
pippin (pi·pin) *s.* BOT. camuesa [manzana].
piquancy (pi·kansi) *s.* lo picante [de una cosa].
piquant (pi·kant) *adj.* picante. *2* travieso, picaresco.
pique (pik) *s.* pique, resentimiento: *in a* ~, resentido.
pique (to) *tr.* picar, ofender, irritar. *2* picar, mover, estimular. *3 to* ~ *oneself on*, picarse, enorgullecerse de. *4 intr.* AVIA. picar.
piqué (pikei·) *s.* TEJ. piqué.
piquet (pike·t) *s.* juego de los cientos.
piracy (pai·rasi) *s.* piratería. *2* robo, plagio.
pirate (pai·rit) *s.* pirata. *2* plagiario.
piratical (pairæ·tikal) *adj.* pirático.
pirogue (pirou·g) *s.* piragua, canoa.
pirouette (pirue·t) *s.* pirueta, girada [en la danza].
pirouette (to) *intr.* piruetear, girar.
Pisan (pi·šan) *adj.-s.* pisano.
pisciculture (pisikø·lchøᵣ) *s.* piscicultura.
pisciculturist (-ist) *s.* piscicultor.
pisciform (pi·sifoᵣm) *adj.* pisciforme.
piscina (pi·sina) *s.* LITURG. piscina.
piscivorous (pisi·vørøs) *adj.* piscívoro.
pish (pish) *interj.* ¡ba!, ¡quita allá!
pisiform (pai·sifoᵣm) *adj.-s.* pisiforme.
piss (pis) *s.* vulg. orina.
piss (to) *intr.* vulg. orinar, mear.
pistachio (pista·chiou) *s.* BOT. alfóncigo, pistacho.
pistil (pi·stil) *s.* BOT. pistilo.
pistol (pi·støl) *s.* doblón de oro.
pistoleer (pistølⁱᵣ) *s.* pistolero.
piston (pi·støn) *s.* MEC. pistón, émbolo: ~ *stroke*, embolada. *2* MÚS. pistón.
pit (pit) *s.* hoyo; hoya, cárcava; excavación, foso, pozo, abismo. *2* boca [del estómago]. *3* cacaraña. *4* mina o sitio de donde se extrae algo. *5* reñidero [de gallos, perros, etc.]. *6* TEAT. parte posterior del patio. *7* (E.U.) corro [de Bolsa]. *8* hueso [de fruta].
pit (to) *tr.* poner en un hoyo. *2* marcar con hoyos, cacarañar. *3* deshuesar [una fruta]. *4 to* ~ *against*, oponer a, poner en competencia con. ¶ Pret. y p. p.: *pitted;* ger.: *-tting*.
pitapat (pi·tapæt) *s.* trip trap; palpitación. *2* adv. con paso o trotecito ligero; con palpitación.
pitch (pich) *s.* pez, brea, alquitrán. *2* echada, lanzamiento, tiro [en ciertos juegos]. *3* grado de inclinación, pendiente, declive. *4* extremo, colmo; grado, punto. *5* MÚS. tono, diapasón. *6* FONÉT. tono. *7* MEC. paso [de rosca; de hélice, etc.]. *8* MAR. cabezada, arfada. *9* ARQ. altura [de un arco].
pitch (to) *tr.* empecinar, embrear. *2* tirar, lanzar, arrojar. *3* levantar [el heno, etc.] con el horcón. *4* clavar, fijar en tierra; armar [una tienda]. *5* poner, colocar. *6* MÚS. graduar el tono de. *7* cantear [una piedra]. *8 intr.* echarse o caer de cabeza. *9* inclinarse, bajar en declive. *10* acampar, instalarse. *11* MEC. engranar, endentar. *12* MAR. cabecear, arfar. *13* fam. *to* ~ *in*, poner manos a la obra. *14 to* ~ *into*, arremeter contra; reprender.
pitch and toss *s.* especie de juego de cara o cruz.
pitch-dark *adj.* oscuro como boca de lobo.
pitched battle (-t) *s.* batalla campal.
pitcher (-øᵣ) *s.* jarro, cántaro. *2* lanzador.
pitchfork (-foᵣk) *s.* AGR. horca, horquilla.
pitchiness (-inis) *s.* oscuridad, negrura.
pitchstone (-stoun) *s.* PETROGR. vidrio volcánico.

pitchy (-i) *adj.* peceño, píceo. *2* empeguntado. *3* negro, oscuro. *4* profunda [oscuridad].

piteous (pi·tiøs) *adj.* lastimoso, lastimero.

pitfall (pi·tfol) *s.* trampa [para cazar]; hoyo disimulado. *2* añagaza; escollo, peligro insospechado.

pith (piz) *s.* BOT., ANAT. meollo, médula. *2* fig. meollo, substancia. *3* fuerza, vigor.

pithy (pi·zi) *adj.* meticuloso. *2* vigoroso. *3* expresivo, enérgico y conciso.

pitiable (pi·tiabøl) *adj.* lastimoso, compasible, lamentable. *2* pobre, despreciable.

pitiful (pi·tiful) *adj.* PITIABLE. *2* compasivo.

pitiless (-lis) *adj.* despiadado, cruel, inhumano, duro de corazón.

pitman (pi·tmæn) *s.* aserrador de foso. *2* MIN. pocero.

pitpit (pi·tpit) *s.* ORN. pitpit.

piton (pito·n) *s.* estaca de hierro usada por los montañeros.

pittance (pi·tɑns) *s.* pitanza. *2* miseria, jornal miserable, renta insuficiente.

pitter-patter *s.* golpeteo ligero y rápido; chapaleteo [de la lluvia].

pituita (pitiuai·tɑ) *s.* pituita.

pituitary (pitiui·teri) *adj.* pituitario: ~ *body,* ~ *gland,* glándula pituitaria.

pituitous (pitiu·itøs) *adj.* pituitoso.

pity (pi·ti) *s.* piedad, misericordia, compasión: *for pity's sake,* ¡por piedad!, ¡por Dios! *2* lástima: *what a* ~!, ¡qué lástima!

pity (to) *tr.* comparecer, tener lástima de, apiadarse de. ¶ Pret. y p. p.: *pitied.*

pitying (-ing) *adj.* compasivo.

pivot (pi·vøt) *s.* eje, gorrón, pivote. *2* fig. eje, punto fundamental. *3* MIL. guía.

pivot (to) *tr.* montar sobre un eje o pivote. *2* proveer de eje o pivote. *3* intr. pivotar: *to* ~ *on,* girar sobre.

pix (piks) *s.* PYX.

pixy, pixie (pi·ksi) *s.* (Ingl.) duende.

pizzle (pi·søl) *s.* vergajo.

placability (pleikabi·liti) *s.* placabilidad.

placable (plei·kabøl) *adj.* placable, clemente.

placard (plæ·ka ͬd) *s.* cartel, anuncio, letrero.

placard (to) *tr.* publicar o anunciar por medio de carteles. *2* fijar [un cartel]; fijar carteles en.

placate (to) (plei·keit) *tr.* aplacar, apaciguar.

place (pleis) *s.* lugar, sitio, paraje; población; parte, punto; local: *in no* ~, en ninguna parte. *2* lugar, sitio, puesto; rango, dignidad; plaza, espacio, cabida: *in the first* ~, en primer lugar; *in* ~ *of,* en lugar de, en vez de; *out of* ~, fuera de lugar o de propósito; *to know one's* ~, no tomarse libertades; ser respetuoso; *to take* ~, verificarse, ocurrir. *3* empleo, cargo. *4* MIL. plaza. *5* plazuela; calle corta. *6* mansión, quinta. *7* ARIT. cifra decimal.

place (to) *tr.* poner, colocar, situar, instalar, fijar. *2* colocar [a una pers.; dinero; mercancías]. *3* intr. colocarse [un caballo en las carreras].

placement (-mønt) *s.* colocación, situación.

placenta (plase·ntɑ) *s.* ANAT., ZOOL., BOT. placenta.

1) placer (plei·sø ͬ) *s.* el que coloca.

2) placer (plæ·sø ͬ) *s.* MIN. placer; lavadero de oro.

placid (plæ·sid) *adj.* plácido, apacible.

placidity (plasi·diti) *s.* placidez, apacibilidad.

plagal (plei·gal) *adj.* MÚS. plagal.

plagiarism (plei·dɏiarišm) *s.* plagio.

plagiarist (-ist) *s.* plagiario.

plagiarize (to) (-aiš) *tr.-intr.* plagiar.

plagiary (-i) *s.* plagiario. *2* plagio.

plague (pleig) *s.* plaga. *2* peste, pestilencia. *3* calamidad. *4 a* ~ *on...,* al demonio...

plague (to) *tr.* plagar; infestar. *2* atormentar, molestar, importunar.

plaguey, plaguy (plei·gi) *adj.* enojoso, molesto.

plaice (pleis) *s.* ICT. platija, acedía.

plaid (plæd) *s.* manta escocesa. *2* tartán. *3* diseño a cuadros. *4 adj.* listado a cuadros.

plain (plein) *adj.* llano, raso, liso. *2* claro, evidente: ~ *as a pickestaff,* claro como la luz. *3* claro, franco, sincero: ~ *dealing,* sinceridad, buena fe; *in* ~ *English,* sin eufemismos. *4* simple, sencillo, corriente, común; humilde. *5* feo, sin atractivo. *6* puro, sin mezcla: *the* ~ *truth,* la pura verdad. *7* MÚS. ~ *song,* canto llano. *8* ~ *clothes,* vestido de paisano. *9 adv.* claro, sin ambigüedad. *10 s.* llano, llanura.

plain-clothes man *s.* agente de policía secreta.

plainness (plei·nnis) *s.* llanura. *2* sencillez; franqueza, claridad. *3* fealdad; vulgaridad.

plain-spoken *adj.* claro, sincero. *2* francote, brusco.

plaint (pleint) *s.* queja. *2* DER. querella.

plaintiff (-if) *s.* DER. demandante, actor.

plaintive (-iv) *adj.* lamentoso, lastimero, triste, elegíaco.

plait (plæt, pleit o plit) *s.* pliegue, plegado. *2* trenza; pleita.

plait (to) *tr.* plegar, alechugar, encañonar. *2* trenzar.

plaiting (-ing) *s.* plegadura, plegado. *2* trenzado.

plan (plæn) *s.* plano, planta, diseño, esquema. *2* PERSP., ESC. plano. *3* plan, proyecto.

plan (to) *tr.* hacer el plano de. *2* planear, proyectar, idear; planificar. *3 intr.* hacer planes. ¶ Pret. y p. p.: *planned;* ger.: *-nning.*

planchette (plænshe·t) *s.* TOP. plancheta. *2* tabla de escritura espiritista.

plane (plein) *adj.* plano: ~ *geometry,* geometría plana. *2 s.* plano [superficie plana]. *3* GEOM., MEC. plano. *4* plano, nivel. *5* aeroplano, avión: ~ *sickness,* mareo en el aire. *6* CARP. cepillo, garlopa. *7* BOT. *plane* o ~ *tree,* plátano [árbol].

plane (to) *tr.* CARP. acepillar, cepillar. *2 intr.* AVIA. volar; viajar en avión. *3* AVIA. planear.

planer (-ø ͬ) *s.* acepillador. *2* acepilladora mecánica. *3* IMPR. tamborilete.

planet (plæ·nit) *s.* ASTR. planeta. *2 adj.* planetario.

planetarium (plænøte·riøm) *s.* planetario.

planetary (plæ·nøteri) *adj.* planetario. *2* mundano, terrestre. *3* errático, inconstante.

planimeter (plæni·metø ͬ) *s.* planímetro.

planimetry (-tri) *s.* planimetría.

planing (plei·ning) *s.* acepilladura: ~ *machine,* acepilladora mecánica.

planish (to) (plæ·nish) *tr.* allanar, aplanar, alisar, pulir.

planisphere (plæ·nisfiø ͬ) *s.* planisferio.

plank (plænk) *s.* tablón, plancha, tabla gruesa. *2 pl.* tablado, entarimado.

plank (to) *tr.* entablar, entarimar. *2* MIN. encofrar. *3 fam. to* ~ *down,* poner firmemente; arrojar con violencia [sobre una mesa, etc.].

planking (-ing) *s.* entarimado, tablazón.

plankton (-tøn) *s.* BIOL. plancton.

planner (plæ·nø ͬ) *s.* proyectista.

plant (plænt) *s.* BOT. planta: ~ *louse,* pulgón. *2* mata, estaca, esqueje. *3* equipo, instalación de fábrica, etc. *4* fábrica, taller.

plant (to) *tr.* plantar, sembrar. *2* plantar, colocar, poner. *3* fundar, establecer. *4* implantar, inculcar.

plantaginaceous (plæntadÿine·shøs) *adj.* BOT. plantagináceo.

plantain (plæ·ntin) *s.* BOT. llantén. *2* BOT. banano; banana.

plantar (plæ·nta^r) *adj.* plantar.

plantation (plæntei·shøn) *s.* plantación, plantío. *2* hacienda, ingenio. *3* [en Terranova] pesquería.

planter (plæ·ntø^r) *s.* plantador; cultivador, hacendado. *2* plantadora [máquina].

plantigrade (plæ·ntigreid) *adj.-s.* plantígrado.

plaque (plæk) *s.* placa [decorativa; condecoración]. *2* MED. placa.

plaquette (plæke·t) *s.* ANAT. plaqueta.

plash (plæsh) *s.* chapaleteo. *2* mancha [de color]. *3* charco, lagunajo.

plash (to) *tr.-intr.* chapalear. *2* PINT. manchar. *3* entretejer [ramas].

plashy (plæ·shi) *adj.* pantanoso. *2* manchado.

plasm (plæsm), **plasma** (-*a*) *s.* ANAT., MINER. plasma. *2* BIOL. protoplasma.

plaster (plæ·stø^r) *s.* yeso; estuco, escayola, argamasa para enlucir: ~ *of Paris*, yeso. *2* FARM. parche, emplasto.

plaster (to) *tr.* enyesar, enlucir, revocar. *2* embadurnar. *3* emplastar. *4* pegar [un cartel, etc.].

plasterer (-ø^r) *s.* yesero. *2* enlucidor, revocador, estuquista.

plasterwork (-uø^rk) *s.* enlucido, enyesado; yesería.

plastic (plæ·stik) *adj.* plástico. *2 s.* plástico. *3* plástica.

plasticity (plæsti·siti) *ṣ.* plasticidad.

plastron (-trøn) *s.* ARM., ZOOL. peto. *2* pechera [de camisa]. *3* ESGR. plastrón.

plat (plæt) *s.* plano, mapa. *2* pedazo de tierra. *3* trenza.

plat (to) *tr.* hacer el plano o mapa de. *2* trenzar. ¶ Pret. y p. p.: *platted;* ger.: *-tting.*

platanaceous (plætanei·shøs) *adj.* platanáceo.

platan(e (plæ·tan) *s.* BOT. plátano [árbol].

platband (plæ·tbænd) *s.* arriate. *2* ARQ. faja de la cornisa.

plate (pleit) *s.* placa, plancha, lámina, hoja, chapa. *2* lámina, grabado, ilustración. *3* ELECT., FOT., BACT., ZOOL. placa: ~ *circuit,* circuito de placa. *4* platina [de la máquina neumática]. *5* ELECT. elemento [de pila]. *6* vajilla [de oro, plata, etc.]. *7* plato, platillo, fuente [vasija]: ~ *rack,* escurreplatos. *8* plato [comida]. *9* DEP. copa o placa [premio]. *10* CARN. falda.

plate (to) *tr.* planchear. *2* dorar, platear, niquelar, chapear [metales]. *3* blindar. *4* IMPR. clisar.

plateau (plætou·) *s.* GEOGR. mesa, meseta, altiplanicie. *2* plato o bandeja decorativos.

plateful (plei·tful) *s.* plato, fuente [su contenido].

plateholder (-jouldø^r) *s.* FOT. chasis, portaplacas.

platen (plæ·tøn) *s.* IMPR., MEC. platina. *2* rodillo [de la máquina de escribir].

plateresque (plætøre·sk) *adj.* ARQ. plateresco.

platform (plæ·tfo^rm) *s.* plataforma. *2* tablado, tribuna. *3* cadalso. *4* FERROC. andén. *5* terraplén. *6* (E.U.) programa; declaración de principios.

plating (plei·ting) *s.* dorado, plateado, niquelado, chapeado; galvanoplastia. *2* blindaje.

platinum (plæ·tinøm) *s.* QUÍM. platino: ~ *blonde,* rubia platinada.

platitude (plæ·titiud) *s.* insulsez, perogrullada, lugar común.

Plato (plei·tou) *n. pr.* Platón.

Platonic (plata·nik) *adj.* platónico.

Platonism (plei·tonišm) *s.* platonismo.

Platonist (plei·tonist) *s.* platónico.

platoon (platu·n) *s.* MIL. sección. *2* pelotón, grupo.

platter (plæ·tø^r) *s.* fuente, platel. *2* (E.U.) plato.

platyhelminth (plætije·lminz) *s.* ZOOL. platelminto.

platyrrhine (plæ·tirain) *adj.-s.* ZOOL. platirrino.

plaudit (plo·dit) *s.* aplauso. *2* aprobación.

plausibility (plošibi·liti) *s.* especiosidad; bondad o credibilidad aparentes.

plausible (plo·šibøl) *adj.* especioso, aparentemente bueno, creíble.

play (plei) *s.* juego [acción de jugar; diversión, entretenimiento, deporte], broma: ~ *upon words,* juego de palabras; *full of* ~, travieso, juguetón. *2* MEC. juego; juego, funcionamiento, acción, operación: *to come into* ~, entrar en juego; *full* ~, juego libre, rienda suelta. *3* juego [de luz, de colores, etc.]. *4* TEAT. representación. *5* TEAT. obra, comedia, drama, etc.

play (to) *tr.* jugar [una partida, una pieza, un naipe, etc.]. *2* jugar a [un juego]. *3* poner en acción, hacer, causar: *to* ~ *a trick on,* hacer una mala jugada a; *to* ~ *havoc with,* hacer estragos en. *4* fingir, hacer o hacerse: *to* ~ *the fool,* hacerse el tonto. *5* TEAT. representar [una obra]; hacer, desempeñar [un papel]. *6* apostar por [un caballo]. *7* dejar que se canse [el pez cogido en el anzuelo]. *8* MÚS. tocar, tañer; ejecutar. *9* malgastar, dilapidar. *10 to* ~ *out,* agotar, cansar. *11 to* ~ *truant* o *the truant,* hacer novillos.
   12 intr. jugar, divertirse; juguetear, retozar, bromear. *13* MÚS. tocar: *to* ~ *on an instrument,* tocar un instrumento. *14* sonar [el instrumento]. *15* obrar, conducirse: *to* ~ *fair,* jugar limpio. *16* jugar, moverse, funcionar. *17* flotar, ondear. *18 to* ~ *into the hands of,* hacer el caldo gordo a. *19 to* ~ *on* o *upon,* jugar con; aprovecharse de, abusar de. *20 to* ~ *up to,* halagar servilmente.

playbill (-bil) *s.* TEAT. cartel, programa.

playboy (-boi) *s.* fam. joven rico y disipado, niño bonito.

player (-ø^r) *s.* jugador. *2* TEAT. actor, representante, tocador; ejecutante.

playfellow (-felou) *s.* compañero de juegos.

playful (-ful) *adj.* juguetón, chancero.

playgoer (-gouø^r) *s.* aficionado al teatro.

playground (-graund) *s.* patio de recreo. *2* campo de juego.

playhouse (-jaus) *s.* teatro, coliseo.

playing card *s.* naipe.

playmate (-meit) *s.* PLAYFELLOW.

plaything (-zing) *s.* juguete [cosa, pers., etc., con que se juega].

playtime (-taim) *s.* hora o tiempo de recreo.

playwright (-rait) *s.* autor dramático.

plea (plі) *s.* argumento, argumentación. *2* defensa, alegato. *3* excusa, disculpa, pretexto. *4* súplica, ruego. *5* proceso, litigio.

pleach (to) (plіch) *tr.* entretejer [ramas, etc.].

plead (to) (plіd) *tr.* DER. defender en juicio. *2* alegar [en defensa, excusa, etc.]. *3 intr.* pleitear, abogar. *4* DER. *to* ~ *guilty,* confesarse culpable; *to* ~ *not guilty,* declararse inocente. *5 to* ~ *with,* rogar, suplicar.

pleader (-ø^r) *s.* abogado; defensor. *2* suplicante.

pleading (-ing) *s.* alegación, defensa. *2* súplica, ruegos.

pleasant (ple·šant) *adj.* agradable, grato, placentero. *2* simpático, afable.

pleasantry (-tri) *s.* broma, chanza, agudeza.
please (to) (plɪš) *tr.-intr.* agradar, gustar, placer, dar gusto, complacer: *to ~ oneself*, darse gusto; hacer uno lo que le guste. *2 to be pleased*, estar contento; *to be pleased to*, tener gusto en; querer, tener a bien: *to be pleased with*, estar contento de. *3 intr.* gustar, servirse, querer, tener a bien; *~ God*, quiera Dios; *as you ~*, como usted quiera o guste; *if you ~* o simplte. *please*, haga usted el favor de.
pleasing (-ing) *adj.* agradable, grato, placentero. *2* afable, cortés.
pleasurable (ple·ȳurabøl) *adj.* agradable, grato, deleitoso, festivo.
pleasurably (-bli) *adj.* agradablemente.
pleasure (ple·ȳøʳ) *s.* placer, deleite, goce, gusto; recreo; gozo, alegría: *~ boat*, embarcación de recreo; *~ trip*, viaje de placer; *with ~*, con mucho gusto. *2* gusto, voluntad, deseo, arbitrio: *what is your ~?*, ¿qué desea usted?
pleat (plɪt) *s.* pliegue, doblez.
pleat (to) *tr.* plegar, hacer pliegues en.
plebeian (plibɪ·an) *adj.-s.* plebeyo.
plebiscite (ple·bisait) *s.* plebiscito.
plebs (plebs) *s.* plebe.
plectrum (ple·ktrøm) *s.* plectro.
pledge (pledȳ) *s.* prenda [señal, garantía], rehén, fianza, caución, empeño: *as a ~ of*, en prenda. *3* brindis.
pledge (to) *tr.* dar en prenda, empeñar, comprometer: *to ~ one's word*, empeñar su palabra. *2* prometer, comprometerse. *3* hacer prometer. *4* brindar por.
pledget (ple·dȳit) *s.* CIR. compresa; tapón.
pleiad (pli·yæd) *s.* pléyade.
Pleiades (pli·yadiš) *n. pr.* MIT., ASTR. Pléyades.
Pleistocene (plais·tosin) *adj.-s.* GEOL. pleistoceno.
plenary (pli·neri) *adj.* pleno, lleno, completo, plenario.
plenipotentiary (plenipøte·nshieri) *adj.-s.* plenipotenciario.
plenitude (ple·nitiud) *s.* plenitud, abundancia.
plenteous (ple·ntiøs) *adj.* PLENTIFUL.
plenteousness (-nis) *s.* abundancia.
plentiful (ple·ntiful) *adj.* abundante, copioso, profuso, pingüe, opulento. *2* fértil, feraz.
plentifulness (-nis) *s.* abundancia, copia. *2* fertilidad.
plenty (ple·nti) *s.* copia, abundancia: *~ of*, mucho, de sobra.
plenum (pli·nøm) *s.* pleno. *2* espacio lleno.
pleonasm (pliønæšm) *s.* pleonasmo, redundancia.
pleonastic (al (pliønæ·stik(al) *adj.* pleonástico.
plesiosaur (plɪ·siøsoʳ) *s.* PALEONT. plesiosauro.
plethora (ple·zora) *s.* plétora.
plethoric (al (ple·zorik(al) *adj.* pletórico.
pleura (plu·ra), *pl.* **rae** (-ri) *s.*, ANAT. pleura.
pleurisy (-risi) *s.* MED. pleuresía; pleuritis.
pleuronectid (plurone·ktid) *adj.-s.* ICT. pleuronecto.
plexiglass (ple·ksiglæs) *s.* plexiglás.
plexus (ple·ksøs) *s.* ANAT. plexo.
pliability (plaiabi·liti) *s.* flexibilidad, docilidad.
pliable (plai·abøl) *adj.* flexible, dócil [fácil de trabajar]. *2* doblegable, dúctil, manejable.
pliancy (-ansi) *s.* flexibilidad, docilidad, ductilidad.
pliant (-ant) *adj.* flexible, cimbreño. *2* blando, dócil. *3* complaciente, obediente, adaptable.
plicate (d (plai·keit(id) *adj.* BOT., ZOOL. plegado.

pliers (plai·øʳš) *s. pl.* alicates, tenazas.
plight (plait) *s.* condición, estado; aprieto, apuro. *2* promesa, compromiso.
plight (to) *tr.* empeñar [la palabra, etc.]; prometer [fidelidad, etc.]. *2* prometer en matrimonio.
plinth (plinz) *s.* ARQ. plinto, orlo; zócalo.
Pliny (pli·ni) *n. pr.* Plinio.
Pliocene (plai·øsin) *adj.-s.* GEOL. plioceno.
plod (to) (plad) *intr.* afanarse, trabajar mucho o pesadamente. ¶ Pret. y p. p.: *plodded;* ger.: *-dding.*
plodder (-øʳ) *s.* el que se afana; el que trabaja con más aplicación que talento.
plop (pla·p) *s.* plaf [ruido sordo].
plot (plat) *s.* porción de terreno; cuadro, bancal; solar, parcela. *2* plano, mapa. *3* conspiración, complot, trama, maquinación. *4* trama, argumento [de una obra literaria].
plot (to) *tr.* (E.U.) dividir [en cuadros o parcelas]. *2* trazar el plano de. *3* tramar, urdir, fraguar. *4* intr.* conspirar. ¶ Pret. y p. p.: *plotted;* ger.: *-tting.*
plotter (-øʳ) *s.* conspirador, tramador.
plough (plau) *s.* arado. *2* ENCUAD. ingenio. *3* ASTR. el Carro, la Osa Mayor.
plough (to) *tr.-intr.* arar. *2 tr.* surcar. *3* arrancar, quitar [con un arado, etc.]. *4 intr.* avanzar como el que ara.
ploughland (-lænd) *s.* tierra labrantía.
ploughman (-mæn) *s.* arador, labrador; rústico, gañán.
ploughshare (-sheʳ) *s.* reja del arado.
ploughstaff (-stæf) *s.* abéstola, aguijada.
ploughtail (-teil) *s.* esteva, mancera.
ploughwright (-rait) *s.* constructor de arados.
plover (plø·vøʳ o plou·vøʳ) *s.* ORN. nombre de varias aves, como el chorlito, el avefría, etc.
plow, to plow, etc. (E.U.) PLOUGH, TO PLOUGH, etc.
pluck (pløk) *s.* valor, resolución. *2* tirón, estirón. *3* asadura. *4* (Ingl.) suspenso, calabazas.
pluck (to) *tr.* coger, arrancar. *2* pelar, desplumar. *3* dar un tirón a. *4* MÚS. puntear, herir las cuerdas de. *5* pop. robar. *6* (Ingl.) catear, calabacear. *7 to ~ up courage*, cobrar ánimo. *8* intr. *to ~ at*, tirar de.
plucky (plø·ki) *adj.* valeroso, denodado.
plug (pløg) *s.* tapón, botana, espita, taco, pieza que entra en un agujero. *2* DENT. empaste. *4* ELECT. clavija; tapón fusible. *5* AUTO. bujía. *6* cala [de melón]. *7* tableta [de tabaco]. *8* fam. chistera. *9* fig. elogio o anuncio interpolado en un texto.
plug (to) *tr.* atarugar, tapar. *2* DENT. empastar. *3* ELECT. *to ~ in*, enchufar. *4* intr.* trabajar con ahínco. ¶ Pret. y p. p.: *plugged;* ger.: *-gging.*
plum (pløm) *s.* BOT. ciruela; ciruelo. *2* pasa [para repostería]: *~ cake*, bizcocho con pasas; *~ pudding*, budín inglés con pasas. *4* fig. lo mejor; cargo provechoso, turrón.
plumage (plu·midȳ) *s.* plumaje.
plumb (pløm) *s.* plomo, plomada. *2* plomo, verticalidad: *in ~*, a plomo, *out of ~*, desaplomado. *3 adj.* vertical. *4* completo. *5 adv.* a plomo. *6* completamente; directamente.
plumb (to) *tr.* sondear. *2* ALBAÑ. aplomar. *3* plomar. *4* instalar cañerías en.
plumbago (plømbei·gou) *s.* plombagina, grafito. *2* BOT. belesa.
plumbeous (plø·mbiøs) *adj.* plomizo. *2* plúmbeo.
plumber (plø·møʳ) *s.* plomero. *2* fontanero.
plumbery (plø·møri) *s.* plomería; fontanería.
plumbic (plø·mbik) *adj.* plúmbico.

plume (plum) *s.* pluma [de ave]. *2* plumaje. *3* penacho, plumero. *4* fig. honor, galardón. *5* BOT. ~ *grass,* carricera.

plume (to) *tr.* desplumar, pelar. *2* emplumar, empenachar. *3* alisar el plumaje de. *4* ref. *to* ~ *oneself,* jactarse, vanagloriarse.

plumeless (-lis) *adj.* implume. *2* fig. sin dinero.

plumiped (plu·miped) *adj.* ORN. calzado.

plummet (plø·mit) *s.* plomo [de la plomada, la sonda, etc.].

plumose (plu·mous) *adj.* plumoso, plúmeo.

plump (plømp) *adj.* regordete, rollizo. *2* brusco, franco. *3* adv. a plomo. *4* de golpe. *5* bruscamente, sin ambages. *6* s. caída brusca, pesada.

plump (to) *tr.* engordar, hinchar. *2* soltar, dejar caer, tirar. *3* intr. engordar; hincharse, llenarse. *4* caer a plomo. *5* dejarse caer, desplomarse.

plumule (plu·miul) *s.* BOT. plúmula. *2* ORN. pluma de plumón.

plumy (plu·mi) *adj.* plumoso, plúmeo.

plunder (plø·ndøʳ) *s.* pillaje, saqueo, robo. *2* botín [de pillaje, robo, etc.].

plunder (to) *tr.* pillar, saquear, robar.

plunderer (-øʳ) *s.* saqueador, ladrón.

plunge (pløndẙ) *s.* zambullida, chapuz, sumersión; salto, caída, acción de arrojarse o lanzarse. *2* MAR. hocicada. *3* MIN. buzamiento.

plunge (to) *tr.* zambullir, chapuzar, sumergir; hundir; arrojar, precipitar. *2* intr. zambullirse, sumergirse; hundirse; abismarse; arrojarse, precipitarse. *3* hocicar [el buque].

plunger (-øʳ) *s.* buzo. *2* MEC. émbolo; chupón. *3* jugador o especulador desenfrenado.

pluperfect (plupø·ʳfikt) *adj.-s.* GRAM. pluscuamperfecto.

plural (plu·ral) *adj.-s.* plural.

pluralism (-išm) *s.* pluralismo.

plurality (pluræ·liti) *s.* pluralidad. *2* mayor número. *3* mayoría de votos.

pluralize (to) (plu·ralaiš) *tr.* pluralizar.

plurally (plu·rali) *adv.* en plural.

plus (plus) *prep.* más. *2* adj. MAT., ELECT. positivo. *3* adicional, de más. *4* s. MAT. el signo más. *5* cosa añadida, de más. *6* ~ *fours,* pantalón de golf.

plush (pløsh) *s.* TEJ. felpa, peluche. *2* adj. de felpa, afelpado. *3* fam. suntuoso.

Plutarch (plu·taʳk) *n. pr.* Plutarco.

plutarchy (plu·taʳki) *s.,* **plutocracy** (pluta·krasi) *s.* plutocracia.

Pluto (plu·tou) *n. pr.* MIT., ASTR. Plutón.

plutocrat (plu·tøkræt) *s.* plutócrata.

Plutonic (pluta·nik) *adj.* plutónico.

Plutonism (plu·tønišm) *s.* plutonismo.

plutonium (plutou·niøm) *s.* QUÍM. plutonio.

pluvial (plu·vial) *adj.* pluvial.

pluviometer (pluvia·mitøʳ) *s.* pluviómetro.

pluvious (plu·viøs) *adj.* lluvioso.

ply (plai) *s.* pliegue, doblez. *2* propensión, inclinación. *3* capa [de una tela, etc.]; cabo [de cuerda].

ply (to) *tr.* usar, manejar [con ardor]. *2* practicar, ejercer. *3* trabajar con ahínco en. *4* *to* ~ *with,* acosar con [preguntas, etc.]; hacer beber o comer [algo]. *5* tr.-intr. ir y venir regularmente, hacer el servicio entre. *7* afanarse; no parar.

plywood (-wud) *s.* CARP. contrachapado.

pneumatic (niumæ·tik) *adj.* neumático: ~ *tire,* neumático. *2* de aire comprimido.

pneumatics (-s) *s.* neumática.

pneumonia (niu·mounia) *s.* MED. neumonía, pulmonía.

pneumothorax (niumozo·ræks) *s.* MED. neumotórax.

poach (to) (pouch) *tr.* invadir [un vedado]; robar [caza o pesca] de un vedado. *2* escalfar [huevos]. *3* intr. cazar o pescar furtivamente.

poacher (-øʳ) *s.* cazador o pescador furtivo.

poachy (-i) *adj.* aguanoso, blando [terreno].

pock (pak) *s.* MED. viruela, pústula eruptiva.

pocket (pa·kit) *s.* bolsillo, faltriquera. *2* fig. bolsa, dinero. *3* bolsa [de papel, etc.]. *4* MIL. bolsa. *5* ANAT., MED. saco, bolsa. *6* BILLAR. tronera. *7* cavidad, hoyo. *8* MIN. depósito de pepitas de oro. *9* AVIA. bache, bolsa de aire. *10* adj. ~ *battleship,* acorazado de bolsillo.

pocket (to) *tr.* embolsar. *2* embolsarse, apropiarse. *3* BILLAR. entronerar. *4* ocultar [el orgullo, el enojo]; tragarse [una injuria].

pocketbook (-buk) *s.* librito de memorias. *2* billetero, carta, portamonedas.

pocketful (-ful) *s.* lo que cabe en un bolsillo o en una bolsa.

pocketknife (-naif) *s.* cortaplumas.

pockmark (-pa·kmaʳk) *s.* hoyo de viruelas, cacaraña.

pock-marked (-t) *adj.* picado de viruelas.

pod (pad) *s.* BOT. vaina, cápsula, silicua.

pod (to) *tr.* desvainar. *2* intr. BOT. criar vainas. *3* hincharse. ¶ Pret. y p. p.: *podded;* ger.: *-dding.*

podagra (pødæ·gra) *s.* MED. podagra, gota.

podgy (pa·dẙi) *adj.* gordinflón, regordete.

podium (pou·diøm) *s.* ARQ. podio.

poem (pou·em o pou·im) *s.* poema. *2* fig. poesía.

poesy (pou·isi) *s.* ant. poesía. *2* inspiración, genio poético.

poet (pou·et o pou·it) *s.* poeta, vate.

poetaster (pouetæ·støʳ) *s.* poetastro.

poetess (pou·tes) *f.* poetisa.

poetic (al (pou·tik(al) *adj.* poético.

poetics (pou·tiks) *s.* poética.

poetize (to) (-taiš) *tr.* poetizar.

poetry (pou·etri) *s.* poesía. *2* No tiene el sentido de verso, poema. *3* poética.

pogrom (pou·gram) *s.* pogrom.

poh (pou) *interj.* ¡puf!, ¡bah!, ¡quía!

poignancy (poi·nansi) *s.* acerbidad. *2* calidad de agudo, penetrante, punzante, conmovedor.

poignant (-ant) *adj.* acerbo. *2* agudo, penetrante, punzante. *3* mordaz. *4* conmovedor.

point (poi·nt) *s.* punta [extremo, esp. agudo]. *2* buril, punzón, puñal; herramienta puntiaguda. *3* GEOGR. punta, promontorio; pico, picacho. *4* punto [en varios sentidos]: ~ *at issue,* punto que se discute; ~ *of honour,* punto o cuestión de honor; ~ *of view,* punto de vista; *at the* ~ *of death,* en el artículo de la muerte; *on,* o *upon, the* ~ *of,* a punto de; *to a certain* ~, hasta cierto punto. *5* tanto, punto [en el juego]. *6* signo [de puntuación], punto final. *7* punto [de cañamazo o encaje; encaje de aguja]. *8* peculiaridad. *9* lo esencial, el quid; la intención, el chiste. *10* fin, propósito: *to carry one's* ~, salirse con la suya. *11* agujeta. *12* BOLSA. entero. *13* MAR. cuarta. *14* grado [de escala]. *15* MÚS. punto. *16* FERROC. aguja. *17* otros sentidos: *beside the* ~, fuera de propósito, que no viene al caso; *in* ~, pertinente, a propósito; *in* ~ *of,* por lo que toca a; *in* ~ *of fact,* de hecho; *to make a* ~ *of,* insistir en; tener por principio o regla; *to come to the* ~, ir al grano; venir al caso; *to speak to the* ~, hablar atinadamente.

point (to) *tr.* aguzar, sacar punta a. *2* apuntar,

asestar, encarar: *to ~ one's finger at*, señalar con el dedo. *3* señalar, indicar, hacer notar. | Gralte. con *out. 4* GRAM. puntuar. *5* ALBAÑ. rejuntar. *6 intr. to ~ at, to* o *toward*, señalar, indicar, apuntar a o hacia. *7* MED. madurar [un absceso]. *8 tr.-intr.* parar, mostrar la caza [el perro].
point-blank (-blænk) *adj.* directo, hecho a quemarropa. *2* claro, categórico. *3 adv.* a quemarropa. *4* clara, categóricamente.
pointed (-tid) *adj.* puntiagudo. *2* intencionado, mordaz. *3* directo, acentuado. *4* punteado. *5* ARQ. apuntado, ojival.
pointer (-tø^r) *s.* ARTILL. apuntador. *2* indicador, índice; manecilla [de reloj]; fiel [de balanza]. *3* puntero, buril. *4* perro de muestra; pachón. *5* fam. indicación u observación útil.
pointless (-list) *adj.* obtuso, sin punta. *2* insubstancial, insulso.
poise (poiš) *s.* equilibrio, estabilidad, reposo. *2* serenidad. *3* contrapeso. *4* indecisión. *5* aire, continente.
poise (to) *tr.* equilibrar, balancear. *2* mantener en equilibrio. *3* contrapesar. *4* llevar [la cabeza de cierto modo]. *5 intr.* posarse, estar suspendido, cernerse.
poison (poi·šøn) *s.* veneno, ponzoña, tósigo: *~ gas*, gas tóxico.
poison (to) *tr.* envenenar, empozoñar.
poisoner (-ø^r) *s.* envenenador.
poisonous (-øs) *adj.* venenoso, ponzoñoso.
poke (pouk) *s.* empujón, codazo. *2* hurgonazo; metido. *3* bolsa, saquito. *4* BOT. hierba, carmín. *5* fam. posma. *6* adj. *~ bonnet*, capota [sombrero].
poke (to) *tr.* picar, aguijonear, atizar, hurgar: *to ~ the fire*, atizar el fuego. *2 to ~ one's nose into*, meter la nariz en. *3 to ~ fun at*, burlarse de. *4 intr.* hurgar [en]. *5* andar buscando, husmear, meterse [en]. *6* haronear. *7* sobresalir, proyectarse.
poker (-ø^r) *s.* hurgón, atizador; espetón. *2* aguja para el pirograbado. *3* poker [juego].
pokeweed (-wid) *s.* BOT. hierba carmín.
polacre (pola·kø^r) *s.* MAR. polacra.
Poland (pou·land) *n. pr.* GEOGR. Polonia.
polar (pou·la^r) *adj.* polar: *~ bear*, oso blanco.
polarimeter (poulari·mitø^r) *s.* polarímetro.
Polaris (pole·ris) *s.* ASTR. la estrella polar.
polariscope (polæ·riskoup) *s.* ÓPT. polariscopio.
polarity (polæ·riti) *s.* polaridad.
polarize (to) (pou·larais) *tr.* polarizar.
pole (poul) *s.* GEOM., GEOGR., ASTR., BIOL., ELECT. polo. *2* palo, pértiga, vara, asta, poste. *3* lanza [de carruaje]. *4* balancín [de volatinero]. *5* TOP. jalón. *6* percha [medida]. *7* (con may.) polaco; polaca.
pole (to) *tr.-intr.* impeler [un barco] con pértiga.
poleax(e (-æks) *s.* hacha de combate o de matadero.
polecat (-lkæt) *s.* ZOOL. turón.
polemarch (pa·lima^rk) *s.* polemarca.
polemic (pole·mik) *adj.* polémico [de la controversia]. *2 s.* polemista. *3* polémica [controversia].
polemical (-kal) *adj.* POLEMIC 1.
polemics (pole·miks) *s.* polémica, dialéctica.
polemist (pa·lemist) *s.* polemista.
polemonium (palimou·niøm) *s.* BOT. polemonio.
polestar (pou·lsta^r) *s.* estrella polar. *2* fig. norte, guía.
police (pøli·s) *s.* policía: *~ court*, tribunal correccional.

police (to) *tr.* mantener el orden en. *2* guarnecer de policía. *3* MIL. asear y ordenar.
policeman (-mæn) *s.* policía; guardia de seguridad o urbano.
policewoman (-wumæn) *s.* mujer policía.
policy (pa·lisi) *s.* política, línea de conducta; trastienda, maña. *2* póliza [de seguro].
policyholder (-jouldø^r) *s.* asegurado, titular de una póliza.
poliomyelitis (paliomaiølai·tis) *s.* MED. poliomielitis.
Polish (pou·lish) *adj.* polaco, polonés. *2 s.* polaco [lengua].
polish (pa·lish) *s.* pulimento. *2* lustre, brillo. *3* acabado. *4* urbanidad, cultura. *5* barniz, betún, lustre para los zapatos.
polish (to) *tr.* pulir, bruñir, lustrar, dar brillo a. *2* pulir, perfeccionar; educar, refinar. *3 intr.* pulirse.
polisher (-ø^r) *s.* pulidor, bruñidor.
polishing (-g) *s.* pulimento, bruñido; *~ wax*, cera de lustrar.
polite (pølai·t) *adj.* cortés, urbano, atento, bien educado. *2* culto, refinado.
politeness (-nis) *s.* cortesía, urbanidad, buena crianza. *2* cultura, refinamiento.
politic (pa·litik) *adj.* sagaz, astuto. *2* político, prudente. *3* POL. constitucional. *4 body ~*, cuerpo político.
political (pøli·tikal) *adj.* político: *~ economy*, economía política.
politician (pøliti·shan) *s.* político. *2* politicastro, politiquero.
politics (pa·litiks) *s. pl.* política.
polity (pa·liti) *s.* constitución política. *2* comunidad, estado.
polka (pou·lka) *s.* polca. *2* adj. *~ dot*, topo o lunar en el dibujo de una tela.
poll (poul) *s.* cabeza [pers.]: *~ tax*, capitación. *2* votación; su resultado. *3* lista electoral. *4 pl.* colegio electoral. *5* urnas electorales.
poll (to) *tr.* recibir y escrutar [los votos]. *2* dar [voto]. *3* obtener [votos]. *4* trasquilar. *5* desmochar. *6* descornar. *7 intr.* votar en las elecciones.
pollack (pa·lak) *s.* ICT. especie de bacalao.
pollard (pa·la^rd) *s.* árbol descopado. *2* res descornada.
pollard (to) *tr.* descopar. *2* descornar.
pollen (pa·løn) *s.* BOT. polen.
pollination (palinei·shøn) *s.* BOT. polinización.
polling (pou·ling) *s.* votación, escrutinio; *~ place*, sección o colegio electoral.
pollinic (pali·nik) *adj.* BOT. polínico.
polliwog (pa·liuag) *s.* ZOOL. renacuajo.
pollute (to) (pøliu·t) *tr.* impurificar, contaminar, manchar, mancillar.
polluted (-id) *adj.* poluto, contaminado.
pollution (poliu·shøn) *s.* ensuciamiento, contaminación, mancillamiento. *2* MED. polución.
Pollux (pa·løks) *s.* ASTR. pólux.
Polly (pa·li) *n. pr.* Mariquita.
polo (pou·lou) *s.* polo [juego].
polonaise (pɑlønei·š) *s.* polonesa [danza, vestido].
polonium (palou·niøm) *s.* QUÍM. polonio.
poltroon (paltru·n) *s.* cobarde.
poltroonery (-øri) *s.* cobardía.
poly (pa·li) *s.* BOT. zamarrilla, polio.
polyandry (pa·liændri) *s.* poliandria.
polycarpic, -pous (palika·^rpik, -pøs) *adj.* BOT. policárpico.

polychrome (pa·likroumi) s. policromía.
polyclinic (paliklí·nik) s. policlínica.
polygamist (pali·gamist) s. polígamo.
polygamous (-gamøs) adj. polígamo.
polygamy (-gami) s. poligamia.
polyglot (pa·liglat) adj.-s. polígloto. 2 poliglota [biblia]. 3 s. mezcla de lenguajes.
polygon (pa·ligan) s. GEOM. polígono.
polygonal (pøli·gønal) adj. poligonal.
polygraph (pa·ligræf) s. polígrafo [escritor]. 2 multicopista.
polyhedral (paliji·dral) adj. poliédrico, poliedro.
polyhedron (-drøn) s. GEOM. poliedro.
polymer (pa·limø^r) s. QUÍM. polímero.
polymorphic (palimo·^rfik) adj. polimorfo.
polymorphism (-fiʃm) s. polimorfismo.
Polynesia (palinı·shia) n. pr. GEOGR. Polinesia.
Polynesian (-an) adj.-s. polinesio.
polynormial (palinou·mial) adj. MAT. de varios términos. 2 m. polinomio.
polyp (pa·lip) s. ZOOL., MED. pólipo.
polypary (pa·liperi) s. polipero.
Polyphemus (palifi·møs) n. pr. Polifemo.
polyphonic (palifa·nik) adj. polifónico.
polyphony (pøli·føni) s. MÚS. polifonía.
polypody (pa·lipoudi) s. BOT. polipodio.
polypus (pa·lipøs) s. ZOOL. pulpo. 2 MED. pólipo.
polysepalous (palise·pałøs) adj. BOT. polisépalo.
polyspermus (palispø·^rmøs) adj. BOT. polispermo.
polysyllabic (al (palisilæ·bik(al) adj. polisílabo.
polysyllable (pa·lisilabøl) s. polisílabo.
polytechnic (palite·knik) adj. politécnico. 2 s. escuela politécnica.
polytheism (pa·liziʃm) s. politeísmo.
polyvalent (-vei·lønt) adj. QUÍM. polivalente.
pomace (pø·mis) s. bagazo de manzanas.
pomaceous (pømei·shøs) adj. BOT. pomáceo.
pomade (pømei·d) s. pomada.
pomander (poumæ·ndø^r) s. pomo [bola olorosa].
pomatum (poumei·tøm) s. pomada.
pome (poum) s. BOT. pomo.
pomegranate (pa·mgrænit) s. BOT. granada. 2 BOT. granado.
pomelo (pa·møłou) s. BOT. toronja, pomelo.
Pomeranian (pamørei·nian) adj.-s. pomerano, pomeranio. 2 s. perro de Pomerania.
pomfret (pa·mfrit) s. ICT. castañola.
pommel (pø·møl) s. pomo [de la espada]. 2 perilla [del arzón]. 3 ARQ. bola, manzana.
pommel (to) tr. aporrear, dar golpes. ¶ Pret. y p. p.: pommel(l)ed; ger.: -l(l)ing.
pomp (pømp) s. pompa, fausto, aparato.
pompadour (pa·mpadø^r) s. copete [peinado].
Pompeian (pampei·an) adj.-s. pompeyano.
Pompeii (pampe·i) n. pr. HIST. Pompeya.
Pompey (pa·mpi) n. pr. Pompeyo.
pompon (pa·mpan) s. pompón.
pomposity (pampa·siti) s. pomposidad.
pompous (pa·mpøs) adj. pomposo. 2 hueco, vanidoso. 3 magnífico, brillante.
poncho (pa·nchou) s. poncho.
pond (pand) s. estanque, alberca, embalse, charca. 2 fam. el océano.
ponder (to) (pa·ndø^r) tr. ponderar, pesar, estudiar. 2 intr. to ~ on o over, reflexionar, acerca de.
ponderable (-abøl) adj. ponderable.
ponderal (-al) adj. ponderal.
ponderosity (pandøra·siti) s. ponderosidad. 2 pesadez.
ponderous (pa·ndørøs) adj. ponderoso, pesado. 2 importante, grave. 3 tedioso, cansado.

poney (pou·ni) s. PONY.
poniard (pa·nia^rd) s. puñal, almarada.
poniard (to) tr. apuñalar.
Pontic (pa·ntik) adj. póntico.
pontifex (pa·ntifeks) s. pontífice, sumo sacerdote.
pontiff (pa·ntif) s. HIST., ECLES. pontífice.
pontifical (panti·fikal) adj. pontifical, pontificio. 2 s. pl. pontifical [ornamentos, libro].
pontificate (-fikit) s. pontificado.
pontificate (to) (-fikeit) intr. pontificar.
pontil (pa·ntil) s. puntel.
pontlevis (pantle·vis) s. puente levadizo.
pontoneer, pontonier (pantø·ni^r) s. MIL. pontonero.
pontoon (pantu·n) s. pontón [para hacer puentes; barcaza]. 2 flotador [de hidroavión].
pony (pou·ni) s. jaquita, caballito. 2 cosa pequeña en su línea; copita, vasito.
poodle (pu·døl) s. perro de lanas.
pooh (pou) interj. ¡bah!, ¡quiá!, ¡uf!
pooh-pooh (to) (pu-pu) tr. desdeñar, quitar importancia a. 2 hacer mofa de.
pool (pul) s. charco, charca, balsa. 2 alberca, estanque: swimming ~, piscina. 3 polla, puesta [en ciertos juegos]. 4 fondos en común; fusión de intereses o de empresas. 5 trucos [juego].
pool (to) tr.-intr. formar una polla. 2 mancomunar [intereses, etc.].
poolroom (pu·lrum) s. (E.U.) sala de billar. 2 sala de apuestas.
poop (pup) s. MAR. popa. 2 MAR. toldilla.
poop (to) tr. MAR. embarcar [agua] por la popa.
poor (pu·ø^r) adj. pobre: ~ in spirit, pobre de espíritu; ~ thing, pobrecito, pobrecita. 2 de mala calidad, malo: ~ health, mala salud. 3 débil, abatido: ~ spirits, abatimiento. 4 enfermo, indispuesto. 5 pl. the ~, los pobres.
poorhouse (-jaus) s. hospicio, casa de caridad, asilo de pobres.
poorly (-li) adv. pobremente. 2 mal. 3 adj. enfermo, indispuesto.
poor-spirited adj. abatido, cobarde.
pop (pap) s. estallido, detonación, taponazo, pistoletazo. 2 bebida gaseosa. 3 fam. (E.U.) papá.
pop (to) tr. hacer estallar o detonar. 2 hacer saltar [un tapón]. 3 sacar, asomar, poner [de sopetón]. 4 soltar, disparar: to ~ the question, declararse, pedir en matrimonio. 5 intr. estallar, detonar; saltar [un tapón]. 6 to ~ in, entrar, meterse [de sopetón]. 7 to ~ off, morir; quedarse dormido. 8 to ~ out, salir [de sopetón]. 9 to ~ up, aparecer [de sopetón]. ¶ Pret. y p. p.: popped; ger.: -pping.
popcorn (pa·pko^rn) s. rosetas de maíz.
Pope (pou·p) s. papa, pontífice. 2 [con min.] pope.
popedom (pou·pdøm) s. papado.
popery (-pøri) s. desp. papismo, catolicismo.
pop-eyed (pa·paid) adj. de ojos saltones.
popgun (pa·pgøn) s. tirabala.
popinjay (pa·pindŷei) s. ORN. loro, papagayo. 2 ORN. picamaderos. 3 pisaverde, petimetre.
popish (pou·pish) adj. desp. católico romano.
poplar (pa·pla^r) s. BOT. álamo, chopo.
poplin (pa·plin) s. TEJ. popelina.
popliteal (popli·tial) adj. ANAT. poplíteo.
poppy (pa·pi) s. BOT. amapola. 2 BOT. adormidera.
poppycork (-kak) s. fam. majadería.
populace (pa·piulis) s. pueblo, plebe, populacho.
popular (-la^r) adj. popular. 2 corriente, general. 3 generalmente estimado; que tiene muchas simpatías. 4 de moda.
popularity (papiulæ·riti) s. popularidad; estimación general.

popularize (to) (pa·piulaṛaiš) *tr.* popularizar, vulgarizar. 2 democratizar.
populate (to) (-leit) *tr.* poblar. 2 *intr.* propagarse, multiplicarse.
population (-ei·shøn) *s.* población, populación. 2 población [habitantes].
populous (-løs) *adj.* populoso.
porbeagle (po·ʳbɪgøl) *s.* ICT. especie de tiburón.
porcelain (po·ʳsølin) *s.* porcelana.
porch (poʳch) *s.* porche, atrio, pórtico. 2 vestíbulo, entrada.
porcine (po·ʳsain) *adj.* porcuno, porcino.
porcupine (po·ʳkiupain) *s.* ZOOL. puerco espín.
pore (poʳ) *s.* poro.
pore (to) *intr. to ~ on, upon* u *over,* mirar fijamente, escudriñar, inspeccionar de cerca; leer con atención; reflexionar, meditar sobre.
porgy (po·ʳdỹi) ICT. pagro, pargo.
pork (poʳk) *s.* cerdo, carne de cerdo.
porker (po·rkøʳ) *s.* cerdo [esp. el de engorde].
pornographic (pɔrnagræ·fik) *adj.* pornográfico.
pornography (poʳna·grafi) *s.* pornografía.
porosity (pora·siti) *s.* porosidad.
porous (po·røs) *adj.* poroso, esponjoso.
porphyry (po·firi) *s.* PETROGR. pórfido.
porpoise (po·ʳpøs) *s.* ZOOL. marsopa, puerco de mar.
porraceous (pørei·shøs) *adj.* porráceo.
porridge (pa·ridỹ) *s.* gachas, puches, potaje.
porringer (pa·rindỹøʳ) *s.* escudilla.
port (poʳt) *s.* puerto [de mar o río]. 2 MAR. porta, cañonera. 3 MEC. abertura, lumbrera. 3 desveno. 5 MAR. babor. 6 porte, aire, continente. 7 vino de Oporto.
port (to) *tr.-intr.* MAR. poner o virar a babor. 2 *tr.* MIL. llevar [el fusil] terciado.
portable (poʳtabøl) *adj.* portátil.
portage (po·ʳtidỹ) *s.* porte, transporte.
portal (po·ʳtal) *s.* portal, portada. 2 vestíbulo. 3 *adj.* ANAT. porta [vena].
portcullis (poʳtkø·lis) *s.* FORT. rastrillo.
porte-cochère (po·ʳt-koshe·ʳ) *s.* puerta cochera.
portend (to) (poʳte·nd) *tr.* anunciar, presagiar.
portent (po·ʳtent) *s.* presagio. 2 portento, prodigio.
portentous (poʳte·ntøs) *adj.* ominoso, presagioso. 2 portentoso. 3 grave, solemne.
porter (po·ʳtøʳ) *s.* portero. 2 portador; faquín; mozo [de estación, hotel, etc.]. 3 (E.U.) camarero de coche cama. 4 cerveza negra y floja.
porterage (-øridỹ) *s.* porte, transporte.
portfolio (-fou·liou) *s.* carpeta, cartera. 2 cartera, ministerio. 3 cartera [de un banco, etc.].
porthole (-joul) *s.* MAR. porta, portilla. 2 FORT. tronera.
portico (po·ʳtikou) *s.* ARQ. pórtico, atrio.
portière (po·ʳtie·ʳ) *s.* portier, antepuerta.
portion (po·ʳshøn) *s.* porción, parte. 2 herencia, patrimonio, dote. 3 sino, suerte.
portion (to) *tr.* dividir, partir, distribuir. 2 dotar.
portly (po·ʳtli) *adj.* voluminoso, corpulento. 2 majestuoso, imponente.
portmanteau (poʳtmæ·ntou) *s.* maleta, maltín.
Porto Rico (po·ʳtori·kou) *n. pr.* GEOGR. Puerto Rico.
Porto Rican (ri·kan) *adj.-s.* portorriqueño.
portrait (po·ʳtrit) *s.* retrato.
portraitist (po·ʳtreitist) *s.* retratista.
portraiture (po·ʳtrei·chuʳ) *s.* retrato. 2 acción o arte de retratar.
portray (to) (poʳtrei·) *intr.* retratar.
portrayal (-al) *s.* retrato, descripción.
portress (po·ʳtris) *f.* portera [de convento].

Portugal (po·ʳchugal) *n. pr.* GEOGR. Portugal.
Portuguese (-ı·š) *adj.-s.* portugués.
portulaca (poʳchulæ·ka) *s.* BOT. verdolaga.
pose (pouš) *s.* actitud. 2 actitud afectada.
pose (to) *tr.* B. ART. colocar en cierta postura. 2 proponer, plantear [un problema, etc.]; hacer, formular [una pregunta]. 3 confundir con preguntas difíciles. 4 *intr.* B. ART. posar. 5 *to ~ as,* darse aires de, hacerse pasar por.
poser (-øʳ) *s.* pregunta difícil, pega. 2 comediante, fachendoso.
posit (to) (po·sit) *tr.* LÓG. afirmar, proponer.
position (poši·shøn) *s.* posición. 2 postura, actitud. 3 situación, ubicación. 4 colocación, empleo. 5 *to be in a ~ to,* estar en situación de.
positive (pa·šitiv) *adj.* positivo. 2 categórico, dogmático; preciso, definido. 3 indudable. 4 terco, porfiado. 5 *s.* lo positivo. 6 GRAM., ELECT., FOT. positivo.
positivism (-išm) *s.* positivismo.
positivist (-ist) *s.* positivista.
positron (pa·šitran) *s.* Fís. positrón.
posology (pøsa·lødỹi) *s.* posología.
posse (pa·si) *s.* destacamento, partida [de gente armada].
possess (to) (pøšue·s) *tr.* poseer. 2 tener, gozar de. 3 posesionar. 4 llenar [de un sentimiento, convicción, etc.]. 5 *to ~ oneself,* dominarse.
possesed (-st) *adj.* dueño; dotado. 2 poseído, poseso. 3 frío, dueño de sí mismo.
possession (-shøn) *s.* posesión. 2 dominio de sí mismo. 3 posesiones; bienes.
possessive (-siv) *adj.* posesional, posesivo. 2 *adj.-s.* GRAM. posesivo.
possessor (-søʳ) *s.* posesor, poseedor. 2 COM. portador.
possessory (-søri) *adj.* posesorio.
possibility (pasibi·liti) *s.* posibilidad. 2 contingencia; cosa posible.
possible (pa·sibøl) *adj.* posible: *as soon as ~,* cuanto antes.
possibly (pa·sibli) *adv.* posiblemente, quizá.
post (pou·st) *s.* poste, pilar, pie derecho. 2 MIL. puesto. 3 puesto, sitio, empleo, cargo. 4 factoría [comercial]. 5 posta [para viajar]: ~ *chaise,* silla de posta. 6 correo, estafeta; correos: ~ *card,* tarjeta postal; ~ *office,* servicio o casa de correo: *by return of ~,* a vuelta de correo. 7 *adv.* por la posta, con rapidez.
post (to) *tr.* anunciar [con carteles]; fijar [carteles]. 2 poner en lista expuesta al público. 3 apostar, situar. 4 enviar por correo, echar al correo. 5 COM. pasar los asientos de un libro al libro mayor. 6 enterar, poner al corriente. 7 *intr.* viajar por la posta.
postage (-idỹ) *s.* porte de correos, franqueo: ~ *stamp,* sello de correos.
postal (-al) *adj.* postal: ~ *order,* giro postal.
postbox (-baks) *s.* buzón de correos.
postboy (-boi) *s.* postillón. 2 cartero.
postdate (-deit) *s.* posfecha.
postdate (to) (poustdei·t) *tr.* posfechar.
poster (pou·støʳ) *s.* cartel, anuncio. 2 fijador de carteles. 3 caballo de posta.
poster (to) *tr.* fijar carteles en.
posterior (pasti·riøʳ) *adj.* posterior. 2 trasero. 3 *s. pl.* trasero, nalgas.
posteriority (pastiria·riti) *s.* posterioridad.
posterity (paste·riti) *s.* posteridad.
postern (pou·støʳn) *s.* FORT. poterna. 2 puerta falsa.

postgraduate (poustgræ·dẏuit) *s.* estudiante que ha recibido un grado y hace estudios superiores.
posthaste (pu·stjei·st) *adv.* a toda prisa, rápidamente.
posthouse (-jaus) *s.* posta, casa de postas.
posthumous (pa·stiumøs) *adj.* póstumo.
postil (po·stil) *s.* nota, apostilla.
postil(l)ion (pousti·lion) *s.* postillón.
postman (pou·stmæn) *s.* cartero.
postmark (-ma·ʳk) *s.* matasellos.
postmaster (-mæstøʳ) *s.* administrador de correos.
postmeridian (-møri·dian) *adj.* postmeridiano, de la tarde.
post mortem (examination) (mo·ʳtem) *s.* autopsia.
post-office *adj.* de correos: ~ *box*, apartado de correos, *casilla postal.
postoperative (-a·pøreitiv) *adj.* postoperatorio.
postpaid (-peid) *adj.* con franqueo pagado.
postpone (to) (poustpou·n) *tr.* aplazar, diferir, suspender. *2* posponer.
postponement (-mønt) *s.* aplazamiento. *2* posposición.
postpose (to) (-pou·s) *tr.* GRAM. posponer.
postposition (-pŏi·shøn) *s.* posposición.
postprandial (-præ·ndial) *adj.* de sobremesa.
postschool (pou·stskul) *adj.* postescolar.
postscript (-skri·pt) *s.* posdata.
postulant (pa·schulant) *s.* postulante. *2* postulanta.
postulate (-leit) *s.* postulado.
postulate (to) *tr.* postular.
postulation (-ei·shøn) *s.* póstula, postulación.
postulator (pa·schuleitøʳ) *s.* postulador.
posture (pa·schuʳ) *s.* postura, actitud, posición. *2* estado, situación. *3* disposición [de ánimo].
posture (to) *tr.* poner en una actitud. *2 intr.* adoptar una actitud.
postwar (pou·stuoʳ) *s.* postguerra. *2 adj.* de postguerra.
posy (pou·ši) *s.* ramillete [de flores]. *2* ant. mote o cifra en verso.
pot (pat) *s.* marmita, olla, puchero, pote, jarro: *to go to the ~*, fracasar, arruinarse; *to keep the ~ boiling*, ganarse la vida; mantener la actividad. *2* maceta, tiesto. *3* orinal. *4* polla [en el juego]. *5* gran cantidad [de dinero]
pot (to) *tr.* cocer en marmita. *2* conservar en potes. *3* poner en macetas. *4* fam. ganar, conseguir. *5* disparar contra. *6 intr.* tirar, disparar. ¶ Pret. y p. p.: *potted;* ger.: *-tting*.
potable (pou·tabøl) *adj.* potable.
potash (pa·tæsh) *s.* QUÍM. potasa.
potassic (pøtæ·sik) *adj.* potásico.
potassium (-siøm) *s.* QUÍM. potasa.
potation (potei·shøn) *s.* potación, bebida. *2* trago.
potato (pøtei·tou) *s.* BOT. patata; *papa: ~ chips*, patatas fritas a la inglesa; *sweet ~*, batata, patata de Málaga, bonito. *2* fam. persona, tipo.
potbellied (pa·tbelid) *adj.* barrigón, panzudo.
potbelly (pa·tbeli) *s.* barriga, panza.
potboy (pa·tboi) *s.* (Ingl.) mozo de taberna.
potence (pou·tøns) *s.* potencia, fuerza.
potency (-i) *s.* potencia, poder. *2* autoridad. *3* fuerza, actividad. *4* potencia [procreadora]. *5* fig. potencia [pers. de poder o autoridad].
potent (tønt) *adj.* potente, poderoso. *2* eficaz.
potentate (-tønteit) *s.* potentado.
potential (pøte·nshal) *adj.-s.* potencial.
potentiality (pøtønshiæ·liti) *s.* potencialidad. *2* potencia, posibilidad.
potentilla (poutønti·la) *s.* BOT. cincoenrama.

potentiometer (pøtenshia·mitøʳ) *s.* ELECT. potenciómetro.
pothanger (pa·tjængøʳ) *s.* llares.
pother (pa·ðøʳ) *s.* nube de polvo o de humo asfixiante. *2* barahúnda, alboroto, agitación.
pother (to) *tr.* preocupar, atormentar. *2* alborotar. *3 intr.* agitarse, alborotarse.
potherb (pa·tjøʳb) *s.* hortaliza.
pothole (pa·tjoul) *s.* GEOL. marmita.
pothook (-juk) *s.* llares. *2* garabato [en la escritura].
pothouse (-jaus) *s.* cervecería; taberna.
potion (pou·shøn) *s.* trago, toma [de medicina, etc.].
potluck (pa·tløk) *s.* comida sin cumplidos; lo que haya: *to take ~*, hacer penitencia, comer de lo que haya.
potpourri (poupuri·) *s.* baturrillo, mezcolanza. *2* MÚS. popurrí.
potsherd (pa·tshøʳd) *s.* tiesto, casco [pedazo de vasija].
pottage (pa·tidẏ) *s.* menestra, potaje.
potter (pa·tøʳ) *s.* alfarero, ollero: *potter's wheel*, torno de alfarero.
potter (to) *intr.* ocuparse en fruslerías. *2* vagar, haraganear.
pottery (-i) *s.* alfarería. *2* vasijas de barro.
pouch (pauch) *s.* bolsa, saquito. *2* faltriquera. *3* cartucho. *4* abazón. *5* ANAT., ZOOL. bolsa, saco.
pouch (to) *tr.* embolsar. *2* fruncir [los labios]; hinchar [los carrillos]. *3* dar forma de bolsa. *4* aguantar, sufrir. *5 intr.* formar bolsa.
poulard (pula·ʳd) *s.* polla cebada.
poulp (e (pulp) *s.* ZOOL. pulpo.
poulterer (pou·ltørøʳ) *s.* pollero, gallinero, recovero.
poultice (pou·ltis) *s.* cataplasma, bizma.
poultice (to) *tr.* bizmar, poner una cataplasma a.
poultry (pou·ltri) *s.* pollería, aves de corral.
punce (pauns) *s.* grasilla, arenilla. *2* polvo para estarcir: *~ bag*, cisquero. *3* garra, zarpa. *4* zarpazo. *5* salto súbito.
pounce (to) *tr.* estarcir. *2* polvorear con grasilla, etc. *3* pulir, apomazar. *4* calar, adornar con agujeros. *5* repujar [oro o plata]. *6 intr. to ~ in* o *into*, entrar de sopetón. *7 to ~ at, on* o *upon*, saltar, abalanzarse sobre.
pound (paund) *s.* libra [peso de 16 onzas]. *2* libra esterlina. *3* corral de concejo, depósito público para el ganado. *4* prisión, encierro. *5* vivero de peces.
pound (to) *tr.* moler, majar, machacar. *2* golpear, aporrear. *3* encerrar, acorralar. *4 intr.* golpear. *5* trabajar duro. *6* andar, etc., pesadamente.
pounder (-øʳ) *s.* golpeador, machacador. *2* mano de almirez; almirez. *3* cosa, pez, etc., que pesa una libra.
pound-foolish *adj.* gastador, derrochador.
pour (poʳ) *s.* vestimiento; caída, lluvia.
pour (to) *tr.* verter, derramar, echar, arrojar, emitir. *2 intr.* fluir, correr, caer. *3* salir a chorros. *4* ir, entrar, salir, etc., en gran número. *5* llover copiosamente, diluviar.
pout (paut) *s.* mohín [con los labios]; puchero. *2* ICT. nombre de varios peces. *3 pl.* berrinche.
pout (to) *intr.* hacer mohínes o pucheros; mostrar mal humor.
pouter (-øʳ) *s.* perrsona que pone mal gesto. *2* ORN. *pouter* o *~ pigeon*, paloma buchona.
poverty (pa·vøʳti) *s.* pobreza, indigencia.
poverty-stricken *adj.* muy pobre, indigente.

powder (pau·dø^r) s. polvo; polvillo. 2 polvos [de tocador]: ~ *box*, polvera; ~ *puff*, borla. 3 pólvora: ~ *magazine*, polvorín, santabárbara.
powder (to) tr. polvorear. 2 empolvar, poner polvos a. 3 pulverizar. 4 intr. empolvarse, ponerse polvos. 5 pulverizarse.
powdered (-d) adj. pulverizado, en polvo.
powdery (-i) adj. pulverulento. 2 friable. 3 polvoriento. 4 empolvado.
power (pau·ø^r) s. poder, facultad, virtud. 2 poder, fuerza, pujanza, poderío. 3 poder, potestad, autoridad, dominio, influencia: *executive* ~, poder ejecutivo; *in one's* ~, en poder de uno; *the powers that be*, las autoridades constituidas. 4 DER. poder: ~ *of attorney*, poder, procuración. 5 facultad [física o moral]. 6 potencia [estado soberano]. 7 MAT., FÍS. potencia. 8 energía, fuerza mecánica o motriz: ~ *plant*, instalación generadora de fuerza motriz; central eléctrica; AUTO. grupo motor; ~ *reactor*, reactor, generador de energía; ~ *shovel*, excavadora mecánica. 9 pl. potestades [angélicas].
power (to) tr. accionar, impulsar.
powerful (-ful) adj. poderoso. 2 fuerte. 3 intenso, potente. 4 fam. grande, considerable.
powerhouse (-jaus) s. central eléctrica.
powerless (-lis) adj. impotente, ineficaz. 2 sin autoridad o capacidad [para un acto].
powwow (pau·uau) s. hechicero indio. 2 (E.U.) ceremonia india, conferencia de los indios o con los indios. 3 fig. reunión, congreso.
pox (paks) s. MED. enfermedad que produce erupciones pustulosas. 2 MED. sífilis.
pozz(u)olana (patsøla·na) s. puzolana.
practicability (præktikabi·liti) s. practicabilidad.
practicable (præ·ktikabøl) adj. practicable. 2 factible, hacedero. 3 transitable.
practical (-al) adj. práctico. 2 virtual, de hecho. 3 ~ *joke*, broma, chasco.
practically (-i) adv. prácticamente. 2 de hecho, casi poco menos que.
practice (præ·ktis) s. práctica: *in* ~, en la práctica. 2 costumbre: *to make a* ~ *of*, tener por costumbre. 3 clientela. 4 arteria, estratagema.
practice (to) tr.-intr., **practiced** adj. s. = TO PRACTISE, PRACTISED.
practician (prækti·shøn) s. persona práctica. 2 PRACTITIONER.
practise (to) (præ·ktis) tr.-intr. practicar. 2 ejercitarse en. 3 ejercer [una profesión]. 4 tr. ejercitar, adiestrar.
practised (-t) adj. práctico, versado.
practising (-ing) adj. en ejercicio [médico, abogado, etc.].
practitioner (prækti·shønø^r) s. médico, etc., que ejerce: *general* ~, médico de medicina general.
praetexta (prite·ksta) s. pretexta.
praetor (prı·to^r) s. pretor.
praetorial (prito·rial) adj. pretorial.
praetorian (prito·rian) adj.-s. pretoriano.
praetorium (prito·riøm) s. pretorio.
pragmatic (al (prægmæ·tik(al) adj. pragmático. 2 oficioso, entrometido. 3 pedante, dogmático. 4 *pragmatic sanction*, pragmática sanción.
pragmatism (præ·gmætišm) s. pragmatismo.
Prague (preig) n. pr. GEOGR. Praga.
prairie (pre·ri) s. pradera, llanura, sabana: ~ *dog*, perro de las praderas; ~ *wolf*, coyote.
praise (preiš) s. alabanza, elogio, encomio, aplauso. 2 celeridad, fama.

praise (to) tr. alabar, encomiar, ensalzar: *to* ~ *to the skies*, poner en las nubes.
praiseworthy (-uø^rdi) adj. laudable, loable, digno de encomio.
praline (pra·lin) s. almendra garapiñada.
pram (pram) s. (Ingl.) cochecito de niño.
prance (præns) s. cabriola, trenzado [del caballo].
prance (to) intr. cabriolar, trenzar [el caballo]. 2 cabalgar o andar pavoneándose.
prancer (-ø^r) s. caballo pisador o trenzador.
prandial (præ·ndial) adj. de la comida.
prank (prænk) s. travesura, retozo, broma.
prank (to) tr. adornar, emperifollar. 2 intr. emperifollarse.
prankish (-ish) adj. travieso, retozón.
prate (preit) s. charla, cháchara.
prate (to) tr. charlar, parlotear.
prater (-ø^r) s. hablador, charlatán.
pratique (prati·k) s. MAR. libre plática.
prattle (præ·tøl) s. charla, cháchara, parloteo.
prattle (to) intr. charlar, chacharear, parlotear. 2 murmurar [un arroyo, etc.].
prawn (pron) s. ZOOL. camarón, quisquilla, langostino.
pray (to) (prei) tr.-intr. rogar, pedir, suplicar. 2 *pray tell me*, haga el favor de decirme. 3 intr. orar, rezar.
prayer (pre·ø^r) s. ruego, súplica, petición. 2 rezo, oración, plegaria; ~ *book*, devocionario; *to say one's prayers*, rezar, decir sus oraciones. 3 pl. preces.
prayerful (-ful) adj. piadoso, devoto.
praying mantis (prei·ing ma·ntis) s. ENT. mantis religiosa.
preach (to) (prı·ch) tr.-intr. predicar, semonear.
preacher (-ø^r) s. predicador.
preachify (to) (-ifai) intr. fam. predicar molestamente, sermonear.
preaching (-ching) s. predicación. 2 sermón.
preachment (-mønt) s. desp. prédica, arenga.
preacquaint (to) (prıakuei·nt) tr. dar a conocer de antemano.
preadamite (prıæ·damait) adj.-s. preadamita.
preadmonition (prıædma·nishøn) s. advertencia previa.
preamble (prıæ·mbøl) s. preámbulo.
prearrange (to) (prıarei·ndỹ) tr. arreglar o disponer de antemano.
prebend (pre·bønd) s. prebenda. 2 prebendado.
prebendary (pre·bønderi) s. prebendado.
precarious (prike·riøs) adj. precario. 2 incierto, inseguro. 3 gratuito, infundado.
precaution (priko·shøn) s. precaución.
precautionary (-eri) adj. de aviso, de precaución.
precede (to) (prısı·d) tr.-intr. preceder. 2 tener derecho a preceder.
precedence, -cy (prısı·døns, -si) s. precedencia; derecho de precedencia. 2 prioridad, anterioridad.
precedent (prısı·dønt) adj. precedente, antecedente, anterior, prior. 2 s. (pre·sødønt) precedente.
preceding (prısı·ding) adj. precedente, que precede.
precentor (prise·ntø^r) s. ECLES. chantre, capiscol.
precept (prı·sept) s. precepto. 2 DER. auto, mandato.
preceptive (prise·ptiv) adj. preceptivo. 2 didáctico.
preceptor (prise·ptø^r) m. preceptor.
preceptorial (-torial) adj. de preceptor.
precession (prise·shøn) s. ASTR. precesión.

precinct (prɪ·sinkt) *s.* recinto; interior de un edificio, etc. 2 distrito. 3 *pl.* inmediaciones.
preciosity (preshia·siti) *s.* LIT. preciosismo.
precious (pre·shøs) *adj.* precioso, preciado. 2 caro, amado. 3 culterano. 4 fig. bueno, considerable. 5 *adv.* mucho, muy: ~ *little*, muy poco.
preciously (-li) *adv.* preciosamente. 2 extremadamente, muy.
precipice (pre·sipis) *s.* precipicio, despeñadero.
precipitance, -cy (prisi·pitans, -si) *s.* precipitación.
precipitant (-pitant) *adj.* precipitado. 2 arrebatado, temerario. 3 *s.* QUÍM. precipitante.
precipitate (-piteit) *adj.* precipitado. 2 súbito. 3 *s.* QUÍM. precipitado.
precipitate (to) *tr.* precipitar, despeñar. 2 precipitar, apresurar. 3 QUÍM., METEOR. precipitar. 4 *intr.* precipitarse.
precipitation (-ei·shøn) *s.* precipitación. 2 derrumbamiento.
precipitous (prisi·pitøs) *adj.* precipitoso, pendiente, escarpado.
precise (prisai·s) *adj.* preciso, claro, distinto; exacto, justo, mismo. 2 rígido, formal, meticuloso.
preciseness (-nis) *s.* precisión, distinción, claridad. 2 rigidez, meticulosidad.
precisian (prisi·ŷan) *s.* rigorista; formulista.
precision (prisi·ŷøn) *s.* precisión, exactitud.
preclude (to) (prikliu·d) *tr.* impedir, excluir, hacer imposible.
precocius (prikou·shøs) *adj.* precoz. 2 temprano.
precocity (prika·siti) *s.* precocidad.
precognition (prɪkagni·shøn) *s.* precognición.
pre-Columbian (prɪkølø·mbian) *adj.* precolombino.
preconception (prɪkønse·pshøn) *s.* prejuicio, preocupación, idea preconcebida.
preconization (prɪkønišei·shøn) *s.* preconización. 2 proclamación, publicación.
preconize (to) (prɪ·kønaiš) *tr.* preconizar. 2 proclamar, pregonar.
precool (prɪku·l) *tr.* preenfriar. 2 enfriar [frutas, etc.] antes de embarcarlas.
precordial (prɪko·ʳdial) *adj.* ANAT. precordial.
precursor (prikø·ʳsøʳ) *s.* precursor.
precursory (-sori) *adj.* precursor; premonitorio.
predaceous, predacious (pridei·shøs) *adj.* rapaz, de presa, de rapiña.
predecease (to) (prɪ·disɪs) *tr.-intr.* premorir.
predecessor (pre·disesøʳ) *s.* predecesor, antecesor. 2 antepasado, abuelo.
predella (prede·la) *s.* predela.
predestinate (prɪde·stinit) *adj.-s.* predestinado.
predestinate (to) (-tineit) *tr.* predestinar.
predestination (-ei·shøn) *s.* predestinación.
predestine (to) (prɪde·stin) *tr.* predestinar.
predeterminate (prɪditø·ʳmineit) *adj.* predeterminado.
predetermination (-ei·shøn) *s.* predeterminación.
predetermine (to) (prɪditø·ʳmin) *tr.* predeterminar.
predicable (pre·dikabøl) *adj.* que puede afirmarse [de]. 2 *adj.-s.* LÓG. predicable.
predicament (pridi·kamønt) *s.* LÓG. predicamento. 2 apuro, aprieto, situación desgraciada.
predicant (pre·dikant) *adj.* de predicadores [orden].
predicate (pre·dikit) *s.* LÓG., GRAM. predicado.
predicate (to) (pre·dikeit) *tr.* afirmar. 2 LÓG., GRAM. predicar.

predication (-ei·shøn) *s.* afirmación, aserción. 2 LÓG., GRAM. predicación.
predict (to) (pridi·kt) *tr.* predecir, vaticinar.
prediction (-kshøn) *s.* predicción, vaticinio.
predictive (-tiv) *adj.* que predice.
predilection (predile·kshøn) *s.* predilección.
predispose (to) (pridispou·š) *tr.* predisponer.
predisposition (prɪdispøsi·shøn) *s.* predisposición.
predominance, -cy (prida·minans, -si) *s.* predominio, predominación.
predominant (-ant) *adj.* predominante.
predominate (to) (-eit) *intr.* predominar, prevalecer.
pre-eminence (prɪ-e·minøns) *s.* superioridad, supremacía.
pre-eminent (-t) *adj.* preeminente.
preen (to) (prɪn) *tr.* limpiar y componer [sus plumas] el ave. 2 componerse, acicalarse.
pre-engage (to) (prɪ-engei·dŷ) *tr.* apalabrar; contratar de antemano.
pre-exist (to) (prɪ-egši·st) *intr.* preexistir.
pre-existence (-øns) *s.* preexistencia.
pre-existent (-ønt) *adj.* preexistente.
prefabricate (to) (prɪfæ·brikeit) *tr.* prefabricar.
preface (pre·fis) *s.* prefacio, prólogo. 2 LITURG. prefacio.
preface (to) *tr.* prologar; introducir, comenzar.
prefatory (pre·fatori) *adj.* de introducción, preliminar.
prefect (prɪ·fekt) *s.* prefecto.
prefect (i) al (prɪfektø·r(i)al) *adj.* prefectoral.
prefecture (prɪfe·kchuʳ) *s.* prefectura.
prefer (to) (prifø·ʳ) *tr.* preferir, anteponer. 2 ascender, elevar, exaltar. 3 ofrecer, presentar. 4 *intr.* escoger [entre]. ¶ Pret. y p. p.: *preferred;* ger.: *-rring.*
preferable (pre·førabøl) *adj.* preferible.
preference (pre·førons) *s.* preferencia. 2 predilección. 3 DER. prioridad.
preferential (-shal) *adj.* preferente, de preferencia.
preferment (prifø·ʳmønt) *s.* ascenso, elevación, adelantamiento. 2 cargo, dignidad. 3 favorecimiento, apoyo. 4 DER. prioridad.
prefiguration (prɪfigurei·shøn) *s.* prefiguración.
prefigure (to) (prɪfi·giøʳ) *tr.* prefigurar. 2 prever, imaginar de antemano.
prefix (prɪ·fiks) *s.* prefijo, afijo.
prefix (to) (prɪfi·ks) *tr.* prefijar, anteponer.
prefloration (prɪflorei·shøn) *s.* BOT. prefloración.
prefoliation (prɪfouliei·shøn) *s.* BOT. prefoliación.
pregnable (pre·gnabøl) *adj.* expugnable.
pregnancy (-nsi) *s.* preñez, embarazo. 2 fertilidad, fecundidad.
pregnant (-ant) *adj.* preñada, embarazada, encinta. 2 fértil, fecundo. 3 preñado, lleno. 4 importante, grave; significativo.
preheat (to) (prɪjɪ·t) *tr.* calentar de antemano.
prehensible (prije·nsil) *adj.* prensil.
prehension (-shøn) *s.* prensión. 2 aprehensión [mental].
prehistoric (al) (prɪjista·rik(al) *adj.* prehistórico.
prehistory (prɪji·stori) *s.* prehistoria.
prejudge (to) (prɪdŷø·dŷ) *tr.* prejuzgar.
prejudg(e)ment (-mønt) *s.* acción de prejuzgar, prejuicio.
prejudice (pre·dŷudis) *s.* prejuicio, prevención, preocupación. 2 perjuicio, detrimento.
prejudice (to) *tr.* prevenir, predisponer. 2 perjudicar, dañar.
prejudicial (predŷudi·shal) *adj.* perjudicial.
prelacy (pre·lasi) *s.* prelacía, prelatura.

prelate (pre·lit) s. prelado.
prelature (pre·lachø^r) s. prelatura. 2 episcopado.
prelect (to) (prile·kt) intr. disertar, hablar en público.
preliminary (prili·mineri) adj.-s. preliminar.
prelude (pre·liud) s. preludio.
prelude (to) tr.-intr. preludiar.
preludial (priliu·dial), **prelusive** (-siv) adj. preliminar, introductorio.
premature (prɪmachu·ø^r) adj. prematuro.
prematurely (-li) adv. prematuramente.
premeditate (to) (prime·diteit) tr. premeditar. 2 intr. reflexionar de antemano.
premeditation (-ei·shøn) s. premeditación.
premier (prɪ·miø^r) adj. primero, principal, el más antiguo. 2 s. primer ministro.
première (premie·^r) s. TEAT. estreno. 2 primera actriz.
premise (pre·mis) s. LÓG. premisa. 2 cosa que se da por supuesta. 3 pl. local, establecimiento, casa, finca.
premise (to) (pre·maiš) tr. sentar, establecer como premisas. 2 suponer preexistente.
premium (prɪ·miøm) s. premio, galardón. 2 COM. premio, prima, interés.
premolar (prɪmou·la^r) adj.-s. premolar [diente].
premonition (prɪmoni·shøn) s. aviso, prenuncio, presentimiento.
premonitory (prɪma·nitori) adj. premonitorio.
prenatal (prɪnei·tal) adj. prenatal.
prentice (pre·ntis) s. fam. aprendiz.
preoccupancy (prɪa·kiupansi) s. ocupación previa. 2 preocupación.
preoccupation (-ei·shøn) s. preocupación. | No tiene el sentido de cuidado. 2 prejuicio. 3 PREOCCUPANCY.
preoccupied (prɪa·kiupaid) adj. preocupado.
preoccupy (to) (prɪa·kiupai) tr. preocupar [ocupar antes que otro]. 2 preocupar, absorber la atención; predisponer.
preordain (to) (prɪo^rdei·n) tr. preordinar.
prepaid (prɪpei·d) adj. pagado por adelantado; con porte pagado.
preparation (preparei·shøn) s. preparación. 2 apresto, preparativo. 3 preparado, confección.
preparative (pripæ·rativ) adj. preparatorio. 2 s. preparativo, apresto.
preparatory (pripæ·ratori) adj. preparatorio.
prepare (to) (pripe·ø^r) tr. preparar. 2 prevenir, disponer, aprestar. 3 equipar, pertrechar. 4 intr. prepararse. 5 hacer preparativos.
preparedness (pripe·ridnis) s. estado de preparación.
preparer (pripe·rø^r) s. preparador.
prepay (to) (prɪpei·) tr. pagar por adelantado. 2 franquear [una carta].
prepayment (-mønt) s. pago adelantado. 2 franqueo.
prepense (pripe·ns) adj. premeditado: with malice ~, DER. maliciosa y premeditadamente.
preponderance, -cy (pripa·ndørans, -si) s. preponderancia.
preponderant (-dørant) adj. preponderante.
preponderate (to) (-døreit) tr. preponderar.
preposition (prepøši·shøn) s. GRAM. preposición.
prepositional (-al) adj. GRAM. prepositivo.
prepositive (pripa·šitiv) adj. GRAM. antepuesto.
prepossess (to) (prɪpøše·s) tr. imbuir [de una idea, etc.]. 3 predisponer favorablemente, causar buena impresión.
prepossessing (-sing) adj. simpático, atractivo.

prepossession (-shøn) s. simpatía, preferencia, predisposición favorable.
preposterous (pripa·størøs) adj. absurdo, descabellado; ridículo.
prepotence, -cy (prɪpou·tøns, -si) s. prepotencia.
prepotent (-ønt) adj. prepotente.
prepuce (prɪ·pius) s. prepucio.
prerequisite (prɪre·kuišit) adj. previamente necesario. 2 s. requisito previo.
prerogative (prira·gativ) adj. privilegiado. 2 s. prerrogativa.
presage (pre·sidỹ) s. presagio. 2 pronóstico.
presage (to) (prisei·dỹ) tr. presagiar. 2 pronosticar.
presbyope (pre·šbioup) s. MED. présbite.
presbyopia (prešbiou·pia) s. MED. presbicia.
presbyter (pre·šbitø^r) s. presbítero.
Presbyterian (presbiti·rian) adj.-s. presbiteriano.
presbytery (pre·šbiteri) s. presbiterio. 2 casa rectoral. 3 sínodo de una iglesia presbiteriana.
prescience (prɪ·shiøns) s. presciencia.
prescient (nt) adj. presciente.
prescind (to) (prisi·nd) tr. abstraer. 2 intr. to ~ from, prescindir, hacer abstracción, de.
prescribe (to) (priskrai·b) tr. prescribir [ordenar; recetar]. 2 tr.-intr. DER. prescribir.
prescription (priskri·pshøn) s. prescripción [orden, precepto, regla; receta]. 3 DER. prescripción.
presence (pre·šøns) s. presencia: ~ of mind, presencia de ánimo; in the ~ of, en presencia de. 2 aire, porte. 3 persona de elevada dignidad; soberano. 4 adj. presence chamber, salón de audiencias.
present (-nt) adj. presente: to be ~, estar presente, asistir. 2 actual: ~ value, valor actual. 3 GRAM. activo [participio]; presente [tiempo]. 4 s. presente, la actualidad: at ~, actualmente; for the ~, por ahora. 5 presente, regalo.
present (to) (priše·nt) tr. presentar: to ~ arms, presentar armas; to ~ oneself, presentarse, personarse. 2 ofrecer [un aspecto, sus respetos, etc.]. 3 apuntar [un arma]. 4 to ~ with, regalar, obsequiar con.
presentable (priše·ntabøl) adj. presentable.
presentation (prešøntei·shøn) s. presentación: on ~, COM. a presentación; the Presentation, fiesta de la Candelaria. 2 regalo, obsequio: ~ copy, ejemplar de regalo con dedicatoria.
present-day adj. actual, de hoy, del día.
presential (priše·nshal) adj. relativo al presente.
presentient (priše·ntiønt) adj. que presiente.
presentiment (prišе·ntimønt) s. presentimiento.
presently (pre·søntli) adv. presentemente. 2 dentro de poco, al poco rato.
presentment (prišе·ntmønt) s. presentación; exhibición. 2 retrato, representación.
preservation (prešø^rvei·shøn) s. preservación. 2 conservación.
preservative (prišø·^rvativ) adj. preservativo. 2 conservativo. 3 s. preservativo.
preserve (to) (prišø·^rv) s. conserva, confitura. 2 vedado.
preserve (to) tr. perseverar, resguardar, proteger. 2 conservar, mantener. 3 conservar, curar, confitar.
preserved (prišø·^rvd) adj. en conserva, confitado.
preserver (prišø·^rvø^r) s. preservador, conservador. 2 conservero; confitero.
preside (to) (prišai·d) tr.-intr. presidir; dirigir: to ~ at o over, presidir.
presidency (pre·šidønsi) s. presidencia.

president (preˈšidønt) s. presidente.
presidential (prešideˈnshal) adj. presidencial.
presidium (prišiˈdiøm) s. presidium [soviético].
press (prés) s. multitud, tropel, muchedumbre. 2 apretura. 3 empuje, presión, apretón. 4 pliegue [de una prenda planchada]. 5 prisa, apremio. 6 prensa [máquina; periódicos]: ~ cutting, ~ clipping, recorte de prensa: in ~, en prensa. 7 imprenta, estampa. 8 armario. 9 FOT. prensa. 10 MIT. leva, enganche.
press (to) tr. apretar. 2 apiñar. 3 impeler. 4 prensar, planchar, laminar. 5 estrujar, exprimir. 6 abrumar, oprimir; apurar: to be pressed for money, estar apurado de dinero. 7 apresurar, apremiar. 8 obligar. 9 instar. 10 insistir en: to ~ one's point, insistir uno en su punto de vista. 11 estrechar, acosar. 12 estrechar [en sus brazos]. 13 MIL. hacer leva de. 14 intr. pesar, ejercer presión. 15 abrirse paso, avanzar; agolparse, apiñarse: to ~ forward, avanzar, arremeter. 16 urgir, apremiar.
pressing (-ing) adj. urgente, apremiante. 2 insistente, importuno.
pressman (-mæn) s. prensador. 2 prensista. 3 (Ingl.) periodista.
pressmark (-maᵣk) s. signatura [de biblioteca].
pressroom (-rum) s. IMPR. sala de prensas.
pressure (preˈshøᵣ) s. presión: ~ gauge, manómetro; ~ group, grupo de presión. 2 prensadura. 3 apretón. 4 impulso, empuje. 5 peso, opresión. 6 urgencia, premura, apremio. 7 ELECT. tensión.
presswork (preˈsuøᵣk) s. IMPR. impresión, tirada.
prestidigitation (prestidiḏyitei·shøn) s. prestidigitación.
prestige (preˈstidẏ) s. prestigio.
presumable (prišiuˈmabøl) adj. presumible. 2 de esperar, probable.
presume (to) (prišiuˈm) tr. presumir, suponer, dar por sentado; contar con. 2 intr. presumir. 3 to ~ to, atreverse a, tomarse la libertad de.
presumption (-šøˈmshøn) s. presunción, suposición. 2 presunción, orgullo.
presumptive (-tiv) adj. presunto, supuesto. 2 presuntivo. 3 probable.
presumptuous (-chuøs) adj. presuntuoso, presumido, atrevido.
presuppose (to) (prisøpouˈš) tr. presuponer.
pretence (prite·ns) s. pretensión. 2 presunción, ostentación. 3 fingimiento, apariencia, pretexto: under false pretences, con engaño; under ~ of, so pretexto.
pretend (to) (prite·nd) tr. aparentar, fingir, simular: to ~ to be, fingirse, dárselas de. 2 intentar. 3 tr.-intr. pretender, aspirar a.
pretended (-id) adj. falso, fingido, supuesto.
pretender (-øᵣ) s. pretendiente [a un trono, etc.]. 2 fingidor, hipócrita.
pretense (prite·ns) s. PRETENCE.
pretension (prite·nshøn) s. pretensión. 2 boato. 3 afirmación gratuita; pretexto.
pretentious (-shøs) adj. pretencioso, ostentoso, de pretensiones. 2 ambicioso, vasto.
preterit(e (pre·tørit) adj. pretérito, pasado. 2 GRAM. pretérito definido.
preterition (pretøri·shøn) s. preterición.
preternatural (pritøᵣnæ·chural) adj. preternatural.
pretext (prite·kst) s. pretexto.
pretext (to) tr. pretextar.
pretor (prɪ·tøᵣ) s. pretor.
pretorial, pretorian adj.-s. PRAETORIAL, PRAETORIAN.

pretiffy (to) (pri·tifai) tr. embellecer, adornar. ¶ Pret. y p. p.: prettified.
prettily (-li) adv. lindamente. 2 considerablemente. 3 bastante.
prettiness (-nis) s. lindeza, gentileza, bonitura.
pretty (pri·ti) adj. lindo, bonito; gracioso, elegante. 2 bueno, regular; considerable: a ~ penny, fam. un dineral, un buen pico. 3 adv. bastante; ~ well, bastante bien.
prevail (to) (privei·l) intr. prevalecer, triunfar. 2 predominar; reinar, ser general o corriente. 3 to ~ upon o with, convencer, persuadir, inducir.
prevalence (pre·valøns) s. predominio. 2 boga, uso o aceptación general.
prevalent (-ønt) adj. reinante, corriente, general, en boga.
prevaricate (to) (privæ·rikeit) intr. usar de equívocos o argucias; deformar la verdad, mentir. 2 DER. prevaricar.
prevent (to) (prive·nt) tr. prevenir, evitar, impedir, estorbar. 2 anticiparse a.
preventative (-tativ) adj.-s. PREVENTIVE.
prevention (-shøn) s. evitación, estorbo, obstáculo, impedimento.
preventive (-tiv) adj. impeditivo. 2 preventivo; profiláctico.
previous (pri·viøs) adj. previo. 2 anterior, precedente. 3 adv. ~ to, antes de.
prevision (privi·ẏøn) s. previsión, presciencia; pronóstico.
prewar (prɪ·uoᵣ) adj. antes de la guerra.
prey (prei) s. presa, rapiña, pillaje: bird of ~, ave de rapiña. 2 presa, botín, víctima: to fall a ~ to, ser presa de.
prey (to) intr. cazar y devorar. 2 rapiñar, pillar, hacer presa. 3 to ~ on, upon o at, consumir, remorder, preocupar: to ~ upon one's mind, preocupar, enloquecer.
Priam (prai·æm) n. pr. Príamo.
price (prais) s. precio; coste, costa: cost ~, precio de coste; set ~, precio fijo; at any ~, a toda costa. 2 valor, importe. 3 curso [en Bolsa].
price (to) tr. apreciar, estimar, tasar, valuar, poner precio a.
priceless (-lis) adj. inapreciable, inestimable, que no tiene precio.
prick (prik) s. pinchazo, punzada, picadura, resquemor, escrúpulo: pricks of conscience, remordimientos. 3 aguijón, púa. 4 estímulo, acicate.
prick (to) tr. pinchar, punzar, picar, agujerear; marcar con agujeros. 2 aguijonear, espolear. Gralte. con o off. 3 avivar, aguzar; enderezar. | Gralte. con up: to ~ up one's ears, aguzar los oídos o las orejas. 4 intr. pinchar, punzar, escocer. 5 agriarse, torcerse. 6 aguzarse, enderezarse.
pricker (-øᵣ) s. punzón, aguijón. 2 espina, púa.
prickle (pri·køl) s. pincho, púa, espina. 2 ardor, comezón.
prickle (to) tr. punzar, producir picazón. 2 intr. sentir una punzada o picazón.
prickly (pri·kli) adj. espinoso, lleno de púas: prickly pear, BOT. chumbera; higo chumbo. 2 que pica: ~ heat, erupción debida al calor.
pride (praid) s. orgullo: to take ~ in, enorgullecerse de. 2 soberbia, altivez, engreimiento. 3 dignidad, amor propio. 4 pompa, esplendor.
pride (to) tr. enorgullecer. 2 to ~ oneself on o upon, enorgullecerse de.
prideful (-ful) adj. orgulloso. 2 altanero.
prier (prai·øᵣ) s. curioso, fisgón, husmeador.

priest (prɪst) *m.* sacerdote. *2* presbítero.
priestcraft (-kræft) *s.* intriga atribuida a los sacerdotes.
priestess (-is) *f.* sacerdotisa.
priesthood (-tjud) *s.* sacerdocio.
prig (prig) *s.* pedante, presuntuoso; gazmoño.
priggish (-ish) *adj.* pedantesco; presuntuoso; gazmoño.
prim (prim) *adj.* relamido, estirado. *2* riguroso, exacto.
prim (to) *intr.* poner gesto estirado. *2 tr.-intr.* vestor con severidad afectada.
primacy (praɪ·masi) *s.* primacía, supremacía. *2* primacía [dignidad de primado].
primal (praɪ·mal) *adj.* prístino, original. *2* principal, fundamental.
primarily (praɪ·merili) *adv.* primariamente.
primary (-meri) *adj.* primario: ~ *coil*, ELECT. bobina primaria de inducción; ~ *school*, escuela primaria. *2* primero, prístino; de origen. *3* principal, fundamental. *4* elemental: ~ *colours*, colores elementales. *5 s.* lo elemental. *6* POL. (E.U.) elección de compromisarios.
primate (-mit) *s.* el primero o superior. *2* primado. *3* ZOOL. primate.
primatial (praimei·shal) *adj.* primacial.
prime (praim) *adj.* primero, primario, principal: ~ *minister*, primer ministro; ~ *mover*, fuente de energía; alma [de una empresa]. *2* superior, excelente. *3* MAT. primo. *4* ~ *cost*, coste de fabricación. *5 s.* prima [hora]. *6* principio, albor, amanecer. *7* flor, nata, lo mejor: *the* ~ *of life*, la flor de la edad; la edad viril. *8* ESGR. prima. *9* MAT. número primo. *10* minuto [de un grado].
prime (to) *tr.* cebar [una arma de fuego, una bomba, etc.]. *2* imprimar, dar la primera mano de color, etc., a. *3* preparar, aleccionar, instruir de antemano. *4* poner el signo (') a.
primer (prɪ·møʳ) *s.* abecedario, cartilla de lectura. *2* compendio [libro]. *3* (praɪ·møʳ) *s.* pistón fulminante.
primeval (praimɪ·val) *adj.* primitivo, prístino.
primigenial (-idẏi·nial) *adj.* primigenio.
priming hole (praɪ·ming) *s.* ART. oído.
primipara (-mi·para) *s.* primípara.
primitive (pri·mitiv) *adj.* primitivo. *2* primero, prístino.
primitivism (-išm) *s.* primitivismo.
primness (pri·mnis) *s.* remilgo, tiesura, afectación.
primogenitor (praimoudẏe·nitøʳ) *s.* antepasado.
primogeniture (-nichøʳ) *s.* primogenitura.
primordial (praimo·ʳdial) *adj.* primordial. *2* original, primitivo.
primp (primp) *tr.* vestir, arreglar. *2 intr.* vestirse, acicalarse.
primrose (pri·mrouš) *s.* BOT. vellorita, primavera. *2* color amarillo verdoso claro. *3 adj.* florido, gayo: ~ *path*, sendero florido, vida dada a los placeres.
Primulaceae (primiulei·shii) *s. pl.* primuláceas.
prince (prins) *s.* príncipe: ~ *consort*, marido de la reina; ~ *royal*, príncipe heredero.
princedom (-døm) *s.* principado.
princeling (pri·nsling) *s.* principillo.
princely (-li) *adj.* principesco, digno de un príncipe; munífico; noble, magnífico, regio.
princeps (-eps) *adj.* príncipe [edición].
princess (-is) *f.* princesa.
principal (prin·sipal) *adj.* principal. *2 s.* principal,

jefe. *3* director [de un colegio]. *4* DER. principal, poderdante. *5* principal [de un rédito].
principality (prinsipæ·liti) *s.* principado. *2 pl.* principados [espíritus angélicos].
principate (pri·nsipeit) *s.* principado.
principle (-pøl) *s.* principio [origen, fundamento; verdad fundamental, regla, ley]. *2* QUÍM. principio. *3 in* ~, en principio; *on* ~, por principio.
print (print) *s.* impresión, huella. *2* impresión, estampa: *in* ~, impreso; en letra de molde; *out of* ~, agotado. *3* lámina, grabado, estampa. *4* TEJ. estampado. *5* FOT. impresión, prueba.
print (to) *tr.-intr.* imprimir, estampar: *printed matter*, impresos; *printed goods*, estampados. *2 tr.* dar a la imprenta, publicar. *3* FOT. tirar [una prueba]. *4* imprimir o grabar [en la mente].
printer (-øʳ) *s.* impresor, tipógrafo: *printer's devil*, aprendiz de impresor. *2* estampador.
printing (-ing) *s.* impresión, estampación, estampado: ~ *office*, imprenta [establecimiento]. *2* imprenta, tipografía [arte]. *3* estampa, impreso. *4* FOT. impresión: ~ *frame*, prensa fotográfica.
prior (praɪ·øʳ) *adj.* anterior, previo. *2* que tiene prioridad. *3 adv. prior to*, antes de. *4 s.* prior.
priorate (-ørit) *s.* priorato.
prioress (-øris) *f.* priora.
priority (praia·riti) *s.* anterioridad. *2* prioridad.
priory (praɪ·øri) *s.* priorato [comunidad].
prism (prišm) *s.* GEOM., ÓPT. cristal, prisma. *2* ÓPT. *prism binocular*, prismáticos.
prismatic (prišmæ·tik) *adj.* prismático. *2* colorido, brillante.
prison (pri·šøn) *s.* prisión, cárcel; encierro: ~ *house*, cárcel; ~ *term*, condena [tiempo]; ~ *van*, coche celular.
prison (to) *tr.* encarcelar.
prisoner (pri·šnøʳ) *s.* preso; prisionero.
pristine (pri·stin) *adj.* prístino, primitivo.
privacy (praɪ·vasi) *s.* retiro, aislamiento, intimidad. *2* reserva, secreto.
private (-vit) *adj.* privado, personal, particular: ~ *affair*, asunto privado; ~ *hospital*, clínica. *2* reservado, confidencial. *3* secreto, excusado. *4* retirado, apartado, solo: *they wish to be* ~, quieren estar solos. *5 in* ~, particularmente, en secreto. *6 s.* soldado raso.
privateer (praivati·øʳ) *s.* MAR. corsario. *2* buque corsario.
privateer (to) *intr.* MAR. hacer el corso.
privately (praɪ·vitli) *adv.* privadamente. *2* reservadamente, secretamente.
privation (praivei·shøn) *s.* privación [carencia; necesidad].
privative (pri·vativ) *adj.* privativo [que causa o significa privación].
privet (pri·vit) *s.* BOT. alheña, ligustro.
privilege (pri·vilidẏ) *s.* privilegio. *2* prerrogativa; inmunidad, exención, derecho; honor.
privilege (to) *tr.* privilegiar. *2* eximir.
privileged (-d) *adj.* privilegiado.
privily (pri·vili) *adv.* privadamente; secretamente.
privity (pri·viti) *s.* conocimiento de algo reservado.
privy (pri·vi) *adj.* privado. | Ús. sólo en denominaciones como: ~ *council*, consejo privado; ~ *seal* (Ingl.) sello privado [del rey]. *2* oculto, secreto. *3 privy to*, enterado, cómplice de.
prize (praiš) *s.* premio, recompensa: ~ *fighter*, boxeador profesional. *2* premio [de lotería]. *3* presa, captura. *4* presa, botín. *5* decomiso.

prize (to) *tr.* apreciar, estimar, valuar. *2* tener en estima. *3* apresar [un buque]. *4* alzaprimar.

pro (prou) *prep.* pro [por]; en pro de: ~ *forma*, COM. pro-forma: ~ *forma invoice*, factura pro-forma; ~ *rata*, a prorrata. *2 s.* pro, razón en favor: *the pros and the cons*, el pro y el contra. *3 fam.* deportista profesional.

probabilism (pra·babilišm) *s.* probabilismo.

probability (prababi·liti) *s.* probabilidad. *2* verosimilitud.

probable (pra·babøl) *adj.* probable. *2* verosímil.

probate (prou·beit) *s.* DER. prueba legal de la validez de un testamento. *2* DER. copia auténtica de un testamento. *3 adj.* DER. testamentario.

probation (probei·shøn) *s.* probación; noviciado. *2* DER. libertad vigilada.

probationer (-øʳ) *s.* el que está a prueba. *2* novicio, delincuente en libertad vigilada.

probative (prou·bativ) *adj.* de prueba. *2* probatorio.

probe (proub) *s.* CIR. tienta, sonda, cala. *2* exploración, sondeo.

probe (to) *tr.* CIR. tentar, sondar. *2* examinar a fondo, sondear.

probity (prou·biti) *s.* probidad.

problem (pra·bløm) *s.* problema.

problematic (al (prablømæ·tik(al) *adj.* problemático. *2* enigmático.

proboscidean, -dian (proubøsi·dian) *adj.-s.* ZOOL. proboscídeo.

proboscis (proba·sis) *s.* ZOOL. probóscide, trompa.

procedure (prosi·dŷøʳ) *s.* proceder. *2* procedimiento. *3* marcha [de una operación, etc.]. *4* DER. procedimiento, tramitación.

proceed (to) (prosi·d) *intr.* proseguir, seguir adelante. *2* proceder, provenir. *3* proceder, obrar; pasar a [hacer algo]. *4* DER. actuar, proceder: *to* ~ *against*, proceder contra.

proceeding (-ing) *s.* proceder, procedimiento. *2* marcha, proceso. *3* diligencia, trámite. *4 pl.* actas. *5* DER. actuaciones, autos.

proceeds (prou·sɪdš) *s. pl.* producto, beneficios.

process (pra·ses) *s.* proceso, progreso, marcha, transcurso: *in* ~ *of time*, con el tiempo. *2* proceso [serie de fenómenos, operaciones, etc.]: *in* ~ *of construction*, en construcción. *3* procedimiento, sistema. *4* ANAT., ZOOL., BOT. apófisis, protuberancia, apéndice. *5* IMPR. procedimiento fotomecánico. *6* DER. auto, citación; proceso.

process (to) *intr.* ir en procesión. *2 tr.* procesar, citar. *3* fotograbar. *4* IND. preparar por algún procedimiento especial.

processal (-sal) *adj.* DER. procesal.

procession (-shøn) *s.* procesión. *2* cortejo, desfile; cabalgata. *3* marcha, curso.

processional (-al) *adj.* procesional. *2 s.* procesionario.

processionary (-eri) *adj.* procesional. *2* ENT. ~ *moth*, procesionaria.

proclaim (to) (proklei·m) *tr.* proclamar. *2* promulgar. *3* pregonar. *4* proscribir, poner fuera de la ley.

proclamation (praklamei·shøn) *s.* proclamación; publicación. *2* proclama, bando, edicto.

proclitic (prokli·tik) *adj.* GRAM. proclítico.

proclivity (prokli·viti) *s.* proclividad.

proconsul (proka·nsøl) *s.* procónsul.

proconsulate (-nsiulit), **proconsulship** (-nsølship) *s.* proconsulado.

procrastinate (to) (prokræ·stineit) *tr.* diferir, aplazar. *2 intr.* pasar el tiempo sin obrar, sin decidirse.

procrastination (-ei·shøn) *s.* dilación, demora.

procreate (to) (prou·krieit) *tr.* procrear.

procreation (-ei·shøn) *s.* procreación.

procreator (prou·krieitøʳ) *s.* procreador.

proctor (pra·ktøʳ) *s.* DER. especie de procurador o abogado. *2* censor [de una universidad].

procumbent (prokø·mbent) *adj.* postrado, inclinado. *2* BOT. rastrero.

procurable (prokiu·rabøl) *adj.* asequible.

procuration (prakiurei·shøn) *s.* DER. procuración, poder. *2* negociación, gestión. *3* alcahuetería.

procurator (pra·kiureitøʳ) *m.* procurador, apoderado.

procure (to) *tr.* lograr, obtener. *2* obtener o proporcionar para un trato ilícito. *3 intr.* alcahuetear.

procurement (-mønt) *s.* obtención, consecución. *2* gestión, manejo.

procurer (prokiu·røʳ) *s.* alcahuete, tercero.

procuress (-ris) *f.* alcahueta.

prod (prad) *s.* pincho, aguijada. *2* aguijonazo.

prod (to) *tr.* pinchar, picar, aguijonear. ¶ Pret. y p. p.: *prodded;* ger.: *-dding*.

prodigal (pra·digal) *adj.-s.* pródigo.

prodigality (pradigæ·liti) *s.* prodigalidad.

prodigious (prodi·dŷøs) *adj.* prodigioso, portentoso. *2* enorme, inmenso.

prodigy (pra·didŷi) *s.* prodigio, portento, maravilla.

produce (prodiu·s) *s.* producto, producción. *2* productos agrícolas.

produce (to) *tr.* presentar, exhibir. *2* producir. *3* criar, generar. *4* presentar al público; poner en escena. *5* GEOM. extender, prolongar.

producer (-øʳ) *s.* productor: *producer's goods*, ECON. bienes de producción. *2* TEAT. director. *3* CINE. productor.

product (pro·døkt) *s.* producto, producción. *2* resultado, efecto. *3* MAT., QUÍM. producto.

productile (-til) *adj.* extensible, dúctil.

production (-shøn) *s.* producción. *2* TEAT. dirección [escénica].

productive (-tiv) *adj.* productivo. *2* productor. *3* fértil, fecundo.

productivity (prodøkti·viti) *s.* productividad. *2* fertilidad.

proem (prou·em) *s.* proemio, prólogo.

proemial (prou·mial) *adj.* proemial.

profanation (profanei·shøn) *s.* profanación.

profane (profei·n) *adj.* profano. *2* irreverente, sacrílego, blasfemo. *3 s.* profano [no entendido].

profane (to) *tr.* profanar. *2* prostituir, envilecer.

profaner (profei·nøʳ) *s.* profanador.

profanity (profæ·niti) *s.* profanidad. *2* irreverencia, blasfemia, reniego.

profess (to) (profe·s) *tr.* profesar. *2* declarar, confesar: *to* ~ *oneself a Catholic*, declararse católico. *3 intr.* profesar [en una orden]. *4* profesar [ser profesor].

professed (-t) *adj.* declarado. *2* ostensible. *3* alegado, supuesto. *4* profeso.

profession (-shøn) *s.* profesión. *2* declaración, manifestación. *3* fe, religión.

professional (-shønal) *adj.-s.* profesional.

professionalism (-išm) *s.* profesionalismo.

professor (profe·søʳ) *s.* el que profesa o declara. *2* profesor, catedrático de Universidad.

professorate (-eit) *s.* profesorado.

professorship (-ship) *s.* profesorado, cátedra.

proffer (pra·fø^r) s. oferta, ofrecimiento, proposición.

proffer (to) tr. ofrecer, brindar, proponer.

proficiency (profi·shønsi) s. pericia, habilidad.

proficient (-shønt) adj. perito, diestro, versado.

profile (prou·fail) s. perfil, contorno. 2 perfil [postura]: in ~, de perfil.

profile (to) tr. dibujar de perfil; perfilar.

profit (pra·fit) s. provecho, ventaja, utilidad. 2 ganancia, beneficio; interés, renta: ~ and loss, COM. ganancias y pérdidas; ~ sharing, participación en los beneficios.

profit (to) tr. servir, aprovechar, ser útil a. 2 intr. aprovecharse, beneficiarse; adelantar, mejorar: to ~ by, aprovechar, sacar partido de.

profitable (-abøl) adj. provechoso, beneficioso, útil, lucrativo.

profiteer (prafiti·ø^r) s. explotador, logrero, acaparador.

profiteer (to) intr. logrear; aprovecharse de las circunstancias de un país para obtener beneficios excesivos.

profitless (pra·fitlis) adj. infructuoso.

profligacy (pra·fligasi) s. libertinaje, disolución.

profligate (pra·figleit) adj.-s. libertino, disoluto.

profound (profau·nd) adj. profundo. 2 hondo. 3 abstruso.

profundity (profø·nditi) s. profundidad, hondura.

profuse (profiu·s) adj. profuso. 2 pródigo, generoso.

profusion (profiu·ÿøn) s. profusión. 2 prodigalidad.

progenitor (prodÿe·nitø^r) s. progenitor.

progeniture (prodÿe·nichø^r), **progeny** (pra·dÿini) s. prole, descendencia, linaje.

prognathism (pra·gnazišm) s. prognatismo.

prognosis (pragnou·sis) s. prognosis. 2 MED. pronóstico.

prognostic (pragna·stik) s. pronóstico, presagio.

prognosticate (to) (-eit) tr. pronosticar.

prognosticator (-ø^r) s. pronosticador.

program (prou·græm) s. (E.U.) PROGRAMME.

programme s. (Ingl.) programa. 2 plan.

programming (-ing) s. programación.

progress (prou·gres) s. progreso. 2 progresos. 3 marcha, curso, carrera.

progress (to) intr. progresar. 2 marchar, avanzar. 3 tr. hacer progresar.

progression (progre·shøn) s. progresión, progreso; curso, marcha. 2 MAT., MÚS. progresión.

progressist (-sist) s. progresista.

progressive (-siv) adj. progresivo.

prohibit (to) (prouji·bit) tr. prohibir. 2 impedir.

prohibition (proujibi·shøn) s. prohibición. 2 (E.U.) prohibición de la fabricación y venta de bebidas alcohólicas: ~ law, ley seca.

prohibitionism (-išm) s. prohibicionismo.

prohibitive (prouji·bitiv) adj. prohibitivo.

project (prodÿe·kt) s. proyecto, plan, traza, idea.

project (to) tr. proyectar, idear. 2 proyectar [sombra, etc.], arrojar, despedir. 3 GEOM. proyectar. 4 intr. volar, salir fuera, sobresalir, resaltar.

projectile (-til) adj. proyectante. 2 arrojadizo. 3 s. proyectil.

projection (-shøn) s. proyección: ~ machine, CINE proyector. 2 proyecto, planeamiento. 3 saliente, resalte.

projector (-tø^r) s. proyectista, arbitrista. 2 proyector, aparato de proyecciones.

projecture (-chø^r) s. ARQ. proyectura, vuelo.

prolegomenon (prouliga·menan), pl. **-na** (-na) s. prolegómeno.

proletarian (proulite·rian) adj.-s. proletario.

proletariat(e (-ræt) s. proletariado.

proliferate (to) (proli·føreit) tr. BIOL. multiplicar [células, etc.]. 2 intr. proliferar.

proliferation (proliførei·shøn) s. proliferación.

prolific (al (proli·fik(al) adj. prolífico.

prolix (pro·liks) adj. prolijo, difuso. 2 pesado, latoso.

prolixity (proli·ksiti) s. prolijidad.

prolocutor (prola·kiutø^r) s. portavoz; representante. 2 presidente [de ciertas asambleas].

prologize (to) (prou·løgaiš) tr. prologar.

prologue (prou·lag) s. prólogo.

prolong (to) (prolo·ng) tr. prolongar, extender, continuar. 2 intr. dilatarse, entretenerse.

prolongation (prolongei·shøn) s. prolongación; continuación.

promenade (pramina·d) s. paseo [acción, lugar]: ~ deck, MAR. cubierta de paseo.

promenade (to) intr. pasear, pasearse. 2 tr. pasear. 3 pasearse por.

Prometheus (promī·ziøs) n. pr. MIT. Prometeo.

prominence, -cy (pra·minøns, -si) s. prominencia. 2 eminencia, altura. 3 relieve, distinción, eminencia.

prominent (-ønt) adj. prominente, saliente: ~ eyes, ojos saltones. 2 visible, notable. 3 distinguido, eminente.

promiscuity (pramiskiu·iti) s. promiscuidad.

promiscuous (prami·skiuøs) adj. promiscuo.

promise (pra·mis) s. promesa, promisión, ofrecimiento, palabra dada: to break one's ~, faltar a la palabra dada. 2 promesa, augurio.

promise (to) tr.-intr. prometer: Promised Land, Tierra prometida o de promisión.

promising (-ing) adj. prometiente. 2 prometedor, halagüeño.

promissory (-ori) adj. promisorio. 2 COM. ~ note, pagaré.

promontory (pra·møntori) s. promontorio.

promote (to) (prømou·t) tr. promover, adelantar, ascender. 2 promover, fomentar. 3 fundar, organizar [una empresa].

promoter (-tø^r) s. promotor, promovedor. 2 organizador de empresas industriales, etc.

promotion (-shøn) s. promoción.

prompt (prampt) adj. pronto, presto, listo, puntual: ~ payment, pronto pago; for ~ cash, al contado. 2 s. plazo para pagar una factura.

prompt (to) tr. mover, incitar, inducir, impulsar. 2 dictar, sugerir, soplar, apuntar. 3 TEAT. apuntar.

prompter (-ø^r) s. TEAT. apuntador, traspunte: prompter's box, concha.

promptitude (pra·mptitiud) s. prontitud, presteza. 2 puntualidad, diligencia.

promulgate (to) (promø·lgeit) tr. promulgar, publicar.

pronation (pronei·shøn) s. pronación.

pronator (-tø^r) s. ANAT. músculo pronador.

prone (proun) adj. prono, inclinado [a una cosa]. 2 prono, boca abajo. 3 inclinado, pendiente.

prong (prang) s. gajo, púa, diente, punta [de horca, tenedor, etc.]. 2 horca, horcón.

pronged (pra·ngd) adj. provisto de gajos o púas.

pronominal (prøna·minal) adj. GRAM. pronominal.

pronoun (prou·naun) s. GRAM. pronombre.

pronounce (to) (prønau·ns) tr. pronunciar [palabras, sentencias]. 2 declarar: to ~ one a brave *man*, declarar que uno es un valiente. *3 intr.* pronunciarse [en pro o en contra].

pronounced (-t) *adj.* pronunciado, marcado, decidido.

pronouncement (-mønt) *s.* juicio, opinión. *2* declaración, proclama, manifiesto.

pronunciamiento (prønønšiamie·ntou) *s.* pronunciamiento militar.

pronunciation (-siei·shøn) *s.* pronunciación.

proof (pruf) *s.* prueba, demostración. *2* prueba, ensayo, experimento: *to put to the ~*, poner a prueba. *3* graduación normal de las bebidas alcohólicas. *4* DER., MAT., IMPR., FOT. prueba. *5 adj.* de prueba o pruebas. *6* a prueba [de], resistente [a]: *to be ~ against*, estar hecho a prueba de, ser resistente a. *7* de graduación alcohólica normal.

proofreader (-ridø^r) *s.* IMPR. corrector de pruebas.

proofreading (-ing) *s.* IMPR. corrección de pruebas.

prop (prap) *s.* puntal, paral, tentemozo; apoyo, sostén. *2* MIN. entibo. *3* AGR. rodrigón.

prop (to) *tr.* apuntalar, sostener, apoyar. *2* MIN. entibar. *3* AGR. rodrigar. ¶ Pret. y p. p.: *propped;* ger.: *propping.*

propaganda (prapægæ·nda) *s.* propaganda.

propagandist (-dist) *s.* propagandista.

propagandize (-daiš) *tr.-intr.* hacer propaganda de o en.

propagate (to) (pra·pageit) *tr.* propagar. *2* espaciar,difundir. *3 intr.* propagarse.

propagation (-eishøn) *s.* propagación.

propagator (pra·pageitø^r) *s.* propagador.

proparoxytone (proupæra·ksitoun) *adj.-s.* GRAM. proparoxítino.

propel (to) (prope·l) *tr.* propulsar, impeler, mover. ¶ Pret. y p. p.: *propelled;* ger.: *propelling.*

propellent (-ønt) *adj.-s.* propulsor, motor.

propeller (-ø^r) *s.* propulsor. *2* hélice [de buque o avión].

propensity (prope·nsiti) *s.* propensión, tendencia. *2* inclinación, afición.

proper (pra·pø^r) *adj.* propio, característico, peculiar. *2* propio, a propósito, apropiado. *3* exacto, correcto [en su uso, aplicación, etc.]. *4* propiamente dicho. *5* GRAM. propio: *~ noun*, nombre propio. *6* MAT. propia [fracción]. *7* correcto, decoroso, conveniente; exigente en cuestiones de decoro o etiqueta. *8 s.* propio [de la misa].

properly (-li) *adv.* propiamente: *more ~*, mejor dicho. *2* convenientemente. *4* decorosamente.

property (pra·pø^rti) *s.* propiedad [atributo, cualidad]. *2* propiedad [derecho]. *3* propiedad, finca. *4* fortuna, bienes, posesiones. *5 pl.* TEAT. guardarropía, accesorios.

prophecy (pra·føsi) *s.* profecía.

prophesy (to) (pra·føsai) *tr.-intr.* profetizar, predecir. ¶ Pret. y p. p.: *prophesied.*

prophet (pra·fit) *s.* profeta.

prophetess (-is) *s.* profetisa.

prophetic (al (profe·tik(al) *adj.* profético.

prophylactic (proufilæ·ktik) *adj.* profiláctico.

prophylaxis (-sis) *s.* profilaxis.

propinquity (propi·nkuiti) *s.* propincuidad. *2* afinidad. *3* parentesco.

propitiate (to) (propi·shieit) *intr.* propiciar.

propitiation (-ei·shøn) *s.* propiciación.

propitiatory (propi·shiatori) *adj.* propiciatorio.

propitious (-shøs) *adj.* propicio. *2* favorable, feliz.

proponent (propou·nønt) *s.* proponedor, proponente.

proportion (prøpo·^rshøn) *s.* proporción [relación, correspondencia debidas]; armonía, correla-

ción: *in ~ as*, a medida que; *in ~ to*, a medida de; *out of ~*, desproporcionado. *2* MAT. proporción. *3 pl.* proporciones, tamaño.

proportion (to) *tr.* proporcionar [una cosa a otra; disponer con proporción o armonía].

proportionable (-abøl) *adj.* proporcionado.

proportional (-al) *adj.* proporcional. *2 s.* MAT. término de una proporción.

proportionate (-it) *adj.* proporcionado.

proportionate (to) (-eit) *tr.* proporcionar, ajustar.

proportioned (-d) *adj.* proporcionado [bien o mal].

proportionless (-lis) *adj.* desproporcionado.

proposal (propou·šal) *s.* propuesta, proposición. *2* oferta. *3* declaración; proposición de matrimonio.

propose (to) (prøpou·š) *tr.* proponer. *2* proponerse, tener intención de. *3* brindar [por]. *4 intr.* declararse [a una mujer].

proposer (-ø^r) *s.* proponedor, proponente.

proposition (prapøši·shøn) *s.* proposición, propuesta. *2* LÓG., MAT., RET. proposición. *3* fam. (E.U.) asunto, negocio, cosa, ocupación, etc.

propound (to) (prøpau·nd) *tr.* proponer. *2* presentar, plantear.

proprietary (prøprai·øteri) *adj.* propietario. *2* de propiedad. *3* registrado [específico]. *4 s.* propiedad, pertenencia. *5* propietarios [en general].

proprietor (-øtø^r) *s.* propietario, dueño, amo.

proprietorship (-øtø^rship) *s.* propiedad [dominio sobre una cosa].

proprietress (-øtris) *f.* propietaria.

propriety (-øti) *s.* propiedad, cualidad de apropiado. *2* corrección, decoro, decencia. *3 pl.* reglas de conducta, urbanidad.

propulsion (propø·lshøn) *s.* propulsión. *2* impulso.

propulsive (-siv) *adj.* propulsor, impelente.

pro rata (prou rei·ta) *adv.* a prorrata.

prorate (to) (prou·reit) *tr.* (E.U.) prorratear.

prorogation (prourougei·shøn) *s.* aplazamiento, suspensión.

prorogue (to) (prourou·g) *tr.* aplazar, suspender.

prosaic (prosei·ic) *adj.* prosaico.

prosaist (-ist) *s.* prosista. *2* persona prosaica.

proscenium (prosi·niøm) *s.* TEAT. proscenio.

proscribe (to) (proskrai·b) *tr.* proscribir.

proscription (proscri·pshøn) *s.* proscripción.

proscriptive (-tiv) *adj.* proscriptivo.

prose (prouš) *s.* prosa. *2* discurso pesado, lata.

prose (to) *tr.* poner en prosa. *2 intr.* escribir o hablar en estilo pesado.

prosecute (pra·sikiut) *tr.* proseguir, seguir, continuar. *2* ejercer [una profesión o actividad]. *3* DER. procesar, enjuiciar, demandar.

prosecution (-shøn) *s.* prosecución. *2* DER. proceso, demanda, acusación. *3* DER. parte actora. *4* DER. ministerio fiscal.

prosecutor (-tø^r) *s.* DER. demandante; acusador privado. *2* DER. *public ~*, fiscal.

proselyte (pra·sølait) *s.* prosélito.

proselytism (-litišm) *s.* proselitismo.

prosenchyma (prase·nkima) *s.* BOT., ZOOL. prosénquima.

prosily (prou·šili) *adv.* prosaicamente. *2* pesadamente, fastidiosamente.

prosodic (prasa·dik) *adj.* métrico [relativo a la métrica].

prosody (pra·sødi) *s.* métrica.

prosopopoeia (prousoupøpi·a) *s.* RET. prosopopeya.

prospect (pra·spekt) *s.* perspectiva, paisaje, panorama. *2* mirada a lo lejos, en el futuro. *3* expectativa, esperanza, probabilidad, perspectiva: *in*

~, en perspectiva, probable; *man of good prospects*, hombre de porvenir. *4* situación, orientación. *5* MIN. indicio de veta.
prospect (to) *tr.* explorar [terrenos] en busca de oro, petróleo, etc. *2* intr. *to* ~ *for*, buscar [oro, petróleo, etc.]
prospecting (-ing) *s.* MIN. prospección.
prospective (-tiv) *adj.* probable, posible, en perspectiva, futuro. *2 s.* vista, perspectiva.
prospector (-tø͡ᵉ) *s.* MIN. buscador.
prospectus (-tøs) *s.* prospecto, programa.
prosper (to) (pra·spø͡ᵉ) *tr.-intr.* prosperar.
prosperity (praspe·riti) *s.* prosperidad.
prosperous (pra·spørøs) *adj.* próspero. *2* favorable.
prostate (pra·steit) *s.* ANAT. próstata.
prosthesis (pra·szesis) *s.* CIR., GRAM. prótesis.
prostitute (pra·stitiut) *s.* prostituta.
prostitute (to) *tr.* prostituir. *2 intr.* prostituirse.
prostitution (prastitiu·shøn) *s.* prostitución.
prostrate (pra·streit) *adj.* postrado, prosternado. *2* postrado, abatido. *3* BOT. tendido.
prostrate (to) *tr.* postrar. *2* abatir. *3* arruinar. *4* *intr.-ref.* postrarse, prosternarse.
prostration (prastrei·shøn) *s.* prostración.
prosy (prou·ši) *adj.* prosaico. *2* latoso, insulso.
protagonist (protæ·gønist) *s.* protagonista.
protasis (pra·tasis) *s.* GRAM. prótasis.
protean (prou·tian) *adj.* proteico.
protect (to) (prøte·kt) *tr.* proteger.
protection (-shøn) *s.* protección. *2* salvoconducto.
protectionism (-shønism) *s.* EC. POL. proteccionismo.
protective (-tiv) *adj.* protector. *2* proteccionista. *3 s.* protección, resguardo [cosa que protege].
protector (-tø͡ᵉ) *s.* protector.
protectorate (-tørit) *s.* protectorado.
protectress (-tris) *s.* protectora.
proteic (prou·tiik) *adj.* QUÍM. proteico.
protein (prou·tiin) *s.* QUÍM. proteína.
pro-tempore *adj.* interino.
protest (prou·test) *s.* protesta: *under* ~, protestando, con reservas. *2* protestación. *3* DER. protesto.
protest (to) (prote·st) *tr.* protestar [declarar, afirmar, confesar]. *2* protestar de o contra; recusar. *3* DER. protestar [una letra]. *4 intr.* protestar, hacer protestas.
Protestant (pra·tistant) *adj.-s.* protestante.
Protestantism (-išm) *s.* protestantismo.
protestation (pratestei·shøn) *s.* protesta; protestación.
protester (prote·stø͡ᵉ) *s.* el que protesta.
prothesis (pra·zisis) *s.* CIR., GRAM. prótesis.
prothonotary (proza·nøteri) *s.* protonotario.
prothorax (prozou·ræks) *s.* ENT. protórax.
protocol (prou·tøkal) *s.* protocolo.
protocol (to) *tr.* protocolizar.
protomartyr (proutøma·ʳtø͡ᵉ) *s.* protomártir.
proton (prou·tan) *s.* FÍS. y QUÍM. protón.
protoplasm (prou·tøplæšm) *s.* BIOL. protoplasma.
prototype (-taip) *s.* prototipo, arquetipo.
protoxid (prouta·ksaid) *s.* QUÍM. protóxido.
protozoan (proutøšo·uan) *adj.-s.* ZOOL. protozoo, protozoario.
protract (to) (protræ·kt) *tr.* alargar, prolongar, dilatar [esp. en el tiempo]. *2* levantar [un plano] por medio del transportador.
protractile (-til) *adj.* protráctil.
protractor (-tø͡ᵉ) *s.* prolongador. *2* transportador [instrumento]. *3* ANAT. músculo extensor.

protrude (to) (protru·d) *tr.* sacar, hacer salir o sobresalir. *2 intr.* salir fuera, sobresalir.
protrusion (protru·ẙøn) *ș.* protrusión.
protuberance (protiu·børans) *s.* protuberancia.
protuberant (-ant) *adj.* prominente, saliente.
protuberate (to) (-reit) *intr.* sobresalir, abultar.
proud (praud) *adj.* orgulloso, soberbio, altanero, arrogante, engreído. *2* orgulloso, satisfecho, ufano: *to be* ~ *of*, enorgullecerse de. *3* magnífico, espléndido, noble, bello.
prove (to) (pruv) *tr.* probar, demostrar, evidenciar, justificar. *2* probar, experimentar, poner a prueba, comprobar. *3.* establecer la validez de [un testamento]. *4* ARIT. hacer la prueba de. *5* IMPR. sacar una prueba de. *6 intr.* salir, resultar [bien, mal, etc.]; demostrar que se es [apto, etc.]. ¶ P. p.: *proved* o *proven.*
provenance (prou·vønans) *s.* PROVENIENCE.
Provençal (prouvansa·l) *adj.-s.* provenzal.
Provence (prouva·nš) *n. pr.* GEOGR. Provenza.
provender (pra·vøndø͡ᵉ) *s.* pienso, forraje.
provenience (provi·niøns) *s.* origen, procedencia.
proverb (pra·vø͡ᵉb) *s.* proverbio, refrán, sentencia. *2* nombre, pers. o cosa proverbial.
proverbial (prouvø·ʳbial) *adj.* proverbial. *2* sentencioso.
provide (to) (prøvai·d) *tr.* proveer, abastecer, equipar: *to* ~ *with*, proveer de. *2* suministrar, proporcionar. *3* estipular. *4 intr. to* ~ *for*, proveer a; sufragar los gastos de; dotar, colocar, proveer de medios de vida; estipular. *5 to* ~ *against*, prevenir, precaverse contra.
provided (-id) *conj.* ~ *that*, con tal que, siempre que, a condición de o que.
providence (pra·vidøns) *s.* providencia, previsión, economía. *2* providencia divina. *3* (con may.) la Providencia, Dios.
provident (-nt) *adj.* próvido, providente, previsor. *2* frugal, económico.
providential (pravide·nshal) *adj.* providencial.
provider (prøvai·dø͡ᵉ) *s.* proveedor.
province (pra·vins) *s.* provincia. *2* región, distrito. *3* esfera, campo [de actividad, etc.]. *4* competencia, incumbencia.
provincial (prøvi·nshal) *adj.* provincial. *2* provinciano, rústico. *3 s.* provincial. *4* provinciano.
provision (prøvi·ẙøn) *s.* provisión, prevención. *2* aprovisionamiento. *3* medida, disposición, providencia: *to make* ~ *for*, proveer a; asegurar el porvenir de. *4* cláusula, estipulación. *5 pl.* provisiones.
provision (to) *tr.* aprovisionar, abastecer.
provisional (-al) *adj.* provisional.
proviso (prøvai·šou) *s.* estipulación, condición, requisito.
provisory (prøvai·šori) *adj.* provisorio. *2* condicional.
provocation (pravøkei·shøn) *s.* provocación. *2* cosa que irrita o exaspera.
provocative (prøva·kativ) *adj.* provocativo. *2* irritante, exasperador.
provoke (to) (prøvou·k) *tr.* provocar. *2* irritar, encolerizar. *3 intr.* ser irritante, causar enojo.
provoking (-ing) *adj.* provocativo. *2* irritante, exasperador.
provost (pra·vøst) *s.* preboste. *2* prepósito, deán. *3* (Ingl.) director de un colegio universitario.
prow (prau) *s.* proa. *2* MAR. tajamar.
prowess (prau·is) *s.* valor, bizarría. *2* proeza. *3* destreza.

prowl (to) (praul) *tr.-intr.* rondar [para robar, hacer presa, etc.], andar acechando, merodear.
proximal (pra·ksimal) *adj.* BIOL. proximal.
proximate (-it) *adj.* próximo, inmediato.
proximity (praksi·miti) *s.* proximidad.
proximo (pra·ksimou) *adv.* del próximo mes.
proxy (pra·ksi) *s.* procuración, poder, delegación: *by ~*, por poderes. *2* apoderado, delegado.
prude (prud) *s.* remilgada, mojigata, gazmoña.
prudence (pru·dəns) *s.* prudencia.
prudent (-dənt) *adj.* prudente.
prudential (prude·nshal) *adj.* prudencial.
prudery (pru·dəri) *s.* remilgo, mojigatería, gazmoñería, pudibundez.
prudish (-ish) *adj.* remilgado, mojigato, gazmoño.
prune (prun) *s.* ciruela pasa; ciruela.
prune (to) *tr.* podar, escamondar, mondar, recortar. *2* TO PREEN.
pruning hook o **knife** (-ing) *s.* podadera, podón.
prurience, -cy (pru·riəns, -si) *s.* comezón, prurito. *2* lascivia.
prurient (-ənt) *adj.* lascivo. *2* deseoso, curioso.
prurigo (prurai·gou) *s.* MED. prurigo.
Prussian (prø·shan) *adj.-s.* prusiano.
prussic (prø·sik) *adj.* prúsico.
pry (prai) *s.* atisbo, fisgoneo. *2* curioso, fisgón, entremetido. *3* palanca, alzaprima.
pry (to) *intr.* espiar, acechar, fisgar, escurdiñar, entremeterse. | Gralte. con *into. 2 tr.* alzaprimar, apalancar: *to ~ open*, abrir, forzar [con palanca]. *3 to ~ out*, arrancar, obtener.
prying (prai·ing) *adj.* curioso, fisgón, entrometido.
psalm (sam) *s.* salmo.
psalmist (sa·mist) *s.* salmista.
psalmody (sæ·lmødi) *s.* salmodia.
psalter (so·ltə^r) *s.* salterio [libro].
psaltery (so·ltøri) *s.* MÚS. salterio.
pseudo (siu·dou) *adj.* pseudo, seudo.
pseudonym (siu·dønim) *s.* seudónimo.
pshaw (shô) *interj.* ¡bah!
psi (si) *s.* psi [letra griega].
psoas (sou·æs) *s.* ANAT. psoas [músculo].
psychasthenia (saikæszi·nia) *s.* MED. psicastenia.
Psyche (sai·ki) *n. pr.* MIT., Psique, Psiquis. *2 s.* (con min.) psiquis, el alma.
psychiater (saikai·ætø^r), **psychiatrist** (-trist) *s.* psiquiatra.
psychiatry (saikai·ætri) *s.* psiquiatría.
psychic (al (sai·kik(al) *adj.* psíquico, anímico.
psychoanalysis (saikoanæ·lisis) *s.* psicoanálisis.
psychoanalyst (saikoæ·nalist) *s.* psicoanalista.
psychologic (al (saikola·dŷik(al) *adj.* psicológico.
psychologist (saika·lodŷist) *s.* psicólogo.
psychology (saika·lodŷi) *s.* psicología.
psychometrics (saikome·triks), **psychometry** (saika·metri), *s.* psicometría.
psychopath (si·kopæz) *s.* psicópata.
psychopaty (saika·pazi) *s.* psicopa-
psychosis (saikou·sis), *pl.* **-ses** (-siš) *s.* MED. psicosis.
psychotherapy (saikoze·rapi) *s.* MED. psicoterapia.
ptarmigan (ta·^rmigøn) *s.* ORN. perdiz blanca.
pteridophyte (te·ridofait) *s.* BOT. pteridofita.
Ptolemaic (talømei·k) *adj.* ptolemaico.
Ptolemy (ta·lømi) *n. pr.* Tolomeo.
pub (pøb) *s.* pop. (Ingl.) cervecería, taberna.
puberty (piu·bø^rti) *s.* pubertad.
pubes (piu·bis) *s.* ANAT. pubis [bajo vientre].
pubescent (piube·sønt) *adj.* pubescente. *2* púber.
pubis (piu·bis) *s.* ANAT. pubis [parte del hueso coxal].
public (pø·blic) *adj.* público: *~ health*, higiene pú-

blica, sanidad; *~ house*, posada; (Ingl.) cervecería, taberna; *~ prosecutor*, DER. fiscal; *~ school* (Ingl.), escuela secundaria con internado, principalmente para clases pudientes; (Esc., E.U.) escuela controlada por el estado; *~ servant*, funcionario público; *~ works*, obras públicas. *2* general, universal. *3 s.* el público: *in ~*, en público.
publican (pø·blikan) *s.* publicano. *2* (Ingl.) taberno, hostelero.
publication (pøblikei·søn) *s.* publicación. *2* edición [acción de editar]. *3* promulgación.
publicist (pø·blisist) *s.* publicista. *2* agente de publicidad.
publicity (pø·blisist) *s.* publicidad: *~ agent*, agente de publicidad; *~ office*, agencia de publicidad. *2* notoriedad.
public-spirited *adj.* cívico, patriótico.
publish (to) (pø·blish) *tr.* publicar. *2* editar; *publishing house*, casa editorial. *3* promulgar; difundir, propalar. *4 to ~ the banns*, correr las amonestaciones.
publisher (-ø^r) *s.* publicador. *2* editor.
puce (pius) *adj.-s.* color de pulga.
puck (pøk) *s.* duende. *2* disco de caucho usado en el hockey sobre hielo.
pucker (pø·kø^r) *s.* arruga, pliegue, frunce, fruncido.
pucker (to) *tr.* arrugar, plegar, coger, fruncir.
puckish (-ish) *adj.* travieso.
pudding (pu·din) *s.* budín, pudín. *2* embuchado: *black ~*, morcilla. *3* GEOL. *~ stone*, pudinga.
puddle (pø·døl) *s.* charco, poza. *2* mezcla de arcilla y arena. *3* fig. confusión, lío.
puddle (to) *tr.* METAL. pudelar. *2* enlodar, enfangar. *3* ensuciar, enturbiar. *4* cubrir con una mezcla de arcilla y arena. *5 intr.* patullar [en el lodo, etc.].
puddly (pø·dli) *adj.* encharcado, cenagoso.
pudency (piu·dønsi) *s.* recato, pudor.
pudge (pø·dŷ) *s.* fam. persona o cosa rechoncha, regordeta.
pudgy (-i) *adj.* rechoncho.
pudicity (piudi·siti) *s.* pudicicia, ardor.
puericulture (piuørikø·lchø^r) *s.* puericultura.
pueriliti (piuøri·liti) *s.* puerilidad.
puerperal (piuø·^rpøral) *adj.-m.* puerperal.
Puerto Rican (pue·^rtouri·kan) *adj.-s.* portorriqueño.
Puerto Rico (-kou) *n. pr.* GEOGR. Puerto Rico.
puff (pøf) *s.* soplo, resoplido, bufido: *~ of wind*, ráfaga de aire. *2* bocanada, fumarada, ventada. *3* COC. bollo: *~ paste*, pasta de hojaldre. *4* COST. bollo, bullón. *5* masa esponjada. *6* chupada [de cigarro]. *7* reclamo, bombo, elogio exagerado. *8* *puff* o *powder ~*, borla [para empolvarse]. *9* interj.* ¡bah!
puff (to) *intr.* soplar, resoplar, jadear; echar bocanadas o fumaradas. *2 to ~ up*, hincharse; ahuecarse. *3 tr.* echar [aliento, aire, humo]; empujar, desvanecer, apagar, etc., con el soplo. *4* hacer jadear. *5* hinchar; ahuecar; abollonar. *6* engreír. *7* bombear, hacer el reclamo de. *8* empolvar [con borla].
puffball (-bol) *s.* BOT. bejín.
puffery (-øri) *s.* bombo, propaganda.
puffin (-in) *s.* ORN. alca, frailecillo.
puffy (-i) *adj.* que sopla a intervalos. *2* jadeante. *3* hinchado. *4* campanudo.
pug (pøg) *s.* barro amasado. *2* ZOOL. *pug* o *~ dog*, perro pequeño y de nariz chata.

pugilism (piu·dy̆lišm) *s.* pugilismo.
pugilist (-list) *s.* pugilista, púgil.
pugnacious (pøgnei·shøs) *adj.* pugnaz, belicoso.
pugnacity (pøgnæ·siti) *s.* pugnacidad.
pug-nosed *adj.* de nariz respingona. *2* chato [perro].
puke (to) (piuk) *tr.-intr.* vomitar.
pulchritude (pø·lkritiud) *s.* pulcritud, belleza.
pule (to) (piul) *intr.* gemir, llorar [con voz débil].
pull (pul) *s.* tirón, sacudida, tracción. *2* tirador [botón, cordón, etc.]. *3* subida, cuesta, ascensión difícil; esfuerzo [prolongado o penoso]. *4* atracción [fuerza que tira o atrae]. *5* trago, tiento. *6* chupada [a un cigarro, etc.]. *7* ventaja, superioridad. *8* influencia, aldabas. *9* acto de refrenar un caballo para que no gane [en una carrera].
pull (to) *tr.* tirar de, halar, estirar, arrastrar. *2* arrancar, sacar, extraer. *3* romper, desgarrar. *4* torcer, distender [un ligamento, etc.]. *5* beber; chupar. *6* DEP. refrenar un caballo para que no gane. *7* (E.U.) sacar [un arma]. *8 to* ~ *apart*, separar con violencia, arrancar. *22 to* ~ *a long face*, poner cara larga. *10 to* ~ *back*, tirar hacia atrás, hacer recular. *11 to* ~ *down*, derribar, demoler, bajar, rebajar, abatir. *12 to* ~ *in*, halar, cobrar [una cuerda]. *13 to* ~ *off*, llevar a cabo. *14 to* ~ *on*, ponerse [las medias, etc.]. *15 to* ~ *oneself together*, recobrarse, serenarse. *16 to* ~ *one's leg*, tomar el pelo a uno. *17 to* ~ *out*, arrancar, sacar. *18 to* ~ *the trigger*, apretar el gatillo. *19 to* ~ *through*, sacar de un apuro; llevar a cabo. *20 to* ~ *up*, arrancar; refrenar [un caballo]; detener, parar; reprender.
21 intr. tirar con esfuerzo, dar un tirón, ejercer tracción; trabajar, esforzarse. *22 to* ~ *apart*, romperse [por tracción]. *23 to* ~ *at*, tirar de, dar chupadas a [una pipa, etc.]; beber de. *24 to* ~ *in*, detenerse; entrar, llegar [un tren] a la estación. *25 to* ~ *on*, tirar de. *26* ~ *out*, salir, partir. *27 to* ~ *round*, restablecerse. *28 to* ~ *through*, salir de un apuro. *29 to* ~ *up*, alcanzar a los demás; detenerse, pararse.
pullet (pu·lit) *s.* ZOOL. polla [gallina joven].
pulley (pu·li) *s.* polea, garrucha, motón; aparejo; polea de transmisión, tambor.
Pullman car (pu·lmæn) *s.* FERROC. vagón Pullman.
pull-over *s.* pulóver, elástica, jersey.
pullulate (to) (pø·liuleit) *intr.* pulular.
pulmonate (pø·lmønit) *adj.* pulmonado.
pulmotor (pø·lmoutøʳ) *s.* MED. pulmón de acero.
pulp (pølp) *s.* pulpa. *2* pasta [de papel]. *3* ANAT. bulbo [de diente].
pulpit (pu·lpit) *s.* púlpito. *2* tribuna, tarima.
pulpous (pø·lpøs), **pulpy** (-pi) *adj.* pulposo, carnoso, mollar.
pulsate (to) (pø·lseit) *intr.* pulsar, latir. *2* vibrar, estar lleno de actividad, etc.
pulsatile (pø·lsatil) *adj.* pulsátil. *2* MÚS. de percusión.
pulsation (pølsei·shøn) *s.* pulsación, latido. *2* vida, vibración.
pulse (pøls) *s.* pulso. *2* latido, vibración, esfuerzo. *3* legumbres [garbanzos, lentejas, etc.].
pulse (to) *intr.* pulsar, latir. *2* vibrar.
pulsimeter (pølsi·mitøʳ) *s.* pulsímetro.
pultaceous (pøltei·shøs) *adj.* pultáceo.
pulverization (pølvørisei·shøn) *s.* pulverización.
pulverize (to) (pø·lvøraiš) *tr.* pulverizar.
pulverizer (pølvøraiˑšøʳ) *s.* pulverizador.

pulverulent (pølve·rulønt) *adj.* pulverulento, polvoriento.
puma (piu·ma) *s.* ZOOL. puma.
pumice o **pumice stone** (pø·mis) *s.* piedra pómez.
pumice (to) *tr.* apomazar.
pummel (to) *tr.* TO POMMEL.
pump (pømp) *s.* MEC. bomba [para fluidos]: *force* ~, bomba impelente; *suction* ~, bomba aspirante. *2* fuente alimentada por una bomba. *3 gasoline* ~, surtidor de gasolina. *4 pl.* zapatos bajos, zapatillas.
pump (to) *tr.* impeler, lanzar, sacar, etc., con bomba o como una bomba. *2* sacar agua, aire, etc. [con bomba]. *3* inyectar aire, hinchar [con bomba o fuelle]. *4* sacar, obtener [noticias, dinero, etc.]. *5* sondear, sonsacar. *6 intr.* dar a la bomba. *7 tr.-intr.* mover o moverse de arriba abajo.
pumper (-øʳ) *s.* el que acciona una bomba. *2* ganzúa, sonsacador.
pumpkin (-kin) *s.* BOT. calabaza; calabacera. *2* fam. (E.U.) personaje; cosa importante.
pump-priming *s.* (E.U.) ayuda económica del Estado al comercio, la industria, etc.
pun (pøn) *s.* retruécano, juego de palabras.
pun (to) *intr.* hacer retruécanos, jugar del vocablo.
punch (pønch) *s.* ponche: ~ *bowl*, ponchera. *2* puñada, puñetazo. *3* empuje, energía, vigor. *4* punzón; contrapunzón. *5* sacabocados; máquina de taladrar. *6* embutidera.
punch (to) *tr.* picar, aguijar. *2* perforar, marcar, embutir, remachar, etc., con punzón, sacabocados, etc. *3* apuñear, dar puñetazos a.
Punch *n. pr.* Polichinela: *Punch-and-Judy show*, función de títeres.
puncheon (-øn) *s.* punzón [para estampar].
punchinello (pønchine·lou) *s.* pulchinela; títere.
punchy (pø·nchi) *adj.* rechoncho.
punctilio (pønkti·liou) *s.* puntillo; detalle nimio.
punctilious (-liøs) *adj.* puntilloso, mirado, meticuloso, etiquetero.
punctual (pø·nkchual) *adj.* puntual, exacto.
punctuality (pønkchuæ·liti) *s.* puntualidad, exactitud, formalidad.
punctuate (to) (pø·nkchueit) *tr.* puntuar. *2* interrumpir a intervalos. *3* acentuar, hacer resaltar.
punctuation (-ei·shøn) *s.* GRAM. puntuación.
puncture (pø·nkchøʳ) *s.* puntura, pinchazo, picadura. *2* CIR. punción.
puncture (to) *tr.* punzar, pinchar, agujerear, picar.
pundit (pø·ndit) *s.* sabio indio. *2* desp. sabihondo.
pungency (pø·ndjønsi) *s.* picante, punta, sabor. *2* acrimonia, mordacidad. *3* agudeza, viveza.
pungent (-ønt) *adj.* picante. *2* acre, mordaz. *3* agudo, vivo, penetrante, pungente.
Punic (piu·nik) *adj.* púnico.
punish (to) (pø·nish) *tr.* castigar, penar.
punisher (-øʳ) *s.* castigador.
punishment (-mønt) *s.* castigo. *2* vapuleo.
punitive, -tory (piu·nitiv, -tori) *adj.* de castigo.
punk (pønk) *s.* yesca; hupe. *2 adj.* zocato [fruto]. *3* pop. (E.U.) inferior, malo.
punster (pø·nstøʳ) *s.* equivoquista.
punt (pønt) *s.* batea, barca plana. *2* MAR. plancha de agua. *3* DEP. puntapié dado al balón en el aire.
punt (to) *tr.* mover [una batea] con percha. *2* dar un puntapié [al balón] en el aire. *3 intr.* ir en batea o barca plana. *5* apuntar [en el juego].
punter (-øʳ) *s.* punto [que apuesta en el juego]. *2* el que mueve una batea o barca plana.

puny (piu·ni) *adj.* endeble, canijo. *2* pequeño, diminuto.

pup (pøp) *s.* cachorro.

pup (to) *intr.* parir [la perra].

pupa (piu·pa) *s.* ENT. ninfa, crisálida.

pupil (piu·pil) *s.* discípulo, alumno. *2* DER. pupilo. *3* ANAT. pupila.

pupilage (-idȳ) *s.* DER. pupilaje. *2* alumnado.

puppet (pø·pit) *s.* títere, muñeco; maniquí. *2* juguete, instrumento [de otro].

puppy (pø·pi) *s.* cachorro, perrito. *2* joven fatuo o casquivano; petimetre.

purblind (pø·ʳblaind) *adj.* cegato. *2* ciego [mentalmente].

purchase (pø·ʳchas) *s.* compra, adquisición. *3* MEC., MAR. acción de mover, tirar de, subir, etc., con algún medio mecánico; este mismo medio: palanca, aparejo, maniobra, etc.

purchase (to) *tr.* comprar, adquirir. *2* mover, tirar de, subir, etc., por medio de palanca, aparejo, etc.

purchaser (pø·ʳchasøʳ) *s.* comprador.

purchasing power (-ing) *s.* poder adquisitivo [de la moneda].

pure (piu·øʳ) *adj.* puro.

purebred (piuʳbre·d) *adj.* de pura raza.

purée (piurei·) *s.* COC. puré.

purgation (pøʳguei·shøn) *s.* purgamiento. *2* DER. purgación.

purgative (pø·ʳgativ) *adj.* purgativo. *2* *adj.-s.* MED. purgante.

purgatory (-tori) *s.* purgatorio.

purge (pø·ʳdȳ) *s.* purga, purgante. *2* purgación.

purge (to) *tr.* purgar, limpiar, purificar. *2* DER., MED., MEC. purgar. *3* *intr.* purgarse.

purification (piurifikei·shøn) *s.* purificación. *2* depuración.

purificator (-tøʳ) *s.* purificador.

purifier (piu·rifaiøʳ) *s.* purificador.

purify (to) (piu·rifai) *tr.* purificar. *2* *intr.* purificarse. ¶ Pret. y p. p.: *purified*.

purism (piu·rišm) *s.* purismo.

purist (-rist) *s.* purista.

Puritan (-ritan) *adj.-s.* puritano.

puritanic (al (piuritæ·niƙ(al) *adj.* puritano.

Puritanism (piu·ritanišm) *s.* puritanismo.

purity (-riti) *s.* pureza.

purl (pø·ʳl) *s.* murmurio del agua. *2* onda, rizo. *3* borde u orla rizada.

purl (to) *tr.* orlar, adornar con fleco o guarnición rizada. *2* *intr.* murmurar [los arroyos, etc.]. *3* ondular, arremolinarse.

purline (pø·ʳlin) *s.* ARQ. correa [de la armadura].

purloin (to) (pøʳloi·n) *tr.* hurtar, robar, substraer.

purloiner (pøʳloi·nøʳ) *s.* ladrón.

purple (pø·ʳpøl) *adj.* purpúreo, morado, rojo. *2* imperial, regio. *3* brillante, magnífico. *4* *s.* púrpura.

purple (to) *tr.* purpurar, teñir de púrpura.

purplish (pø·ʳplish) *adj.* algo purpúreo.

purport (pø·ʳpoʳt) *s.* significado, sentido, tenor.

purport (to) (pøʳpo·ʳt) *tr.* significar, querer decir, dar a entender. *2* *to ~ to be,* querer ser, aparentar ser.

purpose (pø·ʳpøs) *s.* propósito, fin, objeto, mira, intención, designio: *of set ~, on ~,* de propósito. *2* resolución, determinación. *3* efecto, resultado, uso, utilidad: *common purposes,* usos ordinarios; *to no ~,* inútilmente, en vano. *4* *to the ~,* a propósito, al caso.

purpose (to) *tr.-intr.* proponerse, intentar, proyectar, tener designio de.

purposeful (-ful) *adj.* resuelto, determinado. *2* que tiene un sentido, fin u objeto.

purpurin (e (pø·ʳpiurin) *s.* purpurina [colorante].

purr (pøʳ) *s.* ronroneo.

purr (to) *intr.* ronronear.

purse (pøʳs) *s.* bolsa, bolsillo, portamonedas. *2* bolsa, caudal, dinero. *3* bolsa [premio, subvención]. *4* dinero recogido, colecta. *5* bolsa [recipiente; cosa en forma de bolsa].

purse (to) *tr.* fruncir, arrugar [la frente, los labios]. *2* *intr.* fruncirse, arrugarse.

purse-proud *adj.* orgulloso de su dinero.

purser (-øʳ) *s.* MAR. contador, sobrecargo.

purslane (pø·ʳslein) *s.* BOT. verdolaga.

pursuance (pøʳsiu·ans) *s.* persecución, seguimiento. *2* prosecución. *3* cumplimiento, ejecución.

pursuant (-ant) *adj.* consiguiente. *2* conforme [a]. *3* *adv.* de conformidad [con], en cumplimiento [de].

pursue (to) (pøʳsiu·) *tr.* seguir, perseguir. *2* perseguir [un fin]. *3* seguir [una línea de conducta, estudios, etc.]. *4* seguir [con la vista o mentalmente]. *5* *intr.* proseguir, continuar.

pursuit (pøʳsiu·t) *s.* seguimiento, perseguimiento, caza, busca: *~ plane,* avión de caza. *2* pretensión, empeño. *3* prosecución, continuación. *4* ocupación, actividad.

pursuivant (pø·ʳsuivant) *s.* perseverante.

pursy (pø·ʳsi) *adj.* obeso. *2* asmático. *3* engreído por el dinero.

purulent (piu·rulønt) *adj.* purulento.

purvey (to) (pøʳvei·) *tr.* proveer, abastecer. *2* suministrar. *3* *intr.* ser proveedor.

purveyance (-ans) *s.* abastecimiento, suministro.

purveyor (-øʳ) *s.* proveedor, abastecedor.

purview (pø·ʳviu) *s.* esfera, extensión, alcance.

pus (pøs) *s.* MED. pus, materia.

push (push) *s.* empujón. *2* impulso, empuje. *3* embestida. *4* esfuerzo. *5* avance [venciendo obstáculos]. *6* cornada, hurgonazo. *7* fam. apuro, aprieto. *8* apreturas. *9* fam. energía, acometividad. *10 push* o *~ button,* pulsador, botón eléctrico.

push (to) *tr.* empujar, empellar, impeler: *to ~ aside,* hacer a un lado, rechazar, apartar; *to ~ back,* echar atrás, hacer retroceder; *to ~ on,* aguijonear, apresurar. *2* apretar [un botón]. *3* llevar, extender [sus conquistas, etc.]. *4* proseguir. *5* promover, impulsar. *6* apremiar, apretar, estrechar. *7* *intr.* empujar. *8* dar una cornada, un hurgonazo. *9* avanzar [contra obstáculos]: *to ~ forward,* abrirse paso, avanzar. *10 to ~ off,* desatracar; irse, salir. *11 interj. push on!,* ¡adelante!

pushcart (pu·shkaʳt) *s.* carretilla de mano.

pusher (pu·shøʳ) *s.* empujador. *2* fam. persona emprendedora. *3* AVIA. *pusher* o *~ plane,* avión que lleva la hélice en la parte de atrás.

pushpin (pu·shpin) *s.* juego de los alfileres, crucillo. *2* chinche [clavito].

push-pull *adj.* RADIO. de contrafase, simétrico, push-pull.

pusillanimity (piusilani·miti) *s.* pusilanimidad.

pusillanimous (piusilæ·nimøs) *adj.* pusilánime.

puss (pus) *s.* minino, michito, gato: *Puss in Boots,* el gato con botas. *2* chiquilla, mozuela. *3* *~ in the corner,* juego de las cuatro esquinas.

pussy (-i) *s.* minino, michito. *2* chiquilla.

pussyfoot (pu·sifut) *adj.* fam. cauteloso, evasivo [proceder, política]. *2 s.* persona cautelosa, que no se compromete.
pustule (pø·chøl) *s.* MED. pústula.
pustulous (pø·schøløs) *adj.* pustuloso.
put (put) *s.* acción del verbo TO PUT. *2* golpe, tiro, lanzamiento. *3 to stay* ~, estar quieto, en su lugar.
put (to) *tr.* poner, colocar, situar. *2* obligar, incitar. *3* hacer, formular [una pregunta]. *4* presentar [para ser discutido]. *5* exponer, expresar. *6* atribuir [un significado, valor, etc.]. *7* achacar [a una causa o razón]. *8* DEP. arrojar, lanzar. *9 to* ~ *about*, enojar; desconcertar; MAR. hacer virar. *10 to* ~ *aside*, descartar, desechar; poner aparte; ahorrar. *11 to* ~ *away*, guardar [en un cajón, etc.]; ahorrar; rechazar, repudiar; apartar. *12 to* ~ *by*, guardar, ahorrar; desviar, apartar. *13 to* ~ *down*, poner [en el suelo, etc.]; sofocar, reprimir; deprimir, abatir; humillar; apuntar, anotar; rebajar; atribuir; hacer callar. *14 to* ~ *forth*, extender, alargar; mostrar, ejercer, poner en acción; presentar, proponer; echar [hojas, plumas, etc.]. *15 to* ~ *in*, introducir en; pasar, emplear [tiempo] en. *16 to* ~ *in an appearance*, aparecer, ir, dejarse ver. *17 to* ~ *in a word for*, interceder por. *18 to* ~ *in mind*, recordar. *19 to* ~ *into effect*, poner en vigor. *20 to* ~ *off*, diferir, aplazar; desechar; eludir; quitar, quitarse [una prenda]. *21 to* ~ *on*, poner sobre; ponerse, calzarse [ropa, zapatos,etc.]; engañar; fingir; dar [la luz, vapor, etc.]; TEAT. poner en escena. *22 to* ~ *on airs*, darse tono. *23 to* ~ *on weight*, engordar. *24 to* ~ *oneself out of the way*, molestarse, tomarse molestia o trabajo. *25 to* ~ *out*, sacar; echar fuera; alargar, extender; exhibir; invertir, colocar [dinero]; echar [brotes, etc.]; apagar [la luz, un fuego]; molestar, irritar; desconcertar; dislocar. *26 to* ~ *out of countenance*, avergonzar; desconcertar. *27 to* ~ *out of joint*, dislocar. *28 to* ~ *out of the way*, quitar de enmedio; matar; poner [algo] donde no estorbe. *29 to* ~ *over*, aplazar. *30 to* ~ *through*, llevar a cabo; poner en comunicación telefónica. *31 to* ~ *to bed*, acostar. *32 to* ~ *to death*, matar, ajusticiar. *33 to* ~ *together*, reunir, juntar; armar, montar [un artefacto]. *34 to* ~ *to rights*, poner en orden; arreglar; reconciliar. *35 to* ~ *to the sword*, pasar a cuchillo. *36 to* ~ *two and two together*, atar cabos. *37 to* ~ *up*, levantar, elevar, erigir; armar, montar; ahorrar, atesorar; presentar [como candidato]; empaquetar, envolver; ofrecer [dinero] como premio, etc.; urdir, inventar; alojar, dar posada; TEAT. poner en escena. *38 to* ~ *upon oath*, hacer prestar juramento.
39 intr. ir, dirigirse. *40* MAR. *to* ~ *about*, cambiar de rumbo; *to* ~ *in*, entrar en un puerto; *to* ~ *off*, desatracar; *to* ~ *to sea*, hacerse a la mar. *41 to* ~ *out*, irse, salir; MAR. zarpar. *42 to* ~ *up*, parar, hospedarse; presentarse [como candidato]. *43 to* ~ *up with*, aguantar, sufrir, tolerar; conformarse con. ¶ Pret. y p. p.: *put;* ger.: *putting.*
putative (piu·tativ) *adj.* putativo.
putlog (pu·tlag) *s.* ALBAÑ. almojaya.
put-off *adj.* desechado. *2* aplazado. *3 s.* retraso, aplazamiento, dilatorias. *4* excusa, evasiva.

put-out *adj.* enojado, contrariado.
putrefaction (piutrifæ·kshøn) *s.* putrefacción. *2* putridez.
putrefy (to) (piu·trifai) *tr.* pudrir, corromper. *2 intr.* pudrirse, corromperse. ¶ Pret. y p. p.: *putrefied.*
putrescible (piutre·sibøl) *adj.* putrescible.
putrid (piu·trid) *adj.* pútrido. *2* apestoso. *3* corrompido, ponzoñoso [moralmente].
putt (pøt) *s.* GOLF. golpe suave que hace rodar la pelota hasta que se mete en el hoyo.
puttee (pø·ti o pøti·) *s.* polaina.
putter (to) (pu·tø^r) *intr.* TO POTTER.
putting green (-ing) *s.* GOLF. terreno nivelado y cubierto de césped que rodea cada hoyo.
putty (pø·ti) *s.* masilla.
putty (to) *tr.* enmasillar.
put-up *adj.* tramado, urdido, preparado.
puzzle (pø·šøl) *s.* embarazo, perplejidad. *2* enredo, embrollo. *3* acertijo, enigma, rompecabezas: *crossword* ~, crucigrama.
puzzle (to) *tr.* confundir, dejar perplejo. *2* enredar, embrollar. *3 to* ~ *out*, desenredar, descifrar. *4 intr.* estar perplejo o confuso. *5 to* ~ *over*, tratar de descifrar.
puzzlement (pø·sølmønt) *s.* perplejidad, confusión.
puzzler (pø·šlø^r) *s.* lo que confunde o tiene perplejo.
puzzolan (pu·tšolæn) *s.* puzolana.
Pygmalion (pigmei·liøn) *n. pr.* Pigmalión.
pygmean (pigmi·an), **pigmy** (pi·gmi) *adj.-s.* pigmeo, enano.
pyjamas (pidyæ·mæs) *s. pl.* pijama.
pylon (pai·lan) *s.* ARQ. pilón [de templo egipcio]. *2* AVIA., ELECT. torre [de señal, conducción, etc.].
pylorus (pailo·røs) *s.* ANAT. píloro.
pyorrhea, pyorrhae (paiørɪ·a) *s.* MED. piorrea.
pyramid (pi·ramid) *s.* pirámide.
pyramid (to) *tr.* acumular, amontonar. *2 intr.* aumentar, acumularse. *3* aumentar uno la extensión de sus operaciones, empleando el beneficio obtenido en cada una de ellas.
pyramidal (piræ·midal) *adj.* piramidal.
Pyramus (pi·ræmøs) *n. pr.* MIT. Píramo.
pyre (pai·ø^r) *s.* pira, hoguera.
Pyrenean (pirɪnɪ·an) *adj.* pirenaico.
Pyrenees (pi·riniš) *n. pr.* GEOGR. Pirineos.
pyrexla (paire·ksia) *s.* MED. pirexia.
pyriform (pi·rifo^rm) *adj.* piriforme.
pyrites (pirai·tiš) *s.* MIN. pirita.
pyrogenous (paira·dÿenøs) *adj.* pirógeno.
pyrography (paira·grafi) *s.* pirograbado.
pyrolysis (paira·lisis) *s.* QUÍM. pirólisis.
pyrope (pai·ropi) *s.* MIN. piropo.
pyrotechnics (pairotekniks) *s.* pirotecnia.
pyrotechnist (-nist) *s.* pirotécnico.
pyroxylin (paira·ksilin) *s.* piroxilina.
Pyrrhic (pi·rik) *adj.* pírrico. *2 s.* pirriquio.
pyrrhonism (pi·rønišm) *s.* pirronismo.
Pyrrhus (pi·røs) *n. pr.* Pirro.
Pythagoras (pizæ·gørøs) *n. pr.* Pitágoras.
Pythagorean (pizægorɪan) *adj.-s.* pitagórico.
Pythian (pi·zian) *adj.* pitio.
python (pai·zan) *s.* ZOOL., MIT. pitón.
pythoness (pai·zønis) *s.* pitonisa.
pyx (piks) *s.* píxide, copón. *2* caja de la brújula.
pyxidium (piksi·diøm) *s.* BOT. pixidio.

Q

Q, q (kiu) *s.* Q, q, decimoséptima letra del alfabeto inglés.
quack (kuæk) *s.* graznido [del pato]. *2* curandero, charlatán. *3 adj.* falso, de charlatán.
quack (to) *intr.* graznar, parpar. *2* echarlas de entendido, hacer el charlatán.
quackery (-øri) *s.* charlatanismo.
quacksalver (-sælvøʳ) *s.* curandero, charlatán.
quad (kuod) *s.* fam. (E.U.) patio cuadrangular [de una universidad]. *2* pop. cuadrillizo.
quadragenarian (kuadradŷineˑrian) *adj.-s.* cuadragenario.
Quadragesima (-dŷeˑsima) *s.* cuadragésima.
quadrangle (kuaˑdrængøl) *s.* cuadrángulo. *2* ARQ. patio cuadrado.
quadrangular (kuadræˑingiulaʳ) *adj.* cuadrangular.
quadrans (kuaˑdrans) *s.* cuadrante [moneda].
quadrant (-nt) *s.* GEOM., ASTR. cuadrante.
quadrat (kuaˑdræt) *s.* IMPR. cuadrado, cuadratín.
quadrate (-dreit) *adj.-s.* ANAT., ZOOL. cuadrado.
quadrate (to) *intr.* cuadrar, conformarse.
quadratic (kuadræˑtik) *adj.* MAT. cuadrático. *2 s.* MAT. ecuación cuadrática.
quadrature (kuaˑdrachuʳ) *s.* MAT., ASTR. cuadratura.
quadrennium (kuadreˑniøm) *s.* cuadrienio.
quadriga (kuadraiˑga) *s.* cuadriga.
quadrille (kuadriˑl) *s.* contradanza. *2* cuatrillo [juego de naipes]. *3* cuadrilla [de toreros].
quadrillion (kuadriˑliøn) *s.* cuatrillón.
quadripartite (kuadripaˑʳtait) *adj.* cuatripartito.
quadrivium (kuadriˑviøm) *s.* cuadrivio.
quadroon (kuadruˑn) *s.* cuarterón [pers.].
quadrumane (kuadruˑmein) *s.* ZOOL. cuadrúmano.
quadrumanous (-manøs) *adj.* cuadrúmano.
quadruped (kuaˑdruped) *adj.-s.* cuadrúpedo.
quadrupedal (kuadruˑpedal) *adj.* cuadrúpedo.
quadruple (cuaˑdrupøl) *adj.* cuádruple. *2 s.* cuádruplo.
quadruple (to) *tr.* cuadruplicar. *2 intr.* cuadruplicarse.
quadruplet (kuaˑdruplit) *s.* serie de cuatro, cuatrillizo.
quadruplicate (kuadruˑplikit) *adj.* cuadruplicado.
quadruplicate (to) (-plikeit) *tr.* cuadruplicar.
quaestor (kueˑstøʳ) *s.* cuestor [romano].
quaetorship (-ship) *s.* cuestura.

quaff (kuaf) *s.* trago, bebida.
quaff (to) *intr.-tr.* beber, beber a grandes tragos.
quag (kuæg) *s.* lugar pantanoso.
quagga (kuæˑga) *s.* ZOOL. cuaga.
quaggy (-i) *adj.* pantanoso, cenagoso. *2* blando como lodo.
quagmire (-gmaiʳ) *s.* cenagal, tremedal, tembladal. *2* fig. atolladero.
quahog (kuoˑjag) *s.* ZOOL. almeja redonda.
quail (kueil) *s.* ORN. codorniz.
quail (to) *intr.* abatirse, acobardarse. *2* cejar, ceder [por temor].
quaint (kueint) *adj.* raro, singular, curioso; de un primor o gracia anticuados. *2* elegante, afectado.
quake (kueik) *s.* temblor, estremecimiento. *2* terremoto.
quake (to) *intr.* temblar, estremecerse, trepidar.
Quaker (kueiˑkøʳ) *adj.-s.* cuáquero, cuákero. *2 s.* temblador.
Quakeress (-is) *f.* cuáquera, cuákero.
Quakerism (-išm) *s.* cuaquerismo.
quaking (kueiˑking) *adj.* temblador, temblón: ~ *bog*, tremedal; ~ *grass*, BOT. tembladera.
quaky (-i) *adj.* temblón, tembloroso. *2* que tiembla como la gelatina, gelatinoso.
qualifiable (kuaˑlifaiabøl) *adj.* calificable.
qualification (kualifikeiˑshøn) *s.* calificación. | No tiene el sentido de nota. *2* condición, requisito, calidad, cualidad. *3* capacidad, idoneidad. *4* modificación, atenuación, restricción.
qualified (kuaˑlifaid) *adj.* calificado, apto, idóneo, competente. *2* modificado. *3* DER. limitado, restringido.
qualify (to) (-lifai) *tr.* calificar, habilitar, capacitar, hacer idóneo. *2* modificar, limitar, restringir. *3* atenuar, suavizar, templar. *4* GRAM. calificar. *5 intr.* capacitarse, habilitarse. ¶ Pret. y p. p.: *qualified.*
qualifying (-lifaiing) *adj.* calificativo. *2* que capacita, autoriza o prepara.
qualitative (-liteitiv) *adj.* cualitativo.
quality (-liti) *s.* calidad, cualidad: *in ~ of*, en calidad de. *2* clase. *3* excelencia. *4* propiedad, virtud. *5* ant. o vulg. *the ~*, la alta sociedad.
qualm (kuam) *s.* basca, desfallecimiento, angustia. *2* escrúpulo, remordimiento.
qualmish (-ish) *adj.* bascoso. *2* escrupuloso.

quandary (kua·ndari) *s.* incertidumbre, perplejidad. *2* aprieto, brete.

quanta (kua·nta) *s. pl.* de QUANTUM.

quantitative (kua·ntiteitiv) *adj.* cuantitativo.

quantity (-titi) *s.* cantidad, cuantidad; cuantía; tanto. *2* MÉTR., MÚS. cantidad. *3 sing.* y *pl.* gran cantidad, gran número.

quantum (-tøm), *pl.* **quanta** (kua·nta) *s.* tanto, cantidad. *2* FÍS. cuanto, quántum.

quarantine (kua·rantin) *s.* cuarentena [aislamiento]. *2* lazareto, estación de cuarentena.

quarantine (to) *tr.* poner en cuarentena, aislar.

quarrel (kua·røl) *s.* riña, reyerta, disputa, querella, desavenencia. *2* cuadrillo [saeta]. *3* vidrio o loseta cuadrados o en figura de rombo.

quarrel (to) *intr.* reñir, pelear, disputar, contender. *2* reñir, desavenirse. *3* estar disgustado [con], quejarse [de]. ¶ Pret. y p. p.: *quarrel(l)ed;* ger.: *-l(l)ing.*

quarreller (-ø͡r) *s.* quimerista, disputador.

quarrelsome (-søm) *adj.* pendenciero, rencilloso.

quarrier (kua·riø͡r) *s.* cantero, picapedrero.

quarry (kua·ri) *s.* cantera, pedrera. *2* presa, caza [que se persigue]. *3* MONT. carnada. *4* QUARREL 3.

quarry (to) *tr.* sacar [piedra] de una cantera. *2* sacar [datos, etc.] de libros, etc.

1) quart (kuo͡rt) *s.* cuarto de galón [medida].

2) quart (ka͡rt) *s.* ESGR. cuarta. *2* cuarta [en el juego de los cientos].

quartan (kuo·͡rtan) *adj.* cuartanal. *2* MED. cuartana.

quarter (-ø͡r) *s.* cuarto, cuarta [cuarta parte]. *2* cuarto [de hora; de la luna; de un animal]. *3* moneda de veinticinco centavos. *4* MAR. cuarta. *5* trimestre. *6* parte, punto, dirección: *from all quarters,* de todas partes. *7* barrio, vecindad. *8* BLAS. cantón, cuartel. *9* cuartel, clemencia: *to give no ~,* no dar cuartel. *10 pl.* cuartel, oficina; vivienda, alojamiento: *to take up quarters at,* establecerse o alojarse en. *11 m. adv. at close quarters,* muy cerca uno de otro; a las manos.

quarter (to) *tr.* cuartear, dividir en cuatro partes. *2* descuartizar. *3* BLAS. cuartelar. *4* hospedar, alojar. *5* MIL. acuartelar, acantonar. *6 intr.* alojarse.

quarter day *s.* día en que principia o se paga un trimestre.

quarter-deck *s.* MAR. alcázar.

quarter-final *s.* DEP. cuarto de final.

quarterly (-li) *adj.* trimestral. *2 adv.* trimestralmente. *3 s.* publicación trimestral.

quartermaster (-mæ·stø͡r) *s.* MIL. administrador de un regimiento; *~ general,* intendente del ejército. *2* MAR. cabo de mar. *3* MIL. (E.U.) *Quartermaster Corps,* Cuerpo de Intendencia.

quartern (kuo·͡rtø͡rn) *s.* (Ingl.) cuarta [de varias medidas]. *2 quartern* o *~ loaf,* pan de cuatro libras.

quartet(e (kuo͡rte·t) *s.* grupo de cuatro. *2* MÚS. cuarteto.

quarto (kuo·͡rtou) *adj.* IMPR. en cuarto. *2 s.* libro en cuarto.

quartz (kuo͡rts) *s.* MINER. cuarzo.

quash (to) (kuash) *tr.* aplastar, estrellar. *2* sofocar, reprimir. *3* DER. anular, invalidar; revocar.

quasi (kuei·sai) *adj.* cuasi; *~ contract,* cuasicontrato.

Quasimodo (kuei·simoudou) *s.* domingo de Cuasimodo.

quassia (kua·shia) *s.* BOT., FARM. cuasia.

quaternary (kuatø·͡rneri) *adj.* cuaternario. *2* MAT. de base cuatro. *3 s.* grupo de cuatro. *4* (con may.) GEOL. cuaternario.

quaternity (-iti) *s.* cuaternidad.

quatrain (kua·trein) *s.* poét. cuarteta; redondilla.

quatrefoil (kæ·tø͡rfoil) *s.* grupo, flor, ornamento, etc., de cuatro hojas.

quaver (kuei·vø͡r) *s.* temblor [esp. en la voz]; estremecimiento, vibración. *2* MÚS. trémolo; trino. *3* MÚS. corchea.

quaver (to) *intr.* temblar, estremecerse, vibrar. *2* MÚS. trinar, gorjear. *3 intr.-tr.* hablar, decir, etc., con voz trémula.

quavery (kuei·vø͡ri) *adj.* tembloroso, trémulo.

quay (kɪ·) *s.* muelle, desembarcadero.

quean (kuin) *f.* mujerzuela. *2* moza, muchacha.

queasy (kuɪ·si) *adj.* bascoso. *2* nauseabundo. *3* delicado, exigente, escrupuloso, melindroso.

queen (kuɪn) *s.* reina; *~ dowager,* reina viuda; *~ bee,* abeja reina. *2* naipe que equivale al caballo. *3* dama o reina de ajedrez. *4* BOT. *~ of the meadow,* reina de los prados, ulmaría.

queen (to) *tr.* hacer reina. *2* gobernar como reina. *3 intr.* reinar [como reina].

queenly (-li) *adj.* regio, de reina.

queer (kui͡r) *adj.* raro, extraño, curioso, estrafalario. *2* excéntrico; *~ in the head,* fam. tocado, chiflado. *3* débil, indispuesto. *4* dudoso.

queer (to) *tr.* ridiculizar. *2* pop. comprometer; poner en mala situación. *3* pop. estropear; desbaratar: *to ~ the pitch for one,* estropearle a uno el negocio.

quell (to) (kuel) *tr.* reprimir, sofocar, sojuzgar, domar. *2* aquietar. *3* calmar, mitigar.

queller (-ø͡r) *s.* sojuzgador. *2* mitigador.

quench (to) (kuench) *tr.* apagar, extinguir, calmar [el fuego, la luz, la sed, una pasión]; templar el ardor de. *2* templar [el acero].

quenchless (-lis) *adj.* inextinguible; implacable.

quenelle (køne·l) *s.* albondiguilla.

querist (kui·rist) *s.* inquisidor, preguntador.

querulous (kue·ruløs) *adj.* plañidero. *2* quejumbroso, quejicoso, quisquilloso.

query (kui·ri) *s.* pregunta, cuestión. *2* duda. *3* interrogante.

query (to) *tr.* preguntar, inquirir. *2* interrogar. *3* poner en duda. *4 intr.* hacer preguntas. *5* dudar, expresar una duda.

quest (kuest) *s.* busca, demanda: *in ~ of,* en demanda de. *2* pesquisa, indagación.

quest (to) *intr.-tr.* buscar, perseguir. *2* indagar.

question (kue·schøn) *s.* pregunta, interrogación; *~ mark,* signo de interrogación, interrogante. *2* DER. indagación, interrogación; cuestión de tormento. *3* objeción, duda, discusión: *to call in ~,* poner en duda, en tela de juicio; *beyond ~,* fuera de duda, indiscutible; *without ~,* sin duda. *4* cuestión, problema, asunto, caso [punto de que se trata]: *that is the ~,* he ahí el problema; *this is out of the ~,* esto es imposible, está descartado; *beside the ~,* impertinente, ajeno al asunto; *in ~,* de que se trata.

question (to) *tr.* preguntar, examinar, interrogar. *2* hacer objeciones a, recusar; discutir, poner en duda. *3 intr.* hacer preguntas, indagar.

questionable (-øbøl) *adj.* cuestionable. *2* dudoso, sospechoso.

questionary (kue·schøneri) *s.* cuestionario.

questioning (-ing) *s.* interrogatorio. *2* dudas, preguntas. *3 adj.* interrogador. *4* de duda, que pone en duda o discute.

questor (kue·stø͡r) *s.* cuestor.

quetzal (ke·tsal) *s.* ORN. quetzal.

queue (kiu) *s.* coleta. *2* cola, hilera. *3* MÚS. cordal.

queue (to) *intr.* hacer cola. | A veces con *up.*
quibble (kui·bøl) *s.* sutileza; argucia, equívoco, subterfugio.
quibble (to) *intr.* sutilizar, valerse de equivocos o subterfugios; buscar escapatorias.
quibbler (kui·bløᵣ) *s.* sofista, equivoquista.
quick (kuik) *adj.* vivo, animado, rápido, acelerado, pronto, impetuoso: ~ *time,* MIL. paso redoblado. *2* despierto, agudo, perspicaz. *3* vivo, irritable. ~ *temper,* genio vivo. *4* vivo, intenso, penetrante, ardiente. *5* movedizo [suelo, arena]. *6* vivo [agua, fuente]. *7* COM. ~ *assets,* activo fácilmente realizable. *8* BOT. ~ *grass,* grama. *9 s.* carne viva, lo vivo, el alma: *to sting to the* ~, herir en lo vivo. *10* vivo, viviente: *the* ~ *and the dead,* los vivos y los muertos. *11 adv.* QUICKLY.
quick-acting *adj.* de acción rápida.
quilk-change artist *s.* TEAT. transformista.
quicken (to) (-øn) *tr.* vivificar, dar vida, resucitar. *2* avivar, animar, excitar, aguzar. *3* apresurar, acelerar. *5 intr.* revivir. *6* avivarse, animarse. *7* apresurarse, acelerarse.
quick-fire *adj.* ARTILL. de tiro rápido.
quicklime (-laim) *s.* cal viva.
quickly (-li) *adv.* vivamente, prontamente, con presteza, aprisa.
quicksand (-sænd) *s.* arena movediza.
quickset (-set) *s.* BOT. espino; planta para setos.
quickset (to) *tr.* cercar con seto vivo.
quicksilver (-silvøᵣ) *s.* mercurio, azogue.
quickstep (kui·kstep) *s.* MÚS. paso doble, pasacalle. *2* MIL. paso redoblado.
quick-tempered *adj.* de genio vivo, irritable.
quick-witted *adj.* listo, despierto, perspicaz.
quid (kuid) *s.* mascada de tabaco. *2* pop. libra esterlina.
quiddity (-iti) *s.* quid, esencia. *2* argucia. *3* nadería.
quidnunc (-nønk) *s.* curioso, chismoso.
quiescent (kuaie·sønt) *adj.* quieto, en reposo; fijo, sin movimiento.
quiet (kuai·øt) *adj.* quieto, inmóvil. *2* callado, quedo, silencioso: *to be* ~, callar, callarse. *3* tranquilo, sosegado. *4* sencillo, modesto: serio [color, vestido]. *5* COM. encalmado, inactivo. *6 s.* quietud, silencio, sosiego, calma, paz, tranquilidad. *7* pop. *on the* ~, a la chita callando.
quiet (to) *tr.* aquietar, sosegar, calmar, tranquilizar. *2 intr. to* ~ *down,* aquitarse.
quietness (-nis) *s.* quietud. *2* sencillez, modestia.
quietude (-iud) *s.* quietud.
quietus (kuai·tøs) *s.* finiquito. *2* fig. despido; descanso; muerte.
quill (kuil) *s.* pluma [de ave]. *2* cañón [de pluma]. *3* la pluma, la profesión literaria. *4* púa [de puerco espín]. *5* canilla, broca, devanador, canutillo.
quill (to) *tr.* desplumar, pelar. *2* rizar, alechugar, encañonar. *3* encanillar.
quillon (kı·løn) *s.* gavilán [de la espada].
quilt (kuilt) *s.* colcha; cobertor acolchado.
quilt (to) *tr.* acolchar, acojinar. *2* meter [entre dos capas o partes].
quilting (-ing) *s.* colchadura. *2* piqué, tela acolchada.
quina (kı·na) *s.* BOT., FARM. quina.
quince (kuins) *s.* membrillo [árbol y fruto].
quincunx (kui·nkønks) *s.* disposición al tresbolillo.
quindecennial (kuindise·nial) *adj.* quindenial.
quinin(e (kui·nin) *s.* QUÍM. quinina.
quinol (-oul) *s.* QUÍM. hidroquinona.

quinquagenarian (kuinkuadÿine·rian) *adj.-s.* quincuagenario.
Quinquagesima (dÿe·sima) *s.* Quincuagésima.
quinquennial (kuinkue·nial) *adj.* quinquenal. *2 s.* quinto aniversario.
quinquennium (-niøm) *s.* quinquenio.
quinsy (kui·nši) *s.* MED. angina [tonsilar].
quint (kuint) *s.* MÚS., NAIPES. quinta.
quintain (kui·ntin) *s.* estafermo [figura].
quintal (-al) *s.* quintal.
quinte (kæ·nt) *s.* ESGR. quinta.
quintessence (kuinte·søns) *s.* quinta esencia.
quintet(te (kuinte·t) *s.* grupo de cinco. *2* MÚS. quinteto.
quintillion (-ti·liøn) *s.* quintillón.
quintuple (kui·ntiupøl) *adj.-s.* quintuplo.
quintuple (to) *tr.* quintuplicar. *2 intr.* quintuplicarse.
quip (kuip) *s.* pulla, sarcasmo. *2* ocurrencia.
quip (to) *intr.* mofarse, echar pullas. ¶ Pret. y p. p.: *quipped;* ger.: -pping.
quire (kuaiᵣ) *s.* mano [de papel]. *2* pliego [de un libro].
quirk (kuøᵣk) *s.* vuelta, recodo, torcimiento, desviación. *2* rasgo [de pluma]. *3* sutileza, argucia. *4* salida, ocurrencia. *5* arranque, capricho, rareza.
quirt (kuøᵣt) *s.* látigo [de montar].
quirt (to) *tr.* azotar con el látigo de montar.
quit (kuit) *adj.* absuelto, descargado. *2* libre, exento: *to get* ~ *of,* librarse de.
quit (to) *tr.* dejar, abandonar, irse de, separarse de; dejarse de; desistir de; renunciar a: *to* ~ *an employment,* dejar un empleo; *to* ~ *jesting,* dejarse de bromas. *2* librar, descargar. *3* pagar, saldar. *4 intr.* irse: *to give notice to* ~, despedir a un inquilino, arrendatario, etc. *5* parar, dejar de hacer algo. ¶ Pret. y p. p.: *quitted;* ger.: -tting.
quite (kuait) *adv.* completamente, enteramente, totalmente, absolutamente, del todo; realmente, verdaderamente. *2* fam. ~ *a man,* todo un hombre. *3* fam. ~ *so,* así es, en efecto. *4* ~ *a lot,* muchos.
quits (kuits) *adj.-interj.* desquitados, en paz: *to be* ~, estar en paz, haberse desquitado.
quittance (kui·tøns) *s.* quitanza. *2* pago, recompensa.
quiver (-vøᵣ) *s.* aljaba, carcaj. *2* vibración, temblor, estremecimiento.
quiver (to) *intr.* vibrar, temblar, estremecerse.
quixotic (kuiksa·tik) *adj.* quijotesco.
quixotry (kui·ksøtri) *s.* quijotería, quijotismo.
quiz (kuiš) *s.* burla, broma. *2* guasón. *3* (E.U.) interrogatorio, examen [esp. en la escuela].
quiz (to) *tr.* burlarse de. *2* mirar con curiosidad, con burla. *3* (E.U.) examinar, interrogar. ¶ Pret. y p. p.: *quizzed;* ger.: -zzing.
quizzical (-ikal) *adj.* raro, estrambótico, cómico, gracioso. *2* burlón, zumbón.
quodlibet (kua·dlibet) *s.* cuodlibeto. *2* MÚS. fantasía burlesca.
quoin (kuøin) *s.* ARQ. piedra angular. *2* ARQ. ángulo, esquina. *3* MEC., IMPR. cuña.
quoin (to) *tr.* acuñar, meter cuñas.
quoit (kuøit) *s.* tejo, herrón. *2 pl.* juego del tejo.
quondam (kua·ndam) *adj.* antiguo, que fue.
quorum (kuo·røm) *s.* quórum.
quota (kuou·ta) *s.* cuota, cupo.
quotable (-tabøl) *adj.* citable. *2* COM. cotizable.
quotation (kuoutei·shøn) *s.* cita [texto citado]. *2* COM. cotización. *3 adj.* ~ *marks,* comillas (″).

quote (knont) *s.* cita [texto citado]. *2 pl.* comillas (").

quote (to) *tr.* citar [un texto, un autor]. *2* poner entre comillas. *3* COM. cotizar; dar el precio de.

quoth (kuouz) *pret.* del verbo desusado TO QUETH· *quoth I*, dije yo.

quotidian (kuoti·dian) *adj.* cotidiano, diario.

quotient (kuou·shønt) *s.* MAT. cociente.

R

R, r (aʳ) s. R, r, decimoctava letra del alfabeto inglés.
rabbet (ræ·bit) s. CARP. rebajo, ranura, encaje: ~ plane, guillame.
rabbet (to) tr. CARP. ensamblar a rebajo, encajar. 2 CARP. hacer un rebajo en.
rabbi (ræ·bai), **rabbin** (ræ·bin) s. rabí, rabino.
rabbit (ræ·bit) s. ZOOL. conejo: ~ hole, conejera, gazapera: ~ warren, conejar.
rabble (ræ·bøl) s. populacho, chusma, gentuza, canalla. 2 multitud alborotada.
rabic (ræ·bik) adj. MED., VET. rábico.
rabid (ræ·bid) adj. MED., VET. rabioso, rábico. 2 furioso, violento; furibundo, exaltado.
rabies (rei·biš) s. MED., VET. rabia, hidrofobia.
raccoon (ræ·kun) s. ZOOL. mapache.
race (reis) s. raza; casta, estirpe, linaje: human ~, género humano; ~ problem, problema racial. 2 prole, descendencia. 3 carrera, regata: ~ horse, caballo de carreras. 4 competición. 5 curso, carrera [de un astro, de la vida, etc.]. 6 corriente de agua fuerte o rápida. 7 canal, caz, saetín. 8 MEC. canal, ranura, garganta. 9 sabor, fuerza, etc. peculiar de un vino.
race (to) intr. correr [en una carrera, regata, etc.]. 2 correr, moverse, afluir rápidamente. 3 dispararse [el motor]. 4 tr. hacer correr de prisa. 5 competir con [en una carrera].
raceme (ræsı·m) s. BOT. racimo [inflorescencia].
racer (rei·søʳ) s. corredor, carrerista. 2 caballo o coche de carreras. 3 embarcación de regatas.
raceway (-uei) s. RACE 7 y 8. 2 conducto para hilos eléctricos.
rachis (ræ·kis), pl. **-chides** (-kidiš) s. ANAT., ZOOL., BOT. raquis. 2 ástil [de pluma].
rachitic (raki·tic) adj. raquítico.
rachitism (ræ·kitišm) s. MED. raquitismo.
racial (rei·shal) adj. racial.
racily (rei·sili) adv. de manera viva, picante.
raciness (-inis) s. viveza, picante. 2 nariz [del vino].
racing (-ing) s. carrera; regata.
racism (-išm) s. racismo.
rack (ræk) s. aparato de tortura. 2 fig. dolor, tormento. 3 estante, etc., para ciertas cosas: astillero [para lanzas], armero, taquera, espetera, perchero, red para el equipaje. 4 pesebre. 5 cremallera: ~ railway, ferrocarril de cremallera. 6 nube deshilachada. 7 trote cochinero. 8 destrucción: to go to ~ and ruin, perderse, arruinarse completamente.
rack (to) tr. torturar. 2 atormentar. 3 oprimir con exacciones. 4 mover sobre cremallera. 5 to ~ one's brains, devanarse los sesos. 6 intr. andar al trote cochinero.
racket (ræ·kit) s. raqueta [para el juego, para la nieve]. 2 alboroto: to raise a ~, armar alboroto. 3 diversión, holgorio. 4 prueba, dificultad. 5 pop. timo, engaño.
racket (to) intr. andar de fiestas. 2 hacer barullo. 3 tr. sacar dinero con engaños o amenazas.
racketeer (rækitı·ʳ) s. (E.U.) el que saca dinero a personas o empresas comerciales con amenazas de violencia o de perjuicios causados a sus intereses.
rackety (ræ·kiti) adj. bullicioso. 2 jaranero.
racking (-ing) adj. torturador, desgarrador.
rack-rent (-rent) s.arriendo o alquiler exorbitante.
rackwork (-wøʳk) s. mecanismo de cremallera.
racoon (ræ·kun) s. RACCOON.
racquet (ræ·kit) s. RACKET.
racy (rei·si) adj. que tiene el aroma o las cualidades de su clase o casta. 2 vivo, animado, chispeante.
radar (rei·daʳ) s. ELECT. radar: ~ screen, pantalla de radar.
raddle (ræ·døl) s. cañizo. 2 seto de ramas. 3 almagre.
raddle (to) tr. entretejer. 2 pintar con almagre.
radial (rei·dial) adj. radial, radiado.
radian (rei·dian) s. GEOM. radián, ángulo cuyo arco es igual al radio.
radiance, radiancy (rei·dians, -si) s. brillo, resplandor, fulgor, esplendor.
radiant (-iant) adj. FÍS. radiante. 2 radiante, radioso, resplandeciente.
radiate (-ieit) adj. radiado, radial. 2 s. ZOOL. radiado.
radiate (to) tr.-intr. radiar, irradiar. 2 tr. exponer a una radiación; iluminar. 3 difundir. 4 radiar [por radio].
radiation (-iei·shøn) s. radiación.
radiator (-ieitøʳ) s. radiador.
radical (ræ·dikal) adj. radical [en todas sus acepciones]. 2 esencial, fundamental. 3 s. raíz, fundamento. 4 GRAM., QUÍM., POL. radical.

radicalism (-išm) *s.* radicalismo.
radicle (ræ·dikøl) *s.* raicilla. *2* BOT. radícula.
radio (rei·diou) *s.* radio [radiodifusión, radiograma, radiorreceptor]: ~ *amateur*, ~ *fan*, radioaficiondo; ~ *beacon*, AVIA. radiofaro; ~ *listener*, radioescucha, radioyente; ~ *set*, aparato de radio; ~ *wave*, radioonda.
radioactive (-a·ktiv) *adj.* radiactivo.
radiobroadcast (to) (-bro·dkæst) *tr.* radiar, radiodifundir.
radio-frequency *adj.* de radiofrecuencia.
radiogram (rei·diougræm) *s.* radiograma. *2* radiografía [imagen].
radiograph (-græf) *s.* radiografía [imagen]. *2* actinógrafo.
radiograph (to) *tr.* radiografiar. *2* radiotelegrafiar a.
radiography (reidia·grafi) *s.* radiografía [acto, procedimiento].
radiologist (reidia·lodẏist) *s.* radiólogo.
radiology (-lodẏi) *s.* radiología.
radiophony (-foni) *s.* radiofonía.
radioscopy (-skøpi) *s.* radioscopia.
radiosonde (rei·diousand) *s.* radiosonda.
radiotelegraph (reidioute·løgræf) *s.* telégrafo sin hilos.
radiotelegraph (to) *tr.* radiotelegrafiar.
radiotelegraphy (-grafi) *s.* radiotelegrafía.
radiotelephony (-foni) *s.* radiotelefonía.
radiotherapy (-ze·rapi) *s.* radioterapia.
radish (ræ·dish) *s.* BOT. rábano.
radium (rei·diøm) *s.* QUÍM. radio.
radiumtherapy (reidiømze·rapi) *s.* radiumterapia.
radius (rei·diøs) *s.* GEOM., ANAT. radio. *2* radio, rayo. *3* radio [de acción, de influencia, etc.; espacio circular]. *4* ZOOL. plano radial.
radix (rei·diks) *s.* raíz, origen. *2* MAT. base [de un sistema].
radula (ræ·diula), *pl.* **-la** (-li) *s.* ZOOL. rádula.
raffia (ræ·fia) *s.* BOT. rafia.
raffish (ræ·fish) *adj.* canallesco. *2* disoluto.
raffle (ræ·føl) *s.* rifa. *2* fam. desecho, broza.
raffle (to) *intr.* tomar parte en una rifa. *2 tr. to* ~ *off*, rifar, sortear.
raft (raft) *s.* balsa [flotante]. *2* almadía, armadía, jangada. *3* masa flotante [de algas, etc.].
raft (to) *tr.* transportar en balsa. *2 intr.* servir de balsa.
rafter (-ø^r) *s.* ARQ. viga; par.
raftsman (-smæn) *s.* almadiero.
rag (ræg) *s.* trapo, harapo, jirón, pingajo, guiñapo: ~ *doll*, muñeca de trapo; *in rags*, hecho jirones; andrajoso. *2* papelucho. *3* burla, broma, alboroto. *4 pl.* trapos o papeles rotos.
rag (to) *tr.* romper, hacer jirones. *2* reñir, regañar. *3* molestar con burlas o bromas.
ragamuffin (ræ·gamøfin) *s.* golfo, pelagatos.
rage (reidẏ) *s.* rabia, ira; arrebato de cólera. *2* furia, violencia, encarnizamiento. *3* vehemencia, ardor, entusiasmo. *4 to be all the* ~, estar en boga, estar de moda.
rage (to) *intr.* rabiar, encolerizarse. *2* hacer estragos. *3* arder furiosamente [el fuego].
ragged (ræ·gid) *adj.* andrajoso, harapiento. *2* roto, deshilachado; de borde mellado o dentado. *3* áspero, escabroso.
raging (rei·dẏing) *adj.* rabioso, furioso, bramador. *2* entusiasta, vehemente.
raglan (ræ·glæn) *s.* raglán.
ragman (ræ·gmæn) *s.* trapero.
ragout (ræguˑ) *s.* COC. guisado.

ragpicker (ræ·gpikø^r) *s.*trapero.
ragstone (-stoun) *s.* (Ingl.) piedra de amolar.
ragtag (-tæg) *s.* canalla, chusma.
ragtime (-taim) *s.* música de ritmo sincopado.
raid (reid) *s.* correría, incursión, ataque, irrupción.
raid (to) *tr.* hacer una incursión en. *2* BOLSA to ~ *the market*, maniobrar para hacer bajar los precios.
rail (reil) *s.* barra [para apoyo, etc.]; pasamano, barandal; varal [de carro]. *2* antepecho, baranda, barandilla, barrera. *3* bance. *4* CARP. peinazo. *5* carril, rail, riel; ferrocarril: *by* ~, por ferrocarril. *6* ORN. rascón.
rail (to) *tr.* poner barandilla, cercar con valla, verja, etc. *2* transportar por ferrocarril. *3 intr. to* ~ *at*, injuriar, vituperar.
railhead (-jed) *s.* término de vía férrea en construcción. *2* parte superior del riel. *3* MIL. estación ferroviaria de víveres y municiones.
railing (-ing) *adj.* injurioso, vituperioso. *2 s.* barandilla, pasamano, balaustrada, barrera, valla, reja, verja.
raillery (-øri) *s.* burla, fisga. *2* bufonada.
railroad (-roud) *s.* ferrocarril, vía férrea. | Ús. esp. en los E.U.
railroad (to) *tr.* proveer de ferrocarriles. *2* (E.U.) transportar por ferrocarril. *3* (E.U.) apresurar, atropellar; hacer aprobar [una ley, etc.] con precipitación.
railway (-uei) *s.* ferrocarril, vía férrea. | Ús. esp. en Ingl.: ~ *man*, ferroviario. *2* línea de carriles para trasladar algo sobre ruedas.
railway (to) *tr.* (Ingl.) proveer de ferrocarriles.
raiment (rei·mønt) *s.* ropa, indumento, vestidos.
rain (rein) *s.* lluvia: ~ *gauge*, pluviómetro; ~ *water*, agua llovediza; ~ *or shine*, con buen tiempo o con mal tiempo; *the rains*, la época de las lluvias.
rain (to) *intr. impers.* y *tr.* llover: *it is raining*, llueve; *to* ~ *cats and dogs, to* ~ *pitchforks*, llover a cántaros.
rainbow (-bou) *s.* arco iris. *2* espectro solar.
raincoat (-kout) *s.* impermeable, chubasquero.
raindrop (-drap) *s.* gota de lluvia.
rainfall (-føl) *s.* aguacero. *2* lluvia, lluvias.
rainpour (-po^r) *s.* aguacero.
rainproof (to) *tr.* impermeabilizar.
rainstorm (-sto^rm) *s.* tempestad de lluvia.
rainy (rei·ni) *adj.* lluvioso: ~ *day*, día lluvioso; *to save up for a* ~ *day*, ahorrar para el día de mañana; ~ *season*, época de las lluvias.
raise (reiš) *s.* aumento, alza, subida [de precio, salario, etc.]; aumento de sueldo.
raise (to) *tr.* levantar, alzar, elevar; poner derecho, enhestar, erguir, erigir. *2* levantar [polvo, la voz, los ánimos, falsos testimonios, un sitio, etc.]. *3* elevar, subir [la temperatura, el tono, los precios, etc.]. *4* elevar, engrandecer; ascender. *5* despertar. *6* excitar, levantar, sublevar. *7* suscitar, promover, originar; dar lugar a. *8* prorrumpir en [gritos, etc.]. *9* presentar, hacer [una objeción]. *10* cultivar [plantas], criar [animales]. *11* (E.U.) criar, educar. *12* reunir, allegar, obtener. *13* levantar, reclutar. *14* evocar, llamar. *15* hacer surgir o aparecer. *16* leudar. *17* MAT. elevar [a una potencia]. *18 to* ~ *Cain, hell, the devil*, etc., armar un jaleo.
raiser (rei·sšø^r) *s.* cultivador, productor; criador.
raisin (rei·sin) *s.* pasa [uva seca].
raja(h (ra·dẏa) *s.* rajá.

rake (reik) *s.* calavera, libertino. *2* AGR. rastro, rastrillo. *3* raqueta [de mesa de juego]. *4* rascador, raedera. *5* inclinación hacia popa [de un mástil, etc.]; inclinación hacia atrás. *6* MAR. lanzamiento.

rake (to) *tr.* AGR. rastrillar. *2* rascar, raer. *3* recoger, barrer. *4* atizar, hurgar [el fuego]. *5* registrar, buscar en. *6* MIL. barrer. *7* MÚS. rasguear. *8 to ~ over the coals,* criticar severamente. *9 to ~ together,* juntar, acumular. *10 intr.* buscar [en]. *11* estar inclinado hacia atrás.

raker (-ø^r) *s.* rastrillador. *2* AGR. rastrilladora mecánica. *3* raedera, rasqueta.

raking (-ing) *s.* AGR. rastrillaje. *2* reprimenda. *3 adj.* inclinado. *4* rápido, veloz.

rakish (-ish) *adj.* libertino. *2* airoso, gallardo, jacarandoso.

râle (ral) *s.* MED. estertor.

rally (ræ·li) *s.* unión, reunión [de tropas dispersas, de gente]. *2* recobro, restablecimiento.

rally (to) *tr.* reunir y reorganizar [tropas dispersas]. *2* reunir, concentrar [gente, energías, etc.]. *3* reanimar, fortalecer. *4* ridiculizar; embromar. *5 intr.* MIL. reunirse, rehacerse. *6* unirse [para una causa común]; dar su apoyo. *7* reponerse, rehacerse. *9* recobrar firmeza [los precios, el mercado]. ¶ Pret. y p. p.: *rallied.*

Ralph (rælf) *n. pr.* Rodolfo.

ram (ræm) *s.* ZOOL. morueco. *2* MIL. ariete. *3* ariete hidráulico. *4* MEC. martinete, pisón, émbolo percutor. *5* MAR. espolón; buque con espolón. *6* ASTR. (con may.) Aries.

ram (to) *tr.* apisonar. *2* golpear con martinete, pisón, espolón, ariete, etc. *3* hacer chocar [contra]. *4* clavar, meter [a golpes o por la fuerza]; atacar [un arma]; atestar, henchir. *5 intr.* chocar: *to ~ into,* dar contra, chocar con. ¶ Pret. y p. p.: *rammed;* ger.: *-mming.*

ramble (ræ·mbøl) *s.* paseo, excursión, correría, correteo. *2* divagación.

ramble (to) *intr.* pasear, vagar. *2* divagar. *3* extenderse libremente [una planta]. *4* serpentear [un río].

rambling (ræ·mbling) *adj.* paseador. *2* que divaga, incoherente. *3* BOT. trepador, rastrero. *4* grande y de planta irregular [casa].

ramification (ramifikei·shøn) *s.* ramificación.

ramify (to) (ræ·mifai) *tr.* dividir en ramas o ramales. *2 intr.* ramificarse.

rammer (ræ·mø^r) *s.* pisón. *2* atacador, baqueta. *3* MAR. espolón.

rammish (ræ·mish) *adj.* carneruno, maloliente. *2* libidinoso.

ramose (rei·mous), **ramous** (rei·møs) *adj.* ramoso.

ramp (ræmp) *s.* rampa, declive. *2* curva en la barandilla de una escalera. *3* salto o actitud agresiva.

ramp (to) *intr.* ARQ. elevarse o descender [un muro, etc.] a otro nivel. *2* saltar o avanzar amenazadoramente.

rampage (-idÿ) *s.* alboroto, furia, agitación, cólera: *to go on a ~,* alborotarse, enfurecerse.

rampage (to) *intr.* alborotarse, ponerse como un loco.

rampancy (-ansi) *s.* exuberancia, exceso.

rampant (-ant) *adj.* exuberante, excesivo. *2* fiero, violento. *3* general, extendido. *4* BLAS. rampante. *5* ARQ. por tranquil.

rampart (-a^{r}t) *s.* FORT. muralla, baluarte. *2* FORT. terraplén. *3* fig. defensa, amparo.

ramrod (ræ·mrad) *s.* baqueta [de fusil].

ramshackle (-shækøl) *adj.* desvencijado. *2* destartalado, ruinoso. *3* desarreglado, desordenado.

ran (ræn) *pret.* de TO RUN.

ranch (rænch) *s.* rancho, hacienda; *estancia.

rancher (-ø^r), **ranchman** (-mæn) *s.* ranchero, ganadero, vaquero.

rancid (ræ·nsid) *adj.* rancio, rancioso.

ranco(u)r (ræ·nkø^r) *s.* rencor, inquina, encono.

rancorous (-øs) *adj.* rencoroso, malévolo.

random (ræ·ndøm) *s.* azar, acaso: *at ~,* al azar, a la ventura. *2 adj.* ocasional, fortuito, impensado; hecho o dicho al azar.

rang (ræng) *pret.* de TO RING.

range (reindÿ) *s.* fila, línea, hilera: *range o mountain ~,* sierra, cordillera. *2* correría, viaje. *3* espacio [que recorre o cubre un cosa], recorrido. *4* esfera, campo [de una actividad, etc.]. *5* escala, gama, serie. *6* extensión de la voz. *7* alcance [de un arma, etc.]; distancia: *~ finder,* telémetro; *at close ~,* a quema ropa; *within the ~ of,* al alcance de. *8* autonomía [de un buque o avión]. *9* extensión de pastos. *10* clase, orden. *11* campo de tiro; línea de tiro. *12* línea [de dirección]: *in ~ with,* en línea con. *13* cocina económica. *14 pl.* montañas.

range (to) *tr.* alinear. *2* arreglar, ordenar. *3* recorrer, ir y venir por o a lo largo de. *4* pasear [la mirada, etc.] por. *5* tener cierto alcance [un arma]. *6 intr.* alinearse; estar en línea. *7* correr, errar. *8* extenderse, variar, fluctuar [dentro de ciertos límites]. *9* contarse [entre]; ponerse de parte [de].

ranger (-ø^r) *s.* guardabosque. *2* perro ventor.

rank (rænk) *adj.* lozano, lujuriante, exuberante, vicioso. *2* fértil. *3* rancio; ofensivo [sabor, olor]. *4* grosero [lenguaje, etc.]. *5* malo, insalubre. *6* absoluto, extremado, insigne, acabado. *7 s.* línea, hilera, fila. *8* rango, categoría, grado. *9* MIL. graduación. *10* calidad, distinción. *11* la clase alta. *12* MIL. fila: *the ranks, the ~ and file,* la tropa; fig. la gente de abajo.

rank (to) *tr.* alinear, formar, poner en fila. *2* ordenar, arreglar, clasificar. *3* MIL. tener una categoría superior a. *4 intr.* formar o marchar en filas. *6* tener [una categoría]; figurar o contarse entre: *to ~ high,* tener un alto grado o categoría; ser tenido en gran estima, sobresalir; *to ~ with,* contarse entre, tener la misma categoría que.

ranker (-ø^r) *s.* MIL. oficial patatero.

rankle (to) (ræ·nkøl) *intr.* enconarse, ulcerarse, inflamarse, irritarse. *2* fig. roer, escocer.

ransack (to) (-sæk) *tr.* registrar, explorar. *2* saquear, pillar.

ransom (-søm) *s.* rescate, redención.

ransom (to) *tr.* rescatar, redimir. *2* hacer pagar rescate.

rant (rænt) *s.* lenguaje retumbante, declamación sin sentido, monserga; delirio.

rant (to) *intr.* declamar a gritos. *2* desbarrar, delirar; enfurecerse.

ranula (ræ·niula) MED., VET. ránula.

ranunculus (ranø·nkiuløs) *s.* ranúnculo.

rap (ræp) *s.* golpe seco: *~ on a door,* llamada a una puerta. *2* crítica, censura. *3 fam. I don't care a ~,* no me importa un bledo.

rap (to) *tr.-intr.* golpear, dar un golpe seco: *to ~ at a door,* llamar a una puerta. *2 tr.* proferir vivamente. *3* (E.U.) criticar duramente. ¶ Pret. y p. p.: *rapped;* ger.: *-pping.*

rapacious (rapei·shøs) *adj.* rapaz. *2* codicioso. *3* voraz.

rapacity (-pæ·siti) *s.* rapacidad.
rape (reip) *s.* robo, rapiña; rapto. 2 violación, estupro. 3 BOT. colza. 4 *pl.* orujo, brisa.
rape (to) *tr.* robar, raptar. 2 violar, estuprar.
Raphael (ræ·fiǝl) *n. pr.* Rafael.
raphe (rei·fi) *s.* ANAT., BOT. rafe.
raphia (ra·fia) *s.* rafia [fibra].
rapid (ræ·pid) *adj.* rápido. 2 *s.* rápido, rabión.
rapidity (rapi·diti) *s.* rapidez.
rapier (ræ·piǝʳ) *s.* estoque, espadín.
rapier-fish *s.* ICT. pez espada.
rapine (ræ·pin) *s.* rapiña, pilaje.
rapper (ræ·pǝʳ) *s.* golpeador. 2 llamador, aldabón.
rapport (ræ·po·ʳt) *s.* relación, armonía, conformidad.
rapscallion (ræpskæ·liǝn) *s.* golfo, bribón, canalla.
rapt (ræpt) *adj.* arrebatado, transportado, enajenado, absorto.
raptorial (ræptou·rial) *adj.* rapaz, de rapiña.
rapture (ræ·pchǝʳ) *s.* rapto, arrebato, arrobamiento, éxtasis.
rapturous (-ǝs) *adj.* arrobado, embelesado.
rare (re·ǝʳ) *adj.* raro [de poca densidad]; ralo. 2 raro [poco común, escaso]: ~ *bird*, rara avis, mirlo blanco. 3 raro, insigne, excelente, peregrino. 4 COC. poco cocido.
raree-show (re·ri-shou) *s.* tutilimundi, mundonuevo.
rarefy (to) (re·rifai) *tr.* rarefacer, rarificar, enrarecer. 2 *intr.* rarificarse, encarecerse.
rarity (re·riti) *s.* rareza, raridad. 2 tenuidad. 3 preciosidad, primor. 4 curiosidad [cosa].
rascal (ræ·skal) *s.* bribón, pillo, granuja, canalla.
rascally (-i) *adj.* bribonesco. 2 *adv.* ruinmente.
rase (to) (rei·š) *tr.* arrasar. 2 raer. 3 raspar, borrar.
rash (ræsh) *adj.* irreflexivo, precipitado; imprudente, temerario. 2 *s.* salpullido.
rasher (ræ·shǝʳ) *s.* lonja, magra.
rashness (ræ·shnis) *s.* irreflexión, temeridad.
rasp (ræsp) *s.* escofina. 2 rallador. 3 sonido estridente. 4 raspamiento. 5 ronquera, carraspera.
rasp (to) *tr.* raspar, escofinar, raer, rallar: fig. *to ~ the ear*, desgarrar los oídos.
raspberry (ræ·zberi) *s.* BOT. frambuesa; frambueso.
rasper (ræ·spǝʳ) *s.* rallador, raspador.
rasping (-ping) *adj.* raspante. 2 áspero, bronco. 3 irritante, desagradable. 4 *s.* raspamiento.
rasure (rei·šǝʳ) *s.* raspadura, borradura.
rat (ræt) *s.* ZOOL. rata: ~ *trap*, ratonera; *to smell a* ~, sospechar algo malo; oler una intriga, etc. 2 pop. desertor. 3 pop. esquirol [obrero].
rat (to) *intr.* cazar ratas. 2 POL. volver casaca. 3 trabajar como esquirol. 4 *tr.* emplear esquiroles u obreros no sindicados. ¶ Pret. y p. p.: *ratted; ger.: -tting.*
ratable (rei·tabǝl) *adj.* sujeto a contribución, imponible. 2 valuable.
ratafia (rætafi·a) *s.* ratafia.
ratch (ræch), **ratchet** (-it) *s.* MEC. trinquete; cremallera de trinquete: ~ *jack*, gato de cremallera; ~ *wheel*, rueda de trinquete.
rate (reit) *s.* razón, proporción, tanto [por ciento, etc.]; tipo [de interés o cambio]; velocidad. 2 tarifa, precio, tasa, valor, grado. 3 clase, orden: *first* ~, de primer orden, muy bien. 4 modo, manera. 5 arbitrio, impuesto. 6 *at any* ~, al menos, de todos modos. 7 *at the* ~ *of*, a razón de. 8 *at this*, o *that* ~, a este paso, de este modo.
rate (to) *tr.* valuar, tasar, apreciar. 2 clasificar. 3 considerar como, contar entre. 4 reñir, repren-

der. 5 *intr.* valer, ser estimado o considerado: *to* ~ *high*, ser tenido en gran estima.
rather (ra·ðǝʳ) *adv.* bastante, algo, un tanto. 2 mejor, antes, más, más bien: *I had* ~, *I would* ~, me gustaría más, preferiría. 3 antes bien, al contrario. 4 mejor dicho. 5 *the* ~, *the* ~ *as*, *the* ~ *that*, tanto más cuanto que. 6 *interj.* ¡ya lo creo!
ratification (rætifikei·shǝn) *s.* ratificación, confirmación.
ratify (to) (ræ·tifai) *tr.* ratificar, confirmar.
rating (rei·ting) *s.* valuación, justiprecio. 2 clasificación; grado, clase. 4 MEC. capacidad de trabajo. 5 reprimenda, peluca.
ratio (rei·shiou) *s.* relación, proporción. 2 MAT. razón.
ratiocinate (to) (ræshia·sineit) *intr.* raciocinar, razonar.
ration (ræ·shǝn) *s.* MIL. ración. 2 ración, cupo.
ration (to) *tr.* racionar. 2 poner a ración.
rational (ræ·shǝnal) *adj.* racional. 2 cuerdo, razonable. 3 *s.* racional [ser; ornamento].
rationale (ræshǝnæ·li) *s.* fundamento, razón. 2 exposición razonada.
rationalism (ræ·shǝnališm) *s.* racionalismo.
rationality (ræshǝnæ·liti) *s.* racionalidad. 2 lo razonable.
rationalization (ræshǝnališei·shǝn) *s.* acción de hacer racional o explicable. 2 MAT., COM., IND. racionalización.
rationalize (to) (ræ·shǝnalaiš) *tr.* hacer racional o explicable. 2 MAT., COM., IND. racionalizar.
rationing (ræ·shǝning) *s.* racionamiento.
ratlin(e (ræ·tlin), **ratling** (-ling) *s.* MAR. flechaste.
ratsbane (ræ·tsbein) *s.* arsénico.
rattan (rætæ·n) *s.* rota, roten, junquillo, bejuco.
rattle (ræ·tǝl) *s.* tableteo, matraqueo, ruido de algo que rueda, es sacudido, etc. 2 fig. charla, parloteo. 3 estertor. 4 cascabel [de serpiente]. 5 sonajero. 6 matraca, carraca. 7 fig. parlanchín.
rattle (to) *tr.* hacer sonar como una matraca, sacudir, mover, hacer de prisa y con ruido. 2 decir, proferir rápidamente. | Gralte. con *off.* 3 desconcertar, agitar, aturrullar. 5 *intr.* tabletear, matraquear, guachapear, repiquetear. 6 rodar con ruido [un carruaje, etc.]. 7 temblar [la voz, los cristales. 8 parlotear. 9 tener estertor.
rattlebox (-baks) *s.* sonajero. 2 fig. charlatán.
rattle-head *s.* hablador, parlanchín. 2 casquivano.
rattler (ræ·tlǝʳ) *s.* parlanchín, tarabilla. 2 (E.U.) crótalo (serpiente).
rattlesnake (ræ·tǝlsneik) *s.* ZOOL. crótalo, serpiente de cascabel.
rattletrap (-træp) *adj.* desvencijado. 2 *s.* objeto desvencijado, carraca. 3 *pl.* retazos, chucherías.
rattling (ræ·tling) *adj.* ruidoso. 2 vivo, animado. 3 fam. estupendo.
raucity (ro·siti) *s.* ronquedad, bronquedad.
raucous (ro·kǝs) *adj.* rauco, ronco, bronco.
ravage (ræ·vidy̆) *s.* estrago, destrozo, destrucción, ruina, asolamiento. 2 saqueo, pillaje.
ravage (to) *tr.* asolar, talar, arruinar, destruir, hacer estragos en. 2 saquear, pillar.
rave (to) (reiv) *intr.* delirar, desvariarr, disparatar, despotricar. 2 bramar, enfurecerse. 3 *to* ~ *about* u *over*, estar loco por.
ravel (ræ·vǝl) *s.* RAVELLING. 2 RAVELMENT.
ravel (to) *tr.* deshilar, destejer, deshacer. 2 desenredar, desenmarañar. 3 *intr.* deshilarse, destorcerse, deshacerse. 4 desenredarse. ¶ Pret. y p. p.: *ravel(l)ed;* ger.: *-l(l)ing.*
ravelin (ræ·vlin) *s.* FORT. revellín.

ravel(l)ing (ræ·vøling) *s.* hilacha, deshiladura.

ravelment (-mønt) *s.* enredo, maraña.

raven (rei·vn) *s.* ORN. cuervo. *2 adj.* negro y lustroso.

raven (to) *tr.* devorar. *2* apresar, rapiñar.

ravenous (ræ·vnøs) *adj.* voraz. *2* hambriento, famélico. *3* rapaz.

ravin (ræ·vin) *s.* rapacidad. *2* rapiña.

ravine (rɑvi·n) *s.* barranco, barranca, hondonada, quebrada; arroyada.

raving (rei·ving) *s.* delirio, desvarío. *2 adj.* delirante. *3* furioso: ~ *mad,* loco de atar.

ravish (to) (ræ·vish) *tr.* arrebatar, extasiar, embelesar,encantar. *2* arrebatar, robar. *3* raptar, forzar, violar.

ravishment (-mønt) *s.* éxtasis, embeleso, arrobamiento. *2* rapto; forzamiento, violación.

raw (ro) *adj.* crudo [sin cocer, sin preparar], en bruto, en rama: ~ *material,* materia prima. *2* puro, sin diluir [aguardiente, etc.]. *3* tosco, sin refinamiento. *4* llagado, desollado: ~ *flesh,* carne viva. *5* crudo, húmedo, frío [tiempo, viento]. *6* bisoño, novato, inexperto. *7* ~ *deal,* mala pasada. *8 s.* carne viva, llaga, matadura. *9 in the* ~, en estado crudo o natural; al desnudo.

rawboned (-bound) *adj.* esquelético, demacrado.

rawhead (-jed) *s.* coco, espantajo.

rawhide (-jaid) *s.* cuero crudo, sin curtir. *2* látigo de cuero crudo.

ray (rei) *s.* rayo [de luz, calor, etc.]: *X rays,* rayos X. *2* luz [de la luna, de la razón, etc.]. *3* GEOM. radio. *4* BOT. lígula. *5* ICT. raya. *6* BOT. ~ *grass,* ballico.

ray (to) irradiar. *2* exponer a una radiación. *3 intr.* radiar, resplandecer. *4* extenderse en forma radiada.

rayon (rei·øn) *s.* TEJ. rayón.

raze (to) (reiš) *tr.* arrasar, asolar. *2* rascar, rozar. *3* raspar, borrar. *4* afeitar.

razor (rei·šøʳ) *s.* navaja de afeitar: ~ *strop,* suavizador [para la navaja]. *2* ZOOL. ~ *clam,* ~ *shell,* navaja [molusco].

razz (ræš) *s.* (E.U.) burla, irrisión.

razz (to) *tr.-intr.* (E.U.) mofarse [de].

razzia (ræ·šiɑ) *s.* razzia.

razzle-dazzle (ræ·šøl-dæ·šøl) *s.* bullicio, confusión, aturdimiento, borrachera. *2* especie de tíovivo.

re (rei) *s.* MÚS. re. *2 prep.* COM., DER. acerca de, referente a.

reabsorb (to) (riabsoʳb) *tr.* reabsorber.

reabsorption (-pshøn) *s.* reabsorción.

reaccess (riæ·ksis) *s.* MED. recidiva.

reach (rɪch) *s.* acción de alcanzar [con la mano, etc.]. *2* alcance, poder, posibilidad: *within my* ~, a mi alcance. *3* distancia, extensión. *4* tramo, sección. *5* extensión de tierra o agua. *6* MAR. bordada.

reach (to) *tr.* alargar, extender, tender: *to* ~ *out one's hand,* alargar o tender la mano. *2* tocar, llegar a o hasta, alcanzar: *to* ~ *home,* llegar a casa. *3* llegar a las manos, a oídos, etc., de. *4* alargar, dar. *5* largar, atizar. *6* mover, influir sobre. *7* alcanzar, obtener. *8* comprender. *9 intr.* alargar el brazo, la mano, etc. [para tocar, alcanzar, etc.]. *10* extenderse, llegar, alcanzar [a o hasta]. *11* MAR. ceñir el viento. *12 to* ~ *after,* esforzarrse por obtener. *13 to* ~ *into,* meter la mano en, penetrar en.

reach-me-down *adj.* hecho [ropa]; de lance; de segunda mano.

react (to) (riæ·kt) *intr.* reaccionar.

re-act (to) *tr.* TEAT. volver a representar.

reactance (-tans) *s.* ELECT. reactancia.

reaction (-shøn) *s.* reacción.

reactionary (-shøneri) *adj.-s.* reaccionario.

reactivate (to) (-tiveit) *tr.* reactivar.

reactive (-tiv) *adj.* reactivo.

reactor (-øʳ) *s.* FÍS., ELECT. reactor. *2* QUÍM. reactivo.

read (red) *pret.* y *p. p.* de TO READ. *2 adj.* instruido, versado.

read (to) (rɪd) *tr.* leer. *2* interpretar. *3* descifrar [señales, indicios, etc.]. *4* aprender, estudiar. *5* indicar, registrar [dic. de un termómetro, etc.]. *6* IMPR. corregir [pruebas]. *7 to* ~ *one a lecture,* reprender vivamente. *8 to* ~ *out of,* expulsar de [una asociación, etc.]. *9 intr.* leer: *to* ~ *of o about,* leer acerca de, leer que; *to* ~ *through one,* leerle a uno el pensamiento; *to* ~ *for the bar,* prepararse para el foro. *10* decir, rezar [un escrito o impreso]: *the passage reads thus,* el pasage reza así. *11* dar conferencias. *12* leerse: *it reads easily,* se lee con facilidad. ¶ Pret. y p. p.: *read* (red).

readable (-øbøl) *adj.* legible, leíble. *2* interesante, entretenido [libro, etc.].

readapt (to) (rɪadæ·pt) *tr.* readaptar.

reader (rɪ·døʳ) *s.* lector. *2* IMPR. corrector. *3* libro de lectura.

readily (re·dili) *adv.* prontamente. *2* fácilmente, sin esfuerzo. *3* de buena gana.

readiness (-nis) *s.* prontitud, expedición, facilidad. *2* disposición, buena voluntad. *3* disponibilidad.

reading (rɪ·ding) *s.* lectura, lección. *2* conferencia, disertación. *3* indicación [de un termómetro, etc.]. *4* leyenda [materia escrita]. *5 adj.* que lee; de lectura: ~ *book,* libro de lectura; ~ *desk,* atril, facistol; ~ *room,* gabinete de lectura.

readjust (to) (rɪadjø·st) *tr.* reajustar.

readmit (to) (rɪadmi·t) *tr.* readmitir.

ready (re·di) *adj.* preparado, pronto, listo, dispuesto, aparejado: *to make* ~, preparar, disponer; *preparárse. 2* dispuesto, gustoso. *3* vivo, ágil, diestro. *4* fácil [método]. *5* pronto [pago, réplica, etc.]. *6* a la mano, disponible; contante, efectivo. *7* ~ *reckoner,* baremo.

ready (to) *tr.* preparar, apercibir, aprestar.

ready-made *adj.* ya hecho, confeccionado: ~ *clothes,* ropa hecha.

ready-witted *adj.* de ingenio vivo, pronto.

reaffirm (to) (rɪaføʳm) *tr.* reafirmar, reiterar.

reafforest (to) (rɪafo·røst) *tr.* repoblar de árboles.

reagent (rieidyønt) *s.* QUÍM. reactivo.

real (ri·ɑl) *adj.* real, verdadero. *2* sincero. *3* DER., FÍS. real. *4* DER. inmueble, raíz: ~ *estate,* bienes raíces; fincas.

real-estate *adj.* inmobiliario; de fincas.

realgar (riæ·lgaʳ) *s.* rejalgar.

realism (rɪ·ališm) *s.* FIL., B. ART. realismo. *2* realismo, espíritu práctico.

realistic (rɪali·stik) *adj.* FIL., B. ART. realista. *2* práctico, realista.

reality (riæ·liti) *s.* realidad.

realizable (rɪ·alaišabøl) *adj.* realizable. *2* comprensible, perceptible.

realization (rɪališei·shøn) *s.* realización. *2* comprensión.

realize (to) (rɪ·alaiš) *tr.* comprender, ver, sentir, percatarse de. *2* realizar. *3* dar vida o realidad a. *4* obtener [un precio].

really (rɪ·ali) *adv.* realmente, de veras.

realm (relm) *s.* reino. *2* campo, dominio, región.

realty (rɪ·alti) *s.* DER. bienes raíces.
ream (rɪm) *s.* resma. *2* gran cantidad.
ream (to) *tr.* MEC. escariar.
reamer (rɪ·møʳ) *s.* escariador.
reanimate (to) (rɪæ·nimeit) *tr.* reanimar. *2 intr.* reanimarse.
reap (to) (rɪp) *tr.* segar, guadañar. *2* recoger, cosechar.
reaper (rɪ·pøʳ) *s.* segador. *2* segadora mecánica.
reaping machine *s.* segadora mecánica.
reappear (to) (rɪapi·ʳ) *intr.* reaparecer.
reappraise (to) (rɪaprei·ŝ) *tr.* retasar.
rear (rɪ·øʳ) *adj.* trasero, de atrás, de cola, último, posterior: ~ *admiral*, contralmirante; ~ *drive*, AUTO. tracción posterior; ~ *guard*, retaguardia. *2 s.* trasera, zaga, parte de atrás; fondo [de una sala]; cola [de una fila]: *in the* ~, detrás, atrás, a la cola. *3* MIL. retaguardia.
rear (to) *tr.* levantar, alzar; erguir; erigir. *2* criar, cultivar; educar. *3 intr.* empinarse, encabritarse.
rearm (to) (rɪ·aʳm) *tr.* MIL. rearmar. *2 intr.* rearmarse.
rearmost (rɪ·øʳmoust) *adj.* último, de más atrás.
rearrange (to) (rɪarei·ndŷ) *tr.* volver a arreglar, disponer en un nuevo orden; refundir.
rear-view mirror *s.* AUTO. retrovisor.
rearward (rɪ·øʳuøʳd) *adj.* posterior, último. *2 adv.* hacia atrás, hacia la cola. *3 s.* retaguardia.
reason (rɪ·ŝøn) *s.* razón. | No tiene el sentido de razón en MAT. ni el de razón social. *2* ~ *of state*, razón de estado; *to bring to* ~, hacer entrar en razón; *to listen to* ~, atender a razones; *it stands to* ~, es razonable, es justo; *by* ~ *of*, por causa de.
reason (to) *tr.-intr.* razonar. *2 intr.* raciocinar. *3 tr.* discutir, debatir. *4* persuadir o disuadir con razones.
reasonable (-abøl) *adj.* racional [ser]. *2* razonable. *3* módico, de precio módico.
reasoner (-øʳ) *s.* razonador, discutidor.
reasoning (-ing) *s.* razonamiento.
reasonless (-lis) *adj.* irracional [privado de razón]. *2* sin razón o motivo. *3* desrazonable.
reassume (to) (-siu·m) *tr.* reasumir [volver a tomar]. *2* volver a adoptar [una actitud, etc.]; a ocupar [un sitio]. *3* reanudar.
reassurance (-shu·rans) *s.* confianza restablecida. *2* seguridad renovada, afirmación repetida. *3* COM. reaseguro.
reassure (to) (-shu·øʳ) *tr.* tranquilizar. *2* asegurar de nuevo. *3* COM. reasegurar.
reassuring (-ing) *adj.* tranquilizador.
rebaptize (to) (rɪbæ·ptaiŝ) *tr.* rebautizar.
rebate (rɪbei·t) *s.* disminución, rebaja, descuento. *2* ARQ., CARP. rebajo.
rebate (to) *tr.* disminuir, deducir, rebajar, descontar. *2* ARQ., CARP. hacer un rebajo en.
rebatement (-mønt) *s.* rebaja, descuento.
Rebecca (ribe·ka) *n. pr.* Rebeca.
rebeck (rɪ·bek) *s.* MÚS. rabel.
rebel (re·bøl) *adj.-s.* rebelde; insurgente.
rebel (to) (ribe·l) *intr.* rebelarse, sublevarse.
rebellion (-iøn) *s.* rebelión, sublevación.
rebellious (-øs) *adj.* rebelde. *2* insubordinado.
rebind (to) (rɪbai·nd) *tr.* reencuadernar. *2* volver a atar, a vendar. *3* COST. ribetear de nuevo.
rebirth (rɪbø·ʳz) *s.* renacimiento.
reblossom (to) (rɪbla·søm) *intr.* reflorecer.
rebound (rɪbau·nd) *s.* rebote, rechazo. *2* repercusión, eco. *3* salto, bote.

rebound (to) *intr.* rebotar, resurtir. *2* repercutir. *3* volver a adquirir actualidad o interés. *4 tr.* devolver, rechazar, reflejar.
rebounding (-ing) *s.* rebote, rechazo.
rebroadcast (rɪbro·dkæst) *s.* RADIO. retransmisión.
rebroadcast (to) *tr.* RADIO. retransmitir.
rebuff (ribø·f) *s.* sofión, repulsa, desaire.
rebuff (to) *tr.* dar un sofión a, desairar, repulsar.
rebuild (to) (rɪbi·ld) *tr.* reconstruir.
rebuke (ribiu·k) *s.* reproche, censura, increpación, reprimenda.
rebuke (to) *tr.* increpar, reprender, reñir, censurar. *2* ser un reproche para.
rebus (rɪ·bøs) *s.* jeroglífico.
rebut (to) (ribø·t) *tr.* refutar, rebatir. ¶ Pret. y p. p.: *rebutted;* ger.: *-tting.*
rebuttal (ribø·tal) *s.* refutación.
recalcitrant (rikæ·lsitrant) *adj.* recalcitrante, obstinado, rebelde.
recalcitrate (to) (-sitreit) *intr.* recalcitrar.
recall (riko·l) *s.* llamada [para hacer volver]. *2* retirada [de un embajador]. *3* recordación. *4* anulación, revocación: *beyond* ~, irrevocable. *5* MIL. llamada [a la tropa].
recall (to) *tr.* llamar, hacer volver. *2* retirar [un embajador, unas palabras, etc.]. *3* recordar, acordarse de. *4* anular, revocar. *5* destituir.
recant (to) (rikæ·nt) *tr.* retractar, desdecirse de. *2 intr.* retractarse, desdecirse.
recantation (-ei·shøn) *s.* retractación.
recap (to) (rɪkæ·p) *tr.* recauchutar [neumáticos].
recapitulate (to) (rɪkapi·chøleit) *tr.-intr.* recapitular, resumir.
recapitulation (-ei·shøn) *s.* recapitulación, resumen.
recast (to) (rɪkæ·st) *tr.* refundir. *2* reformar, rehacer. *3* calcular de nuevo. ¶ Pret. y p. p.: *recast.*
recede (to) (risi·d) *intr.* retroceder. *2* retirarse, alejarse; inclinarse hacia atrás. *3* desistir, volverse atrás.
receipt (risi·t) *s.* receta, fórmula. *2* recepción, recibo: *to aknowledge* ~, acusar recibo; *on* ~ *of*, al recibo de. *3* cobranza. *4* recibo, carta de pago, recibí. *5 pl.* ingresos, entradas.
receipt (to) *tr.* poner el recibí en.
receivable (risi·vabøl) *adj.* recibidero. *2* cobradero: *bills* ~, cuentas por cobrar.
receive (to) (risi·v) *tr.* recibir: *received payment*, recibí. *2* tomar, aceptar. *3* acoger. *4* percibir, cobrar. *5* comprar, receptar [géneros robados].
receiver (-øʳ) *s.* receptor, recibidor. *2* DER. depositario. *3* cobrador, tesorero. *4* receptador [de géneros robados]. *5* ELECT., RADIO. receptor. *6* TELÉF. auricular. *7* receptáculo, recipiente [de ciertos aparatos]. *8* DER. síndico [de una quiebra].
receiving (-ing) *adj.* receptor: ~ *set*, RADIO. receptor; ~ *teller*, cobrador [de la caja de un banco].
recense (to) (rise·ns) *tr.* revisar [un texto].
recension (-shøn) *s.* revisión crítica. *2* texto revisado.
recent (rɪ·sent) *adj.* reciente. *2* moderno, nuevo.
receptacle (rise·ptakøl) *s.* receptáculo, recipiente. *2* BOT. receptáculo. *3* ELECT. parte fija en un enchufe.
receptibility (riseptibi·liti) *s.* receptividad.
reception (rise·pshøn) *s.* recepción. *2* admisión, aceptación; ingreso.
receptionist (-ist) *s.* recepcionista.
receptive (rise·ptiv) *adj.* receptivo.
receptivity (risepti·viti) *s.* receptividad.

receptor (rise·ptø^r) *s.* DER. receptador. *2* TELÉF. auricular.

recess (rise·s) *s.* hueso, entrada, nicho, alcoba. *2* suspensión, descanso; recreo [escolar]. *3* retiro, lugar recóndito.

recess (to) *tr.* retirar, apartar. *2* hacer un hueco o entrada en. *3 intr.* (E.U.) tomarse una vacación, un descanso.

recession (-shøn) *s.* retroceso, retirada. *2* parte que hace hueco o entrada. *3* DER. retrocesión.

recharge (ri·cha^{r}dÿ) *s.* recarga. *2* carga de recambio.

recharge (to) *tr.* recargar [cargar de nuevo].

recidivist (risi·divist) *s.* criminal reincidente.

recipe (re·sipi) *s.* récipe, receta.

recipient (risi·piønt) *adj.-s.* receptor, recibidor.

reciprocal (risi·prøkal) *adj.* recíproco, mutuo. *2* GRAM. recíproco. *3* intercambiable, permutable; inverso. *4* alternativo, de vaivén. *5* MAT. lo recíproco o inverso.

reciprocate (to) (risi·prøkeit) *tr.* reciprocar. *2* cambiar, intercambiar. *3* corresponder a [un afecto, favor, etc.]. *4* MEC. dar movimiento alternativo o de vaivén a. *5 intr.* ser recíproco o correspondiente. *6* corresponder a un cumplido, etc. *7* MEC. tener movimiento alternativo o de vaivén: *reciprocating engine*, máquina de émbolo o pistón.

reciprocation (-ei·shøn) *s.* reciprocación, reciprocidad. *2* intercambio; correspondencia. *3* MEC. movimiento alternativo.

recision (risi·ÿøn) *s.* rescisión.

recital (risai·tal) *s.* relación, narración; enumeración. *2* recitación. *3* MÚS. recital.

recitation (resitei·shøn) *s.* recitación.

recitative (risai·tativ) *adj.* recitativo. *2 s.* (resitati·v) MÚS. recitado.

recite (to) (risai·t) *tr.-intr.* recitar. *2 tr.* narrar. *3* dar o decir [la lección].

reck (to) (rek) *tr.* preocuparse por, hacer caso de, tener en cuenta. *2 intr.* preocuparse.

reckless (-lis) *adj.* indiferente; que no hace caso. *2* temerario, atolondrado, inconsiderado.

recklessness (-nis) *s.* temeridad, atolondramiento.

reckon (to) (re·køn) *tr.-intr.* contar, calcular. *2 tr.* considerar [como]; tener, reputar [por]; contar [entre]. *3* calcular, suponer, creer. *4 intr. to* ~ *on* o *with*, contar con.

reckoner (-ø^r) *s.* contador, calculador.

reckoning (-ing) *s.* cuenta, cómputo, cálculo. *2* cuenta [que se paga; que se da]; ajuste de cuentas. *3* MAR. estima.

reclaim (to) (riklei·m) *tr.* poner en cultivo, hacer utilizable [un terreno]; ganar [terreno] al mar. *3* salvar, poner a flote. *4* regenerar, redimir [a una pers.]. *5* regenerar [una materia]. *6* DER. reclamar.

reclamation (reclamei·shøn) *s.* regeneración, enmienda [de una pers.]. *2* regeneración [de una materia]. *3* puesta en cultivo, desecación, etc. [de terrenos]. *4* DER. reclamación.

reclination (reklinei·shøn) *s.* reclinación.

recline (to) (riklai·n) *tr.* reclinar, recostar. *2 intr.* reclinarse, recostarse.

recluse (rikliu·s) *adj.* retirado, solitario. *2 s.* pers. retirada del mundo; monje, eremita.

reclusion (riklu·ÿøn) *s.* reclusión; retiro, aislamiento, recogimiento.

recognition (rekøgni·shøn) *s.* reconocimiento. *2* atención, caso [que se hace a uno], saludo amistoso.

recognize (to) (re·køgnaiš) *tr.* reconocer. | No tiene el sentido de examinar o registrar. *2* agradecer.

recoil (rikoi·l) *s.* retroceso, reculada, reacción. *2* rebote, rechazo. *3* coz, culatazo [de un arma]. *4* movimiento de repugnancia, temor, etc.

recoil (to) *intr.* retroceder, recular, retirarse. *2* dar coz o culatazo [un arma]. *3* sobrecogerse, arredrarse.

Recollect (re·kølekt) *adj.-s.* ECLES. recoleto.

recollect (to) (rekøle·kt) *tr.-intr.* recordar, acordarse.

re-collect, recollect (to) (rıkøle·kt) *tr.* recoger, reunir. *2* recobrar. *3 to* ~ *oneself*, reponerse, serenarse; pensarlo mejor. *4 intr.* reunirse, volver a juntarse.

recollection (rekøle·kshøn) *s.* recuerdo, memoria. *2* recolección, recogimiento [espiritual].

recommence (to) (rıkøme·ns) *tr.-intr.* comenzar de nuevo.

recommend (to) (rekøme·nd) *tr.* recomendar. *2* alabar. *3* encomendar [en las oraciones].

recommendation (rekømendei·shøn) *s.* recomendación. *2* consejo.

recompense (re·kømpens) *s.* recompensa. *2* compensación, indemnización.

recompense (to) *tr.* recompensar, pagar, retribuir. *2* compensar, indemnizar.

recompose (to) (rıkømpou·š) *tr.* tranquilizar, serenar de nuevo. *2* recomponer, rehacer.

reconcilable (re·kønsailabøl) *adj.* reconciliable. *2* conciliable, compatible.

reconcile (to) (re·kønsail) *tr.* reconciliar: *to become reconciled*, reconciliarse [dos o más pers.]. *2* conciliar, compaginar, hacer compatible. *3 to* ~ *oneself to*, conformarse con, resignarse a.

recondite (re·køndait) *adj.* recóndito, secreto. *2* abstruso, profundo.

recondition (to) (rıkøndi·shøn) *tr.* reacondicionar.

reconduct (to) (rıkøndø·kt) *tr.* volver a conducir o acompañar.

reconnaissance (rika·nisans) *s.* MIL. reconocimiento.

reconnoitre (to) (rekønoi·tø^r) *tr.* MIL. reconocer. *2 intr.* MIL. hacer un reconocimiento.

reconquer (to) (rıka·nkø^r) *tr.* reconquistar.

reconquest (-kuest) *s.* reconquista.

reconsider (to) (rıkønsi·dø^r) *tr.* repensar. *2* volver a estudiar, a discutir.

reconstitute (to) (rıka·nstitiut) *tr.* reconstituir.

reconstruct (to) (rıkønstrø·kt) *tr.* reconstruir.

reconvention (rıkønve·nshøn) *s.* DER. reconvención.

reconvey (to) (rıkønvei) *tr.* devolver al punto de partida. *2* traspasar [a un propietario anterior].

record (re·ko^{r}d) *s.* inscripción, registro. *2* partida, copia oficial. *3* acta, documento, relación, historia. *4* DER. expediente, autos. *5* hoja de servicios, historial. *6* rollo, disco [de fonógrafo, pianola, etc.]; cinta [magnetofónica]; grabación [en disco, etc.]. *7* DEP. récord, marca: *to beat* o *break the* ~, batir la marca. *8* pl. archivo, protocolo. *9* fastos, anales, memorias. *10 adj.* nunca visto, de récord, de marca.

record (to) (riko·^{r}d) *tr.* asentar, inscribir, registrar. *2* protocolizar [documentos]. *3* fijar en la memoria. *4* grabar en disco fonográfico, etc.

recorder (-ø^r) *s.* archivero, registrador: ~ *of deeds*, registrador de la propiedad. *2* grabador de discos o cintas magnetofónicas. *3* MEC. indicador, contador.

re-count (rı·kaunt) *s.* recuento.

re-count (to) (rıkau·nt) *tr.* recontar.
recount (to) (rikau·nt) *tr.* referir, relatar, contar.
recoup (to) (riku·p) *tr.* resarcirse de. *2* resarcir, indemnizar. *3 intr.* resarcirse, indemnizarse.
recourse (riko·ʳs) *s.* recurso, refugio, auxilio: *to have ~ to,* recurrir a. *2* COM. *without ~,* sin responsabilidad por parte del endosante.
re-cover (to) (rɪka·vøʳ) *tr.* volver a cubrir o tapar.
recover (to) (rika·vøʳ) *tr.* recobrar, recuperar. *2* curar; hacer volver en sí. *3* rescatar, librar. *4* DER. ganar, obtener, reivindicar. *5 to ~ oneself,* reponerse; recobrar el equilibrio. *6 intr.* restablecerse; volver en sí.
recoverable (-abøl) *adj.* recuperable, recobrable; cobrable.
recovery (-i) *s.* recobro, recuperación. *2* cobranza. *3* restablecimiento, convalecencia: *past ~,* sin remedio.
recreant (re·kriant) *adj.-s.* cobarde. *2* falso, desleal; apóstata.
recreate (to) (re·krieit) *tr.* recrear, divertir, deleitar. *2 intr.* recrearse.
re-create (to) (rɪ·criei·t) *tr.* recrear [crear de nuevo].
recreation (recriei·shøn) *s.* recreación, recreo.
recreative (re·krieitiv) *adj.* recreativo.
recriminate (to) (rikri·mineit) *tr.* recriminar.
recrimination (-ei·shøn) *s.* recriminación.
recross (to) (rıkro·s) *tr.* repasar, volver a cruzar.
recrudesce (to) (rıkriude·s) *intr.* recrudecer.
recrudescence (-øns) *s.* recrudecimiento.
recruit (rikriu·t) *s.* recluta, novato.
recruit (to) *tr.* reclutar, alistar. *2* reanimar, rehacer. *3 intr.* recobrarse, reponerse. *4* rehacerse [un ejército].
recruitment (-mønt) *s.* reclutamiento. *2* MIL. refuerzo.
rectal (re·ktal) *adj.* ANAT. rectal.
rectangle (re·ktøngøl) *s.* GEOM. rectángulo.
rectangular (rektæ·ngiulaʳ) *adj.* rectangular.
rectification (rektifikei·shøn) *s.* rectificación, corrección, enmienda. *2* GEOM., QUÍM., ELECT. rectificación.
rectify (to) (re·ktifai) *tr.* rectificar, corregir, enmendar. *2* COM., QUÍM., ELECT. rectificar. ¶ Pret. y p. p.: *rectified.*
rectilineal (rektili·nial), **rectilinear** (-aʳ) *adj.* rectilíneo.
rectitude (re·ktitiud) *s.* rectitud. *2* corrección, exactitud.
recto (re·ktou) *s.* folio recto.
rector (re·ktøʳ) *s.* rector, párroco. *2* rector [de una comunidad, de universidad].
rectorate (-it) *s.* curato. *2* rectorado.
rectory (-i) *s.* curato. *2* casa rectoral.
rectrix (re·ktriks) *s.* timonera [pluma].
rectum (-tøm) *s.* ANAT. recto.
recumbent (rikø·mbønt) *adj.* reclinado, recostado; yacente.
recuperate (to) (rikiu·pøreit) *tr.* recuperar, recobrar. *2 intr.* restablecerse, reponerse, rehacerse.
recuperation (-ei·shøn) *s.* recuperación, recobro. *2* restablecimiento [de la salud].
recur (to) (rikø·ʳ) *intr.* volver [a un tema]. *2* volver a ofrecerse [a la mente, etc.]. *3* volver a ocurrir, repetirse.
recurrence (rikø·røns), **recurrency** (-si) *s.* repetición, reaparición [esp. periódica].
recurrent (-ønt) *adj.* que se repite o reaparece; periódico. *2* ANAT., BOT. recurrente.
recurve (to) (rikø·ʳv) *tr.* recorvar. *2 intr.* recorvarse.

recusation (rekiušei·shøn) *s.* recusación.
red (red) *adj.* encarnado, colorado, rojo; enrojecido, encendido, sanguíneo, sangriento: *~ ball,* mingo [en el billar]; *~ blood,* sangre roja, vitalidad; *~ cabbage,* lombarda [col]; *~ cell, ~ corpuscle,* hematíe, glóbulo rojo; *~ cross,* cruz de San Jorge; *Red Cross,* Cruz Roja; *~ currant,* grosella; *~ hat,* capelo [de cardenal]; (Ingl.) oficial de estado mayor; *~ heat,* calor al rojo; *~ herring,* arenque ahumado; *~ lead,* minio; *~ light,* luz roja; señal de peligro; *~ man,* indio norteamericano; *~ ocher,* almagre; *~ pepper,* pimentón, ají, chile; *~ rag,* trapo rojo; lo que excita o enfurece; *Red Ridinghood,* Caperucita Roja; *~ tape,* balduque; fig. formalismo burocrático, expendienteo; *~ wine,* vino tinto; *to see ~,* enfurecerse; *to turn ~,* ponerse colorado, sonrojarse. *2 adj.-s.* POL. rojo, revolucionario. *3 s.* rojo, encarnado [color, colorante].
redact (to) (rıdæ·kt) *tr.* redactar, escribir. *2* rehacer, revisar [un artículo, etc.].
redaction (-shøn) *s.* redacción [acción de redactar o escribir]. *2* nueva redacción; revisión.
red-bearded *adj.* barbirrojo.
redbird (re·dbøʳd) *s.* ORN. nombre del pinzón real, del cardenal y de otros pájarros.
red-blooded *adj.* animoso. *2* fuerte, viril.
redbreast (-brest) *s.* ORN. petirrojo.
redcap (-kæp) *s.* (E.U.) mozo de estación. *2* (Ingl.) pop. miembro de la policía militar.
redcoat (-kout) *s.* fam. (Ingl.) soldado.
redden (to) (-øn) *tr.* enrojecer, embermejar. *2 intr.* enrojecerse. *3* enrojecer, ruborizarse.
reddish (-ish) *adj.* rojizo.
reddle (re·døl) *s.* almagre.
redeem (to) (ridi·m) *tr.* redimir. *2* cumplir [una promesa]. *3* compensar.
redeemer (-øʳ) *s.* redentor: *The Redeemer,* el Redentor, el Salvador.
redeeming (-ing) *adj.* redentor. *2* que salva o atenúa: *~ feature,* circunstancia atenuante.
redemand (to) (rıdimæ·nd) *tr.* volver a pedir o a preguntar.
redemption (ride·mpshøn) *s.* redención. *2* cumplimiento [de una promesa, etc.].
redescend (to) (rı·disend) *intr.* volver a bajar.
red-haired *adj.* pelirrojo.
red-handed *adj.* con las manos ensangrentadas. *2* con las manos en la masa, en flagrante.
redheaded (re·djedid) *adj.* pelirrojo. *2* de cabeza roja. *3* colérico.
red-hot *adj.* calentado al rojo, muy caliente. *2* acérrimo, muy entusiasta. *3* fresco, reciente [noticia, etc.].
redintegrate (to) (redi·ntigreit) *tr.* reintegrar, restablecer, renovar.
redirect (to) (rıdire·kt) *tr.* volver a dirigir.
rediscount (to) (rıdi·skaunt) *s.* COM. redescuento.
rediscount (to) (rıdi·skaunt) COM. redescontar.
redistribute (to) (rıdistri·biut) *tr.* redistribuir.
red-letter *adj.* marcado con letra roja: *~ day,* día de fiesta; día señalado, feliz, memorable.
redness (-nis) *s.* rojez, rojura, bermejura.
redolent (re·dølønt) *adj.* fragante, oloroso. *2* impregnado. *3* que recuerda o tiene algo [de].
redouble (to) (rıdø·bøl) *tr.* reduplicar, redoblar, aumentar. *2 intr.* redoblarse. *3 tr.-intr.* BRIDGE. recontrar.
redoubt (ridau·t) *s.* FORT. reducto.
redoubtable (-abøl) *adj.* temible, formidable.

redound (to) (ridau·nd) *intr.* redundar, resultar. *2* refluir, recaer.

redpoll (re·dpoul) *s.* ORN. pajarel, pardillo.

redraft (rɪ·dræft) *s.* COM. resaca. *2* nuevo dibujo o borrador.

redraw (to) (rɪdrɔ·) *tr.* COM. recambiar. *2* hacer nuevo dibujo o borrador.

redress (rɪ·dres) *s.* reparación, desagravio. *2* remedio; compensación. *3* corrección, enmienda.

redress (to) (ridre·s) *tr.* deshacer, reparar [injusticias, etc.]. *2* resarcir, compensar, remediar. *3* corregir, enmendar. *4* AVIA. enderezar. *5* equilibrar [una balanza].

re-dress (to) (rɪ-dre·s) *tr.-intr.* vestir o vestirse de nuevo.

redskin (re·dskin) *s.* indio piel roja.

red-tape *adj.* burocrático, de expedienteo.

reduce (to) (ridiu·s) *tr.* reducir [disminuir; someter, obligar; convertir]. *2* rebajar, diluir. *3* MIL. degradar. *4* CIR., QUÍM., MAT. reducir. *5* FOT. rebajar. *6* *intr.* reducirse.

reducer (-ø^r) *s.* reductor. *2* FOT. líquido para rebajar. *3* MEC. manguito o tubo de reducción.

reduction (ridø·kshøn) *s.* reducción. *2* ~ *works,* instalación donde se queman las basuras de una población.

redundance (ridø·ndans), **-cy** (-si) *s.* redundancia.

redundant (-ant) *adj.* redundante.

reduplicate (ridiu·plikeit) *adj.* reduplicado, doblado.

reduplicate (to) *tr.* reduplicar, redoblar.

redwing (re·dwing) *s.* ORN. malvis.

redwood (-wud) *s.* BOT. secoya.

re-echo (to) (rɪe·kou) *intr.-tr.* resonar, repercutir, repetir [como un eco].

reed (rɪd) *s.* BOT. caña; carrizo; junco. *2* caña [material]. *3* MÚS. caramillo. *4* MÚS. lengüeta; instrumento de lengüeta: ~ *organ,* armonio, concertina. *5* MÚS. boquilla. *6* ARQ. junquillo. *7* TEJ. peine. *8* poét. saeta. *9* BOT. ~ *mace,* espadaña.

re-educate (to) (rɪe·dȳøkiet) *tr.* reeducar.

re-education (-eishøn) *s.* reeducación.

reedy (rɪ·di) *adj.* de caña o que lo parece. *2* abundante en cañas. *3* de tono delgado y agudo.

reef (rɪf) *s.* arrecife, bajío, escollo. *2* MIN. filón, vena. *3* MAR. rizo: *to take in a* ~, tomar un rizo.

reef (to) *tr.* MAR. arrizar: *to* ~ *one's sails,* fig. recoger velas.

reefer (-ø^r) *s.* chaquetón de paño grueso. *2* pop. (E.U.) cigarrillo de marihuana.

reefy (-i) *adj.* lleno de escollos.

reek (rɪk) *s.* vaho, vapor, humo, tufo, mal olor.

reek (to) *tr.* exhalar, echar [vaho, humo, tufo, etc.]. *2* ahumar. *3* *intr.* humear, vahear; oler mal: *to* ~ *of,* oler a. *4* salir [un vaho, humo, etc.].

reeky (-i) *adj.* humeante; mal oliente.

reel (rɪl) *s.* devanadera, carrete, broca. *2* CINE. rollo [de película]. *3* danza escocesa muy animada. *4* tambaleo.

reel (to) *tr.* aspar, devanar. *2* hacer dar vueltas a. *3* *to* ~ *off,* contar, recitar, fácil y prestamente. *4* *intr.* dar vueltas [la cabeza]. *5* tambalearse, vacilar, retroceder.

re-elect (to) (rɪile·kt) *tr.* reelegir.

re-embark (to) (rɪemba·^rk) *tr.* reembarcar.

re-enact (to) (rɪenæ·kt) *tr.* revalidar, promulgar de nuevo [una ley]. *2* volver a representar [un papel].

re-engage (to) (rɪengei·dȳ) *tr.* escriturar o contratar de nuevo.

re-enlist (to) (rɪenli·st) *tr.* reenganchar, volver a alistar. *2* *intr.* reengancharse.

re-enter (to) (rɪe·ntø^r) *tr.* volver a entrar en, reingresar en.

re-entering (-ing) *adj.* entrante [ángulo].

re-establish (to) (rɪestæ·blish) *tr.* restablecer, establecer de nuevo, instaurar.

reeve (to) (rɪv) MAR. hacer pasar [un cabo] por; asegurar [un cabo, etc.] en algo. *2* MAR. rozar [un bajío]. *3* *intr.* MAR. laborear.

re-examine (rɪegšæ·min) *tr.* reexaminar, revisar.

re-export (to) (rɪe·kspo^rt) *tr.* reexportar.

refection (rife·kshøn) *s.* refacción, comida.

refer (to) (rifø·^r) *tr.* referir, remitir, enviar, dirigir; someter al juicio o decisión de. *3* referir, relacionar, atribuir. *4* *intr.* referirse, aludir. *5* remitirse. *6* dirigirse, recurrir: ~ *to drawer* (R/D), COM. dirigirse al librador [nota de un banquero, suspendiendo el pago de un cheque]. ¶ Pret. y p. p.: *referred;* ger.: *-rring.*

referee (reførɪ·) *s.* DEP. árbitro, juez. *2* DER. árbitro, componedor. *3* ponente.

referee (to) *tr.* arbitrar [juzgar como árbitro].

reference (re·førøns) *s.* referencia, relación. *2* alusión, mención. *3* referencia, remisión; consulta: ~ *mark,* IMPR. llamada; ~ *work,* obra, de consulta. *4* pers. que da informes de otra; estos informes. *5* COM. referencias. *6* DER. arbitramento.

referendum (reføre·ndøm) *s.* referéndum.

referent (re·førønt) *adj.* referente.

refill (rɪ·fil) *s.* recambio de un producto para rellenar el envase especial con que se expende.

refill (to) (rɪfɪ·l) *tr.* rellenar [volver a llenar].

refine (to) (rifai·n) *tr.* refinar. *2* purificar, clarificar, afinar. *3* pulir, perfeccionar. *4* *intr.* refinarse, pulirse. *5* sutilizar, discurrir sutilmente.

refined (-d) *adj.* refinado. *2* pulido. *3* fino, culto.

refinement (-mønt) *s.* refinamiento. *2* sutileza. *3* finura, urbanidad. *4* afectación. *5* refinación; afinación, afino. *6* perfeccionamiento.

refinery (-øri) *s.* refinería.

refit (to) (rɪfi·t) *tr.* volver a equipar; reparar, renovar.

reflect (to) (rifle·kt) *tr.* reflejar, reflectar. *2* hacer recaer en, traer consigo: *to* ~ *credit on one,* hacer honor a uno. *3* *intr.* reflejarse. *5* reflexionar. *6* *to* ~ *on* o *upon,* desprestigiar, desdorar.

reflection (-shøn) *s.* reflexión, reverberación. *2* reflejo, imagen. *3* tacha, descrédito. *4* ANAT. repliegue. *5* reflexión, consideración: *on* ~, después de reflexionarlo, bien pensado.

reflective (-tiv) *adj.* reflexivo, reflectante. *2* reflexivo, meditativo. *3* GRAM. reflejo [verbo].

reflector (-tø^r) *s.* reflector, reverbero. *2* telescopio de reflexión.

reflex (rɪ·fleks) *adj.-s.* reflejo. *2* *s.* acción refleja.

reflex (to) (rifle·ks) *tr.* doblar, encorvar o dirigir hacia atrás.

reflexive (-siv) *adj.* REFLECTIVE. *2* GRAM. reflexivo.

refloat (to) (rɪflou·t) *tr.* volver a poner a flote. *2* *intr.* volver a flotar.

reflourish (to) (rɪflø·rish) *intr.* reflorecer.

reflow (to) (rɪflou·) *intr.* refluir.

reflux (rɪ·fløks) *s.* reflujo.

reforest (to) (rɪfa·rist) *tr.* repoblar de árboles.

reform (rifo·^rm) *s.* reforma.

reform (to) *tr.* reformar, mejorar, enmendar; convertir [hacer volver a la vida honrada]. *2* *intr.* reformarse, corregirse, enmendarse.

re-form (to) (rɪfo·^rm) *tr.* reformar.

reformation (refoᵣmei·shøn) *s.* reforma [de costumbres, etc.]. *2* (con may.) Reforma [religiosa].
reformatory (rifoᵣmɑtori) *adj.-s.* reformatorio.
reformer (-øᵣ) *s.* reformador.
refract (to) (rifræ·kt) *tr.* ópt. refractar, refringir.
refraction (-shøn) *s.* ópt. refracción.
refractive (-tiv) *adj.* refractivo, de refracción.
refractor (-tøᵣ) *s.* telescopio de refracción.
refractory (-tori) *adj.* terco, obstinado, rebelde. *2* repropio [caballo]. *3* refractario, resistente. *4* med. inmune.
refrain (rifrei·n) *s.* lit., mús. estribillo. *2* fig. cantilena.
refrain (to) *tr.* refrenar, contener, detener. *2 intr.* contenerse; abstenerse.
reframe (to) (rɪfrei·m) *tr.* rehacer, reconstruir. *2* encuadrar de nuevo.
refrangible (rifræ·ndɥibøl) *adj.* refrangible.
refresh (to) (rifre·sh) *tr.* refrescar. *2* orear. *3* renovar, restaurar. *4* reparar las fuerzas de, descansar. *5* vivificar, reanimar. *6 intr.* refrescarse, descansar. *7* refrescar [beber].
refresher (-øᵣ) *s.* refrescador. *2* fam. bebida. *3* recordativo. *4* cursillo de vacaciones.
refreshment (-mønt) *s.* refrescadura. *2* refresco, refrigerio. *3* renovación. *4* descanso, esparcimiento. *5 pl.* refrescos.
refrigerate (to) (rifri·dɥøreit) *tr.* refrigerar, helar.
refrigerating (rifri·dɥøreiting) *adj.* refrigerante, frigorífico: ~ *vault*, cámara frigorífica.
refrigerator (rifri·dɥøreitøᵣ) *s.* refrigerador. *2* nevera, enfriadera. *3* quím. refrigerante.
refringent (rifri·ndɥøn·) *adj.* refringente.
refuge (re·fiudɥ) *s.* refugio, asilo, protección, guarida. *2* refugio, asilo [lugar, institución]. *3* recurso, pretexto, escapatoria.
refugee (refiudɥɪ·) *s.* refugiado. *2* asilado.
refulgent (rifø·ldɥønt) *adj.* refulgente.
refund (rɪ·fønd) *s.* reintegro, reembolso, amortización. *2* consolidación [de una deuda].
refund (to) (rifø·nd) *tr.* restituir, reintegrar, reembolsar, amortizar. *2* consolidar [una deuda].
refurbish (to) (rɪføˑᵣbish) *tr.* volver a pulir. *2* renovar.
refusal (rifiu·šal) *s.* rechazamiento. *2* negativa, denegación, repulsa, desaire. *3* opción, preferencia.
refuse (re·fiuš) *s.* desecho, sobras, barreduras, basura. *2 adj.* de desecho.
refuse (to) (rifiu·š) *tr.* rehusar, rechazar, desechar, denegar, negar. *3* negarse a. *4* renunciar, abandonar.
refutation (refiutei·shøn) *s.* refutación, impugnación.
refute (to) (rifiu·t) *tr.* refutar, impugnar, rebatir.
regain (to) (rigei·n) *tr.* recobrar, recuperar, volver a ganar.
regal (rɪ·gal) *adj.* real, regio.
regale (to) (rigei·l) *tr.* regalar, agasajar. *2* recrear, deleitar. *3 ref.* regalarse.
regalia (rigei·lia) *s. pl.* regalías [del soberano]. *2* insignias, distintivos. *4* atavío.
regality (rɪgæ·liti) *s.* realeza, soberanía.
regard (rigaˑᵣd) *s.* miramiento, consideración, cuidado, atención, caso: ~ *being had to*, en vista de; *without* ~ *to*, sin considerar, sin hacer caso de. *2* afecto, respeto. *3* relación, respecto: *with* ~ *to*, con respecto a, respecto de. *4* mirada. *5 pl.* memorias, recuerdos.
regard (to) *tr.* mirar, contemplar. *2* reparar, observar. *3* mirar, considerar, tener en cuenta. *4* mi-

rar o considerar [como]. *5* estimar, apreciar, respetar. *6* tocar a, concernir, referirse a: *as regards*, en cuanto a.
regardful (-ful) *adj.* atento, cuidadoso; que tiene en cuenta. *2* respetuoso, considerado. *3* observante.
regarding (-ing) *prep.* tocante a, respecto de.
regardless (-lis) *adj.* indiferente; que no hace caso, que no tiene en cuenta.
regatta (rigæ·ta) *s.* dep. regata.
regency (rɪ·dɥønsi) *s.* regencia [del reino].
regenerate (ridɥe·nørit) *adj.* regenerado.
regenerate (to) (-eit) *tr.* regenerar. *2 intr.* regenerarse.
regenerative (-ɑtiv) *adj.* regenerador.
regenerator (-eitøᵣ) *s.* regenerador.
regent (ri·dɥønt) *adj.* regente. *2 s.* pol. regente.
regicide (re·dɥisaid) *s.* regicidio. *2* regicida.
regime (redɥi·m) *s.* pol., med. régimen.
regimen (re·dɥimøn) *s.* régimen [político, de lluvias, etc.]. *2* med., gram. régimen.
regiment (re·dɥimønt) *s.* mil. regimiento.
regiment (to) (-ment) *tr.* regimentar.
regimentals (redɥime·ntals) *s. pl.* mil. uniforme.
region (rɪ·dɥøn) *s.* región.
register (re·dɥistøᵣ) *s.* registro [libro; oficina, asiento]; archivo, protocolo. *2* mar. matrícula. *3* registro [cinta en un libro]. *4* índice [de un libro]. *5* regulador [de calefacción]. *6* mec. indicador, mecanismo registrador. *7* mús., impr. registro.
register (to) *tr.* registrar, inscribir, matricular. *2* registrar, señalar [dic. de un termómetro, etc.]. *3* mar. matricular; abanderar. *4* certificar [una carta, etc.]; facturar [el equipaje]. *5 intr.* registrarse, inscribirse, matricularse.
registrar (re·dɥistraᵣ) *s.* registrador; archivero.
registration (-trei·shøn) *s.* registro, inscripción. *2* facturación [de equipajes], partida [de un registro].
registry (-tri) *s.* registro [inscripción; oficina]. *2* auto., mar. matrícula.
regnant (re·gnɑnt) *adj.* reinante. *2* dominante.
regorge (to) (rɪgoˑᵣdɥ) *tr.* vomitar, devolver.
regress (rɪ·gres) *s.* retroceso. *2* astr. retrogradación.
regress (to) (rigre·s) *intr.* retroceder. *2* astr. retrodradar.
regression (-shøn) *s.* regresión.
regressive (-siv) *adj.* regresivo; retrógrado.
regret (rigre·t) *s.* pesar, sentimiento. *2* remordimiento. *3* añoranza. *4 pl. to send one's regrets*, enviar excusas al rehusar una invitación.
regret (to) *intr.* sentir, lamentar. *2* arrepentirse. *3* llorar, añorar. ¶ Pret. y p. p.: *regretted*; ger.: *-tting*.
regretful (-ful) *adj.* pesaroso.
regrettable (-abøl) *adj.* sensible, lamentable.
regular (re·giulaᵣ) *adj.* regular. | No tiene el sentido de mediano. *2* ordenado, metódico. *3* normal, corriente. *4* fam. acabado, consumado. *5 s.* ecles. regular. *6* soldado regular. *7* obrero permanente.
regularize (to) (re·giularaiš) *tr.* regularizar.
regulate (to) (re·giuleit) *tr.* regular, arreglar, reglamentar. *2* regular, ajustar. *3* regularizar.
regulation (-ei·shøn) *s.* regulación. *2* reglamentación. *3* regla, orden. *4 pl.* reglas, reglamento, ordenanzas. *5 adj.* de reglamento, reglamentario, de rigor.
regulative (re·giulativ) *adj.* regulador, regulativo.

regulator (-leitø^r) *s.* regulador [que regula]. *2* MEC., ELECT. regulador. *3* registro [de reloj].
regulus (re·giuløs) *s.* régulo.
regurgitate (to) (rɪgø·^rdẙiteit) *tr.* regurgitar.
rehabilitate (to) (rɪjabi·liteit) *tr.* rehabilitar.
rehash (rɪ·jæsh) *s.* refundición. *2* fárrago.
rehash (to) (rɪjæ·sh) *tr.* desp. recomponer; refundir.
rehearsal (rijø·^rsal) *s.* ensayo [de una comedia, etc.]. *2* relación, enumeración. *3* repetición, recitación.
rehearse (to) (rijø·^rs) *tr.* ensayar [una comedia, etc.]. *2* repasar [lo estudiado]. *3* repetir, recitar.
reheat (to) (rɪjɪ·t) *tr.* recalentar. *2* recocer.
reign (rein) *s.* reino, soberanía. *2* reinado.
reign (to) *intr.* reinar. *2* imperar, estar en boga.
reimburse (to) (rɪimbø·^rs) *tr.* reembolsar; indemnizar.
reimbursement (-mønt) *s.* reembolso; indemnización.
reimpress (to) (rɪimpre·s) *tr.* reimprimir.
rein (rein) *s.* rienda: *to give* ~, aflojar las riendas, dar rienda suelta; *to take the reins*, fig. tomar las riendas. *2* sujección, freno.
rein (to) *tr.* guiar, gobernar. *2* refrenar, contener. *3 intr.* obedecer a las riendas. *4* detener el caballo, pararse.
reincarnate (to) (rɪinka^rnei·t) *tr.* reencarnar.
reindeer (rei·ndi^r) *s.* ZOOL. reno.
reinforce (rɪinfo·^rs) *s.* refuerzo.
reinforce (to) *tr.* reforzar. *2* armar [el hormigón]: *reinforced concrete*, hormigón armado.
reinforcement (-mønt) *s.* refuerzo. *2 pl.* MIL. refuerzos.
reinstall (to) (rɪinsto·l) *tr.* reinstalar, reponer, rehabilitar.
reinstate (to) (rɪinstei·t) *tr.* reponer [en un cargo]. *2* reparar, renovar.
reinsurance (rɪinshu·rans) *s.* COM. reaseguro.
reinsure (to) (rɪinshu·^r) *tr.* COM. reasegurar.
reinvest (rɪinve·st) *tr.* reinvertir.
reinvestment (-mønt) *s.* reinversión.
reiterate (to) (rɪi·tøreit) *tr.* reiterar, repetir.
reiteration (-ei·shøn) *s.* reiteración, repetición.
reject (rɪ·dẙekt) *s.* desecho.
reject (to) (rɪdẙe·kt) *tr.* rechazar, rehusar, repeler. *2* denegar, desoír. *3* desechar, descartar, arrinconar. *4* arrojar, vomitar.
rejection (-shøn) *s.* rechazamiento. *2* denegación. *3* acción de desechar. *4* desecho. *5 pl.* excremento.
rejoice (to) (rɪdẙoi·s) *tr.* alegrar, regocijar. *2 intr.* alegrarse, regocijarse, gozarse.
rejoicing (rɪdẙoi·sing) *s.* alegría, gozo, regocijo, júbilo. *2* fiesta, festividad.
rejoin (to) (rɪdẙoi·n) *tr.* reunirse con, volver a juntarse con. *2 tr.-intr.* responder, replicar.
rejoinder (-dø^r) *s.* respuesta, réplica. *2* DER. dúplica.
rejoint (to) (-t) *tr.* ALBAÑ. rejuntar.
rejuvenate (to) (rɪdẙu·vøneit) *tr.* rejuvenecer, remozar.
rekindle (to) (rɪki·ndøl) *tr.* volver a encender. *2* reavivar.
relapse (rilæ·ps) *s.* recaída. *2* reincidencia [en un vicio, etc.]. *3* MED. recidiva. *4* relapso.
relapse (to) *intr.* recaer, reincidir [en un vicio, etc.]; volver [a un estado]. *2* MED. recaer.
relate (to) (rilei·t) *tr.* relatar, referir, contar. *2* relacionar [una cosa con otra]. *3 intr.* relacionarse [guardar relación], referirse.

related (-id) *adj.* relacionado, conexo. *2* emparentado, afín.
relating (-ing) *adj.* referente, concerniente.
relation (-shøn) *s.* relación, relato. *2* relación [entre cosas o personas]; respecto: *in* ~ *to*, en relación con, respecto a. *3* parentesco, afinidad. *4* pariente, deudo.
relationship (-ship) *s.* relación [entre cosas o pers.]. *2* parentesco.
relative (re·lativ) *adj.* relativo. *2 s.* GRAM. pronombre relativo. *3* pariente, deudo, allegado.
relatively (-li) *adv.* relativamente.
relativism (-iŝm) *s.* FIL., FÍS. relativismo.
relativity (relati·viti) *s.* relatividad.
relax (to) (rilæ·ks) *tr.* relajar, aflojar, ablandar. *2* mitigar. *3* descansar, esparcir [el ánimo]. *4 intr.* relajarse, aflojarse, ablandarse. *5* remitir, amainar. *6* descansar, esparcirse.
relaxation (-ei·shøn) *s.* relajación, aflojamiento. *2* remisión, mitigación. *3* descanso, solaz, esparcimiento.
relay (rɪ·lei) *s.* parada, posta [caballerías, lugar]. *2* relevo, remuda. *3* ELECT. relevador, relé. *4* MEC. servomotor. *5* DEP. carrera de relevos.
relay (to) *tr.* relevar, mudar. *2* transmitir por relevos. *3* RADIO. retransmitir [una emisión].
release (rilɪ·s) *s.* libertad, excarcelación. *2* descargo, exoneración. *3* quita, finiquito. *4* DER. cesión; escritura de cesión. *5* MEC. disparo, escape; descarga. *6* permiso de publicación, venta, etc., a partir de una fecha determinada.
release (to) *tr.* libertar, soltar. *2* librar, descargar, aliviar. *3* DER. ceder. *4* permitir [a partir de una fecha determinada] la publicación, venta, etc., de una obra.
re-lease (to) (rilɪ·s) *tr.* arrendar de nuevo.
relegate (to) (re·ligeit) *tr.* relegar. *2* confiar, delegar.
relent (to) (rile·nt) *intr.* ablandarse, aplacarse, ceder; enternecerse. *2* mitigarse.
relentless (-lis) *adj.* implacable, inexorable.
relevant (-ant) *adj.* pertinente, aplicable, que hace o viene al caso.
reliable (rilai·abøl) *adj.* confiable, digno de confianza, seguro, formal. *2* fidedigno.
reliance (-ans) *s.* confianza, seguridad.
reliant (-ant) *adj.* confiado [que confía].
relic (re·lik) *s.* reliquia. *2 pl.* restos, ruinas.
relict (re·likt) *s.* viuda [de]. *2* superviviente [de una raza o especie]. *3 pl.* restos [mortales].
relief (rilɪ·f) *s.* ayuda, auxilio, socorro; limosna. *2* alivio. *3* aligeramiento *4* descanso, solaz. *5* MIL. relevo. *6* relieve, realce. *7* DER. remedio, reparación.
relieve (to) (rilɪ·v) *tr.* relevar, remediar, auxiliar, socorrer. *2* consolar. *3* aliviar, mitigar. *4* descargar. *5* desahogar. *6* animar, romper la monotonía de. *7* realzar, hacer resaltar. *8* MIL. relevar. *9* DER. reparar, hacer justicia.
relieving arch (-ing) *s.* ARQ. arco de descarga.
relight (to) (rɪlai·t) *tr.* volver a encender.
religion (rili·dẙøn) *s.* religión.
religionist (-ist) *s.* fanático religioso.
religiosity (rilidẙia·siti) *s.* religiosidad.
religious (rili·dẙøs) *adj.* religioso. *2* devoto, piadoso. *3 s.* religioso.
relinquish (to) (rili·nkuish) *tr.* abandonar, dejar; desistir de. *2* ceder, renunciar a.
reliquary (re·likuæri) *s.* relicario.
relish (re·lish) *s.* buen sabor, gusto, dejo. *2* gusto,

goce, fruición. *3* gusto [para apreciar]. *4* apetencia, inclinación. *5* condimento, entremés.

relish (to) *tr.* saborear, paladear. *2* gustarle a uno [una cosa]; hacer [algo] con fruición. *3* sazonar, condimentar. *4* *intr.* gustar, agradar. *5* saber [a].

reload (to) (rɪlou·d) *tr.* recargar [volver a cargar].

reluctance (rɪlʌ·ktʌns) *s.* repugnancia, renuencia, aversión, mala gana. *2* ELECT. reluctancia.

reluctant (-ʌnt) *adj.* renuente, reacio.

rely (to) (rɪlai·) *intr.* [con *on* o *upon*], confiar o fiar en, contar con, fiarse de.

remain (to) (rimei·n) *intr.* quedar, sobrar, restar, faltar: *to ~ undone,* quedar por hacer. *2* quedarse. *3* permanecer, continuar.

remainder (-dø^r) *s.* resto, remanente, sobrante. *2* MAT. resta, residuo.

remains (rimei·ns) *s. pl.* restos [mortales]. *2* sobras. *3* reliquias, ruinas. *4* obras póstumas.

remake (to) (rɪmei·k) *tr.* rehacer [volver a hacer].

remand (rima·nd) *s.* DER. reencarcelamiento.

remand (to) *tr.* DER. mandar de nuevo a la cárcel.

remark (rima·^rk) *s.* observación [acción de observar o reparar]. *2* observación, nota, dicho, comentario.

remark (to) *tr.* observar, advertir, notar, reparar. *2* observar, hacer notar, decir.

remarkable (-abøl) *adj.* observable. *2* notable, extraordinario.

remarriage (rɪmæ·rid̃) *s.* segundas nupcias.

remarrry (to) (rɪmæ·ri) *tr.-intr.* volver a casar o casarse.

remediable (rimɪ·diabøl) *adj.* remediable.

remedial (-dial) *adj.* terapéutico, reparador.

remedy (re·mødi) *s.* remedio.

remedy (to) *tr.* remediar. *2* curar. *3* arreglar, reparar, corregir.

remember (to) (rime·mbø^r) *tr.* recordar, acordarse de. *2* hacer presente; dar recuerdos: *~ me to him,* déle recuerdos de mi parte.

remembrance (rime·mbrans) *s.* recuerdo, memoria, recordación, rememoración. *2* memoria, retentiva. *3* recuerdo [objeto].

remind (to) (rimai·nd) *tr. to ~ of,* acordar, recordar [una cosa a uno], hacer presente.

reminder (-ø^r) *s.* recordativo, recordatorio.

reminiscence (remini·søns) *s.* reminiscencia. *2 pl.* LIT. recuerdos.

reminiscent (remini·sønt) *adj.* recordativo, evocador. *2* lleno de recuerdos.

remiss (rimi·s) *adj.* remiso, negligente.

remission (-shøn) *s.* remisión [perdón; disminución de intensidad]. *2* COM. remesa. *3* MED. remisión.

remissive (-siv) *adj.* remisivo.

remissness (-snis) *s.* flojedad, negligencia.

remissory (-sori) *adj.* remisorio.

remit (to) (rimi·t) *tr.* remitir [perdonar; someter a la decisión, etc.; diferir, aplazar]. *2* restituir [a un estado o condición]. *3* enviar, remitir, remesar. *4* *tr.-intr.* remitir, disminuir, aflojar. ¶ Pret. y p. p.: *remitted;* ger.: *-tting.*

remittal (-al) *s.* remisión [de una pena].

remittance (-ans) *s.* COM. remesa [de dinero], giro.

remittent (-ønt) *adj.* remitente [fiebre, etc.].

remitter (-ø^r) *s.* remitente.

remnant (re·mnant) *s.* remanente, resto, residuo. *2* vestigio. *3* retal, saldo.

remodel (to) (rima·del) *tr.* modelar de nuevo, rehacer, reconstruir.

remonstrance (rima·nstrans) *s.* protesta, queja, amonestación, reconvención; razonamiento para disuadir. *2* memorial, representación.

remonstrate (to) (rima·nstreit) *intr.* protestar, objetar, reconvenir; tratar de persuadir.

remora (re·møra) *s.* ICT. rémora.

remorse (rimo·^rs) *s.* remordimiento, compunción.

remorseless (-lis) *adj.* implacable, cruel.

remote (rimou·t) *adj.* remoto, lejano, apartado. *2* extraño, ajeno. *3* MEC. *~ control,* mando a distancia.

remount (rimau·nt) *s.* MIL. remonta.

remount (to) *intr.-tr.* volver a montar, volver a subir. *2* remontarse [a una fecha, etc.].

removable (rimu·vabøl) *adj.* trasladable; que se puede quitar. *2* amovible.

removal (rimu·val) *s.* acción de quitar o llevarse; remoción, levantamiento. *2* mudanza, traslado: *~ van,* camión de mudanzas. *3* destitución. *4* eliminación, supresión, alejamiento.

remove (rimu·v) *s.* traslado, mudanza. *2* distancia [que separa]; grado, escalón, intervalo. *3* grado [de parentesco].

remove (to) *tr.* trasladar, mudar. *2* alejar. *3* remover, quitar, sacar, eliminar, extirpar. *4* quitar de enmedio; matar. *5* destituir. *6* *intr.* trasladarse, mudarse; irse.

remunerate (to) (rimiu·nøreit) *tr.* remunerar.

remuneration (-shøn) *s.* remuneración.

remunerative (rimiu·nørativ) *adj.* remuneratorio. *2* remunerador.

Remus (ri·møs) *n. pr.* Remo.

renaissance (renøsa·ns) *s.* renacimiento. *2* HIST. *the Renaissance,* el Renacimiento.

renal (ri·nal) *adj.* ANAT. renal.

renascence (rinæ·søns) *s.* renacimiento.

renascent (-ønt) *adj.* renaciente.

rencounter (rinkau·ntø^r) *s.* encuentro [casual]. *2* encuentro, combate; disputa.

rencounter (to) *tr.-intr.* encontrar; topar, encontrarse con.

rend (to) (rend) *tr.* rasgar, desgarrar, hender, rajar. *2* mesar [los cabellos]. *3* lacerar. *4* dividir, desunir. *5* *intr.* rasgarse, rajarse. ¶ Pret. y p. p.: *rent.*

render (to) (re·ndø^r) *tr.* dar, entregar. *2* devolver. *3* reflejar. *4* dictar [sentencia, etc.]. *5* hacer, administrar [justicia]. *6* rendir [tributo, etc.]. *7* prestar, hacer [ayuda, favor, etc.]. *8* volver, hacer, poner [en un estado]: *to ~ useless,* hacer inútil. *9* dar o rendir [cuenta]. *10* B. ART. representar, expresar, interpretar. *11* traducir [a una lengua]. *12* derretir, clarificar.

rendezvous (ra·ndøvu) *s.* cita [para encontrarse], reunión. *2* lugar de la cita.

rendezvous (to) *tr.-intr.* acudir, juntarse, reunirse.

rendition (rendi·shøn) *s.* rendición, entrega. *2* B. ART. interpretación, ejecución. *3* traducción.

renegade (re·nigeid) *s.* renegado, apóstata.

renege (to) (rini·g) *intr.* renunciar [en el juego de naipes]. *3* fam. volverse atrás, no cumplir lo prometido.

renew (to) (riniu·) *tr.* renovar. *2* reanudar. *3* COM. prorrogar. *4* *intr.* renovarse, reanudarse.

renewal (-al) *s.* renovación, renuevo. *2* reanudación. *3* COM. prórroga.

reniform (re·nifo^rm) *adj.* reniforme, arriñonado.

renitency (reni·tønsi) *s.* renitencia.

rennet (re·nit) *s.* cuajo, cuajaleche: *~ bag,* cuajar.

renounce (to) (rinau·ns) *tr.* renunciar. *2* renegar; abjurar. *3* repudiar, rechazar, desconocer. *4* *tr.-*

intr. no servir [al palo que se juega] por no tener naipe de él.

renouncement (-mønt) *s.* renuncia.

renovate (to) (re·noveit) *tr.* renovar, restaurar. *2* regenerar, revigorizar.

renovation (-ei·shøn) *s.* renovación.

renown (rinau·n) *s.* renombre, fama.

renowned (-d) *adj.* renombrado, famoso.

rent (rent) *s.* renta, arriendo, alquiler. *2* desgarrón; grieta, raja. *3* cisma, división. *4* p. p. de TO REND.

rent (to) *tr.* arrendar, alquilar. *2 intr.* alquilarse, arrendarse.

rentable (-abøl) *adj.* arrendable, alquilable.

rental (-al) *s.* renta, arriendo, alquiler.

renter (-ø^r) *s.* arrendatario, inquilino.

rentier (rantiei·) *s.* rentista.

renunciation (rinønshiei·shøn) *s.* renuncia.

reopen (to) (ɾiou·pøn) *tr.* volver a abrir.

reorganize (to) (ɾio·^{r}ganaiš) *tr.* reorganizar.

rep (rep) *s.* TEJ. reps.

repaint (to) (ɾi·peint) *tr.* repintar.

repair (ɾipe·^{r}) *s.* reparación, restauración, remiendo, compostura. *2* estado, buen estado: *in* ~, *in good* ~, en buen estado; *out of* ~, descompuesto. *3* punto de reunión, lugar que se frecuenta.

repair (to) *tr.* reparar, remendar, componer, recorrer, renovar. *2* remediar, subsanar, restablecer. *3* reparar [daños, injusticias, etc.]. *4 intr. to* ~ *to*, ir o acudir a; refugiarse en.

repairable (-abøl) *adj.* reparable, remendable.

reparable (re·parabøl) *adj.* reparable [pérdida, etc.].

reparation (reparei·shøn) *s.* reparación.

repartee (repa^{r}tı·) *s.* respuesta o réplica pronta y aguda; agudeza. *2* discreteo.

repartee (to) *intr.* dar respuestas prontas y agudas.

repartition (ɾipa^{r}ti·shøn) *s.* reparto, partición. *2* segunda partición.

repass (to) (ɾipæ·s) *tr.* repasar [volver a pasar]. *2* volver a pasar delante de o a cruzarse con. *3 intr.* volver a pasar.

repast (ɾipæ·st) *s.* comida refacción.

repatriate (to) (ɾipei·triet) *tr.* repatriar.

repay (to) (ɾipei·) *tr.* pagar, corresponder a. *2* pagar [lo que se debe]; reembolsar, compensar.

repayment (-mønt) *s.* pago, retorno, desquite.

repeal (ɾipi·l) *s.* abrogación, derogación, revocación, anulación.

repeal (to) *tr.* abrogar, derogar, revocar, anular.

repeat (ɾipi·t) *s.* repetición. *2* MÚS. signo de repetición. *3* TEAT. bisado.

repeat (to) *tr.* repetir, reiterar. *2* recitar. *3* repasar, ensayar. *4 intr.* repetir [lo que se ha comido]. *5* repetirse periódicamente.

repeatedly (-tidli) *adv.* repetidamente.

repeating (-ting) *adj.* repetidor [de repetición.

repel (to) (ɾipe·l) *tr.* repeler, rechazar. *2* repugnar. *3* MED. repercutir. ¶ Pret. y p. p.: *repelled;* ger.: *-lling.*

repellent (-ønt) *adj.* repelente. *2* repulsivo. *3* impermeable. *4 s.* tela impermeable.

repent (to) (ɾipe·nt) *intr.* arrepentirse. *2 tr.* arrepentirse de.

repentance (-ans) *s.* arrepentimiento.

repentant (-ant) *adj.-s.* arrepentido. *2 adj.* de arrepentimiento.

repeople (to) (ɾipı·pøl) *tr.* repoblar.

repercuss (to) (ɾipø^{r}kø·s) *tr.* rechazar, reflejar.

repercussion (ɾipø^{r}kø·shøn) *s.* repercusión. *2* rechazo, reflexión, retumbo.

repertoire (repø^{r}tua·^{r}) *s.* MÚS., TEAT. repertorio.

repertory (re·pø^{r}tori) *s.* repertorio, inventario.

repetend (re·pitend) *s.* MAT. período.

repetition (repiti·shøn) *s.* repetición. *2* repaso [de una lección, etc.]. *4* recitación. *5* copia, reproducción.

repetitious (repiti·shøs) *adj.* redundante; fastidioso.

repine (to) (ɾipai·n) *intr.* quejarse, lamentarse, afligirse. *2* consumirse, decaer.

replace (to) (ɾiplei·s) *tr.* reponer, devolver, volver a poner. *2* reemplazar, substituir. *3* restituir. *4* cambiar [una pieza].

replacement (-mønt) *s.* substitución, cambio. *2* restitución. *3* pieza de recambio.

replant (to) (ɾiplæ·nt) *tr.* replantar.

replenish (to) (ɾiple·nish) *tr.* llenar, henchir. *2* re-llenar, llenar de nuevo, reaprovisionar.

replete (ɾiplı·t) *adj.* lleno, repleto. *2* gordo.

repletion (ɾiplı·shøn) *s.* repleción. *2* ahíto.

replica (re·plika) *s.* B. ART. réplica. *2* MÚS. repetición.

reply (ɾiplai·) *s.* respuesta, contestación.

reply (to) *tr.* responder, contestar. *2* DER. replicar.

report (ɾipo·^{r}t) *s.* voz, rumor. *2* reputación. *3* noticia, información. *4* reseña [de un libro]. *5* relato. *6* parte, comunicado. *7* informe, dictamen. *8* denuncia. *9* DER. apuntamiento. *10* detonación, tiro.

report (to) *tr.* relatar, contar, dar cuenta o parte de. *2* repetir [lo que se ha oído]. *3* hacer reportaje de. *4* reseñar [un libro]. *5* informar sobre, dictaminar. *6* denunciar. *7* rumorear: *it is reported,* se dice. *8 intr.* dar noticias de sí mismo. *9* informar, dictaminar. *10* ser reportero. *11* presentarse.

reporter (-ø^r) *s.* reportero. *2* informador. *3* DER. relator.

reportorial (ɾipo^{r}to·rial) *adj.* reporteril.

repose (ɾipou·š) *s.* reposo. *2* descanso, sueño. *3* tranquilidad, calma, sosiego.

repose (to) *tr.* descansar, reclinar. *2* descansar [dar descanso a]. *3* poner, depositar [confianza, etc.]. *4 intr.* reclinarse, tenderse. *5* reposar, descansar.

reposeful (-ful) *adj.* sosegado, tranquilo.

repository (ɾipa·šitori) *s.* repositorio, depósito, almacén. *2* pers. a quien se confían penas, esperanzas, etc. *4* LITURG. monumento.

repossess (to) (ɾipøše·s) *tr.* recobrar, recuperar. *2* volver a poner en posesión de.

repoussé (røpusei·) *adj.* repujado.

reprehend (to) (reprije·nd) *tr.* reprender, censurar.

reprehension (-nshøn) *s.* reprensión. *2* reprobación, censura.

represent (to) (repriše·nt) *tr.* representar. *2* exponer, hacer presente.

re-present (to) (ɾipriše·nt) *tr.* volver a presentar.

representation (reprišentei·shøn) *s.* representación. | No tiene el sentido de dignidad o autoridad. *2* súplica, protesta, razonamiento.

representative (repriše·ntativ) *adj.* representativo. *2* típico. *3 s.* representante, apoderado, delegado; (E.U.) diputado. *4* tipo, símbolo.

repress (to) (ɾipre·s) *tr.* reprimir, contener, refrenar, dominar, sofocar. *2* cohibir.

repression (-shøn) *s.* represión.

reprieve (ɾiprı·v) *s.* suspensión de la ejecución de una sentencia; indulto. *2* alivio, respiro, tregua.

reprieve (to) *tr.* suspender la ejecución [de un reo]; indultar. *2* aliviar, dar un respiro.
reprimand (re·primænd) *s.* reprimenda, reprensión.
reprimand (to) *tr.* reprender, reconvenir.
reprint (rɪprɪ·nt) *s.* reimpresión. *2* tirada aparte.
reprint (to) *tr.* reprochar. *2* reprender.
reproachful (-ful) *adj.* de reproche.
reproachless (-lis) *adj.* irreprochable.
reprobate (re·probeit) *adj.-s.* réprobo. *2* malvado, vicioso.
reprobate (to) *tr.* reprobar, condenar. *2* desaprobar.
reprobation (reprobei·shøn) *s.* reprobación, desaprobación.
reproduce (to) (rɪprødiu·s) *tr.* reproducir. *2 intr.* reproducirse, propagarse.
reproducer (-ø**ʳ**) *s.* reproductor. *2* aparato reproductor [de sonidos, etc.].
reproduction (rɪprødø·kshøn) *s.* reproducción.
reproof (ripru·f), **reproval** (-val) *s.* reprobación, reprensión.
reprove (to) (ripru·v) *tr.* reprobar, reprender, censurar.
reptant (re·ptant) *adj.* BOT., ZOOL. rastrero, reptante.
reptile (re·ptil) *adj.-s.* ZOOL. reptil. *2 adj.* rastrero, servil.
reptilian (repti·lian) *s.* ZOOL. reptil. *2 adj.* de reptil.
republic (ripø·blik) *s.* república.
republican (-an) *adj.-s.* republicano.
republication (rɪpøblikei·shøn) *s.* nueva publicación o promulgación. *2* reedición.
repudiate (to) (ripiu·dieit) *tr.* repudiar. *2* desconocer, rechazar; recusar.
repudiation (-ei·shøn) *s.* repudiación, repudio. *2* rechazamiento, recusación.
repugn (to) (ripø·gn) *tr.-intr.* repugnar.
repugnance, -cy (-nans, -si) *s.* repugnancia.
repugnant (-ant) *adj.* repugnante. *2* hostil, reacio. *3* opuesto, contradictorio.
repulse (ri·pøls) *s.* repulsión, rechazamiento. *2* repulsa, negativa, desaire.
repulse (to) *tr.* rechazar, repeler. *2* repulsar.
repulsion (-shøn) *s.* repulsión.
repulsive (-siv) *adj.* de repulsión. *2* repulsivo.
reputable (re·piutabøl) *adj.* de buena reputación, estimable, honrado, honroso, lícito.
reputation (repiutei·shøn) *s.* reputación, fama. *2* buena reputación, nota, distinción.
repute (ripiu·t) *s.* reputación, estimación, fama, crédito: *of ill* ~, de mala fama.
repute (to) *tr.* reputar, estimar, juzgar, considerar, tener por.
reputed (-id) *adj.* reputado. *2* supuesto.
reputedly (-li) *adv.* según se cree.
request (rikue·st) *s.* ruego, petición, solicitud: *at the* ~ *of*, a petición, a instancias de. *2* demanda, salida: *in* ~, en boga, solicitado.
request (to) *tr.* rogar, pedir, solicitar, encargar.
requiem (rɪ·kuiem) *s.* LITURG. réquiem.
require (to) (rikuai·ʳ) *tr.-intr.* requerir, pedir, demandar, exigir, necesitar.
requirement (-mønt) *s.* requisito, condición. *2* exigencia, necesidad. *3* demanda, requerimiento.
requisite (re·kuišit) *adj.* requerido, necesario, indispensable. *2 s.* requisito, cosa esencial.
requisition (rekuiši·shøn) *s.* demanda, requerimiento. *2* requisición, requisa. *3* necesidad. *4 to put in*, o *into* ~, poner a contribución.
requisition (to) *tr.* requisar. *2* requerir.

requital (rikuai·tal) *s.* paga, pago, correspondencia, compensación, recompensa. *2* desquite.
requite (to) (rikuai·t) *tr.* pagar, devolver, corresponder, compensar; pagar en la misma moneda.
reredos (ri·øʳdas) *s.* retablo [de altar].
resale (rɪsei·l) *s.* reventa.
rescind (to) (risi·nd) *tr.* rescindir, anular.
rescission (risi·ɣøn) *s.* rescisión, anulación.
rescript (rɪskri·pt) *s.* rescripto. *2* edicto, decreto.
rescue (re·skiu) *s.* liberación, rescate, salvamento, socorro: *to go to the* ~ *of*, acudir en socorro de.
rescue (to) *tr.* librar, libertar, rescatar, salvar.
rescuer (-ø**ʳ**) *s.* libertador, salvador.
research (risø·ʳch) *s.* búsqueda, indagación, investigación.
research (to) *tr.* buscar, indagar, investigar.
reseat (to) (rɪsi·t) *tr.* sentar o asentar de nuevo. *2* poner asiento nuevo a.
resect (to) (risø·kt) *tr.* CIR. resecar.
resection (rise·kshøn) *s.* CIR. resección.
reseda (rɪsi·da) *s.* BOT. reseda.
resell (to) (rise·l) *tr.* revender.
resemblance (riše·mblans) *s.* parecido, semejanza.
resemble (to) (-bøl) *tr.* parecerse, asemejarse a.
resent (to) (riše·nt) *tr.* resentirse u ofenderse de o por; sentirse de, agraviarse por.
resentful (-ful) *adj.* resentido, ofendido. *2* rencoroso.
resentment (-mønt) *s.* resentimiento, enojo.
reservation (rešøʳvei·shøn) *s.* reservación, reserva [acción]. *2* reserva, condición, salvedad. *3* terreno o sitio reservado.
reserve (rišø·ʳv) *s.* reserva, repuesto. *2* terreno reservado. *3* reserva [discreción; sigilo; frialdad]. *4* reservación, reserva, restricción: *without* ~, sin reserva. *5* COM., IND., MIL. reserva.
reserve (to) *tr.* reservar. *2* hacerse reservar [un asiento, etc.].
reserved (-d) *adj.* reservado.
reservist (-ist) *adj.-s.* MIL. reservista.
reservoir (-uaʳ) *s.* depósito [de agua, gas, etc.]. *2* cubeta [de barómetro]. *3* alberca, aljibe. *4* embalse. *5* fig. mina [de datos, saber, etc.].
reset (to) (rɪse·t) *tr.* volver a colocar, volver a engastar o montar; volver a componer [en imprenta].
reshape (to) (rɪshei·p) *tr.* reformar, volver a formar.
reship (to) (rɪshi·p) *tr.-intr.* reembarcar.
reshipment (rɪshi·pmønt) *s.* reembarco, reembarque.
reside (to) (rišai·d) *intr.* residir.
residence (re·sidøns) *s.* residencia; morada, mansión; obligación de residir; período en que se reside.
residency (-si) *s.* residencia del gobernador de un protectorado.
resident (re·šidønt) *adj.* residente. *2* ORN. no migratorio. *3* inherente. *4 s.* residente, morador. *5* ministro residente. *6* gobernador de un protectorado.
residential (-shal) *adj.* residencial.
residual (riši·diual) *adj.* residual, restante.
residuary (riši·diueri) *adj.* residual, restante. *2* DER. ~ *legatee*, heredero universal.
residue (re·šidiu) *s.* residuo, resto, remanente.
residuum (riši·diuøm) *s.* residuo, sobras. *2* hez [de la población].
resign (to) (rišai·n) *tr.* dimitir, renunciar a. *2* resignar, entregar: *to* ~ *oneself*, entregarse a; resig-

narse. *3 intr.* dimitir. *4* resignarse, conformarse. *5* AJED.,abandonar.

resignation (rešignei·shøn) *s.* dimisión, renuncia. *2* resignación, conformidad.

resigned (rišai·nd) *adj.* resignado.

resignee (rišaini·) *s.* resignatario.

resigner (rišai·nø^r) *s.* dimitente. *2* resignante.

resilience, -cy (riši·liøns, -si) *s.* resalto, rebote. *2* resorte, elasticidad. *3* fig. capacidad para reaccionar; animación, viveza.

resilient (-ønt) *adj.* elástico. *2* que reacciona o se recobra fácilmente; alegre, animado,vivo.

resin (re·šin) *s.* resina: *gum* ~, gomorresina.

resiniferous (rešini·førøs) *adj.* resinífero.

resinous (re·šinøs) *adj.* resinoso.

resipiscence (resi·pisøns) *s.* reconocimiento del propio error, retorno al buen sentido.

resist (riši·st) *s.* IND. reserva.

resist (to) *tr.-intr.* resistir. | No tiene el sentido de tolerar, sufrir. *2 tr.* oponerse, resistirse a.

resistance (-øns) *s.* resistencia [acción de resistir o resistirse; capacidad para resistir]: *to offer* ~, oponer resistencia. *2* MEC., ELECT. resistencia. *3* BIOL. defensa.

resistant (-ønt) *adj.* resistente.

resistless (riši·stlis) *adj.* irresistible. *2* indefenso.

resole (to) (risou·l) *tr.* remontar [el calzado].

resolute (re·šoliut) *adj.* resuelto, determinado, decidido. *2* firme, inflexible.

resoluteness (-tnis) *s.* resolución, tesón.

resolution (re·šøliushøn) resolución [acción de resolver o resolverse]. *2* resolución, denuedo. *3* propósito: *good resolutions*, buenos propósitos. *4* solución [de un problema, etc.]. *5* acuerdo [de una asamblea]; propuesta [de acuerdo]; conclusión.

resolve (riša·lv) *s.* resolución, acuerdo. *2* resolución, firmeza de propósito.

resolve (to) *tr.* resolver [en todas sus acepciones]. *2* decidir [a uno a que haga algo]. *3* acordar [en una asamblea]. *4 intr.* resolverse, decidirse. *5 to* ~ *into*, resolverse en.

resolved (-vd) *adj.* resuelto. *2* acordado, decidido. *3* persuadido, convencido.

resonance (re·šønøns) *s.* resonancia. *2* resonación.

resonate (to) (re·šoneit) *intr.* resonar.

resonator (-ø^r) *s.* resonador.

resorb (to) (riso·^rb) *tr.* resorber.

resorption (riso·^rpshøn) *s.* resorción.

resort (rizo·^rt) *s.* recurso, medio, refugio: *to have* ~ *to*, recurrir. *2* concurso, concurrencia. *3* lugar al que se acude: *health* ~, balneario, estación termal, etc.; *summer* ~, punto de veraneo.

resort (to) *intr.* acudir, concurrir, frecuentar. *2* recurrir, apelar, echar mano de.

resound (to) (rišau·nd) *intr.* resonar, retumbar, repercutir, formar eco. *2 tr.* devolver [el sonido]. *3* poét. cantar, celebrar.

resource (riso·^rs) *s.* recurso, medio, expediente, remedio: *without* ~, sin remedio. *2* ingenio, maña. *3 pl.* recursos.

resourceful (-ful) *adj.* listo, ingenioso.

respect (rispe·kt) *s.* respeto, atención, consideración. *2* acepción o aceptación de personas. *3* respeto, relación; concepto, punto de vista: *in* ~ *of*, *with* ~ *to*, respecto a o de; *in all respects*, por todos conceptos. *4 pl.* respetos, saludos [que se mandan].

respect (to) *tr.* respetar. *2* respectar: *as respects*, por lo que respecta a, tocante a.

respectability (rispektabi·liti) *s.* respetabilidad.

respectable (rispe·ktabøl) *adj.* respetable. *2* decente, presentable. *3* honroso. *4* correcto, que respeta las convenciones sociales.

respectful (-ful) *adj.* respetuoso.

respecting (-ing) *prep.* con respecto a, en cuanto a, relativamente a.

respective (-iv) *adj.* respectivo, de cada uno.

respirable (rispai·rabøl) *adj.* respirable.

respiration (respirei·shøn) *s.* respiración, respiro.

respiratory (rispai·ratori) *adj.* respiratorio.

respire (to) (rispai·^r) *tr.-intr.* FISIOL., BOT. respirar. *2 intr.* resollar. *3* respirar [descansar, cobrar aliento].

respite (re·spit) *s.* respiro, tregua, descanso. *2* suspensión [esp. de la pena de muerte].

respite (to) *tr.* dar treguas o respiro a. *2* suspender, diferir, aplazar.

resplendent (risple·ndønt) *adj.* resplandeciente.

respond (to) (rispa·nd) *intr.* responder, contestar. *2* responder, corresponder [a una acción, un estímulo].

respondent (-ønt) *adj.-s.* díc. del que responde; correspondiente. *2* DER. demandado.

response (rispa·ns) *s.* respuesta, contestación, réplica. *2* respuesta [a una acción, un estímulo].

responsibility (rispansibi·liti) *s.* responsabilidad. *2* solvencia.

responsible (rispa·nsibøl) *adj.* responsable: *to be* ~ *for*, ser responsable de; ser la causa u origen de. *2* solvente. *3* autorizado, respetable.

responsibleness (-nis) *s.* responsabilidad.

responsive (rispa·nsiv) *adj.* que responde o corresponde [a una acción, un afecto], sensible; obediente; que se interesa.

rest (rest) *s.* descanso, reposo; sueño, sueño eterno: *to have a* ~, tomarse un descanso; *to lay to* ~, enterrar; *without* ~, descanso. *2* tregua, enterrar; *without* ~, descanso. *2* tregua, paz, tranquilidad. *5* parada, detención. *6* posada, descansadero. *7* apoyo, soporte. *8* diablo [de billar]. *9* cuja [para la lanza]. *10* ristre. *11* MÚS. pausa, silencio. *12* cesura. *13* resta, restante: *the* ~, lo demás; los demás. *14* saldo, superávit. *15* TENIS. rest. *16 at* ~, en reposo; tranquilo; dormido; en paz [muerto].

rest (to) *intr.* descansar, reposar, dormir; yacer; estar quieto, tranquilo. *2* cesar, parar. *3* posarse. *4* descansar, apoyarse, basarse [en], cargar [sobre]. *5* descansar, confiar [en]. *6* quedar, permanecer. *7 to* ~ *with*, depender de. *8 tr.* descansar, dar descanso a: *to* ~ *oneself*. *9* descansar, asentar, poner, apoyar, basar.

restaurant (re·storant) *s.* restaurante.

restful (re·stful) *adj.* quieto, sosegado. *2* que da descanso; reparador.

restharrow (re·stjærou) *s.* BOT. gatuña.

resting place (-ing) *s.* descansadero. *2* última morada. *3* meseta [de escalera].

restitute (to) (re·stitiut) *tr.* restituir.

restitution (restitiu·shøn) *s.* restitución, devolución. *2* indemnización, compensación.

restitutive (resti·tiutiv) *adj.* restitutorio.

restive (re·stiv) *adj.* ingobernable, reacio. *2* repropio [caballo]. *3* inquieto, impaciente, alborotado.

restless (-lis) *adj.* inquieto, intranquilo, agitado, impaciente. *2* bullicioso, revoltoso, levantisco. *3* desvelado, insomne.

restock (to) (rista·k) *tr.* reaprovisionar. *2* repoblar [un acuario, etc.].

restoration (ristorei·shøn) *s.* restauración. *2* reno-

vación. *3* restablecimiento, recobro. *4* restitución, devolución.
restorative (risto·rativ) *adj.-s.* restaurativo. *2* reconstituyente.
restore (to) (risto·ʳ) *tr.* restaurar. *2* restablecer. *3* reponer [en el trono, etc.]. *4* restituir, devolver. *5 to ~ to life,* devolver la vida a.
restrain (to) (ristrei·n) *tr.* refrenar, contener, reprimir, coartar, impedir. *2* restringir, limitar. *3* encerrar, encarcelar.
restraint (ristrei·nt) *s.* refrenamiento, cohibición, restricción. *2* reserva, circunspección. *3* contención, moderación.
restrict (to) (ristri·kt) *tr.* restringir, limitar.
restriction (-shøn) *s.* restricción, limitación.
restrictive (-tiv) *adj.* restrictivo.
result (riso·lt) *s.* resultado. *2* consecuencia: *as a ~ of,* de resultas de, a consecuencia de.
result (to) *intr. to ~ from,* resultar, originarse, inferirse. *2 to ~ in,* dar por resultado, venir a parar en.
resultant (-ænt) *adj.-s.* resultante.
resume (to) (rišiu·m) *tr.* reasumir, volver a tomar, a ocupar. *2* recobrar. *3* reanudar, continuar. *4* resumir, compendiar.
résumé (rešiumei·) *s.* resumen.
resumption (rišø·mpshøn) *s.* reasunción. *2* recobro. *3* reanudación.
resurge (to) (risø·ʳdӯ) *intr.* resurgir, renacer.
resurgence (-øns) *s.* resurgimiento.
resurrect (to) (rešøre·kt) *tr.-intr.* resucitar.
resurrection (-shøn) *s.* resurrección; renacimiento: *the Resurrection,* la Resurrección [del Señor].
resuscitate (to) (risø·siteit) *tr.-intr.* resucitar.
resuscitation (-ei·shøn) *s.* resurrección, restauración, renovación.
ret (to) (ret) enriar [cáñamo, lino, etc.]. ¶ Pret. y p. p.: *retted;* ger.: *-tting.*
retable (ritei·bøl) *s.* retablo.
retail (rıtei·l) *s.* detall, menudeo, venta al por menor: *~ trade,* comercio al por menor; *at ~,* al por menor.
retail (to) *tr.* detallar, vender al por menor.
retailer (-øʳ) *s.* detallista, vendedor al por menor.
retain (to) (ritei·n) *tr.* retener, guardar, quedarse con. *2* detener, contener. *3* tomar o tener a su servicio.
retainer (-øʳ) *s.* criado, dependiente, seguidor. *2* retenedor, mantenedor. *3* ajuste, empleo. *4* DER. retención.
retaining (-ing) *adj.* de retención, de contención, etc.: *~ wall,* muro de contención.
retake (to) (rıtei·k) *tr.* volver a tomar. *2* volver a fotografiar o a firmar.
retaliate (to) (ritæ·lieit) *intr.* desquitarse, vengarse. *2 tr.* devolver [un daño, una injuria].
retaliation (-ei·shøn) *s.* desquite, venganza, represalias.
retaliative, tory (ritæ·liativ, -tori) *adj.* de desquite, de venganza, vengador.
retard (rita·ʳd) *s.* retardo, retraso, demora.
retard (to) *tr.* retardar, retrasar, atrasar. *2* diferir, dilatar, demorar.
retardation (-ei·shøn) *s.* retardación, retardo, retraso, atraso.
retch (to) (rech) *intr.* arquear, tener náuseas. *2 tr.* vomitar.
retention (rite·nshøn) *s.* retención. *2* retentiva. .
retiarius (rısiei·riøs) *s.* reserva, taciturnidad, silencio. *2* RET. reticencia.

reticent (-ønt) *adj.* reservado, callado.
reticle (re·tikøl) *s.* ÓPT. retículo, retícula.
reticular (riti·kiulaʳ) *adj.* reticular.
reticulate (to) (riti·kiuleit) *tr.* dar forma de red. *2* proveer de retícula.
reticule (re·tikiul) *s.* ridículo [bolso]. *2* ÓPT. retículo, retícula.
reticulum (riti·kiuløm) *s.* ANAT., ZOOL. retículo.
retina (re·tina) *s.* ANAT. retina.
retinue (re·tiniu) *s.* séquito, acompañamiento; servidores [de un personaje].
1) retire (to) (ritai·ʳ) *intr.* retirarse, αpartarse, retroceder. *2* retirarse, recogerse, irse a acostar. *3* retraerse. *4* retirarse; jubilarse. *5 tr.* retirar, apartar, sacar. *6* COM. retirar [de la circulación, etc.]. *7* retirar, jubilar.
2) retire (to) (ritai·ʳ) *tr.* poner neumáticos nuevos o llantas nuevas a.
retired (ritai·rd) *adj.* retirado, apartado, solitario. *2* íntimo, recóndito. *3* retraído. *4* retirado, jubilado.
retirement (-mønt) *s.* retiro [recogimiento; lugar retirado]. *2* retirada. *3* retraimiento. *4* retiro, jubilación.
retiring (-ing) *adj.* retraído, tímido, modesto. *2* que se retira. *3* del retiro o jubilación.
retorsion *s.* RETORTION.
retort (rito·ʳt) *s.* réplica mordaz. *2* QUÍM. retorta.
retort (to) *tr.-intr.* replicar. *2 tr.* retorcer, redargüir. *3* devolver [una ofensa, etc.].
retortion (rito·ʳshøn) *s.* retorsión. *2* represalia.
retouch (ritø·ch) *s.* retoque.
retouch (to) (ritø·ch) *tr.* retocar, pulir. *2* FOT. retocar.
retrace (to) (ritrei·s) *tr.* desandar: *to ~ one's steps,* volver sobre sus pasos. *2* seguir las huellas, buscar el origen de. *3* repasar [con los ojos, con la memoria], evocar. *4* relatar, contar.
retract (to) (ritræ·kt) *tr.* retractar, retractarse de. *2* retraer, encoger. *3 intr.* retractarse. *4* retraerse, encogerse.
retractation (-ei·shøn) *s.* retractación. *2* acción de desdecirse.
retractile (ritræ·ktil) *adj.* retráctil.
retraction (ritræ·kshøn) *s.* retractación. *2* retracción [de un órgano retráctil].
retread (rı·tred) *s.* neumático recauchutado.
retread (to) (rıtre·d) *tr.* volver a pisar u hollar. *2* AUTO. recauchutar [neumáticos].
retreat (ritrı·t) *s.* retiro, retirada. *2* retiro, aislamiento. *3* refugio, asilo. *4* ECLES. retiro. *5* MIL. retirada. *6* MIL. retreta [toque]. *7* ARQ. parte entrante.
retreat (to) *intr.* retirarse, retroceder,·cejar. *2* refugiarse. *3* tener inclinación hacia atrás. *4 tr.* retirar, mover hacia atrás.
retrench (to) (ritre·nch) *tr.* cercenar, reducir. *2* quitar, suprimir. *3* atrincherar. *4 intr.* reducirse, economizar.
retrenchment (ritre·nchmønt) *s.* cercenamiento, reducción. *2* MIL. atrincheramiento, trinchera.
retribute (to) (retri·biut) *tr.* dar o hacer en pago o desquite.
retribution (retribiu·shøn) *s.* retribución, recompensa. *2* justo castigo, pago, pena merecida.
retrieval (ritrı·val) *s.* recobro, recuperación. *2* reparación. *3* cobra [en la caza].
retrieve (to) (ritrı·v) *tr.* recobrar, recuperar. *2* restablecer, rehacer, reparar, remediar. *3* desquitarse de. *4* cobrar [la caza]. *5 intr.* cobrar la caza.

retriever (ritrɪ·vøʳ) *s.* perro cobrador. *2* perdiguero.
retroactive (retroæ·ktiv) *adj.* retroactivo.
retroactivity (retroækti·viti) *s.* retroactividad.
retrocede (to) (re·trosid) *intr.* retroceder. *2 tr.* DER. hacer retrocesión de.
retrocession (retrose·shøn) *s.* retrocesión.
retroflex (re·trofleks) *adj.* vuelto hacia atrás.
retrogradation (retrogradei·shøn) *s.* retroceso. *2* ASTR. retrogradación.
retrograde (re·trogreid) *adj.* retrógrado.
retrograde (to) *intr.* retroceder. *2* ASTR. retrogradar.
retrogress (to) (re·trogres) *intr.* retroceder.
retrogression (retrogre·shøn) *s.* retroceso, empeoramiento.
retrospect (re·trospekt) *s.* mirada retrospectiva; *in* ~, retrospectivamente.
retrospective (retrospe·ktiv) *adj.* retrospectivo.
retroussé (røtrusei·) *adj.* respingona [nariz].
retroversion (retrovø·ʳshøn) *s.* retroversión.
retting (re·ting) *s.* enriado, enriamiento.
return (ritø·ʳn) *s.* vuelta, regreso, retorno: ~ *ticket*, billete de vuelta o de ida y vuelta; *many happy returns* [*of the day*], feliz cumpleaños; *by* ~ *mail*, *by* ~ *of post*, a vuelta de correo. *2* devolución, reexpedición: ~ *adress*, señas del remitente [en una carta]. *3* retorno, pago, correspondencia, cambio, desquite: *in* ~, en cambio, en recompensa. *4* respuesta, réplica. *5* vuelta, recodo. *6* beneficio, rédito, fruto; producción. *7* estado, declaración. *8* vuelta [billete]. *9 pl.* datos estadísticos, resultado: *election returns*, resultado del escrutinio.
return (to) *intr.* volver, retornar; regresar, reaparecer. *2* responder, replicar. *3 tr.* volver, devolver, restituir; reflejar; pagar, corresponder a, dar en cambio: *to* ~ *good for evil*, devolver bien por mal. *4* dar [un veredicto, una respuesta, las gracias]. *5* dar oficialmente [un informe, un estado]. *6* (Ingl.) elegir [como diputado]; anunciar como elegido.
reunion (rɪyu·nɪøn) *s.* reunión. *2* reconciliación.
reunite (to) (rɪyunai·t) *tr.* reunir, volver a unir, reconciliar. *2 intr.* reunirse, reconciliarse.
revaccinate (to) (rɪvæ·ksineit) *tr.* revacunar.
revaluation (rɪvaliuei·shøn) *s.* nueva valoración. *2* COM. revalorización.
revalue (to) (rɪvæ·liu) *tr.* revalorizar.
revamp (to) (rɪvæ·mp) *tr.* remendar, componer, renovar.
reveal (to) *tr.* revelar, descubrir, manifestar.
reveille (re·vøli) *s.* MIL. diana [toque].
revel (re·vøl) *s.* holgorio, jarana, francachela, fiesta; *farra.
revel (to) *intr.* jaranear, tomar parte en fiestas u orgías. *2* deleitarse, gozarse [en]. ¶ Pret. y p. p.: *revel(l)ed*; ger.: *-l(l)ing*.
revelation (-ei·shøn) *s.* revelación. *2* (con may.) Apocalipsis.
revel(l)er (re·vøløʳ) *s.* jaranero, juerguista, calavera.
revelry (re·vølri) *s.* jarana, juerga, orgía.
revenant (revna·nt) *s.* aparecido, espectro. *2* el que vuelve tras una larga ausencia.
revenge (rive·ndȳ) *s.* venganza, vindicta. *2* desquite.
revenge (to) *tr.* vengar, vindicar: *to be revenged, to* ~ *oneself*, vengarse. *2 intr.* vengarse.
revengeful (-ful) *adj.* vengativo.
revenue (re·vøniu) *s.* renta, rédito, ingresos. *2* ren-

tas públicas; fisco: ~ *cutter*, escampavia; ~ *officer*, aduanero; agente del fisco; ~ *stamp*, póliza, timbre.
reverberate (to) (rivø·ʳbøreit) *tr.* reflejar [la luz, etc.]. *2 intr.* reverberar, reflejarse, retumbar.
reverberation (-ei·shøn) *s.* reverberación, reflexión. *2* retumbo, eco, repercusión.
reverberator (rivø·ʳbøreitøʳ) *s.* reverbero.
reverberatory (rivø·ʳbørɑtori) *adj.* de reverbero.
revere (to) (rivi·ʳ) *tr.* reverenciar, venerar.
reverence (re·vørøns) *s.* reverencia, respeto. *2* reverencia [saludo; tratamiento].
reverence (to) *tr.* reverenciar, acatar.
reverend (-ønd) *adj.* reverendo, venerable. *2* ECLES. reverendo [tratamiento]. *3 s.* clérigo.
reverent (-ønt) *adj.* reverente. *2* humilde, respetuoso.
reverential (revøre·nshal) *adj.* reverencial.
reverie (re·vøri) *s.* ensueño. *2* visión, fantasía.
revers (røvi·ʳ), *pl.* **-vers** (-vi·ʳš) *s.* vuelta, vista, solapa [de un vestido].
reversal (røvø·ʳsal) *s.* inversión. *2* cambio completo [de la opinión, etc.]. *3* DER. revocación.
reverse (rivø·ʳs) *adj.* inverso, contrario. *2* de inversión, de marcha atrás. *3 s.* lo inverso o contrario: *quite the* ~, todo lo contrario. *4* inversión, cambio completo. *5* revés, contratiempo. *6* ESGR. revés. *7* reverso, revés, dorso. *8* MEC. contramarcha, marcha atrás.
reverse (to) *tr.* invertir, volver al revés, voltear, cambiar completamente. *2* MEC. poner en marcha atrás. *3* DER. revocar, anular. *4* invertirse; moverse en sentido contrario.
reversely (-li) *adv.* inversamente, al revés.
reversible (-ibøl) *adj.* reversible. *2* revocable. *3 s.* tejido de dos caras.
reversion (-shøn) *s.* reversión. *2* inversión, cambio en sentido opuesto. *3* BIOL. salto atrás.
revert (to) (rivø·ʳt) *intr.* DER. revertir. *2* volver [a un estado, lugar o tema]; retroceder. *3 tr.* volver a dirigir hacia atrás.
revet (to) (ri·vet) *tr.* revestir [un muro, etc.]. ¶ Pret. y p. p.: *revetted*; ger.: *-tting*.
revetment (-mønt) *s.* ALBAÑ., FORT., ING. revestimiento. *2* muro de contención.
review (riviu·) *s.* revista, inspección, repaso. *2* crítica, reseña [de una obra]. *3* revisión. *4* MIL. revista. *5* revista [periódico; espectáculo].
review (to) *tr.* rever. *2* revisar, repasar. *3* hacer el juicio crítico o la reseña de; analizar. *4* MIL. revistar.
reviewer (-øʳ) *s.* crítico, revistero. *2* revisor [que revé].
revile (to) (rivai·l) *tr.* ultrajar, denigrar, injuriar, denostar, vilipendiar.
revilement (-mønt) *s.* ultraje, contumelia, denuesto, vilipendio.
revindicate (to) (rɪvi·ndikeit) *tr.* reivindicar.
revisal (rivai·šal) *s.* revisión; corrección.
revise (rivai·š) *s.* revisión. *2* IMPR. segunda prueba.
revise (to) *tr.* revisar, corregir.
reviser (-øʳ) *s.* revisor [de un texto].
revision (revi·ẏøn) *s.* revisión, repaso.
revisit (to) (rɪvi·šit) *tr.* volver a visitar.
revitalize (to) (rɪvai·talaiš) *tr.* hacer revivir, galvanizar.
revival (rivai·val) *s.* reavivamiento, restauración, renacimiento; resurgimiento; despertar: *religious* ~, despertar religioso: *Revival of Learning*, Renacimiento humanístico. *2* TEAT. reposición [de obras antiguas].

revive (to) (rivai·v) *tr.* reanimar, reavivar, despertar. 2 restablecer, renovar, resucitar. 3 TEAT. reponer [obras antiguas]. 4 *intr.* volver en sí. 5 revivir, renacer.

revivify (to) (rivi·vifai) *tr.* reivificar, reanimar, resucitar. 2 QUÍM. reactivar.

revocable (re·vøkabøl) *adj.* revocable.

revocation (-ei·shøn) *s.* revocación, derogación.

revoke (rivou·k) *s.* renuncio [en el juego de naipes].

revoke (to) *tr.* revocar, derogar. 2 renunciar [en el juego de naipes].

revolt (rivou·lt) *s.* revuelta, rebelión.

revolt (to) *intr.* sublevarse, amotinarse. 2 sublevarse, indignarse, sentir asco. 3 *tr.* sublevar, levantar. 4 sublevar, indignar, dar asco.

revolter (-ø^r) *s.* sublevado, amotinado.

revolting (-ing) *adj.* indignante, odioso. 2 repugnante, nauseoso.

revolution (revoliu·shøn) *s.* revolución.

revolutionary (-eri) *adj.-s.* revolucionario.

revolutionist (-ist) *s.* revolucionario.

revolutionize (to) (-naiš) *tr.* revolucionar.

revolvable (riva·lvabøl) *adj.* giratorio, rotatorio.

revolve (to) (riva·lv) *tr.* voltear; hacer girar. 2 revolver [en la mente]. 3 *intr.* rodar, girar, dar vueltas.

revolver (-vø^r) *s.* revólver.

revolving (-ving) *adj.* rotativo, giratorio: ~ *door*, puerta giratoria.

revue (riviu·) *s.* TEAT. revista.

revulsion (rivø·lshøn) *s.* MED. revulsión. 2 cambio repentino, reacción [esp. en los sentimientos o en las ideas].

revulsive (rivø·lsiv) *adj.-s.* revulsivo, revulsorio.

reward (riuo·^{r}d) *s.* premio, recompensa, galardón. 2 pago, merecido.

reward (to) *tr.* premiar, recompensar, pagar.

reweigh (to) (rιueі·) *tr.* repesar.

reword (to) (rі·uø^{r}d) *tr.* redactar de nuevo.

rewrite (to) (rιrai·t) *tr.* volver a escribir. 2 refundir [un escrito]. 3 (E.U.) arreglar [lo escrito por otro] para su publicación.

rhabdomancy (rab·dømansi) *s.* rabdomancia.

rhapsode (ræ·psød), **rhapsodist** (ræ·psødist) *s.* rapsoda. 2 autor de rapsodias.

rhapsodize (to) (ræ·psodaiš) *tr.* recitar como una rapsodia. 2 *intr.* hablar con entusiasmo exagerado.

rhapsody (ræ·psødi) *s.* rapsodia. 2 expresión o discurso entusiástico.

rhea (rι·a) *s.* ORN. ñandú, avestruz americano.

Rhenish (re·nish) *adj.* renano.

rheophore (rι·ofo^r) *s.* ELECT. reóforo.

rheostat (rι·ostæt) *s.* ELECT. reóstato.

rhetoric (re·tørik) *s.* retórica.

rhetorical (rita·rikal) *adj.* retórico.

rhetorician (ritari·shan) *s.* retórico.

rheum (rum) *s.* MED. resfriado, catarro. 2 poét. lágrimas.

rheumatic (rumæ·tik) *adj.-s.* reumático.

rheumatism (ru·matišm) *s.* reumatismo, reuma.

rheumy (ru·mi) *adj.* catarroso. 2 húmedo. 3 legañoso.

Rhineland (rai·nlænd) *n. pr.* GEOGR. Renania.

rhinoceros (raina·sørøs) *s.* ZOOL. rinoceronte. 2 ORN. ~ *hornbill*, cálao rinoceronte.

rhinoplasty (rai·noplæsti) *s.* rinoplastia.

rhizoma (raisou·ma), **rhizome** (rai·šoum) *s.* BOT. rizoma.

rhizopod (rai·šopad) *s.* ZOOL. rizópodo.

Rhodes (rou·dš) *n. pr.* GEOGR. Rodas.

rhodium (rou·diøm) *s.* QUÍM. rodio.

rhododendron (roudode·ndrøn) *s.* BOT. rododendro.

rhomb (ramb) *s.* GEOM. rombo. 2 BLAS. losange.

rhombic (-ik) *adj.* rombal. 2 CRISTAL. rómbico.

rhombohedron (rambouji·drøn) *s.* GEOM. romboedro.

rhomboid (ra·mboid) *s.* GEOM. romboide.

Rhone (roun) *n. pr.* GEOGR. Ródano.

rhotacism (rou·tasišm) *s.* rotacismo.

rhubarb (ru·ba^{r}b) *s.* BOT. ruibarbo. 2 BOT. rapóntico.

rhumb (røm) *s.* MAR. rumbo, cuarta.

rhyme (raim) *s.* LIT. rima. 2 LIT. consonante. 3 *without ~ or reason*, sin ton ni son.

rhyme (to) *tr.* rimar. 2 *intr.* rimar [hacer rima]. 3 consonar, armonizar. 4 versificar.

rhymester (-stø^r) *s.* coplero, poetastro.

rhythm (rizm) *s.* ritmo. 2 MED. periodicidad.

rhythmic(al (-ik(al) *adj.* rítmico.

rialto (riæ·ltou) *s.* mercado, lonja.

rib (rib) *s.* ANAT., BOT., MAR. costilla. 2 ENT. nervio [de ala]. 3 cordoncillo [de tejido]. 4 varilla [de paraguas o abanico]. 5 ARQ. nervadura. 6 surco; caballón. 7 COST. vivo. 8 MEC. pestaña, reborde.

rib (to) *tr.* formar costillas, cordoncillos, etc., en. 2 COST. hacer un vivo en. 3 pop. tomar el pelo. ¶ Pret. y p. p.: *ribbed;* ger.: *-bbing.*

ribald (ri·bald) *adj.* grosero, obsceno. 2 *s.* libertino, ribaldo.

ribaldry (-dri) *s.* lenguaje grosero, obsceno.

riband (ri·band) *s.* cinta [esp. de condecoración].

ribbed (ribd) *adj.* que tiene costillas, nervios, rebordes o pestañas.

ribbing (ri·bing) *s.* costillaje. 2 varillaje. 3 nerviación, nervadura.

ribbon (ri·bøn) *s.* cinta, galón, banda, tira. 2 *pl.* cintas, perifollos.

ribbon (to) *tr.* encintar [adornar con cintas]. 2 *intr.* extenderse como una cinta, serpentear.

rice (rais) *s.* BOT. arroz: ~ *field*, arrozal; ~ *paper*, papel de arroz.

rich (rich) *adj.* rico [en bienes, etc.; abundante; exquisito, costoso, suntuoso]. 2 suculento, muy condimentado. 3 muy dulce. 4 fértil, pingüe. 5 fragante. 6 vivo [color]. 7 lleno y pastoso, melodioso [voz, sonido]. 8 cómico, divertido.

Richard (ri·cha^{r}d) *n. pr.* Ricardo.

riches (-iš) *s. pl.* riqueza, opulencia.

richness (-nis) *s.* riqueza, abundancia, suntuosidad, exquisitez. 2 fertilidad. 3 suculencia. 4 viveza [del color]. 5 plenitud [de la voz, del sonido].

rick (rik) *s.* niara, almiar.

rick (to) *tr.* amontonar [grano, paja, etc.].

rickets (ri·kits) *s.* raquitis, raquitismo.

rickety (ri·kiti) *adj.* raquítico. 2 desvencijado. 3 ruinoso, vacilante.

ricksha (ri·ksha), **rickshaw** (-sho) *s.* cochecito chino o japonés de dos ruedas y tirado por uno o más hombres.

rictus (ri·ktøs) *s.* rictus.

rid (to) (rid) *tr.* librar, desembarazar, zafar: *to get ~ of*, librarse, desembarazarse de; *to be well ~ of*, salir bien de. ¶ Pret. y p. p.: *rid o ridded;* ger.: *-dding.*

riddance (-ans) *s.* acción de librar o desembarazar.

ridden (-øn) *p. p.* de TO RIDE.

riddle (ri·dǝl) *s.* enigma, misterio, acertijo, adivinanza. *2* criba, harnero.
riddle (to) *tr.* resolver, descifrar. *2* cribar. *3* acribillar. *4 intr.* hablar enigmáticamente.
ride (raid) *s.* paseo o viaje a caballo, en bicicleta,
en coche, etc. *2* camino de herradura.
ride (to) *intr.* cabalgar, montar; ir a hombros de
una persona; ir, pasear o viajar a caballo, en
bicicleta, en coche, etc.: *to ~ roughshod*, fig. no
reparar en obstáculos; dominar, tiranizar, imponerse. *2* flotar. *3* ir por el espacio. *4* encabalgar, traslapar. *5* girar, funcionar. *6* andar, marchar [el caballo montado, el vehículo]. *7* MAR. *to
~ at anchor*, estar fondeado.
    8 tr. montar, ir montado en [un caballo, una
bicicleta, etc.]. *9* conducir, ir en [un vehículo].
10 surcar [las olas]. *11* llevar montado, llevar a
cuestas. *12* correr [una carrera]. *13* recorrer,
atravesar, etc. [montado o en vehículo]. *14* llevar, impeler, empujar. *15* criticar, burlarse de.
16 oprimir. *17 to ~ down*, alcanzar [a uno]
yendo montado; atropellar, pisotear, vencer. *18
to ~ out*, sortear, capear [un temporal, etc.]. *19
to ~ shank's mare*, fig. ir a pie. ¶ Pret.: *rode;* p.
p. *ridden;* ger.: *riding.*
rider (-ǝ^r) *s.* jinete, amazona; picador; ciclista; el
que va montado en algo. *2* hojuela pegada a un
documento. *3* aditamento.
ridge (ridž) *s.* espinazo [de cuadrúpedo]. *2* arista,
elevación larga y estrecha. *3* cerro, cresta, cordillera. *4* AGR. caballón, lomo. *5* caballete [de
tejado]. *6* cordoncillo [de tejido].
ridge (to) *tr.* dar forma de lomo o cresta. *2 intr.*
formar lomo o cresta. *3* tener lomos o arrugas;
formar cordoncillo. *4* rizarse [el mar].
ridgepiece (-PIS), **ridgepole** (-poul) *s.* ARQ. parhilera.
ridicule (ri·dikiul) *s.* ridículo, irrisión: *to turn to ~*,
ridiculizar, mofarse de.
ridicule (to) *tr.* ridiculizar, poner en ridículo.
ridiculous (ridi·kiulǝs) *adj.* ridículo.
riding (rai·ding) *s.* cabalgata; paseo a caballo o en
coche. *2* encaballamiento. *3* equitación, manejo: *~ coat*, redingote, capote; *~ habit*, traje de
amazona; *~ school*, picadero. *4* MAR. fondeadero.
rife (raif) *adj.* corriente, común, general, frecuente, abundante. *2 ~ with*, lleno de.
Riff (rif) *n. pr.* GEOGR. Rif. *2 s.* rifeño.
riffle (rai·fǝl) *s.* (E.U.) rápido, rabión. *2* rizo [del
agua].
riffle (to) *tr.* peinar [la baraja].
riffraff (ri·fræf) *s.* canalla, chusma. *2* bahorrina. *3
adj.* ruin, vil.
rifle (rai·fǝl) *s.* rifle, fusil. *2* raya [del fusil].
rifle (to) *tr.* pillar, saquear. *2* robar, llevarse. *3* rayar [un arma].
rifleman (rai·fǝlmæn) *s.* fusilero.
rifler (rai·flǝ^r) *s.* saqueador, salteador.
rift (rift) *s.* hendedura, grieta, raja, rendija. *2* disensión, desavenencia.
rift (to) *tr.* hender, rajar. *2 intr.* henderse, rajarse,
abrirse.
rig (rig) *s.* MAR. aparejo. *2* equipo, avíos, maquinaria. *3* carruaje con sus caballos. *4* traje, atavío, disfraz. *5* timo, engaño, mala partida.
rig (to) *tr.* MAR. aparejar, enjarciar. *2* equipar, preparar. *3* vestir, ataviar, disfrazar. *4* burlar, engañar. *5* arreglar o influir por medios fraudu-
lentos.
rigadoon (rigadu·n) *s.* rigodón.

rigging (-ing) *s.* MAR. aparejo, jarcia. *2* equipo, instrumentos.
right (rait) *adj.* recto, derecho [no torcido]. *2* GEOM.
recto. *3* ASTR. recta [ascensión]. *4* recto, justo,
honrado. *5* bueno, correcto, verdadero, conveniente, apropiado, que se busca, que está bien,
sano, cuerdo: *to be all ~*, estar bien; *in one's ~
mind*, en sus cabales. *6* que tiene razón: *you are
~*, usted tiene razón. *7* derecho, diestro; de la
derecha. *8 the ~ side of*, el derecho, el haz de.
    9 adv. derecho, en derechura. *10* inmediata-
mente: *~ afterwards*, acto seguido; *~ away*, *~
off*, en seguida, en el acto. *11* exactamente, de
lleno. *12* mismo: *~ now*, ahora mismo. *13* muy:
~ reverend, reverendísimo. *14* correctamente,
bien; justamente; con razón: *~ or wrong*, con
razón o sin ella. *15* a la derecha: *~ and left*, a
diestro y siniestro. *16* MIL. *~ about!*, ¡derecha!
17 interj. all ~!, ¡está bien!, ¡conformes!
    18 s. derecho, justicia, razón: *to be in the ~*,
tener razón; *by ~*, *by rights*, de derecho; propiamente. *19* derecho [que se tiene]: *rights of man*,
derechos del hombre; *in one's own ~*, por derecho propio. *20* derecho [de una tela, etc.]. *21*
derecha, diestra. *22* POL. derecha. *23 to put*, o
set, *to rights*, poner en orden, arreglar.
right (to) *tr.* hacer justicia a. *2* enderezar, corregir:
to ~ a wrong, deshacer un entuerto. *3* MAR. adri-
zar.
rightabout-face (rai·tabaut) *s.* vuelta a la derecha.
2 media vuelta.
right-angled *adj.* rectangular, rectángulo.
righteous (rai·chǝs) *adj.* recto, justo. *2* honrado,
virtuoso.
rightful (rai·tful) *adj.* justo, honrado, legítimo.
right-hand *adj.* derecho, de la derecha: *~ drive*,
AUTO. conducción a la derecha; *~ man*, fig. hombre de confianza, brazo derecho.
right-handed *adj.* que no es zurdo. *2* para la mano
derecha. *3* mañoso, hábil. *4* dado o hecho con la
derecha. *5* que gira, fig., de izquierda a derecha.
right-minded *adj.* recto, honrado.
rightness (-nis) *s.* derechura. *2* rectitud, justicia. *3*
corrección, exactitud; propiedad.
right-wing *adj.* POL. derechista, de la derecha.
rigid (ri·džid) *adj.* rígido. *2* preciso, riguroso.
rigidity (ridži·diti) *s.* rigidez.
rigmarole (ri·gmaroul) *s.* galimatías.
rigor (ri·gǝ^r) *s.* rigidez. *2* rigor. *3* austeridad. *4 ~
mortis*, rigidez cadavérica.
rigorism (-išm) *s.* rigorismo.
rigorist (-ist) *s.* rigorista.
rigorous (-ǝs) *adj.* riguroso, rigoroso.
rile (rail) *tr.* fam. irritar, exasperar.
rill (ril) *s.* arroyuelo, riachuelo.
rill (to) *intr.* correr formando arroyuelo.
rim (rim) *s.* borde, margen, canto [esp. de algo
curvo]. *2* reborde, pestaña. *3* aro, llanta [de
rueda].
rim (to) *tr.* proveer de un borde. *2* enllantar [una
rueda]. *3* correr alrededor del borde de; rodear.
¶ Pret. y p. p.: *rimmed;* ger.: *-mming.*
rime (raim) *s.* RHYME. *2* escarcha, helada.
rime (to) *tr.-intr.* TO RHYME. *2* cubrir o cubrirse de
escarcha.
rimester (rai·mstǝ^r) *s.* RHYMESTER.
rimple (ri·mpǝl) *s.* arruga. *2* rizo, onda [en el agua,
etc.].
rimple (to) *tr.* arrugar, plegar. *2* rizar, hacer ondear [el agua, etc.].
rimy (rai·mi) *adj.* helado, cubierto de escarcha.

rind (raind) *s.* corteza. *2* cáscara, piel, hollejo.

rind (to) *tr.* descortezar. *2* pelar, mondar.

ring (ring) *s.* anillo, sortija. *2* ajorca. *3* anilla, anillo, aro, cerco. *4* argáneo. *5* ojera [en el ojo]. *6* grafila. *7* pista, arena, redondel. *8* BOX. ring, cuadrilátero. *9* corro, rueda, círculo. *10* pandilla. *11* sonido vibrante, resonante; clamor, estruendo; tañido [de campana]; sonido [de timbre]; llamada [de teléfono]. *12* juego de campanas. *13* tono especial: ~ *of defiance*, tono de desafío.

1) ring (to) *tr.* cercar, circundar. *2* poner anillo o anillas a. *3* quitar [a un árbol] una tira circular de corteza. *4 intr.* moverse en círculo; formar círculo. ¶ Pret. y p. p.: *ringed*.

2) ring (to) *tr.* hacer sonar [un cuerpo metálico]; tocar, tañer, repicar [campanas]; tocar [un timbre o campanilla]. *2* anunciar, celebrar, convocar [con toque de campanas]. *3* repetir, reiterar. *4 to* ~ *up*, llamar; llamar por teléfono; TEAT. subir el telón. *5 intr.* hacer sonar el timbre o la campanilla, llamar. *6* sonar, tañer, retiñir. *7* resonar. *8* zumbar [los oídos]. *9 to* ~ *true*, sonar bien, sonar como verdadero. ¶ Pret.: *rang* o *rung*; p. p.: *rung*.

ring-around-a-rosy *s.* corro [juego].

ringbolt (-boult) *s.* perno con anillo.

ringdove (ri·ngdøv) *s.* ORN. paloma.

ringer (ri·ngøʳ) *s.* campanero. *2* ELECT. llamador.

ringing (ri·nging) *adj.* resonante; retumbante. *2 s.* campaneo, repique; retintín. *3* zumbido [de oídos]. *4* anillamiento.

ringleader (ri·nglidøʳ) *s.* cabecilla, jefe de banda.

ringlet (ri·nglit) *s.* anillejo, pequeño círculo. *2* sortija, rizo.

ringmaster (ri·ngmæstøʳ) *s.* director de pista [en un circo].

ring-shaped *adj.* circular, en forma de anillo.

ringworm (-wøʳm) *s.* MED. culebrilla.

rink (rink) *s.* pista de patinar, patinadero.

rinse (to) (rins) *tr.* lavar con agua, aclarar, enjuagar.

riot (rai·øt) *s.* tumulto, alboroto, motín, bullanga. *2* desenfreno, exceso. *3* diversión bulliciosa. *4* orgía.

riot (to) *intr.* armar alboroto o motines. *2* entregarse al desenfreno. *3* ser exuberante. *4* moverse tumultuosamente.

rioter (-øʳ) *s.* alborotador, amotinado. *2* desenfrenado, libertino.

riotous (-øs) *adj.* amotinado. *2* desenfrenado, disoluto. *3* alborotado, bullicioso.

rip (rip) *s.* rasgadura, rasgón, hendedura. *2* descosido. *3* agua revuelta por la confluencia de dos corrientes. *4 fam.* jamelgo. *5 fam.* bribón.

rip (to) *tr.* rasgar, romper, abrir, destripar; descoser. | Con *up, open* u *off*. *2* arrancar, cortar. | Gralte. con *out* o *away*. *3* buscar a fondo, sondear, descubrir. | Con *up.* *4 intr.* desgarrarse, abrirse, partirse. *5 fam.* ir a toda marcha. ¶ Pret. y p. p.: *ripped*; ger.: *-pping*.

riparian (raipe·rian) *adj.* ribereño, riberiego.

ripe (raip) *adj.* maduro, sazonado. *2* en sazón, a punto, preparado. *3* hecho, acabado. *4* avanzada [edad]. *5* MED. maduro [tumor, etc.]. *6* rosado, colorado.

ripen (to) (-øn) *tr.* madurar, sazonar. *2 intr.* madurar, sazonarse. *3* MED. madurar.

riposte (to) (ripou·st) *intr.* ESGR. responder. *2* responder, replicar con viveza.

ripper (ri·pøʳ) *s.* rasgador, destripador. *2* arrancaclavos. *3 pop. pers.* o cosa notable.

ripping (-ing) *s.* rasgadura. *2* descosedura. *3 adj.* magnífico, estupendo.

ripple (ri·pøl) *s.* onda, rizo, escarceo [del agua]. *2* pliegue, ondulación. *3* murmullo [de las aguas].

ripple (to) *intr.* rizarse, ondear [la superficie del agua, etc.]. *2* caer en ondas. *3* murmurar [el agua, etc.]. *4 tr.* rizar, formar ondas en.

ripsaw (to) (ri·pso) *tr.* aserrar [madera] al hilo.

rise (raiš) *s.* levantamiento, elevación, ascensión, subida. *2* resurrección. *3* salida [de un astro]. *4* pendiente, cuesta, altura, eminencia. *5* altura [de una cosa sobre otra]. *6* ING. peralte. *7* elevación [de la voz, del tono]. *8* crecida [de un río]. *9* encumbramiento; ascenso. *10* aumento, alza, subida [de precios, la temperatura, etc.]. *11* (Ingl.) aumento de sueldo. *12* fuente, causa, origen: *to give* ~ *to*, dar origen a.

rise (to) *intr.* subir, ascender, elevarse, alzarrse, remontarse. *2* resucitar. *3* salir [un astro]. *4* encumbrarse, ascender. *5* levantarse [de la cama, etc.; ponerse en pie]. *6* erizarse. *7* levantar la sesión. *8* alzarse, sublevarse. *9* subir, aumentar, crecer; encarecerse. *10* leudar. *11* nacer, salir, originarse. *12* surgir, aparecer, presentarse, ocurrir. *13* revolverse [el estómago]. *14 to* ~ *to*, estar o ponerse a la altura de. ¶ Pret.: *rose*; p. p.: *risen*.

risen (-øn) *p. p.* de TO RISE.

riser (rai·søʳ) *s.* el que se levanta. *2* sublevación. *3* conductor o tubo ascendente. *4* ARQ. contrahuella.

risible (ri·šibøl) *adj.* risible. *2* de la risa.

rising (rai·šing) *s.* subida, elevación, ascensión. *2* levantamiento. *3* alzamiento, insurrección. *4* resurrección. *5* ASTR. orto, salida. *6* protuberancia, grano. *7 adj.* ascendente. *8* pendiente, en cuesta. *9* creciente. *10* naciente. *11* próspero.

risk (risk) *s.* riesgo, exposición, peligro, albur.

risk (to) *tr.* arriesgar, aventurar, exponer. *2* correr el riesgo de, exponerse a.

risky (-i) *adj.* arriesgado, expuesto. *2* imprudente, temerario. *3* verde, escabroso.

rite (rait) *s.* rito.

ritual (ri·chuəl) *adj.-s.* ritual. *2* ceremonial.

ritually (-i) *adv.* según el ritual.

rivage (ri·vidy̌) *s.* ribera, costa, playa.

rival (rai·val) *adj.* competidor. *2 s.* rival.

rival (to) *tr.* competir, rivalizar con; emular a. ¶ Pret. y p. p.: *rival(l)ed*; ger.: *-l(l)ing*.

rivalry (-ri) *s.* rivalidad. *2* emulación.

rive (to) (raiv) *tr.* rajar, hender. *2 intr.* henderse. ¶ P. p.: *rived* o *riven*.

river (ri·vøʳ) *s.* río: ~ *basin*, cuenca de río; ~ *horse*, hipopótamo; *up the* ~, río arriba; *down the* ~, río abajo.

riverain (-ein) *adj.-s.* ribereño.

riverhead (-jed) *s.* nacimiento de un río.

riverside (-said) *s.* ribera, orilla de un río. *2 adj.* ribereño.

rivet (ri·vit) *s.* roblón, remache.

rivet (to) *tr.* roblar, remachar. *2* asegurar, afianzar. *3* fijar, absorber [la mirada, la atención, etc.].

riveter (-øʳ) *s.* remachador. *2* remachadora [máquina].

rivulet (ri·viulit) *s.* riachuelo, arroyo.

roach (rouch) *s.* ICT. pez de agua dulce. *2* cucaracha. *3* MAR. alunamiento.

road (roud) *s.* carretera, camino: *high* ~, camino real; ~ *mender*, peón caminero. *2* camino, vía, paso: *to be on the* ~, ir de pueblo en pueblo [un viajante, una compañía teatral, etc.]; *in the ~*, estorbando el paso. *3 sing.* o *pl.* rada, ensenada.

roadbed (-bed) *s.* firme de carretera. *2* FERROC. explanación, balasto.

roadhouse (-jaus) *s.* parador.

roadside (-said) *s.* orilla del camino: *~ inn*, parador, venta.

roadstead (-sted) *s.* MAR. rada, fondeadero.

roadster (-stø^r) *s.* automóvil abierto de turismo. *2* caballo de tiro y silla. *3* MAR. buque que puede fondear en las radas.

roadway (-wei) *s.* carretera, calzada.

roam (to) (roum) *intr.* rodar, vagar, errar. *2 tr.* rodar, vagar por.

roan (roun) *adj.* roano. *2 s.* caballo roano.

roar (ro^r) *s.* rugido, bramido. *2* estruendo: *~ of laughter*, risotada. *3* grito; griterío.

roar (to) *intr.* rugir, bramar. *2* tronar, hacer estruendo. *3* roncar [un motor]. *4* gritar, alborotar. *5* reír a carcajadas.

roaring (-ing) *adj.* rugiente, bramador; ruidoso. *2* tremendo, enorme. *3* próspero, animado [negocio].

roast (roust) *s.* asado. *2* carne para asar. *3* tueste, tostadura. *4* crítica, burla. *5 adj.* asado, tostado: *~ beef*, rosbif.

roast (to) *tr.* asar. *2* tostar. *3* METAL. calcinar. *4* criticar, ridiculizarr. *5 intr.* asarse. *6* tostarse.

roaster (-ø^r) *s.* el que asa, asador. *2* tostador. *3* pollo o lechón propio para asarse.

rob (to) (rab) *tr.* robar, hurtar, pillar, saquear: *to ~ Peter to pay Paul*, desnudar a un santo para vestir a otro. *2* robar [en el juego de naipes]. ¶ Pret.: *robbed*; ger.: *robbing*.

robber (-ø^r) *s.* ladrón: *highway ~*, salteador.

robbery (-øri) *s.* robo, latrocinio.

robe (roub) *s.* ropaje, traje talar, túnica; toga [de juez, letrado, etc.]. *3* bata. *4* vestido de mujer. *5* manta [de coche]. *6* fig. manto, capa.

robe (to) *tr.* vestir, ataviar. *2 intr.* vestirse, ataviarse, cubrir.

robin (ra·bin) *s.* ORN. pechicolorado, petirrojo.

roborate (to) (ra·børeit) *tr.* roborar.

robot (rou·bøt) *s.* robot; autómata.

robust (robø·st) *adj.* robusto. *2* fuerte, sólido.

roc (rak) *s.* rocho [ave fabulosa].

rochet (ra·chit) *s.* ECLES. roquete.

rock (rak) *s.* roca, peña, peñasco; escollo: *~ bottom*, fondo, lo más profundo; *~ crystal*, cristal de roca; *~ dove*, paloma zurita; *~ salt*, sal gema; *in the rocks*, perdido, arruinado. *2* peñón. *3* fig. defensa, sostén, refugio. *4* pop. diamante; piedra preciosa. *5* acción de mecer o mecerse.

rock (to) *tr.* mecer, balancear, acunar. *2* sosegar, aquietar. *3* hacer tambalear, estremecer. *4 intr.* mecerse, balancearse, oscilar. *5* tambalearse.

rocker (-ø^r) *s.* el que mece o balancea. *2* mecedora. *3* columpio. *4* pie de cuna, mecedora, etc. *5* MEC. balancín; eje oscilante.

rocket (-it) *s.* cohete: *~ bomb*, bomba volante; *~ launcher*, MIL. lanzacohetes. *2* BOT. oruga, roqueta.

rocket (to) *intr.* subir o lanzarse como un cohete. *2 tr.* bombardear con cohetes.

rocking (-ing) *adj.* mecedor; vacilante, oscilante: *~ chair*, mecedora; *~ horse*, caballo mecedor.

rock-ribbed (-ribd) *adj.* que tiene costillas de roca. *2* fuerte, firme, inflexible.

rockrose (-rouš) *s.* roca o gruta artificial.

rocky (-i) *adj.* rocoso, roqueño, pedregoso: *Rocky*

Mountains, GEOGR. Montañas Rocosas. *2 fig.* duro, endurecido.

rococo (røkou·kou) *adj.-s.* rococó.

rod (rad) *s.* vara, varilla, barra. *2* varilla de virtudes. *3* vara [de autoridad; para medir; para azotar]: *to give the ~*, dar azotes. *4* bastón de mando; cetro. *5* poder, opresión, castigo. *6* medida de 5'5 yardas. *7* caña [de pescar]. *8* MEC. barra, vástago; tirante. *9* ANAT. bastoncillo.

rode (roud) *pret.* de TO RIDE.

rodent (rou·dønt) *adj.-s.* ZOOL. roedor.

rodeo (rou·diou o roudei·ou) *s.* rodeo [del ganado].

rodomontade (radømantei·d) *s.* bravata, fanfarronada.

rodomontade (to) *intr.* bravear, fanfarronear.

roe (rou) *s.* hueva. *2* ZOOL. corzo. *3* ZOOL. cierva, gama. *4* ZOOL. *~ deer*, corzo.

rogations (rougei·shøns) *s. pl.* LITURG. rogaciones.

rogatory (rou·gatori) *adj.* rogatorio.

rogue (roug) *s.* pícaro, bribón, tunante. *2* fam. picaruelo, pillín. *3* elefante fiero que vive separado del rebaño.

roguery (-øri) *s.* bellaquería, ruindad. *2* picardía, travesura.

roguish (-ish) *adj.* pícaro, ruin. *2* travieso, retozón, burlón.

roll (to) (roil) *tr.* enturbiar. *2* irritar, enojar.

roister (roi·stø^r) *s.* baladrón. *2* jaranero, calavera.

roister (to) *intr.* fanfarronear. *2* tomar parte en orgías o fiestas ruidosas.

roisterer (-ø^r) *s.* ROISTER.

role, róle (roul) *s.* papel [que se hace o representa].

roll *s.* rollo [de papel, etc.]. *2* fajo [de billetes]; dinero: *bank ~*, dinero disponible. *3* pergamino, documento. *4* lista, rol, nómina, catálogo, registro: *to call the ~*, pasar lista. *5* bollo, panecillo. *6* rodillo, cilindro. *7* CIR. mecha. *8* ARQ. voluta. *9* tetumbo [del trueno]; tronar [del cañón]; redoble [del tambor]. *10* trino. *11* ondulación [del terreno]. *12* balanceo. *13* movimiento [de lo que rueda; de las olas], rodadura; *~ of the waves*, oleaje.

roll (to) *tr.* hacer rodar o girar. *2* mover, llevar, recorrer sobre ruedas o como sobre ruedas, con movimiento fácil. *3* arrollar, enrollar. *4* liar [un cigarrillo]. *5* envolver, fajar. *6* laminar, cilindrar; alisar, allanar, pulverizar [con rodillo]. *7* tocar redobles [en el tambor]. *8* pronunciar [la *rr*] con sonido vibrante. *9* cantar con quiebro o trino. *10* mover [los ojos], ponerlos en blanco. *11 to ~ up*, arrollar, enrollar; amontonar [una fortuna]. *12 intr.* rodar, girar. *13* ir, etc. [en carruaje]; ir sobre ruedas. *14* revolverse, revolcarse. *15* ondular [un terreno]. *16* balancearse [un buque, el que anda]. *17* moverse [las olas; como las olas]. *18* arrollarse, hacerse una bola. *19* retumbar, tronar, resonar, retemblar. *20* redoblar [el tambor]. *21* trinar [hacer trinos]. *22* acumularse. *23 to ~ about*, rodar, andar de acá para allá; *to ~ down*, bajar rodando; *to ~ in money*, nadar en posibles.

rolled oats (-d) *s.* copos de avena.

roller (-ø^r) *s.* MEC. rodillo, cilindro, tambor: *~ bearing*, cojinete de rodillos; *~ towel*, toalla continua. *2* rollo [de cocina]. *3* rueda o ruedecita [de patín, etc.]. *4* CIR. venda, faja. *5* MAR. ola larga. *6* canario que trina. *7* ORN. variedad de paloma. *8 ~ coaster*, montañas rusas.

rollick (to) (ra·lik) *intr.* juguetear, retozar, travesear.

rollicking (-ing) *adj.* jovial, juguetón, retozón.

rolling (rou·ling) *adj.* rodante, que rueda; de ruedas; laminador, allanador; ondulado, que retumba, etc. V. TO ROLL: ~ *stock*, FERROC. material rodante; ~ *chair*, sillón de ruedas; ~ *mill*, laminador; taller de laminarr; ~ *pin*, rollo de cocina; ~ *stone*, piedra movediza.

Romaic (roumei·ik) *adj.* romaico.

Roman (rou·man) *adj.* romano, romanesco: ~ *catholic*, católico romano; ~ *law*, derecho romano; ~ *nose*, nariz aguileña; ~ *numeral*, número romano. 2 latina [lengua]. 3 *adj.-s.* IMPR. redonda [letra]. 4 *s.* romano, neolatino.

Romance (romæ·ns) *adj.* romance, neolatino.

romance *s.* romance; novela; literatura novelesca: ~ *of chivalry*, libro de caballerías. 2 lo novelesco; interés, emoción, aventura; espíritu novelesco, idilio amoroso. 3 ficción, invención. 4 MÚS. romanza.

romance (to) *intr.* escribir novelas. 2 contar novelas, mentiras.

romancer (romæ·nsør) *s.* novelista. 2 embustero; visionario.

Romanesque (roumane·sk) *adj.-s.* ARQ. románico.

Romanic (rouma·nik) *adj.* románico, neolatino.

Romanism (rou·manišm) *s.* romanismo. 2 desp. católico romano.

Romanize (to) (rou·manaiš) *tr.-intr.* romanizar. 2 *tr.* catolizar. 3 *intr.* hacerse católico.

Romansh (rou·mænsh) *s.* romanche.

romantic(al (romæ·ntik(al) *adj.* romántico.

romanticism (-tisišm) *s.* romanticismo.

romanticize (-tisaiš) *tr.* hacer romántico. 2 *intr.* obrar, hablar de un modo romántico.

Romany (ra·mani) *adj.-s.* gitano.

Rome (roum) *n. pr.* GEOGR., HIST. Roma.

Romish (-ish) *adj.* desp. romano, católico.

romp (ramp) *s.* juego violento o bullicioso, retozo. 2 muchacha retozona; saltabardales.

romp (to) *intr.* jugar, correr, saltar, retozar, triscar.

rompers (-ørs) *s. pl.* vestido holgado que se pone a los niños pequeños para que jueguen.

rondeau (ra·ndou) *s.* LIT. rondel. 2 MÚS. rondó.

rondel (ra·ndøl) *s.* LIT. rondel.

rood (rud) *s.* cruz, crucifijo. 2 medida de 1/4 de acre. 3 medida de longitud [7 u 8 yardas].

roof (ruf) *s.* techo, techado, tejado, cubierta: *flat* ~, azotea; ~ *garden*, azotea jardín; ~ *truss*, armadura de tejado. 2 techo [casa, habitación]. 3 imperial [de diligencia]. 4 cielo [de la boca].

roof (to) *tr.* cubrir, techar. 2 alojar, abrigar.

roofless (-lis) *adj.* destechado. 2 sin abrigo, sin hogar.

rooftree (-trɪ) *s.* cumbrera, parhilera. 2 techo, tejado. 3 fig. techo, hogar.

rook (ruk) *s.* ORN. grajo, chova. 2 trampista, estafador. 3 torre, roque [de ajedrez].

rookery (-øri) *s.* lugar donde anidan los grajos, los pingüinos, etc.; donde procrean las focas. 2 casa miserable de vecindad.

room (rum) *s.* cuarto, pieza, aposento, habitación, sala. 2 espacio, sitio; cabida: *to make* ~, hacer sitio, abrir paso, despejar. 3 causa, motivo: *there is no* ~ *for doubt*, no cabe duda. 4 ocasión, oportunidad.

room (to) *intr.* alojarse, ocupar una habitación.

roomful (-ful) *s.* los que llenan un aposento; cuanto cabe en él.

roomy (-i) *adj.* espacioso, holgado, amplio.

roost (rust) *s.* percha [de gallinero]; gallinero. 2 lugar de descanso: *at* ~, en la percha [ave]; acostado, retirado a descansar.

roost (to) *intr.* dormir [las aves en la percha]. 2 fig. dormir, pasar la noche. 3 *tr.* albergar, dar posada.

rooster (-ør) *s.* gallo [ave].

root (rut) *s.* raíz [en todos sus sentidos]: *cube* ~, raíz cúbica; *to take* ~, arraigar. 2 tronco [de una raza o familia].

root (to) *intr.-tr.* hozar. 2 *tr.* arraigar, implantar; clavar en el suelo. 3 *to* ~ *up* o *out*, desarraigar, arrancar, estirpar. 4 *intr.* arraigar, echar raíces.

rooted (-id) *adj.* arraigado.

rootlet (lit) *s.* raicilla.

rootstock (-stak) *s.* BOT. rizoma. 2 fig. origen.

rooty (-i) *adj.* lleno de raíces. 2 radicoso.

rope (roup) *s.* cuerda, soga, maroma, cabo, cable: ~ *railway*, ferrocarril aéreo; ~ *yard*, cordelería; *to be at the end of one's* ~, haber agotado todos los recursos; *to know the ropes*, conocer bien un asunto, etc. 2 cuerda, dogal. 3 (E.U.) lazo, cuerda. 4 sarta, ristra; guirnalda.

rope (to) *tr.* atar o cercar con cuerda. 2 ensogar. 3 (E.U.) coger con lazo. 4 fam. (E.U.) *to* ~ *in*, pescar, embaucar. 5 *intr.* hacer madeja [un licor].

ropedancer (-dænsør) *s.* funámbulo, volatín.

ropemaker (-meikør) *s.* cordelero, soguero.

ropewalk (-wok) *s.* atarazana [de cordelería].

ropewalker (-wokør) *s.* funámbulo, volatín.

ropeway (-wei) *s.* ferrocarril aéreo.

ropy (-i) *adj.* que hace hebra o madeja; viscoso. 2 que parece cuerda.

rorqual (ro·ʳkual) *s.* ZOOL. rorcual.

rosace (rou·šas) *s.* ARQ. rosetón [adorno].

rosaceous (roušei·shøs) *adj.* rosáceo.

rosary (rou·šari) *s.* rosario. 2 macizo de rosales; rosaleda.

rose (rouš) *s.* BOT. rosa: ~ *leaf*, pétalo de rosa; ~ *water*, agua de rosas; *under the* ~, secretamente. 3 rosa [color, adorno]. 4 rallo [de regadera]. 5 ARQ. rosetón [ventana]. 6 rosa náutica. 7 ~ *diamond*, diamante rosa. 8 BOT. ~ *apple*, pomarrosa; ~ *laurel*, laurel rosa; ~ *mallow*, malva real.

9 pret. de TO RISE.

Rose *n. pr.* Rosa.

roseate (-lit) *adj.* rosado, róseo; de color de rosa.

rosebay (-bei) *s.* BOT. adelfa. 2 BOT. rododendro.

rosebud (-bød) *s.* capullo de rosa, pimpollo.

rosebush (-bøsh) *s.* BOT. rosal.

rose-coloured *adj.* rosado, de color de rosa.

rosemary (-meri) *s.* BOT. romero, rosmarino.

roseola (rouši·øla) *s.* MED. roseola.

roset (rou·šet) *s.* rosicler.

rosette (rouše·t) *s.* rosa [lazo de cintas]; escarapela. 2 ARQ. rosetón, florón. 3 METAL. roseta.

rosewood (rou·šwud) *s.* palisandro; palo de rosa.

rosily (-ili) *adv.* con color de rosa. 2 con optimismo, lisonjeramente.

rosin (ra·šin) *s.* colofonia.

rosolio (rošo·lio) *s.* rosolí.

roster (ra·støʳ) *s.* MIL. lista. 2 MIL. orden del día. 3 lista, nómina. 4 horario escolar.

rostral (ra·stral) *adj.* rostral.

rostrate (ra·streit) *adj.* rostrado.

rostrum (ra·strøm) *s.* ZOOL., BOT., MAR. rostro. 2 tribuna [de orador].

rosy (rou·ši) *adj.* rosado, sonrosado, color de rosa. 2 sonrojado. 3 risueño, lisonjero. 4 optimista.

rosy-hued *adj.* rosado. 2 de tez rosada.

rot (rat) *s.* putrefacción, podredumbre. 2 BOT. ulceración. *3* VET. modorra. *4* tontería, sandez. *5* *interj.* de disgusto, impaciencia, etc.

rot (to) *intr.* pudrirse, corromperse, echarse a perder. *2* ir a menos. *3 tr.* pudrir. *4* enriar. ¶ Pret. y p. p.: *rotted;* ger.: *-tting.*

Rotarian (røtei·rian) *adj.-s.* rotario.

rotary (rou·tari) *adj.* rotatorio: ~ *press,* rotativa.

rotate (to) (rou·teit) *intr.* rotar, rodar, girar. *2* turnar, alternar. *3 tr.* hacer rodar o girar. *4* hacer turnar o alternar.

rotation (-ei·shøn) *s.* rotación. *2* turno, alternación: *in* ~, *by* ~, por turno.

rotator (-tør) *s.* lo que hace rodar. *2* MAR. hélice [de la corredera].

rotatory (rou·tatori) *adj.* rotatorio. *2* turnante.

rote (rout) *s.* rutina; repetición rutinaria; estudio de memoria mecánica: *by* ~, de rutina.

rotifer (rou·tifør) *s.* ZOOL. rotífero.

rotogravure (rotøgraviu·r) *s.* rotograbado.

rotor (rou·tør) *s.* MEC., ELECT. rotor.

rotten (ra·tøn) *adj.* podrido, corrompido. *2* cariado. *3* fétido. *4* malo, abominable, sucio, ofensivo. *5* poco firme, inseguro.

rotter (ra·tør) *s.* pop. sinvergüenza.

rotula (ra·tiula) *s.* rótula.

rotund (rotø·nd) *adj.* redondo; rechoncho. *2* rotundo [lenguaje].

rotunda (-*a*) *s.* ARQ. rotonda.

rotundity (-iti) *s.* redondez. *2* rotundidad.

roué (ruei·) *s.* libertino.

rouge (ruẙ) *s.* colorete, arrebol. *2* JOY. colcótar.

rouge (to) *tr.* pintar, dar de colorete. *2* arrebolar. *3* *intr.* pintarse. *4* arrebolarse.

rough (røf) *adj.* áspero, rugoso, tosco, basto. *2* peludo, hirsuto. *3* escabroso [terreno]. *4* agitado [mar]. *5* tempestuoso, borrascoso. *6* rudo, inculto. *7* brusco. *8* en bruto, mal acabado, de preparación: ~ *copy,* borrador; ~ *draft,* bosquejo; borrador. *9* aproximativo. *10* duro; penoso; rudo, violento: ~ *usage,* uso poco cuidadoso, maltrato. *11* bronco, discordante. *12 s.* lo áspero, tosco, etc.: *in the* ~, en bruto, sin pulimento. *13* matón, persona brutal. *14* terreno escabroso.

rough (to) *tr.-intr.* poner o ponerse áspero. *2 to* ~ *it,* vivir sin comodidades, hacer vida campestre. *3 tr.* hacer o labrar toscamente. *4* tratar con dureza.

roughage (-idẙ) *s.* material tosco o grosero.

rough-and-ready *adj.* tosco o rudo, pero eficaz.

rough-and-tumble *adj.* irregular, desordenado. *2 s.* lucha violenta y sin sujección a reglas.

roughcast (-kæst) *s.* modelo tosco. *2* ALBAÑ. mezcla o mortero grueso.

roughcast (to) *tr.* bosquejar. *2* ALBAÑ. revocar con mortero grueso.

roughdraw (to) (-dro) *tr.* dibujar toscamente, bosquejar.

roughdress (to) (-dres) *tr.* desbastar, dar [a la piedra] una superficie tosca.

roughdry (-drai) *adj.* seco, sin planchar.

roughdry (to) *tr.* secar [ropa] sin plancharla.

roughen (to) (-øn) *tr.-intr.* poner o ponerrse áspero, rugoso o desapacible.

roughew (to) (-jiu) *tr.* esculpir toscamente.

roughhouse (-jauš) *s.* trapatiesta, alboroto.

roughly (-li) *adv.* ásperamente, bruscamente. *2* toscamente. *3* aproximadamente, en términos generales.

roughride (to) (-raid) *tr.-intr.* domar caballos. *2* dominar, tiranizar, imponerse.

roughrider (raidør) *s.* desbravador o domador de caballos.

roughshod (-shad) *adj.* herrado con ramplones.

roulade (rula·d) *s.* MÚS. trino.

rouleau (rulou·) *s.* cartucho [de dinero]. *2* rollo, cucurucho. *3* MIL. fajina.

roulette (rule·t) *s.* ruleta.

round (raund) *adj.* ·redondo: ~ *table,* mesa redonda; ~ *number,* número redondo; ~ *trip,* viaje redondo, de ida y vuelta. *2* en corro: ~ *dance,* baile en corro. *3* rechoncho. *4* rotundo. *5* completo, cabal. *6* claro, fuerte [tono, voz]. *7* grande, cuantioso, liberal. *8* rápido, vivo. *9* claro, categórico; franco, sincero. *10* recto, honrado.

11 s. círculo, orbe, esfera; parte redonda; rodaja. *12* redondez. *13* corro. *14* circuito, recorrido, ronda: *to go one's rounds,* hacer uno su recorrido. *15* giro, rotación; ciclo, revolución periódica; serie [de sucesos, actos, etc.]; ronda; rutina. *16* salva [de aplausos]. *17* mano, tirada, asalto [en un juego o lucha]. *18* listón, travesaño [de silla], peldaño [de escala]. *19* descarga, salva, andanada, disparo. *20*·cartucho con bala. *21* MÚS. especie de canon.

22 adv. alrededor; por todos lados; siguiendo un circuito o ciclo: *to turn* ~, hacer girar o rodar; *to hand* ~ *the cigars,* pasar los cigarros; *muy head goes* ~, se me va la cabeza; *all the year* ~, todo el año. *23* ~ *about,* alrededor; del lado opuesto; de un modo indirecto; aproximadamente.

24 prep. alrededor de. *25* a la vuelta de: ~ *the corner,* a la vuelta de la esquina.

round (to) *tr.* redondear. *2* moverse alrededor de, rodear, cercar. *3* doblar [un cabo, una esquina]. *4 to* ~ *off* u *out,* redondear, completar, acabar. *5 to* ~ *up,* recoger [pers. o cosas dispersas]. *6* *intr.* redondearse. *7* volverse, revolverse. *8 to* ~ *to,* reponerse; MAR. orzar.

roundabout (-abaut) *adj.* indirecto, hecho con rodeos. *2 s.* rodeo, circunloquio. *3* chaquetilla ajustada. *4* tiovivo.

roundel (-øl) *s.* redondo, círculo. *2* corro. *3* rodela. *4* ARQ. ventana, nicho o panel circular. *5* LIT. rondel.

roundelay (-ølei) *s.* canción con estribillo. *2* danza en corro.

rounders (-ørs) *s.* juego inglés parecido al béisbol.

round-faced *adj.* carirredondo.

roundhand (-jænd) *s.* letra redonda.

roundhead (-jed) *s.* (Ingl.) cabeza redonda [apodo que se daba a los puritanos]

roundhouse (-jaus) *s.* MAR. camareta alta. *2* FERROC. casa de máquinas.

roundish (-ish) *adj.* redondeado.

roundly (-li) *adv.* redondamente. *2* rotundamente. *3* francamente. *4* vigorosamente. *5* en números redondos.

roundsman (-mæn) *s.* (E.U.) policía que hace rondas.

roundup (-øp) *s.* (E.U.) rodeo [del ganado]; recogida, redada.

roup (rup) *s.* pepita [de las aves].

rouse (rauš) *s.* despertar. *2* MIL. (Ingl.) diana [toque].

rouse (to) *tr.* despertar. *2* animar, mover, excitar, provocar. *3* levantar [la caza]. *4* *intr.* despertar.

rousing (-ing) *adj.* administrador, entusiasmador. *2* activo, animado. *3* vigoroso. *4* fam. estupendo.

rout (raut) *s.* rota, derrota, fuga desordenada. *2* turbamulta. *3* alboroto, tumulto. *4* séquito.
rout (to) *tr.* derrotar, poner en fuga. *2* arrancar hozando. *3 to ~ out*, sacar, echar; hacer salir a la fuerza. *4 intr.* huir a la desbandada. *5* hozar.
route (rut) *s.* ruta, camino, vía. *2* itinerario.
route (to) *tr.* encaminar.
routinary (rutì·nari) *adj.* rutinario.
routine (rutì·n) *s.* rutina, hábito. *2* práctica diaria o regular.
routinist (-ist) *s.* rútinario.
rove (rouv) *s.* vagabundeo, correría, paseo. *2* TEJ. mecha; mecha estirada. *3* arandela de remache.
rove (to) *intr.* vagar, errar, corretear. *2* piratear. *3* tr. pasar por un ojete. *4* TEJ. estirar [la mecha].
rover (-ø^r) *s.* vagabundo, el que vaga o corre por el mundo, el mar, etc. *2* ladrón, pirata. *3 boy scout* de cierta categoría.
1) row (rau) *s.* riña, pendencia, pelotera, alboroto.
2) row (rou) *s.* fila, hilera, línea, andana: *in a ~*, seguidos. *2* ALBAÑ. hilada. *3* remadura. *4* paseo en lancha o bote.
1) row (to) (rau·) *tr.* fam. pelearse con. *2* reñir, regañar. *3 intr.* pelearse, alborotar.
2) row (to) (rou·) *intr.* remar, bogar. *2 tr.* conducir o mover al remo.
rowboat (rou·bout) *s.* bote de remos.
rowdy (rau·di) *adj.-s.* camorrista, bravucón, alborotador; bruto, bergante.
rowel (rau·øl) *s.* rodaja de espuela.
rowel (to) *tr.* espolear.
rower (rou·ø^r) *s.* remero, bogador.
rowlock (-lak) *s.* MAR. chumacera. *2* ALBAÑ. sardinel.
royal (ro·ial) *adj.* real, regio. *2* magnífico, espléndido, estupendo. *3* tamaño de papel (19 × 24 pulgs. para escribir y 20 × 25 para imprenta). *4* MAR. sobrejuanete.
royalism (roi·alìsm) *s.* realismo, monarquismo.
royally (-i) *adv.* regiamente.
royalty (-ti) *s.* realeza. *2* persona real. *3* las personas reales. *4* regalía. *5* derechos [que se pagan a un autor o inventor].
rub (røb) *s.* restregón, friega, frote, roce. *2* crítica, sarcasmo. *3* tropiezo, dificultad: *there's the ~*, ahí está la cosa.
rub (to) *tr.* estregar, restregar, fregar, frotar, friccionar. *2* bruñir, pulir. *3* irritar. *4 to ~ away* u *off*, quitar frotando. *5 to ~ in*, hacer penetrar frotando; encasquetar, machacar. *6 to ~ out*, borrar. *7 to ~ the wrong way*, frotar a contrapelo, irritar. *8 intr.* rozar. *9* pasar, penetrar, con fricción o dificultad. *10* fam. *to ~ along, on* o *through*, ir tirando. ¶ Pret. y p. p.: *rubbed*; ger.: -*bbing*.
rubber (-rø·bø^r) *s.* caucho, goma elástica; *~ band*, goma, banda de goma; *~ bulb*, pera de goma; *~ plantation*, cauchal. *2* goma de borrar. *3* frotador. *4* pulidor. *5* estropajo; aljofifa. *6* escofina. *7* [en ciertos juegos] partid entera o manga decisiva. *8 pl.* chanclos de goma.
rubberize (to) (-aiš) *tr.* engomar, cauchutar.
rubberneck (-nek) *s.* fam. (E.U.) turista que quiere verlo todo.
rubberneck (to) *intr.* (E.U.) fam. estirar el cuello o volver la cabeza para ver.
rubber-stamp (to) *tr.* sellar con sello de goma; estampillar. *2* fig. aprobar ciegamente.
rubbish (rø·bish) *s.* basura, desecho, broza, escombros. *2* fam. tonterías.

rubble (rø·bøl) *s.* ripio, cascote, cascajo; mampuestos.
rubblework (-wø^rk) *s.* mampostería.
rubdown (rø·bdaun) *s.* fricción, masaje.
rubefacient (rubifei·shønt) *adj.-s.* rubefaciente.
rubescent (rube·sønt) *adj.* rubicundo, sonrojado.
rubiaceous (rubiei·shøs) *adj.* BOT. rubiáceo.
rubican (ru·bikan) *adj.* rubicán.
rubicund (ru·bikønd) *adj.* rubicundo.
rubidium (rubi·diøm) *s.* QUÍM. rubidio.
rubiginous (rubi·dyinøs) *adj.* ruginoso.
ruble (ru·bøl) *s.* rublo.
rubric (ru·brik) *adj.* rubro, rojo. *2 s.* rúbrica.
rubrical (-al) *adj.* de rúbrica.
rubricate (to) (-ei) *tr.* marcar, iluminar o imprimir con color rojo. *2* poner rúbrica o epígrafe.
ruby (ru·bi) *s.* MINER. rubí: *~ spinel*, rubí espinela. *2 adj.* de color de rubí.
ruby (to) *tr.* rubificar.
ruche (rush) *s.* COST. lechuguilla.
ruck (røk) *s.* arruga, fruncido. *2* DEP. el pelotón [en una carrera]. *3* fig. el vulgo; lo común.
ruck (to) *tr.* arrugar, ajar.
rucksack (-sæk) *s.* mochila, morral.
ruction (-shøn) *s.* fam. alboroto, tumulto.
rudder (rø·dø^r) *s.* timón, gobernalle. *2* fig. timón [dirección, gobierno].
rudderpost (-poust) *s.* MAR. codaste. *2* AVIA. eje del timón.
ruddle (rø·døl) *s.* almagre. *2* color rojo.
ruddle (to) *tr.* marcar con almagre.
ruddy (rø·di) *adj.* rojo, colorado, encendido, rubicundo. *2* fam. maldito, condenado.
rude (rud) *adj.* rudo. *2* tosco. *3* escabroso [terreno]. *4* grande, fuerte. *5* duro, penoso. *6* chapucero, imperfecto. *7* inculto; inhábil. *8* brusco, descortés.
rudeness (-nis) *s.* rudeza. *2* tosquedad. *3* grosería. *4* descortesía. *5* rusticidad, incultura. *6* violencia.
rudiment (ru·dimønt) *s.* rudimento.
rudimentary (rudime·ntari) *adj.* rudimentario.
rue (ru) *s.* BOT. ruda.
rue (to) *tr.-intr.* llorar, lamentar, sentir, pesarle a uno, arrepentirse.
rueful (ru·ful) *adj.* lamentable, lastimoso. *2* triste, lloroso, afligido. *3* compasivo. *4* terrible.
rufescent (rufe·sønt) *adj.* rojizo.
ruff (røf) *s.* gorguera, cuello alechugado. *2* ZOOL., ORN. collar de pelo o pluma. *3* ORN. paloma de toca. *4* fallada [en los naipes]. *5* fam. enojo.
ruff (to) *tr.-intr.* alechugar. *2* fallar [en los naipes].
ruffian (rø·fian) *adj.* brutal, cruel. *2 s.* hombre brutal, matón, forajido.
ruffle (rø·føl) *s.* lechuguilla, volante fruncido. *2* enojo, irritación. *3* rizo [en el agua]. *4* redoble apagado [de tambor].
ruffle (to) *tr.* rizar, alechugar, fruncir. *2* arrugar, ajar, descomponer. *3* irritar, incomodar, hacer perder la calma. *4* encrespar, erizar. *5 intr.* arrugarse, descomponerse; rizarse [el agua]. *6* irritarse, incomodarse.
rufous (ru·føs) *adj.* rufo, bermejo, leonado.
rug (røg) *s.* alfombra, alfombrilla, ruedo, felpudo. *2* (Ingl.) manta [de caballo, de viaje, etc.].
Rugby (football) (rø·gbi) *s.* DEP. rugby.
rugged (rø·gid) *adj.* rugoso, arrugado. *2* áspero, escabroso. *3* desapacible. *4* desgreñado. *5* rudo. *6* severo, regañón. *7* borrascoso. *8* recio.
rugosity (ruga·siti) *s.* rugosidad.

ruin (ruin) *s.* ruina. *2* destrucción. *3* perdición, deshonra. *4 pl.* ruinas.

ruin (to) *tr.* arruinar. *2* destruir. *3* seducir, perder. *4 intr.* arruinarse, perderse.

ruination (-ei·shøn) *s.* arruinamiento, ruina, perdición.

ruinous (rui·nøs) *adj.* ruinoso. *2* fatal, funesto.

rulable (ru·labøl) *adj.* gobernable, regulable. *2* conforme a regla.

rule (rul) *s.* regla, precepto, principio, máxima, pauta, norma: ~ *of three*, regla de tres; *to make it a* ~ *to*, tener por norma; *as a* ~, por regla general. *2* regla [de una orden]. *3* reglamento, régimen: *rules and regulations*, reglamento. *4* fallo [de un tribunal]. *5* gobierno, poder, mando, dominio, autoridad. *6* reinado. *7* regla [para trazar líneas; para medir]. *8* raya [en el papel]. *9* IMPR. filete.

rule (to) *tr.* gobernar, regir, dirigir: *to* ~ *the roast* o *the roost*, fig. ser el que manda. *2* decidir, fallar. *3* regular, reglar. *4* contener, reprimir. *5* reglar, rayar, pautar. *6* tirar [líneas]. *7* ordenar, arreglar. *8 to* ~ *out*, excluir; desechar. *9 intr.* mandar, regir, gobernar, reinar. *10* privar, estar en boga. *11* COM. mantenerse a un tipo.

ruler (-ø*ʳ*) *s.* gobernante, soberano. *2* regla [para trazar líneas].

ruling (-ing) *adj.* gobernante. *2* predominante, imperante. *3* ~ *price*, precio medio. *4* ~ *pen*, tiralíneas.

rum (røm) *s.* ron, aguardiente. *2 adj.* extraño, singular. *3* ~ *customer*, persona o animal con quien no se puede jugar.

Rumania (rumei·nia) *n. pr.* GEOGR. Rumania.

Rumanian (-nian) *adj.-s.* rumano.

rumble (rø·mbøl) *s.* rumor, retumbo, ruido sordo y continuo. *2 rumble* o ~ *seat*, asiento descubierto en la trasera de un automóvil.

rumble (to) *intr.* retumbar, hacer un ruido sordo y continuo. *2* pasar con estruendo o ruido sordo. *3 intr.-tr.* hablar con voz grave y rumorosa.

rumen (ru·min) *s.* panza [del estómago de los rumiantes].

ruminant (ru·minant) *adj.-s.* ZOOL. rumiante. *2 adj.* meditativo, que rumia.

ruminate (to) (-eit) *tr.-intr.* rumiar [masticar por segunda vez]. *2* rumiar, reflexionar.

rumination (-ei·shøn) *s.* rumia, rumiadura. *2* reflexión, meditación.

ruminative (ru·minativ) *adj.* reflexivo, meditativo.

rumly (rø·mli) *adv.* extrañamente, singularmente.

rummage (rø·midȳ) *s.* búsqueda, registro que se hace revolviendo. *2* trastorno, desorden.

rummage (to) *tr.-intr.* registrar, revolver buscando. *2 to* ~ *out* o *up*, hallar [revolviendo], desenterrar.

rummy (rø·mi) *adj.* extraño, singular. *2 s.* pop. (E.U.) borracho. *3* juego de naipes.

rumo (u) r (ru·mø*ʳ*) *s.* rumor, voz que corre.

rumo (u) r (to) *tr.* rumorear, propalar: *it is rumo(u)red*, se rumorea.

rump (rømp) *s.* ancas, cuarto trasero. *2* rabadilla [de ave]. *3* culata [de vaca]. *4* cola, resto, residuo.

rumple (rø·mpøl) *s.* doblez; arruga, arrugamiento, ajamiento.

rumple (to) *tr.* arrugar, chafar, ajar. *2* descomponer, desgreñar. *3 ref.* arrugarse, ajarse.

rumpus (rø·mpøs) *s.* bulla, alboroto, ruido.

run (røn) *s.* corrida, carrera. *2* curso, marcha, tendencia, dirección. *3* serie, continuación, racha. *4* TEAT. serie de representaciones de una obra. *5* asedio [de un banco] por los cuentacorrentistas. *6* funcionamiento. *7* operación, manejo: *to get the* ~ *of*, aprender el manejo de; hallar el modo de. *8* lo que sale, se produce, etc., en un tiempo u operación. *9* recorrido, distancia. *10* vida [de una cosa]. *11* hilo [del discurso]. *12* clase, tipo, etc., usual. *13* MAR. singladura. *14* carrera, competición. *15* viaje, paseo. *16* libertad de andar por un sitio, de hacer uso de algo. *17* terreno, extensión. *18* (E.U.) riachuelo. *19* MIN. buzamiento. *20* MÚS. carrerilla. *21* carrera [en las medias]. *22* TEAT. rampa. *23 in the long* ~, a la larga, tarde o temprano.

24 p. p. de TO RUN.

run (to) *intr.* correr. *2* girar, rodar. *3* extenderse [hacia, hasta, por]; llegar, alcanzar [hasta]. *4* pasar [a cierto estado]: *to* ~ *dry*, secarse [un pozo, etc.]. *5* fluir, manar, chorrear. *6* derretirse. *7* correrse [los colores]. *8* supurar. *9* ir, dirigirse. *10* decir, rezar: *the song runs as follows*, la canción dice así. *11* ser, durar, mantenerse. *12* TEAT. representarse seguidamente. *13* seguir, estar vigente; imperar, estar en boga. *14* funcionar, marchar. *15* POL. presentarse [para]; ser candidato [a]. *16 to* ~ *about*, correr, ir de un lado a otro. *17 to* ~ *across*, encontrar, dar con. *18 to* ~ *against*, chocar con; oponerse [a]. *19 to* ~ *along*, correr a lo largo de; correr, ir: ~ *along!*, ¡lárgate! *20 to* ~ *around with*, andar o juntarse con. *21 to* ~ *away*, huir desbocarse [un caballo], dispararse [un motor]; *to* ~ *away with*, fugarse con, arrebatar; llevarse. *22 to* ~ *down*, escurrir, gotear [un líquido]; pararse, habérsele acabado la cuerda, el vapor, etc. [a un reloj, un aparato]; agotarse, debilitarse. *23* MAR. *to* ~ *foul* o *foul of*, chocar con, abordar. *24 to* ~ *in*, entrar al pasar. *25 to* ~ *in the blood*, estar en la sangre. *26 to* ~ *off the track*, descarrilar. *27 to* ~ *on*, seguir, continuar. *28 to* ~ *out*, salir; salirse, derramarse; expirar; acabarse; extenderse; *to* ~ *out of*, acabársele a uno [una cosa]. *29 to* ~ *over*, rebosar, desbordarse; atropellar, pasar por encima. *30 to* ~ *through*, correr por, pasar por. *31 to* ~ *with*, estar chorreando o empapado de; abundar en.

32 tr. correr [un caballo]. *33* correr, cazar, perseguir. *34* pasar [una cosa por encima o a través de otra]. *35* recorrer, correr por. *36* hacer [un mandado]. *37* seguir [un camino, un curso]. *38* clavar, meter, introducir. *39* mover, empujar, llevar. *40* fundir, vaciar. *41* tirar [una línea]. *42* pasar de contrabando. *43* correr [un riesgo]. *44* derramar, verter, manar. *45* huir de. *46* regentar, dirigir, explotar [un negocio]. *47* conducir [un vehículo o máquina]. *48* MIL. burlar [un bloqueo]. *49* COST. bastear. *50 to* ~ *down*, dar caza a; derribar; atropellar [con un vehículo]; denigrar, difamar. *51 to* ~ *into*, clavar, hundir. *52 to* ~ *off*, escribir o pronunciar rápidamente; imprimir. *53 to* ~ *out*, sacar, extender; agotar. *54 to* ~ *through*, atravesar, pasar de parte a parte; examinar por encima; hojear; dilapidar. *55 to* ~ *to earth*, perseguir hasta su escondite; seguir hasta su origen. *56 to* ~ *up*, hacer subir [una cuenta]; sumar; edificar de prisa; COST. repasar, remendar; MAR. izar.

¶ Pret.: *ran*; p. p.: *run*; ger.: *running*.

runabout (-abaut) *s.* vagabundo. *2* birlocho. *3* automóvil pequeño. *4* canoa, automóvil ligero.

runaway (-auei) *adj.-s.* fugitivo. *2* desertor, tráns-

fuga. *3 adj.* desbocado [caballo]. *4* DEP. ganado fácilmente. *6 s.* fuga, escapatoria. *7* desbocamiento. *8* caballo desbocado.
rundle (rø·ndøl) *s.* RUNG 1. *2* rueda.
rundlet (rø·ndlet) *s.* barrilete, barrilejo.
run-down *adj.* agotado, debilitado; atropellado. *2* sin cuerda [reloj]. *3* ELECT. descargada [batería].
rune (ru·n) *s.* runa. *2* misterio; magia. *3 pl.* poemas rúnicos.
rung (rø·ng) *s.* escalón [de escala]. *2* travesaño [de silla]. *3* rayo [de rueda]. *4 pret.* y *p. p.* de TO RING.
runic (ru·nik) *adj.* rúnico, runo.
runlet (rø·nlit), **runnel** (-nøl) *s.* riachuelo.
runner (-ø[r]) *s.* corredor [que corre]. *2* mensajero. *3* (E.U.) agente [de un hotel, vapor, etc.]. *4* contrabandista. *5* MEC. corredera. *6* anillo corredizo. *7* volandera [muela]. *8* cuchilla [de patín]; patín [de trineo]. *9* carrera [en las medias]. *10* pasillo [alfombra]. *11* camino de mesa. *12* BOT. estolón. *13* BOT. judía [planta].
runner-up, *pl.* **runners-up** *s.* DEP. jugador o equipo que queda en segundo lugar en un torneo.
running (-ing) *s.* carrera, corrida, curso. *2* marcha, funcionamiento. *3* dirección, manejo. *4* flujo. *5* supuración. *6 adj.* corredor. *7* corriente: ~ *water*, agua corriente. *8* corredizo: ~ *knot*, nudo corredizo. *9* corrida [letra]. *10* fluido, fácil [estilo]. *11* AUTO. ~ *board*, estribo. *12* MAR. ~ *lights*, luces de situación. *13* IMPR. ~ *title*, titulillo. *14 adv.* seguido: *three times* ~, tres veces seguidas.
runt (rø·nt) *s.* animal enano. *2* fam. enano, redrojo. *3* paloma de gran tamaño.
runway (rø·nwei) *s.* lecho, cauce. *2* vía; senda. *3* AVIA. pista de aterrizaje. *4* TEAT. pasarela.
rupee (rupi·) *s.* rupia.
rupestrian (rupe·strian) *adj.* rupestre.
rupture (rø·pchø[r]) *s.* ruptura, rotura. *2* MED. hernia. *3* ruptura, desavenencia.
rupture (to) *tr.* romper. *2* producir hernia. *3 intr.* romperse. *4* quebrarse, sufrir hernia.
rural (ru·ral) *adj.* rural, rústico. *2 s.* rústico, campesino.
ruse (ruš) *s.* ardid, astucia, artimaña.
rusé (rušei·) *adj.* astuto.
rush (røsh) *s.* movimiento o avance impetuoso: *with a* ~, de golpe; impetuosamente. *2* torrente, tropel, afluencia: ~ *hour*, hora punta. *3* prisa, precipitación. *4* ímpetu, empuje. *5* ataque, embestida. *6* gran demanda [de una cosa]. *7* BOT. junco. *8* BOT. anea, espadaña. *9* fig. bledo, pito.
rush (to) *intr.* arrojarse, abalanzarse, precipitarse:

to ~ *forward*, avanzar, arrojarse con ímpetu: ~ *to* ~ *in upon*, sorprender; *to* ~ *through*, hacer precipitadamente; arrojarse [a los peligros]. *2 tr.* empujar o arrojar con violencia. *3* despachar con prontitud, apresurar. *4* embestir; tomar por asalto. *5* asediar con atenciones.
rushlight (-lait) *s.* vela de sebo y junco; su luz.
rusk (røsk) *s.* sequillo, galleta.
russet (rø·sit) *adj.* bermejo. *2 s.* color bermejo. *3* variedad de manzana. *4 adj.-s.* burdo [paño].
russety (rø·siti) *s.* bermejizo.
Russia (rø·sha) *n. pr.* GEOGR. Rusia. *2 Russia leather* o simplte. *russia*, piel de Rusia.
Russian (rø·shan) *adj.-s.* ruso.
rust (røst) *s.* moho, orín, herrumbre. *2* inacción, ociosidad. *3* BOT. roya, añublo. *4 adj.* rojizo [color].
rust (to) *tr.* enmohecer [oxidar; embotar]. *2* dar color de herrumbre. *3 intr.* enmohecerse [oxidarse; embotarse]. *4* aherrumbrarse. *5* BOT. arroyarse.
rustic (rø·stik) *adj.-s.* rústico. *2* campesino. *3 adj.* sencillo, campestre.
rusticate (to) (-ikeit) *intr.* rusticar. *2 tr.* enviar al campo. *3* expulsar temporalmente de una universidad.
rusticity (røsti·siti) *s.* rusticidad, rustiquez. *2* simplicidad. *3* grosería, rudeza.
rustle (rø·søl) *s.* susurro, crujido.
rustle (to) *intr.* susurrar, crujir. *2* (E.U.) menearse, obrar con energía. *3 tr.* hacer susurrar o crujir. *4* robar [ganado].
rustler (rø·slø[r]) *s.* pop. (E.U.) persona activa. *2* (E.U.) ladrón de ganado.
rusty (rø·sti) *adj.* mohoso, herrumbroso. *2* enmohecido. *3* rojizo. *4* ronca [voz]. *5* rancio, anticuado.
rut (røt) *s.* brama, celo [de los animales]. *2* carril, rodada, surco. *3* rutina, costumbre, sendero trillado.
rut (to) *tr.* hacer rodadas o surcos en. *2* estar en celo. ¶ Pret. y p. p.: *rutted*; ger.: *-tting*.
rutabaga (rutabei·ga) *s.* BOT. naba.
Ruth (ruz) *n. pr.* Rut.
Ruthenia (ruzi·nia) *n. pr.* GEOGR. Rutenia.
ruthenium (ruzi·niøm) *s.* QUÍM. rutenio.
ruthless (ru·zlis) *adj.* cruel, despiadado, inhumano.
rutile (ru·til) *s.* MINER. rutilo.
rutty (rø·ti) *adj.* lleno de rodadas o surcos.
rye (rai) *s.* BOT. centeno. *2* (E.U.) whisky de centeno. *3* BOT. ~ *grass*, ballico, césped inglés.

S

S, s (es) s. S, s, decimonona letra del alfabeto inglés.

's de, el de (signo del llamado caso posesivo o posesivo sajón): *John's father*, el padre de Juan. *2 abrev.* de IS, HAS y US.

Sabaean (sabɪˈan) *adj.-s.* sabeo.

Sabaism (saˈbaišm) s. sabeísmo.

Sabbath (sæˈbaz) s. día de de descanso [sábado entre los judíos, domingo entre los cristianos].

sabbatic (al (sabæˈtik(al) *adj.* sabático.

saber (seiˈbøʳ) s. sable.

saber (to) *tr.* acuchillar, herir a sablazos.

Sabine (sæˈbin) *adj.-s.* sabino.

sable (seiˈbøl) *adj.-s.* BLAS. sable. *2* negro, obscuro. *3* ZOOL. marta cebellina. *4* su piel. *5 pl.* ropas de luto.

sabot (sæˈbou) s. zueco, almadreña.

sabotage (sæˈbøtidɏ) s. sabotaje.

sabotage (to) *tr.* sabotear.

saboteur (-tøʳ) s. saboteador.

sabre (seiˈbøʳ) s. SABER.

sabre (to) *tr.* TO SABER.

sabulous (sæˈbiuløs) *adj.* sabuloso, arenoso.

saburra (sabøˈra) *adj.* MED. saburra.

sac (sæk) s. ANAT., ZOOL., BOT. saco, cavidad.

saccharimeter (sækariˈmitøʳ) s. sacarímetro.

saccharin(e (sæˈkarin) s. QUÍM. sacarina.

saccharine *adj.* sacarino. *2* azucarado.

saccharose (-ous) s. QUÍM. sacarosa.

saccule (saˈkiul) s. ANAT. sáculo.

sacerdocy (sæˈsøʳdosi) s. sacerdocio.

sacerdotal (sæsøʳdouˈtal) *adj.* sacerdotal. *2* clerical.

sacerdotalism (-išm) s. sacerdocio. *2* clericalismo.

sack (sæk) s. saco, costal. *2* saco, saqueo: *to put to* ~, meter a saco. *3* saco, chaqueta holgada. *4* vino blanco generoso. *5 fam. to give,* o *get, the* ~, despedir o ser despedido; dar o recibir calabazas.

sack (to) *tr.* ensacar, meter en saco. *2* saquear, pillar. *3* despedir; dar calabazas.

sackbut (-bøt) s. MÚS. sacabuche.

sackcloth (-kloz) s. harpillera. *2* cilicio.

sacker (-øʳ) s. ensacador. *2* saqueador.

sacking (-ing) s. tela para sacos, harpillera.

sacque (sæk) s. saco, chaqueta holgada.

sacral (saˈkral) *adj.* ANAT. sacro. *2* sacral.

sacrament (sæˈcramønt) s. sacramento. *2* sacra-

mento del altar, eucaristía. *3* juramento solemne.

sacramental (sækrameˈntal) *adj.* sacramental. *2 s. pl.* sacramentales.

sacrarium (sækreiˈriøm) s. sagrario.

sacred (seiˈkrid) *adj.* sagrado, sacro, santo: *Sacred College,* Sacro Colegio. *2* inviolable.

sacrifice (sæˈkrifais) s. sacrificio; inmolación. *2* COM. *to sell at a* ~, vender sin beneficio.

sacrifice (to) *tr.* sacrificar; inmolar. *2* COM. vender sin beneficio. *3 intr.* sacrificar.

sacrificial (-shal) *adj.* de sacrificio, sacrificatorio.

sacrilege (sæˈkrilidɏ) s. sacrilegio.

sacrilegious (sækriliˈdɏøs) *adj.* sacrílego.

sacring (saˈkring) s. consagración [esp. en la misa]: ~ *tablet,* sacra.

sacristan (sæˈkristan) s. sacristán.

sacristy (-ti) s. sacristía.

sacrosanct (sæˈkrosænct) *adj.* sacrosanto.

sacrum (seiˈkrøm) s. ANAT. sacro.

sad (sæd) *adj.* triste. *2* aciago. *3* malo, pobre, de inferior calidad.

sadden (to) (-øn) *tr.* entristecer. *2* ensombrecer. *3 intr.* entristecerse. *4* ensombrecerse.

saddle (sæˈdøl) s. silla [de montar]: ~ *horse,* caballo de silla; *in the* ~, fig. en el poder; listo, dispuesto. *2* sillín. *3* COC. lomo, cuarto trasero. *4* paso [entre montañas]. *5* cosa o parte en figura de silla de montar.

saddle (to) *tr.* ensillar. *2* enalbardar. *3 to* ~ *with,* hacer cargar con.

saddlebacked (sæˈdølbækt) *adj.* ensillado, de lomo hundido.

saddlebag (sæˈdølbæg) s. alforja [para caballería]; maletín de grupa.

saddlecloth (-kloz) s. mantilla [del caballo].

saddler (sæˈdløʳ) s. guarnicionero, talabartero.

saddlery (sæˈdløri) s. guarnicionería.

saddletree (sæˈdøltrɪ) s. fuste [de la silla de montar].

Sadducee (sæˈdiusɪ) s. saduceo.

sad-iron (sæd-aioʳn) s. plancha [para la ropa].

sadism (seiˈdišm) s. sadismo.

sadistic (seidiˈstik) *adj.* sádico. ·

sadness (sæˈdnis) s. tristeza. *2* melancolía.

safe (seif) *adj.* salvo, ileso, incólume: ~ *and sound,* sano y salvo. *2* seguro [exento de peligro]; pru-

dente. *3* seguro, confiable. *4* ~ *load*, carga máxima. *5 s.* arca, caja de caudales. *7* alacena.
safe-conduct *s.* convoy, salvoconducto.
safeguard (sei·fga^rd) *s.* salvaguardia, resguardo. *2* escolta, salvoconducto.
safeguard (to) *tr.* salvaguardar, proteger.
safe-keeping *s.* guarda, custodia, depósito.
safely (-li) *adv.* seguramente, sin peligro, a salvo, sin novedad.
safeness (-nis) *s.* seguridad [estado o condición]. *2* prudencia [de una conducta].
safety (-ti) *s.* seguridad, protección, salvamento, incolumidad: ~ *belt*, salvavidas, cinturón de seguridad; ~ *island*, burladero [en una calle]; ~ *pin*, imperdible; ~ *razor*, maquinilla de afeitar; ~ *valve*, válvula de seguridad. *2* prudencia [de un proceder]. *3* seguro [de arma].
safflower (sæ·flauø^r) *s.* BOT. alazor.
saffron (sæ·frøn) *s.* BOT. azafrán. *2 adj.* azafranado.
sag (sæg) *s.* combadura, comba, bolsa, hundimiento, depresión. *2* COM. baja [de precios].
sag (to) *tr.* combar, empandar. *2 intr.* combarse, pandear, hacer bolsa. *3* ceder, flojear. *4* bajar [los precios]. ¶ Pret. y p. p.: *sagged;* ger.: *-gging.*
saga (sa·ga) *s.* saga.
sagacious (sagei·shøs) *adj.* sagaz.
sagacity (sagæ·siti) *s.* sagacidad.
sage (seidŷ) *s.* BOT. salvia. *2* sabio, filósofo, hombre prudente. *3 adj.* cuerdo, prudente.
sageness (sei·dŷnis) *s.* sabiduría, cordura, prudencia.
sagittal (sæ·dŷital) *adj.* sagital.
Sagittarius (sædŷite·riøs) *s.* ASTR. Sagitario.
sago (sei·gou) *s.* sagú [fécula]. *2* BOT. *sago* o ~ *palm*, sagú [planta].
Sahara (saje·ra) *n. pr.* GEOGR. Sahara.
sahib (sa·ib) *s.* señor [usado por los persas e hindúes, esp. con el nombre de un europeo].
said (sed) *pret.* y *p. p.* de TO SAY.
sail (seil) *s̃.* MAR. vela: *to set* ~, hacerse a la vela. *2* buque de vela. *3* aspa [de molino].
sail (to) *intr.* navegar: *to* ~ *close to the wind*, ceñir el viento; fig. seguir la corriente; bordear lo ilícito. *2* hacerse a la vela. *3* ir o viajar [en un buque]. *4* deslizarse, flotar, volar. *5* moverse majestuosamente. *6 tr.* gobernar una embarcación. *7* navegar por, surcar.
sailboat (sei·lbout) *s.* buque o barca de vela, velero.
sailcloth (-kloz) *s.* lona, brin. *2* toldo.
sailer (sei·lø^r) *s.* buque de vela, velero.
sailing (sei·ling) *s.* navegación, deporte de vela: ~ *master*, piloto; *plain* ~, fig. progreso fácil, coser y cantar. *2* salida [de un buque]. *3* viaje en barco.
sailmaker (sei·lmeikø^r) *s.* velero [que hace velas de barco].
sailor (-ø^r) *s.* marinero. *2* marino. *3* *sailor* o ~ *hat*, canotié, sombrero de paja.
saint (seint) *s.* santo, santa. *2* santo, san, santa [delante con un nombre]. | Suele escribirse con may. y se abrevia así: *St.: St. Elmo's fire*, fuego de Santelmo; *St. Martin's summer*, veranillo de San Martín; *St. Vitus's dance*, MED. corea, baile de San Vito.
saint (to) *tr.* canonizar. *2 intr.* obrar como un santo.
sainted (-id) *adj.* santo, canonizado. *2* santo, virtuoso, piadoso.
saintliness (-linis) *s.* santidad.
saintly (-li) *adj.* santo, pío, devoto.

sake (seik) *s.* causa, motivo, amor, consideración [que mueve a hacer algo]: *for my* ~, por mí, por mi causa; *for God's* ~, por Dios, por el amor de Dios; *art for art's* ~, el arte por el arte.
saker (-ø^r) *s.* ORN., ARTILL. sacre.
Sal (sæl) *n. pr. dim.* de SARAH.
sal *s.* QUÍM., FARM. sal.
salaam (salæ·m) *s.* zalema.
salaam (to) *tr.-intr.* hacer zalemas.
salability (seilabi·liti) *s.* calidad de vendible, facilidad de venta, salida.
salable (sei·labøl) *adj.* vendible.
salacious (salei·shøs) *adj.* salaz.
salacity (salæ·siti) *s.* salacidad.
salad (sæ·lad) *s.* ensalada: ~ *bowl*, ensaladera; ~ *oil*, aceite de mesa; ~ *days*, fig. juventud inexperta.
salamander (sæ·lamændø^r) *s.* ZOOL., MIT. salamandra. *2* COC. utensilio para calentar o tostar.
salangane (-længein) *s.* ORN. salangana.
salaried (sæ·larid) *adj.* asalariado. *2* retribuido [empleo].
salary (sæ·lari) *s.* salario, sueldo, paga.
sale (seil) *s.* venta; almoneda; liquidación: ~ *tax*, impuesto sobre las ventas; *for* ~, on ~, en venta. *3* salida, demanda [de un género].
salesclerk (-šklø^rk) *s.* vendedor, dependiente.
salesgirl (-sgø^rl·) *s.* vendedora, dependienta.
Salesian (sali·dŷan) *adj.-s.* salesiano.
salesman (-smæn) *s.* vendedor, dependiente. *2* viajante de comercio.
saleswoman (-swuman) *s.* vendedora, dependienta.
salic (sæ·lik) *adj.* sálico: ~ *law*, ley sálica.
salicaceus (sælikei·shøs) *adj.* BOT. salicáceo.
salicylic (sæ·lisilik) *adj.* QUÍM. salicílico.
salient (sei·liønt) *adj.* que brota o surte. *2* saliente, prominente. *3* saliente, notable.
saliferous (sali·førøs) *adj.* salífero.
salification (sælifikei·shøn) *s.* salificación.
salify (to) (sæ·lifai) *tr.* salificar.
saline (sei·lain) *adj.* salino. *2 s.* saladar. *3* salina. *4* substancia salina.
salinity (sali·niti) *s.* salinidad.
salinous (sei·lainøs) *adj.* salino.
saliva (salai·va) *s.* saliva.
salivary (sæ·liveri) *adj.* salival.
salivate (to) (sæ·liveit) *tr.* producir salivación. *2 intr.* salivar.
salivation (-ei·shøn) *s.* salivación.
sallet (sæ·lit) *s.* celada [de la armadura].
sallow (sæ·lou) *adj.* pálido, amarillento, cetrino. *2 s.* BOT. sauce.
sallowness (-nis) *s.* palidez, color amarillento.
Sally (sæ·li) *n. pr. dim.* de SARAH.
sally *s.* MIL. salida. *2* excursión, paseo. *3* arranque, arrebato. *4* salida, ocurrencia. *5* ARQ. saliente, vuelo.
sally (to) *intr.* salir, hacer una salida. *2* salir o avanzar con ímpetu.
salmagundi (sælmagø·ndi) *s.* salpicón. *2* baturrillo, mezcolanza.
salmi (sæ·lmi) *s.* estofado de caza.
salmon (sæ·møn) *s.* ICT. salmón. *2* color de salmón.
Salome (sæ·lomi) *n. pr.* Salomé.
Salomonic (sæloma·nik) *adj.* salomónico [de Salomón].
salon (sæla·n) *s.* salón [pieza de recibir]. *2* salón [literario o artístico].
saloon (salu·n) *s.* salón [gran sala]. *2* cámara [de

un vapor]. *3* (E.U.) taberna, bar. *4* FERROC. (Ingl.)
~ *carriage*, coche salón.
salpa (sæ·lpa) *s.* ICT. salpa.
salsify (sæ·lsifi) *s.* BOT. salsifí.
salt (solt) *s.* QUÍM. sal. *2* sal común: *to be worth
one's* ~, valer uno lo que come; *to take with a
grain of* ~, considerar como exagerado. *3* sal,
ingenio, agudeza. *4 old* ~, lobo de mar. *5 pl.* MED.
sales. *6 adj.* de sal, para la sal; salado, salino;
curado con sal: ~ *lick*, salegar; ~ *marsh*, marisma; ~ *meat*, cecina; ~ *shaker*, salero de mesa;
~ *water*, agua salada. *7* verde [cuento, etc.]. *8*
exagerada [cuenta, factura].
salt (to) *tr.* salar. *2* sazonar con sal, *3* salpresar. *4*
dar sal al ganado. *5* amañar [una cosa]; poner
subrepticiamente mineral en [una mina] para
darle apariencia de valor.
saltatory (sæ·ltatori) *adj.* perteneciente a la danza.
2 saltador. *3* que procede por saltos.
saltcellar (so·ltsela^r) *s.* salero [de mesa].
salted (-id) *adj.* salado. *2* experimentado; perito.
salter (-ø^r) *s.* salador. *2* salinero.
saltern (-ø^rn) *s.* salina.
saltigrade (sæ·ltigreid) *adj.* saltígrado.
salting (so·lting) *s.* saladura, salazón.
saltish (-ish) *adj.* salobre, un poco salado.
saltmaker (-meikø^r) *s.* salinero.
saltness (-nis) *s.* salsedumbre.
salpeter, salpetre (-pɪ·tø^r) *s.* nitro, salitre. *2* nitrato
de Chile.
saltus (sæ·ltøs) *s.* salto, solución de continuidad.
saltworks (so·ltwø^rks) *s.* salina.
saltwort (-wø^rt) *s.* BOT. barrilla, sosa.
salty (-i) *adj.* salado. *2* salobre.
salubrious (saliu·briøs) *adj.* salubre.
salutary (sæ·liuteri) *adj.* saludable; salutífero.
salutation (sæliutei·shøn) *s.* saludo. *2* salutación.
3 bienvenida.
salutatory (sæliu·tatori) *adj.* de salutación. *2 s.*
(E.U.) saludo, discurso de salutación.
salute (saliu·t) *s.* saludo [ademán, actitud, beso].
2 MIL. saludo; salva.
salute (to) *tr.-intr.* saludar. *2 intr.* MIL. cuadrarse.
salvable (sæ·lvabøl) *adj.* que puede salvarse.
Salvador (sæ·lvadø^r) *n. pr.* GEOGR. El Salvador.
salvage (sæ·lvidÿ) *s.* salvamento. *2* derecho de salvamento. *3* lo que se salva de un naufragio,
fuego, etc.
salvage (to) *tr.* salvar [de un naufragio, ruina,
etc.].
salvation (sælvei·shøn) *s.* salvación.
salve (sæv o sav) *s.* ungüento, pomada. *2* remedio,
alivio. *3 fam.* adulación. *4* salve, Salve Regina.
salve (to) *tr.* untar. *2* aquietar, calmar, aliviar. *3*
salvar [un buque, un cargamento, etc.].
salver (sæ·lvø^r) *s.* bandeja. *2* salvilla.
salvia (sæ·lvia) *s.* BOT. salvia.
salvo (sæ·lvou) *s.* salvedad, excepción. *2* excusa,
subterfugio. *3* salva [de artillería, de aplausos].
salvor (sæ·lvø^r) *s.* pers. o buque que efectúa un salvamento.
Sam (sæm) *n. pr. fam.* Samuel.
samara (sæ·mara) *s.* BOT. sámara.
Samaritan (samæ·ritan) *adj.-s.* samaritano.
samarium (same·riøm) *s.* QUÍM. samario.
sambo (sæ·mbou) *s.* zambo [mestizo].
sambuke (sæ·mbiuk) MÚS. sambuca.
same (seim) *adj.-pron.* mismo, misma, etc.: *at the*
~ *time*, a la vez, al mismo tiempo; no obstante:
it is all the ~ *to me*, me da lo mismo. *2 adv. the*

~, del mismo modo, igualmente. *3 all the* ~, a
pesar de todo.
sameness (-nis) *s.* igualdad, identidad. *2* parecido
exacto. *3* monotonía.
samlet (-lit) *s.* ICT. salmón joven.
Samoan (samou·an) *adj.-s.* samoano.
Samotrace (sæ·motreis) *n. pr.* GEOGR. Samotracia.
samovar (sæ·mova^r) *s.* samovar.
sampan (sæ·mpæn) *s.* MAR. sampán.
samphire (-fai^r) *s.* BOT. hinojo marino.
sample (-pøl) *s.* COM. muestra: ~ *case*, muestrario.
2 muestra [para analizar], cala, cata. *3* espécimen, ejemplo.
sample (to) *tr.* sacar una muestra, probar, calar,
catar.
sampler (sæ·mplø^r) *s.* utensilio para sacar muestras. *2* dechado [labor].
Sam(p)son (sæ·mp(s)øn) *n. pr.* Sansón.
sanative (sæ·nativ) *adj.* sanativo, curativo.
sanatorium (sænato·riøm) *s.* sanatorio.
sanctification (sænktifikei·shøn) *s.* santificación.
sanctifier (sæ·nktifaiø^r) *s.* santificador.
sanctify (to) (-ifai) *tr.* santificar. *2* consagrar, hacer
sagrado. ¶ Pret. y p. p.: *sanctified*.
sanctimonious (-imou·niøs) *adj.* santurrón.
sanctimony (-imouni) *s.* santurronería.
sanction (sæ·nkshøn) *s.* sanción.
sanction (to) *tr.* sancionar.
sanctify (sæ·nktiti) *s.* santidad. *2* carácter sagrado,
inviolabilidad.
sanctuary (-chueri) *s.* santuario. *2* asilo, refugio,
sagrado: *to take* ~, acogerse a sagrado.
sanctum (-tøm) *s.* lugar sagrado. *2* estudio, despacho, etc., privado.
Sanctus (-tøs) *s.* LITURG. Sanctus.
sand (sænd) *s.* arena: ~ *bar*, barra de arena; ~ *hill*,
duna; ~ *grouse*, ORN. ganga. *2* playa, arenal. | A
veces en plural. *3 pop.* valor, aguante. *4 pop.*
dinero. *5* MED. arenas. *6* arenas [del reloj]; momentos de vida.
sand (to) *tr.* enarenar. *2* arenar. *3* pulir con arena
o papel de lija.
sandal (sæ·ndal) *s.* sandalia. *2* BOT. sándalo.
sandalwood (-wud) *s.* sándalo [árbol; madera].
sandbag (-dbæg) *s.* saco o porra de arena.
sandbank (-bænk) *s.* banco de arena.
sandblast (-blæst) *s.* chorro de arena.
sandblast (to) *tr.* limpiar, grabar, etc., con chorro
de arena.
sandbox (-baks) *s.* salvadera. *2* FERROC. arenero.
sanders (-ø^rs) *s.* BOT. sándalo rojo.
sandglass (-glæs) *s.* reloj de arena.
sandpaper (-peipø^r) *s.* papel de lija.
sandpaper (to) *tr.* lijar.
sandpiper (-paipø^r) *s.* ORN. lavandera.
sandstone (-stoun) *s.* piedra arenisca.
sandstorm (-sto^rm) *s.* tempestad de arena.
sandwich (-wich) *s.* emparedado, bocadillo: ~
man, hombre sandwich.
sandwich (to) *tr.* poner entre dos cosas iguales, intercalar.
sandy (-i) *adj.* arenoso, arenisco. *2* rufo, rojizo, de
color de arena. *3* inestable.
Sandy *n. pr. dim.* de ALEXANDER.
sane (sein) *adj.* sano. *2* cuerdo. *3* razonable.
sanforize (to) (sæ·nføraiš) *tr.* sanforizar.
sang (sæng) *pret.* de TO SING.
sangaree (sæ·ngarɪ) *t.* sangría [bebida].
sang-froid (san-frua) *s.* sangre fría.
Sangrail (sæ·ngreil) *s.* grial.
sanguify (to) (sæ·ngwifai) *tr.* sanguificar.

sanguinary (-neri) *adj.* sanguinario, cruel. *2* sangriento.
sanguine (-win) *adj.* colorado, rubicundo. *2* sanguíneo. *3* vehemente. *4* optimista. *5 s.* DIB. sanguina.
sanguineous (sangwi·niøs) *adj.* sanguíneo. *2* optimista.
sanguinolent (-nolønt) *adj.* sanguinolento.
Sanhedrim, -drin (sæ·njidrim, -drin) *s.* sanedrin.
sanicle (-nikøl) *s.* BOT. sanícula.
sanify (to) (sæ·nifai) *tr.* sanear [dar condiciones de salubridad]. ¶ Pret. y p. p.: *sanified.*
sanitarian (sænite·rian) *adj.-s.* sanitario.
sanitarium (-riøm) *s.* sanatorio.
sanitary (sæ·niteri) *adj.* sanitario, de sanidad: ~ *corps,* cuerpo de sanidad. *2* higiénico: ~ *napkin,* paño higiénico.
sanitation (sænitei·shøn) *s.* higienización, saneamiento.
sanity (sæ·niti) *s.* sanidad [estado sano]. *2* cordura, sano juicio, sensatez.
Sanscrit, Sanskrit (sæ·nskrit) *adj.-s.* sánscrito.
Santa Claus (sæ·ntiklaš) *n. pr.* San Nicolás [que trae regalos a los niños en Nochebuena].
santon (sæ·ntøn) *s.* santón.
sap (sæp) *s.* savia. *2* vigor, vitalidad. *3* sámago. *4* fig. tonto, bobo. *5* FORT. zapa.
sap (to) *tr.* extraer la savia de; dejar sin savia. *2* zapar, minar. *3 intr.* MIL. hacer trabajos de zapa. *4* obrar bajo mano.
sapful (sæ·pful) *adj.* abundante en savia.
saphead (-jed) *s.* tonto, bobo.
saphenous (safi·nøs) *adj.* ANAT. safena.
sapid (sæ·pid) *adj.* sápido. *2* sabroso, agradable.
sapience, -cy (sei·piøns, -si) *s.* sapiencia.
sapient (-ønt) *v.* sabio.
sapless (sæ·plis) *adj.* sin savia, sin jugo; seco, estéril. *2* débil, sin vitalidad.
sapling (-ling) *s.* arbolillo, renuevo. *2* jovenzuelo.
saponaceous (sæponei·shøs) *adj.* saponáceo.
saponification (sapanifikei·shøn) *s.* saponificación.
saponify (to) (sapa·nifai) *tr.* saponificar. *2 intr.* saponificarse. ¶ Pret. y p. p.: *saponified.*
sapor (sei·pø^r) *s.* sabor.
sapote (sapou·tei) *s.* BOT. zapote. *2* chicozapote, zapotillo.
sapper (sæ·pø^r) *s.* MIL. zapador, gastador.
Sapphic (sæ·fik) *adj.* sáfico. *2 s.* verso cálico.
sapphire (sæ·fai^r) *s.* zafir, zafiro. *2* color de zafiro.
Sappho (sæ·fou) *n. pr.* Safo.
sappy (sæ·pi) *adj.* lleno de savia; jugoso. *2* vigoroso. *3* pueril. *4* ridículamente sentimental.
saprophytic (sæprofi·tik) *adj.* BOT. saprofita.
sapwood (sæ·pwud) *s.* BOT. albura; sámago.
saraband (sæ·rabænd) *s.* zarabanda.
Saracen (sæ·rasen) *s.* sarraceno.
Saragossa (særaga·sa) *n. pr.* GEOGR. Zaragoza.
Sarah (se·ra) *n. pr. f.* Sara.
Saratoga trunk (særatou·ga) *s.* baúl, mundo.
sarbacane (sæ·^{r}bakein) *s.* cerbatana.
sarcasm (-kæšm) *s.* sarcasmo.
sarcastic (al (sa^{r}kæ·stik(al) *adj.* sarcástico.
sarcocarp (-koka^{r}p) *s.* BOT. sarcocarpio.
sarcoma (sa^{r}kou·ma) *s.* MED. sarcoma.
sarcophagus (sa^{r}ka·fagøs), *pl.* **-gi** (-dýai) *o* **-guses** *s.* sarcófago.
Sardanapalus (sa^{r}danapei·løs) *n. pr.* Sardanápalo.
sardine (sa·^{r}din) *s.* ICT. sardina. *2* JOY. sardio.
Sardinia (sa^{r}di·nia) *n. pr.* GEOGR. Cerdeña.
Sardinian (sa^{r}di·nian) *adj.-s.* sardo.

sardonic (sa^{r}da·nik) *adj.* sardónico.
sardonyx (sa·^{r}døniks) *s.* MINER. sardónice.
sargasso (sa^{r}gæ·sou) *s.* BOT. sargazo.
Sarmatian (sa^{r}mei·shan) *adj.-s.* sármata.
sarment (sa·^{r}mønt) *s.* BOT. sarmiento.
sarsaparilla (sa^{r}sapari·la) *s.* BOT. zarzaparrilla.
sartorial (sa^{r}to·rial) *adj.* sartorio. *2* de sastre; de sastrería.
sash (sæsh) *s.* faja, ceñidor, banda [de uniforme o de adorno]. *2* parte movible de la ventana de guillotina: ~ *window,* ventana de guillotina.
sat (-sæt) *pret.* y *p. p.* de TO SIT.
Satan (sei·tan) *n. pr.* Satán, Satanás.
satanic (al (seitæ·nik(al) *adj.* satánico.
satchel (sæ·chøl) *s.* maletín. *2* cartapacio [para llevar los libros, etc.].
sate (to) (seit) *tr.* saciar, hartar. *2* hastiar.
sateen (sætí·n) *s.* satén de algodón.
sateless (sei·tlis) *adj.* insaciable.
satellite (sæ·tølait) *s.* satélite.
satiate (sei·shieit) *adj.* saciado, satisfecho, harto.
satiate (to) *tr.* saciar. *2 intr.* saciarse.
satlety (satai·øti) *s.* saciedad, hartura. *2* hastío.
satin (sæ·tin) *s.* TEJ. raso.
satinet (-et) *s.* TEJ. rasete.
satinwood (-wud) *s.* árbol de madera lustrosa; esta madera; satín, doradillo.
satiny (sæ·tini) *adj.* arrasado, satinado.
satire (sæ·tai^r) *s.* sátira.
satiric (al (sati·rik(al) *adj.* satírico.
satirist (sæ·tirist) *s.* escritor, satírico.
satirize (to) (sæ·tiraiš) *tr.* satirizar.
satisfaction (sætisfæ·kshøn) *s.* satisfacción.
satisfactory (-tori) *adj.* satisfactorio. *2* suficiente, adecuado, ventajoso. *3* expiatorio.
satisfy (to) (sæ·tisfai) *tr.* satisfacer. *2* contentar. *3* librar de duda, convencer: *I am satisfied that,* estoy seguro de que. *4* compensar, pagar. ¶ Pret. y *p. p.:* *satisfied.*
satrap (sei·træp) *s.* sátrapa. *2* tiranuelo.
saturable (sæ·churabøl) *adj.* saturable.
saturate (to) (sæ·chureit) *tr.* saturar. *2* empapar; llenar, colmar. *3* imbuir. *4* QUÍM. neutralizar.
saturation (-rei·shøn) *s.* saturación.
Saturday (sæ·tø^{r}dei) *s.* sábado.
saturn (sæ·tø^{r}n) *n. pr.* MIT., ASTR. Saturno.
Saturnalia (sætø^{r}nei·lia) *s. pl.* saturnales.
saturnine (sæ·tø^{r}nain) *adj.* saturnino, apático, taciturno, melancólico.
satyr (sæ·tø^r) *s.* sátiro.
sauce (sos) *s.* salsa. *2* aderezo, condimento. *3* (E.U.) compota. *4* descaro, insolencia [de lenguaje].
sauce (to) *tr.* aderezar, sazonar. *2* templar, suavizar. *3* desvergonzarse, insolentarse con.
sauceboat (-bout) *s.* salsera.
saucebox (-bøks) *s.* insolente, descarado.
saucepan (-pæn) *s.* cacerola, cazuela.
saucer (-ø^r) *s.* platillo [plato pequeño].
saucily (-ili) *adv.* con descaro.
saucy (-i) *adj.* descarado, respondón. *2* elegante.
sauerkraut (sau·^{r}kraut) *s.* chucruta.
Saul (sol) *n. pr.* Saúl.
saunter (so·ntø^r) *s.* paseo; paso tranquilo [del que pasea].
saunter (to) *intr.* pasear; andar despacio y sin objeto; vagar.
saurian (so·rian) *adj.-s.* saurio.
sausage (so·sidý) *s.* salchicha, embutido.
sauté (sou·tei) *adj.* COC. salteado.
sauté (to) *tr.* COC. saltear.

savage (sæ·vidỹ) *adj.* salvaje. *2* fiero, bárbaro, brutal. *3 s.* salvaje.
savageness (-nis), **savagery** (-ri) *s.* salvajismo. *2* barbarie, ferocidad.
savanna(h) (savæ·na) *s.* GEOGR. sabana, pradera.
savant (sæ·vant) *s.* hombre de letras o de ciencia.
save (seiv) *prep.* salvo, excepto, menos. *2 conj.* si no fuera, a menos [que].
save (to) *tr.* salvar, librar. *2* guardar, preservar: *God ~ the Queen!*, ¡Dios guarde a la Reina! *3* ahorrar [dinero, trabajo, etc.]. *4* guardar; conservar. *5 to ~ appearances*, guardar las apariencias. *6 intr.* ahorrar.
save-all *s.* apuracabos. *2* delantal, mono.
saveloy (sa·vøloi) *s.* especie de salsicha seca.
savin(e (sæ·vin) *s.* BOT. sabina.
saving (sei·ving) *adj.* salvador. *2* ahorrador, económico. *3* que contiene salvedad. *4 s.* economía, ahorro. *5* salvedad. *6 pl.* ahorros: *savings bank,* caja de ahorros. *7 prep.* salvo, excepto.
savio(u)r (-viø^r) *s.* salvador. *2 the Saviour,* el Salvador, el Redentor.
savo(u)r (-vø^r) *s.* sabor; olor. *2* gusto, dejo.
savo(u)r (to) *tr.* saborear, dar sabor a. *2* dar un olor a. *3* saborear [apreciar con deleite]. *4 intr. to ~ of,* saber a, oler a; tener las cualidades de.
savo (u) ry (-vøri) *adj.* sabroso, apetitoso, agradable. *2* fragante. *3 s.* (Ingl.) especie de entremés. *4* BOT. ajedrea.
Savoy (savoi·) *n. pr.* GEOGR. Saboya.
Savoyard (savoi·a^rd) *adj.-s.* saboyano.
saw (so) *s.* sierra [herramienta]. *2* dicho, refrán, proverbio. *3 pret.* de TO SEE.
saw (to) *tr.-intr.* serrar, aserrar. *2* mover o moverse como una sierra. *3 intr.* cortar [una sierra]. *4* aserrarse [bien, mal, etc., una materia]. P. p. *sawed* y *sawn.*
sawbones (-bouns) *s.* pop. cirujano.
sawbuck (-bøk) *s.* SAWHORSE.
sawdust (-døst) *s.* serrín, aserraduras.
sawfish (-fish) *s.* ICT. pez sierra, priste.
sawhorse (-jo^rs) *s.* CARP. caballete, cabrilla, burro.
sawings (-ings) *s. pl.* aserraduras.
sawmill (so·mil) *s.* aserradero.
sawn (-n) *p. p.* de TO SAW.
sawney (so·ni) *adj.* tonto, simple. *2 s.* simplón.
saw-toothed *adj.* BOT. serrado, aserrado.
sawyer (so·iø^r) *s.* aserrador.
saxatile (sæ·ksatil) *adj.* saxátil.
saxhorn (-jø^rn) *s.* MÚS. bombardón.
saxifrage (-ifridỹ) *s.* BOT. saxífraga.
Saxon (-øn) *adj.-s.* sajón. *2* anglosajón.
Saxony (-øni) *n. pr.* GEOGR. Sajonia.
saxophone (-foun) *s.* MÚS. saxofón.
say (sei) *s.* dicho, aserto; opinión. *2* turno para hablar; voz, derecho de hablar.
say (to) *tr.* decir: *to ~ good-bye,* decir adiós, despedir; *to ~ mass,* decir misa; *I should ~ so!,* ¡ya lo creo!; *it is said,* se dice; *no sooner said than done,* dicho y hecho; *say,* digamos, por ejemplo; *that is to ~,* es decir; *you don't ~ so!,* ¡no es posible!, ¿de veras? | No tiene el sentido de convenir o armonizar. *2* recitar, rezar. *3* contar, referir. *4 intr.* decir, hablar: *I say!,* ¡oiga!, ¡escuche! ¶ Pret. y p. p.: *said.*
saying (sei·ing) *s.* dicho, lo que se dice, relato. *2* dicho, sentencia, refrán.
scab (skæb) *s.* MED. costra, postilla. *2* VET. roña, escabro. *3* AGR. escabro. *4* fam. esquirol.
scabbard (skæ·ba^rd) *s.* vaina, funda [de un arma].
scabble (to) (skæ·bøl) *tr.* desbastar.

scabby (skæ·bi) *adj.* costroso, postilloso. *2* VET. roñoso. *3* ruin, vil.
scables (skei·blš) *s.* MED. sarna.
scabious (-biøs) *adj.* SCABBY. *2 s.* BOT. escabiosa.
scabrous (-brøs) *adj.* áspero, rugoso. *2* escabroso [en sentido moral]. *3* difícil.
scaffold (skæ·fould) *s.* andamio. *2* tablado. *3* tribuna [al aire libre]. *4* cadalso, patíbulo.
scaffold (to) *tr.* proveer de andamios.
scaffolding (-ing) *s.* andamiaje. *2* armazón para varios usos.
scagliola (skøliou·la) *s.* escayola, estuco.
scalar (skei·la^r) *adj.* MAT. escalar.
scal(l)awag (skæ·laueg) *s.* res raquítica. *2* fam. pícaro, bribón.
scald (skold) *s.* escaldadura. *2* SKALD.
scald (to) *tr.* escaldar. *2* calentar [un líquido] hasta casi hacerlo hervir.
scald-head *s.* MED. tiña, acores, usagre.
scale (skeil) *s.* platillo [de balanza]: *to turn the scales,* ser decisivo. *2* balanza, báscula, romana. *3* ZOOL., BOT., MED. escama. *4* escama, laminilla, costra, vaina, incrustación: *~ insect,* insecto cóccido. *5* escala [pitipié; serie graduada; proporción]: *on a large ~,* en gran escala; *on a small ~,* en pequeña escala. *6* MÚS. escala. *7 pl.* (con may.) ASTR. Libra.
scale (to) *tr.* pesar. *2* escamar [quitar las escamas]. *3* descostrar, descascarar, desvainar, pelar. *4* cubrir de escamas. *5* escalar, subir. *6* graduar, proporcionar, ajustar a escala. *7 intr.* descamarse; descascararse, pelarse. *8* cubrirse de incrustaciones. *9* subir en escala.
scalene (skeil·n) *adj.* GEOM., ANAT. escaleno.
scaling (skei·ling) *s.* escamadura. *2* escalamiento. *3* imbricación. *4* medición por escala.
scall (skol) *s.* MED. tiña.
scallion (skæ·liøn) *s.* BOT. chalote.
scallop (skæ·løp) *s.* ZOOL. venera, pechina. *2* concha de peregrino. *3* festón, onda, recorte.
scallop (to) *tr.* festonear, recortar en ondas. *2* COC. cocer al horno con pan rallado. *3* COC. cocer [ostras] en su concha.
scalp (skælp) *s.* cuero cabelludo.
scalp (to) *tr.* arrancar la cabellera, el cuero cabelludo a. *2* fig. criticar despiadadamente. *3* (E.U.) comprar y revender [localidades, etc.].
scalpel (-øl) *s.* CIR. escalpelo.
scalper (-ø^r) *s.* (E.U.) revendedor.
scaly (skei·li) *adj.* escamoso. *2* AGR. infestado por insectos cóccidos. *3* vil, ruin. *4* avaro.
scammony (skæ·møni) *s.* BOT. escamonea.
scamp (skæmp) *s.* pícaro, bribón, tuno.
scamp (to) *tr.* hacer [algo] mal o descuidadamente.
scamper (-ø^r) *s.* huida precipitada, carrera rápida.
scamper (to) *intr.* correr o moverse precipitadamente. *2* huir, escaparse.
scan (to) (skæn) *tr.* escandir. *2* examinar, escrutar; recorrer con la vista. *3* TELEV. explorar. ¶ Pret. y p. p.: *scanned;* ger.: *-nning.*
scandal (skæ·ndal) *s.* escándalo. | No tiene el sentido de alboroto. *2* ignominia. *3* vergüenza, cosa escandalosa. *4* difamación, maledicencia.
scandalize (to) (-aiš) *tr.* escandalizar. *2* difamar, murmurar de.
scandalmonger (-møngø^r) *s.* difamador, murmurador.
scandalous (-øs) *adj.* escandaloso, vergonzoso. *3* difamatorio.

Scandinavia (skændinei·via) *n. pr.* GEOGR. Escandinavia.

Scandinavian (-vian) *adj.-s.* escandinavo.

scansion (skæ·nshøn) *s.* escansión.

scant (skænt) *adj.* escaso, corto, limitado, insuficiente, exiguo: ~ *of*, corto de.

scant (to) *tr.* escatimar. *2* reducir, limitar, estrechar. *3 intr.* MAR. caer [el viento].

scantling (-ling) *s.* poco, pequeña cantidad. *2* escantillón, escuadría. *3* cuartón. *4* caballete [para un barril].

scanty (skæ·nti) *adj.* escaso, insuficiente, exiguo. *2* mezquino, cicatero.

scape (skeip) *s.* BOT., ARQ. escapo.

scapegoat (skei·pgout) *s.* víctima propiciatoria, cabeza de turco.

scapegrace (skei·pgreis) *s.* pícaro, travieso.

scapula (skæ·piula) *s.* ANAT. escápula.

scapular (skæ·piula^r) *adj.* escapular. *2 s.* escapulario. *3* ANAT., ZOOL. escápula.

scapular (skæ·piula^r) *adj.* escapular. *2 s.* escapulario. *3* ANAT., ZOOL. escápula.

scar (ska^r) *s.* cicatriz. *2* chirlo, costurón. *3* raya, rasguño. *4* peñasco, farallón, roca pelada.

scar (to) *tr.* marcar con cicatriz, señalar. ¶ Pret. y p. p.: *scarred;* ger.: *-rring.*

scarab (skæ·rab) *s.* ENT. escarabajo, sagrado.

scarce (ske^{r}s) *adj.* escaso, raro, contado.

scarcely (-li) *adv.* escasamente, apenas, difícilmente. *2* apenas, no bien. *3* casi, casi no; ~ *ever*, casi nunca.

scarceness (-nis), **scarcity** (-iti) *s.* escasez, penuria, carestía. *2* rareza, raridad.

scare (ske^r) *s.* susto, alarma. *2* pánico [comercial].

scare (to) *tr.* asustar, amedrentar, alarmar. *2 to* ~ *away*, espantar, ahuyentar.

scarecrow (-krou) *s.* espantapájaros, espantajo.

scaremonger (-møngø^r) *s.* propagador de noticias alarmantes.

scarf (ska^{r}f), *pl.* **scarfs** o **scarves** *s.* echarpe. *2* pañuelo, bufanda, corbata, chalina. *3* banda, faja [de uniforme, etc.]. *4* tapete estrecho. *5* CARP. ensambladura a media madera.

scarf (to) *tr.* CARP. ensamblar a media madera.

scarfpin (-pin) *s.* alfiler de corbata.

scarfskin (-kin) *s.* ANAT. epidermis.

scarification (skærifikei·shøn) *s.* AGR., CIR. escarificación.

scarify (to) (skæ·rifai) *tr.* CIR., AGR. escarificar. *2* fig. flagelar, criticar duramente. ¶ Pret. y p. p.: *scarified.*

scarlatina (ska^{r}latı·na) *s.* MED. escarlatina.

scarless (ska·^{r}lis) *adj.* sin chirlos o cicatrices; ileso.

scarlet (ska·^{r}lit) *adj.* rojo, de color escarlata: ~ *fever*, MED. escarlatina; ~ *oak*, BOT. coscoja. *2 s.* escarlata, grana.

scarp (ska·^{r}p) *s.* escarpa, declive. *2* FORT. escarpa.

scarp (to) *tr.* escarpar [un terreno].

scarred (ska·^{r}d), **scarry** (ska·ri) *adj.* que tiene cicatrices. *2* pelado [roca, etc.].

scary (ske·ri) *adj.* fam. medroso, asustadizo.

scat (skæt) *interp.* ¡zape!

scathe (skeið) *s.* daño, perjuicio.

scatheless (-lis) *adj.* indemne, sano y salvo.

scathing (-ing) *adj.* acerbo, mordaz.

scatology (skata·lødyi) *s.* escatología [estudio de los excrementos].

scatter (to) (skæ·tø^r) *tr.* dispersar, poner en fuga. *2* disipar, desvanecer. *3* esparcir, difundir. *4 intr.* dispersarse. *5* disiparse.

scatterbrain (-brein), *s.,* **scatterbrained** (-breind) *adj.* ligero de cascos, atolondrado.

scavenge (to) (skæ·vindÿ) *tr.* recoger la basura.

scavenger (-ø^r) *s.* basurero, barrendero. *2* animal que se alimenta de basura.

scenario (sine·riou) *s.* TEAT., CINEM. guión.

scenarist (-rist) *s.* CINEM. guionista.

scene (sın) *s.* escena [en todas sus acepciones]: *to make a* ~, hacer una escena. *2* escenario. *3* TEAT. decorado: ~ *shifter*, tramoyista; *behind the scenes*, entre bastidores. *4* cuadro, vista, paisaje.

scenery (-øri) *s.* paisaje, panorama. *2* TEAT. decorado.

scenic (se·nik) *adj.* escénico. *2* pintoresco.

scenographer (sına·grafø^r) *s.* escenógrafo.

scenography (-græfi) *s.* escenografía.

scent (sent) *s.* olfato. *2* olor; fragancia. *3* rastro, pista, indicio. *4* perfume, esencia.

scent (sent) *s.* olfato. *2* olor; fragancia. *3* rastro, pista, indicio. *4* perfume, esencia.

scent (to) *tr.* oler, olfatear, husmear, ventear. *2* sospechar. *3* perfumar. *4 intr. to* ~ *of*, oler a.

scepter (se·ptø^r) *s.* centro [real].

sceptic, scepticism = SKEPTIC, SKEPTICISM.

sceptre *s.* SCEPTER.

schedule (ske·diul) *s.* lista, catálogo, inventario. *2* horario [de trenes, etc.]. *3* programa, plan.

schedule (to) *tr.* incluir en una lista, catálogo, etc. *2* incluir en un horario o programa; fijar el tiempo para.

schema (skı·ma) *s.* esquema, diagrama, cuadro.

schematic (skımæ·tik) *adj.* esquemático.

scheme (skı·m) *s.* esquema, diseño. *2* plan, proyecto, designio. *3* ardid, intriga, maquinación.

scheme (to) *tr.* proyectar, idear, trazar. *2 intr.* formar planes, intrigar.

schemer (-ø^r) *s.* proyectista. *2* maquinador, intrigante.

schism (si·šm) *s.* cisma; escisión.

schismatic (sišmæ·tik) *adj.-s.* cismático.

schist (shist) *s.* GEOL. esquisto.

schizomycete (skišomaisi·t) *s.* BOT. esquizomiceto.

schizophrenia (-frı·nia) *s.* MED. esquizofrenia.

scholar (ska·la^r) *s.* escolar, estudiante. *2* becario. *3* hombre docto, erudito: *classical* ~, humanista. *4 to be no* ~, tener poca instrucción.

scholarly (-li) *adj.* docto, erudito.

scholarship (-ship) *s.* saber, erudición. *2* beca [para estudiar].

scholastic (skølæ·stik) *adj.-s.* escolástico. *2 adj.* de erudito. *3* escolar, estudiantil.

scholasticism (-isišm) *s.* escolasticismo.

scholium (skou·liøm), *pl.* **-lia** (-liø) *s.* escolio.

school (skul) *s.* escuela. *2* colegio [de enseñanza]. *3* clase [sesión]. *4* facultad [de una universidad]. *5* banco de peces. *6 adj.* escolar; de enseñanza: ~ *year*, año escolar; ~ *board*, junta de enseñanza. *7* de clase, lectivo. *8* MAR. ~ *ship*, buque escuela.

school (to) *tr.* enseñar, instruir. *2* amaestrar, adiestrar, disciplinar. *3 intr.* ir en banco [los peces].

schoolbook (-buk) *s.* libro escolar.

schoolboy (-boi) *s.* muchacho de la escuela, colegial.

schoolfellow (-felou) *s.* condiscípulo.

schoolgirl (-gø^r) *s.* muchacha de la escuela, colegiala.

schoolhouse (-jaus) *s.* escuela [edificio].

schooling (-ling) *s.* instrucción, enseñanza. *2* experiencia. *3* precio de la escuela. *4* reprimenda.
schoolman (-mæn) *s.* escolástico. *2* humanista.
schoolmaster (-mæ·støʳ) *s.* profesora de instituto.
schoolmate (-meit) *s.* condiscípulo.
schoolmistress (-mistris) *s.* profesora de instituto.
schoolroom (-rum) *s.* aula, sala de clase.
schoolyard (-yaʳd) *s.* patio de escuela.
schooner (sku·nøʳ) *s.* MAR. goleta. *2* vaso grande para cerveza. *3* (E.U.) galera [carruaje] con toldo.
schottische (sha·tish) *s.* chotis.
sciatica (saiæ·tika) *s.* MED. ciática.
science (sai·øns) *s.* ciencia. *2* ciencias naturales.
scientific (al (saiønti·fik(al) *adj.* científico.
scientist (sai·øntist) *s.* hombre de ciencia.
scimitar, -ter (si·mitaʳ, -øʳ) *s.* cimitarra.
scintilla (sinti·la) *s.* chispa, leve asomo o indicio.
scintillant (si·ntilant) *adj.* centelleante, chispeante.
scintillate (to) (si·ntileit) *intr.* centellear, chispear.
scion (sai·øn) *s.* AGR. vástago, renuevo; esqueje, injerto, púa. *2* vástago, descendiente.
scirrhus (ski·røs) *s.* MED. cirro.
scissel (si·sel) *s.* cizallas, recortes de metal.
scission (si·shøn) *s.* corte, división; escisión.
scissor (to) (si·søʳ) *tr.* cortar [con tijeras].
scissors (-s) *s. pl.* tijeras.
scissure (si·shøʳ) *s.* cisura. *2* escisión.
sclera (skli·ra) *s.* ANAT. esclerótica.
sclerenchyma (sklire·nkima) *s.* BOT. esclerénquima.
sclerosis (sklirou·sis) *s.* MED. esclerosis.
scoff (skaf) *s.* mofa, burla, befa. *2* hazmerreír.
scoff (to) *intr.* mofarse, burlarse, hacer befa: *to ~ at,* mofarse de.
scoffer (-øʳ) *s.* mofador, despreciador.
scold (skould) *s.* mujer regañona, reñidora.
scold (to) *tr.* reñir, regañar.
scolding (-ing) *s.* regaño, represión.
scoliosis (skouliou·sis) *s.* MED. escoliosis.
scolopendra (skalope·ndra) *s.* ZOOL. escolopendra, ciempiés.
scomber (ska·mbøʳ) *s.* ICT. escombro, caballa.
sconce (skans) *s.* abrigo, defensa. *2* FORT. baluarte, reducto. *3* fam. cabeza, seso. *4* multa. *5* candelabro de pared.
sconce (to) *tr.* fortificar con baluarte, proteger. *2* multar.
scone (skan) *s.* COC. especie de bizcocho.
scoop (skup) *s.* cucharón grande, cazo. *2* pala de mano, cogedor, librador. *3* cuchara [de excavadora, draga, etc.]. *4* achicador. *5* instrumento en forma de cuchara. *6* cucharada, palada. *7* hoyo, cavidad. *8* buena ganancia. *9* noticia que da un periódico antes que los demás.
scoop (to) *tr.* sacar con pala o cuchara. *2* ganar, llevarse, obtener. *3* achicar, vaciar. *4* ahuecar, excavar.
scoot (skut) *s.* fam. carrera precipitada.
scoot (to) *intr.* salir, correr, deslizarse [de pronto o velozmente]. *2* fam. largarse.
scooter (-øʳ) *s.* patinete. *2* embarcación rápida y de poco calado. *3* motocicleta ligera.
scope (skoup) *s.* alcance, extensión. *2* campo, radio, esfera, oportunidad, libertad [de acción, etc.]. *3* mira, designio.
scorbutic (skoʳbiu·tik) *adj.-s.* MED. escorbútico.
scorch (skoʳch) *s.* chamusco, quemadura. *2* calor abrasador.
scorch (to) *tr.* chamuscar, socarrar. *2* abrasar, que-

mar, agostar. *3* *intr.* abrasarse, agostarse. *4* correr velozmente.
scorching (-ing) *adj.* ardiente, abrasador. *2* agostador. *3* fig. punzante.
score (skoʳ) *s.* muesca, entalladura. *2* raya, señal. *3* cuenta [de lo que se debe]; agravio: *to settle a ~,* saldar una cuenta. *4* tantos, tanteo [en el dep. o en el juego]: *~ board,* marcador. *5* razón, motivo, consideración: *on that ~,* a este respecto. *6* veintena. *7* MÚS. partitura. *8 pl.* gran número.
score (to) *tr.* marcar con rayas o muescas; rayar. *2* poner en la cuenta. *3* azotar. *4* censurar severamente. *5* contar, marcar, valer [puntos o tantos]; ganar, lograr: *to ~ a point,* apuntarse un tanto. *6* MÚS. orquestar. *7 to ~ out,* borrar, tachar. *8* *intr.* hacer rayas o señales. *9* ganar o marcar tantos; ganar, vencer.
scoria (sko·ria), *pl.* **scoriae** (sko·rii) *s.* escoria.
scoring (sco·ring) *s.* raya, rayado. *2* MÚS. orquestación. *3* CINEM. guión sonoro.
scorn (skoʳn) *s.* desdén, desprecio. *2* escarnio.
scorn (to) *tr.* desdeñar, despreciar. *2* escarnecer. *3* tener a menos.
scornful (-ful) *adj.* despreciativo, insolente.
Scorpio (sko·ʳpiou) *s.* ASTR. Escorpión.
scorpion (sko·ʳpiøn) *s.* ZOOL. escorpión, alacrán. *2* ICT. *~ fish,* escorpión, escorpina.
scorpionwort (-wo·ʳt) *s.* BOT. alacranera.
Scot (skat) *s.* escocés.
scotch (skach) *s.* corte, muesca. *2* calza, cuña. *3* obstáculo, impedimento.
scotch (to) *tr.* cortar, herir ligeramente. *2* calzar, poner cuñas. *3* estorbar, frustrar.
Scotch *adj.-s.* escocés: *~ pine,* pino albar. *2 s.* whisky escocés, idioma escocés.
Scotchman (-mæn) *s.* escocés.
scoter (skou·tøʳ) *s.* ORN. pato negro.
scot-free (ska·tfrɪ) *adj.* impune.
scotia (skou·shan) *s.* ARQ. escocia.
Scotland (ska·tland) *n. pr.* GEOGR. Escocia.
Scotsman (-smæn) *s.* escocés.
Scottish (-ish) *adj.* escocés [de Escocia o de los escoceses].
scoundrel (skau·ndrøl) *s.* granuja, bribón, canalla.
scour (skauʳ) *s.* acción limpiadora de una corriente rápida. *2 pl.* diarrea del ganado.
scour (to) *tr.* fregar, estregar; limpiar, lavar [esp. con un chorro de agua]. *2* desgrasar [el paño]. *3* barrer, expulsar. *4* abrir [cauce] una corriente de agua. *5* purgar [dar una purga]. *6* recorrer, explorar, registrar. *7* batir [el monte].
scourge (sko·ʳdy) *s.* látigo, azote. *2* azote, calamidad.
scourge (to) *tr.* azotar, flagelar. *2* castigar, afligir.
scout (skaut) *s.* MIL. explorador, escucha. *2* buque de observación. *3* avión de reconocimiento. *4* muchacho explorador.
scout (to) *tr.-intr.* explorar, reconocer, espiar. *2* rechazar con desdén, burlarse de.
scow (skäw) *s.* MAR. chalana, barcaza.
scowl (skaul) *s.* ceño, sobrecejo. *2* ceño, aspecto amenazador.
scowl (to) *intr.* mirar con ceño; enfurruñarse. *2* tener aspecto amenazador. *3 tr.* expresar, obligar, rechazar, etc., con el ceño.
scrabble (skræ·bøl) *s.* garabatos. *2* SCRAMBLE.
scrabble (to) *tr.-intr.* garabatear. *2 tr.* arrebañar. *3* *intr.* arañar, escarbar, esforzarse [en busca de algo]. *4* trepar, gatear.
scrag (skræg) *s.* aleluya [pers. o animal flacos]. *2* pescuezo. *3* pedazo delgado y duro.

scrag (to) *tr.* pop. ahorcar, torcer el pescuezo a. ¶ Pret. y p. p.: *scragged;* ger.: *-gaing.*

scragged (skræ·gid) *adj.* flaco, descarnado.

scraggy (-i) *adj.* desigual, escabroso. *2* flaco, huesudo.

scramble (skræ·mbøl) *s.* lucha, arrebatiña. *2* gateamiento.

scramble (to) *intr.* trepar, gatear, arrastrarse. *2* andar a la arrebatiña; correr, luchar [por conseguir algo]. *3* extenderse irregularmente. *4 tr.* recoger precipitadamente. *5* barajar, revolver: *scrambled eggs,* huevos revueltos.

scrap (skræp) *s.* trozo, pedacito, mendrugo. *2* recorte. *3* pop. riña. *4 pl.* sobras, desperdicios; chatarra. *5 pork scraps,* chicharrones. *6* ~ *iron,* hierro viejo.

scrap (to) *tr.* desechar, echar a la basura. *2* desguazar [un buque]. *3* pop. reñir, pelear.

scrapbook (-buk) *s.* álbum de recortes.

scrape (skreip) *s.* raspadura, raedura, rasguño. *2* ruido de raspar. *3* restregadura de pies. *4* lío, aprieto. *5* riña.

scrape (to) *tr.* raspar, rascar, raer; arañar, rayar. *2* fig. rascar [el violín, etc.]. *3* restregar [los pies]. *4 to* ~ *acquaintance,* trabar conocimiento. *5 to* ~ *together* o *up,* rebañar; reunir poco a poco. *6 intr. to* ~ *along,* ir tirando. *7 to* ~ *through,* salir bien [de algo] por milagro.

scraper (skrei·pø^r) *s.* rascador, raspador; raedera. *2* fam. rascatripas. *3* CIR. legra.

scrapings (-ings) *s. pl.* raspaduras, raeduras. *2* ahorros.

scratch (skræch) *s.* arañazo; rasguño, raya; rascadura. *2* tachón, borradura. *3* fam. garabato [escrito]. *4* peluquín, bisoñé. *5* DEP. línea de salida: *to start from the* ~, fig. empezar sin nada, desde el principio. *5* BILL. chiripa. *7 pl.* VET. ajuagas. *8 adj.* casual, improvisado; allegadizo. *9* DEP. sin ventaja.

scratch (to) *tr.* arañar, rasguñar, rayar. *2* rascar, escarbar. *3* reunir [dinero, etc.]. *4* tachar, borrar. *5* garrapatear, borronear. *6 intr.* raspar [la pluma].

scrawl (skrol) *s.* escrito garrapateado. *2 pl.* garabatos, garrapatos.

scrawl (to) *tr.-intr.* garrapatear, borronear.

scrawny (skro·ni) *adj.* (E.U.) flaco, huesudo.

screak (skrik) *s.* chillido. *2* chirrido, rechinido.

screak (to) *intr.* chillar. *2* chirriar, rechinar.

scream (skrim) *s.* chillido, grito, alarido. *2* pitido [de locomotora]. *3* pop. cosa muy cómica.

scream (to) *intr.-tr.* chillar, gritar, vociferar. *2 intr.* pitar [la locomotora]. *3* ser chillón, llamativo.

screamer (-ø^r) *s.* chillón, voceador. *2* titular sensacional [en un periódico].

screaming (-ing) *s.-adj.* chillón, gritador. *2* pop. muy divertido. *3* pop. estupendo.

screech (skrich) *s.* chillido, estridor. *2* alarido. *3* ululato.

screech (to) *intr.* chillar. *2* ulular.

screechy (-i) *adj.* chillón, agudo, estridente.

screen (skrin) *s.* pantalla: *the* ~, la pantalla, el cine. *2* biombo, mampara, cancel, persiana. *3* alambrera, enrejado [de ventana, etc.]. *4* reparo, abrigo, cosa que oculta. *5* criba, harnero. *6* trama [para el fotograbado]. *7* FOT. filtro. *8* tablón de anuncios.

screen (to) *tr.* ocultar, tapar. *2* abrigar, proteger. *3* reparar. *4* proyectar en una pantalla. *5* adaptar para el cine. *6* cribar.

screenings (-ings) *s. pl.* residuos de criba.

screw (skru) *s.* tornillo, rosca; tuerca: *female* ~, tuerca; ~ *eye,* armella; ~ *jack,* cric o gato de rosca; ~ *wrench,* desvolvedor, llave inglesa; *to have a* ~ *loose,* fam. faltarle a uno un tornillo. *2* tornillo [clavo]. *3* hélice [propulsor]. *4* vuelta de tornillo: *to put the screws on,* apretar los tornillos a. *5* pop. tacaño. *6* BILL. efecto.

screw (to) *tr.* atornillar. *2* apretar, oprimir, estrujar. *3* torcer, retorcer. *4* BILL. dar efecto a. *5* arrancar, sacar [dinero, etc.]. *6* dar cierta expresión [al semblante]. *7 to* ~ *down,* atornillar. *8 to* ~ *out,* desatornillar; sacar, sonsacar. *9 to* ~ *up one's courage,* darse ánimo. *10 intr.* atornillarse; retorcerse. *11 to* ~ *into,* insinuarse, introducirse.

screwdriver (-dri·vø^r) *s.* destornillador.

scribble (skri·bøl) *s.* escrito desmañado. *2* garrapatos.

scribble (to) *tr.* escribir de prisa. *2* garrapatear.

scribbler (skri·blø^r) *s.* escritorzuelo.

scribe (skraib) *s.* escriba. *2* escribiente. *3* amanuense, copista. *4* autor, escritor.

scrimmage (skri·midÿ) *s.* escaramuza, refriega, trapatiesta. *2* arrebatiña.

scrimp (skrimp) *adj.* corto, escaso, mezquino. *2 s.* avaro.

scrimp (to) *tr.* escatimar. *2* proveer con escasez.

scrip (skrip) *s.* cédula, documento. *2* título provisional de una acción u obligación. *3* vale, abonaré.

script (skript) *s.* DER. instrumento original. *2* letra, escritura. *3* letra cursiva. *4* TEAT. manuscrito.

scriptural (skri·pchø^r) *adj.* escrito; relativo a la escritura. *2* bíblico.

Scripture (skri·pchø^r) *s.* Sagrada Escritura.

scrofula (skra·fiula) *s.* MED. escrófula.

scrofulous (-løs) *adj.* escrofuloso.

scroll (skroul) *s.* rollo de papel o pergamino [esp. escrito]. *2* voluta. *3* rasgo, rúbrica.

scrotum (skrou·tøm) *s.* ANAT. escroto.

scrub (skrøb) *adj.* desmirriado, achaparrado: ~ *oak,* chaparro. *2* pobre, inferior. *3 s.* fregado, fregoteo. *4* enano. *5* monte bajo.

scrub (to) *tr.* fregar, estregar, aljofifar. ¶ Pret. y p. p.: *scrubbed;* ger.: *-bbing.*

scrubbing (-ing) *s.* fregado, etregón: ~ *brush,* cepillo para fregar.

scrubby (-i) *adj.* desmirriado, achaparrado, bajo. *2* despreciable. *3* hirsuto; mal afeitado. *4* lleno de maleza.

scruff (skrøf) *s.* pescuezo, nuca. *2* cuello [de la chaqueta]. *3* capa, superficie. *4* escoria.

scrummage (skrø·midÿ) *s.* RUGBY melée.

scruple (skru·pøl) *s.* escrúpulo [duda, recelo]. *2* escrúpulo [peso]. *3* cantidad ínfima.

scruple (to) *intr.* tener escrúpulo. *2* escrupulizar. *3 tr.* tener escrúpulo en.

scrupulosity (skrupiula·siti) *s.* escrupulosidad.

scrupulous (skru·piuløs) *adj.* escrupuloso.

scrutineer (skrutini·^r) *s.* escrutador.

scrutinize (to) (skru·tinaiš) *tr.* escrutar, escudriñar, examinar atentamente.

scrutiny (skru·tini) *s.* escrutinio, examen.

scud (skød) *s.* carrera rápida. *2* nubes tenues que corren velozmente. *3* espuma, rocío [del mar].

scud (to) *intr.* correr, volar, deslizarse rápidamente.

scuff (skøf) *tr.* arrastrar [los pies]. *2* pisar, revolver [con los pies]. *3 intr.* arrastrar los pies. *4* ajarse, rayarse.

scuffle (skø·føl) *s.* lucha, riña [en que hay carreras y empujones]; arrebatiña.
scuffle (to) *intr.* luchar, pelear [en confusión]; forcejear [unos con otros].
scull (skøl) *s.* MAR. espadilla; remo.
scull (to) *intr.-tr.* cinglar. *2* remar o mover con remo.
scullery (skø·løri) *s.* fregadero, trascocina.
scullion (skø·liøn) *s.* galopín de cocina, sollastre.
sculptor (skø·lptø^r) *s.* escultor.
sculptress (-tris) *s.* escultora.
sculptural (-chøral) *adj.* escultórico, escultural.
sculpture (skø·lpchø^r) *s.* escultura.
sculpture (to) *tr.* esculpir, cincelar.
sculpturesque (-esk) *adj.* escultural, estatuario.
scum (skøm) *s.* espuma, nata. *2* escoria, hez. *3* canalla, chusma.
scum (to) *tr.* espumar, despumar. *2 intr.* espumar, cubrirse de espuma.
scummy (skø·mi) *adj.* espumoso. *2* cubierto de escoria.
scupper (skø·pø^r) *s.* imbornal.
scurf (skø^rf) *s.* caspa; costra. *2* hez, chusma.
scurfy (skø·^rfi) *adj.* casposo, costroso.
scurrility (skøri·liti) *s.* chabacanería, procacidad, insolencia.
scurrilous (skø·riløs) *adj.* chabacano, grosero, procaz, insolente.
scurry (skø·ri) *s.* carrera [de pasos cortos], fuga precipitada. *2* ventolera, remolino.
scurry (to) *intr.* echar a correr [con pasos cortos y rápidos]; huir, escabullirse. *2 tr.* poner en fuga.
scurvy (skø·^rvi) *s.* MED. escorbuto. *2 adj.* vil, ruin, indigno. *3* grosero.
scut (skøt) *s.* cola corta, rabito.
scutch (skøch) *s.* agramadera, espadilla. *2* agramiza.
scutch (to) *tr.* agramar, espadar.
scutcheon (skø·chøn) *s.* ESCUTCHEON.
scuttle (skø·tøl) *s.* escotillón, abertura. *2* MAR. escotilla pequeña; respiradero. *3* cubo del carbón. *4* cesta plana. *5* paso rápido; huida o partida precipitada.
scuttle (to) *tr.* MAR. barrenar, dar barreno a. *2 intr.* correr, huir.
scythe (saið) *s.* guadaña, dalle.
scythe (to) *tr.* guadañar.
sea (si) *s.* mar; océano, golfo: *Sea of Marmara,* Mar de Mármara; *Sea of Tiberias,* lago de Tiberíades; *high ~,* mar gruesa; *high o open ~,* alta mar; *to go to ~,* embarcar, hacerse marino; *at ~,* en el mar; fig. perdido, perplejo, confuso; *by ~,* por mar. *2* oleaje, marejada. *3* oleada, ola grande. *4 sing.* y *pl.* mar, mares [gran extensión o cantidad].
5 adj. del mar, marino; de las olas; de la marina; naval: *~ bank,* orilla del mar; rompeolas; *~ bread,* galleta de barco; *~ blue,* azul verdoso; *~ captain,* capitán de buque mercante; *~ chart,* carta de marear; *~ front,* paseo o línea de edificios frente al mar; *~ level,* nivel del mar; *~ power,* potencia naval; *~ room,* espacio para maniobrar sin peligro; *~ rover,* corsario, pirata; *~ wall,* rompeolas. *6* ORN. *~ eagle,* halieto; *~ goose,* barnacla. *7* ZOOL., ICT. *~ anemone,* anémone de mar; *~ bream,* besugo, pagro; *~ cow,* vaca marina; morsa; *~ dog,* DOGFISH, fig. lobo de mar; *~ hog,* marsopa; *~ horse,* caballo de mar; morsa; *~ lion,* león marino; *~ star,* estrellamar; *~ urchin,* erizo de mar.
seabeach (-bıch) *s.* playa del mar.

seaboard (-bo^rd) *s.* costa, litoral.
sea-born *adj.* nacido del mar.
sea-borne *adj.* transportado por mar.
seacoast (-koust) *s.* orilla del mar, costa, litoral.
seadrome (-droum) *s.* aeródromo flotante.
seafarer (-ferø^r) *s.* marinero, navegante.
seafaring (-fering) *s.* vida del marino o marinero. *2 adj.* marinero, navegante.
seafolk (-fouk) *s.* gente de mar.
seagirt (-gø^rt) *adj.* rodeado de mar.
seagoing (-gouing) *adj.* de altura [buque]. *2* marinero, navegante.
seal (sıl) *s.* ZOOL. foca; león marino. *2* sello, sigilo: *to set one's ~ to,* sellar, aprobar; *under the hand and ~ of,* firmado y sellado por. *3* timbre [para estampar]. *4* precinto. *5* sigilo, secreto. *6* lo que cierra u obtura: *water ~,* sifón.
seal (to) *tr.* sellar, precintar, marchamar, lacrar: *2* estampar [con sello]. *3* sellar [comunicar un carácter]. *4* confirmar, decidir irrevocablemente. *5* sellar, cerrar. *6* encerrar, aprisionar. *7* fijar, empotrar. *8* contrastar [pesos y medidas]. *9 intr.* cazar focas.
sealer (-ø^r) *s.* sellador; cerrador. *2* cazador de focas.
sealing wax (-ing) *s.* lacre.
sealskin (-skin) *s.* piel de foca.
seam (sım) *s.* costura [serie de puntadas]. *2* grieta, juntura. *3* MAR. costura. *4* arruga. *5* costurón, cicatriz. *6* CIR. sutura. *7* MIN. veta delgada.
seam (to) *tr.* coser. *2* señalar con cicatrices o arrugas. *3 intr.* arrugarse; henderse.
seamaid (sı·meid) *s.* MIT. sirena.
seaman (-mæn) *s.* marinero, marino.
seamanship (-ship) *s.* náutica. *2* pericia náutica.
seamless (sı·mlis) *adj.* inconsútil, sin costura.
seamstress (-stris) *s.* costurera.
seamy (-i) *adj.* con costura o cicatriz: *the ~ side,* fig. el lado peor.
seapiece (sı·pis) *s.* PINT. marina.
seaplane (-plein) *s.* AVIA. hidroplano.
seaport (-po^rt) *s.* puerto de mar.
seaquake (-kueik) *s.* maremoto.
sear (si·ø^r) *adj.* seco, marchito. *2* raído, gastado. *3 s.* chamusco. *4* ARM. muelle real.
sear (to) *tr.* secar, agostar, marchitar. *2* tostar, chamuscar. *3* CIR. cauterizar. *4* fig. endurecer, empedernir.
search (sø^rch) *s.* busca, búsqueda. *2* registro, reconocimiento: *~ warrant,* DER. orden de registro. *3* exploración, examen, indagación.
search (to) *tr.-intr.* buscar. *2* examinar, registrar, explorar. *3* escudriñar, penetrar. *4* indagar, inquirir, investigar. *5* CIR. tentar. *6 to ~ after,* preguntar por, indagar, inquirir. *7 to ~ into,* examinar, investigar. *8 to ~ out,* descubrir buscando.
searcher (-ø^r) *s.* buscador, investigador. *2* vista, inspector. *3* veedor. *4* CIR. tienta, cala. *5* ÓPT. buscador.
searching (-ing) *adj.* escrutador, penetrante. *2* completo, minucioso.
searchlight (-lait) *s.* ELECT. proyector, reflector; foco eléctrico.
seascape (sı·skeip) *s.* vista del mar. *2* PINT. marina.
seashore (-sho^r) *s.* orilla del mar, costa, litoral; playa.
seasick (-sik) *adj.* mareado [en el mar].
seasickness (-nis) *s.* mareo [en el mar].
seaside (-said) *s.* SEASHORE. *2 adj.* costanero; de la playa.

season (sí·søn) s. estación [del año]. *3* estación, tiempo, temporada: ~ *ticket*, abono. *3* sazón, tiempo oportuno: *in due* ~, a su tiempo, en tiempo oportuno; *in* ~, a tiempo; a su tiempo; en sazón; *out of* ~, fuera de sazón, intempestivo.

season (to) *tr.* sazonar. *2* aliñar, aderezar. *3* moderar, templar. *4* habituar, aclimatar. *5* curar [la madera]. *6 intr.* sazonarse. *7* acostumbrarse. *8* curarse [la madera].

seasonable (-abøl) *adj.* oportuno, conveniente. *2* propio de la estación.

seasonal (-al) *adj.* estacional.

seasoning (-ing) s. sazonamiento. *2* condimento, sainete. *3* aclimatación. *4* cura [de la madera]. *5* sazón, punto.

seat (sít) s. asiento [para sentarse]: *to take a* ~, tomar asiento. *2* TEAT. localidad. *3* asiento [de silla, etc.]. *4* asiento, base, sitio, sede, residencia. *5* mansión, quinta. *6* situación. *7* fondillos.

seat (to) *tr.* sentar, asentar. *2* acomodar en asientos; tener asientos para. *3* poner asiento a [una silla]. *4* echar fondillos a [un pantalón]. *5* establecer, instalar. *6* fijar, afianzar.

seating (-ing) s. acción de sentar o de poner asiento. *2* MEC. asiento. *3* adj. ~ *capacity*, cabida, número de asientos.

seaward (sí·ua^rd) *adv.* hacia el mar, mar adentro.

seaway (-uei) s. mar gruesa. *2* ruta marítima.

seaweed (-uid) s. alga marina.

seaworthy (-uø^rði) *adj.* marinero [buque]; en buen estado para navegar.

sebaceous (sibei·shøs) *adj.* sebáceo.

seborrhœa (seborɪ·a) s. MED. seborrea.

secant (sí·kænt) *adj.-s.* GEOM., TRIGON. secante.

secede (to) (sisɪ·d) *intr.* separarse [de una comunión].

secession (sise·shøn) s. secesión, separación.

seclude (to) (sikliu·d) *tr.* apartar, separar, aislar. *2* recluir, encerrar.

seclusion (-ɣøn) s. retraimiento, aislamiento, retiro, soledad. *2* reclusión, encierro.

second (se·kønd) *adj.* segundo: ~ *best*, segundo [en calidad, mérito, etcétera]; mediocre: ~ *cabin*, MAR. segunda clase; ~ *sight*, doble vista, conocimiento de lo futuro. *2* secundario, subordinado. *3* inferior: *to be* ~ *to none*, no ser inferior a nadie. *4* de los segundos: ~ *hand*, segundero [de reloj]. *5* s. segundo [pers.]. *6* padrino [en el duelo]. *7* segundo [división del minuto]. *8* dos [en las fechas]. *9* AUTO., MÚS. segunda. *10 pl.* COM. segundas.

second (to) *tr.* secundar, apoyar, apadrinar. *2* apoyar [una moción o proposición].

secondary (-eri) *adj.* secundario. *2* segunda [enseñanza]. *3* s. ELECT. secundario.

second-class *adj.* de segunda clase; inferior. *2 adv.* en segunda.

seconder (-ø^r) s. el que secunda o apoya.

secondhand (-jænd) *adj.* de segunda mano.

second-rate *adj.* de segunda clase; mediocre.

secrecy (sí·krøsi) s. secreto, sigilo, reserva. *2* clandestinidad. *3* SECRETIVENESS.

secret (sí·krit) *adj.* secreto: ~ *service*; espionaje; policía secreta. *2* recóndito, íntimo. *3* callado, reservado. *5* s. secreto: *in* ~, en secreto. *6* LITURG. secreta.

secretaire (sekrøte·^r) s. escritorio [mueble].

secretariat(e (sekrite·riit) s. secretaría. *2* secretariado.

secretary (se·kriteri) s. secretario, secretaría. *2* escritorio [mueble]. *3* ministro [del gobierno]. *4*

Secretary of State, (E.U.) ministro de asuntos exteriores; (Ingl.) título de varios ministros. *5* ORN. ~ *bird*, serpentario.

secretaryship (-ship) s. secretaría [cargo].

secrete (to) (sikrɪ·t) *tr.* esconder, ocultar, recatar, encubrir. *2* FISIOL. secretar.

secretion (sikrɪ·shøn) s. ocultación. *2* FISIOL. secreción.

secretive (sikrɪ·tiv) *adj.* callado, reservado. *2* FISIOL. secretorio.

sect (sekt) s. secta. *2* grupo, partido.

sectarian (sekte·rian) *adj.-s.* sectario. *2* secuaz.

sectarianism (sekte·rianišm) s. sectarismo.

sectary (sek·tari) s. sectario. *2* disidente.

section (se·kshøn) s. sección [acción de cortar; división, parte, grupo, etc.]. *2* corte microscópico. *4* región; barrio. *5* FERROC. tramo. *6* BIB., GEOM., MIL. sección. *7* H. NAT. grupo. *8* IMPR. párrafo [signo].

sectional (-al) *adj.* de la sección. *2* regional, local. *3* parcial, incompleto.

sectionalism (se·kshønališm) s. localismo.

sector (se·ktø^r) s. sector. *2* compás de proporción.

secular (se·kiula^r) *adj.* secular. *2* s. eclesiástico secular. *3* seglar, lego.

secularism (se·kiularišm) s. POL. laicismo.

secularization (sekiularišei·shøn) s. secularización.

secularize (to) (se·kiularaiš) *tr.* secularizar.

secundo (si·køndou) *adv.* en segundo lugar.

secure (sikiu·^r) *adj.* seguro [libre de peligro o riesgo; que ofrece seguridad; bien guardado; cierto; confiado; confiable]. *2* tranquilo.

secure (to) *tr.* asegurar [resguardar; afianzar; prender]. *2* garantizar. *3* obtener; contratar; apoderarse de.

security (-iti) s. seguridad. *2* protección, salvaguardia. *3* garantía, prenda. *4* fiador, garante. *5* tranquilidad, confianza. *6 pl.* COM. pagarés, valores, efectos.

sedan (sidæ·n) s. silla de manos. *2* AUTO. sedán.

sedate (sidei·t) *adj.* sereno, tranquilo, ecuánime. *2* reposado, juicioso; grave, formal.

sedative (se·dativ) *adj.-s.* MED. sedativo. *2* calmante, sosegador.

sedentary (se·dønteri) *adj.* sedentario.

sedge (sedỹ) s. BOL. juncia, ácoro; chufa.

sediment (se·dimønt) s. sedimento. *2* heces, poso.

sedimentation (-ei·shøn) s. sedimentación.

sedition (sidi·shøn) s. sedición.

seditionary (-shøneri) *adj.-s.* sedicioso.

seditious (-shøs) *adj.* sedicioso, rebelde.

seduce (to) (sidiu·s) *tr.* seducir. *2* inducir, tentar.

seducement (-mønt) s. seducción. *2* tentación, incentivo.

seducer (-ø^r) s. seductor.

seduction (sidø·kshøn) s. seducción. *2* atractivo.

seductive (-tiv) *adj.* seductor, tentador.

sedulity (sidiu·liti) s. asiduidad, diligencia, aplicación.

sedulous (se·diuløs) *adj.* asiduo, aplicado, laborioso.

see (sí) s. ECLES. sede, silla: *Holy* ~, Santa Sede.

see (to) *tr.-intr.* ver: *to* ~ *a thing done*, ver hacer una cosa; *to* ~ *one another*, verse, visitarse; *to* ~ *the back of*, perder de vista, deshacerse; *to* ~ *the light*, ver la luz, salir a luz; *let's* ~, veamos; *I* ~, ya veo; comprendo. *2* mirar, observar. *3* considerar, juzgar: *to* ~ *fit*, tener por conveniente. *4* acompañar: *to* ~ *one off*, ir a despedir a uno. *5 to* ~ *after*, cuidar, cuidar de; buscar. *6 to* ~ *into*, examinar; ver lo interior de. *7 to ~ that, to ~ it that,* cuidar de que. *8 to ~ through,* penetrar; calar las intenciones de; llevar a cabo; ayudar a salir de un apuro. *9 to ~ to,* cuidar de, atender. *10 see!,* ¡mira!, ¡mirad! ¶ Pret.: *saw;* p. p.: *seen.*

seed (sɪd) *s.* BOT. semilla, simiente, grano, pepita: *~ bed,* semillero; *~ plant,* planta fanerógama; *to go,* o *to run, to ~,* dar en grana; fig. agotarse, decaer. *2* fig. semilla, origen.

seed (to) *tr.* sembrar. *2* despepitar, deshuesar. *3 intr.* sembrar, hacer la siembra. *4* granar.

seedcake (-keik) *s.* torta de semillas aromáticas.

seeder (-ǿ^r) *s.* sembradora [máquina]. *2* instrumento para despepitar. *3* pez que desova.

seedling (-liŋ) *s.* planta de semillero. *2* planta joven. *3* fig. semilla, germen.

seedplot (-plat) *s.* semillero.

seedtime (-taim) *s.* sementera [tiempo].

seedy (-i) *adj.* granado. *2* gastado, decaído. *3* andrajoso.

seeing (sɪ·iŋ) *s.* vista, acción de ver. *2* vidente, que ve.

seek (to) (sɪk) *tr.* buscar. *2* pedir. *3* perseguir, ambicionar; solicitar, cortejar. *4* intentar. *5* explorar, registrar. *6 to ~ one's life,* querer matar a uno. *7 intr. to ~ after, for* o *out,* buscar, perseguir, solicitar. ¶ Pret. y p. p.: *sought.*

seem (to) (sɪm) *intr.* parecer: *it seems to me,* me parece. *2* parecerle a uno: *I ~ to see him still,* me parece verlo todavía. *3* fingirse.

seeming (-iŋ) *adj.* aparente, especioso, fingido. *2* parecido. *3 s.* apariencia.

seemingly (-li) *adv.* aparentemente, al parecer.

seemly (sɪ·mli) *adj.* decente, decoroso, correcto. *2* agradable, bien parecido. *3 adv.* decentemente, correctamente.

seen (sɪn) *p. p.* de TO SEE.

seep (to) (sɪp) *intr.* filtrar, rezumarse, escurrirse.

seepage (-idẏ) *s.* filtración; lo que rezuma.

seer (sɪ·ǿ^r) *s.* profeta, vidente, adivino.

seesaw (sɪ·sɔ) *s.* columpio de tabla. *2* balanceo, vaivén. *3 adj.* de balanceo, de vaivén.

seesaw (to) *intr.* columpiarse, oscilar. *2* fig. vacilar, fluctuar.

seethe (to) (sɪd) *intr.* hervir [con el calor]. *2* fig. hervir, estar agitado. *3 tr.* hacer hervir. *4* empapar, macerar. ¶ P. p.: *seethed* o *sodden.*

segment (se·gmønt) *s.* segmento.

segment (to) *tr.* segmentar. *2 intr.* segmentarse.

segmental (segme·ntal) *adj.* segmentario. *2* ARQ. escarzano.

segmentary (-teri) *adj.* segmentario.

segmentation (-ei·shøn) *s.* segmentación.

segregate (se·grøgeit) *adj.* segregado, separado.

segregate (to) *tr.* segregar, separar. *2 intr.* segregarse, separarse.

segregation (-ei·shøn) *s.* segregación, separación.

seigniory (si·ñøri) *s.* señorío [dominio].

Seine (sen) *n. pr.* GEOGR. Sena.

seine *s.* red barredera.

seism (sai·shøm) *s.* seísmo, terremoto.

seismic (-shmik) *adj.* sísmico.

seismograph (sai·shmogræf) *s.* sismógrafo.

seizable (sɪ·shabøl) *adj.* embargable.

seize (to) (sɪsh) *tr.* asir, agarrar, tomar, coger. *2* apoderarse de; prender. *3* confiscar, embargar. *4* atar. *5* comprender. *6* aprovechar [la ocasión]. *7 to be seized of,* estar en posesión de. *8 to be seized with,* tener un ataque de; embargar, sobrecoger a uno [un afecto o pasión].

seizin (sɪ·shin) *s.* DER. posesión. *2* toma de posesión.

seizure (-ẏǿ^r) *s.* asimiento, toma. *2* captura; prendimiento, prisión. *3* embargo, decomiso. *4* MED. ataque, acceso.

selachian (silei·kian) *adj.-s.* ICT. selacio.

seldom (se·ldøm) *adv.* raramente, rara vez.

select (sile·kt) *adj.* selecto, escogido. *2* delicado, exigente [al escoger].

select (to) *tr.* escoger, elegir, seleccionar.

selection (-shøn) *s.* selección. *2* trozo escogido. *3* COM. surtido.

selective (-tiv) *adj.* selectivo.

selectivity (-tiviti) *s.* RADIO. selectividad.

selector (-tǿ^r) *s.* seleccionador. *2* ELECT. selector.

selenium (sɪlɪ·niøm) *s.* QUÍM. selenio.

selenography (selina·grafi) *s.* selenografía.

self (self), *pl.* **selves** *adj.* mismo. | Se une a los pronombres personales, o algunos adjetivos posesivos y al pronombre *one* para formar pronombres reflexivos o para dar más fuerza a la expresión. V. *myself, yourself,* etc. *2 s.* yo, ser; personificación: *my other ~,* mi otro yo; *his former ~,* su ser anterior; *she is beauty's ~,* ella es la belleza misma. *3 one's ~,* ONESELF.

self- elemento de comp. Con el sentido de auto-, de sí mismo, por sí mismo, etc.,entra en gran número de voces.

self-abashed *adj.* avergonzado.

self-acting *adj.* automático.

self-assured, self-reliant *adj.* seguro de sí mismo.

self-binder *s.* AGR. segadora agavilladora.

self-centered o **-centred** *adj.* concentrado en sí mismo, egocéntrico.

self-command *s.* dominio de sí mismo.

self-complacency *s.* satisfacción de sí mismo.

self-conceit *s.* presunción, vanidad, engreimiento.

self-confidence *s.* confianza en sí mismo.

self-concious *adj.* tímido, cohibido, embarazado.

self-consistent *adj.* consecuente [pers.].

self-contained *adj.* completo, independiente, autónomo. *2* callado, reservado. *3* dueño de sí mismo.

self-control *s.* dominio de sí mismo. *2* autonomía.

self-deception *s.* propio engaño; vana ilusión.

self-defeating *adj.* contraproducente.

self-defence *s.* defensa propia.

self-denial *s.* abnegación.

self-destruction *s.* suicidio.

self-determination *s.* POL. libre determinación.

self-effacement *s.* modestia.

self-esteem *s.* propia estimación. *2* presunción.

self-evident *adj.* evidente, patente, palmario.

self-excitation *s.* ELECT. autoexcitación.

self-existent *adj.* existente por sí mismo.

self-explanatory *adj.* que se explica por sí mismo.

self-expression *s.* expresión de la propia personalidad.

self-government *s.* autonomía. *2* dominio de sí mismo.

self-importance *s.* orgullo, presunción.

self-induction *s.* ELECT. autoinducción.

self-indulgence *s.* satisfacción de los propios apetitos, falta de sobriedad, intemperancia.

selfish (se·lfish) *adj.* interesado, egoísta.

selfishness (-nis) *s.* egoísmo.

selfless (se·lflis) *adj.* desinteresado, generoso.

self-love *s.* amor propio, egoísmo.

self-made *adj.* que se ha hecho una posición por su propio esfuerzo.

self-moving *adj.* automotor.

self-portrait *s.* autorretrato.

self-possessed *adj.* sereno, dueño de sí mismo.

self-propelled *adj.* autopropulsado.
self-reliant *adj.* que confía en sí mismo.
self-respect *s.* dignidad, respeto de sí mismo.
self-righteous *adj.* pagado de su propia rectitud, farisaico.
self-sacrifice *s.* sacrificio personal, abnegación.
self-same (se·lfseim) *adj.* idéntico, mismísimo.
self-satisfied *adj.* satisfecho de sí mismo.
self-seeker *s.* egoísta.
self-seeking *s.* egoísmo. *2 adj.* egoísta.
self-service *adj.* de autoservicio.
self-starter *s.* MEC. arranque automático.
self-styled *adj.* que se titula o llama a sí mismo.
self-sufficient *adj.* que se basta a sí mismo. *2* presuntuoso, orgulloso.
self-suggestion *s.* autosugestión.
self-will *s.* voluntariedad, obstinación.
self-willed *adj.* voluntarioso, obstinado.
self-winding *adj.* de cuerda automática [reloj].
sell (sel) *s.* fam. engaño, estafa.
sell (to) *tr.* vender [enajenar; traicionar]: *to ~ oneself,* venderse [por dinero]. *2* pop. engañar. *3 to ~ out,* realizar, saldar; agotar [una edición]; vender, traicionar. *4 intr.* vender: *to ~ off,* liquidar. *5* venderse [un artículo].¶ Pret. y p. p.: *sold.*
seller (-ø^r) *s.* vendedor. *2* cosa que se vende bien: *best ~,* libro de mayor venta.
Seltzer o **Seltzer water** (-tsø^r) *s.* agua de Seltz.
selvage (-vidȳ) *s.* orillo [del paño]. *2* orilla, orla.
semantics (simæ·ntiks) *s.* semántica.
semaphore (se·mafo^r) *s.* semáforo. *2* FERROC. disco de señales.
semasiology (simeisia·lødȳi) *s.* semasiología.
semblance (se·mblans) *s.* semejanza. *2* aspecto, figura, semblante. *3* imagen, retrato. *4* apariencia, simulacro.
semen (sɪ·men) *s.* FISIOL. semen. *2* BOT. semilla.
semester (sime·stø^r) *s.* semestre. *2* semestre escolar.
semi- (se·mi) *pref.* semi-.
semibreve (se·mibrɪv) *s.* MÚS. semibreve.
semicadence (semikei·døns) *s.* mús. semicadencia.
semicircle (se·misø^rkøl) *s.* semicírculo.
semicircular (semisø·^rkiula^r) *adj.* semicircular.
semicolon (semicou·løn) *s.* ORTOG. punto y coma.
semiconsonant (semika·nsønant) *s.* semiconsonante.
semidiameter (semidaiæ·metø^r) *s.* semidiámetro.
semifinal (semifai·nal) *adj.-s.* dep. semifinal.
semifluid (semiflu·id) *adj.* semifluido.
semilunar (semiliu·na^r) *adj.* semilunar.
semimonthly (semimø·nzli) *adj.* quincenal. *2 s.* publicación quincenal.
seminal (se·minal) *adj.* seminal. *2* germinal, originador. *3* embrionario.
seminar (se·mina^r o semina·^r) *s.* seminario [en una Universidad].
seminarist (se·minerist) *s.* seminarista.
seminary (se·mineri) *s.* seminario, plantel. *2* SEMINAR. *3* colegio, academia. *4* ECLES. seminario.
seminiferous (semini·førøs) *adj.* seminífero.
semiofficial (semiofi·shal) *adj.* oficioso.
semiquaver (semikuei·vø^r) *s.* MÚS. semicorchea.
Semiramis (sømi·ramis) *n. pr.* Semíramis.
semispherical (semisfe·rikal) *adj.* semiesférico.
Semite (se·mait) *adj.-s.* semita.
Semitic (simi·tik) *adj.* semítico. *2 s.* semita.
semitone (se·mitoun) *s.* MÚS. semitono.
semivowel (semivau·øl) *s.* letra semivocal.
semolina (semoli·na) *s.* sémola.
sempitern(al (sempitø·^rnal) *adj.* sempiterno.

sempstress (se·mpstris) *s.* SEAMSTRESS.
sen (sen) *s.* sen [moneda japonesa].
senate (se·nit) *s.* senado.
senator (se·natø^r) *s.* senador.
senatorial (senato·rial) *adj.* senatorial.
senatorship (se·natø^rship) *s.* senaduría.
senatus consultum (sinei·tøs consø·ltøm) *s.* senadoconsulto.
send (to) (send) *tr.* enviar, mandar, expedir, despachar. *2* lanzar; exhalar, despedir. *3* lanzar [un golpe]. *4* extender [las ramas, etc.]. *5 to ~ about one's business,* mandar a paseo. *6 to ~ forth,* exhalar, despedir; producir; exportar, publicar. *7 to ~ in one's papers,* dimitir. *8 to ~ word,* mandar recado. *9 tr.-intr.* RADIO [transmitir]. *10 intr. to ~ for,* enviar a buscar, mandar por. ¶ Pret. y p. p.: *sent.*
sender (-ø^r) *s.* remitente, expedidor. *3* TELEGR., RADIO. transmisor.
send-off (send-of) *s.* envío. *2* despedida afectuosa.
Senegalese (senigali·ŝ) *adj.-s.* senegalés.
senescence (sinø·søns) *s.* envejecimiento.
seneschal (se·nishal) *s.* senescal.
senile (si·nail o sɪ·nil) *adj.* senil.
senility (sini·liti) *s.* chochez. *2* senectud.
senior (sɪ·niø^r) *adj.* mayor, primero, padre [calificando a la de más edad de dos personas que llevan el mismo nombre]. *2* de mayor edad, categoría, etc.; más antiguo, decano. *3* (E.U.) del último curso de una facultad. *4 s.* anciano. *5* el que tiene más edad o es más antiguo que otro.
seniority (sinia·riti) *s.* mayor edad, categoría, etc.; antigüedad.
senna (se·na) *s.* BOT. sen, sena.
sensation (sensei·shøn) *s.* sensación. *2* sensacionalismo, efectismo.
sensational (-al) *adj.* sensacional. *2* melodramático. *3* efectista.
sense (sens) *s.* sentido [corporal]. *2* mente, inteligencia. *3* cordura, buen sentido: *common ~,* sentido común. *4* sentido [significado, acepción; razón de ser, finalidad]: *to make ~ out of,* entender, explicarse; *in a ~,* en cierto sentido. *5* sentido [de lo bello, del humor, humor, etc.]. *6* GEOM. sentido. *7* sensación, impresión, conciencia, sentimiento [de una cosa]. *8 to be out of one's senses,* estar loco. *9 to come to one's senses,* volver en sí; recobrar el buen sentido.
sense (to) *tr.* sentir, percibir; darse cuenta de.
senseless (-lis) *adj.* insensible, inerte, sin conocimiento. *2* sin sentido, absurdo. *3* insensato.
sensibility (sensibi·liti) *s.* sensibilidad.
sensible (se·nsibøl) *adj.* sensible. *2* perceptible. *3* cuerdo, razonable, juicioso, sensato. *4 to be ~ of,* sentir, tener conciencia de. *5 s.* MÚS. sensible.
sensitive (se·nsitiv) *adj.* sensitivo. *2* sensible, impresionable. *3* sentido, susceptible. *4* sensorial. *5* sensible [instrumento, placa, etc.]. *6* MED., QUÍM., FOT. sensibilizado. *7* BOT. *~ plant,* sensitiva.
sensitivity (sensiti·viti) *s.* sensibilidad. *2* susceptibilidad.
sensitize (to) (se·nsitaiŝ) *tr.* MED., QUÍM., FOT. sensibilizar. *2* hacer sensible.
sensorial (senso·rial) *adj.* sensorio.
sensorium (-riøm) *s.* sensorio.
sensual (se·nshual) *adj.* sensual. *2* materialista.
sensualism (-iŝm) *s.* sensualismo.
sensuality (senshuæ·liti) *s.* sensualidad.
sensuous (se·nshuøs) *adj.* sensual, sensitivo.
sent (sent) *pret.* y *p. p.* de TO SEND.

sentence (se·ntøns) *s.* sentencia, fallo; condena. *2* sentencia, máxima. *3* GRAM. oración, período.
sentence (to) *tr.* sentenciar, condenar.
sententious (sente·nshøs) *adj.* sentencioso. *2* conciso, enérgico, expresivo, lacónico.
sentience (se·nshiøns) *s.* sensibilidad [facultad de sentir]. *2* conciencia, percepción [de una cosa].
sentient (-ønt) *adj.* sensible [capaz de sentir físicamente]. *2* sensitivo. *3* ~ *of*, consciente de. *4 s.* ser sensible. *5* mente; conciencia.
sentiment (se·ntimønt) *s.* sentimiento. | No tiene el sentido de pena. *2* sensibilidad. *3* parecer, opinión. *4* concepto, frase; brindis.
sentimental (sentime·ntal) *adj.* sentimental.
sentimentalism (-išm) **sentimentality** (-iti) *s.* sentimentalismo.
sentimentalize (to) (-laiš) *tr.* hacer sentimental. *2* tratar sentimentalmente. *3 intr.* hacer el sentimental, afectar sentimiento.
sentinel (se·ntinøl) *s.* centinela: *to stand* ~, hacer centinela.
sentry (se·ntri) *s.* MIL. centinela.
sepal (se·pal) *s.* BOT. sépalo.
separable (se·parabøl) *adj.* separable.
separate (se·parit) *adj.* separado. *2* aparte; suelto. *3* distinto, diferente.
separate (to) (se·pareit) *tr.* separar. *2* despegar, desprender. *3 intr.* separarse. *4* despegarse, desprenderse.
separately (-li) *adv.* separadamente, por separado, aparte, de por sí.
separation (separei·shøn) *s.* separación. *2* porción.
separatism (se·paratišm) *s.* separatismo.
separator (se·pareitø') *s.* separador. *2* desnatadora.
Sephardic (sifa·'dik) *adj.* sefardí, sefardita.
Sephardim (-im) *s. pl.* sefardíes, sefarditas.
sepia (si·pia) *s.* ZOOL. sepia, jibia. *2* sepia [color].
sepoy (si·poi) *s.* cipayo. *2* policía indio.
seps (seps) *s.* ZOOL. eslizón.
sepsis (se·psis) *s.* sepsia.
September (septe·mbø') *s.* septiembre.
septenary (se·ptineri) *adj.-s.* septenario. *2 s.* septena. *3* septenio.
Septentrion (septe·ntriøn) *s.* ASTR. septentrión.
septentrion(al (septe·ntriøn(al) *adj.* septentrional.
septet (septe·t) *s.* septeto.
septicaemia, -cemia (septisɪ·mia) *s.* MED. septicemia.
septicidal (septisai·dal) *adj.* BOT. septicida.
septillion (septi·liøn) *s.* septillón.
septime (se·ptim) *s.* ESGR. séptima.
septimole (se·ptimoul) *s.* MÚS. septillo.
septuagenarian (sepchuadẏine·rian) *adj.-s.* septuagenario.
septuagenary (sepchuæ·dẏineri) *adj.* septuagenario.
septuagesima (sepchuadẏe·sima) *s.* septuagésima.
septum (se·ptøm) *s.* BIOL. septo.
septuor (se·pchuø') *s.* MÚS. septeto.
septuple (se·ptiupøl) *adj.* séptuplo.
septuple (to) *tr.* septuplicar.
sepulchral (sepø·lkral) *adj.* sepulcral.
sepulchre (se·pølkø') *s.* sepulcro, tumba, sepultura.
sepulchre (to) *tr.* enterrar, sepultar.
sepulture (se·pølchø') *s.* sepultura. *2* entierro.
sequel (si·kuøl) *s.* secuela. *2* conclusión, inferencia. *3* continuación, lo que sigue.
sequela (sikui·la) *s.* secuaz, prosélito; grupo de secuaces. *2* secuela. *3* conclusión, inferencia.

sequence (si·kuøns) *s.* sucesión, continuación; serie. *2* consecuencia, secuela. *3* ilación. *5* LITURG., CINEM. secuencia. *5* escalera [en los naipes].
sequent (-ønt) *adj.* siguiente, subsiguiente.
sequential (sikue·nshal) *adj.* SEQUENT. *2* sucesivo, consecutivo. *3* consiguiente.
sequester (to) (sikue·stø') *tr.* separar, apartar, retirar. *2* DER. secuestrar.
sequestered (-d) *adj.* apartado, solitario.
sequestrum (sikue·strøm) *s.* CIR. secuestro.
sequin (sɪ·kuin) *s.* cequi. *2* lentejuela.
sequoia (sikuo·ia) *s.* BOT. secoya.
seraglio (siræ·liou) *s.* serrallo.
seraph (se·raf), *pl.* **-aphs** o **-afim** (-afim) *s.* serafín.
seraphic(al (seræ·fik(al) *adj.* seráfico.
Serb (sø'b) *adj.-s.* servio.
Serbia (sø·'bia) *n. pr.* GEOGR. Servia.
Serbian (sø·'bian) *adj.-s.* servio.
Serbo-Croatian (sø·'bo-krou·shan) *adj.-s.* servocroata.
sere (si') *adj.* seco, marchito; gastado.
serenade (serønei·d) *s.* serenata. *2* fam. cencerrada.
serenade (to) *tr.* obsequiar con una serenata. *2 intr.* dar una serenata.
serene (sirr·n) *adj.* sereno, claro, despejado; plácido, tranquilo.
serene (to) *tr.* serenar, tranquilizar.
sereneness (-nis) *s.* serenidad de ánimo, calma.
serenity (sire·niti) *s.* serenidad, bonanza. *2* sosiego, apacibilidad. *3* serenidad, sangre fría.
serf (sø'f) *s.* siervo. *2* esclavo.
serge (sø·'dẏ) *s.* TEJ. sarga.
sergeancy (sa·'dẏønsi) *s.* SERGEANTCY.
sergeant (-ønt) *s.* MIL. sargento: ~ *major,* sargento auxiliar del ayudante. *2* ~ *at arms,* oficial que mantiene el orden en un cuerpo legislativo.
sergeantcy (-øntsi) *s.* sargentía.
serial (si·rial) *adj.* de serie, en serie. *2* de orden [número, etc.]. *3* consecutivo, sucesivo. *4* publicado por entregas; proyectado o radiado por episodios. *5 s.* obra que se publica por entregas. *6* CINEM., RADIO. serial.
seriate (to) (si·rieit) *tr.* disponer en serie.
seriate (d (si·rieit(id) *adj.* dispuesto en serie.
seriatim (siriei·tim) *adv.* punto por punto.
seric (se·rik) *adj.* de seda.
seri(ci)culture (seri(si)kø·lchø') *s.* seri(ci)cultura.
seri(ci)culturist (-ist) *s.* seri(ci)cultor.
series (si·riš) *s.* serie: *in* ~, ELECT. en serie.
serin (se·rin) *s.* ORN. especie de canario.
seringa (seri·nga) *s.* BOT. jeringuilla. *2* BOT. siringa.
serio-comic(al (siriou-ka·mik(al) *adj.* jocoserio.
serious (si·riøs) *adj.* serio. *2* verdadero, sincero.
seriously (si·riøsli) *adv.* seriamente, gravemente. *2* en serio.
serjeant (sa·'dẏønt) *s.* SERGEANT.
sermon (sø·'møn) *s.* sermón.
sermonize (to) (sø'mønai·š) *intr.-tr.* predicar, sermonear.
sermonizer (sø·'mønaišø') *s.* sermoneador.
serosity (sira·siti) *s.* serosidad.
serous (si·røs) *adj.* seroso.
serpent (sø·'pønt) *s.* ZOOL. serpiente, sierpe. *2* pers. astuta y traidora. *3* PIROT. buscapiés. *4* MÚS. serpentón. *5* ARTILL. serpentín. *6* ASTR. Serpiente.
serpent (to) *intr.* serpentear.
serpentine (sø·'pøntin) *adj.* serpentino. *2* sinuoso. *3 s.* MINER. serpentina.
serpentine (to) *intr.* serpentear.
serpigo (sø'pai·gou) *s.* MED. serpigo.

serrate (d (se·reit(id) *adj.* dentado. *2* BOT. serrado.
serried (se·rid) *adj.* apretado, apiñado, espeso.
serrulated (se·riuleitid) *adj.* denticulado.
serum (si·røm) *s.* suero.
servable (sø·ʳvabøl) *adj.* servible.
servant (sø·ʳvant) *s.* sirviente, criado: ~ *girl,*
criada. *2* servidor. *3* siervo.
serve (sø·ʳv) *s.* TENIS. servicio, saque.
serve (to) *tr.-intr.* servir: *to* ~ *as,* servir de; *to* ~ *for,*
servir de o para. *2* servir, sacar [la pelota]. *3 tr.*
llenar [un objeto]. *4* surtir, abastecer. *5* manejar
[un cañón]. *6* dar cumplimiento a, ejecutar, notificar: *to* ~ *a summons,* entregar una citación.
7 cumplir [una condena]. *8* MAR. aforrar. *9* cubrir [el macho a la hembra]. *10 to* ~ *one's turn,*
bastar, ser suficiente. *11 it serves me (you, him,*
etc.*) right,* me (te, le, etc.) está bien empleado.
server (-vøʳ) *s.* servidor. *2* criado de mesa; mozo
de comedor o de café. *3* saque [en el tenis, etc.].
4 bandeja.
Servia (sø·ʳvia) *pr. n.* SERBIA.
Servian (-an) *adj.-s.* SERBIAN.
service (sø·ʳvis) *s.* servicio: ~ *entrance,* entrada de
servicio; ~ *record,* hoja de servicios; *table* ~, servicio de mesa; *out of* ~, descompuesto; sin empleo. *2* utilidad, ventaja. *3* favor, ayuda. *4* función religiosa, oficio. *5* DER. entrega de una citación. *6* servicio, saque [de pelota]. *7* MAR. aforro. *8* cubrición. *9* reparación, montaje, etc. [de
una máquina] ~ *station,* estación de servicio,
taller de reparaciones. *10* BOT. *service* o ~ *tree,*
serbal.
service (to) *tr.* instalar, conservar, reparar, suministrar lo necesario para; abastecer, surtir.
serviceable (sø·ʳvisabøl) *adj.* servible. *2* útil, provechoso. *3* duradero. *4* servicial.
serviceberry (-beri) *s.* BOT. serba.
serviceman (-mæn) *s.* reparador, mecánico. *2* militar; marino.
servile (sø·ʳvil) *adj.* servil.
servility (sø·vi·liti) *s.* servilismo.
servitor (sø·ʳvitøʳ) *s.* servidor. *2* seguidor, secuaz.
servitude (-tiud) *s.* servidumbre, sujeción. *2* trabajos forzados. *3* DER. servidumbre.
servomotor (sø·ʳvomou·tøʳ) *s.* servomotor.
sesame (se·sami) *s.* BOT. sésamo, ajonjolí. *2 open* ~,
ábrete sésamo.
sesquioxide (seskuia·csaid) *s.* QUÍM. sesquióxido.
sessile (se·sil) *adj.* BOT., ZOOL. sésil.
session (se·shøn) *s.* sesión. *2* período de sesiones;
legislatura. *3* período escolar. *4* (Ingl.) sala de
justicia.
sessional (-al) *adj.* perteneciente a la sesión o período de sesiones.
sesterce (se·støʳs) *s.* sestercio.
set (set) *s.* juego, servicio, surtido, colección; tren,
grupo: ~ *of chairs,* sillería; ~ *of teeth,* dentadura. *2* aderezo [de diamantes]. *3* equipo, cuadrilla. *4* clase, gente, mundo, esfera. *5* aparato
[de radio, etc.]. *6* dirección, curso, tendencia. *7*
colocación, disposición; actitud, postura. *8*
corte [de una prenda]. *9* traba [de una sierra].
10 AGR. pie, estaca, bulbo [para plantar]. *11*
TEAT., CINEM. decoración. *12* TENIS. set. *13* muestra [del perro de caza]. *14* endurecimiento [de
la cola, etc.]; fraguado [de la cal, el yeso, etc.].
15 pret. y p. p. de TO SEAT.
16 adj. resuelto, determinado, empeñado; inflexible. *17* fijo, inmóvil, firme, persistente: ~
price, precio fijo. *18* regular, arreglado. *19* es-

tudiado, preparado. *20* intencionado, premeditado. *21* estrechado, en un aprieto.
set (to) *tr.* poner [en varios sentidos], asentar, colocar, situar, instalar, establecer. *2* poner a empollar. *3* destinar, fijar, señalar. *4* plantar, erigir. *5* preparar, ajustar, arreglar. *6* poner [un
reloj] en hora. *7* azuzar, excitar [contra]. *8* dar
[el tono]. *9* afilar [una navaja]. *10* triscar [una
sierra]. *11* plantar [un terreno]. *12* adornar,
sembrar. *13* engarzar, engastar, montar. *14* dar,
atribuir [valor, precio]. *15* fijar, inmovilizar. *16*
sujetar, apretar. *17* hacer obstinado, inflexible.
18 solidificar, cuajar, coagular. *19* mostrar [la
caza] el perro. *20* IMPR. componer. *21* CIR. encajar [un hueso]. *22* armar, tender [un lazo, una
trampa]. *23 to* ~ *about,* poner a; fam. atacar. *24
to* ~ *afloat,* poner a flote; hacer circular, esparcir. *25 to* ~ *ajar,* entornar, entreabrir. *26 to* ~ *an
example,* dar ejemplo. *27 to* ~ *aside,* poner o dejar a un lado; descartar; reservar, ahorrar. *28 to*
~ *at naught,* despreciar. *29 to* ~ *back,* detener,
estorbar; hacer retroceder; atrasar [el reloj]. *30
to* ~ *by the ears,* hacer reñir, enemistar. *31 to* ~
down, sentar; situar; bajar; humillar; anotar,
poner por escrito; atribuir, achacar. *32 to* ~ *fire
to, to* ~ *on fire,* pegar fuego a; encender, inflamar. *33 to* ~ *forth,* publicar; relatar; exponer,
manifestar. *34 to* ~ *free,* libertar. *35 to* ~ *off,*
adornar, embellecer; hacer resaltar; comparar,
contraponer; compensar; destinar, reservar;
disparar, hacer estallar. *36 to* ~ *one's cap at,*
tratar de conquistar a [uno] para su novio. *37
to* ~ *one's heart on,* poner uno su esperanza en.
38 to ~ *one's teeth,* apretar los dientes. *39 to* ~
one's teeth on edge, dar dentera. *40 to* ~ *out,* extender; exponer; señalar, asignar; trazar, proyectar. *41 to* ~ *right,* enderezar; enmendar. *42*
MAR. to ~ *sail,* hacerse a la vela. *43 to* ~ *store by,*
dar importancia a. *44 to* ~ *the table,* poner la
mesa. *45 to* ~ *to rights,* poner en orden. *46 to* ~
up, ajar, llevar; ensalzar; erigir, levantar, fundar; montar, armar; exponer, presentar; poner
en venta o subasta; IMPR. componer; *to* ~ *upon,*
azuzar; atacar, acometer.
  47 intr. empollar huevos. *48* sentar, caer bien
[una prenda]. *49* ponerse [un astro]; declinar,
acabar. *50* fluir, correr; tender. *51* dedicarse,
ponerse a. *52* fraguar, cuajarse, solidificarse. *53*
fijarse [un color]. *54* estar de muestra [un pe-
rro]. *55 to* ~ *about,* ponerse a. *56 to* ~ *forth,* salir,
ponerse en camino. *57 to* ~ *in,* aparecer; cerrar
[la noche]; correr o soplar hacia tierra. *58 to* ~
off, salir, partir. *59 to* ~ *out for,* salir para. *60 to*
~ *out to, to* ~ *to,* ponerse a. *61 to* ~ *up for,* hacerse pasar por.
  ¶ Pret. y p. p.: *set;* ger.: *setting.*
setaceous (siteis·shøs) *adj.* cerdoso.
setback (se·tbæk) *s.* revés, contrariedad, retroceso.
2 MEC. mecanismo de retroceso.
setoff (se·taf) *s.* adorno. *2* relieve, realce. *3* compensación, contrapeso. *4* ARQ. saliente, retallo. *5*
salida, partida.
seton (si·tøn) *s.* CIR. sedal.
setscrew (-skru) *s.* tornillo de presión.
settee (seti·) *s.* banco [para sentarse]; sofá.
setter (se·tøʳ) *s.* (en comp.) el que prepara, pone,
ajusta, fija, coloca, monta, etc. *2* perro de muestra, perdiguero.
setting (-ing) *s.* puesta, ocaso. *2* fraguado, endurecimiento. *3* engaste, montura. *4* marco, escenario [de una narración, etc.]; medio circun-

dante, ambiente. 5 TEAT. decorado [de una obra]. 6 situación. 7 IMPR. composición. 8 compostura [de huesos]. 9 ~ up, establecimiento; montaje.

settle (se·tǫl) s. escaño, banco. 2 escalón, grada.

settle (to) tr. colocar, asentar, establecer. 2 fijar, afirmar, asegurar. 3 colonizar, poblar. 4 dar estado, colocar, casar. 5 regular, ordenar; arreglar. 6 ajustar [cuentas]; zanjar [una disputa]; decidir, resolver. 7 pagar, liquidar, saldar. 8 sosegar, serenar, pacificar. 9 hacer posar las heces, etc., de. 10 to ~ on o upon, dar en dote, asignar como herencia, pensión, etc., a. 11 intr. posarse, asentarse, establecerse, instalarse. 12 hacer asiento [un edificio]. 13 posarse [las heces, el polvo]; reposarse [un líquido]. 14 fijarse, arraigar. 15 arreglar su vida; tomar estado, casarse. 16 sosegarse, serenarse. 17 to ~ down, asentarse; fijarse; posarse; sentar la cabeza; ponerse [a]. 18 to ~ with, liquidar o ajustar cuentas con.

settle-bed s. sofá cama.

settlement (se·tǫlmǫnt) s. establecimiento, instalación. 2 colonización. 3 colonia, poblado. 4 centro de acción benéfica y social. 5 sedimentación. 6 asignación de bienes, pensión, etc. 7 acomodo, empleo. 8 ajuste [de cuentas]. 9 arreglo, convenio. 10 pago, liquidación.

settler (se·tlǫʳ) s. poblador, colono. 2 establecedor. 3 liquidador. 4 fam. lo que acaba o concluye; golpe de gracia.

settlings (-lings) s. pl. heces, poso, sedimento.

set-to s. fam. lucha, combate, disputa.

setup (se·tǫp) s. cosa levantada o erigida. 2 posición, disposición, arreglo, organización. 3 tren, equipo, etc., de aparatos o instrumentos. 4 fam. (E.U.) invitación a beber.

setwall (se·twol) s. BOT. valeriana.

seven (se·vǫn) adj.-s. siete: ~ hundred, setecientos; ~ o'clock, las siete.

sevenfold (-fould) adj. séptuplo. 2 adv. siete veces.

seventeen (-tin) adj.-s. diecisiete.

seventeenth (-tinz) adj. decimoséptimo. 2 diecisiete [del mes]. 3 diecisieteavo.

seventh (-z) adj. séptimo. 2 siete [del mes]. 3 s. séptimo [séptima parte]. 4 MÚS. séptima.

seventhly (-zli) adv. en séptimo lugar.

seventieth (-tiiz) adj.-s. septuagésimo, setentavo.

seventy (-ti) adj.-s. setenta.

sever (to) (se·vǫʳ) tr. separar, dividir, desunir; cortar, romper. 2 intr. separarse, desunirse, romperse.

several (-al) adj. varios, diversos, algunos. 2 diferentes, distintos. 3 individual, particular. 4 respectivo, respectivos. 5 pron. algunos.

severally (-i) adj. separadamente. 2 respectivamente.

severance (se·vǫrans) s. separación, división, partición. 2 ruptura [de relaciones, etc.].

severe (sivi·ʳ) adj. severo. 2 acerbo, agudo, grave, duro, fuerte, recio. 3 riguroso.

severity (sive·riti) s. severidad. 2 rigor, exactitud, rigorismo. 3 gravedad, agudeza, rigor, dureza, inclemencia.

Sevillian (sivi·lian) adj.-s. sevillano.

Seville (sivi·l) n. pr. GEOGR. Sevilla.

sew (to) (sou) tr.-intr. coser. ¶ P. p.: sewed o sewn.

sewage (siu·idȳ) s. aguas de albañal; aguas inmundas.

1) sewer (sou·ǫʳ) s. cosedor.

2) sewer (siu·ǫʳ) s. alcantarilla, cloaca, albañal. 2 HIST. maestresala.

sewerage (siu·ǫridȳ) s. desagüe de aguas inmundas. 2 alcantarillado. 3 SEWAGE.

sewing (sou·ing) s. costura [acción de coser]: ~ machine, máquina de coser.

sex (se·ks) s. sexo: the fair ~, el bello sexo. 2 adj. sexual: ~ appeal, atracción sexual, encanto femenino.

sexagenarian (seksadȳine·rian) adj.-s. sexagenario.

sexagenary (seksæ·dȳineri) adj. sexagenario.

Sexagesima (seksadȳe·sima) s. sexagésima.

sext (se·kst) s. ECLES. sexta [hora].

sextain (-ain) s. LIT. sextilla.

sextant (-ant) s. sextante. 2 GEOM. sexta parte del círculo.

sextet (sekste·t) s. MÚS. sexteto. 2 LIT. sextilla. 3 grupo de seis.

sexton (se·kstǫn) s. sacristán y enterrador.

sextuple (se·kstiupǫl) adj. séxtuplo.

sexual (se·kshual) adj. sexual.

sexuality (sekshuæ·liti) s. sexualidad.

sgraffito (šgrafi·tou) s. B. ART. esgrafiado.

shabbily (shæ·bili) adv. andrajosamente. 2 mezquinamente.

shabby (shæ·bi) adj. raído, gastado, usado. 2 andrajoso, desaseado. 3 mezquino. 4 ruin, vil.

shabby-genteel adj. de señor tronado, cursi.

shack (shæ·k) s. (E.U. y Can.) cabaña, choza.

shackle (shæ·kǫl) s. grillete, grillo, esposa. 2 maniota, traba. 3 MEC. eslabón giratorio. 4 traba, estorbo. 5 pl. hierros, prisiones.

shackle (to) tr. aherrojar. 2 manear, trabar. 3 estorbar, poner trabas.

shad (shæ·d) s. ICT. sábalo.

shaddock (shæ·dǫk) s. BOT. toronja, pamplemusa.

shade (shei·d) s. sombra [que dan los árboles, etc.]; retiro; protección; aparición. 2 PINT. sombra. 3 matiz, tinte; pequeña diferencia. 4 pantalla [de lámpara o para proteger los ojos]. 5 visillo, cortina, transparente. 6 pl. sombras [de la noche]. 7 infierno, mundo de las sombras.

shade (to) tr. sombrear. 2 resguardar de la luz. 3 obscurecer. 4 matizar. 5 proteger, esconder, velar. 6 intr. modificarse, convertirse gradualmente.

shading (-ing) s. PINT. sombreado, degradación. 2 matización.

shadoof (sha·duf) s. cigoñal [para sacar agua].

shadow (shæ·dou) s. sombra, obscuridad. 2 sombra [de un objeto]. 3 PINT. sombra. 4 sombra [defecto; lo que ensombrece; semejanza; pizca, señal; abrigo, amparo]. 5 sombra, espectro, imagen. 6 sombra [compañero inseparable; el que vigila a uno]. 7 retiro, vida, retirada. 8 ~ play, sombras chinescas.

shadow (to) tr. sombrear, dar sombra a. 2 anublar, ensombrecer. 3 espiar, seguir secretamente. 4 B. ART. sombrear. 5 to ~ forth u out, indicar, representar vagamente, simbolizar.

shadowy (-i) adj. umbroso. 2 oscuro, tenebroso. 3 vago, indistinto. 4 espectral. 5 ilusorio. 6 simbólico.

shady (shei·di) adj. sombreado, umbrío. 2 sombrío. 3 sospechoso, equívoco, de dudosa moralidad. 4 on the ~ side of fifty, pasados los cincuenta años.

shaft (shæft) s. astil [de saeta, herramienta o pluma]. 2 asta [de lanza o bandera]. 3 saeta, dardo. 4 fuste [de columna]. 5 MEC. árbol, eje. 6

lanza, vara [de carruaje]. 7 BOT. tronco, tallo, vástago. 8 ARQ. aguja, obelisco. 9 pozo, chimenea [de mina, etc.].

shag (shæg) s. lana o pelo áspero y enredado. 2 TEJ. pelo áspero y largo. 3 TEJ. felpa. 4 enredijo.

shagbark (-ba^rk) s. BOT. nogal americano.

shagged (-id) adj. peludo, hirsuto. 2 SHAGGY. 3 JAGGED.

shaggy (-i) adj. lanudo, peludo, hirsuto. 2 afelpado. 3 áspero, rugoso. 4 desgreñado.

shagreen (shagrı·n) s. lija, piel de lija. 2 TEN. zapa, piel de zapa; chagrín.

shake (sheik) s. meneo, sacudida; sacudimiento. 2 temblor, estremecimiento. 3 apretón [de manos]. 4 fam. terremoto. 5 periquete, instante. 6 MÚS. trino. 7 grieta, hendedura. 8 acebolladura. 9 batido [de leche]. 10 to be no great shakes, no ser gran cosa.

shake (to) tr. sacudir, menear, agitar, blandir. 2 hacer temblar o retemblar. 3 sacudir, sacudirse, librarse de; dar esquinazo a. | Gralte. con off o out. 4 debilitar, hacer vacilar o flaquear. 5 desalentar; impresionar, afectar. 6 estrechar [la mano]. 7 MÚS. hacer trino en una [nota]. 8 to ~ down, vaciar, o hacer caer sacudiendo; fig. sacar dinero [a uno]. 9 intr. temblar, retemblar, estremecerse, tiritar. 10 vacilar, tambalearse. 11 MÚS. trinar. ¶ Pret.: shook; p. p.: shaken.

shakedown (-daun) s. cama improvisada. 2 acción de sacar dinero a uno.

shaker (shei·kø^r) s. temblador. 2 sacudidor, agitador. 3 coctelera. 4 espolvoreador.

Shakespearian (sheikspi·rian) adj. relativo a Shakespeare.

shako (shæ·kou) s. chacó.

shaky (shæ·ki) adj. trémulo. 2 inseguro, vacilante, ruinoso. 3 agrietado. 4 poco claro; que merece poco crédito.

shale (sheil) s. esquisto.

shall (shæl) aux. def. (con un inf. sin to). Con el pres. forma el futuro del segundo verbo. Al revés de lo que ocurre con to will, en las primeras personas, denota simple acción futura, posibilidad o contingencia, y en las segundas y terceras, voluntad, intención, permiso, mandato o amenaza: I shall go, yo iré; he shall go, tiene que ir. 2 El pret. should se usa a) como signo del subjuntivo: if you should come, si usted viniese; b) para formar el potencial; c) con la significación de deber o haber de: you should come, debería usted venir. V. SHOULD. ¶ Pres., 1.ª y 3.ª pers. sing.: shall; 2.ª pers.: shalt; pl. shall | Pret.: should.

shallop (shæ·løp) s. chalupa.

shallot (shala·t) s. BOT. chalote, ascalonia.

shallow (shæ·lou) adj. bajo, poco profundo, vadoso. 2 superficial, frívolo. 3 s. bajío; paraje vadoso.

shallow (to) tr. hacer menos profundo. 2 intr. hacerse menos profundo.

shallowness (shæ·lounis) s. poca profundidad. 2 superficialidad, ligereza de juicio, frivolidad.

shaly (chei·li) adj. esquistoso.

sham (shæm) s. fingimiento, simulación. 2 imitación, cosa falsa. 3 simulador, farsante. 4 adj. fingido, simulado, falso, postizo.

sham (to) tr.-intr. fingir, simular. ¶ Pret. y p. p.: shammed; ger.: shamming.

shamble (shæ·mbøl) s. paso torpe, vacilante.

shamble (to) intr. andar vacilando, arrastrar los pies.

shambles (shæ·mbøls) s. pl. (a veces construido como sing.) matadero, degolladero.

shame (sheim) s. vergüenza, bochorno; pudor: to put to ~, avergonzar. 2 vergüenza, deshonra: it is a ~, es una vergüenza; for ~!, ¡qué vergüenza!

shame (to) tr. avergonzar, abochornar. 2 afrentar, deshonrar.

shamefaced (-feist) adj. tímido, vergonzoso. 2 avergonzado.

shameful (-ful) adj. vergonzoso, ignominioso. 2 indecente, escandaloso.

shameless (-lis) adj. desvergonzado, descarado, sin vergüenza.

shammer (-ø^r) s. simulador, fingidor.

shammy (shæ·mi) s. CHAMOIS.

shampoo (shæmpu·) s. lavado [de la cabeza]. 2 champú.

shampoo (to) tr. dar champú a, lavar [la cabeza].

shamrock (shæ·mrak) s. BOT. trébol; aleluya; mielga azafranada. 2 emblema de Irlanda.

shank (shænk) s. zanca, pierna. 2 caña [del caballo]; zanca [del ave]; tibia [de insecto]. 3 canilla [de la pierna]. 4 MEC. astil, vástago, espiga. 5 caña [de ancla]. 6 tija [de llave]. 7 enfranque. 8 IMPR. árbol [del tipo]. 9 alacrán [de botón]. 10 cabo, extremo; fin.

shan't (shænt) abrev. fam. de SHALL NOT.

shanty (shæ·nti) s. cabaña, choza, casucha. 2 CHANTEY.

shape (sheip) s. forma, figura, hechura, cuerpo, estado: to put into ~, arreglar, poner en orden; to take ~, tomar forma o cuerpo; in bad ~, mal, en mal estado; out of ~, deformado; desarreglado, descompuesto. 2 giro, aspecto. 3 forma, molde.

shape (to) tr. formar, dar forma a; modelar. 2 expresar. 3 ahormar. 4 amoldar, ajustar. 5 dirigir [el curso, la conducta, etc.]. 6 disponer, idear. 7 concebir, figurarse. 8 intr. formarse, desarrollarse. 9 ocurrir [de cierto modo].

shapeless (-lis) adj. informe. 2 deforme.

shapely (-li) adj. bien formado o proporcionado. 2 de forma definida.

shard (sha·^rd) s. tiesto, casco, fragmento. 2 ENT. élitro.

share (she·ø^r) s. parte, porción, cuota, cupo: to go shares, entrar o ir a la parte. 2 interés, participación. 3 COM. acción. 4 reja [de arado].

share (to) tr. dividir, distribuir, repartir. 2 repartirse, compartir, participar con otros en; usar en común. 3 intr. participar, tener o tomar parte.

sharecropper (-krapø^r) s. AGR. aparcero.

shareholder (-jouldø^r) s. COM. accionista.

sharer (-ø^r) s. partícipe, copartícipe.

shark (sha·^rk) s. ICT. y fig. tiburón. 2 escualo. 3 estafador. 4 as [el que sobresale en algo].

sharp (sha·^rp) adj. agudo, aguzado, afilado, cortante, punzante. 2 puntiagudo. 3 anguloso. 4 distinto, bien marcado. 5 repentino, brusco. 6 abrupto, escarpado. 7 áspero, acre, cáustico. 8 agudo, estridente. 9 vivo, penetrante, agudo, intenso, acerbo. 10 duro, severo, agrio, sarcástico. 11 fino, agudo [sentido]. 12 perspicaz, listo, astuto. 13 vivo, enérgico. 14 empeñado, reñido. 15 violento, impetuoso. 16 grande [apetito]. 17 codicioso. 18 atento, vigilante. 19 MÚS. agudo; sostenido; mayor, aumentado. 20 FONÉT. sordo. 21 ~ practice, estafa, dolo. 22 adv. SHARPLY. : look ~!, ¡ojo alerta! 23 en punto: at three o'clock ~, a las tres en punto. 24 s. pop. experto, perito. 25 estafador, fullero. 26 MÚS. sostenido.

sharp (to) *tr.* engañar, estafar, robar. *2* MÚS. subir el tono de; marcar con sostenido.

sharp-edged *adj.* afilado, aguzado.

sharpen (to) (-øn) *tr.* afilar, aguzar, amolar, adelgazar. *2* aguzar [los sentidos, etc.]. *3* hacer más áspero, severo, intenso, vehemente, etc. *4* hacer distinto o marcado. *5* MÚS. TO SHARP. *6* *intr.* aguzarrse. *7* afilarse.

sharpener (-ønø^r) *s.* afilador, amolador, aguzador. *2* cortalápices. *3* *knife* ~, chaira, afilón.

sharper (-ø^r) *s.* estafador.

sharp-featured *adj.* de facciones enjutas.

sharply (-li) *adv.* grandemente; vivamente; ásperamente; mordazmente; bruscamente; nítidamente, etc.

sharp-pointed *adj.* puntiagudo.

sharp-set *adj.* ávido, ansioso.

sharpshooter (-shutø^r) *s.* buen tirador.

sharp-sighted *adj.* perspicaz; de vista penetrante.

sharp-witted *adj.* agudo, sutil, perspicaz.

shatter (shæ·tø^r) *s.* fragmento, astilla, añico.

shatter (to) *tr.* romper, hacer astillas o añicos. *2* destrozar, destruir. *3* quebrantar [la salud]; trastornar [el juicio]. *4* *intr.* romperse, hacerse añicos.

shatterproof (shæ·tø^rpruf) *adj.* inastillable.

shattery (shæ·tøri) *adj.* quebradizo, friable.

shave (sheiv) *s.* afeitado, rasuración. *2* corte [de la hierba]. *3* rebanada fina; viruta. *4* *to have a close* ~, escaparse o salvarse de milagro.

shave (to) *tr.* afeitar, rasurar. *2* segar de raíz. *3* acepillar, alisar, rascar; cortar, rebanar finamente. *4* rozar [pasar rozando]. *5* *intr.* afeitarse. *6* ser duro en un trato; estafar.

shaver (shei·vø^r) *s.* barbero. *2* máquina de afeitar. *3* fam. jovencito, muchacho.

shaving (-ing) *s.* afeitado; ~ *brush*, brocha de afeitar. *2* viruta.

shawl (shol) *s.* chal, pañolón, mantón.

shawm (shom) *s.* chirimía, dulzaina.

she (shı) *pron. f.* ella [en nominativo]: ~ *who*, la que, aquella que. *2* (en composición) hembra: *she-ass*, borrica.

sheaf (shıf), *pl.* **sheaves** (shıvš) *s.* haz, gavilla. *2* manojo, atado, lío. *3* roldana.

shear (shı^r) *s.* esquila, esquileo. *2* vellón, lana esquilada. *3* hoja de tijera.

shear (to) *tr.* cortar, esquilar, trasquilar. *2* tundir. *3* cizallar, cortar con cizallas. *4* recortar [una planta]. *5* fig. despojar, privar de. ¶ P. p.: *sheared o shorn.*

shearer (-ø^r) *s.* esquilador. *2* tundidor.

shears (-s) *s. pl.* tijeras grandes. *2* cizallas.

shearwater (-wotø^r) *s.* ORN. meauca.

sheatfish (shı·tfish) *s.* ICT. siluro.

sheath (shız) *s.* vaina, funda, estuche, envoltura. *2* BOT. vaina [de hoja]. *3* cama [del arado].

sheathe (to) (shið) *tr.* envainar, enfundar; cubrir, forrar. *2* MAR. aforrar, embonar.

sheathing (shi·ding) *s.* forro exterior, cubierta, revestimiento. *2* MAR. aforro, embono.

sheave (shıv) *s.* roldana, polea. *2* rueda excéntrica.

sheave (to) *tr.* agavillar, reunir en haz.

shed (shed) *s.* cobertizo, alpende. *2* hangar. *3* divisoria de aguas. *4* TEJ. calada.

shed (to) *tr.* verter, derramar. *2* lanzar, emitir, esparcir, despedir. *3* soltar, dejar caer; mudar [las plumas, la piel, etc.]. *4* *intr.* hacer la muda. ¶ Pret. y p. p.: *shed;* ger.: *-dding.*

shedding (-ing) *s.* derramamiento, efusión.

sheen (shın) *s.* lustre, brillo, resplandor.

sheeny (-i) *adj.* lustroso. *2* brillante, radiante.

sheep (shıp) *s. sing.* y *pl.* ZOOL. carnero, oveja; carneros, ovejas: ~ *dog*, perro de pastor; ~ *tick*, garrapata; *to make sheep's eyes at*, fig. mirar lánguida y amorosamente. *2* papanatas, simplón. *3* badana.

sheepcote (-kout), **sheepfold** (-fould) *s.* aprisco, redil.

sheepish (-ish) *adj.* tímido, vergonzoso, encogido. *2* avergonzado.

sheepshead (-sjed) *s.* COC. cabeza de cordero. *2* estúpido, papanatas. *3* ICT. sargo.

sheepshearer (-shirø^r) *s.* esquilador. *2* esquiladora [máquina].

sheepskin (-skin) *s.* piel de cordero, zalea. *2* badana. *3* pergamino. *4* fam. (E.U.) diploma.

sheepwalk (shı·pwok) *s.* dehesa carneril.

sheer (shı^r) *adj.* puro, mero. *2* completo, absoluto. *3* empinado, escarpado. *4* TEJ. fino, ligero, transparente. *5* *adv.* completamente. *6* escarpadamente. *7* de golpe. *8* *s.* MAR. arrufadura. *9* desviación, cambio de rumbo.

sheer (to) *tr.* desviar. *2* *intr.* desviarse: *to* ~ *off*, apartarse, huir de.

sheet (shıt) *s.* hoja, lámina, plancha. *2* hoja [de papel]; pliego [impreso]; carta; periódico. *3* sábana [de cama]. *4* mortaja. *5* extensión [de agua]; cortina [de fuego, de lluvia, etc.]. *6* poét. vela [de barco]; *to be*, o *tohave a* ~ *in the wind*, estar chispo, calamocano. *7* GEOL. capa. *8* MAR. escota. *9* MAR. ~ *anchor*, ancla de la esperanza.

sheet (to) *tr.* ensabanar. *2* disponer en capas. *3* *intr.* caer, extenderse, como una capa u hoja.

sheeting (shı·ting) *s.* lencería para sábanas. *2* acción de cubrir con planchas. *3* laminado. *4* HIDR., MIN. encofrado.

sheik (shık) *s.* jeque.

shekel (she·køl) *s.* siclo. *2* *pl.* fam. dinero.

sheldrake (she·ldreik) *s.* ORN. tadorna; mergánsar.

shelf (shelf) *s.* anaquel, entrepaño, tabla [de armario], repisa. *2* saliente de roca. *3* bajío.

shell (shel) *s.* ZOOL. concha, caparazón, carapacho: *to retire into one's* ~, meterse en su concha. *2* concha [materia]: ~ *comb*, peineta. *3* marisco. *4* cáscara, cascarón [de huevo]. *5* cáscara [de nuez, avellana, etc.]. *6* vaina [de legumbre]. *7* cáscara, concha, caja, cubierta; esqueleto o armazón exterior. *8* forro o casco [de buque]. *9* guarnición [de la espada]. *10* cuerpo [de caldera]. *11* caja [de motón]. *12* MÚS. caja [de tambor, de banjo, etc.]. *13* cubilete [pastel]. *14* MAR. yola. *15* cápsula [de cartucho]. *16* ARTILL. bomba, granada.

shell (to) *tr.* descascarar, desvainar, desgranar; romper [nueces, avellanas]. *2* ARTILL. bombardear. *3* *intr.* desgranarse. *4* descascararse. *5* fam. *to* ~ *out*, aflojar la mosca.

shellac (shølæ·k) *s.* goma laca.

shellac (to) *tr.* barnizar con laca. ¶ Pret. y p. p.: *shellacked;* ger.: *-cking.*

shellbark (she·lba^rk) *s.* BOT. nogal. americano.

shellfire (she·lfai^r) *s.* cañoneo, bombardeo.

shellfish (-fish) *s.* marisco, mariscos.

shellproof (-pruf) *adj.* a prueba de bomba.

shelly (-i) *adj.* de conchas. *2* conchudo.

shelter (she·ltø^r) *s.* resguardo, abrigo, refugio, asilo, albergue, techo: *to take* ~, refugiarse.

shelter (to) *tr.* resguardar, proteger, amparar, guarecer, abrigar. *2* albergar, acoger. *3* *intr.* guarecerse, refugiarse, acogerse.

shelterless (-lis) *adj.* desamparado, sin hogar. 2 desabrigado, al descubierto.
shelve (to) (shelv) *tr.* proveer de anaqueles. 2 poner en un anaquel. 3 fig. arrinconar, archivar, dar carpetazo a. 4 *intr.* estar en declive.
shelves (-š) *s. pl.* de SHELF.
shelving (-ing) *s.* anaquelería, estantería.
shepherd (she·pø*d) *s.* pastor: *the Good Shepherd*, el Buen Pastor. 2 BOT. *shepherd's purse*, bolsa de pastor.
shepherd (to) *tr.* pastorear.
shepherdess (she·pø*dis) *s.* pastora, zagala.
sherbet (shø·*bit) *s.* sorbete.
sherd (shø*d) *s.* tiesto, casco, tejoleta.
sherif (sherı·f) *s.* jerife.
sheriff (she·rif) *s.* funcionario superior de un distrito, encargado de hacer cumplir la ley, ejecutar los mandatos judiciales y mantener el orden.
sherry (she·ri) *s.* vino de Jerez.
she's (shıš) *contr.* de SHE IS y de SHE HAS.
sheth (shez) *s.* dental [del arado].
shew (to) (shou·) *tr.-intr.* (Ingl.) TO SHOW.
shewbread (-bred) *s.* panes de proposición.
shibboleth (shi·boliz) *s.* palabra que sirve de santo y seña.
shield (shıld) *s.* escudo, adarga. 2 escudo, defensa. 3 BLAS., ZOOL. escudo. 4 sobaquera [contra el sudor].
shield (to) *tr.* escudar, proteger, defender.
shield-bearer *s.* escudero.
shift (shift) *s.* recurso, expediente, esfuerzo, artificio, maña: *to make (a)* ~, componérselas [para]; arreglarse, pasar [con o sin]. 2 fraude; subterfugio. 3 muda [de ropa]. 4 tanda, turno [de obreros; de trabajo]. 5 cambio, desviación, sustitución, traslado: ~ *key*, tecla o palanca de mayúsculas.
shift (to) *tr.* cambiar, mudar; cambiar de posición o dirección, mover, trasladar: *to* ~ *gears*, AUTO. cambiar la marcha; *to* ~ *the blame*, echar [a otro] la propia culpa. 2 pop. comer, beber. 3 *intr.* cambiar, mudar; moverse, trasladarse, correrse. 4 usar de subterfugios o evasivas; mañear. 5 ingeniarse: *to* ~ *for oneself*, arreglárselas.
shiftiness (-tinis) *s.* calidad de mudable o movedizo. 2 artificio, astucia; carácter evasivo.
shiftless (-tlis) *adj.* falto de recursos, de inventiva; inútil, perezoso.
shifty (-ti) *adj.* mudable, voluble. 2 movedizo, inquieto. 3 industrioso, mañoso, astuto, evasivo.
shilling (-shi·ling) *s.* chelín [vigésima parte de la libra esterlina].
shilly-shally (shi·li-shæ·li) *s.* irresolución, vacilación. 2 persona irresoluta.
shilly-shally (to) *intr.* vacilar, estar indeciso.
shim (shim) MEC. planchita con que se hacen ajustar entre sí dos partes de una máquina.
shimmer (shi·mø*) *s.* luz trémula, débil resplandor.
shimmer (to) *intr.* rielar, brillar débilmente.
shimmery (-i) *adj.* que luce con débil resplandor. 2 trémulo.
shimmy (shi·mi) *s.* shimmy [baile]. 2 fam. camisa de mujer. 3 AUTO. abaniqueo de las ruedas delanteras.
shimmy (to) *intr.* bailar el SHIMMY.
shin (shin) *s.* espinilla [de la pierna].
shin (to) *intr.-tr.* trepar, subir. 2 *tr.* golpear en la espinilla. ¶ Pret. y p.: *shinned*; ger.: -*nning*.

shindig (shi·ndig) *s.* pop. (E.U.) juerga.
shindy (shi·ndi) *s.* fam. alboroto, trapatiesta.
shine (shai·n) *s.* brillo, resplandor, lustre, esplendor. 2 brillo, lustre [que se saca o se da]. 3 buen tiempo. 4 pop. (E.U.) afición, simpatía.
shine (to) *intr.* brillar, resplandecer, lucir. 2 brillar, distinguirse. 3 hacer sol o buen tiempo. 4 *tr.* hacer brillar. 5 pulir, bruñir, lustrar; limpiar [el calzado]. ¶ Pret. y p.: *shone*.
shiner (-ø*) *s.* persona o cosa brillante. 2 pop. soberano [moneda]. 3 pop. ojo; ojo amoratado.
shingle (shi·ngøl) *s.* guijo, guijarros. 2 guijarro. 3 chilla, ripia [para techar]. 4 fam. (E.U.) letrero de despacho. 5 pelo de mujer corto y en disminución.
shingle (to) *tr.* cubrir con ripia. 2 cortar el cabello dejándolo corto y en disminución. 3 cinglar [el hierro].
shingles (shi·ngøls) *s.* MED. zoster, zona.
shining (shai·ning) *adj.* brillante, resplandeciente. 2 fig. brillante, distinguido.
shinny (shi·ni) *s.* cachava [juego y palo].
shinny (to) *intr.* jugar al *shinny*. 2 (E.U.) *to* ~ *up*, trepar, subir.
Shinto (shi·ntou), **Shintoism** (-išm) *s.* sintoísmo.
shiny (shai·ni) *adj.* brillante, luminoso. 2 claro, radiante. 3 lustroso. 4 raído.
ship (ship) *s.* MAR. buque, barco,nave, bajel, navío: ~ *biscuit*, galleta; ~ *carpenter*, carpintero de ribera; ~ *chandler*, proveedor de buques. 2 nave aérea, aeronave.
ship (to) *tr.* embarcar. 2 enviar, expedir, transportar. 3 armar [los remos, el timón, etc.]. 4 tomar como tripulante. 5 *intr.* embarcarse. ¶ Pret. y p.: *shipped*; ger.: -*pping*.
shipboard (-bo*d) *s.* MAR. bordo: *on* ~, a bordo.
shipbuilder (-bildø*) *s.* constructor de buques.
shipbuilding (-bilding) *s.* arquitectura naval.
shipload (-loud) *s.* MAR. cargamento; todo lo que el buque puede llevar [de una cosa].
shipmaster (-mæstø*) *s.* MAR. patrón, capitán.
shipmate (-meit) *s.* compañero de a bordo.
shipment (-mønt) *s.* embarque, cargamento. 2 envío, remesa, consignación, partida.
shipowner (-ounø*) *s.* naviero, armador.
shipper (-ø*) *s.* COM. cargador, embarcador; expedidor, remitente.
shipping (-ing) *s.* embarque, envío, expedición: ~ *agent*, consignatario de buques. 2 buques, flota, tonelaje [de un puerto, país, etc.].
shipplane (-plein) *s.* avión de cubierta.
shipshape (-sheip) *adj.* en buen orden.
shipworm (-uø*m) *s.* ZOOL. broma, tiñuela.
shipwreck (-rek) *s.* naufragio. 2 buque náufrago.
shipwreck (to) *tr.* hacer naufragar. 2 *intr.* naufragar.
shipwright (-rait) *s.* carpintero de ribera o de buque, calafate.
shipyard (-ya*d) *s.* MAR. astillero, arsenal.
shire (shai*) *s.* (Ingl.) distrito, condado.
shirk (shø*k) *s.* maula, el que huye del trabajo.
shirk (to) *tr.* eludir, evitar. 2 *intr.* huir del trabajo, de hacer algo; faltar a una obligación.
shirr (shø*) *s.* COST. frunce, gandujado.
shirr (to) *tr.* COST. fruncir, gandujar. 2 coc. escalfar huevos en crema de leche.
shirt (shø*t) *s.* camisa [de hombre]: *in one's* ~ *sleeves*, en mangas de camisa.
shirtband (-bænd) *s.* tirilla [del cuello de la camisa].
shirting (-ing) *s.* tela para camisas.

shirtwaist (-weist) *s.* blusa camisera.
shiver (shi·vø^r) *s.* temblor, tiritón, escalofrío, estremecimiento. *2* pedazo, astilla, brizna.
shiver (to) *intr.* temblar, tiritar, estremecerse, vibrar. *2* romperse, hacerse añicos. *3 tr.* hacer temblar, estremecer. *4* romper, hacer añicos.
shivery (shi·vøri) *adj.* trémulo, tembloroso. *2* friolento, friolero. *3* friable, quebradizo.
shoal (shoul) *s.* bajo, bajío, banco de arena. *2* muchedumbre, multitud. *3* banco [de peces]. *4 adj.* poco profundo.
shoal (to) *intr.* MAR. disminuir gradualmente en profundidad. *2* reunirse en gran número.
shoaly (-i) *s.* vadoso, poco profundo. *2* lleno de bajíos.
shoat (shout) *s.* gorrino, cochinillo.
shock (shak) *s.* golpe, choque: ~ *absorber*, amortiguador. *2* conmoción, sacudida. *3* sobresalto, susto, impresión. *4* ofensa, escándalo, horror. *5* MED. choque. *6* hacina, tresnal. *7* greña, maraña.
shock (to) *tr.* chocar, ofender, escandalizar, horrorizar. *2* causar impresión, sobresaltar. *3* MED. someter al choque eléctrico. *4* sacudir, conmover. *5* hacinar. *6 intr.* chocar.
shock-headed *adj.* greñudo.
shocking (-ing) *adj.* chocante, ofensivo, repugnante, vergonzoso, escandaloso. *2* horrible.
shod (shad) *pret.* y *p. p.* de TO SHOE.
shoddy (sha·di) *s.* lana de desecho o regenerada. *2* bambolla, vulgaridad presuntuosa. *3 adj.* falso, de imitación.
shoe (shu) *s.* zapato, bota, botina; calzado: *in another's shoes*, en el pellejo de otro: ~ *polish*, crema o betún para los zapatos. *2* herradura. *3* suela [de trineo]. *4* zapato [de ancla; de freno]; galga [de carruaje]. *5* llanta [de rueda]; cubierta [de neumático]. *6* azuche, contera, regatón.
shoe (to) *tr.* calzar [a una pers.]. *2* herrar [a un animal]. *3* enllantar [una rueda]. *4* poner azuche o regatón a. ¶ *Pret.* y *p. p.: shod.*
shoeblack (-blæk) *s.* limpiabotas.
shoehorn (-jo^rn) *s.* calzador.
shoemaker (-meikø^r) *s.* zapatero.
shoer (shu·ø^r) *s.* herrador.
shoeshine (-shain) *s.* brillo, lustre que se da a los zapatos. *2* limpiabotas.
shone (shoun) *pret.* y *p. p.* de TO SHINE.
shoo (shu) *interj.* ¡so!, ¡oxe!; ¡fuera!
shoo (to) *tr.* oxear; ahuyentar.
shook (shuk) *pret.* de TO SHAKE.
shoot (shut) *s.* BOT. vástago, pimpollo, renuevo, retoño. *2* conducto inclinado [para granos, carbón, etc.]. *3* concurso de tiro; tiro al blanco, tirada. *4* cacería. *5* punzada [dolor].
shoot (to) *tr.* herir o matar [con un proyectil]; fusilar. *2* disparar, tirar, lanzar, arrojar, despedir. *3* vaciar, verter, precipitar. *4* sacar, proyectar, empujar hacia afuera. *5* recorrer, bajar rápidamente. *6* echar [brotes, renuevos]. *7* correr, descorrer [un cerrojo, un pestillo]. *8* disparar [una instantánea], fotografiar, filmar. *9* DEP. chutar, disparar. *10* esmaltar, salpicar. *11 to* ~ *down*, derribar a tiros. *12 to* ~ *off*, descargar [un arma]. *13 to* ~ *out*, extender [sus ramas un árbol]. *14 to* ~ *trouble*, localizar desperfectos o averías.
16 intr. tirar, hacer fuego. *17* cazar, ir de caza. *18* pasar, moverse rápidamente. *19* salir, proyectarse, extenderse, elevarse. *20* salir, en chorro. *21* brotar, retoñar, tallecer, crecer. *22* latir,

punzar [un dolor]. *23 to* ~ *at*, tirar a, disparar contra. *24 to* ~ *up*, crecer, brotar [las plantas]; alzarse, elevarse.
¶ *Pret.* y *p. p.: shot.*
shooting (-ing) *s.* caza con escopeta. *2* acción de tirar o de matar a tiros; tiro, tiros, tiroteo; fusilamiento. *3* CINEM. filmación, rodaje. *4* adj. ~ *gallery*, tiro al blanco [lugar]; ~ *star*, estrella fugaz; ~ *pain*, punzada [dolor].
shop (shap) *s.* tienda, comercio, almacén, taller, negocio, ocupación: *to shut up* ~, cerrar la tienda; fig. dejar de hacer algo; *to talk* ~, hablar de negocios o de asuntos profesionales [fuera de sazón]. *2* fig. institución, establecimiento.
shop (to) *intr.* comprar en tiendas: *to go shopping*, ir de compras. *2 tr.* mandar [un auto, etc.] al taller de reparaciones. ¶ *Pret.* y *p. p.: shopped*; *ger.: -pping.*
shopboard (-bo^rd) *s.* mostrador de tienda.
shopgirl (-gø^rl) *s.* muchacha de tienda, dependienta.
shopkeeper (kipø^r) *s.* tendero.
shoplifter (liftø^r) *s.* rastro de tiendas; mechera.
shoplifting (-lifting) *s.* ratería en una tienda.
shopman (-mæn) *s.* tendero. *2* mancebo de tienda, dependiente.
shopping district *s.* barrio comercial.
shopwalker (-wokø^r) *s.* empleado de un comercio que vigila a los demás y atiende a los compradores.
shopwindow (-windou) *s.* escaparate de tienda.
shore (sho^r) *s.* orilla [del mar, de un río, de un lago], costa, playa, ribera: *in* ~, MAR. junto a tierra; *on* ~, en tierra. *2* ALBAÑ., MAR. puntal, escora *3* MIN. entibo.
shore (to) *tr.* apuntalar, escorar, estibar.
shoreless (sho·^rlis) *adj.* sin ribera, ilimitado.
shoring (sho·ring) *s.* apuntalamiento, puntales.
shorn (sho·^rn) *p. p.* de TO SHEAR. *2 adj.* mocho.
short (sho·^rt) *adj.* corto [de poca extensión, longitud, duración o entidad, que no llega o alcanza]; breve, escaso, poco: ~ *circuit*, ELECT. corto circuito; ~ *cut*, atajo; ~ *ton*, tonelada de 2.000 libras [907 kg.]; ~ *wave*, ELECT. onda corta; *to be* ~ *of*, estar falto o escaso de; estar lejos de, no alcanzar, no corresponder a; *to run* ~ *of*, acabársele a uno algo; *on* ~ *notice*, prontamente; *on* ~ *term*, a corto plazo. *2* bajo [de poca estatura]. *3* breve, sucinto: *to be* ~, para abreviar. *4* ANAT. falsa [costilla]. *5* flaca [memoria]. *6* acelerado [pulso]. *7* anhelosa [respiración]. *8* seco, brusco. *9* pronto [genio]. *10* seco, sin diluir [licor]. *11* quebradizo, friable. *12* FONÉT. breve.
13 adv. brevemente, cortamente; bruscamente, en seco: *to cut* ~, interrumpir bruscamente; abreviar; *to stop* ~, parar en seco. *14* COM. al descubierto. *15 to fall* ~, escasear, faltar; no alcanzar el blanco, el objeto, etc.; fracasar. *16* ~ *of*, excepto, si no, a menos que.
17 s. lo corto, lo breve: *for* ~, para abreviar; *in* ~, en resumen. *18* COM. venta al descubierto. *19* CINEM. película corta. *20* forma abreviada: ~ *for*, forma abreviada de.
shortage (-idÿ) *s.* escasez, falta, carestía. *2* falta, merma, déficit.
shortbread (-bred) *s.* torta dulce y quebradiza.
short-breathed *adj.* corto de resuello, asmático.
shortcoming (-køming) *s.* defecto, falta, negligencia. *2* limitación, insuficiencia.
short-dated *adj.* a corta fecha.

shorten (to) (-øn) *tr.* acortar, reducir, abreviar. *2* cercenar. *3* hacer friable [la pastelería] con mantequilla, manteca, etc. *4 intr.* acortarse.

shorthand (-jænd) *s.* taquigrafía. *2 adj.* taquigráfico.

short-handed *adj.* que carece del número suficiente de criados, operarios, auxiliares, etc.

shortish (-ish) *adj.* algo corto, algo pequeño.

short-legged *adj.* de piernas cortas.

short-lived *adj.* efímero, de breve vida.

shortly (-li) *adv.* brevemente. *2* bruscamente. *3* luego, en breve: ~ *before*, poco antes; ~ *after*, poco después.

short-range *adj.* de poco alcance.

shorts (sho·ʳts) *s. pl.* pantalones cortos para deporte. *2* calzoncillos cortos.

short-sighted *adj.* corto de vista, cegato. *2* poco perspicaz.

short-tempered *adj.* irascible, de mal genio.

short-term *adj.* COM. a corto plazo.

short-winded *adj.* corto de resuello.

short-witted *adj.* limitado, corto de alcances.

shot (sha·t) *pret.* y *p. p.* de TO SHOOT. *2 adj.* tornasolado, matizado. *3 s.* tiro, disparo, balazo, saetazo; fig. tentativa; conjetura: *to take a* ~ *at*, disparar un tiro a; probar a. *4* tiro, alcance; distancia: *not by a long* ~, ni por asomo; ni con mucho. *5* proyectil, bala; perdigones. *6* tirador: *good* ~, buen tirador. *7* pop. inyección; trago. *8* golpe, tirada, tacada, jugada [en ciertos juegos]. *9* fotografía, instantánea. *10* DEP. peso [que se lanza].

shotgun (-gøn) *s.* escopeta de caza.

shot-put *s.* DEP. lanzamiento.

should (shud) *pret.* de TO SHALL. ¶ V. SHALL. | V. el cuadro SUBJUNTIVO.

shoulder (shou·ldøʳ) *s.* hombro: ~ *belt*, tahalí; ~ *blade*, paletilla, escápula; ~ *strap*, correa, etc., que pasa por el hombro; *to turn*, o *to give the cold* ~, tratar fríamente, volver la espalda; ~ *to* ~, hombro a hombro, codo a codo; *straight from the* ~, con toda franqueza. *2* codo [de cuadrúpedo]. *3* espaldilla [de cordero]. *4* CARP. espaldón. *5* parte saliente. *6 pl.* espaldas.

shoulder (to) *tr.* echarse sobre las espaldas o al hombro; llevar a hombros. *2* fig. cargar con, tomar sobre sí. *3* MIL. *shoulder arms*, armas al hombro. *4 intr.* empujar con el hombro.

shout (shaut) *s.* grito, exclamación, griterío, aclamación: ~ *of applause*, aclamación.

shout (to) *intr.-tr.* gritar, vocear, dar gritos. *2* vitorear, dar vivas.

shouting (-ing) *s.* gritería. *2* aclamación.

shove (shøv) *s.* empujón. *2* empuje, impulso.

shove (to) *tr.-intr.* empujar, empellar, impeler, dar empujones. *2 tr.* fam. meter. *3 intr.* avanzar dando empujones o a fuerza de remos: *to* ~ *off*, alejarse de la orilla; fig. salir, irse.

shovel (shø·vøl) *s.* pala [herramienta]. *2* palada [lo que coge una pala]. *3* sombrero de teja.

shovel (to) *tr.* traspalar, mover con palas. *2* cavar con pala. *3* meter a paladas. ¶ Pret. y p. p.: *shovel(l)ed;* ger.: *-l(l)ing.*

shovelboard (-boʳd) *s.* especie de juego del tejo.

shovel(l)er (-øʳ) *s.* palero.

show (shou) *s.* presentación, exhibición, muestra, demostración: ~ *bill*, cartel; ~ *case*, vitrina; ~ *window*, escaparate [de tienda]. *2* exposición [artística, comercial, etc.]. *3* espectáculo; función [de teatro, etc.]; sesión [de cine]: ~ *boat*, barco teatro. *4* ostentación, pompa; alarde,

gala: *to make a fine* ~, hacer gran papel; *to make a* ~ *of*, hacer gala de. *5* ficción, falsa apariencia. *6* señal, indicación, prueba. *7* pop. negocio, organización, conjunto, etc.

show (to) *tr.* mostrar, enseñar, exhibir, lucir: *to* ~ *the heels*, huir. *2* sacar, asomar. *3* hacer ver, demostrar, probar. *4* revelar, descubrir, manifestar. *5* indicar, señalar; dar [señales]. *6* guiar, introducir, acompañar: ~ *him in*, hágale pasar. *7* COM. arrojar [como resultado o saldo]. *8 to* ~ *how to*, enseñar a [hacer algo]. *9 to* ~ *up*, destacar; descubrir, desenmascarar. *10 intr.* mostrarse, aparecer, asomar. *11* TEAT. actuar. *12* TEAT. representarse. *13 to* ~ *off*, fachendear, pavonearse. *14 to* ~ *up*, destacarse; comparecer, dejarse ver. ¶ Pret.: *showed;* p. p.: *shown* o *showed.*

showbread (-bred) *s.* SHEWBREAD.

shower (shau·øʳ) *s.* chubasco, chaparrón. *2* lluvia, copia, abundancia. *3* ~ *bath*, ducha.

shower (to) *tr.* regar, mojar. *2* derramar, hacer llover, dar con abundancia. *3 intr.* llover.

showerless (-lis) *adj.* sin lluvia.

showery (-i) *adj.* lluvioso.

showman (shou·mæn) *s.* director de espectáculos. *2* empresario de teatro, circo, etc.

shown (-n) *p. p.* de TO SHOW.

showroom (-rum) *s.* sala de exposición. *2* sala de muestras.

showy (-i) *adj.* vistoso, ostentoso, lujoso, suntuoso. *2* chillón, llamativo.

shrank (shrænk) *pret.* de TO SHRINK.

shred (shred) *s.* tira, jirón, andrajo, colgajo. *2* triza, fragmento.

shred (to) *tr.* hacer tiras, jirones o trizas. *2* cortar, desmenuzar. ¶ Pret. y p. p.: *shredded* o *shred;* ger.: *shredding.*

shrew (shru) *s.* arpía, mujer de mal genio. *2* ZOOL.ʹ musaraña, musgaño.

shrewd (shrud) *adj.* agudo, sagaz, perspicaz, listo, astuto. *2* vivo, penetrante.

shrewdness (-nis) *s.* agudeza, sagacidad, astucia.

shrewish (shru·ish) *adj.* regañón, mal humorado.

shrewmouse (-maus) *s.* ZOOL. musaraña, musgaño.

shriek (shrik) *s.* chillido, grito agudo, alarido.

shriek (to) *intr.* chillar, gritar.

shrievalty (shri·valti) *s.* cargo de SHERIFF.

shrift (shrift) *s.* confesión [de los pecados]. *2 to make short* ~ *of*, fam. despachar de prisa.

shrike (shraik) *s.* ORN. alcaudón.

shrill (shril) *adj.* agudo, penetrante, estridente, chillón.

shrill (to) *tr.-intr.* chillar.

shrilly (-i) *adv.* chillonamente.

shrimp (shrimp) *s.* ZOOL. camarón, quisquilla. *2* desp. enano, hombrecillo.

shrine (shrain) *s.* urna, relicario, sepulcro de santo; altar, capilla, santuario.

shrine (to) *tr.* TO ENSHRINE.

shrink (shrink) *s.* contracción, encogimiento.

shrink (to) *intr.* escoger, contraerse. *2* acortarse, estrecharse, disminuir, mermar. *3* encogerse, retroceder, estremecerse [por miedo, horror, etc.], huir [de]. *4 tr.* encoger, contraer, reducir, mermar. ¶ Pret.: *shrank* o *shrunk;* p. p.: *shrunk* o *shrunken.*

shrinkage (-idȳ) *s.* encogimiento, reducción. *2* COM. merma, pérdida.

shrive (to) (shraiv) *tr.* ant. confesar, oír en confesión. *3 intr.-ref.* confesarse. ¶ Pret.: *shrived* o *shrove;* p. p.: *shrived* o *shriven.*

shrivel (to) (shri·vøl) *tr.* arrugar, fruncir; encoger. *2* marchitar. *3 intr.* arrugarse, avellanarse, resecarse, encogerse, encarrujarse. *4* marchitarse. ¶ Pret. y p. p.: *shrivel(l)ed*; ger.: *-l(l)ing*.

shriven (shri·vøn) *p. p.* de TO SHRIVE.

shroud (shraud) *s.* mortaja, sudario. *2* manto, envoltura.

shroud (to) *tr.* amortajar. *2* envolver, cubrir.

shrove (shrouv) *pret.* de TO SHRIVE.

Shrove *s.* [sólo en composición] *Shrove Tuesday*, etc., martes, etc., de carnaval.

Shrovetide *s.* carnaval, carnestolendas.

shrub (shrøb) *s.* arbusto. *2* cierto licor.

shrubbery (-øri) *s.* arbustos. *2* plantación o grupo de arbustos.

shrubby (-i) *adj.* arbustivo. *2* cubierto de arbustos. *3* raquítico.

shrug (shrøg) *s.* encogimiento de hombros.

shrug (to) *tr.* encoger [los hombros]. *2 intr.* encogerse de hombros.

shrunk (shrønk) *pret.* y *p. p.* de TO SHRINK.

shrunken (-øn) *p. p.* de TO SHRINK.

shuck (shøk) *s.* cáscara, vaina, hollejo, zurrón. *2* (E.U.) concha [de ostra].

shuck (to) *tr.* descascarar, pelar, desvainar, deshollejar. *2* desbullar.

shudder (shø·dø^r) *s.* temblor, estremecimiento.

shudder (to) *intr.* estremecerse. *2* tiritar.

shuffle (shø·føl) *s.* barajadura. *2* turno de barajar. *3* mezcla, confusión. *4* arrastramiento de pies. *5* evasiva, embuste.

shuffle (to) *tr.* barajar, revolver. *2* meter [entre otras cosas]. *3* arrastrar, restregar [los pies]. *4* mover de un lado a otro. *5 to* ~ *off*, quitarse, desprenderse de. *6 to* ~ *up*, hacer [algo] de cualquier modo. *7 intr.* barajar los naipes. *8* arrastrar o restregar los pies: *to* ~ *along*, ir arrastrando los pies; ir tirando. *9* andar con evasivas o embustes.

shun (to) (shøn) *tr.* rehuir, esquivar, eludir, evitar. *2* retraerse, apartarse de.

shunt (-t) *s.* desviación. *2* FERROC. desvío. *3* ELECT. derivación, shunt.

shunt (to) *tr.* desviar, poner a un lado. *2* FERROC. desviar, apartar. *3* ELECT. poner en derivación. *4 intr.* desviarse.

shunter (shø·ntø^r) *s.* FERROC. (Ingl.) guardaagujas.

shut (shøt) *p. p.* de TO SHUT. *2 adj.* cerrado.

shut (to) *tr.* cerrar [una puerta, un abanico, los ojos, la boca, etc.]. *2* tapar, obstruir. *3* encerrar. *4* pillar, coger [un dedo, etc., en una puerta]. *5* excluir. *6 to* ~ *down*, cerrar [una fábrica]. *7 to* ~ *in*, encerrar. *8 to* ~ *off*, cortar [el gas, el agua, etc.]. *9 to* ~ *out*, impedir la entrada de; ocultar a la vista. *10 to* ~ *up*, cerrar bien; obstruir; encerrar, aprisionar; hacer callar. *11 intr.* cerrarse, cerrar. *12 to* ~ *down*, parar [una fábrica]. *13 to* ~ *up*, callarse. ¶ Pret. y p. p.: *shut*; ger.: *-tting*.

shutdown (-daun) *s.* cierre, paro.

shutout (-aut) *s.* DEP. triunfo en que el contrario no marca ningún tanto.

shutter (-ø^r) *s.* cerrador. *2* postigo, persiana, contraventana; cierre metálico [de escaparate]. *3* cierre, obturador.

shuttle (shø·tøl) *s.* lanzadera.

shuttlecock (-kak) *s.* volante, rehilete.

shy (shai) *adj.* tímido, asustadizo. *2* recatado. *3* retraído, arisco. *4* cauteloso, prudente. *5* que escapa, rehuye o evita. *6* fam. (E.U.) falto, escaso.

7 s. huida, respingo [del caballo]. *8* sobresalto. *9* tiro, echada; ensayo, prueba.

shy (to) *intr.* hacerse a un lado, retroceder [ante algo]; respingar [el caballo]. *2 tr.* evitar, eludir. *3* lanzar, arrojar. ¶ Pret. y p. p.: *shied*.

Shylock (-lak) *s.* fig. usurero.

shyness (-nis) *s.* timidez. *2* vergüenza, recato. *3* esquivez, reserva.

shyster (-stø^r) *s.* (E.U.) trapisondista.

si (si) *s.* MÚS. si.

Siamese (saiami·š) *adj.-s.* siamés.

Siberian (saibi·rian) *adj.-s.* siberiano.

sibilant (si·bilant) *adj.* sibilante.

sibilate (si·bileit) *tr.* pronunciar con *s* inicial.

sibyl (si·bil) *s.* sibila. *2* adivina.

sibylline (si·bilain) *adj.* sibilino, sibilítico.

sic (sik) *adv.* lat. sic.

sicarian (sikei·rian) *s.* sicario.

siccative (si·kativ) *adj.-s.* secante [que seca].

Sicilian (sisi·lian) *adj.-s.* siciliano, sículo.

sick (sik) *adj.-s.* enfermo: *the* ~, los enfermos. *2* de enfermo o de enfermedad. *3* mareado, con náuseas: *to be* ~ *at the stomach*, tener náuseas. *4* anheloso; nostálgico: *to be* ~ *for*, suspirar por. *5* asqueado, cansado, harto. *6* viciado, malsano. *7* pálido, débil. *8* ~ *at heart*, acongojado, angustiado.

sicken (to) (-øn) *tr.* enfermar, poner enfermo. *2* dar asco o náuseas. *3* cansar, hartar; empalagar. *4* debilitar. *5 intr.* enfermar, ponerse enfermo. *6* nausear, tener asco. *7* cansarse, hartarse. *8* debilitarse.

sickening (-øning) *adj.* nauseabundo. *2* hastioso. *3* enfermo. *4* que pone enfermo.

sickish (-ish) *adj.* bascoso. *2* nauseabundo.

sickle (si·køl) *s.* hoz, segadera, segur.

sickly (si·kli) *adj.* enfermizo, achacoso. *2* insaluble. *3* empalagoso. *4* débil, lánguido, pálido.

sickness (-nis) *s.* enfermedad, mal, indisposición. *2* náusea, mareo. *3* hastío.

side (said) *s.* lado, costado, parte: *by the* ~ *of*, al lado de, junto a: *on all sides*, por todos lados, por todas partes; *on his shore* ~, por parte de madre; *right* o *wrong* ~ *of a cloth*, haz o envés [de una tela]. *2* orilla, margen. *3* falda, ladera. *4* GEOM. lado; cara. *5* MAR. costado, borda, banda. *6* lado, parte, partido, facción, bando: *to take sides with*, tomar partido por. *7* ENCUAD. tapa.

8 adj. lateral; de lado, oblicuo; incidental, secundario: ~ *door*, puerta lateral; puerta excusada; ~ *glance*, mirada de soslayo; ~ *issue*, cuestión secundaria; ~ *light*, luz lateral; detalle o ilustración incidental; ~ *table*, mesa auxiliar; trinchero; ~ *wiskers*, patillas, chuletas.

side (to) *tr.* ponerse, ir o estar al lado de. *2* echar a un lado. *3 intr. to* ~ *with*, tomar partido por, ser de la opinión de.

sideboard (sai·dbo^{r}d) *s.* aparador, copero, alacena.

sideburns (-bø·^{r}ns) *s. pl.* patillas, chuletas.

sidecar (sai·dka^r) *s.* sidecar.

sideface (sai·dfeis) *s.* perfil, rostro de perfil.

sidelong (-long) *adj.* lateral; oblicuo. *2* de soslayo. *3 adv.* lateralmente; oblicuamente.

sidereal (saidi·rial) *adj.* sideral, sidéreo.

siderite (si·dørait) *s.* MINER. siderita, siderosa.

siderurgy (si·dørø^{r}ÿi) *s.* siderurgia.

sidesaddle (sai·dsædøl) *s.* silla para montar a mujeriegas. *2 adv.* a mujeriegas.

sideslip (-slip) *s.* AUTO., AVIA. patinazo o deslizamiento lateral.

side-step (to) *intr.* hacerse a un lado. *2 tr.* esquivar, evitar.

sidetrack (sai·dtræk) *s.* FERROC. vía muerta, apartadero.

sidetrack (to) *tr.* FERROC. desviar, apartar.

sidewalk (sai·dwok) *s.* acera, *vereda.

sideward(s (sai·dwø^{r}dš) *adv.* de lado, hacia un lado.

sideways (sai·dueiš), **sidewise** (-uaiš) *adj.* dirigido hacia un lado. *2* indirecto. *3 adv.* de lado. *4* oblicuamente. *5* de soslayo, indirectamente.

siding (sai·aing) *s.* FERROC. apartadero, desvío. *2* adhesión a un partido, a un aopinión.

sidle (to) (sai·døl) *intr.* andar de lado, con timidez o furtivamente.

siege (sidỹ) *s.* sitio, asedio, cerco; ~ *artillery*, artillería de sitio.

sienite (sai·ønait) *s.* GEOL. sienita.

sienna (sie·na) *s.* tierra de Siena.

sierra (sie·ra) *s.* (E.U.) GEOGR. sierra.

siesta (sie·sta) *s.* siesta.

sieve (siv) *s.* cedazo, tamiz.

sieve (to) *tr.* TO SIFT.

sift (to) (sift) *tr.* cerner, tamizar. *2* espolvorear [con cedazo]. *3* separar, entresacar.

sifter (si·ftø^r) *s.* cernedor, tamiz, harnero.

siftings (si·ftings) *s. pl.* cerniduras, granzas.

sigh (sai) *s.* suspiro.

sigh (to) *intr.* suspirar: *to ~ for*, suspirar por, anhelar. *2 tr.* decir suspirando. *3* lamentar.

sight (sait) *s.* vista, visión [sentido, órgano; acción de ver]: *to catch ~ of*, avistar, alcanzar a ver; *to come in ~*, aparecer; *at ~*, *on ~*, a primera vista; *by ~*, de vista; *eight days after ~*, COM. a ocho días vista. *2* vislumbre, atisbo. *3* vista, espectáculo. *4* aspecto. *5* visión, esperpento. *6* pínula. *7* mira, alza [de arma]. *8* opinión, parecer. *9* fam. la mar de. *10 pl.* sitios o cosas interesantes [de un lugar]. *11 adj.* visual. *12* COM. ~ *draft*, giro o letra a la vista. *13* ~ *reading*, lectura a primera vista.

sight (to) *tr.-intr.* ver, mirar, observar. *2 tr.* avistar, vislumbrar. *3* apuntar [un cañón, un fusil].

sightless (-lis) *adj.* ciego [que no ve]. *2* invisible.

sightly (-li) *adj.* hermoso, vistoso, agradable a la vista.

sightseeing (-siing) *s.* turismo; visita de sitios o cosas interesantes.

sigillography (sidỹila·grafi) *s.* sigilografía.

sigla (si·gla) *s.* sigla.

sigma (si·gma) *s.* sigma [letra griega].

sigmoid (sigmoi·d) *adj.* sigmoideo.

sign (sain) *s.* signo, señal, seña; muestra, indicio: ~ *language*, dactilología; ~ *manual*, firma de propio puño; *to show sings of*, dar muestras de; *by signs*, por señas. *2* ASTR. signo [del Zodíaco]. *3* rastro, vestigio. *4* muestra, letrero.

sign (to) *tr.* signar. *2* hacer seña de. *3* firmar la cesión de. *4* contratar [a uno]. *5 intr.* hacer señas. *6* RADIO. *to ~ off*, terminar una emisión.

signal (si·gnal) *s.* señal [para indicar algo]; seña. *2* signo, indicio. *3 adj.* señalado, notable. *4* de señales: ~ *code*, código de señales.

signal (to) *tr.-intr.* señalar, indicar. ¶ Pret. y p. p.: *signal(l)ed*; ger.: *-nal(l)ing*.

signalize (to) (-aiš) *tr.* señalar, distinguir, particularizar.

signalman (-mæn) *s.* FERROC. guardavía.

signalment (-mønt) *s.* filiación, señas personales.

signatory (si·gnatori) *s.-adj.* signatario.

signature (-chø^r) *s.* firma, rúbrica. *2* IMPR., MÚS. signatura. *3* RADIO. notas de sintonía.

signboard (sai·nbo^{r}d) *s.* letrero, muestra.

signer (-ø^r) *s.* firmante.

signet (si·gnit) *s.* sello, signáculo, estampilla.

significance, -cy (signi·fikans, -i) *s.* significación, significado. *2* importancia.

significant (-ant) *adj.* significante, significativo. *2* importante. *3* ARIT. significativa [cifra].

signification (-ei·shøn) *s.* significación, significado. *2* notificación.

significative (signi·fikeitiv) *adj.* significativo. *2* representativo, simbólico.

signify (to) (si·gnifai) *tr.* significar. *2* indicar, manifestar, notificar. *3 intr.* importar: *what does it ~?*, ¿qué importa? ¶ Pret. y p. p.: *signified*.

signory (si·ñøri) *s.* HIST. señoría [de Venecia, etc.].

signpost (sai·npoust) *s.* poste indicador.

silage (sai·lidỹ) *s.* forraje conservado en silo.

silence (sai·løns) *s.* silencio: ~ *gives consent*, quien calle otorga. *2* reserva, secreto. *3 interj.* ¡silencio!

silence (to) *tr.* imponer silencio, hacer callar.

silencer (-ø^r) *s.* silenciador.

silent (sai·lønt) *adj.* silencioso; mudo: ~ *partner*, COM. socio comanditario; *to be ~*, callar, callarse. *2* callado, taciturno. *3* sigiloso.

silex (sai·leks) *s.* MINER. sílex.

silhouette (silue·t) *s.* silueta.

silhouette (to) *tr.* presentar en silueta.

silica (si·lika) *s.* MINER. sílice.

silicate (si·likeit) *s.* QUÍM. silicato.

siliceous (sili·shøs) *adj.* silíceo.

silicon (si·likan) *s.* QUÍM. silicio.

silicosis (silikou·sis) *s.* MED. silicosis.

silique (sili·k) *s.* BOT. silicua.

silk (silk) *s.* seda [materia, hilo, tejido]: ~ *cotton*, seda vegetal; ~ *growing*, sericultura; ~ *hat*, sombrero de copa; ~ *twist*, torzal. *2 pl.* sedería, géneros de seda.

silken (-øn) *adj.* de seda. *2* sedoso, sedeño. *3* suave, delicado. *4* meloso [lenguaje]. *5* lujoso, vestido de seda.

silkman (-mæn) *s.* sedero.

silkworm (-uø^{r}m) *s.* gusano de seda.

silky (-i) *adj.* de seda, sedoso. *2* suave. *3* lustroso.

sill (sil) *s.* umbral. *2* antepecho [de ventana]. *3* ARQ. carrera, solera.

silliness (si·linis) *s.* tontería, simpleza.

silly (si·li) *adj.* tonto, necio. *2* absurdo, disparatado. *3* rústico, sencillo.

silo (sai·lou) *s.* silo, silero.

silt (silt) *s.* cieno, sedimento [de las aguas].

silt (to) *tr.-intr.* obstruir u obstruirse con el cieno.

Silurian (siliu·rian) *adj.-s.* silúrico.

silvan (si·lvan) *adj.-s.* SYLVAN.

silver (si·lvø^r) *s.* plata [metal, moneda; objetos]. *2* color de plata. *3 adj.* de plata, argentado, argentino, plateado: ~ *fox*, zorro plateado; ~ *nitrate*, nitrato de plata; ~ *plating*, plateado, plateadura; ~ *wedding*, bodas de plata.

silver (to) *tr.* platear. *2* azogar [un espejo]. *3 intr.* volverse plateado.

silverfish (-fish) *s.* ENT. lepisma.

silver-haired *adj.* cano, de cabellos blancos.

silvering (-ing) *s.* baño de plata; plateado. *2* azogado [de un espejo].

silver-plated *adj.* plateado.

silversmith (-smiz) *s.* platero, orfebre.

silverware (-ue^r) *s.* objetos de plata.

silvery (-i) *s.* plateado, argentino.

silviculture (silvikø·lchø^r) *s.* silvicultura.
simian (si·mian) *adj.* simiesco. *2 s.* ZOOL. simio.
similar (si·mila^r) *adj.* similar, semejante.
simile (si·mili) *s.* RET. símil.
similitude (simi·litiud) *s.* similitud. *2* símil, alegoría. *3* imagen, semejanza.
similor (si·milø^r) *s.* similor.
simitar (si·mita^r) *s.* cimitarra.
simmer (to) (si·mø^r) *tr.* hacer cocer a fuego lento. *2 intr.* hervir con poco fuego; estar a punto de hervir. *3* fig. hervir [de ira, etc.].
simoniac (simou·niæk) *adj.-s.* simoníaco.
simoom (simu·m), **simoon** (-n) *s.* simún [viento].
simper (si·mpø^r) *s.* sonrisa boba o afectada.
simper (to) *intr.* sonreír tontamente o con afectación.
simple (si·mpøl) *adj.* simple. *2* mero. *3* sencillo. *4* llano [accesible, sin presunción]. *5* humilde, plebeyo. *6* insignificante. *7* ingenuo. *8* mentecato. *9* MAT. de primer grado [ecuación]; incompleja [fracción]. *10 s.* simple, simplón. *11* cosa o idea simple. *12* pers. de humilde condición.
simple-hearted *adj.* sencillo, franco, sincero.
simple-minded *adj.* sencillo, cándido. *2* tonto.
simpleton (-tøn) *s.* simplón, bobo, papanatas.
simplicity (simpli·siti) *s.* simplicidad. *2* sencillez. *3* llaneza. *4* ingenuidad. *5* simpleza, bobería.
simplification (simplifikei·shøn) *s.* simplificación.
simplify (to) (si·mplifai) *tr.* simplificar. ¶ Pret. y p. p.: *simplified.*
simulacrum (simiulei·krøm), *pl.* **-cra** (-kra) *s.* simulacro.
simulate (to) (si·miuleit) *tr.* simular; imitar.
simulation (simiulei·shøn) *s.* simulación; imitación.
simulator (si·miuleitø^r) *s.* simulador.
simultaneity (simøltanı·iti) *s.* simultaneidad.
simultaneous (simøltei·niøs) *adj.* simultáneo.
sin (sin) *s.* pecado: ~ *offering,* sacrificio expiatorio.
sin (to) *intr.* pecar. ¶ Pret. y p. p.: *sinned;* ger.: *-nning.*
sinapism (si·napišm) *s.* sinapismo.
since (sins) *adv.* desde, desde entonces; ha, hace tiempo: ~ *when?,* ¿desde cuándo?; *long* ~, hace mucho tiempo. *2 prep.* desde, después de. *3 conj.* desde que, después que. *4* ya que, puesto que, en vista de.
sincere (sinsı·^r) *adj.* sincero. *2* verdadero, real.
sincereness (sinsı·^rnis), **sincerity** (sinse·riti) *s.* sinceridad, franqueza.
sinciput (si·nsipøt) ANAT. coronilla.
sine (sain) *s.* MAT. seno.
sinecure (sai·nikiu^r) *s.* sinecura, prebenda. *2* ECLES. beneficio simple.
sinew (si·niu) *s.* ANAT. tendón. *2* fuerza muscular. *3* energía, fibra, nervio, fortaleza.
sinew (to) *tr.* fortalecer.
sinewy (-i) *adj.* nervoso, nervudo. *2* fuerte, vigoroso.
sinful (si·nful) *adj.* pecador, pecaminoso.
sing (to) (sing) *tr.-intr.* cantar: *to* ~ *out,* vocear; *to* ~ *out of tune,* desafinar; *to* ~ *to sleep,* arrullar, adormecer. *2 intr.* murmurar [el agua]; silbar [un proyectil, el viento]; zumbar [los oídos]. ¶ Pret.: *sang* o *sung;* p. p.: *sung.*
singe (to) (sindŷ) *tr.* chamuscar, socarrar, sollamar. *2* fig. perjudicar. ¶ Ger.: *singeing.*
singeing (-ing) *s.* chamusco, socarra.
singer (-gø^r) *s.* cantante, cantor, cantatriz. *2* pájaro cantor.
Singhalese (singali·š) *adj.-s.* cingalés.
singing bird (si·nging) *s.* pájaro cantor.
singing master *s.* maestro de canto.
single (si·ngøl) *adj.* único: *not a* ~, ni un solo. *2* célibe, de celibato: ~ *man,* soltero; ~ *life,* vida de celibato. *3* sencillo, simple: COM. ~ *entry,* partida simple. *4* de una sola pieza, movimiento, etc. *5* individual. *6* honrado, sincero. *7* ~ *combat,* singular combate. *8* ~ *file,* hilera, fila india. *9 s. pl.* TENIS. individuales.
single (to) *tr.* singularizar, distinguir; designar especialmente; escoger. | gralte. con *out* o *from.*
single-acting *adj.* MEC. de simple efecto.
single-eyed *adj.* tuerto. *2* perspicaz. *3* sincero.
single-handed *adj.* solo, sin ayuda. *2* con una sola mano.
single-hearted *adj.* sencillo de corazón.
single-minded *adj.* sencillo, sin doblez. *2* de un solo propósito o idea.
single-phase *adj.* ELECT. monofásico.
single-pole *adj.* ELECT. unipolar.
singlet (si·nglit) *s.* camiseta [prenda].
singleton (si·ngøltøn) *s.* BRIDGE única carta de un palo.
singsong (si·nsong) *s.* sonsonete, tonillo. *2* (Ingl.) fam. reunión para cantar. *3 adj.* monótono.
singular (si·ngiula^r) *adj.* singular. *2* curioso, estrafalario. *3* individual. *4 s.* GRAM. número singular.
singularity (singiulæ·riti) *s.* singularidad. *2* individualidad. *3* peculiaridad.
singularize (to) (si·ngiularaiš) *tr.* singularizar, distinguir. *2* particularizar, individualizar.
Sinic (si·nik) *adj.-s.* sínico, chino, chinesco.
sinister (si·nistø^r) *adj.* siniestro, izquierdo. *2* siniestro, avieso, funesto.
sink (sink) *s.* sumidero, sentina, albañal. *2* fregadero. *3* depresión, hoyo.
sink (to) *tr.* hundir, sumir, sumergir, echar a pique. *2* ahondar, excavar, grabar; abrir [un pozo]. *3* bajar [la voz, la mano, etc.]. *5* hundir, arruinar. *6* hundir, clavar. *7* deprimir, abatir. *8* ignorar, olvidar. *9 intr.* hundirse, sumergirse; irse a pique. *10* bajar [descender, disminuir]. *11* desaparecer. *12* decaer, declinar. *13* caer; dejarse caer. *14* abatirse. *15* engolfarse, embeberse. *16* penetrar. *17* grabarse [en la memoria]. *18* ARQ. asentarse. *19 to* ~ *down,* bajar; penetrar profundmente. ¶ Pret.: *sank* o *sunk;* p. p.: *sunk* o *sunken.*
sinker (si·nkø^r) *s.* plomo [de caña de pescar]. *2* grabador en hueco.
sinking fund (-ing) *s.* COM. fondo de amortización.
sinless (si·nlis) *adj.* puro, libre de pecado.
sinner (si·nø^r) *s.* pecador, pecadora.
Sinology (saina·loŷi) *s.* sinología.
sinuate (si·niueit) *adj.* sinuoso. *2* BOT. festoneado.
sinuosity (siniua·siti) *s.* sinuosidad, tortuosidad.
sinuous (si·niuøs) *adj.* sinuoso, tortuoso.
sinus (sai·nøs) *s.* seno [curva]. *2* ZOOL., ANAT., GEOGR. seno.
sinusitis (-aitis) *s.* MED. sinusitis.
sinusoid (-oid) *s.* GEOM. sinusoide.
sip (sip) *s.* sorbo.
sip (to) *tr.-intr.* beber a sorbos. ¶ Pret. y p. p.: *sipped;* ger.: *-pping.*
siphon (sai·føn) *s.* FÍS., ZOOL. sifón.
siphon (to) *tr.* vaciar con sifón. *2 intr.* pasar por un sifón.
sippet (si·pit) *s.* sopita, tostadita [que se moja].
sir (sø^r) *s.* señor [término de cortesía]. *2* (Ingl.) tra-

tamiento que se antepone al nombre de pila de un caballero o baronet.
sire (sai^r) *s.* señor [tratamiento del soberano]. *2* progenitor. *3* animal padre, semental.
siren (sai·røn) *s.* MIT, sirena. *2* buena cantatriz. *3* mujer seductora. *4* sirena [pito].
sirenian (sairi·nian) *adj.-s.* ZOOL. sirenio.
Sirian (si·rian) *adj.-s.* siríaco, sirio.
Sirius (si·riøs) *s.* ASTR. Sirio.
sirloin (sø·^rloin) *s.* solomillo, solomo.
sirocco (sira·kou) *s.* siroco.
sirup (si·røp) *s.* SYRUP.
sisal (si·sal) *s.* sisal, pita.
sister (si·stø^r) *s.* hermana. *2* sor, monja. *3* enfermera jefe; enfermera. *4* adj. ~ *language,* lengua hermana.
sisterhood (-jud) *s.* hermandad [parentesco entre hermanas]. *2* conjunto de hermanas. *3* cofradía de mujeres.
sister-in-law *s.* hermana política, cuñada.
Sistine (si·stin) *adj.* sixtino.
sistrum (si·strøm) *s.* MÚS. sistro.
sit (to) (sit) *tr.* sentar, asentar [colocar en asiento]. *2* montar [un caballo]. *3* to ~ out, aguantar hasta el fin de; estar sin tomar parte en; quedarse más tiempo que [otro]. *4* intr. sentarse, estar sentado. *5* posarse o empollar [las aves]. *6* estar, permanecer. *7* tener asiento [en un cuerpo o tribunal]; actuar [un juez]. *8* descansar, pesar [sobre]. *9* sentar, caer [bien o mal]. *10* to ~ down, sentarse; establecerse; acampar. *11* to ~ for, representar [un distrito] en el Parlamento; posar, servir de modelo para. *12* to ~ in judgement, querer juzgar a los demás, criticar. *13* to ~ on o upon, deliberar sobre; juzgar; fam. hacer callar; poner en su lugar; desairar. *14* to ~ still, estarse quieto. *15* to ~ up, estar bien sentado; incorporarse [el que estaba echado]; velar, estar levantado.
¶ Pret. y p. p.: *sat;* ger.: *sitting.*
sit-down strike *s.* huelga de brazos caídos.
site (sait) *s.* sitio, escenario [de algo]. *2* asiento, situación [de una población, edificio, etc.].
sitter (si·tø^r) *s.* el que está sentado. *2* el que posa o se hace retratar. *3* ave que empolla.
sitting (si·ting) *s.* acción de sentarse o estar sentado. *2* sentada, asentada: *at one* ~, de una sentada. *3* sesión. *4* empolladura; pollazón. *5* adj. sentado. *6* para sentarse: ~ *room,* sala, estancia. *7* BOT. sésil.
situate (si·chueit) *adj.* situado.
situation (sichuei·shøn) *s.* situación. *2* posición, ubicación. *3* colocación, empleo.
sitz bath (sits) *s.* baño de asiento.
six (siks) *adj.-s.* seis: ~ *o'clock,* las seis.
sixfold (-fould) *adj.* séxtuplo. *2 adv.* seis veces.
sixpence (-pøns) *s.* seis peniques.
sixpenny (-peni) *adj.* de a seis peniques. *2* mezquino, de poco valor.
sixteen (-ti·n) *adj.-s.* dieciséis.
sixteenth (-tinz) *adj.-s.* decimosexto, dieciseisavo. *2* dieciséis [día].
sixth (-z) *adj.-s.* sexto. *2* seis [día]. *3 s.* MÚS. sexta.
sixtieth (-tiiz) *adj.-s.* sexagésimo.
sixty (-ti) *adj.-s.* sesenta.
sizable (sai·šabøl) *adj.* regular, de tamaño proporcionado.
sizar (sai·ša^r) *s.* (Ingl.) becario [estudiante].
size (saiš) *s.* medida, tamaño, dimensiones. *2* estatura, talla. *3* número [de calzado, etc.]; talla

[de vestido]; calibre [de un tubo, etc.]. *4* sisa, cola, goma, apresto.
size (to) *tr.* disponer, clasificar según tamaño. *2* medir el tamaño de. *3* apreciar, avaluar. *4* ajustar a un tamaño, medida, etc. *5* encolar, sisar, aprestar.
sizzle (si·søl) *s.* sonido chirriante, chisporroteo.
sizzle (to) *intr.* chirriar [al freírse, etc.].
skald (skold) *s.* escaldo.
skate (skeit) *s.* patín [para los pies]. *2* patinaje.
skate (to) *intr.* patinar [sobre patines]: *to ~ on thin ice,* fig. buscar el peligro.
skater (-ø^r) *s.* patinador.
skating (-ing) *s.* patinaje: ~ *ring,* pista de patinaje.
skedaddle (to) (sikidæ·døl) *intr.* fam. huir a la desbandada.
skein (skein) *s.* madeja, cadejo, capillejo.
skeletal (ske·løtal) *adj.* de esqueleto.
skeleton (ske·løtøn) *s.* esqueleto [osamenta; armazón]: ~ *in the cupboard, family* ~, fig. hecho deshonroso o humillante que se oculta a los extraños. *2* esbozo, esquema. *3 adj.* en esqueleto, en armazón. *4* ~ *key,* llave maestra.
skeptic (ske·ptik) *adj.-s.* escéptico.
skepticism (ske·ptisišm) *s.* escepticismo.
sketch (skech) *s.* boceto, esbozo, apunte, croquis. *2* TEAT., MÚS. pieza corta.
sketch (to) *tr.* esbozar, bosquejar, diseñar, hacer un croquis de. *2 intr.* hacer apuntes o bosquejos.
sketchy (-i) *adj.* abocetado. *2* ligero, incompleto, fragmentario.
skew (skiu·) *adj.* oblicuo, inclinado, sesgado. *2* oblicuidad, esviaje.
skew (to) *tr.* sesgar, poner de través. *2* torcer, tergiversar. *3 intr.* oblicuar; desviarse, girar.
skewback (-bæk) *s.* ARQ. salmer.
skewer (-ø^r) *s.* COC. brocheta. *2* HIL. huso.
skewer (to) *tr.* espetar, clavar.
ski (ski·) *s.* esquí.
ski (to) *intr.* esquiar.
skid (skid) *s.* madero, polín, rodillo. *2* calzo. *3* varadera. *4* AVIA. patín. *5* galga, freno. *6* deslizamiento, patinazo [de ruedas]: ~ *chain,* AUTO. cadena para impedir el deslizamiento.
skid (to) *tr.* hacer deslizar sobre maderos, polines, etc. *2* sostener con calzos. *3* proveer de varaderas. *4 intr.* patinar [una rueda]. ¶ Pret. y p. p.: *skidded;* ger.: *-dding.*
skier (ski·ø^r) *s.* esquiador.
skiff (skif) *s.* esquife, botecillo.
skiff (to) *intr.* navegar en esquife.
skilful (ski·lful) *adj.* diestro, hábil; experto, ducho.
skill (skil) *s.* habilidad, destreza, pericia, maña. *3* arte, ciencia.
skilled (-d) *adj.* práctico, experimentado; hábil, experto.
skil(l)less (-lis) *adj.* inexperto.
skim (skim) *s.* acción de espumar o desnatar. *2* espuma, nata. *3 adj.* desnatada [leche].
skim (to) *tr.* espumar, desnatar. *2* examinar rápida o superficialmente. *3* rasar, rozar [tocar ligeramente]. *4 intr.* cubrirse de espuma o nata. ¶ Pret. y p. p.: *skimmed;* ger.: *-mming.*
skimmer (-ø^r) *s.* espumadera.
skimp (to) (skimp) *tr.* escatimar. *2* chapucear. *3 intr.* tacañear. *4* trabajar con poco cuidado.
skin (skin) *s.* piel, cutis, pellejo [de pers.]: *to be only* ~ *and bone,* estar en los huesos; *to save one's* ~, salvar el pellejo; *by the* ~ *of one's teeth,* por un pelo. *2* piel [de animal]. *3* odre. *4* BOT. piel, cáscara, hollejo. *5* telilla, cutícula, pelí-

cula. *6* fam. avaro. *7* fam. tramposo. *8* ~ *game*, fullería.

skin (to) *tr.* desollar, despellejar. *2* fig. desplumar. *3* pelar, mondar. *4* abrir bien [los ojos]. *5* cubrir de piel. *6 intr.* pelarse. *7* cubrirse de piel o tegumento: *to* ~ *over*, cicatrizarse.

skin-deep *adj.* superficial.

skinflint (-flint) *s.* avaro, vampiro.

skink (-k) *s.* ZOOL. escinco.

skinner (-ø^r) *s.* pellejero. *2* desollador. *3* petardista, estafador.

skinniness (-inis) *s.* flacura.

skinny (-i) *adj.* membranoso. *2* flaco, descarnado. *3* tacaño.

skip (skip) *s.* salto, brinco. *2* salto, omisión.

skip (to) *intr.* saltar, brincar. *2* botar, rebotar. *3* fam. largarse. *4 tr.* saltar [salvar de un salto]. *5* escaparse de. *6* intr.-tr. *to skip* o *to* ~ *over*, saltar, pasar por alto. ¶ Pret. y p. p.: *skipped;* ger.: -*pping.*

skipper (-ø^r) *s.* saltador. *2* gusanillo del queso. *3* patrón, capitán [de barco]. *4* DEP. capitán.

skipping rope (-ing) *s.* comba [para saltar].

skirmish (skø·^{r}mish) *s.* escaramuza.

skirmish (to) *intr.* escaramuzar.

skirmisher (-ø^r) *s.* escaramuzador.

skirt (skø^{r}t) *s.* falda, saya; enaguas, refajo. *2* faldón [de una prenda; de la silla de montar]. *3* orilla, margen: *skirts of a town*, suburbios, alrededores, de una población.

skirt (to) *tr.-intr.* bordear, ladear, rodear, circundar. *2 tr.* evitar, bordear [el peligro].

skirting board (-ing) *s.* zócalo, rodapié.

skit (skit) *s.* paso cómico; cuento satírico; parodia, burla, sátira.

skitter (to) (-ø^r) *intr.* ir rozando el agua [un ave marina]. *2* pescar haciendo deslizar el anzuelo sobre el agua.

skittish (-ish) *tr.* asustadizo [caballo]. *2* tímido. *3* retozón, frívolo, caprichoso.

skittle (ski·tøl) *s.* bolo [para jugar]. *2 pl.* juego de bolos.

skittle (to) *intr.* jugar a los bolos.

skua (skiu·a) *s.* ORN. especie de gaviota.

skulk (to) (skølk) *intr.* esconderse, acechar sin ser visto, moverse furtivamente. *2* tr.-intr. huir del trabajo, etc.

skull (skøl) *s.* cráneo; calavera. *2* ANAT. coronilla. *3* cabeza, cerebro.

skullcap (-kæp) *s.* casquete, gorro.

skunk (skønk) *s.* ZOOL. mofeta; zorrillo, mapurite. *2* fig. canalla.

sky (skai) *s.* cielo [firmamento, atmósfera; mansión celestial]: *out of a clear* ~, inesperadamente, de repente. *2* ~ *blue*, color azul celeste.

sky-blue *adj.* azul celeste.

skyey (-i) *adj.* celeste, etéreo.

skylark (-la^{r}k) *s.* ORN. alondra.

skylark (to) *intr.* retozar, triscar, juguetear.

skylight (-lait) *s.* luz del cielo. *2* claraboya, lumbrera, tragaluz.

skyline (-lain) *s.* línea del horizonte; línea de los edificios, árboles, etc., contra el cielo.

skyrocket (-rakit) *s.* cohete volador.

skyrocket (to) *intr.* fam. subir como un cohete.

skysail (-seil) *s.* MAR. periquito.

skyscraper (skreipø^r) *s.* rascacielos.

skyward (s (ua^{r}d(š) *adv.* hacia el cielo. *2 adj.* dirigido hacia el cielo.

slab (slæb) *s.* tabla, plancha, losa, laja. *2* loncha, tajada. *3* costero [de tronco].

slabber (to) (slæ·bø^r) *intr.* babear, salivar.

slack (slæk) *adj.* flojo, laxo. *2* débil, poco firme. *3* lento, tardo. *4* negligente, remiso. *5* COM. encalmado. *6* ~ *water*, agua mansa; repunte de la marea. *7 s.* seno [de un cabo]. *8* flojedad; inactividad, calma. *9* cisco [carbón]. *10 pl.* pantalones anchos.

slack (to) *tr.* aflojar, relajar. *2* reducir, moderar. *3* apagar [la cal]. *4 intr.* aflojar, amainar, ceder, cejar. *5* flojear. *6* huir del trabajo, remolonear. *7 to* ~ *up*, reducir la marcha.

slacken (to) *tr.* moderar, retardar, hacer más lento. *2* aflojar. *3 intr.* ser lento, remiso o negligente.

slacker (-kø^r) *s.* perezoso; remolón.

slag (-læg) *s.* escoria.

slain (slein) *p. p.* de TO SLAY.

slake (to) (sleik) *tr.* apagar [la sed, la cal, etc.]. *2* mojar, refrescar. *3* moderar, calmar. *4 intr.* apagarse [la cal]. *5* desmenuzarse.

slam (slæm) *s.* golpe, portazo. *2* BRIDGE slam, bola.

slam (to) *tr.* cerrar de golpe; poner, dejar, etc., dando un golpe: *to* ~ *the door*, dar un portazo. *2 tr.-intr.* BRIDGE hacer slam. *3 intr.* cerrarse con estrépito. *4* trabajar con ruido. ¶ Pret. y p. p.: *slammed;* ger.: -*mming.*

slander (slæ·ndø^r) *s.* calumnia, difamación.

slander (to) *tr.* calumniar, difamar, denigrar.

slanderous (-øs) *adj.* calumniador, difamador.

slang (slæng) *s.* lenguaje popular. *2* jerga, argot.

slang (to) *tr.* insultar, maltratar de palabra.

slangy (-i) *adj.* de argot.

slant (slænt) *s.* inclinación, oblicuidad; declive. *2* parecer, punto de vista. *3 adj.* oblicuo, inclinado, en declive.

slant (to) *tr.* sesgar, inclinar. *2 intr.* inclinarse, sesgarse.

slanting (-ing) *adj.-s.* SLANT.

slap (slæp) *s.* palmada, manotazo, bofetón. *2* insulto, desaire. *3 adv.* de sopetón, directamente.

slap (to) *tr.* pegar, abofetear, dar una palmada, un manotazo. *2* poner, meter, etc., con prisa o violencia. ¶ Pret. y p. p.: *slapped;* ger.: -*pping.*

slapdash (-dæsh) *adj.* precipitado, atropellado. *2 s.* cosa hecha atropelladamente. *3 adv.* atropelladamente, impetuosamente.

slash (slash) *s.* cuchillada, tajo. *2* cuchillada [en un vestido]. *3* latigazo.

slash (to) *tr.* acuchillar, dar un tajo a; hacer un corte en. *2* fustigar. *3* hacer restallar [un látigo]. *4* rebajar considerablemente [sueldos, precios, etc.].

slat (slæt) *s.* tablilla, listón.

slate (sleit) *s.* pizarra, esquisto. *2* pizarra [para escribir]: ~ *pencil*, pizarrín. *4* (E.U.) lista de candidatos; programa de partido. *5* pizarra [para techar], teja plana. *6* color de pizarra.

slate (to) *tr.* empizarrar, cubrir. *2* POL. (E.U.) poner en lista o programa. *3* criticar, fustigar.

slater (-ø^r) *s.* pizarrero. *2* crítico severo.

slattern (slæ·tø^{r}n) *adj.* descuidado, desaliñado. *2 s.* mujer desaseada, pazpuerca.

slaty (slei·ti) *adj.* pizarreño, esquistoso.

slaughter (slo·tø^r) *s.* muerte, matanza, mortandad. *2* sacrificio [de reses].

slaughter (to) *tr.* matar. *2* sacrificar [reses].

slaughterer (-ø^r) *s.* asesino. *2* matarife.

slaughterhouse (slo·tø^{r}jaus) *s.* matadero.

Slav (slæ·v) *adj.-s.* eslavo.

slave (sleiv) *s.* esclavo, esclava; ~ *trade*, trata de esclavos.

slip

slave (to) *intr.* trabajar como esclavo. 2 *tr.* esclavizar.
slaveholder (sleiˑvjouldøʳ) *s.* dueño de esclavos.
1) slaver (slæˑvøʳ) *s.* mercader de esclavos; negrero. 2 buque negrero.
2) slaver (slæ·vøʳ) *s.* baba. 2 *fig.* adulación.
slaver (to) *intr.* babear. 2 *tr.* babosear.
slavery (sleiˑvøri) *s.* esclavitud, servidumbre. 2 los esclavos.
Slavic (slæˑvik) *adj.* eslavo.
slavish (sleiˑvish) *adj.* servil. 2 bajo, abyecto. 3 esclavizado. 4 tiránico, opresivo.
Slavism (slaˑvišm) *s.* eslavismo.
Slavonian (slavouˑnian) *adj.-s.* esclavonio.
slay (slei) *s.* SLEY.
slay (to) *tr.* matar [quitar la vida]. ¶ Pret.: *slew;* p. p.: *slain.*
slayer (-øʳ) *s.* matador, asesino.
sleazy (slıˑŝi) *adj.* ligero, tenue, delgado.
sled (sled) *s.* narria, rastra, trineo.
sled (to) *tr.* transportar en rastra o trineo.
sledge (sledŷ) *s.* trineo, rastra, narria. 2 *sledge* o ~ *hammer,* macho [martillo], acotillo.
sledge (to) *tr.-intr.* transportar o viajar en trineo. 2 *tr.* golpear, martillar.
sleek (slık) *adj.* liso, bruñido. 2 zalamero, artero.
sleek (to) *tr.* pulir, alisar, asear.
sleeky (slıˑki) *adj.* liso, lustroso. 2 suave, taimado.
sleep (slıp) *s.* sueño [acto o gana de dormir]; descanso, muerte.
sleep (to) *intr.* dormir; *to ~ like a top,* dormir como un lirón; *to ~ on* o *upon,* consultar con la almohada; *to ~ away* o *on,* seguir durmiendo. 2 *tr. to ~ away* o *out,* pasar [un tiempo durmiendo]. 3 *to be slept in,* haber sido ocupada [una cama]. ¶ Pret. y p. p.: *slept.*
sleeper (-øʳ) *s.* durmiente [pers.]. 2 durmiente, vigueta; traviesa [de vía férrea]. 5 FERROC. coche cama. 6 ZOOL. lirón.
sleepiness (-inis) *s.* somnolencia, sueño.
sleeping (-ing) *adj.* durmiente, dormido: ~ *partner,* COM. socio comanditario. 2 de dormir, que hace dormir: ~ *bag,* saco de dormir; ~ *car,* coche cama; ~ *sickness,* MED. enfermedad del sueño.
sleepless (-lis) *adj.* insomne, desvelado. 2 sin dormir.
sleeplessness (-lisnis) *s.* insomnio.
sleepwalker (-wokøʳ) *s.* sonámbulo.
sleepy (-i) *adj.* soñoliento.
sleet (slıt) *s.* cellisca.
sleet (to) *intr.* cellisquear.
sleeve (slıv) *s.* manga [de vestido]: *to laugh in,* o *up, one's ~,* reírse con disimulo, para sus adentros; *up one's ~,* en reserva. 2 MEC. manguito. 3 camisa [incandescente].
sleeveless (slıˑvlis) *adj.* sin mangas.
sleigh (slei·) *s.* trineo: ~ *bell,* cascabel.
sleigh (to) *tr.-intr.* viajar o transportar en trineo.
sleight (slait) *s.* destreza, habilidad. 2 agilidad. 3 ardid, artificio. 4 ~ *of hand,* juego de manos, prestidigitación.
slender (slenˑdøʳ) *adj.* delgado, fino, esbelto. 2 leve, baladí. 3 corto, escaso. 4 frugal.
slept (slept) *pret.* y p. p. de TO SLEEP.
sleuth (sliuz) *s.* sabueso. 2 (E.U.) detective.
sleuthhound (-jaund) *s.* sabueso.
slew (sliu) *pret.* de TO SLAY.
sley (slei) *s.* TEJ. peine.
slice (slais) *s.* rebanada, lonja, rodaja. 2 COC. pala, estrelladera.
slice (to) *tr.* rebanar. 2 tajar, cortar, dividir.

slick (slik) *adj.* fam. diestro, mañoso. 2 astuto, meloso. 3 liso, lustroso. 4 *s.* parte lisa o lustrosa; lugar aceitoso en el agua. 5 *adv.* astutamente. 6 directamente, completamente.
slick (to) *tr.* alisar, pulir. 2 *intr.* componerse, acicalarse. | Gralte. con *up.*
slicker (-øʳ) *s.* timador, embaucador.
slide (slaid) *s.* resbalamiento, deslizamiento. 2 corrimiento de tierras. 3 MIN. falla. 4 resbaladero, declive. 5 MEC. corredera, ranura: ~ *rest,* soporte de corredera. 6 ÓPT. placa para proyectar; portaobjetos [de microscopio]. 7 MÚS. adorno en escala. 8 *adj.* que se desliza: ~ *bolt,* pestillo, pasador; ~ *caliper,* pie de rey; ~ *rule,* regla de cálculo; ~ *trombon,* trombón de varas; ~ *valve,* corredera [de máquinas de vapor].
slide (to) *intr.* resbalar, deslizarse. 2 escurrirse, escabullirse. 3 cometer un desliz. 4 *to let ~,* dejar correr. 5 *tr.* hacer deslizar. ¶ Pret.: *slid;* p. p.: *slid* o *slidden;* ger.: *slidding.*
slider (-øʳ) *s.* deslizador. 2 MEC. corredera.
sliding (-ing) *adj.* corredizo; variable, móvil: ~ *knot,* nudo, corredizo; ~ *scale,* escala móvil [de salarios, etc.]; regla de cálculo.
slight (slait) *adj.* ligero, leve. 2 pequeño, insignificante, escaso. 3 delgado, frágil, delicado. 4 *s.* desaire, desatención, feo, desprecio.
slight (to) *tr.* despreciar, no hacer caso de. 2 desairar, desdeñar. 3 desatender, descuidar.
slighting (-ing) *s.* desprecio. 2 *adj.* despreciativo.
slim (slim) *adj.* delgado, esbelto. 2 leve, pequeño. 3 fútil, baladí. 4 hábil, astuto.
slime (slaim) *s.* limo, légamo. 2 babaza, viscosidad.
slime (to) *tr.* enlegamar. 2 ensuciar.
sling (sling) *s.* honda. 2 hondazo, golpe. 3 braga, eslinga, balso. 4 CIR. cabestrillo. 5 portafusil; correa para llevar algo a la espalda. 6 *pl.* MAR. grátil [de verga].
sling (to) *tr.* tirar con honda. 2 lanzar, arrojar. 3 embragar, eslingar, suspender. 4 poner en cabestrillo. ¶ Pret. y p. p.: *slung.*
slinger (-øʳ) *s.* hondero.
slingshot (-shat) *s.* tirador [de goma].
slink (to) (slink) *intr.* andar furtivamente: *to ~ away,* escurrirse. 2 *tr.-intr.* VET. abortar. ¶ Pret. y p. p.: *slunk.*
slip (slip) *s.* resbalón, deslizamiento. 2 desliz, tropiezo, error: ~ *of pean, lapsus cálami;* ~ *of tongue, lapsus linguae'.* 2 huida, esquinazo: *to give one the ~,* escaparse de uno, darle esquinazo. 4 AGR. esqueje, estaca. 5 tira [trozo estrecho]; trozo de papel. 6 *fig.* muchacho o muchacha pequeños de cuerpo. 7 funda [de mueble o almohada]. 8 combinación [de mujer]; delantal [de niño]; mono [de trabajo]. 9 slip [calzoncillos]. 10 grada [de astillero]. 11 GEOL. falla. 12 *adj.* que se desliza: ~ *knot,* nudo corredizo; ~ *cover,* sobrecubierta [de libro].
slip (to) *intr.* resbalar, deslizarse, escurrirse, salir de su sitio. 2 escapar; pasar sin ser notado. 3 borrarse de la memoria. 4 tener un desliz, equivocarse. 5 *to ~ away* o *off,* escabullirse, huir, deslizarse. 6 *to ~ by,* pasar inadvertido, pasar rápidamente. 7 *to let ~,* dejar escapar. 8 *tr.* deslizar, meter, introducir. 9 escaparse de o a. 10 dejar escapar, soltar. 11 saltarse, pasar por alto. 12 soltar, desatar; desenganchar. 13 dislocarse [un hueso]. 14 *to ~ off,* quitarse de encima; quitarse [una prenda] precipitada-

mente. *15 to ~ on*, poner o ponerse [una prenda] precipitadamente.
¶ Pret. y p. p.: *slipped;* ger.: *-pping.*
slipcase (-keis) *s.* estuche [para libros].
slipknot (sli·pno) *s.* lazo o nudo corredizo.
slip-on *s.* prenda de vestir que se pone por la cabeza o que se pone y quita con facilidad.
slipper (sli·pø^r) *s.* zapatilla, babucha.
slippered (-ø^rd) *adj.* con zapatillas.
slippery (-i) *adj.* resbaladizo. *2* escurridizo, huidizo. *3* astuto.
slipshod (sli·pshad) *adj.* en chancletas. *2* descuidado, desaliñado.
slipslop (-lap) *s.* aguachirle.
slip-up *s.* error, equivocación.
slit (slit) *s.* abertura, estrecha, corte, hendedura.
slit (to) *tr.* hender, cortar, dividir. ¶ Pret. y p. p.: *slit;* ger.: *-tting.*
slither (to) (sli·de^r) *intr.* bajar, rodar, deslizarse, arrastrarse.
sliver (sli·vø^r) *s.* raja, astilla, tira, brizna. *2* HIL. mecha, cinta.
sliver (to) *tr.* rajar, astillar, cortar en tiras o rodajas. *2* romperse, astillarse.
slobber (sla·bø^r) *s.* baba. *2* fig. sensiblería.
slobber (to) *intr.* babear. *2 tr.* babosear. *3* estropear [un trabajo].
sloe (slou·) *s.* BOT. endrino. *2* endrina.
slog (slag) *s.* golpe, porrazo.
slog (to) *tr.* aporrear. *2 intr.* afanarse.
slogan (slou·gan) *s.* grito de combate. *2* eslogan, lema.
sloop (slup) *s.* MAR. balandra; *~ of war*, corbeta.
slop (slap) *s.* lodo blando; líquido derramado; suciedad líquida. *2* lavazas, agua sucia. *3* aguachirle. *4* vestido holgado. *5* ropa hecha de calidad inferior.
slop (to) *tr.* derramar [un líquido]; ensuciar, enlodar. *2 intr.* derramarse. *3 to ~ over*, estar demasiado efusivo. ¶ Pret. y p. p.: *slopped;* ger.: *-pping.*
slope (sloup) *s.* cuesta, pendiente, declive, inclinación. *2* falda, ladera. *3* GEOGR. vertiente.
slope (to) *intr.* inclinarse, estar en declive. *2 tr.* inclinar, sesgar.
sloping (-ing) *adj.* inclinado, pendiente. *2* deprimida [frente].
sloppy (sla·pi) *adj.* sucio, mojado, lodoso. *2* desaseado. *3* chapucero. *4* mal hecho [vestido].
slosh (slash) *s.* lodo, fango, aguachirle.
slosh (to) *intr.* andar chapoteando. *2* chapotear [el agua, etc.].
slot (slat) *s.* hendedura, abertura: *~ machine*, tragaperras. *2* pista, rastro.
slot (to) *tr.* hacer una hendedura en. *2* pasar por una hendedura.
sloth (sloz) *s.* pereza, galbana. *2* ZOOL. perezoso.
slothful (slo·zful) *adj.* perezoso.
slouch (slauch) *s.* pers. desmañada, perezosa. *2* actitud floja del cuerpo. *3* inclinación, caída. *4 adj.* caído, gacho.
slouch (to) *tr.* poner gacho. *2* bajar [el ala del sombrero]. *3 intr.* caer, estar gacho. *4* tomar una actitud floja; andar con la cabeza baja.
slough (slau·) *s.* cenagal. *2* (sliu·) (E.U.) pantano, marjal. *3* (sløf) piel que muda la serpiente. *4* MED. costra.
slough (to) *tr.* mudar, soltar [la piel, una costra, etc.]. *2 intr.* MED. formar costra. *3* desprenderse, caerse.

sloughy (slau·i) *adj.* fangoso, pantanoso. *2* (slø·fi) MED. que forma costra.
Slovak (slou·væk) *adj.-s.* eslovaco.
sloven (slø·vøn) *adj.* desaseado. *2* inculto. *3 s.* pers. desaseada.
Slovene (slou·vin) *adj.-s.* esloveno.
slovenly (slø·vønli) *adj.* desaliñado, desaseado. *2 adv.* desaliñadamente, descuidadamente.
slow (slou) *adj.* lento, tardo, pausado, detenido: *~ fire*, fuego lento. *2* paulatino. *3* calmoso. *4* lerdo, torpe. *5* que atrasa [reloj]: *to be ~*, atrasar. *6* atrasado [poco progresivo]. *7* aburrido. *8* encalmado. *9 adv.* despacio, lentamente.
slow (to) *tr.* retardar, hacer más lento. *2 intr. to ~ up* o *down*, hacerse más lento, ir más despacio.
slow-motion *adj.* lento, de movimiento lento.
slowness (-nis) *s.* lentitud. *2* cachaza. *3* torpeza, pesadez.
slow-witted *adj.* lerdo, tardo, torpe.
slubber (to) (slø·bø^r) *tr.* manchar, obscurecer. *2* frangollar.
sludge (slødy̆) *s.* lodo, cieno, impurezas. *2* MAR. hielo nuevo que flota en el mar.
sludgy (slø·dyi) *adj.* cenagoso.
slue (sliu·) *s.* giro, vuelta.
slue (to) *tr.* dar vuelta a, hacer girar. *2 intr.* girar, volverse. ¶ Gralte. con *round*.
slug (sløg) *s.* ZOOL. babosa. *2* animal o vehículo lento. *3* bala, posta. *4* IMPR. regleta; línea de linotipia.
slug (to) *tr.* pasar [un tiempo] ocioso. *2* aporrear, apuñear. *3 intr.* andar despacio; pasear.
sluggard (-a^rd) *adj.* lento, perezoso. *2 s.* haragán.
sluggish (-ish) *adj.* flojo, perezoso, indolente. *2* lento. *3* COM. encalmado.
sluice (slius) *s.* acequia, caz. *2* buzón, paradera. *3* compuerta; esclusa; agua detenida por una compuerta, etc., o que sale por ella. *4* lavadero de arenas auríferas.
sluice (to) *tr.* dar salida a, regar, limpiar [abriendo una compuerta]. *2* lavar [arenas auríferas].
slum (sløm) *s.* barrio miserable; barrio bajo.
slum (to) *intr.* visitar los barrios miserables. ¶ Pret. y p. p.: *slummed;* ger.: *-mming.*
slumber (slø·mbø^r) *s.* sueño, sueño ligero. *2* adormecimiento, letargo.
slumber (to) *intr.* dormitar, dormir. *2* dormirse, descuidarse. *3* estar latente.
slumberous (-øs) *adj.* soñoliento. *2* dormido. *3* tranquilo, sosegado. *4* adormecedor.
slump (slømp) *s.* hundimiento, desplome. *2* COM. baja repentina, crisis.
slump (to) *intr.* caer, desplomarse. *2* fracasar. *3* dar un bajón [los precios, etc.]. *4 tr.* hacer bajar [los precios, etc.].
slung (sløng) *pret.* y *p. p.* de TO SLING. *2 ~ shot*, rompecabezas [arma].
slunk (slønk) *pret.* y *p. p.* de TO SLINK.
slur (slø^r) *s.* mancha, borrón; tacha, desdoro. *2* cosa borrosa. *3* farfulla. *4* MÚS. ligadura.
slur (to) *tr.* manchar. *2* desdorar, rebajar. *3* pasar por alto, disimular, ocultar. *4* obscurecer, hacer borroso. *5* comerse [letras, sílabas]; farfullar. *6* MÚS. ligar. *7* IMPR. repintar. ¶ Pret. y p. p.: *slurred;* ger.: *-rring.*
slush (sløsh) *s.* nieve fangosa, lodo. *2* fig. sentimentalismo empalagoso; sensiblería. *3* grasa [para metales].
slushy (-i) *adj.* fangoso. *2* fig. empalagosamente sentimental.
slut (sløt) *s.* pazpuerca. *2* mujerzuela.

sluttish (-ish) *adj.* desaseado. 2 puerco, sucio.
sly (slai·) *adj.* astuto, socarrón, disimulado. 2 travieso. 3 secreto, furtivo: *on the* ~, a hurtadillas, callandito.
slyly (-li) *adv.* astutamente. 2 disimuladamente. 3 a hurtadillas.
smack (smæk) *s.* sabor, dejo, gustillo. 2 poquito, algo, punta. 3 tintura [noción superficial]. 4 restallido, chasquido, golpe, manotazo. 5 beso sonoro. 6 MAR. lancha de pesca. 7 *adv.* de lleno; de golpe.
smack (to) *intr. to* ~ *of*, tener un gustillo de; fig. saber, oler a. 2 *intr.-tr.* chasquear el látigo; chuparse los dedos; besar sonoramente. 3 *tr.* dar un manotazo a.
smacking (-ing) *adj.* vivo, fuerte.
small (smol) *adj.* pequeño, chico, diminuto; insignificante: ~ *capital*, IMPR. versalita; ~ *change*, dinero suelto; ~ *fry*, freza; gente menuda; ~ *matters*, menudencias; ~ *wares*, mercería, artículos pequeños; *in a* ~ *way*, en pequeña escala. 2 menor; ~ *craft*, embarcaciones menores; ~ *game*, caza menor. 3 bajo [estatura]. 4 escaso; *to* ~ *purpose*, con poco resultado. 5 humilde, modesto. 6 mezquino. 7 flojo, diluido. 8 fino, delgado: ~ *intestine*, ANAT. intestino delgado. 9 ~ *hours*, primeras horas de la madrugada. 10 ~ *talk*, habladuría.
11 s. parte pequeña de algo. *12* cosa o cantidad pequeña: *in* ~, en pequeño. *13 pl.* artículos menudos. *14* calzones cortos. *15 adv.* a trocitos: *to cut* ~, desmenuzar. *16* en tono bajo. *17* con desprecio: *to think* ~ *of*, tener en poco.
smallclothes (-klouđš) *s. pl.* calzones cortos. 2 ropa para niños. 3 ropa interior.
smallish (-ish) *adj.* algo pequeño o bajo.
smallness (-nis) *s.* pequeñez. 2 baja esatura. 3 bajeza, ruindad. 4 insignificancia.
smallpox (-paks) *s.* MED. viruelas.
smalt (smolt) *s.* esmalte, esmaltín.
smart (sma⁻t) *adj.* vivo, punzante, picante, acerbo. 2 fuerte, violento. 3 listo, ingenioso, astuto. 4 activo, diligente. 5 vivaracho. 6 agudo, gracioso, mordaz. 7 elegante, a la moda. 8 garrido. 9 distinguido: *the* ~ *set*, la gente distinguida, de buen tono. *10 s.* punzada, escozor. *11* dolor, aflicción.
smart (to) *intr.* escocer, doler. 2 sufrir, padecer. 3 sentir escozor [en el ánimo], sentir pesar o arrepentimiento.
smarten (to) (-tøn) *tr.* poner elegante, embellecer, animar.
smarty (-ti) *s.* (E.U.) el que las echa de agudo o gracioso.
smash (smæsh) *s.* rotura, destrozo. 2 choque [de vehículos]. 3 golpe violento. 4 fracaso, bancarrota. 5 ~ *hit*, éxito ruidoso.
smash (to) *tr.* romper, destrozar, estrellar, aplastar. 2 destruir, arruinar. 3 TENIS golpear la pelota por encima. 4 *intr.* romperse, destrozarse. 5 quebrar, arruinarse.
smatter (smæ·tø⁻), **smattering** (-ing) *s.* barniz, tintura, conocimiento superficial.
smear (smi⁻) *s.* embadurnamiento, mancha. 2 BACT. frotis. 3 fig. mancha, desdoro.
smear (to) *tr.* embadurnar, untar, embarrar, tiznar. 2 fig. manchar, desdorar.
smeary (smi·ri) *adj.* graso, untuoso. 2 manchado.
smell (smel) *s.* olfato [sentido]. 2 olor [aroma, perfume, tufo, hedor]. 3 olor, traza.
smell (to) *tr.* oler [percibir con el olfato]. 2 olfa-

tear, husmear, ventear. 3 oler [adivinar]: *to* ~ *a rat*, sospechar algo malo. 4 *intr.* oler [exhalar olor o hedor]: *to* ~ *of*, oler a. 5 *to* ~ *at a rose*, oler una rosa. ¶ Pret. y p. p.: *smelled* o *smelt*.
smeller (sme·lø⁻) *s.* oledor, husmeador. 2 el que huele o echa un olor. 3 fam. nariz.
smellfeast (-fist) *s.* gorrista, gorrón.
smelling (-ing) *s.* olfato. 2 olfacción; husmeo. 3 olor. 4 *adj.* que huele, oloroso; aromático.
smelt (smelt) *pret.* y *p. p.* de TO SMELL.
smelt (to) *tr.* fundir [minerales]. 2 extraer [metal] por fusión.
smelter (sme·ltø⁻) *s.* fundidor de minerales.
smelting (-ing) *s.* fundición [de metales]: ~ *furnace*, horno de fundición.
smile (smail) *s.* sonrisa. 2 aspecto risueño.
smile (to) *intr.* sonreír: *to* ~ *at*, *on* o *upon*, sonreir a. 2 sonreírse. 3 *tr.* expresar, decir, recibir, etc., con una sonrisa.
smiling (-ing) *adj.* risueño, sonriente.
smirch (smø⁻ch) *s.* borrón, mancha.
smirch (to) *tr.* manchar, ensuciar. 2 mancillar.
smirk (smø⁻k) *s.* sonrisa boba o afectada.
smirk (to) *intr.* sonreírse tontamente o con afectación.
smite (to) (smait) *tr.* golpear, herir, pegar. 2 aplastar. 3 asolar, afligir, castigar. 4 aturdir, sobrecoger; conmover; remorder [la conciencia]. 5 prendar, enamorar. 6 *intr.* dar golpes. ¶ Pret.: *smote;* p. p.: *smitten*.
smith (smiz) *s.* forjador. 2 el que trabaja en metales.
smith (to) *tr.* forjar [metales].
smithereens (smiđøri·nš) *s.* pl. fam. añicos.
smithery (smi·zøri) *s.* forja, herrería.
smithy (-zi) *s.* herrería, taller de herrero.
smitten (smi·tøn) *p. p.* de TO SMITE.
smock (smak) *s.* camisa, bata, delantal [de mujer]. 2 ~ *frock* o simplte. *smock*, blusa [de obrero, de pintor, etc.].
smoke (smouk) *s.* humo: ~ *screen*, cortina de humo. 2 sahumerio. 3 acción de fumar: *to have a* ~, fumar.
smoke (to) *tr.* ahumar. 2 fumigar. 3 sahumar, incensar. 4 fumar. 5 oler, descubrir. 6 *to* ~ *out*, ahuyentar con humo. 7 *intr.* humear, echar humo. 8 fumar.
smoke-dry (to) *tr.* secar o curar al humo.
smokeless (-lis) *adj.* sin humo.
smoker (-ø⁻) *s.* ahumador. 2 fumador. 3 compartimento para fumadores. 4 reunión en que se fuma.
smokestack (-stæk) *s.* chimenea.
smoking (-ing) *s.* acción de fumar: *no* ~, se prohíbe fumar. 2 *adj.* humeante. 3 de fumar: ~ *jacket*, batín; ~ *room*, fumadero.
smoky (-i) *adj.* humeante. 2 humoso. 3 ahumado.
smolt (smoult) *s.* ICT. murgón.
smooth (smuđ) *adj.* liso, terso. 2 llano, igual, parejo. 3 uniforme, regular. 4 fácil, fluido. 5 blando, suave. 6 plácido. 7 afable. 8 meloso, lisonjero, hipócrita. 9 MÚS. ligado. *10 adv.* SMOOTHLY.
smooth (to) *tr.* alisar. 2 allanar, igualar. 3 cepillar, pulir. 4 facilitar [las cosas]. 5 suavizar. 6 calmar, apaciguar. 7 *to* ~ *away*, hacer desaparecer [obstáculos, etc.] suavemente.
smooth-faced *adj.* barbilampiño. 2 liso. 3 meloso.
smoothing (-ing) *adj.* de alisar, cepillar, etc.: ~ *iron*, plancha; ~ *plane*, CARP. cepillo.

smoothly (-li) *adv.* lisamente. *2* fácilmente. *3* suavemente, melosamente.
smooth-shaven *adj.* bien afeitado.
smooth-spoken, smooth-tongued *adj.* meloso, lisonjero, adulador.
smote (smout) *pret.* de TO SMITE.
smother (smø·ðøʳ) *s.* humareda, polvareda, niebla, etc., sofocantes.
smother (to) *tr.* sofocar, ahogar [asfixiar; apagar; reprimir]. *2* COC. estofar. *3* cubrir. *4* ocultar. *5 intr.* ahogarse. *6* estar reprimido.
smothery (-i) *adj.* sofocante, asfixiante.
smo (u) lder (smou·ldøʳ) *s.* fuego sin llama.
smo (u) lder (to) *intr.* arder sin llama, en rescoldo. *2* estar latente, reprimido.
smudge (smødy̆) *s.* mancha, tiznón. *2* humareda sofocante.
smudge (to) *tr.* manchar, tiznar. *2* embadurnar. *3* (E.U.) ahumar, proteger con humo.
smug (smøg) *adj.* compuesto, aseado. *2* satisfecho, pagado de sí mismo.
smuggle (to) (smø·gøl) *tr.* pasar de contrabando. *2 intr.* contrabandear.
smuggler (-gløʳ) *s.* contrabandista.
smuggling (-gling) *s.* contrabando.
smut (smøt) *s.* suciedad, mancha, tiznón. *2* obscenidad. *3* AGR. añublo, tizón.
smut (to) *tr.* ensuciar, manchar, tiznar. *2* mancillar. *3* AGR. producir añublo. *4 intr.* AGR. atizonarse. ¶ Pret. y p. p.: *smutted;* ger.: *-tting.*
smutch (smøch) *s.* mancha, tiznajo.
smutch (to) *tr.* tiznar, manchar. *2* mancillar.
smutty (smø·ti) *adj.* tiznado, holliniento. *2* humoso, obscuro. *3* obsceno. *4* AGR. atizonado.
snack (snæk) *s.* porción, parte; sorbo, bocadito. *2* piscolabis, tentempié: ~ *bar,* bar donde se sirven bocadillos, etc.
snaffle (-bit) (snæ·føl) *s.* bridón [brida pequeña].
snaffle (to) *tr.* enfrenar. *2* refrenar, reprimir.
snag (snæg) *s.* tocón. *2* garrancho. *3* nudo [en la madera]. *4* raigón. *5* tronco o roca sumergidos. *6* obstáculo imprevisto.
snagged (-id), **snaggy** (-i) *adj.* nudoso. *2* lleno de tocones. *3* lleno de troncos o rocas sumergidos. *4* fig. lleno de obstáculos.
snaggletooth (snæ·gøltuz) *s.* sobrediente.
snail (sneil) *s.* ZOOL. caracol [esp. el terrestre]: babosa. *2* persona o cosa lenta.
snake (sneik) *s.* ZOOL. culebra, serpiente: ~ *in the grass,* fig. peligro oculto, enemigo secreto. *2* fig. serpiente [pers.].
snake (to) *tr.* arrastrar, mover sinuosamente. *2 intr.* serpentear.
snakeroot (-rut) *s.* BOT. serpentaria.
snaky (-i) *adj.* serpentino. *2* serpenteante. *3* traidor. *4* lleno de culebras.
snap (snæp) *s.* chasquido, estallido. *2* castañeta [con los dedos]. *3* acción rápida. *4* mordisco, dentellada. *5* disparo rápido, sin apuntar; FOT. instantánea. *6* broche de presión. *7* galletita. *8* energía, vigor, vida. *9* período breve [de frío, etc.]. *10* fam. canonjía; ganga. *11* observación o respuesta brusca. *12* fig. pito, bledo. *13 adj.* precipitado: ~ *judgement,* juicio precipitado. *14* de golpe, de resorte: ~ *bolt,* pestillo de golpe.
snap (to) *intr.* romperse con estallido; cerrarse dando chasquido o golpe. *2* dar chasquido, estallar. *3* echar chispas, llamear. *4 to* ~ *at,* tirar un bocado a; aceptar, asir prontamente. *5 to* ~ *off,* soltarse; abrirse de golpe. *6 tr.* asir, agarrar, arrebatar. *7*

aceptar o tomar en el acto. *8* responder o expresar con acritud. *9* romper, cerrar, etc., con chasquido. *10* hacer chasquear: *to* ~ *one's fingers at,* burlarse de, despreciar. *11* FOT. hacer una instantánea. ¶ Pret. y p. p.: *snapped;* ger.: *-pping.*
snapdragon (-drægøn) *s.* BOT. dragón, becerra.
snapper (-øʳ) *s.* mordedor. *2* pers. gruñona. *3* tralla [del látigo].
snappish (-ish) *adj.* mordedor. *2* gruñón.
snappy (-i) *adj.* SNAPPISH. *2* chispeante, vivo. *3* elegante. *4* rápido.
snapshot (-shat) *s.* FOT. instantánea. *2* disparo rápido, sin apuntar.
snapshot (to) *tr.-intr.* hacer instantáneas. ¶ Pret. y p. p.: *snapshotted;* ger.: *snapshotting.*
snare (sneʳ) *s.* lazo, armadijo. *2* celada, trampa, asechanza. *3* bordón [de tambor]. *4* CIR. lazo.
snare (to) *tr.* atrapar; hacer caer en una trampa, tender celadas o lazos a.
snarl (sna·ʹl) *s.* gruñido. *2* regaño. *3* enredo, maraña; pelo enmarañado.
snarl (to) *intr.* regañar. *2* gruñir. *3* enredarse, enmarañarse. *4 tr.* enredar, enmarañar. *5* repujar [metales].
snarly (-i) *adj.* gruñón, regañón. *2* enredado, enmarañado.
snary (sne·ri) *adj.* enredoso, insidioso.
snatch (snæch) *s.* acción de coger o arrebatar. *2* trozo, pedacito. *3* rato: *by snatches,* a ratos.
snatch (to) *tr.* coger, agarrar precipitadamente; arrebatar, quitar. *2 intr. to* ~ *at,* tratar de agarrar o arrebatar.
snatchy (-i) *adj.* irregular, intermitente.
sneak (snik) *s.* persona ruin, solapada. *2* fam. soplón. *3* movimiento furtivo. *4* sneak o ~ *thief,* ratero, descuidero.
sneak (to) *intr.* moverse furtivamente, escabullirse. | Con *in, out, past, round, off, away,* etc. *2* obrar solapadamente o rastreramente; soplonear. *3 tr.* mover, sacar, meter, etc., furtivamente. *4* hurtar, ratear.
sneaker (-køʳ) *s.* SNEAK 1. *2 pl.* zapatos silenciosos; zapatos de playa o de gimnasia.
sneaking (-ing) *adj.* ruin, cobarde. *2* mezquino. *3* furtivo, husmeador. *4* secreto [no confesado]. *5* vago [idea, sospecha].
sneaky (-i) *adj.* ruin, cobarde. *2* solapado, furtivo.
sneer (snⁱʳ) *s.* sonrisa, gesto o expresión despreciativa; burla, mofa.
sneer (to) *intr.* reírse o mirar con burla o desprecio; burlarse, mofarse. | Gralte. con *at.* *2 tr.* decir o expresar con burla o desprecio.
sneering (-ing) *adj.* burlón, despreciativo.
sneeze (sniš) *s.* estornudo.
sneeze (to) *intr.* estornudar.
snell (snel) *s.* hilo de tripa que une el sedal al anzuelo.
snick (snik) *s.* corte, tijeretazo. *2* ruido seco o metálico.
snick (to) *tr.* cortar. *2* pinchar, atravesar. *3* mover, sacar, etc., con ruido seco o metálico.
snicker (snikøʳ) *s.* risita, risa ahogada.
snicker (to) *intr.* reír con risa ahogada, burlarse. *2* relinchar suavemente.
sniff (snif) *s.* olfato, husmeo. *2* sorbo [por las narices]; resoplido de desprecio.
sniff (to) *tr.* olfatear, husmear, oler. *2 intr.-tr.* absorber ruidosamente por la nariz; dar un resoplido: *to* ~ *at,* husmear; despreciar.
sniffy (sni·fi) *adj.* fam. desdeñoso, estirado.
snifting-valve (sni·fting) *s.* MEC. válvula de purga.

snigger (sni·gøʳ) *s.* SNICKER.
snigger (to) *intr.* TO SNICKER.
snip (snip) *s.* incisión, tijeretazo. *2* recorte, pedacito. *3* fam. persona pequeña o insignificante.
snip (to) *tr.* cortar, recortar [con tijeras o cosa parecida]. ¶ Pret. y p. p.: *snipped;* ger.: *-pping.*
snipe (snaip) *s.* ORN. agachadiza.
snipe (to) *intr.* cazar agachadizas. *2* tirar desde un sitio oculto: *to ~ at,* tirotear, paquear.
sniper (snai·pøʳ) *s.* tiroteador, paco.
snippet (sni·pit) *s.* recorte, pedacito.
snivel (sni·vøl) *s.* moco, moquita. *2* gimoteo.
snivel (to) *intr.* moquear. *2* sorberse la moquita; gimotear, hacer pucheros. ¶ Pret. y p. p.: *snivel(l)ed;* ger.: *-l(l)ing.*
snivel(l)er (sni·vløʳ) *s.* lloraduelos, jeremías.
snivelly (sni·vli) *adj.* llorón, lloroso. *2* mocoso.
snob (snab) *s.* el que, por darse tono, imita a los que les parecen superiores o busca su trato; esnob. *2* el que rehuye el trato de los que tiene por inferiores; orgulloso.
snobbery (sna·børi) *s.* esnobismo. *2* orgullo, presunción.
snooze (snuš) *s.* fam. sueñecito, siestecita.
snooze (to) *intr.* fam. dormitar.
snore (snoʳ) *s.* ronquido [del que duerme, del mar, del viento].
snore (to) *intr.* roncar [el que duerme, el mar, el viento].
snort (snoʳt) *s.* resoplido, bufido.
snort (to) *intr.* resoplar, bufar. *2* reírse ruidosamente con ira o desprecio.
snout (snaut) *s.* trompa [de elefante]. *2* hocico, jeta. *3* pitorro; nariz [de alambique]; lanza [de manguera]; cañón [de fuelle]. *4* MAR. proa. *5* promontorio. *6* ENT. *~ beetle,* gorgojo.
snouted (-id) *adj.* hocicudo. *2* provisto de pitorro, etc. *3* en forma de hocico o pitorro.
snow (snou) *s.* nieve: *~ flurry,* nevisca. *2* nevada. *3* pop. cocaína. *4* n. pr. *Snow White,* Blancanieves.
snow (to) *intr.* nevar. *2* tr. esparcir como nieve. *3* cubrir, obstruir, aprisionar, etc., con nieve. | Con *over, up, in, under. 4* blanquear [el cabello].
snowball (-bol) *s.* bola de nieve. *2* BOT. mundillo.
snowball (to) *tr.-intr.* lanzar bolas de nieve. *2* intr. crecer como una bola de nieve.
snowblind (-blaind) *adj.* cegado por el reflejo de la nieve.
snowbound (-baund) *adj.* sitiado por la nieve.
snowcapped (-kæpt) *adj.* coronado de nieve.
snowdrift (-drift) *s.* nieve que lleva el viento, ventisca. *2* ventisquero.
snowdrop (-drap) *s.* BOT. campanilla blanca. *2* BOT. anémona.
snowfall (-fol) *s.* nevada, nevasca.
snowflake (-fleik) *s.* copo de nieve. *2* ORN. verderón de las nieves. *3* BOT. campanilla.
snowplough, snowplow (-plau) *s.* quitanieves.
snowshoe (-shu) *s.* raqueta para andar sobre la nieve.
snowslide (-laid), **snowslip** (-slip) *s.* alud.
snow-white *adj.* blanco como la nieve.
snowy (-i) *adj.* nevoso; nevado. *2* níveo.
snub (snøb) *s.* repulsa, desaire. *2* represión brusca. *3* fam. nariz chata. *4* adj. chata [nariz].
snub (to) *tr.* dar un sofión; reprender. *2* desairar, despreciar. *3* to ~ *up,* detener de repente.
snub-nosed *adj.* chato.
snuff (snøf) *s.* moco [de vela]. *2* rapé; polvo [que se toma].
snuff (to) *tr.* oler; absorber por la nariz. *2* olfatear,

husmear. *3* despabilar [una vela]. *4* intr. TO SNIFF. *5* tomar rapé.
snuffbox (-baks) *s.* tabaquera, caja de rapé.
snuffers (-øʳs) *s. pl.* despabiladeras.
snuffle (-øl) *s.* respiración o inspiración ruidosa por la nariz. *2* gangueo. *3 pl.* romadizo.
snuffle (to) *intr.* TO SNIFF 2. *2* respirar con la nariz obstruida. *3* ganguear.
snuffy (-i) *adj.* sucio de rapé; tabacoso; desagradable.
snug (snøg) *adj.* cómodo, abrigado. *2* ajustado; apretado, compacto. *3* escondido. *4* tranquilo. *5* limpio, aseado.
snug (to) *tr.* poner cómodo; acomodar. *2* arreglar, asear. *3* hacer próspero.
snuggery (-øri) *s.* aposento cómodo.
snuggle (to) (-øl) *intr.-tr.* arrimar, arrimarse, poner o ponerse juntos, cómodos, abrigados.
so (sou) *adv.* así, de este modo; eso, lo mismo, lo: *if ~,* si es así; *~ be it,* así sea; *I hope ~,* así lo espero; *quite ~, just ~,* eso mismo; *he is not too clever, but he is more ~ than many men,* no es muy listo, pero lo es más que muchos hombres. *2* de modo, de manera: *~ that,* para que; de modo o de manera que. *3* también. *4* tan, tanto: *~ good,* tan bueno; *it is not ~ good as,* no es tan bueno como. *5* y así, por tanto. *6* pron. cosa así, cosa de: *a year or ~,* cosa de un año. *7* conj. con tal que; para que. *8* interj. ¡bueno!; ¿eh? *9* Otras alocuciones: *and ~ forth* (o *on*), etcétera, y así sucesivamente; *how ~?,* ¿cómo es eso?; *~ far as, in ~ far as,* hasta, hasta donde; *~ long,* abur; *~ long as,* mientras, con tal que; *~ many,* tantos; *~ much,* tanto; *~ to say, ~ to speak,* por decirlo así.
soak (souk) *s.* remojo, remojón. *2* borrachín. *3* borrachera.
soak (to) *tr.* empapar, poner en remojo. *2* emborrachar. *3* pop. pegar, zurrar. *4 to ~ up,* embeber, absorber. *5* intr. empaparse, estar en remojo. *6* emborracharse. *7 to ~ into,* penetrar, filtrarse.
soakage (-idỹ) *s.* merma [por absorción].
soaker (-øʳ) *s.* remojador. *2* borrachín. *3* chubasco.
soaky (-i) *adj.* empapado, mojado, calado.
so-and-so *s.* fulano, fulano de tal. *2* tal cosa.
soap (soup) *s.* jabón: *~ dish,* jabonera; *~ flakes,* escamas de jabón. *2* fam. lisonja. *3* fam. dinero. *4* BOT. *~ plant,* jaboncillo.
soap (to) *tr.* jabonar. *2* dar jabón, adular.
soapstone (-stoun) *s.* esteatita, jabón de sastre.
sopasuds (-søds) *s. pl.* jabonaduras.
soapy (-i) *adj.* jabonoso.
soar (soʳ) *s.* vuelo, remonte.
soar (to) *intr.* elevarse, subir, remontarse, volar. *2* cernerse [en el aire]; AVIA. planear. *3 tr.* elevarse, remontarse por.
sob (sab) *s.* sollozo. *2* suspiro [del viento, etc.].
sob (to) *intr.* sollozar.
sober (sou·bøʳ) *adj.* sobrio, moderado, templado. *2* sereno [que no está borracho]. *3* sereno, desapasionado, serio, sensato. *4* serio, discreto [color].
sober (to) *tr.* serenar, aquietar, ajuiciar; poner serio. *2* serenar [quitar la borrachera]. *3 intr. to ~ down,* serenarse, ajuiciarse, sosegarse. *4 to ~ up,* desemborracharse.
soberness (sou·bøʳnes), **sobriety** (sobrai·øti) *s.* sobriedad. *2* moderación. *3* sensatez. *4* serenidad. *5* seriedad, gravedad.
sobriquet (soubrikei·) *s.* apodo, mote.

so-called *adj.* llamado, supuesto, pseudo.
sociability (soushabi·liti) *s.* sociabilidad.
sociable (sou·shabøl) *adj.* sociable, tratable; comunicativo. *2* amistoso, familiar.
social (sou·shal) *adj.* social: ~ *security*, seguro social. *2* de trato o conversación, de sociedad: ~ *gathering*, reunión, fiesta de sociedad. *3* sociable. *4 s.* tertulia, reunión.
socialism (sou·shališm) *s.* socialismo.
socialist (-ist) *adj.* socialista.
socialize (to) (sou·shalaiš) *tr.* socializar.
society (sosai·øti) *s.* sociedad. *2* compañía, reunión, relación, trato social. *3* buena sociedad.
Society Islands *n. pr.* GEOGR. Islas de la Sociedad.
sociology (soshia·lodỹi) *s.* sociología.
sock (sak) *s.* calcetín. *2* sandalia. *3* fig. la comedia. *4* golpe, puñetazo.
socket (-it) *s.* hueco en que encaja algo; caja, cubo, mechero, portalámparas, etc.; cuenca [del ojo]; alvéolo [de diente].
socle (sa·køl) *s.* zócalo.
sod (sad) *s.* césped. *2* terrón; tepe; turba.
sod (to) *tr.* encespedar. ¶ Pret. y p. p.: *sodden;* ger.: *-dding.*
soda (sou·da) *s.* QUÍM. soda, sosa; carbonato de sodio: ~ *plant*, barrilla. *2* soda o ~ *water*, agua carbónica.
sodality (sodæ·liti) *s.* asociación, unión. *2* cofradía, hermandad.
sodden (sa·døn) *p. p.* de TO SEETHE. *2* mojado, empapado. *3* borracho; embrutecido. *4* mal cocido [pan].
sodic (sou·dik) *adj.* QUÍM. sódico.
sodium (sou·diøm) *s.* QUÍM. sodio.
sodomite (sa·dømait) *s.* sodomita.
sodomy (-i) *s.* sodomía.
soever (soe·vø^r) *adv.* que sea; por más que sea: *in any way* ~, de cualquier modo que sea; *how great* ~, por grande que sea. *2* en modo alguno.
sofa (sou·fa) *s.* sofá.
soffit (sa·fit) *s.* ARQ. sofito; intradós.
soft (soft) *adj.* blando, maleable, flexible, mollar, fofo. *2* blando, muelle, suave, delicado. *3* melifluo. *4* dulce, grato. *5* blando, tierno, amoroso. *6* débil [de carácter]. *7* flojo, perezoso. *8* dulce [hierro]. *9* floja [bebida]. *10* FOT. débil. *11* COM. flojo, en baja. *12* FONÉT. suave. *13* MÚS. celeste. *14 adv.* blandamente, suavemente. *15 interj.* ¡quedo!; ¡despacio!
soft-boiled *adj.* pasado por agua [huevo].
soften (to) (so·føn) *tr.* ablandar, reblandecer. *2* dulcificar, mitigar, suavizar, amortiguar, ablandar. *3* bajar [la voz]. *4* debilitar. *5 intr.* ablandarse, resplandecerse. *6* dulcificarse, aplacarse. *7* debilitarse.
softening of the brain (-ning) *s.* MED. reblandecimiento cerebral.
soft-hearted *adj.* bondadoso, de buen corazón.
softish (-ish) *adj.* blanducho.
softly (-li) *adv.* blandamente, suavemente, dulcemente. *2* bajito: *speak* ~, hable usted bajito.
soft-soap (to) *tr.* fig. adular, dar jabón.
soggy (sa·gi) *adj.* empapado. *2* pesado y húmedo.
soil (soil) *s.* tierra, terreno, suelo. *2* suelo, país. *3* suciedad. *4* mancha, baldón. *5* abono, estiércol.
soil (to) *tr.* ensuciar, manchar. *2* mancillar. *3* abonar, estercolar. *4 intr.* ensuciarse.
soirée (suarei·) *s.* reunión nocturna, sarao.
soja (sou·ỹa) *s.* BOT. soja.
sojourn (sou·dỹø^{r}n) *s.* estancia, estada.

sojourn (to) (soudỹø·^{r}n) *intr.* estar, residir [por una temporada].
sol (soul) *s.* MÚS., QUÍM. sol. *2* sol [moneda del Perú].
solace (sa·lis) *s.* consuelo, alivio. *2* solaz.
solace (to) *tr.* consolar, confortar, aliviar. *2* solazar, divertir.
solanaceous (salanei·shøs) *adj.* BOT. solanáceo.
solar (sou·la^r) *adj.* solar [del sol]: ~ *spot*, mancha solar; ~ *system*, sistema solar. *2* ANAT. ~ *plexus*, plexo solar.
solarium (søle·riøm) *s.* solarium.
solatium (sølei·shøm) *s.* compensación.
sold (sould) *pret.* y *p. p.* de TO SELL.
solder (sa·dø^r) *s.* soldadura [material para soldar].
solder (to) *tr.* soldar. *2* unir. *3 intr.* soldarse.
soldering (-ing) *s.* soldadura.
soldier (sou·ldỹø^r) *s.* soldado. *2* militar.
soldier (to) *intr.* servir como militar.
soldierly (-li) *adv.* soldadesco, militar, marcial.
soldiery (-ri) *s.* soldadesca, tropa.
sole (soul) *s.* planta [del pie]; palma [del casco del caballo]. *2* suela [del zapato]. *3* suelo, fondo, base. *4* ICT. lenguado. *5 adj.* solo, único. *6* exclusivo: ~ *right*, exclusiva.
sole (to) *tr.* solar, echar suelas a.
solecism (sa·løsišm) *s.* solecismo. *2* incongruencia. *3* incorrección.
solemn (sa·løm) *adj.* solemne. *2* grave, serio.
solemnity (søle·mniti) *s.* solemnidad. *5* formalidad, requisito.
solemnize (to) (sa·lømnaiš) *tr.* solemnizar. *2* celebrar solemnemente.
solenoid (sou·lønoid) *s.* ELECT. solenoide.
sol-fa (to) *intr.-tr.* solfear.
solfatara (salfata·ra) *s.* solfatara.
solfeggio (salfe·dỹiou) *s.* solfeo.
solicit (to) (søli·sit) *tr.* solicitar. *2* rogar, importunar. *3* inducir, incitar, tentar, atraer.
solicitation (solisitei·shøn) *s.* solicitación. *2* ruego. *3* inclinación, requerimiento.
solicitor (soli·sitø^r) *s.* especie de abogado o procurador.
solicitous (-tøs) *adj.* solícito. *2* inquieto, preocupado. *3* ávido, deseoso. *4* meticuloso.
solicitude (-tiud) *s.* solicitud, cuidado. *2* inquietud. *3 pl.* cuidados, preocupaciones.
solid (sa·lid) *adj.* sólido. *2* macizo. *3* duro, firme. *4* serio, formal; solvente. *5* unánime. *6* continuo, seguido, entero. *7* MAT. cúbico; del espacio. *8 s.* FÍS., GEOM. sólido.
solidarity (salidæ·riti) *s.* solidaridad.
solidary (sa·lideri) *adj.* solidario.
solidify (to) (søli·difai) *tr.* solidificar. *2* consolidar. *3 intr.* solidificarse, consolidarse. ¶ Pret. y p. p.: *solidified.*
solidity (søli·diti) *s.* solidez. *2* macicez. *3* seriedad, solvencia. *4* sensatez.
soliloquize (to) (søli·løkuaiš) *intr.* soliloquiar.
soliloquy (-kui) *s.* soliloquio.
soliped (sa·liped) *s.* ZOOL. solípedo.
solitaire (sa·lite^r) *s.* solitario [diamante; juego]. *2* solitario, ermitaño.
solitariness (-inis) *s.* soledad.
solitary (-i) *adj.* solitario. *2* soledoso. *3* solo, único. *4* DER. ~ *confinement*, incomunicación. *5 s.* solitario, ermitaño.
solitude (-tiud) *s.* soledad, retiro. *2* soledad [lugar solitario].
solmization (salmišei·shøn) *s.* MÚS. solfa.

solo (sou·lou) *s.* MÚS. solo. *2* solo [juego]. *3 adj.* hecho por uno solo.
soloist (-ist) *s.* MÚS. solista.
Solomon (sa·lømøn) *n. pr.* Salomón.
solstice (sa·lstis) *s.* ASTR. solsticio.
solstitial (salsti·shal) *adj.* solsticial.
solubility (saliubi·liti) *s.* solubilidad.
soluble (sa·liubøl) *adj.* soluble.
solution (søliu·shøn) *s.* solución: ~ *of continuity,* solución de continuidad.
solutive (sa·liutiv) *adj.* solutivo.
solvable (sa·lvabøl) *adj.* soluble, resoluble.
solve (to) (salv) *tr.* resolver, aclarar, desentrañar. *2* solventar, solucionar; resolver [un problema].
solvency (sa·lvønsi) *s.* solvencia.
solvent (sa·lvønt) *adj.-s.* solvente, disolvente. *2 adj.* COM. solvente.
somatic(al (somæ·tik(al) *adj.* somático.
somber, sombre (sa·mbø^r) *adj.* obscuro, sombrío. *2* sombrío, tétrico, melancólico.
sombrero (sambre·rou) *s.* sombrero de fieltro de ala ancha.
sombrous (sa·mbrøs) *adj.* sombrío.
some (søm) *adj.* un, algún, cierto, unos, algunos, varios, ciertos: ~ *day,* un día, algún día, cierto día. *2 pop. us.* para encarecer la importancia de algo: *this is ~ war!,* ¡esto es una guerra! *3* algo de, un poco de, una cantidad indeterminada de; unos, cosa de. | A veces no se traduce: *give me ~ bread,* déme pan. *4 pron.* alguno, algunos. *5 adv.* algo, un poco.
somebody (-badi) *pr.* alguien, alguno: ~ *else,* algún otro, otra persona.
somehow (-jau) *adv.* de algún modo. *2* ~ *or other,* de un modo u otro.
someone (so·muøn) *pr.* SOMEBODY.
somersault (sø·mø^rsolt), **somerset** (-set) *s.* salto mortal.
somersault, somerset (to) *intr.* dar un salto mortal, dar saltos mortales.
something (-zing) *s.* algo, alguna cosa. *2* persona o cosa de importancia. *3 to be ~ of a,* TO BE SOMEWHAT OF.
sometime (-taim) *adv.* algún día, alguna vez, en algún momento. *2 adj.* antiguo, ex.
sometimes (-taims) *adv.* algunas veces, a veces.
somewhat (-juat) *s.* algo, un poco. *2 to be ~ of a,* tener algo de. *3 adv.* algo, algún tanto, un poco.
somewhere (-jue^r) *adv.* en alguna parte.
somnambulant (samnæ·mbiulant) *adj.-s.* somnámbulo.
somnambulism (-lišm) *s.* somnambulismo.
somniferous (samni·førøs) *adj.* somnífero.
somnific (samni·fik) *adj.* soporífero.
somnolence, -cy (sa·mnøløns, -si) *s.* somnolencia, soñolencia.
somnolent (-ønt) *adj.* soñoliento. *2* soporífero.'
son (søn) *s.* hijo; descendiente [varón].
sonant (sou·nant) *adj.* FONÉT. sonoro.
sonata (søna·ta) *s.* MÚS. sonata.
sonatina (sønati·na) *s.* MÚS. sonatina.
song (søng o sang) *s.* canto [acción de cantar]. *2* MÚS., LIT. canción, canto, copla, cantar: *the Song of Songs,* el Cantar de los Cantares. *3 an old ~, a (mere) ~,* una bagatela. *4 adj.* ~ *bird,* pájaro cantor; ~ *thrush,* ORN. malvis.
songful (-ful) *adj.* melodioso. *2* canoro.
songster (-tø^r) *s.* cantor. *2* poeta. *3* pájaro cantor.
songstress (-stris) *s.* cantatriz, cantante.
sonic (sa·nik) *adj.* del sonido.
son-in-law, *pl.* **sons-in-law** *s.* yerno.

sonnet (sa·nit) *s.* LIT. soneto.
sonneteer (sanetı·^r) *s.* sonetista.
sonny (sa·ni) *s.* fam. hijito.
sonority (søno·riti) *s.* sonoridad.
sonorous (søno·røs) *adj.* sonoro; armonioso: resonante. ·
soon (sun) *adv.* pronto, luego; temprano: *as ~ as,* tan pronto como; ~ *after,* poco después; *too ~,* demasiado pronto o temprano. *2* prontamente.
sooner (-ø^r) *adv. compar.* de SOON: más pronto, más temprano; antes: ~ *or later,* tarde o temprano; *I would ~ die,* antes quisiera morir.
soonest (-ist) *adv. superl.* de SOON: lo más pronto posible: *at the ~,* cuanto antes.
soot (sut) *s.* hollín. *2* color negro de hollín.
soot (to) *tr.* cubrir o manchar de hollín.
soothe (to) (suð) *tr.* aliviar, mitigar, calmar. *2* apaciguar. *3* agradar, halagar.
soothing (-ing) *adj.* consolador, confortante, calmante, tranquilizador.
soothsayer (su·zseiø^r) *s.* adivino.
sooty (su·ti) *adj.* holliniento, fuliginoso. *2* tiznado.
sop (sap) *s.* sopa [pan empapado en caldo, etc.]. *2* dádiva para apaciguar, sobornar, etc.
sop (to) *tr.* ensopar, empapar: *to ~ up,* absorber.
Sophia (soufai·a) *n. pr.* Sofía.
sophism (sa·fišm) *s.* sofisma.
sophist (sa·fist) *s.* sofista.
sophistic (al (søfi·stik(al) *adj.* sofístico.
sophisticate (søfi·stikeit) *adj.* SOPHISTICATED.
sophisticate (to) *tr.* sofisticar. *2* hacer perder la ingenuidad; hacer complicado, refinado, mundano.
sophisticated (-tid) *adj.* sofisticado. *2* falto de ingenuidad, artificial, complicado, refinado, culto, mundano.
sophistication (-ei·shøn) *s.* sofisticación. *2* falta de espontaneidad o ingenuidad.
sophisticafor (sofi·stikeitø^r) *s.* sofisticador.
sophistry (sa·fistri) *s.* sofistería.
sopor (sou·pø^r) *s.* sopor.
soporiferous (soupøri·førøs) *adj.* soporífero.
soporific (soupøri·fik) *adj.-s.* soporífero.
soppy (sa·pi) *adj.* mojado, empapado. *2 pop.* tontamente sentimental; enamorado, chalado.
soprano (søpræ·nou) *s.* MÚS. soprano, tiple.
sorb (so^rb) *s.* BOT. serbal, serbo: ~ *apple,* serba.
sorbet (sa·^rbet) *s.* sorbete.
sorcerer (so·^rsørø^r) *s.* hechicero, brujo, encantador.
sorceress (so·^rsøris) *s.* hechicera.
sorcery (so·^rsøri) *s.* hechicería, brujería. *2* hechizo, sortilegio.
sordid (so·^rdid) *adj.* sórdido. *2* bajo, vil.
sordine (so·^rdin) *s.* MÚS. sordina.
sore (so^r) *adj.* penoso, doloroso, enojoso. *2* violento. *3* extremo. *4* dolorido, inflamado, llagado: ~ *eyes,* mal de ojos; ~ *throat,* mal de garganta. *5* sensible, irritable. *6* dolorido, enojado, resentido. *7 s.* herida [material o moral]; llaga, úlcera, matadura. *8 adv.* SORELY.
sorely (-li) *adv.* penosamente. *2* sumamente.
sorghum (so·^rgøm) *s.* BOT. sorgo, zahína.
sorrel (sa·røl) *adj.* alazán, rojo, canela. *2 s.* color o caballo alazán. *3* BOT. acedera.
sorrily (sa·rili) *adv.* lastimosamente. *2* mal, malamente, pésimamente.
sorrow (sa·rou o sa·rou) *s.* dolor, pesar, pena, sentimiento. *2* arrepentimiento. *3* luto, duelo. *4* infortunio, sinsabor.
sorrow (to) *intr.* afligirse, sentir pena.

sorrowful (-ful) *adj.* afligido, pesaroso, desconsolado. *2* doloroso, lamentable. *3* triste, melancólico.

sorrow-stricken *adj.* agobiado de dolor.

sorry (sa·ri o so·ri) *adj.* afligido, pesaroso, triste, que siente o compadece: *I am ~*, lo siento; *I am ~ for him*, le compadezco. *2* arrepentido. *3* penoso, lastimoso. *4* malo, pobre, mezquino, ruin.

sort (so^rt) *s.* clase, especie, suerte: *a ~ of*, una especie de; *of sorts*, de varias clases, de clase mediocre. *2* modo, manera: *after a ~*, *in a ~*, en cierto modo. *3 out of sorts*, indispuesto; de mal humor. *4 ~ of*, algo, un tanto.

sort (to) *tr.* ordenar, clasificar. *2* escoger, entresacar. *3 intr.* juntarse, andar con.

sortie (so·^rtɪ) *s.* MIL. salida, surtida.

sortilege (so·^rtɪlɪdӯ) *s.* sortilegio.

sorus (sou·rǫs), *pl.* **-ri** (-rai) *s.* BOT. soro.

S.O.S. (es ou es) *s.* S.O.S., llamada de auxilio.

so-so (sou-sou) *adj.* regular, mediano, pasadero.

sot (sat) *s.* borrachín.

sottish (sa·tish) *adj.* embrutecido por el vicio de la bebida. *2* borracho.

soubrette (subre·t) *s.* TEAT. graciosa, doncella.

soubriquet (sou·brikei) *s.* SOBRIQUET.

Soudan (sudæ·n) *n. pr.* GEOGR. Sudán.

sough (sǫf o sau) *s.* suspiro profundo. *2* murmullo, susurro [del viento].

sough (to) *intr.* suspirar, murmurar, susurrar.

sought (sot) *pret.* y *p. p.* de TO SEEK.

soul (soul) *s.* alma [en todos sus sentidos, menos en los de hueco, madero o pieza interior]: *every living ~*, todo bicho viviente; *poor ~*, pobre, pobrecito; *he is the ~ of honour*, es el honor mismo; *upon my ~*, en mi conciencia.

soulful (sou·lful) *adj.* conmovedor, lleno de sentimiento o que lo expresa; espiritual.

soulless (-lis) *adj.* desalmado, sin conciencia. *2* ruin, sin grandeza de alma.

soul-pained *adj.* afligido.

sound (saund) *adj.* sano: *~ of mind*, en su cabal juicio. *2* ileso, incólume, entero, cabal. *3* cuerdo, sensato. *4* sólido, firme, seguro. *5* COM. solvente. *6* bueno, fuerte: *a ~ beating*, una buena paliza. *7* fiel, leal. *8* profundo [sueño]. *9* de sonido, sonoro: *~ film*, película sonora; *~ wave*, FÍS. onda sonora. *10 s.* son, sonido, tañido; ruido. *11* MAR., MED. sonda. *12* GEOGR. brazo de mar, estrecho.

sound (to) *intr.* sonar. *2* hacer ruido. *3* resonar; divulgarse. *4* echar la sonda. *5* sumergirse [la ballena]. *6 tr.* tocar, tañer [un instrumento]; tocar [un toque, etc.]. *7* cantar, entonar [alabanzas]. *8* sondar; sondear; explorar. *9* auscultar.

Sound *n. pr.* GEOGR. Sund.

soundboard (-bo^rd) *s.* SOUNDING BOARD.

sounder (-ǫ^r) *s.* tañedor. *2* sondeador. *3* CIR. sonda. *4* ELECT. resonador.

sounding (-ing) *adj.* sonoro, sonante, resonante: *~ board*, tabla de armonía, secreto [del órgano]; tornavoz de púlpito. *2* de sondeo: *~ lead*, MAR. escandallo; *~ line*, sonda, sondaleza. *3 s.* acción de sonar. *4* sondeo. *5* braceaje. *6 pl.* MAR. aguas poco profundas.

soundless (-lis) *adj.* silencioso. *2* insondable.

soundly (-li) *adv.* sanamente. *2* cuerdamente. *3* firmemente. *4* vigorosamente. *5* profundamente, a pierna suelta.

soundproof (-pruf) *adj.* insonorizado.

soup (sup) *s.* COC. sopa: *~ dish*, plato sopero; *~ kitchen*, cocina de campaña; comedor de beneficencia; *~ tureen*, sopera. *2* fig. *in the ~*, en apuros.

sour (sau^r) *adj.* ácido, acedo, agrio. *2* rancio; fermentado. *3* verde [fruta]: *~ grapes*, fig. están verdes. *4* agrio, áspero, desabrido, huraño, avinagrado. *5* desagradable. *6* BOT. *~ cherry*, guindo; guinda.

sour (to) *intr.* agriarse. *2* enranciarse, fermentar. *3* malearse [la tierra]. *4 tr.* agriar. *5* enranciar. *6* estropear, amargar.

source (so^rs) *s.* fuente, manantial: *to have from a good ~*, saber de buena tinta.

sourdine (su^rdi·n) *s.* MÚS. sordina.

sourdough (sau·^rdou) *s.* levadura.

sourish (sau·rish) *adj.* agrillo, agrete.

sourness (sau·^rnis) *s.* acidez, agrura. *2* aspereza.

soursop (-sap) *s.* BOT. guanábano; guanábana.

souse (saus) *s.* escabeche, encurtido; cabeza, mano u oreja de cerdo en vinagre. *2* zambullida, remojón.

souse (to) *tr.* escabechar, encurtir. *2* zambullir; remojar. *3* inundar. *4* (E.U.) emborrachar. *5 intr.* mojarse, empaparse. *6* zambullirse. *7* (E.U.) emborracharse.

soutane (suta·n) *s.* sotana.

south (sauz) *s.* sur, mediodía. *2 adj.* del sur, meridional: *South America*, América del Sur; *South American*, sudamericano; *South Pole*, Polo Sur. *3 adv.* al sur; hacia el sur.

southeast (sauzi·st) *adj.-s.* sudeste. *2 adv.* hacia el sudeste, del sudeste.

southeastern (sauzi·stǫ^rn) *adj.* del sudeste.

souther (sau·zǫ^r) *s.* temporal o viento del sur.

southerly (sǫ·ðǫ^rli) *adj.-adv.* del sur.

southern (sǫ·ðǫ^rn) *adj.* del sur, meridional: *Southern Cross*, ASTR. Cruz del Sur.

southernmost (-moust) *adj.* más meridional.

southernwood (-wud) *s.* BOT. abrótano.

southlander (sau·zlændǫ^r) *s.* meridional.

southpaw (-po) *adj.-s.* DEP. zurdo.

southward (-uǫ^rd) *adj.* situado hacia el sur. *2 adv.* al sur, hacia el sur.

southwest (-ue·st) *adj.-s.* sudoeste.

southwester (-ǫ^r) *s.* temporal o viento del sudoeste. *2* MAR. sueste [sombrero].

southwestern (sauzue·stǫ^rn) *adj.* del sudoeste.

souvenir (suveni·^r) *s.* recuerdo.

sovereign (sǫ·vrin) *adj.* soberano. *2* supremo, sumo. *3 s.* soberano [monarca; moneda].

sovereignty (-ti) *s.* soberanía. *2* supremacía.

soviet (sou·viet) *s.* soviet. *2 adj.* soviético: *Soviet Union*, Unión Soviética.

sow (sau) *s.* ZOOL. cerda, marrana. *2* ZOOL. *~ bug*, cochinilla de la humedad.

sow (to) (sou) *tr.* sembrar: fig. *to ~ one's wild oats*, calaverear, pasar las mocedades. ¶ Pret.: *sowed*; *p. p.: sown* o *sowed*.

sowbread (sau·bred) *s.* BOT. pamporcino.

sower (sou·ǫ^r) *s.* sembrador. *2* sembradera.

sown (soun) *p. p.* de TO SOW.

soy (soi), **soya** (sou·ia), **soybean** (soi·bɪn) *s.* BOT. soja [planta y semilla].

spa (spa) *s.* balneario. *2* manantial de agua mineral.

space (speis) *s.* espacio. | No tiene el sentido de lentitud, tardanza: *~ bar*, *~ key*, espaciador [de máquina de escribir]. *2* trecho, distancia. *3* plaza, sitio. *4* tiempo, oportunidad.

space (to) *tr.* espaciar. *2* IMPR. regletear.

spaceless (-lis) *adj.* sin extensión.

spacious (spei·shøs) *adj.* espacioso; vasto, dilatado. *2* amplio, comprensivo.

spadassin (spadæ·sin) *s.* espadachín.

spade (speid) *s.* laya, pala [para remover la tierra]; zapa: *to call a* ~ *a* ~, llamar al pan, pan y al vino, vino. *2 pl.* picas [de la baraja inglesa].

spade (to) *tr.* layar, zapar, remover la tierra.

spadix (spei·diks) *s.* BOT. espádice.

Spain (spein) *n. pr.* GEOGR. España.

spall (spɔl) *s.* astilla.

spall (to) *tr.* romper, astillar [esp. piedra].

span (spæn) *s.* palmo, llave de la mano. *2* extensión; trecho, espacio, lapso; instante. *3* luz [de un arco]; ojo [de puente]. *4* tronco [de caballerías]. *5* envergadura [de aeroplano].

span (to) *tr.* medir por palmos; medir [en general]. *2* extenderse de un lado a otro de; tender un arco o puente sobre. *3* alcanzar, abarcar [en el espacio o en el tiempo]. ¶ Pret. y p. p.: *spanned;* ger.: *-nning.*

spandrel (spæ·ndrøl) *s.* ARQ. enjuta, embecadura.

spangle (spæ·ngøl) *s.* lentejuela; cosa brillante. *2* destello.

spangle (to) *tr.* adornar con lentejuelas o cosas brillantes. *2 intr.* destellar, centellear.

Spaniard (spæ·nia^rd) *s.* español.

spaniel (spæ·niøl) *s.* perro de aguas.

Spanish (spæ·nish) *adj.* español, hispano hispánico: ~ *broom,* retama; ~ *fly,* ENT. cantárida; ~ *leather,* cordobán; ~ *Main,* GEOGR. Tierra Firme; Mar del Caribe; ~ *shawl,* mantón de Manila; ~ *white,* yeso mate. *2 s.* lengua española o castellana. *3 pl. the Spanish,* los españoles.

Spanish-American *adj.-s.* hispanoamericano.

Spanish-speaking *adj.* de habla española.

spank (spæŋk) *s.* golpe, palmada, nalgada.

spank (to) *tr.* azotar, dar nalgadas. *2 intr.* correr, galopar.

spanker (-ø^r) *s.* azotador; azote. *2* pers. o cosa notable. *3* caballo veloz. *4* MAR. cangreja de mesana.

spanking (-ing) *s.* nalgada; azotaina. *2 adj.* rápido, veloz. *3* fuerte [viento]. *4* grande, notable.

spanless (spæ·nlis) *adj.* que no se puede abarcar o medir.

spanner (spæ·nø^r) *s.* MEC. llave de tuerca, llave inglesa.

spanworm (spæ·nwø^rm) *s.* ENT. oruga geómetra.

spar (spa^r) *s.* MINER. espato. *2* MAR. palo; verga; botalón. *3* pértiga. *4* hurgonazo. *5* boxeo, combate de boxeo. *6* riña de gallos. *7* riña, pelea. *8 adj.* MAR. ~ *deck,* cubierta superior sin estructuras altas.

spar (to) *tr.* MAR. proveer de palos, vergas, etc. *2 intr.* boxear. *3* luchar a espolonazos [los gallos]. *4* reñir, disputar. ¶ Pret. y p. p.: *sparred;* ger.: *-rring.*

spare (spe·ø^r) *adj.* de repuesto, de recambio; sobrante; libre, disponible: ~ *parts,* piezas de recambio; ~ *time,* tiempo libre, ratos perdidos. *2* flaco, enjuto. *3* escaso, sobrio, frugal. *4* cicatero. *5 s.* pieza de recambio.

spare (to) *tr.* ahorrar, economizar, evitar, excusar: *to have (something) to* ~, tener [algo] de sobra; *to be spared the labour,* ahorrarse el trabajo. *2* prescindir de, pasar sin. *3* perdonar, hacer gracia de. *4* no maltratar. *5* ~ *oneself,* cuidarse; evitarse molestias. *6 intr.* economizar. *7* ser clemente.

spare-built *adj.* delgado, enjuto.

sparerib (-rib) *s.* chuleta de cerdo casi descarnada.

sparing (-ing) *adj.* económico, parco, sobrio, frugal. *2* escaso. *3* clemente.

spark (spa^rk) *s.* chispa; centella, chispazo: ~ *arrester,* ELECT. parachispas; ~ *coil,* bobina de inducción; ~ *plug,* bujía [del motor]. *2* fig. chispa, átomo, pizca. *3* galán; lechuguino.

spark (to) *intr.* chispear, echar chispas, centellear.

sparkle (-øl) *s.* chispa, destello, brillo, centelleo. *2* viveza, animación. *3* chispa [diamante pequeño]. *4* chispa, átomo, pizca.

sparkle (to) *intr.* chispear, destellar, centellear, brillar. *2* espumar [un vino]. *3* tener viveza, animación.

sparklet (spa^r·kløt) *s.* centellita, chispita.

sparkling (-ing) *adj.* chispeante, centelleante. *2* vivo, animado. *3* espumoso [vino].

sparrow (spæ·rou) *s.* ORN. gorrión. *2* nombre de otros pájaros.

sparrow-hawk *s.* ORN. gavilán, esparver.

sparse (spa^rs) *adj.* esparcido, desparramado. *2* escaso, claro, ralo.

sparsity (-iti) *s.* raleza. *2* escasez, parquedad.

Sparta (spa·^rta) *n. pr.* GEOGR. Esparta.

Spartan (-tan) *adj.-s.* espartano.

spasm (spæšm) *s.* MED. espasmo. *2* paroxismo.

spasmodic (spæsma·dik) *adj.* espasmódico. *2* intermitente.

spat (spæt) *pret.* y *p. p.* de TO SPIT. *2* cría [de los mariscos]. *3* golpecito. *4* gota, salpicadura. *5 pl.* botines [calzado].

spat (to) *intr.-tr.* desovar [los mariscos]. *2 intr.* sonar [la lluvia; un impacto]. *2 tr.* dar un golpecito. ¶ Pret. y p. p.: *spatted;* ger.: *-tting.*

spate (speit) *s.* (Ingl.) chaparrón. *2* (Ingl.) riada. *3* abundancia; torrente [de palabras]; fuerte emoción.

spate (to) *tr.* inundar.

spathe (spei·ð) *s.* BOT. espata.

spathic (spæ·zik) *adj.* MINER. espático.

spatial (spei·shal) *adj.* espacial.

spatter (spæ·tø^r) *s.* salpicadura, rociada. *2* chapoteo.

spatter (to) *tr.* salpicar, rociar. *2* difamar. *3 intr.* echar salpicaduras. *4* caer en gotas gruesas. *5* chapotear.

spatterdashes (-dæshiš) *s. pl.* polainas.

spatula (spæ·chøla) *s.* espátula [instrumento].

spatulate (spæ·chøleit) *adj.* espatulado.

spavin (spæ·vin) *s.* VET. esparaván.

spawn (spɔn) *s.* ICT. freza. *2* huevos de marisco. *3* desp. prole; producto, resultado.

spawn (to) *tr.-intr.* desovar [los peces, los mariscos]. *2* desp. producir, engendrar. *3 intr.* producirse en abundancia.

spay (to) (spei) *tr.* castrar [las hembras de los animales].

speak (to) (spik) *intr.* hablar: *to* ~ *for,* hablar por, ser prueba de; *to* ~ *out,* hablar claro, explicarse; hablar en voz alta; *to through the nose,* ganguear; *to* ~ *well for,* decir mucho en favor de; *so to* ~, por decirlo así. *2 tr.* hablar, decir, expresar, proferir: *to* ~ *one's mind,* decir lo que uno piensa; *to* ~ *volumes,* decir mucho, ser muy significativo. *3* hablar [una lengua]. ¶ Pret.: *spoke*, p. p.: *spoken.*

speakable (-øbøl) *adj.* decible.

speakeasy (-iši) *s.* fam. (E.U.) taberna clandestina.

speaker (-ø^r) *s.* el que habla. *2* orador. *3* presidente [de una asamblea]. *4* RADIO. locutor. *5* RADIO. altavoz.

speaking (-ing) *adj.* que habla, parlante para hablar: ~ *tube,* tubo acústico; *to be on* ~ *terms,* hablarse, tratarse. 2 *s.* habla, acto de hablar, discurso. 3 oratoria.

spear (spiʳ) *s.* lanza, venablo. 2 fisga, arpón [para pescar]. 3 tallo, caña [de hierba].

spear (to) *tr.* alancear. 2 atravesar con arpón. 3 *intr.* BOT. echar un tallo largo.

spearhead (-jed) *s.* moharra, punta de lanza.

spearman (-mæn) *s.* lancero.

spearmint (-mint) *s.* BOT. variedad de menta.

spearwort (-uǝʳt) *s.* BOT. ranúnculo.

special (speˑshǝl) *adj.* especial. 2 particular, peculiar. 3 ~ *delivery,* correo urgente. 4 *s.* tren, autobús, etc., especial. 5 carta urgente.

specialism (-išm) *s.* especialización.

specialist (-ist) *adj.-s.* especialista.

speciality (-iti) *s.* SPECIALTY.

specialize (to) (-aiš) *tr.* especializar. 2 detallar, particularizar. 3 *intr.* especializarse. 4 entrar en detalles.

specialty (-i) *s.* especialidad. 2 peculiaridad, cualidad distintiva.

specie (spiˑshi) *s.* efectivo, metálio.

species (spiˑshiš) *s.* especie [imagen mental; apariencia]. 2 especie sacramental. 3 LÓG., H. NAT. especie. 4 especie, clase, suerte. 5 género humano.

specific (al (spisiˑfik(ǝl) *adj.* específico. 2 preciso, determinado. 3 peculiar, característico. 4 *s.* FARM. específico.

specification (-eishøn) *s.* especificación. 2 *pl.* presupuesto de una obra; pliego de condiciones. 3 instrucciones, detalles técnicos.

specify (to) (spi-sifai) *tr.* especificar, detallar. 2 estipular, prescribir. ¶ Pret. y p. p.: *specified.*

specimen (speˑsimøn) *s.* espécimen, muestra, ejemplar. 2 fam. sujeto, individuo.

specious (spiˑshøs) *adj.* especioso, engañoso.

speck (spek) *s.* manchita; motita, partícula. 2 pizca, átomo.

speck (to) *tr.* manchar, motear.

speckle (-øl) *s.* manchita, punto.

speckle (to) *tr.* manchar, motear, salpicar de manchitas, espolvorear, esmaltar.

specs (-s) *s. pl.* fam. gafas, anteojos.

spectacle (-tøkøl) *s.* espectáculo, exhibición. 2 *pl.* gafas, anteojos.

spectacular (-tæ-kiulaʳ) *adj.* espectacular. 2 sensacional, aparatoso.

spectator (spektei·tøʳ) *m.* espectador.

spectatress (-tris) *s.* espectadora.

specter (speˑktøʳ) *s.* espectro, aparición.

spectral (-trǝl) *adj.* espectral.

spectre (-tøʳ) *s.* SPECTER.

spectroscope (-trøskoup) *s.* espectroscopio.

spectroscopy (spektra·skøpi) *s.* espectroscopia.

spectrum (speˑktrøm) *pl.* **spectra** (-tra) *s.* FÍS. espectro.

speculate (to) (speˑkiuleit) *intr.* especular, meditar, teorizar [sobre]. 2 COM. especular.

speculation (-ei·shøn) *s.* especulación, conjetura, teoría. 2 COM. especulación.

speculative (speˑkiuleitiv) *adj.* especulativo, contemplativo. 2 teórico. 3 COM. especulador.

speculator (-tøʳ) *s.* especulador, teórico. 2 COM. especulador. 3 TEAT. revendedor de billetes.

speculum (speˑkiuløm) *s.* CIR. espéculo.

sped (sped) *pret.* y *p. p.* de TO SPEED.

speech (spıch) *s.* palabra, habla, lenguaje. 2 idioma, dialecto. 3 cosa hablada, oración, discurso. 4 TEAT. parlamento. 5 conversación.

speechify (to) (-ifai) *intr.* fam. discursear.

speechless (-lis) *adj.* mudo, callado, silencioso. 2 estupefacto, cortado, sobrecogido, sin habla.

speechmaker (-meikøʳ) *s.* orador.

speed (spıd) *s.* rapidez, prisa, prontitud, presteza: *with all* ~, a toda prisa; *to make* ~, apresurarse, acelerarse. 2 marcha, andar, velocidad: ~ *gear,* cambio de marchas; ~ *limit,* máxima velocidad permitida; *full* ~, a toda velocidad. 3 *adj.* rápido.

speed (to) *tr.* acelerar, avivar, apresurar, dar prisa a. 2 despachar, expedir. 3 prosperar, favorecer, ayudar. 4 *intr.* apresurarse, correr. 5 llevar una velocidad excesiva. 6 prosperar, tener buen éxito. ¶ Pret. y p. p.: *sped* o *speeded.*

speedboat (-bout) *s.* canoa automóvil.

speedometer (spıda·mitøʳ) *s.* indicador de velocidad; taxímetro; odómetro.

speed-up *s.* aceleración, aumento de velocidad. 2 aumento de producción.

speedway (-wei) *s.* autopista.

speedwell (-wel) *s.* BOT. verónica.

speedy (-i) *adj.* rápido, veloz, ligero. 2 activo, pronto, diligente, expeditivo.

spelean (spili·æn) *adj.* troglodita.

speleology (spilia·lodǝ̈i) *s.* espeleología.

spell (spel) *s.* hechizo, encanto, maleficio. 7 hechizo, fascinación. 3 relevo, turno, tanda. 4 rato, período, temporada: *by spells,* por turnos; *a ratos.*

spell (to) *tr.-intr.* deletrear. 2 escribir correctamente. 3 *tr.* indicar, significar. 4 descifrar. 5 hechizar, encantar. 6 relevar, reemplazar. ¶ Pret. y p. p.: *spelled* o *spelt.*

spellbind (to) (-baind) *tr.* hechizar, encantar, fascinar. ¶ CONJUG. pret. y p. p.: *spellbound.*

spellbinder (-baindøʳ) *s.* orador persuasivo y arrebatador.

spellbound (-baund) *pret.* y *p. p.* de TO SPELLBIND.

speller (-øʳ) *s.* deletreador. 2 silabario, cartilla.

spelling (-ing) *s.* deletreo; ortografía.

spelt (spelt) *p. p.* de TO SPELL. 2 *s.* BOT. espelta.

spelter (speˑltøʳ) *s.* cinc, peltre.

spelt-wheat *s.* BOT. escanda, espelta.

spencer (spe·nsøʳ) *s.* chaqueta corta de punto.

spend (to) (spend) *tr.* gastar, expender. 2 consumir, agotar. 3 pasar [un tiempo]. 4 *intr.* gastar, hacer gastos. 5 consumirse, agotarse. ¶ Pret. y p. p.: *spent.*

spendthrift (-zrift) *s.* derrochador, malgastador, manirroto, pródigo.

spent (spent) *pret.* y *p. p.* de TO SPEND.

sperm (spøʳm) *s.* esperma, semen. 2 espermatozoo. 3 esperma de ballena: ~ *whale,* cachalote.

spermaceti (spøʳmase·ti) *s.* esperma de ballena.

spermatic (al (spøʳmæ·tik(ǝl) *adj.* espermático.

spermatozoön (-tošuˑøn) *s.* BIOL. espermatozoo.

spew (spiu) *tr.-intr.* vomitar, arrojar.

sphenoid (sfiˑnoid) *adj.* esfenoidal. 2 *s.* ANAT. esfenoides.

sphere (sfiʳ) *s.* GEOM., GEOGR., ASTR. esfera. 2 globo, orbe. 3 astro. 4 poét. atmósfera, cielo. 5 esfera [de acción social, etc.].

spheric (sfe·rik) *adj.* esférico.

spherical (sfe·rikǝl) *adj.* esférico. 2 globular, orbicular. 3 de las esferas, celeste, astral.

sphericity (sfiri·siti) *s.* esfericidad.

spheroid (sfi·roid) *s.* esferoide.

spheroidal (sfiroi·dǝl) *adj.* esferoidal.

spherometer (sfira·metøʳ) *s.* esferómetro.

spherule (sfe·riul) *s.* glóbulo.

sphincter (sfi·nktø^r) *s.* ANAT. esfínter.
sphinx (sfinks) *s.* MIT., ARQUEOL., ENT. esfinge. *2* fig. pers. enigmática.
spice (spais) *s.* especia. *2* sainete, picante, interés. *3* aroma, fragancia. *4* punta, algo, un poco.
spice (to) *tr.* condimentar con especias. *2* salpimentar, sazonar, dar picante o interés a.
spicery (-øri) *s.* especiería. *2* aroma, picante.
spick-and-span *adj.* nuevo, flamante, fresco. *2* pulcro, aseado, arreglado.
spicula (spi·kiula) *s.* espícula.
spicule (spi·kiul) *s.* espícula. *2* BOT. espiguilla. *3* aguja del hielo, de la nieve.
spicy (spai·si) *adj.* sazonado con especias, picante, aromático. *2* fig. sabroso, picante. *3* vivo, pronto. *4* elegante, llamativo.
spider (spai·dø^r) *s.* ZOOL. araña: *spider's web*, telaraña; ~ *lines*, ÓPT. retícula. *2* trébedes. *3* cazo o sartén con pies. *4* ZOOL. ~ *monkey*, mono araña.
spidery (-i) *adj.* parecido a una araña.
spiffy (spi·fi) *adj.* fam. guapo, elegante.
spigot (spi·gøt) *s.* espiche, botana, bitoque. *2* macho [de grifo o espita]. *3* (E.U.) grifo, espita.
spike (spaik) *s.* pincho, púa; punta de hierro. *2* clavo grande, alcayata. *3* BOT. espiga. *4* BOT. espliego. *5* (E.U.) gotas [de licor].
spike (to) *tr.* clavar [con clavos grandes]. *2* clavar [un cañón]. *3* atravesar, empalar. *4* acabar, poner fin a; inutilizar. *5* intr. formar espiga.
spikelet (-lit) *s.* BOT. espiguilla.
spikenard (-na^rd) *s.* BOT. espicanardo. *2* nardo [perfume].
spiky (-i) *adj.* puntiagudo. *2* erizado, armado de pinchos o púas.
spile (spail) *s.* botana, espiche. *2* estaca, pilote.
spile (to) *tr.* abrir [un barril]; ponerle botana o espita. *2* poner estacas o pilotes.
spilikin (spi·likin) *s.* SPILLIKIN.
spill (spil) *s.* astilla, alegrador [para encender]. *2* derramamiento. *3* fam. vuelco, caída.
spill (to) *tr.* verter, derramar. *2* contar, divulgar. *3* fam. despedir [de una montura, de un vehículo]. *4* MAR. quitar viento a [una vela]. *5* intr. verterse, derramarse. *6* pop. charlar [revelar lo secreto]. ¶ Pret. y p. p.: *spilled* o *spilt*.
spillikin (spi·likin) *s.* pajita [para jugar]. *2* pl. juego de las pajitas.
spilt (spilt) *pret.* y *p. p.* de TO SPILL.
spin (spin) *s.* giro, vuelta. *2* fam. paseo en coche o bicicleta. *3* AVIA. barrena.
spin (to) *tr.-intr.* hilar. *2* tejer [fantasías, etc.]; hacer, componer [una narración, etc.]: *to* ~ *a yarn*, contar un cuento increíble. *3* hacer girar. *4* hacer bailar [un trompo]. *5* *to* ~ *out*, alargar, prolongar, extender. *6* intr. dar vueltas, girar, pasar, rápidamente. *7* bailar [el trompo]. *8* AVIA. descender en barrena. ¶ Pret. y p. p.: *spun*; ger.: *spinning*.
spinach (spi·nich) *s.* BOT. espinaca. *2* COC. espinacas.
spinal (spai·nal) *adj.* espinal: ~ *column*, espina dorsal; ~ *cord*, médula espinal.
spindle (spi·ndøl) *s.* HIL., BIOL. huso. *2* BOT. raquis, eje. *3* MEC. eje, mandril, varilla. *4* balustre. *5* BOT. ~ *tree*, bonetero.
spindle (to) *intr.* crecer muy alto y delgado.
spindlelegs (-legš) *s.* pl. piernas largas. *2* sing. persona zanquivara.
spindle-shaped *adj.* ahusado, fusiforme.
spindrift (spi·ndrift) *s.* rocío, roción [del mar].

spine (spain) *s.* espinazo. *2* fig. valor, energía. *3* fig. parte saliente y esquinada. *4* espina, púa.
spinel (spine·l) *s.* MINER. espinela.
spineless (spai·nlis) *adj.* invertebrado. *2* fláccido, flojo; sin valor, sin energía. *3* sin espinas.
spinet (spi·nit) *s.* MÚS. espineta.
spinnaker (spi·nakø^r) *s.* MAR. spinnaker.
spinner (spi·nø^r) *s.* hilador, hilandero. *2* máquina de hilar.
spinneret (-øret) *s.* ZOOL. hilera.
spinney (-i) *s.* bosquecillo, soto.
spinning (-spi·ning) *s.* hila, hilado, hilatura. *2* giro rápido. *3* que hila, de hilar: ~ *mill*, fábrica de hilados; ~ *wheel*, torno para hilar. *4* que gira: ~ *top*, trompo. *5* rápido, veloz.
spinose (spi·nous) *adj.* espinoso [que tiene espinas].
spinous (-nøs) *adj.* espinoso.
Spinozism (spinou·šišm) *s.* espinosismo.
spinster (spi·nstø^r) *s.* soltera, solterona. *2* ant. hilandera.
spinstress (-tris) *s.* hilandera.
spiny (spai·ni) *adj.* espinoso. *2* punzante.
spiracle (spi·arakøl) *s.* ZOOL. espiráculo.
spiral (spai·ral) *adj.* espiral. *2* helicoidal. *3* de caracol [escalera]. *4* *s.* GEOM. espiral; hélice; espira.
spiral (to) *intr.* moverse en espiral; tomar forma espiral. *2* AVIA. volar en espiral.
spire (spai^r) *s.* GEOM., ZOOL. espira. *2* GEOM. espiral. *3* cima, cúspide. *4* ARQ. aguja, chapitel. *5* BOT. brizna, caña o tallo largo y delgado.
spire (to) *tr.* elevarse [como un chapitel]; rematar en punta. *2* elevarse en espiral. *3* brotar, germinar.
spirillum (spairi·løm) *s.* BACT. espirilo.
spirit (spi·rit) *s.* espíritu [en todos sus sentidos]: *the Holy Spirit*, el Espíritu Santo; ~ *rapper*, espiritista: *in* ~, en espíritu. *2* aparecido, espectro. *3* estado de ánimo, humor, temple. | A veces en *pl.*: *in good spirits*, alegre, de buen humor. *4* ánimo, valor; vivacidad, animación; energía, ardor, fuego: *to break the* ~ *of*, desalentar; reprimir, domeñar. *5* pl. alcohol, bebida espirituosa. *6* *spirits o high spirits*, alegría, animación, viveza; *out of spirits*, triste, abatido. *7* *animal spirits*, vivacidad, fogosidad, energía.
spirit (to) *tr.* alentar, animar. | A veces con *up*. *2* infundir cierto espíritu. *3* *to* ~ *away* u *off*, llevarse, raptar, escamotear, hacer desaparecer.
spirited (-id) *adj.* vivo, brioso, espiritoso, fogoso.
spiritedly (-idli) *adv.* vivamente, briosamente, fogosamente, animosamente.
spiritism (-išm) *s.* espiritismo.
spiritist (-ist) *s.* espiritista.
spiritless (-lis) *adj.* exánime. *2* abatido, desanimado. *3* cobarde. *4* flojo, sin vigor.
spiritual (spi·richual) *adj.* espiritual. *2* mental, intelectual. *3* eclesiástico. *4* inteligente, agudo. *5* de los espíritus. *6* *s.* espiritual [canto religioso de los negros].
spiritualism (-išm) *s.* espiritualismo. *2* espiritualidad. *3* espiritismo.
spiritualist (-ist) *adj.-s.* espiritualista. *2* espiritista.
spiritualistic (spirichuali·stik) *adj.* espiritista. *2* espiritualista.
spirituality (spirichuæ·liti) *s.* espiritualidad. *2* pl. bienes espirituales o eclesiásticos.
spiritualize (to) (spi·richualaiš) *tr.* espiritualizar.
spirituous (spi·richuøs) *adj.* espirituoso.

spirituousness (-nis) *s.* calidad de espirituoso.
spirometer (spaira·mitø^r) *s.* FISIOL. espirómetro.
spirt (spø^{r}t) *s.* SPURT.
spirt (to) *tr.* TO SPURT.
spit (spit) *s.* espetón, asador. *2* punta de tierra; banco de arena. *3* saliva, salivazo, escupitajo, esputo. *4* llovizna, nevisca.
1) spit (to) *tr.* espetar, ensartar, empalar. ¶ Pret. y p. p.: *spitted;* ger.: *-tting.*
2) spit (to) *tr.* escupir; esputar. *2* escupir, arrojar. *3 intr.* escupir. *4* lloviznar, neviscar. *5* chisporrotear. ¶ Pret. y p. p.: *spat;* ger.: *spitting.*
spitball (-bol) *s.* bolita de papel mascado.
spitchcock (spi·chkak) *s.* COC. anguila abierta o cortada y cocida.
spitchcock (to) *tr.* cortar y cocer. *2* tratar sumariamente.
spite (spait) *s.* despecho, rencor, inquina, resentimiento. *2 in ~ of,* a pesar de, a despecho de.
spite (to) *tr.* molestar, mortificar, irritar.
spiteful (spai·tful) *adj.* rencoroso, maligno, malévolo.
spitfire (spi·tfai^r) *s.* lo que escupe fuego; volcán, cañón, etc. *2* persona violenta, irascible.
spittle (spi·tøl) *s.* saliva, salivazo, escupidura.
spittoon (spitu·n) *s.* escupidera.
spitz (spits) *s.* perro de Pomerania.
splash (splæsh) *s.* salpicadura, rociada. *2* chapoteo. *3* mancha [de color]. *4* fig. *to make a ~,* llamar la atención, hacer sensación.
splash (to) *tr.* salpicar, rociar, manchar. *2* hacer saltar [el agua]. *3* chapotear, humedecer. *4 intr.* chapotear, chapalear.
splashboard (-bo^{r}d) guardabarros, alero.
splashy (-i) *adj.* cenagoso, lodoso. *2* llamativo; sensacional.
splatter (splæ·tø^r) *s.* SPATTER.
splatter (to) *tr.* rociar, salpicar; chapotear.
splay (splei) *adj.* ancho, extendido, desplegado. *2* abocinado, con derrame, capialzado. *3* tosco, pesado. *4 s.* extensión, expansión. *5* ARQ. alféizar, derrame, capialzo. *6* bisel, chaflán.
splay (to) *tr.* extender, desplegar. *2* VET. dislocar. *3* dar derrame, abocinar. *4* achaflanar.
splayfoot(ed (-fut(id) *adj.* de pies planos.
spleen (splin) *s.* ANAT. bazo. *2* bilis, rencor, mal humor. *3* esplín, melancolía.
spleeny (-i) *adj.* bilioso, irritable, enfadadizo. *2* melancólico.
splendent (sple·ndønt) *s.* brillante, esplendoroso.
splendid (-did) *adj.* espléndido [resplandeciente]. *2* ilustre, glorioso.
splendo (u) r (-ø^r) *s.* brillo, resplandor. *2* esplendor, magnificencia.
splenetic (spline·tik) *adj.* esplénico. *2* bilioso, rencoroso, malhumorado.
splenic (sple·nik) *adj.* ANAT. esplénico.
splenius (splı·niøs) *s.* ANAT. esplenio.
splice (splais) *s.* junta, empalme; ayuste.
splice (to) *tr.* empalmar, ayustar. *2* unir, juntar.
splint (splint) *s.* astilla. *2* tira estrecha. *3* CIR. tablilla, férula. *4* VET. sobrehueso.
splint (to) *tr.* CIR. entablillar.
splinter (-ø^r) *s.* astilla, esquirla. *2* rancajo. *3* cacho, añico. *4* CIR. tablilla.
splinter (to) *tr.* astillar. *2* CIR. entablillar. *3 intr.* astillarse, hacerse astillas.
splintery (-øri) *adj.* astilloso.
split (split) *s.* hendedura, grieta. *2* división, cisma, rompimiento. *3* astilla, raja. *4* media botella;

media copa. *5 pl.* despatarrada acrobática. *6 adj.* hendido, partido, rajado, dividido.
split (to) *tr.* hender, partir, rajar, dividir, separar: *to ~ one's sides,* desternillarse de risa. *2* reventar, romper. *3* revelar [un secreto]. *4 intr.* henderse, partirse, rajarse. *5* estallar, romperse. *6* separarse, dividirse. ¶ Pret. y p. p.: *split* o *splitted;* ger.: *-tting.*
splitting (-ing) *adj.* que raja o parte. *2* veloz. *3* muy cómico.
splotch (splach) *s.* mancha, borrón.
splotch (to) *tr.* manchar, salpicar.
splurge (splø^{r}dỹ) *s.* alarde, ostentación.
splutter (splø·tø^r) *s.* balbuceo, farfulla. *2* barullo, confusión. *3* rociada, salpicadura.
splutter (to) *tr.-intr.* balbucir, farfullar. *2* echar rociadas o salpicaduras.
splutterer (-ø^r) *s.* farfullador.
spoil (spoil) *s.* despojo, botín, presa. *2* saqueo, robo. *3 pl.* despojos, sobras.
spoil (to) *tr.* saquear, robar: *to ~ of,* privar de. *2* estropear, echar a perder. *3* viciar, corromper, pudrir. *4* mimar, malcriar. *5 intr.* estropearse, echarse a perder. ¶ Pret. y p. p.: *spoiled* o *spoilt.*
spolit (-t) *pret.* y *p. p.* de TO SPOIL.
spoke (spouk) *pret.* de TO SPEAK. *2 s.* rayo [de rueda]. *3* galga [freno]: *to put a ~ in one's wheel,* poner estorbos a uno. *4* travesaño [de escalera]. *5* cabilla [del timón].
spoke (to) *tr.* enrayar. *2* trabar, frenar.
spoken (-øn) *p. p.* de TO SPEAK.
spokesman (-smæn) *s.* portavoz, vocero. *2* orador.
spoliation (spouliei·shøn) *s.* expoliación, despojo, saqueo, rapiña.
spoliator (-tø^r) *s.* expoliador, saqueador.
spondaic (spandei·k) *adj.* espondaico.
spondee (spa·ndi) *s.* espondeo.
sponge (spøndỹ) *s.* esponja: *~ cake,* bizcocho muy ligero; *to thrown up the ~,* darse por vencido. *2* fig. gorrón, parásito. *3* ARTILL. lanada.
sponge (to) *tr.* lavar con esponja, borrar. *2* absorber, chupar. *3* sacar, exprimir. *4* esponjar [la masa]. *5 intr.* esponjarse. *6* pescar esponjas. *7 to ~ on,* vivir, etc., a costa de.
sponger (-ø^r) *s.* el que lava con esponja. *2* pescador de esponjas. *3* gorrón, sablista.
spongy (-i) *adj.* esponjoso. *2* fungoso. *3* flojo, sin consistencia. *4* mojado, lluvioso.
sponsion (spa·nshøn) *s.* acción de salir fiador o responder por otro.
sponsor (-sø^r) *s.* fiador, responsable. *2* padrino, madrina. *3* patrocinador.
sponsor (to) *tr.* salir fiador de, responder de [otro] o por [otro]. *2* apadrinar. *3* patrocinar.
sponsorship (-ship) *s.* fianza. *2* padrinazgo. *3* patrocinio.
spontaneity (spantanı·iti) *s.* espontaneidad.
spontaneous (spantei·niøs) *adj.* espontáneo.
spook (spuk) *s.* fam. fantasma, aparición.
spool (spul) *s.* carrete, canilla, carretel, bobina.
spool (to) *tr.* devanar en carrete, encanillar.
spoon (spun) *s.* cuchara: *~ hook,* anzuelo de cuchara. *2* cierto bastón de golf. *3* pop. bobo; chalado.
spoon (to) *tr.* cucharear. *2* dar forma de cuchara. *4* ponerse tierno, acaramelado.
spoonbill (-bil) *s.* ORN. cuchareta; espátula.
spoondrift (-drift) *s.* rocío de las olas.
spoonful (-ful) *s.* cucharada.
spoony (-i) *adj.* amartelado, acaramelado. *2 s.* galán acaramelado.

sporadic (sporæ·dik) *adj.* esporádico.
sporangium (sporæ·ndÿiøm) *s.* BOT. esporangio.
spore (spo^r) *s.* BIOL. espora.
sporidium (spori·diøm) *s.* BOT. esporidio.
sporran (spo·ran) *s.* escarcela de los montañeses de Escocia.
sport (spo^{r}t) *s.* deporte. *2* juego, diversión, pasatiempo. *3* broma, burla: *in* ~, en broma; *to make* ~ *of*, burlarse de. *4* irrisión, hazmerreír. *5* juguete [de uno, de las pasiones, etc.]. *6* deportista, aficionado a los deportes. *7 fam.* el que sabe perder; amigo, buen compañero. *8* BIOL. mutación.
sport (to) *tr.* ostentar, lucir. *2 intr.* jugar, divertirse, retozar, holgar. *3* bromear.
sportful (-ful) *adj.* juguetón. *2* chancero. *3* hecho ´ en broma, por juego.
sporting (spo·^{r}ting) *adj.* deportivo. *2* que requiere cualidades deportivas; honrado, leal, arriesgado.
sportive (-iv) *adj.* juguetón. *2* alegre, festivo.
sports (-s) *adj.* deportivo, de deporte.
sportsman (-mæn) *m.* deportista. *2* hombre leal, que juega limpio, que sabe perder.
sportsmanlike (-mænslaik) *adj.* deportivo; leal, honrado.
sportsmanship (-mænship) *s.* destreza en los deportes; afición a ellos. *2* deportividad.
sportswear (-ue·^{r}) *s.* ropa o trajes de deporte.
sportswoman (-wumæn) *s.* mujer deportista.
sporty (spo·^{r}ti) *adj. fam.* deportivo. *2* alegre, disipado. *3* ostentoso, chillón.
spot (spat) *s.* mancha, borrón: ~ *remover*, quitamanchas. *2* lunar, pinta, punto; mácula. *3* sitio, lugar, paraje, punto: *in spots*, aquí y allí; en algunos respectos; *on the* ~, en el sitio mismo; en el acto, al punto; alerta, despierto. *4 adj.* disponible, contante [dinero].
spot (to) *tr.* manchar. *2* motear, tachonar. *3* marcar, señalar. *4* reconocer, descubrir, divisar, observar; localizar. *5* colocar [una bola, etc.]. *6* diseminar. *7 intr.* mancharse. ¶ Pret. y p. p.: *spotted*; ger.: *-tting*.
spotless (-is) *adj.* limpio, inmaculado.
spotlight (-lait) *s.* reflector [de teatro], proyector orientable. *2 fig.* vista o atención del público. *3* AUTO. faro piloto o giratorio.
spotted (-id) *adj.* manchado, moteado, pintado: ~ *fever*, tifus exantemático.
spotter (-ø^r) *s.* pop. (E.U.) detective.
spotty (-i) *adj.* manchado.
spousal (spau·śal) *adj.* nupcial. *2 s. pl.* nupcias, bodas.
spouse (spauš) *s.* esposo; esposa; consorte.
spout (spaut) *s.* caño, espita, canilla [para líquidos]; pico, pitorro [de vasija]; gárgola, canalón. *2* chorro; surtidor. *3* aguacero. *4* pop. casa de empeños.
spout (to) *tr.* echar, arrojar [en chorro]. *2* pop. empeñar [un reloj, etc.]. *3 tr.-intr.* declamar. *4 intr.* chorrear, borbotar; brotar [un líquido].
sprain (sprein) *s.* MED. torcedura, esguince.
sprain (to) *tr.* MED. torcer: *to* ~ *one's ankle*, torcerse el tobillo.
sprang (spræng) *pret.* de TO SPRING.
sprat (spræt) *s.* ICT. arenque pequeño.
sprawl (sprol) *s.* postura del que yace, cae o se arrastra con las extremidades extendidas. *2* desparramamiento [de una planta].
sprawl (to) *intr.* yacer, caer, arrastrarse con las extremidades extendidas. *2* extenderse, despa-

rramarse [una planta]. *3 tr.* abrir, extender [los brazos, piernas, ramas, etc.].
spray (sprei) *s.* líquido pulverizado; rocío [del mar, de una cascada]. *2* ramita, ramaje.
spray (to) *tr.* esparcir [un líquido] en gotas finas. *2* rociar, pulverizar [con un líquido].
sprayer (-ø^r) *s.* pulverizador; rociador.
spread (spred) *pret.* y *p. p.* de TO SPREAD. *2 adj.* extendido, etc. *3* BLAS. exployada [águila]. *4 s.* extensión, despliegue, desarrollo. *5* amplitud. *6* extensión [de terreno, etc.]. *7* difusión, propagación. *8* AVIA. envergadura. *9* cobertor; tapete; mantel. *10* mesa puesta, comida, festín.
spread (to) *tr.* extender, desplegar, desenvolver, alargar. *2* extender, esparcir, desparramar, *3* divulgar, publicar. *4* difundir, propagar. *5* emitir, exhalar. *6* ofrecer a la vista. *7* untar [con]; dar una mano [de]. *8* poner [la mesa], disponer, preparar. *9 fam. to* ~ *oneself*, echar el resto; fachendear. *10 intr.* extenderse. *11* esparcirse, desparramarse. *12* difundirse, propagarse. *13* abrirse, separarse. ¶ Pret. y p. p.: *spread.*
spread-eagle *adj.* (E.U.) patriotero [discurso, etc.].
spree (sprɪ) *s.* diversión, fiesta, juerga, parranda. *2* borrachera.
spree (to) *intr.* divertirse, ir de parranda. *2* emborracharse.
sprig (sprig) *s.* ramita, pimpollo. *2* hita, espiga [clavo].
sprightly (sprai·tli) *adj.* vivo, alegre, animado. *2* brioso, ágil, desenvuelto.
spring (spring) *s.* primavera [estación]. *2* fuente, manantial. *3* origen, principio; móvil. *4* salto, brinco. *5* muelle, resorte, ballesta. *6* resorte, elasticidad. *7* vigor, energía. *8* alabeo, combadura. *9* ARQ. arranque [de un arco]. *10 adj.* primaveral, de primavera. *11* de manantial. *12* de resorte, de muelle: ~ *latch*, cerradura de golpe; ~ *mattress*, colchón de muelles. *13* ~ *tide*, marea viva.
spring (to) *intr.* saltar, brincar; lanzarse, precipitarse, abalanzarse: *to* ~ *to one's feet*, *to* ~ *up*, levantarse de un salto. *2* salir, nacer, brotar; dimanar, provenir. *3* salir, aparecer, elevarse, crecer. | A veces con *forth, out* o *up*. *4* ARQ. arrancar [un arco]. *5* moverse, cerrarse, etc., por resorte, de golpe. *6* torcerse, alabearse, romperse. *7 tr.* hacer saltar. *8* levantar [la caza]. *9* sacar, presentar, dar, etc., de sopetón. *10* soltar [un resorte]; cerrar [con resorte]; meter o encajar haciendo muelle. *11* torcer, alabear, romper, rajar. *12* hacer estallar [una mina]; saltar [una valla, etc.]. *13 to* ~ *a leak*, hacer agua [un buque]. ¶ Pret.: *sprang* o *sprung*; p. p.: *sprung.*
springboard (-bo·^{r}d) *s.* trampolín.
springbook (-bok) *s.* ZOOL. gacela del África del Sur.
springer (-ø^r) *s.* saltador. *2* ojeador. *3* ARQ. imposta; sillar de arranque.
springiness (-inis) *s.* resorte, elasticidad.
springtide (-taid) *s.* primavera [estación].
springy (-i) *adj.* elástico. *2* abundante en fuentes o manantiales.
sprinkle (spri·nkøl) *s.* rocío, rociada. *2* llovizna. *3* pizca, poco.
sprinkle (to) *tr.* rociar, salpicar, regar; espolvorear, asperjar. *2* esparcir. *3 impers.* lloviznar.
sprinkler (spri·nklø^r) *s.* regadera, aparato para regar.
sprinkling (-ing) *s.* rociadura, aspersión. *2* unas gotas, un poco, unos cuantos.

sprint (sprint) *s.* carrera corta y rápida. *2* corto período de esfuerzo.

sprint (to) *intr.* correr a toda velocidad, esp. por un corto espacio.

sprit (sprit) *s.* MAR. verga de vela de abanico.

sprite (sprait) *s.* duende, elfo, trasgo.

spritsail (spri·tseil) *s.* MAR. vela de abanico.

sprocket (spra·kit) *s.* MEC. diente que engrana con una cadena.

sprout (spraut) *s.* retoño, renuevo, brote. *2* pl. *sprouts* o *Brussels sprouts,* coles de Bruselas.

sprout (to) *intr.* germinar, brotar, retoñar, echar renuevos; crecer. *2 tr.* hacer germinar o brotar.

spruce (sprus) *adj.* pulcro, atildado, elegante, peripuesto. *2 s.* BOT. picea, abeto del Norte.

spruce (to) *tr.* asear, componer, vestir con elegancia. | Gralte. con *up.*

sprung (sprøng) *pret.* y *p. p.* de TO SPRING.

spry (sprai) *adj.* vivo, listo, ágil, activo.

spud (spød) *s.* laya larga y estrecha. *2* cosa corta y gruesa. *3* fam. patata.

spue (to) (spiu) *tr.-intr.* TO SPEW.

spume (spium) *s.* espuma. *2* espumarajo.

spume (to) *intr.* espumar, espumear.

spumous (-øs) *adj.* espumoso, espumajoso.

spumy (-i) *adj.* cubierto de espuma, espumoso.

spun (spøn) *pret.* y *p. p.* de TO SPIN.

spun-out *adj.* prolongado, prolijo.

spunk (spønk) *s.* fam. valor, denuedo; enojo. *2* yesca.

spunky (-i) *adj.* vivo, pronto. *2* valiente. *3* irritable, susceptible.

spur (spø[r]) *s.* espuela. *2* aguijón, estímulo, acicate: *on the ~ of the moment,* impulsivamente, sin reflexionar. *3* espolón. *4* uña puntiaguda. *5* pincho. *6* adj. *~ stone,* guardacantón; *~ timber,* MIN. ademe; *~ track,* FERROC. apartadero, vía muerta.

spur (to) *tr.* espolear, picar; aguijar, estimular: *to ~ on,* animar, incitar a seguir adelante. *2* poner o calzar espuelas. *3 intr.* picar espuelas, correr; seguir adelante. ¶ Pret. y p. p.: *spurred;* ger.: -*rring.*

spurge (spø[r]dÿ) *s.* BOT. euforbio; lechetrezna. *2 ~ laurel,* adelfilla.

spurious (spiu·riøs) *adj.* espurio. *2* BOT. falso, aparente.

spurn (spø[r]n) *s.* coz, puntapié. *2* desprecio.

spurn (to) *tr.* rechazar con desprecio, desdeñar, despreciar. *2* rechazar o echar a puntapiés.

spurred (spø[r]d) *p. p.* de TO SPUR.

spurrier (spø·riø[r]) *s.* el que hace espuelas.

spurry (-i) *s.* BOT. espérgula.

spurt (spø[r]rt) *s.* chorretada, borbotón. *2* explosión [de ira, etc.]. *3* esfuerzo o aumento súbito. *4* rato, momento.

spurt (to) *intr.* brotar, salir en chorro. *2* estallar [una pasión], hacer un esfuerzo. *3 tr.* arrojar en chorro. *4* espurriar.

sputter (spø·tø[r]) *s.* rociada, esp. de saliva. *2* chisporroteo. *3* farfulla, barbulla.

sputter (to) *intr.* echar saliva al hablar. *2* chisporrotear. *3 intr.-tr.* farfullar, barbullar. *4 tr.* despedir [gotas o partículas].

sputum (spiu·tøm), *pl.* **sputa** *s.* MED. esputo.

spy (spai) *s.* espía, espión.

spy (to) *tr.* espiar; acechar, observar. *2* divisar, columbrar. *3 intr. to ~ on* o *upon,* espiar a. ¶ Pret. y p. p.: *spied.*

spyglass (spai·glæs) *s.* catalejo, anteojo.

spyhole (spai·joul) *s.* atisbadero.

squab (skuab) *adj.* regordete, rechoncho. *2* im-

plume, recién salido de la cáscara. *3 s.* persona rechoncha. *4* pichoncillo. *5* cojín, almohadón. *6* sofá, otomana. *7 adv.* de golpe; a plomo.

squabble (skua·bøl) *s.* disputa, riña, pelotera.

squabble (to) *intr.* disputar, reñir.

squabbler (skua·blø[r]) *s.* reñidor, pendenciero.

squabby (skua·bi) *adj.* rechoncho.

squad (skuad) *s.* MIL. escuadra; pelotón, piquete.

squadron (skua·drøn) *s.* MAR. escuadra. *2* AVIA. escuadrilla. *3* MIL. escuadrón.

squalid (skua·lid) *adj.* escuálido, sucio, miserable.

squall (skuol) *s.* racha, chubasco, turbonada. *2* chillido.

squall (to) *impers.* hacer rachas, caer chubascos. *2 intr.-tr.* chillar.

squally (skuo·li) *adj.* borrascoso.

squalor (skua·lø[r]) *s.* escualidez, suciedad, miseria.

squama (skuei·ma), *pl.* **-mae** (-mi) *s.* BOT. y ZOOL. escama, escamilla.

squamate (-meit) *adj.* escamoso, con escamas.

squamose, -mous (-mous, -møs) *adj.* escamoso, lamelar.

squander (to) (skua·ndø[r]) *tr.* derrochar, despilfarrar, malgastar, disipar.

squanderer (-dørø[r]) *s.* derrochador, malgastador.

square (skue[r]) *adj.* cuadrado: *~ foot,* pie cuadrado; *~ measure,* medida cuadrada, de superficie; *~ root,* raíz cuadrada. *2* en cuadro: *two feet ~,* dos pies en cuadro. *3* cuadrangular. *4* en ángulo recto, escuadrado. *5* rehecho, fornido. *6* exacto, justo. *7* leal, recto, honrado. *8* saldado, en paz; empatado. *9* rotundo, categórico. *10* abundante [comida]. *11* MAR. de cruz, redonda [vela].

 12 adv. honradamente. *13* directamente. *14* firmemente. *15* en forma de cuadro.

 16 s. GEOM. cuadrado, cuadro. *17* MAT. cuadrado. *18* casilla, escaque. *19* cristal [de ventana]. *20* plaza [espacio abierto]. *21* manzana [de casas]. *22* escuadra, cartabón. *23* MIL. cuadro. *24 on the ~,* honradamente, de buena fe.

square (to) *tr.* cuadrar [dar figura de cuadro]. *2* GEOM., MAT. cuadrar. *3* escuadrar. *4* cuadricular. *5* medir en unidades cuadradas. *6* poner bien. *7* ajustar, saldar [cuentas]. *8* amoldar, ajustar, arreglar, regular. *9* pop. sobornar. *10 to ~ one's shoulders,* enderezar los hombros, cuadrarse. *11 to ~ oneself,* justificarse. *12 to ~ up,* enderezar. *13 intr.* concordar, conformarse [una cosa con otra]. *14* fam. pagar la cuenta. *15 to ~ up to,* tomar una actitud pugilística.

square-toed (-toud) *adj.* de punta ancha y corta [pie, zapato]. *2* fig. de ideas anticuadas.

squash (skuash) *s.* calabaza del gén. *Cucurbita.* *2* pulpa, cosa blanda o machacada. *3* golpe, caída [de algo blando]. *4* apretura [de gente]. *5* juego de pelota. *6* limonada.

squash (to) *tr.* aplastar, estrujar, machacar, despachurrar. *2* aplastar [dejar sin respuesta]. *3 intr.* aplastarse, despachurrarse. *4* apretarse, estrujarse.

squashy (-i) *adj.* blando y húmedo. *2* aplastado; fácil de aplastar.

squat (skuat) *adj.* en cuclillas, agachado. *2* rechoncho. *3 s.* postura del que está en cuclillas.

squat (to) *intr.* sentarse en cuclillas. *2* agacharse, acurrucarse, alebrarse. *3* establecerse como colonizador en tierras baldías o del Estado, sin título o para adquirirlo.

squatter (-ø[r]) *s.* el que se establece como colonizador en tierras baldías o del Estado, sin título o para adquirirlo.

squatty (-i) *adj.* regordete, rechoncho.
squaw (skuo) *s.* (E.U.) mujer o esposa india: ~ *man*, blanco casado con una india.
squawk (skuok) *s.* graznido, chillido. *2* queja.
squawk (to) *intr.* graznar, chillar. *2* quejarse.
squeak (skuik) *s.* chillido, chirrido, rechinido. *2 to have a narrow* ~, escapar por milagro.
squeak (to) *intr.* chillar, chirriar, rechinar. *2* fam. hablar, cantar [confesar lo secreto, delatar].
squeal (skuil) *s.* chillido, grito agudo.
squeal (to) *intr.* chillar, lanzar gritos agudos. *2 to* SQUEAK *2*.
squeamish (skur·mish) *adj.* delicado, escrupuloso, remilgado. *2* propenso a la náusea.
squeegee (skur·dyi) *s.* rodillo o escobilla de goma para restregar y secar superficies mojadas.
squeegee (to) *tr.* restregar con SQUEEGEE.
squeeze (skuiš) *s.* apretón, estrujón, abrazo estrecho. *2* comprensión. *3* apretura. *4* jugo exprimido. *5* facsímil obtenido por presión. *6* presión [para obligar]: *to put the* ~ *on*, apretar los tornillos a. *7* fam. *tight* ~, aprieto, apuro, brete.
squeeze (to) *tr.* apretar, comprimir. *2* estrujar, apretujar, prensar. *3* exprimir. *4* agobiar [con impuestos]. *5* obtener por presión. *6* apretar, obligar. *7 to* ~ *in* o *through*, hacer entrar o hacer pasar apretando. *8 to* ~ *out*, hacer salir apretando; exprimir. *9 intr.* apretujarse. *10* entrar, salir, pasar, apretando o entre apreturas. | Con *in, into, out* o *through*.
squeezer (skur·šøᵣ) *s.* exprimidera.
squelch (skuelch) *s.* aplastamiento, despachurro. *2* chapoteo.
squelch (to) *tr.* aplastar, despachurrar. *2* hacer callar, desconcertar. *3* sofocar, acabar con. *4 intr.* andar chapoteando.
squib (skuib) *s.* PIROT. carretilla, petardo. *2* escrito satírico.
squib (to) *intr.* tirar carretillas o petardos. *2 tr.* atacar con sátiras. ¶ Pret. y p. p.: *squibbed;* ger.: *-bbing.*
squid (skuid) *s.* ZOOL. calamar.
squill (skuil) *s.* BOT. escila, esquila, cebolla albarrana. *2* ZOOL. esquila, quisquilla, camarón.
squint (skuint) *s.* estrabismo; mirada bizca. *2* mirada de soslayo o furtiva. *3 adj.* estrábico [ojo]. *4* que mira de soslayo.
squint (to) *intr.* bizcar. *2* mirar de soslayo. *3* desviarse. *4 tr.* torcer [la mirada]. *5* entornar [los ojos].
squint-eyed (-aid) *adj.* bizco, bisojo, estrábico. *2* desconfiado, avieso, que mira atravesado.
squire (skuaiᵣ) *s.* escudero. *2* (Ingl.) hacendado, esp. el más importante de una localidad. *3* fam. caballero [de una dama].
squire (to) *tr.* escoltar [a una dama].
squirm (to) *intr.* retorcerse, serpear: *to* ~ *out of a difficulty*, salir con trabajo de un aprieto.
squirrel (skuø·rel) *s.* ZOOL. ardilla.
squirt (skuøᵣt) *s.* chorretada, chisguete. *2* jeringazo. *3* jeringa. *4* mequetrefe.
squirt (to) *tr.* lanzar en chorrito. *2* jeringar. *3* rociar. *4 intr.* salir en chorrito.
squirting cucumber *s.* BOT. cohombrillo amargo.
stab (stæb) *s.* puñalada, estocada, cuchillada.
stab (to) *tr.-intr.* herir con arma blanca, apuñalar, pinchar. ¶ Pret. y p. p.: *stabbed;* ger.: *-bbing.*
stability (stabi·liti) *s.* estabilidad. *2* firmeza, constancia. *3* cosa estable.
stabilize (to) (stei·bilaiš) *tr.* estabilizar.
estabilizer (-øᵣ) *s.* estabilizador.

stable (stei·bøl) *adj.* estable. *2 s.* establo, cuadra, caballeriza.
stable (to) *tr.-intr.* poner, tener o estar en un establo o cuadra.
stableboy (-boi) *s.* mozo de cuadra.
stack (stæk) *s.* almiar. *2* pila, montón, rimero. *3* pabellón [de fusiles]. *4* cañón de chimenea. *5* cuba [de alto horno]. *6* montón, gran cantidad.
stack (to) *tr.* apilar, amontonar. *2* poner [los fusiles] en pabellón.
stadholder (sta·tjouldøᵣ) *s.* STADTHOLDER.
stadium (stei·diøm) *s.* estadio.
stadtholder (stæ·tjouldøᵣ) *s.* estatúder.
staff (stæf), *pl.* **staves** (esteivs) o **staffs** *s.* palo, vara, bastón, garrote. *2* báculo. *3* vara, bastón de mando. *4* asta [de bandera, lanza, etc.]. *5* TOP. mira, jalón. *6* MIL. estado mayor; plana mayor. *7* personal [esp. técnico o directivo], cuadro. *8* redacción [de un periódico]. *9* MÚS. pentagrama. *10* cartón piedra.
staff (to) *tr.* proveer de personal técnico, o directivo.
stag (stæg) *s.* ZOOL. ciervo, venado. *2* toro castrado. *3* hombre solo [en una fiesta]. *4* ENT. ~ *beetle*, ciervo volante.
stage (steidy) *s.* TEAT. escenario, escena, tablas: ~ *box*, palco de proscenio; ~ *manager*, director de escena. *2* teatro [arte, profesión]. *3* escena, teatro, campo [de actividades]. *4* piso, alto [de un edificio]. *5* tablado, plataforma, andamio. *6* parada [de diligencia; casa de postas. *7* diligencia [coche]. *8* etapa, jornada: *by easy stages*, por cortas etapas; fig. por grados, gradualmente. *9* estadio, fase, estado, grado, etapa, período. *10* platina [del microscopio]. *11* RADIO. paso.
stage (to) *tr.* poner en escena. *4* preparar [algo] para que ocurra de un modo teatral.
stagecoach (-kouch) *s.* diligencia [coche].
stagecraft (-kræft) *s.* arte escénico.
stagehand (-jænd) *s.* TEAT. tramoyista, metemuertos, metesillas.
stager (-øᵣ) *s.* caballo de diligencia. *3* fig. *old* ~, veterano, perro viejo.
stagger (stæ·gøᵣ) *s.* tambaleo, vacilación.
stagger (to) *intr.* vacilar, tambalearse, temblar; hacer eses [al andar]. *2* vacilar, titubear, flaquear. *3 tr.* hacer vacilar. *4* causar vértigo. *5* asombrar, aturdir, asustar. *6* escalonar.
staggerer (-øᵣ) *s.* cosa que aturde o desconcierta.
staghound (stæ·gjaund) *s.* sabueso.
staging (stei·dying) *s.* andamiaje. *2* tráfico en diligencias. *3* TEAT. puesta en escena.
stagnancy (stæg·gnansi) *s.* estancamiento, paralización [estado].
stagnant (-nant) *adj.* estancado, estantío. *2* paralizado.
stagnate (to) (-neit) *intr.* estancarse, estar estancado; paralizarse.
stagnation (-ei·shøn) *s.* estancamiento; paralización.
stagy (stei·dyi) *adj.* teatral.
staid (steid) *adj.* grave, serio, formal, sentado, juicioso. *2* fijo, decidido.
stain (stein) *s.* mancha, mácula. *2* tinte, tintura [materia colorante].
stain (to) *tr.* manchar. *2* teñir; colorar: *stained glass*, vidriode color. *3* mancillar. *4 intr.* manchar; mancharse.
stainless (-lis) *adj.* limpio, inmaculado, sin mancha. *2* ~ *steel*, acero inoxidable.
stair (steᵣ) *s.* escalón, peldaño. *2 pl.* escalera,

tramo de escalera: *below stairs*, abajo, en el departamento de la servidumbre. *3 adj.* de escalera; ~ *well*, caja de escalera.
staircase (-keis) *s.* escalera; caja de escalera.
stairway (-wei) *s.* escalera.
stake (steik) *s.* estaca, piquete, jalón, estaquilla; poste, pilote. *2* AGR. rodrigón. *3* telero. *4* hoguera [suplicio]. *5* tas, bigorneta. *6* apuesta, puesta [en el juego]. *7* premio [de una contienda]. *8* lo que está en juego o se arriesga. *9 at* ~, en juego, comprometido, en peligro.
stake (to) *tr.* estacar [atar a una estaca; demarcar con estacas]. *2* rodrigar. *3* empalar. *4* apostar, arriesgar: *to* ~ *(one's) all*, jugar el todo por el todo.
stalactite (stalæ·ktait) *s.* estalactita.
stalagmite (stalæ·gmait) *s.* estalagmita.
stale (steil) *adj.* pasado, evaporado; rancio; viejo [pan]; picado [vino]. *2* gastado, viejo, trillado, sabido.
stale (to) *tr.* evaporar, enranciar, alterar. *2 intr.* pasarse, enranciarse. *3* perder la novedad, el interés.
stalemate (-meit) *s.* AJED. tablas por rey ahogado. *2* fig. estancamiento, punto muerto.
stalemate (to) *tr.* AJED. ahogar al rey. *2* estancar, paralizar.
stalk (stok) *s.* BOT., ZOOL. tallo, caña; caballo, pecíolo, pedúnculo. *2* pie [de copa]. *3* paso majestuoso. *5* caza al acecho.
stalk (to) *tr.* andar majestuosamente. *2* acercarse furtivamente a, espiar, acechar. *3* cazar al acecho, ocultándose.
stalking-horse (-ing) *s.* buey de cabestrillo. *2* máscara, capa, disfraz.
stall (stol) *s.* establo, cuadra; compartimento de establo o cuadra. *2* puesto [de venta]. *3* silla de coro. *4* TEAT. luneta, butaca.
stall (to) *tr.* poner o tener en establo o cuadra. *2* atascar, atollar. *3* parar, ahogar [un motor]. *4 intr.* estar en un establo. *5* atascarse, atollarse. *6* pararse, ahogarse [un motor].
stallion (stæ·liøn) *s.* caballo padre.
stalwart (sto·luaʳt) *adj.* fornido, forzudo. *2* valiente. *3* leal, acérrimo. *4 s.* persona forzuda o valiente. *5* POL. partidario acérrimo.
stamen (stei·men) *s.* BOT. estambre.
stamina (stæ·mina) *adj.* fornido, forzudo. *2* valiente. *3* leal, acérrimo. *4 s.* persona forzuda o valiente. *5* POL. partidario acérrimo.
stamen (stei·men) *s.* BOT. estambre.
stamina (stæ·mina) *s.* vitalidad, fibra, fuerza, vigor, resistencia.
staminate (stæ·mineit) *adj.* BOT. estamnífero.
stammer (stæ·møʳ) *s.* tartamudeo. *2* balbuceo, balbucencia.
stammer (to) *intr.* tartamudear. *2* balbucear, balbucir.
stammerer (-øʳ) *s.* tartamudo. *2* farfalloso.
stamp (stæmp) *s.* estampa, huella, señal, impresión. *2* sello, timbre [que se marca]; sello, póliza [que se pega]. *3* sello [utensilio; carácter distintivo]. *4* estampilla. *5* cuño, troquel. *6* carácter, género, suerte.
stamp (to) *tr.* estampar, imprimir, marcar. *2* ditinguir, caracterizar. *3* sellar, timbrar, estampillar. *4* poner sello a. *5* estampar [en relieve]. *6* METAL. triturar. *7* patear; apisonar. *8 to* ~ *one's foot*, patalear. *9 intr.* patear, patalear.
stampede (stæmpɪ·d) *s.* huida en tropel, con pá-

nico; *estampida. *2* determinación repentina y unánime.
stampede (to) *intr.* huir o correr en tropel, con pánico. *2* obrar súbitamente y por común impulso. *3 tr.* hacer huir en desorden.
stance (stæns) *s.* posición, postura.
stanch (stanch) *adj.* estanco. *2* fuerte, sólido, seguro. *3* firme, leal, constante, fiel.
stanch (to) *tr.* estancar, restañar. *2* contener, detener. *3 intr.* restañarse.
stanchion (stæ·nshøn) *s.* poste, puntal, montante, pie derecho. *2* MAR. candelero.
stanchion (to) *tr.* apuntalar, sostener.
stand (stænd) *s.* posición, puesto. *2* parada [de coches, etc.]. *3* alto, parada, detención. *4* resistencia: *to make a* ~, resistir, hacer frente; luchar. *5* tablado, tribuna. *6* puesto [en un mercado, etc.]; quiosco [de venta]. *7* velador, estante, pie, soporte.
stand (to) *intr.* estar o tenerse de pie o en pie. *2* ponerse en pie, levantarse, erguirse. *3* estar situado, hallarse. *4* estar, ponerse [de cierto modo]; tener [cierta altura]. *5* estar, permanecer, quedarse. *6* durar, subsistir; continuar en vigor. *7* pararse, detenerse; estancarse. *8* mantenerse firme, resistir. *9* ser [padrino]; salir [fiador]. *10* consistir. *11* ser compatible [con], conforme [a]. *12* presentarse [como candidato]. *13* descansar, estar sobre. *14* parar [el perro]. *15* MAR. dirigirse, hacer rumbo. *16 to* ~ *alone*, estar solo, ser el único. *17 to* ~ *at attention*, MIL. cuadrarse. *18 to* ~ *back*, retroceder; quedarse atrás. *19 to* ~ *by*, estar cerca, estar presente, quedarse allí; apoyar, defender; atenerse a; MAR., RADIO. estar listo. *20 to* ~ *for*, representar, significar; estar en lugar de, quer por, apoyar; presentarse para; MAR. hacer rumbo a. *21 to* ~ *in with*, estar en buenas relaciones con, gozar del favor de. *22 to* ~ *off*, apartarse, mantenerse apartado. *23 to* ~ *on*, descansar, estar colocado, sobre; depender de; insistir en. *24 to* ~ *on end*, ponerse de punta, erizarse. *25 to* ~ *out*, salir, sobresalir; resaltar, destacarse; mantenerse firme; MAR. alejarse de tierra. *26 to* ~ *to reason*, ser razonable, ser justo. *27 to* ~ *up*, estar derecho; levantarse, ponerse en pie. *28 to* ~ *up for*, defender, apoyar. *29 to* ~ *up to*, afrontar resueltamente.
30 tr. poner derecho, de pie. *31* sufrir, aguantar; soportar, someterse a. *33* atenerse a. *34* pagar, convidar a. *35 to* ~ *a chance*, tener probabilidad. *36 to* ~ *off*, tener a raya. *37 to* ~ *on end*, poner de punta; asentar sobre un extremo. *38 to* ~ *one's ground*, mantenerse firme.
¶ Pret. y p. p.: *stood*.
standard (stæ·ndaʳd) *s.* norma, regla establecida; tipo, nivel, medida: ~ *of living*, nivel de vida. *2* modelo, dechado. *3* marco [depesas y medidas]. *4* ley [de la moneda]. *5* patrón [monetario]. *6* base, pie, sostén; poste, pie derecho. *7* candelero alto. *8* estandarte, enseña. *9 adj.* establecido, de ley, oficial, normal, universal; standard: ~ *keyboard*, teclado universal; ~ *metre*, metro patrón; ~ *time*, hora oficial.
standard-bearer *s.* MIL. portaestandarte, abanderado. *2* jefe [de un movimiento].
standardize (to) (stæ·ndardaiš) *tr.* reducir a un tipo establecido, unificar, regularizar.
stand-by *s.* persona o cosa con quien se puede contar.
stander (stæ·ndøʳ) *s.* persona que está de pie. *2* STANDARD 6.

standing (-ing) *adj.* derecho, en pie, de pie. *2* para estar de pie. *3* parado, estancado. *4* fijo, permanente, duradero: ~ *army*, ejército permanente; ~ *committee*, comisión permanente. *5* DER. vigente. *6* que tiene base o pie. *7 s.* posición del que está en pie. *8* sitio, lugar. *9* reputación, crédito; posición social. *10* duración, antigüedad: *of old* ~, antiguo, de mucho tiempo.
stand-off *s.* reserva, frialdad. *2* empate, tablas. *3 adj.* STAND-OFFISH.
stand-offish *adj.* retraído, frío, reservado.
standpat (-pæt) *adj.-s.* fam. (E.U.) conservador [esp. en política aduanera].
standpoint (-point) *s.* punto de vista.
standstill (-stil) *s.* alto, parada, detención, estacionamiento. *2* pausa, descanso.
stanhope (-joup) *s.* especie de birlocho de un solo asiento.
stank (stænk) *pret.* de TO STINK.
stanniferous (stæni·førøs) *adj.* estannífero.
stanza (stæ·nša) *s.* estancia, estrofa.
stapes (stei·piš) *s.* ANAT. estribo.
staphylococcus (stæfiløka·køs) *s.* BACT. estafilococo.
staple (stei·pøl) *s.* armella, grapa. *2* grapa para sujetar papeles. *3* artículo o producto principal [de un país, etc.]. *4* fig. base; tema principal. *5* materia prima, en bruto. *6* fibra, hebra [de materia textil]. *7 adj.* corriente, de uso general. *8* principal, importante.
staple (to) *tr.* sujetar con grapas. *2* clasificar hebras textiles según su longitud.
stapler (stei·plóʳ) *s.* clasificador de lanas. *2* máquina para coser papeles con grapa.
star (staʳ) *s.* ASTR. estrella, astro. *2* estrella [figura de estrella; asterisco]: *Stars and Stripes*, la bandera de los E.U. *3* placa, gran cruz. *4* estrella, hado, destino. *5* estrella [de cine, etc.]. *6 adj.* ~ *shower*, lluvia de estrellas; ~ *thistle*, BOT. cardo estrellado.
star (to) *tr.* estrellar, tachonar de estrellas. *2* marcar con asterisco. *3* TEAT., CINE. presentar como estrella. *4 intr.* ser estrella. ¶ Pret. y p. p.: *starred*; ger.: *-rring*.
starblind (-blaind) *adj.* medio ciego.
starboard (-boʳd) *s.* MAR. estribor. *2 adj.* de estribor. *3 adv.* a estribor.
starch (staʳch) *s.* almidón, fécula. *2* tiesura, empaque. *3* pop. (E.U.) energía, vigor, actividad.
starch (to) *tr.* almidonar. *2* dar tiesura.
starchy (-i) *adj.* amiláceo, de almidón. *2* almidonado. *3* tieso, entonado.
stare (steʳ) *s.* mirada fija, de hito en hito.
stare (to) *tr.-intr.* mirar fijamente, de hito en hito; clavar la vista. *2 to* ~ *one in the face* saltar a la vista, ser evidente; ser inminente. *3 intr.* ser llamativo o chillón. *4* erizarse [el cabello].
starfish (staʳfish) *s.* ZOOL. estrellamar.
stargaze (to) (-geiš) *intr.* observar las estrellas. *2* estar distraído. *3* soñar despierto.
staring (ste·ring) *adj.* que mira fijamente. *2* chillón, llamativo. *3* que salta a la vista.
stark (staʳk) *adj.* tieso, rígido, yerto. *2* duro, severo. *3* desierto, desolado. *4* puro, completo, absoluto. *5 adv.* completamente, enteramente: ~ *mad*, loco de remate.
starless (staʳlis) *adj.* sin estrellas.
starlet (-lit) *s.* estrellita.
starlight (-lait) *s.* luz de las estrellas. *2 adj.* iluminado por las estrellas. *3* estrella [noche].

starlike (-laic) *adj.* estrellado [de figura de estrella]. *2* brillante, resplandeciente.
starling (-ing) *s.* ORN. estornino.
starred (staʳd) *adj.* estrellado, adornado con estrellas. *2* que tiene buena o mala estrella. *3* CINE., TEAT. presentado como estrella.
starry (sta·ri) *adj.* estrellado [lleno de estrellas; de forma de estrella]. *2* estelar, sidéreo. *3* brillante, resplandeciente.
star-spangled *adj.* estrellado, tachonado de estrellas.
start (staʳt) *s.* sobresalto, repullo, respingo, bote. *2* susto. *3* actividad intermitente: *by starts*, a ratos, a empujones. *4* salida, marcha, partida; principio, comienzo: *at the* ~, al principio. *5* impulso inicial: *to give a* ~ *to*, poner en marcha; ayudar [a uno] a establecerse. *6* ventaja, delantera: *to ge the* ~ *of*, coger la delantera.
start (to) *intr.* sobresaltarse, estremecerse, dar un salto, un respingo. *2* salir, partir, ponerse en marcha, arrancar: ~ *after*, salir en busca de; *to* ~ *for*, salir para. *3* comenzar, empezar: *to* ~ *with*, para empezar. *4* aflojarse, soltarse, salirse de sitio; moverse [un diente]. *5 to* ~ *off*, partir, ponerse en marcha. *6 to* ~ *up*, levantarse precipitadamente; aparecer de pronto; comenzar a funcionar. *7 tr.* levantar [la caza]; desemboscar. *8* poner en marcha, en movimiento; hacer funcionar; hacer o ayudar a empezar. *9* dar la salida a. *10* empezar, comenzar, originar, armar, iniciar, suscitar: *to* ~ *a subject*, sacar un tema [de discusión]. *11* emprender [un negocio, etc.]. *12* aflojar, soltar, desencajar. *13 to* ~ *up*, poner en marcha.
starter (-øʳ) *s.* iniciador, el que comienza o sale. *2* MEC. mecanismo de arranque, motor de arranque. *3* DEP. juez de salida; el que da la salida.
starting (-ing) *s.* principio, comienzo; arranque, puesta en marcha, partida, salida. *2* sobresalto. *3 adj.* ~ *point*, punto de partida; ~ *post*, poste o línea de partida.
startle (to) (sta·ʳtøl) *tr.* asustar, sobresaltar, sorprender, alarmar. *2 intr.* saltar, sobresaltarse.
startling (sta·ʳtling) *adj.* notable, sorprendente.
starvation (staʳvei·shøn) *s.* hambre, inanición.
starve (to) (staʳv) *intr.* morir de hambre. *2* padecer hambre: *to* ~ *for*, sufrir por falta de. *3 tr.* matar de hambre, hambrear: *to* ~ *out*, MIL. rendir por hambre.
starveling (sta·ʳvling) *adj.-s.* extenuado por el hambre.
starving (-ing) *adj.* hambriento, famélico.
starwort (sta·ʳuøʳt) *s.* BOT. álsine, pamplina.
stasis (stei·sis) *s.* MED. éxtasis.
state (steit) *s.* estado, situación, condición: *married* ~, estado matrimonial; ~ *of siege*, estado de sitio. *2* FIS. estado. *3* POL. estado: *State Department*, (E.U.) ministerio de relaciones exteriores; ~ *secret*, secreto de estado. *4* pompa, aparato, ceremonia: ~ *room*, salón de ceremonias; *to lie in* ~, estar en la capilla ardiente. *5* majestad, dignidad.
state (to) *tr.* exponer, enunciar, relatar, declarar, manifestar, decir, expresar, formular. *2* consignar [en un escrito]. *3* plantear [un problema]. *4* fijar, determinar.
statecraft (-kraft) *s.* gobierno, arte de gobernar.
stateliness (-linis) *s.* majestuosidad.
stately (-li) *adj.* majestuoso, imponente. *2* elevado, sublime. *3* digno, ceremonioso.
statement (-mønt) *s.* declaración, manifestación,

afirmación. *2* exposición, relación, resumen, relato, informe, estado. *3* estado de cuentas.

stateroom (-rum) *s.* MAR. camarote. *2* FERROC. departamento individual con cama.

statesman (-smæn) *s.* estadista, hombre de estado.

statemanship (-ship) *s.* calidad de estadista. *2* STATECRAFT.

static (stæ·tik) *s.* RADIO. parásito atmosférico.

static(al (-al) *adj.* estático.

statics(-s) *s.* FÍS. estática.

station (stei·shøn) *s.* estación [de tren, meteorológica, etc.]. *2* parada, apeadero. *3* REL. estación. *4* puesto [militar; de un servicio]. *5* MAR. apostadero. *6* puesto, situación. *7* condición social.

station (to) *tr.* estacionar, situar, apostar.

stationmaster *s.* jefe de estación.

stationary (-eri) *adj.* estacionario; fijo.

stationer (-ø^r) *s.* librero; vendedor de objetos de escritorio.

stationery (-eri) *s.* objetos de escritorio.

statism (stei·tišm) *s.* estatismo.

statist (-ist) *s.* STATITIAN.

statistic (stæti·stik) *adj.* estadístico. *2 s.* estadística.

statistical (-al) *adj.* estadístico.

statistician (stæti·stishan) *s.* estadista [perito en estadística].

statistics (-s) *s.* estadística.

stator (stæ·tø^r) *s.* ELECT. estator.

statuary (stæ·chueri) *adj.* estatuario. *2 s.* estatuario. *3* estatuaria.

statue (stæ·chu) *s.* estatua, imagen.

statuesque (-esk) *adj.* estatuario. *2* escultural.

statuette (stæchue·t) *s.* estatuilla, figurilla.

stature (stæ·chø^r) *s.* estatura, talla.

status (stei·tøs) *s.* estado legal. *2* estado, condición.

statute (stæ·chut) *s.* ley, decreto, ordenanza. *2* estatuto, reglamento. *3* ~ *mile*, milla ordinaria.

statutory (-ori) *adj.* estatuido, legal.

staunch (stonch) *adj.* STANCH.

stave (steiv) *s.* duela [de tonel]. *2* palo, garrote. *3* LIT. estrofa. *4* MÚS. pentagrama.

stave (to) *tr.* poner duelas a. *2* reventar, desfondar. *3* vencer, quebrantar. *4 to* ~ *off*, alejar, evitar. *5 intr.* romperse, desfondarse. ¶ Pret. y p. p.: *staved* o *stove.*

staves (-s) *s. pl.* de STAFF y de STAVE.

stavesacre (-šeikø^r) *s.* BOT. estafisagria.

stay (stei) *s.* MAR. estay. *2* tirante, viento, riostra. *3* sostén. *4* ballena o varilla [de corsé]. *5* parada, detención. *6* suspensión, espera. *7* estancia, morada, permanencia. *8* estabilidad, duración. *9* resistencia, aguante. *10* pl. corsé, cotilla.

stay (to) *tr.* sostener, apoyar, apuntalar. *2* fundar, basar. *3* resistir, soportar. *4* detener, contener, frenar, reprimir. *5* aplazar, suspender. *6* esperar, aguardar. *7* sosegar. *8 intr.* estar de pie. *9* estarse quieto, parar, pararse. *10* estar, permanecer, quedarse en casa; *to* ~ *up*, velar. *11* tardar, detenerse. *12* resistir [tener resistencia].

stead (sted) *s.* (precedido de *in*) lugar, vez; servicio, utilidad: *in* ~ *of*, en lugar de, en vez de; *to stand in (good)* ~, servir, ser útil.

steadfast (-fæst) *adj.* firme, fijo, inmóvil. *2* constante, invariable. *3* firme, resuelto.

steadiness (ste·dinis) *s.* firmeza, estabilidad. *2* constancia, regularidad. *3* morigeración.

steady (ste·di) *adj.* firme, seguro. *2* estable, continuo, regular. *3* tranquilo. *4* grave, juicioso, morigerado.

steady (to) *tr.* afianzar, sostener, dar firmeza. *2* tranquilizar. *3* ajuiciar. *4* hacer continuo, regular. *5 intr.* afianzarse. *6* sentar la cabeza. | Gralte. con *down.*

steak (stek) *s.* tajada [para asar o freír], biftec.

steal (stil) *s.* hurto, robo.

steal (to) *tr.-intr.* hurtar, robar. *2* plagiar. *3* mover, introducir, hacer, etc., furtivamente. *4 to* ~ *a march on*, sorprender, ganar por la mano. *5 intr.* moverse, pasar, deslizarse, etc., furtiva o insensiblemente: *to* ~ *away*, escabullirse; *to* ~ *upon*, aproximarse sin ruido a.

stealing (-ing) *s.* hurto, robo.

stealth (stelz) *s.* disimulo, cautela, secreto: *by* ~, a hurtadillas, a escondidas, con cautela.

stealthy (-zi) *adj.* furtivo, secreto; disimulado, cauteloso.

steam (stim) *s.* vapor [esp. de agua]: ~ *boiler*, caldera de vapor; ~ *engine*, máquina de vapor; ~ *gauge*, manómetro; ~ *roller*, apisonadora; *to blow of* ~, *to let off* ~, descargar vapor; fig. desahogarse; *to get up* ~, dar presión. *2* vaho. *3* fig. vigor, energía. *5* vapor [buque]. *6* guiso hecho al vapor.

steam (to) *tr.* cocer, preparar, etc., al vapor. *2* dar vapor a. *3* transportar por vapor. *4* empañar con vapor. *5 intr.* emitir vaho o vapor, vahear. *6* marchar a vapor. *7* evaporarse.

steamboat (-bout) *s.* vapor [buque].

steamer (-ø^r) *s.* vapor [buque]. *2* máquina o generador, etc., de vapor.

steaming (-ing) *adj.* humeante, vaheante.

steamship (-ship) *s.* vapor [buque].

stearin (stiari·n) *s.* QUÍM. estearina.

steatite (sti·atait) *s.* esteatita.

steed (sti·d) *s.* corcel.

steel (stil) *s.* acero [metal, arma]. *2* afilón, chaira. *3* eslabón [para sacar chispa]. *4* dureza, rigor; frialdad; resistencia. *5 adj.* de acero, acerado; fuerte, duro, insensible: ~ *wool*, estropajo metálico.

steel (to) *tr.* acerar. *2* endurecer, fortalecer, acorazar.

steeliness (-inis) *s.* dureza de acero.

steelwork (-uø^{r}k) *s.* obra de acero.

steelworks (-uø^{r}ks) *s. pl.* acería, fábrica de acero.

steely (-i) *adj.* acerado. *2* duro, fuerte, inflexible.

steelyard (-ya^{r}d) *s.* romana.

steep (stip) *adj.* empinado, pendiente, escarpado. *2* excesivo, exorbitante. *3 s.* cuesta; precipicio. *4* empapamiento; maceración.

steep (to) *tr.* empapar, remojar; macerar. *2 intr.* estar en remojo.

steeple (sti·pøl) *s.* aguja, capitel, campanario.

steeplechase (-cheis) *s.* DEP. carrera [de caballos] de obstáculos.

steer (sti^r) *s.* novillo castrado, buey.

steer (to) *tr.* gobernar [una embarcación]; conducir, pilotar [un vehículo, un avión]. *2* fig. guiar, dirigir, gobernar. *3 intr.* gobernar, obedecer al timón. *4* dirigirse, conducirse.

steerage (-idỹ) *s.* gobierno, dirección. *2* MAR. proa. *3* MAR. ~ *passenger*, pasajero de tercera.

steering (-ing) *s.* dirección, gobierno [esp. de un buque o automóvil]: ~ *gear*, AUTO. dirección; ~ *wheel*, MAR. rueda del timón; AUTO. volante.

steersman (-søn) *s.* timonel, timonero.

stele (sti·li) *s.* ARQUEOL. estela.

stellar (ste·la^r) *adj.* estelar, astral, sidéreo. *2* estrellado [de figura de estrella]. *3* fig. sobresaliente.

stellate (ste·leit) *adj.* estrellado, radiado.

stem (stem) *s.* BOT. tallo, tronco; vástago; pezón, pedúnculo, pecíolo. *2* tronco [de una familia]. *3* raíz [de una palabra]. *4* CARP. espiga. *5* MEC. vástago. *6* pie [de copa]. *7* cañón [de pipa, de pluma]. *8* árbol [de reloj]. *9* palo [de letra]. *10* rabillo [de una nota musical]. *11* MAR. roda; proa.

stem (to) *tr.* desgranar, despalillar. *2* estancar, represar. *3* contener, refrenar. *4* MAR. embestir por la proa; navegar contra [la corriente]. *5* resistir, oponerse a. *6 intr.* provenir, derivar. *7* detenerse, contenerse. ¶ Pret. y p. p.: *stemmed;* ger.: *-mming.*

stemless (-lis) *adj.* BOT. acaule.

stemple (ste·mpøl) *s.* MIN. estemple.

stemson (ste·msøn) *s.* MAR. contrarroda.

stem-winder *s.* remontuar [reloj].

stench (stench) *s.* hedor, tufo, peste.

stencil (-sil) *s.* estarcido. *2* patrón, color o tinta para estarcir.

stencil (to) *tr.* estarcir.

stenograph (ste·nøgræf) *s.* escrito taquigráfico. *2* máquina para escribir en taquigrafía.

stenograph (to) *tr.* taquigrafiar.

stenographer (stena·grafø^r) *s.* taquígrafo.

stenography (stena·grafi) *s.* taquigrafía.

stentorian (ste·ntørian) *adj.* estentóreo.

step (step) *s.* paso [del que anda o baila; manera de andar; acción]: *to keep ~ with,* llevar el mismo paso que; *to watch one's ~,* andarse con tiento; *in ~,* llevando el [mismo] paso; de acuerdo; ELECT. en fase; *~ by ~,* paso a paso. *2* paso [en el progreso]. *3* escalón, peldaño; umbral. *4* estribo [de coche]. *5* grado [de una escala]. *6* huella, pisada. *7* paso, diligencia, medida: *to take steps to,* dar pasos, tomar medidas, para. *8* RADIO. paso. *9* MAR. carlinga. *10* ARQ. resalto. *11* tejuelo. *12* diente de llave. *13 pl.* escalera [de mano]. *14* gradería; escalones de entrada.

step (to) *intr.* dar un paso o pasos; andar, caminar, ir: *to ~ aside,* apartarse; *to ~ back,* retroceder; *to ~ down,* bajar; *to ~ in,* entrar, intervenir; *to ~ out,* salir; *to ~ over,* atravesar; *to ~ up,* subir. *2 fam.* andar de prisa. *3 to ~ on,* pisar, hollar. *4 tr.* poner, sentar [el pie]. *5* plantar [un mástil]. *6* escalonar. *7 to ~ down,* bajar, reducir. *8 to ~ off,* medir por pasos. *9 to ~ up,* elevar, aumentar. ¶ Pret. y p. p.: *stepped* o *stept;* ger.: *stepping.*

stepbrother (-brødø^r) *s.* hermanastro.

stepdaughter (-pdotø^r) *s.* hijastra, entenada.

stepfather (-fadø^r) *s.* padrastro.

Stephen (sti·vøn) *n. pr.* Esteban.

step-ins *s. pl.* pantalones de mujer.

stepladder (ste·plædø^r) *s.* escala, escalera de mano.

stepmother (-mødø^r) *s.* madrastra.

steppe (step) *s.* GEOGR. estepa.

stepping-stone *s.* estriberón, pasadera. *2* montadero. *3 fig.* escabel.

stepsister (-sistø^r) *s.* hermanastra.

stercoraceous (stø^rkørei·shøs) *adj.* estercolizo.

stere (sti^r) *s.* estéreo, metro cúbico.

stereography (steria·grafi) *s.* GEOM. estereografía.

stereometry (steria·metri) *s.* estereometría.

stereophonic (steriøfa·nik) *adj.* estereofónico.

stereoscope (ste·riøskoup) *s.* estereoscopio.

stereotype (ste·riøtaip) *s.* IMPR. estereotipo, clisé.

stereotype (to) *tr.* estereotipar, clisar.

stereotyping (-ing) *s.* estereotipia.

stereotypist (-ist) *s.* estereotipista.

sterile (ste·rail o -ril) *adj.* estéril. *2* improductivo.

sterility (steri·liti) *s.* esterilidad.

sterilization (sterilišei·shøn) *s.* esterilización.

sterilize (to) (ste·rilaiš) *tr.* esterilizar.

sterling (stø·^rling) *adj.* esterlina: *pound ~,* libra esterlina. *2* auténtico, puro, de ley.

stern (stø^rn) *adj.* duro, riguroso. *2* severo, austero. *3* torvo. *4* implacable. *5* firme, resuelto. *6 s.* MAR. popa: *~ chaser,* cañón de popa; *~ frame,* espejo de popa.

sternal (stø·^rnal) *adj.* esternal.

sternmost (stø·^rnmoust) *adj.* popel.

sternpost (-poust) *s.* MAR. codaste.

sternum (stø·^rnøm) *s.* ANAT. esternón.

sternutative (stø^rnui·tiv) *adj.* estornutativo, estornutatorio.

sternway (stø·^rnwei) *s.* MAR. marcha atrás.

stertor (stø·^rtø^r) *s.* estertor. *2* ronquido.

stertorous (-øs) *adj.* estertoroso.

stethoscope (ste·zoskoup) *s.* MED. estetoscopio.

stevedore (sti·vødo^r) *s.* estibador, cargador de muelle.

stew (stiu) *s.* COC. estofado, guisado. *2 fam.* preocupación, apuro.

stew (to) *tr.* estofar, guisar. *2 intr.* cocerse [el estofado]. *3* ahogarse de calor. *4* preocuparse, apurarse.

steward (-a^rd) *s.* mayordomo, administrador. *2* senescal. *3* capataz. *4* despensero. *5* camarero [de buque o avión].

stewardess (-is) *s.* mayordoma, administradora. *2* camarera [de buque].

stewed (stiud) *adj.* estofado, cocido: *~ fruit,* compota de frutas.

stewpan (stiu·pæn) *s.* cazuela, cacerola.

stewpot (stiu·pat) *s.* olla.

St. Gotthard (sei·nt ga·ta^rd) *n. pr.* GEOGR. San Gotardo.

stibium (sti·biøm) *s.* estibio, antimonio.

stick (stik) *s.* palo, garrote, vara: *walking ~,* bastón de paseo. *2* leño. *3* varilla, palito, barrita. *4* batuta. *5* palillo [de escultor, de tambor]. *6* barra [de lacre]. *7* trozo, porción. *8* hurgonazo, estocada; pinchazo. *9* IMPR. componedor. *10* pegajosidad, adhesión. *11* obstáculo, estorbo. *12* demora, duda. *13 pl.* ramitas. *14* trastos. *15 fig.* las piernas.

stick (to) *tr.* clavar, hincar. *2* poner, meter. *3* pegar, adherir. *4* pinchar, matar, punzar, picar. *5* atravesar, ensartar. *6* sacar, asomar. | Con *out* o *up.* *7* levantar, erguir. | Con *up.* *8* sufrir, tolerar. *9* untar. *10 intr.* estar clavado, pegado; clavarse, pegarse, adherirse. *11* aferrarse, mantenerse fiel o afecto; perseverar. *12* salir, sobresalir, resaltar. *13* atascarse. *14* detenerse, vacilar. *15 to ~ around,* estar o quedarse, por allí. *16 to ~ close,* mantenerse juntos. *17 to ~ to one's guns,* mantenerse firme. *18 to ~ up,* salir, proyectarse; estar o punta, erizado.

sticker (-ø^r) *s.* el que clava, fija, pega, etc. *2* espina, aguijón. *3* coma, cola. *4* etiqueta, papel engomado.

stickiness (-inis) *s.* tenacidad, glutinosidad.

sticking (-ing) *adj.* pegajoso, glutinoso, etc.: *~ plaster,* esparadrapo.

stick-in-the-mud *adj.-s.* retrógrado; rutinario [pers.].

stickle (to) (sti·køl) *intr.* disputar; porfiar por menudencias.

stickler (sti·klø^r) *s.* porfiador. *2* rigorista.

sticky (sti·ki) *adj.* pegajoso, viscoso, tenaz.

stiff (stif) *adj.* tieso [rígido; estirado]. *2* yerto, envarado. *3* duro, almidonado. *4* espeso. *5* tirante. *6* recio, fuerte, grande. *7* duro, difícil. *8* torpe, encogido. *9* terco, obstinado. *10* ~ *neck*, tortícolis; obstinación. *11 s.* fam. cadáver.

stiffen (to) (-øn) *tr.* atiesar. *2* envarar. *3* endurecer. *4* espesar. *5 intr.* atiesarse, ponerse tieso. *6* envararse. *7* endurecerse. *8* espesarse. *9* robustecerse. *10* obstinarse. *11* refrescar [el viento].

stiff-necked *adj.* obstinado, testarudo.

stiffness (-nis) *s.* tiesura, rigidez. *2* tirantez. *3* envaramiento.

stifle (stai·føl) *s.* VET. babilla.

stifle (to) *tr.* ahogar, sofocar. *2* apagar. *3* callar, ocultar. *4 intr.* ahogarse.

stifling (stai·fling) *s.* ahogador, sofocante.

stigma (sti·gmə), *pl.* **stigmas** o **-mata** (-tə) *s.* estigma [en todas sus acepciones].

stigmatize (to) (sti·gmataiŝ) *tr.* estigmatizar.

stile (stail) *t.* escalones de un portillo; portillo [en una valla]. *2* larguero, montante.

stiletto (stile·tou) *s.* estilete [puñal].

still (stil) *adj.* quieto, inmóvil: ~ *water runs deep*, fig. no te fíes del agua mansa. *2* tranquilo, sosegado. *3* silencioso, mudo. *4* suave [voz, ruido]. *5* muerto, inanimado: ~ *life*, naturaleza muerta. *6 adv.* aún, todavía. *7 conj.* no obstante, a pesar de eso. *9 s.* silencio, quietud. *10* alambique. *11* destilería.

still (to) *tr.* acallar. *2* aquietar, calmar. *3* detener, parar. *4 intr.* calmarse, aquietarse.

stillborn (sti·lbo'n) *adj.* nacido muerto.

stilly (sti·li) *adj.* silencioso, tranquilo. *2 adv.* quietamente, silenciosamente.

stilt (sti·lt) *s.* zanco. *2* ORN. cigoñuela.

stilted (sti·ltid) *adj.* realzado, elevado. *2* altisonante, hinchado.

stimulant (sti·miulənt) *adj.-s.* estimulante. *2 s. pl.* bebidas alcohólicas.

stimulate (to) (sti·miuleit) *tr.-intr.* estimular. *2* embriagar.

stimulation (stimiulei·shøn) *s.* excitación, estímulo.

stimulus (sti·miuløs) *s.* estímulo, incentivo.

sting (sting) *s.* picadura, punzada; mordedura [de serpiente]. *2* aguijón, estímulo. *3* escozor. *4* ZOOL., BOT. púa, aguijón.

sting (to) *tr.-intr.* picar, punzar, pinchar; morder [la serpiente]. *2* escocer, atormentar, remorder. *3* aguijonear, estimular. ¶ Pret. y p. p.: *stung*.

stingaree (-ATI) *s.* ICT. pastinaca.

stinginess (sti·nŷinis) *s.* avaricia, tacañería.

stingless (sti·nglis) *adj.* sin púa o aguijón.

stingy (sti·nŷi) *adj.* avaro, tacaño. *2* mezquino, escaso.

stink (stink) *s.* hedor, peste.

stink (to) *intr.* heder, oler mal, apestar. ¶ Pret. *stank* o *stunk*; p. p.: *stunk*.

stinkard (sti·nka'd) *s.* cosa o persona hedionda.

stinker (sti·nkø') *s.* cosa o persona hedionda. *2* fam. sujeto despreciable, canalla.

stinking (sti·nking) *adj.* hediondo, apestoso.

stint (stint) *s.* limitación, restricción: *without* ~, sin límite. *2* cuota o tarea asignada.

stint (to) *tr.* limitar, escatimar. *2 intr.* ser económico.

stinted (sti·ntid) *adj.* limitado, restringido. *2* corto, escaso.

stipe (staip) *s.* BOT. estipe; estípite.

stipend (stai·pend) *s.* estipendio, sueldo.

stipendiary (staipe·ndieri) *adj.-s.* estipendiario.

stipple (to) (sti·pøl) *tr.* B. ART., GRAB. puntear, granear.

stipulate (to) (sti·piuleit) *tr.* estipular.

stipulation (stipiulei·shøn) *s.* estipulación.

stipule (sti·piul) *s.* BOT. estípula.

stir (stø') *s.* movimiento, actividad. *2* agitación, revuelo. *3* alboroto.

stir (to) *tr.* mover, menear, bullir. *2* agitar, revolver. *3* atizar, avivar. *4* conmover, inflamar, armar. *5* suscitar, promover; despertar, inspirar. *6* poner en movimiento. *7 intr.* moverse, menearse, agitarse; estar en movimiento. *8* fam. levantarse [por la mañana]. ¶ Pret. y p. p.: *stirred*; ger.: *-rring*.

stirrup (sti·røp) *s.* EQUIT., MEC. estribo: ~ *strap*, acción. *2* ZAP. tirapié. *3* ANAT. ~ *bone*, estribo [del oído].

stitch (stich) *s.* COST. puntada. *2* punto [de costura, bordado, etc.]. *3* CIR. punto. *4* punzada [dolor]. *5* trecho, distancia.

stitch (to) *tr.* coser, adornar con puntadas, pespuntar: *to* ~ *up*, remendar; CIR. dar puntos a. *2 intr.* coser, bordar.

stithy (sti·ði) *s.* yunque. *2* fragua.

stoat (stout) *s.* ZOOL. armiño [en verano].

stock (stak) *s.* BOT. tronco. *2* tronco [del cuerpo]. *3* tronco [origen]; estirpe. *4* zoquete. *5* pilar. *6* acopio, provisión, existencias; material: *in* ~, en existencia; *out of* ~, vendido, agotado. *7* TEAT. repertorio. *8* inventario. *9* ganado: ~ *raising*, ganadería. *10* capital de un negocio. *11* COM. título, acción, obligación; valores: ~ *company*, sociedad anónima; ~ *market*, mercado de valores. *12* muebles, enseres. *13* mango [de látigo, caña de pescar, etc.]; caja [de fusil; de cepillo o garlopa]. *14* patrón [de injerto]. *15* baceta [de la baraja]. *16* BOT. alhelí. *17* corbatín, alzacuello. *18 pl.* valores públicos. *19* cepo [castigo]. *20* VET. potro [máquina]. *21* MAR. basada. *22* común, usual, estereotipado.

stock (to) *tr.* tener en existencia, tener existencias de. *2* proveer, abastecer. *3* poblar [un estanque o río]. *4* sembrar hierba en. *5* almacenar, acoplar. *6* encepar.

stockade (stakei·d) *s.* empalizada, vallado.

stockade (to) *tr.* empalizar.

stockbreeder (stakbri·də') *s.* ganadero.

stockbroker (-broukø') *s.* corredor de Bolsa.

stockfish (-fish) *s.* bacalao seco, pejepalo.

stockholder (-jouldø') *s.* accionista.

Stockholm (-joulm) *n. pr.* GEOGR. Estocolmo.

stocking (-ing) *s.* media, calceta. *2* fig. gato, dinero. *3* calzo [del caballo].

stockish (-ish) *adj.* estúpido.

stockjobber (-dŷabø') *s.* desp. (Ingl.) agente de corredores de Bolsa; (E.U.) bolsista, agiotista.

stockman (-mæn) *s.* ganadero. *2* encargado de las existencias.

stockpile (-pail) *s.* reserva de existencias.

stockpile (to) *tr.* acumular, reunir. *2 intr.* hacer acopio de existencias.

stockroom (-rum) *s.* GEOM. almacén.

stock-still *adj.* completamente inmóvil.

stocky (-i) *adj.* rechoncho. *2* achaparrado.

stodgy (sta·dŷi) *adj.* pesado, indigesto. *2* soso, aburrido. *3* rollizo.

Stoic (stou·ik) *s.* estoico.

stoic (al (stou·ik(al) *adj.* estoico.

stoicism (-isism) *s.* estoicismo.

stoke (to) (stouk) *tr.-intr.* atizar [el fuego]. *2* cargar, alimentar [un horno u hogar].

stokehold (-jould) *s.* MAR. cuarto de calderas. *2* puesto del fogonero.

stokehole (-joul) *s.* boca del horno; puesto del fogonero. *2* cuarto de calderas.

stoker (-ø^r) *s.* fogonero.

stole (stoul) *s.* estola.

stole, stolen (stoul, -øn) *pret.* y *p. p.* de TO STEAL.

stolid (sta·lid) *adj.* estólido. *2* impasible.

stolon (stou·lan) *s.* BOT. estolón.

stoma (-ma), *pl.* **-mata** (-m*a*ta) *s.* BOT. estoma.

stomach (stø·mak) *s.* ANAT. estómago: ~ *ache*, dolor de estómago. *2 fam.* vientre, barriga. *3* apetito, deseo, afición. *4* ánimo, valor.

stomach (to) *tr.* tragar, digerir, sufrir, aguantar.

stomacher (-ø^r) *s.* peto, estomaguero.

stomachic (stømæ·kik) *adj.-s.* estomacal.

stomachless (stø·maklis) *adj.* desganado.

stomatitis (stom*a*tai·tis) *s.* MED. estomatitis.

stone (stoun) *s.* piedra [materia o trozo dě ella], canto, china: *Stone Age*, edad de piedra; ~ *cutter*, picapedrero, cantero: ~ *quarry*, cantera; *stone's throw*, tiro de piedra; *to leave no ~ unturned*, no dejar piedra sin mover. *2* ARQ. sillar. *3* muela [piedra]. *4* piedra preciosa. *5* MED. cálculo. *6* hueso, cuesco [de fruta]: ~ *fruit*, fruta de hueso; ~ *pine*, pino piñonero. *7* (Ingl.) peso de 14 libras. *8* IMPR. platina. *9* ficha [de dominó].

stone (to) *tr.* apedrear, lapidar. *2* despedregar. *3* deshuesar [un fruto]. *4* revestir de piedra.

stone-blind *adj.* completamente ciego.

stone-broke *adj.* arruinado, sin un éntimo.

stonecrop (-krap) *s.* BOT. uva de gato.

stone-deaf *adj.* completamente sordo.

stonewall (-uol) *adj.* fuerte [como una muralla]. *2* obstinado. *3* resuelto.

stoneware (-ue^r) *s.* especie de gres.

stonework (-uø^{r}k) *s.* obra de sillería.

stony (-i) *adj.* pedregoso. *2* de piedra, pétreo. *3* duro, insensible, empedernido.

stony-hearted *adj.* duro de corazón, cruel.

stood (stud) *pret.* y *p. p.* de TO STAND.

stool (stul) *s.* taburete, escabel, banquillo. *2* silico, retrete. *3* deposición, excremento. *4* antepecho [de ventana]. *5* cimillo. *6* cimbel, señuelo: ~ *pigeon*, cimbel [ave]; gancho [pers.]; confidente de la policía.

stool (to) *intr.* brotar, echar renuevos. *2* exonerar el vientre.

stoop (stup) *s.* inclinación del cuerpo, de la cabeza, encorvamiento. *2* dignación; rebajamiento. *4* (E.U.) escalinata de entrada.

stoop (to) *intr.* agacharse, doblar o encorvar el cuerpo. *2* andar encorvado. *3* inclinarse hacia abajo. *4* descender. *5* rebajarse; humillarse. *6* *tr.* inclinar, encorvar.

stop (stap) *s.* alto, parada, estancia; paro, detención; fin, pausa: ~ *light*, luz o señal de parada; *dead* ~, parada súbita; *to put a* ~ *to*, poner fin a; *without* ~, sin parar, sin detenerse. *2* parada, apeadero. *3* posada, parador. *4* obstrucción, estorbo. *5* tapón. *6* GRAM. punto: *full* ~, punto final. *7* MEC. tope, fiador. *8* MÚS. llave [de instrumento]; traste [de guitarra]; registro [de órgano]. *9* FOT. diafragma.

stop (to) *tr.* detener, parar, poner fin a. | *Stop thief!*, ¡al ladrón! *2* dejar de. *3* interrumpir, suspender. *4* refrenar, contener, atajar, poner coto a. *5* impedir, estorbar. *6* cerrar, tapar, cegar, atascar, obstruir; interceptar. *7* empastar [un diente]. *8* estancar, represar. *9* parar [un golpe]. *10* *intr.* pararse, detenerse, cesar; hacer alto, quedarse:

not to ~ *at*, no pararse en; *to* ~ *short*, pararse en seco, quedarse cortado. *11* parar, hospedarse. ¶ Pret. y p. p.: *stopped;* ger.: *-pping*.

stopcock (-kak) *s.* llave o espita de paso.

stopgap (-gæp) *s.* lo que tapa una abertura. *2* recurso temporal, sustitutivo.

stopover (-ouvø^r) *s.* parada intermedia [en un viaje].

stoppage (-idÿ) *s.* detención, cesación, interrupción. *2* obstrucción, interceptación. *3* retención [sobre una paga]. *4* COM. suspensión [de un pago]. *5* MED. oclusión.

stopper (-ø^r) *s.* tapón, obturador.

stopper (to) *tr.* tapar, taponar.

stopple (-øl) *s.* tapón, bitoque.

stopple (to) *tr.* tapar, taponar.

storage (sto·ridÿ) *s.* almacenamiento: ~ *battery*, ELECT. batería de acumuladores, acumulador. *2* almacenaje. *3* espacio para almacenar.

storax (stou·ræks) *s.* estoraque.

store (sto^r) *s.* copia, abundancia; acopio, provisión. *2* tesoro. *3* almacén, depósito: *in* ~, almacenado en reserva. *4* (esp. E.U.) tienda, comercio. *5 to set (great)* ~ *by*, tener en mucha estima. *6 pl.* reservas, provisiones, pertrechos.

store (to) *tr.* proveer, abastecer. *2* guardar, acumular, atesorar, tener en reserva. *3* almacenar.

storehouse (-jaus) *s.* almacén.

storekeeper (sto·^{r}kipø^r) *s.* guardalmacén. *2* (E.U.) tendero.

storeroom (-rum) *s.* almacén. *2* despensa.

storey (sto·ri) *s.* ARQ. piso, alto, planta.

storied (sto·rid) *adj.* B. ART. de temas históricos. *2* histórico, legendario. *3* de [tantos] pisos: *two-storied*, de dos pisos.

storiette (storie·t) *s.* cuento, historieta.

stork (sto^{r}k) *s.* ORN. cigüeña.

storm (sto^{r}m) *s.* tempestad, temporal, tormenta, borrasca: ~ *door*, guardapuerta, cancel. *2 fig.* agitación, tumulto. *3* MIL. asalto: *to take by* ~, tomar por asalto; *fig.* arrebatar, entusiasmar.

storm (to) *tr.* tomar por asalto, atacar. *2 intr.* haber tempestad. *3* rabiar, tempestear; alborotar.

stormy (-i) *adj.* tempestuoso, tormentoso, borrascoso. *2* violento, turbulento.

story (sto·ri) *s.* historia, leyenda, relato, cuento, anécdota, novela: *as the* ~ *goes*, según se cuenta. *2 fam.* chisme, embuste. *3* trama, argumento. *4* ARQ. piso, alto.

story (to) *tr.* historiar. *2* adornar con escenas históricas. ¶ Pret. y p. p.: *storied*.

stoup (stup) *s.* frasco, jarro. *2* pila del agua bendita.

stout (staut) *adj.* fuerte, recio. *2* robusto, grueso, corpulento. *3* valiente, decidido. *4* firme, leal. *5* obstinado. *6 s.* cerveza fuerte.

stouthearted (-ja^{r}tid) *adj.* valiente, intrépido.

stove (stouv) *s.* estufa; hornillo. *2* cocina económica de gas o de electricidad. *3* horno de cerámica. *4* JARD. estufa, invernáculo.

stove *pret.* y *p. p.* de TO STAVE.

stow (to) (stou) *tr.* apretar, hacinar. *2* guardar, esconder. *3* meter, alojar. *4* atestar, abarrotar. *5* MAR. arrimar, estibar. *6 intr. to* ~ *away*, embarcarse clandestinamente.

stowage (-idÿ) *s.* almacenaje. *2* MAR. estiba.

stowaway (-auei) *s.* polizón, pasajero clandestino.

stower (-ø^r) *s.* estibador.

strabismus (strabi·šmøs) *s.* MED. estrabismo.

straddle (stræ·døl) *s.* posición del que se esparranca o monta a horcajadas.

straddle (to) *intr.* esparrancarse. *2* montar o estar a horcajadas sobre. *3* extenderse. *4 tr.-intr.* no comprometerse [entre dos partidos].
stradiot (stra·diat) *s.* estradiote.
strafe (to) (streif) *tr.* fam. bombardear violentamente. *2* ametrallar en vuelo bajo. *3* reprender, castigar.
straggle (to) (stræ·gøl) *intr.* rodar, andar perdido. *2* extraviarse; desbandarse, rezagarse. *3* desparramarse, estar esparcido.
straggler (stræ·gløʳ) *s.* paseante, vagabundo. *2* descarriado, rezagado. *3* el que se aparta o desvía. *4* rama extendida. *5* objeto aislado.
straggly (-i) *adj.* desparramado, esparcido, desordenado.
straight (streit) *adj.* recto, derecho; ~ *line*, línea recta. *2* directo, en línea recta. *3* erguido. *4* lacio [pelo]. *5* seguido. *6* correcto, exacto. *7* franco, sincero. *8* recto, justo, honrado. *9* serio, severo. *10* acérrimo. *11* en orden, arreglado. *12* puro, sin mezcla. *13* formando escalera [naipes]. *14* GEOM. ~ *angle*, ángulo de 180°. *15 adv.* directamente, en línea recta. *16* continuamente. *17* erguidamente. *18* correctamente. *19* honradamente, francamente. *20* ~ *away*, ~ *off*, inmediatamente. *21 s.* recta; plano. *22* escalera [en el poker].
straighten (-øn) *tr.* enderezar. *2* desalabear. *3* arreglar, poner en orden. *4 intr. to* ~ *up*, enderezarse.
straightforward (-fo·ʳuaʳd) *adj.* recto, derecho. *2* honrado, íntegro. *3* franco, sincero.
straightness (strei·tnis) *s.* rectitud, honradez.
straight-out *adj.* fam. (E.U.) sincero, franco; completo, absoluto.
straightway (strei·tuei) *adv.* inmediatamente, al instante, en seguida.
strain (strein) *s.* tensión, tirantez; esfuerzo excesivo; exceso; fatiga. *2* torcedura, esguince. *3* MEC. deformación. *4* estirpe, linaje. *5* clase, suerte. *6* rasgo heredado. *7* vena [de loco, etc.]. *8* tono, acento, modo. *9* MÚS. aire, melodía. *10* estrofa, verso.
strain (to) *tr.* estirar, poner tirante. *2* aguzar [la vista, el oído]; someter a un esfuerzo; sobreexcitar, fatigar. *3* torcer, forzar, violentar, deformar. *4* extremar. *5* apretar, estrechar. *6* colar, tamizar. *7 to* ~ *a point*, excederse, hacer una excepción. *8 intr.* esforzarse. *9* soportar un esfuerzo. *10* pasar [por un filtro, etc.].
strained (-d) *adj.* forzado [risa, etc.]. *2* tirante [situación, relaciones].
strainer (-øʳ) *s.* tensor. *2* colador, cedazo.
strait (streit) *adj.* estrecho, apretado: ~ *jacket*, camisa de fuerza. *2* limitado. *3* difícil, apurado. *4 s.* GEOGR. estrecho. *5* aprieto, apuro.
straiten (to) (-tøn) *tr.* estrechar, contraer. *2* reducir, limitar. *3* agobiar, apurar: *in straitened circumstances*, en situación apurada, sin dinero.
strait-laced *adj.* excesivamente rígido, mojigato.
straitness (-nis) *s.* estrechez. *2* apuro, escasez, penuria.
strake (streik) *s.* STREAK.
stramineous (strami·niøs) *adj.* pajizo. *2* sin valor.
stramonium (-mo·niøm) *s.* BOT. estramonio.
strand (-træn) *s.* playa, ribera. *2* hebra, cabo, ramal [de cuerda]; cuerda, trenza. *3* hilo [de perlas].
strand (to) *tr.-intr.* embarrancar. *2 tr.* dejar perdido, desamparado. *3* romper un ramal de [una cuerda]. *4* torcer formando cuerda.

strange (streindɏ) *adj.* extraño, foráneo, desconocido. *2* ajeno. *3* extraño, raro, singular. *4* retraído, reservado.
stranger (-øʳ) *s.* extraño, forastero, desconocido. *2 to be a* ~ *to*, ignorar, desconocer. *3 you are a* ~, se vende usted muy caro.
strangle (to) (stræ·ngøl) *tr.* estrangular, asfixiar, ahogar. *2* fig. ahogar, sofocar, reprimir. *3 intr.* ahogarse.
strangulate (to) (-giuleit) *tr.* apretar, ahogar. *2* MED. estrangular.
strap (stræp) *s.* correa, tira, faja, banda [esp. para atar o sujetar]. *2* SASTR. trabilla. *3* fleje. *4* ZAP. tirador. *5* suavizador [de navajas].
strap (to) *tr.* atar, sujetar con correas. *2* fajar, precintar. *3* azotar con correa. *4* asentar el filo de [una navaja]. *5* almohazar. ¶ Pret. y p. p.: *strapped;* ger.: *-pping*.
strapper (-øʳ) *s.* mozo de cuadra. *2* pers. o cosa corpulenta. *3* mentira colosal.
strapping (-ing) *adj.* robusto, fuerte: ~ *youth*, mocetón.
Strasbourg (stræ·sbøʳg) *n. pr.* GEOGR. Estrasburgo.
stratagem (stræ·tadɏem) *s.* estratagema, ardid.
strategic(al (strati·dɏik(al) *adj.* estratégico.
strategics (strati·dɏiks) *s.* estrategia.
strategist (stræ·tidɏist) *s.* estratega.
strategy (-tidɏi) *s.* estrategia.
stratification (strætifikei·shøn) *s.* estratificación.
stratify (to) (stræ·tifai) *tr.* estratificar. *2 intr.* estratificarse. ¶ Pret. y p. p.: *stratified.*
stratigraphy (strati·grafi) *s.* estratigrafía.
stratosphere (stræ·tøsfiʳ) *s.* estratosfera.
stratum (strei·tøm) *s.* estrato, capa.
stratus (strei·tus) *s.* METEOR. estrato.
straw (stro) *s.* paja: ~ *hat*, sombrero de paja; *the last* ~, fig. lo que faltaba; *to catch at* ~, fig. arrastrarse a un clavo ardiendo; *I don't care a* ~, me importa un bledo. *2* bálago. *3* fig. señal, indicio.
strawberry (-beri) *s.* BOT. fresa [planta y fruto]. *2* BOT. ~ *tree*, madroño.
strawy (-stro·i) *adj.* pajizo, de paja. *2* sin valor.
stray (strei) *adj.* descarriado, perdido, errante. *2* suelto, aislado, incidental. *3 s.* animal descarriado, perdido. *4 pl.* RADIO. parásitos.
stray (to) *intr.* desviarse. *2* descarriarse, extraviarse, perderse, errar, vagar.
streak (strik) *s.* raya, línea, lista. *2* rayo o raya de luz]: ~ *of lightning*, relámpago. *3* MIN. vena. *4* rastro, rasgo, un algo. *5* MAR. hilada. *6* (E.U.) racha [de suerte].
streak (to) *tr.* rayar, listar, gayar. *2 intr.* ir como un rayo; viajar velozmente.
streaky (stri·ki) *adj.* rayado, listado, abigarrado. *2* desigual, variable [pers., carácter, humor].
stream (strim) *s.* corriente. *2* río, arroyo. *3* torrente, raudal; flujo, chorro: ~ *of words*, flujo de palabras. *4* rayo [de luz, de sol]. *5* curso [de la historia, de la vida].
stream (to) *intr.* correr, fluir, manar, chorrear. *2* salir a torrentes, derramarse. *3* pasar rápidamente. *4* ondear, tremolar. *5* extenderse en línea continua. *6 tr.* verter, derramar. *7* hacer ondear.
streamer (-øʳ) *s.* flámula, gallardete. *2* cola [de un cometa]. *3* titulares de un periódico que ocupan todo el ancho de la página.
streamlet (-lit) *s.* arroyuelo, riachuelo.
streamline (-lain) *s.* línea que sigue una corriente. *2* línea aerodinámica. *3 adj.* aerodinámico.

streamline (to) *tr.* hacer aerodinámico.
streamlined (-laind) *adj.* aerodinámico.
streamy (-i) *adj.* surcado por arroyos. *2* que sale como un chorro; radiante. *3* ondeante.
street (strɪt) *s.* calle, vía pública: ~ *Arab*, golfillo, pilluelo; ~ *cleaner*, ~ *sweeper*, barrendero; barredera [máquina]; ~ *floor*, piso bajo, bajos; ~ *railway*, tranvía.
streetcar (-kaʳ) *s.* (E.U.) tranvía.
streetwalker (-wokøʳ) *s.* prostituta.
strength (strengz) *s.* fuerza, energía, vigor. *2* fortaleza, firmeza, solidez. *3* poder, pujanza. *4* intensidad. *5* concentración, cuerpo [de un líquido]. *6* fuerza legal. *7* MIL. fuerza [número].
strengthen (to) (-øn) *tr.* fortalecer, robustecer. *2* consolidar. *3* confirmar, corroborar. *4* animar, alentar. *5* reforzar. *6 intr.* fortalecerse. *7* hacerse más fuerte.
strenuous (stre·niuøs) *adj.* estrenuo, enérgico, activo, ardiente, celoso. *2* arduo.
strepitous (stre·pitøs) *adj.* estrepitoso, clamoroso.
streptococcus (streptøka·køs) *s.* BACT. streptococo.
streptomycin (-mai·sin) *s.* estreptomicina.
stress (stres) *s.* fuerza [que obliga], presión, coacción, urgencia. *2* peso, importancia; fuerza, énfasis: *to lay* ~ *on*, dar importancia a, subrayar, insistir en. *3* esfuerzo, tensión. *4* MÚS., PROS. acento.
stress (to) *tr.* someter a un esfuerzo, una tensión, un peso. *2* acentuar. *3* recalcar, hacer hincapié en.
stretch (strech) *s.* extensión [acción de extender]. *2* estiramiento, dilatación. *3* tirantez, tensión. *4* estirón, esfuerzo. *5* interpretación forzada; exageración. *6* extensión, trecho, distancia: *at* o *on a* ~, de un tirón. *7* lapso, intervalo. *8* MAR. bordada.
stretch (to) *tr.* extender, alargar, tender. *2* estirar, atesar, distender. *3* ensanchar, dilatar. *4* violentar, forzar; extremar, exagerar. *5 to* ~ *forth*, alargar, extender. *6 to* ~ *oneself*, tenderse; desperezarse. *7 to* ~ *out*, estirar; alargar, tender. *8 to* ~ *a point*, hacer una concesión. *9 intr.* extenderse. *10* alargarse, dar de sí; estirarse; desplegarse. | Gralte. con *out*. *11* esforzarse, menearse. *12* tenderse, tumbarse. *13* desperezarse.
stretcher (-øʳ) *s.* tendedor. *2* estirador, tensor. *3* ensanchador. *4* camilla, parihuelas. *5* CARP. viga, tirante. *6* fam. cuento, exageración.
stretcher-bearer *s.* camillero.
strew (stru) *s.* porción de cosas esparcidas.
strew (to) *tr.* esparcir, desparramar. *2* sembrar, salpicar, regar, espolvorear. ¶ Pret.: *strewed*; p. p.: *strewed* o *strewn*.
stria (strai·a) *s.* estría.
striate (to) (strai·eit) *tr.* estriar.
stricken (stri·køn) *p. p.* de TO STRIKE. *2 adj.* golpeado, herido. *3* gastado, cascado.
strickle (stri·køl) *s.* rasero. *2* escantillón.
strict (strikt) *adj.* estricto. *2* riguroso, escrupuloso. *3* rígido, severo.
stricture (stri·kchøʳ) *s.* crítica, censura. *2* MED. estrechez.
stridden (strai·døn) *p. p.* de TO STRIDE.
stride (straid) *s.* paso largo, tranco, zanzada.
stride (to) *intr.* andar a pasos largos. *2 tr.* pasar, salvar de un tranco. *3* recorrer a paso largo. *4* montar a horcajadas. ¶ Pret.: *strode*; p. p.: *stridden*.
stridency (strai·dønsi) *s.* estridencia.
strident (-ønt) *adj.* estridente.

stridulate (to) (stri·diuleit) *intr.* estridular.
strife (straif) *s.* disputa, contienda, lucha. *2* competición, emulación; porfía.
strike (straik) *s.* golpe. *2* huelga: ~ *breaker*, esquirol; *to go on* ~, declararse en huelga. *3* rasero. *4* descubrimiento de un filón. *5* golpe de suerte; ganga.
strike (to) *tr.* golpear. *2* herir. *3* batir, chocar con, dar contra. *4* hacer chocar. *5* dar [un golpe]. *6* quitar, cortar, etc., de un golpe. *7* embadurnar. *8* afligir, castigar. *9* encender [una cerilla]; sacar [fuego, chispa]. *10* producir un efecto súbito, una emoción: *to* ~ *dumb*, dejar mudo; asombrar; *to* ~ *with horror*, horrorizar. *11* sorprender, extrañar. *12* ocurrir [una idea]; parecer: *how does it* ~ *you?*, ¿qué le parece? *13* acuñar, troquelar. *14* echar [raíces]. *15* MÚS. tocar. *16* dar [la hora]. *17* hallar, dar con. *18* rasar, nivelar. *19* atraer; enamorar. *20* hacer [balance]; sacar [una cuenta]. *21* cerrar [un trato]. *22* bajar, arriar. *23* borrar, tachar. | Con *off* o *out*. *24* tomar [una postura]. *25* levantar [las tiendas]. *26* trazar [una línea]. *27* IMPR. tirar. *28 to* ~ *down*, derribar, tumbar. *29 to* ~ *one's fancy*, antojársele a uno. *30 to* ~ *someone for a loan*, dar un sablazo a uno. *31 to* ~ *up*, ponerse a tocar o a cantar [algo]; trabar [amistad].
32 intr. golpear; luchar; atacar. *33* chocar, tropezar. *34* partir, avanzar, ir, entrar, pasar. *35* sonar, dar la hora. *36* declararse en huelga. *37* arriar el pabellón. *38* picar [el pez]. *39* MAR. arraigar. *40* MAR. embarrancar. *41 to* ~ *at*, amagar un golpe a, acometer. *42 to* ~ *into*, entrar en; echar por; ponerse a. *43 to* ~ *on*, ocurrirse [una idea]; hallar; impresionar.
¶ Pret.: *struck*; p. p.: *struck* o *stricken*.
striker (-øʳ) *s.* golpeador. *2* huelguista. *3* percutor.
striking (-ing) *adj.* notable, sorprendente. *2* manifiesto. *3* llamativo. *4* en huelga.
string (stri·ng) *s.* cordón, cinta, cordel. *2* hilo [con que se mueve una cosa]. *3* ristra, sarta. *4* cuerda [de un arco, de un instrumento]. *5* hebra, fibra, nervio, tendón. *6* BOT. ~ *bean*, judía verde. *7 pl.* MÚS. cuerda [instrumentos].
string (to) *tr.* atar [con cordón, etc.]. *2* encordar. *3* templar [un violín, etc.]. *4* poner tirante, en tensión. *5* sobreexcitar. *6* ensartar, enhebrar. *7* extender, alargar. *8* quitar las hebras a. *9 intr.* formar hilo. *10* marchar en hilera, extenderse en línea; prolongarse. ¶ Pret.: *strung*; p. p.: *strung* o *stringed*.
stringboard (-boʳd) *s.* zanca [de escalera].
stringency (stri·ndyønsi) *s.* fuerza convincente. *2* severidad, rigor. *3* estrechez, penuria.
stringent (-dyønt) *adj.* convincente. *2* rígido, severo. *3* COM. flojo [mercado].
stringy (stri·ngi) *adj.* fibroso, filamentoso. *2* viscoso, correoso.
strip (strip) *s.* tira, lista, cinta, faja, listón.
strip (to) *tr.* despojar, desnudar, desguarnecer. *2* quitar, arrancar [lo que cubre]. *3* privar [de], robar, arrebatar. *4* raer, limpiar. *5* MAR. desmantelar. *6* AGR. desgranar. *7* despalillar [tabaco]. *8* MAR. desnudarse, desgarronarse. *9* soltarse, caer [la piel, la corteza]. ¶ Pret. y p. p.: *stripped* y *stript*; ger.: *-pping*.
stripe (strai·p) *s.* raya, lista, franja, galón.
stripe (to) *tr.* rayar, listar, gayar. *2* azotar.
striped (-d) *adj.* rayado, listado.
striping (-ing) *s.* listas, franjas.
stripling (stri·pling) *s.* mozabete, jovencito.

strip-tease s. espectáculo en que una artista se desnuda total o parcialmente.

stripy (strai·pi) adj. rayado, listado.

strive (to) (straiv) intr. esforzarse. 2 forcejear. 3 luchar, contender. ¶ Pret.: strove; p. p.: striven.

strobile (stra·bil) s. BOT. estróbilo.

strode (stroud) pret. de TO STRIDE.

stroke (strouk) s. golpe: ~ of luck, golpe de suerte; at one ~, de un golpe. 2 brazada [del que nada]; bogada; jugada; tacada. 3 MEC. carrera, embolada. 4 campanada [de reloj]. 5 MED. ataque [de apoplejía, parálisis, etc.]. 6 esfuerzo, acto, rasgo: ~ of wit, rasgo de ingenio. 7 trazo, toque, rasgo, pincelada: ~ of pen, plumada. 8 caricia [con la mano]. 9 DEP. stroke o ~ oar, primer remero.

stroke (to) tr. frotar suavemente; pasar la mano por; acariciar; alisar. 2 tildar, rayar.

stroll (stroul) s. paseo, paseíto, vuelta.

stroll (to) intr. pasear, pasearse [a pie]. 2 andar de un lugar a otro.

stroller (strou·lǿ) s. paseante. 2 vagabundo. 3 cómico ambulante. 4 cochecito de niño.

stroma (strou·ma) s. ANAT. estroma.

strong (strong) adj. fuerte: ~ box, caja fuerte; ~ hand, mano fuerte, dura. 2 robusto, fornido. 3 grande, poderoso. 4 marcado, pronunciado. 5 firme, arraigado. 6 ardiente, acérrimo. 7 espirituosa [bebida]; cargado [café, té]. 8 de olor fuerte u ofensivo. 9 firme [mercado]. 10 an army ten thousand ~, un ejército de diez mil hombres. 11 adv. fuertemente; sumamente.

strong-handed adj. de mano fuerte; duro.

strong-headed adj. obstinado, testarudo.

stronghold (stro·ngjould) s. fortaleza, plaza fuerte.

strong-minded adj. de espíritu independiente.

strontium (stra·nshiøm) s. QUÍM. estroncio.

strop (strap) s. suavizador [para navajas]. 2 MAR. estrobo.

strop (to) tr. suavizar [navajas].

strophe (strou·fi) s. estrofa.

strove (strouv) pret. de TO STRIVE.

struck (strøk) pret. y p. p. de TO STRIKE.

structural (strø·kchøral) adj. estructural. 2 ING. de construcción o construcciones.

structure (strø·kchǿ) s. estructura. 2 hechura, textura. 3 construcción, edificio, máquina.

struggle (strø·gøl) s. esfuerzo, lucha, brega, pugna, forcejeo. 2 contienda, disputa, pelea.

struggle (to) intr. esforzarse, luchar, bregar, pugnar, forcejear, batallar.

strum (to) (strøm) tr. arañar, aporrear [un piano, una guitarra, etc.]. 2 rasguear [la guitarra]. ¶ Pret. y p. p.: strummed; ger.: -mming.

strumpet (strø·mpit) s. ramera.

strung (strøng) pret. y p. p. de TO STRING.

strut (strøt) s. andar arrogante; contoneo, pavoneo. 2 CARP. jabalcón, tornapunta, puntal, ademe.

strut (to) intr. andar con paso arrogante; contonearse, pavonearse. ¶ Pret. y p. p.: strutted; ger.: strutting.

strychnin(e (stri·knin) s. QUÍM. estrictina.

Stuart (stiu·a't) n. pr. Estuardo: Mary ~, María Estuardo.

stub (støb) s. tocón, cepa. 2 zoquete. 3 garrón, tetón. 4 resto, cabo. 5 colilla [de cigarro]. 6 matriz [de talonario]; ~ book, libro talonario.

stub (to) tr. arrancar, desarraigar. 2 limpiar de tocones. 3 aplastar. 4 to ~ one's toe, tropezar [con un tocón, etc.].

stubble (stø·bøl) s. rastrojo. 2 barba sin afeitar.

stubborn (stø·bø'n) adj. obstinado, terco; tenaz, inflexible, irreductible. 2 difícil de trabajar o manejar.

stubby (stø·bi) adj. lleno de tocones. 2 rechoncho. 3 grueso, corto y tieso; cerdoso.

stucco (stø·kou) s. estuco.

stucco (to) tr.-intr. estucar.

stuccowork (-wø'k) s. obra de estuco.

stuck (støk) pret. y p. p. de TO STICK.

stuck-up adj. fam. tieso, estirado, orgulloso.

stud (stød) s. poste, montante [de tabique, de entramado]. 2 tachón, bollón, clavo de adorno. 3 refuerzo de eslabón. 4 gemelo [de camisa]. 5 yeguada, caballada: ~ farm, acaballadero, potrero.

stud (to) tr. tachonar, clavetear; adornar.

studbook (-buk) s. registro genealógico de caballos.

student (stiu·dønt) s. estudiante. 2 estudioso, investigador. 3 ~ lamp, quinqué.

studhorse (stø·djo'rs) s. semental, caballo padre.

studied (stø·did) adj. estudiado, premeditado.

studio (stiu·diou) s. estudio, taller. 2 CINEM., RADIO. estudio.

studious (stiu·diøs) adj. estudioso. 2 de estudio. 3 asiduo, solícito, deseoso. 4 estudiado.

study (stø·di) s. estudio [acción de estudiar]. 2 objeto de estudio. 3 B. ART., LIT. estudio. 4 despacho, estudio. 5 cuidado, esfuerzo, empeño. 6 meditación profunda.

study (to) tr.-intr. estudiar. 2 meditar. 3 discurrir, idear.

stuff (støf) s. material, materia prima. 2 carácter, aptitud, madera. 3 materia, substancia, artículo)s, producto)s : food ~, productos alimenticios. 4 tela, paño. 5 cosa, cosas, chismes, cachivaches. 6 pócima, mejunje. 7 deshecho, broza, tonterías, pataratas. 8 interj. ¡tontería!

stuff (to) tr. llenar, atestar. 2 rellenar; emborrar; disecar [un animal]. 3 embutir, meter de cualquier modo. 4 tapar, atarugar. 5 atracar [de comida]. 6 intr. atracarse, hartarse.

stuffing (stø·fing) s. relleno. 2 MEC. empaquetado: ~ box, prensaestopas.

stuffy (stø·fi) adj. mal ventilado, sofocante. 2 fam. soso, aburrido. 3 fam. (E.U.) malhumorado.

stultify (to) (stø·ltifai) tr. poner en ridículo; hacer parecer ridículo. 2 frustrar, anular.

stumble (stø·mbøl) s. tropiezo, tropezón, trompicón, traspié. 2 desliz.

stumble (to) intr. tropezar, dar un traspié: to ~ on o upon, tropezar con. 2 vacilar, embarullarse, tartamudear.

stumbling-block, stumbling-stone s. tropezadero, escollo; piedra de escándalo.

stump (stømp) s. tocón, tueco, cepa. 2 muñón [de miembro cortado]; raigón [de diente o muela]. 3 colilla [de cigarro]. 4 pequeña parte saliente. 5 DIB. esfumino. 6 fam. (E.U.) reto, desafío. 7 paso pesado. 8 (E.U.) tribuna al aire libre; discurso electoral. 9 pop. pierna. 10 poste [en el criquet]. 11 (E.U.) up a ~, en un brete.

stump (to) tr. cortar, mochar. 2 limpiar de tocones. 3 tropezar. 4 DIB. esfumar. 5 desafiar [a hacer algo]. 6 confundir, aplastar. 7 (E.U.) recorrer haciendo discursos electorales. 8 intr. andar pesadamente; renquear, tropezar. 9 (E.U.) hacer discursos electorales.

stumpy (-i) adj. tozo, rechoncho, cachigordo. 2 lleno de tocones.

stun (to) (støn) *tr.* aturdir, atolondrar, dejar sin sentido. *2* atronar, asordar, ensordecer. *3* pasmar. ¶ Pret. y p. p.: *stunned; ger.: -nning.*

stung (støng) *pret.* y *p. p.* de TO STING.

stunk (stønk) *pret.* y *p. p.* de TO STINK.

stunner (stø·nø^r) *s.* el o lo que aturde o atolondra. *2* fam. cosa pasmosa; mujer guapa.

stunning (-ing) *adj.* aturdidor. *2* fam. estupendo.

stunt (stønt) *s.* falta de crecimiento o desarrollo. *2* animal, planta, etc., raquíticos. *3* ejercicio de habilidad o destreza; acrobacia aérea. *4* truco propagandístico.

stunt (to) *tr.* impedir el crecimiento o desarrollo de. *2 intr.* hacer ejercicios de habilidad; hacer acrobacias aéreas.

stunted (-id) *adj.* desmedrado, raquítico, enano. *2* achaparrado.

stupe (stiup) *s.* MED. compresa, fomento.

stupefacient (stiupifei·shønt) *adj.-s.* estupefaciente.

stupefaction (stiupifæ·kshøn) *s.* estupefacción.

stupefied (stiu·pifaid) *pret.* y *p. p.* de TO STUPEFY.

stupefy (to) (stiu·pifai) *tr.* causar estupor, aturdir, atontar, entorpecer. *2* dejar estupefacto, pasmar. *3 intr.* atontarse, entorpecerse. ¶ Pret. y p. p.: *stupefied.*

stupendous (stiupe·ndøs) *adj.* estupendo, asombroso, enorme.

stupid (stiu·pid) *adj.-s.* estúpido, tonto. *2 adj.* atontado, aturdido.

stupidity (stiupi·diti) *s.* estupidez, tontería.

stupor (stiu·pø^r) *s.* estupor, letargo, atontamiento.

stuporous (-øs) *adj.* letárgico.

sturdiness (stø^{r}dinis) *s.* robustez, fuerza, vigor. *2* firmeza. *3* tenacidad.

sturdy (stø^{r}di) *adj.* robusto, fornido, fuerte. *2* vigoroso. *3* resuelto, firme, tenaz, obstinado.

sturgeon (stø^{r}dÿøn) *s.* ICT. esturión, sollo.

stutter (stø·tø^r) *s.* tartamudeo.

stutter (to) *intr.* tartamudear.

stutterer (-ø^r) *s.* tartamudo.

sty (stai) *s.* pocilga, zahurda. *2* MED. orzuelo.

Stygian (sti·dÿian) *adj.* estigio.

style (stail) *s.* estilo [punzón, gnomon]. *2* BOT. estilo. *3* estilo [de un autor, escuela, etc.; modo, manera]. *4* distinción, elegancia; moda: *in* ~, de moda. *5* nombre, título, tratamiento.

style (to) *tr.* intitular, llamar, nombrar.

stylet (-it) *s.* estilete [puñal, punzón]. *2* CIR. estilete.

stylish (-ish) *adj.* elegante, a la moda.

stylist (-ist) *s.* estilista.

stylistic (-istik) *adj.* estilístico.

stylite (-ait) *s.* estilita.

stylize (-ais) *tr.* estilizar.

stylobate (-øbeit) *s.* ARQ. estilóbato.

stylograph (-øgræf) *s.* estilográfica.

styloid (-oid) *adj.* ANAT. estiloides.

stylus (-øs) *s.* STYLE 1 y 2. *2* aguja [de fonógrafo]. *3* ZOOL. espícula.

stymie (stai·mi) *s.* GOLF. circunstancia de estar una pelota entre la del jugador y el hoyo.

styptic (sti·ptik) *adj.-s.* estíptico.

styrax (stai·raks) *s.* BOT. estoraque.

Styx (stiks) *n. pr.* MIT. Estigia.

suasion (suei·ÿøn) *s.* persuasión.

suasive (-siv) *adj.* persuasivo, suasorio.

suave (sua·v) *adj.* suave, afable. *2* obsequioso, zalamero.

suavity (-iti) *s.* suavidad, afabilidad, dulcedumbre.

sub (søb) *s.* fam. subalterno; substituto. *2* submarino.

sub- *pref.* sub-, -a-, vice-.

subacetate (-æ·siteit) *s.* QUÍM. subacetato.

subalpine (-æ·lpain) *adj.* subalpino.

subaltern (-o·ltø^{r}n) *adj.-s.* subalterno. *2 adj.* subordinado, dependiente.

subaqueous (-ei·kuiøs) *adj.* subacuático.

subchanter (-chæ·ntø^r) *s.* sochantre.

subchasser (-chei·sø^r) *s.* cazasubmarinos.

subclass (-klæs) *s.* subclase.

subclavian (-klei·vian) *adj.* ANAT. subclavio.

subcommittee (sø·bkømiti) *s.* subcomisión.

subconscious (søbka·nshøs) *adj.-s.* subconsciente.

subcostal (-ka·stal) *adj.* ANAT. subcostal.

subcutaneous (-kiutei·niøs) *adj.* subcutáneo, hipodérmico.

subdeacon (-dı·køn) *s.* subdiácono.

subdean (-dıan) *s.* vice-decano.

subdelegate (-de·løgeit) *s.* subdelegado.

subdivide (to) (-divai·d) *tr.* subdividir.

subdivision (-divi·ÿøn) *s.* subdivisión.

subdominant (-da·minant) *adj.-s.* MÚS. subdominante.

subdue (to) (-diu·) *tr.* sojuzgar, someter, dominar, vencer. *2* domar, domeñar, amansar. *3* mitigar, amortiguar, suavizar. *4 subdued tone,* tono sumiso; voz baja; color apagado.

suber (siu·bø^r) *s.* BOT. tejido suberoso.

subereous (siubi·riøs) *adj.* suberoso.

subfamily (søbfæ·mili) *s.* BIOL. subfamilia.

subheading (søbje·ding) *s.* subtítulo.

subitaneous (subitei·niøs) *adj.* súbito.

subjacent (sø·bdÿei·sønt) *adj.* subyacente.

subject (sø·bdÿekt) *adj.* sometido, supeditado. *2* sujeto, expuesto, propenso. *3 adj.-s.* súbdito, vasallo. *4 s.* sujeto, asunto, materia, tema; asignatura: ~ *matter,* materia [de que se trata]. *5* ocasión, motivo. *6* GRAM., LÓG., FIL., PSIC. sujeto. *7* lo sometido a una operación o proceso.

subject (to) (søbdÿe·kt) *tr.* sujetar, someter, sojuzgar. *2* supeditar, subordinar. *3* someter, presentar, exponer.

subjection (-shøn) *s.* sometimiento. *2* sujeción.

subjective (-tiv) *adj.* subjetivo.

subjectivity (søbdÿekti·viti) *s.* subjetividad.

subjoin (to) (søbdÿoi·n) *tr.* añadir.

subjugate (to) (sø·bdÿugeit) *tr.* subyugar.

subjugation (-ei·shøn) *s.* subyugación.

subjunctive (-dÿø·nktiv) *adj.-s.* GRAM. subjuntivo.

subkingdom (sø·bkingdøm) *s.* BIOL. subreino.

sublease (sø·blıs) *s.* subarriendo.

sublease (to) *tr.* subarrendar.

sublet (to) (søble·t) *tr.* subarrendar.

sublimate (sø·blimeit) *adj.-s.* QUÍM. sublimado. *2 adj.* refinado, elevado.

sublimate (to) *tr.* QUÍM. sublimar. *2* refinar, elevar.

sublimation (-ei·shøn) *s.* sublimación.

sublime (søblai·m) *adj.* sublime. *2 s. the* ~, lo sublime.

sublime (to) *tr.* sublimar [engrandecer, ensalzar]; refinar, purificar. *2* QUÍM. sublimar. *3 intr.* sublimarse.

subliminal (søbli·minal) *adj.* subliminar.

sublimity (søbli·miti) *s.* sublimidad.

sublingual (søbli·ngual) *adj.* ANAT. sublingual.

sublunar (-liu·na^r), **sublunary** (-nari) *adj.* sublunar.

submarine (sø·bmarın) *adj.-s.* submarino.

submaxillary (søbmæ·ksilari) *adj.* ANAT. submaxilar.

submerge (to) (-mø·ʳdẙ) *tr.* sumergir. *2* inundar, anegar. *3 intr.* sumergirse.
submergence (-øns) *s.* sumersión.
submergible (-ibøl) *adj.* sumergible. *2 s.* MAR. sumergible, submarino.
submerse (to) (søbmø·ʳs) *tr.* TO SUMMERGE.
submersion (-shøn) *s.* sumersión.
submersible (-ibøl) *adj.-s.* SUBMERGIBLE.
submission (-mi·shøn) *s.* sumisión. *2* sometimiento. *3* DER. sometimiento a arbitraje. *4* conformidad, resignación.
submissive (-siv) *adj.* sumiso.
submit (to) (søbmi·t) *tr.* someter, remitir [a la decisión, etc., de uno]. *2* decir, afirmar. *3 intr.-ref.* someterse, ceder, conformarse, resignarse. ¶ Pret. y p. p.: *submitted;* ger.: *-tting.*
submultiple (-møl·tipøl) *s.* submúltiplo.
subnormal (-no·ʳmal) *adj.-s.* subnormal.
suborder (-o·ʳdø‌ʳ) *s.* suborden.
subordinacy (-o·ʳdinasi) *s.* subordinación, sujeción.
subordinate (-o·ʳdinit) *adj.* subordinado, subalterno, secundario. *2 s.* subordinado.
subordinate (to) (-o·ʳdineit) *tr.* subordinar. *2* supeditar.
subordination (-ei·shøn) *s.* subordinación.
suborn (to) (søbo·ʳn) *tr.* sobornar.
subornation (-ei·shøn) *s.* soborno.
subpoena (søbpɪ·na) *s.* DER. citación, comparendo.
subrogate (to) (sø·brougeit) *tr.* subrogar.
subscribe (to) (-skraib) *tr.-intr.* subscribir, firmar. *2 intr. to ~ for,* suscribirse a. *3 to ~ to,* subscribir, aprobar.
subscription (-skri·pshøn) *s.* firma. *2* subscripción. *3* cantidad subscrita.
subsection (-se·kshøn) *s.* subdivisión.
subsequent (-sikuønt) *adj.* subsecuente, subsiguiente; ulterior.
subserve (to) (søbsø·ʳv) *tr.* servir en condición subordinada. *2* servir, ayudar, favorecer.
subservience, -cy (søbsø·ʳviøns, -si) *s.* subordinación. *2* utilidad, ayuda. *3* servilismo.
subservient (-viønt) *adj.* subordinado. *2* útil. *3* servicial. *4* servil, rastrero.
subside (to) (-sai·d) *intr.* menguar, bajar [de nivel], posarse [un sedimento]. *2* hundirse. *3* calmarse. *4* dejarse caer.
subsidence, -cy (-sai·døns, -si) *s.* hundimiento, descenso. *2* desplome. *3* apaciguamiento.
subsidiary (-si·dieri) *adj.* subsidiario. *2* auxiliar, subordinado. *3 adj.-s.* COM. filial.
subsidize (to) (sø·bsidaiš) *tr.* subvencionar.
subsidy (sø·bsidi) *s.* subvención, subsidio.
subsist (to) (søbsi·st) *intr.* subsistir. *2 tr.* mantener, sustentar.
subsistence (-øns) *s.* subsistencia. *2* manutención, sustento.
subsistent (-ønt) *adj.* subsistente.
subsoil (sø·bsoil) *s.* subsuelo.
substance (-stans) *s.* substancia. *in ~,* en substancia, en lo esencial. *2* realidad, solidez. *3* caudal, bienes: *man of ~,* hombre rico.
substantial (søbstæ·nshal) *adj.* substancial. *2* substantivo. *3* real, positivo. *4* sólido, fuerte. *5* importante, cuantioso, copioso. *6* corpóreo, material. *7* acomodado, rico; solvente. *8 in ~ agreement,* de acuerdo en lo esencial.
substantiality (-shiæ·liti) *s.* substancialidad. *2* corporeidad. *3* solidez.
substantiate (to) (søbstæ·nshiet) *tr.* probar, establecer, demostrar, justificar, comprobar.

substantiation (søbstænshie·shøn) *s.* prueba, demostración, comprobación.
substantival (-tai·val) *adj.* GRAM. substantivo.
substantive (sø·bstɑntiv) *adj.* substantivo, real, positivo. *2* esencial; importante, considerable. *3 adj.-s.* GRAM. substantivo.
substitute (-titiut) *s.* sustitutivo, suplente. *2* substitutivo.
substitute (to) *tr.* sustituir.
substitution (søbstitiu·shøn) *s.* substitución, reemplazo.
substratum (-trei·tøm), *pl.* **substrata** (-ta) *s.* substrato.
substructure (-trø·kchø‌ʳ) *s.* infraestructura.
subtend (to) (-te·nd) *tr.* GEOM. subtender.
subtense (-te·ns) *adj.* GEOM. subtensa.
subterfuge (sø·btø‌ʳfiudẙ) *s.* subterfugio.
subterranean (søbtørei·nian), **subterraneous** (-niøs)*adj.* subterráneo.
subtile (sø·btil) *adj.* SUBTLE.
subtileness (-nis), **subtility** (søbti·liti) *s.* sutileza, sutilidad.
subtilize (-aiš) *tr.-intr.* sutilizar.
subtitle (sø·btaitøl) *s.* subtítulo.
subtle (sø·tøl) *adj.* sutil. *2* disimulado. *3* astuto.
subtleness (-nis), **subtlety** (-ti) *s.* sutileza. *2* agudeza, penetración. *3* astucia.
subtract (to) (søbtræ·kt) *tr.* substraer, deducir, quitar. *2* MAT. restar.
subtraction (-kshøn) *s.* substracción, deducción. *2* MAT. resta, substracción.
subtrahend (sø·btrajønd) *s.* MAT. substraendo.
subtropic (al (søbtra·pikal) *adj.* subtropical.
suburb (sø·bø‌ʳb) *s.* suburbio. *2 pl.* inmediaciones.
suburban (søbø·ʳban) *adj.-s.* suburbano.
suburbicarian (-ø‌ʳbike·rian) *adj.* suburbicario.
subvention (-ve·nshøn) *s.* subvención, ayuda.
subversion (-ve·ʳshøn) *s.* subversión.
subversive (-vø·ʳsiv) *adj.* subversivo.
subvert (to) (-vø·ʳt) *tr.* subvertir.
subway (sø·bwei) *s.* paso subterráneo. *2* (E.U.) metropolitano, ferrocarril, subterráneo.
succedaneous (soksidei·niøs) *adj.* sucedáneo.
succeed (to) (søksi·d) *intr.* suceder [a una persona]. *2* suceder, seguir. *3* tener buen éxito; salir bien.
succeeder (-ø‌ʳ) *s.* sucesor.
succeeding (-ing) *adj.* subsiguiente, futuro.
succentor (-se·ntø‌ʳ) *s.* sochantre.
success (søkse·s) *s.* éxito, buen éxito, logro, triunfo. *2* persona o cosa que tiene éxito.
successful (-ful) *adj.* que tiene éxito, airoso; afortunado, logrado. *2* próspero, venturoso.
succession (søkse·shøn) *s.* sucesión. *2* seguida, serie, continuación: *in ~,* uno tras otro.
successive (-siv) *adj.* sucesivo.
successor (-sø‌ʳ) *s.* sucesor.
succin (søksin) *s.* succino, ámbar.
succinct (søksi·nt) *adj.* sucinto. *2* conciso.
succo(u)r (sø·kø‌ʳ) *s.* socorro, auxilio, asistencia.
succo(u)r (to) *tr.* socorrer, auxiliar.
succubus (sø·kiubøs) *s.* súcubo.
succulence, -cy (sø·kiuløns, -si) *s.* suculencia, jugosidad.
succulent (-ønt) *adj.* suculento, jugoso.
succumb (to) (søkø·m) *tr.* sucumbir. *2* rendirse.
such (sø·ch) *adj.* tal, tales, semejante, semejantes, así: *~ love,* semejante, amor, un amor así; *no ~ a thing,* no hay tal; *~ and ~ thing,* tal y tal cosa. *2 pron.* tal, tales, éste, estos, estas: *~ is the result,* este es el resultado; *as ~,* como a tal. *3 ~ as,* el, la, los, las que; quien, quienes. *4 adv.* tan, así,

tal: ~ *a good man*, un hombre tan bueno; ~ *as it is*, tal cual, o como, es o está.

suck (søˑk) *s.* succión, chupada. *2* mamada, tetada: *to give ~*, amamantar.

suck (to) *tr.-intr.* chapuzar, absorber, sorber, libar. *2* mamar. *3* MEC. aspirar. *4 to ~ dry*, dejar seco o enjuto, agotar.

sucker (-øʳ) *s.* mamón, chupón. *2* lechón; cordero lechal. *3* ZOOL. ventosa. *4* ICT. rémora; lamprea. *5* émbolo o válvula [de bomba]. *6* AGR. retoño, chupón. *7* fig. primo, pagano. *8* fig. borrachín.

suckle (to) (søˑkøl) *tr.* amamantar, lactar, criar. *2 intr.* lactar, mamar, amamantarse.

suckling (søˑkling) *s.* lactación. *2 adj.-s.* niño de teta. *3* mamantón, recental.

sucrose (siuˑkrous) *s.* QUÍM. sacarosa.

suction (søˑkshøn) *s.* succión: *~ cleaner*, aspirador de polvo; *~ pump*, bomba aspirante.

Sudan (sudæˑn) *n. pr.* GEOGR. Sudán.

Sudanese (sudønɪˑs) *adj.-s.* sudanés.

sudatorium (siudatoˑriøm) *s.* sudadero, baño turco.

sudatory (siuˑdatori) *adj.* sudatorio, sudorífico.

sudden (søˑdøn) *adj.* súbito, repentino, inesperado: *all of a ~*, *on a ~*, *of a ~*, de pronto, de repente. *2* súbito, pronto [de genio]; precipitado, violento. *3* improvisado.

suddenness (-nis) *s.* rapidez; precipitación. *2* brusquedad.

sudoriferous (siudoriˑførøs) *adj.* sudorífero.

sudorific (-fik) *adj.-s.* sudorífico.

suds (søds) *s. pl.* jabonaduras; espuma.

sue (to) (siu) *tr.-intr.* DER. demandar, poner pleito. *2* pedir, solicitar, instar. | Con *to* o *for*. *3* hacer la corte, pretender.

suède (sueid) *s.* piel de Suecia.

suet (siuˑit) *s.* saín, sebo.

suffer (to) (søˑføʳ) *tr.-intr.* sufrir, padecer, experimentar: *to ~ from*, padecer de. *2* resistir, soportar, aguantar. *3* sufrir, tolerar.

sufferable (-abøl) *adj.* sufrible, soportable.

sufferance (-ans) *s.* tolerancia, consentimiento tácito. *2* sufrimiento, paciencia, aguante.

suffering (-ing) *s.* sufrimiento, padecimiento, pena. *2 adj.* doliente; enfermo. *3* sufrido.

suffice (to) (søfaiˑs) *intr.* bastar, ser suficiente o bastante, alcanzar. *2 tr.* bastar a.

sufficiency (søfiˑshønsi) *s.* lo suficiente o adecuado. *2* idoneidad, eficacia. *3* presunción. *4* medios suficientes, posición acomodada.

sufficient (-shønt) *adj.* suficiente, adecuado, amplio. *2* satisfactorio. *3* solvente; acomodado.

suffix (søˑfiks) *s.* sufijo.

suffocate (to) (søˑføkeit) *tr.* sofocar, asfixiar. *2 intr.* ahogarse, asfixiarse.

suffocating (-ing) *adj.* sofocante.

suffocation (-eiˑshøn) *s.* sofocación, asfixia.

sufragan (søˑfragan) *adj.-s.* ECLES. sufragáneo.

suffrage (søˑfridẏ) *s.* sufragio, voto.

suffragette (søfradẏeˑt) *t.* sufragista [mujer].

suffragist (søˑfradẏist) *s.* sufragista.

suffuse (to) (søfiuˑs) *tr.* bañar, cubrir, teñir [de un fluido]. *2* difundir.

suffusion (søfiuˑẏøn) *s.* difusión, baño. *2* MED. sufusión.

sugar (shuˑgaʳ) *s.* azúcar: *~ bowl*, azucarero [vasija]; *~ beet*, remolacha; *~ candy*, azúcar cande; *~ cane*, caña de azúcar; *~ mill*, trapiche, ingenio; *~ pea*, tirabeque; *~ tongs*, tenacillas [para el azúcar].

sugar (to) *tr.* azucarar, confitar; endulzar.

sugar-coat (to) *tr.* confitar, cubrir de azúcar. *2* fig. dorar, endulzar [lo desagradable].

sugared (-d) *adj.* endulzado, azucarado. *2* meloso, almibarado.

sugarplum (-pløm) *s.* confite, bombón.

sugary (-i) *adj.* dulce, azucarado. *2* melifluo. *3* goloso.

suggest (to) (søgdẏeˑst) *tr.* sugerir. *2* hacer pensar en, recordar. *3* sugestionar.

suggestible (-tibøl) *adj.* sugestionable. *2* sugerible.

suggestion (-eiˑshøn) *s.* sugestión. *2* indicación, propuesta. *3* señal, indicio.

suggestive (-tiv) *adj.* sugestivo.

suicidal (siuisaiˑdal) *adj.* suicida.

suicide (siuˑsaid) *s.* suicidio: *to commit ~*, suicidarse. *2* suicida.

suint (siuˑint) *s.* churre, grasa de la lana.

suit (siuˑt) *s.* petición, súplica. *2* cortejo, galanteo. *3* DER. demanda; pleito. *4* terno, traje. *5* colección, serie, juego, surtido. *6* palo de la baraja.

suit (to) *tr.* vestir, trajear. *2 tr.-intr.* convenir, acomodar, ir o venir bien. *3* ajustarse, acomodarse. *4* agradar, satisfacer: *~ yourself*, haga usted lo que guste.

suitability (siutabiˑliti) *s.* conformidad, conveniencia.

suitable (siuˑtabøl) *adj.* propio, conveniente, apropiado; conforme, satisfactorio.

suitcase (-keis) *s.* maleta.

suite (suiˑt) *s.* séquito, comitiva. *2* colección, serie: *~ of rooms*, serie de habitaciones. *3* muebles [de una habitación]. *4* MÚS. suite.

suitor (siuˑtøʳ) *s.* DER. demandante. *2* solicitante, aspirante. *3* pretendiente, galán.

sulcate(d (søˑlkeit(ed) *adj.* surcado, acanalado.

sulfate, sulfide, etc. (E.U.) SULPHATE, SULPHIDE, etc.

sulk (søˑlk) *s.* enfurruñamiento, mal humor.

sulk (to) *intr.* estar enfurruñado, de mal humor; encerrarse en un silencio malhumorado.

sulky (-i) *adj.* enfurruñado, hosco, malhumorado. *2 s.* coche de dos ruedas y un solo asiento.

sullage (søˑlidẏ) *s.* basura; escoria.

sullen (søˑløn) *adj.* hosco, huraño, malhumorado. *2* triste, sombrío, lúgubre. *3* lento [río, etc.].

sully (søˑli) *s.* mancha, mancilla.

sully (to) *tr.* manchar, empañar. *2 intr.* mancharse, empañarse.

sulphate (søˑlfeit) *s.* QUÍM. sulfato.

sulphate (to) *tr.* sulfatar.

sulphide (-faid) *s.* QUÍM. sulfuro.

sulphite (-ait) *s.* QUÍM. sulfito.

sulphur (-øʳ) *s.* azufre.

sulphur (to) *tr.* azufrar.

sulphurate (to) (-iureit) *tr.* sulfurar, azufrar.

sulphuret (-rit) *s.* QUÍM. sulfuro.

sulphuric (sølfiuˑrik) *adj.* sulfúrico.

sulphurous (søˑlførøs) *adj.* sulfuroso.

sulphydric (sølfjaiˑdrik) *adj.* sulfhídrico.

sultan (søˑltan) *s.* sultán, soldán.

sultana (søltæˑna) *s.* sultana.

sultanate (søˑltaneit) *s.* sultanía, sultanato.

sultriness (søˑltrinis) *s.* bochorno, calor sofocante.

sultry (søˑltri) *adj.* bochornoso, sofocante.

sum (søm) *s.* MAT. suma. *2* cuenta, problema. *3* suma [cantidad, conjunto]; total, resumen. *4* suma, esencia; lo sumo.

sum (to) *tr.-intr.* sumar. *2 to ~ up*, sumar; resumir, recapitular. *3 to ~ to*, ascender a [un total]. ¶ Pret. y p. p.: *summed*; ger.: *-mming*.

sumac (h (sumæˑk) *s.* zumaque.

Sumatra (suma·tra) *n. pr.* GEOGR. Sumatra.
sumless (sø·mlis) *adj.* innumerable.
summa (sø·ma) *s.* suma [tratado].
summarize (to) (-raiš) *tr.* resumir, compendiar.
summary (-ri) *adj.* sumario, breve. *2 s.* sumario, resumen.
summation (sømei·shøn) *s.* suma [adición; total]. *2* resumen.
summer (sø·møʳ) *s.* estío, verano: ~ *resort*, lugar de veraneo. *2* ARQ. viga maestra; dintel; sotabanco. *3 pl.* años [de una pers.].
summer (to) *intr.* veranear, pasar el verano.
summerhouse (-jaus) *s.* glorieta, cenador.
summering (-ing) *s.* veraneo.
summersault, -set *s.* SOMERSAULT.
summery (-i) *adj.* veraniego, estival.
summit (sø·mit) *s.* ápice, cúspide, punta, cima, cumbre, pináculo.
summon (sø·møn) *tr.* llamar, convocar; evocar. *2* DER. citar. *3* requerir, intimar. *4* hacer acopio de [valor, etc.].
summons (-š) *s.* llamada. *2* convocación. *3* DER. citación. *4* MIL. intimación [de rendición].
sump (sø·mp) *s.* sumidero. *2* MEC. colector de aceite.
sumpter (sø·mptøʳ) *s.* acémila.
sumptuary (-shueri) *adj.* suntuario.
sumptuous (-shuøs) *adj.* suntuoso. *2* espléndido, opíparo.
sun (søn) *s.* sol [astro; luz o calor del sol; día]: ~ *bath*, baño de sol; ~ *blind*, persiana, toldo; *in the* ~, al sol; *under the* ~, debajo del sol.
sun (to) *tr.* asolar, insolar. *2* secar, etc., al sol. *3 intr.* tomar el sol. ¶ Pret. y p. p.: *sunned;* ger.: *sunning.*
sunbeam (-bɪm) *s.* rayo de sol.
sunbeat (-bɪt) *adj.* asoleado.
sunbright (-brait) *adj.* resplandeciente.
sunburn (-bøʳn) *s.* quemadura del sol; bronceado, atezado.
sunburn (to) *tr.-intr.* quemar o quemarse, tostar o tostarse con el sol.
sunburnt (-bøʳnt) *adj.* tostado o bronceado por el sol, atezado.
sunburst (-bøʳst) *s.* salida del sol entre las nubes; rato de sol. *2* broche en figura de sol.
Sunday (-di) *s.* domingo: ~ *school*, escuela dominical; ~ *best*, fam. trapitos de cristianar.
sunder (-døʳ) *s.* separación, división: *in* ~, en dos, en trozos.
sunder (to) *tr.* separar, dividir, cortar. *2 intr.* separarse; romperse.
sundial (-daial) *s.* reloj de sol, cuadrante solar.
sundown (-daun) *s.* puesta del sol.
sundries (-driš) *s. pl.* COM. géneros diversos.
sundry (-dri) *adj.* varios, diversos. *2* sendos.
sunfish (-fish) *s.* ICT. rueda.
sunflower (-flauøʳ) *s.* BOT. girasol.
sung (søng) *pret.* y *p. p.* de TO SING.
sunglasses (sø·nglæsiš) *s.* gafas para el sol.
sunk (sønk) *pret.* y *p. p.* de TO SINK.
sunken (sø·nkøn) *adj.* sumido; hundido.
sunless (sø·nlis) *adj.* sombrío; sin luz; nublado.
sunlight (-lait) *s.* sol, luz del sol.
sunlit (-lit) *adj.* iluminado porʼ el sol.
sunny (-i) *adj.* soleado, lleno de sol. *2* radiante, resplandeciente. *3 it is* ~, hace sol.
sunrise (-raiš) *s.* salida del sol, amanecer.
sunset (-set) *s.* ocaso, puesta del sol.
sunshade (-sheid) *s.* quitasol, sombrilla. *2* toldo. *3* visera contra el sol.

sunshine (-shain) *s.* sol [luz o calor del sol]; solana: *in the* ~, al sol.
sunspot (-spat) *s.* mancha solar.
sunstroke (-strouk) *s.* MED. insolación.
sunstruck (-strøk) *adj.* atacado de insolación.
sunwise (-uaiš) *adv.* como el sol, con el sol.
sup (søp) *s.* sorbo.
sup (to) *intr.-tr.* cenar. *2 tr.* dar de cenar. *3* beber, tomar a sorbos.
super (siu·pøʳ) *adj.* fam. superior, excelente. *2* fam. TEAT. comparsa.
superable (-abøl) *adj.* superable.
superabound (to) (siupørabau·nd) *intr.* superabundar, sobreabundar.
superabundance (-abø·ndans) *s.* superabundancia, sobreabundancia, plétora.
superadd (to) (-æ·d) *tr.* añadir, sobreañadir.
superannuate (-æ·nyueit) *adj.-s.* retirado, jubilado. *2 adj.* anticuado.
superannuate (to) *tr.* retirar, jubilar. *2* anticuar. *3 intr.* retirarse, jubilarse.
superannuated (-tid) *adj.-s.* SUPERANNUATE.
superb (siupøʳb) *adj.* soberbio, magnífico.
supercargo (siupøʳka·ʳgou) *s.* MAR. sobrecargo.
supercilious (-si·liøs) *adj.* arrogante, altanero, desdeñoso.
superdominant (-da·minant) *s.* MÚS. superdominante.
superelevation (-elivei·shøn) *s.* FERROC. peralte.
supereminent (-e·minønt) *s.* supereminente.
supererogatory (-ira·gatori) *adj.* supererogatorio.
superexcellent (-e·ksølønt) *adj.* óptimo.
superficial (-fi·shal) *adj.* superficial. *2* somero. *3* externo.
superficiality (-shiæ·liti) *s.* superficialidad. *2* exterioridad.
superficies (-fi·shiš) *s.* superficie.
superfine (siu·pøʳfain) *adj.* superfino.
superfluity (siupøʳflu·iti) *s.* superfluidad.
superfluous (siupø·ʳfluøs) *adj.* superfluo.
superfortress (siu·pøʳfo·ʳtris) *s.* AVIA. superfortaleza.
superhuman (siupøʳjiu·man) *adj.* sobrehumano.
superimpose (to) (-impou·š) *tr.* sobreponer, superponer.
superincumbent (-inkø·mbønt) *adj.* que pesa o carga sobre; superyacente.
superinduce (to) (-indiu·s) *tr.* sobreañadir.
superintendence, -cy (-inte·ndøns, -si) *s.* superintendencia.
superintendent (-ønt) *s.* superintendente, inspector, director. *2* capataz.
superior (siupi·riøʳ) *adj.-s.* superior. *2* superiora. *3 adj.* de superioridad, orgulloso, desdeñoso.
superioress (-is) *s.* superiora.
superiority (siupiria·riti) *s.* superioridad.
superlative (siupø·ʳlativ) *adj.* superlativo. *2* exagerado. *3 s.* GRAM. superlativo.
superman (siu·pøʳmæn) *s.* superhombre.
supermundane (-mø·ndein) *adj.* supramundano.
supernal (siupø·ʳnal) *adj.* superno, celestial.
supernatural (-næ·chural) *adj.-s.* sobrenatural.
supernumerary (-niu·møreri) *adj.* supernumerario. *2* superfluo. *3 s.* supernumerario.
superphosphate (-fa·sfeit) *s.* QUÍM. superfosfato.
superpose (to) (-pou·š) *tr.* sobreponer, superponer.
supersaturate (to) (-sa·chureit) *tr.* sobresaturar.
superscribe (to) (-skrai·b) *tr.* sobrescribir.
superscription (-skri·pshøn) *s.* sobrescrito.
supersede (to) (-sɪ·d) *tr.* reemplazar, substituir, desalojar. *3* DER. sobreseer.

supersensible (-se·nsibøl) *adj.* suprasensible.
supersensitive (-se·nsitiv) *adj.* supersensible.
supersonic (-sa·nik) *adj.* supersónico.
superstition (-sti·shøn) *s.* superstición.
superstitious (-ti·shøs) *adj.* supersticioso.
superstructure (-strø·kchø^r) *s.* superestructura.
supertax (-æ·ks) *s.* impuesto suplementario.
supervene (to) (siupø^r vi·n) *intr.* sobrevenir, supervenir, seguir.
supervention (-ve·nshøn) *s.* superveniencia.
supervise (to) (-vai·š) *tr.* inspeccionar, revisar, dirigir.
supervisor (-ø^r) *s.* inspector, director. *2* revisor [de una obra literaria].
supination (siupinei·shøn) *s.* supinación.
supinator (-tø^r) *adj.-s.* ANAT. supinador.
supine (siupai·n) *adj.* supino [tendido sobre el dorso, vuelto hacia arriba]. *2* indolente, negligente. *3 s.* GRAM. supino.
supper (sø·pø^r) *s.* cena: *to have* ~, cenar.
supperless (-lis) *adj.* sin cenar.
supplant (to) (søplæ·nt) *tr.* suplantar, desbancar. *2* reemplazar, substituir.
supplanting (-ing) *s.* suplantación.
supple (sø·pøl) *adj.* suave, flexible. *2* elástico, ágil. *3* dócil, complaciente, rastrero, servil.
supple (to) *tr.* suavizar, dar flexibilidad. *2* reducir, aliviar. *3 intr.* hacerse flexible, dócil.
supplement (sø·plimønt) *s.* suplemento.
supplement (to) *tr.* complementar, completar.
supplemental₀-tary (søplime·ntal, -teri) *adj.* suplementario.
suppletory (sø·plitori) *adj.* supletorio.
suppliance (sø·plians) *s.* ruego, súplica.
suppliant (-pliant), **supplicant** (-plikant) *adj.-s.* suplicante.
supplicate (to) (-·plikeit) *tr.-intr.* suplicar, rogar.
supplication (-ei·shøn) *s.* súplica, ruego. *2* plegaria.
supplier (søplai·ø^r) *s.* suministrador, proveedor.
supply (søplai) *s.* suministro, provisión, abastecimiento. *2* respuesto, surtido. *3* COM. oferta, existencia: ~ *and demand*, la oferta y la demanda. *4 pl.* provisiones, pertrechos, víveres, materiales.
supply (to) *tr.* suministrar, proporcionar. *2* proveer, abastecer. *3* suplir. *4* satisfacer [las necesidades, la demanda].
support (søpo·^rt) *s.* soporte, apoyo, sostén: *point of* ~, punto de apoyo. *2* ayuda, protección. *3* sostenimiento. *4* sustento, manutención.
support (to) *tr.* soportar [sostener, aguantar; sufrir, tolerar]. *2* sostener, defender, apoyar, proteger. *3* probar, justificar. *4* sustentar, mantener.
supportable (-abøl) *adj.* soportable, tolerable, llevadero. *2* sostenible, defendible.
supporter (-ø^r) *s.* mantenedor, sostenedor. *2* defensor, partidario. *3* apoyo, sostén. *4* tirante [para medias]. *5* sostén [prenda femenina]. *6* suspensorio.
suppose (to) (søpou·š) *tr.* suponer. *2* creer, pensar, figurarse.
supposed (-d) *adj.* supuesto, presunto.
supposition (søpøši·shøn) *s.* suposición, hipótesis.
suppositional (-al) *adj.* hipotético.
supposititious (søpøšiti·shøs) *adj.* supositicio.
suppositive (søpa·sitiv) *adj.* supositivo. *2* supuesto.
suppository (-sitori) *s.* MED. supositorio.
suppress (to) (søpre·š) *tr.* suprimir. *2* omitir. *3* reprimir, contener. *4* ahogar, sofocar, acabar con. *5* callar, ocultar.
suppression (-shøn) *s.* supresión, omisión. *2* represión, contención. *3* MED. suspensión.
supressive (-siv) *adj.* supresivo. *2* represivo. *3* contentivo.
suppurate (to) (sø·piureit) *intr.* supurar.
suppuration (-ei·shøn) *s.* supuración.
suprarenal (siuprarı·nal) *adj.* ANAT. suprarrenal.
supremacy (siupre·masi) *s.* supremacía.
supreme (siuprı·m) *adj.* supremo, sumo, soberano. *2 s.* el más alto grado. *3 the Supreme,* el Altísimo.
supremely (-li) *adv.* supremamente, soberanamente. *2* sumamente.
surah (sura) *s.* surá.
surbase (sø·^rbeis) *s.* cornisa de pedestal.
surcharge (sø^r cha·^r dÿ) *s.* sobrecarga. *2* recargo.
surcharge (to) *tr.* sobrecargar. *2* recargar.
surcingle (sø·^r singøl) *s.* sobrecincha.
surcoat (-kout) *s.* sobretodo, gabán. *2* sobrevesta.
surd (sø^r d) *adj.* FONÉT. sordo. *2* MAT. irracional.
sure (shu·ø^r) *adj.* seguro [en sus varias acepciones]. *2* salvo. *3* cierto, convencido. *4* firme, estable. *5* seguro de sí mismo. *6 to be* ~, seguramente, sin duda; estar seguro; ser cierto. *7 to make* ~, asegurar (se; cerciorar (se. *8 for* ~, de fijo, a punto fijo. *9 adv.* ciertamente, efectivamente.
sure-footed *adj.* de pie firme, seguro.
surely (-li) *adv.* ciertamente, sin duda.
sureness (-nis) *s.* seguridad [calidad de seguro]. *2* certeza, confianza.
surety (-ti) *s.* SURENES. *2* cosa segura o cierta. *3* seguridad, garantía, fianza. *4* fiador, garante: *to be* ~ *for,* salir fiador por.
surexcitation (søreksitei·shøn) *s.* MED. sobreexcitación.
surf (sø^r f) *s.* oleaje que rompe en la playa, rompiente, resaca.
surface (sø·^r fis) *s.* superficie; cara.
surface (to) *tr.* dar cierta clase de superficie a; alisar, igualar, pulir. *2 intr.* subir a la superficie [un submarino].
surfacer (-ø^r) *s.* máquina de alisar o cepillar.
surfboard (sø·^r fbo^r d) *s.* DEP. esquí acuático.
surfeit (sø·^r fit) *s.* exceso, sobreabundancia. *2* ahíto, empacho. *3* empalago. *4* VET. encebadamiento.
surfeit (to) *tr.* ahitar, hartar, saciar. *2* encebadar. *3* empalagar. *4 intr.* hartarse.
surge (sø^r dÿ) *s.* ola, oleada, oleaje. *2* ELECT. sobretensión.
surge (to) *intr.* hincharse, agitarse [el mar, las olas]. *2* surgir, levantarse, ondular. *3 tr.* hacer ondular. *4* MAR. largar, lascar.
surgeon (sø·^r dÿøn) *s.* cirujano. *2* MIL. médico.
surgery (sø·^r dÿøri) *s.* cirugía. *2* sala de operaciones.
surgical (sø^r ·dÿikal) *adj.* quirúrgico.
surgy (sø·^r dÿi) *adj.* agitado; que se levanta en olas.
surliness (sø·^r linis) *s.* rudeza, brusquedad, hosquedad, desabrimiento, mal genio.
surloin (sø·^r loin) *s.* solomillo.
surly (sø·^r li) *adj.* rudo, brusco, desabrido, hosco, gruñón.
surmise (sø^r mai·š) *s.* conjetura, suposición.
surmise (to) *tr.* conjeturar, suponer.
surmount (to) (sø^r mau·nt) *tr.* vencer, superar. *2* coronar [estar situado sobre]. *3* subir, escalar.
surmullet (sø^r mø·lit) *s.* ICT. salmonete.
surname (sø·^r neim) *s.* apellido. *2* sobrenombre.

surname (to) *tr.* apellidar, llamar.
surpass (to) (sø^rpæ·s) *tr.* sobrepujar, aventajar.
surpassing (sø^rpæ·sing) *adj.* superior, sobresaliente.
surplice (sø·^rplis) *s.* sobrepelliz.
surplus (sø·^rpløs) *s.* sobrante, excedente, exceso. *2* superávit.
surprisal (sø^rprai·śal) *s.* SURPRISE.
surprise (sø^rprai·ś) *s.* sorpresa. *2* extrañeza, asombro, novedad.
surprise (to) *tr.* sorprender. *2* extrañar, maravillar a. *3 to be surprised at,* sorprenderse de.
surprising (sø^rprai·śing) *adj.* sorprendente. *2* asombroso.
surrealism (sørı·ališm) *s.* surrealismo.
surrender (søre·ndø^r) *s.* rendición, sumisión. *2* entrega, renuncia, cesión.
surrender (to) *tr.* rendir, entregar. *2* abandonar, renunciar a. *3 intr.* rendirse, entregarse.
surreptitious (sørepti·shøs) *adj.* subrepticio.
surrey (so·ri) *s.* especie de birlocho.
surrogate (sø·røgeit) *s.* sustituto, delegado.
surround (to) *tr.* rodear, cercar, circundar. *2* MIL. sitiar.
surrounding (-ing) *adj.* circundante. *2 s.* acción de rodear, cerco. *3 pl.* alrededores, contornos. *4* ambiente, medio.
surtax (sø·^rtaks) *s.* impuesto suplementario; recargo.
surveillance (sø^rvei·lans) *s.* vigilancia.
surveillant (sø^rvei·lant) *adj.* y *s.* vigilante.
survey (sø^rvei·) *s.* medición, deslinde; plano [de un terreno]. *2* inspección, examen, estudio. *3* perspectiva, ojeada general.
survey (to) *tr.* medir, deslindar [tierras]. *2* levantar el plano de. *3* inspeccionar, examinar, reconocer. *4* dar una ojeada general. *5 intr.* realizar operaciones de agrimensura o topografía.
surveying (-ing) *s.* agrimensura; topografía.
surveyor (-ø^r) *s.* agrimensor; topógrafo. *2* inspector. *3* vista [de aduanas].
survival (sø^rvai·val) *s.* supervivencia. *2* resto, reliquia.
survive (to) (sø^rvai·v) *tr.* sobrevivir. *2* salir o quedar con vida.
survivor (-ø^r) *s.* sobreviviente.
Susan (su·śan) *n. pr.* Susana.
susceptibility (søseptibi·liti) *s.* susceptibilidad, capacidad. *2* impresionabilidád. *3 pl.* sentimientos.
susceptible (søse·ptibøl) *adj.* susceptible, capaz. *2* sensible, impresionable; enamoradizo.
suspect (søspe·kt) *adj.-s.* sospechoso.
suspect (to) *tr.* sospechar, recelar. *2* presumir, barruntar. *3* sospechar o desconfiar de.
suspected (-id) *adj.* sospechoso. *2* sospechado.
suspend (to) (søspe·nd) *tr.* suspender [colgar; interrumpir, diferir; absortar]. *2* tener en espera, indeciso. *3* suspender [de un cargo, etc.]. *4* COM. *to ~ payment,* hacer suspensión de pagos.
suspenders (-ø^rś) *s. pl.* ligas. *2* tirantes [de pantalón].
suspense (søspe·ns) *s.* suspensión, interrupción. *2* incertidumbre, ansiedad, espera. *3* estado indeciso.
suspension (-shøn) *s.* suspensión; *~ bridge,* puente colgante; *~ points,* puntos suspensivos.
suspensive (-siv) *adj.* suspensivo. *2* suspenso, indeciso.
suspensory (-sori) *adj.* suspensorio.

suspicion (søspi·shøn) *s.* sospecha. *2* recelo, desconfianza. *3* pizca. *4* indicio.
suspicious (-shøs) *adj.* sospechoso, receloso. *2* de sospecha. *3* suspicaz, desconfiado.
suspiration (søspairei·shøn) *s.* suspiro.
suspire (to) (søspai·^r) *tr.* decir suspirando.
sustain (to) (søstei·n) *tr.* sostener. *2* mantener. *3* sustentar. *4* sufrir, experimentar [daño, pérdidas, etc.]. *5* defender, probar.
sustenance (sø·stinans) *s.* sostenimiento. *2* mantenimiento, sustento, alimentos.
sustentation (søstøntei·shøn) *s.* sustentación. *2* sostenimiento. *3* mantenimiento, conservación. *4* apoyo.
susurrate (to) (siusø·reit) *intr.* susurrar, murmurar.
susurration (siusørei·shøn) *s.* susurro.
sutler (sø·tlø^r) *s.* vivandero.
suture (siu·chø^r) *s.* sutura. *2* BOT. rafe.
suzerain (siu·śørin) *adj.* soberano. *2 s.* señor [de vasallos]. *3* estado soberano de otro.
suzerainty (-ti) *s.* soberanía, señoría.
svelte (svelt) *adj.* esbelto.
swab (suab) *s.* estropajo. *2* MAR. lampazo. *3* CIR. compresa, tapón.
swab (to) *tr.* limpiar con estropajo. *2* limpiar, enjugar.
swaddle (sua·døl) *s.* envoltura, faja, vendaje; *swaddling clothes,* pañales.
swaddle (to) *tr.* empañar, envolver [a un niño]. *2* fajar, vendar.
swag (suæg) *s. fam.* botín [de un robo]. *2* B. ART. guirnalda.
swagger (suæ·gø^r) *s.* andar arrogante, contoneo. *2* fanfarronería, jactancia.
swagger (to) *intr.* contonearse, fanfarrear. *2 tr.-intr.* amenazar, intimidar.
swaggerer (-ø^r) *s.* jactancioso, fanfarrón.
swain (suein) *s.* zagal. *2* enamorado.
swale (suei·l) *s.* terreno húmedo y bajo.
swallow (sua·lou) *s.* ORN. golondrina. *2* tragadero, gaznate. *3* engullida, trago.
swallow (to) *tr.-intr.* tragar, deglutir. *2 tr.* tragar, tragarse [absorber, abismar; dar crédito a; aguantar, etc.]. *3* contener [la risa, etc.].
swallowtail (teil) *s. fam. frac.* *2* CARP. cola de milano.
swallowwort (-uø^rt) *s.* BOT. celidonia. *2* BOT. vencetósigo.
swam (suæm) *pret.* de TO SWIM.
swamp (suamp) *s.* pantano, marisma, marjal.
swamp (to) *tr.* atollar. *2* sumergir, hundir. *3* inundar, encharcar. *4* abrumar [de trabajo]. *5 intr.* empantanarse. *6* hundirse, irse a pique.
swampy (-i) *adj.* pantanoso, cenagoso.
swan (suan) *s.* ORN. cisne. *2* fig. poeta. *3* NAT. *~ dive,* salto del ángel.
swap (suap) *s.* cambio, cambalache.
swap (to) *tr.-intr. fam.* cambiar, cambalachear.
sward (suo^rd) *s.* césped, tierra herbosa.
sward (to) *tr.* encespedar. *2 intr.* cubrirse de hierbas.
swarm (suo^rm) *s.* enjambre. *2* multitud, gentío, hormiguero.
swarm (to) *intr.* enjambrar. *2* pulular, hormiguear. *3* llegar en enjambre o multitud. *4 to ~ with,* rebosar de. *5 tr.* enjambrar.
swart (suo^rt), **swarthy** (-di) *adj.* moreno, atezado.
swash (suash) *s.* ruido o golpe del agua; chapoteo, chorro. *2* golpe de una sustancia blanda. *3* ruido, alboroto; fanfarria.

swash (to) *intr.* hacer ruido [el agua]. *2* golpear, etc., haciendo ruido. *3* meter bulla. *4* fanfarronear.

swashbuckle (-bøkøl) *intr.* fanfarronear.

swashbuckler (-bøklø^r), **swasher** (-ø^r) *s.* espadachín, fanfarrón, matasiete.

swastika (sua·stika) *s.* svástica.

swat (suat) *s.* golpazo, golpe abrumador.

swat (to) *tr.* golpear con fuerza; matar [moscas].

swath (suaz) *s.* camba [hierba segada].

swathe (suei·d) *s.* faja, venda. *2 pl.* pañales.

swathe (to) *tr.* fajar, vendar, envolver.

sway (suei) *s.* oscilación, vaivén. *2* inclinación, desviación. *3* poder, dominio, influjo.

sway (to) *intr.* oscilar, cimbrearse. *2* tambalear, flaquear. *3* inclinarse, ladearse, desviarse. *4 tr.-intr.* gobernar, dominar. *5* hacer oscilar. *6* inclinar, desviar. *7* influir en.

swear (to) (sue·ø^r) *intr.* jurar [prestar juramento; renegar, echar maldiciones]: *to ~ at,* maldecir; *to ~ by,* jurar por; poner toda su confianza en. *2 tr.* jurar. *3* pronunciar [un juramento]. *4* tomar juramento, juramentar. ¶ *Pret.: swore;* p. p.: *sworn.*

sweat (suet) *s.* sudor: *to be in a ~,* estar sudando. *2* trasudor. *3* exudación.

sweat (to) *intr.-tr.* sudar. *2* trasudar. *3* exudar. *4 tr.* hacer sudar. *5* explotar [al que trabaja]. *6* soldar, extraer, etc., por el calor.

sweatband (-bænd) *s.* badana [del sombrero].

sweater (-ø^r) *s.* el que suda. *2* explotador [de obreros]. *3* suéter.

sweaty (-i) *adj.* sudado, sudoroso, duro, laborioso.

Swede (suɪd) *s.* sueco.

Sweden (-øn) *n. pr.* GEOGR. Suecia.

Swedish (-ish) *adj.* sueco. *2 s.* idioma sueco.

sweep (suɪp) *s.* barrido, escobada. *2* barrendero. *3* deshollinador. *4* movimiento amplio o rápido en arco de círculo. *5* extensión, alcance, recorrido, golpe. *6* cigoñal [de pozo]. *7* remo largo. *8* cosa que se mueve rozando o barriendo.

sweep (to) *tr.* barrer, escobar. *2* limpiar, deshollinar. *3* pasar rápidamente por. *4* arrebatar, llevarse. *5* rastrear, dragar. *6* MÚS. rasguear, pulsar. *7* arrastrar [la cola]. *8* recorrer [con la vista, los dedos, etc.]; abarcar, dominar. *9* mover con amplio ademán. *10 to ~ one off his feet,* entusiasmar; convencer a uno. *11 tr.* pasar rápidamente. *12* andar majestuosamente. *13* extenderse. *14* describir una curva. ¶ *Pret.* y *p. p.: swept.*

sweeper (-ø^r) *s.* barrendero. *2* escoba mecánica.

sweepstakes (suɪp·steiks) *s. sing.* y *pl.* DEP. combinación en que una sola persona puede ganar todas las apuestas.

sweet (suɪt) *adj.* dulce, azucarado. *2* dulce, grato, suave, amable, bondadoso. *3* benigno, apacible. *4* melodioso. *5* oloroso: *~ herbs,* hierbas aromáticas. *6* bello, lindo. *7* querido. *8* potable. *9 to be ~ on,* estar enamorado de. *10* BOT. *~ basil,* albahaca; *~ clover,* trébol oloroso; *~ flag,* ácoro; *~ potato,* batata, boniato; *~ william,* minutisa. *11 adv.* dulcemente, etc. *12 s.* dulzura. *13 pl.* dulces, golosinas.

sweetbread (-bred) *s.* lechecillas o mollejas de ternera.

sweetbrier (-braiø^r) *s.* BOT. agavanzo.

sweeten (to) (-øn) *tr.* endulzar, dulcificar. *2* suavizar. *3* purificar. *4* embalsamar, perfumar. *5 intr.* endulzarse. *6* dulcificarse.

sweetheart (-ja^{r}t) *s.* novio, amado; novia, amada; ser querido.

sweetish (-ish) *adj.* algo dulce.

sweetly (-li) *adv.* dulcemente.

sweetmeat (-mɪt) *s.* dulce, confitura, golosina.

sweet-scented *adj.* perfumado.

sweet-spoken *adj.* melifluo.

sweet-tempered *adj.* de carácter dulce.

sweet-toothed *adj.* goloso.

swell (suel) *s.* hinchazón. *2* bulto, prominencia. *3* ola, oleaje; crecida. *4* ondulación del terreno. *5* engrosamiento, aumento. *6* MÚS. crescendo y diminuendo. *7* MÚS. pedal de expresión. *8* fam. lechuguino. *9* fam. personaje. *10 adj.* fam. elegante. *11* fam. estupendo.

swell (to) *tr.* hinchar, inflar, dilatar. *2* abultar, engrosar, aumentar. *3* inflar, engreír. *4 intr.* hincharse, inflarse. *5* abultarse, engrosarse, aumentar, crecer. *6* entumecerse [un río]: embravecerse, agitarse [el mar]. *7* aumentar de intensidad [un sonido]. *8* inflarse, engreírse. ¶ *Pret.: swelled;* p. p.: *swelled* o *swollen.*

swelling (-ing) *s.* hinchazón. *2* aumento, crecida. *3* bulto, chichón.

swelter (sue·ltø^r) *s.* calor sofocante. *2* sudor copioso.

swelter (to) *tr.* sofocar [de calor]. *2 intr.* ahogarse de calor; sudar la gota gorda.

swept (suept) *pret.* y *p. p.* de TO SWEEP.

swerve (suø^{r}v) *s.* desviación, viraje. *2* vacilación.

swerve (to) *tr.* desviar, apartar. *2 intr.* desviarse, apartarse, torcer. *3* vacilar, flaquear.

swift (suift) *adj.* veloz, rápido. *2* pronto, presto. *3* repentino. *4* activo, diligente. *5* ORN. vencejo. *6* ZOOL. lagartija. *7* MEC. devanadera, carrete.

swift-footed *adj.* ligero, veloz, de paso rápido.

swiftly (-li) *adv.* velozmente, rápidamente. *2* pronto.

swig (suig) *s.* fam. trago grande.

swig (to) *tr.-intr.* beber a grandes tragos.

swill (suil) *s.* bazofia. *2* tragantada.

swill (to) *tr.* enjuagar, lavar; inundar. *2* beber a grandes tragos. *3 intr.* emborracharse.

swim (suim) *s.* acción o rato de nadar. *2* espacio para nadar. *3* corriente [de los negocios, etc.].

swim (to) *intr.* nadar. *2* sobrenadar, flotar. *3* pasar, deslizarse. *4* anegarse, estar lleno o llenarse [de]. *5 my head swims,* se me va la cabeza. *6 tr.* hacer nadar o flotar. *7* pasar a nado. ¶ *Pret.: swam;* p. p.: *swum.*

swimming (-ing) *s.* natación. *2* vértigo, vahído. *3 adj.* que nada; para nadar: *~ bladder,* vejiga natatoria; *~ pool,* piscina. *4* arrasado [de lágrimas]. *5* desvanecido, con vértigo.

swimmingly (-li) *adv.* lisamente, sin tropiezo; prósperamente.

swindle (sui·ndøl) *s.* estafa, timo.

swindle (to) *tr.* estafar, timar.

swindler (-lø^r) *s.* estafador, timador.

swine (suain) *s. sing.* y *pl.* ZOOL. cerdo; cerdos; ganado de cerda. *2* fig. cerdo, persona sensual.

swineherd (-jø^{r}d) *s.* porquero, porquerizo.

swinery (-ri) *s.* pocilga. *2* conjunto de cerdos.

swing (suing) *s.* oscilación, giro, balance, vaivén; ritmo. *2* impulso, ímpetu. *3* BOX. golpe de lado. *4* columpio, mecedor. *5* juego, operación, marcha; carrese: *full ~,* plena operación; *libre curso;* apogeo. *6* MEC. carrera, recorrido. *7* período [de duración, acción, etc.]. *8* LIT., MÚS. ritmo sostenido.

swing (to) *tr.* balancear, hacer oscilar, hacer girar;

mecer, columpiar. 2 blandir [un bastón, etc.], lanzar con ímpetu. 3 suspender, colgar, engoznar. 4 (E.U.) manejar con éxito. 5 *intr.* balancearse, oscilar, columpiarse. 6 colgar, ser ahorcado. 7 girar, dar vueltas: *to ~ about*, volverse. ¶ Pret. y p. p.: *swung*.

swingeing (sui·ndÿing) *adj.* fam. grande, enorme, estupendo.

swinging (-ging) *adj.* oscilante; colgante: *~ boom*, MAR. tangón; *~ door*, puerta giratoria.

swingle (sui·ngøl) *s.* espadilla [para espadar].

swingle (to) *tr.* espadar, espadillar.

swinish (suai·nish) *adj.* porcuno. 2 cochino, grosero, bestial.

swipe (suaip) *s.* golpe fuerte. 2 trago grande.

swipe (to) *tr.* dar o golpear fuerte. 2 hurtar, robar. 3 *intr.* beber.

swirl (suøᶜl) *s.* remolino, torbellino.

swirl (to) *tr.* hacer girar. 2 *intr.* arremolinarse. 3 girar, dar vueltas.

swish (suish) *s.* silbido del látigo o el bastón al cortar el aire. 2 frufrú; susurro.

swish (to) *tr.* golpear, dar latigazos. 2 *intr.* silbar [el látigo, el bastón] al cortar el aire. 3 producir un frufrú, un susurro; crujir [las sedas, las hojas, etc.].

Swiss (suis) *adj.-s.* suizo, suiza. 2 BOT. *~ chard*, acelga.

switch (suich) *s.* vara flexible, verdasca; látigo, azote. 2 latigazo, verdascazo. 3 añadido [de pelo postizo]. 4 FERROC. aguja, desvío. 5 ELECT. conmutador, interruptor. 6 desviación, conmutación, cambio.

switch (to) *tr.* azotar, fustigar. 2 cambiar, desviar. 3 ELECT. *to ~ on*, conectar; dar [la luz]; *to ~ off*, desconectar; apagar [la luz]. 4 *intr.* cambiar, pasar de una cosa a otra.

switchback (-bæk) *s.* camino o vía férrea en zigzag para subir una pendiente. 2 montaña rusa.

switchboard (-boᶜd) *s.* ELECT., TELÉF. cuadro de distribución.

switchman (-mæn) *s.* guardagujas.

Switzerland (sui·tšøᶜlænd) *n. pr.* GEOGR. Suiza.

swivel (sui·vøl) *s.* pieza o eslabón giratorios: *~ chair*, silla o sillón giratorios; *~ door*, puerta giratoria.

swivel (to) *intr.-tr.* girar o hacer girar [esp. sobre la pieza que sujeta].

swollen (suo·løn) *p. p.* de TO SWELL.

swoon (swun) *s.* desmayo, síncope.

swoon (to) *intr.* desmayarse, desfallecer.

swoop (swup) *s.* descenso súbito; ataque.

swoop (to) *intr.* abatirse, precipitarse [sobre]. 2 *tr.* barrer, arrebatar, llevarse.

swoop *s.*, **swoop (to)** *tr.-intr.* SWAP, TO SWAP.

sword (soᶜd) *s.* espada [arma]: *~ belt*, talabarte, cinturón; *~ lily*, BOT. estoque; *to be at sword's points*, estar a matar.

swordfish (-fish) *s.* ICT. pez espada.

swordplay (-plei) *s.* esgrima.

swordsman (-smæn) *s.* tirador de espada.

swore (suoᶜ) *pret.* de TO SWEAR.

sworn (suoᶜn) *p. p.* de TO SWEAR.

swum (suøm) *p. p.* de TO SWIM.

swung (suøng) *pret.* y *p. p.* de TO SWING.

Sybarite (si·barait) *s.* sibarita.

sybaritism (-išm) *s.* sibaritismo.

sycamore (si·kamoᶜ) *s.* BOT. sicómoro. 2 BOT. (E.U.) plátano falso.

sycon (sai·køn) *s.* ZOOL. sicón.

syconium (saikou·niøm) *s.* BOT. sicono.

sycophant (si·køfant) *s.* adulador; parásito. 2 sicofanta.

syenife (sai·enait) *s.* PETR. sienita.

syllabary (si·labari) *s.* silabario.

syllabic(al (silæ·bik(al) *adj.* silábico.

syllabicate (-bikeit), **syllabify** (-bifai), **syllabize** (-baiš) (to) *tr.* silabear.

syllable (si·labøl) *s.* sílaba. 2 palabra monosílaba.

syllabus (-bøs) *s.* sílabo. 2 sumario, resumen. 3 asignaturas de un curso; plan de estudios.

syllepsis (sile·psis) *s.* GRAM. silepsis.

syllogism (si·lødÿišm) *s.* LÓG. silogismo.

syllogize (to) (-aiš) *intr.* silogizar.

sylph (silf) *s.* silfo. 2 silfide.

sylva (si·lva) *s.* selva. 2 descripción de los árboles de una región. 3 silva [colección].

sylvan (si·lvan) *adj.* selvático. 2 rústico.

Sylvester (silve·støᶜ) *n. pr.* Silvestre.

symbiosis (simbiou·sis) *s.* BIOL. simbiosis.

symbol (si·mbøl) *s.* símbolo.

symbolic(al (simba·lik(al) *adj.* simbólico.

symbolism (si·mbølišm) *s.* simbolismo.

symbolize (to) (-laiš) *tr.* simbolizar.

symmetrical (sime·trikal) *adj.* simétrico.

symmetrize (to) (si·mitraiš) *tr.* hacer simétrico.

symmetry (si·mitri) *s.* simetría. 2 proporción, armonía, conformidad.

sympathetic (simpaze·tik) *adj.* simpático. 2 simpatizante. 3 compasivo, que siente con los demás; comprensivo. 4 favorablemente dispuesto. 5 ANAT. *~ nervous system*, gran simpático.

sympathize (to) (si·mpazais) *intr.* simpatizar. 2 compadecerse, acompañar en un sentimiento. 3 comprender; sentir con los demás. 4 congeniar.

sympathy (-pazi) *s.* simpatía. 2 compasión, condolencia. 3 comprensión, benevolencia. 4 afinidad, armonía. 5 pésame.

symphonic (simfa·nik) *adj.* sinfónico. 2 armonioso. 3 homófono.

symphony (si·mfoni) *s.* sinfonía. 2 consonancia.

symphysis (si·mfisis) *s.* ANAT. sínfisis.

symposium (simpou·siøm) *s.* simpósium.

symptom (si·mptøm) *s.* síntoma.

symptomatic (al (simptømæ·tik(al) *adj.* sintomático.

synaeresis (sine·risis) *s.* sinéresis.

synagogue (si·nagag) *s.* sinagoga.

synalepha (sinali·fa) *s.* sinalefa.

syncarpous (sinka·ᶜpøs) *s.* BOT. sincárpico.

synchronism (si·nkrønišm) *s.* sincronismo. 2 coetaneidad.

synchronize (to) (-naiš) *tr.-intr.* sincronizar.

synchronous (-nøs) *adj.* sincrónico. 2 coetáneo, simultáneo.

synclinal (sinklai·nal) *adj.* GEOL. sinclinal.

syncopate (to) (si·nkøpeit) *tr.* GRAM., MÚS. sincopar.

syncopation (-ei·shøn) *s.* GRAM., MÚS. síncopa.

syncope (sin·køpi) *s.* GRAM., MÚS. síncopa. 2 MED. síncope.

syncretism (si·nkritišm) *s.* sincretismo.

syndic (si·ndik) *s.* síndico.

syndicalism (-ališm) *s.* sindicalismo.

syndicat (sendika·) *t.* sindicato obrero.

syndicate (si·ndikit) *s.* sindicatura. 2 sindicato financiero, trust. 3 empresa distribuidora de artículos, fotografías, etc., para los periódicos.

syndicate (to) (-dikeit) *tr.* sindicar, asociar. 3 *intr.* sindicarse.

syndrome (-drømi) *s.* MED. síndrome.

synecdoche (sine·kdoki) *s.* RET. sinécdoque.

syneresis (sine·risis) *s.* SYNAERESIS.

synergy (si·nø^rdẙi) *s.* sinergia.
synod (si·nød) *s.* ECLES., ASTR. sínodo.
synonym (si·nønim) *s.* sinónimo.
synonymous (sina·nimøs) *adj.* sinónimo.
synonymy (sina·nimi) *s.* sinonimia.
synopsis (sina·psis) *s.* sinopsis.
synovia (sinou·via) *s.* ANAT. sinovia.
syntactic (al (sintæ·ktik(al) *adj.* sintáctico.
syntax (si·ntæks) *s.* GRAM. sintaxis.
synthesis (si·nzisis) *s.* síntesis.
synthesize (to) (si·nziŝaiŝ) *tr.* SYNTHETIZE.
synthetic (al (sinze·tik(al) *adj.* sintético.
synthetize (to) (si·nzitaiŝ) *tr.* sintetizar.
syntonic (sinta·nik) *adj.* sintónico.
syntonize (to) (si·ntønaiŝ) *tr.* RADIO. sintonizar.
syntony (si·ntøni) *s.* RADIO. sintonía.
syphilis (si·filis) *s.* MED. sífilis.

syphon (sai·føn) *s.* SIPHON.
Syracuse (si·rakius) *n. pr.* GEOGR. Siracusa.
Syria (si·ria) *n. pr.* GEOGR. Siria.
Syrian (si·rian) *adj.-s.* sirio.
syringa (siri·nga) *s.* BOT. lila. *2* BOT. jeringuilla.
syringe (si·rindẙ) *s.* jeringa.
syringe (to) *tr.* jeringar. *2* inyectar [con jeringa].
syrinx (si·rinks) *s.* ORN. siringe. *2* ANAT. trompa de Eustaquio. *3* siringa, zampoña.
syrup (si·røp) *s.* jarabe. *2* almíbar.
system (si·støm) *s.* sistema. *2* método, orden.
systematic (al (sistømæ·tik(al) *adj.* sistemático. *2* taxonómico.
systematize (to) (si·stømataiŝ) *tr.* sistematizar. *2* organizar.
systole (si·støli) *s.* sístole.
systyle (-tail) *s.* ARQ. sístilo.
syzygy (si·ŝidẙi) *s.* ASTR. sicigia.

T

T, t (ti) *s.* T, t, vigésima letra del alfabeto inglés.
T *s.* cosa en forma de T: *T square*, te (regla).
't *contr.* de IT.
tab (tæb) *s.* parte saliente; pestaña. *2* oreja [de zapato]. *3* herrete [de cordón]. *4* cuenta [que se lleva].
tabard (tæ·ba^r d) *s.* tabardo.
tabby (tæ·bi) *s.* TEJ. tabí. *2* gato de piel atigrada. *3* fig. mujer chismosa. *4 adj.* atigrado.
tabernacle (tæ·bø^r nækøl) *s.* tabernáculo.
tabes (tei·biš) *s.* MED. tabes.
table (tei·bøl) *s.* mesa [mueble; comida; los que se sientan a una mesa]: ~ *linen*, mantelería; ~ *service*, vajilla; ~ *stone*, dolmen; ~ *tennis*, tenis de mesa. *2* tabla, plancha, losa. *3* tablero [de juego]. *5* ARQ. tablero. *6* PERSP. tabla. *7* mesa [de piedra preciosa]. *8* tabla [lista, índice, cuadro]: ~ *of contents*, índice; *the tables of the law*, las Tablas de la Ley.
table (to) *tr.* poner sobre la mesa. *2* poner en forma de tabla o índice. *3* dejar sobre la mesa, dar carpetazo a.
tableau (tæ·blou), *pl.* **-bleaux** *s.* cuadro vivo.
tablecloth (tei·bølkloz) *s.* mantel [de mesa].
tableland (-lænd) *s.* GEOGR. meseta.
tablespoon (-spun) *s.* cuchara de sopa.
tablet (tæ·blit) *s.* tabla, tablilla. *2* placa, lápida. *3* bloc [de papel]. *4* FARM. tableta, comprimido.
tableware (tei·bølue^r) *s.* artículos para la mesa.
tablier (tablie·) *s.* delantal [de mujer].
tabloid (tæ·bloid) *adj.* breve, conciso, resumido. *2 s.* tableta, comprimido. *3* periódico ilustrado de noticias resumidas.
taboo (tabu·) *adj.-s.* tabú.
taboo (to) *tr.* declarar tabú, prohibir, proscribir.
tabo(u)r (tei·bø^r) *s.* tamboril.
tabo(u)ret (tæbøre·t) *s.* taburete. *2* bastidor [de bordar].
tabourine (tæ·burin) *s.* MÚS. pandero, adufe.
tabu (tabu·) *s.* TABOO.
tabular (tæ·biula^r) *adj.* tabular.
tabulate (to) (-leit) *tr.* disponer en forma de tabla o cuadro.
tabulator (-leitø^r) *s.* tabulador.
tachometer (taka·metø^r) *s.* tacómetro.
tachycardia (tækika·^r dia) *s.* MED. taquicardia.
tachygraphy (tæki·grafi) *s.* taquigrafía.
tachymeter (tæki·mitø^r) *s.* taquímetro.

tacit (tæ·sit) *adj.* tácito.
taciturn (tæ·sitø^r n) *adj.* taciturno.
tack (tæ·k) *s.* tachuela. *2* hilván. *3* MAR. amura [cabo]. *4* MAR. bordada; virada. *5* política, línea de conducta.
tack (to) *tr.* clavar con tachuelas. *2* hilvanar, pegar, unir. *3 intr.-tr.* MAR. virar. *4 intr.* cambiar de política, de línea de conducta.
tackle (tæ·køl) *s.* equipo, aparejos, avíos. *2* MAR. jarcia; motonería. *3* aparejo [sistema de poleas]. *4* agarro, forcejeo.
tackle (to) *tr.* agarrar, forcejear con. *2* luchar, habérselas con. *3* abordar, [un problema, una dificultad].
tackling (-ling) *s.* MAR. jarcia, maniobra.
tact (tæ·kt) *s.* tacto, discreción, tiento, diplomacia.
tactful (-ful) *adj.* hábil, prudente, diplomático.
tactic (al (-ik(al) *adj.* táctico.
tactician (tækti·shan) *s.* táctico.
tactics (tæ·ktiks) *s. pl.* táctica.
tactile (-il) *adj.* táctil. *2* tangible, palpable.
tactless (-lis) *adj.* falto de tacto, impolítico.
tactual (tæ·kchual) *adj.* táctil.
tadpole (tæ·dpoul) *s.* ZOOL. renacuajo.
tael (teil) *s.* tael.
tænia (ti·nia) *s.* ARQ., ZOOL. tenia. *2* ANAT. tira, faja.
taffeta (tæ·fita), **taffety** (tæ·fiti) *s.* TEJ. tafetán.
taffrail (tæ·freil) *s.* MAR. coronamiento.
taffy (tæ·fi) *s.* especie de caramelo. *2* fam. (E.U.) coba.
tag (tæg) *s.* herrete. *2* marbete, etiqueta. *3* tirador [de zapato]. *4* punta [del rabo]. *5* cabo, resto. *6* trozo, cinta, etc., que cuelga; pingajo, colgajo. *7* mechón, vedija. *8* aditamento. *9* estribillo. *10* especie de marro [juego]. *11* TEAT. pie.
tag (to) *tr.* poner herretes a. *2* poner etiqueta a. *3* atar, unir. *4* seguir de cerca, perseguir. *5 intr. to* ~ *after*, andar detrás de [uno]. ¶ Pret. y p. p.: *tagged; ger.*: *tagging.*
Tagal (taga·l), **Tagalog** (-lag) *s.* tagalo.
tagrag (tæ·græg) *s.* RAGTAG.
Tagus (tei·gøs) *n. pr.* GEOGR. Tajo.
Tahitian (tajï·tian) *adj.-s.* tahitiano.
tail (teil) *s.* cola [de animal, de cometa, de vestido, etc.], rabo: ~ *end*, cola, parte de atrás; conclusión, final: ~ *light*, farol trasero, farol de cola. *2* cabo, apéndice. *3* cola, fila [de pers.]. *4* séquito. *5* SASTR. faldón: ~ *coat*, frac. *6* pie [de página]. *7*

LIT. estrambote. *8* DER. limitación de propiedad. *9 pl.* cruz [de moneda].

tail (to) *tr.* proveer de cola. *2* añadir, unir, empalmar, empotrar. *3* quitar los rabos a. *4* seguir, ir detrás de. *5 intr.* formar hilera; moverse en fila. *6 to ~ off* o *away,* dispersarse, desvanecerse.

tailing (-ing) *s.* cola [última parte]. *2* ARQ. cola, entrega [de sillar]. *3 pl.* residuos, restos.

tailor (-ø^r) *s.* sastre.

tailor (to) *tr.* proveer de trajes, vestir. *2 intr.* ser sastre.

tailoress (-is) *s.* sastra, sastresa.

tailoring (-ing) *s.* sastrería [arte, oficio].

tailpiece (tei·lpɪs) *s.* cola, apéndice. *2* MÚS. cordal. *3* IMPR. florón, culo de lámpara.

tain (tein) *s.* hojalata delgada; hoja de estaño.

taint (teint) *s.* punta [de alguna mala cualidad]. *2* mancha, infección, corrupción.

taint (to) *tr.* manchar, inficionar, corromper, viciar. *2* inficionarse, corromperse.

taintless (-lis) *adj.* puro, sin mancha.

take (teik) *s.* toma, tomadura. *2* redada. *3* recaudación [dinero]. *4* atractivo.

take (to) *tr.* tomar. *2* coger. *3* asir, agarrar, apoderarse, posesionarse de. *5* apresar, capturar, prender; cazar, atrapar. *6* asumir. *7* escoger. *8* acometer [a uno una enfermedad, un deseo, etc.]. *9* deleitar, cautivar. *10* inferir, entender, suponer. *11* sacar, quitar; llevarse, robar. *12* restar, substraer. *13* cobrar, percibir. *14* aceptar, recibir, admitir. *15* ocupar, pedir, requerir [espacio, tiempo, etc.]. *16* llevar, conducir. *17* hallar [placer, etc.]. *18* saltar [una valla, etc.]. *19* dar [un golpe, un paseo, un salto, etc.]. *20* hacer [ejercicio, un viaje]. *21* someterse a, sufrir, aguantar. *22* sacar [una fotografía, una copia, etc.]; fotografiar. *23* prestar o tomar [juramento]. *24* forma locuciones equivalentes a un verbo reflexivo: *to ~ cold,* resfriarse; *to ~ offence,* ofenderse. *25 to ~ away,* quitar, sacar, llevarse. *26 to ~ back,* recobrar; devolver, retractar. *27 to ~ care,* cuidar, tener cuidado. *28 to ~ charge,* encargarse, tomar el mando. *29 to ~ down,* bajar, descolgar; desarmar, demoler; tragar; abatir, humillar; escribir, anotar. *30 to ~ fire,* encenderse; encolerizarse. *31 to ~ in,* entrar, llevar adentro; dejar entrar, admitir; recibir [como huésped], acomodar; observar, fijarse en; estrechar [una prenda]; recoger [una vela]; entender; abarcar, incluir; engañar; estar suscrito [a un periódico]. *32 to ~ off,* quitarse [una prenda]; quitar, llevarse; beber; sacar [copias]; saltar; remedar, parodiar. *33 to ~ on,* emprender; tomar [a bordo, a su servicio; como socio]; tomar, adoptar, asumir, arrogarse. *34 to ~ out,* quitar, sacar; sacar fuera; llevar [a comer, a paseo]; sacar, obtener. *35 to ~ up,* alzar, levantar; subir, llevar arriba; recoger; cobrar, recaudar; COST. fruncir; tomar; asumir; emprender; reanudar; absorber; ocupar, llenar; prender, arrestar; reprender; pagar [una letra, etc.]. *36 to ~ wind,* divulgarse. *37 intr.* arraigar [una planta]. *38* prender [el fuego; la vacuna]. *39* ser eficaz. *40* tener éxito. *41* pegar, adherirse. *42 to ~ after,* salir a, parecerse a; seguir el ejemplo de. *43 to ~ off,* partir de súbito; alzar el vuelo; despegar [el avión]. *44 to ~ on,* alborotarse; darse tono. *45 to ~ with,* juntarse con; prendarse de. *46 to ~ to,* dedicarse, entregarse a; retirarse a.

¶ Pret.: *took;* p. p.: *taken.*

take-down *adj.* desmontable. *2 s.* desarmadura, desmontadura. *3* fusil desmontable. *4* fam. humillación.

take-in *s.* fam. fraude, engaño.

taken (tei·kən) *p. p.* de TO TAKE.

take-off *s.* remedo, parodia, caricatura. *2* salto; raya desde donde se salta. *3* punto de partida. *4* AVIA. despegue.

taking (-ing) *adj.* atractivo, seductor. *2* contagioso. *3 s.* toma. *4* capura. *5* afecto, inclinación. *6 pl.* recaudación, ingresos.

talaria (tølei·riə) *s. pl.* talares.

talc (tælk), **talcum** (-øm) *s.* MINER. talco, *talcum powder,* polvos de talco.

tale (teil) *s.* cuento, fábula, conseja. *2* LIT. cuento. *3* relato, informe. *4* cuento, mentira, chisme. *5* cuenta, cómputo. *6* total.

talebearer (-berø^r) *s.* chismoso, soplón.

talent (tæ·lønt) *s.* talento [moneda]. *2* talento, aptitud, don. *3* persona de talento; artista.

talented (-id) *adj.* talentoso, hábil, dotado.

taler (ta·lø^r) *s.* tálero.

taleteller (tei·ltelø^r) *s.* cuentista, narrador de cuentos. *2* chismoso, soplón, enredador.

talion (tæ·liøn) *s.* talión.

talisman (tæ·lismøn) *s.* talismán.

talk (tok) *s.* conversación, plática, charla, conferencia. *2* rumor, hablilla. *3* comidilla, tema de conversación.

talk (to) *intr.* hablar; conversar: *to ~ about,* hablar de; *to ~ back,* a; reprender; *to ~ up,* hablar claro. *2 tr.* hablar [una lengua]. *3* hablar de: *to ~ business,* hablar de negocios. *4 to ~ nonsense,* decir tonterías. *5 to ~ into,* persuadir, inducir a. *6 to ~ out of,* disuadir de. *7 to ~ over,* examinar, discutir. *8 to ~ up,* alabar.

talkative (-ativ) *adj.* hablador, comunicativo.

talked-about *adj.* de que se habla, sonado.

talkie (-i) *s.* película hablada. *2 pl.* cine hablado.

talking (-ing) *adj.* parlante. *2* hablador. *3* hablado [cine, película].

tall (tol) *adj.* alto [pers., árbol, mástil, etc.]; espigado, talludo. *2* fam. altisonante; exagerado, increíble.

tallboy (to·lboi) *s.* mueble con cajones, especie de cómoda.

tallow (tæ·lou) *s.* sebo.

tallow (to) *tr.* ensebar.

tallowy (-i) *adj.* seboso, sebáceo. *2* grasiento.

tally (tæ·li) *s.* tarja [para llevar una cuenta]. *2* cuenta [que se lleva]. *3* marbete, etiqueta. *4* copia, duplicado.

tally (to) *tr.* llevar la cuenta de. *2* marcar, señalar. *3* acomodar, ajustar. *4 intr.* cuadrar, concordar, corresponder.

tallyho (-jou) *interj.-s.* grito del cazador de zorras.

Talmud (tæ·lmød) *s.* Talmud.

talon (tæ·løn) *s.* garra. *2* monte [de la baraja]. *3* ARQ. talón [moldura].

1) talus (tei·løs), *pl.* **-li** (-lai) *s.* ANAT. astrágalo.

2) talus, *pl.* **-luses** (-løsiš) *s.* talud.

tamable (tei·møbøl) *adj.* domable, domesticable.

tamale (tama·li) *s.* tamal.

tamandua (tamandua·) *s.* ZOOL. tamanduá.

tamarack (tæ·maræk) *s.* BOT. alerce americano.

tamarind (tæ·marind) *s.* BOT. tamarindo.

tamarisk (tæ·marisk) *s.* BOT. tamarisco, taray.

tambour (tæ·mbu^r) *s.* MÚS., FORT., ARQ. tambor. *2 tambour* o ~ *frame,* tambor de bordar.

tambourine (tæmbøri·n) *s.* pandero, pandereta.

tame (teim) *adj.* manso, dócil, sumiso. *2* amansado, domesticado. *3* insulso, aburrido.
tame (to) *tr.* domar, domeñar, domesticar, amansar. *2* suavizar [los colores]. *3 intr.* amansarse.
tameless (-lis) *adj.* indomado, indomable.
taming (-ing) *s.* doma, amansamiento.
tamis (tæ·mis) *s.* tamiz, cedazo.
tam-o'-shanter (tæmøshæ·ntøʳ) *s.* boina escocesa.
tamp (to) (tæmp) *tr.* atacar [un barreno; la pipa]. *2* apisonar; llenar apretando.
tamper (-øʳ) *s.* atacador; pisón.
tamper (to) *intr. to ~ with*, meterse en, enredar con; estropear, alterar, falsificar, sobornar.
tampion (-iøn) *s.* ARTILL. tapabocas.
tampon (-an) *s.* CIR. tapón.
tampon (to) *tr.* CIR. taponar.
tamponage (-ønidÿ), **tamponment** (-mønt) *s.* CIR. taponamiento.
tan (tæn) *s.* tanino. *2* casca [para curtir]. *3* tostadura, bronceado [del cutis]. *4* color tostado. *5 adj.* tostado, de color de canela.
tan (to) *tr.* curtir, adobar [las pieles]. *2* curtir, tostar, atezar [el cutis]. *3* fam. zurrar, azotar. ¶ Pret. y p. p.: *tanned*; p. a.: *tanning*.
tanager (tæ·nødÿøʳ) *s.* ORN. tángara.
tanbark (tæ·nbaʳk) *s.* casca.
tandem (tæ·ndøm) *s.* tándem. *adj.-adv.* en tándem.
tang (tæng) *s.* dejo, sabor. *2* olor vivo. *3* sonido vibrante, tañido. *4* punzada. *5* espiga [de una herramienta].
tang (to) *intr.* sonar, retiñir. *2 tr.* hacer retiñir.
tangency (tæ·ndÿønsi) *s.* tangencia.
tangent (-ønt) *adj.-s.* tangente.
Tangerine (tæ·ndÿørin) *adj.-s.* tangerino. *2 s.* (con min.) mandarina [naranja].
tangible (tæ·ndÿibøl) *adj.* tangible, palpable.
Tangier (tænÿi·øʳ) *n. pr.* GEOGR. Tánger.
tangle (tæ·ngøl) *s.* enredo, maraña, confusión.
tangle (to) *tr.* enredar, enmarañar. *2* confundir. *3 intr.* enredarse, enmarañarse. *4* confundirse.
tangly (tæ·ngli) *adj.* enredado, enmarañado.
tango (tæ·ngou) *s.* tango [baile].
tango (to) *intr.* bailar el tango.
tangram (tæ·ngram) *s.* rompecabezas chino.
tank (tæŋk) *s.* tanque, aljibe, cisterna, alberca: ~ *ship*, buque cisterna. *2* MIL. tanque.
tankard (-aʳd) *s.* jarro con tapa para beber.
tanker (-øʳ) *s.* MAR. buque cisterna. *2* camión cuba.
tannage (tæ·nidÿ) *s.* curtido, curtimiento.
tannate (tæ·neit) *s.* QUÍM. tanato.
tanned (tæ·nd) *pret.* y *p. p.* de TO TAN.
tanner (tæ·nøʳ) *s.* curtidor. *2* pop. moneda de seis peniques.
tannery (-øri) *s.* tenería, curtiduría.
tannic (-ic) *adj.* QUÍM. tánico.
tannin (-in) *s.* QUÍM. tanino.
tansy (tæ·nsi) *s.* BOT. tanaceto.
tantalize (to) (tæ·ntalaiš) *tr.* atormentar, exasperar, mostrando lo inasequible.
tantalum (-løm) *s.* QUÍM. tantalio.
Tantalus (-løs) *n. pr.* Tántalo.
tantamount (tæ·ntamaunt) *adj.* equivalente.
tantrum (tæ·ntrøm) *s.* ataque de mal humor, berrinche, rabieta. *2* antojo, capricho.
Taoism (ta·uišm) *s.* taoísmo.
tap (tæp) *s.* grifo, espita, canilla: *on ~*, del barril. *2* tapón, bitoque. *3* calidad, clase [del vino, cerveza, etc.]. *4* mostrador [de taberna]. *5* ELECT. toma, derivación. *6* ZAP. media suela. *7* MEC. macho de aterrajar. *8* golpecito, palmada: ~ *dance*, zapateado. *9 pl.* MIL. silencio [toque].

tap (to) *tr.* poner espita o canilla a; abrir [un barril]; sacar líquido de. *2* CIR. puncionar. *3* sangrar [un árbol]. *4* ELECT. derivar [una corriente]. *5* hacer una acometida en [una conducción]. *6* intervenir [un teléfono].·*7* MEC. aterrajar. *8* horadar; hacer [un agujero]. *9 tr.-intr.* dar golpecitos o palmadas [a o en]: *to ~ at a door*, llamar a una puerta. ¶ Pret. y p. p.: *tapped*; ger.: *-pping*.
tape (teip) *s.* cinta, galón: ~ *line*, ~ *measure*, cinta de medir, cinta métrica; ~ *recorder*, aparato magnetofónico de cinta.
tape (to) *tr.* atar o envolver con cinta. *2* medir con cinta. *3* grabar en cinta magnetofónica.
taper (tei·pøʳ) *s.* candela, velilla, cerilla; cirio. *2* afilamiento, disminución gradual. *3 adj.* afilado, cónico, piramidal.
taper (to) *intr.* afilarse, adelgazarse, ahusarse. *2* ir disminuyendo o cesando. *3 tr.* afilar, adelgazar, ahusar.
tapestry (tæ·pistri) *pl. s.* tapiz, colgadura, tapicería. *2* tela para tapizar. *3* papel que imita la tapicería.
tapeworm (tei·pwøʳm) *s.* ZOOL. tenia, solitaria.
tapioca (tæpiou·ka) *s.* tapioca.
tapir (tei·pøʳ) *s.* ZOOL. tapir, danta.
tapis (tæ·pis) *s. on the ~*, sobre el tapete.
tappet (tæ·pit) *s.* MEC. leva; alzaválvulas.
taproom (tæ·prum) *s.* taberna, bar.
tapster (-støʳ) *s.* mozo de taberna.
tar (taʳ) *s.* alquitrán, brea, pez líquida: ~ *paper*, papel o cartón alquitranado.
tar (to) *tr.* alquitranar, embrear; untar o marcar con pez. ¶ Pret. y p. p.: *tarred*; ger.: *-rring*.
tarantella (tæran·tela) *s.* tarantela.
tarantula (tæræ·nchula) *s.* ZOOL. tarántula.
tardigrade (ta·ʳdigreid) *adj.-s.* ZOOL. tradigrado.
tardy (ta·ʳdi) *adj.* lento, tardo. *2* retrasado, moroso. *3* tardío.
tare (teʳ) *s.* COM. tara. *2* BOT. arveja, algarroba. *3* BIB. cizaña.
tare (to) *tr.* COM. destarar.
tarente (tare·ntei) *s.* ZOOL. salamanquesa.
targe (taʳdÿ) *s.* tarja, escudo.
target (ta·ʳgit) *s.* blanco [al que se tira]; objetivo. *2* blanco, objeto [de críticas, burlas, etc.]. *3* escudo, rodela.
tariff (tæ·rif) *s.* tarifa. *2* arancel [de aduanas]: ~ *protection*, protección arancelaria.
tariff (to) *tr.* tarifar.
tarn (taʳn) *s.* lago pequeño entre montañas.
tarnish (ta·ʳnish) *s.* deslustre, empañadura.
tarnish (to) *tr.* empañar, deslucir; manchar, deshonrar. *2 intr.* empañarse, deslucirse.
tarpaulin (taʳpo·lin) *s.* tela embreada, encerado. *2* sombrero embreado. *3* fam. marinero.
tarpot (ta·ʳpat) *s.* caldero de alquitrán.
tarragon (tæ·ragan) *s.* BOT. estragón.
tarred (taʳd) *adj.* alquitranado, embreado.
tarry (ta·ri) *adj.* alquitranado, embreado. *2* píceo, negro, sucio.
tarry (to) (tæ·ri) *intr.* tardar, demorarse, entretenerse. *2* quedarse, esperar.
tarsal (ta·ʳsal) *adj.* ANAT., ZOOL. tarsal.
tarsus (ta·ʳsøs) *s.* ANAT., ZOOL. tarso.
tart (ta·rt) *adj.* acre, ácido, picante. *2* áspero, agrio; cáustico, mordaz. *3 s.* tarta.
tartan (ta·ʳtan) *s.* tartán. *2* MAR. tartana.
tartar (ta·ʳtaʳ) *s.* tártaro [del mosto]. *2* tártaro, sarro [de los dientes].
Tartar *adj.-s.* tártaro [de Tartaria]. *2* (con min.) persona violenta, intratable.

tartare sauce (ta·ᵗtaʳ) *s.* COC. salsa tártara.
tartaric (taʳtæ·rik) *adj.* tartárico.
Tartarous (ta·ᵗtarøs) *s.* MIT. Tártaro, el infierno.
Tartary (ta·ᵗtari) *n. pr.* GEOGR. Tartaria.
tartlet (ta·ᵗtlit) *s.* tarta o pastel pequeño.
tartrate (ta·ᵗtreit) *s.* QUÍM. tartrato.
task (tæsk) *s.* tarea, labor, trabajo. *2 to take to* ~, reprender, censurar.
task (to) *tr.* atarear, señalar tarea. *2* abrumar [de trabajo]. *3* poner a prueba. *4* acusar, tachar [de].
tassel (tæ·søl) *s.* borla, campanilla [adorno].
tassel (to) *tr.* adornar con borlas. ¶ Pret. y p. p.: *tassel(l)ed;* ger.: *tassel(l)ing.*
tastable (tei·stabøl) *adj.* gustable. *2* sabroso.
taste (teist) *s.* gusto [sentido]: ~ *bud,* ANAT. papila gustativa. *2* gusto, sabor. *3* gusto, afición: *to have a* ~ *for,* gustar de. *4* gusto [discernimiento de lo bello, armónico, etc.]: *in good* ~, de buen gusto; *in bad* ~, de mal gusto; *man of* ~, hombre de gusto. *5* bocadito, sorbo, un poco. *6* muestra, prueba.
taste (to) *tr.* gustar, saborear. *2* probar, catar. *3* gustar, experimentar. *4 intr.* tener cierto sabor o gusto: *to* ~ *of,* saber a.
tasteful (-ful) *adj.* de buen gusto, elegante.
tasteless (-lis) *adj.* insípido, soso, insulso. *2* de mal gusto, falto de gusto.
taster (-tøʳ) *s.* probador, catador. *2* pipeta; catavino.
tasty (-ti) *adj.* de buen gusto. *2* fam. sabroso.
tat (to) (tæt) *intr.* hacer encaje de frivolité.
tatou (tatu·) *s.* ZOOL. tato, tatú [armadillo].
tatter (tæ·tøʳ) *s.* harapo, andrajo, jirón, arambel.
tatterdemalion (tætøʳdimei·liøn) *s.* zarrapastrón.
tattered (tæ·tøʳd) *adj.* roto, desgarrado. *2* andrajoso.
tatting (tæ·ting) *s.* encaje de frivolité.
tattle (tæ·tøl) *s.* charla, parloteo. *2* chismorreo.
tattle (to) *intr.* charlar. *2* chismorrear. *3* soplonear. *4 tr.* descubrir, revelar [charlando].
tattler (tæ·tløʳ) *s.* hablador. *2* chismoso. *3* soplón.
tattoo (tætu·) *s.* retreta [toque; fiesta]. *2* tabaleo, tamborileo. *3* tatuaje [dibujo].
tattoo (to) *tr.* tatuar. *2 intr.* tocar retreta. *3* tabalear, tamborilear.
tattooage (-id y̌) *s.* tatuaje.
tau (tau) *s.* tau [letra griega]. *2* tao.
taught (tot) *pret.* y *p. p.* de TO TEACH.
taunt (tont) *s.* reproche insultante, sarcasmo, insulto, provocación.
taunt (to) *tr.* reprochar con insulto, insultar, provocar.
taurine (to·rin) *adj.* taurino [de toro].
tauromachy (tora·maki) *s.* tauromaquia.
Taurus (to·røs) *n. pr.* ASTR. Tauro.
taut (tot) *adj.* tirante, tenso, tieso. *2* aseado, bien arreglado.
tauten (to) (to·tøn) *tr.* atirantar, tesar. *2 intr.* ponerse tirante, tenso.
tautology (tota·lød y̌i) *s.* RET. tautología.
tavern (tæ·vøʳn) *s.* taberna. *2* hotel, mesón.
taw (to) *s.* canica, bola.
taw (to) *tr.* curtir [pieles] en blanco.
tawdry (to·dri) *adj.* charro, chillón, llamativo.
tawny (to·ni) *adj.* moreno, tostado, atezado. *2* leonado. *3* ORN. ~ *owl,* autillo.
tax (taks) *s.* impuesto, tributo, contribución. *2* carga, esfuerzo gravoso.
tax (to) *tr.* imponer tributo a, gravar. *2* fatigar; abusar de: *to* ~ *one's patience,* abusar de la pa-

ciencia de uno. *3* censurar, tachar, acusar. *4* DER. tasar.
taxable (-abøl) *adj.* imponible; sujeto a tributación.
taxation (-ei·shøn) *s.* imposición de tributos. *2* tributo, impuesto; tributación.
taxer (tæ·ksøʳ) *s.* exactor. *2* acusador.
taxi (-i) *s.* taxi, taxímetro [coche].
taxi (to) *tr.-intr.* llevar o ir en taxi. *2* hacer correr [un avión] o correr [el avión] por tierra.
taxicab (-kæb) *s.* TAXI.
taxidermy (tæksidø·ʳmi) *s.* taxidermia.
taximeter (tæksi·mitøʳ) *s.* taxímetro.
taxonomy (tæksa·nømi) *s.* taxonomía.
taxpayer (ta·kspeiøʳ) *s.* contribuyente.
tea (tɪ) *s.* té: ~ *party,* té [reunión]; ~ *rose,* rosa de té. *2* refacción de la tarde o prima noche. *3* tisana.
teacart (tɪ·kaʳt) *s.* carrito para el té.
teach (to) (tɪ·ch) *tr.-intr.* enseñar, instruir. *2* enseñar, profesar [una materia, etc.]. ¶ Pret. y p. p.: *taught.*
teachable (-abøl) *adj.* enseñable; dócil.
teacher (-øʳ) *s.* maestro, -tra, profesor, -ra.
teaching (-ing) *s.* enseñanza, instrucción. *2 adj.* docente.
teacup (tɪ·køp) *s.* taza para té.
teahouse (-jaus) *s.* salón de té.
teak (tɪ·k) *s.* BOT. teca [árbol].
teakettle (tɪ·ketøl) *s.* tetera.
teal (tɪl) *s.* ORN. trullo.
team (tɪm) *s.* tiro [de animales]; atelaje, tronco, junta. *2* grupo, equipo, cuadrilla. *3* DEP. equipo.
team (to) *tr.* enganchar, uncir. *2 intr.* guiar un tiro, una yunta, etc. *3 to* ~ *up,* formar equipo.
teammate (-meit) *s.* compañero de equipo.
teamwork (-uøʳk) *s.* trabajo de equipo.
teapot (tɪ·pat) *s.* tetera.
1) tear (tɪʳ) *s.* lágrima: ~ *gas,* gas lacrimógeno; ~ *sac,* ANAT. saco lacrimal. *2 pl.* llanto, aflicción.
2) tear (teʳ) *s.* rotura, desgarro. *2* desgarrón. *3* precipitación, furia.
tear (to) *tr.* romper, rasgar, desgarrar: *to* ~ *open,* abrir rompiendo o desgarrando. *2* mesar. *3* arrancar, separar con violencia: *to* ~ *oneself away,* arrancarse de un lugar. *4 to* ~ *down,* desarmar; demoler. *5 to* ~ *up,* arrancar; romper en pedazos. *6 intr.* rasgarse. *7* moverse u obrar con furia, precipitadamente. ¶ Pret.: *tore;* p. p.: *torn.*
teardrop (tɪ·ʳdrap) *s.* lágrima.
tearful (tɪ·ʳful) *adj.* lloroso.
tease (tɪ·š) *s.* importunidad, broma, vaya. *2* embromador.
tease (to) *tr.* fastidiar, importunar, embromar, dar vaya. *2* cardar [el paño].
teasel (tɪ·søl) *s.* BOT. cardencha. *2* carda.
teasel (to) *tr.* cardar [el paño].
teaser (ti·šøʳ) *s.* cardador [de paño]. *2* embromador.
teaspoon (tɪ·spun) *s.* cucharilla, cucharita.
teaspoonful (tɪ·spunful) *s.* cucharadita.
teat (tɪt) *s.* pezón [de teta]; teta.
teazel *s.*, **teazel (to)** *tr.* TEASEL, TO TEASEL.
technic (te·knik) *adj.* técnico. *2 s.* tecnicismo.
technical (te·knikal) *adj.* técnico: ~ *term,* tecnicismo.
technicality (teknikæ·liti) *s.* carácter técnico. *2* tecnicismo. *3* detalle técnico.
technician (te·knishøn) *s.* técnico.

technics (te·kniks) *s.* doctrina de las artes.
technique (tekni·k) *s.* técnica.
technocracy (tekna·krasi) *s.* tecnocracia.
technology (tekna·lodỹ) *s.* tecnología.
techy (te·chi) *adj.* TETCHY.
tectonics (tekta·niks) *s.* tectónica.
Ted (ted), **Teddy** (-i) *n. pr. abrev.* de Theodore y Edward.
Teddy-bear *s.* osito de trapo.
Teddy-boy *s.* gamberro.
Te Deum (tı·-di·øm) *s.* tedéum.
tedious (tı·diøs) *adj.* tedioso, fastidioso, latoso.
tedium (-diøm) *s.* tedio, aburrimiento.
tee (tı) *s.* pieza en forma de T. *2* DEP. meta, hito. *3* GOLF. punto de saque.
tee (to) *tr.* GOLF poner [la pelota] sobre un TEE.
teem (to) (tım) *tr.* producir, engendrar. *2 intr. to ~ with*, abundar en, hervir de.
teen age (tın) *s.* edad de los 13 a los 19 años.
teen-ager (-eidỹø^r) *s.* joven de 13 a 19 años de edad.
teens (tı·nš) *s. pl.* números que terminan en TEEN. *2* edad de los 13 a los 19 años.
teeny (tı·ni) *adj. fam.* pequeñito, diminuto.
teepee (tı·pi) *s.* TEPEE.
teeter (tı·tø^r) *s.* balance, vaivén.
teeter (to) *intr.* balancearse, columpiarse. *2* vacilar, andar vacilando.
teeth (tı·z) *s. pl.* de TOOTH: *to cast*, o *throw, in one's ~*, echar en cara; *in the ~ of*, contra, desafiando.
teethe (to) (tı·ð) *intr.* endentecer, echar los dientes.
teething (-ing) *s.* dentición.
teetotal(l)er (tıtou·talø^r) *s.* abstemio.
teetotum (-tøm) *s.* perinola.
tegmen (te·gmin) *s.* BOT., ZOOL. tegmen.
tegument (te·giumønt) *s.* tegumento.
telamon (te·lamøn) *s.* ARQ. atlante.
telecast (-likæst) *s.* transmisión por televisión.
telecast (to) *tr.* televisar.
telecommunication (telikømiunikei·shøn) *s.* telecomunicación.
telegram (te·ligræm) *s.* telegrama.
telegraph (-græf) *s.* telégrafo. *2* telegrama.
telegrapher (tile·grafø^r) *s.* telegrafista.
telegraphy (-fi) *s.* telegrafía.
Telemachus (tile·makøs) *n. pr.* MIT. Telémaco.
telemeter (tile·mitø^r) *s.* telémetro.
teleology (ıilia·lodỹ) *s.* teleología.
teleost (te·liast) *adj.* ICT. teleósteo.
telepathy (tile·pazi) *s.* telepatía.
telephone (te·lifoun) *s.* teléfono; *~ call*, llamada telefónica; *~ directory*, guía telefónica; *~ exchange*, central telefónica.
telephone (to) *tr.-intr.* telefonear.
telephonist (-nist) *s.* telefonista.
telephony (tile·føni) *s.* telefonía.
telephotography (telifouta·grafi) *s.* telefotografía.
telescope (te·liscoup) *s.* telescopio.
telescope (to) *tr.-intr.* enchufar(se, empotrar(se [una cosa en otra]. *2 tr.* acortar.
teletype (-taip) *s.* teletipo.
teletype (to) *tr.* transmitir por teletipo.
teleview (to) (-viu) *tr.-intr.* ver por televisión.
televiewer (-viuø^r) *s.* telespectador.
televise (to) (-vaiš) *tr.* televisar.
television (-viỹøn) *s.* televisión.
tell (to) (te·l) *tr.* contar, numerar. *2* contar, relatar, narrar: *~ that to the marines*, cuénteselo a su tía. *3* decir: *to ~ volumes*,decir mucho, ser significativo. *4* mandar, ordenar. *5* distinguir, conocer. *6* determinar. *7* MIL. *to ~ off*, destacar [para

un servicio]. *8 intr. to ~ on*, notarse, dejarse ver; hacerse sentir en; delatar. ¶ *Pret.* y p. p.: *told*.
teller (-ø^r) *s.* narrador, relator. *2* escrutador de votos. *3 receiving ~, paying ~*, cobrador, pagador [de la caja de un banco].
telling (-ling) *adj.* eficaz, notable. *2 s.* acción de decir o contar: *there is no ~*, no es posible decir o prever.
telltale (-teil) *adj.-s.* chismoso, soplón. *2 s.* indicador, contador. *3 adj.* indicador, revelador.
tellurian (teliu·rian) *adj.* telúrico [de la Tierra].
tellurium (-riøm) *s.* QUÍM. telurio.
telophase (te·løfeiš) *s.* BIOL. telofase.
temerarious (temørei·riøs) *adj.* temerário.
temerity (time·riti) *s.* temeridad.
temper (te·mpø^r) *s.* temple [del metal]. *2* punto [de una mezcla]. *3* genio; humor, temple. *4* cólera, mal genio. *5 to keep one's ~*, contenerse, dominarse; *to lose one's ~*, perder la calma, encolerizarse.
temper (to) *tr.* templar, moderar, mitigar, atemperar. *2* mezclar, amasar. *3* templar [el metal].
tempera (te·mpøra) *s.* PINT. temple.
temperament (-mønt) *s.* temperamento [de una pers.]. *2* MÚS. temperamento.
temperamental (-al) *adj.* temperamental. *2* muy sensible o excitable.
temperance (te·mpørans) *s.* templanza, sobriedad.
temperate (-it) *adj.* templado [sobrio, moderado; tibio]. *2* templado [clima].
temperature (-achu^r) *s.* temperatura.
tempered (te·mpø^{r}d) *adj.* templado, moderado, suavizado. *2* de genio o disposición: *bad-tempered*, de mal genio. *3* templado [metal, cristal].
tempest (te·mpist) *s.* tempestad.
tempest (to) *tr.* agitar. *2 intr.* moverse con agitación, tempestear.
tempestuous (tempe·schuøs) *adj.* tempestuoso.
Templar (te·mpla^r) *s.* templario.
template (te·mplit) *s.* TEMPLET 2.
temple (te·mpøl) *s.* templo. *2* ANAT. sien. *3* brazo [de anteojos]. *4* TEJ. templazo.
templet (te·mplit) *s.* templete. *2* plantilla, gálibo.
tempo (te·mpou) *s.* MÚS. tiempo. *2* ritmo.
temporal (te·mpøral) *adj.* temporal. *2* ANAT. hueso temporal.
temporality (-iti) *s.* temporalidad.
temporalty (-ti) *s.* propiedad secular. *2* los seglares.
temporary (te·mpøreri) *adj.* temporal, temporario, transitorio, provisional, interino.
temporize (to) (-aiš) *intr.* adaptarse a la ocasión, contemporizar; ganar tiempo; no comprometerse.
tempt (to) (tempt) *tr.* tentar, instigar, atraer.
temptation (-ei·shøn) *s.* tentación. *2* incentivo.
tempter (te·mptø^r) *s.* tentador.
tempting (-ing) *adj.* tentador, atractivo.
temptress (-tris) *s.* tentadora.
ten (ten) *adj.-s.* diez: *~ o'clock*, las diez. *2 s.* decena.
tenable (te·nabøl) *adj.* defendible, sostenible.
tenace (te·neis) *s.* tenaza [en los naipes].
tenacious (tinei·shøs) *adj.* tenaz.
tenacity (tinæ·siti) *s.* tenacidad. *2* tesón.
tenaille (te·neil) *s.* FORT. tenaza.
tenancy (te·nansi) *s.* tenencia, arriendo, inquilinato.
tenant (-t) *s.* inquilino, arrendatario. *2* residente, morador.

tenant (to) *tr.* arrendar, alquilar. *2* tener en arriendo o alquiler.

tenantry (-tri) *s.* arriendo, inquilinato. *2* arrendatarios, inquilinos.

tench (tench) *s.* ICT. tenca.

tend (to) (tend) *tr.* cuidar, atender, guardar, vigilar. *2 intr.* tender [a un fin]; contribuir. *3* propender. *4* ir, dirigirse [a].

tendance (-ans) *s.* cuidado, atención, guarda.

tendency (te·ndønsi), *pl.* **-cies** (-siš) *s.* tendencia. *2* propensión.

tendentious (-shøs) *adj.* tendencioso.

tender (te·ndø^r) *adj.* tierno. *2* delicado [escrupuloso; espinoso]. *3* dolorido. *4* susceptible, sentido. *5 s.* cuidador, guardador. *6* FERROC. ténder. *7* oferta. *8 legal* ~, moneda corriente, de curso legal.

tenderfoot (-fut), **-foots** o **-feet** *s.* novato, poco habituado a los rigores de un clima, una vida.

tenderloin (-loin) *s.* COC. filete. *2* (E.U.) barrio de la vida nocturna.

tenderness (-nis) *s.* terneza, ternura, suavidad. *2* debilidad, fragilidad. *3* sensibilidad.

tendinous (te·ndinøs) *adj.* tendinoso. *2* nervudo.

tendon (te·ndøn) *s.* tendón.

tendril (te·ndril) *s.* BOT. zarcillo, tijereta. *2* rizo [de pelo].

tenebrous (te·nibrøs) *adj.* poét. tenebroso.

tenement (te·nimønt) *s.* habitación, vivienda, piso: ~ *house*, casa de vecindad.

tenet (te·nit) *s.* principio, dogma, credo.

tenfold (te·nfould) *adj.* décuplo. *2 adv.* diez veces.

tennis (te·nis) *s.* tenis: ~ *court*, pista de tenis.

tenon (te·nøn) *s.* CARP. espiga, almilla.

tenor (te·nø^r) *s.* tenor, contenido, significado, carácter, naturaleza. *2* curso, tendencia. *3* MÚS. tenor.

tenpins (te·npins) *s.* (E.U.) juego de bolos.

tense (tens) *adj.* tenso; tirante, tieso. *2* dramático, emocionante. *3 s.* GRAM. tiempo [de verbo].

tensible (-ibøl) *adj.* capaz de tensión.

tensile (-il) *adj.* TENSIBLE. *2* relativo a la tensión.

tension (te·nshøn) *s.* tensión. *2* atirantamiento. *3* tirantez. *4* esfuerzo mental; intensidad de sentimiento; ansiedad.

tensive (-iv) *adj.* tensor.

tensor (-ø^r) *s.* tensor. *2* ANAT. músculo tensor.

tent (tent) *s.* tienda [para alojamiento], tienda de campaña. *2* CIR. lechino, tapón.

tent (to) *intr.* acampar en tiendas. *2 tr.* alojar en tiendas. *3* CIR. poner un lechino a.

tentacle (-økøl) *s.* ZOOL. tentáculo, tiento.

tentacular (tentæ·kiula^r) *adj.* tentacular.

tentative (te·ntativ) *adj.* tentativo. *2 s.* tentativa, ensayo, tanteo.

tenter (te·ntø^r) *s.* rambla, máquina para estirar el paño. *2* TENTERHOOK.

tenter (to) *tr.* estirar, enramblar [el paño].

tenterhook (-juk) *s.* cada uno de los clavos con que se mantiene estirado el paño: *on tenterhooks*, fig. muy inquieto, en ascuas.

tenth (tenz) *adj.-s.* décimo, deceno. *2 s.* diez [día]. *3* MÚS. décima.

tenuirostral (tenuira·stral) *adj.* ORN. tenuirrostro.

tenuity (teniu·iti) *s.* tenuidad. *2* raridad [de un fluido]. *3* debilidad [de un sonido].

tenuous (te·niuøs) *adj.* tenue. *2* raro [poco denso].

tenure (te·niu^r) *s.* tenencia, posesión. *2* ejercicio [de un cargo]; *right of* ~, inamovilidad.

teocalli (tiokæ·li) *s.* toecalí.

tepee (ti·pi) *s.* tienda de los indios norteamericanos.

tepid (te·pid) *adj.* tibio.

tepidity (tipi·diti) *s.* tibieza.

teratology (terata·lodÿi) *s.* teratología.

terbium (tø·^rbiøm) *s.* QUÍM. terbio.

terce (tø^rs) *s.* TIERCE.

tercel (te·^rsøl) *s.* ORN. terzuelo.

tercet (te·^rsit) *s.* LIT. terceto. *2* MÚS. tresillo.

terebinth (te·ribinz) *s.* BOT. terebinto.

teredo (te·ridou) *s.* ZOOL. broma [molusco].

Terence (te·røns) *n. pr.* Terencio.

tergal (tø·^rgal) *adj.* ZOOL. dorsal. *2 s.* tergal.

tergiversate (to) (te·^rdÿivø^rseit) *intr.* usar de evasivas. *2* renegar, apostatar, abandonar una causa.

term (tø^rm) *s.* término, plazo, período, duración. *2* período de sesiones o de clases; período por el cual se hace un arrendamiento. *3* tiempo fijado para el pago de rentas, intereses, etc. *4* término, palabra. *5* LÓG., MAT., ARQ. término. *6 pl.* condiciones, estipulaciones. *7* COM. facilidades de pago. *8* términos o relación mutua: *to be in good terms*, estar en buenas relaciones. *9* acuerdo, arreglo: *to come to terms*, decidirse a un arreglo, ceder.

term (to) *tr.* nombrar, llamar.

termagant (tø·^rmagant) *adj.* turbulento, pendenciero. *2 s.* fiera, furia, arpía.

terminable (tø·^rminabøl) *adj.* limitable.

terminal (-al) *adj.* terminal. *2 s.* término, final. *3* ARQ. coronamiento. *4* ELECT. borne, terminal. *5* estación terminal.

terminate (to) (-eit) *tr.* limitar. *2 tr.-intr.* terminar, acabar.

termination (-ei·shøn) *s.* terminación, fin. *2* GRAM. terminación, desinencia.

terminative (tø·^rminetiv) *adj.* terminativo. *2* terminante, definitivo.

terminology (tø·^rmina·lodÿ) *s.* terminología.

terminus (tø·^rminøs) *s.* término, final. *2* estación terminal. *3 n. pr.* MIT. Término.

termite (tø·^rmait) *s.* ENT. termite.

tern (tø^rn) *s.* ORN. golondrina de mar. *2* terno [en la lotería].

ternary (tø·^rnari) *adj.* ternario. *2* triple. *3 s.* terno [grupo de tres].

terpene (-pin) *s.* QUÍM. terpeno.

Terpsichore (tø^rsi·køri) *n. pr.* MIT. Terpsícore.

terra (te·ra) *s.* tierra [en ciertas denominaciones]: ~ *cotta*, terracota; ~ *firma*, tierra firme.

terrace (te·ris) *s.* terraza. *2* terrado, azotea. *3* hilera de casas sobre un terreno elevado.

terrace (to) *tr.* disponer en terrazas; terraplenar.

terrain (te·rein) *s.* terreno, campo [de batalla, de actividad, etc.]. *2 adj.* terreno, terrestre.

terramycin (teramai·sin) *s.* FARM. terramicina.

terrapin (te·rapin) *s.* ZOOL. tortuga acuática comestible de América.

terraqueous (terei·kuiøs) *adj.* terráqueo.

terrene (teri·n) *adj.* terreno, mundano.

terreplein (te·^rplein) *s.* FORT. terraplén.

terrestrial (tere·strial) *adj.* terrestre, terreno.

terrible (te·ribøl) *adj.* terrible, tremendo.

terribly (te·ribli) *adv.* terriblemente.

terrier (te·riø^r) *s.* terrier [perro].

terrific (teri·fik) *adj.* terrífico, terrorífico. *2* fig. tremendo, grande.

terrify (to) (te·rifai) *tr.* aterrar, aterrorizar. ¶ Pret. y p. p.: *terrified*.

territorial (terito·rial) *adj.* territorial.

territory (te·ritori) *s.* territorio. *2* región, distrito. *3* campo, dominio, esfera.
terror (te·rør) *s.* terror.
terrorism (-ĭšm) *s.* terrorismo.
terrorist (-ist) *s.* terrorista. *2* alarmista.
terrorize (to) (-aiš) *tr.* aterrorizar.
terse (tø·s) *adj.* terso, conciso, limpio [estilo, lenguaje].
tertian (tø·shan) *adj.-s.* MED. terciana.
tertiary (tø·shie·ri) *adj.-s.* terciario.
tessellate (to) (te·søleit) *tr.* cubrir con mosaico; taracear.
tessera (te·søra), *pl.* **-ae** (-i) *s.* tesela. *2* tesera.
tessitura (tesitu·ra) *s.* MÚS. tesitura.
test (test) *s.* copela. *2* prueba, ensayo, examen: ~ *paper*, QUÍM. papel reactivo; ~ *pilot*, AVIA. piloto de pruebas; ~ *tube*, tubo de ensayo; probeta; *to put to the* ~, poner a prueba. *2* medio de prueba, piedra de toque. *3* PSIC., EDUC. test. *4* ZOOL. concha. *5* BOT. tegumento [de semilla].
test (to) *tr.* examinar, probar, ensayar, comprobar, hacer la prueba de, poner a prueba.
testa (te·sta), *pl.* **-tae** (-ti) *s.* TEST 4 y 5.
testacean (testei·shan) *adj.-s.* ZOOL. testáceo.
testacy (te·stasi) *s.* DER. circunstancia de haber testado.
testament (te·stamønt) *s.* testamento. *2 Old, New, Testament*, Antiguo, Nuevo, Testamento.
testate (te·steit) *adj.* testado.
testator (testei·tø) *s.* DER. testador.
testatrix (-triks) *s.* DER. testadora.
tested (te·stid) *adj.* probado, ensayado.
tester (te·stø) *s.* probador, ensayador. *2* QUÍM. reactivo. *3* pabellón de cama. *4* baldaquín, dosel.
testicle (te·stikøl) *s.* testículo.
testify (to) (te·stifai) *tr.* testificar, atestiguar, testimoniar. *2 intr.* dar testimonio: *to* ~ *to*, dar testimonio de. ¶ Pret. y p. p.: *testified*.
testimonial (testimou·nial) *adj.* testimonial. *2* que sirve como testimonio de admiración, etc. *3 s.* certificado de buena conducta, aptitud, etc. *4* testimonio de admiración, respeto, etc.; homenaje.
testimony (te·stimouni) *s.* testimonio, atestación, fe. *2* la divina revelación, las Escrituras.
testiness (te·stinis) *s.* irritabilidad, susceptibilidad, mal humor, mal genio.
testis (te·stis) *s.* ZOOL. testículo.
testudineous (testiu·diniøs) *adj.* testudíneo.
testudo (testiu·dou) *s.* testudo. *2* MED. talpa.
testy (te·sti) *adj.* irritable, susceptible, enojadizo.
tetanus (te·tanøs) *s.* MED. tétano.
tetchy (te·chi) *adj.* quisquilloso, enojadizo.
tête-à-tête (teit-a-teit) *adv.* a solas [dos personas]. *2 adj.* privado, confidencial. *3 s.* entrevista a solas. *4* confidente [mueble].
tether (te·ðø) *s.* cuerda, ramal [con que se tiene atado un animal]. *2* fig. *at the end of one's* ~, habiendo acabado las fuerzas, los recursos.
tether (to) *tr.* atar, estacar [a un animal].
tetrachord (te·trako·d) *s.* MÚS. tetracordio.
tetragon (te·tragan) *s.* GEOM. tetrágono, cuadrilátero.
tetragonal (tetræ·gønal) *adj.* tetragonal.
tetrahedron (tetraji·drøn) *s.* GEOM. tetraedro.
tetralogy (tetræ·lodý) *s.* tetralogía.
tetrameter (tetræ·mitø) *adj.-s.* tetrámetro.
tetrarch (te·tra·k) *s.* tetrarca.
tetrarchy (te·trarki) *s.* tetrarquía.
tetter (te·tø) *s.* herpe; empeine; serpigo.

Teuton (tiu·tøn) *s.* teutón.
Teutonic (tiuta·nik) *adj.-s.* teutónico.
Texan (te·ksan) *adj.-s.* tejano.
Texas (-sas) *n. pr.* GEOGR. Tejas.
text (tekst) *s.* texto. *2* tema [de un discurso, etc.].
textbook (-buk) *s.* libro de texto. *2* libreto.
textile (te·kstil) *adj.-s.* textil.
textual (-chual) *adj.* textual.
texture (-chu) *s.* textura. *2* tejido, obra tejida.
Thailand (tai·land) *n. pr.* GEOGR. Tailandia.
thalamus (zæ·lamøs) *s.* tálamo.
thaler (ta·lø) *s.* tálero.
Thalia (zalai·a) *n. pr.* MIT. Talía.
thallium (zæ·liøm) *s.* QUÍM. talio.
thallophyte (zæ·lofait) *s.* BOT. talofita.
thallus (zæ·løs) *s.* BOT. talo.
thalweg (ta·lveik) *s.* vaguada.
Thames (temš) *n. pr.* GEOGR. Támesis.
than (ðæn) *conj.* que [después de ciertos adverbios o adjetivos]: *softer* ~ *velvet*, más suave que el terciopelo; *nothing else* ~, nada más que. *2* en ciertas expresiones equivale a: de, de lo que, del que, etc.: *more* ~ *two*, más de dos; *more clever* ~ *you think*, más listo de lo que usted se figura. *3* con *whom* y *which*, forma expresiones que hay que traducir libremente: *my father* ~ *whom no one knew better this trade*, mi padre, que conocía este oficio mejor que nadie.
thane (zein) *s.* entre los antiguos anglosajones, gran señor.
thank (to) (zænk) *tr.* dar gracias, agradecer: ~ *you*, gracias; ~ *heaven!*, ¡gracias a Dios!
thankful (-ful) *adj.* agradecido.
thankfulness (-nis) *s.* agradecimiento, gratitud.
thankless (-lis) *adj.* desagradecido. *2* ingrato.
thanks (-s) *s. pl.* gracias, agradecimiento. *2* ~ *to*, gracias a; debido a.
thanksgiving (-sgi·ving) *s.* acción de gracias. *2* (E.U.) *Thanksgiving Day*, día de acción de gracias [cuarto jueves de noviembre].
that (ðæt) *adj.* ese, esa, aquel, aquella. *2 pron. dem.* ése, ésa, eso, aquél, aquélla, aquello: ~ *is*, ~ *is to say*, eso es; es decir; *upon* ~, sobre eso o aquello; luego. *3* a veces se traduce por el, la, lo: ~ *which*, el que, la que, lo que. *4 at* ~, así, como está; aun así, de todos modos. *5 pron. rel.* que: *the money* ~ *you gave me*, el dinero que me diste. *6* en que, donde, cuando. *7 conj.* que: *so* ~, para que. *8 adv.* así, tan: ~ *far*, tan lejos; ~ *much*, tanto.
thatch (zæch) *s.* techo de paja, cañas, etc.
thatch (to) *tr.* techar con paja, cañas, etc.
thaumaturge (zo·matørdý) *s.* taumaturgo.
thaumaturgic (al (-ik(al) *adj.* taumatúrgico.
thaumaturgy (-i) *s.* taumaturgia.
thaw (zo) *s.* deshielo, derretimiento.
thaw (to) *tr.* deshelar, derretir. *2 impers.* deshelar. *3 intr.* deshelarse, derretirse. *5* fig. ablandarse; perder la frialdad, la reserva.
the (ði o ðø) *art.* el, la, lo, los, las. *2 adv.* cuando, mientras, tanto [precediendo a un comparativo]: ~ *more ...*, ~ *more*, cuanto más o mientras más..., más o tanto más. | A veces no se traduce: *so much* ~ *better*, tanto mejor.
theater, theatre (zi·atø) *s.* teatro.
theatrical (ziæ·trikal) *adj.* teatral. *2 s.* representación, comedia. *3 pl.* funciones teatrales. *4* fig. teatro, modo teatral de conducirse.
Thebaid (zibai·d) *n. pr.* GEOGR. Tebaida.
Thebes (zibs) *n. pr.* GEOGR. Tebas.
theca (zi·ka) *s.* BOT. teca [mitad de la antera].

thee (ði) *pron.* te, a ti [caso oblicuo de THOU].
theft (zeft) *s.* robo, hurto, latrocinio.
their (ðeʳ) *adj.* su, sus [de ellos o ellas].
theirs (ðeʳs) *pron. pos.* (el) suyo, (la) suya, (los) suyos, (las) suyas [de ellos o de ellas].
theism (zɪ·iʃm) *s.* teísmo.
theist (zɪ·ist) *s.* teísta.
theistic (al (zɪ·istik(al) *adj.* teísta.
them (ðem) *pron.* [sin prep.] los, las, les [acusativo o dativo de THEY]. *2* [con prep.] ellos, ellas.
thematic (zimæ·tik) *adj.* temático.
theme (zɪm) *s.* tema [asunto; ejercicio]. *2* GRAM., MÚS. tema.
themselves (ðemse·lvš) *pron. pl.* se [reflexivo], si: *they wash* ~, ellos se lavan; *to* ~, a sí mismos o mismas. *2* ellos mismos, ellas mismas.
then (ðen) *adv.* entonces, en aquel tiempo: *by* ~, para entonces; ~ *and there,* en el acto, allí mismo. *2* luego, después. *3* además. *4 conj.* entonces, siendo así, luego pues, por consiguiente. *5 but* ~, pero entonces; pero, es que, pero por otra parte. *6 adj.* de entonces, de aquel tiempo.
thence (ðens) *adv.* de allí, desde allí. *2* desde entonces, de allí en adelante. *3* de ahí, por lo tanto, por eso.
thenceforth (ðensfoˑʳz), **thenceforward** (-foˑʳua⁽r⁾d) *adv.* desde entonces, de allí en adelante, en adelante.
theobromine (zɪøbrou·min) *s.* QUÍM. teobromina.
theocracy (zɪa·krasi) *s.* teocracia.
theodicy (-disi) *s.* teodicea.
theodolite (-dølait) *s.* TOP. teodolito.
Theodore (zɪ·ødoʳ) *n. pr.* Teodoro.
Theodosius (zɪødou·shøs) *n. pr.* Teodosio.
theogony (zɪa·gøni) *s.* teogonía.
theologian (zɪolou·dỹan) *s.* teólogo.
theological (zɪola·dỹikal) *adj.* teológico. *2* teologal: ~ *virtues,* virtudes teologales.
theology (zɪa·lodỹi) *s.* teología.
theorem (zɪ·orem) *s.* teorema.
theoretic (zɪore·tik) *s.* teoría, teórica. *2* teórico.
theoretic(al (zɪore·tik(al) *adj.* teórico.
theorics (zɪa·riks) *s.* teórica.
theorize (to) (zɪ·oraiš) *intr.* teorizar.
theory (zɪ·ori) *s.* teoría.
theosophist (zɪa·søfist) *s.* teósofo.
theosophy (-søfi) *s.* teosofía.
therapeutics (zerapiu·tikts) *s.* terapéutica.
therapeutist (-tist) *s.* terapeuta.
therapy (ze·rapi) *s.* terapia, terapéutica.
there (ðeʳ) *adv.* allí, allá, ahí: ~ *he is,* helo ahí; *who goes there?,* ¿quién va?, ¿quién vive? *2 there* forma con *to be* el verbo impersonal que corresponde al castellano *haber* en su uso impersonal: ~ *is,* ~ *are,* hay. *3* Ús. con otros verbos para dar fuerza a la frase: ~ *came a man,* vino un hombre. *4 interj.* ¡eh!, ¡toma!, ¡vaya!, ¡mira!
thereabout(s (-abauts) *adv.* por allí, cerca de allí. *2* cosa así, poco más o menos. *3* acerca de ello.
thereafter (-æ·ftøʳ) *adv.* después de esto, de allí en adelante. *2* por lo tanto, en consecuencia.
thereat (æ·t) *adv.* allí, ahí. *2* en esto, entonces.
thereby (-bai) *adv.* en relación con esto. *2* así, de este modo; en consecuencia de esto.
therefore (-foʳ) *adv.* por esto, por ende, por lo tanto, por consiguiente.
therefrom (-fram) *adv.* de allí, de allá, de eso, de aquello.
therein (-i·n) *adv.* en esto, en eso, en aquello.
thereinafter (-inæ·ftøʳ) *adv.* más adelante [en un escrito o discurso].

thereof (-a·v) *adv.* de eso, de aquello, de ello.
thereon (-a·n) *adv.* encima, encima de ello, sobre ello. *2* luego, en seguida.
Theresa (tøre·sa) *n. pr.* Teresa.
thereto (ðeʳtu·) *adv.* a aquello, a ello. *2* además.
theretofore (ðeʳtufo·ʳ) *adv.* hasta entonces.
thereunder (-o·ndøʳ) *adv.* debajo de eso o ello. *2* menos de o que.
thereunto (-øntu·) *adv.* THERETO.
thereupon (-øpo·n) *adv.* por lo tanto, por consiguiente. *2* inmediatamente, al instante, en esto.
therewithal (-widol) *adv.* además. *2* al mismo tiempo.
thermæ (zøʳmi) *s. pl.* termas [de los romanos].
thermal (zøˑʳmal) *adj.* termal. *2* térmico.
thermic (zø·ʳmik) *adj.* térmico.
thermionic (zøʳmia·nik) *adj.* FÍS. termiónico.
thermobarometer (zøʳmøbara·mitøʳ) *s.* termobarómetro.
thermocautery (-ko·tøri) *s.* CIR. termocauterio.
thermodynamics (-dainæ·miks) *s.* termodinámica.
thermoelectricity (-ilektri·siti) *s.* termoelectricidad.
thermology (zøʳma·lodỹi) *s.* termología.
thermometer (zøʳma·mitøʳ) *s.* termómetro.
thermometry (zøʳma·metri) *s.* termometría.
thermonuclear (zermoniu·kliaʳ) *adj.* termonuclear.
Thermopylæ (zøʳma·pili) *s. pl.* GEOGR. Termópilas.
thermos bottle o **flask** (zø·ʳmos) *s.* botella termos.
thermosiphon (zøʳmøsai·føn) *s.* termosifón.
thermostat (zø·ʳmøstæt) *s.* termostato.
thesaurus (zeso·røs) *s.* tesauro, diccionario.
these (ðiš) *adj. y pron. pl.* de THIS.
Theseus (zɪ·siøs) *n. pr.* MIT. Teseo.
thesis (zɪ·sis), *pl.* **-ses** (-siš) *s.* tesis.
Thespis (ze·spis) *n. pr.* MIT. Tespis.
Thessalonica (zesalonai·ka) *n. pr.* GEOGR. Tesalónica, Salónica.
Thessaly (ze·sali) *n. pr.* GEOGR. Tesalia.
theurgist (zɪ·øʳdỹist) *s.* teúrgo.
theurgy (-i) *s.* teúrgia.
thews (ziuš) *s.* músculos, fuerza muscular. *2* energía, resolución.
they (ðei) *pron. pl.* de HE, SHE, IT: ellos, ellas [en nominativo].
Thibetan (zi·betan) *adj.-s.* tibetano.
thick (zik) *adj.* espeso, grueso: *two inches* ~, de dos pulgadas de grueso. *2* espeso, tupido, apretado, denso, consistente. *3* lleno: ~ *with,* lleno de. *4* seguido, continuado. *5* turbio; neblinoso, brumoso. *6* torpe, obtuso. *7* ronco, estropajoso, confuso [voz, pronunciación]. *8* duro [de oído]. *9* íntimo, muy amigo. *10 adv.* THICKLY. *11 s.* grueso, espesor. *12 the* ~ *of,* lo más espeso, denso, duro, reñido, etc. de. *13 through* ~ *and thin,* a pesar de todo, incondicionalmente.
thick-bodied *adj.* grueso, corpulento.
thicken (to) (zi·køn) *tr.* espesar, engrosar, reforzar. *2 intr.* espesarse, engrosarse, complicarse, enturbiarse.
thickener (zi·kønøʳ) *s.* sustancia espesativa.
thicket (zi·kit) *s.* soto, espesura, maleza, matorral.
thick-headed *adj.* estúpido; testarudo.
thick-knee *s.* ORN. alcaraván.
thick-lipped *adj.* bezudo.
thickly (zi·kli) *adv.* espesamente, densamente: ~ *settled,* muy poblado. *2* seguido, seguidamente. *3* roncamente, estropajosamente.
thick-necked *adj.* cervigudo, de cuello grueso.

thickness (zi·knis) *s.* espesor, grueso. *2* densidad, consistencia. *3* parte más gruesa, espesa, etc. *4* capa [de una materia].
thick-set *adj.* denso, espeso. *2* grueso, rechoncho.
thick-skinned *adj.* paquidermo. *2* duro, insensible; de cara dura.
thick-skulled *adj.* lerdo, torpe, duro de mollera.
thief (zif) *s.* ladrón, ratero.
thieve (to) (zi·v) *intr.* robar, hurtar.
thievery (-øri) *s.* robo, latrocinio.
thievish (-ish) *adj.* ladrón, rapaz. *2* furtivo.
thigh (zai) *s.* ANAT. muslo.
thighbone (-boun) *s.* ANAT. fémur.
thill (zil) *s.* limonera [de carruaje].
thimble (zi·mbøl) *s.* dedal. *2* MEC. anillo de guía, refuerzo, etc. *3* BOT. digital.
thin (zin) *s.* delgado, fino, tenue. *2* flaco, enjuto. *3* claro, ralo. *4* claro, flojo, aguado. *5* raro, enrarecido. *6* ligero, transparente. *7* escaso, corto. *8* flaco, pobre [argumento, etc.]. *9* débil, agudo [voz, sonido].
thin (to) *tr.* adelgazar. *2* aclarar [hacer menos espeso]; enrarecer. *3* aguar. *4* disminuir. *5 intr.* adelgazarse. *6* aclararse [hacerse menos espeso], ralear, hacerse escaso. ¶ Pret. y p. p.: *thinned;* ger.: *-nning.*
thine (ðain) *pron.* (el) tuyo, (la) tuya, (los) tuyos, (las) tuyas. *2 adj.* tu, tus.
thing (zing) *s.* cosa; lo: *for one ~,* entre otras cosas; *the right ~,* lo justo, lo debido; *the ~,* la cuestión, lo importante, lo conveniente, lo elegante, etc. *2* fam. persona; *poor ~!,* ¡pobre!, ¡pobrecito! *3 pl.* cosas, efectos, bártulos.
think (to) (zink) *tr.-intr.* pensar [en todos sus sentidos, menos en el de echar pienso a]: *to ~ fit, good* o *proper,* tener a bien, estimar conveniente: *to ~ nothing of,* tener en poco, no dar importancia a; creer fácil; *to ~ of,* pensar en; acordarse de; *to ~ over,* pensar bien [una cosa]; *to ~ well* o *ill of,* tener en buen o mal concepto; *I ~ so,* eso creo yo. *2* juzgar, conceptuar, creer. *3* discurrir, idear. ¶ Pret. y p. p.: *thought.*
thinkable (-abøl) *adj.* pensable, concebible.
thinker (-ø^r) *s.* pensador.
thinking (-ing) *s.* pensamiento, reflexión, pensar: *way of ~,* manera de pensar. *2* juicio, concepto.
thinly (zi·nli) *adv.* delgadamente. *2* flacamente. *3* esparcidamente, con poca densidad o espesor.
third (zø^{r}d) *adj.-s.* tercero, tercera. *2* tres [día]. *3 s.* tercio [tercera parte]. *4* MÚS., AUTO. tercera.
third-class *adj.* de tercera clase, de tercera.
thirdly (-li) *adv.* en tercer lugar.
thirst (zø^{r}st) *s.* sed.
thirst (to) *intr.* tener o padecer sed. *2 to ~ after* o *for,* tener sed o ansia de. *3 tr.* hacer padecer sed.
thirsty (-i) *adj.* sediento: *to be ~,* tener sed.
thirteen (zø^{r}tı·n) *adj.-s.* trece.
thirteenth (-nz) *adj.* decimotercio. *2* trezavo. *3* trece.
thirtieth (zø·^{r}tiiz) *adj.* trigésimo. *2* treinta.
thirty (zø·^{r}ti) *adj.-s.* treinta.
this (ðis) *adj.* este, esta. *2 pron.* éste, ésta, esto.
thistle (zi·søl) *s.* BOT. cardo. *2* ORN. *~ finch,* jilguero. *3* (con may.) orden escocesa del Cardo.
thistledown (-daun) *s.* papo del cardo.
thistly (zi·sli) *adj.* lleno de cardos. *2* espinoso.
thither (di·ðø^r) *adv.* allá, hacia allá: *hither and ~,* acá y allá. *2 adj.* de allá, de la parte de allá.
tho' (ðou) *conj.* abr. de THOUGH.
thole (zoul), **tholepin** (-pin) *s.* MAR. escálamo, tolete.

Thomas (ta·mas) *n. pr.* Tomás.
thomism (tou·miŝm) *s.* tomismo.
thong (zang) *s.* correa, tira de cuero, *guasca.
thoracic (zoræ·sik) *adj.* torácico.
thorax (zo·ræks) *s.* ANAT., ZOOL. tórax.
thorium (zo·riøm) *s.* QUÍM. torio.
thorn (zo^{r}n) *s.* espina, púa, pincho. *2* fig. espina, pesadumbre: *to be on thorns,* estar en ascuas. *3* BOT. espino. *4* BOT. abrojo. *5 ~ apple,* estramonio.
thornless (zo·^{r}nlis) *adj.* sin espinas.
thorny (-i) *adj.* espinoso, lleno de espinas. *2* espinoso, arduo.
thorough (zø·rou) *adj.* completo, total, acabado. *2* consumado, perfecto. *3* esmerado, cuidadoso. *4* MÚS. *~ bass,* bajo continuo.
thoroughbred (-bred) *adj.* de pura raza. *2* bien nacido, distinguido. *3 s.* animal de pura raza. *4* pers. bien nacida, distinguida.
thoroughfare (-fe^r) *s.* vía pública, pasaje; camino. *2* paso, tránsito: *no ~,* prohibido el paso.
thoroughgoing (-gouing) *adj.* completo, esmerado, celoso, acérrimo.
thoroughly (-li) *adv.* completamente. *2* concienzudamente, a fondo.
those (ðous) *adj.-pron. pl.* de THAT: esos, esas, aquellos, aquellas; los, las: *~ which, ~ who,* los o las que, quienes.
thou (ðau) *pron.* tú. | Úsase sólo en poesía o en lenguaje dialectal.
thou (to) *tr.* tutear.
though (ðou) *conj.* aunque, aun cuando, si bien; sin embargo. *2 as ~,* como si.
thought (zot) *pret.* y *p. p.* de TO THINK. *2 s.* pensamiento [acción de pensar; cosa pensada; idea, intención]: *~ reading,* adivinación del pensamiento; *on second ~,* pensándolo mejor. *3* consideración, atención, cuidado: *want of ~,* inadvertencia, descuido. *4* un poco, algo.
thoughtful (-ful) *adj.* reflexivo, meditativo. *2* pensativo, meditabundo. *3* atento, considerado. *4* solícito, cuidadoso. *5* previsor.
thoughtless (-lis) *adj.* irreflexivo, atolondrado, descuidado, incauto. *2* imprevido.
thoughtlessness (-nis) *s.* irreflexión, ligereza, indiscreción. *2* descuido, inadvertencia.
thousand (zau·sand) *adj.* mil. *2 s.* mil, millar: *a ~, one ~,* mil.
thousandth (-z) *adj.-s.* milésimo. *2 s.* milésima.
Thrace (zres) *n. pr.* GEOGR. Tracia.
thrall (zrol) *s.* siervo, esclavo. *2* esclavitud, servidumbre.
thrall (to) *tr.* esclavizar, avasallar.
thral(l)dom (-døm) *s.* esclavitud, servidumbre.
thrash (zræsh) *tr.-intr.* AGR. trillar, desgranar: fig. *to ~ out a matter,* ventilar un asunto. *2 tr.* golpear; apalizar; derrotar. *3 intr.* revolcarse, agitarse.
thrasher (-ø^r) *s.* trillador, desgranador. *2* trilladora; máquina de desgranar. *3* apalizador. *4* ORN. malvís americano.
thrashing (-ing) *s.* trilla, desgranamiento; *~ floor,* era. *2* zurra, paliza.
thread (zred) *s.* hilo: *to hang on a ~,* pender de un hilo. *2* fibra, hebra, filamento. *3* MEC. filete [de rosca].
thread (to) *tr.* enhebrar, enhilar, ensartar. *2* pasar o hacer pasar por o entre. *3* MEC. aterrajar, labrar la rosca de [un tornillo]. *4 intr.* pasar, correr, deslizarse.
threadbare (-be^r) *adj.* raído, gastado. *2* fig. manido, trillado, gastado.

threadworm (-wørm) *s.* lombriz intestinal.
threat (zret) *s.* amenaza. *2* amago.
threaten (to) (zre·tøn) *tr.-intr.* amenazar. *2* amagar.
threatening (-ing) *s.* amenaza. *2 adj.* amenazador.
three (zrɪ) *adj.-s.* tres: ~ *o'clock*, las tres.
three-colo(u)r *adj.* tricolor; tricromo.
three-cornered *adj.* triangular. *2* de tres picos.
three-decker *s.* navío de tres puentes. *2* construcción de tres pisos. *3* novela muy larga.
threefold (-fould) *adj.* triplo, triple. *2 adv.* tres veces más.
three-legged *adj.* de tres pies.
threepenny (zre·peni) *adj.* de a tres peniques, barato, despreciable.
three-phase *adj.* ELECT. trifásico.
three-ply *adj.* triple. *2* de tres capas.
three R's (aᶠš) *s. pl.* lectura, escritura y aritmética.
threescore (zrɪ·skoʳ) *adj.-s.* sesenta.
three-way *adj.* de tres pasos, vías o direcciones.
threnody (zre·nodi) *s.* treno.
thresh (to) (zresh) *tr.-intr.* TO THRASH.
thresher (-øʳ) *s.* TRASHER 1, 2 y 3.
threshing (-ing) *s.* THRASHING.
threshold (zre·should) *s.* umbral.
threw (zru) *pret.* de THROW.
thrice (zrais) *adv.* tres veces.
thrift (zrift) *s.* economía, frugalidad. *2* medro, crecimiento, desarrollo vigoroso.
thriftiness (-inis) *s.* economía, frugalidad.
thriftless (-lis) *adj.* manirroto, impróvido.
thrifty (-i) *adj.* económico, ahorrativo, frugal. *2* industrioso. *3* próspero, floreciente.
thrill (zril) *s.* temblor, estremecimiento, escalofrío, emoción.
thrill (to) *tr.* hacer temblar o estremecer, dar escalofríos, emocionar. *2 intr.* temblar, estremecerse.
thriller (-øʳ) *s.* cuento o drama espeluznante.
thrilling (-ing) *adj.* emocionante; espeluznante.
thrive (zraiv) *intr.* crecer, engordar. *2* medrar, prosperar. ¶ Pret.: *throve* o *thrived;* p. p.: *thrived* o *thriven.*
thriving (-ing) *adj.* próspero, floreciente.
thro' (zru·) *adv.* y *prep.* abrev. de THROUGH.
throat (zrout) *s.* garganta, cuello, gaznate: *to clear one's* ~, carraspear; *to cut the* ~ *of*, degollar. *2* fig. garganta, angostamiento. *3* fig. boca, entrada, paso. *5* ARQ. goterón.
throatband (-bænd) *s.* ahogadero [de brida].
throatwort (-uøʳt) *s.* BOT. campanilla.
throaty (-i) *adj.* gutural, ronco.
throb (zrab) *s.* latido, palpitación, vibración.
throb (to) *intr.* latir, pulsar, palpitar, vibrar. ¶ Pret. y p. p.: *throbbed;* ger.: -*bbing.*
throe (zrou) *s.* angustia, agonía, dolor: *throes of childbirth*, dolores del parto.
thrombosis (zrambou·sis) *s.* MED. trombosis.
throne (zrou·n) *s.* trono.
throne (to) *tr.* entronizar, exaltar. *2 intr.* reinar.
throng (zrong) *s.* muchedumbre, gentío, tropel.
throng (to) *intr.* apiñarse, agolparse. *2 tr.* apiñar, apretar. *3* atestar, llenar.
throstle (zra·søl) *s.* ORN. zorzal.
throttle (zra·tøl) *s.* garganta, gaznate. *2* gollete [de botella]. *3* MEC. válvula reguladora; acelerador [de automóvil].
throttle (to) *tr.* ahogar, estrangular. *2* MEC. *to* ~ *down*, disminuir la marcha. *3 intr.* ahogarse.
through (zru) *prep.* por, a lo largo de, a través de, por entre. *2* por medio o conducto de, gracias a,

a causa de. *3 adv.* de un lado a otro, de parte a parte; de cabo a cabo, hasta el fin, completamente. *4* directamente [sin hacer paradas]. *5 adj.* directo [tren, billete]. *6* de paso. *7 to be* ~ *with*, haber acabado con, no querer ocuparse más de.
throughout (-aut) *prep.* por todo, en todo, durante todo, a lo largo de. *2 adv.* de parte a parte; por todas partes; en todo; desde el principio hasta el fin.
throve (zrouv) *pret.* de TO TRIVE.
throw (zrou) *s.* lanzamiento, tiro, tirada, echada. *2* lance [de dados], jugada. *3* MEC. carrera, embolada.
throw (to) *tr.* lanzar, tirar, arrojar, echar, despedir. *2* derribar. *3* impeler, empujar. *4* despojarse de, soltar, perder. *5* poner [en un estado, condición, etc.]. *6* disponer, formar, expresar. *7* torcer [hilo]. *8* proyectar [luz, sombra]. *9* parir [la coneja, etc.]. *10* tender [un puente]. *11 to* ~ *about*, esparcir. *12 to* ~ *away*, tirar, desechar; desperdiciar. *13 to* ~ *back*, devolver; replicar; rechazar. *14 to* ~ *down*, derribar; echar por tierra. *15 to* ~ *in*, intercalar, incluir; añadir, dar de más. *16 to* ~ *off*, quitarse, despojarse de; improvisar [versos, discursos, etc.]. *17 to* ~ *open*, abrir de par en par. *18 to* ~ *out*, echar fuera; proferir, emitir; esparcir, exhalar. *19 to* ~ *over*, echar por la borda, abandonar. *20* ~ *up*, echar al aire; elevar, levantar; abandonar, renunciar; construir precipitadamente; fam. vomitar.
   21 intr. jugar a los dados. *22* fam. *to* ~ *up*, vomitar.
   ¶ Pret.: *threw;* p. p.: *thrown.*
throwback (-bæk) *s.* retroceso. *2* BIOL. reversión, atavismo. *3* CINEM. escena retrospectiva.
thrown (-n) *p. p.* de TO THROW.
thrum (zrøm) *s.* TEJ. cadillos. *2* fleco, borla. *3* hilo basto. *4* tecleo, rasgueo, ruido monótono.
thrum (to) *tr.* teclear, rasguear, producir un ruido monótono en. *2 intr.* sonar monótonamente. ¶ Pret. y p. p.: *thrummed;* ger.: -*mming.*
thrush (zrøsh) *s.* ORN. tordo; zorzal; malvís.
thrust (zrøst) *pret.* y *p. p.* de TO THRUST. *2* golpe de punta, estocada, lanzada, puñalada, cornada. *3* empujón. *4* arremetida. *5* MEC., ARQ. empuje.
thrust (to) *tr.* empujar, impeler: *to* ~ *aside*, rechazar, desechar. *2* extender [sus ramas, raíces, etc.]. *3* meter, introducir, hincar, clavar. *4 to* ~ *out*, echar fuera, sacar. *5 to* ~ *upon*, imponer, hacer aceptar. *6 intr.* meterse, introducirse, abrirse paso. *7* empujar, apiñarse. *8 to* ~ *at*, pinchar, tirar estocadas, dar cuchilladas, etc., a. ¶ Pret. y p. p.: *thrust.*
thud (zød) *s.* porrazo. *2* baque, golpe sordo.
thud (to) *intr.* moverse o golpear con golpe sordo. ¶ Pret. y p. p.: *thudded;* ger.: -*dding.*
thuja (zu·ðýa) *s.* BOT. tuya.
thumb (zøm) *s.* pulgar: ~ *nut*, tuerca de mariposa; *under the* ~ *of*, bajo la férula de.
thumb (to) *tr.* hojear [con el pulgar]. *2* manejar, tocar, ejecutar torpemente, sin arte.
thumbnail (-neil) *s.* uña del pulgar.
thumbscrew (-cru) *s.* tuerca o tornillo de cabeza prismática o moleteada. *2* empulgueras.
thumbtack (-tæk) *s.* chinche [clavito].
thump (zømp) *s.* golpe, porrazo, baque.
thump (to) *tr.-intr.* golpear, aporrear. *2 tr.* meter, encasquetar [a golpes]. *3 intr.* latir fuerte, dar porrazos. *5* andar con pasos resonantes.
thumping (-ing) *adj.* fam. pesado, enorme.

thunder (zø·ndø^r) *s.* trueno. *2* estruendo. *3* fig. rayo, excomunión.

thunder (to) *impers.-intr.* tronar. *2* retumbar, moverse o avanzar con estrépito. *3 tr.* lanzar, fulminar [censuras, excomuniones, etc.]. *4* expresar con aplausos, estrépito, etc.

thunderbolt (-boult) *s.* rayo, centella. *2* fulminación, censura. *3* piedra de rayo.

thunderclap (-klæp) *s.* trueno, estallido.

thundering (-ing) *adj.* atronador; estrepitoso. *2* fam. enorme, extraordinario.

thundershower (-shouø^r) *s.* chubasco con truenos.

thunderstorm (-sto^rm) *s.* tronada.

thunderstruck (-strøk) *adj.* aturdido, atónito, estupefacto.

thurible (ziu·ribøl) *s.* turíbulo.

thurifer (-fø^r) *s.* turiferario.

Thuringia (ziuri·indỹia) *n. pr.* GEOGR. Turingia.

Thursday (zø·^rŝdi) *s.* jueves.

thus (døs) *adv.* así, tal, de este modo. *2* hasta este punto, tanto, tan: ~ *far,* hasta aquí, hasta ahora.

thuya (zu·ya) *s.* BOT. tuya.

thwack (zuæk) *s.* golpe, trastazo.

thwack (to) *tr.* golpear, pegar, zurrar.

thwart (zuø^rt) *s.* MAR. banco de bogar. *2 adj.* transversal, atravesado, oblicuo.

thwart (to) *tr.* desbaratar, frustrar, contrariar, contrarrestar.

thy (ðai) *adj. pos.* tu, tus. | Úsase con THOU.

thyme (taim) *s.* BOT. tomillo.

thymelaeaceous (taimiliei·shøs) *adj.* BOT. timeleáceo.

thymol (tai·moul) *s.* QUÍM. timol.

thymus (tai·møs) *s.* ANAT. timo [glándula].

thyroid (zai·roid) *adj.-s.* ANAT. tiroides. *2 adj.* tiroideo.

thyrse (zø^rs) *s.* BOT. tirso.

thyrsus (zø·^rsøs) *s.* MIT., BOT. tirso.

thyself (ðai·self) *pron.* tú mismo, ti mismo. | Úsase con THOU.

tiara (taie·ra o tia·ra) *s.* tiara. *2* diadema.

Tibetan (tibe·tan) *adj.-s.* tibetano.

tibia (ti·bia), *pl.* **-ae** (-I) o **-as** *s.* ANAT., MÚS. tibia.

tic (tik) *s.* MED. tic.

tick (tik) *s.* ZOOL. garrapata. *2* tela de colchón o almohada; cutí. *3* tictac; latido; clic. *4* fig. momento, segundo. *5* marca, señal. *6* fam. *to buy on* ~, comprar al fiado.

tick (to) *intr.* hacer tictac; hacer un clic; latir [el corazón]. *2 tr.* marcar con señales. *3* señalar, marcar [el reloj, un taxímetro, etc.].

ticker (-ø^r) *s.* teletipo.

ticket (ti·køt) *s.* billete, boleto, entrada, localidad, papeleta, ticket: ~ *office,* despacho de billetes o localidades; ~ *of leave,* (Ingl.) libertad condicional. *2* marbete, etiqueta. *3* POL. (E.U.) candidatura [lista]; programa.

ticket (to) *tr.* rotular, marcar.

ticking (ti·king) *s.* terliz, cutí.

tickle (ti·køl) *s.* cosquillas. *2* toque ligero.

tickle (to) *tr.* hacer cosquillas, cosquillear. *2* agradar, halagar; divertir. *3* coger truchas con la mano. *4 intr.* tener cosquillas.

tickler (ti·klø^r) *s.* el o lo que hace cosquillas. *2* fam. problema difícil.

ticklish (-ish) *adj.* cosquilloso. *2* picajoso, susceptible. *3* inestable, variable. *4* delicado, crítico.

tick-tack (tik-tak) *s.* tictac.

tidal (tai·ðal) *adj.* de la marea o de la corriente: ~ *wave,* aguaje, ola de marea; fig. ola, marejada, conmoción popular. *2* periódico.

tidbit (ti·ðbit) *s.* TITBIT.

tide (taid) *s.* marea; corriente: *high* o *full* ~, pleamar; *ebb* o *low* ~, bajamar; *to go with the* ~, seguir la corriente. *2* flujo [de la marea]. *3* curso, marcha [de las cosas]. *4* época, tiempo, ocasión. *5 pl.* aguas [mareas].

tide (to) *tr.-intr.* llevar, ir, flotar, navegar [con la marea]. *2 to* ~ *over,* ayudar; superar [una dificultad].

tidemark (-ma^rk) *s.* señal que deja la marea.

tidesman (-smæn) *s.* aduanero de puerto.

tidewater (-wotø^r) *s.* aguaje; agua que inunda la playa en la marea alta. *2* playa, litoral.

tideway (-wei) *s.* canal de marea.

tidiness (tai·dinis) *s.* aseo, pulcritud, orden.

tidings (tai·dings) *s. pl.* noticias, nuevas.

tidy (tai·di) *adj.* aseado, limpio, pulcro, ordenado. *2* fam. regular [bastante grande]. *3 s.* cubierta de respaldo. *4* cajón para los retazos.

tidy (to) *tr.* asear, arreglar, poner en orden.

tie (tai) *s.* cinta, cordón, etc., para atar. *2* lazo, nudo, atadura. *3* fig. lazo, vínculo. *4* corbata. *5* MÚS. ligadura. *6* ARQ. tirante. *7* FERROC. traviesa. *8* empate. *9 pl.* zapatos bajos.

tie (to) *tr.* atar. *2* liar, ligar, anudar. *3* unir, enlazar. *4* hacer [un nudo o lazo]. *5 to* ~ *down,* sujetar. *6 to* ~ *up,* atar; liar, envolver; vincular [la propiedad]; impedir, obstruir. *7 tr.-intr.* empatar. ¶ Pret. y p. p.: *tied;* ger.: *tying.*

1) tier (-ø^r) *s.* atador. *2* banda, ligadura.

2) tier (tI^r) *s.* fila, hilera [esp. cuando están unas sobre otras]; capa, tonga. *2* TEAT. fila de palcos.

tier (to) *tr.* disponer en hileras o capas.

tierce (ti^rs) *s.* tercerola [barril]. *2* tercera [en los naipes]. *3* MÚS. tercera. *4* ESGR., LITURG. tercia.

tiercet (ti·^rset) *s.* TERCET.

tie-up *s.* enlace, conexión. *2* contubernio. *3* paro, paralización; embotellamiento.

tiff (tif) *s.* enfado, enojo. *2* pique, disgusto, desavenencia. *3* traguito, sorbo.

tiff (to) *intr.* estar enojado, de mal humor. *2* reñir, desavenirse. *3 tr.* pop. beber.

tiffin (ti·fin) *s.* almuerzo; colación.

tige (tidỹ) *s.* ARQ. fuste [de columna]. *2* BOT. tallo.

tiger (tai·gø^r) *s.* ZOOL. tigre. *2* ZOOL. ~ *cat,* gato cerval; ocelote. *3* BOT. ~ *flower,* flor de la maravilla; ~ *lily,* tigridia.

tigerish (-ish) *adj.* de tigre. *2* feroz, sanguinario.

tight (tait) *s.* bien cerrado, hermético, estanco. *2* tieso; firme; tirante. *3* apretado. *4* compacto. *5* ajustado, estrecho. *6* COM. retraído [dinero, mercado]. *7* listo, capaz. *8* duro, severo. *9* tacaño. *10* DEP. cerrado; igualado [juego]. *11* ~ *squeeze,* apuro, aprieto. *12* pop. borracho. *13 adv.* apretadamente, firmemente, tiesamente.

tighten (to) (-øn) *tr.* apretar, estrechar. *2* estirar, atirantar, atiesar. *3 intr.* apretarse; atirantarse.

tight-fisted *adj.* fam. agarrado, tacaño.

tight-fitting *adj.* muy ajustado.

tightrope (tai·troup) *s.* cuerda de volatinero.

tights (taits) *s. pl.* traje de malla [de los gimnastas, etc.].

tigress (tai·gris) *s. f.* tigresa.

tigrish (tai·grish) *adj.* TIGERISH.

tike (taik) *s.* TYKE.

tilbury (ti·lbøri) *s.* tilburí.

tile (tail) *s.* teja; losa, baldosa, azulejo: *to have a* ~ *loose,* fig. faltarle a uno un tornillo. *2* fam. sombrero de copa.

tile (to) *tr.* tejar. *2* embaldosar. *3* azulejar.

tiler (tai·lø^r) *s.* tejero. *2* azulejero.

tiliaceous (tiliei·shøs) *adj.* BOT. tiliáceo.
tiling (tai·ling) *s.* tejado; embaldosado. 2 tejas, baldosas, azulejos.
till (til) *prep.* hasta. 2 *conj.* hasta que. 3 *s.* cajón o gaveta para el dinero.
till (to) *tr.-intr.* arar, labrar, cultivar.
tillable (ti·labøl) *adj.* arable, cultivable, labrantío.
tillage (ti·lidŷ) *s.* labranza, labor, cultivo.
tiller (ti·lø^r) *s.* labrador, agricultor. 2 MAR. caña [del timón]. 3 palanca, manija. 4 resalvo.
tilt (tilt) *s.* inclinación, ladeo; declive. 2 justa, torneo. 3 lanzada, golpe. 4 disputa. 5 toldo, entalamadura. 6 *full* ~, a toda velocidad.
tilt (to) *tr.* inclinar, ladear. 2 verter, volcar. 3 dar lanzadas, acometer. 4 entoldar. 5 *intr.* inclinarse, volcarse. 6 ajustar.
tilter (ti·ltø^r) *s.* justador. 2 vertedor de carbón.
tilth (tilz) *s.* labranza, cultivo. 2 tierra cultivada.
tilting (ti·lting) *s.* inclinación, ladeo. 2 justa, torneo.
tiltyard (ti·ltya^rd) *s.* liza, lugar de una justa.
Tim (tim) *n. pr. dim.* de TIMOTHY.
timbal (ti·mbal) *s.* MÚS. timbal.
timbale *s.* COC. timbal.
timber (-ø^r) *s.* madera [de construcción o carpintería], maderaje, maderamen. 2 madero, viga. 3 MAR. cuaderna. 4 bosque, árboles maderables.
timber (to) *tr.* enmaderar.
timberland (-lænd) *s.* tierra de bosques maderables.
timbre (ti·mbø^r) *s.* FONÉT., MÚS., BLAS. timbre.
timbrel (ti·mbrøl) *s.* MÚS. pandero, pandereta.
time (taim) *s.* tiempo. | No tiene el sentido de estado de la atmósfera: ~ *clock*, reloj registrador; *to have a good* ~, pasarlo bien; divertirse; *at the same* ~, al mismo tiempo; sin embargo; *behind* ~, atrasado, retrasado, *behind the times*, anticuado; *for the* ~ *being*, por ahora, de momento; *in good* ~, a tiempo; pronto; *in no* ~, en un santiamén; *in* ~, a tiempo; con el tiempo; *in the course of* ~, andando el tiempo; *out of* ~, fuera de tiempo, de sazón. 2 hora, momento: ~ *zone*, GEOGR. huso horario; *what* ~ *is it?*, ¿qué hora es? 3 duración del servicio militar; de una condena, etc.: *to do* ~, cumplir condena. 4 término del embarazo; de un período de trabajo, etc. 5 COM. prórroga, plazo. 6 vez: *at a* ~, de una vez; *at no* ~, nunca: *at times*, a veces; *from* ~ *to* ~, de vez en cuando; ~ *about*, alternadamente. 7 MÚS. compás: *in* ~, a compás; *out of* ~, fuera de compás.
time (to) *tr.* escoger el momento: *well timed*, oportuno. 2 regular, poner a la hora. 3 cronometrar. 4 MÚS. llevar el tiempo a compás.
timeful (-ful) *adj.* oportuno.
time-hono(u)red *adj.* de reputación, consagrado, tradicional.
timekeeper (-kipø^r) *s.* reloj, cronómetro. 2 marcador de tiempo. 3 cronometrador.
timeless (-lis) *adj.* eterno, interminable. 2 independiente del tiempo.
timely (-li) *adv.* oportunamente. 2 *adj.* oportuno, conveniente.
timepiece (-pis) *s.* reloj, cronómetro.
timer (-ø^r) *s.* contador de tiempo. 2 MEC. distribuidor del encendido.
timeserver (-sø^rvø^r) *s.* persona acomodaticia, oportunista.
timetable (-teibøl) *s.* guía, horario, itinerario.
timeworn (-uøn) *adj.* viejo, gastado. 2 anticuado.
timid (ti·mid) *adj.* tímido. 2 medroso.

timidity (timi·diti) *s.* timidez.
timocracy (taima·krasi) *s.* timocracia.
timorous (ti·mørøs) *adj.* temeroso, medroso.
Timothy (ti·mozi) *n. pr.* Timoteo.
timpano (ti·mpanou), *pl.* **-ni** (-ni) *s.* MÚS. tímpano.
tin (tin) *s.* QUÍM. estaño. 2 lata, hojalata: ~ *plate*, hojalata. 3 lata, bote. 4 pop. dinero.
tin (to) *tr.* estañar, cubrir con estaño. 2 enlatar. | Pret. y p. p.: *tinned;* ger.: *-nning.*
tinctorial (tinkto·rial) *adj.* tintóreo.
tincture (ti·nkchø^r) *s.* tintura, color, tinte. 2 FARM. tintura. 3 fig. tinte, algo.
tincture (to) *tr.* teñir, colorar, tinturar.
tinder (ti·ndø^r) *s.* yesca, mecha [para encender].
tinderbox (-baks) *s.* yesquero.
tine (tain) *s.* púa, punta, diente, gajo.
tinea (ti·nia) *s.* MED. tiña.
ting (ting) *s.* tintín.
ting (to) *tr.* hacer tintinear. 2 *intr.* tintinear.
ting-a-ling (tingøli·ng) *s.* tilín, tilín.
tinge (tindŷ) *s.* tinte, matiz. 2 punta, algo, dejo.
tinge (to) *tr.* teñir, matizar; dar un sabor, cualidad, etc., a. ¶ Ger.: *tingeing* o *-ging.*
tingle (ti·ngøl) *s.* hormigueo, picazón. 2 estremecimiento, vibración.
tingle (to) *intr.* hormiguear, picar. 2 estremecerse, vibrar. 3 sonar en los oídos; zumbar [los oídos]. 4 *tr.* producir hormigueo, picar. 5 estremecer, hacer vibrar.
tinker (ti·nkø^r) *s.* calderero remendón. 2 chapucero. 3 remiendo, chapucería.
tinker (to) *tr.-intr.* remendar vasijas de metal. 2 chafallar.
tinkle (ti·nkøl) *s.* tintineo.
tinkle (to) *intr.* retiñir, tintinear. 2 *tr.* hacer sonar o retiñir.
tinman (ti·nmæn) *s.* TINSMITH.
tinned (tind) *adj.* estañado. 2 enlatado, en lata.
tinny (ti·ni) *adj.* de estaño. 2 de hojalata, de relumbrón. 3 que sabe a hojalata [conserva].
tinsel (ti·nsøl) *s.* TEJ. lama [de oro o plata]. 2 oropel, talco, bricho. 3 fig. oropel, relumbrón.
tinsel (to) *tr.* adornar con oropel. ¶ Pret. y p. p.: *tinsel(l)ed;* ger.: *-l(l)ing.*
tinsmith (ti·nsmiz) *s.* hojalatero, estañero.
tint (tint) *s.* tinte, matiz. 2 media tinta.
tint (to) *tr.* teñir, colorar, matizar.
tintinnabulation (tintinæbiulei·shøn) *s.* tintineo, campanilleo.
tinware (ti·nue^r) *s.* objetos de hojalata.
tiny (tai·ni) *adj.* pequeñito, chiquito, diminuto.
tip (tip) *s.* extremo, punta, ápice: *from* ~ *to toe*, de pies a cabeza. 2 casquillo, contera, herrete. 3 BILLAR. suela. 4 ZAP. puntera. 5 propina, gratificación. 6 soplo, aviso confidencial. 7 golpecito. 8 inclinación, vuelco.
tip (to) *tr.* inclinar, ladear, volcar, verter. 2 poner casquillo, contera, etc., a; guarnecer el extremo de. 3 dar propina. 4 dar un soplo o aviso confidencial a. 5 dar un golpecito. 6 *to* ~ *one's hat*, tocarse el sombrero. 7 *intr.* inclinarse, ladearse, volcarse. | A veces con *over*. ¶ Pret. y p. p.: *tipped;* ger.: *-pping.*
tipcart (-ka^rt) *s.* carro de vuelco, volquete.
tipcat (-kæt) *s.* tala [juego].
tippet (ti·pet) *s.* palatina, esclavina.
tipple (ti·pøl) *s.* bebida, licor.
tipple (to) *tr. intr.* beber, beborrotear, libar.
tippler (ti·plør) *s.* bebedor.
tipstaff (ti·pstaf) *s.* vara [de alguacil, etc.]. 2 alguacil.

tipsy (tiˑpsi) *adj.* achispado. *2* vacilante.
tiptoe (tiˑptou) *s.* punta del pie. *2 adv. on* ~, de puntillas; alerta; con expectación.
tiptoe (to) *intr.* andar de puntillas.
tiptop (-tap) *s.* lo más alto, lo mejor.
tipula (tiˑpiulə) *s.* ENT. típula.
tirade (tiˑreid) *s.* andanada, distriba, invectiva.
tire (tai^r) *s.* CARR. llanta, calce: *pneumatic* ~, neumático; ~ *chain*, AUTO. cadena antideslizante.
tire (to) *tr.* cansar, fatigar. *2* aburrir, fastidiar. *3* poner llanta o neumático a. *4 intr.* cansarse, fatigarse, aburrirse.
tired (tai^{r}d) *adj.* cansado, fatigado; aburrido: ~ *out*, muerto de cansancio.
tireless (tai·^{r}lis) *adj.* incansable, infatigable.
tiresome (-søm) *adj.* cansado, pesado, fastidioso.
tiring (-ing) *adj.* cansado, pesado.
Tirol (tiˑroul) *n. pr.* TYROL.
'tis (tiš) *contr.* de IT IS.
tisane (tišaˑn) *s.* tisana.
tissue (tiˑshu) *s.* tisú, gasa: ~ *paper*, papel de seda. *2* tejido [de mentiras, etc.]. *3* BIOL. tejido.
tissue (to) *tr.* tejer, entretejer.
tit (tit) *s.* ORN. paro. *2* pezón [de teta]. *3* ~ *for tat*, golpe por golpe.
Titan (taiˑtan) *n. pr.* MIT. Titán.
titanic (taitæˑnik) *adj.* titánico.
titanium (taiteiˑniøm) *s.* QUÍM. titanio.
titbit (tiˑtbit) *s.* golosina; trozo escogido.
titer (taiˑtø^r) *s.* TITRE.
tithe (taið) *s.* diezmo. *2* décima parte. *3* pizca.
tithe (to) *tr.* diezmar [pagar el diezmo de].
tither (-ø^r) *s.* diezmero.
titi (titiˑ) *s.* ZOOL. tití.
titillate (to) (tiˑtileit) *intr.* titilar. *2 tr.* cosquillear, excitar agradablemente.
titivate (to) (tiˑtiveit) *tr.* ataviar, componer. *2 intr.* ataviarse, componerse.
titlark (tiˑtla^{r}k) *s.* ORN. pitpit.
title (taiˑtøl) *s.* título. | No tiene el sentido de título en química: ~ *page*, portada [de un libro]. *2* DER. ~ *deed*, título de propiedad.
title (to) *tr.* titular, intitular, llamar. *2* conferir un título a.
titling (tiˑtling) *s.* ORN. gorrión silvestre.
titmouse (tiˑtmaus) *s.* ORN. paro.
titrate (to) (taiˑtreit o tiˑtreit) *tr.* QUÍM. titular.
titre (taiˑtø^r) *s.* QUÍM. título.
titter (tiˑtø^r) *s.* TITTERING.
titter (to) *intr.* reír con risa ahogada o disimulada.
tittering (-ing) *s.* risita, risa ahogada o disimulada.
tittle (tiˑtøl) *s.* tilde, punto. *2* partícula, ápice.
tittle-tattle (-tætøl) *s.* charla, chismorreo.
tittle-tattle (to) *intr.* charlar, chismorrear.
titular (tiˑchulə^r) *adj.* del título. *2* honorario, nominal. *3 adj.-s.* titular.
Titus (taiˑtøs) *n. pr.* Tito.
to (tu) *adv.* hacia una posición o estado normal, de contacto, de reposo, etc.: *to come* ~, volver en sí; *to pull a door* ~, entornar una puerta. *2* ~ *and fro*, de un lado a otro, de acá para allá. *3 prep.* a, hacia, para, para con, en comparación con, por, de, en, hasta, etc.: *face* ~ *face*, cara a cara; ~ *the right*, hacia la izquierda; *duty* ~ *humanity*, deber para con la humanidad; *work* ~ *do*, trabajo por hacer; *doctor* ~ *the king*, médico del rey; *from house* ~ *house*, de casa en casa; ~ *the end*, hasta el fin; *a quarter* ~ *five*, las cinco menos cuarto; *I will have* ~ *go*, tendré que irme. *4 to* es

el signo del infinitivo, que generalmente no se traduce: ~ *err is human*, de humanos es errar.
toad (toud) *s.* ZOOL. sapo. *2 fig.* persona odiosa.
toadeater (-itø^r) *s.* parásito, adulador servil.
toadflax (-flæks) *s.* BOT. linaria.
toadstool (-stul) *s.* BOT. hongo; hongo venenoso.
toady (-i) *s.* adulador servil.
toady (to) *tr.-intr.* adular servilmente.
to-and-fro *adj.* alternativo, de vaivén.
toast (toust) *s.* tostada, pan tostado: ~ *water*, agua panada. *2* brindis.
toast (to) *tr.* tostar. *2* brindar por. *3 intr.* tostarse. *4* calentarse. *5* brindar.
toaster (-ø^r) *s.* tostador. *2* el que brinda.
tobacco (tøbæˑkou) *s.* tabaco: ~ *pipe*, pipa para fumar; ~ *pouch*, petaca.
tobaccoism (-išm) *s.* MED. tabaquismo.
tobacconist (tobæˑkønist) *s.* tabaquero, estanquero.
tobacconize (to) (tobæˑkønaiš) *tr.* impregnar de tabaco, fumigar con tabaco.
toboggan (tøbaˑgan) *s.* tobogán [carrito o asiento]. *2* descenso rápido [de precios, etc.].
toboggan (to) *intr.* deslizarse por un tobogán, por una pendiente. *2* caer rápidamente [los precios, etc.].
Toby (touˑbi) *n. pr.* Tobías.
toccata (tøkaˑta) *s.* MÚS. tocata.
tocology (tøkaˑlodýi) *s.* tocología.
tocsin (taˑksin) *s.* campana o toque de rebato.
today, to-day (tuˑdei) *adv.* hoy. *2* hoy en día, actualmente. *3 s.* el día de hoy, la actualidad.
toddle (taˑdøl) *s.* paso corto y vacilante; pinitos.
toddle (to) *intr.* andar con paso corto y vacilante, hacer pinitos.
toddler (taˑdlø^r) *s.* niño pequeño.
toddy (taˑdi) *s.* vino de palmera. *2* ponche.
to-do (tuˑdu) *s.* ruido, bullicio, alboroto.
toe (tou) *s.* dedo del pie: *great* ~, dedo gordo del pie; *on one's toes*, alerta, despabilado. *2* uña, pesuño. *3* punta del pie, del calzado, de la media.
toe (to) *tr.* tocar con la punta del pie: *to* ~ *the line*, fig. obrar como se debe, andar derecho. *2* dar un puntapié a. *3* poner punta o puntera a. *4 intr. to* ~ *in*, andar con las puntas de los pies hacia adentro.
toenail (-neil) *s.* uña de un dedo del pie.
toffee, toffy (toˑfi o taˑfi) *s.* TAFFY.
tog (tag) *s.* fam. prenda de vestir, trapo.
tog (to) *tr.* acicalar, componer. ¶ Pret. y p. p.: *togged;* ger.: -*gging.*
toga (touˑga) *s.* toga [romana].
together (tugeðø^r) *adv.* junto; juntos, reunidos, juntamente; de consumo, de acuerdo; uno con otro, unos con otros; *to get* ~, reunir, juntar; reunirse, juntarse; ponerse de acuerdo; *to hang* ~, tener coherencia; *to sew* ~, coser [unir cosiendo]; ~ *with*, junto con, a una con. *2* al mismo tiempo, simultáneamente. *3* sin interrupción, de seguida.
toggle (taˑgøl) *s.* MAR. cazonete. *2* fiador atravesado. *3* palanca acodillada.
toil (toil) *s.* trabajo, labor, esfuerzo, fatiga, sudor, afán. *2 pl.* red, lazo.
toil (to) *intr.* afanarse, esforzarse. *2* avanzar o moverse con esfuerzo.
toilet (toiˑlit) *s.* acto de vestirse; tocado, peinado; aseo de la persona. *2* tocador; cuarto de baño; retrete: ~ *articles*, artículos de tocador; ~ *paper*, papel higiénico. *3* traje, atavío [de la mujer].
toilful (toiˑlful) *adj.* laborioso, trabajoso.

toilsome (-søm) *adj.* laborioso, trabajoso, cansado, fatigoso, penoso.

token (tou·køn) *s.* señal, signo, indicio, síntoma, prueba, prenda, recuerdo: *as a ~ of*, en señal o en prenda de. *2* distintivo, rasgo característico. *3* moneda, ficha.

Tokio, Tokyo (tou·kiou) *n. pr.* GEOGR. Tokio.

told (tou·ld) *pret.* y *p. p.* de TO TELL.

tolerable (ta·lørabøl) *adj.* tolerable, soportable. *2* pasadero, mediano.

tolerance (ta·lørans) *s.* tolerancia.

tolerant (-ant) *adj.* tolerante.

tolerate (to) (-eit) *tr.* tolerar.

toleration (talørei·shøn) *s.* tolerancia [esp. en materia religiosa].

toil (tou·l) *s.* tañido o doble de campana. *2* peaje, pontazgo, derecho, tributo: *~ bar*, *~ gate*, barrera de peaje o pontazgo; *~ call*, TELÉF. conferencia interurbana. *3* maquilla [del molinero]. *4* fig. número de bajas o víctimas [en una batalla, un siniestro, etc.].

toll (to) *tr.* tañer [la campana] acompasadamente; doblar por. *2 intr.* doblar, sonar [la campana]. *3 tr.-intr.* cobrar o pagar peaje, pontazgo, tributo, etc.

tollable (-abøl) *adj.* sujeto al pago de derecho o tributo.

tollgate (-geit) *s.* barrera de peaje o pontazgo.

tollkeeper (-kɪpøʳ) *s.* peajero, pontazguero.

tolu (tolu·) *s.* bálsamo de Tolú.

toluene (ta·liuin) *s.* QUÍM. tolueno.

Tom (ta·m) *n. pr. abrev.* de THOMAS.

tom *s.* macho de algunos animales: *~ cat*, gato.

tomahawk (ta·majok) *s.* hacha de guerra de los indios norteamericanos.

tomato (toma·tou o tomei·tou) *s.* BOT. tomate.

tomb (tum) *s.* tumba, sepulcro, mausoleo.

tombola (tam·bøla) *s.* tómbola.

tomboy (ta·mboi) *s.* muchacha retozona, traviesa.

tombstone (tu·mstoun) *s.* lápida o piedra sepulcral.

tomcat (ta·mkæt) *s.* ZOOL. gato.

tomcod (ta·mkad) *s.* ICT. pez parecido al bacalao.

tome (tou·m) *s.* tomo, volumen.

tomentose (tome·ntous) *adj.* tomentoso.

tomentum (-tøm) *s.* BOT. tomento.

tomfool (tamfu·l) *s.* necio, mentecato.

tomfoolery (-øri) *s.* tontería, necedad. *2* payasada.

Tommy (ta·mi) *n. pr. dim.* de THOMAS. *2 s.* (con min.) soldado inglés.

tomorrow o **to-morrow** (tuma·rou) *adv.* mañana. *2 s.* día de mañana.

tomtit (ta·mtit) *s.* ORN. paro.

tom-tom (ta·m tam) *s.* gong. *2* tam-tam.

ton (tøn) *s.* tonelada: *long ~*, tonelada de 2.240 libras (1.016 kg); *short ~*, tonelada de 2.000 libras (907 kg); *metric ~*, tonelada métrica.

tonal (tou·nal) *adj.* MÚS. tonal.

tonality (tounæ·liti) *s.* tonalidad.

tone (toun) *s.* sonido [vocal o musical]; voz: *~ control*, RADIO regulación del sonido. *2* MÚS. tono [intervalo]. *3* tono, acento, entonación, tonillo. *4* PINT., MED. tono. *5* tono [energía; nivel moral; carácter dominante].

tone (to) *tr.* dar tono o un tono a. *2* modificar el tono o el color de: *to ~ down*, bajar el tono de; suavizar; *to ~ up*, elevar el tono de; entonar, vigorizar. *3* FOT. virar. *4 intr.* tomar un tono o color; armonizar [con].

tongs (tangs) *s. pl.* tenazas, tenacillas, pinzas, alicates.

tongue (tøng) *s.* ANAT. lengua: *~ twister*, trabalenguas; *to hold one's ~*, callar. *2* palabra, habla; lengua, lenguaje. *3* lengua [de tierra, de fuego, etc.]. *4* hebijón. *5* badajo. *6* MÚS., CARP. lengüeta. *7* fiel [de balanza]. *8* lancha [de coche].

tongue (to) *tr.* lamer. *2* CARP. engargolar. *3 intr.* salir como una lengua. *4 tr.-intr.* MÚS. producir con la lengua.

tongue-lashing *s.* fam. reprensión áspera.

tongueless (-lis) *s.* sin lengua. *2* mudo, sin habla.

tongue-tied *adj.* que tiene impedimento en el habla. *2* mudo, cortado, tímido.

tonic (ta·nik) *adj.* tónico, tonificante. *2* MÚS., FONÉT., PROS. tónico. *3 s.* MED. tónico. *4* MÚS. tónica.

tonicity (touni·siti) *s.* tonicidad.

tonight o **to-night** (tunai·t) *s.* esta noche.

tonish (tou·nish) *adj.* elegante, a la moda.

tonka bean (ta·nka) *s.* BOT. haba tonca; sarapia.

tonnage (tø·nidỹ) *s.* tonelaje, arqueo. *2* tonelaje [derecho]. *3* peso en toneladas.

tonsil (ta·nsil) *s.* ANAT. tonsila, amígdala.

tonsil(l)itis (tansilai·tis) *s.* MED. amigdalitis.

tonsorial (tanso·rial) *adj.* barberil.

tonsure (ta·nshuʳ) *s.* tonsura.

Tony (tou·ni) *n. pr. dim.* de ANTHONY.

too (tu) *adv.* demasiado. *2* fam. mucho. *3* también, además. *4* *~ many*, demasiados. *5* *~ much*, demasiado. *6 it is ~ bad*, es una lástima; *~ bad!*, ¡qué lástima!

took (tuk) *pret.* de TO TAKE.

tool (tul) *s.* instrumento, herramienta, utensilio. *2* fig. instrumento [pers.].

toot (tut) *s.* sonido de trompa; bocinazo; silbido, pitido.

toot (to) *tr.-intr.* tocar o sonar [la trompa, la bocina, el silbato], pitar.

tooth (tuz) *pl.* **teeth** (tiz) *s.* ANAT. diente: *~ decay*, caries dental; *~ powder*, polvos dentífricos; *to cast in one's teeth*, echar a cara; *in the teeth of*, en la cara de; contra, a despecho de; *~ and nail*, furiosamente, desesperadamente. *2* diente [de sierra, de rueda, etc.], púa, gajo, punta. *3* gusto, afición: *to have a sweet ~*, ser goloso.

tooth (to) *tr.* dentar. *2* endentar, engranar.

toothache (tu·zeik) *s.* dolor de muelas.

toothbrush (tu·zbrøsh) *s.* cepillo para los dientes.

toothed (tu·zt) *adj.* dentado, serrado.

toothful (tu·zful) *s.* bocado o trago.

toothing (tu·zing) *s.* ALBAÑ. adarajas.

toothless (tu·zlis) *adj.* desdentado.

toothpick (tu·zpik) *s.* mondadientes, palillo.

toothsome (tu·zsøm) *adj.* sabroso, apetitoso.

toothy (tu·zi) *s.* dentudo. *2* voraz.

tootle (to) (tu·tøl) *tr.* tocar la flauta o silbar suavemente.

top (tap) *s.* parte o superficie superior, lo alto, cima, cumbre, remate, pináculo, tejado, cabeza, tope, cúspide, ápice: *from ~ to bottom*, de arriba abajo; *on (the) ~ of*, encima de, sobre; *on ~*, fig. con bien, con éxito. *2* auge, punto más alto; último grado: *at the ~ of one's voice*, a voz en cuello. *3* cabeza, primer puesto. *4* ANAT. cabeza, coronilla: *from ~ to toe*, de pies a cabeza. *5* copa [de árbol]. *6* tablero [de mesa]. *7* tejadillo o capota [de coche]. *8* MAR. cofa. *9* tapa, cubierta. *10* copete, tupé. *11* trompo, peón. *12* la flor, lo mejor. *13 adj.* superior, primero, principal; alto, de arriba; máximo: *~ hat*, sombrero de copa; *at ~ speed*, a toda velocidad. *14* ZOOL. *~ shell*, trompo [molusco].

top (to) *tr.* descabezar, desmochar. *2* cubrir, coronar. *3* acabar, rematar. *4* exceder, aventajar. *5* dominar. *6* llegar a la cima de. *7 to ~ off*, rematar, completar; MAR. embicar [una verga]. *8 intr.* sobresalir, ser excelente. *9* predominar. ¶ Pret. y p. p.: *topped;* ger.: *-pping*.

topaz (tou·pæš) *s.* MINER. topacio.

topcoat (ta·pkout) *s.* gabán; abrigo de entretiempo.

tope (to) (toup) *intr.* beber con exceso. *2* beber de un trago.

topee (tou·pɪ) *s.* salacot.

toper (tou·pøʳ) *s.* borrachín.

topful (ta·pful) *adj.* lleno hasta el borde.

topgallant (tapgæ·lant) *s.* MAR. juanete.

top-heavy *adj.* demasiado pesado o grande por arriba. *2* COM. capitalizado por encima de su valor real.

topi (tou·pɪ) *s.* TOPEE.

topic (ta·pik) *s.* asunto, tema. *2 pl.* tópicos, lugares comunes.

topic (al (ta·pik(al) *adj.* tópico. *2* del tema o asunto. *3* referente a los asuntos del día. *4* MED. local.

topknot (ta·pnat) *s.* moño [de pelo, de plumas, de cintas].

topman (-mæn) *s.* MAR. gaviero.

topmast (-mæst) *s.* MAR. mastelero.

topmost (-moust) *adj.* más alto [de todos].

topographer (tøpa·graføʳ) *s.* topógrafo.

topographic (al (tapøgræ·fik(al) *adj.* topográfico.

topography (tøpa·grafi) *s.* topografía.

toponymy (-nimi) *s.* toponimia.

topper (ta·pøʳ) *s.* fam. sombrero de copa. *2* persona o cosa excelente.

topping (-ing) *adj.* alto, elevado. *2* eminente, distinguido. *3* excelente, de primera. *4* (E.U.) tiránico, mandón.

topple (to) (ta·pøl) *tr.* hacer caer, derribar, volcar. *2 intr.* tambalearse, caer. | Gralte. con *down* u *over*.

topsail (ta·pseil) *s.* MAR. gavia.

top-shell *s.* ZOOL. trompo [molusco].

topsoil (-soil) *s.* capa superior del suelo.

topsy-turvy (ta·psi·tø·ʳvi) *adv.* patas arriba, en confusión. *2 adj.* trastornado, revuelto, desordenado. *3 s.* desbarajuste, confusión.

toque (touk) *s.* toca [sombrero].

tor (toʳ) *s.* tolmo, tormo.

torch (toʳch) *s.* hacha, antorcha. *2* linterna eléctrica de bolsillo. *3* lámpara de soldar.

torchbearer (-berøʳ) *s.* portador de antorcha.

torchlight (-lait) *s.* luz de antorcha.

tore (toʳ) *pret.* de TO TEAR. *2 s.* ARQ. toro, torés.

toric (ta·rik) *adj.* tórico: *~ lens*, lente tórica.

torment (toʳmønt) *s.* tormento, tortura, pena.

torment (to) (toʳme·nt) *tr.* atormentar, torturar. *2* agitar. *3* molestar, inquietar. *4* violentar, tergiversar.

tormenter, tormentor (-øʳ) *s.* atormentador.

torn (toʳn) *p. p.* de TO TEAR. *2 adj.* roto, rasgado, desgarrado.

tornado (toʳnei·dou) *s.* tornado. *2* manga de viento.

torpedo (toʳpɪ·dou) *s.* MIL., ICT. torpedo: *~ boat*, torpedero.

torpedo (to) *tr.* torpedear. *2* destruir, desbaratar.

torpid (to·ʳpid) *adj.* tórpido. *2* torpe, aletargado, entorpecido, apático.

torpidity (to·ʳpi·diti), **torpidness** (to·ʳpidnis), **torpor** (to·ʳpoʳ) *s.* torpeza, entorpecimiento, letargo, apatía.

torque (toʳk) *s.* torques. *2* MEC. impulso rotativo.

torrefy (to) (ta·rifai) *tr.* tostar, torrar. ¶ Pret. y p. p.: *torrefied*.

torrent (ta·rønt) *s.* torrente. *2* raudal.

torrid (ta·rid) *adj.* tórrido. *2* ardiente, inflamado.

torridity (tari·diti) *s.* calidad de tórrido.

torsion (to·ʳshøn) *s.* torsión.

tort (toʳt) *s.* DER. agravio, perjuicio.

torticollis (to·ʳtika·lis) *s.* tortícolis.

tortoise (to·ʳtøs) *s.* ZOOL. tortuga. *2 tortoise* o *~ shell*, concha, carey.

tortoise-shell *adj.* de concha o carey.

tortuous (to·ʳchuøs) *adj.* tortuoso, torcido, sinuoso. *2* tortuoso, solapado.

torture (to·ʳchuʳ) *s.* tortura, tormento, martirio.

torture (to) *tr.* torturar, martirizar. *2* violentar, tergiversar.

torturer (-øʳ) *s.* atormentador; verdugo.

torus (to·røs) *s.* ARQ. toro.

Tory (to·ri) *s.* POL. (Ingl.) tory, conservador.

toss (tos) *s.* sacudimiento, meneo; agitación. *2* lanzamiento [acción]. *3* tiro [distancia]. *4* cara o cruz; azar.

toss (to) *tr.* sacudir, zarandear, menear, agitar. *2* arrojar, lanzar; mover o levantar vivamente: *to ~ in a blanket*, mantear; *to ~ up*, echar al aire. *3* discutir, dar vueltas a un asunto. *4 intr.* moverse, agitarse; balancearse [un buque]; revolverse [en la cama]. *5 to ~ up for*, echar a cara y cruz.

toss-up *s.* cara y cruz. *2* probabilidad incierta.

tot (tat) *s.* chiquitín, na. *2* fam. suma. *3* fam. traguito.

tot (to) *tr.-intr.* sumar. ¶ Pret. y p. p.: *totted;* ger.: *-tting*.

total (tou·tal) *adj.* total. *2* global. *3* completo, absoluto. *4 s.* total, todo.

total (to) *tr.* sumar, ascender a.

totalitarian (toutælite·rian) *adj.-s.* POL. totalitario.

totalitarianism (-išm) *s.* totalitarismo.

totality (toutæ·liti) *s.* totalidad.

totalize (to) (tou·talaiš) *tr.-intr.* totalizar.

totally (tou·tali) *adv.* totalmente.

totem (tou·tøm) *s.* tótem.

totemism (-išm) *s.* totemismo.

totter (to) (ta·tøʳ) *intr.* vacilar, tambalearse; amenazar ruina. *2* vacilar [al andar].

tottering (-ing) *adj.* vacilante, tambaleante. *2* ruinoso.

toucan (tukæ·n) *s.* ORN. tucán.

touch (tøch) *s.* toque, tocamiento, tiento, palpamiento. *2* pulsación [en música y mecanografía]. *3* tacto [sentido; impresión táctil]. *4* contacto: *in ~ with*, en contacto, en comunicación con. *5* toque, prueba, piedra de toque. *6* toque, pincelada, detalle. *7* señal, huella. *8* sombra, ápice, algo. *9* mano, habilidad. *10* indicación, insinuación. *11 ~ and go*, situación crítica, peligrosa.

touch (to) *tr.* tocar [con la mano, con un objeto] tentar, palpar. *2* tocar [tener contacto con; poner las manos en, ocuparse de, tratar un tema; comer, beber, etc.]. *3* rozar, tropezar. *4* MÚS. tocar, pulsar. *5* tocar, inspirar, aguijonear, conmover, afligir, irritar. *6* alcanzar, llegar a. *7* tocar a, concernir. *8* delinear, esbozar, retocar. *9* pop. robar: dar un sablazo a. *10 to ~ up*, corregir, retocar; espolear.

11 intr. tocar, tocarse, estar contiguo. *12 to ~ at, on, to* o *upon*, tocar; tocar a; frisar en, rayar en. *12* MAR. *to ~ at*, hacer escala en.

touch-and-go *adj.* hecho de prisa, incompleto. *2* crítico, peligroso.
touchhole (-joul) *s.* oído [de un cañón].
touchiness (-inis) *s.* susceptibilidad, irritabilidad.
touching (-ing) *prep.* tocante a, en cuanto a. *2 adj.* patético, conmovedor.
touch-me-not *s.* tema prohibido. *2* persona orgullosa. *3* BOT. balsamina.
touchstone (-stoun) *s.* piedra de toque.
touchwood (-wud) *s.* yesca, hupe.
touchy (-i) *adj.* susceptible, quisquilloso, irritable.
tough (tøf) *adj.* duro, correoso. *2* fuerte, vigoroso. *3* resistente. *4* terco, tenaz. *5* duro, arduo, penoso. *6* mala [suerte]. *7* (E.U.) malvado, pendenciero. *8 s.* (E.U.) matón.
toughen (to) (-øn) *tr.-intr.* endurecer o endurecerse. *2* hacer o hacerse correoso.
toupee (tupɪ·) *s.* peluquín, bisoñé.
tour (tuʳ) *s.* viaje, excursión, vuelta, gira. *2* circuito, recorrido. *3* turno.
tour (to) *intr.* viajar por. *2* hacer turismo.
touring (-ing) *s.* turismo: ~ *car*, turismo [coche].
tourism (-išm) *s.* turismo.
tourist (-ist) *s.* viajero, turista.
tourmalin(e (tu·ʳmalin) *s.* MINER. turmalina.
tournament (tu·ʳnamønt) *s.* torneo, justa. *2* certamen.
tourney (tu·ʳni) *s.* torneo, justa.
tourney (to) *intr.* justar, tomar parte en un torneo.
tourniquet (tu·ʳniket) *s.* CIR. torniquete.
tousle (tau·šøl) *s.* maraña [del cabello], greña.
tousle (to) *tr.* despeinar, desgreñar; desarreglar, maltratar.
tout (taut) *s.* corredor, gancho. *2* espía que vende informes relativos a las carreras de caballos.
tout (to) *tr.-intr.* buscar clientes, votos, etc. *2* espiar para obtener y vender informes relativos a las carreras de caballos.
tow (tou) *s.* estopa. *2* remolque [acción; lo que va remolcado; cabo, sirga]: *to take in* ~, remolcar, llevar a remolque. *3* remolcador.
tow (to) *tr.* remolcar, atoar.
towage (-idỹ) *s.* remolque [acción]. *2* derechos de remolque.
toward (toʳd o tuwo·ʳd), **towards** (-š) *prep.* hacia. *2* cerca de. *3* para. *4* con, para con.
towboat (tou·bout) *s.* remolcador.
towel (tau·øl) *s.* toalla: ~ *horse*, ~ *rack*, toallero.
towel(l)ing (-ing) *s.* género para toallas.
tower (tau·øʳ) *s.* torre, torreón. *2* campanario.
tower (to) *intr.* descollar, sobresalir. *2* elevarse, remontarse.
towered (-d) *adj.* guarnecido de torres.
towering (-ing) *adj.* alto, elevado. *2* que se remonta. *3* grande, exorbitante. *4* violento.
towery (-i) *adj.* guarnecido de torres. *2* alto, elevado.
towheaded (tou·jedid) *adj.* de cabello rubio pajizo.
towhee (tau·jɪ) *s.* ORN. especie de pinzón.
towing (tou·ing) *s.* remolque, atoaje: ~ *service*, AUTO. servicio de remolque.
towline (-lain) *s.* cuerda de remolque; sirga.
town (taun) *s.* población, ciudad, villa, pueblo; municipio: ~ *clerk*, secretario municipal; ~ *council*, ayuntamiento; ~ *hall*, casa del ayuntamiento; ~ *planning*, urbanismo. *2* (sin artículo) la metrópolis, la capital.
township (-ship) *s.* municipio, concejo, distrito municipal.
townsman (-mæn) *s.* ciudadano, vecino. *2* conciudadano.

towpath (tou·pæz) *s.* camino de sirga.
towrope (-roup) *s.* TOWLINE.
tox(a)emia (taksɪ·mia) *s.* MED. toxemia.
toxic (ta·ksik) *s.* tóxico.
toxicity (taksi·siti) *s.* toxicidad.
toxicology (taksika·lodỹ) *s.* toxicología.
toxin(e (ta·ksin) *s.* toxina. *2* ponzoña.
toy (toi·) *s.* juguete [para jugar]. *2* chuchería, fruslería. *3 adj.* de juguete; pequeñito.
toy (to) *intr.* jugar, juguetear, divertirse.
toyshop (toi·shap) *s.* juguetería [tienda].
trace (treis) *s.* huella, pisada, rastro. *2* vestigio, señal, indicio. *3* pizca. *4* trazo. *5* GEOM. traza. *6* tirante [de los arreos].
trace (to) *tr.* trazar, esbozar, escribir. *2* rastrear, seguir la pista de. *3* investigar, descubrir; buscar el origen de; atribuir una causa u origen a: *to* ~ *back to*, hacer remontar a.
tracer (-øʳ) *s.* trazador. *2* calcador. *3* punzón; tiralíneas. *4* rastreador, buscador. *5* MIL. ~ *bullet*, bala trazante.
tracery (-søri) *s.* ARQ. tracería.
trachea (trei·kia) *s.* ANAT., ZOOL., BOT. tráquea.
tracheotomy (trekia·tømi) *s.* CIR. traqueotomía.
trachoma (tracou·ma) *s.* MED. tracoma.
tracing (trei·sing) *s.* trazado, trazo. *2* calco: ~ *paper*, papel de calcar. *3* descubrimiento, rastreo.
track (træk) *s.* rastro, pista, huellas; señal, vestigio: *to keep* ~ *of*, fig. no perder de vista, estar al corriente de. *2* carril, rodada. *3* MAR. estela. *4* reguero. *5* camino, senda. *6* curso, rumbo, trayectoria. *7* DEP. pista. *8* banda [de tractor de oruga]. *9* vía [de tren, tranvía, etc.]. *10* *off the* ~, descarrilado; fuera de camino, despistado.
track (to) *tr.* rastrear, seguir la pista de: *to* ~ *down*, llegar a descubrir o capturar. *2* trazar, trillar [un camino]. *3* sirgar.
trackless (-lis) *adj.* sin rastro. *2* sin caminos. *3* sin vías.
tract (trækt) *s.* área, región, espacio, trecho. *2* FISIOL. aparato, sistema. *4* LITURG. tracto. *5* folleto [esp. político o religioso].
tractable (-tabøl) *adj.* dócil, complaciente, tratable.
tractate (-teit) *s.* tratado, opúsculo, ensayo.
tractile (-til) *adj.* dúctil.
traction (-shøn) *s.* tracción. *2* servicio público de transportes. *3* FISIOL. contracción. *4* MEC. fricción adhesiva.
tractive (-tiv) *adj.* de tracción.
tractor (-tøʳ) *s.* tractor. *2* aeroplano de hélice delantera.
Tracy (tra·si) *n. pr. dim.* de THERESA.
trade (treid) *s.* profesión, ocupación; oficio, arte mecánica: ~ *union*, sindicato obrero. *2* gremio. *3* comercio, tráfico, trato, negocio: ~ *mark*, marca registrada. *4* parroquia, clientela. *5 the trades*, *the* ~ *winds*, los vientos alisios.
trade (to) *intr.* comerciar, traficar, negociar, tratar: *to* ~ *in*, tratar en; *to* ~ *on*, explotar, aprovecharse de. *2 tr.* comerciar o tratar en; vender; trocar, cambiar.
trader (-øʳ) *s.* comerciante, mercader, tratante, negociante. *2* buque mercante.
tradesfolk (-sfouk) *s.* tenderos. *2* artesanos; gentes del oficio.
tradesman (-mæn) *s.* comerciante, mercader, tendero. *2* artesano.
tradespeople (-spipøl) *s. pl.* TRADESFOLK.
trading (-ing) *s.* comercio, tráfico. *2 adj.* comer-

cial, mercantil: ~ *post*, factoría; ~ *stamp*, cupón prima.
tradition (tradi·shøn) *s.* tradición.
traditional (-al) *adj.* tradicional.
traduce (to) (tradiu·s) *tr.* difamar, calumniar.
traffic (træ·fik) *s.* tráfico, comercio. 2 tránsito, circulación, transporte, tráfico: ~ *jam*, embotellamiento del tráfico; ~ *light*, semáforo.
traffic (to) *intr.* comerciar, traficar. ¶ Pret. y p. p.: *trafficked;* ger.: *-cking.*
trafficker (-ø^r) *s.* traficante.
tragacanth (træ·gakænz) *s.* BOT. tragacanto. 2 goma adragante.
tragedian (tradÿı·dian) *s.* trágico [autor; actor].
tragedienne (tradÿıdie·n) *s.* actriz trágica.
tragedy (træ·dÿidi) *s.* tragedia.
tragic (al (-k(al) *adj.* trágico.
tragicomedy (trædÿika·mødi) *s.* tragicomedia.
tragicomic (al (-mik(al) *adj.* tragicómico.
tragus (trei·gøs) *s.* ANAT. trago.
trail (treil) *s.* cola [de vestido, cometa, etc.]. 2 rastro, huella, pista. 3 reguero. 4 estela [de luz]. 5 senda [esp. en una región deshabitada].
trail (to) *tr.* arrastrar, llevar arrastrando. 2 alargar, hacer durar. 3 rastrear, seguir la pista de. 4 ir detrás de. 5 dejar [un rastro]; trillar [un camino]. 6 *intr.* arrastrar, ir arrastrando. 7 arrastrarse. 8 rezagarse. 9 extenderse [un camino, etc.]. 10 dejar rastro. 11 *to* ~ *off*, perderse, ir desapareciendo.
trailer (-ø^r) *s.* AUTO. remolque, coche habitación. 2 cosa que arrastra; planta rastrera. 3 rastreador, cazador. 4 rezagado. 5 CINEM. trailer.
trailing (-ing) *adj.* colgante, que arrastra. 2 BOT. rastrero. 3 MEC. trasero.
train (trein) *s.* FERROC. tren. 2 tren [de máquina, ondas, etc.]. 3 fila, recua; séquito, comitiva. 4 reguero [de pólvora]. 5 serie, encadenamiento. 6 cola [de cometa, vestido, etcétera].
train (to) *tr.* adiestrar, amaestrar, enseñar, educar. 2 DEP. entrenar. 3 AGR. poner en espaldera. 4 apuntar [un cañón, etc.]. 5 *intr.* adiestrarse, ejercitarse, entrenarse.
trainbearer (-berø^r) *s.* caudatario.
trainee (treinı·) *s.* el que se adiestra. 2 MIL. quinto.
trainer (trei·nø^r) *s.* adiestrador, amaestrador. 2 DEP. preparador. 3 AVIA. avión de prácticas. 4 AGR. espaldera.
training (-ning) *s.* adiestramiento, instrucción, preparación, educación. 2 DEP. entrenamiento.
trainman (-mæn) *s.* FERROC. ferroviario.
trait (treit) *s.* toque, pincelada. 2 rasgo, peculiaridad. 3 rasgo,facción.
traitor (trei·tø^r) *adj.-s.* traidor.
traitorous (-ørøs) *adj.* traidor, pérfido, alevoso.
traitress (trei·tris) *s.* traidora.
trajectory (tradÿe·ktori) *s.* trayectoria.
tram (træm) *s.* (Ingl.) tranvía. 2 vagoneta [de mina]. 3 carril, riel plano.
tram (to) *intr.* ir en tranvía.
tramcar (-ka^r) *s.* tranvía.
trammel (træ·møl) *s.* trasmallo. 2 llares [de chimenea]. 3 compás de varas. 4 elipsógrafo. 5 traba, maniota. 6 traba, impedimento.
trammel (to) *tr.* trabar, sujetar, impedir, estorbar.
tramp (træmp) *s.* viajero a pie, viandante. 2 vagabundo. 3 caminata. 4 marcha pesada; ruido de pisadas. 5 MAR. vapor volandero.
tramp (to) *intr.* andar con paso fuerte. 2 viajar a pie, vagabundear. 3 *tr.* pisar, pisotear, apisonar. 4 recorrer a pie.

tramper (-ø^r) *s.* vagabundo. 2 buen andador.
trample (træ·mpøl) *s.* pisoteo. 2 ruido de pisadas. 3 atropello.
trample (to) *tr.* hollar, pisar, pisotear. 2 *intr.* patullar, pisar fuerte. 3 *to* ~ *on*, pisotear, maltratar, atropellar.
tramway (træ·muei) *s.* (Ingl.) tranvía. 2 transbordador, funicular aéreo.
trance (træns) *s.* éxtasis, enajenamiento, ensimismamiento. 2 catalepsia; estado hipnótico.
tranquil (træ·nkuil) *adj.* tranquilo, apacible.
tranquillize (to) (-aiš) *tr.* tranquilizar.
tranquillity (trænkui·liti) *s.* tranquilidad, sosiego, paz, calma.
transact (to) (trænšæ·kt) *tr.* llevar a cabo, hacer, despachar [un negocio]. 2 *intr.* negociar, pactar.
transaction (-kshøn) *s.* despacho, negociación. 2 COM. transacción, operación. 3 DER. transacción, arreglo. 4 *pl.* actas, memorias [de una sociedad docta].
transalpine (trænsæ·lpin o -pain) *adj.* transalpino.
transatlantic (-ætlæ·ntik) *adj.* transatlántico.
transcend (to) (trænse·nd) *tr.* sobrepujar, sobrepasar; ir más allá de [los límites o facultades]. 2 *intr.* FIL., TEOL. transcender. 3 sobresalir.
transcendence, transcendency (-øns, -si) *s.* excelencia, superioridad. 2 FIL. transcendencia.
transcendent (-ønt) *adj.* sobresaliente, extraordinario. 2 FIL., TEOL. transcendente.
transcendental (trænsønde·ntal) *adj.* FIL. transcendental. 2 sobrenatural, sobrehumano.
transcontinental (trænskantine·ntal) *adj.* transcontinental.
transcribe (to) (-krai·b) *tr.* transcribir. 2 RADIO. grabar en disco.
transcript (træ·nskript) *s.* copia, traslado, trasunto. 2 transcripción [de taquigrafía].
transcription (trænskri·pshøn) *s.* transcripción. 2 copia.
transept (træ·nsept) *s.* ARQ. crucero, transepto.
transfer (træ·nsfø^r) *s.* transferencia, traslado, transporte, transbordo. 2 DER. traspaso, cesión. 3 cosa o persona trasladada. 4 calco. 5 LITOG. reporte.
transfer (to) *tr.* transferir, trasladar, transportar, transbordar. 2 DER. traspasar, ceder. 3 LITOG. reportar. ¶ Pret. y p. p.: *transferred;* ger.: *-rring.*
transferable (trænsfø·rabøl) *adj.* transferible. 2 trasladable.
transference (-fø·røns) *s.* transferencia, traslado.
transfiguration (-figiurei·shøn) *s.* transfiguración.
transfigure (to) (-fi·giu^r) *tr.* transfigurar.
transfix (to) (-fi·ks) *tr.* traspasar, atravesar.
transfixion (-fi·kshøn) *s.* transfixión.
transform (to) (-fo·^rm) *tr.* transformar. 2 *intr.* transformarse.
transformation (-fo·^rmei·shøn) *s.* transformación.
transformer (-fo·^rmø^r) *s.* transformador.
transformism (-fo·^rmišm) *s.* BIOL. transformismo.
transfuse (to) (-fiu·š) *tr.* transfundir. 2 infundir, instilar.
transfusion (-fiu·ÿøn) *s.* transfusión.
transgress (to) (-gre·s) *tr.* transgredir, infringir, quebrantar. 2 traspasar los límites de. 3 *intr.* quebrantar la ley, pecar; propasarse.
transgression (-shøn) *s.* transgresión. 2 delito, pecado.
transgressor (-sø^r) *s.* transgresor.
tranship (to) (træ·nship) *tr.* TRANSSHIP.
transient (træ·nshønt) *adj.* transitorio, pasajero;

rápido, momentáneo. 2 transeúnte, migratorio. 3 s. huésped o viajero de paso.

transiently (-li) adv. transitoriamente, temporalmente, de paso.

transistor (trænsi·stø^r) s. ELECT. transistor.

transit (træ·nsit) s. tránsito, paso, pasaje. 2 tránsito, muerte. 3 ASTR., TOP. tránsito.

transit (to) tr.-intr. ASTR., TOP. pasar [por].

transition (trænsi·shøn) s. transición.

transitional (-shønal) adj. de transición.

transitive (træ·nsitiv) adj.-s. GRAM. transitivo.

transitory (træ·nsitori) adj. transitorio, pasajero.

translatable (trænslei·tabøl) adj. traducible.

translate (to) (trænslei·t) tr. traducir. 2 descifrar, interpretar. 3 trasladar [de un lugar a otro]. 4 TELEGR. retransmitir.

translation (-shøn) s. traducción, versión. 2 traslado. 3 B. ART. copia, interpretación.

translator (-tø^r) s. traductor. 2 TELEGR. repetidor.

translucence, translucency (trænsliu·søns, -si) s. translucidez.

translucent (-sønt), **translucid** (-sid) adj. translúcido, trasluciente.

transmigrate (to) (-mai·greit) intr. transmigrar.

transmigration (-maigrei·shøn) s. transmigración.

transmission (-mi·shøn) s. transmisión. 2 AUTO. cambio de marchas.

transmit (to) (-mi·t) tr. transmitir. 2 enviar, remitir.

transmitter (-ø^r) s. transmisor.

transmitting (-ing) adj. transmisor: ~ set, RADIO. aparato transmisor; ~ station, emisora.

transmutable (miu·tabøl) adj. transmutable.

transmutation (-miutei·shøn) s. transmutación.

transmute (to) (miu·t) tr. transmutar.

transoceanic (-oushiæ·nik) adj. transoceánico.

transom (træ·nsøm) s. CARP. travesaño. 2 ARQ. dintel, puente. 3 montante [ventana]. 4 MAR. yugo.

transpacific (trænspasi·fik) adj. transpacífico.

transpadane (-pei·dein) adj. transpadano.

transparence (trænspe·røns) s. transparencia.

transparency (-rønsi) s. transparencia. 2 pintura, dibujo, etc., hechos para ser vistos por transparencia.

transparent (-rønt) adj. transparente, diáfano. 2 franco, ingenuo.

transpierce (to) (transpi·^rs) tr. traspasar, atravesar.

transpiration (-pirei·shøn) s. transpiración.

transpire (to) (-pai·^r) tr.-intr. transpirar, sudar. 2 tr. exhalar. 3 intr. exhalarse, rezumarse. 4 transpirar, traslucirse. 5 fam. acaecer, suceder.

transplant (to) (-plæ·nt) tr. trasplantar.

transplantation (-plantei·shøn) s. trasplante.

transport (træ·nspo^r t) s. transporte, acarreo. 2 transporte [buque]. 3 transporte, rapto, éxtasis. 4 deportado.

transport (to) (trænspo·^r t) tr. transportar, acarrear. 2 transportar, enajenar. 3 deportar.

transportation (-ei·shøn) s. transporte, acarreo, sistemas de transporte. 2 (E.U.) coste del transporte; billete, pasaje. 3 deportación.

transposal (trænspou·šal) s. transposición.

transpose (to) (-pou·š) tr. transponer [mudar el orden o la posición relativa de]. 2 MÚS. transportar.

transposition (-pouši·shøn) s. transposición. 2 MÚS. transporte.

transship (to) (-shi·p) tr. MAR. transbordar.

transshipment (-mønt) s. MAR. transbordo.

transubstantiation (-søbstænshiei·shøn) s. transubstanciación.

transude (to) (-siud) intr. resudar, rezumar.

transversal (-vø·^r sal) adj. transversal. 2 s. GEOM. línea transversal.

transverse (-vø·^r s) adj. transverso, travesero. 2 adv. transversalmente.

Transylvania (trænsilvei·nia) n. pr. GEOGR. Transilvania.

trap (træp) s. trampa, armadijo, lazo. 2 bombillo, sifón [de desagüe]. 3 coche ligero. 4 DEP. lanzaplatos. 5 pop. (Ingl.) policía. 6 fam. la boca. 7 ~ door, trampa [puerta]; escotillón. 8 pl. MÚS. instrumentos de percusión. 9 equipaje, bártulos.

trap (to) tr. entrampar, hacer caer en la trampa, atrapar. 2 proveer de sifón. 3 engualdrapar. 4 intr. cazar con trampa. ¶ Pret. y p. p.: trapped; ger.: -pping.

trapan (træpæ·n) s. TREPAN.

trapeze (trapı·š) s. GEOM., GIMN. trapecio.

trapezing (-šing) s. ejercicios en el trapecio.

trapezist (-šist) s. trapecista.

trapezium (-šiøm) s. GEOM. trapezoide; trapecio. 2 ANAT. trapecio [hueso].

trapezius (-šiøs) s. ANAT. trapecio [músculo].

trapezoid (træpišoi·d) s. GEOM. trapecio; trapezoide.

trapper (træ·pø^r) s. trampero, cazador de pieles.

trappings (-ingš) s. pl. jaeces, caparazón, gualdrapa. 2 adornos, atavíos.

traprock (-rak) s. GEOL. roca volcánica, basalto.

Trappist (-ist) s. trapense.

trash (træsh) s. bagazo, hojarasca, broza, basura, desecho. 2 trastos, cosa inútil. 3 tontería, patarata. 4 gentuza.

trashy (-i) adj. inútil, malo, despreciable.

trauma (tro·ma) s. MED. trauma, herida.

traumatism (-tišm) s. MED. traumatismo.

travail (træ·veil) s. afán, trabajo, pena. 2 dolores del parto.

travail (to) intr. trabajar, afanarse. 2 estar de parto.

travel (træ·vøl) s. viaje, camino: ~ bureau, agencia de viajes. 2 MEC. curso, carrera. 3 tráfico, movimiento de viajeros.

travel (to) intr. viajar. 2 MEC. moverse, trasladarse. 3 propagarse [la luz, el sonido, etc.]. 4 tr. viajar por, recorrer.

travel(l)ed (-d) adj. que ha viajado mucho. 2 frecuentado, recorrido por los viajeros.

travel(l)er (-ø^r) s. viajero, viajador: travel(l)er's check, cheque de viajero. 2 viajante. 3 MEC. carro.

travel(l)ing (-ing) adj. de viaje; que viaja. 2 MEC. móvil: ~ crane, grúa corredora.

travelogue (træ·vølog) s. conferencia sobre un viaje.

traverse (træ·vø^r s) s. travesaño. 2 cruce, paso, pasaje. 3 ARQ. galería transversal. 4 GEOM. línea transversal. 5 camino en zigzag [para una pendiente]. 6 MAR. bordada o ruta oblicua. 7 FORT. través. 8 DER. negación [de un hecho alegado]. 9 obstáculo, contrariedad, revés. 10 adj. atravesado, transversal. 11 adv. de través, transversalmente.

traverse (to) tr. cruzar, atravesar, recorrer. 2 estudiar detenidamente. 3 contrariar, oponerse a. 4 mover lateralmente. 5 DER. negar [un hecho alegado]. 6 ir y venir. 7 girar, dar vueltas.

travesty (træ·visti) s. disfraz, parodia.

travesty (to) tr. disfrazar, parodiar.

trawl (trol) *s.* especie de jábega. *2 ~ line*, palangre.

trawl (to) *tr.* pescar a la rastra o con palangre.

tray (trei) *s.* bandeja. *2* cubeta [de baúl o maleta]. *3* FOT. cubeta.

treacherous (tre·chørøs) *adj.* traidor, traicionero, falso, engañoso.

treachery (tre·chøri) *s.* traición. *2* deslealtad, perfidia, alevosía.

treacle (trī·køl) *s.* melado. *2* fig. melosidad.

tread (tred) *s.* paso, pisada. *2* huella, rastro. *3* huella [del peldaño]. *4* suela [del zapato]. *5* superficie de rodadura [de la rueda, el neumático, etc.]. *6* galladura. *7* chalaza. *8* ORN. pisa.

tread (to) *tr.* pisar, hollar. *2* pisotear. *3* trillar, andar, seguir [un camino]. *4* ORN. pisar, gallear. *5* *intr.* pisar, andar, bailar. *6 to ~ on* o *upon*, pisar, pisotear. *7 to ~ on the heels of*, pisar los talones a. ¶ Pret.: *trod;* p. p.: *trodden* o *trod.*

treadle (-øl) *s.* cárcola, pedal. *2* chalaza.

treadmill (-mil) *s.* rueda de andar. *2* especie de noria. *3* rutina fatigosa, tráfago.

treason (trī·šøn) *s.* traición.

treasonable (-abøl) *adj.* traidor, traicionero.

treasure (tre·ȳøᵣ) *s.* tesoro. *2* preciosidad.

treasure (to) *tr.* atesorar. *2* guardar como un tesoro.

treasurer (tre·ȳurøᵣ) *s.* tesorero.

treasurership (-ship) *s.* tesorería [cargo].

treasury (tre·ȳuri) *s.* tesoro, erario, hacienda; ministerio de hacienda. *2* tesorería [oficina]. *3* tesoro [de noticias, etc.].

treat (trīt) *s.* agasajo, obsequio, convite, convidada. *2* regalo, placer, deleite.

treat (to) *tr.* tratar. *2* convidar, invitar, obsequiar, agasajar. *3* *intr.* tratar, negociar: *to ~ for peace*, negociar la paz. *4 to ~ of*, tratar de.

treatise (-is) *s.* tratado [libro u opúsculo].

treatment (-mønt) *s.* trato, tratamiento [manera de tratar]. *2* MED., QUÍM., IND. tratamiento.

treaty (-i) *s.* tratado, convenio.

treble (tre·bøl) *adj.* triple, triplo, tríplice. *2* MÚS. de tiple, atiplado. *3* agudo, chillón [voz, sonido]. *4* *s.* MÚS. tiple.

treble (to) *tr.* triplicar. *2* *intr.* triplicarse.

trecento (treishe·ntou) *s.* el siglo XIV.

tree (trī) *s.* BOT. y fig. árbol: *~ of life*, árbol de la vida, tuya; *~ of the knowledge of good and evil*, árbol de la ciencia del bien y del mal; *up a tree*, en un aprieto. *2* palo, pieza de madera [esp. en composición]: *shoe ~*, horma de zapato. *3* *adj.* arborescente, arbóreo.

tree (to) *tr.* obligar [a una pers. o animal] a refugiarse en un árbol. *2* fam. acorralar. *3* poner [un zapato] en la horma.

treeless (-les) *adj.* pelado, sin árboles.

treenail (-neil) *s.* CARP. espiga, clavija.

treetop (-tap) *s.* cima, copa [de árbol].

trefoil (-foil) *s.* BOT. trébol, trifolio. *2* ARQ. trébol.

trek (trek) *s.* (Áf. del S.) viaje, migración [esp. en carromato].

trek (to) *tr.* tirar [de una carga]. *2* *intr.* viajar, emigrar en carromatos. ¶ Pret. y p. p.: *trekked;* ger.: *-kking.*

trellis (tre·lis), **trelliswork** (-uoᵣk) *s.* enrejado, espaldera. *2* glorieta, emparrado.

tremble (tre·mbøl) *s.* temblor, estremecimiento.

tremble (to) *intr.* temblar. *2* tiritar. *3* estremecerse, trepidar.

trembler (tre·mbløᵣ) *s.* temblador. *2* cuáquero. *3* ELECT. vibrador automático.

tremendous (trime·ndøs) *adj.* tremendo.

tremolo (tre·mølou) *s.* MÚS. trémolo.

tremor (tre·møᵣ) *s.* tremor, temblor, estremecimiento.

tremulous (tre·miuløs) *adj.* trémulo, tembloroso. *2* palpitante. *3* tímido, medroso.

trench (trench) *s.* foso, zanja. *2* MIL. trinchera. *3 ~ coat*, trinchera [abrigo].

trench (to) *tr.* abrir fosos o zanjas en. *2* avenar [un terreno]. *3* atrincherar. *4* *intr.* hacer surco, abrir cauce. *5* atrincherarse. *6 to ~ on* o *upon*, usurpar, invadir, bordear, rayar en.

trenchant (-ønt) *adj.* tajante, bien definido. *2* mordaz, incisivo, penetrante.

trencher (-øᵣ) *s.* trinchero, plato trinchero.

trencherman (-mæn) *s.* comilón. *2* compañero de mesa, parásito.

trend (trend) *s.* dirección, rumbo, curso, giro. *2* inclinación, tendencia.

trend (to) *intr.* dirigirse, tender.

Trent (trent) *n. pr.* GEOGR. Trento.

trepan (tripæ·n) *s.* CIR. trépano.

trepan (to) *tr.* CIR. trepanar.

trepanation (trepanei·shøn) *s.* CIR. trepanación.

trepidation (trepidei·shøn) *s.* trepidación, temblor. *2* sobresalto, alarma, agitación.

trespass (tre·spas) *s.* transgresión, infracción. *2* delito, pecado. *3* invasión, intrusión.

trespass (to) *intr.* *to ~ against*, infringir, violar; delinquir o pecar contra. *2 to ~ on* o *upon*, traspasar los límites de, entrar sin derecho en; invadir, usurpar; abusar de.

tress (tres) *s.* trenza [de pelo]; rizo, bucle.

tressed (-t) *adj.* trenzado.

trestle (tre·søl) *s.* caballete, asnilla. *2* bastidor de mesa. *3* TRESTLEWORK.

trestlework (-uøᵣk) *s.* obra de caballetes y riostras para sostener un puente, etc.

trey (trei) *s.* tres [en naipes, dados y dominó].

triad (trai·æd) *s.* tríada. *2* MÚS. acorde de tres notas.

trial (trai·al) *s.* prueba, ensayo, experimento: *~ balloon*, globo sonda; *~ trip*, viaje de prueba; *on ~*, a prueba. *2* probatura, tentativa. *3* prueba, aflicción, desgracia. *4* DER. juicio, vista de una causa.

triangle (-æŋgøl) *s.* GEOM., MÚS. triángulo. *2* escuadra [de dibujo]. *3* ASTR. Triángulo.

triangled (traiæ·ŋgøld), **triangular** (-giulaᵣ) *adj.* triangular; triangulado.

triangulate (to) (-giuleit) *tr.* triangular.

triangulation (-ei·shøn) *s.* triangulación.

Triassic (traiæ·sik) *adj.-s.* GEOL. triásico.

tribal (trai·bal) *adj.* tribal.

tribasic (traibei·sik) *adj.* QUÍM. tribásico.

tribe (traib) *s.* tribu.

tribesman (-smæn) *s.* miembro de una tribu.

tribulation (tribiulei·shøn) *s.* tribulación.

tribunal (traibiu·nal) *s.* tribunal. *2* juzgado.

tribune (tri·biun) *s.* tribuno. *2* tribuna.

tribuneship (-ship) *s.* tribunado.

tributary (tri·biuteri) *adj.-s.* tributario.

tribute (tri·biut) *s.* tributo. *2* homenaje, obsequio, elogio, encomio.

trice (trais) *s.* momento, instante: *in a ~*, en un santiamén.

trice (to) *tr.* MAR. izar y amarrar o trincar.

tricennial (traise·nial) *adj.* tricenal.

triceps (trai·seps) *adj.-s.* ANAT. triceps.

trichina (trikai·na) *s.* ZOOL. triquina.

trichinosis (trikinou·sis) *s.* MED. triquinosis.

trichotomy (traika·tømi) *s.* tricotomía.

trick (trik) *s.* treta, ardid, maña, trampa, engaño. *2* burla, travesura. *3* acción: *dirty* ~, mala pasada, jugarreta. *4* suerte [de destreza], truco, ilusión. *5* manera, arte, habilidad. *6* hábito, vicio. *7* baza [en los naipes]. *8* turno, guardia. *9 to do the* ~, servir, resolver el problema. *10 to play tricks*, hacer suertes; hacer travesuras, burlarse.

trick (to) *tr.-intr.* engañar, estafar, burlar. *2 tr.* inducir con engaño. *3 to* ~ *out* o *up*, vestir, ataviar.

trickery (-øri) *s.*engaño, superchería, malas artes.

trickish (-ish) *adj.* engañoso, trapacero. *2* habilidoso.

trickle (-øl) *s.* goteo, chorrillo, hilillo [de líquido].

trickle (to) *intr.* gotear, escurrir, destilar. *2* moverse, ir o salir de uno en uno.

trickster (-stø^r) *s.* trampista, embaucador.

tricksy (-si) *adj.* travieso, juguetón. *2* marrullero.

tricky (-i) *adj.* trapacero, marrullero. *2* delicado, difícil, intrincado.

triclinic (traikli·nik) *adj.* CRISTAL. triclínico.

triclinium (-niøm) *pl.* **-a** (-a) *s.* triclinio.

tricolo(u)r (trai·kølø^r) *adj.* tricolor. *2 s.* bandera tricolor.

tricot (tri·kou) *s.* tejido de punto.

tricuspid (traikø·spid) *adj.* tricúspide.

tricycle (trai·sikøl) *s.* triciclo.

trident (trai·dønt) *s.* tridente.

tridentate (-eit) *adj.* tridente.

triduum (tri·duøm) *s.* triduo.

tried (traid) *pret.* y *p. p.* de TO TRY. *2 adj.* probado, fiel, seguro.

triennial (traie·niøl) *adj.* trienal.

triennium (-niøm) *s.* trienio.

Triest (trie·st) *n. pr.* Trieste.

trifid (trai·fid) *adj.* BOT. trífido.

trifle (-føl) *s.* fruslería, friolera, bagatela, baratija, nadería. *2* cierto plato de dulce.

trifle (to) *intr.* bromear, burlar, hablar u obrar con frivolidad. *2* holgar. *3 to* ~ *with*, jugar con; burlarse de [uno], engañarlo. *4 tr. to* ~ *away*, malgastar [el tiempo, etc.].

trifler (-flø^r) *s.* persona frívola.

trifling (-ing) *adj.* fútil, ligero. *2* frívolo.

trifoliate(d (traifou·lieit(id) *adj.* BOT. trifoliado.

trig (trig) *adj.* arreglado, aseado. *2* peripuesto. *3* metódico; estirado. *4* sano, firme. *5 s.* calzo.

trig (to) *tr.* calzar o trabar [una rueda]. *2* acicalar, ataviar. ¶ Pret. y p. p.: *trigged;* ger.: *-gging.*

trigeminal (traidÿe·minal) *adj.-s.* ANAT. trigémino.

trigger (tri·gø^r) *s.* gatillo, disparador.

triglyph (trai·glif) *s.* ARQ. triglifo.

trigon (-gan) *s.* GEOM., ASTROL. trígono. *2* MÚS. trigón.

trigonometry (trigøna·metri) *s.* trigonometría.

trihedral (traiji·dral) *adj.* GEOM. triedro.

trihedron (-ji·drøn) *s.* GEOM. ángulo triedro.

trilingual (li·ngual) *adj.* trilingüe.

triliteral (-li·tøral) *adj.* trilítero.

trilithon (tri·lizøn) *s.* ARQUEOL. trilito.

trill (tril) *s.* FONÉT. vibración, sonido vibrante. *2* MÚS. trino. *3* quiebro, gorjeo.

trill (to) *tr.* pronunciar con vibración. *2* hacer trinos en. *3 intr.* trinar, gorjear. *4* gotear [caer gota a gota].

trillion (tri·liøn) *s.* (Ingl.) trillón. *2* (E.U.) billón.

trilobate(d (trailou·beit(id) *adj.* trilobulado.

trilocular (traila·kiula^r) *adj.* trilocular.

trilogy (tri·lødÿ) *s.* trilogía.

trim (trim) *adj.* bien arreglado; en buen estado. *2* bonito, elegante. *3* pulcro, aseado, acicalado. *4 s.* disposición, condición, estado. *5* buen estado.

6 adorno, aderezo. *7* traje, vestido. *8* MAR. asiento, disposición de un buque para navegar. *9* MAR. orientación [de las velas].

trim (to) *tr.* arreglar, disponer, adaptar. *2* cortar, recortar [arreglar cortando], atusar, podar. *3* CARP. alisar, desbastar. *4* despabilar, arreglar [una luz]. *5* pulir, componer; adornar, ribetear, guarnecer. *6* MAR. equilibrar [pesos]: *to* ~ *the hold*, estibar. *7* MAR. orientar las velas; disponer para la navegación. *8* reprender, castigar. *9 intr.* mantenerse neutral, nadar entre dos aguas. ¶ Pret. y p. p.: *trimmed;* ger.: *-mming.*

trimester (trai·mestø^r) *s.* trimestre.

trimestr(i)al (-tr(i)al) *adj.* trimestral.

trimmer (tri·mø^r) *s.* arreglador; guarnecedor. *2* máquina de recortar. *3* pastelero, oportunista. *4* RADIO. condensador de compensación.

trimming (-ing) *s.* acción de TO TRIM. *2* COST. guarnición, ribete, orla, franja. *3* reprensión, paliza. *4 pl.* adornos, accesorios. *5* recortes.

trine (train) *adj.* trino, triple. *2* (con may.) Trinidad.

tringle (tri·ngøl) *s.* vara de cortina. *2* ARQ. listel.

Trinitarian (trini·teriøn) *adj.-s.* trinitario. *2* que cree en la Trinidad. *3 adj.* (con min.) trino.

trinity (tri·niti) *s.* trinca, trío. *2* (con may.) Trinidad.

trinket (tri·nkit) *s.* joya, dije. *2* baratija.

trinomial (trinou·miøl) *adj.* de tres nombres o términos. *2 s.* MAT. trinomio.

trio (tri·ou) *s.* trío.

triode (trai·oud) *s.* RADIO. triodo.

trip (trip) *s.* viaje, excursión. *2* paso ágil o vivo. *3* tropezón, traspié. *4* tropiezo, desliz. *5* zancadilla. *6* MEC. trinquete, escape, disparo.

trip (to) *intr.* andar ligero, saltar, brincar. *2* tropezar, dar un traspié; equivocarse. *3 tr.* hacer tropezar o caer, echar la zancadilla a. *4* coger en falta, en error, etc. *5* MEC. soltar, disparar. *6* MAR. levar [el ancla]; inclinar [una verga]. ¶ Pret. y p. p.: *tripped;* ger.: *-pping.*

tripartite (trai·pa^{r}tait) *s.* tripartito.

tripe (traip) *s.* COC. tripas, callos. *2* fig. cosa sin valor; tontería. *3* ΙΕJ. tripe.

trip-hammer *s.* martillo pilón, martinete de fragua.

triphthong (tri·fzang) *s.* triptongo.

tripinnate (trai·pineit) *adj.* BOT. tripinado.

triple (tri·pøl) *adj.* triple, triplo, tresdoble.

triple (to) *tr.* triplicar, tresdoblar.

triplet (tri·plit) *s.* trinca, terno. *2* trillizo. *3* MÚS. tresillo. *4* LIT. terceto.

triplex (trai·pleks) *adj.* triple, tríplice. *2* MEC. de triple efecto.

triplicate (tri·plikit) *adj.-s.* triplicado.

triplicate (to) (-keit) *tr.* triplicar.

tripod (trai·pad) *s.* trípode.

Tripolitan (tripa·litan) *adj.-s.* tripolitano.

tripper (tri·pø^r) *s.* (Ingl.) excursionista, turista. *2* saltarín. *3* tropezador. *4* MEC. disparador.

tripping (-ing) *adj.* ágil, ligero, vivo. *2* MEC. disparador.

triptych (tri·ptik) *s.* B. ART. tríptico.

triptyque (triptı·k) *s.* AUTO. tríptico.

trireme (trai·rim) *s.* trirreme.

Trisagion (trisei·giøn) *s.* ECLES. Trisagio.

trisect (to) (traise·kt) *tr.* trisecar.

trisection (-kshøn) *s.* trisección.

Tristram (tri·stram) *n. pr.* Tristán.

trisyllable (traisi·labøl) *s.* palabra trisílaba.

trite (trait) *adj.* gastado, trillado, trivial.

triton (trai·tøn) s. MIT., ZOOL. tritón.
tritone (trai·toun) s. MÚS. trítono.
triturate (to) (tri·chøreit) tr. triturar.
triumph (trai·ømf) s. triunfo, victoria. 2 júbilo, exultación.
triumph (to) intr. triunfar [recibir el triunfo]. 2 triunfar, vencer. 3 exultar, gozarse [en].
triumphal (traiø·mfal) adj. triunfal.
triumphant (-fant) adj. triunfante. 2 victorioso.
triumvir (-vø^r) s. triunviro.
triumvirate (-virit) s. triunvirato.
triune (trai·un) adj. TEOL. trino y uno.
trivet (tri·vit) s. trébedes, trípode.
trivial (tri·vial) adj. trivial [del trivio]. 2 trivial, fútil, insignificante, frívolo, vulgar.
triviality (triviæ·liti) s. trivialidad, futilidad, frivolidad, insignificancia.
trivium (tri·viøm) s. trivio [las tres artes liberales].
trocar (trou·ka^r) s. CIR. trocar.
trochaic(al (trokei·k(al) adj.-s. trocaico.
trochanter (trokæ·ntø^r) s. ANAT., ENT. trocánter.
trochee (trou·ki) s. troqueo.
trochoid (trou·koid) adj. trocoideo. 2 s. GEOM. trocoide.
trod (tra·d) pret. y p. p. de TO TREAD.
trodden (tra·døn) p. p. de TO TREAD.
troglodyte (tra·glødait) s. troglodita. 2 ZOOL. mono antropoide.
trogon (trou·gan) s. ORN. ave de la familia del quetzal.
troika (troi·ka) s. troica.
Trojan (trou·dÿan) adj.-s. troyano. 2 s. persona valiente, esforzada.
troll (troul) s. MÚS. especie de canon. 2 repetición, rutina. 3 sedal y anzuelo rotatorios. 8 MIT. gnomo; gigante.
troll (to) tr. cantar por turno. 2 cantar, celebrar. 3 recitar sonora o rápidamente. 4 pescar con anzuelo desde un bote en movimiento. 5 intr. voltear, girar. 6 corretear. 7 cantar alegremente.
trolley (tra·li) s. polea del trole: ~ bus, trolebús; ~ pole, trole. 2 carrito, carretilla. 3 carrito aéreo.
trollop (tra·løp) s. pazpuerca. 2 ramera.
trombone (tra·mboun) s. MÚS. trombón [instrumento].
trombonist (-ist) s. trombón [músico].
troop (trup) s. tropa, cuadrilla, banda, tropel. 2 bandada, manada. 3 MIL. escuadrón [de caballería]. 4 pl. tropas, soldados.
troop (to) intr. atroparse, ir en grupo, en tropel: to ~ away, to ~ off, alejarse, retirarse en tropel.
trooper (-ø^r) s. soldado de caballería; su caballo. 2 MAR. transporte de tropas [buque].
troopial (tru·pial) s. TROUPIAL.
trope (troup) s. RET. tropo.
trophy (trou·fi) s. trofeo.
tropic (tra·pik) adj. tropical. 2 BIOL. del tropismo. 3 adj.-s. ASTR., GEOGR. trópico.
tropical (tra·pik(al) adj. tropical. 2 RET. trópico.
◄tropism (trou·pišm) s. BIOL. tropismo.
troposphere (tra·pøsfi^r) s. troposfera.
trot (trat) s. trote: at a ~, al trote. 2 niñito.
trot (to) intr. trotar. 2 tr. hacer trotar.
troth (troz) s. fe, fidelidad; verdad, veracidad. 2 ant. esponsales.
trotline (-lain) s. especie de palangre.
trotter (tra·tø^r) s. trotador, trotón. 2 COC. pie, mano [de carnero, cerdo, etc.].
troubadour (tru·bado^r) s. trovador.
trouble (trø·bøl) s. perturbación, desorden, agita-

ción, inquietud. 2 pena, congoja; apuro, dificultad: to be in ~, estar en un apuro. 3 molestia, incomodidad, engorro. 4 inconveniente. 5 molestia, trabajo, pena [que se toma uno]: to go to the ~ to, to take the ~ to, molestarse en, tomarse la molestia de. 6 avería, accidente [en un mecanismo]: ~ shooting, localización de averías. 7 MED. afección, desarreglo, trastorno: lung ~, afección pulmonar.
trouble (to) tr. turbar, perturbar. 2 revolver, agitar, enturbiar. 3 inquietar, afligir, atribular. 4 incomodar, molestar. 5 intr.-ref. preocuparse, apurarse. 6 molestarse, tomarse trabajo o molestia.
troublemaker (-meikø^r) s. agitador, alborotador.
troublesome (-søm) adj. molesto, gravoso, dificultoso, pesado, fatigoso. 2 enojoso, incómodo, fastidioso. 3 inquieto, enredador.
troublous (trø·bløs) adj. agitado, revuelto.
trough (trof) s. comedero; abrevadero. 2 artesa, batea, cubeta. 3 seno o depresión entre dos olas, montañas, etc. 4 canalón de tejado.
trounce (to) (trauns) tr. pegar, zurrar. 2 derrotar.
troupe (trup) s. TEAT. compañía.
trouper (-ø^r) s. miembro de una compañía teatral. 2 actor veterano.
troupial (tru·pial) s. ORN. trupial.
trousers (trau·šø^rs) s. pl. pantalones, calzones.
trousseau (trousou·) s. ajuar de novia.
trout (traut) s. ICT. trucha.
trouvère (truve·^r) s. trovero.
trowel (trau·øl) s. ALBAÑ. trulla, llana; paleta, palustre. 2 JARD. desplantador.
trowel (to) tr. alisar o aplicar con llana.
Troy (troi) n. pr. GEOGR. Troya.
troy, troy-weight s. sistema de pesos para oro, plata y drogas medicinales cuya unidad es la libra de 12 onzas [373 gramos].
truancy (tru·ansi) s. acción o costumbre de hacer novillos; ociosidad.
truant (-ant) s. tunante, holgazán: to play ~, hacer novillos. 2 adj. ocioso; perezoso, errabundo.
truant (to) intr. hacer novillos; holgazanear.
truce (trus) s. tregua.
truck (trøk) s. carretilla [carro de mano]. 2 rueda pequeña y fuerte. 3 carro grande, camión: ~ driver, camionero. 4 FERROC. (Ingl.) furgón; batea. 5 cambio, trueque, trato. 6 efectos para trocar o vender. 7 artículos sin valor; desecho. 8 pl. trucos [juego].
truck (to) tr. trocar, traficar. 2 pagar los salarios en especie. 3 transportar en camión.
truckage (-idÿ) s. camionaje.
trucker (-ø^r) s. carretero, camionero.
truckle (trø·køl) s. ruedecita. 2 ~ bed, TRUNDLE BED.
truckle (to) intr. rodar sobre ruedecitas. 2 someterse servilmente.
truckman (trø·kmæn) s. carretero, camionero. 2 chamarilero.
truculence (trø·kiuløns) s. truculencia, crueldad.
truculent (- lønt) adj. truculento.
trudge (trødÿ) s. caminata; marcha penosa.
trudge (to) intr.-tr. andar, caminar, recorrer [esp. con fatiga o esfuerzo].
true (tru) adj. verdadero, cierto, real: ~ ribs, ANAT., costillas verdaderas; it is true, es cierto, es verdad. 2 verídico, veraz. 3 fiel, leal. 4 exacto, fiel, correcto: ~ copy, copia fiel. 5 puro, legítimo, genuino. 6 adv. TRULY.
true (to) tr. arreglar, corregir, rectificar.
true-blue adj. fiel, constante, leal.

true-born *adj.* legítimo, verdadero, de nacimiento.
true-bred *adj.* de casta legítima.
true-hearted *adj.* sincero, leal.
truelove (-lav) *s.* fiel amante. *2* amado, amada: ~ *knot*, lazada, lazo.
truffle (trø·føl) *s.* BOT. trufa.
truffled (-d) *adj.* trufado.
truism (tru·išm) *s.* verdad manifiesta; perogrullada.
truly (tru·li) *adv.* verdaderamente, realmente, en verdad. *2* sinceramente. *3* fielmente. *4* exactamente, correctamente, debidamente. *5* *yours (very) truly*, su afectísimo o su seguro servidor.
trump (trømp) *s.* NAIPES triunfo; palo de triunfo: ~ *card*, triunfo [naipe]; fig. valioso recurso; *no* ~, sin triunfo. *2* poét. trompeta.
trump (to) *tr.* triunfar, fallar, jugar triunfo. *2 to* ~ *up*, inventar, forjar.
trumpery (trø·mpøri) *s.* oropel, relumbrón; vaciedades, tonterías. *2* ant. engaño, fraude.
trumpet (trø·mpit) *s.* trompeta, clarín: ~ *blast*, trompetazo. *2* sonido de la trompeta. *3* barrito, berrido [del elefante]. *4* zumbido [del mosquito].
trumpet (to) *tr.* pregonar a son de trompeta. *2* gritar, decir gritando. *3* abocardar. *4* intr. trompetear. *5* berrear [el elefante].
trumpeter (-ø^r) *s.* trompetero, trompeta. *2* pregonero. *3* ORN. agamí.
truncate (to) *tr.* truncar, troncar. *2* mutilar. *3* abreviar.
truncheon (trø·nchøn) *s.* garrote, porra, cachiporra. *2* porra de policía.
truncheon (to) *tr.* golpear con cachiporra.
trundle (trø·ndøl) *s.* ruedecilla [esp. de mueble]. *2* carretilla de ruedas pequeñas. *3 trundle* o ~ *bed*, cama baja con ruedas.
trundle (to) *tr.* hacer rodar. *2* intr. rodar.
trunk (trønk) *s.* tronco [de árbol; del cuerpo; de una familia, etc.]. *2* FERROC. línea principal. *3* cofre, baúl; portaequipaje [de automóvil]. *4* trompa de elefante. *5* pl. pantalones cortos de deporte. *6* adj. TELÉF. interurbano: ~ *call*, conferencia interurbana.
trunkfish (-fish) *s.* ICT. pez cofre.
trunnion (trø·ñøn) *s.* ARTILL. muñón.
truss (trøs) *s.* ING. armazón o armadura de sostén, viga de celosía. *2* mazorca. *3* CIR. braguero. *4* haz [de paja].
truss (to) *tr.* atar, liar. *2* recoger, empaquetar. *3* COC. atar [un ave] para asarla. *4* ARQ., ING. sostener; atirantar.
trust (trøst) *s.* confianza, fe [en una pers. o cosa]; esperanza. *2* depósito, cargo, cuidado, custodia; *Trust Company*, Banco de depósitos. *3* DER. fideicomiso. *4* COM. crédito: *to sell on* ~, vender a crédito. *5* trust, asociación de empresas.
trust (to) *tr.* confiar en, tener confianza o fe en. *2* confiar [algo] al cargo, custodia, etc., de alguno. *3* confiar, esperar [que]. *4* COM. hacer crédito a, fiar a. *5* intr. confiar, esperar. *6* COM. fiar.
trustee (trøsti·) *s.* fideicomisario, fiduciario, depositario; administrador legal. *2 board of trustees*, patronato, consejo [de una universidad].
trustful (trø·stful) *adj.* confiado.
trustworthy (-uø^rdi) *adj.* fiable, confiable, fidedigno, seguro.
trusty (-i) *adj.* fiel, leal, honrado, fidedigno. *2* firme, fuerte, seguro. *3* confiado. *4* s. persona honrada, digna de confianza.

truth (truz) *s.* verdad: *in* ~, en verdad. *2* exactitud, realidad. *3* veracidad. *4* fidelidad, constancia.
truthful (-ful) *adj.* veraz, verídico. *2* verdadero, exacto.
truthless (-lis) *adj.* falso; fementido.
try (trai) *s.* prueba, ensayo. *2* tentativa.
try (to) *tr.* probar a, intentar, tratar de. *2* probar, ensayar, hacer la prueba de: *to* ~ *on*, probarse [una prenda]. *3* poner a prueba, exasperar, cansar: *to* ~ *someone's patience*, poner a prueba la paciencia de uno. *4* DER. juzgar [a uno]; ver [una causa o litigio]. *5* CARP., MEC. ajustar, acabar. *6 to* ~ *out*, probar, someter a prueba. *7* intr. probar, esforzarse. ¶ Pret. y p. p.: *tried*.
trying (-ing) *adj.* de prueba. *2* molesto, irritante, fatigoso.
tryout (-aut) *s.* prueba [que se hace de una persona o cosa].
Tsar (tsa^r) *s.* zar.
tub (tøb) *s.* tina, dornajo, batea. *2* bañera, baño. *4* cuñete, barrilito.
tub (to) *tr.* poner en tina. ¶ Pret. y p. p.: *tubbed;* ger.: *tubbing.*
tuba (tiu·ba) *s.* MÚS. tuba.
tubage (tiu·bidÿ) *s.* CIR. intubación.
tubby (tø·bi) *adj.* en forma de cubo, rechoncho.
tube (tiub) *s.* tubo: *inner* ~, cámara de neumático. *2* caño, cañuto. *3* ANAT. conducto, tubo. *4* RADIO. lámpara, válvula. *5 tube* o ~ *railway*, metro, ferrocarril subterráneo.
tube (to) *tr.* proveer de tubos. *2* entubar, conducir por tubos. *3* dar forma de tubo.
tubercle (tiu·bø^rkøl) *s.* ANAT., ZOOL., MED. tubérculo. *2* raíz tuberosa.
tubercular (tiubø·^rkula^r) *adj.* tuberculoso, parecido a un tubérculo. *2* adj.-s. tuberculoso.
tuberculosis (tiubø^rkiuløu·sis) *s.* MED. tuberculosis.
tuberculous (tiubø·^rkiuløs) *adj.* MED. tuberculoso.
tuberose (tiu·børouš) *s.* BOT. tuberosa, nardo.
tuberosity (tiubøra·siti) *s.* tuberosidad.
tuberous (tiu·børøs) *adj.* tuberoso.
tubing (tiu·bing) *s.* tubería, material para tubos.
tubular (tiu·biula^r) *adj.* tubular.
tubulate (d (tiu·biuleit(id) *adj.* tubular. *2* provisto de tubos.
tuck (tøk) *s.* alforza, pliegue, lorza. *2* ENCUAD. tapa con cartera. *3* pop. buena comida, golosinas.
tuck (to) *tr.* alforzar, recoger, arremangar. | Gralte. con *up*. *2* envolver, arropar. | Con *in, up,* etc. *3* meter: *to* ~ *in*, remeter bien [la ropa de la cama, etc.]; pop. engullir; *to* ~ *away*, esconder.
Tuesday (tiu·šdi) *s.* martes.
tufa (tiu·fa) *s.* toba, tufo.
tufaceous (tiufei·šøs) *adj.* tobáceo, toboso.
tuft (tøft) *s.* penacho, cresta, moño, copete, tupé. *2* mechón, borla. *3* manojo; grupo [de plantas]; mata espesa.
tuft (to) *tr.* empenachar. *2* adornar con borlas.
tug (tøg) *s.* tirón, estirón; lucha, forcejeo: ~ *of war*, DEP. juego de la cuerda. *2* tirante [guarnición]; cuerda [para arrastrar]. *3* remolcador.
tug (to) *tr.* tirar de, arrastrar. *2* halar, remolcar. *3* intr. tirar con fuerza, trabajar con esfuerzo.
tuition (tiui·šøn) *s.* enseñanza, instrucción. *2* lo que se paga por la enseñanza.
tulip (tiu·lip) *s.* BOT. tulipán. *2* BOT. ~ *tree*, tulipero.
tulipwood (-wud) *s.* palo de rosa [árbol y madera].
tulle (tul) *s.* tul.
tumble (tø·mbøl) *s.* caída, tumbo, vuelco, voltereta. *2* desorden, confusión.

tumble (to) *intr.* voltear, dar volteretas. *2* caerse, derrumbarse; dejarse caer. *3* hundirse, desplomarse. *4* correr, precipitarse. *5* agitarse, revolverse, revolcarse. *6 to* ~ *into, on* o *upon*, tropezar con, dar con, encontrar. *7 to* ~ *to*, comprender, entender, percatarse. *8 tr.* hacer caer, derribar, tumbar. *9* volcar. *10* desarreglar, trastornar. *11* zarandear, empujar de un lado a otro. *12* secar, pulir, etc., en un tambor giratorio.

tumblebug (-bøg) *s.* ENT. escarabajo pelotero.

tumble-down *adj.* destartalado, ruinoso.

tumbler (-ø^r) *s.* vaso [para beber], cubilete. *2* volteador, volatinero. *3* dominguillo. *4* tambor giratorio [para secar ropa, pulir metales, etc.]. *5* ORN. pichón volteador.

tumbrel, tumbril (tø·mbrøl) *s.* carro, carreta. *2* carro de artillería.

tumefaction (tiumifæ·kshøn) *s.* tumefacción.

tumefy (to) (tiu·mifai) *tr.* hinchar, producir tumefacción. *2 intr.* hincharse. ¶ CONJUG. pret. y p. p.: *tumefied.*

tumid (tiu·mid) *adj.* túmido, hinchado.

tummy (-mi) *s.* fam. estómago.

tumo(u)r (-mø^r) *s.* MED. tumor.

tumular (-miula^r) *adj.* tumulario.

tumult (-mølt) *s.* tumulto.

tumultuary (tiumø·lchueri) *adj.* tumultuario.

tumultuous (-chuøs) *adj.* tumultuoso.

tumulus (tiu·miuløs) *s.* túmulo [montecillo].

tun (tøn) *s.* tonel, cuba.

tun (to) *tr.* entonelar, encubar.

tuna (tu·na) *s.* BOT. tuna, higo chumbo. *2* ICT. atún.

tunable (tiu·nabøl) *adj.* afinable, templable. *2* armonioso, melodioso, agradable.

tune (tiun) *s.* aire, melodía, canción. *2* MÚS. afinación: *out of* ~, desafinado, destemplado. *3* concordancia, armonía: *in* ~ *with*, a tono con. *4* tono [con que se habla], actitud. *5* humor, disposición.

tune (to) *tr.* templar, afinar, acordar. *2* cantar, entonar. *3* ajustar, adaptar. *4* RADIO *to* ~ *in*, sintonizar. *5 to* ~ *up*, acordar [instrumentos]; poner a punto [un motor]. *6 intr.* armonizar.

tuneful (-ful) *adj.* armonioso, melodioso.

tuneless (-lis) *adj.* disonante, discordante.

tuner (-ø^r) *s.* afinador, templador. *2* ajustador. *3* RADIO. sintonizador.

tungsten (tøn·gstøn) *s.* QUÍM. tungsteno, volframio.

tunic (tiu·nik) *s.* túnica [vestidura]; blusa, guerrera. *2* ANAT., ZOOL., BOT. túnica.

Tunicata (tiunikei·ta) *s. pl.* ZOOL. tunicados.

tunicle (tiu·nikøl) *s.* ECLES. tunicela.

tuning (tiu·ning) *s.* MÚS. afinación, templadura. *2* RADIO. sintonización. *3 adj.* que sirve para afinar o sintonizar: ~ *fork*, diapasón; ~ *hammer*, ~ *key*, llave de afinador; ~ *coil*, bobina sintonizadora.

Tunis (tu·nis) *n. pr.* GEOGR. Túnez [ciudad].

Tunisian (tuni·shan) *adj.-s.* tunecí, tunecino.

tunnel (tø·nøl) *s.* túnel. *2* MIN. galería, socavón.

tunnel (to) *tr.* abrir un túnel a través de o debajo de; excavar. *2 intr.* abrir túnel o galería. ¶ Pret. y p. p.: *tunnel(l)ed;* ger.: *-l(l)ing.*

tunny (tø·ni) *s.* ICT. atún.

turban (tø·^{r}ban) *s.* turbante.

turbary (tiu·^{r}bæri) *s.* turbera.

turbid (tø·^{r}bid) *adj.* turbio, túrbido, turbulento.

turbine (tø·^{r}bin) *s.* MEC. turbina.

turbojet (tø·^{r}boudÿet) *s.* turborreactor.

turbomotor (-moutø^r) *s.* turbomotor.

turbot (tø·^{r}bot) *s.* ICT. rodaballo, rombo.

turbulence, -cy (tø·^{r}biuløns, -si) *s.* turbulencia, alboroto, tumulto.

turbulent (-ønt) *adj.* turbulento, agitado, tempestuoso. *2* levantisco, revoltoso.

tureen (tiuri·n) *s.* sopera. *2* salsera.

turf (tø·^{r}f) *s.* césped; tepe. *2* turba. *3 the* ~, el hipódromo; las carreras de caballos.

turf (to) *tr.* encespedar.

turfy (tø·^{r}fi) *adj.* abundante en césped o turba.

turgescence (tø·^{r}dÿe·søns) *s.* turgencia. *2* fig. hinchazón, pomposidad.

turgescent (-sønt), **turgid** (tø·^{r}dÿid) *adj.* turgente. *2* hinchado, ampuloso, pomposo.

turion (tiu·riøn) *s.* BOT. turión.

Turk (tø·^{r}k) *s.* turco, otomano.

Turkestan (tø·^{r}kø·stan) *n. pr.* GEOGR. el Turquestán.

Turkey (tø·^{r}k) *n. pr.* GEOGR. Turquía.

turkey *s.* ORN. pavo, gallipavo, *guajolote. *2* ORN. ~ *buzzard*, aura, gallinazo, *zopilote.

Turkish (-ish) *adj.* turco, turquí: ~ *blue*, azul turquí: ~ *towel*, toalla rusa. *2* ANAT. ~ *saddle*, silla turca. *3 s.* idioma turco.

Turk's-head *s.* escobón, deshollinador.

turmalin(e (tu·^{r}malin) *s.* TOURMALIN.

turmeric (tø·^{r}merik) *s.* BOT. cúrcuma.

turmoil (tø·^{r}moil) *s.* tumulto, agitación, alboroto, confusión, barahúnda.

turmoil (to) *tr.* agitar, inquietar, trastornar.

turn (tø·^{r}n) *s.* vuelta, giro, revolución. *2* vuelta, paseo. *3* recodo, vuelta; cambío, variación, desviación: ~ *of life*, FISIOL. menopausia. *4* viraje. *5* sobresalto, impresión. *6* aspecto, sesgo, giro, curso: *to take another* ~, tomar otro sesgo, cambiar de aspecto. *7* forma, hechura, estilo. *8* giro [de la frase]. *9* acción, comportamiento [respecto de otra pers.]: *friendly* ~, *good* ~, favor, servicio; *bad* ~, *ill* ~, mala pasada, jugarreta, trastada. *10* turno, tanda: *to take turns,* turnarse. *11* acto de destreza. *12* MÚS. grupeto. *13* COC. *to a turn*, en su punto.

turn (to) *tr.* volver, dar vuelta a; voltear, hacer rodar. *2* tornear [labrar al torno]. *3* formar, moldear, hacer, pergeñar. *4* volver, dirigir, encaminar. *5* remover [la tierra]. *6* trastornar, revolver: *to* ~ *the brain of,* trastornar el juicio a; *to* ~ *the stomach,* revolver el estómago. *7* volver del revés: *to* ~ *coat,* fig. volver casaca. *8* desviar, apartar, disuadir. *9* encauzar, dirigir. *10* aplicar, destinar. *11* rechazar, expulsar. *12* doblar [un cabo, una esquina], rebasar, dar la vuelta a: *to* ~ *the corner,* doblar la esquina. *13* cambiar, transformar, traducir. *14* poner [pálido, enfermo, etc.]. *15* encorvar, doblar, torcer. *16 to* ~ *a deaf ear,* hacerse sordo. *17 to* ~ *an honest penny,* ganar dinero honradamente. *18 to* ~ *around,* dar vuelta o la vuelta; hacer girar. *19 to* ~ *aside,* desviar. *20 to* ~ *away,* despedir, echar; desviar. *21 to* ~ *back,* volver atrás; devolver. *22 to* ~ *bridle,* volver grupas. *23 to* ~ *down,* poner boca abajo; bajar [el gas]. *24 to* ~ *on,* abrir [una llave o espita]; dar [la luz, el gas, etc.]; poner, abrir [la radio]. *25 to* ~ *out,* echar, expulsar, arrojar; producir, hacer; volver del revés; apagar [la luz]. *26 to* ~ *over,* volcar, invertir; revolver; revolver en la mente; traspasar, transferir; volver una hoja. *27 to* ~ *the scale (s,* fig. pesar, ser decisivo. *28 to* ~ *the tables,* volver las tornas. *29 to* ~ *to account, advantage* o *profit,* aprovechar, sacar partido de. *30 to* ~ *up,* volver, doblar o dirigir hacia arriba, subir [el cuello]; poner

más fuerte [la radio]; *to* ~ *up one's nose at*, desdeñar, hacer ascos a.
31 intr. girar, rodar, dar vueltas, voltear. *32* volverse [volver el cuerpo, el rostro]. *33* desviarse, torcer, virar. *34* dirigirse, tomar una dirección. *35* volverse, ponerse, hacerse: *to* ~ *pale*, ponerse pálido, palidecer. *36* volverse [contra]. *37* girar, versar [sobre]. *38* apartar la vista, la atención. *39* caer [la balanza]. *40* agriarse, torcerse, cortarse [un líquido]. *41* torcerse, doblarse. *42 to* ~ *about* o *around*, volver la cara, volverse, dar una vuelta. *43 to* ~ *aside*, desviarse. *44 to* ~ *away*, alejarse; volver la cara, la espalda. *45 to* ~ *from*, apartarse de, huir de. *46 to* ~ *in*, entrar; irse a la cama, acostarse. *47 to* ~ *into*, entrar en; volverse, convertirse en. *48 to* ~ *off*, desviarse, torcer. *49 to* ~ *out*, salir, resultar: *to* ~ *out badly*, salir mal; *to* ~ *out well*, salir bien. *50 to* ~ *over*, dar vueltas, revolverse; volcar [un vehículo]. *51 to* ~ *to*, tender, dirigirse a; ponerse, aplicarse a; acudir, recurrir a; volverse hacia; redundar en. *52 to* ~ *turtle*, zozobrar. *53 to* ~ *up*, estar vuelto hacia arriba; aparecer de pronto, reaparecer. *54 to* ~ *upside down*, volcarse, zozobrar.
turnbuckle (-bøkøl) *s.* tornillo tensor. *2* tarabilla [para tener abierta una ventana].
turncoat (-kout) *s.* POL. desertor, renegado.
turndown (-daun) *adj.* doblado hacia abajo, vuelto [cuello, etc.].
turner (-ø^r) *s.* tornero, torneador.
turning (-ing) *s.* giro, vuelta. *2* viraje. *3* revuelta, recodo, esquina. *4* tornería. *5 pl.* torneaduras. *6* piezas torneadas. *7 adj.* giratorio. *8* ~ *point*, punto crucial o decisivo, crisis.
turnip (tø·^{r}nip) *s.* BOT. nabo. *2* BOT. colinabo.
turnkey (tø·^{r}nki) *s.* carcelero, llavero de cárcel.
turnout (tø·^{r}naut) *s.* salida [acción]. *2* reunión, concurrencia. *3* apartadero [en un camino o vía férrea]. *4* producción [de una fábrica, etc.]. *5* acabado, presentación. *6* vestido, atuendo.
turnover (-ouvø^r) *adj.* doblado o vuelto hacia abajo. *2 s.* vuelco. *3* voltereta. *4* vuelta, parte doblada sobre otra. *5* empanadilla. *6* COC. estrelladera, pala. *7* cambio completo. *8* reorganización, cambio [de personal]. *9* COM. giro, movimiento. *10* COM. ciclo de compra y venta.
turnpike (-paik) *s.* barrera o camino de portazgo. *2* (E.U.) gran autopista de peaje.
turnspit (-spit) *s.* el que da vueltas al asador.
turnstile (-stail) *s.* torniquete [en un paso].
turnstone (-stoun) *s.* ORN. revuelvepiedras.
turntable (-teibøl) *s.* FERROC. placa giratoria. *2* disco giratorio del microscopio o del fonógrafo.
turpentine (tø·^{r}pentain) *s.* trementina.
turpitude (tø·^{r}pitiud) *s.* vileza, depravación.
turquoise (tø·^{r}kois) *s.* MINER. turquesa.
turret (tø·rit) *s.* torrecilla. *2* MAR. torre blindada.
turtle (tø·^{r}tøl) *s.* ZOOL. tortuga [esp. de mar]. *2 adj.* de tortuga: ~ *shell*, carey.
turtledove (-døv) *s.* ORN. tórtola.
Tuscan (tø·skan) *adj.-s.* toscano.
Tuscany (tø·skani) *n. pr.* GEOGR. Toscana.
tusk (tøsk) *s.* colmillo, defensa [de elefante, jabalí, morsa, narval, etc.].
tussle (tø·søl) *s.* pelea. *2* discusión, agarrada.
tussle (to) *intr.* luchar, pelear, forcejear.
tussock (tø·søk) *s.* mechón, penacho. *2* macizo de hierba espesa.
tutelage (tiu·tølidӯ) *s.* tutela.
tutelar (-la^r) *adj.* tutelar.

tutelary (-leri) *adj.* TUTELAR. *2 s.* divinidad o santo tutelar.
tutor (tiu·tø^r) *s.* preceptor, ayo. *2* tutor, curador.
tutor (to) *tr.* enseñar, instruir. *2* ser tutor de. *3* disciplinar, dominar. *4 intr.* ser preceptor, dar lecciones particulares.
tutorial (-ial) *adj.* preceptoral. *2* tutelar.
tutorship (-ship) *s.* preceptoría. *2* tutoría.
tuxedo (tuksi·dou) *s.* (E.U.) traje de esmoquing.
tuyere (tuiye·^{r}) *s.* tobera, alcribís.
twaddle (tua·døl) *s.* charla, palabreo, palabrería.
twaddle (to) *intr.* charlar, decir tonterías.
twain (tuein) *adj.-s.* poét. dos.
twang (tuæng) *s.* sonido vibrante, como el de una cuerda punteada. *2* gangueo, tonillo nasal.
twang (to) *tr.* puntear [una cuerda, un instrumento]. *2* decir gangueando. *3 intr.* producir un sonido vibrante; sonar [una cuerda]. *4* ganguear.
tweak (tuik) *s.* pellizco retorcido.
tweed (tuid) *s.* TEJ. cierto paño de lana o mezcla y de dos o más colores. *2 pl.* ropa hecha de este paño. *3 adj.* hecho de este paño.
tweedle (to) (-øl) *intr.-tr.* cantar, silbar. *2* tocar un instrumento. *3 tr.* engaitar.
tweet (tuit) *s.* pío, gorjeo [de pájaro].
tweezers (tui·sø^{r}š) *s. pl.* pinzas, tenacillas [para objetos menudos].
twelfth (tuelf) *adj.* duodécimo, doceno, doce. *2 adj.-s.* duodécimo. *3 s.* doce [del mes]. *4* MÚS. duodécima.
Twelfth-day *s.* día de Reyes, Epifanía.
Twelfth-night *s.* noche de Reyes.
twelve (tue·lv) *adj.-s.* doce: ~ *o'clock;* las doce.
twelvemonth (-manz) *s.* año, doce meses.
twentieth (tue·ntiiz) *adj.-s.* vigésimo, veintavo. *2 adj.* veinte [capítulo, etc.]. *3 s.* veinte [del mes].
twenty (tue·nti) *adj.-s.* veinte.
twice (tuais) *adv.* dos veces. *2* el doble: ~ *as much*, ~ *as many*, el doble.
twiddle (to) (tui·døl) *tr.* jugar, entretenerse con. *2* hacer dar vueltas [esp. a los pulgares para entretenerse]. *3 intr.* entretenerse, estar ocioso.
twig (tuig) *s.* BOT. ramita. *2* varita, vergueta. *3* ANAT. pequeña ramificación.
twilight (tuai·lait) *s.* crepúsculo, media luz: *at* ~, entre dos luces. *2 adj.* crepuscular; débilmente iluminado.
twill (tuil) *s.* tela cruzada o asargada.
twill (to) *tr.* TEJ. cruzar, asargar.
twin (tuin) *s.* gemelo, mellizo. *2 pl.* ASTR. Géminis. *3 adj.* gemelo. *4* doble, de dos.
twin (to) *tr.* juntar, emparejar, unir [dos cosas].
twine (tuain) *s.* cordel, bramante, guita. *2* abrazo, enroscadura, entrelazamiento.
twine (to) *tr.* torcer [hilos, hebras, etc., juntos]; tejer. *2* enroscar, enlazar, abrazar. *4 intr.* entrelazarse. *4* enroscarse. *5* serpentear.
twin-engined *adj.* AVIA. bimotor.
twinge (tuindӯ) *s.* punzada, dolor agudo. *2* remordimiento.
twinge (to) *tr.* punzar, causar dolor agudo. *2 intr.* sentir una punzada, un dolor agudo.
twinkle (tui·nkøl) *s.* titilación, centelleo, destello. *2* parpadeo. *3* instante.
twinkle (to) *intr.* titilar, centellear, destellar, chispear. *2* parpadear; guiñar. *3 tr.* hacer centellear. *4* abrir y cerrar [los ojos].
twinkling (-kling) *s.* TWINKLE: *in a* ~, *in the* ~ *of an eye*, en un abrir y cerrar de ojos.

twirl (tuøᵣl) *s.* giro o vuelta rápidos; molinete. *2* rasgo [hecho con la pluma].

twirl (to) *tr.* hacer girar o dar vueltas rápidamente. *2* retorcer, ensortijar. *3 intr.* girar rápidamente. *4* retorcerse, enroscarse.

twist (tuist) *s.* torsión, torcedura. *2* enroscadura, vuelta. *3* sesgo, inclinación; propensión, tendencia. *4* rosca [de pan]. *5* rollo [de tabaco].

twist (to) *tr.* torcer, retorcer. *2* enroscar, enrollar. *3* entrelazar, trenzar. *4* estrujar, oprimir [torciendo]. *5* doblar, doblegar. *6 intr.* torcerse, retorcerse. *7* enroscarse, arrollarse, ensortijarse. *8* serpentear. *9* dar vueltas.

twisting (tui·sting) *s.* TWIST. *2 adj.* que tuerce, que se enrosca; serpenteante.

twit (to) (tuit) *tr.* reprochar, echar en cara. ¶ Pret. y p. p.: *twitted;* ger.: *-tting.*

twitch (tuich) *s.* crispamiento, temblor, contracción nerviosa. *2* tirón, sacudida. *3* VET. acial.

twitch (to) *tr.* tirar de, dar un tirón a. *2 intr.* crisparse, moverse convulsivamente. *3 to ~ at,* tirar de.

twitter (tui·tøᵣ) *s.* gorjeo, piar [de los pájaros]. *2* charla alegre. *3* risa ahogada. *4* agitación, inquietud.

twitter (to) *intr.* gorjear, piar. *2* reír con risa ahogada. *3* temblar, agitarse.

two (tu) *adj.-s.* dos: *~ o'clock,* las dos; *~ of a kind,* tal para cual.

two-colo (u) r *adj.* de dos colores, bicromático.

two-cycle *adj.* MEC. de dos tiempos.

two-decker *s.* MAR. navío de dos puentes.

two-edged *adj.* de dos filos.

twofold (-fould) *adj.* doble [duplo; de dos]. *2 adv.* doble, doblemente.

two-four *adj.* MÚS. de dos por cuatro.

two-legged *adj.* de dos pies o patas. *2* bípedo.

twopence (tu·pøns) *s.* dos peniques.

two-penny *adj.* de dos peniques. *2* de tres al cuarto.

two-phase *adj.* ELECT. bifásico.

two-ply *adj.* de dos cabos o hilos. *2* de dos capas.

two-seater *s.* coche, aeroplano, etc., de dos asientos.

two-step *s.* paso doble [baile y música].

two-stroke *adj.* MEC. de dos tiempos.

two-way *adj.* de dos sentidos o direcciones.

two-wheeler *s.* vehículo de dos ruedas.

tycoon (taiku·n) *s.* magnate [de la industria, etcétera].

tyke (taik) *s.* fam. gozque. *2* fam. tipo, sujeto.

tympan (ti·mpạn) *s.* MÚS. tambor. *2* ARQ., IMPR. tímpano.

tympanic (timpæ·nik) *adj.* ANAT., MED. timpánico.

tympanist (ti·mpạnist) *s.* MÚS. timbalero.

tympanites (timpạnai·tiš) *s.* MED. timpanitis.

tympanitis (-tis) *s.* MED. inflamación del tímpano.

tympanum (ti·mpạnøm) *s.* ANAT., ZOOL., ARQ. tímpano. *2* TELEF. diafragma.

type (taip) *s.* tipo [símbolo, modelo, género, ejemplo característico]. *2* BIOL., H. NAT., IMPR. tipo. *3* NUMIS. figura.

type (to) *tr.* representar, ser el tipo de. *2* mecanografiar. *3* MED. determinar el grupo o tipo [de una sangre].

typesetter (-setøᵣ) *s.* IMPR. cajista, tipógrafo.

typesetting (-seting) *s.* IMPR. composición. *2 adj.* IMPR. de componer.

typewrite (to) (-rait) *tr.* mecanografiar.

typewriter (-øᵣ) *s.* máquina de escribir. *2* mecanógrafo, fa.

typewriting (-ting) *s.* mecanografía.

typhoid (tai·foid) *adj.* tifoideo. *2 s.* fiebre tifoidea.

typhoon (taifu·n) *s.* METEOR. tifón.

typhous (tai·føs) *adj.* MED. tífico.

typhus (tai·føs) *s.* MED. tifo, tifus.

typical (ti·pikạl) *adj.* típico; característico.

typify (to) (ti·pifai) *tr.* representar, simbolizar. *2* ser el tipo o ejemplo de. ¶ Pret. y p. p.: *tipified.*

typist (tai·pist) *s.* mecanógrafo, fa; dactilógrafo, fa.

typographer (taipa·graføᵣ) *s.* tipógrafo, impresor.

typographic (al (taipogræ·fik(ạl) *adj.* tipográfico.

typography (-grafi) *s.* tipografía, imprenta.

tyrannic(al (tiræ·nik(ạl) *adj.* tiránico, despótico.

tyrannicide (-nisaid) *s.* tiranicidio. *2* tiranicida.

tyrannize (to) (ti·ranaiš) *tr.* tiranizar. *2 intr.* obrar con tiranía.

tyrannous (-nøs) *adj.* tiránico.

tyranny (ti·rạni) *s.* tiranía. *2* acto tiránico.

tyrant (tai·rạnt) *s.* tirano, déspota.

Tyre (taiᵣ) *n. pr.* GEOGR. Tiro.

tyre *s.* TIRE.

Tyrian (ti·rian) *adj.-s.* tirio.

tyro (tai·rou) *s.* tirón, novicio.

Tyrol (the) (ti·roul) *n. pr.* GEOGR. el Tirol.

Tyrolese (tirøli·š) *adj.-s.* tirolés.

Tyrrhenian (tirr·nian) *adj.* tirreno: *~ Sea,* Mar Tirreno.

tzigane (tši·gạn) *s.* cíngaro, zíngaro.

U

U, u (yu) *s.* U, u, vigésima primera letra del alfabeto inglés.
ubiquitous (yubi·kuitøs) *adj.* obicuo, omnipresente.
ubiquity (-ti) *s.* ubicuidad, omnipresencia.
udder (ø·døʳ) *s.* ZOOL. ubre, teta.
udometer (yuda·mitøʳ) *s.* udómetro.
ugh (øg) *interj.* ¡uf!, ¡puf!, ¡fu!
ugly (ø·gli) *adj.* feo. *2* horroroso, horrible. *3* odioso, repugnante; malo, desagradable. *4* (E.U.) de mal genio.
uhlan (u·lan) *s.* MIL. ulano.
ukase (yu·keis) *s.* ucase.
Ukraine (yu·krein) *n. pr.* GEOGR. Ucrania.
Ukrainian (yukreini·an) *adj.-s.* ucranio, ucraniano.
ulcer (ø·lsøʳ) *s.* úlcera, llaga.
ulcerate (to) (-eit) *tr.* ulcerar. *2 intr.* ulcerarse.
ulceration (ølsørei·shøn) *s.* ulceración.
ulcerous (ø·lsørøs) *adj.* ulceroso.
ulema (uløma·) *s.* ulema.
uliginous (yuli·dẏinøs) *s.* uliginoso.
ulmaceous (ølmei·shøs) *adj.* BOT. ulmáceo.
ulmic (ø·lmik) *adj.* QUÍM. úlmico.
ulna (ø·lna) *s.* ANAT. cúbito. *2* ana [medida].
ulster (ø·lstøʳ) *s.* ruso [abrigo].
ulterior (ølti·riøʳ) *adj.* ulterior.
ultima (ø·ltima) *s.* última sílaba.
ultimate (ø·ltimit) *adj.* último, final. *2* fundamental, esencial, elemental. *3* MEC. máximo.
ultimatum (øltimei·tøm) *s.* ultimátum.
ultimo (ø·ltimou) *adj.* del mes próximo pasado.
ultra- (ø·ltra) *pref.* ultra-.
ultra *adj.* exagerado, extremo. *2* fanático, acérrimo. *3 s.* extremista, exaltado.
ultraism (-išm) *s.* extremismo, radicalismo.
ultraist (-ist) *s.* extremista, radical.
ultramarine (øltramarɪ·n) *adj.* ultramarino. *2 s.* azul ultramaro o de ultramar.
ultramicroscope (-mai·kroskoup) *s.* ultramicroscopio.
ultramontane (-ma·ntein) *adj.-s.* ultramontano.
ultramundane (-ma·ndein) *adj.* ultramundano.
ultravioleta (-vai·ølit) *adj.* ultravioleta.
ultravirus (-vai·røs) *s.* ultravirus.
ululate (to) (ø·liuleit) *intr.* ulular, aullar.
ululation (øliulei·shøn) *s.* ululato. *2* aullido.
Ulysses (yuli·sis) *n. pr.* Ulises.

umbel (ø·mbøl) *s.* BOT. umbela.
umbellate(d (-eit(id) *adj.* umbelado.
umbellifer (ømbøli·føʳ) *s.* BOT. umbelífera.
umbelliferous (-øs) *adj.* umbelífero.
umber (ø·mbøʳ) *s.* PINT. tierra de sombra. *2* ICT. tímalo. *3 adj.* de color pardo oscuro.
umbilical (ømbi·likal) *adj.* umbilical.
umbilicate (ømbi·likit) *adj.* umbilicado.
umbo (ø·mbou) *s.* cazoleta de broquel.
umbra (ø·mbra), *pl.* **-brae** (-brɪ) *s.* sombra. *2* ASTR. cono de sombra. *3* ASTR. núcleo [de las manchas solares].
umbrage (ø·mbridẏ) *s.* sombra, umbría. *2* sombraje. *3* pique, resentimiento: *to take ~ at*, resentirse por.
umbrage (to) *tr.* sombrear, dar sombra a. *2* picar, ofender.
umbrageous (ømbrei·dẏøs) *adj.* sombrío, umbroso. *2* receloso, resentido.
umbrella (ømbre·la) *s.* paraguas: *~ stand*, paragüero [mueble]. *2* sombrilla. *3* ZOOL. umbrela.
umbrous (ø·mbrøs) *adj.* umbrátil, umbroso.
umpire (ø·mpaiʳ) *s.* árbitro, juez árbitro. *2* DEP. árbitro.
umpire (to) *tr.-intr.* arbitrar [juzgar como árbitro].
un- (øn) *pref.* que denota contrariedad, oposición, negación, privación y equivale en muchos casos a des-, in-, no, sin, etc.
unabashed (ønabe·sht) *adj.* no avergonzado.
unable (-ei·bøl) *adj.* incapaz, imposibilitado. *2 to be ~ to*, no poder [hacer una cosa].
unabridged (-abri·dẏd) *adj.* sin abreviar, íntegro.
unacceptable (-akse·ptabøl) *adj.* inaceptable.
unaccommodating (-æka·mødeiting) *adj.* poco complaciente, poco servicial.
unaccountable (-ækau·ntabøl) *adj.* inexplicable, extraño, misterioso; irresponsable.
unaccounted-for (-tid) *adj.* no explicado.
unadaptable (-adæptabøl) *adj.* inadaptable.
unaddressed (-ædre·st) *adj.* sin dirección [carta, etc.].
unadorned (-ado·ʳnd) *adj.* sencillo, sin adornos.
unadvisable (-advai·šabøl) *adj.* que no es de aconsejar; poco cuerdo o prudente.
unadvised (-advai·šd) *adj.* sin consejo. *2* imprudente, precipitado, irreflexivo.
unaffected (-afe·ktid) *adj.* sencillo, natural, libre de afectación. *2* impasible, inalterado.

unaided (-ei·did) *adj.* sin ayuda.
unalloyed (-*a*loi·d) *adj.* puro, sin mezcla.
unalterable (-o·ltørabøl) *adj.* inalterable, inmutable.
unaltered (-o·ltø^rd) *adj.* inalterado.
unanimity (yunani·miti) *s.* unanimidad.
unanimous (yunæ·nimøs) *adj.* unánime. 2 de acuerdo.
unannounced (ønanau·nst) *adj.* sin ser anunciado. 2 de improviso.
unanswerable (-æ·nsørabøl) *adj.* incontrovertible, incontestable, indisputable.
unanswered (-ø^rd) *adj.* por contestar, no contestado. 2 no correspondido.
unappreciated (-apri·shieitid) *adj.* no apreciado; mal comprendido.
unapproachable (-aprou·chabøl) *adj.* inaccesible, inabordable.
unappropriate(d (-aprou·pieit(id) *adj.* no concedido o aplicado [crédito, fondos]. 2 libre, baldío.
unarmed (-a·^rmd) *adj.* desarmado, indefenso.
unartistic (-a^rti·stik) *adj.* nada artístico, poco artístico.
unasked (-a·skt) *adj.* no pedido o solicitado. 2 sin ser llamado o invitado.
unassailable (-asei·labøl) *adj.* inexpugnable.
unassisted (-asi·stid) *adj.* sin ayuda.
unassuming (-asiu·ming) *adj.* modesto, sin presunción.
unattached (-atæ·cht) *adj.* suelto, despegado. 2 libre, sin compromiso. 3 DER. no embargado. 4 MIL. disponible.
unattainable (-atei·nabøl) *adj.* inasequible.
unattended (-ate·ndid) *adj.* no acompañado, solo.
unattractive (-atræ·ktiv) *adj.* poco atractivo.
unau (yu·nou) *s.* ZOOL. perezoso.
unauthorized (øno·zøraišd) *adj.* no autorizado.
unavailable (-avei·labøl) *adj.* no utilizable, no disponible. 2 agotado [libro].
unavailing (-avei·ling) *adj.* inútil, infructuoso, vano, ineficaz.
unavoidable (-avoi·dabøl) *adj.* inevitable, ineludible.
unaware (-aue·^r) *adj.* desprevenido, ignorante [de una cosa]; que no recela o hace caso [de ella].
unaware(s (-aue·^r(š) *adv.* sin premeditación, inadvertidamente. 2 inopinadamente, de improviso: *to catch unawares*, coger desprevenido.
unbacked (-bæ·kt) *adj.* sin ayuda, sin apoyo. 2 sin respaldo. 3 sin domar [potro].
unbalanced (-bæ·lanst) *adj.* desequilibrado.
unbar (to) (-ba·^r) *tr.* desatrancar, quitar la barra de.
unbearable (-be·rabøl) *adj.* insufrible, insoportable, inaguantable.
unbeaten (-bɪ·tøn) *adj.* no pisado o frecuentado. 2 invicto, imbatido.
unbecoming (-bika·ming) *adj.* que sienta o cae mal. 2 impropio, indecoroso.
unbelief (-bilɪ·f) *s.* descreimiento.
unbeliever (-vø^r) *s.* descreído; infiel.
unbend (to) (-be·nd) *tr.* enderezar, desencorvar. 2 aflojar, relajar. 3 MAR. desenvergar. 4 *intr.* enderezarse. 5 ablandar, humanizarse. 6 descansar, solazarse.
unbending (-ing) *adj.* inflexible.
unbias(s)ed (-bai·ast) *adj.* imparcial.
unbind (to) (-bai·nd) *tr.* desatar, desligar. 2 *intr.* desatarse, desligarse.
unblemished (-ble·misht) *adj.* puro, perfecto.

unblushing (-blø·shing) *adj.* que no se ruboriza. 2 sin rubor, desvergonzado.
unbolt (to) (-bou·lt) *tr.* desclavar [lo sujetado con pernos]. 2 abrir [corriendo el cerrojo]; desatrancar.
unborn (-bo^rn) *adj.* no nacido, por nacer, futuro.
unbosom (to) (-bu·søm) *tr.* revelar, confesar: *to ~ oneself*, abrir su pecho, desahogarse.
unbottomed (-ba·tømd) *adj.* sin fondo. 2 insondable. 3 infundado.
unbound (-bau·nd) *pret.* y *p. p.* de TO UNBIND. 2 *adj.* desatado, suelto. 3 sin encuadernar.
unbounded (-id) *adj.* ilimitado, infinito. 2 libre, sin freno.
unbraid (to) (-brei·d) *tr.* destrenzar, destejer. 2 desembrollar.
unbreakable (-brei·kabøl) *adj.* irrompible.
unbred (-bre·d) *adj.* malcriado, grosero.
unbridle (to) (-brai·døl) *tr.* desembridar. 2 soltar, dar rienda suelta a.
unbroken (-brou·køn) *adj.* entero, intacto. 2 inviolado. 3 continuo, ininterrumpido. 4 indomado, indómito. 5 no labrado o cultivado [suelo].
unbuckle (to) (-bø·køl) *tr.* deshebillar, desatar, desabrochar.
unburden (to) (-bø·^rdøn) *tr.* descargar [quitar un peso]; aliviar.
unburied (-be·rid) *adj.* insepulto.
unbury (to) (-be·ri) *tr.* desenterrar, exhumar.
unbusinesslike (-bi·šnislaik) *adj.* contrario a la práctica mercantil. 2 poco práctico.
unbutton (to) (-bø·tøn) *tr.* desabotonar, desabrochar.
uncage (to) (-kei·dӯ) *tr.* desenjaular.
uncalled-for (-ko·ld) *adj.* no requerido, innecesario, gratuito. 2 inmerecido.
uncanny (-kæ·ni) *adj.* misterioso, extraño, sobrenatural; del mundo de los fantasmas, duendes, etc.
uncap (to) (-kæ·p) *tr.* descubrir, destapar, quitar el casquillo.
uncared-for (ke·^rd) *adj.* descuidado, abandonado, desatendido.
unceasing (-sɪ·sing) *adj.* incesante.
unceremonious (-serimou·niøs) *adj.* sin ceremonia; familiar, llano. 2 brusco, descortés.
uncertain (-sø·^rtøn) *adj.* incierto, dudoso. 2 vago, indeterminado. 3 poco seguro o confiable. 4 precario. 5 variable, inconstante. 6 indeciso, irresoluto.
uncertainty (-ti) *s.* incertidumbre. 2 vaguedad. 3 precariedad. 4 inestabilidad. 5 indecisión.
unchain (to) (-chei·n) *tr.* desencadenar.
unchangeable (-chei·ndӯabøl) *adj.* inmutable, invariable, inalterable.
unchanged (-chei·ndӯd) *adj.* inalterado, igual.
unchanging (-chei·ndӯing) *adj.* inmutable, uniforme.
uncharitable (-chæritabøl) *adj.* poco caritativo, falto de caridad, duro.
unchaste (-chei·st) *adj.* incasto, deshonesto, impúdico, lascivo.
unchastity (-chei·stiti) *s.* deshonestidad, impureza, lascivia.
unchecked (-che·kt) *adj.* desenfrenado. 2 libre, sin que nada o nadie lo contenga. 3 COM. no comprobado.
unchristened (-kri·sønd) *adj.* no bautizado. 2 sin nombre.
unchristian (-stshan) *adj.* poco cristiano.
uncinate (ø·nsineit) *adj.* ganchudo.

uncivil (ønsi·vil) *adj.* incivil, descortés.

uncivilized (-sivilai·šd) *adj.* salvaje, tosco, inculto.

unclad (-klæ·d) *adj.* no vestido, desnudo.

unclasp (to) (-klæ·šp) *tr.* desabrochar.

uncle (ø·nkøl) *s.* tío. 2 *Uncle Sam*, el tío Sam [los Estados Unidos].

unclean (ønklɪ·n) *adj.* sucio, desaseado. 2 inmundo. 3 impuro.

uncleanly (-kle·nli) *adj.* UNCLEAN. 2 *adv.* suciamente.

unclog (to) (-cla·g) *tr.* desembarazar, desobstruir.

unclose (to) (-klou·š) *tr.* abrir. 2 descubrir, revelar.

unclothe (to) (-klou·ð) *tr.* quitar la ropa a, desnudar.

unclouded (-klau·did) *adj.* claro, despejado, sin nubes.

uncock (to) (-ka·k) *tr.* desmontar [un arma de fuego].

uncoil (to) (-koi·l) *tr.* desarrollar, desenrollar.

uncollected (-køle·ktid) *adj.* disperso. 2 por cobrar. 3 perturbado, desconcertado.

uncombed (-kou·md) *adj.* despeinado, sin peinar.

uncomfortable (-kø·mfø'tabøl) *adj.* penoso, incómodo, desagradable, molesto. 2 incómodo, molesto, embarazado; que no se siente bien.

uncommon (-ka·møn) *adj.* poco común o frecuente, insólito, raro, notable, extraordinario, excepcional.

uncommunicative (-kømiu·nikeitiv) *adj.* reservado, poco comunicativo.

uncomplimentary (-kamplime·ntɑri) *adj.* poco halagüeño o amable; ofensivo; desfavorable.

uncompromising (-kamprømai·šing) *adj.* inflexible, firme, intransigente.

unconcerned (-kønsø·'nd) *adj.* indiferente, frío, desinteresado. 2 no interesado.

unconcluded (-kliu·did) *adj.* inconcluso.

unconditional (-ndi·shønal) *adj.* incondicional.

unconditioned (-ndi·shønd) *adj.* no condicionado. 2 FIL. ilimitado, infinito, absoluto.

unconformable (-fo·'mabøl) *adj.* no conforme, proporcionado o correspondiente.

unconformity (-fø·'miti) *s.* disconformidad, contradicción, incompatibilidad.

uncongenial (-køndÿi·nial) *adj.* incompatible. 2 antipático, desagradable. 3 impropio, inadecuado;

unconnected (-køne·ktid) *adj.* inconexo. 2 incoherente. 3 desconectado.

unconquerable (-ka·nkørabøl) *adj.* inconquistable, invencible, indomable.

unconscionable (-shønabøl) *adj.* injusto, irrazonable. 2 desmedido. 3 sin conciencia.

unconscious (-shøs) *adj.* inconsciente. 2 desmayado, sin sentido. 3 ignorante, no sabedor o que no se percata [de]. 4 inanimado. 5 *s. the ~*, lo inconsciente.

unconstitutional (-stitiu·shønal) *adj.* inconstitucional, anticonstitucional.

uncontaminated (-tæ·mineitid) *adj.* incontaminado.

uncontrollable (-trou·labøl) *adj.* ingobernable, indomable, irrefrenable.

uncontrolled (-trou·ld) *adj.* libre, sin freno.

unconventional (-ve·nshønal) *adj.* libre de trabas o reglas; que no sujeta a convenciones o costumbres, despreocupado; original.

unconvincing (-vi·nsing) *adj.* que no convence, poco convicente.

uncork (to) (ønko·'k) *tr.* descorchar, destapar.

uncorrupted (ønkørø·ptid) *adj.* incorrupto.

uncouth (-ku·z) *adj.* tosco, grosero. 2 rudo, rústico, inculto. 3 torpe, desmañado. 4 raro, extraño.

uncover (to) (-kø·vø') *tr.* destapar, descubrir. 2 desabrigar, desarropar. 3 poner al descubierto, revelar. 4 *intr.* descubrirse. 5 desabrigarse.

uncreated (-kriei·tid) *adj.* increado.

uncrown (to) (-krau·n) *tr.* destronar.

unction (ø·ncshøn) *s.* unción, ungimiento. 2 untamiento, untadura. 3 untura, ungüento. 4 lenitivo. 5 unción, fervor. 6 hipocresía.

unctuous (-chuøs) *adj.* untuoso. 2 meloso, zalamero, hipócrita.

uncurl (to) (ønkø·'l) *tr.* desrizar, desenroscar.

uncut (-køt) *adj.* sin cortar. 2 sin tallar, en bruto.

undamaged (-dæ·midÿd) *adj.* indemne, ileso.

undaunted (-do·ntid) *adj.* impávido, impertérrito, intrépido.

undecagon (-de·kagøn) *s.* GEOM. undecágono.

undeceive (to) (-disɪ·v) *tr.* desengañar, desimpresionar, sacar de un engaño o error.

undecipherable (-disai·førabol) *adj.* indescifrable.

undeclinable (-diklai·nabøl) *adj.* indeclinable. 2 inevitable.

undefeated (-difɪ·tid) *adj.* invicto.

undefensible (-dife·nsibøl) *adj.* indefendible.

undefiled (-difai·ld) *adj.* impoluto, limpio, libre de mancha.

undefined (-difai·nd) *adj.* indefinido.

undeniable (-dinai·abøl) *adj.* innegable, indiscutible, irrefragable.

under (ø·ndø') *prep.* bajo, debajo de. 2 de menos de; en menos de, dentro; menos de, inferior o de grado inferior a: *all weights ~ two pounds*, todos los pesos de menos de dos libras; *~ an hour*, en menos de una hora, dentro de una hora. 3 en tiempo de, durante el reinado de. 4 conforme a, según: *~ the terms of*, según las condiciones de. 5 bajo la dirección o enseñanza de. 6 a o en, en frases como: *~ the care of*, al cuidado de; *~ discussion*, en discusión. 7 Otros usos: *~ arms*, MIL. sirviendo en el ejército; *~ cover*, al abrigo, a cubierto; *~ one's nose*, fam. en las barbas de uno; *~ sail*, navegando, con las velas desplegadas; *~ way*, en camino; en marcha; *to be ~ age*, ser menor de edad. 8 *adv.* abajo, debajo, más abajo. 9 *adj.* inferior. 10 subalterno, subordinado.

under- *pref.* que denota inferioridad, subordinación, etc., y que en muchos casos corresponde al español *sub-*.

underbred (øndø'bre·d) *adj.* que no es de pura raza. 2 tosco, vulgar.

underbrush (-brøsh) *s.* maleza [de un bosque].

undercarriage (ø·ndø'kæridÿ) *s.* soporte o armazón inferior. 2 AVIA. tren de aterrizaje.

underclothes (ø·ndø'kloudš), **underclothing** (-klou·ding) *s.* ropa interior.

undercurrent (-kørønt) *s.* corriente que pasa debajo de otra. 2 tendencia oculta. 3 *adj.* que corre bajo la superficie; secreto, oculto.

undercut (-køt) *adj.* cortado por debajo. 2 *s.* corte dado o hecho por la parte de abajo. 3 solomillo. 4 TENIS, BOX. golpe dado por debajo o de abajo arriba.

undercut (to) *tr.* cortar o vaciar por debajo, socavar. 2 TENIS, BOX. golpear por debajo o de abajo arriba.

underdeveloped (øndø'dive·løpt) *adj.* poco desarrollado. 2 subdesarrollado.

underdog (ø·ndø'dog) *s.* el que pierde [en una contienda]. 2 fig. oprimido, desvalido: *the underdogs*, los desvalidos, los de abajo.

underdone (-dǫn) *adj.* coc. poco asado, a medio asar.

underdress (to) (øndøʳdre·s) *intr.* vestirse menos de lo conveniente. *2* vestirse demasiado sencillamente para lo que requiere la ocasión.

underestimate (to) (-e·stimeit) *tr.* menospreciar, tener en poco. *2* valuar o calcular en menos del valor real.

underexpose (to) (-ekspou·š) *tr.* FOT. dar poca exposición a.

underfeed (to) (-fɪ·d) *tr.* alimentar insuficientemente, desnutrir.

underfoot (ø·ndʳfut) *adv.* bajo los pies. *2* en sujeción. *3* en secreto. *4 adj.* pisoteado, oprimido.

undergo (to) (øndø·ʳgou) *tr.* sufrir, padecer, aguantar. *2* experimentar, ser sometido a.

undergraduate (-græ·diuit) *s.* estudiante que aún no tiene ningún grado académico.

underground (ø·ndøʳgraund) *adj.* subterráneo. *2* secreto, clandestino. *3 s.* subterráneo. *4* subsuelo. *5* metro, ferrocarril subterráneo. *6 adv.* bajo tierra. *7* en secreto, ocultamente.

undergrown (-groun) *s.* pequeño, raquítico. *2* cubierto de maleza.

undergrowth (-grouz) *s.* maleza, matas, hierbas [del bosque].

underhand (øndøʳjæ·nd) *adv.* bajo mano, por bajo cuerda, clandestinamente. *2 adj.* secreto, clandestino.

underhanded (-id) *adj.* secreto, clandestino, disimulado, solapado.

underlay (-lei) *s.* IMPR. alza. *2* pieza que realza o sostiene. *3* UNDERCURRENT.

underlay (to) *tr.* reforzar por debajo. *2* IMPR. calzar. *3* realzar [poniendo algo debajo].

underlet (to) (-lei·t) *tr.* subarrendar.

underlie (to) (-lai) *tr.* estar debajo de. *2* ser la base, fundamento o sostén de.

underline (ø·ndøʳlain) *s.* línea puesta debajo.

underline (to) (øndøʳlai·n) *tr.* subrayar.

underling (øndøʳling) *s.* subordinado, inferior.

underlying (øndøʳlai·ing) *adj.* subyacente. *2* fundamental.

undermine (to) (-mai·n) *tr.* minar, socavar, zapar. *2* fig. minar [la salud, etc.].

undermost (ø·ndøʳmoust) *adj.* el más bajo. *2* ínfimo. *3 adv.* debajo de todo.

underneath (øndøʳnɪ·z) *adv.* debajo. *2 prep.* debajo de, bajo.

undernourish (to) (-nø·rish) *tr.* alimentar insuficientemente.

underpass (ø·ndøʳpæs) *s.* paso inferior.

underpay (to) (øndøʳpei·) *tr.* pagar poco, pagar mal.

underpin (to) (-pi·n) *tr.* socalzar, apuntalar.

underprivileged (-pri·vilidýd) *adj.* menesteroso, desheredado.

underrate (to) (ø·ndøʳreit) *tr.* desestimar, menospreciar, valorar demasiado bajo.

underrun (to) (øndøʳrøn) *tr.* correr por debajo de. *2* MAR. resacar.

underscore (to) (-sko·ʳ) *tr.* subrayar.

undersecretary (-se·krøteri) *s.* subsecretario.

underset (to) (-se·t) *tr.* apuntalar, sostener.

undershirt (ø·ndøʳshøʳt) *s.* camiseta.

undershot (-shot) *adj.* impulsada por debajo [rueda hidráulica]. *2* que tiene saliente la mandíbula inferior.

undersign (to) (øndøʳsai·n) *tr.* firmar, subscribir. *2 the undersigned,* el infrascrito, el abajo-firmado.

undersized (ø·ndøʳsai·šd) *adj.* pequeño, de estatura o tamaño menor que los normales.

underskirt (-skøʳt) *s.* enaguas; refajo.

understand (to) (øndøʳstæ·nd) *tr.* entender, comprender: *to give to ~,* dar a entender; *to ~ each other,* entenderse, ir de acuerdo. *2* entender en. *3* ser sabedor de, tener entendido. *4* sobrentender.

understanding (-ing) *s.* inteligencia, comprensión, conocimiento [de una cosa]. *2* entendimiento, inteligencia [facultad]. *3* inteligencia, armonía, acuerdo: *to come to an ~,* llegar a un acuerdo. *4 adj.* inteligente; comprensivo.

understatement (-stei·tmønt) *s.* declaración incompleta, en la que se dice menos de lo que hay.

understood (-stu·d) *pret. y p. p.* de TO UNDERSTAND.

understudy (ø·ndøʳstødi) *s.* TEAT. sobresaliente, suplente.

understudy (to) *tr.* aprender [un papel] para poder suplir a [otro actor].

undertake (to) (øndøʳtei·k) *tr.* emprender, acometer, intentar. *2* tomar por su cuenta, a su cargo; comprometerse a, encargarse de.

undertaker (-øʳ) *s.* empresario, contratista. *2* empresario de pompas fúnebres, dueño de una funeraria.

undertaking (-ing) *s.* empresa [acción de emprender, cosa que se emprende]. *2* contrata. *3* funeraria, empresa de pompas fúnebres. *4* DER. promesa, garantía.

undertone (ø·ndøʳtoun) *s.* voz baja. *2* color apagado.

undertow (-tou) *s.* MAR. resaca; contracorriente.

undervalue (to) (øndøʳvæ·liu) *tr.* desestimar, valuar por debajo del valor real.

underwater (-uø·tøʳ) *adj.* subacuático. *2* que se usa debajo del agua.

underwear (-ue·ʳ) *s.* ropa interior.

underwood (ø·ndøʳwud) *s.* maleza, monte bajo.

underworld (-uøʳld) *s.* los profundos. *2* mundo subterráneo o submarino, de los insectos, de la vida inferior. *3* los antípodas. *4* el hampa, los bajos fondos de la sociedad.

underwrite (to) (øndøʳrai·t) *tr.* subscribir, firmar. *2* COM. subscribir [una emisión]. *3* COM. asegurar.

underwriter (-øʳ) *s.* firmante. *2* COM. suscriptor de una emisión. *3* COM. asegurador.

undeserved (-dišø·ʳvd) *adj.* inmerecido.

undeserving (-disø·ʳving) *adj.* desmerecedor, indigno.

undesigning (dišai·ning) *adj.* sencillo, sin astucia, sincero, de buena fe.

undesirable (-dišai·rabøl) *adj.* indeseable, poco deseable.

undetected (-dite·ktid) *adj.* no descubierto.

undetermined (-dite·ʳmind) *adj.* indeterminado. *2* indeciso, irresoluto.

undeviating (-dɪ·vieiting) *adj.* directo, sin rodeos; invariable, siempre igual.

undies (ø·ndɪš) *s. pl.* fam. ropa interior femenina.

undigested (-didýe·stid) *adj.* no digerido.

undignified (-di·gnifaid) *adj.* poco digno o decoroso. *2* falto de seriedad, de gravedad.

undine (øndɪ·n) *s.* ondina.

undisciplined (-di·siplind) *adj.* no sujeto a disciplina. *2* rebelde, indócil, indisciplinado.

undisguised (-disgai·šd) *adj.* manifiesto, no disimulado.

undismayed (-dismei·d) *adj.* firme, impertérrito, no desanimado.

undisturbed (distø·ʳbd) *adj.* quieto, tranquilo. *2* impasible, sereno.

undivided (-divai·did) *adj.* entero, indiviso.

undo (to) (-du·) *tr.* abrir, desatar, desliar, soltar, desabrochar: *to ~ one's hair,* soltarse el cabello. *2* deshacer. *3* anular, desvirtuar. *4* destruir, arruinar, perder.

undoing (-du·ing) *s.* destrucción, pérdida, ruina.

undone (-døn) *p. p.* de TO UNDO: *to come ~,* desatarse, soltarse, desabrocharse; *to leave ~,* dejar por hacer.

undoubted (-dau·tid) *adj.* cierto, indudable, fuera de duda, indiscutido.

undraw (to) (-dro·) *tr.* abrir, descorrer [una cortina, etc.].

undress (-dre·s) *s.* traje de casa, deshabillé. *2* vestido de calle. *3* MIL. traje de diario.

undress (to) *tr.* desnudar, desvestir. *2* vestir a la ligera. *3* CIR. desvendar. *4 intr.* desnudarse.

undressed (-dre·st) *adj.* sin preparar, sin curtir; en rama, en bruto. *2* de trapillo. *3* vestido con traje de calle.

undrinkable (-dri·nkabøl) *adj.* impotable.

undue (-diu·) *adj.* indebido, excesivo, desmedido. *2* impropio. *3* ilegal, injusto. *4* COM. no vencido.

undulant (ø·ndiulant) *adj.* ondulante, undulante.

undulate (-diuleit) *adj.* ondulado, ondeado.

undulate (to) *intr.* ondular, ondear. *2* fluctuar. *3 tr.* hacer ondear o fluctuar. *4* ondular.

undulation (øndiulei·shøn) *s.* ondulación, ondeo.

undulatory (ø·ndiulatori) *adj.* ondulatorio, undoso.

undutiful (øndiu·tiful) *adj.* que falta a sus deberes; desobediente, irrespetuoso.

undying (-dai·ng) *adj.* imperecedero, eterno.

unearned (-ø·ʳnd) *s.* no ganado; inmerecido: *~ increment,* plusvalía.

unearth (to) (-ø·ʳz) *tr.* desenterrar.

unearthly (-ø·ʳzli) *adj.* no terrenal. *2* sobrenatural, supernatural. *3* terrible, fantástico.

uneasiness (-ɪ·šinis) *s.* intranquilidad, inquietud, desasosiego. *2* malestar, incomodidad.

uneasy (-ɪ·si) *adj.* intranquilo, inquieto, desasosegado. *2* molesto, incómodo. *3* torpe, cohibido.

unedifying (-e·difaiing) *adj.* poco edificante.

uneducated (-e·diukeitid) *adj.* inculto, indocto.

unemployed (-imploi·d) *adj.* desocupado, ocioso. *2* sin trabajo, parado. *3* no empleado.

unemployment (-mønt) *s.* desocupación, falta de trabajo, paro.

unending (-e·nding) *adj.* inacabable, interminable, perpetuo, eterno.

unendurable (-endiu·rabøl) *adj.* insoportable.

unenlightened (-enlai·tønd) *adj.* sin instrucción, ignorante.

unequal (-i·kual) *s.* desigual. *2* diferente. *3* desproporcionado. *4* insuficiente. *5* falto de fuerzas, capacidad, etc. [para algo].

unequalled (-d) *adj.* inigualado, sin par.

unequivocal (-ikui·vøkal) *adj.* inequívoco.

unerring (-ø·ring) *adj.* infalible. *2* certero.

unessential (-ese·nshal) *adj.* no esencial.

unethical (øne·zical) *adj.* contrario a la moral, o a las normas de la conducta profesional.

uneven (-ɪ·vn) *adj.* desigual, desnivelado, irregular, accidentado. *2* de longitud diferente. *3* impar, non.

uneventful (-ive·ntful) *adj.* exento de acontecimientos notables; tranquilo.

unexampled (-egšæ·mpøld) *adj.* sin ejemplo.

unexceptionable (ekse·pshønabøl) *adj.* intachable, irreprochable.

unexpected (-ekspe·ktid) *adj.* inesperado, imprevisto, inopinado. *2* repentino.

unexperienced (-pi·riønst) *adj.* inexperto. *2* no experimentado.

unexplained (-plei·nd) *adj.* inexplicado.

unexplored (-plo·ʳd) *adj.* inexplorado.

unexpressive (-pre·siv) *adj.* inexpresivo.

unextinguishable (-tingwi·shabøl) *adj.* inextinguible.

unfading (-fei·ding) *adj.* inmarcesible.

unfailing (-fei·ling) *adj.* inagotable. *2* cierto, seguro, indefectible. *3* infalible.

unfair (-fe·ʳ) *adj.* injusto, desleal, de mala fe.

unfaithful (-fei·zful) *adj.-s.* infiel.

unfaltering (-fo·ltøring) *adj.* resuelto, firme, inquebrantable.

unfamiliar (-fami·liaʳ) *adj.* poco familiar, desconocido. *2* que no conoce una cosa, que está poco familiarizado con ella.

unfashionable (-fæ·shønabøl) *adj.* no ajustado a la moda, que no la sigue.

unfasten (to) (-fæ·søn) *tr.* abrir, desatar, desabrochar, desprender, soltar, aflojar.

unfathomable (-fæ·dømabøl) *adj.* insondable. *2* impenetrable, inescrutable.

unfavo(u)rable (-fei·vørabøl) *adj.* desfavorable, contrario, adverso.

unfeasible (-fi·søbøl) *adj.* impracticable, no hacedero.

unfed (-fe·d) *adj.* falto de alimento; sin comer.

unfeeling (-fɪ·ling) *adj.* insensible, duro, cruel.

unfeigned (-fei·nd) *adj.* verdadero, no fingido.

unfelt (-fe·lt) *adj.* no percibido o sentido.

unfetter (to) (-fe·tøʳ) *tr.* quitar los hierros a; libertar.

unfinished (-fi·nisht) *adj.* inacabado, incompleto. *2* TEJ. sin acabar.

unfit (-fi·t) *adj.* incapaz, inepto. *2* inadecuado, impropio. *3* inservible, inútil. *4* en malas condiciones físicas.

unfitting (-fi·ting) *adj.* impropio. *2* indecoroso.

unfix (to) (-fi·ks) *tr.* desfijar, desprender.

unflagging (-flæ·gaing) *adj.* persistente, incansable.

unfledged (-fle·dyd) *adj.* ORN. implume. *2* fig. novel, inexperto.

unflinching (-flɪ·nching) *adj.* firme, resuelto.

unfold (to) (-fou·ld) *tr.* desplegar, desdoblar, extender, abrir. *2* descubrir, revelar, explicar. *3 intr.* abrirse, desplegarse, extenderse.

unforeseen (-fo·ʳsin) *adj.* imprevisto.

unforgettable (-foʳge·tabøl) *adj.* inolvidable.

unforgiving (-foʳgi·ving) *adj.* implacable, rencoroso, que no perdona.

unfortunate (-fo·ʳchønit) *adj.-s.* infortunado, desgraciado, desdichado. *2 adj.* infausto, aciago.

unfortunately (-li) *adv.* desgraciadamente, por desgracia.

unfounded (-fau·ndid) *adj.* infundado.

unfrequently (-frikue·ntli) *adv.* raramente, pocas veces.

unfriendly (-fre·ndli) *adj.* poco amistoso, hostil, enemigo. *2* desfavorable, perjudicial.

unfruitful (-fru·tful) *adj.* estéril, infecundo. *2* infructuoso.

unfulfilled (-fulfi·ld) *adj.* incumplido.

unfurl (to) (-fø·ʳl) *tr.* desplegar, extender.

unfurnished (-fø·ʳnisht) *adj.* desamueblado. *2* desprovisto.

ungainly (-gei·nli) *adj.* desgarbado, torpe, sin gracia.
ungenerous (-dȳe·nørøs) *adj.* poco generoso.
ungentle (-dȳe·ntøl) *adj.* rudo, brusco, duro.
ungentlemanlike, ungentlemanly (-ønȳe·ntølmanlaik, -li) *adj.* impropio de un caballero; incorrecto, descortés.
ungird (to) (-gø·ʳd) *tr.* desceñir. *2* descinchar.
unglazed (-glei·šd) *adj.* sin vidrios. *2* sin vidriar. *3* deslustrado.
unglue (to) (-gliu·) *tr.* despegar [lo pegado]. *2* desencolar.
ungodly (-ga·dli) *adj.* impío. *2* malvado. *3* fam. atroz, enorme.
ungraceful (-grei·sful) *adj.* desgarbado, torpe, falto de gracia.
ungracious (grei·shøs) *adj.* brusco, desabrido.
ungrammatical (-gramæ·tikal) *adj.* antigramatical.
ungrateful (-grei·tful) *adj.* ingrato, desagradecido. *2* ingrato, desagradable.
ungrounded (-grau·ndid) *adj.* infundado, inmotivado. *2* ELECT. no conectado con la tierra.
unguarded (-ga·ʳdid) *adj.* no guardado, indefenso. *2* desprevenido, descuidado. *3* imprudente.
unguent (ø·ngwønt) *s.* ungüento, unto.
unguiculate (øngwi·kiuleit) *adj.-s.* ZOOL. unguiculado.
unguided (-gai·did) *adj.* no dirigido, sin guía.
unguis (ø·ngwis) *s.* ANAT. unguis.
ungulate (-giuleit) *adj.-s.* ungulado.
unhallowed (ønjæ·loud) *adj.* no consagrado. *2* profano, impío.
unhandy (-jæ·ndi) *adj.* torpe, desmañado. *2* incómodo, de mal manejar.
unhang (to) (ø·njæng) *tr.* descolgar, desprender.
unhappily (ønjæ·pili) *adv.* infelizmente. *2* desgraciadamente, por desgracia.
unhappiness (-pinis) *s.* infelicidad, desdicha.
unhappy (-pi) *adj.* infeliz, desgraciado, desdichado. *2* poco oportuno o acertado. *3* triste.
unharmed (ønja·ʳmd) *adj.* ileso, incólume.
unharness (to) (-ja·ʳnis) *tr.* despojar de la armadura. *2* desenjaezar; desenganchar.
unhealthy (-je·lzi) *adj.* enfermo, enfermizo, achacoso. *2* malsano, insalubre.
unheard (-jø·ʳd) *adj.* no oído; sin que se le haya oído. *2* ~ *of*, inaudito, nunca oído, extraño; obscuro, desconocido.
unheeded (- jɪ·did) *adj.* desatendido, sin que se le haga caso, inadvertido.
unheeding (-jɪ·ding) *adj.* desatento, descuidado, distraído.
unhesitating (-je·šiteiting) *adj.* resuelto, que no vacila. *2* hecho sin vacilar, rápido, pronto.
unhinge (to) (-ji·ndȳ) *intr.* desgoznar, desquiciar. *2* fig. trastornar, desequilibrar.
unhitch (to) (-jɪ·ch) *tr.* descolgar, desatar. *2* desenganchar [animales].
unholy (-jou·li) *adj.* profano [no sagrado].
unhook (to) (-ju·k) *tr.* desenganchar, desabrochar. *2* descolgar [de un gancho]. *3 intr.* desengancharse, desabrocharse, descolgarse.
unhoped-for (-jou·pt) *adj.* inesperado.
unhorse (to) (-jo·ʳs) *tr.* desmontar, desarzonar.
unhurt (-jø·ʳt) *adj.* ileso, indemne.
unicameral (yunikæ·møral) *adj.* unicameral.
unicellular (-se·liulaʳ) *adj.* unicelular.
unicity (yuni·siti) *s.* unicidad.
unicorn (yu·nikoʳn) *s.* unicornio.
unification (yunifikei·shøn) *s.* unificación.

uniform (yu·nifoʳm) *adj.* uniforme. *2* semejante, concorde, consonante. *4 s.* uniforme.
uniformity (yunifo·ʳmiti) *s.* uniformidad.
unify (to) (yu·nifai) *tr.* unificar, unir. *2 intr.* unificarse, unirse.
unilateral (yunilæ·tøral) *adj.* unilateral.
unimaginable (ønimæ·dȳinabøl) *adj.* inimaginable.
unimpaired (-impe·ʳd) *adj.* intacto, incólume, inalterado.
unimpeachable (-impɪ·chabøl) *adj.* intachable, irreprochable. *2* irrecusable.
unimportant (-impo·ʳtant) *adj.* insignificante, sin importancia.
uninflammable (-inflæ·mabøl) *adj.* no inflamable.
uninformed (-infoʳmd) *adj.* ignorante, indocto. *2* no informado.
uninhabited (-injæ·bitid) *adj.* inhabitado, desierto, despoblado.
uninjured (-indȳøʳd) *adj.* indemne, incólume, sin daño.
uninsured (-inshu·ʳd) *adj.* COM. no asegurado.
unintelligible (-inte·lidȳibøl) *adj.* ininteligible.
unintentional (-inte·nshønal) *adj.* involuntario.
uninterested (-i·ntørestid) *adj.* indiferente, distraído, apático.
uninteresting (-intøre·sting) *adj.* poco interesante, falto de interés, soso.
uninterrupted (-intøro·ptid) *adj.* ininterrumpido, continuo, incesante.
union (yu·niøn) *s.* unión: *the Union,* los Estados Unidos de América. *2* junta, juntura. *3* MEC. conexión, tubo de unión, etc. *4* (Ingl.) asociación o sindicato obrero. *5* emblema de la unión [en una bandera]: *Union Jack,* pabellón nacional de la Gran Bretaña.
unionism (-išm) *s.* unionismo. *2* (Ingl.) principios y sistema de los sindicatos obreros.
unionist (-ist) *s.* unionista. *2* (Ingl.) miembro de un sindicato obrero.
unipersonal (yunipø·ʳsønal) *adj.* unipersonal.
unique (yuni·k) *adj.* único, solo. *2* sin igual, extraordinario. *3* extraño, raro.
unisexual (-se·kschual) *adj.* unisexual.
unison (yu·nisøn) *adj.* unísono. *2 s.* MÚS. unisonancia: *in ~,* fig. al unísono.
unisonous (yuni·sønøs) *adj.* unísono.
unit (-nit) *s.* unidad: ~ *figure,* cifra de las unidades. *2* MEC., ELECT. grupo.
Unitarian (yunite·rian) *s.* unitario [partidario del unitarismo].
Unitarianism (yunite·rianišm) *s.* unitarismo.
unitary (yu·niteri) *adj.* unitario.
unite (to) (yunai·t) *tr.* unir. *2* juntar, asociar. *3 intr.* unirse. *4* juntarse,· asociarse. *5* obrar de acuerdo, concertarse.
united (-id) *adj.* unido: *United States,* Estados Unidos.
unity (yu·niti) *s.* unidad. *2* unión, concierto, armonía. *3* continuidad [de propósito o acción].
univalence (yuni·valøns) *s.* QUÍM. univalencia.
univalve (yu·nivælv) *adj.* univalvo.
universal (yunivø·ʳsal) *adj.* universal. *2* general [de todos].
universality (-vø·ʳsæ·liti) *s.* universalidad.
universe (yu·nivø·s) *s.* universo, mundo.
university (yunivø·ʳsiti) *s.* universidad. *2 adj.* universitario.
univocal (yuni·vøkal) *adj.* unívoco.
unjudged (øndȳø·dȳd) *adj.* no juzgado, pendiente de juicio, en litigio.

unjust (-dy̆ø·st) *adj.* injusto, inicuo. *2 s.* pecador.

unjustifiable (-dy̆østifai·abøl) *adj.* injustificable, inexcusable.

unjustified (-dy̆ø·stifaid) *adj.* injustificado.

unkempt (-ke·mpt) *adj.* desaliñado. *2* desgreñado, despeinado.

unkind (-kai·nd) *adj.* duro, cruel, falto de bondad. *2* adusto, seco, poco amable.

unkindly (-li) *adj.* UNKIND. *2 adv.* duramente, ásperamente.

unknown (-nau·n) *adj.* desconocido, ignorado, no sabido; ignoto: ~ *quantity,* incógnita; ~ *to me,* sin mi consentimiento, sin saberlo yo. *2* extraño. *3* incalculable, indecible.

unladylike (-lei·dilaik) *adj.* impropio de una dama. *2* poco femenino.

unlawful (-lo·ful) *adj.* ilegal, ilícito, ilegítimo.

unlearned (-lø·ʳnd) *adj.* indocto, ignorante. *2* no aprendido, ignorado. *3* natural, instintivo.

unleavened (-le·vønd) *adj.* ázimo.

unless (-le·s) *conj.* a menos que, a no ser que, como no sea, no siendo. *2* salvo, excepto, si no es.

unlevel (to) (-le·vøl) *tr.* desnivelar.

unlevelled (-d) *adj.* desnivelado.

unlike (-lai·k) *adj.* desemejante, diferente, distinto. *2 adv.* diferentemente, otramente, de diferente modo que. *3 prep.* a diferencia de.

unlikelihood (-lijud) *s.* improbabilidad. *2* inverosimilitud.

unlikely (-li) *adj.* improbable, remoto. *2* incierto, inseguro. *3* inverosímil. *4 adv.* improbablemente.

unlimited (ønli·mitid) *adj.* ilimitado. *2* vago, indefinido.

unload (to) (-lou·d) *tr.* descargar [un buque, una bestia, mercancías, etc.]. *2* descargar, exonerar, aligerar.

unlock (to) (-la·k) *tr.* abrir [una puerta, cajón, etc.], descubrir, revelar. *2* IMPR. desapretar [las formas].

unlooked-for (-lu·kt) *adj.* inopinado.

unloose (n (-lu·s(øn) *tr.* desatar, aflojar, soltar. *2 intr.* aflojarse, deshacerse.

unlucky (-lø·ki) *adj.* desafortunado, desgraciado, de mala suerte. *2* nefasto, aciago. *3* siniestro, de mal agüero.

unmake (to) (-mei·k) *tr.* deshacer, destruir, aniquilar.

unman (to) (-mæ·n) *tr.* dejar sin hombres, sin tripulación. *2* acobardar, desanimar, afeminar.

unmanageable (-mæ·nidy̆abøl) *adj.* inmanejable, ingobernable, indomable.

unmanly (-mæ·nli) *adj.* impropio de un hombre. *2* falto de las cualidades de un hombre.

unmannerly (-mæ·nøʳli) *adj.* mal educado, grosero. *2 adv.* descortésmente.

unmarried (-mæ·rid) *adj.* soltero, soltera.

unmask (to) (-mæ·sk) *tr.* desenmascarar, quitar la careta. *2* descubrir, mostrar. *3 intr.* quitarse la careta.

unmast (to) (-mæ·st) *tr.* MAR. desarbolar.

unmatched (-mæ·cht) *adj.* único, sin par. *2* desapareado.

unmeasurable (-me·y̆ørabøl) *adj.* inmensurable, incomensurable.

unmentionable (-me·nshønabøl) *adj.* que no se puede mencionar.

unmerciful (-mø·ʳsiful) *adj.* implacable, inclemente, despiadado, riguroso, cruel.

unmerited (-me·ritid) *adj.* inmerecido.

unmindful (-mai·ndful) *adj.* que olvida, que no atiende o considera.

unmistakable (-mistei·kabøl) *adj.* inequívoco, inconfundible, claro, evidente.

unmitigated (-mi̧·tigeitid) *adj.* no mitigado, duro. *2* acabado, de siete suelas.

unmixed (-mi·kst) *adj.* puro, sin mezcla.

unmoor (to) (-mu·ʳ) *tr.* MAR. desamarrar.

unmoral (-ma·ral) *adj.* amoral.

unmounted (-mau·ntid) *adj.* no montado, sin montar. *2* de a pie.

unmoved (-mu·vd) *adj.* firme, inmoble, en el mismo sitio. *2* impasible, frío, indiferente. *3* inflexible, inexorable.

unmuzzle (to) (-mø·s̆øl) *tr.* quitar el bozal a.

unnatural (-næ·chøral) *adj.* no natural, antinatural. *2* desnaturalizado, inhumano. *3* artificial, afectado, forzado.

unnecessary (-ne·søseri) *adj.* innecesario, inútil, superfluo.

unnerve (to) (-nø·ʳv) *tr.* enervar, acobardar, debilitar. *2* hacer perder la serenidad.

unnoticed (-nou·tist) *adj.* inadvertido, desadvertido, no observado.

unnumbered (-nø·mbøʳd) *adj.* innumerable; sin número.

unobservant (-øbsø·ʳvant) *adj.* distraído, poco observador.

unobtainable (-øbtei·nabøl) *adj.* inasequible.

unobtrusive (-øbtru·siv) *adj.* modesto, discreto.

unoccupied (øna·kiupaid) *adj.* desocupado, vacante, vacío. *2* desocupado [sin ocupación].

unofficial (-nøfi·shal) *adj.* no oficial; oficioso.

unorthodox (-o·ʳzødaks) *adj.* poco ortodoxo.

unostentatious (ønastentei·shøs) *adj.* sencillo, llano, modesto, no ostentoso.

unpack (to) (-pæ·k) *tr.* desempaquetar, desembalar, deshacer [baúles, maletas, etc.]. *2 intr.* deshacer los bultos o maletas.

unpaid (-pei·d) *adj.* sin pagar, por pagar, pendiente.

unpalatable (-pæ·latabøl) *adj.* ingustable, desagradable al gusto, fig. desagradable.

unparalleled (-pæ·raleld) *adj.* sin paralelo, único, sin par, sin igual.

unpardonable (-pa·ʳdønabøl) *adj.* imperdonable, inexcusable.

unpaved (-pei·vid) *adj.* sin empedrar.

unpeople (to) (-pi·pøl) *tr.* despoblar.

unpleasant (-ple·s̆ant) *adj.* desagradable, ingrato, enfadoso, molesto.

unploughed, unplowed (-plau·d) *adj.* inculto, sin arar.

unpolished (-pa·lisht) *adj.* áspero, tosco. *2* sin pulir. *3* mate.

unpolluted (-pøliu·tid) *adj.* impoluto, limpio.

unpopular (-pa·piula^r) *adj.* impopular. *2* que no goza de simpatías [en un mundo o esfera].

unpractical (-præ·ktikal) *adj.* poco práctico.

unpractised (-præ·ktist) *adj.* inexperto. *2* no practicado.

unprecedented (-pre·sidentid) *adj.* sin precedente, nunca visto, inaudito.

unprejudiced (-pre·dy̆udist) *adj.* imparcial.

unpremeditated (-prime·diteitid) *adj.* impremeditado.

unprepossessing (-pripøs̆e·sing) *adj.* poco atractivo.

unpresentable (-pris̆e·ntabøl) *adj.* impresentable.

unpretending, unpretentious (-prite·nding, -shøs) *adj.* modesto, sencillo, sin pretensiones.

unprincipled (-pri·nsipøld) *adj.* inmoral, sin con-·ciencia.

unprofitable (-pra·fitabøl) *adj.* improductivo, inútil, nada provechoso o lucrativo.

unpronounceable (-pronau·nsabøl) *adj.* impronunciable.

unpropitious (-prøpi·shøs) *adj.* desfavorable, adverso, poco propicio.

unprotected (-prøte·ktid) *adj.* sin protección, indefenso.

unprovided (-prøvai·did) *adj.* desproveído, desprovisto. *2* desprevenido.

unpublished (-pø·blisht) *adj.* inédito.

unpunished (-pø·nisht) *adj.* impune, sin castigo.

unqualified (-kua·lifaid) *adj.* inhábil, incapaz, incompetente. *2* absoluto, categórico; no modificado o condicionado; completo, entero.

unquenchable (-kue·nchabøl) *adj.* inextinguible.

unquestionable (-kue·schønabøl) *adj.* incuestionable, indiscutible, indudable.

unquiet (-kuai·øt) *adj.* inquieto, desasosegado, agitado, turbado. *2* nada silencioso.

unravel (to) (-ræ·vøl) *tr.* desenredar, desenmarañar. *2* aclarar, explicar, descifrar. *3* deshacer, deshilar. *4 intr.* desenredarse, desenmarañarse.

unread (-re·d) *adj.* no leído, por leer. *2* indocto.

unready (-re·di) *adj.* no listo o preparado.

unreal (-rr·al) *adj.* irreal, ilusorio, imaginario.

unreasonable (-rr·sønabøl) *adj.* irrazonable, desrazonable. *2* inmoderado, exorbitante.

unrecognizable (-re·køgnaišabøl) *adj.* desconocido, imposible de reconocer.

unrecovered (-ri·køvø{r}d) *adj.* no recuperado.

unreeve (to) (-rr·v) *tr.* MAR. despasar.

unrefined (-rifai·nd) *adj.* no refinado. *2* inculto, rudo.

unregenerate (-ridȳe·nørit) *adj.* no regenerado.

unrelenting (-rile·nting) *adj.* inexorable, implacable, inflexible. *2* que no cede o disminuye, tenaz.

unreliable (-rilai·abøl) *adj.* no confiable, de poca confianza. *2* informal.

unreligious (-rili·dȳøs) *adj.* irreligioso.

unremitting (-rimi·ting) *adj.* incesante, constante. *2* sostenido, incansable.

unrepentant (-ripe·ntant) *adj.* impenitente.

unreserved (-rišø·{r}vd) *adj.* no reservado, franco, abierto. *2* absoluto, ilimitado, incondicional.

unresisting (-riši·sting) *adj.* que no resiste, que no ofrece resistencia.

unresolved (-rišo·lvd) *adj.* no resuelto, sin solución. *2* irresoluto.

unresponsive (-rispa·nsiv) *adj.* que no responde [esp. a un sentimiento]; frío, insensible.

unrest (-re·st) *s.* inquietud, desasosiego.

unrestrained (-ristrei·nd) *adj.* libre, desenfrenado. *2* suelto, desembarazado.

unriddle (to) (-ri·døl) *tr.* resolver, descifrar, desembrollar.

unrig (to) (-ri·g) *tr.* MAR. desaparejar.

unrighteous (-rai·chøs) *adj.* malo, perverso. *2* injusto, inicuo.

unripe (-rai·p) *adj.* verde, en agraz; inmaduro.

unrivalled (-rai·vald) *adj.* sin rival, sin par.

unrivet (to) (-ri·vit) *tr.* desroblar.

unrobe (to) (-rou·b) *tr.* desnudar. *2 intr.* desnudarse.

unroll (to) (-rou·l) *tr.* desenrollar, desenvolver, desplegar. *2 intr.* abrirse, desenrollarse.

unroot (to) (-ru·t) *tr.* desarraigar, extirpar.

unruffled (-rø·føld) *adj.* tranquilo, sereno.

unruly (-ru·li) *adj.* indócil, díscolo, desobediente, indómito. *2* turbulento, levantisco.

unsaddle (to) (-sæ·døl) *tr.* desensillar. *2* desarzonar, derribar del caballo.

unsafe (-sei·f) *adj.* inseguro, peligroso.

unsaid (-se·d) *adj.* no dicho, por decir.

unsal(e)able (-sei·labøl) *adj.* invendible.

unsalted (-so·ltid) *adj.* no salado, sin salar.

unsatisfactory (-sætisfæ·ktori) *adj.* que no satisface, poco satisfactorio, inaceptable.

unsatisfied (-sæ·tisfaid) *adj.* no satisfecho. *2* descontento.

unsavo(u)ry (-sei·vøri) *adj.* insípido, soso, desabrido, de mal gusto. *2* mal oliente. *3* malo, desagradable.

unscathed (-skæ·did) *adj.* indemne, ileso.

unscrew (to) (-kru·) *tr.* destornillar.

unscrupulous (-skru·piuløs) *adj.* poco escrupuloso, inmoral.

unseal (to) (-sı·l) *tr.* abrir, desellar.

unseasonable (-sı·šønabøl) *adj.* intempestivo, inoportuno, prematuro o tardío.

unseat (to) (-sı·t) *tr.* quitar de un asiento. *2* desarzonar. *3* echar abajo [un ministerio].

unseaworthy (-sı·vø{r}dı) *adj.* MAR. sin condiciones marineras; innavegable [buque].

unseemly (-sı·mli) *adj.* impropio, indecoroso.

unseen (-sı·n) *adj.* no visto, inadvertido. *2* invisible.

unselfish (-se·lfish) *adj.* altruista, generoso, abnegado, desinteresado.

unserviceable (-sø·{r}visabøl) *adj.* inútil, inservible.

unsettle (to) (-se·tøl) *tr.* desquiciar, descomponer, desarreglar. *2* trastornar, agitar, turbar, alterar.

unsettled (-se·tøld) *adj.* desarreglado, descompuesto. *2* trastornado, inquieto, agitado. *3* turbio, revuelto. *4* inestable. *5* errante, sin residencia fija. *6* inhabitado. *7* irresuelto, indeterminado. *8* COM. pendiente, por pagar.

unsew (to) (-sou·) *tr.* descoser.

unshackle (to) (-shæ·køl) *tr.* libertar.

unshaded (-shei·did) *adj.* no sombreado, sin sombra.

unshaken (-shei·køn) *adj.* firme, inalterado, no conmovido.

unshaven (-shei·vøn) *adj.* sin afeitar.

unsheathe (to) (-shı·d) *tr.* desenvainar, sacar.

unsheltered (-sh·eltø{r}d) *adj.* desabrigado, sin abrigo, sin protección.

unship (to) (-shi·p) *tr.* MAR. desembarcar, descargar. *2* MAR. desmontar, desarmar [el timón, los remos, etc.].

unshod (-sha·d) *adj.* descalzo. *2* desherrado, sin herraduras.

unshorn (-sho·{r}n) *adj.* intonso; sin esquilar.

unshrinkable (shri·nkabøl) *adj.* inencogible.

unsightly (-sai·tli) *adj.* feo, deforme.

unskilled (-ski·ld) *adj.* UNSKILLFUL. *2* ~ *labo(u)rer*, obrero no especializado.

unskillful (-ful) *adj.* torpe, inhábil, inexperto, imperito.

unsling (to) (-sli·ng) *tr.* descolgar [lo que se lleva colgado].

unsociable (-sou·shabøl) *adj.* insociable, huraño, reservado.

unsoiled (-so·noild) *adj.* limpio, sin mancha.

unsold (ønsou·ld) *adj.* no vendido, por vender.

unsoldierlike, unsoldierly (-sou·lyø{r}laik, -li) *adv.* poco militar o marcial. *2* impropio de un militar.

unsolvable (-sa·lvabøl) *adj.* insoluble, irresoluble.

unsophisticated (-søfi·stikeitid) *adj.* puro, no sofisticado. *2* ingenuo, natural, sencillo.

unsought (ø·nsot) *adj.* no buscado, no solicitado.

unsound (-sau·nd) *adj.* enfermo, achacoso. *2* defectuoso, erróneo, falso. *3* malsano, pernicioso. *4* insano, perturbado. *5* inseguro, poco sólido, rajado, podrido.

unsparing (-spe·ring) *adj.* liberal, generoso, profuso. *2* implacable, despiadado; cruel.

unspeakable (-spɪ·kabøl) *adj.* inefable, indecible. *2* atroz, execrable.

unspecified (-spe·sifaid) *adj.* no especificado o detallado.

unspotted (-spa·tid) *adj.* limpio, inmaculado.

unstable (-tei·bøl) *adj.* inestable. *2* inconstante, variable. *3* poco sólido.

unstamped (-stæ·mpt) *adj.* sin sellar. *2* sin franquear [carta].

unsteadily (-te·dili) *adv.* inseguramente. *2* con fluctuación, irregularmente. *3* inconstantemente.

unsteady (-ste·di) *adj.* inseguro, vacilante, inestable, movedizo. *2* fluctuante. *3* inconstante, irregular. *4* veleidoso.

unstitch (to) (-tɪ·ch) *tr.* descoser.

unstop (to) (-sta·p) *tr.* destapar, descorchar. *3* desobstruir.

unstrained (-strei·nd) *adj.* natural, no forzado.

unstring (to) (-stri·ng) *tr.* desensartar. *2* desencordar. *3* aflojar. *4* debilitar, aturdir.

unstudied (-stø·did) *adj.* no estudiado, no aprendido. *2* natural, no afectado.

unsubstantial (-søbstæ·nshal) *adj.* etéreo, incorpóreo; fantástico. *2* flojo, inconsistente.

unsuccessful (-søkse·sful) *adj.* infructuoso, desgraciado. *2* fracasado, sin éxito, sin suerte.

unsufferable (-sø·førabøl) *adj.* insoportable, insufrible.

unsuitable (ønsiu·tabøl), **unsuited** (-id) *adj.* impropio, inadecuado, poco apropiado o conveniente.

unsupported (-søpoˑᵣtid) *adj.* sin apoyo, sin sostén.

unsure (-shu·ᵣ) *adj.* inseguro. *2* incierto, precario.

unsurmountable (-søᵣmau·ntabøl) *adj.* insuperable, invencible.

unsurpassed (-søᵣpa·st) *adj.* excelente, insuperado.

unsuspected (-søspe·ktid) *adj.* insospechado. *2* que no es objeto de sospecha.

unsuspecting (-søspe·kting), **unsuspicious** (-søspi·shøs) *adj.* confiado, que no sospecha.

unswerving (-suøˑᵣving) *adj.* firme, inmutable, resoluto.

unsympathetic (-simpaze·tik) *adj.* incompasivo, frío.

untainted (-tei·ntid) *adj.* impoluto, no inficionado.

untamed (-tei·md) *adj.* indomado, indómito, cerril, bravío.

untasted (-tei·stid) *adj.* sin probar, no gustado.

untaught (-toˑt) *adj.* no aprendido, natural, espontáneo. *2* sin instrucción.

untenable (-te·nabøl) *adj.* insostenible.

untenanted (-te·nantid) *adj.* desalquilado, desocupado.

unthinkable (-zi·nkabøl) *adj.* inconcebible.

unthought-of (-zoˑt) *adj.* inimaginado. *2* impensado, inesperado.

unthoughtful (-zoˑtful) *adj.* irreflexivo, inconsiderado.

unthread (to) (-zreˑd) *tr.* desenhebrar, desensartar.

untidy (-tai·di) *adj.* desaliñado, desaseado, desordenado.

untie (to) (-tai·) *tr.* desatar, desligar, desanudar. *2* deshacer [un nudo]. *3* aflojar, soltar, zafar.

until (-ti·l) *prep.* hasta [con sentido temporal]. *2 conj.* hasta que.

untilled (-ti·ld) *adj.* inculto, baldío.

untimely (-tai·mli) *adj.* intempestivo, inoportuno. *2* prematuro. *3 adv.* intempestivamente. *4* prematuramente.

untiring (-tai·ring) *adj.* incansable, infatigable.

unto (ø·ntu) *prep.* poét. y ant. hacia, a, hasta, contra, en.

untold (øntou·ld) *adj.* no dicho, contado o narrado. *2* no revelado. *3* incontable, incalculable, vasto.

untouchable (-tø·chabøl) *adj.* intangible. *2 s.* intocable.

untoward (-toˑaᵣd) *adj.* indócil, terco, inmanejable. *2* inconveniente, indecoroso. *3* desgraciado, contrario, adverso.

untractable (-træ·ktabøl) *adj.* indócil, insumiso.

untrained (-trei·nd) *adj.* no ejercitado o entrenado, inexperto; indisciplinado. *2* MIL. bisoño.

untranslatable (-trænslei·tabøl) *adj.* intraducible.

untravelled (-træ·vøld) *adj.* no transitado, inexplorado, virgen. *2* que no ha visto mundo, provinciano.

untried (-trai·d) *adj.* no probado, no ensayado.

untrimmed (-tri·md) *adj.* desguarnecido, sin adornos. *2* sin cortar, sin arreglar.

untrod(den (-tra·d(øn) *adj.* no hollado.

untroubled (-trø·bøld) *adj.* quieto, sosegado, tranquilo.

untrue (-tu·) *adj.* falso, inexacto. *2* infiel, desleal.

untrustworthy (-trø·stuøᵣdi) *adj.* poco fiable, poco seguro.

untruth (-tru·z) *s.* falsedad, error.

untruthful (-ful) *adj.* falso, mentiroso.

untutored (-tiu·tøᵣd) *adj.* inculto, sin instrucción.

untwine (to) (-tuai·n) *tr.* desenlazar, desenroscar.

untwist (to) (-tui·st) *tr.* destorcer, desenroscar.

unused (-yu·šd) *adj.* no usado. *2* no habituado. *3* desusado.

unusual (-yu·ŷual) *adj.* extraordinario, excepcional, raro, insólito, no acostumbrado.

unutterable (-ø·tørabøl) *adj.* indecible.

unvanquished (-væ·nkuisht) *adj.* invicto.

unvarying (-ve·riing) *adj.* invariable, constante.

unveil (to) (-vei·l) *tr.* quitar el velo a, descubrir, revelar. *2* quitarse el velo, descubrirse.

unvoiced (-voi·sd) *adj.* mudo [no expresado en palabras].

unwarned (-woˑrnd) *adj.* no avisado. *2* desprevenido.

unwarrantable (-wa·rantabøl) *adj.* insostenible, injustificable, inexcusable.

unwarranted (-wa·rantid) *adj.* injustificado. *2* no autorizado. *3* sin garantía.

unwary (-we·ri) *adj.* descuidado, desprevenido, incauto. *2* imprudente, irreflexivo.

unwatered (-woˑtøᵣd) *adj.* no regado, de secano.

unwavering (-wei·vøring) *adj.* que no tiembla o vacila; firme, determinado, resuelto.

unwearied (-wɪ·rid) *adj.* infatigable.

unweave (to) (-wɪ·v) *tr.* destejer, deshacer.

unwelcome (-we·lkøm) *adj.* mal acogido, mal recibido. *2* desagradable, inoportuno, indeseable.

unwell (-weˑl) *adj.* enfermo, indispuesto, achacoso. *2* fam. que tiene la regla o menstruo.

unwholesome (-jou·lsøm) *adj.* insalubre, malsano. *2* dañino, pernicioso, nocivo.

unwieldy (-wɪ·ldi) *adj.* pesado, difícil de manejar,

embarazoso. *2* torpe, desmañado. *3* rebelde, ingobernable.

unwilling (-wi·ling) *adj.* reacio, renuente, mal dispuesto.

unwind (to) (-wai·nd) *tr.* devanar. *2* desenrollar. *3* desenredar, desenmarañar, desenvolver. ¶ Pret. y p. p.: *unwound*.

unwise (-wai·s̄) *adj.* imprudente, poco cuerdo, necio. *2* ignorante.

unwitting (-wi·ting) *adj.* inconsciente, que no se percata, distraído.

unwomanly (-wu·manli) *adj.* impropio de una mujer.

unwonted (-wø·ntid) *adj.* desusado, desacostumbrado, inusitado, raro, poco común.

unwooded (-wu·did) *adj.* sin árboles.

unworldly (-wø·ʳldli) *adj.* no mundano, no terrenal, espiritual.

unworn (-wo·ʳn) *adj.* nuevo, no llevado, sin estrenar. *2* no usado o gastado.

unworthy (-wø·ʳdi) *adj.* indigno, desmerecedor.

unwrap (to) (-ræ·p) *tr.* desenvolver [quitar lo que envuelve], desabrigar.

unwritten (-ri·tøn) *adj.* no escrito. *2* en blanco. *3* oral, tradicional.

unwrought (-ro·t) *adj.* en bruto, no trabajado.

unyielding (-yɪ·lding) *adj.* inflexible, firme, inexorable. *2* terco, reacio.

unyoke (to) (-you·k) *tr.* desuncir; desunir. *2* *intr.* libertarse de un yugo.

up (øp) *adv.* hacia arriba, arriba, en lo alto, en o hacia una posición superior: ~ *above*, arriba, más arriba. *2* en o hacia una posición derecha, en pie. *3* en o hacia el centro más importante, la dirección, la oficina principal, etc. *4* en o hacia un estado de mayor actividad, fuerza, excitación, resolución, etc.: *to stir* ~, excitar, avivar. *5* en o hacia un estado de evidencia; manifestación o aparición. *6* a la altura, a la par de. *7* enteramente, completamente: *to burn* ~, quemar del todo. *8* de cara, en contacto, en proximidad: *to run* ~ *against*, topar con; *close* ~ *to*, tocando a. *9* a un lado, en reserva: *to lay* ~, guardar, acumular. *10* hasta: ~ *to now*, hasta ahora; ~ *to date*, hasta la fecha; al día, al corriente. *11* ~ *and down*, arriba y abajo, de un lado a otro. *12 up*, con estos y otros sentidos modifica gran número de verbos formando locuciones que se encontrarán en los artículos respectivos.

13 prep. subido a, en o a lo alto de, hacia arriba de, a lo largo de [subiendo], hacia el interior de: ~ *a tree*, subido en un árbol; fig. en apuros; ~ *the river*, río arriba; ~ *the country*, hacia el interior del país.

14 adj. de arriba, dirigido hacia arriba, ascendente. *15* alto, levantado, derecho, en pie. *16* levantado [no acostado]. *17* vuelto hacia arriba. *18* en estado de actividad, excitado; levantado, sublevado. *19* que está en curso, en marcha: *what is* ~?, ¿qué ocurre?, ¿qué pasa? *20* igualado [con otro]. *21* entendido, enterado. *22* capaz, dispuesto. *23* acabado, terminado; *time is* ~, expiró el plazo; ha llegado la hora. *24* que está haciendo o se propone [algo]: *to be* ~ *to one's old tricks*, hacer uno de las suyas. *25* fam. ~ *against*, abocado a. *26* ~ *against it*, ante un obstáculo insuperable. *27 hard* ~, apurado, a la cuarta pregunta. *28 s.* movimiento o curva ascendente. *29* alza [de precios]. *30 ups and downs*, altibajos, vaivenes.

31 interj. ¡arriba!, ¡aúpa!, ¡sus! *32* ~ *there!*, ¡alto ahí!

33 up and, seguido de infinitivo, indica que se inicia bruscamente la acción indicada por el verbo: ponerse de repente a + infinitivo.

up-and-coming *adj.* fam. (E.U.) listo, activo.

upas (yu·pas) *s.* BOT. antiar. *2* upas [veneno]. *3* ponzoña.

upbraid (to) (øpbrei·d) *tr.* reconvenir, reprender.

upbraiding (-ing) *s.* reconvención, reproche.

upbringing (øpbri·nging) *s.* educación.

upcast (ø·pkæst) *adj.* lanzado o dirigido hacia arriba.

upcountry (ø·pkøntri) *s.* fam. interior [del país]. *2 adj.* del interior [del país]. *3 adv.* en el interior, hacia el interior, tierra adentro.

upgrowth (ø·pgrouz) *s.* crecimiento, desarrollo.

upheaval (øpjɪ·val) *s.* solevamiento, levantamiento [esp. de la corteza terrestre]. *2* trastorno, conmoción, cataclismo.

upheave (to) (-jɪ·v) *tr.* solevar, levantar. *2 intr.* solevarse, levantarse.

uphill (ø·pjil) *adv.* cuesta arriba. *2 adj.* que sube, ascendente. *3* penoso, trabajoso, dificultoso.

uphold (to) (øpjou·ld) *tr.* levantar; mantener derecho. *2* sostener, apoyar. *3* mantener, defender.

upholster (to) (øpjou·lstøʳ) *tr.* tapizar y emborrar [muebles]. *2* tapizar, colgar [habitaciones].

upholsterer (-øʳ) *s.* tapicero.

upholstery (-i) *s.* tapicería; colgaduras.

upkeep (ø·pkɪp) *s.* conservación, manutención, entretenimiento.

upland (ø·plænd) *s.* altiplanicie, tierra alta. *2* tierra adentro, el interior.

uplift (øpli·ft) *s.* levantamiento, elevación.

upon (øpa·n) *prep.* sobre, encima. *2* corresponde a otras preposiciones, según los casos: *nothing to live* ~, nada con qué vivir; *to to turn* ~ *him*, volverse contra él; ~ *my honour*, por mi honor, a fe mía; ~ *pain of*, bajo pena de. *3* no se traduce cuando precede a una fecha o a algunos gerundios: ~ *the tenth of June*, el diez de junio; ~ *seeing this*, viendo esto.

upper (ø·pøʳ) *adj. compar.* de UP: superior, alto, más elevado, de encima, de arriba: ~ *case*, IMPR. caja alta; ~ *classes*, la clase alta; *Upper House*, cámara alta; ~ *works*, MAR. obra muerta. *2* dirigido hacia arriba. *3 s.* pala y caña del zapato: *on one's uppers*, con las suelas gastadas; fig. tronado; apurado.

uppercut (-køt) BOX. golpe dirigido hacia arriba.

uppermost (-moust) *adj.* el más alto o elevado; supremo, predominante. *2* el de encima de todo. *3 adv.* en lo más alto; en primer lugar.

uppish (ø·pish) *adj.* fam. orgulloso, arrogante.

upright (ø·prait) *adj.* derecho, erguido, vertical, enhiesto: ~ *piano*, plano vertical. *2* recto, íntegro, honrado.

uprise (øprai·s̄) *s.* levantamiento, ascensión. *2* pendiente enhiesta. *3* levantamiento, insurrección.

uprise (to) *intr.* levantarse [de la cama, etc.]. *2* levantarse, sublevarse. *3* elevarse, ascender. *4* crecer, aumentar [un sonido].

uprising (-ing) *s.* levantamiento; solevantamiento. *2* levantamiento, insurrección.

uproar (ø·proʳ) *s.* gritería, alboroto, tumulto.

uproarious (øpro·riøs) *adj.* estruendoso; ruidoso; bullicioso. *2* tumultuoso.

uproot (to) (øpru·t) *tr.* desarraigar, extirpar.

upset (-se·t) *adj.* volcado, tumbado. *2* trastornado, desarreglado, turbado. *3* indispuesto [malo]. *4*

~ *price*, precio inicial en una subasta. *5 s.*
vuelco. *6* trastorno; desorden; indisposición. *7*
contratiempo.
upset (to) *tr.* volcar. *2* trastornar, descomponer,
desarreglar. *3* turbar, alterar, conmover. *4* contrariar, desbaratar. *5* indisponer, poner enfermo. *6 intr.* volcar.
upshot (ø·pshat) *s.* resultado final, conclusión.
upside (-said) *s.* lado o parte superior: ~ *down*, lo
de arriba abajo, al revés, patas arriba.
upstairs (øpste·ᶠš) *adv.* arriba, a o en el piso de
arriba. *2 adj.* de arriba.
upstanding (-stæ·nding) *adj.* derecho, en pie. *2*
recto, honrado.
upstart (øpsta·ᶠt) *adj.-s.* advenedizo; presuntuoso.
upstream (øpstrɪ·m) *adv.* aguas arriba, río arriba.
upthrust (ø·pzrøst) *s.* GEOL. solevantamiento.
up-to-date *adj.* que llega hasta la fecha, al corriente. *2* moderno, del día; de última moda.
upturn (-tøᶠn) *s.* alza [de precios]. *2* mejoramiento.
upturn (to) (øptø·ᶠn) *tr.* volver hacia arriba. *2* revolver, trastornar, volcar.
upward (ø·pwaᶠd) *adj.* dirigido hacia arriba, ascendente.
upward(s *adv.* hacia arriba, para arriba, arriba.
uraemia (yurɪ·mi*a*) *s.* (Ingl.) uremia.
Ural Mountains (yu·ral) *n. pr.* GEOGR. Montes Urales.
Urania (yurei·ni*a*) *n. pr.* MIT. Urania.
uranite (yu·ranait) *s.* MINER. uranita.
uranium (yurei·niøm) *s.* QUÍM. uranio.
uranography (yurana·grafi) *s.* uranografía.
Uranus (yu·ranøs) *s.* ASTR. Urano.
urate (yu·reit) *s.* QUÍM. urato.
urban (ø·ᶠban) *adj.* urbano [de la ciudad].
Urban *n. pr.* Urbano.
urbane (ø·ᶠbei·n) *adj.* urbano, cortés.
urbanity (ø·ᶠbæ·niti) *s.* urbanidad. *2* fineza.
urchin (ø·ᶠchin) *s.* pilluelo, granuja, bribonzuelo,
rapaz. *2* ZOOL. erizo: *sea* ~, erizo de mar.
urea (yurɪ·*a*) *s.* QUÍM. urea.
uremia (yurɪ·mi*a*) *s.* (E.U.) uremia.
ureter (yurɪ·tøᶠ) *s.* ANAT. y ZOOL. uréter.
urethra (yurɪ·zra) *s.* ANAT., ZOOL. uretra.
urge (ø·ᶠdȳ) *s.* impulso. *2* ganas, deseo, estímulo.
urge (to) *tr.* encarecer, insistir en. *2* alegar. *3* proponer, recomendar. *4* instar, apremiar. *5* mo-
ver, incitar. *6* apresurar, acelerar.
urgency (-ønsi) *s.* urgencia. *2* insistencia; instancia. *3* URGE.
urgent (-ønt) *adj.* urgente. *2* insistente, apremiante.
Uriah (yurai·*a*) *n. pr.* Urías.
uric (yu·rik) *adj.* QUÍM. úrico.
urinal (yu·rinal) *s.* orinal. *2* urinario, mingitorio.
urinary (yu·rineri) *adj.* urinario: ~ *tract*, vías urinarias.
urinate (to) (yu·rineit) *intr.* orinar, mear.
urine (yu·rin) *s.* orina, orines.
urn (øᶠn) *s.* urna. *2* jarrón.
urodelan (yurodi·lan) *adj.-s.* ZOOL. urodelo.
urologist (yura·lødȳist) *s.* urólogo.
urology (-i) *s.* urología.
Ursa (ø·ᶠsa) *s.* ASTR. Osa: ~ *Major*, Osa mayor; ~
Minor, Osa menor.
Ursidae (ø·ᶠsidɪ) *s. pl.* ZOOL. úrsidos.
ursine (-sin) *adj.* osuno. *2* peludo.
Ursuline (ø·rsiulin) *n. pr.* Ursulina.
urticaceous (ø·ᶠtikei·šøs) *adj.* urticáceo.
urticant (ø·ᶠtikant) *adj.* urticante.

urticaria (ø·ᶠtike·ri*a*) *s.* MED. urticaria.
urubu (ø·rubu) *s.* ORN. urubú.
Uruguayan (yurugwi·*a*n) *adj.-s.* uruguayo.
us (øs) *pron.* [sin prep.] nos [acusativo o dativo de
WE]. *2* [con prep.] nosotros, nosotras.
usable (yu·šabøl) *adj.* que se puede usar.
usage (yu·sidȳ) *s.* trato, tratamiento. *2* uso, costumbre.
use (yus) *s.* uso, empleo, goce, aprovechamiento:
out of ~, desusado, pasado de moda. *2* utilidad,
servicio, provecho, objeto: *to put to* ~, aprovechar, sacar partido de; *of no* ~, inútil; *to have
no (further)* ~ *for*, no necesitar; no querer saber
nada o nada más de. *3* uso, usanza, práctica,
costumbre. *4* DER. uso.
use (to) *tr.* usar, emplear, gastar, servirse o valerse
de. *2* hacer, practicar. *3* tratar [bien, mal, etc.].
4 acostumbrar, habituar. *5* soler ir o andar por.
6 to ~ *up*, gastar, consumir, agotar. *7 intr.* soler,
acostumbrar.
used (-d) *adj.* usado. *2* usual, acostumbrado. *3*
acostumbrado, habituado: ~ *to*, acostumbrado
a.
useful (-ful) *adj.* útil. *2* conveniente, provechoso,
beneficioso.
useless (-lis) *adj.* inútil. *2* inservible.
usher (yu·shøᶠ) *s.* ujier, portero, introductor. *2*
TEAT. acomodador. *3* (Ingl.) ayudante de escuela.
usher (to) *tr.* introducir, anunciar, guiar.
usherette (-et) *s.* TEAT. acomodadora.
ustion (ø·schiøn) *s.* ustión.
usual (yu·ȳual) *adj.*· usual, habitual, acostumbrado, ordinario, de costumbre: *as* ~, como de
costumbre, como de ordinario.
usufruct (yu·šiufrøkt) *s.* usufructo.
usufructuary (yusiufrø·kchueri) *adj.-s.* usufructuario.
usurer (yu·ȳørøᶠ) *s.* usurero.
usurious (yuȳu·riøs) *adj.* usurario.
usurp (to) (yušø·ᶠp) *tr.* usurpar.
usurpation (yušøᶠpei·shøn) *s.* usurpación.
usurper (yušø·ᶠpøᶠ) *s.* usurpador.
usury (yu·ȳuri) *s.* usura.
ut (ut) *s.* MÚS. ut, do.
utensil (yute·nsil) *s.* utensilio. *2* útil, herramienta.
uterine (yu·tørin) *adj.* uterino.
uterus (-øs) *s.* ANAT., ZOOL. útero.
utilitarian (yutilite·rian) *adj.* utilitario.
utilitarianism (-išm) *s.* FIL. utilitarismo.
utility (yuti·liti) *s.* utilidad, ventaja, provecho. *2*
empresa de servicio público [agua, gas, electricidad, etc.]. *3* TEAT. ~ *man*, racionista.
utilize (to) (yu·tilaiš) *tr.* utilizar, emplear, aprovechar, explotar.
utmost (ø·tmoust) *adj.* sumo, extremo; más
grande, mayor, más alto, más distante, último.
2 s. lo más posible, lo sumo: *to do one's* ~, hacer
cuanto uno puede.
utopia, Utopia (yutou·pia) *s.* utopía.
utopian, Utopian (-n) *adj.* utópico. *2* utopista.
utricle (yu·trikøl) *s.* ANAT., BOT. utrículo.
utter (ø·tøᶠ) *adj.* absoluto, completo, total. *2* categórico, terminante.
utter (to) *tr.* pronunciar, articular, proferir. *2* dar,
lanzar [un grito]. *3* decir, expresar, manifestar.
utterance (øtæ·rans) *s.* pronunciación, articulación, emisión [de sonidos, palabras, etc.]. *2* expresión, manera de hablar. *3* declaración, discurso.
utterly (-li) *adv.* absolutamente, completamente,
totalmente, del todo.

uvate (yu·veit) *s.* uvate.
uvea (yu·vi*a*) *s.* ANAT. úvea.
uvula (yu·viul*a*) *s.* ANAT. úvula.
uvular (-la^r) *adj.* uvular.

uxorial (øxo·rial) *adj.* uxorial.
uxoricide (-isaid) *s.* uxoricidio. *2* uxoricida.
uxorious (-iøs) *adj.* gurrumino.

V

V, v (vi) *s.* V, v, vigésima segunda letra del alfabeto inglés. *2* V, cifra romana.
vacancy (vei·kansi) *s.* ocio. *2* vacante, vacatura. *3* vacío, hueco, laguna. *4* vacuidad.
vacant (-kant) *adj.* vacante. *2* vacío, despreocupado. *3* ocioso, de ocio. *4* inexpresivo, vago. *5* distraído.
vacate (to) (vei·keit) *tr.* dejar vacante. *2* evacuar, desocupar. *3* anular, invalidar. *4 intr.* vacar, dedicarse.
vacation (veikei·shøn) *s.* vacación, descanso. *2* vacante. *3* DER. anulación.
vaccinate (to) (væ·ksineit) *tr.* vacunar.
vaccination (væksinei·shøn) *s.* vacunación.
vaccine (væ·ksin) *adj.* vacuno. *2* de vacuna: ~ *therapy,* vacunoterapia. *3 s.* vacuna.
vacillate (to) (væ·sileit) *tr.* vacilar. *2* fluctuar.
vacillation (væsilei·shøn) *s.* vacilación. *2* fluctuación.
vacuity (vakiu·iti) *s.* vacío. *2* hueco, blanco. *3* vaciedad. *4* ausencia [de ideas, emociones, etc.]; vaguedad.
vacuole (væ·kiuol) *s.* BIOL. vacuola.
vacuous (væ·kiuøs) *adj.* vacuo, vacío. *2* estúpido. *3* insulso. *4* ocioso, frívolo.
vacuum (va·kiuøm) *s.* vacío, vacuo: ~ *bottle* o *flask,* termos; ~ *cleaner,* aspirador eléctrico; ~ *tube,* ELECT. tubo o lámparra de vacío.
vade mecum (vei·di mi·køm) *s.* vademécum, manual.
vagabond (væ·gaband) *adj.* errabundo, nómada, vagabundo. *2 s.* vagabundo; vago.
vagabondize (to) (væ·gabandaiš) *intr.* vagabundear.
vagary (veige·ri) *s.* capricho, extravagancia, antojo, extravío, vagabundeo.
vagina (vadÿai·na) *s.* ANAT. vagina.
vaginate (væ·dÿineit) *s.* BOT. envainado.
vagrancy (vei·gransi) *s.* vagabundeo, vagancia. *2* extravío, capricho.
vagrant (-ant) *adj.* vagabundo, vagaroso, errante, errático. *2 s.* vago, vagabundo.
vague (veig) *adj.* vago, indefinido, indistinto. *2* incierto, dudoso.
vain (vein) *adj.* vano, fútil. *2* vano, infructuoso: *in* ~, en vano. *3* vano, vanidoso.
vainglorious (veinglo·riøs) *adj.* vanaglorioso.
vainglory (-ri) *s.* vanagloria.

vair (ve^r) *s.* vero [piel]. *2* BLAS. veros.
valance (væ·lans) *s.* cenefa colgante, doselera, sobrepuerta.
vale (veil) *s.* poét. valle: ~ *of tears,* valle de lágrimas.
valediction (vælidi·kshøn) *s.* adiós, despedida.
valedictory (-tori) *adj.* de despedida. *2 s.* discurso de despedida a fin de curso.
valence, -cy (vei·løns, -si) *s.* QUÍM. valencia.
Valentine (væ·løntain) *n. pr.* Valentín.
valentine *s.* tarjeta amorosa o jocosa enviada a una persona del sexo contrario el día de San Valentín. *2* novio o novia.
valerian (valɪ·rian) *s.* BOT., FARM. valeriana.
valerianate (-eit) *s.* QUÍM. valerianato.
valet (væ·lit o væ·lei) *s.* criado, ayuda de cámara. *2* planchador de trajes [en un hotel].
valetudinarian (vælitiudine·rian) *s.* valetudinario.
valiant (væ·liant) *adj.* valiente, valeroso.
valid (væ·lid) *adj.* válido. *2* valedero. *3* eficaz.
validate (to) (va·lideit) *tr.* validar.
validity (vali·diti) *s.* validez.
valise (valɪ·s) *s.* maleta, valija; *petaca.
Valkyrie (væ·lkiri) *s.* valquiria.
valley (væ·li) *s.* GEOGR. valle, cuenca, hoya. *2* ARQ. lima hoya.
valor (væ·lø^r) *s.* VALOUR.
valorous (-lørøs) *adj.* valeroso, valiente.
valour (væ·lø^r) *s.* valor, valentía, fortaleza.
valuable (væ·liuabøl) *adj.* valioso, costoso, preciado. *2 s. pl.* joyas, objetos de valor.
valuation (væliuei·shøn) *s.* valoración, avalúo. *2* estimación, apreciación.
value (væ·liu) *s.* valor [de una cosa]; precio, mérito, valía, estimación, aprecio. *2* entidad, importancia. *3* MÚS., PINT. valor.
value (to) *tr.* valorar, valuar, tasar. *2* dar valor a, tener en mucho, estimar, considerar.
valueless (-lis) *adj.* sin valor, insignificante.
valval, valvar (væ·lval, -a^r) *adj.* BIOL. valvar.
valve (væ·lv) *s.* ANAT., MEC., RADIO. válvula. *2* BOT. ventalla. *3* ZOOL. valva. *4* compuerta [de canal, presa, etc.].
valvular (væ·lviula^r) *adj.* valvular.
valvule (-viul) *s.* válvulilla.
vamp (væmp) *s.* ZAP. pala, empella. *2* remiendo. *3* arreglo, improvisación. *4* fam. vampiresa, mujer fatal.

vamp (to) *tr.* remendar, componer. *2* arreglar, improvisar. *3* pop. conquistar [una mujer a un hombre], coquetear con. *4 intr.* coquetear, hacer de mujer fatal.

vamper (-ø^r) *s.* remendón.

vampire (væ·mpai^r) *s.* vampiro. *2* vampiresa. *3* TEAT. escotillón.

van (væn) *s.* carromato. *2* carro de mudanzas; camión. *3* (Ingl.) furgón de equipajes. *4* vanguardia.

vanadium (vanei·diøm) *s.* QUÍM. vanadio.

Vandal (væ·ndal) *adj.-s.* vándalo.

vandalism (væ·ndɑlišm) *s.* vandalismo.

vane (vein) *s.* veleta. *2* MAR. grímpola. *3* aspa [de molino]. *4* paleta, álabe. *5* barbas [de la pluma]. *6* pínula.

vanguard (væ·ngɑ^rd) *s.* vanguardia.

vanilla (vani·la) *s.* BOT. vainilla.

vanish (to) (væ·nish) *intr.* desaparecer, desvanecerse, disiparse, esfumarse.

vanity (væ·niti) *s.* vanidad, envanecimiento: ~ *case*, polvera. *2* vanidad, inutilidad, futilidad.

vanquish (to) (væ·nkuish) *tr.* vencer, derrotar. *2* vencer, dominar.

vantage (væ·ntidÿ) *s.* ventaja, superioridad; situación favorable: ~ *ground*, posición ventajosa. *2* TENIS ventaja.

vapid (væ·pid) *adj.* soso, insípido, insulso.

vapor (vei·pø^r) *s.* VAPOUR.

vapor (to) *intr.-tr.* TO VAPOUR.

vaporer (vei·pørø^r) *s.* fanfarrón.

vaporish (-ish) *adj.* vaporoso. *2* histérico.

vaporize (to) (-aiš) *tr.* vaporizar. *2* volatilizar. *3* evaporar. *4 intr.* vaporizarse.

vaporizer (-aisø^r) *s.* vaporizador. *2* pulverizador.

vaporose (vei·pørous) *adj.* vaporoso, volátil.

vaporous (-øs) *adj.* calinoso, brumoso. *2* vaporoso, etéreo, fantástico. *3* vago, nebuloso.

vapour (-pø^r) *s.* vapor, gas, humo, vaho, exhalación. *2* niebla ligera. *3* fig. humo, fantasía.

vapour (to) *intr.* evaporarse, vahear. *2* fanfarronear. *3 tr.* evaporar. *4* exhalar.

vapo(u)ry (-i) *adj.* vaporoso, calinoso.

vapulate (to) (vei·piulet) *tr.* vapulear.

variability (veriabi·liti) *s.* variabilidad.

variable (ve·riabøl) *adj.* variable. *2* inconstante, mudable. *3 s.* cosa variable. *4* MAT. variable. *5* GRAM. parte variable.

variance (ve·rians) *s.* variación, cambio. *2* discrepancia. *3* desavenencia, desacuerdo. *4 at* ~, en desacuerdo; desavenidos.

variant (ve·riant) *adj.* vario, distinto, diferente. *2 s.* variante.

variation (veriei·shøn) *s.* variación. *2* AJED. variante.

varicolo (u) red (ve·rikølø^rd) *adj.* multicolor.

varicose (væ·rikous) *adj.* varicoso.

varied (ve·rid) *adj.* vario, variado.

variegate (to) (ve·rigeit) *tr.* abigarrar, jaspear, vetear, matizar. *2* dar variedad a.

variegated (-id) *adj.* abigarrado, jaspeado, veteado, matizado, variado.

variety (varai·iti) *s.* variedad. *2* TEAT. variedades.

variform (varai·fo^rm) *adj.* diversiforme.

variolous (varai·oløs) *adj.* varioloso. *2* picado de viruelas.

variometer (veria·mitø^r) *s.* ELECT. variómetro.

various (ve·riøs) *adj.* vario [diverso; variable]. *2* variado. *3* varios, algunos.

varix (ve·riks), *pl.* **varices (ve·risiš)** *s.* MED. variz.

varlet (va·^rlit) *s.* ant. lacayo. *2* ant. bribón.

varnish (va·^rnish) *s.* barniz. *2* charol. *3* CERÁM. vidriado.

varnish (to) *tr.* barnizar; charolar. *2* CERÁM. vidriar. *3* fig. disimular, encubrir, paliar.

varnishing (-ing) *s.* barnizado [acción]: ~ *day*, B. ART. barnizado [de una exposición].

varsity (va·^rsiti) *s.* fam. universidad.

vary (to) (ve·ri) *tr.-intr.* variar. *2 intr.* discrepar, diferenciarse. *3* desviarse, apartarse.

varying (ve·riing) *adj.* variante; variable.

vascular (væ·skiula^r) *adj.* vascular.

vasculose (-lous) *adj.* vasculoso.

vase (veis) *s.* jarrón; florero; jarro.

vaseline (væ·sølin) *s.* vaselina.

vasomotor (væsømou·tø^r) *s.* FISIOL., ANAT. vasomotor.

vassal (væ·sal) *adj.-s.* vasallo.

vassalage (væ·sølidÿ) *s.* vasallaje.

vast (væst) *adj.* vasto. *2* anchuroso. *3* inmenso; enorme, atroz. *4 s.* vastedad, inmensidad.

vastly (-li) *adv.* inmensamente, enormemente, muy, mucho, en sumo grado.

vasty (-i) *adj.* vasto, inmenso.

vat (væt) *s.* tina, cubo grande, tanque.

Vatican (væ·tikan) *n. pr.* Vaticano.

vaticinal (væti·sinal) *adj.* vatídico, profético.

vaticinate (to) (væti·sineit) *intr.* vaticinar.

vaticination (-ei·shøn) *s.* vaticinio.

vaudeville (vou·dvil) *s.* espectáculo de variedades. *2* especie de zarzuela. *3* canción popular satírica.

vault (volt) *s.* ARQ., ANAT. bóveda. *2* fig. bóveda celeste. *3* sótano; cripta; tumba o panteón subterráneo. *4* salto [con pértiga, etc.].

vault (to) *tr.* abovedar, cubrir con bóveda. *2 tr.-intr.* saltar [por encima], voltear, saltar con pértiga.

vaulted (-id) *adj.* abovedado.

vaunt (vont) *s.* jactancia, vanagloria, alarde.

vaunt (to) *intr.* jactarse, vanagloriarse. *2 tr.* jactarse de, ostentar.

vaunter (-ø^r) *s.* jactancioso, fanfarrón.

veal (vil) *s.* ternera [carne].

vector (ve·ktø^r) *s.* MAT. radio vector.

vectorial (vekto·rial) *adj.* vector.

Veda (vei·da) *s.* Veda.

vedette (vide·t) *s.* MIL. centinela o escucha a caballo. *2* MAR. escampavía.

veer (to) (vi^r) *intr.* virar, girar, desviarse. *2* METEOR. cambiar [el viento]. *3 tr.* cambiar el rumbo o la dirección de.

veering (-ing) *s.* virada.

veery (vi·ri) *s.* ORN. tordo americano.

vegetable (ve·dÿitabøl) *adj.* vegetal: ~ *kingdom*, reino vegetal. *2* de hortalizas: ~ *garden*, huerto. *3 s.* vegetal, planta. *4* legumbre, hortaliza.

vegetal (ve·dÿital) *adj.* vegetal.

vegetarian (vedÿite·rian) *adj.-s.* vegetariano.

vegetate (to) (ve·dÿiteit) *intr.* vegetar.

vegetation (-shøn) *s.* vegetación. *2* vida monótona, vegetante.

vegetative (-tiv) *adj.* vegetativo.

vehemence (vɪ·jimøns) *s.* vehemencia. *2* violencia, intensidad.

vehement (-mønt) *adj.* vehemente. *2* violento, intenso.

vehicle (vɪ·jikøl) *s.* vehículo. *2* FARM. excipiente.

veil (veil) *s.* velo: *to take the* ~, tomar el velo, profesar. *2* disfraz, pretexto. *3* FOT. veladura.

veil (to) *tr.* velar [cubrir con velo]. *2* velar, ocultar, disimular, oscurecer.

veilless (-lis) *adj.* sin velo.
vein (vein) *s.* ANAT. vena. 2 BOT. vena, nervio. 2 ENT. nervio [de ala]. 4 vena, veta [de la piedra, la madera, etc.]. 5 MIN. vena, veta, filón. 2 humor, disposición.
vein (to) *tr.* cubrir de venas. 2 vetear, jaspear.
veined (-d) *adj.* venoso. 2 veteado.
veinstone (-stoun) *s.* MIN. ganga.
velar (vɪ·laʳ) *adj.* ANAT., FONÉT. velar.
veld, veldt (velt) *s.* en África del Sur, extensión de tierras cubiertas de hierba, arbustos o maleza.
vellum (vɪ·løm) *s.* pergamino, vitela.
velocipede (vila·sipid) *s.* velocípedo.
velocity (vila·siti) *s.* velocidad. 2 celeridad, rapidez.
velodrome (vɪ·lødroum) *s.* velódromo.
velours (velu·ʳ) *s.* felpa aterciopelada.
velvet (ve·lvit) *s.* terciopelo, velludo. 2 ZOOL. vellosidad. 3 pop. ganancia, ventaja.
velveteen (velvøtɪ·n) *s.* velludillo.
velvety (-i) *adj.* aterciopelado. 2 suave.
venal (vɪ·nal) *adj.* venal.
venality (vinæ·liti) *s.* venalidad.
venatic (vinæ·tik) *adj.* venatorio.
vend (to) (vend) *tr.* vender.
vendee (vendɪ·) *s.* DER. comprador.
vender (ve·ndøʳ) *s.* vendedor.
vendible (-ibøl) *adj.* vendible. 2 venal.
vendor (-øʳ) *s.* vendedor.
vendue (vendiu·) *s.* almoneda, subasta, *venduta.
veneer (vønɪ·ʳ) *s.* hoja para chapear, chapa. 2 revestimiento. 3 fig. apariencia.
veneer (to) *tr.* chapear, enchapar; revestir. 2 encubrir.
venerable (ve·nørabøl) *adj.* venerable. 2 venerado.
venerate (to) (-eit) *tr.* venerar, reverenciar.
veneration (venørei·shøn) *s.* veneración, reverencia.
venereal (vinɪ·rial) *adj.* venéreo.
venery (ve·nøri) *s.* venus, deleite sensual. 2 ant. montería.
Venetia (vinɪ·sha) *n. pr.* GEOGR. Venecia [comarca].
Venetian (vinɪ·shan) *adj.-s.* veneciano: ~ *blind*, persiana.
Venezuelan (venišui·lan) *adj.-s.* venezolano.
vengeance (ve·ndȳans) *s.* venganza. 2 *with a* ~, con furia; extremadamente; con creces.
vengeful (-ful) *adj.* vengativo.
venial (vɪ·nial) *adj.* venial.
Venice (venis) *n. pr.* GEOGR. Venecia [ciudad].
venison (ve·nišøn) *s.* venado, carne de venado.
venom (ve·nøm) *s.* veneno. 2 ponzoña, rencor.
venomous (ve·nømøs) *adj.* venenoso. 2 rencoroso.
venous (vɪ·nøs) *adj.* venoso.
vent (vent) *s.* orificio, abertura, paso [para dar salida al aire, un fluido]; escape, respiradero. 3 oído, fogón [de un arma]. 4 ZOOL. ano. 5 salida, expansión, desahogo.
vent (to) *tr.* dar salida, expresión o libre curso a; desahogar, descargar.
venter (-øʳ) *s.* vientre.
venthole (-joul) *s.* orificio de escape; respiradero.
ventilate (to) (ve·ntileit) *tr.* ventilar, airear. 2 ventilar, discutir.
ventilation (-ei·shøn) *s.* ventilación.
ventilator (ve·ntileitøʳ) *s.* ventilador.
ventose (ve·ntous) *adj.* ventoso, flatulento.
ventral (ve·ntral) *adj.* ventral. 2 abdominal.
ventricle (ve·ntrikøl) *s.* ANAT., ZOOL. ventrículo.
ventriloquism (ventri·løkuišm) *s.* ventriloquía.
ventriloquist (-ist) *s.* ventrílocuo.

venture (ve·nchøʳ) *s.* ventura, azar, riesgo: *at a* ~, al azar. 2 especulación, empresa arriesgada.
venture (to) *tr.* aventurar, arriesgar. 2 *intr.* aventurarse, arriesgarse, atreverse.
venturesome (-søm), **venturous** (-øs) *adj.* atrevido, temerario, emprendedor. 2 aventurado, arriesgado, azaroso.
Venus (vɪ·nøs) *n. pr.* ASTR., MIT. Venus. 2 fig. encanto, gracia.
Venus'-comb *s.* BOT. aguja de pastor o de Venus. 2 ZOOL. molusco del género *murex*.
Venus's-flytrap *s.* BOT. atrapamoscas, dionea.
veracious (virei·shøs) *adj.* veraz. 2 verídico.
veracity (viræ·siti) *s.* veracidad.
veranda(h (vøræ·nda) *s.* veranda.
verb (vøʳb) *s.* GRAM. verbo.
verbal (vø·ʳbal) *adj.* verbal: ~ *noun*, GRAM. sustantivo verbal. 2 literal.
verbalism (-išm) *s.* verbalismo. 2 palabrería.
verbalize (to) (-aiš) *tr.* convertir en verbo. 2 gastar muchas palabras, ser verboso.
verbatim (vøʳbei·tim) *adv.* literalmente, al pie de la letra.
verbena (vøʳbɪ·na) *s.* BOT. verbena.
verbiage (vø·ʳbiidȳ) *s.* verbosidad, palabrería.
verbose (vøʳbou·s) *adj.* verboso. 2 difuso, prolijo.
verbosity (vøʳba·siti) *s.* verbosidad.
verdancy (vø·ʳdansi) *s.* verdor. 2 fig. inocencia, sencillez, ingenuidad.
verdant (-dant) *adj.* verde [planta, campo, etc.]. 2 fam. ingenuo, sencillo.
verdict (vø·ʳdikt) *s.* veredicto. 2 dictamen.
verdigris (vø·ʳdigris) *s.* verdete. 2 cardenillo, verdín.
verdure (vø·ʳdȳuʳ) *s.* verde, verdura, verdor [de la vegetación]. 2 verdor, lozanía.
verge (vøʳdȳ) *s.* borde, orilla, límite: *on the* ~ *of*, al borde de, a punto de. 2 círculo, anillo. 3 ámbito, esfera. 4 vara [insignia], varilla. 5 fuste [de columna].
verge (to) *intr.* inclinarse, acercarse [a o hacia]. 2 *to* ~ *on*, estar próximo a, estar al borde de, rayar en.
verger (-øʳ) *s.* macero. 2 pertiguero.
veridical (viri·dikal) *adj.* verídico.
verification (verifikei·shøn) *s.* verificación, comprobación, demostración.
verify (to) (ve·rifai) *tr.* verificar, comprobar, demostrar. 2 justificar, acreditar. 3 cumplir [una predicción, una promesa]. ¶ Pret. y p. p.: *verified*.
verily (ve·rili) *adv.* verdaderamente, en verdad.
verisimilar (verisi·milaʳ) *adj.* verosímil, verisímil.
verisimilitude (verisimi·litiud) *s.* verosimilitud.
verism (viri·šm) *s.* verismo.
veritable (ve·ritabøl) *adj.* verdadero.
verity (ve·riti) *s.* verdad, realidad.
verjuice (vø·ʳyus) *s.* agraz. 2 agrazada. 3 acritud, aspereza [de carácter].
vermicelli (vø·ʳmise·li o -che·li) *s.* fideos.
vermicide (vø·ʳmisaid) *s.* vermicida.
vermicular (vøʳmi·kiulaʳ) *adj.* vermicular. 2 vermiforme.
vermiculation (vøʳmikiulei·shøn) *s.* movimiento vermicular. 2 dibujo u ornamentación vermiforme.
vermiform (vø·ʳmifoʳm) *adj.* vermiforme.
vermifuge (-fiuȳ) *s.* vermífugo.
vermillion (vøʳmi·liøn) *s.* bermellón. 2 rojo, carmín.

vermin (vø·ʳmin) *s.* bicho, sabandija. *2* bichos, sabandijas; alimañas.
verminous (-øs) *adj.* verminoso. *2* infestado de bichos o sabandijas.
vermis (vø·ʳmis) *s.* ANAT. vermis.
verm(o)uth (vø·ʳmuz) *s.* vermut.
vernacular (vøʳnæ·kiulaʳ) *adj.* vernáculo. *2 s.* lenguaje vernáculo o, por ext., profesional.
vernal (vø·ʳnɑl) *adj.* vernal. *2* BOT. ~ *grass,* grama de olor.
vernier (vø·ʳniøʳ) *s.* vernier, nonio.
veronal (ve·rønɑl) *s.* veronal.
Veronica (vira·nika) *n. pr.* Verónica. *2* la Santa Faz. *3* (con min.) BOT. verónica.
Versailles (veʳsai· o veʳse·lš) *n. pr.* GEOGR. Versalles.
versatile (vø·ʳsatil) *adj.* BOT., ZOOL. versátil. *2* versátil, voluble, inconstante. *3* vario, universal, de conocimientos variados.
verse (vøʳs) *s.* LIT. verso. *2* versículo.
verse (to) *intr.* versificar, hacer versos.
versed (vøʳst) *adj.* versado, instruido. *2* MAT. verso: ~ *sine,* seno verso.
versemonger (vø·ʳsmøngøʳ) *s.* coplero, poetastro.
versicle (vø·ʳsikøl) *s.* versículo. *2* verso corto.
versification (vø·ʳsifikei·shøn) *s.* versificación.
versify (to) (vø·ʳsifai) *tr.-intr.* versificar.
version (vø·ʳshøn) *s.* versión.
verso (vø·ʳsou) *s.* reverso. *2* folio verso.
verst (vøʳst) *s.* versta.
versus (vø·ʳsøs) *prep.* DER., DEP. contra.
vertebra (vø·ʳtibra), *pl.* **-bræ** (-brı) o **-bras** *s.* vértebra. *2 pl.* espinazo.
vertebral (vø·ʳtibral) *adj.* vertebral. *2* vertebrado.
Vertebrata (vøʳtibrei·ta) *s. pl.* ZOOL. vertebrados.
vertebrate (vø·ʳtibreit) *adj.-s.* ZOOL. vertebrado.
vertebrated (-id) *adj.* vertebrado.
vertex (vø·ʳteks) *s.* vértice. *2* cima, cumbre, cúspide, ápice. *3* ASTR. cenit.
vertical (vø·ʳtikal) *adj.* vertical.
verticil (vø·ʳtisil) *s.* BIOL. verticilo.
vertiginous (vøʳti·dÿinøs) *adj.* vertiginoso.
vertigo (vø·ʳtigou) *s.* vértigo.
vervain (vø·ʳvein) *s.* BOT. verbena.
verve (vøʳv) *s.* inspiración, brío.
very (ve·ri) *adj.* mismo, idéntico: *at the ~ moment,* en aquel mismo instante. *2* verdadero, exacto, puro, mero, solo: *the ~ truth,* la pura verdad. *3 adv.* muy, sumamente. *4* ~ *much,* mucho, muchísimo, muy.
vesania (visei·nia) *s.* MED. vesania.
vesica (visai·ka) *s.* ANAT. vejiga.
vesicant (ve·sikant) *adj.-s.* vesicante.
vesicatory (-tori) *adj.-s.* vejigatorio.
vesicle (ve·sikøl) *s.* vesícula, vejiguilla.
vesicular (visi·kiulaʳ) *adj.* vesicular.
Vesper (ve·spøʳ) *n. pr.* Vespero. *2 s.* (con min.) anochecer. *3 pl.* LITURG. vísperas. *4 adj.* vespertino.
vespertine (-tin) *adj.* vespertino.
vespiary (ve·spieri) *s.* avispero [de avispas].
vessel (ve·søl) *s.* vasija, vaso. *2* nave, embarcación. *3* AÑAT., ZOOL., BOT. vaso.
vest (vest) *s.* chaleco. *2* camiseta de punto; chaqueta [de mujer].
vest (to) *tr.* poét. vestir. *2 to ~ with,* investir con o de. *3 to ~ in,* dar, atribuir, conferir a. *4 intr.* poét. vestirse. *5* pasar, recaer [un derecho, propiedad, etc.].
vestal (ve·stal) *s.* vestal. *2* virgen, monja.
vested interests (ve·stid) *s. pl.* intereses creados.
vestibule (ve·stibiul) *s.* vestíbulo; zaguán, recibimiento. *3* ANAT. vestíbulo.

vestige (ve·stidÿ) *s.* vestigio.
vestigial (vesti·dÿial) *adj.* BIOL. rudimentario.
vestment (ve·stmønt) *s.* vestidura, vestido. *2* vestidura sagrada, ornamento.
vestry (ve·stri) *s.* sacristía. *2* junta parroquial.
vestryman (-mæn) *s.* miembro de la junta parroquial.
Vesuvius (visiu·viøs) *n. pr.* GEOGR. Vesubio.
vetch (vech) *s.* BOT. arveja, algarroba, veza.
vetchling (-ling) *s.* BOT. almorta.
veteran (ve·tøran) *s.-adj.* veterano.
veterinarian (vetørine·rian) *s.* veterinario, albéitar.
veterinary (ve·tørineri) *adj.* veterinario.
veto (vi·tou) *s.* veto.
veto (to) *tr.* poner el veto a. *2* vedar, prohibir.
vex (to) (veks) *tr.* vejar, molestar, incomodar, irritar, exasperar. *2* disgustar, desazonar. *3* discutir: *vexed point,* punto discutido.
vexation (veksei·shøn) *s.* molestia, mal trato. *2* chinchorrería. *3* disgusto, enojo, desazón.
vexatious (shøs) *adj.* molesto, enfadoso, enojoso, irritante.
via (vai·a) *prep.* vía, por la vía de, por.
viability (vaiabi·liti) *s.* viabilidad.
viable (-abøl) *adj.* viable [que puede vivir].
viaduct (-adøkt) *s.* viaducto.
vial (-al) *s.* redoma, frasco, ampolleta.
viands (-ands) *s. pl.* vituallas.
viaticum (vaiæ·tikøm) *s.* HIST., ECLES. viático.
vibrant (vai·brant) *adj.* vibrante.
vibrate (to) (-breit) *tr.* vibrar, hacer vibrar. *2 intr.* vibrar. *3* oscilar. *4* palpitar, trepidar.
vibratile (-bratil) *adj.* vibrátil.
vibration (vaibrei·shøn) *s.* vibración. *2* oscilación. *3* palpitación, trepidación.
vibrator (vai·breitøʳ) *s.* vibrador.
vibratory (-bratori) *adj.* vibratorio.
vibrion (vi·brian) *s.* BACT. vibrión.
viburnum (vaibø·ʳnøm) *s.* BOT. viburno; mundillo.
vicar (vi·kaʳ) *s.* vicario. *2* párroco anglicano que no cobra diezmos.
vicarage (vi·karidÿ) *s.* beneficio y casa del VICAR *2.*
vicarial (vike·rial) *adj.* delegado.
vicarious (vaike·riøs) *adj.* delegado. *2* hecho o sufrido por cuenta de otro o en su beneficio.
vice (vais) *s.* vicio. *2* VISE. *3* fam. sustituto, suplente.
vice- *pref.* vice-.
vicegerent (vaisdÿi·rent) *adj.-s.* lugarteniente, vicario: ~ *of God,* Vicario de Dios, el Papa.
viceregal (vaisrı·gal) *adj.* virreinal.
viceroy (vai·sroi) *s.* virrey.
vice versa (vai·sivøʳsa) *adv.* viceversa.
vicinage (vi·sinidÿ) *s.* vecindad; vecindario.
vicinal (vi·sinal) *adj.* vecino, adyacente. *2* vecinal.
vicinity (visi·niti) *s.* vecindad, cercanía, proximidad. *2* alrededores, contornos.
vicious (vi·shøs) *adj.* vicioso [depravado; defectuoso]. *2* resabiado. *3* maligno, sañudo, rencoroso.
vicissitude (visi·sitiud) *s.* vicisitud.
Vicky (vi·ki) *n. pr. dim.* de VICTORIA.
victim (vi·ktim) *s.* víctima. *2* interfecto.
victimize (to) (-aiš) *tr.* hacer víctima, sacrificar. *2* estafar, embaucar.
victor (vi·ktøʳ) *m.* vencedor, triunfador. *2 n. pr.* Víctor.
Victoria (vikto·ria) *n. pr.* Victoria. *2 s.* (con min.) victoria [coche].
Victorian (-rian) *adj.-s.* victoriano.

victorious (-riøs) *adj.* victorioso. *2* triunfal.
victory (vi·ktori) *s.* victoria, triunfo.
victress (vi·ktris) *s.* vencedora, triunfadora.
victual (to) (vi·tøl) *tr.* avituallar. *2 intr.* avituallarse. ¶ Pret. y p. p.: *victual(l)ed;* ger.: *-l(l)ing.*
victual(l)er (-ø^r) *s.* abastecedor. *2* tabernero.
victuals (-s) *s. pl.* vitualla, víveres.
vicugna, vicuña (viku·ña) *s.* ZOOL. vicuña.
vide (vai·di) *voz lat.* vide, véase.
videlicet (vide·liset) *adv.* a saber.
video (vi·diou) *s.* televisión (aparato); video. *2 adj.* de televisión.
vie (to) (vai) *tr.* emular, competir, rivalizar. ¶ Pret. y p. p.: *vied;* ger.: *vying.*
Vienna (vie·na) *n. pr.* GEOGR. Viena [de Austria].
Viennese (vieni·ŝ) *adj.-s.* vienés.
view (viu) *s.* vista, visión, contemplación, inspección, consideración; mirada: *to take a ~ of,* ver, examinar; *in ~ of,* en vista de; *on ~,* a la vista. *2* vista, panorama, escena, perspectiva: *~ finder,* FOT. visor. *3* modo de ver, opinión, punto de vista, aspecto. *4* mira, propósito: *with a ~ to,* con el propósito de. *5* DIB. proyección.
view (to) *tr.* ver, mirar. *2* examinar, inspeccionar. *3* considerar.
viewer (-ø^r) *s.* espectador. *2* inspector. *3* TELEV. telespectador.
viewpoint (-point) *s.* punto de vista.
vigesimal (vaidŷe·simal) *adj.* vigésimo. *2* vigesimal.
vigil (vi·dŷil) *s.* vigilia, desvelo, vela, velación. *2* vigilancia. *3* ECLES. vigilia.
vigilance, vigilancy (-ans, -si) *s.* vigilancia.
vigilant (-ant) *adj.* vigilante, atento.
vignette (viñe·t) *s.* IMPR., FOT., GRAB. viñeta. *2* bosquejo literario.
vigor (vi·gø^r) *s.* VIGOUR.
vigorous (vi·gørøs) *adj.* vigoroso. *2* fuerte, enérgico.
vigour (vi·gø^r) *s.* vigor, fuerza, energía.
viking (vai·king) *s.* vikingo.
vile (vail) *adj.* vil, ruin. *2* malo, pésimo.
vilification (vilifikei·shøn) *s.* vilipendio, denigración.
vilify (to) (vi·lifai) *tr.* vilipendiar, denigrar.
village (vi·lidŷ) *s.* lugar, aldea, pueblo.
villager (-ø^r) *s.* lugareño, aldeano.
villa (vi·la) *s.* villa, quinta, hotel.
villain (vi·løn) *s.* bribón, canalla. *2* VILLEIN. *3* malo, traidor [de un drama o novela].
villainous (-nøs) *adj.* villano, ruin, vil. *2* malo, detestable.
villainy (vi·løni) *s.* villanía, maldad, infamia.
villein (vi·lin) *s.* villano, pechero.
villei(i)nage (-idŷ) *s.* villanaje [condición].
villosity (vila·siti) *s.* vellosidad.
villous (vi·løs) *adj.* velloso. *2* BOT. pubescente.
vim (vim) *s.* fam. fuerza, vigor, energía.
vinaceous (vainei·shøs) *adj.* vinoso. *2* vinario.
vinaigrette (vineigre·t) *s.* COC. vinagreta.
Vincent (vi·nsønt) *n. pr.* Vicente.
vincible (vi·nsibøl) *adj.* vencible.
vinculum (vi·nkiuløm) *s.* vínculo.
vindicate (to) (vi·ndikeit) *tr.* vindicar, justificar. *2* mantener, defender. *3* reivindicar.
vindication (-ei·shøn) *s.* vindicación, defensa.
vindicative (vindi·kativ) *adj.* vindicativo, justificativo.
vindicatory (-tori) *adj.* vindicatorio.
vindictive (vindi·ktiv) *adj.* vindicativo, vengativo.

vine (vain) *s.* BOT. planta rastrera o enredadera. *2* vid, parra: *~ pest,* filoxera.
vinedresser (vai·ndresø^r) *s.* viñador.
vinegar (vi·niga^r) *s.* vinagre.
vinegarish, vinegary (vi·nigarish, -ri) *adj.* vinagroso. *2* avinagrado, agrio.
vineyard (vi·nya^rd) *s.* viña, viñedo.
vinic (vai·nik o vi·nik) *adj.* vínico.
vinification (vinifikei·shøn) *s.* vinificación.
vinous (vai·nøs) *adj.* vinoso. *2* vínico. *3* de color de vino. *4* borracho.
vintage (vi·ntidŷ) *s.* vendimia. *2* cosecha [de vino]. *3* vino [esp. de calidad].
vintager (-ø^r) *s.* vendimiador, cosechero.
vintner (vi·ntnø^r) *s.* vinatero, tratante en vinos.
viny (vai·ni) *adj.* de vides o enredaderas. *2* sarmentoso.
vinyl (vi·nil) *s.* QUÍM. vinilo.
viol (vai·øl) *s.* MÚS. viola. *2* MAR. virador.
viola (viou·la) *s.* MÚS. viola, alto.
violaceous (vaiølei·shøs) *adj.* violáceo, violado.
violate (to) (vai·øleit) *tr.* violar.
violation (vaiølei·shøn) *s.* violación.
violence (vai·øløns) *s.* violencia. *2* ímpetu, ardor, vehemencia.
violent (-lønt) *adj.* violento. *2* impetuoso, furioso. *3* grande, extremo, intenso.
violet (vai·ølit) *s.* BOT. violeta. *2* color de violeta. *3 adj.* violado, de color de violeta.
violin (vaiøli·n) *s.* MÚS. violín.
violinist (-ist) *s.* violinista.
violoncellist (vaiølønche·list) *s.* violoncelista.
violoncello (-che·lou) *MÚS.* violoncelo.
viper (vai·pø^r) *s.* ZOOL. víbora. *2* persona mala o traidora. *3* BOT. *~ grass,* escorzonera.
viperine, viperish, viperous (vai·pørin, -ish, -øs) *adj.* viperino.
virago (virei·gou) *s.* virago. *2* arpía, mujer regañona.
vire (vi^r) *s.* vira [saeta].
vireo (vi·riou) *s.* ORN. víreo.
virescent (vaire·sønt) *adj.* verdoso.
Virgil (vø·^rdŷil) *n. pr.* Virgilio.
virgin (vø·^rdŷin) *s.* virgen, doncella: *the Virgin,* la Santa Virgen. *2* ASTR. Virgo. *3 adj.* virgen. *4* virginal. *5* primero, inicial.
virginal (-al) *adj.* virgen, intacto. *2* virginal. *3* MÚS. virginal.
Virginia (vø·^rŷi·nia) *n. pr.* Virginia.
virginity (-niti) *s.* virginidad.
virgin's-bower *s.* BOT. clemátide.
Virgo (vø·^rgou) *s.* ASTR. Virgo.
viridescent (viride·sønt) *adj.* verdoso.
virile (vi·ril) *adj.* viril, masculino, varonil.
virility (viri·liti) *s.* virilidad.
virose (vai·rous) *adj.* ponzoñoso. *2* fétido.
virtu (vø·^rtu·) *s.* afición a las curiosidades y objetos de arte. *2* curiosidades, objetos de arte.
virtual (vø·^rchual) *adj.* virtual.
virtue (vø·^rchu) *s.* virtud: *by,* o *in,* *~ of,* en virtud de. *2 pl.* virtudes [espíritus angélicos].
virtuosity (vø·^rchua·siti) *s.* virtuosismo, maestría.
virtuoso (vø·^rchuou·sou) *s.* B. ART. virtuoso. *2* entendido en curiosidades u objetos de arte.
virtuous (vø·^rchuøs) *adj.* virtuoso [que practica la virtud o inspirado por ella]. *2* poderoso, eficaz.
virulence (vi·riuløns) *s.* virulencia.
virulent (-lønt) *adj.* virulento.
virus (vai·røs) *s.* virus.
visa (vi·ŝa) *s.* visado, visto bueno.

visa (to) *tr.* visar, refrendar. ¶ Pret. y p. p.: *visaed;* ger.: *visaing.*
visage (vi·sidў) *s.* rostro, semblante. *2* aspecto.
viscacha (viska·cha) *s.* VIZCACHA.
viscera (vi·søra) *s. pl.* vísceras.
viscid (vi·sid) *adj.* viscoso, pegajoso, glutinoso.
viscose (vi·skous) *s.* viscosa.
viscosity (viska·siti) *s.* viscosidad.
viscount (vai·kaunt) *s.* vizconde.
viscountess (-is) *s.* vizcondesa.
viscous (vi·skøs) *adj.* viscoso.
vise (vais) *s.* MEC. tornillo de banco.
visé (visei·) *s.* VISA.
visibility (višibi·liti) *s.* visibilidad.
visible (vi·šibøl) *adj.* visible.
Visigoth (vi·šigaz) *s.* visigodo.
vision (vi·ỹøn) *s.* vista [sentido]. *2* visión [acción o facultad de ver; cosa vista; aparición].
visionary (-eri) *adj.-s.* visionario. *2 adj.* imaginario, quimérico.
visit (vi·šit) *s.* visita [que se hace; registro, reconocimiento].
visit (to) *tr.* visitar. *2* afligir, castigar [con una desgracia, calamidad, etc.]. *2 intr.* hacer visitas. *3* visitarse.
visitant (-ɑnt) *s.* visitante.
visitation (višitei·shøn) *s.* visita, visitación. *2* inspección. *3* TEOL. consuelo o trabajo que Dios envía. *4* aflicción, calamidad, castigo.
visiting card (vi·šiting) *s.* tarjeta de visita.
visitor (-ø^{r}) *s.* visita, visitante. *2* visitador.
visor (vai·šø^{r}) *s.* visera. *2* fig. máscara, disfraz.
visor (to) *tr.* cubrir con visera. *2* fig. cubrir, disimular.
vista (vi·sta) *s.* vista, panorama, perspectiva.
visual (vi·ỹual) *adj.* visual. *2* visible. *3 s.* visual.
visuality (viỹuæ·liti) *s.* visibilidad. *2* imagen, vislumbre.
visualize (to) (vi·ỹuælaiš) *tr.* hacer visible. *2* representarse en la mente.
vital (vai·tal) *adj.* vital. *2* fatal, mortal. *2* demográfico.
vitalism (-lišm) *s.* vitalismo.
vitality (vaitæ·liti) *s.* vitalidad. *2* animación, vigor.
vitalize (to) (vai·talaiš) *tr.* vivificar.
vitals (vai·tals) *s. pl.* órganos vitales, entrañas.
vitamin(e (vai·tamin) *s.* QUÍM. vitamina.
vitaminize (to) (-aiš) *tr.* vitaminar.
vitelline (vite·lin) *adj.* vitelino.
vitellus (-løs) *s.* BIOL. vitelo.
vitiate (to) (vi·shieit) *tr.* viciar [dañar, corromper; invalidar].
vitiation (-ei·shøn) *s.* corrupción. *2* invalidación.
viticulture (vitikø·lchø^{r}) *s.* viticultura.
viticulturist (-chørist) *s.* viticultor.
vitreous (vi·triøs) *adj.* vítreo, vidrioso.
vitrification (vitrifikei·shøn) *s.* vitrificación.
vitrify (to) (vi·trifai) *tr.* vitrificar. ¶ Pret. y p. p.: *vitrified.*
vitriol (vi·triøl) *s.* vitriolo. *2* virulencia, causticidad.
vitriolic (vitria·lik) *adj.* vitriólico. *2* fig. ferozmente cáustico o mordaz.
vituperate (to) (vaitiu·pøreit) *tr.* vituperar. *2* denostar.
vituperation (-ei·shøn) *s.* vituperación, vituperio.
vivacious (vaivei·shøs) *adj.* vivaz, vivaracho, vivo, alegre, animado. *2* vivaz [que vive mucho].
vivacity (vaivæ·siti) *s.* vivacidad, viveza, animación.

vivandiere (vivandie·^{r}) *s.* cantinera, vivandera.
vivarium (vaive·riøm) *s.* vivario.
viva voce (vai·va vou·si) *adj.* de viva voz.
vivid (vi·vid) *adj.* vívido. *2* vivo, intenso. *3* gráfico [que expresa vivamente].
vividness (-nis) *s.* viveza, intensidad.
vivify (to) (vi·vifai) *tr.* vivificar. *2* avivar, animar. ¶ Pret. y p. p.: *vivified.*
viviparous (vaivi·parøs) *adj.* vivíparo.
vivisect (to) (vi·visekt) *tr.* hacer la vivisección de.
vivisection (vivise·kshøn) *s.* vivisección.
vixen (vi·ksøn) *s.* ZOOL. zorra, raposa. *2* arpía, mujer colérica.
viz (viš) *abrev.* de VIDELICET, a saber. | Gralte. se lee *namely* o *to wit.*
vizcacha (viska·cha) *s.* ZOOL. viscacha, vizcacha.
vizler, vizir (viši·^{r}) *s.* visir, gran visir.
vizor (vi·šø^{r}) *s.* VISOR.
vizor (to) *tr.* TO VISOR.
vocable (vou·kabøl) *adj.* vocablo, voz, término.
vocabulary (vokæ·biuleri) *s.* vocabulario. *2* léxico.
vocal (vou·kal) *adj.* vocal: ~ *cords,* cuerdas vocales. *2* oral. *3* vocálico. *4* fig. hablador, elocuente. *5 s.* FONÉT. vocal.
vocalic (vokæ·lik) *adj.* vocálico.
vocalist (-ist) *s.* vocalista.
vocalization (voukališei·shøn) *s.* vocalización.
vocalize (to) (vou·kalais) *tr.* articular; cantar. *2* FONÉT. convertir en vocal. *3 intr.* MÚS. vocalizar.
vocally (-kali) *adv.* vocalmente. *2* oralmente.
vocation (vokei·shøn) *s.* vocación. *2* oficio, profesión.
vocational (-al) *adj.* de la vocación. *2* profesional. *3* de artes y oficios.
vocative (va·kativ) *s.* vocativo.
vociferate (to) (vosi·føreit) *intr.* vociferar.
vociferation (-ei·shøn) *s.* vociferación, griterío.
vociferous (vosi·førøs) *adj.* vociferante, vocinglero.
vogue (voug) *s.* boga, moda.
voice (vois) *s.* voz [del hombre, de los animales, etc.]. *2* habla, palabra. *3* voz, opinión, voto: *with one* ~, unánimemente. *4* GRAM. voz [del verbo].
voice (to) *tr.* expresar, decir, anunciar, rumorear; interpretar. *2* MÚS. regular el tono de. *3* FONÉT. hacer sonoro.
voiceless (-lis) *adj.* sin voz. *2* sin voto. *3* mudo, silencioso. *4* FONÉT. sordo.
void (voi·d) *adj.* vacío; desocupado, vacante. *2* desprovisto, falto [de]. *3* vano, inútil. *4* DER. nulo, inválido. *5 s.* vacío, hueco, claro. *6 the* ~, el vacío.
void (to) *tr.* vaciar, desocupar. *2* expeler, evacuar. *3* DER. anular.
voidance (-ans) *s.* vaciamiento, evacuación. *2* DER. anulación.
volant (vo·lant) *adj.* volador. *2* ágil, ligero.
volatile (va·latil) *adj.* volátil. *2* ágil, ligero, fugaz.
volatility (valati·liti) *s.* volatilidad. *2* fugacidad.
volatilize (to) (va·latilaiš) *tr.* volatilizar. *2 intr.* volatilizarse.
volcanic (valkæ·nik) *adj.* volcánico.
volcano (valkei·nou) *s.* volcán.
vole (voul) *s.* ZOOL. rata de agua; campañol. *2* bola [en el juego de naipes].
volition (voli·shøn) *s.* volición; voluntad.
volitive (va·litiv) *adj.* volitivo.
volley (va·li) *s.* descarga, andanada. *2* lluvia [de flechas, balas, etc.]. *3* DEP. voleo [de la pelota].
volley (to) *tr.* lanzar una descarga, una lluvia de. *2*

DEP. volear [la pelota]. *3 intr.* ser lanzado en descarga, volear.

volplane (va·lplein) *s.* vuelo planeado.

volplane (to) *intr.* planear, volar planeando.

volt (voult) *s.* ELECT. volt, voltio.

voltage (vou·ltidÿ) *s.* ELECT. voltaje, tensión.

voltaic (valtei·ik) *adj.* voltaico.

Voltairian (valte·rian) *adj.-s.* volteriano.

voltameter (valtæ·mitøʳ) ELECT. voltámetro.

voltmeter (vou·ltmitøʳ) *s.* ELECT. voltímetro.

volubility (valiubi·liti) *s.* ZOOL., BOT. volubilidad. *2* verbosidad, afluencia, facundia.

voluble (va·tiubøl) *2* verboso, afluente, fecundo.

volume (va·lium) *s.* volumen, tomo, libro. *2* GEOM., MÚS. volumen. *3* volumen, bulto, masa.

volumetry (voliu·metri) *s.* volumetría.

voluminous (voliu·minøs) *adj.* voluminoso. *2* copioso, prolijo.

voluntary (va·lønteri) *adj.* voluntario. *2* espontáneo, libre. *3 s.* ECLES. sólo de órgano.

volunteer (valønti·ʳ) *adj.* voluntario, espontáneo. *2* de voluntarios. *3 s.* voluntario.

volunteer (to) *tr.* ofrecer, dar voluntariamente. *2 intr.* ofrecerse o contribuir voluntariamente. *3* servir como voluntario.

voluptuary (volø·pchueri) *s.* voluptuoso, sibarita.

voluptuous (volø·pchuøs) *adj.* voluptuoso, sensual.

volute (voliu·t) *adj.* enroscado, en espiral. *2 s.* voluta, espiral. *3* ZOOL. espira.

vomer (vou·møʳ) *s.* ANAT. vómer.

vomit (va·mit) *s.* vómito. *2* vomitivo, emético.

vomit (to) *tr.-intr.* vomitar.

vomitive (va·mitiv) *adj.* vomitivo, emético.

vomitory (va·mitori) *adj.-s.* vomitorio, vomitivo. *2 s.* ARQ. vomitorio.

voodoo (vu·du) *s.* brujería, magia [esp. la de los negros de los E.U. y de las Antillas].

voracious (vorei·shøs) *adj.* voraz. *2* insaciable, ávido.

voracity (voræ·siti) *s.* voracidad.

vortex (vo·ʳteks), *pl.* **-texes** o **-tices** (-tisiš) *s.* vórtice. *2* vorágine, torbellino.

vortical (vo·ʳtikal) *adj.* vortiginoso.

vorticella (voʳtise·la) *s.* ZOOL. vorticela.

votaress (vou·taris) *s.* mujer dedicada o consagrada a; adepta, partidaria.

votary (-ari) *s.* persona dedicada o consagrada a

[Dios, etc.]. *2* adepto, devoto, partidario.

vote (vout) *s.* voto, votación, sufragio. *2* voto [derecho de votar].

vote (to) *tr.-intr.* votar [dar su voto]: *to ~ down,* rechazar por votación; *to ~ in,* elegir por votación.

voter (vou·tøʳ) *s.* votante. *2* elector.

voting (-ing) *s.* votación, acción de votar.

votive (-iv) *adj.* votivo.

vouch (to) (vauch) *tr.* testificar, certificar, dar fe de. *2* garantizar, responder de. *3 intr. to ~ for,* responder de o por.

voucher (-øʳ) *s.* garante, fiador. *2* documento justificativo, comprobante, resguardo, recibo.

vouchsafe (to) (vauchsei·f) *tr.* conceder, permitir, dignarse dar o hacer. *2* dignarse.

voussoir (vusua·ʳ) *s.* ARQ. dovela.

vow (vau) *s.* voto, promesa solemne. *2* voto, deseo; súplica.

vow (to) *tr.* hacer voto de; prometer solemnemente; consagrar.

vowel (va·uøl) *adj.-s.* GRAM. vocal.

voyage (voi·idÿ) *s.* viaje por mar, o por el aire, travesía.

voyage (to) *intr.* viajar, navegar. *2 tr.* recorrer o cruzar [un mar] viajando.

voyager (-øʳ) *s.* viajero, pasajero.

Vulcan (vø·lkan) *n. pr.* MIT. Vulcano.

Vulcanism (vø·lkanišm) *s.* vulcanismo.

vulcanite (-nait) *s.* vulcanita, ebonita.

vulcanization (vølkanišei·shøn) *s.* vulcanización.

vulcanize (to) (vø·lkanaiš) *tr.* vulcanizar.

vulgar (vø·lgaʳ) *adj.* vulgar. *2* común, ordinario, plebeyo, de mal gusto. *4 s. the ~,* el vulgo.

vulgarism (-išm) *s.* vulgarismo. *2* ordinariez.

vulgarity (vølgæ·riti) *s.* vulgaridad. *2* ordinariez.

vulgarization (vølgarišei·shøn) *s.* vulgarización.

vulgarize (to) (vø·lgaraiš) *tr.* vulgarizar. *2* adocenar.

vulnerable (vø·lnørabøl) *adj.* vulnerable.

vulnerary (vø·lnøræri) *adj.-s.* vulnerario.

vulpine (vø·lpain o -pin) *adj.* vulpino, zorruno. *2* astuto, taimado.

vulture (vø·lchuʳ) *s.* ORN. buitre, cóndor.

Vulturidæ (vølchu·ridi) *s. pl.* ORN. vultúridos.

vulva (vø·lva) *s.* ANAT. vulva.

vying (vai·ing) *ger.* de TO VIE.

W

W, w (dø·bøliu) *s.* W, w, vigésima tercera letra del alfabeto inglés.
wabble (ua·bøl) *s.* WOBBLE.
wabble (to) *intr.* TO WOBBLE.
wabbly (ua·bli) *adj.* WOBBLY.
wad (uad) *s.* porción de borra, algodón, etc., para rellenar, acolchar, etc. 2 guata. 3 ARTILL. taco. 4 fam. (E.U.) fajo [de billetes].
wad (to) *tr.* rellenar, acolchar, tapar, destruir. 2 atacar [un arma de fuego]. ¶ Pret. y p. p.: *wadded;* ger.: *wadding.*
wadding (-ing) *s.* relleno, borra, guata.
waddle (ua·døl) *s.* anadeo. 2 marcha torpe o vacilante.
waddle (to) *intr.* anadear, nanear. 2 andar o moverse con marcha torpe o vacilante.
wade (to) (ueid) *intr.* andar sobre terreno cubierto de agua, sobre lodo, nieve, arena, etc.; avanzar con dificultad. 2 *to ~ in* o *into,* atacar, emprender resueltamente. 3 *tr.* vadear.
wadeable (-abøl) *adj.* vadeable.
wading bird (ing) *s.* ORN. ave zancuda.
wafer (uei·fø^r) *s.* hostia, oblea. 2 barquillo.
wafer (to) *tr.* pegar o cerrar con oblea.
wafery (-i) *adj.* delgado y ligero.
waffle (ua·føl) *s.* coc. barquillo plano.
waft (uaft) *s.* mecedura, fluctuación, ondeo. 2 soplo, ráfaga [de aire o de olor].
waft (to) *tr.* mecer, hacer flotar, ondear. 2 llevar o enviar por el agua o el aire. 3 *intr.* mecerse, flotar, ir flotando.
wag (uæg) *s.* meneo. 2 movimiento de cabeza. 3 bromista, guasón.
wag (to) *tr.* mover, menear [la cabeza, la cola, etc.]. 2 *intr.* moverse, menearse; oscilar. 3 fam. irse. ¶ Pret. y p. p.: *wagged;* ger.: *-gging.*
wage (ueidý) *s.* paga, jornal, sueldo, salario. | Ús. gralte. en plural.
wage (to) *tr.* emprender, sostener, empeñar, hacer: *to ~ war,* hacer guerra.
wager (uei·dÿø^r) *s.* apuesta: *to lay a ~,* hacer una apuesta, apostar.
wager (to) *tr.-intr.* apostar [hacer una apuesta].
waggery (uæ·gøri) *s.* jocosidad, travesura. 2 broma, guasa, bufonada.
waggish (-gish) *adj.* juguetón.
waggle (-gøl) *s.* meneo, oscilación, balanceo.

waggle (to) *tr.* menear, mover de un lado a otro. 2 menearse, moverse de un lado a otro.
Wagnerian (vagni·rian) *adj.-s.* vagneriano.
wag (g) on (-gøn) *s.* carromato, furgón, camión. 2 FERROC. vagón de mercancías.
wag (g) oner (-ø^r) *s.* carretero, carromatero.
wag (g) onette (uægøne·t) *s.* carricoche.
wagtail (uæ·gteil) *s.* ORN. aguzanieves, motacilla, nevatilla, pizpita.
waif (ueif) *s.* cosa o animal sin dueño. 2 cosa o fragmento encontrado. 3 niño abandonado, golfillo, granuja.
wail (ueil) *s.* lamento, gemido, lloro.
wail (to) *tr.* lamentar, deplorar, llorar. 2 *intr.* lamentarse, gemir, llorar.
wailing (-ing) *s.* WAIL.
wainscot (uei·nskat) *s.* revestimiento interior de una pared; zócalo, friso, arrimadillo.
wainscot (to) *tr.* enmaderar; poner friso o arrimadillo a.
waist (ueist) *s.* cintura, talle. 2 cinto, cinturón. 3 corpiño, jubón. 4 MAR. combés.
waistband (-bænd) *s.* pretina, cintura.
waistcoat (-kout o køt) *s.* chaleco. 2 justillo.
wait (ueit) *s.* espera, plantón. 2 pausa, detención, demora. 3 *to lie in ~,* estar al acecho, en emboscada. 4 *pl.* cantores de Nochebuena.
wait (to) *intr.-tr.* esperar, aguardar. | a veces con *for.* 2 *intr.* estar esperando órdenes, servir; ser mozo o camarero [de restaurante, etc.]: *to ~ at table,* servir a la mesa. 3 *to ~ on* o *upon,* servir, atender, despachar; estar de servicio cerca de [alguien]; visitar; presentar sus respetos a; escoltar, acompañar.
waiter (-tø^r) *s.* mozo, camarero [de café, restaurante, etc.]. 2 bandeja.
waiting (-ting) *s.* espera. 2 servicio. 3 *adj.* de espera; de servicio: ~ *room,* sala de espera; ~ *maid* o *woman,* doncella [de una señora].
waitress (-tris) *s.* camarera [de restaurante, etcétera].
waive (to) (ueiv) *tr.* renunciar, abandonar; desechar. 2 desaprovechar. 3 abstenerse de. 4 diferir, aplazar.
waiver (-ø^r) *s.* DER. renuncia, abandono.
wake (ueik) *s.* MAR. estela, aguaje: *in the ~ of,* fig. detrás de. 2 vela, velatorio.
wake (to) [a veces con *up*] *intr.* despertar, desper-

tarse, despabilarse. 2 resucitar. 3 velar [no dormir]. 4 tr. despertar. 5 excitar. 6 resucitar. 7 velar [un muerto]. ¶ Pret.: *waked* o *woke;* p. p.: *waked* o *woken.*

wakeful (-ful) *adj.* desvelado, insomne. 2 vigilante, alerta.

waken (to) (-øn) *tr.-intr.* despertar.

wake-robin *s.* BOT. aro, alcatraz.

wale (ueil) *s.* roncha, verdugo. 2 MAR. cinta. 3 TEJ. cordoncillo.

wale (to) *tr.* levantar roncha en; azotar.

Wales (ueilś) *n. pr.* GEOGR. Gales.

walk (uok) *s.* paso, andar [del que camina o pasea]. 2 paso [de un cuadrúpedo]. 3 paseo, caminata. 4 sitio para andar; paseo, alameda, acera, terraza, etc. 5 campo, esfera. 6 vida, conducta. 7 ~ *of life,* condición social; profesión, ocupación.

walk (to) *intr.* andar, caminar, marchar, ir a pie: *to ~ away,* irse, marcharse; *to ~ in,* entrar, pasar adelante; *to ~ on air,* fig. estar muy contento o ufano; *to ~ up to,* acercarse a. 2 pasear, pasearse: *to ~ with,* o *out with,* salir con, ser novio de. 3 ir al paso [la caballería]. 4 aparecer [fantasmas, espectros]. 5 obrar, conducirse.

6 *tr.* andar, pasear por, recorrer; hacer [un recorrido]: *to ~ the boards,* TEAT. pisar las tablas, ser actor; *to ~ the hospitals,* estudiar medicina. 7 hacer andar o pasear; sacar a paseo. 8 llevar [una caballería] al paso. 9 medir a pasos. *10 to ~ off a headache,* quitarse una jaqueca andando. *11 to ~ one off his legs,* rendir de fatiga a uno haciéndole andar.

walkie-talkie (uo·ki-to·ki) transmisor-receptor portátil.

walking (uo·king) *s.* marcha, paseo. 2 piso [de un camino, etc.]. 3 *adj.* de paseo; para andar, que anda, ambulante: ~ *cane,* ~ *stick,* bastón; ~ *papers,* fam. despido [de un empleo].

walkout (-aut) *s.* fam. (E.U.) huelga [de obreros].

walkover (-ouvø^r) *s.* fam. pan comido, victoria fácil.

wall (uol) *s.* pared, muro, tapia, seto: ~ *clock,* reloj de pared; ~ *fruit,* fruta de espaldera; ~ *louse,* ENT. chinche; ~ *paper,* papel pintado [de empapelar]; *to drive,* o *push,·to the ~,* poner en un aprieto, poner entre la espada y la pared; *to take the ~,* tomarse la acera; *with one's back to the ~,* acorralado. 2 muralla. 3 pared [de un tubo, vasija o cavidad].

wall (to) *tr.* emparedar, tapiar. 2 cercar, murar. 3 amurallar. 4 separar con pared.

wallaby (ua·labi) *s.* ZOOL. especie de canguro.

wallet (ua·lit) *s.* zurrón, bolsa de cuero. 3 cartera [de bolsillo].

wallflower (uo·lflauø^r) *s.* BOT. alhelí.

Walloon (ualu·n) *adj.-s.* valón.

wallop (ua·løp) *s.* golpe o puñada fuerte.

wallop (to) *tr.* pegar, zurrar. 2 dar un golpe fuerte.

walloping (-ing) *s.* zurra, tunda. 2 *adj.* fam. grande, tremendo.

wallow (ua·lou) *s.* revuelco, revolcadero.

wallow (to) *intr.* revolcarse [en el agua, en el fango, etc.]. 2 nadar [en la abundancia]. 3 estar encenagado [en un vicio].

wallwort (uo·lwø^rt) *s.* BOT. parietaria, cañarroya.

walnut (uo·lnøt) *s.* BOT. nuez [del nogal]; nogal: ~ *tree,* nogal [árbol]; ~ *wood,* nogal [madera].

walrus (uo·lrøs) *s.* ZOOL. morsa.

Walter (uo·ltø^r) *n. pr.* Gualterio.

waltz (uolts) *s.* vals.

waltz (to) *intr.* valsar. 2 dar vueltas rápidas. 3 *tr.* hacer valsar.

wan (uan) *adj.* pálido, descolorido. 2 lánguido, triste, enfermizo.

wand (uand) *s.* vara, vergueta. 2 varita de virtudes. 3 vara [insignia]. 4 batuta.

wander (ua·ndø^r) *s.* paseo, correría.

wander (to) *intr.* errar, vagar, rodar, corretear: *to ~ away,* extraviarse, perderse. 2 desviarse, apartarse. 3 delirar, divagar. 4 *tr.* errar o vagar por.

wanderer (-ø^r) *s.* paseante, vagabundo, viajero.

wandering (-ing) *s.* correteo, viaje. 2 extravío, aberración. 3 delirio; divagación. 4 *adj.* errante, errabundo: ~ *Jew,* judío errante. 5 extraviado, descaminado. 6 delirante; que divaga.

wane (uein) *s.* mengua, disminución. 2 declinación, decadencia. 3 marchitamiento. 4 menguante [de la luna]. 5 *on the ~,* acabándose, declinando, en decadencia.

wane (to) *intr.* menguar, disminuir, decrecer. 2 declinar, decaer. 3 marchitarse.

wangle (to) (uæ·ngøl) *tr.* fam. sacar u obtener con maña, astucia o superchería. 2 fam. arreglar, amañar, falsear.

wannish (ua·nish) *adj.* algo pálido o macilento.

want (uant o uont) *s.* falta, necesidad, carencia, escasez: *for ~ of,* por falta de. 2 necesidad, indigencia, miseria.

want (to) *tr.* necesitar, tener falta o necesidad de. 2 carecer de. 3 querer, desear, anhelar. 4 buscar, reclamar [a uno]. 5 faltar [minutos, etc., para]. 6 *intr.* pasar necesidad. 7 *to ~ for,* necesitar.

want ad *s.* fam. anuncio clasificado.

wantage (-idÿ) *s.* falta, déficit, merma.

wanting (-ing) *adj.* falto, defectuoso, deficiente, escaso. 2 necesitado. 3 *que falta: to be ~,* faltar.

wanton (ua·ntøn) *adj.* alegre, juguetón, travieso. 2 irreflexivo, caprichoso. 3 lascivo. 4 licencioso, disoluto. 5 brutal, desconsiderado, injustificado, arbitrario. 6 pródigo, exuberante, lujuriante. 7 *s.* mujer disoluta. 8 niño travieso.

wanton (to) *intr.* juguetear, jugar,retozar.

wantonness (-nis) *s.* retozo, picardía. 2 libertinaje. 3 brutalidad. 4 exuberancia.

wapiti (ua·piti) *s.* ZOOL. uapití.

war (uo^r) *s.* guerra: ~ *dance,* danza guerrera; *War Department* (E.U.), *War Office* (Ingl.), Ministerio de la Guerra; ~ *horse,* corcel de batalla; fig. veterano; ~ *memorial,* monumento a los caídos. 2 arte de la guerra. 3 milicia, armas [profesión militar].

war (to) *intr.* guerrear, estar en guerra. ¶ Pret. y p. p.¡ *warred;* ger.: *warring.*

warble (uo·^rbøl) *s.* trino, gorjeo, quiebro.

warble (to) *tr.-intr.* cantar con trinos y gorjeos; trinar, gorjear. 2 murmurar [un arroyo].

warbler (uo·^rblø^r) *s.* gorjeador. 2 pájaro cantor.

ward (uo^rd) *s.* guarda, custodia. 2 tutela. 3 pupilo, persona bajo tutela. 4 barrio, distrito [de una población]. 5 sala, cuadra [de hospital]. 6 ala, sección [de una cárcel]. 7 guarda [de llave o cerradura].

ward (to) *tr.* guardar, proteger. 2 *to ~ off,* resguardarse de, parar, evitar, desviar.

warden (-øn) *s.* vigilante, guardián. 2 gobernador, jefe, director, alcaide. 3 fabriquero [de una parroquia].

warder (-ø^r) *s.* guarda, centinela. 2 carcelero.

wardmaid (-meid) *s.* camarera de hospital.

wardrobe (-roub) *s.* armario, guardarropa, ropero. *2* TEAT. guardarropía. *3* vestuario, ropa.

wardroom (-rum) *s.* MAR. cámara de oficiales [en un buque de guerra].

wardship (-ship) *s.* DER. tutela; pupilaje.

ware (ue·æ^r) *s. sing.* o *pl.* géneros, artículos, mercancías; vajilla, cacharrería.

warehouse (ue·^rjaus) *s.* almacén, depósito. *2* guardamuebles.

warfare (uo·^rfeø^r) *s.* guerra, lucha. *2* arte militar.

warfare (to) *intr.* guerrear, combatir.

warily (ue·rili) *adv.* cautamente.

wariness (ue·rinis) *s.* cautela, precaución, prudencia.

warlike (uo·^rlaik) *adj.* bélico, belicoso, marcial.

warm (uo^rm) *adj.* caliente, cálido, caluroso: *I am* ~, tengo calor; *it is* ~, hace calor; se está caliente. *2* de abrigo. *3* acalorado. *4* caluroso, ferviente, afectuoso, cordial. *5* ardiente, vivo, celoso, fogoso, apasionado, violento. *6* cómodo, confortable. *7* duro, difícil. *8* reciente, fresco. *9* PINT. cálido [color].

warm (to) *tr.* calentar. *2* caldear. *3* abrigar. *4* animar, enardecer, acalorar. *5 to* ~ *over*, o *up*, recalentar [la comida]; AUTO. calentar [el motor]. *6 intr.* calentarse. *7* animarse, acalorarse. *8 to* ~ *up*, irse calentando, animando, etc. *9 to* ~ *to, to* ~ *up to*, cobrar afecto a; sentir compasión de.

warm-blooded *adj.* ardiente, entusiasta. *2* ZOOL. de sangre caliente.

warm-hearted *adj.* de buen corazón, afectuoso.

warming pad (-ing) *s.* esterilla eléctrica.

warming pan *s.* calentador de cama.

warmth (-z) *s.* calor moderado. *2* calor, celo, ardor, afecto, cordialidad, entusiasmo, viveza.

warn (to) (uo^rn) *tr.* avisar, advertir, prevenir. *2* amonestar, exhortar. *3* DER. desahuciar. *4 to* ~ *off*, prohibir el paso, la entrada, etc.

warning (uo·^rning) *s.* aviso, advertencia. *2* amonestación. *3* lección, escarmiento. *4* despido [entre propietario e inquilino].

warp (uo^rp) *s.* TEJ. urdimbre. *2* MAR. espía [cabo]. *3* alabeo. *4* torcimiento, deformación; prejuicio. *5* AGR. tarquín.

warp (to) *tr.* TEJ. urdir. *2* MAR. espiar. *3* alabear, abarquillar. *4* torcer, deformar, falsear, desviar. *5* AGR. entarquinar. *6 intr.* alabearse, abarquillarse; torcerse, deformarse.

warplane (uo·^rplein) *s.* avión militar.

warrant (ua·rant) *s.* autorización, poder. *2* orden, mandamiento, libramiento, despacho. *3* DER. orden de prisión, registro, etc. *4* justificante, comprobante. *5* COM. warrant. *6* garantía, seguridad. *7* derecho, razón, fundamento, autoridad.

warrant (to) *tr.* autorizar. *2* garantizar. *3* responder de, asegurar, certificar. *4* justificar.

warrantee (-ı) *s.* persona en favor de la cual se establece una garantía.

warranter, warrantor (-ø^r) *s.* garante.

warranty (-ı) *s.* garantía. *2* autoridad, justificación.

warren (ua·røn) *s.* vedado. *2* conejar, vivar. *3* lugar donde habita mucha gente.

warrior (uo·riø^r) *s.* guerrero, soldado.

Warsaw (uo·^rso) *n. pr.* GEOGR. Varsovia.

warship (-ship) *s.* buque de guerra.

wart (uo^rt) *s.* verruga, excrecencia. *2* ZOOL. ~ *hog*, facóquero.

wartime (uo·^rtaim) *s.* tiempo de guerra.

warty (uo·^rti) *adj.* verrugoso, averrugado.

wary (ue·ri) *adj.* cauto, cauteloso, prudente.

was (uaš o uøš) *pret.* de TO BE.

wash (uash) *s.* lavado, lavatorio, ablución. *2* WASHING *3.* *3* lavazas; aguachirle. *4* loción. *5* chapaleo [del agua]: conmoción producida por la hélice en el agua o en el aire. *6* pincelada grande. *7* baño, capa. *8* PINT. lavado. *9* estuario; marjal. *10* aluvión.

wash (to) *tr.* lavar. *2* bañar, regar. *3* lamer [las aguas]. *4* barrer, arrastrar, llevarse [el agua]. *5* dar un baño o capa a. *6 to* ~ *away, off* o *out*, quitar lavando; borrar; derrubiar; llevarse [el agua]. *7 intr.* lavarse. *8* ser resistente al lavado. *9* correr, chapalear [el agua]. *10* ser arrastrado, llevado o desgastado por el agua. *11 to* ~ *up*, lavar los platos.

washable (ua·shabøl) *adj.* lavable.

washbasin (-beisin) *s.* jofaina, palangana. *2* lavamanos.

washboard (-bo^rd) *s.* tabla de lavar. *2* friso, rodapié. *3* MAR. falca.

washbowl (-boul) *s.* WASHBASIN.

washcloth (-kloz) *s.* paño [para lavarse].

washed-out *adj.* descolorido. *2* fig. extenuado.

washed-up *adj.* fam. extenuado. *2* fracasado [pers.].

washer (ua·shø^r) *s.* lavador. *2* lavadora, máquina de lavar. *3* MEC. arandela.

washerwoman (-wumæn) *s.* lavandera.

washhouse (ua·shjaus) *s.* lavadero.

washing (ua·shing) *s.* acción de TO WASH. *2* MIN. lave. *3* colada, ropa lavada o para lavar. *4* adj. de lavar, que lava: ~ *machine*, lavadora.

washy (ua·shi) *adj.* aguado. *2* mojado. *3* flojo, débil. *4* insulso.

wasn't (ua·šønt) *contr.* de WAS NOT.

wasp (uasp) *s.* ENT. avispa: *wasp's nest*, avispero.

waspish (ua·spish) *adj.* de avispa. *2* irascible, gruñón.

wast (uast) *2.ª pers. sing. pret. de ind.* de TO BE. | Ús. cuando se usa THOU.

wastage (uei·stidÿ) *s.* merma, desgaste. *2* gasto inútil, desperdicio.

waste (ueist) *adj.* yermo, inculto. *2* desierto, desolado. *3* triste, sombrío. *4* devastado, arruinado. *5* inútil, desechado, sobrante, que se pierde: ~ *paper*, papeles rotos o usados. *6 s.* extensión, inmensidad. *7* erial, desierto. *8* devastación, destrucción. *9* gasto inútil, pérdida, derroche. *10* desgaste, merma, consunción. *11* desechos, desperdicios; aguas sucias.

waste (to) *tr.* devastar, arruinar, destruir. *2* gastar, consumir, mermar, agotar. *3* debilitar, enflaquecer. *4* malgastar, desperdiciar, derrochar. *5 intr.* gastarse, consumirse; debilitarse, demacrarse. | A veces con *away*.

wasteful (-ful) *adj.* asolador. *2* destructivo, ruinoso. *3* malgastador, pródigo, manirroto.

waster (-ø^r) *s.* WASTREL *2* y *3.* *2* cosa inútil, defectuosa.

wastrel (uei·strøl) *s.* desperdicio, desecho. *2* gastador, pródigo. *3* vago, golfo, perdido.

watch (uach) *s.* reloj de bolsillo: ~ *strap*, pulsera de reloj. *2* vela, vigilia: ~ *night*, noche vieja. *3* velatorio. *4* vigilancia, observación, cuidado: *on the* ~, alerta, sobre sí; de vigilancia. *5* centinela, vigilante; atalaya, vigía: ~ *box*, garita. *6* guardia [grupo que vigila o está de servicio]. *7* MAR., MIL. cuarto, guardia.

watch (to) *intr.* velar [estar despierto]. *2* velar, vigilar, estar alerta; tener cuidado: *to* ~ *for*, esperar, aguardar; *to ~ over*, velar por, cuidar de, vigilar, inspeccionar; *watch out!*, ¡cuidado! *3 tr.* vigilar, observar, contemplar, tener cuidado con: *to ~ one's step*, andarse con tiento. *4* esperar, aguardar. *5* seguir, espiar. *6* guardar, custodiar.

watchdog (-dog) *s.* perro guardián.

watcher (-ø^r) *s.* velador [que vela]. *2* observador. *3* vigilante.

watchful (-ful) *adj.* desvelado; en vela. *2* atento, vigilante, en guardia, cuidadoso.

watching (-ing) *s.* vigilia, desvelo. *2* vigilancia.

watchmaker (-meikø^r) *s.* relojero.

watchman (-mæn) *s.* vigilante, sereno, guardián.

watchtower (-tauø^r) *s.* atalaya, garita.

watchword (-wø^{r}d) *s.* MIL. santo y seña, consigna.

watchwork (-wø^{r}k) *s.* mecanismo de relojería.

water (uo·tø^r) *s.* agua: *to pour o throw cold ~ on*, fig. echar un jarro de agua fría; desanimar; *above ~*, a flote; *by ~*, por mar, por barco; *in deep ~ o waters*, en apuros; *in smooth ~*, sin dificultades. *2* marea. *3* FISIOL. linfa. *4* orina. *5* limpidez [de una piedra preciosa]; fig. calidad, clase: *of the first ~*, de lo mejor. *6* aguas, visos, reflejos. *7 pl.* aguas [territoriales; termales, etc.].
8 adj. de agua, acuático, hidráulico, para el agua: *~ bath*, baño de María; *~ carriage*, transporte por agua; conducción de agua; *~ channel*, cuneta; *~ clock*, reloj de agua; *~ closet*, retrete con descarga de agua; *~ colo(u)r*, acuarela; aguada; *~ fowl*, ave o aves acuáticas; *~ front*, orilla, ribera; barrio ribereño; *~ gate*, compuerta, paradera; *~ hammer*, martillo de agua; *~ level*, nivel de agua; *~ line*, MAR. línea de flotación, orilla del agua; *~ parting*, divisoria de aguas; *~ plane*, hidroavión; *~ polo*, DEP. waterpolo; *~ pot*, jarro, regadera; *~ power*, energía hidráulica; *~ spring*, manantial de agua; *~ wave*, ondulación al agua [en el peinado]; *~ wheel*, rueda hidráulica, turbina; *~ wings*, nadaderas. *9* BOT. *~ cress*, berro; *~ fennel*, enante; *~ germander*, escordio; *~ lily*, nenúfar; *~ parsnip*, berrera; *~ plantain*, alisma. *10* ENT. *~ skipper*, tejedor, zapatero. *11* ORN. *~ hen*, polla de agua, gallineta. *12* ZOOL. *~ flea*, pulga de agua; *~ rat*, rata de agua; rata almizclada; *~ snake*, culebra de agua.

water (to) *tr.* regar, rociar, mojar. *2* proveer de agua. *3* abrevar [el ganado]. *4* aguar, bautizar [el vino, etc.]. *5* dar visos a [una tela]. *6 intr.* chorrear agua o humedad. *7* llenar o llenarse de agua, lágrimas, etc.; llorar [los ojos], hacerse agua [la boca]. *8* abrevarse. *9* tomar agua. *10* MAR. hacer aguada.

water-cooling *s.* refrigeración por agua.

watercourse (-kø^{r}s) *s.* corriente de agua, río, arroyo. *2* lecho de un río. *3* vaguada.

waterfall (-fol) *s.* cascada, catarata, salto de agua.

wateriness (-inis) *s.* acuosidad, humedad.

watering (-ing) *s.* riego, irrigación: *~ can o pot*, regadera. *2* provisión o uso de agua; *~ place*, abrevadero; aguada; balneario. *3* dilución. *4* acción de abrevar [a los animales]. *5* lagrimeo.

waterish (-ish) *adj.* acuoso, aguanoso. *2* húmedo, insípido.

waterman (-mæn) *s.* barquero. *2* el que cuida del agua o de dar agua.

watermark (-ma^{r}k) *s.* señal indicadora del nivel del agua. *2* filigrana [en el papel].

watermelon (-meløn) *s.* BOT. sandía, melón de agua.

waterproff (-pruf) *adj.* impermeable. *2 s.* tela o abrigo impermeable.

watershed (-shed) *s.* GEOGR. divisoria de aguas. *2* GEOGR. cuenca; vertiente.

waterside (-said) *s.* orilla del agua, litoral.

waterspout (-spaut) *s.* manga, tromba marina. *2* turbión.

watertight (-tait) *adj.* estanco, hermético.

waterworks (-wø^{r}ks) *s. sing.* o *pl.* instalación o sistema de abastecimiento de agua. *2* fuente, juegos de agua.

watery (-i) *adj.* acuoso; aguanoso. *2* seroso. *3* lloroso. *4* húmedo. *5* claro [líquido]. *6* evaporado, insípido.

watt (uat) *s.* ELECT. vatio.

wattle (ua·tøl) *s.* zarzo. *2* sebe. *3* barbas [de ave]. *4* barba [de pez].

wattle (to) *tr.* cubrir o cercar con zarzos. *2* tejer, entretejer, entrelazar.

wattmeter (ua·tmitø^r) *s.* vatímetro.

wave (ueiv) *s.* ola. *2* onda: *~ band*, RADIO. banda de ondas; *~ length*, RADIO. longitud de onda; *~ motion*, FÍS. movimiento ondulatorio. *3* ondulación. *4* temblor, oscilación. *5* aguas, visos. *6* ademán, señal [con la cabeza, la mano, una bandera].

wave (to) *intr.* flotar, ondear, ondular. *2* hacer señales. *3 tr.* blandir, agitar, tremolar. *4* mover [haciendo señales]; indicar, señalar [con la mano, un pañuelo, etc.]: *to ~ aside*, apartar; desechar. *5* ondular. *6* formar aguas [en una tela].

wavelet (-lit) *s.* ola u onda pequeña.

waver (-ø^r·) *s.* ondeo, oscilación, temblor. *2* ondulación [del cabello]. *3* tenacillas para ondular.

waver (to) *intr.* ondear, oscilar, temblar. *2* vacilar. *3* flaquear, ceder.

wavy (uei·vi) *adj.* ondoso, ondulante. *2* ondulado.

wax (uæks) *s.* cera: *~ candle*, vela, cirio; *~ end*, hilo encerado; *~ paper*, papel parafinado; *~ taper*, velita, candela. *2* objeto de cera. *3* cerumen. *4* fam. berrinche.

wax (to) *tr.* encerar. *2 intr.* crecer, aumentar. *3* hacerse, volverse, ponerse: *to ~ old*, envejecer.

waxchandler (uæ·kschændlø^r) *s.* cerero.

waxen (-øn) *adj.* de cera; encerado.

waxwork (-uø^{r}k) *s.* obra o figura de cera.

waxy (-i) *adj.* céreo, ceroso. *2* blando, plástico.

way (uei) *s.* vía, camino, calle, canal, conducto. *2* camino, viaje, rumbo, curso, dirección, sentido: *~ down*, bajada; *~ up*, subida; *to go one's ~*, seguir uno su camino; irse, partir; *to look the other ~*, mirar a otro lado, desviar la mirada; *all the ~*, todo el camino; *on the ~*, de paso, al pasar; de camino; *the other ~ around*, al revés; *this ~*, por aquí. *3* paso [espacio o libertad para pasar]: *~ in*, entrada; *~ through*, paso, pasaje; *~ out*, salida; *to be in the ~*, estorbar; *to get out of the ~*, quitarse de en medio, quitarse de encima [un trabajo, etc.]. *4* espacio, distancia, trecho: *a good ~*, *a long ~*, un buen trecho; *a long ~ off*, muy lejos. *5* marcha, progreso: *to make no ~*, no adelantar, no prosperar. *6* modo, manera: *any ~*, de cualquier modo o manera, de todos modos, como se quiera; *in a ~*, en cierto modo; *in a big ~*, en gran escala; *in a small ~*, en pequeña escala; *no ~*, nada, de ningún modo. *7* punto, lado, aspecto, respecto: *in a ~*, por un lado, en un aspecto; *in every ~*, en todos respectos. *8* medio, arbitrio. *9* sistema de vida, oficio, ocupa-

ción, hábito, costumbre: *it is not my ~ to*, ya no acostumbro a. *10* estado, condición: *in a bad ~*, mal, en mal estado. *11* impulso recibido. *12* MAR. marcha, andar, velocidad: *to gather ~*, ganar velocidad; *to get under ~*, levar, zarpar; *under ~*, en marcha, navegando; fig. empezando, haciéndose. *13 pl.* maneras, peculiaridades [de una pers.]. *14 to have a ~ with*, tener atractivo o poder de persuasión para; *to have one's ~*, salirse con la suya. *15 by ~ of*, pasando por; por vía de, a modo de, como. *16 by the ~*, a propósito, dicho sea de paso. *17 out of the ~*, fuera de camino; fuera del paso; impropio, inconveniente, extraordinario.
18 adj. de camino, de tránsito: *~ train*, tren tranvía.

waybill (uei·bil) *s.* hoja de ruta. *2* lista de pasajeros. *3* itinerario.

wayfarer (uei·feɹøʳ) *s.* caminante. *2* viajero.

waylay (to) (uei·lei) *tr.* aguardar, acechar, asaltar [en el camino].

waymark (uei·maʳk), **waypost** (uei·poust) *s.* hito o poste indicador.

wayside (uei·said) *s.* orilla del camino.

wayward (uei·uaʳd) *adj.* díscolo, voluntarioso. *2* adverso. *3* irregular, caprichoso.

we (uɪ) *pron. pers. pl.* de I; nosotros, nosotras.

weak (uɪk) *adj.* débil, flojo, flaco. *2* enclenque, delicado. *3* frágil, endeble, pobre, baladí. *4* ineficaz, impotente. *5* simple, recio. *6* GRAM., FONÉT. débil.

weaken (to) (-øn) *tr.* debilitar, enervar. *2* disminuir. *3 intr.* debilitarse. *4* flaquear, desfallecer.

weak-headed *adj.* de poca inteligencia.

weak-hearted *adj.* pusilánime.

weak-kneed *adj.* falto de energía, irresoluto.

weakling (uɪ·kling) *adj.-s.* persona débil, canija.

weakly (uɪ·kli) *adj.* débil, enclenque, enfermizo. *2 adv.* débilmente. *3* defectuosamente.

weak-minded *adj.* pobre de espíritu. *2* simple, mentecato.

weaker sex *s.* sexo débil.

weakness (uɪ·knis) *s.* debilidad, flaqueza. *2* flojedad. *3* fragilidad, endeblez. *4* decaimiento. *5* futilidad. *6* defecto. *7* lado débil.

weal (uɪl) *s.* cardenal, verdugón. *2* bien, salud, prosperidad: *public ~*, bien público.

wealth (uɪlz) *s.* riqueza. *2* fortuna, caudal. *3* opulencia. *4* copia, abundancia.

wealthy (uɪ·lzi) *adj.* rico, adinerado, opulento. *2* rico, abundante.

wean (to) (uɪn) *tr.* destetar. *2 to ~ away from*, apartar gradualmente [de un afecto, hábito, etc.].

weaning (-ing) *s.* destete.

weapon (ue·pøn) *s.* arma [para atacar o defenderse].

wear (ueʳ) *s.* uso [de ropa, calzado, etc.]: *for everyday ~*, de uso diario; *in general ~*, de moda, que se lleva mucho: *the worse for the ~*, usado, deteriorado por el uso. *2* ropa, vestidos: *foot ~*, calzado! *3* gasto, desgaste: *~ an tear*, uso, deterioro causado por el uso. *4* duración, resistencia.

wear (to) *tr.* traer puesto, usar, llevar: *to ~ the breeches*, llevar los calzones [la mujer]; *to ~ one's heart on one's sleeve*, llevar el corazón en la mano. *2* llevar, gastar [bigote, barba, etc.]. *3* llevar de cierto modo, color, etc. [el vestido, el pelo, etc.]. *4* tener [cierto aire o aspecto]. *5* gastar, desgastar, deteriorar. *6* agotar, fatigar, debilitar. *7 to ~ away*, gastar, consumir. *8 to ~*

down, desgastar con el roce; fig. gastar, acabar, convencer. *9 to ~ out*, desgastar; acabar con; cansar, fatigar; durar más que. *10 intr.* gastarse, consumirse, decaer. *11* pasar [un tiempo]. *12* resistir el uso. *13 to ~ away*, gastarse; pasar, decaer. *14 to ~ off*, borrarse; pasar; desaparecer. *15 to ~ out*, gastarse, inutilizarse. ¶ Pret.: *wore*; p. p.: *worn*.

wearied (uɪ·rid) *adj.* cansado, fatigado, agotado. *2* aburrido, fastidiado.

weariness (uɪ·rinis) *s.* cansancio, fatiga. *2* aburrimiento.

wearing apparel (we·ring) *s.* prendas de vestir.

wearisome (uɪ·risøm) *adj.* cansado, fatigoso. *2* pesado, aburrido, fastidioso.

weary (uɪ·ri) *adj.* cansado, fatigado. *2* abrumado, afligido. *3* cansado, aburrido, hastiado. *4* pesado, fatigoso, fastidioso.

weary (to) *tr.* cansar [fatigar, abrumar; aburrir, fastidiar]. *2 intr.* cansarse. *3* aburrirse. *4* hacerse pesado, aburrido.

weasel (uɪ·søl) *s.* ZOOL. comadreja.

weather (ue·ðøʳ) *s.* tiempo [estado de la atmósfera]: *~ forecast(ing*, pronóstico del tiempo; *~ report*, boletín meteorológico; *~ strip*, burlete; *~ vane*, veleta; *how is the ~ like?*, ¿qué tiempo hace? *2* mal tiempo, temporal, viento. *3* MAR. barlovento: *~ side*, costado de barlovento. *4 pl.* vicisitudes de la suerte.

weather (to) *tr.* curar, secar, etc., a la intemperie. *2* capear, aguantar [el temporal; dificultades, etc.]. *3* MAR. doblar [un cabo]. *4 intr.* curarse, secarse, curtirse, etc., a la intemperie. *5* durar, resistir.

weather-beaten *adj.* curtido por la intemperie.

weathercock (kak) *s.* veleta.

weathering (-ing) *s.* acción de los agentes atmosféricos; desgaste, alteración que produce.

weatherman (-mæn) *s.* hombre del tiempo, meteorólogo.

weatherproof (-pruf) *adj.* a prueba de intemperie o de mal tiempo.

weather-wise *adj.* experto en prever los cambios de tiempo.

weave (uɪv) *s.* TEJ. tejido, textura, ligado.

weave (to) *tr.* tejer. *2* hilar [la araña, un insecto]. *3* entretejer. *4* urdir, trama. *5 to ~ one's way*, avanzar zigzagueando. *6 intr.* tejer. Pret.: *wove*; p. p.: *woven* o *wove*.

weaver (-øʳ) *s.* ORN. tejedor, tejedora. *2* tramador.

weaverbird (-bøʳd) *s.* ORN. tejedor [pájaro].

web (ueb) *s.* tejido, tela, tejido; tela, tejido. *2* enredo, red, trama. *3* ANAT. membrana. *4* ZOOL. membrana interdigital. *5* barbas [de una pluma]. *6* MEC. alma [de carril, etc.]; paletón [de llave]. *7* rollo [de papel continuo].

webbed (-d) *adj.* unido por una membrana; palmeado, palmípedo.

webfoot (-fut) *s.* ORN. pie palmeado. *2* palmípedo.

web-footed *adj.* ORN. palmípedo.

we'd (uɪd) *contr.* de WE HAD, WE SHOULD y WE WOULD.

wed (to) (ued) *tr.* casarse con. *2* casar [unir, dar en matrimonio]. *3* casarse. ¶ Pret. y p. p.: *wedded* o *wed*; ger.: *wedding*.

wedded (-id) *pret.* y *p. p.* de TO WED.

wedding (ue·ding) *s.* casamiento, boda, unión, enlace: *~ cake*, pastel de boda. *2* aniversario de la boda: *silver ~*, bodas de plata; *golden ~*, bodas de oro.

wedge (uedž) *s.* cuña, calza, calce, alzaprima. *2*

GEOM. prisma triangular. *3* ZOOL. ~ *shell*, coquina.
wedge (to) *tr.* acuñar, apretar, partir o separar con cuña. *2* clavar, encajar o aprisionar [como una cuña]. *3 intr.* entrar o clavarse [como una cuña].
wedlock (ue·dlak) *s.* matrimonio, nupcias.
Wednesday (ue·nšdi) *s.* miércoles.
wee (uɪ) *adj.* fam. pequeño, chiquito.
weed (uɪd) *s.* yerbajo, mala hierba. *2* alga, planta acuática. *3* fam. tabaco; marihuana. *4 pl.* gasas, vestidos de luto.
weed (to) *tr.* escardar, desyerbar, limpiar; arrancar las malas hierbas. *2* quitar, extirpar.
weedy (uɪ·di) *adj.* lleno de yerbajos; parecido a un yerbajo. *2* algoso. *3* flaco, desgarbado.
week (uɪk) *s.* semana: ~ *end*, fin de semana; ~ *in*, ~ *out*, semana tras semana.
weekday (uɪ·kdei) *s.* día laborable.
week-end (to) *intr.* pasar el fin de semana.
weekly (uɪ·kli) *adj.* semanal, hebdomadario. *2 adv.* semanalmente, por semana. *3 s.* semanario [periódico].
weep (to) (uɪp) *intr.* llorar. *2 tr.* llorar, lamentar. *3* llorar, verter [lágrimas]. *4 to* ~ *one's eyes out*, hartarse de llorar. ¶ Pret. y p. p.: *wept.*
weeper (-ør) *s.* llorador, llorón. *2* plañidera. *3 pl.* velo de viuda.
weeping (uɪ·ping) *s.* llanto. *2 adj.* llorón: ~ *willow*, sauce llorón.
weever (uɪ·vør) *s.* ICT. dragón marino.
weevil (uɪ·vøl) *s.* ENT. gorgojo.
weft (ueft) *s.* TEJ. trama. *2* tejido. *3* velo [de humo, niebla, etc.].
weigh (to) (uei) *tr.* pesar [determinar el peso de; ponderar, examinar]: *to* ~ *out*, pesar y distribuir. *2* sopesar. *3* contrapesar. *4* MAR. levar [un ancla]: *to* ~ *anchor*, levar anclas. *5 to* ~ *down*, abrumar, agobiar. *6 intr.* pesar [tener peso; hacer peso]. *7* pesarse. *8* MAR. levar anclas.
weight (ueit) *s.* peso, gravedad. *2* peso [de una cosa: *standard* ~, peso legal o normal; *to put on* ~, ganar peso, engordar; *by* ~, al peso. *3* unidad de peso. *4* sistema de pesos. *5* pesa. *6* peso, carga. *7* peso, importancia, fuerza, autoridad, influencia. *8* pisapapeles.
weight (to) *tr.* cargar con peso; aumentar el peso de; sobrecargar.
weightless (-lis) *adj.* ingrávido, ligero, leve.
weighty (-i) *adj.* pesado, ponderoso. *2* de peso, importante, serio, grave. *3* corpulento.
weir (uɪr) *s.* azud, presa [en un río]. *2* cañal, encañizada.
weird (uɪ·rd) *adj.* sobrenatural, fantástico, misterioso. *2* raro, extraño.
welcome (ue·lkøm) *adj.* bien venido, bien acogido, bien recibido. *2* grato, agradable, oportuno. *3 you are* ~, no hay de qué, de nada [en respuesta a *thank you*]. *4 you are* ~ *here*, está usted en su casa. *5 you are* ~ *to it*, está a su disposición. *6 s.* bienvenida, buena acogida. *7 interj.* ¡bien venido!
welcome (to) *s.* dar la bienvenida. *2* acoger con agasajo. *3* recibir con gusto, aceptar.
weld (ueld) *s.* soldadura, unión. *2* BOT. gualda.
weld (to) *tr.* soldar [esp. a martillo]. *2* unir íntimamente, unificar. *3 intr.* soldarse.
welder (-ør) *s.* soldador.
welding (ue·lding) *s.* soldadura: ~ *torch*, lámpara de soldar.
welfare (-fer) *s.* bienestar, bien, felicidad, salud: ~ *work*, obra social o de beneficencia.

we'll (uɪl) *contr.* de WE SHALL y WE WILL.
well (uel) *s.* fuente, manantial, venero. *2* pozo [de agua, de petróleo, etc.]. *3* MAR. pozo; caja de bombas. *4* aljibe, cisterna. *5* ARQ. [caja de escalera o ascensor]. *6* vaso [de tintero]; depósito [de estilográfica].
well *adj.* bien hecho, satisfactorio, agradable, conveniente, bueno, sano, dichoso, apto, adecuado. | Us. gralte. como predicado y, en muchos casos, equivale al adverbio castellano «bien»: *all is* ~, todo va bien, no hay novedad: *is your father* ~?, ¿está bien su padre?; *very* ~, muy bien. *2 adv.* bien, felizmente, favorablemente, completamente, del todo; ~ *done*, bien hecho; COC. bien asado; ~ *off*, próspero, acomodado; *as* ~, además, también; ~ *then*, pues bien, conque. *3 interj.* ¡bien!, ¡bueno!, ¡vamos!
well (to) *intr.* manar, brotar. *2 tr.* manar.
well-balanced *adj.* bien equilibrado. *2* fig. equilibrado, cuerdo, sensato.
well-behaved *adj.* de buena conducta. *2* atento, cortés.
well-being *s.* bienestar.
well-bred *adj.* bien educado, bien criado.
well-disposed *adj.* bien dispuesto, favorable.
well-favoured *adj.* agraciado, bien parecido.
well-founded *adj.* bien fundado.
wellhole (ue·ljoul) *s.* caja u ojo de escalera. *2* boca de pozo.
well-informed *adj.* bien enterado. *2* culto, ilustrado.
well-known *adj.* conocido, bien conocido; familiar.
well-meaning *adj.* bienintencionado.
well-nigh *adv.* casi, cerca de.
well-off *adj.* próspero, acomodado.
well-read *adj.* leído, docto, erudito.
wellspring (ue·lspring) *s.* fuente, manantial.
well-timed *adj.* oportuno.
well-to-do *adj.* acomodado, próspero.
well-worn *adj.* gastado, raído. *2* fig. trillado.
Welsh (uelsh) *adj.* galés: ~ *rabbit* o *rarebit*, tostada cubierta de queso derretido en cerveza. *2 s.* idioma galés. *3 pl. the* ~, los galeses.
Welshman (ue·lshmæn) *s.* galés.
welt (uelt) *s.* COST. vivo, ribete. *2* ZAP. vira. *3* CARP. refuerzo. *4* roncha, verdugón.
welt (to) *tr.* ribetear. *2* ZAP. poner viras a. *3* CARP. reforzar. *4* levantar ronchas; zurriagar.
welter (ue·ltør) *s.* agitación, tumulto. *2* confusión, revoltijo.
welter (to) *intr.* revolcarse. *2* encenagarse.
welterweight (ue·ltørueit) *s.* DEP. peso «welter».
wen (uen) *s.* lobanillo, lupia.
wench (uench) *s.* muchacha, jovencita. *2* moza, criada. *3* ant. ramera, coima.
wend (to) (uend) *tr.* dirigir, encaminar: *to* ~ *one's way*, dirigir sus pasos.
went (uent) *pret.* de TO GO.
wept (uept) *pret.* y *p. p.* de TO WEEP.
we're (uɪr) *contr.* de WE ARE.
were (uør) *pret. pl.* de *ind.* y *sing.* y *pl.* de *subj.* de TO BE.
Wesleyan (ue·slian) *adj.-s.* wesleyano, metodista.
west (uest) *s.* oeste, occidente, poniente. *2* ~ *northwest*, oesnoroeste; ~ *southwest*, oessudoeste. *3 adj.* occidental, del oeste: *West Indies*, las Antillas. *4 adv.* al oeste, en el oeste o hacia el oeste.
wester (-ør) *s.* viento o temporal del oeste.
westerly (-ørli) *adj.* occidental, del oeste. *2* que va

hacia el oeste; que viene del oeste. *3 adv.* hacia el oeste. *4* viniendo del oeste.

western (-øʳn) *adj.* occidental, de occidente, del oeste: *Western Empire,* Imperio de Occidente. *3 s.* novela, cuento o película de la vida del Oeste [de los E.U.].

westerner (-øʳnøʳ) *s.* natural o habitante del oeste.

Westphalia (uestfei·lia) *n. pr.* GEOGR. Vestfalia.

westward (ue·stwaʳd) *adj.* que se dirige o está hacia el oeste; que mira al oeste. *2 s.* el Occidente [regiones, países].

westwards (-s) *adv.* hacia el oeste.

wet (uet) *adj.* mojado: ~ *blanket,* fig. aguafiestas, jarro de agua fría. *2* húmedo: ~ *cell,* ELECT. pila húmeda. *3* humedecido. *4* lluvioso. *5* que crece en terreno húmedo. *6* fam. achispado. *7* (E.U.) antiprohibicionista. *8* ~ *nurse,* ama de cría. *9 s.* humedad; tiempo lluvioso; agua, lluvia.

wet (to) *tr.* mojar: *to* ~ *one's whistle,* fam. mojar el gaznate, beber. *2* humedecer, humectar. ¶ Pret. y p. p.: *wet* o *wetted;* ger.: *-tting.*

wether (ue·ðøʳ) *s.* carnero castrado.

whack (juæk) *s.* fam. golpe, garrotazo. *2* pop. prueba, tentativa. *3* pop. porción, parte.

whack (to) *tr.* fam. golpear, pegar.

whacking (-ing) *adj.* fam. enorme, desmesurado.

whale (jueil) *s.* ZOOL. ballena, cachalote. *2* fig. (E.U.) cosa enorme, extraordinaria.

whale (to) *intr.* ir a la pesca de la ballena. *2* (E.U.) zurrar, apalizar.

whaleboat (-bout) *s.* MAR. ballenero [embarcación].

whalebone (-boun) *s.* ballena [lámina]. *2* ballena [de corsé].

whaler (-øʳ) *s.* ballenero. *2* buque ballenero. *3* WHALEBOAT.

whaling (-ing) *s.* pesca de la ballena.

whang (juæng) *s.* golpe fuerte, que resuena.

whang (to) *tr.* golpear con fuerza.

wharf (juoʳf) *s.* muelle, embarcadero.

wharfage (-idȳ) *s.* muellaje.

wharfinger (-ingøʳ) *s.* dueño o encargado de un muelle.

what (juat) *adj. y pron. interr.* qué; cuál: ~ *a man!,* ¡qué hombre!; ~ *is this?,* ¿qué es esto?; ~ *for?,* ¿para qué?; ~ *is his name?,* ¿cuál es su nombre?, ¿cómo se llama? *2* a veces tiene el sentido de ¿y qué?», «¿qué importa?», «¿qué le parece?». *3 pron. rel.* lo que: ~ *followed,* lo que siguió; ~ *is* ~, lo que hay. *4 and* ~ *not,* y qué sé yo qué más. *5 adj. rel.* el, la, los, las... que; cuanto, cuantos, cuantas: *take* ~ *money you need,* tome el dinero que (o cuanto dinero) necesite. *6 adv.* parte, entre: ~ *with drink and* ~ *with fright,* entre la bebida y el miedo. *7 interj.* ¡eh!, ¡qué!

whatever (juate·vøʳ) *pron.* cualquier cosa que, sea, lo que sea que, cuanto, todo lo que. *2* fam. qué [interrogativo]: ~ *do you want?,* ¿qué quiere usted? *3 adj.* cualquiera que; de ninguna clase, en absoluto: ~ *be the issue,* cualquiera que sea el resultado; *no food* ~, ninguna clase de comida.

whatnot (jua·tnat) *s.* cosa, chisme. *2* estante, rinconera.

whatsoever (juatsoue·vøʳ) *pron. y adj.* WHATEVER.

wheal (juil) *s.* haba, roncha.

wheat (juIt) *s.* BOT. trigo: ~ *field,* trigal.

wheatear (iøʳ) *s.* ORN. culiblanco.

wheaten (-øn) *adj.* de trigo.

wheedle (to) (juI·døl) *tr.* halagar, engatusar. *2* conseguir por medio de halagos.

wheel (juIl) *s.* rueda [de carro, de reloj, etc.]: *on*

wheels, sobre ruedas. *2* rodaja, disco, polea. *3* rodezno. *4* torno [de alfarero o de hilar]. *5* PIROT. rueda. *6* rueda [suplicio]. *7* MAR. rueda del timón. *8* AUTO. volante. *9* fam. bicicleta. *10* giro, revolución. *11* MIL. conversión. *12 adj.* de ruedas, de figura de ruedas; del timón; que gira: ~ *base,* batalla [de un carruaje]; ~ *chair,* silla de ruedas; ~ *horse,* caballo de varas; ~ *window,* ARQ. rosa, rosetón.

wheel (to) *tr.* mover, llevar sobre ruedas; hacer rodar; hacer girar. *2* poner ruedas a. *3* labrar en el torno del alfarero. *4 intr.* girar, rodar, dar vueltas. *5* MIL. girar, efectuar una conversión. *6* ir en bicicleta. *7* rodar, marchar fácilmente.

wheelbarrow (-bærou) *s.* carretilla de mano.

wheeler (-øʳ) *s.* rodador, girador. *2* caballo de varas. *3* buque de ruedas. *4* fam. ciclista; motociclista.

wheelhouse (-jaus) *s.* MAR. timonera.

wheelrace (-reis) *s.* cárcavo.

wheelwork (-wøʳk) *s.* MEC. rodaje, ruedas.

wheelwright (-rait) *s.* CARTWRIGHT.

wheeze (juis) *s.* jadeo, silbido de la respiración fatigosa. *2* pop. chiste, broma, etc., gastados.

wheeze (to) *intr.* jadear, respirar produciendo un silbido.

wheezy (-i) *adj.* asmático, jadeante.

whelk (juelk) *s.* ZOOL. buccino, caracol de mar. *2* pápula, pústula, grano.

whelp (juelp) *s.* cachorro. *2* desp. mozalbete, granuja.

whelp (to) *intr.* parir [la perra, la loba, etc.].

when (juen) *adv. y conj.* cuando, al tiempo que, en cuanto, así que: *since* ~?, ¿desde cuándo? *2* en cuyo momento, y entonces. *3* en que: *the moment* ~, el momento en que. *4* estando, en caso de: ~ *in doubt,* en caso de duda. *5* aunque, a pesar de que.

whence (juens) *adv.* de donde, de qué lugar, origen, etc. *2* de donde, de ahí, por lo cual.

whenever (juene·vøʳ) *adv.* cuando quiera que, siempre que, en cualquier tiempo o que sea, todas las veces que.

where (jueʳ) *adv. y conj.* donde, en donde, adonde, por donde. *2 pron.* donde.

whereabout (jue·rabaut) *adv.* dónde, hacia dónde.

whereabouts (jue·rabauts) *s.* paradero.

whereas (jueræ·š) *conj.* considerando que. *2* mientras que, cuando por el contrario.

whereby (-bai) *adv.* con que, por medio de lo cual. *2* ¿cómo?

wherefore (-foʳ) *adv.* ¿por qué? *2* por lo cual, por consiguiente. *3 s.* porqué, razón, motivo.

wherein (jueri·n) *adv.* donde, en qué, con lo cual.

whereto (-tu·), **whereunto** (juerøntu·) *adv.* a lo cual, a que.

whereupon (-øpa·n) *adv.* entonces, después de lo cual. *2* sobre que, en que.

wherever (-e·vøʳ) *adv.* dondequiera que, adondequiera que, por dondequiera que.

wherewith (jue·ʳwid) *adv.* con que, con lo cual.

wherry (jue·ri) *s.* bote; chalana.

whet (juet) *s.* afiladura, amoladura, aguzadura. *2* filo [cortante].

whet (to) *tr.* afilar, amolar. *2* excitar, aguzar; abrir [el apetito].

whether (jue·ðøʳ) *conj.* si: *I don't know* ~ *he will be there,* yo no sé si estará allí. *2* sea, sea que, ora, ya, tanto si... (como): ~ *we go or not,* tanto si vamos como si no vamos.

whetstone (jue·tstoun) *s.* piedra de afilar.

whetter (-ø^r) s. amolador, afilador. 2 estimulante.
whew (jiu) interj. ¡eh!, ¡uf!, ¡cáspita!
whey (juei·) s. suero [de la leche].
which (juich) adj. y pron. interrog. ¿qué?, ¿cuál?, ¿cuáles?: ~ way?, ¿por qué camino?, ¿por dónde?; ~ is ~, quién, o cuál, es el uno y quién, o cuál, es el otro. 2 pron. rel. lo que, lo cual: all of ~, all ~, todo lo cual. 3 que, el cual, los o las cuales [con referencia o cosas]: both of ~, los cuales, que [refiriéndose a dos]. 4 cualquiera que; el, los, etc., que: take ~ you will, tome el que quiera. 5 adj. rel. Hay que traducirlo libremente: three days, during ~ time, tres días, durante los cuales.
whichever (-e·vø^r) pron. y adj. cualquiera, cualesquiera, quienquiera; el que.
whidah-bird (jui·da·bø^{r}d) s. ORN. viuda.
whiff (juif) s. soplo [de aire]. 2 vaharada, bocanada, fumarada, hálito, tufo; olor o hedor repentino.
whiff (to) tr. echar, exhalar [humo, olor, etc.]. 2 llevar o disipar con el soplo.
whiffle (to) (jui·føl) tr. soplar, exhalar, disipar, desvanecer. 2 intr. soplar a rachas [el viento]. 3 vacilar, fluctuar.
whiffletree (-trī) s. CARR. volea, balancín.
Whig (juig) adj.-s. POL. (Ingl.) liberal, del partido liberal.
while (juail) s. rato, tiempo: a little ~, a short ~, un ratito; for a ~, por algún tiempo; in a ~, dentro de poco; the ~, entretanto; to be worth ~, o one's ~, valer la pena. 2 conj. mientras, mientras que. 3 aun, aun cuando, si bien.
while (to) tr. pasar, entretener, distraer [el tiempo, el aburrimiento, etc.]. | Gralte. con away.
whilst (-st) conj. mientras, mientras que.
whim (juim) s. antojo, capricho, fantasía. 2 MIN. malacate.
whimper (-pø^r) s. gemido, gimoteo, lloriqueo.
whimper (to) intr. gemir, gimotear, lloriquear.
whimsey (-ši) s. WHIM.
whimsical (-šikal) adj. caprichoso, antojadizo. 2 caprichoso, fantástico, raro, extravagante.
whimsy (-ši) s. WHIM.
whin (juin) s. roca basáltica. 2 BOT. tojo.
whine (juain) s. gemido, plañido, gimoteo.
whine (to) intr. gemir, quejarse, gimotear.
whinny (jui·ni) s. relincho [esp. suave].
whinny (to) intr. relinchar [esp. suavemente].
whip (juip) s. látigo, fusta, zurriago, azote. 2 latigazo. 3 COC. batido de nata, huevos, etc. 4 movimiento de vaivén en arco de círculo. 5 MAR. tecle, andarivel. 6 POL. (Ingl.) miembro de una cámara encargado de velar por la disciplina de su grupo. 7 ~ top, peonza.
whip (to) tr. fustigar, zurriagar, azotar, dar latigazos a; zurrar, dar una paliza a. 2 COC. batir [huevos, nata, etc.]. 3 mover, sacar, meter, asir, etc., bruscamente, vivamente, con presteza. | Con away, into, off, out, etc. 4 sacudir [una alfombra, etc.]. 5 envolver [un cabo, palo, etc.] con cuerda o cordel. 6 COST. sobrecoser. 7 intr. moverse, obrar, volverse, ir, pasar, etc., rápida o súbitamente. | Con away, down, into, out, up, etc. 8 ondear, restallar. ¶ Pret. y p. p.: whipped; ger.: whipping.
whipcord (-ko^{r}d) s. tralla [de látigo]. 2 catgut. 3 tela fuerte de estambre.
whippersnapper (jui·pø^{r}snæ·pø^r) s. quídam, mequetrefe.

whippet (-it) s. perro de una raza inglesa, muy corredora. 2 MIL. carro de asalto ligero.
whipping (-ing) s. azotamiento, flagelación, vapuleo, paliza. 2 ~ top, peonza.
whippletree (-øltrī) s. CARR. volea, balancín.
whipstitch (-stich) s. sobrecostura.
whipstitch (to) tr. sobrecoser.
whir (juø^r) s. zumbido; aleteo.
whir (to) intr. zumbar, rehilar. 2 moverse, volar, girar con zumbido. ¶ Pret. y p. p.: whirred; ger.: rring.
whirl (juø^{r}l) s. giro o vuelta rápidos; remolino, confusión. 2 espiral [de humo].
whirl (to) intr. girar, dar vueltas, volverse, pasar rápidamente; remolinar. 3 tr.hacer girar, voltear. 4 arremolinar.
whirligig (-igig) s. perinola. 2 tiovivo. 3 fig. torbellino. 4 ENT. girino.
whirlpool (-pul) s. vórtice, vorágine, remolino de agua.
wirlwind (-uind) s. torbellino, remolino de viento.
whirr s. y **whirr (to)** intr. WHIR y TO WHIR.
whish (juish) interj. ¡zas! 2 ¡chitón!
whish (to) intr. TO SWISH. 2 TO WHIZ.
whisk (juisk) s. movimiento rápido, ligero [como el del que barre o roza algo]. 2 escobita, manojo [de paja, etc.]. 3 COC. batidor. 4 panoja [de mijo].
whisk (to) tr. barrer, arrastrar, cepillar. 2 mover, llevar, arrebatar: to ~ out of sight, escamotear. 3 COC. batir. 4 intr. moverse rápidamente.
whisker (-ø^r) s. patilla; barba: side whiskers, patillas. 2 pl. bigotes [del gato, el león, etc.].
whiskey s. WHISKY.
whisky (-i) s. whisky.
whisper (jui·spø^r) s. susurro, murmullo, cuchicheo.
whisper (to) intr.-tr. susurrar, murmurar, cuchichear; hablar o decir al oído.
whispering (-ing) s. susurro, rumor. 2 adj. susurrador, murmurador. 3 cuchicheador.
whist (juist) s. whist [juego de naipes].
whistle (jui·søl) s. silbato, pito, chiflato. 2 fam. gaznate. 3 silbido, silbo, pitido.
whistle (to) intr.-tr. silbar, pitar: to ~ for, llamar con un silbido; fig. pedir en vano.
whit (juit) s. pizca: not a ~, nada.
white (juait) adj. blanco; albo: ~ ant, ENT. hormiga blanca; ~ coal, hulla blanca; ~ corpuscle FISIOL. glóbulo blanco; ~ elephant, elefante blanco; fig. carga, estorbo; cosa gravosa e improductiva; ~ feather, pluma blanca, símbolo de cobardía; ~ friar, carmelita; ~ heat, temperatura al rojo blanco; ~ lead, albayalde; ~ lie, mentirilla; ~ matter, ANAT. substancia blanca; ~ monk, monje cisterciense; ~ oak, roble albar; ~ paper, (Ingl.) informe oficial; White Russia, GEOGR. Rusia Blanca; White Sea, GEOGR. Mar Blanco; ~ slavery, trata de blancas. 2 cano. 3 pálido, descolorido. 4 rubio [trigo]. 5 puro, inmaculado. 6 feliz, propicio. 7 en blanco.
8 s. color blanco, blancura. 9 pureza, inocencia. 10 blanco [del ojo]. 11 clara [de huevo]. 12 vestido blanco. 13 blanco, blanca [pers.]. 14 AJED. las blancas. 15 pl. leucorrea. 16 flor de harina.
whitebait (-beit) s. boquerones.
whitebeam (-bim) s. BOT. mostellar.
whitecaps (-kæps) s. MAR. cabrillas.
whitefish (-fish) s. ICT. coregóno.
white-handed adj. de manos blancas. 2 de manos limpias, inocente, puro.

white-hot *adj.* calentado al rojo blanco.
white-livered *adj.* cobarde. *2* envidioso.
whiten (to) (-øn) *tr.* blanquear, emblanquecer. *2* platear. *3 intr.* emblanquecerse, volverse blanco, blanquear.
whitening (-ning) *s.* blanqueo; emblanquecimiento. *2* enjalbegadura; lechada.
whitethorn (-zo^r n) *s.* BOT. espino blanco.
whitewash (-uash) *s.* preparación para blanquear, lechada. *2* blanquete, afeite.
whitewash (to) *tr.* blanquear, enjalbegar, encalar. *2* encubrir los vicios o faltas de uno o de algo.
whitewood (juai·twud) *s.* BOT. tulipero.
whither (jui·ðø^r) *adv.* adonde, al lugar o punto donde. *2* ¿adónde?
whiting (juai·ting) *s.* blanco de España. *2* ICT. pescadilla. *3* ICT. ~ *pout*, faneca.
whitish (-ish) *adj.* blanquecino, blancuzco.
whitlow (jui·tlou) *s.* MED. panadizo.
whitlowwort (-louwø^r t) *s.* BOT. nevadilla.
Witsun (-søn) *adj.* de Pentecostés.
Whitsunday (-dei) *s.* domingo de Pentecostés.
Whitsuntide (-taid) *s.* Pascua de Pentecostés.
whittle (jui·tøl) *s.* ant. cuchillo, cuchilla.
whittle (to) *tr.* dar forma, sacar pedazos, sacar punta [a un trozo de madera] con el cuchillo. *2 to* ~ *away* o *down*, fig. reducir, cercenar poco a poco.
whity (juai·ti) *adj.* blanquizco.
whiz o **whizz** (juiš) *s.* zumbido; sonido entre zumbido y silbido.
whiz o **whizz** (o) *intr.* zumbar, silbar, rehilar, ir zumbando por el aire.
who (ju) *pron. rel.* quien, quienes, que, el que, los que, las que [refiriéndose a pers. y gralte. como sujeto]. *2 he* ~, el que, quien. *3 pron. interr.* ¿quién?, ¿quiénes?
whoa (juou) *interj.* ¡so!, ¡cho!
whoever (jue·vø^r) *pron. rel.* quienquiera que, cualquiera que, quien.
whole (joul) *adj.* todo, entero, completo, total: *the* ~ *story*, toda la historia; ~ *note*, MÚS. semibreve, redonda; ~ *number*, número entero. *2* enterizo. *3* íntegro, intacto, sano, ileso. *4* s. todo, total, totalidad, conjunto: *as a* ~, en conjunto; *on the* ~, en suma, en general.
whole-hearted *adj.* sincero, cordial.
wholesale (-seil) *adj.-adv.* al por mayor, por mayor: ~ *dealer*, mayorista. *2 adj.* extenso, general. *3 s.* venta al por mayor.
wholesome (-søm) *adj.* sano, saludable; salutífero. *2* sano [en buena salud].
whole-wheat *adj.* integral, de todo el trigo.
wholly (-i) *adv.* totalmente, enteramente, del todo, completamente.
whom (jum) *pron.* (caso oblicuo de WHO) quien, quienes; que, el que, la que, etc.; el cual, la cual, etc. [precedidos de preposición].
whoop (jup) *s.* grito, alarido. *2* inspiración ruidosa propia de la tosferina.
whoop (to) *intr.* gritar, vocear. *2* silbar [el búho]. *3* inspirar ruidosamente después de un acceso de tos. *4 tr.* decir, llamar, insultar, alabar, etc., a gritos.
whooping cough (-pin) *s.* MED. tos ferina.
whop (to) (juap) *tr.* zurrar, dar una paliza a.
whopper (-ø^r) *s.* fam. cosa enorme. *2* mentira colosal.
whopping (-ing) *adj.* fam. enorme, colosal.
whore (jo^r) *s.* prostituta, ramera, puta.
wore (to) *intr.* fornicar.

whorl (juø^r l) *s.* tortera [del huso]. *2* espiral, circunvolución. *3* BOT. verticilo. *4* ZOOL. espira [de caracol].
whorled (-d) *adj.* verticilado.
whortleberry (juø·r tølberi) *s.* BOT. arándano.
who's (ju·š) *contr.* de WHO IS.
whose *pron.* (genitivo de WHO y WHICH) cuyo, cuya, cuyos, cuyas, del que, de la que, de los que, de las que, de quien, de quienes.
why (juai) *adv.* y *conj.* ¿por qué?, ¿cómo?; por qué, por el cual, por lo que, por... que. *2 interj.* ¡cómo!, ¡toma!, ¡qué! *3 s.* porqué, causa, razón.
wick (uik) *s.* pábilo, mecha torcida.
wicked (ui·kid) *adj.* malo, malvado, perverso. *2* maligno, mal intencionado. *3* travieso, revoltoso.
wicker (ui·kø^r) *s.* mimbre. *2* tejido de mimbres. *3 adj.* de mimbres, de cestería, recubierto de mimbres.
wickerwork (-uø^r k) *s.* tejido de mimbres, obra de cestería.
wicket (ui·kit) *s.* postigo, portillo; ventanilla. *2* CRICQUET meta; turno de cada jugador con el palo.
wide (uaid) *adj.* ancho. *2* de ancho: *two feet* ~, de dos pies de ancho. *3* anchuroso, espacioso. *4* amplio, dilatado, extenso, variado. *5* alejado, desviado. *6* muy abierto. *7 adv.* ampliamente. *8* lejos a distancia: ~ *of the mark*, sin dar en el blanco. *9* muy: ~ *apart*, muy separado; ~ *open*, muy abierto; de par en par.
wide-awake *adj.* muy despierto, despabilado.
wide-eyed *adj.* con los ojos abiertos. *2* asombrado.
widely (-li) *adv.* extensamente. *2* muy, mucho, ampliamente, holgadamente.
widen (to) (-øn) *tr.* ensanchar, dilatar, extender. *2 intr.* ensancharse, extenderse.
widespread (-spred) *adj.* extendido [alas, brazos, etc.]. *2* muy difundido; general, extenso.
widgeon (ui·dÿøn) *s.* ORN. cierto pato silvestre.
widow (ui·dou) *s.* viuda.
widow (to)*tr.* dejar viuda o viudo.
widower (-ø^r) *s.* viudo.
widowhood (-jud) *s.* viudez.
width (uidz) *s.* anchura, ancho.
wield (to) (uild) *tr.* manejar, esgrimir, empuñar. *2* ejercer [poder, autoridad].
wieldy (-i) *adj.* manejable.
wife (uaif), *pl.* **wives** (uai·vš) *s.* esposa, mujer.
wifely (-li) *adj.* de esposa.
wig (uig) *s.* peluca, peluquín. *2* fam. (Ingl.) juez.
wigged (-d) *adj.* con peluca.
wigging (-ing) *s.* fam. peluca, reprensión.
wiggle (-øl) *tr.-intr.* culebrear.
wiggle (to) *tr.* menear [la cola, los dedos, etc.]. *2 intr.* menearse, culebrear.
wigwag (-wæk) *s.* counicación con banderas.
wigwam (-wam) *s.* tienda o cabaña de ciertos indios norteamericanos.
wild (uaild) *adj.* salvaje, montaraz, silvestre [animal, planta]: ~ *ass*, onagro; ~ *boar*, jabalí; ~ *duck*, pato salvaje; ~ *fig*, cabrahigo; ~ *goat*, cabra montés; ~ *goose*, ánsar, ganso bravo; ~ *hazel*, nochizo; ~ *olive tree*, acebuche. *2* cimarrón. *3* inculto, sin cultivo, desierto. *4* salvaje [no civilizado]. *5* bravo, indómito, fiero. *6* turbulento, alborotado, borrascoso. *7* violento, impetuoso. *8* desenfrenado, desordenado. *9* alocado. *10* extraño, extravagante, disparato, loco. *11 adv.* WILDLY. *12* sin gobierno, sin freno. *13 s.* desierto, yermo, selva, tierra virgen.

wildcat (-kæt) *s.* ZOOL. gato montés. 2 (E.U.) locomotora suelta, sin tren. 3 pozo [de petróleo] de exploración. 4 *adj.* poco seguro, arriesgado; fantástico, quimérico; ilícito.

wilderness (ui·ldø^rnis) *s.* tierra inculta, desierto, soledad, extensión, inmensidad.

wild-eyed *adj.* con la mirada extraviada.

wildfire (uai·ldfai^r) *s.* fuego griego. 2 fuego fatuo. 3 fucilazo.

wld-goose *adj.* quimérico, inútil:~ *chase*, búsqueda o empresa inútil, quimérica.

wildly (-dli) *adv.* en estado salvaje, sin cultivo. 2 salvajemente, furiosamente, locamente,etc.

wile (uail) *s. pl.* ardid, maña, engaño, astucia.

wile (to) *tr.* inducir, atraer, engañar. 2 *to* ~ *away*, pasar, entretener [el tiempo].

wilful (ui·lful) *adj.* voluntarioso, testarudo. 2 voluntario, intencionado.

wilfully (-li) *adv.* voluntariosamente. 2 voluntariamente, intencionadamente.

wilfulness (-nis) *s.* obstinación, terquedad. 2 voluntariedad.

Wilhelmina (uiljelmi·na) *n. pr.* Guillermina.

will (ui·l) *s.* voluntad. No tiene el sentido de amor, cariño: ~ *power*, fuerza de voluntad; *at* ~, a voluntad, a discreción; *with a* ~, con toda el alma. 2 albedrío. 3 poder, arbitrio. 4 gana, inclinación, deseo. 5 DER. testamento.

1) will (to) *tr.* querer, determinar, ordenar, mandar. 2 legar, dejar en testamento. ¶ Pret. y p. p.: *willed;* ger.: *-lling.*

2) will *tr.-intr.* querer, desear, anhelar, gustar: *if you* ~, si usted quiere; *would (to) God*, plegue, o pluguiera, a Dios; ojalá. 2 *aux.* (con un infinitivo sin *to*). Forma el futuro y el potencial del segundo verbo. En las primeras personas, denota especialmente voluntad, intención, promesa o amenaza; en las segundas y terceras, simple acción futura, posibilidad o contingencia: *I* ~ *not do it*, no lo haré, no quiero hacerlo; *it* ~ *be very pleasant*, será muy agradable. | A veces indica que la acción del segundo verbo es habitual, frecuente o persistente y se traduce por soler, acostumbrar, o se traduce libremente: *he would take nightly walks*, solía dar (o daba) paseos nocturnos. ¶ Pret. y SUBJ.: *would.* | Carece de INF. e IMPERS.

willed (-d) *pret.* y *p. p.* de TO WILL.

willful *adj.* **willfully** *adv.*, **willfulness** *s.* = WILFUL, WILFULLY, WILFULNESS.

William (ui·liam) *n. pr.* Guillermo.

willing (ui·ling) *adj.* deseoso, dispuesto, inclinado, pronto. 2 gustoso, complaciente. 3 voluntario. 4 ger. de TO WILL: *God* ~, Dios mediante.

willingly (-li) *adv.* de buena gana, con gusto.

willingness (-nis) *s.* buena gana, gusto, complacencia.

will-o'-the-wisp *s.* fuego fatuo.

willow (ui·lou) *s.* BOT. sauce. 2 BOT. mimbrera.

willowy (-i) *adj.* abundante en sauces o mimbres. 2 cimbreño, flexible, esbelto, juncal.

willy-nilly (ui·li-ni·li) *adv.* velis nolis, de grado o por fuerza.

wilt (to) (uilt) *tr.* marchitar, secar. 2 *intr.* marchitarse. 3 languidecer, descaecer. 4 acobardarse.

wily (uai·li) *adj.* astuto, artero, marrullero.

wimble (ui·mbøl) *s.* berbiquí, barrena.

wimple (-pøl) *s.* toca, griñón.

wimple (to) *tr.* ondular, rizar [la superficie del agua]. 2 *intr.* caer en pliegues. 3 rizarse [la superficie del agua].

win (to) (uin) *tr.* ganar, obtener, alcanzar, conquistar, lograr. 2 persuadir, atraer, convencer, ganar el afecto de. 3 *intr.* vencer, triunfar, ganar. ¶ Pret. y p. p.: *won;* ger.: *winning.*

wince (uins) *s.* respingo.

wince (to) *intr.* cejar, retroceder, encogerse, acobardarse [ante una dificultad, un golpe, el dolor, etc.]; dar un respingo, respingar.

winch (uinch) *s.* manubrio, cigüeña. 2 torno, montacargas. 3 carrete [de caña de pescar].

1) wind (uind, *en poesía* uaind) *s.* viento, aire: ~ *sail*, MAR. manga [de ventilación]; ~ *sock*, AVIA. manga de viento; *to be in the* ~, tramarse; *to cast to the* ~, *to the winds*, esparcir, arrojar; *abandonar; to get o have the* ~ *up*, asustarse, ponerse nervioso; *against* o *up the* ~, contra el viento; *before the* ~, viento en popa; *between* ~ *and water*, en la línea de flotación; en sitio delicado o peligroso; *by the* ~, ciñendo el viento; *in* o *into, the wind's eye* o *the teeth of the* ~, de cara al viento; *under the* ~, a sotavento. 2 viento, rumbo, punto cardinal. 3 viento [olor que deja la caza]: *to get* ~ *of*, fig. oler, tener noticia de. 4 aliento, respiración, resuello. 5 flato, ventosidad: *to break* ~, ventosear. 6 BOX. boca del estómago. 7 *sing.* y *pl.* MÚS. instrumento de viento.

2) wind (uaind) *s.* mecanismo para devanar. 2 devanado; espiral, vuelta, sinuosidad.

1) wind (to) (uind) *tr.-intr.* ventear, husmear, olfatear. 2 *tr.* orear, airear. 3 quitar el resuello. 4 dejar recobrar el aliento. ¶ CONJUG. pret. y p. p.: *winded.*

2) wind (to) (uaind) *tr.* soplar. 2 tocar, hacer sonar [un instrumento de viento]. ¶ Pret. y p. p.: *wound.*

3) wind (to) *tr.* devanar, ovillar, encanillar. 2 arrollar, envolver, retorcer, ensortijar: *to* ~ *someone around one's fingers*, fig. manejar o gobernar a uno. 3 torcer; manejar. 4 dar cuerda a. 5 atirantar. 6 izar, elevar [con máquina]. 7 *to* ~ *off*, desenrollar, desovillar. 8 *to* ~ *one's way*, zigzaguear, serpentear. 9 *to* ~ *up*, devanar, ovillar; dar cuerda a; atirantar; excitar; izar, elevar [con máquina]. 10 *intr.* arrollarse, enrollarse, enroscarse. 11 serpentear, culebrear. 12 alabearse. 13 *tr.-intr. to* ~ *up*, acabar, concluir, finalizar. ¶ Pret. y p. p.: *wound* (en términos náuticos, *winded*).

windage (ui·ndidy) *s.* ARTILL. viento. 2 ARTILL. desvío de un proyectil por efecto del viento.

windbag (-bæg) *s.* fam. palabrero, charlatán.

wind-blown *adj.* llevado o desarreglado por el viento.

windbreak (-brek) *s.* abrigo contra el viento.

winded (-id) *adj.* venteado. 2 sin aliento, sin resuello.

winder (uai·ndø^r) *s.* devanador. 2 argadillo, devanadera; carrete. 3 llave para dar cuerda. 4 ARQ. escalón de abanico.

windfall (ui·ndfol) *s.* fruta caída del árbol por la fuerza del viento. 2 suerte inesperada.

winding (uai·nding) *s.* arrollamiento, enroscamiento, devanado, bobinado. 2 vuelta, revuelta, recodo, sinuosidad. 3 ELECT. arrollamiento. 4 alabeo. 5 ~ *up*, acción de dar cuerda o de atirantar; final, conclusión. 6 *adj.* sinuoso, tortuoso, etc. 7 ~ *frame*, devanadera; ~ *sheet*, mortaja, sudario; ~ *stairs*, escalera de caracol.

windlass (ui·ndlas) *s.* torno [para elevar pesos]; malacate. 2 MAR. molinete.

windmill (-mil) *s.* molino de viento. *2* molinete [juguete]. *3* AVIA. turbina de aire.

window (ui·ndou) *s.* ventana: ~ *case*, ~ *frame*, marco de ventana; ~ *envelope*, sobre de ventanilla; ~ *screen*, sobrevidriera. *3* ventanilla. *4* escaparate [de tienda]: ~ *dresser*, decorador de escaparates; ~ *dressing*, arreglo de escaparates; fig. amaño para dar a ciertas cosas un aspecto favorable.

windpipe (ui·ndpaip) *s.* tráquea, gaznate.

windscreen (-skrin), **windshield** (-shild) *s.* AUTO. parabrisas: ~ *wiper*, limpiaparabrisas.

wnd-up *s.* conclusión, final, desenlace. *2* fam. estado de excitación, ansiedad, miedo, etc.

windward (-a^rd) *s.* barlovento: *to sail to the* ~, barloventear. *2 adj.* de barlovento: *Windward Islands*, Islas de Barlovento. *3 adv.* hacia barlovento.

windy (-i) *adj.* ventoso. *2* ampuloso, hinchado. *3* palabrero. *4* vano, inconsistente.

wine (uain) *s.* vino: ~ *bag*, odre, pellejo; ~ *cellar*, bodega; ~ *press*, prensa para uva, lagar.

wine-colo(u)red *adj.* de color de vino, rojo oscuro.

wineglass (-glæs) *s.* copa para vino.

winegrower (-grouø^r) *s.* viticultor, vinicultor.

winesap (-sæp) *s.* manzana roja de invierno.

wineskin (-skin) *s.* odre, pellejo.

wing (uing) *s.* ORN., ENT., ANAT., ARQ., FORT., MIL., POL. ala: *on*, o *upon, the* ~, volando; viajando con un pie en el estribo; *under the* ~ *of*, bajo la protección de. *2* vuelo [acción de volar]. *3* MEC. aleta, oreja: ~ *nut*, tuerca de orejas. *4* TEAT. bastidor.

winged (-d o -id) *adj.* alado, aligero. *2* herido del ala. *3* lleno de pájaros.

winglet (-lit) *s.* alita.

wingspread (-pred) *s.* ORN. envergadura.

wink (uink) *s.* parpadeo, pestañeo, abrir y cerrar de ojos. *2* guiño. *3* sueño corto: *not to steep a* ~, no pegar los ojos. *4* relámpago, destello.

wink (to) *intr.* pestañear, parpadear, abrir y cerrar los ojos. *2* hacer guiños, un guiño. *3* centellear, dar luz trémula. *4 to* ~ *at*, hacer la vista gorda, disimular.

winker (-ø^r) *s.* guiñador. *2* BLINKER. *3* pop. pestaña.

winkle (ui·nkøl) *s.* PERIWINKLE.

winner (ui·nø^r) *s.* ganador. *2* vencedor.

winning (-ing) *adj.* triunfante, ganador; ganancioso. *2* atractivo, encantador, persuasivo. *3* DEP. ~ *post*, poste de llegada.

winnow (to) (ui·nou) *tr.* aventar, ahechar. *2* fig. cerner, analizar, entresacar. *3* poét. batir [el aire] con las alas; recorrer volando.

winsome (ui·nsøm) *adj.* agradable, atractivo, simpático, seductor.

winter (ui·ntø^r) *s.* invierno. *2 adj.* de invierno, invernal: ~ *cherry*, BOT. alquequenje; ~ *season*, invierno, invernada; ~ *solstice*, solsticio de invierno.

winter (to) *intr.* invernar, pasar el invierno.

wintergreen (-grin) *s.* BOT. gaultería.

wintering (-ing) *s.* invernada.

winterly (-li), **wintry** (ui·ntri) *adj.* de invierno, invernizo; invernal, hiemal. *2* fig. frío, helado, triste.

winy (uai·ni) *adj.* vinoso. *2* embriagado.

wipe (uaip) *s.* limpión, limpiadura. *2* golpe, revés, manotazo.

wipe (to) *tr.* limpiar, secar, enjugar, restregar. *2* quitar, lavar, borrar, extirpar, destruir. | Con

away, off o *out*. *3* pasar [la mano, un trapo, etc.] por.

wiper (-ø^r) *s.* limpiador, enjugador. *2* fam. paño, trapo, toalla, pañuelo. *3* pop. WIPE *2*. *4* ELECT. contacto deslizante.

wire (uai^r) *s.* alambre; hilo o cuerda de alambre: ~ *cutter*, cortaalambres; ~ *edge*, filván; ~ *entanglement*, FORT. alambrada; ~ *fence*, alambrado; ~ *nail*, alfiler de París; ~ *rope*, cordón o cable metálico; ~ *screen*, alambrera, tela metálica. *2* alambrado. *3* telégrafo eléctrico. *4* telegrama. *5 pl.* hilos [con que se mueve una cosa]: *to pull the wires*, mover los hilos.

wire (to) *tr.* proveer de alambres; alambrar. *2* coger, atar, etc. con alambre. *3 tr.-intr.* telegrafiar.

wiredraw (to) (uai·^rdro) *tr.* tirar [metales]. *2* alargar, hacer durar. *3* alambicar, sutilizar. ¶ Pret.: *-drew*; p. p.: *-drawn*.

wiredrawing (-droing) *s.* tirado [de metales].

wire-haired *adj.* de pelo áspero [perro].

wireless (-lis) *adj.* ELECT. inalámbrico, sin hilos; de telegrafía o telefonía sin hilos. *4* (Ingl.) radio, radiotelefonía; aparato de radio.

wireless (to) *tr.-intr.* comunicar o transmitir por radiotelegrafía o radiofonía.

wiring (-ing) *s.* ELECT. sistema e instalación de hilos y cables de distribución; conducción [eléctrica].

wiry (-i) *adj.* de alambre; como alambre. *2* delgado y fuerte; nervudo.

wisdom (ui·sdøm) *s.* sabiduría, sapiencia. *2* prudencia, cordura, juicio, discreción: ~ *tooth*, muela del juicio.

wise (uaiš) *adj.* cuerdo, prudente, juicioso, sensato. *2* fam. enterado, noticioso. *3* sabio, docto: *the Wise Men of the East*, los Magos de Oriente. *4 s.* modo, manera: *in no* ~, de ningún modo.

wiseacre (-eikø^r) *s.* sabihondo.

wisecrack (-kræk) *s.* fam. chiste, bufonada.

wish (uish) *s.* deseo, anhelo.

wish (to) *tr.* desear, anhelar, ansiar, querer: *to* ~ *one good morning*, dar los buenos días; *I* ~ *it were true!*, ¡ojalá fuera verdad! *2* intr. *to* ~ *for* o *after*, anhelar, desear.

wishbone (-boun) *s.* espoleta [de ave].

wshful (ui·shful) *adj.* deseoso, anheloso, ansioso.

wishy-washy (ui·shi-ua·shi) *adj.* ñoño, insípido. *2* flojo, aguado [líquido].

wisp (uisp) *s.* mechón, manojito, trocito, jirón, pizca.

wisteria (uistir·ria) *s.* BOT. ¿ icina.

wistful (ui·stful) *adj.* anhelante, ansioso. *2* pensativo, tristón.

wit (uit) *s.* agudeza, ingenio, sal, chispa. *2* ingenio [pers. ingeniosa], chistoso; conceptista. *3* talento, imaginación, inventiva: *to be at one's wits' end*, no saber qué hacer. *4* buen sentido. *5 pl.* juicio, razón, equilibrio mental: *to loose one's wits*, perder el juicio. *6* ingenio, habilidad, industria.

wit (to) *tr.* ant. saber. | Ús. sólo en *to* ~, a saber, es decir.

witch (uitch) *s.* bruja, hechicera. *2* bruja [mujer fea y vieja].

witch (to) hechizar.

witchcraft (-kræft); **witchery** (-øri) *s.* brujería, hechicería, encantamiento. *2* encanto, fascinación.

witching (-ing) *adj.* encantador. *2* brujesco.

with (uið) *prep.* con; contra; para con; a, de, en, entre, etc., expresando relaciones varias: ~ *me*, conmigo; ~ *all speed*, a toda prisa; *charged* ~, acusado de; *filled* ~, lleno de; *to abound* ~, abundar en; *it was customary* ~ *the Greeks*, era costumbre entre los griegos; *away* ~ *you!*, ¡fuera de ahí!, ¡anda!

whital (ui·ðo·l) *adv.* ant. además, también, al mismo tiempo; con todo. *2 prep.* ant. con.

withdraw (to) (uiðdro·) *tr.* retirar. *2* apartar, separar, quitar, sacar. *3* descorrer [una cortina]. *4* distraer [de una ocupación]. *5 to* ~ *a statement*, retractarse. *6 intr.* retirarse.

withdrawal (-al) *s.* retiro, retirada. *2* recogida. *3* retractación.

withe (uai·d) *s.* mimbre, junco, vencejo.

wither (to) (ui·ðøʳ) *tr.* marchitar, secar, poner mustio, ajar. *2* debilitar, enflaquecer. *3* avergonzar. *4* marchitarse, secarse, ajarse. *5* debilitarse.

withered (-d) *adj.* marchito, mustio, seco.

withers (ui·ðøʳš) *s. pl.* cruz [de un cuadrúpedo].

withhold (to) (ui·djould) *tr.* detener, contener; impedir. *2* suspender [un pago]. *3* negar, rehusar. ¶ Pret. y p. p.: *withheld*.

within (ui·ðin) *prep.* dentro de, dentro de los límites de, en. *2* a, o a menos de [cierta distancia]. *3* al alcance de: ~ *hearing*, al alcance del oído. *4 adv.* dentro, adentro, en o al interior. *5* por dentro. *6* en la casa, en la habitación.

without (-out) *prep.* sin. *2* falto de. *3* fuera de. *4 adv.* fuera, en el exterior, afuera. *5* por fuera, exteriormente. *6 conj.* fam. si no, a menos que.

withstand (to) (ui·zstænd) *tr.* resistir, aguantar, oponerse a, hacer resistencia a.

withy (ui·ďi) *s.* WHITE.

witless (ui·tlis) *adj.* necio, tonto, mentecato.

witness (-nis) *s.* testigo [pers.]. *2* testimonio, atestación, prueba: *to call to* ~, tomar por testigo; *in* ~ *whereof*, en fe de lo cual.

witness (to) *tr.* dar testimonio de, atestiguar, dar fe de. *2* presenciar, ver. *3* mostrar, demostrar. *4 intr.* dar testimonio, declarar.

witted (ui·tid) *adj.* ingenioso, inteligente.

witticism (ui·tisišm) *s.* agudeza, rasgo de ingenio, chiste, ocurrencia.

wittiness (-inis) *s.* ingenio, agudeza, gracia.

witty (-i) *adj.* ingenioso, agudo, chistoso, ocurrente.

wivern (uai·vøʳn) *s.* BLAS. dragón alado.

wives (uai·vs) *s. pl.* de WIFE.

wizard (ui·šaʳd) *s.* brujo, hechicero.

wizardry (-ri) *s.* hechicería, magia.

wizen (to) (ui·šøn) *tr.* marchitar, secar, arrugar. *2 intr.* marchitarse, secarse, arrugarse, acartonarrse.

wizened (-d) *adj.* seco, marchito; arrugado, acartonado.

woad (uoud) *s.* BOT. y TINT. glasto, pastel.

wobble (ua·bøl) *s.* tambaleo, vacilación.

wobble (to) *intr.* balancearse, tambalear, vacilar. *2* cambiar, ser inconstante.

wobbly (ua·bli) *adj.* tambaleante, vacilante.

woe (uou) *s.* pena, aflicción, calamidad, infortunio. *2 interj.* ¡ay!: ~ *is me!*, ¡ay de mí!

wo(e)begone (-bigon) *adj.* miserable, triste, abatido.

wo(e)ful (-ful) *adj.* triste, afligido. *2* desdichado. *3* lastimero, doloroso. *4* ruin, pobre.

wold (uould) *s.* llanura; campiña ondulada.

wolf (wulf), *pl.* **wolves** (-š) *s.* ZOOL. lobo: ~ *cub*, lobezno; *to keep the* ~ *from the door*, ponerse a cubierto de la miseria.

wolf (to) *tr.* fam. engullir.

wolfhound (-jaund) *s.* mastín, perro lobero.

wolfish (-ish) *adj.* lobuno. *2* feroz, voraz.

wolfram (wu·lfram) *s.* QUÍM., MINER. volframio.

wolfsbane (wu·lfsbein) *s.* BOT. acónito.

wolf's-milk *s.* BOT. lechetrezna.

wolverene, -rine (wulvøri·n) *s.* ZOOL. carcayú.

woman (wu·mæn), *pl.* **women** (ui·min) *s.* mujer: ~ *writer*, escritora. *2* criada. *3 adj.* femenino, de mujer.

womanhood (-jud) *s.* condición de mujer. *2* feminidad. *3* el sexo femenino.

womanish (-ish) *adj.* femenil, mujeril. *2* afeminado.

womankind (-kaind) *s.* las mujeres, el sexo femenino. *2* las mujeres de una familia o grupo.

womanlike (-laik) *adj.* WOMANLY.

womanly (-li) *adj.* femenino, femenil, mujeril. *2* propio de la mujer adulta. *3 adv.* como mujer.

womb (wu·m) *s.* útero, matriz. *2* seno, entrañas.

won (uøn) *pret.* y *p. p.* de TO WIN.

wonder (uø·ndøʳ) *s.* admiración, asombro, sorpresa: *no* ~, no es de extrañar. *2* incertidumbre, perplejidad. *3* portento, prodigio, maravilla: *to do wonders*, hacer maravillas.

wonder (to) *tr.* desear saber, preguntarse: *I* ~ *if it will rain*, me pregunto si va a llover. | A veces no se traduce y su sentido se expresa en forma de pregunta: *I* ~ *what he wants*, ¿qué querrá? *2 intr.* sentir duda y curiosidad. *3* extrañarse, sorprenderse, maravillarse.

wonderful (-ful) *adj.* admirable, maravilloso, asombroso, portentoso, prodigioso.

wondering (-ing) *adj.* asombrado, maravillado.

wonderland (uø·ndøʳlænd) *s.* país de las maravillas; reino de las hadas.

wonderment (-mønt) *s.* admiración, asombro. *2* milagro, maravilla.

wondrous (uø·ndrøs) *adj.* sorprendente, asombroso, maravilloso, portentoso.

wont (uønt) *adj.* acostumbrado, sólito *to be* ~, soler, acostumbrar. *2 s.* costumbre, hábito.

wont (to) *intr.* acostumbrar, soler. ¶ Pret.: *wont;* p. p.: *wont* o *wonted*.

won't *contr.* de WILL NOT.

wonted (-id) *adj.* acostumbrado, usual.

woo (to) (wu) *tr.* cortejar, pretender [a una mujer]. *2* buscar, perseguir [tratar de obtener]. *3 intr.* cortejar.

wood (wud) *s.* bosque, selva, monte: *he cannot see the* ~ *for the trees*, los árboles no le dejan ver el bosque. *2* madera, palo, leña: *small* ~, chasca, leña menuda. *3 adj.* de los bosques: ~ *louse*, cochinilla de humedad; ~ *pigeon*, paloma torcaz; ~ *sorrel*, acederilla. *4* de madera, en madera, etc.: ~ *carver*, tallista; ~ *carving*, talla de la madera; ~ *engraving*, grabado en madera.

wood (to) *tr.* cubrir de bosque. *2* proveer de leña.

woodbine (-bain) *s.* BOT. madreselva.

woodchuck (-chøk) *s.* ZOOL. marmota de Norteamérica.

woodcock (-kak) *s.* ORN. chocha, becada.

woodcraft (-kræft) *s.* conocimiento y práctica de todo lo referente a los bosques y a la vida en ellos. *2* arte de trabajar la madera.

woodcut (-køt) *s.* grabado en madera.

woodcutter (-køtøʳ) *s.* leñador. *2* grabador en madera.

wooded (-id) *adj.* arbolado, cubierto de bosques.

wooden (-øn) *adj.* de madera, de palo. *2* vago, sin

expresión [mirada, etc.]. *3* embotado, torpe; tosco, sin gracia.

wooden-headed *adj.* torpe, estúpido.

woodland (-lænd) *s.* monte, bosque, selva.

wodlander (-lændø^r) *s.* habitante del bosque.

woodless (-lis) *adj.* sin árboles, sin bosques.

woodman (-mæn) *s.* leñador. *2* (Ingl.) guardabosque. *3* habitante del bosque.

woodpecker (-pekø^r) *s.* ORN. pico, picamaderos, pájaro carpintero.

woodpile (-pail) *s.* pila de leña, leñera.

woodruff (-drøf) *s.* BOT. asperilla.

woodshed (-shed) *s.* leñera.

woodsman (-smæn) *s.* habitante del bosque; cazador, trampero, etc.

wood-wind *s.* MÚS. madera [instrumentos de viento].

woodwork (-uø^{r}k) *s.* maderaje. *2* obra de carpintería.

woody (-i) *adj.* arbolado, selvoso. *2* leñoso.

wooer (wu·ø^r) *s.* cortejador, pretendiente.

woof (wuf) *s.* TEJ. trama. *2* tejido, textura.

wooing (wu·ing) *s.* cortejo, galanteo.

wool (wul) *s.* lana: ~ *bearing*, lanar; *all* ~, pura lana; *to pull the* ~ *over one's eyes*, engañar. *2* cabello crespo.

wooled (-d) *adj.* lanudo.

woolen (-øn) *adj.* de lana; lanero. *2 s.* paño o tejido de lana. *3 pl.* géneros de lana.

woolgatherer (-gædørø^r) *s.* distraido; visionario.

woolgathering (-gæðoring) *s.* ensimismamiento.

woollen (-øn) *adj.-s.* WOOLEN.

woolly (-i) *adj.* de lana. *2* lanudo, lanoso. *3* coposo. *4* crespo, cabello. *5* confuso. *6 s.* prenda de lana.

woolsack (-sæk) *s.* saco de lana. *2* (Ingl.) asiento del Lord Canciller en la Cámara de los lores.

word (uø^{r}d) *s.* palabra, vocablo, voz, término; cosa dicha: *the last* ~, la última palabra; *to have a* ~ *with*, hablar un poco con; *in a* ~, en una palabra; *in other words*, en otros términos; *in so many words*, literalmente; sin ambages. *2* palabra [expresión oral o escrita]: *in* ~, de palabra; *by* ~ *of mouth*, oralmente, verbalmente. *3* dicho, sentencia, adagio. *4* palabra [promesa, seguridad]: *to keep one's word*, cumplir su palabra; *to take one at his* ~, coger la palabra a uno; *on* o *upon my* ~, palabra de honor; a fe mía. *5* aviso, recado, noticia: *to leave* ~, dejar dicho, decar recado. *6* contraseña, santo y seña. *7* orden, voz de mando. *8 the Word*, el Verbo. *9 pl.* letra [de una canción]. *10* palabras, disputa: *to have words*, disputar.

word (to) *tr.* expresar [con palabras]; formular, redactar.

wordiness (-inis) *s.* verbosidad, palabrería.

wording (-ing) *s.* redacción, estilo, fraseología.

wordy (-i) *adj.* verbal. *2* verboso.

wore (uo^r) *pret.* de TO WEAR.

work (uø^{r}k) *s.* trabajo, labor, obra, tarea, faena; ocupación, empleo; operación, funcionamiento: *piece of* ~, trabajo, obra; *at* ~, trabajando; *en operación*; *out of* ~, sin trabajo. *2* obra [literaria, artística, etc.]. *3* COST. labor, bordado. *4* FORT. obra, trabajo. *5* obra, acto, acción. *6 pl.* fábrica, taller. *7* obras [públicas o de ingeniería]. *8* maquinaria [de un artefacto].

work (to) *intr.* trabajar; laborar: *to* ~ *at*, trabajar en. *2* obrar, surtir efecto, dar resultado. *3* funcionar, marchar. *4* moverse, avanzar, salir, entrar, etc. [gradualmente, con esfuerzo o por el uso, el movimiento, etc.]: *to* ~ *loose* o *free*, sol-

tarse, aflojarse. *5* moverse nerviosamente, agitarse. *6 to* ~ *out*, salir, resultar [bien o mal]; resolverse; DEP. entrenarse.

7 tr. trabajar, labrar, manufacturar. *8* formar, crear, fabricar, preparar, producir, causar, obrar, hacer. *9* explotar [una mina, etc.]. *10* hacer trabajar. *11* manejar, hacer funcionar. *12* obrar sobre, influir. *13* excitar, ir poniendo en cierto estado. *14* bordar. *15* resolver un problema. *16 to* ~ *in*, hacer entrar; intercalar. *17 to* ~ *off*, eliminar gradualmente; deshacerse de. *18 to* ~ *out*, hacer, realizar; borrar, expropiar; agotar [una mina]. *19 to* ~ *up*, excitar, inflamar; elaborar [un plan, etc.]; lograr, adquirir [con esfuerzo].

workable (-abøl) *adj.* explotable, laborable. *2* factible, viable.

workaday (-adei) *adj.* de diario. *2* prosaico.

workbag (-bæg) *s.* saco de labor.

workbasket (-bæskit) *s.* neceser, costurero.

workday (-dei) *s.* día laborable. *2* jornada [de trabajo]. *3 adj.* WORKADAY.

worker (-ø^r) *s.* obrero, operario. *2* ENT. obrera·

workhouse (-jaus) *s.* (Ingl.) hospicio. *2* (E.U.) casa de corrección, taller penitenciario.

working (-ing) *adj.* de trabajo, trabajador, que trabaja: ~ *class*, clase obrera; ~ *day*, día laborable; jornada [de trabajo]. *2* activo, laborioso. *3* que se mueve o contrae nerviosamente [rostro, facciones]. *4* suficiente, eficaz. *5* MEC. motor. *6* MEC. de régimen. *7* que sirve de guía o modelo: ~ *drawing*, plano; ARQ. montea. *8* COM. ~ *capital*, capital circulante.

workman (-mæn) *s.* obrero, trabajador, oficial. *2* artesano. *3* artífice.

workmanlike (-laik), **workmanly** (-li) *adj.* primoroso, bien hecho, bien acabado.

workmanship (-ship) *s.* hechura, ejecución, obra. *2* arte o habilidad en el trabajo.

workout (uø^{r}kaut) *s.* prueba, ensayo. *2* DEP. ejercicio de entrenamiento.

workroom (-rum), **workshop** (-shap) *s.* taller, obrador.

workwoman (-wumæn) *s.* obrera, trabajadora.

world (uø^{r}ld) *s.* mundo. | No tiene el sentido de baúl, mundo: *the* ~ *beyond*, el otro mundo; *for all the* ~, por nada del mundo; bajo todos los conceptos; ~ *without end*, por los siglos de los siglos. *2 adj.* mundano; mundial: ~ *map*, mapa mundi.

worldling (-ling) *s.* persona mundana.

worldly (-li) *adj.* mundano, mundanal. *2* terrenal. *3* seglar, secular.

worldly-minded *adj.* mundano, apegado a las cosas del mundo.

worldly-wise *adj.* que tiene mucho mundo.

world-wide *adj.* mundial, universal.

worm (uø^{r}m) *s.* gusano, lombriz: fig. *the* ~ *of conscience*, el gusano de la conciencia. *2* oruga. *3* polilla, carcoma, coco. *4* rosca de barrena o de tornillo. *5* MEC. tornillo sin fin: ~ *gear*, engranaje de tornillo sin fin.

worm (to) *intr.-ref.* introducirse, insinuarse, deslizarse. *2 tr.* limpiar de cocos o lombrices. *3 to* ~ *one's way*, serpentear, arrastrarse. *4 to* ~ *out*, arrancar mañosamente, sonsacar.

worm-eaten *adj.* agusanado. *2* carcomido, apolillado.

wormhole (-joul) *s.* picadura de gusano, carcoma, etc.

wormseed (-sid) *s.* BOT. santónico.

wormwood (-wud) *s.* BOT. ajenjo.

wormy (-i) *adj.* agusanado, gusaniento. *2* bajo, rastrero.

worn (uoᵗn) *p. p.* de TO WEAR. *2 adj.* ~ *out,* usado, raído, gastado. *3* cansado, agotado.

worried (uø·rid) *adj.* angustiado, preocupado, inquieto.

worrier (uø·riøʳ) *s.* pesimista; aprensivo.

worry (uø·ri) *s.* cuidado, ansiedad, preocupación; molestia, tormento. *2* mordedura, desgarro.

worry (to) *tr.* inquietar, preocupar, apurar. *2* molestar, acosar. *3* morder, desgarrar, asir con los dientes y sacudir. *4* ajar, arrugar. *5 to* ~ *out,* hallar solución a. *6 intr.* inquietarse, preocuparse, apurarse.

worse (uøᵗs) *adj.* y *adv. compar.* peor: *to get* ~, empeorarse; ~ *and* ~, cada vez peor; *from bad to* ~, de mal en peor. *2 s.* lo peor; la peor parte: *to change for the* ~, empeorar; *to put to the* ~, derrotar.

worsen (to) *tr.* empeorar. *2 intr.* empeorarse.

worship (uø·ʳship) *s.* culto, adoración. *2* veneración. *3 Your Worship,* su señoría, usía.

worship (to) *tr.* rendir culto a, adorar. *2* venerar. *3* idolatrar [querer mucho]. *4 intr.* hacer actos de culto. ¶ Pret. y p. p.: *worship(p)ed;* ger.: -*p(p)ing.*

worshipful (-ful) *adj.* adorable. *2* venerable, respetable, honorable. | Ús. como tratamiento. *3* adorador.

worship (p) er (-øʳ) *s.* adorador. *2* fiel [que asiste a un acto religioso].

worst (uøᵗst) *adj. superl.* peor [en sentido absoluto]: *the* ~, el peor. *2 adv. superl.* peor, pésimamente, de la peor manera posible. *3 s.* lo peor: *the* ~ *(of it) is,* lo malo es, lo peor es; *at (the)* ~, en el peor estado; en el peor de los casos; *if the* ~ *comes to (the)* ~, si sucede lo peor.

worst (to) *tr.* vencer, derrotar, triunfar de.

worsted (wu·ʳstid) *s.* TEJ. estambre, lana peinada.

worth (uøᵗz) *s.* valor, valía, precio: *twopence* ~ *of,* dos peniques de. *2* valor, valía, mérito. *3* utilidad, importancia. *4* riqueza, caudal. *5 adj.* que vale o posee: *to be* ~, valer; poseer [por valor de cierta cantidad]; *to be* ~ *while,* valer la pena. *6* digno, merecedor de; *to be* ~ *seeing,* ser digno de verse.

worthily (uø·ʳdili) *adv.* merecidamente.

worthiness (uø·ʳdinis) *s.* valía, mérito, dignidad.

worthless (uø·ʳzlis) *adj.* sin valor, inútil, despreciable. *2* indigno.

worthy (uø·ʳdi) *adj.* estimable, excelente, digno. *2* digno, merecedor, acreedor. *3 s.* persona ilustre, notable, personaje.

would (wud) *pret.* y *subj.* de TO WILL.

would-be *adj.* supuesto, seudo, presumido de. *2* aspirante, que quisiera ser.

wouldn't (wu·dønt) *contr.* de WOULD NOT.

1) wound (uaund) *pret.* y *p. p.* de TO WIND.

2) wound (wund) *s.* herida, llaga, lesión. *2* daño, ofensa.

wound (to) *tr.* herir, lastimar. *2* ofender, dañar.

wounded (-id) *adj.* herido, lastimado. *2 s.* herido; heridos.

wove (uouv) *pret.* y *p. p.* de TO WEAVE.

woven (uou·vøn) *p. p.* de TO WEAVE.

wrack (ræk) *s.* naufragio, ruina: *to go to* ~, arruinarse. *2* WRECKAGE 2. *3* alga que se recoge en la playa.

wrack (to) *tr.* hacer naufragar. *2* arruinar, perder.

wraith (reiz) *s.* espectro, aparecido.

wrangle (ræ·ngøl) *s.* disputa, altercado, discusión.

wrangle (to) *intr.* disputar, altercar. *2 tr.-intr.* debatir, discutir.

wrangler (ræ·ngløʳ) *s.* pendenciero, quimerista. *2* discutidor.

wrangling (-ing) *s.* disputa. *2* discusión.

wrap (ræp) *s.* envoltura. *2* abrigo, manta, capa, chal.

wrap (to) *tr.-intr.* cubrir (se, envolver (se, arropar (se; ocultar. | A veces con *up.* 2* enrollar (se, enroscar (se [alrededor de algo]. ¶ Pret. y p. p.: *wrapped;* ger.: -*pping.*

wrapper (-øʳ) *s.* envolvedor. *2* cubierta, envoltura. *3* sobrecubierta [de libro]. *4* faja [de periódico]. *5* capa [de cigarro]. *6* bata, peinador.

wrapping (-ing) *s.* cubierta, envoltura.

wrasse (ræs) *s.* ICT. labro.

wrath (raez) *s.* cólera, ira, rabia, furor.

wrathful (-ful) *adj.* colérico, airado, furioso.

wreak (to) *tr.* infligir. *2* descargar [un golpe, etc.]; desahogar [la cólera, etc.]; satisfacer. *3* tomar [venganza]. *4* aplicar, dedicar.

wreath (riz) *s.* corona, guirnalda. *2* anillo, espiral [de humo, etc.].

wreathe (to) (rið) *tr.* entrelazar. *2* tejer [coronas o guirnaldas]. *3* enguirnaldar. *4* ceñir, rodear. *5 wreathed in smiles,* sonriente [rostro]. *6 intr.* entrelazarse; enroscarse. *7* formar anillos o espirales [el humo].

wreck (rek) *s.* naufragio; choque, descarrilamiento; ruina, destrucción, destrozo: *to go to* ~, naufragar, arruinarse. *2* restos de un naufragio. *3* ruina, cosa arruinada.

wreck (to) *tr.* hacer naufragar. *2* destruir, arruinar; hacer fracasar. *3* hacer chocar o descarrilar [un tren]. *4 intr.* naufragar. *5* arruinarse; fracasar. *6* raquear.

wreckage (-idÿ) *s.* naufragio, ruina. *2* pecio. *3* ruinas, escombros.

wrecker (-øʳ) *s.* el que hace naufragar; arruinador. *2* raquero. *3* salvador de buques. *4* WRECKING CAR.

wrecking car (-ing) *s.* AUTO. camión de auxilio.

wren (ren) *s.* ORN. reyezuelo. *2* mujer perteneciente al servicio auxiliar femenino de la Armada.

wrench (rench) *s.* tirón o torcedura violenta. *2* torcedura, esguince. *3* MEC. llave, desvolvedor.

wrench (to) *tr.* tirar de [torciendo]; arrancar, arrebatar. *2* torcer, dislocar. *3* torcer [el sentido de una frase].

wrest (rest) *s.* WRENCH 1. *2* MÚS. llave, templador.

wrest (to) *tr.* torcer violentamente. *2* arrancar; arrebatar. *3* torcer, pervertir, tergiversar.

wrestle (to) (re·søl) *intr.* luchar a brazo partido. *2* luchar, contender. *3* esforzarse. *4* disputar.

wrestling (re·sling) *s.* lucha. *2* DEP. lucha grecorromana.

wretch (rech) *s.* miserable, desdichado. *2* miserable, canalla.

wretched (-id) *adj.* infeliz, desdichado. *2* miserable. *3* calamitoso. *4* vil. *5* malo, ruin.

wriggle (to) (ri·gøl) *tr.* retorcer, menear. *2* retorcerse. *3* serpentear, culebrear: *to* ~ *into,* insinuarse en; *to* ~ *out of,* escaparse, deslizarse, escurrirse.

wriggling (-ing) *s.* retorcimiento; culebreo, serpenteo.

wright (rait) *s.* artífice, artesano.

wring (to) (ring) *tr.* torcer, retorcer: *to* ~ *the neck of,* torcer el pescuezo a. *2* estrujar, exprimir, es-

currir. *3* arrancar. *4* oprimir, punzar, atormentar. *5* torcer, tergiversar. ¶ Pret. y p. p.: *wrung.*
wrinkle (ri·nkøl) *s.* arruga, surco.
wrinkly (ri·nkli) *adj.* arrugado, lleno de arrugas.
wrist (rist) *s.* ANAT. muñeca: ~ *watch*, reloj de pulsera. *2* puño [de una prenda].
wristlet (-lit) *s.* mitón. *2* pulsera de reloj.
writ (rit) *s.* escrito, escritura: *The Holy Writ*, la Sagrada Escritura. *2* DER. auto, mandamiento.
write (to) (rait) *tr.-intr.* escribir: *to ~ down*, anotar, poner por escrito; *to ~ off*, escribir de corrido; cancelar [en una cuenta]; *to ~ out*, redactar; escribir sin abreviar; *to ~ up*, describir extensamente por escrito; poner al día; dar bombo a. *2* decretar, ordenar. ¶ Pret.: *wrote;* p. p.: *written.*
writer (-ø^r) *s.* escritor, autor. *2* escribiente.
write-up *s.* relato; crónica. *2* bombo [elogio].
writhe (to) (raid) *tr.* torcer, retorcer [el cuerpo, etc.]. *2 intr.* serpentear. *3* contorcerse, retorcerse [esp. de dolor o angustia]; sufrir.
writing (rai·ting) *s.* escritura, letra: *in one's own* ~, de su puño y letra. *2* acción de escribir. *3* escrito. *4 adj.* de escribir: ~ *desk*, escritorio, pupitre; ~ *materials*, ~ *set*, recado de escribir.
written (ri·tøn) *p. p.* de TO WRITE.
wrong (rong) *adj.* malo, pecaminoso, injusto, que no está bien. *2* erróneo, equivocado, defectuoso; inconveniente, inoportuno; que no es el que corresponde, el que se busca, el que debería ser, etc.: *to take the ~ train*, equivocarse de tren; *in*

the ~ place, mal colocado, fuera de lugar. *3 the* ~ *side*, el revés [de una tela]. *4 to be ~*, no tener razón, estar equivocado; ser un error. *5 to be ~ with*, pasarle algo a. *6 adv.* mal, al revés, equivocadamente: *to go ~*, descaminarse; resultar mal. *7 s.* agravio, injusticia, daño, perjuicio. *8* mal, pecado, mala acción. *9* culpa. *10* error, falta de razón: *to be in the ~*, no tener razón; tener culpa.
wrong (to) *tr.* agraviar, ofender, perjudicar, hacer mal a, ser injusto con. *2* calumniar.
wrongdoer (-duø^r) *s.* el que obra mal.
wrongful (-ful) *adj.* injusto, inicuo. *2* perjudicial. *3* ilegítimo, ilegal.
wrongheaded (-jedid) *adj.* terco, obstinado.
wrongly (-li) *adv.* injustamente. *2* mal. *3* equivocadamente.
wrote (rout) *pret.* de TO WRITE.
wroth (roz) *adj.* enojado, furioso, exasperado.
wrought (rot) *pret.* y *p. p. irreg.* de TO WORK. *2 adj.* trabajado, labrado, forjado, manufacturado: ~ *iron*, hierro forjado.
wrung (røng) *pret.* y *p. p.* de TO WRING.
wry (rai) *adj.* torcido, ladeado: ~ *face*, gesto, mueca. *2* de desagrado, de disgusto. *3* deformado, tergiversado.
wryly (-li) *adv.* torcidamente.
wryneck (-nek) *s.* MED. tortícolis. *2* ORN. torcecuello.
wye (uai) *s.* i griega. *2* cosa en forma de Y

X, x (eks) *s*. X, x vigésimo cuarta letra del alfabeto inglés.
xanthein(e (šæ·nziin) *s*. QUÍM. xanteína, janteína.
xanthic (šæ·nzik) *adj*. QUÍM. xántico, jántico.
Xanthipe (šænzi·pi) *n. pr*. Jantipa. 2 *s*. fig. esposa regañona.
Xanthophyl(l (šæ·nzofil) *s*. QUÍM. xantofila, jantofila.
Xavier (šæ·viøᵣ) *n. pr*. Javier.
xebec (ši·bek) *s*. MAR. jebeque.
xenon (ši·nan) *s*. QUÍM. xeno, xenón.
xenophobia (šenofou·bia) *s*. xenofobia.
Xenophon (še·nøføn) *n. pr*. Jenofonte.

xerophil(e (ši·rofil) *adj*. BOT. xerófilo.
xerophthalmia (širafzæ·lmia), **xerophthalmy** (ši·rafzæ·lmi) *s*. MED. xeroftalmía.
xerophyte (ši·rofait) *s*. BOT. planta xerófila.
xiphoid (ši·foid) *adj*. ANAT. xifoideo. 2 *adj.-s*. ANAT. xifoides.
Xmas (kri·smas) *s*. abrev. de CHRISTMAS.
X-ray *adj*. radiográfico.
X rays (i·ks-reiš) *s. pl*. rayos X.
xylem (šai·lem) *s*. BOT. leño [parte del tallo].
xylograph (šai·løgræf) *s*. grabado en madera.
xylography (šaila·grafi) *s*. xilografía.
xylophagous (šaila·fagøs) *adj*. xilófago.
Xylophone (šai·lofoun) *s*. xilófono, xilórgano.

Y

Y, y (uai) *s.* Y, y, vigésimo quinta letra del alfabeto inglés.

yacht (yat) *s.* MAR. yate.

yacht (to) *intr.* manejar un yate o navegar en él.

yacht(s)man (ya·t(s)mæn) *s.* dueño de un yate. *2* marinero especializado en tripular yates.

yagua (ya·gua) *s.* BOT. yagua.

yak (yak) *s.* ZOOL. yak [buey del Asia].

yam (yæm) *s.* BOT. ñame.

yank (yænk) *s.* fam. (E.U.) tirón, sacudida.

yank (to) *tr.* fam. (E.U.) dar un tirón; sacar de un tirón.

Yankee (yæ·nki) *adj.-s.* yanqui.

Yankeedom (-døm) *s.* Yanquilandia. *2* los yanquis.

yap (yæp) *s.* ladrido corto, gañido. *2* fig. parloteo.

yap (to) *intr.* ladrar con ladrido corto. *2* fig. parlotear.

yard (ya⸁d) *s.* yarda [medida ingl. de longitud = 0'914 m.]. *2* MAR. verga. *3* patio, corral, cercado, terreno.

yard (to) *tr.* acorralar [encerrar en corral]. *2* almacenar, guardar, reunir [en patio o depósito].

yardarm (ya·⸁da⸁m) *s.* MAR. penol.

yardstick (ya·⸁dstik) *s.* vara de medir [de una yarda].

yarn (ya⸁n) *s.* hebra, hilo, hilado, hilaza. *2* narración extraordinaria; cuento o historia increíble: *to spin a ~,* contar un cuento.

yarrow (yæ·rou) *s.* BOT. milenrama.

yataghan (yæ·tagæn) *s.* yatagán.

yaw (yo·) *s.* MAR. guiñada. *2* AVIA. desviación.

yaw(to) *intr.* MAR. guiñar. *2* AVIA. desviarse.

yawl (yol) *s.* MAR. yola; bote.

yawn (yon) *s.* bostezo. *2* abertura, boquete.

yawn (to) *intr.* bostezar. *2* abrir la boca [con avidez]. *3* abrirse, formar una abertura.

yawning (-ing) *adj.* bostezante. *2* abierto.

ye (yɪ) *pron. pers.* plural de THOU.

yea (yei) *adv.* sí, ciertamente; y es más. *2 s.* sí [consentimiento].

yean (to) (yɪn) *intr.* parir [la cabra o la oveja].

yeanling (-ling) *s.* cabritillo, corderillo.

year (yi·ø⸁) *s.* año: *once a ~,* una vez al año; *~ in, ~ out,* año tras año. *2 pl.* años, edad: *to grow in years,* envejecer.

yearbook (-buk) *s.* anuario.

yearling (-ling) *adj.* primal, añal, añojo. *2 s.* niño, planta, etc., de un año.

yearly (-li) *adj.* anual. *2 adv.* anualmente.

yearn (yø⸁n) *intr.* anhelar:*to ~ for* o *after,* anhelar, suspirar por. *2* sentir ternura o compasión.

yearning (-ing) *s.* anhelo, deseo ardiente. *2* ternura.

yeast (yɪst) *s.* levadura.

yeasty (-i) *adj.* de levadura. *2* espumoso. *3* ligero, frívolo.

Yeddo (ye·dou) *n. pr.* GEOGR. Yedo.

yell (yel) *s.* grito, alarido, aullido.

yell (to) *intr.* gritar, dar alaridos, aullar, vociferar. *2 tr.* decir a gritos.

yellow (ye·lou) *adj.* amarillo: *~ bark, ~ chinchona,* calisaya; *~ fever,* fiebre amarilla; *~ spot,* ANAT. mácula lútea. *2* de raza amarilla. *3* bilioso, celoso, melancólico. *4* de cobarde o traidor; vil, ruin. *5* sensacionalista: *~ press,* prensa sensacionalista. *6 s.* color amarillo. *7* yema [de huevo].

yellow (to) *tr.* poner amarillo. *2 intr.* amarillecer.

yellowbird (-bø⸁d) *s.* ORN. jilguero americano. *2* ORN. oropéndola.

yelloish (-ish) *adj.* amarillento.

yelp (yelp) *s.* latido, gañido, ladrido.

yelp (to) *intr.* latir, gañir, ladrar. *2* gritar [el pavo salvaje].

yen (yen) *s.* yen [moneda japonesa].

yeoman (you·mæn) *s.* labrador acomodado. *2* hidalgo que servía en una casa real o noble. *3 ~ of the guard,* alabardero de palacio. *4* miembro de una antigua milicia. *5* oficinista de un buque de guerra.

yeomanry (-ri) *s.* HIST. conjunto de los labradores acomodados. *2* ant. milicia. *3* guardia del rey.

yes (yes) *adv.* sí. *2 s.* sí [respuesta afirmativa].

yesterday (ye·stø⸁dei) *s.* y *adv.* ayer.

yet (yet) *adv.* todavía, aún: *as ~,* todavía, hasta ahora; *not ~,* todavía no, aún no. *2 conj.* aun así, no obstante, sin embargo.

yew (yu) *s.* BOT. tejo.

Yiddish (yi·dish) *s.* yiddish [dialecto judío].

yield (yɪld) *s.* producto, rendimiento, rédito, producción, cosecha. *2* rendición. *3* ING. acción de ceder o deformarse.

yield (to) *tr.* producir, rendir, dar. *2* exhalar, despedir. *3* dar de sí. *4* rendir, entregar, ceder. *5* otorgar, dar. *6 intr.* dar fruto, rendir. *7* rendirse, someterse. *8* sujetarse, conformarse. *9* ceder, deferir. *10* consentir, asentir. *11* ceder [a una fuerza o presión], doblegarse, flaquear.

yielding (-ing) *adj.* productivo, que rinde. *2* dúctil, complaciente, condescendiente.

yodel (you·døl) *s.* modo de cantar de los tiroleses.

yodel (to) *tr.* cantar, como los tiroleses, modulando la voz desde el tono natural al falsete y viceversa.

yoga (you·ga) *s.* yoga.

yogi (you·gi) *s.* yogi [asceta de la India].

yoke (youk) *s.* yugo [para uncir; para los vencidos; sujeción, esclavitud]. *2* yunta. *3* yugada. *4* yugo [de campana]. *5* MEC. horquilla. *6* culata [de imán]. *7* percha [para elevar pesos]. *8* hombrillo [de camisa].

yoke (to) *tr.* uncir, acoyundar. *2* acoplar, unir, casar.

yoke-elm *s.* BOT. carpe.

yokel (you·køl) *s.* rústico, patán.

yolk (youk) *s.* yema [de huevo]. *2* churre [de la lana].

yon (yan) *adj.* y *adv.* YONDER.

yonder (ya·ndøʳ) *adj.* aquel, aquella, aquellos, aquellas. *2* de más allá. *3 adv.* allí, allá; más allá.

yore (yoʳ) *s.* otro tiempo: *of ~*, en otro tiempo, antaño.

you (yu) *pron.* de *2.ª pers. sing.* y *pl.* tú, usted, vosotros, ustedes. *2* te, a ti; le, a usted; os, a vosotros; les, a ustedes. *3 for ~*, para ti, usted, vosotros o ustedes.

young (yøng) *adj.* joven: *a ~ lady*, una señorita; *a ~ man*, un joven. *2* mozo, juvenil. *3* nuevo, tierno, verde; reciente; que empieza. *4 s. the ~*,

los jóvenes. *5* hijuelos, cría [de los animales]. *6 with ~*, encinta; preñada.

younger (-øʳ) *adj. comp.* de YOUNG: más joven, menor. *2 Pliny the ~*, Plinio el joven.

youngest (-ist) *adj. superl.* de YOUNG: el más joven, el menor.

youngling (-ling) *s.* pequeñuelo. *2* jovencito.

youngster (-støʳ) *s.* muchacho joven, niño.

your (yuʳ) *adj. pos.* tu, tus, vuestro, vuestra, vuestros, vuestras; su, de usted, de ustedes.

yours (yuʳš) *pron. pos.* (el) tuyo o vuestro, (la) tuya o vuestra, (los) tuyos o vuestros, (las) tuyas o vuestras; (el) suyo, (la) suya, (los) suyos, (las) suyas [de usted o ustedes]: *you and ~*, usted y los suyos; *a friend of ~*, un amigo suyo, o vuestro. *2* la suya [su carta de usted]; *~ faithfully, ~ sincerely, ~ (very) truly*, su afectísimo, su atento, s. s., etc. [en las cartas].

yourself (yuʳse·lf) *pron. pers.* tú, ti, usted, tú mismo, usted mismo; te, se [reflexivos].

yourselves (youʳse·lvš) *pron. pl.* de YOURSELF.

youth (yuz) *s.* juventud, mocedad, adolescencia. *2* primer período de existencia. *3* joven, mozalbete. *4 sing.* y *pl.* la juventud, los jóvenes.

youthful (-ful) *adj.* joven. *2* mozo, juvenil. *3* fresco, vigoroso.

you've (yuv) *contr.* de YOU HAVE.

yowl (yaul) *s.* aullido, alarido.

yowl (to) *intr.* aullar, gritar.

ytterbium (itø·ʳbiøm) *s.* QUÍM. iterbio.

yttrium (i·triøm) *s.* QUÍM. itrio.

yucca (yø·ka) *s.* BOT. yuca.

Yugoslav (yu·gouslav) *adj.-s.* yugoeslavo.

Yugoslavia (yu·gousla·via) *n. pr.* Yugoeslavia.

yule (yul) *s.* Navidad; Pascua de Navidad: *~ log*, nochebueno [leño].

yuletide (-taid) *s.* Pascua de Navidad, Navidades.

Z

Z, z (ši·) *s.* Z, z, vigésimo sexta y última letra del alfabeto inglés.
Zaccheus (šæki·øs) *n. pr.* Zaqueo.
zany (še·ni) *s.* bufón, truhán. 2 simplón.
Zanzibar (šænši·ba^r) *n. pr.* GEOGR. Zanzíbar.
zeal (šɪ·l) *s.* celo, ardor, fervor, entusiasmo.
Zealand (šɪ·land) *n. pr.* GEOGR. Zelandia.
zealot (še·løt) *s.* partidario acérrimo; fanático.
zealotry (-ri) *s.* fanatismo.
zealous (še·løs) *adj.* celoso, entusiasta.
Zebedee (še·bidɪ) *n. pr.* Zebedeo.
zebra (šɪ·bra) *s.* ZOOL. cebra.
Zebu (šɪ·biu) *n. pr.* GEOGR. Cebú.
zebu *s.* ZOOL. cebú.
Zechariah (šekarai·a) *n. pr.* Zacarías.
zed (šed) *s.* (Ingl.) zeda, zeta, ceda [letra Z].
Zend-Avesta (šend-*avesta*) *s.* zendavesta.
zenith (šɪ·niz) *s.* cenit. 2 culminación, apogeo.
zenithal (ši·nizal) *adj.* cenital.
zephyr (še·fø^r) *s.* céfiro [viento; tela].
Zeppelin (še·pælin) *s.* zepelín.
zero (ši·rou) *s.* cero.
zest (šest) *s.* luquete [de limón o naranja]. 2 sabor, sainete. 3 deleite, gusto, entusiasmo.
zeta (šɪ·ta) *s.* zeta [letra griega].
zeugma (šiu·gma) *s.* RET. zeugma.
Zeus (šius) *n. pr.* Zeus, Júpiter.
zigzag (ši·gšæg) *s.* zigzag. 2 *adj.* en zigzag.
zigzag (to) *intr.* zigzaguear.
zinc (šink) *s.* QUÍM. cinc, zinc.
zincite (ši·nksait) *s.* MINER. cincita.
zincograph (-øgraf) *s.* cincograbado.
zincography (šinka·grafi) *s.* cincografía.
zingaro (ši·ngarou) *s.* cíngaro.
Zion (šai·øn) *n. pr.* Sion.
Zionism (šai·ønišm) *s.* sionismo.
zip (šip) *s.* silbido, zumbido [de una bala]. 2 fam. energía, vigor.
zip (to) *intr.* silbar o zumbar [como una bala].

zipper (ši·p^r) *s.* cierre relámpago, cremallera.
zircon (šø·^rkan) *s.* MINER. circón.
zirconium (šø^rkou·niøm) *s.* QUÍM. circonio.
zither(n (ši·zø^r(n) *s.* MÚS. cítara.
zoanthropy (šouæ·nzroupi) *s.* zoantropía.
zodiac (šou·diæk) *s.* ASTR. zodíaco. 2 circuito.
zoetrope (šoui·troup) *s.* zootropo.
zonal (šou·nal) *adj.* zonal.
zone (šoun) *s.* zona. | No tiene el sentido de erupción.
zoned (-d) *adj.* dividido en zonas. 2 marcado con fajas.
zoo (šu) *s.* parque zoológico; colección zoológica.
zoogeography (šouodýia·grafi) *s.* zoogeografía.
zoography (šoua·grafi) *s.* zoografía.
zooid (šou·oid) *adj.-s.* zooide.
zoolatry (šoua·latri) *s.* zoolatría.
zoolite (šou·olait) *s.* GEOL. zoolito.
zoological (šouola·dýkal) *adj.* zoológico.
zoology (šoua·lodýi) *s.* zoología.
zoom (to) (šum) *intr.* AVIA. elevarse rápidamente.
zoophagous (šoua·fagøs) *adj.* zoófago.
Zoophyta (šou·ofita) *s. pl.* ZOOL. zoófitos.
zoophyte (-ofait) *s.* zoófito.
zoospore (-ospo^r) *s.* zoospora.
zootechny (-otecni) *s.* zootecnia.
Zoroaster (šouroæ·stø^r) *n. pr.* Zoroastro.
Zoroastrian (šouroæ·strian) *adj.* zoroástrico.
zoster (ša·stø^r) *s.* MED. zoster, zona.
Zouave (šua·v) *s.* zuavo.
Zulu (šu·lu) *adj.-s.* zulú.
Zululand (-lænd) *n. pr.* Zululandia.
Zwinglian (šui·nglian) *adj.-s.* zuingliano.
zygomatic (šaigømæ·tik) *adj.* ANAT. cigomático.
zygomorphic (šaigømo·^rfik), **zygomorphous** (-føs) *adj.* cigomorfo.
zygospore (šai·gøspø^r) *s.* zigospora.
zygote (šai·gout) *s.* BIOL. cigoto, zigoto.
zymogen (šai·modýøn) *s.* BIOQUÍM. cimógeno.

IDIOMS AND EXPRESSIONS / MODISMOS Y EXPRESIONES

A

A boca llena
Openly, plainly

A bordo
On board

A buena hora
On time

A buen santo te encomiendas
To bark up the wrong tree

A buen seguro
Certainly, very probably

A cada momento
Continually, frequently

A cada paso
At every turn (or step)

A cada rato
Each time, all the time

A cambio de
In exchange for

A campo raso
In the open

A campo traviesa
Cross-country

A casa
Home

A causa de
On account of

A ciegas
Blindly

A (or de) ciencia cierta
With certainty

A contrapelo
Against the grain

¿A cuánto(s) estamos?
What is the date?

A deshora(s)
At all hours, unexpectedly; at an untimely moment

A despecho de
In spite of, despite

A duras penas
With great difficulty, hardly, scarcely

A escape
Rapidly, at full speed

A escondidas
On the sly, undercover

A escondidas de
Without the knowledge of

A eso de
At about

A espaldas de
Behind one's back

A estas alturas
At this point or juncture

A falta de
For want of, lacking

A fin de cuentas
After all, in the final analysis

A fin de que
In order that, so that

A fines de
Late, towards the end of a period (week, etc.)

A flor de
Flush with

A fondo
Fully, thoroughly

A fuerza de
By force of, by dint of

A gatas
On all fours, crawling

A guisa de
Like, in the manner of

A hurto
On the sly, stealthily

A instancias de
At the request of

A la antigüita
Old-fashioned

A la buena (mala)
Willingly (unwillingly)

A la buena de Dios
Without malice, without plan, at random

A la carrera
In haste, on the run

A la fuerza
By force

A la larga
In the long run

A la moda
Up to date, in the latest fashion

A la noche
Tonight, at night

A la postre
At last, when all is said and done

A la redonda (or en redondo)
All around, round about

A la sazón
Then, at that time

A la ventura
Aimlessly, haphazardly, at random

A la verdad
In truth, in earnest, truly

A la vez
Together, at the same time

A la vista de
In plain view of

A la voluntad
At will, as you like

A la vuelta de
Around the corner, on returning

A la vuelta de la esquina
Around the corner

A la vuelta de los años
Within a few years

A lado de
Beside

A las claras
Clearly, openly, frankly, publicly

A las mil maravillas
Beautifully, wonderfully well

A lo largo (de)
Along, alongside of, lengthwise, at full length

A lo lejos
In the distance

A lo más
At most, at worst

A lo mejor
Perhaps, maybe

A lo sumo
At most

A los cuatro vientos
In all directions

A los pocos meses
After a few months

A (la) manera de
Like, in the style of

A mano
By hand, at hand, handmade

A mar de
A lot of, lots of

A más no poder
To the utmost, full blast

A más tardar
At the very latest

A más ver (or hasta más ver)
Goodbye

A mediados de
About the middle of the (day, week, etc.), during the (week, etc.)

A medida que
As, in proportion to

A medio camino
Halfway (to a place)

A medio hacer
Incomplete, half-done

A menos que
Unless

A menudo
Often

A merced de
At the mercy (or expense) of

A mi entender
In my opinion, as I understand it

A mi modo de ver
In my opinion

¡A mí qué!
What's that to me? So what!

A montones
In abundance, heaps

A ninguna parte
Nowhere

A no ser que
Unless

A ojo
By sight, by guess

A ojos cerrados
Blindly

A ojos vistas
Visibly, clearly; before one's eyes

A oscuras (or a obscuras)
In the dark

A partir de
As of, beginning on

A partir de hoy
From today on

A pedir de boca
Exactly as desired, to one's heart's content

A pesar de (todo)
In spite of (everything)

A pesar de que
In spite of the fact that

A pie
On foot, by foot

A piedra y lodo
Shut tight

A pie(s) juntillas
With both feet together; believe strongly

A poco
Shortly after

A pocos pasos
At a short distance

A porfía
In competition

A primera luz
At dawn

A principios de
Towards, early in, about the first of (day, week, etc.)

A propósito
By the way, apropos; on purpose

A prueba de
—proof, safe against

A puerta cerrada
Secretly, behind closed doors

A punto fijo
With certainty

A pura fuerza
By sheer force

A puros gritos
By just shouting

A que
I bet…(not a real wager)

¡A que no!
I bet you don't!

¿A qué viene eso?
What is the point of that?

A quema ropa (or a quemarropa)
Very close, point blank, without warning

A raíz de
Soon after, close to

A ras de (or al ras con)
Flush (or even) with

A ratos
From time to time, at times

A ratos perdidos
In (at) odd or spare moments

A rienda suelta
Free rein, violently, swiftly

A saber
Namely, that is

A sabiendas
Knowingly, consciously

A salvo
Safe, unharmed

A sangre fría
In cold blood

A secas
Plain, alone, simply, to the point

A semejanza de
Like, as

A su (debido) tiempo
In due course or time

A tiempo
On time, in time

A tientas
Blindly

A toda costa
By all means, at whatever cost

A toda hora
At any time, at all times

A toda prisa
At greatest speed

A toda vela
Under full sail, at full speed

A todas luces
By all means, any way you look at it

A todo correr
At full speed

A todo trance
At all costs

A todo trapo
Under full sail, speedily

A traición
Deceitfully, treacherously

A través de, al través de
Across, through

A última hora
At the last moment

A una brazada
At arm's length

A una voz
Unanimously

A un tiempo
At one (the same) time

A veces
At times

A ver (si)
Let's see (if)

A vista de
Within view, in the presence of

A vistas
On approval

A voluntad
At will

A vuelo de pájaro
As the crow flies

Abrir paso
To make way, to clear the way

Acabar de
To have just (done something)

Acabar por
To end up by (doing something)

Acerca de
About, with regard to

Acordar con
To be on good terms with

Acostarse con las gallinas
To go to bed early

¿Adónde va?
Where are you going?

Adondequiera que
Wherever

Agachar las orejas
To hang one's head

Aguantar el chubasco
To weather the storm

Águila o pico
Heads or tails

Águila o sello
Heads or tails

Aguzar las orejas (los oídos)
To prick up one's ears

¡Ahí está el detalle!
That's the point!

Ahogarse en poca agua
To worry about nothing

Ahora bien
Now then, well now, however

Ahora es cuando
Now is the time; now is your chance

Ahora mismo
Right now, at once

Al aire libre
In the open air, outdoors

Al azar
By chance, at random

Al cabo (de)
Finally or after

Al caer de la noche
At nightfall

Al centavo
Just right, to the letter

Al contado
Cash

Al contrario
On the contrary

Al cuidado de
In care of

Al derecho
Right side out

Al (or en) derredor
Around

Al descubierto
Openly

Al día
Per day

Al día siguiente
On the following day

Al filo de (las cinco)
At about (5 o'clock)

Al fin
At the end, at last

Al fin de cuentas
In any case

Al fin y al cabo
In short, at last, anyway

Al frente de
In front of

Al habla
Within speaking distance;
speaking! (in answering a
telephone)

Al igual
Equally

Al instante
At once

Al lado (de)
At one's side, near at hand,
next to

Al menos (or a lo menos)
At least, at the least

Al menudeo (or al por menor)
At retail, in small quantities

Al mismo tiempo
At the same time

Al oído
Confidentially

Al otro día
On the following day

Al otro lado de
On the other side of

Al pan, pan y al vino, vino
Call a spade a spade

Al parecer
Apparently

Al pelo
Perfectly, agreed, just right

Al pie de la letra
Literally, to the letter

Al (or a) poco rato
In a short while, soon after

Al presente
Now, at present

Al principio
At first

Al punto
At once

Al raso
In the open air

Al (or en) rededor
Around, about

Al remo
At hard labor

Al revés
Backwards, wrong side out, in
the opposite way

Al sereno
In the night air

Al sesgo
On the bias, diagonally,
obliquely

Al soslayo
On the bias, slanting, obliquely

Al tanteo
Hit or miss, by guess

Al través de
Through, throughout

Al trote
Quickly

Algo por el estilo
Similar, something of the sort

Algo sordo
Hard of hearing

Algo tarde
Rather late

Algún otro
Somebody else, some other

Alrededor de
Around about, more or less

Alzar el codo
To drink too much

Allá a las quinientas
Once in a blue moon

¡Allí está el toque!
There is the heart of the matter!

Amante de
Fond of

Amigo de
Fond of (friend of)

Amor propio
Self-esteem, pride, vanity

Andar a gatas
To creep, crawl

Andar agitado
To be out of sorts

Andar bien
To keep good time (e.g., a
watch), to work well, to be right

Andar (or ir) de parranda (or de fiesta en fiesta)
To go on a spree

Andarse con rodeos
To beat around the bush

Andarse el tiempo
Meantime, as time goes on

Andarse por las ramas
To beat around the bush

Ante todo
Especially, first of all, above all

Antes de que
Before

Antes hoy que mañana
The sooner the better

Antes que
Rather than

Año antepasado
Year before last

Año entrante
Next year

Año bisiesto
Leap year

Aparte de eso
Besides that, aside from that

Aprender de memoria
To learn by heart

Aprendiz de todo y oficial de nada
Jack of all trades

Aprovechar la ocasión
To take advantage of the
situation

Aquí cerca
Around (near) here

Aquí mismo
Right here

Arranque de cólera
Fit of anger

Así así
So-so

Así como
Just as, the same as, as well as

Así de largo
That long

Así es que
So that, as soon as

Así está bien
This will do (be OK)

Así nada más
Just plain, just as is

Así pues
So then, therefore

Así que
So that, as soon as, so,
therefore

¡Así se hace!
Well done!, Bully for you!

Así y todo
In spite of that, even so,
anyhow

Atrás de
Behind, in back of

Aun así
Even so

Aun cuando
Even if, even though

Aún no
Not yet

Ayer mismo
Just yesterday

Ayer por la tarde
Yesterday afternoon

Azotar el aire
To work in vain

B

Bailar a secas
To dance without music

Baja el radio
Turn down the radio

Bajo techo
Indoors

Barrios bajos
Slums

Beber a pulso
To gulp down

Bien arreglado
Neatly dressed

Bien asado
Well-done (well-cooked)

Bien cocido
Well-done (well-cooked)

Bien me lo merezco
It serves me right

Bien parecido
Good-looking

Bien peinado
Well-groomed, trim

Bien que
Although

Boca abajo
Face down, prone

Boca arriba
Face up, supine

Bromas aparte
All joking aside

Buen mozo
Handsome man

¡Buen provecho!
Good appetite! Enjoy your meal!

Buen rato
Pleasant (or long) time

Buen tipo
Good fellow

Burlarse de
To make fun of

Buscarle tres (cuatro) pies al gato
To look for trouble

Buscar una aguja en un pajar
To look for a needle in a haystack

C

Cada cual (or cada uno)
Each one

¿Cada cuánto tiempo?
How often?

Cada dos días
Every other day

Cada uno
Apiece

Cada vez menos
Less and less

Caer bien
To fit well, to be becoming, to please

Caer enfermo
To fall ill

Caer en gracia
To please

Caer en la cuenta
To realize, to get the point

Caer mal
To fit badly, displease

Caliente de cascos
Hot-headed

¡Cállate la trompa!
Shut up!

Calle abajo
Down the street

Calle arriba
Up the street

Callejón sin salida
Blind alley, dead end

Cambiar de tema
To change the subject

Caminar con pies de plomo
To go cautiously

Camino de
On the way to, on the road to

Camino trillado
Beaten path

Cara a cara
Face to face

Cara o cruz
Heads or tails

Cargar con
To carry away, assume responsibility

Cargar con el muerto
To get the blame unjustly

Carne de gallina
Goosebumps

Casarse con
To marry (someone)

Casi nunca
Hardly ever

Castañetear con los dedos
To snap one's fingers

Cerca de
Near to, close to

Cerrarse el cielo
To become overcast, cloudy

Cifrar la esperanza en
To place one's hope in

Claro que no
Of course not, certainly not

Claro que sí
Of course, naturally

Colmo de la locura
Height of folly

Como a costumbre
At about

Como de costumbre
As usual

Como dijo el otro
As someone said, as the saying goes

Como Dios manda
According to Hoyle (the rules)

Como en
In about

Como mínimo
At least

Como no
Unless

¡Cómo no!
Of course, why not!

Como por ensalmo
As if by magic, in a jiffy

Como que
Since, inasmuch as

Como quiera que
Since, inasmuch as

Como quiera que sea
At any rate

Como si
As if

Como si fuera
As if it were

Como siempre
As usual, like always

Como sigue
As follows

Como último recurso
As a last resort

Como una seda
As smooth as silk, soft as silk

Como visita de obispo
Once in a blue moon

Con anticipación
In advance

Con delirio
Madly

Con el propósito de
With the aim of

Con (or en o por) extremo
Very much, extremely

Con fuerzas para...(la tarea)
Equal to...(the task)

Con la lengua de corbata (or con la lengua de pechera)
Out of breath, with tongue hanging out

Con motivo de
With the idea of, because of, on the occasion of, on account of

¿Con qué cara?
How can I (one) have the nerve?

¡Con razón!
No wonder!

Con respecto a
With regard to

Con rumbo a
In the direction of

Con tal (de) que
Provided that, so that

Con tiempo
In advance, in good time

Con todo (or con todos) los obstáculos
In spite of that

Conciliar el sueño
To get to sleep

Confiar en
To trust, rely on

Conforme a
In accordance with

Conocer de vista
To know by sight

Consigo mismo
To oneself

Conspirar contra una persona
To frame someone

Consultar con la almohada
To sleep on it

Contar con
To reckon with, rely on, count on

Contra viento y marea
Against all odds, come hell or high water, come what may

Convenirle a uno
To be to one's advantage

Correr por cuenta de uno
To be one's own affair, to be up to oneself

Correr riesgo
To take a chance, to risk

Corrida del tiempo
Swiftness of time

Cortar el hilo
To break the thread of a story, to interrupt

Corto de oído
Hard of hearing

Corto de vista
Nearsighted

Cosa de
Approximately, about

Costar trabajo
To be very difficult

Costar un ojo de la cara
To cost an arm and a leg, be very expensive

Cruzarse con
To meet

Cualquier cosa
Anything at all

Cualquiera (or cualesquiera) de los dos
Either of the two

Cuando más tarde
At the latest

Cuando menos
At least

Cuando quiera
Whenever

Cuanto antes
As soon as possible

Cuatro letras
A few lines

Cuatro palabras
A few words

Cuento alegre
Spicy story

Cuento chino
Cock and bull story

Cueste lo que cueste
At any cost

Cumplir años
To have a birthday

Cumplir su palabra
To keep one's word

CH

Chueco o derecho
Hit or miss, happy-go-lucky

D

Dado caso
Supposing

Dado el caso que
Provided that

Dar a
To face, look towards, give to

Dar a conocer
To make known

Dar a entender
To pretend

Dar alas a
To embolden, give courage

Dar aliento
To encourage

Dar al traste con
To ruin, destroy

Dar al través con
To ruin, destroy

Dar ánimo
To cheer up

Dar atención
To pay attention

Dar batería
To raise a rumpus, to work hard

Dar calabazas
To reject, to jilt

Dar caza
To pursue, track down

Dar cima
To complete, carry out

Dar coba
To flatter, play up to, softsoap

Dar cuenta de
To give a report on

Dar de comer
To feed, be fed

Dar disgustos a
To cause distress or grief to

Dar el pésame por
To extend condolences to or for

Dar el visto bueno
To approve, OK

Dar en
To hit or to hit upon

Dar en cara
To reproach, blame

Dar en el clavo
To hit the nail on the head

Dar en (or dar con) el chiste
To guess right, hit the nail on the head

Dar en tierra con alguien
To overthrow someone

Dar esquinazo
To "ditch," avoid meeting someone

Dar fe de
To vouch for

Dar fin (a)
To complete

Dar gato por liebre
To cheat or swindle

Dar grasa
To polish (shoes)

Dar guerra
To make trouble

Dar la hora
To strike the hour

Dar la lata
To annoy

Dar la mano
To help, shake hands

Dar la noticia
To break the news

Dar la razón
To agree, to be of same opinion

Dar la razón a una persona
To admit a person is right

Dar (or darse) la vuelta
To turn (to turn around)

Dar largas
To postpone or delay, or give someone the run around

Dar las espaldas a
To turn one's back on

Dar las gracias
To give thanks, to thank

Dar lástima (de)
To arouse pity or sorrow

Dar lo mismo
To make no difference

Dar los recuerdos
To give regards

Dar lugar a
To give cause for

Dar lustre
To polish

Dar marcha atrás
To back up

Dar mucha pena
To cause sorrow, to be
disconcerting

Dar parte
To inform

Dar pie
To give opportunity (or
occasion to)

Dar por
To consider as

Dar por descontado
To take for granted

Dar por hecho
To take for granted, to consider
as done

Dar por sabido
To take for granted

Dar por sentado
To take for granted

Dar por supuesto
To take for granted

Dar prestado
To lend

Dar propina
To tip (give a gratuity)

Dar que hacer
To cause extra work

Dar rabia
To anger

Dar razón
To inform, give account

Dar realce
To enhance, emphasize

Dar sepultura
To bury

Dar un paseo
To take a walk or ride

Dar un paseo en barco
To go for a sail

Dar un paso
To take a step

Dar un pisotón
To step hard upon

Dar un portazo
To slam the door

Dar un salto (or dar saltos)
To leap, jump

Dar un traspié
To trip, stumble

Dar un vistazo a
To glance over, peruse

Dar una cita
To make an appointment

Dar una fiesta
To give (throw) a party

Dar una pasada por
To pass by, walk by

Dar una pisada
To step (stomp) on (upon)

Dar una satisfacción
To apologize

Dar una vuelta
To take a stroll

Dar uno en la tecla
To hit the nail on the head, find
the right way to do something

Darle a uno mala espina
To arouse one's suspicion

Darle lo mismo
It makes no difference

Darse aires a
To put on airs

Darse cuenta de (que)
To realize (that), to notice

Darse de baja
To drop out

Darse farol
To show off, put on airs

Darse la mano
To shake hands

Darse por vencido (or me doy)
To give up (or I give up)

Darse prisa
To hurry

Darse tono
To put on airs

Darse un tropezón
To trip, stumble

Darse un encontrón
To collide with, bump into each
other

Darse un resbalón
To slip

Dárselas de
To pose as

De acuerdo con
In accordance with

De ahí en adelante
From then on

De ahí que
Hence

De ahora en adelante
From now on, in the future

De algún modo
Somehow

De algún tiempo para acá
For some time now

De alguna manera
Somehow

De arriba abajo
From top to bottom

De aquel tiempo en adelante
From that time on

De aquí en adelante
From now on

De aquí para allá
To and fro, back and forth

De broma
Jokingly, in jest

De buen tomo y lomo
Bulky, important

De buen tono
In good taste, stylish

De buen ver
Good-looking

De buena cepa
Of good stock or quality

De buena fe
In good faith

**De buena gana (or de buen
grado)**
Willingly, gladly

De buena ley
Of good quality

De buenas a primeras
All of a sudden, unexpectedly,
on the spur of the moment

De burla
In jest

De cabo a rabo
From beginning to end

De camino (or de camino real)
On the way

De canto
On edge

De copete
High rank, important, proud

De corrida
Without stopping

De cualquier modo
At any rate

De cuando en cuando
Sometimes, occasionally

De día
By day, before dark

De dientes afuera
Insincerely

¡De dónde!
Nonsense!

De dos caras
Two-faced

De dos en dos
By twos, two by two

De dos sentidos
Two-way

De ese modo (or de esa manera)
In that way

De espaldas
On one's back, supine

**De este modo (or de esta
manera)**
In this way

De etiqueta
Formal

De golpe
Suddenly

De gorra
At another's expense

De grado en grado
By degrees

De hecho
In fact

De hilo
Without stopping

De hoy en adelante
From now on

De hoy en ocho días
One week from today

De hoy en quince días
Two weeks from today

De improviso
Unexpectedly

De lado
Tilted, oblique, sideways

De la noche a la mañana
Overnight

De lejos
From a distance

De lo contrario
If not, otherwise

De lo lindo
Wonderfully, very much, to the
utmost

De mal en peor
From bad to worse

De mal grado
Reluctantly, unwillingly

De mal gusto
In poor taste

De mal temple
In a bad humor

De mala fe
In bad faith, deceitfully

De mala gana
Unwillingly

De mala suerte
Unlucky

De manera que
So that

De marca
Of excellent quality

De memoria
By heart

De moda
In vogue, stylish

De modo que
So what?, so that, and so

De momento
For the time being

De nada
Don't mention it; you're
welcome

De ningún modo
By no means

¡De ninguna manera!
By no means!, I should say not!

De noche
By (at) night

De nuevo
Again, once again

De ocasión
Reduced price, a bargain

De (or al) oído
By ear

De oídos
Rumor, hearsay

De ordinario
Ordinary, usual

De otro modo
Otherwise

De palabra
By word of mouth

De par en par
Wide open

De parte a parte
Through, from one side to
the other

De parte de
On behalf of, in favor of

De paso
In passing, at the same time, by
the way, in transit

De pie
Standing

De pilón
To boot, besides, in addition

De poca monta
Of little value or importance

De poquito
In small amounts

De por sí
Separately, by itself

De prisa
Quickly

De pronto
At once, suddenly

De propósito
On purpose

De punta
On end

De puntillas (or de puntas)
On tiptoes

De punto
By the minute

De pura casualidad
By pure chance

De rebote
On the rebound, indirectly

De relieve
In relief, outstanding,
prominent

De remate
Absolutely, without remedy

De repente
Suddenly, all of a sudden

De repuesto
Spare, extra

De resultas
As a result, consequently

De rigor
A "must," it must

De rodillas
On one's knees

De seguida
Continuously, without
interruption

De segunda mano
Secondhand

De seguro
For certain, for sure

De sobra
More than enough,
unnecessary

De sol a sol
Sunrise to sunset

De soslayo
Slanting, sideways

De subida
On the way up

De súbito
Suddenly

De suerte que
So that, and so, in such a way

De su (propia) cosecha
Of one's own making or
invention

De suyo
Naturally, by nature

De tarde en tarde
From time to time, now and
then, once in a blue moon

De tejas abajo
Here below, in this world

De todas maneras
Anyway, at any rate

De todos modos
At any rate, in any case,
anyhow, by all means

De tránsito
In transit, on the way, passing
through

De través
Across

De un golpe
All at once

De un modo u otro
Somehow, in some way or other

De un momento a otro
At any moment

De un salto
Quickly

De un solo sentido
One way (e.g., one-way street)

De un tirón
All at once

De una pieza
Solid, of one piece

De una tirada
All at once, in one fell swoop

De una vez
At once, at one time, at one
stroke, once and for all

De una vez por todas
Once and for all

De uno en uno
One at a time

De unos
Of about

De uso
Secondhand

De veras (¿De veras?)
Really, in truth, in earnest
(really?, is that so?)

De verdad (¿De verdad?)
Truly, truthfully (really?, is
that so?)

De vez en cuando
Now and then, occasionally

De vicio
As a (bad) habit

De viva voz
By word of mouth

De (buena) voluntad
Willingly, with pleasure

De vuelta
Again

Debajo de
Under, beneath

Debe de ser
It must be, it probably is

Decir para sí
To say to one's self

Decir para su coleto (or capote)
To say to one's self

Dejar a uno plantado
To "stand someone up," leave
someone in the lurch

Dejar caer
To drop

Dejar de
To stop

Dejar de asistir
To drop out

Dejar de la mano
To leave, abandon

Dejar dicho
To leave word

Dejar en las astas del toro
To leave in the lurch

Dejar en paz
To let be, to leave alone

Dejar saber
To let on, pretend

Dejar tranquilo
To leave alone

Dejarse de cuentos
Come to the point, stop beating
around the bush

Dejarse de rodeos
Stop the excuses, stop beating
around the bush

Del mismo modo
Of the same sort, in the
same way

Del próximo pasado
Of last month

Del todo
Wholly, at all

Delante de
In front of

Dentro de
Inside of, within

Dentro de poco
In a little while

Dentro de un momento
In a short time

Dentro de una semana
Within a week

Desayunarse con la noticia
To hear a piece of news early or
for the first time

Descabezar el sueño
To take a nap

Desde ahora
From now on

Desde el principio
All along, from the beginning

Desde entonces
Since then, ever since

Desde hace
Dating from, over a period of...

Desde lejos
From a distance, from afar

Desde luego
Actually, of course, at once

Desde que
Since

Desde un principio
From the beginning

Desempeñar un papel
To play a part

Despedirse de
To say goodbye to

Después de eso
Thereafter

Después de todo
After all

Detrás de
Behind, in back of

Devanarse los sesos
To rack one's brain

Día de raya
Payday

Día de semana (or día de trabajo)
Weekday

Día hábil
Weekday, workday

Día tras día
Day after day

Días de antaño
Days of old

Días de semana
Weekdays

Dicho y hecho
Sure enough, no sooner said
than done

Dificultar el paso
To obstruct, impede

Digno de
Well worth it

Digno de confianza
Reliable, trustworthy

Dinero contante y sonante
Ready (or hard) cash

Dinero menudo
Change (re money)

Doblar a la esquina
To turn the corner

Dolerle a uno la garganta
To have a sore throat

Dolor de cabeza
Headache

Donde no
Otherwise, if not

Dondequiera que (or por dondequiera que)
Wherever

Dormir a pierna suelta
To sleep soundly

Dormir la mona
To sleep it off

Dormir la siesta
To take an afternoon nap

E

Echar a correr (or echarse a correr)
To begin running (to run away)

Echar(se) a perder
To spoil, to ruin

Echar a pique
To sink

Echar al olvido
To forget on purpose

Echar de menos
To miss

Echar de ver
To notice, to observe

Echar en cara
To reproach, blame

Echar espumarajos
To froth at the mouth, to be
very angry

Echar flores
To throw bouquets, to flatter,
to compliment

Echar la casa por la ventana
To spare no expense, squander
everything

Echar la culpa a
To blame

Echar la garra
To arrest, grab

Echar la llave
To lock the door

Echar la uña
To steal

Echar la zarpa
To grasp, to seize

Echar leña al fuego
To add fuel to the fire

Echar mano
To seize

Echar pajas
To draw lots

Echar papas
To fib

Echar por tierra
To knock down, demolish

Echar raíces
To take root, become firmly fixed

Echar suertes
To draw lots

Echar un piropo
To compliment, flatter

Echar un sueño
To take a nap

Echar (or soltar) un terno
To say a bad word, to swear, curse

Echar un trago
To take a drink

Echar una cana al aire
To go out for a good time or fling

Echar (una carta) al correo
To mail (a letter)

Echar una siesta
To take a nap

Echarle la bendición a una cosa
To give something up for lost

Echarse a
To begin to (do something)

Echarse al coleto
To drink down, devour

Echarse para atrás
To back out, go back on one's word

El caso es
The fact is

El común de las gentes
The majority of the people, the average person

El cuento del tío
Deceitful story told to get money

El de
The one with

El día menos pensado
When least expected, unexpectedly

El gusto es mío
The pleasure is mine

El más reciente
The latter

El mismísimo hombre
The very man

El mismo que (or lo mismo que)
The same as

El pro y el contra
Pro and con

El que
The one who, the one which

El sol poniente
The setting sun

El tren llegó con (x) minutos de retraso
The train was (x) minutes late

El uno al otro
Each other

El uno o el otro (or uno u otro)
Either, one or the other

Empeñar la palabra
To promise, pledge

Empinar el codo
To drink (too much)

En abonos
On installments

En absoluto
Absolutely (not)

En adelante
In the future, from now on

En alguna otra parte
Somewhere else

En alguna parte
Somewhere

En ambos casos
In either case

En aquel tiempo (en aquel entonces)
At that time, in those days

En balde
In vain

En breve
Shortly

En broma
In jest, as a joke

En buen romance
In plain language

En cambio
On the other hand

En casa
At home, indoors

En caso afirmativo
If so

En caso de
In the event of

En caso de que
In case of (that)

En concreto
Concretely, to sum up

En conformidad con
In compliance with

En conjunto
As a whole

En contra de
Against, opposed to

En cualquier caso
Anyway

En cuanto
As soon as

En cuanto a
As for, with regard to

En curso
In progress

En descubierto
Uncovered, unpaid

En días pasados
In days gone by

En efecto
In fact, indeed, really

En el acto
Right away, at once

En el extranjero
Abroad, out of the country

En el fondo
At bottom, at heart, in substance

En el momento preciso
In the nick of time

En el quinto infierno (or los quintos infiernos)
Very far away

En el sigilo (or silencio) de la noche
In the dead of the night

En especial
Especially, in particular

En espera de
Awaiting

En fecha a próxima
At an early date

En fin
In short, finally, in conclusion

En fragante
In the act

En grande
On a large scale

En grueso
In bulk, by wholesale

En junto (or en conjunto)
All together, in all

En la actualidad
At the present time

En libertad
Free

En lo futuro
In the future

En lo más crudo del invierno
In the dead of winter

En lo sucesivo
Hereafter, in future

En lontananza
In the distance, in the background

En lugar de
Instead of, in place of

En manga de camisa
In shirtsleeves

En marcha
In progress

En muchos puntos
In many respects

En (or a) ninguna parte
Nowhere

En obsequio de
In honor of, for the sake of

En otros términos
In other words

En parte
Partly

En particular
Especially

En pleno día
In broad daylight

En pleno rostro (or en plena cara)
Right on the face

En poder de
In the hands of

En prenda de
As proof of, as a pledge

En pro de
On behalf of

En pro y en contra
For and against

En punto
On the dot, sharp

En rama
Crude, raw

En realidad
As a matter of fact

En regla
In order

En resolución
In brief

En resumen
Summing up, in brief

En resumidas cuentas
In short, after all

En rigor
In fact, in reality

En rueda
In turn, in a circle

En salvo
In safety, out of danger

En sazón
Ripe, in season

En secreto
Secretly

En seguida
At once, right now

En señal de
In proof of, in token of

En serio
Seriously

En sueños
In one's sleep

En tal caso
In such a case

En tanto que
While

En todas partes
Everywhere

En todo caso
In any event

En un credo
In a jiffy, in a minute

En un chiflido
In a jiffy, in a second

En un improviso
In a moment

En un salto
Quickly

En un santiamén
Instantly, in the twinkling of an eye

En un soplo
In a jiffy, in a second

En vela
On watch, without sleep

En verdad
Really, truly

En vez de
Instead of

En vigor
In force, in effect

En vista de que
Since, in view of

En voz alta
Aloud, loud voice

En voz baja
In a low voice, whispering

Encargarse de
To take charge of

Encima de
On, upon

Encogerse de hombros
To shrug one's shoulders

Encontrarse con
To come across, to meet

Enfrentarse con
To confront, meet face to face

Enredarse con
To have an affair with

Entablar una conversación
To start a conversation

Entre azul y buenas noches
Undecided, on the fence

Entre bastidores
Behind the scenes, offstage

Entre la espada y la pared
Between the devil and the deep blue sea

Entre paréntesis
By the way

Entre semana
During the week

Entre tanto
Meanwhile, all the while, at the same time

Es cierto
It's true

Es decir
That is to say, in other words

Es (la) hora de (partir)
It is time for, it is time to (go)

Es lo de menos
It makes no difference, that's the least of the trouble

Eso corre prisa
That is urgent

Eso es
That is it, that's right

¡Eso es el colmo!
That is the limit!

Eso es harina de otro costal
That's a horse of a different color

Eso estriba en que
The basis for it is that

Eso no tiene quite
That can't be helped

Eso sí
That was (or is) true

Esperar en alguien
To place hope (or confidence) in someone

Esperar todo el santo día
To wait the whole blessed day

Está de más
It is unnecessary, superfluous

Está por hacer
It is yet to be done

Estamos a mano
We are even, quits

Estar a buen recaudo
To be safe

Estar a cargo de
To be in charge of

Estar a gusto
To be contented or comfortable

Estar a la altura de
To be equal to (a task)

Estar a la mira de
To be alert for, on the lookout for

Estar a punto de
To be about to

Estar al cabo de
To be well-informed, up-to-date

Estar al corriente de
To be informed, to be up-to-date

Estar afecto a
To be fond of

Estar afilando con (or afilar con)
To flirt with

Estar (or ponerse) ancho
To swell with pride

Estar arreglado
To be in order

Estar bien
To be all right, OK. Ex.: Está bien. (It is) all right, (it's) OK

Estar bien de salud
To be in good health

Estar bruja
To be broke

Estar con el agua al cuello
To be in big trouble

Estar de acuerdo
To agree

Estar de bote en bote
To be crowded, be completely
filled up

Estar de buen humor (or de buen genio)
To be in a good mood

Estar de conformidad con
To be in compliance with

Estar de duelo
To mourn, be in mourning

Estar de luto
To be in mourning

Estar de malas
To be out of luck

Estar de mal humor (or de mal genio)
To be in a bad mood

Estar (or quedar) de non
To be left alone, without a
partner or companion

Estar de paso
To be passing through

Estar de prisa
To be in a hurry

Estar de regreso
To be back

Estar de sobra
To be in the way

Estar de turno
To be on duty

Estar de vacaciones
To be on vacation

Estar de (or estar en) vena (para)
To be in the mood (for)

Estar de venta
To be on sale

Estar de viaje
To be traveling, on the road

Estar de vuelta
To be back

Estar desahogado
To be well off

Estar dispuesto
To be willing

Estar en buen uso
To be in good condition (re a
thing)

Estar en camino
To be on the way

Estar en curso
To be going on, be under way

Estar en las mismas
To be in the same boat

Estar en las nubes
To daydream

Estar en las últimas
To be on one's last legs, to be at
the end of one's rope, out of
resources

Estar en pañales
To be in infancy, to possess
scant knowledge

Estar en peligro
To be in danger

Estar en pugna con
To be opposed to, to be in
conflict with, to be against

Estar en todo
To have a finger in everything

Estar en un aprieto
To be in a jam, to be in trouble

Estar en un error
To be wrong, to be mistaken

Estar encargado de
To have charge of, to be in
charge of

Estar entre la espada y la pared
To be between the devil and the
deep blue sea

Estar (or andar) escaso de dinero
To be just about out of money,
be short of money

Estar fuera de la casa
To be out of the house, away
from home

Estar fuera de la ley
To be against the law

Estar harto de
To be fed up with

Estar hasta los topes
To be filled up

Estar hecho un costal de huesos
To be very thin, nothing but skin
and bones

Estar hecho una sopa
To be sopping wet, soaked
through

Estar mal templado
To be in a bad humor

Estar muy metido en
To be deeply involved in

Estar para
To be about to

Estar peor que antes
To be worse off

Estar por
To be in favor of

Estar ras con ras
To be flush, perfectly even

Estar regular
To feel OK

Estar salado
To be unlucky; to be witty, salty

Estar sobre sí (...sobre aviso)
To be on the alert, cautious

Estar torcido con
To be on unfriendly terms with

Estar uno en sus cabales
To be in one's right mind

Estar uno hasta el copete
To be stuffed, fed up

Estar uno hasta la coronilla
To be fed up, satisfied

Estarse parado
To stand still

Estirar la pata
To die

Estrechar la mano (a)
To shake hands, grasp (or
squeeze) a hand

Explicar una cátedra
To teach a course

F

Falta de conocimientos
Lack of instructions

Falta de saber
Lack of instructions

Faltar a clase
To cut class

Faltar a su palabra
To break one's word

Faltar poco
To be almost time

Faltarle a uno un tornillo
To have little sense, "to have a
screw loose"

Fijarse en
To notice, pay attention to

Formar parte de
To be a part (or member) of

Forzar la entrada
To break into

Frente a
In front of

Fruncir el ceño
To frown, scowl

Fruncir el entrecejo
To wrinkle one's brow

Fruncir las cejas
To frown, knit the eyebrows

Fuera de broma
All joking aside

Fuera de lo corriente
Unusual, out of the ordinary

Fuera de propósito
Irrelevant

Fuera de sí
Beside oneself

G

Ganar para comer
To earn a living

Ganar tiempo
To save time

Ganarse la vida
To make one's living

Gente de baja estofa
Low-class people, rabble

Guardar cama
To stay in bed, to be confined in
bed

Guardar rencor
To bear or hold a grudge

Guardar silencio
To keep silent

Gusano de la conciencia
Remorse

H

Había una vez (or érase que se era; érase una vez; y va de cuento)
Once upon a time

Hablar al alma
To speak frankly

Hablar al caso
To speak to the point, or in plain language

Hablar alto (or en voz alta)
To speak loudly

Hablar en secreto
To whisper

Hablar para sus adentros
To talk to oneself

Hablar por los codos
To talk too much, chatter constantly

Hace (dos, tres, etc.) años
(Two, three, etc.) years ago

Hace buen (mal) tiempo
It is good (bad) weather

Hace caso omiso
It (he, etc.) ignores

Hace mucho que no (juego, etc.)
It's been a long time since (I played, etc.)

Hace mucho tiempo
Long ago

Hacer alto
To stop

Hacer arreglos
To make arrangements

Hacer buen papel
To make a good showing

Hacer burla de
To make fun of

Hacer caso a (or hacer caso de)
To take into account, pay attention to

Hacer caso omiso de
To ignore

Hacer cocos
To make eyes at, flirt

Hacer cola
To form a line, wait in line

Hacer como si
To act as if

Hacer cuco a
To fool, make fun of

Hacer de
To act as

Hacer de nuevo
To do again, to do over

Hacer deducciones precipitadas
To jump to conclusions

Hacer destacar
To emphasize

Hacer ejercicio
To take exercise

Hacer el favor de
Please

Hacer el (or hacer un) papel
To play a role

Hacer el ridículo
To be ridiculous, act a fool

Hacer escala (en)
To stop over at

Hacer falta
To lack, be in need of

Hacer favoritismos en prejuicio de
To discriminate against

Hacer frente (a)
To face

Hacer gala de
To boast of

Hacer garras
To tear to pieces

Hacer gestos
To make faces at

Hacer gracia
To amuse, to make laugh

Hacer juego
To match

Hacer la corte
To court, woo

Hacer la zanguanga
To feign illness

Hacer las maletas
To pack, get ready to leave

Hacer las paces
To make up after a quarrel

Hacer lo posible
To do one's best

Hacer mal papel
To make a poor showing

Hacer mala obra
To hinder, interfere

Hacer mella
To make a dent or impression, to cause pain or worry

Hacer memoria
To remember, recollect

Hacer muecas
To make faces

Hacer otra vez
To do over

Hacer pedazos
To break into pieces

Hacer pinta
To play hooky, cut class

Hacer por escrito
To put in writing

Hacer preguntas (or hacer una pregunta)
To ask questions, to ask a question

Hacer presa
To seize

Hacer puente
To take a long weekend

Hacer rajas
To slice, to tear or cut into strips

Hacer rostro
To face

Hacer rumbo a
To head (or sail) towards

Hacer sombra
To shade, cast a shadow

Hacer su agosto
To make hay while the sun shines

Hacer teatro
To show off

Hacer trizas
To tear to pieces, to shred

Hacer un pedido
To place an order

Hacer un trato
To make a deal

Hacer un viaje
To go on a journey

Hacer una mala jugada
To play a mean trick

Hacer una perrada
To play a mean trick

Hacer una plancha
To make a ridiculous blunder

Hacer una visita
To pay a visit

Hacer vida
To live together

Hacerle daño a uno
To hurt or harm someone

Hacerse a
To get used to

Hacerse a la derecha
To pull over to the right

Hacerse a un lado
To step aside, move over

Hacerse amigo
To make friends with

Hacerse cargo
To take charge, to be responsible for

Hacerse de rogar
To be coaxed, to let oneself (or want to) be coaxed

Hacerse duro
To resist stubbornly

Hacerse el desentendido
To pretend not to notice

Hacerse el sordo
To pretend not to hear, turn a deaf ear

Hacerse el tonto
To play dumb, to act the fool

Hacerse entender
To make oneself understood

Hacerse ilusiones
To fool oneself

Hacerse noche
To grow late, get late in the evening

Hacerse tarde
To get late

Hacerse un lío
To get tangled up, become confused

Hacerse uno rajas
To wear oneself out

Hacia adelante
Forward

Hacia atrás
Backward

Hasta aquí (or hasta ahí)
Up to now, so far

Hasta cierto punto
In a way, up to a point

¿Hasta dónde?
How far?

Hasta más no poder
To the limit, utmost

Hasta el tope
Up to the top

Hasta la fecha
Up to date, up to now

Hasta que
Until

Hasta que se llene
Until full

Hay gato encerrado
There is more than meets the eye

Hay moros en la costa
Something is wrong; the coast is not clear; little pitchers have big ears

Hay que
One must, it is necessary to

He aquí
Behold, here is...

Hecho y derecho
Mature, full-fledged, grown up

Hincarse de rodillas
To kneel down

Hoy (en) día
Nowadays

I

Ida y vuelta
Round trip

Idas y venidas
Comings and goings

Igual que
The same as

Impedir el paso
To block the door, to obstruct the way

Ímpetu de ira
Fit of anger

Inaplicable al caso
Irrelevant

Incurrir en el odio de
To incur the hatred of

Incurrir en un error
To fall into (or commit) an error

Ingresar en
To join (a club, etc.)

Ir a caballo
To ride horseback

Ir a medias (or ir a la mitad)
To go halves (50-50)

Ir a pie
To walk, to go on foot

Ir al centro
To go downtown

Ir al grano
To get down to cases, come to the point

Ir corriendo
To be running

Ir de compras
To go shopping

Ir de jarana
To go on a spree

Ir de pesca
To go fishing

Ir de vacaciones
To go on vacation

Ir del brazo
To go arm in arm

Ir entendiendo
To begin to understand

Ir para atrás
To back up

Irse (or andar) a la deriva
To drift, be adrift

Irse abajo
To fall down

J

Juego de palabras
Pun, play on words

Juego limpio
Fair play

Juego sucio
Foul play

Jugar limpio
To play fair

Jugarle una mala partida
To play a bad trick on one

Junto a
Near to, or next to

Junto con
With, along with

L

La comidilla de la vecindad
The talk of the town

La cosa no cuajó
The thing did not jell (or work well)

La cuestión palpitante
The burning question

La gota que derrama el vaso
The last straw, the straw that broke the camel's back

La mayoría (de)
The majority (of), most of

La mayor parte (de)
The majority (of), most of

La mera idea de
The very thought of

La mera verdad
The real truth

La rutina diaria
The daily grind

La verdad clara y desnuda
The whole truth, the plain and simple truth

Lado flaco
Weak side

Largas uñas
A thief

¡Largo de aquí!
Get out of here!

Largos años
A long time, many years

Lavarse las manos de
To wash one's hands of

Levantar a pulso
To lift (something heavy) with the hand

Levantar la mesa
To clear the table

Levantarse de malas (or levantarse con las malas, or levantarse con el santo de espaldas)
To get up on (or out of) the wrong side of the bed

Ligero de cascos (or alegre de cascos)
Featherbrained

Limpio de polvo y paja
Net, entirely free, clear profit

Lo antes posible
The earliest possible

Lo de menos
Of little importance, the least of it

Lo expuesto
What has been said

Lo más pronto posible
As soon as possible

Lo menos posible
As little as possible

Lo mismo da
It makes no difference

Lo que
That which

Lo que hizo
Which caused

Lo recién llegado
A new arrival

Lo siento mucho
I'm very sorry

Loco de remate
Stark raving mad

Los (las) demás
The others, the rest of them

Los que
Those which, those who, the ones

Luego que
As soon as

LL

Llamar al pan pan, y al vino vino
Call a spade a spade

Llamar por teléfono
To call on the telephone

Llegar a saber
To come to know

Llegar a ser
To become, to get to be

Llenar un vacío
To bridge a gap

Lleno de bote en bote
Full to the brim

Llevar a cabo
To carry through, to accomplish

Llevar a efecto
To carry out

Llevar cuentas
To keep accounts

Llevar el compás
To beat time

Llevar la contra
To oppose, to object to

Llevar la cuenta (or llevar cuenta de)
To keep track of

Llevar puesto
To wear

Llevar ventaja
To have the lead, to be ahead

Llevarse adelante
To carry out

Llevarse bien (con)
To get along well with

Llevarse un chasco
To be disappointed

Llover a cántaros
To rain cats and dogs (pitchforks)

Llover sobre mojado
To come one after another (bad luck, misfortune)

M

Mal genio
Bad temper

Mal mandado (or muy mandado)
Ill-behaved

Mal sufrido
Impatient

Malas tretas
Bad tricks, bad habits

Mandar una bofetada
To slap

Mandar una pedrada
To throw a stone

Mañana Dios dirá
Tomorrow is another day

Mañana por la mañana (temprano)
Tomorrow morning (early)

Mañana por la noche
Tomorrow night

Mañana por la tarde
Tomorrow afternoon

Más acá
Closer

Más acá de
This side of, before you get to

Más adelante
Farther on, later on

Más ahorita
Right now

Más allá (de)
Beyond, farther away

Más aún
Furthermore, what is more

Más bien
Rather

Más bien que
Rather than

Más de
More than

Más de una vez
More than once

Más pesado que una mosca
Pesky as a fly

Más que
More than

Más que nadie
More than anyone

Más que nunca
More than ever

Más vale...
It is better...

Más vale tarde que nunca
Better late than never

Matar dos pájaros de un tiro
To kill two birds with one stone

Matar el gusano
To satisfy a need or desire (hunger, etc.)

Me entró miedo
I became afraid

Me hace falta
I need it

Me lloran los ojos
My eyes water

Media cuchara
A mediocre person

Medio sordo
Hard of hearing

Medir las calles
To walk the streets, be out of a job

Mejor dicho
Better yet, rather

Memoria de gallo
Poor memory

Menor de edad
A minor (person)

Menos de (or menos que)
Less than

Menos mal
At least

Merecer la pena
To be worthwhile

Meter la pata
To put one's foot in one's mouth

Meterse con
To pick a quarrel or fight with

Meterse de por medio
To intervene, meddle in a dispute

Meterse en un lío
To get oneself in a mess

Mientras más...menos
The more...the less...

Mientras tanto
Meanwhile

Mil gracias
A thousand thanks

Mirada de soslayo
Side glance

Mirar con el rabo del ojo
To look out of the corner of one's eye

Mirar por alguien
To take care of someone

Mirar por encima
To glance at

Mirar por encima del hombro
To look down on; despise

Molestarse en (con)
To bother about

Muchas subidas y bajadas
Many ups and downs, much going up and down

Mudar de casa
To move (change residence)

Muy a menudo
Very often

Muy de mañana
Very early in the morning

Muy trabajador
Hard-working

N

Nacer de pie (or pies)
To be born lucky

Nada de eso
Nothing like that

Nada de particular
Nothing unusual

Nada en absoluto
Nothing at all

Nada más
Just, only

Negarse a (contestar)
To refuse to (answer)

Ni con mucho
Not by far, not by a long shot,
far from

Ni esto ni aquello
Neither this nor that

Ni mucho menos
Not by any means, not anything
like it

Ni siquiera
Not even, even though

Ni yo tampoco
Nor I either

Ningún otro
Nobody else

No cabe duda (que)
There is no doubt (that)

No caer bien
To displease, (with direct
object) not to fit well

No da abasto a
To be unable to cope with

No dar pie con bola
To make a mistake, not to get
things right

No darse cuenta
Not to realize

No despegar los labios
Not to say a word, not to open
one's mouth

¡No diga!
Is that so? You don't say!

No es asunto mío (suyo, etc.)
It's none of my (your, etc.)
business

No es mucho que
It is no wonder that

No estar de humor
To be out of sorts, not in a
laughing mood

No estoy de acuerdo
I disagree

¡No faltaba más!
That's the last straw! Why, the
very idea!

No hallar vado
To find no way out

No hay de que
You're welcome; don't mention
it

No hay más remedio que
There's no other way but to;
there's nothing to do except

No hay para que
There's no need to

No hay prisa
There's no hurry

No hay que darle vueltas
There's no way around it; there
are no two ways about it

¡No importa!
Never mind!

No irle ni venirle a uno
To make no difference to one

No le hace
It doesn't matter, it makes no
difference

No más que
Only

No le haga caso
Pay no attention to him

No me da la gana
I don't want to

No nos debemos nada
We are even (quits)

No obstante
Notwithstanding, nevertheless

No pararse en pelillos
Not to bother about trifles

No poder con
Not to be able to stand, endure,
control, carry

No poder con la carga
Not to be able to lift the load,
not equal to the burden

No poder más
To be exhausted, "all in"

No poder menos de
Not to be able to help... Ex.: No
puede menos de hacerlo;
he can't help doing it

No quedar otro recurso
No way out, no alternative

No querer hacerlo
To be unwilling to do it

No saber ni papa (de eso)
To know absolutely nothing
(about that)

No saber una (or ni) jota
Not to know anything

No se dé usted prisa
Don't hurry

¡No se ocupe!
Never mind! Don't worry!

¡No se preocupe usted!
Don't worry!

No se trata de eso
That's not the point; that's not
the question

No sea que
Or else, because

No ser cosa de juego
Not to be a laughing matter

No ser ni chicha ni limonada
To be worthless, neither fish nor
fowl

No servir para nada
To be good for nothing

No sólo...sino también
Not only...but also

No tan a menudo
Not so often

No tener alternativa (or elección)
To have no alternative, no way
out

No tener entrañas
To be cruel

No tener nada que ver con
To have nothing to do with

No tener pelillos en la lengua
To speak frankly

No tener razón
To be wrong

No tener remedio
To be beyond help or repair

No tener sal en la mollera
To be dull, stupid

No tenga usted cuidado
Don't worry about it; forget it

No tiene remedio
It can't be helped; it is hopeless

No tiene vuelta de hoja
There's no two ways about it

No vale la pena
It's not worthwhile

No vale un pito
Not worth a straw

No vale una cuartilla
Not worth a penny

No ver la hora de
To be anxious to

**No viene al cuento (or no viene
al caso)**
It is not opportune, or to the
point

O

O sea que
That is to say

O si no...
Or else...

Oír decir que
To hear that

Oír hablar de
To hear about

Oler a
To smell like

Optar por
To choose, decide upon

¡Otra, otra!
Encore!

Otra vez
Again

P

Pagado de sí mismo
To be pleased with oneself

Pagar el pato
To be the scapegoat, get the
blame

Pagarse de
To be proud of, or boast of

¡Palabrita de honor!
Word of honor, honestly; no kidding?

Para mis adentros
To myself

Para que
In order that

¿Para qué?
What for? For what use?

Para (or por) siempre (+ jamás)
Forever (forever and ever)

Para todos lados
To right and left, on all sides

Para unos fines u otros
For one purpose or another

Para variar
For a change

Parar en seco
To stop short or suddenly

Parar mientes en
To consider, reflect on

Pararse en pelillos
To split hairs

Parece mentira
It seems to be impossible

Parecido a
Like, similar to

Pasado de moda
Out of style, out of date

Pasado mañana
Day after tomorrow

Pasar a mejor vida
To die

Pasar como un relámpago
To flash by

Pasar de la raya
To overstep bounds, take undue liberties

Pasar de moda
To go out of style

Pasar el rato
To while away time

Pasar la noche en claro (or en blanco)
Not to sleep a wink

Pasar lista
To call the roll

Pasar por alto
To omit, overlook

Pasar revista a
To review, to go over carefully

Pasar un buen rato
To have a good time

Pasarse sin
To do without

Pasear a pie
To take a walk

Pasear en coche
To go for a drive (by auto)

Pata de gallo
Crow's foot wrinkles

Patas arriba
Upside down

Pecar de bueno
To be too good

Pecar de oscuro
To be very unclear, too complicated

Pedir prestado
To borrow

Pegar de soslayo
To glance, to hit at a slant

Pegar fuego
To set afire

Pegar un chasco
To play a trick, surprise, disappoint

Pegar un salto
To take a jump

Pegar un susto
To give a scare

Pensar en
To intend, to think about

Peor que
Worse than

Peor que peor
That is even worse

Perder cuidado
Not to worry

Perder de vista
To lose sight of

Perder el juicio
To lose one's mind, go crazy

Perder el tiempo
To lose time

Perder la razón
To lose one's mind

Perder la vista
To go blind

Perder prestigio
To lose face

Perderse de vista
To vanish, to be lost from view, to drop out of sight

Pesarle a uno
To be sorry for someone, to regret

Picar en
To dabble in

Picar muy alto
To aim very high

(X) Pies de altura (or de alto)
(X) Feet tall

(X) Pies de largo
(X) Feet long

Pillar una mona
To get drunk

Pintar venado
To play hooky

Pintarle un violín
To break one's word

Planchar el asiento
To be a wallflower

Poca cosa
Not much

Poco a poco
Gradually, little by little

Poco después (de)
Shortly thereafter

Poco para las (tres)
To be nearly (3) o'clock

Poco rato
Very soon

Poner a buen recaudo
To place in safety

Poner adelantado
To set forward (e.g., a clock)

Poner al corriente
To inform, to bring up to date

Poner casa
To set up housekeeping

Poner defectos
To find fault with

Poner el grito en el cielo
To complain loudly, to ''hit the ceiling''

Poner en claro
To clear up, to clarify

Poner en conocimiento
To inform

Poner en duda
To question, to doubt

Poner en el cielo
To praise, extol

Poner en juego
To set in motion, to coordinate

Poner en limpio
To make a clean copy, to recopy

Poner en marcha
To get going

Poner en razón
To pacify

Poner en ridículo
To humiliate, make a fool of

Poner faltas
To find fault with

Poner la luz, (el radio, etc.)
To turn on the light (radio, etc.)

Poner la mesa
To set the table

Poner la mira
To fix one's eyes on, aim at

Poner por las nubes
To praise to the skies

Poner por obra
To undertake, put into practice

Poner todo de su parte
To do one's best

Poner una queja
To file a complaint

Ponerse a
To begin, start

Ponerse bien
To get well

Ponerse colorado
To blush

Ponerse de acuerdo
To come to an agreement

Ponerse de pie
To get to one's feet

Ponerse de rodillas
To kneel

Ponerse duro
To resist stubbornly

Ponerse en
To reach

Ponerse en camino
To set out (on a trip, etc.)

Ponerse en contra de
To oppose, be against

Ponerse en marcha
To start, start out

Ponerse en pie
To get up, or rise

Por acá (or por aquí)
This way, over here

Por accidente
By accident

Por adelantado
In advance

Por ahí (or por allá)
Over there, about that

Por ahora
For the time being, for now

Por algo
For some reason; that's why

Por allí
That way

Por amor de
For the sake of

Por aquí
This way

Por aquí cerca
Around here, in this vicinity

Por arriba
Above

Por casualidad
By chance, by accident

Por completo
Completely

Por (or en) consecuencia de
Therefore, consequently

Por consiguiente
Consequently, therefore

Por de (or por lo) pronto
For the present

Por delante
Ahead

Por dentro
On the inside

Por desgracia
Unfortunately

Por despecho
Out of spite

Por detrás
From the rear

Por día
By the day

¿Por dónde?
Where, through, which? Which way?

Por el estilo
Such as that, of that kind

Por el (or por la or por lo) presente
For the present

Por encima de
On top of

Por encima de todo
Above all

Por ende
Hence, therefore

Por entre
Among, between

Por esa razón
For that reason, that is why

Por escrito
In writing

Por eso
For that reason, therefore

Por extenso
In detail, at length

Por favor
Please

Por fin
At last, finally

Por fuera
From the outside, on the outside

Por hoy
At present

Por instantes
Continually, moment to moment

Por la mañana (or por la tarde, etc.)
In the morning (afternoon, etc.)

Por la mitad
In half, in the middle

Por la noche (or en la noche)
At night, in the evening

Por las buenas o por las malas
Whether one likes it or not

Por las nubes
Sky-high

Por lo común
Generally

Por lo cual
Therefore

Por lo demás
Moreover, as for the rest (of us), aside from this

Por lo general
Usually, generally

Por lo menos
At least

Por lo pronto
For the time being

Por lo regular
Usually, as a rule

Por lo que
Because of which

Por lo que pueda tronar
Just in case

Por lo tanto
Therefore

Por lo visto
Apparently, by the looks of, evidently

Por más que
However much

Por medio de
By means of

Por menudo
In detail, retail

Por mi parte
As far as I'm concerned

Por motivo
On account of

Por mucho que
No matter how much

Por ningún lado
Nowhere

Por ningún motivo
Under no circumstances, no matter what

Por otra parte
On the other hand

Por otro lado
On the other hand (or side)

Por poco
Almost, nearly. Ex.: Por poco se muere; he almost died

Por primera vez
For the first time

¿Por qué?
Why?

Por rareza
Seldom

Por regla general
As a general rule, usually

Por separado
Separately

Por si acaso
In case, just in case

Por sí solo
By oneself

Por su cuenta
All by himself (oneself)

Por su mano
By oneself

Por supuesto
Of course

Por término medio
On an average

Por (or a or en) todas partes
All over, everywhere

Por toda suerte de penalidades
Through thick and thin

Por todo el mundo
All over the world

Por todo lo alto
Not sparing expense

Por todos lados
All over, everywhere, all sides

Por última vez
For the last time, finally

Por último
Finally, at last

Porque si no
Otherwise

Preguntar por
To ask about

Prender el fuego
To start the fire

Prender fuego a
To set fire to

Preocuparse de
To take care of

Preocuparse por
To worry about, to be concerned about or for

Presencia de ánimo
Presence of mind, serenity

Prestar atención
To pay attention

Profundamente dormido
Fast asleep

Prohibida la entrada
No trespassing

Prohibido el paso
No trespassing, keep out

Prohibido estacionarse
No parking

Puede ser que
It may be that

Pues bien
Now then, well then, all right then

Pues mire
Well, look

Pues que(?)
Since, so what?

Puesta del sol
Sunset

Puesto que
Although, since

Q

¡Qué barbaridad!
What nonsense! What an atrocity!

¡Qué batingue!
What a mess!

¡Qué de!
What a lot! How much!

¡Qué desgracia!
How unfortunate!

¡Qué divino!
What a beauty!

¡Qué gusto!
What a pleasure! I am delighted!

¿Qué haces?
What's the matter? What is it?

¿Qué hay?
What's the matter?

¿Qué hay de malo con eso?
What's wrong with that? So, what's so bad about that?

¿Qué hay de nuevo?
What's new(s)?

¿Qué hora es? (or ¿qué horas son?)
What time is it?

¡Qué horror!
How awful!

¿Qué hubo?
How goes it? What's up?

¡Qué lástima!
Too bad! What a pity!

¿Qué le pasa (a Ud.)?
What's the matter with you?

Que le vaya bien
Good luck

Que lo pase bien
Have a good day, etc.

¿Qué mosca te ha picado?
What's eating you?

¡Qué nombrecito!
What a tonguetwister!

¿Qué pasa?
What's up? What's going on?

¿Qué pasó?
What happened?

¿Qué quiere decir?
What does it mean?

¡Que se divierta!
Have a good time

¿Qué tal?
Hello! How are you?

¿Qué tiene de malo?
What's wrong with...?

Quebrarse uno la cabeza
To rack one's brain

Quedar bien (con)
To come out well, to get along well (with)

Quedar contento con
To be pleased with

Quedar en
To agree (to)

Quedar entendido que
To be understood, agreed to

Quedarle bien
To be becoming

Quedarse con (re una cosa)
To keep, to take (e.g., I'll take it.)

Quedarse en la casa
To stay in

Quejarse de
To complain of

Quemarse hasta el suelo
To burn down

Quemarse las pestañas (or las cejas)
To burn the midnight oil, study hard

Querer decir
To mean, signify

¿Quién sabe?
Who knows? I don't know

¿Quién te mete, Juan Copete?
Mind your own business. What's it to you?

Quieras que no
Whether you wish or not

Quiere llover
It is trying (is about) to rain

Quince días
Two weeks

¡Quita allá!
Don't tell me that!

Quitar la mesa
To clear the table

Quitarse uno un peso de encima
To be relieved of, to be a load off one's mind

Quitarse de una cosa
To give up (or get rid of) something

¡Quítese de aquí!
Get out of here!

R

Rabiar por
To be very eager to (or for)

Rara vez (or raras veces)
Seldom

Ratos perdidos
Leisure hours

Recibir noticias (de)
To hear from

Recuerdos a
Regards to...

Rechinar los dientes
To gnash one's teeth

Reírse para sus adentros
To laugh up one's sleeve

Remolino de gente
Throng, crowd

Repetidas veces
Over and over again, various times

Repetir de carretilla
To rattle off, repeat mechanically

Resarcirse de
To make up for

Respecto a
With regard to, concerning, about

Reunión de confianza
Informal gathering or party

Reventar de risa
To burst with laughter

Romper a
To start to

Romper el alba
To dawn

Romperse los cascos
To rack one's brain

Rosario de desdichas
Chain of misfortunes

Rozarse con alguien
To have connections (or dealings) with someone

S

Saber a
To taste like

Saber de memoria
To know by heart

Sacar a bailar
To ask to dance

Sacar a uno de quicio
To exasperate someone

Sacar el cuerpo
To dodge

Sacar en claro (or en limpio)
To deduce, conclude

Salida de pie de banco
Silly remark, nonsense

Salida del sol
Sunrise

Salir a
To resemble, take after

Salir a gatas
To crawl out of a difficulty

Salir al encuentro de
To go out to meet, to oppose, take a stand against

Salir bien
To be successful, to come out well

Salir de
To leave, depart

Salir del paso
To get out of a difficulty

Salir fiador de
To vouch for

Salir ganando
To win, to come out ahead

Salir mal
To fail, to come out poorly

Salirse con la suya
To have one's own way

Saltar a la vista
To be obvious

Saltar a tierra
To disembark, to land

Saltar las trancas
To lose patience, lose one's head

Salvar el pellejo
To save one's skin

Sano y salvo
Safe and sound

Santo y bueno
Well and good

Se aguó la fiesta
The party was spoiled

Se conoce (que)
It is obvious

Se dice
It is said, they say

Se ha acabado
It is all over

Se prohibe (fumar)
It is forbidden (to smoke); no (smoking)

Se solicita
Wanted

Se suena que
It is rumored that

Se ve que
It is obvious that

Se venció el plazo
The time limit expired

Seguir las pisadas
To follow in the footsteps (of), emulate

Según y conforme (or según y como)
Exactly as, just as, that depends

Seguro que están
I bet they are

Seguro que sí
Of course

Sentar bien a
To fit well

Sentarle bien
To be becoming

Sentarse en cuclillas
To squat

Sentir en el alma
To be terribly sorry, to regret very much

Sentirse destemplado
Not to feel well, to feel feverish

Ser aficionado a
To be a fan, a buff

Ser como un puño
To be close-fisted

Ser conocedor
To be a judge of

Ser de carne y hueso
To be only human

Ser de rigor
To be indispensable, to be required by custom

Ser de (or ser para) ver
Worth seeing

Ser duro de mollera
To be stubborn

Ser fuerza
To be necessary

Ser gente
To be cultured, socially important

Ser huésped en su casa
To be seldom at home

Ser oriundo de
To hail from, come from

Ser piedra de escándalo
To be the object of scandal

Ser plato de segunda mesa
To play second fiddle

Ser tan fuerte como un león
To be as strong as a horse

Ser tempranero
To be an early riser

Ser un cero a la izquierda
To be of no account

Ser un erizo
To be irritable; a grouchy person

Servir de
To serve, act as, be used as

Servir la mesa
To wait table

Servir para
To be good for, used for

Si acaso
If at all

Si alguna vez
If even

Si bien
Although

Si mal no recuerdo
If I remember correctly

Si me hace el favor
If you would do me the favor

Si no
Or else

Si no fuera por
Except for

Si no fuera porque
Except for

Siempre que
Whenever, provided that, as long as

Siempre y cuando
Provided

Sin ceremonia
Informal

Sin comentarios
No comment

Sin contar
Exclusive of

Sin disputa
Without question

Sin embargo
However, nevertheless

Sin falta
By all means, without fail, without fault

Sin fin
An infinite quantity

Sin hacer caso de
Regardless of

Sin igual
Unequaled

Sin novedad
As usual (to be well, in good health)

Sin par
Peerless, without equal

Sin que
Without

Sin qué ni para qué
Without rhyme or reason

Sin querer
Unwillingly

Sin rebozo
Openly, frankly

Sin recurso
Without remedy, without appeal

Sin remedio
Unavoidable, without help

Sin reserva
Unreserved, frankly

Sin sentir
Without realizing, inadvertently, unnoticed

Sin ton ni son
Without rhyme or reason

Sino que
But

Sobradas veces
Repeatedly, many times

Sobre manera
Excessively

Sobre mi palabra
Upon my honor

Sobre que
Besides, in addition to

Sobre seguro
Without risk

Sobre todo
Especially, above all

Soltar el hervor
To come to a boil

Soltar la rienda
To let loose, act without restraint

Sonar a
To sound like, seem like

Soñar con (or soñar en)
To dream of

Soñar despierto
To daydream

Su punto flaco
His weakness, her weak side

Subidas y bajadas
Ups and downs

Subir al tren
To get on the train

Subir de punto
To increase, get worse

Subirse de tono
To put on airs

Suceda lo que suceda
Come what may, no matter what

Sudar la gota gorda
To sweat profusely, work hard, sweat blood, have a bad time

Suerte negra
Very bad luck

Suma atención
Close attention

Supuesto que
Supposing that, since

Surtir efecto
To come out as desired or expected, to give good results

T

Tal como (or tales como)
Such as

Tal cual
Such as, so-so, fair

Tal para cual
Two of a kind

Tal vez
Maybe, perhaps

Tal vez sea que
It may be that

Tan pronto como
As soon as

Tanto...como
As much...as

Tanto mejor
So much the better

Tanto peor
So much the worse

Tardar en
To be long in, take a long time (in doing)

Tarde o temprano
Sooner or later

Tener a la vista
To have in sight

Tener a raya
To keep in bounds, hold in check

Tener al corriente
To keep up-to-date (informed, posted)

Tener...años
To be...years old

Tener buena cara
To look well

Tener cabida con alguien
To have influence with someone

Tener calor
To be hot

Tener celos
To be jealous

Tener confianza con
To be on intimate terms with

Tener cosquillas
To be ticklish

Tener cuidado (con)
To take care, watch out (for)

Tener deseos de
To want to, to be eager to

Tener el pico de oro
To be eloquent

Tener en cuenta
To consider, to take into account

Tener en la mente
To have in mind

Tener en la punta de la lengua
To have on the tip of one's tongue

Tener en mucho
To esteem highly

Tener en poco a
To hold in low esteem

Tener entendido que
To understand that...

Tener éxito
To be successful

Tener frío
To be cold

Tener gana(s) de
To feel like

Tener gancho
To be attractive, alluring

Tener gracia
To be funny

Tener gusto en
To be glad to

Tener hambre
To be hungry

Tener la bondad de
To be good enough to

Tener la costumbre de
To be used (accustomed) to...

Tener la culpa
To be to blame

Tener la intención de
To intend or mean to

Tener la lengua larga
To have a big mouth

Tener la pena de
To have the misfortune to

Tener la vida en un hilo
To be in great danger

Tener lástima de
To feel sorry for, take pity on

Tener lugar
To take place

Tener miedo
To be afraid

Tener mucho copete
To be arrogant, haughty

Tener murria
To be sulky, to have the blues

Tener para sí
To think, to be of the opinion

Tener por
To believe, judge, consider, to take for a...

Tener presente (de or que)
To bear in mind

Tener prisa
To be in a hurry

Tener probabilidad
To stand a chance

Tener que
To have to (do something)

Tener que ver (con)
To have to do with

Tener razón
To be right

Tener roce con
To have contact with a person

Tener sed
To be thirsty

Tener sueño
To be sleepy

Tener suerte
To be lucky

Tener tiempo libre
To have time off

Tener vergüenza
To be ashamed

Tenerle tirria a una persona
To have a dislike for (or grudge against) a person

Tenerse en pie
To keep one's feet

Tirar de
To pull

Tirar las riendas
To restrain, tighten the reins

Tirarse una plancha
To put oneself in a ridiculous situation

Tocar de oído
To play by ear

Tocar en lo vivo
To hurt to the quick, hit a nerve, touch a sore spot

Tocar por fantasía
To play by ear

Tocarle a uno
To be one's turn

Tocarle a uno la suerte
To be one's turn, to fall to one's lot, to be lucky

Tocarse el sombrero
To tip one's hat

Toda clase de
All kinds of

Todas las veces (que)
Every time, whenever

Todavía no
Not yet

Todo el año
All year round

Todo el día
All day

Todo el mundo
Everybody

Todo el que
Everybody who

Todo el tiempo
All the time

Todo hombre
Everyone

Todo lo contrario
Exactly the opposite

Todo lo demás
Everything else

Todo lo posible
All that is possible

Todo sigue bien
All goes well

Todos los días
Every day

Tomar a broma
To take as a joke

Tomar a pecho(s)
To take to heart, to take seriously

Tomar a risa
To laugh off, take lightly

Tomarle el pelo
To tease, pull one's leg

Tomar el rábano por las hojas
To put the cart before the horse, to misinterpret or misconstrue

Tomar el sol
To sunbathe

Tomar en cuenta
To consider, take into account

Tomar en serio
To take to heart

Tomar la delantera
To take the lead

Tomar por cierto
To take for granted

Tomar por su cuenta
To attend to personally

Tomar tiempo libre
To take time off

Tomarlo con calma
To take it easy

Tonto de capirote
Dunce, plain fool

Traer puesto
To wear, to have on

Transporte de locura
Fit of madness

Tras de
Behind, after, beside

Tratar con
To have dealings with

Tratar de
To try to; to treat, to deal with

Tratar en
To deal in

Tratarse de
To be a question of

¡Trato hecho!
It's a deal!

Tronar los dedos
To snap one's fingers

Tropezar con
To meet, come across, encounter

U

Un buen pasar
Enough to live on

Un día sí y otro no
Every other day

Un día sí y un día no
Every other day

Un hervidero de gente
A swarm of people

Un no sé qué
Something indefinable

Un nudo en la garganta
A lump in the throat

Un rato desagradable
A hard time

Un tanto
Somewhat

Una buena carcajada
A hearty laugh

Una infinidad de
A large number of

Una mala pasada
A mean trick

Una negativa rotunda
A flat denial

Una negativa terminante
A flat denial

Una que otra vez
Once in a while

Una y otra vez
More than once, over and over again

Unas cuantas (or unos cuantos)
A few

Uno a la vez
One at a time

Uno por uno
One by one

Unos a otros
Each other

Unos pocos
A few

V

Valer la pena
To be worthwhile. Ex.: No vale la pena, it's not worth the trouble

Valer más
To be better

Valer por
To be worth

Valerse de
To make use of

Varias veces
Several times

Venir a las manos
To come to blows

Venir a menos
To decline

Venir a parar
To turn out to be, to end up (as)

Venir a (or al) pelo
To come at the right moment, to
suit perfectly, to be opportune

Venir a ser
To turn out to be

Venir bien
To suit

Venir en
To agree to

Venir sobre
To fall upon

Venirse abajo
To fall down, collapse, fail

Ver de (or ver que)
To try to, see to it that

Verse obligado a
To be obliged to or forced to

Visto que
Whereas, considering that

Vivir de sus uñas
To live by stealing

Voltear la espalda
To turn one's back

Volver a
To do...again

Volver a las andadas
To fall back into old habits

Volver corriendo
To hurry back

Volver en sí
To come to, regain
consciousness

Volver loco
To drive crazy

Volver por
To return for, to defend

Volverse atrás
To go back, back out, go back
on one's word

Volverse loco
To go crazy

Y

Y así sucesivamente
And so on, et cetera

Y pico
(A) little more

¿Y qué?
So what?

¿Y si?
What if...?

Ya es hora de
It's time to

Ya es tarde
It's too late now

Ya mero
Very soon, just about to...

¡Ya lo creo!
I should say so! Yes, of course

Ya no
No longer

Ya no sopla
To be no good, of no use as...

Ya que
Since, although

Ya se acabó
It is all over

Ya se ve
Of course; it is clear

Ya voy
I am coming

MODISMOS Y EXPRESIONES / IDIOMS AND EXPRESSIONS

A

About
Acerca de, al (or en) rededor, alrededor de, cosa de, respecto a

About that
Por ahí, por allá

About the first of...
A principios de...

About the middle of...
A mediados de

Above
Por arriba

Above all
Ante todo, por encima de todo, sobre todo

Abroad
En el extranjero

Absolutely
De remate

Absolutely (not)
En absoluto

Accomplish
Llevar a cabo

According to Hoyle; according to the rules
Como Dios manda

Across
A través de, de través

Act a fool
Hacer el ridículo, hacerse el tonto

Act as
Hacer de, servir de

Act as if
Hacer como si

Actually
Desde luego

Act without restraint
Soltar la rienda

Add fuel to the fire
Echar leña al fuego

Admit a person is right
Dar la razón a una persona

After (in position)
Tras de

After a few months (etc.)
A los pocos meses

After all
A fin de cuentas, después de todo, en resumidas cuentas

Again
De nuevo, de vuelta, otra vez

Against
En contra de

Against all odds
Contra viento y marea

Against the grain
A contrapelo

Agree
Dar la razón, estar de acuerdo, quedar en

Agree to
Quedar en, venir en

Ahead
Por delante

Aim at
Poner la mira

Aimlessly
A la ventura

Aim very high
Picar muy alto

A little more
Y pico

All along
Desde el principio

All around
A la redonda, en redondo

All at once
De un golpe, de un tirón, de una tirada

All by oneself (himself)
Por su cuenta

All day
Todo el día

All goes well
Todo sigue bien

All joking aside
Bromas a un lado, fuera de broma

All kinds of
Toda clase de

All of a sudden
De buenas a primeras, de repente

All over
En todas partes, por todas partes, por todos lados

All that is possible
Todo lo posible

All the time
A cada rato, todo el tiempo

All the while
Entre tanto

All together
En conjunto, en junto

All year round
Todo el año

Almost
Por poco

Alone
A secas

Along, alongside of
A lo largo (de)

Along with
Junto con

Aloud
En voz alta, voz alta

Although
Bien que, puesto que, si bien, ya que

Among
Por entre

Amuse
Hacer gracia

And so
De modo que, de suerte que

And so on
Y así sucesivamente

Anger, to make angry
Dar rabia

Annoy
Dar la lata

Anyhow
Así y todo, de todos modos

Anything at all
Cualquier cosa

Anyway
Al fin y al cabo, de todas maneras, en cualquier caso

Any way you look at it
A todas luces

Apiece
Cada uno

Apologize
Dar una satisfacción

Apparently
Al parecer, por lo visto

Approve
Dar el visto bueno

Approximately
Cosa de

Apropos
A propósito

Around (about)
Al derredor, en derredor, al rededor, en rededor, alrededor de

Around here
Aquí cerca, por aquí cerca

Around the corner
A la vuelta de, a la vuelta de la esquina

Arouse one's suspicions
Darle a uno mala espina

Arouse pity (or sorrow)
Dar lástima (de)

Arrest
Echar la garra

As
A medida que, a semejanza de, según y conforme, según y como

As a general rule
Por regla general; por lo general

As a last resort
Como último recurso

As a matter of fact
En realidad

As a result (of)
A consecuencia de, de resultas

As a rule
Por lo regular

As a whole
En conjunto

As far as I'm concerned
Por mi parte

As follows
A continuación, como sigue

As for
En cuanto a

As for the rest (of us)
Por lo demás

Aside from that
Aparte de eso

Aside from this
Por lo demás

As if
Como si

As if by magic
Como por ensalmo

As if it were
Como si fuera

As I understand it
A mi entender

Ask about
Preguntar por

Ask a question (or questions)
Hacer una pregunta (preguntas)

Ask to dance
Sacar a bailar

As little as possible
Lo menos posible

As long as
Siempre que

As much as
Tanto como

As of
A partir de

As proof of
En prenda de

As smooth as silk
Como una seda

As soon as
Así es que, así que, en cuanto, luego que, tan pronto como

As soon as possible
Cuanto antes, lo más pronto posible

Assume responsibility
Cargar con

As the crow flies
A vuelo de pájaro

As the saying goes
Como dijo el otro

As time goes on
Andarse el tiempo

As usual
Como de costumbre, como siempre, sin novedad

As well as
Así como

As you like
A la voluntad

At about
A eso de, como a costumbre

At about...(time)
Al filo de...

At all
Del todo

At all costs
A toda costa, a todo trance

At all hours
A deshora(s)

At all times
A toda hora

At an early date
En fecha a próxima

At another's expense
De gorra

At an untimely moment
A deshora(s)

At any cost
Cueste lo que cueste

At any moment
De un momento a otro

At any rate
Como quiera que sea, de cualquier modo, de todas maneras, de todos modos

At any time
A toda hora

At arm's length
A una brazada

At a short distance
A pocos pasos

At bottom
En el fondo

At every turn
A cada paso

At first
Al principio

At full length
A lo largo (de)

At full speed (or greatest speed)
A escape, a toda prisa, a toda vela, a todo correr

At hand
A mano

At hard labor
Al remo

At heart
En el fondo

At home
En casa

At last
A la postre, al fin, al fin y al cabo, por fin, por último

At (the) least
Al menos, a lo menos, como mínimo, menos mal, por lo menos

At length
Por extenso

At most
A lo más, a lo sumo

At once
Ahora mismo, al instante, al punto, de pronto, de una vez, desde luego, en el acto, en seguida

At one stroke
De una vez

At one time
A un tiempo, de una vez

At present
Al presente, por hoy

At random
A la buena de Dios, a la ventura, al azar

Attend to personally
Tomar por su cuenta

At that time
A la sazón, en aquel tiempo

At the end
Al fin

At the last moment
A última hora

At the mercy of
A merced de

At the most
A lo sumo

At the present time
En la actualidad

At the request of
A instancias de

At the same time
A la vez, al mismo tiempo, de paso, entre tanto

At the very latest
A más tardar

At this point or juncture
A estas alturas

At times
A ratos, a veces

At whatever cost
A toda costa

At will
A la voluntad, a voluntad

At worst
A lo más

At your service
A sus órdenes, servidor de usted

Average person
El común de las gentes

Avoid someone
Dar esquinazo

Awaiting
En espera de

B

Back and forth
De aquí para allá

Back out
Echarse para atrás, volverse atrás

Back up
Dar marcha atrás, ir para atrás

Backward(s)
Al revés, hacia atrás

Bad habits
Malas tretas

Bad temper
Mal genio

Bark up the wrong tree
A buen santo te encomiendas

Be a buff
Ser aficionado a

Be about to
Estar a punto de, estar para

Be a fan of
Ser aficionado a

Be afraid
Tener miedo

Be against
Estar en pugna con, ponerse en contra de

Be agreed to
Quedar entendido que

Be ahead
Llevar ventaja

Be alert
Estar a la mira de, ponerse chango

Be all right, OK
Estar bien

Be alluring
Tener gancho

Be a load off one's mind
Quitarse uno un peso de encima

Be an early riser
Ser tempranero

Be anxious to
No ver la hora de

Be a part of
Formar parte de

Be a question of
Tratarse de

Bear or hold a grudge
Guardar rencor

Bear in mind
Tener presente (de lo que)

Be arrogant
Tener mucho copete

Be ashamed
Tener vergüenza

Be as strong as a horse
Ser tan fuerte como un león

Beat around the bush
Andarse con rodeos, andarse por las ramas

Beaten path
Camino trillado

Be at the end of one's rope or resources
Estar en las últimas

Beat (or mark) time
Llevar el compás

Be attractive
Tener gancho

Beautifully
A las mil maravillas

Be a wallflower
Planchar el asiento

Be away from home
Estar fuera de casa

Be back
Estar de regreso, estar de vuelta

Be becoming
Caer bien, quedarle bien, sentarle bien

Be beyond help or repair
No tener remedio

Be born lucky
Nacer de pie (...de pies)

Be broke
Estar bruja

Because
No sea que

Because of
Con motivo de

Because of which
Por lo que

Be cautious
Estar sobre sí, estar sobre aviso

Be close-fisted
Ser como un puño

Be coaxed
Hacerse del rogar

Become
Llegar a ser

Become confused
Hacerse un lío

Become effective
Entrar en vigor (e.g., a law)

Be contented
Estar a gusto

Be courageous
Tener puños

Be crowded
Estar de bote en bote

Be cruel
No tener entrañas

Be cultured
Ser gente

Be deeply involved in
Estar muy metido en

Be disappointed
Llevarse un chasco

Be disconcerting
Dar mucha pena

Be dull
No tener sal en la mollera

Be eager to
Tener deseos de

Be eloquent
Tener el pico de oro

Be equal to (a task)
Estar a la altura de

Be exhausted
No poder más

Be fed
Dar de comer

Be fed up
Estar uno hasta el copete, estar uno hasta la coronilla

Be fed up with
Estar harto de

Be filled up
Estar hasta los topes

Be flush (even with)
Estar ras con ras

Be fond of
Estar afecto a

Be forced to
Verse obligado a

Before
Antes de que

Before dark
De día

Beforehand
Con tiempo

Before one's (very) eyes
A ojos vistas

Be funny
Tener gracia

Begin
Echarse a, ponerse a, romper a

Beginning on
A partir de

Begin running
Echar(se) a correr

Begin to understand
Ir entendiendo

Be glad to
Tener gusto en

Be good for
Servir para

Be good for nothing
No servir para nada

Be haughty
Tener mucho copete

Behind
Atrás de, detrás de, tras de

Behind closed doors
A puerta cerrada

Behind one's back
A espaldas de

Behind the scenes
Entre bastidores

Behold
He aquí

Be in a bad mood
Estar mal templado, estar de mal humor, mal genio

Be in a good mood
Estar de buen humor, buen genio

Be in a hurry
Estar (or andar) de prisa, tener prisa

Be in a jam
Estar en un aprieto

Be in big trouble
Estar con el agua al cuello

Be in charge of
Estar a cargo de, estar encargado de

Be indebted to
Estar en deuda con

Be indispensable
Ser de rigor

Be in favor of
Estar por

Be in good condition (a thing)
Estar en buen uso

Be in good health
Estar bien de salud, sin novedad

Be in great danger
Tener la vida en un hilo

Be in infancy
Estar en pañales

Be in mourning
Estar de duelo, estar de luto

Be in need of
Hacer falta

Be in one's right mind
Estar uno en sus cabales

Be in order
Estar arreglado

Be in the mood (for)
Estar de (or en) vena (para)

Be in the same boat
Estar en las mismas

Be in the way
Estar de sobra

Be in trouble
Estar en un aprieto

Be irritable (or a grouchy person)
Ser un erizo

Be jealous
Tener celos

Be a judge of
Ser conocedor

Be just about out of money
Estar (or andar) escaso de dinero

Be left alone
Estar de non, quedar de non

Believe
Tener por

Believe strongly
A pie(s) juntillas

Be long (in doing)
Tardar en

Below
A continuación

Be lucky
Tener suerte, tocarle a uno la suerte

Be mistaken
Estar en un error

Be nearly...(o'clock)
Faltar un poco para las...(horas)

Beneath
Debajo de

Be necessary
Ser fuerza

Be obliged to
Verse obligado a

Be obvious
Saltar a la vista

Be of no account
Ser un cero a la izquierda

Be of no use
Ya no sopla

Be of the opinion
Dar la razón, tener para sí

Be on duty
Estar de turno

Be one's own affair
Correr por cuenta de uno

Be one's turn
Tocarle a uno, tocarle a uno la suerte

Be on good terms with
Acordar con

Be on intimate terms with
Tener confianza con

Be only human
Ser de carne y hueso

Be on one's last legs
Estar en las últimas

Be on the alert for
Estar a la mira de, estar sobre sí, estar sobre aviso

Be on the lookout for
Estar a la mira de

Be on unfriendly terms with
Estar torcido con

Be on vacation
Estar de vacaciones

Be opportune
Venir a (or al) pelo

Be opposed to
Estar en pugna con

Be out of a job
Medir las calles

Be out of luck
Andar de malas, estar de malas, tener la de malas

Be out of resources
Estar en las últimas

Be out of sorts
Andar agitado, no estar de humor

Be out of the house
Estar fuera de la casa

Be passing through
Estar de paso

Be perfectly even
Estar ras con ras

Be pleased with
Quedar contento con

Be pleased with oneself
Pagado de sí mismo

Be proud of (or vain about) something
Pagarse de algo

Be a question of
Tratarse de

Be relieved of
Quitarse uno un peso de encima

Be required by custom
Ser de rigor

Be responsible for
Hacerse cargo de

Be ridiculous
Hacer el ridículo

Be right
Andar bien; tener razón

Be safe
Estar a buen recaudo

Be satisfied
Estar uno hasta la coronilla

Be seldom at home
Ser huésped en su casa

Be short of money
Estar (or andar) escaso de dinero

Beside
A lado de, tras de

Beside oneself
Fuera de sí

Besides (to boot)
Además de, de pilón, sobre que

Beside that
Aparte de eso

Be sleepy
Tener sueño

Be soaked through
Estar hecho una sopa

Be sorry for someone
Pesarle a uno

Be stubborn
Ser duro de mollera

Be stuffed
Estar uno hasta el copete

Be stupid
No tener sal en la mollera

Be successful
Salir bien, tener éxito

Be sulky
Tener murria

Be terribly sorry
Sentir en el alma

Be the scapegoat
Pagar el pato

Be the object of scandal
Ser piedra de escándalo

Be thirsty
Tener sed

Be ticklish
Tener cosquillas

Be to blame
Tener la culpa

Be too complicated
Pecar de oscuro

Be too good
Pecar de bueno

Be to one's advantage
Convenirle a uno

Better late than never
Más vale tarde que nunca

Better yet
Mejor dicho

Between
Por entre

Between the devil and the deep blue sea
Entre la espada y la pared

Be unable to cope with
No da abasto a

Be understood
Quedar entendido que

Be unlucky
Estar salado

Be unwilling to do it
No querer hacerlo

Be up to date
Estar al cabo de, estar al corriente de, estar en corriente

Be up to oneself
Correr por cuenta de uno

Be used as
Servir de

Be used for
Servir para

Be used (or accustomed) to...
Tener la costumbre de...

Be very angry
Echar espumarajos

Be very eager to (or for)
Rabiar por

Be very difficult
Costar trabajo

Be very thin
Estar hecho un costal de huesos

Be very unclear
Pecar de oscuro

Be a wallflower
Planchar el asiento

Be well
Sin novedad

Be well-informed
Estar al cabo de, estar al corriente de, estar en corriente

Be well off
Estar desahogado

Be willing
Estar dispuesto

Be witty or salty
Estar salado

Be worse off
Estar peor que antes

Be worth
Valer por

Be worthless
No ser ni chicha ni limonada

Be worthwhile
Merecer la pena, valer la pena

Be wrong
Estar en un error, no tener razón

Be...years old
Tener...años

Beyond
Más allá (de)

Blame
Dar en cara, echar en cara, echar la culpa a

Blindly
A ciegas, a ojos cerrados, a tientas

Block the door
Impedir el paso

Blush
Ponerse colorado

Boast of
Hacer gala de, pagarse de

Borrow
Pedir prestado

Bother about
Molestarse en

Brand as (or accuse)
Motejar de

Break into
Forzar la entrada

Break into pieces
Hacer pedazos

Break one's word
Faltar a su palabra, pintarle un violín

Break the news
Dar la noticia

Break the thread of a story
Cortar el hilo

Bridge a gap
Llenar un vacío

Bring up to date
Poner al corriente

Bulky
De buen tomo y lomo

Bully for you!
¡Así se hace!

Bump into each other
Darse un encontrón

Burn down
Quemarse hasta el suelo

Burning question
La cuestión palpitante

Burn the midnight oil
Quemarse las pestañas (or las cejas)

Burst with laughter
Reventar de risa

Bury
Dar sepultura

But
Sino que

By all means
A toda costa, a todas luces, de todos modos, sin falta

By chance
Al azar, por casualidad

By dint of
A fuerza de

By ear
Al oído, de oído

By foot
A pie

By force (of)
A fuerza (de), a la fuerza

By guess
A ojo, al tanteo

By hand
A mano

By heart
De memoria

By itself
De por sí

By just shouting
A puros gritos

By means of
Por medio de

By mistake
Por equivocación, por descuido

By no means
De ningún modo, de ninguna manera, ni modo

By oneself
Por sí solo, por su mano

By pure chance
De pura casualidad

By sheer force
A pura fuerza

By sight
A ojo

By the looks of
Por lo visto

By the minute
De punto

By the roots
De raíz

By the way
A propósito, de paso, entre paréntesis

By twos
De dos en dos

By word of mouth
De palabra, de viva voz

C

Call a spade a spade
Al pan, pan y al vino, vino;
llamar al pan pan y al vino vino

Call on the phone (telephone)
Llamar por teléfono

Call the roll
Pasar lista

Carry away
Cargar con -

Carry out
Dar cima, llevar a efecto,
llevarse adelante

Carry through
Llevar a cabo

Cast a shadow
Hacer sombra

Catch cold
Coger catarro, coger un
resfriado

Catch fire
Coger fuego

Cause distress or grief to
Dar disgustos a

Cause extra work
Dar que hacer

Cause pain or worry
Hacer mella

Cause sorrow
Dar mucha pena

Cents off
Rebaja de...centavos

Certainly
A buen seguro

Certainly not
Claro que no

Chain of misfortunes
Rosario de desdichas

Change one's mind
Cambiar de idea (...opinión,
...pensamiento)

Change the subject
Cambiar de tema

Chatter constantly
Hablar por los codos, hablar a
chorros

Cheat (in a bargain or exchange)
Dar gato por liebre

Cheer up
Dar ánimo

Choose
Optar por

Clarify
Poner en claro

Clearly
A las claras, a ojos vistas

Clear the table
Levantar la mesa, quitar la
mesa

Clear the way
Abrir paso

Clear up
Poner en claro

Close attention
Suma atención

Closer
Más acá

Close to
A raíz de, cerca de

Coast is not clear, the
Hay moros en la costa

Cock and bull story
Cuento chino

Collide with
Darse un encontrón

Collapse
Venirse abajo

**Come across (someone or
something)**
Encontrarse con, tropezar con

Come at the right moment
Venir a (or al) pelo

Come from
Ser oriundo de

Come hell or high water
Contra viento y marea

**Come one after another (bad
luck or misfortunes)**
Llover sobre mojado

Come out ahead
Salir ganando

Come out as desired
Surtir efecto

Come out poorly
Salir mal

Come out well
Quedar bien, salir bien, surtir
efecto

Come to (regain consciousness)
Volver en sí

Come to a boil
Soltar (or alzar) el hervor

Come to an agreement
Ponerse de acuerdo

Come to blows
Venir a las manos

Come to know
Llegar a saber

Come to pass
Llegar a suceder, ocurrir

Come to the point
Dejarse de cuentos, ir al grano

Come what may
Contra viento y marea, suceda
lo que suceda

Comings and goings
Idas y venidas

Complain loudly
Poner el grito en el cielo

Complain of
Quejarse de

Complete
Dar cima, dar fin (a)

Completely
De raíz, por completo

Compliment
Echar flores, echar un
piropo

Concerning
Respecto a

Confidentially
Al oído

Confront
Enfrentarse con

Consciously
A sabiendas

Consequently
De resultas, en consecuencia
de, por consecuencia de, por
consiguiente

Consider
Parar mientes en, tener en
cuenta, tener por, tomar en
cuenta

Consider as
Dar por

Consider as done
Dar por hecho

Considering that
Visto que

Continually
A cada momento, por instante

Continuously
De seguida

Coordinate
Poner en juego

Cost an arm and a leg
Costar un ojo de la cara

Count on
Contar con

Crawl (or creep)
Andar a gatas

Crawling
A gatas

Crawl out of a difficulty
Salir a gatas

Cross-country
A campo traviesa

Crowd
Hervidero de gente, remolino
de gente

Crowded
De bote en bote

Crow's feet (wrinkles)
Pata de gallo

Crude
En rama

Curse
Echar ternos, soltar un terno

Cut class
Faltar a (la) clase, hacer
pinta

Cut into strips
Hacer rajas

D

Dabble in
Picar en

Daily grind
La rutina diaria

Dance without music
Bailar a secas

Dating from
Desde hace

Day after day
Día tras día

Daydream
Estar en las nubes, soñar despierto

Days of old
Días de antaño

Dead end
Callejón sin salida

Deal in
Tratar en

Deal with
Tratar de

Deceitfully
A traición, de mala fe

Deceitful story told to get money
El cuento del tío

Decide upon
Optar por

Decline
Venir a menos

Delay
Dar largas

Demolish
Echar por tierra

Depart
Salir de

Despite
A despecho de

Destroy
Dar al traste con, dar al través con

Devour (eat up or drink down)
Echarse al coleto

Diagonally
Al sesgo

Die
Estirar la pata, pasar a mejor vida

Disappoint
Pegar un chasco

Displease
Caer mal, no caer bien

Ditch (avoid)
Dar esquinazo

Do...again
Hacer...de nuevo, volver a...

Dodge the issue
Evadir el tema

Don't worry
¡No se ocupe!, ¡No se preocupe usted!

Don't worry about it
No tenga usted cuidado

Do one's best
Hacer lo posible, poner todo de su parte

Do over
Hacer de nuevo, hacer otra vez, volver a hacer

Doubt
Poner en duda

Do without
Pasarse sin, prescindir de

Draw lots
Echar pajas, echar suertes

Dream of
Soñar con (or en)

Drift
Andar a la deriva, irse a la deriva

Drink too much
Alzar el codo, empinar el codo

Drive someone crazy
Volver loco a uno

Drop
Dejar caer

Drop out (of)
Darse de baja, dejar de asistir, retirarse (de)

Drop out of sight
Perderse de vista

Dunce
Tonto de capirote, zopenco

During the week
A mediados de la semana, entre semana

E

Each one
Cada cual, cada uno

Each other
El uno al otro, unos a otros

Each time
A cada rato, cada vez

Earliest possible, the
Lo antes posible

Early in (a period of time)
A principios de

Earn a living
Ganar para comer, ganarse la vida

Either
El uno o el otro, uno u otro

Either of the two
Cualesquiera (or cualquiera) de los dos

Emphasize
Dar realce, hacer destacar

Encore!
¡Otra, otra!

Encounter
Tropezar con

Encourage
Dar aliento, dar alas a

Endanger
Poner al tablero, poner en peligro

End up as
Venir a parar

End up by (doing something)
Acabar por

Enhance
Dar realce

Enjoy your meal!
¡Buen provecho!

Equally
Al igual

Equal to or up to
Con fuerzas para, estar a la altura de

Especially
Ante todo, en especial, en particular, sobre todo

Esteem highly
Tener en mucho, poner en (or sobre) las nubes

Et cetera
Y así sucesivamente

Even if
Aun cuando

Even so
Así y todo

Even though
Aun cuando, ni siquiera

Even with (flush)
Al ras con, a ras de

Ever since
Desde entonces

Everybody
Todo el mundo

Everybody who
Todo el que

Every day
Todos los días

Everyone
Todo hombre

Every other day
Cada dos días, un día sí y otro no, un día sí y un día no

Everything else
Todo lo demás

Every time
Todas las veces (que)

Everywhere
A todas partes, en todas partes, por todas partes, por todos lados

Evidently
Por lo visto

Exactly as
Según y como, según y conforme

Exactly as desired
A pedir de boca

Exactly the opposite
Todo lo contrario

Exasperate (someone)
Sacar (a uno) de quicio

Except for
Si no fuera por, si no fuera
porque

Excessively
Sobre manera

Exclusive of
Sin contar

Extend condolences to or for
Dar el pésame por

Extra
De repuesto

Extremely
Con (or en or por) extremo

F

Face
Dar a, hacer frente (a), hacer
rostro

Face to face
Cara a cara

Fail
Dejar de, salir mal, venirse
abajo

Fair (or such as it is)
Tal cual

Fair play
Juego limpio

Fall back into old habits
Volver a las andadas

Fall down
Irse abajo, venirse abajo

Fall ill
Caer enfermo, ponerse enfermo

Fall to one's lot
Tocarle a uno la suerte

Fall upon
Venir sobre

Far from
Ni con mucho

Farther away
Más allá de

Farther on
Más adelante

Fast asleep
Profundamente dormido

Featherbrained
Alegre de cascos, ligero de
cascos

Feed
Dar de comer

Feel feverish
Sentirse destemplado

Feel like
Tener gana(s) de

Feel OK
Estar regular

Feel sorry for
Tener lástima de

Feign illness, to
Hacer la zanguanga

Few, a
Unas cuantas, unos cuantos

Few lines, a
Cuatro letras

Few words, a
Cuatro palabras

Fib
Echar papas

Finally
Al cabo, en fin, por fin, por
última vez, por último

Find fault with
Poner defectos, poner faltas

Find no way out
No hallar vado

First of all
Ante todo

Fit badly
Caer mal

Fit of anger
Arranque de cólera, ímpetu
de ira

Fit of madness
Transporte de locura

Fit well
Caer bien, sentar bien a

Fix one's eyes on
Poner la mira

Flash by
Pasar como un relámpago

Flat denial
Una negativa rotunda, una
negativa terminante

Flatter
Dar coba, dar jabón (a), echar
flores, echar un piropo

Flirt (with)
Afilar con, coquetear, hacer
cocos

Flush with
A flor de, al ras con, a ras de

Follow in the footsteps (of)
Seguir las pisadas

Fond of
Amante de, amigo de

Fool, to
Hacer cuco a

Fool oneself
Hacerse ilusiones

Foot the bill
Pagar los gastos

For a change
Para variar

For and against
En pro y en contra

For certain
De seguro

Forever
Para siempre, por siempre

For example
Por ejemplo

Form a line
Hacer cola

For now
Por ahora

For one purpose or another
Para unos fines u otros

For some reason
Por algo

For some time now
De algún tiempo para acá

For sure
De seguro

For that reason
Por esa razón, por eso

For the first time
Por primera vez

For the last time
Por última vez

For the present
Por de pronto, por lo pronto,
por el (or la or lo) presente

For the sake of
En obsequio de, por amor de

For the time being
De momento, por ahora, por el
momento, por lo pronto

For want of
A falta de

Forward
Hacia adelante

Foul play
Juego sucio

Frame someone
Conspirar contra una persona

Frankly
A las claras, sin rebozo, sin
reserva

Free
En libertad

Free rein
A rienda suelta

Frequently
A cada momento, a menudo,
con mucha frecuencia

Frighten
Dar horror

From a distance
De lejos, desde lejos

From afar
Desde lejos

From bad to worse
De mal en peor

From beginning to end
De cabo a rabo

From now on
De ahora en adelante, de aquí
en adelante, de hoy en adelante,
desde ahora en adelante

From one side to the other
De parte a parte

From that time on
De aquel tiempo en adelante, de
aquel entonces

From the beginning
Desde el principio

From then on
De ahí en adelante

From the outside
Por fuera

From the rear
Por detrás

From time to time
A ratos, de tarde en tarde

From today on
A partir de hoy

From top to bottom
De arriba abajo

Full-fledged
Hecho y derecho

Full to the brim
Lleno de bote en bote

Fully
A fondo

Furthermore
Más aún

G

Generally
Por lo común, por lo general

Get along well with
Llevarse bien con, quedar bien con

Get down to cases
Ir al grano

Get drunk
Pillar una mona

Get going
Poner en marcha

Get late
Hacerse tarde

Get late in the evening
Hacerse noche

Get lost!
¡Vete a bañar!

Get married
Contraer matrimonio

Get oneself in a mess
Meterse en un lío

Get out of a difficulty
Salir del paso

Get out of here!
¡Largo de aquí!, ¡Quítese de aquí!

Get ready to leave
Hacer las maletas

Get tangled up
Hacerse un lío

Get the blame
Pagar el pato

Get the blame unjustly
Cargar con el muerto

Get the point
Caer en la cuenta

Get to one's feet
Ponerse de pie

Get to sleep
Conciliar el sueño

Get up
Ponerse de pie, ponerse en pie

Get up on the wrong side of the bed
Levantarse de malas, levantarse con las malas, levantarse con el santo de espaldas

Get well
Ponerse bien

Get worse
Subir de punto

Give account
Dar razón

Give a party
Dar una fiesta

Give a report on
Dar cuenta de

Give a scare
Pegar un susto

Give cause for
Dar lugar a

Give courage
Dar alas a

Give good results
Surtir efecto

Give it up
Darlo por abandonado

Given name
Nombre de bautismo, nombre de pila

Give opportunity (or occasion) to
Dar pie

Give regards
Dar los recuerdos

Give someone the run around
Dar largas

Give something up for lost
Echarle la bendición a una cosa

Give thanks
Dar las gracias

Give to
Dar a

Give up
Darse por vencido

Give up (or get rid of) something
Quitarse de una cosa

Gladly
Con mucho gusto, de buena gana, de buen grado, de (buena) voluntad

Glance at
Mirar por encima

Glance off
Pegar de soslayo

Glance over
Dar un vistazo a

Gnash one's teeth
Rechinar los dientes

Go arm in arm
Ir del brazo

Go back
Volverse atrás

Go back on one's word
Echarse para atrás, volverse atrás

Go blind
Perder la vista

Go cautiously
Caminar con pies de plomo

Go crazy
Perder el juicio, volverse loco

Go halves
Ir a medias, ir a la mitad

Go jump in the lake!
¡Vete a bañar!

Good-looking
Bien parecido, de buen ver

Good luck
Que le vaya bien

Go on a journey
Hacer un viaje

Go on a spree
Andar (or ir) de parranda, andar (or ir) de fiesta en fiesta, ir de jarana

Go on foot
Ir a pie

Go on vacation
Ir de vacaciones

Goosebumps
Carne de gallina

Go out for a good time or fling
Echar una cana al aire

Go out of style
Pasar de moda

Go out to meet
Salir al encuentro de

Go over carefully
Pasar revista a

Go over like a lead balloon
Caer mal, caer gordo

Go shopping
Ir de compras

Go to bed early
Acostarse con las gallinas

Grab
Echar la garra

Gradually
Poco a poco

Grasp
Echar la zarpa

Grow late
Hacerse noche

Grown up
Hecho y derecho

Guess right
Dar en (or con) el chiste

H

Hail from
Ser oriundo de

Half done
A medio hacer

Halfway (to a place)
A medio camino

Hang one's head
Agachar las orejas

Haphazardly
A la ventura

Happy-go-lucky
Chueco o derecho

Hard cash
Dinero contante y sonante

Hardly
A duras penas

Hardly ever
Casi nunca

Hard of hearing
Algo sordo, corto de oído,
medio sordo

Hard time
Un rato desagradable

Hard-working
Muy trabajador

Have a bad time
Sudar la gota gorda

Have a big mouth
Tener la lengua larga

Have a birthday
Cumplir años

Have a finger in everything
Estar en todo

Have a good day
Que lo pase bien

Have a good time
Pasar un buen rato

Have (an illness)
Estar con (una enfermedad)

Have a screw loose
Faltarle a uno un tornillo

**Have contact (or a lot to do)
with a person**
Tener roce con alguien

Have dealings with
Tratar con

Have a dislike for someone
Tenerle tirria a una persona

Have influence with someone
Tener cabida con alguien

Have in mind
Tener en la mente

Have in sight
Tener a la vista

Have just (done something)
Acabar de

Have little sense
Faltarle a uno un tornillo

Have nothing to do with
No tener nada que ver con

Have no way out
No tener alternativa (or
elección)

Have on
Traer puesto

Have one's own way
Salirse con la suya

Have on the tip of one's tongue
Tener en la punta de la lengua

Have the blues
Tener murria

Have the lead
Llevar ventaja

Have the misfortune to
Tener la pena de

Have time off
Tener tiempo libre

Have to (do something)
Tener que...

Have to do with
Tener que ver con

Heads or tails
Águila o pico, águila o sello,
cara o cruz

Head toward
Hacer rumbo a

Heaps
A montones

Hear about
Oír hablar de

**Hear news early or for the
first time**
Desayunarse con la noticia

Hear from
Recibir noticias de

Hearsay
De oídos

Hear that
Oír decir que

Hearty laugh
Una buena carcajada

Height of folly
El colmo de la locura

Help
Dar la mano

Help yourself
Sírvase usted

Hence
De ahí que, por ende

Here!
A sus órdenes

Hereafter
En lo sucesivo

Here below
De tejas abajo

Hinder
Hacer mala obra

Hit (upon)
Dar en

Hit a nerve
Tocar en lo vivo

Hit at a slant
Pegar de soslayo

Hit or miss
Al tanteo, chueco o derecho

Hit the ceiling
Poner el grito en el cielo

Hit the nail on the head
Dar en el clavo, dar en (or con)
el chiste, dar uno en la tecla

Hold in check
Tener a raya

Hold in low esteem
Tener en poco a

Honestly!
¡Palabrita de honor!

Horrify
Dar horror

Hot-headed
Caliente de cascos

How awful!
¡Qué horror!

How can I (one) have the nerve?
¿Con qué cara?

How do you like...?
¿Qué le parece...?

How do you say...?
¿Cómo se dice...?

However
Ahora bien, sin embargo

However much
Por más que

How far?
¿Hasta dónde?

**How goes it? (or how is it
going?)**
¿Qué hubo?

How often?
¿Cada cuánto tiempo?

How should I know?
¿Qué sé yo?

How unfortunate!
¡Qué desgracia!

Humiliate
Poner en ridículo

Hurry
Darse prisa

Hurry back
Volver corriendo

Hurt or harm someone
Hacerle daño a uno

Hurt to the quick
Tocar en lo vivo

I

I bet... (not a real wager)
A que...

I bet they are...
Seguro que están

I bet you don't!
¡A que no!

If at all
Si acaso

If even
Si alguna vez

If I remember correctly
Si mal no recuerdo

If not
De lo contrario, donde no

I forgot to tell you
Se me pasó decirte

If so
En caso afirmativo

Ignore
Hacer caso omiso de

Ill-behaved
Mal mandado, muy mandado

Impatient
Mal sufrido

Impede
Dificultar el paso

Important
De buen tomo y lomo, de
copete

In a bad humor
De mal temple

In about
Como en

In abundance
A montones

In accordance with
Conforme a, de acuerdo con

In addition to
Además de, a más de, sobre que

In advance
Con anticipación, con tiempo,
de antemano, por adelantado

Inadvertently
Sin sentir

In a jiffy
Como por ensalmo, en un
credo, en un chiflido, en un
soplo

In a little while
Dentro de poco

In all
En junto, en conjunto

In all directions
A los cuatro vientos

In a loud voice
En voz alta

In a low voice
En voz baja

In a minute
En un credo

In a moment
En un improviso

In a month of Sundays
Como visita de obispo

In any case
Al fin de cuentas, de todos
modos

In any event
En todo caso

In a second
En un chiflido, en un soplo

In a short time
Dentro de un momento

In a short while
A (or al) poco rato, dentro
de poco

Inasmuch as
Como que, como quiera que

In a way
Hasta cierto punto

In back of
Atrás de, detrás de

In bad faith
De mala fe

In brief
En resolución, en resumen

In broad daylight
En pleno día

In case
Por si acaso

In case of (that)
En caso de (que)

In cold blood
En sangre fría

In competition
A porfía

Incomplete
A medio hacer

In compliance with
En conformidad con, estar de
conformidad con

In conclusion
En fin

In conflict with
Estar en pugna con

Increase
Subir de punto

In days gone by
En días pasados

Indeed
En efecto

In detail
Por extenso, por menudo

Indirectly
De rebote

Indoors
Bajo techo, en casa

In due course or time
A su (debido) tiempo

In earnest
A la verdad, de veras

In either case
En ambos casos

In exchange for
A cambio de

In fact
De hecho, en efecto, en rigor

In favor of
De parte de

Inform
Dar parte, dar razón, poner al
corriente, poner en
conocimiento

Informal
Sin ceremonia

Informal gathering or party
Reunión de confianza

In front of
Al frente de, delante de, frente a

In good faith
De buena fe

In good taste
De buen tono, de buen gusto

In good time
Con tiempo

In half
Por la mitad

In haste
A la carrera

In honor of
En obsequio de

In jest
De broma, de burla, en broma

In many respects
En muchos puntos

In my opinion
A mi entender, a mi modo
de ver

In (at) odd moments
A ratos perdidos

In one fell swoop
De una tirada

In one's sleep
En sueños

In order
En regla

In order that
A fin de que, para que

In other words
En otros términos, es decir

In particular
En especial

In passing
De paso

In place of
En lugar de

In plain language
En buen romance

In plain view (of)
A la vista (de)

In poor taste
De mal gusto

In the presence of
A vista de

In progress
En curso, en marcha

In proof of
En señal de

In proportion to
A medida que

In safety
En salvo

In season
En sazón

In shirtsleeves
En mangas de camisa

In short
Al fin y al cabo, en fin, en
resumidas cuentas

Inside of
Dentro de

Insincerely
De dientes afuera

In small quantities
Al menudeo, al por menor, de poquito

In some way or other
De un modo u otro

In (at) spare moments
A ratos perdidos

In spite of
A despecho de, a pesar de

In spite of everything
A pesar de todo

In spite of that
Así y todo, con todo, con todos los obstáculos

In spite of the fact that
A pesar de que

Instantly
En un santiamén

Instead of
En lugar de, en vez de

In such a case
En tal caso

In such a way
De suerte que

Intend or mean to
Pensar en, tener la intención de

Interfere
Hacer mala obra

Interrupt
Cortar el hilo

Intervene
Meterse de por medio

In that way
De esa manera, de ese modo

In the act
En fragante

In the background
En lontananza

In the dark
A oscuras, a obscuras

In the dead of the night
En el sigilo (or silencio) de la noche, en las altas horas

In the dead of winter
En lo más crudo del invierno

In the direction of
Con rumbo a

In the distance
A lo lejos, en lontananza

In the evening
En la noche, por la noche

In the event of
En caso de

In the final analysis
A fin de cuentas

In the future
De ahora en adelante, en adelante, en lo futuro, en lo sucesivo

In the hands of
En poder de

In the latest fashion
A la moda

In the long run
A la larga

In the manner of
A guisa de

In the middle
Por la mitad

In the morning (afternoon, etc.)
Por la mañana (la tarde, etc.)

In the nick of time
En el momento preciso

In the night air
Al sereno

In the open
A campo raso

In the open air
Al aire libre, al raso

In the opposite way
Al revés

In the same way
Del mismo modo

In the style of
A (la) manera de

In the twinkling of an eye
En un abrir y cerrar de ojos, en un santiamén

In this vicinity
Por aquí cerca

In this way
De esta manera, de este modo

In this world
De tejas abajo

In those days
En aquel tiempo, en aquel entonces

In time
A tiempo

In transit
De paso, de tránsito

In truth
A la verdad, de veras

In turn
En rueda

In vain
En balde

In view of
En vista de que

In vogue
De moda

In writing
Por escrito

Irrelevant
Fuera de propósito, inaplicable al caso

I should say not!
¡De ninguna manera!

I should say so!
¡Ya lo creo!

Is that so?
¿De veras?, ¿de verdad?, ¡no diga!

It can't be helped
No hay remedio, no tiene remedio

It doesn't matter
No le hace, no tiene importancia

It is all over
Ha pasado, ha terminado, se ha acabado, ya se acabó

It is all right
Está bien

It is better...
Más vale...

It is clear
Ya se ve

It is forbidden
Se prohíbe

It is good (bad) weather
Hace buen (mal) clima

It is hopeless
No tiene remedio

It is necessary to
Hay que

It is not worth the trouble
No vale la pena

It is no wonder that
No es mucho que

It is obvious
Se conoce (que)

It is obvious that
Se ve que

It is rumored that
Se suena que

It is said
Se dice

It is time for
Es (la) hora de

It is time to go
Es (la) hora de partir

It is unnecessary (superfluous)
Está de más

It is yet to be done
Está por hacer

It makes no difference
Darle lo mismo, es lo de menos, lo mismo da, no le hace

It may be that
Puede ser que, tal vez sea que

It must
De rigor

It must be
Debe de ser

It must be true
Ha de ser verdad

It probably is
Debe de ser

It's a deal!
¡Trato hecho!

It's almost time
Falta poco

It's been a long time since (I played)
Hace mucho que no (juego)

It seems to be impossible
Parece mentira

It seems to me that
Me parece que

It serves me right
Bien me lo merezco

It's none of your (my) business
No es asunto suyo (mío)

It's not important
No tiene importancia

It's not opportune (not to the point)
No viene al caso, no viene al cuento

It's not worthwhile
No vale la pena

It's time to...
Ya es hora de...

It's too late now
Ya es tarde

It's true
Es cierto

It won't be long now
Ya mero, ya merito

J

Jack of all trades
Aprendiz de todo y oficial de nada

Jilt
Dar calabazas

Join (a club, etc.)
Ingresar en

Jokingly
De broma

Judge
Tener por

Jump
Dar un salto, dar saltos

Jump to conclusions
Hacer deducciones precipitadas

Just
Nada más

Just about to
Ya mero

Just as
Así como, según y como, según y conforme

Just as is
Así nada más

Just in case
Por lo que pueda tronar, por si acaso

Just plain
Así nada más

Just right
Al centavo, al pelo

Just yesterday
Ayer mismo

K

Keep (something)
Quedarse con (una cosa)

Keep accounts
Llevar cuentas

Keep good time (a watch)
Andar bien

Keep in bounds
Tener a raya

Keep one's feet
Tenerse en pie

Keep one's word
Cumplir (con) su palabra

Keep out!
¡Prohibido el paso!

Keep silent
Guardar silencio

Keep track of
Llevar la cuenta, llevar cuenta de

Keep up to date, informed, posted
Tener al corriente

Kick out
Dar de baja

Kill two birds with one stone
Matar dos pájaros de un tiro

Kneel
Ponerse de rodillas

Kneel down
Hincarse de rodillas

Knit the eyebrows
Fruncir las cejas

Knock down
Echar por tierra

Know absolutely nothing (about that)
No saber ni papa (de eso)

Know by heart
Saber de memoria

Know by sight
Conocer de vista

Know how to (sew, dance, etc.)
Saber (coser, bailar, etc.)

Knowingly
A sabiendas

L

Lack
Hacer falta

Lacking
A falta de

Lame excuse
Disculpa pobre

Large number of
Una infinidad de

Last month
El mes pasado

Last straw
La gota que derrama el vaso

Last week
La semana pasada

Last year
El año pasado

Late
A fines de

Later on
Más adelante

Latter
El más reciente

Laugh at
Reírse de

Laugh off
Tomar a risa

Laugh up one's sleeve
Reírse para sus adentros

Leap year
Año bisiesto

Learn by heart
Aprender de memoria

Least of it
Lo de menos

Leave
Dejar de la mano; salir de

Leave alone
Dejar en paz, dejar tranquilo

Leave (someone) in the lurch
Dejar (a uno) plantado, dejar en las astas del toro

Leave word
Dejar dicho

Leisure hours
Ratos perdidos

Lend
Dar prestado

Lengthwise
A lo largo (de)

Less and less
Cada vez menos

Less than
Menos de, menos que

Let be
Dejar en paz

Let loose
Soltar la rienda

Let on
Dejar saber

Let oneself be coaxed
Hacerse del rogar

Let's see (if)
A ver (si)

Like
A guisa de, a (la) manera de, a semejanza de, parecido a

Like always
Como siempre

Literally
Al pie de la letra

Little by little
Poco a poco

Little more
Y pico

Little pitchers have big ears
Hay moros en la costa

Live by stealing
Vivir de sus uñas

Live together
Hacer vida

Long ago
Hace mucho tiempo

Long time
Largos años

Look
Pues, mire

Look down on
Mirar por encima del hombro

Look for a needle in a haystack
Buscar una aguja en un pajar

Look for trouble
Buscarle tres (or cuatro) pies
al gato

Look out of the corner of one's
eye
Mirar con el rabo del ojo

Look towards
Dar a

Look well
Tener buena cara

Lose face
Perder prestigio

Lose one's head
Saltar las trancas

Lose one's mind
Perder el juicio, perder la razón

Lose patience
Saltar las trancas

Lose sight of
Perder de vista

Lose time
Perder el tiempo

Lots of
A mar de

Loud voice
En voz alta

Lump in the throat
Un nudo en la garganta

M

Madly
Con delirio

Mail (a letter)
Echar (una carta) al correo

Majority of
La mayoría (de), la mayor
parte (de)

Majority of the people
El común de las gentes

Make a deal
Hacer un trato

Make a dent
Hacer mella

Make a fool of
Poner en ridículo

Make a good showing
Hacer buen papel

Make a mistake
No dar pie con bola

Make an appointment
Dar una cita

Make a poor showing
Hacer mal papel

Make a ridiculous blunder
Hacer una plancha

Make arrangements
Hacer arreglos

Make eyes at
Hacer cocos

Make faces
Hacer gestos, hacer muecas

Make friends with
Hacerse amigo de

Make fun of
Burlarse de, hacer cuco a, hacer
burla de

Make good
Tener buen éxito

Make hay while the sun shines
Hacer su agosto

Make known
Dar a conocer

Make laugh
Hacer gracia

Make no difference
Dar lo mismo, no irle ni venirle
a uno

Make oneself understood
Hacerse entender

Make one's living
Ganarse la vida

Make trouble
Dar guerra

Make up
Inventar, imaginar

Make up (after a quarrel)
Hacer las paces

Make up for
Resarcirse de

Make use of
Valerse de

Make way for
Abrir paso para

Many years
Largos años

Match, to
Hacer juego

Mature
Hecho y derecho

Maybe
A lo mejor, tal vez

Mean (intend)
Querer decir

Meantime
Andarse el tiempo

Mean trick
Una mala pasada

Meanwhile
Entre tanto, mientras tanto

Measure
Tomar una providencia

Meddle
Meterse de por medio

Mediocre person
Media cuchara

Meet
Cruzarse con, encontrarse con,
tropezar con

Meet face to face
Enfrentarse con

Mind your own business!
¿Quién te mete, Juan Copete?

Minor (in age)
Menor de edad

Misconstrue or misinterpret
Tomar el rábano por las hojas

Miss
Echar de menos

Moment to moment
Por instante

More or less
Alrededor de

Moreover
Por lo demás

More than
Más de, más que

More than anyone
Más que nadie

More than enough
De sobra

More than ever
Más que nunca

More than once
Más de una vez, una y otra vez

Most of
La mayoría de, la mayor
parte de

Mourn
Estar de duelo

Move over
Hacerse a un lado

N

Namely
A saber

Naturally
Claro que sí

Near at hand
Al lado (de)

Nearly
Por poco

Neatly dressed
Bien arreglado(a)

Neither fish nor fowl
No ser ni chicha ni limonada

Neither this nor that
Ni esto ni aquello

Never mind
¡No importa!, ¡no se ocupe!

Nevertheless
No obstante, sin embargo

Next to
Al lado de, junto a

No...(smoking, eating, etc.)
Se prohibe...(fumar, comer, etc.)

Nobody else
Ningún otro

No comment
Sin comentarios

No kidding!
¡Palabrita de honor!

No longer
Ya no

No matter how much
Por mucho que

No matter what
Por ningún motivo, suceda lo que suceda

Nonsense
¡De dónde!; salida de pie de banco

No parking
Prohibido estacionarse

Nor I either
Ni yo tampoco

No sooner said than done
Dicho y hecho

Not by a long shot
Ni con mucho

Not by any means
Ni mucho menos

Not by far
Ni con mucho

Not equal to the burden
No poder con la carga

Not even
Ni siquiera

Nothing at all
Nada en absoluto

Nothing like that
Nada de eso

Nothing unusual
Nada de particular

Notice
Darse cuenta de, echar de ver, fijarse en

Not in a laughing mood
No estar de humor

Not much
Poca cosa

Not only...but also
No sólo...sino también

No trespassing
Prohibida la entrada, prohibido el paso, se prohibe entrar (pasar)

Not so often
No tan a menudo

Not to be a laughing matter
No ser cosa de juego

Not to bother about trifles
No pararse en pelillos

Not to feel well
Sentirse destemplado

Not to fit well
No caer bien

Not to get things right
No dar pie con bola

Not to know anything
No saber una (or ni) jota

Not to my knowledge
No que yo sepa

Not to open one's mouth
No despegar los labios

Not to realize
No darse cuenta

Not to say a word
No despegar los labios

Not to sleep a wink
Pasar la noche en claro (or en blanco)

Not to worry
Perder cuidado

Notwithstanding
No obstante

Not worth a red cent
No vale una cuartilla

Not worth a straw
No vale un pito

Not yet
Aún no, todavía no

Now
Al presente

Nowadays
Hoy (en) día

Now and then
De tarde en tarde, de vez en cuando

No way out
No quedar otro

No way out of it
No hay tu tía

Nowhere
A ninguna parte, en (or a) ninguna parte, por ningún lado

No wonder!
¡Con razón!

Now then
Ahora bien, pues bien

O

Object to
Levantar la contra

Obstruct (the way)
Dificultar (el paso), impedir (el paso)

Occasionally
De cuando en cuando, de vez en cuando

Of about
De unos

Of age
Mayor de edad

Of course
Claro que sí, ¿cómo no?, desde luego, por supuesto, seguro que sí, ya se ve

Of course not
Claro que no

Of last month
Del próximo pasado

Of little value or importance
De poca monta, lo de menos

Of one piece
De una pieza

Of one's own making or invention
De su (propia) cosecha

Often
A menudo

Of that kind
Por el estilo

Of the same sort
Del mismo modo

OK (to approve)
Dar el visto bueno

Omit
Pasar por alto

On (upon)
Encima de

On account of
A causa de, con motivo de, por motivo

On a large scale
En grande

On all fours
A gatas

On all sides
Para todos lados

On an average
Por término medio

On approval
A vistas

On behalf of
De parte de, en pro de

Once again
De nuevo

Once and for all
De una vez, de una vez por todas

Once in a blue moon
Allá a las quinientas, como visita de obispo, de tarde en tarde

Once in a while
Una que otra vez

Once upon a time
Había una vez, érase que se era, érase una vez, y va de cuento

One at a time
De uno en uno, uno a la vez

One by one
Uno por uno

On edge
De canto

One must
Hay que

On end
De punta

One of these (fine) days
Un día de estos

One or the other
El uno o el otro, uno u otro

One way
De un solo sentido

One week from today
De hoy en ocho días

On foot
A pie

Only
Nada más, no más que

Only yesterday
Ayer mismo

On one's back
De espaldas

On one's knees
De rodillas

On purpose
A propósito, de propósito

On returning
A la vuelta de

On the contrary
Al contrario, por el contrario

On the dot
En punto

On the fence
Entre azul y buenas noches

On the following day
Al día siguiente, al otro día

On the inside
Por dentro

On the lookout for
Estar a la mira de

On the occasion of
Con motivo de

On the other hand
En cambio, por otra parte, por otro lado

On the other side of
Al otro lado de

On the outside
Por fuera

On the rebound
De rebote

On the road to
Camino de

On the run
A la carrera

On the sly
A escondidas, a hurto

On the spur of the moment
De buenas a primeras

On the way
De camino, de tránsito, (estar) en camino

On time
A buena hora, a tiempo

On tiptoes
De puntillas, de puntas

On top of
Por encima de

On vacation
De vacaciones

On watch
En vela

Openly
A boca llena, a las claras, al descubierto, sin rebozo

Oppose
Llevar la contra, ponerse en contra de, salir al encuentro de

Opposed to
En contra de

Ordinary
De ordinario

Or else
No sea que, o si no, si no

Others
Los (las) demás

Otherwise
De lo contrario, de otro modo, donde no, porque si no

Out of breath
Con la lengua de corbata, con la lengua de pechera

Out of danger
En salvo

Out of date
Pasado de moda

Out of sorts
No estar de humor

Out of spite
Por despecho

Out of style
Pasado de moda

Out of the country
En el extranjero

Out of the ordinary
Fuera de lo corriente

Over and over again
Repetidas veces, una y otra vez

Over a period of (time)
Desde hace

Over here
Por acá, por aquí

Overlook
Pasar por alto

Overnight
De la noche a la mañana

Overstep the bounds
Pasar de la raya

Over there
Por ahí, por allá

Overthrow someone
Dar en tierra con alguien

P

Pacify
Poner en razón

Pack
Hacer las maletas

Partly
En parte

Pass by
Dar una pasada por

Passing through
De tránsito

Pay attention (to)
Dar atención, fijarse en, hacer caso (a or de), prestar atención

Pay a visit
Hacer una visita

Pay by cash
Pagar al contado

Payday
Día de raya

Peerless
Sin par

Perchance
Por ventura

Per day
Al día

Perhaps
A lo mejor, tal vez

Pesky as a fly
Más pesado que una mosca

Pick a fight or quarrel with
Meterse con

Place hope in someone
Esperar en alguien

Place in safety
Poner a buen recaudo

Place one's hope in
Cifrar la esperanza en

Plain
A secas

Plain and simple truth
La verdad clara y desnuda

Plain fool
Tonto de capirote

Plainly
A boca llena

Play a bad (or mean) trick (on someone)
Hacer una mala jugada, hacer una perrada, jugarle una mala partida

Play a part
Desempeñar un papel

Play a role
Hacer el (or un) papel

Play a trick
Pegar un chasco

Play by ear
Tocar de oído, tocar por
fantasía

Play dumb
Hacerse el tonto

Play fair
Jugar limpio

Play hooky
Hacer pinta, pintar venado

Play on words
Juego de palabras

Play second fiddle
Ser plato de segunda mesa

Play up to (someone)
Dar coba a (alguien)

Please (make contented)
Caer bien, caer en gracia,
dar gusto

Pledge
Empeñar la palabra

Point blank
A quema ropa, a quemarropa

Poor memory
Memoria de gallo

Pose as
Dárselas de

Praise (to the skies)
Poner en el cielo, poner por
las nubes

Presence of mind
Presencia de ánimo

Present!
¡A sus órdenes!

Pretend
Dar a entender, dejar saber

Pretend not to hear
Hacerse el sordo

Pretend not to notice
Hacerse el desentendido

Pretend to be dead
Hacerse muerto

Prick up one's ears
Aguzar las orejas (or los oídos)

Pride
Amor propio

Proud
De copete

Provided
Siempre y cuando

Provided that
Con tal (de) que, dado el caso
que, siempre que

Publicly
A las claras

Pull
Tirar de

Pull one's leg
Tomarle el pelo

Pull over to the right
Desviarse hacia la derecha,
hacerse a la derecha

Pun
Juego de palabras

Pursue
Dar caza

Put into practice
Poner por obra

Put in writing
Hacer por escrito

Put on airs
Darse aires a, darse farol, darse
tono, subirse de tono

**Put oneself in a ridiculous
situation**
Tirarse una plancha

Put one's foot in one's mouth
Meter la pata

Put the cart before the horse
Tomar el rábano por las hojas

Q

Quarrel with
Meterse con

Question
Poner en duda

Quickly
Al trote, de prisa, de un salto,
en un salto

R

Rabble
Gente de baja estofa

Rack one's brain
Devanarse los sesos, quebrarse
uno la cabeza, romperse los
cascos

Rain cats and dogs
Llover a cántaros

Rain or shine
Que llueva o no

Raise a rumpus
Dar batería

Rapidly
A escape

Rather
Más bien, mejor dicho

Rather late
Algo tarde

Rather than
Antes que, más bien que

Rattle off
Repetir de carretilla

Reach
Ponerse en

Realize (that)
Caer en la cuenta, darse cuenta
de (que)

Really
De veras, en efecto, en verdad

Real truth, the
La mera verdad

Reckon with
Contar con

Reflect on (think about)
Parar mientes en

Regardless of
Sin hacer caso de

Regards to
Recuerdos a

Regret
Pesarle a uno

Regret very much
Sentir en el alma

Reject
Dar calabazas

Reliable
Digno de confianza

Reluctantly
De mal grado

Rely on
Confiar en, contar con

Remember (or recollect)
Hacer memoria

Remorse
Gusano de la conciencia

Repeatedly
Sobradas veces

Repeat mechanically
Repetir de carretilla

Reproach
Dar en cara, echar en cara

Resemble
Salir a

Resist stubbornly
Hacerse duro, ponerse duro

Rest of them, the
Los (las) demás

Restrain
Tirar las riendas

Return for
Volver por

Right away
En el acto

Right here
Aquí mismo

Right now
Ahora mismo, en seguida, más
ahorita

Right side out
Al derecho

Ripe
En sazón

Rise
Ponerse en pie

Risk
Correr riesgo, poner al tablero

Round about
A la redonda, en redondo

Ruin
Dar al traste con, dar al través
con, echar(se) a perder

Rumor
De oídos

Run away
Echar(se) a correr

S

Safe
A salvo

Safe against
A prueba de

Safe and sound
Sano y salvo

Same as, the
El (or lo) mismo que, igual que

Satisfy a need or desire
Matar el gusano

Save one's skin
Salvar el pellejo

Save time
Ganar tiempo

Say a bad word
Echar (or saltar) un terno

Say goodbye to
Despedirse de

Say to oneself
Decir para sí

Scarcely
A duras penas

Scowl
Fruncir el ceño

Secondhand
De segunda mano, de uso

Secretly
A puerta cerrada, en secreto

Seem like
Sonar a

See to it that
Ver de, ver que

Seize
Echar la zarpa, echar mano, hacer presa

Seldom
Por rareza, rara vez, raras veces

Self-esteem
Amor propio

Separately
De por sí, por separado

Serenity
Presencia de ánimo

Seriously
En serio

Serve
Servir de

Serve as
Oficiar de

Set forward (e.g., a clock)
Poner adelantado

Set in motion
Poner en juego

Set out (on a trip, etc.)
Ponerse en camino

Set the table
Poner la mesa

Set up housekeeping
Poner casa

Several times
Varias veces

Shake hands (with)
Dar la mano, darse la mano, estrechar la mano (a)

Sharp (on time)
En punto

Shortly
En breve

Shortly after
A poco

Shortly thereafter
Poco después de

Show off
Darse farol, hacer teatro

Shred
Hacer trizas

Shrug one's shoulders
Encogerse de hombros

Shut tight
A piedra y lodo

Sideways
De lado, de soslayo

Signify
Querer decir

Silly remark
Salida de pie de banco

Similar
Algo por el estilo, parecido a

Simply
A secas

Since
Como que, como quiera que, desde que, en vista de que, pues que, puesto que, supuesto que, ya que

Since then
Desde entonces

Sky high
Por las nubes

Slam the door
Dar un portazo

Slanting
Al soslayo, de soslayo

Slap
Mandar una bofetada

Sleep it off
Dormir la mona

Sleep on it
Consultar con la almohada

Sleep soundly
Dormir a pierna suelta

Slice
Hacer rajas

Slip
Darse un resbalón

Slowly
A la larga

Smell like
Oler a

Snap one's fingers
Castañetear con los dedos, tronar los dedos

So
Así que

So far
Hasta aquí, hasta ahí

Soft (or smooth) as silk
Como una seda

Softsoap or flatter (someone)
Dar coba a, dar jabón a

Somebody else
Algún otro

Someday
Algún día

Somehow
De algún modo, de alguna manera, de un modo u otro

Something indefinable
Un no sé qué

Something is wrong
Hay moros en la costa

Something of the sort
Algo por el estilo

Sometime
Algún día, algún tiempo, alguna vez

Sometimes
Algunas veces, de cuando en cuando

Somewhat
Un tanto

Somewhere
En alguna parte

Somewhere else
En alguna otra parte

So much the better
Tanto mejor

So much the worse
Tanto peor

Soon after
A raíz de, al (or a) poco rato

Sooner or later
A la corta o a la larga, tarde o temprano

Sooner the better, the
Antes hoy que mañana

So-so
Así así, tal cual

So that
A fin de que, así es que, así que, con tal (de) que, de manera que, de modo que, de suerte que

So then
Así pues

Sound like
Sonar a

So what?
¡A mí qué!, ¿de modo que?, ¿pues qué?, ¿y qué?

Spare (extra)
De repuesto

Spare no expense
Echar la casa por la ventana

Speak frankly
Hablar al alma, no tener pelillos en la lengua

Speaking! (in answering a telephone)
Al habla

Speak loudly
Hablar alto, hablar en voz alta

Speak to the point
Hablar al caso

Speedily
A todo trapo

Spicy story
Un cuento alegre

Split hairs
Pararse en pelillos

Spoil
Echar(se) a perder

Stand a chance
Tener probabilidad

Standing
De pie

Stand someone up
Dejar a uno plantado

Stand still
Estarse parado

Stark raving mad
Loco de remate

Start to
Ponerse a, ponerse en marcha, romper a

Start a conversation
Entablar una conversación

Start a fire
Prender el fuego

Start out
Ponerse en marcha

Stay in
Quedarse en la casa

Stay in bed
Guardar (la) cama

Stealthily
A hurto

Step aside
Hacerse a un lado

Step hard upon
Dar un pisotón

Stomp or step on
Dar una pisada

Stop (smoking, etc.)
Dejar de (fumar, etc.)

Stop beating around the bush
Dejarse de cuentos, dejarse de rodeos

Stop over at
Hacer escala en

Stop short (or suddenly)
Parar en seco

Stop the excuses
Dejarse de rodeos

Straw that broke the camel's back
La gota que derrama el vaso

Strike the hour
Dar la hora

Study hard
Quemarse las pestañas (or las cejas)

Stumble
Dar un traspié, darse un tropezón

Stylish
De buen tono, de moda

Succeed
Tener éxito

Such as
Tal como, tales como, tal cual

Such as that
Por el estilo

Suddenly
De golpe, de pronto, de repente, de súbito

Suit
Venir bien

Suit perfectly
Venir a (or al) pelo

Summing up
En resumen

Superfluous
Está de más

Supposing
Dado caso, supuesto que

Sure enough
Dicho y hecho

Surprise
Pegar un chasco

Swarm of people
Un hervidero de gente, un remolino de gente

Swear (curse)
Echar un terno, soltar un terno

Sweat blood
Sudar la gota gorda

Sweat profusely
Sudar la gota gorda

Swell with pride
Estar (or ponerse) ancho

Swiftly
A rienda suelta

Swiftness of time
Corrida del tiempo

Swindle
Dar gato por liebre

T

Take (something)
Quedarse con (una cosa)

Take a chance
Correr riesgo

Take a drink
Echar un trago

Take advantage of the situation
Aprovechar la ocasión

Take after (someone)
Salir a

Take a jump
Pegar un salto

Take a long time (in doing something)
Tardar en (hacer algo)

Take a long weekend
Hacer puente

Take an afternoon nap
Dormir la siesta

Take a nap
Descabezar el sueño, echar un sueño, echar una siesta

Take a stand against
Salir al encuentro de

Take a step
Dar un paso, tomar una providencia

Take a stroll
Dar una vuelta

Take a walk
Pasear a pie

Take a walk or ride
Dar un paseo

Take care
Tener cuidado (con)

Take care of
Preocuparse de

Take care of someone
Mirar por alguien

Take charge (of)
Encargarse (de), hacerse cargo (de)

Take exercise
Hacer ejercicios

Take for a...
Tener por...

Take for granted
Dar por descontado, dar por hecho, dar por sabido (or sentado or supuesto), tomar por cierto

Take into account
Hacer caso a (or de), tener en cuenta, tomar en cuenta

Take it easy
Tomarlo con calma

Take lightly
Tomar a risa

Take pity on
Tener lástima de

Take place
Tener lugar

Take root
Echar raíces

Take seriously
Tomar a pecho(s)

Take the lead
Tomar la delantera

Take time off
Tomar tiempo libre

Take to heart
Tomar a (or en) pecho(s), tomar en serio

Take undue liberties
Pasar de la raya

Talk of the town
La comidilla de la vecindad

Talk too much
Hablar por los codos

Talk to oneself
Hablar para sus adentros

Tear into strips
Hacer rajas

Tear to pieces
Hacer garras, hacer trizas

Tease
Tomarle el pelo

Thank (or give thanks)
Dar las gracias

That can't be helped
Eso no tiene quite

That depends
Según y conforme, según y como

That is
A saber

That is a horse of a different color
Eso es harina de otro costal

That is even worse
Peor que peor

That is it
Eso es

That is the limit!
¡Eso es el colmo!

That is to say
Es decir, o sea que

That is urgent
Eso corre prisa

That is why
Por algo, por esa razón

That long
Así de largo

That's not the point (or the question)
No se trata de eso

That's right
Eso es

That's the last straw!
¡No faltaba más!

That's the least of the trouble
Es lo de menos

That's the point
¡Ahí está el detalle!

That was (is) true
Eso sí

That way
Por allí

That which
Lo que

The coast is not clear
Hay moros en la costa

The fact is
El caso es

The more...the less
Mientras más...mientras menos

Then
A la sazón

The ones
Los que

Thereafter
Después de eso

There are no two ways about it
No hay que darle vueltas, no tiene vuelta de hoja

Therefore
Así pues, así que, por (or en) consecuencia de, por consiguiente, por ende, por eso, por lo cual, por lo tanto

There is more than meets the eye
Hay gato encerrado

There is no doubt (that)
No cabe duda (que)

There is no way around it
No hay que darle vueltas

There is the heart of the matter!
¡Allí está el toque!

There's no hurry
No hay prisa

There's no need to
No hay para que

There's no other way but to...
No hay más remedio que...

There's nothing to do except...
No hay más remedio que...

The same as
Así como, el (or lo) mismo que

They say
Se dice

Think (be of the opinion)
Tener para sí

Think about
Pensar en

Think not
Creer que no

Think so
Creer que sí

This side of
Más acá de

This way
Por acá, por aquí

This will do
Así está bien

Thoroughly
Por completo

Those which (or those who)
Los (or las) que

Thousand thanks, a
Mil gracias

Throng (of people)
Remolino de gente

Through or throughout
A través de, al través de, de parte a parte, por conducto de, por donde

Through thick and thin
Por toda suerte de penalidades

Throw a party
Dar una fiesta

Throw a stone
Mandar una pedrada

Tilted
De lado

Tip (give a gratuity)
Dar propina

Tip one's hat
Tocarse el sombrero

To and fro
De aquí para allá

To boot
De pilón

Together
A la vez

Tomorrow afternoon
Mañana por la tarde

Tomorrow is another day
Mañana Dios dirá

Tomorrow morning
Mañana por la mañana, mañana temprano

Tomorrow night
Mañana por la noche

To myself
Para mis adentros

Tonight
A la noche, por la noche

Too bad!
¡Qué lástima!

To oneself
Consigo mismo

To one's heart's content
A pedir de boca

To the letter (just right)
Al centavo, al pie de la letra

To the limit
Hasta más no poder

To the point
A secas, de perlas

To the utmost
A más no poder, de lo lindo, hasta más no poder

Touch a sore spot
Tocar en lo vivo

Towards (a period of time)
A principios de

Towards the end of (a period of time)
A fines de

Track down
Dar caza

Train was x minutes late
El tren llegó con x minutos de retraso

Treacherously
A traición

Treat (deal with)
Tratar de

Trip (or stumble)
Dar un traspié, darse un tropezón

Truly or truthfully
A la verdad, de veras, de verdad, en verdad

Trust
Confiar en

Trustworthy
Digno de confianza

Try to (attempt)
Tratar de, ver de, ver que

Turn (around)
Dar(se) la vuelta

Turn a deaf ear
Hacerse el sordo

Turn one's back (on)
Dar las espaldas (a), voltear la espalda

Turn out to be
Venir a parar, venir a ser

Turn the corner
Doblar a la esquina

Turn the page
Darle vuelta a la hoja

Two by two
De dos en dos

Two-faced
De dos caras

Two of a kind
Tal para cual

Two-way
De dos sentidos

Two weeks from today
De hoy en quince días

U

Unanimously
A una vez

Unavoidable
Sin remedio

Uncovered
En descubierto

Undecided
Entre azul y buenas noches

Under
Debajo de

Undercover
A escondidas

Understand that...
Tener entendido que...

Undertake
Poner por obra

Under the table (underhanded)
Bajo cuerda

Unequaled
Sin igual

Unexpectedly
A deshora(s), de buenas a primeras, de improviso, el día menos pensado

Unfortunately
Por desgracia

Unharmed
A salvo

Unless
A menos que, a no ser que, como no

Unlucky
De mala suerte

Unnecessary
De sobra

Unnoticed
Sin sentir

Unpaid
En descubierto

Unreserved
Sin reserva

Until
Hasta que

Unusual
Fuera de lo corriente

Unwillingly
A la mala, de mal grado, de mala gana, sin querer

Upon
Encima de

Upon my honor
Sobre mi palabra

Ups and downs
Subidas y bajadas

Upside down
Patas arriba

Up to a point
Hasta cierto punto

Up to date
A la moda, hasta la fecha

Up to now
Hasta aquí, hasta ahí, hasta la fecha

Up to the top
Hasta el tope

Usual
De ordinario

Usually
Por lo general, por lo regular, por regla general

V

Vanish
Perderse de vista

Vanity
Amor propio

Various times
Repetidas veces

Very bad luck
Suerte negra

Very close
A quema ropa, a quemarropa

Very early in the morning
Muy de mañana

Very far away
En el quinto infierno

Very much
Con (or en or por) extremo, de lo lindo

Very often
Con mucha frecuencia, muy a menudo

Very probably
A buen seguro

Very soon
Poco rato, ya mero

Very thought of, the
La mera idea de

Violently
A rienda suelta

Visibly
A ojos vistas

Vouch for
Dar fe de, salir fiador de

W

Wait in line
Hacer cola

Wait table
Servir la mesa

Wait the whole blessed day
Esperar todo el santo día

Walk
Ir a pie

Walk by
Dar una pasada por

Walk the streets
Medir las calles

Wanted
Se solicita

Want to
Tener deseos de

Wash one's hands of
Lavarse las manos de

Watch out (for)
Tener cuidado (con)

Weakness (or weak side)
Lado flaco, punto flaco

Wear
Llevar puesto, traer puesto

Wear oneself out
Hacerse uno rajas

Weather the storm
Aguantar el chubasco

Week before last
La semana antepasada

Weekday(s)
Día(s) de semana, día de trabajo, día hábil

Weekend
El fin de semana

Welcome
Dar la bienvenida

Well and good
Santo y bueno

Well done!
¡Así se hace!

Well-done (well-cooked)
Bien asado, bien cocido

Well-groomed
Bien peinado

Well now
Ahora bien

Well then
Pues bien

Well worth it
Digno de

What a mess!
¡Qué batingue!

What an atrocity!
¡Qué barbaridad!

What a pleasure!
¡Qué gusto!

What does it mean?
¿Qué quiere decir?, ¿qué
significa?

What do you think of it?
¿Qué le parece?

What for?
¿Para qué?

What happened?
¿Qué pasó?

What has been said
Lo expuesto

What if...?
¿Y si...?

What is it?
¿Qué haces?

What is it about?
¿De qué se trata?

What is it good for?
¿Para qué sirve?

What is more
Más aún

What is the date?
¿A cuánto(s) estamos?

What is the point of that?
¿A qué viene eso?

What is the use of it?
¿Qué ventaja tiene?

What nonsense!
¡Qué barbaridad!

What's eating you?
¿Qué mosca te ha picado?

What's it to you?
¿Quién te mete, Juan Copete?

What's going on?
¿Qué pasa?

What's new?
¿Qué hay de nuevo?

What's so bad about that?
¿Qué hay de malo con eso?

What's that to me?
¿A mí qué?

What's the difference?
¡Qué más da!

What's the matter with you?
¿Qué le (or te) pasa?

What's up?
¿Qué hubo?, ¿qué pasa?

What's wrong with...?
¿Qué tiene de malo...?

What's wrong with that?
¿Qué hay de malo con eso?

What time is it?
¿Qué hora es?, ¿qué horas son?

When all is said and done
A la postre

Whenever
Cuando quiera, siempre que,
todas las veces (que)

When least expected
El día menos pensado

Whereas
Visto que

Wherever
Adondequiera que,
dondequiera que, por
dondequiera que

Whether one likes it or not
Por las buenas o por las malas

Whether you wish or not
Quieras que no, quiera o no

While
En tanto que

While away the time
Pasar el rato

Whisper
Hablar en secreto

Whispering
En voz baja

Whole truth, the
La verdad clara y desnuda

Wholly
Del todo

Wide open
De par en par

Willingly
A la buena, con mucho gusto,
de buena gana, de buen grado,
de (buena) voluntad

Win
Salir ganando

With
Junto con

**With both feet together (or on
the ground)**
A pie(s) juntillas

With certainty
A (or de) ciencia cierta, a punto
fijo

With great difficulty
A duras penas

Within
Dentro de

Within a few years
A la vuelta de los años

Within a week
Dentro de una semana

Within speaking distance
Al habla

Within view
A vista de

With no confidence
De mala fe

Without
Sin que

Without a plan
A la buena de Dios

Without equal
Sin par

Without fail
Sin falta

Without help
Sin remedio

Without interruption
De seguida

Without question
Sin disputa

Without realizing
Sin sentir

Without remedy
De remate, sin recurso

Without rhyme or reason
Sin qué ni para qué, sin ton
ni son

Without risk
Sobre seguro

Without sleep
En vela

Without stopping
De corrida, de hilo

Without the knowledge of
A escondidas de

Without warning
A quema ropa, a quemarropa

With pleasure
De (buena) voluntad

With regard to
Acerca de, con respecto a, en
cuanto a, respecto a

With the aim of
Con el propósito de

With the idea of
Con motivo de

With tongue hanging out
Con la lengua de corbata, con
la lengua de pechera

With your permission
Con permiso

Wonderfully
De lo lindo

Wonderfully well
A las mil maravillas

Word of honor!
¡Palabrita de honor!

Workday
Día hábil

Work hard
Dar batería, sudar la gota
gorda

Work in vain
Azotar el aire

Work well
Andar bien

Worry about
Preocuparse por

Worry about nothing
Ahogarse en poca agua

Worse than
Peor que

Worth seeing
Ser de ver, ser para ver

Wrinkle one's brow
Fruncir el entrecejo

Wrong side out
Al revés

Y

Year before last
Año antepasado

Years ago
Hace años

Yes, of course
Ya lo creo

Yesterday afternoon
Ayer por la tarde

You don't say!
¡No diga!

You're welcome
De nada, no hay de que

SPANISH-ENGLISH
ESPAÑOL-INGLÉS

REMARKS

For ease of reference, the reader should note the following:

- Within each entry, the word or group of words corresponding to each of the meanings of the Spanish word constitutes a separate numbered subentry.

- Examples of usage, phrases, and idioms are included in each entry immediately following the meaning of the word to which they correspond.

- Examples of usage, phrases, and idioms are given in a fixed sequence within each item of the entry: word groups not containing a verb; expressions containing a verb; phrases or locutions (adverbial, prepositional, etc.).

- Expressions, phrases, etc. that do not directly correspond to a specific meaning of the word are numbered separately within the entry.

- Words given as equivalents of the main entry are clarified further, when necessary, by synonyms and definitions enclosed in brackets.

- Abbreviations indicate meaning and usage in specific subject areas and geographical regions, as well as in grammar. See "Abbreviations Used in This Dictionary."

- The letters *ch* and *ll*, which are distinct letters in the Spanish alphabet, are listed as such.

In addition to the explanations of grammar within individual entries, certain points of grammar have been explained in greater detail in an overview preceding the lexicon. These summaries treat specific instances of Spanish grammar that have proven most troublesome to English-speaking readers (e.g., direct and indirect object pronouns, the subjunctive). (An asterisk in one of the grammar notes signals a reference to another note on a related subject.)

- An asterisk in the body of an entry indicates that the word it precedes is used only in the Americas.

In order to assist the reader, reference sections on a variety of topics are included in this dictionary. Idioms and expressions—both Spanish-to-English and English-to-Spanish—can be found in the center of the dictionary.

The appendices include:

- False Cognates and "Part-Time" Cognates
- Monetary Units / Unidades monetarias
- Weights and Measures / Pesas y medidas
- Numbers / Numerales
- Temperature / La temperatura
- Abreviaturas más usadas en inglés
- Abbreviations Most Commonly Used in Spanish
- Business Correspondence in Spanish / La carta comercial en español
- Maps / Mapas

ABBREVIATIONS USED IN THIS DICTIONARY

abs.	absolute	GEOG.	geography
ACC.	accounting	GEOL.	geology
adj.	adjective	GEOM.	geometry
adv.	adverb	GER.	Gerund
AER.	aeronautics	GRAM.	grammar
AGR.	agriculture	GYM.	gymnastics
ALG.	algebra		
Am.	Spanish America	HIST.	history
ANAT.	anatomy		
ARCH.	architecture		
ARCHEOL.	archeology	ICHTH.	ichthyology
Arg.	Argentina	*imper.*	imperative
ARITH.	arithmetic	imperf.	imperfect
art.	article	*impers.*	impersonal verb
ARTILL.	artillery	*indef.*	indefinite
ASTR.	astronomy	INDIC.	Indicative
aug.	augmentative	IND.	industry
AUTO.	automobile	INF.	Infinitive
aux.	auxiliary verb	INSUR.	insurance
		interj.	interjection
BACT.	bacteriology	*interrog.*	interrogative
BIBL.	Bible; Biblical	*intr.*	intransitive verb
BILL.	billiards	iron.	ironic
BIOCHEM.	biochemistry	*irr., irreg.*	irregular
BIOL.	biology		
BOOKBIND.	bookbinding	JEWEL.	jewelry
BOOKKEEP.	bookkeeping		
BOT.	botany	Lat.	Latin
BULL.	bullfighting	LIT.	literature
		LITURG.	liturgy
CARP.	carpentry	LOG.	logic
CHEM.	chemistry		
coll.	colloquial	*m.*	masculine; masculine noun
collect.	collectively	MACH.	machinery
COM.	commerce	MATH.	mathematics
comp.	comparative	MECH.	mechanics
COND.	Conditional	MED.	medicine
conj.	conjunction	METAL.	metallurgy
CONJUG.	conjugation	Mex.	Mexico
COOK.	cooking	MIL.	military
cop.	copulative verb	MIN.	mining
		MINER.	mineralogy
def.	defective; definite	MUS.	music
dim.	diminutive	MYTH.	mythology
ECCL.	ecclesiastic	*n.*	noun; masculine and feminine noun
ELEC.	electricity		
ENG.	engineering	NAUT.	nautical
ENT.	entomology	NAV.	naval; navy
exclam.	exclamatory	*neut.*	neuter
		not cap.	not capitalized
f.	feminine; feminine noun		
F. ARTS.	fine arts	obs.	obsolete
FENC.	fencing	OPT.	optics
fig.	figuratively	ORN.	ornithology
FISH.	fishing		
Fut.	Future		

pers., pers.	person; personal		scorn.	scornful
PHIL.	philosophy		SUBJ.	Subjunctive
PHOT.	photography		*superl.*	superlative
PHYS.	physics		SURG.	surgery
pl.	plural		SURV.	surveying
POET.	poetry			
POL.	politics		TELEV.	television
poss.	possessive		THEAT.	theater
p. p.	past participle		THEOL.	theology
prep.	preposition		TOP.	topography
Pres.	Present		*tr.*	transitive verb
pres. p.	present participle			
Pret.	preterit			
PRINT.	printing		usu.	usually
pr. n.	proper noun			
pron.	pronoun		V.	Vide; See
			vul.	vulgar
RADIO.	radio; broadcasting			
ref.	reflexive verb		WEAV.	weaving
reg.	regular			
REL.	religion			
RLY.	railway; railroad		ZOOL.	zoology

KEY TO PRONUNCIATION IN SPANISH

VOWELS

Letter	Approximate sound
a	Like *a* in English *far, father,* e.g., **casa, mano.**
e	When stressed, like *a* in English *pay,* e.g., **dedo, cerca.** When unstressed, it has a shorter sound like in English *bet, net,* e.g., **estado, decidir.**
i	Like *i* in English *machine* or *ee* in *feet,* e.g., **fin, salí.**
o	Like *o* in English *obey,* e.g., **mona, poner.**
u	Like *u* in English *rule* or *oo* in *boot,* e.g., **atún, luna.** It is silent in **gue** and **gui,** e.g., **guerra, guisado.** If it carries a diaeresis (ü), it is pronounced (see Diphthongs), e.g., **bilingüe, bilingüismo.** It is also silent in **que** and **qui,** e.g., **querer, quinto.**
y	When used as a vowel, it sounds like the Spanish **i,** e.g., **y, rey.**

DIPHTHONGS

Diphthong	Approximate sound
ai, ay	Like *i* in English *light,* e.g., **caigo, hay.**
au	Like *ou* in English *sound,* e.g., **cauto, paular.**
ei, ey	Like *ey* in English *they* or *a* in *ale,* e.g., **reina, ley.**
eu	Like the *a* in English *pay* combined with the sound of *ew* in English *knew,* e.g., **deuda, feudal.**
oi, oy	Like *oy* in English *toy,* e.g., **oiga, soy.**
ia, ya	Like *ya* in English *yarn,* e.g., **rabia, raya.**
ua	Like *wa* in English *wand,* e.g., **cuatro, cual.**
ie, ye	Like *ye* in English *yet,* e.g., **bien, yeso.**
ue	Like *wa* in English *wake,* e.g., **buena, fue, bilingüe.**
io, yo	Like *yo* in English *yoke,* without the following sound of *w* in this word, e.g., **región, yodo.**
uo	Like *uo* in English *quote,* e.g., **cuota, oblicuo.**
iu, yu	Like *yu* in English *Yule,* e.g., **ciudad, triunfo, yunta.**
ui	Like *wee* in English *week,* e.g., **ruido, bilingüismo.**

TRIPHTHONGS

Triphthong	Approximate sound
iai	Like *ya* in English *yard* combined with the *i* in *fight,* e.g., **estudiáis.**
iei	Like the English word *yea,* e.g., **estudiéis.**
uai, uay	Like *wi* in English *wide,* e.g., **averiguáis, guay.**
uei, uey	Like *wei* in English *weigh,* e.g., **amortigüéis, buey.**

CONSONANTS

Letter	Approximate sound
b	Generally like the English *b* in *boat, bring, obsolete,* when it is at the beginning of a word or preceded by *m,* e.g., **baile, bomba.** Between two vowels and when followed by *l* or *r,* it has a softer sound, almost like the English *v* but formed by pressing both lips together, e.g., **acaba, haber, cable.**
c	Before *a, o, u,* or a consonant, it sounds like the English *c* in *coal,* e.g., **casa, saco, cuba, acto.** Before *e* or *i,* it is pronounced like the English *s* in *six* in American Spanish and like the English *th* in *thin* in Castillian Spanish, e.g., **cerdo, cine.** If a word contains two *c*s, the first is pronounced like *c* in *coal,* and the second like *s* or *th* accordingly, e.g., **acción.**
ch	Like *ch* in English *cheese* or *such,* e.g., **chato, mucho.**
d	Generally like *d* in English *dog* or *th* in English *this,* e.g., **dedo, digo.** When ending a syllable, it is pronounced like the English *th,* e.g., **usted, libertad.**
f	Like *f* in English *fine, life,* e.g., **final.**
g	Before *a, o,* and *u;* the groups *ue* and *ui;* or a consonant, it sounds like *g* in English *gain,* e.g., **gato, gorra, aguja, guerra, guitar, digno.** Before *e* or *i,* like a strongly aspirated English *h,* e.g., **general, región.**
h	Always silent, e.g., **hoyo, historia.**
j	Like *h* in English *hat,* e.g., **joven, reja.**
k	Like *c* in English *coal,* e.g., **kilo.** It is found only in words of foreign origin.
l	Like *l* in English *lion,* e.g., **libro, límite.**
ll	In some parts of Spain and Spanish America, like the English *y* in *yet;* generally in Castillian Spanish, like the *lli* in English *million;* e.g., **castillo, silla.**
m	Like *m* in English *map,* e.g., **moneda, tomo.**
n	Like *n* in English *nine,* e.g., **nuevo, canto, determinación.**
ñ	Like *ni* in English *onion* or *ny* in English *canyon,* e.g., **cañón, paño.**
p	Like *p* in English *parent,* e.g., **pipa, pollo.**
q	Like *c* in English *coal.* This letter is only used in the combinations *que* and *qui* in which the *u* is silent, e.g., **queso, aquí.**
r	At the beginning of a word and when preceded by *l, n,* or *s,* it is strongly trilled, e.g., **roca, alrota, Enrique, desrabar.** In all other positions, it is pronounced with a single tap of the tongue, e.g., **era, padre.**
rr	Strongly trilled, e.g., **carro, arriba.**
s	Like *s* in English *so,* e.g., **cosa, das.**
t	Like *t* in English *tip* but generally softer, e.g., **toma, carta.**
v	Like *v* in English *mauve,* but in many parts of Spain and the Americas, like the Spanish **b,** e.g., **variar, mover.**
x	Generally like *x* in English *expand,* e.g., **examen.** Before a consonant, it is sometimes pronounced like *s* in English *so,* e.g., **excepción, extensión.** In the word **México,** and in other place names of that country, it is pronounced like the Spanish **j.**
y	When used as a consonant between vowels or at the beginning of a word, like the *y* in English *yet,* e.g., **yate, yeso, hoyo.**
z	Like Spanish **c** when it precedes *e* or *i,* e.g., **zapato, cazo, azul.**

ACCENTUATION / ACENTUACIÓN

Rules of accentuation

All words in Spanish (except adverbs ending in -mente) only have one stressed syllable. The stressed syllable is sometimes indicated by a written accent.

In words with no written accent, the ending of the word determines the placement of stress.

- Words that end in a consonant (except *n* or *s*) stress the last syllable: pared, añil, capaz.
  —The final y as part of a diphthong is treated as a consonant: carey, Paraguay.

- Words that end in a vowel or in *n* or *s* stress the next to the last (penultimate) syllable: casa, pasan, libros.

Note: Adverbs ending in -mente retain the original stress (and written accent) of the root word as well as stress the first syllable of the adverbial ending: claramente, difícilmente, últimamente.

The written accent is used in the following cases:

- Words that end in a vowel or the consonants *n* or *s* and that stress the last syllable: café, talón, anís.

- Words that end in a consonant (except *n* or *s*) and that stress the next to the last syllable: árbol, quídam.

- All words that stress the third from the last (antepenultimate) syllable: párvulo, máximo, ánimo.

Note: Verbs having unstressed pronouns attached to them preserve the written accent when they ordinarily carry one: llevóme, apuréla.

Other uses of the written accent

- The written accent is used to distinguish between two words with the same spelling but different meanings or functions:

él (pronoun)	el (article)
tú (pronoun)	tu (possessive adjective)
mí (pronoun)	{ mi (possessive adjective) { mi (musical note)
sí (adverb) } sí (pronoun) }	si (conjunction)
sé (of the verb *ser*) } sé (of the verb *saber*) }	se (reflexive pronoun)
más (adverb)	mas (conjunction)
dé (of the verb *dar*)	de (preposition)
té (noun)	te (pronoun)
éste } ése } (pronouns) aquél }	este } ese } (adjectives) aquel }
sólo (adverb)	solo (adjective)

- The written accent is also used in the following cases:
  —Quién, cuál, cúyo, cuánto, cuán, cuándo, cómo, and dónde in interrogative and exclamatory sentences.
  —Qué, cúyo, cuándo, cómo, and porqué used as nouns: sin qué ni para qué, el cómo y el cuándo.
  —Quién, cuál, and cuándo having a distributive sense: quién más, quién menos.
  —Aún when it is interchangeable with todavía: no ha llegado aún.
  —The vowels *i* and *u* are accented when they are preceded or followed by another vowel and form a separate stressed syllable: llovía, baúl.
  —The conjunction o takes an accent when it comes between two arabic numerals to avoid mistaking it for zero (0): 3 ó 4.

ARTICLES / ARTÍCULOS

The article in Spanish is a variable part of speech, agreeing with the noun in gender and number.

Definite articles

	Masculine	Feminine
Singular	**el** libro (the book)	**la** cara (the face)
Plural	**los** libros (the books)	**las** caras (the faces)

The neuter article **lo** is used to give a substantive value to some adjectives: **lo** bello (the beautiful, what is beautiful, beautiful things); **lo** profundo de sus pensamientos (the profoundness of his thoughts).

Indefinite articles

	Masculine	Feminine
Singular	**un** hombre (a man)	**una** naranja (an orange)
Plural	**unos** hombres (some men)	**unas** naranjas (some oranges)

Special cases

- The masculine article is used with feminine nouns that begin with a stressed **a**: **el** alma (the soul); **un** ave (a bird).

- With reflexive verbs, the definite article is equivalent to an English possessive adjective in sentences like: me lavo **las** manos, I wash my hands; ponte **el** sombrero, put on your hat.

- When followed by **de** or an adjective, the Spanish definite article may be used as a pronoun equivalent to *the one* or *the ones:* el **del** sombrero blanco, the one in the white hat.

GENDER / GÉNERO

All nouns in Spanish have a gender: masculine, feminine, common, or epicene. Some adjectives having the value of a noun are in the neuter gender.

Note: For all practical purposes, common and epicene nouns are masculine or feminine and are treated as such in the entries of this dictionary.

Some observations

- Nouns denoting living beings usually have a different form for the masculine or feminine gender: **trabajador, trabajadora**, working man, working woman; **actor, actriz**, actor, actress; **oso, osa**, bear (male), bear (female); **buey, vaca**, ox, cow; **caballo, yegua**, horse, mare.

- Some nouns that denote persons have only one ending for both masculine and feminine genders. They are in the common gender, and the sex is indicated solely by the article: **un** pianista, **una** pianista, a pianist.

- Some masculine nouns and feminine nouns are used to denote animals of either sex. They are in the epicene gender, and the sex is indicated by the word **macho** or **hembra** following the noun: una serpiente **macho**, a male serpent; un rinoceronte **hembra**, a female rhinoceros.

- Nouns denoting material or spiritual things are never in the neuter gender but have either the masculine or feminine gender attributed to them. The reader is advised to look for the gender in the corresponding entries of this dictionary whenever a question arises.

FORMATION OF THE PLURAL / PLURAL

The plural of Spanish nouns and adjectives is formed by adding s or es to the singular word.

The plural is formed by adding s to:

- Words ending in an unstressed vowel: casa, **casas**; blanco, **blancos**.
- Words ending in an accented é: café, **cafés**.

The plural is formed by adding es to:

- Words ending in an accented á, í, ó, or ú: bajá, **bajaes**; rubí, **rubíes**.
  Exception: **Papá, mamá, chacó,** and **chapó** add s; maravedí has three forms for the plural: **maravedis, maravedíes,** and **maravedises.**
- The names of the vowels: a, **aes**; e, **ees**; i, **íes**, etc.
- Nouns and adjectives ending in a consonant: árbol, **árboles**; anís, **anises**; cañón, **cañones**.
  Exception: Nouns of more than one syllable ending in an s preceded by an unstressed vowel do not change in the plural: lunes, **lunes**; crisis, **crisis**. Observe that nouns and adjectives ending in z change the z to c in their written plurals: vez, **veces**; feliz, **felices**.

Proper names

When a proper name is used in the plural, all the preceding rules and exceptions are observed. Exception: Family names ending in z (Núñez, Pérez, etc.) do not change in the plural.

Nouns of foreign origin

Usually nouns of foreign origin form the plural according to the preceding rules. However, the plural of lord is **lores**, and the plural of cinc or zinc is **cincs** or **zincs**.
Latin words, such as ultimátum, déficit, fiat, and exequátur, have no plural form.

Compound nouns and adjectives

- When the elements of the compound noun or adjective are separate, only the first element takes the plural form: ojos de buey, **patas de gallo**.
- When the compound is imperfect, such as ricahembra, mediacaña, both the elements take the plural form: **ricashembras, mediascañas.**
- When the compound is perfect, the plural is formed at the end of the word: **ferrocarriles, patitiesos.**
- The plurals of cualquiera and quienquiera are **cualesquiera** and **quienesquiera.**

DIRECT AND INDIRECT OBJECTS / COMPLEMENTOS DIRECTO E INDIRECTO

Direct object

As a rule, the direct object is not preceded by a preposition. However, the positions of the subject and object in Spanish are often reversed, and the direct object is sometimes preceded by the preposition a to avoid confusion.

Examples and exceptions:

Construction with a	Construction without a
César venció a Pompeyo. (Proper noun—name of a person)	Plutarco os dará mil Alejandros. (Proper noun used as a common noun)
Ensilló a Rocinante. (Proper noun—name of an animal)	Ensilló el caballo. (Common noun of an animal)
Conquistó a Sevilla. Conozco Madrid. Uncertain use. (Proper nouns—names of places without the article)	Visitó La Coruña. Veremos El Escorial. (Proper nouns—names of places preceded by the article)

Busco al criado de mi casa.
(Common noun of a specified person)

Busco criados diligentes.
(Common noun of nonspecified persons)

Tienen por Dios al viento.
Temo al agua.
(Noun of a personified thing or of a thing to which an active quality is attributed)

Partiremos esta leña. Recojo el agua.
(Nouns of things in general)

No conozco a nadie.
Yo busco a otros, a alguien, a ti.
(Indefinite pronoun representing a person or personal pronoun)

No sabía nada. Di algo.
(Indefinite pronouns representing things)

Aquel a quien amo.

No sé quién vendrá.

Indirect object

The indirect object is always preceded by the prepositions **a** or **para**: Escribo una carta a mi madre. Compro un libro **para** mi hijo. (I write a letter to my mother. I buy a book for my son.)

ADJECTIVES / ADJETIVOS

The adjective in Spanish is a variable part of speech and must agree in gender and number with the noun it qualifies: libro **pequeño**, casa **pequeña**; libros **pequeños**, casas **pequeñas**.

Some adjectives, however, have the same ending for both masculine and feminine genders: hombre **fiel**, mujer **fiel**; hombres **fieles**, mujeres **fieles**.

Placement of the adjective
Predicate adjectives usually follow the verb: la nieve es **blanca**, the snow is white.

Nevertheless, the order of the sentence can be reversed for emphasis or in some fixed expressions: ¡**buena** es ésta!, that is a good one!; ¡**bueno** está lo bueno!, leave well enough alone.

Adjectives that directly modify a noun may either precede or follow it.

Special cases
- Adjectives that express a natural quality or a quality associated with a person or thing are placed before the noun: el **fiero** león, la **blanca** nieve.

- Indefinite, interrogative, and exclamative adjectives; the adjectives **medio, buen, mal, poco, mucho,** and **mero**; and adjectives expressing cardinal numbers are placed before the noun: **algún** día, some day; ¿**qué** libro prefiere usted?, which book do you prefer?; **dos** hombres, two men.

  Alguno, when placed after a noun, has a negative sense: no hay remedio **alguno**, there is no remedy.

- Some adjectives change meaning or connotation when they precede or follow a noun: un **simple** hombre, a mere man; un hombre **simple**, a simpleton.

- Some adjectives change in form when used before a noun. **Grande** may be shortened to **gran** when used in the sense of extraordinary or distinguished: un **gran** rey, a great king; una **gran** nación, a great nation.

- The masculine adjectives **alguno, ninguno, bueno, malo, primero,** and **tercero** drop the final o when placed before a noun: **algún** día, some day; **ningún** hombre, no man; **primer** lugar, first place; **tercer** piso, third floor.

- The masculine adjective **Santo** is shortened to **San** before all names of saints except Tomás, Toribio, and Domingo: **San** Juan, Saint John; **Santo** Tomás, Saint Thomas.

Comparative degree
The English comparatives—*more...than, less...than,* and adjective + *er than*—are expressed in Spanish as **más...que, menos...que**: Pedro es **más** (or **menos**) atlético **que** Juan, Peter is more (or less) athletic than John.

In a comparative expression, when **que** is followed by a conjugated verb or a number, it is replaced by **de lo que** and **de**, respectively: esto es más difícil **de lo que** parece, this is more difficult than it seems; hay más **de** diez personas, there are more than ten people.

The English comparatives, *as...as* and *so...as,* are expressed in Spanish as **tan...como**: mi casa es **tan** hermosa **como** la de usted, my house is as beautiful as yours.

Superlative degree

The English superlatives—*the most* (or *the least)...in* or *of* and adjective + *est...in* or *of*—are expressed in Spanish as **el más** (or **el menos)...de**: el barrio **más** populoso **de** la ciudad, the most populous quarter in the town.

- The absolute superlative is formed by placing **muy** before the adjective or by adding the ending **-ísimo** to the adjective: **muy** excelente, **excelentísimo**, most excellent.

- Adjectives ending in a vowel drop the vowel and add **-ísimo**: grande, **grandísimo**; alto, **altísimo**.

- Adjectives ending in **co** or **go**, change **c** to **qu** and **g** to **gu** and add **-ísimo**: poco, **poquísimo**; largo, **larguísimo**.

- Adjectives ending in **io** drop the ending and add **-ísimo**: limpio, **limpísimo**.

- Adjectives containing an accented diphthong—**ie** or **ue**—change **ie** to **e** and **ue** to **o** and add **-ísimo**: valiente, **valentísimo**; fuerte, **fortísimo**.

- Adjectives ending in **ble** change this ending to **bilísimo**: amable, **amabilísimo**.

- Some adjectives have special forms for the comparative and superlative degrees: bueno, mejor, óptimo; malo, peor, pésimo; grande, mayor, máximo; pequeño, menor, mínimo.

NUMERALS / NUMERALES

Observations

1) Uno, when it precedes a masculine noun, and **ciento**, when it precedes any noun and when used in a cardinal number, take the shortened forms **un** and **cien**: un libro; **cien** hombres; **cien** mil soldados.

2) The cardinal numbers between 20 and 30 are spelled **veintiuno, veintidós, veintitrés,** etc.

3) The cardinal numbers between 30 and 40, 40 and 50, etc. (under 100), use the conjunction **y**: treinta y uno, ochenta y tres.

4) The preceding rules apply to the spelling of any cardinal number over 100: **ciento veintiuno,** 121; **seiscientos** cuarenta y dos, 642; **cien mil** cuarenta, 100.040. Note that:
—**Millón, billón,** and the like take the indefinite article **un**; however, **ciento, cien,** and **mil** do not: un millón, a million; **ciento,** a hundred; **mil,** a thousand; **cien mil,** one hundred thousand.

5) Ordinal numbers between 10th and 20th are: **undécimo, duodécimo, decimotercero** or **decimotercio, decimocuarto, decimoquinto, decimosexto, decimoséptimo, decimoctavo,** and **decimonoveno** or **decimonono.**

6) The ordinal numbers between 20th and 30th, 30th and 40th, etc. are formed by adding the first nine ordinal numbers to **vigésimo, trigésimo, cuadragésimo,** etc.: **vigésimo primero,** twenty-first; **trigésimo segundo,** thirty-second; **cuadragésimo tercero,** forty-third.

7) Most ordinal numbers may also be formed by adding the endings **-eno, -ena,** and **-avo, -ava** to the cardinal numbers. The ordinal numbers ending in **-avo** (except octavo) are used only to express fractions: una **dozava** parte, one twelfth part; el **dozavo** de, a twelfth of.

8) The cardinal numbers (except **uno**) may be used as ordinals. However, from 2 to 10, preference is given to the ordinal numbers for the names of kings, chapters of books, etc.
—For the days of the month (except the first), only cardinal numbers are used: el **primero** de junio, el **dos** de octubre, el **catorce** de diciembre.

9) As a rule, cardinal numbers are placed before the noun; but when they are used as ordinal numbers, they are placed after the noun: dos libros, capítulo **quince**.

10) All the ordinal numbers and the cardinal numbers uno, **doscientos, trescientos,** through **novecientos** agree with the noun they qualify: la **primera** puerta, el **tercer** hombre, una casa, **doscientos** libros, **trescientas cuatro** personas.

PERSONAL PRONOUNS / PRONOMBRES PERSONALES
Subject pronouns

Person	Singular	Plural
1st	yo	nosotros, nosotras, nos
2nd	usted, tú	ustedes, vosotros, vosotras, vos
3rd	él, ella	ellos, ellas

- The subject pronoun in Spanish is used only for emphasis or to prevent ambiguity. When neither of these reasons for its use exists, its presence in the sentence makes the style heavy and should be avoided.

- Usted and **ustedes** are technically second person pronouns used out of courtesy. However, they take the verb in the third person.

- Nos is used by kings, bishops, etc. in their writings or proclamations in the same way as the English *royal we* and *us*. Nosotros is used by writers in the same way as the *editorial we* in English.

- Vos is used to address God, a saint, a king, etc. In some American countries tú is used.

Object pronouns

Direct Object Pronouns

Person	Singular	Plural
1st	me	nos
2nd	te, le, lo, la	os, los, las
3rd	le, lo, la	los, las

Indirect Object Pronouns (without a preposition)

Person	Singular	Plural
1st	me	nos
2nd	te, le	os, les
3rd	le	les

Object Pronouns (with a preposition)

Person	Singular	Plural
1st	mí	nosotros, nosotras
2nd	usted, ti	ustedes, vosotros, vosotras
3rd	él, ella, sí	ellos, ellas, sí

- Sí is equivalent to *himself, herself, itself,* and *themselves* relating to the subject of the sentence: esto es malo de sí, this is bad in itself; habla de sí **mismo**, he speaks of himself.

- When the indirect object pronouns le and les must precede another third person pronoun, they are replaced by se. Incorrect: le lo mandaron, les las quitaron. Correct: se lo mandaron, se las quitaron.

Reflexive Pronouns

Person	Singular	Plural
1st	me	nos
2nd	te	os
3rd	se	se

- Se may also be:
  —An indication of the passive voice.
  —An impersonal subject equivalent to the English *one, you, they, people:* se habló de todo, they talked about everything. However, when the verb is reflexive, se cannot be used this way. Instead, **uno, alguno,** or **alguien** may be substituted as the impersonal subject.

Observations:
- When the verb is a gerund or a form of the imperative or infinitive mood, the object pronoun or pronouns are placed after the verb: diciéndolo, dámelo, observarnos. In compound tenses, they are placed after the auxiliary verb: habiéndome dado, haberos comprendido.
  When the gerund or infinitive is subordinate to another verb, the pronouns may pass to the main verb: quieren molestarte or te quieren molestar; iban diciéndolo or lo iban diciendo.

- Direct and indirect object pronouns may be placed before or after the verb when the verb is in the indicative, subjunctive, or conditional mood. In everyday language, it is usual to place them before the verb.

- When there are two object pronouns, the indirect precedes the direct, and a reflexive pronoun precedes another pronoun: me lo dio, se las prometí.

- Object pronouns that follow the verb are incorporated into the verb: **diciéndolo, molestarte.**
  Sometimes in this union, the final letter of the verb must be dropped to avoid a metaplasm: correct: **unámonos,** incorrect: **unamosnos;** correct: **sentaos,** incorrect: **sentados.**

Order of placement
  When two or more pronouns accompany the verb, either preceding or following it, the second person pronoun is placed before the first person pronoun, and this before the third person pronoun. The pronoun se always precedes the others. (Te me quieren arrebatar. Nos lo ofrecen. Se te conoce en la cara.)

POSSESSIVE PRONOUNS AND ADJECTIVES / POSESIVO (Adjetivo y pronombre)

- The Spanish possessive adjective and pronoun agree with the noun representing the possessed thing: **mi** sombrero, my hat; **mis** libros, my books; **tus** caballos, **vuestros** caballos, your horses.

- The third person possessive adjective or noun, especially in the form of **su,** is very ambiguous because it can mean *his, her, its,* and *their.* It is also equivalent to *your* when used in correlation with **usted** or **ustedes.** To prevent misunderstanding, the practice had been to add the possessor's name (or a pronoun representing it) preceded by **de:** su casa **de** Luis; su libro **de ellos;** su madre **de usted.** However, this use is now restricted to su...**de usted** or su...**de ustedes:** su libro **de usted,** su madre **de ustedes.** In most cases, it is preferable to reword the sentence to avoid ambiguity.

- **Nuestro** and **vuestro** denote only one possessor when the corresponding personal pronoun (**nosotros, nos,** or **vos**) denotes one person.

- In some sentences, the definite article replaces the possessive adjective: he dejado **los** guantes sobre la mesa, I have left my gloves on the table; te has olvidado **el** paraguas, you have forgotten your umbrella.

CONJUGATION OF VERBS / CONJUGACIÓN

Regular verbs in Spanish fall into three groups: -ar verbs (first conjugation), -er verbs (second conjugation), and -ir verbs (third conjugation).

Models of the three conjugations (simple tenses)

amar (to love)   temer (to fear)   recibir (to receive)

Indicative Mood

Present

am-o, -as, -a; -amos, -áis, -an
tem-o, -es, -e; -emos, -éis, -en
recib-o, -es, -e; -imos, -ís, -en

Preterite

am-é, -aste, -ó; -amos, -asteis, -aron
tem ⎱
recib ⎰ -í, -iste, -ió; -imos, -isteis, -ieron

Imperfect

am-aba, -abas, -aba; -ábamos, -abais, -aban
tem ⎱
recib ⎰ -ía, -ías, -ía; -íamos, -íais, -ían

Future

amar ⎱
temer ⎬ -é, -ás, -á; -emos, -éis, -án
recibir ⎰

Conditional

amar ⎱
temer ⎬ -ía, -ías, -ía; -íamos, -íais, -ían
recibir ⎰

Subjunctive Mood

Present

am-e, -es, -e; -emos, -éis, -en
tem ⎱
recib ⎰ -a, -as, -a; -amos, -áis, -an

**Imperfect
(s-form)**

am-ase, -ases, -ase; -ásemos, -aseis, -asen
tem ⎱ -iese, -ieses, -iese; -iésemos, -ieseis,
recib ⎰ -iesen

**Imperfect
(r-form)**

am-ara, -aras, -ara; -áramos, -arais, -aran
tem ⎱ -iera, -ieras, -iera; -iéramos, -ierais,
recib ⎰ -ieran

Future

am-are, -ares, -are; -áremos, -areis, -aren
tem ⎱ -iere, -ieres, -iere; -iéremos, -iereis,
recib ⎰ -ieren

Past Participle

amado   temido   recibido

Gerund

amando   temiendo   recibiendo

Compound tenses are formed by the auxiliary verb **haber** and the past participle of the conjugated verb: **he comido**, I have eaten; **habrá llegado**, he will have arrived; **habías temido**, you had feared.

Irregular verbs

The conjugations of irregular verbs are given in the entries corresponding to their infinitives.

Orthographic-changing verbs

Some verbs undergo spelling changes to preserve their regularity to the ear: tocar, **toque**; llegar, **llegue**; vencer, **venzo**; lanzar, **lance**, etc. These orthographic-changing verbs are neither considered nor treated as irregular verbs in this dictionary.

PASSIVE VOICE / VOZ PASIVA

The Spanish language expresses the passive voice in two different ways:
1) By a form of the verb ser and a past participle: la serpiente **fue muerta** por Pedro, the snake was killed by Peter.
2) By the pronoun se preceding the verb: aquí **se habla** español, Spanish is spoken here.
The second form of the passive voice is often difficult to distinguish from the active voice in sentences where se is an impersonal subject.

EXPRESSING NEGATION / NEGACIÓN

Negation is expressed by the adverb no, which is equivalent to the English *no* and *not*.

- No is always placed before the verb: la casa **no** es mía, the house is not mine; el niño **no** come, the child does not eat.
  —Other words, even whole sentences, may be placed between no and the verb: no **se lo** daré, I will not give it to him; no **todos los presentes** estaban conformes, not all those present agreed.
  —Whenever the meaning may not be clearly understood, no must accompany the words it modifies. For example: tu madre **no puede** venir, your mother cannot come; tu madre **puede no** venir, your mother may not come.

- Words expressing negation: jamás, nunca, nada, nadie, ninguno, and the phrases en mi vida, en todo el día, etc. are substituted for no when they precede the verb: jamás volveré, nunca lo sabrás, nada me falta, a nadie veo, ninguno sobra.
  —However, when these words follow the verb, no must be used in the sentence and precede the verb: no volveré **jamás**, no lo sabrás **nunca**, no me falta **nada**, no veo a **nadie**, no sobra **ninguno**.
  —When the sentence contains many words that express negation, only one of them can be placed before the verb: **nadie** me ayudó nunca en nada, **nunca** me ayudó nadie en nada.
  —If the verb is preceded by no, all other negative words must follow the verb: No me ayudó **nunca nadie** en nada.

- No may be used without expressing negation:
  —In sentences subordinate to a verb expressing fear or possibility, **no** is substituted for a que: temía **no** viniese, I feared that he should come.
  —As an expletive in sentences like: Nadie dudará que la falta de precisión... **no** dimane de..., No one will doubt that the lack of precision comes from (or is due to)....

INTERROGATIVES / INTERROGACIÓN

Construction of the interrogative sentence

Sentences with no interrogative word:
- The subject is placed after the verb. If a compound tense is used, the subject follows the participle. Remember that in Spanish the subject is expressed only for emphasis or when its presence is necessary for meaning.

¿Ha llegado tu padre?
¿Viene alguien?
¿Trae cada uno su libro?
Llaman.— ¿Será él?
¿Vienes?
¿Viene usted?
¿Viene ella?

Sentences with an interrogative word:
- When the interrogative word is the subject, the sentence order is not reversed.
- When the interrogative word is an attribute, an object, or a complement, the sentence order is reversed.

¿Quién llama?
¿Qué dolor es comparable al mío?
¿Cuál es tu libro?
¿Qué quiere tu hermano?
¿Con quién habla usted?

Complement, object, or subject placed at the beginning of the sentence:

- For emphasis, a complement or object is placed at the beginning of a sentence. If a direct or indirect object is emphasized, it may be repeated by means of a pronoun: A este hombre, ¿lo conocían ustedes? A tu padre, ¿le has escrito? De este asunto, ¿han hablado ustedes?

- The subject can also be placed at the beginning of an interrogative sentence, but then the question is indicated only by the question marks and vocal intonation: ¿Los estudiantes estaban contentos? or Los estudiantes, ¿estaban contentos?

Interrogative sentences are punctuated with two question marks: the one (¿) at the beginning of the question and the other (?) at the end of the question.

THE INFINITIVE / INFINITIVO

The infinitive in Spanish has practically the same uses as the infinitive in English.

Exception: In some subordinate sentences that express what is ordered, expected, desired, etc., the subjunctive or indicative mood is used; whereas in English, the infinitive would be used: El capitán ordenó a los soldados **que trajesen** al prisionero. (The captain ordered the soldiers *to bring* the prisoner.) Me pidió **que pagase** la cuenta. (He asked me *to pay* the bill.) Esperan **que se irá** pronto. (They expect him *to go* away soon.)

The Spanish infinitive is used as a noun in the same way as the English infinitive and sometimes gerund are used as nouns. **Errar** es humano. (To err is human.) El **comer** es necesario para la vida. (Eating is necessary for life.)

PARTICIPLES / PARTICIPIOS

Past participle

- The past participle is always invariable when it is used to form a compound tense: he **recibido** una carta, los libros que **he recibido**.
  —When the past participle is used as an adjective or an attribute, it agrees with its noun in number and gender: un problema **resuelto**, la obra está **terminada**.
  —When the past participle is used with the verbs **tener, llevar, dejar**, etc., it is made to agree in number and gender with a related noun: tengo **resueltos** los problemas, I have the problems solved; llevo **escritas** cuatro cartas, I have four letters written; la dejó **hecha** una furia, when he left her, she was in a rage.

- Many past participles in Spanish have both a regular and an irregular form. As a rule, the irregular forms of the past participles are only used as adjectives and sometimes as nouns: Dios le ha **bendecido**, God has blessed him; una medalla **bendita**, a blessed medal.

Present participle

Very few Spanish verbs have a present participle (in the Latin sense). This participle has become an adjective. Only **concerniente, condescendiente, conducente, correspondiente**, and some others that can have the same complements and objects as the verb, retain something of their participial nature.

THE GERUND / GERUNDIO

Formation

The first conjugation adds **-ando** to the stem of the infinitive (amar, **amando**). The second and third conjugations add **-iendo** (temer, **temiendo**; recibir, **recibiendo**). The gerund does not change for number and gender.

Observations

- The gerund in Spanish never acts as a noun. It expresses an action occurring at the same time as or immediately preceding the action of the main verb: Lee **paseándose**, he reads while strolling; **viendo** a su padre, corrió hacia él, on seeing his father, he ran toward him; **habiendo estudiado** la proposición, me resuelvo a aceptarla, having studied the proposition, I resolve to accept it.

The gerund never expresses an action that occurs after the action of the main verb.

- When the gerund is related to the subject of the main sentence, it may be used only in an explanatory sense: el lobo, **huyendo de los perros**, se metió en el bosque. (The wolf, fleeing from the dogs, went into the woods.)

  The gerund is never used restrictively. *It is correct to say*: Los pasajeros, **llevando pasaporte**, pudieron desembarcar. (The passengers, having their passports, were able to disembark.) *It is incorrect to say*: Los pasajeros **llevando pasaporte** pudieron desembarcar. (Only the passengers having their passports could disembark.) This can be expressed as: Los pasajeros **que llevaban** pasaporte....

- When the gerund is related to the object of the main verb, the object then acts as the subject of the gerund. This use is only correct when the gerund expresses an action perceptible in its course, never a state, quality, or action not perceptible in its course. *It is correct to say*: Vi a un hombre **plantando** coles. (I saw a man planting cabbages.) *It is incorrect to say*: Envió una caja **conteniendo** libros. (He sent a box containing books.) In this case, it is necessary to say: Envió una caja **que contiene** libros.

- The gerund is often used in phrases that are independent of a main sentence, as in titles, captions, inscriptions on engravings, photographs, paintings, etc.: César **pasando** el Rubicón (Caesar passing the Rubicon); las ranas **pidiendo** rey (the frogs asking for a king).

- The gerund is frequently used as an adverb: Ella se fue **llorando** (she went away in tears); el tiempo pasa **volando** (time passes swiftly).

  As an adverb, the gerund may also express the way in which something is done or attained: hizo una cuerda **uniendo varias sábanas** (he made a rope by tying several sheets together).

ADVERBS / ADVERBIOS

Adverbs ending in -mente

Some adverbs are formed by adding -**mente** to the end of an adjective: fiel, **fielmente**. If the adjective can change gender, -**mente** is added to the feminine form: rico, rica, **ricamente**.

Placement of the adverb

Generally, when the adverb is qualifying an adjective or another adverb, it immediately precedes the word it qualifies: un libro **bien** escrito, a well-written book; tan **lindamente** ilustrado, so beautifully illustrated.

When the adverb modifies a verb, it may precede or follow the verb: **mañana** llegará mi padre or mi padre llegará **mañana**; my father will arrive tomorrow.

The negative adverb is always placed before the verb: **no** conozco a este hombre, I don't know this man; **no** lo conozco, I don't know him.

When a direct or indirect object pronoun precedes the verb, the adverb cannot separate the pronoun from the verb: **ayer** la vi or la vi **ayer**, I saw her yesterday. The adverb usually never separates an auxiliary verb from the principal verb: ha vencido **fácilmente** a su adversario, he has easily defeated his opponent.

Note: When a word is qualified by two or more adverbs that end in -**mente**, only the last adverb has the ending -**mente**, the others retain the adjective form: ella habló **clara, concisa** y **elegantemente**; she spoke clearly, concisely, and elegantly.

Comparative and superlative degrees

Adverbs can also be expressed in comparative and superlative degrees: **más claramente**, more clearly; **clarísimamente**, very clearly or most clearly.

SYNTAX / SINTAXIS

Sentence construction in Spanish is very free. As a general rule its elements, with the exception of object pronouns may be placed in any order.

Examples:

Pedro llegará a las tres.
Pedro a las tres llegará.
Llegará a las tres Pedro.
A las tres llegará Pedro.
A las tres Pedro llegará.

Traigo un regalo para ti.
Traigo para ti un regalo.
Un regalo traigo para ti.
Un regalo para ti traigo.
Para ti traigo un regalo.
Para ti un regalo traigo.

The use of any one of these constructions is a matter of style or of psychological or emotional intent. Nevertheless, the placement of the verb at the end of the sentence is considered affected, even though it is grammatically correct. It is rarely used in writing and not used at all in conversation.

Special cases

There are some cases in which the subject must be placed after the verb. The more important ones are:

- In some interrogative sentences.

- In exclamatory sentences beginning with **qué, cuál, cuán, cuánto**: ¡Qué alegría tendrá **Juan!** ¡Cuál sería **su sorpresa!**

- After **cualquiera que** and **quienquiera que**, used with the verb **ser**, and after **por...que** and **por muy...que**, when the intervening word is an attribute: Cualquiera que fuese **su estado.** Por muy hábil que sea **tu hermano.**

- In parenthetic sentences using the verbs **decir, preguntar, responder, exclamar**, etc.: Nadie — dijo **Juan** — lo creería.

- In sentences expressing a wish or desire, a condition, or a supposition: ¡Viva **la Reina!** Si se presenta **la ocasión.** Si lo quiere **usted** así.

- In sentences beginning with the adverbs or phrases **cuando, apenas, en cuanto**, etc.: Cuando llegue **tu padre.** Apenas lo oyó **Juan.** En cuanto estemos **todos** reunidos.

- In imperative sentences having **usted** as a subject or having a subject that is to be emphasized: Oiga **usted.** Ven **tú** si no viene él.

A

A, a *f.* A, a, the first letter of the Spanish alphabet.
a *prep.* to [governing the indirect object]: *dáselo ~ Pedro*, give it to Peter. *2* at, by, in, on, to, after, like, etc.: *~ la mesa*, at table; *~ la una*, at one o'clock; *~ dos pesetas la libra*, at two pesetas a pound; *~ mano*, by hand; *~ fuerza de*, by dint of; *~ oscuras*, in the dark; *~ tiempo*, in time; *~ bordo*, on board; *~ caballo*, on horseback; *~ la mañana siguiente*, on the next morning; *~ mi gusto*, to my taste; *de diez ~ doce*, from ten to twelve; *voy ~ jugar*, I am going to play; *~ los ocho días de*, eight days after; *~ la inglesa*, English style; after the English fashion; *~ lo loco*, like a madman, recklessly, widly; *~ no ser que*, unless. *3* if, had, but: *~ no ser por José*, but for Joseph. *3* Generally it is not translated when used with the direct object of a verb: *César venció ~ Pompeyo*, Caesar defeated Pompey. See DIRECT OBJECT diagram. *5* It coalesces with the article *el*, forming *al*: *al niño*, to the child; *al contrario*, on the contrary; *al menos*, at least; *al principio*, at first; *al llegar yo*, on my arrival.
Aaron *pr. n.* Aaron.
abacá *m.* abaca, Manila hemp.
abacería *f.* grocer's shop, grocery store.
abacero, -ra *m.-f.* grocer, retail grocer.
abacial *adj.* abbatial.
ábaco *m.* ARCH. abacus. *2* abacus [calculating frame]. *3* MIN. washing trough.
abad *m.* abbot.
abadejo *m.* codfish.
abadengo, -ga *adj.* abbatial. *2 m.* abbatial states.
abadesa *f.* abbess.
abadía *f.* Abbey. *2* abbacy. *3* abbotship.
abajeño, -ña *adj.* (Am.) lowland. *2 n.* (Am.) lowlander.
abajo *adv.* down: *boca ~*, face down; *cuesta ~*, downhill; *hacia ~*, downwards; *muy ~*, low down. *2* below, under: *el hombre que está ~*, the man below. *3 interj.* down with!
abalanzar *tr.* to balance [a scale]. *2 ref.* to fall, pounce, throw oneself, rush impetuously.
abalaustrado, -da *adj.* BALAUSTRADO.
abalizamiento *m.* buoy-laying. *2* AER. airways marking.
abalizar *tr.* to buoy, buoy off. *2 ref.* NAUT. to take bearings.
abalorio *m.* glass bead. *2* glass beads, beadwork.

abaluartar *tr.* ABASTIONAR.
abanderado *m.* colour bearer, standard-bearer.
abanderar *tr.* to register [a ship].
abanderizar *tr.* to divide into parties or factions.
abandonado, -da *adj.* abandoned, forsaken. *2* forlorn. *3* negligent, slovenly.
abandonar *tr.* to abandon, leave, forsake. *2* to give up. *3 intr.* CHESS, DRAUGHTS to resign. *4 ref.* to give oneself up (to). *5* to despair, give in. *6* to neglect oneself, one's duties.
abandono *m.* abandon, abandonment. *2* forlornness. *3* CHESS, DRAUGHTS. resigning.
abanicar *tr.* to fan. *2 ref.* to fan oneself.
abanico *m.* fan [instrument]: *en ~*, fan-shaped; fan-like. *2* NAUT. derrick, crane.
abaniqueo *m.* fanning.
abaniquero *m.* fanmaker.
abanto *adj.* shy, timid [bull]. *2 m.* ORN. Egyptian vulture.
abaratamiento *m.* cheapening.
abaratar *tr.* to cheapen, lower the price of. *2 ref.* to cheapen, become cheap, fall in price.
abarca *f.* brogue, sandal.
abarcar *tr.* to clasp, grasp, take in, embrace, comprise, include. *2* to undertake [too many things at once]. *3* (Am.) to monopolize.
abarloar *tr.* to bring alongside.
abarquillar *tr.-ref.* to curl up, warp, curve, turn up at the edges.
abarraganamiento *m.* concubinage.
abarrajarse *ref.* (Am.) to stumble, fall. *2* (Am.) to become a ruffian.
abarrancar *tr.* to ravine. *2 ref.* to fall into a ravine. *3 intr.-ref.* to get into a jam.
abarrotado, -da *adj.* full, crammed; *~ de gente*, crowded.
abarrotar *tr.* to bar, strengthen with bars. *2* to cram, pack; to overstock. *3* CARDS to finesse.
abarrote *m.* NAUT. stopgap, small package. *2 pl.* (Am.) groceries.
Abasidas *pr. n. pl.* HIST. Abbasids.
abastardar *intr.* fig. to degenerate, to degrade.
abastecedor, -ra *m.-f.* purveyor, supplier.
abastecer *tr.* to provision, purvey, supply. ¶ CONJUG. like *agradecer*.
abastecimiento *m.* supply, provision, purveyance.
abastionar *tr.* to fortify with bastions.

abasto *m.* purveyance, supply. *2* abundance. *3 dar*
~ *a*, to be sufficent for; to be able to attend to.
abatanar *tr.* WEAV. to full, beat [cloth].
abatatar *tr.* (Am.) coll. to frighten, to scare, to intimidate. *2 ref.* coll. to become listless or lethargic. *3 ref.* (Am.) coll. to become frightened, to
lose one's nerve.
abate *m.* abbé.
abatible *adj.* folding, collapsible.
abatido, -da *adj.* dejected, despondent, dispirited,
downcast. *2* low, weakened. *3* humbled. *4* abject, mean.
abatimiento *m.* dejection, low spirits. *2* abjected-
ness. *3* humiliation. *4* lowness, prostration. *5*
NAUT., AER. drift, leeway.
abatir *tr.* to bring down, throw down, overthrow.
2 NAUT. to lower [a sail]. *3* to depress, dishearten. *4* to humble. *5 intr.* NAUT., AER. to drift. *6 ref.*
to humble oneself. *7* to be disheartened. *8* [of a
bird of prey] to swoop down.
abazón *m.* ZOOL. cheek pouch.
abdicación *f.* abdication.
abdicar *tr.* to abdicate, to renounce.
abdomen *m.* abdomen.
abdominal *adj.* abdominal.
abducción *f.* LOG., PHYSIOL. abduction.
abductor *adj.* ANAT. abducent. *2 m.* ANAT. abductor.
abecé *m.* ABC. *2* abecedary, primer.
abecedario *m.* alphabet. *2* abecedary, primer.
abedul *m.* BOT. birch, birch tree.
abeja *f.* ENT. bee, honeybee: ~ *reina*, queen bee; ~
obrera, worker [bee].
abejarrón *m.* ENT. bumblebee.
abejaruco *m.* ORN. bee eater.
abejero *m.* beekeeper. *2* ABEJARUCO.
abejón *m.* ENT. drone. *2* ENT. bumblebee.
abejorro *m.* ENT. bumblebee. *2* ENT. cockchafer.
Abel *pr. n. m.* Abel.
abellacado, -da *adj.* knavish.
abellotado *adj.* acorn-shaped.
abemolar *tr.* to soften [the voice]. *2* MUS. to flat.
aberenjenado, -da *adj.* eggplant-shaped. *2* egg-
plant-coloured.
aberración *f.* aberration [deviation].
aberrante *adj.* aberrant.
aberrar *intr.* to aberrate.
abertura *f.* opening, aperture, hole, slit, gap. *2*
cove, inlet, small bay. *3* frankness.
abestiado, -da *adj.* beast-like.
abetal *m.* fir wood or grove.
abeto *m.* BOT. fir, silver fir: ~ *del Canadá*, hemlock.
abetunado, -da *adj.* bitumen-like, bituminous.
abiertamente *adv.* openly, declaredly, frankly.
abierto, -ta *p. p.* of ABRIR; opened. *2* open. *3* sincere,
frank.
abigarrado, -da *adj.* variegated; motley, many-
coloured.
abigeato *m.* gentle, light sound; rustling.
abigarrar *tr.* to variegate, motley.
ab intestato *adv.* intestate.
abintestato *m.* LAW settlement of an intestate
state.
abisal *adj.* abyssal.
Abisinia *pr. n.* Abyssinia.
abisinio, -a *adj.-n.* Abyssinian.
abismal *adj.* abysmal, abyssal.
abismar *tr.* to plunge into an abyss. *2* to depress.
3 ref. to plunge, be plunged [into]; to be buried
or sunk [in thought, grief, etc.].
abismático, -ca *adj.* abysmal.
abismo *m.* abysm, abyss, gulf.

abitar *tr.* NAUT. to bitt.
abjuración *f.* abjuration; recantation.
abjurar *tr.* to abjure, forswear.
ablación *f.* SURG. ablation.
ablandabrevas *m.-f.* good-for-nothing.
ablandamiento *m.* softening. *2* mollification.
ablandar *tr.* to soften. *2* to mollify. *3* to loosen [the
bowels]. *4* to appease [temper, anger]; to melt.
5 intr.-ref. [of weather] to moderate. *6 ref.* to soften, become soft. *7* to relent, melt.
ablande *m.* (Am.) AUTO. running-in.
ablativo *m.* GRAM. ablative.
ablución *f.* ablution.
ablusado, -da *adj.* blouse- like.
abnegación *f.* abnegation, self-denial.
abnegado, -da *adj.* self-denying.
abobado, -da *adj.* silly, stupid. *2* stupefied.
abobar *tr.* to make silly. *2 ref.* to become silly. *3 tr.-
ref.* EMBOBAR.
abobamiento *m.* amazement, stupefaction. *2* foolishness, stupidity.
abocado *adj.* dry-sweet [wine].
abocar *tr.* to mouth, seize with the mouth. *2* to
bring near: *verse abocado a*, to be on the verge
of. *3* to pour from one vessel to another. *4 intr.*
NAUT. to enter the mouth of a channel, a strait,
etc.
abocardado, -da *adj.* bell-mouthed.
abocardar *tr.* to widen the mouth of [a hole, tube,
etc.]; to ream, trumpet.
abocelado, -da *adj.* torus- shaped.
abocetado, -da *adj.* sketchy, roughly outlined.
abocetar *tr.* to sketch; to make a rough model of.
abocinado, -da *adj.* trumpet-shaped. *2* ARCH. splayed [arch]. *3* droop-headed [horse].
abocinar *tr.* to shape like a trumpet, to flare. *2 intr.*
coll. to fall on one's face.
abochornado, -da *adj.* blushing, ashamed.
abochornar *tr.* to overheat. *2* to shame, put to the
blush. *3 ref.* to blush, be ashamed. *4* AGR. to wilt
from excessive heat.
abofetear *tr.* to buffet, cuff, slap in the face.
abogacía *f.* law, legal profession.
abogada *f.* a female lawyer. *2* advocatress, mediatrix.
abogado *m.* advocate, lawyer, barrister: ~ *de secano*, quack lawyer. *2* advocate, intercessor.
abogar *intr.* to plead [in favour of]: to intercede.
abolengo *m.* ancestry, descent. *2* inheritance.
abolición *f.* abolition, abrogation.
abolicionismo *m.* abolitionism.
abolir *tr.* to abolish, abrogate. ¶ Only used in the
forms having *i* in their terminations.
abolsado, -da *adj.* loose, baggy.
abolsarse *ref.* to become purse-shaped, to bag.
abolladura *f.* dent, bruise, bump.
abollar *tr.* to dent, batter, bruise, bump.
abollón *m.* ABOLLADURA.
abollonar *tr.* to emboss, to raise bosses on.
abombado, -da *adj.* convex. *2* (Am.) stunned, dan-
zed. *3* merry, tipsy, fuddled.
abombar *tr.* to curve, make convex. *2* coll. to deafen, stun. *3 ref.* (Am.) to get drunk. *4* (Am.) to
taint, become putrid.
abominable *adj.* abominable. *2* very bad.
abominación *f.* abomination.
abominar *tr.* to abominate. *2* to detest, abhor.
abonable *adj.* payable. *2* COM. creditable.
abonado, -da *m.-f.* subscriber; *commuter, sea-
son-ticket holder. *2 adj.* apt, capable.
abonanzar *intr.* [of the weather] to calm, clear up.

abonar *tr.* to approve, *approbate. *2* to guarantee, answer for. *3* to improve. *4* to fertilize, manure [soil]. *5* COM. to credit; to discount; to pay. *6 tr.-ref.* to subscribe [for], to buy a season or commutation ticket [for].

abonaré *m.* COM. credit note.

abono *m.* approbation. *2* guarantee. *3* payment. *4* COM. discount, allowance. *5* COM. credit. *6* fertilizer. *7* subscription; season or commutation ticket.

aboquillado, -da *adj.* with a mouthpiece. *2* bell-shaped, wide-mouthed. *3* bevelled, chamfered.

aboquillar *tr.* to make bell-shaped.

abordaje *m.* NAUT. collision. *2* NAUT. the act of boarding a ship.

abordable *adj.* affordable, reasonable, within one's means. *2* within reach, attainable, accesible. *3* approachable.

abordar *tr.* NAUT. to board, come up against [a ship]. *2* to run foul of [a ship]. *3* to approach [a person, a matter, etc.]. *4 intr.* NAUT. to land.

aborigen *adj.* aboriginal.

aborígenes *m. pl.* aboriginals, aborigines.

aborrajarse *ref.* to dry prematurely, to go bad or off.

aborrascarse *ref.* [of weather] to become stormy.

aborrecer *tr.* to abhor, hate. *2* to desert [brood or nest]. *3* to bore, annoy. ¶ CONJUG. like *agradecer.*

aborrecible *adj.* hateful, detestable.

aborrecimiento *m.* abhorrence, hate, dislike.

aborregado *adj.* fleecy, mackerel [sky].

aborregarse *ref.* to become covered with fleecy clouds (the sky). *2* (Am.) fig. to lose one's nerve, to get frightened.

aborricarse *ref.* to become coarse, to grow stupid.

abortar *intr.* to abort, miscarry. *2* BIOL. to abort.

abortivo, -va *adj.-m.* abortive.

aborto *m.* abortion, miscarriage. *2* monster.

abotagado, -da *adj.* bloated, swollen.

abotagamiento *m.* bloating, swelling.

abotagarse *ref.* to become bloted, swollen.

abotonador *m.* buttonhook.

abotonadura *f.* fastening [buttons].

abotonar *tr.* to button, button up. *2 intr.* to bud. *3 ref.* to button up [one's coat].

abovedado, -da *adj.* vaulted, fornicate(d.

abovedar *tr.* to vault, cove, make vault-shaped.

aboyar *tr.* to lay buoys in. *2 intr.* to float.

abozalar *tr.* to muzzle.

abra *f.* GEOL. bay, cove, haven. *2* dale, valley. *3* fissure.

abracadabra *m.* abracadabra.

Abrahán *pr. n.* Abraham.

abrasador, -ra *adj.* burning, scorching, very hot.

abrasar *t.* to burn, sear, scorch, parch. *2* [of cold or frost] to nip [a plant]. *3* fig. to squander. *4 ref.* to swelter, feel very hot. *5* AGR. to be nipped [by cold]. *6 abrasarse de* o *en*, to burn with [thirst, love, etc.].

abrasión *f.* abrasion.

abrasivo, -va *adj.-m.* abrasive.

abrazadera *f.* clasp, clamp, cleat, brace. *2* band [of a gun]. *3* PRINT. brace, bracket.

abrazamiento *m.* embracing.

abrazar *tr.* to embrace, hug, clasp. *2* to include, comprise. *3* to embrace, espouse, adopt, follow [a cause, opinion, etc.]. *4 ref.* to embrace, hug each other; to cling [to].

abrazo *m.* hug, embrace, clasp.

ábrego *m.* south wind.

abrelatas *m.* can or tin opener.

abrevadero, abrevador *m.* drinking trough. *2* watering, place for cattle.

abrevar *tr.* to water [cattle]. *2 ref.* to drink.

abreviación *f.* abbreviation. *2* abridgement. *3* shortening. *4* hastening, acceleration.

abreviadamente *adv.* briefly, in short.

abreviar *tr.* to abridge, abbreviate, shorten. *2* to hasten, speed up.

abreviatura *f.* abbreviation.

abridor *m.* opener. *2* grafting knife.

abrigadero *m.* sheltered place for ships.

abrigado, -da *adj.* protected, covered, sheltered. *2* wrapped-up, warmly dressed. *3* cosy.

abrigaño *m.* place sheltered from the wind.

abrigar *tr.* to cover, wrap, keep warm. *2* to shelter, protect. *3* to entertain, harbour [fears, hopes, etc.]. *4 ref.* to wrap oneself up. *5* to take shelter.

abrigo *m.* protection against the cold, keeping warm: *ropa de ~*, warm clothing. *2* shelter. *3* protection. *4* overcoat, wrap. *5* NAUT. haven.

abril *m.* April. *2 pl.* years of early youth.

abrileño, -ña *adj.* [pertaining to] April, like April.

abrillantador, -ra *n.* polisher, lapidary, person who polishes. *2 m.* polishing tool. *3 m.* polishing substance or product.

abrir *tr.* to open. *2* to unfasten, uncover, unlock, unseal. *3* to cut or tear open; to split. *4* to bore [a hole, a well], to dig [a trench]. *5* to head, lead [a procession, etc.]. *6* to whet [the appetite]. *7 ~ paso*, to make way; to clear the way. *8 tr.-ref.* to spread out, to unfold. *9 ref.* to open (be opened). *10* to split, to burst open. *11* [of flowers] to blossom. *12* to open up [to], confide [in]. ¶ Past. p.: *abierto.*

abrochar *tr.-ref.* to button, clasp, buckle; to fasten with hooks and eyes.

abrogación *f.* abrogation, repeal.

abrogar *tr.* to abrogate, repeal [an act, a bill, etc.].

abrojal *m.* ground abounding in caltrops.

abrojo *m.* BOT., MIL. caltrop. *2 pl.* NAUT. hidden rocks. *3* fig. difficulties.

abroncar *tr.-ref.* to vex, annoy. *2* pop. to dress down.

abroquelado, -da *adj.* BOT. shield-shaped.

abroquelar *tr.* NAUT. to boxhaul. *2* to shield. *3 ref.* to shield oneself.

abrótano *m.* BOT. abrotanum, southernwood.

abrumado, -da *adj.* overwhelmed, overcome.

abrumador, -ra *adj.* overwhelming, crushing. *2* oppressive, fatiguing.

abrumar *tr.* to overwhelm, crush. *2* to oppress, weary, fatigue. *3 ref.* [of the weather] to become foggy.

abrupto, -ta *adj.* abrupt, steep, craggy.

abrutado, -da *adj.* brutish.

absceso *m.* MED. abscess.

abscisa *f.* GEOM. abscissa.

abscisión *f.* abscission.

absentismo *m.* absenteeism.

ábside *m.-f.* ARCH. apse, apsis.

absidiola *f.* ARCH. apse chapel.

absidiolo *m.* ARCH. apsidiole.

absintio *m.* absinthe, absinth.

absolución *f.* absolution. *2* LAW acquittal.

absoluta *f.* dogmatic statement. *2* MIL. discharge.

absolutamente *adv.* absolutely, completely, in every way. *2* not at all, in no way. *3 ~ nada*, nothing at all, absolutely nothing.

absolutismo *m.* POL. absolutism.

absoluto, -ta *adj.* absolute. *2 m. lo ~*, the absolute. *3 en ~*, absolutely, by no means, at all.

absolutorio, -ria *adj.* absolutory, absolving.
absolvederas *f. pl.* coll. readiness to absolve.
absolver *tr.* to absolve. *2* to acquit. ¶ Conjug. like *mover.*
absorbente *adj.-m.* absorbent. *2 adj.* absorbing, engrossing.
absorber *tr.* to absorb. *2* to engross.
absorción *f.* absorption.
absorto, -ta *adj.* amazed, ecstatic. *2* absorbed in thought.
abstemio, -mia *adj.* abstemious. *2 m.-f.* teetotal(l)er.
abstención *f.* abstention, refraining.
abstencionismo *m.* POL. abstentionism.
abstencionista *adj.* abstentionist. *2 n* abstentionist person.
abstenerse *ref.* to abstain, refrain, forbear.
abstinencia *f.* abstinence.
abstinente *adj.* abstinent.
abstracción *f.* abstraction. *2 hacer ~ de,* to leave aside.
abstracto, -ta *adj.* abstract: *en ~,* in the abstract.
abstraer *tr.* to abstract. *2 ref.* to be abstracted, lost in thought. *3 abstraerse de,* to become oblivious of, to leave aside.
abstraído, -da *adj.* abstracted, lost in thought.
abstruso, -sa *adj.* abstruse.
absuelto, -ta *irreg. p. p.* of ABSOLVER.
absurdidad *f.* absurdity.
absurdo, -da *adj.* absurd, nonsensical. *2 m.* absurdity, nonsense.
abubilla *f.* ORN. hoopoe.
abuchear *tr.* to boo, hoot.
abucheo *m.* booing, hooting.
abuela *f.* grandmother: *cuénteselo a su ~,* fig. tell that to the marines. *2* old woman.
abuelo *m.* grandfather. *2* ancestor. *3* old man.
abuhardillado, -da *adj.* garret-like.
abulense *adj.-n.* AVILÉS.
abulia *f.* abulia.
abúlico, -ca *adj.* abulic.
abultado, -da *adj.* bulky, large, big.
abultamiento *m.* swelling, protuberance. *2* enlarging, exaggeration.
abultar *tr.* to enlarge, increase. *2* to exaggerate. *3 intr.* to bulge, be bulky.
abundamiento *m.* abundance. *2 a mayor ~,* moreover, furthermore, by the same token.
abundancia *f.* abundance, plenty.
abundante *adj.* abundant, copious, plentiful.
abundar *intr.* to abound [the plentiful]. *2* to abound, teem, be rich [in]. *3 ~ en una opinión,* to adhere to, or have, an opinion.
¡abur! *interj.* ¡AGUR!
aburguesamiento *m.* adoption of bourgeois customs and manners.
aburguesarse *ref.* to become or act as a bourgeois.
aburrido, -da *adj.* bored, weary. *2* boring, tedious, weary, irksome, tiresome.
aburrimiento *m.* boredom, weariness, ennui.
aburrir *tr.* to annoy, bore, tire, weary. *2* to hazard, to spend. *3 ref.* to get bored.
abusar *intr.* to go too far, to abuse. *2 ~ de,* to abuse [misuse, make bad use of]; to take advantage of; to impose upon.
abusivo, -va *adj.* abusive [implying misuse].
abuso *m.* abuse [misuse, bad use, immoderate use]. *2 ~ de confianza,* breach of faith or trust.
abyección *f.* abjection, abjectness.
abyecto, -ta *adj.* abject, base, servile.
acá *adv.* here, over here, hither, this way, this side;

~ y acullá, here and there; *de ~ para allá,* hither and thither. *2 desde entonces ~,* since that time; *¿de cuándo ~?,* since when?
acabable *adj.* which can be finished.
acabado, -da *adj.* finished. *2* complete, perfect, consummate; arrant. *3* spent, worn out, ruined. *4 ~ de hacer,* freshly done. *5 m.* last touch, touching up. *6* F. ARTS., WEAV. finish.
acabador, -ra *m.-f.* finisher.
acaballadero *m.* place and time for covering mares.
acaballado, -da *adj.* horselike.
acaballar *tr.* to cover [a mare].
acaballonar *tr.* AGR. to ridge.
acabamiento *m.* finish, finishing, completion. *2* end, death.
acabar *tr.* to finish, end, complete. *2* to make, achieve. *3* to consume, exhaust. *4* to finish, kill. *5 intr.* to end, finish. *6* to die. *7 ~ con,* to obtain; to use up; to destroy, put an end to. *8 ~ de,* to have just: *acaba de salir,* he has just come out. *9 ~ por,* to end by. *10 ¡acabáramos!,* at last! *11 ref.* to end, be over; to diminish, run out: *se acaba el pan,* the bread is running out; *¡se acabó!,* it is all up!
acabestrar *tr.* to accustom to a halter.
acabóse *m.* coll, limit, end: *ser el ~,* to be the limit, to be the end.
acacalote *m.* (Am.) ORN. cormorant.
acacia *f.* BOT. acacia.
acachetear *tr.* to slap.
academia *f.* academy. *2* special school. *3* F. ARTS academy figure.
academicismo *m.* academicism.
académico, -ca *adj.* academic, academical. *2* it is said of official studies, titles, degrees, etc. *3 m.* academic. *4* academician.
acaecedero, -ra *adj.* possible, that may happen.
acaecer *impers.* to happen, come to pass. ¶ Conjug. like *agradecer.*
acaecimiento *m.* happening, event, occurrence.
acalabrotar *tr.* NAUT. to make a cable-laid rope.
acalambrarse *ref.* to get a cramp.
acalefo *adj.-n.* ZOOL. acalephan. *2 pl.* ZOOL. Acalephae.
acalía *f.* BOT. marshmallow.
acaloradamente *adv.* heatedly.
acalorado, -da *adj.* heated, excited, fiery.
acaloramiento *m.* heat, ardour, excitement.
acalorar *tr.* to warm, heat [with work or exercise]. *2* to excite, inflame. *3 ref.* to get overheated. *4* to become heated, excited.
acallar *tr.* to silence, hush, still, quiet.
acamar *tr.* [of rain or wind] to lay [plants] flat. *2 ref.* [of plants] to be laid flat [by rain or wind].
acampanado, -da *adj.* bell-shaped, flaring.
acampanar *tr.* to shape like a bell.
acampar *intr.-tr.* to camp, encamp.
acanalado, -da *adj.* blowing through a narrow place [wind]. *2* channeled, grooved, fluted.
acanaladura *f.* ARCH. flute, stria, striation.
acanalar *tr.* to shape like a gutter. *2* to groove, flute, striate, corrugate.
acanallado, -da *adj.* base, rabble-like.
acanelado, -da *adj.* cinnamon-coloured or flavoured.
acantáceo, -a *adj.* BOT. acanthaceous.
acantilado, -da *adj.* sheer, cliffy. *2* stepped [sea floor]. *3 m.* cliff, bluff.
acanto *m.* BOT., ARCH. acanthus.
acantonamiento *m.* cantonment.

acantonar *tr.* to canton, quarter [troops].
acantopterigio, -a *adj.-m.* ICHTH. acanthopterygian.
acaparador, -ra *adj.* monopolizer; one who corners.
acaparamiento *m.* monopolizing, cornering.
acaparar *tr.* to monopolize. *2* COM. to corner.
acápite *m* (Am.) paragraph. *2* (Am.) *punto* ~, full stop, new paragraph; period, new paragraph.
acaracolado, -da *adj.* spiral-shaped.
acaramelado, -da *p. p.* of ACARAMELAR. *2* overpolite, spoony, oversweet.
acaramelar *tr.* to cover with caramel. *2 ref.* to get over-polite, spoony, oversweet.
acardenalar *tr.* to bruise; to beat black and blue.
acariciador, -ra *adj.* caressing, fondling. *2 m.-f.* caresser, fondler.
acariciar *tr.* to caress, fondle. *2* to stroke, brush lightly. *3* to cherish [hopes, etc.].
ácaro *m.* ZOOL. mite, acarus.
acarreador, -ra *m.-f.* carrier, transporter.
acarreamiento *m.* ACARREO.
acarrear *tr.* to carry, cart, haul, transport. *2* to cause, occasion. *3 ref.* to bring upon oneself.
acarreo *m.* carriage, cartage, haulage. *2 de* ~, transported; alluvial: *tierras de* ~, alluvium.
acarroñarse *ref.* obs. to decay, to rot. *2* (Am.) coll. to get scared or intimidated, to lose one's nerve.
acartonado, -da *adj.* cardboard-like. *2* dried up, wizened [with age].
cartonarse *ref.* to become cardboard-like. *2* to dry up, become wizened [with age].
caso *m.* chance, accident. *2 adv.* by chance; maybe, perhaps: *por si* ~, just in case.
acatable *adj.* worthy of, or deserving respect.
acatadamente *adv.* obediently and respectfully.
acatamiento *m.* obedience and respect.
acatar *tr.* to obey and respect.
acatarrado, -da *adj.* MED. having a cold.
acatarrar *tr.* to give a cold. *2 ref.* to catch a cold.
acaudalado, -da *adj.* rich, opulent, wealthy.
acaudalar *tr.* to accumulate, acquire [money, knowledge, etc.].
acaudillar *tr.* to lead, command [troops, men].
acaule *m.-f.* BOT. acaulescent.
Acaya *pr. n.* Achaea.
acceder *intr.* to accede, agree, consent.
accesible *adj.* accessible.
accesión *f.* acceeding. *2* LAW. accession.
accésit *m.* accessit.
acceso *m.* access [approach; entry]. *2* access, attack, fit, outburst [of illness, anger, etc.]. *3* sexual intercourse.
accesoria *f.* outbuilding, outhouse.
accesorio, -a *adj.* accessory [said of things]; secondary. *2 m.* accessory, fixture.
accidentado, -da *adj.* stormy, agitated. *2* broken, uneven, rough. *3* GEOG. accidented.
accidental *adj.* accidental. *2* acting [doing duty temporarily]. *3 m.* MUS. accidental.
accidentarse *ref.* to have or to be involved in an accident.
accidente *m.* accident. *2* MED. sudden fit. *3* MUS. accidental.
acción *f.* action [acting, doing, operation], act: ~ *de gracias*, thanksgiving; *en* ~, in action, at work. *2* attitude. *3* action [of an actor or speaker]. *4* COM. share, *stock. *5* PHYS., CHEM., MIL. action. *6* LAW lawsuit. *7* THEAT. plot.
accionamiento *m.* working.

accionar *tr.* to gesticulate, gesture. *2* MECH. to move, drive, operate, work.
accionista *m.-f.* shareholder, stockholder.
acebo *m.* BOT. holly tree.
acebolladura *f.* shake [in wood].
acebrado, -da *adj.* striped.
acebuche *m.* BOT. oleaster, wild olive tree.
acebuchina *f.* wild olive [fruit].
acecinar *tr.* to salt and dry [meat].
acechadero *m.* lurking or spying place.
acechanza *f.* ACECHO.
acechar *tr.* to lurk, to watch stealthily. *2* to lie in wait, look out for.
aceche *m.* copperas.
acecho *m.* lurking, spying: *al* ~, in wait, on the watch.
acedar *tr.* to sour, acidify. *2* to sour, embitter. *3 ref.* to sour [become sour or acid].
acedera *f.* BOT. sorrel, sorrel dock.
acederaque *m.* BOT. azederach.
acedía *f.* acidity, sourness. *2* sournes of temper. *3* heartburn. *4* PLATIJA.
acedo, -da *adj.* acid, sour, tart. *2* sour, crabbed, harsh, disagreeable.
acefalía *f.* acephalia.
acéfalo, -la *adj.* acephalous.
aceitar *tr.* to oil.
aceite *m.* olive oil, salad oil: ~ *virgen*, crude olive oil. *2* oil: ~ *de hígado de bacalao*, codliver oil; ~ *de linaza*, linseed oil; *echar* ~ *al fuego*, fig. to add fuel to the flames.
aceitera *f.* oil can. *2* MEC. oil cup. *3* ENT. oil beetle. *4 pl.* cruet, cruetstand.
aceitería *f.* olive-oil shop.
aceitero, -ra *adj.* [pertaining to] oil. *2 m.-f.* olive-oil dealer.
aceitoso, -sa *adj.* oily, oleaginous; greasy.
aceituna *f.* olive [fruit]: ~ *zapatera*, stale olive.
aceitunado, -da *adj.* olive, olivaceous.
aceitunero, -ra *m.-f.* olive dealer. *2* olive picker.
aceituní *m.* an ancient oriental fabric. *2* ARCH. a kind of arabesque work.
aceituno *m.* BOT. olive tree.
aceleración *f.* acceleration. *2* haste.
aceleradamente *adv.* quickly, fast, rapidly.
acelerado, -da *adj.* quick, fast. *2* PHYS. accelerated, increasing speed gradually. *3* acceleration. *4* quick motion.
acelerador, triz *adj.* accelerating. *2* accelerative. *3 m.* ANAT., AUTO. accelerator.
aceleramiento *m.* ACELERACIÓN.
acelerar *tr.* to accelerate, hasten, quicken, hurry. *2 ref.* to accelerate [move or act faster].
aceleratriz *f. adj.* accelerative [power].
acelerón *m.* sudden acceleration.
acelga *f.* BOT. chard, swiss chard.
acémila *f.* mule, pack mule.
acemilero, -ra *adj.* of the muleteer's trade. *2 m.* muleteer.
acendrado, -da *adj.* pure, stainless.
acendramiento *m.* purifying. *2* purity, stainlessness.
acendrar *tr.* to purify. *2* to fine, refine [metals].
acensar, acensuar *tr.* to tax [a property].
acento *m.* accent [in every sense]; stress; ~ *ortográfico*, written accent; ~ *prosódico*, stress accent.
acentuación *f.* accentuation.
acentuado, -da *adj.* accented. *2* accentuated.
acentuar *tr.* to accent. *2* to accentuate, emphasize.
aceña *f.* water mill. *2* AZUD 1.

acepción *f.* acceptation, meaning. *2* respect [of persons].
acepilladora *f.* ENG. planer, planing machine.
acepilladura *f.* brushing [of clothes]. *2* planing, shaving. *2 pl.* shavings.
acepillar *tr.* to brush [clothes, etc.]. *2* to plane, smooth [wood, metals].
aceptabilidad *f.* acceptability.
aceptable *adj.* acceptable, admissible.
aceptación *f.* acceptance. *2* approbation. *3* respect [of persons].
aceptador, -ra *m.-f.* accepter, acceptant. *2* acceptor.
aceptante *adj.* accepting. *2 m.-f.* ACEPTADOR.
aceptar *tr.* to accept, receive. *2* to approve of. *3* COM. to accept [a bill].
acequia *f.* irrigation canal or ditch.
acera *f.* sidewalk, pavement. *2* side of a street: *en la otra ~,* across the street.
aceráceas *f. pl.* BOT. Aceraceae.
acerado, -da *adj.* steel, made of steel; steely. *2* sharp, incisive, mordant.
acerar *tr.* to acierate. *2* to steel.
acerbidad *f.* acerbity, harshness, bitterness, cruelty.
acerbo, -ba *adj.* harsh to the taste. *2* harsh, bitter, cruel.
acerca de *adv.* about, concerning, with regard to.
acercamiento *m.* approach, approximation. *2* rapprochement.
acercar *tr.* to bring or place near or nearer. *2 ref.* to approach, come near or nearer; to come up [to]; gain [upon].
acería *f.* steel works.
acerico, acerillo *m.* pincushion.
acero *m.* steel. *2* sword; weapon. *3 pl.* spirit, courage. *4* coll. appetite.
acerola *f.* azarole [fruit].
acerolo *m.* BOT. azarole tree.
acérrimo, -ma *adj.* very acrid. *2* very strong, utter [enemy], staunch [friend, supporter].
acerrojar *tr.* to bolt [fasten or lock with a bolt].
acertado, -da *adj.* right, fit, proper, opportune; successful, well-aimed, apposite.
acertante *adj.* winning, just right, to the point. *2 n.* winner.
acertar *tr.* to hit [the mark]. *2* to hit upon, find. *3* to guess right; to divine. *4* to do well, right; to succeed in. *5 intr.* to happen, chance: *yo acertaba a estar allí,* I chanced to be there. ¶ CONJUG. INDIC. Pres.: *acierto, aciertas, acierta, aciertan.* | SUBJ. Pres.: *acierte, aciertes, acierte, acierten.* | IMPER.: *acierta, acierte, acierten.*
acertijo *m.* riddle; conundrum.
acervo *m.* heap, pile. *2* common property.
acetato *m.* CHEM. acetate.
acético, -ca *adj.* CHEM. acetic.
acetificar *tr.* to acetify.
acetileno *m.* CHEM. acetylene.
acetona *f.* CHEM. acetone.
acetre *m.* small bucket. *2* holy-water vessel.
aciago, -ga *adj.* ill-fated, unlucky, sad, ominous.
acial *m.* VET. barnacles, twitch [for horses].
aciano *m.* BOT. bluet, bluebottle, cornflower.
acíbar *m.* BOT. aloe. *2* aloes. *3* bitterness, displeasure.
acibarar *tr.* to put aloes into. *2* to embitter.
acicalado, -da *p. p.* of ACICALAR. *2 adj.* wellgroomed; trim, neat. *3 m.* ACICALADURA.
acicaladura *f.,* **acicalamiento** *m.* burnishing. *2* dressing, embellishing, adorning, trimming.

acicalar *tr.* to burnish, polish. *2* to dress, embellish, trim. *3 ref.* to embellish oneself.
acicate *m.* one-pointed spur. *2* spur, incitement.
acicatear *tr.* to stimulate, to spur on, to motivate.
acíclico, -ca *adj.* acyclic.
acidez *f.* acidity, sourness.
acidificar *tr.* to acidify.
acidímetro *m.* acidimeter.
ácido *adj.* acid, sour, tart. *2* harsh, mordant. *3 adj.-m.* CHEM. acid.
acidosis *f.* MED. acidosis.
aciculado, -da *adj.* acidulated.
acidular *tr.* to acidulate.
acídulo, -la *adj.* acidulous.
acierto *m.* good aim, hit. *2* good guess. *3* wisdom, prudence. *4* ability, address. *5* success.
acierto, acierte, etc. *irr.* V. ACERTAR.
acije *m.* ACECHE.
ácimo, -ma *adj.* ÁZIMO.
acimut *m.* ASTR. azimuth.
ación *f.* stirrup leather or strap.
acirate *m.* raised earthen boundary. *2* CABALLÓN. *3* walk between two rows of trees.
aclamación *f.* acclamation. *2* acclaim.
aclamador, -ra *m.-f.* acclaimer, applauder.
aclamar *tr.* to acclaim, cheer, hail, applaud. *2* to acclaim, proclaim.
aclaración *f.* explanation, elucidation. *2* rinsing.
aclarar *tr.* to clear, clarify. *2* to thin, thin out. *3* to rinse. *4* to clear, sharpen [faculties, etc.]. *5* to explain, elucidate. *6 intr.* [of weather] to clear up. *7* to dawn. *8 ref.* to become clear, to brighten up.
aclaratorio, -ria *adj.* explanatory.
aclavelado, -da *adj.* carnation-like.
aclimatación *f.* acclimatization, acclimation.
aclimatable *adj.* that can be acclimatized.
aclimatar *tr.-ref.* to acclimatize..
aclínico, -ca *adj.* aclinic.
acmé *f.* MED. acme.
acné *f.* MED. acne.
acobardar *tr.* to cow, daunt, dishearten. *2 ref.* to be daunted, to lose courage.
acobrado, -da *adj.* copper-coloured.
acochambrar *tr.* (Am.) to dirty, to soil, to befoul, to defile.
acochinar *tr.* to murder, slaughter like a pig. *2* ACOQUINAR. *3* to corner [in draughts].
acodado, -da *adj.* elbow-shaped, elbowed, cranked.
acodadura *f.* HORT. layerage.
acodalar *tr.* ARCH. to prop, stay.
acodamiento *m.* leaning upon one's elbows.
acodar *tr.-ref.* to lean or rest the elbow. *2 tr.* HORT. to layer. *3* ACODALAR.
acodillar *tr.* to bend into an elbow or angle.
acodo *m.* HORT. layer. *2* HORT. laying [of shoots].
acogedor, -ra *adj.* welcoming, inviting, cozy.
acoger *tr.* to receive, admit, take into one's house or company. *2* to shelter, protect. *3* to receive, accept [ideas, etc.]. *4 ref.* to take refuge [in]; to resort [to]; to claim the benefit [of].
acogida *f.* reception; hospitality: *dar buena ~,* to receive favourably. *2* refuge, shelter. *3* acceptance, approval.
acogido, -da *m.-f.* inmate [in a home or asylum].
acogimiento *m.* ACOGIDA 1, 2 & 3.
acogollar *tr.* to cover up [plants]. *2 intr.* [of plants] to sprout, bud.
acogotar *tr.* to kill by a blow on the back of the neck. *2* to overpower, to cow.

acojinar *tr.* to quilt. *2* MACH. to cushion.
acojonamiento *m.* vul. jitters.
acojonar *tr.* vul. to give someone the jitters, to put the wind up. *2 ref.* to get the jitters, to get the wind up. ¶
acolada *f.* accolade.
acolchado, -da *adj.* padded, quilted, upholstered. *2* stuffing, padding. *3* (Am.) mattress.
acolchar *tr.* to quilt. *2* CORCHAR.
acolitado *m.* acolythate.
acólito *m.* acolyte.
acología *f.* acology.
acollador *m.* NAUT. lanyard.
acollarar *tr.* to collar, put a collar on [an animal]. *2* to fasten dogs together by the collar.
acollonar *tr.-ref.* ACOBARDAR.
acombar *tr.* COMBAR.
acometedor, -ra *adj.* enterprising, go-ahead. *2* aggressive.
acometer *tr.* to attack, assail, charge, go at. *2* to undertake. *3* [of fear, sleep, an illness] to seize, overtake: *le acometió el miedo*, he was seized by fear.
acometida *f.* attack, assault. *2* intake [of a pipe or power line].
acometividad *f.* aggressiveness.
acomodable *adj.* adaptable. *2* suitable.
acomodación *f.* accommodation, adaptation.
acomodadizo, -za *adj.* adaptable, pliable.
acomodado, -da *adj.* convenient, fit, apt. *2* well off, well-to-do. *3* moderate [in price].
acomodador, -ra *m.-f.* THEAT. usher, usherette.
acomodamiento *m.* transaction, agreement. *2* convenience.
acomodar *tr.* to accommodate [adapt; supply; harmonize; reconcile]. *2* to take in, lodge. *3* to place, settle, usher. *4* to suit, fit. *5 ref.* to come to an arrangement. *6* to install oneself. *7* to adapt oneself.
acomodaticio, -cia *adj.* adaptable, pliable.
acomodo *m.* employment, situation, place. *2* lodgings.
acompañado, -da *adj.* accompanied. *2* frequented.
acompañamiento *m.* accompaniment; attendance. *2* retinue, train, cortege. *3* MUS. accompaniment. *4* THEAT. supernumeraries.
acompañanta *f.* female companion; chaperon. *2* MUS. woman accompanist.
acompañante *m.* accompanier, attendant. *2* MUS. accompanist.
acompañar *tr.* to keep [someone] company. *2* to accompany, go with, attend, escort. *3* to enclose. *4* MUS. to accompany. *5* to share [feelings] with. *6 ref.* to join, be accompanied. *7* MUS. to accompany oneself.
acompasado, -da *adj.* rhythmic, measured. *2* leisurely [in speech or action].
acompasar *tr.* to keep in time or in pace. *2* MUS. to mark the rhythm, to beat time. *3* fig. to adjust, to adapt.
acomplejar *tr.* to give a complex, to make someone feel inferior. *2 ref.* to get a complex, to feel inferior.
aconchabarse *ref.* to gather together, to gang up.
acondicionado, -da *adj.* [well, ill] conditioned. *2* fitted, conditioned: *con aire ~*, air-conditioned.
acondicionamiento *m.* conditioning: *~ de aire*, air conditioning.
acondicionar *tr.* to fit, condition, arrange.
acongojar *tr.* to distress, to anguish.
acónito *m.* BOT. aconite, wolf's-bane.

aconsejable *adj.* advisable.
aconsejar *tr.* to advise, counsel. *2 ref.* to take advice.
aconsonantar *tr.-intr.* to rhyme.
acontecer *impers.* to happen, occur, befall. ¶ CONJUG. like *agradecer*.
acontecimiento *m.* event, happening, occurrence.
acopado, -da *adj.* shaped like the top of a tree. *2* VET. cup-shaped [hoof].
acopar *tr.* to trim [a tree] to a crown. *3* NAUT. to hollow.
acopiar *tr.* to gather, store up, stock.
acopio *m.* gathering, storing. *2* store, stock, supply.
acopladura *f.*, **acoplamiento** *m.* coupling, joining.
acoplar *tr.* to couple; to join, connect, yoke. *2* to fit together. *3 tr.-ref.* to pair, mate. *4* to become intimate.
acoquinar *tr.-ref.* ACOBARDAR.
acorazado, -da *adj.* ironclad, armoured. *2 m.* battleship.
acorazar *tr.* to armour [ships, forts, etc.].
acorazonado, -da *adj.* heart-shaped, cordate.
acorcharse *tr.* to become spongy, corklike.
acordadamente *adv.* by common consent. *2* with mature deliberation.
acordado, -da *p. p.* of ACORDAR. *2* wise, judicious.
acordar *tr.* to decide, agree upon. *2* to reconcile. *3* MUS. to attune. *4* PAINT. to harmonize. *5* to agree, correspond. *6 ref.* to come to an agreement. *7* to remember, recall, recollect. ¶ CONJUG. like *contar*.
acorde *adj.* agreeing; coincident in opinion. *3* conformable, consonant. *3* MUS. in harmony. *4 m.* MUS. chord.
acordeón *m.* accordion.
acordeonista *m.-f.* accordionist.
acordonamiento *m.* milling [of a coin]. *2* surrounding [by a cordon of men].
acordonar *tr.* to lace, to tie. *2* to mill, knurl [coins]. *3* to surround with a cordon of men, to draw a cordon round.
acornar, acornear *tr.* to horn [gore with the horns].
ácoro *m.* BOT. sweet flag.
acorralar *tr.* to corral, pen [cattle]. *2* to drive at bay, to corner. *3* to intimidate.
acorrer *tr.* to help, succour.
acortamiento *m.* shortening, reduction.
acortar *tr.* to shorten, diminish, abridge. *2 ref.* to shorten [become short or shorter].
acosamiento *m.* close pursuit, persecution.
acosar *tr.* to pursue closely. *2* to persecute, harass, worry.
acoso *m.* ACOSAMIENTO.
acostado, -da *adj.* abed, in bed. *2* lying down. *3* HER. couchant.
acostar *tr.* to put to bed; to lay down. *2* NAUT. to bring alongside. *3 intr.* to lean, have a list. *4* to reach the coast. *5 ref.* to go to bed. ¶ CONJUG. like *contar*.
acostumbrado, -da *adj.* accustomed, used. *2* usual, habitual, customary.
acostumbrar *tr.* to accustom. *2 intr.* to be wont, be used [to]. *3 ref.* to accustom oneself, get used [to].
acotación *f.* annotation, marginal note. *2* THEAT. stage directions. *3* ACOTAMIENTO. *4* TOP. elevation marked on a map.
acotamiento *m.* boundary mark, landmark.
acotar *tr.* to preserve [ground]. *2* to delimitate,

restrict. *3* to accept, choose, take. *4* to mark elevations on [a map].
acotiledóneo, -a *adj.* acotyledonous. *2 f.* acotyledon.
acotillo *m.* sledge hammer.
acoyuntar *tr.* to yoke [oxen].
acracia *f.* acracy.
ácrata *adj.-n.* anarchist.
acre *adj.* acrid, tart, pungent. *2* acrimonious. *3 m.* acre.
acrecencia *f.* ACRECENTAMIENTO. *2* LAW accretion.
acrecentamiento *m.* increase, growth.
acrecentar *tr.* to increase, augment. *2* to advance, promote. *3 ref.* to increase [become greater].
acrecer *tr.* to increase. *2 intr.* to acquire by accretion. ¶ CONJUG. like *agradecer.*
acrecimiento *m.* increase.
acreditado, -da *adj.* of good repute, well-known.
acreditar *tr.* to accredit, authorize. *2* to prove to be. *3* to bring fame or credit. *4* ACC. to credit. *5 ref.* to win credit or fame; to gain reputation.
acreditativo, -va *adj.* crediting, proving.
acreedor, -ra *adj.* deserving, worthy. *2* ACC. favourable [balance]. *3 m.* COM. creditor.
acribillar *tr.* to riddle [pierce with many holes]. *2* to harass, plague, pester.
acriminar *tr.* to criminate, accuse.
acrimonia *f.* acridity. *2* acrimony.
acrisolado, -da *adj.* proven, unblemished.
acrisolar *tr.* to purify, refine. *2* to ascertain, prove [truth, virtue, etc.].
acritud *f.* ACRIMONIA.
acrobacia *f.* acrobatics; acrobatism.
acróbata *m.-f.* acrobat.
acrobático, -ca *adj.* acrobatic.
acromático, -ca *adj.* achromatic.
acromatismo *m.* achromatism.
acromio, acromión *m.* ANAT. acromion.
acrópolis *f.* acropolis.
acróstico *adj.-m.* acrostic.
acrotera *f.* ARCH. acroterium.
acta *f.* minutes [of a meeting, etc.]. *2* certificate of election. *3* statement of facts: ~ *notarial,* affidavit. *4* records, proceedings [of a learned society]. *5 actas de los mártires,* acta martyrum.
actínico, -ca *adj.* actinic.
actinio *m.* CHEM. actinium.
actitud *f.* attitude. *2* posture, position, pose.
activar *tr.* to activate. *2* to hasten, quicken.
actividad *f.* activity.
activo, -va *adj.* active. *2 m.* COM. assets. *3 en activo,* in active service.
acto *m.* act, action, deed: *en el* ~, at once; ~ *seguido,* inmediately afterwards. *2* ceremony, meeting, public function. *3* act [of a play]. *4* THEOL. act [of faith, etc.]. *5 Actos de los Apóstoles,* Acts of the Apostles.
actor *m.* THEAT. actor. *2* actor [in an affair].
actor, -ra *m.-f.* LAW actor, plaintiff, claimant.
actriz *f.* actress.
actuación *f.* action [of any agent], performance. *2 pl.* law proceedings.
actual *adj.* present, current, of the day. *2* THEOL. actual.
actualidad *f.* present time: *en la* ~, at present. *2* the state of being present, of the day: *ser de* ~, to be the topic of the day. *3* current events. *4 pl.* CINEM. newsreel.
actualizar *tr.* to bring up-to-date.
actualmente *adv.* at present, now, nowadays.
actuar *tr.* to put into action. *2 intr.* to act, to per-

form, to take action: ~ *de,* to act as. *3* LAW to perform judicial acts.
actuario *m.* clerk of a court of justice. *2* ~ *de seguros,* actuary.
acuadrillar *tr.* to band [unite in a band]. *2* to lead a band. *3 ref.* to band together.
acuarela *f.* PAINT. water colour, aquarelle.
acuarelista *m.-f.* aquarellist.
acuario *m.* aquarium. *2* ASTR. Aquarius.
acuartelar *tr.* to quarter [troops]. *2* to confine [troops] to barracks. *3* to quarter [to divide]. *4* NAUT. to flat in [sails]. *5 ref.* [of troops] to take quarters.
acuático, -ca or **acuátil** *adj.* aquatic, water.
acucia *f.* diligence, haste. *2* longing, eagerness.
acuciamiento *m.* stimulation, urge. *2* longing.
acuciante *adj.* pressing, urging.
acuciar *tr.* to stimulate, urge, incite, goad, hasten. *2* to long for.
acucioso, -sa *adj.* diligent, eager. *2* longing for.
acuclillarse *ref.* to squat, to crouch.
acuchillado, -da *adj.* slashed [garments].
acuchillar *tr.* to knife, stab, put to the sword. *2* to slash [a garment].
acudir *intr.* to go or come to: ~ *a una llamada,* to answer a call. *2* to frequent. *3* to come or go to the aid, or rescue [of]. *4* to have recourse [to], to resort [to].
acueducto *m.* aqueduct.
ácueo, -a *adj.* aqueous.
acuerdo *m.* accord, agreement, understanding, convention: *de* ~ *con,* in agreement with, in accordance with; *de común* ~, by mutual agreement: *estar de* ~, to agree; *poner de* ~, to make agree, to harmonize. *2* resolution: *tomar un* ~, to pass a resolution. *3* resolve. *4* advice, opinion. *5* reflection, prudence. *6* PAINT. accord. *7 estar uno en su* ~, to be in one's right senses.
acuerdo, acuerde, etc. *irr.* V. ACORDAR.
acuesto, acueste, etc. *irr.* V. ACOSTAR.
acuífero, -ra *adj.* aquiferous, that contains water.
acuitar *tr.* to distress, afflict, grieve.
acular *tr.* to back [a horse, a cart, etc.] against. *2* to corner [somebody].
acullá *adv.* yonder, over there, there.
acuminado, -da *adj.* BOT. acuminate.
acumulación *f.* accumulation, gathering.
acumulador, -ra *adj.* accumulating. *2 m.-f.* accumulator. *3 m.* MACH., ELECT. accumulator; storage battery.
acumular *tr.* to accumulate.
acumulativo, -va *adj.* accumulative, growing by additions. *2* LAW cumulative, non-concurring.
acunar *tr.* to rock, cradle [a child].
acuñación *f.* coinage, mintage.
acuñador, -ra *m.-f.* coiner, minter.
acuñar *tr.* to coin, mint. *2* to wedge, key.
acuosidad *f.* wateriness.
acuoso, -sa *adj.* watery, aqueous.
acupuntura *f.* MED. acupuncture.
acurrucarse *ref.* to huddle up, tu cuddle, nestle.
acusación *f.* accusation, charge, impeachment.
acusado, -da *adj.* accused. *2 m.-f.* accused, defendant.
acusador, -ra *adj.* accusing. *2 m.-f.* accuser: ~ *privado,* prosecutor.
acusar *tr.* to accuse, to charge [with], to prosecute, indict. *2* to denounce. *3* to acknowledge [receipt]. *4 ref.* to acknowledge one's sins.
acusativo *m.* GRAM. accusative.
acusatorio, -ria *adj.* accusatory.

acuse *m.* acknowledgement [of receipt].
acusón, -na *adj.* sneak, talebearer, telltale.
acústica *f.* PHYS. acoustics.
acústico, -ca *adj.* acoustic.
acutángulo *adj.* GEOM. acute-angled.
achacar *tr.* to impute, ascribe.
achacoso, -sa *adj.* sickly, ailing, unhealthy, infirm.
achaflanar *tr.* to chamfer, bevel.
achampañado, -da *adj.* champagne-like [wine].
achantarse *ref.* to submit, be daunted. *2* to hide during danger.
achaparrado, -da *adj.* low and spreading. *2* stumpy, stubby [person].
achaque *m.* ailment, indisposition. *2* weakness, habitual failing. *3* matter, subject. *4* excuse, pretext.
achares *m. pl.* coll. *dar ~,* to make jealous.
achatamiento *m.* flattening.
achatar *tr.* to flatten. *2 ref.* to become flat.
achicado, -da *adj.* diminished. *2* childish.
achicador, -ra *adj.* diminishing. *2 m.-f.* diminisher. *3 m.* NAUT. bailer, scooper.
achicamiento *m.* diminution, reduction. *2* humiliation.
achicar *tr.* to diminish, belittle. *2* to bail, bale, scoop [water]. *3* to humiliate, to cow. *4 ref.* to diminish. *6* to humble oneself; to be daunted.
achicoria *f.* BOT. chicory.
achicharradero *m.* inferno, hot place.
achicharrar *tr.* COOK. to burn. *2* to swelter, scorch with heat. *3* to bother. *4 ref.* to swelter, be scorched.
achinelado, -da *adj.* slipper-shaped.
achique *m.* NAUT., MIN. bailing, baling, scooping.
achispado, -da *adj.* tipsy.
achispar *tr.* to make tipsy. *2 ref.* to get tipsy.
achocharse *ref.* to begin to dote, to enter one's dotage.
achubascarse *ref.* to get showery.
achuchar *tr.* AZUZAR. *2* to crush [by a blow or weight]. *3* to push [a person] violently.
achuchón *m.* push, squeeze. *2* fit.
achulado, -da *adj.* jaunty, cocky.
achulaparse, achularse *ref.* to become or get jaunty or cocky.
adagio *m.* adage, proverb, saying. *2 adv.-m.* MUS. adagio.
adalid *m.* leader, chief.
adamado, -da *adj.* womanish, delicate [man].
adamantino, -na *adj.* adamantine.
adamascado, -da *adj.* WEAV. damasked.
adamascar *tr.* WEAV. to damask.
Adán *m. pr. n.* Adam.
adán *m.* coll. slovenly man.
adaptable *adj.* adaptable.
adaptación *f.* adaptation, fitting, accommodation.
adaptador, -ra *adj.* adapting. *2 m.-f.* adapter.
adaptar *tr.* to adapt, fit, suit, accommodate. *2 ref.* to adapt oneself, to fit, to suit.
adaraja *f.* ARCH. toothing.
adarga *f.* oval or heart-shaped leather shield.
adarme *m.* ancient weight [179 centigrams]. *2* whit, jot: *por adarmes,* very sparingly.
adarve *m.* FORT. walk behind the parapet on top of wall. *2* rampart.
adaza *f.* BOT. sorghum.
adecentar *tr.* to tidy. *2* to make decent. *3 ref.* to tidy oneself.
adecuación *f.* adequation. *2* adequacy, suitableness.

adecuadamente *adv.* appropriately, adequately, conveniently. *2* sufficiently.
adecuado, -da *adj.* adequate, fit, suitable.
adecuar *tr.* to fit, adapt, make suitable.
adefesio *m.* nonsense, absurdity. *2* ridiculous attire. *3* scarecrow, fright.
adehala *f.* bonus, extra, gratuity.
adehesar *tr.* to turn [land] into pasture.
Adelaida *pr. n.* Adelaide.
adelantado, -da *adj.* anticipated: *por ~,* in advance. *2* advanced. *3* proficient. *4* precocious. *5* fast [clock]. *6 m.* formerly, the governor of a province.
adelantamiento *m.* advance, advancing. *2* advancement, furtherance, promotion. *3* progress, improvement.
adelantar *tr.* to advance [move forward; hasten; further, promote]. *2* to advance [money, an event]. *3 tr.-ref.* to be in advance of; to outstrip, overtake; get ahead of. *4 intr.-ref.* [of a clock] to be fast. *5 intr.* to make progress, improve.
adelante *adv.* forward, ahead, onward, farther on: *ir ~, pasar ~,* to go on or further; *de tres libras en ~,* from three pounds up. *2 en ~, de aquí en ~,* henceforth; *más ~,* later on. *3 interj.* forward!, onward!, go on!, come in!
adelanto *m.* advance. *2* progress, improvement. *3* COM. advance, payment.
adelfa *f.* BOT. oleander, rosebay.
adelfilla *f.* BOT. spurge laurel.
adelgazamiento *m.* thinness, slenderness.
adelgazar *tr.* to attenuate, make thin or slender. *2* to subtilize. *3 intr.-ref.* to become thin or slender. *4* to taper off.
Adelina *pr. n.* Adeline.
Adelita *pr. n.* dim. of ADELA.
ademán *m.* gesture, attitude: *en ~ de,* in the attitude of. *2 pl.* manners.
además *adv.* moreover, besides, furthermore, yet, too, as well. *2 ~ de,* besides.
adenoideo, -a *adj.* ANAT. adenoid.
adenoma *m.* MED. adenoma.
adentellar *tr.* to bite, to set one's teeth in. *2* to leave a toothing in [a wall].
adentrarse *ref.* to penetrate, go into.
adentro *adv.* within, inside, in: *mar ~,* out at sea; *tierra ~,* inland. *2 m. pl.* inward mind or thoughts: *para sus adentros,* to oneself. *3 interj.* come in!; let's go in!
adepto *m.* adept, initiated. *2* adherent, follower.
aderezamiento *m.* dressing, seasoning. *2* adornment, embellishing.
aderezar *tr.* to adorn, embellish, dress. *2* to cook. *3* to season. *4* to arrange, prepare. *5* to repair. *6* to dress [salad]. *7* to direct.
aderezo *m.* adornment, dressing. *2* cooking, seasoning. *3* preparation. *4* set of jewelry. *5* trappings [of a horse].
adeudado, -da *adj.* owing, still to be paid. *2* indebted.
adeudar *tr.* to owe. *2* to be dutiable. *3* ACC. to debit, to charge. *4 intr.* EMPARENTAR.
adeudo *m.* debt. *2* customs duty. *3* ACC. charge debit.
adherencia *f.* adhesion [sticking together]. *2* BOT., PHYS., MED. adhesion. *3* adhesiveness.
adherente *adj.* adherent, adhesive. *2* adherent, attached. *3 m. pl.* equipment, accessories.
adherido, -da *p. p.* of ADHERIR. *2 m.-f.* adherent, follower.

adherir *intr.-ref.* to adhere, to stick (to). ¶ CONJUG. like *hervir*.
adhesión *f.* adherence, adhesion. 2 PHYS. adhesion.
adhesivo, -va *adj.-m.* adhesive.
adiar *tr.* to fix a date.
adición *f.* addition, adding, addendum. 2 MATH. addition.
adicional *adj.* additional.
adicionar *tr.* to add, join; to make additions to.
adicto, -ta *adj.* attached, devoted. 2 *m.* supporter, follower.
adiestrado, -da *adj.* instructed, taught, trained. 2 HER. dexter.
adiestrador, -ra *adj.* who instructs or trains. 2 *n.* instructor, trainer, teacher.
adiestramiento *m.* training, drilling, teaching.
adiestrar *tr.* to train, drill, school, teach, guide. 2 *ref.* to train oneself, practise.
adinerado, -da *adj.* rich, moneyed.
adintelado, -da *adj.* ARCH. straight [arch].
adiós *interj.* good-by or -bye!, farewell!, adieu!
adiposidad *f.* adiposity.
adiposo, -sa *adj.* adipose.
aditamento *m.* addition, addendum.
adivas *f. pl.* VET. vives.
adive *m.* ZOOL. corsac.
adivinación *f.* divination.
adivinanza *f.* ADIVINACIÓN. 2 ACERTIJO.
adivinar *tr.* to divine, guess, foresee. 2 to solve [a riddle].
adivino, -na *m.-f.* diviner, soothsayer.
adjetivación *f.* use in adjectival form.
adjetival *adj.* GRAM. adjectival.
adjetivar *tr.* to make an adjective of. 2 to apply adjectives to.
adjetivo, -va *adj.-s.* adjective. 2 *adj.* adjectival.
adjudicación *f.* awarding, adjudgement.
adjudicador, -ra *m.-f.* awarder.
adjudicar *tr.* to adjudge, award, assign. 2 *ref.* to appropriate.
adjudicatario, -ria *m.-f.* awardee.
adjuntar *tr.* to attach, to join, to append. 2 to enclose, to include. 3 to give.
adjunto, -ta *adj.* adjunct, joined. 2 enclosed [in a letter]. 3 *m.-f.* adjunct, associate. 4 *m.* ADITAMENTO.
adminículo *m.* adminicle. 2 *pl.* articles carried for emergency use.
administración *f.* administration, administering. 2 office of an administrator, manager, steward or trustee. 3 ~ *de Correos*, Post Office; ~ *militar*, Commissariat.
administrador, -ra *m.-f.* administrator, manager, steward, trustee. 2 ~ *de Correos*, postmaster.
administrar *tr.* to administer, manage. 2 to administer.
administrativo, -va *adj.* administrative.
admirable *adj.* admirable. 2 wonderful.
admiración *f.* admiration. 2 wonder, astonishment. 3 exclamation mark (¡ !).
admirado, -da *adj.* wondering, astonished.
admirador, -ra *m.-f.* admirer.
admirar *tr.* to astonish, surprise. 2 to admire. 3 *ref.* to wonder, be astonished, surprised: *admirarse de*, to wonder at.
admirativo, -va *adj.* admirative; of admiration; of wonder. 2 astonished.
admisible *adj.* admissible, allowable.
admisión *f.* admission.
admitir *tr.* to admit [in every sense except «to acknowledge»]. 2 to accept. 3 to allow, suffer.

admonición *f.* admonition, admonishment.
admonitor *m.* admonisher, admonitor.
adnato, -ta *adj.* BOT., ZOOL. adnate.
adobado *m.* pickled meat [esp. pork].
adobar *tr.* to dress, prepare. 2 to pickle, souse [meat]. 3 to cook. 4 to tan and dress [hides].
adobe *m.* adobe.
adobo *m.* dressing, preparing; tanning. 2 sauce for seasoning or pickling. 3 mixture for dressing skins or cloth.
adocenado, -da *adj.* common, ordinary, vulgar.
adocenar *tr.* to dozen. 2 *ref.* to become common, ordinary, vulgar.
adoctrinamiento *m.* indoctrination, filling someone's mind with particular ideas or beliefs. 2 teaching.
adoctrinar *tr.* to indoctrinate, teach, instruct.
adolecer *intr.* to be ill. 2 ~ *de*, to have [a specified defect, vice etc.].′3 *ref.* CONDOLERSE. ¶ CONJUG. like *agradecer*.
adolescencia *f.* adolescence.
adolescente *adj.-n.* adolescent.
Adolfo *pr. n.* Adolphus.
adonde *adv.* where. 2 *interr.* where?, whither?
adondequiera *adv.* wherever, anywhere.
Adonis *m.* Adonis.
adopción *f.* adoption.
adoptador, -ra; adoptante *adj.* adopting. 2 *m.-f.* adopter.
adoptar *tr.* to adopt. 2 to embrace [an opinion]. 3 to take [an attitude, a decision].
adoptivo, -va *adj.* adoptive.
adoquín *m.* paving stone. 2 fig. blockhead.
adoquinado *m.* cobblestone paving; stone-block pavement.
adorable *adj.* adorable.
adoración *f.* adoration, worship.
adorador, -ra *adj.* adoring. 2 *m.-f.* adorer. 3 worshipper.
adorar *tr.* to adore; worship.
adormecedor, -ra *adj.* soporific, sleep-inducing. 2 fig. sedative.
adormecer *tr.* to make sleepy, to lull to sleep. 2 to lull, allay. 3 *ref.* to drowse, fall asleep. 4 to grow benumbed. ¶ CONJUG. like *agradecer*.
adormecimiento *m.* drowsiness, slumber. 2 numbness.
adormidera *f.* BOT. opium poppy. 2 poppy-head.
adormilarse *ref.* to drowse.
adormitarse *ref.* ADORMILARSE.
adornado, -da *adj.* adorned, ornamented.
adornar *tr.* to adorn, beautify, grace, decorate, embellish, deck, garnish.
adorno *m.* adornment, ornament, decoration, embellishment, garnishment, trimming.
adosar *tr.* to back or lean [something] against. 2 HER. to place back to back.
adquiero, adquiera, etc. *V.* ADQUIRIR.
adquirente; adquiridor, -ra *adj.* acquiring. 2 *m.-f.* acquirer.
adquirido, -da *adj.* acquired, not inherent. 2 bought, purchased.
adquirir *tr.* to acquire. 2 to obtain, to buy. ¶ CONJUG. INDIC. Pres.: *adquiero, adquieres, adquiere, adquieren.* | SUBJ. Pres.: *adquiera, adquieras, adquiera, adquieran.* | IMPER.: *adquiere, adquiera, adquieran.*
adquisición *f.* acquisition; acquirement.
adquisidor, -ra *adj.* ADQUIRENTE.
adquisitivo, -va *adj.* LAW acquisitive.
adragante *adj. goma* ~, tragacanth [gum].

adrales *adv.* hurdles on the sides of cart.
adrede *adv.* purposely, on purpose.
adrenalina *f.* CHEM. adrenaline.
Adrián *m. pr. n.* Adrian.
Adriático *pr. n.* GEOGR. Adriatic Sea.
adscribir *tr.* to attribute, assign, ascribe. *2* to attach, or appoint [a person] to a service.
adscrito, -ta *p. p.* of ADSCRIBIR.
adscripción *f.* attachment, appointment.
adsorbente *m.-adj.* CHEM. adsorbent.
adsorción *f.* CHEM. adsorption.
aduana *f.* customhouse.
aduanero, -ra *adj.* [pertaining to] customs or the customhouse. *2 m.* customhouse officer.
aduar *m.* douar. *2* gipsy camp.
aducción *f.* PHYSIOL. adduction.
aducir *tr.* to adduce, cite, allegre. ¶ CONJUG. like *conducir.*
aductor *adj.-m.* ANAT. adductor.
adueñarse *ref. ~ de,* to seize, take possession of.
aduja NAUT. rope coil, fake.
adujar *tr.* NAUT. to coil, fake.
adulación *f.* adulation, flattery.
adulador, -ra *adj.* adulating, flattering. *2 m.-f.* adulator, flatterer.
adular *tr.* to adulate, flatter, fawn upon.
adulón, -na *m.-f.* adulator, gross flatterer.
adúltera *f.* adulteress.
adulteración *f.* adulteration.
adulterado, -da *adj.* adulterated, sophisticated.
adulterar *tr.* to adulterate, corrupt, sophisticate. *2 intr.* to commit adultery.
adulterino, -na *adj.* adulterine.
adulterio *m.* adultery.
adúltero, -ra *adj.* adulterous. *2 m.* adulterer. *3 f.* adulteress.
adulto, -ta *adj.-n.* adult, grown-up.
adulzar *tr.* to soften [metals]. *2* ENDULZAR.
adustez *f.* gloominess, sulleness, sternness.
adusto, -ta *adj.* burnt, hot. *2* gloomy, sullen, stern.
advenedizo, -za *adj.* foreign. *2 m.-f.* foreigner, stranger, newcomer. *3* upstart, parvenu.
advenimiento *m.* advent, arrival, coming. *2* accession [to the throne].
advenir *intr.* to come, to arrive.
adventista *adj.-n.* adventist.
adventicio, -cia *adj.* adventitious.
adverbial *adj.* adverbial.
adverbio *m.* GRAM. adverb.
adversario, -ria *m.-f.* adversary, opponent; foe.
adversativo, -va *adj.* GRAM. adversative.
adversidad *f.* adversity.
adverso, -sa *adj.* adverse.
advertencia *f.* admonition, warning, advice. *2* foreword. *3* notice. *4* awareness, knowledge.
advertido, -da *adj.* capable, knowing, clever.
advertir *tr.* to notice, observe, perceive, realize. *2* to advise, instruct, recommend, point out; to warn. *3* to admonish. ¶ CONJUG. like *discernir.*
adviento *m.* ECCL. advent.
advierto, advierta etc. *irr.* V. ADVERTIR.
advocación *f.* name under wich a church, altar, saint, etc., is known.
adyacente *adj.* adjacent, adjoining.
adyuvante *adj.* adjuvant.
aeración *f.* aeration.
aéreo, -rea *adj.* aerial. *2* air. *3* airy, ethereal, insubstantial.
aeriforme *adj.* aeriform.
aerobio, -a *adj.* aerobic, aerobious. *2 m.* aerobe.
aerobús *m.* airbus.

aeroclub *m.* flying club.
aerodeslizador *m.* hovercraft, anphibian craft supported on air cushions.
aerodinámica *f.* aerodynamics.
aerodinámico, -ca *adj.* aerodynamic. *2* streamline.
aeródromo *m.* aerodrome.
aerograma *m.* aerogram.
aerolito *m.* aerolite.
aeromancia *f.* aeromancy.
aerómetro *m.* aerometer.
aeromodelismo *m.* aeroplane modelling, aeromodelling.
aeronauta *m.* aeronaut.
aeronáutica *f.* aeronautics.
aeronáutico, -ca *adj.* aeronautic(al.
aeronave *f.* airship.
aeroplano *m.* aeroplane, airplane.
aeropuerto *m.* airport.
aeroscopio *m.* aeroscope.
aerostación *f.* aerostation.
aerostática *f.* aerostatics.
aerostático, -ca *adj.* aerostatic.
aerostato *m.* aerostat, air balloon.
afabilidad *f.* affability.
afable *adj.* affable.
afamado, -da *adj.* famous, renowned.
afamar *tr.* to make famous, give fame to.
afán *m.* toil, labour. *2* anxiety, eagerness, ardour, solicitude; desire.
afanar *tr.* to harass, worry. *2 intr.* to drudge. *3 ref.* to toil, labour, strive: *afanarse por,* to strive to.
afanoso, -sa *adj.* toilsome, laborious. *2* eager, anxious, desirous.
afasia *f.* MED. aphasia.
afeamiento *m.* disfiguring, making ugly. *2* blaming, reproaching.
afear *tr.* to disfigure, deface, make ugly. *2* to blame, reproach.
afección *f.* affection, inclination. *2* MED. affection.
afectación *f.* affectation, affectedness. *2* affecting. *3* impression, emotion.
afectado, -da *adj.* affected.
afectar *tr.* to make a show of; to feign. *3* to annex, áttach. *3* to affect [move; influence; concern]. *4* LAW to encumber. *5* MED. to affect. *6 ref.* to be affected, moved.
afectivo, -va *adj.* affective.
afecto, -ta *adj.* attached, fond. *2* LAW ~ *a,* subject to [some charge]. *3 m.* affection, love, attachment. *4* affect, feeling, passion.
afectuosidad *f.* affectionateness.
afectuoso, -sa *adj.* fond, affectionate, loving; kind.
afeitar *tr.* to shave [with razor]. *2* to beautify; to make up. *3* to trim [a plant; a horse's tail or mane]. *4 ref.* to shave. *5* to put on cosmetics, make up.
afeite *m.* cosmetics, paint, rouge, make-up.
afelio *m.* ASTR. aphelion.
afelpado, -da *adj.* plushy, velvety.
afeminación *f.* effeminacy.
afeminado, -da *adj.* effeminate, ladylike.
afeminar *tr.-ref.* to effeminate.
aferente *adj.* PHYSIOL. afferent.
aféresis *f.* GRAM. aphaeresis, apheresis.
aferradamente *adv.* obstinately.
aferrado, -da *adj.* clinging, holding fast [to an opinion or purpose].
aferramiento *m.* grasping, seizing, grappling. *2* NAUT. furling. *3* obstinacy, tenacity.
aferrar *tr.* to grasp, seize, grapple. *2* NAUT. to furl. *3* NAUT. to moor, anchor. *4 ref. aferrarse a,* to hold

fast to, cling to; to stick to [an opinion]. *5* [of boats] to grapple.
afestonado, -da *adj.* festooned.
Afganistán *pr. n.* GEOG. Afghanistan.
afianzar *tr.* to stand surety for. *2* to make firm or fast, to prop, to strengthen. *3 ref.* to become firm or fast, to steady oneself, to hold fast [to].
afición *f.* fondness, liking, leaning. *2* ardour. *3* hobby. *4* coll. *la* ~, the fans, the public.
aficionado, -da *m.-f.* amateur. *2* fan, devotee.
aficionar *tr.* to give a liking for. *2 ref.* to grow fond of, to take a liking to.
afidávit *m.* affidavit.
áfido *m.* ENT. aphid, aphis.
afijo, -ja GRAM. affixed. *2 m.* GRAM. affix.
afiladera *f.* whetstone.
afilado, -da *adj.* sharp, keen, pointed. *2* taper.
afiladura *f.* sharpening, grinding, whetting.
afilador, -ra *adj.* sharpening, whetting. *2 m.* tool or knife grinder.
afilamiento *m.* sharpness [of the face or nose], tapering [of fingers].
afilar *tr.* to sharpen, grind, whet, hedge, point; to taper. *2 ref.* to grow thin; to taper.
afiliación *f.* affiliation [with a party, etc.].
afiliado, -da *adj.-s.* affiliate, member.
afiliar *tr.* to affiliate, associate. *2 ref. afiliarse a,* to join, to affiliate with.
afiligranado, -da *adj.* filigree, filigreed. *2* delicate, slender, thin.
afiligranar *tr.* to filigree. *2* to give an exquisite finish to.
afín *adj.* contiguous, adjacent. *2* kindred, related, allied. *3 m.-f.* relative by marriage.
afinación *f.* perfecting, finishing touch. *2* MUS. tune; tuning.
afinado, -da *adj.* well finished, perfected. *2* MUS. in tune, well tuned.
afinamiento *m.* AFINACIÓN. *2* FINURA.
afinar *tr.* to perfect, polish, refine. *2* to refine, try [metals]. *3* MUS. to tune. *4* MUS. to sing or play in tune. *5 ref.* to become refined, polished.
afincar *intr.-ref.* FINCAR.
afinidad *f.* affinity.
afino *m.* refining, trying [of metals].
afirmación *f.* affirmation, assertion.
afirmado *m.* roadbed.
afirmar *tr.* to make firm, to firm, secure, steady. *2* to affirm, say. *3 ref.* to steady oneself, to lean [upon]. *4* to maintain firmly.
afirmativa *f.* affirmative, affirmative proposition.
afirmativo, -va *adj.* affirmative, affirming.
aflamencado, -da *adj.* flamenco-like.
aflautado, -da *adj.* fluted, flutelike.
aflechado, -da *adj.* arrow-shaped.
aflicción *f.* affliction, grief, sorrow, distress.
aflictivo, -va *adj.* afflictive.
afligido, -da *adj.* afflicted, sorrowing, grieving.
afligir *tr.* to afflict. *2* to distress, grieve. *3 ref.* to grieve, repine, sorrow.
aflojadura *f.*, **aflojamiento** *m.* slackening, relaxation, loosening.
aflojamiento *m.* loosening, slackening. *2* relaxation, laxity [of discipline, severity...]. *3* loosening [of ties, bonds...]. *4* abatement [of the wind, of a storm].
aflojar *tr.* to slacken, slack, loose, loosen, relax, ease, let out. *2* coll, to pay up. *3 intr.* to slack, slacken, relent, let up, abate, weaken. *4 ref.* to become slack, loose, relaxed.
afloramiento *m.* MIN. outcrop, outcropping.

aflorar *intr.* MIN. to outcrop, crop out.
afluencia *f.* affluence, inflow, flowing to. *2* affluence, abundance, plenty.
afluente *adj.* inflowing. *2* fluent, voluble. *3 m.* affluent.
afluir *intr.* ~ *a,* to flow in, into, to or towards; to congregate in; [of a stream] to discharge into. ¶ CONJUG. like *huir.*
aflujo *m.* MED. afflux, affluxion.
afluyo, afluyó, afluya, etc. *irr.* V. AFLUIR.
afofarse *ref.* to soften, to become or to turn soft.
afonía *f.* MED. aphonia.
afónico, -ca *adj.* aphonic.
áfono, -na *adj.* PHONET. aphonic.
aforar *tr.* to appraise [goods]. *2* to gauge [a stream, a vessel, etc.].
aforismo *m.* aphorism.
aforo *m.* gauging; appraisement. *2* capacity [of a theatre, cinema, etc.].
afortunado, -da *adj.* lucky, fortunate, happy.
afrancesado, -da *adj.* Frenchified. *2 adj.-n.* Francophile [during the Peninsular War].
afrancesar *tr.* to Frenchify. *2 ref.* to become a Francophile [during Peninsular War].
afrecho *m.* SALVADO.
afrenta *f.* affront, outrage, dishonour.
afrentar *tr.* to affront, outrage, dishonour.
África *pr. n.* GEOG. Africa.
africano, -na *adj.* African.
áfrico *adj.* african. *2 m.* ÁBREGO.
afro, afra *adj.* AFRICANO.
afrodisíaco *adj.-m.* aphrodisiac.
afrontamiento *m.* confrontation, facing.
afrontar *tr.* to put face [to]; to bring face to face. *2* to confront, face.
afta *f.* MED. aphta.
afuera *adv.* out, outside. *2* outward. *3 interj.* out of the way! *4 f. pl.* outskirts, environs.
afusión *f.* affusion.
afuste *m.* gun-carriage.
agabachar *tr.* to Frenchify.
agachadiza *f.* ORN. snipe.
agachar *tr.* to lower, bend down [a part of the body]: fig. ~ *las orejas,* to hang one's head. *2 ref.* to stoop; to duck, cower; to crouch, squat [as a partridge].
agáloco *m.* BOT. agalloch, aloes wood.
agalla *f.* BOT. gall, gall-nut. *2* ~ *de ciprés,* cypress nut. *3* tonsil. *4* gill [of a fish]. *5* each side of a bird's head. *6 pl.* coll. courage, guts.
agallón *m.* large gall-nut. *2* hollow silver bead. *3* large wooden bead of a rosary.
agamí *m.* ORN. agami, trumpeter.
ágape *m.* agape. *2* banquet, feast.
agarbanzado, -da *adj.* chick-pea coloured.
agarbillar *tr.* AGR. to sheaf, sheave.
agareno, -na *adj.-n.* Mohammedan.
agárico *m.* BOT. agaric.
agarrada *f.* altercation, wrangle, tussle.
agarradero *m.* hold, handle, grip. *2* fig. protection, pull. *3* NAUT. anchorage.
agarrado, -da *adj.* close-fisted, stingy, niggardly.
agarrador *m.* flatiron holder.
agarrar *tr.* to seize, take, catch; to clutch, grab, grasp. *2* to get, obtain. *3 ref.* to grapple, take hold of each other. *4 agarrarse a,* to take hold of, cling to, catch at.
agarrotado, -da *adj.* tied up tightly. *2* rigid, stiff. *3* stuck, jammed, seized-up [a motor]. *4* fig. restricted, tied down.
agarrotamiento *m.* tying up, bundling up, bin-

ding. *2* seizing up [of a mòtor]. *3* stiffness, rigidity. *4* garrotting, garotting.

agarrotar *tr.* to tighten; to hold tight, to press tightly. *2* to garrotte. *3* to oppress. *4 ref.* to stiffen.

agasajar *tr.* to fête, make much of. *2* to regale, entertain, feast.

agasajo *m.* attention shown, affectionate reception. *2* gift, treat, refreshment.

ágata *f.* agate.

agaucharse *ref.* (Am.) to adopt the gauchos' way of life.

agavanza *f.* BOT. hip [dog rose fruit].

agavanzo *m.* BOT. dog rose. *2* AGAVANZA.

agave *m.* BOT. agave, century plant.

agavillar *tr.* to sheave. *2* to band, collect in bands. *3 ref.* to band together.

agazapar *tr.* coll. to nab, seize. *2 ref.* to crouch, squat.

agencia *f.* agency, bureau. *2* (Am.) pawnshop.

agenciar *tr.* to carry out, negotiate. *2 tr.-ref.* to manage to get.

agencioso, -sa *adj.* diligent, active.

agenda *f.* note-book, memorandum book.

agente *m.* agent. *2* ~ *de cambio y bolsa,* stockbroker; ~ *de negocios,* business agent; ~ *de policía,* plain-clothes man or officer.

agibílibus *m.* industry, smartness.

agigantado, -da *adj.* gigantic. *2* uncommon, extraordinary.

agigantar *tr.* to enlarge, aggrandize. *2* to exaggerate.

ágil *adj.* agile, nimble, limber, quick.

agilidad *f.* agility, nimbleness, quickness.

agilitar *tr.* to make someone agile. *2* to make easy, to facilitate. *3* (Am.) to activate.

agio, agiotaje *m.* agio. *2* agiotage, stockjobbing.

agiotador, agiotista *m.* agioter, stockjobber.

agitación *f.* agitation, flurry, flutter, excitement.

agitador, -ra *adj.* agitating. *2 m.* agitator.

agitanado, -da *adj.* gypsylike.

agitar *tr.* to agitate; to flurry, excite. *2* to shake, to stir; to wave. *3 ref.* to be agitated, to flurry [of the sea] to be rough.

aglomeración *f.* agglomeration, crowding, crowd.

aglomerado, -da *adj.-m.* agglomerate. *2 m.* coal briquette.

aglomerar *tr.* to agglomerate. *2 ref.* to agglomerate [be agglomerated].

aglutinación *f.* agglutination.

aglutinante *adj.* agglutinating, agglutinative. *2 m.* agglutinating agent.

aglutinar *tr.* to agglutinate. *2 ref.* to be agglutinated.

agnación *f.* agnation.

agnado, -da *adj.-m.* agnate.

agnosticismo *m.* agnosticism.

agnóstico, -ca *adj.* agnostic(al. *2 m.-f.* agnostic.

Agnusdéi *m.* Agnus Dei.

agobiado, -da *adj.* bent over, weighed down, bowed. *2* overwhelmed, over burdened, loaded with worries. *3* too tired, exhausted. *4* round-shouldered, with the shoulders bent forward.

agobiar *tr.* to bow down, weigh down, overburden; to oppress.

agobio *m.* burden, oppression, fatigue.

agolpamiento *m.* crowding, thronging.

agolpar *tr.* to gather suddenly. *2 ref.* to crowd, throng; to rush [to].

agonía *f.* agony, death agony. *2* agony, anguish.

agónico, -ca *adj.* dying, in the death agony. *2* pertaining to the death agony.

agonizante *adj.* dying. *2 m.-f.* dying person. *3 m.* monk who assists the dying.

agonizar *intr.* to be dying. *2 tr.* to press, hurry. *3* to assist the dying.

ágora *f.* agora.

agorafobia *f.* MED. agoraphobia.

agorar *tr.* to predict superstitiously. ¶ CONJUG. like *contar.*

agorero, -ra *adj.* of ill omen [bird]. *2 m.-f.* diviner. *3* a prophet of evil. *4* a believer in omens.

agorgojarse *ref.* [of grains, seeds] to get weeviled.

agostamiento *m.* parching, drying up [plants].

agostar *tr.* to parch, dry up [plants]. *2 ref.* [of plants] to be parched, dried up.

agostero *m.* harvest-worker.

agosto *m.* August. *2* harvest time; harvest, reaping: *hacer uno su* ~, to feather one's nest.

agotable *adj.* exhaustible.

agotador, -ra *adj.* exhausting, tiresome.

agotamiento *m.* exhaustion.

agotar *tr.* to exhaust, to drain off, use up, work out, sell out, tire out. *2 ref.* to exhaust oneself; to be exhausted, to run out; to become sold out.

agracejina *f.* BOT. barberry [fruit].

agracejo *m.* stunted grape. *2* BOT. barberry [tree].

agraciado, -da *adj.* graceful, well-favoured, genteel. *2* having [a gift, etc.] bestowed on him; winner [of a lottery prize].

agraciar *tr.* to grace, adorn. *2* to bestow [on], to favour [with].

agradable *adj.* agreeable, pleasant, enjoyable.

agradar *tr.* to please, be agreeable to; to suit, gratify: *esto me agrada,* I like this. *2 ref.* to like, to be pleased with. *3* to like each other.

agradecer *tr.* to acknowledge [a favour]; to thank for, be grateful for. ¶ CONJUG. INDIC. Pres.: *agradezco.* | SUBJ. PRES.: *agradezco, agradezcas, agradezca; agradezcamos, agradezcáis, agradezcan.* IMPER.: *agradezca; agradezcamos, agradezcan.*

agradecido, -da *adj.* acknowledged [favour]. *2* grateful, thankful, obliged.

agradecimiento *m.* gratitude, thankfulness.

agradezco, agradezca, etc. *irr.* V. AGRADECER.

agrado *m.* affability, amiableness, graciousness. *2* pleasure, liking.

agramadera *f.* scutch, brake, breaker.

agramado *m.* scutching, braking.

agramar *tr.* to brake [flax or hemp].

agramiza *f.* scutch, flax or hemp tow.

agrandamiento *m.* enlargement, aggrandizement.

agrandar *tr.* to enlarge, aggrandize, magnify. *2 ref.* to enlarge [grow larger].

agranujado, -da *adj.* pimply. *2* rascally; urchin-like.

agrario, -ria *adj.* agrarian.

agravación *f.,* **agravamiento** *m.* aggravation. *2* getting worse.

agravante *adj.* aggravating, making worse. *2* aggravative.

agravar *tr.* to aggravate, make heavier or worse. *2* to burden with taxes. *3 ref.* to become more grave; to get worse.

agraviador, -a *m.-f.* offender, wronger.

agraviar *tr.* to offend, insult. *2* to injure, hurt, wrong. *3 ref.* to take offence.

agravio *m.* grievance, offence, insult. *2* injury, harm, wrong.

agravioso, -sa *adj.* offensive, insulting.

agraz *m.* unripe grape: *en* ~, fig. prematurely. *2*

grape verjuice. *3* AGRAZADA. *4* bitterness, sorrow.
agrazada *f.* drink made of grape verjuice.
agrazón *m.* wild grape. *2* gooseberry bush. *3* annoyance, vexation.
agredir *tr.* to assail, assault, attack. ¶ Def.: only used in forms having *i* in their terminations.
agregable *adj.* aggregable.
agregación *f.* aggregation, addition, joining.
agregado *m.* aggregate, collection. *2* annex. *3* attaché.
agregar *tr.* to aggregate, add, join, attach. *2 ref.* to join, to attach oneself.
agremán *m.* insertion, attachment.
agremiación *f.* forming into a guild or association.
agremiar *tr.-ref.* to form a guild or tradesmen's union.
agresión *f.* aggression, assault, attack.
agresividad *f.* aggressiveness.
agresivo, -va *adj.* aggresive.
agresor, -ra *adj.* aggressing. *2 m.-f.* aggressor, assaulter.
agreste *adj.* rustic, rural, wild. *2* rude, uncouth.
agrete *adj.* sourish.
agriamente *adv.* fig. sourly, sharply, harshly. *2* bitterly.
agriar *tr.* to sour [make sour]. *2* to exasperate, embitter. *3 ref.* to sour, turn sour.
agrícola *adj.* agricultural. *2 m.-f.* agriculturist.
agricultor, -ra *m.-f.* agriculturist, farmer.
agricultura *f.* agriculture.
agridulce *adj.* bittersweet.
agrietar *tr.* to crack, fissure, chap. *2 ref.* to crack, fissure, chap [be cracked].
Agrigento *pr. n.* GEOG. Agrigento.
agrillo, -lla *adj.* sourish, acidulous.
agrimensor *m.* land surveyor.
agrimensura *f.* survey, land surveying.
agrimonia *f.* BOT. agrimony.
agrio, -gria *adj.* sour, acid, crab. *2* bitter [orange]. *3* rough, uneven. *4* sour, tart, sharp, ungracious. *5* brittle [metal]. *6* PAINT. harsh. *7 m.* acid juice. *8 pl.* citrus fruits.
agripalma *f.* BOT. motherwort.
agrisado, -da *adj.* grayish.
agro *m.* land, countryside.
agronomía *f.* agronomics, agronomy.
agrónomo *m.* agronomist.
agropecuario *adj.* land and cattle.
agrumar *tr.* to clot, coagulate. *2 ref.* to clot [become clotted].
agrupación *f.* grouping. *2* groupment, group, union, association. *3* cluster.
agrupar *tr.* to group. *2* to cluster, bunch. *3 ref.* to group, cluster, crowd together.
agrura *f.* sourness, acidity. *2* acid juice. *3* citrus trees.
agua *f.* water [liquid, body of water, sea, stream, etc.]: ~ *bendita,* holy water; ~ *carbónica,* soda water; ~ *corriente,* running water; ~ *dulce,* fresh water; ~ *mansa,* still water; ~ *salada,* salt water; *aguas jurisdiccionales,* territorial waters; *¡hombre al agua!,* man overboard!; *estar con el ~ al cuello,* fig. to be in deep water, in great difficulties; *guárdate del ~ mansa,* fig. still waters run deep; *tan claro como el ~,* obvious, manifest; *aguas abajo,* downstream; *aguas arriba,* upstream. *2* water [solution, infusion, distillation, etc.]: ~ *de azahar,* orangeflower water; ~ *de borrajas* or *de cerrajas,* fig. unsubstantial thing; ~ *de Colonia,* eau-de-Cologne; ~

de rosas, rose water; ~ *fuerte,* agua fortis, nitric acid; AGUAFUERTE; ~ *oxigenada,* hydrogen peroxide; ~ *regia,* agua regia. *3* rain: ~ *nieve,* sleet; ~ *viento,* wind and rain. *4* slope of a roof. *5* NAUT. water leakage: *via de* ~, leak. *6* water, saliva: *se me hace la boca* ~, fig. my mouth waters. *7 pl.* tide, tides [in the sea]: *aguas de creciente,* rising tide; *aguas de menguante,* ebb tide. *8* water, urine. *9* water [of a precious stone, etc.].
aguacatal *m.* plantation of avocadoes.
aguacate *m.* BOT. avocado, alligator pear [tree and fruit]. *3* pear-shaped emerald.
aguacero *m.* rainstorm, heavy shower.
aguacha *f.* foul, stagnant water.
aguachar *m.* pool, puddle.
aguachirle *f.* inferior wine. *2* weak liquor; unsubstantial thing.
aguada *f.* watering place [place where water may be obtained]. *2* NAUT. supply of drinking water: *hacer* ~, take fresh water. *3* PAINT. water colour.
aguaderas *f. pl.* frame for carrying water-pitchers on horses.
aguadero, -ra *adj.* water, for water; waterproof [cloak]. *2 m.* watering place [for animals].
aguado, -da *adj.* watered, watery. *2* teetotaller.
aguador, -ra *m.-f.* water carrier.
aguaducho *m.* water-seller's stall. *2* freshet. *3* flood.
aguafiestas *m.-f.* kill-joy, marplot.
aguafuerte *m.* etching; etched plate.
aguaje *m.* AGUADERO *2. 2* NAUT. spring tide; tidal wave. *3* sea stream or current. *4* NAUT. wake.
aguamala *f.* MEDUSA *1.*
aguamanil *m.* pitcher, ewer. *2* wash-basin. *3* washstand.
aguamanos *m.* water for washing the hands. *2* AGUAMANIL *1.*
aguamar *m.* MEDUSA *1.*
aguamarina *f.* aquamarina, aquamarine.
aguamiel *f.* hydromel.
aguanieve *f.* sleet.
aguanoso, -sa *adj.* waterish, watery.
aguantar *tr.* to restrain, hold, hold back, control. *2* to bear, endure, suffer, sustain, support, stand, abide, resist. *3* to swallow [an affront, etc]. *4* NAUT. to haul tight. *ref.* to restrain oneself.
aguante *m.* patience, endurance. *2* strength, firmness.
aguapié *m.* small wine.
aguar *tr.* to water [dilute with water]. *2* to spoil, mar [fun, pleasure]. *3 ref.* to be spoiled, marred.
aguará *m.* ZOOL. a South-American fox.
aguardada *f.* awaiting, wait.
aguardar *tr.* to wait, to await or wait for. *2* to expect. *3 intr.* to stay, hold on, stop. *4* ~ *a,* to wait, to wait for.
aguardentoso, -sa *adj.* mixed with spirits. *2* harsh, hoarse [voice].
aguardiente *m.* spirit, firewater: ~ *de caña,* rum.
aguarrás *m.* turpentine, oil of turpentine.
aguaturma *f.* BOT. Jerusalem artichoke.
aguaviento *m.* rainy wind.
aguazal *m.* fen. swamp.
aguazar *tr.* ENCHARCAR.
agudeza *f.* acuteness, sharpness, acuity, keenness. *2* perspicacity. *3* wit, smartness. *4* witticism, sally.
agudizar *tr.* to render more acute.
agudo, -da *adj.* acute [sharp-pointed; sharp; keen; high-pitched; shrill; perspicacious]. *2* witty,

smart, clever. *3* GEOM., GRAM., MED. acute. *4* oxytone [word].
Agueda *f. pr. n.* Agatha.
agüero *m.* augury, prediction. *2* sign, omen: *de mal* ~, of ill omen.
aguerrido, -da *adj.* inured to war; veteran.
aguerrir *tr.* to inure to war. ¶ Only used in forms having *i* in their terminations.
aguijada *f.* goad. *2* ploughstaff.
aguijar *tr.* to goad, spur, prick. *2* to incite, stimulate. *3 intr.* hurry along.
aguijón *m.* point of a goad: *dar coces contra el* ~, to kick against the pricks. *2* ZOOL., BOT. sting. *3* fig. spur, goad, stimulus.
aguijonazo *m.* thrust with a goad or prick; sting.
aguijonear *tr.* to goad, prick. *2* to sting. *3* to incite, stimulate.
águila *f.* eagle [bird; emblem; coin]: ~ *barbuda*, lammergeyer; ~ *caudal*, golden eagle; *ser un* ~, fig. to be very clever. *2* ICHTH. eagle ray.
aguileña *f.* BOT. columbine.
aguileño, -ña *adj.* aquiline. *2* hawk-nosed.
aguilón *m. aug.* of ÁGUILA. *2* jib of a crane. *3* ARCH. gable angle.
aguilucho *m.* eaglet.
aguinaldo *m.* Christmas box, Christmas gift.
agüista *m.* resorter, frequenter of a spa.
aguja *f.* needle: ~ *de hacer calceta*, knitting needle; ~ *mechera*, larding pin; ~ *saquera*, pack needle; ~ *de marear*, NAUT. compass; *buscar una* ~ *en un pajar*, to look for a needle in a haystack. *2* bodkin, hatpin. *3* hand [of clock]; pointer, index. *4* style [of dial, etc.]. *5* ARCH. spire, steeple. *6* ICHTH. needlefish. *7* BOT. Lady's-comb. *8* switch rail. *9 pl.* RLY. switch. *10* fore ribs [of an animal].
agujereado, -da *adj.* with a hole or full of holes.
agujerear *tr.* to pierce, bore, perforate.
agujero *m.* hole. *2* needle maker or seller.
agujeta *f.* costume point, tagged lace. *2 pl.* pains from overexercise.
aguosidad *f.* lymph, serosity.
¡agur! *interj.* coll. good-bye!, farewell!
agusanamiento *m.* maggotiness, grubbiness.
agusanarse *ref.* to get or become maggoty, grubby or wormy; to become worm-eaten.
Agustín *pr. n.* Augustin, Austin.
agustino, -na *adj.-n.* Augustinian, Austin [friar].
agutí *m.* ZOOL. (Arg., Par.) agouti.
aguzadero, -ra *adj.* whetting, sharpening.
aguzado, -da *adj.* sharp-edged or -pointed, keen.
aguzamiento *m.* sharpening, whetting.
aguzanieves *f.* ORN. wagtail.
aguzar *tr.* to sharpen, point, whet. *2* to spur, goad, estimulate. *3* to sharpen [the wits, the senses]. *4* to prick up [one's ears].
¡ah! *interj.* oh!, ha!
ahebrado, -da *adj.* fibrous, thready.
ahechador, -ra *adj.* sieving, sifting. *2 n.* sifter, small utensil used for sifting.
ahechaduras *f. pl.* siftings of grain.
ahechar *tr.* to sift [grain].
aherrojamiento *m.* chaining, putting in irons.
aherrojar *tr.* to iron, fetter, put in irons. *2* to oppress, hold in subjection.
aherrumbrarse *ref.* [of water] to become ferruginous. *2* [of iron] to rust.
ahí *adv.* there, in that place: *de* ~ *que*, hence, therefore; *por* ~, somewhere around; that way; *por* ~ *por* ~, more or less.
ahijada *f.* goddaughter.
ahijado *m.* godchild, godson. *2* protégé.

ahijar *tr.* to adopt [a person]. *2* to impute. *3 intr.* to procreate. *4* AGR. to bud.
ahilar *intr.* to go in single file. *2 ref.* to grow thin [from illness]. *3* [of wine] to turn ropy. *4* [of plants] to become etiolated; [of trees] to grow slender.
ahincadamente *adv.* hard, eagerly, earnestly.
ahínco *m.* eagerness, earnestness, ardour.
ahitar *tr.* to surfeit, cloy, satiate, pall. *2 ref.* to gorge oneself.
ahíto, -ta *adj.* cloyed, surfeited, gorged. *2* fed up, disgusted. *3 m.* surfeit, indigestion.
ahogadero *m.* crowded, stifling place. *2* throatband.
ahogadilla *f.* ducking.
ahogado, -da *adj.* choked, suffocated, stifled, smothered. *2* drowned. *3* close, stuffy, illventilated. *4 m.-f.* drowned person.
ahogamiento *m.* suffocation, choking. *2* drowning.
ahogar *tr.* to chocke, stifle, smother, suffocate, strangle, quench. *2* to drown. *3* to oppress. *4 ref.* to chocke, stifle, etc. [be choked, etc.]. *5* to be drowned.
ahogo *m.* anguish, oppression, suffocation. *2* pinch, financial difficulties.
ahoguijo, ahoguío *m.* constriction of the chest.
ahondamiento *m.* deepening, excavation, digging, penetration. *2* fig. investigation.
ahondar *tr.* to deepen [a hole or cavity]; to excavate. *2 intr.-tr.* to go deep into, to penetrate.
ahonde *m.* deepening.
ahora *adv.-conj.* now; ~ *mismo*, just now, right now; *por* ~, for the present; ~ *bien*, now, now then. *2 conj.* whether... or.
ahorcado, -da *m.-f.* hanged man (woman).
ahorcadura *f.* hanging [of a person].
ahorcajarse *ref.* to sit astride.
ahorcar *tr.* to hang [kill by hanging]. *2* to give up [books, studies]: ~ *los hábitos*, to give up clerical life. *3 ref.* to hang [oneself].
ahorita *adv.* (Am.) instantly, this very minute.
ahormar *tr.* to adjust, shape, mould; to block [a hat], to last [a shoe].
ahornagarse *ref.* [of soil & plants] to become parched or scorched.
ahorquillado, -da *adj.* forked, furcate.
ahorquillar *tr.* AGR. to stay, prop up [with a forked pole]. *2* to fork [give a forklike shape].
ahorrado, -da *adj.* saving, thrifty.
ahorrador, -ra *adj.* saving, thrifty. *2 m.-f.* economizer.
ahorrar *tr.* to save, economize, lay by, spare. *2 tr.-ref.* to spare, to spare oneself [trouble, labour, etc.].
ahorrativo, -va *adj.* saving, thrifty.
ahorro *m.* saving, economy. *2 pl.* savings.
ahuecado, -da *adj.* deep, deep, low [voice]. *2* hollow, empty. *3* bouffant, full, flared [a dress].
ahuecar *tr.* to hollow; to inflate, puff out. *2* to loosen, soften, fluff. *3* to make [the voice] hollow or pompous. *4* fig. ~ *el ala*, to beat it, go away. *5 ref.* to become puffed up.
ahuesado, -da *adj.* bone-coloured. *2* bone-hard.
ahumado, -da *adj.* smoked, smoky. *2 f.* smoke signal.
ahumar *tr.* to smoke [blacken, cure, etc., with smoke]; to fill with smoke. *2 intr.* to smoke [emit smoke]. *3 ref.* to be smoked. *4* fig. to get drunk.
ahusado, -da *adj.* spindle-shaped, fusiform.
ahuyentar *tr.* to drive away, to scare away, to put to flight. *2 ref.* to flee.

ailanto *m.* BOT. ailanthus.
airadamente *adv.* angrily.
airado, -da *adj.* angry, irate, wrathful. *2* loose, depraved [life].
airar *tr.* to anger, irritate. *2 ref.* to get angry.
aire *m.* air [fluid, atmosphere, wind]; ~ *colado,* cold draught; ~ *comprimido,* compressed air; *beber los aires por,* fig. to sight or long for or after; to be madly in love with; *hacer ~ a uno,* to fan someone; *mudar de aires,* to go for a change; *tomar el ~,* to take the air, take a walk; *al ~ libre,* in the open air, outdoors; *por el ~, por los aires,* fig. swiftly, rapidly. *2* appearance, air, airs: *tener aires de salud,* to have a healthy appearance. *3* resemblance: *darse un ~ a,* to resemble. *4* pace, gait [of a horse]. *5* humour, temper. *6* ease, dexterity. *7* elegance, gracefulness. *8* vigor, violence. *9* MUS. movement. *10* MUS. air, melody.
aireación *f.* VENTILACIÓN.
aireado, -da *adj.* aired, ventilated. *2* sour, bitter, fermented.
airear *tr.* to air, ventilate. *2 ref.* to take the air.
airón *m.* ORN. European heron. *2* ORN. crest of feathers. *3* aigrette, panache, crest.
airosamente *adv.* gracefully, lively.
airosidad *f.* graceful deportment.
airoso, -sa *adj.* airy, windy [place]. *2* graceful, lively [in carriage or deportment]. *3 salir ~,* to acquit oneself well; to be successful.
aislacionismo *m.* isolationism.
aislacionista *adj.-n.* isolationist, supporter of isolationism.
aisladamente *adv.* isolatedly, singly, separately.
aislado, -da *adj.* isolate(d, separate. *2* insulate(d.
aislador *m.* PHYS., ELEC. isolator, insulator.
aislamiento *m.* isolation; insulation. *2* seclusion.
aislante *adj.* non-conducting, insulating. *2 m.* insulator.
aislar *tr.* to isolate, insulate. *2 ref.* to isolate or seclude oneself.
¡ajá! *interj.* aha!, that is right!
ajada *f.* a garlic sauce.
ajamiento *m.* withering, fading, crumpling.
ajamonarse *ref.* [of a woman] to grow plump and buxon.
ajar *tr.* to crumple, rumple, spoil, wither, fade. *2 ref.* to become spoiled, to wither.
ajardinado, -da *adj.* landscaped, arranged as a garden.
aje *m.* ACHAQUE 1. *2* BOT. a plant of the yam family.
ajebe *m.* alum.
ajedrea *f.* BOT. savory, savoury.
ajedrecista *m.-f.* chess player.
ajedrez *m.* chess [game].
ajedrezado, -da *adj.* checkered, chequered.
ajenjo *m.* BOT. wormwood. *2* absinth.
ajeno, -na *adj.* another's, alien, strange. *2* alien, foreign [to], inconsistent [with], improper [of]. *3* ignorant [of]. *4 ~ de cuidados,* free from care.
ajerezado, -da *adj.* sherry-like.
ajete *m.* BOT. young garlic. *2* garlic sauce.
ajetrearse *ref.* to tire oneself out; to bustle about.
ajetreo *m.* fatigue; bustle.
ají *m.* (Am.) chili, chili pepper. *2* chili sauce.
ajiaceite *m.* a garlic and oil sauce.
ajipuerro *m.* BOT. wild leek.
ajo *m.* BOT. garlic. *2* garlic clove. *3* garlic sauce. *4* secret affair. *5* PALABROTA. *6* BOT. ~ *chalote,* shallot.
ajobar *tr.* to carry on the back.

ajofaina *f.* washbasin, washboul, washhand basin.
ajolote *m.* ZOOL. axolotl.
ajomate *m.* a green filamentous alga.
ajonjera *f.* BOT. carline thistle.
ajonjolí *m.* BOT. sesame [plant & seeds].
ajorca *f.* ring bracelet, anklet, bangle.
ajornalar *tr.* to hire [a person] by the day.
ajuar *m.* household furniture. *2* trousseau.
ajuiciado, -da *adj.* sensible, wise.
ajuiciar *tr.-intr.* to make or become sensible, wise.
ajumarse *ref.* to get canned or drunk.
ajustado, -da *adj.* adjusted. *2* just, right. *3* tight, close-fitting.
ajustador *m.* close-fitting waistcoat. *3* MEC. adjuster, fitter. *4* PRINT. pager.
ajustar *tr.* to adjust, adapt, fit, regulate. *2* to fit tight, to tighten. *3* to make [an agreement]: to agree upon, to arrange. *4* to reconcile. *5* to settle [accounts]. *6* to hire, engage. *7* PRINT. to page. *8 intr.* to fit tight. *9 ref.* to conform [to]. *10* to hire oneself. *11* to come to an agreement.
ajuste *m.* adjustement, fitting, fit. *2* agreement, contract. *3* settlement [of accounts]. *4* hire, engagement. *5* PRINT. paging.
ajusticiado, -da *adj.-n.* executed [person].
ajusticiamiento *m.* execution [of a culprit].
ajusticiar *tr.* to execute, put to death.
al *contr.* of A EL: to the; at or at the [foll. by a masc. noun]. *2* when used with an inf. it is equivalent to «on», «about», «on the point of»: ~ *verlo,* on seeing it; *está ~ llegar,* he is about to arrive.
ala *f.* ORN., ENT., ANAT., ARCH., FORT., MIL., POL. wing: *cortar las alas,* fig. to clip the wings. *2* ANAT. auricle [of the heart]: *caérsele a uno las alas del corazón,* fig. to be dismayed. *3* brim [of a hat]. *4* flap [of a table]. *5* blade [of a propeller]. *6* NAUT. studding sail. *7* row, line. *8* eaves. *9 pl.* courage, boldness: *dar alas,* to embolden.
¡ala! *interj.* come on!, hup hup la! *2* hey!
Alá *pr. n.* Allah.
alabado *m.* motet in praise of the Sacrament.
alabador, -ra *m.-f.* praiser.
alabancioso, -sa *adj.* boastful, vainglorious.
alabanza *f.* praise, commendation, eulogy.
alabar *tr.* to praise, commend, extol, applaud. *2 ref.* to praise oneself. *3* to boast.
alabarda *f.* halberd.
alabardero *m.* halberdier. *2* THEAT. clapper.
alabastrado, -da *adj.* alabastrine, alabaster-like.
alabastrino, -na *adj.* alabaster, alabastrine.
alabastro *m.* MINER. alabaster.
álabe *m.* drooping branch of a tree. *2* side mat [in carts]. *3* float, paddle [of a water wheel].
alabear *tr.* to warp, camber. *2 ref.* to have a camber.
alabeo *m.* warp, warping, camber.
alacena *f.* cupboard, closet.
alacrán *m.* ZOOL. scorpion. *2* shank [of button].
alacranado, -da *adj.* bitten by a scorpion. *2* tainted with some vice or disease.
alacranera *f.* BOT. scorpionwort.
alacridad *f.* alacrity, cheerful readiness.
alacha *f.* BOQUERÓN 2.
alada *f.* wing stroke or beat.
aladares *m. pl.* hair falling over the temples.
Aladino *m. pr. n.* Aladdin.
aladierna *f.,* **aladierno** *m.* BOT. alatern.
alado, -da *adj.* winged [having wings; swift]. *2* BOT. alate.
alalimón *m.* a children's game.

alama *f.* BOT. a fodder plant.
alamar *m.* frog [ornamental braiding]. 2 fringe, tassel.
alambicado, -da *adj.* distilled. 3 parsimoniously given. 4 subtle, finedrawn.
alambicamiento *m.* distillation. 2 subtility.
alambicar *tr.* to distill, rectify. 2 to investigate closely. 3 to subtilize, fine-draw.
alambique *m.* still, alembic: *por* ~, sparingly.
alambrado, -da *adj.* wired [fenced with wires]. 2 *f.* FORT. wire entanglement. 3 *m.* wire screen; wire cover; wire fence.
alambrar *tr.* to fence with wire.
alambre *m.* wire [metallic thread].
alambrera *f.* wire screen. 2 wire cover.
alameda *f.* poplar grove. 2 avenue, mall.
álamo *m.* BOT. poplar: ~ *blanco*, white poplar; ~ *negro*, black poplar; ~ *temblón*, aspen.
alamparse *ref.* to crave after, long for, be very fond of.
alancear *tr.* to lance, to spear. 2 ZAHERIR.
alano *m.* a large dog. 2 *pl.* Alans.
alantoides *adj.-m.* ANAT. allantoid.
alar *m.* eaves. 2 horse-hair snare for partridges.
alarde *m.* display, show, ostentation.
alardear *intr.* to boast.
alargadera *f.* CHEM. adapter. 2 lengthening bar, tube, etc.
alargado, -da *adj.* long, elongated, oblong.
alargador, -ra *adj.* lengthening, extending, stretching.
alargar *tr.* to lengthen, elongate, extend, prolong, protract. 2 to increase. 3 to reach, stretch out. 4 to hand, pass [something to somebody]. 5 to pay out [a rope]. 6 *ref.* to lengthen, grow longer. 7 to expatiate.
Alarico *pr. n.* Alaric.
alarido *m.* yell, howl, scream.
alarife *m.* formerly, an architect or builder.
alarije *m.* variety of grape.
alarma *f.* MIL. alarm. 2 alarm [warning or apprehension of danger]: *timbre de* ~, alarm bell.
alarmado, -da *adj.* alarmed.
alarmante *adj.* alarming.
alarmar *tr.* to call to arms. 2 to alarm. 3 *ref.* to be alarmed.
alarmista *m.-f.* alarmist, scaremonger.
Álava *pr. n.* GEOG. Alava, a Basque province of Spain.
alavés, -sa *adj.-s.* of or from Álava.
alazán, -na *adj.-n.* sorrel [horse].
alazor *m.* BOT. safflower, bastard saffron.
alba *f.* dawn, daybreak. 2 beginning. 3 ECCL. alb.
albacea *m.* LAW testamentary executor. 2 *f.* LAW testamentary executrix.
albaceazgo *m.* LAW executorship.
albaceteño, -ña, albacetense *adj.* of or from Albacete, Spain. 2 *n.* inhabitant of Albacete.
albacora *f.* ICHTH. albacore. 2 BREVA 1.
albahaca *f.* BOT. sweet basil.
albahaquero *m.* flowerpot. 2 a stand for flowerpots.
albaida *f.* BOT. a leguminous plant.
albalá *m.-f.* royal letters patent. 2 voucher.
albanés, -sa *adj.-n.* Albanian.
Albania *pr. n.* GEOG. Albania.
albañal, albañar *m.* drain, sewer.
albañil *m.* mason, bricklayer.
albañilería *f.* masonry.
albar *adj.* white [plant or tree].

albarán *m.* white paper in window implying that the place is to let. 2 voucher. 3 delivery note.
albarazado, -da *adj.* variegated. 2 affected with white leprosy.
albarda *f.* pack saddle. 2 ALBARDILLA 6.
albardado, -da *adj.* characteristic of some animals which consists in having the back a different color from the rest of the body.
albardilla *f.* small saddle for breaking in colts. 2 coping. 3 flatiron handle-pad. 4 a pad on the eyes of shears. 5 water-carrier's cushion. 6 COOK. bard.
albardín *m.* BOT. hooded matweed.
albardón *m.* a large pack-saddle for riding.
albaricoque *m.* BOT. apricot.
albaricoquero *m.* BOT. apricot tree.
albarillo *m.* BOT. white apricot. 2 tune on the guitar.
albarizo, -za *adj.* whitish [soil].
albarrada *f.* dry wall. 2 earth fence.
albarrana *adj.* see CEBOLLA & TORRE.
albarranilla *f.* BOT. squill.
albatros *m.* ORN. albatross.
albayalde *m.* ceruse, white lead.
albazano, -na *adj.* dark chestnut [horse].
albear *intr.* to whiten, show white.
albedrío *m.* free will: *libre* ~, free will. 2 will, pleasure: *al* ~ *de uno*, at one's pleasure.
albéitar *m.* farrier, veterinarian.
alberca *f.* pond, pool, millpond, water reservoir.
albérchigo *m.* BOT. peach-tree. 2 peach [fruit].
alberchiguero *m.* BOT. peach tree.
albergar *tr.* to house, shelter, lodge, harbour. 2 *ref.* to take shelter; to lodge, harbour.
albergue *m.* housing, shelter, lodging, harbour, refuge. 2 lair, den. 3 orphanage, home.
albero *m.* a tract of whitish soil. 2 dishcloth.
Alberto *pr. n.* Albert.
albigense *adj.* albigensian. 2 *m. pl.* Albigenses.
albinismo *m.* albinism, albinoism.
albino, -na *adj.* albinic. 2 *m.* albino. 3 *f.* albiness.
Albión *pr. n.* GEOG. Albion.
albitana *f.* GARD. fence for plants. 2 NAUT. apron or inner post [in small boats].
albo, -ba *adj.* poet, white.
albohol *m.* BOT. the lesser bindweed.
albóndiga, albondiguilla *f.* COOK. meat ball.
albor *m.* whiteness. 2 *pl.* dawn, beginning.
alborada *f.* dawn, break of day. 2 MIL. action fought at dawn. 3 reveille. 4 aubade.
alborear *intr.* [of the day] to dawn.
albornoz *m.* burnoose, burnous. 2 bathing gown.
alboronía *f.* dish of tomatoes, pumpkins, sweet peppers, etc.
alboroque *m.* treat given at the close of a deal.
alborotadamente *adv.* disorderly, excitedly, noisily.
alborotadizo, -za *adj.* easily agitated, excitable.
alborotado, -da *adj.* hasty, thoughtless, rash.
alborotador, -ra *m.-f.* agitator, rioter. 2 noisy person.
alborotar *tr.* to disturb, agitate, excite. 2 to incite to riot. 3 ALBOROZAR. 4 *intr.* to make a racket, to shout. 5 *ref.* [of the sea] to get rough. 6 to get excited. 7 to riot.
alboroto *m.* uproar, noise. 2 excitement, agitation. 3 disturbance, disorder. 4 tumult, riot.
alborozado, -da *adj.* rejoicing, joyful, jubilant.
alborozar *tr.* to gladden, cheer, exhilarate.
alborozo *m.* joy, joyfulness, exhilaration.

albricias f. pl. reward for good news. 2 interj. joy!, joy!
albufera f. lagoon, salt lake by the sea.
álbum m. album.
albumen m. BOT. albumen.
albúmina f. BIOCHEM. albumin.
albuminoide m. BIOCHEM. albuminoid.
albuminoideo, -a adj. albuminoid.
albuminuria f. MED. albuminuria.
albur m. chance, hazard. 2 ICHTH. dace.
albura f. whiteness. 2 ALBURNO.
alburno m. alburnum, sapwood.
alca f. ORN. auk, razorbill.
alcabala f. an ancient excise.
alcacel, alcacer m. green barley. 2 barley field.
alcachofa f. BOT. artichoke. 2 cardoon or thistle head.
alcachofera f. BOT. artichocke [plant].
alcahueta f. procuress, bawd, go-between.
alcahuete m. procurer, pander. 2 screener, concealer.
alcahuetear tr.-intr. to procure, pander, bawd. 2 intr. to act as a screen or concealer [for something dishonourable].
alcahuetería f. bawdry, pandering. 2 screening, concealing.
alcaico adj. alcaic.
alcaide m. formerly, a warden [of a prison or castle].
alcaidía f. wardenship [of a prison or castle].
alcaldada f. abuse of authority.
alcalde m. Mayor, Lord Mayor; head of a town council.
alcaldesa f. Mayoress.
alcaldía f. Mayoralty. 2 the Mayor's office.
alcalescencia f. alkalescence or -cy.
alcalescente adj. alkalescent.
álcali m. CHEM. alkali.
alcalinidad f. alkalinity.
alcalino, -na adj. alkaline.
alcalizar tr. CHEM. to alkalize, alkalify or alkalinize.
alcaloide m. CHEM. alkaloid.
alcaloideo, -a adj. alkaloidal.
alcance m. pursuit, overtaking: dar ~, to overtake. 2 reach: fuera del ~ de uno, out of one's reach. 3 scope, range [of missile]; import, consequence; de gran ~, far-reaching. 4 stop-press [news]. 5 intellect, understanding: cortos alcances, meagre intellect. 6 COM. balance due. 7 POST. buzón de ~, late collection post-box.
alcancía f. child's bank, money box.
alcándara f. perch [for falcons].
alcandía f. ZAHÍNA.
alcanfor m. camphor. 2 BOT. camphor tree.
alcanforar tr. to camphorate.
alcanforero m. BOT. camphor tree.
alcantarilla f. sewer, drains. 2 culvert.
alcantarillado m. sewage [system of sewers].
alcanzable o **alcanzadizo, -za** adj. attainable, reachable, accessible.
alcanzado, -da adj. in debt. 2 short of, lacking in.
alcanzadura f. VET. attaint.
alcanzar tr. to overtake, catch up with. 2 to reach. 3 to get, obtain. 4 to understand. 5 COM. to find [one] debtor of. 6 to reach back to, to have known. 7 intr. [of a weapon] to carry. 8 to reach, arrive [to]. 9 to suffice, be sufficient [to or for]. 10 ~ a ver, a oír, to se, to hear. 11 ref. VET. [of horses] to overreach.
alcaparra f. BOT. caper [plant]. 2 caper [bud].

alcaparro m. BOT. caper [plant].
alcaparrón m. caper berry.
alcaraván m. ORN. thick-knee, stone curlew.
alcaravea f. BOT. caraway.
alcarraza f. porous earthenware water vessel.
alcarria f. high, barren land.
alcatifa f. carpet.
alcatraz m. CUCURUCHO. 2 BOT. cuckoopint. 3 ORN. white pelican.
alcaucil m. BOT. artichoke. 2 wild artichoke.
alcaudón m. ORN. shrike.
alcayata f. ESCARPIA.
alcazaba f. fortress [within a walled town].
alcázar m. fortress. 2 royal palace. 3 NAUT. quarterdeck.
alce m. ZOOL. elk; moose. 2 cut [at carts].
Alcestes m. pr. n. Alcestis.
Alcibíades m. pr. n. Alcibiades.
alción m. ORN. kingfisher, halcyon. 2 ASTR. Alcyone.
alcionarios m. pl. ZOOL. Alcyonaria.
alcista f. bull [stock speculator].
alcoba f. alcove [recess for bed], bedroom.
alcohol m. alcohol. 2 kohl. 3 GALENA.
alcoholar tr. CHEM. alcoholize. 2 to blacken with kohl.
alcoholato m. CHEM. alcoholate.
alcohólico, -ca adj.-n. alcoholic.
alcoholímetro m. alcoholometer.
alcoholismo m. alcoholism.
alcoholizado, -da adj. alcoholized. 2 adj.-m. MED. alcoholic.
alcoholizar tr. to alcoholize.
alcor m. hill, hillock.
Alcorán m. Alcoran.
alcornocal m. plantation of cork oaks.
alcornoque m. cork oak. 2 fig. blockhead, dolt.
alcorza f. sugar and starch paste, sugar icing.
alcorzar tr. to ice [cakes] with ALCORZA.
alcotán m. ORN. lanner.
alcotana f. bricklayer's hammer.
alcurnia f. lineage, ancestry, parentage, blood.
alcuza f. can for oil used in kitchens.
alcuzcuz m. couscous.
aldaba f. door-knocker. 2 bolt, crossbar. 3 hitching ring. 4 fig. tener buenas aldabas, to have powerful protectors.
aldabada f. knock, knocking [at the street door].
aldabilla f. latching hook, fastening hook.
aldabón m. door knocker. 2 large handle [of a chest, coffer, etc.].
aldabonazo m. ALDABA.
aldea f. hamlet, village.
aldeaniego, -ga adj. ALDEANO 1 & 2.
aldeano, -na adj. of a hamlet. 2 village, rustic. 3 m.-f. villager, countryman, countrywoman.
aldehído, -da m.-f. CHEM. aldehyde.
aldehuela f. hamlet, small village.
aldeorrio, aldeorro m. miserable hamlet.
alderredor adv. ALREDEDOR.
¡ale! interj. come on!
álea m. risk.
aleación f. alloyage. 2 alloy [of metals].
alear tr. to alloy [metals]. 2 intr. to flutter, flap the wings [or the arms].
aleatorio, -ria adj. aleatory, contingent, uncertain.
alebrarse ref. [of a rabbit] to squat. 2 to cower.
aleccionar tr. to teach, instruct, drill, coach.
aleche m. fresh anchovy.
alechugar tr. to plait, flute, frill, curl in the shape of a lettuce leaf.

aledaño, -ña *adj.* bordering, adjacent. 2 *m. pl.* borders, surroundings.
alegación *f.* allegation, plea, argument.
alegar *tr.* to allege, quote, adduce, plead, urge.
alegato *m.* plea, pleading. 2 reasoned allegation.
alegoría *f.* allegory, emblem.
alegórico, -ca *adj.* allegoric(al, allegoristic.
alegorizar *tr.* to allegorize.
alegrar *tr.* to cheer, gladden, make joyful. 2 to brighten, enliven. 3 to incite [the bull]. 4 *ref.* to be glad. 5 to rejoice, cheer. 6 coll. to get tipsy.
alegre *adj.* glad, joyful. 2 cheerful, merry, jolly, light-hearted. 3 beaming, bright, gay. 4 tipsy. 5 reckless. 6 light, wanton. 7 ~ *de cascos,* scatter-brained.
alegremente *adv.* happily, merrily.
alegreto *adj., adv. & m.* MUS. allegretto.
alegría *f.* joy, pleasure. 2 glee, merriment, mirth, gaiety. 3 brightness. 4 BOT. sesame.
alegro *adj., adv. & m.* MUS. allegro.
alegrón *m.* a sudden intense joy. 2 flash, transitory blaze.
alejado, -da *adj.* far away, distant, remote, far-off. 2 far away from, a long way from. 3 aloof, apart, isolated.
alejamiento *m.* removal to a distance, distance, absence. 2 withdrawal, estrangement, aloofness.
Alejandría *pr. n.* GEOG. Alexandria.
alejandrino, -na *adj.* Alexandrine.
Alejandro *pr. n.* Alexander.
alejar *tr.* to remove to a distance, to move away. 2 to separate, estrange. 3 *ref.* to go away, move away.
Alejo *pr. n.* Alexis.
alelado, -da *adj.* bewildered, dazed, stupefied. 2 stupid, slow-witted.
alelar *tr.* to bewilder. 2 to stupefy.
alelí *m.* ALHELÍ.
aleluya *f.* or *m.* hallelujah. 2 *m.* Easter time. 3 *f.* poor verses, doggerel. 4 BOT. wood sorrel.
alemán, -na *adj.-n.* German. 2 *m.* German language.
alemana, alemanda *f.* allemande [a dance].
Alemania *pr. n.* GEOG. Germany.
alemanisco, -ca *adj.* germanic. 2 damask.
alentada *f.* long breath: *de uña ~,* without interruption, at one go.
alentado, -da *adj.* brave, courageous, spirited.
alentador, -ra *adj.* encouraging, cheering, heartening. 2 *m.-f.* encourager.
alentar *intr.* to breathe. 2 *tr.* to encourage, cheer, hearten. ¶ CONJUG. like *acertar.*
alerce *m.* BOT. larch tree.
alergia *f.* allergy.
alérgico, -ca *adj.* allergic.
alero *m.* eaves. 2 splashboard, mudguard [of a carriage].
alerón *m.* AER. aileron.
alerta *adv.* on the watch, on the alert. 2 *interj.* look out! 3 *m.* sentinel's call.
alertar *tr.* to alert, put on guard.
alerto, -ta *adj.* watchful, careful.
aleta *f.* small wing. 2 fin [of a fish]. 3 ARCH. alette. 4 MACH. wing. 5 ALA 5.
aletada *f.* a motion of the wings.
aletargado, -da *adj.* lethargic, drowsy.
aletargamiento *m.* lethargy.
aletargar *tr.* to lethargize. 2 *ref.* to fall into a lethargy, to get drowsy.
aletazo *m.* stroke of wing or fin; flap.

aletear *intr.* to flutter, to flap the wings or the fins.
aleteo *m.* flapping of wings or fins. 2 palpitation [of the heart].
aleudar *tr.* to leaven. 2 *ref.* to rise [the dough].
aleve *adj.* ALEVOSO.
alevino *m.* alevin, fry.
alevosamente *adv.* treacherously, wickedly, mischievously. 2 in cold blood.
alevosía *f.* treachery, perfidy.
alevoso, -sa *adj.* treacherous, perfidious.
aleya *f.* koran verse.
alfa *f.* alpha.
alfabético, -ca *adj.* alphabetical.
alfabetización *f.* teaching to read and write, teaching literacy. 2 literacy.
alfabetizar *tr.* to teach literacy, to alphabetize [someone]. 2 to put in alphabetical order.
alfabeto *m.* alphabet.
alfajor *m.* sort of gingerbread. 2 (Am.) macaroon.
alfalfa *f.* BOT. lucerne, lucern, alfalfa.
alfalfal, alfalfar *m.* lucerne field.
alfaneque *m.* ORN. buzzard.
alfanje *m.* kind of short scimitar.
alfaque *m.* bar of sand at a river's mouth.
alfaquí *m.* alfaqui.
1) alfar *m.* pottery [factory]. 3 clay, argil.
2) alfar *intr.* [of horses] to rear.
alfarda *f.* ARCH. rafter.
alfarería *f.* pottery [shop, factory, art].
alfarero *m.* potter [pottery maker].
alfarje *m.* grinding mill for olives. 2 carved and panelled ceiling.
alfayate *m.* obs. tailor.
alféizar *m.* ARCH. splay; embrasure.
alfeñicado, -da *adj.* weakly, delicate.
alfeñique *m.* sugar paste in thin bars. 2 frail, delicate person. 3 REMILGO.
alferazgo *m.* ensigncy; second lieutenancy.
alferecía *f.* MED. epilepsy [in children]. 2 ALFERAZGO.
alférez *m.* second lieutenant, ensign.
alfil *m.* CHESS. bishop.
alfiler *m.* pin [pointed metal piece]: ~ *de corbata,* tie-pin; *de veinticinco alfiles,* dressed up. 2 brooch. 3 ~ *de París,* wire nail. 4 *pl.* pin money.
alfilerazo *m.* prick [with a pin].
alfiletero *m.* needlecase, pincase.
alfombra *f.* floor carpet, rug. 2 fig. carpet.
alfombrar *tr.* to carpet.
alfombrilla *f.* small carpet or rug.
alfombrista *m.* carpet seller. 2 carpet layer.
alfoncigo, alfónsigo *m.* BOT. pistachio [tree and nut].
alfonsino, -na *adj.* Alphonsine.
Alfonso *pr. n.* Alphonse.
alforfón *m.* BOT. buckwheat.
alforja *f.* wallet [long bag open at the middle and closed at the ends].
alforjón *m.* ALFORFÓN.
alforza *f.* tuck, pleat [in a garment].
alga *f.* BOT. alga; sea-weed. 2 *pl.* BOT. Algae.
algaida *f.* thick forest. 2 MÉDANO.
algalia *f.* civet [a perfume]. 2 SURG. catheter. 3 *m.* ZOOL. civet, cat.
algara *f.* old-time raiding cavalry party. 2 raid of an ALGARA.
algarabía *f.* arabic language. 2 jargon. 3 hubbub, uproar.
algarada *f.* ALGARA 2. 2 outcry. 3 ancient war engine for throwing stones.
algarroba *f.* carob bean. 2 BOT. vetch.

algarrobilla f. BOT. vetch, tare.
algarrobo m. BOT. carob tree, locuşt tree.
algazara f. din, clamour, joyful uproar.
algazul m. BOT. ice plant.
álgebra f. algebra. 2 bonesetting.
algebrista m. algebraist. 2 bonesetter.
algidez f. algidity.
álgido, -da adj. algid.
algo pron. something; aught, anything. 2 adv. somewhat, a little.
algodón m. cotton: ~ en rama, cotton wool, raw cotton; ~ hidrófilo, absorbent cotton; ~ pólvora, guncotton. 2 cotton plant.
algodonal m. cotton plantation. 2 cotton plant.
algodonar tr. to fill with cotton.
algodonero, -ra adj. cotton. 2 m.-f. cotton dealer. 3 m. BOT. cotton plant.
algodonoso, -sa adj. cottony.
algorín m. place in oilmills for receiving olives.
algoritmo m. algorism, algorithm.
alguacil m. beadle, court apparitor. 2 obs. a kind of judge. 3 obs. a peace-officer. 4 ZOOL. jumping spider.
alguacilillo m. rider at the head of bullfighter's parade.
alguien pron. somebody, someone.
algún adj. some. | Used before sing. masc. noun. 2 adv. ~ tanto, a little, somewhat.
alguno, -na adj. some, any: ~ vez, sometimes; ~ que otro, some, a few. 2 pron. someone, anyone.
alhaja f. jewel. 2 a valuable thing, or ornament. 3 iron. buena ~, a bad one, a sly one.
alhajar tr. to jewel. 2 to furnish [a house or room].
alharaca f. fuss, ado, exaggerated show of feeling.
alhárgama, alharma f. BOT. African rue.
alhelí m. BOT. gillyflower.
alheña f. BOT. privet, henna. 2 privet powder.
alheñar tr. to dye with privet.
alholva f. BOT. fenugreek.
alhóndiga f. public granary or grain market.
alhucema f. ESPLIEGO.
aliacán m. ICTERICIA.
aliado, -da adj. allied, confederated. 2 m.-f. ally.
aliadófilo, -la adj. allied. 2 n. sympathiser of the allied in world wars I and II.
aliaga f. AULAGA.
alianza f. alliance, league. 2 alliance [by marriage].
aliar tr. to ally. 2 ref. to ally [become allied].
aliaria f. BOT. hedge garlic.
alias lat. adv. alias.
alicaído, -da adj. weak, drooping. 2 sad, crestfallen. 3 downfallen.
alicántara f., **alicante** m. ZOOL. a viper.
alicantina f. coll, artifice, stratagem.
alicantino, -na adj.-n. of Alicante.
alicatado m. a glazed-tile work in Moorish style.
alicates m. pl. pliers.
Alicia pr. n. Alice.
aliciente m. incentive, inducement, attraction.
alicortar tr. to cut the winds off. 2 to wound in the wing. 3 to clip someone's wings.
alicuanta adj. aliquant.
alícuota adj. aliquot; proportional.
alidada f. alidade.
alienación f. alienation. 2 MED. mental alienation.
alienado, -da adj. alienated. 2 m.-f. MED. alienated [person].
alienar tr. ENAJENAR.
alienista m. alienist.
aliento m. breath, breathing; respiration: tomar

~, to breathe, take breath: sin aliento, breathless, out of breath. 2 spirit, courage: dar ~, to encourage.
aliento, aliente, etc. irr. V. ALENTAR.
alifafe m. VET. tumour on a horse's hock. 2 chronic complaint.
aliforme adj. wing-shaped, aliform.
aligación f. alligation: regla de ~, MATH. alligation.
aligeramiento m. lightening, making lighter [of a burden, a load]. 2 reduction, cutting down [taxes, fees]. 3 lessening; reduction, diminution [of responsibilities]. 4 relief, ease, alleviation.
aligerar tr. to lighten [make less heavy]. 2 to alleviate. 3 to hasten. 4 ref. to lighten [become lighter].
aligero, -ra adj. poet. aligerous, winged. 2 fast, fleet.
aligustre m. ALHEÑA 1.
alijador, -ra m.-f. ginner. 2 NAUT. unloader. 3 m. NAUT. lighter.
1) **alijar** tr. NAUT. to lighten or unload [a ship]. 2 to gin [cotton].
2) **alijar** m. untilled land. 2 pl. common land.
alijo m. NAUT. unloading. 2 smuggled goods.
alimaña f. beast that destroys game, vermin.
alimentación f. alimentation, feeding, nourishment.
alimentador, -ra adj. nourishing. 2 m.-f. nourisher. 3 m. MECH. feeder.
alimentar tr. to feed, nourish, sustain, aliment. 2 MECH. to feed; to stoke. 3 to entertain, cherish, nurture, foster. 4 ref. to feed, nourish oneself: ~ de, to feed on.
alimenticio, -cia adj. alimentary, nourishing, nutritious.
alimento m. aliment, food, nourishment. 2 pabulum. 3 pl. LAW allowance for sustenance, alimony.
alimentoso, -sa adj. nourishing.
alimoche m. ABANTO 2.
alimón (al) adv. BULLF. with the cape held by two bullfighters. 2 together, conjointly.
alindamiento m. boundary marking or setting.
alindar tr. set landmarks to. 2 to embellish. 3 intr. LINDAR.
alineación f., **alineamiento** m. alignment, alinement.
alineamiento m. alignment, arrangement in a straight line, lining up; no ~, nonalignment.
alinear tr. to align, aline, put into line, range. 2 ref. to align, aline, fall in line, be in line.
aliñar tr. to adorn, dress, tidy. 2 to dress, season [food, drink]. 3 to prepare, arrange. 4 (Am.) to set [bones].
aliño m. adornment, tidiness. 2 dressing, seasoning. 3 arrangement.
alioli m. AJIACEITE.
alípede adj. poet. wing-footed, swift, fleet.
alípedo, -da adj. ALÍPEDE. 2 ZOOL. aliped.
aliquebrado, -da adj. broken-winged. 2 ALICAÍDO.
alisador, -ra adj. smoothing, polishing. 2 m.-f. smoother, polisher, planer.
alisadura f. smoothing, planing. 2 pl. shavings.
1) **alisar** tr. to smooth, slick, sleek. 2 to polish, plane; to surface. 3 ref. to become smooth.
2) **alisar** m. plantation of alder trees.
alisios adj. vientos ~, trade winds.
alisma f. BOT. water plantain.
aliso m. BOT. alder tree.
alistado, -da adj. enlisted, enrolled, recruited. 2 striped. 3 m. volunteer, recruit.

alistamiento *m.* enlistment, enrollment. *2* MIL. conscription. *3* conscripts of a year.
alistar *tr.-ref.* to enlist, enroll [a person]. *2* to prepare, make ready.
aliteración *f.* alliteration.
aliterado, -da *adj.* alliterate.
aliviador, -ra *adj.* alleviating, allaying, relieving. *2 m.-f.* alleviator, allayer, reliever. *3* helper.
aliviar *tr.* to lighten [make less heavy]. *2* to unburden. *3* to alleviate, allay, relieve, ease, assuage. *4* to hasten. *5 ref.* to ease up, subside. *6* to get better.
alivio *m.* alleviation, allay, relief, ease, assuagement, mitigation. *2* improvement [in an illness].
aljaba *f.* quiver [case for holding arrows].
aljama *f.* a Jewish or Moorish community in medieval Spain; a mosque, a synagogue.
aljamía *f.* Spanish written in Arabic characters.
aljez *m.* crude gypsum.
aljibe *m.* cistern; water tank. *2* NAUT. tank boat; tanker.
aljofaina *f.* washboul, washbasin, washhand basin.
aljófar *m.* seed pearl. *2* poet. drops of dew.
aljofarar *tr.* to adorn or cover with ALJÓFAR.
aljofifa *f.* mop [for floors].
aljofifar *tr.* to mop [floors].
aljuba *f.* a Moorish garment.
alma *f.* soul, spirit, ghost: ~ *de cántaro*, fig. senseless fool; ~ *de Dios*, fig. good soul; ~ *en pena*, soul in purgatory; fig. lonely, dejected person; ~ *mía, mi* ~, my dearest, my love; *entregar* or *rendir el* ~ *a Dios*, to die, give up the ghost; *estar con el* ~ *en un hilo*, fig. to have one's heart in one's mouth; to be on tenterhooks; *romper el* ~ *a uno*, fig. to break someone's head or neck; *como* ~ *que lleva el diablo*, as if the devil were after one; *con el* ~ *y la vida*, very willingly. *2* soul, person, inhabitant. *3* soul [leader, moving spirit]. *4* soul, strength, vigour. *5* bore [of a gun]. *6* core, heart [of a rope, a casting, etc.]. *7* web [of a rail, etc.]. *8* MUS. sound post.
almacén *m.* store, storehouse, warehouse, shop. *2* storeroom. *3* depot. *4* magazine, repository, reservoir. *5 pl.* department store.
almacenaje *m.* storage [charges].
almacenamiento *m.* storage, warehousing, keeping of goods. *2* supply, stock, goods available.
almacenar *tr.* to store, store up. *2* to hoard.
almacenero *m.* warehouse keeper.
almacenista *m.* storekeeper, wholesale merchant.
almáciga *f.* mastic. *2* seedbed [for later transplantation].
almacigar *tr.* to perfume with mastic.
almácigo *m.* ALMÁCIGA 2. *2* BOT. mastic tree.
almádana, almádena *f.* stone hammer.
almadraba *f.* tunny fishing or fishery. *2* net for catching tunnies.
almadrabero *m.* tunny fisher.
almadreña *f.* sabot, wooden shoe.
almagesto *m.* almagest.
almagral *m.* reddle deposit.
almagrar *tr.* to reddle, ruddle. *2* to stigmatize.
almagre *m.* reddle, ruddle, red ocher.
almajaneque *m.* MAGANEL.
almalafa *f.* haik, haick.
almanaque *m.* almanac, calendar.
almandina *f.* MINER. almandine, almandite.
almarada *f.* triangular poniard.
almarjal *m.* marshy land.

almarjo *m.* any plant yielding barilla.
almazara *f.* oil mill.
almea *f.* alme, almeh. *2* storax; storax bark.
almecina *f.* hackberry, fruit of the nettle plant.
almeja *f.* ZOOL. quahog, round clam.
almena *f.* FORT. merlon.
almenado, -da *adj.* embattled, battlemented. *2 m.* FORT. battlement.
almenaje *m.* FORT. battlement.
almenar *tr.* FORT. to embattle, to crenel(l)ate.
almenara *f.* beacon, signal fire.
almendra *f.* BOT. almond: ~ *confitada*, sugar almond; ~ *garrapiñada*, praline. *2* BOT. kernel [of a drupe]. *3* cutglass drop. *4* coll, pebble.
almendrado, -da *adj.* almond-shaped. *2 m.* macaroon. *3 f.* almond milk.
almendral *m.* plantation of almond trees.
almendro *m.* BOT. almond tree.
almendruco *m.* green almond.
almeriense *adj.-n.* of Almería.
almete *m.* armet.
almez *m.* BOT. hackberry, nettle tree.
almeza *f.* hackberry [fruit].
almezo *m.* ALMEZ.
almiar *m.* haystack, straw stack.
almíbar *m.* syrup [as used in confectionery].
almibarado, -da *adj.* sugary, honeyed.
almibarar *tr.* to preserve in syrup. *2* to sweeten, honey [one's words].
almidón *m.* starch. *2* (Am.) paste [for gluing].
almidonado, -da *adj.* starched. *2* coll. spruce, dapper.
almidonar *tr.* to starch.
almijar *m.* place where olives and grapes are put to dry before pressing them.
almilla *f.* under waistcoat.
alminar *m.* minaret.
almiranta *f.* NAUT. obs. vice-almiral's ship. *2* admiral's wife.
almirantazgo *m.* NAV. court of Admiralty. *2* admiralship, admiralty.
almirante NAV. admiral.
almirez *m.* brass mortar.
almizcate *m.* space for land between two houses.
almizcle *m.* musk [the substance].
almizcleño, -ña *adj.* musky. *2 f.* BOT. grapehyacinth.
almizclera *f.* ZOOL. musk rat.
almizclero, -ra *adj.* ALMIZCLEÑO. *2 m.* musk deer.
almo, -ma *adj.* nourishing, vivifying. *2* holy.
almocafre *m.* hoe, weeding hoe.
almocárabe *m.* ARCH. knotted ornament.
almocela *f.* hood.
almocrí *m.* reader of the Koran in a mosque.
almófar *m.* ARM. hood of mail, camail.
almogávar *m.* a medieval foot soldier or adventurer.
almohada *f.* pillow, bolster; cushion: *consultar con la* ~, to sleep on [something]. *2* pillowcase.
almohadilla *f.* small cushion, pad. *2* sewing cushion. *3* (Am.) pincushion. *4* ARCH. bulging front or cushion [in an ashlar].
almohadillado, -da *adj.* ARCH. cushioned. *2 m.* ARCH. bolsterwork.
almohadón *m.* cushion, large cushion. *2* ARCH. springer.
almohaza *f.* currycomb.
almohazar *tr.* to currycomb, curry [a horse].
almojarifazgo *m.* obs. former payment demanded by the government on certain goods imported or exported.

almóndiga, almondiguilla *f.* ALBÓNDIGA, ALBONDI-
GUILLA.
almoneda *f.* auction, auction sale. *2* bargain sale.
almonedar, almonedear *tr.* to sell by auction.
almoraduj, almoradux *m.* BOT. sweet marjoram.
almorávides *m.* Almoravides.
almorranas *f. pl.* MED. piles, haemorrhoids.
almorta *f.* BOT. bitter vetch.
almorzado, -da *adj.* having breakfasted.
almorzar *intr.* to breakfast, to lunch. *2 tr.* to eat at
breakfast or lunch. ¶ CONJUNG. like *contar.*
almotacén *m.* inspector of weights and measures.
2 (Morocco) overseer of markets.
almud *m.* a dry measure.
almuecín, almuédano *m.* muezzin.
almuerzo *m.* breakfast, lunch.
almuerzo, almuerce, etc. *irr.* V. ALMORZAR.
alocación *f.* allocation, distribution, assignment.
alocadamente *adv.* wildly, recklessly.
alocado, -da *adj.* mad, foolish, wild, reckless.
alocución *f.* allocution, harangue, address.
alodio *m.* al(l)odium.
áloe *m.* BOT. aloe. *2* PHARM. aloes. *3* agalloch.
aloja *f.* drink made of water, honey and spices.
alojado *m.* MIL. billeted man. *2* (Am.) lodger, guest.
alojamiento *m.* lodging, quartering, billeting. *2*
lodgings, lodgement, quarters, billet; housing.
alojar *tr.* to lodge, give lodgings, to house, to quarter, to billet. *2 ref.* to lodge, lodge oneself or itself, to put up.
alomado, -da *adj.* ridged. *2* high-backed [horse].
alomar *tr.* to plough leaving wide ridges.
alón *m.* COOK. wing of fowl.
alondra *f.* ORN. lark, skylark.
Alonso *pr. n.* Alphonse.
alópata *adj.-n.* allopath, allopathist.
alopatía *f.* allopathy.
alopecia *f.* MED. alopecia.
aloque *adj.-n.* light red [wine].
alotropia *f.* CHEM. allotropy, allotropism.
alotrópico, -ca *adj.* allotropic.
alpaca *f.* ZOOL. alpaca. *2* alpaca [wool and cloth].
3 German silver.
alpargata *f.* rope-soled sandal.
alpargatería *f.* ALPARGATA shop or factory.
alpargatero, -ra *m.-f.* maker or seller of ALPARGA-
TAS.
alpargatilla *f.* crafty, artful, insinuating person.
alpechín *m.* dark, fetid liquid which runs from
piled-up olives before being pressed.
Alpes *pr. n.* GEOG. Alps.
alpestre *adj.* Alpestrine.
alpinismo *m.* alpinism.
alpinista *m.-f.* alpinist, alpestrian.
alpino, -na *adj.* alpine.
alpiste *m.* BOT. canary grass. *2* alpist, canary seed.
alquequenje *m.* BOT. winter cherry.
alquería *f.* grange, farmhouse.
alquilable *adj.* rentable, that may be rented or
hired.
alquiladizo, -za *adj.* for rent, for hire. *2 adj.-n.* hireling.
alquilador, -ra *m.-f.* hirer.
alquilar *tr.* to let, rent; to hire. *2 ref.* to hire out,
serve for wages. *3* to be let or rented.
alquiler *m.* letting, renting. *2* rent, rental, hire
[price]. *3 de ~,* for rent, for hire; hack, hackney.
alquimia *f.* alchemy.
alquimista *m.* alchemist.
alquitara *f.* ALAMBIQUE.

alquitarar *tr.* to distil. *2* fig. *alquitarado,* over refined, affected.
alquitrán *m.* tar; pitch: ~ *mineral,* coal tar.
alquitranado, -da *adj.* tarred, covered with tar. *2*
m. NAUT. tarpaulin, tarred canvas. *3 m.* tarring
[of the road, the roof, etc.]. *4* tarmac, tar and
gravel mixture used for paving roads, paths,
etc.
alquitranar *tr.* to tar.
alrededor *adv.* ~ *de,* around, about [on all sides of;
approximately]; *a su* ~, around or about him or
it. *2 m. pl.* outskirts, surroundings.
Alsacia *pr. n.* GEOG. Alsace.
alsaciano, -na *adj.-n.* Alsatian.
alta *f.* an old court dance. *2* discharge [from hospital, etc]. *3* registration for fiscal purposes. *4*
MIL. inscription in the muster book. *5 dar de* ~,
to discharge [a patient from hospital, etc.]; MIL.
to enter or inscribe in the muster book. *6 darse
de* ~, to register for fiscal purposes; to join [a
club, society, etc.].
altaico, -ca *adj.* altaic.
altamente *adv.* highly, strongly, extremely.
altanería *f.* haughtiness, arrogance. *2* falconry,
hawking.
altanero, -ra *adj.* haughty, arrogant. *2* flying high
[as a falcon].
altar *m.* altar; ~ *mayor,* high altar; *el Sacramento
del* ~, the Holy Eucharist. *2* altar stone.
altavoz *m.* RADIO. loudspeaker.
alterable *adj.* alterable, changeable.
alteración *f.* alteration, change. *2* unevennes [of
the pulse]. *3* strong emotion, agitation. *4* disturbance: ~ *del orden público,* breach of the peace.
alterado, -da *adj.* altered, changed. *2* disturbed,
agitated, upset.
alterar *tr.* to alter, change. *2* to excite, unsettle. *3*
to disturb, upset. *4 ref.* to become altered, changed, excited, disturbed, agitated.
altercación *f.,* **altercado** *m.* altercation, dispute,
wrangle.
altercar *tr.* to altercate, dispute, wrangle.
alternación *f.* alternation.
alternadamente *adv.* ALTERNATIVAMENTE.
alternado, -da *adj.* alternate, altern.
alternador *m.* ELECT. alternator.
alternancia *f.* alternation, alternance.
alternante *adj.* alternating, alternate. *2 m.* MATH.
alternant.
alternar *tr.-intr.* to alternate. *2 intr.* to have social
intercourse, to mix.
alternativa *f.* alternative, option. *2* alternation. *3*
admission of a bullfighter as a MATADOR.
alternativo, -va *adj.* alternate, alternating.
alterno, -na *adj.* ALTERNATIVO. *2* ELEC. alternating
[current]. *3* BOT., GEOM. alternate.
alteza *f.* height. *2* elevation, sublimity: ~ *de miras,*
high-mindedness. *3* Highness [a title].
altibajo *m.* FENC. downright blow. *2 pl.* ups and
downs.
altilocuente; altilocuo, -cua *adj.* grandiloquent.
altillo *m.* hillock. *2* (Am.) garret.
altimetría *f.* altimetry.
altímetro *m.* altimeter.
altiplanicie *f.* plateau, tableland.
altiplano *m.* (Am.) high plateau, tableland.
altísimo, -ma *adj. superl.* of ALTO. *2 m. El Altísimo,*
The Most High, God.
altisonancia *f.* pompousness, bombast.
altisonante, altísono, -na *adj.* altisonant, high
sounding, bombastic.

altitud *f.* height [above ground, from base to top, in the air]. *2* GEOG. altitude [above sea level].
altivecer *tr.* to make haughty. *2 ref.* to become haughty.
altivez, altiveza *f.* haughtiness, arrogance, pride.
altivo, -va *adj.* haughty, arrogant, proud, lofty.
alto, -ta *adj.* high: ~ *precio*, high price; ~ *relieve*, high relief, alto-relievo; *alta mar*, high seas; *alta traición*, high treason; *lo* ~, the top; *de lo* ~, from above. *2* tall. *3* upper: ~ *Egipto*, Upper Egypt. *4* [of things] elevated, noble, excellent. *5* [of time] high, late, advanced. *6* ACCUST. high, loud. *7* ~ *hornos*, blast furnace. *8 m.* high: *un metro de* ~, a metre high. *9* height, hillock, eminence. *10* storey, floor [of a house]. *11* MUS. viola. *12* halt, stop: *dar el* ~, to call to a halt, stop. *13 altos y bajos*, ups and downs. *14 adv.* high, on high, raised: *en* ~, on high, raised. *15* loudly. *16 interj.* halt!, stop!: *¡alto ahí!*, stop there!
altoparlante *m.* (Am.) loudspeaker.
altozano *m.* height, hill. *2* highest part of a town.
altramuz *m.* BOT. lupine.
altruismo *m.* altruism.
altruista *adj.* altruistic.
altura *f.* height, hillock. *2* height, tallness. *3* summit, top. *4* elevation, excellence. *5* altitude [above sea level]. *6* ASTR., GEOM. altitude. *7* GEOM. height. *8* MUS. pitch. *9* NAUT. latitude. *10 a la* ~ *de*, opposite; on the same level as; *estar a la* ~ *de*, to be equal to [a task, etc.]. *11* NAUT. *de* ~, sea-going. *12 pl.* heights. *13* heavens. *14 a estas alturas*, at this point or juncture.
alubia *f.* BOT. bean, French bean.
alucinación *f.* hallucination.
alucinador, -ra *adj.* hallucinating, fascinating, deluding. *2 m.-f.* hallucinator, deluder.
alucinante *adj.* hallucinating, hallucinatory.
alucinar *tr.* to hallucinate. *2* to fascinate, delude. *3 ref.* to delude oneself.
alucinógeno, -na *adj.* hallucinogenic. *2 m.* hallucinogen.
alud *m.* avalanche, snowslip.
aluda *f.* ENT. winged ant.
aludido, -da *adj.* mentioned, talked about, above mentioned. *2 darse por* ~, to consider oneself object of allusion, to get the hint, to take it personal.
aludir *intr.* to allude, refer to, hint at.
alumbrado, -da *p. p.* of ALUMBRAR. *2 adj.* coll. tipsy. *3 m.* lighting, lights.
alumbramiento *m.* illumination, enlightening. *2* drawing out of subterranean waters. *3* childbirth.
alumbrar *tr.* to light, illuminate. *2* to light the way [for someone]. *4* to illuminate, enlighten. *5* to give or launch [a blow]. *7* to alum. *8 intr.* to shed light. *9* to be delivered of a child. *10 ref.* to get tipsy.
alumbre *m.* alum: ~ *de pluma*, feather alum.
alúmina *f.* CHEM. alumina, alumine.
aluminio *m.* CHEM. aluminium, aluminum.
aluminita *f.* MINER. aluminite.
alumnado *m.* pupils [in school] students, student body [in university].
alumno, -na *m.-f.* pupil, scholar, alumnus.
alunado, -da *adj.* whimsical, quaint, fanciful. *2* lunatic, mad, insane, extremely foolish.
alunarse *ref.* [of bacon] to become spoiled.
alunizaje *m.* landing on the moon.
alunizar *intr.* to land on the moon.
alusión *f.* allusion, reference, hint, mention.

alusivo, -va *adj.* allusive, hinting.
aluvial *adj.* alluvial.
aluvión *f.* alluvion. *2* alluvium, silt, wash.
álveo *m.* channel, bed, runway [of a stream].
alveolado *adj.* honeycombed, faveolate, alveolate.
alveolar *adj.* alveolar, alveolary.
alvéolo *m.* alveole, alveolus.
alverja, alverjana *f.* ARVEJA. *2* (Am.) GUISANTE.
alza *f.* advance, rise, lift [in prices]. *2* PRINT. overlay. *3* FIREARMS. leaf sight, rear sight. *4* flashboard.
alzacuello *m.* neck stock.
alzada *f.* height, stature [of horses]. *2* appeal to a higher administrative body or official.
alzadamente *adv.* for a lump sum.
alzado, -da *adj.* lump [sum]: *por un tanto* ~, for a lump sum. *2 m.* ARCH., DRAW. elevation. *3* BOOKBIND. gathering.
alzamiento *m.* raising, lifting. *2* uprising, insurrection. *3* ~ *de bienes*, fraudulent bankruptcy.
alzapaño *m.* curtain holder or loop.
alzaprima *f.* lever, pry, crowbar. *2* wedge [for raising something]. *3* MUS. bridge.
alzaprimar *tr.* to lever, pry [raise with a lever].
alzar *tr.* to raise, lift, hoist, uplift, heave. *2* to elevate [the Host]. *3* to erect, build. *4* to remove, carry off. *5* to clear [the table]. *6* to gather [a crop]. *7* to strike [tents]. *8* PRINT. to gather [signatures for binding]. *9* ~ *el vuelo*, to take wing. *10* ~ *velas*, to set sail; to flee, depart. *11 ref.* to rise; to get up, stand up. *12* to rise, rebel. *13* LAW to appeal. *14 alzarse con*, to appropriate, to run away with.
allá *adv.* there [in or at that place]: *más* ~, farther; *el más* ~, the Beyond, the future life; *por* ~, thereabouts. *2* ~ *en Francia*, over in France; ~ *por el año 1800*, about 1800; ~ *veremos*, we shall see; ~ *vosotros*, that's up to you; that's your lookout.
allanamiento *m.* levelling, smoothing, razing. *2* submission, consent. *3* LAW ~ *de morada*, forcing an entry into a house.
allanar *tr.* to level, smooth, flatten. *2* to raze, level to the ground. *3* to smooth out [difficulties, etc.]. *4* to pacify, subdue. *5* to force an entry into [a house]. *7 ref.* [of a building] to tumble down. *8* to yield, submit, consent.
allegado, -da *adj.* near, related, allied. *2 m.-f.* relative, friend; follower.
allegar *tr.* to gather, raise, collect. *2* to put [a thing] near another. *3* to add.
allende *adv.* on the other side. *2 prep.* beyond, over.
allí *adv.* there, in that place, yonder: ~ *mismo*, in that very place; *por* ~, that way; there, thereabouts. *2* then, at that moment.
allozo *m.* BOT. almond tree. *2* wild almond tree.
ama *f.* mistress, lady of the house: ~ *de casa*, housewife. *2* mistress, owner. *3* ~ *de gobierno*, ~ *de llaves*, housekeeper. *4* nurse [of a child]: ~ *de leche*, wet nurse; ~ *seca*, dry nurse.
amabilidad *f.* kindness, affability, amiability.
amable *adj.* kind, affable, nice, amiable, obliging. *2* lovable.
amachetear *tr.* to strike with a machete.
Amadeo *m. pr. n.* Amadeus.
amado, -da *m.-f.* love, loved one, beloved.
amador, -ra *m.-f.* lover.
amadrinar *tr.* to act as godmother to, to sponsor. *2* to couple [horses]. *3* NAUT. to join or couple [two things].
amaestrado, -da *adj.* taught, trained, drilled.

amaestramiento *m.* teaching, training, drill.
amaestrar *tr.* to teach, coach, train, drill.
amagar *tr.* to threaten, to show intention of [doing something]. *2 intr.* to threaten, impend, to show signs or symptoms.
amago *m.* threatening gesture, feint. *2* sign, hint, symptom.
amainar *tr.* NAUT. to lower or shorten [the sails]. *2 intr.* [of wind, anger, etc.] to abate, subside, die down. *3* to relax.
amaine *m.* NAUT. lowering [the sails]. *2* abating, subsiding, dying down.
amajadar *tr.* to fold [land] with sheep. *2* to fold [sheep] on a land. *3 intr.* [of sheep] to have fold in.
amalecita *adj.-n.* amalekite.
amalgama *f.* amalgam.
amalgamación *f.* amalgamation.
amalgamiento *m.* amalgamating.
amalgamar *tr.* CHEM. to amalgamate. *2* to amalgamate, mix.
amamantamiento *m.* nursing, suckling, lactation.
amamantar *tr.* to nurse, suckle, lactate.
amán *m.* in Morocco, pardon, amnesty.
amancebamiento *m.* concubinage.
amancebarse *ref.* to enter into concubinage.
1) **amanecer** *intr.* to dawn, to get light. *2* to be, or appear [at or in some place or state] at dawn. ¶ CONJUG. like *agradecer*.
2) **amanecer** *m.*, **amanecida** *f.* dawn, dawning, daybreak: *al* ~, at dawn.
amaneradamente *adv.* affectedly, in a manneristic way.
amanerado, -da *adj.* mannered, affected.
amaneramiento *m.* mannerism; affectation.
amanerarse *ref.* to fall into mannerism; to be or become affected.
amanezco, amanezca, etc. *irr.* V. AMANECER.
amanita *f.* BOT. amanita.
amanojar *tr.* to bunch, gather in a handful.
amansador, -ra *m.-f.* tamer. *3* (Am.) horsebreaker.
amansamiento *m.* taming subduing; appeasing.
amansar *tr.* to tame, domesticate. *2* to tame, subdue, soften. *3 ref.* to become tame; to soften [in character].
amante *adj.* loving, fond. *2 m.-f.* lover. *3* paramour; mistress. *4 m.* NAUT. pendant.
amantillo *m.* NAUT. lift.
amanuense *m.* amanuensis, clerk.
amañado, -da *adj.* skilful, clever, crafty. *2* fake. *3* fixed, rigged [a contest, a fight].
amañar *tr.* to arrange artfully, to cook, to fake. *2 ref.* to manage.
amaño *m.* cleverness, skill. *2* artifice, trick. *3 pl.* tools, implements. *4* machinations.
amapola *f.* BOT. red poppy, corn poppy.
amar *tr.* to love. *2* to like, be fond of.
amaraje *m.* AER. alighting on water.
amarantina BOT. globe amaranth.
amaranto *m.* BOT. amaranth.
amarar *tr.* AER. to alight on water.
amargado, -da *adj.-n.* embittered, soured [person].
amargamente *adv.* bitterly.
amargar *intr.* to taste bitter. *2 tr.* to embitter. *3* to spoil [an evening, a feast, etc.]. *4 ref.* to become embittered, to sour.
amargo, -ga *adj.* bitter [tasting bitter; painful; expressing pain or grief]. *2* sour [temper]. *3 s.* bitterness. *4* bitters [liquor].
amargón *m.* BOT. dandelion.

amargor *m.* AMARGURA. *2* bitterness. *3* sorrow, grief.
amargura *f.* bitterness. *2* sorrow, grief.
amaricado, -da; amariconado, -da *adj.* coll. effeminate, queer.
amarilidáceas *f. pl.* BOT. Amaryllidaceae.
amarillear *intr.* to show yellow, to be yellowish. *2* to pale.
amarillecer *intr.* to yellow, turn yellow.
amarillento, -ta *adj.* yellowish. *2* sallow, pale.
amarilleo *m.* showing yellow; yellowishness.
amarillez *f.* yellowness. *2* sallowness, paleness.
amarillo, -lla *adj.* yellow. *2* sallow, pale. *3 m.* yellow colour.
amariposado, -da *adj.* papilionaceous.
amarro *m.* BOT. clary.
amarra *f.* martingale [for horses]. *2* NAUT. mooring cable, fast. *3 pl.* friends at court, protection.
amarradero *m.* fastening or mooring post, ring, etc. *2* NAUT. moorings.
amarrado, -da *adj.* fig. tied down.
amarradura *f.* tying. *2* NAUT. circumvolution. *3* mooring.
amarraje *m.* NAUT. moorage [charge for mooring].
amarrar *tr.* to tie, fasten, rope. *2* NAUT. to moor [a ship].
amarre *m.* NAUT., AER. mooring, fastening.
amartelado, -da *adj.* infatuated, in love, starryeyed.
amartelamiento *m.* making love. *2* absorption [of lovers in each other].
amartelar *tr.* to make jealous. *2* to make love to. *3* to charm, enamour. *4 ref.* to fall in love.
amartillar *tr.* MARTILLAR. *2* to cock [a gun, a pistol].
amasadera *f.* kneading trough.
amasamiento *m.* kneading; mixing. *2* MED. massage.
amasar *tr.* to knead, mould, mix. *2* to amass. *3* MED. to massage. *4* to arrange [matters] for some purpose.
amasijo *m.* batch of dough. *2* kneading, mixing. *3* mixed material; medley. *4* plot, machination.
amatista *f.* MINER. amethyst.
amatorio, -ria *adj.* amatorial, amatory.
amaurosis *f.* MED. amaurosis.
amazacotado, -da *adj.* heavy, thick, clumsy.
amazona *f.* MYTH. Amazon. *2* a courageous woman. *3* horsewoman, lady rider. *4* habit, riding habit.
Amazonas *pr. n.* GEOG. Amazon [river].
amazónico, -ca *adj.* Amazonian.
ambages *m. pl.* ambages: *hablar sin* ~, to speak plainly.
ámbar *m.* amber: ~ *gris*, amber, ambergris. *2* ~ *negro*, jet.
ambarino, -na *adj.* amber, amber-like.
Amberes *pr. n.* GEOG. Antwerp.
ambición *f.* ambition.
ambicionar *tr.* to desire ambitiously.
ambicioso, -sa *adj.* ambitious.
ambidextro, -tra *adj.* ambidexter, ambidextrous.
ambientación *f.* atmosphere, environment. *2* setting, scene. *3* RADIO. sound effects.
ambiental *adj.* environmental.
ambientar *tr.* to give an appropriate atmosphere or setting to.
ambiente *adj.-m.* ambient. *2 m.* atmosphere, environment, setting.
ambigú *m.* buffet [at a party, dance, etc.]. *2* bar [in a theater, etc.].
ambiguamente *adv.* ambiguously.
ambigüedad *f.* ambiguity, ambiguousness.

ambiguo, -gua *adj.* ambiguous.
ámbito *m.* circuit, compass, field, area, precinct.
ambivalencia *f.* ambivalence.
ambivalente *adj.* ambivalent.
ambladura *f.* ambling [of horses].
amblar *tr.* [of animals] to amble, to pace.
ambo *m.* two-number combination in lotto.
ambón *m.* ambo [a reading pulpit].
ambos, bas *adj.-pron.* both: ~ *a dos,* both, both together.
ambrosía *f.* ambrosia. *2* BOT. ragweed.
ambrosíaco, -ca *adj.* ambrosial.
Ambrosio *pr. n.* Ambrose.
ambulancia *f.* ambulance. *2* ~ *de correos,* RLY. mail car, *postal car.
ambulante *adj.* ambulatory, itinerant, walking, travelling. *2 m.* ~ *de correos,* railway mail clerk.
ambulatorio, -ria *adj.* MED. ambulatory.
ameba *f.* AMIBA.
amedrentamiento *m.* fright, fear, terror.
amedrentar *tr.* to frighten, scare, intimidate.
amelocotonado, -da *adj.* peachy.
amén *m.* amen, so be it. *2* ~ *de,* excepting, save; besides, not to mention.
amenaza *f.* threat, menace.
amenazador, -a *adj.* threatening, menacing, lowering.
amenazar *tr.* to threaten, menace. *2 intr.* to be impending.
amenguar *tr.* to diminish, lessen. *2* to dishonour, disgrace.
amenidad *f.* amenity, pleasantness.
amenizar *tr.* to render pleasant, to brighten. *2* to adorn [a speech, etc.].
ameno, -na *adj.* agreeable, pleasant, delightful.
amenorrea *f.* MED. amenorrhœa.
amentáceo, -a; amentífero, -ra *adj.* BOT. amentaceous or amentiferous.
amento *m.* BOT. ament, catkin.
ameos *m.* BOT. bishop's weed.
amerengado, -da *adj.* meringue-like. *2* fig. sugary, syrupy.
América *pr. n.* GEOG. America.
americana *f.* coat, sack coat [of a man's suit].
americanismo *m.* Americanism.
americanista *n.* americanist.
americanización *f.* americanization.
americano, -na *adj.-n.* American.
amerindio, -a *adj.* amerindian. *2 n.* american indian, amerind.
amerizaje *m.* landing on the sea. *2* splashdown, landing of a spacecraft in the sea.
amerizar *int.* to land on the sea. *2* to splashdown [a spacecraft].
amestizado, -da *adj.* like a half-breed or half-caste.
ametralladora *f.* machine gun.
ametrallar *tr.* to shrapnel. *2* to machine-gun.
amianto *m.* amianthus, earth flax, asbestos.
amiba *f.,* **amibo** *m.* ZOOL. amœba.
amida *f.* CHEM. amide.
amiga *f.* friend [female f.]. *2* mistress, concubine.
amigable *adj.* amicable, friendly. *2* LAW ~ *componedor,* arbitrator.
amigacho *m.* AMIGOTE.
amigar *tr.-ref.* AMISTAR. *2 ref.* AMANCEBARSE.
amígdala *f.* tonsil, amygdala.
amigdaláceo, -a *adj.* BOT. amygdalaceous.
amigdalitis *f.* MED. tonsilitis.
amigo, -ga *adj.* friendly. *2* fond of or advocating [something]. *3 m.-f.* friend: ~ *del alma,* bosom

friend; *hacerse* ~ *de,* to make friends with. *4* paramour [man].
amigote *m.* coll. friend, pal.
amiláceo, -a *adj.* amilaceous.
amilanamiento *m.* daunting. *2* spiritlessness.
amilanar *tr.* to daunt, cow. *2 ref.* to be daunted.
amilasa *f.* BIOL. amylase.
Amílcar *pr. n.* Hamilcar.
amílico, -ca *adj.* CHEM. amylic.
amilo *m.* CHEM. amyl.
amillarar *tr.* to assess [property] for taxes.
aminorar *tr.* MINORAR.
amistad *f.* friendship. *2* amity. *3* favour, good graces. *4* concubinage. *5 pl.* friends. *6 hacer las amistades,* to make up, to become reconciled.
amistar *tr.* to make [others] friends. *2* to reconcile. *3 ref.* to become friends. *4* to be reconciled.
amistoso, -sa *adj.* friendly, amicable.
amito *m.* amice.
amnesia *f.* MED. amnesia.
amnios *f.* ANAT., ZOOL. amnion.
amnistía *f.* amnesty.
amnistiar *tr.* to amnesty.
amo *m.* master [of a house], lord, owner. *2* master [of servants]; boss.
amoblar *tr.* to furnish, fit up with furniture. ¶ CONJUG. like *contar.*
amodorrado, -da *adj.* drowsy, sleepy.
amodorramiento *m.* drowsiness, sleepiness.
amodorrarse *ref.* to drowse, become drowsy.
amojamar *tr.* to salt and dry [tunny fish]. *2 ref.* ACECINARSE.
amojonar *tr.* to set landmarks marks to.
amoladera *f.* whetstone, grindstone.
amolador *m.* whetter, knife grinder or sharpener.
amoladura *f.* whetting, grinding, sharpening.
amolar *tr.* to whet, grind, sharpen. *2* to bother, annoy. ¶ CONJUG. like *contar.*
amoldamiento *m.* mo(u)lding, modelling, adjusting, adapting.
amoldar *tr.* to mo(u)ld, shape, model, adapt, adjust. *2 ref.* to adjust, adapt oneself.
amomo *m.* BOT. amomum. *2* grains of Paradise.
amonedar *tr.* to monetize, coin.
amonestación *f.* admonition, reproof, warning. *2 pl.* marriage banns.
amonestar *tr.* to admonish, reprove, warn. *2* to publish banns of, to ask.
amoniacal *adj.* ammoniacal.
amoníaco *m.* CHEM. ammonia. *2* ammoniac.
amonio *m.* CHEM. ammonium.
amonita *f.* ZOOL. ammonite. *2 m.-f.* BIBL. Ammonite.
amontillado *m.* pale dry sherry.
amontonamiento *m.* heaping, accumulation, pile, heap. *2* crowding [of people].
amontonar *tr.* to heap, pile, accumulate; to crowd. *2 ref.* to heap, be piled; to crowd, throng. *3* to fly into a passion.
amor *m.* love: ~ *mío,* my love; ~ *propio,* amour propre, pride; *hacer el* ~ *a,* to woo, court; *al* ~ *del agua,* with the current; *al* ~ *del fuego,* or *de la lumbre,* by the fire, at the fireside; *por* ~ *de,* for the sake of. *2* care, careful attention [in work]. *3 pl.* love, love affair: *mal de amores,* love sickness; *requerir de amores,* to woo. *4* willingness: *con,* or *de mil amores,* willingly. *5* BOT. hedgehog parsley.
amoral *adj.* amoral.
amoratado, -da *adj.* purplish. *2* livid, black-and-blue.

amorcillo *m.* dim. of AMOR. *2 F.* ARTS cupid.
amordazar *tr.* to gag, muzzle.
amorfo, -fa *adj.* amorphous.
amorío *m.* love affair, amour.
amormío *m.* BOT. sea daffodil.
amoroso, -sa *adj.* loving, amorous, tender, affectionate; gentle. *2* love, of love.
amortajar *tr.* to shroud [a corpse], to dress for burial.
amortecer *tr.* to deaden. *2 ref.* to swoon, faint. ¶ CONJUG. like *agradecer*.
amortiguador, -ra *adj.* deadening, muffling, softening, damping. *2 m.* deadener, muffler. *3* MACH. shock absorber, buffer. *4* ELECT. damper.
amortiguamiento *m.* deadening, muffling, softening, damping.
amortiguar *tr.* to deaden [a blow, etc.], to muffle [a sound]; to lessen, soften, tone down. *2* to absorb [a shock]. *3* ELECT. to damp.
amortización *f.* amortization.
amortizable *adj.* amortizable.
amortizar *tr.* to amortize.
amoscarse *ref.* to get angry, take offence.
amostazar *tr.* to anger, irritate. *2 ref.* to get angry or irritated.
amotinado, -da *m.-f.* mutineer, rioter.
amotinador, -ra *m.-f.* mutineer, inciter to rebellion.
amotinamiento *m.* mutiny.
amotinar *tr.* to mutiny, incite to rebellion. *2 ref.* to mutiny, rebel.
amovible *adj.* removable.
amparador, -ra *adj.* protecting. *2 m.-f.* protector.
amparar *tr.* to protect, shelter, help, support. *2 ref.* to shelter, protect oneself; to avail oneself of the protection [of].
amparo *m.* protection, shelter, help, support: *al ~ de*, under cover of, protected by.
amperímetro *m.* ammeter, amperemeter.
amperio *m.* ELECT. ampere.
ampliación *f.* enlargement, ampliation, extension. *2* PHOT. enlargement.
ampliador, -ra *adj.* enlarging. *2 m.-f.* enlarger. *3 f.* PHOT. enlarger [camera].
ampliamente *adv.* largely, extensively.
ampliar *tr.* to enlarge, amplify, extend.
amplificación *f.* enlargement, amplification. *2* RHET. amplification.
amplificador, -ra *adj.* enlarging, amplifying. *2 m.-f.* enlarger, amplifier. *3* PHYS. amplifier.
amplificar *tr.* to enlarge, amplify, extend, magnify.
amplio, -plia *adj.* ample, extensive. *2* spacious, roomy, wide. *3* large, plentiful.
amplísimo, -ma *adj.* superl. of AMPLIO.
amplitud *f.* amplitude, extent. *2* ASTR., PHYS. amplitude.
ampo *s.* shining whiteness. *2* snowflake.
ampolla *f.* blister [on the skin]. *2* water bubble. *3* round-bellied bottle. *4* cruet. *5* MED. ampoule.
ampollar *tr.* to blister. *2* to make hollow. *3 ref.* to become blistered. *4* to bubble out.
ampolleta *f.* phial, smal cruet. *2* hourglass, sandglass.
ampulosidad *f.* turgidness, pompousness.
ampuloso, -sa *adj.* turgid, inflated, pompous.
amputación *adj.* amputation.
amputar *tr.* to amputate.
Amsterdam *pr. n.* GEOG. Amsterdam.
amuchachado, -da *adj.* boyish, childish.
amueblar *tr.* AMOBLAR.

amueblo, amueble, etc. *irr.* V. AMOBLAR.
amuelar *tr.* to gather grain into a pile.
amulatado, -da *adj.* mulatto-like.
amuleto *m.* amulet.
amura *f.* NAUT. bow [part of the side of a vessel]. *2* NAUT. tack [rope].
amurada *f.* NAUT. interior side of a ship.
amurallar *tr.* to wall [defend with walls].
amusgar *tr.* [of a horse, a bull, etc.] to throw back [the ears]. *2* to half-close [the eyes] to see better.
Ana *pr. n.* Ann, Anne, Hannah.
ana *f.* ell [a measure].
anabaptismo *m.* Anabaptism.
anabaptista *adj.-n.* Anabaptist.
anacarado, -da *adj.* pearly, pearl-coloured, like mother-of-pearl.
anacardo *m.* BOT. cashew. *2* cashew nut.
anaconda *f.* ZOOL. anaconda.
anacoreta *m.* anchoret, anchorite, hermit.
Anacreonte *m. pr. n.* Anacreon.
anacreóntico, -ca *adj.* Anacreontic.
anacrónico, -ca *adj.* anachronic, anachronistic.
anacronismo *m.* anachronism.
ánade *m.* ORN. duck, drake.
anadear *intr.* to waddle.
anaerobio, -bia *adj.* BIOL. anaerobic. *2 m.* anaerobe.
anafe *m.* portable cooker.
anafilaxis *f.* MED., BIOL. anaphylaxis.
anafrodisíaco, -ca *adj.-m.* anaphrodisiac.
anáglifo *m.* anaglyph.
anagoge *m.*, **anagogía** *f.* anagoge.
anagrama *f.* anagram.
anal *adj.* ZOOL. anal.
analectas *f. pl.* analects, analecta.
anales *m. pl.* annals.
analfabetismo *m.* illiteracy.
analfabeto, -ta *adj.-m.* illiterate.
analgesia *f.* MED. analgesia.
analgésico, -ca *adj.-m.* analgesic.
análisis *m.* analysis. *2* GRAM. parsing.
analista *m.* analyst. *2* annalist.
analítico, -ca *adj.* analytic(al.
analizable *adj.* analysable, analyzable.
analizar *tr.* to analyse, analyze. *2* GRAM. to parse.
analogía *f.* analogy. *2* GRAM. part of grammar studying parts of speech as such.
analógico, -ca *adj.* analogous. *2* GRAM. pertaining to ANALOGIA 2.
análogo, -ga *adj.* analogous, similar, parallel.
Anam *pr. n.* GEOG. Annam.
anamita *adj.-n.* Annamese.
ananá, ananás *f.* BOT. pineapple, ananas.
anapesto *m.* PROS. anapaest.
anaquel *m.* shelf [on a wall, in a cabinet, etc.].
anaquelería *f.* shelving, shelves.
anaranjado, -da *adj.* orange-coloured. *2* orange [colour].
anarquía *f.* anarchy.
anárquico, -ca *adj.* anarchic(al.
anarquismo *m.* anarchism.
anarquista *adj.-n.* anarchist. *2 adj.* anarchistic.
anastasia *f.* BOT. mugwort.
anastomosis *f.* ANAT., BOT. anastomosis.
anatema *m.-f.* anathema.
anatematizar *tr.* to anathematize.
anatomía *f.* anatomy.
anatómico, -ca *adj.* anatomical.
anatomista *m.* anatomist.
anatomizar *tr.* to anatomize.

anca *f.* haunch. *2* croup [in horses]: *a (las) ancas,* pillion riding [on horseback]. *3* hip [in men].
ancianidad *f.* old age.
anciano, -na *adj.* old, aged. *2 m.-f.* old man, woman or person; ancient; elder.
ancla *f.* NAUT. anchor: *~ de leva,* bower anchor, bower; *~ de la esperanza,* sheet or waist anchor; *sobre el ~,* at anchor.
ancladero *m.* NAUT. anchorage [anchoring place].
anclaje *m.* NAUT. anchorage.
anclar *intr.* to anchor, cast anchor.
anclote *m.* kedge anchor, kedge.
ancón *m.* little bay, cove. *2* (Am.) corner, nook.
áncora *f.* ANCLA. *2* HOROL. anchor.
ancusa *f.* BOT. bugloss, alkanet.
ancho, -cha *adj.* broad, wide. *2* too broad or wide. *3* loose fitting [garment, etc.]. *4* lax, elastic [conscience]. *5 m.* breadth, width: *~ de vía,* gauge. *6 f. pl. a sus anchas,* free, comfortable, at one's ease.
anchoa, anchova *f.* ICHTH. anchovy.
anchor *m.* ANCHURA.
anchura *f.* breadth, width. *2* freedom, ease, comfort.
anchuroso, -sa *adj.* broad, wide, spacious.
andadas *f. pl.* traces [of game]. *2 volver a las andadas,* to go back to one's old tricks.
andaderas *f. pl.* gocart for learning to walk.
andadero, -ra *adj.* [of ground] easy. *2* gadding about.
andador, -ra *adj.* good at walking. *2* gadding about. *3 m.* good walker. *4* gadabout. *5* messenger. *6 pl.* leading strings.
andadura *f.* galt, pace. *2 paso de ~,* amble.
Andalucía *pr. n.* GEOG. Andalusia.
andaluz, -za *adj.-n.* Andalusian.
andaluzada *f.* exaggeration.
andamiaje *m.* scaffolding.
andamio *m.* scaffold [for workmen or spectators].
andana *f.* row, tier. *2 llamarse ~,* to go back on one's word.
andanada *f.* NAUT. broadside [discharge]. *2* reprimand. *3* covered, grandstand in bull-ring.
andante *adj.* walking. *2* errant [knight]. *3* MUS. andante.
andanza *f.* event. *2* [good or bad] fortune. *3 pl.* adventures.
1) **andar** *intr.* to walk, to go, to move; to ride: *~ a gatas,* to go on all fours; *~ a caballo, en coche,* to ride on horseback, in a carriage. *2* [of a clock] to go; [of a machine] to run, to work. *3* to be: *~ enfermo,* to be ill; *~ con cuidado,* to be careful. *4* to tamper, touch, handle. | With *con* or *en.* *5* NAUT. to sail. *6* Other senses: *~ a derechas,* to act uprightly; *~ en los treinta años,* to be about thirty; *~ en los negocios,* to be engaged in business; *andando el tiempo,* in the course of time; *a todo ~,* at full speed; *¡anda!,* go on!; move ahead!; gracious! *7 tr.* to walk, cover [a distance]. *8 ref. andarse con,* to employ, indulge in. *9 andarse por las ramas,* to beat about the bush. ¶ CONJUG.: INDIC. Pret.: *anduve, anduviste, anduvo; anduvimos, anduvisteis, anduvieron.* | SUBJ. Imperf.: *anduviera, anduvieras, anduviera; anduviéramos, anduvierais, anduvieran,* or *anduviese, anduvieses,* etc. | Fut.: *anduviere, anduvieres,* etc.
2) **andar** *m.* gait, pace: *a largo ~,* in the long run.
andariego, -ga *adj.* good at walking. *2* gadding about.
andarín *m.* good walker.

andarivel *m.* ferry cable. *2* NAUT. safety rope.
andas *f. pl.* bier. *2* stretcher, portable plataform: *en ~* in triumph.
andén *m.* platform [of a railway station]. *2* banquette [of bridge]. *3* footwalk. *4* quay.
Andes *pr. n.* GEOG. Andes.
andino, -na *adj.* Andean.
andorga *f.* coll, belly.
Andorra *pr. n.* GEOG. Andorra.
andorra *f.* gadder, gadabout [woman].
andorrano, -na *adj.-n.* Andorran.
andorrear *intr.* to gad about.
andorrero, -ra *adj.* gadabout. *2 m.-f.* gadder.
andrajo *m.* rag, tatter. *2* despicable person or thing.
andrajoso, -sa *adj.* ragged, in rags, in tatters.
Andrés *pr. n.* Andrew.
androceo *m.* BOT. androecium.
andrógino, -na *adj.* BIOL. androgynous, androgyne. *2 n.* BIOL. androgyne.
androide *m.* android.
Andrómaca *f. pr. n.* Andromache.
Andrómeda *f. pr. n.* ASTR. Andromeda.
andrómina *f.* humbug, artifice, lie.
andullo *m.* rolled tobacco leaf. *2* NAUT. canvas shield on harpings and blocks.
andurriales *m. pl.* out-of-the-way places.
anduve, anduviera, anduviese, etc., irr. V. ANDAR.
anea *f.* BOT. cattail, cattail flag, rush.
aneblar *tr.* to befog. *2* to cloud, darken. *3 ref.* to become foggy or cloudy. ¶ CONJUG. like *acertar.*
anécdota *f.* anecdote.
anecdótico, -ca *adj.* anecdotical.
anegadizo, -za *adj.* frequently inundated.
anegar *tr.* to flood, overflow, inundate. *2* to drown. *3 ref.* to be inundated. *4* to drown; to sink.
anejar *tr.* ANEXAR.
anejo, -ja *adj.* ANEXO. *2 m.* sucursal church. *3* hamlet annexed to a town.
anélido *m.* ZOOL. annelid.
anemia *f.* anaemia, anemia.
anémico, -ca *adj.* anaemic, anemic.
anemófilo, -la *adj.* BOT. anemophilous.
anemómetro *m.* anemometer.
anémona, anémone *f.* BOT. anemone. *2* ZOOL. *~ de mar,* sea anemone.
aneroide *adj.-n.* aneroid [barometer].
anestesia *f.* anaesthesia.
anestesiar *tr.* anaesthetize.
anestésico, -ca *adj.-m.* anaesthetic.
anestesista *n.* anaesthetist, anesthetist.
aneurisma *m.* MED. aneurism.
anexar *tr.* to annex [a territory, etc.].
anexión *f.* annexion, annexation.
anexionar *tr.* to annex.
anexionismo *m.* annexationism.
anexo, -xa *adj.* annexed, joined. *2 m.* annex.
anfibio, -bia *adj.* amphibious. *2 adj.-n.* ZOOL. amphibian.
anfíbol *m.* MINER. amphibole.
anfibología *f.* amphibology.
anfictión *m.* amphyction.
anfisbena *f.* ZOOL. amphisbaena.
anfiscios *m. pl.* amphiscians, amphiscii.
anfiteatro *m.* amphitheatre.
anfitrión *m.* amphitryon, host, entertainer.
ánfora *f.* amphora.
anfractuosidad *f.* anfractuosity.
anfractuoso, -sa *adj.* anfractuous.
angarillas *f. pl.* handbarrow. *2* panniers [for pack animals]. *3* cruet stand, set of casters.

ángel *m.* angel; ~ *custodio* or *de la guarda,* guardian angel. 2 crossbar shot. 3 *tèner* ~, to be charming.
angélica *f.* BOT. angelica.
angelical *adj.* angelic(al, cherubic(al.
angélico, -ca *adj.* angelic.
angelico, angelito *m. dim.* little angel. 2 fig. baby.
angelote *m.* large figure of an angel. 2 ICHTH. angelfish. 3 a fat, sweet child.
ángelus *m.* Angelus.
angina *f.* MED. angina, sorethroat. 2 MED. ~ *de pecho,* angina pectoris.
angiospermas *f. pl.* BOT. angiospermae.
anglesita *f.* MINER. anglesite.
anglicanismo *m.* Anglicanism.
anglicano, -na *adj.-n.* Anglican.
anglicismo *m.* Anglicism.
anglo, -gla *adj.-n.* Anglian. 2 English. 3 *m. pl.* Angles.
anglófilo, -la *adj.-n.* Anglophil(e.
anglófobo, -ba *adj.-n.* Anglophobe.
anglosajón, -na *adj.-n.* Anglo-saxon.
Angora *f. pr. n.* GEOG. Angora.
angora *f.* angora wool.
angorina *f.* a light fluffy wool for knitting.
angostar *tr.* to narrow [lessen the breadth]. 2 *ref.* to narrow [become less broad].
angosto, -ta *adj.* narrow.
angostura *f.* narrowness. 2 narrows, narrow passage. 3 angostura [medicinal bark].
angrelado *adj.* HER. engrailed.
anguila *f.* ICHTH. eel. 2 NAUT. ~ *de cabo,* REBENQUE 1.
angula *f.* elver, young eel.
angular *adj.* angular. 2 *piedra* ~, corner stone.
ángulo *m.* GEOM. angle: ~ *agudo, recto, obtuso,* acute, right, obtuse angle; ~ *de mira,* angle of sight; ~ *horario,* ASTR. hour angle. 2 angle, corner, quoin.
anguloso, -sa *adj.* angular, angulated, angulous.
angustia *f.* anguish, affliction, distress.
angustiado, -da *adj.* anguished, afflicted, distressed.
angustiar *tr.* to afflict, distress, worry.
angustioso, -sa *adj.* anguishing, distressing.
anhelante *adj.* panting. 2 desirous, longing.
anhelar *intr.* to pant, gasp. 2 *tr.* to desire, to long or yearn for or to.
anhelo *m.* longing, yearning, desire.
anheloso, -sa *adj.* hard [breathing]. 2 painting. 3 anxious, desirous, wishful, eager.
anhídrido *m.* CHEM. anhydrid.
anhidro, -dra *adj.* CHEM. anhydrous.
Aníbal *pr. n.* Hannibal.
anidar *intr.* to nest, nidify. 2 to dwell, reside. 3 *tr.* to harbour, cherish.
anilina *f.* CHEM. aniline.
anilla *f.* curtain ring; strap ring. 2 *pl.* GYM. rings.
anillado, -da *adj.* curled. 2 ringed, annulated. 3 *m.* ZOOL. annulate.
anillar *tr.* to form into rings. 2 to fasten with rings.
anillo *m.* ring, circlet, finger ring: ~ *de boda,* wedding ring; *venir como* ~ *al dedo,* to fit, to be opportune. 2 cigar band. 3 ARCH., ZOOL., BOT. annulet, annulus. 4 NAUT. grommet. 5 MACH. ring, collar.
ánima *f.* human soul. 2 soul in Purgatory. 3 bore [of a gun]. 4 *pl.* ringing of bells at night for prayers for souls in Purgatory.
animación *f.* animation, liveliness, life. 3 bustle, movement.

animado, -da *adj.* animate. 2 animated, lively. 3 prompted. 4 heartened. 5 full of people.
animador, -ra *adj.* animating; comforting, inspiring; encouraging. 2 *m.-f.* animator; comforter; inspirer; encourager.
animadversión *f.* hatred, ill will, antagonism. 2 animadversion.
animal *adj.* animal. 2 stupid. 3 *m.* animal. 4 fig. stupid, rude person.
animalada *f.* stupidity.
animálculo *m.* animalcule.
animalejo *m.* small animal.
animalidad *f.* animality.
animalizar *tr.* to animalize.
animalote *m. aug.* big animal. 2 fig. very stupid person.
animalucho *m.* ugly, hideous animal.
animar *tr.* to animate. 2 to cheer up. 3 to encourage, impel, decide. 4 to enliven, brighten. 5 *ref.* to become animated, enlivened. 6 to take heart. 7 to make up one's mind.
anime BOT. courbaril. 2 courbaril copal.
anímico *adj.* PSÍQUICO.
animismo *m.* animism.
ánimo *m.* mind, spirit. 2 courage, energy: *cobrar* ~, to take courage. 3 intention, purpose: *hacer* or *tener* ~ *de,* to mean, to purpose. 4 attention, thought. 5 *interj.* ¡*ánimo!,* cheer up!
animosidad *f.* animosity, ill will. 2 courage.
animoso, -sa *adj.* brave, courageous.
aniñado, -da *adj.* childlish; girlish.
anión *m.* CHEM., PHYS. anion.
aniquilación *f.* annihilation, destruction.
aniquilador, -ra *adj.* annihilating, destroying; crushing. 2 *m.-f.* annihilator.
aniquilamiento *m.* annihilation, complete destruction.
aniquilar *tr.* to annihilate, destroy, crush. 2 *ref.* to be annihilated.
anís *m.* BOT. anise. 2 aniseed. 3 sugar-coated aniseed. 4 ANISADO 2.
anisado, -da *adj.* anise-flavoured. 2 *m.* anise-flavoured brandy.
anisar *tr.* to flavour with anise.
anisete *m.* anisette.
anisopétalo, -la *adj.* BOT. anisopetalous.
aniversario, -ria *adj.* ANUAL. 2 *m.* anniversary. 3 annual memorial service.
Ankara *f. pr. n.* GEOG. Ankara.
ano *m.* ANAT. anus.
anoche *adv.* last night, last evening, yesternight.
1) **anochecer** *intr.* to grow dark. 2 to be or reach somewhere at nightfall. ¶ CONJUG. like *agradecer.*
2) **anochecer** *m.,* **anochecida** *f.* nightfall, dusk, evening.
anodino, -na *adj.-n.* anodyne. 2 inane, ineffective.
anódico, -ca *adj.* PHYS. anodic.
ánodo *m.* ELECT. anode.
anomalía *f.* anomaly, irregularity. 2 ASTR. anomaly.
anómalo, -la *adj.* anomalous.
anona *f.* BOT. soursop.
anonadado, -da *adj.* crushed, thunderstruck.
anonadamiento *m.* annihilation. 2 humiliation. 3 prostration.
anonadar *tr.* to annihilite; to crush, overwhelm. 2 to humiliate. 3 *ref.* to humble oneself; to be crushed.
anonimato *m.* anonimity.
anónimo, -ma *adj.* anonymous. 2 COM. joint-stock

[company]. *3 m.* annonym(e [person, author]. *4* anonymous letter. *5* anonymity.
anorexia *f.* MED. anorexia.
anormal *adj.* abnormal. *2 m.-f.* abnormal person.
anormalidad *f.* abnormality, abnormity.
anosmia *f.* anosmia.
anotación *f.* annotation. *2* note, entry.
anotador, -ra *m.-f.* annotator.
anotar *tr.* to annotate, note. *2* to write, put down; to enter, inscribe.
anquilosamiento *m.* MED. ankylosis, anchylosis. *2* fig. paralysis, inmobility; ~ *de las negociaciones,* paralysis of the negotiations.
anquilosarse *ref.* to ankylose.
anquilosis *f.* MED. ankylosis, stiff joint.
ansa *f.* Hanse.
ánsar *m.* ORN. graylag. *2* ORN. goose, gander.
ansarino, -na *adj.* anserine. *2 m.* ORN. gosling.
ansarón *m.* ORN. ÁNSAR. *2* ORN. gosling.
anseático, -ca *adj.* Hanseatic.
ansia *f.* throe, anguish, pang. *2* eagerness, avidity, longing, hankering. *3 pl.* NÁUSEAS.
ansiar *tr.* to wish, long for, covet.
ansiedad *f.* anxiety, uneasiness, worry. *2* MED. anxiety.
ansioso, -sa *adj.* anguished. *2* desirous, anxious, eager; greedy.
anta *f.* ZOOL. elk, moose. *2* ARCH. anta. *3* menhir.
antagónico, -ca *adj.* antagonistic(al.
antagonismo *m.* antagonism.
antagonista *m.* antagonist, adversary, opponent.
antaño *adv.* last year. *2* formerly, in olden times; of yore.
antañón, -na *adj.* very old.
antártico, -ca *adj.* antarctic.
Antártida *f. pr. n.* GEOG. Antarctica.
1) **ante** *m.* ZOOL. elk, moose. *2* ZOOL. bubal. *3* buff [leather], buckskin.
2) **ante** *prep.* before, in the presence of. *2* ~ *todo,* first of all; above all.
antealtar *m.* chancel.
anteanoche *adv.* night before last.
anteayer *adv.* day before yesterday.
antebrazo *m.* forearm.
antecámara *f.* antechamber, anteroom.
antecedente *adj.-m.* antecedent.
antecedentemente *adv.* antecedently, previously.
anteceder *tr.* to antecede, precede.
antecesor, -ra *m.-f.* antecessor. *2* ancestor, forefather.
antecocina *f.* pantry, scullery.
antecolumna *f.* ARCH. column of a porch.
antecoro *m.* antechoir.
Antecristo *m.* Antichrist.
antedata *f.* antedate.
antedatar *tr.* to antedate [a document].
antedicho, -cha *adj.* a)foresaid; a(forenamed.
antediluviano, -na *adj.* antediluvian.
antefirma *f.* description of the signatory before the signature.
anteiglesia *f.* church porch.
antelación *f.* anteriority, previousness.
antemano (de) *adv.* beforehand.
antemeridiano, -na *adj.* antemeridian.
antena *f.* NAUT. lateen yard. *2* ZOOL. antenna, horn. *3* RADIO. antenna, aerial.
anteojera *f.* spectacle case. *2* blinder, blinker [for horses].
anteojo *m.* spyglass. *2 pl.* binocular fieldglasses, opera glasses. *3* eyeglasses, spectacles.
antepalco *m.* THEAT. small anteroom to a box.

antepasado, -da *adj.* foregone. *2 m.* ancestor, forefather.
antepecho *m.* parapet, railing; window sill. *2* FORT., MAR. breastwork. *3* breastband [of harness]. *4* breast beam [of loom].
antepenúltimo, -ma *adj.* antepenultimate.
anteponer *tr.* to place before, to prefix. *2* to place before, give the preference to. ¶ CONJUG. like *poner.*
anteportada *f.* bastard title page.
anteposición *f.* putting before, anteposition.
anteproyecto *m.* first draft or a project.
antepuerta *f.* portière. *2* FORT. anteport.
antepuerto *m.* NAUT. outer port.
antepuesto, -ta *p. p.* of ANTEPONER.
antera *f.* BOT. anther.
anteridio *m.* BOT. antheridium.
anterior *adj.* anterior, foregoing, former, previous: *el día* ~, the day before. *2* anterior, fore, front, forward.
anterioridad *f.* anteriority, priority: *con* ~, previously; *con* ~ *a,* previously to, prior to.
anteriormente *adv.* previously, before.
antes *adv.* before, first, previously, formerly; soon, sooner; ~ *de,* ~ *de que,* ~ *que,* previous to, before; *cuanto* ~, as soon as possible; *de* ~, from before; of old. *2* sooner, rather: ~ *morir que mentir,* sooner die than lie. *3 conj. antes,* or ~ *bien,* rather, on the contrary. *4 adj.* before, previous: *el día* ~, the previous day.
antesala *f.* anteroom, antechamber: *hacer* ~, to wait in an antechamber.
antevíspera *f.* the day before the eve [of]; two days before.
anti- *pref.* anti-.
antiaéreo, -a *adj.* anti-aircraft.
antiafrodisíaco, -ca *adj.* antiaphrodisiac.
antialcohólico, -ca *adj.* antialcoholic.
antiar *m.* BOT. antiar.
antiartístico, -ca *adj.* inartistic.
antibiótico, -ca *adj.-n.* antibiotic.
anticatarral *adj.* MED. anticatarrhal.
anticiclón *m.* METEOR. anticyclone.
anticipación *f.* anticipation, advance: *con* ~, in advance.
anticipadamente *adv.* in advance, beforehand, previously. *2* prematurely.
anticipado, -da *adj.* advanced, in advance; advance [payment]. *3* early, premature.
anticipar *tr.* to anticipate, advance, hasten. *2* to advance [money], to lend; to pay in advance. *3 ref.,* to occur before the regular time. *4 anticiparse a,* to anticipate, forestall, to get ahead of.
anticipo *m.* ANTICIPACIÓN. *2* advance, advance payment, money advanced.
anticlerical *adj.-n.* anticlerical.
anticlinal *adj.* GEOL. anticlinal.
anticolonialismo *m.* anticolonialism.
anticonceptivo, -va *adj.* birth-controlling, contraceptive. *2 m.* contraceptive.
anticongelante *adj.* antifreeze.
anticonstitucional *adj.* anticonstitutional.
Anticristo *m.* Antichrist.
anticuado, -da *adj.* antiquated, old-fashioned, obsolete.
anticuar *tr.* to antiquate. *2 ref.* to become antiquated.
anticuario *m.* antiquarian, antiquary. *2* antique dealer; old curiosity dealer.
anticuerpo *m.* BACT. antibody.
antidemocrático, -ca *adj.* antidemocratic.

antideportivo, -va *adj.* unsportmanlike; unsporting, unsporty.
antideslizante *adj.* AUTO. antiskid.
antidetonante *adj.* anti-knock [gasoline].
antidiftérico, -ca *adj.-m.* MED. antidiphteritic.
antídoto *m.* antidote.
antiespasmódico, -ca *adj.-n.* antispasmodic.
antiestético, -c *adj.* unaesthetic.
antifaz *m.* mask, veil, etc., covering the face.
antífona *f.* ECCL. antiphon, anthem.
antífrasis *f.* RHET. antiphrasis.
antifricción *adj.* MACH. anti-friction.
antígeno *m.* PHYSIOL. antigen.
antigualla *f.* antique; old-fashioned or out-of-date custom, object, etc.
antiguamente *adv.* anciently, in old times.
antigüedad *f.* antiquity. 2 seniority. 3 *pl.* antiquities, antiques.
antiguo, -gua *adj.* ancient, old; antique: *Antiguo Testamento*, Old Testament; *a la antigua*, in the ancient manner. 2 of long standing, old. 3 *más* ~, senior [in employments, etc.]. 4 *m.* old [old time]: *de* ~, of old. 5 senior. 6 *pl. los antiguos*, the ancients.
antihigiénico, -ca *adj.* unhygienic, unhealthy.
antilogaritmo *m.* MATH. antilogarithm.
antilogía *f.* antilogy.
antílope *m.* ZOOL. antelope.
antillano, -na *adj.-n.* Antillean, West-Indian.
Antillas *f. pl.* GEOG. Antilles, West Indies.
antimilitarismo *m.* antimilitarism.
antimonio *m.* CHEM. antimony.
antinacional *adj.* antinational.
antinatural *adj.* unnatural
antinomia *f.* antinomy.
Antíoco *n. pr.* Antiochus.
Antioquía *f. pr. n.* GEOG. Antioch.
antipapa *m.* antipope.
antípara *f.* screen, folding screen. 2 legging.
antiparras *f. pl.* coll, spectacles, barnacles.
antipatía *f.* antipathy, dislike, aversion.
antipático, -ca *adj.* antipathetic, disagreeable.
antipatriótico, -ca *adj.* unpatriotic.
antipirético, -ca *adj.-m.* MED. antipyretic.
antipirina *f.* CHEM. antipyrine.
antípoda *adj.* antipodal. 2 *m. pl.* antipodes.
antiquísimo, -ma *adj. superl.* very ancient, very old.
antirrábico, -ca *adj.* antihydrophobic.
antirreglamentario, -ria *adj.* against the rules.
antirreligioso, -sa *adj.* antireligious; irreligious.
antirrevolucionario, -ria *adj.-n.* antirevolucionary.
antiscios *m. pl.* GEOG. antiscians, antiscii.
antisemita *m.-f.* anti-Semite.
antisemítico, -ca *adj.* anti-Semitic.
antisemitismo *m.* anti-Semitism.
antisepsia *f.* MED. antisepsis.
antiséptico, -ca *adj.-n.* antiseptic.
antisocial *adj.* antisocial.
antistrofa *f.* antistrophe.
antitanque *adj.* MIL. antitank.
antítesis *f.* antithesis.
antitético, -ca *adj.* antithetic.
antitoxina *f.* MED. antitoxin.
antituberculoso, -sa *adj.* antituberculous.
antojadizo, -za *adj.* capricious, whimsical, fickle.
antojarse *ref.* (used with a pers. pron.: *me, te, le, nos, os, les*) to arouse a whimsical desire, a fancy: *se le antoja este juguete*, he wants this toy.

2 to seem probable, occur to the mind, be imagined: *se me antoja que*, I think or imagine that.
antojo *m.* caprice, whim, notion, fancy, freak, will: *a su* ~, as one pleases; arbitrarily. 2 birthmark.
antología *f.* anthology.
antológico, -ca *adj.* anthological.
Antón *pr. n.* ANTONIO.
antónimo, -ma *adj.* antonymous. 2 *m.* antonym.
Antonio *m. pr. n.* Anthony.
antonomasia *f.* antonomasia.
antorcha *f.* torch, flambeau, cresset.
antozoario, antozoo *adj.-n.* ZOOL. anthozoan.
antraceno *m.* CHEM. anthracene.
antracita *n.* anthracite, hard coal.
ántrax *m.* MED. anthrax.
antro *m.* cavern, den.
antropocéntrico, -ca *adj.* anthropocentric.
antropofagia *f.* anthropophagy.
antropófago, -ga *adj.* anthropophagous. 2 *m.-f.* anthropophagite. 3 *pl.* anthropophagi.
antropoide *adj.* ZOOL. anthropoid.
antropología *f.* anthropology.
antropológico, -ca *adj.* anthropologic(al.
antropólogo *m.* anthropologist.
antropometría *f.* anthropometry.
antropomorfismo *m.* anthropomorphism.
antropomorfo, -fa *adj.* anthropomorphous.
antruejo *m.* carnival days.
anual *adj.* annual, yearly.
anualidad *f.* annual recurrence. 2 annuity, yearly rent; year's pay.
anualmente *adv.* every year, yearly, annually.
anuario *m.* annual, yearbook, trade directory.
anubarrado, -da *adj.* clouded, cloudy [sky].
anublar *tr.* to cloud, darken, obscure, dim. 2 AGR. to blast, blight. 3 *ref.* to become clouded, dimmed. 4 AGR. to become blasted, blighted.
anublo *m.* AÑUBLO.
anudar *tr.* to knot [make nots in; join, unite]. 2 to take up, resume. 3 *ref.* to be knotted, united. 4 to be stunted. 5 *anudársele a uno la voz*, to become speechless with emotion.
anuencia *f.* consent, permission.
anuente *adj.* consenting.
anulable *adj.* revocable, that can be annulled, revoked, cancelled or invalidated.
anulación *f.* annulment, voiding, nullification.
1) **anular** *tr.* to annul, make void, nullify. 2 to deprive of authority or influence.
2) **anular** *adj.* annular. 2 *dedo* ~, ring finger.
anunciación *f.* announcement, annunciation. 2 Annunciation [to the Virgin Mary].
anunciador, -ra *adj.* announcing. 2 advertising. 3 *m.-f.* announcer. 4 advertiser. 5 ELEC. annunciator.
anunciante *adj.* advertising. 2 *m.-f.* advertiser.
anunciar *tr.* to announce. 2 to indicate, foretell. 3 to advertise, to bill.
anuncio *m.* announcement, notice. 2 presage, sign. 3 advertisement. 4 COM. advice.
anuo, -a *adj.* annual.
anuro, -ra *adj.-m.* ZOOL. anuran.
anverso *m.* obverse [as opposed to reverse]. 2 PRINT. recto [of a page].
anzuelo *m.* fishhook. 2 fig. lure, allurement, incitement: *picar en el* ~, *tragar el* ~, to swallow the bait.
añada *f.* AGR. good or bad year.
añadido *m.* hair switch. 2 PRINT. addition.

añadidura *f.* addition, additament: *por ~*, into the bargain; to boot.
añadir *tr.* to add, join. 2 to augment, increase.
añagaza *f.* lure, decoy [for birds]. 2 snare, trick.
añalejo *m.* ordinal, liturgical calendar.
añejar *tr.* to age [a thing]. 2 *ref.* [of wine, etc.] to grow old, to age.
añejo, -ja *adj.* old, aged, of old vintage [wine]; old [bacon, vice, custom, etc.].
añicos *m. pl.* bits, shatters, smithereens: *hacerse ~*, to be smashed; fig. to take great pains.
añil *m.* anil, indigo [shrub, dye]. 2 indigo blue.
año *m.* year: *~ bisiesto*, leap year; *~ de luz*, light year; *~ económico*, fiscal year; *~ escolar*, school year; *día de ~ nuevo*, New Year's Day; *el ~ de la nanita*, donkey's years ago; *estar de buen ~*, to be healthy and fleshy; *al ~ de...*, a year after...; *por años*, by the year; *por muchos años*, many happy returns [of the day]. 2 AGRIC. crop, harvest. 3 *pl.* years, age; *tener años*, to be old; *tener diez años [de edad]*, to be ten years old; *¿cuántos años tiene usted?*, how old are you?
añojal *m.* fallow land.
añojo, -ja *m.-f.* yearling calf or lamb.
añoranza *f.* regret, nostalgia, homesickness.
añorar *tr.* to pine for, miss [a lost or absent person, etc.].
añoso, -sa *adj.* old, stricken in years.
añublo *m.* BOT. smut; rust.
aojar *tr.* to cast the evil eye on, to bewitch.
aojo *m.* casting the evil eye, bewitching.
aoristo *m.* GRAM. aorist.
aorta *f.* ANAT. aorta.
aovado, -da *adj.* ovate, oviform, egg-shaped.
aovar *tr.* to lay eggs.
apabullar *tr.* to crush, flatten. 2 to squelch, disconcert, silence.
apacentamiento *m.* pasturage, grazing. 2 pasture, food.
apacentar *tr.* to pasture, graze [cattle]. 2 to feed [spiritually]. 3 *ref.* [of cattle] to pasture, graze. 4 to feed one's spirit or mind. ¶ CONJUG. like *acertar*.
apacibilidad *f.* gentleness, mildness, placidity.
apacible *adj.* gentle, mild, sweet. 2 pleasant, placid, tranquil, untroubled.
apaciguador, -ra *adj.* pacifying, appeasing. 2 *m.-f.* pacifier, appeaser.
apaciguamiento *m.* pacification, appeasement.
apaciguar *tr.* to pacify, appease, calm, placate. 2 *ref.* to be appeased.
apaciento, apaciente, etc. *irr.* V. APACENTAR.
apache *adj.-n.* Apache [indian]. 2 *m.* apache [ruffian].
apadrinamiento *m.* sponsoring, acting as a godfather or a second. 2 protection, support, patronage.
apadrinar *tr.* to sponsor, to act as godfather to; to act as second of [in a duel]. 2 to protect, favour, patronize, support.
apagado, -da *adj.* out, extinguished, quenched. 2 meek, dull [person]. 3 faint, pale, dead, dull, muffled. 4 dead [volcano]. 5 slaked [lime].
apagador *m.* extinguisher. 2 damper [in a piano].
apagar *tr.* to extinguish, to put out, blow out, turn out. 2 to quench. 3 to slake [lime]. 4 to dull, soften [colours]. 5 to deaden, muffle [sound]. 6 *ref.* [of fire, light, etc.] to die out, go out. 7 to be quenched. 8 [of colours, sound] to deaden.
apagavelas *m.* candle extinguisher.

apagón *m.* sudden failure of lights. 2 blackout [as when electricity fails].
apainelado *adj.* ARCH. basket-handle [arch].
apaisado, -da *adj.* oblong [rectangular with the horizontal dimension the greater].
apalabrar *tr.* to agree [to something]. 2 to bespeak, reserve, engage, beforehand.
apalancamiento *m.* levering, leverage.
apalancar *tr.* to lever, pry.
apaleado, -da *adj.* beaten, hit repeatedly.
apaleamiento *m.* beating, cudgelling, thrashing.
apalear *tr.* to beat, cane, cudgel, thrash. 2 AGR. to winnow [grain] with a shovel.
apaleo *m.* winnowing grain with a shovel.
apanalado, -da *adj.* honeycombed.
apancora *f.* ZOOL. a Chilean crab.
apandillar *tr.-ref.* to form a gang or league.
apanojado, -da *adj.* BOT. paniculate(d.
apañado, -da *adj.* clothlike. 2 dexterous, skilful. 4 suitable.
apañadura *f.*, **apañamiento** *m.* act of taking or grasping. 2 mending. 3 managing.
apañar *tr.* to take, seize; to steal. 2 to dress, adorn. 3 to wrap up [for warmth]. 4 to patch, mend. 5 *ref.* to manage, contrive.
apaño *m.* patch, repair, mending. 2 knack, skill.
apañuscar *tr.* to crumple. 2 to seize, pilfer.
aparador *m.* sideboard, cupboard, buffet; dresser. 2 credence. 3 shop window, show window.
aparasolado, -da *adj.* umbrella-shaped.
aparato *m.* apparatus, appliance, device: *~ de radio*, wireless set; *~ de relojería*, clockwork; *~ fotográfico*, camera. 2 coll. machine [airplane]. 3 coll. phone. 4 SURG. application, bandage. 5 PHYSIOL. apparatus, system: *~ digestivo*, digestive system. 6 exaggeration. 7 pomp. ostentation, display, show. 8 signs, symptoms. 9 assemblage, paraphernalia.
aparatosamente *adv.* ostentaciously, showily, pretentiously. 2 spectacularly.
aparatosidad *f.* show, ostentation, pomposity.
aparatoso, -sa *adj.* pompous, showy. 2 exaggerating, fussy. 3 spectacular.
aparcamiento *m.* parking. 2 parking place, car park, parking lot. 3 lay-by [on the road].
aparcar *tr.* to park [cars, artillery, etc.].
aparcería *f.* share tenancy, partnership.
aparcero, -ra *m.-f.* share tenant, partner.
apareamiento *m.* pairing, matching, mating.
aparear *tr.* to pair, match [things]. 2 to pair, mate [animals]. 3 *ref.* to form a pair. 4 [of animals] to pair, mate, couple.
aparecer *intr.-ref.* to appear, show up, turn up; to arise, heave in sight. 2 [of a ghost] to walk. ¶ CONJUG. like *agradecer*.
aparecido *m.* ghost, spectre, specter, wraith.
aparejado, -da *adj.* apt, fit, competent, ready.
aparejador *m.* architect's assistant. 2 NAUT. rigger.
aparejar *tr.* to prepare, get ready. 2 to saddle [horses, mules, etc.]. 3 NAUT. to rig, rig out. 4 to size, to prime [before gilding or painting]. 5 *ref.* to get [oneself] ready.
aparejo *m.* preparation, arrangement. 2 gear, equipment. 3 riding gear; packsaddle. 4 NAUT. masts, rigging, sails, tackle [on a ship]. 5 tackle [pulleys]: *~ de gata*, cat tackle. 6 MAS. bond. 7 PAINT., GILD. sizing, priming.
aparentar *tr.* to feign, pretend. 2 to look, seem.
aparente *adj.* apparent [not real], seeming. 2 apparent, visible. 3 fit, suitable.
aparezco, aparezca etc. *irr.* V. APARECER.

aparición f. apparition, appearance. 2 apparition, ghost, vision.
apariencia f. appearance, aspect, look, semblance. 2 likelihood. 3 pretence, show. 4 pl. appearances: *guardar las apariencias*, to keep up appearances.
apartadero m. RLY. sidetrack, siding. 2 turnout [beside a road, etc.]. 3 place where bulls are boxed.
apartadizo m. partitioned off space.
apartado, -da adj. retired, aloof; distant, remote, out-of-the-way. 2 different. 3 m. side room. 4 post-office box; mail for it. 5 penning of bulls. 6 section [of a law, bill, etc.].
apartador, -ra m.-f. sorter, separator.
apartamiento m. retirement, separation. 2 aloofness. 3 putting aside. 4 sorting. 5 secluded place. 6 apartment, flat.
apartar tr. to separate, divide part. 2 to push, draw or turn aside; to remove, move away. 3 to dissuade. 4 to sort. 5 RLY. to shunt. 6 ref. to part, become separated. 7 to move away, withadraw, hold off. 8 to stray [from path, etc.].
aparte adj. separate, other: *esto es cuestión* ~, this is another matter. 2 adv. apart, aside. 3 separately. 4 m. THEAT. aside. 5 paragraph: *punto y* ~, paragraph.
apartidar tr. to form a party or faction.
aparvadera f. wooden rake.
aparvar tr. to heap [grain].
apasionadamente adv. ardently, passionately. 2 in a biased way, with partiality.
apasionado, -da adj. ardent, fervid, impassioned. 2 loving. 3 devoted, passionately fond. 4 biased.
apasionamiento m. ardour, fervour, enthusiasm, vehemence. 2 bias, partiality.
apasionante adj. exciting, thrilling, stirring.
apasionar tr. to impassion, excite strongly, to appeal deeply to. 2 ref. to become impassioned, strongly excited; to become passionately fond [of]. 3 to be biased in one's judgement.
apatía f. apathy.
apático, -ca adj. apathetic.
apátrida adj. without a country, stateless [person].
apeadero m. horse block. 2 wayside rest. 3 RLY. stop, wayside station, flag stop. 4 temporary quarters.
apeador m. land surveyor.
apear tr. to dismount, bring down, help down or out [from horse or carriage]. 2 to hobble [a horse]. 3 to scotch [a wheel]. 4 to survey [land]. 5 to fell [a tree]. 6 to dissuade. 7 ARCH. to prop up. 8 ~ *el tratamiento*, to drop the title. 9 ref. to dismount, alight, get of, get out. 10 to be dissuaded.
apechugar intr. to push with the chest. 2 ~ *con*, to take or accept [something distasteful].
apedreado, -da adj. stoned. 2 variegated, mottled, spotted. 3 pockmarked.
apedreamiento m. stone-throwing. 2 stoning, lapidation. 3 damage from hail.
apedrear tr. to throw stones at. 2 to stone, lapidate. 3 impers. to hail. 4 ref. to be injured by hail.
apedreo m. stoning. 2 damage caused by hail [to the crop].
apegadamente adv. devotedly.
apegado, -da adj. attached, devoted.
apegarse ref. to become attached, to attach oneself [to].
apego m. attachment, affection, liking.

apelable adj. LAW appealable.
apelación f. LAW appeal: *interponer* ~, to appeal. 2 coll. remedy, help.
apelado, -da m.-f. LAW appellee.
apelambrar tr. to remove hair from [hides].
apelante adj. LAW appealing. 2 m.-f. LAW appellant.
apelar intr. LAW to appeal. 2 call upon, have recourse to.
apelativo adj.-m. GRAM. appellative.
apelmazado, -da adj. heavy, compact, compressed.
apelmazamiento m. sogginess, stodginess, clumpiness. 2 compressing, flattening [the soil].
apelmazar tr. to make heavy, compact, thick; to compress, to render less spongy or porous.
apelotonar tr. to form [hair, wool, etc.] into knots, tufts or balls. 2 ref. to form knots, tufts or balls. 3 [of people] to cluster.
apellidar tr. to call, name, surname. 2 to proclaim. 3 ref. to be called [have the name].
apellido m. family name. 2 surname, name.
apenar tr. to pain, cause sorrow to. 2 ref. to grieve.
apenas adv. scarcely, hardly. 2 as soon as, no sooner than.
apencar intr. ~ *con*, to take or accept [something distasteful].
apendectomía f. MED. appendicectomy, appendectomy.
apéndice m. appendage, appendix.
apendicitis f. MED. appendicitis.
Apeninos pr. n. GEOG. Apennines.
apeñuscar tr. to pack together, to cram together, to press something together.
apeo m. landmarking, surveying. 2 ARCH. proping; prop. 3 tree felling.
apeonar intr. [of partridges] to run.
apercibimiento m. preparedness. 2 admonishing, warning, admonition.
apercibir tr. to prepare. 2 to admonish, warn, advise. 3 to perceive, see. 4 ref. to prepare oneself, to get ready.
apercollar tr. to grab by the neck.
apergaminado, -da adj. parchment-like. 2 fig. wizened, dry and wrinkled: *piel apergaminada* wizened, old-looking skin.
apergaminarse ref. to dry up, become yellow and wrinkled.
aperitivo, -va m. apéritif, appetizer. 2 adj.-m. MED. aperitive.
apero m. farm implements. 2 equipment of a farm. 3 kit, tools. 4 (Am.) riding gear.
aperreado, -da adj. harassed, worried.
aperreador, -ra adj. harassing, fatiguing, worrisome.
aperrear tr. to set the dogs on. 2 to harass, worry, fatigue. 3 ref. EMPERRARSE.
aperreo m. harassment, worry, toil.
apersogar tr. to tether [an animal].
apersonado, -da adj. *bien* or *mal* ~, of good or bad appearance.
apersonamiento m. LAW. appearance.
apertura f. opening [of an assembly, a shop, etc.]. 2 reading [of a will]. 3 CHESS. opening.
apesadumbrado, -da adj. pained, distressed.
apesadumbrar tr. to pain, distress. 2 ref. to be pained, to grieve.
apesaradamente adv. grievingly, sorrowfully.
apesarar tr. APESADUMBRAR.
apestado, -da adj. infected with the plague. 2 *estar* ~ *de*, to be infested with; to be full of.

apestar *tr.* to infect with the plague. *2* to corrupt, vitiate. *3* to sicken, plague. *4 intr.* to stink.
apestoso, -sa *adj.* stinking. *2* sickening. *3* pestilent.
apétalo, -la *adj.* BOT. apetalous.
apetecedor, -ra *adj.* desirous.
apetecer *tr.* to desire, to feel an appetite for. *2 esto me apetece,* I wish to have or to do this. ¶ CONJUG. like *agradecer.*
apetezco, apetezca, etc. *irr.* V. APETECER.
apetecible *adj.* desirable.
apetecido, -da *adj.* desired, *resultado ~,* desired result.
apetencia *f.* appetence, appetency, desire. *2* appetite.
apetitivo, -va *adj.* appetitive.
apetito *m.* appetite: *abrir el ~,* to whet the appetite. *2* appetence.
apetitoso, -sa *adj.* appetizing, savoury, palatable, tasty.
apezonado, -da *adj.* nipple-shaped.
apiadar *tr.* to inspire pity. *2 ref. apiadarse de,* to pity, have pity on.
apical *adj.* apical.
apicarado, -da *adj.* roguish, knavish.
ápice *m.* apex, summit, top. *2* whit, iota. *3* crux.
apícola *adj.* apicultural, apiarian.
apicultor, -ra *m.-f.* apiculturist, bee-keeper.
apicultura *f.* apiculture, bee-keeping.
apilada *adj.* dried [chestnut].
apilamiento *m.* piling, heaping.
apilar *tr.* to pile, pile up, heap, heap up.
apimplarse *ref.* coll. to get merry or tipsy, to get tight.
apiñado, -da *adj.* shaped like a pine-cone. *2* packed, crowded, pressed together.
apiñamiento *m.* packing, crowding together. *2* crowd, press.
apiñar *tr.* to pack, press together, jam. *2 ref.* to press [become pressed together].
apio *m.* BOT. celery.
apiolar *tr.* to jess, gyve. *2* to tie [game] by the legs. *3* coll. to arrest [a person]. *4* coll. to kill.
apiparse *ref.* coll. to stuff oneself.
apirexia MED. apyrexia.
apisonadora *f.* road roller, steam roller.
apisonar *tr.* to tamp, pack down [earth, etc.]; to roll [roadways].
apitonar *intr.* [of a deer, etc.] to begin to grow horns. *2* [of trees] to bud, sprout. *3 tr.* to break with bill or point.
apizarrado, -da *adj.* slate-coloured.
aplacamiento *m.* appeasement, placation, calming.
aplacar *tr.* to appease, placate, calm. *2 ref.* to become appeased.
aplacer *tr.* to please, satisfy. ¶ CONJUG. like *agradecer.*
aplanadera *f.* levelling board, road drag.
aplanador, -ra *adj.* smoothing, levelling. *2* crushing. *3* disheartening.
aplanamiento *m.* smoothing, levelling, flattening. *2* depression, prostration.
aplanar *tr.* to smooth, level, make even; to planish. *2* to astound. *3 ref.* to tumble down, collapse. *4* to be discouraged or depressed.
aplastado, -da *adj.* flat, flattened. *2* dumbfounded.
aplastamiento *m.* flattening. *2* crushing, quashing. *3* dumbfounding.
aplastante *adj.* crushing. *2* dumbfounding.
aplastar *tr.* to flatten. *2* to crush, to quash. *3* to dumbfound. *4 ref.* to become flat.

aplatanarse *ref.* coll. to become lethargic, to get listless, to become apathetic.
aplaudir *tr.-intr.* to applaud.
aplauso *m.* applause. *2* handclapping.
aplazamiento *m.* postponement. *2* summons.
aplazar *tr.* to adjourn, put off, postpone. *2* to summon, convene.
aplebeyar *tr.-ref.* to render, or to become, coarse, base.
aplicación *f.* application [in every sense but the one of marking a request]. *2* assiduity, sedulousness, studiousness. *3* SEW. appliqué.
aplicado, -da *adj.* applied. *2* studious, industrious, sedulous.
aplicar *tr.* to apply. *2* to impute, attribute. *3* LAW to adjudge. *4 ref.* to apply [have a bearing]. *5* to apply or devote oneself. *6* to be diligent, studious.
aplique *m.* wall light, wall lamp.
aplomado, -da *adj.* self-possessed, calm, prudent. *2* plumb, perpendicular. *3* lead-coloured.
aplomar *tr.* MAS., ARCH. to plumb. *2 ref.* DESPLOMARSE. *3* to acquire aplomb.
aplomo *m.* aplomb, self-possession, gravity. *2* verticality, aplomb.
apnea *f.* MED. apnœa.
apocado, -da *adj.* diffident, timid. *2* humble, lowly.
Apocalipsis *m.* Apocalypse, Book of Revelation.
apocalíptico, -ca *adj.* apocalyptic(al.
apocamiento *m.* diffidence, timidity, pusillanimity. *2* dejection, depression.
apocar *tr.* to lessen. *2* to contract, restrict. *3* to humble, belittle. *4 ref.* to become diffident.
apocináceo, -a *adj.* BOT. apocynaceous.
apocopar *tr.* GRAM. to apocopate.
apócope *f.* GRAM. apocope; apocopation.
apócrifo, -fa *adj.* apocryphal. *2 m. pl.* Apocrypha.
apodar *tr.* to nickname, give a nickname to.
apoderado, -da *m.* proxy, [private] attorney, manager.
apoderar *tr.* to empower, grant power of attorney to. *2 ref. apoderarse de,* to seize, take hold or possesion of.
apodo *m.* nickname, sobriquet.
ápodo, -da *adj.* ZOOL. apodal.
apódosis *f.* GRAM. apodosis.
apófisis *f.* ANAT. apophysis, process.
apogeo *m.* ASTR. apogee. *2* fig. apogee, height.
apolillado, -da *adj.* moth-eaten, mothy.
apolilladura *f.* moth hole.
apolillar *tr.* [of moths] to eat or infest [clothes, wool, etc.]. *2 ref.* to become moth-eaten.
apolíneo, -a *adj.* Apolline, Apollonian.
apolítico, -ca *adj.* apolitical.
Apolo *pr. n.* Apollo.
apologético, -ca *adj.* apologetic [defending]. *2 f.* apologetics.
apología *f.* apology, defence, eulogy.
apologista *m.* apologist.
apólogo *m.* apologue.
apoltronarse *ref.* to grow lazy.
apomazar *tr.* to pumice.
aponeurosis *f.* ANAT. aponeurosis.
apoplejía *f.* MED. apoplexy.
apoplético, -ca *adj.-n.* apoplectic.
aporcar *tr.* AGR. to hill, bank up. ¶ CONJUG. like *contar.*
aporreado, -da *adj.* cudgelled. *2* wretched, miserable.
aporreante *adj.* bothering.

aporrear *tr.* to cudgel, club; to beat, pound. *2* to bother, annoy. *3 ref.* to drudge, toil.
aporreo *m.* cudgelling, beating, pounding. *2* bother, bothering. *3* toiling, drudgery.
aportación *f.* contribution [to a fund, an enterprise, etc.].
aportar *tr.* to bring, furnish; to contribute [as one's share]. *2 intr.* ~ *a*, NAUT. to arrive at [a port]; to reach [an unexpected place].
aposentamiento *m.* lodging.
aposentar *tr.* to put up, lodge. *2 ref.* to take lodging.
aposento *m.* room or apartment. *2* lodging.
aposición *f.* GRAM. apposition.
apósito MED. bandaged application.
aposta, apostadamente *adv.* designedly, on purpose.
apostadero *m.* stand, station, post. *2* NAUT. naval station. *3* NAUT. naval district.
apostador, -ra *m.-f.* better, bettor.
1) **apostar** *tr.-ref.-intr.* to bet, wager: ~ *a* or *por*, to bet on, to back [a horse, etc.]; ~ *a que*, to bet that; *apostárseles a* or *con*, to compete with. ¶ CONJUG. like *contar*.
2) **apostar** *tr.-ref.* to place, post, station.
apostasía *f.* apostasy.
apóstata *m.-f.* apostate.
apostatar *intr.* apostatize.
apostema *f.* MED. aposteme, abscess.
apostemarse *ref.* to become abscessed.
a posteriori *Lat. adv.* a posteriori.
apostilla *f.* marginal note, annotation.
apostillar *tr.* to annotate [a text]. *2 ref.* to break out in pimples.
apóstol *m.* apostle.
apostolado *m.* apostolate, apostleship.
apostólico, -ca *adj.* apostolic(al.
apostrofar *tr.* RHET. to apostrophize. *2* to scold.
apóstrofe *m.-f.* RHET. apostrophe. *2* taunt, insult.
apóstrofo *m.* GRAM. apostrophe.
apostura *f.* handsomeness, good looks [of a person].
apotegma *m.* apophthegm, apothegm.
apotema *m.* GEOM. apothem.
apoteósico, -ca *adj.* glorifying. *2* glorious, great.
apoteosis, *pl.* **-sis** *f.* apotheosis.
apoyar *tr.* to rest, lean [something on]. *2* to back, favour, support, countenance, abet. *3* to prove, confirm. *4* to prop. *5 intr.-ref.* to rest lean [on]; to be supported [on or by]; to depend, be based [on]. *6 ref.* to base one's arguments.
apoyatura *f.* MUS. appoggiatura.
apoyo *m.* prop, stay, support. *2* protection, help, support, countenance.
apreciable *adj.* appraisable, evaluable. *2* appreciable. *3* estimable, nice, fine.
apreciación *f.* appraisal; appreciation.
apreciar *tr.* to appraise, estimate, value. *2* to esteem, like. *3* to appreciate.
apreciativo, -va *adj.* appreciative. *2* appraising.
aprecio *m.* appraisement, valuation. *2* esteem, regard, liking.
aprehender *tr.* to apprehend, arrest. *2* to seize [contraband]. *3* PHIL. to apprehend.
aprehensión *f.* apprehension, arrest. *2* seizure [of contraband]. *3* PHIL. apprehension.
aprehensor, -ra *adj.* apprehending. *2 m.-f.* apprehender, seizer.
apremiante *adj.* urgent, pressing.
apremiar *tr.* to urge, press. *2* to compel, constrain. *3* to dun.

apremio *m.* pressure, urgency. *2* constraint, judicial compulsion.
aprendedor, -ra *adj.* learning. *2 m.-f.* learner.
aprender *tr.* to learn: ~ *a leer*, to learn to read.
aprendiz, -za *m.-f.* apprentice.
aprendizaje *m.* apprenticeship; act of learning.
aprensar *tr.* to press, to calender.
aprensión *f.* APREHENSIÓN. *2* scruple, squeamishness. *3* dread of contagion or illness. *4* unfounded opinion or idea.
aprensivo, -va *adj.* fearing contagion or illness.
apresador, -ra *adj.* capturing. *2 m.-f.* captor.
apresar *tr.* NAUT. to seize, capture [a ship]. *2* to seize, cluth [with claws or teeth]. *3* APRISIONAR.
aprestar *tr.-ref.* to prepare, make ready. *2 tr.* to dress [cloth].
apresto *m.* preparation, making ready. *2* outfit, equipment. *3* WEAV. dressing, sizing.
apresuradamente *adv.* hastily, hurriedly.
apresurado, -da *adj.* hasty, hurried, lively.
apresuramiento *m.* hastening. *2* haste.
apresurar *tr.* to hasten, quicken, hurry. *2 ref.* to hasten, hurry, make haste.
apretadamente *adv.* tightly. *2* eagerly.
apretado, -da *adj.* tight [knot, screw, etc.]. *2* dense, compact. *3* difficult, dangerous. *4* coll. stingy. *5* coll. badly off.
apretadura *f.,* **apretamiento** *m.* compression, constriction. *2* tightening.
apretar *tr.* to squeeze, to hug. *2* to press, press down. *3* to tighten [bonds, screws]: *apretarse el cinturón*, to tighten or take in one's belt. *4* to clench [the fist], to set [the teeth]. *5* [of garments] to fit tight; [of shoes] to pinch. *6* to grip, clutch. *7* to compress, constrict; to press together, pack tight; to crowd. *8* to spur, urge, press. *9* to pursue, press closely. *10* to afflict, distress. *11* to treat with severity; to make more severe. *12* ~ *el paso*, to quicken the pace. *13* ~ *las clavijas*, fig. to put the screw on. *14* ~ *los talones*, to take to one's heels. *15 intr.* to get more severe. *16* to insist. *17* ~ *a correr*, to start running. *18 ref.* to crowd, throng, become pressed together. ¶ CONJUG. like *acertar*.
apretón *m.* squeeze, quick pressure: ~ *de manos*, handshake. *2* effort, dash, spurt. *3* press [of people]. *4* difficulty, fix.
apretujar *tr.* to press or squeeze hard.
apretujón *m.* hard pressure or squeeze.
apretura *f.* press [of people], jam, crush. *2* narrow place. *3* difficulty, fix.
aprieto *m.* straits, difficulty, scrape, fix. *2* press [of people], jam, crush.
aprieto, apriete, etc. *irr.* V. APRETAR.
apriorismo *m.* apriorism.
aprisa *adv.* fast, quickly, swiftly.
apriscar *tr.* to gather [sheep] in the fold.
aprisco *m.* sheepfold.
aprisionar *tr.* to imprison. *2* to shackle. *3* to hold fast.
aproar *intr.* NAUT. to turn the prow.
aprobación *f.* approbation, approval; applause.
aprobado *m.* EDUC. pass mark.
aprobar *tr.* to approve, approve of. *2* to pass [an examination; a student]. *3* to pass, adopt [a bill, a resolution, etc.]. ¶ CONJUG. like *contar*.
aprobatorio, -ria *adj.* approbative, approving.
aproches *m. pl.* FORT. approaches.
aprontar *tr.* to prepare, have ready. *2* to pay, deliver.

apropiación f. appropriation [taking to oneself]. 2 fitting, applying.
apropiadamente adv. fitly, appropriately.
apropiado, -da adj. fit, proper, appropriate.
apropiar tr. to make [something] the possession of one. 2 to fit, make suitable. 3 to apply fitly. 4 ref. to appropriate, take to oneself.
aprovechable adj. utilizable, available.
aprovechado, -da adj. made use of. 2 well spent [time]. 3 studious, advanced, proficient. 4 m.-f. ser un ~ or una aprovechada, to look after the main chance.
aprovechamiento m. utilization, use, exploitation, development. 2 progress, improvement, proficiency.
aprovechar tr. to utilize, make use or good use of, benefit from, profit by, improve, spend profitably. 2 to use up [remaining material, etc.]. 3 intr. to be useful, to avail. 4 ref. to avail oneself of, to take advantage of.
aprovechón, -ona adj. opportunist, selfish. 2 n. profiteer, advantage-taker, opportunist.
aprovisionamiento m. supplying. 2 supply, supplies.
aprovisionar tr. to supply, furnish, provision.
aproximación f. nearing, nearness. 2 aproximation.
aproximadamente adv. approximately.
aproximado, -da adj. approximate.
aproximar tr. to bring near. 2 to approximate. 3 ref. to approach, come near, approximate.
aproximativo, -va adj. approximate.
ápside m. ASTR. apsis.
áptero, -ra adj. ENT. apterous, wingless.
aptitud f. aptitude, fitness, ability, talent.
apto, -ta adj. able, competent. 2 apt, fit, suitable.
apuesta f. bet, wager.
apuesto, -ta, adj. handsome, good-looking. 2 elegant, spruce.
apuesto, apueste, etc. irr. V. APOSTAR.
apuntación f. note, memorandum. 2 MUS. notation. 3 share in a lottery ticket.
apuntado, -da adj. pointed: arco ~, pointed arch.
apuntador m. one who notes or marks. 2 THEAT. prompter. 3 ARTILL. pointer [gunner].
apuntalamiento m. propping.
apuntalar tr. to prop, prop up, shore, underpin.
apuntamiento m. pointing, aiming. 2 note, memorandum. 3 sketch. 4 judicial report.
apuntar tr. to aim, level, point [a gun, etc.]. 2 to point at, point out, indicate, mark. 3 to note, jot down, inscribe. 4 to point, sharpen. 5 to sketch. 6 to stitch, pin or tack lightly. 7 to prompt [at the theatre, etc.]. 8 to hint at, insinuate. 9 to stake [a sum] on a card. 10 intr. to break, dawn, begin to appear. 11 [of wine] to begin to turn.
apunte m. note, memorandum. 2 rough sketch. 3 THEAT. prompter; prompt-book. 4 punter [gambler]. 5 coll. rogue.
apuntillar tr. BULLF. to finish off or deal the coup de grâce to the bull with a dagger.
apuñalar tr. to poniard, stab with a dagger.
apuñear tr. to punch, strike with the fist.
apuracabos m. save-all [in a candlestick].
apuradamente adv. exactly. 2 with difficulty.
apurado, -da p. p. of APURAR. 2 adj. exhausted. 3 needy, hard up. 4 difficult, dangerous. 5 accurate, precise. 6 hard-pressed.
apurador, -ra adj. exhausting. 2 worrying.
apurar tr. to purify, refine. 2 to investigate or expound minutely. 3 to carry to extremes. 4 to

drain, use up, exhaust. 5 to hurry, press. 6 to worry, annoy. 7 ref. to grieve, worry, fret. 8 to exert oneself.
apuro m. fix, predicament, difficulty. 2 need, want. 3 worry. 4 (Am.) haste, urgency.
aquejado, -da adj. having, suffering [an illness].
aquejar tr. to ail, afflict.
aquel, aquella, pl. **aquellos, aquellas** adj. that, that... there, those, those... there.
aquél, aquélla, pl. **aquéllos, aquéllas** pron. dem. that one, those ones: ~, or aquélla, que, he, or she, who. 2 the former, the first mentioned. 3 m. coll. charm, appeal, it.
aquelarre m. witche's Sabbath.
aquello pron. dem. neuter that, it; that thing, that matter.
aquende adv. on this side of.
aquenio m. BOT. achene.
aqueo, -a adj.-n. Achean.
aquerenciarse ref. [of animals] to become fond of [a place].
aquí adv. here: ~ dentro, in here; de ~, from here, hence; por ~, here, hereabouts; this way. 2 now: de ~ en adelante, from now on. 3 then, at that moment.
aquiescencia f. acquiescence, consent.
aquietar tr. to quiet, calm, lull, pacify. 2 ref. to quiet down, become calm.
aquilatado, -da adj. proven, tested, demonstrated.
aquilatar tr. to estimate the carats of. 2 to weigh the merit or character of. 3 to purify.
aquilea f. BOT. yarrow.
Aquiles pr. n. Achilles.
aquilino, -na adj. poet, aquiline.
aquilón m. north wind; north.
aquillado, -da adj. keel-shaped, keel-like.
Aquisgrán pr. n. Aix-la-Chapelle.
Aquitania f. pr. n. GEOG. Aquitaine. 2 HIST. Aquitania.
ara f. altar; altar slab. 2 (cap.) ASTR. Ara. 3 ORN. macaw. 4 en aras de, for the sake of.
árabe adj.-n. Arab, Arabic, Arabian. 2 m. Arabic [language]. 3 adj. ARCH. Moresque.
arabesco, -ca adj. Arabic. 2 m. F. ARTS arabesque.
Arabia pr. n. GEOG. Arabia.
arábigo, -ga adj. Arabic, Arabian. 2 m. Arabic [language].
arabismo m. Arabism, Arabicism.
arabización f. arabicization.
arable adj. arable, suitable for ploughing.
arabista m.-f. Arabist, Arabic scholar.
aráceo, -a adj. BOT. araceous. 2 f. pl. BOT. Araceae.
arácnido, -da adj.-n. ZOOL. arachnid, arachnidan.
aracnoides adj.-f. ANAT. arachnoid.
arado m. AGR. plough, *plow. 2 ploughing, *plowing.
arador m. ploughman, *plowman. 2 ZOOL. itch mite.
Aragón pr. n. GEOG. Aragon.
aragonés, -sa adj.-n. Aragonese.
araguato m. ursine howler, an american monkey.
aralia f. BOT. American spikenard.
arambel m. rag, tatter.
arameo, -a adj. Aramaean, Aramaic. 2 m.-f. Aramaean. 3 m. Aramaic [language].
arana f. trick, imposition, cheat.
arancel m. tariff [of fees, duties or customs].
arancelario, -ria adj. [pertaining to] tariff, customs.
arándano m. BOT. bilberry, whortleberry.

arandela *f.* socket pan [of candlestick]. 2 MECH. washer. *3* burr [on a lance].
arandillo *m.* ORN. marsh warbler.
araña *f.* ZOOL. spider. *2* fig. go-getter, thrifty person. *3* chandelier. *4* ICHTH. weaver, stingbull. *5* ARAÑUELA 2. *6* ZOOL. ~ *de mar*, spider crab.
arañar *tr.* to scratch. *2* to scrape together, scrape up.
arañazo *m.* scratch [mark or injury].
arañuela *f.* little spider. *2* BOT. love-in-a-mist.
arar *tr.* to plough, plow; to furrow.
araucano, -na *adj.-n.* Araucanian.
araucaria *f.* BOT. araucaria.
arbitraje *m.* arbitration, arbitrage. *2* umpiring; refereeing. *3* COM. arbitrage.
arbitral *adj.* arbitral.
arbitrar *tr.* to arbitrate; to umpire; to referee. *2* to act freely. *3* to contrive, find [ways, means]; to raise [funds].
arbitrariedad *f.* arbitrary act. *2* arbitrariness.
arbitrario, -ria *adj.* arbitrary.
arbitrio *m.* free will. *2* power, choice, discretion: *al ~ de*, at the discretion of. *3* means, device. *4* arbitrament. *5 pl.* excise, taxes.
arbitrista *m.* utopic planner or schemer.
árbitro, -tra *adj.-n.* sole master, free to do. *2 m.* arbiter, arbitrator, umpire, referee.
árbol *m.* BOT. tree: ~ *de Judas*, Judas tree; ~ *de la ciencia del bien y del mal*, BIBL. tree of knowledge (of good and evil); ~ *de la cruz*, tree of the cross; ~ *de la vida*, BIBL., BOT. tree of life; ANAT. arborvitae; ~ *de Navidad*, Christmas tree; ~ *frutal*, fruit tree. *2* MECH. arbor, shaft, axle, spindle: ~ *de levas*, camshaft. *3* NAUT. mast. *4* PRINT. shank. *5* newel [of winding stairs]. *6* ~ *genealógico*, genealogical tree.
arbolado, -da *adj.* wooded. *2* NAUT. masted. *3 m.* trees [in a place].
arboladura *f.* NAUT. masting, mast and yards.
arbolar *tr.* to hoist, raise aloft. *2* to set upright against a wall, etc. *3* NAUT. to mast [a ship]. *4 ref.* [of a horse] to rear.
arboleda *f.* grove, wooded ground.
arborecer *intr.* to grow into a tree.
arbóreo, -a *adj.* arboreal.
arborescencia *f.* BOT. arborescence.
arborescente *adj.* arborescent.
arborícola *adj.* ZOOL. arboreal, living in the trees, tree-dwelling.
arboricultor *m.* arboriculturist.
arboricultura *f.* arboriculture.
arbotante *m.* ARCH. flying buttress.
arbustivo, -va *adj.* BOT. shrubby.
arbusto *m.* BOT. shrub.
arca *f.* coffer, chest, box. *2* strong-box, safe. *3* annealing oven [for glass]. *4* ark: ~ *de la Alianza*, Ark of the Covenant; ~ *de Noé*, Noah's ark. *5* ~ *de agua*, water tower, reservoir. *6 pl.* ANAT. costal cavities.
arcabucear *f.* to shoot with a harquebus.
arcabucería *f.* trop of harquebusiers. *2* harquebuses. *3* harquebus factory.
arcabucero *m.* harquebusier. *2* harquebus maker.
arcabuz, *pl.* -buces *m.* harquebus.
arcada *f.* ARCH. arcade. *2* arch [of a bridge]. *3 pl.* retching.
Arcadia *pr. n.* Arcadia.
arcaduz *m.* pipe, conduit. *2* bucket [of waterwheel].
arcaico, -ca *adj.* archaic. *2* GEOL. Archeozoic.
arcaísmo *m.* archaism.

arcaizante *adj.* archaistic.
arcaizar *tr.-intr.* to archaize.
arcángel *m.* archangel.
arcano, -na *adj.* arcane. *2 m.* arcanum.
arce *m.* BOT. maple tree: ~ *sacarino*, sugar maple.
arcediano *m.* archdeacon.
arcén *m.* border, brim, edge. *2* curbstone [of well].
arcilla *f.* clay: ~ *figulina*, potter's clay, argil.
arcilloso, -sa *adj.* clayey, argillaceous.
arciprestazgo *m.* archpriesthood.
arcipreste *m.* archpriest.
arco *m.* GEOM., ELEC. arc: ~ *voltaico*, voltaic arc. *2* ARCH., ANAT. arch.: ~ *de herradura*, horseshoe arch: ~ *de medio punto*, round arc. *3* bow [weapon]. *4* MUS. bow, fiddle-bow. *5* hoop [of a cask]. *6* METEOR. ~ *iris*, rainbow.
arcón *m.* large chest or bin.
arconte *m.* archon.
archicofradía *f.* arch-brotherhood.
archiconocido, -da *adj.* coll. well-known, known by everyone.
archidiácono *m.* archdeacon.
archidiócesis *f.* archdiocese.
archiducado *m.* archduchy, archdukedom.
archiducal *adj.* archducal.
archiduque *m.* archduke.
archiduquesa *f.* archduchess.
archifamoso, -sa *adj.* coll. world famous.
archimandrita *m.* archimandrite.
archimillonario, -ria *n.* multimillionaire, multimillionairess.
archipiélago *m.* archipelago.
archisabido *adj.* coll. very well-known.
archivador *m.* letter file, filing cabinet.
archivar *tr.* to deposit in the archives. *2* to file, file away [papers, etc.]. *3* coll. to pigeonhole.
archivero, -ra *m.-f.* archivist.
archivo *m.* archives; file, files.
archivolta *f.* ARCH. archivolt.
Ardenas *pr. n.* Ardennes.
ardentía *f.* ardour. *2* heartburn. *3* phosphorescence [of sea].
arder *tr.* to burn, to blaze. *2* POÉT. to shine. *3* ~ *de*, or *en*, to burn with [love, etc.]; ~ *en*, to be ablaze with [war, discord, etc.]. *4 ref.* to burn, be burning. *5* [of grain, tobacco, etc.] to be heated up.
ardid *m.* stratagem, trick, artifice.
ardido *-da adj.* bold, intrepid.
ardiente *adj.* ardent, burning, fiery, hot. *2* red. *3* ardent, feverish, eager, vehement.
ardientemente *adv.* ardently, fervently, earnestly.
ardilla *f.* ZOOL. squirrel.
ardimiento *m.* burning. *2* intrepidity, courage.
ardite *m.* old spanish coin of little value: *no me importa un* ~, fig. I don't care a hang.
ardor *m.* ardour, heat. *2* ardour, vehemence, eagerness. *3* intrepidity, courage.
ardorosamente *adv.* ardently.
ardoroso, -sa *adj.* burning, ardent, vehement, eager.
arduo, -dua *adj.* arduous, hard, difficult.
área *f.* area [superficial extent]. *2* are [measure].
areca *f.* BOT. areca, betel palm.
arena *f.* sand, grit: ~ *movediza*, quicksand. *2* arena, circus. *3 pl.* MED. gravel, bladder stones.
arenáceo, -a *adj.* arenaceous, sandy.
arenal *m.* sandy ground, extent of quicksands. *2* sand pit.
arenar *tr.* ENARENAR. *2* to rub or polish with sand.
arenero *m.* RLY. sandbox.
arenga *f.* harangue, speech, address.

arengar *intr.-tr.* to harangue.
arenilla *f.* powder to dry writing. *2 pl.* MED. stones, gravel.
arenisca *f.* PETROG. sandstone.
arenisco, -ca *adj.* sandy, gritty.
arenoso, -sa *adj.* sandy.
arenque *m.* ICHTH. herring.
aréola *f.* ANAT., ZOOL., MED. areola, areole.
areometría *f.* areometry.
areómetro *m.* areometer, hydrometer.
areopagita *m.* areopagite.
areópago *m.* Aeropagus.
arepa *f.* (Am.) corn griddle cake.
arestín *m.* BOT. an umbelliferous plant. *2* VET. thrush.
arete *m.* small hoop or ring. *2* earring.
arfada *f.* NAUT. pitching [of a ship].
arfar *intr.* NAUT. [of a ship] to pitch.
argadijo *m.* ARGADILLO. *2* ARGAMANDIJO.
argadillo *m.* DEVANADERA. *2* bustling, restless person.
argallera *f.* croze, crozing saw.
argamasa *f.* MAS. mortar.
argamasón *m.* large dry piece of mortar.
árgana *f.* MECH. crane.
árganas *f. pl.* wicker baskets for packsaddle.
arganeo *m.* NAUT. anchor ring.
Argel *pr. n.* GEOG. Algiers.
Argelia *pr. n.* Algeria.
argelino, -na *adj.-n.* Algerian, Algerine.
aregmone *f.* BOT. aregmone, prickly poppy.
argén *m.* HER. argent.
argentado, -da *adj.* silver-plated. *2* silvery.
argénteo, -a *adj.* silvery, silver-white.
argentería *f.* embroidery in gold or silver.
argentero *m.* silversmith.
argentífero, -ra *adj.* argentiferous.
Argentina (la) *pr. n.* GEOG. the Argentine.
argentinismo *m.* argentine word, phrase or locution.
argentino, -na *adj.* argentine, silvery. *2* Argentine. *3 m.-f.* Argentine, Argentinean.
argento *m.* poet. silver. *2* ~ *vivo*, quicksilver.
argivo, -va *adj.-n.* Argive.
argo *m.* CHEM. argon.
Argólida (la) *pr. n.* HIST. GEOG. Argolis.
argolla *f.* ring, metal ring. *2* bracelet. *3* old game similar to croquet.
argón *m.* CHEM. argon.
argonauta *m.* MYTH. Argonaut. *2* ZOOL. paper nautilus.
Argos *pr. n.* HIST. GEOG. Argos. *2* MITH. Argus. *3* MYTH., ASTR. Argo. *4 m.* Argus [watchful person].
argucia *f.* subtlety, sophistry.
árguenas *f. pl.* handbarrow. *2* ALFORJAS.
argüir *tr.* to infer. *2* to argue [imply, prove; accuse]. *3 intr.* to argue, reason. ¶ CONJUG. like *huir*.
argumentación *f.* argumentation.
argumentador, -ra *m.-f.* arguer, argumentator.
argumentar *tr.* to argue, dispute, reason.
argumento *m.* argument. *2* plot [of a story or play].
aria *f.* MUS. aria.
Ariadna *f. pr. n.* MYTH. Ariadne.
aridecer *tr.* to render aid. *2 ref.* to become arid. ¶ CONJUG. like *agradecer*.
aridez *f.* aridity, aridness.
árido, -da *adj.* arid. *2 m. pl.* dry commodities [esp. grains].
Aries *m.* ASTR. Aries.

ariete *m.* battering ram. *2* NAUT. ram. *3* PHYS. ~ *hidráulico*, hydraulic ram.
arijo, -ja *adj.* AGR. light, easily tilled.
arilo *m.* BOT. aril.
arillo *m.* earring.
arimez *m.* ARCH. projection [in a building].
ario, -ria *adj.-n.* Aryan.
arisaro *m.* BOT. wake-robin.
arisco, -ca *adj.* unsociable, surly, shy.
arista *f.* arris, edge. *2* BOT. awn, beard [of grain].
aristado, -da *adj.* BOT. bearded [wheat].
aristarco *m.* Aristarch, severe critic.
Arístides *m. pr n.* Aristides.
aristocracia *f.* aristocracy.
aristócrata *m.-f.* aristocrat.
aristocrático, -ca *adj.* aristocratic.
aristocratizar *tr.* to make aristocratic.
Aristófanes *pr. n.* Aristophanes.
aristoloquia *f.* BOT. birthwort.
Aristóteles *pr. n.* Aristotle.
aristotélico, -ca *adj.-n.* Aristotelian.
aritmética *f.* arithmetic.
aritmético, -ca *adj.* arithmetic(al. *2 m.-f.* arithmetician.
arlequín *m.* harlequin. *2* (cap.) Harlequin.
arlequinado, -da *adj.* parti-coloured [clothes].
arlequinada *f.* harlequinade, buffoonery.
arlo *m.* BOT. barberry.
arma *f.* weapon, arm; ~ *atómica*, atomic weapon; ~ *blanca*, steel, cold steel; ~ *de fuego*, firearm; *¡a las armas!*, to arms!; *alzarse en armas*, to rise up in arms; *medir las armas*, to fight; *presentar las armas*, to present arms; *tomar las armas*, to take up arms; *sobre las armas*, under arms. *2* MIL. arm [combatant branch of an army]. *3 pl.* arms [military profession]. *6* HER. arms, armorial bearings.
armada *f.* navy, naval forces. *2* fleet [of warships].
armadía *f.* raft, float.
armadijo *m.* trap, snare [for game]. *2* wooden frame.
armadillo *m.* ZOOL. armadillo.
armado *m.* man dressed as a Roman soldier [in Holy Week processions].
armador *m.* shipowner, ship-charterer. *2* assembler, adjuster. *3* jerkin.
armadura *f.* armo(u)r [defensive covering]. *2* frame, framework, truss. *3* ARCH. roof frame. *4* ELECT., MAGN. armature. *5* MUS. key signature.
armajo *m.* ALMARJO.
armamentista *adj.* arms, armaments: *política* ~, arms policy; *carrera* ~, arms race.
armamento *m.* armament. *2* arms [of a soldier]. *3* outfitting [a ship].
Armando *m. pr. n.* Herman.
armar *tr.* to array in armour. *2* to arm. *3* to fix [a bayonet]. *4* NAUT. to outfit, fit out [a ship]. *5* to supply [with]. *6* to assemble, set up, adjust. *7* to build, establish [on]. *8* to set [a trap]. *9* to start, make, rise, stir up: ~ *ruido*, to raise a disturbance; *armarla*, to kick up a shindy. *10* to form, prepare. *11* SEW. to stiffen. *12* ~ *caballero*, to knight. *13 ref.* to array oneself in armour. *14* to arm oneself. *15* to happen, arise, be raised or started. *16 armarse de valor*, to gather up one's courage; *armarse de paciencia*, to arm oneself with patience.
armario *m.* press, wardrobe, cabinet, closet.
armatoste *m.* hulk, cumbersome machine or object; big, clumsy person.

armazón *f.* assemblage, setting up. *2* frame, framework, structure. *3* ANAT. skeleton.
armella *f.* screw eye, eyebolt.
Armenia *pr. n.* GEOG. Armenia.
armenio, -nia *adj.-n.* Armenian.
armería *f.* arms museum. *2* armo(u)ry. *3* gunsmith craft or shop; arms shop.
armero *m.* armo(u)rer; gunsmith. *2* rack or stand for arms, armrack.
armilar *adj.* armillary.
armilla *f.* ARCH. astragal [of a column]. *2* ASTR. armilary sphere.
armiñado, -da *adj.* trimmed or lined with ermine fur. *2* ermine-white.
armiño *m.* ZOOL., HER. ermine. *2* ermine fur.
armisticio *m.* armistice.
armón *m.* ARTILL. limber.
armonía *f.* harmony. *2* MUS. harmonization.
armónica *f.* MUS. harmonica, mouth organ.
armónicamente *adv.* harmoniously, in a harmonic way, in harmony.
armónico, -ca *adj.* harmonic. *2 m.* MUS., PHYS. harmonic.
armonio *m.* MUS. harmonium.
armonioso, -sa *adj.* harmonious.
armonista *m.-f.* harmonist.
armonización *f.* harmonization.
armonizar *tr.-intr.* to harmonize.
armuelle *m.* BOT. orach, orache.
arnés *m.* harness, armour. *2 pl.* harness [of horses]. *3* gear, tackle, implements, tools.
árnica *f.* BOT., PHARM. arnica.
aro *m.* hoop, ring, rim. *2* hoop [plaything]: *entrar por el* ~, to be forced to yield. *3* BOT. cuckoopint.
aroma *f.* flower of the huisache. *2* aroma, fragrance. *3 m.-f.* aromatic.
aromático, -ca *adj.* aromatic.
aromatizador *m.* (Am.) spray, atomizer.
aromatizar *tr.* to aromatize.
aromo BOT. huisache, sponge tree.
aromoso, -sa *adj.* aromatic.
arpa *f.* MUS. harp: ~ *eolia,* aeolian harp.
arpado, -da *adj.* serrated, toothed. *2* poet. singing [bird].
arpar *tr.* to scratch. *2* to tear, rend.
arpegiar *intr.* to arpeggio.
arpegio *m.* MUS. arpeggio.
arpella *f.* ORN. marsh harrier.
arpeo *m.* NAUT. grappling iron.
arpía *f.* MYTH. harpy. *2* harpy [rapacious person]. *3* shrew [woman]. *4* hag.
arpillera *f.* burlap, sackcloth.
arpista *m.-f.* harper, harpist.
arpón *m.* harpoon. *2* ARCH. clamp.
arponear *tr.* to harpoon.
arponero *m.* harpoon maker. *2* harpooner.
arqueador *m.* ship gauger. *2* wool beater.
arqueamiento *m.* NAUT. gauging, tonnage, standard measurement of a ship's capacity.
arquear *tr.* to arch, bend. *2* to beat [wool]. *3* to gauge [a ship]. *4 intr.* to retch, be nauseated. *5 ref.* to arch.
arquegonio *m.* BOT. archegonium.
arqueo *m.* arching, bending. *2* NAUT. gauging. *3* NAUT. tonnage. *4* COM. checking the contents of a cashbox.
arqueología *f.* archaeology.
arqueológico, -ca *adj.* archaeological.
arqueólogo *m.* archaeologist.
arquería *f.* ARCH. series of arches.
arquero *m.* archer, bowman. *2* bow maker.

arqueta *f.* small coffer.
arquetipo *m.* archetype.
arquiepiscopal *adj.* archiepiscopal.
Arquímedes *pr. n.* Archimedes.
arquitecto *m.* architect.
arquitectónico, -ca *adj.* architectonic, architectural.
arquitectura *f.* architecture; architectonics.
arquitrabe *m.* ARCH. architrave.
arquivolta *f.* ARCHIVOLTA.
arrabal *m.* suburb. *2 pl.* environs, outskirts.
arracada *f.* earring with a pendant, eardrop.
arracimarse *ref.* to cluster, bunch.
arraclán *m.* BOT. alder buckthorn.
arraigado, -da *adj.* rooted, deep-rooted. *2* owning real estate, landed.
arraigar *intr.-ref.* to take root. *2 tr.* to establish, to strengthen.
arraigo *m.* taking root. *2* root, settling [in a place]; landed property, connexions.
arramblar *tr.* [of streams] to cover [ground] with sand or gravel. *2* to sweep away. *3 ref.* [of ground] to be covered with sand or gravel.
arrancaclavos *m.* nail puller.
arrancada *f.* sudden departure. *2* NAUT. starting speed. *3* sudden increase in speed. *4* sudden charge [of a bull].
arrancadura *f.*, **arrancamiento** *m.* pulling out, extraction.
arrancar *tr.* to root up or out, to pull out, extract, extirpate: ~ *de cuajo* or *de raíz,* to uproot, eradicate. *2* to pluck [feathers, hairs, etc.]. *3* to tear out, snatch, snatch away. *4* to wrest, wrench, wring, extort, force [from]. *5 intr.* to start: ~ *a correr,* to start running. *6* to set sail. *7* to come [from], originate [in]. *8* ARCH. [of an arch or vault] to spring.
arrancarse *ref.* ENRANCIARSE.
arranque *m.* pulling up. *2* start [of a motor, a car, etc.]. *3* MECH. starter, starting gear: ~ *automático,* self-starter. *4* impulse, outburst [of piety, anger, etc.]. *5* sally, lively remark. *6* ARCH. spring [of an arch]. *7* ANAT., BOT. base, root.
arrapiezo *m.* child, urchin. *2* rag, tatter.
arras *f.* security, earnest [of a contract], earnest money, handsel. *2* thirteen coins given by bridegroom to bride at weeding.
arrasamiento *m.* razing to the ground.
arrasar *tr.* to level, flatten. *2* to raze, demolish. *3* to level with a strickle. *4* to fill to the brim. *5 ref.-intr.* [of the sky] to clear up. *6 ref. arrasarse los ojos de,* or *en, lágrimas,* [of the eyes] to become filled with tears.
arrastradamente *adv.* coll. badly, poorly. *2* coll. miserably, wretchedly.
arrastradero *m.* log path. *2* BULLF. spot through which dead animals are dragged from the ring.
arrastradizo, -za *adj.* dangling, -trailing.
arrastrado, -da *adj.* wretched, miserable. *3* rascally. *4* suit-following [card game]. *5 m.-f.* rascal, scamp.
arrastrar *tr.* to drag, drag along, on or down, to trail, to have: ~ *los pies,* to shuffle, drag one's feet. *2* to carry after oneself. *3* to drive, impel; to carry away, to wash down, urge along. *4 intr.* to drag, trail [hang down to the ground]. *5* CARDS. to lead trumps. *6 intr.* to crawl, creep, trail. *7 ref.* fig. to crawl, cringe.
arrastre *m.* drag, dragging; haulage. *2* washing down [by waters]. *3* dragging dead bull from ring. *4* CARDS. leading a trump.

arrayán *m.* BOT. myrtle. *2* BOT. ~ *brabántico*, wax myrtle, bayberry.

¡arre! *interj.* gee!, gee up! *2* get away!

arrear *tr.* to urge on [horses, mules, etc.]. *2* to spur, to hurry. *3* to deliver [a blow]. *4* to dress, adorn. *5* *intr.* to hurry: *¡arrea!*, get moving!; nonsense!

arrebatadamente *adv.* hurriedly, hastily. *2* impulsively, rashly.

arrebatado, -da *adj.* hasty, rash, impetuous, violent. *2* ruddy, flushed, inflamed [face].

arrebatador, -ra *adj.* captivating. *2* stirring, exciting, inflaming, enrapturing.

arrebatamiento *m.* carrying off. *2* fury, rage. *3* rapture, ecstasy.

arrebatar *tr.* to snatch, to carry or take away [by force]. *2* to carry away, move, captivate, enrapture. *3* *ref.* to be led away [by emotionl, passion, etc.]. *4* COOK. to be burned.

arrebatiña *f.* scramble, scrimmage [to pick up something].

arrebato *m.* fit, rage, fury. *2* rapture.

arrebol *m.* red tinge in the clouds. *2* rouge, paint. *3* *pl.* red clouds.

arrebolar *tr.* to give a red tinge to. *2* *ref.* take a red tinge, to flush.

arrebozar *tr.* to coat, to cover [with flour, crumbs, etc.]. *2* *ref.* to cover oneself, to muffle or wrap oneself. *3* to swarm, to hive [the bees, wasps, etc.].

arrebujadamente *adv.* confusedly.

arrebujar *tr.* to pick up [clothes, etc.] in a huddle or heap. *2* to tuck in; to wrap up. *3* *ref.* to tuck oneself in; to wrap oneself up.

arreciar *intr.-ref.* to increase in strength or intensity, to wax stronger. *2* *ref.* ARRECIRSE.

arrecife *m.* reef [in the sea]. *2* stone-paved road.

arrecirse *ref.* to grow stiff with cold. ¶ Only used in forms having *i* in their terminations.

arrechucho *m.* sudden impulse, fit, outburst. *2* sudden and passing indisposition.

arredramiento *m.* backing out, fright, intimidation.

arredrar *tr.* to frighten, intimidate; to make [one] draw back or back out through fear. *2* *ref.* to be frightened; to flinch, draw back.

arredro *adv.* backwards.

arregazado, -da *adj.* tucked up. *2* turned up.

arregazar *tr.* to tuck up [the skirts].

arreglado, -da *p. p.* of ARREGLAR. *2* *adj.* orderly, neat. *3* regular [without excesses]. *4* moderate, reasonable [price, etc.].

arreglar *tr.-ref.* to adjust, regulate. *2* to settle, arrange. *3* to put in order. *4* to dress, smarten up. *5* to mend, fix up. *6* *ref.* *arreglarse con*, to come to an understanding with; to manage with. *7* *arreglárselas*, to manage, to shift.

arreglo *m.* order, orderly state. *2* settlement arrangement; agreement, compromise. *3* arrangement, putting in order. *4* mending, fixing up. *5* MUS. arrangement. *6* *con* ~ *a*, according to.

arrellanarse *ref.* to sit at ease, to make oneself comfortable [in a seat].

arremangar *tr.-ref.* to tuck up [one's] sleeves. *2* to take a firm decision.

arremetedor, -ra *adj.* attacking.

arremeter *intr.* to attack, rush [upon].

arremetida *f.* attack, rushing upon. *2* sudden start [of a horse].

arremolinarse *ref.* to crowd, press together.

arrendable *adj.* suitable for renting, rentable. *2* LAW. leasable.

arrendado, -da *adj.* rented, leased, farmed. *2* obedient to the reins.

arrendador, -ra *m.-f.* landlord, landlady, lessor. *2* lessee, tenant, farmer.

arrendajo *m.* ORN. jay. *2* fig. aper, mimic.

arrendamiento *m.* renting; leasing, letting, farming; lease. *2* rent.

arrendar *tr.* to rent, to lease, to farm [to someone or by someone]; to let. *2* to tie [a horse] by the reins. *3* to break [a horse] to the reins. ¶ CONJUG. like *acertar*.

arrendatario, -ria *m.-f.* lessee, tenant, farmer.

1) arreo *m.* dress, ornament. *2* *pl.* harness, riding gear. *3* appurtenances.

2) arreo *adv.* successively, without interruption.

arrepanchingarse *ref.* to lounge, to sit back, to make oneself comfortable.

arrepentido, -da *adj.* repentant; regretful.

arrepentimiento *m.* repentance; regret.

arrepentirse *ref.* to repent: ~ *de*, to repent of, be sorry for, to regret. *2* to back down or out. ¶ CONJUG. like *hervir*.

arrepiento, arrepintió, arrepienta, etc. *irr.* V. ARREPENTIR.

arrequesonarse *ref.* [of milk] to curdle.

arrequives *m. pl.* finery, adornments. *2* circumstances or requisites.

arrestado, -da *adj.* bold, daring.

arrestar *tr.* to arrest, imprison. *2* MIL. to detain, confine. *3* *ref.* *arrestarse a*, to dare, venture.

arresto *m.* arrest, detention. *2* MIL. confinement. *3* *pl.* pluck, spirit.

arrevesado, -da *adj.* intricate, obscure.

arrezagar *tr.* to tuck up [sleeves, etc.].

arriada *f.* flood, overflowing, freshet. *2* NAUT. lowering of the sails.

arrianismo *m.* Arianism.

arriano, -na *adj.-n.* Arian.

arriar *tr.* NAUT. to lower, to strike. *2* NAUT. to pay out [a rope]. *3* to strike [a flag, etc.].

arriate *m.* narrow bed along the wall of a garden. *2* causeway. *3* trellis.

arriba *adv.* up, upwards: *cuesta* ~, uphill; *río* ~, upstream; *de cuatro pesetas* ~, from four pesetas up. *2* above, on high, at the top, aloft: *de* ~ *abajo*, from top to bottom; from beginning to end. *3* afore, before, above: ~ *dicho*, above mentioned! *4* *interj.* up!

arribada *f.* NAUT. arrival, putting in: ~ *forzosa*, putting in by stress.

arribaje *m.* NAUT. arrival, putting into port.

arribar *intr.* to arrive. *2* NAUT. to put into port. *3* NAUT. to fall off to leeward.

arribazón *f.* seasonal influx of fish to coasts.

arribismo *m.* arrivism.

arribista *adj.* profit-seeking, self-seeking. *2* *n.* arrivist, arriviste.

arribo *m.* NAUT. arrival [of a ship, of merchandise].

arricés *m.* buckle of a stirrup strap.

arriendo *m.* ARRENDAMIENTO.

arriero *m.* muleteer.

arriesgado, -da *adj.* risky, dangerous. *2* daring, bold, rash.

arriesgar *tr.* to risk, hazard, venture. *2* *ref.* to expose oneself to danger. *3* *arriesgarse a*, to dare, risk [to do something].

arrimadero *m.* support. *2* wainscot.

arrimar *tr.* to bring close [to], draw up [to], place [against]. *2* to put away, shelve. *3* to give [a blow, etc.]. *4* NAUT. to stow [the cargo]. *5* *ref.* *arrimarse a*, to go near, to lean against, to press oneself close to; to seek the protection of; to associate with.

arrimo *m.* placing beside, near, against. *2* support, help, protection. *3* attachment, leaning.

arrinconado, -da *adj.* out-of-the-way. *2* shelved, ignored, forgotten.

arrinconamiento *m.* discarding, laying aside, ruling out.

arrinconar *tr.* to put in a corner. *2* to corner [a person]. *3* to shelve, ignore, neglect. *4* to lay aside, discard. *5 ref.* to retire, become a recluse.

arriñonado, -da *adj.* kidney-shaped.

arriostrar *tr.* ARCH. to shore up, to support, to prop up, to stay.

Arrio *pr. n.* Arius.

arriscado, -da *adj.* craggy. *2* bold, resolute. *3* easy, free, brisk.

arriscamiento *m.* boldness, resolution.

arriscar *tr.-ref.* ARRIESGAR. *2 ref.* [of sheep or cattle] to plunge over a crag.

arritmia *f.* MED. arrhythmy.

arrítmico, -ca *adj.* MED. arrhythmic.

arrizar *tr.* NAUT. to reef. *2* NAUT. to fasten, lash.

arroaz *m.* ZOOL. dolphin.

arroba *f.* weight of about 11½ kg. *2* liquid measure of varying value.

arrobador, -ra *adj.* enchanting, entrancing.

arrobamiento *m.* bliss, entrancement, ecstasy, rapture.

arrobar *tr.* to entrance, to enrapture. *2 ref.* to be entranced, enraptured.

arrocero, -ra *adj.* [pertaining to] rice. *2 m.-f.* rice grower; rice dealer.

arrodilladura *f.*, **arrodillamiento** *m.* kneeling.

arrodillar *tr.* to make kneel down. *2 ref.* to kneel, kneel down.

arrodigrar, arrodrigonar *tr.* to prop [vines].

arrogación *f.* arrogation.

arrogancia *f.* arrogance, haughtiness. *2* courage, spirit. *3* handsomeness, stately carriage.

arrogante *adj.* arrogant, haughty. *2* courageous, spirited. *3* handsome, stately.

arrogantemente *adv.* arrogantly. *2* bravely, courageously. *3* proudly, with dignity.

arrogarse *ref.* to arrogate to oneself.

arrojadizo, -za *adj.* easily thrown; for throwing, missile.

arrojado, -da *adj.* bold, intrepid, dashing, rash.

arrojar *tr.* to throw, fling, hurl, cast. *2* to shed, emit. *3* to put forth [leaves, shoots]. *4* to expel, throw out; to turn out, dismiss. *5* NAUT. to drive or cast [on rocks, etc.]. *6* to vomit. *7* to show [a total, a balance]. *8 ref.* to throw oneself. *9* to rush [at], fall [upon]. *10* to launch out upon [an enterprise].

arrojo *m.* boldness, dash, bravery.

arrollador *m.* rolling, winding. *2* violent, sweeping.

arrollamiento *m.* rolling, winding. *2* ELECT. winding.

arrollar *tr.* to roll, roll up. *2* to wind, coil. *3* to roll or sweep away. *4* to rout [the enemy]. *5* to trample down, to run over. *6* to confound [an opponent]. *7* to rock [a child].

arromanzar *tr.* to translate into Spanish.

arropar *tr.-ref.* to cover, wrap, wrap up [in clothes].

arrope *m.* must boiled to a syrup. *2* honey syrup.

arropea *f.* fetter. *2* hopple [for horses].

arropía *f.* kind of taffy made of honey.

arrostrar *tr.* to face, stand, brave. *2 ref.* to fight face to face.

arroyar *tr.* [of rain] to form gullies in. *2 ref.* AGR. [of grain] to become smutted.

arroyo *m.* brook, rivulet, stream. *2* gutter [in a street], street: *poner en el* ~, to put out in the street. *3* stream [of tears, etc.].

arroyuelo *m.* rill, small brook.

arroz *m.* BOT. rice.

arrozal *m.* rice field.

arrufadura *f.* NAUT. sheer [of a ship].

arrufar *tr.* NAUT. to form the sheer of. *2 intr.* [of a ship] to have a sheer.

arrufianado, -da *adj.* rascally, dishonest, mischeavous. *2* vulgar, coarse, uncouth.

arruga *f.* wrinkle; crease, crumple, rumple.

arrugamiento *m.* wrinkling, creasing, crumpling.

arrugar *tr.* to wrinkle; to crease, crumple, rumple. *2* SEW. to gather, fold. *3* ~ *el entrecejo, la frente*, to frown, to knit the brow. *4 ref.* to wrinkle, crumple, shrivel [become wrinkled].

arruinar *tr.* to ruin, ruinate, demolish, destroy. *2* to become ruined; to fall into ruins.

arrullador, -ra *adj.* cooing. *2* lulling.

arrullar *tr.* to coo; to bill and coo. *2* to lull or sing to sleep, to croon.

arrullo *m.* coo. *2* billing and cooing. *3* lullaby.

arrumaco *m.* caress, show of affection.

arrumaje *m.* NAUT. stowage.

arrumar *tr.* NAUT. to stow. *2 ref.* NAUT. [of the horizon] to become overcast.

arrumazón *f.* NAUT. stowage. *2* overcast horizon.

arrumbar *tr.* to lay aside, put out of the way, reject, discard. *2* to confound [an opponent]. *3* to shelve, cast into oblivion. *4 intr.* NAUT. to fix the course. *6 ref.* NAUT. to take bearings.

arrurruz *m.* arrowroot [starch].

arsenal *m.* shipyard, dockyard, navy yard. *2* arsenal.

arseniato *m.* CHEM. arseniate.

arsénico *adj.-m.* CHEM. arsenic.

Artajerjes *m. pr. n.* Artaxerxes.

arte *m.-f.* art: *artes mecánicas*, manual arts; *bellas artes*, fine arts; *por* ~ *de birlibirloque* or *de encantamiento*, as if by magic; *no tener* ~ *ni parte en*, to have nothing to do with. *2* craft, skill, knack; cunning: *con malas artes*, by evil means. *3* fishing appliance.

artefacto *m.* manufacture, mechanical handiwork. *2* device, contrivance, appliance.

artejo *m.* knuckle [of finger]. *2* ZOOL. article.

Artemisa *f. pr. n.* MYTH. Artemis.

artemisa, artemisia *f.* BOT. mugwort; sagebrush.

arteramente *adv.* artfully, craftily, slyly.

arteria *f.* ANAT. artery. *2* fig. artery [main thoroughfare].

artería *f.* artfulness, craftiness; cunning, trick.

arterial *adj.* arterial.

arteriola *f.* ANAT. arteriole.

arteriosclerosis *f.* MED. arteriosclerosis.

arteritis *f.* MED. arteritis.

artero, -ra *adj.* artful, crafty, sly.

artesa *f.* trough [for kneading, washing ore, etc.].

artesanado *m.* craftmen, artisans.

artesanía *f.* craftsmanship. *2* craftsmen.

artesano, -na *m.-f.* artisan, craftsman, mechanic.

artesiano, -na *adj.-n.* Artesian.

artesón *m.* kitchen tub. *2* ARCH. caisson, coffer.

artesonado, -da *adj.* panelled [ceiling]. *2 m.* panelwork [in a ceiling].

ártico, -ca *adj.* arctic: *Océano* ~, Arctic Ocean.

articulación *f.* articulation. *2* MECH. joint.
articulado, -da *adj.* articulate, articulated. *2 m.* the articles [of an act, law, etc.]. *3 adj.-m.* articulate.
1) **articular** *tr.* to articulate. *2 ref.* to articulate, be connected.
2) **articular & articulario, -ria** *adj.* articular.
articulista *m.-f.* writer of articles.
artículo *m.* article [in a writing, contract, law, act, etc.; literary composition]: ~ *de fondo*, leader, editorial. *2* entry [in a dictionary]. *3* article [of faith]. *4* article, commodity: *artículos de consumo*, consumer's goods. *5* GRAM. article. *6* ZOOL. articulation. *7 en el* ~ *de la muerte*, in articulo mortis.
artífice *m.* artificier, craftsman, artist. *2* maker.
artificial *adj.* artificial.
artificiero *m.* MIL. artificer.
artificio *m.* artifice, skill. *2* artifice, cunning, trick. *3* device, contrivance.
artificioso, -sa *adj.* skilful, ingenious. *2* crafty, artful.
artilugio *m.* contraption, worthless mechanical contrivance.
artillar *tr.* to equip with artillery.
artillería *f.* artillery; ordnance.
artillero *m.* gunner, artilleryman.
artimaña *f.* trick, stratagem. *2* trap, snare.
artiodáctilo, -la *adj.-m.* ZOOL. artiodactyl.
artista *m.-f.* artist.
artísticamente *adv.* artistically.
artístico, -ca *adj.* artistic.
artocarpáceo, -a *adj.* BOT. artocarpous.
artritis *f.* MED. arthritis.
artritismo *m.* MED. arthritism.
artrópodo, -da *adj.-m.* ZOOL. arthropod. *2 m.-pl.* ZOOL. Arthropoda.
arturiano, -na; artúrico, -ca *adj.* arthurian.
Arturo *pr. n.* Arthur.
arúspice *m.* haruspex.
arveja *f.* BOT. spring vetch, tare.
arvejal, arvejar *m.* vetch field.
arzobispado *m.* archbishopric.
arzobispal *adj.* archiepiscopal.
arzobispo *m.* archbishop.
arzolla *f.* BOT. kind of centaury. *2* BOT. milk thistle.
arzón *m.* ~ *delantero*, saddlebow; ~ *trasero*, cantle [in saddles].
as *m.* ace [in cards or dice]. *2* ace, king [good performer].
asa *f.* handle [of a basket, cup, valise, etc.]: *en asas*, fig. akimbo. *2* ASIDERO. *3* BOT. ~ *fétida*, asafœtida.
asadero, -ra *adj.* fit for roasting.
asado, -da *adj.* roasted: ~ *al horno*, baked [meat]; ~ *a la parrilla*, broiled. *2 m.* roast.
asador *m.* spit [for roasting]. *2* roasting jack.
asadura *f.* entrails, haslet; liver. *2* coll. slowness, phlegm.
asaetear *tr.* to shoot, wound or kill with arrows. *2* to bother, harass.
asalariado, -da *adj.* salaried. *2 m.* wage-earner.
asalariar *tr.* to employ, hire [a person].
asalmonado, -da *adj.* salmon-coloured.
asaltante *adj.* assailing. *2 m.-f.* assailant.
asaltar *tr.* to assail, assault, storm. *2* to surprise, hold up. *3* [of a thought, fear, etc.] to strike, to assail; [of death] to overtake.
asalto *m.* assault, storm: *tomar por* ~, to take by storm. *2* FENC. assault. *3* BOX. round.
asamblea *f.* assembly [for deliberation or legislation]. *2* MIL. assembly.

asambleísta *m.-f.* member of an assembly. *2 m.* assemblyman.
asar *tr.* to roast: ~ *a la parrilla*, to broil. *2 ref.* fig. to roast [be roasted].
asargado, -da *adj.* twiled, sergelike.
ásaro *m.* BOT. asarabacca.
asaz *adv.* poet. enough; much, very.
asbesto *m.* MINER. asbestos.
ascalonia *f.* BOT. shallot.
ascáride *f.* ZOOL. ascarid.
ascendencia *f.* ancestry, line of ancestors.
ascendente *adj.* ascending, ascendant. *2* up [train].
ascender *intr.* to ascend. *2* to accede [to the throne]. *3* to amount or add up [to]. *4* to be promoted. *5 tr.* to promote. ¶ CONJUG. like *entender*.
ascendido, -da *adj.* promoted.
ascendiente *adj.* ascending, ascendant. *2 m.-f.* ancestor. *3* ascendancy, ascendency.
ascensión *f.* ascension, ascent. *2* ASTR. ascension. *3 la Ascensión*, the Ascension, Ascension Day. *4* accession [to the throne].
ascensional *adj.* ascensional.
ascenso *m.* promotion.
ascensor *m.* lift, elevator.
ascensorista *m.* lift maker or operator.
asceta *m.* ascetic.
ascético, -ca *adj.* ascetic(al. *2 f.* ascetics.
ascetismo *m.* ascetism.
ascidia *f.* ZOOL. ascidian.
asciendo, ascienda, etc. *irr.* V. ASCENDER.
asco *m.* nausea, loathing, disgust: *dar* ~, to turn the stomach, to disgust; *hacer ascos a*, to turn up one's nose at. *2* disgusting thing.
ascomiceto *s.* BOT. ascomycete.
ascón *s.* BOT. ascon.
ascua *f.* ember, live coal: ~ *de oro*, resplendent thing; *estar en ascuas*, to be on tenterhooks; *arrimar uno el ascua a su sardina*, to further one's own interests.
Asdrúbal *pr. n.* Hasdrubal.
aseadamente *adv.* neatly, tidily, in an orderly way. *2* cleanly.
aseado, -da *adj.* clean, neat, tidy.
asear *tr.* to clean, to tidy. *2 ref.* to make [oneself] clean, to tidy [oneself] up.
asechanza *f.* snare, trap, pitfall.
asechar *tr.* to set traps [for somebody].
asecho *m.* ASECHANZA.
asediador, -ra *adj.* besieging. *2 m.-f.* besieger.
asediar *tr.* to besiege, lay siege to. *2* fig. to besiege, beset, importunate.
asedio *m.* siege, blockade.
aseguración *f.* insurance.
asegurado, -da *adj.-n.* insured.
asegurador, -ra *adj.* assuring. *2* insuring. *3 m.-f.* assurer. *4* insurer, underwriter.
aseguramiento *m.* securing; security. *2* insurance.
asegurar *tr.* to secure, fasten, fix. *2* to secure [make safe; guarantee; seize and confine]; to ensure. *3* to assure. *4* to assert, affirm. *5* COM. to insure. *6 ref.* to make sure. *7* to hold fast. *8* to insure oneself.
asemejar *tr.* to liken, to compare. *2 intr.-ref.* to resemble, be like or alike.
asendereado, -da *adj.* beaten, frequented. *2* overwhelmed with hardships.
asenso *m.* assent, credence.
asentaderas *f. pl.* coll, buttocks.
asentado, -da *adj.* situated, located. *2* fig. stable, settled, established.

asentador *m.* razor 'strop. 2 wholesale provisionner.

asentamiento *m.* sitting down. 2 settling, establishment, situation. 3 location, emplacement. 4 COM. registration, entry, record of facts.

asentar *tr.* to seat. 2 to place, fix establish, found. 3 to give [a blow]. 4 to tamp down. 5 to iron [seams]. 6 to affirm, asume. 7 to enter [in a ledger, etc.]; to note down. 8 to make [a deal, a bargain]. 9 to strop, hone. 10 ref. to sit down. 11 to settle, become established. 12 [of birds] to alight. 13 [of liquids, a building] to settle. 14 [of food] not to be digested. 15 [of a packsaddle] to hurt the horse, mule, etc. ¶ CONJUG. like *acertar*.

asentimiento *m.* assent.

asentir *intr.* to assent, to agree. ¶ CONJUG. like *hervir*.

asentista *m.* government, contractor.

aseñorado, -da *adj.* gentlemanly.

aseo *m.* cleanliness, tidiness. 2 cleaning, tidying: *cuarto de* ~, toilet room.

asepsia *f.* asepsis.

aséptico, -ca *adj.* aseptic.

asequible *adj.* accesible, obtainable, reachable.

aserción *f.* assertion, affirmation.

aserradero *m.* sawmill, sawing place.

aserrador, -ra *adj.* sawing. 2 *m.* sawer, sawyer.

aserradura *f.* saw cut. 2 *pl.* sawings, sawdust.

aserrar *tr.* to saw. ¶ CONJUG. like *acertar*.

aserrín *m.* sawdust.

asertivo, -va *adj.* assertive, affirmative, positive.

aserto *m.* assertion, affirmation, statement.

asertorio *m.* affirmatory.

asesinar *tr.* to assassinate, murder.

asesinato *m.* assassination, murder.

asesino, -na *adj.* murderous. 2 *m.-f.* assassin, murderer.

asesor, -ra *m.-f.* adviser; assessor.

asesoramiento *m.* advice [esp. professional advice].

asesorar *tr.* to advise, give professional advice to. 2 *ref.* to take advice.

asesoría *f.* the post or office of an adviser, assessorship.

asestar *tr.* to aim, point, level, direct. 2 to strike, deal [a blow]; to fire [a shot].

aseveración *f.* asseveration.

aseverar *tr.* to asseverate.

asexual *adj.* asexual.

asexuado, -da *adj.* asexual.

asfaltado, -da *adj.* asphalt, asphalted. 2 *m.* asphalting. 3 asphalt pavement.

asfaltar *tr.* to asphalt.

asfalto *m.* asphalt, asphaltum.

asfixia *f.* asphyxia; asphyxiation.

asfixiado, -da *adj.* suffocated, asphyxiated.

asfixiante *adj.* asphyxiating; suffocating.

asfixiar *tr.* to asphyxiate; to suffocate. 2 *ref.* to be asphyxiated.

asfódelo *m.* BOT. asphodel.

asgo, asga, etc. *irr.* V. ASIR.

así *adv.* so, thus, in this way: *así, así,* so so, middling; ~ *como* ~, anyway; ~ *sea,* so be it; *así y todo,* yet, notwithstanding. 2 in the same manner, as well. 3 as soon: ~ *como,* ~ *que,* as soon as. 4 *adj.* such: *un hombre* ~, such a man. 5 *conj.* would that. 6 *así,* ~ *pues,* ~ *que,* so then, therefore.

Asia *pr. n.* GEOG. Asia: ~ *Menor,* Asia Minor.

asiático, -ca *adj.-n.* Asiatic, Asian.

asidero *m.* handle, hold. 2 occasion, pretext.

asiduamente *adv.* assiduously. 2 frequently, regularly, often.

asiduidad *f.* assiduity, sedulity.

asiduo, -dua *adj.* assiduous, sedulous, frequent.

asiento *m.* seat [chair, etc.; place]: *tomar* ~, to take a seat. 2 site [of building, town, etc.]. 3 ARCH. settling [of materials or building]. 4 sediment. 5 settlement, establishment. 6 contract for supplies. 7 entry [in a ledger or register]. 8 indigestion. 9 stability, permanence. 10 judgment, wisdom.

asiento, asiente, etc. *irr.* V. ASENTAR.

asiento, asienta, etc. *irr.* V. ASENTIR.

asierro, asierre, etc. *irr.* V. ASERRAR.

asignación *f.* assignation, assignment, allotment. 2 assignation, amount assigned [as wages, etc.].

asignado *m.* assignat.

asignar *tr.* to assign, allot. 2 to assign, fix, appoint.

asignatario, -ria *n.* Am. legatee, heir, inheritor.

asignatura *f.* subject or course of study.

asilar *tr.* to place in a home or asylum.

asilo *m.* asylum, home [for the poor, etc.].

asimetría *f.* asymmetry.

asimétrico, -ca *adj.* asymmetric(al).

asimiento *m.* seizing, grasping. 2 affection, attachment.

asimilación *f.* assimilation.

asimilar *tr.* to assimilate. 2 *intr.* to be similar. 3 *ref.* to be assimilated. 4 to resemble.

asimismo *adv.* in like manner, likewise, also.

asincrónico, -ca *adj.* asynchronous.

asíndeton *m.* RHET. asyndeton.

asintió, asintiera, etc. *irr.* V. ASENTIR.

asíntota *f.* GEOM. asymptote.

asir *tr.* to seize, grasp, take: *asidos del brazo,* arm in arm. 2 *intr.* to take root. 3 *ref.* to take hold [of]; to hold [to]. 4 to avail oneself [of]. 5 to dispute, grapple. ¶ CONJUG.: INDIC. Pres.: *asgo, ases,* etc. | SUBJ. Pres.: *asga, asgas, asga; asgamos, asgáis, asgan.* | IMPER.: *ase, asga; asgamos, asid, asgan.*

Asiria *f. pr.* HIST. GEOG. Assyria.

asirio, -ria *adj.-n.* Assyrian.

Asís *m. pr. n.* Assisi.

asistencia *f.* attendance, presence. 2 assistance, aid: ~ *social,* social service. 3 *pl.* allowance; alimony.

asistenta *f.* charwoman.

asistente *adj.-n.* attendant, present. 2 *m.* assistant, helper. 3 MIL. a soldier assigned as a servant to an officer.

asistido, -da *adj.* assisted, helped, aided: *dirección* ~, power steering; *frenos* ~, power brakes.

asistir *intr.* to attend, be present, go: ~ *a la escuela,* to attend school. 2 CARDS to follow suit. 3 *tr.* to assist, aid, help. 4 to attend, take care of [the sick]. 5 *me asiste la razón,* I am right.

asma *f.* MED. asthma.

asmático, -ca *adj.-n.* asthmatic.

asna *f.* she-ass, jenny ass. 2 *pl.* rafters.

asnacho *m.* BOT. restharrow.

asnada *f.* stupidity, foolish act.

asnal *adj.* donkey, asinine.

asnería *f.* asses. 2 stupidity, nonsense.

asno *m.* ZOOL. ass, donkey, jackass.

asociación *f.* association.

asociacionismo *m.* associationism.

asociado, -da *adj.* associated, associate. 2 *m.-f.* associate, partner. 3 member [of an association].

asociar *tr.* to associate. 2 *ref.* to associate, become associated; to join, enter into partnership.

asolador, -ra *adj.* razing, ravaging, devastating.
asolamiento *m.* ravage, desolation, devastation.
asolar *tr.* to raze, level with the ground, lay waste, desolate, devastate. *2 ref.* [of liquids] to settle. ¶ CONJUG. like *contar.*
asolear *tr.* to sun. *2 ref.* to become heated in the sun. *3* to become sun-tanned.
asomada *f.* peep, short appearance. *2* point from which something is first seen.
asomar *intr.* to begin to appear or to show. *2 tr.* to show, put out [through, behind or over an opening or a wall]. *3 ref.* to peep out, put one's head out, look out.
asombradizo, -za *adj.* ESPANTADIZO.
asombrado, -da *adj.* surprised. *2* amazed, astonished, astounded.
asombrar *tr.* to shade [throw a shadow on]. *2* to frighten. *3* to amaze, astonish. *4 ref.* to take fright. *5* to be astonished, amazed.
asombro *m.* fright. *2* amazement, astonishment.
asombrosamente *adv.* amazingly, surprisingly, wonderfully.
asombroso, -sa *adj.* amazing, astonishing, wonderful.
asomo *m.* peep, looking out. *2* sign, indication: *ni por ~*, by no means.
asonada *f.* riot, tumult, disturbance.
asonancia *f.* as'~nance.
asonantar *tr.* to make assonant. *2 intr.* to assonate.
asonante *adj.-n.* assonant.
asonar *intr.* to assonate. ¶ CONJUG. like *contar.*
aspa *f.* X-shaped figure or cross: *~ de San Andrés*, St. Andrew's cross. *2* reel [for skeining]. *3* sail, vane [for windmill]. *5* HER. saltier.
aspadera *f.* reel [for skeining].
aspado, -da *adj.* X-shaped.
aspar *tr.* to skein [yarn]. *2* to crucify. *3* to vex, annoy. *4 ref.* to cry and writhe [with pain, anger, etc.].
aspaviento *m.* exaggerated demonstration of terror, admiration, or feeling.
aspecto *m.* aspect, look. *2* ARCH., ASTROL. aspect.
aspereza *f.* asperity, roughness. *2* tartness; harshness. *3* rudeness, gruffness. *4* rough place.
asperges *m.* coll. sprinkling, aspersion. *2* coll. aspergillum.
asperilla *f.* BOT. woodruff.
asperillo *m.* slight sour taste.
asperjar *tr.* to sprinkle; to sprinkle with holy water.
áspero, -ra *adj.* rough. *2* harsh. *3* sour, tart. *4* rude, gruff.
asperón *m.* sandstone; grindstone.
aspersión *f.* aspersion, sprinkling.
aspersorio *m.* sprinkler, aspergillum.
áspid, áspide *m.* ZOOL. asp, aspic.
aspidistra *f.* BOT. aspidistra.
aspillera *f.* MIL. loophole.
aspiración *f.* aspiration. *2* MUS. short pause.
aspirado, -da *adj.* PHON. aspirate.
aspirador, -ra *adj.* sucking. *2 m. ~ de polvo*, vacuum cleaner.
aspirante *adj.* suction, sucking. *2 m.* aspirant, candidate.
aspirar *tr.* to inhale. *2* to suck, draw in. *3* PHYS., PHON. to aspirate. *5 intr. ~ a*, to aspire after or to; to be a candidate for.
aspiratorio, -ria *adj.* aspiratory.
aspirina *f.* PHARM. aspirin.
asquear *tr.* to loathe, be nauseated at. *2* to disgust, nauseate.

asquerosidad *f.* dirtiness, filthiness.
asqueroso, -sa *adj.* loathsome, dirty, filthy.
asta *f.* shaft [of a lance or pike]. *2* lance, pike. *3* flagstaff: *a media ~*, at half mast. *4* horn, antler. *5* handle [of a brush].
astado *m.* bull. *2* Roman pikeman.
astático, -ca *adj.* PHYS. astatic.
astenia *f.* MED. asthenia.
asténico, -ca *adj.-n.* asthenic.
asterisco *m.* asterisc (*).
asteroide *adj.* asteroid, starlike. *2 m.* ASTR. asteroid.
astigmático, -ca *adj.* astigmatic.
astigmatismo *m.* astigmatism.
astil *m.* handle, helve [of hoe, ax, etc.]. *2* beam [of balance]. *3* shaft [of arrow, of feaher]. *4* neck [of guitar].
astilla *f.* chip, splinter.
astillar *tr.* to chip, to splinter. *2 ref.* to splinter [be splintered].
astillero *m.* shipyard, dockyard. *2* rack for lances or pikes.
astracán *m.* astrakhan, astrachan.
astracanada *f.* THEAT. cheap farce.
astrágalo *m.* ANAT., ARCH., ARTILL. astragal. *2* BOT. milk vetch.
astral *adj.* astral.
astreñir *tr.* ASTRINGIR.
astricción *f.* astriction.
astringencia *f.* astringency.
astringente *adj.* astringent.
astringir *tr.* to astringe. *2* to astrict, bind.
astro *m.* star, heavenly body. *2* fig. star, luminary.
astrofísica *f.* astrophysics.
astrofísico, -ca *n.* astrophysicist. *2 f.* astrophysics.
astrolabio *m.* astrolabe.
astrología *f.* astrology.
astrológico, -ca *adj.* astrological.
astrólogo, -ga *m.-f.* astrologer. *2 adj.* astrological.
astronauta *m.-f.* astronaut.
astronáutica *f.* astronautics.
astronave *f.* spacecraft, spaceship.
astronomía *f.* astronomy.
astronómico, -ca *adj.* astronomic(al.
astrónomo *m.* astronomer.
astrosamente *adv.* uncleanly, slovenly, shabbily.
astroso, -sa *adj.* unclean, shabby. *3* vile, contemptible.
astucia *f.* astuteness, cunning. *2* trick, artifice.
astur, asturiano, -na *adj.-n.* Asturian.
Asturias *f. pr. n.* GEOG. Asturias.
astuto, -ta *adj.* astute, cunning, sly, crafty.
asueto *m.* brief vacation, day off, school holiday.
asumir *tr.* to assume [responsibilities, command, great proportions, etc.].
asunción *f.* assumption [taking to oneself]. *2* elevation [to a great dignity]. *3* (cap.) ECCLES. Assumption [of the Virgin].
asunto *m.* matter, subject. *2* affair, business. *3* LIT. theme or plot.
asustadizo, -za *adj.* easily frightened, scary, skittish.
asustar *tr.* to frighten, scare. *2 ref.* to be frightened, to take fright.
atabal *m.* kettledrum. *2* kettledrummer. *3* timbrel.
atacador *m.* rammer, ramroad.
atacante *adj.* attacking, assaulting, assailing. *2 m.* attacker, assailant, aggressor.
atacar *tr.* to attack. *2* to assail. *3* to impugn. *4* to

fasten, button [a garment]. *5* to ram, tamp, pack, stuff.

atadero *m.* tying cord, rope, etc. *2* part of a thing by which it is tied: *no tiene* ~, there is nothing to do with him [or it].

atadijo *m.* small bundle.

atado, -da *adj.* spiritless, irresolute. *2 m.* pack, bundle.

atador, -ra *adj.* binding. *2* string, rope, bond.

atadura *f.* tying, binding, fastening. *2* string, rope, bond. *3* union, connection.

atafagar *tr.* to stun [by strong odours]. *2* to pester, plague.

ataguía *f.* cofferdam.

atajar *intr.* to take a short cut. *2 tr.* to head off. *3* to stop, interrupt. *4* to cut [someone] short. *5* to partition off. *6 ref.* to stop short in confusion.

atajo *m.* short cut: *echar por el* ~, to take the easiest way out. *2* small herd or flock. *3* collection, lot.

atalaya *f.* watchtower; high lookout. *2 m.* guard, lookout [man].

atalayar *tr.* to watch [from a watchtower]. *2* to spy on.

ataludar *tr.* to slope, batter.

atanasia *f.* BOT. costmary. *2* PRINT. English type.

atanor *m.* earthen water pipe.

atañer *impers.* to concern, respect, regard.

ataque *m.* attack. *2* impugnation. *3* fit, access, stroke.

atar *tr.* to tie, fasten, lace, knot, bind; ~ *cabos*, to put two and two together. *2* to tie, stop: ~ *la lengua*, to prevent from speaking. *3 ref.* to bind oneself. *4* to become embarrassed or tied.

atarantado, -da *adj.* bitten by a tarantula. *2* restless, bustling. *3* bewildered, confused.

atarantar *tr.* to stun, to daze. *2* to bewilder.

ataraxia *f.* ataraxia, ataraxy, imperturbability.

atarazana *f.* shipyard, dockyard. *2* ropewalk.

1) **atardecer** *impers.* to draw towards the evening.

2) **atardecer** *m.* late afternoon, evenfall.

atareado, -da *adj.* busy.

atarear *tr.* to task, assign work to. *2 ref.* to toil, busy oneself.

atarjea *f.* drain pipe, sewer.

atarugamiento *m.* confusion, dumbfoundedness.

atarugar *tr.* CARP. to fasten with pegs or wedges. *2* to plug [a cask]. *3* to stuff, fill. *4* to silence, confuse. *5 ref.* to get confused.

atasajar *tr.* to jerk [meat].

atascadero *m.* mudhole. *2* difficulty, obstruction, blind alley, dead end.

atascamiento *m.* ATASCO.

atascar *tr.* to stop, clog, obstruct. *2* fig. to arrest [an affair]. *3 ref.* to be bogged. *4* to get stuck.

atasco *m.* sticking in the mud. *2* obstruction.

ataúd *m.* coffin [for a corpse].

ataujía *f.* damascene work.

ataviar *tr.* to dress, dress up, deck out, adorn. *2 ref.* to dress or adorn oneself.

atávico, -ca *adj.* atavistic.

atavío *m.* dress, adornment. *2 pl.* adornments.

atavismo *m.* atavism.

ataxia *f.* MED. ataxia.

ateísmo *m.* atheism.

atelaje *m.* harness [for horses]; team [of horses].

atemorizar *tr.* to intimidate, to frighten. *2 ref.* to become frightened.

atemperar *tr.* to temper, soften, moderate. *2* to adjust, accommodate.

atenacear *tr.* to tear off the flesh [of a person] with pincers. *2* to torture.

Atenas *f. pr. n.* GEOG. Athens.

atenazar *tr.* ATENACEAR. *2* to clench [one's teeth]. *3* to grip, tightly.

atención *f.* attention: *en* ~ *a*, considering, in view of. *2* civility, kindness. *3 pl.* affairs, duties, obligations. *4 interj.* ¡atención!, attention!

atender *intr.-tr.* to attend, pay attention. *2* to heed. *3* to take care [of]. *4* to attend, receive, serve, wait [upon]. *5 tr.* to listen to [entreaties, advice, etc.]; to comply with [someone's wishes]. ¶ CONJUG. like *entender*.

atendible *adj.* worthy of consideration.

atendré, atendría, etc. *irr.* V. ATENERSE.

ateneo *m.* athenaeum [literary club].

atenerse *ref.* ~ *a*, to abide by, stick to, keep to [an opinion, one's instructions, etc.]. ¶ CONJUG. like *tener*.

ateniense *adj.-n.* Athenian.

atenta *f. su* ~, yours, your favour [letter].

atentado, -da *adj.* prudent, moderate. *2 m.* abuse of power. *3* outrage, crime. *4* murder or attempted murder [of a high-placed person].

atentamente *adv.* attentively. *2* politely.

atentar *intr.* atentar contra, to commit outrage against; to attempt the life of.

atentatorio, -ria *adj.* contrary to [morals, law, etc.].

atento, -ta *adj.* attentive; watchful. *2* polite, courteous: *su* ~ *seguro servidor*, yours truly, yours faithfully.

atenuación *f.* attenuation, extenuation. *2* RHET. litotes.

atenuante *adj.* attenuating, extenuating. *2 m.* extenuating circumstance.

atenuar *tr.* to attenuate; to extenuate, diminish.

ateo, -a *adj.* atheist, atheistic. *2 m.-f.* atheist.

aterciopelado, -da *adj.* velvety.

aterido, -da *adj.* stiff with cold.

aterirse *tr. def.* to become stiff with cold.

aterrador, -ra *adj.* terrifying, dreadful.

aterrajar *tr.* MACH. to thread [a screw], to tap [a nut].

1) **aterrar** *intr.* AER. to land. *2* NAUT. to stand inshore. *3 tr.* to pull down, to demolish. ¶ CONJUG. like *acertar*.

2) **aterrar** *tr.-ref.* ATERRORIZAR.

aterrizaje *m.* AER. landing, alighting.

aterrizar *tr.* AER. to land, alight.

aterrorizador, -ra *adj.* terrifying, frightening, scary, terrific.

aterrorizar *tr.* to terrify. *2* to terrorize. *3 ref.* to be terrified.

atesorador *m.* hoarder.

atesoramiento *m.* hoarding, amassing, treasuring-up.

atesorar *tr.* to treasure, hoard up. *2* to possess [virtues, perfections, etc.].

atestación *f.* attestation, testimony.

atestado, -da *adj.* crammed. *2* obstinate, stubborn. *3 m.* LAW attestation, statement, certificate.

1) **atestar** *tr.* to pack, cram, stuff; to crowd. *2 ref.* to stuff oneself. ¶ CONJUG. like *acertar*.

2) **atestar** *tr.* to attest, witness.

atestiguar *tr.* to attest, testify, bear witness to.

atezado, -da *adj.* tan, tanned [by sun], sunburnt. *2* black, blackened.

atezar *tr.* to tan, make sunburnt. *2* to blacken. *3 ref.* to become sunburnt.

atiborrar *tr.* to pack, cram, stuff. *2* to stuff [with food]. *3 ref.* to stuff oneself.

ático, -ca *adj.-n.* Attic: *sal ática*, Attic salt. *3 m.* ARCH. attic.

atiendo, atienda, etc. *irr.* V. ATENDER.

atiento, atiente, etc. *irr.* V. ATENTARSE.

atiesar *tr.* to stiffen. *2* to tighten, tauten.

atiesto, atieste, etc. V. ATESTAR I).

atigrado, -da *adj.* marked like a tiger's skin.

Atila *m. pr. n.* Attila.

atildado, -da *adj.* neat, elegant.

atildamiento *m.* neatness, elegance. *2* rendering neat or elegant, tidying.

atildar *tr.* to render neat, to tidy, trim.

atinado, -da *adj.* right, judicious.

atinar *intr.-tr.* to hit [the mark]. *2* to hit upon, find, find out, guess, guess right.

atinente *adj.* concerning.

atiplado, -da *adj.* high-pitched, shrill, sharp; *voz* ~, high-pitched voice.

atiplar *tr.* MUS. to raise the pitch of [an instrument] to treble. *2 ref.* to rise to treble.

atirantar *tr.* to tighten, tauten. *2* ARCH. to stay, brace with ties.

atisbar *tr.* to peep, spy, observe.

atisbo *m.* ATISBADURA. *2* inkling.

¡atiza! *interj.* goodness me! oh my goodness! good Lord!

atizador, -ra *adj.* inciting, stirring. *2 m.* poker, fire poker.

atizar *tr.* to poke, stir [the fire]. *2* to trim [a lamp]. *3* to fan, stir up [passions, etc.]. *4* coll. to give [a blow]. *5 interj. ¡atiza!*, good gracious!

atizonarse *ref.* AGR. [of corn] to smut.

atlantes *m. pl.* ARCH. atlantes.

atlántico, -ca *adj. m. pr. n.* Atlantic.

atlas *m.* atlas [book of maps]. *2* ANAT. atlas.

Atlas *pr. n.* MYTH. Atlas. *2* GEOG. Atlas Mountains.

atleta *m.* athlete.

atlético, -ca *adj.* athletic. *2* robust [person].

atletismo *m.* athletics.

atmósfera *f.* atmosphere [in every sense].

atmosférico, -ca *adj.* atmospheric.

atoar *tr.* NAUT. to tow. *2* NAUT. to warp.

atocinado, -da *adj.* fig. coll. fat, fleshy, obese.

atocinar *tr.* to cut up [a pig]. *2* to make into bacon. *3* coll. to assassinate.

atocha *f.* ESPARTO.

atole *m.* (Am.) corn-flour gruel.

atolón *m.* GEOG. atoll.

atolondrado, -da *adj.* scatterbrained, giddy, thoughtless, inconsiderate. *3* bewildered, confused.

atolondramiento *m.* giddiness, thoughtlessness, inconsideration. *2* stunned state, bewilderment.

atolondrar *tr.* ATURDIR. *2 ref.* to become bewildered, confused.

atolladero *m.* ATASCADERO.

atollar *intr.-ref.* to get stuck in the mud. *2 ref.* to get stuck, obstructed.

atómico, -ca *adj.* atomic.

atomismo *m.* atomism.

atomización *f.* atomization, spraying.

atomizador *m.* atomizer, spray, pulverizer [for liquids].

atomizar *tr.* to atomize.

átomo *m.* atom.

atonal *adj.* MUS. atonal, toneless, atonic.

atonalidad *f.* MUS. atonality, tonelessness.

atonía *f.* MED. atony.

atónito, -ta *adj.* astonished, amazed, aghast.

átono, -na *adj.* GRAM., MED. atonic.

atontado, -da *adj.* stunned, confused. *2* stupid, silly.

atontamiento *m.* stunning, stunned state, stupefaction, bewilderment, confusion. *2* stupidity.

atontar *tr.* to stun, to stupefy. *2* to confuse, bewilder. *3 ref.* to become stunned, stupefied.

atorar *tr.* to obstruct, choke. *2 ref.* to become obstructed. *3* ATRAGANTARSE 2.

atormentador, -ra *adj.* tormenting. *2 m.-f.* tormentor, tormentress, torturer.

atormentar *tr.* to torment. *2* to torture. *3 ref.* to torment oneself, worry.

atornillar *tr.* to screw [turn a screw]. *2* to screw [on].

atorrante *m.* (Arg.) vagabond, loafer, beggar.

atorrantismo *m.* (Am.) vagrancy, vagabondage.

atortolar *tr.* to confound, rattle, intimidate.

atosigamiento *m.* poisoning. *2* pestering, annoyance, harassing.

atosigar *tr.* to poison. *2* to press, rush, harass. *3 ref.* to trouble, toil.

atrabancar *tr.-intr.* to hurry over, jump over.

atrabiliario, -ria *adj.* MED. atrabiliary, atrabilious. *2* bad-tempered. *3 m.-f.* bad-tempered person.

atrabilis *f.* black bile.

atracadero *m.* NAUT. landfall, landing place.

atracador, -ra *m.* bandit, robber, thief, raider.

atracar *tr.* to gorge [with food]. *2* to assault, *hold up. *3* NAUT. to bring alongside. *4 intr.* NAUT. to come alongside. *5 ref.* to gorge oneself.

atracción *f.* attraction.

atraco *m.* assault, robbery, *holdup.

atracón *m.* overeating, gorging.

atractivo, -va *adj.* attractive. *2* engaging, charming. *3 m.* charm, grace. *4* inducement, attraction.

atraer *tr.* to attract, draw. *2* to lure, allure. *3* to charm, captivate. ¶ CONJUG. like *traer*.

atragantarse *ref.* to chocke, stick in the throat. *2* to be choked [by something sticking in the throat]. *3* to get mixed up [in one's speech].

atraigo, atraiga, etc. *irreg.* V. ATRAER.

atraillar *tr.* to leash [dogs]. *2* to dominate, subjugate.

atrampar *tr.* to trap, entrap. *2 ref.* to fall in a trap. *3* [of a pipe] to become choked. *4* [of a lock] to become jammed. *5* to get stuck [in an affair].

atrancar *tr.* to bar [a door]. *2* to choke, obstruct. *3 intr.* coll. to take long strides. *4 ref.* to bar oneself in.

atranco *m.* ATOLLADERO. *2* snag, hole, difficulty.

atrapamoscas *m.* BOT. Venu's-fly-trap.

atrapar *tr.* to overtake, catch. *2* to catch, take; to get. *3* to trap, entrap, ensnare.

atrás *adv.* back, in the rear, behind: *dejar* ~, to leave behind; *volverse* ~, to turn back; *hacia* ~, backwards; *de* ~, back [adj.]; *la parte de* ~, the back. *2* ago: *días* ~, some days ago. *3 interj.* back!, go back!, back up!; go behind!

atrasado, -da *adj.* in debt, in arrears. *2* behindhand. *3* backward, dull. *4* behind the times. *5* slow [clock]. *6 número* ~, back number or copy. *7* ~ *de noticias*, ignorant of common things.

atrasar *tr.* to delay, postpone, retard. *2* to postdate [an event]. *3* to set back [a clock]. *4 intr.* [of a clock], to be slow. *5 ref.* to remain behind, lag, fall, back. *6* to be late. *7* to be in arrears, in debt.

atraso *m.* backwardness. *2* delay, lateness: *con*

diez minutos de ~, ten minutes late. *3* slowness [of a clock]. *4 pl.* arrearages, arrears.
atravesado, -da *adj.* pierced. *2* crossed, laid or stretched across. *4* cross-eyed, squint-eyed. *5* crossbred [animal]. *6* fig. wicked, treacherous.
atravesar *tr.* to cross [go across]. *2* to cross, span, bridge, lie across. *3* to put or lay across, athwart or crosswise. *4* to pierce; to transfix, run through; to pass through. *5* to interpose. *6* to bet, stake. *7 ref.* to come between; to be or come in the way of. *8* to butt in. *9* [of an obstacle, etc.] to interfere, arise, spring up. ¶ CONJUG. like *acertar.*
atravieso, atraviese, etc. *irr.* V. ATRAVESAR.
atrayente *adj.* attractive.
atreverse *ref.* to dare, venture, make bold. *2* ~ *con,* to be insolent to; to feel equal to.
atrevidamente *adv.* daringly, boldly, fearlessly. *2* insolently, rudely, shamelessly.
atrevido, -da *adj.* daring, bold. *2* forward, impudent.
atrevimiento *m.* daring, boldness. *2* forwardness, effrontery, impudence.
atribución *f.* attribution. *2* power, authority.
atribuir *tr.* to attribute. *2* to ascribe, impute. *3 ref.* to assume, take to oneself. ¶ CONJUG. like *huir.*
atribulado, -da *adj.* full of tribulation, distressed.
atribular *tr.* to grieve, afflict. *2 ref.* to be worried.
atributivo, -va *adj.* attributive.
atributo *m.* attribute.
atrición *f.* THEOL. attrition.
atril *m.* music stand; reading desk, lectern.
atrincheramiento *m.* MIL. entrenchment.
atrincherar *tr.* MIL. to entrench [surround with a trench]. *2 ref.* to entrench oneself, to dig in.
atrio *m.* ARCH., ZOOL. atrium.
atrito, -ta *adj.* THEOL. attrite.
atrocidad *f.* atrocity, atrociousness. *2* enormity, excess. *3* stupidity, foolish action.
atrofia *f.* atrophy.
atrofiarse *ref.* to atrophy [undergo atrophy].
atronado, -da *adj.* harebrained, reckless.
atronador, -ra *adj.* deafening, thundering.
atronar *tr.* to deafen. *2* to stun. *3* to kill [a bull] by a stab on the nape of the neck. ¶ CONJUG. like *contar.*
atropar *tr.-ref.* to troop, assemble in troops. *2 tr.* to pile [grain, hay, etc.].
atropelladamente *adv.* helter-skelter; hastily.
atropellado, -da *adj.* badly off. *2 adj.* headlong, hasty, impetuous, precipitate.
atropellador, -ra *adj.* brusque, precipitate, rash, hasty.
atropellar *tr.* to run down or over, trample, drive over. *2* to knock down, to push violently down or away. *3* to outrage, oppress, bully. *4* [of age, misfortune, etc.], to crush. *5* to do hastily. *6 tr.-intr.* to disregard [rights, difficulties, etc.]; to ride roughshod over. *7 ref.* to be hasty.
atropello *m.* running over [accident]. *2* high-handed proceeding, outrage, abuse.
atropina *f.* CHEM. atropine.
atroz *adj.* atrocious. *2* enormous, huge.
atrozmente *adj.* atrociously. *2* fig. awfully, terribly, horribly, dreadfully.
atrueno, atruene, etc. *irr.* V. ATRONAR.
atuendo *m.* dress. *2* pomp, ostentation.
atufar *tr.* to anger, irritate. *2 tr.-ref.* to overcome or be overcome [by fumes]. *3 ref.* to get angry. *4* [of food] to get smelly.
atufo *m.* anger, irritation.

atún *m.* ICHTH. tunny, tunny fish, tuna.
atunero, -ra *m.-f.* tunny dealer. *2 m.* tunny fisher.
aturdido, -da *p. p.* of ATURDIR. *2 adj.* ATOLONDRADO.
aturdimiento *m.* stunning. *2* bewilderment, giddiness. *3* amazement. *4* awkwardness.
aturdir *tr.* to stun, to deafen. *2* to make giddy. *3* to rattle, bewilder. *4* to amaze. *5 ref.* to be stunned, rattled, bewildered.
aturrullamiento *m.* ATOLONDRAMIENTO.
aturrullar *tr.* to rattle, confound.
atusar *tr.* to trim [the hair]; to comb or smooth [the hair]. *2* to trim [plants]. *3 ref.* to make oneself neat or trim, to dress elaborately.
atuve, atuviste, etc. *irr.* V. ATENERSE.
audacia *f.* audacity, boldness.
audaz, *pl.* audaces *adj.* audacious, bold.
audible *adj.* audible.
audición *f.* audition, hearing. *2* concert.
audiencia *f.* audience [formal interview]. *2* Spanish provincial or colonial high court.
audífonos *m. pl.* (Am.) earphones.
audiofrecuencia *f.* RADIO. audio-frequency.
audiovisual *adj.* audio-visual.
auditivo, -va *adj.* auditive.
auditor *m.* judge advocate. *2* ECCL. ~ *de la Rota,* auditor of the Rota.
auditorio, -ria *adj.* auditory. *2 m.* audience, auditory.
auge *m.* acme, culmination. *2* ASTR. apogee.
augur *m.* augur.
augurar *tr.* to augur, to augur of.
augurio *m.* augury; omen.
Augusto *m. pr. n.* Augustus.
augusto, -ta *adj.* august. *2 m.* august [clown].
aula *f.* class room, lecture room: ~ *magna,* assembly hall. *2* poet. palace.
aulaga *f.* BOT. furze, gorse.
áulico, -ca *adj.* aulic. *2 m.* courtier.
aullador, -ra *adj.* howling.
aullar *intr.* to howl.
aullido *m.* howl. *2* RADIO. howling, squealing.
aúllo *m.* AULLIDO.
aumentar *tr.-intr.-ref.* to augment, increase, magnify. *2 intr.-ref.* to grow, grow larger.
aumentativo, -va *adj.-n.* GRAM. augmentative.
aumento *m.* augmentation, increase, magnifying. *2* OPT. magnifying power.
aun *adv.* even, still: ~ *cuando,* although.
aún *adv.* yet, as yet, still.
aunar *tr.-ref.* to join, unite, combine. *2* to unify.
aunque *conj.* though, although, even though.
¡aúpa! *interj.* up, up! *2 de* ~, important.
aupar *tr.* to lift, to help up, give a leg up.
aura *f.* gentle breeze. *2* breath. *3* general favour, popularity. *4* MED., ORN. aura.
áureo, -a *adj.* golden, gold, aureous.
aureola, auréola *f.* THEOL., METEOR., ASTR. aureole. *2* fig. aureole, halo. *3* areola.
aureolar *tr.* to aureole.
aureomicina *f.* PHARM. aureomycin.
aurícula *f.* ANAT., BOT. auricle.
auricular *adj.* auricular. *2 m.* TELEPH. receiver, ear-piece. *3* RADIO. earphone.
aurífero, -ra *adj.* auriferous, gold-bearing.
auriga *m.* poet, coachman, charioteer. *2* (cap.) ASTR. Auriga, Wagoner.
aurora *f.* aurora, dawn. *2* fig. dawn, beginning. *3* METEOR. ~ *austral,* aurora australis; ~ *boreal,* aurora borealis.
auscultación *f.* MED. auscultation.
auscultar *tr.* MED. to auscultate.

ausencia *f.* absence. *2* lack.
ausentarse *ref.* to absent oneself.
ausente *adj.* absent. *2 m.-f.* absentee. *3* LAW missing person.
ausentismo *m.* absenteeism.
auspiciar *tr.* to patronize, to favour.
auspicio *m.* omen, auspice, augury. *2* sponsorship: *bajo los ~ de...* sponsored by...
austeridad *f.* austerity.
austero, -ra *adj.* austere.
austral *adj.* austral.
Australia *f. pr. n.* GEOG. Australia.
australiano, -na *adj.-n.* Australian.
Austria *f. pr. n.* GEOG. Austria.
austríaco, -ca *adj.-n.* Austrian.
austro *m.* south. *2* south wind.
autarquía *f.* autarchy, self-sufficiency.
auténtica *f.* certification. *2* LAW authentic copy.
autenticar *tr.* to authenticate.
autenticidad *f.* authenticity, genuineness.
auténtico, -ca *adj.* authentic, genuine.
autillo *m.* ORN. tawny owl.
auto *m.* judicial decree, writ, warrant. *2* coll. auto, car. *3* religious or biblical play. *4 ~ de fe,* auto-da-fé. *5 pl.* LAW proceeding: fig. *poner en autos,* to inform.
autobiografía *f.* autobiography.
autobombo *m.* self-glorification.
autobús *m.* bus, autobus.
autocamión *m.* autotruck, motor truck.
autocar *m.* coach, bus.
autoclave *f.* autoclave.
autocracia *f.* autocracy.
autócrata *m.* autocrat.
autocrítica *f.* self-examination, self-criticism.
autóctono, -na *adj.* autochthonous. *7 m.-f.* autochthon.
autodeterminación *f.* POL. self-determination.
autodidacto, -ta *adj.* self-taught.
autógeno, -na *adj.* autogenous [welding].
autogiro *m.* autogiro.
autografía *f.* autography.
autógrafo, -fa *adj.-m.* autograph.
autoinducción *f.* ELEC. self-induction.
automación *f.* automation.
autómata *m.* automaton.
automático, -ca *adj.* automatic(al.
automatismo *m.* automatism.
automatizar *tr.* to automate: *~ la fábrica,* to automate the factory.
automotor, triz *adj.* automotive. *2 m.* railway motor coach.
automóvil *adj.-m.* automobile.
automovilismo *m.* automobilism, motoring.
automovilista *adj.* automobile, automobilist. *2 m.-f.* automobilist, motorist.
autonomía *f.* autonomy. *2* home rule. *3* cruising radius [of a boat, airplane, etc.].
autonomista *adj.* autonomous. *2 n.* autonomist.
autonómico, -ca *adj.* autonomic.
autónomo, -ma *adj.* autonomous, autonomic.
autopista *f.* expressway, motorway.
autopropulsión *f.* self-propulsion.
autopsia *f.* autopsy, post-mortem examination.
autor, -ra *m.-f.* author, maker. *2* author, authoress [writer]. *3* perpetrator [of a crime].
autoría *f.* THEAT. treasurership.
autoridad *f.* authority. *2* person exercising power or command. *3* ostentation, pomp.
autoritario, -ria *adj.* authoritative, overbearing. *2 adj.-n.* authoritarian.

autoritarismo *m.* authoritarianism.
autorización *f.* authorization. *2* permit, license.
autorizadamente *adv.* with authority.
autorizado, -da *adj.* authorized. *2* empowered. *3* legalized. *4* respectable, responsible.
autorizar *tr.* to authorize. *2* to empower. *3* to permit. *4* to legalize. *5* to approve.
autorregulación *f.* self-regulation.
autorretrato *m.* self-portrait.
autostop *m.* hitchhiking: *hacer ~,* to hitchhike.
autosuficiencia *f.* self-sufficiency.
autosugestión *f.* autosuggestion.
autovía *f.* railway motor coach. *2* AUTOPISTA.
autumnal *adj.* OTOÑAL.
Auvernia *f. pr. n.* Auvergne.
auxiliador, -ra *adj.* helping, aiding. *2 m.-f.* helper, aider.
1) **auxiliar** *tr.* to help, aid; to assist. *2* to succour. *3* to attend [a dying person].
2) **auxiliar** *adj.* auxiliary. *2 m.* GRAM. auxiliary verb. *3* second class clerk. *4* professor's assistant.
auxilio *m.* help, aid, relief, assistance.
aval *m.* COM. guarantor's signature [in a bill of exchange]. *2* POL. guarantee of conduct.
avalancha *f.* avalanche.
avalar *tr.* to put an AVAL on [a bill of exchange]. *2* to answer for [a person].
avalentonado, -da *adj.* swaggering, bullying.
avalorar *tr.* to render valuable.
avaluar *tr.* VALUAR.
avalúo *m.* VALUACIÓN.
avance *m.* advance [going forward; payment beforehand]. *2* COM. balance sheet. *3* COM. estimate.
avantrén *m.* ARTILL. limber.
avanzada *f.* MIL. outpost; advance guard.
avanzado, -da *adj.* advanced [in age, in ideas]. *2* far into [the night, etc.].
avanzar *intr.* to advance [move forward]. *2* to advance, progress. *3 intr.-ref.* [of night, winter, etc.] to be approaching its end.
avaramente *adv.* avariciously, niggardly.
avaricia *f.* avarice.
avaricioso, -sa *adj.* AVARIENTO.
avariento, -ta *adj.* avaricious, miserly. *2 m.-f.* miser.
avaro, -ra *adj.-n.* AVARIENTO. *2 m.-f.* stinter.
avasallador, -ra *adj.* overwhelming. *2* domineering. *3 m.-f.* subjugator.
avasallar *tr.* to subjugate. *2 ref.* to become a vassal; to submit.
ave *f.* ORN. bird: *~ de corral,* domestic fowl; *~ de paso,* bird of passage; *~ del Paraíso,* bird of Paradise; *~ de rapiña,* or *rapaz,* bird of prey; *~ lira,* lyrebird.
avecilla *f. dim.* little bird.
avecinar *tr.* AVECINDAR. *2 ref.* to approach, be coming.
avecindar *tr.* to domicile. *2 ref.* to take up residence [at or in].
avechucho *m.* ugly bird.
avefría *f.* ORN. lapwing.
avejentar *tr.-ref.* to age [before one's time].
avejigar *tr.* to blister. *2 ref.* to blister [become blistered].
avellana *f.* BOT. hazel nut; filbert [nut].
avellanado, -da *adj.* shriveled; wizened.
avellanador *m.* countersink [bit].
avellanal, avellanar *m.* hazel plantation.
avellanar *tr.* MACH. to countersink. *2 ref.* to shrivel.
avellaneda *f.,* **avellanedo** *m.* AVELLANAL.

avellano *m.* BOT. hazel, hazel tree, filbert.
avemaría *f.* Hail Mary: *en un* ~, in a twinkle. *2* Angelus bell; *al* ~, at dusk.
¡Ave María! *interj.* gracious goodnes!
avena *f.* BOT. oats. *2* ~ *loca*, wild oats.
avenar *tr.* to drain [land].
avenate *m.* drink made with oatmeal.
avendré, avendría, etc. *irr.* V. AVENIR.
avenencia *f.* agreement, compact, coming to terms. *2* harmony, concord.
avengo, avenga, etc. *irr.* V. AVENIR.
avenida *f.* flood, freshet. *2* avenue. *3* wide street.
avenido, -da *adj. bien o mal* ~, *con*, on good or bad terms with; agreeing or disagreeing with.
avenir *tr.* to make agree, to reconcile. *2 ref.* to agree, to get along well together. *3* to agree, come to an agreement. *4* to consent, resign oneself to.
aventador, -ra *m.-f.* winnower. *2 f.* winnowing machine. *3 m.* winnowin fork. *4* esparto fan [for fanning fire].
aventajado, -da *adj.* notable, excellent. *2* advantageous.
aventajar *tr.* to surpass, excel. *2* to advance, better. *3 ref.* to better oneself.
aventar *tr.* to fan, to blow. *2* to winnow. *3* to strew to the wind. *4* fig. to expel, drive away. *5 ref.* to swell up [with air]. *6* coll. to flee. ¶ CONJUG. like *acertar.*
aventura *f.* adventure. *2* hazard, chance, risk.
aventurado, -da *adj.* venturesome, risky.
aventurar *tr.* to venture, hazard, risk. *2 ref.* to adventure, risk, take the risk.
aventurero, -ra *adj.* adventure-seeking. *2 m.* adventurer; gentleman of fortune. *3* mercenary. *4 f.* adventuress.
avergonzar *tr.* to shame, put to shame, confound; to abash. *2 ref.* to be ashamed or abashed, to blush. ¶ CONJ. like *contar.*
avergüenzo, avergüence etc. *irr.* V. AVERGONZAR.
avería *f.* COM. damage. *2* NAUT. average. *3* MACH. failure, breakdown. *4* AVERÍO.
averiado, -da *adj.* damaged [esp. said of goods].
averiarse *ref.* to be damaged [esp. said of goods].
averiguación *f.* inquiry, acertainment.
averiguar *tr.* to inquire, ascertain, find out.
averno *m.* Avernus. *2* poet, hell.
averrugado, -da *adj.* full of warts, warty.
aversión *f.* aversion, dislike, loathing.
avestruz *f.* ORN. ostrich.
avetoro *m.* ORN. bittern, European bittern.
avezar *tr.* to accustom, inure. *2 ref.* to become accustomed, inured.
aviación *f.* aviation. *2* aviation corps, air force.
aviador, -ra *adj.* preparing, equipping. *2* AER. air [pilot]. *3 m.-f.* preparer, equipper. *4* AER. aviator, aviatrix, airman, airwoman.
aviar *tr.* to prepare, arrange. *2* to equip, provide. *3* to hasten. *4 estar uno aviado*, to be in a mess.
avícola *adj.* bird-rearing.
avicultor, -ra *m.-f.* aviculturist.
avicultura *f.* aviculture.
avidez *f.* avidity, greed. *2* eagerness.
ávido, -da *adj.* avid, eager, greedy.
aviene, avienes, etc. *irr.* V. AVENIR.
avieso, -sa *adj.* crooked, irregular. *2* evil-minded, perverse, malicious, wicked.
avilés, -a *adj.-n.* of Ávila.
avinagrado, -da *adj.* vinegary, sour, crabbed.
avinagrar *tr.* to sour, make sour. *2 ref.* to sour, to turn sour or vinegary.

avine, aviniera, etc. *irr.* V. AVENIR.
Aviñón *m. pr. n.* GEOG. Avignon.
avío *m.* preparation, provision. *2 pl.* tools, tackel, equipment. *3 interj. ¡al avío!,* hurry up!
avión *m.* AER. airplane: ~ *de caza*, pursuit plane; ~ *de combate*, fighter; ~ *de reacción*, jet plane; ~ *de línea*, air liner. *2* ORN. martin.
avioneta *f.* AER. light airplane.
avisado, -da *adj.* prudent, wise, shrewd: *mal* ~, ill-advised.
avisador *m.* adviser. *2* warner. *3* ~ *de incendios*, fire alarm.
avisar *tr.* to inform. *2* to send word. *3* to warn; to advise, admonish.
aviso *m.* notice, information; warning. *2* admonishment, advice. *3* prudence, attention, caution: *sobre* ~, on the alert. *4* NAUT. dispatch boat.
avispa *f.* ENT. wasp.
avispado, -da *adj.* keen-witted, clever, smart.
avispar *tr.* to whip, urge [horses]. *2* to make clever. *4 ref.* to become lively or clever.
avispero *m.* wasp's nest. *2* swarm of wasps. *3* MED. carbuncle.
avispón *m.* ENT. hornet.
avistar *tr.* to sight, descry, get sight of. *2 ref.* to have an interview.
avitaminosis *f.* MED. avitaminosis.
avituallamiento *m.* provisioning, food-supplying. *2* NAUT. victualling.
avituallar *tr.* to victual, to provision.
avivado, -da *adj.* quick, lively, bright, spirited. *2* made brighter or livelier [a color]. *3* made quicker, livelier [the pace]. *4* excited, provoked, roused [the anger].
avivador, -ra *adj.* enlivening, stirring up.
avivar *tr.* to enliven, to stir up. *2* to heat, inflame, intensify. *3* to quicken, hasten. *4* to revive [the fire]. *5* to heighten, brighten [light, colours]. *6* intr.-ref. to acquire life, vigour; to revive.
avizor *adj.* watching: *ojo* ~, on the alert.
avizorar *tr.* to watch, spy.
avocar *tr.* LAW. to remove [a lawsuit] to a superior court.
avoceta *f.* ORN. avocet.
avutarda *f.* ORN. great bustard.
axial, axil *adj.* axial, axile.
axila *f.* ANAT. axilla, armpit. *2* BOT. axil.
axilar *adj.* axillar, axillary.
axioma *m.* axiom.
axiomático, -ca *adj.* axiomatic.
axis *m.* ANAT. axis.
ay, *pl.* **ayes** *m.* sigh, moan.
¡ay! *interj.* alas!, ouch!: *¡~ de...!,* woe to ...!; *¡~ de mí!*, woe is me!, ah me!
aya *f.* governess. *2* dry nurse.
ayeaye *m.* ZOOL. aye-aye.
ayer *adv.-m.* yesterday.
ayo *m.* tutor [private teacher].
ayuda *f.* help, aid, assistance. *2* MED. enema. *3* ~ *de cámara*, valet, valet de chambre.
ayudante *m.* aid, assistant. *2* substitute teacher. *3* MIL. aid, aide; adjutant.
ayudantía *f.* assistantship. *2* MIL. adjutancy.
ayudar *tr.* to help, aid, assist.
ayuga *f.* BOT. mock cypress.
ayunar *intr.* to fast.
ayunas (en) *adv.* fasting. *2* without [or before] eating breakfast: *estar en* ~, not to have eaten breakfast, to have no idea; *quedarse en* ~, not to understand a thing.
ayuno, -na *adj.* having taken no food. *2* deprived.

3 uninformed. *4 adv. en ayunas* or *en ayuno*, before, breakfasting; having taken no food; uninformed; not understanding. *5 m.* fast, fasting.

ayuntamiento *m.* town or city council. *2* town or city hall. *3* sexual intercourse.

ayustar *tr.* NAUT. to splice.

azabachado, -da *adj.* jet, jet-black.

azabache *m.* MINER. jet. *2* ORN. coal titmouse.

azacán, -na *adj.* menial, drudging. *2 m.-f.* drudge.

azada *f.* AGR. hoe.

azadilla *f.* ALMOCAFRE.

azadón *m.* AGR. hoe. *2 ~ de pico*, mattock.

azadonada *f.* stroke with a hoe.

azadonar *tr.* to hoe, hoe up, dig with a hoe.

azafata *f.* lady of the queen's wardrobe. *2* AER. air hostess.

azafate *m.* flat basket, tray.

azafrán *m.* BOT. saffron [plant and dried stigmas].

azafranado, -da *adj.* saffron, saffroned.

azafranal *m.* saffron plantation.

azafranar *tr.* to saffron.

azagaya *f.* assagai, javelin.

azahar *m.* orange, lemon or citron blossom.

azalea *f.* BOT. azalea.

azamboa *f.* BOT. kind of citron [fruit].

azamboero, azamboo *m.* BOT. kind of citron [tree].

azar *m.* hazard, chance: *al ~*, at random, haphazard. *2* accident, mishap.

azarado, -da *adj.* troubled, rattled, flustered.

azarosamente *adv.* with difficulties.

azaroso, -sa *adj.* misfortunate, unlucky.

ázimo, -ma *adj.* azymous, unleavened.

azimut *m.* ACIMUT.

aznacho *m.* BOT. pinaster, cluster pine.

azoar *tr.* to azotize.

ázoe *m.* CHEM. azote.

azófar *m.* brass, latten.

azogadamente *adv.* agitatedly.

azogado, -da *adj.-n.* [person] affected with mercurialism: *temblar como un ~*, to shake like a leaf. *2 m.* quicksilvering [in a mirror].

azogamiento *m.* quicksilvering. *2* MED. mercurialism. *3* shaking, agitation.

azogar *tr.* to quicksilver, to silver [a mirror]. *2 ref.* to be affected with mercurialism. *3* to get troubled, agitated.

azogue *m.* mercury, quicksilver: *ser un ~*, to be restless. *2* market place.

azoico, -ca *adj.* CHEM., GEOL. azoic.

azolar *tr.* to adze. ¶ CONJUG. like *contar.*

azor *m.* ORN. goshawk.

azorado, -da *adj.* embarrassed, flustered, confused and ashamed.

azoramiento *m.* trouble, fluster, embarrassment.

azorar *tr.* to trouble, rattle, startle. *2 ref.* to get troubled, rattled, startled.

Azores *f. pr. n.* GEOG. Azores.

azorrarse *ref.* to be drowsy from heaviness.

azotacalles *m.* gadabout, loafer, street lounger.

azotado, -da *adj.* variegated.

azotaina *f.* flogging; spanking.

azotamiento *m.* whipping, flogging.

azotar *tr.* to whip, flog. *2* to flagellate. *3* to spank. *4* [of sea, rain, etc.] to beat, lash.

azotazo *m.* troke, lash, lashing. *2* spank.

azote *m.* birch, thong, scourge, etc. [for flogging]. *2* AZOTAZO. *3* fig. scourge. *4 pl.* public flogging.

azotea *f.* flat roof [of a house].

azteca *adj.-n.* Aztec.

azúcar *m.-f.* sugar: *~ blanco*, refined sugar; *~ cande*, rock candy; *~ de cortadillo*, lump sugar; *~ moreno*, brown sugar.

azucarado, -da *adj.* sugared, sweedtened, made sweet: *yogur ~*, sugared yogurt. *2* sweet. *3* fig. sugary, syrupy, sweet.

azucarar *tr.* to sugar. *2* to coat or ice with sugar.

azucarera *f.* sugar bowl. *2* sugar factory.

azucarero, -ra *adj.* [pertaining to] sugar. *2 m.* sugar producer. *3* sugar bowl.

azucarillo *m.* spongy sugar bar.

azucena *f.* BOT. Madonna lily, white lily.

azud, azuda *f.* irrigation water wheel. *2* irrigation dam.

azuela *f.* adze.

azufaifa *f.* jujube [fruit].

azufaifo *m.* BOT. jujube [tree].

azufrado, -da *adj.* sulphured. *2* sulphur, sulphureous. *3 m.* sulphuring.

azufrar *tr.* to sulphur, sulphurate, sulphurize.

azufre *m.* CHEM. sulphur, brimstone.

azufrera *f.* sulphur mine.

azul *adj.-m.* blue: *~ celeste*, sky blue; *~ marino*, navy blue; *~ turquí*, indigo.

azulado, -da *adj.* blue, bluish.

azular *tr.* to colour blue, to dye blue.

azulear *tr.* to have a bluish cast. *2* to show blue.

azulejo *m.* Dutch tile, glazed tile.

azulete *m.* blue, bluing [powder].

azulino, -na *adj.* bluish.

azumbre *m.* a liquid measure [about 2 litres].

azur *adj.-m.* HER. azure.

azurita *f.* MINER. azurite.

azuzar *tr.* to set [the dogs] on. *2* to incite.

B

B, b *f.* B, b, second letter of the Spanish alphabet.
Baal *m. pr. n.* Baal.
baba *f.* drivel, slaver, slobber: *caérsele a uno la* ~, to be silly; to be delighted. *2* BABAZA 1.
babada *f.* BABILLA.
babaza *f.* mucus, slime. *2* ZOOL. slug.
babear *intr.* to drivel, slaver, slobber, drool.
babel *f.* babel, bedlam. *2 pr. n.* (cap.) Babel.
babeo *m.* drivelling, slobbering [flow of saliva].
babera *f.* beaver [of helmet]. *2* BABERO.
babero *m.* bib, chin-cloth.
Babia *f. estar en* ~, to be absent in mind.
babieca *adj.* silly. *2 m.-f.* simpleton.
Babilonia *f. pr. n.* HIST. GEOG. Babylon. *2* (not cap.) babel, bedlam, uproar.
babilónico, -ca *adj.* Babylonian.
babilonio, -nia *adj.-n.* Babylonian.
babilla *f.* VET. stifle.
babirusa *m.* ZOOL. babirusa.
bable *m.* Asturian [dialect].
babor *m.* port, larboard.
babosa *f.* ZOOL. slug.
babosear *tr.* to cover with saliva, to slaver. *2 intr.* coll. BABEAR.
baboseo *m.* dribbling [a baby] slobbering, slavering. *2* foaming, frothing. *3* slime. *4* fig. drooling, drivelling.
baboso, -sa *adj.* slavering, drooling. *2 m.-f.* slaverer, drooler. *3 adj.-m.* spoony. *4 m.* brat.
babucha *f.* babouche.
babuino, -na *n.* ZOOL. baboon.
baca *f.* top [of stagecoach]. *2* rainproof cover [for a stagecoach].
bacalao *m.* ICHTH. codfish.
bacanal *adj.* bacchanal, bacchanalian. *2 f.* bacchanalia. *3 pl. bacanales,* Bacchanalia.
bacante *f.* bacchante. *2* drunken, riotous woman.
bacará *m.* baccarat.
bacelar *m.* arbour with grapevines.
bacía *f.* basin; shaving basin.
bacilar *adj.* bacillary.
baciliforme *adj.* bacilliform, rod-shaped.
bacilo *m.* bacillus.
bacín *m.* chamber pot. *2* cur, despicable man.
bacineta *f.* small basin; alms plate.
bacinete *m.* basinet. *2* ANAT. pelvis.
Baco *m. pr. n.* Bacchus.

baconiano, -na *adj.-n.* baconian [of Francis Bacon].
bacteria *f.* bacterium. *2 pl.* bacteria.
bactericida *adj.* bactericidal, germ-kill-ing. *2 m.* bactericide, germicide.
bacteriología *f.* bacteriology.
bacteriólogo *m.* bacteriologist.
báculo *m.* stick, staff. *2* fig. support, relief, comfort, aid. *3* ~ *pastoral,* crozier, pastoral staff.
bache *m.* hole [in a road]. *2* AER. ~ *de aire,* air pocket.
bachiller, -ra *adj.* garrulous. *2 m.-f.* babbler, gossip. *3* bachelor [holder of degree].
bachillerato *m.* baccalaureate.
bachillerear *intr.* to babble, to gossip.
bachillería *f.* babbling, gossiping.
badajada *f.* stroke [of bell]. *2* stupidity, nonsense.
badajo *m.* clapper [of bell]. *2* coll, stupid babbler.
badajocense *adj.-n.* of Badajoz.
badana *f.* basan, dressed sheepskin: fig. *zurrarle a uno la* ~, to tan someone's hide.
badén *m.* channel made by rain water. *2* paved trench for a stream across a road.
badián *m.* BOT. Chinese anise.
badil *m.,* **badila** *f.* small fire shovel.
badulaque *m.* nincompoop, simpleton.
baga *f.* flax boll.
bagaje *m.* MIL. baggage. *2* MIL. beast of burden. *3* coll. a person's store of knowledge or information.
bagatela *f.* bagatelle, trifle.
bagazo *m.* flax chaff. *2* bagasse. *3* waste pulp [of olives, oranges, etc.].
bagre *m.* ICHTH. South American catfish.
baguarí *m.* ORN. (Am.) kind of stork.
¡bah! *interj.* bah!
baharí *m.* ORN. sparrow hawk.
bahía *f.* [sea] bay.
bailable *adj.* dance [music]. *2 m.* THEAT. dance number.
bailador, -ra *adj.* dancing. *2 m.-f.* dancer.
bailar *intr.* to dance. *2* [of a top] to spin. *3 tr.* to dance [some dance]. *4* to dance; dandle.
bailarín, -na *adj.* dancing. *2 m.-f.* dancer.
baile *m.* dance; ball: ~ *casero,* informal dance; ~ *de etiqueta,* dress ball, formal dance; ~ *de máscaras,* masked ball, masquerade; ~ *de San Vito,* MED. St. Vitu's dance. *2* obs. bailiff [in Aragon].

bailiaje *m.* bailiage. *2* commandery in the order of Malta.

bailío *m.* knight commander of Malta.

bailotear *intr.* to dance a lot and ungracefully.

bailoteo *m.* ungraceful dancing.

baivel *m.* bevel square with a curved leg.

bajá, *pl.* **bajaes** *m.* pasha.

baja *f.* fall, drop [in prices, in value, etc.]: *jugar a la ~,* COM. to bear [speculate for a fall]; *ir de ~,* to decline. *2* MIL. casualty. *3* cancelled subscription. *4 dar de ~,* to cross out from a list of members, subscribers, etc.; MIL. to muster out; *darse de ~,* to cease to be a subscriber; to resign membership [of] voluntarily.

bajada *f.* descent. *2 ~ de aguas,* rainwater pipe, leader. *3* sloping street.

bajamar *f.* low tide, low water.

bajar *intr.* to descend, come down, go down. *2* to fall, drop, lessen, diminish. *3* to descend, sink, slope downwards. *4* to alight, get down. *5 tr.* to bring down, get down, lower, drop. *6* to descend [stairs, a slope, etc.]. *7* to lower, bow [one's head, body, etc.]: *~ los ojos,* to cast one's eyes down. *8* to lower reduce [the price, etc.]. *9 ref.* to stoop, bend down. *10* to alight [from carriage, etc.].

bajel *m.* ship, boat, vessel.

bajete *m.* MUS. bariton. *2* MUS. counterpoint exercise.

bajeza *f.* baseness, meanness; lowliness. *2* low action.

bajío *m.* shoal, sand bank. *2* (Am.) lowland.

bajista *m.* bear [in stock market].

bajo *adv.* softly, in a low voice. *2 prep.* beneath, under; on: *~ mano,* underhandly, secretly; *~ pena de muerte,* on pain of death; *~ techado,* under a roof, sheltered.

bajo, -ja *adj.* low [in practically every sense]: *~ latín,* low latin; *~ relieve,* bass-relief; *por lo ~,* secretly. *2* short [not tall]. *3* downcast [head, eyes, etc.]. *4* base [gold, metal]. *5* dull [colour]. *6* base, vile. *7* lower: *la clase ~,* the lower classes. *8 piso ~, planta baja,* ground floor. *9 m.* hollow, deep. *10* shoal, sand-bank. *11 pl.* lower part of trousers or skirts. *12* ground floor; ground-floor rooms.

bajón *m.* MUS. bassoon. *2* bassoonist. *3* decline, drop [in health, wealth, etc.]. *4* great fall [in prices].

bajonista *m.* bassoonist.

bajorrelieve *m.* low relief, bas relief.

bajuno, -na *adj.* low, coarse [people].

bajura *f.* lowness.

bakelita *f.* bakelite.

bala *f.* bullet, ball, shot: *~ perdida,* stray bullet; fig. flighty person; *~ rasa,* solid cannon ball. *2* bale [of goods]. *3* ten reams [of paper].

balada *f.* ballad [poem].

baladí *adj.* trivial, trifling.

baladrón *m.* braggart, bully, rodomont.

baladronada *f.* boast, brag, bravado, rodomontade.

baladronear *intr.* to brag, to play the bully.

bálago *m.* straw, grain stalk.

balaj, balaje *m.* balas, balas ruby.

balance *m.* oscillation; [a single movement of] swinging, rocking, rolling. *2* vacillation. *3* COM. balancing, balance, balance sheet.

balancear *intr.-ref.* to rock, swing, roll. *2 intr.* to hesitate, waver. *3 tr.* to balance, counterpoise.

balanceo *m.* swinging, rocking, rolling.

balancín, *pl.* **-nes** *m.* whippletree. *2* MACH. walking beam. *3* ropewalker's balancing pole. *4* small coining press. *5* balancer, halter [of insect].

balandra *f.* NAUT. sloop.

balandro *m.* NAUT. small sloop.

bálano *m.* ANAT. glans. *2* ZOOL. acorn barnacle.

balanza *f.* balance, scales. *2* comparative estimate, judgment. *3 ~ comercial,* balance of trade. *4 en ~,* undecided, in danger.

balar *intr.* to bleat, baa.

balastar *tr.* RLY. to ballast.

balasto *m.* RLY. ballast.

balaustrada *f.* balustrade, banisters.

balaustrado, -da *adj.* baluster-shaped.

balaustre, balaústre *m.* baluster.

balazo *m.* shot; bullet wound.

balbucear *intr.* to stammer, hesitate in speech. *2* [of a child] to babble.

balbucencia *f.,* **balbuceo** *m.* stammering. *2* babble [of a child].

balbuciente *adj.* stuttering, stammering. *2* babbling.

balbucir *intr.* BALBUCEAR. ¶ Only used in forms having *i* in their terminations.

Balcanes (los) *m. pr. n.* GEOG. the Balkans.

balcánico, -ca *adj.-n.* Balkan.

balcón *m.* balcony [of a house].

balconaje *m.* balconies [of a house].

baldadura *f.,* **baldamiento** *m.* physical disability.

baldado, -da *adj.* invalid, physically disabled.

baldaquín, baldaquino *m.* baldachin.

baldar *tr.* to cripple, disable physically. *2* to annoy.

balde *m.* bucket, pail. *2 adv. de ~,* free, for nothing. *3 en ~,* in vain.

baldear *tr.* to wash [decks or floors] with buckets of water. *2* NAUT. to bail.

baldeo *m.* washing the decks. *2* washing, cleaning.

baldíamente *adv.* in vain, vainly; idly.

baldío, -día *adj.* untilled, uncultivated. *2* vain, idle. *3* idle, lazy.

baldón *m.* insult, affront. *2* blot, disgrace.

baldonar *tr.* to insult, to affront.

baldosa *f.* floor tile.

baldosado *m.* tiling, flagging, paving with tiles or flagstones. *2* tiled floor flooring.

baldosar *tr.* to tile, to flag, to pave with tiles or flagstones.

baldosín *m.* small floor tile.

baldragas *m.* weak, soft fellow.

balduque *m.* red tape.

balear *tr.* (Am.) to shoot [wound or kill].

balear, baleárico *adj.* Balearic.

balénidos *m. pl.* ZOOL. whales.

baleo *m.* round mat.

balido *m.* bleat, bleating, baa.

balín *m.* small bullet, buckshot.

balista *f.* ballista.

balístico, -ca *adj.* ballistic. *2 f.* ballistics.

baliza *f.* buoy, beacon.

balizar *tr.* ABALIZAR.

balneario, -ria *adj.* [pertaining to] bath. *2 m.* [medicinal] baths; watering place, spa.

balompié *m.* football [game].

balón *m.* [a large inflated] ball; a football. *2* bag [for holding a gas]. *3* CHEM. balloon.

baloncesto *m.* basketball.

balonmano *m.* handball.

balonvolea *m.* volleyball.

balota *f.* ballot [small voting ball].

balotaje *m.* (Am.) voting. *2* tie, draw [in an election].
balsa *f.* pool, pond. *2* NAUT. raft, float. *3* ~ *de aceite*, fig. quiet place or assembly.
balsadera *f.*, **balsadero** *m.* ferry.
balsámico, -ca *adj.* balsamic, balmy.
balsamina *f.* BOT. balsam apple. *2* BOT. impatiens, garden balsam.
bálsamo *m.* BOT., PHARM. balsam, balm. *2* fig. balm [something soothing].
balsear *tr.* to ferry [a river] on rafts.
balsero *m.* ferryman.
Baltasar *m. pr. n.* Balthasar. *2* Belshazzar [from Babylonia].
báltico, -ca *adj.* Baltic. *2 pr. n.* (cap.) Baltic Sea.
baluarte *m.* FORT. bastion. *2* fig. bulwark, defence.
balumba *f.* bulk, mass of many things thrown together.
ballena *f.* ZOOL. whale. *2* whalebone. *3* bone [of corset]. *4 pr. n.* ASTR. Whale, Cetus.
ballenato *m.* young whale, whale calf.
ballenera *f.* NAUT. whaleboat.
ballenero, -ra *adj.* whale, whaling: *barco* ~, whaler. *2 m.* whaler, whaleman.
ballesta *f.* crossbow, arbalest. *2* carriage spring.
ballestería *f.* hunting, chase. *2* crossbows. *3* cross-bowmen. *4* crossbowmen's quarters.
ballestero *m.* crossbowman, arbalester. *2* maker of crossbows. *3* royal armourer.
ballestilla *f.* small singletree. *2* NAUT. cross-staff, forestaff. *3* VET. fleam.
ballet *m.* ballet [dance and music].
ballico *m.* BOT. Italian rye grass.
ballueca *f.* BOT. wild oats.
bambalear *intr.-ref.* BAMBOLEAR.
bambalinas *f. pl.* THEAT. flies, borders.
bambarria *m.-f.* dolt, fool. *2 f.* fluke [at billiards].
bamboche *m.* short and chubby person.
bambolear *intr.-ref.* to sway, swing.
bamboleo *m.* swaying, swinging.
bambolla *f.* show, sham, pretence.
bambollero, -ra *adj.* bragging, boastful, swanky. *2* showy, flashy.
bambú *m.* BOT. bamboo.
banal *adj.* banal, commonplace, trivial, uninteresting.
banalidad *f.* banality, triviality, triteness.
banana *f.* BOT. banana.
banano *m.* BOT. banana [plant].
banasta *f.* large basket.
banasto *m.* large round basket.
banca *f.* COM. banking. *2* a card game. *3* bank [in gambling]. *4* bench. *5* washing box.
bancada *f.* MACH. bed, bedplate; sideframe. *2* NAUT. thwart, bank. *3* portion of masonry. *4* MIN. shelf.
bancal *m.* AGR. terrace. *2* AGR. oblong plot. *3* bench cover.
bancario, -ria *adj.* COM. bank, banking.
bancarrota *f.* bankruptcy: *hacer* ~, to go bankrupt.
banco *m.* bench, form; pew. *2* bench [working table]. *3* bank, shoal. *4* school [of fishes]. *5* MIN. bench. *6* GEOL. stratum. *7* COM. bank.
banda *f.* scarf, sash [worn baldric-wise]. *2* band, strip. *3* band, gang; flock, herd. *4* side, border: *cerrarse a la* ~, to stand firm. *5* side [of ship]; *dar a la* ~, to careen. *6* cushion [of billiard table]. *7* MUS., RADIO. band: ~ *de tambores*, drum corps. *8* CINEM. ~ *de sonido*, sound track.
bandada *f.* flock [of birds], covey.
bandazo *m.* NAUT. lurch [sudden roll to one side].

bandear *tr.* to cross, to go across. *2* to shoot through. *3* to pursue, to chase, to run after. *4* to wound, to harm. *5* to court, to woo [a woman]. *6 ref.* to manage, to get by, to take care of oneself.
bandeja *f.* tray.
bandera *f.* flag, banner, ensign, colours: ~ *blanca*, white flag; ~ *negra*, black jack; *a banderas desplegadas*, openly; *con banderas desplegadas*, with flying colours; *de* ~, wonderful, extraordinary.
bandería *f.* faction, party.
banderilla *f.* BANDERITA. *2* barbed dart used in bull-fighting: *clavar, poner una* ~ fig. to taunt, to be sarcastic to.
banderillear *tr.* to thrust banderillas into the neck of [a bull].
banderillero *m.* banderillero.
banderín *m.* small flag; camp colour. *2* recruiting post. *4* RLY. flag.
banderita *f.* small flag.
banderizo, -za *adj.* factional. *2* seditious. *3 m.* factionist, partisan.
banderola *f.* banderole. *2* SURV. fanion.
bandidaje *m.* BANDOLERISMO.
bandido *m.* outlaw. *2* bandit. *3* rascal.
bando *m.* faction, party. *2* edict, proclamation.
bandola *f.* MUS. mandore. *2* NAUT. jury mast.
bandolera *f.* female brigand. *2* bandoleer, bandolier.
bandolerismo *m.* brigandage.
bandolero *m.* brigand, robber, highwayman.
bandolina *f.* bandoline.
bandoneón *m.* MUS. concertina.
bandullo *m.* coll. guts, bowels.
bandurria *f.* MUS. bandurria, bandore.
baniano *m.* banian.
banjo *m.* MUS. banjo.
banquero *m.* COM. banker. *2* banker [in gambling].
banqueta *f.* stool, footstool. *2* FORT. banquette. *3* little bench. *4* (Mex.) sidewalk.
banquete *m.* banquet, feast.
banquetear *intr.-tr.* to banquet.
banquillo *m.* stool, little bench. *2* prisoner's seat [in court], dock.
banquisa *f.* ice field, ice floe, sheet of floating ice.
banzo *m.* cheek [of a frame].
bañadera *f.* (Am.) bathtub.
bañadero *m.* place where wild animals bathe.
bañado *m.* (Am.) marsh, swamp, soft wet land.
bañador *m.* bathing suit.
bañar *tr.* to bathe. *2* to give a coating to. *3 ref.* to bathe, take a bath.
bañera *f.* bath, bathtub.
bañero, -ra *m.* bathhouse owner or keeper. *2 m.-f.* bath attendant.
bañil *m.* BAÑADERO.
bañista *m.* bather. *2* resorter, frequenter of a spa or a seaside resort.
baño *m.* bath: ~ *de asiento*, sitz bath; ~ *María*, double boiler. *2* bathtub. *3* coating. *4* bagnio [oriental prison]. *5 pl.* bathing place. *6* spa.
bao *m.* NAUT. beam [cross timber].
baobab *m.* BOT. baobab.
baptisterio *m.* baptist(e)ry.
baque *m.* blow in falling, thud, thump, bump.
baqueta *f.* ramrod. *2* switch used as a whip. *3* ARCH. bead. *4 pl.* drumsticks. *5 carrera de baquetas*, running the gauntlet. *6 a* ~, harshly, despotically.
baqueteado, -da *adj.* experienced [person].

baquetear *tr.* fig. to treat roughly, 2 to train, to harden, to season, to drill. 3 to bother, to put out, to upset, to disturb.

baqueteo *m.* bother, trouble, annoyance. 2 training, hardening, seasoning, drilling. 3 jolting, jerking, shaking.

baquía *f.* familiarity with roads, paths, rivers, etc., of a region. 2 (Am.) skill, manual dexterity.

baquiano, -na *adj.* skillful. 2 *m.* expert guide.

báquico, -ca *adj.* Bacchic. 2 bacchic.

báquira *f.*, **báquiro** *m.* ZOOL. peccary.

bar *m.* bar, barroom.

barahúnda *f.* uproar, tumult.

baraja *f.* pack, *deck [of cards].

barajar *tr.* to shuffle [cards]. 2 to mingle, jumble together. 3 *intr.* to quarrel. 4 *ref.* to get mingled.

baranda *f.* BARANDILLA. 2 border [of billiard table].

barandado, barandaje *m.* BARANDILLA.

barandal *m.* upper or lower support [of a balustrade]; handrail. 2 BARANDILLA.

barandilla *f.* balustrade, railing, banisters.

baratería *f.* MAR., LAW barratry.

baratija *f.* trinket, trifle, gewgaw.

baratillero *m.* seller of cheap articles.

baratillo *m.* cheap or second-hand goods or shop.

barato, -ta *adj.* cheap. 2 *adv.* cheaply. 3 *m.* bargain sale. 4 money exacted from winning gamblers. 5 *dar de* ~, to grant [for the sake of argument].

báratro *m.* poet, barathrum, hell.

baratura *f.* cheapness [of goods].

baraúnda *f.* BARAHÚNDA.

barba *f.* chin. 2 beard, whiskers: ~ *cerrada*, thick beard; *Barba Azul*, Bluebeard; *hacer la* ~, to shave; to annoy; to fawn on; *en las barbas de uno*, apiece. 3 beard [of goat]. 4 wattle [of fowl]. 5 ~ *de ballena*, whalebone. 6 *m.* THEAT. old man. 7 *f. pl.* barbs [of feather]. 8 BOT. slender roots. 9 deckle edge [of paper].

barbacana *f.* FORT. barbican.

barbacoa *f.* barbecue.

barbada *f.* lower jaw [of horse]. 2 bridle curb. 3 ICHTH. a Mediterranean fish.

barbado, -da *adj.* bearded. 2 deckle-edged.

Barbados *pr. n.* GEOG. Barbados.

Bárbara *f. pr. n.* Barbara.

bárbaramente *adv.* barbarously. 2 enormously.

barbaridad *f.* barbarousness. 2 barbarity; atrocity; rash or preposterous act or saying. 3 awful amount.

barbarie *f.* barbarism, barbarousness. 2 barbarity, cruelty.

barbarismo *m.* barbarism [impurity of language]. 2 BARBARIE.

barbarizar *tr.* to fill with barbarisms.

bárbaro, -ra *adj.* barbarian, barbaric, barbarous. 2 rude, cruel, savage. 3 coll. rash. 4 coll. enormous. 5 *m.-f.* barbarian.

barbechar *tr.* to fallow.

barbechera *f.* series of fallows. 2 fallowing.

barbecho *m.* fallow. 2 ploughed land ready for sowing.

barbería *f.* barber's shop. 2 barbering.

barberil *adj.* tonsorial.

barbero *m.* barber.

barbeta *f.* barbette.

barbián, -na *adj.* coll, dashing, bold, handsome.

barbicano, -na *adj.* white-bearded.

barbilampiño *adj.* smooth-faced, beardless.

barbilindo, barbilucio *adj.* foppish [young man].

barbilla *f.* point of the chin. 2 barbel [of fish]. 3 CARP. bevel end for joining.

barbinegro, -gra *adj.* black-bearded.

barbiquejo *m.* chin strap. 2 NAUT. bobstay.

barbirrojo *adj.-m.* red-bearded, ginger-bearded.

barbitúrico *adj.-m.* CHEM. barbiturate.

barbo *m.* ICHTH. barbel: ~ *de mar*, red mullet.

barbón *m.* bearded man.

barboquejo *m.* chin strap.

barbotar *intr.-tr.* to mumble, to mutter.

barboteo *m.* mumbling, muttering, grumbling.

barbudo, -da *adj.* bearded, long-bearded.

barbulla *f.* hubbub.

barbullar *intr.* to jabber noisily and in spurts.

barbullón *m.* jabberer.

barbuquejo *m.* BARBOQUEJO.

barca *f.* boat, small boat: ~ *de pasaje*, ferry-boat.

barcada *f.* boatload. 2 boat trip.

barcaje *m.* transport by boat. 2 boat freight. 3 ferrying, ferriage.

barcarola *f.* MUS. barcarole.

barcaza *f.* lighter, barge.

Barcelona *pr. n.* GEOG. Barcelona.

barcelonés, -sa *adj.-n.* of Barcelona.

barcia *f.* chaff [from grain].

barco *m.* NAUT. boat, vessel, ship.

barda *f.* bard [horse armour]. 2 thatched top [of a wall or fence].

bardaguera *f.* BOT. kind of osier.

bardal *m.* BARDA 2.

bardana *f.* BOT. burdock.

bardo *m.* bard [poet.].

baremo *m.* ready reckoner.

bargueño *m.* a painted and inlaid cabinet.

bario *m.* CHEM. barium.

barita *f.* CHEM. baryta.

barítono *m.* MUS. baritone.

barloventear *intr.* NAUT. to beat to windward, to beat. 2 coll. to rove about.

barlovento *m.* NAUT. windward.

barnacla *f.* ORN. barnacle, barnacle goose.

barniz *m.* varnish. 2 glaze [on pottery]. 3 fig. smattering.

barnizado *m.* varnishing.

barnizador, -ra *m.-f.* varnisher.

barnizar *tr.* to varnish.

barógrafo *m.* barograph.

barométrico, -ca *adj.* barometrical, barometric.

barómetro *m.* barometer.

barón *m.* baron.

baronesa *f.* baroness.

baronía *f.* barony, baronage.

baroscopio *m.* baroscope.

barquear *tr.* to cross [a river, etc.] by boat. 2 *intr.* to go about in a boat.

barquero *m.* boatman; ferryman.

barquichuelo *m.* small boat or ship.

barquilla *f.* AER. basket; nacelle. 2 NAUT. ~ *de la corredera*, log, log chip.

barquillero *m.* maker or seller o BARQUILLOS.

barquillo *m.* thin rolled waffle; cone.

barquín *m.* large bellows.

barquinazo *m.* hard jolt or upset of a carriage.

barra *f.* bar. 2 MECH. lever, bar; beam, rod. 3 ingot, bar [of metal]. 4 bar, rail [in lawcourt]. 5 SPORT. bar. 6 sand-bar. 7 WEAV. gross-spun thread in cloth. 8 HER. stripe, bar. 9 NAUT. irons. 10 ~ *colectora*, ELECT. bus bar. 11 *sin pararse en barras*, regardless of obstacles.

Barrabás *m. pr. n.* BIBL. Barabas. 2 (non cap.) devil [evil or mischievous person].

barrabasada *f.* wrong, hasty, inconsiderate action.

barraca *f.* cabin, hut, booth, shanty. *2* farmhouse [in the Valencian countryside].

barracón *m.* large hut or booth.

barracuda *f.* barracuda.

barrado, -da *adj.* striped, lined, streaked. *2* HER. barred.

barragana *f.* concubine.

barranca *f.* BARRANCO 1 & 2.

barranco *m.* precipice. *2* ravine, gorge. *3* difficulty, setback.

barrancoso, -sa *adj.* full of ravines, broken.

barredero, -ra *adj.* sweeping: *red barredera,* dragnet, seine. *2 m.* baker's mop.

barredor, -ra *adj.* sweeping. *2 m.-f.* sweeper.

barreminas *m.* mine sweeper [ship].

barrena *f.* drill, auger, gimlet. *2* rock drill. *3* AER. spin: *entrar en ~,* to go into a spin.

barrenado, -da [de cascos] *adj.* scatter-brained.

barrenar *tr.* to drill, bore. *2* to scuttle [a ship]. *3* to foil, sap, thwart. *4* to violate, infringe.

barrendero, -ra *m.-f.* street sweeper.

barrenillo *m.* ENT. borer [insect].

barreno *m.* large drill. *2* bored hole: *dar ~,* to scuttle [a ship]. *3* blast hole.

barreño *m.* earthen tub, dishpan.

barrer *tr.* to sweep; to sweep away; to sweep clean. *2* NAUT. to rake.

barrera *f.* barrier: *~ del sonido,* sound barrier. *2* RLY. crossing gate. *3* FORT. parapet. *4* MIL. barrage. *5* BULLF. fence around inside of bullring. *6* BULLF. first row of seats. *7* clay pit.

barreta *f.* small bar. *2* shoe lining.

barretear *tr.* to fasten with bars.

barretina *f.* Catalan cap.

barriada *f.* city ward or district; suburb.

barrial *m.* claypit. *2* muddy place, mire, swampy ground.

barrica *f.* cask, barrel.

barricada *f.* barricade.

barrido *m.* sweeping.

barriga *f.* belly. *2* bulge [in a wall].

barrigón, -na, barrigudo, -da *adj.* big-bellied.

barriguera *f.* belly-band.

barril *m.* barrel, keg. *2* earthen water jug.

barrilamen *m.* stock of barrels or casks.

barrilete *m.* keg. *2* CARP. dog, clamp. *3* NAUT. mouse. *4* ZOOL. fiddler crab.

barrilla *f.* BOT., CHEM. barilla.

barrio *m.* town ward, quarter or district: *~ extremo,* suburb; *barrios bajos,* slums; fig. *el otro ~,* the other world.

barriobajero, -ra, *adj.* vulgar, low-class, cheap, common.

barrizal *m.* muddy ground, muddy place.

barro *m.* mud. *2 pl.* pimples [on the face].

barroco, -ca *adj.* baroque.

barroquismo *m.* baroque style; baroque taste.

barroso, -sa *adj.* muddy. *2* pimpled, pimply.

barrote *m.* heavy bar. *2* bar [in a window, etc.]. *3* rung [of a chair]; crosspiece.

barruntar *tr.* to conjecture guess, suspect.

barrunto *m.* feeling, guess. *2* inkling, sign.

bartola (a la) *adv. tumbarse a la ~,* to lie back lazily; to do nothing.

bartolillo *m.* little custard pie.

Bartolo, Bartolomé *m. pr. n.* Bartholomew.

bártulos *m. pl.* tools, traps: *liar los ~,* coll. to pack up.

barullo *m.* noise, confusion, tumult, medley.

barzón *m.* saunter, stroll.

barzonear *intr.* to walk idly, to stroll about.

basa *f.* basis, foundation. *2* ARCH. base.

basada *f.* stocks [for shipbuilding].

basal *adj.* basal.

basáltico, -ca *adj.* basalt, basaltic.

basalto *m.* PETROG. basalt.

basamento *m.* ARCH. base and pedestal, basement.

basar *tr.* to base, found. *2 ref.* to be based. *4* to base oneself, one's statement, etc.

basáride *f.* ZOOL. cacomistle.

basca *f.* nausea, squeamishness.

bascosidad *f.* filth, dirt.

báscula *f.* platform scale or balance. *2* bascule.

bascular *intr.* to tilt, seesaw.

basculante *adj.* bascule: *puente ~,* bascule bridge.

base *f.* basis, base: *a ~ de,* on the basis of. *2* MATH., GEOM., CHEM., MIL., SURV. base.

básico, -ca *adj.* basic.

basidio *m.* BOT. basidium.

basilar *adj.* basilar.

Basilea *f. pr. n.* GEOG. Basle.

basílica *f.* basilica. *2 adj.* basilic [vein].

Basilio *m. pr. n.* Basil.

basilisco *m.* MYTH. basilisk, cockatrice: *estar hecho un ~,* to be furious. *2* ZOOL., MIL. basilisk.

basquear *intr.* to be nauseated. *2 tr.* to nauseate.

basquiña *f.* black outer skirt.

basta *f.* basting stitch.

bastante *adj.* enough, sufficient. *2 adv.* enough, fairly, pretty, rather, sufficiently.

bastar *intr.* to suffice, be enough. *2 ref. bastarse a sí mismo,* to be sufficient unto oneself. *3 ¡basta!,* that wil do; stop!

bastardear *tr.* to debase, to adulterate. *2 intr.* to bastardize, degenerate.

bastardía *f.* bastardy. *2* meanness, indignity.

bastardilla *adj.* italic [letter]. *2 f.* italics.

bastardo, -da *adj.* bastard. *2* mean, base. *3 m.-f.* bastard.

baste *m.* basting stitch. *2* saddle pad.

bastear *tr.* SEW. to baste.

bastedad *f.* coarseness, lack of polish.

bastidor *m.* sash, frame. *2* embroidery frame. *3* PHOT. plate holder. *4* chassis [of a car]. *5* wing [of stage scenery]: *entre bastidores,* behind the scenes.

bastilla *f.* SEW. hem.

bastimento *m.* supply of provisions. *2* NAUT. vessel.

bastión *m.* FORT. bastion.

basto, -ta *adj.* coarse, rough, inferior. *2* unpolished [person]. *3 m.* packsaddle. *4* ace of clubs. *5 pl.* clubs [in Spanish cards].

bastón *m.* cane, walking stick. *2* baton, staff, truncheon.

bastonada *f.,* **bastonazo** *m.* blow with a cane.

bastoncillo *m. dim.* stick, small cane. *2* ANAT. rod [in retina].

bastonera *f.* cane stand, umbrella stand.

bastonero *m.* cane maker or seller.

basura *f.* sweepings, rubbish, garbage.

basurero *m.* dustman, garbage man. *2* rubbish dump.

bata *f.* dressing gown, morning gown. *2* white coat [for doctors, etc.]. *3* obs. frock with train.

batacazo *m.* violent bump [in falling].

batahola *f.* din, hubbub, hurly-burly.

batalla *f.* battle: *~ campal,* pitched battle. *2* joust, tournament. *3* PAINT. battle piece.

batallador, -ra *adj.* battling, fighting.

batallar *intr.* to battle, fight; to struggle. *2* to fence. *3* to waver, hesitate.

batallón *m.* battalion.

batán *m.* fulling mill. *2* WEAV. lathe, lay.

batanar *tr.* to full [cloth].

batanear *tr.* fig. coll. to beat, to give someone a thrashing or a hiding.

batanero *m.* cloth fuller.

bataola *f.* BATAHOLA.

batata *f.* BOT. sweet potato.

bátavo, -va *adj.-n.* Batavian.

batayola *f.* NAUT. fender rail.

batea *f.* painted wooden tray. *2* small tub. *3* NAUT. SCOW. *4* RLY. flatcar, platform car.

bateador *m.* batsman [in cricket], *2* batter [in baseball].

bate *m.* (Am.) baseball bat.

batel *m.* small boat.

batelero *m.* boatman.

batería *f.* MIL., NAV., ELECT., MUS. battery. *2* battery [set of instruments, etc.]: ~ *de cocina*, kitchen utensils. *3* THEAT. footlights. *4* MIL. breach.

batiborrillo, batiburillo *m.* hodgepodge.

baticola *f.* crupper.

batida *f.* HUNT. battue, beat. *2* combing, search.

batidero *m.* constant beating or striking. *2* beating place. *3* rough ground. *4* NAUT. washboard.

batido, -da *adj.* beaten [path]. *2* shot [silk]. *3* *m.* COOK. batter. *4* beaten eggs; milk shake.

batidor *m.* beater. *2* COOK. whisk. *3* MIL. scout. *4* one of the cavalry men heading a regiment on parade. *5* comb [for cleaning hair].

batiente *adj.* beating. *2* *m.* jamb against which a door closes. *3* spot where the sea beats. *4* damper [of piano]. *5* leaf [of door].

batihoja *m.* goldbeater, silverbeater.

batimetría *f.* bathymetry.

batín *m.* smoking jacket.

batintín *m.* gong.

batir *tr.* to beat, to strike. *2* to batter, beat down. *3* [of water, waves, wind, etc.], to beat, dash against. *4* to flap [wings]. *5* to beat [a metal] into sheets. *7* to coin [money]. *8* to beat, defeat. *9* HUNT. to beat. *10* MIL. to range, reconnoitre. *11* MED. to couch [the cataract]. *12* ~ *la marca*, to beat the record. *13* ~ *palmas*, to clap hands. *14* *ref.* to fight.

batista *f.* cambric.

batracio, -cia *adj.-m.* ZOOL. batrachian.

baturrillo *m.* hodgepodge, medley.

baturro, -rra *m.-f.* a rustic or peasant of Aragon.

batuta *f.* MUS. baton: *llevar la* ~, to lead.

baúl *m.* luggage trunk: ~ *mundo*, Saratoga trunk.

bauprés *m.* NAUT. bowsprit.

bautismal *adj.* baptismal.

bautismo *m.* baptism. *2* christening.

bautista *m.* baptizer: *el Bautista*, John the Baptist.

bautisterio *m.* baptistery.

bautizar *tr.* to baptize, to christen. *2* to name, give a name to. *3* to water [wine].

bautizo *m.* christening; christening party.

bávaro, -ra *adj.-n.* Bavarian.

Baviera *pr. n.* GEOG. Bavaria.

baya *f.* BOT. berry.

bayadera *f.* bayadere [dancer].

bayeta *f.* baize.

bayetón *m.* kind of duffel [cloth].

bayo, -ya *adj.* bay. *2* *m.* bay horse.

Bayona *f. pr. n.* GEOG. Bayonne.

bayoneta *f.* bayonet.

bayonetazo *m.* bayonet thrust. *2* bayonet wound.

baza *f.* trick [in cards]: *meter* ~ *en*, coll. to butt in.

bazar *m.* baza(a)r [in the East]. *2* baza(a)r, department store.

1) **bazo** *m.* ANAT. spleen.

2) **bazo, -za** *adj.* yellowish-brown.

bazofia *f.* refuse, scraps of food. *2* garbage.

bazooka, bazuka *m.* MIL. bazooka.

bazucar, bazuquear *tr.* to stir [a liquid] by shaking.

be *f.* name of the letter *b*: ~ *por* ~, in detail.

beatería *f.* sanctimoniusness.

beaterio *m.* kind of beguinage.

beatificación *f.* beatification.

beatificar *tr.* to beatify.

beatífico, -ca *adj.* beatific(al.

beatísimo, -ma *adj.* most holy. *2 beatísimo Padre.* Holy Father.

beatitud *f.* beatitude, blessedness. *2* (cap.) Beatitude [title given to the Pope].

beato, -ta *adj.* happy, blessed. *2* blessed [beatified]. *3* devout; sanctimonious. *4* *m.* beatus. *5* *m.-f.* devout or sanctimonious person. *6* *f.* beata. *7* woman who lives in pious retirement.

Beatriz *pr. n.* Beatrice.

bebé *m.* baby. *2* doll.

bebedero, -ra *adj.* drinkable. *2* *m.* drinking bowl, dish, etc. [for birds]. *3* spout [of a drinking vessel].

bebedizo, -za *adj.* drinkable. *2* *m.* potion; philtre.

bebedor, -ra *adj.* drinking. *2* *m.-f.* drinker; hard drinker, toper.

1) **beber** *m.* drink, drinking.

2) **beber** *tr.-ref.* to drink: ~ *a la salud de uno*, to drink someone's health; ~ *los vientos por*, to sigh or long for or after, to be madly in love with.

bebible *adj.* pleasant to drink, drinkable.

bebida *f.* drink; beverage, potion.

bebido, -da *adj.* drunk, intoxicated, tipsy.

bebistrajo *m.* unpalatable drink, nasty drink.

beborrotear *intr.* to sip often.

beca *f.* sash worn over the ancient academic gown. *2* scholarship, sizarship [allowance].

becacina *f.* AGACHADIZA.

becada *f.* ORN. woodcock.

becafigo *m.* ORN. figpecker.

becario *m.* holder of a scholarship; sizar.

becerra *f.* BOT. snapdragon. *2* calf, young cow.

becerrada *f.* BULLF. fight with young bulls.

becerrillo, -lla *m.-f.* young calf. *2* calfskin.

becerro *m.* calf, young bull: ~ *de oro*, golden calf, wealth. *2* calfskin. *3* ZOOL. ~ *marino*, seal.

becuadro *m.* MUS. natural sign.

bechamela *f.* béchamel sauce.

bedel *m.* beadle, apparitor [in a University].

beduino, -na *adj.-n.* Bedouin. *2* *m.* barbarian.

befa *f.* jeer, flout, scoff.

befar *tr.* to jeer, flout, scoff at.

befo, -fa *adj.* blobber-lipped. *2* knock-kneed. *3* *m.* lip [of an animal]. *4* a kind of monkey.

begonia *f.* BOT. begonia.

beguina *f.* beguine.

Beirut *f. pr. n.* GEOG. Beyrouth.

béisbol *m.* baseball.

bejín *m.* BOT. puffball.

bejuco *m.* BOT. liana, liane; rattan.

Belcebú *m. pr. n.* Beelzebub.

belcho *m.* BOT. joint fir.

beldad *f.* beauty [of a woman]. *2* beauty, belle.

Belén *m. pr. n.* GEOG. Bethlehem. *2* *m.* (not cap.)

Christmas crib. *3* confusion, bedlam. *4* bad business.
beleño *m.* BOT. henbane.
belérico *m.* BOT. myrobalan.
belesa *f.* BOT. leadwort.
belfo, -fa *adj.* blobber-lipped. *2 m.* lip (of an animal).
belga *adj.-n.* Belgian.
Bélgica *f. pr. n.* GEOG. Belgium.
Belgrado *f. pr. n.* GEOG. Belgrade.
bélico, -ca *adj.* warlike, martial.
belicosidad *f.* bellicosity.
belicoso, -sa *adj.* bellicose, pugnacious.
beligerancia *f.* belligerency.
beligerante *adj.-n.* belligerent.
belígero, -ra *adj.* poet. warlike.
Beluchistán *m. pr. n.* GEOG. Beluchistan.
belvedere *m.* ARCH. belvedere.
bellaco, -ca *adj.* wicked, knavish. *2* cunning, sly. *3 m.-f.* knave, scoundrel.
belladona BOT. belladonna, deadly nightshade.
bellamente *adv.* beautifully, prettily.
bellaquería *f.* knavery, knavish act. *2* slyness.
belleza *f.* beauty.
bellido, -da *adj.* beautiful, handsome.
bello, -lla *adj.* beautiful, fair, fine: ~ *sexo,* fair sex; *bellas artes,* fine arts.
bellota *f.* BOT. acorn. *2* acorn-shaped tassel. *3* ZOOL. ~ *de mar,* acorn barnacle.
bellote *m.* large round-headed nail.
bemol *adj.-m.* MUS. flat: *doble* ~, double flat.
bemolado, -da *adj.* MUS. flat [lowered a semitone].
benceno *m.* CHEM. benzene.
bencina *f.* benzine. *2* petrol [for motor-cars].
bendecir *tr.* to bless. *2* to consecrate; to invoke a blessing upon. ¶ CONJUG. like *decir,* except for the INDIC. fut.: *bendeciré;* the COND.: *bendeciría,* and the IMPER.: *bendice.*
bendigo, bendije, bendiga, etc. *irr. V.* BENDECIR.
bendición *f.* benediction, blessing: *que es una* ~, abundantly; with the greatest ease. *2 pl.* wedding ceremony.
bendito, -ta *adj.* sainted, holy, blessed: *agua bendita,* holy water. *2* happy. *3* annoying, bothersome. *4 m.* simple-minded soul.
benedícite *m.* benedicite.
benedictino, -na *adj.-n.* Benedictine. *2 m.* benedictine [liqueur].
benefactor; -ra *adj.* beneficent, beneficial. *2 n.* benefactor, benefactress.
beneficencia *f.* beneficence. *2* charity, poor relief, social service.
beneficiado *m.* ECCL. beneficiary. *2* THEAT. person, charity, etc., to whom the proceeds of a benefit go.
beneficiar *tr.* to benefit, to do good to. *2* to cultivate, improve [land]; to exploit, work [a mine]; to beneficiate, process [ores]. *3* COM. to sell [bills, etc.] at a discount. *4 ref.* to benefit, to profit.
beneficiario *m.* [feudatory or insurance] beneficiary.
beneficio *m.* benefaction. *2* benefit, advantage, profit. *3* COM. profit: ~ *neto,* clear profit. *4* THEAT. benefit. *5* [feudal] benefice. *6* ECCL. benefice. *7* cultivation [of land]; exploitation [of mines]; beneficiation, processing [of ores]. *8* LAW ~ *de inventario,* benefit of inventory.
beneficioso, -sa *adj.* beneficial, profitable.
benéfico, -ca beneficent, charitable. *2* beneficial.

benemérito, -ta *adj.* well deserving, worthy, meritorious.
beneplácito *m.* approval, consent.
benevolencia *f.* benevolence, kindness, goodwill.
benévolo, -la *adj.* benevolent, kind.
Bengala *pr. n.* GEOG. Bengal.
bengala *f.* rattan. *2* MIL. baton. *3* Bengal light.
bengalí *adj.-n.* Bengalese, Bengali. *2 m.* Bengali [language]. *3* ORN. Bengali.
benignidad *f.* benignity, benignancy.
benigno, -na *adj.* benign. *2* benignant.
Benito *pr. n.* Benedict.
Benjamín *pr. n.* Benjamín. *2 m.* (not cap.) baby [the youngest son].
benjuí *m.* benzoin.
Beocia *pr. n.* GEOG. Boeotia.
beocio, -cia *adj.-n.* Boeotian.
beodo, -da *adj.* drunk. *2 m.-f.* drunkard.
beorí *m.* ZOOL. American tapir.
berberecho *m.* ZOOL. cockle.
Berbería *pr. n.* GEOG. Barbary.
berberí *adj.-n.* BEREBER.
berberís *m.* BÉRBERO.
berberisco, -ca *adj.-n.* BEREBER.
bérbero *m.* BOT. barberry. *2* a barberry confection.
berbiquí *m.* brace, carpenter's brace, wimble.
bereber *adj.-n.* Berber.
berenjena *f.* BOT. eggplant.
berenjenal *m.* bed of eggplants: *meterse en un* ~, fig. to get into a mess.
bergamota *m.* bergamot [pear, lime, perfume].
bergamote, bergamoto *m.* BOT. bergamot [tree].
bergante *adj.* scoundrel, rascal.
bergantín *m.* NAUT. brig: ~ *goleta,* brigantine.
beriberi *m.* MED. beriberi.
berilo *m.* MINER. beryl.
Berlín *pr. n.* GEOG. Berlín.
berlina *f.* berlin [carriage]. *2* closed front compartment [of stagecoach]. *3 en* ~, in a ridiculous position.
berlinés, -sa *adj.* of Berlin. *2 m.-f.* Berliner.
berma *f.* FORT. berm, berme.
bermejear *intr.* to be or show red.
bermejizo, -za *adj.* reddish.
bermejo, -ja *adj.* bright reddish.
bermellón *m.* vermilion.
Bermudas (las) *pr. n.* GEOG. Bermudas Islands.
Berna *pr. n.* GEOG. Bern.
Bernabé *pr. n.* Barnaby.
Bernardo *pr. n.* Bernard.
bernardo, -da *adj.* Bernardine. *2 m.* Bernardine monk. *3 f.* Bernardine nun.
bernés, -sa *adj.-n.* Bernese.
berra *f.* BOT. tall water cress.
berrear *intr.* to low [as a calf]. *2* to bawl.
berreo *m.* lowing, bawling.
berrinchín *m.* BERRINCHE.
berrendo, -da *adj.* two-coloured. *2* dappled [bull].
berrera *f.* BOT. water parsnip.
berrido *m.* cry of the calf; low. *2* bawl.
berrinche *m.* rage, tantrum. *2* child's rage.
berrizal *m.* water cress patch.
berro *m.* BOT. water cress.
berroqueña *adj.* *piedra* ~, granite.
berrueco *m.* granite rock. *2* baroque pearl.
Berta *pr. n.* Bertha.
berza *f.* BOT. cabbage.
besalamano *m.* unsigned note, beginning with B.L.M. [kisses the hand].
besamanos *m.* reception at court.
besante *m.* bezant [coin]. *2* HER. bezant.

besar *tr.* to kiss. *2 ref.* to kiss [one another].
besico, besito *m. dim.* little kiss.
beso *m.* kiss. *2* bump [collision].
bestezuela *f.* little beast.
bestia *f.* beast: ~ *de carga,* beast of burden. *2* boor, dunce, idiot. *3 adj.* stupid, idiot.
bestial *adj.* beastly, bestial. *2* coll. enormous, colossal.
bestialidad *f.* beastliness, bestiality. *2* stupidity.
bestiario *m.* bestiary.
bestseller *m.* best seller.
besucar *tr.* BESUQUEAR.
besucón, -na *adj.* fond of kissing.
besugo *m.* ICHTH. sea bream.
besuguera *f.* fish kettle.
besuquear *tr.* to kiss repeatedly.
beta *f.* beta [Greek letter]. *2* MAR. small rope.
Betania *pr. n.* GEOG. Bethany.
betel *m.* BOT. betel.
Bética *f. pr. n.* GEOG. Betica.
bético, -ca *adj.* Andalusian.
betónica *f.* BOT. betony.
betún *m.* bitumen. *2* shoe blaking. *3* ZULAQUE.
bey *m.* bey.
bezo *m.* blubber lip. *2* lip. *3* proud flesh.
bezoar *m.* bezoar.
bezudo, -da *adj.* thick-lipped, blobber-lipped.
bibásico, -ca *adj.* CHEM. dibasic.
biberón *m.* feeding bottle, nursing bottle.
Biblia *f.* Bible.
bíblico, -ca *adj.* Biblical.
bibliofilia *f.* bibliophilism.
bibliófilo *m.* bibliophile.
bibliografía *f.* bibliography.
bibliomanía *f.* bibliomania.
biblioteca *f.* library: ~ *circulante,* lending library.
bibliotecario, -ria *m.-f.* librarian.
bical *m.* ICHTH. male salmon.
bicameral *adj.* bicameral.
bicarbonato *m.* CHEM. bicarbonate.
bicéfalo, -la *adj.* bicephalous.
bíceps *m.* ANAT. biceps.
bicerra *f.* ZOOL. ibex, wild goat.
bicicleta *f.* bicycle.
bicloruro *m.* CHEM. dichloride, bichloride.·
bicoca *f.* obs. small fort. *2* fig. trifle, bagatelle.
bicolor *adj.* bicolor, bicolour, two-tone, two-colour.
bicóncavo, -va *adj.* biconcave.
biconvexo, -xa *adj.* biconvex.
bicorne *adj.* poet, bicorn, two-horned.
bicornio *m.* two-cornered hat.
bicúspide *adj.* bicuspid.
bicha *f.* shake [in superstitious use]. *2* ARCH. grotesque animal figure.
bicharraco *m.* insect, ugly animal.
bichero *m.* boat hook.
bicho *m.* little animal, vermin. *2* domestic animal. *3* BULLF. bull. *4* ~ *raro,* odd fellow; *mal* ~, wicked person; *todo* ~ *viviente,* all living soul.
bidé *m.* bidet [a form of sitz bath].
bidentado, -da *adj.* bidentate, double-toothed. *2 m.* AGR. pitchfork.
bidón *m.* can, drum [for petrol, etc.].
biela *f.* MACH. connecting rod.
bieldo, bielgo *m.* winnowing fork.
1) **bien** *adv.* well, properly, right, perfectly, happily, successfully. *2* willingly, readily: *yo* ~ *lo haría, pero...,* I'd willingly do it, but... *3* very much, a good deal, fully, enough. *4* easily: ~ *se ve que...,* it is easy to see that... *5 tener a* ~, to see

fit, to deign. *6* ~... ~, either... or. *7 ahora* ~, now, now then. *8 bien a* ~, *de* ~ *a* ~, willingly. *9* ~ *que,* although. *10 más* ~, rather. *11 no* ~, as soon as, just as. *12 si* ~, although. *13 y* ~, well, now then.
2) **bien,** *pl.* **bienes** *m.* good [as opposed to evil]: *hombre de* ~, honest, straight man. *2* good, welfare, benefit: *hacer* ~, to do good; *en* ~ *de,* for the sake, good or benefit of. *3* fig. *mi* ~, my dearest, my love. *4 pl.* property, possessions, estate: *bienes de fortuna,* worldly possessions; *bienes inmuebles* or *raíces,* real estate; *bienes muebles,* movables, personal property.
bienal *adj.* biennial.
bienamado, -da *adj.-n.* well-loved.
bienandante *adj.* happy, fortunate.
bienandanza *f.* happiness, fortune.
bienaventurado, -da *adj.* happy, blessed. *2* simple, guileless.
bienaventuranza *f.* blessedness. *2* happiness. *3 pl. Las bienaventuranzas,* the Beatitudes.
bienestar *m.* well-being, comfort. *2* comfortable living. *3* happiness, peace of mind.
bienhablado, -da *adj.* well-spoken, civil.
bienhadado, -da *adj.* fortunate.
bienhechor, -ra *adj.* beneficent, beneficial. *2 m.* benefactor. *3 f.* benefactress.
bienintencionado, -da *adj.* well-meaning.
bienio *m.* biennium.
bienmandado, -da *adj.* obedient, submissive.
bienoliente *adj.* fragrant.
bienquerencia *f.,* **bienquerer** *m.* affection, good will.
bienquerer *tr.* to love, like, esteem.
bienquistar *tr.-ref.* to gain the esteem [of somebody].
bienquisto, -ta *adj.* well-liked; generally esteemed.
bienvenida *f.* happy arrival. *2* welcome: *dar la* ~, to welcome.
bienvenido, -da *adj.* welcome.
bies *m.* bias [obliquity].
bifásico, -ca *adj.* ELEC. diphase, twophase.
bife *m.* (Am.) beefsteak.
bífido, -da *adj.* BOT. bifid.
bifocal *adj.* bifocal.
biftec *m.* beefsteak.
bifurcación *f.* bifurcation, forking. *2* branch.
bifurcado, -da *adj.* bifurcated, forked.
bifurcarse *ref.* to fork, bifurcate.
bigamia *f.* bigamy.
bígamo, -ma *adj.* bigamous. *2 m.-f.* bigamist.
bigardo *m.* obs. licentious friar. *2* licentious vagabond.
bigardón, -a *m.-f.* licentious vagabond.
bígaro, bigarro *m.* a sea snail.
bigornia *f.* two-pointed anvil.
bigote *m.* m(o)ustache, mustachio. *2* whiskers [of cat]. *3* PRINT. dash rule.
bigotera *f.* mustache protector. *2* smear on upper lip. *3* folding carriage seat. *4* bow compass.
bigotudo *adj.* mustachioed.
bija *f.* BOT. annatto tree. *2* annatto [dyestuff].
bilabial *adj.* PHON. bilabial.
bilateral *adj.* bilateral.
bilbaíno, -na *adj.-n.* of Bilbao.
Bilbao *m. pr. n.* GEOG. Bilbao.
biliar; biliario, -ria *adj.* biliary.
bilingüe *adj.* bilingual.
bilioso, -sa *adj.* bilious.

bilis f. bile, gall: fig. *descargar la* ~, to vent one's spleen.
bilobulado, -da adj. bilobate.
billa f. BILLIARDS hazard.
billar m. billiards. 2 billiard table. 3 billiard room. 4 billiard hall.
billarista m. billiardist, billiard player.
billete m. note, short letter. 2 love letter. 3 ticket [railway, theater, lottery, etc., ticket]: ~ *de ida*, one-way ticket; ~ *de ida y vuelta*, return ticket; ~ *kilométrico*, mileage book. 4 ~ *de banco*, bank note.
billón m. [British] billion; [U.S.A.] trillion.
bimano, -na adj. bimanous. 2 m. ZOOL. bimane.
bimba f. coll. high hat, top hat.
bimensual adj. semimonthly.
bimestral adj. bimestral, bimonthly.
bimestre adj. BIMESTRAL. 2 m. period of two months.
bimetalismo m. bimetallism.
bimotor adj. AER. two-motor.
binar tr. AGR. to plough a second time. 2 intr. to celebrate two Masses on the same day.
binario, -ria adj. binary.
binocular adj. binocular.
binóculo m. binocle, binocular. 2 lorgnette.
binomio m. ALG. binomial.
binza f. pellicle [of eggshell or onion]. 2 any thin membrane.
biofísica f. biophysics.
biogenia f. biogeny.
biografía f. biography.
biográfico, -ca adj. biographic(al).
biógrafo m. biographer.
biología f. biology.
biológico, -ca adj. biologic(al).
biólogo m. biologist.
biombo f. folding screen.
bioquímica f. biochemistry.
bióxido m. CHEM. dioxide.
bipartido, da; bipartito, -ta adj. bipartite.
bípede; bípedo, -da adj. bipedal. 2 m. biped.
biplano m. AER. biplane.
bipolar adj. bipolar.
biricú m. sword belt.
birimbao m. MUS. Jew's harp.
birlar tr. coll. ~ *la novia, un empleo*, etc., to pinch [somebody's] sweetheart, job, etc.
birlibirloque m. *por arte de* ~, by magic.
birlocha f. kite [toy].
birlocho m. barouche.
Birmania f. pr. n. GEOG. Burma.
birmano, -na adj.-n. Burmese.
birrefringente adj. OPT. birefringent.
birreme adj.-f. bireme.
birreta f. scarlet biretta. 2 cardinalate.
birrete m. scarlet biretta. 2 academic cap. 3 cap worn by judges, barristers, etc., with official dress.
birretina f. MIL. bearskin, hussar or grenadier's cap.
birria f. horror, horrible person or thing. 2 lousy, unworthy thing, piece of junk. 3 (Am.) mania.
bis adv.-adj. bis.
bisabuelo, -la m.-f. great-grandfather; great-grandmother. 2 m. pl. great-grandparents.
bisagra f. hinge. 2 shoemaker's polisher.
bisar tr. to repeat [a song, performance, etc.].
bisbisar tr. to mutter, mumble.
bisbiseo m. muttering, mumbling.
bisecar tr. GEOM. to bisect.

bisección f. MATH. bisection.
bisector, bisectriz adj. GEOM. bisecting. 2 m. bisector. 3 f. bisectrix.
bisel m. bevel, bevel edge.
biselado m. bevelling. 2 adj. bevel, bevelled.
biselar tr. to bevel.
bisemanal adj. semiweekly.
bisexual adj. bisexual.
bisiesto adj. bissextile, leap [year].
bisílabo, -ba adj. disyllabic. 2 m. disyllable.
bismuto m. CHEM. bismuth.
bisnieto, -ta m.-f. great-grandchild. 2 m. great-grandson. 3 f. great-granddaughter.
bisojo, -ja adj.-n. BIZCO.
bisonte m. ZOOL. bison.
bisoñé m. toupee or small wig for front of head.
bisoño, -ña adj. green, inexperienced. 2 MIL. raw. 3 m.-f. greenhorn, novice. 4 raw recruit.
bistec m. beefsteak.
bistorta f. BOT. bistort.
bistre m. bistre.
bisturí m. SURG. bistoury.
bisulco, -ca adj. bisulcate, cloven-footed.
bisulfato m. bisulphate.
bisulfito m. CHEM. bisulphite.
bisutería f. imitation jewelry.
bita f. NAUT. bitt.
bitácora f. NAUT. binnacle.
bitongo adj. *niño* ~, boy fond of acting like a child.
bitoque m. spigot [in a cask].
bituminoso, -sa adj. bituminous.
bivalencia f. CHEM. bivalence.
bivalente adj. CHEM. bivalent.
bivalvo, -va adj. bivalve.
Bizancio f. pr. n. GEOG., HIST. Byzantium.
bizantinismo m. Byzantinism. 2 idle discussion.
bizantino, -na adj.-n. Byzantine. 2 adj. idle [discussion].
bizarría f. gallantry, courage. 2 generosity, grandness, splendour.
bizarro, -rra adj. gallant, courageous. 2 generous, grand, splendid.
bizcar intr. to squint. 2 tr. to wink [the eye].
bizco, -ca adj. squint-eyed, cross-eyed. 2 m.-f. cross-eyed person, squinter.
bizcocho m. biscuit, hardtack. 2 sponge cake. 3 biscuit, bisque [unglazed porcelain].
bizcotela f. frosted sponge cake.
biznaga f. BOT. bishop's-weed.
biznieto, -ta m.-f. BISNIETO, TA.
bizquear intr. to squint.
blanca f. old copper and silver coin: *estar sin* ~, to be broke. 2 MUS. minim.
blanco, -ca adj. white, hoar, hoary. 2 white, pale. 3 fair [complexion]. 4 white [person, race, metal]. 5 POL. white. 6 m.-f. white person. 7 m. white colour. 8 target, mark: *dar en el* ~, to hit the mark. 9 aim, goal. 10 gap, interval. 11 blank, blank space: *en* ~, blank [page, check, etc.]. 12 white [of the eye]. 13 ~ *de España*, whiting. 14 *quedarse en* ~, to fail to grasp the point, to be disappointed.
blancor m. BLANCURA.
blancura f. whiteness. 2 fairness [of skin].
blancuzco, -ca adj. whitish.
blandamente adv. softly, gently.
blandear intr.-ref. to yield, give in. 2 tr. to make [someone] change his mind.
blandengue adj. soft, weak, without energy.
blandicia f. flattery. 2 love of luxury, luxury.
blandir tr. to brandish, flourish, swing.

blando, -da *adj.* soft [yielding to pressure]. *2* soft, gentle, mild, bland. *3* soft, delicate. *4* cowardly. *5* watery [eyes]. *6* ~ *de boca,* tendermouthed [horse].

blandón *m.* thick wax candle. *2* large candlestick.

blanducho, -cha; blandujo, -ja *adj.* softish.

blandura *f.* softness. *2* gentleness, sweetness, blandness. *3* endearing word. *4* luxury, delicacy.

blanqueador, -ra *adj.* whitening; whitewashing; bleaching. *2 m.-f.* whitener; whitewasher; bleacher.

blanquear *tr.* to whiten, blanch. *2* to bleach. *3* to whitewash. *4 intr.* to whiten, turn white. *5* to show white.

blanquecedor *m.* blancher [of metals].

blanquecer *tr.* to whiten, to bleach. *2* to blanch [metals]. ¶ Conjug. like *agradecer.*

blanquecino, -na *adj.* whitish.

blanqueo *m.* whitening, bleaching. *2* whitewashing.

blanquete *m.* white cosmetic.

blanquillo, -lla *adj.* whitish.

blanquizco, -ca *adj.* blanquecino.

Blas *m. pr. n.* Blase.

blasfemador, -ra *m.-f.* blasphemer.

blasfemar *intr.* to blaspheme.

blasfematorio, -ria *f.* blasphemous.

blasfemia *f.* blasphemy.

blasfemo, -ma *adj.* blasphemous. *2 m.-f.* blasphemer.

blasón *m.* heraldry, blazon. *2* armorial bearings. *3* her. charge. *4* honour, glory.

blasonar *tr.* her. to emblazon. *2 intr.* to boast: *blasonar de,* to boast of being.

blasonería *f.* boasting, bragging.

blástula *f.* biol. blastula.

bledo *m.* bot. blite: *no me importa un* ~, I don't care a straw.

blenda *f.* miner. blende.

blinda *f.* fort. blind.

blindado, -da *adj.* armoured [car, ship], steel-jacketed [bullet]. *2* elect. shielded.

blindaje *m.* fort. blindage. *2* armour plate. *3* elect. shield.

blindar *tr.* to armour, armour-plate. *2* elect. to shield.

blocao *m.* fort. blockhouse.

blonda *f.* blond lace.

blondo, -da *adj.* blond, blonde, fair.

bloque *m.* block [of stone, wood, paper, etc.].

bloquear *tr.* mil., naut. to blockade. *2* med., print. to block. *3* com. to block [an account].

bloqueo *m.* mil., naut. blockade. *2* print., com. blocking. *3* med. block.

blusa *f.* smock. *2* blouse.

boa *f.* zool. boa. *2* boa [neckpiece].

boato *m.* show, pomp.

bobalicón, -na *adj.* silly, simple. *2 m.-f.* nitwit.

bobear *intr.* to talk nonsense, play the fool; to fool around.

bobería *f.* silliness, foolishness. *2* silly action or remark; nonsense, trifle, foolery.

bóbilis, bóbilis (de) *adv.* for nothing.

bobina *f.* bobbin. *2* elect. coil: ~ *de encendido,* spark coil, ignition coil.

bobinado *m.* winding [yarn or wire].

bobinadora *f.* winder, winding machine.

bobinar *tr.* to wind [yarn or wire].

bobo, -ba *adj.* silly, foolish, gullible. *2 m.-f.* fool, simpleton. *3 m.* theat. fool.·

bobote *m.* coll. great fool.

boca *f.* mouth [of man or animal; speech]: ~ *de escorpión,* fig. evil tongue [person]; ~ *de oro,* fig. very eloquent person; *andar en* ~ *de todos, andar de* ~ *en* ~, to be the talk of the place, to be generally known; *hacer* ~, to work up an appetite [by eating or drinking something]; *írsele a uno la* ~, to talk imprudently; *meterse en la* ~ *del lobo,* to put one's head into the lion's mouth; *no decir esta* ~ *es mía,* not to say a word; *oscuro como* ~ *de lobo,* pitchdark; *quitárselo uno de la* ~, to deprive oneself for the sake of another; *torcer la* ~, to make a wry mouth; ~ *abajo,* face downwards, flat on one's face, prone; ~ *arriba,* face upwards, flat on one's back, supine; *a pedir de* ~, very well, according to one's desire. *2* mouth, entrance, opening; ~, or *bocas, de un río,* mouth of a river; ~ *del metro,* subway entrance; ~ *de agua,* hydrant; *a* ~ *de jarro,* [drinking] without measure; at close range; suddenly. *3* beginning: *a* ~ *de noche,* at nightfall. *4* approaches [of a tunnel]. *5* muzzle [of a gun]. *6* zool. pincers [of a crustacean]. *7* cutting part of some tools. *8* peen [of hammer]. *8* ~ *del estómago,* pit of the stomach. *10* ~ *de fuego,* firearm [esp. artillery];·*11* bot. ~ *de dragón,* snapdragon.

bocacalle *f.* street entrance.

bocacaz *f.* a dam's outlet for irrigation.

bocacha *f.* wide-mouthed blunderbuss.

bocadillo *m.* sandwich.

bocadito *m.* little bit.

bocado *m.* mouthful [of food], morsel, bit. *2* bit [of the bridle].

bocajarro [a] *adv.* point-blank.

bocal *m.* wide-mouthed pitcher.

bocamanga *f.* bottom part of a sleeve.

bocamina *f.* mine entrance.

bocanada *f.* mouthful [of liquid]. *2* puff [of tobacco smoke]. *3* ~ *de aire* or *de viento,* gust, blast of wind. *4 echar bocanadas,* to boast, brag.

bocaza *f.* large mouth. *2 m.* indiscreet talker.

bocazo *m.* fizzle [in blasting].

bocel *m.* arch. torus [molding]: *medio* ~, half round; *cuarto* ~, quarter round.

bocelar *tr.* to cut a round molding on.

bocera *f.* smear on lips [after eating or drinking].

boceto *m.* paint. sketch. *2* sculp. rough model.

bocina *f.* mus. horn [instrument made of a horn]. *2* sea shell used as a horn. *3* foghorn, auto horn. *4* speaking trumpet, megaphone. *5* phonograph horn. *6* mech. bushing.

bocinar *tr.* to blow the horn.

bocinazo *m.* honk, toot. *2* coll. scolding, telling off, rebuke.

bocio *m.* med. goitre.

bocón, -na *adj.* bigmouthed, boastful. *2 m.-f.* braggard.

bocoy *m.* large barrel [for goods]; hogshead.

bocudo, -da *adj.* bigmouthed.

bocha *f.* bowl [ball]. *2 pl.* bowls, bowling.

bochar *tr.* bowl. to hit and dislodge [a ball].

boche *m.* small hole in the ground [for boys games].

bochinche *m.* noise, row, riot, tumult.

bochinchero, -ra *adj.-n.* coll. rowdy, rough and noisy.

bochorno *m.* hot summer breeze. *2* sultry weather, suffocating heat. *3* blush, blushing. *4* embarrassment, shame.

bochornoso, -sa *adj.* hot, sultry. *2* disgraceful, shameful.

boda *f.* marriage, wedding: *bodas de plata, de oro,* silver, golden wedding; *bodas de Camacho,* banquet, lavish feast.
bodega *f.* cellar, wine cellar, wine vault. *2* wine shop. *3* pantry. *4* dock-warehouse. *5* NAUT. hold [of a ship].
bodegón *m.* cheap eating house. *2* still-life painting [esp. of edibles].
bodeguero, -ra *m.-f.* cellarer, keeper of a wine cellar. *2 m.* NAUT. one in charge of the hold.
bodijo *m.* coll. mesalliance. *2* coll. wedding with little ceremony.
bodoque *m.* clay ball or pellet shot from crossbow. *2* lump. *3* fig. dolt, dunce.
bodoquera *f.* mould for clay balls. *2* cradle [of a crossbow]. *3* blowgun, peashooter.
bodorrio *m.* BODIJO.
bodrio *m.* soup made of leavings; poorly cooked food.
bóer *adj.-n.* Boer.
bofe *m.* coll. lung; *echar el ~* or *los bofes,* to toil; to pant. *2 pl.* lights [of sheep, hogs, etc.].
bofetada *f.* slap in the face; buffet.
bofetón *m.* slap in the face.
boga *f.* vogue [acceptation, popularity]. *2* rowing. *3* ICHTH. boce.
bogada *f.* distance covered at one oar-stroke.
bogador *m.* rower.
bogar *intr.* to row. *2* to sail.
bogavante *m.* first rower [in a galley]. *2* ZOOL. homard, lobster.
bogui *m.* RLY. bogie.
Bohemia *pr. n.* Bohemia [country].
bohemio, -mia *adj.-n.* Bohemian [in every sense]. *2 f.* Bohemia; Bohemian life.
bohío *m.* (Am.) hut, *shack.
bohordo *m.* short spear or reed, formerly used in tournaments. *2* BOT. scape.
boicot *m.* boycott.
boicotear *tr.* to boycott.
boicoteo *m.* boycott, boycotting.
boina *f.* beret.
boj, boje *m.* BOT. box, boxwood. *2* boxwood [wood].
bol *m.* punch bowl. *2* bowl [cup without a handle]. *3 ~ arménico,* Armenian bole.
bola *f.* ball [spherical body]: *~ de nieve,* snowball; BOT. snowball; *~ negra,* blackball. *2* marble. *3* CARDS slam. *4* NAUT. ball [for signals]. *5* shoe blacking. *6* fib.
bolada *f.* throw [of a ball].
bolardo *m.* NAUT. bollard.
bolchevique *adj.-n.* Bolshevist.
bolchevismo *m.* Bolshevism.
boleadoras *f. pl.* bolas, lariat with balls at the ends used by South American cowboys.
bolear *intr.* BILL. to knock the balls about. *2 tr.* to throw, flunk. *3* (Am.) to lasso with bolas.
bolero, -ra *adj.* lying. *2 m.-f.* fibber, liar. *3 m.* bolero [dance; short jacket]. *4* bowling alley.
boleta *f.* MIL. billet. *2* (Am.) ballot.
boletería *f.* (Am.) box office, ticket office [theatre]. *2* ticket office, booking office [station].
boletín *m.* subscription form. *2* bulletin.
boleto *m.* (Am.) ticket.
boliche *m.* jack [small ball for bowling]. *2* bowls, skittles. *3* bowling alley. *4* cup and ball [toy]. *5* small dragnet. *6* NAUT. bowline of a small sail.
bólido *m.* bolide, meteor.
bolígrafo *m.* ball-point pen.
bolilla *f.* small ball. *2* marble.

bolillo *m.* bobbin [for making lace]. *2* VET. coffin bone.
bolina *f.* NAUT. bowline: *de ~,* close-hauled; *navegar de ~,* to sail close to the wind. *2* NAUT. sounding line. *3* noise, tumult.
bolinear *tr.* NAUT. to sail close-hauled, to sail close to the wind.
bolívar *m.* bolivar [Venezuelan coin].
Bolivia *f. pr. n.* GEOGR. Bolivia.
boliviano, -na *adj.-n.* of Bolivia.
bolo *m.* skittle, ninepin, tenpin. *2* dunce, idiot. *3* THEAT. snap; tour [in the country]. *4* newel [of winding stairs]. *5* large pill. *6* bolus. *7 ~ arménico,* Armenian bole. *8 pl.* skittles.
Bolonia *pr. n.* GEOG. Bologna.
bolonio *adj.* stupid, ignorant. *2 m.* dunce, donkey.
boloñés, -sa *adj.-n.* Bolognese.
bolsa *f.* bag, pouch [receptacle]. *2* purse [for carrying money; money, funds]: *la ~ o la vida,* your money or your life. *3* bag, pucker [in cloth, etc.]. *4* ZOOL. pouch. *5* MED. pouch, pocket. *6* MIN. pocket. *7* stock exchange, stock market: *jugar a la bolsa,* to speculate in stocks. *8 ~ del trabajo,* employment bureau. *9* BOT. *~ de pastor,* shepherd's-purse.
bolsero, -ra *m.-f.* maker or seller of bags or pouches.
bolsillo *m.* pocket [in a garment]: *de ~,* pocket, pocket-size. *2* purse [for money].
bolsín *m.* curb market.
bolsista *m.-f.* stockbroker; stock speculator.
bolsita *f. dim.* small purse.
bolso *m.* purse [for carrying money]: *~ de mano,* ladie's handbag. *2* NAUT. bulge [in a sail].
bollar *tr.* to bump. *2* to dent.
bollería *f.* bakery, pastry shop.
bollo *m.* bun, roll. *2* puff [in a dress]. *3* dent: *~ de relieve,* boss [round embossment]. *4* bump [swelling]. *5* row, shindy; confusion.
bollón *m.* stud [ornamental nail]. *2* button earring. *3* boss [round embossment].
bollonado, -da *adj.* studded [with nails or bosses].
bomba *f.* pump: *~ aspirante,* suction pump; *~ impelente,* force pump; *~ neumática,* air pump. *2* bomb: *~ atómica,* atomic bomb; *~ de mano,* handbomb; *~ volante,* flying bomb; *a prueba de ~,* bombproof; *caer como una ~,* to drop or to burst upon like a bombshell; *noticia ~,* surprising news. *3* globe [of lamp]. *4* MUS. slide [of an instrument].
bombáceo, -a *adj.* BOT. bombacaceous. *2 f. pl.* Bombacaceae.
bombacho *adj. calzón ~,* short, wide breeches; *pantalón ~,* loose-fitting trousers, fastened at the ankles.
bombarda *f.* bombard.
bombardear *tr.* MIL. to bombard; to bomb. *2* PHYS. to bombard.
bombardeo *m.* bombardment; bombing; *~ en picado,* AER. dive bombing.
bombardero *m.* bombardier. *2* bomber.
bombardino *m.* MUS. alto saxhorn.
bombardón *m.* MUS. bombardon.
bombazo *m.* explosion, detonation [of a bomb].
bombear *tr.* ARTILL. to bombard. *2* to puff, write up [praise exaggeratedly].
bombeo *m.* bulging, convexity.
bombero *m.* fireman [who puts out fires]. *2* pumpman.
bombilla *f.* ELECT. light bulb. *2* thief tube. *3* (Am.) small tube for drinking mate.

bombillo *m.* water-closet trap. 2 thief tube.
bombín *m.* coll. derby, bowler [hat]. 2 pump [of a bicycle].
bombo, -ba *adj.* dumfounded, stunned. 2 *m.* MUS. bass drum. 3 bass-drum player. 4 puffing, writing up: *dar ~*, to puff, to write up [praise exaggerately]. 5 revolving lottery box.
bombón *m.* bonbon, sweetmeat, chocolate.
bombona *f.* carboy.
bombonaje *m.* BOT. jipijapa.
bombonera *f.* box for bonbons.
bombonería *f.* sweet shop, confectioner's shop.
bonachón, -na *adj.* kind, good-natured. 2 *m.-f.* good soul.
bonaerense *adj.-n.* of Buenos Aires.
bonancible *adj.* fair [weather]; calm [sea]; moderate [wind].
bonanza *f.* NAUT. fair weather; calm sea. 2 MIN. bonanza. 3 prosperity.
bonapartista *adj.-n.* Bonapartist.
bondad *f.* goodness. 2 kindness, kindliness, good nature. 3 kindness, favour: *tenga la ~ de*, kindly, please to.
bondadoso, -sa *adj.* kind, good, good-natured.
boneta *f.* NAUT. bonnet.
bonete *m.* biretta. 2 college cap. 3 cap, skull cap. 4 FORT. bonnet. 5 ZOOL. bonnet, reticulum.
bonetero *m.* BOT. spindle tree.
boniato *m.* BUNIATO.
Bonifacio *pr. n.* Boniface.
bonificación *f.* allowance, discount.
bonificar *tr.* to improve. 2 COM. to credit.
bonísimo, -ma *adj. superl.* very good.
bonitamente *adv.* easily, artfully.
bonito, -ta *adj.* pretty, nice, dainty. 2 goodly, pretty good. 3 *m.* ICHTH. bonito.
bono *m.* COM. bond, debenture. 2 charity foodticket.
bonzo *m.* bonze.
boñiga *f.* cow dung.
boñigo *m.* cake of cow dung.
boqueada *f.* gasp [of death].
boquear *intr.* to gape, to gasp. 2 to be dying; to be at the last gasp. 3 *tr.* to utter.
boquera *f.* opening in an irrigation canal. 2 window in a hayloft. 3 MED. sore at angle of lips.
boquerón *m.* wide opening. 2 ICHTH. anchovy.
boquete *m.* gap, breach, opening, narrow entrance.
boquiabierto, -ta *adj.* open-mouthed, gaping.
boquiduro, -ra *adj.* hard-mouthed [horse].
boquifresco, -ca *adj.* tender-mouthed [horse]. 2 outspoken.
boquilla *f.* stem [of pipe]. 2 cigar holder; cigarette holder; tip [of cigarette]. 3 mouthpiece [of musical instrument]. 4 burner [of lamp]. 5 upper chape [of scabbard].
boquirrubio, -bia *adj.* loose-tongued, babbling. 2 simple, naive. 3 *m.* pretty boy, conceited youth.
borato *m.* CHEM. borate.
bórax *m.* CHEM. borax.
borbollar, borbollear *intr.* to bubble up.
borbollón *m.* bubbling up [of water]: *a borbollones*, hastily, tumultuously.
borbollonear *intr.* BORBOLLAR.
borbónico, -ca *adj.* Bourbonian, Bourbonic.
borbor *m.* bubble, bubbling.
borborigmo *m.* rumbling of the bowels.
boboritar *intr.* BORBOTAR, BORBOLLAR.
borbotar *intr.* [of water] to bubble up, to burble.

borbotón *m.* BORBOLLÓN: *a borbotones*, bubbling, gushing.
borceguí *m.* half boot, buskin.
borda *f.* NAUT. gunwale: *arrojar por la ~*, to throw overboard. 2 CHOZA.
bordada *f.* NAUT. tack, board: *dar bordadas*, to beat to windward, to tack.
bordado *m.* embroidering; embroidery.
bordador, -ra *m.-f.* embroiderer.
bordar *tr.* to embroider. 2 to perform exquisitely.
borde *adj.* bastard [person]. 2 wild [plant]. 3 *m.* border, edge, fringe, verge, brink; fig. *al ~ de*, on the verge of. 4 hem [of a garment]. 5 brim [of a vessel]. 6 NAUT. board.
bordear *intr.-tr.* to border, skirt. 2 *tr.* to border, to verge. 4 *intr.* NAUT. to beat to windward.
bordelés, -sa *adj.-n.* of Bordeaux.
bordillo *m.* ENCINTADO.
bordo *m.* NAUT. board [ship's side]: *a ~*, aboard; *de alto ~*, large [ship]; fig. of importance, high-up. 2 NAUT. tack.
bordón *m.* pilgrim's staff. 2 MUS. snare [of drum]; bass string; bourdon [in organ]. 4 refrain, burden [of poem]. 5 pet word, pet phrase.
bordonear *intr.* to pluck a guitar's bass string.
bordoneo *m.* sound of the guitar's bass string.
boreal *adj.* boreal, northern.
bóreas *m.* Boreas [north wind].
Borgoña *f. pr. n.* GEOG. Burgundy. 2 *m.* Burgundy [wine].
borgoñón, -na *adj.-n.* Burgundian.
bórico, -ca *adj.* CHEM. boric.
borinqueño, -ña *adj.-n.* Puerto Rican.
borla *f.* tassel, tuft. 2 tassel in academic cap. 3 powder puff.
borne *m.* tip of a jousting lance. 2 ELECT. terminal, binding post. 3 BOT. cytisus. 4 *adj.* hard and brittle [wood].
bornear *tr.* to turn, move, shift. 2 to model and carve [a column]. 3 *intr.* NAUT. to swing at anchor. 4 *ref.* to warp, to bulge.
borní *m.* ORN. marsh harrier.
boro *m.* CHEM. boron.
borona *f.* BOT. millet. 2 BOT. Indian corn.
borra *f.* yearling ewe. 2 coarse wool. 3 goat's hair [for stuffing]. 4 floss, fluff, fuzz, waste: *~ de algodón*, cotton waste. 5 lees. 6 fig. trash.
borrachera *f.* drunkenness, intoxication. 2 carousal. 3 high exaltation. 4 coll. great folly.
borrachín *m.* drunkard.
borracho, -cha *adj.* drunk, drunken, intoxicated. 2 violet-coloured. 3 *m.-f.* drunk man or woman, drunkard.
borrador *m.* draft, rough copy. 2 blotter [book].
borragináceo, -a *adj.* BOT. boraginaceous.
borraja *f.* BOT. borage.
borrajear *tr.* to scribble, scrawl.
borrar *tr.* to cross, strike, rub or blot out; to obliterate, efface, erase. 2 to smudge, blur.
borrasca *f.* storm, tempest. 2 coll. orgy, revelry.
borrascoso, -sa *adj.* stormy, tempestuous.
borregada *f.* flock of sheep.
borrego, -ga *m.-f.* yearly lamb. 2 simpleton.
borreguil *adj.* [pertaining to] lamb; of lambs.
borrica *f.* she-ass. 2 stupid woman.
borricada *f.* drove of donkeys. 2 stupidity, asininity.
borrico *m.* ZOOL. ass, donkey. 2 fig. ass. 3 CARP. sawhorse.
borrilla *f.* fuzz, fur [of fruits].
borriquillo, -lla *m.* young ass. 2 *f.* young she-ass.

borrón *m.* ink blot. *2* blot, blemish. *3* draft, rough copy. *4* first sketch.
borronear *tr.* BORRAJEAR. *2* to sketch.
borroso, -sa *adj.* smudgy, blurred, blurry, faded. *2* thick with sediment.
borujo *m.* BURUJO.
borujón *m.* BURUJÓN.
boscaje *m.* boscage. *2* PAINT. woodland scene.
boscoso, -sa *adj.* wooded.
Bósforo *m. pr. n.* GEOG. Bosphorus.
bosnio, -nia *adj.-n.* Bosnian.
bosorola *f.* dregs, sediment.
bosque *m.* forest, wood, grove, thicket; woodland.
bosquecillo *m.* small wood, grove, copse, copice.
bosquejar *tr.* to sketch, to outline.
bosquejo *m.* sketch, outline: *en* ~, sketchy.
bosquimano, -na *adj.-n.* Bushman.
bosta *f.* dung, manure.
bostezar *intr.* to yawn, gape [with drowsiness, etc.].
bostezo *m.* yawn.
bota *f.* small leather wine bag. *2* cask, butt [for liquids]. *3* boot: ~ *de montar*, riding boot; *ponerse las botas*, fig. to make money.
botador *m.* pole [for pushing a boat]. *2* CARP. nail puller; nail set.
botadura *f.* NAUT. launching.
botafuego *m.* linstock, match staff. *2* quicktempered person.
botafumeiro *m.* incense burner, censer [in Santiago de Compostela].
botalón *m.* NAUT. boom.
botana *f.* plug, stopper. *2* patch, plaster. *3* scar.
botánica *f.* botany.
botánico, -ca *adj.* botanical. *2* *m.-f.* botanist.
botar *tr.* to throw, fling out. *2* to launch [a boat]. *3* *intr.* to bound, bounce. *4* to jump. *5* *ref.* [of horses] to buck.
botaratada *f.* folly, nonsense.
botarate *m.* fool, harebrain. *2* (Am.) spendthrift.
botarel *m.* ARCH. buttress, counterfort.
botarga *f.* old large breeches. *2* ridiculous costume.
botasilla *f.* MIL. boots and saddles.
botavara *f.* NAUT. spanker boom.
bote *m.* NAUT. small boat: ~ *salvavidas*, lifeboat. *2* bound, bounce, jump. *3* jar, pot, canister; tin can. *4* MIL. ~ *de metralla*, canister shot. *5* *de* ~ *en* ~, crowded, crammed with people.
botella *f.* bottle. *2* ELECT. ~ *de Leyden*, Leyden jar.
botellazo *m.* blow with a bottle.
botellero *m.* bottle maker or dealer. *2* bottle rack.
botero *m.* NAUT. boatman.
botica *f.* chemist's; apothecary's shop, *drug store. *2* medicines.
boticaria *f.* chemist wife. *2* female pharmacist.
boticario *m.* chemist, druggist, apothecary.
botija *f.* earthen jug with a narrow mouth.
botijo *m.* round earthen jug with spout and handle.
botilla *f.* booty, ankle boot. *2* half boot.
botillería *f.* obs. icecream and light drinks saloon.
botín *m.* spat [short gaiter]. *2* boot. *3* booty, spoils.
botina *f.* high shoe.
botiquín *m.* medicine case; first-aid kit. *2* (Am.) retail wine store.
botivoleo *m.* SPORT. hitting the ball on the bounce.
boto, -ta *adj.* blunt, dull.
botón *m.* button [of garment, foil, electric bell, etc.]. *2* knob: ~ *de puerta*, doorknob. *3* BOT. but-

ton, bud. *4* SURG. ~ *de fuego*, hot iron cautery. *5* BOT. ~ *de oro*, buttercup.
botonadura *f.* set of buttons.
botonazo *m.* FENC. thrust with a foil.
botonería *f.* button maker's shop.
botonero, -ra *m.-f.* button maker or seller.
botones *m.* buttons, pageboy, bell boy.
botulismo *m.* MED. botulism.
bou *m.* fishing by casting a net between two boats.
bóveda *f.* ARCH., ANAT. vault: ~ *esquifada*, cross vault; ~ *en cañón*, barrel vault; ~ *palatina*, ANAT. palatine vault. *2* crypt. *3* ~ *celeste*, canopy of heaven.
bovedilla *f.* ARCH. cove, small vault. *2* NAUT. counter.
bóvido, -da *adj.-n.* ZOOL. bovid.
bovino, -na *adj.* bovine.
boxeador *m.* SPORT. boxer.
boxear *intr.* SPORT. to box.
boxeo *m.* SPORT. boxing.
boya *f.* NAUT. buoy. *2* float [of fishing net].
boyada *f.* drove of oxen.
boyante *adj.* NAUT. [of a ship] riding light. *2* prosperous, successful.
boyar *intr.* [of a ship] to float, be afloat again.
boyardo *m.* boyar.
boyera, boyeriza *f.* ox stable.
boyero, boyerizo *m.* ox driver; oxherd.
boyuno, -na *adj.* bovine.
bozal *m.* muzzle [mouth covering]. *2* muzzle bells.
bozo *m.* down [on upper lip]. *2* mouth, lips.
braceada *f.* impetuous movement of the arms.
braceaje *m.* coining, minting. *2* NAUT. depth of water.
bracear *intr.* to move or swing the arms. *2* to struggle. *3* to swim with overhead strokes. *4* [of horses] to step high. *5* NAUT. to brace.
braceo *m.* waving of the arms. *2* stroke [swimming].
bracero *m.* labourer [unskilled workman]. *2* *adv. de* ~, arm in arm.
bracmán *m.* BRAHMÁN.
bráctea *f.* BOT. bract.
bractéola *f.* BOT. bractlet, bracteole.
braga *f.* hoisting rope. *2* diaper [infant breechcloth]. *3* *pl.* wide breeches. *4* panties, step-ins.
bragado, -da *adj.* having the BRAGADURA of a different colour from the rest of the body [animal]. *2* wicked, ill-disposed. *3* firm, resolute.
bragadura *f.* crotch [of the body, of the trousers]. *2* inner surface of the thighs [in animals].
bragazas *m.* man without energy; henpecked man.
braguero *m.* SURG. truss [for a rupture]. *2* breeching [rope] of a gun.
bragueta *f.* fly [of trousers].
braguetazo *m.* coll. marriage of convenience: *dar un* ~, to marry money.
brahmán *m.* Brahman.
brahmánico, -ca *adj.* Brahmanic(al.
brahmanismo *m.* Brahmanism.
brahmin *m.* BRAHMÁN.
brama *f.* rut [of deers].
bramadera *f.* bull-roarer [toy]. *2* shepherd's horn.
bramador, -ra *adj.* lowing [a cow]; bellowing, roaring [a bull].
bramante *m.* thin twine or hemp string. *2* *adj.* roaring.
bramar *intr.* to bellow, roar.
bramido *m.* bellow, roar.
brancada *f.* trammel net, trammel.

branca ursina *f.* BOT. acanthus.
brancal *m.* frame [of a gun carriage].
brandal *m.* NAUT. side-rope [of ladder]. 2 NAUT. backstay.
branquia *f.* ZOOL. branchia. 2 *pl.* branchiae.
branquial *adj.* branchial.
braquial *adj.* ANAT. brachial.
braquicéfalo, -la *adj.* ANTHROP. brachycephalic.
braquiópodos *m. pl.* brachiopodes.
braquiuro *m.* brachyuran.
brasa *f.* live coal: *estar en brasas*, to be on tenter-hooks; *estar hecho unas brasas*, to be flushed; *pasar como sobre brasas*, to mention or touch upon superficially.
brasca *f.* lute.
braserillo *m.* small pan for burning coals.
brasero *m.* brazier [pan for burning coals].
Brasil *m. pr. n.* GEOG. Brazil.
brasil *m.* BOT. brazil tree. 2 brazil, brazilwood.
brasileño, -ña *adj.-n.* Brazilian.
brasilete *m.* BOT. brazilette tree. 2 braziletto.
bravamente *adv.* bravely, gallantly. 2 cruelly. 3 finely, extremely well. 4 abundantly.
bravata *f.* bluster, swagger, brag.
bravear *intr.* to talk big, bluster, swagger.
braveza *f.* bravery. 2 fierceness, ferocity [of animals]. 3 fury [of the sea, wind, etc.].
bravío, -a *adj.* ferocious, wild, untamed. 2 rustic [person]. 3 wild [plant].
bravo, -va *adj.* brave, courageous. 2 fine, excellent. 3 fierce, ferocious [animal]. 4 rough [sea, land]. 5 angry, violent. 6 sumptuous, magnificent. 7 *interj.* bravo!
bravucón, -na *adj.* swaggering. 2 *f.* swaggerer.
bravuconada *f.* bluster, swagger.
bravura *f.* bravery, courage. 2 fierceness, ferocity [of animals]. 3 BRAVATA.
braza *f.* NAUT. fathom. 2 NAUT. brace [rope].
brazada *f.* stroke [with arms]. 2 BRAZADO.
brazado *m.* armful, armload.
brazal *m.* ARM. brassart. 2 brassard, arm band. 3 irrigation ditch. 4 NAUT. headrail. 5 EMBRAZA-DURA.
brazalete *m.* bracelet, armlet.
brazo *m.* arm [of the body, a chair, lever, etc.]: *cruzarse de brazos*, to fold one's arms; fig. to remain idle; *no dar su ~ a torcer*, not to yield; *ser el ~ derecho de uno*, to be someone's right-hand man; *a ~ partido*, hand to hand; tooth and nail; *asidos del ~*, arm in arm; *con los brazos abiertos*, with open arms. 2 arm, power, might. 3 foreleg [of a quadruped]. 4 branch [of a river]. 5 *pl.* hands, workers.
brazuelo *m.* small arm. 2 forearm [of quadrupeds].
brea *f.* tar, wood tar: *~ seca*, rosin. 2 NAUT. pitch.
brear *tr.* to ill-treat. 2 to make fun of, to tease.
brebaje *m.* beverage, unpalatable drink.
breca *f.* ICHTH. bleak.
brécol *m.*, **brecolera** *f.* BOT. broccoli.
brecha *f.* breach, gap, opening [in wall or fortification]; fig. impression [on the mind].
brega *f.* fight, scrap. 2 struggle: *andar a la ~*, to work hard, to toil. 3 *dar ~*, to tease.
bregar *intr.* to fight. 2 to struggle. 3 to work hard, toil. 4 *tr.* to knead.
Brema *pr. n.* Bremen.
breña *f.*, **breñal, breñar** *m.* bushy and craggy ground.
breñoso, -sa *adj.* bushy an craggy.

breque *m.* sea bream. 2 (Am.) handbrake, emergency brake.
bresca *f.* honeycomb.
Bretaña *f. pr. n.* Bretagne, Brittany. 2 *Gran ~*, Great Britain, Britain.
brete *m.* tight spot, difficult situation.
bretón, -na *adj.-n.* Breton. 2 *m. pl.* BOT. Brussels sprouts.
breva *f.* early fig. 2 flat cigar. 3 fig. plum, good thing.
breve *adj.* short, brief. 2 PHON. short. 3 *m.* apostolic brief. 4 *f.* MUS. breve. 5 *adv. en ~*, soon, shortly.
brevedad *f.* brevity, briefness. 2 *a la mayor ~*, as soon as possible.
breviario *m.* breviary. 2 PRINT. brevier.
brezal *m.* heath, moor.
brezo *m.* BOT. heath, heather.
briba *f.* vagrant life, loafing about.
bribón, -na *adj.* loafing. 2 rascally. 3 *m.-f.* loafer. 4 rascal, knave, scoundrel.
bribonada *f.* knavery, dirty trick.
bribonería *f.* life of loafing. 2 rascality.
bribonzuelo, -la *m.-f.* little rascal, rogue.
bricbarca *f.* NAUT. bark.
brida *f.* bridle [of riding gear]: *a toda ~*, at to speed. 2 MEC. splice bar, clamp; flange. 3 RLY. fishplate. 4 *pl.* SURG. filaments around the lips of a wound.
bridón *m.* small bridle. 2 snaffle bit. 3 steed, spirited horse.
brigada *f.* MIL. brigade. 2 MIL. train [of beasts]. 3 squad, gang. 4 MIL. sergeant-major.
brigadier *m.* brigadier, brigadier general.
Brígida *f. pr. n.* Bridget.
brillante *adj.* brilliant, shining, bright. 2 sparkling, glittering, glossy. 3 *m.* brilliant [diamond].
brillantez *f.* brillance. 2 success, splendour.
brillantina *f.* brilliantine. 2 metal polish.
brillar *intr.* to shine. 2 to sparkle, glitter, be glossy. 3 fig. *~ por su ausencia*, to be lacking.
brillo *m.* brilliance, brightness, lustre; splendor.
brin *m.* fine canvas.
brincar *intr.* to spring, skip, leap, jump. 2 to take offence, to get excited.
brinco *m.* spring, skip, leap jump.
brindar *intr.* to toast: *~ por*, to drink [a person's] health; to toast. 2 *tr.-intr.* to offer, present, afford; to invite: *~ a uno con una cosa*, to offer something to someone. 3 *ref. brindarse a*, to offer to [do something].
brindis *m.* toast, drinking the health.
brío *m.* strength, spirit, determination. 2 grace, elegance, vivacity.
briofita *adj.* BOT. bryophyitic.
briol *m.* NAUT. buntline.
brionia *f.* BOT. bryony.
bríos *interj.* ¡*voto a ~!*, by the Almighty!
briosamente *adv.* bravely, courageously, valiantly. 2 resolutely, firmly. 3 vigorously, energetically, with spirit.
brioso, -sa *adj.* vigorous, spirited, lively.
briqueta *f.* briquet, briquette [of coal].
brisa *f.* northeast wind. 2 breeze. 3 bagasse of pressed grapes.
brisca *f.* a Spanish card game.
briscar *tr.* to brocade.
brisote *m.* stormy breeze.
bristol *m.* Bristol board, Bristol paper.
británico, -ca *adj.* British, Britannic.
britano, -na *adj.* British. 2 *m.-f.* Briton.
briza *f.* BOT. quaking grass.

brizna f. slender particle, filament; leaf [of grass]; string [in pods].

broca f. WEAV., SPIN. spindle, skewer: ~ de lanzadera, shuttle spindle. 2 conical drill bit. 3 shoemaker's tack.

brocado, -da adj. brocaded. 2 m. brocade.

brocal m. curbstone [of a well]. 2 steel rim [of a shield]; metal mouth [of a scabbard]. 3 mouthpiece [of a leather wine bag].

brocamantón m. diamond brooch.

brocatel m. brocatel, brocatelle [fabric; marble].

bróculi m. BRÉCOL.

brocha f. stubby brush [for painting]: de ~ gorda, house [painter]; crude, heavyhanded [literary work]. 2 ~ de afeitar, shaving brush.

brochada f. dab, stroke [with a stubby brush].

brochazo m. BROCHADA.

broche m. clasp, fastener, hook and eye; brooch. 2 hasp [for book covers].

brocheta f. COOK. skewer.

brocho adj.-m. BULLF. having horns close together.

broma f. fun, merriment; joke, jest, practical joke: gastar una ~ a, to play a joke on; en ~, in fun, jokingly. 2 ZOOL. shipworm.

bromato m. CHEM. bromate.

bromatología f. bromatology.

bromazo m. practical joke.

bromear intr. to joke, jest, make fun.

bromeliáceo, -a adj. BOT. bromeliaceous.

brómico adj. CHEM. bromic.

bromista adj. full of fun. 2 m.-f. merry person, joker, practical joker.

bromo m. CHEM. bromin(e. 2 BOT. brome grass.

bromuro m. CHEM. bromide.

bronca f. row, shindy. 2 harsh reprehension.

bronce m. bronze: la Edad de ~, the Bronze Age. 2 poet. cannon, bell, trumpet.

bronceado, -da adj. bronze, bronze coloured. 2 tanned, sunburnt. 3 m. bronzing, bronze finish; bronze [colour].

bronceador m. suntan product.

broncear tr. to bronze. 2 to tan [the skin].

broncíneo, -a adj. brazen; bronzelike.

broncista m. bronzesmith.

bronco, -ca adj. coarse, rough. 2 brittle [metal]. 3 gruff, rude. 4 harsh, hoarse [sound, voice].

bronconeumonía f. MED. bronchopneumonia.

broncoscopio m. bronchoscope.

bronquedad f. coarseness, roughness. 2 brittleness [of metals]. 3 gruffness. 4 hoarseness.

bronquial adj. bronchial.

bronquio m. ANAT. bronchus. 2 pl. bronchi.

bronquiolo m. ANAT. bronchiole.

bronquitis f. MED. bronchitis.

broquel m. shield, buckler. 2 shield, protection.

broqueta f. COOK. skewer.

brotadura f. budding, sprouting. 2 springing, gushing. 3 eruption, rash.

brotar intr. to germinate, to sprout; to bud, burgeon, shoot. 2 [of water, tears, etc.] to spring, gush. 3 [of pimples, etc.] to break out. 4 tr. to put forth [plants, gras, etc.]. 5 to shed.

brote m. bud, sprout. 2 outbreak, appearance.

broza f. underbrush. 2 brush, brushwood. 3 rubbish, trash.

brozno, -na adj. BRONCO. 2 slow-witted.

bruces (a or de) adv. face downward, on one's face.

brucita f. MINER. brucite.

bruja f. witch, sorceress. 2 coll. hag, shrew.

Brujas pr. n. GEOG. Bruges.

brujería f. witchcraft, sorcery, magic.

brujir tr. to trim the edge of a glass.

brujo m. wizard, sorcerer.

brújula f. magnetic needle, compass.

brujulear tr. to guess, smell out.

brulote m. fire ship.

bruma f. mist, fog [in the sea].

brumazón m. heavy fog, thick mist.

brumoso, -sa adj. foggy, hazy, misty.

bruno, -na adj. dark, brown.

bruñido, -da adj. burnished. 2 m. burnishing.

bruñidura f., **bruñimiento** m. burnishing.

bruñir tr. to burnish.

bruño m. BOT. black plum.

brusco, -ca adj. brusque, rude, blunt, gruff. 2 sudden. 3 sharp [curve]. 4 m. BOT. butcher's-broom.

Bruselas pr. n. GEOG. Brussels.

brusquedad f. brusqueness, rudeness, bluntness, gruffness; rude action or treatment. 2 suddenness.

brutal adj. brutal, brutish. 2 coll. colossal. 3 m. brute, beast.

brutalidad f. brutality. 2 stupidity. 3 fig. me gusta una ~, I like it enormously.

brutalizarse ref. to brutalize [become like a brute].

bruteza f. brutality. 2 roughness, want of polish.

1) **bruto** m. brute, beast. 2 fig. brute; blockhead. 3 pr. n. (cap.) Brutus.

2) **bruto, -ta** adj. brute, brutish. 2 stupid, ignorant. 3 rough, unpolished. 4 bruto or en ~, in the rough, unwrought, crude; gross [without any deduction].

bruza f. horse brush. 2 printer's brush.

bruzar tr. to brush [horses or printing forms].

bu m. bogey man: hacer el ~, to scare, frighten.

búa f. pimple. 2 m. bubo.

buba f. MED. bubo.

búbalo m. ZOOL. bubal, bubale.

bubón m. MED. bubo.

bubónico, -ca adj. bubonic.

bucal adj. buccal.

bucanero m. buccaneer.

Bucarest pr. n. GEOG. Bucharest.

búcaro m. an odoriferous clay. 2 flower vase.

buccino m. ZOOL. whelk.

buceador m. diver. 2 pearl diver.

bucear intr. to dive; to swim under water. 2 fig. to dive [in], to explore.

Bucéfalo m. Bucephalus.

buceo m. diving.

bucinador m. ANAT. buccinator.

bucle m. long curl [of hair]. 2 AER. loop.

buco m. ZOOL. billy goat, buck. 2 opening, gap.

bucólica f. bucolic [poem]. 2 coll. food; meal.

bucólico, -ca adj. bucolic. 2 m. bucolic poet.

buchada f. mouthful.

buche m. craw [of animals]. 2 stomach [of man]. 3 bosom [thoughts, secrets]. 4 suckling ass.

buchon, -na adj. pouter [pigeon].

Buda m. pr. n. Buddha.

budin m. pudding.

budión m. ICHTH. peacock fish.

budismo m. Buddhism.

budista adj.-n. Buddhist.

buen adj. apocopated form of BUENO, used only before a masculine substantive.

buenamente adv. easily, without difficulty. 2 voluntarily, spontaneously.

buenaventura f. good luck, happiness. 2 fortune [as told by a fortuneteller]: decirle a uno la ~, to tell someone his fortune.

Buenaventura *m. pr. n.* Bonaventure.
bueno, -na *adj.* good. *2* kind. *3* fit, suitable. *4* well [in good health or condition]. *5* iron. extraordinary, fine: ~ *fuera que...*, it would be fine if... *6 a buenas, por la buena*, willingly, without reluctance; *¡buena es ésta!*, that is a good one! [surprise or disapproval]; *buenos días*, good day, good morning; *buenas noches*, good evening, good night; *buenas tardes*, good afternoon.; *de buenas a primeras*, from the very start. *7 adv. ¡bueno!*, well!, very well!; al right! that is enough!
Buenos Aires *m. pr. n.* GEOG. Buenos Aires.
buey *m.* ZOOL. ox, bullock, steer: *carne de ~*, beef. *2* ZOOL. ~ *del Tibet*, yak. *3* ~ *de cabestrillo*, stalking-horse.
bufado, -da *adj.* blown'very thin [glass].
búfalo *m.* ZOOL. buffalo.
bufanda *f.* muffler [for the neck], scarf.
bufar *intr.* to puff and blow, to snort [with anger].
bufete *m.* writing desk. *2* lawyer's office or practice. *3* (Am.) snack, refreshment.
bufido *m.* angry snort or roar.
bufo, -fa *adj.* farcical bouffe: *ópera ~*, opera bouffe. *2 m.* buffoon. *3* buffo [actor].
bufón, -na *adj.* buffoon. *2 m.-f.* buffoon, jester.
bufonada *f.* buffoonery.
bufonesco, -ca *adj.* buffoon, farcical.
buganvilla *f.* BOT. bougainvillea.
bugle *m.* MUS. bugle [wind instrument with pistons].
buglosa *f.* BOT. bugloss.
buharda, buhardilla *f.* dormer, dormer window. *2* garret. *3* (Am.) skylight.
buharro *m.* ORN. scops owl.
búho *m.* ORN. eagle owl.
buhonería *f.* pedlary, peddlery [pedlar wares].
buhonero *m.* pedlar, peddler, hawker.
buido, -da *adj.* pointed, sharp. *2* grooved, striated.
buitre *m.* ORN. vulture.
buitrón *m.* fish trap [made of osier]. *2* partridge net. *3* snare for game.
buje *m.* axle box [bushing].
bujería *f.* gewgaw, knick-knack.
bujía *f.* wax or stearine candle. *2* candlestick. *3* PHYS. candlepower. *4* spark plug.
bula *f.* [papal] bull. *2* bulla.
bulbillo *m.* BOT. bulbil.
bulbo'm. ANAT., BOT. bulb.
bulboso, -sa *adj.* bulbous.
buldog *m.* bulldog.
buldozer *m.* bulldozer.
bulerías *f. pl.* bulerias, dance and song from Andalusia.
bulevar *m,* boulevard.
Bulgaria *f. pr. n.* GEOG. Bulgaria.
búlgaro, -ra *adj.-n.* Bulgar, Bulgarian.
bulo *m.* canard, hoax, false report.
bulto *m.* volume, size, bulk: *de ~*, in sculpture; fig. obvious, striking. *2* shade, form, body: *buscar el ~ a uno*, to persecute, provoke [someone]; *escurrir el ~*, to evade a task, danger, etc. *3* swelling, lump. *4* statue. *5* bundle, pack, piece of luggage. *6 a ~*, broadly, roughly.
bulla *f.* noise, uproar, racket. *2* crowd.
bullabesa *f.* bouillabaisse.
bullanga *f.* tumult, racket, disturbance.
bullanguero, -ra *adj.* fond of noise. *2 m.-f.* noisy person, rioter.
bullebulle *m.-f.* coll. a lively, bustling person.
bullicio *m.* hubbub, noise, stir. *2* riot.

bullicioso, -sa *adj.* noisy, boisterous, restless, lively, merry. *2* riotous. *3 m.-f.* rioter.
bullidor, -ra *adj.* bustling, lively.
bullir *intr.* to boil. *2* to bubble up. *3* to seethe. *4* to bustle about. *5 intr.-ref.-tr.* to move, stir, budge.
bullón *m.* stud [for bookbindings]. *2* puff [in a dress].
bumerang *m.* boomerang.
bungalow *m.* bungalow.
buniato *m.* BOT. sweet potato.
bunker *m.* bunker.
buñolería *f.* fried cake shop.
buñolero, -ra *m.-f.* maker or seller of BUÑUELOS.
buñuelo *m.* doughnut, cruller; fritter. *2* botch, bungle.
buque *m.* NAUT. ship, vessel: ~ *de cabotaje*, coaster; ~ *de guerra*, warship; ~ *de vapor*, steamer, steamboat; ~ *de vela*, sailboat; ~ *cisterna*, tanker; ~ *escuela*, training ship; ~ *mercante*, merchant vessel; ~ *transbordador*, train ferry. *2* hull [of a ship]. *3* capacity.
burbuja *f.* bubble.
burbujear *intr.* to bubble.
burbujeo *m.* bubbling.
burdégano *m.* ZOOL. hinny.
burdel *m.* brothel, disorderly house.
Burdeos *pr. n. & m.* Bordeaux [town and wine].
burdo, -da *adj.* coarse. *2* clumsy [lie, work].
bureo *m.* amusement, diversion.
bureta *f.* CHEM. burette.
burga *f.* hot springs.
burgado *m.* ZOOL. a brown edible snail.
burgalés, -sa *adj.-n.* of Burgos.
burgo *m.* obs. hamlet.
burgomaestre *m.* burgomaster.
burgrave *m.* burgrave.
burgués, -sa *m.-f.* burgher. *2* bourgeois.
burguesía *f.* burgeoisie.
buriel *adj.* chestnut red. *2 m.* coarse woollen cloth.
buril *m.* burin.
burilar *tr.* to engrave with a burin.
burjaca *f.* pilgrim's scrip. *23* leather bag carried by pilgrims and beggars for carrying food and alms.
burla *f.* mockery, gibe, jeer, scoff: *hacer ~ de*, to mock, scoff, make fun of. *2* joke, jest: *de burlas*, in fun. *3* deception, trick.
burladero *m.* refuge in a bull ring. *2* safety island.
burlador, -ra *adj.* mocking, deceiving. *2 m.* mocker, deceiver. *3* seducer of women.
burlar *tr.* to mock. *2* to deceive. *3* to disappoint, to frustrate, to evade. *4 intr.-ref.* to make fun: *burlarse de*, to make fun of, to laugh at; *burla, burlando*, without noticing it; on the quiet.
burlería *f.* mockery. *2* illusion. *3* derision.
burlesco, -ca *adj.* burlesque, comical, jocular.
burlete *m.* weather strip or stripping.
burlón, -na *adj.* mocking. *2 m.-f.* mocker, joker.
buró *m.* writing desk, bureau.
burocracia *f.* bureaucracy.
burócrata *m.-f.* bureaucrat.
burra *f.* she-ass. *2* ignorant, stupid woman. *3* strong hardworking woman.
burrada *f.* drove of asses. *2* stupid act or expression.
burrero *m.* ass keeper who sells asses' milk.
burro *m.* ZOOL. donkey, ass: fig. ~ *de carga*, strong, hardworking man. *2* ignorant, stupid man. *3* sawbuck, sawhorse. *4* card game.
bursátil *adj.* stock, stock-market.

burujo *m.* knot [in wool], lump [in a matter]. *2* bagasse of pressed olives.

burujón *m.* aug. of BURUJO. *2* lump, swelling.

busardo *m.* ORN. buzzard.

busca *f.* search, hunt, quest: *en ~ de*, in quest of. *2* HUNT. party of beaters.

buscador, -ra *adj.* searching. *2 m.-f.* searcher, seeker; prospector. *3 m.* OPT. finder.

buscapié *m.* sounding remark [in conversation].

buscapiés *m.* serpent, snake [firework].

buscapleitos *m. pl.* troublemaker, litigious fellow.

buscar *tr.* to look for, search for, hunt for, seek. *2* to prospect. *3 ref.* to get; to bring upon oneself.

buscarruidos *m.-f.* troublemaker.

buscavidas *m.-f.* busybody. *2* hustler.

busco *m.* miter sill [of canal-lock gate].

buscón, -na *m.-f.* searcher, seeker. *2* petty thief. *3 f.* harlot.

busilis *m.* coll. rub, point: *ahí está el ~*, there's the rub; *dar en el ~*, to see the point.

búsqueda *f.* search, hunt, quest.

busto *m.* bust.

butaca *f.* easy chair. *2* THEAT. orchestra seat.

butano *m.* CHEM. butane.

buten (de) *adj.* coll, first-rate, ripping.

butifarra *f.* a kind of pork sausage.

butilo *m.* CHEM. butyl.

butírico, -ca *adj.* CHEM. butyric.

buxáceo, -a *adj.* BOT. buxaceous.

buyo *m.* buyo [chewing paste].

buzamiento *m.* GEOL. dip.

buzar *intr.* GEOL. to dip.

buzo *m.* diver: *campana de ~*, diving bell.

buzón *m.* outlet [of a pond]. *2* letter drop; letter box, mailbox, postbox; *~ de alcance*, late-collection postbox. *3* stopper, plug, bung.

C

C, c *f.* C, c., third letter of the Spanish alphabet.

¡ca! *interj.* oh no! not at all!, no indeed!

cabal *adj.* exact, full, complete. 2 perfect, faultless. 3 *adv.* exactly. 4 *m. pl. no estar uno en sus cabales*, not to be in one's right mind.

cábala *f.* cabala. 2 cabal. 3 guess, divination.

cabalgada *f.* [in old times] raid by horsemen.

cabalgador, -ra *m.-f.* rider [on horseback].

cabalgadura *f.* mount, riding horse or animal. 2 beast of burden.

cabalgar *intr.* to horse, ride on horseback. 2 *tr.* to ride, mount [a horse, mule o ass]. 3 to cover [a mare].

cabalgata *f.* cavalcade.

cabalista *adj.-n.* cabalist, cabbalist. 2 intriguer, schemer.

cabalístico, -ca *adj.* cabalistic.

cabalmente *adv.* exactly, completely, fully. 2 just.

caballa *m.* ICHTH. mackerel.

caballada *f.* drove of horses. 2 (Am.) stupidity.

caballar *adj.* equine.

caballejo *m.* little horse. 2 nag.

caballeresco, -ca *adj.* chivalric, chivalrous, chivalresque.

caballerete *m.* little gentleman, little dandy.

caballería *f.* riding animal; horse, mule, ass. 2 MIL. horse, cavalry. 3 knights, knighthood, chivalry, order of knights: ~ *andante*, errantry, knight errantry. 4 chivalric act.

caballeriza *f.* stable [for horses]. 2 royal mews. 3 stable, stud [horses kept]. 4 stable hands.

caballerizo *m.* head groom of a stable. 2 equerry: ~ *mayor del rey*, royal master of the horse.

caballero, -ra *adj.* riding, mounted. 2 *m.* knight: ~ *andante*, knight errant; *armar* ~, to knight. 3 gentleman: fig. ~ *de industria*, gentleman crook, chevalier of industry; ~ *en plaza*, mounted toreador. 4 sir [in addressing a man].

caballerosamente *adv.* chivalrously.

caballerosidad *f.* chivalry, gentlemanly behaviour.

caballeroso, -sa *adj.* chivalrous, gentlemanly.

caballete *m.* small horse. 2 ridge [of a roof]. 3 horse [instrument of torture]. 4 trestle, carpenter's horse, gantry. 5 easel. 6 ridge [between furrows]. 7 chimney cap. 8 bridge [of nose]. 9 stand for saddles.

caballista *m.* horseman, good rider. 2 mounted highwayman.

caballito *m. dim.* little horse. 2 rocking-horse, hobby-horse. 3 ENT. ~ *del diablo*, dragonfly. 4 *pl.* merry-go-round. 5 petits chevaux [game].

caballo *m.* ZOOL. horse: ~ *de batalla*, battle horse; fig. forte, specialty; fig. main point [in controversy]; ~ *de silla*, saddle horse; ~ *padre* or *semental*, stallion; *a* ~, on horse-back; *a* ~ *de*, astride. 2 knight [in chess]. 3 CARDS. queen. 4 ~ *de agua* or *marino*, ZOOL. river horse; ICHTH. sea horse. 5 MECH. ~ *de fuerza* or *de vapor*, horsepower. 6 MIL. ~ *de Frisa* or *de Frisia*, cheval-de-frise. 7 *pl.* MIL. horse, cavalry.

caballón *m.* ridge [between furrows]. 2 small ridge for dividing plots, directing water, etc.

caballuno, -na *adj.* equine; horselike.

cabaña *f.* cabin, hut, hovel. 2 large number of sheep or cattle. 7 balk [in billiards].

cabañal *adj.* sheep-and-cattle [path]. 2 *m.* village of cabins.

cabañuela *f.* little cabin.

cabaretera *f.* cabaret entertainer.

cabe *m.* stroke on a ball: *dar un* ~ *a*, to hurt, harm. 2 *prep.* poét. near, at the side of.

cabecear *intr.* to nod [in drowsiness]. 2 [of horses] to raise and lower the head. 3 NAUT. to pitch. 4 *tr.* to strengthen [new wine] with old wine. 5 to blend [wines]. 6 to bind the edge [of a carpet, etc.]. 7 to put the headband to [a book].

cabeceo *m.* nodding [of the head]. 2 NAUT. pitching.

cabecera *f.* beginning or principal part; upper end; head [of a table, bed, etc.]. 2 seat of honour. 3 headboard [of a bed]. 4 bedside. 5 headwaters. 6 main town. 7 PRINT. headpiece. 8 head or tail of the back [of a book].

cabecero *m.* headrest.

cabecilla *f.* little head. 2 wrong-headed person. 3 *m.* ringleader, rebel leader.

cabellera *f.* hair, head of hair. 2 wig. 3 ASTR. tail [of comet].

cabello *m.* hair [of the human head, singly or collectively]: *asirse de un* ~, to seize upon any trivial pretext; *partir un* ~ *en el aire*, to be very shrewd; *traído por los cabellos*, farfetched. 2 corn silk. 3 ~ *de ángel*, sweetmeat made from a squash. 4 *pl.* hair, head of hair.

cabelludo, -da *adj.* with an abundant head of hair. 2 BOT. hairy.

caber *intr.* to be containable [in], to go [in or into]; to have room or room enough: *en esta lata caben diez litros,* this can will hold ten litres; *usted no cabe entre nosotros,* there is no room for you among us; *no me cabe en la cabeza que,* fig. I never would have believed that. 2 *me cabe el honor de,* I have the hono(u)r of. 3 *todo cabe en,* all is possible in. 4 *no cabe duda,* there is no doubt. 5 *no caber en sí de,* to be bursting with [joy, etc.]. ¶ CONJUG.: IND. Pres.: *quepo, cabes, cabe,* etc. | Pret.: *cupe, cupiste, cupo; cupimos, cupisteis, cupieron.* | Fut.: *cabré, cabrás,* etc. | COND.: *cabría, cabrías,* etc. | SUBJ. Pres.: *quepa, quepas, quepa; quepamos, quepáis, quepan.* | Imperf.: *cupiera, cupieras,* etc., or *cupiese, cupieses,* etc. | Fut.: *cupiere, cupieres,* etc. | IMPER.: *cabe, quepa; quepamos, cabed, quepan.*

cabestrante *m.* capstan.

cabestrar *tr.* to put a halter on [a beast].

cabestrillo *m.* sing [for injured arm]. 2 little chain worn as a necklace.

cabestro *m.* halter [for horses]: *llevar* or *traer del cabestro,* to lead by the halter; fig. to lead by the nose. 3 leading ox.

cabeza *f.* head [of man or animal; mind, understanding; top part of end]: ~ *de chorlito,* scatterbrains; ~ *de puente,* bridgehead; ~ *de turco,* scapegoat; *mala* ~, ne'er-do-well; scapegrace; *de* ~, by heart; head first; *calentarse la* ~ to rack one's brains; *írsele a uno la* ~, to feel giddy; *levantar* ~, to get on one's feet [after misfortune]; to recover [from illness]; *pasarle a uno por la* ~ [*una cosa*], to cross one's mind; to come into one's head; *romperse la* ~, to cudgel or to rack one's brains; *sentar la* ~, to settle down; *subirse una cosa a la* ~, to go to one's head. 2 head [chief, leader; first place]: *a la* ~, at the head, in the lead. 3 headwaters, head [of a river]. 4 head, individual: *por* ~, per head. 5 main town: ~ *de partido,* country seat. 6 ~ *de ajo,* bulb of garlic.

cabezada *f.* blow with the head, butt. 2 nod [from drowsiness or in salutation]: *dar cabezadas,* to nod. 3 NAUT., AER. pitch, pitching, plunge. 4 headgear [of harness], headstall [of bridle]. 5 headband [of book].

cabezal *m.* small pillow. 2 long pillow, bolster. 3 SURG. bolster. 4 MIN., MACH. headstock.

cabezazo *m.* blow with the head, butt.

cabezón, -na *adj.-n.* CABEZUDO 1 & 2. 2 *m.* opening for the head [in a garment]. 3 ~ *de serreta,* cavesson.

cabezonada *f.* obstinate act.

cabezota *f.* large head. 3 *m.-f.* big-headed or obstinate person.

cabezudo, -da *adj.* big-headed. 2 obstinate. 3 *m.-f.* big-headed or obstinate person. 4 *m.* figure of a big-headed dwarf [in some processions]. 5 ICHTH. mullet.

cabezuela *f. dim.* small head. 2 coarse flour, middling. 3 BOT. capitulum, head [inflorescence].

cabida *f.* espace, room, capacity: *dar* ~ *a,* to make room for; *tener* ~, to apply, be applicable. 2 extent [of a field]. 3 favour, influence.

cabildante *m.* town councillor.

cabildear *intr.* to lobby.

cabildeo *m.* lobbying, intriguing.

cabildo *m.* chapter [of a cathedral or collegiate church]. 2 town council. 3 meeting of a CABILDO.

cabilla *f.* NAUT. driftbolt. 2 NAUT. belaying pin. 3 NAUT. wheel handle.

cabillo *m.* BOT. stem [of leaf, flower or fruit].

cabina *f.* AER., TELEPH. cabin.

cabio *m.* ARCH. joist. 2 ARCH. trimmer. 3 top piece or bottom piece [of a door frame].

cabizbajo, -ja *adj.* crestfallen; pensive.

cable *m.* cable, rope, hawser. 2 cable [cable's length; submarine cable; cablegram].

cablegrafiar *tr.* to cable.

cablegráfico, -ca *adj.* cable: *dirección cablegráfica,* cable address.

cablegrama *m.* cablegram.

cabo *m.* end, extremity: ~ *suelto,* fig. loose end; *atar cabos,* fig. to put two and two together; *estar al* ~ *de la calle,* to be informed [about something]; *de* ~ *a rabo,* from head to tail, from beginning to end. 2 end, termination, conclusion: *llevar a* ~, to carry out; *al* ~, finally; *al* ~ *de,* at the end of; *al* ~ *de un mes,* in a month. 3 bit, stump: ~ *de vela,* stump of candle. 4 strand [of rope or thread]. 5 haft. 6 NAUT. rope, cordage. 7 GEOG. cape: ~ *de Buena Esperanza,* Cape of Good Hope; ~ *de Hornos,* Cape Horn. 8 MIL. corporal. 9 mane, muzzle and feet [of horses].

cabotaje *m.* NAUT. cabotage, coasting trade.

cabra *f.* ZOOL. goat: ~ *de almizcle,* musk deer; ~ *montés,* wild goat. 2 *pl.* marks on the legs from sitting near the fire.

cabrahigar *tr.* to caprificate.

cabrahigo *m.* BOT. caprifig, goat fig, wild fig.

cabreado, -da *adj.* coll. angry, furious, livid.

cabrear *tr.* coll. to get worked up, to get one's back up, to become annoyed. 2 *intr.* (Am.) to prance about, to scamper about. 3 *ref.* coll. to see red, to get furious, to get worked up.

cabreo *m. coger un* ~, to fly of the handle; *tener un* ~, to be annoyed, to be worked up; *dar un* ~ *a alguien,* to get someone worked up.

cabrera *f.* goatherdess. 2 goatherd's wife.

cabrería *f.* goat's milk dairy. 2 stable for goats.

cabreriza *f.* goatherd's cabin. 2 goatherd's wife.

cabrerizo, cabrero *m.* goatherd.

cabrestante *m.* capstan.

cabria *f.* crab, derrik [hoisting machine].

cabrilla *f.* ICHTH. cabrilla. 2 sawbuck. 3 *pl.* CABRAS 2. 4 whitecaps [in the sea]. 5 ASTR. Pleiades.

cabrillear *intr.* [of the sea] to form whitecaps.

cabrilleo *m.* the forming of whitecaps.

cabrio *m.* common rafter.

cabrío *adj.* hircine, goat. 2 *m.* herd of goats.

cabriola *f.* caper, sikp, gambol, tumble; capriole.

cabriolar *intr.* CABRIOLEAR.

cabriolé *m.* cabriolet.

cabriolear *intr.* to caper, gambol; to capriole.

cabrita *f.* she-kid.

cabritilla *f.* [dressed] kidskin.

cabrito *m.* kid [young of goat].

cabrón *m.* ZOOL. buck, billy-goat. 2 fig. acquiescing cuckold.

cabronada *f.* vulg. dirty trick, foul trick. 2 tough job.

cabruno, -na *adj.* hircine, goat, goatish.

cabujón *m.* JEWEL. cabochon.

cabuya *f.* BOT. century plant. 2 pita [fiber]. 3 pita rope. 4 NAUT. small ropes, cordages.

caca *f.* coll. human excrement. 2 dirt, filth.

cacahual *m.* cacao plantation.

cacahuete *m.* BOT. peanut.

cacao *m.* cacao [tree, seed]; cocoa [tree, powder, drink]. 2 (Am.) *pedir* ~, to beg mercy.

cacaraña f. pit [in the face], pockmark.
cacarañado, -da adj. pitted, pock-marked.
cacarañar tr. to pockmark, to scar. 2 (Am.) to pinch, to scratch.
cacarear intr. [of fowls] to cackle, crow. 2 coll. to boast, brag.
cacareo m. cackling, crowing [of fowls]. 2 coll. boasting, bragging.
cacatúa f. ORN. cockatoo.
cacera f. irrigation ditch.
cacería f. hunt, hunting party. 2 bag [game shot]. 3 PAINT. hunting scene.
cacerina f. cartridge pouch.
cacerola f. casserole, saucepan.
cacicato, cacicazgo m. dignity or territory of a cacique. 2 political fief.
cacillo m. dim. small dipper or ladle.
cacique m. cacique, Indian chief. 2 political boss.
caciquismo m. bossism.
caco m. thief, burglar. 2 coll, coward.
cacodilato m. CHEM. cacodylate.
cacofonía f. cacophony.
cactáceo, -a, cácteo, -a adj. BOT. cactaceous.
cacto m. BOT. cactus.
cacumen m. coll. acumen, brains, head.
cacha f. side of a razor or knife handle. 2 cheek. 3 buttock [of a rabbit].
cachada f. stroke of one top [toy] against another.
cachafaz m. (Am.) rogue, scoundrel, rascal.
cachalote m. ZOOL. cachalot, sperm whale.
cachar tr. to break in pieces, to split.
cacharrería f. crockery shop.
cacharrero, -ra m.-f. crockery seller.
cacharro m. crock, piece of crockery. 2 coll. rattletrap; rickety machine or car.
cachava f. shinny [game and stick]. 2 crook, hooked staff.
cachaza f. slowness, phlegm, coolness.
cachazudo, -da adj. slow, leisurely, phlegmatic, cool.
cachear tr. to search, frisk [a person].
cachemir m., cachemira f. CASIMIR.
Cachemira f. pr. n. Kashmir.
cacheo m. searching, frisking [a person].
cacheta f. spring-catch [of a lock].
cachetada, f. cachetazo m. slap, whack, smack.
cachete m. punch [in the face or the head]. 2 plump cheek. 3 short dagger.
cachetear tr. to slap, to whack, to smack.
cachetudo, -da adj. plum-cheeked.
cachifollar tr. to squash, humiliate.
cachimba f. smoking pipe.
cachipolla f. ENT. dayfly, May fly.
cachiporra f. club, bludgeon.
cachirulo m. liquor container. 2 NAUT. small three-masted vessel.
cachivache m. vessel, pot, utensil.
cacho, -cha adj. GACHO. 2 m. bit. piece, fragment. 3 a fresh-water fish. 4 card game.
cachondearse ref. to poke fun at somebody.
cachondeo m. coll. ragging, leg- pulling, jeering, joking, teasing: armar ~, to mess about, to lark about; sin ~, no messing about, no joking; tomárselo a ~, to take it as a joke.
cachondez f. heat, rut, readiness to mate. 2 lust, randiness, lechery.
cachondo, -da adj. on heat, in rut, rutting. 2 coll. randy, lusty. 3 hilarious, funny.
cachorrillo m. obs. small pistol.
cachorro, -rra m.-f. pup, puppy, whelp, cub. 2 CACHORRILLO.

cachú m. catechu.
cachucha f. small rowboat. 2 man's cap. 3 Andalusian dance.
cachuchear tr. to caress, to fondle.
cachuela f. stew.
cachumbo m. GACHUMBO.
cachunde f. cachou. 2 catechu.
cachupín m. (Am.) Spaniard who settles in Spanish America.
cada adj. each, every: ~ cual, ~ uno, each one, every one, ~ y cuando que, provided; as soon as; ~ dos días, every other day. 2 m. ENEBRO.
cadalso m. scaffold, platform, stage, stand. 2 scaffold for capital punishment.
cadáver m. corpse, cadaver.
cadavérico, -ca adj. cadaverous.
cadejo m. small skein. 2 tangled hair.
cadena f. chain [connected series of links; restraining force; sequence, series of events, mountains, etc.]: ~ de neumático, tire chain; ~ de agrimensor, surveyor's chain; ~ de montañas, range, chain of mountains; ~ sin fin, endless chain. 2 chain gang. 3 ARCH. pier [in a wall]. 4 LAW. imprisonment; ~ perpetua, imprisonment for life. 5 CHEM. chain.
cadencia f. cadence, cadency, rhythm, rhythmical flow. 2 MUS. cadence.
cadencioso, -sa adj. cadenced, rhythmical.
cadeneta f. chain stitch.
cadera f. ANAT. hip. 2 coxa [of arthropod].
cadete m. MIL. cadet.
cadí m. cadi [Mohammedan judge].
Cádiz pr. n. GEOG. Cadiz.
cadillo m. BOT. hedgehog parsley. 2 BOT. burdock. 3 wart. 4 pl. WEAV. [warp] thrums.
cadmio m. CHEM. cadmium.
caducar intr. to dote [from old age]. 2 to fall into disuse. 3 LAW., COM. TO LAPSE, TO EXPIRE.
caduceo m. caduceus, Mercury's staff.
caducidad f. caducity, lapse.
caduco, -ca adj. caducous.
caedizo, -za adj. easily falling. 2 BOT. deciduous.
caer intr.-ref. to fall, drop, fall down, come down; to tumble down; to fall off or out: ~ al suelo or en tierra, to fall to the ground; ~ enfermo, to fall ill; ~ en una trampa, en la miseria, to fall into a trap, into poverty: caerse de viejo, to totter with age. 2 to realize; ~ en la cuenta de, to realize; ya caigo, I see it, I understand now. 3 [of interests] to become due. 4 to fall, to come [by lot, inheritance, etc.]: ~ en suerte, to fall to one's lot. 5 to lie, be located: el camino cae a la derecha, the way lies to the right. 6 [of the sun] to go down. 7 to fall, occur: ~ en viernes, to fall on friday. 8 caerse de su peso or de suyo, to be self-evident. 9 [of the day] to decline; [of the night] to fall: al ~ de la noche, at nightfall. 10 caérsele a uno la cara de vergüenza, to be ashamed. 11 to fall [in battle]. 12 ~ bien or mal, to suit, fit, become, or not to suit, fit, become. 13 estar al ~ [of an event] to be imminent, about to happen. ¶ CONJUG.: IND. Pres.: caigo, caes, etc. | Pret.: caí, caíste, cayó; caímos, caísteis, cayeron. | SUBJ. Pres.: caiga, caigas, caiga; caigamos, caigáis, caigan. | Imperf.: cayera, cayeras, etc., or cayese, cayeses, etc. | Fut.: cayere, cayeres, etc. | IMPER.: cae, caiga; caigamos, caed, caigan. | GER.: cayendo.
café m. coffee [tree; seeds; beverage]. 2 café: ~ cantante, café-chantant, cabaret.
cafeína f. CHEM. caffein.

cafetal *m.* coffee plantation.
cafetera *f.* coffee-pot: ~ *de filtro*, percolator.
cafetería *f.* coffee house, bar.
cafetero, -ra *adj.* [pertaining to] coffee. *2 m.-f.* coffee gatherer. *3* keeper of a café.
cafetín *m.* small café.
cafeto *m.* BOT. coffee tree or plant.
cáfila *m.* coll. multitude, large number.
cafre *adj.-n.* Kaffir. *2* savage, inhuman [person]. *3* rude, rustic [person].
caftán *m.* caftan.
cagaaceite *m.* ORN. missel thrush.
cagachín *m.* ENT. small reddish mosquito.
cagada *f.* flyspeck. *2* droppings. *3* coll. shit. *4* coll. crap.
cagadero *m.* coll. bog, loo, latrine, john.
cagado, -da *adj.* coll. cowardly, yellow, yellow-bellied. *2 estar* ~, to be shit-scared.
cagafierro *m.* iron slag or scoria.
cagajón *m.* horse, mule or ass dung.
cagalera, cagaleta *f.* coll. diarrhea, the runs. *2 tener* ~, to be shit-scared.
cagar *intr., tr.-ref.* vulg. to defecate, go to stool. *2 tr.* vulg. to soil, defile; to make a botch of. *3 ref.* vulg. to be cowed.
cagarria *f.* BOT. morel.
cagarruta *f.* goat or sheep dung.
cagatinta *m.* coll. penpusher.
cagón, -na *adj.* cowardly. *2 m.-f.* coward.
cagueta *adj.* yellow, yellow-bellied. *2* diarrheic. *3 n.* chicken. *4* diarrheic child.
caid *m.* kaid.
caída *f.* fall, drop; downfall; falling off or out. *2* fall, descent [on ground]. *3* lapse, spiritual ruin. *4* arrangement of folds [of drapery]. *5* NAUT. depth, hoist [of a sail]. *6 a la ~ del sol*, at sunset; *a la ~ de la tarde*, in the late afternoon. *7 pl.* witty remarks; native wit.
caído, -da *adj.* fallen. *2* weak, downhearted. *3* drooping [eyelids, shoulders, etc.]. *4 m. pl.* interest due. *5 los caídos*, the fallen [in battle].
Caifás *m. pr. n.* Caiaphas.
caigo, caiga etc. *irr.* V. CAER.
caimán *m.* ZOOL. alligator, cayman.
caimiento *m.* fall. *2* downheartedness, languidness.
caimito *m.* BOT. star apple.
Caín *m. pr. n.* Cain: *pasar las de Caín*, to have a terrible time.
cairel *m.* crown of false hair. *2* fringe trimming.
Cairo (El) *m. pr. n.* Cairo.
caja *f.* box, chest, case, casing: ~ *de cambios de marcha*, AUTO. gearshift box; ~ *de ingletes*, mitre box; ~ *del tambor o del tímpano*, ANAT. eardrum; ~ *de música*, musical box. *2* cash box, safe; cashier's office or desk: ~ *fuerte* or *de caudales*, safe, strong box; ~ *registradora*, cash register. *3* name of some institutions: ~ *de ahorros*, savings bank; ~ *de reclutamiento*, MIL. induction centre. *4* frame, shell [of pulley]. *5* coffin. *6* body [of carriage; of a violin, guitar, etc.]. *8* stock [of firearm]. *9* well [of staircase]. *10* MUS. drum. *11* socket, mortise; ~ *y espiga*, mortise and tenon. *12* BOT. capsule. *13* PRINT. case: ~ *alta*, upper case; ~ *baja*, lower case.
cajel *adj.* bittersweet [orange].
cajero *m.* box maker. *2* cashier.
cajetilla *f.* packet, pack [of cigarettes].
cajetín *m.* rubber stamp. *2* box [in a printing case].
cajiga *f.* QUEJIGO.

cajigal *m.* QUEJIGAL.
cajista *m.* PRINT. compositor.
cajón *m.* large box, bin. *2* drawer, till, locker: ~ *de sastre*, miscellany, odds and ends. *3* wooden stand or shed [for selling or working]. *4* (Am.) grocer's shop. *5* ENG. ~ *hidráulico*, caisson. *6 ser de* ~, to be customary, be a matter of course.
cal *f.* lime [burned limestone]: ~ *viva*, quicklime; ~ *muerta*, slaked lime; *de* ~ *y canto*, fig. firm. solid.
cala *f.* cove, small bay. *2* fishing ground. *3* plugging [a melon, etc.]. *4* plug [cut out of a melon, etc.]. *5* hole made in a wall to try its thickness. *6* suppository. *7* SURG. probe. *8* NAUT. hold. *9* BOT. calla, calla lily.
calabacear *tr.* to fail, turn down [in examination]. *2* to refuse [a lover], to give the mitten to.
calabacín *m.* BOT. vegetable marrow. *2* fig. dolt.
calabacino *m.* gourd [used as a bottle].
calabaza *f.* calabash, gourd, pumpkin, squash [plant and fruit]: ~ *confitera*, pumpkin; ~ *vinatera*, bottle gourd; *dar calabazas*, fig. CALABACEAR. *2* fig. dolt.
calabazada *f.* knock with the head: *darse de calabazadas*, to rack one's brains.
calabazar *m.* AGR. pumpkin field, gourd field.
calabazazo *m.* knock on the head.
calabazo *m.* gourd, pumpkin. *2* calabash.
calabobos *m.* drizzle.
calabocero *m.* jailer.
calabozo *m.* dungeon. *2* cell [of jail]. *3* pruning sickle.
calabrés, -sa *adj.-n.* Calabrian.
calabriada *f.* mixture of wines. *2* medley.
calabrote *m.* NAUT. cable, laid rope.
calada *f.* soaking. *2* sinking [of a fishing net]. *3* swoop [of a bird of prey]. *4* WEAV. shed.
caladio *m.* BOT. caladium.
calado *m.* drawn work [in linen]; openwork [in metal, stone, etc.]; fretwork. *3* NAUT. draught. *4* NAUT. depth [of water].
calafate *m.* NAUT. caulker. *2* shipwright.
calafateado *m.* CALAFATEO.
calafatear *tr.* to caulk [a boat or crevice].
calafateo *m.* NAUT. caulking.
calamar *m.* ZOOL. squid, calamary.
calambac *m.* BOT. calambac.
calambre *m.* MED. cramp.
calambuco *m.* BOT. calaba tree.
calamento *m.* BOT. calamint.
calamidad *f.* calamity, grievous disaster. *2* fig. *ser una* ~, to be a nuisance.
calamina *f.* MINER. calamine.
calaminta *f.* BOT. calamint.
calamita *f.* MINER. lodestone.
calamite *m.* ZOOL. green toad.
calamitoso, -sa *adj.* calamitous.
cálamo *m.* ancient flute. *2* poet, reed. *3* poet. writing pen. *4* BOT. smooth stem [as in rushes]. *5* BOT. a graminaceous plant.
calamocano *adj.* coll. tipsy. *2* coll. doting.
calamoco *m.* icicle.
calamón *m.* ORN. purple gallinule. *2* roundheaded brass nail.
calamorra *f.* coll. head.
calandrado *m.* calendering.
calandrajo *m.* rag, talter. *2* despicable person.
calandrar *tr.* to calender.
calandrero *m.* calenderer.
calandria *f.* ORN. calander, lark. *2* calender, mangle [machine]. *3* hoisting treadmill.

calaña *f.* pattern, model. *2* kind, sort, nature.
calañés *adj.* designating a kind of Andalusian hat.
cálao *m.* ORN. hornbill.
1) **calar** *tr.* to soak, drench. *2* to go through, pierce, penetrate. *3* to make drawn work in [linen]; to cut open work in [paper, metal, etc.]. *4* to plug [a melon]. *5* to incline [pikes, etc.] ready to use them. *6* to fix [the bayonet]. *7* to size up, to see through [a person, his intentions, etc.]. *8* NAUT. to lower [a yard]. *9* to sink [a fishing net, etc.]. *10 intr.* NAUT. [of a ship] to draw. *11 ref.* to get soaked or drenched. *12* to enter, get in. *13* to pull on or down [one's hat or cap]. *14* [of birds] to swoop.
2) **calar** *adj.* calcareous. *2 m.* limestone quarry.
calavera *f.* [fleshless] skull; death's head. *2* madcap, gay blade, profligate.
calaverada *f.* reckless action, escapade.
calaverear *intr.* to act recklessly. *2* to have a ball, to whoop it up.
calcado *m.* calking, calquing, tracing.
calcador, -ra *n.* tracer.
calcáneo *m.* ANAT. calcaneum, calcaneus.
calcañal, calcañar *m.* heel [of the human foot].
calcar *tr.* to calk or calque; to trace, transfer [a drawing]. *2* fig. to imitate.
calcáreo, -a *adj.* calcareous.
calce *m.* steel tire [of a wheel]. *2* shim, wedge; chock.
calcedonia *f.* MINER. chalcedony.
calceolado, -da *adj.* BOT. calceolate.
calceolaria *f.* BOT. calceolaria.
calcés *m.* NAUT. masthead.
calceta *f.* stocking, hose: *hacer* ~, to knit.
calcetería *f.* hosiery.
calcetín *m.* sock.
cálcico, -ca *adj.* CHEM. calcic.
calcificación *f.* calcification.
calcificar *tr.* to calcify.
calcinación *f.* calcination.
calcina *f.* concrete.
calcinar *tr.* to calcine. *2 ref.* to calcine [undergo calcination].
calcio *m.* CHEM. calcium.
calcita *f.* MINER. calcite, calcspar.
calcitrapa *f.* BOT. star thistle.
calco *m.* copy made by tracing. *2* copy, imitation.
calcografía *f.* chalcography.
calcomanía *f.* decalcomania.
calculable *adj.* calculable.
calculadamente *adv.* in a calculating way.
calculador, -ra *adj.* calculating. *2 m.-f.* calculator [person]. *3 f.* calculator [machine].
calcular *tr.-intr.* to calculate. *2 tr.* to conjecture, guess.
calculista *m.-f.* calculator, designer.
cálculo *m.* calculation, computation, estimate. *2* conjecture, guess. *3* MATH., MED. calculus.
calculoso, -sa *adj.* MED. calculous.
calda *f.* warming, heating. *2 pl.* hot springs, hot mineral-water baths.
caldaico, -ca *adj.* Chaldaic, Chaldean.
Caldea *f. pr. n.* Chaldea.
caldeamiento *m.* heating.
caldear *tr.* to warm, heat. *2 ref.* to heat [grow ot].
1) **caldeo** *m.* warming, heating.
2) **caldeo, -a** *adj.-n.* Chaldean.
caldera *f.* cauldron, cooper, kettle: *calderas de Pedro Botero,* coll. hell. *2* MACH. boiler: ~ *de vapor,* steam boiler. *3* shell of a kettle-drum.
calderada *f.* cauldron [contents of cauldron].

calderería *f.* boilermaker trade or shop.
calderero *m.* boilermaker, coppersmith.
caldereta *f.* small cauldron. *2* holy-water pot. *3* fish-stew. *4* lamb-stew.
calderilla *f.* holy-water pot. *2* copper coins.
caldero *m.* semispherical kettle or small cauldron.
calderón *m.* large cauldron. *2* PRINT. paragraph mark [¶]. *3* MUS. hold, pause; its symbol.
caldo *m.* broth, bouillon: ~ *de cultivo,* BACT. broth; ~ *de la Reina,* eggnog; *hacer el* ~ *gordo a,* to play into the hands of. *2 pl.* COM. vegetable juices, as wine, oil, etc.
caldoso, -sa *adj.* having plenty of broth.
calducho *m.* hogwash.
calé *m.* Spanish gypsy.
Caledonia *f. pr. n.* GEOG. Caledonia. *Nueva* ~, New Caledonia.
calefacción *f.* heating; heating system.
calefactor *m.* heating engineer.
caleidoscopio *m.* kaleidoscope.
calendario *m.* calendar: *hacer calendarios,* fig. to muse; to make hasty forecasts.
calendas *f. pl.* calends: ~ *griegas,* Greek calends.
caléndula *f.* BOT. pot marigold.
calentador *m.* heater; warming pan: ~ *a gas,* gas heater ~ *de cama,* warming pan.
calentamiento *m.* warming, heating.
calentar *tr.* to warm, heat, warm up, heat up: ~ *las orejas a,* fig. to chide, dress down. *2* to beat, spank. *3 ref.* to warm oneself; to warm or heat up. *4* [of animals] to be in heat. ¶ CONJUG. like *acertar.*
calentón *m. darse un* ~, to take a bit of a warming.
calentura *f.* MED. fever, temperature.
calenturiento, -ta *adj.* feverish.
calenturón *m.* high fever.
calesa *f.* kind of calash.
calesero *m.* driver of a CALESA.
caleta *f.* small cove or creek.
caletre *m.* coll, judgement, acumen, brains.
calibración *f.* calibration.
calibrado *m.* boring [a cylinder]. *2* gauging.
calibrador *m.* cal(l)ipers, gauge.
calibrar *tr.* to calibrate; to gauge.
calibre *m.* calibre, bore, gauge. *2* fig. size, importance.
calicata *f.* MIN. test pit.
calicó *m.* calico.
calículo *m.* BOT. calycle.
calidad *f.* quality. *2* capacity, position: *en* ~ *de,* in the capacity of. *3* character, nature. *4* rank, importance. *6 pl.* moral qualities, gifts.
cálido, -da *adj.* warm, hot [climate, country]. *2* hot, burning [as pepper]. *3* PAINT. warm [colour].
calidoscopio *m.* kaleidoscope.
calientapiés *m.* foot warmer.
calientaplatos *m.* hot plate, chaffing dish.
caliente *adj.* warm, hot. *2* in heat, in rut. *3* PAINT. warm [colour]. *4 adv. en* ~, while hot, at once.
caliento, caliente, etc. *irr.* V. CALENTAR.
califa *m.* caliph.
califato *m.* caliphate.
calificable *adj.* qualifiable.
calificación *f.* qualification, rating. *2* judgement, grading [of marks]. *3* mark [in examination].
calificado, -da *adj.* qualified, competent. *2* [of a thing] having all the necessary conditions.
calificador, -ra *m.-f.* qualifier, examiner, judge. *2 m.* ECCL. qualificator.
calificar *tr.* to determine, express or denote the

qualities or attributes of; to apply an.epithet to: ~ *de*, to qualify, rate or class as, to call. *2* to ennoble, give credit to. *3* to award marks to [in examination].

calificativo, -va *adj.* GRAM. qualifying [adjective]. *2 m.* GRAM. qualifier [adjective]; epithet.

California *f. pr. n.* GEOG. California.

californiano, -na *adj.-n.* Californian.

calígine *f.* gloom, darkness.

caliginoso, -sa *adj.* misty, caliginous.

caligrafía *f.* calligraphy.

calígrafo *m.* calligrapher, calligraphist.

calina *f.* haze.

calinoso, -sa *adj.* hazy.

Calíope *f. pr. n.* MYTH. Calliope.

calipso *m.* calypso.

calistenia *f.* calisthenics.

cáliz *m.* chalice [cup]. *2* BOT. calyx, chalice. *3* ANAT. calyx. *4* fig. cup of sorrow.

caliza *f.* limestone.

calizo, -za *adj.* calcareous, limy.

calma *f.* METEOR. calm: ~ *chicha*, dead calm. *2* calm, inactivity, let-up. *3* allayment, cessation [of pain]. *4* peace, calmness. *5* calmness, composure. *6* slowness, phlegm. *7 en* ~, calm, quiet; motionless [sea].

calmante *adj.* assuaging, soothing. *2 m.* MED. calmative, sedative.

calmar *tr.* to calm, quiet, pacify. *2* to allay, soothe. *3 intr.* [of wind] to abate. *4 intr.-ref.* to abate, calm down. *5* to calm oneself; to be allayed.

calmo, -ma *adj.* barren, treeless. *2* at rest.

calmoso, -sa *adj.* calm, quiet. *2* slow, sluggard.

calmuco, -ca *adj.-n.* Kalmuck.

caló *m.* slang of gypsies and low-class people.

calofrío *m.* ESCALOFRÍO.

calomelanos *m. pl.* calomel.

calor *m.* heat, warmth, hotness: *hacer* ~, [of weather], to be hot: *tener* ~, [of a person] to feel warm, hot. *2* glow, heat, warmth [excitement, enthusiasm], ardour, fire, animation. *3* heat [of a battle, a debate, etc.].

caloría *f.* PHYS., PHYSIOL. calorie.

calórico *m.* caloric.

calorífero, -ra *adj.* heat-conducting. *2 m.* heater [for a room]. *3* foot warmer.

calorífico, -ca *adj.* calorific.

calorífugo, -ga *adj.* heat-resistant, uninflammable.

calorimetría *f.* calorimetry.

calorimétrico, -ca *adj.* calorimetric, calorimetrical.

calostro *m.* colostrum.

calta *f.* BOT. caltha, marsh marigold.

calumet *m.* calumet, peace pipe.

calumnia *f.* calumny, slander.

calumniar *tr.* to calumniate, to slander.

calumnioso, -sa *adj.* calumnious, slanderous.

calurosamente *adj.* warmly, heartily, enthusiastically. *2* hotly, passionately.

caluroso, -sa *adj.* hot [weather]. *2* [of a person] sensitive to heat. *3* warm, hearty, enthusiastic.

calva *f.* bald head, bald pate. *2* bald spot or patch [in head, fields, woods, fur, or velvet].

Calvario *m. pr. n.* Calvary. *2 m.* (not cap.) calvary. *3* series of debts.

calvero *m.* clearing, bare spot [in a wood].

calvez, calvicie *f.* baldness.

calvinismo *m.* Calvinism.

calvinista *adj.* Calvinistic. *2 adj.-n.* Calvinist.

Calvino *m. pr. n.* HIST. Calvin.

calvo, -va *adj.* bald, hairless, bald-headed, baldpated. *2* bare, barren [land].

calza *f.* coll. stocking: ~ *de arena*, sandbag. *2* wedge. *3 pl.* hose; breeches: *calzas atacadas*, laced breeches.

calzada *f.* paved road, causey, causeway: ~ *romana*, Roman road.

calzado, -da *adj.* shod. *2* calced, calceate. *3* with feet of a different colour to the rest of the body [animal]. *4* braccate [bird]. *5 m.* footwear.

calzador *m.* shoehorn.

calzadura *f.* putting on shoes.

calzapiés *m.* toe clip.

calzar *tr.-ref.* to put on [any article of footwear; gloves; spurs]. *2 ref.* to put one's shoes on. *3 tr.* to shoe, put the shoes on [a person]. *4* to supply with shoes. *5* to wear [gloves or spurs]. *6* to take [a certain size of shoe or glove]: fig. ~ *poco* or *pocos puntos*, not to be very intelligent. *7* to shim, wedge up. *8* to scotch [a wheel]. *9* PRINT. to underclay.

calzo *m.* shim, wedge, chock, scotch. *2* NAUT. quoin, chuck. *3 pl.* stockings [of horses].

calzón, calzones *m. sing.* or *pl.* breeches, trousers: ~ *corto*, knee breeches; *llevar los calzones* [of a woman], to wear the trousers.

calzonazos *m.* weak, soft fellow.

calzoncillos *m. pl.* drawers, pants [for men].

calzorras *m.* coll. henpecked husband.

callada *m.* a meal of tripe. *2* silence, keeping silent: *dar la* ~ *por respuesta,* to give no answer; *a las calladas, de* ~, on the quiet, secretly.

calladamente *adj.* silently, quietly, secretly.

callado, -da *adj.* silent, quiet. *2* reserved, reticent.

callandico, -dito *adv.* silently, stealthily, softly.

callar *intr.-ref.* to be, keep or become silent; to shut up, be quiet: *callarse la boca*, to shut up; *quien calla otorga*, silence gives consent. *2 tr.-ref.* to keep to oneself, keep secret, not to mention. *3 interj.* ¡calla! or ¡calle!, why!, don't tell me!

calle *f.* street: ~ *mayor*, high street, main street; *dejar en la* ~, fig. to deprive of one's livelihood; *echar, poner* or *plantar a uno en la* ~, to dismiss someone; *echarse a la* ~, to go out into the street; to mutiny, rebel, riot; *llevarse a uno de* ~, to sweep away; to convince someone. *3* ~ *de árboles*, alley, glade. *4 abrir* ~, to make way, clear a passage.

calleja *f.* CALLEJUELA.

callejear *intr.* to lounge about the streets.

callejeo *m.* lounging about the streets.

callejero, -ra *adj.* [pertaining to the] street. *2* fond of lounging about the streets. *3 m.* street guide.

callejón *m.* lane, alley: ~ *sin salida*, blind alley, impasse.

callejuela *f.* little street, by-street, alley, lane.

callicida *m.* corn remover, corn eradicator.

callista *m.-f.* chiropodist, corn doctor.

callo *m.* callus, callosity; corn. *2 pl.* tripe.

callosidad *f.* callosity.

calloso, -sa *adj.* callous, horny.

cama *f.* bed, couch; bedstead; ~ *turca*, day bed; *estar en* ~, to be sick in bed; *guardar* ~, to keep one's bed. *2* lair [of wild animals]. *3* part of a melon resting on the ground. *4* brood, litter [young animals]. *5* sheath [of the plough]. *6* COOK. layer or thickness [of food]. *7* MACH. cam.

camada *f.* brood, litter [young animals]. *2* bed, layer. *3* gang, band [of thieves, etc.].

camafeo *m.* cameo.

camal *m.* halter. *2* (Am.) slaughterhouse.

camaleón *m.* ZOOL. & fig. chameleon.
camalote *m.* BOT. South-American river plant.
camamila *f.* CAMOMILA.
camándula *f.* trickery, hypocrisy: *tener muchas camándulas*, to be full of tricks.
camandulería *f.* prudery, hypocrisy.
camandulero, -ra *adj.* hypocritical, sly, tricky.
cámara *f.* chamber, room [in some cases]: ~ *nupcial*, nuptial chamber. 2 royal chamber. 3 grain loft; granary. 4 NAUT. stateroom ward-room; cabin. 5 chamber, house [legislative body]: ~ *alta*, senate; ~ *baja*, Chamber of Deputies; ~ *de compensación*, COM. clearing house. 6 chamber [cavity]; ~ *de aire*, air chamber. 7 OPT. camera: ~ *oscura*, camera obscura. 8 inner tube [of tire]. 9 PHYSIOL. stool.
camarada *m.* comrade, companion, pal, chum.
camaradería *f.* camaraderie, good-fellowship.
camarera *f.* head maid. 2 waitress. 4 stewardess [on ship]. 5 lady in waiting.
camarero *m.* waiter. 2 steward [in a ship]. 3 papal chamberlain.
camareta *f.* NAUT. cabin [of a small ship]. 2 NAUT. mess-room. 3 NAUT. ~ *alta*, deckhouse.
camarilla *f.* coterie, clique, cabal.
camarín *m.* little chapel behind an altar. 2 THEAT. dressing room. 3 closet [private room]. 4 car [of a lift or elevator].
camarista *f.* lady in waiting.
camarlengo *m.* papal chamberlain.
camarón *m.* ZOOL. a marine shrimp or prawn.
camaronero, -ra *m.-f.* shrimp seller.
camarote *m.* NAUT. cabin, stateroom [for passengers].
camarroya *f.* BOT. wild chicory.
camastro *m.* wretched bed. 2 MIL. sleeping boards in a guardhouse.
camastrón *m.* cunning, sly person.
cambalache *m.* barter of cheap things. 2 (Am.) second-hand shop.
cambalachear *tr.* to barter, exchange.
cámbaro *m.* ZOOL. crab, green crab.
cambiable *adj.* changeable. 2 exchangeable.
cambiadiscos *m.* record changer.
cambiadizo, -za *adj.* inconsistent, changeable, variable.
cambiador, -ra *adj.* changing; exchanging. 2 *s.* changer.
cambiante *adj.* changing; fickle. 2 *m.-f.* money-changer. 3 *m. pl.* iridescence.
cambiar *intr.-tr.* to change, alter. 2 to change, shift: ~ *de ropa*, to change clothes. 3 *tr.* to change, convert: ~ *en*, to change into. 4 to change, exchange; ~ *por*, to exchange for. 5 to exchange [money]. 6 *intr.-ref.* [of the wind] to veer.
cambiazo *m.* dar el ~, to make a fraudulent substitution.
cambio *m.* change [alteration; substitution, etc.]; shift, shifting: ~ *de domicilio*, change of address. 2 change [of money]. 3 small change, exchange, barter: *libre* ~, free trade; *a* ~ *de*, in exchange for; *en* ~, in exchange. 4 market price [of bonds, shares, etc.]. 5 BOT. cambium. 6 AUTO., MECH. shift: ~ *de marchas*, gearshift. 7 RLY. switch.
cambista *m.-f.* money-changer. 2 *m.* banker.
cambium *m.* BOT. cambium.
Camboya *f. pr. n.* GEOG. Cambodia.
camboyano, -na *adj.-n.* Cambodian.
cambray *m.* cambric [linen].

cambriano, -na; cámbrico, -ca *adj.-n.* Cambrian.
cambrón *m.* BOT. boxthorn. 2 BOT. buckthorn. 3 BOT. bramble. 4 *pl.* BOT. Christ's-thorn.
cambronal *m.* thicket of boxthorn, buckthorn or brambles.
cambronera *f.* BOT. boxthorn.
cambur *m.* BOT. kind of banana.
camedrio *m.* BOT. germander, wall germander.
camelar *tr.* to court, flirt with. 2 to cajole.
cameleo *m.* coll. flattery.
camelia *f.* BOT. camellia.
camelo *m.* courting, flirtation. 2 deception.
camelote *m.* camlet. 2 BOT. a tropical weed.
camella *f.* ZOOL. she-camel. 2 GAMELLA.
camellero *m.* camel driver, camel keeper.
camello *m.* ZOOL., NAUT. camel.
camellón *m.* CABALLÓN.
camerino *m.* THEAT. dressing room.
camero, -ra *adj.* full-sized [bed]. 2 suitable for a full-sized bed.
Camerún *m. pr. n.* GEOG. Cameroons.
Camilo *m. pr. n.* Camillus.
camilla *f.* stretcher, litter. 2 small bed, couch. 3 table with a heater underneath.
camillero *m.* stretcher-bearer.
caminador, -ra *adj.* good-walking. 2 *m.-f.* good walker.
caminante *m.-f.* traveller, wayfarer.
caminar *intr.* to travel, journey. 2 to walk, march, go, move along. 3 fig. ~ *derecho*, to act uprightly. 4 *tr.* to cover [a distance] walking.
caminata *f.* long walk, hike, march, excursion.
caminero, -ra *adj.* [pertaining to] road: *peón* ~, road mender.
camino *m.* path, road, way, -track, course: ~ *cubierto*, FORT. cover or covered way; ~ *de herradura*, bridle path; ~ *de hierro*, railway; *abrirse* ~, to make a way for oneself; *allanar el* ~, to smooth the way; *ir por buen* ~, to be on the right track; *llevar* ~ *de*, to be on the way to. 2 way, journey, travel: *ponerse en* ~, to start, set off on a journey; *de* ~, in passing, by the way; *en* ~, on the way. 3 ~ *de mesa*, runner [on a table].
camión *m.* camion, lorry, truck, motor truck.
camionaje *m.* trucking, truck transport. 2 truckage.
camionero *m.* truck driver, lorry driver.
camioneta *f.* light motor van.
camisa *f.* shirt; chemise: ~ *de dormir*, nightgown, nightdress; ~ *de fuerza*, strait jacket; *dejar a uno sin* ~, to clean someone out; *meterse en* ~ *de once varas*, to meddle in something that is not one's concern; *no llegarle a uno la* ~ *al cuerpo*, to be frightened; to be anxious. 2 BOT. tegmen [of a seed]. 3 slough [of a serpent]. 4 FORT. chemise. 5 MECH. jacket, casing, lining. 6 folder [for papers]. 7 incandescent gas mantle. 8 PRINT. linen case [for roller].
camisería *f.* shirt factory. 2 shirt shop.
camisero, -ra *n.* shirt maker, outfitter. 2 *adj.* shirt-like: *blusa* ~, shirt blouse.
camiseta *f.* vest, undervest, undershirt.
camisola *f.* ruffled shirt. 2 shirt of fine linen.
camisolín *m.* dicky, dickey [false shirt front].
camisón *m.* nightshirt, nightgown, nightdress.
camomila *f.* BOT., PHARM. camomile, chamomile.
camorra *f.* row, quarrel: *armar* ~, to raise a row; *buscar* ~, to look for trouble. 2 Camorra.
camorrista *adj.* quarrelsome. 2 *m.-f.* quarrelsome person.
campal *adj.* pitched [battle].

campamento *m.* camp, camping; encampment.
campana *f.* bell [of church, tower, etc.]: *echar las campanas al vuelo*, to publish [something] jubilantly; 2 bell-shaped object: ~ *de buzo*, diving bell; ~ *de chimenea* or *de hogar*, mantel [of a chimney], hood [of a fireplace]; ~ *de vidrio*, bell glass, bell jar. 3 parish church, parish.
campanada *f.* stroke of a bell. 2 scandal; sensational happening.
campanario *m.* belfry, bell tower, campanile: *de ~*, fig. local, mean, narrow-minded.
campanear *intr.* to ring bells frequently.
campaneo *m.* bell ringing, chime.
campanero *m.* bell founder. 2 bell ringer. 3 ENT. praying cricket, mantis. 4 ORN. bellbird.
campaniforme *adj.* campanulate.
campanil *m.* CAMPANARIO. 2 *adj.* bell [metal].
campanilo *m.* bell tower, belfry, campanile.
campanilla *f.* small bell; hand bell, doorbell: *persona de campanillas*, person of great importance or distinction. 2 ANAT. uvula. 3 small tassel. 4 BOT. bellshaped flower.
campanillazo *m.* loud ring of a bell.
campanillear *intr.* [of a hand bell or a doorbell] to ring, keep on ringing.
campanilleo *m.* ringing of a hand bell or a doorbell.
campanillero *m.* bellman.
campanología *f.* campanology.
campante *adj.* satisfied, contented, cheerful.
campanudo, -da *adj.* pompous, high-sounding.
campánula *f.* BOT. campanula, bell flower.
campaña *f.* level country. 2 (Am.) fields, country. 3 [military, commercial, political, etc.] campaign.
campañol *m.* ZOOL. vole, meadow mouse.
campar *intr.* to excel, to stand out. 2 to camp, encamp. 3 ~ *por sus respetos*, to act according to one's will or fancy; [of things] to prevail.
campeador *m.* champion in battle.
campear *intr.* to go to pasture. 2 [of wild animals] to go about. 3 [of fields] to grow green. 4 to excel, stand out. 5 MIL. to be in the field.
campechanía *f.* frankness, heartiness, good humor.
campechano, -na *adj.* frank, open, hearty, good-humored. 2 generous.
campeche *m. palo* ~ or *de Campeche*, campeachy-wood, logwood.
campeón *m.* champion. 2 defender.
campeona *f.* championess.
campeonato *m.* SPORT. championship.
campero, -ra *adj.* unsheltered, in the open field. 2 sleeping in the open [cattle]. 4 (Arg.) good at farming.
campesinado *m.* peasantry, peasants [pl.].
campesino, -na *adj.* country, rural, peasant. 2 *m.-f.* peasant, countryman, countrywoman.
campestre *adj.* campestrian, field, rural, country.
camping *m.* camping: *ir de* ~, to go camping. 2 camping site or ground.
campiña *f.* stretch of arable land; fields, country.
campista *m.* camper. 2 (Am.) herdsman, livestock keeper.
campo *m.* fields, country, countryside: ~ *raso*, open fields; *a* ~ *raso*, in the open; *a* ~ *traviesa*, across the fields. 2 cultivated land, crops. 3 field, ground: ~ *de Agramante*, bedlam [place of confusion]; ~ *de instrucción*, MIL. drill ground; ~ *del honor*, field of honour; ~ *de minas*, MIL., NAV. mine field; ~ *santo*, cemetery. 4 GOLF. links.

5 ground [in painted stuffs, engravings, etc.]. 6 MIL. camp: *levantar el* ~, to raise camp. 7 MIL. army, side. 8 ~ *de concentración*, concentration camp.
camposanto *m.* cemetery, graveyard.
camuflaje *m.* MIL. camouflage.
camuflar *tr.* MIL. to camouflage. 2 to hide, to cover up, to conceal.
can *m.* ZOOL. dog. 2 trigger [of firearm]. 3 ARCH. bracket, corbel [projecting timber]; modillion. 4 Khan. 5 ASTR. *Can mayor*, Canis Major, Great Dog; *Can Menor*, Canis Minor, Little Dog.
cana *f.* white hair: *peinar canas*, to be old; *echar una* ~ *al aire*, fig. to have a gay time.
canáceo, -a *adj.* BOT. cannaceous.
canaco, -ca *m.-f.* Kanaka.
Canadá (el) *m. pr. n.* GEOG. Canada.
canadiense *adj.-s.* Canadian.
canal *m.* canal [artificial channel]: ~ *de Suez*, Suez Canal. 2 GEOG. channel, strait: ~ *de la Mancha*, English Channel. 3 channel [deeper part of a river, harbour, etc.]. 4 *m.-f.* natural underground watercourse or duct. 5 ANAT. canal, duct. 6 long, narrow dell. 7 valley, gutter [in a roof]; gutter tile. 8 ARCH. flute. 9 groove. 10 front edge [of a book]. 11 *abrir en* ~, to cut open from top to bottom.
canalado *adj.* grooved, fluted.
canaladura *f.* ARCH. vertical groove, flute.
canalera *f.* roof gutter.
canalete *m.* paddle [for canoeing].
canalización *f.* canalization, channeling. 2 mains, piping, wiring.
canalizar *tr.* to canalize. 2 to channel, pipe, wire.
canalizo *m.* NAUT. narrow channel.
canalón *m.* rain water pipe; roof gutter. 2 gargoyle.
canalones *m. pl.* canneloni, cannelons.
canalla *f.* rabble, riffraff. 2 *m.* cad, rascal, scoundrel.
canallada *f.* dirty trick, caddish trick.
canallesco, -ca *adj.* low, rabblelike. 2 low, caddish, rascally.
canana *f.* cartridge belt.
cananeo, -a *adj.-n.* Canaanite.
canapé *m.* couch, sofa. 2 canapé [appetizer].
Canarias (islas) *f. pr. n.* GEOG. Canary Islands.
canario, -ria *adj.-n.* Canarian. 2 *m.* ORN. canary, canary bird. 3 *interj.* by Jove!, Great Scott!, *gee!
canasta *f.* large round basket. 2 canasta [card game].
canastilla *f.* small basket: ~ *de la costura*, sewing basket. 2 layette. 3 trousseau.
canastillo *m.* wicker tray. 2 small basket.
canasto *m.* large basket. 2 *interj.* ¡*canastos!*, expression of surprise and annoyance.
cáncamo *m.* NAUT. eyebolt, ringbolt.
cancamurria *f.* coll gloominess, blues.
cancamusa *f.* ruse, trick.
cancán *m.* cancan.
cáncana *f.* ZOOL. kind of spider.
cancanear *intr.* to loiter about.
cancaneo *m.* (Am.) stuttering, stammering. 2 faltering.
cáncano *m.* coll. louse.
cancel *m.* storm door, wooden screen in the entrance of a church, hall, etc. 2 (Mx.) folding screen.
cancela *f.* entrance grating.
cancelación *f.* cancellation.

cancelar tr. to cancel, annul.
cancelaria f. papal chancery.
cáncer m. MED. cancer. 2 (cap.) ASTR. Cancer.
cancerado, -da adj. MED. cancerous, affected with cancer. 2 evil, corrupt [heart, soul].
Cancerbero m. MYTH. & fig. Cerberus.
cancerígeno adj. MED. cancerigenic, cancerogenic.
canceroso, -sa adj. MED. cancerous.
cancilla f. gate, barrier [in a garden, barnyard, etc.].
canciller m. chancellor.
cancillería f. chancellery, chancery.
canción f. song: ~ de cuna, lullaby, cradlesong; ~ popular, folk-song. 2 lyric poem.
cancionero m. collection of lyrics. 2 song-book.
cancionista m.-f. song composer. 2 singer of songs.
cancro m. MED. cancer. 2 canker [of trees].
cancroide m. MED. cancroid tumor.
cancha f. court for playing pelota. 2 cockpit. 3 (Am.) game ground; tennis court; racecourse.
canchal m. rocky ground or region.
cancho m. rock, boulder. 2 rocky ground.
candado m. padlock.
candaliza f. NAUT. brail.
cande adj. azúcar ~, rock candy, sugar candy.
candeal adj. white [wheat]; pan ~, bread made of white wheat.
candela f. candle, taper. 2 candlestick. 3 chestnut flower. 4 fire [burning coals or wood]. 5 arrimar ~ a, to beat, trash. 6 NAUT. en ~, in a vertical position.
candelabro m. candelabrum.
candelada f. bonfire.
candelaria f. BOT. great mullein. 2 (cap.) Candlemas.
candelero m. candlestick. 2 metal olive-oil lamp. 3 fishing torch. 4 NAUT. stanchion. 5 en ~, in a position of authority.
candelilla f. dim. thin candle. 2 SURG. bougie. 3 BOT. catkin. 4 coll. le hacen candelillas los ojos, his eyes sparkle with the fumes of wine.
candente adj. candent, candescent. 2 cuestion ~, burning question.
candi adj. candied, formed into sugar crystals, crystalized, rock candy.
candidato, -ta m.-f. candidate [to post or election].
candidatura f. list of candidates [to post, election, etc.]. 2 candidacy, *candidature. 3 ballot paper, voting paper.
candidez f. whiteness. 2 simplicity, naïvety.
cándido, -da adj. white, snowy. 2 guileless, naïve simple; easy to deceive.
candil m. open oil lamp. 2 Greek or Roman oil lamp. 3 tine [of antler]. 4 corner [of a cocked hat].
candileja f. inner receptacle of an oil lamp. 2 pl. THEAT. footlights.
candiota adj.-n. Candiot, Candiote. 2 f. wine barrel. 3 large earthen vessel for wine.
candiotera f. wine cellar.
candonga f. ruse, trick. 2 banter, mockery.
candongo, -ga adj. cunning, wheedling. 2 workshy.
candonguear tr. to tease, banter, mock. 2 intr. to shirk work, swing the lead.
candonguero, -ra adj. jocose, reasing, mocking. 2 s. teaser, mocker. 3 wheedler.
candor m. pure whiteness. 2 candour, ingenuousness.
candoroso, -sa adj. ingenuous, pure, naïve, innocent.
caneca f. glazed earthen bottle.

canecillo m. ARCH. bracket, corbel, modillion.
canela f. cinnamon [bark and spice]. 2 fig. anything exquisite, very fine.
canelo, -la adj. cinnamon-coloured [dog, horse]. 2 m. BOT. cinnamon tree.
canelón m. CANALÓN. 2 icicle. 3 cinnamon candy. 4 tubular element of a fringe.
canesú m. a woman's corsage. 2 yoke of a shirt or blouse.
cangilón m. earthen or metal vessel for liquids. 2 bucket [of a wheel]. 3 dredge bucket, scoop. 4 fluting [of a ruff].
cangreja adj. NAUT. vela ~, boom-sail, gaff-sail.
cangrejero, -ra m.-f. crab or crayfish catcher or seller. 2 f. nest of crabs or crayfish.
cangrejo m. ZOOL. crab or crayfish: ~ de río, freshwater crayfish; ~ de mar, crab. 2 NAUT. gaff.
canguelo m. coll. fear.
canguro m. ZOOL. kangaroo.
caníbal adj.-n. Cannibal.
canibalismo m. Cannibalism.
canica f. marble [little ball]. 2 pl. marbles [game].
canicie f. whiteness of the hair.
canícula f. dog days. 2 (cap.) ASTR. Canicula, Dog Star.
canicular adj. canicular.
cánido, -da adj. ZOOL. canine [animal]. 2 m. ZOOL. canid. 3 pl. ZOOL. Canidae.
canijo, -ja adj. weak, infirm, sickly.
canilla f. long bone of either extremity; arm bone, leg bone, shinbone. 2 tap, spigot [in a cask or barrel]. 3 WEAV. bobbin, spool, quill. 4 WEAV. unevenness of the woof in thickness or colour.
canillera f. ESPINILLERA.
canino, -na adj. canine. 2 m. ANAT. canine tooth.
canje m. MIL., DIP., COM. exchange.
canjeable adj. exchangeable.
canjear tr. to exchange [prisoners, diplomatic notes, newspapers, etc.].
cano, -na adj. gray, gray-haired, hoary, white.
canoa f. canoe: ~ automóvil, motor boat.
canódromo m. dog track.
canoero, canoísta m. canoeist.
canon, pl. cánones m. canon [rule, law]. 2 ECCL., BIBL., MUS., PRINT. canon. 3 Canon [of the Mass]. 4 F. ARTS standard measurements of the human figure. 5 rent, rate, royalty. 6 pl. canon law.
canonesa f. canoness.
canonical adj. canonical [pertaining to a canon or member of a chapter].
canonicato m. canonicate, canonry.
canónico, -ca adj. canonical, canonic. 2 derecho ~, canon law.
canónigo m. canon, prebendary.
canonista m. canonist, canon lawyer.
canonización f. canonization.
canonizar tr. to canonize.
canonjía f. canonry. 2 coll. sinecure.
canoro, -ra adj. canorous. 2 sweet-singing, tuneful [bird].
canoso, -sa adj. gray-haired, hoary.
canotié m. straw hat with a low, flat crown.
cansadamente adv. wearily. 2 wearingly.
cansado, -da adj. tired, weary. 2 spent, worn-out, exhausted. 3 tiresome, wearisome.
cansancio m. fatigue, tiredness, weariness.
cansar tr. to fatigue, tire, weary. 2 to bore, harass. 3 to wear out, exhaust. 4 ref. to fatigue, tire, grow weary; to become exhausted. 5 intr. to be tiring or tiresome.

cansera *f.* coll. bother, nuisance. *2* tiredness, weariness.

cansino, -na *adj.* tired, exhausted [animal].

cantable *adj.* singable. *2* MUS. to be sung slowly. *3 m.* musical passage [of a ZARZUELA]; words for it.

cantábrico, ca; cántabro, bra *adj.-n.* Cantabrian.

cantador, -ra *m.-f.* singer [of popular songs].

cantalupo *m.* BOT. cantaloupe, cantaloup.

cantante *adj.* singing. *2 m.-f.* singer, professional singer.

cantaor, -ra *n.* flamenco singer.

1) **cantar** *m.* short poem apt for a folk song: fig. *éste es otro ~*, that's another story. *2 ~ de gesta*, chanson de geste. *3* BIBL. *Cantar de los Cantares*, Song of Songs, Canticles.

2) **cantar** *tr.-intr.* to sing: *cantarlas claras*, fig. to call a spade a spade. *2* POET. to chant. *3* [at cards] to declare. *4 ~ misa*, [of a priest] to say Mass for the first time. *5 intr.* coll. to speak, squeak, confess: *~ de plano*, to make a full confession. *6* [of cocks] to crow: *en menos que canta un gallo*, in a twinkling. *7* [of insects] to chirp, chirr. *8* NAUT. to chantey.

cántara *f.* CÁNTARO. *2* wine measure [32 pints].

cantarela *f.* MUS. treble string [of violin or guitar].

cantarera *f.* shelf for jars, or jugs

cantarero, -ra *n.* potter, dealer in earthenware.

cantárida *f.* ENT. cantharis, Spanish fly. *2* PHARM. cantharides. *3* blister raised by cantharides.

cantarín, -na *adj.* fond of singing; always singing. *2 m.-f.* singer.

cántaro *m.* water jar. *2* variable liquid measure. *3* ballot box.

cantata *f.* MUS. cantata.

cantatriz, *pl.* **-trices** *f.* professional singer [woman].

cantazo *m.* blow given with a stone.

cante *m.* Andalousian singing or song.

cantera *f.* quarry, stone pit. *2* fig. talent, capacity.

cantería *f.* stone cutting [for building]. *2* cutstone work. *3* cut or dressed stone.

cantero *m.* stone cutter. *2* easy-to-break extremity of something hard: *~ de pan*, crust of bread.

cántico *m.* canticle, song.

cantidad *f.* MATH., PHON., PROS. quantity. *2* quantity, amount. *3* sum [of money].

cantiga *f.* old poetical composition to be sung.

cantil *m.* shelf, ledge [on coast or under sea].

cantilena *f.* short lyric. *2* song, annoying repetition: *la misma ~*, the same old song.

cantiléver *adj.-n.* cantilever.

cantillo *m.* small pebble.

cantimplora *f.* siphon [to transfer liquids]. *2* water cooler. *3* canteen, water bottle.

cantina *f.* canteen [in barracks, etc.], railway buffet. *2* (Am.) barroom. *3* lunch box.

cantinela *f.* CANTILENA.

cantinera *f.* vivandière.

cantinero *m.* canteen-keeper.

canto *m.* singing, chant, song: *~ llano*, plain chant, plain song. *2* poet. canto. *3* crow [of cock]; chirp, chirr [of insects]. *4* edge, arris. *5* corner, point. *6* edge, thickness: *de ~*, on edge. *7* back [of knife]. *8* stone: *~ rodado*, boulder. *9* · *~ de pan*, crust of bread.

cantón *m.* canton, district, region. *2* corner. *3* HER. canton. *4* cantonment.

cantonal *adj.* cantonal.

cantonero, -ra *adj.* loafing. *2 f.* corner-plate, rein-

forcement or protection for a corner. *3* RINCONERA. *4* streetwalker.

cantor, -ra *adj.* singing: *pájaro ~*, song bird. *2 m.-f.* singer, songster, songstress. *3* cantor.

cantoral *m.* choir book.

Cantórbery *m. pr. n.* GEOG. Canterbury.

cantueso *m.* BOT. French lavender.

canturrear *intr.* to hum, sing in a low voice.

canturreo *m.* humming, singing in a low voice.

canturriar *intr.* CANTURREAR.

cánula *f.* cannula.

canutero *m.* barrel of pen. *2* pin box, pin case. *3* fountain pen.

canutillo *m.* CAÑUTILLO.

canzonetista *f.* singer, vocalist.

caña *f.* cane [stem]; culm, stem of any graminaceous plant. *2* reed [plant and stem]: *correr cañas*, formerly, to joust with reed spears. *3* any reedlike plant: *~ de azúcar*, cane, sugar cane; *~ de Bengala* or *de Indias*, rotang, rattan palm. *4* long bone [of arm or leg]. *5* shank, cannon [of horse]. *6* leg [of boot]. *7* tall, narrow wine tumbler. *8* tipstock [of firearm]. *9 ~ de pescar*, fishing rod. *10* NAUT. *~ del timón*, tiller, helm.

cañacoro *m.* BOT. Indian shot, Indian reed.

cañada *f.* glen, dell, hollow. *2* cattle path.

cañadilla *f.* ZOOL. purple shell.

cañaduz *f.* sugar cane.

cañafístola or **cañafístula** *f.* BOT. drumstick tree. *2* PHARM. cassia fistula.

cañaheja, cañaherla *f.* BOT. giant fennel.

cañamazo *m.* hemp tow. *2* burlap. *3* canvas for embroidery. *4* embroidered canvas.

cañamiel *f.* BOT. sugar cane.

cáñamo *m.* hemp [plant and fiber]. *2* hempen cloth.

cañamón *m.* hempseed.

cañaveral *m.* reed plantation. *2* canebrake. *3* sugar plantation.

cañería *f.* conduit, water or gas pipe.

cañí *m.* coll. gypsy.

cañizal, cañizar *m.* CAÑAVERAL.

cañizo *m.* hurdle of reeds [for drying fruit, rearing silkworms, etc.].

caño *m.* short tube or pipe. *2* sewer. *3* spout. *4* wind trunk [of the organ]. *5* jet [of water]. *6* NAUT. narrow channel [of a harbour].

cañón *m.* tube, pipe. *2* barrel [of gun]. *3* organ pipe. *4* flue [of chimney]. *5* quill [of feather]. *6* pinfeather. *7* canyon. *8* ARTILL. cannon, gun: *~ antiaéreo*, anti-aircraft gun.

cañonazo *m.* cannon shot; report of a gun.

cañonear *tr.* to shell, to bombard.

cañoneo *m.* cannonade, cannonading, cannonry.

cañonera *f.* FORT. NAUT. embrasure, porthole. *2* NAUT. armed launch. *3* (Am.) holster.

cañonería *f.* MUS. pipework [of organ]. *2* cannon; cannonry, ordnance.

cañonero, -ra *adj.* NAUT. armed [boat]. *2 m.* gunboat.

cañota *f.* BOT. a reedlike grass.

cañuto *m.* internode [of cane or reed]. *2* small tube. *3* tale-bearer, squealer.

caoba *f.* BOT. mahogany [tree and wood].

caobo *m.* BOT. mahogany [tree].

caolín *m.* kaolin, kaoline.

caos *m.* chaos.

caótico, -ca *adj.* chaotic.

capa *f.* cloak, mantle, cape: *~ rota*, fig. person sent under cover for an important affair; *andar de ~ caída*, to be on the decline; *hacer uno de su ~ un* *sayo*, to do as one pleases in one's own affairs; *de* ~ *y espada*, cloak-and-sword. *2* ECCL. cope, cloak: ~ *magna*, pontifical cope. *3* cope, canopy [of heaven]. *4* cloak, pretence, disguise. *5* coat, coating, couch [of paint, etc.]. *6* stratum. *7* wrapper [of a cigar]. *8* colour [of an animal]. *9* hider, concealer. *10* NAUT. primage, hat money. *11* NAUT. *estar* or *ponerse a la capa*, to lie to.

capacidad *f.* capacity [power of holding, etc.], content, capaciousness. *2* capacity, capability, ableness, ability. *3* LAW., ELECT., PHYS. capacity.

capacitado, -da *adj.* qualified *2* LAW. competent, qualified, capable.

capacitación *f.* enabling, qualification, capacitation.

capacitar *tr.* to enable, qualify, capacitate.

capacho *m.* flexible two-eared basket of palmetto, esparto grass or rushes.

capador *m.* gelder, castrator. *2* gelder's whistle.

capadura *f.* gelding, castration.

capar *tr.* to geld, castrate, emasculate.

caparazón *m.* caparison. *2* covering [for a coach, etc.]. *3* nose bag. *6* carcass [of a fowl]. *5* carapace, shell [of tortoise and crustaceans].

caparrosa *f.* CHEM. vitriol; ~ *azul*, blue vitriol; ~ *blanca*, white vitriol; ~ *verde*, copperas.

capataz *m.* foreman, overseer, steward.

capaz *adj.* having room or capacity [for]. *2* capacious, roomy. *3* capable. *4* able, competent.

capazo *m.* large flexible basket. *2* blow given with a cloak.

capciosidad *f.* captiousness, insidiousness.

capcioso, -sa *adj.* captious, insidious, deceiving.

capea *f.* exciting the bull with a cloak. *2* amateur free-for-all bullfight.

capeador *m.* BULLF. novice bullfighter. *2* BULLF. cape man, bullfighter who uses the cape.

capear *tr.* BULLF. to play the bull with the cape. *2* to beguile. *3* to weather [a storm]. *4* *intr.* NAUT. to lie to.

capelán *m.* ICHTH. capelin.

capelina *f.* SURG. capeline.

capelo *m.* cardinal's hat. *2* cardinalate.

capellada *f.* toe piece [of a shoe].

capellán *m.* priest, clergyman. *2* chaplain: ~ *castrense*, army chaplain.

capellanía *f.* chaplaincy.

capellina *f.* ARMOUR., SURG. capeline. *2* formerly a peasant's hood.

capeo *m.* CAPEA.

caperuceta, caperucita *f. dim.* small pointed hood: *Caperucita Roja*, Little Red Ridinghood.

caperuza *f.* pointed hood. *2* chimney cap. *3* MACH. hood.

Capeto *m. pr. n.* Capetian.

capialzado *adj.* ARCH. splayed [arch].

capialzar *tr.* ARCH. to splay.

capibara *f.* ZOOL. capybara.

capicúa *m.* palindromic number.

capilar *adj.* [pertaining to] hair. *2* capillary.

capilaridad *f.* capillarity. *2* capillary atraction.

capilla *f.* hod, cowl [attached to a garment]. *2* chapel; oratory: ~ *ardiente*, chamber where a dead body lies in state; *estar en* ~, to be sentenced to death and awaiting execution; to be awaiting an important issue. *3* MUS. chapel. *4* coll. friar, monk. *7* PRINT. proof sheet.

capillita *f. dim.* little chapel.

capillo *m.* baby cap. *2* baptismal cap. *3* hood [of hawk]. *4* toe-piece lining [of shoe]. *5* bud, rosebud. *6* cocoon. *7* ANAT. prepuce.

capirotazo *m.* fillip [stroke with the finger].

capirote *m.* chaperon [medieval hood]. *2* conical hood or cap [worn in processions]. *3* doctoral hooded mozzetta. *4* hood [of hawk]. *5* hood [of carriage]. *6* CAPIROTAZO.

capirucho *m.* coll. CAPIROTE.

capisayo *m.* cloaklike garment. *2* bishop's vestment.

capitación *f.* capitation, poll tax.

capital *adj.* capital [pertaining to the head, chief, main, great]: *pena* ~, capital punishment. *2* *m.* property, fortune. *3* ECON., SOCIOL. capital: ~ *social*, nominal capital, capital stock. *4* principal [sum invested or lent]. *5* *f.* capital, chief town. *6* FORT. capital.

capitalino, -na *adj.* of the capital. *2* *n.* native or inhabitant of the capital.

capitalismo *m.* capitalism.

capitalista *adj.* capitalist, capitalistic. *2* *m.-f.* capitalist.

capitalizable *adj.* capitalizable.

capitalización *f.* capitalization.

capitalizar *tr.* to capitalize [compute the present value of an income]. *2* to compound [interest].

capitán *m.* captain, chief, leader, great soldier. *2* MIL. captain: ~ *general del ejército*, field marshal; ~ *general de una región*, commander of a large military district. *3* NAV. captain: ~ *de navío*, captain; ~ *de fragata*, junior captain, commander; ~ *de corbeta*, senior lieutenant, *lieutenant commander. *4* NAUT. captain, master [of a ship]. *5* SPORT. captain. *6* ~ *del puerto*, harbour master.

capitana *f.* admiral's ship. *2* captain's wife. *3* female leader.

capitanear *tr.* to captain, lead, command.

capitanía *f.* captaincy, captainship. *2* ~ *general*, post and office of a CAPITÁN GENERAL. *6* ~ *de puerto*, harbour-master's office.

capitel *m.* ARCH. capital. *2* ARCH. spire. *3* capital [of a still].

Capitolio *m. pr. n.* Capitol. *2* *m.* capitol.

capitoné *m.* furniture van, removal van. *2* *adj.* (Am.) quilted, upholstered.

capitoste *m.* big chief, big boss, petty tyrant.

capitulación *f.* capitulation, agreement. *2* MIL. capitulation. *3* *pl.* articles of marriage.

capitular *adj.-m.* capitular, capitulary. *2* *pl.* HIST. capitularies.

capitular *intr.* to agree, conclude an agreement. *2* to capitulate [surrender on terms]. *3* to order, decree.

capítulo *m.* chapter [of a book]. *2* fig. chapter, subject, matter. *3* charge, impeachment: *llamar* or *traer a* ~, to call to account, bring to book. *4* chapter [meeting of members of a monastic or knightly order]. *5* *pl. capítulos matrimoniales*, articles of marriage.

capó *m.* AUTO. hood, bonnet.

capoc *m.*, **capoca** *f.* Kapok.

capón *adj.* castrated, gelded. *2* *m.* castrated man. *3* capon. *4* rap on the head.

caponera *f.* fattening coop for capons. *2* FORT. caponier. *3* coll. coop, jail.

caporal *m.* chief, leader. *2* (Am.) headman in a ranch.

capot *m.* AUT. hood, bonnet.

capota *f.* bonnet with strings, poke bonnet. *2* hood [of carriage]. *3* AER. cowling.

capotar *intr.* [of a car or airplane] to capsize, turn turtle, nose over.

capotazo *m.* a flick with the cloak to stop the bull.
capote *m.* kind of cloak with sleeves: *decir para su* ~, to say to oneself. *2* MIL. capote, greatcoat. *3* bullfighter's cape. *4 dar* ~, [in some card games] to win all the tricks.
capotear *tr.* CAPEAR 1 & 2. *2* to dodge, elude, evade difficulties, etc.
capoteo *m.* BULLF. passes with the cape. *2* coll. trickery, wiles. *3* shirking.
capotillo *m.* cape, mantlet.
Capricornio *pr. n.* ASTR. Capricorn.
capricho *m.* caprice, freak, whim, fancy. *2* longing, keen desire. *3* F. ARTS., MUS. caprice.
caprichoso, -sa *adj.* capricious, freakish, whimsical, fanciful.
caprichudo, -da *adj.* whimsical, willful.
cápsico *m.* BOT. capsicum.
cápsula *f.* capsule. *2* cartridge shell.
capsulado *m.* capping.
capsulador *f.* capping machine.
1) **capsular** *adj.* capsular.
2) **capsular** *tr.* to put a capsule on [a bottle].
captación *f.* winning, securing [good will, attention, etc.]. *2* collecting [spring waters]. *3* RADIO. picking up [signals].
captar *tr.-ref.* to win, secure [good will, esteem, attention, etc.]. *2 tr.* to collect [spring waters]. *3* RADIO, to get, pick up [signals].
captura *f.* capture, seizure.
capturar *tr.* to capture, seize.
capucha *f.* hood, cowl. *2* PRINT. circumflex accent.
capuchina *f.* BOT. capucine. *2* Capuchin nun.
capuchino, -na *adj.* pertaining to the Capuchin order. *2* ZOOL. *mono* ~, capuchin [monkey]. *3 m.* Capuchin [monk].
capuchón *m.* capuchin, cloak and hood [for women]. *2* short domino. *3* AUTO. valve cap. *4* cap [of fountain pen].
capullo *m.* cocoon: ~ *ocal*, double cocoon. *2* flower bud. *3* acorn cup. *4* foreskin.
capuz *m.* cowl. *2* hooded mantle. *3* dive, ducking.
caquéctico, -ca *adj.* MED. cachectic.
caquexia *f.* MED. cachexia.
caqui *m.* BOT. kaki, japanese persimmon. *2 adj.-m.* khaki [material and colour].
cara *f.* face, visage, countenance: ~ *de pascua*, cheerful face: ~ *de pocos amigos*, stern, forbidding countenance; *echar en* ~, to reproach, to throw in one's face; *dar la* ~, to face the consequences of one's actions; *dar la* ~ *por otro*, to answer for someone, to defend him; *hacer* ~, to face, resist; *verse las caras*, to meet in order to fight or dispute; to settle a difference; *a* ~ *descubierta*, openly; *de* ~ *a*, opposite, facing; ~ *a* ~, face to face. *2* look, aspect: *tener* ~ *de*, to look as if; *tener buena* ~, to look well; to look good. *3* face, front, façade; outside, surface. *5* face, obverse, right side. *6* face, head [of a coin]: ~ *y cruz*, heads or tails. *7* side [of phonograph record]. *8 adv.* facing, towards.
caraba *f.* coll. *esto es la* ~, this is the limit, this is the last straw.
carabao *m.* ZOOL. carabao.
cárabe *m.* amber.
carabela *f.* NAUT. caravel.
carabina *f.* carbine: *ser la* ~ *de Ambrosio*, to be useless. *2* coll. chaperon.
carabinero *m.* carabineer. *2* revenue guard. *3* coll. kind of crayfish.
cárabo *m.* a small moorish vessel. *2* ENT. carabus. *3* ORN. tawny owl.

caracal *m.* ZOOL. caracal.
caracará *m.* ORN. caracara.
Caracas *f. pr. n.* GEOG. Caracas.
caracol *m.* ZOOL. snail. *2* snail shell. *3* spit curl. *4* HOROL. fusee. *5* caracole [of horse]. *6* ARCH. spiral: *escalera de* ~, winding staircase.
caracola *f.* conch or triton shell [used as a horn].
caracolada *f.* dish of snails.
caracolear *intr.* [of horses] to caracole.
caracoleo *m.* caracoling.
¡caracoles! *interj.* ¡CARAMBA!
caracolillo *m. dim.* of CARACOL. *2* BOT. garden flower. *3* a variety of coffee. *4* veined mahogany.
carácter, *pl.* **caracteres** *m.* character [sign, type, letter, hand]: ~ *de letra*, hand, handwriting. *2* character [distinctive qualities; moral strength]. *3* nature, disposition. *4* character, status. *5* F. ARTS, BIOL., THEOL. character.
característica *f.* characteristic [distinctive trait]. *2* LOG., MATH. characteristic. *3* THEAT. actress who enacts elderly characters.
característico, -ca *adj.* characteristic(al. *2 m.* THEAT. old man.
caracterización *f.* characterization. *2* THEAT. make-up.
caracterizado, -da *adj.* qualified, competent, distinguished.
caracterizar *tr.* to characterize [be characteristic of]. *2* to give distinction, honour, etc. *3* THEAT. to act a part properly. *4 ref.* THEAT. to dress and make up for a rôle.
caracterología *f.* characterology.
caracul *m.* karakul.
caradura *n.* coll. cad, rotter, shameless person, cheeky devil. *2* coll. cheek, nerve: *es muy* ~, he's got a lot of cheek!
carajo *m.* prick. *2* coll. ¡~! shit! hell! ¡*vete al* ~, go to hell!
caramanchel *m.* NAUT. shed over the hatchways.
¡caramba! *interj.* confound it!, gracious me!
carámbano *m.* icicle.
carambola *f.* BILL. cannon, carom: fig. *por* ~, indirectly. *2* double effect of a single act. *3* BOT. carambola [fruit].
carambolear *intr.* BILL. to cannon, to carom.
carambolista *m.-f.* BILL. cannon or carom player.
carambolo *m.* BOT. carambola [tree].
caramelizar *tr.* to caramelize.
caramelo *m.* caramel [burnt sugar; sweetmeat].
caramillo *m.* flageolet; rustic flute. *2* BOT. kind of saltwort. *3* confused heap of things. *4* tale, lie, malicious gossip.
carantoña *f.* coll. ugly person. *2* coll. painted hag. *3 pl.* caresses, wheedling, cajolery.
carantoñero, -ra *m.-f.* wheedler, cajoler.
carapacho *m.* ZOOL. carapace.
¡carape! *interj.* ¡CARAMBA!
caraqueño, -ña *adj.-n.* of Caracas.
carátula *f.* mask [false face]. *2* wire mask [of beekeeper].
caravana *f.* caravan [of pilgrims, travellers, etc.].
caravanero *m.* caravaneer [leader of a caravan].
caravaning *m.* caravanning.
caravasar *m.* caravanserai.
caray *interj.* ¡CARAMBA!
carbohidrato *m.* carbohydrate.
carbón *m.* coal; charcoal: ~ *animal*, animal charcoal; bone black; ~ *mineral* or *de piedra*, coal, mineral coal; ~ *vegetal*, charcoal. *2* F. ARTS charcoal. *3* ELECT. carbon, crayon.

carbonada *f.* charge of coal [for a furnace]. *2* broiled mincemeat. *3* kind of pancake.
carbonado *m.* black diamond.
carbonar *tr.* to turn into charcoal, to make charcoal of.
carbonario *m.* Carbonaro, Carbonarist.
carbonatación *f.* carbonatation, carbonation.
carbonatado, -da *adj.* CHEM. carbonated.
carbonatar *tr.* to carbonate.
carbonato *m.* CHEM. carbonate.
carboncillo *m.* F. ARTS charcoal, charcoal pencil. *2* black sand. *3* wheat smut.
carbonear *tr.* to burn [wood] into charcoal. *2 intr.* NAUT. to coal [take in coal].
carboneo *m.* charcoal making. *2* NAUT. coaling.
carbonera *f.* wood prepared for burning into charcoal. *2* coal cellar, coal shed, coal bunker, coal bin.
carbonería *f.* coalyard; charcoal shop or store.
carbonero, -ra *adj.* [pertaining to] coal or charcoal; coaling. *2 m.* charcoal burner. *3* coal dealer, collier. *4 m.-f.* charcoal seller.
carbónico, -ca *adj.* carbonic.
carbonífero, -ra *adj.* carboniferous.
carbonilla *f.* fine coal; coal dust; cinders.
carbonización *f.* carbonization.
carbonizar *tr.* to carbonize, char. *2 ref.* to become carbonized.
carbono *m.* CHEM. carbon.
carbonoso, -sa *adj.* carbonaceous.
carbunclo *m.* CARBÚNCULO. *2* CARBUNCO.
carbunco *m.* MED., VET. carbuncle, anthrax.
carbúnculo *m.* carbuncle, ruby.
carburación *f.* carburation, carburetion.
carburador *m.* carburet(t)er, carburet(t)or.
carburante *adj.-m.* carburant.
carburar *tr.* to carburet.
carburo *m.* CHEM. carbide.
carca *adj.-n.* coll. square. *2* coll. carlist. *3* coll. reactionary.
carcaj *m.* quiver [for carrying arrows].
carcajada *f.* burst of laughter, cachinnation, guffaw.
carcajearse *ref.* to roar with laughter, to have a good laugh.
carcamal *m. adj.* coll. infirm, decrepit. *2 m.* infirm, decrepit person.
cárcel *f.* jail, gaol, prison. *2* coulisse [of a sluice gate]. *3* carpenter's clamp.
carcelario, -ria *adj.* [relating to] jail or prison.
carcelero, -ra *adj.* CARCELARIO. *2 m.* jailer, gaoler, warder. *3 f.* gaoleress, wardress.
carcinógeno, -na *adj.* MED. carcinogen.
carcinoma *m.* MED. carcinoma.
carcinomatoso, -sa *adj.* carcinomatous.
cárcola *f.* treadle [of a loom].
carcoma *f.* ENT. woodworm. *2* dust made by the woodworm. *3* fig. gnawing care. *4* fig. fritterer, corroder.
carcomer *tr.* [of the woodworm] to eat, gnaw. *2* fig. to gnaw away, consume, undermine.
carcomido, -da *adj.* worm-eaten. *2* consumed, decayed.
carda *f.* carding. *2* teaseling. *3* card [for carding wool, etc.]; carding machine. *4* card, teasel [for teaseling]. *5* coll. severe reproof.
cardado *m.* carding, combing. *2* back-combing [hair].
cardador, -ra *m.-f.* carder [of wool]. *2 m.* ZOOL. millepede.
cardadura *f.* carding [of wool].

cardamina *f.* BOT. MASTUERZO.
cardamomo *m.* BOT. cardamom.
cardán *adj.* MECH. Cardan.
cardar *tr.* to card. *2* to teasel, raise a nap.
cardenal *m.* ECCL., ORN. cardinal. *2* black-and-blue mark, ecchymosis.
cardenalato *m.* cardinalate.
cardenalicio, -cia *adj.* cardinalitian.
cardencha *f.* BOT. teasel, fuller's teasel.
cardenillo *m.* verdigris. *2* verditer, Paris green.
cárdeno, -na *adj.* purple, livid. *2* piebald [bull]. *3* opaline [water].
cardíaco, -ca *adj.* cardiac.
cardialgia *f.* MED. cardialgia.
cardias *m.* ANAT. cardiac orifice [of the stomach].
cardillo *m.* BOT. golden thistle.
cardinal *adj.* cardinal.
cardiografía *f.* cardiography.
cardiográfico, -ca *adj.* MED. cardiographic.
cardiograma *m.* cardiogram.
cardiología *f.* cardiology.
cardiólogo, -ga *m.* cardiologist.
cardiotónico *m.* MED. heart tonic.
carditis *f.* MED. carditis.
cardizal *m.* land covered with thistles and weeds.
cardo *m.* BOT. cardoon. *2* BOT. thistle: ~ *ajonjero*, carline thistle; ~ *borriqueño*, cotton thistle, scotch thistle; ~ *estrellado*, star thistle.
cardón *m.* card, teasel. *2* carding, teasing. *3* (Am.) giant cactus.
cardoncillo *m.* BOT. milk thistle.
cardume, cardumen *m.* school, shoal [of fishes].
carear *tr.* to confront, bring face to face. *2* to confront, compare. *3* to lead [cattle] toward some place. *4 ref.* to meet face to face.
carecer de *intr.* to lack, be without. ¶ CONJUG. like *agradecer*.
carena *f.* NAUT. careen, careening [caulking and repairing].
carenadura *f.* NAUT. careenage.
carenar *tr.* NAUT. to careen [caulk and repair].
carencia *f.* lack, want, deficiency, deprivation.
carenero *m.* NAUT. careenage [place for careening].
carente *adj.* ~ *de*, lacking, wanting.
careo *m.* confrontation [esp. of criminals or witness].
carero, -ra *adj.* selling dearly, charging high prices.
carestía *f.* scarcity, want; famine. *2* high cost.
careta *f.* mask [covering for the face]: *quitar la* ~, to unmask, expose. *2* fencing mask, face-guard.
carey *m.* ZOOL. tortoise-shell, turtle. *2* tortoise shell.
carezco, carezca, etc. *irr.* V. CARECER.
carga *f.* loading, lading; charging. *2* load, burden. *3* cargo, freight: *buque de* ~, freighter, cargo ship. *4* tax, impost. *5* duty, obligation, expenses. *6* charge [on real estate]. *7* charge [of gun, furnace, etc.]. *8* ELECT. charge, load. *9* ENG., ARCH. load. *10* HYDR. head. *11* MIL. charge: *volver a la* ~, fig. to insist. *12* measure for charcoal, fruit, grain, etc.
cargadero *m.* loading place, freight station. *2* ARCH. lintel.
cargado, -da *adj.* full, fraught. *3* sultry, cloudy [weather]. *4* strong, saturated: *café* ~, strong coffee. *5* ~ *de años*, up in years; ~ *de espaldas*, round-shouldered.
cargador *m.* shipper; freighter. *2* carrier, porter. *3* loader, charger. *4* clip [of cartridges]. *5* (Am.) street-porter.

cargamento *m.* NAUT. cargo, shipment.
cargante *adj.* coll. boring, annoying, tiresome.
cargar *tr.* to load. *2* to burden. *3* to charge [a furnace, battery, etc.]. *4* to impose or lay [taxes]. *5* to impute, ascribe. *6* to bore, annoy, tire. *7* ACCOUNT. to charge, to debit. *8* NAUT. to brail up [a sail]. *9* MIL. to charge. *10* ~ *la mano*, to pursue something eagerly; to overdo; to be too exacting. *11 intr.* to lean, incline towards. *12* to load up, take on a load: ~ *mucho* or *demasiado*, coll. to eat or drink too much. *13* PHON. [of an accent] to fall, have its place. *14* ~ *con*, to take, carry away; to assume [a responsibility]; to bear [the blame]. *15* ~ *en* or *sobre*, to bear, rest or lean on; to fall on. *16 ref.* to lean the body [towards]. *17* to burden oneself. *18* to get cloudy, overcast. *19* [of a patient] to run up a temperature. *20* ELEC. to become charged. *21 cargarse de*, to fill oneself (or itself) up with: *cargarse de paciencia*, to arm oneself with patience.
cargazón *f.* NAUT. cargo, shipment. *2* heaviness [of head or stomach]. *3* mass of heavy clouds.
cargo *m.* loading. *2* burden, weight: ~ *de conciencia*, a load on one's conscience, responsibility. *3* ACCOUNT. charge, debit. *4* employment, post, office. *5* duty, charge, responsibility: *a* ~ *de*, under the charge of. *6* charge, accusation, reproach: *hacer cargos*, to lay charges, accuse. *7 hacerse* ~, to take charge; to be understanding; *hacerse* ~ *de*, to take charge of; to take into consideration, understand, realize.
cargoso, -sa *adj.* burdensome, onerous. *2* annoying, bothersome.
carguero, -ra *adj.* freight, freight carrying. *2 m.* (Arg.) beast of burden.
cariacontecido, -da *adj.* sad, troubled, crestfallen.
cariado, -da *adj.* carious [tooth, bone].
cariancho, -cha *adj.* broad-faced.
cariar *tr.* to cause caries. *2 ref.* to become carious, to decay.
cariátide *f. f.* ARCH. caryatid.
Caribdis *f. pr. n.* Charybdis.
caribe *adj.* Caribbean. *2 m.-f.* Carib. *3 m.* fig. brute, savage.
caribú, *pl.* **-búes** *m.* ZOOL. caribou.
caricato *m.* baso buffo [opera singer].
caricatura *f.* caricature; cartoon.
caricaturesco, -ca *adj.* caricatural.
caricaturista *m.-f.* caricaturist.
caricaturizar *tr.* to caricature.
caricia *f.* caress, petting, endearment.
caridad *f.* charity [virtue]; gift, alms] charitableness.
caridoliente *adj.* sad-looking.
caries *f.* MED., DENT. caries, decay.
carigordo, -da *adj.* fat-faced.
carilampiño, -ña *adj.* beardless, smoothfaced, clean-shaven.
carilargo, -ga *adj.* long-faced.
carilla *f.* mask [of beekeeper]. *2* page, side [of writing paper].
carilleno, -na *adj.* plump-faced.
carillo, -lla *adj. dim.* rather dear or expensive.
carillón *m.* carillon.
carimba *f.*, **carimbo** *m.* branding iron. *2* brand.
cariño *m.* love, affection, fondness, tenderness; care, solicitude. *2 pl.* caresses, endearments.
cariñoso, -sa *adj.* loving, affectionate, kind; endearing.
carioca *adj.* of Rio de Janeiro. *2 n.* native or inhabitant of Rio de Janeiro.

cariofiláceo, -a *adj.* BOT. caryophylaceous.
carioplasma *m.* karyoplasm.
cariópside *f.* BOT. caryopsis.
carirredondo, -da *adj.* round-faced.
carisma *m.* THEOL. charism.
carismático, -ca *adj.* charismatic.
caritativo, -va *adj.* charitable.
cariz *m.* aspect, look [of weather, a business, etc.].
carlanca *f.* spiked collar [for dogs]. *2 pl.* fig. *tener muchas carlancas*, to be very crafty.
carlina *f.* BOT. carline thistle.
carlinga *f.* AER. cockpit. *2* NAUT. mast step.
carlismo *m.* Carlism.
carlista *m.* Carlist.
Carlomagno *m. pr. n.* Charlemagne.
Carlos *m. pr. n.* Charles.
Carlota *f. pr. n.* Charlotte.
carmañola *f.* carmagnole.
carmelita *adj.-m.* Carmelite. *2 f.* Carmelite nun.
carmelitano, -na *adj.* Carmelite.
Carmen *m.* carmen [song, poem]. *2* country house and garden [in Granada].
Carmen *f. pr. n.* Carmen. *2 m.* order of Our Lady of Mount Carmel.
carmenador *m.* large toothed comb. *2* carder, teasel.
carmenadura *f.* disentangling, combing [hair]. *2* carding, teasing [wool], unraveling [silk].
carmenar *tr.* to comb, disentangle [the hair: wool, silk, etc.]. *2* to rob, clean out.
carmesí *adj.-m.* crimson. *2 m.* crimson silk fabric.
carmín *m.* carmine.
carminativo, -va *adj.-m.* MED. carminative.
carmíneo, -a *adj.* carmine-coloured.
carnación *f.* flesh colour.
carnada *f.* bait [to entice prey].
carnadura *f.* flesh, robustness. *2* ENCARNADURA.
carnal *adj.* carnal. *2 hermano* ~, full brother; *primo* ~, cousin-german.
carnaval *m.* carnival [feast before Lent].
carnavalada *f.* carnival trick or frolic.
carnavalesco, -ca *adj.* carnivalesque.
carnaza *f.* bait. *3* abundance of flesh, fleshiness.
carne *f.* flesh [of man, animal or fruit]: fig. ~ *de gallina*, goose flesh, goose skin; *estar metido en carnes*, to be plump, stout; *criar carnes*, to put on flesh; *ser de* ~ *y hueso*, to be only human; *en* ~ *viva*, raw [skin or sore]. *2* flesh [human nature, carnality). *3* meat, flesh [as food]: ~ *asada*, roasted meat; *carnes blancas*, meat of fowl and young animals; ~ *de pluma*, fowl flesh; ~ *de vaca*, beef; *ni* ~ *ni pescado*, neither fish, flesh nor good red herring. *4* fig. ~ *de cañón*, cannon fodder. *5* ~ *de membrillo*, quince jelly.
carné, carnet *m.* card: ~ *de conducir*, driving license; ~ *de socio*, membership card; ~ *de identidad*, identity card. *2* pocket notebook, bankbook.
carneada *f.* (Am.) slaughtering.
carnear *f.* (Am.) to slaughter [for food].
carnicería *f.* butcher's shop.
carnerada *f.* flock of sheep.
carnerear *tr.* to kill [trepassing sheep] for damage done.
1) **carnero** *m.* ZOOL. sheep; mutton: ~ *padre*, ram. *2* ~ *del Cabo*, albatross.
2) **carnero** *m.* charnel, charnel house, sepulchre.
carneruno, -na *adj.* [pertaining to] sheep. *2* sheeplike.
carnestolendas *f. pl.* carnival, Shrovetide.
carnet *m.* notebook. *2* dance or membership card.

3 ~ *de chófer,* driver's licence; ~ *de periodista,* reporter's card.

carnicería *f.* butcher's shop. 2 carnage, massacre.

carnicero, -ra *adj.* carnivorous [animal]. 2 bloodthirsty, sanguinary. *3 m.-f.* butcher [meat seller]. *5 m. pl.* ZOOL. Carnivora.

cárnico, -ca *adj.* meat; *productos* ~, meat products.

carnicol *m.* hoof [half of a cloven foot].

carnívoro, -ra *adj.* carnivorous. *2 m.* ZOOL. carnivore. *3 pl.* ZOOL. Carnivora.

carnosidad *f.* MED. proud flesh. 2 carnosity. 3 fleshiness.

carnoso, -sa *adj.* carnose.

carnudo, -da *adj.* fleshy.

1) **caro** *adv.* dear, dearly.

2) **caro, -ra** *adj.* dear, costly, high-priced; expensive. 2 dear, beloved: *cara mitad,* better half.

carocha *f.* some insects'eggs [pl.].

Carolina *f. pr. n.* Caroline. 2 GEOG. Carolina. *3 Islas Carolinas,* Caroline Islands.

carolingio, -gia *adj.-n.* Carolingian.

Caron *m. pr. n.* MYTH. Charon.

carota *n.* coll. cheeky devil.

caroteno *m.* CHEM. carotin, carrotin, carotene, carrotene.

carotenoide *adj.-n.* CHEM. carotinoid, carotenoid.

carótida *f.* ANAT. carotid, carotid artery.

carozo *m.* cob of maize, corncob.

carpa *f.* ICHTH. carp: ~ *dorada,* goldfish. 2 (Am.) awning, tent.

carpanel *adj.* ARCH. basket-handle [arch].

carpanta *f.* coll, hunger, keen appetite.

Cárpatos (Montes) *m. pr. n.* Carpathian Mountains.

carpe *m.* BOT. hornbeam, witch-hazel.

carpelo *m.* BOT. carpel.

carpeta *f.* writing-table cover. 2 writing case. 3 portfolio. 4 folder, letter file.

carpetazo *m.* dar ~, to shelve, pigeonhole, lay aside.

carpetovetónico, -ca *adj.* Spanish to the core, terribly Spanish.

carpiano, -na *adj.* ANAT. carpal.

carpincho *m.* ZOOL. capybara.

carpintería *f.* carpentry, carpentering. 2 carpenter's shop.

carpintero *m.* carpenter: ~ *de carretas,* cartwright; ~ *de ribera,* ship carpenter, shipwright.

carpo *m.* ANAT. carpus.

carpología *f.* BOT. carpology.

carpólogo *m.* BOT. carpologist.

carraca *f.* NAUT. carrack [galleon]. 2 fig. clumsy old boat; rattletrap. 3 rattle [instrument]. 5 ratchet brace.

carraco, -ca *adj.* old, decrepit.

carrada *f.* cartload. 2 loads, heaps, a lot.

carraleja *f.* ENT. oil beetle, blister beetle.

carranza *f.* iron spike [in a dog collar].

carrasca *f.* BOT. small holm oak.

carrascal *m.* ground covered with CARRASCAS.

carraspear *intr.* to hawk, clear one's throat. 2 to suffer from hoarseness.

carraspeo *m.* clearing the throat. 2 hoarseness.

carraspera *f.* hoarseness, frog-in-the-throat.

carrasposo, -sa *adj.* very hoarse, having a sore throat. 2 (Am.) harsh, rough.

carraspique *m.* BOT. candytuft.

carrasqueño, -ña *adj.* rough, harsh.

carrera *f.* run, running: ~ *de baquetas,* MIL. gauntlet, running the gauntlet; *a* ~ *tendida, a la* ~, at full speed; *de* ~, speedily, without thinking. 2 road, highway. 3 course [of a star]. 4 route [followed by pageant or procession]. 5 race [contest of speed]: ~ *de armamento,* armament race. 6 row; line, range. 7 run, ladder [in a stocking]. 8 parting [in hair]. 9 career. 10 profession. *11* ARCH. girder. *12* MACH. stroke [of piston], travel [of valve]. *13 pl.* horse racing, turf.

carrerilla *f.* short run. 2 MUS. run of an octave.

carrerista *m.-f.* racegoer, turfman; race fan. 2 bicycle racer.

carrero *m.* cart driver, carter, cartman.

carreta *f.* long, narrow cart.

carretada *f.* cartful, cartload. 2 great quantity.

carrete *m.* spool, reel, bobbin. 2 ELECT. coil.

carretear *tr.* to cart, haul [goods]. 2 to drive [a cart].

carretel *m.* NAUT. log reel.

carretera *f.* road, high road, highway.

carretería *f.* carting business. 2 carts, wagons. 3 cartwright's yard.

carretero *m.* carter, cartman, teamster. 2 cartwright, wheelwright. *3 adj. camino* ~, cartway.

carretilla *f.* wheelbarrow; truck, baggage truck, handcart. 2 gocart [for learning to walk]. *3* BUSCAPIÉS. *4 de* ~, by heart, mechanically.

carretillero *m.* wheelbarrow man.

carretón *m.* small cart. 2 handcart. 3 wheeled frame for a portable grindstone.

carricera *f.* BOT. plume grass.

carricoche *m.* old coach.

carricuba *f.* street-watering cart.

carril *m.* rut, track, furrow. 2 cartway. *3* RLY. rail.

carrillera *f.* ZOOL. jaw. 2 chin strap.

carrillada *f.* fat of hog's jowls.

carrillera *f.* jaw [of some animals]. 2 chin strap.

carrillo *m.* cheek, jowl: *comer a dos carrillos,* to eat greedily; to have two sources of income.

carrilludo, -da *adj.* round-cheeked.

carrizal *m.* ground covered with ditch reeds.

carrizo *m.* BOT. ditch reed grass.

carro *m.* cart: ~ *de mudanzas,* moving van; *untar el* ~, to grease the palm, to bribe; *pare usted el* ~, hold your horses, restrain yourself. 2 (Am.) automobile; streetcar; railway car. 3 chariot. 4 MIL. car, tank. 5 cartload. 6 running gear [of carriage]. *7* ASTR. *Carro,* or *Carro Mayor,* Great Bear. 8 MACH. carriage [of typewriter, etc.]. *9* ~ *de tierra,* a land measure.

carrocería *f.* coachmaker's shop. 2 body [of motorcar].

carrocero *m.* coachmaker, coach builder.

carrocín *m.* chaise, gig [light carriage].

carrocha *f.* insect eggs.

carrochar *intr.* to lay eggs [an insect].

carromato *m.* long two-wheeled cart with a tilt.

carroña *f.* carrion [corrupted flesh].

carroño, -ña *adj.* carrion, corrupt, rotten.

carroza *f.* coach, stately carriage. 2 float [in processions]. 3 (Am.) hearse. 4 NAUT. companion [covering]; awning, tilt.

carruaje *m.* carriage, car, vehicle.

carrusel *m.* merry-go-round, carrousel, roundabout. 2 horse tattoo.

carta *f.* letter [written communication]: ~ *certificada,* registered letter; ~ *credencial* or *de creencia,* letters of credence, credentials; ~ *de presentación,* letters of introduction. 2 charter, chart, letters patent; deed: ~ *de fletamento,* ~ *partida,* charter party; ~ *de marca,* letters of marque; ~ *de venta,* deed of sale; *Carta Magna,* Magna

Charta. *3* chart, map: ~ *de marear*, marine chart. *4* playing card: ~ *falsa*, card of no value; *jugar a cartas vistas*, to act frankly, openly; to act on inside information; *poner las cartas boca arriba*, to put or lay one's cards on the table; *tomar cartas en un asunto*, to take a hand in an affair. *5* bill of fare: *a la* ~, à la carte. *6* ~ *blanca*, carte blanche, full powers. *7* ~ *de naturaleza*, privilege of naturalization; *adquirir* ~ *de naturaleza*, to become naturalized. *8* ~ *de pago*, acquittance, receipt, discharge in full. *9* ~ *partida por a, b, c*, indenture [indented document]. *10 a* ~ *cabal*, thoroughly.

cartabón *m.* drawing triangle. *2* carpenter's square. *3* size stick. *4* topographic octagonal prism.

Cartagena *f. pr. n.* GEOG. Cartagena.

cartagenero, -ra *adj.-n.* of Cartagena.

cartaginense; cartaginés, -sa *adj.-n.* Carthaginian.

Cartago *f. pr. n.* GEOG. Carthage.

cártama *f.*, **cártamo** *m.* BOT. safflower.

cartapacio *m.* notebook; schoolboy's copy book. *2* schoolboy's satchel. *3* papers in a folder.

cartear *intr.* to play low cards [to see how the game stands]. *2 ref.* to correspond by letter.

cartel *m.* poster, placard, bill: fig. *tener* ~, to have a reputation. *2* mural reading chart [for teaching children]. *3* cartel.

cartelera *f.* billboard, hoarding.

cartelista *n.* poster designer.

cartelón *m.* large poster.

carteo *m.* correspondence, intercourse by letters.

cárter *m.* MACH. housing, case.

cartera *f.* pocketbook, wallet. *2* portfolio [portable case for papers; office of cabinet minister; list of securities]. *3* brief case, letter-case. *4* satchel. *5* pocket flap.

cartería *f.* sorting room [in post office].

carterista *m.* pickpocket.

cartero *m.* postman, letter, carrier.

cartesiano, -na *adj.-n.* Cartesian.

cartilaginoso, -a *adj.* cartilaginous.

cartílago *m.* ANAT. cartilage, gristle.

cartilla *f.* primer, *speller [spelling book]. *2* short treatise [about some trade or art]. *3* identity book. *4* ~ *de la caja de ahorros*, deposit book of savings bank; ~ *de racionamiento*, ration book.

cartografía *f.* cartography.

cartógrafo *m.* cartographer.

cartomancia *f.* cartomancy.

cartón *m.* cardboard, pasteboard; ~ *piedra;* staff, papier mâché. *2* cartoon [model for frescoes, tapestry, etc.].

cartonaje *m.* cardboard articles.

cartoné *m.* BOOKBIND. *en* ~, in boards.

cartonería *f.* cardboard factory or shop.

cartuchera *f.* cartridge box. *2* cartridge belt.

cartucho *m.* cartridge: *quemar el último* ~, fig. to use up one's last resource. *2* roll of coins. *3* paper cone or bag [for sweets].

cartuja *f.* Carthusian order or monastery.

cartujo *adj.* Carthusian. *2 m.* Carthusian monk. *3* fig. taciturn fellow, recluse.

cartulario *m.* cartulary.

cartulina *f.* light or fine cardboard, Bristol board.

carúncula *f.* ANAT., ZOOL. caruncle, wattle.

carvi *m.* BOT. caraway. *2* caraway seeds.

casa *f.* house, building, establishment, institution, office: ~ *central*, head office; ~ *consistorial*, or *de la villa*, town hall; ~ *cuna* or *de expósitos*, founding hospital; ~ *de banca*, banking house;

~ *de caridad*, alms house, poorhouse; ~ *de empeños* or *de préstamos*, pawn shop; ~ *de huéspedes*, boarding house; ~ *de juego*, gambling house; ~ *de labor*, or *de labranza*, farming house; ~ *de locos* or *de orates*, madhouse, lunatic asylum; bedlam; ~ *de maternidad*, maternity hospital; ~ *de moneda*, mint; ~ *de salud*, private hospital; ~ *de socorro*, first-aid station; emergency hospital; ~ *de vecindad*, tenement house; ~ *editorial*, publishing house; ~ *matriz*, head office, mother house; ~ *mortuoria*, house of mourning, of deceased person; ~ *pública*, brothel; ~ *real*, royal palace; royal family; ~ *solariega*, manor. *2* home; house, household, family: *en* ~, at home; *en* ~ *de*, at the home, office, shop, etc., of; *la* ~ *de Borbón*, the house of Bourbon; *echar la* ~ *por la ventana*, to go to a lot of expense [to entertain, etc.]; *poner* ~, to set up housekeeping. *3* house, commercial house, firm. *4* square [of chessboard]. *5* ba(u)lk [in billards]. *6* ASTROL. house.

casabe *m.* cassava flour or bread.

Casablanca *pr. n.* GEOG. Casablanca.

casaca *f.* old long coat: *volver uno* ~, to become a turncoat. *2* diplomat's coat.

casación *f.* LAW cassation, -quashing.

casacón *m.* large CASACA; cassock.

casadero, -ra *adj.* marriageable.

casado, -da *adj.* married. *2 m.-f.* married person.

casal *m.* country house. *2* ancestral mansion.

casamata *f.* FORT. casemate.

casamentero, -ra *adj.* matchmaking. *2 m.-f.* matchmaker, marriage maker.

casamiento *m.* marriage, wedding.

casaquilla *f.* kind of coat with short tails.

1) **casar** *m.* hamlet.

2) **casar** *intr.-ref.* to marry, get married: ~ or *casarse con*, to marry, to be married to. *2* to marry [unite in wedlock; give in marriage]. *3* to marry, match, harmonize [things]. *4* to quash, annul. *5 intr.* [of things] to match, suit, correspond.

casca *f.* tanning bark. *2* skin of pressed grapes. *3* CÁSCARA.

cascabel *m.* small spherical bell: *poner el* ~ *al gato*, to bell the cat; *ser un* ~, to be a rattlebrain; to be merry, gay. *2* cascabel [of cannon]. *3* ZOOL. *serpiente de* ~, rattlesnake.

cascabelear *tr.* to incite with vain hopes. *2 intr.* to behave in a featherbrained manner.

cascabeleo *m.* jingle, jingling of bells.

cascabelero, -ra *adj.* thoughtless, featherbrained.

cascabelillo *m.* BOT. a small sweet plum.

cascada *m.* cascade, waterfall.

cascado, -da *adj.* broken, cracked. *2* worn out, infirm, decayed. *3* weak, cracked [voice].

cascadura *f.* breaking, cracking.

cascajal, cascajar *m.* place full of gravel.

cascajo *m.* gravel, fragments of stone, rubbish. *2* a broken piece of crockery: *estar hecho un* ~, to be decrepit.

cascanueces, *pl.* **-ces** *m.* nutcracker [instrument]. *2* ORN. nutcracker.

cascar *tr.* to break, crack, chink. *2* to beat, thrash. *3* to break the health of. *4 intr.* to chatter. *5 ref.* to crack. *6* to become infirm, decrepit.

cáscara *f.* rind, peel [of orange, melon, etc.]; shell [of egg or seed]. *2* bark [of tree]. *3* hard covering, hull, shell crust: *ser de la* ~ *amarga*, to hold advanced views. *5 interj.* ¡*cáscaras!*, by Jove!

cascarela *f.* a card game.

cascarilla *f.* thin metal shell or covering. *2* BOT. cascarilla, bark. *3* PHARM. thin cinchona bark.
cascarillo *m.* BOT. a cinchona shrub.
cascarón *m.* aug. of CÁSCARA. *2* eggshell; broken eggshell [from which chick has emerged]. *3* ~ *de nuez*, cockleshell [flimsy boat].
cascarrabias *m.-f.* coll, crab, irritable person.
casco *m.* casque, helmet. *2* crown [of hat]. *3* skull, cranium. *4* coat [of onion]. *5* fragment of broken crockery. *6* cask, bottle [for liquids]. *7* hull [of ship]. *8* hoof [of horse, mule or donkey]. *9* ~ *de población*, a city excluding its suburbs. *10 pl.* brains [of a person]: *levantar de cascos*, to incite with false hopes: *ser alegre de cascos*, to be scatterbrained.
cascote *m.* piece of rubble. *2* rubble, debris.
caseína *f.* casein.
cáseo *adj.* caseous, cheesy. *2 m.* curd.
caseoso, -sa *adj.* caseous, cheesy.
caserío *m.* group of houses. *2* hamlet. *3* CASERÍA.
caserna *f.* FORT. casern.
casero, -ra *adj.* house, home, informal [dress, gathering, etc.]. *2* domestic; homemade; homespun. *3* home-loving. *4 m.-f.* landlord, landlady [who leases houses or flats]. *5* house-agent. *6* caretaker. *7* renter, tenant.
caserón *m.* large house. *2* large ramshackle house.
caseta *f.* small house, hut. *2* ~ *de baño*, bathhouse, bathing cabin.
casi *adv.* almost, nearly.
casia *f.* BOT. cassia.
casicontrato *m.* LAW quasi contract.
casilla *f.* booth, cabin, hut [of railway guard, etc.]; keeper's lodge. *2* square [of chess board]; point [of backgammon board]. *3* column or square [on sheet of paper]. *4* pigeonhole. *5 sacar a uno de sus casillas*, to jolt someone out of his old habits; to vex someone beyond patience; *salir uno de sus casillas*, to lose one's temper.
casillero *m.* set of pigeonholes, rack.
casimir *m.*, **casimira** *f.* cashmere; cassimere.
Casimiro *m. pr. n.* Casimir.
casino *m.* casino, club; clubhouse.
Casio *m. pr. n.* Cassius.
casis *f.* BOT. cassis, black currant.
casita *f. dim.* little house.
caso *m.* GRAM., MED. case. *2* case, event, happening, instance, circumstances: ~ *de conciencia*, case of conscience: ~ *fortuito*, chance, accident; LAW force majeure; *hacer* or *venir al* ~, to be to the purpose, to be relevant; *poner por* ~, to take as an example; *vamos al* ~, let's come to the point; *el* ~ *es que*, the fact or the thing is that; ~ *que*, *en* ~ *de que*, in case; *de* ~ *pensado*, on purpose; *en todo* ~, anyhow. *3* heed, notice, attention: *hacer* ~ *de*, to heed, mind, notice; to listen, pay attention to, take into account; to esteem; *hacer* ~ *omiso*, to take no notice, to leave aside.
casón *m.* large house.
casorio *m.* unwise marriage. *2* informal wedding.
caspa *f.* dandruff, scurf.
caspio, -pia *adj.* Caspian: *Mar Caspio*, Caspian.
¡cáspita! *interj.* gracious!, by Jove!
casposo, -sa *adj.* scurfy, full of dandruff.
casquería *f.* tripe shop.
casquero *m.* tripe seller.
casquete *m.* skullcap, calotte. *3* MACH. cap. *4* GEOM. ~ *esférico*, one-base spherical segment.
casquillo *m.* ferrule, socket, metal tip or cap. *2* cartridge case; cartridge cap. *3* iron arrowhead.
casquivano, -na *adj.* featherbrained, frivolous.

cassette *f.* cassette.
casta *f.* caste. *2* race, stock, breed. *3* lineage, kindred. *4* kind quality [of things].
Castálidas *f. pl.* MYTH. Castalides.
castamente *adv.* chastely.
castaña *f.* chestnut [fruit]: *sacar las castañas del fuego*, to pull the chestnuts out of the fire; *dar la* ~ *a uno*, fig. to play a trick on one. *2* demijohn. *3* knot of hair, chignon.
castañal, castañar *m.*, **castañeda** *f.* chestnut grove or plantation.
castañazo *m.* coll. bash, punch, thump.
castañero, -ra *m.-f.* chestnut seller.
castañeta *f.* castanet. *2* snapping of the fingers.
castañetazo *m.* clap of castanets. *2* craking of a chestnut in the fire. *3* cracking of the joints.
castañetear *tr.* to play [a tune] with the castanets. *2 intr.* [of teeth] to chatter; [of kness] to crackle. *3* [of partridges] to cry.
castañeteo *m.* sound of the castanets. *2* chattering [teeth], cracking [bones], clicking, clattering.
castaño, -ña *adj.* chestnut, chestnut-coloured, brown, hazel. *2 m.* BOT. chestnut tree: ~ *de Indias*, horse-chestnut tree. *3* chestnut, brown, hazel [colour]: *pasar de* ~ *oscuro*, fig. to be the limit, be intolerable.
castañola *f.* ICHTH. pomfret.
castañuela *f.* castanet.
castañuelo, -la *adj.* chestnut, hazel [horse].
castellana *f.* mistress of a castle, chatelaine. *2* wife of a castellan.
castellanismo *m.* word or phrase characteristic of Castile.
castellanizar *tr.* to give Castilian form to.
castellano, -na *adj.-n.* Castilian. *2 m.* Castilian or Spanish language. *3* castellan; lord of a castle.
casticidad *f.* purity, correctness [in language].
casticismo *m.* love of purity [in language], of pure national nature [in customs, fashions, etc.].
casticista *adj.-n.* purist.
castidad *f.* chastity, continence.
castigable *adj.* punishable.
castigador, -ra *adj.* punishing. *2 m.-f.* punisher; castigator. *3 m.* coll. ladykiller.
castigar *tr.* to punish, chastise, penalize. *2* to chasten, castigate. *3* to mortify [the flesh]. *4* to cut down [expenses].
castigo *m.* punishment, chastisement; penance, penalty. *2* afliction, mortification. *3* castigation.
Castilla *f. pr. n.* GEOG. Castile.
castillejo *m.* small castle. *2* scaffolding [for hoisting heavy materials].
castillo *m.* castle: ~ *en el aire*, castle in the air, castle in Spain; ~ *de naipes*, house of cards. *3* ~ *de fuego*, fireworks. *4* NAUT. ~ *de proa*, forecastle.
castina *f.* limestone flux.
castizo, -za *adj.* of good breed; of good origin. *2* pure, correct [style, language, writer]. *3* prolific.
casto, -ta *adj.* chaste, pure.
castor *m.* ZOOL. beaver. *2* beaver [fur, hair, cloth].
Cástor *m. pr. n.* MYTH., ASTR. Castor.
castoreño, -ña *adj. sombrero* ~, beaver hat.
castóreo *m.* castor, castoreum.
castración *f.* castration, gelding; spaying. *2* extraction of honeycombs.
castrado, -da *adj.* castrated. *2* gelded [a horse]. *3 m.* eunuch.
castrador *m.* castrator, gelder.
castrar *tr.* to castrate, geld; to spay. *2* to prune. *3*

to extract combs from [hive]. 4 to weaken, emasculate.

castrazón f. extraction of honeycombs.

castrense adj. [pertaining to the] army; military.

casual adj. chance, accidental, fortuitous, casual.

casualidad f. chance, accident, coincidence: por ~, by chance. 2 chance event.

casualmente adv. by chance, by accident. 2 as it happens.

casuario m. ORN. cassowary.

casucha f., **casucho** m. small, miserable house.

casuista adj. casuistic. 2 m.-f. casuist.

casuística f. casuistry.

casulla f. chasuble.

cata f. tasting, sampling. 2 taste, small portion, sample. 3 (Am.) MIN. prospection.

catacaldos m.-f. one who starts many things and concentrates on none. 2 busybody.

cataclismo m. cataclysm.

catacumbas f. pl. catacombs.

catador, -ra m.-f. taster, sampler.

catadura f. tasting, sampling. 2 aspect, face, countenance.

catafalco m. catafalque.

catalán, -na adj. Catalan, Catalonian. 2 m.-f. Catalan.

catalanismo m. Catalanism.

catalejo m. spyglass.

catalepsia f. MED. catalepsis, catalepsy.

cataléptico, -ca adj.-n. cataleptic.

Catalina f. pr. n. Catherine.

catálisis f. CHEM. catalysis.

catalizador m. CHEM. catalyzer, catalytic agent.

catalogar tr. to catalogue, cataloguize.

catálogo m. catalogue.

catalpa f. BOT. catalpa.

Cataluña f. pr. n. GEOG. Catalonia.

cataplasma f. poultice.

cataplum interj. bang!, boom!

catapulta f. catapult.

catar tr. to taste, try by the taste; to sample. 2 to look at, to examine. 3 to think, judge. 4 to cut combs out of [hive].

cataraña f. ORN. whithe heron. 2 ZOOL. a West Indian lizard.

catarata f. cataract, waterfall.

catarral adj. catarrhal.

catarro m. MED. catarrh; head cold.

catarsis f. catharsis.

catártico, -ca adj. MED. cathartic.

catastral adj. cadastral.

catastro m. cadastre, cadaster.

catástrofe f. catastrophe.

catastrófico, -ca adj. catastrophic, disastrous, calamitous.

cataviento m. NAUT. dogvane.

catavino m. cup for tasting wine.

Catay m. pr. n. GEOG. Cathay.

cate m. blow, slap. 2 dar ~, to reject, *flunk [in an examination].

catear tr. to reject [in an examination]. 2 (Am.) to prospect [a district] for minerals.

catecismo m. catechism.

catecú m. catechu.

catecúmeno, -na m.-f. catechumen.

cátedra f. chair [seat of the professor; professorship]. 2 cathedra: ~ del Espíritu Santo, pulpit; ~ de San Pedro, Chair of Saint Peter [papal office].

catedral adj.-f. cathedral [church].

catedralicio, -cia adj. [pertaining to a] cathedral.

catedrática f. woman professor. 2 professor's wife.

catedrático m. university professor.

categoría f. category. 2 class, condition, kind; quality: de ~, of importance; prominent.

categórico, -ca adj. categoric(al).

catenaria adj.-f. MATH. catenary.

cateo m. (Am.) prospection.

catequesis f., **catequismo** m. catechesis.

catequista m.-f. catechist.

catequístico, -ca adj. catechistic. 2 catechetical.

catequizar tr. to catechize, catechise. 3 to bring around, persuade.

caterva f. multitude, lot, great number.

catéter m. SURG. catheter.

cateterismo m. MED. catheterism.

cateto m. GEOM. leg [of a right-angled triangle]. 2 coll. yokel, rustic.

catilinaria f. oration of Cicero against Catiline. 2 vehement denunciation.

catión f. ELECT. cation.

catirrino, -na adj.-m. ZOOL. catarrhine.

catite m. light blow or slap.

cato m. catechu.

catódico, -ca adj. cathode, cathodic.

cátodo m. ELECT. cathode.

catolicismo m. catholicism. 2 Catholicism; Catholicity.

católico, -ca adj. catholic. 2 adj.-n. Catholic, Roman Catholic. 3 no estar muy ~, to feel out of sorts.

catolizar tr. to catholicize.

Catón m. pr. n. Cato.

catón m. severe censor. 2 primer, reading book.

catóptrica f. catoptrics.

catorce adj.-n. fourteen.

catorceno, -na adj. fourteenth.

catorzavo, -va adj.-m. fourteenth [part].

catre m. cot, light bed: ~ de tijera, folding cot.

catrecillo m. dim. camp canvas chair.

Cátulo m. pr. n. Catullus.

caucásico, -ca adj.-n. Caucasian [white].

Cáucaso m. pr. n. GEOG. Caucasus.

cauce m. bed [of watercourse]. 2 channel, ditch.

caución f. caution, precaution. 2 LAW surety.

caucionar tr. LAW to bail. 2 LAW to guard against loss or harm.

cauchera f. BOT. rubber plant.

cauchero, -ra adj. [pertaining to] rubber. 2 m. rubber gatherer or worker.

caucho m. rubber, india-rubber, caoutchouc. 2 BOT. rubber plant.

cauchutado m. rubberizing, covering or furnishing with rubber.

cauchutar tr. to rubberize, to cover or furnish with rubber.

caudal adj. of great volume [river]. 2 ZOOL. caudal. 3 m. fortune, wealth, means; plenty, abundance. 4 volume [of water].

caudaloso, -sa adj. of great volume of water, carrying much water. 2 rich, wealthy.

caudatario m. ECCL. train-bearer.

caudillaje m. leadership.

caudillo m. chief, leader. 2 military leader.

caudinas adj. f. pl. HIST. Caudine.

caulescente adj. BOT. caulescent.

causa f. cause, origin, reason, motive: a ~ de, por ~ de, because of, on account of. 2 cause [espoused or advocated]: hacer ~ común con, to make common cause with. 3 lawsuit. 4 case, trial at law.

causahabiente m. LAW asignee, trustee, executor.

causal *adj.* GRAM. causal, causative.
causalidad *f.* causality.
causante *adj.* causing, causative; occasioning. 2 *m.-f.* causer, doer, occasioner, originator.
causar *tr.* to cause, do, create, occasion, originate.
causativo, -va *adj.* causative.
causticidad *f.* causticity.
cáustico, -ca *adj.* caustic(al. 2 *m.* caustic. 3 vesicatory.
cautamente *adv.* cautiously.
cautela *f.* caution, wariness. 2 craft, cunning.
cautelar *tr.* to prevent. 2 *ref. cautelarse de*, to guard against.
cautelosamente *adv.* cautiously, heedfully, warily, carefully.
cauteloso, -sa *adj.* cautious, wary, guarded.
cauterio *m.* cautery.
cauterización *f.* cauterization.
cauterizar *tr.* to cauterize.
cautivador, -ra *adj.* captivating, charming.
cautivante *adj.* captivating, fascinating.
cautivar *tr.* to take prisoner. 2 to win, hold [the attention, etc.]. 3 to captivate, charm.
cautiverio *m.*, **cautividad** *f.* captivity.
cautivo, -va *adj.-n.* captive.
cauto, -ta *adj.* cautious, wary, prudent.
cava *f.* digging, hoeing. 2 royal wine cellar.
cavador *m.* digger.
cavar *tr.* to dig, to hoe. 2 *intr.* to dig [in]. 3 to go to the bottom [of a subject, etc.].
cavatina *f.* MUS. cavatina.
cavazón *m.* digging.
caverna *f.* cavern, cave. 2 MED. morbid cavity.
cavernario, -ria *adj.* cave, cavern.
cavernícola *adj.* cave-dwelling. 2 *m.-f.* cave dweller. 3 coll. political reactionary.
cavernoso, -sa *adj.* cavernous. 2 hollow [voice, sound].
caveto *m.* ARCH. cavetto.
cavia *f.* ZOOL. guinea pig.
cavial, caviar *m.* caviar.
cavicornio, -na *adj.* ZOOL. cavicorn.
cavidad *f.* cavity.
cavilación *f.* rumination, brooding over. 2 unfounded apprehension; fancy.
cavilar *tr.* to ruminate, brood over, muse on.
caviloso, -sa *adj.* given to anxious ruminations.
cayado *m.* hooked staff, crook, shepherd's hook. 2 crozier [of bishop].
Cayena *f. pr. n.* GEOG. Cayenne.
Cayetano *m. pr. n.* Gaetan.
cayo *m.* cay, key.
caz *m.* millrace, flume, channel.
caza *f.* hunting, chase: *dar ~ a*, to hunt, give chase to; *a la ~ de*, hunting for. 2 game [animals]: *~ mayor* big game; *~ menor*, small game. 3 *m.* AER. pursuit plane, fighter.
cazabe *m.* cassava bread.
cazabombardero *m.* fighter bomber.
cazador, -ra *adj.* hunting. 2 *m.* hunter; huntsman, fowler: *~ furtivo*, poacher. 3 MIL. chasseur. 4 *f.* huntress. 5 jacket, hunting jacket.
cazar *intr.* to hunt, to fowl. 2 *~ largo*, to be perspicacious. 3 *tr.* to hunt, chase, to hunt for. 4 to catch, get: *cazarlas al vuelo*, fig. to be quick-witted. 5 NAUT. to haul tight [a sheet].
cazasubmarinos, *pl.* **-nos** *m.* NAV. submarine chaser.
cazatorpedero *m.* NAV. torpedo-boat destroyer.
cazcarrias *f. pl.* dried mud splashings on clothes.
cazo *m.* dipper; little saucepan. 2 back [of knife].

cazolada *f.* contents of a cooking pan.
cazoleta *f.* small cooking pan. 2 flashpan [of firearm]. 3 bowl [of tobacco pipe]. 4 hand guard [of sword]. 5 boss [of buckler].
cazón *m.* ICHTH. dogfish [a small shark].
cazuela *f.* earthen cooking pan; large casserole. 2 THEAT. gallery.
cazumbre *m.* cooper's oakum.
cazurro, -rra *adj.* taciturn, reticent.
ce *f.* name of the letter *c*: *~ por be*, minutely, circumstantially.
ceba *f.* fattening [of animals]. 2 feeding [of a furnace].
cebada *f.* BOT. barley: *~ perlada*, pearl barley.
cebadal *m.* barley field.
cebadera *f.* barley bin. 2 nose bag. 3 METAL. furnace charger. 4 NAUT. spritsail.
cebadero *m.* barley dealer. 2 MIN. the mouth of a furnace. 3 lead mule. 4 feeding place.
cebadilla *f.* BOT. wall barley. 2 BOT. sabadilla.
cebador *adj.* fattening; feeding, priming. 2 *m.* priming horn, powder flask.
cebadura *f.* fattening [animal]. 2 stoking [furnace]. 3 priming [gun]. 4 (Am.) load of mate leaves. 5 brewing, making [mate].
cebar *tr.* to fatten, to feed [animals]. 2 to feed [a furnace, fire, etc.]; to prime [a gun, pump, steam engine, etc.]; to bait [a fishook, a trap]; to lure with bait. 3 to nourish [sentiments, passions]. 4 *intr.* [of a nut, a nail] to catch, take hold. 5 *ref. cebarse en*, to be firmly bent upon [a thing]; to vent one's fury on.
cebellina *f.* ZOOL. sable. 2 sable fur.
cebo *m.* food given to animals; fattening food. 2 bait. 3 lure, incentive. 4 primer charge, priming. 5 ZOOL. an African monkey.
cebolla *f.* BOT. onion [plant and bulb]. 2 BOT. bulb. 3 BOT. *~ albarrana*, squill.
cebollana *f.* BOT. chive.
cebollar *m.* onion patch.
cebolleta *f.* tender onion. 2 BOT. Welsh onion.
cebollino *m.* onion seedling. 2 onion seeds. 3 CEBOLLANA.
cebollona *f.* (Am.) coll. spinster, old maid.
cebolludo, -da *adj.* bulbous, bulbaceous. 2 coarse, rude.
cebón, -na *adj.* fattened. 2 *m.-f.* fattened animal.
cebra *f.* ZOOL. zebra.
cebrado, -da *adj.* striped [like the zebra].
cebruno, -na *adj.* deer-coloured.
cebú, *pl.* **cebúes** *m.* ZOOL. zebu.
ceca *f.* obs. mint [where money is coined].
Ceca *f. andar de Ceca en Meca* or *de la Ceca a la Meca*, to go hither and thither.
cecear *intr.* to lisp.
ceceo *m.* lisping.
ceceoso, -sa *adj.* lisping. 2 *m.-f.* lisper.
Cecilia *f. pr. n.* Cecilia.
Cecilio *m. pr. n.* Cecil.
cecina *f.* cornet and dried meat.
cecinar *tr.* to jerk, to cure, to cut into strips and dry in the sun.
ceda *f.* CERDA 1. 2 ZEDA.
cedacero *m.* sieve maker.
cedacillo *m.* BOT. quacking grass.
cedazo *m.* sieve, bolt, bolter.
cedente *adj.* grating, assigning, transferring. 2 *n.* grantor, assignor.
ceder *tr.* to cede, transfer, yield, give up, resign. 2 *intr.* to yield, submit, give in, give way. 3 [of wind, fever, etc.]. to abate, slacken. 4 [of a floor,

a rope, etc.] to fall, give way. 5 ~ *en*, to redound to. 6 *no ~ en nada a*, to be by no means inferior to.
cedilla *f*. cedilla.
cedrino, -na *adj*. cedrine.
cedro *m*. BOT. cedar: ~ *deodara*, deodar. 2 cedar wood.
cédula *f*. piece or slip of paper or parchment written or to write upon; order, bill, certificate.
cefalalgia *f*. MED. cephalalgia.
cefalea *f*. headache.
cefálico, -ca *adj*. cephalic.
cefalópodo *adj.-m*. cephalopod.
cefalotórax *m*. ZOOL. cephalothorax.
Cefeo *n. pr*. ASTR., MYTH. Cepheus.
céfiro *m*. zephyr [wind; cloth].
cefo *m*. an African monkey.
cegado, -da *adj*. blinded. 2 blocked, walled up.
cegador, -ra *adj*. dazzling, blinding.
cegar *intr*. to go blind. 2 *tr*. to blind [make blind]; to obfuscate. 3 to dazzle. 4 to wall up, close up, stop up [a door, well, channel, passage, etc.]. 5 *ref*. to be blinded [by passion, love, etc.] ¶ CONJUG. like *acertar*.
cegarra *adj.-n*. cegato.
cegarrita *f*. weak-eyed.
cegato, -ta *adj*. short-sighted, weak-eyed.
cegesimal *adj*. PHYS. centimeter-gram-second, C.G.S.
ceguedad *f*. blindness.
ceguera *f*. blindness. 2 obfuscation [of mind].
ceiba *f*. BOT. silk-cotton tree. 2 BOT. sea moss.
Ceilán *m. pr. n*. Ceylon.
ceilanés, -sa *adj.-n*. Ceylonese.
ceja *f*. ANAT. brow, eyebrow: *quemarse las cejas*, to burn the midnight oil: *tener entre ~ y ~*, to dislike [someone]; to persist in [a purpose]. 2 projecting part, flange. 3 brow [of a hill]. 4 cloud cap. 5 MUS. nut [of guitar, etc.]. 6 MUS. capotasto.
cejar *intr*. to back up, go backward. 2 to relax, desist: *no ~*, to persist.
cejijunto, -ta *adj*. bushy-browed, with thick, heavy eyebrows. 2 frowning, grim, scowling.
cejilla *f*. MUS. nut [of a guitar]. 2 capotasto.
cejo *m*. morning mist over a river or stream.
cejudo, -da *adj*. beetle-browed.
celacanto *m*. ZOOL. coelacanth.
celada *f*. ambush, trap, snare. 2 ARM. sallet, helmet.
celador, -ra *adj*. watching. 2 *m.-f*. watcher, inspector; warden, wardress.
celaje *m*. NAUT. mass of clouds. 2 cloud scenery, cloud effect. 3 skylight, window. 5 *pl*. sky covered with many-coloured clouds.
celandés, -sa *adj.-n*. ZEELANDÉS.
celar *tr*. to see to [the observance of law, duties, etc.]. 2 to watch over [employees, etc.]. 3 to watch, spy on [through suspicion or jealousy]. 4 to hide, conceal. 5 to carve, engrave.
celastro *m*. BOT. staff tree.
celda *f*. cell [in convent, prison, honeycomb].
celdilla *f*. cell [in honeycomb]. 2 BIOL., BOT. cell. 3 niche, cavity.
celebérrimo, -ma *adj*. superl. most celebrated.
celebración *f*. celebration. 2 holding [of a meeting, etc.]. 3 praise, applause.
celebrado, -da *adj*. popular.
calebrante *m*. celebrant.
celebrar *tr*. to celebrate [a ceremony, a birthday, etc.]; to make [a festival]; to perform [a contract]; to hold [a meeting]. 2 to celebrate, ap-

plaud; to extol, to honour. 3 to be glad of. 4 *intr*. to celebrate, say Mass.
célebre *adj*. celebrated, famous. 2 coll. funny, witty.
celebridad *f*. celebrity. 2 celebration, festival.
celemín *m*. a dry measure [about half a peck].
celenterado, celenterio *adj.-n*. ZOOL. cœlenterate.
celeridad *f*. celerity.
celeste *adj*. celestial. 2 sky-blue. 3 Celestial [Empire]. 4 MUS. celeste. 5 MUS. soft [pedal].
celestial *adj*. celestial. 2 heavenly; perfect, delightful.
celestina *f*. bawd, procuress.
celíaco, -ca *adj*. ANAT. cœliac.
celibato *m*. celibacy. 2 coll. bachelor, single man.
célibe *adj*. celibate, single, unmarried. 2 *m.-f*. bachelor or spinster, unmarried person.
celidonia *f*. BOT. celandine.
celinda *f*. syringa.
celo *m*. zeal. 2 heat, rut. 3 *pl*. jealousy.
celofana *f*. cellophane.
celosía *f*. lattice; lattice window. 2 jealousy.
celoso, -sa *adj*. zealous. 2 jealous. 3 suspicious.
celsitud *f*. elevation, grandeur.
celta *adj*. Celtic. 2 *m.-f*. Celt.
celtibérico, -ca; celtíbero, -ra *adj.-n*. Celtiberian.
céltico, -ca *adj*. Celtic.
célula *f*. BIOL., ELECT. cell. 2 ~ *comunista*, communist cell.
celulado, -da *adj*. celled, cellated, cellular.
celular *adj*. cellular.
celulitis *f*. MED. cellulitis.
celuloide *m*. celluloid.
celulosa *f*. cellulose.
celuloso, -sa *adj*. cellulose, cellulous.
cellisca *f*. sleet, sleet storm.
cellisquear *intr*. to sleet.
cello *m*. hoop [of a barrel].
cementación *f*. METAL. cementation.
cementar *tr*. METAL. to cement.
cementerio *m*. cemetery, churchyard, graveyard.
cemento *m*. cement. 2 ~ *armado*, reinforced concrete.
cementoso, -sa *adj*. cement-like.
cena *f*. supper. 2 *la Santa Cena*, the Last Supper.
cenáculo *m*. Cenacle. 2 cenacle [literary group].
cenacho *m*. esparto or palm bag.
cenador, -ra *adj*. supping. 2 *m.-f*. supper [pers.]. 3 *m*. arbo(u)r, bower, summerhouse.
cenagal *m*. slough, miry place. 2 fig. quagmire.
cenagoso, -sa *adj*. miry, muddy.
cenar *intr*. to sup [have supper]. 2 *tr*. to have for supper.
cenceño, -ña *adj*. lean, slender, thin.
cencerrada *f*. charivari, tin-pan serenade.
cencerrear *intr*. to jingle cowbells continually. 2 to jangle, rattle. 3 to play out of tune.
cencerreo *m*. jingle of cowbells. 2 jangle, rattle.
cencerro *m*. cowbell: *a cencerros tapados*, stealthily, cautiously.
cencuate *m*. poisonous snake from Mexico.
cendal *m*. sendal, gauze, transparent fabric. 2 ECCL. humeral veil. 3 barbs of a feather.
cendolilla *f*. madcap [girl].
cenefa *f*. list or stripe on the border of a stuff, garment, etc.; border. 2 middle stripe in a chasuble. 3 ARCH. ornamental band or fret.
cenicero *m*. ash tray. 2 ash pan, ashpit; ash dump.
ceniciento, -ta *adj*. ashen, ash-gray. 2 *f*. Cinderella.
cenit *m*. ASTR. zenith.
cenital *adj*. zenith, zenithal.

ceniza f. ash, ashes. 2 BOT. oidium. 3 pl. ashes, cinders. 4 ashes [mortal remains].
cenizo, -za adj. CENICIENTO. 2 m. BOT. goosefoot. 3 BOT. oidium. 4 hoodoo, jinx, Jonah [person who brings ill-luck].
cenobial adj. coenobitic, cenobitic, coenobitical, cenobitical.
cenobio m. cenoby, cenobium.
cenobita m. cenobite.
cenotafio m. cenotaph.
censal adj. CENSUAL. 2 m. rent charge.
cenozoico, -ca adj. GEOL. cenozoic, caenozoic.
censar tr. to take a census of.
censatario m. person paying a rent charge.
censo m. census [official enumeration of population, etc.]. 2 LAW census, rent charge.
censor m. censor. 2 censorious person.
censorio, -ria adj. censorial.
censual adj. [pertaining to the] rent-charge.
censualista m. rent charger.
censura f. censure. 2 censorship. 3 body of censors.
censurable adj. censurable, blamable, reprehensible.
censurador, -ra adj. censorious.
censurar tr. to censor. 2 to censure, blame, critizice.
centaura, centaurea f. BOT. centaury, knapweed.
centauro m. MYTH. centaur.
centavo, -va adj. hundredth. 2 m. hundredth; one-hundredth part. 3 cent [money].
centella f. lightning, thunderbolt. 2 spark, flash.
centelleante adj. sparkling, glittering, flashing.
centellar, centellear intr. to sparkle, glitter, flash, scintillate; to twinkle.
centelleante adj. CENTELLANTE.
centelleo m. sparkling, glittering, scintillation.
centén m. old Spanish gold coin.
centena f. a hundred.
centenada f. hundred: a ~, by the hundred.
centenal m. hundred. 2 rye field.
centenar m. hundred: a centenares, by hundreds. 2 rye field.
centenario, -ria adj. centenary, centennial, centenarian. 2 m.-f. centenarian [person]. 3 m. centenary, centennial [centennial aniversary].
1) **centeno** m. BOT. rye.
2) **centeno, -na** adj. hundredth.
centesimal adj. centesimal.
centésimo, -ma adj. centesimal, hundredth. 2 m.-f. hundredth.
centiárea f. centiare, square metre.
centígrado, -da adj. centigrade.
centigramo m. centigram.
centilitro m. centilitre.
centímetro m. centimetre.
céntimo m. hundredth part. 2 centime, one-hundredth part of a peseta.
centinela m.-f. sentinel, sentry: ~ de vista, prisoner's guard; estar de ~, hacer ~, to be on sentry duty, to watch.
centinodia f. BOT. knotgrass.
centolla f. ZOOL. thornback [crab].
centón m. crazy quilt, patchwork. 2 LITER. cento.
centrado, -da adj. centred, centered. 2 balanced. 3 m. centring, centering.
central adj. central. 2 f. main office, headquarters. 3 TELEPH. exchange, central. 4 ELECT. powerhouse, generating station.
centralilla, centralita f. TELEPH. local exchange.
centralismo m. centralism.
centralización f. centralization.

centralizador, -ra adj. centralizing. 2 m. centralizer.
centralizar tr.-ref. to centralize.
centrar tr. to centre, to center. 2 to point, to aim, to focus [beam, ray]. 3 to base. 4 ref. to center, to centre, to be based. 5 ref. find one's feet, to concentrate.
céntrico, -ca adj. centric, central. 2 downtown.
centrifugador, -ra adj.-f. centrifugal [machine].
centrifugar tr. to centrifuge.
centrífugo, -ga adj. centrifugal.
centrípeto, -ta adj. centripetal.
centrista n. centrist, middle-of-the-roader. 2 adj. centre, center, belonging to the center.
centro m. center, centre: ~ de gravedad, center of gravity; estar en su ~, to be in one's element. 2 the central part of a town, city. 3 goal, aim. 4 club, association, social meeting place. 5 main office, headquarters. 6 ~ de mesa, centrepiece [of table].
centroamericano, -na adj.-n. Central American.
centroeuropeo, -a adj.-n. Central European.
centrosfera f. BIOL. centrosphere.
centrosoma m. BIOL. centrosome.
centunviro m. centumvir.
centuplicar tr. to centuple, centuplicate.
céntuplo, -pla adj.-m. centuple, hundredfold.
centuria f. century [a hundred years]. 2 HIST. [Roman] century.
centurión m. centurion.
cénzalo m. ENT. mosquito.
ceñido, -da adj. close-fitting. 2 thrifty, economical. 4 reduced, condensed.
ceñidor m. girdle, belt, sash [for the waist].
ceñir tr. to gird; to girdle, encircle. 2 to fasten around the waist. 3 to fit tight. 4 to shorten, to condense. 5 ~ espada, to wear a sword. 6 NAUT. to haul [the wind]. 7 ref. to reduce one's expenses. 8 to be concise. ¶ CONJUG. like reír.
ceño m. frown. 2 threatening aspect [of clouds, sea, etc.].
ceñudo, -da adj. frowning, stern, grim.
ceo m. ICHTH. dory.
cepa f. underground part of the stock [of tree or plant]. 2 grapevine; vine stem. 3 butt or root [of horn, tail, etc.]. 4 stock [of lineage]. 5 de buena ~, of good quality.
cepillado, -m. cepilladura f. planing [carpintry]. 2 brushing [a suit]. 2 pl. shavings.
cepillar tr. ACEPILLAR.
cepillo m. brush [for cleaning]: ~ de dientes, toothbrush; ~ para el pelo, hairbrush. 2 CARP. plane; ~ bocel, fluting plane. 3 alms box, poor box.
cepo m. bough, branch [of tree]. 2 stock [of anvil]. 3 stocks, pillory. 4 iron trap. 5 alms box. 6 stock [of anchor]. 7 CEFO. 8 ¡cepos quedos!, hands off!
cequí m. sequin, zequin [old golden coin].
cera f. wax; beeswax: ~ aleda, bee glue; ~ de los oídos, earwax; figuras de ~, waxworks. 2 ORN. cere. 3 pl. honeycomb.
cerafolio m. BOT. chervil.
cerámica f. ceramics. 2 ARCHEOL. study of ceramics.
cerámico, -ca adj. ceramic.
ceramista m.-f. ceramist.
cerapez f. cobbler's wax.
cerasta f., **ceraste, cerastes** m. ZOOL. cerastes.
cerato m. PHARM. ointment containing wax.
cerbatana f. blowgun. 2 peashooter, popgun. 3 ear trumpet. 4 small culverin.
cerbero m. CANCERBERO.

cerca

1) **cerca** *f.* enclosure, hedge, fence.
2) **cerca** *adv.* near, close, nigh: *aquí* ~, near here; *de* ~, from near; *seguir de* ~, to follow closely. | Before a noun, pron. or adv., it requires *de:* ~ *de Madrid*, near Madrid. *2* ~ *de*, nearly, about: ~ *de un año*, nearly a year. *3* to, at the court of. *4 pl.* PAINT. objects in the foreground.
cercado, -da *adj.* fenced-in, walled-in. *2* MIL. surrounded. *3 m.* enclosure, fenced-in or walled-in garden or field. *4* fence, enclosure.
cercanamente *adv.* nearby, close by. *2* shortly, soon, in a short time.
cercanía *f.* nearness, proximity. *2 pl.* neighbourhood, vicinity; surroundings.
cercano, -na *adj.* near, close, nearing. *2* neighbouring, adjoining.
cercar *tr.* to fence, hedge, pale, wall in. *2* to encircle, surround, hem in; to crowd around. *3* MIL. to invest, lay siege to.
cercén, a cercén *adv.* to the root. *2* completely.
cercenador *m.* clipper. *2* curtailer, reducer.
cercenamiento *m.* clipping, retrenchment. *2* curtailment, reduction.
cercenar *tr.* to clip, to cut off the point or edges of. *2* to curtail, lessen, reduce.
cerceta *f.* ORN. garganey. *2 pl.* buds [of antlers].
cerciorar *tr.* to make [someone] sure of a fact. *2 ref.* ˈcerciorarse de, to ascertain, make sure of.
cerco *m.* circle [about a thing]; hoop, ring, edge. *2* rim [of wheel]. *3* casing, frame [of door or window]. *4* halo. *5* circle, ring [of persons]. *6* MIL., siege, blockade.
cerchar *tr.* AGR. to layer [the vine].
cerchearse *ref.* to warp.
cerchón *m.* ARCH. truss.
cerda *f.* horsehair; bristle, hog bristle. *2* ZOOL. sow. *3 ganado de* ~, swine (collec.).
cerdada *f.* coll. foul trick, lousy trick, dirty trick. *2* mess.
cerdamen *m.* tuft of bristle or horsehair.
Cerdaña *f. pr. n.* GEOG. Cerdagne valley.
cerdear *intr.* [of horses or bulls] to falter in the forelegs. *2* [of stringed instruments] to sound harsh, to rasp. *3* to show reluctance.
Cerdeña *f. pr. n.* Sardinia.
cerdito *m. dim.* little pig.
cerdo *m.* ZOOL. swine [domestic] hog, pig. *2* pork [meat]. *3* fig. pig, swine [person].
cerdoso, -sa *adj.* bristly.
cereal *adj.-m.* cereal.
cerealista *adj.* pertaining to cereals. *2 m.-f.* grain producer; grain dealer.
cerebelo *m.* ANAT. cerebellum.
cerebral *adj.* cerebral.
cerebro *m.* ANAT. cerebrum. *2* fig. head, brains.
cerebroespinal *adj.* cerebrospinal.
cereceda *f.* cherry orchard.
ceremonia *f.* ceremony. *2* formality. *3* ceremoniousness. *4 de* ~, formal, with all due ceremony; *por* ~, as a matter of form.
ceremonial *adj.-m.* ceremonial.
ceremonioso, -sa *adj.* ceremonious.
céreo, -a *adj.* cereous, waxen.
cerería *f.* waxchandlery, waxchandler's shop.
cerero *m.* waxchandler; waxdealer.
Ceres *f. pr. n.* MYTH. Ceres.
cereza *f.* cherry [fruit]: ~ *gordal*, bigaroon.
cerezal *m.* cherry orchard.
cerezo *m.* BOT. cherry tree: ~ *silvestre*, dogwood.
ceriflor *f.* BOT. honeywort.
cerilla *f.* wax match, paper match. *2* wax taper.

cerillera *f.*, **cerillero** *m.* matchbox.
cerillo *m.* wax taper.
cerio *m.* CHEM. cerium.
cermeña *f.* BOT. a variety of pear.
cermeño *m.* BOT. a variety of pear tree.
cernada *f.* leached ashes.
cerne *m.* heart [of tree].
cernedero *m.* place for sifting flour.
cernedor *m.* sifter, bolter [person]. *2* bolter [machine].
cerneja *f.* fetlock [tuft of hair in horses].
cerner *tr.* to sift, bolt [flour, etc.]. *2* to scan, observe. *3 intr.* [of some plants] to have flowers in a state of pollination. *4* to drizzle, mizzle. *5 ref.* to swing the body in walking. *6* [of birds] to soar, hover. *7* [of evil, storm, etc.] to impend, to hang [over], to gather, to threaten. ¶ CONJUG. like *entender*.
cernícalo *m.* ORN. kestrel, sparrow hawk. *2* fig. rude ignoramus.
cernidillo *m.* drizzle. *2* short minced pace.
cernidura *f.* sifting, bolting. *2 pl.* siftings.
cernir *tr.* CERNER.
cero *m.* zero, naught, nought, cipher: *ser un* ~ *a la izquierda*, to be a mere cipher.
cerón *m.* dross of honeycombs.
ceroso, -sa *adj.* waxen, waxy.
cerote *m.* shoemaker's wak. *2* coll. fright, fear.
cerquillo *m.* fringe of hair around tonsure. *2* welt [of shoe].
cerquita *adv. dim.* not far off, very near.
cerrado, -da *adj.* shut; close, closed; fastened; locked. *2* obscure, incomprehensible. *3* cloudy, overcast. *4* secretive, reserved. *5* sharp [curve]. *6* thick [beard]. *7* PHONET. close. *8* with a heavy local accent. *9* ~ *de mollera*, dense, stupid. *10 m.* CERCADO.
cerrador *m.-f.* shutter, closer, fastener. *2 m.* fastening, lock, etc.
cerradura *f.* CERRAMIENTO. *2* lock [fastening]: ~ *de golpe*, spring lock; ~ *de seguridad*, safety lock.
cerraja *f.* lock [fastening]. *2* BOT. sow thistle.
cerrajería *f.* locksmith trade. *2* locksmith's shop.
cerrajero *m.* locksmith.
cerramiento *m.* shutting, closing. *2* occlusion. *3* enclosure. *4* partition, partition wall.
cerrar *tr.* to close, shut: ~ *la boca*, to shut up; ~ *los oídos*, to turn a deaf ear. *2* to fasten, bolt, lock; ~ *de golpe*, to slam. *2* to clench [the fist]. *4* to block up, stop, obstruct, bar. *5* to wall, to fence. *6* to seal [a letter]. *7* to close [a shop, a business; a bargain, etc.]. *8* ELECT. to close [a circuit]. *9* to turn off [the water, the gas, etc.]. *10 intr.* [of a shop, theatre, etc.] to shut, to close its doors. *11* to shut [to admit of closing]. *12* ~ *con*, to attack. *13* ~ *la noche*, to get dark. *14 ref.* to close, to close itself. *15* to persist, to stand firm. ¶ CONJUG. like *acertar*.
cerrazón *f.* dark and cloudy weather. *2* ~ *de mollera*, density, stupidity.
cerrejón *m.* hillock.
cerrero, -ra *adj.* wild, roaming, untamed. *2* uncouth, coarse, rough. *3* (Am.) bitter.
cerril *adj.* broken, uneven [ground]. *2* unbroken, untamed [cattle]. *3* coll. unpolished, boorish.
cerrillo *m.* hillock. *2* BOT. couch grass.
cerro *m.* neck [of animal]. *2* back, backbone. *3* hill: *irse por los cerros de Úbeda*, to talk irrelevantly.
cerrojazo *m.* slamming the bolt.
cerrojillo *m.* ORN. coal titmouse.
cerrojo *m.* bolt [fastening]. *2* bolt [of a rifle].

certamen *m.* literary contest. *2* competition for a literary, artistic or scientific prize.
certeramente *adv.* surely, unerringly.
certero, -ra *adj.* good [shot]. *2* well-aimed well-directed, unerring. *3* certain, sure, well-informed.
certeza, certidumbre *f.* certainty, certitude.
certificable *adj.* certifiable, registrable.
certificación *f.* certification.
certificado *adj.* registered [letter, package]. *2 m.* registered letter or package. *2* certification, certificate.
certificador *m.* certifier.
certificar *tr.* to certify, to certificate [assure; attest formally]. *2* to register [a letter or package].
certísimo, -ma *adj. superl.* very or most certain.
certitud *f.* certainty, certitude.
cerúleo, -lea *adj.* cerulean, sky-blue.
cerumen *m.* cerumen, earwax.
cerusa *f.* CHEM. ceruse.
cerval *adj.* deer, deerlike: *miedo* ~, great fear.
cervantino, -na *adj.* pertaining or peculiar to Cervantes; in the style of Cervantes.
cervantista *adj.* Cervantist.
cervatillo *m.* new-born fawn. *2* ZOOL. musk deer.
cervato *m.* fawn.
cervecería *f.* brewery. *2* alehouse, beer saloon.
cervecero, -ra *adj.* [pertaining to] beer. *2 m.-f.* brewer. *3* alehouse keeper.
cerveza *f.* beer, ale.
cervicabra *f.* ZOOL. an Indian antelope.
cervical, cervicular *adj.* cervical.
cérvidos *m. pl.* ZOOL. Cervidae.
cerviguillo *m.* thick nape of the neck.
Cervino *pr. n. el monte* ~, the Matterhorn.
cervino, -na *adj.* cervine.
cerviz, *pl.* -**vices** *f.* cerviz, neck, nape of the neck: *bajar* or *doblar la* ~, to humble oneself.
cervuno, -na *adj.* cervine. *2* deerlike.
cesación *f.*, **cesamiento** *m.* cessation, ceasing.
cesante *adj.* ceasing. *2* [of a civil servant] out of office; on part pay. *3 m.* civil servant out of office or put on part pay.
cesantía *f.* dismissal of public employment. *2* part pay, pension of a dismissed civil servant.
cesar *intr.* to cease, stop; to leave off [doing something]; *sin* ~, unceasingly, without cease. *2* [of a civil servant] to go out of office, leave a post.
César *m. pr. n.* Caesar.
cesáreo, -rea *adj.* Caesarean.
cesarismo *m.* Caesarism.
cese *m.* cessation of a civil servant in his functions.
cesibilidad *f.* LAW transferability.
cesible *adj.* LAW transferable.
cesio *m.* CHEM. cesium.
cesión *f.* cession; transfer, conveyance, assignment.
cesionario, -ria *m.-f.* cessionary.
cesionista *m.* transferrer, assigner.
césped, céspede *m.* thick short grass, sward. *2* turf, sod. *3* BOT. ~ *inglés*, Italian rye grass.
cesta *f.* basket, hamper: ~ *de costura*, sewing basket. *2* wicker scoop used in playing the game of pelota.
cestada *f.* basketfull.
cestería *f.* basketmaking; basketwork. *2* basket shop.
cestero, -ra *m.-f.* basketmaker. *2* basket dealer.
cestilla, cestita *f.*, **cestillo, cestito** *m.* small basket.
cesto *m.* basket, washbasket. *2* HIST. cestus.

cestodo *m.* ZOOL. cestode.
cestón *m.* large basket. *2* FORT. gabion.
cesura *f.* PROS. cæsure.
ceta *f.* ZETA.
cetáceo, -cea *adj.* ZOOL. cetacean, cetaceous. *2 m.* ZOOL. cetacean. *3 m. pl.* ZOOL. Cetacea.
cetona *f.* CHEM. ketone.
cetrería *f.* falconry, hawking.
cetrero *m.* falconer. *2* ECCL. verger.
cetrino, -na *adj.* sallow, greenish yellow. *2* melancholy. *3* citrine; made with citron.
cetro *m.* scepter: *empuñar el* ~, to ascend the throne. *2* ECCL. verge. *3* FALCON. perch.
ceugma *f.* zeugma.
ceutí *adj.-n.* of Ceuta.
cía *f.* hipbone.
ciaboga *f.* NAUT. *hacer* ~, to put [a boat] about.
cianhídrico *adj.* CHEM. hydrocyanic.
cianosis *f.* MED. cyanosis.
cianotipo *m.* cyanotype, blueprint.
cianuro *m.* CHEM. cyanide.
ciar *tr.* NAUT. to back water. *2* to go backwards. *3* to back out.
ciático, -ca *adj.* sciatic. *2 f.* MED. sciatica.
Cibeles *f. pr. n.* MYTH. Cybele.
cibelina *f* zool. sable.
cibernética *f.* cybernetics.
ciborio *m.* ARCH. ciborium.
cicatear *intr.* coll. to act niggardly.
cicatería *f.* niggardliness, stinginess.
cicatero, -ra *adj.* niggardly, stingy. *2 m.-f.* niggard.
cicatriz, *pl.* -**trices** *f.* cicatrice, cicatrix, scar.
cicatrizable *adj.* likely to heal, that may heal.
cicatrización *f.* cicatrization.
cicatrizante *adj.* MED. cicatrizing, healing.
cicatrizar *tr.* to cicatrize, to heal [a wound or ulcer]. *2 ref.* [of a wound or ulcer] to cicatrize, heal, scar.
cícero *m.* PRINT. pica.
Cicerón *m. pr. n.* Cicero.
cicerone *m.* cicerone.
cicindela *f.* ENT. tiger beetle.
Cícladas *f. pr. n.* Cyclades.
ciclamino *m.* BOT. cyclamen.
ciclamor *m.* BOT. Judas tree.
cíclico, -ca *adj.* cyclic(al.
ciclismo *m.* cycling, cyclism.
ciclista *m.-f.* cyclist.
ciclo *m.* cycle. *2* series [of lectures].
cicloidal, cicloideo *adj.* MATH. cycloidal.
cicloide *f.* GEOM. cycloid.
ciclomotor *m.* autocycle, moped, small motorcycle.
ciclón *m.* cyclone.
cíclope *m.* MYTH. Cyclops.
ciclópeo, -ea; ciclópico, -ca *adj.* Cyclopean, Cyclopic.
ciclorama *m.* cyclorama.
ciclotimia *f.* MED. cyclothymia.
ciclostilo *m.* cyclostile, mimeograph.
ciclotrón *m.* PHYS. cyclotron.
cicuta *f.* BOT. hemlock, poison hemlock. *2* hemlock [poison]. *3* BOT. ~ *menor*, water hemlock.
cid *m.* strong, courageous man. *2 El Cid Campeador*, a medieval Spanish hero.
cidra *f.* BOT. citron [fruit]. *2* BOT. ~ *cayote*, a variety of squash.
cidrada *f.* preserved citron.
cidro *m.* BOT. citron tree.
cidronela *f.* BOT. balm [*Melissa officinalis*].

ciegamente *adv.* blindly. *2* fearlessly. *3 confiar* ~, to have blind faith.

ciego, -ga *adj.* blind [in practically every sense]; blinded: ~ *de ira*, blind with anger. *2* [of a channel, pipe, etc.] stopped, blocked. *3 m.-f.* blind man, blind woman. *4 m.* ANAT. caecum, blind gut. *5 adv. a ciegas*, blindly; thoughtlessly.

ciego, ciegue, etc. *irr.* V. CEGAR.

cielito *m.* darling, dearest, dearie.

cielo *m.* sky, heaven: *llovido del* ~, heaven sent; *despejarse el* ~, [of the weather] to clear up; *estar hecho un* ~, to be splendid, brilliant; *poner por los cielos*, to praise to the sky; *ver uno el* ~ *abierto*, to see one's way out [of a difficulty]; *a* ~ *abierto*, open to the sky; *a* ~ *descubierto*, in the open air. *2* heaven, Heaven [celestial abode; God]; *bajado del* ~, excellent, perfect. *3* skies, climate, weather. *4* top, roof, covering: ~ *de la cama*, canopy of bed; ~ *de la boca*, roof of mouth; ~ *raso*, flat celling [of room].

ciempiés, *pl.* **-piés** m. ZOOL. centipede, scolopendra. *2* coll. preposterous, disconnected work.

cien *adj.* hundred, a hundred, one hundred [used before nouns].

ciénaga *f.* marsh, miry or marshy place.

ciencia *f.* science; knowledge, learning; certainty; *a* ~ *y paciencia de*, with the knowledge or sufferance of.

cienmilésimo, -ma *adj.-n.* hundred-thousandth.

cienmillonésimo, -ma *adj.-n.* hundred-millionth.

cieno *m.* silt, slime, mire.

científico, -ca *adj.* scientific. *2 m.-f.* scientist.

cientifismo *m.* scientism.

ciento *adj.-m.* hundred, a hundred, one hundred [used when not before the noun]: *por* ~, per cent.

cierne *m.* fecundation of flowers [of some plants]: *en* ~, BOT. blossoming; fig. in the bud.

cierno, cierna, *etc. irr.* V. CERNER.

cierre *m.* closing, shutting [act of closing]. *2* fastening, snap, clasp; closing or shutting device: ~ *de cremallera*, zipper; ~ *metálico*, sliding metal shutter.

cierro *m.* closing, shutting. *2* ~ *de cristales*, glass-enclosed balcony.

cierro, cierre, etc. *irr.* V. CERRAR.

ciertamente *adj.* certainly, surely.

cierto, -ta *adj.* certain, sure: *estar* ~, to be sure; *estar en lo* ~, to be right; *no, por* ~, certainly not; *sí, por* ~, certainly, surely; *por* ~ *que*, by the way. *2* certain, a certain, some: ~ *día*, a certain day, one day.

cierva *f.* ZOOL. hind.

ciervo *m.* ZOOL. red deer; stag, hart. *2* ENT. ~ *volante*, stag beetle.

cierzo *m.* cold north wind.

cifosis *f.* MED. kyphosis.

cifra *f.* cipher, figure, number. *2* amount. *3* cipher [secret writing], code. *4* cipher, monogram. *5* abbreviation. *6* sum, summary. *7 en* ~, in code; enigmatically; in brief.

cifrado, -da *adj.* ciphered, in code.

cifrar *tr.* to cipher [write in cipher]. *2* to summarize. *3* to base, to place: ~ *la dicha en*, to base one's happiness on; ~ *sus esperanzas en*, to place one's hope in.

cigala *f.* ZOOL. crustacean of the *Scyllarus* genus.

cigarra *f.* ENTOM. cicada, harvest fly, *locust.

cigarral *m.* country house with orchard [in Toledo].

cigarrera *f.* cigar maker or seller [woman]. *2* cigar cabinet. *3* pocket cigar case.

cigarrillo *m.* cigarette.

cigarro *m.* cigar: ~ *puro*, cigar; ~ *de papel*, cigarette.

cigarrón *m.* ENT. cicada. *2* ENT. grasshopper.

cigomático, -ca *adj.* ANAT. zygomatic.

cigoñal *m.* well sweep.

cigoñino *m.* ORN. young stork.

cigoñuela *f.* ORN. stilt.

cigoto *m.* BIOL. zygote.

cigua *f.* BOT. a tropical tree.

cigüeña *m.* ORN. stork. *2* MACH. crank, winch. *3* crank [of a bell].

cigüeñal *m.* CIGOÑAL. *2* MACH. crankshaft.

cilantro *m.* BOT. coriander.

ciliado, -da *adj.* ciliate, ciliated.

ciliar *adj.* ANAT. ciliary.

cilicio *m.* cilice.

cilindrada *f.* AUTO. cylinder capacity.

cilíndrico, -ca *adj.* cylindric(al).

cilindro *m.* GEOM., MACH., HOROL., PRINT. cylinder. *2* PRINT. roller, in roller.

cilindroeje *m.* ANAT. axon, axone.

cilio *m.* BIOL. cilium.

cima *f.* summit, top, head [of mountain]; top [of tree]. *2* top, height: *por* ~, POR ENCIMA. *3* BOT. cyme. *4 dar* ~ *a*, to carry out, to achieve.

cimacio *m.* ARCH. cymatium, cyma recta.

cimarrón, -na *adj.* (Am.) runaway [slave]; gone wild [animal]; wild [plant]. *2 m.* (Am.) maroon [slave].

cimbalaria *f.* BOT. Kenilwort ivy, ivywort.

cimbalero, cimbalista *m.* MUS. cymbalist.

cimbalillo *m.* small bell.

címbalo *m.* small bell. *2* MUS. cymbal.

cimbel *m.* decoy [bird]. *2* cord by which the decoy is tied.

cimborio, cimborrio *m.* ARCH. dome.

cimbra *f.* ARCH. centre, center, centring, centering. *2* ARCH. inside curvature of an arch or vault. *3* NAUT. bending of a board.

cimbrado, -da *adj.* centred. *2 m.* bend from the waist [dancing].

cimbrar *tr.* to vibrate [a flexible thing]. *2* to bend, sway [the body]. *3* ARCH. to build the centering for. *4 ref.* to vibrate, to sway. *5* to bend or sway one's body.

cimbreante *adj.* flexible, lithe, pliant; swaying.

cimbrear *tr.* CIMBRAR.

cimbreño, -ña *adj.* flexible, pliant.

cimbreo *m.* act of vibrating, bending, swaying.

címbrico, -ca *adj.* Cimbrian.

cimentación *f.* foundation; laying the foundation.

cimentar *tr.* to lay the foundation for; to found, ground, establish. ¶ CONJUG. like *acertar*.

cimera *f.* crest [of helmet]. *2* HER. crest.

cimero, -ra *adj.* top, uppermost, crowning.

cimicaria *f.* BOT. danewort.

cimiento *m.* foundation [of a building, etc.]; groundwork, basis.

cimiento, cimiente etc. *irr.* V. CIMENTAR.

cimitarra *f.* scimitar.

cinabrio *m.* MINER. cinnabar. *2* cinnabar, vermilion.

cinamomo *m.* BOT. bead tree, China tree. *2* an aromatic substance.

cinc *m.* CHEM. zinc.

cincel *m.* chisel.

cincelado *m.* chisel(l)ing.

cinceladura *f.* carving, chiselling.

cincelador *m.* chisel(l)er, sculptor, engraver.
cincelar *tr.* to chisel, carve, engrave.
cinco *adj.* five: *las* ~, five o'clock; *decir cuántas son* ~, to tell one what's what. *2 m.* five. *3* fifth [in dates].
cincoenrama *f.* BOT. cinquefoil.
cincograbado *m.* zincography. *2* zincograph.
cincografía *f.* zincography.
cincuenta *adj.-m.* fifty. *2* fiftieth.
cincuentavo, -va *adj.-n.* fiftieth.
cincuentena *f.* group of fifty.
cincuentenario *m.* semicentennial.
cincuentón, -na *adj.-n.* quinquagenarian.
cincha *f.* saddle girth, cinch.
cinchar *tr.* to girth, cinch up. *2* to band, hoop.
cincho *m.* belly band. *2* iron band or hoop. *3* ARCH. transverse rib.
cine *m.* cine, movies, pictures: ~ *sonoro*, talkies; ~ *mudo*, silent movies. *2* cinema, picture house.
cineasta *m.-f.* movie producer, actor or actress.
cineclub *m.* cine club, film club, film society.
cinegético, -ca *adj.* cynegetic. *2 f.* cynegetics.
cinemateca *f.* film library.
cinemática *f.* kinematics.
cinematografía *f.* cinematography.
cinematográfico, -ca *adj.* cinematographic.
cinematógrafo *m.* cinematograph. *2* cinema, movies [show]. *3* film projector.
cineraria *f.* BOT. cineraria.
cinerario, -ria *adj.* cinerary.
cinéreo, -a *adj.* cinereous, ash-gray.
cinestesia *f.* kinaesthesis, kinesthesis.
cinético, -ca *adj.* kinetic. *2 f.* kinetics.
cingalés, -sa *adj.-n.* Cingalese.
cíngaro, -ra *adj.* gypsy. *2 m.-f.* zíngaro.
cingiberáceas *f. pl.* BOT. zingiberaceae.
cinglar *tr.* to shingle [iron]. *2* NAUT. to propel [a boat] with only one oar aft.
cíngulo *m.* cingulum.
cínico, -ca *adj.* cynical. *2* barefaced, impudent. *3 m.-f.* cynic. *4 m.* Cynic.
cínife *m.* MOSQUITO.
cinismo *m.* cynicism. *2* barefacedness, impudence.
cinocéfalo *m.* ZOOL. baboon.
cinoglosa *f.* BOT. hound's tongue.
cinta *f.* ribbon, tape, band: ~ *magnetofónica*, recording tape; ~ *métrica*, decimal tape measure. *2* CINEM. film. *3* ARCH. fillet. *4* NAUT. wale.
cintarazo *m.* blow with the flat of the sword.
cinteado, -da *adj.* beribboned.
cintería *f.* ribbons. *2* ribbon trade. *3* ribbon shop.
cintillo *m.* ornamental hat cord. *2* small ring with precious stones.
cinto, -ta *adj.* girdled. *2 m.* belt, girdle. *3* waist [of a person].
cintra *f.* ARCH. curvature [of an arch or vault].
cintrado, -da *adj.* ARCH. arched.
cintura *f.* waist, waistline. *2* waistband [of dress]. *3* throat [of chimney]. *4* *meter en* ~, to discipline, bring into subjection.
cinturón *m.* belt [around the waist; around something]: ~ *de seguridad*, safety belt; ~ life belt.
cipayo *m.* sepoy.
ciperáceo, -a *adj.* BOT. cyperaceous.
cipolino *m.* cipolin, onion marble.
ciprés *m.* BOT. cypress.
ciprino *m.* cyprinid. *pl.* cyprinidae.
Cipriano *m. pr. n.* Cyprian.
ciprio, -pria *adj.-n.* Cyprian [of Cyprus].
circense *adj.* Circensian.

circo *m.* [Roman] circus. *2* GEOL. circus, cirque. *2 circo* or ~ *equestre*, circus [show].
circón *m.* MINER. zircon.
circonio *m.* CHEM. zirconium.
circuito *m.* circuit: *corto* ~, ELECT. short circuit.
circulación *f.* circulation; currency. *2* traffic, movement [of vehicles, etc.].
circulante *adj.* circulating.
1) **circular** *adj.* circular. *2 f.* circular, circular letter.
2) **circular** *intr.* to circulate. *2* to walk, move, pass.
circulatorio, -ria *adj.* circulatory.
círculo *m.* circle: ~ *máximo;* ~ *polar*, ASTR. great circle; polar circle; ~ *vicioso*, vicious circle. *2* circumference. *3* club, casino.
circumpolar *adj.* circumpolar.
circuncidar *tr.* to circumcise.
circuncisión *f.* circumcision.
circunciso, -sa *adj.* circumcised.
circundante *adj.* surrounding.
circundar *tr.* to surround.
circunferencia *f.* circumference.
circunferente *adj.* circumscribing, surrounding, limiting.
circunferir *tr.* to circumscribe, to limit.
circunflejo *adj.* circumflex [accent].
circunlocución *f.*, **circunloquio** *m.* circumlocution.
circunnavegación *f.* circumnavigation.
circunnavegar *tr.* to circumnavigate.
circunscribir *tr.* to circumscribe. *3 ref.* to confine oneself [to].
circunscripción *f.* circumscription. *2* district, territory.
circunscripto, -ta; circunscrito, -ta *adj.* circumscribed; circumscript.
circunspección *f.* circumspection. *2* decorousness, decorum, dignity.
circunspecto, -ta *adj.* circumspect.
circunstancia *f.* circumstance: *en las circunstancias presentes*, under the circumstances. *2* particular, detail.
circunstanciado, -da *adj.* circumstancial, minute, particular.
circunstancial *adj.* circumstantial [pertaining to, or depending on, circumstances].
circunstancialmente *adv.* temporarily, provisionally.
circunstante *adj.* present, surrounding. *2 m. pl.* persons that are present, bystanders, audience.
circunvalación *f.* circumvallation: *carretera de* ~, bypass, ring road.
circunvalar *tr.* to circumvallate.
circunvecino, -na *adj.* neighbouring, adjacent, surrounding.
circunvolar *tr.* to fly around.
circunvolución *f.* circumvolution.
cirial *m.* ECCL. processional candlestick.
Cirilo *pr. n.* Cyril.
cirineo, -da *adj.* CIRENEO. *2 m.* fig. helper, candle.
cirio *m.* ECCL. wax candle.
Ciro *m. pr. n.* Cyrus.
cirrípedo, -da *adj.* CIRRÓPODO.
cirro *m.* BOT., METEOR., ZOOL. cirrus. *2* MED. scirrhus.
cirrópodo, -da *adj.-m.* cirriped.
cirrosis *f.* MED. cirrhosis.
cirrótico, -ca *adj.* cirrhotic.
ciruela *f.* plum [fruit]: ~ *damascena*, damson; ~ *claudia*, greengage; ~ *pasa*, dry plum, prune.
ciruelo *m.* BOT. plum tree. *2* coll. dolt.

cirugía f. surgery [science or art].
cirujano m. surgeon.
cisalpino, -na adj. cisalpine.
cisca f. BOT. sedge.
ciscar tr. to dirty, soil. 2 ref. to ease nature.
cisco m. broken up charcoal: hacer ~, to shatter, smash. 2 row, breeze, shindy.
ciscón m. clinker, ashes, a piece of slag. 2 (Am.) easily offended.
cisión f. cutting, cut, incision.
cisma m. schism. 2 discord.
cismático, -ca adj.-n. schismatic.
cisne m. ZOOL. swan. 2 fig. swan, poet.
cisoide f. GEOM. cissoid.
cisoria adj. arte ~, art of carving meat.
cisquero m. pounce bag.
cista f. cist, kist.
cistel, císter m. Cistercian order.
cisterciense adj.-m. Cistercian.
cisterna f. cistern, reservoir. 2 water tank.
cístico adj. ANAT. cystic [duct].
cistitis f. MED. cystitis.
cisto m. BOT. cistus.
cistotomía f. cystotomy.
cisura f. fissure. 2 ANAT. sulcus.
cita f. appointment, engagement, date [for a meeting]: darse ~, to make an appointment. 2 [in a bad sense] assignation. 3 citation, quotation.
citación f. citation, quotation. 2 LAW citation, summons.
citador, -ra m.-f. citator.
citar tr. to make an appointment with. 2 LAW to cite, summon. 3 to cite, quote. 4 BULLF. to incite [the bull].
cítara f. MUS. cithara. 2 MUS. cithern, cittern. 3 MUS. zithern.
citarista m.-f. citharist. 2 zithern player.
Citerea pr. n. MYTH. Cytherea.
citerior adj. hither, nearer: España ~, the northeastern part of Roman Spain.
citiso m. BOT. cytisus.
cítola f. clapper [in a corn mill], millclapper.
citoplasma m. BIOL. cytoplasm.
citrato m. CHEM. citrate.
cítrico, -ca adj. CHEM. citric.
ciudad f. city, town: Ciudad del Cabo, Cape Town; ~ jardín, garden city. 2 city council.
ciudadanía f. citizenship.
ciudadano, -na adj. [pertaining to the] city or town. 2 civic. 3 citizenly. 4 m.-f. citizen, urbanite.
ciudadela f. FORT. citadel.
civeta f. ZOOL. civet cat.
civeto m. civet.
cívico, -ca adj. civic. 2 civil, polite.
civilidad f. civility, politeness, sociability.
civil adj. civil. 2 adj.-n. civilian [non military person]. 3 m. a member of the Guardia civil.
civilización f. civilization.
civilizado, -da adj. civilized.
civilizar tr. to civilize. 2 ref. to become civilized.
civismo m. civism, good citizenship.
cizalla f. or **cizallas** f. pl. sheet-metal shears. 2 paper cutter. 3 metal clippings.
cizallar tr. to shear [metal sheets or paper].
cizaña f. BOT. darnel. 2 BIBL. tare. 3 corrupting vice, bad influence. 4 discord.
cizañar tr. to sow discord in.
clac m. opera hat, claque, collapsible hat.
clamar tr.-intr. to clamour, cry, cry out: ~ contra, to clamour against; ~ al cielo, to cry to heaven. 2 intr. [of things] to want, require, demand.
clámide f. chlamys.
clamor m. clamour, outcry. 2 plaint, cry of affliction. 3 knell, toll of bells.
clamorear tr. to clamour. 2 intr. [of bells] to knell, toll.
clamoreo m. clamour, clamouring.
clamoroso, -sa adj. clamourous; crying.
clan m. clan.
clandestinidad f. clandestinity.
clandestino, -na adj. clandestine.
claque f. THEAT. claque.
Clara f. pr. n. Clara, Claire.
clara f. white of egg. 2 bald spot. 3 thinly woven spot [in cloth]. 4 break [in a rainy day]. 5 adv. a la ~, a las claras, openly, manifestly.
claraboya f. skylight. 2 clerestory.
clarear tr. to make clear. 2 intr. to dawn. 3 [of weather] to clear, clear up. 4 ref. to be transparent. 5 to disclose one's intentions.
clarecer intr. to dawn. ¶ CONJUG. like agradecer.
clareo m. clearing [a thicket or woods].
clarete m. claret wine.
claridad f. light. 2 clarity. 3 clearness; distinctness; plainness. 4 brightness. 5 pl. home truths, plain truths.
clarificar tr. to clarify.
clarín m. BUS. clarion; bugle. 2 clarion player.
clarinete m. MUS. clarinet. 2 clarinet(t)ist.
clarión m. white crayon, chalk.
clarisa f. Clare [nun].
clarísimo, -ma m. very clear. 2 most illustrious.
clarividencia f. clairvoyance, clear-sightedness.
clarividente adj. clairvoyant, clear-sighted.
claro, -ra adj. bright, full of light. 2 clear [pure, nitid, transparent]. 3 clear, plain, obvious, distinct, intelligible. 4 clear [vision, intellect, day, night, weather, etc.]. 5 thin [liquid]; thin, sparse [hair, vegetation, etc.]. 6 light [colour; in colour]. 7 outspoken. 8 clear, illustrious. 9 adv. clearly, plainly, outspokenly. 10 interj. ¡claro!, ¡claro está!, of course!, sure! 11 m. gap, break, space, interval. 12 clearing [in woods]. 13 PAINT. light. 14 ARCH. light, opening. 15 poner en ~, to make plain, to clear up, elucidate. 16 pasar la noche de ~ en ~, not to sleep a wink.
claroscuro m. PAINT. clear obscure, chiaroscuro.
clarucho, -cha adj. coll. thin, watery.
clase f. class, classes, order: ~ alta, upper classes; clases pasivas, pensioners. 2 HIST. NAT., RLY., NAUT. class. 3 class, kind, sort: toda ~ de, all kind of. 4 EDUC. class; classroom. 5 MIL. clases de tropa, non commissioned officers.
clasicismo m. classicism.
clasicista adj. classicistic. 2 m.-f. classicist.
clásico, -ca adj. classic(al. 2 m. classic [author].
clasificable adj. classifiable.
clasificación f. classification. 2 sorting, filing.
clasificado, -da adj. classified.
clasificador, -ra adj. classifying. 2 m.-f. classifier. 3 m. filing cabinet, file.
clasificar tr. to class, classify. 2 to sort, file.
claudia adj. f. ciruela ~, reina ~, greengage.
Claudia f. pr. n. Claudia, Claudette.
claudicación f. limping. 2 being untrue to one's professed principles.
claudicante adj. halting, limping.
claudicar intr. to halt, limp. 2 to be untrue to one's professed principles.
Claudio m. pr. n. Claude, Claudius.

claustral *adj.* claustral; cloistral.
claustro *m.* ARCH., ECCL. cloister. *2* faculty, academic staff. *3* ~ *materno*, womb, matrix.
claustrofobia *f.* MED. claustrophobia.
cláusula *f.* clause [in a document], proviso. *2* GRAM. sentence, period.
clausura *f.* inner part of a monastery or convent. *2* cloister, monastic confinement. *3* official closing of a congress, court sessions, etc.
clausurar *tr.* to close [sessions, a congress, etc.].
clava *f.* club [stick].
clavado, -da *adj.* nailed. *2* nail-studded. *3* exact, precise. *4* fitting exactly, apposite.
clavadura *f.* prick in a horse's hoof.
clavar *tr.* to drive, stick, thrust [something pointed], to prick or stab with. *2* to nail, to pin. *3* to fix [eyes, etc.]. *4* to set [a precious stone]. *5* to spike [a cannon]. *6 tr.-ref.* to deceive.
clave *f.* key [to a riddle, etc.]. *2* code, cryptography: ~ *telegráfica*, telegraphic code. *3* ARCH. keystone. *4* MUS. clef. *5 m.* MUS. clavichord.
clavecín *m.* MUS. clavecin, harpsichord.
clavel *m.* BOT. pink, carnation; ~ *coronado*, grass pink; ~ *doble*, carnation; ~ *reventón*, large carnation.
clavelito *m.* BOT. sweet william.
clavelón *m.* BOT. marigold, African marigold.
clavellina *f.* BOT. pink: ~ *de pluma*, grass pink.
clavero, -ra *m.-f.* keeper of the keys. *2 m.* BOT. clove tree.
claveteado *m.* studding.
clavetear *tr.* to stud, nail [stud with nails]. *2* to tip, tag [a lace]. *3* to wind up, settle.
clavicémbalo *m.* MUS. clavicymbal, harpsichord.
clavicordio *m.* MUS. clavichord.
clavícula *f.* ANAT. clavicle, collar bone.
clavija *f.* pin, peg, dowel, treenail. *2* MEC. pintle. *3* MUS. peg, wrest pin [of a stringed instrument]. *4* ELECT. plug.
clavijero *m.* MUS. pegbox [of guitar, etc.]. *2* wrest block, wrest plank [of piano].
clavillo *m.* rivet, pin [of scissors or fan]. *2* clove [spice].
clavo *m.* nail [of metal]: ~ *de adorno*, stud; ~ *de rosca*, screw; *agarrarse a un* ~ *ardiendo*, to catch at a straw; *dar en el* ~, to hit the nail on the head; *de* ~ *pasado*, self-evident; easy. *2* corn [on the foot]. *3* headache. *4* grief, pain. *5* core [of boil]. *6* SURG. tent. *7 clavo* or ~ *de especia*, clove [spice].
clemátide *f.* BOT. clematis, virgin's bower.
clemencia *f.* clemency, mercy, forbearance.
clemente *adj.* clement, merciful.
clepsidra *f.* clepsydra, water clock.
cleptomanía *f.* kleptomania.
clerecía *f.* clergy.
clerical *adj.* clerical [pertaining to the clergy]. *2 adj.-n.* POL. clerical.
clericalismo *m.* clericalism.
clerigalla *f.* [contempt.] priests, priesthood.
clérigo *m.* clergyman, priest. *2* HIST. clerk, scholar.
clero *m.* clergy.
clerofobia *f.* hatred of priests.
cliché *m.* cliché, stereotyped expression.
cliente *m.-f.* client. *2* customer.
clientela *f.* clientele, practice, customers.
clima *m.* climate. *2* clime.
climatérico, -ca *adj.* climacteric.
climático, -ca *f.* climatic(cal.
climatología *f.* climatology.
climax *m.* RHET. climax.

clin *f.* CRIN.
clínica *f.* clinic. *2* private hospital. *3* clinical medicine.
clínico, -ca *adj.* clinical. *2 m.-f.* clinician.
Clío *f. pr. n.* MYTH. Clio.
clip *m.* clip, paper clip. *2* clip, hairclip, hairpin. *3* earclip, earring.
clíper *m.* NAUT., AER. clipper.
clisado *m.* PRINT. plating, stereotyping.
clisar *tr.* PRINT. to plate, stereotype.
clisé *m.* PRINT. plate, stereotype plate.
clistel, clister *m.* MED. clyster, enema.
clivoso, -sa *adj.* poet. sloping.
cloaca *f.* sewer, cloaca. *2* ZOOL. cloaca.
clocar *intr.* CLOQUEAR.
Clodoveo *m. pr. n.* Clovis.
cloquear *intr.* [of a hen] to cluck.
cloqueo *m.* cluck, clucking.
cloral *m.* CHEM. chloral.
clorato *m.* CHEM. chlorate.
clorhídrico, -ca *adj.* CHEM. hydrochloric.
cloro *m.* CHEM. chlorine.
clorofila *f.* BOT., BIOCHEM. chlorophyll.
cloroformizar *tr.* to chloroform, chloroformize.
cloroformo *m.* CHEM. chloroform.
cloroplasto *m.* BOT. chloroplast.
clorosis *f.* MED. chlorosis.
clorótico, -ca *adj.* chlorotic.
cloruro *m.* CHEM. chloride.
Clotilde *f. pr. n.* Clotilda.
clown *m.* circus clown.
club *m.* club [association].
clueco, -ca *adj.* broody [hen]. *2* coll. decrepit, *f.* broody hen.
cluniacense *adj.-n.* Cluniac.
coacción *f.* coaction, coercion, compulsion.
coaccionar *tr.* to coerce, compel.
coactivo, -va *adj.* coactive, compelling.
coacusado, -da *m.-f.* LAW codefendant.
coadjutor *m.* coadjutor. *2* assistant to a parish priest.
coadjutora *f.* coadjutrix.
coadministrador *m.* coadministrator.
coadquisición *f.* joint purchase.
coadyutorio, -ria *adj.* helping, aiding.
coadyuvante *adj.* coadjuvant, co-operating.
coadyuvar *intr.* to aid, co-operate, contribute.
coagente *m.* helper, assistant, coadjutant.
coagulable *adj.* coagulable, likely to coagulate.
coagulación *f.* coagulation; curdling.
coagulador, -ra *adj.* coagulative, coagulant. *2* coagulator, coagulant.
coagulante *adj.* coagulative. *2 m.* coagulant.
coagular *tr.* to coagulate; to curdle, to clot. *2 ref.* to coagulate [undergo coagulation].
coágulo *m.* coagulum, curd, clot.
coaita *m.* MONO ARAÑA.
coalición *f.* coalition, league.
coaligarse *ref.* to associate, to ally, to unite. *2* to form a coalition, to coalesce.
coana *f.* ANAT. choana.
coarrendador *m.* joint lessor.
coartación *f.* limitation, restriction.
coartada *f.* alibi: *probar la* ~, to prove an alibi.
coartar *tr.* to limit, to restrict.
coatí *m.* ZOOL. coati.
coautor, -ra *m.-f.* co-author; joint doer.
coaxial *adj.* MATH. coaxial, coaxal.
coba *f.* humorous lie. *2* soft soap, flattery.
cobalto *m.* CHEM. cobalt.

cobarde *adj.* cowardly; timid. *2 m.-f.* coward, yellow.

cobardear *intr.* to be cowardly.

cobardía *f.* cowardice, faint-heartedness.

cobayo *m.* ZOOL. guinea pig.

cobear *tr.* coll. to play up to, to butter up to, to suck up to, to soap up.

cobertera *f.* lid, cover [of pot, pan, etc.]. *2 fig.* ALCAHUETA. *3* ORN. tail covert [feather].

cobertizo *m.* shed; lean-to. *2* penthouse.

cobertor *m.* bedcover, coverlet; counterpane.

cobertura *f.* cover, covering. *2* FINANCE coverage.

cobija *f.* ridge tile. *2* ORN. covert [feather]. *3* cover, covering. *4 pl.* (Am.) bedclothes.

cobijar *tr.* to cover, to shelter, give shelter. *2 ref.* to take shelter.

cobijo *m.* covering, sheltering, shelter: *hallar ~,* to find shelter. *2* lodgings.

cobra *f.* ZOOL. cobra. *2* HUNT. retrieving, retrieval. *3* yoke strap. *4* mares employed in threshing.

cobrable; cobradero, -ra *adj.* collectable, collectible.

cobrador *m.* collector [of money]; receiving teller. *2* tram or bus conductor. *3 adj.* retriever [dog].

cobranza *f.* recovery, collection, cashing.

cobrar *tr.* to collect, receive [money, taxes]; to cash [cheques]; to get paid. *2* coll. to catch it. *3* to charge [a price]. *4* to recover. *5* to take, acquire, gather: *~ ánimo,* to take courage; *~ cariño,* to take a liking; *~ fuerzas,* to gather strength . *6* to pull in [a rope]. *7* HUNT. to retrieve. *8* HUNT. to take [game]. *9 ref.* to recover, to come to.

cobre *m.* CHEM. copper. *2* brasses [kitchen utensils]. *3* MUS. brass, brasses.

cobreño, -ña *adj.* copper [of copper].

cobrizo, -za *adj.* coppery. *2* copper-coloured.

cobro *m.* cashing, collection. *2 poner en ~,* to put in a safe place; *poner ~ en,* to be careful, to be cautious about.

coca *f.* BOT. coca. *2* coca leaf. *3* little round berry. *4* a medieval boat. *5* kink [in a rope]. *6* coll. head, bean. *7* side hair of women. *8* BOT. *~ de Levante,* India berry tree.

cocaína *f.* CHEM. cocaine.

cocción *f.* cooking, boiling. *2* baking [of bread, bricks, pottery, etc.].

cóccix *m.* ANAT. coccix.

coceador, -ra *adj.* kicking [animal].

coceadura *f.*, **coceamiento** *m.* kicking.

cocear *intr.* [of animals] to kick.

cocedero, -ra *adj.* easily cooked, boiled or baked.

cocer *tr.* to cook [food]. *2* to boil [a substance]. *3* to bake [bread, bricks, pottery, etc.]. *4* to digest [in the stomach]. *5 intr.* [of a liquid] to boil. *6* [of wine] to ferment. *7 ref.* to cook, to be cooked, boiled or baked. ¶ CONJUG. like *mover.*

cocido, -da *adj.* cooked, boiled, baked, done. *2 m.* Spanish dish of boiled meat and vegetables.

cociente *m.* MATH. quotient.

cocimiento *m.* COCCIÓN. *2* decoction.

cocina *f.* kitchen. *2* NAUT. galley. *3* kitchen stove: *~ económica,* cooking range. *4* cookery, cooking, cuisine.

cocinar *tr.* to cook [food]. *2 intr.* to cook, do the cooking. *3* coll. to meddle.

cocinero, -ra *m.-f.* cook.

cocinilla *f.* dim. alcohol stove, camping stove.

cóclea *f.* Archimedean screw. *2* ANAT., BOT. cochlea.

coclearia *f.* BOT. scurvy grass.

coco *m.* BOT. coco, coconut palm or tree. *2* BOT. coconut. *3* grub [larva]. *4* BACT. coccus. *5* bogey, bogy, bugbear. *6* face, grimace: *hacer cocos,* to cajole; to make eyes, to flirt.

cocodrilo *m.* ZOOL. crocodile.

cócora *adj.* bothersome, annoying. *2 m.-f.* bothersome person.

cocotal *m.* coconut grove.

cocotero *m.* BOT. coco palm, coconut palm or tree.

coctel *m.* cocktail; cocktail party.

coctelera *f.* cocktail shaker.

cochambre *m.* coll, greasy, stinking filth.

cochambroso, -sa *adj.* coll. filthy and stinking.

coche *m.* coach, carriage, car: *~ de alquiler, de punto,* cab, hack; *~ de camino,* stage-coach; *~ fúnebre,* hearse. *2* AUT. car: *~ de turismo,* touring car. *3* RLY. car, carriage: *~ cama,* sleeping car; *~ restaurante,* dining car. *4* tram car; omnibus.

cochera *f.* coach house, livery stable. *2* tramway depot. *3* coachman's wife.

cochero *m.* coachman, carriage driver: *~ de punto,* cabby, hackman.

cochevis *m.* COGUJADA.

cochifrito *m.* fricassee of lamb or kid.

cochina *f.* ZOOL. sow.

cochinada *f.* dirty thing. *2* dirty trick.

Cochinchina *f. pr. n.* GEOG. Cochin China.

cochinería *f.* filth, dirt; dirty thing. *2* dirty, base, indecorous action.

cochinero, -ra *adj.* of hog; for hogs.

cochinilla *f.* ENT. cochineal insect. *2* cochineal [dyestuff]. *3* ZOOL. *~ de la humedad,* sow bug.

cochinillo *m.* sucking pig.

cochino, -na *adj.* filthy, dirty; piggish. *2* paltry. *3 m.* ZOOL. pig, hog. *5 m.-f.* dirty person.

cochitril *m.* pigsty. *2* filthy room, hovel.

cochura *f.* COCCIÓN. *2* dough for a batch of bread.

coda *f.* MUS. coda. *2* CARP. corner block.

codal *m.* ARM. elbow-piece. *2* ARCH. horizontal strut. *3* frame side of bow saw.

codaste *m.* NAUT. sternpost.

codazo *m.* poke with the elbow; nudge.

codear *intr.* to elbow, move the elbows. *2 ref. codearse con,* to mix or hobnob with.

codeína *f.* CHEM. codein, codeine.

codeo *m.* elbowing, nudging. *2* hobnobbing.

codera *f.* elbow patch. *2* itch on the elbow. *3* NAUT. stern fast.

codeso *m.* BOT. a Spanish cytisus.

codeudor, -ra *m.-f.* joint debtor.

códice *m.* codex.

codicia *f.* covetousness, cupidity, greed.

codiciable *adj.* covetable.

codiciado, -da *adj.* much desired, coveted, yearned for.

codiciar *tr.* to covet.

codicilo *m.* LAW codicil.

codiciosamente *adv.* covetously, greedily.

codicioso, -sa *adj.* covetous, greedy, grasping. *2* desirous. *3* coll. industrious, hard-working.

codificación *f.* codification.

codificar *tr.* to codify.

codificador *n.* codifier.

código *m.* code [collection or body of laws; system of principles or rules]: *~ civil,* civil code; *~ militar,* military law; *~ del honor,* code of honour. *2* NAUT. *~ de señales,* signal code.

codillera *f.* tumour in a horse's elbow.

codillo *m.* elbow, shoulder [of quadruped]. *2* elbow, bend [in tube or pipe]. *4* stump [of branch]. *5* NAUT. end [of keel]. *6* a term at ombre, used when the game is lost by the challen-

ger; *tirar a uno al* ~, to do one's best to harm somebody.
codirección *f.* co-direction, joint management.
codirector, -ra *n.* co-director, co-directress, co-manager, co-manageress.
codo *m.* ANAT. elbow; *dar de* ~, or *del* ~, to nudge; to spurn. *2* CODILLO I. *3* elbow, bend [in tube or pipe]. *4* cubit [measure].
codoñate *m.* quince sweet.
codorniz, *pl.* -nices *f.* ORN. quail.
coeducación *f.* coeducation.
coeficiente *adj.-m.* coefficient.
coercer *tr.* to coerce.
coerción *f.* coertion.
coercitivo, -va *adj.* coercive.
coetáneo, -a *adj.-n.* contemporary.
coexistencia *f.* coexistence.
coexistente *adj.* coexisting, coexistent.
coexistir *intr.* to coexist.
cofa *f.* NAUT. top [platform].
cofia *f.* hair net. *2* women's cap. *3* ARM. coif.
cofrade *m.-f.* member of a confraternity.
cofradía *f.* confraternity, brotherhood, guild.
cofre *m.* coffer; trunk, chest. *2* ICHTH. trunkfish.
cogedera *f.* forked pole for gathering fruits.
cogedor *m.* dustpan. *2* coal or ash shovel.
coger *tr.* to take, seize, grasp; to take hold of; ~ *a uno de la mano*, to take someone by the hand. *2* to catch: ~ *un resfriado*, to catch a cold. *3* to get: ~ *la delantera*, to get the start. *4* to overtake. *5* to take, surprise: ~ *desprevenido*, to take unawares. *6* to find: ~ *a uno en casa*, to find someone at home. *7* to pick, gather, collect [flowers, fruits, etc.]. *8* to take up, absorb. *9* to hold [have capacity for]. *10* to cover, occupy. *11* BULLF. [of the bull] to gore [the bullfighter]. *12* ~ *la palabra a uno*, to hold someone to his promise.
cogestión *f.* co-partnership.
cogida *f.* picking, gathering, harvest. *2* act of the bull goring the bullfighter.
cogido *m.* gather [in cloth].
cogitabundo, -da *adj.* pensive, quietly thoughtful.
cogitación *f.* cogitation.
cogitativo, -va *adj.* cogitative.
cognación *f.* cognation [blood relationship].
cognado, -da *adj.* GRAM. cognate. *2 m.-f.* cognate.
cognición *f.* cognition.
cognomento *m.* cognomen, appellation.
cognoscible *adj.* cognoscible.
cognoscitivo, -va *adj.* cognoscitive.
cogollo *m.* heart [of lettuce, cabbage, etc.]. *2* shoot [of plant]. *3* fig. cream, the best.
cogorza *f.* coll. drunkeness.
cogotazo *m.* slap on the back of the neck.
cogote *m.* back of the neck.
cogotera *f.* havelock. *2* sun-bonnet for carriage horses.
cogotudo, -da *adj.* thick-necked. *2* coll. proud, haughty. *3 m.* (Am.) enriched commoner.
cogujada *f.* ORN. crested lark.
cogulla *f.* cowl, frock [of monk].
cogullada *f.* dewlap [of pig].
cohabitar *intr.* to cohabit.
cohechar *tr.* to bribe [a judge, etc.].
cohecho *m.* bribing, bribery.
coheredar *tr.* to inherit jointly.
coheredero *m.* coheir.
coherencia *f.* coherence. *2* PHYS. cohesion.
coherente *adj.* coherent.
cohesión *f.* cohesion.

cohesivo, -va *adj.* cohesive.
cohesor *m.* RADIO. coherer.
cohete *m.* rocket, skyrocket.
cohibición *f.* restraint; embarrassment.
cohibido, -da *adj.* restrained; embarrassed, ill at ease.
cohibir *tr.* to restrain. *2* to constrain, embarrass.
cohombro *m.* BOT. cucumber. *2* ZOOL. ~ *de mar*, sea cucumber.
cohonestar *tr.* to give an honest appearance to [an action].
cohorte *f.* cohort.
coima *f.* concubine.
coincidencia *f.* coincidence.
coincidente *adj.* coincident.
coincidir *intr.* to coincide.
coito *m.* coition, coitus.
cojear *intr.* to limp, halt, hobble. *2* [of a table, chair, etc.] to be unsteady. *3* to have a failing or a weakness: *saber de qué pie cojea uno*, to know someone's weakness.
cojera *f.* lameness, halt, limp, hobble.
cojín *m.* cushion.
cojinete *m.* small cushion; pad. *2* RLY. chair. *3* MAC. bearing, pillow block: ~ *de bolas*, ball bearing; ~ *de rodillos*, roller bearing.
cojitranco, -ca *adj.* bustling lame person.
cojo, -ja *adj.* lame [person, animal, leg]. *2* unsteady [table, chair, etc.]. *3* out of scan [line]. *4 m.-f.* lame person, cripple.
cojudo, -da *adj.* not castrated.
cojuelo, -la *adj.* dim. of COJO.
col *f.* BOT. cabbage: *coles de Bruselas*, Brussels sprouts.
cola *f.* tail [of animal, bird or comet]: fig. *tener* or *traer* ~ *una cosa*, to have serious consequences. *2* train [of gown]. *3* tail, tail end. *4* queue, line: *hacer* ~, to queue up. *5* last place, end, rear [of queue, line, etc.]: *a la* ~, behind, in the rear. *6* ARQ. back [of ashlar]. *7* glue: ~ *de pescado*, fish glue, isinglass. *8* BOT. cola, kola [tree and nut]. *9* BOT. ~ *de caballo*, horsetail. *10* CARP. ~ *de milano* or *de pato*, dovetail.
colaboración *f.* collaboration.
colaborador, -ra *m.-f.* collaborator. *2* contributor [to a publication].
colaborar *intr.* to collaborate. *2* to contribute articles [to a publication].
colación *f.* conferring [of a degree, of an ecclesiastical benefice]. *2* collation [comparison]. *3* collation, light meal. *4* *sacar a* ~, to mention.
colacionar *tr.* to confer [an ecclesiastical benefice]. *2* to collate, compare. *3* LAW to collate.
colada *f.* bucking, bleaching [of washed clothes]. *2* buck, lye. *3* washing [washed clothes]. *4* cattle run. *5* narrow mountain pass. *6* tap [of blast furnace].
coladera *f.* strainer for liquors.
coladero *m.* strainer, colander. *2* narrow pass.
colado, -da *adj. hierro* ~, cast iron; *aire* ~, draught. *2 estar colado por* ~, to be mad or crazy about, to have a crush on.
colador *m.* strainer, colander.
coladura *f.* straining [of liquids]. *2* slip, faux pas, blunder.
colapez *f.* fish glue, isinglass.
colapso *m.* MED. collapse. *2* fig. collapse, breakdown.
colar *tr.* ECCL. to confer [a benefice]. *2* to strain [pass through a strainer]. *3* to buck, bleach [washed clothes]. *4 intr.* to pass through inters-

tices or a narrow space. *5* to pass [be accepted]: fig. *ésta no cuela*, I don't believe that. *6 ref.* to slip or sneak in. *7* to make a slip, to blunder. ¶ CONJUG. like *contar*.

colateral *adj.* side, lateral. *2* collateral [relative].

colcótar *m.* CHEM. colcothar.

colcrén *f.* cold cream.

colcha *f.* counterpane, quilt.

colchón *m.* mattress: ~ *de muelles*, bedspring; ~ *de pluma*, feather mattress.

colchonería *f.* mattress shop. *2* wool shop.

colchonero, -ra *m.-f.* mattress maker.

colchoneta *f.* long cushion [for a bench, a lounge, etc.]. *2* NAUT. mattress [for a berth].

cole *m.* coll. school.

coleada *f.* shake of the tail.

colear *intr.* to shake or wag the tail. *2* fig. *todavía colea*, we haven't seen the end of it yet. *3* AER. to fishtail. *4 tr.* (Am.) to throw [cattle] by pulling at their tails.

colección *f.* collection [of objects, etc.].

coleccionar *tr.* to collect [form a collection of].

coleccionista *m.* collector [of objects or specimens].

colecta *f.* collection [act of collecting money for charity, in church, etc.]. *2* LITURG. collect.

colectar *tr.* RECAUDAR.

colectividad *f.* collectivity; community, group.

colectivismo *m.* collectivism.

colectivista *adj.* collectivistic. *2 m.-f.* collectivist.

colectivización *f.* collectivization.

colectivizar *tr.* to collectivize.

colectivo, -va *adj.* collective [pertaining to a group]. *2* GRAM. collective.

colector *adj.* collecting. *2 m.* main sewer. *4 canal* ~, collecting waters. *5* ELECT. collector; commutator.

colédoco *m.-adj. m.* choledoch.

colega *m.* colleague. *2* contemporary [newspaper].

colegatario, -ria *n.* col-legatee, joint legatee.

colegiado, -da *adj.* collegiate. *2 m.* member of a professional association.

colegial *adj.-f.* collegiate [church]. *2* [pertaining to a] school. *3 m.* schoolboy. *4* collegian.

colegiala *f.* schoolgirl.

colegiarse *ref.* to form a professional association. *2* to join a professional association.

colegiata *f.* collegial church.

colegio *m.* school, academy. *2* college, body, association: ~ *cardenalicio*, College of Cardinals. *3* ~ *electoral*, polling station.

colegir *tr.* to collect, assemble. *2* to collect, infer, conclude. ¶ CONJUG. like *servir*.

coleóptero, -ra *adj.* ENT. coleopterous. *2 m.* ENT. coleopteran. *3 m. pl.* ENT. Coleoptera.

cólera *f.* PHYSIOL. bile. *2* anger, rage, wrath: *montar en* ~, to fly into a rage. *3 m.* MED. cholera.

colérico, -ca *adj.* choleric, irascible; angry. *2* MED. choleric.

colesterina *f.* BIOCHEM. cholesterin.

colesterol *m.* BIOL. cholesterol.

coleta *f.* pigtail, queue: *cortarse la* ~, to give up bullfighting. *2* additional remark, rider.

coletazo *m.* blow, slash with the tail.

coletilla *f.* COLETA.

coleto *m.* buff coat. *2* fig. one's body, oneself: *echarse al* ~, to drink or eat [something]: to read through.

colgadero *m.* peg, hook, etc., to hang things on; clothes rack; hanger.

colgadizo *m.* penthouse [over a door, etc.].

colgado, -da *adj.* pending, uncertain. *2 dejar* ~ *a uno*, to disappoint, to frustrate someone.

colgador *m.* PRINT. peel. *2* hanger, coat hanger.

colgadura *f.* hangings, drapery.

colgajo *m.* tatter, rag. *2* bunch of fruit hung up for keeping.

colgamiento *m.* hanging, suspending.

colgante *adj.* hanging, suspended; suspension. *2 m.* pendant [jewel]. *3* ARCH. festoon.

colgar *tr.* to hang, suspend. *2* to hang [kill by hanging]. *3* to hang [adorn with hangings]. *4* to attribute, impute. *5 intr.* to hang [be suspended], to dangle, to droop. ¶ CONJUG. like *contar*.

colibrí *m.* ORN. humming bird.

cólico, -ca *adj.* ANAT., MED. colic. *2 m.* MED. colic.

coliflor *f.* BOT. cauliflower.

coligación *f.* union, alliance. *2* colligation.

coligado, -da *m.-f.* ally, confederate, leaguer.

coligarse *ref.* to confederate, ally: ~ *con*, to ally oneself with.

colilla *f.* butt, stub, stump of cigar or cigarette.

colillero, -ra *m.-f.* cigar-butt picker.

colimador *m.* OPT. collimator.

colín *adj.* bobtail (horse). *2 m.* bread stick.

colina *f.* hill, small mountain. *2* cabbage seed. *3* cabbage nursery. *4* BIOCHEM. choline.

colinabo *m.* BOT. rutabaga.

colindante *adj.* adjacent, contiguous.

colindar *intr.* to be adjacent, to be contiguous, to adjoin.

colipava *adj.* fantail [pigeon].

colirio *m.* MED. collyrium, eyewash.

coliseo *m.* coliseum. *2* (cap.) Coliseum, Colosseum.

colisión *f.* collision. *2* clashing [of ideas, interests, etc.].

colista *m.-f.* queuer.

colitigante *m.-f.* co-litigant.

colitis *f.* MED. colitis.

colmado, -da *adj.* full, abundant. *2 m.* wine shop, eating house. *3* grocer's,* foodstore.

colmar *m.* to fill to overflowing. *2* to fulfill [one's hopes, etc.]. *3* ~ *de*, to fill with, to shower, overwhelm with.

colmena *f.* beehive.

colmenar *f.* apiary.

colmenero, -ra *m.-f.* beekeeper.

colmenilla *f.* BOT. morel.

colmillada *f.* injury made with an eyetooth or tusk.

colmillar *adj.* [pertaining to] eyetooth.

colmillo *m.* canine tooth, eyetooth, fang; tusk: *escupir por el* ~, fig. to brag; *tener los colmillos retorcidos*, fig. to be an old dog, be astute.

colmilludo, -da *m.-f.* having large eyeteeth; bigtusked. *2* fig. shrewd, astute.

colmo, -ma *adj.* brimful, full to the top. *2 m.* fill, completion, crowning. *3* height, limit: *es el* ~, it's the limit. *4* thatched roof.

colocación *f.* placing, laying, putting [in place or in a place], location, emplacement. *2* placement. *3* investment [of capital]. *4* employment; place, situation, job.

colocar *tr.* to place, to put [in place, in a place]; to set, lay. *2* to place, to find or give [someone] a situation or job. *3 ref.* to place oneself. *4* to get a situation, a job.

colocasia *f.* BOT. taro.

colodión *m.* CHEM. collodion.

colofón *m.* colophon.

colofonia *f.* colophony; rosin.

coloidal *adj.* colloidal.
coloide *adj.-m.* CHEM. colloid.
Colombia *f. pr. n.* GEOG. Colombia.
colombiano, -na *adj.* Colombian.
colombino, -na *adj.* of Christopher Columbus.
colombofilia *f.* pigeon breeding.
colombófilo, -la *m.-f.* pigeon fancier.
colon *m.* ANAT., GRAM. colon. *2* GRAM. principal part of a period.
Colón *m. pr. n.* Columbus.
colón *m.* silver coin of Costa Rica and El Salvador.
colonato *m.* cultivation of lands by tenant farmers.
Colonia *f. pr. n.* GEOG. Cologne: *agua de Colonia,* cologne, eau-de-Cologne.
colonia *f.* colony. *2* cologne, eau-de-Cologne.
coloniaje *m.* (Am.) colonial period.
colonial *adj.* colonial. *2 m. pl.* colonial products.
colonialismo *m.* colonialism.
colonialista *adj.-n.* colonialist.
colonización *f.* colonization.
colonizador, -ra *adj.* colonizing. *2 m.-f.* colonizer, colonist.
colonizar *tr.* to colonize, to settle.
colono *m.* colonist, settler. *2* tenant farmer.
coloquial *adj.* of the colloquy. *2* colloquial.
coloquíntida *f.* BOT. colocynth, bitter apple.
coloquio *m.* colloquy. *2* talk, conversation.
color *m.* colo(u)r [of things]: *colores nacionales,* colo(u)rs of the flag; *de ~,* colo(u)red [dress, person]: *salirle a uno los colores a la cara,* to blush, be ashamed. *2* colo(u)r [colo(u)ring matter]: *~ al óleo,* oil colo(u)r; *~ sólido,* fast colo(u)r. *3* colo(u)r, pretext: *so ~,* under colo(u)r.
coloración *f.* colo(u)ration, colo(u)ring.
colorado, -da *adj.* colo(u)red. *2* red, ruddy: *ponerse ~,* to blush, redden. *3* risqué, off-colour.
colorante *adj.* colo(u)ring. *2 m.* colo(u)ring matter, colo(u)rant, dye, pigment.
colorar *tr.* to colo(u)r, tint.
colorear *tr.* COLORAR. *2* to colo(u)r, gloss, make plausible. *3 intr.* to show red. *4 intr.-ref.* [of fruit] to redden, begin to ripen.
colorete *m.* rouge.
colorido *m.* colo(u)r [of things]. *2* colo(u)r, false appearance.
colorímetro *m.* colorimeter.
colorín *m.* ORN. goldfinch, linnet. *2 pl.* gaudy colo(u)rs.
colorista *m.* colo(u)rist.
colosal *adj.* colossal, gigantic, enormous.
colosalmente *adv.* coll. marvellously, wonderfully, fabulously.
coloso *m.* colossus.
cólquico *m.* BOT. colchicum, autumn crocus. *2* PHARM. colchicum.
Cólquida (la) *f. pr. n.* Colchis.
columbario *m.* columbarium.
columbino, -na *adj.* columbine, dovelike; pure, innocent.
columbrar *tr.* to descry, glimpse. *2* to guess.
columelar *m.* ANAT. canine [tooth].
columna *f.* column [in practically every sense]: *~ salomónica,* ARCH. wreathed column; *~ cerrada,* MIL. close column; *~ vertebral,* vertebral column. *2* fig. *quinta ~,* fifth column.
columnata *f.* colonnade.
columnista *n.* columnist [journalist].
columpiar *tr.* to swing. *2 ref.* to swing, to seesaw. *3* to swing the body in walking.
columpio *m.* swing [apparatus], seesaw.

colusión *f.* LAW collusion.
colza *f.* BOT. colza, rape.
colla *f.* gorget, throatpiece [armor]. *2* fish trap, line of fishing nets. *3* leash. *4* storm, tempest. *5* team of dockers. *6 n.* inhabitant of Argentinian or Bolivian Andes mountains.
collado *m.* hill, hillock. *2* mountain pass, col.
collar *m.* necklace. *2* collar [of knighthood]; chain of office. *3* collar [of dog, serf, etc.]. *4* ORN., MACH. collar.
collarín, collarino *m.* ARCH. gorgerin.
colleja *f.* BOT. a salad herb.
collera *f.* horse collar. *2* chain gang.
coma *f.* GRAM. comma: *sin faltar una ~,* down to the last detail. *2* MUS. comma. *3 m.* MED. coma.
comadre *f.* midwife. *2* mother and godmother with respect to each other; godmother with respect to father. *3* gossip [woman]. *4* female gossip, crony.
comadrear *intr.* to gossip, go around gossiping.
comadreja *f.* ZOOL. weasel.
comadreo *m.* gossiping.
comadrería *f.* gossip, tittle tattle.
comadrón *m.* obstetrician, accoucheur.
comadrona *f.* midwife.
comanche *adj.-n.* comanche.
comandancia *f.* command [office, district of commander]. *2 ~ de marina,* naval district. *3* MIL. majority.
comandanta *f.* coll. major's wife.
comandante MIL. commander, commandant: *~ en jefe,* commander in chief. *2* MIL. major.
comandita *f.* COM. limited or silent partnership.
comanditar *tr.* to enter as a sleeping partner or a silent partner.
comanditario, -ria *adj.* pertaining to a COMANDITA. *2 m.* silent partner.
comando *m.* MIL. command. *2* MIL. commando.
comarca *f.* district, region, country.
comarcal *adj.* district, regional.
comarcano, -na *adj.* neighbouring.
comatoso, -sa *adj.* comatose.
comátula *f.* ZOOL. feather star.
comba *f.* curvature, bend, warp, bulge. *2* skipping rope. *3* game of skipping rope.
combadura *f.* curvature, bend, camber.
combar *tr.* to curve, bend, camber. *2 ref.* to become curved, bent, cambered.
combate *m.* combat, fight. *2* BOX. fight.
combatible *adj.* that may be attacked, open to attack.
combatiente *adj.-n.* combatant.
combatir *intr.* to combat, to fight. *2 tr.* to combat, fight, oppose. *3* to cotest, impugn. *4* [of wind, sea, etc.] to beat, buffet. *5* [of passions] to shake, agitate, buffet.
combatividad *f.* combativeness.
combativo, -va *adj.* aggressive, combative, full of fighting spirit.
combinación *f.* combining; combination. *2* CHEM., MATH. combination. *3* combination [undergarment]. *4* RLY. connection.
combinado *m.* cocktail.
combinar *tr.* to combine. *2 ref.* to combine [be combined]. *3 intr.* RLY. to connect.
combinatorio, -ria *adj.* MATH. combinatorial.
combo, -ba *adj.* curved, bent, cambered. *2 m.* stand for casks.
combustible *adj.* combustible. *2 m.* combustible; fuel.
combustión *f.* combustion.

comedero, -ra *adj.* eatable. *2 m.* feeding vessel [for birds]; feeding trough.
comedia *f.* comedy, play: ~ *de capa y espada*, cloak-and-sword comedy. *2* farce, pretence: *hacer la* ~, to feign, pretend.
comedianta *f.* comedienne, actress.
comediante, -ta *m.-f.* hypocrite. *2 m.* comedian, actor.
comedido, -da *adj.* courteous, polite. *2* moderate.
comedimiento *m.* courtesy, politeness. *2* moderation.
comediógrafo *m.* playwright, writer of comedies.
comedirse *ref.* to restrain oneself, be moderate. *2* to be courteous.
comedón *m.* MED. comedo, blackhead.
comedor, -ra *adj.* heavy-eating. *2 m.* dining room. *3* eating place, restaurant.
comején *m.* ENT. kind of white ant.
comejenera *f.* nest of COMEJÉN.
comendador *m.* knight commander [of a military order]. *2* head of some religious houses.
comendadora *f.* mother superior of some convents.
comendatario *adj. m.* REL. commendatory.
comensal *m.-f.* commensal.
comentador, -ra *m.-f.* commenter, commentator.
comentar *tr.* to comment on.
comentario *m.* commentary. *2* comment. *3* talk, gossip.
comentarista *m.-f.* commentator.
comento *m.* commentation. *2* commentary, comment.
comenzar *tr.-intr.* to commence, to begin. ¶ CONJUG. like *acertar*.
1) comer *tr.-ref.* to eat [chew and swallow; take as food; consume, corrode], to eat up: ~ or *comerse vivo a uno*, [of passions, vermin, debts, etc.] to devour, to eat one up; *no tener qué* ~, to have nothing to live on; *sin comerlo ni beberlo*, having nothing to do with it. *2* to spend, waste, use up. *3* to omit [words]. *4* CHESS, DRAUGHTS to take. *5 intr.* to eat, feed [take food]. *6* fig. to cause expenditure. *7* to dine; to take a meal.
2) comer *m.* eating; food.
comerciable *adj.* marketable. *2* affable, sociable.
comercial *adj.* commercial, mercantile.
comercialización *f.* commercialization, marketing.
comercializar *tr.* to commercialize.
comerciante *adj.* mercantile, trading. *2 m.* merchant, trader, tradesman: ~ *al por mayor*, wholesaler; ~ *al por menor*, retailer.
comerciar *intr.* to trade, to deal.
comercio *m.* commerce, trade: ~ *exterior*, foreign trade; ~ *interior*, domestic trade. *2* merchants, tradesmen. *3* shop, store. *4* commerce, intercourse. *5* a card game.
comestible *adj.* eatable, comestible. *2 m.* eatable, comestible, foodstuff.
cometa *m.* ASTR. comet. *2 f.* kite [toy].
cometer *tr.* to entrust, to commit [an undertaking to someone]. *2* to commit, do, perpetrate.
cometido *m.* commission, charge, duty.
comezón *f.* itch. itching. *2* hankering, longing.
comible *adj.* coll. fit to eat.
comicastro *m.* THEAT. poor actor.
comicial *adj.* comitial.
comicios *m. pl.* comitia. *2* POL. elections, polls.
cómico, -ca *adj.* comic, dramatic [pertaining to the comedy]. *2* comic, comical, ludicrous,

funny. *3 m.* comedian, actor: ~ *de la legua*, strolling player. *5 f.* comedienne, actress.
comida *f.* food, dressed food; fare. *2* eating, meal, repast. *3* diner.
comidilla *f.* gossip, talk. *2* hobby.
comido, -da *adj.* eaten. *2* having eaten.
comienzo *m.* commencement, beginning, opening, initiation, start.
comienzo, comience etc. irr. V. COMENZAR.
comilón, -na *adj.-n.* great eater, glutton.
comilona *f.* big meal, plentiful repast, spread.
comillas *f. pl.* quotation marks.
comino *m.* BOT. cumin. *2* cumin seed: *no valer un* ~, not to be worth a rush.
comisar *tr.* to seize, confiscate, forfeit.
comisaría *f.*, **comisariato** *m.* commissariat [function, office of commissioner]: ~ *de policía*, police station.
comisario *m.* commissary, commissioner, delegate: *alto* ~, high commissioner. *2* commissar.
comiscar *tr.* to eat in small quantities.
comisión *f.* commission, trust, charge, order. *2* COM. commission. *3* commitee; deputation. *4* commission, perpetration.
comisionado *m.* commissioner, commissioned person.
comisionar *tr.* to commission.
comisionista *m.* COM. commission agent or merchant.
comiso *m.* seizure, confiscation. *2* confiscated goods.
comisura *f.* ANAT. commissure. *2* ANAT. suture.
comité *m.* committee.
comitente *m.-f.* committent.
comitiva *f.* suite, retinue, procession.
cómitre *m.* NAUT. galley slave driver.
como *adv.* how [the manner in which]. | Sometimes it is not translated: *la manera* ~ *lo hizo*, the way he did it. *2* as, like: *se portó* ~ *un héroe*, he behaved like a hero; ~ *usted dice*, as you say; *tanto* ~, as much as. *3 conj.* the moment, as soon as: *así* ~, *tan luego* ~, as soon as. *4* if: ~ *lo vuelvas a hacer...*, if you do it again... *5* because, since, as [offen with *que*]: ~, or ~ *que*, *estábamos a oscuras...*, as we were in the dark... *6* ~ *quiera que*, since, as, inasmuch as. *7* ~ *no sea*, unless it be.
cómo *adv. interr.* how [in what manner]: *¿~ está usted?*, how do you do?; *¡~ corre!*, how he runs! *2* why, how is it that: *¿cómo no viniste?*, why did you not come?; *¿cómo?*, what?, what did you say? *4 interj.* why!, how now!, you don't say! *5 m.* the how.
cómoda *f.* chest of drawers.
cómodamente *adv.* comfortably.
comodidad *f.* comfortableness, comfort, convenience, ease, leisure. *2* commodiousness.
comodín *m.* CARDS joker, wild card. *2* something of general utility. *3* habitual pretext or excuse.
cómodo, -da *adj.* comfortable. *2* convenient, easy. *3* commodious.
comodón, -na *adj.* comfort-loving, ease-loving. *2 m.-f.* comfort lover, ease lover.
comodoro *m.* NAV. commodore.
compacidad, compactibilidad *f.* compactness.
compacto *adj.* compact, solid, close, dense.
compadecer *tr.* to pity, to feel sorry for, to sympathize with. *2 ref. compadecerse de*, to pity, to have pity on. *3 compadecerse con*, to agree, be consistent with.

compadraje *m.* league for mutual protection or benefit [used in a bad sense].

compadrazgo *m.* spiritual relationship between godfather and parents of a child. 2 COMPADRAJE.

compadre *m.* father and godfather with respect to each other; godfather with respect to mother. 2 comrade, pal. 3 (Arg.) bully.

compadrear *intr.* coll. to be on familiar terms.

compadrito *m.* (Am.) bully.

compaginación *f.* making [things] compatible. 2 PRINT. paging.

compaginador *m.* PRINT. pager.

compaginar *tr.* to arrange, connect. 2 to make compatible. 3 PRINT. to page, page up. 4 *ref.* to fit, agree, be consistent.

compaña *f.* coll. COMPAÑÍA 1 & 2.

compañerismo *m.* good fellowship; companionship.

compañero, -ra *m.-f.* companion, fellow, mate, comrade, partner, associate. 2 [of things] one of a pair or set, mate.

compañía *f.* company [act of accompanying]: *hacer ~ a uno,* to give or keep somebody company. 2 company [accompanying persons]. 3 company, society. 4 COM., MIL., THEAT. company: *~ anónima,* joint-stock company.

comparable *adj.* comparable.

comparación *f.* comparison.

comparar *tr.* to compare. 2 to confront, collate.

comparativo, -va *adj.* comparative.

comparecencia *f.* LAW appearance [in court].

comparecer *intr.* LAW to appear [before a judge, etc.]. ¶ CONJUG. like *agradecer.*

compareciente *adj.* LAW appearing. 2 *n.* person appearing before a tribunal.

comparendo *m.* LAW summons.

comparezco, comparezca, etc. *irr.* V. COMPARECER.

comparsa *f.* THEAT. supernumeraries [as a body]. 2 masquerade. 3 THEAT. supernumerary.

compartimentado, -da *adj.* partitioned.

compartimiento *m.* division [of a whole in parts]. 2 compartment.

compartir *tr.* to divide [a whole in parts]. 2 to share [partake of, participate in].

compás *m.* compass, compasses, dividers: *~ de calibres,* or *de espesores,* caliper(s. 2 NAUT. compass. 3 MUS. bar, measure: *~ de espera,* whole rest; fig. brief interruption. 4 MUS. time, measure, rhythm: *llevar el ~,* to keep time, to beat time; *a ~,* in time. 5 rule, measure. 6 springs of a coach hood.

compasado, -da *adj.* moderate, prudent.

compasar *tr.* to measure with a compass. 2 to regulate. 3 MUS. to bar, divide into measures.

compasible *adj.* compassionate. 2 pitiable.

compasillo *m.* MUS. quadruple time measure.

compasión *f.* compassion, pity: *tener ~ de,* to have pity on; *¡por ~!,* for pity's sake.

compasivo, -va *adj.* compassionate, merciful.

compatibilidad *f.* compatibility.

compatible *adj.* compatible, consistent.

compatricio, -cia, compatriota *m.-f.* compatriot.

compatriota *n.* felow countryman or countrywoman, compatriot.

compeler *tr.* to compel, force, constrain.

compendiar *tr.* to epitomize, summarize, abridge.

compendio *m.* compendium, epitome, abstract.

compendioso, -sa *adj.* compendious, brief, succinct.

compenetración *f.* mutual understanding. 2 full accordance or agreement in thought, feeling, etc.

compenetrarse *ref.* to penetrate or pervade lach other. 2 to be in full agreement of thought, feeling, etc.

compensación *f.* compensation.

compensador, -ra *adj.* compensating. 2 *m.* compensador.

compensar *tr.* to compensate. 2 to compensate for, make up for. 3 *ref.* to be compensated.

compensatorio, -ria *adj.* compensatory, compensating.

competencia *f.* competence, fitness, ability. 2 competence [legal authority], qualification. 3 province, jurisdiction. 4 competition.

competente *adj.* competent, fit, able. 2 adequate. 3 competent, qualified [with due authority for].

competer *intr.* to behove, belong; be incumbent [on].

competición *f.* competition.

competidor, -ra *adj.* competing, rival. 2 *m.-f.* competitor, rival.

competir *intr.* to compete. ¶ CONJUG. like *servir.*

competitivo, -va *adj.* competitive.

compilación *f.* compilation, compilement.

compilador, -ra *m.-f.* compiler, compilator.

compilar *tr.* to compile.

compinche *m.* coll. comrade, chum, pal, associate.

complacencia *f.* pleasure, satisfaction.

complacer *tr.* to please, to oblige, to humour. 2 *ref.* to be pleased: *~ en,* to be pleased to, to delight in. ¶ CONJUG. like *agradecer.*

complaciente *adj.* complaisant, compliant, obliging. 2 indulgent.

complazco, complazca, etc. *irr.* V. COMPLACER.

complejidad *f.* complexity.

complejo, -ja *adj.* complex. 2 compound [number]. 3 *m.* complex.

complementar *tr.* to complement.

complementario, -ria *adj.* complementary.

complemento *m.* complement. 2 GRAM. object: *~ directo,* direct object; *~ indirecto,* indirect object. 4 completion, perfection.

completar *tr.* to complete. 2 to finish, to perfect.

completas *f. pl.* LITURG. compline.

completivo, -va *adj.* completive.

completo, -ta *adj.* complete: *por ~,* completely. 2 full [bus, tram, etc.].

complexión *f.* PHYSIOL. constitution.

complexo, -xa *adj.* complex.

complicación *f.* complicating. 2 complication, complicacy.

complicado, -da *adj.* complicated, complicate.

complicar *tr.* to complicate. 2 to implicate, involve. 3 *ref.* to become complicated. 4 to become involved.

cómplice *m.-f.* accomplice, accesory.

complicidad *f.* complicity.

complot *m.* complot, plot, conspiracy; intrigue.

complotar *intr.* to complot, to conspire.

compondré, compondría, etc. *irr.* V. COMPONER.

componedor, -ra *m.-f.* arranger, mender, repairer. 2 conciliator: *amigable ~,* LAW arbitrator. 3 composer. 4 *m.* PRINT. stick, composing. stick.

componenda *f.* shady or dubious compromise.

componente *adj.-n.* component.

componer *tr.* to compose, compound, make up. 2 to compose, constitute. 3 LIT., MUS., F. ARTS. GRAM. to compose. 4 to prepare, mix [a drink]. 5 to repair, mend, put in order. 6 to adorn, trim, spruce. 7 to make up [the face]. 8 to reconcile. 9

PRINT. to compose, set [type]. *10* coll. to restore, fortify. *11 ref.* to adorn oneself, to dress up, to make up. *12* to make up differences. *13 componerse de*, to be composed of, to consist in. *14 componérselas*, to manage, make shift, shift for oneself. ¶ CONJUG. line *poner*.

compongo, componga etc. *irr.* V. COMPONER.

comportamiento *m.* behavior, comportment.

comportar *tr.* to bear, to tolerate. *2 ref.* to behave, to comport oneself.

composición *f.* composition [in practically every sense]. *2* agreement, compromise. *3* PRINT. type that has been set. *4 hacer ~ de lugar*, to weigh the pros and cons.

compositivo, -va *adj.* GRAM. combining [particle].

compositor, -ra *m.-f.* MUS. composer.

compostelano, -na *adj.-n.* of Santiago de Compostela.

compostura *f.* making, mixing. *2* repair, reparation, mending. *3* making neat, adorning, making up. *4* modesty, circumspection.

compota *f.* compote [fruit cooked in syrup].

compotera *f.* compotier, compote.

compra *f.* buying, purchasing, purchase; day's marketing, shopping; *ir de compras*, to go shopping. *2* purchase [that which is bought].

comprable *adj.* purchasable, buyable.

comprador- ra, *n.* purchaser, buyer. *2* customer, shopper.

comprar *tr.* to purchase, to buy. *2* to buy [by bribing].

compraventa *f.* LAW *contrato de ~*, contract of sale.

comprender *tr.* to comprehend, comprise, embrace. *2* to comprehend, understand.

comprensibilidad *f.* comprehensibility, understandability.

comprensible *adj.* comprehensible, understandable.

comprensión *f.* comprehension, inclusion. *2* comprehension, understanding.

comprensivo, -va *adj.* comprehensive; comprising. *2* understanding, large-minded.

compresa *f.* MED. compress.

compresibilidad *f.* compressibility.

compresible *adj.* compressible.

compresión *f.* compression, compressure.

compresivo, -va *adj.* compressive.

compresor, -ra *adj.* compressing. *2 m.* compressor.

comprimible *adj.* compressible.

comprimido, -da *adj.* compressed. *2 m.* PHARM. tablet.

comprimir *tr.* to compress. *2* to control, restrain. *3 ref.* to become compressed. *4* to control, restrain oneself.

comprobable *adj.* verificable, ascertainable.

comprobación *f.* verification, checking, substantiation. *2* proof.

comprobante *adj.* proving. *2 m.* proof, evidence. *3* voucher.

comprobar *tr.* to verify, check, control, ascertain, substantiate. *2* to prove, confirm.

comprometedor, -ra *adj.* compromising, committing.

comprometer *tr.* to arbitrate [submit to arbitration]. *2* to compromise, risk, jeopardize. *3* to bind, engage; to render accountable or answerable. *4 ref.* to commit oneself; to undertake, to engage or pledge oneself [to do something]; to become involved. *5* to become engaged, betrothed.

comprometido, -da *adj.* implicated, involved. *2*

embarassing, compromising: *situación ~*, embarassing situation. *3* committed, engaged.

compromisario *m.* delegate, representative. *2* electoral delegate.

compromiso *m.* power given to an electoral delegate. *2* commitment to arbitration. *3* commitment, pledge, engagement, obligation. *4* fix, predicament.

compuerta *f.* hatch, half door. *2* sluice, floodgate.

compuestamente *adv.* with modesty or circumspection. *2* orderly.

compuesto, -ta *adj.* composed. *2* composite, compound, compounded. *3* ARCH., BOT. composite. *4* GRAM., MATH. compound. *5* repaired, mended. *6* dressed up, bedecked. *7 m.* compound, composite. *8* preparation, mixture. *9* CHEM., GRAM. compound. *10 p. p.* of COMPONER.

compulsa *f.* collation [of documents].

compulsar *tr.* to collate [documents].

compulsión *f.* compulsion.

compulsivo, -va *adj.* compulsory.

compunción *f.* compunction. *2* sorrow, pity.

compungido, -da *adj.* remorseful. *2* sorrowful.

compungir *tr.* to make remorseful. *2 ref.* to feel compunction. *3* to be sorry, to feel pity.

computable *adj.* computable.

compuse, compusiera, etc. *irr.* V. COMPONER.

computación *f.* CÓMPUTO.

computador *m.* computer.

computadora *f.* computer.

computar *tr.* to compute.

cómputo *m.* computation, calculation.

comulgante *m.-f.* ECCL. communicant.

comulgar *tr.* to administer Holy Communion. *2 intr.* to communicate, to take Holy Communion.

comulgatorio *m.* communion rail, altar rail.

común *adj.* common: *por lo ~*, in general, generally. *2* public. *3* current, ordinary, usual. *4* mean, low, inferior. *5 m.* community, commonalty: *el ~ de las gentes*, most people; *en ~*, in common.

comuna *f.* (Am.) municipality.

comunal *adj.* common, communal.

comunero, -ra *adj.* popular, pleasing to the people. *2 m.* member of the party that rose in Castile against Charles I.

comunicabilidad *f.* communicability.

comunicable *adj.* communicable. *2* sociable.

comunicación *f.* communication. *2* official letter. *3 pl.* communications [means of communication].

comunicado *m.* communiqué.

comunicante *m.-f.* communicant [one who communicates something].

comunicar *tr.* to communicate. *2 ref.* to communicate [hold communication]. *3* [of rooms, etc.] to communicate. *4* [of the telephone] to be engaged.

comunicativo, -va *adj.* communicative. *2* open, unreserved.

comunidad *f.* community. *2* commonwealth. *3 pl. comunidades de Castilla*, uprisings in Castile under Charles I.

comunión *f.* communion. *2 la Comunión, la Sagrada Comunión*, the Holy Communion.

comunismo *m.* communism.

comunista *adj.* communist, communistic. *2 m.-f.* communist.

comunistoide *adj.* coll. communistic. *2 n.* coll. communist sympathiser.

comunitario, -ria *adj.* of the community.

comunizar *tr.* to communize.
comúnmente *adv.* commonly, usually, generally. 2 frequently.
con *prep.* with [on nearly every sense]. 2 [before an infinitive]: a) in spite of: ~ *ser tan fuerte, no lo pudo resistir*, in spite of his being so strong, he could not resist it; b) by: ~ *enseñar la carta, disipó sus dudas*, by showing the letter, he dispelled his doubts. 3 ~ *que*, as long as, if. 4 ~ *tal que*, provided that. 5 ~ *todo*, nevertheless. 6 *para* ~, towards, to.
conato *m.* endeavour, effort, exertion. 2 act or crime attempted but not committed.
concadenar *tr.* to concatenate.
concatenación *f.*, **concatenamiento** *m.* concatenation.
concatenado, -da *adj.* linked up, concatenate.
concausa *f.* factor, cause, motive.
concavidad *f.* concavity.
cóncavo, -va *adj.* concave. 2 *m.* concavity, hollow.
concebible *adj.* mentally conceivable.
concebir *tr.-intr.* to conceive [become pregnant]. 2 *tr.* to conceive mentally. 3 to conceive, formulate, express. 4 to conceive, begin to have [a dislike, etc.]. ¶ CONJUG. like *servir*.
conceder *tr.* to grant, bestow, award. 2 to concede, admit.
concedido, -da *adj.* conceded, granted.
concejal *m.* alderman, town councillor.
concejalía *f.* aldermanship, town councillorship.
concejil *adj.* pertaining to a town council.
concejo *m.* municipal council of a small town or village; municipality. 2 council meeting.
concentración *f.* concentration.
concentrado, -da *adj.* concentrate(d.
concentrar *tr.* to concentrate, concenter. 2 *ref.* to concentrate, concenter [in intr. sense]. 3 to be absorbed [mentally].
concéntrico, -ca *adj.* concentric(al).
concepción *f.* conception. 2 *La Inmaculada Concepción*, the Immaculate Conception.
conceptismo *m.* conceptism.
concepto *m.* concept. 2 witty thought, concept. 3 opinion, judgement: *en mi* ~, in my opinion. 4 *en* ~ *de*, as: *en* ~ *de remuneración*, as a remuneration. 5 *bajo este* ~, from this point of view. 6 *por este* ~, on this head, on this score.
conceptual *adj.* conceptual.
conceptualismo *m.* conceptualism.
conceptuar *tr.* to deem, judge, think, to form an opinion of.
conceptuoso, -sa *adj.* sententious, full of conceits or witty turns of expression.
concerniente *adj.* concerning, relating: *en lo* ~ *a*, as for; with regard to.
concernir *intr.* (with *a*) to concern [belong to, relate to]: *por lo que concierne a*, as concerns. ¶ Def., only used in third persons and the forms *concerniendo* and *concerniente*.
concertadamente *adv.* orderly, regularly. 2 concertedly.
concertado, -da *adj.* concerted, planned, agreed upon.
concertante *adj.* MUS. concerted.
concertar *tr.* to assemble, fit together, to adjust; to put in order. 2 to harmonize. 3 to concert, to arrange [a marriage, a treaty]; to conclude [a bargain]; to agree upon [a price, etc.]. 4 to unite [efforts, means, etc.]. 5 MUS. to tune, attune, put in tune. 6 *intr.* to agree, be in concordance. 7

GRAM. to agree. 8 *ref.* to agree [come to an agreement]. ¶ CONJUG. like *acertar*.
concertina *f.* MUS. concertina.
concertino *m.* MUS. concertmaster.
concertista *m.-f.* MUS. concertist.
concesión *f.* concession. 2 grant.
concesionario *m.* concessionary, grantee.
concesivo, -va *adj.* concessive.
concibo, conciba, concibiera, etc. *irr.* V. CONCEBIR.
conciencia *f.* conscience: *en* ~, in conscience, in good faith. 2 consciousness; awareness: *tener* ~ *de*, to be conscious of. 3 conscientiousness: *a* ~, conscienciously.
concienzudo, -da *adj.* conscientious, thorough.
concierne, concierna, etc. *irr.* V. CONCERNIR.
concierto *m.* good order and arrangement. 2 agreement, covenant. 3 concert, agreement: *de* ~, in concert. 4 MUS. concert. 5 MUS. concerto.
conciliable *adj.* conciliable, reconciliable, capable of being conciliated.
conciliábulo *m.* secret meeting.
conciliación *f.* conciliation. 2 winning of good will, favor, estime, etc.
conciliador, -ra *adj.* conciliating, conciliatory. 2 *m.-f.* conciliator.
1) **conciliar** *adj.* conciliar. 2 *m.* ECCL. member of a council.
2) **conciliar** *tr.* to conciliate. 2 to reconcile. 3 ~ *el sueño*, to get some sleep. 4 *ref.* to win, conciliate.
conciliatorio, -ria *adj.* conciliatory.
concilio *m.* ECCL. council.
concisión *f.* conciseness, concision.
conciso, -sa *adj.* concise.
concitar *tr.* to excite [one against another], to instigate, stir up, raise [opposition, sedition, etc.].
conciudadano, -na *adj.* fellow citizen.
cónclave *m.* conclave.
concluir *tr.* to conclude, finish, end. 2 to conclude [a treaty, etc.]. 3 to conclude, to infer. 4 to silence [by reason or argument]. 5 *intr.-ref.* to conclude, finish, end [come to an end]. ¶ CONJUG. like *huir*.
conclusión *f.* conclusion: *en* ~, in conclusion.
conclusivo, -va *adj.* conclusive.
concluso, -sa *adj.* concluded, closed. 2 [of a trial] ready for sentence.
concluyente *adj.* conclusive, convincing.
concluyo, concluyó, concluya, etc. *irr.* V. CONCLUIR.
concoide *adj.* conchoidal. 2 *f.* GEOM. conchoid.
concoideo, -a *adj.* conchoidal.
concomerse *ref.* to shrug one's shoulders and wriggle. 2 fig. to be eaten up [with impatience, sorrow, etc.].
concomitancia *f.* concomitance.
concomitante *adj.* concomitant, accompanying.
concordancia *f.* concordance, conformity, agreement. 2 GRAM. concord. 3 MUS. accord, concord. 4 *pl.* concordance [verbal index].
concordante *adj.* concordant, agreeing.
concordar *tr.* to make agree, to harmonize. 2 GRAM. to make agree. 3 *intr.* to agree, accord, tally. 4 GRAM. to agree. ¶ CONJUG. like *contar*.
concordatario, -ria *adj.* [pertaining to a] concordat.
concordato *m.* concordat.
concorde *adj.* concordant, in agreement.
concordia *f.* concord, harmony, peace.
concreción *f.* concretion [concreted mass].
concretamente *adv.* concretely. 2 specifically, particulary. 3 exactly, accurately.
concretar *tr.* to combine, unite. 2 to summarize,

condense; to express concretely; to fix details. *4 ref.* to limit or confine oneself [to].
concreto, -ta *adj.* concrete [not abstract]; definite. *2* concrete [formed by concretion]. *3 m.* concretion, concrete. *4 adv. en ~*, to sum up; *nada en ~*, nothing definite.
concubina *f.* concubine.
concubinato *m.* concubinage.
concuerdo, concuerde, etc. *irr.* V. CONCORDAR.
conculcación *f.* violation [of rights, law, etc.].
conculcar *tr.* to tread upon. *2* to violate, infringe [rights, law, etc.].
concupiscencia *f.* concupiscence. *2* cupidity.
concupiscente *adj.* concupiscent.
concurrencia *f.* concurrence, coincidence. *2* concourse [of people]; attendance, audience. *3* aid, cooperation.
concurrente *adj.* concurrent. *2* attending, present. *3 m.-f.* attendant, present. *4* frequenter, habitué.
concurrido, -da *adj.* [of a place] frequented; [of a meeting, etc.] attended.
concurrir *intr.* to concur [happen together, coincide, act jointly; agree in opinion]. *2* to converge. *3* to be present [at], to attend, to frequent. *4* to contribute [money]. *5* to take part in a competition for a prize, a post, etc.
concursante *n.* participant, competitor, contestant. *2* candidate [for a job, a post].
concursar *tr.* LAW to declare insolvent.
concurso *f.* concourse [of people]. *2* concurrence, coincidence. *3* aid, co-operation, assistance. *4* call for tenders [for contracts]. *5* competition [for a prize, a post, etc.]. *7* LAW *~ de acreedores*, meeting of creditors.
concusión *f.* MED. concussion. *2* LAW extortion.
concusionario, -ria *adj.* extortioner.
Concha *f. pr. n.* coll. Conception.
concha *f.* ZOOL. shell; concha: *~ de peregrino*, scallop shell; *tener muchas conchas*, to be reserved, sly, cunning. *2* oyster. *3* tortoise-shell. *4* any shell-shaped object. *5* THEAT. prompter's box. *6* enclosed bay. *7* ARCH. concha.
conchabanza *f.* comfort. *2*-leaguing, banding together.
conchabarse *ref.* to plot, band together.
conchífero, -ra *adj.* conchiferous.
condado *m.* earldom; countship. *2* county.
condal *adj.* pertaining to an earl or count.
conde *m.* earl, count. *2* gypsy chief.
condecoración *f.* decoration [act of investing with an order, medal, etc.]. *2* decoration [order, medal, badge of honour].
condecorar *tr.* to decorate [award a decoration].
condena *f.* LAW sentence; term [of imprisonment]. *2* transcript of a sentence.
condenable *adj.* condemnable, blameworthy, reprehensible, worthy of disapproval. *2* damnable, deserving condemnation.
condenación *f.* condemnation. *2* damnation.
condenado, -da *adj.* sentenced, condemned. *2* doomed. *3* damned. *4* wicked, accursed. *5 m.-f.* sentenced person. *6* damned person.
condenar *tr.* to condemn [a pers.]. *2* to condemn, blame. *3* THEOL. to damn. *4* to wall up [a door or window]. *5 ref.* to condemn oneself. *6* THEOL. to be condemned.
condenatorio, -ria *adj.* condemnatory.
condensación *f.* condensation.
condensador, -ra *adj.* condensing. *2 m.* condenser.
condensar *tr.* to condense. *2 ref.* to condense [become condensed].

condesa *f.* countess.
condescendencia *f.* complaisance, obligingness.
condescender *intr.* to comply, to accede or yield [out of kindness]. ¶ CONJUG. like *descender*.
condescendiente *adj.* complaisant, obliging.
condesciendo, condescienda, etc. *irr.* V. CONDESCENDER.
condestable *m.* HIST. constable. *2* NAUT. master gunner.
condición *f.* condition, rank, class; abs. high bird. *2* nature, disposition. *3* condition [requisite, stipulation, etc.]: *a ~ de que, con la ~ de que*, on condition that, provided that. *4 pl.* condition [of a thing]: *en buenas condiciones*, in good condition. *5* position; trim: *estar en condiciones de*, to be in a position to; to be in trim for. *6* conditions, terms. *7* conditions, circumstances.
condicionado, -da *adj.* conditionated, conditional.
condicional *adj.* conditional.
condicionamiento *m.* conditioning.
condicionar *tr.* to condition. *2* to conditionate.
cóndilo *m.* ANAT. condyle.
condimentación *f.* seasoning.
condimentar *tr.* to dress, to season [foods].
condimento *m.* condiment, seasoning.
condiscípulo, -la *m.-f.* classmate, schoolfellow.
condolencia *f.* condolence.
condolerse *ref.* to condole, sympathize, feel sorry: *~ de*, to sympathize with, feel sorry for. ¶ CONJUG. like *mover*.
condominio *m.* LAW condominium.
condonación *f.* remission, pardon.
condonar *t.* to remit, pardon.
cóndor *m.* ORN. condor. *2* condor [coin].
conducción *f.* conduction. *2* conveyance, transportation. *3* piping, wiring. *4* driving [of vehicles]. *5* AUTO. drive: *~ interior*, enclosed drive.
conducente *adj.* conducing, leading, conducive.
conducir *tr.* to convey, transport. *2* to conduct, lead. *3* to conduct, direct, manage. *4* PHYS. to conduct. *5* to conduce. *6* to drive [a vehicle]. *7* to engage [services]. *8 ref.* to behave, conduct oneself. ¶ CONJUG. INDIC. Pres.: *conduzco*, *conduces*, etc. | Pret.: *conduje, condujiste, condujo; condujimos, condujisteis, condujeron.* | SUBJ. Pres.: *conduzca, conduzcas, conduzca; conduzcamos, conduzcáis, conduzcan.* | Imperf.: *condujera, -as,* or *condujese*, etc. | Fut.: *condujere*, etc. | IMPER.: *conduce, conduzca; conduzcamos, conducid, conduzcan.*
conducta *f.* conduct, behaviour. *2* conduct, direction, management. *3* medical services contracted for a fixed subscription.
conductibilidad *f.* PHYS. conductivity.
conductivo, -va *adj.* conductive, conducting.
conducto *m.* conduit, pipe, duct, -channel. *2* ZOOL., BOT. duct, canal: *~ auditivo*, auditory canal. *3* channel, mediation, intermediary: *por ~ de*, through.
conductor, -ra *adj.* conducting, leading, guiding. *2* PHYS. conducting. *3 m.-f.* conductor, leader, guide. *4* driver [of a vehicle]; motorist. *5* PHYS., RLY. conductor.
conduelo, conduela, etc. *irr.* V. CONDOLERSE.
condueño *m.* joint owner.
conduje, condujera, etc. *irr.* V. CONDUCIR.
condumio *m.* food, food to be eaten with bread.
conduzco, conduzca, etc. *irr.* V. CONDUCIR.
conectar *tr.* to unite, connect, gear.
coneja *f.* ZOOL. female rabbit, doe rabbit.
conejal, conejar *m.* rabbit warren.

conejera *f.* burrow, rabbit hole. *2* rabbit warren. *3* fig. den, low haunt; warren.
conejero, -ra *adj.* rabbit-hunting [dog].
conejillo *m.* young rabbit. *2* ZOOL. ~ *de Indias*, guinea pig, cavy.
conejo *adj.* ZOOL. rabbit.
conexión *f.* connection, relation, coherence. *2* ELECT. connection. *3 pl.* [social] connections.
conexo, -xa *adj.* connected, related.
confabulación *f.* confabulation. *2* league, plot.
confabular *intr.* to confabulate. *2 ref.* to plot, enter into a secret understanding.
confalón *m.* gonfalon.
confección *m.* making, confection. *2* confection [ready-made article]. *3* PHARM. confection.
confeccionar *tr.* to make, to prepare, to form [esp. by hand]. *3* PHARM. confection.
confeccionista *m.-f.* manufacturer of articles of dress.
confederación *f.* confederation, federation; league.
confederado, -da *adj.-n.* confederate, federate.
confederar *tr.-ref.* to confederate, federate.
conferencia *f.* conference. *2* public lecture. *3* TELEPH. trunk-call.
conferenciante *m.-f.* lecturer.
conferenciar *intr.* to confer [converse, hold conference].
conferir *tr.* to confer [bestow; consult about; compare]. *2 intr.* to confer [hold conference]. ¶ CONJUG. like *hervir*.
confesar *tr.* to confess. *2* to confess [one's sins]. *3* to confess [hear in confession]. *4 intr.-ref.* to confess [make confession]. *5 ref.* to confess oneself [guilty, etc.]. ¶ CONJUG. like *acertar*.
confesión *f.* confession [act of confessing; avowal, admission].
confesional *adj.* confessional.
confesionario *m.* CONFESONARIO.
confeso, -sa *adj.* having confessed his or her guilt. *2* converted [Jew]. *3 m.* converted Jew. *4* lay brother.
confesonario *m.* confessional.
confesor *m.* confessor.
confeti *m.* confetti.
confiable *adj.* reliable, trustworthy.
confiado, -da *adj.* confiding, unsuspecting. *2* self-confident, presumptuous.
confianza *f.* confidence, reliance, trust: *de* ~, reliable; *en* ~, confidentially. *2* courage, enterprise. *3* self-confidence, assurance. *4* familiarity, informality: *de* ~, informal. *5 pl.* liberties, familiarities.
confiar *intr.* to confide, to trust, to rely. *2 tr.* to confide, entrust, commit [something to somebody]. *3 ref.* to be trustful. *4* to make confidences.
confidencia *f.* confidence, trust. *2* confidence, secret, confidential information.
confidencial *adj.* confidential.
confidente, -ta *adj.* trustworthy, reliable. *2 m.* confidant. *3* secret informer, police informer. *4* love seat, tête-à-tête. *5 f.* confidante.
confiero, confiera, etc. *irr.* V. CONFERIR.
confieso, confiese, *irr.* V. CONFESAR.
configuración *f.* configuration.
configurar *tr.* to configurate, form, shame.
confín *adj.* bordering. *2 m.* confine, border, boundary.
confinamiento *m.* LAW banishement to a definite place.

confinar *intr.* to border: ~ *con*, to border on. *2 tr.* LAW to banish [somebody] to a definite place.
confinidad *f.* proximity, contiguity.
confirmación *f.* confirmation.
confirmadamente *adv.* firmly, surely.
confirmar *tr.* to confirm [strengthen, sanction; ratify; corroborate]. *2* ECCL. to confirm.
confirmatorio, -ria *adj.* confirmatory.
confiscable *adj.* confiscable.
confiscación *f.* confiscation.
confiscar *tr.* to confiscate.
confitado, -da *adj.* candied, glacé, covered with sugar, iced.
confitar *tr.* to candy, to preserve [fruit]. *2* fig. to dulcify, sweeten.
confite *m.* small round sweet, sugarplum.
confiteor *m.* confiteor.
confitera *f.* sweet box or jar.
confitería *f.* confectionery. *2* confectioner's shop.
confitero, -ra *m.-f.* confectioner.
confitura *f.* candied or preserved fruit, jam, confection, comfit.
conflagración *f.* conflagration.
conflictivo *adj.* that has conflict. *2* conflicting.
conflicto *m.* conflict. *2* fix, dilemma.
confluencia *f.* confluence.
confluente *adj.* confluent. *2 m.* confluence.
confluir *intr.* [of streams or roads] to flow together, converge, meet. *2* [of people] to crowd, assemble [coming from different parts]. ¶ CONJUG. like *huir*.
conformación *f.* conformation, form, structure.
conformar *tr.* to conform, adapt. *2 intr.* to conform, agree. *3 ref.* to conform, to adapt oneself or itself. *4* to submit, yield, comply; to resign oneself. *5* to content oneself.
conforme *adj.* according, accordant, agreeable, conformable, consistent. *2* agreeing, of a mind. *3* correct, in order. *4* resigned, patient. *5 adv.* in accordance [with], according or agreeably [to]. *6* as: ~ *había estado*, as it had been.
conformidad *f.* conformity. *2* accordance: *en* ~ *con*, in accordance with, according to. *3* union, harmony: *de* ~, agreeing, at one. *4* symmetry. *5* patience, resignation.
conformismo *m.* conformism, conventionalism, orthodoxy. *2* REL. conformism.
confort *m.* comfort.
confortable *adj.* comforting; comfortable.
confortación *f.* comfort, consolation. *2* strengthening, invigoration.
confortador, -ra *adj.* comforting, comfortable. *2* invigorating. *3 m.-f.* comforter, consoler.
confortante *adj.* comforting, comfortable. *2* tonic, invigorating. *3 m.-f.* comforter. *4 m.* mitten.
confortar *tr.* to confort [console, cheer, encourage]. *2* to strengthen, invigorate.
confortativo, -va *adj.* comforting. *2 m.* comfort, consolation. *4* cordial, restorative.
confraternidad *f.* confraternity, brotherhood.
confraternizar *intr.* to fraternize.
confrontación *f.* confrontation.
confrontar *tr.* to confront [put face to face]. *2* to confront, collate, compare. *3 intr.* to border: ~ *con*, to border on. *4 intr.-ref.* to face [be facing]; place oneself facing].
confucianismo *m.* Confucianism.
Confucio *m. pr. n.* Confucius.
confundido, -da *adj.* embarassed, confounded, bewildered. *2* mistaken, confused.
confundir *tr.* to mix, mingle. *2* to confuse. *3* to con-

found. *4* to defeat [in argument]. *5* to mistake: ~ *con*, to mistake for. *6 ref.* to get mixed. *7* to get lost or mingled [in a crowd, etc.]. *8* to be confused or confounded. *9* to make a mistake.

confusamente *adv.* confusedly.

confusión *f.* confusion. *2* humiliation, shame.

confuso, -sa *adj.* confused. *2* troubled, bewildered, awed. *3* obscure, unintelligible. *4* blurred, indistinct.

congelación *f.* congelation, congealment, freezing.

congelador *m.* freezer.

congelar *tr.* to congeal, freeze. *2* COM. to freeze [credits, etc.]. *3 ref.* to congeal, freeze [become congealed].

congénere *adj.* congeneric. *2 m.-f.* congener.

congeniar *intr.* to get along well together.

congénito, -ta *adj.* congenital.

congestión *f.* congestion.

congestionar *tr.* to congest. *2 ref.* to become congested.

congestivo, -va *adj.* congestive.

conglobar *tr.-ref.* to conglobate, conglobe.

conglomerado, -da *adj.* conglomerate(d. *2 m.* conglomerate.

conglomerar *tr.* to conglomerate. *2 ref.* to conglomerate [be conglomerated].

conglutinación *f.* conglutination.

conglutinar *tr.* to conglutinate. *2 ref.* to conglutinate [be conglutinated].

Congo *m. pr. n.* GEOG. Congo.

congoja *f.* anguish, agony.

congojoso, -sa *adj.* anguishing. *2* anguished.

congoleño, -ña *adj.-n.* Congoese, Congolese.

congraciar *tr.* to win the good will of. *2 ref.* to ingratiate oneself [with].

congratulación *f.* congratulation.

congratular *tr.* to congratulate. *2 ref. congratularse de*, to be glad of, be rejoiced at.

congratulatorio, -ria *adj.* congratulatory.

congregación *f.* congregation, assembly. *2* ECCL. congregation.

congregante, -ta *m.-f.* member of a congregation.

congregar *tr.* to congregate, to assemble. *2 ref.* to congregate, assemble, meet.

congresista *m.-f.* member of a congress or assembly; congressist.

congreso *m.* congress, assembly. *2 Congreso de los diputados*, Chamber of deputies.

congrio *m.* ICHTH. conger eel, congre.

congrua *f.* adequate income for one who is to be ordained a priest. *2* suplementary emolument.

congruencia *f.* congruence, congruity. *2* MATH. congruence.

congruente *adj.* congruent, congruous.

congruo, -a *adj.* congruous, fitting.

conicidad *f.* conicalness.

cónico, -ca *adj.* conic(al.

conífero, -ra *adj.* BOT. coniferous. *2 f.* BOT. conifer. *3 pl.* BOT. Coniferae.

coniza *f.* BOT. fleawort.

conjetura *f.* conjecture, surmise, guesswork.

conjetural *adj.* conjectural.

conjeturar *tr.* to conjecture, surmise, guess.

conjugable *adj.* conjugable, that can be conjugated.

conjugación *f.* conjugation.

conjugado, -da *adj.* conjugate(d. *2 f.* BOT. conjugate.

conjugar *tr.* to conjugate.

conjunción *f.* conjunction, union. *2* ASTR., ASTROL., GRAM. conjunction.

conjuntamente *adj.* conjointly, jointly.

conjuntiva *f.* ANAT. conjunctiva.

conjuntivitis *f.* MED. conjunctivitis.

conjuntivo, -va *adj.* conjunctive, uniting. *2* GRAM. conjunctive. *3* ANAT. conjunctive, connective.

conjunto, -ta *adj.* conjoint, conjunct, united. *2 m.* whole, ensemble: *de* ~, general; *en* ~, as a whole; *en su* ~, all together. *5 m.* MUS. ensemble. *6* THEAT. chorus.

conjura, conjuración *f.* plot, conspiracy.

conjurado, -da *m.-f.* conspirator.

conjurador *m.* conjurer [one who entreats].

conjurar *intr.* or *ref.* to swear together; to conspire, join in a conspiracy. *2 tr.* to swear in. *3* to conjure, entreat. *4* to exorcise. *5* to avert, ward off.

conjuro *m.* exorcism. *2* conjuration.

conllevar *tr.* to help somebody to bear [hardships, etc.]. *2* to bear with [somebody]. *3* to suffer with patience [hardships, etc.].

conmemorable *adj.* memorable, worthy of being remembered.

conmemoración *f.* commemoration.

conmemorar *tr.* to commemorate.

conmemorativo, -va *adj.* commemorative; memorial.

conmensurable *adj.* commensurable. *2* mensurable, measurable.

conmigo *pron.* with me, with myself.

conminación *f.* commination. *2* threatening order or summons.

conminar *tr.* to threaten. *2* to order or summon [under threat of punishment].

conmiseración *f.* commiseration, pity.

conmoción *f.* commotion, agitation, shock. *2* commotion, disturbance, riot. *3* MED. concussion.

conmocionar *tr.* MED. to concusse, to shock. *2* to upset, to disturb, to cause turmoil.

conmovedor, -ra *adj.* moving, touching, pathetic.

conmover *tr.* to move, touch, affect, stir. *2* to shake, to upset. *3 ref.* to be moved, touched, affected. *4* to be shaken. ¶ CONJUG. like *mover*.

conmuevo, conmueva, etc. *irr.* V. CONMOVER.

conmutabilidad *f.* commutability.

conmutable *adj.* commutable.

conmutación *f.* commutation, exchange, substitution.

conmutador *m.* ELECT. commutator; switch, change-over switch.

connatural *adj.* connatural, inherent, natural.

connaturalizarse *ref.* to become adapted, accustumed [to], acclimated.

connivencia *f.* connivance. *2* secret understanding.

connivente *adj.* conniving. *2* ANAT., BOT. connivent.

connotación *f.* connotation.

connotar *tr.* to connote.

connubial *adj.* connubial.

connubio *m.* poet. marriage.

cono *m.* GEOM., BOT. cone.

conocedor, -ra *adj.* knowing, expert. *2 m.-f.* knower, connoiseur, judge.

conocer *tr.* to know [by the senses or by the mind]. *2* to be or get acquainted with, to meet [a person]. *3* LAW to have cognizance of. *4* to know [carnally]. *5* to own, avow. *6 intr.* ~ *de*, to be versed in. *7 ref.* to know oneself. *8* to be or get acquainted with each other. ¶ CONJUG. like *agradecer*.

conocido, -da *adj.* known, familiar. *2* wellknown, distinguished. *3 m.-f.* acquaintance [person].

conocimiento *m.* knowledge, cognition, cognizance; notice, information: *poner una cosa en ~ de uno*, to inform someone of something. *2* understanding, intelligence, sense. *3* skill, ability. *4* consciousness: *perder el ~*, to lose consciousness. *5* acquaintance [with a person or thing]. *6* COM. bill of lading [also called *~ de embarque*]. *7 pl.* knowledge, learning.

conoidal *adj.* conoidal.

conoide *adj.* conoid. *2 m.* GEOM. conoid.

conozco, conozca, etc. *irr.* V. CONOCER.

conque *conj.* so, so then, and so; well then. *2 m.* condition, terms.

conquista *f.* conquest.

conquistable *adj.* conquerable. *2* attainable.

conquistador, -ra *adj.* conquering. *2 m.-f.* conqueror. *3 m.* lady-killer. *4* conquistador.

conquistar *tr.* to conquer [by force of arms]; win, gain, attain. *2* to win the love of; to win over.

Conrado *m. pr. n.* Conrad.

consabido, -da *adj.* before-mentioned, in question.

consagración *f.* consecration.

consagrado, -da *adj.* consecrate, consecrated. *2* sanctioned, established. *3* stock [phrase]. *4* *autor ~*, autor of established fame.

consagrante *adj.* consecrating. *2 m.* consecrator.

consagrar *tr.* to consecrate, hallow. *2* to consecrate, devote. *3* to authorize [a word or meaning]. *4* to erect [a monument] to. *5 tr.-intr.* to consecrate [in the Mass]. *6 ref.* to devote oneself.

consanguíneo, -a *adj.* consanguineous.

consanguinidad *f.* consanguinity.

consciente *adj.* conscious, aware. *2* responsible, knowing what he is about.

conscripción *f.* (Am.) conscription.

conscripto *adj. padre ~*, conscript father.

consecución *f.* obtainment, attainment.

consecuencia *f.* consequence, inference: *en ~, por ~*, consequently, therefore. *2* consequence, issue, result: *a ~ de*, because of, owing to. *3* consistency [of conduct]. *4 ser de ~*, to be important.

consecuente *adj.* following. *2* consistent [conduct, person]. *3 m.* LOG., MATH. consequent.

consecutivo, -va *adj.* consecutive.

conseguir *tr.* to obtain, attain, get. *2* [with an inf.] to succeed in, to manage to. ¶ CONJUG. like *servir*.

conseja *f.* fable, old wive's tale.

consejero, -ra *m.-f.* adviser. *2 m.* counselor, councilor. *3* COM. director. *4 f.* counselor's wife.

consejo *m.* advice, counsel; piece of advice. *2* council, board: *~ de administración*, COM. board of directors; *~ de guerra*, council of war; court-martial; *~ de ministros*, cabinet, council of ministers. *2* meeting of a council or board.

consenso *m.* consensus, assent, consent.

consensual *adj.* LAW consensual.

consentido, -da *adj.* spoiled, pampered [child]. *2* complaisant [husband]. *3* cracked, slightly disjointed, unsound.

consentidor, -ra *adj.* conniving. *2 m.-f.* conniver.

consentimiento *m.* consent, permission. *2* spoiling, pampering.

consentir *tr.* to allow, permit, tolerate. *2* to admit of. *3* to spoil, pamper. *4 intr. ~ en*, to consent to. *5 ref.* to begin to split, crack, or become unsound. ¶ CONJUG. like *hervir*.

conserje *m.* concierge, keeper, caretaker [of a palace or public building].

conserjería *f.* conciergerie.

conserva *f.* preserve, preserved food, conserve:

conservas alimenticias, canned goods. *2* NAUT. convoy, consort.

conservación *f.* conservation, maintenance, upkeep. *2* preservation; self-preservation.

conservador, -ra *adj.* preserving, preservative. *2 adj.-n.* POL. conservative. *3 m.-f.* conserver. *4 m.* conservator, curator.

conservaduría *f.* conservatorship, curatorship [of a museum, etc.].

conservadurismo *m.* conservatism.

conservar *tr.* to conserve, keep, maintain, preserve: *bien conservado*, well-preserved [pers.]. *2* to preserve, can, pickle.

conservatorio, -ria *adj.* conservatory. *2 m.* conservatoire, conservatory.

conservería *f.* art of making preserves.

conservero, -ra *adj.* preserve-making, canning. *2 m.-f.* preserve maker, canner.

considerable *adj.* considerable, great, important.

consideración *f.* consideration [considering; reflection; esteem; respect; thoughtfulness]: *tomar en ~*, to take into consideration; *en ~ a*, considering; *tener consideraciones*, to show consideration; to be considerate. *2* meditation. *3 de ~*, severe, important.

considerado, -da *adj.* considerate. *2* considered, esteemed.

considerando *conj.* whereas. *2 m.* whereas [introductory clause or item in a law, etc.].

considerar *tr.* to consider [think over; bear in mind]. *2* to consider [treat with consideration]. *3* to consider [believe, judge].

consigna *f.* MIL. orders, instructions, watchword. *2* luggage room, *checkroom.

consiento, consintió, consienta, etc. *irr.* V. CONSENTIR.

consignación *f.* consignation. *2* COM. consignment. *3* assignment [on a budget], appropriation.

consignador *m.* COM. consignor.

consignar *tr.* to assign [a sum on a budget] to a specified use, to appropriate. *2* to consign, deposit. *3* to state in writing. *4* COM. to consign.

consignatario *m.* consignatary. *2* COM. consignee. *3* NAUT. shipping agent.

consigo *pron.* with him, with her, with one, with it; with them; with himself, with herself, with itself, with themselves, with oneself. *2* with you or yourselves [with people adressed as *usted*].

consigo, consiguió, consiga, etc. *irr.* V. CONSEGUIR.

consiguiente *adj.* consequent [following, resulting]. *2 m.* LOG. consequent. *3 por ~*, therefore.

consistencia *f.* consistence, consistency [firmness; solidity; density].

consistente *adj.* consistent, firm, solid. *2* consistent [as a syrup]. *3* consisting.

consistir *intr. ~ en*, to consist, lie, reside in.

consistorial *adj.* consistorial. *2 casas consistoriales*, town hall, city hall.

consistorio *m.* consistory. *2* town council.

consocio *m.* fellow member. *2* COM. partner.

consola *f.* console, console table, pier table.

consolación *f.* consolation.

consolador, -ra *adj.* consoling. *2 m.-f.* consoler.

consolar *tr.* to console, comfort, cheer, soothe. *2 ref.* to be consoled. ¶ CONJUG. like *contar*.

consolidación *f.* consolidation.

consolidado, -da *adj.* consolidated. *2* funded [debt]. *3 m. pl.* consols.

consolidar *tr.* to consolidate [make firm, solid]. *2* to fund [a floating debt]. *3 ref.* to consolidate [become firm, solid].

consonancia *f.* consonance, consonancy, accord, conformity. *2* MUS. consonance, consonancy. *3* PROS. rhyme.

consonante *adj.* consonant. *2* rhyming. *3 m.* PROS. rhyme word. *4 f.* GRAM. consonant.

consonar *intr.* to agree, harmonize. *2* PROS. to rhyme.

consorcio *m.* union, fellowship. *2* marital association. *3* consortium.

consorte *m.-f.* consort, partner. *2* consort [husband or wife]. *3 pl.* LAW join-parties. *4* LAW confederates.

conspicuo, -cua *adj.* conspicuous, eminent.

conspiración *f.* conspiracy, plot.

conspirador, -ra *m.-f.* conspirer, conspirator.

conspirar *intr.* to conspire, plot. *2* to conspire, concur [to an end].

constancia *f.* constancy, perseverance. *2* certainty, proof.

Constancia *f. pr. n.* Constance.

Constancio *m. pr. n.* Constance.

constante *adj.* constant. *2* known for certain. *3* consisting [of]. *4 f.* MATH. constant.

constantemente *adv.* constantly.

Constantino *m. pr. n.* Constantine.

Constantinopla *f. pr. n.* Constantinople.

constar *intr.* to be certain, proved; to be on record: *hacer ~,* to state, to put on record. *2* to consist of, be composed of. *3* [of verses] to scan.

constatación *f.* verification, proof. *2* recording.

constatar *tr.* GAL. to verify. *2* to state, to record.

constelación *f.* ASTR., ASTROL. constellation.

constelado, -da *adj.* starry, star-spangled, full of stars. *2* strewn, studded.

constelar *tr.* to spangle, to constellate.

consternación *f.* consternation, dismay.

consternar *tr.* to consternate, dismay.

constipado, -da *adj.* MED. suffering from a cold. *2 m.* MED. cold, chill.

constipar *tr.* MED. to constrict, to close the pores of. *2 ref.* to catch a cold.

constitución *f.* constitution [in every sense].

constitucional *adj.* constitutional. *2 m.* constitutionalist.

constitucionalidad *f.* constitutionality.

constitucionalizar *tr.* to constitutionalize.

constituir *tr.* to constitute. *2 ref.* to constitute oneself. *3 constituirse en sociedad, en república,* to form an association, a republic. ¶ CONJUG. like *huir.*

constitutivo, -va *adj.* constitutive, essential. *2 m.* constituent [essential part].

constituyente *adj.* constituent, component. *2* POL. constituent.

constituyo, constituyó, constituya, etc. *irr.* V. CONSTITUIR.

constreñimiento *m.* constraint, compulsion. *2* MED. constriction, stricture.

constreñir *tr.* to constrain, compel, force. *2* MED. to constrict. ¶ CONJUG. like *ceñir.*

constricción *f.* constriction.

constrictor, -ra *adj.* constricting. *2 m.* constrictor.

constringente *adj.* constringent.

construcción *f.* construction, building [act or art of constructing; thing constructed], erection, structure. *2* GRAM. construction.

constructivo, -va *adj.* constructive.

constructor, -ra *m.-f.* constructor, builder.

construir *tr.* to construct, build, make. *2* GRAM. to construct, construe. ¶ CONJUG. like *huir.*

construyo, construyó, construya, etc. *irr.* V. CONSTRUIR.

consubstanciación *f.* THEOL. consubstantiation.

consubstancial *adj.* consubstantial.

consubstancialidad *f.* consubstantiality.

consuegra *f.* mother-in-law of one's child.

consuegro *m.* father-in-law of one's child.

consuelda *f.* BOT. comfrey.

consuelo *m.* consolation, comfort, alleviation: *sin ~,* inconsolably: coll. without measure. *2* joy.

consuelo, consuele, etc. *irr.* V. CONSOLAR.

consuetudinario, -ria *adj.* consuetudinary, customary: *derecho ~,* common law.

cónsul *m.* consul: *~ general,* consul general.

consulado *m.* consulate.

consular *adj.* consular.

consulta *f.* consultation, consulting. *2* opinion, information given or asked. *3* MED. consultation.

consultación *f.* consultation [conference].

consultante *adj.* consulting [asking advice]. *2 m.-f.* consulter.

consultar *tr.-intr.* to consult.

consultivo, -va *adj.* consultative.

consultor, -ra *adj.* consulting. *2 m.-f.* consultant, adviser, counsellor. *3* consulter.

consultorio *m.* technical advising bureau. *2* MED. clinic, institution where outpatients are treated; doctor's room or office.

consumación *f.* consummation. *2* end, extinction.

consumado, -da *adj.* consummated. *2* consummate, perfect, complete. *3 m.* consommé.

consumar *tr.* to consummate, accomplish, complete. *2* to commit [a crime].

consumible *adj.* consumable.

consumición *f.* consuming, consumption. *2* service [drink, etc., taken in a café, restaurant, etc.].

consumido, -da *adj.* consumed. *2* thin, emaciated.

consumidor, -ra *adj.* consuming. *2 m.-f.* consumer.

consumir *tr.* to consume. *2* to waste away, eat up, use up. *3* to worry, afflict, vex. *4* to take [the Eucharist] in the mass. *5 ref.* to be consumed. *6* to waste away, to be vexed, to fret.

consumo *m.* consumption [of food, full, goods, etc.]: *artículos de ~,* commodities, consumers' goods. *2 pl.* municipal customs.

consunción *f.* consumption, consuming. *2* MED. consumption.

consuno (de) *adv.* together, in accord.

consuntivo, -va *adj.* MED. consumptive.

contabilidad *f.* accounting, accountancy, bookkeeping.

contabilizar *tr.* ACCOUNT. to enter [as an item] into a book.

contable *adj.* countable. *2 m.* accountant.

contacto *m.* contact. *2* touch: *mantenerse en ~ con,* to keep in touch with.

contado, -da *adj.* counted, numbered. *2* scarce, rare, few: *contadas veces,* rarely. *3 m. al ~,* for cash, cash down. *4 de ~,* at once, right away. *5 por de ~,* of course, certainly.

contador, -ra *adj.* counting. *2 m.-f.* counter, computer. *3 m.* accountant, auditor. *4* counter, meter: *~ de gas,* gas meter; *~ de Geiger,* Geiger counter.

contaduría *f.* accountant's office. *2* THEAT. box office for advance booking.

contagiar *tr.* to communicate by contagion. *2* to infect with. *3* to corrupt, pervert. *4 ref.* to be contagious, infectious. *5 contagiarse de,* to be infected with.

contagio *m.* contagion. *2* contagious disease.
contagioso, -sa *adj.* contagious, infectious.
contaminación *f.* contamination, pollution.
contaminador, -ra *adj.* contaminating, polluting, infecting.
contaminante *adj.* polluting, defiling. *2 m.* polluting agent.
contaminar *tr.* to contaminate, pollute, infect. *2 ref.* to be contaminated.
contante *adj.* ready [money].
contar *tr.* to count, number, tell, reckon. *2* to number, rate, reckon [among]. *3* to charge [a price for]. *4* to tell, relate, narrate, spin: *cuéntuselo a su abuela*, fig. tell that to the marines. *5 cuéntelo por hecho*, count it as done. *6 contar [tantos] años*, to be [so many] years old. *7 intr.* to count, to do sums. *8 ~ con*, to count, reckon, rely, depend on or upon; to have. ¶ CONJUG.: INDIC. Pres.: *cuento, cuentas, cuenta;* contamos, contáis, *cuentan.* | SUBJ. Pres.: *cuente, cuentes, cuente;* contemos, contéis, *cuenten.* | IMPER.: *cuenta, cuente;* contemos, contad, *cuenten.*
contemplación *f.* contemplation. *2 pl.* complaisance, leniency.
contemplar *tr.* to contemplate, view, look at. *2* THEOL. to contemplate. *3* to be complaisant or lenient towards [somebody], to pamper.
contemplativo, -va *adj.* contemplative.
contemporaneidad *f.* contemporariness.
contemporáneo, -a *adj.* contemporaneous, contemporary, coeval. *2 m.-f.* contemporary.
contemporización *f.* temporizing, compliance.
contemporizador, -ra *adj.* temporizing, yielding, complying.
contemporizar *intr.* to temporize, to yield, comply.
contención *f.* holding back, restraint, restraining, checking. *2* contention, contest. *5* LAW litigation.
contencioso, -sa *adj.* contentious.
contender *int.* to contend, contest. *2* to fight, combat, strive. ¶ CONJUG. like *entender*.
contendiente *adj.* contending. *2 m.-f.* contender, contestant.
contendré, contendría, etc. *irr.* V. CONTENER.
contenedor, -ra *adj.* containing. *2 m.* container.
contener *tr.* to contain, hold, comprise. *2* to contain, restrain, refrain, curb, check, stop. *3* to hold back. *4 ref.* to be contained. *5* to contain oneself. ¶ CONJUG. like *tener*.
contengo, contenga, etc. *irr.* V. CONTENER.
contenido, -da *adj.* moderate, prudent, temperate. *2 m.* contents. *3* tenor, context.
contentadizo *adj.* easily pleased, easily satisfied.
contentamiento *m.* contentment, joy, content.
contentar *tr.* to content, please, satisfy. *2 ref.* to be contented.
contento, -ta *adj.* contented, pleased, satisfied, glad. *2 m.* contentment, content, joy, gladness.
contera *f.* ferrule, tip [of cane, umbrella, etc.]; chape [at scabard's point]. *2 por ~*, coll. to clinch it.
conterráneo, -a *m.-f.* compatriot, fellow countryman or countrywoman.
contertulio, -lia *m.-f.* fellow member of a coterie.
contestable *adj.* contestable. *2* answerable.
contestación *f.* answer, reply. *2* debate.
contestador *m.* ~ *automático*, answering machine, answer phone.
contestar *tr.* to answer, to reply. *2* to answer [a

summons, a letter]. *3* to confirm [another's statement].
contexto *m.* context. *2* intertexture.
contextura *f.* contexture.
contienda *f.* contest, fight, battle, dispute.
contiendo, contienda, etc. *irr.* V. CONTENDER.
contigo *pron.* with thee, with you, with thyself or yourself.
contigüidad *f.* contiguity.
contiguo, -gua *adj.* contiguous, adjoining.
continencia *f.* continence. *2* containing.
continental *adj.* continental.
continente *adj.* containing. *2* continent [temperate, chaste]. *3 m.* container. *4* countenance, bearing. *5* GEOG. continent.
contingencia *f.* contingency.
contingente *adj.* contingent [chance, that may happen]. *2 m.* contingent.
continuación *f.* continuation, continuance; prolongation; literary sequel: *a ~*, immediately, immediately afterwards.
continuado, -da *adj.* continued, constant.
continuamente *adv.* continuously, continually, incessantly.
continuar *tr.* to continue [pursue, carry on]. *2 intr.* to continue, go on, keep. *3 ref.* to be continued, to extend: *se continuará*, to be continued.
continuativo, -va *adj.* continuative. *2* GRAM. illative.
continuidad *f.* continuity.
continuo, -a *adj.* continuous. *2* continued, constant, continual. *3* MACH. endless. *4* ELECT. direct [current]. *5 de ~*, continually. *6 m.* continuum.
contonearse *ref.* to swing the hips and shoulders in walking.
contoneo *m.* swinging of the hips and shoulders in walking.
contorcerse *ref.* to twist oneself, to writhe.
contornar, contornear *tr.* to circle, go around [a place]. *2* to contour, outline.
contorno *m.* contour, outline: *en ~*, around. *2 sing.-pl.* environs, neighbourhood.
contorsión *f.* contortion.
contorsionista *m.-f.* contortionist.
contra *prep.* against; athwart, counter: *~ viento y marea*, stubbornly, in spite of all difficulties. *2* contrarily to. *3* facing: *~ oriente*, facing east. *4 m.* con, against. *5* MUS. organ pedal; lower bass [of organ]. *6 f.* opposition: *hacer, o llevar, la ~*, to oppose, contradict; *ir en ~ de*, to run counter to. *7* snag, drawback. *8* FENC. counter.
contraalmirante *m.* rear admiral.
contraamura *f.* NAUT. preventer-tack.
contraatacar *tr.-intr.* to counterattack.
contrabajo *m.* MUS. contrabass. *2* contrabassist. *3* MUS. double-bass [voice; singer].
contrabalancear *tr.* to counterbalance, counterpoise. *2* to compensate.
contrabandear *intr.* to smuggle.
contrabandista *m.-f.* smuggler, contrabandist.
contrabando *m.* smuggling, contraband: *pasar de ~*, to smuggle [goods].
contrabarrera *f.* BULLF. second barrier in the bullring.
contracarril *m.* RLY. guardrail.
contracción *f.* contraction, contracting, shrinking [drawing together, making smaller]. *2* GRAM. contraction.
contracepción *f.* MED. contraception.
contraceptivo, -va *adj.-n.* contraceptive.
contracifra *f.* key to a cipher.

contraclave f. ARCH. voussoir next to the keystone.
contracorriente f. countercurrent; back water.
contráctil adj. contractile.
contracto, -ta irreg. p. p. of CONTRAER.
contractual adj. contractual.
contrachapado m. plywood.
contradanza f. contradance, country-dance.
contradecir tr.-ref. to contradict, to gainsay.
contradicción f. contradiction, gainsaying. 2 opposition, inconsistency.
contradictorio, -ria adj. contradictory.
contradique m. counterdike.
contraer tr. to contract [draw together; cause to shrink; wrinkle, knit]. 2 GRAM. to contract. 3 to contract [marriage, debts, a disease, etc.]. 4 to limit, confine [to one idea, point, etc.]. 5 ref. to contract [be contracted], to shrink. 6 to limit, confine, oneself. ¶ CONJUG. like traer.
contraescarpa f. FORT. counterscarp.
contraespionaje m. counterespionage.
contrafagot m. US. double bassoon, contrabassoon.
contrafilo m. back edge near the point [of a weapon].
contrafirma f. countersignature.
contrafirmar tr. to countersign.
contrafoque m. NAUT. fore-topmast staysail.
contrafoso m. THEAT. subcellar. 2 FORT. outer ditch.
contrafuego m. backfire.
contrafuero m. infringement or violation of a charter, right or privilege.
contrafuerte m. counter [of shoe]. 2 spur [of mountain range]. 3 FORT. counterfort. 4 ARCH. counterfort, buttress.
contrafuga f. MUS. counterfuge.
contragolpe m. MED. counterstroke. 2 kick-back. 3 counterblow.
contraguerrilla f. anti-guerrilla warfare. 2 anti-guerrilla force or troops.
contrahacer tr. to counterfeit. 2 to imitate, to mimic. 3 ref. to feign oneself. ¶ CONJUG. like hacer.
contrahecho, -cha p. p. de CONTRAHACER. 2 adj. counterfeit. 3 deformed, hunchbacked.
contrahilo m. a ~, across the grain.
contrahuella f. riser [of a step].
contraindicación m. MED. contraindication.
contraindicar tr. MED. to contraindicate.
contralmirante m. CONTRAALMIRANTE.
contralor m. comptroller, auditor.
contralto m.-f. MUS. contralto.
contraluz f. view [of a thing] against the light: a ~, against the light.
contramaestre m. foreman. 2 NAUT. boatswain.
contramano (a) adv. in the wrong direction.
contramarca f. countermark.
contramarcar tr. to countermark.
contramarcha f. countermarch. 2 MACH. reverse.
contramarchar tr. to countermarch.
contramarea f. NAUT. opposing tide.
contramina f. MIL. countermine.
contraminar tr. to countermine.
contramuralla f., **contramuro** m. FORT. countermure.
contraofensiva f. MIL. counteroffensive.
contraoferta f. counteroffer.
contraorden f. countermand, counterorder.
contrapartida f. emendatory entry [in book-keeping]. 2 compensation.
contrapaso m. back step. 2 MUS. second part.
contrapelo (a) adv. against the hair, against the grain.

contrapesar tr. to counterbalance, counterpoise, compensate, offset, setoff.
contrapeso m. counterweight. 2 counterpoise, counterbalance. 3 makeweight. 4 ropedancer's pole.
contraponer tr. to set against, to compare. 2 tr.-ref. to oppose. ¶ CONJUG. like poner.
contraposición f. contraposition. 2 opposition.
contraproducente adj. self-defeating, producing the opposite of the desired effect.
contraproposición f. counterproposition.
contraproyecto m. alternative project or plan, counterplan.
contrapuerta f. storm door. 2 second door.
contrapuesto, -ta adj. set against, compared. 3 opposed.
contrapuntear tr. MUS. to sing in counterpoint. 2 ref. [of two persons] to be at odds.
contrapunto m. MUS. counterpoint.
contrariamente adv. contrarily.
contrariar tr. to oppose, run counter to, cross, thwart. 2 to mortify, chagrin, vex, disappoint.
contrariedad f. contrariety, opposition. 2 mortification, vexation. 3 set back, disappointment.
contrario, -ria adj. contrary, opposed, adverse, hostile. 2 harmful, unfavourable. 3 opposite, reverse. 4 m.-f. opponent, adversary. 5 m. the contrary, the opposite: al ~, por el ~, on the contrary; de lo ~, otherwise. 6 f. llevar la contraria, to contradict; to oppose.
contrarreforma f. Counter Reformation.
contrarregistro m. second examination.
contrarréplica f. rejoinder.
contrarrestar tr. to resist, oppose, counteract, neutralize.
contrarresto m. resistance, counteraction.
contrarrevolución f. counterrevolution.
contrarrevolucionario, -ria adj. counterrevolutionary. 2 m.-f. counterrevolutionist.
contrarriel m. check rail, guard rail.
contrarroda f. NAUT. apron.
contrasellar tr. to counterseal.
contrasello m. counterseal.
contrasentido m. contradiction in terms, inconsistency.
contraseña f. countersign, countermark. 2 MIL. countersign, watchword. 3 check [for a coat, hat, etc.].
contrastable adj. contrastable. 2 comparable.
contrastar tr. to resist, oppose. 2 to hall-mark. 3 to check [weights and measures]. 4 intr. to contrast.
contraste m. resistance, opposition. 2 contrast. 3 hall mark. 4 hallmarker. 5 assay office. 6 inspector of weights and measures; his office.
contrata f. contract [esp. for works, supplies, etc.]. 2 engagement [of an actor, artist, etc.].
contratación f. contracting [marking contracts]. 2 commerce, trade, business transaction.
contratante adj. contracting. 2 m.-f. contracting party, contractor.
contratar tr. to contract for. 2 to engage, hire.
contratiempo m. mishap, hitch, disappointment. 2 MUS. contretemps.
contratista m. contractor: ~ de obras, building contractor.
contrato m. contract [agreement]: ~ leonino, one-sided, unfair contract.
contratorpedero m. NAUT. torpedo-boat destroyer.
contratuerca f. check nut, lock nut.
contravapor m. MACH. back-pressure steam.

contravención f. contravention, infringement.
contraveneno m. counterpoison, antidote.
contravenir tr. to contravene, infringe.
contraventana f. window shutter.
contraventor, -ra adj. contravening. 2 m.-f. contravener, transgressor.
contraviento m. ARCH. windbrace.
contrayente adj. contracting marriage. 2 m.-f. contracting party [to a marriage].
contribución f. contribution [act of contributing]. 2 contribution, tax.
contribuir tr. to pay as a tax. 2 tr.-intr. to contribute [a sum]. 3 intr. ~ a, to contribute to. ¶ CONJUG. like huir.
contributivo, -va adj. [pertaining to] tax, imposition.
contribuyente adj. contributing, taxpaying. 2 m.-f. contributor, taxpayer.
contrición f. contrition.
contrincante m. competidor, opponent, rival.
contristar tr. to sadden, grieve.
contrito, -ta adj. contrite.
control m. GAL. control, check.
controlable adj. controlable, regulable. 2 verifiable, checkable.
controlador m. controller; ~ del tráfico aéreo, air traffic controller.
controlar tr. GAL. to control, check, verify.
controversia f. controversy, disputation.
controversista m. controversialist.
controvertible adj. controversial, polemical. 2 questionable, debatable, disputable.
controvertir tr.-intr. to controvert, to dispute. ¶ CONJUG. like hervir.
contubernio m. cohabitation, concubinage. 2 base or evil alliance.
contumacia f. contumacy, stubborn persistency in one's error. 2 LAW default.
contumaz adj. contumacious, stubborn in maintaining an error. 2 LAW guilty of default.
contumelia f. contumely, insult, abuse.
contundencia f. contusive properties of a weapon. 2 weight [of a reason].
contundente adj. contusive. 2 blunt [instrument]. 3 forceful, impressive [argument, proof, etc.].
contundir tr. to bruise, beat; to contuse.
conturbación f. disturbance, trouble, disquiet.
conturbar tr. to disturb, trouble, disquiet. 2 ref. to become disturbed, troubled.
contusión f. contusion.
contusionar tr. to contuse [cause contusion].
contuso, -sa adj. contused, bruised.
contuve, contuviera, etc. irr. V. CONTENER.
convalecencia f. convalescence.
convalecer intr. to convalesce, be convalescent, recover. ¶ CONJUG. like agradecer.
convaleciente adj. convalescent.
convalezco, convalezca, etc. irr. V. CONVALECER.
convalidación f. LAW confirmation.
convalidar tr. LAW to confirm.
convecino, -na adj. neighbouring. 2 m.-f. fellow neighbour.
convencer tr. to convince. 2 ref. to become convinced.
convencido, -da adj. convinced.
convencimiento m. conviction [convincing; being convinced]; belief.
convención f. convention, agreement. 2 convention, conventionality. 3 POL. convention.
conventional adj. conventional. 2 m. member of a convention.

convencionalismo m. conventionalism, conventionality.
convencionalmente adv. conventionally.
convenido, -da adj. agreed, settled by agreement.
conveniencia f. conformity, agreement. 2 fitness, suitability, desirability. 3 convenience, advantage, interest. 4 place, situation [as a servant]. 5 pl. income, property.
conveniente adj. convenient, fit, suitable, expedient, opportune. 2 good, useful, advantageous.
convenio m. covenant, agreement, pact.
convenir intr. to agree [be of the same mind]. 2 to meet, convene. 3 to befit, harmonize, agree. 4 to be convenient, advantageous, necessary; to suit one's interests: me conviene, it suits me. 5 conviene a saber, namely, to wit. 6 ref. to agree, come to an agreement. ¶ CONJUG. like venir.
conventículo m. conventicle.
conventillo m. (Am.) tenement house.
convento m. convent, monastery; nunnery.
conventual adj.-m. conventual.
convergencia f. convergence, concurrence.
convergente adj. convergent, converging.
converger, convergir intr. to converge, to concur.
conversación f. conversation, talk.
conversador, -ra m.-f. good conversationalist.
conversar intr. to converse, talk, chat. 2 to have intercourse. 3 MIL. to effect a conversion.
conversión f. conversion; transformation, change. 2 THEOL., MATH., FENC., FINANCE conversion.
converso, -sa adj. converted. 2 m. convert. 3 lay brother.
conversor m. PHYS. converter.
convertible adj. convertible, transformable.
convertido, -da adj. converted. 2 m.-f. convert.
convertidor m. ELECT., METAL. converter.
convertir tr. to convert. 2 ref. to be or become converted, to turn [into]. ¶ CONJUG. like discernir.
convexidad f. convexity.
convexo, -xa adj. convex.
convicción f. conviction, belief.
convicto, -ta adj. convicted [found guilty].
convidada f. coll. invitation to drink, treat.
convidado, -da m.-f. invited person, guest.
convidar tr. to invite [as a guest or participant]; to treat: ~ a uno con una cosa, to offer something to someone. 2 to move, incite, invite, tempt. 3 ref. to invite oneself.
conviene, convienes, etc. irr. V. CONVENIR.
convierto, convierta, etc. irr. V. CONVERTIR.
convincente adj. convincing.
convite m. invitation. 2 treat, entertainment, banquet.
convivencia f. living together with others.
convivir intr. to cohabit, to live together. 2 to co-exist.
convocación f. convocation, summoning, summons.
convocar tr. to convoke, convene, summon.
convocatorio, -ria adj. convoking, convocative. 2 f. letter of convocation, call, notice of meeting.
convolvuláceo, -a adj. BOT. convolvulaceous.
convólvulo m. BOT. bindweed. 2 ENT. vine inchworm.
convoy m. convoy. 2 railway train. 4 retinue. 5 cruet stand.
convoyar tr. to convoy, escort.
convulsión f. convulsion.
convulsionar tr. to convulse.
convulsivo, -va adj. convulsive.
convulso, -sa adj. convulsed.

conyugal *adj.* conjugal, matrimonial.
cónyuge *m.-f.* spouse, consort, husband or wife.
coña *f.* coll. joke; *tomárselo en* ~, to take it as a joke.
coñac *m.* cognac, brandy.
coño *m.* coll. cunt. *2 interj.* coll. shit! damn! Christ!
coolí *m.* coolie.
cooperación *f.* co-operation.
cooperador, -ra *adj.* co-operative. *2 m.-f.* cooperator.
cooperar *tr.* to co-operate.
cooperativo, -va *adj.* co-operative. *2 f.* co-operative [co-operative society, store or enterprise].
cooptación *f.* co-optation, co-option.
coordenado, -da *adj.* MATH. co-ordinate. *2 f.* MATH. co-ordinate.
coordinación *f.* co-ordination.
coordinado, -da *adj.* co-ordinate(d. *2* GRAM. co-ordinate.
coordinamiento *m.* co-ordinating, co-ordination.
coordinar *tr.* to co-ordinate.
copa *f.* cup, glass [with stem and foot], goblet, wineglass. *2* drink [of liquor]. *3* cup [trophy]. *4* brazier. *5* head, top [branches and foliage of a tree]. *6* crown [of a hat]. *7* CARDS suit corresponding to hearts.
copado, -da *adj.* having a head [tree].
copaiba *f.* BOT. copaiba [tree]. *2* PHARM. copaiba.
copal *m.* copal.
copar *tr.* to sweep [all posts in an election]. *2* MIL. to cut off the retreat of [a force] and capture it. *3* GAMBLING ~ *la banca,* to go banco.
coparticipación *f.* copartnership, joint partnership.
copartícipe *m.-f.* joint participator, copartaker.
copayero *m.* BOT. copaiba [tree].
copear *intr.* to sell wine or liquor by the glass. *2* to drink, have drinks.
copeck *m.* kopeck.
copela *f.* cupel.
copelación *f.* cupellation.
copelar *tr.* to cupel.
Copenhague *f. pr. n.* Copenhaguen.
Copérnico *m. pr. n.* Copernicus.
copero *m.* cupbearer. *2* cabinet for wineglasses.
copete *m.* topping, topknot; tuft, pompadour; crest [of a bird]; forelock [of a horse]. *2* ornamental top [on a piece of furniture]. *3* fig. arrogance, uppishness. *4 de alto* ~, of high rank, aristocratic.
copetín *m.* small drinking glass. *2* (Am.) cocktail, drink.
copetudo, -da *adj.* tufted, crested. *2* vain, uppish.
copia *f.* abundance, plenty. *2* copy [transcript, reproduction, imitation]. *3* duplicate.
copiador, -ra *adj.* copying. *2 m.-f.* copier. *3* letter book.
copiar *tr.* to copy [transcribe, make copy of, imitate]. *2* to mimic, ape.
copiloto *m.* copilot. *2* co-driver.
copión *m.* coll. poorly made copy.
copiosidad *f.* copiousness, abundance.
copioso, -sa *adj.* copious, plentiful, abundant.
copista *m.-f.* copyist.
copla *f.* stanza. *2* short poetical composition; song, folk song, ballad. *3 pl.* rhymes, poetry; *coplas de ciego,* doggerel.
coplear *intr.* to rhyme [make verses].
coplero, -ra *adj.* ballad seller. *2* poetaster.
coplista *m.* poetaster.
copo *m.* flake [of snow]. *2* clot. *3* bunch of wool,

flax, etc. [to be spun]. *4* bottom of purse net. *5* GAMBLING banco. *6* sweeping all posts [in an election]. *7* MIL. cutting off the retreat of a force and capturing it.
copón *m.* large goblet. *2* ECCL. ciborium, pyx.
copra *f.* copra.
copropietario, -ria *m.-f.* joint owner, coproprietor.
copto, -ta *adj.* Coptic. *2 m.-f.* Copt.
copudo, -da *adj.* thick-topped [tree].
cópula *f.* copula, link. *2* copulation. *3* GRAM., LOG. copula.
copularse *ref.* to copulate.
copulativo, -va *adj.* joining. *2* GRAM. copulative.
coque *m.* coke.
coqueluche *f.* MED. whooping cough.
coqueta *adj.* coquettish, flirtatious. *2 f.* coquette, flirt [woman].
coquetear *intr.* to coquet, flirt.
coqueteo *m.* coquetting, flirting, flirtation.
coquetería *f.* coquetry.
coquetón, -na *adj.* [of things], pretty, charming. *2* flirtatious [man]. *3 m.* flirt [man].
coquina *f.* ZOOL. wedge shell.
coquito *m.* gesture, face [to amuse a baby]. *2* BOT. a palm of Chile; its fruit.
coracero *m.* cuirassier. *2* coll. strong cigar.
coracoides *adj.-m.* ANAT. coracoid.
coracha *f.* leather sack.
coraje *m.* courage, mettle. *2* anger, irritation.
corajina *f.* fit of anger.
corajudo, -da *adj.* choleric, irritable.
coral *adj.* MUS. choral. *2 m.* MUS. choral, chorale. *3* coral, red coral [polyp and secretion]. *4 f.* ZOOL. coral snake. *5 m. pl.* coral beads.
coralero, -ra *m.-f.* worker or dealer in corals.
coralífero, -ra *adj.* coralliferous.
coralillo *m.* ZOOL. coral snake.
coralina *f.* ZOOL., BOT. coralline.
coralino, -na *adj.* coralline, coral-like, coral-red.
corambre *f.* hides, skins, pelts. *2* wineskin.
Corán *m.* Koran.
coránico, -ca *adj.* Koranic.
coraza *f.* cuirass. *2* armour [of a ship].
corazón *m.* ANAT., ZOOL. heart. *2* heart [soul, sensibility, love, cordiality, good will; courage, spirit]: *llevar el* ~ *en la mano,* to wear one's heart on one's sleeve; *me da* or *me dice el* ~, I have a feeling that; *no caberle a uno el* ~ *en el pecho,* to be bursting with anger, anxiety, etc.; *to be bighearted; no tener* ~, to have no heart, be insensible; *se me parte el* ~, my heart bleeds; *tocarle a uno en el* ~, to move one for the best; *de* ~, heartily, sincerely. *3* heart, core, middle [of a thing]. *4* core [of apple, pear, etc.].
corazonada *f.* presentiment, foreboding, *hunch. *2* impulse [that moves to act]. *3* coll. ASADURA 1.
corazoncillo *m.* BOT. St.-John's-wort.
corbata *f.* tie, necktie, cravat, scarf: ~ *de lazo,* bow tie; ~ *de pala,* four-in-hand tie.
corbatería *f.* necktie shop.
corbatero, -ra *m.* necktie maker or dealer.
corbatín *m.* bow tie. *2* stock [for the neck].
corbeta *f.* NAUT. corvette, sloop of war.
Córcega *f. pr. n.* Corsica.
corcel *m.* steed, charger.
corcino *m.* ZOOL. fawn [of roe deer].
corcova *f.* hump, hunch, crooked back or chest.
corcovado, -da *adj.* humpbacked, hunchbacked. *2 m.-f.* humpback, hunchback.
corcovar *tr.* to crook.
corcovear *intr.* [of a horse] to buck.

corcoveta *f.* small hump. *2 m.-f.* CORCOVADO 2.
corcovo *m.* buck [of a horse]. *2* bend, crook.
corchar *tr.* NAUT. to lay [strands of rope].
corchea *m.* MUS. quaver, eighth note.
corchero, -ra *adj.* cork [industry, etc.]. *2 m.* cork-tree peeler. *3 f.* CORCHO 3.
corcheta *f.* eye [of a hook and eye].
corchete *m.* hook and eye. *2* hook [of a hook and eye]. *3* CARP. bench hook. *4* MUS., PRINT. brace, bracket. *5* bumbailiff, catchpole.
corcho *m.* cork. *2* cork mat. *3* cork bucket [for cooling drinks]. *4* cork-soled clog. *5* beehive.
¡córcholis! *interj.* gracious me!, by Jove!
corchoso, -sa *adj.* corky, corklike.
corchotaponero, -ra *adj.* corkmaking.
cordaje *m.* NAUT. rigging, cordage.
cordal *m.* MUS. tailpiece [of stringed instrument]. *2 adj. muela* ~, wisdom tooth.
cordel *m.* string, twine, fine cord: ~ *de la corredera*, NAUT. log line; *a* ~, in a straight line.
cordelería *f.* ropemaking. *2* ropewalk. *3* rope shop.
cordelero, -ra *adj.* ropemaking. *2 m.-f.* ropemaker, cordmaker. *2* rope seller.
cordera *f.* ewe lamb. *2* fig. lamb [meek woman].
cordería *f.* roping, cordage.
corderillo *m.* little lamb. *2* lambskin dressed with wool on it.
cordero *m.* ZOOL. lamb: ~ *lechal*, sucking lamb. *2* fig. lamb [meek man]. *3* lamb meat. *4* lambskin. *5* (cap.) Lamb [Christ]: *Cordero de Dios, Divino Cordero,* Lamb of God.
cordezuela *f.* dim. small rope.
cordial *adj.* cordial, invigorating. *2* cordial, hearty, warm, affectionate, sincere. *3* middle [finger]. *4 m.* cordial [drink].
cordialidad *f.* cordiality, heartiness, warmth.
cordillera *f.* chain of mountains, mountain range.
cordita *f.* cordite [explosive].
Córdoba *f. pr. n.* Cordova.
cordobán *m.* cordovan, tanned goatskin.
cordobés, -sa *adj.-n.* Cordovan.
cordón *m.* cordon, cord, string [mostly ornamental]. *2* lace [of shoe, corset, etc.]. *3* string [of purse]. *4* cord girdle [of a monk]. *5* cordon [of an order]. *6* NAUT. sfrand [of rope]. *7* ELECT., ANAT. cord. *8* ARCH. torus. *9* cordon [line, circle of persons or posts]. *10 pl.* MIL. aglets.
cordonazo *m.* blow with a cord.
cordoncillo *m.* dim. small cord. *2* rib, cord [on a textile fabric]. *3* milling [on edge of a coin].
cordura *f.* soundness of mind, sanity. *2* prudence, wisdom.
Corea *f. pr. n.* Corea, Korea.
corea *f.* MED. chorea, St. Vitus dance.
corear *tr.* to compose chorus music. *2* to chorus.
coreo *m.* PROS. choreus. *2* MUS. harmony of choruses.
coreografía *f.* choreography.
coriáceo, -a *adj.* coriaceous.
coriambo *m.* PROS. choriamb.
corifeo *m.* coryphaeus. *2* leader.
corimbo *m.* BOT. corymb.
corindón *m.* MINER. corundum.
corintio, -tia *adj.-n.* Corinthian.
Corinto *f. pr. n.* Corinth.
corión *m.* EMBR. chorion.
corista *m.-f.* chorist, chorister. *2* choir priest. *3 m.* THEAT. chorus man. *4 f.* THEAT. chorus girl.
coriza *f.* MED. coryza, cold in the head.
cormofita *adj.* BOT. cormophytic.
cormorán *m.* ORN. cormorant.

cornac, cornaca *m.* mahout.
cornada *f.* thrust with the horns.
cornalina *f.* MINER. carnelian, cornelian.
cornalón *adj.* big-horned [bull].
cornamenta *f.* horns, antlers [of an animal].
cornamusa *f.* MUS. cornemuse, bagpipe. *2* MUS. kind of brass horn. *3* NAUT. chock, cleat.
córnea *f.* ANAT. cornea: ~ *opaca,* sclera.
cornear *tr.* to horn [gore with the horns].
corneja *f.* ORN. jackdaw, daw. *2* ORN. scops owl.
cornejo *m.* BOT. cornel, dogwood, red dogwood.
Cornelio *m. pr. n.* Cornelius.
córneo, -a *adj.* horny, corneous.
corneta *f.* MUS. bugle: ~ *de llaves,* cornet. *2* swineherd's horn. *3* NAUT. broad pennant. *4* bugler. *5* cornetist.
cornete *m.* ANAT. turbinated bone.
cornetilla *f.* BOT. hot pepper.
cornetín *m.* MUS. cornet. *2* cornetist.
cornezuelo *m. dim.* small horn. *2* BOT., FARM. ergot.
corniabierto, -ta *adj.* with widespread horns.
corniapretado, -da *adj.* with close-set horns.
cornicabra *f.* BOT. terebinth tree. *2* BOT. wild fig tree.
corniforme *adj.* horn-shaped.
cornijal *m.* corner [of building, mattress, etc.]. *2* ECCL. altar napkin.
cornisa *f.* ARCH. cornice.
cornisamento, cornisamiento *m.* ARCH. entablature.
corniveleto, -ta *adj.* with high, straight horns.
Cornualles *f. pr. n.* GEOG. Cornwall.
cornucopia *f.* cornucopia. *2* sconce with mirror.
cornudo, -da *adj.* horned, antlered. *2* cuckolded. *3 m.* cuckold [man].
cornúpeta *m.* coll. bull.
coro *m.* choir. *2* chorus: *a* ~, in chorus; *hacer* ~ *a,* to chorus, echo. *3* choir loft. *4 de* ~, by heart.
corografía *f.* chorography.
coroides *adj.-f.* ANAT. choroid.
corola *f.* BOT. corolla.
corolario *m.* corollary.
corona *f.* crown; wreath. *2* crown [regal power; monarchy; reward, glory]. *3* coronet [of nobility; of horse's pastern]. *4* halo, nimbus. *5* clerical tonsure. *6* crown [of a tooth]. *7* crown [coin]. *8* ASTR., METEOR. corona. *9* FORT. crownwork. *10* crown, summit. *11* crowning, end.
coronamento, coronamiento *m.* coronation. *2* crowning, completion. *3* ARCH. crown, crest. *4* NAUT. taffrail.
coronar *tr.* to crown [in every sense].
coronario, -ria *adj.* coronary. *2* fine [gold].
corondel *m.* PRINT. column rule.
coronel *m.* MIL. colonel. *2* HER. coronet. *3* ARCH. top moulding.
coronela *f.* colonel's wife.
coronilla *f.* dim. little crown. *2* crown [of the head]: *estar hasta la* ~, coll. to be fed up.
corosol *m.* BOT. kind of soursop.
coroza *f.* conical pasteboard hat worn as a mark of infamy.
corpachón, corpanchón *m.* big body, big carcass.
corpazo *m.* big body.
corpiño *m.* sleeveless bodice, waist.
corporación *f.* corporation, official corporation or institution. *2* guild.
corporal *adj.* corporal, bodily. *2 m.* ECCL. corporal.
corporativamente *adv.* as a body.
corporativo, -va *adj.* corporative.
corporeidad *f.* corporeity.

corpóreo, -a *adj.* corporeal.
corpulencia *f.* corpulence.
corpulento, -ta *adj.* corpulent, bulky.
Corpus *m.* Corpus Christi [festival].
corpuscular *adj.* corpuscular.
corpúsculo *m.* corpuscle.
corral *m.* yard, farm yard, poultry yard, barnyard. 2 corral, enclosure, fold. 3 weir [to take fish]. 4 formerly, a playhouse.
corraliza *f.* yard, farm yard, poultry yard.
correa *f.* leather strap, thong, leash. 2 MACH. belt, belting. 3 flexibility [of a pliant thing]. 4 CARP. purlin. 5 *tener* ~, to bear raillery; to have endurance for work.
correaje *m.* straps, leather straps, belting.
correazo *m.* blow, lash or stroke with a belt.
correcalles *m. pl.* coll. loafer, lazybones, loiterer.
corrección *f.* correction. 2 correctness. 3 correctitude, honesty. 4 adjustement [of an instrument].
correccional *adj.* correctional. 2 *m.* correctional, prison.
correctivo, -va *adj.* corrective, correcting. 2 *m.* corrective. 3 punishment.
correcto, -ta *adj.* correct. 2 properly behaved.
corrector, -ra *adj.* correcting, corrective. 2 *m.* corrector. 3 PRINT. proofreader. 4 *f.* correctress.
corredera *f.* runner, groove, rail, track [on which something slides]: 2 sliding panel. 3 NAUT. log [chip and line]; log line. 4 slide valve [of steam engine]. 5 ENT. cockroach.
corredizo, -za *adj.* running, sliding, slip [easy to be untied]: *nudo* ~, slipknot.
corredor, -ra *adj.* fast running. 2 *adj.-f.* ORN. ratite. 3 *m.* SPORT runner. 4 COM. broker, commercial agent, canvasser. 5 corridor, passage, gallery. 6 FORT. covert way.
corredura *f.* overflow [in measuring].
correduría *f.* profession of the broker or commercial agent. 2 brokerage.
corregente *m.* co-regent.
corregible *adj.* corrigible.
corregidor, -ra *adj.* correcting. 2 corregidor [Spanish magistrate]. 2 wife of a corregidor.
corregir *tr.* to correct. 2 to adjust [an instrument]. 3 to temper, mitigate. 4 PRINT. ~ *pruebas*, to read proofs. 5 *ref.* to mend; to cure oneself. ¶ CONJUG. like *servir*.
correinante *adj.* jointly reigning.
correlación *f.* correlation.
correlacionar *tr.* to correlate.
correlativo, -va *adj.* correlative.
correligionario, -ria *m.-f.* one of the same religion or political opinions.
correntío, -tía *adj.* [of liquids] running. 2 easy, agile.
correntón, -na *adj.* gadabout. 2 jolly, full of fun.
correntoso, -sa *adj.* (Am.) rapid, having a strong current, swift [river].
correo *m.* courier. 2 post, post office, mail, mail service: ~ *aéreo*, airmail; ~ *urgente*, special delivery; *echar al* ~, to post, to mail [a letter]. 3 correspondence, mail [letters].
correón *m.* large leather strap.
correoso, -sa *adj.* leathery, tough [food]. 2 pliant, stringy.
correr *intr.* to run [move swiftly, go fast; contend in race; slide, roll; extend]: *a todo* ~, at full speed. 2 [of wind] to blow, move. 3 to ramble, roam, rove. 4 [of rumours, news, etc.] to spread, run. 5 to be accepted, circulate. 6 [of time] to

pass. 7 [of interest, rent, etc.] to run. 8 to hasten, hurry. 9 *corría el mes de mayo*, it was the month of May. 10 ~ *una cosa por cuenta de*, to be the concern of; ~ *uno con una cosa*, to take charge of something. 11 *tr.* to run [a distance]. 12 to go about, to travel, to wander or rove over: ~ *los mares*, to rove over the seas. 13 to run [a horse]. 14 to chase, hunt, run. 15 to fight [a bull]. 16 to run [a chance, a risk]; to have, seek [adventures]. 17 to slide, to move to a side; to turn [a key]; to draw [a bolt, a curtain]. 18 to abash, confound. 19 to publish [the banns]. 20 ~ *prisa*, to be pressing, urgent. 21 ~ *un artículo*, COM. to take orders for a merchandise, acting as a commercial agent. 22 *correrla*, to go on a spree. 23 *ref.* to move to the right or left, to shift. 24 to slide, to slip. 25 [of candles] to gutter. 26 [of ink, colours] to run. 27 to go too far [in talking, offering, etc.].
correría *f.* wandering, excursion. 2 raid, foray.
correspondencia *f.* correspondence [of a thing to another]. 2 correspondence [intercourse by letters; letters]. 3 return, reciprocation. 4 connection [of subway, etc.].
corresponder *intr.* to correspond, to answer [to or with]. 2 to pertain, belong, fall [to], devolve [upon]. 3 to fall to one's lot. 4 to return, reciprocate, repay. 5 *ref.* [of things] to correspond with each other. 6 to correspond [by letters]. 7 to love each other.
correspondiente *adj.* corresponding. 2 respective. 3 *m.* correspondent [by letters]. 4 correspondent [corresponding member].
corresponsal *m.* newspaper's correspondent. 2 COM. correspondent.
corresponsalía *f.* correspondent's post [in a newspaper]. 2 correspondent's office.
corretaje *m.* brokerage.
corretear *tr.* to walk around, to ramble, wander, romp.
correteo *m.* walking around, ramble, wandering, romp.
correvedile, correveidile *m.-f.* gossip monger. 2 go-between.
corrida *f.* run [spell of running]. 2 coll. reprehension. 3 ~ *de toros*, bullfight. 4 *de* ~, fast, easily, fluently.
corrido, -da *adj.* long, exceeding a specified weight or measure. 2 abashed, confused. 3 wordlywise. 4 dissipate [man]. 5 continuous, unbroken [balcony, eaves, etc.]. 6 flowing [handwriting]. 7 *de* ~, DE CORRIDA.
corriente *adj.* flowing, running: *agua* ~, running water. 2 current. 3 ordinary, average, common, usual: ~ *y moliente*, plain, usual. 4 correct, afable. 5 *adv.* all right, O.K. 6 *f.* current, stream: ~ *de aire*, air draft; ~ *del Golfo*, Gulf stream; *seguir la* ~, to swim with the current. 7 ELECT. current. 8 *m.* current month. 9 *al* ~, up to date; informed.
corrientemente *adv.* currently, usually.
corrijo, corrija, etc. *irr.* V. CORREGIR.
corrillo *m.* group of talkers, clique.
corrimiento *m.* running [of colour or ink]. 2 guttering [of a candle]. 3 shame, confusion. 4 vine blight. 5 ~ *de tierras*, landslide.
corro *m.* circle, ring of people [talkers, spectators, etc.]: *hacer* ~, to make place. 2 ring-around-a-rosy. 3 ring, circular space.
corroboración *f.* corroboration. 2 strengthening.

corroborante *adj.* corroborative. *2 adj.-m.* corroborant.

corroborar *tr.* to corroborate. *2* to strengthen.

corroborativo, -va *adj.* corroborative, corroborating.

corroer *tr.* to corrode. *2 ref.* to become corroded.

corrompedor, -ra *adj.* corrupting. *2 m.-f.* corrupter.

corromper *tr.* to corrupt. *2* to bribe. *3* to seduce, debauch. *4* to mar, spoil, vitiate. *5* to annoy. *6 intr.* to smell bad. *7 ref.* to corrupt [become corrupted]; to rot. ¶ P. P.: *corrompido* and *corrupto.*

corrompido, -da *adj.* corrupted. *2* depraved.

corrosal *m.* BOT. soursop.

corrosión *f.* corrosion.

corrosivo, -va *adj.-m.* corrosive.

corrupción *f.* corruption; corruptness. *2* vitiation, depravation. *3* pollution, filth. *4* stench.

corruptela *f.* corruption. *2* abuse, corrupt practice.

corruptibilidad *f.* corruptibility.

corrupto, -ta *adj.* corrupt, corrupted.

corruptor, -ra *adj.* corrupting. *2 m.-f.* corrupter.

corrusco *m.* coll. crust of bread.

corsario *m.* corsair, privateer; pirate.

corsé *m.* corset, stays.

corsetería *f.* corset shop.

corsetero, -ra *m.-f.* corset maker or seller.

1) **corso** *m.* privateering: *armar en ~*, NAUT. to arm as a privateer.

2) **corso, -sa** *adj.-n.* Corsican.

corta *f.* cutting, felling [of trees].

cortaalambres *m.* wire cutter.

cortabolsas *m.-f.* pickpocket, cutpurse.

cortacallos *m.* corn cutter, corn parer.

cortacésped *m.* lawnmower.

cortacircuitos *m.* ELECT. circuit breaker.

cortada *f.* (Am.) cut: *~ de pelo*, haircut.

cortadillo *m.* small tumbler [drinking glass].

cortado, -da *adj.* cut. *2* chapped [skin]. *3* adapted, proportioned. *4* broken, in short sentences [style]. *5* abashed, confused. *6* HER. parted.

cortador, -ra *adj.* cutting. *2 m.* butcher. *3* cutter [esp. one who cuts out garments, etc.]. *4 f.* cutting or slicing machine.

cortadura *f.* cut, incision, slit, slash. *2* cut between two mountains. *3 pl.* cuttings, trimmings.

cortafrío *m.* cold chisel.

cortafuego *m.* FORESTRY fireguard. *2* ARCH. fire wall.

cortalápices *m.* pencil sharpener.

cortamente *adv.* scantily, sparingly.

cortante *adj.* cutting, sharp. *2* biting [air, cold]. *3 m.* butcher.

cortapapeles *m.* paper knife, paper cutter. *2* letter opener.

cortapicos *m.* ENT. earwig.

cortapisa *f.* condition, restriction, interference.

cortaplumas *m.* penknife, pocketknife.

cortapuros *m.* cigar cutter.

cortar *tr.* to cut, to slash; to cut away, off, out or up [make an incision in; divide, sever; remove or shape by cutting]. *2* to cut [carve, chop, cleave]. *3* to trim, pare, clip. *4* to hew, hack. *5* to cut, fell [trees]. *6* to cut, cross, intersect. *7* to cut [a deck of cards]. *8* to cut off, intercept: *~ la retirada*, to cut the retreat. *9* to interrupt, cut short. *10* to stop, bar [the passage]; to stop the progress [of something]. *11* to cut off [the steam, the gas, etc.]. *12* to chap [the skin]. *13* to settle, decide. *14 tr.-intr.* [of air or cold] to cut,

pierce. *15 ref.* to stop short in confusion. *16* [of milk] to curdle. *17* [of the skin] to chap. *18* [of leather or cloth] to crack, to slit. *19* GEOM. to intersect each other.

cortaúñas *m.* nail clipper.

cortavidrio *m.* glass cutter.

cortaviento *m.* windshield, windbreak.

1) **corte** *m.* cutting edge. *2* cut, cutting. *3* art of cutting clothes. *4* length [of material for a garment]. *5* felling [of trees]. *6* compromise [to settle differences]. *7* ARCH. section, sectional view. *8* ELECT. break [of current]. *9* edge [of a book].

2) **corte** *f.* court [of sovereign]. *2* fig. suite, retinue. *3* city where the sovereign resides. *4* barnyard; stable; sheepfold. *5* (Am.) court [of justice]. *6* court [paid to someone]; courtship, wooing: *hacer la ~ a*, to court, pay court to. *7 pl.* Parliament. *8 Cortes Constituyentes*, Constituent Assembly.

cortedad *f.* shortness, scantiness, insufficiency. *2* bashfulness, timidity, diffidence.

cortejador, -ra; cortejante *adj.* courting; wooing. *2 m.-f.* courter; wooer.

cortejar *tr.* to court, woo.

cortejo *m.* court, paying court, hommage. *2* courtship, wooing. *3* sweetheart. *4* paramour. *5* train, procession: *~ fúnebre*, funeral procession.

cortés *adj.* courteous, civil, polite, gracious.

cortesana *f.* courtesan.

cortesanía *f.* courtesy, politeness, civility.

cortesano, -na *adj.* of the court, courtlike. *2* courteous, polite. *3 m.* courtier.

cortesía *f.* courtesy, courteousness, politeness. *2* compliment, attention, present, favor. *3* COM. days of grace. *4* curtsey, curtsy.

corteza *f.* bark, rind [of tree]; crust [of bread, a pie, etc.]; rind [of cheese, melon, etc.]; rind, peel [of orange, lemon, etc.]: *~ terrestre*, crust of the earth. *2* crust, exterior surface. *3* rusticity [in a person].

cortical *adj.* cortical.

cortijada *f.* group of farm houses.

cortijero, -ra *m.-f.* caretaker of a CORTIJO.

cortijo *m.* farm, grange.

cortina *f.* curtain, shade, screen: *~ de humo*, smoke screen. *3* FORT. curtain. *4 ~ de muelle*, wharf, jetty.

cortinaje *m.* set or pair of curtains.

cortinilla *f.* little curtain; window shade or blind; carriage curtain.

cortinón *m.* large heavy curtain.

cortisona *f.* BIOL. cortisone.

corto, -ta *adj.* short [not long or not sufficiently long; brief]. *2* scant, scanty, wanting. *3* bashful, timid. *4* dull, short-witted. *5* ELECT. *~ circuito*, short circuit. *6 ~ de alcances*, short-witted; *~ de genio*, timid, spiritless; *~ de vista*, short-sighted. *7 de corta edad*, tender in years. *8 quedarse ~*, to underrate, to ask too little. *9 a la corta o a la larga*, sooner or later.

cortón *m.* ENT. mole cricket.

Coruña (La) *f. pr. n.* Corunna.

coruñés, -sa *adj.-n.* of Corunna.

coruscante *adj.* coruscant, shining.

coruscar *intr.* to coruscate, shine.

corva *f.* back of the knee.

corvadura *f.* bend, curvature.

corvejón *m.* VET. hock, gambrel. *2* ORN. cormorant.

corveta *f.* curvet.

corvetear *intr.* to curvet.

córvido, -da *adj.* ZOOL. corvine.
corvina *f.* ICHTH. a food fish in the Mediterranean.
corvo, -va *adj.* arched, curved. *2 m.* hook, gaff.
corzo, -za *m.-f.* ZOOL. roe deer.
cosa *f.* thing, matter: ~ *de*, about, a matter of; ~ *de ver*, something worth seeing; ~ *de risa*, laughing matter; ~ *rara*, strange thing; strange to say; *alguna* ~, something; *poquita* ~, weak, little person; *como el que no quiere la* ~, feigning unconcern, casually; *como si tal* ~, as if nothing had happened; *no hay tal* ~, this is not so; *no sea* ~ *que*, lest; *no ser* ~ *del otro jueves*, or *del otro mundo*, to be nothing out of the common, or out of the world; *ser* ~ *hecha*, to be as good as done. *2* affair: *esto es* ~ *tuya*, that is your affair. *3 pl.* peculiarities, oddities [of a person]. *4* coll. regards.
cosaco, -ca *adj.-n.* Cossack.
cosario *m.* carrier, messenger.
coscoja *f.* BOT. kermes, kermes oak. *2* dry leaves of the evergreen oak.
coscojal, coscojar *m.* plantation of kermes oaks.
coscojo *m.* kermes gall.
coscorrón *m.* bump, blow on the head.
cosecante *f.* TRIG. cosecant.
cosecha *f.* harvest, crop, yield. *2* harvest, harvesting, reaping: *de su propia* ~, fig. of one's own invention. *3* vintage. *4* harvest, harvest time.
cosechadora *f.* AGR. reaping machine, combine.
cosechar *tr.* to harvest, crop, reap, gather. *2 intr.* to harvest [gather the crop].
cosechero, -ra *m.* grower, crop grower.
cosedora *f.* sewing machine. *2* stitching machine.
coselete *m.* corselet [piece of armour]. *2* pikeman. *3* ENT. corselet, thorax [of insect].
coseno *m.* TRIG. cosine: ~ *verso*, coversed sine.
coser *tr.* to sew; to stitch: *esto es* ~ *y cantar*, this is very easy, it's a child's play. *2* to join, unite. *3* to stab repeatedly. *4 ref. coserse con* or *contra*, to stick close to.
cosido, -da *adj.* sewed, sewn. *2* sticking close [to]. *3 m.* sewing.
cosilla, cosita *f.* small thing, trifle.
cosmético, -ca *adj.-m.* cosmetic.
cósmico, -ca *adj.* cosmic(al.
cosmogonía *f.* cosmogony.
cosmografía *f.* cosmography.
cosmógrafo *m.* cosmographer.
cosmología *f.* cosmology.
cosmonauta *n.* cosmonaut, astronaut.
cosmonave *f.* spaceship.
cosmopolita *adj.-n.* cosmopolitan, cosmopolite.
cosmopolitismo *m.* cosmopolitanism, cosmopolitism.
cosmorama *m.* cosmorama.
cosmos *m.* cosmos [universe].
coso *m.* enclosure for bullfights or other public spectacles. *2* main street.
cospel *m.* blank [coin-disk before stamping].
cosque *m.* coll. COSCORRÓN.
cosquillar *tr.* COSQUILLEAR.
cosquillas *f.* tickling, ticklishness: *buscarle a uno las* ~, fig. to try to irritate someone; *hacer* ~, to tickle.
cosquillear *tr.* to tickle.
cosquilleo *m.* tickling, tickling sensation.
cosquilloso, -sa *adj.* ticklish [sensitive to tickling]. *2* touchy, easily offended.
1) **costa** *f.* cost, price, expense: *a* ~ *de*, at the expense of; by dint of; *a mi* ~, at my expense; *a toda* ~, at any cost, at any price. *2 pl.* LAW costs.

2) **costa** *f.* coast, shore. *2* GEOG. *Costa Azul*, Côte d'Azur; *Costa de Marfil*, Ivory Coast; *Costa de Oro*, Gold Coast.
costado *m.* side [of the human body, of a ship, of a thing]. *2* MIL. flank. *3 pl.* lines of descent, ascendance.
costal *adj.* ANAT. costal. *2 m.* large sack [for grain, flour, etc.].
costalada *f.*, **costalazo** *m.* blow one gets when falling on the back or the side.
costanera *f.* slope, steep ground. *2 pl.* CARP. rafters.
costanero, -ra *adj.* steep, sloping. *2* coastal, coasting; of the coast.
costanilla *f.* gentle slope. *2* short steep street.
costar *intr.* to cost [be had at a price; involve expenditure of, penalty, etc.]: *costarle a uno caro*, or *cara*, *una cosa*, to pay dearly for a thing; *cueste lo que cueste*, at any price; *cuesta trabajo creerlo*, it is hard to believe it. ¶ CONJUG. like *contar*.
Costa Rica *f. pr. n.* GEOG. Costa Rica.
costarricense *adj.-n.* Costa Rican.
coste *m.* cost, price.
costear *intr.* NAUT. to coast, to sail along the coast. *2 tr.* to defray the cost of. *3 ref.* to pay one's own [studies, travel, etc.]. *4* to pay for itself.
costeño, -ña *adj.* COSTANERO.
costero, -ra *adj.* coastal, coasting. *2 m.* slab [taken from a log]. *3* side wall [of blast furnace].
costilla *f.* ANAT., ZOOL., NAUT. rib. *2* rib [of a leaf, a fruit, etc.]; rib-like thing. *3* coll. wife, better half. *4 pl.* shoulders, back.
costillaje, costillar *m.* ANAT. ribs. *2* ribs, ribbing, framework.
costilludo, -da *adj.* coll. broad-shouldered.
costo *m.* cost, price, expense. *2* BOT. costusroot.
costoso, -sa *adj.* costly, expensive, dear. *2* hard, difficult to obtain.
costra *f.* crust [hard dry formation, incrustation]; scab, scale [on cut, wound, etc.].
costroso, -sa *adj.* crusty, scabby.
costumbre *f.* custom [usual practice]; habit: *de* ~, usual, customary; usually. *2 pl.* customs, ways, habits.
costumbrista *m.-f.* genre writer.
costura *f.* sewing, needlework: *hacer* ~, to do sewing. *2* seam [formed by sewing]: *sentar las costuras*, to press the seams; to take [someone] to task; *sin* ~, seamless. *3* NAUT. seam. *4* MACH. seam, joint.
costurera *f.* seamstress.
costurero *m.* sewing case or table. *2* sewing room.
costurón *m.* large or coarse seam. *2* large scar.
cota *f.* coat [of arms or mail]. *2* quota. *3* TOPOGR. figure indicating height above datum line.
cotangente *f.* TRIG. cotangent.
cotarrera *f.* gossipy woman.
cotarro *m.* formerly, night lodging for beggars: *alborotar el* ~, fig. to raise a rumpus.
cotejable *adj.* comparable.
cotejar *tr.* to collate, compare.
cotejo *m.* collation, comparison.
coterráneo, -a *adj.-n.* CONTERRÁNEO.
cotí *m.* CUTÍ.
cotidiano, -na *adj.* daily, everyday, quotidian.
cotiledón *m.* BOT. cotyledon.
cotillear *tr.* to gossip.
cotilleo *m.* gossiping.
cotillero, -ra *m.-f.* gossiper.
cotillo *m.* face [of hammer].
cotillón *m.* cotillion.

cotizable *adj.* COM. quotable.
cotización *f.* COM. quotation, current price, price list. *2* act of paying or collecting subscription fees to a trade union, etc.
cotizar *tr.* COM. to quote; to value at a price. *2* to pay or collect subscription fees to a trade union, etc.
coto *m.* reserved ground, preserve. *2* boundary mark. *3* limit, boundary. *4* stop, restriction: *poner ~ a*, to stop, check, put a limit to. *5* set of billiard games. *6* ICHTH. chub.
cotorra *f.* ORN. parrot, small parrot. *2* fig. chatterbox, magpie.
cotorrear *intr.* to chatter, to gossip.
cotorreo *m.* gossiping, chattering [of women].
cotorrón, -na *adj.* affecting youth [old person].
cotudo, -da *adj.* cottony, hairy. *2* (Am.) goitrous.
cotufa *f.* Jerusalem artichoke [tuber]. *2* tidbit, delicacy.
coturno *m.* cothurnus, buskin: *de alto ~*, of high standing.
cotutela *f.* LAW joint guardianship.
covacha *f.* small cave.
covachuela *f.* dim. small cave. *2* coll. public office.
covachuelista *m.* coll. public servant, clerk.
coxal *adj.* ANAT. coxal.
coxcojilla, -jita *f.* hopscotch [child's game]: *a coxcojita*, jumping on one foot.
coxis *m.* CÓCCIX.
coy *m.* NAUT. sailor's cot or hammock.
coyote *m.* ZOOL. coyote, prairie wolf.
coyunda *f.* strap for yoking oxen. *2* yoke, dominion, tyranny. *3* matrimonial union.
coyuntura *f.* ANAT. joint, articulation. *2* conjuncture, juncture, occasion, opportunity.
coz *f.* kick [from a beast], backward kick [of a person]: *dar coces contra el aguijón*, to kick against the pricks. *2* churlish act or word. *3* kick, kickback, recoil [of a firearm]. *4* butt [of a musket, pistol, etc.].
crac *m.* crash, failure, bankruptcy.
cran *m.* PRINT. nick [of a type].
craneal; craneano, -na *adj.* cranial.
cráneo *m.* ANAT. cranium, skull.
craniano *adj.* CRANEAL.
crápula *f.* crapulence, debauchery.
crapuloso, -sa *adj.* crapulous; debauched.
crascitar *intr.* [of a raven] to croak.
crasitud *f.* fat, greasiness.
Craso *m. pr. n.* Crassus.
craso, -sa *adj.* thick, fat, greasy. *2* crass, gross [ignorance, error, etc.].
crasuláceo, -a *adj.* BOT. crasulaceous.
cráter *m.* GEOL., MIL. crater. *2* ASTR. Crater, Cup.
crátera *f.* ARCHEOL. crater [vessel].
creación *f.* creation. *2 La Creación*, the Creation.
creador, -ra *adj.* creating. *2 m.-f.* creator. *3 El Creador*, the Creator.
crear *tr.* to create. *2* to make: *crearse una posición*, to make a position for oneself. *3* to institute, establish. *4* to invent, design.
creativo, -va *adj.* creative.
crecedero, -ra *adj.* able to grow. *2* [of a child's garment] large enough to allow for growth.
crecer *intr.* [of natural beings] to grow. *2* to grow, increase. *3* [of a stream] to rise, to swell. *4 ref.* to take courage; to grow daring. ¶ CONJUG. like *agradecer*.
creces *f. pl. con ~*, amply, with interest.
crecida *f.* freshet, flood, swelling [of a river].
crecido, -da *adj.* grown. *2* swollen [stream]. *3*

large, big, numerous. *4 m. pl.* widening stitches [in knitting].
creciente *adj.* growing, increasing. *2* ASTR. *cuarto ~*, first quarter [of moon]. *3 m.* HER. crescent. *4 f.* CRECIDA. *5 ~ de la Luna*, crescent. *6 ~ del mar*, flood.
crecimiento *m.* growth, growing.
credencia *f.* ECCL. credence.
credencial *adj.-f.* credential. *2 f. pl.* credential, credential letters.
credibilidad *f.* credibility.
crediticio, -cia *adj.* credit.
crédito *m.* credit, credence: *dar ~ a*, to believe. *2* credit, good reputation. *3* COM. credit: *a ~*, on credit. *4* bank-credit.
credo *m.* creed, credo: *en un ~*, fig. in a trice. *2* creed [set of opinions or beliefs].
credulidad *f.* credulity.
crédulo, -la *adj.* credulous.
creedero, -ra *adj.* believable, credible.
creencia *f.* belief, creed, tenet. *2* credence, credit.
creer *tr.-intr.-ref.* to believe: *~ en*, to believe in; *no me lo creo*, I don't believe it: *¡ya lo creo!*, coll. I should say so. *2 tr.* to think [think probable]. *3 ref.* to believe or think oneself.
creíble *adj.* credible, believable.
creído, -da *adj.* confident. *2* credulous. *3* vain, conceited.
crema *f.* cream [of milk]. *2* fig. cream [of society]. *3* custard. *4* cream [cosmetic]. *5* GRAM. diaeresis.
cremación *f.* cremation, incineration.
cremallera *f.* MACH. ratch, ratchet. *2* rack, rack rail: *ferrocarril de ~*, rack railway. *3* zipper.
crematístico, -ca *adj.* chrematistic. *2 f.* chrematistics.
crematorio, -ria *adj.* crematory, incinerating.
cremoso, -sa *adj.* creamy.
crémor *m.* cream [of tartar].
crencha *f.* parting of the hair [line]. *2* hair at each side of the parting.
creosota *f.* CHEM. creosote.
crepitación *f.* crepitation, crackling. *2* MED. crepitation.
crepitar *intr.* to crepitate.
crepuscular *adj.* crepuscular.
crepúsculo *m.* crepuscle, twilight; dawn; dusk.
cresa *f.* eggs of the queen bee. *2* flyblow.
crescendo *adv.-m.* MUS. crescendo.
Creso *pr. n. & fig.* Croesus.
crespo, -pa *adj.* crispy, curly [hair]. *2* BOT. crisp, crisped [leaves]. *3* angry, irritated.
crespón *m.* crape. *2 ~ de China*, crêpe de Chine.
cresta *f.* crest, comb [of a bird], cock's comb. *2* ZOOL. crest. *3* crest [of helmet, of mountain, of wave]. *4* FORT. crest [of the glacis]. *5* BOT. *~ de gallo*, wild sage; cockscomb.
crestería *f.* ARCH. cresting. *2* FORT. battlement.
crestón *m.* large crest. *2* crest [of helmet]. *3* MIN. outcrop.
Creta *f. pr. n.* Crete.
creta *f.* chalk.
cretáceo, -a *adj.* cretaceous. *2 adj.-m.* GEOL. Cretaceous.
cretense *adj.-n.* Cretan.
cretinismo *m.* cretinism.
cretino, -na *adj.* cretinic. *2 m.-f.* cretin.
cretona *f.* cretonne.
creyente *adj.* believing. *2 m.-f.* believer.
crezco, crezca, etc. *irr.* V. CRECER.
cría *f.* nursing, suckling, fostering, bringing up. *2* rearing, breeding: *~ caballar*, horse breeding. *3*

suckling [child or animal]. *4* brood, litter, young [animals].
criada *f.* female servant, maid, housemaid.
criadero, -ra *adj.* prolific. *2 m.* tree nursery. *3* breeding place [for animals]; fish hatchery. *4* MIN. seam, vein.
criadilla *f.* testicle: ~ *de carnero,* lamb's fry. *2* potato. *3* ~ *de tierra,* truffle.
criado, -da *adj.* bred: *bien* ~, well-bred; *mal* ~, illbred. *2 m.* manservant.
criador, -ra *adj.* nursing, nurturing. *2 adj.-m.* [of God] creator: *el Criador,* the Creator. *3* rearer, raiser, breeder. *4* ~ *de vinos,* viniculturist.
crianza *f.* nursing, lactation. *2* rearing, bringing up, education. *3* breeding, manners: *buena* ~, good breeding.
criar *tr.* to create [said only of God]. *2* to nurse, suckle. *3* to raise, rear, breed, grow. *4* to produce, put forth: ~ *carnes,* to put on flesh. *5* to bring up, to educate.
criatura *f.* creature [anything created; one owing his position to another]. *2* baby, infant, child.
criba *f.* cribble, screen, sieve.
cribado *m.* screening, sifting.
cribar *tr.* to screen, to sift.
cric *m.* jack, jackscrew, lifting jack.
cricoides *adj.-m.* ANAT. cricoid.
cricquet *m.* SPORT. cricket.
crimen *m.* serious crime, felony.
criminal *adj.-n.* criminal.
criminalista *m.* criminalist.
criminar *tr.* to criminate; to censure.
criminología *f.* criminology.
crin *f.* mane [of horse, lion, etc.]. *2* horsehair: ~ *vegetal,* vegetable horsehair.
crinado, -da *adj.* poet. long-haired.
crinolina *f.* crinoline.
crío *m.* baby, infant.
criolita *f.* MINER. cryolite.
criollo, -lla *adj.-n.* Creole.
cripta *f.* crypt.
criptógamo, -ma *adj.* BOT. cryptogamous. *2 f. pl.* BOT. Cryptogamia.
criptografía *f.* cryptography.
criptograma *m.* cryptogram, cryptograph.
cris *m.* kris [Malayan dagger].
crisálida *f.* ENT. chrysalis, pupa.
crisantema *f.*, **crisantemo** *m.* BOT. chrysanthemum.
crisis *f.* crisis: ~ *de la vivienda,* housing shortage. *2* COM. depression.
crisma *m.-f.* ECCL. chrism. *2 f.* coll. head: *romper la* ~ *a uno,* to break someone's head.
crismera *f.* chrismatory.
crismón *m.* chrismon.
crisoberilo *m.* MINER. chrysoberyl.
crisol *m.* crucible.
crispadura *f.*, **crispamiento** *m.* muscular contraction, twitch.
crispar *tr.* to cause contraction or twitching: ~ *los nervios,* coll. to set the nerves on edge. *2 ref.* to be contracted, to twitch.
cristal *m.* CHEM., MINER., RADIO. crystal: ~ *de roca,* rock crystal. *2* crystal [glass], flint glass; ~ *de aumento,* magnifying glass; ~ *tallado,* cut glass. *3* window pane, pane of glass. *4* poet. crystal [clear water].
cristalera *f.* sideboard. *2* glass door.
cristalería *f.* glassworks. *2* glass shop. *3* glassware. *3* glass service.

cristalino, -na *adj.* crystalline. *2 m.* ANAT. crystalline lens.
cristalización *f.* crystallization.
cristalizar *tr.* to crystallize. *2 intr.-ref.* to crystallize [become crystallized].
cristalografía *f.* crystallography.
Cristián *m. pr. n.* Christian [man's name].
cristianar *tr.* coll. to christen, baptize.
cristiandad *f.* Christendom, Christianity. *2* observance of Christ's law.
cristianismo *m.* Christianism, Christianity. *2* Christendom. *3* baptism.
cristianizar *tr.* to Christianize.
cristiano, -na *adj.-n.* Christian. *2 m.* soul, person. *3 hablar en* ~, to speak clearly.
Cristina *f. pr. n.* Christine.
cristino *m.* supporter of Queen Regent Maria Cristina against the Carlists.
Cristo *m. pr. n.* Christ. *2 m.* crucifix.
Cristóbal *m. pr. n.* Christopher.
criterio *m.* criterion. *2* judgement, discernment.
crítica *f.* criticism, critique. *2* criticism, faultfinding, censure. *3* the critics [as a body].
criticable *adj.* blameworthy.
criticador, -ra *adj.* criticizing, faultfinding. *2 m.-f.* criticizer, faultfinder.
criticar *tr.* to criticize. *2* to blame.
criticastro *m.* criticaster.
crítico, -ca *adj.* critical. *2 m.* critic.
criticón, -na *adj.* censorious, faultfinding. *2 m.-f.* faultfinder.
crizneja *f.* braid of hair. *2* rope or plait of esparto, etc.
Croacia *f. pr. n.* Croatia.
croar *intr.* [of frogs] to croak.
croata *adj.-n.* Croatian.
crocante *m.* almond brittle.
crol *m.* crawl [swimming].
cromar *tr.* to cromium plate.
cromático, -ca *adj.* MUS., OPT. chromatic. *2 f.* PHYS. chromatics.
cromo *m.* CHEM. chromium, chrome. *2* chromo, chromolithograph.
cromolitografía *f.* chromolithography.
cromosfera *f.* ASTR. chromosphere.
cromosoma *m.* BIOL. chromosome.
crónica *f.* chronicle. *2* news chronicle.
crónico, -ca *adj.* chronic.
cronicón *m.* brief chronicle.
cronista *m.* chronicler; reporter.
crónlech *m.* ARCHEOL. cromlech.
cronógrafo *m.* chronographer. *2* chronograph.
cronología *f.* chronology.
cronológico, -ca *adj.* chronologic(al.
cronólogo *m.* chronologist.
cronometrador, -ra *m.-f.* SPORT. timekeeper.
cronometraje *m.* SPORT. clocking, timing.
cronometrar *tr.* SPORT. to clock, time.
cronometría *f.* chronometry.
cronómetro *m.* chronometer.
Cronos *m. pr. n.* MYTH. Cronus.
croquet *m.* croquet [game].
croqueta *f.* croquette.
croquis *m.* sketch, rough drawing.
crótalo *m.* ZOOL. rattlesnake. *2* MUS. crotalum, castanet.
cruce *m.* cross, crossing. *2* intersection. *3* crossing [of roads, etc.]. *4* ELECT. cross.
crucería *f.* ARCH. intersecting ribs [in Gothic vaulting]; Gothic architecture.
crucero *m.* crucifer, cross-bearer. *2* crossroads. *3*

ARCH. crossing. *4* NAUT., AER. cruise, cruising. *5* NAV. cruiser. *6* PRINT. crossbar of a chase. *7* MIN. cleavage plane.
cruceta *f.* MACH. crosshead [of connecting rod]. *2* NAUT. crosstree.
crucial *adj.* crucial.
cruciata *f.* BOT. kind of crosswort.
cruciferario *m.* crucifer, cross-bearer.
crucífero, -ra *adj.* cruciferous [bearing a cross]. *2* BOT. cruciferous. *3 m.* crucifer, cross-bearer. *4 f.* BOT. crucifer.
crucificado, -da *adj.* crucified.
crucificar *tr.* to crucify. *2* fig. to vex, torment.
crucifijo *m.* crucifix.
crucifixión *f.* crucifixion.
cruciforme *adj.* cruciform, cross-shaped.
crucigrama *m.* crossword puzzle.
crudeza *f.* crudity, rawness. *2* bluntness, rudeness, roughness. *3* bitterness [of weather].
crudo, -da *adj.* raw, uncooked, underdone [food]. *2* unripe [fruit]. *3* hard [water]. *4* ecru, unbleached [silk, linen]. *5* raw [leather]. *6* raw, bitter [weather]. *7* harsh, rough. *8* crude, blunt.
cruel *adj.* cruel.
crueldad *f.* cruelty.
cruentamente *adv.* with effusion of blood.
cruento, -ta *adj.* bloody, involving bloodshed.
crujía *f.* corridor, passage [in some buildings]. *2* hospital ward. *3* NAUT. midship gangway.
crujido *m.* creak, creaking, crackle, crackling. *2* rustle [of silk]. *3* gnash, gnashing [of teeth]. *4* flaw [in a sword blade].
crujiente *adj.* creaking, crackling. *2* rustling.
crujir *intr.* to creak, to crackle. *2* [of silk] to rustle. *3* [of teeth] to gnash.
crúor *m.* POET. blood. *2* MED. cruor, blood clot.
crup *m.* MED. croup.
crural *adj.* ANAT. crural.
crustáceo, -a *adj.* ZOOL. crustaceous. *2 adj.-m.* crustacean.
cruz *f.* cross: ~ *de Malta*, Maltese cross; ~ *gamada*, swastica; *Cruz Roja*, Red Cross; *hacerse cruces de*, to be astonished at; *de la ~ a la fecha*, from beginning to end; *en ~*, with the arms extended; crosswise; ~ *y raya*, no more of this. *2* tails [of coin]. *3* withers [of quadruped]. *4* PRINT. dagger. *5* crown [of anchor]. *6* NAUT. middle [of yard]. *7* ASTR. *Cruz del Sur*, Southern Cross.
cruzada *f.* crusade. *2* crossroads.
cruzado, -da *adj.* crossed. *2* engaged in a crusade. *3* WEAV. twilled. *4* cross, crossbred. *5* double-breasted [garment]. *6 m.* crusader.
cruzamiento *m.* crossing. *2* cross-breeding.
cruzar *tr.* to cross [place crosswise; cause to intersect; lie across, intersect; go across]: ~ *la cara a uno*, to slap or slash someone in the face. *2* to cross [breeds]. *3* WEAV. to twill. *4* NAUT. to cruise. *5 ref.* to take the cross. *6* to cross, pass each other. *7 cruzarse de brazos*, to cross one's arms, do nothing.
cu *m.* name of the letter *q*.
cuaderna *f.* NAUT. frame. *2 cuaderna via*, a Spanish medieval stance.
cuadernal *m.* NAUT. block.
cuadernillo *m.* quinternion.
cuaderno *m.* notebook, exercise book, writing book: ~ *de bitácora*, NAUT. log book.
cuadra *f.* stable [for horses]. *2* hall, ward, dormitory [in works, hospital, etc.]. *3* NAUT. quarter [of ship]. *4* croup [of horse]. *5* (Am.) block [of houses].

cuadrada *f.* MUS. breve.
cuadradillo *m.* square ruler. *2* sugar in cubes.
cuadrado, -da *adj.* square, quadrate. *2* square [measure; root]. *3* square-shouldered. *4* perfect, complete. *5 m.* GEOM., MATH. square. *6* square ruler. *7* clock [of stocking]; gusset [of shirt]. *8* PRINT. quadrat.
cuadragenario, -ria *adj.-n.* quadragenarian.
cuadragésima *f.* CUARESMA.
cuadragesimal *adj.* quadragesimal.
cuadragésimo, -ma *adj.-m.* fortieth.
cuadrangular *adj.* quadrangular.
cuadrante *m.* ASTR., GEOM. quadrant. *2* sundial. *3* quarter [of the compass]. *4* quadrans [Roman coin].
cuadrar *tr.* to square [give a square shape]. *2* to square [the shoulders]. *3* MATH., GEOM. to square. *4* PAINT. to graticulate. *5 intr.* to fit, suit. *6* to please. *7 ref.* MIL. to stand at attention. *8* to assume a firm attitude.
cuadratura *f.* ASTR., MATH., ELECT. quadrature.
cuadrícula *f.* quadrille ruling, graticule.
cuadriculado, -da *adj.* cross-section squared [paper].
cuadricular *tr.* to graticulate, to rule in squares.
cuadrienal *adj.* quadrennial.
cuadrienio *m.* quadrennium.
cuadriga *f.* quadriga.
cuadril *m.* haunch bone. *2* haunch; hip.
cuadrilátero, -ra *adj.-m.* quadrilateral.
cuadrilongo, -ga *adj.* oblong, rectangular. *2 m.* oblong, rectangle.
cuadrilla *f.* party, crew, gang, band, squad, troop. *2* BULLF. quadrille.
cuadrimotor *adj.-m.* AER. four-motor [plane].
cuadrigentésimo, -ma *adj.-m.* four-hundredth.
cuadrinomio *m.* ALG. quadrinomial.
cuadripartito, -ta *adj.* quadripartite.
cuadriplicado, -da *adj.* quadrupled.
cruadriplicar *tr-intr.* to quadruple, to quadruplicate.
cuadrisílabo, -ba *adj.* quadrisyllabic. *2 m.* quadrisyllable.
cuadrivalente *adj.* CHEM. quadrivalent, tetravalent. ·
cuadrivio *m.* quadrivium.
cuadro *adj.* square, square-shaped. *2 m.* square or rectangle: *a cuadros*, checkered, chequered. *3* picture, painting. *4* frame [of picture, door, bicycle, etc.]. *5* LIT. picture, description. *6* THEAT. tableau. *7* picture, scene, view, spectacle. *8* THEAT. a division of the act. *9* [flower] bed. *10* PRINT. platen. *11* MIL. square. *12* MIL. cadre, staff [of a regiment]. *13* table, synopsis. *14* ELECT., TELEPH. ~ *de distribución*, switchboard; ~ *indicador*, anunciator. *15 en ~*, square: *dos metros en ~*, two meters square. *16 quedarse en ~*, to be left friendless; to be broke, ruined; MIL. [of a body of troops] to be left with officers only.
cuadrumano, -na; cuadrúmano, -na *adj.* ZOOL. quadrumanous. *2 m.* ZOOL. quadrumane.
cuadrúpedo *adj.-m.* quadruped.
cuádruple *adj.* quadruple, fourfold.
cuádruplex *adj.* TELEG. quadruplex.
cuadruplicar *tr.* to quadruple, quadruplicate.
cuádruplo, -pla *adj.-m.* CUÁDRUPLE.
cuaga *f.* ZOOL. quagga.
cuajada *f.* curd [of milk]. *2* cottage cheese.
cuajaleche *f.* BOT. yellow bedstraw, cheese rennet.
cuajamiento *m.* curdling, coagulation.
1) **cuajar** *tr.* to curd, curdle, coagulate. *2* to fill

[with adornments]. *3 intr.* [of a thing] to be successful. *4* to please, suit. *5 ref.* to curd, curdle, coagulate [be coagulated]. *6* to become crowded.

2) cuajar *m.* ZOOL. rennet bag, abomasum.

cuajarón *m.* clot, grume.

cuajo *m.* rennet [for curling milk]. *2* ZOOL. rennet bag. *3* curdling, coagulation. *4* phlegm, sluggishness, patience. *5 de* ~, by the roots.

cual, cuales *rel. pron.* who, which. *2* as, such as. *3 el, la* ~, *los, las cuales*, who, which; *lo* ~, which. *4 por lo* ~, for which reason. *5 adv.* as, like: ~ *lo exigen las circunstancias*, as circumstances demand.

cuál *interr. pron.* which, what. *2* [in distributive sense] some: ~ *más*, ~ *menos*, some more, some less. *3 adv.* how [exclamative].

cualidad *f.* quality [distinctive character, trait, etc.].

cualificado, -da *adj.* skilled [worker].

cualitativo, -va *adj.* qualitative.

cualquier, *pl.* **cualesquier** *indef. adj.* apocopated form of CUALQUIERA used only before nouns.

cualquiera, *pl.* **cualesquiera** *pron.* anyone, anybody. *2* ~ *que*, whatever, whichever, whoever; ~ *que sea el resultado*, whatever the result may be; ~ *que lo diga*, whoever says so. *3 ¡*~ *se acuerda!*, who's going to remember that! *4 un, una* ~, despicable person. *5 adj.* any; any whatever.

cuan *adv.* as: *el castigo será tan grande* ~ *grande fue la culpa*, the punishment will be as great as great was the sin.

cuán *adv.* how: *¡*~ *grande es mi dolor!*, how great is my pain!

cuando *adv.* when. *2* even when, even though. *3* since: ~ *tú lo dices*, since you say it. *4* at the time of: ~ *la peste*, at the time of the plague. *5* ~ *más*, ~ *mucho*, at most; ~ *menos*, at least; ~ *no*, if not; ~ *quiera*, whenever; *de* ~ *en* ~, now and then.

cuándo *adv. interr.* when. *2* sometimes, now: ~ *con motivo*, ~ *sin él*, sometimes (or now) with a reason, sometimes [or now] without it.

cuantía *f.* amount, quantity. *2* distinction, importance.

cuántico, -ca *adj.* quantum, quantic.

cuantificación *f.* PHIL. quantification. *2* PHYS. quantization.

cuantimás *adv.* all the more.

cuantioso, -sa *adj.* large, substantial, numerous.

cuantitativo, -va *adj.* quantitative.

1) cuanto *adv.* as far as concerns or regards: ~ *a eso, en* ~ *a eso*, as far as regards that. *2* as long as: *durará la alegría* ~ *dure el dinero*, joy will last as long as the money lasts. *3* ~ *antes*, as soon as possible. *4* ~ *más* ..., *menos* [or *más*], the more... the less [or the more]. *5* ~ *más que*, all the more because. *6 en* ~, no sooner. *7 por* ~, since, seeing that. *8 m.* quantum.

2) cuanto, ta; cuantos, tas *adj.* all the, every, as much, as many. *2 pron.* all [that], everything, as much as. *3* as many as; all who. *4 adj.-pron. unos cuantos, unas cuantas*, some, a few.

1) cuánto *adv.* how: *¡*~ *me duele!*, how it pains me! *2 pron.* how much; how long.

2) cuánto, -ta; cuántos, -tas [with interr. or exclam.] *adj.* how many, how much, what.

cuáquero, -ra *adj.-n.* Quaker. *2 f.* Quakeress.

cuarenta *adj.-n.* forty. *2* fortieth.

cuarentavo, -va *adj.-m.* fortieth.

cuarentena *f.* forty, two score. *2* forty days, months or years. *3* Lent. *4* quarantine. *5* fig. *poner en* ~, to entertain doubts about.

cuarentón, -na *m.-f.* person forty years old.

cuaresma *f.* Lent.

cuaresmal *adj.* Lenten.

cuarta *f.* fourth part, quarter. *2* span [measure]. *3* quart [in piquet]. *4* NAUT. point [of the compass]. *5* MUS. fourth. *6* FENC. carte. *7* (Am.) short whip.

cuartana *f.* MED. quartan.

cuartear *tr.* to quarter, to divide in four parts. *2* to zigzag up steep places. *3* (Mex.) to whip, lash. *4* NAUT. ~ *la aguja*, to box the compass. *5 intr.-ref.* BULLF. to dodge. *6 ref.* [of a wall, roof, etc.] to crack.

cuartel *m.* quarter, fourth part. *2* ward [of a town]. *3* plot, section [of land]. *4* HER. quarter. *5* MIL. barracks. *6* MIL. quarters: ~ *general*, headquarters. *7* MIL. quarter [granted to enemy]. *8* NAUT. hatch [trap-door].

cuartelada *f.* military insurrection or coup d'état.

cuartelar *tr.* HER. to quarter.

cuartelazo *m.* putsch.

cuartelero, -ra *adj.* [pertaining to] barracks.

cuartelillo *m.* MIL. station: ~ *de bomberos*, fire station, *firehouse.

cuarteo *m.* quartering. *2* zigzagging up steep places. *3* BULLF. dodging. *4* crack [in wall or roof].

cuarterón, -na *m.-f.* quadroon. *2 m.* fourth part, quarter. *3* quarter pound. *4* panel [of door]. *5* shutter [of window]. *6* HER. quarter.

cuarteta *f.* REDONDILLA. *2* stanza of four octosyllabic lines the second and last of which are in assonance.

cuarteto *m.* quatrain [poem]. *2* MUS. quartet, quartette.

cuartilla *f.* sheet of writing paper. *2* pastern [of horse].

cuartillo *m.* dry measure (1.156 l.). *2* liquid measure (0.504 l.). *3* fourth part of a REAL.

cuarto, -ta *adj.* fourth. *2 m.* quarter [fourth part]. *3* flat, rooms. *4* room, chamber: ~ *de baño*, bathroom; ~ *de estar*, living room; ~ *excusado*, water-closet. *4* ASTR. quarter [of the moon]: ~ *creciente*, first quarter; ~ *menguante*, last quarter. *5* quarter [of an hour, of a quadruped; of a quartered criminal]. *6* old copper coin of little value: *de tres al* ~, of little importance; *echar su* ~ *a espadas*, to butt into the conversation; *no tener un* ~, to be penniless. *7* ~ *militar*, military attendants to a sovereign or chief of State. *8 en* ~, quarto [volume]. *9 pl.* cash, money. *10 tener buenos cuartos*, to be strong, sturdy.

cuartucho *m.* hovel, miserable dwelling or room.

cuarzo *m.* MINER. quartz. *2* ~ *hialino*, rock crystal.

cuasi *adv.* CASI.

cuasia *f.* BOT., PHARM. quassia.

cuasicontrato *m.* LAW quasi contract.

cuasidelito *m.* LAW quasi delict, technical offence.

cuasimodo *m.* ECCL. Quasimodo.

cuaternario, -ria *adj.* quaternary. *2 adj.-m.* GEOL. quaternary.

cuatrero *m.* horse thief, cattlethief.

cuatrifolio *m.* ARCH. quatrefoil.

cuatrillizos, -zas *m. pl.* quadruplets.

cuatrillo *m.* a card game.

cuatrillón *m.* quadrillion.

cuatrimestral *adj.* four-monthly, every four months. *2* lasting four months.

cuatrimestre *adj.* four-month. *2 m.* period of four months.

cuatrimotor *m.-adj.* four engined, four engined airplane.

cuatrirreactor *adj.* four-engined. *2 m.* four-engined jet.

cuatrisílabo *adj.* quadrisyllabic, four-syllable. *2 m.* quadrisyllable.

cuatro *adj.* four. *2* fig. a few: ~ *letras*, a few lines. *3 las* ~, four o'clock. *4 más de* ~, many, many people. *5 m.* four. *6* fourth [in dates].

cuatrocientos, -tas *adj.-m.* four hundred.

cuba *f.* cask, barrel: *estar hecho una* ~, fig. to be drunk. *2* tub, vat. *3* fig. big-bellied person, tubby. *4* stack [of blast furnace].

cubano, -na *adj.-n.* Cuban.

cubeba *f.* BOT. cubeb.

cubero *m.* cooper.

cubeta *f.* small cask. *2* pail, bucket. *3* toilet bowl. *4* cup, cistern [of barometer]. *5* MUS. pedestal [of harp]. *6* PHOT., CHEM. tank, cuvette.

cubicación *f.* cubing. *2* calculation of volumes.

cubicar *tr.* to cube.

cúbico, -ca *adj.* cubic(al).

cubículo *m.* cubicle.

cubierta *f.* cover, covering. *2* envelope, cover [of letter]. *3* cover [of a paper-bound book]. *4* roof, roofing [of a building]. *5* MACH. case, casing. *6* shoe [of a pneumatic tire]. *7* pretext. *8* NAUT. deck.

cubierto, -ta *p. p.* of CUBRIR. *2 m.-f.* cover, roof, shelter, protection: *a* ~, *bajo* ~, sheltered, indoors; *a* ~ *de*, protected from; under cover of. *3* set of fork, spoon and knife. *4* cover, plate [service of food for one at a meal]. *5* meal for one at a fixed price.

cubil *m.* lair, den [of wild animals].

cubilete *m.* goblet. *2* dicebox. *3* COOK. a thimble-shaped mould. *4* small round mince pie.

cubileteo *m.* jugglery. *2* scheming, intrigue.

cubilote *m.* METAL. cupola [furnace].

cubismo *m.* F. ARTS cubism.

cubista *adj.-n.* F. ARTS cubist.

cubital *adj.* cubital.

cúbito *m.* ANAT. ulna, cubit.

cubo *m.* bucket, pail, tub. *2* hub, nave [of wheel]. *3* socket [of bayonet or candlestick]. *4* water reservoir [for a mill]. *5* barrel [of watch]. *6* FORT. round tower. *7* GEOM., MATH. cube.

cuboides *adj.-m.* ANAT. cuboid.

cubrecadena *m.* chain cover [on bicycle].

cubrecama *m.* counterpane, coverlet, bedspread.

cubrecorsé *m.* corset cover, underbodice.

cubreobjeto *m.* cover glass, cover slip [for microscopic preparations].

cubrir *tr.* to cover, cover up; to wrap, envelop, clak, clothe, drape, shroud, veil; to coat, face, overlay, spread, spread over. *2* to hide, mask, disguise. *3* MIL. to cover, protect. *4* to roof [a building]. *5* to cover [expenses, a shortage, etc.]. *6* to cover [a distance]. *7* to cover, serve [a female]. *8 ref.* to cover [oneself]; to be or become covered. *9* to cover one's expenses. *10* to protect or guard oneself [against losses, etc.]. ¶ Past. p.: *cubierto.*

cucamonas *f. pl.* CARANTOÑAS.

cucaña *f.* greased pole to be walked on or climbed for a prize; the sport itself.

cucaracha *f.* ENT. cockroach, black beetle. *2* ZOOL. pill bug, wood louse.

cucarda *f.* cockade.

cuclillas (en) *adv.* in a squatting or crouching position, sitting on one's heels.

cuclillo *m.* ORN. cuckoo. *2* fig. cuckold.

cuco, -ca *adj.* nice, pretty, dainty. *2* crafty, cunning. *3 m.* ORN. cuckoo. *4 m.-f.* crafty, cunning person.

cucú *m.* cuckoo [call of the cuckoo].

cucurbita *f.* cucurbit, retort.

cucurbitáceo, -a *adj.* BOT. cucurbitaceous.

cucurucho *m.* paper cone, cornet.

cuchara *f.* spoon: ~ *de sopa*, table spoon; *meter uno su* ~, to meddle, to put in one's oar. *2* ladle. *3* NAUT. scoop [for bailing water]. *4* scoop, bucket [of dredging machine]; dipper [of excavator].

cucharada *f.* spoonful: *meter uno su* ~, to meddle, to put in one's oar.

cucharadita *f.* teaspoonful.

cuchareta *f.* little spoon. *2* ORN. (Am.) shoveller.

cucharetear *intr.* coll. to meddle in other people's affairs.

cucharilla *f.* small spoon, teaspoon.

cucharón *m.* large spoon; soup ladle, kitchen ladle. *2* MACH. bucket, grab bucket.

cuchichear *intr.* to whisper, speak in whispers [to another].

cuchicheo *m.* whispering, talking in whispers.

cuchichiar *intr.* [of a partridge] to call or cry.

cuchilla *f.* large knife. *2* cutting tool. *3* blade [of cutting tool or weapon]. *4* POET. sword. *5* runner [of skate, sledge, etc.]. *6* ELECT. blade [of switch].

cuchillada *f.* stab, slash, gash [from a knife, sword, etc.]. *2 pl.* slashes [ornamental slits in a garment].

cuchillería *f.* cutlery. *2* cutler's shop.

cuchillero *m.* cutler.

cuchillo *m.* knife: ~ *de monte*, hunting knife; *pasar a* ~, to put to the sword. *2* gore [in a garment]. *3* ENG., ARCH. truss [of a bridge]; frame [of a roof]. *4* NAUT. *vela de* ~, fore-and-aft sail.

cuchipanda *f.* merry feast, banquet.

cuchitril *m.* COCHITRIL.

cuchufleta *f.* jest, quip.

cuchufletero, -ra *adj.* given to poking fun at others.

cuelgacapas *adj.* cloak hanger.

cuelgo, cuelga, etc. *irr.* V. COLGAR.

cuelmo *m.* pine torch.

cuelo, cuele, etc. *irr.* V. COLAR.

cuellicorto, -ta *adj.* short-necked.

cuellilargo, -ga *adj.* long-necked.

cuello *m.* ANAT., ZOOL. neck; throat. *2* neck [of a vessel, of an object]. *3* collar [of a garment; detachable collar]: ~ *blando*, soft collar; ~ *duro*, stiff collar; ~ *de pajarita*, wing collar; ~ *alechugado* or *escarolado*, ruff.

cuenca *f.* wooden bowl. *2* socket [of eye]. *3* walley. *4* GEOG. basin, river basin, watershed.

cuenco *m.* earthen bowl. *2* hollow, concavity.

cuenta *f.* bead [of rosary, etc.]. *2* account, count, counting, reckoning; bill, note; arithmetical operation: *cuentas del Gran Capitán*, fig. overcharged bill; *cuentas galanas*, castles in the air; *hacer cuentas*, to cast accounts; to do one's sums; *a fin de cuentas*, after all; *en resumidas cuentas*, in short, to sum up; *más de la* ~, too much. *3* account [in the commercial and kindred senses]: ~ *corriente*, current account, checking account; *abonar en* ~, *adeudar* or *cargar en* ~, to credit or to charge to [someone's account]; *a* ~, *a buena* ~, on account. *4* account [given or taken]; *dar* ~, *rendir cuentas, de*, to answer for; give account of. *5* account, behalf, care, duty, responsibility: *tomar uno por su cuenta [una cosa]*, to take upon oneself, to assume responsibility for; *esto es ~ mía*, that is my affair; *por ~ de*, for account of; on the behalf of. *6* report, information: *dar ~ de*, to inform of. *7 caer en la ~, darse ~*, to see, realize. *8 dar ~ de*, to use up, waste, destroy. *9 hacer* or *hacerse ~*, or *la ~*, to imagine; to take for granted. *10 tener en ~*, to take into account, to bear in mind. *11 tener ~*, to be profitable, advantageous. *12 a la ~, por la ~*, as it seems.

cuentacorrentista *m.-f.* depositor, person having a current account in a bank.

cuentagotas *m.* PHARM. dropper, medicine dropper.

cuentahílos *m.* cloth prover.

cuentakilómetros *m.* AUTO. speedometer.

cuentarrevoluciones, cuentavueltas *m.* revolution counter.

cuentero, -ra *adj.-n.* CUENTISTA 1 & 2.

cuentista *adj.* gossipy. *2 m.-f.* gossip, talebearer. *3* narrator or writer of tales; story writer.

cuento *m.* tale, narrative, story, short story: *~ de hadas*, fairy tale; *~ de nunca acabar*, endless affair; *~ de viejas*, old-wives' tale; *dejarse de cuentos*, to come to the point; *venir a ~*, to be pertinent; *traer a ~*, to drag in [a subject]. *2* tale, gossip; yarn, falsehood. *3* gist, difficulty. *4* quarrel, disagreement. *5* count, number: *sin ~*, numberless. *6* million. *7* ferrule, tip [of cane, pike, etc.]. *8* prop, support.

cuento, cuente, etc. *irr.* V. CONTAR.

cuerda *f.* rope, cord, string: *~ floja*, tight rope, acrobat's rope; *por debajo de ~*, secretly, underhandedly. *2* MUS. string, chord [of an instrument]. *3* MUS. voice [bass, tenor, contralto, soprano]; compass [of a voice]. *4* spring or chain [of clock or watch]: *dar ~ a un reloj*, to wind a clock or watch. *5* GEOM. chord. *6 ~ de presos*, chain gang. *9 pl.* ANAT. cords, tendons. *10* ANAT. *cuerdas vocales*, vocal cords.

cuerdo, -da *adj.* sane [mentally sound]. *2* sane, wise, prudent, discreet, sensible.

cuerna *f.* horn vessel or trumpet. *2* ZOOL. antler. *3* ZOOL. horns, antlers [óf an ox, deer, etc.].

cuerno *m.* horn [of an animal, of the moon]. *2* horn [material]: *saber a ~ quemado*, to be unpleasant, distasteful. *3* ENT. horn, feeler. *4* MUS. *cuerno* or *~ de caza*, horn [made of a horn]. *5* PALEONT. *~ de Amon*, ammonite. *6 ~ de la abundancia*, horn of plenty. *7* GEOG. *Cuerno de Oro*, Golden Horn. *8 pl.* hornlike ends of some object.

cuero *m.* hide, rawhide, pelt. *2* leather. *3* wine bag, wineskin. *4* (Am.) whip. *5* skin: *~ cabelludo*, scalp; *en cueros, en cueros vivos*, stark naked.

cuerpo *m.* body [distinct mass or portion of matter]: *~ celeste*, heavenly body. *2* GEOM. body, solid. *3* CHEM. body, substance. *4* body [of a person or animal; trunk]: *~ sin alma*, fig. dull, inactive person; *echar el ~ fuera*, fig. to side-step a difficulty, an obligation, etc.; *hacer del ~*, to go to stool; *huir* or *hurtar el ~*, to dodge, avoid a blow, a person, a difficulty, etc.; *pedirle a uno el ~ una cosa*, fig. to want, desire something; *a ~, en ~*, without overcoat or cloak; *a ~ de rey*, like a king, with all comfort; *a ~ descubierto*, unprotected; manifestly; *~ a ~*, at close quarters, hand to hand; *de ~ entero*, full-length [portrait]; *de medio ~*, half-length [portrait]. *5* figure, build [of a person]. *6* corpse: *estar de ~ presente*, [of a corpse] to lie in state. *7* body [of a garment],

bodice: *en ~ de camisa*, in shirt sleeves. *8* ANAT. corpus, body. *9* body [of a church, a structure, a document, etc.]. *10* corpus [of laws]. *11* body, thickness, bulk, importance: *tomar ~*, to grow, take shape, gather importance. *12* body politic. *13* body [of persons], corps, company, staff: *~ de ejército*, army corps; *~ de redacción*, editorial staff; *~ diplomático*, diplomatic corps. *14* MACH. *~ de bomba*, pump barrel. *15* MIL. *~ de guardia*, guard, post of guard, guardroom. *16* LAW *~ del delito*, corpus delicti.

cuervo *m.* ORN. raven, crow. *2* ORN. *~ marino*, cormorant. *3* ORN. *~ merendero*, rook.

cuesco *m.* stone [of fruit]. *2* coll. PEDO.

cuesta *f.* slope, rising ground, sloping ground: *~ abajo*, downhill; *~ arriba*, uphill; *hacérsele a uno ~ arriba una cosa* [of a thing], to be repugnant to one. *2* CUESTACIÓN. *3 adv. a cuestas*, on one's back or shoulders; to one's charge or care.

cuestación *f.* collection for a charitable purpose.

cuestión *f.* question [problem, matter in discussion]; affair, business. *2* dispute, quarrel. *3* LAW *~ de tormento*, torture.

cuestionable *adj.* questionable, doubtful.

cuestionar *tr.* to controvert.

cuestionario *m.* questionnaire.

cuesto, cueste, etc. *irr.* V. COSTAR.

cuestor *m.* quaestor. *2* solicitor of contributions for a charitable purpose.

cuestura *f.* questorship.

cueto *m.* defended tor. *2* rocky hill.

cueva *f.* cave. *2* cellar. *3* den.

cuévano *m.* round basket or pannier.

cuezo *m.* mortar trough.

cuezo, cueza, etc. *irr.* V. COCER.

cuidado *m.* care, carefulness. *2* care, charge, keeping: *tener uno una cosa a su ~*, to have care or charge of a thing. *3* care, fear, anxiety, worry: *estar con ~*, to be worried, uneasy; *de ~*, dangerous; *estar uno de ~*, to be seriously ill. *5 no hay ~*, there is no danger. *6 interj.* take care!, beware!

cuidador, -ra *adj.* taking care. *2 m.-f.* caretaker; keeper, tender.

cuidadoso, -sa *adj.* careful, painstaking. *2* watchful.

cuidar *tr.* to execute with care. *2 tr.-intr. cuidar* or *~ de*, to take care of, to tend, keep, mind, look after, nurse; *~ de que*, to see that. *3 ref.* to take care of oneself. *4 cuidarse de*, to care, to mind, to take notice.

cuita *f.* trouble, sorrow, misfortune.

cuitado, -da *adj.* unfortunate. *2* spiritless.

cuja *f.* lance bucket. *2* bedstead.

culantrillo *m.* BOT. maidenhair fern.

culantro *m.* CILANTRO.

culata *f.* butt [of a firearm]. *2* breech [of a gun]. *3* MACH. head [of a cylinder]. *4* buttock, haunch. *5* rear part [of some things].

culatazo *m.* blow with the butt of a firearm. *2* kick, recoil [of a firearm].

culebra *f.* ZOOL. snake: *~ de cascabel*, rattlesnake.

culebrear *intr.* to twist, wriggle, wind along.

culebreo *m.* twisting, wriggling, winding along.

culebrilla *f.* MED. ringworm. *2* BOT. green dragon.

culebrina *f.* culverin [cannon].

culebrona *f.* intriguing woman.

culera *f.* dirty spot in a baby's swaddling clothes. *2* patch on the seat of trousers.

culero, -ra *adj.* lazy. *2 m.* baby's diaper.

culinario, -ria *adj.* culinary.

culminación f. culmination.
culminante adj. culminating. 2 predominant.
culminar intr. to culminate.
culo m. behind, bottom, seat, backside, buttocks, rump. 2 anus. 3 seat [of trousers]. 4 bottom [of anything]: ~ de vaso, fig. imitation stone.
culombio m. ELECT. coulomb.
culón, -ona adj. coll. big-bottomed, broad-bottomed. 2 m. disabled soldier.
culote m. base [of a projectile].
culpa f. guilt, fault, sin, blame: echar a uno la ~, to put the blame on; tener la ~ de, to be to blame for; esto es culpa mía, it's my fault.
culpabilidad f. culpability, guilt.
culpable adj. guilty. 2 culpable, blamable, blameworthy. 3 m.-f. culprit. 4 the one to blame.
culpado, -da adj. guilty. 2 m.-f. culprit.
culpar tr. to blame, to accuse. 2 ref. to blame oneself, to take the blame.
cultalatiniparla f. euphuistic language.
cultedad f. hum. affectation [in style].
culteranismo m. euphuism, cultism.
culterano, -na adj. euphuistic. 2 m.-f. euphuist, cultist.
cultismo m. euphuism, cultism.
cultivado, -da adj. cultured.
cultivador, -ra adj. cultivating. 2 m.-f. cultivator; tiller, farmer. 3 f. cultivator [implement].
cultivar tr. to cultivate, labour, till, farm [land, soil]. 2 to cultivate [plants, a branch of learning, etc.]. 3 BACT. to culture.
cultivo m. cultivation, culture. 2 BACT. culture.
1) **culto** m. cult, worship: ~ divino, public worship. 2 veneration, homage [to beauty, etc.]. 3 pl. acts or ceremonies of public worship.
2) **culto, -ta** adj. cultured, cultivated, educated. 2 enlightened, civilized. 3 learned [language].
cultor, -ra m.-f. worshiper.
cultura f. CULTIVO. 2 cultivation, refinement, learning; culture.
cultural adj. cultural.
cumbre f. summit, top [of mountain]. 2 fig. summit, top, acme, pinnacle.
cumbrera f. ARCH. ridge [of a ceiling], lintel. 2 (Am.) top, peak, summit, acme.
cúmel m. kümmel.
cumpleaños m. birthday.
cumplidamente adv. completely.
cumplidero, -ra adj. expiring [by a specified date]. 2 necessary [to some purpose].
cumplido, -da adj. full, complete, through, perfect. 3 large, ample, abundant. 4 courteous, polite. 5 m. act of courtesy, compliment, ceremony: visita de ~, formal call.
cumplidor, -ra adj. conscientious, dependable. 2 trustworthy, true to one's word. 3 m.-f. one who executes [an order], keeps [a promise], does [his duty], observes [a law, a precept].
cumplimentar tr. to compliment, to pay a complimentary visit to. 2 to carry out [an order].
cumplimiento m. accomplishment, carrying out, fulfilment. 2 observance [of law or precepts]. 3 lapse, expiration [of a term]. 4 perfection. 5 CUMPLIDO 5: por ~, as a matter of pure form.
cumplir tr. to accomplish, perform, fulfil. 2 to keep [a promise]. 3 to do [one's duty]. 4 to observe [a law, a precept]. 5 ~ una condena, to serve or finish a term in prison. 6 hoy cumplo treinta años, I am thirty today. 7 intr. to do one's duty: ~ con Dios, to do one's duty to God; por ~, as a matter of form. 8 to have served the time

required in the Army. 9 to behove: cúmpleme decir, it behoves me to say. 10 intr.-ref. [of a term or period of time] to expire. 11 ref. to be fulfilled, to come true.
cumquibus m. coll. money, wherewithal.
cumulativo, -va adj. cumulative.
cúmulo m. heap, pile. 2 METEOR. cumulus.
cuna f. cradle [for a baby; infancy]. 2 place of birth [of a person]. 3 birth, family, lineage. 4 foundling hospital. 5 pl. cat's cradle.
cundir intr. [of liquids; of news, etc.] to spread. 2 to increase in volume; to go a long way.
cunear tr. to rock [in the cradle]. 2 ref. coll. to rock, sway.
cuneiforme adj. cuneiform. 2 BOT. cuneate.
cúneo m. ARCHEOL. cuneus.
cunero, -ra adj.-m. foundling. 2 BULLF. unpedigreed [bull].
cuneta f. ditch [at the side of a road].
cunicultura f. rabbit raising, rabbit breeding.
cuña m. wedge, quoin. 2 ANAT. cuneiform [bone].
cuñada f. sister-in-law.
cuñado m. brother-in-law.
cuñete m. keg.
cuño m. die [for stamping coins, medals, etc.]. 2 stamp made by the die: de nuevo ~, fig. newly minted, newly made.
cuota f. quota, share. 2 membership fee.
cuotidiano, -na adj. COTIDIANO.
cupe, cupiera, etc. irr. V. CABER.
cupé m. coupé [automobile, carriage]. 2 coupé [of a Continental diligence].
cupido m. cupid. 2 (cap.) MYTH. Cupid.
cuplé m. variety song, music-hall song.
cupletista f. variety singer, music-hall singer.
cupo m. quota, contingent.
cupón m. coupon.
cupresáceo, -a adj. BOT. cupressineous.
cúprico, -ca adj. CHEM. cupric.
cuprífero, -ra adj. cupriferous.
cuprita f. MINER. cuprite.
cuproníquel m. cupronickel.
cúpula f. ARCH. cupola, dome. 2 NAUT. cupola, turret. 3 BOT. cupule.
cupulífero, -ra adj. BOT. cupuliferous.
cura m. Roman Catholic priest; parish priest: ~ párroco, parish priest; este ~, fig. I, myself. 2 cure, healing, treatment: no tener ~, to be incurable. 3 dressing [of a wound]. 4 ~ de almas, care of souls.
curable adj. MED. curable.
curación f. cure, curing, healing.
curadillo m. ICHTH. codfish.
curador, -ra adj. curing, healing. 2 caretaking. 3 m.-f. curer, healer. 4 curer, seasoner, tanner. 5 caretaker, overseer. 6 LAW curator, guardian.
curaduría f. LAW curatorship.
curalotodo m. cure-all.
curanderismo m. quackery, quack medicine.
curandero m. quack doctor.
curar intr.-ref. to cure, heal, recover, be cured. 2 to take care [of]; to mind. 3 tr. cure, heal. 4 MED. to treat; to dress [a wound]. 5 to cure [meat, fish]; to season [lumber]; to tan [hides]. 6 ref. to take treatment: curarse en salud, to guard against possible danger.
curare m. curare, curari.
curasao m. curaçao [liqueur].
curatela f. CURADURÍA.
curativo, -va adj. curative.
curato m. office of a parish priest. 2 parish.

curda *f.* drunkenness, drunken fit.
curdo, -da *adj.* Kurdish. *2 m.-f.* Kurd.
cureña *f.* gun carriage. *2* gunstock in the rough. *3* stock [of crossbow].
curia *f.* HIST. curia. *2* barristers, solicitors and court clerks as a whole. *3* ecclesiastical court: *Curia romana*, Roman Curia.
curialesco, -ca *adj.* legal [language, style].
curiana *f.* CUCARACHA 1.
curiosamente *adv.* curiously. *2* neatly, tidily, cleanly. *3* carefully.
curiosear *intr.* to act with curiosity; to inquire, snoop.
curiosidad *f.* curiosity [inquisitiveness; strangeness]. *2* cleanliness, tidiness. *3* curiosity [curious thing]: curio.
curioso, -sa *adj.* curious. *2* clean, tidy. *3 m.-f.* curious person.
Curlandia *f. pr. n.* Kurland.
Curra, Currita *f. pr. n.* Francis.
currelar *intr.* coll. to slog away, to toil, to drudge.
Curro, Currito *m. pr. n.* Frank.
curruca *f.* ORN. whitethroat.
currutaco, -ca *adj.* dandified. *2 m.* fop, dandy, dude. *3 f.* woman of fashion.
cursado, -da *adj.* versed, experienced.
cursar *tr.* to frequent. *2* EDUC. to attend lectures of, to study [a subject]. *3* to make [a petition, etc.] pass through the regular administrative channels.
cursi *adj.-s.* [person] poorly affecting distinction and elegance; shabby-genteel.
cursilón, -ona *adj.* pretentious, showy, flashy, affected, pseudo-refined, snobish. *2 n.* flashy type, common but pretentious person, genteel person, snob.
cursilería *f.* poor afectation of distinction and elegance; shabby-gentility.
cursillo *m.* EDUC. short course of lectures on a subject.
cursivo, -va *adj.* cursive. *2 f.* italics.
curso *m.* course [career, direction, progress]; lapse, succession. *2* route [of a procession]. *3* MACH. run, -travel [of part or device]. *4* passing of a petition or affair through the regular chan-

nels. *5* EDUC. course [of lectures]. *6* school year. *7* course, run, flow, circulation: *dar libre* ~, to give free course. *8* COM. current rate. *9 pl.* diarrhœa.
cursor *m.* MECH. slide.
curtido, -da *adj.* tanned, curried [leather]. *2* tanned, sunburnt, weather-beaten. *3* hardened, experienced. *4 m.* tanning. *5* tanning bark. *6 m. pl.* tanned leather.
curtidor *m.* tanner, currier, leather dresser.
curtiduría *f.* tannery, tanyard.
curtiembre *f.* tannery.
curtir *tr.* to tan [hides]. *2* to tan, to sunburn. *3* to harden, to inure. *4 ref.* to become tanned. *5* to be hardened or inured; to gain experience.
curuguá *m.* BOT. cassabanana.
curul *adj.* curule.
curva *f.* curve. *2* NAUT. knee.
curvatura, curvidad *f.* curvature, bend.
curvilíneo, -a *adj.* curvilinear.
curvo, -va *adj.* curve, curved, bent.
cuscurro *m.* crust of bread.
cuscuta *f.* BOT. common dodder.
cuscús, cuzcuz *m.* couscous.
cúspide *f.* GEOM. vertex [of cone or pyramid]. *2* peak [of mountain]. *3* cusp, apex, summit.
custodia *f.* custody, care, safe-keeping. *2* escort or guard [to a prisoner]. *3* ECCL. monstrance. *4* ECCL. tabernacle. *5* custody [of the Franciscan order].
custodiar *tr.* to guard, keep, take care of.
custodio *m.* custodian, guard.
cutáneo, -a *adj.* cutaneous.
cúter *m.* NAUT. cutter [vessel with one mast].
cutí *m.* ticking [fabric].
cutícula *f.* cuticle.
cutis *m.* skin [of the human body], complexion.
cutre *adj.* stingy, miserly. *2 m.-f.* miser.
cuyo, -ya, *pl.* **cuyos, -yas** *poss. pron.* whose, of which; *mi hermana, cuyo marido es inglés*, my sister, whose husband is an Englishman. *2 m.* coll. lover [of a woman].
cuzco *m.* small dog.
czar *m.* ZAR.
czarevitz *m.* ZAREVITZ.
czarina *f.* ZARINA.

CH

Ch, ch *f.* fourth letter of the Spanish alphabet.

chabacanada, chabacanería *f.* coarseness, vulgarity, bad taste.

chabacano, -na *adj.* coarse, vulgar, in bad taste.

chabola *f.* hut, cabin, shanty.

chabolismo *m.* shanty or shacky towns, slums.

chacal *m.* ZOOL. jackal.

chacarero, -ra *adj.-n.* farmer, peasant, grower. *2 f.* peasant dance in Argentina, Uruguay and Bolivia.

chacina *f.* CECINA. *2* pork seasoned for sausages.

chacinería *f.* porkbutcher's shop.

chacó *pl.* **-cós** *m.* shako.

chacolí *m.* light sour wine of Vizcaya.

chacolotear *intr.* [of a loose horseshoe] to clatter.

chacoloteo *m.* clatter [of a loose horseshoe].

chacona *f.* MUS. chaconne.

chaconá, chaconada *f.* jaconet [fabric].

chacota *f.* fun, noisy mirth: *hacer* ~ *de*, coll. to make fun of.

chacoteo *m.* fun, noisy mirth, mockery.

chacra *f.* (Am.) farm, country estate, cultivated land. *2* farmhouse. *3* farm products.

chacha *f.* coll. nurse, nursemaid.

cháchara *f.* prattle, idle talk. *2* chitchat.

chacharear *intr.* to chatter, prate, prattle.

chacharero, -ra *adj.* chattering. *2 m.-f.* chatterer, prattler.

chacho *m.* coll. boy, lad.

chafaldita *f.* jest, banter.

chafalmejas *m.-f.* dauber [bad painter].

chafalonía *f.* (Am.) scrap gold or silver, worn out gold jewellery.

chafallar *tr.* to botch, to make or mend clumsily.

chafallo *m.* botch, clumsy mending.

chafallón, -na *adj.* botching. *2 m.-f.* botcher.

chafandín *m.* conceited ass.

chafar *tr.* to flatten, crush, crumple, rumple. *2* fig. to squash, cut short, silence.

chafarote *f.* cutlass. *2* sword, sabre.

chafarrinar *tr.* to blot, to stain.

chafarrinón *m.* CHAFARRINADA.

chaflán *m.* chamfer, bevel.

chaflanar *tr.* to chamfer, to bevel.

chah *m.* shah.

chaira *f.* steel [for sharpening knives]. *2* shoemaker's blade.

chal *m.* shawl.

chalado, -da *adj.* fool, addlepated. *2* infatuated: *estar* ~ *por*, to be madly in love with.

chaladura *f.* coll. fancy or crazy idea, whim. *2* craze, old habit, mania. *3* stupid thing. *4* crush.

chalán, -na *m.-f.* horse dealer; wily, crafty dealer. *2 m.* (Am.) horsebreaker.

chalana *f.* scow, flatboat.

chalanear *tr.* coll. to drive [deals] craftily.

chalaneo *m.* horse dealing; crafty dealing.

chalanesco, -ca *adj.* pertaining to craftiness in buying and selling.

chalar *tr.* to drive mad. *2 ref.* to lose one's head. *3* to become madly in love.

chalaza *f.* EMBRYOL., BOT. chalaza.

chaleco *m.* waistcoat, vest.

chalet *m.* chalet.

chalina *f.* bowtie with long ends.

chalote BOT. shallot, scallion.

chalupa *f.* NAUT. a small two-mast boat. *2* NAUT. launch, lifeboat. *3* (Mex.) a small canoe.

chámara, chamarasca *f.* brushwood. *2* brush fire.

chamarilero, -ra *m.-f.* dealer in second-hand goods.

chamariz *m.* ORN. greenfinch.

chamarra *f.* jacket of coarse woollen cloth.

chamba *f.* coll. CHIRIPA.

chambelán *m.* chamberlain.

chambergo *m.* an old broad-brimmed hat with a cocked side. *2* (Arg.) soft hat.

chambón, -na *adj.* coll. clumsy, awkward [in games]; unskilled. *2* coll. lucky [attaining something by a fluke]. *3 m.-f.* coll. blunderer. *4* lucky person.

chambonada *f.* blunder. *2* fluke, stroke of luck.

chambra *f.* femenine dressing jacket.

chambrana *f.* ARCH. trim [around a door, window, etc.].

chamicera *f.* strip of half-burnt woodland.

chamiza *f.* BOT. chamiso. *2* brushwood [for fuel].

chamizo *m.* half-burnt tree or log. *2* chamiso-thatched hut. *3* fig. den.

chamorro, -rra *adj.* with the head shorn. *2* beardless [wheat].

champán *m.* NAUT. sampan. *2* champagne [wine].

champaña *m.* champagne [wine].

champiñón *m.* mushroom.

champú *m.* shampoo.

champurrar *tr.* to mix [liquors].

chamullar *tr.* to speak, to talk: ~ *algo de inglés*, to speak some English.
chamuscado, -da *adj.* singed, scorched.
chamuscar *tr.* to singe, sear, scorch. 2 *ref.* to be singed, scorched.
chamusquina *f.* singe, singeing, scorching. 2 row, quarrel. 3 *oler a chamusquina*, coll. to look like a fight; coll. to smack of heresy.
chancear *intr.-ref.* to joke, jest, fool.
chancero, -ra *adj.* joking, jesting.
chancla *f.* old shoe worn down at the heel.
chancleta *f.* slipper: *en chancleta*, with shoes worn slipper-like.
chancletear *intr.* to go about wearing the shoes slipper-like.
chancleteo *m.* clatter of slipper.
chanclo *m.* clog, patten. 2 overshoe, galosh, *gum.
chancro *m.* MED. chancre.
chanchada *f.* (Am.) coll. dirty trick, vile ed.
chanchería *f.* (Am.) pork-butcher's shop.
chancho, -cha *adj.* (Am.) dirty, unclean. 2 (Am.) pig, hog.
chanchullero, -ra *m.-f.* underhand dealer.
chanchullo *m.* underhand deal.
chandal *m.* track suit.
chanfaina *f.* COOK. stew of chopped lights.
changüí *m.* coll. joke. 2 trick, hoax, swindle: *dar* ~, to trick, to swindle.
chantaje *m.* blackmail.
chantajista *m.-f.* blackmailer.
chantar *tr.* to put on [clothes]. 2 to tell [someone something] to his face.
chantre *m.* precentor [in a cathedral].
chanza *f.* joke, jest, fun.
chanzoneta *f.* old little song. 2 coll. CHANZA.
chapa *f.* sheet, plate, veneer. 2 small piece of metal plate, used as a badge, sign, token, etc. 3 rosy spot on the cheek. 4 *hombre de* ~, serious man. 5 *pl.* game of tossing up coins.
chapado, -da *adj.* plated, veneered. 2 ~ *a la antigua*, old-fashioned [person].
chapalear *intr.* [of water] to splash. 2 CHACOLOTEAR.
chapaleo *m.* splashing [of water]. 2 CHACOLOTEO.
chapaleta *f.* flap valve, clack valve.
chapaleteo *m.* dash, splashing [of water]. 3 patter [of rain].
chapar *tr.* CHAPEAR.
chaparra *f.* BOT. kermes oak. 2 CHAPARRO.
chaparral *m.* thicket of dwarf oaks.
chaparreras *f. pl.* (Am.) chaps [worn by cowboys].
chaparro *m.* BOT. dwarf oak, dwarf evergreen oak.
chaparrón *m.* downpour, violent shower.
chapear *tr.* to plate [cover with metal sheets]; to veneer. 2 *intr.* CHACOLOTEAR.
chapeo *m.* hat.
chapería *f.* sheet-metal ornament.
chapeta *f.* small metal plate. 2 rosy spot on the cheek.
chapín *m.* chopine [kind of patten].
chápiro *m.* coll. *¡voto al* ~*!*, by Jove!, by thunder!
chapitel *m.* ARCH. spire. 2 ARCH. capital. 3 NAUT. agate socket [of the needle].
chapodar *tr.* to trim, clear of branches [a tree].
chapodo *m.* branch lopped off a tree.
chapotear *tr.* to moisten [by dabbing at with a wet, sponge or cloth]. 2 *intr.* [of water] to make a splashing sound.
chapoteo *m.* moistening, dabbing. 2 splashing.
chapucear *tr.* to botch, bungle.
chapucería *f.* clumsiness [of a work]. 2 botch, bungle, clumsy work.

chapucero, -ra *adj.* botched, bungled. 2 botching, bungling. 3 *m.-f.* botcher, bungler.
chapurrar, chapurrear *tr.* to jabber [a language]; to speak [a language] brokenly.
chapuz *m.* duck, ducking [sudden dip of head under water]. 2 CHAPUZA.
chapuza *f.* slight work. 2 botch, bungle.
chapuzar *tr.-intr.-ref.* to duck [under water].
chapuzón *m.* coll. duck, ducking, diving.
chaqué *m.* cutaway coat, morning coat.
chaqueta *f.* jacket, sack coat.
chaquete *m.* backgammon.
chaquetear *intr.* coll. to take fright, to flee.
chaquetilla *f.* short jacket.
chaquetón *m.* pea-jacket. 2 short overcoat.
charabán *m.* charabanc.
charada *f.* charade.
charanga *f.* MUS. military brass band.
charca *f.* pool, pond [of stagnant water].
charco *m.* puddle, pool. 2 fig. *pasar el* ~, to cross the pond [the sea].
charcutería *f.* pork butcher's shop.
charla *f.* chatter, prattle. 2 chat, chatting. 3 talk, lecture. 4 ORN. missel thrush.
charladuría *f.* indiscreet talk, gossip, prattle.
charlar *intr.* to chatter, prattle. 2 to chat.
charlatán, -na *adj.* chattering, prattling, loquacious. 2 babbling. 3 *m.-f.* chatterer, chatterbox. 4 charlatan, quack, mountebank; humbug.
charlatanería *f.* garrulity. 2 charlatanry.
charlatanismo *m.* charlatanism.
charnela *f.* hinge [of door, box, etc.]. 2 MACH. knuckle. 3 ZOOL. hinge [of bivalve shell].
charol *m.* varnish, japan. 2 patent leather.
charolado, -da *adj.* shiny, lustrous. 2 varnished.
charolar *tr.* to varnish, to japan.
charpa *f.* formerly, a baldric for carrying pistols. 2 sling [for a broken arm].
charquear *tr.* (Am.) to jerk, dry [beef].
charqui *m.* (Am.) jerked beef, dry beef.
charrada *f.* tawdriness, gaudiness.
charrán *adj.* knave, rogue.
charranada *f.* dirty trick, knavery.
charrasca *f.* coll. trailing sword or sabre.
charrería *f.* tawdriness, gaudiness.
charretera *f.* epaulet. 2 garter.
charro, -rra *adj.* pertaining to the countryfolk of Salamanca. 2 rustic. 3 tawdry, gaudy, flashy. 4 *m.-f.* Salamanca countryman or countrywoman. 5 *m.* (Mex.) cowboy.
chasca *f.* small wood [for fuel].
chascar *intr.* to crack [emit a splitting sound]. 2 *tr.* to click [one's tongue]. 3 to crunch [food].
chascarrillo *m.* joke, funny story.
chasco *m.* trick, deceit. 2 disappointment. 3 *dar un* ~, to play a trick upon; to disappoint; *llevarse un* ~, to be disappointed.
chasis *m.* AUTO., RADIO. chassis. 2 PHOT. plate-holder.
chasponazo *m.* scratch made by a bullet.
chasquear *tr.* to play a trick on, to fool, deceive. 2 to disappoint. 3 to crack, snap [a whip]. 4 *intr.* to crack, snap. 5 *ref.* to be frustrated.
chasquido *m.* crack, snap, click [sound].
chata *f.* CHALANA. 2 bedpan.
chatarra *f.* scrap iron. 2 iron slag.
chatarrero, -ra *m.-f.* scrap-iron dealer.
chato, -ta *adj.* flat-nosed. 2 flat [nose and other things]. 3 *m.-f.* flat-nosed person.
chatón *m.* JEWEL. the stone in a bezel or chaton.
¡chau! *interj.* (Am.) so long.

chauvinismo *m.* chauvinism.
chauvinista *adj.* chauvinistic. 2 *m.-f.* chauvinist.
chaval, -la *adj.* coll. young. 2 *m.* coll. lad. 3 *f.* coll. lass.
chavea *f.* coll, boy, lad.
chaveta *f.* cotter pin; key, forelock, linchpin. 2 coll. *perder la* ~, to go off one's head.
chayote *m.* BOT. edible fruit of an American vine.
che *f.* name of the letter *ch.*
checo, -ca *adj.-n.* Czech.
checoeslovaco, -ca *adj.-n.* Czecho-Slovakian.
Checoeslovaquia *f. pr. n.* GEOG. Czecho-Slovakia.
chelín *m.* shilling.
chepa *f.* coll. hump, hunch.
cheque *m.* COM. cheque, check: ~ *cruzado*, crossed check; ~ *de viajero*, traveler's check.
chequeo *m.* MED. checkup. 2 AUTO. servicing, overhauling. 3 checking, verifying.
cherna *f.* ICHTH. a mediterranean grouper.
cheviot *m.* cheviot [fabric, wool].
chibalete *m.* PRINT. frame.
chibuquí *m.* chibouk [turkish pipe].
chicada *f.* childish action.
chicle *m.* chicle gum; chewing gum.
chico, -ca *adj.* small, little. 2 very young [person]. 3 *m.* child, kid, youngster, boy, lad. 4 coll. fellow; old chap. 5 *f.* child, kid, girl, lass. 6 coll. old girl.
chicolear *intr.* to address compliments to a woman.
chicoleo *m.* compliment [addressed to a woman].
chicorro *m.* sturdy youngster.
chicote *m.* sturdy boy. 2 coll, cigar. 3 (Am.) whip. 4 NAUT. end of rope; piece of rope.
chicozapote *m.* BOT. sapodilla, sapote.
chicuelo, -la *adj. dim.* little, small, very small. 2 *m.* child, little boy. 3 *f.* child; girl, little girl.
chicha *f.* alcoholic drink made from maize: *no ser* ~ *ni limonada*, to be neither fish nor fowl. 2 *adj.* NAUT. *calma* ~, dead calm.
chicharra *f.* ENT. cicada. 2 a noisy toy.
chicharrón *m.* crackling, scratching [residue of hog fat]. 2 burned meat.
chichón *m.* bump [swelling on the head].
chichonera *f.* cap for protecting child's head.
chifla *f.* hissing, whistling [to express disapproval]. 2 whistle. 3 paring knife.
chiflado, -da *adj.* off one's head, crazy. 2 *estar* ~ *por*, to be in love with, to dote on; to have a craze for. 3 *m.-f.* crackbrain, crank.
chifladura *f.* craziness. 2 love, doting. 3 craze, mania.
chiflar *intr.* to whistle. 2 *tr.-ref.* to hiss, to scoff. 3 *tr.* to pare [leather]. 4 to gulp down [wine, liquors]. 5 *ref.* to become crazy, unbalanced. 6 *chiflarse por*, to go crazy on.
chiflato *m.* whistle [instrument].
chiflido *m.* whistle [instrument and sound].
chilaba *f.* Moorish hooded garment.
Chile *m. pr. n.* Chile.
chile *m.* chil(l)i; red pepper.
chileno, -na; chileño, -ña *adj.-n.* Chilean.
chilindrina *f.* trifle. 2 joke; jest, banter.
chilindrinero, -ra *adj.* waggish. 2 *m.-f.* wag, joker.
chilindrón *m.* a card game.
chillador, -ra *adj.* shrieking, squeaking, screaming.
chillar *intr.* to shriek, screech, squeak, scream. 2 fig. to shout. 3 [of colours] to clash, to glare, be garish. 4 CHIRRIAR.
chillería *f.* screaming, shouting. 2 scolding.

chillido *m.* shriek, screech, squeak, scream.
chillón, -na *adj.* shrieking, screaming. 2 shrill, screechy. 3 loud, garish [colour].
chimenea *f.* chimney; smokestack. 2 NAUT. funnel. 3 hearth, fireplace, chimney: ~ *francesa*, fireplace. 4 MIN. shaft.
chimpancé *m.* ZOOL. chimpanzee.
China *f. pr. n.* China.
china *f.* pebble, small stone. 2 BOT. chinaroot. 3 China silk or cotton stuff. 4 China, porcelain. 5 Chinese woman. 6 (Am.) Indian or half-breed maidservant.
chinazo *m.* blow with a pebble.
chinchar *tr.* coll. to bother, annoy. 2 coll. to kill.
chincharrero *m.* place swarming with bedbugs. 2 (Am.) fishing smack.
chinche *f.* ENT. bedbug. 2 drawing pin, thumb tack. 3 bore, nuisance [person].
chincheta *f.* drawing pin, thumbtack.
chinchilla *f.* ZOOL. chinchilla. 2 chinchilla [fur].
chinchín *m.* street music. 2 ballyhoo.
chinchona *f.* CHEM. cinchona, cinchona bark.
chinchorrería *f.* annoyance. 2 tale, gossip.
chinchorrero, -ra *adj.* annoying, pestering.
chinchorro *m.* kind of fishing net. 2 small rowing boat.
chinchoso, -sa *adj.* annoying, pestering [person].
chinela *f.* slipper, chopine.
chinero *m.* china cabinet.
chinesco, -ca *adj.* Chinese. 2 *m.* MUS. bell tree.
chingar *tr.* coll. to drink, tipple. 2 *ref.* to get drunk.
chino, -na *adj.* Chinese. 2 *adj.-n.* (Am.) offspring of Indian and mestizo. 3 *m.* Chinaman, Chinese. 4 Chinese language. 5 (Am.) manservant.
chipé *f.* coll. truth, goodness.
chipén *f.* coll. life, excitement. 2 *de* ~, first-class, excellent.
chipirón *m.* ZOOL. squid, calamary.
Chipre *f. pr. n.* Cyprus.
chipriota, chiprote *adj.-n.* Cyprian.
chiquero *m.* pigsty. 2 in a bull ring, place where bulls are shut up.
chiquilicuatro *m.* CHISGARABÍS.
chiquillada *f.* childish action.
chiquillería *f.* children, crowd of children.
chiquillo, -lla *adj.* small. 2 *m.-f.* little boy or girl, child, little one, youngster.
chiquirritín, -na; chiquitín, -na *adj.* tiny, small. 2 *m.-f.* tiny child, tot, infant.
chiquito, -ta *adj.* tiny, very small: *hacerse* ~, to be modest. 2 *m.-f.* CHIQUILLO 2. 3 *f. no andarse con chiquitas*, not to shift, to be clear, direct.
chiribita *f.* BOT. daisy. 2 *pl.* sparks. 3 *hacer chiribitas los ojos*, to see spots before the eyes.
chiribitil *m.* crib, hovel, den, small narrow room.
chirigota *f.* joke, jest, banter.
chirigotero, -ra *adj.* fond of jesting or bantering.
chirimbolo *m.* utensil, implement, vessel.
chirimía *f.* MUS. kind of flageolet, hornpipe.
chirimoya *f.* cherimoya.
chirinola *f.* trifle. 2 *estar de* ~, to be in good spirits.
chiripa *f.* fluke, piece of luck.
chirivía *f.* BOT. parsnip. 2 ORN. wagtail.
chirla *f.* ZOOL. a small clam.
chirle *adj.* coll. dull, insipid, tasteless, wishy-washy, flat. 2 *m.* droppings.
chirlata *f.* gambling den.
chirlo *m.* long slash or scar in the face.
chirona *f.* coll. jug, jail, prison.
chirriar *intr.* to hiss, sizzle. 2 [of a wheel, etc.] to

squeak. *3* [of birds] to chirr, screech. *4* [of insects] to chirr, chirp.
chirrido *m.* hiss, sizzle. *2* squeak [of a wheel, etc.] *3* chirr, screech [of birds]. *4* chirr, chirping [of insects].
chirrión *m.* squeaky, two-wheeled dray.
chirumen *m.* coll. acumen, brains.
¡chis! *interj.* hush!, sh!, silence!
chisgarabís *m.* whippersnapper, insignificant meddlesome fellow.
chisguete *m.* drink, swallow, swig [of wine]. *2* squirt [of a liquid].
chisme *m.* mischievous tale, piece of gossip. *2* coll. implement, utensil.
chismear *tr.* to gossip, tattle, bear tales.
chismografía *f.* gossip, tattle.
chismorrear *intr.* CHISMEAR.
chismorreo *m.* gossip, gossiping, tale-bearing.
chismoso, -sa *adj.* gossipy. *2 m.-f.* gossip, tale bearer.
chispa *f.* spark, sparkle: *echar chispas*, fig. to be raging, hit the ceiling. *2* sparkle [little bit; small diamond]. *3* drop [of drizzling rain]. *4* sparkle, wit: *tener ~*, to be witty. *5* coll. *coger una ~*, to get drunk.
chispazo *m.* spark, flying off of a spark, flash.
chispeante *adj.* sparkling, scintillant.
chispear *intr.* to spark, to sparkle. *2* to scintillate. *3* to drizzle, sprinkle [rain lightly].
chispero *m.* blacksmith. *2* formerly, in Madrid, man of the lower classes.
chispo, -pa *adj.* tipsy, drunk.
chisporrotear *intr.* to spark, sputter.
chisporroteo *m.* sparking, sputtering.
chistar *intr.* to speak: *no ~*, not to say a word.
chiste *m.* joke, funny story: *contar chistes*, to crack jokes. *2* fun: *hacer ~ de*, to make fun of. *3 caer en el ~*, to see the point.
chistera *f.* top hat. *2* fish basket. *3* CESTA 2.
chistoso, -sa *adj.* witty, funny. *2 m.* wit, funny fellow.
chita *f.* ANAT. ankle bone. *2* knucklebone [of sheep]. *3* a game like, quoits. *4 adv. a la ~ callando*, on the quiet, stealthily.
chiticalla *m.-f.* coll. reticent person, oyster, *clam. *2* coll. secret.
chito *m.* CHITA.
¡chito!, ¡chitón! *interj.* hush!, silence!
chitón *m.* ZOOL. chiton.
chiva *f.* ZOOL. female kid.
chivar *tr.* to annoy, to upset, to get on someone's nerves. *2 ref.* to tell, to split, to squeal, to inform [against].
chivata *f.* shepherd's club or stick. *2* coll. female informer or talebearer.
chivatazo *m.* coll. tip-off, telling, informing: *dar el ~*, to spill the beans, to split, to give a tip-off.
chivato *m.* ZOOL. kid. *2* coll. informer, talebearer.
chivo *m.* ZOOL. male kid.
chocante *adj.* provoking. *2* surprising. *3* funny.
chocar *intr.* to collide, come into collision; to clash, bump together. *2* to meet, fight. *3* to annoy, vex. *4* to surprise: *esto me choca*, I am surprised at this.
chocarrear *intr.* to crack vulgar jokes.
chocarrería *f.* vulgar joke, coarse humour.
chocarrero, -ra *adj.* coarse vulgar [joke humour]. *2 m.-f.* vulgar joker.
choclo *m.* clog, patten. *2* (Am.) green ear of maize.
chocolate *m.* chocolate.

chocolatería *f.* chocolate factory. *2* chocolate shop.
chocolatero, -ra *adj.* fond of drinking chocolate. *2 m.-f.* chocolate maker or seller. *3 f.* chocolate pot.
chocolatín *m.* chocolate tablet or drop.
chocha, chochaperdiz *f.* ORN. woodcock.
chochear *intr.* to dote, to be in one's dotage.
chochera, chochez *f.* dotage. *2* doting act or word.
chocho, -cha *adj.* dotard, doddering. *2* doting: *estar ~ por*, to dote on. *3 m.-f.* dotard.
chófer *m.* AUT. chauffeur, driver.
chola *f.* CHOLLA.
cholla *f.* coll. head, noodle, pate.
chollo *m.* soft job, plum, good number. *2* bargain, snip. *3* luck.
chopo *m.* BOT. black poplar. *2* coll. musket, gun.
choque *m.* collision, clash; shock, impact. *2* MIL. encounter, skirmish. *3* dispute, quarrel. *4* MED. shock [depression].
choquezuela *f.* ANAT. kneecap, kneepan.
choricería *f.* sausage shop.
choricero, -ra *m.-f.* sausage maker or seller.
chorizo *m.* smoked-pork sausage.
chorlito *m.* ORN. golden plover. *2* coll. scatter-brains.
chorrada *f.* extra dash of a liquid [for good measure].
chorreado, -da *adj.* [of cattle] with dark vertical stripes.
chorrear *intr.* to spout, to gush. *2* to drip. *3* to be dripping wet. *4* [of some things] to come trickling.
chorreo *m.* spouting, gushing. *2* dripping.
chorrera *f.* place whence a liquid drips. *2* mark left by dripping or running water. *3* rapid [in a stream]. *4* jabot, shirt frill. *5* coll. (Am.) string, stream [of things or people].
chorretada *f.* squirt, spurt. *2* CHORRADA.
chorrillo *m.* small jet or flow, trickle. *2* continual trickle [of some things]: *sembrar a ~*, to sow in a trickle.
chorrito *m.* small jet, trickle. *2* dash [of a liquid].
chorro *m.* jet, spout, gush, flow, stream [of liquid, etc.]: *~ de arena*, sandblast; *a chorros*, in abundance. *2 ~ de voz*, voice of large volume.
chortal *m.* pool fed by a spring at the bottom.
chotacabras *f.* ORN. goatsucker.
chotearse *ref.* to make fun [of someone].
choteo *m.* fun, mockery.
chotis *m.* schottische [dance].
choto, -ta *m.-f.* sucking kid. *2* calf.
chova *f.* ORN. chough. *2* ORN. jackdaw.
choza *f.* hut, cabin, hovel, shanty.
chozo *m.* small hut.
chozpo *m.* gambol.
chubasco *m.* shower, squall: fig. *aguantar el ~*, to stand a storm of words, difficulties, etc.
chubasquero *m.* raincoat.
chucha *f.* bitch [female dog]. *2* (Am.) opossum.
chuchería *f.* trinquet, knick-nack. *2* titbit, delicacy.
chucho *m.* coll. dog.
chueca *f.* stump [of tree]. *2* head [of a bone]. *3* game played with a ball and sticks.
chueta *m.-f.* in the Balearic Islands, a descendant of Christianized Jews.
chufa *f.* BOT. chufa, groundnut.
chufero, -ra *adj.* chufa or orgeat seller.
chufleta *f.* CUCHUFLETA.
chufletear *intr.* to poke fun [at others].

chulada *f.* low action. *2* pert, droll saying.
chulapo, -pa *m.-f.* CHULO 3.
chulear *tr.* to banter, rally wittily. *2 ref.* to make fun, be facetious.
chulería *f.* pertness. *2* assemblage of CHULOS.
chulesco, -ca *adj.* pertaining to CHULOS.
chuleta *f.* chop, cutlet. *2* coll. slap in the face.
chulo, -la *adj.* pert and droll. *2* CHULESCO. *3 m.-f.* man or woman of the lower class of Madrid who affects special airs and manners. *4 m.* bullfighter's assistant. *5* pimp, procurer. *6* man kept by a woman. *7* fig. knave.
chumacera *f.* MACH. journal bearing, pillow block. *2* NAUT. rowlock.
chumbera *f.* BOT. Indian fig, prickly pear [plant].
chumbo, -ba *adj. higo* ~, Indian fig, prickly pear [fruit]; *higuera* ~, CHUMBERA.
chunga *f.* fun, banter: *estar de* ~, to be joking; *tomar a* ~, to make fun of.
chunguearse *ref.* to joke, to make fun [of].
chupa *f.* an old undercoat or jacket: *poner como* ~ *de dómine*, to upbraid, to abuse.
chupada *f.* suck, sucking. *2* pull [at a pipe].
chupadero, -ra *adj.* sucking. *2 m.* CHUPADOR 2.
chupado, -da *adj.* lean, emaciated.
chupador, -ra *adj.* sucking; absorbent. *2 m.* pacifier, teething ring, baby's coral.
chupadura *f.* suck, sucking.
chupaflor *m.* ORN. a humming bird.
chupar *tr.* to suck, draw; fig. *chuparse los dedos*, to eat, do or say something with much pleasure. *2* to absorb, imbibe. *3* to drain [money, etc.]; to

sponge. *4* (Am.) to smoke. *5* (Am.) to drink. *6 ref.* to become lean, emaciated.
chupatintas *m.* coll. office clerk.
chupete *m.* pacifier [nipplelike device for babies to suck]. *2 de* ~, fine, splendid.
chupetear *tr.* to suck gently and by starts.
chupeteo *m.* frequent sucking.
chupetón *m.* hard suck.
chupón, -na *adj.* sucking. *2* blotting [paper]. *3 m.* sucker, sponger, parasite. *4* HORT. sucker. *5* MACH. sucker [piston].
churrasco *m.* (Am.) barbecued steak. *2* steak, choice piece of meat.
churrasquear *tr.* (Am.) to barbecue.
churre *m.* thick, dirty grease. *2* greasy dirt.
churretada *f.* large dirty spot [on hands or face].
churrete *m.* dirty spot [on hands or face].
churrería *f.* shop where CHURROS are made and sold.
churrero, -ra *m.-f.* maker or seller of CHURROS.
churriento, -ta *adj.* dirty, greasy.
churrigueresco, -ca *adj.* F. ARTS Churrigueresque.
churro, -rra *adj.* coarse-wooled [sheep]. *2* coarse [wool]. *3 m.* a long cylindrical fritter.
churrusco *m.* burnt piece of bread.
churumbel *m.* coll. child.
churumbela *f.* MUS. kind of flageolet.
chuscada *f.* joke, pleasantry.
chusco, -ca *adj.* droll, funny. *2 m.* funny [person].
chusma *f.* rabble, mob. *2* galley slaves.
chutar *intr.* FOOTBALL to shoot.
chuzo *m.* short pike: fig. *caer* or *llover chuzos*, to rain pitchforks.
chuzón, -na *adj.* crafty, sly. *2* BURLÓN.

D

D, d *f*. D, d, the fifth letter of the Spanish alphabet.
daca (word formed by *da*, and *acá*) give me.
Dacia *f. pr. n.* GEOG. Dacia.
dacio, -cia *adj.-m.* Dacian.
dactilar *adj.* digital, finger: *huella* ~, fingerprint.
dáctilo *m.* dactyl.
dactilografía *f.* typewriting.
dactilógrafo, -fa *m.-f.* typist.
dactilología *f.* dactylology.
dactiloscopia *f.* dactyloscopy.
dádiva *f.* gift, present.
dadivoso, -sa *adj.* bounteous, liberal.
dado, -da *adj.* given. *2 conj. dado que*, assuming that, if. *3 m.* ARCH. dado, die. *4* MACH. block. *5* die [used in gaming].
dador, -ra *m.-f.* giver. *2* bearer [of a letter]. *3* drawer [of a bill of exchange].
daga *f.* dagger. *2* line of bricks in a kiln.
daguerrotipo *m.* daguerreotype.
daifa *f.* concubine.
¡dale! or **¡dale que dale!** *interj.* at it again! [expressing displeasure at another's obstinacy]. *2 estar* ~ *que* ~, to insist, to persist.
dalia *f.* BOT. dahlia.
Dalila *f. pr. n.* Delilah.
Dalmacia *f. pr. n.* GEOG. Dalmatia.
dálmata *adj.-n.* Dalmatian.
dalmática *f.* dalmatic [vestment].
dalmático, -ca *adj.* Dalmatian.
daltonismo *m.* MED. Daltonism.
dallar *tr.* to scythe [mow with a scythe].
dalle *m.* scythe.
dama *f.* lady, dame. *2* lady in waiting. *3* mistress, concubine. *4* king [in draughts]. *5* queen [in chess]. *6* THEAT. actress: *primera* ~, leading lady. *7* FOUN. dam. *8* GAMO. *9* BOT. ~ *de noche*, night jasmine. *10 pl.* draughts, *checkers.
damaceno, -na *adj.* DAMASCENO.
damajuana *f.* demijohn.
damasceno, -na *adj.-n.* Damascene. *2 adj.-f.* BOT. damson [plum].
Damasco *f. pr. n.* GEOG. Damascus.
damasco *m.* damask [fabric]. *2* BOT. a variety of apricot.
damasquinado, -da *adj.* damascened. *2 m.* damascene work.
damasquinar *tr.* to damascene.
damasquino, -na *adj.* Damascene.

damería *f.* affected nicety, mincing. *2* scruple.
damisela *f.* young lady, damsel. *2* courtesan.
damnificado, -da *m.-f.* injured party.
damnificar *tr.* to damage, hurt, injure.
dandi *m.* dandy.
danés, -sa *adj.* Danish. *2 m.-f.* Dane. *3 m.* Danish [language].
dango *m.* ORN. gannet.
danta *f.* ZOOL. elk. *2* ZOOL. tapir.
dantesco, -ca *adj.* Dantesque.
danubiano, -na *adj.-n.* Danubian.
Danubio *m. pr. n.* Danube.
danza *f.* dance; dancing: ~ *de cintas*, maypole dance. *2* HABANERA. *3* dubious or entangled affair.
danzador, -ra *adj.* dancing. *2 m.-f.* dancer.
danzante, -ta *m.-f.* dancer. *2* coll. active person, hustler. *3* coll. whippersnapper.
danzar *intr.* to dance. *2* to be [in an affair].
danzarín, -na *m.-f.* good dancer. *2* professional dancer. *3* coll. whippersnapper.
danzón *m.* a Cuban dance.
dañable *adj.* harmful. *2* condemnable.
dañado, -da *adj.* evil, wicked. *2* [of food, fruits, etc.] damaged, spoiled, tainted.
dañar *tr.* to harm, damage, injure, hurt. *2* to spoil, taint. *3 ref.* to become damaged, to spoil; to get hurt.
dañino, -na *adj.* harmful, destructive. *2* evil, wicked.
daño *m.* harm, damage, detriment, injury: *daños y perjuicios*, damages; *en* ~ *de*, to the detriment of. *2* hurt.
dañoso, -sa *adj.* harmful, noxious, damaging.
dar *tr.* to give [in nearly every sense], hand, deliver, grant, confer. *2* to produce, bear, yield [fruits, profits, etc.]. *3* to deal [cards]. *4* to produce, cause, excite; ~ *lástima*, to excite pity. *5* to strike [the hours]: *el reloj da las cinco*, the clock strikes five. *6* to show [at theatre, etc.]. *7* with some nouns it expresses the action implied by the noun: ~ *cabezadas*, to nod; ~ *comienzo*, or *principio*, to begin; ~ *gritos* or *voces*, to shout; ~ *un abrazo*, to embrace; ~ *un paseo*, to take a walk. *8 dar como* or *por*, to suppose, assume, consider, hold: ~ *como cierto*, to hold as true; ~ *por bueno*, to approve. *9* ~ *de puñetazos, tiros*, etc., to punch, shoot, etc.; ~ *de barniz, de pin-*

tura, etc., to overlay with varnish, paint, etc. *10* other senses: ~ *a conocer*, to make known; ~ *a entender*, to hint; ~ *a luz*, to give birth to; to publish: ~ *crédito a*, to believe; ~ *de lado*, to shun; ~ *de mano*, to leave, abandon; ~ *la enhorabuena*, to congratulate; ~ *que decir*, to set tongues wagging; ~ *que hacer*, to give trouble; ~ *que pensar*, to arouse suspicions, to set one thinking; ~ *señales*, to show sign; *no da pie con bola*, he does nothing right.
11 intr. to feel, to be stricken with or by: *me dio un dolor*, I was stricken by or with a pain. *12* ~ *a:* a) to overlook, open on, face: *esta ventana da a la calle*, the window overlooks the street. b) to work: ~ *a la bomba*, to work the pump. *13* ~ *con*, to meet, to find. *14* ~ *consigo en*, to land in. *15* ~ *contra*, to knock against. *16* ~ *de:* a) to fall on [one's head, etc.]. b) to give [food or drink]: ~ *de comer*, to feed. *17* ~ *en:* a) to take to, to acquire the habit of: *dio en salir todos los días*, he took to going out every day. b) to strike, hit, fall against: ~ *en el clavo*, to hit the nail on the head. c) to hit upon, to guess. *18 darle a uno por*, to take it into one's head; to take to. *19* other senses: ~ *al traste con*, to spoil, destroy, shatter; ~ *con uno en tierra*, to throw or bring one to the ground; ~ *de sí*, to give, yield, stretch. *20 ref.* to give oneself. *21* to yield, surrender, give in. *22* to take to: *darse a la bebida*, to take to drink. *23* [of things, events, etc.] to happen, exist, to be, to be given: *se da el caso*, (as) it happens, the case is. *24* other senses: *darse [uno] a conocer*, to identify oneself, to make oneself known; to allow one's real character to be seen; *darse la mano*, to shake hands; *darse por muerto*, to give oneself up for dead; *darse por vencido*, to give up. ¶ CONJUG.: INDIC. Pres.: *doy, das, da; damos, dais, dan.* | Imperf.: *daba, dabas*, etc. | Pret.: *di, diste, dio; dimos, disteis, dieron.* | Fut.: *daré, darás*, etc. | COND.: *daría, darías*, etc. | SUBJ. Pres.: *dé, des, dé; demos, deis, den.* | Imperf.: *diera, dieras*, etc., or *diese, dieses*, etc. | Fut.: *diere, dieres*, etc. | IMPER.: *da, dé; demos, dad, den.* | PAST. P.: *dado.* | GER.: *dando.*

dardabasí *m.* ORN. kite.
Dardanelos *m. pr. n.* GEOG. Dardanelles.
dardo *m.* dart [missile]. *2* cutting remark. *3* ICHTH. bleak.
dares y tomares *m. pl.* coll. disputes, discussions.
Darío *m. pr. n.* Darius.
dársena *f.* inner harbour, dock, basin.
darvinismo *m.* Darwinism.
dasocracia, dasonomía *f.* science of forestry.
data *f.* date [in documents, etc.]. *2* ACC. credit. *3 de larga* ~, very ancient.
datar *tr.* to date [mark with date]. *2* ACC. to credit on an account. *3 intr.* ~ *de*, to date from.
dátil *m.* BOT. date [fruit]. *2* ZOOL. date shell.
datilera *f.* BOT. date palm.
dativo *m.* GRAM. dative.
dato *m.* datum, fact. *2* document, testimony. *3* MAT. datum.
David *m. pr. n.* David.
1) **de** *f.* name of the letter *d*.
2) **de** *prep.* of [in practically every sense]. *2* from, about, for, on, by, at, out of, with: *viene* ~ *Madrid*, he comes from Madrid; *goma* ~ *mascar*, gum for chewing; *llorar* ~ *alegría*, to weep for joy; *un libro* ~ *matemáticas*, a book on mathematics; *la casa* ~ *la derecha*, the house on the

right; *un cuadro* ~ *Velázquez*, a painting by Velázquez; ~ *día*, by day; ~ *noche*, at night; ~ *diez uno*, one out of ten; *loco* ~ *rabia*, mad with anger. *3* if, should [conditional]: ~ *ir a pie, llegaríamos tarde*, if we went on foot, we'd arrive late. *4* [preceded by *más* or *menos*] than. *5* Other uses: *María Suárez* ~ *López*, Mrs. López, née Suárez; *este diablillo* ~ *criatura*, this imp of a child; *el bueno* ~ *Juan*, that good fellow John; ~ *pie*, standing up; ~ *un*, ~ *una*, at a, in one; ~ *uno en uno*, one by one; *¡pobre* ~ *mí!*, woe is me!
dé *irr.* V. DAR.
deambular *tr.* to walk, stroll.
deán *m.* ECCL. dean.
deanato, deanazgo *m.* ECCL. deanship.
debajo *adv.* underneath: ~ *de*, under, beneath; *por* ~, underneath; *por* ~ *de*, under, below.
debate *m.* debate. *3* altercation.
debatir *tr.* to debate, discuss.
debe *m.* COM. debit, debtor side of an account.
debelador, -ra *m.-f.* conqueror.
debelar *tr.* to conquer, to vanquish [in war].
1) **deber** *m.* duty obligation. *2* school work, homework.
2) **deber** *tr.* to owe. *2 aux.* [with an inf.] must, have to; ought to, should: *debo salir*, I must go out. *3* ~ *de*, must [expressing conjecture]: *deben de ser las cinco*, it must be five o'clock.
debidamente *adv.* duly, properly.
debido, -da *adj.* owed. *2* due, just, proper, right: *como es* ~, rightly, well, as it should be.
débil *adj.* weak, feeble. *2* slight, faint. *3* faint, sickly.
debilidad *f.* weakness, debility, feebleness.
debilitación *f.* debilitation. *2* weakness.
debilitar *tr.* to weaken, enfeeble, debilitate. *2 ref.* to weaken, become feeble, lose strength.
débito *m.* debt. *2* ~ *conyugal*, conjugal duty.
debut *m.* GALL. debut [first performance].
debutante *n.* débutante. *2* beginner.
debutar *intr.* GALL. to make one's debut.
década *f.* decade.
decadencia *f.* decadence, decline, decay.
decadente *adj.* decadent, declining.
decaedro *m.* GEOM. decahedron.
decaer *intr.* to decline, decay, to be in decadence, fall, fall off, lessen.
decágono, -na *adj.-m.* GEOM. decagon.
decagramo *m.* decagram.
decaído, -da *adj.* declining. *2* low [sick person]. *3* ~ *de ánimo*, disheartened.
decaimiento *m.* decline, decay. *2* weakness.
decalitro *m.* decaliter.
decálogo *m.* decalogue.
decampar *intr.* [of an army] to decamp.
decanato *m.* deanship, deanery [of a faculty]; doyenship [of a body].
decano *m.* dean [of a faculty]. *2* doyen, dean [of a body].
decantación *f.* decantation.
decantar *tr.* to decant. *2* to overpraise.
decapante *adj.* scaling. *2* scaling product, scaler [metals], remover [paint].
decapitación *f.* beheading, decapitation.
decapitar *tr.* to behead, decapitate.
decápodo, -da *adj.-n.* ZOOL. decapod.
decárea *f.* decare.
decasílabo, -ba *adj.* decasyllabic. *2 m.* decasyllable.
decena *f.* ten [ten unities]. *2 pl.* ARITH. tens.

decenal *adj.* decennial.
decencia *f.* decency, propriety. *2* decorum, modesty. *3* cleanliness, tidiness. *4* honesty.
deceno, -na *adj.* tenth.
decentar *tr.* to begin the use of, to cut the first slice of. *2* to begin to impair [the health, etc.]. *3 ref.* to get bedsores. ¶ CONJUG. like *acertar.*
decente *adj.* decent. *2* proper, decorous, modest. *3* clean, tidy. *4* correct, hono(u)rable.
decenviro *m.* decemvir.
decepción *f.* disappointment, disillusionment. *2* deceit.
decepcionar *tr.* to disappoint, disillusion.
deciárea *f.* deciare.
decibel, decibelio *m.* PHYS. decibel.
decididamente *adv.* decidedly. *2* resolutely.
decidido, -da *adj.* decided. *2* determined.
decidir *tr.* to decide, settle. *2* to decide, determine, resolve [bring or come to a resolution]. *3 ref.* to make up one's mind.
decidor, -ra *adj. m.-f.* good talker, witty talker.
decigramo *m.* decigram.
decilitro *m.* deciliter.
décima *f.* tenth [tenth part]. *2* a ten-line stanza.
decimal *adj.-m.* decimal. *2* pertaining to tithes.
decímetro *m.* decimetre, decimeter.
décimo, -ma *adj.* tenth. *2 m.-f.* tenth. *3 m.* tenth part of lottery ticket.
decimoctavo, -va *adj.* eighteenth.
decimocuarto, -ta *adj.* fourteenth.
decimonono, -na *adj.* nineteenth.
decimoquinto, -ta *adj.* fifteenth.
decimoséptimo, -ma *adj.* seventeenth.
decimosexto, -ta *adj.* sixteenth.
decimotercero, -ra; decimotercio, -cia *adj.* thirteenth.
1) decir *tr.* to say, to talk, tell, speak: ~ *bien de,* to say well of, to speak well of; ~ *entre sí* or *para sí,* to say to oneself; ~ *mentiras,* to tell lies; ~ *misa,* to say mass; ~ *por* ~, to talk for talking's sake; ~ *verdad,* to speak the truth; ¡*diga!,* hello! [answering the telephone]; *el qué dirán,* what people will say; *querer* ~, to mean; *como quien dice, como si dijéramos,* so to speak; *es* ~, that is to say; *mejor dicho,* more properly speaking, rather. *2* to denote, show. *3* [with *bien* or *mal*] to suit, become, or not to suit, not to become. *4 ref.* to say to oneself. *5* to pretend to be. *6 se dice,* they say, it is said. ¶ CONJUG.: INDIC. Pres.: *digo, dices, dice;* decimos, decís, *dicen.* | Imperf.: *decía, decías,* etc. | Pret.: *dije, dijiste, dijo; dijimos, dijisteis, dijeron.* | Fut.: *diré, dirás,* etc. | COND.: *diría, dirías,* etc. | SUBJ. Pres.: *diga, digas, diga; digamos, digáis, digan.* | Imperf.: *dijera, dijeras, dijera; dijéramos, dijerais, dijeran* or *dijese, dijeses, dijese; dijésemos, dijeseis, dijesen.* | Fut.: *dijere, dijeres,* etc. | IMPER.: *di, diga; digamos,* decid, *digan.* | PAST. PART.: *dicho.* | GER.: *diciendo.*
2) decir *m.* say, saying, language: *al* ~ *de,* according to [someone]; *es un* ~, it is a manner of speaking. *2 el* ~ *de las gentes,* the opinion of the people.
decisión *f.* decision [act]; issue; judgement, verdict; order, command. *2* decision, resoluteness.
decisivo, -va *adj.* decisive, final, conclusive.
declamación *f.* declamation.
declamar *intr.-tr.* to declaim.
declamatorio, -ria *adj.* declamatory.
declaración *f.* declaration. *2* statement. *3* LAW deposition. *4* expounding, explanation. *5* proposal, declaration of love. *6* BRIDGE bid.

declaradamente *adv.* openly, declaredly.
declarado, -da *adj.* declared.
declarante *m.-f.* LAW deponent. *2* BRIDGE bidder.
declarar *tr.* to declare. *2* to state, make known, avow. *3* to expound, explain. *4* LAW to find [guilty or not guilty]; to decide. *5 intr.* to testify, make a statement. *6 ref.* to declare oneself. *7* to let one's feelings, purposes, etc., be known; to propose [to a woman]. *8* [of war] to be declared. *9* [of a fire, an epidemic, etc.] to start, break out.
declaratorio, -ria *adj.* explanatory. *2* LAW declaratory.
declinable *adj.* GRAM. declinable.
declinación *f.* decline, fall, descent. *2* ASTR., MAGN. declination. *3* GRAM. declension.
declinante *adj.* declining.
declinar *intr.* to decline, lean, deviate. *4* to decline, decay, sink, fall off, decrease; draw to close. *4* ASTR., MAGN. to have declination. *5 tr.* to decline, renounce. *6* GRAM. to decline.
declive *m.* declivity, slope, descent.
decocción *f.* decoction.
decolorar *tr.* to decolo(u)rize.
decolorante *adj.-m.* decolorant.
decomisar *tr.* COMISAR.
decomiso *m.* COMISO.
decoración *f.,* **decorado** *m.* decoration, adorning. *2* decoration, adornment. *3* THEAT. scenery, setting.
decorador, -ra *m.-f.* decorator.
decorar *tr.* to decorate, adorn, embellish.
decorativo, -va *adj.* decorative.
decoro *m.* decorum, propriety, decency, dignity. *2* circumspection, gravity. *3* modesty, honour. *5* honour, respect, reverence [due to a person].
decoroso, -sa *adj.* decorous, decent.
decrecer *intr.* to decrease, diminish.
decreciente *adj.* decreasing, diminishing.
decrecimiento *m.* decrease, diminution.
decremento *m.* decrement, decrease.
decrepitar *intr.* to decrepitate [crackle under heat].
decrépito, -ta *adj.* decrepit.
decrepitud *f.* decrepitude.
decretal *adj.-f.* decretal.
decretar *tr.* to decree, ordain, resolve, determine.
decreto *m.* decree. *2* an order of a judge.
decúbito *m.* decubitus, lying down position.
décuplo, -pla *adj.-m.* decuple.
decurión *m.* decurion.
decurso *m.* course, lapse [of time].
decusado, -da; decuso, -sa *adj.* BOT. decussate(d.
dechado *m.* example, model, pattern. *2* sampler [to learn needlework].
dedada *f.* small portion [of honey, etc.].
dedal *m.* thimble. *2* thimbleful. *3* leather fingerstail.
dedalera *f.* BOT. foxglove.
Dédalo *m. pr. n.* MYTH. Daedalus.
dédalo *m.* labyrinth, maze.
dedicación *f.* dedication, consecration. *2* dedication [dedicatory inscription on a building].
dedicar *tr.* to dedicate [a church, a book, etc.]. *2* to autograph [a photograph]. *3* to dedicate, devote. *4 ref. dedicarse a,* to devote oneself to, to make a specialty of.
dedicatoria *f.* dedication [in a book, etc.]; autograph [on a photograph].
dedil *m.* fingerstall.
dedillo *m.* little finger. *2 saber una cosa al* ~, to have something at one's finger tips.

dedo *m.* finger; toe: ~ *de la mano,* finger; ~ *del pie,* toe; ~ *anular,* ring finger; ~ *meñique,* little finger; ~ *del medio* or *del corazón,* middle finger; ~ *gordo,* thumb; big toe; ~ *pulgar,* thumb; ~ *índice,* forefinger, index; *cogerse los dedos,* to burn one's fingers; *chuparse los dedos,* to enjoy, relish [something] greatly; *no mamarse el* ~, to be no fool; *poner el* ~ *en la llaga,* to put one's finger on the sore spot; *señalar a uno con el* ~, to point one's finger at someone. *2* finger's breath; fig. very small distance: *estar a dos dedos de,* to be within an ace of.
deducción *f.* deduction, inference, conclusion. *2* deduction, rebate, discount.
deducible *adj.* deducible, inferable. *2* COM. deductible, allowable.
deducir *tr.* to deduce, deduct, infer. *2* to deduct, rebate, discount. *3* LAW to put forward, allege. ¶ CONJUG. like *conducir.*
deductivo, -va *adj.* deductive.
deduje, dedujera, deduzco, deduzca, etc. *irr.* V. DEDUCIR.
defalcar *tr.* DESFALCAR.
defecación *f.* defecation.
defecar *tr.-intr.* to defecate.
defasaje *m.* ELECT. dephasing, phaseshift, phase difference. *2* gap, difference.
defección *f.* defection, desertion.
defectillo *m. dim.* slight fault or defect.
defectivo, -va *adj.* defective, faulty. *2* GRAM. defective.
defecto *m.* defect, fault, failing, blemish, imperfection. *2* default, lack: *en* ~ *de,* in default of.
defectuoso, -sa *adj.* defective, faulty.
defendedor, -ra *adj.* defending. *2 m.-f.* defender.
defender *tr.-ref.* to defend. ¶ CONJUG. like *entender.*
defendible *adj.* defensible.
defensa *f.* defence, *defense. *2* protection, guard. *3 m.* FOOTBALL back. *4 f. pl.* FORT. defences. *5* NAUT. fenders, skids. *6* horns [of bull], antlers [of deer], tusks [of elephant or boar].
defensión *f.* defence, protection.
defensivo, -va *adj.* defensive. *2 f.* defensive: *estar a la* ~, to be on the defensive.
defensor, -ra *adj.* defending, protecting. *2 m.-f.* defender. *3* advocate, supporter. *4* LAW counsel for the defence.
deferencia *f.* deference.
deferente *adj.* deferential. *2* deferring [to another's opinion]. *3* ANAT. deferent.
deferir *intr.* to defer [to another's wishes, opinions, etc.]. ¶ CONJUG. like *hervir.*
deficiencia *f.* defect, fault, deficiency.
deficiente *adj.* deficient, faulty.
deficientemente *adv.* insufficiently, poorly.
déficit *m.* deficit, shortage.
deficitario, -ria *adj.* showing a deficit.
defiendo, defienda, etc. *irr.* V. DEFENDER.
defiero, defiera, etc. *irr.* V. DEFERIR.
definición *f.* definition.
definido, -da *adj.* definite. *2* defined, sharp. *3 m.* defined thing.
definidor, -ra *adj.* defining. *2 m.-f.* definer. *3* ECCL. definitor.
definir *tr.* to define. *2* PAINT. to finish, complete.
definitivamente *adv.* finally. *2* for good, once and for all. *3* decisively.
definitivo, -va *adj.* definitive. *2 f. en definitiva,* after all, in conclusion, in short.
deflación *f.* ECON. deflation.
deflagración *f.* deflagration.

deflagrar *intr.* to deflagrate.
deflector *m.* deflector, baffle. *2* NAUT. deflector.
deflegmar *tr.* CHEM. to dephlegmate.
defoliación *f.* BOT. defoliation.
deformación *f.* deformation. *2* MECH. distorsion.
deformar *tr.* to deform, misshape, put out of shape. *2 ref.* to become deformed.
deforme *adj.* deformed, misshapen, ugly.
deformidad *f.* deformity, ugliness. *2* gross error.
defraudación *f.* defraudation.
defraudador, -ra *m.-f.* defrauder.
defraudar *tr.* to defraud, rob, cheat. *2* to frustrate, disappoint. *3* to deceive [hopes].
defunción *f.* death, decease, demise.
degeneración *f.* degeneration. *2* degeneracy.
degenerado, -da *adj.-n.* degenerate.
degenerar *intr.* to degenerate.
deglución *f.* deglutition, swallowing.
deglutir *tr.* to swallow.
degollación *f.* decollation, beheading.
degolladero *m.* neck [of animals]. *2* slaughter-house. *3* scaffold where people were beheaded.
degolladura *f.* slash, gash in the throat. *2* joint [between bricks]. *3* slender part of balusters.
degollante *adj.* presumptuous, boring. *2 m.-f.* bore, nuisance.
degollar *tr.* to decollate, behead; to cut the throat. *2* to cut [a garment] low in the neck. *3* fig. to destroy, ruin. ¶ CONJUG. like *contar.*
degollina *f.* massacre, slaughter, butchery.
degradación *f.* degradation.
degradante *adj.* degrading.
degradar *tr.* to degrade. *2 ref.* to degrade oneself, to become degraded.
degüello *m.* decollation; throat-cutting: *entrar a* ~, MIL. to take a town without giving quarter. *2* slender part, neck [of dart, etc.].
degüello, degüelle, etc. *irr.* V. DEGOLLAR.
degustación *f.* tasting, degustation.
dehesa *f.* pasture ground.
dehiscente *adj.* BOT. dehiscent.
deicida *adj.* deicidal. *2 m.-f.* deicide [person].
deicidio *m.* deicide, slaying of Jesus.
deidad *f.* deity.
deificar *tr.* to deify. *2 ref.* THEOL. to become deified [by divine union].
deífico, -ca *adj.* deific.
deísmo *m.* deism.
deísta *adj.* deistic. *2 m.-f.* deist.
dejación *f.* abandonment, relinquishment.
dejadez *f.* laziness, negligence. *2* slovenliness, neglect [of one's things or oneself].
dejado, -da *adj.* lazy, negligent, slovenly. *2* lowspirited. *3 p. p.* of DEJAR.
dejamiento *m.* DEJACIÓN. *2* laziness, slovenliness. *3* lassitude. *4* dejection. *5* indifference.
dejar *tr.* to leave: ~ *aparte,* to leave aside; ~ *atrás,* to leave behind; to excel, surpass; ~ *en paz,* to leave alone, let be; ~ *por hacer,* to leave undone, put off doing. *2* to abandon, relinquish, let go. *3* to quit, depart from. *4* to permit, consent, allow, let: ~ *caer,* to let fall; ~ *que ruede la bola,* to let things alone. *5* to abandon, forsake. *6* to commit, entrust, leave in charge. *7* to give up. *8* to deposit. *9* to yield, bring [as a profit]. *10* to lend, *loan. *11* to bequeath. *12* ~ *de,* to omit, to stop, cease, desist; ~ *de escribir,* to stop writing; *no* ~ *de tener,* not to lack, not to be without. *13* COM. ~ *de cuenta,* to refuse delivery [of goods]. *14* ~ *frío* or *helado,* to surprise, astound. *15* ~ *plantado,* to abandon; to disappoint. *16* ~ *seco,* to

kill dead. *17 ref.* to abandon oneself; to neglect oneself. *18* to allow or let oneself [die, be seen, etc.]. *19 dejarse caer* [of a person], to drop or fall down purposely; fig. to turn up unexpectedly; fig. to let drop, to hint something. *20 dejarse de rodeos*, to come to the point; *déjate de tonterías*, quit your nonsense. *21 dejarse olvidado*, to forget; to omit, leave out. *22 dejarse ver*, to show, be easy to see; to appear in public, at friend's homes, etc.

deje *m.* slight accent, lilt, special inflection.

dejillo *m.* DEJO 2. 2 DEJO 3.

dejo *m.* DEJACIÓN I. *2* peculiar accent or inflexion in speaking. *3* aftertaste. *4* lassitude.

de jure *adv.* de jure.

del contraction of DE AND EL; OF THE.

delación *f.* accusation, denunciation, information.

delantal *m.* apron; pinafore.

delante *adv.* before, in front; ahead: ~ *de*, before, in front of, in the presence of: ahead of; in preference to; *por* ~, before; ahead.

delantera *f.* front, fore part. *2* front row [in theaters, etc.]. *3* lead, advance, advantage; *coger or tomar la* ~ *a*, to get ahead of, to outstrip, to get the start of: *tomar la* ~, to take the lead.

delantero, -ra *adj.* fore, front, foremost, first. *2 m.* SPORT. forward.

delatar *tr.* to accuse, denounce, inform against. *2* to betray, disclose. *3 ref.* to betray oneself.

delator, -ra *adj.* accusing, denouncing. *2* betraying, disclosing. *3 m.-f.* accuser, denouncer, informer.

delco *m.* AUTO. distributor.

dele *m.* PRINT. dele.

delectación *f.* delectation, pleasure.

delegación *f.* delegation. *2* office of a delegate. *3* COM. branch.

delegado, -da *adj.* delegated. *2 m.-f.* delegate, representative, commissioner, deputy.

delegar *tr.* to delegate.

deleitable *adj.* DELEITOSO.

deleitar *tr.* to delight, please. *2 ref.* to delight, take delight or pleasure.

deleite *m.* pleasure, delight, gratification.

deleitoso, -sa *adj.* delightful, pleasing, pleasurable.

deletéreo, -a *adj.* deleterious, poisonous.

deletrear *tr.* to spell, spell out [read by spelling].

deletreo *m.* spelling out [of words].

deleznable *adj.* frail, perishable, weak. *2* crumbly. *3* slippery.

délfico, -ca *adj.* Delphian, Delphic.

delfín *m.* dauphin. *2* ZOOL., ASTR. dolphin.

delfina *f.* dauphiness.

delga *f.* ELECT. commutator bar.

delgadez *f.* thinness, leanness, slenderness, tenuity. *3* acuteness, subtlety.

delgado, -da *adj.* thin, lean, slender, slim, lank. *2* tenuous, delicate. *3* acute, subtle. *4 m.* NAUT. dead rise. *5* flank [of an animal].

delgaducho, -cha *adj.* thinnish, rather emaciated.

deliberación *f.* deliberation [weighing in mind]. *2* deliberation, discussion, debate.

deliberadamente *adv.* deliberately, on purpose.

deliberado, -da *adj.* deliberate, intentional.

deliberante *adj.* deliberating, deliberative.

deliberar *intr.* to deliberate, consider, weigh in mind. *2* to deliberate, take counsel together, hold debate. *3 tr.* to determine, resolve.

deliberativo, -va *adj.* deliberative [pertaining to deliberation].

delicadeza *f.* delicateness, delicacy. *2* fineness. *3* softness, tenderness. *4* scrupulousness, honesty.

delicado, -da *adj.* delicate. *2* poor [health]. *3* subtle, ingenious. *4* touchy, fastidious. *5* scrupulous, honest.

delicaducho, -cha *adj.* sickly, of weak health.

delicia *f.* delight.

delicioso, -sa *adj.* delicious, delightful.

delictivo, -va; delictuoso, -sa *adj.* criminal, unlawful.

delicuescente *adj.* deliquescent.

delimitación *f.* delimitation.

delimitar *tr.* to delimit, delimitate.

delincuencia *f.* delinquency, criminality.

delincuente *adj.* delinquent, offending. *2 m.-f.* delinquent, criminal, offender.

delineación *f.* delineation, draft, drawing in outline.

delineante *adj.* delineating. *2* draughtsman, draftsman [who draws plans, etc.].

delinear *tr.* to delineate.

delinquir *intr.* to commit a transgression, offence or crime.

deliquio *m.* fainting, ecstasy, rapture.

delirante *adj.* delirious, raving.

delirar *intr.* to rave, wander, be delirious. *2* to rant, talk nonsense. *3* ~ *por*, to be mad for.

delirio *m.* delirium, raving.

delirium tremens *m.* MED. delirium tremens.

delito *m.* transgression, offence, crime.

delta *f.* delta [Greek letter]. *2* GEOG. delta.

deltoides *adj. m.* ANAT. deltoid [muscle].

deludir *tr.* to delude.

delusorio, -ria *adj.* delusive, delusory.

demacración *f.* emaciation.

demacrar *tr.* to emaciate. *2 ref.* to waste away become emaciated.

demagogia *f.* demagogism; demagogy.

demagógico, -ca *adj.* demagogic.

demagogo, -ga *m.-f.* demagogue.

demanda *f.* petition, request. *2* COM. demand. *3* question, inquiry. *4* enterprise, endeavour. *5* LAW claim, plaint, complaint: *entablar* ~, to begin an action at law. *6* search, quest: *ir en* ~ *de*, to go in search of, go looking for.

demandadero, -ra *m.-f.* messenger [in a convent, etc.].

demandado, -da *m.-f.* LAW. defendant.

demandante *m.-f.* LAW claimant, plaintiff.

demandar *tr.* to demand, ask for, beg, request. *2* to ask, inquire. *3* to wish for. *4* LAW to sue.

demarcación *f.* demarcation.

demarcar *tr.* to demarcate. *2* NAUT. to determine the bearings of [a ship].

demás *adj.* [with *lo, la, los, las*] the other, the rest of the. *2* in plural, may be used without article: *y* ~ *vehículos*, and other vehicles. *3 pron.* other, others, the rest: *los* ~, others, other people; *lo* ~, the rest; *por lo* ~, as to the rest, apart from this; *y* ~, and so on, etcetera. *4 adv.* besides. *5 por* ~, in vain; excessively.

demasía *f.* excess, superabundance: *en* ~, too much, excessively. *2* boldness, audacity. *3* insolence, disrespect. *4* outrage. *5* iniquity, misdeed.

1) **demasiado** *adv.* too, excessively; too much. *2 pron.* too much.

2) **demasiado, -da** *adj.* too much, too many.

demencia *f.* insanity, madness.

demente *adj.* demented, mad, insane. *2 m.-f.* lunatic, maniac, insane person.

demérito *m.* want of worth or merit. *2* demerit, that which divests of worth or merit.
demiurgo *m.* demiurge.
democracia *f.* democracy.
demócrata *adj.* democratic. *2 m.-f.* democrat.
democrático, -ca *adj.* democratic.
democratizar *tr.* to democratize.
Demócrito *m. pr. n.* Democritus.
demografía *f.* demography.
demoledor, -ra *adj.* demolishing, destructive. *2 m.-f.* demolisher.
demoler *tr.* to demolish, pull down, destroy.
demolición *f.* demolition, destruction.
demoníaco, -ca *adj.* demoniac(al.
demonio *m.* demon, devil, evil spirit: *ser un ~*, fig. to be very wicked, roguish or cleever. *2 interj.* the deuce!
demonolatría *f.* demonolatry.
demontre *m.* coll. devil. *2 interj.* the deuce!
demora *f.* delay: *sin ~*, without delay. *2* NAUT. bearing.
demorar *tr.* to delay, retard. *2 intr.* to delay, tarry, linger. *3* NAUT. to bear.
Demóstenes *m. pr. n.* Demosthenes.
demostrable *adj.* demonstrable.
demostración *f.* demonstration, show. *2* demonstration, proof, evidence.
demostrador, -ra *m.-f.* demonstrator.
demostrar *tr.* to demonstrate, show, prove. *2 ref.* to show oneself. ¶ CONJUG. like *contar*.
demostrativo, -va *adj.* demonstrative. *2 adj.-m.* GRAM. demonstrative.
demótico, -ca *adj.* demotic.
demudar *tr.* to change, alter, vary. *2 ref.* to become disturbed, change colour or countenance.
demuelo, demuela, etc. *irr.* V. DEMOLER.
demuestro, demuestre, etc. *irr.* V. DEMOSTRAR.
denario, -ria *adj.* denary. *2 m.* denarius.
dendrita *f.* ANAT., GEOL. dendrite.
denegación *f.* denial, refusal.
denegar *tr.* to deny, refuse. ¶ CONJUG. like *acertar*.
denegatorio, -ria *adj.* denying.
dengoso, -sa *adj.* finicky, mincing, affected.
dengue *m.* mincing, affectation of delicacy. *2* MED. dengue, influenza.
deniego, deniegue, etc. *irr.* V. DENEGAR.
denigrante *adj.* denigrating; insulting.
denigrar *tr.* to denigrate, debase, vilify. *2* to insult.
denodadamente *adv.* bravely, boldly, intrepidly. *2* stoutly, determinedly.
denodado, -da *adj.* bold, brave, intrepid, resolute.
denominación *f.* denomination, name, designation.
denominado *adj.* MAT. compoud [number].
denominador, -ra *adj.* denominating. *2 m.* MATH. denominator.
denominar *tr.* to denominate, call, give a name to.
denostador *m.-f.* reviler, railer, insulter.
denostar *tr.* to revile, rail, insult. ¶ CONJUG. like *contar*.
denotación *f.* denotation.
denotar *tr.* to denote.
densidad *f.* density [closeness, compactness]. *2* obscurity, confusion. *3* PHYS. density. *4 ~ de población*, density of population.
densificar *tr.* to densify.
denso, -sa *adj.* dense, close, compact, thick. *2* dark, confused.
dentado, -da *adj.* dentate, toothed, cogged: *rueda dentada*, cogwheel. *2 m.* MACH. teeth [of a wheel]. *3* PHILAT. perforation.

dentadura *f.* denture, set of teeth.
dental *adj.* dental. *2 m.* ploughshare bed.
dentar *tr.* to tooth, furnish with teeth or cogs; to indent, cut into teeth. *2 intr.* to teethe, cut one's teeth. ¶ CONJUG. like *acertar*.
dentario, -ria *adj.* dental.
dentellada *f.* bite, biting: *a dentelladas*, with the teeth. *2* mark made by the teeth.
dentellado, -da *adj.* dentated. *2* HER. dentelated.
dentellar *intr.* to have the teeth chattering.
dentellear *tr.* to bite, nibble at.
dentellón *m.* cam, tooth [of lock]. *2* ARCH. dentil. *3* ARCH. tooth [of toothing].
dentera *f.* tooth edge. *2* coll. envy. *3* coll. desire. *4 dar ~*, to set the teeth on edge; to awaken desire
dentición *f.* dentition, teething.
denticulado, -da *adj.* denticulate.
denticulo *m.* ARCH. dentil. *2* denticle, dentation.
dentífrico, -ca *adj.* tooth [paste, powder, etc.]. *2 m.* dentifrice.
dentina *f.* ANAT. dentine.
dentirrostro, -tra *adj.* ORN. dentirostral, dentirostrate. *2 m.* ORN. dentiroster.
dentista *m.* dentist.
dentón, -na *adj.* DENTUDO. *2 m.* ICHTH. dentex.
dentro *adv.* in, inside, within: *~ de un sobre*, in an envelope; *~ de una hora*, within an hour; *~ de poco*, soon, shortly; *de ~*, from the inside; *por ~*, inside, inwardly, on the inside.
dentudo, -da *adj.* big-toothed.
denudación *f.* denudation.
denudar *tr.* ZOOL., BOOT., GEOL. to denude, lay bare. *2 ref.* to be denuded.
denuedo *m.* bravery, intrepidity, vigor.
denuesto *m.* insult, abuse.
denuncia *f.* denouncement. *2* report [of a transgression]. *3* denunciation [of a treaty]. *4* MIN. registration [of a mine or claim].
denunciación *f.* denouncing, denouncement.
denunciante *adj.* denouncing. *2 m.-f.* denouncer.
denunciar *tr.* to denounce. *2* to inform against, to accuse. *3* to report [the commission of a transgression or offence]. *4* to denounce [a treaty], etc.]. *5* MIN. to denounce.
deontología *f.* deontology.
deontológico, -ca *adj.* deontological.
deparar *tr.* to afford, furnish, offer, present.
departamental *adj.* departmental.
departamento *m.* department. *2* district. *3* compartment, section. *4* naval district. *5* (Am.) apartment.
departir *intr.* to chat, talk, converse.
depauperar *tr.* to depauperate, impoverish, weaken, exhaust. *2 ref.* to become depauperate.
dependencia *f.* dependence, dependency [subordination, subjection]. *2* branch office, section. *3* affair, errand. *4* staff, personnel, employees. *6 pl.* accessories. *7* outbuildings.
depender *intr.* *~ de*, to depend on; be subordinate to.
dependienta *f.* female employee or shop assistant.
dependiente *adj.* depending, dependent, subordinate. *2 m.* clerk, salesman, shop assistant, employee. *3* subordinate.
depilación *f.* depilation.
depilar *tr.* to depilate.
depilatorio, -ria *adj.-m.* depilatory.
deplorable *adj.* deplorable, sad, lamentable.
deplorar *tr.* to deplore, lament, regret.
depondré, depondría, etc. *irr.* V. DEPONER.

deponente *adj.* GRAM. deponent. *2 m.-f.* LAW deponent.

deponer *tr.* to lay aside, set aside [fears, etc.]. *2* to lay down [one's arms]. *3* to depose, remove from office. *4* to take down. *5 tr.-intr.* LAW to depose, depone. *6 intr.* to go to stool. ¶ CONJUG. like *poner.*

depongo, deponga, etc. *irr.* V. DEPONER.

deportación *f.* deportation, exile, transportation.

deportar *tr.* to deport, exile, transport.

deporte *m.* sport [outdoor pastime]. *2* amusement, recreation.

deportismo *m.* sports, sporting.

deportista *m.* sportsman. *2 f.* sportswoman. *3 m.-f.* sport fan.

deportividad *f.* sportsmanship.

deportivo, -va *adj.* sports, sporting, sportive. *2* sportsmanlike.

deposición *f.* exposition, declaration. *2* deposal, deposition [removal from office]. *3* LAW deposition; sworn evidence. *4* evacuation of bowels.

depositante *m. f.* depositor.

depositar *tr.* to deposit. *2* to place, put. *3* to check [luggage]. *4 intr.* [of dust, a sediment, etc.] to settle, deposit.

depositaria *f.* place where deposits are made. *2* public treasury.

depositario, -ria *m.-f.* depositary. *2* public treasurer.

depósito *m.* deposit; trust: *en ~*, on deposit; in trust. *2* precipitation, sediment. *3* depot, store, storehouse, warehouse, depository, repository. *4* tank, reservoir: *~ de gasolina,* AUTO. gas tank. *5* well [of a fountain pen]. *6 ~ de equipajes,* checkroom.

depravación *f.* depravation, depravity.

depravado, -da *adj.* bad, depraved.

depravar *tr.* to deprave, corrupt. *2 ref.* to become depraved, dissolute.

deprecación *f.* entreaty, prayer, imploration.

deprecar *tr.* to entreat, pray, implore.

deprecativo, -va; deprecatorio, -ria *adj.* entreating.

depreciación *f.* depreciation [in value].

depreciar *tr.* to depreciate [lessen in value]. *2 ref.* to depreciate [become depreciated].

depredación *f.* depredation. *2* malversation.

depredar *tr.* to depredate, plunder, pillage.

depresión *f.* depression [act of depressing]. *2* pression [sunken place], hollow, dip. *3* dejection, low spirits. *4* ASTR., MED., METEOR. depression.

depresivo, -va *adj.* depressive.

depresor, -ra *adj.* depressing. *2 m.* ANAT., SURG. depressor.

deprimente *adj.* depressing, depressive. *2* humiliating.

deprimir *tr.* to depress [press down, cause to sink]. *2* to humiliate, belittle. *3 ref.* to become depressed, sunken. *4* to feel humiliated. *5* [of a line or a surface] to dip.

depuesto *p. p.* of DEPONER.

depuración *f.* depuration, purification. *2* POL. purge.

depurado, -da *adj.* pure, purified.

depurar *tr.* to depurate, purify. *2* POL. to purge.

depurativo, -va *adj.-m.* MED. depurative.

depuse, depusiera, etc. *irr.* V. DEPONER.

derecha *f.* right; right-hand side, right side; *a la ~,* to the right, on the right-hand side. *2* right hand. *3* POL. right. *4 adv. a derechas,* well, right, rightly.

derechazo *m.* BULLF. pass with the right hand. *2* BOX. right.

derechista *m.-f.* POL. member of the right.

derecho, -cha *adj.* right, right-hand [opposite to left]. *2* straight. *3* standing, upright. *4* just, reasonable. *5* right-handed. *6 adv.* straight, straight on, directly. *7 m.* right [that to which one is entitled]: justice, equity: *~ de propiedad literaria,* copyright; *derechos del hombre,* rights of man; *tener ~ a,* to be entitled to; *de ~,* de jure, by right. *8* law [body of rules or laws]: *~ canónico,* canon law; *~ civil,* civil law; *~ mercantil,* commercial law; *~ natural,* natural law. *9* law [legal science or learning]. *10* exemption, grant, privilege. *11* right side, outside [of cloth, etc.]. *12* straight way; *ir por derecho,* to go straight. *13 pl.* fees, dues, taxes, duties: *derechos de aduana,* customs duties; *derechos de autor,* royalties, copyright; *derechos reales,* inheritance tax; duty on transfer of property.

derechura *f.* straightness, right way: *en ~,* directly, straight.

deriva *f.* NAUT., AER. drift, drifting: *ir a la ~,* to drift, be adrift.

derivable *adj.* derivable.

derivación *f.* derivation, descent. *2* inference. *3* drawing off [water, etc.] from a stream or source. *4* GRAM., MATH., MED. derivation. *5* ELECT. branch. *6* ELECT. shunt, shunt connection: *en ~,* shunt, shunted.

derivado, -da *adj.* derived, derivative. *2 m.* GRAM., CHEM. derivative. *3 f.* MATH. derivate, derivative.

derivar *tr.* to lead, conduct. *2* to derive. *3* ELECT. to shunt. *4 intr.-ref.* to derive, be derived. *5* AER., NAUT. to drift.

derivativo, -va *adj.* GRAM. derivative. *2 adj.-m.* MED. derivative.

derivo *m.* derivation, origin.

dermatoesqueleto *m.* ZOOL. dermatoskeleton.

dermatología *f.* dermatology.

dermatólogo *m.* dermatologist.

dérmico, -ca *adj.* dermic, dermal.

dermis *f.* ANAT. derma, dermis.

derogable *adj.* repealable, that can be abolished or annulled.

derogación *f.* abolishment, repeal, revocation.

derogar *tr.* to abolish, repeal, revoke. *2* to destroy, reform.

derrama *f.* apportionment of a tax, assessment or contribution. *3* special tax.

derramamiento *m.* overflowing, spilling. *2* outpouring. *3* shedding [of tears, etc.]. *4* scattering.

derramar *tr.* to pour out, to spill. *2* to shed [blood, tears, etc.]. *3* to scatter. *4* to spread [news]. *5 ref.* to overflow, run over; to spill [be spilled]. *6* to scatter, disperse [be dispersed].

derrame *m.* DERRAMAMIENTO. *2* leakage [of liquids]. *3* ARCH. splay. *4* declivity, slope. *5* NAUT. draft [of a sail]. *6* MED. effusion; discharge; *~ cerebral,* cerebral haemorrhage.

derramo *m.* ARCH. splay.

derrapar *intr.* AUTO. to skid.

derredor *m. al ~, en ~,* around, round about.

derrelicto *m.* NAUT. derelict.

derrengado, -da *adj.* coll. done up, aching all over.

derrengadura *f.* hip dislocation or hurt. *2* hurt or wound in the spine.

derrengar *tr.* to hurt seriously the spine or the hip of; to dislocate the hip of. *2* to tilt, inclinate. *3 ref.* to hurt one's spine or hip.

derretimiento *m.* fusion, melting, thaw, thawing. 2 consuming love.

derretir *tr.* to fuse, melt, thaw. 2 to consume, expend, waste. 3 *ref.* to fuse, melt, thaw [become liquid]. 4 to burn, be consumed [with love, with impatience]. ¶ Conjug. like *servir*.

derribar *tr.* to pull down, tear down, demolish. 2 to fell, knock down, throw, throw down. 3 to overthrow. 4 to bring down [game, etc.]. 5 *ref.* to tumble down, to throw oneself on the ground.

derribo *m.* pulling down, demolition. 2 *pl.* materials from demolished buildings.

derrito, derrita, etc. *irr.* V. DERRETIR.

derrocamiento *m.* throwing down. 2 pulling down, demolition. 3 overthrow.

derrocar *tr.* to precipitate from a rock. 2 to pull down, demolish. 3 to overthrow [from office, etc.].

derrochador, -ra *adj.* spending, extravagant. 2 *m.-f.* prodigal, spendthrift, squanderer, wastrel.

derrochar *tr.* to waste, squander, spend lavishly.

derroche *m.* waste, extravagance. 2 profusion.

derrota *f.* defeat, rout. 2 path, road. 3 NAUT. ship's curse.

derrotar *tr.* to defeat, rout. 2 to waste, dilapidate. 3 *ref.* NAUT. to drift from the course.

derrote *m.* upward thrust of a bull's horn.

derrotero *m.* NAUT. ship's course. 2 NAUT. navigation track. 3 route, course, way.

derrotismo *m.* defeatism.

derrotista *adj.-n.* defeatist.

derrubiar *tr.* to wash away [river banks].

derrubio *m.* washing away of banks by a stream.

derruido, -da *adj.* in ruins.

derruir *tr.* to pull down, demolish. ¶ Conjug. like *huir*.

derrumbadero *m.* precipice.

derrumbamiento *m.* fall [over a precipice]. 2 collapse, abrupt falling. 3 MIN. caving in.

derrumbar *tr.* to precipitate, throw down. 2 *ref.* to fall over a precipice. 3 to collapse, tumble down. 4 MIN. to cave in.

derrumbe *m.* precipice. 2 MIN. landslide, cave in.

derviche *m.* dervish.

desabastecer *tr.* to leave unprovided, unsupplied. ¶ Conjug. like *agradecer*.

desabollar *tr.* to knock the dents or bruises out of.

desabonarse *ref.* to drop one's subscription, to discontinue a subscription.

desaborido, -da *adj.* tasteless, insipid. 2 dull, insipid [person].

desabotonar *tr.* unbutton. 2 *ref.* to undo one's buttons. 4 to become unbuttoned.

desabrido, -da *adj.* tasteless, insipid. 2 gruff, surly, rude, disagreeable. 3 dirty [weather].

desabrigado, -da *adj.* lightly, dressed, uncovered. 2 unsheltered, unprotected, exposed.

desabrigar *tr.* to uncover, undress, to take off someone's warm clothes. 2 to deprive of shelter or protection. 3 *ref.* to uncover oneself, to take off one's warm clothes.

desabrigo *m.* lack of covering, clothing, sheltering or protection. 2 desertion, destitution.

desabrimiento *m.* insipidity, flatness. 2 gruffness, surliness. 3 displeasure, bitterness.

desabrir *tr.* to give a bad taste to. 2 to displease, annoy. 3 *ref.* to be annoyed.

desabrochar *tr.* to unclasp, unfasten, unbutton. 2 *ref.* to undo one's buttons or fastenings. 3 to become unfastened or unbuttoned.

desacalorarse *ref.* to cool off.

desacatar *tr.-ref.* to be disrespectful or irreverent toward; to disobey.

desacato *m.* disrespect, irreverence, contempt. 2 disobedience.

desacedar *tr.* to remove the acidity from.

desacertadamente *adv.* unwisely, wrongly, erroneously.

desacertado, -da *adj.* unwise, wrong, mistaken.

desacertar *tr.* to be wrong, err, make a mistake. ¶ Conjug. like *acertar*.

desacierto *m.* error, mistake, blunder.

declimatado, -da *adj.* unacclimatized.

desacobardar *tr.* to free from fear.

desacomodamiento *m.* uncomfortableness.

desacomodar *tr.* to deprive of ease or convenience. 2 to deprive [a servant] of his place. 3 *ref.* [of a servant] to lose his place.

desacomodo *m.* inconvenience. 2 unemployment.

desacompañar *tr.* to abandon, leave the company of.

desaconsejado, -da *adj.* ill-advised, imprudent.

desaconsejar *tr.* to dissuade.

desacoplar *tr.* to uncouple, disconnect.

desacordar *tr.* MUS. to put out of tune; to make discordant. 2 *ref.* MUS. to get out of tune. 3 to forget, be forgetful. ¶ Conjug. like *contar*.

desacorde *adj.* MUS. discordant. 2 disagreeing, incongruous.

desacostumbrado, -da *adj.* disaccustomed. 2 unusual.

desacostumbrar *tr.* to disaccustom. 2 *ref.* to lose a habit.

desacotar *tr.* to open up a preserved or reserved ground; to remove boundary marks of.

desacreditado, -da *adj.* discredited.

desacreditar *tr.* to discredit, bring discredit on. 2 *ref.* to lose credit, good repute or estimation.

desacuerdo *m.* disagreement, disaccord. 2 error, mistake.

desaderezar *tr.* to disarrange, ruffle.

desadormecer *tr.* to awaken. 2 to free from numbness. ¶ Conjug. like *agradecer*.

desadornar *tr.* to divest of adornments.

desafecto, -ta *adj.* disaffected; opposed. 2 *m.* disaffection, dislike.

desaferrar *tr.* to loosen, unfasten. 2 NAUT. to unfurl. 3 NAUT. to weigh anchor. 4 to bring [a person] to a change of mind or opinion.

desafiador, -ra *adj.* defiant, defying. 2 *m.-f.* challenger, defier.

desafiante *adj.* defiant. 2 challenging.

desafiar *tr.* to challenge, defy; to dare. 2 to rival, compete with.

desafición *f.* disaffection, indifference.

desaficionar *tr.* ~ *de,* to cause [one] to lose his liking, or inclination for.

desafinación *f.* being out of tune.

desafinadamente *adv.* out of tune.

desafinado, -da *adj.* out of tune.

desafinar *intr.* MUS. to be out of tune. 2 to speak indiscreetly or irrelevantly.

desafío *m.* challenge, defiance; daring. 2 rivalry, competition. 3 duel, combat.

desaforado, -da *adj.* reckless, lawless, outrageous. 2 huge, enormous.

desaforar *tr.* to encroach on the rights of someone, to deprive of one's privileges. 2 to act violently, to behave outrageously, to lose control, to get worked up.

desafortunado, -da *adj.* unlucky; unfortunate.

desafuero *m.* excess, outrage, violence.

desagraciado, -da *adj.* graceless, ungraceful.
desagradable *adj.* disagreeable, unpleasant.
desagradar *tr.* to be unpleasant to; to displease, offend. *2 ref.* to be displeased.
desagradecer *tr.* to be ungrateful for. ¶ Conjug. like *agradecer.*
desagradecido, -da *adj.* ungrateful.
desagradecimiento *m.* ungratefulness, ingratitude.
desagrado *m.* displeasure.
desagraviar *tr.* to make amends to, to right a wrong made to.
desagravio *m.* satisfaction for an injury, righting of a wrong, amends.
desagregación *f.* separation, disgregation.
desagregar *tr.* to separate, disgregate.
desaguadero, desaguador *m.* water oulet, drain.
desaguar *tr.* to drain [free of water], to empty. *2* to waste, to squander. *3 intr.* [of streams] to empty, flow [into].
desagüe *m.* drainage, drain. *2* water outlet.
desaguisado, -da *adj.* unjust, unreasonable. *2 m.* wrong, offence, outrage.
desaherrojar *tr.* to unchain, to unshackle.
desahogadamente *adv.* easily, comfortably. *2* impudently.
desahogado, -da *adj.* forward, impudent, cheeky, fresh. *2* roomy, unencumbered. *3 posición desahogada,* comfortable circumstances.
desahogar *tr.* to relieve [one] from care, worry, etc.; to relieve, alleviate [care, worry, etc.]. *2* to give free rein to [passions]; to vent [anger, etc.]. *3 ref.* to find relief from heat, fatigue, etc. *4* to relieve oneself from worry, debt, etc. *5* to vent one's anger, etc.; to relieve one's feelings; to unbosom oneself.
desahogo *m.* relief, respite [from care, worry, etc.]. *2* comfort, ease. *3* comfortable circumstances. *4* ample room. *5* forwardness, impudence, cheek. *6* relieving one's feelings; unbosoming oneself.
desahuciadamente *adv.* without hope.
desahuciar *tr.* to take away all hope from. *2* to condemn [a patient]. *3* LAW to evict, disposses [a tenant].
desahucio *m.* LAW eviction [of a tenant].
desairadamente *adv.* gracelessly, clumsily.
desairado, -da *adj.* graceless, unattractive. *2* unsuccessful, slighted, cutting a poor figure.
desairar *tr.* to slight, disregard, snub. *2* to reject, ignore [a petition].
desaire *m.* gracelessness. *2* slight, disregard.
desajustar *tr.* to disarrange, to disadjust.
desajuste *m.* disarrangement, lack of adjustment.
desalabear *tr.* to straighten, unwarp.
desalado, -da *adj.* desalted. *2* hasty, swift. *3* anxious, eager.
desalar *tr.* to desalt. *2* to cut off the wings of. *3 ref.* to hurry, to go swiftly. *4 desalarse por,* to be eager to, to yearn for.
desalentadamente *adv.* with discouragement.
desalentador, -ra *adj.* discouraging.
desalentar *tr.* to put out of breath. *2* to discourage. *3 ref.* to be discouraged. ¶ Conjug. like *acertar.*
desalfombrar *tr.* to take up the carpets from.
desalhajar *tr.* to dismantle [a room, a house].
desaliento *m.* discouragement. *2* faintness, weakness.
desaliento, desaliente, etc. *irr.* V. DESALENTAR.
desalineación *f.* desalignment.
desalinear *tr.* to desalign, to put out of alignment.

desaliñado, -da *adj.* untidy, unkempt, slovenly, slipshod. *2* untidy, careless, neglectful [person].
desaliñar *tr.* to disarrange, disorder, ruffle, make untidy. *2 ref.* to become disarranged, untidy.
desaliño *m.* untidiness, slovenliness; carelessness.
desalmado, -da *adj.* wicked, cruel, inhuman.
desalmar *tr.* to weaken [a thing]. *2* to disquiet, worry. *3 ref.* to be eager, to yearn [to or for].
desalojamiento *m.* dislodging, evacuation.
desalojar *tr.* to dislodge. *2* to evacuate. *3* NAUT., PHYS. to displace. *4* to empty. *5 intr.* to move out.
desalojo *m.* DESALOJAMIENTO.
desalquilado, -da *adj.* unrented, untenanted, vacant.
desalquilar *tr.* to leave, to vacate [a rented room or house].
desalterar *tr.* to calm, quiet.
desamable *adj.* unlovable.
desamar *tr.* to love no more. *2* to hate, dislike.
desamarrar *tr.* to untie, unfasten, loosen. *2* NAUT. to unmoor.
desambientado, -da *adj.* out of place. *2* that lacks athmosphere.
desamistarse *ref.* to quarrel, to become estranged.
desamoblar *m.* DESAMUEBLAR.
desamor *m.* disaffection, lack of love. *2* dislike, hate.
desamorado, -da *adj.* indifferent, cold.
desamortización *f.* freeing from mortmain.
desamortizar *tr.* to free from mortmain.
desamotinarse *ref.* to cease mutinying.
desamparado, -da *adj.* abandoned, deserted, helpless, unprotected. *2* needy, destitute.
desamparar *tr.* to abandon, forsake, desert, leave, helpless or unprotected. *2* to leave, quit [a place]. *3* NAUT. to dismantle.
desamparo *m.* abandonment, desertion; lack of protection; need, destitution.
desamueblado, -da *adj.* unfurnished.
desamueblar *tr.* to remove the furniture from.
desandar *tr.* to retrace, to go back over [the way travelled]: ~ *lo andado,* to retrace one's steps. ¶ Conjug. like *andar.*
desangelado, -da *adj.* dull, insipid.
desangrado, -da *adj. estar* ~, to have lost blood; *morir* ~, to bleed to death.
desangramiento *m.* bleeding to excess.
desangrar *tr.* to bleed to excess. *2* to drain [a lake, etc.]. *3 fig.* to bleed, to impoverish. *4 ref.* to bleed copiously, to lose much blood.
desanidar *intr.* to leave the nest. *2 tr.* to dislodge from a haunt.
desanimación *f.* discouragement, downheartedness. *2* lack of animation, dullness, unliveliness.
desanimado, -da *adj.* discouraged, downhearted, dispirited. *2* lacking in animation, dull. *3* poorly attended [party, etc.].
desanimar *tr.* to discourage, dishearten. *3 ref.* to become discouraged, disheartened.
desánimo *m.* discouragement, downheartedness.
desanudar *tr.* to untie, unknot. *2* to clear up, disentangle.
desaojar *tr.* to dispel the evil eye for.
desapacibilidad *f.* disagreeableness.
desapacible *adj.* unpleasant, disagreeable, harsh.
desaparear *tr.* to separate [the two of a pair].
desaparecer *intr.-ref.* to disappear.
desaparejar *tr.* to unsaddle [a pack animal]. *2* NAUT. to unrig.
desaparición *f.* disappearance.
desapasionado, -da *adj.* dispassionate, unbiased.

desapasionarse *ref.* to free oneself of love or fondness, to become indifferent.

desapegar *tr.* to detach, loosen, unglue. *2 ref.* to detach or unglue itself. *3* to lose one's love or liking [for]; to become indifferent [to].

desapego *m.* lack of affection, indifference.

desapercibido, -da *adj.* unprovided, unprepared, unguarded, unaware. *2 m.-f.* unnoticed.

desapercibimiento *m.* unpreparedness.

desaplicación *f.* lack of studiousness, laziness.

desaplicado, -da *adj.* not studious, lazy. *2 m.-f.* bad student.

desaplicarse *ref.* to become a bad student.

desaplomar *tr.* to put out of plumb. *2 ref.* to get out of plumb.

desapoderado, -da *adj.* impetuous, precipitate. *2* unbridled, wild, violent.

desapoderamiento *m.* dispossession of powers. *2* boundless freedom or licence.

desapoderar *tr.-ref.* to dispossess.

desapolillar *tr.* to clear of moths.

desapreciar *tr.* not to appreciate.

desaprender *tr.* to unlearn.

desaprensión *f.* unscrupulousness.

desaprensivo, -va *adj.* unscrupulous.

desapretar *tr.* to loosen. ¶ Conjug. like *acertar*.

desaprobación *f.* disapproval.

desaprobar *tr.* to disapprove, to disapprove of; to censure, blame. ¶ Conjug. like *contar*.

desapropiarse *ref.* to divest oneself [of property].

desaprovechado, -da *adj.* wasted, unproductive. *2* unprofiting, unproficient, backward.

desaprovechamiento *m.* waste, ill use, poor use. *2* lack of progress in studies, etc.

desaprovechar *tr.* to waste, to make no use of; to use to no advantage. *2 intr.* to make little or no progress in studies, etc.

desapuntalar *tr.* to remove the props or supports of.

desarbolar *tr.* NAUT. to dismast.

desarenar *tr.* to clear of sand.

desarmable *adj.* dismountable, collapsible.

desarmado, -da *adj.* unarmed. *2* dismounted, disassembled, taken to pieces.

desarmar *tr.* to disarm. *2* to dismount, take apart, disassemble. *3* NAUT. to lay up [a ship]. *4 intr.* to disarm.

desarme *m.* disarmament, disarming. *2* dismounting, disassembling. *3* NAUT. laying up.

desarmonizar *tr.* to disharmonize.

desarraigar *tr.* to uproot, root out, eradicate. *2* to exile. *3 ref.* to be uprooted. *4* to leave one's country or place of abode.

desarraigado, -da *adj.* uprooted [tree], uprooted, rootless [person]. *2* wiped out, erradicated.

desarraigo *m.* uprooting, eradication.

desarrapado, -da *adj.* DESHARRAPADO.

desarrebujar *tr.* to uncover, unbundle [a person]. *2* to disentangle. *3* to explain, elucidate.

desarregladamente *adv.* disorderly.

desarreglado, -da *adj.* disarranged, disorderly. *2* dishevelled, slovenly. *3* intemperate, extravagant, immoderate.

desarreglar *tr.* to disarrange, put out of order, to derange. *2 ref.* to become disarranged. *3* to become disorderly.

desarreglo *m.* disarrangement, disorder.

desarrimar *tr.* to move [a thing] away [from something]. *2* to dissuade.

desarrollado, -da *adj.* developed: *poco* ~, underdeveloped [country].

desarrollar *tr.* to unroll, to unwind, to unfurl. *2* to develop [form or expand by a process of growth]. *3* to develop, expound, work out [a theory, etc.]. *4* MATH., MEC. to develop. *5 ref.* to unroll, unwind, unfurl. *6* to develop, to grow. *7* [of a scene, action, etc.] to take place.

desarrollo *m.* unrolling, unwinding, unfurling. *2* development, growth, increase. *3* development, unfolding, working out [of a theory, etc.]. *4* MATH., MEC. development.

desarropar *tr.-ref.* to uncover, to take off covering clothes.

desarrugar *tr.* to smooth out, unwrinkle: ~ *el entrecejo*, to unknit the brow.

desarticular *tr.* to disarticulate, to put out of joint. *2* to take apart, disconnect, disjoint. *3 ref.* to come out of joint.

desartillar *tr.* to take the guns out of [a fort or ship].

desarzonar *tr.* to unhorse, unsaddle.

desaseado, -da *adj.* untidy, dirty, slovenly.

desasear *tr.* to make untidy, dirty, slovenly.

desasentar *tr.* to displace, move, remove. ¶ Conjug. like *acertar*.

desaseo *m.* untidiness, dirtiness, slovenliness.

desasimiento *m.* loosening, letting loose. *2* detachment, disinterest, disaffection.

desasimilación *f.* PHYSIOL. disassimilation.

desasir *tr.* to detach, to loosen. *2 ref. desasirse [de]*, to get loose, free oneself [of]; to let go; to give up. ¶ Conjug. like *asir*.

desasistir *tr.* to abandon, forsake.

desasnar *tr.* to educate, polish, civilize.

desasosegadamente *adv.* uneasily, anxiously.

desasosegar *tr.* to disquiet, worry, disturb, make uneasy or anxious. ¶ Conjug. like *acertar*.

desasosiego *m.* disquiet, uneasiness, anxiety.

desastrado, -da *adj.* wretched, unfortunate. *2* shabby, ragged, untidy.

desastre *m.* disaster, catastrophe.

desastrosamente *adv.* disastrously.

desastroso, -sa *adj.* disastrous, unfortunate. *2* very bad.

desatadamente *adv.* loosely, freely.

desatado, -da *adj.* loose, untied. *2* wild, fierce, violent.

desatalentado, -da *adj.* out of one's senses.

desatancar *tr.* to unclog [a pipe or channel].

desatar *tr.* to untie, undo, loose, loosen, unbind, unfasten. *2* to undo, solve, unravel. *3 ref.* to come untied. *4* to lose one's timidity or fear. *5* to burst forth, lose all restraint. *6* [of a storm, etc.] to break out, break loose.

desatascar *tr.* to pull out of the mud. *2* to unclog [a pipe, etc.]. *3* to extricate from difficulties. *4 ref.* to get out of the mud.

desatención *f.* inattention. *2* disregard, disrespect, discourtesy, slight.

desatender *tr.* to pay no attention to. *2* to be unheedful or unmindful of. *3* to neglect. *4* to disregard. ¶ Conjug. like *entender*.

desatentado, -da *adj.* unjudicious, unwise. *2* excessive, wild, disorderly.

desatentar *tr.* to derange, perturb the mind. ¶ Conjug. like *acertar*.

desatentamente *adv.* inattentively, carelessly. *2* rudely, impolitely, discourteously.

desatento, -ta *adj.* inattentive. *2* discourteous, impolite, unmannerly.

desatinado, -da *adj.* deranged, perturbed. *2* nonsensical, foolish, senseless.

desatinar *tr.* to perturb, rattle, derange. *2 intr.* to talk nonsense, to act foolishly. *3* to lose one's sense of direction or bearings.
desatino *m.* absurdity, nonsense, folly, error.
desatollar *tr.* to pull out of the mud.
desatornillar *tr.* to unscrew.
desatracar *tr.* NAUT. to move [a boat] away [from]. *2 ref.* [of a boat] to move away [from].
desatraillar *tr.* to unleash [dogs].
desatrancar *tr.* to unbar, unbolt [a door].
desatufarse *ref.* to get out of the close air; to clear one's head. *2* to calm down, to put off anger.
desaturdir *tr.-ref.* to rouse from a state of dizziness or stupor.
desautorización *f.* withdrawal of authority, disavowal.
desautorizado, -da *adj.* disauthorized, discredited.
desautorizar *tr.* to deprive of authority or credit, to disauthorize, to disavow.
desavenencia *f.* discord, disagreement, quarrel.
desavenido, -da *adj.* discordant, disagreeing, in bad terms.
desavenir *tr.* to make disagree. *2 ref.* to disagree, be at variance, quarrel. ¶ CONJUG. like *venir.*
desaventajado, -da *adj.* disadvantageous, inferior.
desavezar *tr.-ref.* DESACOSTUMBRAR.
desavisado, -da *adj.* unadvised; uninformed.
desavisar *tr.* to cancel a notice or summons.
desayunarse *ref.* to breakfast; ~ *con,* to breakfast on. *2 fig.* ~ *de,* to have first intelligence of.
desayuno *m.* breakfast.
desazogar *tr.* to remove the backing of [a mirror].
desazón *f.* insipidity. *2* displeasure, vexation, worry. *3* discomfort, uneasiness. *4* indisposition.
desazonado, -da *adj.* insipid. *2* annoyed, vexed. *3* uneasy. *4* indisposed.
desazonar *tr.* to render tasteless. *2* to displease, annoy; to cause discomfort or uneasiness. *3 ref.* to be displeased, annoyed. *4* to feel ill.
desbancar *tr.* NAUT. to clear of benches. *2* [in gambling] to break the bank. *3* to supplant in the affection of another, to cut out.
desbandada *f.* disbandment: *a la* ~, helter-skelter, in disorder.
desbandarse *ref.* to disperse [be dispersed]. *2* to disband, to flee in disorder.
desbarajuste *m.* disorder, confusion, confused medley.
desbaratado, -da *adj.* disorderly; debauched.
desbaratamiento *m.* destruction, ruin. *2* frustration. *3* defeat.
desbaratar *tr.* to destroy, ruin, take to pieces. *2* to waste, squander. *3* to frustrate, foil, thwart. *4* MIL. to disperse, rout, break up. *5 intr.-ref.* to talk nonsense, to act unreasonably.
desbarbar *tr.* to cut off filaments, slender roots, etc., of. *2* coll. to shave.
desbarrar *intr.* to glide, slide. *2* to talk nonsense, to act foolishly.
desbarro *m.* gliding. *2* nonsensical talk; foolish act.
desbastar *tr.* to take off the rough parts of a thing; to plane, roughdress, rough down. *2* to spend, consume. *3* to polish [a person].
desbaste *m.* roughdressing. *2* roughdressed state.
desbecerrar *tr.* to wean calves.
desbloquear *tr.* COM. to unfreeze.
desbloqueo *m.* COM. unfreezing.
desbocado, -da *adj.* wide-mouthed [gun]. *2* broken-

faced [tool]. *3* broken-lipped, broken-mouthed [jar, vessel]. *4* runaway [horse]. *5* foul-mouthed.
desbocamiento *m.* running away [of a horse]. *2* foulmouthedness, abusiveness, obscenity.
desbocar *tr.* to break the lips or mouth of [a jar, etc.]; to break the face [of a tool]. *2 ref.* [of a horse], to run away. *3* [of a person] to become insolent.
desbordamiento *m.* overflowing. *2* breaking all bounds.
desbordante *adj.* overflowing.
desbordar *intr.-ref.* to overflow. *2 ref.* [of passions] to break all bounds.
desborrar *tr.* to burl [cloth].
desbravador *m.* horse breaker.
desbravar *tr.* to tame, break in [horses]. *2 intr.-ref.* to become less wild or fierce. *3* [of a liquor] to go flat.
desbridar *tr.* SURG. to débride.
desbriznar *tr.* to shred, to divide in small shreds. *2* to remove the strings [of vegetables]. *3* to pluck the stamens [of saffron].
desbrozar *tr.* to clear [lands, etc.] of rubbish, underbrush, obstructions, etc.: ~ *el camino,* to clear the way.
desbrozo *m.* the act of clearing lands, etc., of rubbish, obstructions, etc. *2* rubbish from clearing lands, trenches, etc.
desbulla *f.* oyster shell.
desbullador *m.* oyster fork.
desbullar *tr.* to take [oysters] out of shell.
descabal *adj.* incomplete.
descabalar *tr.* to make incomplete, to take out a part of, to impair.
descabalgar *intr.* to dismount, to alight from a horse. *2 tr.* to dismount [a gun].
descabellado, -da *adj.* dishevelled. *2* preposterous, wild, absurd.
descabellar *tr.* to dishevel, tousle the hair. *2* BULLF. to kill [the bull] by stabbing him in the back of the neck.
descabello *m.* BULLF. killing the bull by stabbing him in the back of the neck.
descabestrar *tr.* to unhalter.
descabezado, -da *adj.* decapitated, headless, beheaded. *2* light-headed, reckless, crazy, wild. *3* absurd, ridiculous. *4* absentminded, forgetful.
descabezar *tr.* to behead. *2* to top, lop, cut off the top of. *3* to begin to overcome [a difficulty]. *4* ~ *el sueño,* to take a nap. *5 ref.* to cudgel one's brains.
descabullirse *ref.* ESCABULLIRSE. *2* to slip out of a difficulty; to elude the strenght of an argument.
descacharrante *adj.* coll. hilarious, killing, terribly funny.
descaderar *tr.* to injure the hips of. *2 ref.* to injure one's hips.
descaecer *intr.* to decline, droop, languish. ¶ CONJUG. like *agradecer.*
descaecimiento *m.* weakness, debility. *2* dejection.
descalabazarse *ref.* coll. to cudgel one's brains.
descalabrado, -da *adj.* wounded in the head. *2* injured, worsted: *salir* ~, to come out worsted.
descalabradura *f.* wound in the head.
descalabrar *tr.* to wound in the head. *2* to hurt, injure. *3* to occasion losses to. *4 ref.* to hurt one's head.
descalabro *m.* misfortune, damage, loss, defeat.
descalcar *tr.* NAUT. to remove oakum from [seams].
descalce *m.* undermining.

descalcificación f. MED. decalcification.
descalificación f. disqualification. 2 discrediting, discredit.
descalificar tr. to disqualify [render unfit]. 2 to discredit. 3 SPORT. to disqualify.
descalzador m. bootjack.
descalzar tr. to take off [somebody's] shoes or stockings. 2 to remove wedges or chocks from. 3 to dig under, undermine. 4 ref. to take off one's shoes or stockings. 5 to take off [one's shoes, stockings or gloves]. 6 [of a horse] to lose a shoe.
descalzo, -za adj. unshod, barefooted, in stockinged feet. 2 discalced, barefooted [friar, nun].
descamar tr. ESCAMAR 1. 2 ref. MED. to desquamate.
descaminado, -da adj. lost, on the wrong road. 2 mistaken, wrong. 3 misguided, ill-advised.
descaminar tr. to lead astray, mislead, misguide. 2 ref. to lose one's way, to go astray. 3 to go wrong.
descamino m. leading astray, going astray. 2 misguidance, error.
descamisado, -da adj. shirtless, ragged. 2 m.-f. poor person, ragamuffin.
descampado, -da adj.-m. open, clear [ground]: en ~, in the open country.
descansadero m. resting place.
descansado, -da adj. rested, refreshed. 2 free of toil, easy, tranquil, peaceful.
descansar intr. to rest [get repose; lie in sleep or death; stop work]. 2 to feel alleviation. 3 AGR. [of land] to rest. 4 to rest, rely, put trust [in a person]. 5 to rest [be supported]. 6 tr. to give rest to, to aid, help [someone] in labour. 7 to rest, lean [one's head, etc.].
descansillo m. landing [of stairs].
descanso m. rest, repose, refreshment. 2 sleep. 3 rest, alleviation. 4 aid, help. 5 peace, quiet. 6 landing [of stairs]. 7 MEC. rest, seat, support.
descantear tr. to smooth corners or edges in.
descantillar tr. to break the arris or edge of. 2 to substract [a part] of an amount.
descañonar tr. to take off the quills left on [a plucked fowl]. 2 to shave against the grain.
descapotable adj. convertible [car].
descapotar tr. to fold or take down the hood of [a carriage].
descaradamente adv. barefacedly. 2 openly.
descarado, -da adj. impudent, barefaced; saucy.
descararse ref. to behave in an impudent manner, to be saucy. 2 to lose all decency.
descarbonatar tr. CHEM. to decarbonate.
descarburar tr. to decarbonize.
descarga f. unloading, unburdening, discharge. 2 ARCH., ELECT. discharge. 3 discharge [of firearms], volley, round.
descargadero m. unloading place.
descargador m. unloader; ~ del muelle, dock labourer.
descargar tr. to unload, unburden, disburden, discharge. 2 to ease [one's conscience]. 3 to free, discharge [of a debt, etc.]. 4 to clear [of an accusation]. 5 to dump, empty. 6 to deal, strike [a blow]. 7 to vent [one's fury, etc.]. 8 to unload; to fire, discharge [a firearm]. 9 ELECT. to discharge. 10 intr. [of streams] to flow into, to empty. 11 [of a storm] to burst. 12 ref. to unburden oneself; to get rid of. 12 ref. to unburden oneself; to get rid of. 13 to clear oneself [of an accusation]. 14 to disburden one's cares, duties, etc. [upon another].
descargo m. unburdening. 2 COM. acquittance. 3

easement [of one's conscience]. 4 clearing, justification. 5 discharge [of an obligation].
descargue m. unloading [of goods, etc.].
descariño m. lack of affection, coolness.
descarnadamente adv. bluntly, without euphemisms.
descarnado, -da adj. thin, lean. 2 bare [bone]. 3 fig. bare, unadorned, crude, blunt.
descarnador m. DENT. scraper.
descarnar tr. to remove the flesh from. 2 to wear away, corrode, denudate. 3 to detach from earthly things. 4 ref. to lose flesh.
descaro m. impudence, effrontery, sauciness, nerve, cheek.
descarriar tr. to lead astray, mislead. 2 to separate [cattle] from the herd. 3 ref. to stray, go astray. 4 to go wrong.
descarrilamiento m. derailment.
descarrilar intr. to derail, to run off the track.
descarrío m. going astray or wrong; error, sin.
descartar tr. to leave aside, leave out. 2 ref. CARDS descartarse [de], to discard.
descarte m. leaving aside. 2 CARDS discard.
descasamiento m. annulment of marriage.
descasar tr. to annul the marriage of. 2 to disturb the arrangement of [well matched things].
descascarar tr. to peel, to shell. 2 ref. to peel off, to shell off.
descascarillar tr. to peel [rice]. 2 to remove the thin metal plate covering [an object]. 2 ref. [of an object] to lose its thin metal plate covering.
descaspar tr. to remove the dandruff of.
descastado, -da adj. showing little natural afection. 2 ungrateful.
descendencia f. descent, descendants, issue. 2 descent, lineage.
descendente adj. descendent, descending; down: tren ~, down train.
descender intr. to descend, to come or go down. 2 to stoop [to something mean, etc.]. 3 [of temperature] to drop. 4 to descend [from a stock, etc.]; to derive. 5 tr. to take down, bring, down. ¶ CONJUG. like entender.
descendiente adj. descendent. 2 m.-f. descendant, offspring.
descendimiento m. descent, taking down. 2 Descent from the Cross.
descenso m. descent, coming down. 2 drop, fall [of temperature, prices, etc.]. 3 decline, fall [in station, dignity, etc.].
descentrado, -da adj. out of centre, decentred.
descentralización f. decentralization.
descentralizar tr. to decentralize.
descentrar tr. to decentre, uncentre, place out of centre. 2 ref. to become uncentred.
desceñir tr. to ungird; to unbelt. 2 tr.-ref. to take off one's girdle, belt, etc. ¶ CONJUG. like reír.
descepar tr. to uproot [trees, shrubs]. 2 to exterminate.
descercado, -da adj. open, unfenced.
descercar tr. to destroy or tear down the wall or fence of. 2 MIL. to raise the siege of. 3 MIL. to force the enemy to raise the siege of.
descerco m. raising the siege.
descerezar tr. to pulp [coffee berries].
descerrajadura f. lock breaking, lock bursting.
descerrajar tr. to burst or force the lock. 2 ~ un tiro a, to shoot, let go a shot at.
desciendo, descienda, etc. irr. V. DESCENDER.
descifrable adj. decipherable.
descifrador m. decipherer; decoder.

desciframiento *m.* deciphering. 2 decoding.
descifrar *tr.* to decipher, make out; to decode.
descinchar *tr.* to ungirth [a horse or pack animal].
desciño, desciña, etc. *irr.* V. DESCEÑIR.
desclavador *m.* nail puller.
desclavar *tr.* to remove the nails from. 2 to unnail. 3 to take [a precious stone] out of setting.
descoagulante *adj.* decoagulating.
descoagular *tr.* to decoagulate.
descobajar *tr.* to separate [grapes] from the stem.
descocado, -da *adj.* bold, forward, brazen.
descocar *tr.* to clear [trees] of grubs. 2 *ref.* to become bold, forward.
descoco *f. m.* boldness, forwardness, excessive freedom in manners.
descoger *tr.* to unfold, extend, spread.
descogollar *tr.* to strip [a tree or plant] of shoots. 2 to take the heart out of [vegetables].
descolar *tr.* to dock or crop the tail of [an animal].
descolgar *tr.* to unhang, take down. 2 to lower, let down [something suspended from a rope, etc.]. 3 to unhang, divest of hangings [a room, etc.]. 4 *ref.* to show up unexpectedly. 5 to slip or let oneself down [from a window, etc.]; to come down [from a steep place]. 6 *descolgarse con*, to say [something unexpected]. ¶ CONJUG. like *contar*.
descolocado, -da *adj.* out of place.
descolonizar *tr.* to decolonize.
descoloramiento *m.* decolourization.
descolorante *adj.* decolourizing. 2 *m.* decolourizer.
descolorar *tr.* DESCOLORIR 1.
descolorido, -da *adj.* decolourized. 2 pale, colourless, faded.
descolorimiento *m.* decoloration, fading, paleness.
descolorir *tr.* to decolourize, to discolour. 2 to fade, render pale.
descolladamente *adv.* haughtily, loftily.
descollamiento *m.* superiority.
descollante *adj.* outstanding.
descollar *intr.* to stand out, be prominent or conspicuous: ~ *entre* or *sobre*, to excel, surpass, tower above. ¶ CONJUG. like *contar*.
descombrar *tr.* to disencumber, to clear of obstacles.
descombro *m.* disencumbering, clearing of obstacles.
descomedido, -da *adj.* excessive, disproportionate, immoderate. 2 rude, disrespectful, impolite.
descomedimiento *m.* disrespect, impoliteness.
descomedirse *ref.* to be rude, disrespectful, impolite.
descompaginar *tr.* to disarrange, upset.
descompás *m.* excess, want of measure or proportion.
descompasado, -da *adj.* excessive, immoderate.
descomponer *tr.* to decompose. 2 MEC. to resolve [forces]. 3 to put out of order; to disarrange, disturb, unsettle, upset. 4 fig. to alienate, set at odds. 5 *ref.* to decompose [be decomposed]; to become putrid or tainted. 6 to get out of order. 7 [of the body] to be indisposed. 8 [of the face] to be altered by emotions. 9 to lose one's temper. 10 [of the weather, etc.] to change for the worse. ¶ CONJUG. like *poner*.
descomposición *f.* decomposition. 2 MEC. resolution [of forces]. 3 ~ *de vientre*, looseness of bowels.
descompostura *f.* decomposition. 2 disarrange-

ment. 3 slovenliness, untidiness. 4 lack of restraint, of moderation. 5 disrespect, insolence.
descompresión *f.* decompression.
descompuesto, -ta *adj.* decomposed. 2 disarranged, out of order. 3 wild, insolent, impolite.
descomulgado, -da *adj.* coll. perverse, wicked.
descomulgar *tr.* to excommunicate.
descomunal *adj.* extraordinary, huge, enormous.
desconceptuar *tr.* to discredit. 2 *ref.* to become discredited.
desconcertadamente *adv.* disorderly, in disorder. 2 disconcertedly.
desconcertado, -da *adj.* disorderly. 2 out of order. 3 dislocate [bones]. 4 disconcerted, baffled.
desconcertante *adj.* disconcerting, baffling.
desconcertar *tr.* to disconcert. 2 to disarrange, disturb, put out of order. 3 to dislocate [a bone]. 4 *ref.* to become disarranged, to get out of order. 5 to disagree. 6 to be disconcerted. 7 [of a bone] to become dislocated. ¶ CONJUG. like *acertar*.
desconcierto *m.* disarrangement, disorder, confusion. 2 mismanagement. 3 disagreement. 4 disarrangement, disrepair. 5 disconcertment. 6 lack of restraint. 8 looseness of bowels.
desconchado *m.* scaled or peeled off part [of wall, etc.].
desconchar *tr.* to remove part of the coating, varnish, etc., of. 2 *ref.* to lose part of its coating, varnish, etc.
desconchón *m.* DESCONCHADO.
desconectar *tr.* MACH., ELECT. to disconnect. 2 *ref.* to become disconnected.
desconfiadamente *adv.* distrustfully, suspiciously.
desconfiado, -da *adj.* distrustful, suspicious.
desconfianza *f.* distrust, mistrust. 2 suspicious fear. 3 diffidence.
desconfiar *intr.* to have no confidence: ~ *de*, to distrust, to have little hope of.
descongelar *tr.* to defreeze.
descongestión *f.* removing or relieving of congestion.
descongestionar *tr.* to remove or relieve the congestion of. 2 *ref.* to become less congested.
desconocedor *m.* not knowing, ignorant.
desconocer *tr.* not to know, to ignore, be unacquainted with. 2 to fail to recognize. 3 to disown, disavow, deny. 4 to disregard, ignore. 5 *ref.* to be ignored. 6 to become unrecognizable. ¶ CONJUG. like *agradecer*.
desconocido, -da *adj.* unknown. 2 strange, unfamiliar. 3 ungrateful. 4 unrecognizable. 5 *m.-f.* stranger, unknown person.
desconocimiento *m.* ignorance [of something]. 2 disregard. 3 ungratefulness, ingratitude.
desconozco, desconozca, etc. *irr.* V. DESCONOCER.
desconsideración *f.* inconsiderateness, disregard, inattention.
desconsiderado, -da *adj.* inconsiderate, rude, discourteous. 2 inconsiderate, rash, imprudent.
desconsiderar *tr.* to have no regard for.
desconsolado, -da *adj.* disconsolate, griefstricken.
desconsolador, -ra *adj.* distressing.
desconsolar *tr.* to distress, grieve. 2 *ref.* to be distressed, to grieve. ¶ CONJUG. like *contar*.
desconsuelo *m.* disconsolation, disconsolateness, grief. 2 empty feeling [in the stomach].
descontar *tr.* to discount, deduct, abate. 2 to discount [a bill, etc.]. 3 to allow [for exaggeration, etc.]. 4 to take for granted. 5 *ref.* to miscount. ¶ CONJUG. like *contar*.

descontentadizo, -za *adj.* hard to please, easily displeased, fastidious.

descontentar *tr.* to discontent, dissatisfy, displease. *2 ref.* to be displeased.

descontento, -ta *adj.* discontent, dissatisfied, displeased. *2 m.* discontent, displeasure.

desconvenir *tr.* to disagree, differ [in opinion]. *2* to disagree, be dissimilar, not to suit. ¶ CONJUG. like *venir*.

descorazonadamente *adv.* despondently.

descorazonamiento *adv.* discouragement, despondency.

descorazonar *tr.* to dishearten, discourage.

descorchador *m.* corkscrew. *2* bark stripper.

descorchar *tr.* to bark [a cork tree]. *2* to uncork.

descorche *m.* barking [of cork oaks]. *2* uncorking.

descornar *tr.* to dehorn. *2 ref.* to be dehorned. *3* coll. to rack one's brains. ¶ CONJUG. like *contar*.

descoronar *tr.* to uncrown.

descorrer *tr.* to draw back [a curtain, a bolt, etc.]. *2* to run back over [the same ground]. *3 intr.* [of a liquid] to drip, trickle.

descortés *adj.* discourteous, impolite, uncivil.

descortesía *f.* discourtesy, impoliteness.

descortezador *m.* decorticator.

descortezamiento *m.* removal of bark, rind or crust.

descortezar *tr.* to bark [a tree]; to peel, to unrind; to remove the crust of. *2* coll. to polish, civilize. *3 ref.* to peel [lose the bark or rind].

descortezo *m.* removing of bark.

descosedura *f.* unseaming, ripping.

descoser *tr.* to unstitch, to unseam, to rip. *2* fig. *no ~ los labios*, to be silent. *3 ref.* [of a garment, etc.] to rip. *4* fig. to babble.

descosidamente *adv.* excessively. *2* disorderly, desultorily.

descosido, -da *adj.* ripped, unstitched. *2* disorderly, disconnected. *3 m.* open seam, rip. *4 como un ~*, immoderately.

descostillar *tr.* to beat [someone] on the ribs. *2 ref.* to fall violently on one's back.

descostrar *tr.* to remove the crust, or the scab, from.

descotar *tr.* to cut low in the neck. *2 ref.* to wear a low-neck dress.

descote *m.* ESCOTE 1.

descoyuntado, -da *adj.* disjointed, disconnected.

descoyuntamiento *m.* dislocation [of a joint]. *2* pain through overexertion.

descoyuntar *tr.* to dislocate, disjoint. *2* to annoy, bore. *3 ref.* to be dislocate: *descoyuntarse de risa*, to split one's sides with laughter.

descrédito *m.* discredit, loss of repute.

descreer *tr.* to disbelieve.

descreído, -da *adj.* unbelieving. *2 m.-f.* disbeliever, unbeliever.

descreimiento *m.* unbelief, lack of faith.

descremar *tr.* to skim.

describir *tr.* to describe.

descripción *f.* description [in every sense, except sort, kind, class]. *2* LAW inventory, schedule.

descriptible *adj.* describable.

descriptivo, -va *adj.* descriptive.

descrismar *tr.* to remove the chrism from. *2* coll. to hit violently on the head. *3 ref.* coll. to break one's skull. *4* to cudgel one's brains.

descristianizar *tr.* to dechristianize. *2 ref.* to become dechristianized.

descrito, -ta *irr. p. p.* of DESCRIBIR.

descruzar *tr.* to uncross.

descuadernar *tr.* to unbind [a book]. *2* to derange, upset, put out of order.

descuajar *tr.* to decoagulate, to liquefy. *2* AGR. to uproot. *3* to dishearten.

descuajaringarse *ref.* coll. to be broken down with fatigue, to fall to pieces.

descuartizamiento *m.* quartering, dividing into pieces. *2* quartering [punishment].

descuartizar *tr.* to quarter, to divide into pieces. *2* to quarter [as punishment].

descubierta *f.* MIL. reconnoitering. *2* NAUT. scanning of the horizon. *3 adv. a la ~*, openly.

descubierto, -ta *irr. p. p.* of descubrir. *2 adj.* patent, manifest. *3* bareheaded, uncovered. *4* open to attack, charges or accusations. *5 m.* deficit, overdraft: *en ~*, overdrawn; fig. unable to justify one's conduct. *6 adv. al ~*, in the open; openly. *7* COM. short.

descubridor, -ra *adj.* discovering. *2 m.-f.* discoverer. *3 m.* MIL. scout.

descubrimiento *m.* discovery. *2* uncovering. *3* revealing, disclosure.

descubrir *tr.* to discover, disclose, reveal, exhibit. *2* to make known, to betray [a secret, etc.]. *3* to uncover, lay bare, expose to view. *4* to discover [find out; suddenly realize]. *6* to catch sight of, descry, make out. *6 ref.* to uncover, to take off one's hat or cap. *7* to betray oneself.

descuello *m.* overtopping. *2* superiority, eminence. *3* haughtiness, loftiness.

descuello, descuelle, etc. *irr.* V. DESCOLLAR.

descuento *m.* discount, deduction, rebate. *2* BANK. discount.

descuento, descuente, etc. *irr.* V. DESCONTAR.

descuernacabras *m.* strong, cold north wind.

descuidado, -da *adj.* neglected. *2* careless, negligent. *3* slovenly, untidy. *4* unaware, off his guard.

descuidar *tr.* to relieve from care. *2* to divert the attention of. *3 tr.-intr. ref. descuidar, descuidar de, descuidarse de o en*, to neglect, to fail to attend with due care. *4 intr. descuide usted*, depend on lit.

descuidero *m.* sneak thief.

descuido *m.* neglect. *2* negligence, carelessness. *3* slovenliness. *4* oversight, inadvertence. *5* slip, faux pas. *6* slight, lack of attention.

descuitado, -da *adj.* carefree.

descular *tr.* to break the bottom of.

desde *prep.* from, since: *~ ... hasta*, from... to; *~ ahora*, from now on; *~ entonces*, since then, ever since; *~ niño*, from a child: *~ que*, since; *está enfermo ~ hace un año*, he has been ill for a year. *2 adv. ~ luego*, immediately; of course.

desdecir *intr. ~ de*, to be unbecoming to; not to be in keeping with. *2 ref.* to retract, to unsay.

desdén *m.* disdain, scorn. *2* slight, disdainful behaviour.

desdentado, -da *adj.* toothless. *2 adj.-m.* ZOOL. edentate.

desdeñable *adj.* contemptible.

desdeñar *tr.* to disdain, scorn. *2 ref.* to disdain, scorn [doing something], not to deign to.

desdeñoso, -sa *adj.* disdainful, contemptuous.

desdibujado, -da *adj.* poorly drawn, badly outlined, blurred.

desdibujarse *ref.* to become blurred.

desdicha *f.* misfortune; unhappiness, misery.

desdichado, -da *adj.* unfortunate, unlucky. *2* miserable, unhappy, wretched. *3 m.-f.* wretch, unfortunate one. *4* spiritless person, poor devil.

desdoblamiento *m.* unfolding. *2* splitting, originating two things out of one: ~ *de la personalidad,* desintegration of the personality.
desdoblar *tr.* to unfold, to spread open. *2 tr.-ref.* to split, to originate two things out of one.
desdorar *tr.* to take off the gilding of. *2* to tarnish, to sully [reputation, etc.].
desdoro *m.* dishonor, blemish, blot.
desdoroso, -sa *adj.* disgraceful.
deseable *adj.* desirable.
deseado, -da *adj.* desired.
desear *tr.* to desire, to wish.
desecación *f.* DESECAMIENTO.
desecamiento *m.* desiccation, drying, draining.
desecar *tr.* to desiccate, exsiccate; to dry, dry up; to drain: ~ *un pantano,* to drain a swamp.
desecativo, -va *adj.-n.* dessicative.
desechar *tr.* to cast aside, banish, refuse, decline, reject. *2* to cast off. *3* to underrate. *4* to draw back [a bolt].
desecho *m.* refuse, rubbish, reject, remainder, scrap: *de* ~, cast off, discarded; scrap [iron, etc.]. *2* contempt. *3 pl.* MIN. tailings.
deselectrizar *tr.* to dielectrify.
desellar *tr.* to unseal.
desembalaje *m.* unpacking [of goods].
desembalar *tr.* to unpack [goods].
desembaldosar *tr.* to untile [a floor].
desembarazado, -da *adj.* clear, free, open, unobstructed. *2* easy, unrestrained [air, manners, etc.].
desembarazar *tr.* to clear, disembarrass, disencumber: ~ *de,* to clear, rid of. *2* to empty [a room]. *3 ref.* to get rid [of].
desembarazo *m.* disembarrassment. *2* freedom, lack of restraint, ease, naturalness.
desembarcadero *m.* landing place, wharf, pier.
desembarcar *tr.* to disembark, debark, land, put ashore. *2 intr.-ref.* to disembark, debark, land, go ashore. *3 intr.* [of a stairs] to end at a landing.
desembarco *m.* disembarkation, landing.
desembargar *tr.* to free, to remove impediments from. *2* LAW to raise the attachment or seizure of.
desembargo *m.* LAW raising of an attachment or seizure.
desembarque *m.* debarkation, landing, unloading.
desembarrancar *tr.* to refloat [a stranded ship]. *2 intr.* [of a stranded ship] to float again.
desembarrar *tr.* to clear of mud.
desembaular *tr.* to take out of a trunk, box, etc.
desembebecerse *ref.* to come out of one's absorption. ¶ CONJUG. like *agradecer.*
desembelesarse *ref.* to come out of one's rapture.
desembocadura *f.* mouth [of a river]. *2* outlet, exit [of a street, road, etc.].
desembocar *intr.* [of streams] to flow, disembogue. *2* [of streets, etc.] to end [at], lead [to].
desembolsar *tr.* to take out of a bag or purse. *2* to disburse, pay out.
desembolso *m.* disbursement, payment; expenditure.
desemboscarse *ref.* to come out of the thicket or woods. *2* to come out of ambush.
desembotar *tr.* to remove the dullness of wits, senses, etc.
desembozar *tr.* to unmuffle, to uncover. *2 intr.* to unmuffle, to uncover one's face.
desembragar *tr.* MACH. to unclutch, ungear, disconnect.

desembrague *m.* MACH. unclutching.
desembriagar *tr.* to sober, cure from intoxication. *2 ref.* to sober up, recover from intoxication.
desembridar *tr.* to unbridle.
desembrollar *tr.* to unravel, disentangle, disembroil.
desembuchar *tr.* [of birds] to disgorge. *2* coll. to speak out, to tell all one knows.
desemejante *adj.* dissimilar, unlike.
desemejanza *f.* dissimilarity, unlikeness, difference.
desemejar *intr.* to be dissimilar, be unlike. *2 tr.* to disfigure.
desempacar *tr.* to unpack, to unwrap [goods].
desempachar *tr.-ref.* to relieve or be relieved from indigestion. *2 ref.* to lose one's bashfulness or timidity.
desempacho *m.* ease, unconstraint.
desempalagar *tr.* to uncloy.
desempalmar *tr.* to disconnect, to unsplice.
desempañar *tr.* to clean [a glass, mirror, etc.] of steam or tarnish; to make recover its luster to. *2* to remove swaddling clothes from [children].
desempapelar *tr.* to unwrap [from paper]. *2* to strip [a wall, a room, etc.] of paper hangings.
desempaque *m.* unpacking.
desempaquetar *tr.* to unpack.
desemparejar *tr.* to make uneven or unequal.
desempastar *tr.* to remove the filling.
desempatar *tr.* SPORT. to break a tie between. *2* to break a tie-vote.
desempate *m.* breaking the tie between.
desempedrar *tr.* to unpave, to remove the paving stones of. ¶ CONJUG. like *acertar.*
desempeñar *tr.* to redeem [what was pledged], to take out of pawn. *2* to free from debt or obligation. *3* to discharge [a duty]; to acquit oneself of [a commission]. *4* to fill [an office]. *5* to act, play [a part]. *6 ref.* to get out of debts. *7* to get out of a difficulty.
desempeño *m.* redeeming a pledge; tacking out of pawn. *2* discharging [of debt]. *3* performance [of an obligation]; discharging [of duty]; fulfilment [of a function]; filling [an office]. *4* acting [a part].
desempleado, -da *adj.* unemployed, out of work. *2 n.* unemployed man or woman.
desempleo *m.* unemployment.
desempolvadura *f.* removal of dust or powder.
desempolvar *tr.* to dust, remove the dust from. *2* to remove the powder from [face, etc.].
desemponzoñar *tr.* to free from poison.
desempotrar *tr.* to remove, take out [something embedded in a wall, etc.].
desenalbardar *tr.* to unsaddle [a pack animal].
desenamorar *tr.* to destroy the love [for]. *2 ref.* to lose the love [for].
desencabalgar *tr.* MIL. to dismount [a gun].
desencadenamiento *m.* unchaining.
desencadenar *tr.* to unchain, to unfetter. *2* to free, unleash. *3 ref.* [of passions] to become unleashed, run wild; [of wind] to break loose; [of a storm] to break; [of a war] to break out.
desencajado, -da *adj.* disjointed, out of joint. *2* [of features] distorted.
desencajamiento *m.* disjointing, dislocation, unhingement. *2* distortion [of face or features].
desencajar *tr.* to disjoint, dislocate; to unhinge. *2 ref.* to be disjointed. *3* [of face or features] to become distorted.

desencajonar *tr.* to take out of a box. *2* BULLF. to remove [bulls] from the travelling boxes.

desencalabrinar *tr.-ref.* to clear [somebody's] head, or [one's] head, of fumes.

desencallar *tr.* to set [a stranded ship] afloat. *2 intr.* [of a stranded ship] to float again.

desencaminar *tr.* to mislead, lead astray.

desencantar *tr.* to disenchant. *2* to disillusion. *3 ref.* to be disenchanted. *4* to become disillusioned.

desencanto *m.* disenchantment, disillusionment.

desencapotar *tr.* to strip [one] of his great coat. *2* to reveal. *3* to make [a horse] keep its head up. *4 ref.* [of the sky] to clear up. *5* to smooth one's brow.

desencaprichar *tr.* to dissuade from or cure of a whim or fancy. *2 ref.* to give up or get over a whim or fancy.

desencarcelar *tr.* to set free, release from prison.

desencargar *tr.* to countermand.

desenclavar *tr.* DESCLAVAR. *2* to put [someone] violently out of his place.

desenclavijar *tr.* to take the pins or pegs out of. *2* to separate, disjoint.

desencoger *tr.* to unfold, to spread out, to extend. *2 ref.* to lose one's timidity or constraint.

desencogimiento *m.* unfolding. *2* ease, naturalness.

desencolar *tr.* to unglue. *2* to unsize [fabrics].

desencolerizarse *ref.* to cool off, be appeased.

desenconar *tr.* to allay the inflammation of. *2* to appease. *3 ref.* to abate, calm down, soften up.

desencono *m.* mitigation of anger, passion or bitterness.

desencordar *tr.* MUS. to unstring.

desencorvar *tr.* to straighten, unbend.

desencrespar *tr.* to uncurl, to unfrizzle.

desencuadernar *tr.* to unbind, take the binding off [a book].

desenchufar *tr.* to unplug, to disconnect.

desendemoniar *tr.* to drive evil spirits out of.

desendiosar *tr.* to humble the vanity of.

desenfadaderas *f. pl. tener buenas* ~, to be resourceful.

desenfadadamente *adv.* without inhibition, casually, confidently.

desenfadado, -da *adj.* easy, unconstrained, bold.

desenfadar *tr.* to appease, pacify [an angry person]. *2 ref.* to calm down, cease to be angry.

desenfado *m.* ease, freedom, naturalness.

desenfardar *tr.* to unpack [bales of goods].

desenfilar *tr.* MIL., FORT. to defilade.

desenfocado, -da *adj.* out of focus.

desenfocar *tr.* to put out of focus, not to focus properly. *2 ref.* to get out of focus.

desenfoque *m.* out of focus.

desenfrenadamente *adv.* wildly; unrestrainedly: *correr* ~, to run wildly. *2* licentiously, wantonly.

desenfrenado, -da *adj.* unbridled. *2* wild [course, run, etc.]. *3* licentious, wanton.

desenfrenar *tr.* to unbridle. *2 ref.* [of passion, vices, etc.] to run wild. *3* to give oneself up to vice; to give rein to one's passions or desires.

desenfreno *m.* licentiousness, wantonness. *2* boundless freedom or licence. *3* unbridling [of passions].

desenfundar *tr.* to take out of a sheath, case, cover, etc.

desenfurecer *tr.* to quiet the fury or anger of. *2 ref.* to calm down, quiet down.

desenfurruñar *tr.* to appease [someone], make [someone] cease being angry or sulking.

desenganchar *tr.* to unhook, unfasten, disengage. *2* to uncouple, to unhitch, to unharness.

desengañadamente *adv.* clearly, openly, frankly.

desengañado, -da *adj.* disabused, disillusioned.

desengañar *tr.* to undeceive, disabuse. *2* to disillusion. *3 ref.* to be undeceived, to be desillusioned.

desengaño *m.* undeceiving, disabusal. *2* disillusion, disappointment; bitter lesson of experience.

desengarzar *tr.* to take [precious stones, etc.] out of a setting. *2* to unstring [pearls, etc.].

desengastar *tr.* DESENGARZAR 1.

desengomar *tr.* DESGOMAR.

desengoznar *tr.* DESGOZNAR.

desengranar *tr.* MACH. to unmesh, disengage.

desengrasar *tr.* to take the grease out of.

desengrase *m.* removal of grease.

desenhebrar *tr.* to unthread.

desenhornar *tr.* to take out of the oven.

desenjaezar *tr.* to take the trappings off [a horse].

desenjalmar *tr.* to unsaddle [a pack animal].

desenjaular *tr.* to uncage, let out of the cage.

desenlace *m.* outcome, issue, end. *2* denouement, unravelling [of drama, plot, etc.].

desenladrillar *tr.* to untile [a floor].

desenlatar *tr.* to open, to take out [of a can].

desenlazar *tr.* to untie. *2* to solve, to bring to an issue. *3* to unravel [a drama or plot]. *4 ref.* to come untied. *5* to come to a denouement.

desenlodar *tr.* to clear of mud.

desenlosar *tr.* to take up the flagstones from.

desenlutar *tr.* to strip of mourning hangings. *2 ref.* to leave off mourning garments.

desenmallar *tr.* to disentangle [fish] from the net.

desenmarañar *tr.* to disentangle, unravel. *2* to disembroil.

desenmascaramiento *m.* unmasking, exposure.

desenmascarar *tr.* to unmask, expose. *2 ref.* to unmask, take off one's mask.

desenmohecer *tr.* to unrust, clear of rust.

desenmudecer *tr.* to make [someone] recover speech. *2 intr.* to recover speech. *3* to break a long silence. ¶ CONJUG. like *agradecer*.

desenojar *tr.* to appease, dispel the displeasure of. *2 ref.* to cease to be angry or displeased.

desenojo *m.* appeasement of anger.

desenredar *tr.* to disentangle. *2* to unravel, clear, free from confusion. *3 ref.* to disentangle oneself or itself; to extricate oneself.

desenredo *m.* disentangling, unravelling.

desenrollar *tr.* to unroll, to unwind. *2 ref.* to unroll, to unwind [itself].

desenroscar *tr.* to uncoil, to untwist. *2* to unscrew.

desensamblar *tr.* CARP. to disjoint.

desensartar *tr.* to unstring, unthread. *2* to unskewer.

desensibilizar *tr.* to desensitize. *2 ref.* to become desensitized.

desensillar *tr.* to unsaddle [a horse].

desensoberbecer *tr.* to make humble. *3 ref.* to become humble. ¶ CONJUG. like *agradecer*.

desentablar *tr.* to take up the boards from.

desentarimar *tr.* to take up the flooring boards from.

desentenderse *ref.* ~ *de*, to pretend not to understand, affect ignorance of; to take no part in, cease to be interested in. ¶ CONJUG. like *entender*.

desentendido, -da *adj.* desinterested [in]. *2 s. ha-*

cerse el ~, to pretend not to understand or not to notice.

desenterrador *m.* exhumer, unearther.

desenterramiento *m.* unearthing. *2* disinterment, exhumation.

desenterrar *tr.* to unearth. *2* to disinter, exhume. *3* to recall [long-forgotten things]. ¶ Conjug. like *acertar.*

desentoldar *tr.* to take off the awning from. *2* strip of ornaments.

desentonado, -da *adj.* out of tune. *2* disrespectful.

desentonar *tr.* to humble the pride of. *2 intr.* mus. to be out of tune. *3* to be out of harmony, to discord.

desentono *m.* mus. being out of tune, discordance. *3* rude, disrespectful tone of voice.

desentorpecer *tr.* to free from numbness or torpor. *2* to make smart, to polish [a clumsy person]. *3 ref.* to shake off numbness or torpor. *4* to become smart, lively. ¶ Conjug. like *agradecer.*

desentrampar *tr.* to free of debts. *2 ref.* to get out of debt.

desentrañar *tr.* to eviscerate, to disembowel. *2* to find out, solve, decipher. *3 ref. desentrañarse por,* to give one's all to [someone], out of love.

desentrenado, -da *adj.* sport. out of training.

desentrenamiento *m.* sport. lack of training.

desentrenarse *ref.* sport. to go or get out of training.

desentronizar *tr.* to dethrone.

desentumecer *tr.* to free [a limb] from numbness. *2 ref.* to shake off numbness.

desentumecimiento *m.* freeing from numbness.

desentumir *tr.-ref.* desentumecer.

desenvainar *tr.* to unsheathe. *2* [of an animal] to stretch out or bare [the claws].

desenvergar *tr.* naut. to unbend [a sail].

desenvoltura *f.* easy and graceful delivery in talking; ease in acts or manners. *2* boldness, wantonness [chiefly in women].

desenvolver *tr.* to unfold. *2* to develop. *3* to develop [a theme, etc.], to evolve. *4* to unravel, decipher; to clear up. *5 ref.* to develop [be developed]. *6* to come out [of a difficulty]. *7* to act or behave with ease or assurance. ¶ Conjug. like *mover.*

desenvolvimiento *m.* unfolding, development.

desenvueltamente *adv.* with ease, naturally, confidently, gracefully. *2* boldly, rudely. *3* shamelessly, brazenly. *4* openly.

desenvuelto, -ta *p. p.* of desenvolver. *2* easy, free [in talk or manners]. *3* brazen, excessively free.

desenyesar *tr.* to remove plaster from.

desenzarzar *tr.* to disentangle from brambles. *2* to separate or appease [quarrelers].

deseo *m.* desire; wish.

deseoso, -sa *adj.* desirous.

desequilibrado, -da *adj.* unbalanced, unpoinsed, disequilibrated. *2* unbalanced [mind; person]. *3 m.-f.* unbalanced person.

desequilibrar *tr.* to unbalance. *2 ref.* to become unbalanced.

desequilibrio *m.* lack of equilibrium; unbalanced condition. *2* ~ *mental,* unbalanced mental condition.

deserción *f.* mil. desertion.

desertar *tr.-intr.* mil. to desert. *2 tr.* coll. to give up frequenting [friends, a place of meeting].

desértico, -ca *adj.* barren, desert, uncultivated. *2* deserted, uninhabited. *3* geog. desert.

desertor *m.* deserter.

deseslabonar *tr.* deslabonar.

desespaldar *tr.-ref.* to break or dislocate the shoulder of.

desesperación *f.* despair, desperation. *2 ser una* ~, to be unbearable.

desesperado, -da *adj.* despairing. *2* hopeless. *3* desperate. *4* furious, mad. *5 m.-f.* desperate person.

desesperante *adj.* exasperating, maddening.

desesperanza *f.* despair, want of hope.

desesperanzar *tr.* to deprive of hope, to discourage. *2 ref.* to lose hope.

desesperar *tr.* to cause to despair. *2* to exasperate, drive mad or wild. *3 intr.* to despair, to have no hope [of]. *4 ref.* to be exasperate. *5* to be driven to despair.

desespero *m.* desesperación.

desestañar *tr.* to untin, to detin. *2* to unsolder.

desesterar *tr.* to remove the mates from [floor].

desestima, desestimación *f.* disesteem, misestimation, undervaluation. *2* refusal, denial.

desestimar *tr.* to disesteem, misestimate, undervalue. *2* to reject [a petition].

desfacedor *m.* ~ *de entuertos,* righter of wrongs.

desfachatado, -da *adj.* impudent, brazen, shameless.

desfachatez *f.* impudence, brazenness, effrontery.

desfajar *tr.* to ungird.

desfalcador, -ra *m.-f.* embezzler, defalcator.

desfalcar *tr.* to detract a part of. *2* to embezzle.

desfalco *m.* detracting, diminution. *2* embezzlement, defalcation.

desfallecer *tr.* to weaken, debilitate. *2 intr.* to faint, faint away. *3* to lose courage or vigour.

desfalleciente *adj.* weak, fainting.

desfallecimiento *m.* faintness, languor. *2* fainting fit.

desfasado, -da *adj.* out of date, antiquated, old fashioned. *2* out of place. *3* out of phase.

desfase *m.* elect. phase difference, phase shift. *2* gap. *3* imbalance.

desfavorecer *tr.* to disregard, to cease favouring. *2* to disfavour, to discountenance; to oppose. *3* to injure, hurt.

desfigurar *tr.* to disfigure, change, alter. *2* to disguise. *3* to blur, to obscure. *4* to distort, to misrepresent. *5 ref.* to become disfigured.

desfiladero *m.* defile, gorge, long narrow pass.

desfilar *tr.* to defile [march in file]. *2* to march past [in review, etc.] to parade. *3* to file out.

desfile *m.* defiling; marching past, parade.

desflecar *tr.* to form fringes by loosening threads.

desflemar *tr.* chem. to dephlegmate. *2 intr.* to expel phlegm.

desflocar *tr.* desflecar. ¶ Conjug. like *contar.*

desfloración *f.* defloration.

desfloramiento *m.* defloration, violation.

desflorar *tr.* to deflower. *2* to treat [a matter] superficially.

desfogar *tr.* to vent, to make an opening in [a furnace, etc.] for fire. *2* to slack [lime]. *3 tr.-ref.* to give vent [to one's anger or feelings].

desfogue *m.* opening a vent [in a furnace, etc.]. *2* venting [of anger or feelings].

desfondar *tr.* to break or remove the bottom of. *2* naut. to bilge [a ship]. *3* agr. to dig [the soil] to a great depth. *4 ref.* naut. [of a ship] to bilge.

desfonde *m.* breaking of the bottom. *2* agr. digging of the soil to a great depth.

desfrenar *tr.-ref.* desenfrenar. *2 tr.* to take the breaks off [a carriage].

desfruncir *tr.* to unpucker. *2* to unknit [the brow].

desgaire *m.* affected carelessness in dress and deportment: *al* ~, with affected carelessness. *2* scornful attitude.

desgajar *tr.* to tear off [a branch of a tree]. *2* to break, to rent, to separate. *3 ref.* [of a branch] to break off. *4* to come off, break off, break away.

desgaje *m.* act of tearing or breaking off.

desgalichado, -da *adj.* coll. untidy. *2* ungainly.

desgana *f.* lack of appetite. *2* indifference, reluctance: *a* ~, reluctantly.

desganado, -da *adj.* having no appetite.

desganar *tr.* to take away one's taste [for]. *2 ref.* to lose one's appetite. *3* to lose one's taste [for].

desgano *m.* DESGANA.

desgañitarse *ref.* to shout oneself hoarse.

desgarbado, -da *adj.* ungainly, ungraceful, gawky.

desgarbo *m.* clumsiness.

desgaritar *intr.-ref.* NAUT. to lose the course. *2* to lose the way, to go astray.

desgarradamente *adv.* with effrontery.

desgarrado, -da *adj.* torn, ripped. *2* brazen, shameless, licentious.

desgarrador, -ra *adj.* rending. *2* heart-rending.

desgarrar *tr.* to tear, rend. *2* to cough up [phlegm]. *3 ref.* to tear oneself away.

desgarro *m.* tear, rent. *2* effrontery, impudence. *3* swagger, swaggering.

desgarrón *m.* large rent or rip. *2* shred, tatter.

desgastar *tr.* to wear away, abrade, erode, consume. *2 ref.* to wear down or away.

desgaste *m.* wear, wearing down, abrasion, attrition.

desglosar *tr.* to separate [a question, matter, etc.] of others. *2* to detach [a part] of a book.

desglose *m.* separation, detachment [of questions, etc.].

desgobernado, -da *adj.* disorderly.

desgobernar *tr.* to upset the government of, to misgovern. *2* to dislocate [bones]. *4 ref.* to go through contortions. ¶ CONJUG. like *acertar.*

desgobierno *m.* disorder, mismanagement, misgovernment.

desgomar *tr.* to ungum, unsize [silk fabrics].

desgonzar *tr.* DESGOZNAR. *2* to disjoint, to upset.

desgoznar *tr.* to unhinge.

desgracia *f.* misfortune: *por* ~, unfortunately. *2* bad luck, mischance. *3* disfavour, loss of favour. *5* gracelessness, awkwardness. *6* accident, casualty.

desgraciadamente *adv.* unfortunately.

desgraciado, -da *adj.* unfortunate, unhappy, unlucky. *2* graceless. *3* disagreeable. *4 m.-f.* wretch, unfortunate.

desgraciar *tr.* to displease. *2* to spoil, mar; to cripple. *3 ref.* to spoil [be spoiled]; to fail, fall through. *4* to be crippled. *5* to fall out [with a pers.].

desgranar *tr.* to beat or shake out the grain [from cereals, etc.], to thresh, to flail; to shell [peas, beans, etc.]; to remove grapes [from bunch]. *2 ref.* [of cereals, etc.] to shed the grains. *3* [of a necklace, a string of beads, etc.] to come loose [scattering pearls, beads, etc.].

desgrasar *tr.* to remove the grease from [wool].

desgrase *s.* removal of grease.

desgravación *f.* lowering of duties or taxes.

desgravar *tr.* to lower the duties or taxes on.

desgreñado, -da *adj.* dishevelled, with disordered hair.

desgreñar *tr.* to dishevel [the hair]. *2 ref.* to get dishevelled. *3* to pull each other's hair, to quarrel.

desguace *m.* NAUT. breaking up [of a ship].

desguarnecer *tr.* to strip of trimming or ornaments. *2* to dismantle [a fort]; to leave without garrison. *3* to remove the accessories from. *4* to unharness [a horse].

desguazar *tr.* to roughdress [timber]. *2* NAUT. to break up [a ship].

deshabitado, -da *adj.* uninhabited, deserted. *2* untenanted.

deshabituar *tr.* to disaccustom, free from a habit. *2 ref.* to leave off a habit.

deshacedor *m.* undoer: ~ *de agravios*, righter of wrongs.

deshacer *tr.* to undo, unmake. *2* to undo, untie, open [a parcel]; to undo, loosen [a knot]. *3* to consume, destroy. *4* to divide, cut to pieces; to take apart. *5* to upset [plans]. *6* MIL. to rout. *7* to melt, liquefy; to dissolve. *8* to cancel [a deal]. *9* to right [wrongs]. *10 ref.* to come undone. *11* to be consumed, destroyed, to wear itself out. *12* to dissipate, evanesce. *13* to melt, dissolve: *deshacerse en la boca,* to melt in the mouth. *14* to work hard. *15* [of a deal] to fall through. *16 deshacerse de,* to dispose of; to get rid of. *17 deshacerse en cumplidos,* to be all civility. *18 deshacerse en lágrimas,* to melt into tears. ¶ CONJUG. like *hacer.*

desharrapado, -da *adj.* ragged, in tatters. *2 m.-f.* tatterdemalion.

desharrapamiento *m.* misery, poverty.

deshebillar *tr.* to unbuckle.

deshebrar *tr.* to ravel into threads. *2* to separate into filaments.

deshecha *f.* dissimulation, dissembling.

deshechizar *tr.* to uncharm, disenchant.

deshecho, -cha *adj.* undone, destroyed, in pieces, melted, dissolved. *2* fig. broken, crushed, exhausted [person]. *3* violent [storm]. *4 p. p.* of DESHACER.

deshelar *tr.* to thaw, melt the ice of. *2 ref.* (of a thing) to thaw. ¶ CONJUG. like *acertar.*

desherbar *tr.* to weed [ground]. ¶ CONJUG. like *acertar.*

desheredado, -da *adj.* disinherited. *2* poor, destitute.

desheredar *tr.* to disinherit.

desherrar *tr.* to unshoe [a horse]. *2 ref.* [of a horse] to lose a shoe. ¶ CONJUG. like *acertar.*

desherrumbrar *tr.* to clean of rust.

deshidratación *f.* dehydration.

deshidratado, -da *adj.* dehydrated.

deshidratar *tr.* to dehydrate, deprive of water.

deshielo *m.* thaw, thawing.

deshilachar *tr.* to ravel out [a fabric]; to fray. *2 ref.* to fray, become ravelled out.

deshilado, -da *adj.* going in single file. *2 m.* drawn-work [in embroidery].

deshiladura *f.* ravelling out.

deshilar *tr.* to ravel out; to fray. *2* to shred [meat].

deshilvanado, -da *adj.* disjointed, disconnected, lose, desultory [speech, writing, thinking, etc.].

deshilvanar *tr.* SEW. to unbaste, remove basting threads from.

deshinchar *tr.* to deflate [a balloon, etc.]. *2* to reduce the swelling of. *3* to appease [anger]. *4 ref.* to become deflated. *5* to unpuff.

deshipotecar *tr.* to cancel the mortgage on.

deshojar *tr.* to strip [a tree] of its leaves, [a flower] of its petals. *2* to tear the leaves out of [a book]. *3 ref.* to defoliate.

deshoje *m.* defoliation, fall of leaves.

deshollejar *tr.* to skin [grapes]; to shell [beans].
deshollinadera *f.* DESHOLLINADOR 2.
deshollinador *m.* chimney sweeper. *2* longhanded broom or brush, Turk's-head.
deshollinar *tr.* to sweep [a chimney]. *2* to sweep or clean [ceilings] with a Turk's-head.
deshonestidad *f.* immodesty, indecency, lewdness.
deshonesto, -ta *adj.* immodest, indecent, lewd.
deshonor *m.* dishonour, disgrace.
deshonorar *tr.* to dishonour, disgrace. *2* to deprive of office or dignity.
deshonra *f.* dishonour, disgrace, shame. *2* seduction or violation [of a woman].
deshonrabuenos *m.* defamer. *2* degenerate.
deshonrador, -ra *m.-f.* dishonourer, disgracer, defamer. *2* violator, seducer.
deshonrar *tr.* to dishonour, disgrace. *2* to insult, defame. *3* to violate or seduce [a woman]. *4 ref.* to disgrace or dishonour oneself.
deshonroso, -sa *adj.* dishonourable, disgraceful.
deshora *f.* unseasonable or inconvenient time: *a ~, a deshoras,* untimely, inopportunely.
deshornar *tr.* DESENHORNAR.
deshuesado, -da *adj.* boned [meat], pitted, stoned [fruit].
deshuesar *tr.* to bone [meat, an animal]. *2* to stone [fruits].
deshumanizar *tr.* to dehumanize.
deshumedecer *tr.* to dehumidify, dry up. ¶ CONJUG. like *agradecer.*
desiderativo, -va *adj.* desiderative, expressing desire.
desiderátum, *pl.* **-data** *m.* desideratum.
desidia *f.* carelessness, negligence, indolence.
desidioso, -sa *adj.* careless, negligent, indolent.
desierto, -ta *adj.* deserted, uninhabited, lonely. *2 m.* desert, waste, wilderness.
designación *f.* designation, appointment.
designar *tr.* to design, purpose. *2* to design, designate, appoint. *3* to designate, denote.
designio *m.* design, purpose, intention.
desigual *adj.* unequal, unlike. *2* uneven; irregular, rough, broken. *3* arduous, difficult. *4* changeable, variable. *5* unsuitable [marriage]. *6 salir ~ una cosa,* to fail, fall through.
desigualar *tr.* to make unequal. *2* to make uneven.
desigualdad *f.* inequality, unequality, difference. *2* roughness, unevenness. *3* changeableness. *4* MATH. inequality.
desilusión *f.* disillusion, disillusionment, disenchantment, disappointment.
desilusionar *tr.* to disillusion, disenchant, disappoint. *2 ref.* to become disillusioned.
desimanar, desimantar *tr.* to demagnetize. *2 ref.* to become demagnetized.
desimpresionar *tr.* to undeceive.
desinencia *f.* GRAM. desinence, termination, inflection.
desinencial *adj.* desinential.
desinfección *f.* disinfection.
desinfectante *adj.-m.* disinfectant.
desinfectar *tr.* to disinfect.
desinflamar *tr.* to remove the inflammation from. *2 ref.* [of a wound, part of the body, etc.] to be cured of inflammation.
desinflar *tr.* to deflate.
desinsectación *f.* fumigation, freeing from insects.
desinsectar *tr.* to fumigate, free from insects.
desintegración *f.* disintegration.

desintegrar *tr.* to disintegrate. *2 intr.* to disintegrate [become disintegrated].
desinterés *m.* disinterest, disinterestedness.
desinteresadamente *adv.* disinterestedly, generously.
desinteresado, -da *adj.* disinterested. *2* uninterested.
desinteresarse *ref.* to lose interest [in something].
desintoxicar *tr.* MED. to cure of intoxication.
desistimiento *m.* desistance. *2* LAW waiving a right.
desistir *intr.* to desist: *~ de,* to desist from or to. *2* LAW to waive [a right].
desjarretar *tr.* to hamstring, hock [animals].
desjuiciado, -da *adj.* lacking judgment, senseless.
desjuntar *tr.* to disjoin, sever, separate.
deslabonar *tr.* to unlink; to disjoint, disconnect.
deslavado, -da *adj.* weak, faded, pale. *2* barefaced.
deslavar *tr.* to wash superficially. *2* to weaken, fade; to take away the colour or force of.
deslavazar *tr.* DESLAVAR.
deslazar *tr.* DESENLAZAR.
desleal *adj.* disloyal.
deslealtad *f.* disloyalty.
desleimiento *m.* dissolving [with a liquid].
desleír *tr.* to dissolve [with a liquid]. *2* to dilute [expressions, ideas, etc.]. ¶ CONJUG. like *reír.*
deslenguado, -da *adj.* impudent, insolent, foulmouthed.
deslenguar *tr.* to cut out the tongue of. *2 ref.* to speak impudently or insolently.
desliar *tr.* to untie [a package, etc.]. *2* to separate less from [wine]. *2 ref.* to come untied.
desligadura *f.* untying, unbinding.
desligar *tr.* to untie, unbind. *2* to unravel [immaterial things]. *3* to absolve, free [from obligation]. *4* MUS. to play or sing [a note] staccato. *5 ref.* to come untied. *6* to free oneself [from obligation, bonds, etc.].
deslindamiento *m.* DESLINDE.
deslindar *tr.* to demarcate, delimitate, fix the boundaries or limits of. *2* to explain, define.
deslinde *m.* demarcation, delimitation.
deslío, deslía, desliera, etc. *irr.* V. DESLEÍR.
desliz *m.* sliding, slipping. *2* fig. slip, blunder, false step, frailty.
deslizadero *m.* slippery place.
deslizadizo, -za *adj.* sliding. *2* slippery.
deslizamiento *m.* sliding, slipping, skidding.
deslizante *adj.* gliding.
deslizar *intr.-ref.* to slide, glide, skid; to slip. *2 tr.* to slip, to glide. *3 ref.* to make a slip or blunder. *4* to slip away.
deslomadura *f.* injuring or straining of the loins.
deslomar *tr.-ref.* to injure or strain the loins of. *2 tr.* to beat, thrash.
deslucido, -da *adj.* tarnished, spoilt, lacklustre. *2* dull, poor, flat, being a failure.
deslucimiento *m.* tarnishing, lack of brilliancy; dullness, flatness, failure.
deslucir *tr.* to tarnish, mar, spoil, to impair the lustre or splendour of. *2 ref.* to become tarnished, to get spoilt, to lose lustre. ¶ CONJUG. like *lucir.*
deslumbrador, -ra *adj.* dazzling, glaring.
deslumbramiento *m.* dazzle, dazzling.
deslumbrante *adj.* dazzling, glaring.
deslumbrar *tr.* to dazzle, daze.
deslustrado, -da *adj.* frosted, ground [glass]. *2 m.* frosting [of glass].
deslustrar *tr.* to tarnish, dull; to unglaze, remove

the luster from; to frost [glass]. 2 to impair the beauty, the fame, etc., of.

deslustre *m.* tarnishing, dulling. 2 unglazing, removal of the luster. 3 discredit, stain.

desmadejamiento *m.* lassitude.

desmadejar *tr.* to cause languor or lassitude. 2 *ref.* to feel languor or lassitude.

desmadrar *tr.* to separate [young animals] from their mothers.

desmagnetización *f.* demagnetization.

desmagnetizar *tr.* to demagnetize.

desmajolar *tr.* to pull up [new vines].

desmallar *tr.* to cut or undo the meshes of. 2 DESENMALLAR.

desmán *m.* excess, outrage. 2 mishap. 3 ZOOL. desman, muskrat.

desmanarse *ref.* to stray from a flock or herd.

desmandado, -da *adj.* disobedient, unruly. 2 insolent. 3 strayed, stray.

desmandar *tr.* to repeal an order. 2 to revoke a legacy. 3 *ref.* to be insolent. 4 to take undue liberties, to lose moderation. 5 to break away from [group, ranks, etc.].

desmangado, -da *adj.* handleless, without a handle.

desmanotado, -da *adj.* awkward, unhandy.

desmantelado, -da *adj.* dismantled, ill-furnished.

desmantelar *tr.* to dismantle. 2 NAUT. to unmast. 3 NAUT. to unrig.

desmaña *f.* clumsiness, awkwardness.

desmañado, -da *adj.* clumsy, awkward, unhandy.

desmaño *m.* untidiness, slovenliness.

desmarcar *tr.* to remove marks from. 2 *ref.* FOOTBALL to evade the marking of an opponent.

desmarrido, -da *adj.* sad, languid, weak.

desmayado, -da *adj.* faint, languid. 2 discouraged. 3 pale; wan [colour, light].

desmayar *tr.* to dismay, discourage. 2 *intr.* to lose courage. 3 *ref.* to faint, swoon.

desmayo *m.* languor, weakness. 2 discouragement. 3 fainting fit, swoon. 4 BOT. weeping willow.

desmedido, -da *adj.* excessive, disproportionate, out of measure.

desmedirse *ref.* to forget oneself, act insolently. ¶ CONJUG. like *servir*.

desmedrado, -da *adj.* small, stunted.

desmedrar *tr.* to deteriorate. 2 *intr.-ref.* to decay, lose strength.

desmedro *m.* deterioration, decline.

desmejora *f.*, **desmejoramiento** *m.* impairment, loss of health.

desmejorar *tr.* to impair the beauty or perfection of. 2 to impair the health of. 3 *intr.-ref.* to lose beauty or perfection. 4 to decline [in health].

desmelenado, -da *adj.* dishevelled, tousled.

desmelenar *tr.* to dishevel, disarrange the hair of.

desmembración *m.* dismemberment.

desmembrar *tr.* to dismember. 2 to divide, segregate. ¶ CONJUG. like *acertar*.

desmemoriado, -da *adj.* forgetful, having a poor memory.

desmemoriarse *ref.* to forget, lose the memory.

desmenguar *tr.* to lessen, to reduce, to decrease, to lower.

desmentida *f.* denial, act of giving the lie to.

desmentir *tr.* to give the lie to. 2 to contradict, deny. 3 to belie [give the lie to in conduct; be false to]. ¶ CONJUG. like *hervir*.

desmenuzable *adj.* crumbly, easily crumbled.

desmenuzamiento *m.* crumbling, breaking into small pieces or shreds. 2 minute scrutinizing.

desmenuzar *tr.* to crumble, to break into small pieces or shreds, to fritter. 2 to scrutinize.

desmerecedor, -ra *adj.* unworthy.

desmerecer *tr.* to be or become unworthy of. 2 *intr.* to lose worth. 3 ~ *de*, to be inferior to [another thing]. ¶ CONJUG. like *agradecer*.

desmerecimiento *m.* demerit.

desmesura *f.* excess, lack of moderation.

desmesuradamente *adv.* beyond measure.

desmesurado, -da *adj.* excessive, disproportionate. 2 impudent, discourteous, forward.

desmesurar *tr.* to disorder, disarrange. 2 *ref.* to be insolent, lose restraint, go too far.

desmiento, desmienta, etc. *irr.* V. DESMENTIR.

desmigajar *tr.* to crumb, break into small pieces. 2 *ref.* to crumble, fall into small pieces.

desmigar *tr.* to crumb [bread].

desmilitarización *f.* demilitarization.

desmilitarizar *tr.* to demilitarize.

desmineralización *f.* MED. demineralization.

desmirriado, -da *adj.* lean, emaciated, run-down.

desmochar *tr.* to lop or cut off the top of [a tree, etc.]; to dehorn [an animal]. 2 to cut [a literary work, a musical composition, etc.].

desmoche *m.* lopping or cutting off.

desmonetizar *tr.* to demonetize.

desmontable *adj.* that can be taken to pieces, dismountable, knockdown. 2 collapsible. 3 detachable. 4 ARCH. sectional, in sections, portable. 5 *n.* tyre lever.

desmontadura *f.* dismounting, demounting. 2 disassembling.

desmontar *tr.* to clear [a wood]. 2 to level [ground]. 3 to dismount, take, apart, disassemble. 4 to uncock [firearms]. 5 to dismount [deprive of horses]; to unhorse. 6 to dismount [cannon]. 7 *intr.* to dismount, alight.

desmonte *m.* clearing from trees or bushes. 2 levelling [of ground]; cut [for a railway, road, etc.]. 3 cleared or levelled ground.

desmoralización *f.* demoralization.

desmoralizador, -ra *adj.* demoralizing. 2 *m.-f.* demoralizer.

desmoralizar *tr.* to demoralize. 2 *ref.* to become demoralized. 3 MIL. to lose the morale.

desmoronamiento *m.* crumbling, disintegration.

desmoronar *tr.* to crumble, disintegrate, erode; to destroy little by little. 2 *ref.* to crumble, fall to pieces.

desmostarse *ref.* [of grapes] to lose must.

desmotar *tr.* to burl [cloth].

desmovilización *f.* demobilization.

desmovilizar *tr.* to demobilize.

desnacionalización *f.* denationalization.

desnacionalizar *tr.* to denationalize.

desnarigado, -da *adj.* noseless; small-nosed.

desnarigar *tr.* to cut off the nose of. 2 *ref.* to bump one's nose.

desnatadora *f.* cream separator.

desnatar *tr.* to cream, draw off the cream from.

desnaturalizado, -da *adj.* denaturalized. 2 denatured. 3 unnatural [parent, child, etc.].

desnaturalizar *tr.* to denaturalize. 2 to denature.

desnivel *m.* unevenness, difference of level, drop.

desnivelado, -da *adj.* unlevelled, uneven.

desnivelar *tr.* to unlevel, make uneven. 2 *ref.* to become uneven.

desnucamiento *m.* breaking of the neck.

desnucar *tr.-ref.* to break or dislocate the neck of.

desnudamente *adv.* nakedly; clearly, plainly.
desnudamiento *m.* undressing. *2* denuding.
desnudar *tr.* to undress, unclothe. *2* to draw [the sword]. *4 ref.* to undress. *5* to become denuded; to divest oneself or itself.
desnudez *f.* nudity, nakedness.
desnudo, -da *adj.* naked, nude. *2* ill-clothed. *3* bare, uncovered, stripped. *4* destitute. *5 m.* F. ARTS nude; nude figure.
desnutrición *f.* MED. denutrition.
desnutrirse *ref.* to suffer from denutrition.
desobedecer *tr.* to disobey. ¶ CONJUG. like *agradecer.*
desobediencia *f.* disobedience.
desobediente *adj.* disobedient.
desobstrucción *f.* removal of obstructions.
desobstruir *tr.* to clear, remove obstructions from. *2* MED. to deobstruct. ¶ CONG. like *huir.*
desocupación *f.* leisure. *2* unemployment.
desocupado, -da *adj.* free, vacant, unoccupied. *2* at leisure, idle. *3* unemployed [person]. *4 m.-f.* idle or unemployed person.
desocupar *tr.* to vacate, leave, empty; to evacuate.
desodorante *adj.-m.* deodorant.
desoír *tr.* not to hear, not to heed, to be deaf to.
desojarse *ref.* to strain one's eyes, to look hard.
desolación *f.* desolation, destruction; solitariness. *2* desolation, grief.
desolado, -da *adj.* desolate. *2* disconsolate.
desolador, -ra *adj.* desolating. *2* grieving.
desolar *tr.* to desolate, lay waste. *2 ref.* to be desolate, disconsolate. ¶ CONJUG. like *contar.*
desoldar *tr.* to unsolder. *2 ref.* to come unsoldered. ¶ CONJUG. like *contar.*
desolladero *m.* slaughterhouse.
desollado, -da *adj.* skinned, flayed. *2* impudent, brazen, shameless.
desollador, -ra *m.-f.* skinner, flayer. *3* fleecer, extortioner.
desolladura *f.* skinning, flaying. *2* excoriation.
desollar *tr.* to skin, flay. *2* to excoriate. *3* to cause great harm or injure to [a person]. *4 ~ vivo*, fig. to skin alive; fig. to backbite. ¶ CONJUG. like *contar.*
desollón *m.* excoriation.
desopilar *tr.* MED. to deoppilate.
desopinar *tr.* to discredit.
desorden *m.* disorder [want of order], confusion, disarray. *2* disorder, disturbance, riot. *3* disorder, licence, excess.
desordenado, -da *adj.* disorderly. *2* disarranged. *3* careless, slovenly. *4* inordinate, immoderate. *5* licentious [life].
desordenar *tr.* to disorder, throw into disorder, disarrange, upset. *2 ref.* to become disarranged.
desorejado, -da *adj.* infamous, dissolute, degraded.
desorejar *tr.* to crop the ears of.
desorganización *f.* disorganization.
desorganizar *tr.* to disorganize. *2 ref.* to become disorganized.
desorientación *f.* disorientation, loss of one's bearings. *2* confusion, bafflement.
desorientador, -ra *adj.* confusing, baffling.
desorientar *tr.* to disorientate. *2* to confuse, bewilder. *3 ref.* to become disorientated.
desosar *tr.* DESHUESAR.
desovar *intr.* [of aquatic animals] to spawn.
desove *m.* spawning. *2* spawning season.
desovillar *tr.* to unwind [a ball of yarn]. *2* to clear up, unravel.

desoxidación *f.* deoxidization. *2* removal of the rust.
desoxidar *tr.* to deoxidize. *2* to remove the rust of.
desoxigenar *tr.* to deoxygenate, to deoxidize.
despabiladeras *f. pl.* snuffers.
despabilado, -da *adj.* wakeful, awake. *2* smart, quick-witted.
despabilar *tr.* to trim or snuff [a candle]. *2* to finish quickly. *3* to steal. *4* to smarten, enliven, sharpen the wits of. *5* coll. to kill. *6 ref.* to wake up, shake sleepiness. *7* to become alert.
despacio *adv.* slowly, deliberately. *2* (Am.) in a low voice. *3 interj.* easy there!, gently!
despacioso, -sa *adj.* slow, deliberate, phlegmatic.
despacito *adv.* slowly, gently. *2 interj.* DESPACIO 3.
despachaderas *f. pl.* coll. surly manner of replying. *2* coll. resourcefulness.
despachado, -da *adj.* impudent, brazen. *2* resourceful.
despachar *tr.* to dispatch [get promptly done; send off; kill]. *2* to attend to [correspondence]. *3* to attend to, settle [business]. *4* to sell [goods]. *5* to wait upon [customers]. *6* to dismiss, discharge. *7* to clear [at the custom-house]. *8 intr.-ref.* to hasten, be quick. *9 ref.* to talk without restraint.
despacho *m.* dispatch, promptness. *2* attending [to correspondence]; settling [of business]. *3* sale [of goods]. *4* clearance [at the custom-house]. *5* dismissal. *6* shipment. *7* office, bureau, counting house: *~ de billetes*, ticket-office; *~ de localidades*, box-office. *8* library, study. *9* dispatch [message]. *10* title, commission, warrant.
despachurrar *tr.* to crush, squash. *2* fig. to make a mess of [a speech, etc.].
despajar *tr.* to separate straw from [grain].
despaldillar *tr.* to break or dislocate the shoulder of [an animal].
despalmar *tr.* NAUT. to careen, clean the bottom of [a ship]. *2* to pare [a horse's hoof].
despampanante *adj.* astounding; stunning, splendid, ripping.
despampanar *tr.* to prune [vines]. *2* coll. to astound. *3 ref.* to give oneself a hard bump.
despancijar, despanzurrar *tr.* to burst the belly of; to squash.
desparejar *tr.* to break the pair of.
desparpajado, -da *adj.* easy in speech and deportment.
desparpajo *m.* easiness in speech and deportment, unembarrassment.
desparramado, -da *adj.* spread, scattered.
desparramamiento *m.* spreading, scattering. *2* squandering, extravagance. *3* dissipation.
desparramar *tr.* to spread, scatter. *2* to squander, dissipate. *3 ref.* to spread, scatter. *4* to amuse , oneself, have a wild time.
despasar *tr.* NAUT. to unreeve. *2* SEW. to take [a string, etc.] out of a casing.
despatarrada *f.* split [in dancing].
despatarrar *tr.* to make [a person] open his legs wide. *2* coll. to astound, to dumbfound. *3 ref.* to fall flat with legs spread out.
despatillar *tr.* CARP. to tenon.
despavesar *tr.* to snuff [candles]. *2* to blow the ashes off [embers].
despavorido, -da *adj.* terrified.
despavorir *intr.-ref.* to feel dread, terror; to be or become terrified. ¶ Only used in the forms having *i* in their terminations.

despearse *ref.* to get one's feet or hoofs sore [by much walking].

despectivamente *adj.* contemptuously, scornfully. 2 pejoratively.

despectivo, -va *adj.* contemptuous. 2 GRAM. pejorative.

despechadamente *adv.* spitefully; despairingly.

despechar *tr.* to irritate, enrage; to cause despair.

despecho *m.* spite born from disappointment. 2 despair. 3 *a ~ de*, in spite of, despite.

despechugar *tr.* to carve off the breast of a [fowl]. 2 *ref.* coll. to bare one's breast.

despedazamiento *m.* tearing to pieces, cutting into pieces.

despedazar *tr.* to tear to pieces, cut into pieces. 2 to break [one's heart]; to tear to shreds [a reputation].

despedida *f.* farewell. 2 leave-taking.

despedir *tr.* to throw. 2 to emit, send forth, eject, discharge, dart. 3 to reject, expel, throw back. 4 to dismiss; discharge, give notice to. 5 to see off, escort to the door, say good-bye to. 6 *ref.* to part, say good-bye to: *despedirse de*, to take leave of; *despedirse a la francesa*, to take French leave. 7 to give up one's job, give notice. ¶ CONJUG. like *servir*.

despedregar *tr.* to clear of stones.

despegado, -da *adj.* detached, unglued. 2 cool, indifferent, detached, unaffectionate. 3 surly.

despegar *tr.* to detach, unglue, unstick; to separate. 2 *intr.* AER. to take off. 3 *ref.* to detach itself. 4 to move away from. 5 to lose affection for. 6 not to suit, not to go well with.

despego *m.* coolness, indifference.

despegue *m.* AER. take-off.

despeinado, -da *adj.* dishevelled, unkempt.

despeinar *tr.-ref.* to dishevel, disarrange, ruffle the hair of.

despejado, -da *adj.* assured, self-confident. 2 [of person, intelligence, etc.] bright. 3 [of space, forehead, etc.] clear, wide; [of the sky] cloudless.

despejar *tr.* to clear, free from encumbrance. 2 to clear up [a situation, etc.]. 3 ALG. to find value of [unknown quantify]. 4 *ref.* to acquire assurance, ease. 5 [of weather, the head, etc.] to clear up. 6 MED. to get rid of fever.

despejo *m.* clearing, freeing from encumbrance. 2 clearing up. 3 assurance, ease. 4 intelligence.

despelotado, -da *adj.* coll. stark-naked.

despelotarse *ref.* coll. to strip naked. 2 to take care of oneself.

despeluzar *tr.* to dishevel. 2 to make the hair [of a person] stand on end. 3 *ref.* to be horrified.

despeluznante *adj.* hair-raising, horrifying.

despeluznar *tr.* DESPELUZAR.

despellejar *tr.* to skin, flay. 2 fig. to flay, speak ill of.

despenar *tr.* to relieve from sorrow. 2 coll. to kill.

despensa *f.* pantry, larder, storeroom. 2 store of provisions.

despensería *f.* pantryman's post.

despensero, -ra *m.* pantryman, butler. 2 *f.* pantrywoman.

despeñadero *m.* precipice, craggy slope. 2 fig. danger [to which one exposes oneself].

despeñar *tr.* to precipitate, fling down a precipice.

despepitar *tr.* to remove the pips from [a fruit]; to gin [cotton]. 2 *ref. despepitarse por*, to be mad about.

desperdiciar *tr.* to waste, squander, misspend. 2 to fail to take advantage of; to lose, miss [an opportunity, etc.].

desperdicio *m.* waste, squander, misspending. 2 (spec. *pl.*) waste, waste material, remains.

desperdigar *tr.* to scatter, disperse. 2 *ref.* to scatter, disperse [go in different directions].

desperezarse *ref.* to stretch, to stretch one's limbs.

desperezo *m.* stretching [one's limbs].

desperfecto *m.* slight damage, deterioration.

desperfilar *tr.* PAINT. to soften the contours of.

despernar *tr.* to cut or injure the legs of.

despersonalizar *tr.* to depersonalize.

despertador, -ra *adj.* awaking. 2 *m.-f.* awakener. 3 *m.* alarm clock, alarum-clock.

despertar *tr.* to wake, awaken, rouse [from sleep]. 2 awaken, rouse, stir up, excite. 3 *intr.-ref.* to wake up, awake; to revive. ¶ CONJUG. like *acertar*.

despestañarse *ref.* to look hard, strain one's eyes.

despezonar *tr.* to take off the stem [of a fruit].

despiadado, -da *adj.* pitiless, ruthless, unmerciful.

despicar *tr.* to satisfy, gratify. 2 *ref.* to have one's own back, to take revenge.

despichar *tr.* to expel [juice or moisture].

despidiente *m.* ARCH. *~ de aguas*, flashing.

despido *m.* farewell; leave taking. 2 dismissal, discharge, layoff.

despido, despida, etc. *irr.* V. DESPEDIR.

despiertamente *adv.* smartly, ingeniously.

despierto, -ta *adj.* awake. 2 lively, smart, quickwitted.

despierto, despierte, etc. *irr.* V. DESPERTAR.

despilfarradamente *adv.* lavishly, prodigally.

despilfarrado, -da *adj.* wasted, squandered. 2 ragged, in rags. 3 *adj.-n.* prodigal, spendthrift.

despilfarrador, -ra *adj.* squanderer, prodigal.

despilfarrar *tr.* to waste, squander, spend lavishly. 2 *ref.* to be prodigal of his money.

despilfarro *m.* waste, extravagance, lavishness.

despimpollar *tr.* to clear [a vine] of useless shoots.

despintar *tr.* to take the paint off. 2 to cause to turn out differently. 3 *ref.* [of a thing] to lose its paint, lose colour. 4 *no despintársele a uno una persona*, not to forget what a person is like.

despinzar *tr.* to burl [cloth].

despiojar *tr.* to delouse.

despique *m.* satisfaction, requital.

despistar *tr.* to throw off the scent. 2 *ref.* to loose the scent. 3 coll. to go off the track, get lost.

despiste *m.* swerve (car). 2 absentmindedness, confusion, bewilderment. 3 mistake; *tener un gran ~*, to be terribly absentminded.

1) **desplacer** *m.* pain, displeasure.

2) **desplacer** *tr.* to pain, to displease.

desplanchar *tr.* to rumple [something that was ironed].

desplantador *m.* garden trowel.

desplantar *tr.* to uproot. 2 to throw out of plumb.

desplante *m.* irregular posture [in dancing or fencing]. 2 arrogant or insolent act or words.

desplayar *intr.* [of the sea] to recede from the beach.

desplazamiento *m.* NAUT. displacement [of water].

desplazar *tr.* NAUT. to displace.

desplegable *m.* brochure, folder, pamphlet.

desplegar *tr.* to unfold, spread, lay out, open out. 2 to unfurl. 3 to unfold, explain. 4 to display [activity, etc.]. 5 MIL. to deploy. 6 *ref.* to unfold, open, expand, spread out. 7 MIL. [of troops] to deploy. ¶ CONJUG. like *acertar*.

despliegue *m.* unfolding; displaying. *2* MIL. deployment.

desplomar *tr.* to throw out of plumb. *2 ref.* to get out of plumb. *3* [of a wall] to tumble down. *4* to crash down. *5* [of a pers.] to collapse.

desplome *m.* getting out of plumb. *2* tumbling down. *3* collapse, fall.

desplomo *m.* ARCH. deviation from the vertical.

desplumar *tr.* to pluck [a bird]. *2* fig. to pluck, fleece [someone]. *3 ref.* [of a bird] to lose its feathers.

desplume *m.* plucking, deplumation.

despoblación *f.* depopulation. *2* stripping [a land] of trees; emptying [a river] of fishes.

despoblado *m.* uninhabited tract of land; open country.

despoblar *tr.* to depopulate. *2* to strip [a land] of trees, to deprive [the head, a spot] of hair; to empty [a river, etc.] of fishes. *3 ref.* to become depopulated, desert. *4* to become bald, treeless or empty of fishes. ¶ CONJUG. like *contar*.

despojar *tr.* to despoil, deprive; to strip, divest. *2* LAW to dispossess. *3 ref. despojarse de*, to take off [a garment]; to give up, to divest oneself of.

despojo *m.* depoilment, despoilation; stripping; divesting; dispossession. *2* spoils, booty. *3 pl.* head, pluck and feet [of slaughtered animals]; gizzard, pinions, legs, head and neck [of fowl]. *4* leavings, scraps. *5* mortal remains.

despolarizar *tr.* PHYS., CHEM. depolarize.

despolvorear *tr.* to dust, dust off.

desportillar *tr.* to chip or break the edge of.

desposado, -da *adj.* newly married. *2* handcuffed. *3 m.-f.* newlywed.

desposar *tr.* to marry [unite in wedlock]. *2 ref.* to get married. *3* to be betrothed.

desposeer *tr.-ref.* to disposses, to divest.

desposeimiento *m.* disposession.

desposorios *m. pl.* nuptials, marriage. *2* betrothal.

déspota *m.* despot, tyrant.

despótico, -ca *adj.* despotic.

despotismo *m.* despotism.

despotricar *intr.* to talk without restraint, to rant.

despotrique *m.* wild talk, ranting.

despreciable *adj.* despicable, contemptible. *2* negligible.

despreciar *tr.* to despise, contemn, scorn, slight. *2* to lay aside, to reject. *3* to set to nought, to undervalue.

despreciativo, -va *adj.* contemptuous, scornful.

desprecio *m.* contempt, scorn, disregard. *2* slight.

desprender *tr.* to detach, loose, separate. *2* to emit, send, give out [light, heat, etc.]. *3 ref.* to come loose, detach itself; to detach or extricate oneself. *4* [of light, heat, etc.] to issue, come forth. *5* to dispossess oneself. *6* to follow, be inferred.

desprendido, -da *adj.* generous, disinterested.

desprendimiento *m.* detaching, coming loose. *2* emission [of light, heat, etc.]. *3* disinterestedness. *4* indifference. *5* PAINT. descent from the Cross. *6* landslide.

despreocupación *f.* freedom from bias. *2* unconventionality. *3* unconcernedness. *4* openmindedness.

despreocupado, -da *adj.* unprejudiced. *2* carefree, unconcerned. *3* unconventional. *4* broadminded.

despreocuparse *ref.* to abandon a prejudice. *2 ~ de*, not to care or worry anymore about.

desprestigiar *tr.* to discredit, impair the prestige of. *3 ref.* to fall into discredit, lose prestige.

desprestigio *m.* discredit, loss of prestige.

desprevenido, -da *adj.* unprovided, unprepared: *coger a uno ~*, to catch somebody unawares.

desproporción *f.* disproportion.

desproporcionado, -da *adj.* disproportionate.

desproporcionar *tr.* to disproportion.

despropósito *m.* absurdity, nonsense.

desproveer *tr.* to deprive of provisions, supplies or the necessaries of life.

desprovisto, -ta *adj.* unprovided. *2* deprived, void [of]; lacking [in].

después *adv.* after, afterwards, later; next. *2 ~ de*, after, next to; *~ (de) que*, after; *~ de todo*, after all.

despulpar *tr.* to extract the pulp from [a fruit].

despuntar *tr.* to blunt, to break or wear out the point of. *2 intr.* to show wit or intelligence; to excel. *4 ~ el alba, ~ el día*, to dawn.

desquejar *tr.* HORT. to slip.

desqueje *f.* HORT. slipping.

desquiciamiento *m.* unhinging. *2* upsetting, unsetting, downfall.

desquiciar *tr.* to unhinge. *2* to disjoint, to upset, to unsettle. *3 ref.* to become unhinged, disjointed, upset, unsettled.

desquitar *tr.* to compensate [someone] for loss, etc. *2 ref.* to retrieve a loss, to win back one's money. *3* to take revenge, get even.

desquite *m.* retrieving [of one's loss], compensation. *2* revenge, requital, retaliation.

desramar *tr.* to strip of branches.

desratizar *tr.* to derat.

desratización *f.* deratting, deratization.

desrizar *tr.* to uncurl, unfrizzle.

destacado, -da *adj.* outstanding, distinguished.

destacamento *m.* MIL. detachment.

destacar *tr.* MIL. detach, detail. *2* PAINT. to make stand out, emphasize. *3 ref.* MIL. [of a troop] to detach itself. *4* to stand out, be conspicuous.

destaconar *tr.* to wear down the heels of [shoes].

destajador *m.* forging hammer.

destajar *tr.* to settle the terms for [a job]. *2* to cut [cards].

destajero, -ra & destajista *m.-f.* pieceworker.

destajo *m.* piecework, taskwork: *a ~*, by the job; fig. eagerly, rapidly.

destapar *tr.* to uncover. *2* to take off the cover, lid or cap of; to uncork, unplug, open. *3* to reveal. *4 ref.* to get uncovered.

destapiar *tr.* to pull down the walls enclosing [an open space].

destaponar *tr.* to remove the stopper from.

destarar *tr.* COM. to deduct the tare on.

destartalado, -da *adj.* ramshackle. *2* poorly furnished [house, room].

destazar *tr.* BUTCH. to cut up carcasses.

destechar *tr.* to unroof.

destejar *tr.* to untile the roof of.

destejer *tr.* to unweave or ravel, to unknit, to unbraid.

destellar *tr.* to sparkle, twinkle, flash, scintillate.

destello *m.* sparkling, twinkling. *2* sparkle, flash, scintillation; beam [of light].

destemplado, -da *adj.* MUS. out of tune. *2* PAINT. inharmonious. *3* intemperate, disagreeable.

destemplanza *f.* intemperance, unsteadiness [of the weather]. *2* MED. malaise. *3* want of moderation [in language or actions], rudeness.

destemplar *tr.* to disturb the harmony of. *2* MUS. to put out of tune. *3 ref.* MUS. [of instruments] to get out of tune. *4* MED. to feel a malaise. *5* [of a metal] to lose its temper. *6* to lose moderation in language or actions.

destemple *m.* MUS. [of instruments] being out of tune. *2* MED. malaise. *3* unpleasantness [of weather]. *4* untempering. *5* want of moderation [in words, etc.]; rudeness.

desteñir *tr.* to undye; to discolour, fade. *2 ref.* to lose the dye; to fade. ¶ CONJUG. like *teñir*.

desternillarse *ref.* to break one's gristles: ~ *de risa*, coll. to split one's sides with laughter.

desterrado, -da *adj.* exiled. *2 m.-f.* exile, outcast.

desterrar *tr.* to exile, banish [a person]. *2* to banish [sadness, uses, etc.]. *3 ref.* to go into exile. ¶ CONJUG. like *acertar*.

desterronar *tr.* to break or crumb the clods of.

destetar *tr.* to wean.

destete *m.* weaning.

destiempo (a) *adv.* inopportunely, untimely, out of season.

destierro *m.* banishment, exile. *2* place of exile. *3* remote and solitary place.

destierro, destierre, etc. *irr.* V. DESTERRAR.

destilación *f.* distillation. *2* catarrhal discharge.

destilado, -da *adj.* distilled.

destilador, -ra *adj.* distilling. *2 m.-f.* distiller. *3 m.* ALAMBIQUE.

destilar *tr.* to distil. *2* to filter. *3 intr.* to distil, trickle down.

destilería *f.* distillery, distilling plant.

destinación *f.* destination, destining.

destinar *tr.* to destine. *2* to designate, appoint [to a post]. *3* to allot, assign.

destinatario, -ria *m.-f.* addressee. *2* consignee.

destino *m.* destiny, fate, fortune, doom. *2* destination: *con* ~ *a*, bound for, going to. *3* employment, post, job.

destitución *f.* dismissal, removal from office. *2* destitution, depriving.

destituir *tr.* to dismiss or remove from office. *2* to destitute, deprive. ¶ CONJUG. like *huir*.

destocar *tr.-ref.* to undo the coiffure of; to uncover the head of.

destorcer *tr.* to untwist. *2* to straighten. *3 ref.* to untwist [become untwisted]. ¶ CONJUG. like *mover*.

destornillado, -da *adj.* unscrewed. *2* brainless, thoughtless, with a screw loose.

destornillador *m.* screwdriver.

destornillamiento *m.* unscrewing. *2* craziness.

destornillar *tr.* to unscrew. *2 ref.* to go crazy.

destrabar *tr.* to unshackle, untie. *2* to loosen, separate.

destraillar *tr.* to uncouple, unleash [dogs].

destral *m.* hatchet, small axe.

destramar *tr.* to unweave.

destrenzar *tr.* to unbraid, to undo [a tress].

destreza *f.* skill, dexterity, address, mastery.

destripacuentos *m.-f.* untimely interrupter of an account or narrative.

destripar *tr.* to gut, disembowel. *2* to take the inside out of, to crush.

destripaterrones *m.* clodhopper, rustic.

destriunfar *tr.* CARDS to draw out the trumps from.

destronamiento *m.* dethronement.

destronar *tr.* to dethrone. *2* to overthrow [from power].

destroncar *tr.* to detruncate; to maim, to dislocate. *2* to cut [trees] at the trunk. *3* to deprive of means, bring to ruin. *4* to tire out, exhaust.

destrozar *tr.* to break in pieces, shatter, rend, des-

troy. *2* to spoil, ill-treat. *3* fig. to anihilate. *4* MIL. to destroy, inflict great losses.

destrozo *m.* breakage, destruction, havoc.

destrozón, -na *m.-f.* one who wears out clothes and shoes too quickly.

destrucción *f.* destruction.

destructible *adj.* destructible.

destructivo, -va *adj.* destructive.

destructor, -ra *adj.* destructive. *2 m.-f.* destroyer. *3 m.* NAV. destroyer.

destruible *adj.* destructible.

destruir *tr.* to destroy. *2* to deprive of means, bring to ruin. *3* to waste, dissipate. *4 ref.* to destroy each other. *5* ALG. to cancel each other. ¶ CONJUG. like *huir*.

destruyente *adj.* destructive.

destruyo, destruyó, destruya, etc. *irr.* V. DESTRUIR.

desubstanciar *tr.* DESUSTANCIAR.

desudación *f.* topping the sweating.

desudar *tr.* to stop the sweating of.

desuello *m.* skinning, flaying. *2* effrontery.

desuello, desuelle, etc. *irr.* V. DESOLLAR.

desuncir *tr.* to unyoke.

desunión *f.* disunion.

desunir *tr.* to disunite. *2 ref.* to disunite, fall apart.

desuñar *tr.* to tear off the nails or claws of. *2* to pull up the dead roots of [plants]. *3 ref.* coll. to work hard with one's hands.

desurdir *tr.* to remove the warp from [a fabric]; to unweave. *2* to upset [a plot, etc.].

desusado, -da *adj.* out of use, obsolete. *2* unusual.

desusar *tr.* to discontinue the use of.

desuso *m.* disuse, obsoleteness, desuetude: *caer en* ~, to become obsolete.

desustanciar *tr.* to deprive of substance, to weaken. *2 ref.* to lose substance, weaken.

desvaído, -da *adj.* pale, dull [colour]. *2* lank, ungainly [person].

desvainar *tr.* to shell [beans, peas, etc.].

desvalido, -da *adj.* helpless, unprotected, destitute.

desvalijador, -ra *n.* thief, robber. *2* burglar.

desvalijar *tr.* to take out or steal the contents of [a valise, suitcase, etc.]. *2* to rob, plunder, fleece.

desvalimiento *m.* helplessness, abandonment, destitution.

desvalorización *f.* devaluation.

desvalorizar *tr.* to devalue.

desván *m.* garret, loft.

desvanecedor *m.* PHOT. mask.

desvanecer *tr.* to melt, cause to vanish. *2* to dispel, dissipate [clouds, doubts, etc.]. *3* to efface [a recollection]. *4* to swell [with pride]. *5 ref.* to melt, vanish, evanesce, evaporate. *6* to be dispelled, dissipated, effaced. *7* to swell [with pride]. *8* to faint, swoon. *9* RADIO. to fade. ¶ CONJUG. like *agradecer*.

desvanecidamente *adv.* proudly, with presumption.

desvanecido, -da *adj.* vain, proud, conceited, haughty. *2* smug, self-satisfied. *3* MED. fainted.

desvanecimiento *m.* melting, vanishing, dispelling. *2* pride, presumption. *3* giddiness, swoon, fainting fit. *4* RADIO. fading.

desvarar *intr.-ref.* to glide, slip. *2 tr.* NAUT. to refloat, set afloat [a stranded ship].

desvariado, -da *adj.* delirious, raving. *2* wild, nonsensical.

desvariar *intr.* to be delirious, rave, rant.

desvarío *m.* delirium, raving. *2* wild act or speech,

nonsense. *3* monstrosity. *4* inconstancy, caprice, whim.

desvelado, -da *adj.* wakeful, sleepless. *2* careful, solicitous.

desvelar *tr.* to keep awake, make sleepless. *2 ref.* to be unable to sleep. *3* to spare no pains, watch carefully [over].

desvelo *m.* sleeplessness, wakefulness. *2* care, solicitude, concern.

desvencijado, -da *adj.* rickety, loose-jointed.

desvencijar *tr.* to disjoint, make rickety. *2 ref.* to become rickety.

desvendar *tr.* to take off a bandage from.

desventaja *f.* disadvantage; drawback.

desventajoso, -sa *adj.* disadvantageous, detrimental.

desventura *f.* unhappiness, misery. *2* misfortune.

desventurado, -da *adj.* unfortunate, wretched. *2* timid, spiritless. *3* miserly. *4 m.-f.* poor, spiritless person. *5* miser.

desvergonzado, -da *adj.* shameless; impudent. *2 m.-f.* shameless or impudent person.

desvergonzarse *ref.* to lose shame. *2 ~ con*, to be impudent or insolent to. ¶ CONJUG. like *contar*.

desvergüenza *f.* shamelessness, effrontery. *2* impudence, insolence.

desvestir *tr.-ref.* to undress.

desviación *f.* deviation, deflection, diversion. *2* turning aside or away, wandering away, swerving, swerve. *3* MAGN. deviation.

desviacionismo *m.* deviationism.

desviacionista *adj.* deviationist.

desviado, -da *adj.* deviated; devious.

desviar *tr.* to deviate, deflect. *2* to turn aside, turn away, swerve. *3* to dissuade. *4* RLY. to switch. *5* to ward off [in fencing]. *6 ref.* to deviate, be deflected, turn aside, swerve, wander away.

desvinculación *f.* freeing, releasing. *2* breaking one's links with, severing one's connections with, discharging [from an obligation or commitment], separation, cutting-off.

desvincular *tr.* to free, to discharge, to release. *2* to break one's links with, to cut-off, to separate.

desvío *m.* deviation, deflection, turning aside or away. *2* coldness, indifference, dislike. *3* RLY. siding, sidetrack.

desvirar *tr.* to pare off the edges of [a sole]. *2* to trim [a book]. *3* NAUT. to reverse [a capstan].

desvirgar *tr.* to deflower [a woman].

desvirtuar *tr.* to deprive of import, meaning, force or efficacity.

desvivirse *ref. ~ por*, to do one's utmost for; to long for.

desyemar *tr.* AGR. to remove the buds from [plants].

desyerbar *tr.* DESHERBAR.

deszumar *tr.* to extract the juice from.

detall *m.* retail: *al ~*, retail, at retail.

detalladamente *adv.* in detail.

detallar *tr.* to detail, particularize; to work in detail. *2* to retail, sell at retail.

detalle *m.* detail, particular. *2* detailed account.

detallista *m.-f.* painter or writer fond of, or skilled in, detail. *2* retailer.

detección *f.* RADIO. detection.

detectar *tr.* RADIO. to detect.

detective *m.* detective.

detector *m.* RADIO. detector.

detención *f.* detainment, detention, stopping. *2* halt, stop, delay. *3* detention [in jail]. *4* arrest, capture [of a person]. *5* care, thoroughness.

detendré, detendría, etc. *irr.* V. DETENER.

detener *tr.* to detain, stop; to check, hold, hold back, keep, refrain. *2* to arrest, capture, take into custody. *3* to keep, retain. *4 ref.* to stop, halt. *5* to delay, linger, tarry, pause. *6 detenerse a considerar*, to stop to consider. ¶ CONJUG. like *tener*.

detengo, detenga, etc. *irr.* V. DETENER.

detenido, -da *adj.* careful, minute, thorough. *2* in custody, under arrest. *5 m.-f.* LAW prisoner.

detenimiento *m.* care, thoroughness.

detentar *tr.* to retain unlawfully, to deforce.

detergente *adj.-n.* detergent, detersive.

deterger *tr.* to deterge.

deterioración *f.* impairing, damaging, spoiling, deterioration.

deteriorar *tr.* to impair, damage, spoil, deteriorate. *2 ref.* to become damaged, spoiled.

deterioro *m.* DETERIORACIÓN. *2* injury, damage.

determinación *f.* determination, determining. *2* determination, decision, resolve. *2* resoluteness, firmness, daring.

determinado, -da *adj.* determinate. *3* fixed, appointed. *4* given, specified. *5* determined. *6* GRAM. definite [article].

determinante *adj.-m.* determinant.

determinar *tr.* to determine. *2* to fix, appoint [time or place]. *3* to determine on, resolve. *4 ref.* to determine, make up one's mind.

determinativo, -va *adj.* determinative.

determinismo *m.* PHILOS. determinism.

determinista *adj.-n.* PHIL. determinist.

detersión *f.* detersion.

detersivo, -va; detersorio, -ria *adj.* detersive.

detestable *adj.* detestable. *2* very bad.

detestación *f.* detestation.

detestar *tr.* to detest.

detonación *f.* detonation, report.

detonador *m.* detonator.

detonante *adj.* detonating, explosive. *2* stunning, shattering. *3 m.* explosive.

detonar *tr.* to detonate.

detorsión *f.* MED. sprain.

detracción *f.* detraction.

detractar *tr.* to detract, defame, denigrate.

detractor, -ra *m.-f.* detractor.

detraer *tr.* to detract. ¶ CONJUG. like *traer*.

detrás *adv.* behind, back, in the rear. *2 ~ de*, behind, after, in pursuit of: *~ de la puerta*, behind the door; *ir ~ de*, to go after. *3 por ~*, from behind; behind one's back.

detrimento *m.* detriment, damage, harm.

detrítico, -ca *adj.* GEOL. detrital.

detrito *m.* detritus.

detuve, detuviera, etc. *irr.* V. DETENER.

deuda *f.* debt. *2* sin, fault, offence. *3* public debt; *~ consolidada*, funded debt.

deudo, -da *m.-f.* relative. *2* relationship.

deudor, -ra *adj.* indebted. *2 m.-f.* debtor.

Deuteronomio *m.* Deuteronomy.

devalar *intr.* NAUT. to drift from the course.

devaluación *f.* devaluation.

devanadera *f.* reel, winding frame.

devanado *m.* winding [of yarn, etc.].

devanador, -ra *adj.* winding. *2 m.-f.* winder.

devanar *tr.* to wind, reel, spool. *2 ref. devanarse los sesos*, to rack one's brains.

devanear *intr.* to rave, to act or talk nonsense.

devaneo *m.* raving, delirium, nonsense. *2* dissipation. *3* flirtation.

devastación *f.* devastation, destruction, waste, ruin.

devastador, -ra *adj.* devastating. *2 m.-f.* devastator.

devastar *tr.* to devastate, lay waste, ruin.

devengar *tr.* to earn [wages]; to draw [interest].

devenir *intr.* to happen. *2* PHIL. to become. ¶ CON-JUG. like *venir.*

devoción *f.* devotion, devoutness. *2* strong attachment. *3 pl.* devotions, prayers.

devocionario *m.* prayer book.

devolución *f.* return, restitution.

devolver *tr.* to give back, pay back, put back, send back, return, restore. *2* to return [give in requital or recompense]. *3* coll. to vomit.

devónico, -ca *adj.-n.* GEOL. Devonian.

devorador, -ra *adj.* devouring. *2 m.-f.* devourer.

devorar *tr.* to devour.

devotería *f.* sanctimony.

devoto, -ta *adj.* devout, pious. *2* devotional. *3* devoted [to a person]. *4 m.-f.* devout person.

dextrógiro, -ra *adj.* PHYS. dextrorotary, dextrorotatory.

dextrina *f.* CHIM. dextrine.

dextrorso, -sa *adj.* BOT. dextrorse.

dextrosa *f.* CHEM. dextrose.

dey *m.* dey [ruler of Algiers].

deyección *f.* PHYSIOL. dejection. *2* GEOL. debris.

dezmable *adj.* tithable.

di *irr.* V. DAR & DECIR.

día *m.* day: ~ *de abstinencia* or *de vigilia,* day of abstinence; ~ *de año nuevo,* New Year's day; ~ *de asueto,* day off; ~ *de ayuno,* fast day; ~ *de fiesta,* feast day, holiday; ~ *del juicio,* Judgement day; ~ *de los difuntos,* All-Soul's Day; ~ *de los inocentes,* Innocents' Day; ~ *de Reyes;* Epiphany; ~ *de Todos los Santos,* All-Saint's Day, Hallowmass; ~ *feriado,* LAW court holyday; ~ *festivo,* holyday; ~ *laborable,* workday, weekday; *quince días,* a fortnight; *a días,* now and then; *al* ~, a day, per day; up to date; *antes del* ~, at dawn; *de* ~ *en* ~, from day to day; *el* ~ *de hoy, hoy* ~, today; now, the present time; *el* ~ *menos pensado,* when least expected; *el mejor* ~, some fine day; *en cuatro días,* in few days; *en su* ~, at the proper time; *¡buenos días!,* good morning!; *dar los buenos días,* to pass the time of day. *2* daytime, daylight. *3 pl.* birthday; saint's day [of a person]: *dar los días,* to wish [someone] many happy returns of the day.

diabetes *f.* MED. diabetes.

diabético, -ca *adj.-n.* diabetic.

diablear *intr.* to play pranks.

diablejo *m.* little devil; imp.

diablesa *f.* she-devil.

diablillo *m.* little devil, devilkin; imp. *2* mischievous, waggish person, rogue.

diablo *m.* devil [evil spirit]; wicked person: *como un* ~, like the deuce, like the devil; *darse al* ~, to get angry, to get wild; *del* ~, *de mil diablos, de todos los diablos,* the devil of a; *¡diablos!,* the devil! *2* bad-tempered, reckless, mischievous, shrewd or skilled person. *3 pobre* ~, poor devil. *4* BILL. rest, *bridge.

diablura *f.* devilry, mischievous or daring act.

diabólico, -ca *adj.* diabolic, diabolical, devilish.

diábolo *m.* diabolo [game].

diaconado *m.* DIACONATO.

diaconato *m.* deaconry, diaconate.

diaconisa *f.* deaconess.

diácono *m.* deacon.

diacrítico, -ca *adj.* diacritic(al.

diacústica *f.* diacoustics.

diadelfo, -fa *adj.* BOT. diadelphous.

diadema *f.* diadem. *2* tiara, coronet [worn by women]. *3* glory, halo.

diafanidad *f.* diaphaneity.

diáfano, -na *adj.* diaphane. *2* clear, transparent.

diáfisis *f.* ANAT. diaphysis.

diafragma *m.* diaphragm.

diagnosis *f.* MED. diagnosis.

diagnosticar *tr.* to diagnose.

diagnóstico, -ca *adj.* diagnostic. *2 m.* diagnostic.

diagonal *adj.* diagonal. *2 f.* GEOM. diagonal.

diagrama *m.* diagram.

dial *m.* dial [radio].

dialectal *adj.* dialectal.

dialéctica *f.* dialectics.

dialéctico, -ca *adj.* dialectic(al. *2 m.* dialectician.

dialecto *m.* dialect.

diálisis *f.* CHEM. dialysis.

dializador *m.* CHEM. dialyzer.

dializar *tr.* CHEM. to dialyze.

dialogar *intr.-tr.* to dialogue, dialogize.

dialogismo *m.* RHET. dialogism.

diálogo *m.* dialogue.

dialoguista *m.* dialogist [writer].

diamante *m.* MINER. diamond: ~ *rosa,* rose diamond.

diamantífero, -ra *adj.* diamantiferous.

diamantino, -na *adj.* diamantine. *2* adamantine.

diamantista *m.* diamond cutter or merchant.

diametral *adj.* diametral, diametrical.

diametralmente *adv.* diametrically.

diámetro *m.* diameter.

Diana *f. pr. n.* MYTH. Diana.

diana *f.* MIL. reveille. *2* bull's eye [of a target].

dianche *m.* coll. devil. *2 interj.* the deuce!

diandro, -dra *adj.* BOT. diandrous.

diantre *m.* DIANCHE.

diapasón *m.* MUS. diapason. *2* MUS. fingerboard [of violin, etc.]. *3* MUS. tuning fork; pitch pipe.

diapente *m.* MUS. diapente.

diapositiva *f.* PHOT. diapositive; lantern slide.

diariamente *adv.* daily, every day.

diario, -ria *adj.* daily; *a* ~, daily, every day. *2 m.* daily newspaper. *3* diary, journal: ~ *de navegación,* NAUT. log book. *4* BOOKKEEP. day book.

diarismo *m.* (Am.) journalism.

diarista *m.* diarist.

diarrea *f.* MED. diarrhœa, diarrhea.

diartrosis *f.* ANAT. diarthrosis.

Diáspora *f.* Diaspora.

diastasa *f.* BIOCHEM. diastase.

diástilo *m.* ARCH. diastyle.

diástole *f.* PHYSIOL., PROS. diastole.

diatermia *f.* MED. diathermia, diathermy.

diatomea *f.* BOT. diatom.

diatónico, -ca *adj.* MUS. diatonic.

diatriba *f.* diatribe.

dibujante *m.-f.* draftsman, draftswoman. *2* sketcher, designer, illustrator.

dibujar *tr.* to draw, make a drawing of; to sketch, to design. *2* to depict, describe vividly. *3 ref.* to be outlined. *4* to appear, be revealed.

dibujo *m.* drawing [act or art of drawing; product of this]: ~ *animado,* animated cartoon. *2* description. *3* pattern [of an embroidery, wall paper, etc.].

dicción *f.* word. *2* diction.

diccionario *m.* dictionary.

diccionarista *m.-f.* lexicographer.

diciembre *m.* December.
dicotiledóneo, -a *adj.* BOT. dicotyledonous. *2 f.* dicotyledon. *3 pl.* Dicotyledones.
dicotomía *f.* dichotomy.
dicroísmo *m.* PHYS. dichroism.
dictado *m.* dictation: *escribir al ~*, to take dictation. *2* title, epithet, appellation. *3 pl.* dictates.
dictador *m.* dictator.
dictadura *f.* dictatorship.
dictáfono *m.* dictaphone.
dictamen *m.* opinion, judgment, advice. *2* expert's report; findings.
dictaminar *intr.* to give an opinion [on]. *2* [of an expert] ro report.
dictamo *m.* BOT. dittany.
dictar *tr.* to dictate [a letter, terms, etc.]. *2* to inspire, suggest. *3* to give [laws, precepts]; to pass [judgment].
dictatorial *adj.* dictatorial.
dicterio *m.* taunt, insult, insulting word.
dicha *f.* happiness. *2* fortune, good luck.
dicharachero, -ra *adj.* fond of using vulgar expressions.
dicharacho *m.* vulgar expression.
dicho, -cha *p. p.* of DECIR.: *~ y hecho*, no sooner said than done. *2 adj.* said, mentioned: *arriba ~*, above mentioned. *3 m.* saying, proverb, sentence; remark, statement; *del ~ al hecho, hay gran trecho*, saying and doing are different things. *4* amusing sally.
dichoso, -sa *adj.* happy, fortunate, lucky. *2* coll. annoying, bothersome, wretched.
didáctica *f.* didactics.
didáctico, -ca *adj.* didactic(al.
diecinueve *adj.-m.* nineteen. *2 m.* nineteenth.
diecinueveavo, -va *adj.-m.* nineteenth.
dieciochavo, -va; dieciocheno, -na *adj.-m.* eighteenth.
dieciocho *adj.-m.* eighteen. *2 m.* eighteenth.
dieciséis *adj.-m.* sixteen. *2 m.* sixteenth.
dieciseisavo -va *adj.-m.* sixteenth.
diecisiete *adj.-m.* seventeen. *2 m.* seventeenth.
diecisieteavo, -va *adj.-m.* seventeenth.
diedro, -dra *adj.* GEOM. dihedral.
Diego *m. pr. n.* James.
dieléctrico, -ca *adj.-m.* dielectric.
diente *m.* ANAT., ZOOL. tooth: *~ canino*, canine tooth, eyetooth; *~ incisivo*, incisor, cutting tooth; *~ molar*, molar, back tooth; *aguzar los dientes*, to whet one's appetite; *apretar los dientes*, to set one's teeth; *dar ~ con ~*, to be with teeth chattering; *hablar*, or *decir, entre dientes*, to mutter, mumble; *hincar el ~ en*, to misappropriate a part of [another's property]; to backbite, slander; to attack [a task, etc.]; *tener buen ~*, to be a hearty eater; *a regañadientes*, reluctantly, most unwillingly; *de dientes afuera*, insincerely. *2* fang [of serpent]. *3* tooth [of a comb, saw, etc.]; cog. *4* MAS. tooth. *5* clove [of garlic]. *6* BOT. *~ de león*, dandelion.
dientimellado, -da *adj.* nick-toothed.
diera, diese, etc. *irr.* V. DAR.
diéresis *f.* diaeresis.
diesi *f.* MUS. diesis. *2* MUS. sharp.
diestra *f.* right side. *2* right hand.
diestramente *adv.* skilfully, cleverly.
diestro, -tra *adj.* right, right-hand. *2* dexterous, skilful, able, clever. *3 m.* right, right hand; *a ~ y siniestro*, right and left, wildly. *4* skilful fencer. *5* bullfighter; matador. *6* halter or bridle.
dieta *f.* diet [prescribed or regulated food; assembly]. *2* allowance to public officials and members of Parliament.
dietario *m.* family acount book. *2* chronicler's record book.
dietético, -ca *adj.* dietetic(al. *2 f.* dietetics.
diez *adj.-m.* ten; *las ~*, ten o'clock. *2 m.* tenth [in dates].
diezmar *tr.* to decimate. *2* to tithe.
diezmilésimo, -ma *adj.-m.* then-thousandth.
diezmo *m.* tithe.
difamación *f.* defamation.
difamador, -ra *adj.* defaming. *2 m.-f.* defamer.
difamar *tr.* to defame.
difamatorio, -ria *adj.* defamatory.
diferencia *f.* difference: *hacer diferencias*, to treat differently; *a ~ de*, unlike.
diferenciación *f.* differentiation.
diferencial *adj.-f.* differential.
diferenciar *tr.* to differentiate. *2 ref.* to differ [be different]. *5* to make oneself noticeable. *3* BIOL. to differentiate.
diferente *adj.* different. *2 adv.* differently.
diferir *tr.* to defer, delay, adjourn, postpone, put off. *2 intr.* to differ [be different]. ¶ CONJUG. like *hervir*.
difícil *adj.* difficult, hard: *~ de creer*, hard to believe. *2* improbable.
difícilmente *adv.* with difficulty, hardly.
dificultad *f.* difficulty. *2* objection.
dificultar *tr.* to make difficult; to hinder. *2* to consider difficult or improbable.
dificultoso, -sa *adj.* difficult. *2 m.-f.* raiser of difficulties.
difidente *adj.* distrustful.
difiero, difiera, etc. *irr.* V. DIFERIR.
difluir *intr.* to be diffused. ¶ CONJUG. like *fluir*.
difracción *f.* PHYS. diffraction.
difteria *f.* MED. diphteria.
difumar *tr.* ESFUMAR.
difuminar *tr.* ESFUMINAR.
difumino *f.* ESFUMINO.
difundir *tr.* to diffuse. *2* to spread, divulge. *3* RADIO. to broadcast. *4 ref.* to diffuse itself; to spread.
difunto, -ta *adj.* deceased, defunct, late. *2 m.-f.* deceased.
difusión *f.* diffusion. *2* diffuseness. *3* spreading. *4* RADIO. broadcasting.
difuso, -sa *adj.* diffuse. *2* broad, widespread.
difusor, -ra *adj.* diffusing. *2* RADIO. broadcasting. *3 m.* diffuser.
digerible *adj.* digestible.
digerir *tr.* PHYSIOL., CHEM. to digest. *2* to digest [assimilate mentally; bear, put up with]. ¶ CONJUG. like *hervir*.
digestión *f.* PHYSIOL., CHEM. digestion.
digestivo, -va *adj.* digestive.
digesto *m.* LAW digest.
digestor *m.* digester [apparatus].
digiero, digiera, etc. *irr.* V. DIGERIR.
digitación *f.* MUS. fingering.
digitado, -da *adj.* BOT., ZOOL. digitate.
digital *adj.* digital. *2 f.* BOT. digitalis, foxglove.
digitalina *f.* CHEM., PHARM. digitalin.
digitígrado, -da *adj.-m.* ZOOL. digitigrade.
dígito *adj.* ARITH. *número ~*, digit.
dignarse *ref.* to deign, condescend.
dignatario *m.* dignitary, high official.
dignidad *f.* dignity. *2* dignified bearing. *3* ECCL. dignitary.
dignificación *f.* dignification.
dignificar *tr.* to dignify.

digno, -na *adj.* worthy, honorable. *2* worthy, deserving. *3* suitable, appropriate. *4* dignified.
digo, diga, etc. *irr.* V. DECIR.
dígrafo *m.* digraph.
digresión *f.* digression.
dije *m.* trinket, locket, small piece of jewelry.
dije, dijera, etc. *irr.* V. DECIR.
dilaceración *f.* rending, tearing; laceration.
dilacerar *tr.* to rend, tear, lacerate.
dilación *f.* delay, procrastination.
dilapidación *f.* dilapidation, squandering.
dilapidador, -ra *m.-f.* dilapidator, squanderer.
dilapidar *tr.* to dilapidate, squander.
dilatabilidad *f.* dilatability.
dilatación *f.* dilatation, dilation, expansion. *2* delay, prolongation. *3* diffuseness, prolixity.
dilatado, -da *adj.* vast, extensive, large; numerous.
dilatar *tr.* to dilate, expand, widen. *2* to spread [fame, etc.]. *3* to delay, retard. *4* ~ *el ánimo,* to comfort, cheer up. *5 ref.* to dilate, expand, spread, etc. [be dilated, expanded, etc.]. *6* to expatiate.
dilatorio, -ria *adj.* dilatory, delaying. *2 f.* delay, procrastination.
dilección *f.* love, affection.
dilecto, -ta *adj.* beloved, loved.
dilema *m.* dilemma.
diletantismo *m.* dilettantism.
diligencia *f.* diligence, activity, dispatch, speed. *2* errand; step, action. *3* judicial proceeding. *4* diligence, stagecoach.
diligenciar *tr.* to take the necessary steps to acomplish or obtain [something].
diligente *adj.* diligent; prompt, active.
dilucidación *f.* clearing up, elucidation.
dilucidar *tr.* to clear up, to elucidate.
dilución *f.* dilution.
diluente *adj.-m.* diluent.
diluir *tr.* to dilute. *2 ref.* to dilute [become diluted].
¶ CONJUG. like *huir.*
diluvial *adj.* diluvial, diluvian. *2* GEOL. diluvial.
diluviar *impers.* to pour, rain hard.
diluvio *m.* deluge. *2* hard raining, downpour. *3 el Diluvio,* the Deluge, the Flood.
dimanante *adj.* springing, originating, issuing.
dimanar *intr.* ~ *de,* to spring, issue, arise from; originate in.
dimensión *f.* dimension.
dimensional *adj.* dimensional.
dimes *m. pl. andar en dimes y diretes,* to bicker.
diminutivo, -va *adj.* diminishing. *2 adj.-m.* GRAM. diminutive.
diminuto, -ta *adj.* diminutive, minute, tiny.
dimisión *f.* resignation [of office].
dimisionario, -ria; dimitente *adj.* resigning [an office].
dimitir *tr.* to resign, to give up [office].
dimorfismo *m.* dimorphism.
dimorfo, -fa *adj.* dimorphous.
dina *f.* PHYS., dyne.
Dinamarca *f. pr. n.* GEOG. Denmark.
dinamarqués, -sa *adj.* Danish. *2 m.-f.* Dane.
dinámica *f.* dynamics.
dinámico, -ca *adj.* dynamic.
dinamismo *m.* dynamism.
dinamita *f.* dynamite.
dinamitar *tr.* to dynamite.
dinamitero, -ra *m.-f.* dynamiter.
dinamo *f.* ELECT. dynamo.
dinamómetro *m.* dynamometer.
dinasta *m.* dynast.

dinastía *f.* dynasty.
dinástico, -ca *adj.* dynastic(al.
dineral *m.* large sum of money.
dinerillo *m.* dim. coll. some money.
dinero *m.* money, currency, wealth: ~ *contante,* ~ *contante y sonante,* ready money; cash; *hombre de* ~, wealthy man. *2* ancient silver coin. *3* denier.
dingo *m.* ZOOL. dingo.
dinosauro *m.* PALEONT. dinosaur.
dinoterio *m.* PALEONT. dinothere.
dintel *m.* ARCH. lintel, doorhead.
diñar *tr.* vulg. to give: *diñarla,* to die.
diocesano, -na *adj.-m.* diocesan.
diócesi, diócesis *f.* diocese.
Diocleciano *m. pr. n.* Diocletian.
diodo *m.* diode.
dioico, -ca *adj.* BOT. diœcious.
dionea *f.* BOT. Venus's-flytrap.
dionisíaco, -ca *adj.* Dionysiac.
Dionisio *m. pr. n.* Dionysius, Denis.
Dionisios, Dionisos *m. pr. n.* MYTH. Dionysos, Dionysus.
dioptría *f.* OPT. diopter [unit].
dióptrico, -ca *adj.* dioptric(al. *2 f.* dioptrics.
diorama *m.* diorama.
dios *m.* MYTH. god. *2 pr. n.* (cap.) God: ~ *Hombre,* Jesus Christ; ~ *Padre,* God the Father; *¡adiós!,* adieu!, farewell, good-bye; *a la buena de* ~, artlessly; *¡anda con* ~!, *¡vaya con* ~!, good-bye; *¡bendito sea* ~!, bless me!; ~ *dirá,* we shall see; ~ *los cría y ellos se juntan,* birds of a feather flock together; ~ *mediante,* God willing; *¡~ mío!,* my God!, good Heavens!; ~ *me libre,* God forbid; *sabe* ~, goodness knows; *plegue a* ~, please God; *¡válgame* ~!, good God!
diosa *f.* goddess.
diplodoco *m.* PALEONT. diplodocus.
diploma *m.* diploma.
diplomacia *f.* diplomacy.
diplomática *f.* diplomatics.
diplomático, -ca *adj.* diplomatic. *2 m.-f.* diplomat. *3* diplomatist.
dipsomanía *f.* dipsomania.
dipsómano, -na *adj.-s.* dipsomaniac.
díptero, -ra *adj.* ENT. dipteran, dipterous. *2* ARCH. dipteros.
díptica *f.* diptych [tablets].
díptico *m.* diptych [tablets; picture].
diptongar *tr.* to diphthongize.
diptongo *m.* diphthong.
diputación *f.* deputation. *2* object of a deputation.
diputado *m.* deputy, delegate, representative. *2* POL. deputy, member of a Chamber of Deputies.
diputar *tr.* to delegate, to commission. *2* to consider, to judge to be.
dique *m.* dam, mole, dike. *2* fig. barrier, check. *3* NAUT. dry dock: ~ *flotante,* floating dock.
diré, diría, etc. *irr.* V. DECIR.
dirección *f.* direction [line of course, point to which one moves, looks, etc.]; ~ *única,* one way. *2* direction, management; leadership. *3* office of a director or a manager. *6* address [on a letter, etc.]. *7* AUTO. steering.
directamente *adv.* directly in a direct manner.
directivo, -va *adj.* directive, managing. *2 f.* board of directors. *3 m.* member of a board of directors, *executive.
directo, -ta *adj.* direct, straight. *2* GRAM. direct.
director, -ra *adj.* directing, leading, managing. *2 m.-f.* director, manager, *executive: ~ *de es-*

cena, stage manager. *3* editor [of a paper]. *4* principal, headmaster [of a school]. *5* MUS. conductor.

directorio *m.* directory [body of rules]. *2* POL. directory. *3* Directoire.

directriz *f.* GEOM. directrix.

dirigente *adj.* leading, governing. *2 m.-f.* leader, director, *executive.

dirigible *adj.* dirigible. *2 m.* AER. dirigible.

dirigir *tr.* to direct [in every sense, except to give an order or instruction to]. *2* to manage, govern; to lead, to head. *3* AUT. to steer. *4* MUS. to conduct. *5* to point [a gun, etc]. *6* to address [a letter, one's word, etc]. *7 ref. dirigirse a*, to be directed to; to go to; to address [a person], to apply, resort to.

dirimente *adj.* diriment.

dirimir *tr.* to annul, dissolve. *2* to settle [a quarrel, a controversy].

discerniente *adj.* discerning.

discernimiento *m.* discernment, judgment. *2* discrimination.

discernir *tr.* to discern, distinguish. *2* LAW to appoint [a guardian]. ¶ CONJUG.: INDIC. Pres.: *discierno, disciernes, discierne; disciernen.* | SUBJ. Pres.: *discierna, disciernas, discierna; disciernan.* | IMPER.: *discierne, discierna; disciernan.* | All other forms are regular.

disciplina *f.* discipline. *2* teaching, instruction. *3* art, science. *4 pl.* scourge [for flogging].

disciplinadamente *adv.* with discipline.

disciplinado, -da *adj.* disciplined.

disciplinante *m.* disciplinant.

disciplinar *tr.* to discipline. *2 ref.* to scourge oneself [as penance].

disciplinario, -ria *adj.* disciplinary.

discípulo, -la *m.-f.* disciple. *2* pupil [of a teacher].

disco *m.* disk. *2* SPORT. discus. *3* record [of phonograph].

discóbolo *m.* discobolous, discus thrower.

díscolo, -la *adj.* ungovernable, refractory, wayward.

disconforme *adj.* disagreeing.

disconformidad *f.* disagreement. *2* disconformity.

discontinuación *f.* discontinuance, discontinuation.

discontinuar *tr.* to discontinue.

discontinuidad *f.* discontinuity.

discontinuo, -nua *adj.* discontinuous.

discordancia *f.* discordance, disagreement.

discordante *adj.* discordant.

discordar *intr.* to discord [be discordant]. *2* to disagree [in opinion]. *3* MUS. to discord. ¶ CONJUG. like *contar*.

discorde *adj.* discordant, in disagreement. *2* MUS. discordant, dissonant.

discordia *f.* discord, disagreement, disunion.

discoteca *f.* collection of phonograph records.

discreción *f.* discretion: *a ~*, at discretion. *2* wit, gracefulness [in talk or expression].

discrecional *adj.* discretionary.

discrepancia *f.* discrepancy. *2* dissent, disagreement.

discrepante *adj.* discrepant; disagreeing.

discrepar *intr.* to differ, disagree. *2* to dissent.

discretear *intr.* to make a show of graceful talk.

discreteo *m.* show of graceful talk.

discreto, -ta *adj.* discret. *2* graceful in talk or expression. *3* MATH. discrete [quantity]. *4* coll. not bad; fairly good.

discriminación *f.* discrimination.

discriminar *tr.* to discriminate.

disculpa *f.* excuse, apology. *2* exculpation.

disculpar *tr.* to exculpate; to excuse. *2 ref.* to excuse oneself, apologize.

discurrir *intr.* to go about, roam. *2* [of a river, etc.] to flow. *3* [of time] to pass. *4* to reflect, reason, discourse [about a thing]. *5 tr.* to invent, think out, devise. *6* to infer.

discursear *intr.* coll. to perorate, make speeches.

discursivo, -va *adj.* meditative.

discurso *m.* discourse. *2* use of reason. *3* talk, speech. *4* course [of time].

discusión *f.* discussion, argument.

discutible *adj.* disputable, debatable; uncertain.

discutidor, -ra *adj.* argumentative [person].

discutir *tr.* to discuss, argue about, dispute. *2 intr.* to discuss, argue.

disecador *m.* dissecter; taxidermist.

disecar *tr.* to dissect. *2* to stuff [dead animals].

disección *f.* dissection, anatomy. *2* stuffing [of dead animals], taxidermy.

disector *m.* dissector.

diseminación *f.* dissemination, scattering.

diseminar *tr.* to disseminate, scatter. *2 ref.* to disseminate, scatter [be disseminated].

disensión *f.* dissension. *2* division, strife.

disentería *f.* MED. dysentery.

disentimiento *m.* dissent, disagreement.

disentir *intr.* to dissent, disagree. ¶ CONJUG. like *sentir*.

diseñador *m.* designer, delineator, sketcher.

diseñar *tr.* to design, draw, sketch, outline.

diseño *m.* design, drawing, sketch, outline.

disertación *f.* dissertation, disquisition.

disertar *tr.* to dissert, dissertate.

diserto, -ta *adj.* eloquent, fluent.

disfasia *f.* MED. dysphasia.

disfavor *m.* disfavour. *2* bad turn.

disforme *adj.* misshapen, hideous. *2* huge, monstruous.

disfraz *m.* disguise. *2* costume, fancy dress. *3* dissimulation, dissembling.

disfrazar *tr.* to disguise. *2* to dissemble. *3 ref.* to disguise oneself, to masquerade.

disfrutar *tr.* to enjoy, possess, have the use or benefit of. *2 intr.* to enjoy oneself, take enjoyment. *3 ~ de*, to enjoy, have the use of. *4 ~ con*, to take or find enjoyment in.

disfumino *m.* stump.

disfrute *m.* enjoyment, benefit, use.

disgregación *f.* scattering, disgregation.

disgregar *tr.* to scatter, disintegrate, disperse.

disgustado, -da *adj.* tasteless. *2* displeased. *3* sorry.

disgustar *tr.* to render tasteless, disagreeable. *2* to displease, annoy, anger; to pain, give sorrow. *3 ref.* to be displeased, or hurt. *4* to fall out, have a difference [with].

disgustillo *m. dim.* slight displeasure or difference.

disgusto *m.* unpleasantness [to the palate]. *2* displeasure, annoyance, vexation. *3* sorrow. *4* quarrel. *5 a ~*, against one's will; ill at ease.

disidencia *f.* dissidence. *2* dissent, nonconformity.

disidente *adj.* dissident. *2 m.-f.* dissenter.

disidir *intr.* to dissent, separate [from a creed, etc.].

disiento, disienta, etc. *irr.* V. DISENTIR.

disimetría *f.* dissymmetry.

disímil *adj.* dissimilar.

disimilación *f.* PHON. dissimilation.

disimilitud *f.* dissimilitude, dissimilarity.
disimulable *adj.* excusable.
disimulación *f.* dissimulation. *2* DISIMULO.
disimuladamente *adv.* stealthily, slyly.
disimulado, -da *adj.* dissembling, reserved, sly.
disimulador, -ra *m.-f.* dissembler. *2* tolerator.
disimular *tr.* to dissimulate, dissemble. *2* to disguise; conceal. *3* to overlook, excuse, pardon.
disimulo *m.* dissimulation. *2* sly proceeding: *con* ~, stealthily, slyly. *3* tolerance, indulgence.
disipación *f.* dissipation.
disipado, -da *adj.* dissipated. *2 m.-f.* dissipated person.
disipador, -ra *adj.* squandering. *2 m.-f.* squanderer, spendthrift.
disipar *tr.* to dissipate [dispel; squander]. *2 ref.* to dissipate, envanesce, disappear.
dislate *m.* nonsense, absurdity.
dislocación, dislocadura *f.* dislocation.
dislocar *tr.* to dislocate. *2 ref.* to come out of joint.
disloque *m.* coll. the (giddy) limit.
disminución *f.* diminution.
disminuir *tr.-intr.-ref.* to diminish, lessen, decrease. *2* to taper. ¶ CONJUG. like *huir*.
disminuyo, disminuyó, disminuya, etc. irr. V. DISMINUIR.
disnea *f.* MED. dyspnea.
disociación *f.* dissociation.
disociar *tr.* to dissociate. *2 ref.* to dissociate [undergo dissociation].
disolubilidad *f.* dissolubility.
disoluble *adj.* dissoluble.
disolución *f.* dissolution, dissolving. *2* dissolution, solution [in a solvent]. *3* dissoluteness.
disoluto, -ta *adj.* dissolute. *2 m.-f.* debauchee.
disolvente *adj.* dissolving. *2 m.* dissolvent, dissolver.
disolver *tr.* to dissolve.*2 ref.* to dissolve [be dissolved]. ¶ CONJUG. like *mover*.
disón *m.* MUS. dissonance, harsh sound.
disonancia *f.* harsh sound. *2* dissonance.
disonante *adj.* harsh, dissonant, discordant.
disonar *intr.* MUS. to sound harshly, be dissonant or discordant. *2* to disagree, be incongruous.
dispar *adj.* unlike, different, disparate.
disparada *f.* (Am.) flight, stampede, wild rush; *a la* ~, flat out, full plet; *de una* ~, at once, right away.
disparadero *m.* trigger: *poner en el* ~, PONER EN EL DISPARADOR.
disparador *m.* shooter. *2* trigger: *poner en el* ~, to drive one to do something rash. *3* escapement [of watch]. *4* release [of camera]. *5* NAUT. anchor tripper.
disparar *tr.* to discharge, fire, let off [a firearm; a bow]: ~ *un tiro,* to fire a shot. *2* to hurl, throw. *3 ref.* to dash off: to bolt. *4* [of a gun, alarm, clock, etc.] to go off. *5* to lose self-control.
disparatado, -da *adj.* absurd, nonsensical, foolish.
disparatar *tr.* to talk nonsense; to act foolishly.
disparate *m.* absurdity, nonsense; crazy idea. *2* foolish or preposterous act, blunder, mistake.
disparejo, -ja *adj.* DISPAR.
disparidad *f.* disparity, unlikeness, dissimilarity.
disparo *m.* shot, discharge. *2* MACH. release, trip, start.
dispendio *m.* excessive expenditure.
dispendioso, -sa *adj.* costly, expensive.
dispensa *f.* dispensation, exemption.
dispensable *adj.* dispensable. *2* excusable.

dispensación *f.* dispensation [granting; exemption].
dispensador, -a *m.-f.* dispenser.
dispensar *tr.* to dispense, give, grant. *2* to dispense, exempt. *3* to excuse, pardon: *¡dispense!, ¡dispénseme!,* excuse me!, beg pardon! *4 ref.* to excuse oneself [from doing something].
dispensario *m.* clinic [for the poor].
dispepsia *f.* MED. dyspepsia.
dispéptico, -ca *adj.-n.* dyspeptic.
dispersar *tr.* to disperse, scatter. *2* MIL. to put to flight. *3 ref.* to disperse [be dispersed].
dispersión *f.* dispersion, dispersal. *2* PHYS. dispersion.
disperso, -sa *adj.* dispersed, scattered.
displicencia *f.* coolness, indifference, disdain.
displicente *adj.* cool, disdainful. *2* peevish.
dispondré, dispondría, etc. irr. V. DISPONER.
disponer *tr.* to dispose, arrange. *2* to dispose [incline; bring into certain state; determine course of events]. *3* to prepare, get ready. *4* to order, decree. *5 intr.* ~ *de,* to have. *6 ref.* to get ready [for]; to be about [to]. ¶ CONJUG. like *poner.*
dispongo, disponga, etc. irr. V. DISPONER.
disponibilidades *f. pl.* resources, money on hand.
disponible *adj.* disposable. *2* available.
disposición *f.* disposition. *2* disposal. *3* state of health. *4* gift, natural aptitude. *5* figure [of a pers.]. *6* order, command, provision. *7 pl.* dispositions, steps, measures. *8 últimas disposiciones,* last will and testament.
dispositivo, -va *adj.* preceptive. *2 m.* MACH. device, contrivance.
dispuesto, -ta *p. p.* of DISPONER. *2 adj.* disposed: *bien* ~, favourably disposed; *mal* ~, unfavourably disposed. *3* prepared, ready. *4* comely. *5* able, clever.
dispuse, dispusiera, etc. irr. V. DISPONER.
disputa *f.* dispute; disputation: *sin* ~, beyond dispute.
disputable *adj.* disputable, contestable.
disputar *tr.* to dispute, contest. *2 intr.* to argue, dispute; to altercate.
disquisición *f.* disquisition.
distal *adj.* ANAT., BOT. distal.
distancia *f.* distance: *a* ~, at a distance. *2* difference, disparity.
distanciar *tr.* to distance [place at a distance]. *2* to separate, estrange. *3 ref.* to become distant or estranged.
distante *adj.* distant, far, remote.
distar *intr.* ~ *de,* to be [so many miles, etc.] distant from; to be different from; ~ *mucho de,* to be far from.
distender *tr.* MED. to distend.
distensión *f.* MED. distension, distention.
dístico, -ca *adj.* BOT. distichous. *2 m.* POET. distich.
distinción *f.* distinction. *2* distinctness. *3 a* ~ *de,* in distinction from or to.
distingo *m.* LOG. distinction. *2* coll. subtle distinction.
distinguido, -da *adj.* distinguished, prominent.
distinguir *tr.* to distinguish. *2* to discriminate. *3* to show regard for. *4 ref.* to distinguish oneself. *5* to make oneself different. *6* to be distinguished or characterized.
distintivo, -va *adj.* distinctive. *2 m.* distinctive peculiarity. *3* distinctive mark; badge, sign.
distinto, -ta *adj.* distinct. *2* different, separate.
distorsión *f.* distortion.
distracción *f.* distraction, diversion, amusement.

2 absent-mindedness. 3 oversight. *4 ~ de fondos*, embezzlement. *5 por ~*, for amusement; through an oversight.
distraer *tr.* to divert, amuse, entertain. 2 to distract [the attention, the mind, etc.]. 2 to lead astray. *4 ~ fondos*, to embezzle. *5 ref.* to amuse oneself. 6 to be inattentive, absent-minded.
distraídamente *adv.* without thinking.
distraído, -da *adj.* absent-minded, inattentive.
distribución *f.* distribution. 2 apportionment.
distribuidor, -ra *adj.* distributing. 2 *m.-f.* distributer, distributor: *~ automático*, slot machine.
distribuir *tr.* to distribute. 2 to sort [mail]. ¶ CONJUG. like *huir*.
distributivo, -va *adj.* distributive.
distrito *m.* district.
disturbio *m.* disturbance, outbreak, riot.
disuadir *tr.* to dissuade.
disuasión *f.* dissuasion.
disuasivo, -va *adj.* dissuasive.
disuelto, -ta *p. p.* of DISOLVER.
disuelvo, disuelva, etc. *irr.* V. DISOLVER.
disuria *f.* MED. dysuria.
disyunción *f.* disjunction.
disyuntiva *f.* disjunctive, dilemma.
disyuntivo, -va *adj.* disjunctive.
disyuntor *m.* ELECT. circuit-breaker.
ditirambo *m.* dithyramb.
dítono *m.* MUS. ditone.
diurético, -ca *adj.-m.* MED. diuretic.
diurno, -na *adj.* diurnal.
diuturno, -na *adj.* diuturnal.
diva *f.* poet. goddess. 2 diva [great woman singer].
divagación *f.* divagation, rambling, digression.
divagar *intr.* to divagate, ramble, digress.
diván *m.* divan.
divergencia *f.* divergence; divergency.
divergente *adj.* divergent.
divergir *intr.* to diverge. 2 to differ, disagree.
diversidad *f.* diversity. 2 variety, abundance.
diversificar *tr.* to diversify.
diversión *f.* diversion, amusement. 2 MIL. diversion.
diverso, -sa *adj.* diverse, different, various. 2 *pl.* several, many.
divertido, -da *adj.* amusing, funny.
divertimiento *m.* diversion, amusement.
divertir *tr.* to divert, amuse, entertain. 2 to divert, turn away. *3 ref.* to amuse oneself, have a good time. ¶ CONJUG. like *hervir*.
dividendo *m.* MATH., COM. dividend.
dividir *tr.* to divide. *2 ref.* to divide [separate, be at odds].
dividivi *m.* BOT. dividivi.
divierto, divierta, etc. *irr.* V. DIVERTIR.
divieso *m.* MED. furuncle, boil.
divinamente *adv.* divinely. 2 admirably.
divinatorio, -ria *adj.* divinatory.
divinidad *f.* divinity, godhead. 2 MYTH. divinity. 3 beauty, very beautiful person or thing.
divinizar *tr.* to divinize, deify.
divino, -na *adj.* divine.
divisa *f.* badge, emblem. 2 BULLF. coloured bow serving as brand on bull. 3 HER. device. 4 principle. 5 foreign currency.
divisar *tr.* to descry, espy, perceive.
divisibilidad *f.* divisibility.
divisible *adj.* divisible.
división *f.* division [dividing; distribution; discord]. 2 LOG., MATH., MIL. division.
divisional *adj.* divisional.

divisionario, -ria *adj.* divisional, divisionary. 2 fractional [currency].
divisor, -ra *adj.* dividing. 2 *m.* MATH. divisor: *máximo común ~*, greatest common divisor.
divisorio, -ria *adj.* dividing. 2 *f.* GEOG. divide.
divo, -va *adj.* poet. divine. 2 *m.* poet. god. 3 great singer [man]. 4 *f.* diva.
divorciado, -da *adj.* divorced. 2 *n.* divorcee.
divorciar *tr.* to divorce. *2 ref.* to divorce [get divorced]: *~ de*, to divorce [one's husband or wife]; to become divorced from.
divorcio *m.* divorce. 2 disunion, breach.
divulgación *f.* divulgation. 2 popularization [of knowledge].
divulgar *tr.* to divulge, publish abroad. 2 to popularize [knowledge]. *3 ref.* to be spread about.
do *m.* MUS. C, do, ut. 2 *adv.* poet. DONDE.
dobladillar *tr.* SEW. to hem.
dobladillo *m.* SEW. hem.
doblado, -da *p. p.* of DOBLAR. 2 *adj.* thick-set. 3 uneven [land]. 4 deceitful, dissembling.
doblaje *m.* CINEM. dubbing.
doblar *tr.* to double [make double; amount to twice as much as]. 2 to double, fold. 3 to bend [curve; cause to yield]; to bow [one's head]; *~ la rodilla*, to go down on one's knee; to humble oneself. 4 to turn [a page]. 5 to turn, double [a corner, a cape]. 6 CINEM. to dub; to double. 7 *intr.* to toll, knell. 8 *ref.* to double, double up. 9 to bend, yield, give in.
doble *adj.* double, twofold: *al ~*, doubly. 2 thick, heavy [cloth, etc.]. 3 thick-set, sturdy. 4 BOT. double [flower]. 5 two-faced, deceitful. 6 *adv.* doubly. 7 *m.* fold, crease. 8 toll, knell.
doblegable *adj.* easily bent; pliable, pliant.
doblegar *tr.* to bend, curve. 2 to bend, force to yield, subdue. *3 ref.* to yield, give in, submit.
doblete *m.* doublet [false stone]. 2 a stroke in billiards.
doblez *m.* fold, crease, ply. 2 cuff [of trousers]. 3 *f.* duplicity, deceitfulness.
doblón *m.* doubloon [old Spanish gold coin].
doce *adj.-m.* twelve: *las ~*, twelve o'clock. 2 *m.* twelfth [in dates].
docena *f.* dozen: *~ de fraile*, baker's dozen.
docente *adj.* educational, teaching.
dócil *adj.* docile, obedient. 2 tame. 3 soft, easily worked.
docilidad *f.* docility, meekness.
dócilmente *adv.* docilely, meekly. 2 obediently.
docto, -ta *adj.* learned [person].
doctor, -ra *m.-f.* doctor, doctoress. *2 Doctor de la Iglesia*, Doctor of the Church.
doctorado *m.* doctorate, doctorship.
doctoral *adj.* doctoral.
doctorar *tr.* to doctor [confer a doctorate upon]. *2 ref.* to take the degree of doctor.
doctrina *f.* doctrine. 2 learning, knowledge. 3 catechism. 4 Sunday School.
doctrinal *m.* doctrinal.
doctrinar *tr.* to teach, instruct.
doctrinario, -ria *adj.-n.* doctrinaire, doctrinarian.
doctrinarismo *m.* doctrinairism, doctrinarianism.
doctrino *m.* charity boy.
documentación *f.* documentation. 2 papers [proving identity, authorization, etc.].
documentado, -da *adj.* documented. 2 well-documented, well-informed.
documental *adj.* documental, documentary. 2 *m.* CINEM. documentary [film].
documentar *tr.-ref.* to document.

documento *m.* document.
dodecaedro *m.* GEOM. dodecahedron.
dodecágono *m.* GEOM. dodecagon.
dodecafónico, -ca *adj.* MUS. dodecaphonic.
dodecasílabo, -ba *adj.* dodecasyllabic. *2 m.* dodecasyllabic verse.
dogal *m.* halter, hangman's rope; *estar con el ~ al cuello*, to be in a tight spot.
dogaresa *f.* dogaressa.
dogma *m.* dogma.
dogmático, -ca *adj.* dogmatic(al.
dogmatismo *m.* dogmatism.
dogmatizar *tr.-intr.* to dogmatize.
dogo, -ga *adj.-n.* bulldog. *2 m.* doge.
dogre *m.* NAUT. dogger.
doladera *f.* cooper's adze.
dolar *tr.* to dress wood or stone.
dólar *m.* dollar [U.S. money].
dolencia *f.* ailment, complaint, disease, illness.
doler *intr.* to ache, hurt, pain: *me duele la cabeza*, my head aches. *2* to pain, be hateful to one: *me duele hacer esto*, I hate, to do this. *3 ref. dolerse de*, to repent; to be moved by [another's misfortune]; to complain of. ¶ CONJUG. like *mover*.
dolicocéfalo, -la *adj.* dolichocephalous.
dolido, -da *adj.* hurt, pained, grieved.
doliente *adj.* aching, suffering. *2* ill, sick. *3* sorrowful. *4 m.-f.* sufferer, sick person.
dolmen *m.* ARCHEOL. dolmen.
dolo *m.* guile, deceit, fraud.
dolomía, dolomita *f.* MINER. dolomite.
dolor *m.* pain, ache, aching; *~ de cabeza*, headache. *2* pain, sorrow, grief: *la Virgen de los Dolores*, Mary of the Sorrows. *3* repentance. *4 pl. dolores del parto*, labour pains, throes of childbirth.
dolora *f.* short sentimental and philosophic poem.
dolorido, -da *adj.* sore, aching, tender, painful. *2* sorrowful, grieving, pained.
Dolorosa *f.* Mater Dolorosa.
doloroso, -sa *adj.* painful. *2* dolorous, distressing; pitiful, regrettable.
doloso, -sa *adj.* guileful, deceitful, fraudulent.
doma *f.* taming, breaking in.
domable *adj.* tamable. *2* conquerable.
domador, -ra *m.-f.* tamer. *2* horsebreaker.
domar *tr.* to tame. *2* to break, break in [horses, etc.]. *3* to curb, subdue, conquer.
domeñar *tr.* to master, conquer, subdue.
domesticación *f.* domestication.
domesticar *tr.* to tame, domesticate. *2 ref.* to become tame.
domesticidad *f.* domesticity.
doméstico, -ca *adj.* domestic [of the home]. *2* domestic [animal]. *3 m.-f.* domestic, servant.
Domiciano *m. pr. n.* Domitian.
domiciliado, -da *adj.* resident. *2* domiciled: *letra domiciliada*, domiciled draft.
domiciliar *tr.* to domicile, domiciliate. *2 ref.* to domiciliate, take up residence.
domiciliario, -ria *adj.* domiciliary.
domicilio *m.* domicile, home, residence.
dominación *f.* domination. *2 pl.* dominations [order of angels].
dominador, -ra *adj.* dominating; domineering. *2 m.-f.* dominator.
dominante *adj.* domineering. *2* dominant. *3* commanding [height, position]. *4 adj.-f.* MUS. dominant.
dominar *tr.* to dominate *2* to domineer. *3* to rule

over. *4* to control, restrain. *5* to master [a subject]. *6 ref.* to control oneself.
dómine *m.* coll. latin teacher. *2* coll. pedant.
Domingo *m. pr. n.* Dominic.
domingo *m.* Sunday: *~ de Pasión*, Passion Sunday; *~ de Ramos*, Palm Sunday.
dominguero, -ra *adj.* Sunday [used on Sundays].
domínica *f.* ECCL. Lord's day, Sunday.
dominical *adj.* dominical. *2* feudal [fees].
dominicano, -na *adj.-n.* Dominican.
dominico, -ca *adj.* Dominican [pertaining to the Dominican order]. *2 m.* Dominican friar.
dominio *m.* dominium. *2* domination, control, rule. *3* mastery [of a subject]. *4* domain. *5 ~ público*, public property; public knowledge.
dómino *m.* dominoes [game]; domino [piece].
dominó *m.* DÓMINO. *2* domino [cloak].
domo *m.* ARCH. dome, cupola.
dompedro *m.* BOT. DONDIEGO. *2* coll. chamber pot.
don *m.* gift, present, donation. *2* natural gift or talent, knack: *~ de gentes*, charm, winning manners. *3* Don, Spanish title prefixed to Christian names of men.
donación *f.* donation, gift, bestowal. *2* LAW donation.
donado, -da *m.-f.* lay brother or sister.
donador, -ra *m.-f.* donor, giver.
donaire *m.* nimble-wit. *2* sally, lively remark. *3* graceful carriage.
donante *m.-f.* donor.
donar *tr.* to donate, bestow, make donation of.
donatario *m.* donee, grantee.
donativo *m.* gift, donative, donation, contribution.
doncel *m.* virgin man. *2* king's page.
doncella *f.* virgin, maiden, maid. *2* maidservant, lady's maid.
doncellería, doncellez *f.* virginity, maidenhood.
donde *adv.-pron.* where, wherein, whither, in which: *a ~*, *en ~*, where; *de ~*, from where, whence; *hasta ~*, up to where, how far; *¿por dónde?* whereabouts? [by] wich way?; why? | The *o* is accented in interrogative or exclamatory sentences.
dondequiera *adv.* anywhere, wherever.
dondiego *m.* BOT. *dondiego* or *~ de noche*, four-o'clock, marvel-of-Peru; *~ de día*, morning glory.
donguindo *m.* variety of pear tree.
donjuanismo *m.* Don Juanism.
donosamente *adv.* wittily, amusingly. *2* gracefully, elegantly.
donoso, -sa *adj.* nimble-witted; graceful.
donostiarra *adj.-n.* of San Sebastián.
donosura *f.* grace, gracefulness.
doña *f.* Spanish title used before the Christian name of a lady.
dopar *tr.* to dope, to drug.
doquier, doquiera *adv.* anywhere, wherever.
dorada *f.* ICHTH. gilthead.
doradillo *m.* fine brass wire. *2* satinwood.
dorado, -da *adj.* gilt, golden. *2 m.* gilt, gilding.
dorador *m.* gilder.
doradura *f.* gilding.
dorar *tr.* to gild. *2 ref.* to take a golden tinge. *4* COOK. to turn brown.
dórico, -ca *adj.* Doric. *2 m.* Doric [dialect].
dorio, -ria *adj.-n.* Dorian.
dormida *f.* night's sleep. *2* sleeping period [of silkworms].
dormidera *f.* BOT. garden poppy, opium poppy.

dormidero, -ra *adj.* soporific. *2 m.* sleeping place for cattle.
dormilón, -na *adj.* sleepy. *2 m.-f.* sleepyhead. *3 f.* armchair for napping. *4* earring.
dormir *intr.* to sleep, to rest; ~ *a pierna suelta*, to sleep soundly and peacefully; ~ *la mona*, to sleep oneself sober. *2* to pass the night. *3 tr.* to put to sleep. *4 intr.-ref.* to be careless, to be unwary or inactive. *5 ref.* to go to sleep, fall asleep. *6* to get benumbed. ¶ CONJUG.: INDIC. Pres.: *duermo, duermes, duerme;* dormimos, dormís, *duermen.* | Pret.: dormí, dormiste, *durmió;* dormimos, dormisteis, *durmieron.* | SUBJ. Pres.: *duerma, duermas, duerma;* durmamos, durmáis, *duerman.* | Imperf.: *durmiera, durmieras,* etc.; or *durmiese, durmieses,* etc. | Fut.: *durmiere, durmieres,* etc. | IMPER.: *duerme, duerma; durmamos, dormid, duerman.* | GER.: *durmiendo.*
dormitar *intr.* to doze, to nap.
dormitorio *m.* bedroom. *2* dormitory.
dornajo *m.* small round trough.
dornillo *m.* DORNAJO. *2* wooden bowl.
Dorotea *f. pr. n.* Dorothy.
dorsal *adj.* dorsal.
dorso *m.* back [of a thing]. *2* dorsum.
dos *adj.* two: *las ~,* two o'clock; *los ~, las ~,* both; *de ~ en ~,* two abreast; by twos; *en un ~ por tres,* in a flash, in a twinkling. *2* second [of the month]. *3 m.* two [number]. *4* deuce.
doscientos, -tas *adj.-m.* two hundred.
dosel *m.* canopy, dais.
doselete *m.* ARCH. canopy.
dosificación *f.* dosage. *2* CHEM. titration.
dosificar *tr.* to dose [a medicine]; to proportion [ingredients].
dosimétrico, -ca *adj.* dosimetric.
dosis *f.* MED. dose. *2* quantity [of something].
dotación *f.* endowment [endowing; funds]. *2* dowering. *3* NAV. complement. *4* staff, personnel.
dotado, -da *adj.* endowed; gifted.
dotal *adj.* dotal.
dotar *tr.* to endow, dower, portion [with money, a dowry, gifts, talents, etc.]; to gift. *2* NAV. to man [a ship]. *3* to staff [an office, etc.].
dote *m.* or *f.* dowry, dower, marriage portion. *2 f. pl.* endowments, gifts, virtues, talents.
dovela *f.* ARCH. voussoir.
doy *irr.* V. DAR.
dozavo, -va *adj.-m.* twelfth.
dracma *f.* drachm, drachma [coin]. *2* drachma, dram [weight].
draconiano, -na *adj.* Draconian.
draga *f.* dredge [machine]. *2* dredger [boat].
dragado *m.* dredging.
dragaminas *m.* NAV. mine sweeper.
dragar *tr.* to dredge.
drago *m.* BOT. dragon tree.
dragón *m.* MYTH., ZOOL., BOT. dragon. *2* MIL. dragoon. *3* ASTR. Draco. *4* ICHTH. ~ *marino,* greater weever.
dragona *f.* female dragon. *2* MIL. shoulder knot.
dragontea *f.* BOT. green dragon.
drama *m.* drama.
dramática *f.* drama, dramatic art or literature.
dramático, -ca *adj.* dramatic. *2 m.-f.* dramatist. *3* dramatic actor or actress.
dramatismo *m.* dramatic effect.
dramatizar *tr.* to dramatize.
dramaturgia *f.* drama, dramatic art.
dramaturgo, -ga *m.-f.* dramatist, playwright.
dramón *m.* a badly written sensational drama.

drapeado *m.* drapery.
drapear *tr.* to drape.
drástico, -ca *adj.* drastic.
drenaje *m.* SURG. drainage.
drenar *tr.* SURG. to drain.
Dresde *f. pr. n.* GEOG. Dresden.
dríada, dríade *f.* MYTH. dryad.
driblar *tr.* SPORT. to dribble.
dril *m.* drill [fabric]. *2* ZOOL. drill [baboon].
driza *f.* NAUT. halyard.
droga *f.* drug. *2* chemical substance. *3* fib, lie.
drogadicto, -ta *adj.-n.* drug addict.
drogado, -da *adj.* doped, drugged. *2 n.* drug addict. *3 m.* doping.
droguería *f.* drugstore.
droguero *m.* druggist.
dromedario *m.* ZOOL. dromedary.
druida *m.* Druid.
druidismo *m.* Druidism.
drupa *f.* BOT. drupe, stone fruit.
dual *adj.-m.* GRAM. dual.
dualidad *f.* duality.
dualismo *m.* dualism.
dubitativo, -va *adj.* dubitative.
ducado *m.* duchy. *2* dukedom. *3* ducat.
ducal *adj.* ducal.
dúctil *adj.* ductile.
ductilidad *f.* ductility.
ducha *f.* douche, shower bath.
duchar *tr.* to douche, give a shower bath. *2 ref.* to douche, take a shower bath.
ducho, -cha *adj.* skilful, expert, experienced.
duda *f.* doubt; *sin ~,* doubtless, no doubt.
dudable *adj.* dubitable.
dudar *intr.-tr.* to doubt, question. *2 intr.* to doubt, waver, hesitate.
dudoso, -sa *adj.* doubtful, dubious.
duela *f.* stave [of barrel]. *2* ZOOL. fluke.
duelista *m.* duelist.
duelo *m.* duel: ~ *judiciario,* judicial combat. *2* grief, sorrow. *3* pity, compassion: fig. *sin ~,* abundantly. *4* mourning; bereavement. *5* mourners [at a funeral]. *6 pl.* hardships.
duelo, duela, etc. *irr.* V. DOLER.
duende *m.* goblin, hobgoblin.
dueña *f.* owner, proprietress, mistress. *2* duenna.
dueño, -ña *m.-f.* owner, proprietor, master, landlord: *hacerse ~* or *dueña de,* to appropriate to oneself; to master; *ser ~ de,* to own; to be master of; to be at liberty to [do, etc.]; *ser ~ de sí mismo,* to be self-controlled. *2 mi ~,* my love.
duermevela *m.* doze, light sleep.
duermo, duerma, etc. *irr.* V. DORMIR.
Duero *m. pr. n.* GEOG. Douro.
dueto *m.* MUS. short duet.
dulcamara *f.* BOT. bittersweet.
dulce *adj.* sweet. *2* saltless, insipid. *3* fresh [water]. *4* soft [iron]. *5* PAINT. soft, agreeably coloured. *6 adv.* sweetly, softly. *7 m.* sweet [dessert]. *8* sweetmeat, confection.
dulcémele *m.* MUS. dulcimer.
dulcera *f.* preserve dish, compotier.
dulcería *f.* confectionery shop.
dulcero, -ra *m.-f.* confectioner.
dulcificar *tr.* to sweeten, dulcify.
dulcinea *f.* coll. sweetheart, beloved one [woman].
dulcísono, -na *adj.* poet, sweet-toned.
dulía *f.* dulia, worship of angels and saints.
dulzaina *f.* MUS. kind of flageolet.
dulzarrón, -na; dulzón, -na *adj.* sickeningly sweet.
dulzor *m.* sweetness.

dulzura *f.* sweetness. *2* mildness [of temper, of weather]. *3* gentleness, kindliness. *4* pleasantness. *5 pl.* endearments.
dumdum *adj.* dumdum: *bala* ~, dumdum bullet.
duna *f.* dune.
Dunquerque *f. pr. n.* GEOG. Dunkirk.
dúo *m.* MUS. duet.
duodecimal *adj.* duodecimal.
duodécimo, -ma *adj.-m.* twelfth.
duodeno, -na *adj.* twelfth. *2 m.* ANAT. duodenum.
duplex *adj.* TELEG. duplex.
duplicado, -da *adj.-m.* duplicate.
duplicador, -ra *adj.* duplicating. *2 m.* duplicator.
duplicar *tr.* to double, duplicate.
duplicidad *f.* duplicity.
duplo *adj.-m.* double [twice as much].
duque *m.* duke.
duquesa *f.* duchess.
durabilidad *f.* durability.
durable *adj.* durable, lasting.
duración *f.* duration, endurance, lasting.
duradero, -ra *adj.* durable, enduring, lasting.
duramadre, duramater *f.* ANAT. dura mater.

duramen *m.* BOT. duramen.
durante *prep.* during.
durar *intr.* to endure, last, continue. *2* [of clothes, etc.] to wear well.
duraznero *m.* BOT. peach tree.
durazno *m.* BOT. peach tree. *2* peach [fruit].
dureza *f.* hardness. *2* harshness, severity. *3* obstinacy. *4* MED. callosity.
durillo, -lla *adj.* rather hard. *2 m.* BOT. laurustine. *3* BOT. dogwood. *4* a small golden coin.
durmiente *adj.* sleeping, dormant. *2 m.-f.* sleeper [pers.]. *3 m.* ARCH. dormant.
durmiera, durmiere, etc. *irr.* V. DORMIR.
duro, -ra *adj.* hard: ~ *de corazón,* hard-hearted; ~ *de oído,* hard of hearing; *ser* ~ *para* or *para con,* to be hard on. *2* harsh, severe, rigorous, unbearable. *3* obdurate, unfeeling. *4* obstinate. *5* strong, hardy. *6* stingy. *7* stiff [collar]. *8 a duras penas,* hardly, scarcely. *9 adv.* hard. *10* Spanish dollar [coin worth 5 pesetas].
duunvirato *m.* duumvirate.
duunviro *m.* duumvir.
dux *m.* doge.

E

E, e *f.* E, e, sixth letter of the Spanish alphabet.
e *conj.* and [used for *y* before words beginning with *i* or *hi* not followed by *e*].
¡ea! *interj.* used as an encouragement or to express determination.
ebanista *m.* cabinetmaker.
ebanistería *f.* cabinetwork. 2 cabinetmaker's shop.
ébano *m.* BOT. ebony. 2 ebony wood.
ebonita *f.* ebonite.
ebriedad *f.* drunkenness, intoxication.
ebrio, ebria *adj.* drunk, intoxicated. 2 fig. blind [with anger, etc.].
ebullición *f.* ebullition, boiling.
eburnación *f.* MED. eburnation.
ebúrneo, -a *adj.* eburnean, ivorylike.
Eccehomo *m.* Ecce Homo.
Ezequiel *m. pr. n.* Ezekiel.
eclecticismo *m.* eclecticism.
ecléctico, -ca *adj.-n.* eclectic.
Eclesiastés *m.* BIBL. Ecclesiastes.
eclesiástico, -ca *adj.* ecclesiastic(al. 2 *m.* ecclesiastic, clergyman.
eclipsar *tr.* ASTR. & fig. to eclipse. 2 *ref.* to disappear.
eclipse *m.* eclipse.
eclíptica *f.* ASTR. ecliptic.
eclisa *f.* RLY. fishplate.
eco *m.* echo: *tener ~*, fig. to spread, to be widely accepted. 2 distant sound. 3 (cap.) MYTH. Echo.
economato *m.* company store, commissary; cooperative shop.
economía *f.* economy: *~ dirigida*, planned economy. 2 economics. 3 saving, thrift. 4 sparingness, scantiness. 5 *pl.* savings: *hacer economías*, to save up.
económico, -ca *adj.* economic. 2 economical. 3 thrifty, saving. 4 cheap, uncostly. 5 cheap [price].
economista *m.* economist.
economizar *tr.* to economize; to save, spare.
ecónomo *m.* acting parish priest.
ectoblasto *m.* BIOL. ectoblast.
ectodermo *m.* BIOL. ectoderm.
ectropión *m.* MED. ectropion.
ecuación *f.* MATH., ASTR. equation.
Ecuador *m. pr. n.* GEOG. Ecuador.
ecuador *m.* GEOM., GEOG., ASTR. equator.

ecuánime *adj.* equanimous. 2 just, impartial.
ecuanimidad *f.* equanimity. 2 impartiality.
ecuatorial *adj.-m.* equatorial.
ecuatoriano, -na *adj.-n.* Ecuadorian.
ecuestre *adj.* equestrian.
ecuménico, -ca *adj.* ecumenic(al.
eczema *f.* MED. eczema.
echada *f.* throw, cast. 2 SPORT. man's length.
echar *tr.* to throw, cast, fling, pitch, toss; to heave, drop: *~ anclas*, to cast anchor; *~ la culpa a*, to throw the blame on. 2 to put in or into, to add: *~ leña al fuego*, to add fuel to the flame. 3 to emit, give off or out [sparks, smell, etc.]: *~ chispas*, fig. to be wild with anger. 4 to dismiss, discharge, fire, expel, throw out: *~ con cajas destempladas*, fig. to dismiss or turn away without ceremony. 5 to grow, begin to have [hair, teeth, feathers]. 6 to put forth, sprout, bear [leaves, fruit, etc.]. 7 to give, deliver [a speech, a sermon]. 8 to turn [a key]; to shoot home [a bolt]. 9 to pour [wine, etc.]. 10 to move, push: *~ a un lado*, to push aside. 11 followed by some nouns, it expresses the idea implied by the noun: *~ cuentas*, to reckon; *~ maldiciones*, to utter curses; *~ suertes*, to draw lots; *~ un trago*, to take a drink. 12 Other senses: *~ abajo* or *por tierra*, to throw down, overthrow, demolish; *~ a broma*, to take as a joke; *~ a perder*, to spoil, to ruin; *~ a pique*, to sink [a vessel]; *~ de menos*, to miss; *~ de ver*, to notice, observe; *~ las cartas*, to tell fortunes by cards; *~ mano a*, to seize, take hold of; *~ mano de*, to resort to; *~ raíces*, to take root; *~ una mano*, to lend a hand; *¿cuántos años le echa?*, how old would you say he is?
13 *intr. ~ calle arriba*, to go or start up the street. 14 *~ por*, to take [a road, etc.]; to turn to [the right, the left, etc.].
15 *intr.-ref. ~* or *echarse a correr, a reír, a saltar*, etc., to begin to run, laugh, jump, etc., to start running, laughing, jumping, etc.
16 *ref.* to lie down, to throw oneself down, to stretch oneself at full length. 17 to throw oneself into. 18 *echarse a perder*, to spoil, get spoiled, to become stale, to go bad. 19 *echarse atrás*, to draw back, to back out. 20 *echarse a un lado*, to move aside. 21 *echarse encima* or *sobre*, to rush at, fall upon; to throw on or upon oneself. 22

echárselas de, to pretend or claim to be, to boast of being.

echarpe *f*. scarf, stole, shawl.

echazón *f*. throwing. 2 NAUT. jettison; jetsam.

edad *f*. age: ~ *madura* or *provecta*, mature age, maturity; *mayor* ~, majority, full age; *menor* ~, minority; ~ *de oro*, golden age; ~ *media*, Middle Ages; *¿qué* ~ *tiene usted?*, how old are you?

edafología *f*. edaphology.

edecán *m*. MIL. aide-de-camp.

edema *f*. MED. œdema, edema.

Edén *m*. Eden, paradise.

edénico, -ca *adj*. paradisiac.

edición *f*. edition. 2 issue [of a newspaper]. 3 publication [of a book].

edicto *m*. edict.

edículo *m*. ARCH. small building or niche.

edificación *f*. building, construction. 2 edification.

edificante *adj*. edifying.

edificar *tr*. to build, construct. 2 to edify.

edificio *m*. edifice, building, structure.

edil *m*. aedile, edile. 2 town councillor.

Edimburgo *m. pr. n*. GEOGR. Edinburgh.

Edipo *m. pr. n*. MYTH. Oedipus.

editar *tr*. to publish [a book, a newspaper, etc.].

editor *m*. publisher.

editorial *adj*. publishing. 2 leading [article]. 3 *f*. publishing house. 4 editorial, leader [article].

editorialista *m.-f*. writer of editorials.

edredón *m*. eider down. 2 down quilt.

Eduardo *m. pr. n*. Edward.

educación *f*. education. 2 breeding, manners; good breeding, good manners; politeness.

educador, -ra *adj*. educating. 2 *m.-f*. educator.

educando, -da *m.-f*. student, pupil.

educar *tr*. to educate; to train. 2 to give good breeding.

educativo, -va *adj*. educative.

educción *f*. eduction.

educir *tr*. to educe. ¶ CONJUG. like *conducir*.

edulcorar *tr*. PHARM. to edulcorate, sweeten.

efe *f*. Spanish name of the letter *f*.

efebo *m*. ephebus.

efectismo *m*. F. ARTS striving after effect.

efectivamente *adv*. really, actually. 2 as a matter of fact; indeed. 3 effectually.

efectividad *f*. reality, actuality. 2 effectuality.

efectivo, -va *adj*. effective, real, actual. 2 permanent [employment]. 3 *dinero* ~, cash. 4 *hacer* ~, to carry out; to cash. 5 *m*. cash, specie: *en* ~, in cash. 6 *pl*. MIL. effectives, troops.

efecto *m*. effect: *surtir* ~, to have the desired effect, to work; *poner en* ~, to put into effect, to carry out; *con* ~, *en* ~, in fact, indeed, really; *de simple* ~, *de doble* ~, MACH. single acting, double acting. 2 purpose, end: *al* ~, for the purpose. 3 impression; *hacer* ~, to be impressive. 5 BILL. side, *English. 6 COM. article of merchandise. 7 COM. draft, bill, security: *efectos a cobrar*, bills receivable; *efectos públicos*, public securities. 8 *pl*. effects, goods, movables.

efectuar *tr*. to effect, effectuate, do, carry out. 2 *ref*. to take place.

efemérides *pl*. diary, daily record. 2 events of the same day in former years.

efendi *m*. Effendi [Turkish title].

eferente *adj*. PHYSIOL. efferent.

efervescencia *f*. effervescence. 2 agitation.

efervescente *adj*. effervescent.

Efeso *f. pr. n*. HIST., GEOG. Ephesus.

eficacia *f*. efficacity, efficacy.

eficaz *adj*. efficacious, effective, effectual.

eficiencia *f*. efficiency.

eficiente *adj*. efficient.

efigie *f*. effigy, image.

efímero, -ra *adj*. ephemeral.

eflorecerse *ref*. CHEM. to effloresce.

eflorescencia *f*. CHEM., MED. efflorescence.

efluvio *m*. effluvium, emanation, exhalation.

Efraín *m. pr. n*. Ephraim.

efugio *m*. evasion, subterfuge, shift, way out.

efundir *tr*. to effuse, to pour.

efusión *f*. effusion, pouring out, shedding. 2 fig. warmth, effusion.

efusivo, -va *adj*. effusive, warm.

Egeo (Mar) *m. pr. n*. GEOG. Ægean Sea.

égida, egida *f*. aegis, egis.

egipcio, -cia *adj.-n*. Egyptian. 2 *m*. Egyptian [language].

Egipto *m. pr. n*. GEOG. Egypt.

egiptología *f*. Egyptology.

égira *f*. HÉGIRA.

égloga *f*. eclogue.

egocéntrico, -ca *adj.-n*. egocentric.

egocentrismo *m*. egocentrism, self-centredness, egocentrity.

egoísmo *m*. egoism, selfishness.

egoísta *adj*. egoistic, selfish. 2 *m.-f*. egoist.

egolatría *f*. self-worship.

egotismo *m*. egotism.

egregio, -gia *adj*. illustrious, eminent, egregious.

egresado, da *adj.-n*. graduate.

egresar *intr*. (Am.) to go away, to leave. 2 to graduate, to take one's degree. 3 to pass out [military academy].

¡eh! *interj*. he!, here!

eider *m*. ORN. eider, eider duck.

eje *m*. axis. 2 axle, axletree, shaft, spindle, arbor. 3 fig. main or central point, subject, idea, etc.

ejecución *f*. execution. 2 LAW distraint.

ejecutante *adj*. executing. 2 *m.-f*. performer, executant. 3 LAW distrainor.

ejecutar *tr*. to execute, carry out, perform. 2 to execute [put to death]. 3 LAW to distrain.

ejecutivo, -va *adj*. executive. 2 pressing. 3 prompt, active. 4 *m*. (Am.) executive.

ejecutor, -ra *m.-f*. executer, executor. 2 *m*. ~ *de la justicia*, executioner.

ejecutoria *f*. letters pattent of nobility. 2 glorious deed.

ejecutorio, -ria *adj*. LAW firm.

ejemplar *adj*. exemplary. 2 *m*. exemplar, pattern, model. 3 exemplar, specimen. 4 copy [of a book, magazine, etc.]. 5 precedent: *sin* ~, exceptional. 6 example, warning.

ejemplaridad *f*. exemplary quality or character.

ejemplarizar *tr*. to exemplify, to set an example to, to demonstrate by example.

ejemplificar *tr*. to exemplify, illustrate.

ejemplo *m*. example: *dar* ~, to set an example; *sin* ~, unexampled. 2 instance: *por* ~, for instance, for example.

ejercer *tr*. to exercise [authority, a right, etc.]. 2 to exercise, discharge, perform [functions]. 3 to exercise, practice, follow [a profession]. 4 to exercise, exert [influence, etc.].

ejercicio *m*. exercise. 2 MIL. drill. 3 practice [of a virtue, ability, or profession]; holding, tenure [of an office]. 4 fiscal year.

ejercitación *f*. exercise, practice.

ejercitante *adj*. exercising. 2 *m.-f*. exercitant.

ejercitar *tr.* to practice [a trade, profession, etc.].
2 tr.-ref. to exercise, drill, train.
ejército *m.* army.
ejido *m.* commons, public land [nearing a village].
el *def. art. masc. sing.* the.
él *pers. pron. masc. sing.* he, him; it.
elaboración *f.* elaboration, manufacturing.
elaborar *tr.* to elaborate, manufacture, work. *2* to work [a material].
elástica *f.* knit vest, undervest.
elasticidad *f.* elasticity. *2* resilience.
elástico, -ca *adj.* elastic. *2 m.* elastic [fabric].
Elba *f. pr. n.* Elbe [river].
ele *f.* Spanish name of the letter *l*.
eléboro *m.* BOT. hellebore.
elección *f.* election. *2* choice. *3* free election. *4 pl.* POL. election.
electivo, -va *adj.* elective.
electo, -ta *adj.* elected, chosen. *2* elect [chosen for office].
elector, -ra *adj.* electing. *2 m.-f.* elector, electress. *3 m.* Elector [German prince].
electorado *m.* electorate.
electoral *adj.* electoral.
electricidad *f.* electricity.
electricista *m.-f.* electrician.
eléctrico, -ca *adj.* electric(al.
electrificación *f.* electrification [of a railroad, etc.].
electrificar *tr.* to electrify [a railroad, etc.].
electrización *f.* electrification, electrization.
electrizante *adj.* electrifying.
electrizar *tr.* to electrify, to electrize.
electro *m.* amber. *2* electrum, electron.
electrocardiografía *f.* electrocardiography.
electrocardiograma *m.* electrocardiogram.
electrocinética *f.* electrokinetics.
electrocución *f.* electrocution.
electrocutar *tr.* to electrocute.
electrodinámica *f.* electrodynamics.
electrodo *m.* electrode.
electroencefalograma *m.* electro-encephalogram.
electróforo *m.* electrophorus.
electrógeno, -na *adj.* generating electricity. *2 m.* electric generator.
electroimán *m.* electromagnet.
electrólisis *f.* electrolysis.
electrólito *m.* electrolyte.
electrolizar *tr.* to electrolyze.
electromagnetismo *m.* electromagnetism.
electromecánico, -ca *adj.* electromechanical.
electrometría *f.* electrometry.
electrómetro *m.* electrometer.
electromotor, -ra *adj.* electromotive. *2 m.* electro-motor.
electromotriz *adj.-f.* electromotive [force].
electrón *m.* PHYS., CHEM. electron.
electrónico, -ca *adj.* electronic, electron: *microscopio* ~, electron microscope. *2 f.* electronics.
electroquímica *f.* electrochemistry.
electroscopio *m.* PHYS. electroscope.
electrostático, -ca *adj.* electrostatic. *2 f.* electrostatics.
electroterapia *f.* MED. electrotherapy.
electrotérmico, -ca *adj.* electrothermic.
electrotipia *f.* electrotypy.
electrotipo *m.* electrotype.
elefancía *f.* MED. elephantiasis.
elefanta *f.* ZOOL. female elephant.
elefante *m.* ZOOL. elephant.

elegancia *f.* elegance, gracefulness, neatness, style.
elegante *adj.* elegant, graceful, smart, stylish. *2 m.-f.* elegant, dandy.
elegantizar *tr.* to make elegant, give style to.
elegía *f.* elegy.
elegíaco, -ca *adj.* elegiac, mournful.
elegible *adj.* eligible.
elegido, -da *adj.* elected, chosen. *2 m.* THEOL., one of the elect.
elegir *tr.* to elect. *2* to choose, select. ¶ CONJUG. like *servir*.
elemental *adj.* elemental, elementary. *2* fundamental.
elemento *m.* element. *2 pl.* elements [atmospheric forces]. *3* elements, rudiments. *4* means, resources.
Elena *f. pr. n.* Helen, Elaine.
elenco *m.* catalogue, index. *2* THEAT. company.
elevación *f.* elevation, raising, rise, ascent. *2* elevation, height. *3* elevation [of mind, of the style]. *4* ecstasy, transport. *5* exaltation [to a dignity]. *6* elevation [in the Mass].
elevado, -da *adj.* elevated, raised, lifted; high. *2* exalted. *3* sublime.
elevador, -ra *adj.* elevating. *2 m.* elevator.
elevamiento *m.* elevation, ecstasy, rapture.
elevar *tr.* to elevate, raise, lift. *2* to hoist. *3* to exalt [to a dignity]. *4* MATH. to raise [to a power]. *5 ref.* to rise, ascend, soar.
elfo *m.* elf.
elidir *tr.* GRAM. to elide.
elijo, elija, etc. *irr.* V. ELEGIR.
eliminación *f.* elimination.
eliminar *tr.* to eliminate.
eliminatorio, -ria *adj.* eliminating.
elipse *f.* GEOM. ellipse.
elipsis *f.* GRAM. ellipsis.
elipsoide *m.* GEOM. ellipsoid.
elíptico, -ca *adj.* GEOM., GRAM. elliptic(al.
Elisa *f. pr. n.* Eliza.
Eliseo *m. pr. n.* BIBL. Elisha. *2* MYTH. Elysium.
elíseo, -a *adj.* Elysian.
elisión *f.* elision.
élitro *m.* ENT. elytron, shard.
elixir, elíxir *m.* elixir.
elocución *f.* elocution.
elocuencia *f.* eloquence.
elocuente *adj.* eloquent.
elogiable *adj.* praiseworthy.
elogiar *tr.* to praise, commend, eulogize.
elogio *m.* praise, eulogy.
elogioso, -sa *adj.* praising, eulogistic.
elongación *f.* ASTR., MED. elongation.
elote *m.* (Am.) ear of green Indian corn.
elucidación *f.* elucidation.
elucidar *tr.* to elucidate.
elucubración *f.* lucubration.
eludir *tr.* to elude, avoid, evade.
ella *pron. f. sing.* she, her, it.
elle *f.* Spanish name of the letter *ll*.
ello *pron. neuter sing.* it: ~ *es que*, the fact is that.
ellos, ellas *pron. m. & f. pl.* they, them.
Ema *f. pr. n.* Emma.
emaciación *f.* MED. emaciation.
emanación *f.* emanation.
emanar *intr.* to emanate, issue.
emancipación *f.* emancipation.
emancipar *tr.* to emancipate. *2 ref.* to free oneself.
Emanuel *m. pr. n.* BIBL. Immanuel.
emasculación *f.* emasculation.

embabiamiento *m.* absorption, fit of abstraction.

embadurnador, -ra *adj.* daubing. 2 *m.-f.* dauber.

embadurnar *tr.* to daub, bedaub, besmear.

embaír *tr.* to deceive, humbug. ¶ Only used in the forms having *i* in their terminations.

embajada *f.* embassy. 2 ambassadorship. 3 message, errand.

embajador *m.* ambassador.

embajadora *f.* ambassadress.

embalaje *m.* packing [of goods]. 2 packing case.

embalar *tr.* to pack, bale [goods]. 2 *intr.* SPORT. to sprint. 3 AUTO. to step on the gas.

embaldosado *m.* paving with tiles. 2 tile floor.

embaldosar *tr.* to tile, pave with tiles.

embalsamador, -ra *adj.* embalming. 2 *m.-f.* embalmer.

embalsamamiento *m.* embalming.

embalsamar *tr.* to embalm [a corpse]. 2 to embalm, to perfume.

embalsar *tr.* to gather in a pond or pool. 2 to dam up [water]. 3 *ref.* [of water] to gather in a pond or pool. '

embalse *m.* damming [of water]. 2 dam [for water].

emballenar *tr.* to bone [stiffen with whalebone].

embanastar *tr.* to put into a basket. 2 to huddle, crowd together, pack.

embanderar *tr.* to bedeck with flags or banners.

embarazada *adj.* pregnant, with child. 2 *f.* pregnant woman.

embarazar *tr.-ref.* to embarrass, encumber, hinder. 2 *tr.* to make pregnant.

embarazo *m.* obstruction, hindrance. 2 embarrassment, constraint. 3 pregnancy.

embarazoso, -sa *adj.* embarrassing, difficult. 2 cumbersome.

embarbillar *tr.* CARP. to join obliquely.

embarcación *f.* NAUT. boat, craft, ship, vessel.

embarcadero *m.* wharf, pier, jetty.

embarcador *m.* shipper.

embarcar *tr.* NAUT. to embark; to ship. 2 *tr.-ref.* to embark [engage or become engaged in an enterprise]. 3 *intr.-ref.* to embark [go on board].

embarco *m.* embarkation [of people].

embardar *tr.* BARDAR.

embargable *adj.* LAW attachable.

embargar *tr.* to impede, restrain. 2 [of emotions] to overcome, to paralyse. 3 LAW to attach, seize [property]. 4 to lay an embargo on.

embargo *m.* LAW attachment, seizure [of property]. 2 embargo. 3 *adv. sin* ~, notwithstanding, nevertheless, however.

embarque *m.* shipment [of goods].

embarrancar *tr.* NAUT. to run [a ship] aground. 2 *intr.* NAUT. [of a ship] to run aground. 3 *ref.* fig. to stick in the mud.

embarrar *tr.* to bemud; to splash with mud. 2 to bedaub, besmear.

embarrilar *tr.* to pack in barrels or kegs.

embarullador, -ra *adj.* muddling. 2 *m.-f.* muddler.

embarullar *tr.* to muddle, mix up, make a mess of. 2 *ref.* to muddle, act in a confused way.

embasamiento *m.* ARCH. foundation.

embastar *tr.* SEW. to baste.

embaste *m.* SEW. basting.

embastecer *intr.* to put on flesh. 2 *ref.* to become gross or coarse. ¶ CONJUG. like *agradecer.*

embate *m.* dash, buffet, dashing, buffeting [of waves, wind, etc.].

embaucador, -ra *adj.* deceiving. 2 *m.-f.* deceiver, humbug, bamboozler.

embaucamiento *m.* deceiving, humbugging.

embaucar *tr.* to deceive, humbug, bamboozle.

embaular *tr.* to pack in a trunk. 2 to gobble, eat greedily.

embausamiento *m.* absorption, abstraction.

embebecer *tr.* to enrapture, absorb, delight. 2 *ref.* to become enraptured, be absorbed. ¶ CONJUG. like *agradecer.*

embebecimiento *m.* rapture, absorption.

embeber *tr.* to absorb, imbibe, soak up. 2 to soak [in]. 3 to embed, insert, fit in. 4 SEW. to take in. 5 *intr.* [of cloth] to shrink. 6 *ref.* to become absorbed. 7 *fig. embeberse de,* to get well acquainted with [a subject].

embebezco, embebezca, irr. V. EMBEBECER.

embelecar *tr.* to delude, deceive, humbug.

embeleco *m.* deception, trick, humbug.

embelesador, -ra *adj.* charming, captivating.

embelesamiento *m.* EMBELESO.

embelesar *tr.* to charm, entrance, delight, captivate. 2 *ref.* to be charmed, become entranced.

embeleso *m.* delight, enchantment. 2 charm; charming thing.

embellecer *tr.* to embellish, beautify. ¶ CONJUG. like *agradecer.*

embellecimiento *m.* embellishment, beautifying.

embermejar *tr.* EMBERMEJECER.

embermejecer *tr.* to dye red; to redden. 2 *ref.* to redden, blush. ¶ CONJUG. like *agradecer.*

emberrenchinarse, emberrincharse *ref.* fam. to be enraged, fly into a rage.

embestida *f.* assault, attack, charge, onset.

embestidor, -ra *adj.* attacking. 2 charging [a bull].

embestir *tr.* to assail, attack, charge. 2 to accost [someone]. 3 *intr.* ~ *contra,* to rush against or upon. ¶ CONJUG. like *servir.*

embetunar *tr.* to bituminize. 2 to black [shoes].

embicar *tr.* NAUT. to top [a yard].

embisto, embista, etc. irr. V. EMBESTIR.

emblandecer *tr.* to soften. 2 *ref.* to soften, to turn soft. 3 to relent.

emblanquecer *tr.* to whiten. 2 *ref.* to turn white. ¶ CONJUG. like *agradecer.*

emblanquecimiento *m.* whitening.

emblema *m.* emblem.

emblemático, -ca *adj.* emblematic(al.

embobado, -sa *adj.* dumbfounded, flabbergasted, agape. 2 bewildered, dazed, stupefied.

embobamiento *m.* absorption, enchantment.

embobar *tr.* to enchant, hold in suspense. 2 *ref.* to be enchanted, absorbed; to stand gaping.

embobecer *tr.* to make foolish, make silly. 2 *ref.* to become foolish, get silly. ¶ CONJUG. like *agradecer.*

embocado, -da *adj.* dry-sweet [wine].

embocadura *f.* entrance by a narrow passage. MUS. embouchure, mouthpiece. 3 mouthpiece [of a bridle]. 4 flavour [of wine]. 5 rivermouth. 6 THEAT. proscenium arch.

embocar *tr.* to mouth, put into the mouth. 2 to enter or to put through [a narrow place]. 3 to gobble up. 4 MUS. to mouth [as instrument].

embocinado, -da *adj.* shaped like a trumpet.

embodegar *tr.* to store [wine, olive oil, etc.].

embojar *tr.* to put on branches, encouraging the formation of cocoons [silkworms].

embolada *f.* MACH. stroke [of piston].

embolado *m.* THEAT. minor role. 2 BULLF. bull with wooden balls on horns. 3 coll. trick, deception.

embolar *tr.* BULLF. to tip horns of [bull] with wooden balls.

embolia *f.* MED. embolism.
embolismar *tr.* to carry tales, to make mischief.
embolismo *m.* ASTR. embolism. *2* muddle, confusion, difficulty. *3* gossip, falsehood.
émbolo *m.* MECH. piston, plunger. *2* MED. embolus.
embolsar *tr.* to pocket [money].
embonar *tr.* to improve. *2* to sheathe [a ship].
embono *m.* sheathing [of a ship].
emboquillar *tr.* to tip, put a tip on [a cigarette].
emborrachamiento *m.* intoxication, drunkenness.
emborrachar *tr.* to intoxicate, make drunk. *2 ref.* to become intoxicated, to get drunk. *3* [of colours] to run together.
emborrascar *tr.* to anger, irritate. *2 ref.* to get angry. *3* [of weather] to get stormy.
emborrazamiento *m.* COOK. barding.
emborrazar *tr.* COOK. to bard [a fowl].
emborronar *tr.* to blot [paper]; to scribble.
emborrullarse *ref.* to wrangle.
emboscada *f.* ambuscade, ambush.
emboscar *tr.-ref.* to ambuscade, ambush [station or lie in ambush]. *2 ref.* to enter or hide in the woods. *3* fig. to shirk work or danger by taking an easy job.
embotado, -da *adj.* blunt, dull.
embotamiento *m.* blunting, dulling. *2* bluntness, dullness.
embotar *tr.* to blunt, to dull. *2* to put [tobacco] in a jar. *3 ref.* to become blunt or dull.
embotellado, -da *p. p.* of EMBOTELLAR. *2 adj.* fig. prepared [speech, etc]. *3 m.* bottling.
embotelladora *f.* bottling machine.
embotellamiento *m.* stoppage, jam, traffic jam.
embotellar *tr.* to bottle. *2* to bottle up. *3* fig. to stop, obstruct.
embovedar *tr.* to arch, vault. *2* to enclose in a vault.
embozadamente *adv.* covertly.
embozado, -da *adj.* muffled, wrapped up to the eyes. *2* covert, disguised. *3 m.-f.* person wrapped up to the eyes.
embozar *tr.-ref.* to muffle or wrap up to the eyes. *2 tr.* to mask, disguise [the meaning of]. *3* to muzzle [dogs, horses, etc.].
embozo *m.* part of cloak, etc., held over the face: *quitarse el ~*, fig. to remove one's mask. *2* strip of wool, silk, etc., lining the side of a cloak. *3* fold in top part of bedsheet. *4* disguise [of meaning, etc.]: *sin ~*, openly, frankly.
embragar *tr.* to sling [for hoisting]. *2* MECH. to engage the clutch, throw the clutch in.
embrague *m.* slinging [for hoisting]. *2* MECH. clutch. *3* MECH. throwing the clutch in.
embravecer *tr.* to irritate, enrage. *2 ref.* to get angry. *3* [of the sea] to get rough; [of a storm] to gather violence. ¶ CONJUG. like *agradecer*.
embravecido, -da *adj.* furious, enraged [person.], wild, rough [sea], wild [wind].
embravecimiento *m.* anger, fury, rage.
embrazadura *f.* handle [of shield].
embrazar *tr.* to clasp [a shield].
embreadura *f.* tarring, pitching.
embrear *tr.* to tar, pitch.
embriagado, -da *adj.* intoxicated, inebriated; drunk.
embriagador, -ra *adj.* intoxicating, inebriating.
embriagar *tr.* to intoxicate, inebriate. *2* to make drunk. *3 ref.* to get drunk, become inebriated.
embriaguez *f.* intoxication, inebriation, drunkenness.
embridar *tr.* to bridle [a horse].

embriología *f.* embryology.
embrión *m.* embryo: *en ~*, in embryo.
embrionario, -ria *adj.* embryonic.
embrocación *f.* MED. embrocation; embrocating.
embrocar *tr.* to empty [a vessel] into another. *2* BULLF. to catch between the horns.
embrolladamente *adv.* confusedly.
embrollar *tr.* to entangle, confuse, muddle; to embroil. *2 ref.* to get muddled or confused.
embrollo *m.* tangle, muddle, mess. *2* lie, deception. *3* imbroglio.
embrollón, -na *m.-f.* embroiler, confuser. *2* liar, mischief-maker.
embromado, -da *adj. estar ~*, to be in a fix, having a tough time.
embromar *tr.* to play jokes on, to banter, chaff. *2* to fool, deceive. *3* (Am.) to annoy, vex; to do a bad turn.
embrujamiento *m.* bewitchment.
embrujar *tr.* to bewitch.
embrujo *m.* EMBRUJAMIENTO.
embrutecedor, -ra *adj.* besotting, brutifying.
embrutecer *tr.* to besot, brutify. *2 ref.* to become besotted. ¶ CONJUG. like *agradecer*.
embrutezco, embrutezca, etc. *irr.* V. EMBRUTECER.
embrutecimiento *m.* sottishness, stupidity.
embuchado *m.* any kind of sausage. *2* stuffing [of a ballot-box]. *3* fraudulent affair.
embuchar *tr.* to stuff [guts] to make sausages. *2* to stuff [food] into a fowl's crop. *3* to gobble up [one's food].
embudar *tr.* to put a funnel into. *2* to trick, deceive.
embudo *m.* funnel. *2* trick, deception.
emburujar *tr.* to tangle [threads, etc.]. *2* to make lumpy. *3* to jumble.
embuste *m.* lie, falsehood, invention.
embustería *f.* lying, deceit.
embustero, -ra *adj.* lying. *2 m.-f.* liar, deceiver.
embutido *m.* inlaid work, marquetry. *2* any kind of sausage.
embutir *tr.* to stuff [guts] to make sausages. *2* to inlay, set flush. *3* to stuff, cram. *4* to insert, put [into]. *5 tr.-ref.* to gobble up [food].
eme *f.* Spanish name of the letter *m*.
emergencia *f.* emergence, emersion [act of emerging]. *2* happening, incident.
emergente *adj.* emergent.
emerger *intr.* to emerge.
emérito *adj.* emeritus.
emersión *f.* ASTR. emersion.
emético, -ca *adj.-m.* emetic.
emetropía *f.* MED. emmetropia.
emigración *f.* emigration.
emigrado, -da *m.-f.* emigree, émigré.
emigrante *adj.-n.* emigrant.
emigrar *intr.* to emigrate.
emigratorio, -ria *adj.* migratory, emigratory.
Emilia *f. pr. n.* Emily.
Emilio *m. pr. n.* Æmilius.
eminencia *f.* eminence. *2* (cap.) Eminence [cardinal's title].
eminente *adj.* eminent.
eminentísimo, -ma *adj. superl.* most eminent.
emirato *m.* emirate.
emir *m.* emir, ameer.
emisario *m.* emissary; envoy, messenger.
emisión *f.* emission. *2* COM. issuance, issue [of bonds, shares, etc.]. *3* RADIO. broadcasting, broadcast.

emisor, -ra *adj.* emitting. *2* broadcasting. *3 m.* wireless transmitter. *4 f.* broadcasting station.
emitir *tr.* to emit. *2* to issue [bonds, shares, etc.]. *3* RADIO. to broadcast.
emoción *f.* emotion [agitation of mind].
emocionado, -da *adj.* touched, moved, stirred. *2* upset.
emocional *adj.* emotional [of the emotions].
emocionante *adj.* moving, touching, thrilling.
emocionar *tr.* to move, touch, thrill, arouse emotion in. *2 ref.* to be moved.
emoliente *adj.-m.* emollient.
emolumento *m.* emolument.
emotividad *f.* emotionality.
emotivo, -va *adj.* emotive, emotional.
empacador, -ra *m.-f.* packer, baler.
empacar *tr.* to pack, bale. *2 ref.* to get obstinate, stubborn or sulky [about].
empachado, -da *adj.* surfeited. *2* troubled, ashamed. *3* awkward, timid.
empachar *tr.* to impede, embarrass. *2* to surfeit, give indigestion. *3 ref.* to be embarrassed; to be ashamed. *4* to have an indigestion.
empacho *m.* awkwardness, embarrassment, shame. *2* hindrance, obstacle. *3* surfeit, overeating.
empachoso, -sa *adj.* embarrassing. *2* bashful.
empadronamiento *m.* census; taking of the census.
empadronar *tr.* to register in a census.
empajar *tr.* to cover or stuff with straw.
empalagar *tr.* to cloy, sicken, pall. *2* to weary, bore.
empalago *m.* cloying, sickening, palling. *2* boring.
empalagoso, -sa *adj.* cloying, sickening, palling.
empalar *tr.* to impale [on a stake].
empaliar *tr.* to adorn with hangings.
empalizada *f.* palisade, stockade.
empalizar *tr.* to palisade, strockade.
empalmar *tr.* to join end to end, to splice. *2* to join, connect. *3 intr.* [of roads or railways] to connect.
empalme *m.* joint, connection, join, union. *2* junction [train, road], intersection. *3* connection [train, bus]. *4* kick on the volley [football].
empalletado *m.* NAUT. barricade.
empanada *f.* COOK. pie.
empanadilla *f. dim.* turnover, small pie.
empanar *tr.* COOK. to put into a pie. *2* COOK. to bread. *3* AGR. to sow with wheat.
empantanar *tr.* to make swampy. *2* to swamp [plunge into a swamp]. *3* to obstruct [a business]. *4 ref.* to become swampy. *5* to stick in the mud.
empañar *tr.* to swaddle. *2* to dim, blur, dull, tarnish. *3* to sully [reputation, etc.]. *4 ref.* to become dim, dull, tarnished.
empapar *tr.* to soak, drench, steep, saturate. *2* to soak up, absorb, imbibe. *3 ref.* fig. to acquire a full knowledge [of]; to enter into the spirit [of]. *4* to get soaked, or soaked up.
empapelado *m.* papering, paper hanging. *2* wallpaper.
empapelador, -ra *m.* paper hanger.
empapelar *tr.* to wrap in paper. *2* to paper [a wall]; to wallpaper. *3* coll. to prosecute [a person].
empaque *m.* packing. *2* coll. mien, appearance. *3* stiffness, affected gravity.
empaquetado *m.* packing.
empaquetadura *f.* packing. *2* MACH. gasket.

empaquetar *tr.* to pack [goods]. *2* to pack, crowd.
emparchar *tr.* to cover with plasters.
emparedado, -da *adj.* immured. *2 m.-f.* recluse. *3 m.* sandwich.
emparedar *tr.* to immure, wall in.
emparejar *tr.* to pair, match. *2* to make [a thing] level with another. *3* to close [doors] flush. *4 intr.* to come abreast, catch up [with another]. *5* to equal. *6 ref.* to pair.
emparentado, -da *adj.* related [by marriage].
emparentar *intr.* to become related by marriage. ¶ CONJUG. like *acertar*.
emparrado *m.* vine arbour, bower.
emparrar *tr.* to form into a bower. *2* to embower.
emparrillado *m.* ARCH. & ENG. grillage.
empastar *tr.* to cover with paste. *2* to bind [books] in a stiff cover. *3* to fill [a tooth]. *4* PAINT. to impaste.
empaste *m.* covering with paste. *2* filling [of a tooth]. *3* PAINT. impasto.
empastelar *tr.* PRINT. to pi, pie.
empatar *tr.-intr.-ref.* to tie, be in a tie, equal, draw [in games or voting].
empate *m.* tie, draw [in games or voting].
empavesada *f.* NAUT. armings, waistcloths.
empavesado *m.* NAUT. dressing [of a ship], bunting.
empavesar *tr.* NAUT. to dress [a ship]. *2* to veil [a monument].
empavonado, empavonamiento *m.* blueing [of a metal].
empecatado, -da *adj.* confounded, incorrigible. *2* ill-starred, unlucky.
empecer *intr.* to be an obstacle. ¶ CONJUG. like *agradecer*.
empecinado, -da *adj.* (Am.) stubborn.
empecinamiento *m.* stubbornness, obstinacy, pigheadedness.
empecinar *tr.* to smear with pitch or slime. *2 ref.* (Am.) to get obstinate [about].
empedernido, -da *adj.* hardened, hard-hearted. *2* inveterate.
empedernir *tr.* to harden. *2 ref.* to harden; to become hard-hearted. ¶ Only used in the forms having *i* in their terminations.
empedrado, -da *adj.* stone-paved. *2* strewn. *3* cloud-flecked. *4 m.* stone pavement.
empedrador *m.* stone paver.
empedrar *tr.* to pave with stones. *2* fig. ~ *de*, to strew, bespatter with.
empegado *m.* tarpaulin.
empegar *tr.* to coat with pitch. *2* to mark [sheep] with pitch.
empeine *m.* lower part of the abdomen. *2* instep. *3* vamp [of shoe]. *4* MED. tetter.
empelotarse *ref.* coll. to get muddled. *2* coll. to get into a row. *3* coll. to strip naked, to undress. *4* to be mad or crazy about, to fall in love with.
empellar *tr.* to push, shove, jostle.
empellón *m.* push, shove: *a empellones*, by pushing, roughly.
empenachar *tr.* to plume, adorn with plumes.
empenaje *m.* AER. empennage, tail unit.
empeñadamente *adv.* with a will, hard, insistently.
empeñado, -da *adj.* pledged. *2* pawned. *3* eager [to], bent [on]. *4* [of a dispute, etc.] hard, hot.
empeñar *tr.* to pledge; plight; to pawn. *2* to engage, compel. *3* to join [battle]; to start [a dispute]. *4 ref.* to get into debt. *5* to bind oneself. *6* [of a battle, dispute, etc.] to begin. *7 empeñarse*

en, to insist on, to set one's mind on. *8 empeñarse por*, to intercede for.

empeño *m.* pledging [of one's word, etc.]. *2* pawning, pawn: *casa de empeños*, pawnshop. *3* pledge, obligation. *4* insistence, determination. *5* undertaking. *6* protector, recommender.

empeoramiento *m.* deterioration, worsening.

empeorar *tr.-intr.-ref.* to deteriorate, worsen [make or get worse].

empequeñecer *tr.* to make smaller, belittle, diminish. ¶ CONJUG. like *agradecer*.

emperador *m.* emperor.

emperatriz *f.* empress.

emperejilar *tr.* to dress up, adorn. *2 ref.* to dress up, adorn oneself.

emperezar *intr.-ref.* to grow lazy.

empergaminar *tr.* to cover or bind with parchment.

emperifollar *tr.* EMPEREJILAR.

empernar *tr.* to bolt [secure with bolts].

empero *conj.* yet, however, notwithstanding.

emperrarse *ref.* to get obstinate; to stick doggedly [to an idea or purpose].

empezar *tr.-intr.* to begin: ~ *a*, to begin to, to start [doing something]; ~ *por*, to begin by. ¶ CONJUG. like *acertar*.

empiezo, empiece, etc. *irr.* V. EMPEZAR.

empinada *f.* AER. zooming. *2 irse a la* ~, [of a horse] to rear.

empinado, -da *adj.* high; steep. *2* stiff, stuck-up.

empinar *tr.* to raise, lift. *2* ~ *el codo*, to crook the elbow, to tipple. *3 intr.* to drink much. *4 ref.* to stand on tiptoe. *5* [of a horse] to rear. *6* AER. to zoom. *7* to tower, rise high.

empingorotado, -da *adj.* of high social standing; stuck-up.

empíreo, -a *adj.-m.* empyrean.

empírico, -ca *adj.* empirical, empiric. *2 m.-f.* empiric, empiricist.

empirismo *m.* empiricism.

empitonar *tr.* BULLF. to catch with the horns.

empizarrado *m.* slate roof.

empizarrar *tr.* to roof with slate.

emplastar *tr.* to apply plasters to. *2* to paint the face of. *3 ref.* to paint one's face.

emplástico, -ca *adj.* sticky, glutinous.

emplasto *m.* PHARM. plaster; poultice. *2 coll.* unsatisfactory compromise.

emplazamiento *m.* summoning, summons. *2* location, emplacement.

emplazar *tr.* to summon at a specified time. *2* to locate, place.

empleado, -da *m.-f.* employee; clerk; officeholder.

emplear *tr.* to employ [a person, time, etc.]. *2* to employ, use. *3* to spend, invest [money]. *4 le está bien empleado*, it serves him right. *5 ref.* to take employment. *6* to occupy oneself.

empleo *m.* employ, employment, post, job; occupation. *2* employment, use. *3* investment [of money].

empleomanía *f.* eagerness for civil employment.

emplomado *m.* leads [of roof or latticed windows].

emplomar *tr.* to lead [cover, fix, etc., with lead]. *2* to plumb [seal with lead].

emplumar *tr.* to feather [cover, adorn with feathers]. *2* to tar and feather.

emplumecer *intr.* to fledge, grow feathers. ¶ CONJUG. like *agradecer*.

empobrecer *tr.* to impoverish. *2 intr.-ref.* to become poor. ¶ CONJUG. like *agradecer*.

empobrecimiento *m.* impoverishment.

empobrezco, empobrezca, etc. *irr.* V. EMPOBRECER.

empolvar *tr.* to cover with dust. *2* to powder [put powder on]. *3 ref.* to get dusty. *4* to powder [one's face].

empollado, -da *adj.* hatched, incubated. *2 coll.* primed for an examination.

empollar *tr.* to brood, hatch [eggs]. *2 coll.* to grind, swot up [a subject]. *3 intr.* [of bees] to brood.

empollón, -na *adj.* swotting. *2 m.-f.* swot, grind [student].

emponchado, -da *adj.* (Am.) wearing a poncho. *2* suspicious.

emponcharse *ref.* (Am.) to put on a poncho.

emponzoñamiento *m.* poisoning.

emponzoñar *tr.* to poison. *2 ref.* to become poisoned.

emporcar *tr.* to dirty, foul, soil. *2* to get dirty. ¶ CONJUG. like *contar*.

emporio *m.* emporium. *2* center of arts or culture.

empotrar *tr.* ARCH. to embed [in a wall or floor].

emprendedor, -ra *adj.* enterprising.

emprender *tr.* to undertake, engage in, enter upon; to begin: ~ *la marcha*, to start out. *2* ~ *a uno*, to accost, address someone; *emprenderla con*, to attack, set upon.

empresa *f.* enterprise, undertaking. *2* concern, firm, company. *3* management [of a theater]. *4* HER. device.

empresarial *adj.* management, managerial.

empresario *m.* contractor. *2* theatrical manager; impresario; showman. *3* ~ *de pompas fúnebres*, undertaker.

empréstito *m.* government or corporation loan.

empujar *tr.* to push, shove; to impel.

empuje *m.* push, pushing. *2* ARCH., ENG. pressure, thrust. *3* push, energy, enterprise.

empujón *m.* push, shove, violent push. *2* push [to a work, etc.]. *3 a empujones*, pushing, roughly; by fits and starts.

empuñadura *f.* hilt [of sword].

empuñar *tr.* to take [a sword, cane, etc.] by the hilt or the handle: ~ *el cetro*, to begin to reing. *2* to clutch, grasp, grip.

empuñidura *f.* NAUT. earing.

emú *m.* ORN. emu.

emulación *f.* emulation.

emular *tr.* to emulate.

émulo, -la *adj.* emulous. *2 m.-f.* emulator.

emulsión *f.* emulsion.

emulsionar *tr.* to emulsify.

emulsor *m.* emulsifier.

en *prep.* in, at, on, upon: ~ *la caja*, in the box; ~ *casa*, at home; ~ *aquella ocasión*, on that occasion. *2* into: *convertir* ~, to change or turn into. *3* for: ~ *adelante*, for the future. *4* [followed by infinitive] by: *le conocí* ~ *el andar*, I recognized him by his gait. *5* [followed by gerund] on, upon, once, no sooner, right after.

enaceitar *tr.* to oil.

enaguachar *tr.* to fill with water, make watery.

enaguas *f. pl.* petticoat, underskirt.

enaguazar *tr.* to flood, make swampy. *2 ref.* to become swampy.

enagüillas *f. pl.* short skirt or petticoat; kilt.

enajenable *adj.* alienable.

enajenación *f.* alienation. *2* abstraction, rapture. *3* ~ *mental*, mental derangement, madness.

enajenamiento *m.* ENAJENACIÓN.

enajenar *tr.* to alienate. *2* [of emotions] to transport, carry away. *3 ref.* to dispossess oneself of. *4* to become estranged. *5* to become enraptured.

enálage *f.* GRAM. enallage.

enalbardar *tr.* to put a packsaddle on. *2* COOK. to bread, to cover with batter.

enaltecedor, -ra *adj.* ennobling. *2* exalting, extolling.

enaltecer *tr.* to ennoble. *2* to exalt, extoll. *3 ref.* to become exalted. ¶ CONJUG. like *agradecer.*

enaltecimiento *m.* ennobling. *2* exalting, extolling.

enamoradizo, -za *adj.* inclined to love, amorous.

enamorado, -da *adj.* in love, loving, enamoured. *2 m.-f.* lover; sweetheart.

enamoramiento *m.* love, infatuation. *2* enamouring, love-making.

enamorar *tr.* to make love to. *2* to infatuate, enamour; to charm. *3 ref.* to fall in love.

enamoricarse *ref.* coll. to be slightly in love.

enanito, -ta *m.-f.* little dwarf; gnome.

enano, -na *adj.* dwarf, dwarfish. *2 m.-f.* dwarf.

enarbolar *tr.* to raise on high, to hoist [a flag, etc.]. *2* to brandish [a cane, a pike, etc.]. *3 ref.* [of a horse] to rear. *4* to hoop [barrels].

enarcar *tr.* to raise [one's eyebrows], to arch. *2* to hoop, to put a hoop on.

enardecer *tr.* to inflame, fire, heat, kindle, excite. *2 ref.* to heat, to become inflamed, kindled. *3* [of a dispute] to become heated. *4* [of a part of the body] to burn. ¶ CONJUG. like *agradecer.*

enardecimiento *m.* inflaming, heating, excitement.

enarenar *tr.* to sand, cover with sand; to gravel. *2 ref.* NAUT. to run aground.

enarmónico, -ca *adj.* MUS. enharmonic.

enastado, -da *adj.* horned [having horns].

enastar *tr.* to put a handle or shaft on.

encabalgar *intr.* [of some things] to rest upon another thing. *2 tr.* to provide horses for.

encaballar *tr.* to lap over [as tiles]. *2 intr.* to rest upon another thing.

encabestrar *tr.* to halter [a horse, etc.]. *2* to make [wild bulls] be lead by tame ones.

encabezamiento *m.* heading, first words [of a letter, deed, etc.], caption. *2* tax roll. *3* registering on a tax roll.

encabezar *tr.* to head, put a heading to [a letter, deed, etc.]. *2* to head [a subscription list]. *3* to head, lead. *4* to register on a tax roll. *5* to fortify [wine] with another wine or alcohol.

encabritarse *ref.* [of horses] to rear. *2* AER., NAUT. to shoot up.

encachado *m.* stone or concrete lining in the bed of a canal, ditch, etc.

encadenamiento *m.* chaining. *2* enchainment, connection, linking, concatenation.

encadenar *tr.* to chain, enchain. *2* to enslave. *3* to connect, link together, concatenate.

éncajar *tr.* to make [a thing] fit into another; to fit in, insert. *2* to put or force in. *3* to put in [a joke, a remark, etc.], to drop [a hint]. *4* to force or palm off [something] on someone. *5* to land [a blow, etc.]; to take [a blow, etc.]. *6 intr.* to fit: ~ *en* or *con,* to fit into. *7* to be relevant, to the purpose. *8 ref.* to squeeze [oneself into]. *9* to butt in. *10* to put on [a garment].

encaje *m.* fitting in, insertion. *2* socket, cavity, frame, etc., into which a thing is fitted or inserted. *3* lace [openwork tissue]. *4* inlaid work.

encajero, -ra *m.-f.* lacemaker. *2* lace dealer.

encajonado *m.* cofferdam. *2* MAS. wall made of packed earth.

encajonamiento *m.* boxing [putting in boxes]. *2* narrowing of rivers between steep banks.

encajonar *tr.* to box, put in boxes. *2* to put in a narrow place. *3 ref.* [of rivers] to narrow between steep banks.

encalabrinado, -da *adj.* obstinate about a thing.

encalabrinar *tr.* [of a vapour or odour] to affect the head, make dizzy. *2* to excite, irritate. *3 ref.* to get dizzy. *4* to get obstinate.

encalador *m.* whitewasher. *2* lime pit or vat [for liming hides].

encaladura *f.* whitewashing.

encalar *tr.* to whitewash. *2* to lime [treat with lime].

encalmarse *ref.* VET. to be overheated. *2* [of weather or wind] to become calm, still.

encalladero *m.* NAUT. shoal.

encalladura *f.* NAUT. grounding, stranding.

encallar *intr.* NAUT. to run aground. *2* fig. to get stuck.

encallecer *intr.-ref.* to get corns or callosities. *2 ref.* to become hardened or callous. ¶ CONJUG. like *agradecer.*

encallecido, -da *adj.* hardened, callous.

encamarse *ref.* coll. to take to bed, fall ill. *2* [of cattle and game] to lie down. *3* [of wheat, etc.] to be beaten down by rain, wind, etc.

encaminar *tr.* to direct, set on the way, put on the right road. *2* to bend [one's steps]. *3* to direct [to an end]. *4 ref.* to betake oneself, be on one's way [to]. *5* to be intended [to].

encanallamiento *m.* becoming base, vile.

encanallar *tr.* to make base, vile. *2 ref.* to contract base habits, to become base, vile.

encanastar *tr.* to put in baskets.

encandelar *intr.* to blossom with catkin.

encandilado, -da *adj.* hight, erect. *2* cocked [hat].

encandilar *tr.* to dazzle, daze. *2* coll. to stir [the fire]. *3 ref.* [of the eyes] to shine with lust or drink.

encanecer *intr.* to grow white, hoary, gray or gray-haired. *2* to become old. *3 tr.* to turn hoary. ¶ CONJUG. like *agradecer.*

encanijamiento *m.* weakness, sickliness.

encanijar *m.* to make [an infant] lean and sickly. *2 ref.* [of infants] to grow lean and sickly.

encanillar *tr.* WEAV. to wind on a quill.

encantación *f.* ENCANTAMIENTO.

encantado, -da *adj.* enchanted. *2* delighted, satisfied. *3* coll. abstracted. *4* hautned, rambling [house].

encantador, -ra *adj.* enchanting, charming, delightful. *2 m.-f.* charmer. *3 m.* enchanter. *4 f.* enchantress.

encantamiento *m.* enchantment.

encantar *tr.* to enchant, cast a spell on. *2* to enchant, charm, delight.

encante *m.* auction, public sale.

encanto *m.* enchantment. *2* charm, delight. *3* delightful thing. *4 pl.* charms [of a woman].

encanutar *tr.* to shape like a tube. *2* to put into a tube.

encañado *m.* conduit for water. *2* trellis of reeds.

encañar *tr.* to pipe [water]. *2* to drain [a land]. *3* to prop up [plants] with reeds.

encañizada *f.* weir [for fish]. *2* trellis of reeds.

encañonar *tr.* to convey through pipes. *2* to cover [with a firearm]. *3* to quill, ruff. *4 intr.* [of birds] to fledge out.

encaperuzar *tr.* to put a hood on.
encapillar *tr.* to hood [a falcon].
encapirotar *tr.* to put a hood on.
encapotar *tr.-ref.* to put a capote on. *2 ref.* to frown, look grim. *4* to become cloudy. *5* [of horses] to lower the head too much.
encapricharse *ref.* to take it into one's head. *2* ~ *por*, to take a fancy to.
encapuchar *tr.* to cover with a cowl or hood. *2 ref.* to put on one's cowl or hood.
encarado, -da *adj. bien* (or *mal*) ~, well- (or ill-) favoured [in looks].
encaramar *tr.* to raise, hoist. *2* to elevate [to a high post]. *3 ref.* to climb, mount. *4* to reach a high post.
encarar *tr.* to aim, point [a weapon]. *2 intr.-ref.* ~ or *encararse con*, to face, to place oneself face to face with.
encarcelación *f.* **encarcelamiento** *m.* imprisonment, incarceration.
encarcelar *tr.* to incarcerate, imprison.
encarecedor, -ra *adj.* extolling, praising. *2* extoller, praiser.
encarecer *tr.* to raise the price of. *2* to emphasize, enhance, exaggerate; to praise. *3* to recommend strongly. *4 intr.-ref.* to become dearer. ¶ CONJUG. like *agradecer.*
encarecidamente *adv.* earnestly, insistently.
encarecimiento *m.* increase in price. *2* emphasizing; praising. *3* earnestness: *con* ~, earnestly.
encarezco, encarezca, etc. *irr.* V. ENCARECER.
encargado, -da *m.-f.* person in charge, manager, foreman, forewoman. *2 m.* ~ *de negocios*, chargé d'affaires.
encargar *tr.* to entrust, put under the care of. *2* to recommend, charge, urge. *3* to order [goods, etc.]. *4 ref. encargarse de*, to take charge of; to attend, see to.
encargo *m.* charge, commission, job. *2* errand. *3* recommendation, warning. *4* order [for goods].
encariñado, -da *adj.* attached, fond of.
encariñar *tr.* to awaken affection or liking. *2 ref. encariñarse con*, to get fond of.
encarnación *f.* THEOL., incarnation. *2* incarnation, embodiment. *3* PAINT., SCULP. flesh colour.
encarnado, -da *adj.* incarnate. *2* flesh-coloured, incarnadine. *3* red. *4 m.* flesh colour, incarnadine, red.
encarnadura *f. buena* (or *mala*) ~, quick- (or slow) healing flesh.
encarnar *intr.* THEOL. to be incarnate. *2* SURG. to heal over, incarn. *3 tr.* to incarnate, embody, personify. *4* to bait [a fishhook]. *5* to give flesh colour to [a sculpture]. *6 ref.* to unite, incorporate with one another.
encarnizadamente *adv.* bloodily, fiercely, bitterly, brutally, cruelly.
encarnizado, -da *adj.* blood-shot. *2* bloody, fierce, furious, bitter, hard fought.
encarnizamiento *m.* cruelty, fierceness, fury, rage.
encarnizar *tr.* to make cruel, to infuriate. *2 ref.* to become infuriated; to fight bitterly. *3 encarnizarse con*, to persecute, treat mercilessly.
encarpetar *tr.* to put in a file or portfolio.
encarrilar *tr.* to put back on the rails. *2* to put [a matter] on the right track; to set right.
encarrujarse *ref.* to curl, kink. *2* to become corrugated, to shrivel.
encartar *tr.* to indict. *2* [in card games] to play a suit that opponent can follow.

encarte *m.* [in card games] having to follow suit. *2* order of cards at the close of a hand.
encartonar *tr.* to put cadboard on; to protect with cardboard. *3* to bind [books] in boards.
encascabelar *tr.* to bell, put sleigh bells on.
encasillado *m.* set of squares or pigeonholes. *2* list of government candidates.
encasillar *tr.* to classify, to distribute. *2* to assign [a government candidate] to a voting district.
encasquetar *tr.* to pull on or down [a hat, cap, etc.]. *2* to hammer [an idea, etc.] into one's head. *4 ref.* to pull on [a hat, etc.]. *5* to get it into one's head.
encasquillar *tr.* to put a cap or ferrule on. *2* (Am.) to shoe [horses]. *3 ref.* [of a bullet in a gun] to stick, get stuck.
encastillado, -da *adj.* castellated. *2* haughty, proud.
encastillar *tr.* to fortify with castles. *2* to pile up. *3 ref.* to make a stand in a castle or lofty place. *4* to take refuge in some high spot. *5* to stick to one's own opinion.
encastrar *tr.* MECH. to engage, mesh.
encauchar *tr.* to cover with rubber.
encausar *tr.* LAW to arraign, indict, prosecute.
encauste, encausto *m.* PAINT. *pintura al* ~, encaustic.
encáustico, -ca *adj.* encaustic. *2 m.* wax polish.
encauzamiento *m.* channeling [directing by a channel]. *2* directing, guiding, guidance.
encauzar *tr.* to channel [direct by, or confine in, a channel]. *2* to direct, guide.
encebollado *m.* beef stew with onions.
encefálico, -ca *adj.* encephalic.
encefalitis *f.* MED. encephalitis.
encéfalo *m.* ANAT. encephalon.
encefalograma *m.* MED. encephalogram, encephalograph.
encelamiento *m.* jealousy. *2* rut.
encelar *tr.* to make jealous. *2 ref.* to become jealous. *3* to be in rut.
enceldar *tr.* to put in a cell.
encella *f.* cheese mould.
encenagamiento *m.* bemudding. *2* wallowing in vice.
encenagarse *ref.* to get into the mud. *2* to get covered with mud. *3* to give oneself up to, or to wallow [in vice].
encendaja *f.* kindling [for starting a fire].
encendedor, -ra *adj.* lighting, kindling. *2 m.* lighter, lighting device: ~ *automático*, cigarette lighter.
encender *tr.* to light, set fire to, ignite, kindle. *2* to burn [the mouth, etc.]. *3* to inflame, excite. *5 ref.* to burn, be kindled, catch fire. *6* [of war] to break out. *7* to become inflamed. *8* to blush, to redden. ¶ CONJUG. like *entender.*
encendidamente *adv.* ardently.
encendido, -da *adj.* high [colour], high-coloured. *3* red, flushed. *4* ardent, inflamed. *5 m.* AUTO. ignition.
encendimiento *m.* ignition; kindling, lighting. *2* flush, ruddy colour. *3* ardour, inflammation.
encentadura *f.* bed sore.
encentar *tr.-ref.* DECENTAR.
encerado, -da *adj.* waxed. *2* wax-coloured. *3 m.* oilcloth, oilskin, tarpaulin. *4* blackboard. *5* waxing [of floors and furniture].
encerador, -ra *m.-f.* waxer [of floors].
encerar *tr.* to wax.

encerradero *m.* sheep pen. *2* pen holding bulls before fight.
encerrar *tr.* to shut in, confine, hem in, lock up or in. *2* to enclose, contain. *3 ref.* to shut oneself in. *2* to retire, go into seclusion. *5* to be closeted. ¶ CONJUG. like *acertar.*
encerrona *f.* voluntary confinement. *2* plant, trap.
encespedar *tr.* to sward, turf.
encestar *tr.* to put in a basket.
enceste *m.* basket [in basketball].
encía *f.* gum [of the mouth].
encíclica *f.* encyclical.
enciclopedia *f.* encyclop(a)edia.
enciclopedismo *m.* Encyclop(a)edism.
enciendo, encienda, etc. *irr.* V. ENCENDER.
encierro *m.* shutting in or up, locking up, enclosing, penning, confinement. *2* seclusion, retirement. *3* place of confinement, prison.
encierro, encierre, etc. *irr.* V. ENCERRAR.
encima *adv.* on, upon, over, at the top: ~ *de,* on, upon; *por* ~, superficially, hastily; *por* ~ *de,* over, above; in spite of; *blanco por* ~, white at the top. *2* on, upon, with [a person, oneself]: *echarse* ~ *[ropas, una responsabilidad],* to throw [clothes] on, to take upon oneself [a responsability]; *quitarse [una cosa] de* ~, to be rid of [a thing]. *3* in addition, on top, to boot.
encimar *tr.* to raise hight, to put on top. *2 ref.* to rise above.
encina *f.* BOT. evergreen oak, holm oak.
encinal, encinar *m.* evergreen-oak grove.
encinta *adj.* pregnant, with child.
encintado *m.* curb [of a sidewalk, etc.].
encintar *tr.* to adorn with ribbons. *2* ENG. to put the curb or curbs on.
enclaustrar *tr.* to cloister.
enclavado, -da *adj.* enclaved. *2 m.* enclave.
enclavar *tr.* to nail. *2* to pierce, transfix. *3* coll. to deceive.
enclave *m.* enclave, small area, isolated area. *2* setting, situation, location.
enclavijar *tr.* to join, interlock. *2* to peg [a stringed instrument].
enclenque *adj.* weak, feeble, sickly.
enclítico, -ca *adj.-f.* GRAM. enclitic.
encocorar *tr.* to vex, annoy, nag.
encofrado *m.* MIN. plank lining. *2* form [for concrete].
encofrar *tr.* MIN. to plank, timber. *2* to build a form for [concrete].
encoger *tr.* to contract, draw back, draw in [a limb, etc.]. *2* to dispirit. *3 intr.* [of cloth, wood, etc.] to shrink. *4 ref.* to shrink. *5* to lose courage. *6 encogerse de hombros,* to shrug one's shoulders.
encogido, -da *adj.* awkward, timid, bashful.
encogimiento *adj.* contraction, shrinking, shrinkage. *2* awkwardness, timidity. *3* ~ *de hombros,* shrug.
encolado *m.* clarification [of wine]. *2* WEAV. dressing.
encoladura *f.,* **encolamiento** *m.* gluing. *2* PAINT. sizing. *3* ENCOLADO.
encolar *tr.* to glue. *2* WEAV. to dress. *3* PAINT. to size. *4* to clarify [wine].
encolerizar *tr.* to anger, irritate. *2 ref.* to become angry.
encomendar *tr.* to entrust, commit, commend, recommend. *2* to make [somebody] a knight commander. *3 ref.* to commend oneself [to]. ¶ CONJUG. like *acertar.*

encomendero *m.* holder of an ENCOMIENDA.
encomiar *tr.* to praise, eulogize, extol.
encomiasta *m.-f.* panegyrist.
encomiástico, -ca *adj.* encomiastic.
encomienda *f.* charge, commission. *2* commandery [of a military order]. *3* knight's cross. *4* HIST. grant of land made by a Spanish king. *5* HIST. Indian territory committed to the care of a Spanish colonist. *6* praise, commendation. *7* care, protection. *8* (Am.) postal parcel. *9 pl.* regards [sent].
encomiendo, encomiende, etc. *irr.* V. ENCOMENDAR.
encomio *m.* encomium.
enconamiento *m.* inflammation [of a wound or sore]. *2* bitterness, rancour.
enconar *tr.* to inflame, aggravate [a wound or sore]. *2* to embitter [the feelings]. *3 ref.* to become inflamed, to rankle, fester. *4* to become embittered. *5 enconarse con uno,* to treat someone bitterly.
encono *m.* bitterness, rancour.
encontradamente *adv.* oppositely.
encontradizo, -za *adj. hacerse el* ~, to try to meet someone seemingly by chance.
encontrado, -da *adj.* contrary, opposed.
encontrar *tr.* to find, meet, encounter. *2* to find [good, disagreable, etc.]. *3 intr.* to meet, collide. *4 ref.* to meet [come together]; to collide, be in opposition. *5* to be [in a place]. *6* to find oneself. *7* to feel [ill, well, at ease, etc.]. *8 encontrarse con,* to meet with, run across; to find. ¶ CONJUG. like *contar.*
encontrón, encontronazo *m.* bump, collision.
encopetado, -da *adj.* presumptuous, stuck-up. *2* noble, aristocratic, of high social standing.
encorajar *tr.* to give courage to. *2 ref.* to become enraged.
encorajinarse *ref.* to become enraged.
encorar *tr.* to cover with leather. *2* to grow a skin over [a sore]. *3 intr.-ref.* [of a sore], to grow a new skin. ¶ CONJUG. like *contar.*
encordadura *f.* MUS. strings [on an instrument].
encordar *tr.* to string [a musical instrument or a tennis racket]. *2* to bind or wrap with a rope. ¶ CONJUG. like *contar.*
encordonar *tr.* to lace, tie with laces. *2* to adorn with cords.
encornado, -da *adj.* [of a bull or cow] horned.
encornadura *f.* horns; set of the horns.
encorralar *tr.* to corral, shut in [cattle].
encorsetar *tr.-ref.* to put a corset on.
encortinar *tr.* to put up curtains on or in.
encorvadura *f.,* **encorvamiento** *m.* bending, curving, curvature. *2* stoop [bend of back and shoulderss].
encorvar *tr.* to bend, curve. *2 ref.* to bend over, to stoop. *3* [of horses] to buck.
encostarse *ref.* NAUT. to approach the coast.
encostrar *tr.* to encrust, cover with a crust. *2 intr.-ref.* to crust; to develop a crust or a scab.
encovar *tr.* to put in a cave. *2* to keep, hide away. *3* to force to hide oneself. *4 ref.* to hide oneself. ¶ CONJUG. like *contar.*
encrespado, -da *adj.* curly [hair]. *2* rough [sea].
encrespador *m.* curling iron.
encrespadura *f.* curling, crimping, crisping, frizzling.
encrespamiento *m.* curling, crisping, frizzling. *2* bristling, ruffling. *3* roughness [of the sea]. *4* anger, irritation.
encrespar *tr.* to curl, crisp, frizzle. *2* to bristle, ruf-

fle. *3* to stir up [the waves]. *4* to anger, irritate. *5 ref.* to curl, crisp, frizzle [become curled, etc.]. *6* [of hair, feathers] to bristle, ruffle. *7* [of the sea] to become rough. *8* to bristle with anger, be infuriated.

encrestarse *ref.* [of birds] to stiffen the crest or comb.

encrucijada *f.* crossroads; street intersection. *2* ambush, snare.

encrudecer *tr.* to make raw; to make hard to cook. *2* to exasperate, irritate. *3 ref.* to become exasperated, irritated. ¶ Conjug. like *agradecer.*

encruelecer *tr.* to make cruel. *2 ref.* to become cruel. ¶ Conjug. like *agradecer.*

encuadernación *f.* bookbinding. *2* binding [of a book]: ~ *a la holandesa,* half binding; ~ *en pasta,* carboard binding. *3* bindery.

encuadernador *m.* bookbinder.

encuadernar *tr.* to bind [a book]: *sin* ~, unbound.

encuadramiento *m.* framing.

encuadrar *tr.* to frame [provide with a frame; enclose in a frame; serve as a frame to].

encuadre *m.* CINEM. framing. *2* setting, background. *3* MILL. officering [troop].

encubar *tr.* to cask [wine, etc.]. *2* MIN. to timber [a shaft].

encubierta *f.* fraudulent concealment.

encubiertamente *adv.* secretly, on the sly.

encubierto, -ta *p. p.* of ENCUBRIR: *palabras encubiertas,* veiled words.

encubridor, -ra *m.-f.* concealer, one who covers up. *3* LAW accessory after the fact.

encubrimiento *m.* concealment. *2* LAW being an accesory after the fact.

encubrir *tr.* to conceal, hide. *2* to cover up. *3* LAW to become an accesory after the fact.

encuentro *m.* meeting [act of meeting]; encounter: *mal* ~, unlucky encounter; *salir al* ~ *de,* to go to meet; to oppose; to meet half way. *2* clash, collision, opposition. *3* MIL. encounter. *4* ARCH. angle, nook, corner. *5* ZOOL. axilla. *6 pl.* [in quadrupeds] points of the shoulder blades.

encuentro, encuentre, etc. *irr.* V. ENCONTRAR.

encuesta *f.* inquiry.

encuestador, -ra *n.* pollster.

encumbrado, -da *adj.* high, lofty. *2* elevated, sublime. *3* mighty, high-placed.

encumbramiento *m.* elevation, height. *2* exaltation, climbing or rising to high station.

encumbrar *tr.* to raise high. *2* to exalt, elevate. *3* to climb on the top of. *4 ref.* to rise high. *5* to raise oneself [to high station]. *6* to become proud, haughty.

encunar *tr.* to put [a child] in the cradle. *2* BULLF. to catch between the horns.

encurtidos *m. pl.* pickles.

encurtir *tr.* to pickle.

enchalecar *tr.* coll. to pocket, to pinch. *2* to put sómeone into a straightjacket. *3 ref.* to pocket.

enchancletar *tr.* to put slippers on. *2* to drag shoes. *3 ref.* to put slippers on.

enchapado *m.* veneer, veneering, covering of thin plates or sheets.

encharcar *tr.* to inundate, turn into a pool. *2 ref.* to be covered with puddles. *3* to upset the stomach by much drinking.

enchiquerar *tr.* BULLF. to pen [the bull] before the fight. *2* coll. to jail.

enchironar *tr.* coll. to jail.

enchufado, -da *adj. p.p.* of ENCHUFAR. *2* coll. well in; *estar* ~, to have useful contacts, to have

friends in the right places, to have a cushy lob. *3* coll. *n.* wirepuller, one who has succeeded through contacts. *4* slacker [soldier].

enchufar *tr.* to fit [a tube or pipe] into another. *2* ELECT. to connect, to plug in. *3 ref.* to get a sinecure.

enchufe *m.* fitting [of a pipe into another]; joint [of two pipes]. *2* ELECT. plug; plug and receptacle. *3* sinecure, easy job.

ende *adv. por* ~, therefore.

endeble *adj.* weak, feeble, frail, flimsy.

endeblez *f.* feebleness, fragility, flimsiness.

endecágono *m.* GEOM. hendecagon, undecagon.

endecasílabo, -ba *adj.* hendecasyllabic. *2 m.* hendecasyllabe.

endecha *f.* dirge, doleful song. *2* assonanced sevensyllabled quatrain.

endemia *f.* MED. endemic.

endémico, -ca *adj.* endemic.

endemoniado, -da *adj.* demoniac. *2* fig. devilish, very bad. *3* fig. tremendous, awful. *4 m.-f.* demoniac, possessed.

endemoniar *tr.* to possess with an evil spirit. *2* coll. to irritate, enrage.

endentar *tr.* MACH. to furnish with teeth. *2 tr.-intr.* to engage, mesh. ¶ Conjug. like *acertar.*

endentecer *intr.* to teethe, cut one's teeth. ¶ Conjug. like *agradecer.*

enderezamiento *m.* straightening. *2* setting right.

enderezar *tr.* to straighten, unbend. *2* to right, set upright. *3* to address, dedicate. *4* to right, correct, put in order. *5* to fix, punish. *6* to bend [one's steps]. *7 ref.* to straighten up. *8* to be directed [to an end].

endeudarse *ref.* to fall into debt.

endiablado, -da *adj.* devilish. *2* ugly, deformed. *3* very bad. *4* furious, wild. *5* complicated, difficult.

endibia *f.* BOT. endive.

endiento, endiente, etc. *irr.* V. ENDENTAR.

endilgar *tr.* coll. to direct, guide. *2* coll. to put, lodge. *3* coll. to land [a blow]; to spring [something unpleasant] on [a person].

endino, -na *adj.* coll. wicked, perverse.

endiosamiento *m.* haughtiness, pride, conceit.

endiosarse *ref.* to become haughty, proud.

endocardio *m.* ANAT. endocardium.

endocarpio *m.* BOT. endocarp.

endocrino, -na *adj.* PHYSIOL. endocrine.

endodermo *m.* BIOL. endoderm. *2* BOT. endodermis.

endógeno, -na *adj.* endogenous.

endolinfa *f.* PHYSIOL. endolymph.

endomingado, -da *adj.* in his Sunday best.

endomingarse *ref.* to put on one's Sunday best.

endosante *m.-f.* COM. endorser.

endosar *tr.* COM. to endorse, indorse. *2* to transfer [a burden, task, etc.] to another person, to saddle with.

endosatario, -ria *m.-f.* endorsee.

endoselar *tr.* to canopy.

endósmosis *f.* PHYS., CHEM. endosmosis.

endoso *m.* COM. endorsement.

endospermo *m.* BOT. endosperm.

endrina *f.* BOT. sloe plum.

endrino, -na *adj.* sloe-coloured. *2 m.* BOT. blackthorn, sloe tree.

endulzar *tr.* to sweeten. *2* to soften, make bearable.

endurecer *tr.* to harden. *2* to inure. *3 ref.* to harden [become hard]. *4* to become hardened, cruel. ¶ Conjug. like *agradecer*.

endurecido, -da *adj.* hard, hardened. *2* obdurate.

endurecimiento *m.* hardening. *2* hardness. *3* obduracy. *4* hard-heartedness.

endurezco, endurezca, etc. *irr.* V. ENDURECER.

ene *f.* Spanish name of the letter *n*. *2* x [unknown quantity].

enea *f.* BOT. cattail, bulrush.

eneágono, -na *m.* GEOM. nonagon.

Eneas *m. pr. n.* MYTH. Æneas.

enebrina *f.* juniper berry.

enebro *m.* BOT. juniper.

Eneida *f.* Æneid.

eneldo *m.* BOT. dill.

enema *f.* enema, clyster.

enemiga *f.* enmity, hatred, ill-will.

enemigo, -ga *adj.* adverse, opposed [to]. *2* enemy, hostile. *3 m.-f.* enemy, foe: *el ~ malo*, the Evil one.

enemistad *f.* enmity.

enemistar *tr.* to make enemices of. *2 ref.* to become enemies: *enemistarse con*, to fall out with.

energético, -ca *adj.* energy. *2 f.* energetics. *3 m. pl.* fuels.

energía *f.* energy: *~ atómica*, PHYS. atomic energy. *2* MECH. power: *~ eléctrica*, electric power.

enérgico, -ca *adj.* energetic, vigorous, active, lively.

energúmeno, -na *m.-f.* energumen. *2* wild, frantic person.

enero *m.* January.

enervación *f.* enervation. *2* MED. nervous prostration.

enervamiento *m.* enervation.

enervante *adj.* enervating.

enervar *tr.* to enervate. *2 ref.* to become enervate.

enésimo, -ma *adj.* MATH. nth.

enfadadizo, -za *adj.* easily displeased, peevish.

enfadar *tr.* to displease, annoy, anger. *2* to bore. *3 ref.* to be displeased, get angry.

enfado *m.* displeasure, annoyance, irritation. *2* trouble, bother.

enfadoso, -sa *adj.* annoying, bothersome, boring.

enfangar *tr.* to bemud. *2 ref.* to sink in the mud. *3* to mix [in dirty business]. *4* to sink [into vice].

enfardar *tr.* to pack, to bale.

enfardelar *tr.* to bundle, to pack.

énfasis *m.* emphasis [special impressiveness of expression]. *2* affectation in delivery.

enfático, -ca *adj.* emphatic, impressive.

enfatizar *tr.* to emphasize.

enfatuarse *ref.* to become vain or conceited.

enfermar *intr.* to fall ill, be taken ill. *2 tr.* to make ill.

enfermedad *f.* illness, sickness, disease.

enfermera *f.* woman nurse [for the sick].

enfermería *f.* infirmary, sick-quarters.

enfermero *m.* male nurse [for the sick].

enfermizo, -za *adj.* sickly, unhealthy.

enfermo, -ma *adj.* sick, ill, diseased. *2 m.-f.* sick person, patient.

enfermucho, -cha *adj.* sickish, sickly.

enfervorizar *tr.* to inspire fervour. *2 ref.* to become inflamed with fervour.

enfeudación *tr.* infeudation, enfeoffment.

enfeudar *tr.* to enfeoff.

enfilar *tr.* to line up. *2* to aim, sight. *3* to go straight down or up [a street, etc.]. *4* to string [beads, etc.]. *5* ARTILL. to enfilade.

enfisema *m.* MED. emphysema.

enfiteusis *f.* LAW emphyteusis.

enflaquecer *tr.* to make thin or lean. *2* to weaken. *3 intr.-ref.* to become thin or lean. ¶ Conjug. like *agradecer*.

enflaquecimiento *m.* loss of flesh, emaciation.

enflorar *tr.* to flower [adorn with flowers].

enfocar *tr.* to focus. *2* to envisage, direct [an affair]; to approach [a problem, etc.].

enfoque *m.* focussing. *2* approach [to a problem, etc.].

enfrascamiento *m.* absorption.

enfrascar *tr.* to put in bottles. *2 ref.* to become absorbed, become deeply engaged [in].

enfrenamiento *m.* bridling. *2* checking, restraining.

enfrentar *tr.* to confront, cause to face; to bring face to face. *2 tr.-ref.* to face: *enfrentarse con*, to face, oppose, stand up to; to cope with.

enfrente *adv.* in front, opposite: *~ de*, in front of, opposite, facing, against.

enfriadera *f.* bottle cooler.

enfriamiento *m.* cooling, refrigeration. *2* MED. cold.

enfriar *tr.* to cool, make cool. *2 ref.* to cool [become cool], cool off. *3* to get chilled.

enfrontar *tr.* to come face to. *2 tr.-intr.* to face, oppose.

enfundar *tr.* to sheathe, case. *2* to muffle [a drum].

enfurecer *tr.* to infuriate, enrage. *2 ref.* to rage, become infuriated. ¶ Conjug. like *agradecer*.

enfurecimiento *m.* infuriation, fury.

enfurezco, enfurezca, etc. *irr.* V. ENFURECER.

enfurruñamiento *m.* anger, sulkiness.

enfurruñarse *ref.* to get angry, to sulk.

enfurtir *tr.* to full [cloth].

engaitar *tr.* to deceive, cozen, humbug, wheedle.

engalanar *tr.* to adorn, bedeck. *2* NAUT. to dress.

engalgar *tr.* to brake [a cart wheel].

engallado, -da *adj.* erect, upright. *2* haughty.

engallador *m.* checkrein.

engallarse *ref.* to draw oneself up arrogantly; to get cocky. *2* [of a horse] to have the head pulled up.

enganchar *tr.* to hook [grasp with a hook]; to hook on or up. *2* to hitch, harness. *3* RLY. to couple [carriages]. *4* to attract, hook [a person]. *5* MIL. to recruit, enlist. *6* BULLF. to hook with the horns. *7 ref.* to get caught [on a hook, a nail, etc.]. *8* MIL. to enlist [enroll oneself].

enganche *m.* hooking. *2* hitching [of horses]. *3* RLY. coupling, coupler. *4* MIL. enlistment.

engañabobos *m.-f.* bamboozler. *2 m.* catchpenny.

engañador, -ra *adj.* deceptive, deluding. *2 m.-f.* deceiver.

engañar *tr.* to deceive, beguile, delude, dupe, fool, hoax, mislead, impose upon, take in. *2* to wheedle. *3* to beguile, while away [time, etc.]. *4 ref.* to deceive oneself, be mistaken.

engañifa *f.* coll. deception, trick. *2* catchpenny.

engaño *m.* deception, deceit; falsehood; fraud imposition: *llamarse a ~*, to revoke an agreement, alleging fraud. *2* error, mistake. *3* lure, bait.

engañoso, -sa *adj.* deceptive, delusive. *2* deceitful.

engarabatar *tr.* to hook. *2* to crook, gnarl, twist. *3 ref.* to get crooked or gnarled.

engarabitar *intr.-ref.* to climb. *2 ref.* [of fingers] to get crooked and stiff [from cold].

engarce *m.* JEWEL. linking, wiring; setting.

engargantar *tr.* to put into the throat. *2 intr.* MACH. to mesh, engage.

engargante *m.* MACH. mesh, meshing.

engargolado *m.* groove for a sliding door.
engargolar *tr.* CARP. to groove [fix in a groove].
engarzar *tr.* JEWEL. to link, wire. 2 JEWEL. to enchase, set, mount. 3 to curl [hair].
engastar *tr.* JEWEL. to enchase, set, mount.
engaste *m.* JEWEL. enchasing, setting, mounting. 2 setting [of a gem]. 3 pearl flat on one side.
engatillado, -da *adj.* having a high, thick neck [horse or bull]. 2 *m.* flat-lock seaming.
engatillar *tr.* to joint with flat-lock seams.
engatusador, -ra *m.-f.* cajoler, wheedler.
engatusamiento *m.* coaxing, wheedling, inveigleing.
engatusar *tr.* to cajole, coax, wheedle.
engazar *tr.* ENGARZAR. 2 NAUT. to strap [blocks].
engendramiento *m.* engendering, begetting, generation.
engendrar *tr.* engender, beget. 2 to generate, originate. 3 GEOM. to generate.
engendro *m.* foetus. 2 abortion, freak. 3 poor literary or artistic work. 4 *mal* ~, perverse child.
englobar *tr.* to lump together, to include.
engolado, -da *adj.* HER. engouled. 2 presumptuous, pompous.
engolamiento *m.* arrogance, presumption, pretentiousness.
engolfar *intr.-ref.* NAUT. to go far out on the sea. 2 *ref.* to be deeply engaged or absorbed.
engolosinar *tr.* to allure, tempt. 2 *ref. engolosinarse con*, to get fond of.
engomadura *f.* gumming.
engomar *tr.* to gum [papers, fabrics, etc.].
engordar *tr.* to fatten. 2 *intr.* to fatten [grow fat; become rich].
engorde *m.* fattening.
engorro *m.* encumbrance, nuisance, bother.
engorroso, -sa *adj.* cumbersome, annoying.
engoznar *tr.* to hinge.
engranaje *m.* MACH. mesh, meshing. 2 MACH. gear, gearing. 3 teeth of a gear.
engranar *intr.* MACH. to mesh, gear. 2 to interlock.
engrandecer *tr.* to enlarge, aggrandize. 2 to extol. 3 to enhance, exaggerate. 4 to elevate, exalt. 5 *ref.* to be exalted. ¶ CONJUG. like *agradecer.*
engrandecimiento *m.* enlargement. 2 praise. 3 enhancement. 4 exaltation.
engrane *m.* MACH. mesh, meshing.
engrapar *tr.* MAS., CARP. to cramp.
engrasador, -ra *adj.* greasing. 2 *m.-f.* greaser, oiler.
engrasar *tr.* to make greasy. 2 to grease, oil, lubricate. 3 to fertilize. 4 to dress [cloth].
engrase *m.* greasing, lubrication. 2 grease [for lubrication]. 3 fertilization [of land].
engreído, -da *adj.* vain, conceited.
engreimiento *m.* vanity, presumption, conceit.
engreír *tr.* to make vain or conceited. 2 *ref.* to become vain or conceited. ¶ CONJUG. like *reír.*
engrescar *tr.* to incite to quarrel. 2 to incite to merriment. 3 *ref.* to get into a row. 4 to get merry.
engrifarse *ref.* to take drugs, to drug oneself.
engrosamiento *m.* thickening. 2 enlargening [of a number].
engrosar *tr.* to thicken; to make fat or corpulent. 2 to enlarge [the number of]. 3 *ref.* to thicken [grow thick]. 4 to grow fat or corpulent. ¶ CONJUG. like *contar.*
engrudar *tr.* to paste.
engrudo *m.* paste [of flour or starch and water].
engruesar *tr.-r.* ENGROSAR.
engrueso, engruese, etc. *irr.* V. ENGROSAR.

engrumecerse *ref.* to clot, to curdle.
engualdrapar *tr.* to caparison [a horse].
enguantado, -da *adj.* wearing gloves.
enguijarrado *m.* cobblestone paving.
enguijarrar *tr.* to cobble [pave with cobblestones].
enguirnaldar *tr.* to garland.
engullir *tr.* to swallow, gulp, gobble.
enharinar *tr.* to cover or smear with flour.
enhebillar *tr.* to bucle [a strap].
enhebrar *tr.* to thread [a needle]; to thread, string [beads].
enhestadura *f.* raising high; setting upright.
enhestar *tr.* to raise high. 2 to set upright. ¶ CONJUG. like *acertar.*
enhiesto, -ta *adj.* erect, upright, raised.
enhilar *tr.* ENHEBRAR. 2 ENFILAR. 3 to marshal, arrange [ideas] in order. 4 to direct to an end.
enhorabuena *f.* congratulations: *dar la* ~ *a*, to congratulate. 2 *adv.* happily. 3 all right; well and good.
enhoramala *adv.* in an evil hour. 2 *vete* ~, go to blazes!
enhorcar *tr.* to string [onions].
enhornar *tr.* to put into an oven.
enigma *m.* enigma, riddle.
enigmático, -ca *adj.* enigmatic(al.
enjabonar *tr.* to soap, to lather. 2 coll. to softsoap. 3 coll. to give a rubbing to.
enjaezar *tr.* to put trappings on [a horse].
enjalbegadura *f.* whitewashing.
enjalbegar *tr.* to whitewash. 2 to paint [the face]. 3 *ref.* to paint one's face.
enjalma *f.* light packsaddle.
enjambrar *tr.* to hive, swarm [bees]. 2 *intr.* [of bees] to swarm, to breed a new hive.
enjambrazón *f.* swarming [of bees].
enjambre *m.* swarm. 2 crowd, multitude.
enjarciar *tr.* NAUT. to equip with rigging.
enjaretado *m.* grating, lattice work.
enjaretar *tr.* to run [a string] through a casing. 2 to rattle off [a speech, etc.]; to do [something] in a rush. 3 to spring [something] on [a person].
enjaular *tr.* to cage. 2 coll. to imprison, confine.
enjoyar *tr.* to bejewel, adorn or cover with jewels. 2 to embellish. 3 to set with precious stones.
enjuagadientes *m.* mouthwash.
enjuagadura *f.* rinse, rinsing, wash.
enjuagar *tr.* to rinse [mouth, vessels, etc.].
enjuague *m.* rinse, rinsing. 2 rinsing water; mouthwash. 3 washbowl, rinsing cup. 4 fig. scheme, plot.
enjugador, -ra *m.-f.* drier. 2 *m.* clotheshorse.
enjugar *tr.* to dry [free from moisture]; to wipe. 2 to dry [tears, sweat, etc.]. 3 to cancel, wipe out [a debt, etc.].
enjuiciamiento *m.* examining, judging. 2 LAW act of instituting and carrying out a judicial proceeding. 3 LAW prosecution.
enjuiciar *tr.* to submit [a matter] to study and judgment; to judge of. 2 LAW to institute a judicial proceeding against, to prosecute.
enjundia *f.* fat in the ovary of fowls. 2 fat of any animal. 3 substance, force.
enjundioso, -sa *adj.* having much fat. 2 substantial, important, solid.
enjunque *m.* NAUT. pig-iron, ballast, kentledge.
enjuta *f.* ARCH. spandrel.
enjuto, -ta *adj.* dry [free from moisture]. 2 lean, thin, skinny.
enlace *m.* lacing, interlacing, linking. 2 link,

union. 3 RLY. junction; connection. 4 wedding. 5 oficial de ~, MIL. liaison officer.

enlaciar tr.-ref. to render or to become lax or flabby.

enladrillado, -da adj. paved with bricks. 2 m. brick pavement.

enladrillar tr. to pave with bricks.

enlatar tr. to can [food, etc.]. 2 to roof or cover with battens.

enlazadura f., **enlazamiento** m. linking, connection.

enlazar tr. to lace, to interlace. 2 to link, join. 3 to lasso. 4 ref. to marry. 5 to become laced or linked. 6 to be connected together.

enligar tr. to smear with birdlime. 2 ref. to be caught with birdlime.

enlistonado m. CARP. lathing, lath work.

enlistonar tr. to lath, lay lathwork on.

enlobreguecer tr. to make dark or gloomy.

enlodar tr. to bemud, bemire. 2 to smirch. 3 ref. to get muddy. 4 to soil oneself.

enloquecedor, -ra adj. maddening.

enloquecer tr. to madden, drive insane, distract. 2 intr. to go mad, become insane. ¶ CONJUG. like agradecer.

enloquecimiento m. going mad. 2 madness, distraction.

enlosado m. flagstone paving.

enlosar tr. to pave with flagstones.

enlozar tr. (Am.) to enamel [iron, etc.].

enlucido, -da adj. MAS. plastered. 2 m. MAS. plastering [of a wall]; coat of plaster.

enlucimiento m. MAS. plastering. 2 polishing.

enlucir tr. MAS. to plaster [walls]. 2 to polish [metals].

enlutar tr. to put in mourning, to crape. 2 to darken. 3 to sadden. 4 ref. to put on mourning; to dress oneself in mourning.

enllantar tr. to rim, to shoe [a wheel].

enmaderar tr. to plank, board, wainscot. 2 to timber [a building].

enmagrecer intr. to grow lean, lose flesh. ¶ CONJUG. like agradecer.

enmallarse ref. [of a fish] to be caught in the meshes of a net.

enmarañamiento m. entanglement, tangle. 2 embroilment, confusion.

enmarañar tr. to entangle, tangle, ravel. 2 to embroil, confuse. 3 ref. to get tangled, embroiled.

enmararse ref. NAUT. to take to the open sea.

enmarcar tr. to frame. 2 to surround, to provide the setting for.

enmascaramiento m. MIL. camouflage.

enmascarar tr. to mask. 2 ref. to put on a mask.

enmasillar tr. to putty.

enmendable adj. emendable.

enmendadura f. emendation, correction.

enmendar tr. to emend, correct, amend. 2 to repair, make amends for. 3 ref. to reform, mend. ¶ CONJUG. like acertar.

enmienda f. emendation, correction. 2 amends, reparation. 3 [in parliamentary procedure] amendment. 4 pl. AGR. amendments.

enmiendo, enmiende, etc. irr. V. ENMENDAR.

enmohecer tr. to make mouldy, to mildew. 2 to rust. 3 ref. to get mouldy. 4 to get rusty. ¶ CONJUG. like agradecer.

enmohecido, -da adj. mouldy, rusty.

enmohecimiento m. mouldiness, rustiness.

enmohezco, enmohezca, etc. irr. V. ENMOHECER.

enmonarse ref. (Am.) to get drunk.

enmudecer tr. to hush, silence. 2 intr. to become dumb. 3 to be silent. ¶ CONJUG. like agradecer.

enmudezco, enmudezca, etc. irr. V. ENMUDECER.

enmugrecer tr. to soil, make greasy. ¶ CONJUG. like agradecer.

ennegrecer tr. to blacken, to darken. ¶ CONJUG. like agradecer.

ennegrecimiento m. blackening, darkening.

ennegrezco, ennegrezca, etc. irr. V. ENNEGRECER.

ennoblecedor, -ra adj. ennobling.

ennoblecer tr. to ennoble. ¶ CONJUG. like agradecer.

ennoblezco, ennoblezca, etc. irr. V. ENNOBLECER.

ennoblecimiento m. ennoblement.

enojadizo, -za adj. irritable, peevish, easily angered.

enojar tr. to anger, make angry. 2 to annoy, displease. 3 ref. to become angry, get cross.

enojo m. anger, irritation, displeasure. 2 annoyance.

enojosamente adv. angrily.

enojoso, -sa adj. annoying, vexatious, bothersome.

enología f. œnology.

enólogo, -ga n. oenologist.

enorgullecer tr. to make proud. 2 ref. to be or become proud; enorgullecerse de, to pride oneself on. ¶ CONJUG. like agradecer.

enorgullecimiento m. pride, haughtiness.

enorgullezco, enorgullezca, etc. irr. V. ENORGULLECER.

enorme adj. enormous. 2 wicked, heinous.

enormemente adv. enormously, extremely, tremendously, vastly.

enormidad f. enormousness. 2 enormity. 3 absurdity, nonsense.

enquistarse ref. MED. to encyst

enrabiar tr. to anger, enrage.

enraizar intr. to take root.

enramada f. bower; shelter of branches.

enranciar tr.-ref. to make or to become rancid or stale.

enrarecer tr. to rarefy [make less dense]. 2 ref. to rarefy [become less dense]. 3 intr.-ref. to become scarce. ¶ CONJUG. like agradecer.

enrarecido, -da adj. rarefied.

enrarecimiento m. rarefaction.

enrasar tr. MAS. to make level or flush. 2 intr. to become level or flush.

enrase m. making or being level or flush.

enrayar tr. to spoke [a wheel].

enredadera adj. BOT. climbing. 2 f. BOT. climbing vine, climber. 3 BOT. bindweed.

enredador, -ra adj. entangling, embroiling. 2 mischievous.

enredar tr. to tangle, entangle, mat, ravel. 2 to net [catch in a net]. 3 to set [nets] for birds, etc. 4 to embroil, sow discord between. 5 to involve, implicate. 6 intr. [of children] to be mischievous, play pranks. 7 to fumble, meddle. 8 ref. to be caught [in a net, etc.]. 9 to get entangled; to get involved. 10 to become complicated, embroiled. 11 [of an anchor] to foul.

enredijo m. tangle, entanglement.

enredo m. tangle, entanglement. 2 complication. 3 imbroglio. 4 falsehood, gossip, mischief.

enredoso, -sa adj. complicated, full of difficulties.

enrejado m. iron railing, grille. 2 grating, latticework, trellis.

enrejar tr. to close with a grille. 2 to fence with railing or trellis. 3 to fix the share to [a plough].

enrevesado, -da adj. REVESADO.

enriar tr. to ret [flox or hemp].

Enrique *m. pr. n.* Henry.
enriquecedor, -ra *adj.* enriching.
enriquecer *tr.* to enrich. *2 ref.* to become wealthy. *3* to be enriched. ¶ CONJUG. like *agradecer.*
enriquezco, enriquezca, etc. *irr.* V. ENRIQUECER.
enriquecimiento *m.* enrichment.
Enriqueta *f. pr. n.* Henrietta, Harriet.
enriscado, -da *adj.* craggy [full of crags].
enriscar *tr.* to raise. *2 ref.* to go or take refuge among the rocks.
enristrar *tr.* to couch [the lance]. *2* to string [onions, etc.]. *3* to go straight to.
enrocar *tr.-intr.* CHESS to castle. *2 tr.* to put [flak or hemp] on the distaff.
enrojar *tr.* to redden. *2* to make red-hot.
enrojecer *tr.* to redden. *2* to make red-hot. *3 ref.* to redden, turn red. *4 intr.* to blush. ¶ CONJUG. like *agradecer.*
enrojecimiento *m.* reddening, blushing, blush [face]. *2* reddening, glowing [metal].
enrolamiento *m.* enrolment, enrollment, signing-up. *2* MIL. enlistment.
enrolar *tr.* to enroll, to sign-up. *2* MIL. to enlist.
enrollable *adj.* roll-up.
enrollar *tr.* to roll, coil.
enronquecer *tr.* to make hoarse. *2 intr.-ref.* to get hoarse. ¶ CONJUG. like *agradecer.*
enroque *m.* CHESS. castling.
enroscar *tr.* to coil, twist. *2* to screw on or in. *3 ref.* to coil, twist itself.
ensacar *tr.* to bag, sack [put in bags or sacks].
ensaimada *f.* cake made of a coiled lenght of puff paste.
ensalada *f.* salad. *2* hodge-podge, medley.
ensaladera *f.* salad bowl.
ensaladilla *f.* kind of salad with mayonnaise sauce. *2* hodge-podge.
ensalivar *tr.* to moisten with saliva.
ensalmador, -ra *m.-f.* bonesetter. *2* one who pretends to cure by spells.
ensalmar *tr.* to set [bones]. *2* to cure by spells.
ensalmo *m.* curing by spells: *como por ~,* as if it were by magic, in a jiffy.
ensalzamiento *m.* exalting, elevation. *2* extolling.
ensalzar *tr.* to exalt, elevate. *2* to praise, extoll.
ensambladura *f.,* **ensamblaje** *m.* CARP. joining, assembling; joint.
ensamblar *tr.* to join, fit together. *2* CARP. to joint.
ensamble *m.* joining. *2* joint.
ensanchador *m.* glove stretcher.
ensanchamiento *m.* widening, enlarging.
ensanchar *tr.* to widen, broaden, enlarge. *2* to let out [a garment]. *3 ~ el corazón,* to relieve, cheer up. *4 ref.* to widen, to expand. *5* to put on airs.
ensanche *m.* widening, enlargement, extension. *2* SEW. allowance [in seams] for future enlargement. *3* suburban development.
ensangrentar *tr.-ref.* to stain with blood. *2 ref.* to get violent or furious. ¶ CONJUG. like *acertar.*
ensañamiento *m.* cruelty, ferocity.
ensañar *tr.* to irritate, enrage. *2 ref. ensañarse con,* to be cruel to, to wend one's fury on.
ensartar *tr.* to string [beads, etc]. *2* to spit, skew, pierce. *3* coll. to rattle off, say disconnectedly.
ensayar *tr.* to assay [metals]. *2* to try, try out, test. *3* to rehearse [a play, etc.]. *4* to train, practise. *5 ref.* to practise, train oneself.
ensaye *m.* assay [of metals].
ensayista *m.-f.* essayist, essay-writer.
ensayo *m.* assay [of metals]. *2* trying, testing, trial, test, experiment. *3* preparatory practice; rehearsal: *~ general,* THEAT. dress rehearsal. *4* LIT. essay.
ensebar *tr.* to grease, tallow.
enseguida *adv.* at once, right away, inmediately.
ensenada *f.* cove, inlet, small bay.
enseña *f.* standard, ensign.
enseñado, -da *adj.* trained, accustomed, educated.
enseñanza *f.* teaching, instruction, education: *primera ~,* primary education; *~ superior,* higher education. *2* lesson, example.
enseñar *tr.* to teach. *2* to instruct, train, school. *3* to show [exhibit, let be seen]. *4* to show, point out.
enseñoreamiento *m.* mastery, domination.
enseñorearse *ref.* to make oneself the master [of], take possession [of].
enseres *m. pl.* chattels, household goods. *2* implements, utensils.
ensilaje *m.* ensilage, silage.
ensilar *tr.* to ensilage, to ensile.
ensillado, -da *adj.* saddle-backed.
ensillar *tr.* to saddle [a horse, etc.].
ensimismado, -da *adj.* pensive, lost in thought, thoughtful, absorbed.
ensimismamiento *m.* absorption in thought.
ensimismarse *ref.* to become absorbed in thought.
ensoberbecer *tr.* to make haughty, arrogant. *2 ref.* to become haughty, arrogant. ¶ CONJUG. like *agradecer.*
ensoberbecimiento *m.* haughtiness, arrogance.
ensombrecer *tr.* to darken, cloud. *2 ref.* to darken [become dark or gloomy]. ¶ CONJUG. like *agradecer.*
ensombrezco, ensombrezca, etc. *irr.* V. ENSOMBRECER.
ensopar *tr.* to dunk, to soak.
ensordecedor, -ra *adj.* deafening.
ensordecer *tr.* to deafen [make deaf]. *2 ref.* to become deaf. ¶ CONJUG. like *agradecer.*
ensordecimiento *m.* deafening; deafness.
ensordezco, ensordezca, etc. *irr.* V. ENSORDECER.
ensortijar *tr.* to curl, crisp [hair, etc.]. *2 ref.* [of hair, etc.] to curl.
ensuciamiento *m.* soiling, staining.
ensuciar *tr.* to dirty, soil, stain, defile, pollute. *2 ref.* to get dirty. *3* to soil one's bed, clothes, etc. *4* to soil oneself.
ensueño *m.* dream, day-dream, fantasy.
entablado *m.* flooring [of boards]. *2* wooden framework.
entablamento *m.* ARCH. entablature.
entablar *tr.* to plank, board, cover with boards. *2* to start [a conversation, etc.]; to bring [a suit or action]. *3* SURG. to splint. *4 ref.* [of wind] to settle.
entablillar *tr.* SURG. to splint.
entalamadura *f.* awning [of cart or wagon].
entalegar *tr.* to put in a bag, to bag. *2* to save, to hoard, to stash away. *3* to pocket. *4 ref.* coll. to make, to earn.
entalladura *f.,* **entallamiento** *m.* carving, sculpture; engraving. *2* notch, mortise, incision.
entallar *tr.* to carve, sculpture, engrave. *2* to notch, make a cut in. *3* to make [a garment] fit to the waist. *4 intr.* [of a garment] to fit to the waist.
entapizar *tr.* to upholster. *2* to carpet [cover as with a carpet].
entarimado *m.* boarded or parqueted floor.
entarimar *tr.* to floor with boards.
entarquinar *tr.* to fertilize with slime. *2* to soil with slime. *3* to reclaim [a swamp] by siltation.

entarugado *m.* pavement of wooden blocks.
ente *m.* entity, being. 2 coll, fellow *guy.
enteco, -ca *adj.* weakly, sickly.
entelequia *f.* PHILOS. entelechy.
entena *f.* NAUT. lateen yard.
entenada *f.* stepdaughter.
entenado *m.* stepson.
entendederas *f. pl.* brains, understanding.
entendedor, -ra *m.-f.* one who understands: *al buen ~ pocas palabras*, a word to the wise is enough.
1) **entender** *m.* understanding; opinion: *a mi ~*, in my opinion.
2) **entender** *tr.* to understand, conceive, comprehend. 2 to intend, mean. 3 to think, believe; infer. 4 *intr. ~ de* or *en*, to be an expert on; to be in charge [of an affair]; to have authority to pass on. 5 *ref.* to be understandable. 6 to be understood. 7 to know what one's about. 8 to understand each other. 9 to have a secret understanding. ¶ CONJUG. IND. Pres.: *entiendo, entiendes, entiende;* entendemos, entendéis, *entienden.* | SUBJ. Pres.: *entienda, entiendas, entienda;* entendamos, entendáis, *entiendan.* | IMPER.: *entiende, entienda;* entendamos, entended, *entiendan.*
entendido, -da *p. p.* of ENTENDER: *tener ~*, to understand. 2 *adj.* that understands; *no darse por ~*, to pretend not to understand. 3 able, expert, learned.
entendimiento *m.* understanding, comprehension. 2 understanding, intellect, mind, sense.
entenebrecer *tr.* to darken, obscure. 2 *ref.* to get dark. ¶ CONJUG. like *agradecer.*
enterado *adj.* informed, well informed.
enteramente *adv.* completely, fully, entirely, quite.
enterar *tr.* to inform, acquaint, make cognizant. 2 *ref. enterarse de*, to learn, be informed of; to inquire about.
entercarse *ref.* to get obstinate.
entereza *f.* entirety. 2 integrity. 3 fortitude, firmness, presence of mind. 4 *~ virginal*, virginity.
enteritis *f.* MED. enteritis.
enterizo, -za *adj.* in one piece.
enternecedor, -ra *adj.* affecting, moving, touching.
enternecer *tr.* to soften. 2 to touch, move to pity. 3 *ref.* to be touched, be moved to pity. ¶ CONJUG. like *agradecer.*
enternecimiento *m.* tenderness, pity, compassion.
entero, -ra *adj.* entire, whole, complete. 2 sound, robust. 3 honest, upright. 4 firm, constant. 5 ARITH. whole [number]. 6 BOT. entire. 7 uncastrated. 8 *m.* ARITH. integer. 9 *por ~*, entirely, completely, fully.
enterocolitis *f.* MED. enterocolitis.
enterrador *m.* gravedigger, sexton.
enterramiento *m.* interment, burial. 2 sepulchre, tomb, grave.
enterrar *tr.* to bury; to inter. 2 to survive. 3 *ref.* to retire, bury oneself. ¶ CONJUG. like *acertar.*
entesar *tr.* to stretch, tighten, tauten.
entestado, -da *adj.* stubborn, obstinate.
entibación *f.* MIN. timbering.
entibar *tr.* MIN. to shore up, timber. 2 *intr.* to rest, lean.
entibiar *tr.* to cool, to make lukewarm. 2 to temper, moderate. 3 *ref.* to become lukewarm, cool down.
entibo *m.* MIN. timber, prop, strut.
entidad *f.* entity. 2 consequence, importance, moment. 3 association, corporation.

entiendo, entienda, etc. *irr.* V. ENTENDER.
entierro *m.* interment, burial, funeral. 2 grave, tomb. 3 buried treasure.
entierro, entierre, etc. *irr.* V. ENTERRAR.
entimema *m.* LOG. enthymeme.
entintar *tr.* to ink. 2 to stain with ink. 3 to dye.
entoldado *m.* covering with awnings. 2 awnings; overhead shelter made of awnings.
entoldar *tr.* to cover with awnings. 2 to adorn with hangings. 3 *ref.* to get cloudy, become overcast.
entomología *f.* entomology.
entomólogo *m.* entomologist.
entonación *f.* ENTONO. 2 intonation, modulation, tone. 3 MED., PAINT. toning.
entonado, -da *adj.* haughty, stuck-up.
entonamiento *m.* ENTONACIÓN.
entonar *tr.* to sing in tune. 2 to sing [a song]. 3 to intone [for others to follow]. 4 MUS., PAINT., PHOT. to tone. 5 MED. to tone up. 6 *ref.* to become stuck-up.
entonces *adv.* then, at that time: *por ~, por aquel ~*, at that time. 2 then, this being the case.
entonelar *tr.* to put in casks or barrels.
entono *m.* singing in tune. 2 haughtiness, arrogance, airs.
entontecer *tr.* to besot, hebetate, make silly. ¶ CONJUG. like *agradecer.*
entorchada *adj.* ARCH. wreathed [column].
entorchado *m.* bullion lace [in the cuffs of some uniforms]. 2 string covered with silk or wire.
entornar *tr.* to half-close [the eyes]; to set ajar [a door]. 2 to tilt, upset.
entorpecedor *adj.* dulling, blunting, benumbing. 2 delaying, obstructing.
entorpecer *tr.* to dull, blunt [the mind, the senses], to benumb. 2 to clog, delay, obstruct. 3 *ref.* to become dull, blunt, awkward. 4 to get delayed, obstructed. ¶ CONJUG. like *agradecer.*
entorpecimiento *m.* dullness, bluntness, numbness; torpidity. 2 obstruction, delay.
entorpezco, entorpezca, etc. *irr.* V. ENTORPECER.
entozoario *m.* ZOOL. entozoan.
entrada *f.* entrance, gate, place of entrance, access; MIN. adit; MACH. intake, inlet. 2 entrance, entering, entry, ingress. 3 admission [to society, club, etc.]; admittance, opening. 4 entrance fee; admission ticket. 5 THEAT. house [audience]: *gran ~*, full house. 6 THEAT. receipt, takings. 7 first payment. 8 beginning [of a book, year, etc.]. 9 intimacy with. *10* COOK. entrée. *11* cash receipts. *12* invasion. *13* MUS. entrance. *14* THEAT. *~ general*, gallery. *15 pl.* income. *16* receding hair at the temples.
entrado, -da *adj. ~ en años*, advanced in years.
entramado *m.* MAR. timber framework, studwork.
entrambos, -bas *adj. pl.* both, both the.
entrampar *tr.* to trap, entrap, ensnare. 2 to trick. 3 to entangle [matters]. 4 to burden with debt. 5 *ref.* to stick in the mud. 6 to run into debt.
entrante *adj.* entrant, entering, incoming. 2 coming, next: *el mes ~*, the next month. 3 re-entering [angle]. 4 *m.-f. entrantes y salientes*, goers and comers.
entraña *f.* ANAT. vital or internal organ. 2 the innermost part, the bottom, the core. 3 *pl.* vitals. 4 entrails. 5 heart, feeling: *no tener entrañas*, to be heartless. 6 temper, disposition: *de buenas entrañas*, kind, human.
entrañable *adj.* most affectionate. 2 deep [affection].
entrañablemente *adv.* dearly, deeply.

entrañar *tr.* to bury deep. *2* to contain, involve. *3 ref.* to penetrate to the core. *4* to become deeply attached.

entrar *intr.* to enter, go in, come in. *2* to charge, attack. *3* [of seasons, writings, etc.] to begin. *4* to play for the stakes [at cards]. *5* MUS. to strike in. *6* ~ *a*, to enter, begin, start: ~ *a reinar*, to begin to reign. *7* ~ *en*, to go into, enter, penetrate; to have access to; to join, become a member of; to enter into, to engage in; to be numbered among. *8* ~ *en deseo*, to be seized by a desire. *9* ~ *en juego*, to come into play. *10 entran cuatro peras en libra*, there's four pears to the pound. *11 no entrarle a uno una persona*, not to be able to bear somebody. *12 tr.* to introduce, bring, put in. *13* MIL. to invade. *14* to attack, to influence. *15 ref.* to enter, go in, penetrate.

entre *prep.* between, among, amongst. *2* ~ *mí*, ~ *sí*, in my, his, heart; to myself, to himself. *3* ~ *tanto*, meanwhile, in the interim.

entreabierto, -ta *adj.* half-open, ajar.

entreabrir *tr.* to half-open; to set ajar. ¶ Past. p.: *entreabierto*.

entreacto *m.* THEAT. entr'acte, interval.

entreancho, -cha *adj.* neither broad nor narrow.

entrecano, -na *adj.* grayish [hair or beard].

entrecava *f.* AGR. shallow digging.

entrecejo *m.* space between the eyebrows: *fruncir el* ~, to knit one's brow. *2* frown, frowning.

entreclaro, -ra *adj.* lightish.

entrecoger *tr.* to catch, corner.

entrecoro *m.* ECCL. chancel.

entrecortado, -da *adj.* broken, faltering [voice, sound].

entrecortar *tr.* to cut without severing.

entrecruzar *tr.* to intercross. *2 ref.* to intercross [be intercrossed].

entrecubiertas *f. pl.* NAUT. between decks.

entrechocar *intr.-ref.* to collide with one another, to clash.

entredicho *m.* interdiction, prohibition. *2* ECCL. interdict.

entredós *m.* SEW. insertion. *2* PRINT. long primer.

entrefilete *m.* short feature [in a newspaper].

entrefino, -na *adj.* of medium quality.

entrega *f.* delivery, handing over. *2* surrender. *3* fascicle, instalment [of a novel, etc.].

entregar *tr.* to deliver, hand over; to give up: ~ *el alma a Dios*, to give up the ghost. *2* to surrender. *3 ref.* to surrender, give oneself up. *4* to yield, submit. *5* to abandon oneself [to a feeling, etc.]. *6* to devote oneself [to something].

entrelazamiento *m.* interlacing, interweaving.

entrelazar *tr.* to interlace, braid, entwine, interweave.

entrelínea *f.* writing between the lines.

entrelinear *tr.* to interline, write between lines.

entreliño *m.* space between rows of trees or vines.

entrelucir *intr.* to show through. ¶ CONJUG. like *lucir*.

entremediar *tr.* to put between.

entremedias *adv.* in between; in the mean time: ~ *de*, between; among.

entremés *m.* hors d'oeuvre, side dish. *2* THEAT. short farce inserted between two acts of a play.

entremeter *tr.* to insert, place between. *2 ref.* to butt in, meddle, intermeddle, obtrude.

entremetido, -da *adj.* meddlesome, officious. *2 m.-f.* meddler, busybody.

entremetimiento *m.* meddling, meddlesomeness.

entremezclar *tr.* to intermingle, intermix.

entrenador *m.* SPORT. trainer, coach.

entrenamiento *m.* SPORT. training, coaching.

entrenar *tr.* SPORT. to train, coach. *2 ref.* SPORT. to train, be in training.

entrenudo *m.* BOT. internode.

entreoír *tr.* to hear vaguely; to half-ear. ¶ CONJUG. like *oír*.

entrepaño *m.* ARCH. pier [piece of wall]. *2* panel [of door]. *3* shelf.

entrepernar *intr.* to put one's legs between those of another. ¶ CONJUG. like *acertar*.

entrepiernas *f. pl.* inner surface of the thights.

entrepiso *m.* MIN. space between galleries. *2* Am. mezzanine, entresol.

entrepuente *m.* or *pl.* -tes NAUT. between-decks.

entrerrenglonar *tr.* to pick out, select. *2* to thin out [trees, hair, etc.].

entresacar *tr.* to select, to pick out, to sift out, to prune [tree], to thin out [plants], to thin [hair, woods].

entresijo *m.* ANAT. mesentery. *2* anything secret or hidden: *tener muchos entresijos*, to be complicated; to be reserved, sly.

entresuelo *m.* entresol, mezzanine.

entretalla, entretalladura *f.* bas-relief.

entretallar *tr.* to carve in bas-relief. *2* to sculpture, engrave. *3* to make openwork on.

entretanto *adv.* meanwhile. *2 m.* meanwhile, meantime: *en el* ~, in the meantime.

entretejer *tr.* to interweave, intertwine. *2* to insert, mix, intermix.

entretejido *m.* intertwining, interweaving, entwining.

entretejimiento *m.* interweaving.

entretela *f.* SEW. interlining. *2 pl.* heartstrings.

entretelar *tr.* SEW. to interline.

entretener *tr.* to delay, detain. *2* to make bearable [hunger, etc.]. *3* to entertain, amuse. *4* to maintain, keep up. *5* to delay, put off. *6 ref.* to delay, dally, linter. *7* to amuse oneself. ¶ CONJUG. like *tener*.

entretenido, -da *adj.* entertaining, amusing.

entretenimiento *m.* entertainment, amusement, pastime. *2* maintenance, upkeep.

entretiempo *m.* spring or autumn: *ropa de* ~, light clothing.

entrever *tr.* to glimpse, see imperfectly. *2* to guess, divine.

entreverado, -da *adj.* intermingled, intermixed; interlarded. *2 tocino* ~, streaky bacon.

entreverar *tr.* to intermingle, intermix. *2* to streak, to interlard.

entrevero *m.* (Am.) crowd, throng. *2* confusion, muddle, mix-up, jumble. *3* hand-to-hand fight [horse soldiers].

entrevía *f.* RLY. space between rails.

entrevista *f.* interview, meeting, conference.

entrevistarse *ref.* to meet, hold an interwiew.

entripado *m.* bellyache. *2* suppressed anger or displeasure.

entristecedor, -ra *adj.* sad, saddening.

entristecer *tr.* to sadden; to make gloomy. *2 ref.* to sadden, become sad. ¶ CONJUG. like *agradecer*.

entristecimiento *m.* saddening, sadness.

entrojar *tr.* to garner [grain].

entrometer *tr.-ref.* ENTREMETER.

entrometido, -da *adj.* meddlesome, interfering. *2 n.* meddler, interferer, busybody, intruder.

entromparse *ref.* coll. to get stewed, canned, tight. *2* (Am.) to get angry, to get cross.

entroncar *intr.* to be or become related [to a family] by marriage. *2* (Am.) [of railways, roads, etc.] to connect.
entronerar *tr.* BILL. to pocket [a ball].
entronización *f.* enthronement, enthronization.
entronizar *tr.* to enthrone, enthronize. *2* to exalt.
entronque *m.* relationship between people of the same stock.
entropión *m.* MED. entropion.
entruchada *f.*, **entruchado** *m.* coll. plot, intrigue, dirty affair.
entruchar *tr.* to lure into a business.
entubar *tr.* to tube, to pipe. *2* to tube, to case. *3* MED. to tube.
entuerto *m.* wrong, injustice. *2 pl.* afterpains.
entumecer *tr.* to benumb, make torpid [a limb, etc.]. *2 ref.* [of limbs] to become numb. *3* [of sea, etc.] to swell. ¶ CONJUG. like *agradecer.*
entumecimiento *m.* numbness, torpor [of limbs]. *2* swelling [of sea, etc.].
entumezco, entumezca, etc. *irr.* V. ENTUMECER.
entumirse *ref.* [of a limb] to become numb.
enturbiar *tr.* to render turbid, to muddy. *2* to cloud, obscure, muddle, dim, confuse; to trouble [waters]. *3 ref.* to get or become turbid. *4* to get obscured.
entusiasmar *tr.* to awake the enthusiasm of; to enrapture. *2 ref.* to be filled with enthusiasm, be enraptured.
entusiasmo *m.* enthusiasm.
entusiasta *m.-f.* enthusiast.
entusiástico, -ca *adj.* enthusiastic.
enumeración *f.* enumeration.
enumerar *tr.* to enumerate.
enunciación *f.*, **enunciado** *m.* enouncement, enunciation, statement.
enunciar *tr.* to enounce, enunciate, state.
envainador, -ra *adj.* sheathing.
envainar *tr.* to sheathe.
envalentonamiento *m.* emboldening. *2* boldness.
envalentonar *tr.* to embolden, to make bold, daring. *2 ref.* to grow bold or daring.
envanecer *tr.* to make vain, conceited. *2 ref.* to become vain, conceited; to be proud [of], to boast [of]. ¶ CONJUG. like *agradecer.*
envanecimiento *m.* vanity, conceit, conceitedness.
envanezco, envanezca, etc. *irr.* V. ENVANECER.
envaramiento *m.* stiffness, numbness.
envarar *tr.* to stiffen, benumb.
envasador, -ra *m.-f.* filler, packer.
envasar *tr.* to pack, bottle, can, sack, put into a container. *2* to drink [wine, etc.].
envase *m.* packing, bottling, canning, etc. *2* container [package, bottle, can, sack, etc.].
envejecer *tr.* to age; to make look old. *2 intr.-ref.* to age, grow old. *3* to go out-of-date. ¶ CONJUG. like *agradecer.*
envejecido, -da *adj.* aged, looking old. *2* tried, experienced.
envejecimiento *m.* ageing, growing or looking old.
envejezco, envejezca, etc. *irr.* V. ENVEJECER.
envenenador, -ra *m.-f.* poisoner.
envenenamiento *m.* poisoning.
envenenar *tr.* to poison, to envenom.
enverar *intr.* to take on ripe colour.
envergadura *f.* breadth [of a sail]. *2* AER. span, spread. *3* wingspread [of birds].
envergar *tr.* NAUT. to bend [a sail].
enverjado *m.* iron railing [for closing or fencing].
envés *m.* back, wrong side, underside.
enviado *m.* messenger, envoy.

enviajado, -da *adj.* ARCH. oblique, sloping.
enviar *tr.* to send, dispatch; to ship.
enviciamiento *m.* corruption. *2* taking bad habits.
enviciar *tr.* to corrupt; to make [one] acquire bad habits. *2 intr.* [of plants] to have luxuriant foliage and little fruit. *3 ref.* to take [to], to become addicted [to].
envidar *intr.-tr.* to bid or bet against [at cards].
envidia *f.* envy, enviousness, jealousy.
envidiar *tr.* to envy.
envidioso, -sa *adj.* envious. *2 m.-f.* envious person.
envigar *tr.* to put the beams [in a building].
envilecer *tr.* to debase, degrade, vilify. *2 ref.* to degrade oneself. ¶ CONJUG. like *agradecer.*
envilecimiento *m.* debasement, degradation, vilification.
envinagrar *tr.* to put vinegar into.
envío *m.* sending, remittance; shipment.
envión *m.* push, shove.
enviscar *tr.* to smear with birdlime. *2* to irritate, anger. *3* AZUZAR.
envite *m.* bid, rise on the stake [at cards]. *2* offer, proffer. *3* push: *al primer ~,* right off.
enviudar *intr.* to become a widower or widow.
envoltorio *m.* bundle, parcel.
envoltura *f.* cover, envelope, wrapper. *2* AER., BOT. envelope. *3 pl.* swaddling clothes.
envolvente *adj.* enveloping.
envolver *tr.* to cover, envelop, wrap, wrap up; to make up in a packet. *2* to swaddle [an infant]. *3* to wind [thread, etc.]. *4* to floor [an opponent]. *5* to involve [in an affair]. *6* to contain, imply. *7* MIL. to envelop. *8 ref.* to wrap oneself up. *9* to become involved. ¶ CONJUG. like *mover.* | PAST. P.: *envuelto.*
envolvimiento *m.* wrapping, enveloping. *2* winding. *3* MIL. envelopment.
envuelvo, envuelva, etc. *irr.* V. ENVOLVER.
envuelto, -ta *p. p.* of ENVOLVER.
enyesado *m.* plastering [of wine]. *2* plasterwork.
enyesar *tr.* to plaster [walls, etc.]. *2* to treat with gypsum. *3* SURG. to put a plaster cast on.
enzarzar *tr.* to cover with brambles. *2* to set [people] disputing. *3 ref.* to get entangled in brambles. *4* to engage [in difficult business]. *5* to dispute, quarrel.
enzima *f.* BIOCHEM. enzyme.
eñe *f.* name of the letter *ñ.*
eoceno, -na *adj.-m.* GEOL. Eocene.
eólico, -ca *adj.* Æolian. *2 m.* Æolic [dialect].
Eólida (la) *f. pr. n.* GEOG. Æolis.
eolio, lia *adj.-n.* Æolian.
eolítico, -ca *adj.* eolithic.
Eolo *m. pr. n.* MYTH. Æolus.
eón *m.* æon.
eoperlano *m.* ICHTH. smelt.
¡epa! *interj.* (Am.) hello! *2* come on!
épica *f.* epic poetry.
epicarpio *m.* BOT. epicarp.
epiceno, -na *adj.* GRAM. epicene.
epicentro *m.* epicentre.
epicicloide *f.* GEOM. epicycloid.
épico, -ca *adj.* epic, epical.
epicureísmo *m.* Epicureanism.
epicúreo, -a *adj.-s.* epicurean. *2* Epicurean.
epidemia *f.* epidemic.
epidémico, -ca *adj.* epidemic(al).
epidérmico, -ca *adj.* epidermal, epidermic.
epidermis *f.* ANAT., BOT. epidermis.
Epifanía *f.* Epiphany.
epifenómeno *m.* epiphenomenon.

epífisis *f.* ANAT. epiphysis.
epífito, -ta *adj.* epiphytic. *2 f.* BOT. epiphyte.
epifonema *m.* RHET. epiphonema.
epigastrio *m.* ANAT. epigastrium.
epiglotis *f.* ANAT. epiglottis.
epígrafe *m.* epigraph. *2* title, headline.
epigrafía *f.* epigraphy.
epigrama *m.* epigram.
epigramático, -ca *adj.* epigrammatic(al.
epilepsia *f.* MED. epilepsy.
epiléptico, -ca *adj.-s.* epileptic.
epilogar *tr.* to epilogize. *2* to sum up.
epílogo *m.* epilogue. *2* summing up.
Epiro (el) *m. pr. n.* GEOG. Epirus.
episcopado *m.* episcopacy, episcopate, bishopric.
episcopal *adj.* episcopal. *2* Episcopal.
episódico, -ca *adj.* episodic(al.
episodio *m.* episode.
epístola *f.* epistle, letter. *2* ECCL. Epistle.
epistolar *adj.* epistolary.
epistolario *m.* collection of letters. *2* ECCL. epistolary.
epitafio *m.* epitaph.
epitalamio *m.* epithalamium.
epitelio *m.* ANAT. epithelium.
epitelioma *m.* MED. epithelioma.
epíteto *m.* GRAM. epithet.
epítimo *m.* BOT. clover dodder.
epítome *m.* epitome, abstract, summary.
epizootia *f.* epizootic.
época *f.* epoch, age, time.
epodo *m.* epode.
epónimo, -ma *adj.* eponymous.
epopeya *f.* epopee. *2* epic poem.
épsilon *f.* epsilon.
eptágono, -na *adj.* MATH. heptagonal. *2 m.* MATH. heptagon.
equidad *f.* equity; equitableness. *2* reasonableness [in prices, terms, etc.].
equidistancia *f.* equidistance, equal distance.
equidistante *adj.* equidistant.
equidna *m.* ZOOL. echidna.
équido *m.* ZOOL. equid.
equilátero, -ra *adj.* equilateral.
equilibrado, -da *adj.* sensible, well-balanced.
equilibrar *tr.* to equilibrate, balance, equipoise, equalize. *2 ref.* to balance [be equal].
equilibrio *m.* equilibrium, balance, equipoise: ~ *europeo*, European balance of power.
equilibrista *m.-f.* equilibrist.
equimosis *m.* ecchymosis.
equino, -na *adj.* equine. *2 m.* ZOOL., ARCH. echinus.
equinoccial *adj.* equinoctial.
equinoccio *m.* ASTR. equinox.
equinodermo *adj.-m.* ZOOL. echinoderm.
equipaje *m.* luggage, baggage. *2* equipment. *3* NAUT. crew.
equipar *tr.* to equip, fit out.
equiparable *adj.* comparable.
equiparar *tr.* to compare, to put on the same level.
equipo *m.* equipment, fitting out. *2* equipment, outfit: ~ *de novia*, trousseau. *3* crew, gang, squad [of workmen]. *4* SPORT. team.
equiponderar *intr.* to equiponderate.
equis *f.* Spanish name of the letter *x.*
equisetáceo, -a *adj.* BOT. equisetaceous.
equitación *f.* equitation, horsemanship, riding.
equitativo, -va *adj.* equitable. *2* reasonable [price].
equivalencia *f.* equivalence.
equivalente *adj.-m.* equivalent.

equivaler *intr.* to be equivalent; to be equal, tantamount. ¶ CONJUG. like *valer.*
equivocación *f.* mistake, error.
equivocadamente *adv.* by mistake. *2* erroneously.
equivocado, -da *adj.* mistaken. *2* erroneous.
equívocamente *adv.* ambiguously, equivocally.
equivocar *tr.-ref.* to mistake. *2* to make a mistake in, to take wrongly: ~ *la carrera*, to miss one's calling; *equivocarse de camino*, to take the wrong way. *3 ref.* to be mistaken.
equívoco, -ca *adj.* equivocal. *2 m.* equivocation quibble, ambiguity.
era *f.* era, age : ~ *cristiana*, Christian era. *2* GEOL. era. *3* threshing floor. *4* vegetable patch; garden bed.
era, éramos, etc. *irr.* V. SER.
eral *m.* two-year-old ox.
erario *m.* exchequer, public treasury; provincial or municipal treasury.
ere *f.* Spanish name of the letter *r.*
eres *2nd pers. sing. pres.* of SER.
erebo *m.* MYTH. Erebus.
erección *f.* erection [raising, building]. *2* PHYSIOL. erection. *3* foundation, establishment.
eréctil *adj.* erectile.
eremita *m.* eremite, hermit.
eremítico, -ca *adj.* eremite.
erg *m.* ERGIO.
ergástula *m.* slave prison.
ergio *m.* PHYS. erg.
ergotismo *m.* LOG., MED. ergotism.
ergotizar *intr.* to ergotize.
erguimiento *m.* raising, straightening up.
erguir *tr.* to raise, lift up, erect [the head, the body, etc.] *2 ref.* to stand erect. *3* to become arrogant. ¶ CONJUG.: INDIC. Pres.: *irgo* or *yergo, irgues* or *yergues, irgue* or *yergue;* erguimos, erguís, *irguen* or *yerguen.* | Pret.: erguí, erguiste, *irguió;* erguimos, erguisteis, *irguieron.* | SUBJ. Pres.: *irga* or *yerga, irgas* or *yergas, irga* or *yerga; irgamos* or *yergamos, irgáis* or *yergáis, irgan* or *yergan.* | Imperf.: *irguiera, irguieras,* etc., or *irguiese, irguieses,* etc. | Fut.: *irguiere, irguieres,* etc. | IMPER.: *irgue* or *yergue, irga* or *yerga; irgamos* or *yergamos,* erguid, *irgan* or *yergan.* | PAST. P.: erguido. | GER.: *irguiendo.*
erial *adj.* untilled, uncultivated. *2 m.* uncultivated land.
ericáceo, -a *adj.* BOT. ericaceous.
erigir *tr.* to erect, build. *2* to found, establish. *3 tr.-ref.* ~, or *erigirse en,* to set, or set oneself up as.
erisipela *f.* MED. erysipelas.
Eritreo, -a *adj.* Eritraean.
erizado, -da *adj.* bristled, bristling. *2* covered with bristles. *3* ~ *de,* bristling with [difficulties, etc.].
erizar *tr.* to set on end; to bristle. *2* to cause to be bristling [with difficulties, etc.]. *3 ref.* to stand on end, to bristle.
erizo *m.* ZOOL. hedgehog. *2* fig. hedgehog [person]. *3* BOT. a prickly pant. *4* BOT. bur [of chestnut, etc.]. *5* ZOOL. ~ *de mar,* sea urchin.
ermita *f.* hermitage. *2* isolated sanctuary or chapel.
ermitaño *m.* hermit. *2* keeper of an isolated sanctuary or chapel. *3* ZOOL. hermit crab.
Ernesto *m. pr. n.* Ernest.
erogación *f.* distribution. *2* (Am.) expenditure, payment. *3* (Am.) contribution.
erogar *tr.* to distribute. *2* (Am.) to pay, to spend. *3* (Am.) to contribute.
Eros *m. pr. n.* MYTH. Eros.

erosión f. erosion.
erótico, -ca adj. erotic. 2 f. erotic poetry.
erotismo m. erotism.
errabundo, -da adj. wandering.
errada f. BILL. miscue.
erradicación f. eradication.
erradicar tr. to eradicate.
errado, -da adj. mistaken, in error. 2 erroneous.
erraj m. fine coal made of crushed olive stones.
errante adj. errant, wandering. 2 errant, erring.
errar tr. to miss [the target, a blow, one's calling, etc.]. 2 to wander, roam. 3 intr.-ref. to err, to be mistaken. ¶ CONJUG. like acertar, changing the i for y in the irregular forms.
errata f. erratum.
errático, -ca adj. wandering. 2 GEOL., MED. erratic.
errátil adj. erratic, variable.
erre f. Spanish name of the letter rr.
erróneo, -a adj. erroneous.
error m. error. 2 mistake.
eructar intr. to belch, eructate.
eructo m. belching, eructation.
erudición f. erudition, learning.
erudito, -ta adj.-n. erudite.
erupción f. MED., GEOL. eruption.
eruptivo, -va adj. eruptive.
esa adj. f. of ESE.
ésa pron. f. of ÉSE.
esbatimentar tr. PAINT. to shade.
esbatimento m. PAINT. shade.
esbeltez, esbelteza f. graceful slenderness.
esbelto, -ta adj. slender and graceful, svelte.
esbirro m. catchpoll, myrmidon.
esbozar tr. to sketch, outline.
esbozo m. sketch, outline.
escabechar tr. to pickle [fish, meat]. 2 coll. to kill.
escabeche m. pickle [of fish, etc.]. 2 pickled fish.
escabechina f. coll. ravage.
escabel m. stool; footstool. 2 fig. stepping stone.
escabiosa f. BOT. scabious.
escabrosidad f. roughness, unevenness [of a ground]. 2 asperity [of temper]. 3 scabrousness.
escabroso, -sa adj. rough, rugged, uneven [ground]. 2 harsh, rude. 3 scabrous, risqué.
escabullirse ref. to slip.
escacado, -da adj. HER. checkered.
escacharrar tr. to break, smash.
escafandra f., **escafandro** m. diving suit.
escala f. ladder, stepladder: ~ de cuerda, rope ladder. 2 scale [series of degrees; size, proportion; ratio, etc.]: en grande ~, on a large scale. 3 MUS. scale. 4 NAUT. port of call: hacer ~ en, to call at. 5 MIL. army list.
escalada f. escalade. 2 scaling, climbing.
escalador, -ra m.-f. scaler, climber, mountain climber.
escalafón m. roll, list [showing rank, seniority, etc.]; army list.
escalamiento m. escalading. 2 scaling, climbing.
escálamo m. NAUT. thole, tholepin.
escalar tr. to escalade. 2 to scale, climb. 3 to break into or out of [a place] through a wall, roof, etc.
Escalda m. pr. n. Scheldt [river].
escaldado, -da adj. cautious, wary.
escaldadura f. scalding, scald. 2 chafing [of the skin].
escaldar tr. to scald. 2 to make red-hot. 3 to chafe [the skin].
escaleno adj. GEOM. scalene.
escalera f. stair, staircase: ~ mecánica, escalator; ~ de caracol, winding stairs; ~ de escape, fire

escape. 2 ladder; ~ de incendio, fire ladder; ~ de mano, ladder; ~ de tijera, stepladder. 3 irregular cut in hair. 4 sequence; straight [at cards].
escalerilla f. dim. short ladder, steps. 2 sequence of three or five [at cards].
escalfado adj. COOK. poached [egg].
escalfador m. barber's kettle. 2 chaffing dish.
escalfeta f. CHOFETA.
escalinata f. ARCH. perron, front steps.
escalo m. breaking a way into or out of a place. 2 breaking in: robo con ~, burglary.
escalofriante adj. chilling, blood-curdling.
escalofrío m. chill [feverish shivering], shudder.
escalón m. stair, step, rung. 2 fig. step, degree. 3 MIL. echelon.
escalonado, -da adj. spaced out, spread out. 2 staggered. 3 in stages, escheloned.
escalonar tr. to place at intervals. 2 MIL. to echelon. 3 to space, to string out.
escalonia, escaloña f. BOT. scallion.
escalope m. escalope, veal cutlet.
escalpelo m. SURG. scalpel.
escama f. ZOOL., BOT. scale. 2 scale [of armour, etc.]. 3 distrust, suspicion.
escamado, -da p. p. of ESCAMAR. 2 adj. distrustful, suspicious. 3 m. scalework.
escamar tr. to scale [fish]. 2 to cause distrust or suspicion. 3 to adorn with scalework. 4 ref. to become distrustful or suspicious.
escamón, -na adj. distrustful, suspicious.
escamonda f. ESCAMONDO.
escamondar tr. to trim, to prune [a tree, etc.].
escamondo m. trimming, pruning.
escamonea f. BOT. scammony.
escamoso, -sa adj. scaly, squamous.
escamoteador, -ra m.-f. conjurer, prestidigitator.
escamotear tr. to make disappear by sleight of hand. 2 to whisk out of sight; to spirit away.
escamoteo m. sleight of hand. 2 spiriting away.
escampada f. clear spell [on a rainy day].
escampar tr. to clear out [a place]. 2 intr. to stop raining. 3 [of weather] to clear up.
escampavía f. NAUT. scout. 2 NAUT. revenue cutter.
escanciador, -ra m.-f. cupbearer.
escanciar tr. to pour, serve [wine]. 2 intr. to drink wine.
escandalera f. racket, uproar.
escandalizador, -ra adj. scandalizing. 2 m.-f. scandalizer. 3 noisy, boisterous person.
escandalizar tr. to give scandal to. 2 to scandalize, shock. 3 to make a lot of noise. 4 ref. to be scandalized, be shocked.
escándalo m. scandal: dar ~, to give scandal; dar un ~, to make a scene. 2 tumult, noise, disturbance; shouting.
escandaloso, -sa adj. scandalous. 2 noisy. 3 shameful.
escandallar tr. NAUT. to sound.
escandallo m. NAUT. sounding lead.
Escandinavia f. pr. n. GEOG. Scandinavia.
escandinavo, -va adj.-n. Scandinavian.
escandir tr. to scan [verse].
escantillar tr. ARCH. to measure off.
escantillón m. pattern, scantling. 2 ESCUADRÍA.
escaño m. settle, bench with a back.
escapada f. escape, flight. 2 en una ~, in a jiffy.
escapar intr.-ref. to escape; to flee, run away, make one's escape; to slip away: ~ a, to escape [death, danger, etc.]: escapársele a uno [una cosa], not to notice; to let slip, say inadvertently. 2 ref. [of gas, water, etc.]. to escape, leak out.

escaparate *m.* show window. *2* glass cabinet.
escapatoria *f.* escape, getaway. *2* evasion, way out [of difficulty, etc.].
escape *m.* escape, flight: *a ~*, at full speed, in great haste. *2* escape, leak, leakage. *3* exhaust, valve. *4* HOROL. escapement.
escapo *m.* ARCH., BOT. scape.
escápula *f.* ANAT. scapula, shoulder blade.
escapular *adj.* scapular.
escapulario *m.* ECCL. scapular, scapulary.
escaque *m.* square [of chessboard]. *2* HER. square.
escara *f.* SURG. eschar, slough.
escarabajear *intr.* to crawl around. *2* to scribble, scrawl. *3* coll. [of worry, care, etc.] to gnaw.
escarabajo *m.* ENT. beetle, scarab: *~ pelotero*, tumblebug. *2 pl.* fig. scrawl, scribbling.
escaramujo *m.* BOT. dog rose. *2* BOT. hip. *3* ZOOL. goose barnacle.
escaramuza *f.* skirmish. *2* dispute, quarrel.
escaramuzar *intr.* to skirmish.
escarapela *f.* cockade. *2* dispute, quarrel.
escarbadientes *m.* toothpick.
escarbaorejas *m.* earpick.
escarbar *tr.* to scratch [the ground]. *2* to clean out, pick [one's ears or teeth]. *3* to poke [the fire]. *4* to dig into, to investigate.
escarcela *f.* a pouch hanging from the waist. *2* game bag. *3* skirt [of plate armour].
escarceo *m.* small bubbling waves. *2 pl.* turns of spirited horses. *3* detour, circumlocution.
escarcha *f.* rime, hoarfrost, white frost.
escarchada *f.* BOT. ice plant.
escarchar *tr.* to frost [fruit; glass]. *2 impers.* to freeze, to rime: *anoche escarchó*, it froze last night.
escarda *f.* AGR. weeding. *2* weeding time. *3* weeding hoe.
escardar, escardillar *tr.* to weed. *2* to weed out.
escardillo *m.* weeding hoe.
escariador *m.* reamer [tool].
escariar *tr.* to ream [a hole].
escarificador *m.* SURG. scarifier, scarificator. *2* AGR. scarifier, cultivator.
escarificar *tr.* AGR., SURG. to scarify.
escarlata *adj.-f.* scarlet [colour; cloth].
escarlatina *f.* MED. scarlatina, scarlet fever.
escarmenar *tr.* CARMENAR. *2* to cheat.
escarmentado, -da *adj.* taught or warned by punishment or experience.
escarmentar *tr.* to inflict an exemplary punishment on. *2 intr.* to learn one's lesson, take warning. ¶ CONJUG. like *acertar*.
escarmiento *m.* lesson, warning; punishment.
escarmiento, escarmiente, etc. *irr.* V. ESCARMENTAR.
escarnecedor, -ra *adj.* mocking, jeering, scoffing. *2* shameful. *3 n.* mocker, jeerer, scoffer.
escarnecer *tr.* to mock, to jeer at, to scoff at, to ridicule.
escarnio *m.* scoffing, derision, mock.
escaro *m.* ICHTH. scarus, parrot fish.
escarola *f.* BOT. endive. *2* ruff [collar].
escarpa *f.* scarp, steep slope. *2* FORT. scarp.
escarpado, -da *adj.* abrupt, steep, cliffy.
escarpadura *f.* scarp, escarpment.
escarpar *tr.* to scarp, escarp. *2* SCULPT. to rasp.
escarpelo *m.* SURG. scalpel. *2* rasp.
escarpia *f.* hooked nail.
escarpidor *m.* wide toothed comb.
escarpín *m.* sock, thin-soled shoe. *2* woollen slipper.
escarzano *adj.* ARCH. segmental [arch].

escasamente *adv.* scarcely, hardly.
escasear *tr.* to give sparingly, to spare. *2 intr.* to be or become scarce.
escasez *f.* scarcity, dearth, shortness. *2* stinginess. *3* want, poverty.
escaso, -sa *adj.* scant, scanty, scarce. *2* stingy. *3* short: *andar ~ de*, to be short of. *4 dos millas escasas*, less than two miles.
escatimar *tr.* to stint, curtail, give sparingly.
escatología *f.* THEOL. eschatology. *2* scatology.
escayola *f.* scagliola. *2* stucco.
escena *f.* THEAT. stage: *poner en ~*, to stage [a play]. *2* scene. *3* THEAT. scenery.
escenario *m.* THEAT. stage, boards. *2* setting, environment.
escénico, -ca *adj.* scenic [pertaining to the stage].
escenificación *f.* adaptation for the scene.
escenificar *tr.* to adapt for the scene.
escenografía *f.* scenography. *2* scene painting.
escenógrafo *m.* scenographer. *2* scene painter.
escepticismo *m.* scepticism, skepticism.
escéptico, -ca *adj.* sceptical, skeptical. *2 m.-f.* sceptic, skeptic.
escila *f.* BOT. squill.
escinco *m.* ZOOL. skink.
escindible *adj.* divisible. *2* PHYS. fissionable.
escindir *tr.* to cut, divide, split.
Escipión *m. pr. n.* Scipio.
escisión *f.* scission, division, schism. *2* BIOL. fishion.
esclarea *f.* BOT. clary.
esclarecer *tr.* to light up, brighten. *2* to enlighten. *3* to ennoble, make illustrious. *4* to clear up, elucidate. ¶ CONJUG. like *agradecer*.
esclarecido, -da *adj.* noble, illustrious.
esclarecimiento *m.* enlightening. *2* clearing up, elucidation.
esclarezco, esclarezca, etc. *irr.* V. ESCLARECER.
esclavina *f.* cape, pelerine, tippet. *2* pilgrim's cloak.
esclavitud *f.* slavery.
esclavizar *tr.* to enslave.
esclavo, -va *adj.* enslaved. *2 m.-f.* slave. *3 f.* kind of bracelet.
esclerénquima *m.* BOT. sclerenchyma.
esclerosis *f.* MED. sclerosis.
esclerótica *f.* ANAT. sclera.
esclusa *f.* lock, canal lock, sluice.
escoba *f.* broom, besom. *2* BOT. broom.
escobajo *f.* old broom. *2* grape stem [with grapes removed].
escobazo *m.* blow with a broom.
escobén *m.* NAUT. hawsehole.
escobilla *f.* brush [for cleaning]. *2* ELECT. brush [of a dynamo]. *3* BOT. fuller's teasel. *4* BOT. broom heath.
escobillar *tr.* to brush.
escobillón *m.* brush or cleaner for firearms; swab.
escobón *m.* large broom.
escocedura *f.* chafe, soreness [skin irritation].
escocer *intr.* to smart, cause a burning sensation. *2* fig. to smart, to annoy. *3 ref.* to feel hurt. *4* [of skin] to chafe. ¶ CONJUG. like *mover*.
escocés, -sa *adj.* Scotch, Scottish. *2* plaid [fabric]. *3 m.-f.* Scot. *4 m.* Scotchman. *5* Scotch [language]. *6 f.* Scotchwoman.
Escocia *f. pr. n.* GEOG. Scotland.
escocia *f.* ARCH. scotia.
escocimiento *m.* ESCOZOR.
escofieta *f.* coif, woman's headdress of gauze.
escofina *f.* rough rasp.

escoger *tr.* to choose, select, pick, pick out, sort.
escogido, -da *adj.* chosen. *2* choice, select.
escogimiento *m.* choosing, choice, selection, picking out, sorting.
escolanía *f.* choir school. *2* choirboys.
escolapio, -pia *adj.* pertaining to the *Scuole Pie. 2 m.* piarist.
escolar *adj.* [pertaining to] school, scholastic. *2 m.* pupil, student.
escolaridad *f.* schooling: ~ *obligatoria,* compulsory schooling.
escolarización *f.* schooling.
escolasticismo *m.* scholasticism.
escolástico, -ca *adj.* scholastic(al. *2 m.* PHIL. Scholastic. *3 f.* Scholasticism.
escolio *m.* scholium.
escoliosis *f.* MED. scoliosis.
escolopendra *f.* ZOOL. scolopendra, centipede. *2* BOT. hart's tongue.
escolta *f.* escort. *2* NAUT. convoy, convoying ship.
escoltar *tr.* to escort. *2* NAUT. to convoy.
escollera *f.* breakwater.
escollo *m.* NAUT. reef, rock. *2* fig. danger, difficulty.
escombrar *tr.* to clear of rubbish, obstacles, etc.
escombro *m.* debris, rubbish. *2* MIN. deads.
esconce *m.* angle, corner.
esconder *tr.* to hide, conceal. *2* to harbour, contain. *3 ref.* to hide, be hidden; to lurk, skulk.
escondidas (a) *adv.* secretly, on the sly. *2 a escondidas de,* without the knowledge of.
escondite *m.* hiding place, cache. *2* hide-and-seek.
escondrijo *m.* hiding place, cache.
escopeta *f.* shotgun, gun; fowling piece: ~ *de viento,* air gun.
escopetazo *m.* gunshot.
escopetear *tr.* to fire a gun [at someone] repeatedly. *2 ref.* to exchange compliments or insults.
escopetería *f.* musketry. *2* musketry fire.
escopetero *m.* musketeer. *2* gun-maker, gunsmith.
escopetón *m.* (scorn.) big musket or shotgun.
escopleadura *f.* chisel cut, mortise, notch.
escoplear *tr.* CARP. to chisel, mortise, notch.
escoplo *m.* CARP. chisel.
escora *f.* NAUT. shore [prop]. *2* NAUT. list, heel.
escorar *tr.* NAUT. to shore up. *2 intr.* NAUT. to list, heel.
escorbuto *m.* MED. scurvy, scorbutus.
escordio *m.* BOT. water germander.
escoria *f.* scoria, dross, slag. *2* fig. dregs [worthless part, refuse]. *3* scoria [cinderlike lava].
escoriación *f.* excoriation.
escorial *m.* slag dump; slag heap.
Escorial (el) *m. pr. n.* Escorial or Escurial.
escoriar *tr.* to excoriate.
escorpena, escorpina *f.* ICHTH. scorpion fish.
escorpión *m.* ZOOL. scorpion. *2* ICHTH. scorpion fish. *3* ASTR. Scorpio.
escorzar *tr.* PAINT. to foreshorten.
escorzo *m.* PAINT. foreshortening.
escorzonera *f.* BOT. viper's-grass.
escota *f.* NAUT. sheet.
escotado, -da *adj.* low-necked. *2* indented.
escotadura *f.* low cut in the neck [of a garment]. *2* THEAT. large stage trap. *3* indentation, cut.
escotar *tr.* to cut the neck of [a garment]; to cut an indentation in. *2* to club, pay one's share of a common expense.
escote *m.* low-neck. *2* tucker. *3* share, part paid [of a common expense].
escotera *f.* NAUT. sheet hole.

escotero, -ra *adj.* walking or travelling unburdened. *2* NAUT. sailing alone [ship].
escotilla *f.* NAUT. hatchway.
escotillón *m.* trap door. *2* THEAT. stage trap. *3* NAUT. scuttle.
escozor *m.* irritation, burning pain or sensation.
escriba *m.* scribe [teacher of Jewish law].
escribanía *f.* court clerkship. *2* court clerk's office. *3* inkstand. *4* writing desk.
escribano *m.* court clerk. *2* obs. notary.
escribiente *m.* amanuensis; clerk.
escribir *tr.-intr.* to write. *2 ref.* to hold correspondence. ¶ PAST. p. irreg.: *escrito.*
escriño *m.* casket, jewel case. *2* straw basket.
escrito, -ta *p. p. irreg.* of ESCRIBIR. *2 m.* writing [written paper, etc.]: *por* ~, in writing. *3* LAW brief, bill, written plea.
escritor, -ra *m.-f.* writer.
escritorio *m.* writing desk; cabinet. *2* office, study; countinghouse.
escritorzuelo *m. dim.* scribbler.
escritura *f.* writing: ~ *a máquina,* typewriting. *2* handwriting, hand, script. *3* LAW deed, instrument. *4 La Escritura,* the Scripture.
escriturar *tr.* LAW to establish by deed or legal instrument. *2* to engage [an artist].
escrófula *f.* MED. scrofula.
escrofularia *f.* BOT. figwort.
escrofuloso, -sa *adj.* scrofulous.
escroto *m.* ANAT. scrotum.
escrúpulo *m.* scruple. *2* ESCRUPULOSIDAD.
escrupulosidad *f.* scrupulosity, scrupulousness.
escrupuloso, -sa *adj.* scrupulous. *2* squeamish.
escrutador, -ra *adj.* searching. *2 m.-f.* searcher, examiner, scrutinizer. *3* teller of votes.
escrutar *tr.* to search, examine, scrutinize. *2* to tell the votes [at an election].
escrutinio *m.* scrutiny, examination. *2* telling or counting of votes [at an election].
escuadra *f.* NAV. fleet, squadron. *2* MIL. squad. *3* squad, gang. *4* angle iron. *5* carpenter's square, drawing triangle: *falsa* ~, bevel square; *a* ~, square, at right angles.
escuadrar *tr.* to square [form with right angles].
escuadría *f.* scantling [of timber].
escuadrilla *f.* NAV., AER. escadrille.
escuadrón *m.* MIL. squadron [of cavalry].
escualidez *f.* leanness, emaciation. *2* squalor.
escuálido, -da *adj.* lean, pale, emaciate. *2* squalid, filthy. *3 m. pl.* ICHTH. Squalidae.
escualo *m.* ICHTH. shark.
escucha *f.* act of listening: *estar a la* ~, to be listening. *2* MIL. night scout.
escuchar *tr.* to listen to. *2* to mind, heed [advice, etc.]. *3 intr.* to listen.
escuchimizado, -da *adj.* lean, weak.
escudar *tr.* to shield, protect. *2 ref.* to protect oneself. *3* to take refuge in [a law, authority, etc.].
escudería *f.* squiredom, squire post. *2* AUTO. stable.
escudero *m.* HIST. shield bearer, squire. *2* HIST. nobleman. *3* HIST. lady's page.
escudete *m.* escutcheon. *2* SEW. gusset.
escudilla *f.* bowl [hemispherical cup].
escudo *m.* shield, buckler. *2* shield, protection. *3* escutcheon. *4* ZOOL. scute. *5* escudo [money]. *6* ~ *de armas,* coat of arms.
escudriñar *tr.* to scrutinize, search; to investigate; to pry into.
escuece, escueza, etc. *irr.* V. ESCOCER.
escuela *f.* school [teaching establishment]: ~ *de artes y oficios,* trade school; ~ *dominical,* Sun-

day school; ~ *de la experiencia, de la vida*, fig. school of experience, of life. *2* school [philosophic, artistic, etc.]. *3* school-house.

escuerzo *m.* toad. *2* fig. little runt [person].

escueto, -ta *adj.* bare, plain, unadorned, strict, unqualified.

Esculapio *pr. n.* MYTH. Aesculapius.

esculpir *tr.* to sculpture, carve; to engrave.

escultora *f.* sculptress.

escultor *m.* sculptor.

escultórico, -ca *adj.* sculptural [of sculpture].

escultura *f.* sculpture [art and work].

escultural *adj.* sculptural, sculpturesque.

escupidera *f.* cuspidor, spittoon.

escupir *intr.* to spit [eject saliva, etc.]. *2 tr.* to spit [saliva, etc.]. *3* to spit at. *4* to throw off, discharge.

escupitajo *m.,* **escupitina** *f.* spit [spitted saliva].

escurreplatos *m.* plate rack, dish-draining rack.

escurridero *m.* draining place.

escurridizo, -za *adj.* slippery.

escurrido, -da *adj.* narrow-hipped.

escurridor *m.* colander. *2* ESCURREPLATOS.

escurriduras, escurrimbres *f. pl.* heeltap, last dregs.

escurrir *tr.* to drain [a vessel, plates, a liquid, etc.]. *2* to wring [moisture out of]. *3 intr.* to drip, ooze, trickle. *4 intr.-ref.* to slip, glide. *5 ref.* to slip away, slip out. *6* to say too much.

esdrújulo, -la *adj.-m.* GRAM. accented on the antepenult, proparoxytonic [word].

1) **ese** *f.* name of the letter *s*. *2* S-shaped link [of chain]. *3* MUS. sound hole [of violin]. *4 hacer eses,* [of a drunken man] to zigzag.

2) **ese, esa,** *pl.* **esos, esas** *adj.* that, those [nearest to the one addressed].

ése, ésa, *pl.* **ésos, ésas** *pron.* that one, those [nearest to the one addressed]. *2 ésa,* your town or city. *3 ni por ésas,* nothing doing. *4 ¡a ése!,* at him!

esencia *f.* essence. *2* CHEM. essence, perfume. *3 quinta* ~, quintessence.

esencial *adj.* essential.

esenciero *m.* scent bottle.

esfenoides *m.* ANAT. sphenoid, sphenoid bone.

esfera *f.* GEOM., ASTR., GEOG. sphere. *2* sphere [of action, influence, etc.]. *3* sphere, rank, social class. *4* dial [of clock].

esfericidad *f.* sphericity.

esférico, -ca *adj.* spherical.

esferoidal *adj.* spheroidal.

esferoide *f.* GEOM. spheroid.

esfinge *f.* sphinx. *2* ENT. hawk moth.

esfínter *m.* ANAT. sphincter.

esforzadamente *adv.* vigorously, bravely.

esforzado, -da *adj.* brave, courageous.

esforzar *tr.* to give strength. *2* to give courage. *3 ref.* to exert oneself, try hard, strive.

esfuerzo *m.* effort, exertion. *2* ENG. stress. *3* courage, spirit, vigor.

esfumar *tr.* DRAW. to stump. *2* PAINT. to tone down, soften. *3 ref.* to disappear, evanesce.

esfuminar *tr.* ESFUMAR.

esfumino *m.* DRAW. stump.

esgrima *f.* fencing [art].

esgrimidor *m.* fencer, swordsman.

esgrimir *tr.* to wield, brandish [a weapon]; to enforce, urge, make use of [arguments, reasons, etc.]. *2 intr.* to fence, practice fencing.

esguín *m.* ICHTH. parr, young salmon.

esguince *m.* dodge [to avoid a blow]. *2* frown, wry face. *3* sprain [of a joint].

eslabón *m.* link [of a chain]. *2* steel [for sharpening knives; for striking sparks from flint].

eslabonamiento *m.* linking, sequence, concatenation.

eslabonar *tr.* to link, interlink, concatenate. *2 ref.* to be linked or concatenated.

eslavo, -va *adj.* Slav, Slavic. *2 m.-f.* Slavish. *3 m.* Slavic [language].

eslinga *f.* NAUT. sling.

eslingar *tr.* NAUT. to sling up.

eslizón *m.* ZOOL. seps.

eslogan *m.* slogan.

eslora *f.* NAUT. length [of ship]. *2* NAUT. carling.

eslovaco, -ca *adj.-n.* Slovak, Slovakian.

esloveno, -na *adj.-n.* Slovene, Slovenian.

esmaltado *m.* enamelling.

esmaltador *m.* enameller.

esmaltadura *f.* enamelling.

esmaltar *tr.* to enamel. *2* to variegate with bright colors. *2* to adorn, embellish.

esmalte *m.* enamel. *2* enamel work. *3* smalt. *4* HER. tincture.

esmaltín *m.* smalt.

esmeradamente *adv.* carefully, with great care, neatly. *2* elegantly.

esmerado, -da *adj.* careful, conscientious, painstaking. *2* conscientiously done.

esmeralda *f.* emerald. *2* ~ *oriental*, corundum.

esmeraldino, -na *adj.* emeraldlike.

esmerar *tr.* to polish, brighten. *2 ref. esmerarse en* or *por*, to do one's best to, to take pains to.

esmerejón *m.* ORN. goshawk. *2* ancient small cannon.

esmeril *m.* emery. *2* ancient small cannon.

esmerilar *tr.* to emery, to grind with emery.

esmero *m.* great care, conscientiousness, neatness.

Esmirna *pr. n.* GEOG. Smyrna.

esmirriado, -da *adj.* DESMIRRIADO.

esmoquin *m.* tuxedo, dinner jacket.

esnob *m.-f.* snob, foolish admirer of new things.

esnobismo *m.* snobism, fawning admiration of new things.

esnórquel *m.* snorkel.

eso *pron. neut.* that, that thing; that matter: ~ *es,* that is it; *por* ~, for that reason; *a* ~ *de la una,* about one o'clock.

esófago *m.* ANAT. esophagus.

Esopo *m. pr. n.* Aesop.

esos, esas *adj. pl.* of *ese, esa*.

ésos, ésas *pr. pl.* of *ése, ésa*.

esotérico, -ca *adj.* esoteric.

esotro, -tra *adj.-pron.* that other.

espabiladeras *f. pl.* snuffers.

espabilado, -da *adj.* wide-awake. *2* quick, smart, sharp.

espaciador *m.* spacer, space bar, spacing key.

espacial *adj.* spatial, space.

espaciar *tr.* to space, space out. *2* PRINT. to space, lead. *3 tr.-ref.* to spread, diffuse. *4 ref.* to expatiate. *5* to relax, amuse oneself.

espacio *m.* space. *2* room, capacity. *3* blank [empty space]. *4* delay, slowness.

espacioso, -sa *adj.* spacious, roomy. *2* slow, deliberate.

espada *f.* sword, rapier; *entre la* ~ *y la pared*, between the devil and the deep blue sea. *2* swordsman. *3* BULLF. matador. *4* ace of ESPADAS. *5 pl.* CARDS suit equivalent to spades.

espadachín *m.* swordsman. *2* spadassin, bravo.

espadaña *f.* BOT. cattail, reed mace. *2* bell gable.

espadar *tr.* to scutch, swingle [flax or hemp].
espádice *m.* BOT. spadix.
espadilla *f.* scutch, swingle. *2* scull [oar]. *3* ace of ESPADAS. *4* hair bodkin.
espadillar *tr.* ESPADAR.
espadín *m.* narrow gala sword; rapier.
espadón *m.* *aug.* large sword. *2* high-up [person].
espaguetis *m. pl.* spaghetti.
espalda *f. sing.* & *pl.* back [of the human body, of a garment, etc.]; shoulders: *cargado de espaldas,* round-shouldered; *a espaldas de,* behind someone's back; *de espaldas,* backwards; *echarse una cosa a las espaldas,* not to bother oneself about a thing; *echarse una cosa sobre las espaldas,* to take on, assume something as a responsibility; *guardar las espaldas a uno,* to protect someone.
espaldar *m.* backpiece [of cuirass]. *2* carapace [of turtle]. *3* back [of a seat]. *4* HORT. spalier.
espaldarazo *m.* accolade; slap on the back.
espaldera *f.* HORT. spalier.
espaldilla *f.* shoulder blade. *2* shoulder [of mutton, pork, etc.].
espaldón *m.* CARP. shoulder. *2* FORT. entrenchment.
espalmar *tr.* DESPALMAR.
espalto *m.* PAINT. dark glaze.
espantada *f.* sudden flight [of an animal]. *2* sudden scare, sudden giving up from fear.
espantadizo, -za *adj.* scary, shy.
espantajo *m.* scarecrow; fright.
espantamoscas *m.* flyflap.
espantapájaros *m.* scarecrow.
espantar *tr.* to frighten, scare. *2* to chase, drive away, scare away. *3 ref.* to take fright. *4* to marvel, be astonished.
espanto *m.* fright, terror. *2* astonishment.
espantoso, -sa *adj.* fearful, frightful, dreadful, awful. *2* astonishing, astounding.
España *f. pr. n.* GEOG. Spain.
español, -la *adj.* Spanish. *2 m.-f.* Spaniard. *3 m.* Spanish [language].
españolismo *m.* love of Spain, Spanish patriotism. *2* Spanishness. *3* Hispanicism.
españolizar *tr.* to make Spanish or Spanishlike.
esparadrapo *m.* court plaster, sticking plaster.
esparaván *m.* GAVILÁN 1. *2* VET. spavin.
esparcido, -da *adj.* scattered. *2* merry, gay, frank.
esparcimiento *m.* scattering, spreading, dissemination. *2* relaxation, recreation, amusement.
esparcir *tr.* to scatter, spread, disseminate. *2* to recreate, entertain. *3 ref.* to scatter, spread [be spread]. *4* to amuse oneself.
espárrago *m.* BOT. asparagus. *2* awning pole. *3* peg ladder.
esparraguera *f.* BOT. asparagus [plant]. *2* asparagus bed. *3* asparagus dish.
esparrancado, -da *adj.* with one's legs wide apart. *2* spread apart.
esparrancarse *ref.* to spread the legs apart.
Esparta *f. pr. n.* HIST. Sparta.
espartano, -na *adj.-n.* Spartan.
espartería *f.* esparto goods. *2* esparto goods' shop.
espartero, -ra *m.-f.* maker or seller of esparto goods.
esparto *m.* esparto, esparto grass.
espasmo *m.* MED. spasm.
espasmódico, -ca *adj.* MED. spasmodic.
espata *f.* BOT. spathe.
espatarrarse *ref.* to open one's legs wide, to do the splits.
espático, -ca *adj.* spathic.
espato *m.* MINER. spar: ~ *flúor,* fluor spar.

espátula *f.* spatula; palette knife. *2* ORN. spoonbill.
especería *f.* ESPECIERÍA.
especia *f.* spice [condiment].
especial *adj.* especial. *2* special: *en* ~, specially.
especialidad *f.* speciality; specialty.
especialista *adj.-n.* specialist.
especialización *f.* specialization.
especializar *intr.-ref.-tr.* to specialize: *especializarse en,* to specialize in.
especiar *tr.* to spice.
especie *f.* NAT. HIST., PHIL. species. *2* species, kind, sort. *3* matter, notion, piece of news. *4* pretext, show. *5* THEOL. *especies sacramentales,* species. *6 en* ~, in kind, not in money.
especiería *f.* epicery, spices. *2* spice shop.
especiero *m.* spice dealer. *2* spice box.
especificación *f.* specification [stating precisely, in detail].
específicamente *adv.* specifically.
especificar *tr.* to specify [state precisely, in detail]; to itemize.
específico, -ca *adj.* specific. *2 m.* MED. specific. *3* patent medicine.
espécimen *m.* specimen.
especioso, -sa *adj.* specious. *2* neat, beautiful.
espectacular *adj.* spectacular.
espectáculo *m.* spectacle; show, pageant: *dar un* ~, to make a scene.
espectador, -ra *m.-f.* spectator. *2 pl.* audience.
espectral *adj.* spectral, ghostly. *2* PHYS. spectral.
espectro *m.* spectre, ghost. *2* PHYS. spectrum.
espectrograma *m.* PHYS. spectrogram.
espectroscopia *f.* spectroscopy.
especulación *f.* speculation, consideration, reflection. *2* COM. speculation, venture.
especulador, -ra *adj.* speculating. *2 m.-f.* speculator.
especular *tr.* to speculate about, consider attentively. *2 intr.* COM. to speculate.
especulativo, -va *adj.* speculative.
espéculo *m.* SURG., MED. speculum.
espejear *intr.* to shine like a mirror.
espejería *f.* mirror factory or shop.
espejismo *m.* mirage. *2* fig. illusion.
espejo *m.* mirror, looking glass: ~ *de cuerpo entero,* pier glass. *2* mirror, model. *3* NAUT. ~ *de popa,* escutcheon.
espejuelo *m.* small looking glass. *2* MINER. selenite. *3* leaf of talc. *4* a lure for larks. *5 pl.* spectacles.
espeleología *f.* speleology.
espelta *f.* BOT. spelt.
espeluznante *adj.* hair-raising, dreadful, horrifying.
espeluznar *tr.-ref.* DESPELUZAR.
espeluzno *m.* shuddering.
espeque *m.* handspike, lever. *2* prop.
espera *f.* wait, waiting; expectation: *sala de* ~, waiting room. *2* delay, respite: *esto no tiene* ~, this admits of no delay. *3* LAW stay. *4* patience, restraint.
esperantismo *m.* Esperantism.
esperanto *m.* Esperanto.
esperanza *f.* hope, hopes, hopefulness.
esperanzado, -da *adj.* hopeful [having hopes].
esperanzar *tr.* to give hopes.
esperar *tr.* to hope, hope for; to expect: ~ *que,* to hope that. *2* to look forward to. *3 tr.-intr.* to await, wait [for]: ~ *a que,* to wait until. *4 intr.* to hope, to trust: ~ *en Dios,* to trust in God. *5* to wait, stay.
esperma *f.* sperm. *2* ~ *de ballena,* spermaceti.

espermatozoo *m.* BIOL. spermatozoid.
espernada *f.* open end link [of chain].
esperpento *m.* fright, sight [ugly, slovenly person or thing]. *2* absurdity.
1) **espesar** *m.* thickness, deep [of a wooded land].
2) **espesar** *tr.* to thicken [inspissate; make closer]. *2 ref.* to thicken [become thick or thicker].
espeso, -sa *adj.* thick, dense, close, heavy, thickset. *2* close-woven. *3* thick [wall, etc.]. *4* dirty, untidy.
espesor *m.* thickness.
espesura *f.* thickness. *2* thicket, dense wood. *3* dirtiness, untidiness.
espetar *tr.* to spit, skewer. *2* to run [a knife, etc.] through. *3* coll. to spring [something] on [one]. *4 ref.* to stiffen, assume a solemn air. *5* to thrust oneself [into a place].
espetón *m.* spit; pocker; rapier. *2* large pin.
espía *m.-f.* spy [person]. *2 f.* NAUT. warp.
espiar *tr.* to spy, spy on. *2 intr.* NAUT. to warp.
espicanardo *m.* BOT. spikenard.
espícula *f.* ZOOL. spicule.
espichar *tr.* to prick. *2 intr.* coll. to die.
espiche *m.* pointed instrument. *2* peg, spigot.
espiga *f.* BOT. spike, ear. *2* shank, tang [of knife, etc.]. *3* CARP. tenon. *4* brad, peg, treenail. *5* clapper [of bell]. *6* fuse [of bomb]. *7* NAUT. masthead.
espigado, -da *adj.* spikelike. *2* AGR. seeded. *3* tall, grown [young person or tree].
espigador, -ra *m.-f.* gleaner.
espigar *tr.-intr.* to glean. *2 tr.* CARP. to tenon. *3 intr.* [of grain] to ear. *4 ref.* AGR. to run to seed. *5* [of a person] to grow tall.
espigón *m.* point of sharp tool or nail. *2* peaky hill. *3* breakwater, jetty.
espigueo *m.* gleaning. *2* gleaning season.
espiguilla *f.* spikelet. *2* BOT. meadow grass.
espín *m.* ZOOL. porcupine.
espina *f.* thorn: fig. *sacarse la ~,* to get even. *2* splinter. *3* fishbone. *4* spine, backbone: *~ dorsal,* spinal column. *5* scruple, suspicion: *dar mala ~,* to make one suspicious. *6* worry, pain.
espinaca *f.* BOT. spinach.
espinal *adj.* spinal.
espinapez *m.* herringbone [in parquetry floors].
1) **espinar** *m.* place full of thornbushes.
2) **espinar** *tr.* to prick with thorns. *2* fig. to prick, wound. *3 ref.* to get pricked [with a thorn].
espinazo *m.* spine, backbone. *2* ARCH. keystone.
espinel *m.* FISH. trawl line.
espinela *f.* MINER. spinel ruby. *2* ten-line stanza.
espineta *f.* MUS. spinet.
espingarda *f.* long Moorish gun. *2* a small cannon.
espinilla *f.* shin bone. *2* MED. blackhead.
espinillera *f.* ARMOUR. greave, jambe. *2* shin guard.
espino *m.* BOT. thornbush, hawthorn: *~ albar* or *blanco,* hawthorn; *~ cerval,* buckthorn; *~ negro,* blackthorn. *2 ~ artificial,* barbed wire.
espinosismo *m.* Spinozism.
espinoso, -sa *adj.* spiny, thorny. *2* arduous, delicate.
espionaje *m.* spying, espionage.
espira *f.* GEOM. spiral; spire. *2* turn [of a winding]. *3* ZOOL. spire [of a shell].
espiración *f.* PHYSIOL. expiration. *2* THEOL. spiration.
espiral *adj.-f.* GEOM. spiral. *2 f.* HOROL. hairspring.
espirar *tr.-intr.* PHYSIOL. to expire. *2 tr.* to exhale [an odour]. *3* to infuse a divine spirit in.
espirilo *m.* BACT. spirillum.

espiritado, -da *adj.* coll. ghostlike [extremely thin].
espiritismo *m.* spiritualism, spiritism.
espiritista *adj.* spiritualistic, spiritistic. *2 m.-f.* spiritualist, spiritist.
espiritoso, -sa *adj.* spirited, lively. *2* spirituous.
espíritu *m.* spirit [in practically every sense]: *~ de cuerpo,* esprit de corps; *el ~ y la letra,* the letter and the spirit; *pobre de ~,* poor in spirit, pusillanimous. *2* ghost: *Espíritu Santo,* Holy Ghost.
espiritual *adj.* spiritual, ghostly.
espiritualidad *f.* spirituality.
espiritualismo *m.* PHIL. spiritualism; idealism.
espiritualista *adj.* PHIL. spiritualistic. *2 m.-f.* PHIL. spiritualist.
espiritualizar *tr.* to spiritualize.
espiritualmente *adv.* spiritually. *2* wittily.
espirituoso, -sa *adj.* ESPIRITOSO.
espirómetro *m.* spirometer.
espiroqueta *f.* ZOOL. spirochaete, spirochete.
espita *f.* cock, tap, faucet [for a cask, etc.].
espitar *tr.* to tap, to put a cock on [a cask, etc.].
espito *m.* PRINT. peel, hanger.
esplendente *adj.* resplendent, shining.
esplender *intr.* poet. to shine.
esplendidez *f.* splendour, magnificence. *2* abundance, liberality, generosity.
espléndido, -da *adj.* splendid, magnificent, grand. *2* liberal, generous. *3* resplendent.
esplendor *m.* splendour. *2* fulgency, radiance.
esplendoroso, -sa *adj.* splendid, resplendent, radiant.
esplenio *m.* ANAT. splenius.
espliego *m.* BOT. lavender.
esplín *m.* melancholy, spleen, the blues.
espolada *f.,* **espolazo** *m.* prick with a spur.
espolear *tr.* to spur; to incite, to stimulate.
espoleta *f.* fuse [of bomb]. *2* wishbone [of bird].
espolín *m.* spur fixed to the heel of boot.
espolio *m.* ECCL. spolium.
espolique *m.* groom who walks in front of his master's horse.
espolón *m.* spur [of bird; of flower; of a range of mountains]. *2* beak, ram [of warship]. *3* cutwater [of bridge]. *4* ARCH. buttress. *5* breakwater, jetty.
espolvorear *tr.* DESPOLVOREAR. *2* to sprinkle with a powdered substance.
espondaico, -ca *adj.* spondaic.
espondeo *m.* spondee.
espongiarios *m. pl.* ZOOL. spongiae.
esponja *f.* sponge.
esponjado, -da *adj.* spongy, fluffy [wool, hair]. *2 m.* sugar bar.
esponjar *tr.* to make spongious or fluffy. *2 ref.* to become elated, proud. *3* to glow with health.
esponjera *f.* sponge tray.
esponjosidad *f.* sponginess, spongiousness.
esponjoso, -sa *adj.* spongy, spongious, porous.
esponsales *m. pl.* betrothal, spousals.
espontanearse *ref.* to speak frankly.
espontaneidad *f.* spontaneity, spontaneousness.
espontáneo, -a *adj.* spontaneous.
espora *f.* BIOL. spore.
esporádico, -ca *adj.* sporadic.
esporangio *m.* BOT. sporangium.
esporidio *m.* BOT. sporidium.
esportilla *f.* ESPUERTA.
esportillo *m.* esparto basket.
esposa *f.* spouse, wife. *2 pl.* handcuffs, manacles.
esposar *tr.* to handcuff.

esposo *m.* spouse, husband. *2 pl.* husband and wife.

esprint *m.* sprint.

espuela *f.* spur [pricking instrument; incitement]. *2* BOT. ~ *de caballero*, larkspur.

espuerta *f.* two-handed esparto basket.

espulgar *tr.* to delouse, to clean of lice or fleas. *2* to examine closely.

espulgo *m.* delousing. *2* close examination, scrutiny.

espuma *f.* foam, froth, lather, spume. *2* scum. *3* ~ *de mar*, meerschaum.

espumadera *f.* COOK. skimmer [utensil].

espumajear *intr.* to foam [at the mouth].

espumajo *m.* ESPUMARAJO.

espumante *adj.* ESPUMOSO.

espumar *tr.* to skim, scum. *2 intr.* to foam, froth. *3* [of wine] to sparkle.

espumarajo *m.* froth from the mouth: *echar espumarajos*, to be furious.

espumoso, -sa *adj.* foamy, frothy, lathery. *2* sparkling [wine].

espurio, -ria *adj.* spurious.

espurrear, espurriar *tr.* to sprinkle with water, etc. squirted from the mouth.

esputar *tr.* EXPECTORAR.

esputo *m.* spittle, sputum.

esqueje *m.* HORT. cutting, slip.

esquela *f.* note, short letter. *2* ~ *mortuoria*, death note, death notice.

esquelético, -ca *adj.* skeletal, thin, wasted.

esqueleto *m.* ANAT., ZOOL. skeleton. *2* skeleton [thin person]. *3* framework.

esquema *m.* schema, scheme.

esquemático, -ca *adj.* schematic.

esquematizar *tr.* to sketch, outline.

esquenanto *m.* BOT. camel grass.

esquí *m.* ski. *2* skiing.

esquiador, -ra *m.-f.* skier.

esquiar *intr.* to ski.

esquiciar *tr.* PAINT. to sketch.

esquicio *m.* PAINT. sketch, outline.

esquife *m.* skiff, small boat.

esquila *f.* sheepshearing. *2* cattle bell. *3* call bell. *4* ZOOL. marine prawn. *5* BOT. squill.

esquilador, -ra *m.-f.* shearer [of sheep, etc.]; clipper [of horses]; trimmer [of dogs].

esquilar *tr.* to shear, clip [animals].

esquileo *m.* shearing, clipping [of animals], sheepshearing. *2* shearing pen. *3* shearing time.

esquilmar *tr.* to harvest. *2* to impoverish [the soil]. *3* to squeeze dry [a source of wealth].

esquilón *m.* large cattle bell or cattle bell.

esquimal *adj.-n.* Eskimo.

esquina *f.* corner, outside angle: *las cuatro esquinas*, puss in the corner.

esquinado, -da *adj.* cornered, angular. *2* difficult [person].

esquinar *tr.-intr.* to form a corner with, to be on the corner of. *2 tr.* to square [timber]. *3* to set [one] against [another]. *4 ref.* to quarrel, fall out.

esquinazo *m.* corner: *dar ~ a*, to avoid [someone], to give the slip [to].

esquirla *f.* splinter [of bone, stone, glass, etc.].

esquirol *m.* coll. blackleg, scab, strike breaker.

esquisto *m.* GEOL. schist, slate.

esquivar *tr.* to avoid, elude, evade, shun, dodge. *2 ref.* to withdraw, shy off.

esquivez *f.* disdain, coldness; gruffness.

esquivo, -va *adj.* disdainful, cold, shy. *2* elusive.

esquizofrenia *f.* MED. schizophrenia.

esquizofrénico, -ca *adj.-n.* MED. schizophrenic.

esquizoide *adj.-n.* MED. schizoid.

estabilidad *f.* stability.

estabilización *f.* stabilization.

estabilizador, -ra *adj.* stabilizing. *2 m.* stabilizer.

estabilizar *tr.* to stabilize. *2 ref.* to become stabilized.

estable *adj.* stable, steady, firm, permanent.

establecer *tr.* to establish. *2* to decree, order. *3 ref.* to settle, establish oneself, to take up residence, to set up in business. ¶ CONJUG. like *agradecer*.

establecimiento *m.* establishment, establishing. *2* establishment [institution, house], shop, store. *3* statute, ordinance.

establezco, establezca, etc. *irr.* V. ESTABLECER.

establo *m.* stable; cattle barn.

estabular *tr.* to stable, to raise in a stable.

estaca *f.* stake, pale, picket. *2* HORT. cutting. *3* stick, cudgel. *4* clamp nail.

estacada *f.* stockade, palisade, paling. *2* lists; battlefield: *dejar en la ~*, to leave in the lurch.

estacar *tr.* to tie [an animal] to a stake. *2* to stake off.

estacazo *m.* blow with a stick or cudgel.

estación *f.* state, position. *2* season [of the year]; season, time. *3* halt, stop. *4* RLY., RADIO., TEL., SURG., BIOL., ASTR. station. *5* ~ *balnearia*, bathing resort.

estacional *adj.* seasonal. *2* ASTR. stationary.

estacionamiento *m.* stationing. *2* AUTO. parking. *3* remaining stationary.

estacionar *tr.* to station. *2* to park [a car, etc.]. *3 ref.* to station, be stationed, stop; [of a car, etc.] to park. *4* to remain stationary.

estacionario, -ria *adj.* stationary.

estacha *f.* harpoon rope. *2* NAUT. line, hawser.

estada *f.* stay, sojourn.

estadal *m.* linear measure of about 10 ft. 9 in.

estadía *f.* stop, stay. *2* COM. demurrage.

estadio *m.* stadium.

estadista *m.* statesman. *2* statistician.

estadística *f.* statistics.

estado *m.* state, condition: ~ *de guerra*, martial law; ~ *líquido*, liquid state; ~ *civil*, status [celibacy, married state, etc.]; *tomar ~*, to marry, take orders, become a nun; *en ~*, *en ~ interesante*, with child; *en mal ~*, in bad condition. *2* estate, order, class: ~ *llano*, the commons. *3* POL. state, government, State, Nation. *4* lineal measure. *5* statement [of accounts, etc.]. *6* MIL. ~ *mayor*, staff. *7 pl.* HIST. *Estados Generales*, States General.

Estados Unidos de América *m. pr. n.* GEOG. United States of America.

estadounidense *adj.-n.* [citizen] of the U.S.

estafa *f.* cheat, swindle.

estafador, -ra *m.-f.* cheat, swindler.

estafar *tr.* to cheat, swindle.

estafermo *m.* quintain. *2* fig. person who stands like a dummy.

estafeta *f.* courier, post. *2* post-office branch. *3* diplomatic mail.

estafilococo *m.* BACT. staphylococcus.

estafisagria *f.* BOT. stavesacre.

estalactita *f.* stalactite.

estalagmita *f.* stalagmite.

estallar *intr.* to burst, to explode. *2* [of a fire, a war, etc.] to break out. *3* to burst [with anger, joy, etc.]. *4* RESTALLAR.

estallido *m.* explosion, outburst; snap, crack, crash: *dar un* ~, to explode, to crash.

estambre *m.* worsted, woolen yarn. *2* WEAV. varp. *3* BOT. stamen.

Estambul *m. pr. n.* GEOG. Istanbul.

estamento *m.* state. *2* each of the four estates of Aragon. *3* each of the two legislative bodies in Spain in the nineteenth century. *4* stratum, class.

estaminífero, -ra *adj.* BOT. staminate.

estampa *f.* stamped picture, print, engraving. *2* fig. appearance, figure. *3* likeness, image; *la mismísima ~ de*, the very image of. *4* printing; *dar a la* ~, to publish. *5* footstep, imprint.

estampación *f.* print(ing), stamp(ing).

estampado *m.* impression, stamping. *2* cotton print. *3* stamped object.

estampador *m.* stamper. *2* printer [of fabrics].

estampar *tr.* to print. *2* to stamp [metals]. *3* to stamp, impress, imprint, mark. *4* coll. to dash against.

estampero *m.* picture or print maker or seller.

estampía (de) *adv.* suddenly.

estampida *f.* ESTAMPIDO. *2* (Am.) rush, stampede.

estampido *m.* explosion, report, crack, crash.

estampilla *f.* rubber stamp [for signature]. *2* (Am.) postage or revenue stamp.

estampillar *tr.* to stamp [with a rubber stamp].

estancamiento *m.* stagnation, stagnancy.

estancado, -da *adj.* stagnant [water]. *2* bogged down, at a standstill, deadlocked, blocked.

estancar *tr.* to make stagnant, to hold up or back, to stop. *2* [of the government] to monopolize the sale of certain goods. *3 ref.* to stagnate.

estancia *f.* stay, sojourn. *2* room, living room. *3* day in hospital. *4* stanza. *5* (Am.) ranch.

estanciero *m.* (Am.) rancher.

estanco, -ca *adj.* stanch, watertight. *2 m.* shop for selling government monopolized goods, tobacconist's.

estándar *m.* standard.

estandarte *m.* standard, banner.

estannífero, -ra *adj.* stanniferous.

estanque *m.* reservoir, basin, pond.

estanquero, -ra *m.* pond-keeper. *2 m.-f.* tobacconist.

estantal *m.* MAS. abutment, buttress.

estantalar *tr.* MAS. to buttress.

estante *adj.* veing [in a place], fixed, permanent. *2 m.* shelving, bookcase.

estantería *f.* shelving.

estantigua *f.* phantom, vision; scarecrow.

estañadura *f.* tinning, tinwork.

estañar *tr.* to tin. *2* to solder with tin.

estaño *m.* CHEM. tin.

estaquilla *f.* brad [nail]. *2* CARP. clamp nail.

estaquillar *tr.* to fasten with pegs.

estar *tr.-ref.* to be, to keep, stay, remain [in or at some place; in some condition or state]: ~ *en casa*, to be at home; ~ *enfermo*, to be ill; ~ *or estarse quieto*, to be or keep still; *están verdes*, fig. sour grapes. *2 intr.* followed by gerund it constitutes the progressive form; ~ *comiendo*, to be dining. *3* [of garments] to be too [wide, large, long, etc.] for one. *4* ~ *a*, to abide by; to be the; to be selling for: ~ *a lo que resulte*, to abide by the result; *estamos a 4 de abril*, it is the fourth of April; *las peras están a diez pesetas*, pears are selling at ten pesetas. *5* ~ *al caer*, to be about to happen. *6* ~ *a matar*, to be at daggers drawn. *7* ~ *bien*, to be good, all right, to

suit, fit, become [one]; [of a person] to be in a good way; to be well off; to be in good health; *¡está bien!*, all right! *8* ~ *bien con*, to be on good terms with. *9* ~ *de paseo*, to be taking a walk; ~ *de vacaciones*, to be on holiday. *10* ~ *de más*, to be unnecessary; to be in the way. *11 estar en*, to lie; to understand: *en eso está*, that is where it lies; *¿está usted?*, do you understand? *12* ~ *en mí, en ti, en sí*, to know what one is saying or doing. *13 no está en mí hacerlo*, it is not in my power to do it. *14* ~ *en que*, to believe, be of opinion that. *15* ~ *mal*, to be wrong, improper, incorrect, unbecoming; not to suit, fit or become one; [of a person] to be in a bad way, badly off. *16* ~ *mal con*, to be on bad terms with. *17* ~ *sobre mí, sobre ti, sobre sí*, to be on one's guard, be wary. *18* ~ *para*, to be about to, on the point of; to be in a humour for. *19* ~ *por*, to be for, to advocate; to have half a mind to; to be still to be [seen, done, etc.]. *20 le está bien empleado*, serve him right. *21 ¿estamos?*, do you understand?

¶ CONJUG.: IND. Pres.: *estoy, estás, está; estamos, estáis, están* | Pret.: *estuve, estuviste, estuvo; estuvimos, estuvisteis, estuvieron*. | SUBJ. Pres.: *esté, estés, esté; estemos, estéis, estén*. | Imperf.: *estuviera, estuvieras, estuviera; estuviéramos, estuvierais, estuvieran, or estuviese, estuvieses, estuviese; estuviésemos, estuvieseis, estuviesen*. | Fut.: *estuviere, estuvieres, estuviere; estuviéremos, estuviereis, estuvieren*. | IMPER.: *está, esté; estemos, estad, estén*. | PAST. P.: estado. | GER.: estando.

estarcido *m.* pounce drawing, stencil.

estarcir *tr.* to stencil.

estarna *f.* ORN. gray partridge.

estatal *adj.* [pertaining to] the state.

estático, -ca *adj.* static(al. *2* dumfounded, speechless. *3 f.* statics.

estatismo *m.* statism. *2* static state.

estator *m.* MACH., ELECT. stator.

estatorreactor *m.* AER. ramjet.

estatua *f.* statue.

estatuaria *f.* statuary [art].

estatuario, -ria *adj. n.* statuary.

estatúder *m.* stadholder.

estatuilla *f. dim.* statuette.

estatuir *tr.* to establish, order, decree. ¶ CONJUG. like *huir*.

estatura *f.* stature.

estatuto *m.* statutes, regulations [of a corporation, society, etc.]. *2* statute [in international and Roman law].

estay *m.* NAUT. stay.

1) **este** *m.* east, orient. *2* east wind.

2) **este** *adj. m.*, **esta** *adj. f.* this.

éste *pron. m.*, **ésta** *pron. f.* this, this one, the latter. *2 ésta*, this town [from where I am writing].

esté, etc. *irr.* V. ESTAR.

estearina *f.* CHEM. stearin.

esteatita *f.* MINER. steatite.

Esteban *m. pr. n.* Stephen.

estela *f.* wake [of a ship]; trail [of a luminous body]. *2* ARCH. stele. *3* ESTELARIA.

estelar *adj.* stellar, sidereal.

estelaria *f.* BOT. lady's mantle.

estemple *m.* MIN. stemple.

estenografía *f.* stenography.

estenografiar *tr.* to stenograph.

estenordeste *m.* east-northeast.

estenotipia *f.* stenotypy, stenotype.

estentóreo, -a *adj.* stentorian.
estepa *f.* steppe. *2* BOT. rockrose.
estepario, -ria *adj.* [pertaining to the] steppe.
estepilla *f.* BOT. white-leaved rockrose.
Ester *f. pr. n.* Esther.
éster, ester *m.* CHEM. ester.
estera *f.* mat, matting.
esterar *tr.* to cover [the floor] with a mat.
1) estercolar *m.* dunghill.
2) estercolar *tr.* to dung, manure. *2 intr.* [of animals] to void the excrements.
estercolero *m.* dunghill. *2* dung collector.
estéreo *m.* stere [one cubic metre].
estereofonía *f.* stereo, stereophony.
estereofónico, -ca *adj.* stereophonic.
estereografía *f.* stereography.
estereometría *f.* stereometry.
estereoscopio *m.* stereoscope.
estereotipado, -da *adj.* stereotyped.
estereotipar *tr.* to stereotype.
estereotipia *f.* stereotypography, stereotypy.
estereotipista *m.* stereotypist.
esterería *f.* mat factory or shop.
esterero, -ra *m.-f.* mat maker or seller.
estéril *adj.* sterile, barren, fruitless. *2* futile, vain.
esterilidad *f.* sterility, barrenness. *2* futility.
esterilización *f.* sterilization.
esterilizador, -ra *adj.* sterilizing. *2 m.* sterilizer.
esterilizar *tr.* to sterilize.
esterilla *f.* small mat, door mat: ~ *eléctrica*, electric mat. *2* straw plait. *3* gold or silver braid.
esterlina *adj. libra* ~, sterling pound.
esternón *m.* ANAT. sternum, breastbone.
estero *m.* matting, act of laying mats on [floors]; matting season. *2* estuary, tideland.
estertor *m.* MED. stertor. *2* death rattle.
estertoroso, -sa *adj.* stertorous.
esteta *n.* aesthete.
estética *f.* aesthetics.
esteticismo *m.* aestheticism.
estético, -ca *adj.* aesthetic. *2* beautiful, having an artistic effect. *3 m.-f.* aesthete.
estetoscopio *m.* stethoscope.
esteva *f.* plough handle, stilt.
estevado, -da *adj.* bowlegged.
estiaje *m.* low water [in a river, lake, etc.]; low-water season.
estiba *f.* NAUT. stowage. *2* ORD. rammer.
estibador *m.* stevedore.
estibar *tr.* NAUT. to stow. *2* to pack, to stuff.
estiércol *m.* dung, manure.
Estige *f. pr. n.* MYTH. Styx.
estigio, -gia *adj.* Stygian.
estigma *m.* stigma.
estigmatizar *tr.* to stigmatize.
estilar *tr.* to draw [a document, etc.], in due style. *2 intr.* to use, to be in the habit of. *3 ref.* to be the fashion, the style, to be usual.
estilete *m.* stylet. *2* stiletto. *3* style [tool].
estilista *m.* stylist, mater of style.
estilita *m.* ECCL., HIST. stylite.
estilización *f.* stylizing, stylization, styling.
estilizar *tr.* to stylize.
estilo *m.* style, stylus [instrument for writing]. *2* style, gnomon. *3* BOT., ARCH., LIT., ART. style. *4* style, manner; use, custom, fashion: *al* ~ *de*, after the custom or style of; *por el* ~, *por este* ~, like that, of that kind.
estilóbato *m.* ARCH. stylobate.
estilográfica *adj. pluma* ~ or *f. estilográfica*, fountain pen.

estima *f.* esteem. *2* NAUT. dead reckoning.
estimable *adj.* estimable.
estimación *f.* esteem, estimation, regard: *propia* ~, self-respect. *2* estimation, estimate, valuation.
estimar *tr.* to esteem, hold in regard, set a high value on: ~ *en poco*, to hold in low esteem. *2* to judge, think. *3* to estimate, value.
estimativa *f.* power of judging. *2* instinct.
estimulación *f.* stimulation.
estimulante *adj.* stimulating. *2 m.* stimulant.
estimular *tr.* to stimulate. *2* to incite, encourage.
estímulo *m.* stimulus. *2* inducement, incentive. *3* encouragement.
estío *m.* summer, summer time.
estipe *m.* BOT. stipe.
estipendiario *m.* stipendiary.
estipendio *m.* stipend, salary, pay, fee.
estípite *m.* ARCH. pilaster in the form of an inverted truncated pyramid. *2* BOT. columnar trunk.
estíptico, -ca *adj.* styptic. *2* costive. *3* miserly.
estípula *f.* BOT. stipule.
estipulación *f.* stipulation.
estipular *tr.* to stipulate.
estirado, -da *adj.* stretched, expanded, lengthened, drawn. *2* stiff, prim; stuck-up.
estiramiento *m.* stretching. *2* drawing [of wire].
estirar *tr.* to stretch [by pulling]. *2* to stretch, extend, lengthen, expand: ~ *la pierna*, coll. to die; ~ *las piernas*, coll. to stretch one's legs. *3* to draw [wire]. *4* to iron lightly. *5 ref.* to stretch, stretch one's limbs.
estirón *m.* pull, tug. *2* coll. *dar un* ~, to grow tall in a short time.
estirpe *f.* stock, lineage, family.
estival; estivo, -va *adj.* aestival, estival, summer.
esto *dem. pron. neut.* this; this subject, this matter, this point: *en* ~, at this point; *por* ~, for this reason.
estocada *f.* stab, thrust, lunge [with a sword].
Estocolmo *m. pr. n.* GEOG. Stockholm.
estofa *f.* quality, class.
estofado, -da *adj.* stewed. *2* quilted. *3* ornamented. *4 m.* COOK. stew, ragout.
estofar *tr.* COOK. to stew, ragout. *2* to paint on burnished gold. *3* to size [wood carvings] for gilding.
estoicismo *m.* stoicism. *2* Stoicism.
estoico, -ca *adj.* stoic(al).
estola *f.* stole [garment]. *2* ECCL. stole.
estolidez *f.* stupidity, imbecility.
estólido, -da *adj.* stupid, imbecile.
estolón *m.* BOT. stolon. *2* ECCL. deacon's stole.
estoma *m.* BOT. stoma.
estomacal *adj.-m.* stomachic.
estomagar *tr.* to give indigestion. *2* coll. to disgust.
estómago *m.* ANAT. stomach: *revolver el* ~, to turn the stomach.
estomatitis *f.* MED. stomatitis.
estonio, -nia *adj.-n.* Estonian.
estopa *f.* tow [of flax, hemp, etc.]. *2* burlap. *3* oakum.
estopilla *f.* finest part of tow. *2* lawn [fabric]. *3* coarse cotton cloth.
estopor *m.* NAUT. stopper.
estoque *m.* estoc, rapier, narrow sword. *4* BULLF. sword. *3* BOT. sword lily, gladiolus.
estoquear *tr.* to stab, with an estoc or sword.
estoraque *m.* BOT. storax tree. *2* storax [balsam].
estorbar *tr.* to hinder, obstruct, hamper, impede;

to be in the way of; to prevent [someone] from. 2 to annoy, inconvenience.

estorbo *m.* hindrance, obstruction, nuisance.

estornija *f.* washer [under linchpin].

estornino *m.* ORN. starling.

estornudar *intr.* to sneeze.

estornudo *m.* sneeze.

estoy *irr.* V. ESTAR.

estrábico, -ca *adj.* strabismic, strabismal.

estrabismo *m.* MED. strabismus, squint.

estrada *f.* road, way.

estradiote *m.* stradiot.

estrado *m.* formerly, a lady's drawing-room. 2 dais. 3 *pl.* courtrooms, halls of justice.

estrafalario, -ria *adj.* ridiculous, queer, eccentric, edd. 2 *m.-f.* queer fish, eccentric person.

estragamiento *m.* disorderr and corruption.

estragar *tr.* to corrupt, vitiate, deprave. 2 to ruin, spoil, ravage.

estrago *m.* havoc, ruin, ravage: *hacer estragos,* to play havoc.

estragón *m.* BOT. tarragon.

estrambote *m.* LIT. tail [of a sonnet, etc.].

estrambótico, -ca *adj.* odd, queer, strange.

estramonio *m.* BOT. stramonium, thorn apple.

estrangulación *f.* throttling, strangulation. 2 SURG. strangulation. 3 MACH. throttling, chocke.

estrangular *tr.* to strangle, throttle, chocke. 2 SURG., MED. to strangulate. 3 MACH. to throttle, choke.

estraperlista *m.-f.* black marketeer.

estraperlo *m.* black market.

estrás *m.* strass [glass].

Estrasburgo *f. pr. n.* GEOG. Strasbourg.

estratagema *f.* stratagem, ruse.

estratega *m.* strategist.

estrategia *f.* strategy, strategics.

estratégico, -ca *adj.* strategic(al. 2 *m.* strategist.

estratificación *f.* stratification.

estratificar *tr.-ref.* GEOL. to stratify.

estratigrafía *f.* stratigraphy.

estrato *m.* GEOL., ANAT. stratum, layer. 2 METEOR. stratus.

estratosfera *f.* METEOR. stratosphere.

estraza *f.* rag. 2 *papel de* ~, brown paper.

estrechamiento *m.* narrowing. 2 closing [making close]. 3 pressing [of siege, etc.].

estrechar *tr.* to narrow, contract, make less wide. 2 to take in [a garment]. 3 to constrain, compel. 4 to press, to follow or besiege closely. 5 to tighten [bonds, etc.]. 6 ~ *la mano de,* to shake hands with; ~ *entre los brazos,* to embrace, clasp in one's arms. 7 *ref.* to narrow [become narrower]. 8 to press together. 9 to cut down expenses. 10 to become more intimate.

estrechez *f.* narrowness. 2 tightness [of shoes, garments, etc.]. 3 strictness. 4 pressure [of time]. 5 closeness, intimacy. 6 jam, predicament. 7 penury, poverty.

estrecho, -cha *adj.* narrow. 2 tight [shoes, garments, etc.]. 3 close [relation, friendship, etc.]. 4 strict. 5 miserly. 6 *m.* jam, predicament. 7 GEOG. straits: ~ *de Gibraltar,* Straits of Gibraltar.

estrechura *f.* narrowness, narrow passage. 2 closeness, intimacy. 3 jam, predicament.

estregadera *f.* scrubbing brush.

estregadura *f.,* **estregamiento** *m.* rubbing, scrubbing.

estregar *tr.* to rub, scrub, scour. 2 to strike [matches]. ¶ CONJUG. like *acertar.*

estregón *m.* hard or rough rub.

estrella *f.* ASTR. star: ~ *fugaz,* shooting star; ~ *polar,* polestar; *poner sobre las estrellas,* to praise to the skies; *ver las estrellas,* fig. to see stars. 2 star [starlike figure or object]. 3 star [of the screen, etc.]. 4 stars, destiny, luck: *tener buena* ~, to be lucky. 5 ZOOL. ~ *de mar,* starfish.

estrellado, -da *adj.* starry, star-spangled. 2 star-shaped. 3 fried [egg].

estrellamar *f.* ZOOL. starfish.

estrellar *tr.* to strew with stars. 2 to smash [against], dash to pieces. 3 to fry [eggs]. 4 *ref.* to become strewn with stars. 5 to smash, dash, be smashed [against]; to fail.

estremecedor, -ra *adj.* frightful, fearful; thrilling.

estremecer *tr.* to shake, make tremble or shudder; to thrill. 2 *ref.* to shake, tremble, shudder; to thrill. ¶ CONJUG. like *agradecer.*

estremecimiento *m.* shaking, trembling, shuddering, shudder; thrill, thrilling.

estrenar *tr.* to use or wear for the first time; to handsel. 2 to perform [a play] or to show [a film] for the first time. 3 *ref.* to make one's debut. 4 to make the first sale of day. 5 [of a play] to open.

estreno *m.* first use. 2 THEAT. première. 3 début; first performance. 4 handsel.

estreñido, -da *adj.* constipated, costive. 2 stingy.

estreñimiento *m.* constipation, costiveness.

estreñir *tr.* to bind, constipate. 2 *ref.* to become constipated. ¶ CONJUG. like *ceñir.*

estrépito *m.* clatter, crash, din, loud noise. 2 display, show.

estrepitosamente *adv.* noisily, loudly, rowdily, deafeningly.

estrepitoso, -sa *adj.* deafening, crashing, loud, boisterous, noisy, obstreperous. 2 spectacular.

estreptococo *m.* BACT. streptococcus.

estreptomicina *f.* PHARM. streptomycin.

estría *f.* stria, flute, groove.

estriar *tr.* to striate, flute.

estribación *f.* GEOG. spur, counterfort.

estribar *intr.* ~ *en,* [of things] to rest on or upon; to be based on; to lie in.

estribera *f.* stirrup.

estribillo *m.* burden, refrain, chorus. 2 pet word, pet phrase.

estribo *m.* stirrup: *perder los estribos,* fig. to lose one's head. 2 footboard, step [of a carriage]. 3 AUTO. running board. 4 GEOG. spur. 5 ARCH. abuttment, buttress. 6 ANAT. stapes. 7 fig. base, support.

estribor *m.* NAUT. starboard.

estricnina *f.* CHEM. strychnine.

estricto, -ta *adj.* strict.

estridencia *f.* stridence; stridor.

estridente *adj.* strident; shrill.

estridor *m.* stridor, harsh screeching noise.

estridular *intr.* to stridulate, to chirp, to chirr.

estro *m.* inspiration, afflatus. 2 ENT. botfly.

estróbilo *m.* BOT. strobile.

estrobo *m.* NAUT. grommet, grummet, becket.

estroboscopio *m.* stroboscope.

estrofa *f.* stanza, strophe.

estroncio *m.* CHEM. strontium.

estropajo *m.* esparto scrub; dishcloth. 2 fig. worthless thing. 3 BOT. dishcloth gourd.

estropajoso, -sa *adj.* fig. thick, indistinct [utterance]. 2 fig. untidy, ragged. 3 coll. tough, stringy [meat, vegetables, etc.].

estropear *tr.* to spoil, ruin, damage, put out of or-

der. *2* to maim, cripple. *3 ref.* to get spoiled, ruined, out of order. *4* to get maimed or crippled.
estropicio *m.* coll, breakage, smash, crash [of fragile things]. *2* upset, mess.
estructura *f.* structure, make.
estructuración *f.* structuration.
estructural *adj.* structural.
estructuralismo *m.* structuralism.
estructurar *tr.* to structure, to build.
estruendo *m.* great noise, clangor, crash. *2* uproar, clamour, din, confusion. *3* ostentation, pomp.
estruendoso, -sa *adj.* noisy, loud, uproarius, clamorous. *2* showy.
estrujamiento *m.* squeezing, pressing, crushing.
estrujar *tr.* to squeeze, press, crush, jam. *2* to squeeze, drain, exhaust.
estrujón *m.* squeeze, crush.
estuación *f.* flow of the tide, flood tide.
Estuardo *pr. n.* Stuart: *María ~,* Mary Stuart.
estuario *m.* estuary.
estucado *m.* stuccoing, stuccowork.
estucar *tr.* to stucco.
estuco *m.* stucco.
estuche *m.* case [for jewels, instruments, etc.]. *2* case, cover, etui, etwee.
estudiado, -da *adj.* studied, affected, mannered.
estudiante *m.* student [of a university, etc.].
estudiantil *adj.* [pertaining to] students, college.
estudiantina *f.* musical band of students.
estudiar *tr.* to study; to read or study for. *2* to read lesson to. *3* ART. to draw from nature. *4 intr.* to be a student.
estudio *m.* study [act or process of studying]. *2* study, paper [article, writing]. *3* F. ARTS, CINEM., RADIO. studio. *4* studio, library. *5* studied manner. *6* F. ARTS study, sketch. *7 pl.* studies, learning, education.
estudioso, -sa *adj.* studious.
estufa *f.* stove, heater: *~ de desinfección,* sterilizer. *2* heated room. *3* sweating room. *4* HORT. hothouse. *5* foot stove. *6* drying chamber.
estufilla *f.* foot stove. *2* small fire pan.
estulticia *f.* foolishness, stupidity.
estulto, -ta *adj.* foolish, stupid.
estupefacción *f.* stupefaction, amazement.
estupefaciente *adj.-m.* stupefacient, narcotic.
estupefacto, -ta *adj.* amazed, dumbfounded.
estupendo, -da *adj.* stupendous, wonderful, grand.
estupidez *f.* stupidity. *2* stupid act or remark, folly.
estúpido, -da *adj.* stupid, foolish, witless. *2 m.-f.* stupid [person].
estupor *m.* MED. stupor. *2* amazement.
estuprar *tr.* to rape, violate.
estupro *m.* rape, violation.
estuquista *m.* stucco plasterer.
esturión *m.* ICHTH. sturgeon.
estuve, estuviste, etc. *irr.* V. ESTAR.
esvarar *intr.* to slide, glide.
esvástica *f.* swastika.
esviaje *m.* ARCH. obliquity, skew.
eta *f.* eta [greek letter].
etalaje *m.* bosh.
etamín *f.* etamine [fabric].
etano *m.* CHEM. ethane.
etapa *f.* MIL. stage [of journey]. *2* stage [of development, process, etc.].
etcétera *f.* et cetera.
éter *m.* PHYS., CHEM. ether. *2* poet. ether, heavens.
etéreo, -a *adj.* ethereal.
eterificar *tr.* CHEM. to etherify.

eterizar *tr.* to etherize.
eternal *adj.* eternal.
eternidad *f.* eternity. *2* fig. long time.
eternizar *tr.* to eternize, perpetuate; to prolong indefinitely. *2 ref.* to become interminable.
eterno, -na *adj.* eternal, endless, everlasting. *2 m.* *el Eterno,* the Eternal, God.
etesio *adj.-m.* etesian [wind].
ética *f.* ethics.
ético, -ca *adj.* ethical, moral. *2 m.* ethicist, moralist. *3 adj.-n.* HÉTICO.
etileno *m.* CHEAM. ethylene.
etílico, -ca *adj.* ethylic.
etilo *m.* CHEM. ethyl.
etimología *f.* etymology.
etimólogo *m.* etymologist.
etiología *f.* aetiology.
etíope *adj.-n.* Ethiopian. *2 adj.* Ethiopic.
Etiopía *f. pr. n.* GEOG. Ethiopia.
etiqueta *f.* label, tag. *2* etiquette, ceremony, formality: *de ~,* full dress, formal.
etiquetado *m.* labelling.
etiquetero, -ra *adj.* ceremonious [person].
etmoides *adj.-m.* ANAT. ethmoid.
Etna *m. pr. n.* GEOG. Etna.
etnia *f.* ethnos.
étnico, -ca *adj.* ethnic(al). *2* GRAM. gentilic.
etnografía *f.* ethnography.
etnología *f.* ethnology.
etnólogo *m.* ethnologist.
etrusco, -ca *adj.-n.* Etruscan.
eucalipto *m.* BOT. eucalyptus.
eucaristía *f.* THEOL. Eucharist.
eucarístico, -ca *adj.* Eucharistic.
Euclides *m. pr. n.* Euclid.
eucologio *m.* euchology.
eudiómetro *m.* eudiometer.
eufemismo *m.* euphemism.
eufonía *f.* euphony.
eufónico, -ca *adj.* euphonic, euphonious.
euforbiáceo, -a *adj.* BOT. euphorbiaceous.
euforia *f.* euphoria, euphory.
eufuismo *m.* euphuism.
eugenesia *f.* eugenics.
Eugenia *f. pr. n.* Eugenia.
Eugenio *m. pr. n.* Eugene.
eunuco *m.* eunuch.
eurasiático, -ca *adj.-n.* Eurasian.
euritmia *f.* eurythmy.
euro *m.* east wind.
Europa *f. pr. n.* GEOG. Europe. *2* MYTH. Europa.
europeizar *tr.* to Europeanize.
europeo, -a *adj.-n.* European.
euscalduna; euscaro, -ra *adj.-m.* Basque [language].
Eustaquio *m. pr. n.* Eustace.
eutanasia *f.* euthanasia.
eutrapelia *f.* moderation in pleasures.
Eva *f. pr. n.* Eve.
evacuación *f.* evacuation. *2* discharge, carrying out [of commission, etc.].
evacuar *tr.* to evacuate, empty, vacate. *2* to discharge [bowels, etc.]. *3* to discharge, carry out, fulfil [comission, etc.]. *4* MED., MIL. to evacuate.
evadido, -da *adj.* escaped. *2 m.-f.* escapee.
evadir *tr.* to evade, elude, avoid. *2 ref.* to escape, sneak away.
evaluación *f.* evaluation.
evaluar *tr.* to evaluate.
evangélico, -ca *adj.* evangelical.

evangelio *m.* gospel, Gospel, Evangel. *2* fig. gospel truth.
evangelista *m.* Evangelist. *2* gospel chanter.
evangelización *f.* evangelization.
evangelizar *tr.* to evangelize.
evaporación *f.* evaporation.
evaporar *tr.* to evaporate. *2* to cause to vanish. *3 ref.* to evaporate; to vanish, disappear.
evasión *f.* escape. *2* evasion.
evasiva *f.* evasion, subterfuge.
evasivo, -va *adj.* evasive.
evento *m.* event, contingency: *a todo* ~, against every contingency.
eventual *adj.* eventual, contingent.
eventualidad *f.* eventuality, case, contingency.
evicción *f.* LAW eviction.
evidencia *f.* evidence, obviousness.
evidenciar *tr.* to evidence, show, render evident.
evidente *adj.* evident, obvious.
evidentemente *adv.* evidently, obviously, clearly.
evisceración *f.* SURG. evisceration.
evitable *adj.* avoidable.
evitación *f.* avoidance.
evitar *tr.* to avoid, elude, shun. *2* to prevent [keep from happening]. *3* to save [trouble, etc.].
evo *m.* poet, age, æon.
evocación *f.* evocation, evoking.
evocar *tr.* to evoke, call up; to conjure up.
evocativo, -va *adj.* evocative.
evolución *f.* evolution [development, change]. *2* BIOL., PHIL., MIL., NAV. evolution.
evolucionar *intr.* to evolve. *2* to change [in conduct, etc.]. *3* MIL., NAV. to perform evolutions.
evolucionismo *m.* evolutionism.
evolutivo, -va *adj.* evolutional, evolutive.
ex *prep.* ex-, former, late.
ex abrupto *adv.* abruptly, suddenly. *2 m.* impolite or misplaced outburst.
exacción *f.* exaction. *2* extortion.
exacerbar *tr.* to exacerbate. *2* to irritate, exasperate. *3 ref.* to become exacerbate.
exacerbante *adj.* exasperating, irritating, provoking.
exactitud *f.* exactness, accuracy. *2* punctuality.
exacto, -ta *adj.* exact, accurate, precise, punctual.
exageración *f.* exaggeration.
exageradamente *adv.* exaggeratedly. *2* exceedingly, exorbitantly.
exagerado, -da *adj.* exaggerated. *2* excessive. *3* exaggerative.
exagerador, -ra *adj.* exaggerating. *2 m.-f.* exaggerator.
exagerar *tr.* to exaggerate.
exaltación *f.* exaltation. *2* passion, excitement; hot-headedness.
exaltado, -da *adj.* exalted. *2* hot-headed, extreme.
exaltar *tr.* to exalt. *2* to extol. *3 ref.* to become excited, worked up.
examen *m.* examination. *2* inspection, survey.
examinador, -ra *adj.* examining. *2 m.-f.* examiner.
examinando, -da *m.-f.* examinee.
examinar *tr.* to examine. *2* to inspect, survey, look into, inquire into, search, scan. *3 ref.* to sit for examination.
exangüe *adj.* bloodless, pale. *2* exhausted, worn out. *3* lifeless, dead.
exánime *adj.* exanimate, lifeless. *2* weak, faint.
exasperación *f.* exasperation.
exasperante *adj.* exasperating.
exasperar *tr.* to exasperate. *2 ref.* to become exasperated.

excarcelar *tr.* LAW to relase, set [a prisoner] free.
exavación *f.* excavation.
excavador, -ra *adj.* excavating. *2 m.-f.* excavator [person]. *3 f.* excavator, power shovel.
excavar *tr.* to excavate [hollow out, make a hole]. *2* AGR. to loosen the soil around [a plant].
excedencia *f.* temporary retirement [from post].
excedente *adj.* excessive. *2* left over; surplus. *3* temporarily retiring [employee]. *4 m.* surplus.
exceder *tr.* to exceed, surpass, outdo. *2 intr.-ref.* to go too far: *excederse en sus atribuciones*, to exceed one's powers. *3 excederse a sí mismo*, to outdo oneself.
excelencia *f.* excellence, excellency: *por* ~, preeminently. *2* Excellency [title].
excelente *adj.* excellent, very good, very fine.
excelentísimo, -ma *adj. superl.* most excellent.
excelsitud *f.* loftiness, sublimity.
excelso, -sa *adj.* lofty, elevated, sublime.
excentricidad *f.* eccentricity.
excéntrico, -ca *adj.* eccentric(al. *2 m.-f.* eccentric, crank [person]. *3 f.* MACH. eccentric.
excepción *f.* exception.
excepcional *adj.* exceptional, uncommon, unusual.
excepto *adv.* except, excepting, save.
exceptuar *tr.* to except.
excesivo, -va *adj.* excessive.
exceso *m.* excess, surplus: *en* ~, excessively, to excess. *2* excess, intemperance, outrage.
excipiente *m.* PHARM. excipient.
excisión *f.* MED. excision.
excitable *adj.* excitable.
excitación *f.* exciting, excitation, excitement. *2* ELEC., PHYSIOL. excitation.
excitador, -ra *adj.* exciting, excitant. *2 m.* ELEC. exciter.
excitante *adj.* exciting. *2 adj.-m.* excitant.
excitar *tr.* to excite, stir up, move. *2* ELEC., PHYSIOL. to excite. *3 ref.* to get excited.
exclamación *f.* exclamation.
exclamar *intr.* to exclaim, cry out.
exclamativo, -va *adj.* exclamatory.
exclaustrar *tr.* to secularize [a monk or nun].
excluir *tr.* to exclude, bar, debar. ¶ CONJUG. like *huir.*
exclusión *f.* exclusion.
exclusiva *f.* sole or exclusive right, special privilege. *2* rejection, exclusion.
exclusivamente *adv.* exclusively, solely.
exclusive *adv.* exclusively, exclusive.
exclusivismo *m.* exclusive attachment to an idea, person, etc.
exclusivo, -va *adj.* exclusive, excluding. *2* sole: *agente* ~, sole agent.
excogitar *tr.* to excogitate, find, devise.
excomulgado, -da *adj.-n.* excomunicate. *2* fig. & coll. imp of mischief.
excomulgar *tr.* to excommunicate. *2* to anathematize.
excomunión *f.* excommunication.
excoriación *f.* excoriation.
excoriar *tr.* to excoriate. *2 ref.* to be excoriated.
excrecencia *f.* excrescence, excrescency.
excreción *f.* PHYSIOL. excretion.
excremento *m.* excrement.
excretar *intr.* to excrete. *2* to void excrements.
excreto, -ta *adj.* excreted.
exculpación *f.* exculpation, exoneration.
exculpar *tr.* to exculpate, exonerate.
excursión *f.* excursion, trip, outing, tour.

excursionista *adj.* [pertaining to] excursion. *2 m.-f.* excursionist, tripper.
excusa *f.* excuse, excusing. *2* excuse, apology.
excusable *adj.* excusable, pardonable. *2* that may be omitted.
excusado, -da *adj.* exempt. *2* superfluous, unnecessary. *3* private: *puerta excusada*, side door, private door. *4 m.* water-closet, toilet.
excusar *tr.* to excuse. *2* to avoid, prevent. *3* to exempt from. *4 excuso decir*, needless to say. *5 ref.* to excuse oneself, to apologize. *6 excusarse de*, to excuse oneself from.
execrable *adj.* execrable.
execración *f.* execration.
execrando, -da *adj.* execrable.
execrar *tr.* to execrate.
exedra *f.* ARCH. exedra.
exégesis *f.* exegesis.
exégeta *m.* exegete.
exención *f.* exemption.
exentar *tr.* to exempt.
exento, -ta *adj.* exempt. *2* free [from]; deprived, bare. *3* ARCH. isolated, disengaged.
exequátur *m.* esequatur.
exequias *f.* exequies, obsequies.
exergo *m.* NUMIS. exergue.
exfoliación *f.* exfoliation.
exfoliar *tr.* to exfoliate.
exhalación *f.* exhalation. *2* shooting star. *3* bolt of lightning. *4* fume, vapour.
exhalar *tr.* to exhale, breathe forth, emit. *2* to heave [a sigh]. *3 ref.* to exhale [be exhaled].
exhaustivo, -va *adj.* exhaustive.
exhausto, -ta *adj.* exhausted.
exhibición *f.* exhibition, exhibiting. *2* show off.
exhibicionismo *m.* showing off. *2* exhibitionism.
exhibicionista *n.* exhibitionist.
exhibir *tr.* to exhibit, show, display. *2* to produce [documents, etc.]. *3 ref.* to show oneself. *4* to show off.
exhortación *f.* exhortation.
exhortar *tr.* to exhort.
exhorto *m.* LAW letters rogatory.
exhumación *f.* exhumation.
exhumar *tr.* to exhume, disinter, dig up.
exigencia *f.* exactingness; fastidiousness. *2* exigency, demand, requirement.
exigente *adj.* exigent, exacting; fastidious.
exigibilidad *f.* liability to be demanded or required.
exigible & exigidero, -ra *adj.* exigible.
exigir *tr.* to exact. *2* to require, demand, need.
exigüidad *f.* exiguity.
exiguo, gua *adj.* exiguous.
exiliado, -da *adj.* exiled. *2 n.* exile.
exilio *m.* DESTIERRO.
eximente *adj.* exempting. *2* exonerating.
eximio, -mia *adj.* eminent, most excellent.
eximir *tr.* to exempt.
existencia *f.* existence. *2* life [of man]. *3 sing. & pl.* COM. stock [goods in hand]: *en ~*, in stock.
existencialismo *m.* PHIL. existentialism.
existente *adj.* existent, extant. *2* COM. in stock.
existir *tr.* to exist, to be.
exitazo *m.* great success.
éxito *m.* issue, end: *buen ~*, success; *mal ~*, failure. *2* success; hit: *tener ~*, to be successful; to be a hit.
ex libris *m.* ex libris, bookplate.
éxodo *m.* exodus. *2* (cap.) BIB. Exodus.
exoneración *f.* exoneration. *2* dismissal, deposal.

exonerar *tr.* to exonerate. *2* to unburden. *3* to dismiss, depose, deprive of office.
exorar *tr.* to beg, entreat.
exorbitancia *f.* exorbitance, exorbitancy.
exorbitante *adj.* exorbitant.
exorcismo *m.* exorcism.
exorcizar *tr.* to exorcise.
exordio *m.* exordium.
exornar *tr.* to adorn, embellish.
exósmosis *f.* PHYS. exosmosis.
exotérico, -ca *adj.* exoteric.
exótico, -ca *adj.* exotic, foreign. *3* odd, bizarre.
exotismo *m.* exoticism.
expansibilidad *f.* PHYS. expansibility.
expansión *f.* PHYS., ANAT., BOT. expansion. *2* emotional effusion. *3* relaxation, recreation.
expansionarse *ref.* to open one's heart.
expansivo, -va *adj.* PHYS. expansive. *2* expansive, effusive.
expatriación *f.* expatriation.
expatriarse *ref.* to expatriate [leave one's country].
expectación *f.* expectancy, suspense.
expectante *adj.* expectant.
expectativa *f.* expectancy, hope. *2 a la ~*, on the look out.
expectoración *f.* expectoration.
expectorar *tr.* to expectorate.
expedición *f.* dispatch, shipment. *2* issuance [of a certificate, etc.]. *3* expedition, dispatch, speed, ease, readiness. *4* [military, scientific, etc.] expedition.
expedicionario, -ria *adj.* expeditionary. *2 m.-f.* expeditionist.
expedidor, -ra *adj.* sender, dispatcher, shipper. *2* issuer [of a certificate, etc.].
expediente *m.* action, proceeding: *formar ~ a uno*, to investigate an official's conduct. *2* dossier, file of papers bearing on a case. *3* device, resource, expedient. *4* excuse, motive, reason. *5* *cubrir el ~*, to keep up appearances.
expedienteo *m.* red tape [in public business].
expedir *tr.* to issue [a certificate, etc.]. *2* to send, ship. *3* to expedite, dispatch. ¶ CONJUG. like *servir*.
expeditivo, -va *adj.* expeditious, expeditive.
expedito, -ta *adj.* clear, free from encumbrance, open [way, etc.]. *2* expeditious. *3* ready to act.
expeler *tr.* to expel, eject, throw out.
expendedor, -ra *adj.* spending. *2 m.-f.* spender. *3* seller, retailer. *4 ~ de moneda falsa*, counterfeit distributor.
expendeduría *f.* [tobacco] shop.
expender *tr.* to spend. *2* to sell, retail. *3* to pass [counterfeit money].
expendición *f.* sale, retailing. *2* spending. *3* distribution [of counterfeit money].
expensas *f. pl.* expenses: *a ~ de*, at the expense of.
experiencia *f.* experience [knowledge, skill, etc., resulting from experience]. *2* experiment.
experimentación *f.* experimentation.
experimentado, -da *adj.* experienced [person].
experimental *adj.* experimental.
experimentar *tr.* to experiment, test, try. *2* to experience, feel, undergo.
experto, -ta *adj.* expert, skilful. *2 m.* expert.
expiación *f.* expiation, atonement.
expiar *tr.* to expiate.
expiatorio, -ria *adj.* expiatory.
expido, expida, etc. *irr.* V. EXPEDIR.
expiración *f.* expiration, end.

expirar *intr.* to expire [come to an end; die].
explanación *f.* levelling, grading [of ground]. *2* explanation, elucidation.
explanada *f.* esplanade.
explanar *tr.* to level, grade [ground]. *2* to explain, elucidate.
explayar *tr.* to extend, widen, dilate. *2 ref.* to extend, spread out; to dwell [upon a subject]. *3* to amuse oneself. *4* to open one's heart.
expletivo, -va *adj.-m.* expletive.
explicable *adj.* explicable, explainable, accountable.
explicación *f.* explanation. *2* accounting for.
explicar *tr.* to explain, expound. *2* to account for. *3 ref.* to express oneself. *4* to explain oneself. *5 explicarse una cosa,* to account for a thing.
explicativo, -va *adj.* explanatory.
explícito, -ta *adj.* explicit.
exploración *f.* exploration. *2* scanning [of the horizon, etc.]. *3* MIL. scouting.
explorador *m.-f.* explorer. *2 m.* MIL. scout. *4* boy scout. *5* TELEV. scanning disk.
explorar *tr.* to explore. *2* to scan [the horizon, etc.]. *3* MIL. to scout.
exploratorio, -ria *adj.* exploratory.
explosión *f.* explosion [exploding; outburst]: *hacer* ~, to explode; *motor de* ~, combustion engine. *2* PHON. explosion. *3* MIN. blast.
explosivo, -va *adj.* explosive.
explotación *f.* exploitation. *2* development [of natural resources], cultivation [of soil]; working [of a mine]. *3* works, plantation, etc.
explotar *tr.* to run, operate, work, exploit [a business, mine, etc.]; to develop [natural resources]; to cultivate [soil]. *2* to exploit [a person].
expoliación *f.* spoliation.
expondré, expondría, etc. *irr.* V. EXPONER.
exponente *m.-f.* exponent, expounder. *2 m.* MATH. exponent.
exponer *tr.* to expound, explain, set forth, state. *2* to expose, show, put on view. *3* to exhibit [goods, painting, etc.]. *4* PHOT. to expose. *5* to expose [put in danger], imperil, jeopardize; to stake. *6* to expose [an infant]. *7 ref.* to expone oneself. ¶ CONJUG. like *poner.*
expongo, exponga, etc. *irr.* V. EXPONER.
exportable *adj.* exportable.
exportación *f.* exportation, export: *derechos de* ~, export duties.
exportador, -ra *adj.* exporting. *2 m.-f.* exporter.
exportar *tr.* to export.
exposición *f.* exposition, expounding, explanation, statement. *2* address, petition. *3* exposition, exposure. *4* PHOT. exposure. *5* peril, risk, jeopardy. *6* exposition, public exhibition, show.
expositivo, -va *adj.* expositive.
expósito *m.-f.* foundling.
expositor, -ra *adj.* expounding. *2* exhibiting. *3 m.-f.* expositor, expunder. *4* exhibitor.
exprés *m.* express [train]. *2* espresso [coffee].
expresado, -da *adj.* aforesaid.
expresamente *adv.* expressly. *2* on purpose.
expresar *tr.* to express [in words, etc.]. *2 ref.* to express oneself.
expresión *f.* expression. *2* expressiveness. *3* squeezing [of fruits, etc.]. *4 pl.* regards.
expresivo, -va *adj.* expressive. *2* affectionate, kind.
expreso, -sa *adj.* expressed. *2* express. *3 m.* RLY. express. *4* express messenger.
exprimidera *f.* squeezer, lemon squeezer.
exprimidor *m.* squeezer.

exprimir *tr.* to express, squeeze, press out, wring, wring out. *2* to express, state, show.
ex profeso *adv.* expressly; on purpose.
expropiación *f.* expropriation.
expropiar *tr.* to expropriate.
expuesto, -ta *p. p.* of EXPONER. *2 adj.* exposed. *3* on view, exhibited. *4* liable, open [to]; in danger. *5* dangerous, hazardous.
expugnable *adj.* expugnable, pregnable.
expugnar *tr.* MIL. to take by storm.
expulsar *tr.* to expel, eject, drive out. *2* to remove from membership; to cashier.
expulsión *f.* expulsion.
expulsor *m.* ejector [of firearm].
expurgación *f.* expurgation.
expuse, expusiera, etc. *irr.* V. EXPONER.
exquisitez *f.* exquisiteness, excellence.
exquisito, -ta *adj.* exquisite [of consummate excellence or beauty]; delicious.
extasiarse *ref.* to go into ecstasies, be enraptured.
éxtasis *m.* ecstasy, rapture. *2* MED. ecstasy.
extático, -ca *adj.* ecstatic.
extemporáneo, -a *adj.* untimely, inopportune.
extender *tr.* to spread, extend. *2* to spread out, unfold. *3* to stretch out [a limb]. *4* to extend, make extensive, enlarge, widen, expand. *5* to draw up [a document]. *6 ref.* to extend spread; become extensive; become general or popular. *7* to stretch, extend [in time or space], to reach. *8* to expatiate, speak at lenght. ¶ CONJUG. like *entender.*
extensamente *adv.* extensively, at length.
extensible *adj.* extensible.
extensión *f.* extension, extending. *2* extent; range. *3* expanse, stretch. *4* length [of a discourse, etc.]. *5* GEOM., LOG., GRAM. extension.
extensivo, -va *adj.* ample, loose [sense]. *2* extensive.
extenso, -sa *adj.* extensive, vast. *2* long, lengthy: *por* ~, extensively, at length.
extenuación *f.* emaciation, wasting, exhaustion.
extenuar *tr.* to emaciate, exhaust, weaken, wear out. *2 ref.* to exhaust oneself.
exterior *adj.* exterior, external, outer, outside, outward. *2* foreing [commerce, debt, etc.]. *3 m.* exterior, outside. *4* [personal] appearance. *5* foreing countries.
exterioridad *f.* externals, outside things. *2* outward appearance, outward show. *3 pl.* pomp, show.
exteriorizar *tr.* to externalize, reveal, show, make manifest. *2 ref.* to apear outwardly.
exterminador, -ra *adj.* exterminating. *2 m.-f.* exterminator.
exterminar *tr.* to exterminate.
exterminio *m.* extermination.
externado *m.* day school.
externo, -na *adj.* external, outside. *2* day [scholar, pupil]. *3 m.-f.* day scholar, day pupil.
extinción *f.* extinction, extinguishment.
extinguible *adj.* extinguishable.
extinguir *tr.* to extinguish. *2* to quench, put out [fire, etc.]. *3 ref.* to become extinct; to die, go out.
extinto, -ta *adj.* extinct. *2* (Am.) late, deceased.
extintor *m.* extinctor, fire extinguisher.
extirpación *f.* extirpation.
extirpador, -ra *adj.* extirpating. *2 m.-f.* extirpator. *3 m.* AGR. cultivator [implement].
extirpar *tr.* to extirpate.
extorsión *f.* extortion. *2* damage, trouble.

extra *adj.* extra. *2 m.* extra [gratuity]. *3 m.-f.* CINEM. extra.

extracción *f.* extraction. 2 birth, origin. 3 drawing numbers [in lottery].

extracorta *adj.* RADIO. ultrashort.

extractar *tr.* to abstract, epitomize.

extracto *m.* abstract, summary. *2* PHARM. extract.

extractor, -ra *adj.* extracting. *2 m.-f.* extractor [person]. *3 m.* extractor [device, machine].

extradición *f.* extradition.

extradós *m.* ARCH. extrados.

extraer *tr.* to extract, draw out. *2* MATH. to extract [a root]. ¶ CONJUG. like *traer.*

extraigo, extraiga, extraje, etc. *irr.* V. EXTRAER.

extrajudicial *adj.* extrajudicial.

extralimitarse *ref.* to overstep one's power or authority, exceed the limit, go too far.

extramuros *adv.* outside the town or city.

extranjerismo *m.* foreignism.

extranjerizar *tr.* to introduce foreign customs in. *2 ref.* to adopt foreign ways.

extranjero, -ra *adj.* foreign [of another country], outlandish. *2 m.-f.* alien, foreigner. *3 m.* any foreign country: *al* or *en el* ~, abroad.

extranjis (de) *adv.* secretly.

extrañamiento *m.* banishment, exile.

extrañar *tr.* to banish, exile. 2 to surprise: *me extraña su actitud,* I am surprised at his attitude. 3 not to feel at home in [an unfamiliar place, etc.]. *4 ref.* to exile oneself. 5 *extrañarse de,* to be surprised, or wonder, at.

extrañeza *f.* strangeness, oddity. 2 wonder, surprise, astonishment.

extraño, -ña *adj.* strange, foreign, alien, extraneous. 2 strange, odd, queer, peculiar.

extraoficial *adj.* extraofficial, unofficial.

extraordinario *adj.* extraordinary, uncommon. 2 *m.* extra dish [at a meal]. 3 special messenger or courier.

extrarradio *m.* outskirts [of a town].

extraterritorial *adj.* extraterritorial.

extraterritorialidad *f.* extraterritoriality.

extravagancia *f.* oddness, wildness, folly, nonsense.

extravagante *adj.* odd, queer, wild, nonsensical.

extravasarse *ref.* to extravasate.

extraversión *f.* PSICH. extroversion.

extraviado, -da *adj.* out-of-the-way.

extraviar *tr.* to lead astray. 2 to mislay. *3* ~ *la vista, la mirada,* to have a set unseeing look. *4 ref.* to stray, to miss or lose one's way, to get lost. 5 to be mislaid. 6 [of a letter] to miscarry. 6 to go astray.

extravío *m.* straying, going astray. 2 mislaying, loss. 3 error, wrong, disorderly life.

extremado, -da *adj.* extreme, extremely good or bad.

extremar *tr.* to carry to extremes, carry to the limit. *2 ref.* to do one's best, strive hard.

extremaunción *f.* ECCL. extreme unction.

extremeño, -ña *adj.-n.* Extremenian.

extremidad *f.* extremity, end, tip. 2 extremity [the highest degree]. *3 pl.* extremities [limbs, hands, feet].

extremismo *m.* extremism.

extremista *adj.-n.* extremist.

extremo, -ma *adj.* extreme. 2 great, excessive. *3 m.* extreme, tip, end, extremity. 4 extreme, extremity [highest degree]; *en, con* or *por* ~, extremely, very much; *hasta tal* ~, to such a point. 5 utmost care. 6 point [of a conversation, letters, etc.]. 7 MATH., LOG. extreme. *8 pl. hacer extremos,* to make a great show [of pain, joy, love, etc.], to gush.

extremoso, -sa *adj.* demonstrative, effusive.

extrínseco, -ca *adj.* extrinsic.

extroversión *f.* MED. extroversion.

exuberancia *f.* exuberance.

exuberante *adj.* exuberant. 2 luxuriant.

exudar *intr.-ref.* to exude; ooze out.

exultación *f.* exultation.

exultar *intr.* to exult.

exutorio *m.* MED. issue [artificial ulcer].

exvoto *m.* ex-voto, votive offering.

eyaculación *f.* ejaculation.

eyacular *tr.* PHYSIOL. to ejaculate.

Ezequías *m. pr. n.* BIBL. Hezekiah.

Ezequiel *m. pr. n.* BIBL. Ezekiel.

F

F, f *f*. F, f, seventh letter of the Spanish alphabet.
fa *m*. MUS. fa.
fabada *f*. in Asturias, stew made of pork and beans.
fabiano, -na *adj.-n*. Fabian.
fabla *f*. literary imitation of Old Spanish.
fábrica *f*. factory, works, mill, plant. 2 manufacture, fabrication, invention. 3 building, fabric. 4 masonry [brick of stone work]. 5 church funds.
fabricación *f*. manufacture, fabrication, make.
fabricante *m*. manufacturer, maker. 2 factory owner.
fabricar *tr*. to make, manufacture. 2 to build. 3 to fabricate, construct, invent, forge.
fabril *adj*. manufacturing; pertaining to factories or workmen.
fabriquero *m*. FABRICANTE. 2 church warden.
fabuco *m*. BOT. beechnut.
fábula *f*. fable. 2 rumor, gossip. 3 talk [of the town]. 4 mythology.
fabulista *m.-f*. fabulist, writer of fables.
fabuloso, -sa *adj*. fabulous. 2 enormous, extraordinary.
faca *f*. curved knife; large pointed knife.
facción *f*. faction. 2 insurgent party. 3 MIL. action, combat. 4 MIL. *estar de* ~, to be on duty. 5 *pl*. features [of the face].
faccioso, -sa *adj*. factious, insurgent. 2 *m*. rebel.
faceta *f*. facet.
facial *adj*. facial. 2 intuitive.
fácil *adj*. easy, facile. 2 easy, fluent [speech, style]. 3 probable, likely. 4 frail, wanton [woman].
facilidad *f*. ease, easiness, facility: ~ *de palabra*, fluency. 2 *pl*. facilities: *facilidades de pago*, easy payments.
facilitar *tr*. to facilitate, make easy, expedite. 2 to furnish, provide with.
facilón, -na *adj*. coll. dead easy, very simple.
facineroso, -sa *m.-f*. habitual criminal. 2 villain, evil person.
facistol *m*. lectern, chorister's desk.
facón *m*. (Am.) gaucho's knife.
facsímil, facsimile *m*. facsimile.
factible *adj*. feasible, practicable.
facticio, -cia *adj*. factitious, artificial.
factitivo, -va *adj*. GRAM. factitive.

factor *m*. COM. factor, agent. 2 RLY. luggage clerk. 3 factor [for a result]. 4 MATH. factor.
factoría *f*. COM. factorage, agency. 2 commercial factory; commercial establishment in a colony.
factótum *m*. factotum. 2 busybody.
factura *f*. facture, execution. 2 COM. invoice, bill.
facturación *f*. invoicing, billing. 2 RLY. registration [of luggage].
facturar *tr*. COM. to invoice, to bill. 2 RLY. to register [luggage]; to remit [goods] by rail.
fácula *f*. ASTR. facula.
facultad *f*. faculty. 2 power, permission. 3 ability, skill. 4 science, art. 5 branch or college [of University]. 6 *pl. facultades del alma*, mental powers.
facultar *tr*. to empower, authorize.
facultativo *adj*. facultative, optional. 2 [pertaining to a] faculty. 3 *adj.-n*. professional. 4 *m*. doctor, physician, surgeon.
facundia *f*. fluency, eloquency.
facundo, -da *adj*. fluent, eloquent.
facha *f*. appearance, look. 2 ridiculous figure, fright. 3 NAUT. *ponerse en* ~, to lie to.
fachada *f*. ARCH. façade, front. 2 appearance [of a person].
fachenda *f*. vanity, ostentation. 2 *m*. boaster.
fachendear *intr*. to boast, show off.
fachendoso, -sa *adj*. vain, boastful, ostentatious. 2 *m.-f*. boaster.
fachoso, -sa *adj*. odd-looking, weird-looking. 2 (Am.) swanky, snooty, conceited.
fado *m*. Portuguese popular song.
faena *f*. work, toil. 2 task, job, *chore.
faenar *intr*. to fish.
faetón *m*. phaeton.
fagocito *m*. PHYSIOL. phagocyte.
fagot *m*. MUS. bassoon.
faisán *m*. ORN. pheasant.
faisana *f*. hen pheasant.
faja *f*. sash, scarf [around the waist]; girder. 2 swaddling band. 3 newspaper, wrapper. 4 stripe, band, zone. 5 strip [of land]. 6 ARCH. fascia.
fajamiento *m*. banding, bandaging. 2 swaddling.
fajar *tr*. to band, bandage, girdle. 2 to swaddle.
fajín *m*. sash [worn by generals, etc., with their civilian clothes].

fajina f. brushwood, kindling. 2 FORT. fascine. 3 MIL. call to mess; call to quarters.
fajo m. bundle, sheaf, roll.
falacia f. fallacy, deception, deceit. 2 deceitfulness.
falange f. phalanx. 2 ANAT., ZOOL. phalange, phalanx. 3 (cap.) POL. Falange.
falangero m. ZOOL. phalanger.
falangeta f. ANAT. phalangette.
falangina f. ANAT. second phalanx.
falangista adj.-n. POL. Falangist.
falansterio m. phalanstery.
falaz adj. deceitful. 2 deceptive, fallacious.
falcado, -da adj. falcate. 2 carro ~, scythed chariot.
falciforme m. falciform.
falcón m. ARTILL. falcon.
falda f. skirt [of dress; woman's garment]. 2 lap [of a person]. 3 ARM. skirt. 4 BUTCH. plate. 5 foot [of a mountain]. 6 brim [of hat]. 7 pl. skirts; women.
faldamenta f., **faldamento** m. skirt, long skirt.
faldar m. ARM. skirt of tasses.
faldear tr. to skirt [a hill or mountain].
faldero, -ra adj. [pertaining to] skirt. 2 fond of the company of women. 3 lap [dog].
faldillas f. pl. skirts of some dresses.
faldistorio m. faldstool.
faldón m. skirt, tall [of a garment], coat tail. 2 shirt tail. 3 flap [of a saddle]. 4 ARCH. triangular slope [of roof]. 5 mantel [of chimney].
faldriquera f. FALTRIQUERA.
falibilidad f. fallibility.
falible adj. fallible.
fálico adj. phallic.
falo m. phallus.
falsario, -ria adj. liar. 2 forger, counterfeiter.
falsarregla f. bevel square.
falseamiento m. counterfeiting. 2 adulteration, misrepresentation.
falsear tr. to counterfeit, falsify; to misrepresent. 2 CARDS to lead with a low card. 3 to pierce or split [armour]. 4 ARCH. to slant a surface. 5 intr. [of things] to weaken, give way. 7 MUS. [of a string] to be out of tune.
falsedad f. falseness, falsity. 2 falsehood.
falsete m. MUS. falsetto, head voice. 2 plug, spigot [in barrels]. 3 smalll communication door.
falsía f. falseness, duplicity, perfidy.
falsificación f. falsification, forgery.
falsificador, -ra m.-f. falsifier, counterfeiter, forger, faker.
falsificar tr. to falsify, counterfeit, forge, fake.
falsilla f. guide-lines [for writing].
falso, -sa adj. false. 2 untrue. 3 sham, imitated. 4 treacherous, perfidious [person]. 5 vicious [horse]. 6 counterfeit [money]. 7 ~ testimonio, false witness, slander. 8 m. SEW. reinforcement. 9 en ~, falsely. 10 en ~, sobre ~, without proper support. 11 envidiar en ~, to bluff.
falta f. lack, want, abscence, deficiency, shortage: ~ de pago, nonpayment; ~ de respeto, disrespect; a ~ de, lacking, for want of. 2 fail: sin ~, without fail. 3 fault, infraction. 4 absence, non attendance. 5 SPORT. fault. 6 LAW fault, misdeed, slight offence. 7 mistake, error: ~ de ortografía, misspelling. 8 fault, defect, failing. 9 hacer ~, to be necessary, to be needed; me hizo usted mucha ~, I missed you very much.
faltante adj. wanting, missing.
faltar intr. to be lacking, wanting or missing; to be short of: faltan los víveres, victuals are lacking; faltaban dos tenedores, two forks were missing. 2 to die. 3 not to go, not to attend, to be absent from. 4 [of a gun, a rope, etc.] to fail. 5 to be false to, untrue to; to sin or offend against; ~ a la verdad, to lie. 6 to fail somebody; to offend somebody. 7 to break [an appointment, one's word, etc.], fail to fulfil [one's engagement]. 8 impers. faltan tres días para Navidad, it is three days till Christmas; faltó poco para que cayese, he almost fell. 9 falta algo por hacer, something remains to be done. 10 ¡no faltaba más!, that goes without saying!; that would be the last straw!
falto, -ta adj. devoid, wanting, lacking, short: ~ de, devoid of, wanting in, short of, lacking.
faltriquera f. pocket [of a garment].
falúa f. NAUT. barge [of a flagship], harbour tender.
falucho m. NAT. felucca.
falla f. fault, flaw [in things]. 2 GEOL. fault, break. 3 one of the bonfires made in Valencia on St. Joseph's eve.
fallar tr. to judge, pass sentence. 2 to ruff, trump [at cards]. 3 intr. to fail, miss, be deficient or wanting; to fail, break, give way.
falleba f. shutter bolt.
fallecer intr. to decease, die. ¶ CONJUG. like agradecer.
fallecimiento m. decease, death, demise.
fallezco, fallezca, etc. irr. V. FALLECER.
fallido, -da adj. unsuccessful, ineffectual. 2 irrecoverable, uncollectable. 3 adj.-n. bankrupt.
fallo, -lla adj. out of a certain suit [at cards]. 2 m. lack of a certain suit [at cards]. 3 decision, judgment, verdict.
fama f. fame, renown, reputation. 2 report, rumor: es ~, it is said.
famélico, -ca adj. hungry, famished.
familia f. family. 2 household. 3 relatives, kin.
familiar adj. [pertaining to the] family. 2 familiar [well-known]. 3 familiar, unceremonious, informal. 4 colloquial. 5 familiar [spirit]. 6 m. friend; relative. 7 familiar spirit. 8 familiar [of a bishop; of the Inquisition].
familiaridad f. familiarity.
familiarizar tr. to familiarize. 2 ref. familiarizarse con, to familiarize oneself with.
familiarmente adv. familiarly. 2 colloquially.
familión m. aug. large family.
famoso, -sa adj. famous. 2 iron, priceless.
fámula f. coll. maidservant.
fámulo m. famulus. 2 coll. manservant.
fanal m. harbour beacon. 2 light or lamp globe. 3 bell-shaped glass case.
fanático, -ca adj. fanatic(al. 2 m.-f. fanatic.
fanatismo m. fanaticism.
fanatizar tr. to fanaticize.
fandango m. a lively Spanish dance. 2 coll. shindy.
fanega f. grain measure [about 1.60 bu.]. 2 ~ de tierra, land measure [about 1.59 acres].
fanerógamo, -ma adj. BOT. phanerogamous. 2 f. BOT. phanerogam.
fanfarrear intr. FANFARRONEAR.
fanfarria f. coll. bravado, braggadocio, boast.
fanfarrón, -na adj. swaggering, bragging, boasting. 2 m.-f. swaggerer, braggart, boaster.
fanfarronada f. fanfaronade, swagger, boast.
fanfarronear intr. to bluster, boast swagger.
fanfarronería f. blustering, boasting.
fanfurriña f. pet, huff.
fangal, fangar m. miry place, mudhole, slough.

fango *m.* mud, mire.

fangoso, -sa *adj.* muddy, miry.

fantasear *intr.* to let one's imagination run free. *2* to boast. *3 tr.* to fancy, imagine.

fantasía *f.* fancy, imagination. *2* fancy [mental image]. *3* fantastic fiction, tale, etc. *4* vanity, airs, conceit. *6* MUS. fantasía. *7 de* ~, fancy, not plain.

fantasioso, -sa *adj.* vain, conceited.

fantasma *m.* phantom. *2* ghost, apparition. *3* solemn, conceited person. *4* TELEV. ghost.

fantasmagoría *f.* phantasmagoria.

fantasmagórico, -ca *adj.* phantasmagoric.

fantasmal *adj.* phantasmal, ghostly, irreal. *2* phantasmal [of ghosts].

fantasmón, -na *m.* solemn, conceited person.

fantástico, -ca *adj.* fantastic, fanciful. *2* vain, conceited.

fantoche *m.* puppet, marionette. *2* coll. jackanapes; ridiculous and presumptuous fellow.

faquín *m.* porter, carrier, street porter.

faquir *m.* fakir.

farad, faradio *m.* ELEC. farad.

faralá *m.* SEW. flounce. *2* tawdry ornament.

farallón *m.* cliff, headland. *2* MIN. outcrop.

faramalla *f.* blarney, eyewash, claptrap. *2* empty show, hollow sham. *3* coll. blarneyer, boaster.

faramallero, -ra *adj.* coll. tattling, blarneying. *2 m.-f.* tattler, blarneyer.

farandola *f.* farandole [dance].

farándula *f.* obs. profession of farce players. *2* troupe of strolling players. *3* FARAMALLA.

farandulear *intr.* to boast, show off.

farandulero, -ra *m.-f.* comedian. *2* blarneyer.

faraón *m.* Pharaoh. *2* faro [card game].

faraónico, -ca *adj.* Pharaonic.

faraute *m.* herald, messenger.

fardar *tr.* to outfit, to dress. *2* to be classy: *farda mucho este coche,* this car looks classy. *3* to show off, to swank, to boast.

fardel *m.* bundle, package.

fardo *m.* bundle, bale, package.

farfallón *adj.* bungler, botcher.

farfante, farfantón *m.* braggadocio, boaster.

fárfara *f.* shell membrane [of egg].

farfolla *f.* husk [of Indian corn]. *2* empty show.

farfulla *f.* spluttering, shuttering. *2 m.-f.* splutterer, slutterer.

farfullar *tr.* fo splutter, stutter. *2* to stumble through [a task, etc.].

farináceo, -a *adj.* farinaceous.

faringe *f.* ANAT. pharynx.

faríngeo, -a *adj.* pharyngeal.

faringitis *f.* MED. pharyngitis.

farisaico, -ca *adj.* pharisaic(al. *2* Pharisaic.

farisaísmo, fariseísmo *m.* pharisaism. *2* Pharisaism.

fariseo *m.* pharise. *2* Pharisee.

farmacéutico, -ca *adj.* pharmaceutic(al. *2 m.-f.* chemist, *druggist, pharmacist, apothecary.

farmacia *f.* pharmacy. *2* chemist's, *drug-store.

fármaco *m.* medicine.

farmacopea *f.* pharmacopoeia.

faro *m.* lighthouse, beacon: ~ *aéreo,* air beacon. *2* headlight [of car]: ~ *piloto,* spotlight.

farol *m.* street lamp, lamppost. *2* lantern. *3* carriage lamp. *4* NAUT. light: ~ *de situación,* position light. *5* boaster, show-off. *6* bluff: *echar un* ~, to bluff. *7* a feat in bullfighting.

farola *f.* many-branched lamppost. *2* harbour beacon.

farolear *intr.* to show off, to boast.

farolería *f.* lantern shop. *2* showing off, boast.

farolero, -ra *adj.* showing off, boasting. *2 m.* lamplighter. *3* show-off; boaster.

farolillo *m.* dim. small lantern. *2* BOT. Canterbury bell. *3* BOT. heartseed.

farolón *m.* FAROLERO 3. *2* large lamp of lantern.

farpa *f.* point of a scallop.

farra *f.* ICHTH. lavaret. *2* (Am.) spree, revelry.

fárrago *m.* farrago, medley.

farragoso, -sa *adj.* confused, disordered.

farraguista *m.-f.* muddlehead.

farro *m.* barley soaked, peeled and broken.

farruco, -ca *adj.* bold, fearless.

farsa *f.* THEAT. farce. *2* troupe of farce players. *3* farce, empty show, mockery, humbug.

farsante *adj.-n.* THEAT. farce player. *2* hypocrite.

fas *por* ~ or *por nefas,* rightly or wrongly, for one thing or for another.

fasces *f. pl.* fasces.

fascículo *m.* fascicle, instalment [of a book]. *2* ANAT. fascicle.

fascinación *f.* fascination, bewitching, spell.

fascinador, -ra *adj.* fascinating. *2 m.-f.* fascinator.

fascinante *adj.* fascinating.

fascinar *tr.* to fascinate, bewitch.

fascismo *m.* Fascism.

fascista *adj.* fascist, fascistic. *2 m.-f.* fascist.

fase *f.* phase.

fastidiar *tr.* to cloy, sicken. *2* to do a bad turn to. *3* to bore. *4 ref.* to become annoyed or bored; to be disappointed.

fastidio *m.* distaste, nausea. *2* annoyance, botheration. *3* boredom, ennui.

fastidioso, -sa *adj.* cloying. *2* annoying, bothersome. *3* boring, tedious, tiresome.

fastigio *m.* apex, summit. *2* ARCH. fastigium.

fasto, -ta *adj.* lucky, happy [day, year]. *2 m.* pomp, magnificence. *3 pl.* fasti.

fastuoso, -sa *adj.* pompous, magnificent.

fatal *adj.* fatal, unavoidable. *2* fateful. *3* bad, evil, deadly, destructive. *4* LAW unpostponable.

fatalidad *f.* fatality. *2* mischance, misfortune.

fatalismo *m.* fatalism.

fatídico, -ca *adj.* fatidic, ominous.

fatiga *f.* fatigue [weariness, labour, toil]. *2* hard breathing. *3 pl.* hardships, pains, anguish.

fatigante *adj.* fatiguing, tiring, annoying.

fatigar *tr.* to fatigue, weary, tire. *2* to annoy, harass. *3 ref.* to get tired, weary oneself.

fatigoso, -sa *adj.* fatiguing, wearisome. *2* hard [breathing].

fatuidad *f.* fatuity, stupidity. *2* foolishness, inanity. *3* ridiculous, presumption.

fatuo, -tua *adj.* fatuous, half-witted. *2* vain, conceited.

fauces *f. pl.* ANAT. fauces.

fauna *f.* fauna.

fauno *m.* MYTH. faun.

fausto, -ta *adj.* happy, fortunate [event, etc.]. *2 m.* pomp, magnificence.

fautor, -ra *adj.* helper, abettor.

favor *m.* help, succour. *2* favour, service, good turn: *hacer el* ~ *de,* to do [one] the favour of. *3* favour, good will, good graces. *4* favour [ribbon, etc.]. *5 a* ~ *de,* for, pro, in favour of; *a* ~ *del viento,* with the wind [taking advantage of the wind]; *a* ~ *de la oscuridad,* under cover of darkness.

favorable *adj.* favourable. *2* advantageous.

favorecedor, -ra *adj.* favouring. *2 m.-f.* favourer. *3* helper, supported. *4* client, customer.
favorecer *tr.* to help, aid, favour. *2* to favour, support. *3* to bestow a favour to. *4* to become, improve the appearance of. ¶ CONJUG. like *agradecer.*
favorezco, favorezca, etc. *irr.* V. FAVORECER.
favoritismo *m.* favoritism.
favorito, -ta *adj.* favorite, preferred, best liked, pet. *2 m.-f.* favorite.
faz *f.* face, visage. *2* face, aspect. *3* obverse.
fe *f.* faith: *dar* or *prestar ~ a,* to give credit to, to believe; *tener ~ en,* to have faith in; *de buena ~,* in good faith; *a ~ mía,* upon my faith. *2* assurance, certification: *~ de bautismo,* certificate of baptism; *dar ~,* to attest, to certify; *hacer ~,* to be a valid assurance or certification. *3* PRINT. *~ de erratas,* errata, list of errata.
fealdad *f.* ugliness, hideousness. *2* plainness, homeliness. *3* badness, foulness [of deeds, words, etc.].
Febe *f. pr. n.* MYTH. Phœbus.
febrero *m.* February.
febricitante *adj.* MED. feverish.
febrífugo, -ga *adj.-m.* febrifuge.
febril *adj.* febrile. *2* feverish.
fecal *adj.* faecal, fecal.
fécula *f.* fecula, starch.
feculento, -ta *adj.* starchy [food]. *2* feculent.
fecundación *f.* fecundation.
fecundante *adj.* fecundating.
fecundar *tr.* to fecundate, to fertilize.
fecundidad *f.* fecundity, fertility.
fecundizar *tr.* to fertilize.
fecundo, -da *adj.* fecund. *2* abundant.
fecha *f.* date [time]: *con ~ de,* under date of; *hasta la ~,* to date. *2* day [elapsed].
fechar *tr.* to date [a letter, etc.].
fechoría *f.* misdeed, villainy.
federación *f.* federation.
federal *adj.* federal. *2* federalistic.
federalismo *m.* federalism.
federar *tr.* to federate, federalize. *2 ref.* to federate [become federated].
federativo, -va *adj.* federative.
Federica *f. pr. n.* Frederica.
Federico *m. pr. n.* Frederick.
Fedra *f. pr. n.* MYTH. Phaedra.
fehaciente *adj.* LAW. authentic.
feldespato *m.* MINER. feldspar.
felice *adj.* poet. happy.
felicidad *f.* felicity, happiness. *2* good fortune.
felicitación *f.* felicitation, congratulation.
felicitar *tr.* to felicitate, wish joy to, congratulate.
félidos *m.* ZOOL. Felidœ.
feligrés, -sa *m.-f.* ECCL. parishioner.
feligresía *f.* parish.
felino, -na *adj.* feline. *2 m.* ZOOL. feline.
Felipe *m. pr. n.* Philip.
feliz *adj.* happy, fortunate. *2* felicitous.
felón, -na *adj.* perfidious, treacherous, felonious. *2 m.-f.* traitor, felon, wicked person.
felonía *f.* perfidy, treachery, felony.
felpa *f.* plush. *2* coll. drubbing. *3* reprimand.
felpilla *f.* chenille.
felpudo, -da *adj.* plushy. *2 m.* plush mat, doormat.
femenil *adj.* feminine, womanish.
femenino, -na *adj.* female, feminine. *2* GRAM. feminine.
fementido, -da *adj.* false, unfaithful, treacherous.
femineidad *f.* feminity.

feminismo *m.* feminism.
feminista *adj.* feminist, feministic. *2 m.-f.* feminist.
femoral *adj.* femoral.
fémur *m.* ANAT. ENT. femur.
fenecer *tr.* to finish, conclude. *2 intr.* to die. *3* to come to an end. ¶ CONJUG. like *agradecer.*
fenecimiento *m.* death. *2* finish, termination.
fenezco, fenezca, etc. *irr.* V. FENECER.
fenianismo *m.* Fenianism.
feniano *m.* Fenian.
fenicado, -da *adj.* carbolized.
Fenicia *f. pr. n.* Phoenicia.
fenicio, -cia *adj.-n.* Phoenician.
fénico *adj.* CHEM. phenic, carbolic.
fénix *m.* MYTH. phœnix. *2* fig. phœnix, paragon.
fenol *m.* CHEM. phenol.
fenomenal *adj.* phenomenal. *2* great, enormous.
fenómeno *m.* phenomenon. *2* monster, freak.
feo, -a *adj.* ugly. *2* plain, homely. *3* unbecoming. *4* bad, dirty [word, deed]. *5* bad, serious, alarming. *6 m.* slight, affront.
feracidad *f.* feracity, fertility.
feraz *adj.* feracious, fertile.
féretro *m.* bier, coffin.
feria *f.* fair [gathering, exhibition]. *2* deal, agreement. *3* ECCL. feria. *4* rest, holiday.
ferial *adj.* ferial. *2 m.* fair; fairground.
feriante *adj.* fairgoing. *2 m.-f.* fairgoer. *3* trader at fairs.
feriar *tr.* to buy at a fair. *2* to buy, sell or barter.
ferino, -na *adj.* ferine. *2* MED. whooping [cough].
fermentación *f.* fermentation.
fermentar *intr.* to ferment. *2 tr.* to produce fermentation.
fermento *m.* CHEM. ferment.
Fernando *m. pr. n.* Ferdinand.
ferocidad *f.* ferocity.
feroz *adj.* ferocious. *2* fig. ravenous.
ferrar *tr.* to put an iron on; to garnish, cover or shoe with iron. ¶ CONJUG. like *acertar.*
férreo, -a *adj.* ferreous, iron: *vía férrea,* railroad. *2* strong, harsh, severe.
ferrería *f.* ironworks, foundry.
ferretería *f.* FERRERÍA. *2* ironmongery. *3* hardware.
ferretero, -ra *m.-f.* hardware dealer.
férrico, -ca *adj.* CHEM. ferric.
ferrocarril *m.* railway, railroad: *~ aéreo,* aerial railway; *~ de cremallera,* rack railway; *~ funicular,* funicular railway.
ferrocianuro *m.* CHEM. ferrocyanide.
ferroso, -sa *adj.* CHEM. ferrous.
ferroviario *adj.* [pertaining to the] railway, railroad. *2 m.* railwayman, *railroader.
ferruginoso, -sa *adj.* ferruginous.
fértil *adj.* fertile.
fertilidad *f.* fertility.
fertilizante *adj.* fertilizing. *2 m.* fertilizer.
fertilizar *tr.* to fertilize [the soil].
férula *f.* ferule. *2* fig. authority, rule, yoke. *3* BOT. giant, fennel. *4* SURG. flexible splint.
férvido, -da *adj.* fervid, ardent.
ferviente *adj.* FERVOROSO.
fervor *m.* fervour.
fervorín *m.* short prayer.
fervoroso, -sa *adj.* fervent.
festejar *tr.* to feast, fête, celebrate, honour with a celebration. *2* to court, to woo.
festejo *m.* fête, fêting. *2* courting, courtship. *3 pl.* public rejoicings.
festín *m.* feast, banquet.

festival *m.* festival.
festividad *f.* feast, celebration. *2* feast day, holiday. *3* humour, esprit.
festivo, -va *adj.* humourous, witty. *2* merry, joyful. *3 día ~,* feast day, holiday.
festón *m.* festoon. *2* scalloped border.
festonar, festonear *tr.* to festoon. *2* to scallop.
fetal *adj.* fœtal, fetal.
fetén *adj.* coll. fantastic, terrific, smashing, super. *2* hundred per cent, through and through, from head to toe.
fetiche *m.* fetish.
fetichismo *m.* fetishism.
fetidez *f.* fetidity: *~ de aliento,* foul breath.
fétido, -da *adj.* fetid. *2* foul [breath].
feto *m.* fœtus, fetus.
feúco, ca; feúcho, -cha *adj.* rather ugly, plain.
feudal *adj.* feudal. *2* feudalistic.
feudalismo *m.* feudalism.
feudatario, -ria *adj.-n.* feudatory.
feudo *m.* LAW feud, fief. *2* vassalage.
fez *m.* fez.
fi *f.* phi [greek letter].
fiable *adj.* trustworthy, responsible.
fiado *m. al ~,* on credit.
fiador, -ra *m.-f.* guarantor, surety, bail: *salir ~,* to stand surety. *2* safety cord, strap; safety catch; catch, pawl, stop.
fiambre *adj.* cold [meat]. *2* fig. stale [news, etc.]. *3 m.* cold meat, cold cut.
fiambrera *f.* lunch basket. *2* dinner pail.
fiambrería *f.* (Am.) sausage store, coldmeat store. *2* (Am.) delicatessen store.
fianza *f.* bail, guaranty, security, bond: *bajo ~,* on bail. *2* guarantor, guarantee, surety, bond.
fiar *tr.* to answer for, go surety for; to bail. *2* to entrust, confide. *3 tr.-intr.* to sell on credit. *4 intr.* to trust: *~ en,* to trust in. *5 ref. fiarse de,* to trust, to rely on.
fiasco *m.* failure, fiasco.
fiat *m.* fiat.
fibra *f.* fibre, fiber; staple. *2* grain [of wood]. *3* fig. energy, vigour, stamina.
fibrilla *f.* fibril.
fibrina *f.* CHEM. fibrin, fibrine.
fibroma *m.* MED. fibroma.
fibroso, -sa *adj.* fibrous.
fíbula *f.* ARCHEOL. fibula.
ficción *f.* fiction.
ficticio, -cia *adj.* fictitious.
ficha *f.* counter, chip. *2* domino [piece]. *3* filing card: *~ catalográfica,* index card [of a library].
fichar *tr.* to play [a domino]. *2* to file particulars of [a person] in the police record.
fichero *m.* card index; filing cabinet.
fideicomiso *m.* LAW fideicommissum.
fidelidad *f.* fidelity, faithfulness, loyalty. *2* fealty. *3* fidelity, faithfulness, accuracy.
fideos *m. pl.* vermicelli.
fiduciario, -ria *adj.-n.* fiduciary.
fiebre *f.* MED. fever. *2* fever, excitement, agitation.
fiel *adj.* faithful, loyal, true, trustworthy. *2* faithful, true, accurate. *3 m.* faithful [church member]. *4* pointer [of scales]. *5* public inspector: *~ contraste,* inspector of weights and measures; hallmarker.
fielato *m.* office of the FIEL. *2* octroi [office].
fieltro *m.* felt. *2* felt hat. *3* felt rug.
fiera *f.* wild beast. *2* BULLF. bull. *3* cruel, fierce person. *4 ser una ~ para,* to be the devil for [work, etc.].

fierabrás *m.* devil [wicked person or child].
fiereza *f.* fierceness, cruelty, ferocity. *2* ugliness.
fiero, -ra *adj.* fierce, cruel, ferocious. *2* wild [beast]. *3* ugly, hideous. *4* great, violent. *5* rough, rude. *6 m.* bluster, threat: *echar fieros,* to bluster, to threaten.
fiesta *f.* feast, entertainment, party: fête, festival, public rejoicing; *la ~ brava, la ~ nacional,* bullfight; *fin de ~,* THEAT. grand finale; *aguar la ~,* to spoil the feast; *tengamos la ~ en paz,* let's have no disturbance. *2* feast, holiday, feast day: *~ de guardar* or *de precepto,* holiday of obligation; *~ de la hispanidad, ~ de la raza,* Columbus Day, Discovery Day; *~ del Trabajo,* Labour Day; *~ nacional,* national feast day, bank holiday; *hacer ~,* to take a day off. *3* merrymaking. *4* endearment, caress: *hacer fiestas a,* to caress, fondle; [of a dog, etc.] to fawn on. *5 pl.* holidays. *6* public rejoicings.
fiestero, -ra *adj.* gay, jolly, fond of feasts.
fígaro *m.* fig. barber. *2* short jacket.
figle *m.* MUS. ophicleide. *2* ophicleidist.
figón *m.* cheap eating house.
figulino, -na *adj.* figuline.
figura *f.* figure [external form; person; representation]. *2* figure [of the human body]. *3* figure, drawing. *4* GEOM., F. ARTS, RHET., LOG., GRAM., DANC. figure: *~ retórica,* figure of speech. *5* MUS. note. *6* THEAT. character; actor. *7* ridiculous person. *8* court card. *9 hacer ~,* to cut a figure.
figuración *f.* figuration. *2* imagining; fancy: *eso son figuraciones tuyas,* that's wat you imagine.
figuradamente *adv.* figuratively.
figurado, -da *adj.* figured, represented, imagined. *2* figurative [language, sense, etc.].
figurante, -ta *m.-f.* THEAT. figurant.
figurar *tr.* to figure, depict, represent. *2* to feign. *3 intr.* to be counted [among, in the number of]. *4* to cut a figure. *5 ref.* to fancy, imagine.
figurativo, -va *adj.* figurative, representative.
figurilla *f.* figurine, statuette. *2* small person.
figurín *m.* fashion plate [design; person]. *2* small model [of dress].
figurón *m.* large figure: *~ de proa,* NAUT. figurehead. *2* pretentious nobody.
fijación *f.* fixation, fixing. *2* appointment [of time or place]. *3* posting [of bills]. *4* immobilizing. *5* CHEM., PHOT. fixation.
fijador, -ra *adj.* fixing. *2 m.* fixer, poster. *3* PHOT. fixing bath. *4* PAINT. fixing liquid.
fijamente *adv.* firmly, steadfastly, attentively.
fijar *tr.* to fix, nail, make fast. *2* to stick, paste up, placard, post [bills, etc.]. *3* PHOT., F. ARTS. to fix. *4* to fix, make firm, set, determine. *5 ref.* to become fixed or set. *6* to pay attention, notice, observe.
fijeza *f.* firmness. *2* fixity, steadfastness.
fijo, -ja *adj.* fixed. *2* firm, immovable, set, intent: *mirada fija,* set look. *3* fast [colour]. *4* MACH. stationary. *5 de ~,* surely. *6 ésa es la fija,* that is a fact.
fila *f.* row, line, tier; file: *~ india,* single file, Indian file; *en ~,* in a row; in single file. *2* MIL. rank [of soldiers]: *estar en filas,* to be in the Army. *3* coll. dislike, hatred.
filacteria *f.* phylactery.
Filadelfia *f. pr. n.* GEOG. Philadelphia.
filamento *m.* filament.
filamentoso, -sa *adj.* filamentous.
filandria *f.* ZOOL. filander.
filantropía *f.* philanthropy.

filántropo *m.* philanthropist.
filaria *f.* ZOOL. filaria.
filarmonía *f.* love of music.
filarmónico, -ca *adj.-n.* philharmonic.
filástica *f.* NAUT. rope yarn.
filatelia *f.* philately.
filatélico, -ca *adj.* philatelic. 2 *m.-f.* philatelist.
filete *m.* ARCH. fillet, listel. 2 BOOKB., PRINT. fillet, ornamental line. 3 SEW. narrow hem. 4 small spit. 5 MACH. narrow edge; thread [of a screw]. 6 snaffle bit. 7 COOK. fillet. 8 COOK. sirloin.
filetear *tr.* to fillet. 2 BOOKB. to tool.
filfa *f.* lie, humbug, false news.
filiación *f.* filiation. 2 personal description.
filial *adj.* filial. 2 COM. branch, affiliated. 3 *f.* branch of a commercial house.
filiar *tr.* to note down the personal description of. 2 *ref.* to enlist.
filibustero *m.* filibuster, freebooter.
filicales *f. pl.* BOT. Filicales.
filiforme *adj.* filiform, threadlike.
filigrana *f.* filigree. 2 delicate, fanciful thing or work. 3 watermark [in paper].
filipéndula *f.* BOT. dropwort.
filipense *adj.-n.* Philippian. 2 Oratorian.
filípica *f.* Philippic. 2 philippic [invective].
Filipinas *f. pr. n.* GEOG. Philippine [islands].
filipino, -na *adj.-n.* Philippine.
Filipo *m. pr. n.* Philip [of Macedonia].
filisteo, -a *adj.-n.* BIBL. Philistine. 2 *m.* tall, corpulent fellow.
filmación *f.* CINEM. filming.
filmar *tr.* CINEM. to film.
filme *m.* CINEM. film.
filmoteca *f.* film library.
filo *m.* [cutting] edge. 2 point or line dividing something in two equal-parts. 3 NAUT. ~ *del viento*, direction of the wind.
filocomunista *adj.-n.* procommunist.
filodio *m.* BOT. phyllode.
filología, filológica *f.* philology.
filólogo *m.* philologist.
filomela, filomena *f.* poet. philomel, nightingale.
filón *m.* MIN. vein, lode. 2 fig. mine.
filosofal *adj. piedra* ~, philosopher's stone.
filosofar *intr.* to philosophize.
filosofía *f.* philosophy.
filosófico, -ca *adj.* philosophic(al).
filósofo, -fa *adj.* philosophic. 2 *m.* philosopher.
filoxera *f.* ENT. phylloxera.
filtración *f.* filtration. 2 fig. leakage.
filtrador, -ra *adj.* filtering. 2 *m.* filter.
filtrante *adj.* filtering. 2 porous.
filtrar *tr.-intr.* to filtrate, filter, percolate. 2 *intr.* to leak. 3 *ref.* to ooze out or through; [of money] to leak away.
filtro *m.* filter, percolator. 2 ELEC., OPT. filter. 3 seaside fresh-water spring. 4 philtre, philter.
filustre *m.* coll. fineness, elegance.
filló, filloa *f.* kind of pancake.
fimbria *f.* border [of a skirt].
fimosis *f.* MED. phimosis.
fin *m.* end [conclusion, close, finish; extremity]: *dar* ~ *a*, to end, finish; *poner* ~ *a*, to put an end to; *a fines de*, towards the end of; *al* ~, at the end; finally, at last: *al* ~ *y al cabo*, in the end; after all; *en* ~, finally; in short; well [as an expletive]: *por* ~, at last, lastly. 2 end, purpose: *a* ~ *de*, in order to; *a* ~ *de que*, in order that, so that.
finado, -da *adj.* late, deceased. 2 *m.-f.* deceased.

final *adj.* final, last, ultimate. 2 GRAM. final. 3 *m.* end, termination. 4 MUS. finale. 5 *f.* SPORT. finals.
finalidad *f.* PHILOS. finality. 2 end, purpose.
finalista *m.-f.* PHILOS., SPORT finalist.
finalizar *tr.-intr.* to end, finish, conclude.
finamente *adv.* finely, nicely, delicately. 2 politely.
financiar *tr.* to finance.
financiero, -ra *adj.* financial. 2 *m.-f.* financier.
finanzas *f. pl.* finances.
finar *intr.* to die. 2 *ref.* to long, yearn.
finca *f.* property [piece of real estate], land, house, farm, ranch.
fincar *intr.-ref.* to buy up real estate.
finés, -sa *adj.* Finnic, Finnish. 2 *m.* Finnish [language]. 3 *m.-f.* Finn [person].
fineza *f.* fineness [goodness, purity], delicacy, perfection. 2 civility, kindness, favour, little gift.
fingido, -da *adj.* feigned, sham, affected. 2 false, deceitful.
fingidor, -ra *adj.* feigning, dissembling. 2 *m.-f.* feigner, dissembler.
fingimiento *m.* feigning, simulation, pretence.
fingir *tr.* to feign, simulate, sham, pretend. 2 *ref.* to feign to be; to pretend to be.
finiquitar *tr.* to settle, to close [an account]. 2 to finish, conclude, close, end.
finiquito *m.* settlement [of an account].
finito, -ta *adj.* finite.
finlandés, -sa *adj.* Finnish. 2 *m.* Finnish [language]. 3 *m.-f.* Finn, Finlander.
Finlandia *f. pr. n.* GEOG. Finland.
fino, -na *adj.* fine [of high quality; pure, refined]. 2 thin; sheer; slender. 3 polite, wellbred. 4 affectionate, true. 5 shrewd. 6 subtle, nice. 7 sharp [point; sense].
finta *f.* feint [sham attack or blow].
finura *f.* fineness, perfection. 2 politeness, courtesy.
fiord, fiordo *m.* fiord.
fioritura *f.* MUS. fioritura. 2 embellishment.
firma *f.* signature, subscription; hand: ~ *en blanco*, blank signature. 2 [act of] signing. 3 letters, etc., brought to be signed. 4 COM. firm.
firmamento *m.* firmament.
firmante *adj.* signer, subscriber, signatory.
firmar *tr.* to sign, subscribe.
firme *adj.* firm [stable, strong, solid, steady]: *tierra* ~, mainland. 2 steadfast, unflinching. 3 *m.* roadbed. 4 *adv.* firmly. 5 *de* ~, with a will, hard; violently. 6 *en* ~, COM. firm: *oferta en* ~, firm offer. 7 *¡firmes!* MIL. attention!
firmeza *f.* firmness [stability; steadfastness].
firuletes *m. pl.* (Am.) ornaments, elaborate adornments, flourishes.
fiscal *adj.* fiscal. 2 *m.* LAW public prosecutor; *district attorney. 3 busybody, prier. 4 ~ *de tasas*, official in charge of price control.
fiscalía *f.* office and post of a FISCAL.
fiscalización *f.* control, inspection. 2 prying.
fiscalizar *tr.* to control, to inspect. 2 to pry into [somebody's conduct], to censure.
fisco *m.* fisc, fisk, state treasury.
fisga *f.* fish-spear. 2 sly mockery, raillery.
fisgar *tr.* to fish, fish spear. 2 to smell out, pry, peep. 3 *ref. fisgarse de*, to make fun of.
fisgón, -na *m.-f.* sly mocker. 2 prier, peeper.
fisgonear *tr.* to keep prying [into other people's business].
fisgoneo *m.* prying, constant prying.
física *f.* physics.

físico, -ca *adj.* physical. *2 m.* physicist. *3* physique, looks [of a person].
fisicoquímica *f.* physicochemistry.
fisil *adj.* fissile.
fisiócrata *m.-f.* physiocrat.
fisiología *f.* physiology.
fisiológico, -ca *adj.* physiological.
fisiólogo *m.* physiologist.
fisión *f.* PHYS., CHEM. fission.
fisionomía *f.* FISONOMÍA.
fisioterapia *f.* physiotherapy.
fisípedo, -da *adj.-n.* ZOOL. fissiped.
fisirrostro, -tra *adj.* ORN. fissirostral.
fisonomía *f.* physiognomy. *2* features, face.
fisonómico, -ca *adj.* physiognomic(al.
fisonomista *m.-f.*, **fisónomo** *m.* physiognomist. *2* one who has a good memory for faces.
fístula *f.* fistula, tube. *2* MED. fistula.
fistular *adj.* fistular.
fisura *f.* MED., MIN. fissure.
fitófago, -ga *adj.* ZOOL. phytophagous.
fitografía *adj.* phytography.
fitopatología *f.* plant pathology.
flabelífero, -ra *adj.* fan-carrying [in ceremonies].
flabelo *m.* flabellum.
flaccidez *f.* flaccidity, flabbiness.
fláccido, -da *adj.* flaccid, flabby.
flaco, -ca *adj.* lean, thin, lank, meagre. *2* weak, feeble. *3* frail, weak in resolution. *4 m.* weak point, foible.
flacucho, -cha *adj.* rather lean, thinnish.
flacura *f.* leanness, thinness [lack of flesh]. *2* weakness, feebleness.
flagelación *f.* flagellation, scourging.
flagelado, -da *adj.-n.* BIOL., BOT. flagellate.
flagelante *m.-f.* flagellant. *2* Flagellant.
flagelar *tr.* to flagellate, scourge. *2* to lash, flay [vice, etc.].
flagelo *m.* scourge. *2* BIOL. flagellum.
flagrante *adj.* blazing, flaming. *2 en ~* or *en delito*, in the very act.
flama *f.* flame. *2* reverberation.
flamante *adj.* blazing, flaming, brilliant. *2* splendid, magnificent, remarkable. *3* brand new.
flamear *intr.* to flame, blaze. *2* [of flags, etc.] to wave, flutter. *3 tr.* to flame [sterilize with flame].
flamen *m.* flamen.
flamenco, -ca *adj.-n.* Flemish. *2 adj.* Andalousian gypsy [dance, song, etc.]. *3* buxom. *4 m.* Flemish [language]. *5* ORN. flamingo. *6 ponerse ~*, to get cocky.
flamenquería *f.* swagger.
flamígero, -ra poet. flaming. *2* ARCH. flamboyant.
flámula *f.* streamer, pennon.
flan *m.* flan, solid custard.
flanco *m.* flank, side. *2* FORT., MIL., NAV. flank.
Flandes *f. pr. n.* GEOG. Flanders.
flanquear *tr.* to flank.
flanqueo *m.* flanking.
flaquear *intr.* to weaken, give way; to lose strength. *2* fig. to lose heart, weaken, flag.
flaqueza *f.* leanness, emaciation. *2* weakness [lack or strength]. *3* weakness, frailty, failing.
flash *m.* PHOT. flash, flashlight. *2* RADIO. newsflash.
flato *m.* flatus [gas].
flatulencia *f.* flatulence.
flatulento, -ta *adj.* flatulent.
flauta *f.* MUS. flute. *2* flautist, flutist.
flautado, -da *adj.* flutelike. *2 m.* flute [organ stop].
flauteado, -da *adj.* flutelike, sweet.

flautín *m.* MUS. piccolo, octave flute.
flautista *m.* flautist, flutist.
flavo, -va *adj.* flavid, golden yellow.
flébil *adj.* poet. sad, tearful, plaintive.
flebitis *f.* MED. phlebitis.
fleco *m.* fringe [ornamental border]. *2* ragged edge. *3* fringe [of hair].
flecha *f.* arrow. *2* FORT. flèche. *3* ASTR. Sagita. *4* AER. sweepback. *5* ENG., ARCH. deflection [of a beam, etc.].
flechadura *f.* NAUT. ratlines.
flechar *tr.* to fit an arrow to [the bow]. *2* to wound or kill with arrows. *3* coll. to inspire sudden love.
flechaste NAUT. ratline.
flechazo *m.* arrow shot. *2* arrow wound. *3* coll. sudden love, love at first sight.
fleje *m.* iron hoop or strap.
flema *f.* physiol., chem. phlegm. *2* phlegm, calmness: *gastar ~*, to be cold, phlegmatic.
flemático, -ca *adj.* phlegmatic(al.
flemón *m.* MED. phlegmon. *2* MED. gumboil.
flequillo *m.* small fringe. *2* FLECO *3*.
fletador *m.* NAUT. freighter, charterer.
fletamento *m.* NAUT. freightment, charterage. *2* freight, charter party.
fletante *m.* shipowner [in the charter party].
fletar *tr.* NAUT. to freight, charter [a ship].
flete *m.* NAUT. freight, cargo. *2* NAUT. freightage.
flexibilidad *f.* flexibility.
flexible *adj.* flexible, pliant, lithe, supple. *2* soft [hat]. *3 m.* ELEC. cord, flex. *4* soft hat.
flexión *f.* flexion, bending. *2* GRAM. flexion.
flexor, -ra *adj.* bending. *2 m.* ANAT. flexor.
flexuoso, -sa *adj.* flexuous.
flirtear *intr.* to flirt.
flirteo *m.* flirtation.
flocadura *f.* SEW. fringe trimming.
flojamente *adv.* laxly, carelessly, negligently.
flojear *intr.* to slack. *2* to weaken [in one's efforts, etc.]. *3* FLAQUEAR.
flojedad *f.* laxity, weakness. *2* slackness, carelessness.
flojera *f.* FLOJEDAD.
flojo, -ja *adj.* loose [only lightly secured], slack [not tight]; flaccid. *2* weak [wine, tea, etc.]. *3* weak [spring]. *4* light [wind]. *5* lax, careless, negligent.
floqueado, -da *adj.* fringed, trimmed with fringe.
flor *f.* BOT. flower, bloom, blossom; *~ compuesta*, composite flower; *~ de amor*, amaranth; *~ de la maravilla*, tigerflower; *~ de la Trinidad*, pansy; *~ de lis*, fleur-de-lis; *en ~*, in flower, in bloom, in blossom. *2* bloom [dust covering certain fruits]. *3* flower, cream, elite: *la ~ y nata*, the pick and choice, the cream. *4* flowers [of wine]. *5* CHEM. flower: *flores de cinc*, zinc oxide. *6* flower [of life, youth, etc.]: *en la ~ de la edad*, in the prime. *7* METAL. floss. *8* iridescence on quenched metal sheets. *9* compliment, flattering remark: *decir* or *echar flores*, to say flattering things to a lady. *10* a card game. *11* face [of leather]. *12* GAMBLING. trick. *12 a ~*, flush; *a ~ de agua*, close to, or on the surface of, the water; awash; *a ~ de tierra*, close to the ground. *13 dar uno en la ~ de*, to acquire the habit of.
flora *f.* flora. *2* (cap.) MYTH. Flora.
floración *f.* BOT. flowerring, florescence.
floral *adj.* floral. *2 Juegos florales*, Floral Games.
flordelisado, -da *adj.* HER. fleury.
florear *tr.* to flower [decorate with flowers]. *2* to

stack [cards]. *3* to bolt [flour]. *4 intr.* to strike a continuous flourish on the guitar. *5* to vibrate the sword. *6* to pay compliments. *7* (Am.) to choose the best.

florecer *intr.* to flower, bloom, blossom. *2* to flourish, prosper. *3 ref.* to become mouldy. ¶ CONJUG. like *agradecer.*

floreciente *adj.* flowering, florescent. *2* flourishing.

florecimiento *m.* flowering, blossoming. *2* flourishing, prosperity. *3* mouldiness.

Florencia *f. pr. n.* Florence. *2* GEOG. Florence.

florentino, -na *adj.-n.* Florentine.

floreo *m.* idle talk. *2* idle compliment. *3* act of vibrating the sword. *4* continuous flourish on the guitar.

florería *f.* florist's [shop].

florero, -ra *m.-f.* flower seller. *2 m.* flower vase. *3* flower pot, flower box. *4* PAINT. flower piece.

florescencia *f.* MED., CHEM. efflorescence. *2* BOT. florescence.

floresta *f.* pleasant woods or grove.

florete *m.* foil, fencing foil.

florezco, florezca, etc. *irr.* V. FLORECER.

floricultor, -ra *m.-f.* floriculturist.

floricultura *f.* floriculture.

florido, -da *adj.* flowery, blossomy. *2* flowery, florid. *3* choice, select. *4 Pascua florida,* Easter.

florífero, -ra *adj.* floriferous.

florilegio *m.* florilegium, anthology.

florín *m.* florin [coin].

florista *m.-f.* florist, flower seller, flower girl.

florón *m.* ARCH. rosette. *2* HER. fleuron [in a crown]. *3* glorious feat.

flósculo *m.* BOT. floscule.

flota *f.* NAUT. fleet. *2 ~ aérea,* air fleet.

flotación *f.* flotation, floating: *línea de ~,* NAUT. waterline.

flotador, -ra *adj.* floating, swimming. *2 m.* floater, float.

flotante *adj.* floating.

flotar *intr.* to float [on a liquid, in the air]. *2* [of a flag, etc.] to wave.

flote *m.* flotation: *a ~,* afloat.

flotilla *f.* flotilla, small fleet.

fluctuación *f.* fluctuation, wavering.

fluctuante *adj.* fluctuating, fluctuant.

fluctuar *intr.* to fluctuate, to bob up and down. *2* to fluctuate, waver, hesitate. *3* to wave [to the wind]. *4* to totter, be in danger.

fluencia *f.* flowing, running. *2* source, spring.

fluente *adj.* flowing, running.

fluidez *f.* fluidity. *2* flowingness, fluidness.

fluido, -da *adj.* fluid [body]. *2* flowing, fluid [style]. *3 m.* fluid. *4 ~ eléctrico,* electric current.

fluir *intr.* to flow. ¶ CONJUG. like *huir.*

flujo *m.* flowing, flux: *~ magnético,* magnetic flux. *2* flow, rising tide. *3* MED. flux, discharge. *4* CHEM., METAL. flux.

flúor *m.* CHEM. fluorin, fluorine. *2* MINER. fluor spar.

fluorescencia *f.* fluorescence.

fluorescente *adj.* fluorescent.

fluoruro *m.* CHEM. fluoride.

fluvial *adj.* fluvial, river.

flux *m.* flush [at cards].

fluxión *f.* MED. fluxion. *2* cold in the head.

foca *f.* ZOOL. seal.

focal *adj.* focal.

focalizar *tr.* PHYS. to focalize.

focense *adj.-n.* Phocian.

Fócida (la) *f. pr. n.* HIST., GEOG. Phocis.

focino *m.* goad for elephants.

foco *m.* GEOM., OPT., PHYS., MED., SEISM. focus. *2* fig. focus, source. *3* AUTO., THEAT. headlight, spotlight. *4* (Am.) electric light.

fofo, -fa *adj.* soft, spongy, flabby.

fogata *f.* blaze, bonfire. *2* MIL. fougasse.

fogón *m.* open fire for cooking. *2* touch-hole [of cannon]. *3* fire-box [of steam-engine boiler].

fogonadura *f.* NAUT. mast-hole.

fogonazo *m.* powder flash.

fogonero *m.* fireman, stoker.

fogosidad *f.* fire, spirit, vehemence.

fogoso, -sa *adj.* ardent, vehement. *2* fierce, spirited, mettlesome.

foguear *tr.* to scale [a gun]. *2* MIL. to accustom to the discharge of firearms. *3* to accustom to the hardships of a trade or state. *4* VET. to cauterize.

fogueo *m.* habituation to the discharge of firearms.

foja *f.* ORN. European coot.

folía *f.* light popular music. *2 pl.* Portuguese dance.

foliáceo, -a *adj.* foliaceous.

foliación *f.* foliation.

foliar *tr.* to foliate, folio [a book].

folicular *adj.* follicular.

foliculario *f.* scorn, pamphleteer, news writer.

folículo *m.* ANAT., BOT. follicle.

folio *m.* folio: *~ recto,* recto; *~ vuelto,* verso; *de a ~,* fig. great, enormous; *en ~,* in folio. *2* PRINT. running head.

folíolo *m.* BOT. foliole.

folklore *m.* folklore.

folklórico, -ca *adj.* folkloric, folkloristic.

follaje *m.* foliage, leafage. *2* ARCH. foliage. *3* gaudy ornament. *4* rhetoric trash.

follar *tr.* to blow (up) with bellows. *2* tr.-intr. to fuck. *3* ref. coll. to drop a silent one, to fart silently.

folletín *m.* feuilleton, newspaper serial.

folletinesco, -ca *adj.* serial, romantic, sensational.

folletinista *m.-f.* serial writer.

folletista *m.-f.* pamphleteer.

folleto *m.* pamphlet, brochure, tract.

follón, -na *adj.* lazy, indolent. *2* cowardly and knavish. *3 m.-f.* lazy person. *4* cowardly knave. *5 m.* noiseless rocket. *6* coll. shindy.

fomentación *f.* MED. fomentation.

fomentar *tr.* to foment, promote, encourage, foster. *2* MED. to foment.

fomento *m.* fomentation, promoting, encouraging, fostering; encouragement. *2* MED. fomentation.

fonación *f.* phonation, uttering of voice.

fonda *f.* inn, restaurant, eating house.

fondeadero *m.* NAUT. anchorage [place].

fondear *tr.* NAUT. to sound. *2* to search [a ship]. *3* to examine closely. *4 intr.* to cast anchor.

fondeo *m.* NAUT. searching. *2* NAUT. anchorage.

fondillos *m. pl.* seat [of trousers].

fondista *m.-f.* innkeeper, hotel keeper.

fondo *m.* bottom [of a cavity or hollow; of sea, river, etc.; farthest or inmost point]: *dar ~,* NAUT. to cast anchor. *2* NAUT. bottom. *3* bottom, essence: *en el ~,* at bottom. *4* depth [down or inwards]. *5* farthest end [of a room]. *6* background. *7* ground [of a painting, etc.]. *8* disposition, nature: *tener buen ~,* to have a good disposition. *9* head [of a cask]. *10* FENC. *tirarse a ~,* to lunge. *11 s.-pl.* fund [of wisdom, knowledge, money, etc.]; common fund [in gambling];

funds [money, resources]: *fondos de amortización*, sinking funds: *estar en fondos*, to have available money. *12 adv.* thoroughly.

fonducho *m.* cheap eating house.

fonema *m.* phoneme.

fonética *f.* phonetics.

fonético, -ca *adj.* phonetic(al).

foniatra *m.* MED. phoniatrician.

fónico, -ca *adj.* phonic.

fonocaptor *m.* ELEC. pickup.

fonográfico, -ca *adj.* phonographic.

fonógrafo *m.* phonograph.

fonograma *m.* phonogram.

fonolita *f.* MINER. phonolite.

fonología *f.* phonology.

fonoscopio *m.* PHYS. phonoscope.

fontana *f.* poet. spring; fountain.

fontanal *adj.* fontal. *2 m.* spring, source [of water]. *3* place abounding in springs.

fontanar *m.* springs, source [of water].

fontanela *f.* ANAT. fontanel.

fontanería *f.* plumbing, pipelaying. *2* water supply system.

fontanero *m.* plumber, pipelayer.

foque *m.* NAUT. jib.

forajido *m.* outlaw, bandit, malefactor.

foral *adj.* pertaining to the rights and privileges of a region. *2* pertaining to a special jurisdiction.

forámen *m.* foramen.

foráneo, -a *adj.* foreign, strange.

forastero, -ra *adj.* foreign, outside. *2 m.-f.* stranger, outsider; guest, visitor [of a town].

forcejar, forcejear *intr.* to struggle, strive, make violent efforts. *2* to contend [with].

forcejeo *m.* struggle, strife, struggling, striving.

fórceps *m.* SURG. forceps.

forense *adj.* forensic, legal.

forestal *adj.* forest, forestal.

forja *f.* METAL. forge; forging: ~ *a la catalana,* Catalan forge or furnace. *2* ironworks, foundry. *3* silversmith's forge.

forjado, -da *adj.* wrought, forged [metal].

forjador *m.* forger [of metals]. *2* forger, inventer.

forjar *tr.* to forge, hammer into shape. *2* to forge, invent: *forjarse ilusiones,* to have false illusions.

forma *f.* form, shape: *en ~ de,* in the shape of. *2* form, style, mode of being. *3* form [of a sacrament]. *4* SPORT., PRINT. form. *5* small host [for giving Holy Communion]. *6* mould. *7* format. *8* manner, way, method, means: *de ~ que,* so that, in such a manner that; *en debida ~,* in due form; *en toda ~,* properly. *9 pl.* figure, configuration [of the human body].

formación *f.* formation, forming. *2* form, shape. *3* training, education. *4* GEOL., MIL. formation.

formal *adj.* formal [pertaining to the form]. *2* serious, steadygoing, reliable [person, firm, ‣etc.]; grave, sedate. *3* formal, explicit, definite.

formalidad *f.* seriousness, exactitude, reliability. *2* restraint, composure, gravity. *3* formality, established practice.

formalismo *m.* formalism.

formalista *adj.-n.* formalist.

formalizar *tr.* to put in final form. *2* to formalize, give definite shape or legal form to. *3* to formulate, state. *4 ref.* to become serious or earnest; to take offence.

formalmente *adv.* formally. *2* seriously.

formar *tr.* to form [in practically every sense]. *2* to shape, fashion, make, frame, model, mould. *3* to constitute, make out or up. *4* to train, educate,

develop. *5 tr.-intr.* MIL. to form, draw up. *6 ref.* to form, take form. *7* to grow, develop, become trained or educated.

formativo, -va *adj.* formative.

formato *m.* format.

fornero *m.* ARCH. side arch of a vault.

fórmico *adj.* CHEM. formic.

formidable *adj.* formidable. *2* great, enormous, huge, immense. *3* coll. fantastic, magnificent.

formol *m.* CHEM. formol.

formón *m.* CARP. chisel.

fórmula *f.* formula. *2 por ~,* as a matter of form.

formular *tr.* to formulate, express, make: ~ *cargos,* to make charges. *2* MED. to prescribe.

formulario, -ria *adj.* formulary. *2* perfunctory. *3 m.* formulary, form.

formulismo *m.* formulism.

fornicación *f.* fornication.

fornicar *tr.* to fornicate.

fornido, -da *adj.* robust, sturdy.

foro *m.* forum. *2* bar [legal profession]. *3* THEAT. back [of the stage]. *4* LAW kind of leasehold.

forofo, -fa *n.* coll. supporter, fan.

forraje *m.* forage, green fodder [for animals]. *2* foraging. *3* unsubstantial hodgepodge.

forrajeador *m.* MIL. forager.

forrajear *tr.* to gather forage. *2 intr.* MIL. to forage.

forrajera *f.* shako guard.

forrar *tr.* to line [a garment, box, etc.]. *2* to cover [a book, etc.]; to plank [a ship].

forro *m.* lining [of a garment, etc.]. *2* protective cover [on a book]: *ni por el ~,* not in the least. *3* NAUT. sheathing, planking.

fortachón, -na *adj.* coll. strong, sturdy, burly.

fortalecedor, -ra *adj.* fortifying, strengthening.

fortalecer *tr.* to fortify, strenghten. *2* MIL. to fortify. *3 ref.* to grow strong. ¶ CONJUG. like *agradecer.*

fortalecimiento *m.* fortification, strengthening.

fortaleza *f.* fortitude. *2* strength, vigour. *3* fortress, stronghold. *4* AER. ~ *volante,* flying fortress.

fortalezca, fortalezco, etc. *irr.* V. FORTALECER.

fortificable *adj.* fortifiable.

fortificante *adj.* fortifying. *2 m.* fortifier, tonic.

fortificar *tr.* to fortify, strengthen. *2* MIL. to fortify.

fortín *m.* MIL. small fort.

fortísimo, -ma *adj. super.* very strong.

fortuito, -ta *adj.* fortuitous.

fortuna *f.* fortune, -chance, luck, good luck: *por ~,* fortunately, luckily. *2* fortune, fate. *3* fortune, wealth. *4 de ~,* makeshift.

fortunón *m. aug.* great fortune [wealth].

forúnculo *m.* FURÚNCULO.

forzadamente *adv.* by force, forcibly, forcedly. *2* with difficulty.

forzado, -da *adj.* forced, compelled, constrained. *2* forced, strained [not spontaneous, not natural]. *3 trabajos forzados,* hard labour. *4 m.* galley slave.

forzamiento *m.* forcing. *2* ravishing, violation.

forzar *tr.* to force, compel, constrain. *2* to force, break [a door, lock, etc.]. *3* MIL. to force, storm, take. *4* to strain [one's ears, eyes, etc.]. *5* to ravish, violate. ¶ CONJUG. like *contar.*

forzosamente *adv.* against one's will. *2* necessarily, per force.

forzoso, -sa *adj.* necessary, unavoidable. *2 heredero ~,* legal heir. *3 paro ~,* unemployment.

forzudo, -da *adj.* strong, vigorous.

fosa *f.* grave, sepulture. *2* ANAT. fossa.

fosco, -ca *adj.* sullen, frowning. *2* dark.

fosfato *m.* CHEM. phosphate.

fosfaturia *f*. MED. phosphaturia.
fosfito *m*. CHEM. phosphite.
fosforado, -da *adj*. phosphoretted or phosphoretted, phosphuretted or phosphureted.
fosforecer *intr*. to phosphoresce. ¶ CONJUG. like *agradecer*.
fosforera *f*. matchbox.
fosforero, -ra *m.-f*. match seller.
fosforescencia *f*. phosphorescence.
fosforescente *adj*. phosphorescent.
fosfórico, -ca *adj*. CHEM. phosphoric.
fosforita *f*. MINER. phosphorite.
fósforo *m*. CHEM. phosphorus. *2* match, friction match. *3* (cap.) Phosphor [morning star].
fósil *adj.-m*. fossil.
fosilización *f*. fossilization.
fosilizarse *ref*. to fossilize.
foso *m*. pit, hole [in the ground]. *2* FORT. ditch, moat, fosse, foss. *3* THEAT. cellar under the stage.
fotingo *m*. (Am.) jalopy.
foto *f*. col. photo.
fotocalco *m*. photoprint.
fotocomposición *f*. phototypesetting.
fotocopia *f*. photocopy.
fotocopiadora *f*. photocopier.
fotoeléctrico, -ca *adj*. photoelectric.
fotofobia *f*. MED. photophobia.
fotogénico, -ca *adj*. photogenic.
fotógeno, -na *adj*. photogenic.
fotograbado *m*. photoengraving, photogravure.
fotograbador, -ra *m.-f*. photoengraver.
fotograbar *tr*. to photoengrave.
fotografía *f*. photography. *2* photograph.
fotografiar *tr*. to photograph.
fotógrafo *m*. photographer.
fotograma *m*. photogram. *2* CINEM. still, shot.
fotolito *m*. photolitho, photolith.
fotolitografía *f*. photolithography. *2* photolithograph.
fotometría *f*. photometry.
fotómetro *m*. PHOT. exposuremeter, photometer.
fotón *m*. PHYS. photon.
fotoquímica *f*. photochemistry.
fotosfera *f*. ASTR. photosphere.
fotosíntesis *f*. BOT., CHEM. photosynthesis.
fototerapia *f*. phototherapeutics, phototherapy.
fototipografía *f*. phototypography.
fototropismo *m*. BIOL. phototropism.
frac, *pl*. **fraques** *m*. full-dress coat, swallow-tailed coat.
fracasado, -da *adj*. unsuccessful. *2* *m.-f*. failure, person who has failed in life.
fracasar *intr*. to fail, be unsuccessful, to fall through.
fracaso *m*. failure, unsuccess. *2* disaster, calamity.
fracción *f*. fraction part. *2* breaking into parts. *3* LITURG. fraction. *4* MATH. fraction. *5* faction, party.
fraccionamiento *m*. breaking up, fractioning. *2* CHEM. fractionation.
fraccionar *tr*. to break up, fraction. *2* CHEM. to fractionate.
fraccionario, -ria *adj*. fractional, fractionary.
fractura *f*. breaking, fracture. *2* MINER., SURG. fracture: ~ *conminuta*, comminution.
fracturar *tr*. to break, fracture.
fragancia *f*. fragrance.
fragante *adj*. fragrant. *2* FLAGRANTE: *en* ~, in the very act.
fragata *f*. NAUT. frigate: ~ *ligera*, corvette.
frágil *adj*. fragile, brittle, breakable. *2* frail, weak.

fragilidad *f*. fragility, brittleness. *2* frailty.
fragmentación *f*. fragmentation.
fragmentar *tr*. to break into fragments. *2* *ref*. to fragment.
fragmento *m*. fragment.
fragor *m*. noise, roar, crash, thunder.
fragoroso, -sa *adj*. noisy, thundering.
fragosidad *f*. roughness and thickness [of woods]. *2* rough and brambly spot.
fragoso, -sa *adj*. rough and brambly. *2* FRAGOROSO.
fragua *f*. forge [furnace].
fraguar *tr*. to forge [metals]. *2* to plan, plot, brew, concoct. *3* *intr*. MAS. [of mortar, etc.] to set.
fraile *m*. friar, monk. *2* PRINT. friar.
frailecillo *m*. *dim*. little friar. *2* ORN. lapwing. *3* ORN. puffin.
frailesco, -ca *adj*. monkish.
frailuno, -na *adj*. monkish, friarlike.
frambuesa *f*. BOT. raspberry [fruit].
frambueso *m*. BOT. raspberry bush.
francachela *f*. merry meal, carousal, spread.
francés, -sa *adj*. French: *despedirse a la francesa*, to take French leave. *2* *m*. Frenchman. *3* French [language]. *4* *f*. Frenchwoman. *5* *m. pl. los franceses*, the French [people].
francesada *f*. Frenchism. *2* French invasion of Spain in 1808.
Francia *f. pr. n*. GEOG. France.
Francisca *f. pr. n*. Frances.
franciscano, -na *adj.-n*. Franciscan.
Francisco *m. pr. n*. Francis.
francmasón, -na *m.-f*. Freemason.
francmasonería *f*. Freemasonry.
franco, -ca *adj*. frank, open, candid. *2* generous, liberal. *3* free, open, unobstruced. *4* free, exempt [of duty, tax, etc.]: ~ *de servicio*, off duty; ~ *a bordo*, free on board. *5* Frankish. *6* *m*. franc [coin]. *7* *pl*. HIST. *los francos*, the Franks.
francófilo, -la *adj.-n*. Francophile.
francófobo *adj.-n*. Francophobe.
francolín *m*. ORN. francolin, black partridge.
francote, -ta *adj*. frank, open-hearted.
franela *f*. flannel.
frangollar *tr*. coll. to bungle.
frangollón, -na *adj*. bungling, botching.
franja *f*. ornamental band or braid; stripe. *2* strip [of land].
franjar, franjear *tr*. to trim with bands, braids or stripes.
franquear *tr*. to free, exempt. *2* to grant liberally. *3* to clear, open [the way]. *4* to stamp, prepay [a letter or parcel]. *5* to free [a slave]. *6* *ref*. to yield to another's wishes. *7* *franquearse con*, to open one's heart to.
franqueo *m*. postage [of a letter or parcel].
franqueza *f*. frankness, candour: *con* ~, frankly, candidly. *2* freedom, liberty, exception.
franquía *f*. NAUT. sea-room: *en* ~, ready to sail.
franquicia *f*. exemption of taxes, duties, etc.: ~ *postal*, frank. *2* franchise, privilege.
fraque *m*. FRAC.
frasco *m*. vial, bottle, flask. *2* powder flask.
frase *f*. phrase, sentence: ~ *hecha*, set expression, cliché. *2* MUS. phrase.
frasear *tr*. to phrase.
fraseología *f*. phraseology. *2* verbosity.
frasquera *f*. bottle frame or case.
fratás *m*. MAS. plastering trowel.
fraternal *adj*. fraternal, brotherly.
fraternidad *f*. fraternity, brotherhood.

fraternizar *intr.* to fraternize.
fraterno, -na *adj.* fraternal, brotherly.
fratricida *adj.* fratricidal. *2 m.-f.* fratricide [person].
fratricidio *m.* fratricide [crime].
fraude *m.* fraud [criminal deception].
fraudulencia *f.* fraudulence.
fraudulento, -ta *adj.* fraudulent.
fray *m.* brother [prefixed to the names of friars].
frazada *f.* blanket [bed covering].
frecuencia *f.* frequency: *con ~,* frequently.
frecuentación *f.* frecuentation. *2* frequent practice.
frecuentar *tr.* to frequent. *2* to practice, or partake of, frequently.
frecuente *adj.* frequent.
fregadero *m.* scullery; kitchen sink.
fregado *m.* scrubbing. *2* doubtul affair.
fregadura *f.* scrubbing.
fregamiento *m.* friction.
fregar *tr.* to rub, scrub, scour. *2* to mop [the floor]; to wash [dishes]. *3* (Am.) to annoy, bother. ¶ Conjug. like *acertar.*
fregatriz, fregrona *f.* coll. kitchenmaid.
fregotear *tr.* to scrub or wash up quickly and carelessly.
fregoteo *m.* quick, carreless scrub or wash up.
freidura *f.* frying in a pan.
freiduría *f.* fried-fish shop.
freír *tr.* to fry in a pan: *al ~ será el reír,* he laughs best who laughs last. *2* to bother, pester. *3 ref.* [of food] to fry. *4 freírsela a uno,* to deceive someone premeditatedly. ¶ Conjug. like *reír.*
frenaje *m.* braking.
frenar *tr.* to brake [apply the brake to]. *2* to bridle [a horse].
frenesí *m.* frenzy. *2* vehemence, distraction.
frenético, -ca *adj.* frantic, frenzied, mad.
frenillo *m.* ANAT. frenum. *2* muzzle [for an animal]. *3* NAUT. tarred rope, lobstay.
freno *m.* bridle, bit of the bridle: *tascar el ~,* to champ the bit; fig. to bear something with impatience. *2* MACH. brake. *3* fig. curb check, restraint: *sin ~,* without restraint.
frenópata *m.* alienist.
frenopatía *f.* phrenopathy.
frente *f.* forehead, brow, face, countenance: *hacer ~ a,* to face, to meet; *con la ~ levantada,* serenely, brazenly; *~ a ~,* face to face. *2 m.* front, face, fore part: *al ~ de,* fig. at the head of, in charge of; *~ por ~,* directly opposite. *3* obverse. *4* FORT. face [of a bastion]. *5* MIL., POL., METEOR. front. *6 de ~,* forward: facing, abreast. *7 adv.* before, opposite: *~ a,* before, face to; *en ~,* opposite.
freo *m.* channel, strait.
fresa *f.* BOT. strawberry [plant and fruit]. *2* MACH. milling cutter.
fresado *m.* milling [of metals].
fresadora *f.* MACH. milling machine.
fresal *m.* strawberry patch.
fresar *tr.* to mill [metals].
fresca *f.* cool air; cool of the early morning or the evening. *2* blunt remark, piece of one's mind.
frescachón, -na *adj.* robust and fresh-looking. *2 viento ~,* fresh gale.
frescal *adj.* slightly salted [fish].
frescales *m.-f.* forward, careless person.
fresco, -ca *adj.* cool, fresh, moderately cold. *2* light [clothing]. *3* fresh [recent; not preserved or salted; not faded; not stale]. *4* fresh [wind]. *5* fresh

[complexion]; fresh,-buxom [person]. *6* cool, calm, unconcerned: *se quedó tan ~,* it left him unconcerned. *7* bold, cheeky, *fresh. *8 estar ~,* coll. to be in a pretty pickle. *9 m.* cool, coolness, cool air: *hacer ~* [of weather], to be cool; *tomar el ~,* to get a bit of cool air. *10* fresh fish, fresh bacon. *11* PAINT. fresco: *al ~,* in fresco.
frescor *m.* cool, coolness, freshness. *2* PAINT. freshness of flesh-colour.
frescote, -ta *adj.* fresh, buxom, looking healthy.
frescura *f.* freshness, coolness [of things; of a verdant place]. *2* freshness [of complexion]. *4* cheek, forwardness, freshness. *5* coolness, unconcern.
fresneda *f.* plantation of ash trees.
fresnillo *m.* BOT. fraxinella.
fresno *m.* BOT. ash, ash tree. *2* ash [wood].
fresón *m.* BOT. Chilean strawberry.
fresquera *f.* meat-safe.
fresquista *m.-f.* fresco painter.
fresquito, -ta *adj.* rather cool, coolish. *2* recent, fresh, freshly made. *3 m.* cool, cool breeze.
freza *f.* dung, droppings. *2* spawning. *3* spawning season. *4* spawn [of fishes, etc.]; fry.
frezar *intr.* to eject the dung. *2* to spawn.
friable *adj.* friable.
frialdad *f.* coldness, frigidity. *2* coolness, calmness, indifference, unconcern. *3* dullness, gracelessness.
fricandó *m.* COOK. fricandeau.
fricasé *m.* COOK. fricassee.
fricativo, -va *adj.* PHON. fricative.
fricción *f.* friction, rubbing. *2* MEC. friction.
friccionar *tr.* MED. to rub.
friega *f.* medicinal rubbing or friction.
friego, friegue, etc. *irr.* V. FREGAR.
Frigia *f. pr. n.* GEOG. Phrygia.
frigidez *f.* frigidity.
frígido, -da *adj.* cold, frigid.
frigio, -gia *adj.-n.* Phrygian.
frigorífico, -ca *adj.* refrigerating: *cámara frigorífica,* cold-storage room. *2 m.* refrigerator.
frijol *m.* BOT. kidney bean.
fringílidos *m. pl.* ORN. Fringillidae.
frío, fría *adj.* cold, frigid. *2* cool, calm. *3* cold, chill, indifferent, unconcerned, unmoved, unemotional. *4* dull, graceless, inexpressive. *5 m.* cold, coldness [of temperature]: *hacer ~* [of the weather], to be cold; *tener ~* [of a person], to be cold.
frío, fría, friera, etc. *irr.* V. FREÍR.
friolento, -ta *adj.* FRIOLERO.
friolera *f.* trifle.
friolero, -ra *adj.* chilly, very sensitive to cold.
frisa *f.* frieze [coarse cloth]. *2* FORT. fraise.
frisado *m.* frizzing [of cloth].
frisar *tr.* to frieze, frizz [cloth]. *2* to rub. *3 intr.* to be close to, to border, approach.
Frisia *f. pr. n.* GEOG. Friesland.
friso *m.* ARCH. frieze. *2* dado, mopboard, ornamental band [on a wall].
frisón, -na *adj.-n.* Frisian.
fritada, fritanga *f.* fry [dish of anything fried].
frito, frita *adj.* fried. *2* worried to death, exasperated. *3 m.* fry, fried food.
fritura *f.* FRITADA.
frivolidad *f.* frivolity, frivolousness.
frívolo, -la *adj.* frivolous. *2* trifling.
fronda *f.* BOT. frond; leaf. *2* SURG. sling-shaped bandage. *3 pl.* foliage, frondage.
fronde *m.* BOT. frond [of fern].
frondosidad *f.* abundance of foliage, leafiness.

frondoso, -sa *adj.* leafy, luxuriant.
frontal *adj.* frontal. *2 m.* ANAT., ECCL. frontal.
frontalera *f.* front [of a bridle]. *2* yoke pad [for oxen].
frontera *f.* frontier, boundary, border. *2* ARCH. façade.
fronterizo, -za *adj.* frontier, border [situated on the frontier]. *2* facing, opposite.
frontero, -ra *adj.* facing, opposite, placed in front. *2 adv.* in front.
frontil *m.* FRONTALERA 2.
frontis *m.* ARCH. frontispiece, façade.
frontispicio *m.* frontispiece. *2* coll. face [of person].
frontón *m.* ARCH. fronton, pediment. *2* main wall of pelota court. *3* pelota court.
frotación *f.* rubbing.
frotar *tr.* to rub.
frote *m.* rubbing, friction.
fructífero, -ra *adj.* fructiferous. *2* fruitful.
fructificación *f.* fructification.
fructificar *intr.* to fructify. *2* to yield profit.
fructosa *f.* CHEM. fructose.
fructuoso, -sa *adj.* fruitful, fructuous, profitable.
frugal *adj.* frugal.
frugalidad *f.* frugality.
frugívoro, -ra *adj.* frugivorous.
fruición *f.* fruition, pleasure, enjoyment.
frunce *m.* SEW. gather, gathering, *shirr, shirring.
fruncido *m.* SEW. gathering, *shirring.
fruncimiento *m.* knitting [of brow]; puckering [of mouth]. *2* FRUNCIDO.
fruncir *tr.* to knit [the brow]; to pucker [the mouth]. *2* SEW. to gather, *shirr.
fruslería *f.* trifle, triviality.
frustración *f.* frustration.
frustrar *tr.* to frustrate, baulk, foil, defeat, thwart. *2 ref.* to miscarry, fail, fall through.
frustratorio, -ria *adj.* frustrative, defeating.
fruta *f.* fruit [edible fruit or piece of fruit]: ~ *prohibida*, forbidden fruit; ~ *seca*, dry fruits. *2* ~ *de sartén*, fritter.
frutaje *m.* PAINT. fruit piece.
frutal *adj.* fruit [tree]. *2 m.* fruit tree.
frutar *intr.* to bear fruit.
frutería *f.* fruit shop; *fruit store.
frutero, -ra *adj.* fruit [boat, dish, etc.]. *2 m.-f.* fruit seller. *3 m.* fruit dish. *4* table centrepiece imitating fruit. *5* PAINT. fruit piece.
frutescente *adj.* FRUTICOSO.
frútice *m.* BOT. frutex.
fruticoso, -sa *adj.* BOT. frutescent, fruticose.
frutilla *f.* (Am.) strawberry.
fruto *m.* BOT. fruit. *2* any useful produce of the earth. *3* fruit, product, consequence: *sin* ~, fruitlessly, in vain.
fu *interj.* faugh!, fie! *2 no hacer ni* ~ *ni fa*, to leave one indifferent.
fucilar *intr.* to flash with heat lightning. *2* to flash, to twinkle.
fucilazo *m.* heat lightning.
fucsia *f.* BOT. fuchsia.
fuego *m.* fire [in practically every sense]: ~ *de Santelmo*, St. Elmo's fire; ~ *fatuo*, ignis fatuus; ~ *graneado*, MIL. drumfire; *fuegos artificiales*, fireworks; *abrir* ~, to open fire; *atizar el* ~, to stir the fire; *echar* ~ *por los ojos*, to look daggers; *hacer* ~, to fire [discharge firearms]; *pegar* ~, to set fire to, to set on fire; *a* ~ *lento*, by slow fire. *2* light [to light a cigarette, etc.]. *3* beacon fire.

4 rash, skin eruption. *5* hearth, house. *6 interj.* MIL. fire!
fuelle *m.* bellows [for blowing]. *2* PHOT. bellows [of a folding camera]. *3* folding carriage hood. *4* folding side of some things. *5* fold, pucker. *6* bag [of a bagpipe]. *7* coll. talebearer.
fuente *f.* water spring, spring, source; fountain: ~ *luminosa*, illuminated fountain. *2* fig. source, origin: *beber en buenas fuentes*, to be well informed. *3* font, baptismal font. *4* dish [for serving up food; dishful]. *5* SURG. issue. *6 pl.* headwaters, source [of a stream].
fuer *m.* *a* ~ *de*, as, as behoves, in the manner of.
fuera, fuere, etc. *irr.* V. IR and SER.
fuera *adv.* out, outside, without; away, out of town: *de fuera*, exterior; *desde* ~, from the outside; *hacia* ~, outward(s); *por* ~, in the outside. *2* ~ *de*, out of, outside of; away from; apart from, short of, except, save. *3* ~ *de sí*, beside oneself. *4 interj.* out! *5* off with...!
fuero *m.* exception, privilege. *2* jurisdiction. *3* name for some codes of laws. *4* ~ *interior, interno*, conscience, inmost heart. *5 pl.* coll. arrogance.
fuerte *adj.* strong. [in practically every sense]. *2* intense, severe [pain]. *3* heavy [blow]. *4* healthy, serious, vigorous, extreme. *5* active, eficacious [remedy, etc.]. *6* loud [voice, sound]. *7* good, proficient. *8 hacerse* ~, to entrench oneself, make a stand. *9 m.* fort, fortress. *10 adv.* strongly; heavily.
fuerza *f.* strength, force power [capacity to raise, move, resist, etc.]: ~ *bruta*, brute force; *hacer* ~, to struggle; to apply force; to carry weight; *hacer* ~ *de velas*, NAUT. to crowd sail: *sacar fuerzas de flaqueza*, to make an extraordinary effort. *2* MECH., PHYS. force, power: ~ *centrífuga*, centrifugal force; ~ *hidráulica*, water power; ~ *motriz*, motive power. *3* strength [innate quality of things]. *4* force, duress, compulsion: *ser* ~, to be necessary; *de por* ~, *por* ~, by force, forcibly; perforce, undoubtedly; *a viva* ~, by sheer or main force. *5* force, violence. *6* strength, vigour [of youth, etc.]. *7* force, efficacy [of an argument, etc.]. *8* ~ *mayor*, force majeure, act of God. *9 a* ~ *de*, by dint of. *10 sing.-pl.* MIL. force, forces: ~ *pública*, police force; *fuerzas armadas*, armed forces.
fuerzo, fuerce, etc. *irr.* V. FORZAR.
fuetazo *m.* (Am.) lash.
fuete *m.* (Am.) whip, horsewhip.
fuga *f.* flight, escape: *poner en* ~, to put to flight. *2* elopement. *3* leak, leakage. *4* ardour, impetuousity. *5* MUS. fugue.
fugacidad *f.* fugacity.
fugarse *ref.* to escape, run away. *2* to elope.
fugaz *adj.* fugacious, fugitive, fleeting, brief, transitory. *2* ASTR. *estrella* ~, shooting star.
fugitivo, -va *adj.* fugitive, fleeting. *2 adj.-n.* fugitive, runaway.
fuguillas *m.* coll. hustler.
fui, fuiste, etc. *irr.* V. IR and SER.
fuina *f.* ZOOL. stone marten, beech marten.
ful *adj.* (slan.) bogus, sham.
fulanito, -ta *m.-f.* dim. of FULANO.
fulano, -na *m.-f.* so-and-so, what's-his-name. *2* fellow; woman. *3 f.* mistress, paramour.
fular *m.* foulard [silk fabric].
fulcro *m.* MECH. fulcrum.
fulero *adj.* bungling. *2 n.* bungler.
fulgente & fúlgido, -da *adj.* fulgent, resplendent.

fulgor *m.* light, brillancy.
fulguración *f.* flash, flashing.
fulgurante *adj.* flashing, shining.
fulgurar *intr.* to flash, shine, fulgurate.
fulgurita *f.* GEOL. fulgurite.
fúlica *f.* ORN. fulica, coot.
fulminación *f.* fulmination.
fulminado, -da *adj.* struck by lightning.
fulminante *adj.* fulminating, fulminant. *2* sudden.
3 MED. fulminant. *4 m.* explosive; fulminating
powder [in a percussion cap].
fulminar *tr.* to fulminate, thunder, hurl [censures,
excommunions, etc.]. *2* to strike with lightning.
fulminato *m.* CHEM. fulminate.
fullería *f.* cheating [esp. at games], trickery.
fullero, -ra *adj.* cheating, tricky. *2 m.-f.* cheat,
sharper.
fumada *f.* puff [of tobacco smoke].
fumadero *m.* smoking room. *2* ~ *de opio*, opium
den.
fumador, -ra *m.-f.* smoker.
fumar *tr.-intr.* to smoke [a cigar, etc.]. *2 ref.* coll.
to spend, blow. *3* coll. *fumarse la clase*, to play
truant. *4 intr.* HUMEAR.
fumarada *f.* puff, whiff or blast of smoke.
fumaria *f.* BOT. fumitory.
fumarola *f.* GEOL. fumarole.
fumigación *f.* fumigation.
fumigar *tr.* to fumigate.
fumista *m.* stove maker, repairer or seller.
fumistería *f.* stove or heater shop.
funámbulo, -la *m.-f.* funambulist, ropewalker.
función *f.* function. *2* show, performance [in a
theater, circus, etc.]. *3* MIL. action, battle.
funcional *adj.* functional.
funcionamiento *m.* functioning, operation, working, running.
funcionar *intr.* to function, work, run.
funcionario *m.* functionary, civil servant.
funda *f.* case, sheath, envelope, cover, slip: ~ *de
almohada*, pillowcase; ~ *para la pistola*, holster.
fundación *f.* foundation, founding, establishing. *2*
foundation [endowed institution].
fundadamente *adv.* with good reason or proof.
fundador, -ra *adj.* founding. *2 m.-f.* founder.
fundamental *adj.* fundamental. *2* foundation.
fundamentar *tr.* to lay the foundations of. *2* to establish on a basis, to base, ground, set firm.
fundamento *m.* foundation, groundwork. *2* foundation, basis, ground. *3* root, origine. *4* seriousness, sense.
fundar *tr.* to found [build, erect; set up, establish,
base, ground]. *2 ref. fundarse en*, to be based on,
to base oneself on.
fundente *adj.* CHEM. fusing, melting. *2 adj.-m.* MED.
dissolvent. *3 m.* CHEM. flux.
fundición *f.* founding, melting, casting. *2* foundry
[of metals]. *3* cast iron. *4* PRINT. font.
fundidor *m.* founder, foundryman, smelter.
fundir *tr.* to fuse, melt. *2* to found, smelt, cast. *3
ref.* [of interests, parties, etc.] to merge, fuse. *4*
(Am.) to be or become ruined.
fundo *m.* LAW land, country property.
fúnebre *adj.* funeral: *honras fúnebres*, obsequies. *2*
funereal, sad, lugubrious.
funeral *adj.* funeral. *2 m.* funeral pomp. *3 pl.* obsequies.

funerala (a la) *adv.* MIL. with arms inverted [as a
token of mourning].
funerario, -ria *adj.* funerary, funeral. *2 f.* undertaker's shop.
funéreo, -a *adj.* poet, funereal, sad, mornful.
funesto, -ta *adj.* fatal, baneful, pernicious. *2* sad,
unfortunate.
fungicida *adj.* fungicidal. *2 n.* fungicide.
fungo *m.* MED. fungus.
fungoso, -sa *adj.* fungous, spongy.
funicular *adj.* funicular. *2 m.* funicular railway.
funículo *m.* BOT., ZOOL. funicle, funiculus.
furente *adj.* poet, furious, raging.
furgón *m.* van, waggon. *2* RLY. waggon, boxcar.
furgoneta *f.* van, station wagon, shooting brake,
estate car.
furia *f.* fury, rage. *2* fit of madness. *3* hurry, speed,
violence [of action]. *4* (cap.) MYTH. Fury. *5 estar
hecho una* ~, to be raging.
furibundo, -da *adj.* furious, angry, choleric.
furioso, -sa *adj.* furious, in a fury. *2* violently insane. *3* tremendous, excessive.
furor *m.* furor, fury, rage. *2* furor, enthusiasm [of
poets]. *3* fury, violence, vehemence. *4* fig. *hacer*
~, to be the rage.
furriel, furrier *m.* MIL. fourrier quartermaster.
furtivo, -va *adj.* furtive, clandestine: *cazador* ~,
poacher.
furúnculo *m.* MED. furuncle, boil.
fusa *f.* MUS. demisemiquaver.
fusco, -ca *adj.* fuscous, dark.
fuselaje *m.* AER. fuselage.
fusibilidad *f.* fusibility.
fusible *adj.* fusible. *2 m.* ELEC. fuse.
fusiforme *adj.* fusiform, spindle-shaped.
fusil *m.* rifle, gun, musket: ~ *ametralladora*, submachine gun; ~ *de chispa*, flintlock gun; ~ *rayado*, rifle.
fusilamiento *m.* execution by shooting.
fusilar *tr.* to shoot [execute by shooting]. *2* coll. to
plagiarize.
fusilería *f.* musketry. *2* body of fusiliers.
fusilero *m.* fusilier, musketeer.
fusión *f.* fusion. *2* COM. merger, amalgamation.
fusionar *tr.-ref.* to unite, merge, amalgamate.
fusta *f.* brushwood. *2* coachman's whip. *3* a wool-
en fabric. *4* NAUT. an ancient two-mast boat.
fustal, fustán *m.* fustian [cotton cloth].
fuste *m.* wood, timber. *2* saddle-tree. *3* shaft [of a
lance]. *4* fust, shaft [of a column]. *5* importance,
substance.
fustete *m.* BOT. fustic.
fustigar *tr.* to whip, lash.
fútbol *m.* football.
futbolín *m.* table football.
futbolista *m.* football player.
futesa *f.* trifle, bagatelle.
fútil *adj.* futile, trifling, unimportant.
futileza *f.* triviality, futility, trifling nature. *2*
worthlessness. *3* trifle, unimportant thing.
futilidad *f.* futility, triviality.
futura *f.* coll. fiancée, bride-to-be.
futurismo *m.* futurism.
futurista *adj.* futuristic. *2 m.-f.* futurist.
futuro, -ra *adj.* future. *2 m.* future [time]. *3* GRAM.
future. *4 m.-f.* future, fiancé, fiancée. *5 pl.* COM.
futures.

G

G, g f. G, g, eighth letter of the Spanish alphabet.
gabacho, -cha adj.-n. scorn. French; Frenchman, Frenchwoman.
gabán m. greatcoat, overcoat.
gabardina f. gabardine. 2 raincoat.
gabarra f. NAUT. barge, lighter.
gabarrero m. NAUT. lighterman.
gabarro m. GEOL. nodule. 2 fault [in a fabric].
gabela f. tax, duty, gabelle. 2 fig. burden.
gabinete m. lady's private sitting room. 2 library, study, room: ~ de lectura, reading room; de ~, parlour, theoretical. 3 collection [of art, science, etc]. 4 POL. cabinet [Ministry, Government].
gablete m. ARCH. gablet.
gacel m. ZOOL. male gazelle.
gacela f. ZOOL. gazelle.
gaceta f. gazette; politic or literary newspaper.
gacetilla f. column of short news, news in brief. 2 short news, news item. 3 coll. newsmonger.
gacetillero m. paragrapher, short new's writer.
gacha f. watery mass. 2 pl. porridge, mush, pap. 3 coll. mud, mire.
gacheta f. spring catch [of lock].
gachí f. [in Andalousian slang] woman, girl.
gacho, -cha adj. turned or bent downwards. 2 down-curved [horn]. 3 slouch [hat]. 4 having down-curved horns. 5 a gachas, on all fours.
gachón, -na adj. coll. sweet and graceful [person].
gachupín m. CACHUPÍN.
gádido, -da adj. ICHTH. gadid.
gaditano, -na adj.-n. Gaditan.
gaélico, -ca adj.-m. Gaelic. 2 m.-f. Gael.
gafa f. hook [for bending a crossbow]. 2 cramp [for holding together]. 3 NAUT. grapple fork. 4 pl. can hooks. 5 spectacles. 6 spectacle bows.
gafe m. coll. jinx.
gafedad f. MED. claw hand.
gafete m. hook and eye.
gaita f. MUS. large flageolet. 2 MUS. hurdy-gurdy. 3 coll. neck. 4 coll. bother. 5 MUS. ~ gallega, bagpipe. 6 templar gaitas, to act in a smoothing way.
gaitero m. piper, bagpipe player.
gaje m. gage [symbol or challenge]. 2 pl. emoluments, perquisites: gajes del oficio, unpleasant things that go with a job.
gajo m. branch, broken off branch [of tree]. 2 cluster [of cherries, plums, etc.]. 3 division of an

orange, a pomegranate, a bunch of grapes, etc. 4 prong, tine. 5 spur [of a mountain]. 6 BOT. lobe.
gala f. best dress: de ~, in gala dress, in full dress. 2 grace and elegance in speaking and doing. 3 ser la ~ de, to be the flower or the pride of. 4 hacer ~ de, to make a show of; tener a ~, to pride oneself on, to glory in. 5 pl. regalia, dresses, jewels, ornaments.
galabardera f. BOT. dog rose [plant and fruit].
galactogogo adj.-m. MED. galactagogue.
galáctico, -ca adj. ASTR. galactic.
galactita, galactites f. MINER. galactite.
galaico, -ca adj. Galician.
galán adj. GALANO. 2 m. handsome man. 3 gallant, lover, suitor. 4 THEAT. primer ~, leading man; ~ joven, juvenile. 5 BOT. ~ de día, day jasmine; ~ de noche, night jasmine.
galancete m. young man. 2 THEAT. juvenile.
galano, -na adj. spruce, smartly dressed. 2 beautiful, elegant, adorned. 3 beautifully turned [style].
galante adj. courteous, obliging; gallant [attentive to women]. 2 mujer ~, courtesan.
galanteador m. courter, wooer. 2 flatterer.
galantear tr. to pay compliments [to a lady]. 2 to court, woo, pay attentions to.
galanteo m. paying compliments [to a lady]. 2 courtship, wooing.
galantería f. gallantry, polite attention, compliment. 2 generosity, liberality. 3 gracefulness.
galantina f. COOK. galantine.
galanura f. beauty, grace, elegance.
galápago m. ZOOL. tortoise, fresh-water tortoise. 2 NAUT. block flat on a side. 3 ingot [of copper, lead or tin]. 4 light saddle. 5 MIL. testudo.
galardón m. guerdon, reward, recompense.
galardonar tr. to reward, recompense.
gálata adj.-n. Galatian.
galaxia f. MINER. galactite. 2 ASTR. Galaxy.
galbana f. sloth, laziness.
gálbano m. galbanum.
gálbula f. BOT. cone of cypress.
gálea f. galea [Roman helmet].
galeaza f. NAUT. galleass.
galena f. MINER. galena.
Galeno m. pr. n. Galen.
galeno, -na adj. gentle, soft [breeze]. 2 m. coll. Galen, physician.

galeón *m.* NAUT. galleon.
galeota *f.* NAUT. galliot.
galeote *m.* galley slave.
galera *f.* NAUT. galley [vessel]. *2* covered wagon. *3* ward [of hospital]. *4* women's prison. *5* PRINT. galley. *6* CARP. large plane. *7* ZOOL. mantis shrimp. *8 pl.* rowing on a galley [as punishment].
galerada *f.* wagonload. *2* PRINT. galley proof.
galería *f.* ARCH., FORT., MIN., NAUT., THEAT. gallery. *2* gallery, collection [of paintings]. *3* gallery, burrow.
galerín *m.* PRINT. small galley.
galerita *f.* ORN. crested lark.
galerna *f.* stormy northwest wind [on northern coast of Spain].
Gales *f. pr. n.* GEOG. Wales.
galés, -sa *adj.* Welsh. *2 m.* Welshman. *3* Welsh [language]. *4 f.* Welshwoman.
galga *f.* greyhound bitch. *2* large falling stone. *3* kind of brake for carts. *4* NAUT. back [of an anchor].
galgo *m.* greyhound.
Galia (la) *f. pr. n.* HIST., GEOG. Gaul.
gálibo *m.* NAUT. pattern, template. *2* RLY. gabarit. *3* fig. elegance.
galicanismo *m.* Gallicanism.
galicano, -na *adj.-n.* Gallican.
Galicia *f. pr. n.* GEOG. Galicia [in Spain].
galicismo *m.* Gallicism.
gálico *adj.* Gallic.
Galilea *f. pr. n.* HIST., GEOG. Galilee.
galileo, -a *adj.-n.* Galilean. *2 f.* galilee [porch].
galillo *m.* ANAT. uvula.
galimatías *m.* gibberish, rigmarole.
galio *m.* CHEM. gallium. *2* BOT. cheese rennet.
galiparla *f.* Frenchified Spanish.
galo, -la *adj.* Gallic. *2 m.-f.* Gaul. *3 m.* Gaulish [language].
galocha *f.* clog, wooden shoe.
galón *m.* galloon, braid. *2* MIL. stripe. *3* gallon [English measure].
galoneadura *f.* galloons, trimming.
galonear *tr.* to trim with galloons or braid.
galop *m.*, **galopa** *f.* galop [dance].
galopada *f.* a spell of galloping.
galopante *adj.* galloping.
galopar *intr.* to gallop.
galope *m.* gallop: *a* or *de* ~, at a gallop; in great haste; *a* ~ *tendido*, at full speed.
galopeado, -da *adj.* hastily done, botched. *2 m.* beating, punching.
galopín *m.* ragamuffin. *2* scoundrel. *3* shrewd fellow. *4* NAUT. cabin boy. *5* ~ *de cocina*, scullion.
galvánico, -ca *adj.* galvanic.
galvanismo *m.* galvanism.
galvanizar *tr.* to galvanize. *2* to electroplate.
galvano *m.* PRINT. electroplate.
galvanómetro *m.* galvanometer.
galvanoplastia, galvanoplástica *f.* galvanoplasty, galvanoplastics. *2* electroplating.
galladura *f.* cicatricle, tread [of an egg].
gallardamente *adv.* gracefully, elegantly. *2* valiantly, bravely, dashingly. *3* nobly.
gallardear *intr.* to do things with grace and ease.
gallardete *m.* NAUT. pennant, streamer.
gallardía *f.* good carriage, graceful deportment. *2* gallantry, bravery.
gallardo, -da *adj.* handsome, graceful. *2* bold, brave, gallant. *3* great, excellent.

gallareta *f.* ORN. European coot.
gallarón *m.* ORN. little bustard.
gallear *tr.* [of a cock] to tread. *2 intr.* coll. to cock, crow. *3* coll. to stand out, excel.
gallegada *f.* number of Galicians. *2* action or saying peculiar to a Galician.
gallego, -ga *adj.-n.* Galician [of Spain]. *2 m.* northwest wind [in Castile].
galleo *m.* FOUND. flaw in casting.
gallera *f.* cockpit.
gallero *m.* breeder of gamecocks. *3* (Am.) cockfighting fan.
galleta *f.* hardtack, ship biscuit or bread. *2* briquet [of anthracite]. *3* biscuit [small cake], *cookie, *cracker. *4* coll. slap, buffet.
galletería *f.* biscuit shop.
galletero *m.* biscuit dish. *2* biscuit maker.
gallina *f.* hen: ~ *de Guinea*, guinea hen; *acostarse con las gallinas*, to go to bed very early. *2* chicken-hearted person. *3* ~ *ciega*, blindman's buff. *4 adj.* chicken-hearted.
gallináceo, -a *adj.* ORN. gallinaceous.
gallinaza *f.* GALLINAZO. *2* hen dung.
gallinazo *m.* ORN. turkey buzzard.
gallinería *f.* hens, poultry. *2* cowardice.
gallinero, -ra *m.-f.* poultry dealer. *2 m.* hencoop, henhouse, henroost. *3* THEAT. coll. paradise, top gallery. *6* fig. madhouse.
gallineta *f.* ORN. European coot. *2* ORN. woodcock. *3* (Am.) guinea hen.
gallipato *m.* ZOOL. an European salamandroid.
gallipava *f.* large variety of hen.
gallipavo *m.* ORN. turkey. *2* false note [in singing].
gallito *m.* cockerel. *2* fig. cock, cock of the walk.
gallo *m.* ORN. cock, rooster: ~ *de pelea*, gamecock, fighting cock; ~ *silvestre*, cock of the wood; *en menos que canta un* ~, in a short time; *otro* ~ *me, te, le, nos, os, les cantara*, how differently I, you, etc., should or would, have fared. *2* fig. cock, boss, cock of the walk. *3* false note [in singing]. *4* ICHTH. dory. *5* *alzar el* ~, to show arrogance; *bajar el* ~, to lower one's tone.
gallocresta *f.* BOT. wild sage, vervain sage.
gallofero, ra; gallofo, -fa *m.-f.* tramp, vagabond.
gallón *m.* sod [piece of turf]. *2* ARCH. ecchinus.
gama *f.* ZOOL. doe, female of the fallow deer. *2* MUS. gamut. *3* fig. gamut.
gamarra *f.* martingale [of harness].
gamba *f.* ZOOL. a Mediterranean prawn.
gamberrada *f.* loutish act, piece of hooliganism, act of vandalism.
gamberrear *intr.* to behave loutishly, to act like a hooligan, to go around causing trouble.
gámbaro *m.* CAMARÓN.
gamberro, -rra *adj.-n.* libertine. *2* uncivil, illbred. *3 m.-f.* uncivil or ill-bred person.
gambeta *f.* DANCE crosscaper. *2* caper, prance.
gambetear *intr.* to caper, prance.
gambito *m.* CHESS GAMBIT.
gamella *f.* bow [of yoke]. *2* feed trough.
gameto *m.* BIOL. gamete.
gamma *f.* gamma [Greek letter].
gamo *m.* ZOOL. fallow deer.
gamón *m.* BOT. asphodel.
gamopétalo, -la *adj.* BOT. gamopetalous.
gamosépalo, -la *adj.* BOT. gamosepalous.
gamuza *f.* ZOOL. chamois. *2* chamois [leather].
gamuzado, -da *adj.* chamois-coloured.
gana *f.* apetite, desire, will: ~ *de comer*, appetite; *darle a uno la* ~ or *la real* ~ *de*, to choose to; *no me da la* ~, I won't; *tener* ~ or *ganas de*, to wish,

to feel like; *de buena* ~, willingly; *de mala* ~, reluctantly.

ganadería *f.* cattle raising. *2* cattle, livestock. *3* breed, brand, stock [of cattle].

ganadero, -ra *adj.* cattle, cattle raising. *2 m.-f.* cattle raiser or dealer.

ganado *m.* cattle, livestock: ~ *caballar*, horses; ~ *cabrío*, goats; ~ *de cerda*, swine; ~ *lanar*, sheep; ~ *mayor*, cows and bulls, horses, asses mules; ~ *menor*, sheep, goats, etc. *2* stock of bees.

ganador, -ra *adj.* winning. *2 m.-f.* winner. *3* gainer; earner.

ganancia *f.* gaining. *2* gain, profit: *ganancias y pérdidas*, COM. profit and loss.

ganancioso, -sa *adj.* lucrative, profitable. *2* profiting, winning. *3 m.-f.* gainer, winner.

ganapán *m.* odd-job man. *2* rough coarse man.

ganapierde *m.* giveaway [game].

ganar *tr.-ref.* to gain, earn, win: *ganarse la vida*, to earn one's living; *ganársela*, coll. to get it. *2* to gain or win over. *3* to earn [wages, etc.]. *4 tr.* to gain, reach, arrive at. *5* to make, win [money]. *6* to win, take [a city, etc.]. *7* to gain [land from the sea]. *8* to defeat [in war or competition]; to surpass, to outstrip. *9* to draw [interest]. *10 intr.* to gain, improve.

ganchero *m.* raftsman, log driver.

ganchillo *m.* small hook. *2* crochet needle. *2* crochet work.

gancho *m.* hook, crook. *2* fig. attractiveness; *tener* ~ [of a woman], to have a way with the men. *3* fig. enticer, decoy. *4* fig. pimp. *5* shepherd's crook. *6* snag [branch stump]. *7* coll. pothook, scrawl. *8* (Am.) hairpin.

ganchoso, -sa; ganchudo, -da *adj.* hooked, curved.

gándara *f.* low wasteland.

gandul, -la *adj.* idling, loafing. *2 m.-f.* idler, loafer, vagabond.

gandulear *intr.* to idle, loaf.

gandulería *f.* idleness, loafing, laziness.

ganga *f.* MIN. gangue. *2* ORN. pin-tailed sand grouse. *3* bargain [advantageous purchase]; something obtained easily, *snap, *cinch.

ganglio *m.* ANAT., MED. ganglion.

gangosidad *f.* snuffe, snuffling, nasal twang.

gangoso, -sa *adj.* snuffling, nasal.

gangrena *f.* MED. gangrene.

gangrenarse *ref.* to gangrene [become gangrenous].

gangrenoso, -sa *adj.* gangrenous.

gangsterismo *m.* gangsterism.

ganguear *intr.* to snuffle, speak through the nose.

gangueo *m.* snuffle, speaking through the nose.

Ganimedes *m. pr. n.* MYTH. Ganymede.

ganoso, -sa *adj.* desirous, wishing.

gansada *f.* coll. stupidity, silly act, remark, etc.

gansarón *m.* ORN. male goose. *2* ORN. gosling. *3* coll. tall, lanky fellow.

ganso, -sa *m.* ORN. goose, gander. *2 m.-f.* slow, lazy person. *3* rustic person. *4 f.* ORN. female goose.

Gante *m. pr. n.* GEOG. Ghent.

ganzúa *f.* picklock [tool; thief]. *2* pumper of secrets.

gañán *m.* farm hand. *2* strong rough man.

gañanía *f.* farm hands. *2* lodge for farm hands.

gañido *m.* yelp.

gañiles *m. pl.* throat [of animals].

gañir *intr.* to yelp. *2* [of some birds] to croak.

gañón, gañote *m.* coll. throat, gullet.

garabatear *intr.* to throw a hook or graple [to

catch a thing]. *2 intr.-tr.* to scrawl, scribble. *3* coll. to beat about the bush.

garabateo *m.* hooking, grappling. *2* scrawling, scribbling.

garabato *m.* hook; meathook, pothook. *2* grappling iron. *3* weeding hoe. *4* charm, winsomeness, it [of a woman]. *5 pl.* pothooks, scrawls. *6* disorderly movements of hand or fingers.

garaje *m.* garage [for motor cars].

garajista *m.* garage owner, garage attendant, garage man.

garambaina *f.* frippery, tawdry ornament. *2 pl.* ridiculous grimacing or affectation.

garante *adj.* responsible. *2 m.-f.* guarantor.

garantía *f.* guarantee, guaranty. *2* COM. warranty, security, collateral. *3* LAW *garantías constitucionales*, constitutional rights.

garantizar *tr.* to guarantee, guaranty; to warrant. *2* to indorse, vouch for.

garañón *m.* stud jackass. *2* stud camel.

garapiña *f.* state of a liquid frozen or coagulated into grumes.

garapiñado, -da *adj.* frozen into grumes. *2* coated with grumous sugar: *almendra garapiñada*, praline [almond].

garapiñera *f.* ice-cream freezer.

garapullo *m.* small dart or arrow.

garba *f.* sheaf [of wheat, etc.].

garbanzal *m.* chickpea field.

garbanzo *m.* BOT. chickpea [plant and seed].

garbar *tr.* AGR. to sheaf, sheave.

garbear *intr.* to affect grace or elegance. *2 intr.-ref.* coll. to get or pull along.

garbeo *m.* coll. stroll. *2* trip, tour.

garbera *f.* AGR. shock [of sheaves].

garbo *m.* gracefulness, easy and graceful bearing; jauntiness. *2* grace and ease [in doing something]. *3* liberality, generosity.

garbón *m.* ORN. male partridge.

garbosamente *adv.* gracefully, elegantly, stylishly. *2* proudly and gracefully. *3* generously.

garboso, -sa *adj.* easy and graceful, airy, sprightly; jaunty. *2* liberal, openhanded, generous.

garceta *f.* ORN. lesser egret. *2* side lock [of hair]. *3* brow antler.

gardenia *f.* BOT. gardenia.

garduña *f.* ZOOL. beech marten, stone marten.

garduño, -ña *m.-f.* sneak thief.

garete *m.* NAUT. *al* ~, adrift.

garfa *f.* claw [sharp, curved nail].

garfio *m.* hook; drag hook; gaff.

gargajear *intr.* to expectorate, spit phlegm.

gargajo *m.* [expectorated] phlegm.

garganta *f.* ANAT. throat, gullet: *tener a uno atravesado en la* ~, not to be able to bear someone. *2* voice [of a singer]. *3* throat [front of neck]. *4* instep. *5* throat [of a river], gorge; narrow mountain pass; neck, throat [of some things]. *6* MECH. gorge, groove [of a sheave].

gargantear *intr.* to warble, quaver, trill [in singing]. *2 tr.* NAUT. to strap [a deadeye].

gargantilla *f.* necklace.

gárgaras *f. pl.* gargling: *hacer* ~, to gargle.

gargarismo *m.* gargle, gargling. *2* gargle [liquid].

gárgol *adj. m.* CARP. groove, gain, croze.

gárgola *f.* ARCH. gargoyle. *2* flax boll.

garguero *m.* gullet; windpipe.

garita *f.* fortification turret. *2* sentry box. *3* box [for a guard]; railway-crossing box. *4* porter's lodge.

garitero m. keeper or frequenter of a gambling den.

garito m. gambling den.

garla f. coll. talk, -chat.

garlar intr. to chatter.

garlito m. fishtrap. 2 fig. trap, snare: *coger en el ~*, to catch in the act.

garlopa f. CARP. jack plane, trying plane.

garnacha f. gown, robe [worn by lawyers, judges, etc.]. 2 a sweet purple grape; wine made from it.

Garona m. pr. n. GEOG. Garonne.

garra f. paw, claw [of wild beast]; talon [of bird of prey]. 2 fig. claw, hand, clutch: *caer en las garras de*, to fall into the clutches of. 3 NAUT. hook [of the grappling iron].

garrafa f. carafe, decanter.

garrafal adj. great, big, whopping.

garrafón m. demijohn, carboy.

garrancha f. coll. sword. 2 BOT. spathe.

garrancho m. snag [branch stump].

garrapata f. ZOOL. tick. 2 MIL. disabled horse.

garrapatear intr. to scribble, scrawl.

garrapato m. pothook, scrawl.

garrar, garrear intr. NAUT. to drag the anchor.

garrido, -da adj. handsome, beautiful, elegant.

garrocha f. BULLF. picador's pike or lance. 2 staff with a barbed point.

garrochazo m. prick or blow with a GARROCHA.

garrón m. spur [of bird]. 2 heel of a dead animal by which it is hung. 2 snag [on a tree branch].

garrotazo m. blow with a stick or cudgel.

garrote m. thick stick, cudgel. 2 AGR. olive cutting. 3 garrote [for capital punishment].

garrotillo m. MED. croup.

garrotín m. a Spanish dance.

garrucha f. pulley.

garrucho m. NAUT. cringle.

garrulería f. prattle, chatter.

garrulidad f. garrulity.

gárrulo, -la adj. garrulous, loquacious. 2 [of bird, stream, etc.] garrulous, chirping, babbling.

garúa f. (Am.) NAUT. drizzle.

garza f. ORN. heron, purple heron: ~ *real*, gray heron.

garzo, -za adj. blue [eye]; blue-eyed.

garzón m. boy, lad, youth. 2 male child.

garzota f. ORN. night heron. 2 aigrette, plume.

gas m. gas: ~ *de los pantanos*, marsh gas; *gases asfixiantes*, MIL. poison gas; *gases lacrimógenos*, tear gas. 2 gaslight.

gasa f. gauze, chiffon. 2 antiseptic gauze. 3 crape [worn round a hat].

gascón, -na; gasconés, -na adj.-n. Gascon.

Gascuña f. pr. n. GEOG. Gascony.

gasear tr. to gas [treat or attack with gas].

gaseiforme adj. gasiform.

gaseosa f. soda water.

gaseoso, -sa adj. gaseous.

gasificar tr. to gasify.

gasógeno m. gasogene, gazogene. 2 gas generator.

gasolina f. gasoline, petrol.

gasolinera f. NAUT. boat with petrol engine. 2 gas station.

gasómetro m. gasometer. 2 gasholder.

Gaspar m. pr. n. Jasper.

gastado, -da adj. spent. 2 used-up, worn-out. 3 trite, hackneyed, stale.

gastador, -ra adj.-n. spendthrift. 2 m. MIL. sapper. 3 MIL. pioneer.

gastamiento m. consumption, wearing out.

gastar tr. to expend, spend [money, time, etc.]. 2 to consume, use up, exhaust, wear out, fret. 3 to waste. 4 to lay waste. 5 to be, have, enjoy, use, etc., habitually: ~ *mal humor*, to be bad tempered. 6 to wear: ~ *bigote*, to wear a moustache. 7 to play [a joke or jokes]. 8 *gastarlas*, coll. to act, behave, conduct oneself. 9 ref. to be expended. 10 to become used up, to wear out, fray. 11 to become trite.

gasterópodo, -da adj. ZOOL. gast(e)ropodous. 2 m. ZOOL. gast(e)ropod. 3 pl. ZOOL. Gast(e)ropoda.

gasto m. expenditure, expense. 2 consumption, waste, use, wear. 3 PHYS. flow, rate of flow [of water, gas, electricity, etc.]. 4 pl. expenses: *gastos de conservación* or *mantenimiento*, upkeep, maintenance [expenses]; *gastos de explotación*, operating expenses; *gastos generales*, overhead charges or expenses; *gastos menores*, petty expenses; *cubrir gastos*, to cover expenses.

gastoso, -sa adj. spendthrift.

gastralgia f. MED. gastralgia.

gástrico, -ca adj. gastric.

gastritis f. MED. gastritis.

gastronomía f. gastronomy.

gastrónomo, -ma m.-f. gastronomer, gourmet.

gastrovascular adj. ZOOL. gastrovascular.

gástrula f. BIOL. gastrula.

gata f. she-cat. 2 Madrilene [woman].

gatada f. catlike act. 2 mean trick.

gatas (a) adv. on all fours.

gatatumba f. dissembling, pretence.

gatazo m. aug. big cat.

gatear intr. to climb [a pole, tree, etc.]. 2 to go on all fours; [of children] to creep. 3 tr. [of a cat] to scratch. 4 coll. to pilfer.

gatera f. cat's hole. 2 NAUT. cathole.

gatería f. cats, number of cats. 2 gang of ill-bred boys. 3 fake humility, cajolery.

gatesco, -ca adj. catlike, feline.

gatillo m. trigger, hammer, cock [of firearm]. 2 pelican, dentist's forceps. 3 nape [of bull, cow, etc.]. 4 clamping piece.

gatita f. dim. little she-cat, pussy, kitten.

gatito m. dim. little cat, pussy, kitten.

gato m. ZOOL. cat; tomcat: ~ *cerval*, tiger cat, serval; ~ *de algalia*, civet cat; ~ *montés*, wild cat; *cuatro gatos*, fig. a few people; ~ *encerrado*, fig. nigger in the woodpile; *dar ~ por liebre*, fig. to cheat [in a bargain]. 2 stocking, money [of a person]. 3 MECH. jack, lifting jack. 4 CARP. clamp. 5 Madrilene [man]. 6 fig. fox [shrewd fellow]. 7 sneak thief.

gatuno, -na adj. cat, catlike, feline.

gatuña f. BOT. restharrow.

gatuperio m. hodgepodge. 2 intrigue.

gaucho, -cha adj.-s. Gaucho.

gaudeamus, pl. **-mus** m. feast, merrymaking.

gaultería f. BOT. wintergreen.

gavanza f. dog rose [flower].

gavanzo m. BOT. dog rose [plant].

gaveta f. drawer [of writing desk].

gavia f. NAUT. topsail. 2 NAUT. maintopsail. 3 ditch. 4 ORN. gull. 5 MIN. gang of basket passers.

gavial m. ZOOL. gavial.

gaviero m. NAUT. topman.

gavilán m. ORN. sparrow hawk. 2 nib [of a quill pen]. 3 hair stroke [ending a letter]. 4 quillon [of swords]. 5 pappus.

gavilla f. sheaf, bundle, gavel. 2 gang: ~ *de pícaros*, gang of rogues.

gavina f. GAVIOTA.

gavinote *m.* ORN. young sea gull.
gavión *m.* FORT., HYD. gabion. *2* coll. large hat.
gaviota *f.* ORN. gull, sea gull.
gavota *f.* gavotte [dance and tune].
gaya *f.* stripe [on fabrics, etc.]. *2* ORN. magpie.
gayar *tr.* to trim or adorn with coloured stripes.
gayo, -ya *adj.* gay, bright, showy. *2* ~ *ciencia*, art of poetry.
gayomba *f.* BOT. kind of Spanish broom.
gayuba *f.* BOT. bearberry.
gaza *f.* NAT. strap, strop, eye.
gazapa *f.* coll. lie, fib.
gazapatón *m.* blunder, slip [in talking].
gazapera *f.* rabbit, hole, burrow or warren. *2* fig. den. *3* fig. brawl, row.
gazapo *m.* young rabbit. *2* sly fellow. *3* lie. *4* blunder, slip [in talking or writing].
gazmoñería *f.* prudery; demureness, affected modesty; sanctimony.
gazmoño, -ña *adj.* prude, prudish; demure, affectedly modest, sanctimonious.
gaznápiro, -ra *m.-f.* bumpkin, booby, simpleton.
gaznate *m.* gullet, throttle, windpipe.
gazpacho *m.* cold vegetable soup.
gazuza *f.* (coll.) keen appetite, hunger.
ge *f.* Spanish name of the letter *g*.
gea *f.* mineral kingdom of a region or country.
Gedeón *m. pr. n.* BIBL. Gideon.
gedeonada *f.* platitude, self-evident truth.
gehena *m.* Gehenna, hell.
géiser *m.* geyser [spring].
gel *m.* CHEM. gel.
gelatina *f.* gelatin(e, jelly.
gelatinoso, -sa *adj.* gelatinous.
gélido, -da *adj.* poet, gelid, chilly.
gema *f.* gem, precious stone. *2* BOT. bud, gemma.
gemación *f.* BOT., ZOOL. gemmation.
gemebundo, -da *adj.* groaning, moaning.
gemelo, -la *adj.-n.* twin. *2 m.* ANAT. gemellus. *3 pl.* cuff links. *4* binocular: *gemelos de campaña*, field glasses; *gemelos de teatro*, opera glasses. *5* ASTR. (cap.) Gemini.
gemido *m.* lamentation, moan, groan, wail.
geminado, -da *adj.* geminate(d.
geminar *tr.* to geminate.
Géminis *m.* ASTR. Gemini.
gemir *intr.* to moan, groan, wail, grieve. *2* [of wind, etc.] to wail. ¶ CONJUG. like *servir*.
gen *m.* BIOL. gene.
genciana *f.* BOT. gentian.
gendarme *m.* gendarme.
gendarmería *f.* gendarmerie.
genealogía *f.* genealogy.
genealógico, -ca *adj.* genealogical.
genealogista *m.* genealogist.
generación *f.* generation. *2* succession, lineage.
generador, -ra *adj.* generating. *2 m.* ELEC., MACH generator.
general *adj.* general: *en* ~, *por lo* ~, in general, generally. *2* common, usual. *3 m.* MIL., ECCL. general: ~ *de brigada*, brigadier general; ~ *de división*, major general; ~ *en jefe*, general in chief.
generala *f.* general's wife. *2* MIL. call to arms.
generalato *m.* generalship. *2* generals of an army.
generalidad *f.* generality.
generalísimo *m.* generalissimo.
generalización *f.* generalization.
generalizar *tr.-intr.* to generalize. *2 ref.* to become general, usual or prevalent; to spread.
generalmente *adj.* generally.
generar *tr.* to generate.

generativo, -va *adj.* generative.
generatriz, *pl.* **-trices** *f.* GEOM. generatrix.
genérico, -ca *adj.* generic.
género *m.* kind, sort, description. *2* manner, way. *3* kind, race: ~ *humano*, mankind. *4* GRAM. gender. *5* BIOL., LOG. genus. *6* F. ARTS, LIT. genre. *7* COM. cloth, stuff, material, goods, merchandise: ~ *de punto*, knit goods, knitwear.
generosidad *f.* generosity.
generoso, -sa *adj.* generous, magnanimous, nobleminded. *2* generous, liberal, munificent. *3* excellent. *4* generous [wine].
genésico, -ca *adj.* genesic.
génesis *f.* genesis. *2 m.* (cap.) BIBL. Genesis.
genético, -ca *adj.* genetic. *2 f.* genetics.
genial *adj.* genial [denoting or marked with genius]. *2* endowed with genius, brilliant, inspired. *3* temperamental. *4* cheerful, pleasant.
genialidad *f.* eccentricity, peculiarity.
geniazo *m.* strong or fiery temper.
genio *m.* temper, disposition, nature; *de buen* ~, good-tempered; *de mal* ~, evil-tempered. *2* coll. fire, spirit: *corto de* ~, timid. *3* hot temper. *4* genius. *5* peculiarities [of an language]. *6* MYTH. genie, jinnee, jinni. *7* ~ *del mal*, evil spirit.
genital *adj.* genital.
genitivo, -va *adj.* generative. *2 adj.-m.* GRAM. genitive.
genitor *m.* begetter.
genízaro, -ra *adj.* JENÍZARO.
genol *m.* NAUT. futtok.
genovés, -sa *adj.* Genoese.
gente *f.* people, folk, folks: ~ *bien*, smart set; ~ *de bien*, honest people; ~ *de mar*, seamen; ~ *de pluma*, clerks; ~ *menuda*, children; ~ *principal*, important people. *2* troops. *3* retinue. *4* coll. family, folks. *5* clan, nation. *6 pl.* Gentiles.
gentecilla *f.* dim. contemptible people.
gentil *adj.-n.* gentile, heathen, pagan. *2 adj.* handsome, graceful, lively.
gentileza *f.* handsomeness, gracefulness, elegance. *2* show, splendour. *3* courtesy, graciousness.
gentilhombre *m.* obs. my good man. *2* gentleman [attendant to a person of high rank].
gentilicio, -cia *adj.* GRAM. gentile, gentilic.
gentílico, -ca *adj.* gentilic, heathen, pagan.
gentilidad *f.*, **gentilismo** *m.* gentilism, heathenism. *2* heathendom.
gentilmente *adv.* gracefully, elegantly. *2* courteously. *3* generously. *4* heathenishly.
gentío *m.* crowd, throng, multitude.
gentuza *f.* riff-raff, rabble.
genuflexión *f.* genuflexion.
genuino, -na *adj.* genuine, true, pure, real.
geocéntrico, -ca *adj.* geocentric(al.
geoda *f.* GEOL. geode.
geodesia *f.* geodesy.
geofísica *f.* geophysics.
geogenia *f.* geogeny.
geognosia *f.* geognosy.
geografía *f.* geography.
geográfico, -ca *adj.* geographic(al.
geógrafo *m.* geographer.
geología *f.* geology.
geológico, -ca *adj.* geologic(al.
geólogo *m.* geologist.
geómetra *m.* geometer, geometrician. *2* ZOOL. measuring worm.
geometría *f.* geometry.
geométrico, -ca *adj.* geometric(al.

geopolítica *f.* geopolitics.
geórgica *f.* georgic [poem].
geotactismo *m.*, **geotaxia** *f.* BIOL. geotaxis.
geotropismo *m.* BIOL. geotropism.
geraniáceo, -a *adj.* BOT. geraniaceous.
geranio *m.* BOT. geranium.
Gerardo *m. pr. n.* Gerald.
gerbo *m.* JERBO.
gerencia *f.* COM. management, managership. *2* manager's office.
gerente *m.* COM. manager.
gerifalte *m.* ORN. gerfalcon: *como un* ~, wonderfully.
germanía *f.* slang or jargon of the gypsies, thieves, etc.
germánico, -ca *adj.* Germanic. *2 m.* Germanic [language].
germanio *m.* CHEM. germanium.
germanismo *m.* Germanism.
germanizar *tr.* to Germanize.
germano, -na *adj.* Germanic, Teutonic. *2 m.-f.* German, Teuton [of ancient Germany].
germen *m.* germ. *2* fig. spring, origin.
germinación *f.* germination.
germinal *adj.* germinal.
germinar *intr.* to germinate.
gerontología *f.* gerontology.
Gertrudis *f. pr. n.* Gertrude.
gerundense *adj.-n.* of or from Gerona.
gerundio *m.* GRAM. gerund. *2* bombastic writer or speaker [esp. a preacher or theologist].
Gervasio *m. pr. n.* Gervas.
gesta *f.* gest, geste: *cantar de* ~, chanson de geste.
gestación *f.* gestation.
gestatorio, -ria *adj.* gestatorial.
gestear *intr.* to make faces or grimaces.
gesticulación *f.* expressive movement of the features.
gesticular *intr.* to make faces or expressive movements of the features.
gestión *f.* action, negotiation, steps, exertions. *2* administration, management.
gestionar *tr.* to take steps to; to negotiate.
gesto *m.* distortion of one's countenance; face, grimace: *hacer gestos a una cosa,* to make faces at a thing; *poner* ~, to look annoyed. *2* face, countenance.
gestor *m.* COM. manager, director. *2* COM. ~ *de negocios,* agent.
Getsemaní *pr. n.* BIBL. Gethsemane.
giba *f.* hump, hunch. *2* coll. annoyance, inconvenience.
gibado, -da *adj.* humped; hunchbacked.
gibelino, -na *adj.-n.* Ghibelline.
gibosidad *f.* gibbosity.
giboso, -sa *adj.* gibbous, crookbacked, hunchbacked.
Gibraltar *m. pr. n.* GEOG. Gibraltar.
gibraltareño, -ña *adj.-n.* of Gibraltar.
giga *f.* jig [dance].
giganta *f.* giantess. *2* BOT. sunflower.
gigante *adj.* giant, gigantic. *2 m.* giant. *3* giant pasteboard figure [borne in processions].
gigantesco, -ca *adj.* gigantic.
gigantismo *m.* MED. giantism, gigantism.
gigantón, -na *m.-f.* huge giant. *2* GIGANTE 3.
gigote *m.* chopped-meat stew.
Gil *m. pr. n.* Giles.
Gilberto *m. pr. n.* Gilbert.
gilvo, -va *adj.* honey-coloured.
gimnasia *f.* gymnastics.

gimnasio *m.* gymnasium.
gimnasta *m.* gymnast.
gimnástico, -ca *adj.* gymnastic. *2 f.* GIMNASIA.
gimnoto *m.* ICHTH. electric eel.
gimotear *intr.* to whine, to moan.
gimoteo *m.* whining.
gindama *f.* JINDAMA.
Ginebra *f. pr. n.* GEOG. Geneva. *2* MYTH. Guinevere.
ginebra *f.* gin [liquor].
ginebrino, -na *adj.-n.* Genevan, Genevese.
gineceo *m.* gynaeceum, gynaecium.
ginecología *f.* gynecology.
ginecólogo *m.* gynecologist.
ginesta *f.* RETAMA.
gineta *f.* ZOOL. genet.
gira *f.* trip, excursion, tour.
girado, -da *m.-f.* COM. drawee.
girador, -ra *m.-f.* COM. drawer.
giralda *f.* weathercock in the form of an animal or human figure. *2 la Giralda,* the Giralda.
girándula *f.* girandole [fireworks; fountain].
girante *m.* gyrating.
girar *intr.* to gyrate, revolve, rotate, turn, spin, swivel; to turn [to the right, the left, etc.]. *2* ~ *en torno de,* [of a discussion, etc.] to turn on, to center round. *3* COM. to trade. *4 tr.-intr.* COM. to draw.
girasol *m.* BOT. sunflower.
giratorio, -ria *adj.* gyratory, revolving, swivel.
girino *m.* ENT. whirligig.
giro *m.* gyration, revolution, turn. *2* turn, course, bias: *tomar otro* ~, to take another course. *3* turn [of expression]. *4* COM. draft: ~ *postal,* money order. *5* COM. trade, circulation, bulk of business.
girola *f.* ARCH. apse aisle.
girondino, -na *adj.-n.* HIST. Girondist.
giroscopio *m.* gyroscope.
giróstato *m.* gyrostat.
giste *m.* froth of beer.
gitana *f.* gypsy woman or girl.
gitanada *f.* gypsylike trick, mean trick. *2* cajolerie.
gitanería *f.* gypsylike cajolery or wheedling. *2* gypsydom; assembly of gypsies.
gitanesco, -ca *adj.* gypsylike, gypsy.
gitano, -na *adj.* gypsy. *2* sly, honeymouthed. *3 m.-f.* gypsy, Spanish gypsy.
glabro, -bra *adj.* glabrous.
glacial *adj.* glacial. *2* fig. cold, chilly.
glacis *m.* FORT. glacis.
gladiador *m.* gladiator.
gladio, gladiolo *m.* BOT. gladiolus.
glande *m.* ANAT. glans penis.
glándula *f.* ANAT., BOT. gland: ~ *pineal,* pineal body, pineal gland.
glandular *adj.* glandular.
glanduloso, -sa *adj.* glandulous.
glasé *m.* glacé silk.
glasear *tr.* to calender, satin; to glaze.
glasto *m.* BOT. woad.
glauco, -ca *adj.* glaucous, light green.
glaucoma *m.* MED. glaucoma.
gleba *f.* clod or lump of earth.
glena *f.* ANAT. glenoid cavity.
glicerina *m.* glycerin.
glicina *f.* BOT., CHEM. glycine. *2* BOT. wisteria.
glicógeno *m.* GLUCÓGENO.
glíptica *f.* glyptics.
gliptografía *f.* glyptography.
global *adj.* taken in a lump, in all.
globo *m.* globe, ball, orb, sphere: ~ *terráqueo,*

globe, terrestrial globe. 2 globe [lampshade]. 3 balloon, air balloon: ~ *aerostático*, air balloon; ~ *sonda*, sounding balloon. 4 ANAT. ~ *del ojo*, eyeball. 5 *en* ~, in bulk, as a whole, without details.

globoso, -sa *adj.* globose, globate.

globular *adj.* globular, globulous.

globulina *f.* BIOCHEM. globulina.

glóbulo *m.* globule. 2 PHYSIOL. corpuscle.

glomérulo *m.* BOT. glomerule.

gloria *f.* glory. 2 heaven, eternal bliss. 3 bliss, delight, keen pleasure: *estar en sus glorias*, to delight in what one is doing; *saber a* ~, to taste heavenly. 4 boast, pride. 5 gloria [fabric]. 6 a gauzy silk tissue. 7 *m.* ECCL. Glory.

gloriarse *ref.* ~ *de*, to pride oneself on, boast of; ~ *en*, to glory in.

glorieta *f.* arbour, bower, summerhouse. 2 circus [circle or square with streets converging on it].

glorificación *f.* glorification. 2 praise, extolling.

glorificar *tr.* to glorify. 2 *ref.* GLORIARSE.

glorioso, -sa *adj.* glorious [possessing or conferring glory; illustrious, praseworthy]. 2 holy, blessed. 3 proud, boastful.

glosa *f.* gloss, comment, explanation. 2 gloss [poem]. 3 MUS. variation.

glosar *tr.* to gloss, annotate, comment. 2 to compose a gloss to [a stanza]. 3 MUS. to vary [a theme].

glosario *m.* glossary.

glosopeda *f.* VET. foot-and-mouth disease.

glotis *f.* ANAT. glottis.

glotón, -na *adj.* gluttonous. 2 *m.-f.* glutton. 3 *m.* ZOOL. glutton.

glotonear *intr.* to gluttonize, gormandize.

glotonería *f.* gluttony.

glucemia *f.* MED. glucemia, glucaemia.

glucinio *m.* CHEM. glucinium.

glucógeno *m.* CHEM. glycogen.

glucosa *f.* CHEM. glucose.

glugú *m.* gurgle, glug.

gluma *f.* BOT. glume.

gluten *m.* gluten. 2 glue.

glúteo, -a *adj.* ANAT. gluteal.

glutinoso, -sa *adj.* glutinous.

gneis *m.* GEOL. gneiss.

gnomo *m.* gnome.

gnomon *m.* gnomon.

gnomónico, -ca *adj.* gnomonic(al. 2 *f.* gnomonics.

gnosticismo *m.* Gnosticism.

gnóstico *adj.-n.* Gnostic.

gobernación *f.* governing. 2 *ministerio de la* ~, Home Office; *Department of the Interior.

gobernador, -ra *adj.* governing. 2 *m.* governor [official; ruler]. 3 *f.* woman governor. 4 governor's wife.

gobernalle *m.* NAUT. rudder, helm.

gobernante *adj.* governing, ruling. 2 *m.-f.* ruler, member of a government.

gobernar *tr.-intr.* to govern, rule. 2 *tr.* to direct, manage, control. 3 NAUT. to steer [a ship]. 4 *intr.* NAUT. to steer, obey the helm. 5 *ref.* to manage one's affairs. ¶ CONJUG. like *acertar*.

gobierno *m.* governing, government, ruling. 2 direction, guidance, management, control: ~ *de la casa*, nousekeeping; *para tu* ~, for your guidance. 3 NAUT. steering. 4 NAUT. rudder, helm. 5 control [of an automobile, an airplane, etc.]. 6 POL. government, cabinet, administration. 7 governorship; governor's office. 8 government [district].

gobierno, gobierne, etc. *irr.* V. GOBERNAR.

gobio *m.* ICHTH. gudgeon.

goce *m.* enjoyment, fruition.

godo, -da *adj.-n.* Goth.

Godofredo *m. pr. n.* Godfrey.

goflo *m.* (Am.) roasted flour or maize meal.

gofo, -fa *adj.* ignorant and rude. 2 PAINT. dwarf [figure].

gol *m.* SPORT. goal [making a goal].

gola *f.* ANAT. throat. 2 ARM., MIL. gorget. 3 ruff; ruche [collar]. 4 FORT. gorge. 5 ARCH. cyma.

goleta *f.* NAUT. schooner.

golf *m.* SPORT. golf.

golfear *intr.* to loaf, idle.

golfería *f.* street Arabs, loafers, ᐧ agabonds.

golfillo *m.* street Arab, guttersnipe.

golfín *m.* DELFÍN 2.

golfista *m.-f.* SPORT. golfer.

1) **golfo** *m.* GEOG. gulf, large bay. 2 sea, main. 3 a card game.

2) **golfo, -fa** *m.-f.* loafer, vagabond, ragamuffin. 2 *m.* street Arab, guttersnipe.

Gólgota *m. pr. n.* BIBL. Golgotha.

Goliat *m. pr. n.* BIBL. Goliath.

golilla *f.* collar formerly worn by magistrates or court clerks.

golondrina *f.* ORN. swallow. 2 ICHTH. swallow fish. 3 ORN. ~ *de mar*, tern.

golondrino *m.* young swallow. 2 wanderer, vagabond. 3 MIL. deserter. 4 MED. tumor in the armpit.

golondro *m.* *campar de* ~, to live at another's expense.

golosamente *adv.* eagerly, with relish.

golosear *tr.* GOLOSINAR.

golosina *f.* dainty, delicacy, sweet, titbit. 2 sweet tooth, appetite for delicacies; appetite; yearning; greediness. 3 pleasing trifle.

golosinar, golosinear *intr.* to eat, or look for, delicacies and sweetmeats.

golosmear *intr.* GULUSMEAR.

goloso, -sa *adj.* sweet-toothed, fond of delicacies. 2 fond of [something].

golpazo *m.* heavy blow or knock.

golpe *m.* blow, bump, hit, knock, stroke; coup: ~ *de Estado*, coup d'état; ~ *de fortuna*, stroke of luck; ~ *de gracia*, coup de grâce; finishing blow; ~ *de mar*, heavy sea [striking a ship, etc.]; ~ *de remo*, oar stroke; ~ *de vista*, glance; view, sight; *errar el* ~, to miss one's aim, to fail; *parar el* ~, to stop or ward off the blow; *a golpes*, by knocking; brutally; at intervals; *de* ~, suddenly, quickly; *de* ~ *y porrazo*, all of a sudden. 2 impact, impingement. 3 hurt, bruise. 4 abundance, great number or quantity [of something]. 5 hard blow, shock [sudden misfortune]. 6 *dar* ~, to astonish. take, create a sensation. 7 witty sally or remark. 8 GAMBLING coup. 9 spring bolt. 10 SEW. trimming of braid, beads, etc. [on a dress]. 11 pocket flap. 12 MECH. stroke [of piston]; travel [of a valve].

golpeadura *f.* striking, beating, hitting, knocking.

golpear *tr.-intr.* to strike, beat, knock [repeatedly], to pummel, pound.

golpecito *m. dim.* slight blow or stroke.

golpeo *m.* GOLPEADURA.

golpete *m.* door or window catch [to keep it open].

golpetear *tr.-intr.* to beat, knock, hammer or strike repeatedly; to rattle.

golpeteo *m.* repeated beating; rattling.

gollería *f.* dainty, delicacy, superfluity.

golletazo *m.* blow on the neck of a bottle [to break it open]. *2* sudden termination of an affair. *3* BULLF. stab in the neck of bull.
gollete *m.* throat, neck. *2* neck [of bottle].
goma *f.* gum; rubber: ~ *adragante*, gum dragon, tragacanth; ~ *arábiga*, gum arabic; ~ *de mascar*, chewing gum; ~ *elástica*, gum elastic; ~ *laca*, lacker. *2* rubber band. *3* rubber eraser. *4* MED. gumma.
gomero, -ra *adj.* [pertaining to] gum, rubber. *2 m.* (Am.) rubber producer.
gomia *f.* bugbear. *2* glutton. *3* fig. waster.
gomífero, -ra *adj.* gummiferous.
gomorresina *f.* gum resin.
gomosería *f.* dandyism, foppishness.
gomosidad *f.* gumminess, stickiness.
gomoso, -sa *adj.* gummy, viscous. *2 m.* dandy, fop.
gonce *m.* GOZNE.
góndola *f.* gondola [boat]. *2* kind of omnibus.
gondolero *m.* gondolier.
gonfalón *m.* gonfalon.
gonfalonier, -ro *m.* gonfalonier.
gong *m.* gong.
gongorismo *m.* Gongorism.
goniometría *f.* goniometry.
goniómetro *m.* goniometer.
gordal *adj.* big, large-sized.
gordiano *adj.* Gordian.
gordinflón, -na *adj.* chubby, fat and flabby.
gordito, -ta *adj. dim.* somewhat fat, plump.
gordo, -da *adj.* fat, obese, stout. *2* bulky. *3* fat, greasy, oily. *4* thick [thread, paper, cloth, etc.]. *5* big, large, of importance: *premio* ~, first prize [in lotery]. *6* hard [water]. *7 dedo* ~, thumb; big toe. *8 hacer la vista gorda*, to pretend not to see, to wink at. *9 m.* fat, grease, suet. *10 f. se armó la gorda*, there was the devil of a row.
gordolobo *m.* BOT. mullein, great mullein.
gordura *f.* fatness. *2* fat, grease.
gorgojo *m.* ENT. weevil. *2* fig. tiny person.
Gorgona *f.* MYTH. Gorgon.
gorgor *m.* GORGOTEO.
gorgoritear *intr.* to trill, quaver [in singing].
gorgorito *m.* trill, quaver [in singing]: *hacer gorgoritos*, to trill.
gorgoteo *m.* gurgle, gurgling sound.
gorguera *f.* ruff [collar]. *2* ARM. gorget.
gorigori *m.* coll. chant at funerals.
gorila *m.* ZOOL. gorilla.
gorja *f.* gorje, throat.
gorjal *m.* ARM. gorget.
gorjear *intr.* to trill, warble. *2* [of a baby] to gurgle.
gorjeo *m.* trill, warble, warbling. *2* gurgle [of a baby].
gormar *tr.* to vomit.
gorra *f.* cap [headgear without a brim]: ~ *de visera*, cap [with a visor]. *2* bearskin, hussar's cap. *3* baby's bonnet. *4* coll. sponging: *de* ~, at other people's expense.
gorrería *f.* cap factory or shop.
gorrero, -ra *m.-f.* cap maker or seller. *2 m.* parasite, sponger.
gorretada *f.* doffing the cap [in greeting].
gorrín *m.* GORRINO.
gorrinada *f.* pigs, number of pigs. *2* dirty action.
gorrinera *f.* pigsty.
gorrinería *f.* dirt, dirtiness. *2* dirty action.
gorrino, -na *m.-f.* sucking pig. *2* hog; sow. *3* fig. slovenly person; pig.
gorrión *m.* ORN. sparrow.

gorriona *f.* female sparrow.
gorrionera *f.* den of vice.
gorrista *m.-f.* parasite, sponger.
gorro *m.* cap [without a visor]; coif: ~ *de dormir*, nightcap; ~ *frigio*, liberty cap. *2* baby's bonnet.
gorrón, -na *adj.* sponging. *2 m.-f.* sponger, parasite. *3 m.* large round pebble. *4* MACH. journal, gudgeon, pivot. *5 f.* harlot, strumpet.
gorronería *f.* sponging, parasitism.
gorullo *m.* BURUJO.
gota *f.* drop [of a liquid]; raindrop: ~ *a* ~, drop by drop; *no ver* ~, fig. to see nothing; *sudar la* ~ *gorda*, fig. to work one's head off. *2* ARCH. drop, gutta. *3* MED. gout. *4* MED. ~ *serena*, amaurosis.
goteado, -da *adj.* spotted, speckled.
gotear *intr.* to dribble, drip [fall in drops]. *2* to sprinkle [begin to rain].
goteo *m.* dribbling, dripping.
gotera *f.* leak, leakage [in a roof]. *2* dripping [from a roof]; mark left by dripping water. *3* valance [of canopy]. *4* chronical ailment.
goterón *m.* big raindrop. *2* ARCH. throat.
gótico, -ca *adj.* Gothic: *letra gótica*, black letter. *2* noble, illustrious. *3 m.* Gothic art.
gotón, -na *adj.-n.* Goth.
gotoso, -sa *adj.* gouty. *2 m.-f.* gout sufferer.
goyesco, -ca *adj.* [pertaining to] Goya; in the style of Goya.
gozar *tr.-intr.* to enjoy [have, posess, have the benefit of]: ~ *de buena salud*, to enjoy good health. *2 tr.* to have carnal knowledge of [a woman]. *3 intr.-ref.* to enjoy oneself; to enjoy, rejoice, take a pleasure: *gozarse en*, to take pleasure in.
gozne *m.* hinge.
gozo *m.* joy, gladness, glee, pleasure: *no caber en sí de* ~, to be bursting with joy. *2 pl.* couplets in praise of the Virgin or a Saint.
gozoso, -sa *adj.* joyous, joyful, glad, gleeful.
gozque *m.* a little yapping dog.
grabación *f.* recording: ~ *en disco*, recording on phonograph record; ~ *en cinta magnetofónica*, wire or tape recording.
grabado *m.* engraving [art, process, plate, picture]; cut, print; gravure: ~ *al agua fuerte*, etching; ~ *al agua tinta*, aquatint. *2* picture [in a book, newspaper, etc.].
grabador, -ra *m.-f.* engraver; woodcutter; diesinker.
grabadura *f.* engraving [act].
grabar *tr.* to engrave; ~ *al agua fuerte*, to etch; ~ *en la mente*, to engrave in the mind. *2* to sink [a punch or die]. *3* to record [for reproduction]. *4 ref.* to become engraved.
grabazón *f.* engraved onlays.
gracia *f.* THEOL. grace: *estar en* ~, to be in state of grace. *2* grace, charm; gracefulness. *3* grace, favour, kindness: *de* ~, for nothing; *hacer* ~ *de*, to excuse from, to free from. *4* graciousness, affability. *5* grace, favour, good graces: *caer en* ~, to find favour with; to please, be liked; *más vale caer en* ~ *que ser gracioso*, better to be lucky than wise. *6* grace, pardon, mercy. *7* witticism; point [of a joke]. *8* comicalness, funniness, pleasantness: *hacer* ~, to raise a laugh, amuse, be funny; fig. to please, be liked: *¡qué* ~*!*, iron. how funny!, how fine! *9* name [of a person]. *10* facility, dexterity. *11 en* ~ *a*, in consideration of, for the sake of. *12 pl.* thanks: *¡gracias!*, thank you; *gracias a*, thanks to [owing to]; *gracias a Dios*, thank God. *13* grace [thanksgiving after a meal]: *dar gracias*, to say grace. *14* charms, ac-

complishments. *15* MYTH. *las Gracias,* the Graces.

grácil *adj.* gracile, slender, small.

graciosidad *f.* grace, gracefulness, beauty.

gracioso, -sa *adj.* graceful, charming. *2* gracious, gratuitous. *3* witty, facetious. *4* comical, funny. *5 m.-f.* THEAT. actor, actress playing the funny rôles.

Graco *m. pr. n.* HIST. Graccus.

grada *f.* step [of stairs]. *2* gradin, tier of seats. *3* gradins of an amphitheatre, etc. *4* footpace [of altar]. *5* NAUT. slip [of shipyard]. *6* AGR. harrow. *7 pl.* stone steps [in front of a building].

gradación *f.* gradation. *2* RHET. climax.

gradar *tr.* AGR. to harrow.

gradería *f.* gradins, tier of seats [in an amphitheatre, etc.]; series of steps.

gradiente *m.* METEOR. gradient. *2* gradient, slope.

gradilla *f.* small stepladder. *2* brick mould. *3* CHEM. tube, rack. *4* gradin [of altar].

gradina *f.* gradine, sculptor's chisel.

grado *m.* step [of stairs]. *2* degree [in a scale or process]. *3* grade [degree in quality, value, etc.]. *4* [academic] degree. *5* EDUC. section of an elementary school, *grade. *6* ALG., GEOM., MUS., GRAM. degree. *7* degree, measure: *en sumo ~,* in the highest degree. *8* degree [of relationship]. *9* MIL. brevet. *10* will, willingness: *de ~, de buen ~,* willingly; *de ~ o por fuerza,* willy-nilly; *mal de mi ~,* against my wishes, much to my regret. *11 pl.* ECCL. minor orders.

graduable *adj.* adjustable.

graduación *f.* graduation, grading. *2* strength [of spirituous liquors]. *3* MIL. rank, degree of rank. *4* EDUC. admission to a degree.

graduado, -da *adj.* graduated, graded. *2* MIL. brevetted. *3 m.-f.* graduate.

gradual *adj.* gradual. *2 m.* ECCL. gradual.

graduando, -da *m.-f.* candidate for a degree.

graduar *tr.* to regulate, adjust, set. *2* to graduate [in nearly every sense]. *3* to determine the degree or quality of. *4* MIL. to brevet. *5 ref.* EDUC. to *graduate, receive a degree.

grafía *f.* GRAM. graph.

gráfico, -ca *adj.* graphic, graphical. *2* ilustrated [newspaper, magazine, etc.]. *3 m.* diagram. *4 f.* graph.

gráfila, grafila *f.* circle of dots around field of coin.

grafito *m.* MINER. graphite.

grafología *f.* graphology.

gragea *f.* small coloured sugarplums. *2* PHARM. sugar-coated pill.

graja *f.* female rook.

grajear *intr.* to caw. *2* [of a baby] to gurgle.

grajo *m.* ORN. rook, crow, common rook.

grama *f.* BOT. Bermuda grass, scutch grass. *2* BOT. *~ del Norte,* couch grass, scutch grass. *3* BOT. *~ de color,* or *de los prados,* vernal grass.

gramalla *f.* an ancient robe. *2* coat of mail.

gramática *f.* grammar. *2* coll. *~ parda,* shrewdness.

gramatical *adj.* grammatical.

gramático, -ca *adj.* grammatical. *2 m.-f.* grammarian.

gramil *m.* CARP. gauge, marking gauge.

gramináceo, -a *adj.* BOT. graminaceous.

gramo *m.* gram, gramme [weight].

gramófono *m.* gramophone.

gramola *f.* console phonograph. *2* portable gramophone.

gran *adj.* contr. of GRANDE, used before *m.* or *f.*

nouns in the singular: *~ bestia,* ZOOL. elk; *~ cruz,* grand cross; *~ visir,* grand vizier.

grana *f.* seeding. *2* seeding time. *3* small seed of some plants. *4* cochineal. *5* kermes [dyestuff]. *6* kermes berry. *7* scarlet colour. *8* a fine cloth. *9* BOT. *~ del Paraíso,* cardamom.

Granada *f. pr. n.* GEOG. Granada. *2 Nueva ~,* New Granada.

granada *f.* BOT. pomegranate [fruit]. *2* MIL. grenade, shell: *~ de mano,* hand grenade.

granadera *f.* grenadier's pouch.

granadero *m.* MIL. grenadier.

granadilla *f.* BOT. passionflower. *2* passion fruit.

granadillo *m.* BOT. granadilla tree, red ebony.

granadina *f.* grenadine [fabric; syrup].

granadino, -na *adj.* [pertaining to] pomegranate. *2 adj.-n.* of Granada [Spain]. *3 m.* pomegranate flower.

granado, -da *adj.* choice, select. *2* distinguished, illustrious. *3* mature, expert. *4* tall, grown. *5* AGR. seedy. *6 m.* BOT. pomegranate [tree].

granalla *f.* FOUND. granulated metal.

granar *intr.* [of plants] to seed.

granate *m.* garnet [stone and colour].

granazón *f.* seeding [forming seeds].

Gran Bretaña *f. pr. n.* GEOG. Great Britain.

grande *adj.* large, big; great, grand: *en ~,* as a whole; in a big way; grandly. *2 m.* grandee; *~ de España,* Spanish grandee.

grandeza *f.* bigness, largeness. *2* size, magnitude. *3* greatness, grandeur. *4* magnificence. *5* grandeeship. *6* the grandees.

grandilocuencia *f.* grandiloquence.

grandilocuente; grandílocuo, -cua *adj.* grandiloquent, grandiloquous.

grandiosidad *f.* grandeur, magnificence.

grandioso, -sa *adj.* grandiose, grand, magnificent.

grandor *m.* size, magnitude.

grandote *adj.* biggish.

grandullón, -na *adj.* overgrown.

graneado, -da *adj.* grained. *2* spotted. *3* MIL. *fuego ~,* drumfire.

granear *tr.* to grain [powder; a lithographic stone]; to stipple [in engraving].

granel (a) *adv.* loose, in bulk. *2* in abundance.

granelar *tr.* to grain [leather].

granero *m.* granary, barn. *2* fig. granary [region].

granillo *m.* small grain. *2* small pimple.

granítico, -ca *adj.* granitic.

granito *m.* small grain or pimple. *2* MINER. granite.

granívoro, -ra *adj.* granivorous.

granizada *f.* hailstorm. *2* fig. hail, shower.

granizado *m.* iced drink: *~ de café,* iced coffee.

granizar *intr.* to hail. *2 tr.* to hail, shower as hail.

granizo *m.* hail; hailstorm.

granja *f.* grange, farm. *2* dairy [farm or shop].

granjear *tr.* to gain, earn, acquire. *2 tr.-ref.* to win [the affection, etc., of].

granjería *f.* gain, profit.

granjero, -ra *m.-f.* granger, farmer.

grano *m.* grain [of cereals]. *2* small seed. *3* berry, grape, bean: *~ de café,* coffee bean. *4* grain [small hard particle]. *5* grain [of the wood, the stone, the leather, etc.]. *6* grain [weight]. *7* pimple. *8* *ir al ~,* to come to the point. *9 pl.* COM. grain, corn, small seeds.

granoso, -sa *adj.* grained.

granuja *f.* loose grapes. *2* grapeseed. *3 m.* gamin, waif, street Arab. *4* knave, rascal.

granujada *f.* scurvy trick, knavery.

granujería *f.* lot of gamins. *2* lot of rascals, rascaldom. *3* GRANUJADA.
granulación *f.* granulation.
granulado, -da *adj.* granulated.
1) **granular** *adj.* granular.
2) **granular** *tr.* to granulate. *2 ref.* MED. to granulate.
gránulo *m.* granule.
granuloso, -sa *adj.* granulose.
granza *f.* BOT. madder.
granzas *f. pl.* chaff, shiftings, screenings. *2* dross of metals.
grao *m.* beach used as a landing place.
grapa *f.* staple, cramp, cramp-iron.
grapón *m.* large staple or cramp.
grasa *f.* grease, fat. *2* lubricant grease. *3* greasy dirt.
grasera *f.* vessel for grease. *2* COOK. dripping pan.
graseza *f.* fattiness, greasiness.
grasiento, -ta *adj.* greasy, oily.
grasilla *f.* pounce [powder].
graso, -sa *adj.* greasy, fat. *2* CHEM. fat [acid]. *3 m.* GRASEZA.
grasoso, -sa *adj.* greasy [permeated with grease].
grasura *f.* GROSURA.
grata *f.* wire brush.
gratificación *f.* gratification, gratuity, tip; bonus.
gratificar *tr.* to gratify, reward, tip. *2* to gratify, please.
grátil, gratil *m.* NAUT. head [of sail]. *2* NAUT. slings [of a yard].
gratitud *f.* gratitude, gratefulness.
gratis *adv.* gratis.
grato, -ta *adj.* agreeable, pleasant, pleasing. *2* acceptable. *3 f. su grata,* your favour [letter].
gratuito, -ta *adj.* gratuitous.
gratulación *f.* congratulation. *2* rejoicing.
grava *f.* pebble gravel. *2* broken stone [for roadbeds].
gravamen *m.* burden, obligation. *2* tax, impost, duty. *3* mortgage, lien, encumbrance.
gravar *tr.* to weigh on or upon. *2* to burden [with taxes, etc.], to tax. *3* to encumber [property].
grave *adj.* heavy [heaving weight]. *2* grave, weighty, important, serious. *3* difficult, troublesome. *4* grave, dignified, solemn. *5* elevated [style]. *6* grave [sound]; deep [voice]. *7* GRAM. grave [accent]. *8* GRAM. having the stress on the penultimate syllable [word]. *9* MED. serious, dangerous [illness, wound]; in a dangerous condition [patient].
gravedad *f.* PHYS. gravity. *2* MUS. gravity. *3* gravity, importance, seriousness: *herido de ~,* dangerously wounded. *4* gravity, graveness.
gravidez *f.* pregnancy, gravidity.
grávido, -da *adj.* gravid. *2* full [of], abundant [in].
gravimetría *f.* gravimetry.
gravímetro *m.* PHYS. gravimeter.
gravitación *f.* gravitation.
gravitar *intr.* to gravitate. *2* to weigh [upon].
gravoso, -sa *adj.* burdensome, onerous. *2* annoying, hard to bear.
graznar *intr.* [of a crow, rook or raven] to caw, croak. *2* [of a goose] to cackle, gaggle.
graznido *m.* caw, croak [of crow, rook or raven]. *2* cackle, gaggle [of goose].
greba *f.* ARM. greave.
greca *f.* fret, Greek fret.
Grecia *f. pr. n.* GEOG. Greece.
grecizar *tr.-intr.* to Grecize.
greco, -ca *adj.-n.* Greek.

grecolatino, -na *adj.* Greco-Latin.
grecorromano, -na *adj.* Greco-Roman.
greda *f.* clay, fuller's earth.
gredoso, -sa *adj.* clayey.
gregal *m.* northeast wind [in the Mediterranean].
gregario, -ria *adj.* gregarious [pertaining to a crowd]. *2* servilely following other people's initiatives.
gregoriano, -na *adj.* Gregorian.
Gregorio *m. pr. n.* Gregory.
greguería *f.* hubbub, uproar.
gregüescos *m. pl.* wide breeches.
greguizar *intr.* to Grecize.
gremial *adj.* (pertaining to a) guild. *2 m.* guildsman. *3* ECCL. gremial.
gremio *m.* guild, corporation. *2* body, pale [of the Church].
greña *f.* [usually *pl.*] shock, head of dishevelled hair: *andar a la ~* [of women], to pull each other's hair; to wrangle. *2* something tangled or matted.
greñudo, -da *adj.* shock-headed.
gres *m.* material for making pottery refractory to heat and acids.
gresca *f.* merry noise, hubbub. *2* shindy, brawl.
grey *f.* flock, herd. *2* fig. flock [Christian body; congregation; people, race, nation].
grial *m.* grail: *el Santo Grial,* the Holy Grail.
griego, -ga *adj.-n.* Greek, Grecian. *2 m.* Greek [Greek language; inintelligible language].
grieta *f.* crack, crevice, cleft, flaw. *2* chap [in skin].
grifo, -fa *adj.* kinky, tangled [hair]. *2 adj.-f.* PRINT. script [type]. *3 m.* faucet, tap, cock. *4* MYTH. griffin.
grillarse *ref.* [of a seed, potato, etc.] to sprout.
grillete *m.* fetter, shackle.
grillo *m.* ENT. cricket: *~ cebollero* or *real,* mole cricket. *2* sprout [of a seed, potato, etc.]. *3 pl.* fetters, irons.
grillotalpa *m.* ENT. mole cricket.
grima *f.* horror; vexation, irritation: *dar ~,* to cause horror; to vex, irritate.
grímpola *f.* NAUT. pennant, streamer.
gringo, -ga *m.-f.* scorn. (Am.) foreigner [esp. English or American]. *2 m.* coll. gibberish.
griñón *m.* wimple. *2* BOT. nectarine.
gripal *adj.* MED. grippal.
gripe *f.* MED. grippe, flu.
gris *adj.* grey, gray. *2* dull, cloudy [day]. *3* dull, monotonous. *4 m.* ZOOL. a Siberian squirrel and its fur. *5* cold, cold wind.
grisáceo, -a *adj.* greyish.
grisalla *f.* grisaille [decorative painting].
gríseo, -a *adj.* greyish.
grisú *m.* MIN. firedamp.
grita *f.* shouting. *2* hooting [in disapproval].
gritador, -ra *adj.* shouting. *2 m.-f.* shouter.
gritar *intr.-tr.* to shout, cry out; scream. *2* to hoot [in disapproval].
gritería *f.,* **griterío** *m.* shouting, outcry, uproar.
grito *m.* shout, cry, scream, hoot: *alzar el ~,* to talk loud and haughtily; *poner el ~ en el cielo,* to complain vehemently; *a ~ herido* or *pelado, a voz en ~,* at the top of one's voice. *2* cry [of an animal].
gritón, -na *adj.* bawling, vociferous. *2 m.-f.* shouter.
groelandés, -sa; groenlandés, -sa *adj.* Greenlandic. *2 m.-f.* Greenlander.
Groenlandia *f. pr. n.* GEOG. Greenland.
groera *f.* NAUT. rope hole.

grog *m.* grog [drink].
grosella *f.* currant, red currant [fruit]. *2 ~ silvestre,* gooseberry [fruit].
grosellero *m.* BOT. currant, red currant [plant]. *2 ~ silvestre,* gooseberry [plant].
grosería *f.* coarseness, roughness. *2* rusticity. *3* rudeness, ill-breeding; discourtesy, incivility.
grosero, -ra *adj.* coarse, rough. *2* gross [error, etc.]. *3* rustic, unpolished. *4* rude, uncivil, discourteous. *5 m.-f.* ill-bred person, boor, churl.
grosor *m.* thickness.
grosura *f.* fat, suet, grease.
grotesco, -ca *adj.* grotesque, ridiculous. *2 adj.-m.* F. ARTS. grotesque.
grúa *f.* MACH. crane, derrick crane.
gruesa *f.* gross [twelve dozen].
grueso, -sa *adj.* thick [not thin or slender]. *2* corpulent, bulky, stout. *3* big, heavy. *4* dull, slow [mind]. *5* ANAT. large [intestine]. *6 m.* bulk, mass, corpulence. *7* main body or part. *8* thickness [of a wall, etc.]. *9* GEOM. thickness. *10* heavy stroke [in writing]. *11* COM. *en ~,* in gross, in the gross.
gruir *intr.* [of a crane] to cry, crunk. ¶ CONJUG. like *huir.*
grujidor *m.* glazier's trimmer.
grujir *tr.* to trim [glass] with the GRUJIDOR.
grulla *f.* ORN. crane.
grumete *m.* NAUT. cabin boy, ship boy.
brumo *m.* clot, lump [coagulated mass]. *2* thick cluster.
grumoso, -sa *adj.* full of clots, clotted.
gruñido *m.* grunt, growl, grumble.
gruñidor, -ra *adj.* grunting, growling.
gruñir *intr.* to grunt. *2* to growl; to grumble. *3* to creak, squeak. ¶ CONJUG. like *mullir.*
gruñón, -na *adj.* grumbling, grumpy, cranky.
grupa *f.* croup, rump [of horse].
grupada *f.* squall, burst of wind or rain.
grupera *f.* crupper [of harness].
grupo *m.* group, set, knot, clump, cluster: *~ de presión,* pressure group. *2* MACH., ELEC. set, unit.
gruta *f.* grot, grotto.
grutesco, -ca *adj.-m.* F. ARTS. grotesque.
guacamayo *m.* ORN. red-and-blue macaw.
guaco *m.* BOT. guaco. *2* ORN. curassow.
guachapear *tr.* to dabble in [water] with the feet. *2* to botch, bungle. *3 intr.* to clap, clatter.
guácharo, -ra *adj.* sickly. *2* dropsical. *3 m.* birdling.
guadalajareño, -ña *adj.-n.* of Guadalajara.
Gudalupe *f. pr. n.* Guadeloupe.
guadamací, guadamacil *m.* GUADAMECÍ.
guadamacilero *m.* embossed-leather maker.
guadamecí, guadamecil *m.* embossed leather.
guadaña *f.* scythe.
guadañar *tr.* to scythe, mow.
guadarnés *m.* harness room. *2* harness keeper.
guagua *f.* trifle: *de ~,* free, for nothing.
guaita *f.* MIL. obs. night watch.
guaja *m.* coll, rogue, knave.
guájar *m.* or *f.,* **guájaras** *f. pl.* fastness, roughest part of a mountain.
guajira *f.* Cuban popular song.
guajiro, -ra *m.-f.* Cuban peasant.
guajolote *m.* (Am.) ORN. turkey.
gualda *f.* weld, woad, dyer's rocket.
gualdera *f.* sidepiece [of a ladder, of the stock of a gun-carriage, etc.].
gualdo, -da *adj.* yellow, weld.

gualdrapa *f.* housing, horse trappings. *2* coll. dirty rag hanging from clothes.
gualdrapazo *m.* NAUT. flap [of sail against rigging].
gualdrapear *intr.* NAUT. [of sails] to flap. *2 tr.* to place [things] head to tail.
Gualterio, Gualtero *m. pr. n.* Walter.
guanábana *f.* BOT. soursop, custard-apple [fruit].
guanábano *m.* BOT. soursop, custard-apple [tree].
guanaco *m.* ZOOL. guanaco.
guanche *m.-f.* ancient inhabitant of the Canary Islands.
guanera *f.* guano deposit.
guanero, -ra *adj.* [pertaining to] guano.
guano *m.* guano [fertilizer]. *2* (Am.) palm tree.
guantada *f.,* **guantazo** *m.* slap [blow with the open hand].
guante *m.* glove: *arrojar el ~,* to throw down the glove, or the gauntlet; *echar el ~ a,* to take, to seize; *poner a uno más suave que un ~,* to render tractable. *2 pl.* tip, bonus.
guantelete *m.* gauntlet [armoured glove].
guantería *f.* glove shop. *2* glovemaking.
guantero, -ra *m.-f.* glovemaker, glover.
guañir *intr.* [of little pigs] to grunt.
guapamente *adv.* coll. bravely. *2* coll. very well.
guapear *intr.* coll. to be courageous; to brag, swagger. *2* to dress in a showy manner.
guapería *f.* blustering, bullying.
guapetón, -na *adj.* coll. handsome, good-looking, buxom. *2 m.* blusterer, bully, rough.
guapeza *f.* coll. bravery, daring. *2* coll. showiness [in dress]. *3* blustering, swagger.
guapo, -pa *adj.* handsome, good-looking. *2* coll. well-dressed, smart. *3 m.* blusterer, bully, rough.
guapote, -ta *adj.* good-natured. *2* handsome, good-looking.
guapura *f.* coll. good looks.
guaraní *adj.-n.* Guaraní.
guarapo *m.* juice of the sugar cane.
guarda *m.-f.* guard, keeper, custodian: *~ de coto,* gamekeeper. *2 m.* (Am.) street-car conductor. *3 f.* ward, guard, care, trust, custody, safe-keeping. *4* observance [of law, etc.]. *5* guard [of sword]. *6* ward [of lock or key]. *7* BOOKBIND. flyleaf. *8* outside rib [of a fan]. *9* MEC. guard plate.
¡guarda! *interj.* look out!, beware!
guardabarrera *m.* RLY. gatekeeper.
guardabarros, *pl.* **-rros** *m.* mudguard, fender.
guardabosque *m.* forester, gamekeeper.
guardabrazo *m.* ARM. brassard.
guardabrisa *m.* AUTO. windshield. *2* glass shade [for candles].
guardacabo *m.* NAUT. thimble.
guardacantón *m.* spur stone; corner spur stone.
guardacostas *m.* NAUT. revenue cutter. *2* NAUT. coast-guard ship.
guardado, -da *adj.* reserved, reticent.
guardador, -ra *adj.* thrifty, careful. *2* observant [of law, etc.]. *3* stingy. *4 m.-f.* thrifty person. *5* observer [of law, etc.]. *6* niggard.
guardafrenos *m.* RLY. brakeman.
guardagujas *m.* RLY. switchman.
guardainfante *m.* farthingale. *2* NAUT. whelp [of capstan].
guardalado *m.* railling, parapet.
guardalmacén *m.* storekeeper, warehouseman.
guardamalleta *f.* lambrequin [over a curtain].
guardamano *f.* guard [of sword].
guardameta *m.* SPORT. goalkeeper.
guardamonte *m.* trigger guard. *2* kind of poncho.

guardamuebles *m.* warehouse for storing furniture.

guardapelo *m.* locket [little case].

guardapesca *m.* NAUT. boat used by officials controlling the observance of fishing laws.

guardaplés *m.* BRIAL.

guardapolvo *m.* dust cover. *2* dust coat, duster. *3* inner lid [of watch]. *4* flashing [over a door or window].

guardapuerta *f.* hangings before a door.

guardar *tr.* to keep, watch over, take care of. *2* to tend [a flock, etc.]. *3* to keep, guard, preserve, protect, shield, keep safe, save: *Dios os guarde,* God save you. *4* to keep, hold, retain. *5* to put away, lay up, store, save. *6* to keep [one's word, a secret, etc.]. *7* to keep, observe [commandments, etc.]. *8* to show [respect, regard, etc.]. *9* ~ *rencor,* to bear a grudge. *10* ~ *cama,* to keep one's bed; ~ *silencio,* to be silent. *11* *guardársela a uno,* to bild one's time to take revenge on. *12* *ref. guardarse de,* to guard, protect oneself against, avoid, beware; to take care not to [say, do, etc.].

guardarropa *m.* wardrobe, clothespress. *2* cloakroom, checkroom. *3* *m.-f.* cloakroom attendant. *4* THEAT. property man or woman.

guardarropía *f.* THEAT. wardrobe.

guardarruedas *m.* GUARDACANTÓN.

guardasilla *f.* chair rail.

guardavía *m.* RLY. trackwalker, flagman, signalman.

guardería *f.* guardship, keepership. *2* ~ *infantil,* day nursery.

guardesa *f.* female guard. *2* guard's wife.

guardia *f.* guard [body of armed men]: ~ *civil,* gendarmery; ~ *de honor,* guard of honour; ~ *urbana,* city police; *montar la* ~, MIL. to mount guard. *2* guard, defence, protection. *3* guard duty; turn of persons on duty; *estar de* ~, to be on duty. *4* FENC. guard: *estar en* ~, to be on guard; fig. to be on one's guard. *5* NAUT. watch. *6* *m.* guard; member of a GUARDIA: ~ *civil,* gendarme; ~ *urbano,* policeman. *7* NAV. ~ *marina,* midshipman.

guardián, -na *m.-f.* guardian, keep, watchman. *2* guardian [of a convent of Franciscans].

guardilla *f.* buhardilla.

guarecer *tr.* to shelter, protect. *2* to preserve [from harm]. *3* *ref.* to take shelter or refuge. ¶ CONJUG. like *agradecer.*

guarezco, guarezca, etc. *irr.* V. GUARECER.

guarida *f.* haunt, den, lair [of wild animals]. *2* shelter, cover. *3* fig. haunt, lurking place.

guarismo *m.* ARITH. cipher, figure, number.

guarnecer *tr.* to adorn, decorate, garnish. *2* to equip, furnish, provide. *3* to trim, bind, edge, face [clothes]. *4* to enchase [a jewel]. *8* [of nails, a lining, ferrule, etc.] to adorn, protect, reinforce. *6* to harness [horses]. *7* MIL. to garrison. ¶ CONJUG. like *agradecer.*

guarnés *m.* GUADARNÉS.

guarnezco, guarnezca, etc. *irr.* V. GUARNECER.

guarnición *f.* SEW. trimming, binding, edge, facing, flounce, garniture. *2* JEWEL. setting. *3* guard [of a sword]. *4* MACH. packing [of a piston]. *5* MIL. garrison. *6* *pl.* gear, harness [of mules and horses].

guarnicionar *tr.* to garrison [put a garrison in].

guarnicionería *f.* harness making. *2* harness maker's shop.

guarnicionero *m.* harness maker.

guarnigón *m.* young quail.

guarnir *tr.* GUARNECER. *2* NAUT. to rig [a tackle].

guarro, -rra *adj.* dirty, filthy. *2* *m.* ZOOL. hog. *3* *f.* ZOOL., SOW. *4* *m.-f.* fig. unclean person.

¡guarte! *interj.* look out!, beware!

guasa *f.* jest, fun; mocking, irony: *estar de* ~, to be in a jesting mood.

guasca *f.* (Am.) thong, piece of rope; whip.

guasearse *ref.* to make fun, to joke.

guaso, -sa *adj.* (Am.) coarse, unpolished; uncivil. *2* *m.* (Am.) peasant.

guasón, -na *adj.* mocking. *2* *m.-f.* jester, mocker.

guata *f.* wadding, cotton wool.

Guatemala *f. pr. n.* GEOG. Guatemala.

guatemalteco, -ca *adj.-n.* Guatemalan.

guateque *m.* noisy ball or dancing party. *2* fig. frolic, spree.

guau *m.* bowwow [of a dog].

¡guay! *interj.* poet. alack!, woe!

guayaba *f.* BOT. guava, guava apple. *2* guava jelly.

guayabo *m.* BOT. guava tree.

guayacán, guayaco *m.* BOT. guaiac, guaiacum.

Guayana *f. pr. n.* GEOG. Guiana.

gubernamental *adj.* governmental. *2* gubernatorial.

gubernativo, -va *adj.* government, governmental, administrative. *2* gubernatorial.

gubia *f.* gouge [chisel].

guedeja *f.* long hair. *2* lion's mane.

güelfo, -fa *m.-f.* Guelf, Guelph.

guerra *f.* war, warfare: ~ *a muerte,* war to death; ~ *bacteriológica,* germ war; ~ *civil,* civil war; ~ *fría,* cold war; *Guerra Mundial,* World War; *dar* ~, to annoy, cause trouble.

guerreador, -ra *adj.* warlike, warring. *2* *m.-f.* warrior.

guerrear *intr.* to war, wage war; to struggle.

guerrera *f.* MIL. tunic.

guerrero, -ra *adj.* martial, warlike. *2* warring. *3* *m.-f.* warrior, soldier.

guerrilla *f.* MIL. party of skirmishers. *2* band of guerrillas. *3* a card game.

guerrillear *intr.* to fight guerrilla warfare.

guerrillero *m.* guerrilla, partisan. *2* guerrilla leader.

guía *m.-f.* guide [leader; adviser; mentor]. *2* guide, cicerone. *3* *m.* MIL. guide [in evolutions]. *4* *f.* guide, guidance. *5* guide [manual]; guidebook; directory: ~ *de ferrocarriles,* RLY. timetable. *6* MACH. guide rope, etc. *7* NAUT. guy. *8* road marker [on mountain paths]. *9* HORT., MIN. leader. *10* leader [horse]. *11* MUS. lead [of a fugue]. *12* curled-up end [of moustache]. *13* handle bar [of bicycle]. *14* customhouse docket. *15* *pl.* reins for driving the leading horses.

guiadera *f.* MACH. guide, guide bar.

guiar *tr.* to guide, lead. *2* to guide [advise; direct the course of]. *3* to train [plants]. *4* to drive, steer [a car, etc.]. *5* AER. to pilot. *6* *ref. guiarse por,* to be guided by, to follow.

Guido *m. pr. n.* Guy.

guija *f.* pebble. *2* BOT. blue vetch.

guijarral *m.* place full of cobbles or large pebbles.

guijarro *m.* large pebble, cobble, cobblestone.

guijarroso, -sa *adj.* full of cobbles, cobbly.

guijo *m.* pebble gravel. *2* MACH. gudgeon.

guijoso, -sa *adj.* pebbly, gravelly.

guilladura *f.* CHIFLADURA.

guillame *m.* CARP. rabbet plane.

guillarse *ref.* to leave, to flee. *2* to become crazy.

Guillermo *m. pr. n.* William.

guillotina *f.* guillotine.
guillotinar *tr.* to guillotine.
guimbalete *m.* pump handle.
guimbarda *f.* CARP. grooving plane.
guincho *m.* prod, pointed stick.
guinda *f.* BOT. sour cherry [fruit]. *2* NAUT. height of masts.
guindalera *f.* sour-cherry plantation.
guindaleza *f.* NAUT. hawser.
guindamaina *f.* NAUT. dipping the flag [as a salute].
guindar *tr.* to hoist, hang up. *2 ref.* to hoist oneself up. *3* to let oneself down by a rope, etc.
guindaste *m.* NAUT. frame; sheet bitt.
guindilla *f.* BOT. Guinea pepper [fruit]. *2* BOT. a very pungent pepper. *3* coll. policeman.
guindo *m.* BOT. sour cherry [tree].
guindola *f.* NAUT. boatswain's chair. *2* NAUT. life buoy. *3* NAUT. log chip.
guinea *f.* guinea [coin; money]. *2 f. pr. n.* GEOG. Guinea.
guineo, -a *adj.* Guinea, Guinean. *2 m.-f.* Guinean.
guinga *f.* gingham.
guinja *f.* jujube.
guinjo *m.* BOT. jujube tree.
guinjolero *m.* GUINJO.
guiñada *f.* wink [with one eye]. *2* NAUT. yaw, lurch.
guiñapo *m.* rag, tatter. *2* ragged person, tatterdemalion. *3* degraded, despicable person.
guiñar *tr.* to wink [one eye]. *2* NAUT. to yaw, lurch. *3 ref.* to wink at each other.
guiño *m.* wink [with one eye].
guión *m.* hyphen; dash. *2* notes [for a speech]. *3* CINEM., RADIO. scenario, script. *4* cross [carried before a prelate]. *5* banner [carried before procession]. *6* leader, guide. *7* NAUT. loom [of an oar].
guionista *m.-f.* CINEM., RADIO. script writer.
guipar *tr.* vulg. to see.
guipur *m.* guipure.
guipuzcoano, -na *adj.-n.* of Guipuzcoa.
güira *f.* BOT. calabash [tree and fruit].
guirigay *m.* gibberish. *2* hubbub, confusion.
guirindola *f.* frill of a shirt.
guirlache *m.* roast almond brittle.
guirlanda *f.* garland, wreath [of flowers, leaves, etc.]. *2* BOT. globe amaranth.
guisa *f.* manner, fashion, way, wise: *a ~ de*, as, like, in the manner of.
guisado, -da *adj.* cooked. *2* fig. prepared. *3 m.* COOK. cooked dish; stew, ragout, fricassee.
guisandero, -ra *m.-f.* cook [one who cooks food].
guisante *m.* BOT. pea [plant and seed]: *~ de olor*, sweet pea.
guisar *tr.* to cook [food]. *2* to stew, to make into a ragout or fricassee. *3* fig. to arrange, cook.
guiso *m.* cooked dish.
guisote *m.* coarse, poorly cooked dish.
guita *f.* packthread, twine. *2* coll. money, tin.
guitarra *f.* MUS. guitar.
guitarrazo *m.* blow with a guitar.
guitarreo *m.* strumming on the guitar.
guitarrería *f.* lutherie.
guitarrero, -ra *m.-f.* luthier.

guitarrillo *m.* MUS. small four-stringed guitar. *2* MUS. small treble guitar.
guitarrista *m.-f.* guitarist.
guitarro *m.* GUITARRILLO.
guitón, -na *m.-f.* vagabond, vagrant.
guitonear *intr.* to loaf, lead a vagrant life.
guizacillo *m.* BOT. hedgehog grass.
guizque *m.* pole with a hook for reaching things.
gula *f.* gluttony, gormandize.
gules *m. pl.* HER. gules.
gulusmear *intr.* to eat titbits. *2* to sniff the cooking.
gúmena *f.* NAUT. cable, thick rope.
gumia *f.* Moorish dagger or poniard.
gumífero, -ra *adj.* gum-bearing, gummiferous.
gurriato *m.* ORN. young sparrow.
gurrumina *f.* uxoriousness.
gurrumino, -na *adj.* small, poor, stunty, puny. *2 m.* uxorious man, henpecked husband.
gurullada *f.* gang of good-for-nothings.
gurullo *m.* BURUJO.
gusanear *intr.* HORMIGUEAR.
gusanera *f.* nest of worms, wormy place. *2* coll. ruling passion.
gusanería *f.* multitude of worms.
gusaniento, -ta *adj.* wormy, grubby, maggoty.
gusanillo *m.* small worm: *matar el ~*, fig. to take a shot of liquor before breakfast. *2* SEW. gold, silver or silk twist. *3* screw point of gimlet or bit.
gusano *m.* ZOOL. worm. *2* worm, grub, maggot, caterpillar: *~ de luz*, glowworm; *~ de seda*, silkworm. *3* fig. worm, miserable, wretch. *4 ~ de la conciencia*, worm of conscience, remorse.
gusarapiento, -ta *adj.* wormy [liquid]. *2* rotten, filthy.
gusarapo *m.* any worm found in liquids.
gustación, gustadura *f.* gustation, tasting.
gustar *tr.* to taste [perceive by the sense of taste]. *2* to taste, experience. *3 intr.* to please, be pleasing [to]. | often to be rendered by a sentence with «to like»: *me gusta el café*, I like coffee; *a nadie gustó la obra*, nobody liked the play. *4* to like, please, will: have a liking for: *gusta de leer*, he likes to read.
gustativo, -va *adj.* gustative, gustatory.
gustazo *m.* coll. great pleasure.
gustillo *m.* a lingering taste or flavour.
gusto *m.* taste [sense]. *2* taste, relish, flavour. *3* taste [discernment or appreciation of beauty, fitness, etc.]: *de buen ~, de mal ~*, in good taste, in bad taste; *de gustos no hay nada escrito*, there is no accounting for tastes. *4* pleasure, gratification: *dar ~*, to please, gratify, oblige; *hallarse a ~ en*, to be pleased or comfortable in; *tengo mucho ~ en conocerlo*, I am very glad to meet you; *con mucho ~*, with pleasure; gladly. *5* will, choice, liking, fancy, whim: *hacer uno su ~*, to do one's own will; *ser del ~ de*, to be to the liking of; *tomar ~ a*, to take a liking for.
gustoso, -sa *adj.* tasty, savoury, palatable. *2* agreeable, pleasant, pleasing. *3* glad, willing, ready.
gutapercha *f.* gutta-percha.
gutífero, -ra *adj.* guttiferous.
gutural *adj.* guttural.
guzla *f.* MUS. gusla.

H

H, h *f.* H, h, ninth letter of the Spanish alphabet.
ha *irr.* V. HABER & HACER.
haba *f.* BOT. bean, broad bean [plant, pod and seed]: ~ *panosa*, horse bean; *son habas contadas*, it is a sure thing; it is that and no more. *2* bean [of coffee, cocoa, etc.]. *3* GEOL., MIN. nodule. *4* welt, papule.
habado, -da *adj.* dappled [horse, etc.]. *2* mottled [fowl].
Habana (La) *f. pr. n.* GEOG. Havana.
habanero, -ra *adj.-n.* Havanese. *2 f.* habanera [dance and tune].
habano, -na *adj.* Havanese, Havana. *2 m.* Havana [cigar].
habar *m.* broad-bean patch.
1) **haber**, *pl.* **haberes** *m.* BOOKKEEP. credit side. *2* salary, pay, wages. *3 sing.-pl.* property, fortune [of a person].
2) **haber** *tr.* obs. to have, own, possess. *2* to catch, get, lay hands on: *los ladrones no pudieron ser habidos*, the thiefs could not be caught.
3 aux. to have. *4* (with *de*) to have to, to be obliged to, to be to: *he de trabajar*, I have to work, I must work.
5 impers. (3rd. pers. pres. ind. *hay*) to be [with *there* as a subject]; to take place: *hay un puente sobre el río*, there is a bridge on the river. | Sometimes it requires a different translation: *¿cuánto hay de aquí a...?* how far is it to...?; *·lo que hay es*, the fact is; *no hay de qué*, you are welcome, don't mention it [when thanked]; *¿qué hay?*, how's things? *6* (with *que*) it is necessary to, it's got to: *hay que trabajar*, it is necessary to work; *hay que hacerlo*, it's got to be done. *7 ¡hay que ver!*, fancy!, look! *8* (3rd. pers. pres. ind. *ha*) It is used to express a lapse of time, often with the adverbial value of *ago*: *cinco días ha*, five days ago.
9 ref. *habérselas con*, to deal with, dispute or contend with, cope with. *10 ¡habráse visto!*, fancy!
¶ CONJUG: IND. Pres.: *he, has, ha* or *hay; hemos* or *habemos, habéis, han*. | Imperf.: *había, habías*, etc. | Pret.: *hube, hubiste, hubo; hubimos, hubisteis, hubieron*. | Fut.: *habré, habrás, habrá; habremos, habréis, habrán*. | COND: *habría, habrías, habría; habríamos, habríais, habrían*. | SUBJ. Pres.: *haya, hayas, haya; hayamos, hayáis,* *hayan*. | Imperf.: *hubiera, hubieras, hubiera; hubiéramos, hubierais, hubieran* or *hubiese, hubieses, hubiese; hubiésemos, hubieseis, hubiesen*. | Fut.: *hubiere, hubieres, hubiere; hubiéremos, hubiereis, hubieren.* | IMPER : *he, haya; hayamos, habed, hayan*. | PAST. P.: *habido*. | GER.: *habiendo*.

habichuela *f.* BOT. kidney bean, French bean.
habiente *adj.* LAW having, possessing.
hábil *adj.* skilful, clever, dexterous. *2* LAW able, legally qualified. *3* LAW lawful [day].
habilidad *f.* ability, skill, cleverness. *2* talent [special aptitude].
habilidoso, -sa *adj.* skilful.
habilitación *f.* habilitation, act of qualifying or making apt. *2* making [a place, etc.] available for a specified use. *3* financing, outfitting. *4* employment or office of a paymaster.
habilitado, -da *adj.* habilitated, qualified. *2* made available for a specified use [place, etc.]. *3 m.* paymaster [appointed by a body, regiment, etc.].
habilitar *tr.* to habilitate, qualify; to make apt. *2* to make [a place, etc.] available for a specified use. *3* to finance; to outfit.
habitabilidad *f.* habitability, habitableness.
habitable *adj.* habitable.
habitación *f.* habitation, inhabiting. *2* habitation, dwelling, abode. *3* room, chamber, apartment. *4* BOT. habitat.
habitáculo *m.* habitation, dwelling [place].
habitante *adj.* inhabiting, residing. *2 m.-f.* inhabitant, dweller, citizen.
habitar *tr.-intr.* to inhabit; to dwell, live, reside in.
hábito *m.* habit, custom: *tener el ~ de*, to be in the habit of. *2 sing.* or *pl.* habit, dress, esp. dress of a religious or military order: *tomar el ~*, to profess, to take vows.
habituación *f.* habituation, inurement.
habitual *adj.* habitual.
habituar *tr.* to habituate, accustom, inure. *2 ref.* to become habituated, accustomed, inured; to get used.

habla *f.* speech [faculty of speaking]: *perder el ~*, to lose one's speech. *2* speaking, act of speaking: *al ~*, NAUT. within speaking distance; in comunication, in negotiations: *¡al ~!*, speaking! [ans-

wer to telephone]. *3* speech, talk. *4* speech, language, tongue, dialect.
hablado, -da *adj.* spoken: *bien* ~, well-spoken; polite; *mal* ~, ill-tongued, foul-mouthed.
hablador, -ra *adj.* talkative. *2* chattering, babbling. *3 m.-f.* chatterer. *4* gossip, babbler.
habladuría *f.* impertinent talk. *2* gossip, piece of gossip, idle rumour.
hablanchín, -na *adj.-n.* HABLADOR.
hablar *intr.* to speak, talk: ~ *a*, to speak, talk to; ~ *al alma*, to speak movingly, touchingly; ~ *bien*, to speak well; ~ *bien de*, to speak favourably of, to commend; ~ *claro*, to speak plainly; to call a spade a spade; ~ *con sentido*, to speak sense; ~ *de*, to speak or talk of, on or about; to mention; ~ *en plata*, to speak plainly; ~ *entre dientes*, to mutter, mumble; ~ *por*, to speak for; to speak in behalf of, intercede for; ~ *por boca de ganso*, to speak at second hand; ~ *por* ~, to talk to no purpose; ~ *por los codos*, to chatter, talk incessantly; ~ *por señas*, to talk by signs. *2* to converse, chat, speak, talk: ~ *con*, to talk with; to woo, court, go out with. *3 tr.* to speak, utter, talk: ~ *disparates*, to talk nonsense. *4* to speak, talk [a language]; *se habla inglés*, English spoken. *5 ref.* to speak to each other: *no hablarse con*, not to be on speaking terms with.
hablilla *f.* idle rumour, piece of gossip.
hablista *m.-f.* one who writes or talks with elegance and purity of language.
habré, habrás, etc. *irr.* V. HABER.
hacanea *f.* nag, sturdy small horse.
hacecico, -llo, -to *m.* dim. small sheaf; fascicle. *2* pencil [of luminous rays].
hacedero, -ra *adj.* feasible, practicable.
hacedor *m.* manager [of a farm]. *2* (cap.) Maker: *el Supremo Hacedor*, the Maker, the Creator.
hacendado, -da *adj.* landed, property-owning. *2 m.-f.* landholder; owner of real estate.
hacendero, -ra *adj.* industrious, thrifty.
hacendista *m.* financier, one skilled in the management of the public finances.
hacendoso, -sa *adj.* assiduous, industrious [in household works].
hacer *tr.* to make [create, construct, build, form, frame, compose, draw up, produce, inflict, cause to exist, bring about]: ~ *una casa*, to build a house; ~ *testamento*, to make a will; ~ *ruido*, to make a noise. *2* to make, do [perform, execute, carry out]: ~ *un mandado*, to make an errand; *no sabe qué* ~, he doesn't know what to do. *3* to do, bring: *esto le hace honor*, this does him credit. *4* to make, deliver [a speech, etc.]. *5* to make, prepare [a meal, a bed, etc.]. *6* to pack [luggage]. *7* to make [cause to be or become]: ~ *famoso a uno*, to make someone famous. *8* to make, amount to: *dos y dos hacen cuatro*, two and two make four. *9* to make [compose, constitute]. *10* to make [cause to act in a certain way, compel]: *no me hagas hablar*, don't make me talk. *11* to make [grimaces, signs]. *12* to make [money]. *13* to do, work [wonders, miracles, etc.]. *14* to project, shed, cast, raise [shadow, smoke, dust, etc.]. *15* to habituate, inure. *16* to lead [a life]. *17* to provide, supply [with]. *18 no lo hacía tan tonto*, I did not suppose him to be so silly. *19* ~ *agua*, NAUT. to leak. *20* ~ *aguas* or *aguas menores*, to make water [void urine]; ~ *aguas mayores*, to evacuate the bowels. *21* ~ *alarde*, to boast; ~ *burla de*, to mock. *22* ~ *pedazos*, to break to pieces. *23* ~

juego, [of things] to match. *24 hacerlo bien, mal*, to do it rightly, wrongly, to perform or acquit oneself well, badly. *25* ~ *de las suyas*, to be up to one's old tricks. *26 ¡buena la has hecho!*, now you have done it!
27 tr.-intr.-ref. to act, play, pretend to be, boast of being: ~ *el hombre*, to act the man; *hacerse el olvidadizo*, to pretend to forget.
28 intr. to suit, be relevant, be to the purpose: *esto no hace al caso*, that is irrelevant. *29* [with *de*] to act or work as: ~ *de presidente*, to act as a chairman. *30* [with *por* o *para*] to do one's best, to try: *haré por venir*, I'll try to come.
31 ref. to grow, develop. *32* to turn to, to grow, become: *hacerse vinagre*, to turn to vinegar; *hacerse más fuerte*, to grow stronger; *hacerse fraile, médico*, etc., to become a monk, a doctor, etc. *33* to make oneself: *hacerse obedecer*, to make oneself obeyed. *34* to order or have [something] made for oneself. *35* to inflict upon oneself [a wound, etc.]. *36* to move, step, retire: *hacerse a un lado*, to move or step aside. *37 hacerse con*, to get, obtain, get hold of. *38 hacerse de rogar*, to like to be coaxed.
39 impers. [referring to the weather] to be [with *it as* a subject]: *hace frío*, it is cold; *hace buen día*, it is a fine day.
40 When used to express a lapse of time it is rendered by *ago, since, for* or by *to be* [sometimes with *it* as a subject]: *hace tres días*, three days ago; *hace un año que no lo veo*, it is a year since I saw him; *hace un mes que estoy aquí*, I have been here a month. *41 se hace tarde*, it is getting, growing or becoming late.
¶ IRREG. CONJUG.: INDIC. Pres.: *hago, haces, hace; hacemos, hacéis, hacen.* | Imperf.: *hacía, hacías,* etc. | Pret.: *hice, hiciste, hizo; hicimos, hicisteis, hicieron.* | Fut.: *haré, harás, hará; haremos, haréis, harán.* | CONDIC.: *haría, harías, haría; haríamos, haríais, harían.* | SUBJ. Pres.: *haga, hagas, haga; hagamos, hagáis, hagan.* | Imperf.: *hiciera, hicieras, hiciera; hiciéremos, hicierais, hicieran* or *hiciese, hicieses, hiciese; hiciésemos, hicieseis, hiciesen.* | Fut.: *hiciere, hicieres, hiciere; hiciéremos, hiciereis, hicieren.* | IMPER. *haz, haga; hagamos, haced hagan.* | PAST. P.: *hecho.* | GER.: *haciendo.*
hacia *prep.* towards, toward, to, for [in the direction of]: ~ *abajo*, downward; ~ *adelante*, forward; ~ *atrás*, backward; ~ *el mar*, seaward; *partir* ~, to leave for. *2* towards, toward, to, for [as regards, in relation to]: *su actitud* ~ *mí*, his attitude toward me. *3* toward, near, about: ~ *las tres*, toward three o'clock.
hacienda *f.* landed property, farm. *2* (Am.) ranch. *3* property, possessions: ~ *pública*, public finances, public treasury. *4* management or science of public finance. *5 pl.* household work.
hacina *f.* pile of sheaves, shock. *2* heap.
hacinamiento *m.* heaping, piling. *2* packing, crowding together. *3* heap, pile, accumulation.
hacinar *tr.* to pile sheaves. *2* to heap, pile, stack, accumulate. *3* to pack, crowd together. *4 ref.* to pile up. *5* to be packed, crowded together.
hacha *f.* ax, axe, hatchet; ~ *de armas*, battleax. *2* heavy wax candle with four wicks. *3* torch, flambeau.
hachazo *m.* blow or stroke with an axe.
hache *f.* name of the letter *h*.
hachear *tr.* to dress [wood] with an axe.
hachero *m.* torch stand. *2* axman, axeman.

hacho *m.* torch, link. 2 beacon hill.
hachón *m.* large torch. 2 cresset.
hada *f.* MYTH. fairy [supernatural female being].
hado *m.* fage, destiny.
hagiografía *f.* hagiography.
hagiógrafo *m.* hagiographer.
hago, haga, etc., *irr.* V. HACER.
Haití *m. pr. n.* GEOM. Haiti.
haitiano, -na *adj.-n.* Haitian.
¡hala! *interj.* get up!, go on!, move on!
halagador, -ra *adj.* flattering. 2 pleasing, gratifying. 3 alluring. 4 promising, bright, rosy.
halagar *tr.* to flatter. 2 to adulate. 3 to please, gratify.
halago *m.* flattering. 2 flattery. 3 pleasure, gratification. 4 *pl.* caresses, blandishments.
halagüeño, -ña *adj.* HALAGADOR.
halar *tr.* NAUT. to haul [on a rope, etc.]; to pull [an oar]. 2 to pull or draw to oneself.
halcón *m.* ORN. falcon, hawk: ~ *niego*, eyas.
halconería *f.* falconry.
halconero *m.* falconer.
halda *f.* skirt [garment]; skirt [of a garment].
haldada *f.* skirtful.
haldeta *f.* small skirt, flap [of a garment].
haleche *m.* BOQUERÓN 2.
halieto *m.* ORN. osprey, sea eagle.
hálito *m.* breath [from the mouth]. 2 vapour, effluvium. 3 poet. breath, gentle breeze.
halo *m.* METEOR., PHOT. halo. 2 F. ARTS halo, nimbus.
hallado, -da *adj.* found. 2 *bien* ~, at ease, contented; *mal* ~, displeased [in or with a place, situation, etc.] 3 *¡bien* ~!, welcome!
hallar *tr.* to find, come across, light upon. 2 to find out, discover, detect, catch. 3 to find, ascertain. 4 to find [favour, means, leisure, expression, one's way, etc.]. 5 to find, think. 6 to see, observe. 7 ~ *la solución de un problema*, to solve a problem. 8 *ref.* to be, be present, be found [in some place]. 9 to be, feel [in some state, condition, etc.]: *hallarse enfermo*, to be ill; *hallarse incómodo*, to feel uncomfortable.
hallazgo *m.* find, finding, discovery [act of finding; something found]. 2 reward [for finding].
hamaca *f.* hammock [hanging bed].
hamadríada *f.* MYTH. hamadryad.
hambre *f.* hunger; starvation, famine: ~ *canina*, canine hunger; *matar de* ~, to starve [someone]; *morirse de* ~, [of someone] to starve; *tener* ~, to be hungry. 2 hunger [strong desire]: *tener* ~ *de*, to hunger for or after.
hambrear *tr.* to starve, famish. 2 *intr.* to starve, go hungry.
hambriento, -ta *adj.* hungry: ~ *de*, hungry for. 2 *m.-f.* hungerer, starveling.
hambrón, -na *adj.* hungry, greedy for food. 2 *m.-f.* glutton.
Hamburgo *f. pr. n.* GEOG. Hamburg.
hamburgués, -sa *adj.-n.* of Hamburg.
hampa *f.* underworld [low or criminal people]. 2 underworld life.
hampón *m.* rowdy, bully, gangster, vagrant.
hanega *f.* FANEGA.
hangar *m.* AER. hangar.
Hansa *f.* Hanse.
hanseático, -ca *adj.* Hanseatic.
haragán, -na *adj.* idle, lazy, slothful. 2 *m.-f.* idler, loafer, loiterer, idle or lazy person.
haraganear *intr.* to idle, loaf, hang around.
haraganería *f.* idleness, loafing, laziness.
harapiento, -ta *adj.* ragged, tattered.

harapo *m.* rag, tatter.
haraposo, -sa *adj.* ragged, tattered.
haré, harás, etc. *irr.* V. HACER.
harem, harén *m.* harem.
harina *f.* flour [wheat meal]: *ser* ~ *de otro costal*, to be a horse of another colour. 2 flour, meal, powder: ~ *de linaza*, linseed meal; ~ *de maíz*, corn meal.
harinero, -ra *adj.* [pertaining to] flour. 2 *m.* flour dealer. 3 flour bin or chest.
harinoso, -sa *adj.* floury, mealy, farinaceous.
harmonía, harmónico, harmonioso, etc. ARMONÍA, ARMÓNICO, ARMONIOSO, etc.
harmonio *m.* ARMONIO.
harnero *m.* sieve, sifter.
harón, -na *adj.* lazy, slothful, sluggish. 2 balky.
haronear *intr.* to be slow or lazy; to dawdle.
harpa *f.* ARPA.
harpado, -da *adj.* ARPADO.
harpía *f.* ARPÍA.
harpillera *f.* burlap, sackcloth.
hartar *tr.* to sate, satiate, glut. 2 to fill, gorge [with]. 3 to give in abundance: ~ *de palos*, to beat soundly. 4 to tire, sicken. 5 *ref.* to satiate; to stuff oneself. 6 to have or get one's fill [of]. 7 to tire, sicken, become fed up.
hartazgo, hartazón *m.* fill, glut, bellyful. 2 *darse un hartazgo*, to eat out one's fill: *darse un hartazgo de*, to have or get one's fill of.
harto, -ta *adj.* satiated, glutted. 2 tired, sick [of]; fed up [with]. 3 enough, more than enough. 4 *adv.* enough, well, well enough.
hartura *f.* fill, satiety, repletion. 2 abundance. 3 full gratification.
has *irr.* V. HABER.
hasta *prep.* till, until; to, as far as; as much as, up to, down to: ~ *ahora*, till now, up to now; ~ *aquí*, so far; ~ *la vista*, so long, see you later; ~ *más no poder*, to the utmost; ~ *que*, till, until; *iremos* ~ *el punte*, we'll go so far as the bridge. 2 *conj.* even: ~ *un niño lo haría*, even a child could do it.
hastial *m.* ARCH. gable wall. 2 MIN. side wall. 3 big coarse man.
hastiar *tr.* to cloy, sate, surfeit. 2 to weary, bore. 3 *ref. hastiarse de*, to weary of.
hastío *m.* surfeit, disgust. 2 weariness, boredom, ennui.
hatajo *m.* small herd or flock. 2 coll. lot, bunch, set: *un* ~ *de mentiras*, a bunch of lies.
hatillo *m.* small bundle [made with one's belongings]: *tomar el* ~, to leave, depart.
hato *m.* outfit, belongings: *liar el* ~, to pack up; *menear el* ~ *a*, to beat up. 2 herd [of cattle], flock [of sheep]. 3 shepherd's place of sojourn. 4 provisions for shepherds. 5 lot, bunch, set [of knaves, lies, etc.].
hawaiano, -na *adj.-n.* Hawaiian.
haxix *m.* hasheesh, hashish.
hay, haya, etc. *irr.* V. HABER.
Haya (La) *f. pr. n.* GEOG. The Hague.
haya *f.* BOT. beech [tree]. 2 beech [wood].
hayal, hayedo *m.* beech forest or grove.
hayuco *m.* beechnut. 2 *pl.* beech mast.
1) **haz** *m.* bunch, bundle [of sticks, etc., fastened together]; fagot, faggot; gavel, sheaf. 2 beam, pencil [of rays]. 3 BOT. fascicle. 4 *f.* face, visage. 5 face [of the earth]; right side [of cloth, etc.]. 6 *m. pl.* fasces.
2) **haz** *irr.* V. HACER.
haza *f.* AGR. piece of tillable land.

hazaña *f.* deed, feat, exploit, achievement.
hazmerreír *m.* laughing-stock.
1) **he** *adv.* used generally, as a demonstrative, with the adverbs *aquí, allí,* and the pronouns *me, te, la, le, lo, los, las:* ~ *aquí que,* behold; *heme aquí,* here I am.
2) **he** *irr.* V. HABER.
hebdomadario, -ria *adj.* hebdomadary.
hebilla *f.* buckle, clasp.
hebillaje *m.* buckles, set of buckles.
hebra *f.* needleful of thread. *2* TEXT. fibre, staple. *3* thread, filament. *4* fibre [of meat]. *5* grain [of wood]. *6* thread [of discourse]. *7 pl.* poet. threads, the hair. *8 pegar la* ~, to chat.
hebraico, -ca *adj.* Hebraic, Hebrew.
hebraísmo *m.* Hebraism.
hebraísta *m.* Hebraist [Hebrew scholar].
hebraizante *adj.* hebraizing. *2 m.* HEBRAÍSTA. *3* Hebraist, Judaizer.
hebraizar *intr.* to Hebraize [use Hebraisms].
hebreo, -a *adj.-n.* Hebrew. *2 m.* Hebrew [language]. *3* coll. usurer.
Hébridas (las) *f. pr. n.* GEOG. the Hebrides. *2 Las Nuevas Hébridas,* the New Hebrides.
hebroso, -sa *adj.* fibrous, stringy.
hecatombe *f.* hecatomb.
hectárea *f.* hectare.
hectogramo *m.* hectogram.
hectolitro *m.* hectolitre, hectoliter.
hectómetro *m.* hectometre, hectometer.
hechicería *f.* sorcery, witchcraft, witchery, wizardry, enchantment. *2* charm, fascination.
hechicero, -ra *adj.* bewitching, -charming, fascinating. *2 m.-f.* bewitcher. *3 m.* enchanter, sorcerer, wizard. *4 f.* enchantress, sorceress, witch. *5* enchantress, witch [charming woman].
hechizar *tr.* to bewitch, charm, enchant. *2* to entrance, fascinate.
hechizo, -za *adj.* false, artificial. *2 m.* charm, spell, magic ointment, etc. *3* charm, fascination, glamour. *4 pl.* charms [of a woman].
1) **hecho, -cha** *irr. p. p.* of HACER.
2) **hecho, -cha** *adj.* made, done, finished: ~ *de encargo,* made to order. *2* grown, full matured, ripe. *3* build, shaped, proportioned [animal, body, limbs]. *4* ready-made [clothing]. *5* turned into, quite, like: *el niño está* ~ *un hombrecito,* the boy is quite a little man; *se volvió hacia él* ~ *un león,* he turned on him like a lion. *6* accustomed, inured, used. *7* ~ *y derecho,* complete, finished, in every respect. *8 m.* fact: *de* ~, in fact, as a matter of fact; actually; *de facto; de* ~ *y de derecho,* by deed and right. *9* happening. *10* deed act, action, feat. *11 Hechos de los Apóstoles,* Acts of the Apostles.
hechura *f.* make, making. *2* form, shape, cut, build. *3* creation, creature [of someone]. *4 sing. -pl.* workmanship, work, making [of a dress, etc.]; money paid for it.
hedentina *f.* stench, stink.
heder *intr.* to stink. *2 tr.* to be insufferable [to one]. ¶ CONJUG. like *entender.*
hediondez *f.* stench, evil smell, fetidness.
hediondo, -da *adj.* stinking, fetid. *2* annoying. *3* filthy, dirty, obscene.
hedonismo *m.* hedonism.
hedonista *adj.* hedonistic. *2 m.-f.* hedonist.
hedor *m.* stench, stink, foul smell.
hegeliano, -na *adj.-n.* Hegelian.
hegemonía *f.* hegemony.
hégira, hejira *f.* hegira, hejira.

helada *f.* freeze, freezing, frost: ~ *blanca,* hoarfrost, white frost.
Hélade *f. pr. n.* GEOG. Hellas [Greece].
heladera *f.* (Am.) freezer, refrigerator.
helado, -da *adj.* frozen. *2* frostbitten. *3* frigid, cold, chilly. *4* fig. *quedarse* ~, to be frozen [with amazement, fear, etc.]. *5 m.* frozen food, ice cream, sherbet, water ice.
helamiento *m.* congealment, congelation, freezing.
helar *tr.* to freeze, congeal, chill, ice. *2* to frostbite. *3* to astound, amaze. *4* to chill, discourage. *5 ref.* to freeze, congeal, be frozen. *6* to become frostbitten. *7 impers.* to freeze: *está helado,* it is freezing. ¶ CONJUG. like *acertar.*
helechal *m.* fern land, fernery.
helecho *m.* BOT. fern: ~ *arbóreo,* tree fern.
helénico, -ca *adj.* Hellenic.
helenio *m.* BOT. elecampane.
helenismo *m.* Hellenism.
helenístico, -ca *adj.* Hellenistic(al.
heleno, -na *adj.* Hellenic. *2 m.-f.* Hellene.
helero *m.* GEL. glacier.
Helesponto *m. pr. n.* GEOG. Hellespont.
helgado, -da *adj.* jagged-toothed.
helíaco, -ca *adj.* ASTR. heliacal.
helianto *m.* BOT. helianthus.
hélice *f.* ANAT., ARCH., GEOM. helix. *2* GEOM. spiral. *3* AER., NAUT. propeller, screw-propeller.
helicoidal *adj.* helicoidal.
helicóptero *m.* AER. helicopter.
helio *m.* CHEM. helium.
heliocéntrico, -ca *adj.* heliocentric.
heliograbado *m.* heliogravure.
heliógrafo *m.* heliograph.
helióstato *m.* heliostat.
helioterapia *f.* heliotherapy.
heliotropo *m.* BOT., MINER. heliotrope.
helminto *m.* ZOOL. helminth.
Helvecia *f. pr. n.* GEOGR. Helvetia.
helvecio, -cia or **helvético, -ca** *adj.* Helvetic. *2 adj. -n.* Helvetian.
hematíe *m.* PHYSIOL. red cell.
hematina *f.* CHEM. haematin, hematin.
hematites *f.* MINER. haematite, hematite.
hematoma *m.* MED. haematoma, hematoma.
hematuria *f.* MED. haematuria, hematuria.
hembra *adj.* female [animal or plant]. *2 f.* female [of an animal]. *3* BOT. female plant. *4* coll. female, woman. *5* eye [of hook an eye]. *6* MACH. nut [for a bolt or screw]; bolt staple; female part, tool, etc. *7* NAUT. *hembras del timón,* gudgeons of the rudder.
hembrilla *f.* MACH. small nut or staple; small female part or piece. *2* eyescrew.
hemélitro *m.* hemelytron.
hemeroteca *f.* newspaper and magazine library.
hemiciclo *m.* hemicycle. *2* in Spain, floor [of the House of Deputies].
hemicránea *f.* MED. hemicrania, megrim.
hemihédrico, -ca *adj.* CRYST. hemihedral.
hemihedro *m.* CRYST. hemihedron.
hemiplejia *f.* MED. hemiplegia.
hemíptero, -ra *adj.* ENT. hemipteran. *2 m.* ENT. hemipteran. *3 pl.* ENT. Hemiptera.
hemisférico, -ca *adj.* hemispherical.
hemisferio *m.* hemisphere.
hemistiquio *m.* PROS. hemistich.
hemofilia *f.* MED. haemophilia, hemophilia.
hemoglobina *f.* PHYSIOL. haemoglobin, hemoglobin.

hemoptisis *f.* MED. haemoptysis, hemoptysis.
hemorragia *f.* MED. haemorrhage, hemorrhage.
hemostático, -ca *adj.* haemostatic, hemostatic.
henal *m.* hayloft.
henar *m.* hayfield.
henchidura *f.*, **henchimiento** *m.* filling, stuffing.
henchir *tr.* to fill, stuff. *2 ref.* to be filled. *3* to stuff oneself. ¶ CONJUG. like *servir.*
hendedura *f.* HENDIDURA.
hender *tr.* to cleave, split, slit, crack, chink. *2* to cut through, to cleave [the air, the water]. *3 ref.* to cleave, split, crack [become cleaved, etc.]. ¶ CONJUG. like *entender.*
hendidura *f.* cleft, crevice, crack, fissure, slit, slot.
hendiente *m.* downstroke of a sword.
hendimiento *m.* cleaving, splitting, cracking.
henequén *m.* BOT. henequen, sisal.
henificar *tr.* to hay [cut and cure grass for hay].
henil *m.* hayloft, hay barn.
henné *m.* henna [dye].
heno *m.* hay. *2* BOT. an hay plant.
heñir *tr.* to knead [work up into dough]. ¶ CONJUG. like *reir.*
hepático, -ca *adj.* MED. hepatic(al. *2* BOT. hepatic. *3 f.* BOT. hepatica, liverwort.
hepatitis *f.* MED. hepatitis.
heptacordio, heptacordo *m.* MUS. heptachord.
heptagonal *adj.* heptagonal.
heptágono, -na *adj.* heptagonal. *2 m.* GEOM. heptagon.
heptámetro *m.* PROS. heptameter.
heptarquía *f.* heptarchy.
heptasílabo, -ba *adj.* heptasyllabic.
Heptateuco *m.* Heptateuc.
heráldica *f.* Heraldry.
heráldico, -ca *adj.* heraldic. *2 m.-f.* heraldist.
heraldo *m.* herald. *2* harbinger.
herbáceo, -a *adj.* herbaceous.
herbaje *m.* herbage, grass, pasture.
herbario, -ria *adj.* herbal. *2 m.* botanist; herbalist. *3* herbarium. *4* ZOOL. rumen [of ruminant].
herbazal *m.* grassland. *2* weedy place.
herbecer *intr.* [of grass] to begin to grow.
herbero *m.* gullet [of ruminants].
herbívoro, -ra *adj.* herbivorous.
herbolario, -ria *adj.* scatterbrained. *2 m.-f.* scatterbrain. *3 m.* herbalist. *4* herbman shop.
herborización *f.* herborization, botanizing.
herborizar *intr.* to herborize, botanize.
herboso, -sa *adj.* herby, grassy.
hercúleo, -a *adj.* Herculean. *2* herculean.
heredable *adj.* inheritable; hereditable.
heredad *f.* country property, country estate.
heredado, -da *adj.* inherited. *2* landed, owning real state. *3* having inherited.
heredamiento *m.* landed property.
heredar *tr.* to inherit. *2* to give possessions or real estate to. *3* to institute heir.
heredero, -ra *adj.* inheriting. *2 m.-f.* heir, heiress, inheritor.
hereditario, -ria *adj.* hereditary.
hereje *m.* heretic. *2* fig. shameless person.
herejía *f.* heresy. *2* insult, injurious expression.
herencia *f.* heritage, inheritance. *2* heredity.
heresiarca *m.* heresiarch.
heretical; herético, -ca *adj.* heretical.
Heriberto *m. pr.* Herbert.
herida *f.* wound, injury: *renovar la* ~, to open an old sore.
herido, -da *adj.* wounded, injured hurt: *mal* ~, se-

riously wounded, seriously injured. *2* struck. *3 m.-f.* wounded or injured person.
herir *tr.* to wound, injure, hurt [bodily or morally]. *2* to offend, pique. *3* to touch, move. *4* to strike, hit. *5* MUS. to finger, pluck. ¶ CONJUG. like *hervir.*
hermafrodita *adj.* hermaphrodite.
hermana *f.* sister; V. HERMANO.
hermanable *adj.* fraternal, brotherly. *2* compatible.
hermanado, -da *adj.* matched, mated, like, uniform.
hermanamiento *adj.* matching, mating, joining, making compatible.
hermanar *tr.* to join, match, mate; to harmonize, make compatible. *2* to make brothers or sisters [in a spiritual sense]. *3 ref.* to match, harmonize, be compatible. *4* to become brothers or sisters [in a spiritual sense].
hermanastro, -tra *m.* stepbrother. *2 f.* stepsister.
hermandad *f.* fraternity, brotherhood, sisterhood [fraternal tie; intimate friendship]. *2* correspondence, harmony. *3* confraternity, guild, religious association. *4 Santa Hermandad,* a Spanish rural police instituted in the fifteenth century.
hermano, -na *m.-f.* brother, sister: ~ or *hermana carnal,* full brother or sister; ~ or *hermana de leche,* foster brother, foster sister; ~, or *hermana, de madre* or *de padre,* half brother by the same mother or father; ~ *político,* brother-in-law, sister-in-law; *hermanos siameses,* Siamese twins; *Hermanos de la Doctrina Cristiana,* Brothers of the Christian Schools; *Hermanas de la Caridad,* Sisters of Charity. *2 adj. lenguas hermanas,* sister languages; *primo* ~, *prima hermana,* cousin german.
hermenéutica *f.* hermeneutics.
hermenéutico, -ca *adj.* hermeneutic(al.
hermético, -ca *adj.* hermetic(al, airtight. *2* impenetrable.
hermetismo *m.* secretiveness, secrecy.
hermosamente *adv.* beautifully. *2* perfectly.
hermosear *tr.* to beautify, embellish. *2 ref.* to beautify oneself.
hermoso, -sa *adj.* beautiful, beauteous, fair, lovely. *2* handsome, good-looking.
hermosura *f.* beauty, fairness, loveliness. *2* handsomeness, good looks. *3* belle, beauty.
hernia *f.* MED. hernia; rupture.
herniado, -da *adj.* MED. herniated, ruptured. *2 m.-f.* ruptured person.
hernista *m.* hernia surgeon.
Herodes *m. pr. n.* BIBL. Herod: *ir de* ~ *a Pilatos,* to go from pillar to post; from bad to worse.
herodiano, -na *adj.* Herodian.
Herodías *f. pr. n.* BIBL. Herodias.
héroe *m.* hero.
heroicidad *f.* heroicity, heroism. *2* heroic deed.
heroico, -ca *adj.* heroic: *verso heroico,* heroics.
heroína *f.* heroine. *2* CHEM. heroin.
heroísmo *m.* heroism.
herpe, herpes *m.-f.* MED. herpes.
herpético, -ca *adj.* MED. herpetic. *2 m.-f.* one who suffers from herpes.
herpetología *f.* herpetology.
herrada *f.* wooden bucket or pail.
herradero *m.* branding of cattle. *2* place where cattle are branded. *3* season for branding cattle.
herrado *m.* horseshoeing.

herrador *m.* horseshoer, farrier.
herradura *f.* horseshoe.
herraje *m.* ironwork, pieces of iron put on a door, coffer, etc. *2* horseshoes and their nails. *3* ERRAJ.
herramental *adj.-m.* tool bag, tool box.
herramienta *f.* tool, implement. *2* tools, set of tools. *3* coll, horns [of bull, cow, deer, etc.]. *4* coll. teeth, set of teeth, grinders.
herrar *tr.* to shoe [an animal]. *2* to brand [cattle, etc.]. *3* to cover or ornament with iron. ¶ CONJUG. like *acertar.*
herrén *m.* mixed grain for fodder.
herrera *f.* coll. blacksmith's wife.
herrería *f.* forge, ironworks. *2* smithy, blacksmith's shop; blacksmith's trade.
herrerillo *m.* ORN. blue titmouse. *2* ORN. great titmouse.
herrero *m.* blacksmith; iron forger, iron worker.
herreruelo *m.* ORN. coal titmouse.
herrete *m.* tag, aglet [of a lace, etc.].
herretear *tr.* to tag, to tip [a lace, etc.] with a tag.
herrín *m.* HERRUMBRE 1.
herrón *m.* quoit.
herrumbre *f.* rust, iron rust. *2* iron taste. *3* rust [plant disease].
herrumbroso, -sa *adj.* rusty, rusted.
hertziano, -na *adj.* Hertzian.
herventar *tr.* COOK. to bring to a boil.
hervidero *m.* noise and agitation of a boiling liquid. *2* boiling spring. *3* MED. rumbling in the chest. *4* crowd, swarm, seething mass.
hervir *intr.* [of a liquid] to boil: *hacer ~,* to make boil: to boil [something]. *2* to bubble, effervesce. *3* [of sea, etc.] to boil, seethe, be agitated. *4* to seethe [with emotion, etc.]. *5 ~ en,* to swarm or teem with. ‖ IRREG. CONJUG.: INDIC. Pres.: hiervo, hierves, hierve; hervimos, hervís, *hierven.* ‖ Pret.: herví, herviste, *hirvió;* hervimos, hervisteis, *hirvieron.* ‖ SUBJ. Pres.: *hierva, hiervas, hierva; hirvamos, hirváis, hiervan.* ‖ Imper.: *hirviera, hirvieras,* etc., or *hirviese, hirvieses,* etc. Fut.: *hirviere, hirvieres,* etc. ‖ IMPER. *hierve, hierva; hirvamos, hervid, hiervan.* ‖ PAST. P.: hervido. ‖ GER.: *hirviendo.*
hervor *m.* boiling, reaching the boiling point. *2* vehemence, ardour [of youth].
hervoroso, -sa *adj.* ardent, impetuous.
Hesíodo *m. pr. n.* Hesiod.
Hesperia *f. pr. n.* GEOG. Hesperia [Spain or Italy].
Hespérides *f. pl.* MYTH. Hesperides. *2* ASTR. Pleiades.
hesperidio *m.* BOT. hesperidium.
Héspero *m.* ASTR. Hesperus, the evening star.
heteo, -a *adj.-n.* Hittite.
heterocerca *adj.* ICHTH. heterocercal.
heteróclito, -ta *adj.* heteroclite.
heterodino, -na *adj.* RADIO. heterodyne.
heterodoxia *f.* heterodoxy.
heterodoxo, -xa *adj.* heterodox.
heterogeneidad *f.* heterogeneity.
heterogéneo, -a *adj.* heterogeneous.
heterónomo, -ma *adj.* heteronomous.
heteroscios *m. pl.* GEOG. heteroscians.
hético, -ca *adj.-n.* hectic, consumptive.
hexacordo *m.* MUS. hexacord.
hexaedro *m.* GEOM. hexahedron.
hexagonal *adj.* hexagonal.
hexágono, -na *adj.* hexagonal. *2 m.* GEOM. hexagon.
hexámetro *m.* PROS. hexameter.
hexápodo, -da *adj.-m.* hexapod.

hexasílabo, -ba *adj.* hexasyllabic.
hexástilo *m.* ARQ. hexastyle.
hez *f.* scum, dregs [vilest part]. *2 pl.* **heces** dregs, grounds, lees, sediment. *3* fœces, excrement.
hialino, -na *adj.* hyaline.
hialografía *f.* hyalography.
hiato *m.* GRAM., PROS. hiatus.
hibernación *f.* hibernation.
hibernal *adj.* hibernal.
hibernés, -sa *adj.-s.* Hibernian.
hibridación *f.* hybridization.
híbrido, -da *adj.-n.* hybrid.
hice, hiciera, hiciese, etc., *irr.* V. HACER.
hidalgo, -ga *adj.* noble, generous [person, act, etc.]. *2* of noble birth. *3 m.* hidalgo, nobleman. *4 f.* hidalga, noblewoman.
hidalguía *f.* quality, state or status of being an hidalgo. *2* nobility, nobleness, generosity.
hidra *f.* ZOOL. a poisonous sea snake. *2* ZOOL. hydra [polyp]. *3* (cap.) ASTR., MYTH. Hydra.
hidrácido *m.* CHEM. hydracid.
hidrargirio *m.* HIDRARGIRO.
hidrargirismo *m.* MED. mercurialism.
hidrargiro *m.* CHEM. hydrargyrum, mercury.
hidratación *f.* hydration, hydrating.
hidratado, -da *adj.* hydrated.
hidratar *tr.* CHEM. to hydrate.
hidrato *m.* CHEM. hydrate.
hidráulica *f.* hydraulics.
hidráulico, -ca *adj.* hydraulic. *2 m.* expert in hidraulics.
hidria *f.* hydria [ancient jar].
hidroavión *m.* AER. hydroplane, seaplane.
hidrocarburo *m.* CHEM. hydrocarbon.
hidrodinámica *f.* hydrodynamics.
hidrodinámico, -ca *adj.* hydrodynamic.
hidroeléctrico, -ca *adj.* hidroelectric.
hidrófilo, -la *adj.* absorbent: *algodón ~,* absorbent cotton.
hidrofobia *f.* MED. hydrophobia; rabies.
hidrófobo, -ba *adj.* MED. hydrophobe.
hidrófugo, -ga *adj.* nonabsorbent, moistureproof.
hidrogenar *tr.* to hydrogenate.
hidrógeno *m.* CHEM. hydrogen.
hidrografía *f.* hydrography.
hidrográfico, -ca *adj.* hydrographical.
hidrólisis *f.* CHEM. hydrolysis.
hidrolizar *tr.* CHEM. to hydrolyze.
hidrología *f.* hydrology.
hidromel *m.* hydromel.
hidrómetro *m.* hydrometer.
hidromiel *m.* HIDROMEL.
hidropatía *f.* MED. hydropathy, water cure.
hidropesía *f.* MED. dropsy.
hidrópico, -ca *adj.* dropsical, dropsied, hydropic(al. *2 m.-f.* dropsied person.
hidroplano *m.* AER. hydroplane, seaplane.
hidroscopio *m.* hydroscope.
hidrosfera *f.* hydrosphere.
hidrostática *f.* hydrostatics.
hidrostático, -ca *adj.* hydrostatic(al.
hidrostato *m.* hydrostat.
hidrosulfuro *m.* CHEM. hydrosulphide.
hidroterapia *f.* hydrotherapeutics.
hidróxido *m.* CHEM. hydroxide.
hidroxilo *m.* CHEM. hydroxil.
hiedra *f.* BOT. ivy.
hiel *f.* bile, gall: *echar la ~,* fig. to work hard. *2* fig. gall, bitterness, asperity, rancour.
hielo *m.* ice [frozen water]. *2* freezing, frost. *3*

ice, reserve, coldness: *romper el* ~, to break the ice.

hielo, hiele, etc., *irr.* V. HELAR.

hiemación *f.* wintering. 2 BOT. winter blooming.

hiemal *adj.* hibernal.

hiena *f.* ZOOL. hyena, hyaena.

hiendo, hienda, etc. *irr.* V. HENDER.

hierático, -ca *adj.* hieratic(al.

hierba *f.* herb, grass, weed: *mala* ~, weed; *sentir crecer,* or *nacer, la* ~, to be very sagacious; *en* ~, [of grain] green; *y otras hierbas,* fig. and many other things. 2 grass, herbage. 3 *pl.* years of age [of grazing cattle or horse]: *un potro de dos yerbas,* a colt two years old.
4 BOT. the word *hierba* forms the name of a great number of herbs and plants: ~ *buena,* mint; ~ *cana,* groundsel; ~ *de Santa María,* costmary, tansy; ~ *jabonera,* soapwort; ~ *luisa,* lemon verbena; ~ *pastel,* woad; ~ *sagrada,* vervain.

hierbabuena *f.* BOT. mind.

hierbezuela *f. dim.* small herb.

hierofanta or **hierofante** *m.* hierophant.

hieroglífico, -ca *adj.-m.* JEROGLÍFICO.

hierosolimitano, -na *adj.* JEROSOLIMITANO.

hierro *m.* iron [metal]: ~ *colado,* cast iron; ~ *dulce,* wrought iron; ~ *ondulado,* corrugated iron; *machacar en* ~ *frío,* to labour in vain. 2 iron, branding iron. 3 brand [mark]. 4 iron, head [of an arrow, lance, etc.]. 5 iron piece; steel, weapon: *quien a* ~ *mata, a* ~ *muere,* he who lives by the sword, will die by the sword. 6 *pl.* irons [fetters, chains, etc.].

hierro, hierre, etc. *irr.* V. HERRAR.

hiervo, hierva, hirviera, hirviere, etc. *irr.* V. HERVIR.

higa *f.* baby's fist-shaped amulet. 2 derisive gesture. 3 contempt, derision. 4 coll. *no dar dos higas por,* not to care a rap for. 5 *dar* ~ [of firearms] to miss fire.

higadillo *m.* liver [of birds and other small animals].

hígado *m.* liver. 2 *pl.* fig. courage. 3 *malos hígados,* evil disposition; *echar uno los hígados,* to work to excess; *hasta los hígados,* deeply, vehemently.

higiene *f.* hygiene, hygienics. 2 hygiene, cleanliness; sanitation.

higiénico, -ca *adj.* hygienic.

higienista *m.* hygienist.

higienizar *tr.* to sanitate, make sanitary.

higo *m.* fig: *no dársele a uno un* ~, not to care a fig; *de higos a brevas,* once in a while.

higrometría *f.* hygrometry.

higrómetro *m.* hygrometer.

higroscopio *m.* hygroscope.

higuera *f.* BOT. fig tree: ~ *chumba, de Indias* or *de tuna,* prickly pear; ~ *de Egipto,* caprifig, wild fig; *estar en la* ~, to be dreaming, to be in the clouds.

higueral *m.* plantation of fig trees.

higuereta *f.* BOT. castor-oil plant.

hija *f.* daughter. V. HIJO.

hijastro, -tra *m.-f.* stepson, stepdaughter.

hijito, -ta *m.-f. dim.* little son, sonny; little daughter; little child. 2 my son, my girl, my child, my dear. 3 young [of all animals].

hijo, -ja *m.-f.* son, daughter; child: ~ *adoptivo,* adopted child; citizen of honour; ~ *de confesión,* spiritual son; *Hijo de Dios,* Son of God, the Word; ~ *de leche,* foster child; ~ *legítimo,* legi-

timate child; ~ *natural,* illegitimate child; ~ *político,* son-in-law. 2 native [of a town or country]. 3 young [of an animal]. 4 fig. child, offspring, fruit, result. 5 junior: *Alejandro Dumas hijo,* Alexander Dumas Junior. 6 *m. pl.* sons, descendants.

hijodalgo *m.* HIDALGO.

hijuela *f.* dim. of HIJA. 2 accesory thing. 3 chalice pall. 4 irrigation channel. 5 BOT. palm seed; palmetto seed.

hijuelo *m.* dim. of HIJO. 2 BOT. offshoot, shoot.

hila *f.* file, row. 2 thin gut. 3 spinning [operation]. 4 *pl.* SURG. lint.

hilacha *f.,* **hilacho** *m.* thread, filament or shred ravelled out of cloth.

hilada *f.* file, row. 2 MAS. layer [of bricks], course. 3 NAUT. streak.

hilado *adj.* spun. 2 *m.* spinning [operation]. 3 yarn, spun yarn, thread.

hilador, -ra *m.-f.* spinner.

hilandera *f.* woman spinner.

hilandería *f.* spinning [art, business]. 2 spinning mill, spinnery.

hilandero, -ra *m.-f.* spinner. 2 *m.* spinning room.

hilar *tr.* to spin [wool, flax, silk, etc.]. 2 ~ *delgado,* to be exceedingly particular.

hilarante *adj.* laughable. 2 laughing [gas].

hilaridad *f.* hilarity.

Hilario *m. pr. n.* Hilary.

hilaza *f.* yarn, thread. 2 uneven thread. 3 *descubrir uno la* ~, to show one's true nature.

hilera *f.* file, line, row. 2 drawplate [for drawing wire]. 3 fine yarn. 4 ARCH. ridgepole. 5 MIL. file, single file. 6 *pl.* ZOOL. spinnerets.

hilillo *m. dim.* small thread. 2 trickle.

hilo *m.* thread [of flax, wool, hemp, etc.]: ~ *de empalomar,* packthread; ~ *de la vida,* thread of life; ~ *de perlas,* string of pearls; *pender de un* ~, to hang by a thread; *por el* ~ *se saca el ovillo,* a known detail leads to the knowledge of the whole. 2 thread [of conversation, narrative, etc.]. 3 fibre, grain. 4 direction, current: *irse tras el* ~ *de la gente,* to follow the current. 5 thin wire, wire thread. 6 trickle, thread [of water, etc.]. 7 linen [cloth]. 8 *al* ~, with the thread, with the grain. 9 *al* ~ *de medianoche,* on the stroke of midnight; *al* ~ *del mediodía,* at noon sharp.

hilván *m.* basting, tacking.

hilvanar *tr.* to baste, tack. 2 to string together, coordinate [phrases, ideas, etc.]. 3 to plan something hurriedly.

himen *m.* ANAT. hymen.

himeneo *m.* hymen, nuptials, marriage, wedding.

himenóptero, -ra *adj.* ENT. hymenopterous. 2 *m.* ENT. hymenopter.

himnario *m.* hymnal.

himno *m.* hymn, anthem: ~ *nacional,* national anthem.

himplar *intr.* [of a panther] to roar, bellow.

hincadura *f.* sticking, driving, thrusting in or into.

hincapié *m. hacer* ~ *en,* to insist upon, emphasize, lay emphatic stress on.

hincar *tr.* to stick, introduce, drive, thrust in or into: ~ *el diente,* to bite, set one's teeth into. 2 to plant, set [a post, etc.]. 3 ~ *la rodilla,* to go down on one's knee. 4 *ref. hincarse de rodillas,* to kneel down.

hincha *f.* hatred, enmity. 2 *m.-f.* coll. football-club fan.

hinchado, -da *adj.* swollen, inflated, bloated, tumid. 2 vain, puffed up. 3 high-flown, tumid, turgid [style].

hinchamiento *m.* swelling.

hinchar *tr.* to inflate, puff up, blow up, bloat, swell. 2 to swell [a river, brook, etc.]. 3 to pad, puff up [news, etc.]. 4 ref. to swell, blot [become swelled]. 5 to swell [with pride].

hinchazón *f.* swelling, tumefaction. 2 vanity, pride, haughtiness. 3 tumidness [of style].

hincho, hinche, etc. *irr.* V. HENCHIR.

hindú *adj.-n.* Hindu, Hindoo.

hinduismo *m.* Hinduism.

hinojo *m.* BOT. fennel: ~ *marino,* samphire.

hinojos *m. pl.* knees: *de hinojos,* on one's knees.

hintero *m.* baker's kneading table.

hioideo, -a *adj.* hyoid.

hioides *adj.* hyoid: *hueso* ~, hyoid bone.

hipar *intr.* to hiccup. 2 [of dogs on the scent] to pant, snuffle. 3 to whimper.

hiper- *pref.* hyper-.

hipérbaton *m.* RHET. hyperbaton.

hipérbola *f.* GEOM. hyperbola.

hipérbole *f.* RHET. hyperbole.

hiperbólico, -ca *adj.* hyperbolic.

hiperbóreo, -a *adj.* hyperborean.

hiperclorhidria *f.* hyperchlorhydria.

hipercrítico, -ca *adj.* hypercritical.

hiperdulia *f.* ECCL. hyperdulia.

hiperestesia *f.* hyperaesthesia.

hipérico *m.* BOT. hypericum, St. John's wort.

hipermetropía *f.* hypermetropia.

hipersensible *adj.* MED. hypersensitive.

hipertensión *f.* MED. hypertension.

hipertrofia *f.* hypertrophy.

hipertrofiarse *ref.* to hypertrophy.

hipertrófico, -ca *adj.* hypertrophic.

hípico, -ca *adj.* equine, pertaining to horses: *concurso* ~, riding competition.

hipido *m.* action of hiccuping. 2 whine, whimper.

hipnosis *f.* hypnosis.

hipnótico, -ca *adj.-n.* hypnotic.

hipnotismo *m.* hypnotism.

hipnotizador, -ra *adj.* hypnotizing. 2 *m.-f.* hypnotizer, hypnotist.

hipnotizar *tr.* to hypnotize.

hipo *m.* hiccup. 2 fig. longing. 3 fig. dislike, hatred.

hipocampo *m.* ICHTH. sea-horse, hippocampus.

hipocausto *m.* hypocaust.

hipoclorito *m.* CHEM. hypochlorite.

hipocondria *f.* hypochondria.

hipocondríaco, -ca *adj.-n.* hypochondriac.

hipocondrio *m.* ANAT. hypochondrium.

hipocrás *m.* hippocras, spiced wine.

Hipócrates *m. pr. n.* Hippocrates.

hipocresía *f.* hypocrisy.

hipócrita *adj.* hypocritical. 2 *m.-f.* hypocrite.

hipocritón, -na *m.-f.* coll. great hypocrite.

hipodérmico, -ca *adj.* hypodermic.

hipódromo *m.* hippodrome.

hipófisis *f.* ANAT. hypophysis.

hipofosfito *m.* CHEM. hypophosphite.

hipogastrio *m.* ANAT. hypogastrium.

hipogeo *m.* ARCH. hypogeum.

hipogrifo *m.* MYTH. hippogriff, hippogryph.

Hipólito *pr. n.* Hyppolytus.

hipopótamo *m.* ZOOL. hippopotamus.

hiposo, -sa *adj.* hiccuping, having hiccups.

hipóstasis *f.* hypostasis.

hipostático, -ca *adj.* hypostatic, hipostatical.

hipoteca *f.* mortgage, pledge. 2 LAW hypothec, hypothecation.

hipotecar *tr.* to mortgage, hypothecate, pledge.

hipotecario, -ria *adj.* hypothecary.

hipotenusa *f.* GEOM. hypotenuse.

hipótesis *f.* hypothesis.

hipotético, -ca *adj.* hypothetic(al.

hipsometría *f.* hypsometry.

hipsómetro *m.* hypsometer.

hirco *m.* ZOOL. wild goat.

hircocervo *m.* MYTH. hircocervus. 2 chimera, fantasy.

hiriente *adj.* cutting, smarting, offensive.

hirsuto, -ta *adj.* hirsute, hairy, bristly.

hirviente *adj.* boiling, seething.

hisopada *f.* a sprinkle with the aspergillum, aspersion.

hisopar, hisopear *tr.* to asperse, to sprinkle with the aspergillum.

hisopo *m.* BOT. hyssop. 2 aspergillum, sprinkler.

hispalense *adj.* Sevillan.

hispánico, -ca *adj.* Hispanic.

Hispaniola *f. pr. n.* GEOG. Haiti Island.

hispanicismo *m.* hispanicism; interest in language, literature, and other Spanish things.

hispanista *m.-f.* Hispanist.

hispano, -na *adj.-n.* Hispanic, Spanish, Hispano.

hispanoamericano, -na *adj.* Spanish-American.

hispanófilo, -la *adj.* Hispanophile.

híspido, -da *adj.* BOT., ZOOL. hispid, shaggy, bristly.

histéresis *f.* PHYS. hysteresis.

histérico, -ca *adj.* hysteric, hysterical. 2 *m.-f.* hysterical person. 3 *m.* HISTERISMO.

histerismo *m.* hysteria.

histología *f.* histology.

historia *f.* history: ~ *natural,* Natural History; ~ *sacra* or *sagrada,* Sacred History; ~ *universal,* Universal History; *hacer* ~ *de,* to relate, to give an account of; *picar en* ~, to be more serious than it seems. 2 story, tale, fable; gossip: *dejarse de historias,* to come to the point.

historiado, -da *adj.* historiated [letter]. 2 F. ARTS storied. 3 excessively and badly adorned.

historiador, -ra *m.-f.* historian.

historial *adj.* historical. 2 *m.* account of an affair, event, etc. 3 dossier, record [of a person].

historiar *tr.* to write or tell the history of; to chronicle, relate, give an account of.

histórico, -ca *adj.* historic, historical.

historieta *f.* short story or tale: ~ *cómica,* comic strip.

historiografía *f.* historiography.

historiógrafo *m.* historiographer.

histrión *m.* histrion.

histriónico, -ca *adj.* histrionic.

histrionismo *m.* histrionism.

hita *f.* headless nail. 2 landmark, mile-stone.

hito, -ta *adj.* fixed, firm. 2 *m.* landmark. 3 game like quoits. 4 target, aim: *dar en el* ~, fig. to see the point, the difficulty. 5 *mirar de* ~ *en* ~, to look fixedly, to stare at.

hizo *irr.* V. HACER.

hobachón, -na *adj.* fat, soft and lazy.

hocicada *f.* blow with the snout.

hocicar *tr.* [of hogs] to root. 2 coll. to kiss repeatedly. 3 *intr.* to fall on one's face. 4 to knock one's face [against an object]. 5 NAUT. to pitch.

hocico *m.* snout, muzzle, nose [of animal]. 2 blubber-lipped mouth. 3 coll. pouting, sullen look: *estar de* ~, to be sulky. 4 *sing. & pl.* coll. face [of

a person]: *caer de hocicos*, to fall on one's face; *meter el ~ en*, to poke one's nose into.
hocino *m.* billhook. *2* glen, den; narrow gorge. *3 pl.* gardens in glens.
hogaño *adv.* this year. *2* nowadays, at present.
hogar *m.* hearth, fireplace. *2* furnace [of steam engine]. *3* home [house; family life].
hogareño, -ña *adj.* home [of the home]. *2* home-loving.
hogaza *f.* large loaf.
hoguera *f.* bonfire, fire, blaze.
hoja *f.* BOT. leaf [of tree or plant], blade [of grass]; petal: *~ de parra*, fig. leaf [on a statue]. *2* leaf [of a book, door, table, etc.]: *volver la ~*, to turn the page; to change the subject [of conversation]. *3* sheet [of paper], printed or written sheet; blank form: *~ de pedidos*, COM. order blank; *~ de ruta*, RLY. waybill; *~ de servicios*, service record; *~ suelta* or *volante*, leaflet, handbill, fly sheet. *4* leaf, sheet, foil, pane [of metal, wood, etc.]. *5* blade [of sword, knife, etc.]: *~ de afeitar*, razor blade. *6* blade, sword. *7* layer, flake [of pastry]. *8* flitch, side [of bacon]. *9* ground cultivated every other year. *10* flaw [in a coin].
hojalata *f.* tin, tinplate.
hojalatería *f.* tinware. *2* tin-shop.
hojalatero *m.* tinman, tinsmith.
hojaldrado, -da *adj.* flaky [paste, pastry].
hojaldre *m.* or *f.* flaky or puff paste or pastry.
hojarasca *f.* dead leaves. *2* excessive foliage. *3* empty or superfluous words, rubbish, trash.
hojear *tr.* to leaf through, to skim the pages of.
hojita *f.* dim. small leaf, leaflet. *2* small blade, sheet, foil, layer or flake.
hojoso, -sa; hojudo, -da *adj.* leafy.
hojuela *f.* dim. HOJITA.
¡hola! *interj.* hello! *2* NAUT. hoy!, ahoy!
Holanda *f. pr. n.* GEOG. Holland. *2 f.* (not cap.) holland [fabric].
holandés, -sa *adj.* Dutch. *2 m.-f.* Dutchman, Dutchwoman, hollander.
holgachón, -na *adj.* ease-loving.
holgadamente *adv.* amply, fully. *2* quite. *3* comfortably.
holgado, -da *adj.* idle. *2* large, ample, roomy. *3* loose [clothing]. *4* comfortable, well-to-do.
holganza *f.* leisure, rest. *2* idleness. *3* pleasure, amusement.
holgar *intr.* to rest [after exertion]. *2* to be idle. *3* to be needless: *huelga decir*, needless to say. *4 ref.* to enjoy oneself. *5 intr.-ref.* to be glad: *huélgome de ello*, I am glad of it. ¶ CONJUG. like *contar*.
holgazán, -na *adj.* idle, lazy, slothful. *2 m.-f.* idler, loafer, lazy person.
holgazanear *intr.* to idle, lounge.
holgazanería *f.* idleness, laziness, slothfulness.
holgorio *m.* merrymaking, frolic.
holgura *f.* roominess, ampleness. *2* ease, comfort. *3* merrymaking.
holocausto *m.* holocaust, burnt offering; sacrifice.
hológrafo, -fa *adj.-m.* OLÓGRAFO.
holohedro *m.* CRYST. holohedron.
holoturia *f.* ZOOL. holoturian.
holladero *m.* trampled part of a path or place.
hollar *tr.* to tread, tread on or upon, trample. *2* fig. to tread upon, to humiliate, scorn.
hollejo *m.* thin skin covering some fruits [as grapes, beans, etc.].

hollín *m.* soot.
holliniento, -ta *adj.* sooty, fuliginous.
hombrachón *m.* big sturdy man.
hombrada *f.* manly action.
hombradía *f.* manliness. *2* courage, firmness.
hombre *m.* man [male member of the human race; human being; mankind]: *~ bueno*, LAW conciliator; *~ de armas*, man-at-arms; *~ de bien*, honest man; *~ de corazón*, courageous, magnanimous man; *~ de dinero*, man of means; *~ de estado*, statesman; *~ de letras*, man of letters; *~ de mar*, seaman; *~ de mundo*, man of the world; *~ de negocios*, businessman; *~ de palabra*, man of his word; *~ de pelo en pecho*, strong, daring man; *~ de pro* or *de provecho*, honest, steady man; *~ público*, politician; *buen ~*, good man; *pobre ~*, poor fellow; *ser todo un ~*, to be every inch a man: *como un solo ~*, at one, unanimously; *~ prevenido vale por dos*, forewarned is forearmed. *2* coll. man, husband. *3* CARDS ombre. *4 interj.* why!, well!, well I never!
hombrear *intr.* [of a boy] to try to act fullgrown. *2 intr.-ref.* hombrearse con, to strive to equal.
hombrecillo *m.* dim. little man, manikin. *2* BOT. hop.
hombrera *f.* ARM. pauldron. *2* shoulder strap. *3* shoulder pad.
hombretón *m.* big man.
hombría de bien *f.* probity, honesty.
hombrillo *m.* yoke [of a shirt].
hombro *m.* ANAT., ZOOL., PRINT. shoulder: *arrimar el ~*, to put one's shoulder to the wheel; *cargado de hombros*, round-shouldered; *echar al ~*, to take upon oneself; to shoulder the responsibility for something; *encogerse de hombros*, to shrug one's shoulders; not to be able or willing to answer; *llevar a hombros*, to carry on the shoulders; *mirar a uno por encima del ~*, to look down upon one.
hombrón *m.* big, sturdy man.
hombruno, -na *adj.* mannish, masculine.
homenaje *m.* homage: *rendir ~*, to pay or do homage to. *2* tribute, attention.
homenajear *tr.* to pay homage to. *2* to show respect, admiration, etc., through a public ceremony.
homeópata *m.* homoeopath, homoeopathist.
homeopatía *f.* homoeopathy.
homérico, -ca *adj.* Homeric.
Homero *m. pr. n.* Homer.
homicida *adj.* homicide [killing].
homilía *f.* homily.
hominicaco *m.* ugly, worthless man.
homocerca *adj.* ICHTH. homocercal.
homófono, -na *adj.* homophonous.
homogeneidad *f.* homogeneity.
homogéneo, -a *adj.* homogeneous.
homologación *f.* homologation.
homologar *tr.* to homologate.
homólogo, -ga *adj.* homologous.
homónimo, -ma *adj.* homonymous. *2 m.* homonym. *3 m.-f.* namesake.
homóptero, -ra *adj.* ENT. homopterous.
homosexual *adj.-n.* homosexual.
homúnculo *m.* homunculus.
honda *f.* sling [for hurling stones; hoisting rope].
hondamente *adv.* deeply, profoundly. *2* with deep insight.
hondazo *m.* shot with a sling.
hondero *m.* HIST. slinger.

hondo, -da *adj.* deep, profound. *2* low [ground]. *3 m.* depth, bottom: *de ~,* in depth.

hondón *m.* bottom [of a hollow thing]. *2* hollow, dell. *3* footpiece [of a stirrup].

hondonada *f.* hollow, dell, ravine, bottom land.

hondura *f.* depth, profundity: *meterse en honduras,* fig. to go beyond one's depth.

Honduras *f. pr. n.* GEOG. Honduras.

hondureño, -ña *adj.-n.* Honduran.

honestidad *f.* purity, chastity; modesty, decency.

honesto, -ta *adj.* pure, chaste, modest, decent. *2* honest, upright. *3* reasonable, just.

hongo *m.* BOT. fungus, mushroom. *2* bowler, Derby [hat]. *3* MED. fungus.

honor *m.* honour: *hacer ~ a uno,* to do one credit; *hacer uno ~ a sus compromisos,* to fulfill one's engagements. *2* honesty. *3 pl.* honours [civilities]. *4* dignity, rank, office. *5 honores de guerra,* honours of war.

honorabilidad *f.* honourability.

honorable *adj.* honourable [worthy of honour].

honorario, -ria *adj.* honorary. *2 pl.* honorarium, professional fee.

honorífico, -ca *adj.* honorific. *2* honorary.

honra *f.* honour [reputation, good name], dignity. *2* honour, purity [of women]. *3* honour, respect. *4 tener a mucha ~,* to be proud of. *5 pl.* obsequies.

honradez *f.* honesty, probity, integrity, uprightness.

honrado, -da *adj.* honest, honourable, upright, fair.

honramiento *m.* honouring.

honrar *tr.* to honour. *2* to do honour to, be a credit to. *3 ref.* to deem it an honour [to oneself], be proud [of].

honrilla *f.* keen sense of honour [*por la negra ~,* out of concern for what people will say.

honroso, -sa *adj.* honourable [behaviour, etc.]. *2* creditable, honour-giving. *3* decent, decorous.

hontanal, hontanar *m.* place with water springs.

hopa *f.* long cassock.

hopalanda *f.* houppelande.

hoplita *m.* hoplite.

hopo *m.* bushy or woolly tail. *2* tuft [of hair].

hora *f.* hour; time of day; time, season [of doing something, for something to happen]: *~ de comer,* mealtime, dinnertime; *~ de verano,* daylight-saving time; *~ oficial,* standard time; *horas de ocio,* leisure hours; *horas de trabajo,* working hours; *horas extraordinarias,* overtime; *horas punta,* rush hours; *noticias de última ~,* last-minute news: stop-press; *no ver la ~ de,* to be impatient for; *¿qué ~ es?,* what time is it?; *a estas horas,* coll. at this time, by now; *a última ~,* at the last moment, at the eleventh hour; *de ~ en ~,* unceasingly; *en buen* or *buena ~,* happily, luckily; all right; *en mal* or *mala ~,* in an evil hour, unluckily; *por horas,* by instants; by the hour. *2 pl.* ECCL. hours. *3* (cap.) MYTH. Hours. *4 adv.* now.

horaciano, -na *adj.* Horatian.

Horacio *m. pr. n.* Horace, Horatio.

horadado, -da *adj.* perforated, bored, pierced.

horadar *tr.* to perforate, bore, drill, pierce.

horario, -ria *adj.* horary, horal, hour. *2 m.* hour hand. *3* timepiece. *4* timetable, schedule of times: *~ escolar,* school hours.

horca *f.* gallows, gibbet. *2* AGR. hayfork, pitchfork. *3* crotch, forked prop [for trees]. *4* sting [of

onions or garlic]. *5 Horcas Caudinas,* Caudine Forks.

horcado, -da *adj.* forked, forklike.

horcadura *f.* crotch, fork [of a tree].

horcajadas (a) *adv.* astride, astraddle.

horcajadura *f.* crotch [of human body].

horcajo *m.* yoke [for mules]. *2* fork [made by two streams].

horcate *m.* hames [of harness].

horco *m.* string [of onions or garlic].

horcón *m.* large pitchfork.

horchata *f.* orgeat.

horchatería *f.* orgeat shop.

horda *f.* orde.

horizontal *adj.-f.* horizontal.

horizontalidad *f.* horizontality.

horizonte *m.* horizon.

horma *f.* form, mould. *2* shoe tree, shoemaker's last: *hallar la ~ de su zapato,* to meet one's match. *3* hatter's block. *4* MAS. dry wall.

hormaza *f.* MAS. dry wall.

hormiga *f.* ENT. ant: *~ blanca,* white ant; *~ león,* lion ant; *ser una ~,* fig. to be very thrifty.

hormigón *m.* ENG. concrete: *~ armado,* reinforced concrete.

hormigonera *f.* concrete mixer.

hormiguear *intr.* [of a part of the body] to creep. *2* [of people or animals] to swarm, to move in a swarm.

hormigueo *m.* crawling or creeping sensation. *2* swarming.

hormiguero, -ra *adj.* pertaining to the ants. *2 m.* anthill. *3* place swarming with people. *4* AGR. pile of dry leaves burned to serve as manure.

hormiguillo *m.* VET. disease of horses' hoofs. *2* line of people who pass materials or loads from hand to hand. *3* tickling or creeping sensation; itching.

hormiguita *f. dim.* small ant. *2* fig. very thrifty person.

hormilla *f.* buttonmould.

hormón *m.,* **hormona** *f.* PHYSIOL. hormone.

hornablenda *f.* MINER. hornblende.

hornacina *f.* ARCH. niche.

hornachuela *f.* cave or hut.

hornada *f.* batch, baking [quantity of bread, bricks, etc., baked at once]; melt [of a blast furnace].

hornaguera *f.* coal, hard coal, pit coal.

hornaguero, -ra *adj.* loose, too large. *2* spacious. *3* coal-bearing [ground].

hornazo *m.* Easter cake with hard-boiled eggs.

hornear *intr.* to bake bread, be a baker.

hornera *f.* baker's wife.

hornero, -ra *m.-f.* baker [one who makes bread].

hornija *f.* brushwood for an oven.

hornilla *f.* kitchen grate. *2* pigeonhole [for pigeons to nest in].

hornillo *m.* portable furnace or stove: *~ de gas,* gas-ring.

horno *m.* oven; furnace; kiln: *~ de cal,* limekiln; *~ de cuba, alto ~,* blast furnace; *no está el ~ para bollos,* fig. this is not the moment for doing that.

horópter(o *m.* OPT. horopter.

horóscopo *m.* horoscope.

horqueta *f.* crotch, forked prop. *2* crotch [of a tree].

horquilla *f.* small forked piece. *2* hooked pole for propping or hanging things. *3* hairpin. *4* fork [of bicycle]. *5* cradle [of telephone]. *6* MACH. gab, jaw [of connecting rod].

horrendo, -da *adj.* horrendous, horrible, frightful.

hórreo *m.* granary, mow. *2* granary built on pillars.

horrible *adj.* horrible, fearful, hideous, heinous.

hórrido, -da *adj.* horrid, horrible.

horrífico, -ca *adj.* horrific, horrifying.

horripilación *f.* horror, fright. *2* MED. horripilation.

horripilante *adj.* hair-raising, horrifying.

horripilar *tr.* to horripilate. *2* to horrify. *3 ref.* to feel horripilation. *4* to be horrified.

horrisonante, horrísono, -na *adj.* horrisonant.

horro, -rra *adj.* enfranchised. *2* free, untrammelled.

horror *m.* horror. *2* horrid thing.

horrorizar *tr.* to horrify. *2 ref.* to be horrified.

horroroso, -sa *adj.* horrible, horrid. *2* hideous, frightful, ugly.

horrura *f.* filth, dirt, dross.

hortaliza *f.* vegetables, garden produce.

hortelano, -na *adj.* [pertaining to] garden or orchard. *2 m.-f.* gardener, horticulturist. *3 m.* ORN. ortolan.

hortense *adj.* garden, hortensial: *plantas hortenses*, vegetables.

Hortensia *f. pr. n.* Hortense.

hortensia *f.* BOT. hydrangea.

hortera *f.* wooden bowl. *2 m.* in Madrid, shop clerk.

hortícola *adj.* horticultural.

horticultor, -ra *m.-f.* horticulturist.

hosanna *m.* ECCL. hosanna.

hosco, -ca *adj.* dark [colour of skin]. *2* sullen, surly; gloomy.

hospedador, -ra *m.-f.* host, one who gives lodging.

hospedaje, hospedamiento *m.* lodging, board. *2* cost of lodging or board.

hospedar *tr.* to lodge; to lodge an board. *2 ref.* to lodge [in]; to stop, put up [at].

hospedería *f.* hostelry, inn. *2* hospice, place for guests [in a monastery].

hospedero, -ra *m.-f.* host, innkeeper.

hospiciano, -na *m.-f.* inmate of a poor-house.

hospicio *m.* hospice, poor-house; orphanage.

hospital *m.* hospital.

hospitalariamente *adv.* hospitably.

hospitalario, -ria *adj.* hospitable. *2* ECCL. charitable [order]. *3* [pertaining to] hospital.

hospitalicio, -cia *adj.* [pertaining to] hospitality.

hospitalidad *f.* hospitality. *2* hospitableness.

hospitalizar *tr.* to hospitalize.

hosquedad *f.* sullenness, surliness.

hostal *m.* HOSTERÍA.

hostelero, -ra *m.-f.* host, inkeeper.

hostería *f.* hostelry, inn, tavern.

hostia *f.* sacrificial victim or offering. *2* ECCL. Host; wafer. *2* sugar wafer.

hostiario *m.* ECCL. wafer box; wafer mould.

hostigamiento *m.* harassing, worrying, plaguing. *2* lashing, whipping, flogging.

hostigar *tr.* to harass, worry, plague. *2* to lash, whip, flog.

hostil *adj.* hostile.

hostilidad *f.* hostility. *2 pl.* hostilities, warfare: *romper las hostilidades*, to start hostilities.

hostilizar *tr.* to harry, worry [the enemy]; to commit hostilities against.

hotel *m.* hotel. *2* villa, detached house.

hotelería *f.* keeping of hotels.

hotelero, -ra *adj.* [pertaining to] hotel. *2 m.-f.* hotelkeeper.

hotentote *adj.-n.* Hottentot.

hoy *adv.* today; now; nowadays, at the present time: *de ~ en adelante*, from now on, henceforth; *~ día, ~ en día*, nowadays; *~ por ~*, at the present time.

hoya *f.* hole, hollow, pit [in the ground]. *2* grave. *3* valley, dale.

hoyada *f.* dip, hollow, depression [in the ground].

hoyo *m.* hole, pit, hollow. *2* dent. *3* pockmark. *4* grave.

hoyuela *f.* the depression at the front of the neck.

hoyuelo *m.* small hole or pit. *2* dimple. *3* a boys' game. *4* HOYUELA.

hoz *f.* AGR. sickle: *de ~ y de coz*, headlong. *2* gorge, ravine.

hozadero *m.* hogs' rooting place.

hozadura *f.* hole made by a rooting hog.

hozar *tr.* [of hogs] to root.

Huberto *m. pr. n.* Hobart, Hubert.

hube, hubiera, hubiese, etc. *irr.* V. HABER.

hucha *f.* large chest or coffer. *2* money-box, money bank. *3* savings, nest egg.

huchear *tr.-intr.* to hoot at, to hoot.

hueco, -ca *adj.* hollow [not solid]. *2* empty: *cabeza hueca*, empty brains. *3* vain, conceited, proud. *4* hollow, deep [voice]. *5* affected, pompous [style]. *6* puffed, inflated. *7* soft, spongy [soil, wool, etc.]. *8 m.* hollow, cavity: *~ del ascensor*, elevator or lift shaft. *9* gap, void, interval. *10* socket [of bone]. *11* ARCH. opening [for a door, etc.]. *12* vacancy.

huecograbado *m.* photogravure for a rotary press.

huélfago *m.* VET. heaves.

huelga *f.* strike [of workmen]: *~ de brazos caídos*, sit-down strike; *~ de hambre*, hunger strike; *declararse en ~*, to go on strike. *2* leisure, recreation. *3* HUELGO *3*.

huelgo *m.* breath, respiration. *2* room, space. *3* MACH. play, allowance [between two pieces].

huelgo, huelga, etc. *irr.* V. HOLGAR.

huelguista *m.-f.* striker [workman].

huelguístico, -ca *adj.* [pertaining to a] workers' strike.

huella *f.* tread, treading. *2* print, impression; trace, track, rut, footprint, footstep: *~ dactilar*, fingerprint; *seguir las huellas de*, to follow in the footsteps of. *3* ARCH. tread [of a stair].

huemul *m.* ZOOL. the Andes deer.

huequecito *m. dim.* small hollow, space or interval.

huérfano, -na *adj.-n.* orphan. *2 adj.* orphaned.

huero, -ra *adj.* addle [egg]. *2* fig. addle, empty: *salir ~*, to flop, fall through.

huerta *f.* large vegetable garden or orchard. *2* irrigated region.

huertano, -na *m.-f.* inhabitant of some irrigated regions.

huerto *m.* orchard, fruit garden. *2* kitchen garden, vegetable garden.

huesa *f.* grave, tomb.

huesarrón *m. augm.* large bone.

hueso *m.* bone [piece of the skeleton]: *~ sacro*, sacrum; *la sin ~*, fig. the tongue; *calarse hasta los huesos*, to get soaked to the skin; *estar en los huesos*, to be nothing but skin and bones; *no dejar ~ sano a uno*, to pick somebody to pieces, to backbite; *tener los huesos molidos*, to be tired out. *2* bone [material]. *3* BOT. stone, pit [of fruit]. *4* fig. hard or unwelcome job: *~ duro* *de roer*, hard nut to crack. *5 pl.* bones, mortal remains.

huesoso, -sa *adj.* bony, osseous.

huésped, -da *m.-f.* guest; lodger, boarder: *casa de huéspedes*, boarding house. *2* host, hostess: *echar la cuenta sin la huéspeda*, to reckon without one's host. *3* BOT., ZOOL. host.

hueste or *pl.* **huestes** *f.* army, host. *2* followers.

huesudo, -da *adj.* bony, big-boned.

hueva *f.* roe [fish eggs].

huevera *f.* egg dealer [woman]. *2* oviduct [of birds]. *3* eggcup. *4* eggdish.

huevería *f.* egg shop.

huevero, -ra *m.-f.* egg dealer. *2 m.* eggcup.

huevo *m.* egg: ~ *de zurcir*, darning egg; ~ *duro*, hard-boiled egg; ~ *pasado por agua*, (Am.) ~ *tibio*, soft-boiled egg; ~ *escalfado*, poached egg; ~ *estrellado*, or *frito*, fried egg; *huevos revueltos*, (Am.) *huevos pericos*, scrambled eggs; *parecerse como un ~ a una castaña*, not to be alike at all. *2* ZOOL. ~ *de pulpo*, sea hare.

Hugo *m. pr. n.* Hugh.

hugonote *adj.-n.* Huguenot.

huida *f.* flight, escape. *2* shying [of a horse].

huidero *m.* cover, shelter [of animals].

huidizo, -za *adj.* fugitive, evasive.

huir *intr.* to flee, fly, escape, run away, slip away: ~ *de*, to run away from, to flee, fly, avoid, shun, evade. *2* [of the time, days, etc.] to fly, pass rapidly. *3 tr.* to flee, fly, avoid, shun. *3* ~ *la cara*, to avoid [someone]. ¶ CONJUG. INDIC. Pres.: *huyo, huyes, huye; huimos, huís, huyen.* | Pret.: *hui, huiste, huyó; huimos, huisteis, huyeron.* | SUBJ. Pres.: *huya, huyas*, etc. | Imperf.: *huyera, huyeras*, etc., or *huyese, huyeses*, etc. | Fut.: *huyere, huyeres*, etc. | IMPER.: *huye, huya; huyamos, huid, huyan.* | GER.: *huyendo.*

hule *m.* oilcloth, oilskin. *2* rubber, India rubber. *3* BOT. (Am.) rubber tree. *4* BULLF. blood, goring.

hulla *f.* coal, mineral [gen. bituminous] coal. *2* fig. ~ *blanca*, white coal, water power.

hullero, -ra *adj.* [containing or pertaining to] coal.

humanamente *adv.* humanely. *2* humanly.

humanal *adj.* human.

humanar *tr.-ref.* HUMANIZAR. *2 ref.* to become man [said of Jesus Christ].

humanidad *f.* humanity. *2* mankind. *3* humaneness. *4* human weakness. *5* coll. corpulence, fleshiness. *6 pl.* humanities [classic literature].

humanista *m.-f.* humanist, classical scholar.

humanitario, -ria *adj.* humanitarian. *2* humane, charitable, benevolent.

humanitarismo *m.* humanitarism, humaneness.

humanizar *tr.* to humanize, soften [make humane]. *2 ref.* to humanize, soften [become humane].

humano, -na *adj.* human. *2* humane, compassionate. *3 m.* human, human being.

humareda *f.* cloud of smoke, a great deal of smoke.

humazo *m.* dense smoke. *2* smoke made to drive rats from ship or animals out of their lair.

Humberto *m. pr. n.* Humbert.

humeante *adj.* smoky, smoking [emiting smoke]. *2* steaming.

humear *intr.* to smoke [emit smoke]. *2* to steam [emit steam]; to emit fumes or vapours. *3* to get proud, take on airs. *4 tr.* (Am.) to fumigate.

humectación *f.* humidification.

humectar *tr.* to humidify, moisten.

humedad *f.* humidity, moisture, dampness.

humedal *m.* humid ground, marsh.

humedecer *tr.* to humidify, moisten, dampen, wet. *2 ref.* to become humid, moist. ¶ CONJUG. like *agradecer.*

humedezco, humedezca, etc. *irr.* V. HUMEDECER.

húmedo, -da *adj.* humid, moist, damp, wet.

humeral *adj.* ANAT. humeral. *2 m.* ECCL. humeral veil.

húmero *m.* ANAT. humerus.

humildad *f.* humility. *2* humbleness, lowliness.

humilde *adj.* humble; lowly. *2* meek, submissive.

humillación *f.* humiliation; humbling.

humilladero *m.* roadside crucifix or shrine.

humillante *adj.* humiliating.

humillar *tr.* to humiliate. *2* to humble, abase, crush, lower. *3* to bow [one's head], to bend [one's body or knees]. *4 ref.* to humble oneself.

humillos *m. pl.* vanity, pride.

humo *m.* smoke: *la del* ~, good riddance; *a* ~ *de pajas*, without a reason. *2* steam, vapour, fume. *3 pl.* conceit, pride, vanity: *bajarle a uno los humos*, to humble someone's pride.

humor *m.* PHYSIOL. humour. *2* humour, temper, mood: *buen* ~, good humour; *mal* ~, bad humour; *no estar de* ~ *para*, not to be in the mood to or for. *3* merry disposition. *4* humour, wit.

humorada *f.* whim. *2* whimsical or witty act or saying.

humoral *adj.* PHYSIOL. humoural.

humorismo *m.* humour [in speaking or writing]; humorous literature. *2* humorousness.

humorista *m.-f.* humorist [writer].

humorístico, -ca *adj.* humorous, jocular, funny.

humosidad *f.* smokiness.

humoso, -sa *adj.* smoky.

hundimiento *m.* sinking. *2* cave-in. *3* NAUT. foundering. *4* collapse, downfall, ruin.

hundir *tr.* to sink, submerge, plunge. *2* NAUT. to founder. *3* to cave in, stave in. *4* to drive in. *5* to confound, confute. *6* to crush, destroy, ruin. *7* *ref.* to sink, go down, be submerged; to subside, cave in. *8* to collapse, be ruined.

húngaro, -ra *adj.-n.* Hungarian.

Hungría *f. pr. n.* GEOG. Hungary.

huno, -na *m.-f.* Hun.

hupe *f.* punk, touchwood.

huracán *m.* hurricane.

huracanado, -da *adj.* hurricane-like [wind].

huraña *f.* sullenness, unsociableness.

huraño, -ña *adj.* sullen, unsociable.

hurgar *tr.* to poke, stir: *hurgarse la nariz*, to pick one's nose. *2* to stir up, incite.

hurgón *m.* poke [for poking the fire].

hurgonazo *m.* thrust with a poker. *2* coll. ESTOCADA.

hurgonear *tr.* to poke [the fire]. *2* coll. to make a thrust at.

hurí *f.* houri.

hurón, -na *adj.* sullen, unsociable. *2 m.* ZOOL. ferret. *3* fig. ferreter, prier. *4* fig. unsociable person. *5* ZOOL. female ferret.

huronear *intr.* to ferret.

huronera *f.* ferret hole. *2* lair, hiding place.

huronero *m.* ferret keeper.

¡hurra! *interj.* hurrah!

hurtadillas (a) *adv.* stealthily, on the sly.

hurtar *tr.* to steal, thieve, pilfer. *2* to cheat [in weight or measure]. *3* to plagiarize. *4* to move away: ~ *el cuerpo*, to dodge, shy away. *5 ref.* to withdraw, hide.

hurto *m.* stealing, theft, pilferage. *2* stolen thing. *3 adv. a hurto*, by stealth, on the sly.

husada *f.* spindleful [of yarn].

húsar *m.* MIL. hussar.

husero *m.* brow antler [of a yearling fallow deer].

husillo *m. dim.* small spindle. *2* MACH. screw pin.

husma *f.* HUSMEO: *andar a la ~*, to nose around.

husmeador, -ra *adj.* scenting, nosing around. *2 m.-f.* scenter. *3* prier, inquisitive person.

husmear *tr.* to scent, wind, smell out. *2* to pry out, nose out. *3 intr.* [of meat] to become gamy or high, to smell bad.

husmeo *m.* scenting, smelling. *2* nosing around.

husmo *m.* high odour, gaminess. *2 andar al ~*, to go scenting or prying.

huso *m.* spindle [for hand spinning]. *2* TEXT. spindle. *3* HER. narrow lozenge. *4* MIN. drum of a windlass. *5* GEOM. ~ *esférico*, spherical lune. *6* GEOG. ~ *horario*, time zone.

¡huy! *interj.* of pain, grief, surprise, etc.

huyo, huyó, huya, huyera, etc. *irr.* V. HUIR.

I, i *f.* I, i, tenth letter of the Spanish alphabet.
iba, etc., *imperf.* of IR.
Iberia *f. pr. n.* GEOG. Iberia.
ibérico, -ca; iberio, -ria *adj.* Iberian.
ibero, -ra *adj.-n.* Iberian.
iberoamericano, -na *adj.-n.* Latin-American.
ibice *m.* ZOOL. ibex, wild goat.
ibis, *pl.* **ibis** *f.* ORN. ibis.
Ibiza *f. pr. n.* GEOG. Iviza [Balearic Island].
icáreo, -a; icario, -ria *adj.* Icarian.
iceberg *m.* iceberg.
icneumón *m.* ZOOL., ENT. ichneumon.
icnografía *f.* ARCH. ichnography.
icono *m.* icon.
iconoclasta *adj.* iconoclastic. *2 m.-f.* iconoclast.
iconografía *f.* iconography.
iconología *f.* iconology.
iconostasio *m.* ECCL. iconostasis.
icor *m.* MED. ichor.
icosaedro *m.* GEOM. icosahedron.
ictericia *f.* MED. jaundice.
ictérico, -ca *adj.* icteric(al. *2* jaundiced.
ictíneo *m.* submarine vessel.
ictiófago, -ga *adj.* ichthyophagous.
ictiología *f.* ichthyology.
ictiosauro *m.* PALEONT. ichthyosaurus.
ida *f.* going [to a place], departure: *viaje de ~ y vuelta,* round trip; *idas y venidas,* comings and goings. *2* FENC. attack. *3* HUNT. track, trail [of game].
idea *f.* idea; notion. *2* intent, purpose: *llevar ~ de,* to intend to; *mudar de ~,* to change one's mind. *3* opinion, estimate. *4* ingenuity, inventiveness.
ideación *f.* ideation.
ideal *adj.-m.* ideal. *2 adj.* perfectly suitable or proper.
idealismo *m.* idealism.
idealista *adj.* idealist, idealistic. *2 m.-f.* idealist.
idealizar *tr.* to idealize.
idear *tr.* to form an idea of. *2* to devise, contrive, plan, invent, *think up.
ídem *pron.* idem, ditto.
idéntico, -ca *adj.* identic(al.
identidad *f.* identity. *2* identicalness.
identificación *f.* identification.
identificar *tr.* to identify. *2 ref.* to be identified. *3 identificarse con,* to identify oneself with.
ideografía *f.* ideography.

ideograma *m.* ideogram.
ideología *f.* ideology.
ideólogo *m.* ideologist.
idílico, -ca *adj.* idyllic.
idilio *m.* idyll. *2* amorous talk. *3* love relations.
idioma *m.* idiom, language, tongue.
idiomático, -ca *adj.* idiomatic [pertaining to an idiom or language].
idiosincrasia *f.* idiosyncrasy.
idiota *adj.* idiotic. *2 m.-f.* idiot.
idiotez *f.* idiocy.
idiotismo *m.* ignorance. *2* idiom [peculiar expression].
idólatra *adj.* idolatrous. *2 m.* idolater. *3 f.* idolatress.
idolatrar *tr.-intr.* to idolize.
idolatría *f.* idolatry.
idolátrico, -ca *adj.* idolatrous.
ídolo *m.* idol.
idoneidad *f.* fitness, suitability; competence.
idóneo, -a *adj.* fit, suitable; able, competent.
idus *m.* ides.
iglesia *f.* church [in every sense]: *~ anglicana,* Anglican Church, Church of England; *~ católica,* Roman Catholic Church.
Ignacio *m. pr. n.* Ignatius.
ignaro, -ra *adj.* ignorant.
ígneo, -a *adj.* igneous.
ignición *f.* ignition [burning state].
ignífugo, -ga *adj.* ignifuge, protecting from fire.
ignipotente *adj.* poet. ignipotent.
ignívomo, -ma *adj.* poet. ignivomous.
ignominia *f.* ignominy.
ignominioso, -sa *adj.* ignominious.
ignorado, -da *adj.* unknown. *2* fameless, obscure.
ignorancia *f.* ignorance.
ignorante *adj.* ignorant. *2 m.-f.* ignoramus.
ignorantón, -na *adj.* ignorant. *2 m.-f.* ignoramus.
ignorar *tr.* not to know, be ignorant of.
ignoto, -ta *adj.* unknown; undiscovered.
igual *adj.* equal [the same in value, size, etc.]: *~ a,* equal to, the same as. *2* the same, indifferent: *es ~, me es ~,* it is all the same [to me]. *3* level, even, uniform. *4* equal, commensurate. *5* equable. *6* constant, unchanging. *7 m.* MATH. equality sign (=). *8* equal. *sin ~,* matchless, unrivalled. *9 adv. al ~,* equally; *~ que,* as well as; *por ~, por un ~,* equally, evenly.

iguala *f.* equalizing, equalization. *2* monthly or annual fee.
igualación *f.* equalization. *2* leveling, making even.
igualado, -da *adj.* equal, level, even.
igualar *tr.* to equalize; to equate. *2* to even, level, smooth, face. *3* to deem equal, match. *4 intr.-ref.* ~ *a, igualarse con*, to equal [be equal to]; to compare with. *5 ref.* to become equal. *6* SPORT. to tie [in scoring].
igualdad *f.* equality, sameness. *2* MATH. equality. *3* evenness, smoothness, uniformity. *4* ~ *de ánimo*, equability, equanimity.
igualitario, -ria *adj.* equalizing. *2* equalitarian.
igualmente *adv.* equally. *2* evenly, uniformly. *3* likewise, also. *4* coll. the same to you.
iguana *f.* ZOOL. iguana.
iguanodonte *m.* PALEONT. iguanodont.
ijada *f.* flank [of an animal]. *2* side [of a pers.]; pain in the side, stitch.
ijar *m.* IJADA I.
ilación *f.* illation. *2* connectedness.
ilativo, -va illative.
Ildefonso *m. pr. n.* Alphonso.
ilegal *adj.* illegal, unlawful.
ilegalidad *s.* illegality, unlawfulness.
ilegible *adj.* illegible.
ilegitimar *tr.* to illegitimate.
ilegitimidad *f.* illegitimacy.
ilegítimo, -ma *adj.* illegitimate. *2* false, spurious.
íleo *m.* MED. ileus.
ileon *m.* ANAT. ileum. *2* ANAT. ilium.
ileso, -sa *adj.* unharmed, sound, unhurt, unscathed.
iletrado, -da *adj.* illiterate, uneducated.
ilíaco, -ca *adj.* ANAT. iliac. *2* Iliac, Trojan.
Ilíada *f.* Iliad.
iliberal *adj.* illiberal, stingy.
ilícito, -ta *adj.* illicit, unlawful.
ilíquido, -da *adj.* COM. unliquidated.
iliterato *adj.* illiterate, unlearned.
ilógico, -ca *adj.* illogical.
ilota *m.* helot.
iluminación *f.* illumination, lighting. *2* illumination, enlightenment. *3* F. ARTS illumination.
iluminado, -da *adj.* illuminated, lighted. *2* illuminated [mentally or spiritually]. *3* illuminated [manuscript, book, etc.]. *4 m.-f.* one of the illuminati. *5 pl.* illuminati.
iluminador, -ra *adj.* illuminating. *2 m.-f.* illuminator.
iluminar *tr.* to illuminate, illumine, light, light up. *2* to illuminate, illumine, enlighten. *3* F. ARTS to illuminate. *4 ref.* to illuminate; to light up, brighten.
iluminarias *f. pl.* LUMINARIAS.
iluminismo *m.* illuminism.
ilusión *f.* illusion. *2* false or groundless hope: *hacerse ilusiones,* to deceive oneself with false hopes. *3* hopeful anticipation.
ilusionarse *ref.* to indulge in groundless hopes or in hopeful anticipations.
ilusionista *m.-f.* illusionist, prestidigitator.
ilusionismo *m.* illusionism, prestidigitation.
ilusivo, -va *adj.* illusive, deceiving.
iluso, -sa *adj.* deluded, deceived, beguiled. *2* dreamer, visionary.
ilusorio, -ria *adj.* illusive, illusory. *2* vain, ineffectual.
ilustración *f.* illustration, illustrating. *2* enlightenment. *3* learning, erudition. *4* making illus-

trious. *5* illustration picture. *6* illustrated or pictorial magazine.
ilustrado, -da *adj.* illustrated. *2* enlightened. *3* learned, informed, cultivated.
ilustrar *tr.* to illustrate. *2* to enlighten. *3* to educate, civilize. *4* THEOL. to illuminate. *5* to make illustrious. *6 ref.* to learn, become educated. *7* to distinguish oneself.
ilustrativo, -va *adj.* illustrative.
ilustre *adj.* illustrious, distinguished.
ilustrísimo, -ma *adj.* most illustrious: *su ilustrísima,* form of address when talking to a bishop.
imagen *f.* image: ~ *de bulto,* image in sculpture; ~ *real,* ~ *virtual,* PHYS. real image, virtual image; *a su* ~, in his own image.
imaginación *f.* imagination, imagining. *2* imagination, fancy [mental faculty]. *3* fancy, unfounded belief, arbitrary supposition.
imaginar *tr.* to imagine, conceive. *2 tr.-ref.* to imagine [represent to oneself], fancy, suppose, conjecture: *¡imagínese!,* just imagine!
imaginaria *f.* MIL. reserve guard.
imaginario, -ria *adj.* imaginary, fancied. *2* MATH. imaginary. *3* of account [money].
imaginativa *f.* imagination, fancy [faculty].
imaginativo, -va *adj.* imaginative.
imaginería *f.* religious imagery or statuary. *2* fancy embroidery in colours.
imaginero *m.* painter or sculptor of religious images.
imago *m.* ENT. imago.
imán *m.* magnet. *2* loadstone, lodestone. *3* fig. attraction, charm. *4* imam [Mohammedan priest].
imanación *f.* magnetization [of a needle, etc.].
imanar *tr.* to magnetize [a needle, etc.]. *2 ref.* to become magnetized.
imantación *f.* IMANACIÓN.
imantar *tr.-ref.* IMANAR.
imbatido, -da *adj.* SPORT. unbeaten.
imbécil *adj.-n.* imbecile.
imbecilidad *f.* imbecility; stupidity.
imberbe *m.* beardless.
imbornal *m.* scupper [of roof]. *2* NAUT. scupper.
imborrable *adj.* indelible, ineffaceable.
imbricación *f.* imbrication.
imbricado, -da *adj.* imbricate, imbricated.
imbuir *tr.* to imbue, infuse. ¶ CONJUG. like *huir.*
imbuyo, imbuyó, imbuya, etc. *irr.* V. IMBUIR.
imitable *adj.* imitable.
imitación *f.* imitation: *a* ~ *de,* in imitation of; *de* ~, imitation [as adj.].
imitado, -da *adj.* imitated; imitation, mock, sham.
imitador, -ra *adj.* imitating. *2 m.-f.* imitator.
imitar *tr.* to imitate. *2* to ape, mimic. *3* to counterfeit.
imitativo, -va *adj.* imitative.
impaciencia *f.* impatience. *2* anxiousness, eagerness.
impacientar *tr.* to make [one] lose patience; to vex, irritate. *2 ref.* to lose patience, become impatient, -chafe.
impaciente *adj.* impatient; anxious, eager.
impacto *m.* impact.
impalpable *adj.* impalpable.
impar *adj.* unmatched. *2* MATH. odd, uneven [number].
imparcial *adj.* impartial, fair, unbiassed.
imparcialidad *f.* impartiality.
imparisílabo, -ba *adj.* GRAM. imparisyllabic.
impartir *tr.* to impart.
impasable *adj.* impassable.

impasible *adj.* impassible. *2* impassive, unmoved.
impavidez *f.* fearlessness, intrepidity.
impávido, -da *adj.* dauntless, fearless, undaunted.
impecabilidad *f.* impeccability. *2* faultlessness.
impecable *adj.* impeccable. *2* faultless.
impedancia *f.* ELECT. impedance.
impedido, -da *adj.* disabled, crippled, paralytic. *2 m.-f.* cripple; paralytic person.
impediente *adj.* impeding.
impedimenta *f.* MIL. impedimenta.
impedimento *m.* impediment, hindrance, obstacle.
impedir *tr.* to impede, hinder, obstruct, prevent; ~ *el paso*, to block the way. ¶ CONJUG. like *servir*.
impelente *adj.* impellent. *2* force [pump].
impeler *tr.* to impel, drive forward, propel. *2* to impel, drive [to action, to do something].
impenetrabilidad *f.* impenetrability.
impenetrable *adj.* impenetrable.
impenitente *adj.* impenitent, obdurate.
impensado, -da *adj.* unexpected, unforeseen.
imperante *adj.* ruling, commanding. *2* prevailing.
imperar *intr.* to rule, command, hold sway. *2* to prevail, be prevailing, reign.
imperativo, -va *adj.* imperative, commanding. *2 adj.-n.* GRAM. imperative. *3 m.* PHIL. ~ *categórico*, categorical imperative.
imperceptible *adj.* imperceptible.
imperdible *adj.* unlosable. *2 m.* safety pin.
imperdonable *adj.* unpardonable, unforgivable.
imperecedero, -ra *adj.* imperishable, undying.
imperfección *f.* imperfection; fault, blemish.
imperfecto, -ta *adj.* imperfect, defective, faulty. *2 adj.-n.* GRAM. imperfect.
imperial *adj.* imperial. *2 f.* imperial, upper-deck [of a coach, diligence, etc.].
imperialismo *m.* imperialism.
impericia *f.* inexpertness, unskilfulness.
imperio *m.* empire. *2* command, sway. *3* haughtiness, imperiousness.
imperiosidad *f.* imperiousness.
imperioso, -sa *adj.* imperious, imperative.
imperito, -ta *adj.* inexpert, unskilful.
impermeabilidad *f.* impermeability.
impermeabilizar *tr.* to waterproof; to make impermeable.
impermeable *adj.* impermeable; impervious. *2* waterproof. *3 m.* raincoat, mackintosh, waterproof.
impersonal *adj.* impersonal.
impertérrito, -ta *adj.* dauntless, intrepid; unmoved.
impertinencia *f.* impertinence. *2* annoyance, importunity.
impertinente *adj.* impertinent. *2* annoying, peevish. *3 m.-f.* impertinent [person]. *4 m. pl.* lorgnette.
imperturbable *adj.* imperturbable, unperturbed.
impétigo *m.* MED. impetigo.
impetración *f.* impetration; beseeching.
impetrante *adj.* impetrating; beseeching.
impetrar *tr.* to impetrate. *2* to beseech.
ímpetu *m.* impetus, impulse, momentum. *2* impetuousness, violence.
impetuosidad *f.* impetuosity, impetuousness.
impetuoso, -sa *adj.* impetuous.
impido, impida, etc. *irr.* V. IMPEDIR.
impiedad *f.* impiety, ungodliness.
impío, -pía *adj.* impious, irreligious, godless. *2* cruel, pitiless. *3 m.-f.* impious person.
implacabilidad *f.* implacability.
implacable *adj.* implacable, inexorable.
implantación *f.* implantation.

implantar *tr.* to implant, introduce [doctrines, customs, etc.]. *2* SURG. to implant.
implicación *f.* contradiction. *2* implication, involving.
implicar *tr.* to implicate, involve, entangle. *2* to imply. *3 intr.* to contradict, be an obstacle.
implícito, -ta *adj.* implicit.
imploración *f.* imploration, supplication.
implorar *tr.* to implore.
implume *adj.* featherless, unfeathered; unfledged.
impluvio *m.* impluvium.
impolítica *f.* impoliteness, incivility, discourtesy.
impolítico, -ca *adj.* impolite. *2* impolitic.
impoluto, -ta *adj.* unpollute, untarnished.
imponderable *adj.* imponderable. *2* great, extraordinary, beyond all exaggeration or praise.
impondré, impondría, impongo, imponga, etc. *irr.* V. IMPONER.
imponente *adj.* imposing. *2 m.-f.* depositor [one who deposits money in a bank].
imponer *tr.* to impose [taxes, penalties, silence, etc.]. *2* ECCL. to impose [the hands]. *3* to impute falsely. *4* to acquaint, instruct. *5* to command, inspire [respect, awe]. *6* to deposit [money in a bank]. *7* PRINT. to impose. *8 ref.* to assert oneself. *9* to be imperative or necessary. *10 imponerse a*, to impose one's authority on. *11 imponerse de*, to learn, find out. ¶ CONJUG. like *poner*.
imponible *adj.* taxable, dutiable.
impopular *adj.* unpopular.
impopularidad *f.* unpopularity.
importación *f.* COM. importation, imports.
importador, -ra *adj.* COM. importing. *2 m.-f.* importer.
importancia *f.* importance, consequence.
importante *adj.* important, material, momentous.
importar *intr.* to import, be important, be of consequence; to matter, concern: *no me importa*, I don't care; *¿qué importa?*, what does it matter? *2 tr.* to amount to, to be worth. *3* to carry, involve, imply. *4* COM. to import.
importe *m.* COM. amount, value, cost.
importunación *f.* importuning, pestering.
importunar *tr.* to importune, pester.
importunidad *f.* importunity, importunateness.
importuno, -na *adj.* importunate. *2* inopportune.
imposibilidad *f.* impossibility.
imposibilitado, -da *adj.* unable. *2* disabled, crippled, paralytic.
imposibilitar *tr.* to make unable. *2* to make impossible; to prevent. *3* to disable, cripple.
imposible *adj.* impossible. *2 m.* impossible thing, impossibility: *hacer los imposibles*, to do one's utmost.
imposición *f.* imposition. *2* false imputation. *3* sum which a person, deposits in a bank.
imposta *f.* ARCH. impost.
impostor, -ra *m.* impostor. *2 f.* impostress. *3 m.-f.* slanderer.
impostura *f.* imposture. *2* false imputation, slander.
impotable *adj.* undrinkable.
impotencia *f.* impotence, inability. *2* MED. impotence.
impotente *adj.* impotent, powerless, unable. *2* MED. impotent.
impracticable *adj.* impracticable, infeasible. *2* impracticable, impassable [road, etc.].
imprecación *f.* imprecation.
imprecar *tr.* to imprecate.
imprecisión *f.* imprecision, vagueness.
impreciso *adj.* imprecise, vague, indefinite.

impregnar *tr.* to impregnate, interpenetrate. *2 ref.* to become impregnate or interpenetrated.
impremeditación *f.* unpremeditation.
impremeditado, -da *adj.* unpremeditated.
imprenta *f.* printing [art of printing books, etc.]. *2* printing office or house, press. *3* press, printed matter: *libertad de ~,* freedom of the press.
imprescindible *adj.* essential, indispensable.
imprescriptible *adj.* imprescriptible.
impresentable *adj.* unpresentable.
impresión *f.* impression, impressing, stamping [of a mark]. *2* impression, impress, imprint, print [mark impressed]. *3* PRINT. print, printing, press-work. *4* PHOT. print. *5* impression [physical or moral effect]. *6* impression [vague notion, belief, etc.].
impresionable *adj.* emotional, impressionable.
impresionante *adj.* impressive.
impresionar *tr.* to impress [affect, influence]. *2* to touch, move deeply. *3* PHOT. to produce images on [a plate]. *4* to record sounds on [a gramophone disk, etc.]. *5* CINEMA. to film, to shoot [a film]. *6 ref.* to be impressed or moved.
impresionismo *m.* F. ARTS impressionism.
impresionista *adj.* impressionistic. *2 m.-f.* impressionist.
impreso, -sa *adj.* impressed, printed, stamped. *2 m.* print, printed paper or book. *3 pl.* printed matter, publications.
impresor, -ra *m.-f.* PRINT. printer [workman or owner]. *2 f.* printer's wife.
imprevisible *adj.* unforeseeable.
imprevisión *f.* lack of foresight, improvidence.
imprevisor, -ra *adj.* unforeseeing, improvident.
imprevisto, -ta *adj.* unforeseen, unexpected. *2 m. pl.* incidental or unforeseen expenses.
imprimación *f.* priming [of a surface].
imprimar *tr.* to prime [a surface].
imprimir *tr.* to impress, imprint, stamp. *2* PRINT. to print [a book, etc.]. *3* to impart, communicate [a motion, etc.].
improbabilidad *f.* improbability, unlikelihood.
improbable *adj.* improbable, unlikely.
improbar *tr.* to disapprove, reprobate.
improbidad *f.* improbity, dishonesty.
improbo, -ba *adj.* dishonest. *2* arduous, laborious.
improcedencia *f.* inappropriateness, unsuitability, inexpedience. *2* non-conformableness to law.
improcedente *adj.* inappropriate, unsuitable, inexpedient. *2* not conformable to law.
improductivo, -va *adj.* unproductive, unprofitable. *2* unemployed [money].
impronta *f.* cast, impression.
impronunciable *adj.* unpronounceable.
improperio *m.* insult, affront, taunt.
impropiedad *f.* impropriety [in the use of language].
impropio, -pia *adj.* improper, unsuited. *2* unfitting, unbecoming. *3* MATH. improper [fraction].
improrrogable *adj.* unextendible [term, time].
impróvido, -da *adj.* improvident, thoughtless.
improvisación *f.* improvisation, extemporization, impromptu.
improvisado, -da *adj.* improvised, extempore, off-hand. *2* extemporaneous.
improvisador, -ra *m.-f.* improviser, extemporizer.
improvisar *tr.* to improvise, to extemporize.
improviso, -sa; improvisto, -ta *adj.* unforeseen, unexpected: *al ~, de ~, a la improvista,* suddenly.
imprudencia *f.* imprudence, indiscretion.
imprudente *adj.* imprudent, indiscret, unwise.
impúber; impúbero, -ra *adj.* impuberate, immature.

impublicable *adj.* unpublishable.
impudencia *f.* impudence, shamelessness.
impudente *adj.* impudent, shameless.
impudicia, impudicicia *f.* impudicity, immodesty.
impúdico, -ca *adj.* immodest; shameless.
impudor *m.* immodesty. *2* barefacedness.
impuesto, -ta *p. p.* of IMPONER. *2 adj.* imposed. *3* informed, cognizant. *4 m.* tax, duty, impost.
impugnación *f.* impugnation, challenge, refutation.
impugnar *tr.* to impugn, challenge, refute.
impulsar *tr.* to impel. *2* to actuate, move, prompt. *3* MECH. to drive, force.
impulsión *adj.* impulsion, impulse, drive.
impulsivo, -va *adj.* impulsive.
impulso *m.* impulse [in every sense]. *2* prompting. *3* impetus, momentum.
impulsor, -ra *adj.* impelling. *2 m.-f.* impeller.
impune *adj.* unpunished.
impunidad *f.* impunity.
impureza *f.* impurity. *2* unchasteness.
impurificar *tr.* to make impure, defile; to adulterate.
impuro, -ra *adj.* impure. *2* defiled, adulterated. *3* unchaste, lewd.
impuse, impusiera, etc. *irr.* V. IMPONER.
imputable *adj.* imputable.
imputación *f.* imputation.
imputar *tr.* to impute, ascribe, lay at the door of.
inabordable *adj.* unapproachable.
inacabable *adj.* interminable, endless, everlasting.
inaccesible *adj.* inaccessible.
inacción *f.* inaction, inactivity, idleness.
inaceptable *adj.* unacceptable.
inactividad *f.* inactivity.
inactivo, -va *adj.* inactive. *2* idle, doing nothing.
inadaptación *f.* inadaptation.
inadecuado, -da *adj.* unsuited, unsuitable.
inadmisible *adj.* inadmissible.
inadvertencia *f.* inadvertence, oversight.
inadvertido, -da *adj.* unseen, unnoticed, unobserved.
inagotable *adj.* inexhaustible, exhaustless.
inaguantable *adj.* intolerable, unbearable.
inalámbrico, -ca *adj.* wireless.
inalcanzable *adj.* unattainable, unreachable.
inalienable *adj.* inalienable.
inalterable *adj.* unalterable, unchangeable.
inalterado, -da *adj.* unaltered, unchanged.
inamovible *adj.* irremovable, unremovable.
inane *adj.* inane, empty, void.
inanición *f.* MED. inanition.
inanidad *f.* inanity.
inanimado, -da *adj.* inanimate, lifeless.
inapelable *adj.* unappealable. *2* inevitable.
inapetencia *f.* inappetence, lack of appetite.
inapetente *adj.* inappetent, having no appetite.
inaplazable *adj.* undeferable.
inaplicable *adj.* inapplicable.
inapreciable *adj.* invaluable. *2* inappreciable.
inarticulado, -da *adj.* inarticulate.
inartístico, -ca *adj.* inartistic.
inasequible *adj.* unattainable, inaccessible.
inastillable *adj.* nonshatterable.
inatacable *adj.* unattackable.
inaudible *adj.* inaudible.
inaudito, -ta *adj.* unheard-of, extraordinary. *2* outrageous, monstrous.
inauguración *f.* inauguration, opening. *2* unveiling [of a statue].
inaugural *adj.* inaugural.

inaugurar *tr.* to inaugurate [enter upon; initiate public use of]; to open [an exhibition, etc.]; to unveil [a statue].

inca *m.* Inca. *2* a gold Peruvian coin.

incaico, -ca *adj.* Inca.

incalculable *adj.* incalculable.

incalificable *adj.* very bad, most reprehensible.

incandescencia *f.* incandescence.

incandescente *adj.* incandescent.

incansable *adj.* indefatigable, untiring.

incapacidad *f.* incapacity. *2* incompetence, disability. *3* incapability, stupidity.

incapacitar *tr.* to incapacitate. *2* to disqualify, disable. *3* LAW to declare incapable.

incapaz, pl. -ces *adj.* incapable. *2* unable.

incasable *adj.* unmarriageable.

incasto, -ta *adj.* unchaste.

incautarse *ref.* ~ *de* [of a court, the government, etc.], to seize [money or property].

incauto, -ta *adj.* incautious, unwary, innocent.

incendiar *tr.* to set on fire, set fire to. *2 ref.* to catch fire, be burnt.

incendiario, -ria *adj.-n.* incendiary.

incendio *m.* fire, conflagration [destructive burning]. *2* fig. fire, passion.

incensada *f.* swing of the thurible. *2* flattery.

incensar *tr.* to incense [burn incense to]. *2* fig. to flatter, overpraise. ¶ CONJUG. like *acertar*.

incensario *m.* censer, incensory, thurible.

incentivo, -va *adj.* incentive. *2 m.* incentive, inducement.

incertidumbre *f.* uncertainty, doubt.

incesante *adj.* incessant, unceasing, continual.

incesto *m.* incest.

incestuoso, -sa *adj.* incestuous.

incidencia *f.* incident. *2* GEOM., PHYS. incidence.

incidental *adj.* INCIDENTE 1.

incidente *adj.* incidental, happening as a subordinate event. *2* GEOM., PHYS. incident. *3 m.* incident.

incidir *intr.* PHYS. [of a ray] to fall [upon]. *2* to fall [into error, etc.].

incienso *m.* incense [gum, spice], frankincense. *2* fig. incense, flattery.

incienso, inciense, etc. *irr.* V. INCENSAR.

incierto, -ta *adj.* not certain, untrue. *2* uncertain, doubtful, problematical.

incineración *f.* incineration, cremation.

incinerar *tr.* to incinerate, cremate.

incipiente *adj.* incipient.

incircunciso *adj.* uncircumcised.

incisión *f.* incision, cut.

incisivo, -va *adj.* incisive, cutting: *diente* ~, incisor. *2* incisive, sarcastic. *3 m.* ANAT. incisor.

inciso, -sa *adj.* cut, incised. *2 m.* GRAM. parenthetic sentence.

incitación *f.* incitation, incitement.

incitador, -ra *adj.* inciting. *2 m.-f.* inciter.

incitante *adj.* inciting, exciting.

incitar *tr.* to incite.

incivil *adj.* uncivil.

incivilidad *f.* incivillity.

inclasificable *adj.* unclassifiable.

inclemencia *f.* inclemency, unmercifulness. *2* inclemency [of weather or climate].

inclemente *adj.* inclement.

inclinación *f.* inclination [inclining; slant, slope; leaning; propension, liking]. *2* bow, nod, obeisance.

inclinado, -da *adj.* inclined, slanting, sloping. *2* inclined, disposed.

inclinar *tr.* to incline, tilt, slant, bow. *2* to incline, dispose, move. *3 ref.* to incline, tilt, lean, slope, bow [as intr.]. *4* to incline, lean, tend, be disposed. *5* to yield, defer.

ínclito, -ta *adj.* illustrious, renowned.

incluir *tr.* to include. *2* to enclose [in an envelope]. ¶ CONJUG. like *huir*.

inclusa *f.* foundling hospital.

inclusero, -ra *adj. m.-f.* foundling.

inclusión *f.* inclusion.

inclusivamente, inclusive *adv.* inclusively, inclusive.

incluso, -sa *adj.* included. *2* enclosed [in an envelope]. *3 adv.* including, even.

incoar *tr.* LAW to inchoate, initiate.

incoativo, -va *adj.* inchoative, inceptive.

incobrable *adj.* COM. irrecoverable, uncollectable.

incoercible *adj.* incoercible.

incógnita *f.* unknown quantity.

incógnito *adj.* unknown. *2 adj.-m.* incognito. *3 adv. de* ~, incognito.

incognoscible *adj.* unknowable.

incoherencia *f.* incoherence, disconnectedness.

incoherente *adj.* incoherent, disconnected.

incoloro, -ra *adj.* colourless.

incólume *adj.* unharmed, sound, safe, whole.

incolumidad *f.* soundness, safety, wholeness.

incombustibilidad *f.* incombustibility.

incombustible *adj.* incombustible, fireproof.

incomible *adj.* uneatable, inedible.

incomodar *tr.* to inconvenience, put to inconvenience, incommode, bother. *2* to annoy, anger. *3 ref.* to get annoyed or angered.

incomodidad *f.* inconvenience, uncomfortableness, discomfort. *2* annoyance.

incómodo, -da *adj.* [of things] incommodious, inconvenient, uncomfortable, unhandy, cumbersome. *2* [of persons] uncomfortable, ill at ease.

incomparable *adj.* incomparable, matchless.

incompatibilidad *f.* incompatibility, inconsistency; uncongeniality.

incompatible *adj.* incompatible, inconsistent; uncongenial.

incompetencia *f.* incompetence, incompetency.

incompetente *adj.* incompetent.

incompleto, -ta *adj.* incomplete.

incomportable *adj.* intolerable, unbearable.

incomprensibilidad *f.* incomprehensibility.

incomprensible *adj.* incomprehensible, inconceivable.

incompresible *adj.* incompressible.

incomunicable *adj.* incommunicable.

incomunicación *f.* isolation, lack of comunication. *2* solitary confinement.

incomunicado, -da *adj.* isolated, without communication. *2* in solitary confinement.

incomunicar *tr.* to isolate; to deprive of communication. *2* to put in solitary confinement.

inconcebible *adj.* inconceivable.

inconciliable *adj.* unconciliable. *2* irreconciliable.

inconcluso, -sa *adj.* unfinished.

inconcuso, -sa *adj.* incontrovertible, indisputable.

incondicional *adj.* unconditional.

inconexión *f.* lack of connection, disconnection.

inconexo, -xa *adj.* inconnected, disconnected.

inconfesable *adj.* unavowable, dishonourable.

inconfeso, -sa *adj.* unconfessing [that has not admitted his guilt].

inconfidente *adj.* unreliable.

inconfundible *adj.* unmistakable.

incongruencia *f.* incongruity, incongruousness.

incongruente; incongruo, -grua *adj.* incongruous, incongruent.
inconmensurable *adj.* incommensurable, incommensurate.
inconmovible *adj.* immovable, unmovable, firm. *2* unyielding, inexorable.
inconquistable *adj.* unconquerable.
inconsciencia *f.* unconciousness. *2* thoughtlessness.
inconsciente *adj.* unconcious. *2* unaware, unwitting. *3* thoughtless, unthinking.
inconsecuencia *f.* inconsistency [lack of harmony between conduct and principles].
inconsecuente *adj.* not consequent. *2* inconsistent [acting at variance with one's own principles]. *3 m.-f.* inconsistent person.
inconsideración *f.* inconsiderateness. *2* thoughtlessness, rashness.
inconsiderado, -da *adj.* inconsiderate, thougthless, rash.
inconsistencia *f.* inconsistency, flimsiness, unsubstantiality.
inconsistente *adj.* inconsistent; flimsy, unsubstantial.
inconsolable *adj.* inconsolable.
inconstancia *f.* inconstancy.
inconstante *adj.* inconstant.
inconstitucional *adj.* unconstitutional.
inconsútil *adj.* seamless.
incontable *adj.* uncountable, countless.
incontaminado, -da *adj.* uncontaminated, undefiled.
incontestable *adj.* incontestable, indisputable.
incontinencia *f.* incontinence.
incontinente *adj.* incontinent. *2 adv.* INCONTINENTI.
incontinenti *adv.* at once, immediately, instantly.
incontrastable *adj.* invincible, irresistible, unaswerable.
incontrovertible *adj.* incontrovertible.
inconveniencia *f.* inconvenience, uncomfortableness. *2* unsuitableness. *3* impoliteness. *4* impolite act or remark.
inconveniente *adj.* inconvenient. *2* impolite. *3 m.* drawback, obstacle, disadvantage, objection: *no tengo ~*, I have no objection.
incordio *m.* MED. bubo. *2 vulg.* nuisance.
incorporación *f.* incorporation [union, combination]. *2* sitting up. *3* joining a body, regiment, etc.
incorporar *tr.* to incorporate [unite, combine]. *2* to raise to a sitting position. *3 ref.* to incorporate [become incorporated with]. *4* to join a body, regiment, etc. *5* to sit up [from a reclining position].
incorpóreo, rea *adj.* incorporeal.
incorrección *f.* incorrectness. *2* incorrect act.
incorrecto, -ta *adj.* incorrect.
incorregible *adj.* incorrigible.
incorruptible *adj.* incorruptible.
incorrupto, -ta *adj.* incorrupt.
increado, -da *adj.* uncreated.
incredibilidad *f.* incredibility.
incredulidad *f.* incredulity; unbelief.
incrédulo, -la *adj.* incredulous; unbelieving. *2 m. -f.* unbeliever, disbeliever.
increíble *adj.* incredible, unbelievable.
incremento *m.* increment, increase.
increpación *f.* upbraiding.
increpar *tr.* to upraid.
incriminación *f.* incrimination.
incriminar *tr.* to incriminate.
incruento, -ta *adj.* bloodless [offering].

incrustación *f.* incrustation, encrusting. *2* scale [in a boiler]. *3* F. ARTS inlaying, inlay.
incrustar *tr.* to incrust. *2* F. ARTS to inlay.
incubación *f.* incubation.
incubadora *f.* incubator [apparatus].
incubar *tr.* to incubate, hatch.
íncubo *m.* incubus.
incuestionable *adj.* unquestionable.
inculcar *tr.* to inculcate.
inculpabilidad *f.* inculpability, guiltlessness: *veredicto de ~*, verdict of not guilty.
inculpación *f.* inculpation.
inculpar *tr.* to inculpate. *2* to blame.
inculto, -ta *adj.* incult, uncultivated, untilled. *2* incult, uncultured, uneducated, uncivilized.
incultura *f.* lack of culture.
incumbencia *f.* incumbency, duty, concern.
incumbir *intr.* to be incumbent [on], be the duty [of].
incumplido, -da *adj.* unfulfilled, nonexecuted.
incumplimiento *m.* unfulfilment, nonexecution, breach.
incumplir *tr.* not to fulfil, fail to fulfil.
incunable *adj.* incunabular. *2 m.* incunabulum.
incurable *adj.* incurable, hopeless.
incuria *f.* negligence, carelessness.
incurrimiento *m.* incurring.
incurrir en *intr.* to incur, become liable to. *2* to commit [a fault, etc.], to fall into [error].
incursión *f.* MIL. incursion. *2* INCURRIMIENTO.
incurso, -sa *adj.* having incurred.
incuso, -sa *adj.* incuse.
indagación *f.* investigation, search, inquiry, inquest.
indagar *tr.* to investigate, search, inquire.
indebido, -da *adj.* undue, improper, illegal, illicit.
indecencia *f.* indecency.
indecente *adj.* indecent. *2* low, dirty [act, conduct].
indecible *adj.* unspeakable, unutterable.
indecisión *f.* indecision, irresolution.
indeciso, -sa *adj.* undecided [not yet determined]. *2* undecided, hesitant, irresolute.
indeclinable *adj.* undeclinable. *2* GRAM. indeclinable, undeclinable.
indecoro *m.* indecorum, indecorousness.
indecoroso, -sa *adj.* indecorous, improper. *2* indecent.
indefectible *adj.* indefectible, unfailing, certain.
indefendible, indefensible *adj.* indefensible.
indefensión *f.* defencelessness.
indefenso, -sa *adj.* defenceless.
indeficiente *adj.* unfailing, certain.
indefinible *adj.* undefinable.
indefinido, -da *adj.* indefinite, undefined, vague. *2* GRAM. indefinite.
indehiscente *adj.* BOT. indehiscent.
indeleble *adj.* indelible, ineffaceable.
indeliberado, -da *adj.* indeliberate, unpremeditated.
indelicadeza *f.* indelicacy; unscrupulousness.
indelicado, -da *adj.* indelicate; unscrupulous.
indemne *adj.* unharmed, unhurt, undamaged.
indemnidad *f.* indemnity, freedom from damage.
indemnización *f.* indemnification, indemnity.
indemnizar *tr.* to indemnify, compensate.
indemostrable *adj.* indemonstrable, undemonstrable.
independencia *f.* independence.
independiente *adj.* independent.
independizar *tr.-ref.* EMANCIPAR.

indescifrable *adj.* undecipherable.
indescriptible *adj.* indescribable.
indeseable *adj.* undesirable [pers.].
indestructible *adj.* indestructible.
indeterminación *f.* indetermination. *2* irresolution.
indeterminado, -da *adj.* indeterminate, undetermined. *2* undetermined, irresolute, hesitating. *3* GRAM. indefinite [article].
indevoción *f.* indevotion, lack of devotion.
indevoto, -ta *adj.* undevout. *2* undevoted.
India *f. pr. n.* GEOG. India. *2 pl.* Indies: *Indias Occidentales,* Spanish America; West Indies; *Indias Orientales,* India.
indiada *f.* (Am.) multitude of Indians.
indiana *f.* printed calico.
indiano, -na *adj.* of the Spanish America. *2* Indian [of India]. *3 adj.-n.* Spanish American. *4 m.-f.* one who returns rich from America.
indicación *f.* indication, sign. *2* hint, suggestion. *3* direction, instruction. *4* MED. indication.
indicado, -da *adj.* indicated. *2* proper, appropriate, suitable.
indicador, -ra *adj.* indicating, indicatory. *2 m.* indicator, pointer, index, gauge. *3* ELECT. annunciator disc.
indicar *tr.* to indicate, point out, show. *2* to indicate, betoken, be sign of. *3* to indicate [state briefly]. *4* to hint, suggest.
indicativo, -va *adj.* indicative. *2 adj.-m.* GRAM. indicative.
índice *m.* ANAT. index, forefinger. *2* sign, indication. *3* index [table of contents, list; pointer, hand; ratio]: ~ *cefálico,* cephalic index. *4* MATH. index. *5* ECCL. Index.
indicio *m.* sign, indication, clue, evidence. *2 pl.* CHEM. traces. *3* LAW *indicios vehementes,* circumstantial evidence.
índico, -ca *adj.* Indian, East-Indian: *Océano Índico,* Indian Ocean.
indiferencia *f.* indifference.
indiferente *adj.* indifferent: *me es* ~, it is all the same to me.
indiferentismo *m.* indifferentism.
indígena *adj.* indigenous, native. *2 m.-f.* native [person].
indigencia *f.* indigence, destitution, need.
indigente *adj.* indigent, destitute, needy.
indigestarse *ref.* to cause indigestion. *2* [of persons] to be disagreeable, cause aversion or dislike.
indigestión *f.* indigestion.
indigesto, -ta *adj.* indigestible. *2* indigested, undigested. *3* disagreeable [person].
indignación *f.* indignation.
indignado, -da *adj.* indignant, angry.
indignamente *adv.* unworthily. *2* with indignity.
indignante *adj.* irritating, causing indignation.
indignar *tr.* to irritate, make indignant, cause indignation. *2 ref.* to become indignant.
indignidad *f.* unworthiness. *2* indignity.
indigno, -na *adj.* unworthy. *2* low, contemptible.
índigo *m.* indigo.
indino, -na *adj.* mischievous, saucy.
indio, dia *adj.-n.* Indian [of Asia or America]. *2 m.* CHEM. indium. *3 adj.* blue, azure.
indirecta *f.* hint, insinuation, innuendo.
indirectamente *adv.* indirectly.
indirecto, -ta *adj.* indirect.
indisciplina *f.* indiscipline, lack of discipline.
indisciplinado, -da *adj.* undisciplined, unruly.

indisciplinarse *ref.* to become undisciplined.
indiscreción *f.* indiscretion [want of discretion].
indiscreto, -ta *adj.* indiscreet [wanting in discretion].
indiscutible *adj.* unquestionable, indisputable.
indisolubilidad *f.* indissolubility.
indisoluble *adj.* indissoluble.
indispensable *adj.* indispensable, necessary, essential.
indisponer *tr.* to indispose [make sick or ill]. *2* ~ *a una persona con otra,* to set a person against another. *3 ref.* to be indisposed, out of health. *4* [of two persons] to fall out. *5 indisponerse con,* to quarrel with.
indisposición *f.* lack of fitness, unpreparation. *2* indisposition, passing ailment.
indispuesto, -ta *adj.* indisposed, slightly ill. *3* on bad terms, at variance.
indisputable *adj.* indisputable.
indistinguible *adj.* undistinguishable.
indistintamente *adv.* indistinctly, indiscriminately.
indistinto, -ta *adj.* indistinct.
individual *adj.* individual.
individualidad *f.* individuality.
individualismo *m.* individualism.
individualista *adj.* individualistic. *2 m.-f.* individualist.
individualizar *tr.* to individualize.
individuo, -dua *adj.* individual. *2* indivisible. *3 m.* individual [single member of a class]. *4* member, fellow [of a board, society, etc.]. *5* individual, fellow, person. *6 f.* despicable woman.
indivisibilidad *f.* indivisibility.
indivisible *adj.* indivisible.
indiviso, -sa *adj.* LAW undivided.
Indo *m. pr. n.* GEOG. Indus.
indo, -da *adj.-n.* Indian, East-Indian.
indócil *adj.* indocile.
indocilidad *f.* indocility.
indocto, -ta *adj.* unlearned, uneducated.
indocumentado, -da *adj.* lacking the documents for identification. *2 m.-f.* nobody [person of no account].
Indochina *f. pr. n.* GEOG. Indo-China.
indochino, -na *adj.-n.* Indo-Chinese.
indoeuropeo, -a *adj.-n.* Indo-European.
índole *f.* disposition, nature. *2* class, kind.
indolencia *f.* indolence. *2* painlessness.
indolente *adj.* indolent.
indoloro *adj.* MED. indolent.
indomable *adj.* untamable, indomitable.
indomado, -da *adj.* untamed.
indómito, -ta *adj.* untamed. *2* indomitable. *3* unruly.
Indostán *m. pr. n.* GEOG. Hindustan.
indostanés, -sa *adj.-n.* Hindustani, Hidoostani.
indostánico, -ca *adj.* Hindustani [of Hindustan].
indostano, -na *adj.* INDOSTANÉS.
indubitable *adj.* indubitable, doubtless.
inducción *f.* inducing, instigation. *2* ELECT., LOG. induction.
inducido *m.* ELECT. armature [of motor or dynamo].
inducir *tr.* to induce, persuade, instigate. *2* ELECT., LOG. to induce. ¶ CONJUG. like *conducir.*
inductancia *f.* ELECT. inductance.
inductivo, -va *adj.* LOG., ELECT. inductive.
inductor, -ra *adj.* inducing. *2 m.-f.* inducer, instigator. *3 m.* ELECT. inductor, field.
indudable *adj.* indubitable, doubtless, certain.

indujo, indujera, etc. *irr.* V. INDUCIR.
indulgencia *f.* indulgence, leniency, forbearance. 2 ECCL. indulgence.
indulgente *adj.* indulgent, lenient, forbearing.
indultar *tr.* to pardon [free from penalty]. 2 to exempt [from an obligation].
indulto *m.* LAW pardon, commutation. 2 indult.
indumentaria *f.* clothing, dress, garb.
indumento *m.* VESTIDURA.
induración *f.* MED. induration.
industria *f.* industry. 2 ingenuity. 3 *de* ~, designedly, on purpose.
industrial *adj.* industrial. 2 *m.* industrialist, manufacturer.
industrialismo *m.* industrialism.
industrializar *tr.* to industrialize.
industriar *tr.* to train, teach. 2 *ref.* to manage; to get along.
industrioso, -sa *adj.* industrious. 2 ingenious.
induzco, induzca, etc. *irr.* V. INDUCIR.
inedia *f.* inanition.
inédito, -ta *adj.* unpublished.
inefabilidad *f.* ineffability.
inefable *adj.* ineffable, unutterable.
ineficacia *f.* inefficacy, inefficiency, ineffectualness.
ineficaz *adj.* inefficacious, inefficient, ineffectual.
inelegante *adj.* inelegant.
ineluctable *adj.* ineluctable, inevitable.
ineludible *adj.* ineludible, unavoidable.
inenarrable *adj.* ineffable, inexpressible.
inencogible *adj.* unshrinkable.
inepcia *f.* silliness, ineptitude.
ineptitud *f.* incompetence. 2 ineptitude.
inepto, -ta *adj.* incompetent, incapable. 2 inept. 3 *m.-f.* incapable [person].
inequívoco, -ca *adj.* unequivocal, unmistakable.
inercia *f.* inertia.
inerme *adj.* unarmed. 2 BOT., ZOOL. inerm, inermous.
inerte *adj.* inert.
inervación *f.* innervation.
Inés *f. pr. n.* Agnes.
inescrutabilidad *f.* inscrutability.
inescrutable, inescudriñable *adj.* inscrutable.
inesperado, -da *adj.* unexpected, unforeseen.
inestabilidad *f.* instability.
inestable *adj.* unstable, instable.
inestimable *adj.* inestimable, invaluable, priceless.
inevitable *adj.* inevitable, unavoidable.
inexactitud *f.* inexactness; inaccuracy.
inexacto, -ta *adj.* inexact; inaccurate. 2 untrue.
inexcusable *adj.* inexcusable. 2 unavoidable.
inexhausto, -ta *adj.* unexhausted; unexhaustible.
inexistencia *f.* inexistence.
inexistente *adj.* inexistent, nonexistent.
inexorable *adj.* inexorable, relentless.
inexperiencia *f.* inexperience.
inexperto, -ta *adj.* inexpert, inexperienced.
inexplicable *adj.* inexplicable, unaccountable.
inexplorado, -da *adj.* unexplored.
inexpresable *adj.* inexpressible.
inexpresivo, -va *adj.* inexpressive.
inexpugnable *adj.* inexpugnable, impregnable. 2 firm, stubborn.
inextenso, -sa *adj.* unextended [having no extension].
inextinguible *adj.* inextinguishable, unquenchable.
inextricable *adj.* inextricable.

infalibilidad *f.* infallibility.
infalible *adj.* infallible.
infamación *f.* defamation.
infamador, -ra *adj.* defaming. 2 *m.-f.* defamer.
infamante *adj.* causing infamy, opprobious.
infamar *tr.* to defame, infamize, dishonour.
infamatorio, -ria *adj.* defamatory, libellous.
infame *adj.* infamous. 2 fig. very bad. 3 *m.-f.* infamous, wicked person.
infamia *f.* infamy. 2 infamous act.
infancia *f.* infancy, babyhood.
infando, -da *adj.* frightful, unspeakable.
infanta *f.* female child. 2 infanta.
infantado *m.* territory assigned to an INFANTE or INFANTA.
infante *m.* male infant. 2 infante. 3 infantry soldier.
infantería *f.* MIL. infantry: ~ *de marina,* marines.
infanticida *m.* infanticide [murderer of an infant].
infanticidio *m.* infanticide [act].
infantil *adj.* infantile, infant. 2 infantile, childish, innocent. 3 children's.
infantilismo *m.* infantility. 2 MED. infantilism.
infanzón *m.* ancient nobleman.
infanzona *f.* ancient noblewoman.
infarto *m.* MED. infarct, infarction.
infatigable *adj.* indefatigable, untiring.
infatuación *f.* conceit, presumption.
infatuar *tr.* to make conceited or vain. 2 *ref.* to become conceited or vain.
infausto, -ta *adj.* unlucky, unhappy, fatal.
infección *f.* infection.
infeccioso, -sa *adj.* MED. infectious.
infectar *tr.* to infect. 2 *ref.* to become infected.
infectivo, -va *adj.* infective.
infecto, -ta *adj.* infected, foul, corrupt.
infecundo, -da *adj.* infecund, barren, sterile.
infelice *adj.* poet. unhappy, wretched.
infelicidad *f.* infelicity, unhappiness.
infeliz *adj.* unhappy, unfortunate, wretched. 2 *m.-f.* unhappy person, wretch. 3 *adj.-n.* coll. simple, good-natured [person].
inferencia *f.* inference.
inferior *adj.-n.* inferior. 2 *adj.* lower, under [part].
inferioridad *f.* inferiority.
inferir *tr.* to infer, conclude. 2 to cause, inflict [a wound]; to offer [an insult]; to do [an injury]. ¶ CONJUG. like *hervir.*
infernáculo *m.* hopscotch [game].
infernal *adj.* infernal, hellish. 2 coll. infernal, confounded, detestable.
infernalmente *adv.* infernally, hellishly.
infestación *f.* infestation.
infestar *tr.* to infest, overrun. 2 to infect.
infesto, -ta *adj.* poet. harmful, prejudicial.
infeudación *f.* ENFEUDACIÓN.
infeudar *tr.* ENFEUDAR.
inficionar *tr.* to infect, corrupt, taint. 2 *ref.* to be infected.
infidelidad *f.* infidelity, unfaithfulness. 2 the infidels as a whole.
infidencia *f.* breach of trust, unfaithfulness.
infidente *adj.* unfaithful, dishonest.
infiel *adj.* unfaithful, disloyal. 2 inaccurate, inexact. 3 *adj.-n.* infidel, pagan.
infiernillo *m.* small alcohol stove.
infierno *m.* [often in the *pl.*] hell, inferno: *en los quintos infiernos,* fig. very far; far away.
infiltración *f.* infiltration.
infiero, infiera, etc. *irr.* V. INFERIR.
infiltrar *tr.* infiltrate. 2 to infuse, instill [ideas,

etc.]. *3 ref.* to infiltrate [be infiltrated]. *4* to insinuate itself.
ínfimo, -ma *adj.* lowest, least. *2* vilest, most abject. *3* most inferior [in quality].
infinidad *f.* infinity, infinitude; infinite number, no end.
infinitesimal *adj.* infinitesimal.
infinitivo *adj.-n.* GRAM. infinitive.
infinito, -ta *adj.* infinite. *2 m.* infinite, infinite space. *3* MATH. infinity. *4 adv.* infinitely.
infinitud *f.* infinitude, infiniteness.
inflación *f.* inflation. *2* conceit, vanity.
inflacionista *adj.* inflationary.
inflamable *adj.* inflammable.
inflamación *f.* inflammation.
inflamar *tr.* to inflame. *2 ref.* to inflame [become inflamed].
inflamatorio, -ria *adj.* inflammatory.
inflar *tr.* to inflate. *2* to exaggerate [news, etc.]. *3 ref.* to inflate. *4* to be puffed up with pride.
inflexibilidad *f.* inflexibility.
inflexible *adj.* inflexible.
inflexión *f.* inflection, bend. *2* GEOM., GRAM. inflection. *3* inflection, modulation [of the voice].
infligir *tr.* to inflict.
inflorescencia *f.* BOT. inflorescence.
influencia *f.* influence.
influenciar *tr.* (Am.) to influence.
influenza *f.* MED. influenza.
influir *tr.* to influence. *2 intr.* ~ *en* or *sobre*, to influence, have influence on; to affect. ¶ CONJUG. like *huir.*
influjo *m.* influence. *2* NAUT. rising tide.
influyente *adj.* influential.
infolio *m.* folio book, book in folio form.
información *f.* information [informing, telling, being told, intelligence, news]: *oficina de informaciones,* information bureau. *2* reportage. *3* inquiry, investigation. *4* PHILOS. information.
informador, -ra *m.-f.* newspaper reporter.
informal *adj.* informal [not according to due form]. *2* [of a pers.] not serious, unreliable.
informalidad *f.* informality [want of regular or prescribed form]. *2* lack of seriousness, unreliability. *3* nonfulfilment of a promise, engagement, etc.
informante *adj.* informing, reporting. *2 m.-f.* one who reports on something.
informar *tr.* to inform [tell, notify, make acquainted]. *2* PHIL. to inform. *3 intr.* to report [on something]. *4* LAW [of a lawyer] to plead before a court. *5 ref.* to inquire, find out: *informarse de,* to inquire into, find out about.
informativo, -va *adj.* informative, giving news. *2* PHIL. informative.
informe *adj.* shapeless, formless. *2 m.* information, report, account. *3* report [of an expert, a commitee]. *4* LAW plea. *5 pl.* references, character.
infortunado, -da *adj.* unfortunate, unlucky. *2 m.-f.* unfortunate [person].
infortunio *m.* misfortune, misery. *2* mishap, mischance.
infracción *f.* infraction, infringement, breach.
infractor, -ra *m.-f.* infractor, breaker, transgressor.
infraestructura *f.* AER. nonflying structures.
in fraganti *adv.* in the very act.
infrangible *adj.* infrangible, inviolable.
infranqueable *adj.* insurmountable.
infrarrojo, -ja *adj.* infrared.

infrascripto, -ta; infrascrito, -ta *adj.-n.* undersigned.
infrecuente *adj.* infrequent.
infringir *tr.* to infringe, break, transgress.
infructífero, -ra *adj.* unfruitful, unprofitable.
infructuoso, -sa *adj.* fruitless, unfruitful, unsuccessful.
ínfula *f.* infula. *2 pl.* conceit, airs: *darse ínfulas,* to put on airs.
infumable *adj.* unsmokable, bad [tobacco].
infundado, -da *adj.* groundless, baseless, unfounded.
infundio *m.* lie, canard, false report.
infundir *tr.* to infuse, instil [life, spirit, etc.], to imbue with. *2* to infuse [steep in liquid].
infusible *adj.* infusible.
infusión *f.* infusion.
infuso, -sa *adj.* infused [by God].
infusorio, -ria *adj.-n.* ZOOL. infusory.
ingeniar *tr.* to think up, contrive, devise. *2 ref.* to manage, to find a way.
ingeniería *f.* engineering [art, science, profession].
ingeniero *m.* engineer [one who follows as profession any branch of engineering]. *2* MIL. engineer [soldier].
ingenio *m.* inventive faculty, mind, talent. *2* talented person, talent [esp. author]. *3* ingenuity, cleverness, wit: *aguzar el* ~, to sharpen one's wits. *4* engine, machine, mechanical device. *5* BOOKBIND. plough. *6* ~ *de azúcar,* sugar mill; sugar plantation.
ingeniosidad *f.* ingeniousness, ingenuity.
ingenioso, -sa *adj.* ingenious.
ingénito, -ta *adj.* unbegotten. *2* innate, inborn.
ingente *adj.* huge, prodigious, very large.
ingenuidad *f.* ingenuousness, candour.
ingenuo, -nua *adj.* ingenuous, candid, guileless.
ingerencia *f.* INJERENCIA.
ingerir *tr.* to ingest. ¶ CONJUG. like *hervir.*
ingiero, ingiera, etc. *irr.* V. INGERIR.
ingestión *f.* ingestion, ingesting of food.
Inglaterra *f. pr. n.* GEOG. England. *2 la Nueva* ~, New England.
ingle *f.* ANAT. groin.
inglés, -sa *adj.* English. *2 m.* Englishman. *3* English [language]. *4 f.* Englishwoman. *5 m. pl. los ingleses,* the English [people].
inglesismo *m.* Anglicism.
inglete *m.* mitre, miter [angle of 45°].
ingobernable *adj.* ungovernable, uncontrollable, unruly.
ingratitud *f.* ingratitude, ungratefulness.
ingrato, -ta *adj.* ungrateful, thankless. *2* ungrateful, harsh, unpleasant. *3 m.-f.* ungrateful person.
ingravidez *f.* weightlessness. *2* lightness, tenuousness.
ingrávido, -da *adj.* weightless. *2* light, tenuous.
ingresar *intr.* to enter: ~ *en,* to enter [a school, etc.]; to become a member of; to join [a political party, etc.]. *2* [of money] to come in. *3 tr.* to deposit [money], to pay in.
ingreso *m.* entrance, ingress. *2* entrance [into a school, etc.]; joining, admision to [a political party, society, etc.]. *3* COM. coming in [of money]. *4 pl.* income, revenue. *5* COM. receipts, incomings.
inguinal; inguinario, -ria *adj.* ANAT. inguinal.
ingurgitar *tr.* MED. to ingurgitate.
inhábil *adj.* unable, unskilful. *2* tactless. *3* unfit, unqualified, incompetent: *día* ~, dies non.

inhabilidad f. unskilfulness. 2 inability, disability.
inhabilitación f. disqualification, incapacitation.
inhabilitar tr. to disable, disqualify, incapacitate. 2 to render unfit.
inhabitable adj. uninhabitable.
inhabitado, -da adj. uninhabited.
inhalación f. inhalation.
inhalar tr. to inhale.
inherencia f. inherence.
inherente adj. inherent.
inhibición f. LAW, PHYSIOL., PSYCHOL. inhibition. 2 act of keeping out of [an affair].
inhibir tr. LAW, PHYSIOL., PSYCHOL. to inhibit. 2 ref. to keep out of [an affair].
inhospitalario, -ria adj. inhospitable.
inhospitalidad f. inhospitableness.
inhóspito, -ta adj. inhospitable [affording no shelter].
inhumación f. inhumation, burial, interment.
inhumanidad f. inhumanity.
inhumano, -na adj. inhuman, barbarous, cruel.
inhumar tr. to inhume, bury, inter.
iniciación f. initiation.
iniciado, -da adj. initiate, initiated. 2 m.-f. initiate.
iniciador, -ra adj. initiating. 2 starting. 3 m.-f. initiator, initiatrix. 3 starter, originator.
inicial adj. initial. 2 f. initial, initial letter.
iniciar tr. to initiate, begin. 2 to initiate [a person]. 3 ref. [of a thing] to initiate, begin, commence. 4 [of a person] to be initiated.
iniciativo, -va adj. initiative. 2 f. initiative: tomar la ~, to take the initiative.
inicuo, -cua adj. iniquitous.
inigualado, -da adj. unequaled, unrivaled.
inimaginable adj. unimaginable, inconceivable.
inimitable adj. inimitable.
inimitablemente adv. inimitably.
ininteligible adj. unintelligible.
iniquidad f. iniquity.
injerencia f. interference, intermeddling.
injerir tr. to insert, introduce. 2 ref. to interfere, intermeddle. ¶ CONJUG. like hervir.
injertador m. HORT., SURG. grafter.
injertar tr. HORT., SURG. to graft, engraft.
injerto adj. HORT. grafted. 2 m. HORT., SURG. grafting. 3 HORT. graft, scion. 4 HORT. stock [grafted plant]. 5 SURG. graft.
injiero, injiera, etc. irr. V. INJERIR.
injuria f. offence, affront, insult, abuse. 2 wrong, injustice. 3 injury, damage.
injuriante adj. injuring, offending, insulting.
injuriar tr. to offend, insult, abuse. 2 to injure, damage.
injurioso, -sa adj. injurious, insulting, abusive.
injusticia f. injustice.
injustificable adj. unjustifiable, unwarrantable.
injustificado, -da adj. unjustified.
injusto, -ta adj. unjust.
*'**inmaculado, -da** adj. immaculate: Inmaculada Concepción, Immaculate Conception.
inmanejable adj. unmanageable.
inmanencia f. immanence, immanency.
inmanente adj. immanent, inherent.
inmarcesible adj. unfading, unwithering.
inmaterial adj. immaterial, incorporeal.
inmaturo, -ra adj. immature.
inmediación f. immediacy. 2 contiguity. 3 pl. environs, neighbourhood.
inmediato, -ta adj. immediate. 2 contiguous, adjoining, close, next: ~ a, close to, next to.

inmejorable adj. that cannot be better, unsurpassable; most excellent.
inmemorial adj. immemorial.
inmensidad f. immensity, immenseness. 2 vastness. 3 great multitude or number.
inmenso, -sa adj. immense. 2 unbounded, infinite.
inmensurable adj. immensurable, unmeasurable.
inmerecido, -da adj. undeserved, unmerited.
inmersión f. immersion.
inmerso adj. immersed.
inmigración f. immigration.
inmigrante adj. immigrating, immigrant. 2 m.-f. immigrant.
inmigrar intr. to immigrate.
inmigratorio, -ria adj. [of] immigration.
inminencia f. imminence, nearness.
inminente adj. imminent, impending, near.
inmiscuir tr. to mix. 2 ref. to interfere, meddle, intermeddle. ¶ CONJUG. regular or like huir.
inmobiliario, -ria adj. real-estate.
inmoble adj. unmovable. 2 motionless. 3 firm, constant.
inmoderado, -da adj. immoderated.
inmodestia f. immodesty.
inmodesto, -ta adj. immodest.
inmolación f. immolation, sacrifice.
inmolar tr. to immolate. 2 to sacrifice. 3 ref. to sacrifice oneself.
inmoral adj. immoral.
inmoralidad f. immorality.
inmortal adj. immortal.
inmortalidad f. immortality.
inmortalizar tr. to immortalize. 2 ref. to become immortal.
inmotivado, -da adj. unmotivated.
inmoto, -ta adj. unmoved, motionless.
inmóvil adj. immobile, motionless, stationary, still, fixed, set. 2 constant, unchanging.
inmovilidad f. immobility.
inmovilizar tr. to immobilize.
inmueble adj. immovable, real [property] 2 m. building [as a property]. 3 pl. immovables, real property.
inmundicia f. dirt, filth, lewdness. 2 impurity.
inmundo, -da adj. dirty, filthy. 2 unclean, impure.
inmune adj. immune, exempt. 2 MED. immune.
inmunidad f. immunity, exemption. 2 MED. immunity.
inmunización f. immunization.
inmunizar tr. to immunize.
inmunología f. immunology.
inmutabilidad f. immutability.
inmutable adj. immutable.
inmutar tr. to change, alter. 2 ref. to change countenance, become disturbed.
innato, -ta adj. innate, inborn.
innavegable adj. unnavigable. 2 unseaworthy.
innecesario, -ria adj. unnecessary.
innegable adj. undeniable.
innoble adj. ignoble.
innocuo, -cua adj. INOCUO.
innominado, -da adj. nameless, innominate.
innovación f. innovation.
innovador, -ra adj. innovating. 2 m.-f. innovator.
innovar tr. to innovate.
innumerable adj. innumerable, numberless.
innúmero, -ra adj. INNUMERABLE.
inobediente adj. inobedient, disobedient.
inobservancia f. inobservance, nonobservance.
inocencia f. innocence, innocency.
Inocencio m. pr. n. Innocent.

inocentada *f.* simple, silly act or words. *2* practical, joke, esp. when played on Holy Innocents' Day.

inocente *adj.-n.* innocent: *día de los Inocentes,* Holy Innocents' Day.

inocentón, -na, *adj.-n.* innocent, simple, credulous. *2 m.-f.* simple and credulous person.

inocuidad *f.* innocuity.

inoculación *f.* inoculation.

inocular *tr.* to inoculate; to inoculate with. *2 ref.* to become inoculated with.

inocuo, -cua *adj.* innocuous, harmless.

inodoro, -ra *adj.* inodorous, odourless. *2 m.* water closet, toilet.

inofensivo, -va *adj.* inoffensive, harmless.

inolvidable *adj.* unforgettable.

inoperable *adj.* MED. inoperable.

inoperante *adj.* inoperative, producing no effect.

inopia *f.* poverty, indigence, penury.

inopinado, -da *adj.* unexpected, unforeseen.

inoportunidad *f.* inopportuneness, inopportunity.

inoportuno, -na *adj.* inopportune, unseasonable.

inorgánico, -ca *adj.* inorganic.

inoxidable *adj.* inoxidable; stainless [steel].

in promptu (Lat.) *adv.* impromptu, offhand.

inquebrantable *adj.* unbreakable. *2* unyielding. *3* firm, irrevocable.

inquiero, inquiera, etc. *irr.* V. INQUIRIR.

inquietante *adj.* disquieting, disturbing.

inquietar *tr.* to disquiet, disturb, worry, make uneasy. *2* to vex, harass, trouble. *3 ref.* to worry, be anxious, be uneasy.

inquieto, -ta *adj.* restless, never still. *2* restless, agitated. *3* worried, anxious, uneasy.

inquietud *f.* inquietude, disquietude, restlessness, anxiety, concern, worry. *2* disturbance, riot.

inquilinato *m.* tenancy [of house or apartment].

inquilino, -na *m.-f.* tenant [of house or apartment].

inquina *f.* aversion, dislike, ill will, grudge.

inquinar *tr.* to infect, contaminate.

inquirir *tr.* to inquire into, search, investigate. ¶ CONJUG. like *adquirir.*

inquisición *f.* inquisition, investigation. *2 pr. n.* Inquisition, Holy Office.

inquisidor, -ra *f.* inquiring, inquisitive. *2m.-f.* inquirer, examiner. *3 m.* Inquisitor.

inquisitivo, -va *adj.* inquisitive.

inquisitorial *adj.* inquisitional, inquisitorial.

inri *m.* I.N.R.I. [inscription on the cross]: *poner el ~ a,* to deride, to insult.

insaciable *adj.* insatiable.

insalivación *f.* insalivation.

insalivar *tr.* to insalivate.

insalubre *adj.* insalubrious, unhealthy.

insalubridad *f.* insalubrity, unhealthiness.

insania *f.* insanity, madness.

insatisfecho, -cha *adj.* unsatisfied.

insano, -na *adj.* insane, mad, crazy.

inscribir *tr.* to inscribe [words, etc., on metal, stone, etc.]. *2* GEOM. to inscribe. *3 ref.* to inscribe oneself; to register.

inscripción *f.* inscription. *2* registration.

inscripto, -ta; inscrito, -ta *irreg. p. p.* of INSCRIBIR.

insecticida *adj.* insecticidal. *2 m.* insecticide.

insectívoro, -ra *adj.* insectivorous.

insecto *m.* ZOOL. insect. *2 pl.* ZOOL. Insecta.

inseguridad *f.* insecurity, unsafety. *2* uncertainty.

inseguro, -ra *adj.* insecure, unsafe. *2* uncertain. *3* not firm.

inseminación *f.* insemination, impregnation.

inseminar *tr.* to inseminate, impregnate.

insensatez *f.* insensateness, stupidity, folly.

insensato, -ta *adj.* insensate, stupid, foolish.

insensibilidad *f.* insensibility, insensitiveness. *2* hard-heartedness, callousness.

insensibilizar *tr.* to insensibilize. *2 ref.* to become insensible.

insensible *adj.* insensible [incapable of sensation; unconscious; imperceptible]. *2* insentient. *3* insensible, unfeeling, callous.

inseparable *adj.-n.* inseparable. *2 adj.* undetachable.

insepulto, -ta *adj.* unburied, uninterred.

inserción *f.* insertion.

inserir *tr.* to insert, introduce. *2* HORT. to graft. ¶ CONJUG. like *hervir.*

insertar *tr.* to insert, introduce [esp. in written or printed matter]. *2 ref.* BOT., ZOOL. to be inserted.

inservible *adj.* unserviceable, useless.

insidia *f.* snare, insidious act.

insidiar *tr.* to insidiate, put snares for.

insidioso, -sa *adj.* insidious.

insigne *adj.* illustrious, eminent. *2* egregious.

insignia *f.* badge, emblem. *2* standard of a Roman legion. *3* NAUT. pennant. *4 pl.* insignia.

insignificancia *f.* insignificance, insignificancy.

insignificante *adj.* insignificant.

insinceridad *f.* insincerity.

insinuación *f.* insinuation, hint, innuendo, intimation. *2* insinuation [insinuating oneself].

insinuante *adj.* insinuating, ingratiating, engaging.

insinuar *tr.* to insinuate, hint, suggest. *2 ref.* to insinuate oneself. *3* [of feelings, virtues, etc.] to be instilled into [a person].

insipidez *f.* insipidity, insipidness.

insípido, -da *adj.* insipid, tasteless, flat, vapid.

insistencia *f.* insistence, insistency.

insistente *adj.* insistent.

insistir *intr.* to insist: *~ en,* to insist on; *~ en que,* to insist that.

ínsito, -ta *adj.* connatural, inborn, inherent.

insociable, insocial *adj.* unsociable.

insolación *f.* insolation. *2* MED. sunstroke.

insolar *tr.* to insolate. *2 ref.* to be sunstruck.

insolencia *f.* insolence.

insolentar *tr.* to make insolent. *2 ref.* to become insolent.

insolente *adj.* insolent. *2 m.-f.* insolent person.

insólito, -ta *adj.* unusual, unaccustomed.

insoluble *adj.* insoluble. *2* unsolvable.

insolvente *adj.* insolvent.

insomne *adj.* insomnious, sleepless.

insomnio *m.* insomnia, sleeplessness.

insondable *adj.* fathomless. *2* inscrutable.

insonorizado, -da *adj.* soundproof.

insoportable *adj.* insupportable, unbearable.

insostenible *adj.* untenable, indefensible.

inspección *f.* inspection, overseeing, survey. *2* inspectorship. *3* inspector's office.

inspeccionar *tr.* to inspect, oversee, survey.

inspector, -ra *adj.* inspecting. *2 m.-f.* inspector, overseer, surveyor, supervisor.

inspiración *f.* inspiration.

inspirado, -da *adj.* inspired: *~ poeta,* inspired poet.

inspirador, -ra *adj.* inspiring. *2 m.-f.* inspirer.

inspirar *tr.* PHYSIOL. to inspire. *2* to inspire [infuse thought, create feeling, animate, suggest, etc.], to awaken, excite. *3 ref.* to become inspired. *4*

inspirarse en, to take as a model or subject [in literary or artistic work].
instable *adj.* INESTABLE.
instalación *f.* installation, instalment. *2* installation, plant; fittings, appointments.
instalar *tr.* to install, induct. *2* to install, lay, set up, put in place. *3 ref.* to install or establish oneself.
instancia *f.* instance, request: *a ~ de,* at the request of. *2* earnestness, urgency [in asking]. *3* petition, memorial. *4* LAW instance.
instantáneo, -a *adj.* instantaneous. *2 f.* PHOT. snapshot.
instante *adj.* pressing, soliciting. *2 m.* instant, moment: *al ~,* immediately; *por instantes,* incessantly, every moment.
instar *tr.* to request, beg, press, urge. *2 intr.* to be pressing, urgent.
instauración *f.* restoration, renewal. *2* establishment, foundation [of a monarchy, etc.].
instaurar *tr.* to restore, re-establish, renew. *2* to establish, found [a monarchy, etc.].
instigación *f.* instigation.
instigador, -ra *adj.* instigating. *2 m.-f.* instigator.
instigar *tr.* to instigate, incite, urge.
instilación *f.* instillation.
instilar *tr.* to instil, instill.
instintivo, -va *adj.* instinctive.
instinto *m.* instinct: *por ~,* instinctively.
institución *f.* institution [instituting; established thing; establishment, foundation]. *2 pl.* institutes. *3* constitutional organs of the soverain power.
institucional *adj.* institutional.
instituir *tr.* to institute, establish, found. *2* LAW to institute, appoint [heir]. ¶ CONJUG. like *huir.*
instituto *m.* constitution, rule [esp. of a religious order]. *2* institute [society, organization]. *3 ~ de enseñanza media,* high school, secondary school.
institutriz *f.* governess [of a young person].
instituyente *adj.* instituting.
instrucción *f.* instruction, teaching, education. *2* instruction, knowledge, learning. *2* MIL. drill. *4* LAW institution or carrying out of proceedings. *5 pl.* instructions, directions, orders.
instructivo, -va *adj.* instructive.
instructor *m.* instructor. *2* LAW *juez ~,* examining magistrate.
instruido, -da *adj.* learned, informed, educated.
instruir *tr.* to instruct, teach, educate. *2* MIL. to drill. *3* to instruct, inform, advise. *4* LAW to institute or carry out proceedings. *5 ref.* to learn, to educate oneself. ¶ CONJUG. like *huir.*
instrumentación *f.* MUS. instrumentation, orchestration.
instrumental *adj.* MUS. instrumental. *2 m.* MUS. instruments of an orchestra, etc. *3* SURG. kit of instruments.
instrumentar *tr.* MUS. to instrument, instrumentate.
instrumentista *m.* instrument maker. *2* MUS. instrumentalist.
instrumento *m.* instrument, implement, tool, appliance, contrivance, apparatus. *2* instrument, medium, means. *3* MUS. instrument: *~ de cuerda,* stringed instrument. *4* LAW instrument.
insuave *adj.* rough, unpleasant.
insubordinación *f.* insubordination.
insubordinar *tr.* to incite to insubordination. *2 ref.* to become insubordinate, to rebel.

insubstancial *adj.* unsubstantial, insubstantial. *2* inane, vapid, pointless, trivial.
insubstancialidad *f.* insubstantiality. *2* inanity, vapidness, triviality.
insubstituible *adj.* irreplaceable.
insuficiencia *f.* insufficiency, inadequacy.
insuficiente *adj.* insufficient, inadequate.
insuflar *tr.* MED. to insufflate.
insufrible *adj.* unbearabie, intolerable, insufferable.
ínsula *f.* obs. isle, island. *2* fig. small village.
insular *adj.* insular. *2 m.-f.* islander.
insulina *f.* MED. insulin.
insulsez *f.* insipidity, vapidity, flatness, dullness.
insulso, -sa *adj.* insipid, vapid, flat, dull.
insultante *adj.* insulting.
insultar *tr.* to insult; to call names.
insulto *m.* insult, affront.
insumergible *adj.* insubmergible, unsinkable.
insumiso, -sa *adj.* disobedient, rebellious.
insuperable *adj.* insuperable, insurmontable, invincible. *2* unsurpassable.
insurgente *adj.-n.* insurgent.
insurrección *f.* insurrection, rebellion.
insurreccionar *tr.* to incite to insurrection. *2 ref.* to rise up, rebel.
insurrecto, -ta *adj.* insurgent, rebellious. *2 m.-f.* insurgent, insurrectionist, rebel.
insustancial *adj.* INSUBSTANCIAL.
insustancialidad *f.* INSUBSTANCIALIDAD.
insustituible *adj.* INSUBSTITUIBLE.
intacto, -ta *adj.* intact, unimpaired, whole, pure.
intachable *adj.* blameless, faultless, irreprochable.
intangibilidad *f.* intangibility.
intangible *adj.* intangible. *2* not to be touched.
integérrimo, -ma *adj.* superl. of ÍNTEGRO: most honest or upright, irreproachable.
integración *f.* integration.
integrado, -da *adj. ~ por,* consisting of.
integral *adj.* integral, constituent. *2 adj.-f.* MATH. integral.
íntegramente *adv.* entirely, wholly.
integrante *adj.* integral, integrant.
integrar *tr.* to integrate, compose, form, make up. *2* MATH. to integrate.
integridad *f.* integrity, wholeness. *2* integrity, honesty, uprightness.
íntegro, gra *adj.* integral, whole, complete. *2* honest, upright.
integumento *m.* integument.
intelección *f.* intellection.
intelecto *m.* intellect.
intelectual *adj.-n.* intellectual.
intelectualidad *f.* intellectuality. *2* the intellectuals.
inteligencia *f.* intelligence, intellect, mind, understanding. *2* intelligence, sagacity, ability. *3* understanding, comprehension, interpretation. *4* sense, meaning. *5* understanding [between persons]. *6 en la ~ de que,* on the understanding that.
inteligente *adj.* intelligent.
inteligible *adj.* intelligible.
intemperancia *f.* intemperance.
intemperante *adj.* intemperate [person].
intemperie *f.* inclemency [of weather]: *a la ~,* in the open air, outdoors, unsheltered.
intempestivo, -va *adj.* untimely, ill-timed, unseasonable.
intención *f.* intention, purpose, mind, meaning:

segunda ~, duplicity of meaning or purpose; *mudar de* ~·, to change one's mind; *tener* ~ *de*, to intend, have in mind; *con* ~, *con toda* ~, deliberately, on purpose; *de primera* ~, on the first impulse. 2 pointed way of saying something. 3 THEOL., SURG. intention.
intencionadamente *adv.* deliberately, on purpose.
intencionado, -da *adj.* deliberate, made on purpose. 2 inclined, disposed: *mal* ~, evil-minded.
intencional *adj.* intentional.
intendencia *f.* intendance, intendancy. 2 MIL. administrative corps of the army.
intendente *m.* intendant. 2 administrator.
intensidad *f.* intensity, intenseness, vehemence. 2 PHYS., MUS. PHONET. intensity.
intensificar *tr.* to intensify. 2 *ref.* to intensify [become more intense].
intensión *f.* intension, intensity.
intensivo, -va *adj.* intensive.
intenso, -sa *adj.* intense, intensive, vehement.
intentar *tr.* to try, attempt, endeavour. 2 to intend, mean, purpose. 3 LAW to enter [an action].
intento *m.* intent, purpose: *de* ~, purposely, on purpose. 2 attempt, try, trial, effort.
intentona *f.* rash attempt.
intercalación *f.* intercalation, interpolation.
1) **intercalar** *tr.* to intercalate, interpolate.
2) **intercalar** *adj.* intercalary. 2 leap [day or year].
intercambiable *adj.* interchangeable.
intercambio *m.* interchange, reciprocation [of services, etc.].
interceder *intr.* to intercede.
intercelular *adj.* intercellular.
interceptación *f.* interception.
interceptar *tr.* to intercept.
intercesión *f.* intercession.
intercesor, -ra *m.-f.* intercessor.
intercolumnio *m.* ARCH. intercolumniation.
intercontinental *adj.* intercontinental.
intercostal *adj.* ANAT. intercostal.
interdecir *tr.* to interdict, forbid.
interdicción *f.* interdiction.
interdicto *m.* interdict.
interdigital *adj.* interdigital.
interés *m.* interest [advantage, profit, concern]. 2 interest [value of thing in itself]. 3 interest [on capital]: ~ *legal*, legal rate of interest. 4 interest [attention, curiosity, inclination towards pers. or thing; quality exciting them]. 5 *pl.* worldly possessions. 6 interests; *intereses creados*, vested interests.
interesado, -da *p. p.* of INTERESAR. 2 *adj.* interested, concerned. 3 mercenary, selfish. 4 *m.-f.* person or party concerned.
interesante *adj.* interesting.
interesar *tr.* to interest. 2 to concern. 3 MED. to affect [an organ, etc.]. 4 ~ *en*, to interest [invest with a share; cause to share]. 5 *intr.* to be interesting. 6 to be advantageous, or necessary. 7 to have a pecuniary share [in]. 8 *ref. interesarse en* or *por*, to be interested.
interfecto, -ta *m.-f.* LAW murdered person, victim.
interferencia *f.* PHYS. interference.
interferir *intr.-ref.* PHYS. interfere.
ínterin *adv.-m.* interim, meanwhile.
interinidad *f.* provisionality, temporariness. 2 duration of temporary job or office.
interino, -na *adj.* provisional, temporary. 2 acting, holding a temporary job or office. 3 *m.-f.* holder of a temporary job or office.
interior *adj.* interior, internal, inner, inside, in-

ward; home, domestic [not foreign]: *comercio* ~, domestic trade. 2 *m.* interior, inside, inner part; inland. 3 mind, soul.
interioridad *f.* interiority, inwardness.
interioridades *f. pl.* private matters.
interjección *f.* GRAM. interjection.
interlínea *f.* PRINT. lead, space line.
interlineación *f.* interlineation.
interlinear *tr.* to interline, interlineate.
interlocución *f.* interlocution, dialogue.
interlocutor, -ra *m.-f.* interlocutor.
interludio *m.* MUS. interlude.
intermediar *intr.* to be in the middle. 2 to intermediate, mediate.
intermediario, -ria *adj.* intermediary. 2 *m.-f.* intermediary, mediator. 3 COM. middleman.
intermedio, -dia *adj.* intermediate, intervening. 2 *m.* interval, interim. 3 THEAT. interlude.
interminable *adj.* interminable, endless.
intermisión *f.* intermission.
intermitencia *f.* intermittence.
intermitente *adj.* intermittent.
internación *f.* internment.
internacional *adj.* international.
internacionalismo *m.* internationalism.
internacionalizar *tr.* to internationalize.
internado *m.* boarding school; boarding school system. 2 state of being a boarding student.
internar *tr.* to lead or send inland. 2 to intern. 3 *ref.* to go into the interior of. 4 to go deeply [into a subject].
internista *m.-f.* MED. internist.
interno, -na *adj.* internal, interior, inside. 2 boarding [student]. 3 *m.-f.* boarding student. 4 *m.* intern [in a hospital].
internuncio *m.* interlocutor. 2 internuncio.
interparlamentario, -ria *adj.* interparliamentary.
interpelación *f.* act of addressing oneself to another [asking for aid or explanations, etc.]. 2 interpellation [in parliamentary practice].
interpelar *tr.* to address oneself to [another] asking for aid or explanations. 2 to interpellate.
interplanetario, -ria *adj.* interplanetary.
interpolación *f.* interpolation.
interpolar *tr.* to interpolate.
interponer *tr.* to interpose, place between. 2 to set as a mediator. 3 LAW to present [an appeal]. 4 *ref.* to interpose [be or come between]. 5 to interpose, intervene, mediate. ¶ CONJUG. like *poner*.
interposición *f.* interposition, interposal.
interpretación *f.* interpretation.
interpretar *tr.* to interpret.
intérprete *m.-f.* interpreter.
interpuesto, -ta *adj.* interposed, intervening.
interregno *m.* interregnum.
interrogación *f.* interrogation, question. 2 GRAM. interrogation mark, question mark.
interrogante *adj.* interrogating, questioning. 2 *m.* GRAM. *interrogante* or *punto* ~, interrogation mark; question mark.
interrogar *tr.* to interrogate, question.
interrogativo, -va *adj.* interrogative.
interrogatorio *m.* interrogatory, questioning.
interrumpido, -da *adj.* interrupted, broken, discontinued.
interrumpir *tr.* to interrupt. 2 to obstruct, hinder. 3 *ref.* to be interrupted, pause, break off.
interrupción *f.* interruption.

interruptor, -ra *adj.* interrupting. *2 m.-f.* interrupter. *3 m.* ELECT. switch, circuitbreaker.
intersecarse *ref.* GEOM. [of two lines, planes, etc.] to intersect.
intersección *f.* intersection.
intersticio *m.* interstice. *2* interval.
intervalo *m.* interval [intervening time or space]; break, gap. *2* MUS. interval.
intervención *f.* intervention, taking part; interference. *2* mediation. *3* supervision, control. *4* auditing [of accounts]. *5* SURG., INTERN., LAW intervention.
intervencionismo *m.* interventionism.
intervenir *intr.* to take part. *2* to intervene. *3* to intercede, plead [for another]. *4* to mediate [between parties]. *5 tr.* to audit [accounts]. *6* SURG. to operate upon [someone].
interventor, -ra *m.-f.* supervisor. *2* auditor [of accounts]. *3* election supervisor.
interviev *m.* Angl. journalistic interview.
intervievar *tr.* to interview [for journalistic purposes].
intestado, -da *adj.* intestate. *2 m.* intestate.
intestinal *adj.* intestinal.
intestino, -na *adj.* internal. *2* intestine, domestic, civil. *3 m.* ANAT. intestine. *4 pl.* ANAT. intestines.
intimación *f.* notification; order, calling upon.
intimar *tr.* to intimate, notify authoritatively. *2* to order, call upon. *3 intr.-ref.* to become intimate.
intimidación *f.* intimidation.
intimidad *f.* intimacy, closeness. *2* inwardness.
intimidar *tr.* to intimidate, daunt. *2 ref.* to become intimidated, daunted.
íntimo, -ma *adj.* intimate. *2* internal, innermost. *3* private, personal. *4* close [contact, relation].
intitular *tr.* to entitle [give the title of]. *2 ref.* to be called; to call oneself.
intolerable *adj.* intolerable, unbearable.
intolerancia *adj.* intolerance.
intolerante *adj.* intolerant.
intonso, -sa *adj.* poet. unshorn. *2* fig. ignorant. *3* [of a book] with untrimmed leaves.
intoxicación *f.* MED. intoxication, poisoning.
intoxicar *tr.* to poison. *2 ref.* MED. to suffer intoxication.
intradós *m.* ARCH. intrados.
intraducible *adj.* untranslatable.
intramuros *adv.* within the walls [of a town].
intranquilidad *f.* unrest, restlessness, uneasiness.
intranquilizar *tr.* to worry, disquiet, make uneasy. *2 ref.* to worry, to become uneasy.
intranquilo, -la *adj.* restless, worried, uneasy.
intransferible *adj.* untransferable.
intransigencia *f.* intransigence, intransigency, uncompromisingness.
intransigente *adj.* intransigent, uncompromising.
intransitable *adj.* impassable [road, etc.].
intransitivo, -va *adj.-n.* GRAM. intransitive.
intratable *adj.* intractable. *2* cantankerous, crossgrained, unsociable.
intravenoso, -sa *adj.* intravenous.
intrepidez *f.* intrepidity, courage, bravery.
intrépido, -da *adj.* intrepid.
intriga *f.* intrigue. *2* plot [of a play]; imbroglio.
intrigante *adj.* intriguing. *2 m.-f.* intriguer.
intrigar *intr.* to intrigue, plot, scheme. *2 tr.* to intrigue [arouse the interest or curiosity of].
intrincación *f.* intricacy, intricateness.
intrincado, -da *adj.* intricate.
intrincar *tr.* to complicate, entangle, confuse.

intríngulis, *pl.* **-lis** *m.* hidden reason or motive, enigma, mystery.
intrínseco, -ca *adj.* intrinsic, intrinsical.
introducción *f.* introduction [in every sense except introduction of a bill; of a person]. *2* preliminary step, preparation. *3* exordium.
introducir *tr.* to introduce [in every sense except introducing a person to another or a bill, etc., before Parliament]. *2* to insert. *3* to usher in. *4 ref.* to introduce oneself or itself; to enter, gain access [to]; worm oneself [into]. ¶ CONJUG. like *conducir.*
introductor, -ra *adj.* introducing. *2 m.-f.* introducer, introductor. *3* usherer.
introito *m.* introduction, beginning. *2* ECCL. introito.
intromisión *f.* interference, meddling.
introspección *f.* introspection.
introspectivo, -va *adj.* introspective.
introversión *f.* introversion.
introverso, -sa *adj.-n.* introverted.
intrusarse *ref.* to usurp [an office, authority, etc.].
intrusión *f.* intrusion [in office, profession, etc.].
intrusismo *m.* practice of a profession without authority.
intruso, -sa *adj.* intruding, usurping. *2 m.-f.* intruder, usurper. *3* unauthorized practitioner.
intuición *f.* intuition.
intuir *tr.* to intuit. ¶ CONJUG. like *huir.*
intuitivo, -va *adj.* intuitive.
intumescencia *f.* intumescence, swelling.
inulto, -ta *adj.* poet, unavenged.
inundación *f.* inundation, flood, deluge.
inundar *tr.* to inundate, flood, overflow, deluge. *2 ref.* to be flooded.
inurbano, -na *adj.* inurbane, uncivil, discourteous.
inusitado, -da *adj.* unusual.
inútil *adj.* useless. *2 adj.-n.* good for nothing.
inutilidad *f.* uselessness, inutility. *2* useless person.
inutilizar *tr.* to render useless; to disable; to spoil. *2 ref.* to become useless; to be disabled.
inútilmente *adv.* uselessly, to no purpose, in vain.
invadeable *adj.* unfordable.
invadir *tr.* to invade. *2* to encroach upon.
invaginación *f.* invagination.
invaginar *tr.* to invaginate.
invalidación *f.* invalidation.
invalidar *tr.* to invalidate, void, nullify.
invalidez *f.* invalidity.
inválido, -da *adj.* invalid, void, null. *2* invalid, disabled. *3 m.* invalid [pers. disabled for active service].
invariable *adj.* invariable, constant.
invasión *f.* invasion.
invasor, -ra *adj.* invading. *2 m.-f.* invader.
invectiva *f.* invective.
invencible *adj.* invincible, unconquerable.
invención *f.* invention. *2 Invención de la Santa Cruz,* Invention of the Cross.
invendible *adj.* unsalable.
inventar *tr.* to invent.
inventariar *tr.* to inventory.
inventario *m.* inventory: *hacer* ~, to take inventory.
inventiva *f.* faculty of invention, inventiveness.
invento *m.* invention.
inventor, -ra *adj.* inventing, inventive. *2 m.-f.* inventor.
inverecundia *f.* shamelessness, impudence.
inverecundo, -da *adj.* shameless, impudent.

invernáculo *m.* greenhouse, hothouse, conservatory.

invernada *f.* winter season.

invernadero *m.* winter quarters. *2* winter pastureland. *3* INVERNÁCULO.

invernal *adj.* hibernal, hiemal, wintry, winter.

invernar *intr.* to hibernate, winter. *2* to be winter. ¶ CONJUG. like *acertar*.

invernizo, -za *adj.* wintry, hiemal.

inverosímil *adj.* not verisimilar, unlikely.

inverosimilitud *f.* inverisimilitude, unlikeliness.

inversión *f.* inversion. *2* COM. investment.

inverso, -sa *adj.* inverse, inverted, opposite. *2 a,* or *por, la inversa,* on the contrary.

inversor, -ra *adj.* inversing; reversing. *2* COM. investing. *3 m.* reversing mecanism. *4* ELECT. reverser. *5* COM. investor.

invertebrado, -da *adj.-n.* invertebrate.

invertido, -da *adj.* inverted, reversed. *2* COM. invested [money or capital]. *3 adj.-m.* invert.

invertir *tr.* to invert. *2* to reverse. *3* to spend [time]. *4* COM. to invest [money or capital]. ¶ CONJUG. like *hervir*.

investidura *f.* investiture.

investigación *f.* investigation, research, enquiry.

investigador, -ra *adj.* investigating. *2 m.-f.* investigator, researcher.

investigar *tr.* to investigate, inquire into.

investir *tr.* to invest [endow, establish legally]: ~ *de,* or *con,* to invest with. ¶ CONJUG. like *servir*.

inveterado, -da *adj.* inveterate; confirmed.

inveterarse *ref.* to become inveterate.

invicto, -ta *adj.* unconquered, unvanquished.

invierno *m.* winter.

inviolabilidad *f.* inviolability.

inviolable *adj.* inviolable.

invisibilidad *f.* invisibility.

invisible *adj.* invisible.

invitación *f.* invitation.

invitado, -da *m.-f.* person invited, guest.

invitar *tr.* to invite.

invocación *f.* invocation, invoking.

invocar *tr.* to invoke.

involución *f.* BIOL. involution.

involucrar *tr.* to introduce irrelevantly.

involucro *m.* BOT. involucre.

involuntario, -ria *adj.* involuntary.

involuto, -ta *adj.* involute. *2 f.* GEOM. involute.

invulnerable *adj.* invulnerable.

inyección *f.* injection.

inyectable *adj.* injectable. *2 m.* MED. ampoule.

inyectado, -da *adj.* injected. *2 ojos inyectados en sangre,* bloodshot eyes.

inyectar *tr.* to inject.

inyector *m.* MECH. injector.

ión *m.* CHEM., PHYS. ion.

ionización *f.* ionization.

iota *f.* iota [Greek letter].

ipsilon *f.* upsilon [Greek letter].

ipso facto *adv.* at once, right away.

ir *intr.* to go, proceed, make one's way, move, walk, ride, travel: ~ *a casa,* to go home; ~ *de prisa,* to go, move or walk fast; ~ *a pie,* to go on foot; ~ *a caballo,* to ride, go on horseback; ~ *en tren,* to travel by train. *2* to go, go about, be: ~ *descalzo,* to be barefooted; ~ *sin afeitar,* to go unshaved. *3* to go, happen, be, be doing, fare: *las cosas van despacio,* things go slowly; ~ *bien,* to be all right, to be doing well; ~ *de mal en peor,* to grow worse and worse; *¿cómo le va?, ¿cómo vamos?,* how are you? *4* to fit, suit, become: *esto*

no me va, that doesn't suit me. *5* to go, lead: *esta carretera va a Madrid,* this road goes or leads to Madrid. *6* to go, extend [from point to point]. *7* to be at stake, to depend on; to affect, concern: *le va la vida en ello,* his life depends on that; *nada te va en ello,* it doesn't concern you in the least. *8* to be, elapse: *de mayo a julio van dos meses,* it is two months from May to July. *9* ARITH. to leave: *de 2 a 5 van 3,* 2 from 5 leaves 3. *10* to bet, lay, wager: *¿cuánto va...?,* what do you bet...? *11* to act: ~ *a una,* to act in unison; ~ *de buena fe,* to act sincerely. *12* to go, frequent, attend: ~ *a la escuela,* to go to school. *13* followed by a gerund, it constitutes the progressive form: *va oscureciendo,* it is getting dark. *14* ~ *a* [followed by an inf.], to go to; to be going to, to intend to; to go and: *ir a esperar a uno,* to go to meet someone; *iba a decir,* I was going to say; *vaya a verlo,* go and see it. *15* ~ *de,* to be clad in; to perform the action implied by the following noun: ~ *de uniforme,* to be in uniform; ~ *de caza,* to go hunting. *16* ~ *para largo,* to take time. *17* ~ *por,* to go for, to go to fetch. *18 ¿quién va?,* who is there?, who goes there? *19 ¡vamos!,* let's go, come on!; come!, why!, well! *20 vamos a ver,* let's see. *21 ¡vaya una idea!,* what an idea! *22 vaya usted con Dios,* farewell, God be with you. *23 vaya* or *vete a paseo,* go away, go and chop chips. *24 ref.* to be going, go away, depart. *25* to wear out. *26* [followed by a gerund] to be, to be gradually: *se va acercando,* it is getting near. *27 irse abajo,* to fall down, topple down. *28* NAUT. *irse a pique,* to sink, founder. *29 írsele a uno la cabeza,* to become dizzy. *30 írsele a uno la mano,* to overdo oneself; to put too much [salt, etc.]: *írsele a uno los pies,* to slip. *31 irse todo en humo,* to go up in smoke.

¶ IRREG. CONJUG.: INDIC. Pres.: *voy, vas, va; vamos, vais, van.* | Imperf.: *iba, ibas, iba; íbamos, ibais, iban.* | Pret. *fui, fuiste, fue; fuimos, fuisteis, fueron.* | Fut.: *iré, irás,* etc. | COND.: *iría, irías,* etc. | SUBJ. Pres.: *vaya, vayas, vaya; vayamos, vayáis, vayan.* | Imperf.: *fuera, fueras,* etc., *or fuese, fueses,* etc. | Fut.: *fuere, fueres,* etc. | IMPER.: *ve, vaya; vayamos, id, vayan.* | PAST. P.: *ido.* | GER.: *yendo.*

ira *f.* ire, anger, wrath.

iracundia *f.* irascibility. *2* anger, wrath.

iracundo, -da *adj.* irascible. *2* angry, wrathful.

Irak (el) *m. pr. n.* GEOG. Irak, Iraq.

Irán (el) *m. pr. n.* GEOG. Iran.

iranio, nia *adj.-n.* Iranian.

irascible *adj.* irascible, irritable.

Irene *f. pr. n.* Irene.

irgo, irga, irguió, irguiera, etc. *irr.* V. ERGUIR.

iridáceo, -a *adj.* BOT. iridaceous.

iridio *m.* CHEM. iridium.

iridiscencia *f.* iridescence.

iridiscente *adj.* iridescent.

iris *m.* iris, rainbow: ~ *de paz,* fig. peacemaker. *2* ANAT., OPT. iris. *3* MINER. noble opal.

irisación *f.* iridiscence.

irisado, -da *adj.* irised, rainbow-hued.

Irlanda *f. pr. n.* GEOG. Ireland.

irlandés, -sa *adj.* Irish. *2 m.* Irishman. *3* Irish [language]. *4 f.* Irishwoman. *5 m. pl. los irlandeses,* the Irish.

ironía *f.* irony.

irónico, -ca *adj.* ironic, ironical.

irracional *adj.* irrational [not endowed with rea-

son]. *2* irrational, absurd. *3* MATH. irrational. *4*
m. irrational being.
Irracionalidad *f.* irrationality.
Irradiación *f.* irradiation, radiation.
Irradiar *tr.* to irradiate, radiate [light, heat, etc.].
Irrazonable *adj.* unreasonable.
Irreal *adj.* unreal.
Irrealidad *f.* unreality.
Irrealizable *adj.* unrealizable, impracticable.
Irrebatible *adj.* irrefutable.
Irreconciliable *adj.* irreconcilable.
Irrecuperable *adj.* irrecoverable, irretrievable.
Irrecusable *adj.* irrecusable.
Irredentismo *m.* irredentism.
Irredento, -ta *adj.* unredeemed [region].
Irreductible *adj.* irreducible. *2* stubborn, unyiel-
ding.
Irreemplazable *adj.* irreplaceable.
Irreflexión *f.* rashness, thoughtlessness.
Irreflexivo, -va *adj.* unreflecting, inconsiderate,
rash, thoughtless.
Irrefragable *adj.* irrefragable.
Irrefrenable *adj.* irrepressible, uncontrollable.
Irrefutable *adj.* irrefutable.
Irregular *adj.* irregular.
Irregularidad *f.* irregularity.
Irreligión *f.* irreligion.
Irreligioso, -sa *adj.* irreligious.
Irremediable *adj.* irremediable, hopeless.
Irremisible *adj.* irremissible.
Irrenunciable *adj.* unrenounceable.
Irreparable *adj.* irreparable, irretrievable.
Irreprensible *adj.* irreprehensible, blameless.
Irreprimible *adj.* irrepressible.
Irreprochable *adj.* irreproachable.
Irresistible *adj.* irresistible.
Irresoluble *adj.* unsolvable.
Irresolución *f.* irresolution, indecision.
Irresoluto, -ta *adj.* irresolute, wavering.
Irrespetuoso, -sa *adj.* disrespectful.
Irrespirable *adj.* unbreathable, suffocating.
Irresponsable *adj.* irresponsible.
Irreverencia *f.* irreverence.
Irreverente *adj.* irreverent.
Irreversible *adj.* LAW, MACH., BIOL. irreversible.
Irrevocable *adj.* irrevocable.
Irrigación *f.* MED. irrigation.
Irrigar *tr.* MED. to irrigate.
Irrisible *adj.* laughable, ridicule.
Irrisión *f.* derision, ridicule. *2* laughing stock.
Irrisorio, -ria *adj.* derisory, ridiculous. *2* insignifi-
cant, ridiculously small.
Irritabilidad *f.* irritability.
Irritable *adj.* irritable.
Irritación *f.* irritation.
Irritante *adj.* irritating, irritant. *2* LAW irritant. *3*
m. MED., PHYSIOL. irritant.
Irritar *tr.* to irritate, anger, annoy. *2* MED., PHY-
SIOL., LAW to irritate. *4 ref.* to become irritated.
Irrogar *tr.* to cause, occasion [harm, damage].
Irrompible *adj.* unbreakable.
Irrumpir *intr.* to make an irruption.
Irrupción *f.* irruption, bursting in, invasion.
Irubú *m.* ORN. (Am.) turkey buzzard.
Isaac *m. pr. n.* Isaac.
Isabel *f. pr. n.* Isabela, Elizabeth.
Isabelino, -na *adj.* Isabelline; Elizabethan. *2 adj.*

-n. HIST. defender of Isabella II against the Car-
lists.
Isaías *m. pr. n.* BIBL. Isaiah.
Isidoro *m. pr. n.* Isidore.
Isidro *m. pr. n.* Isidore.
Isla *f.* GEOG. isle, island: *islas Baleares,* Balearic Is-
lands; *islas Británicas,* British Isles; *islas Cana-
rias,* Canary Islands; *islas Filipinas,* Philipine Is-
lands. *2* block [of houses]. *3* isolated grove or
woodland.
Islam *m.* Islam.
Islámico, -ca *adj.* Islamic.
Islamismo *m.* Islamism.
Islandés, -sa *adj.* Icelandic. *2 m.-f.* Icelander. *3 m.*
Icelandic [language].
Islandia *f. pr. n.* GEOG. Iceland.
Isleño, -ña *adj.* insular. *2 m.-f.* islander.
Isleta *f. dim.* small island, islet.
Islote *m.* small barren island.
Ismael *m. pr. n.* Ishmael.
Ismaelita *adj.* Ishmaelitic. *2 m.-f.* Ishmaelite.
Isobara *f.* METEOR. isobar.
Isobárico, -ca *adj.* METEOR. isobaric: *línea isobárica,*
isobar.
Isoclino, -na *adj.* isoclinal, isoclinic.
Isocromático, -ca *adj.* OPT. isochromatic.
Isócrono *adj.* isochronal, isochrone, isochronic.
Isodáctilo, -la *adj.* ZOOL. isodactylous.
Isógono, -na *adj.* CRIST. isogonic.
Isómero, -ra *adj.* CHEM., BIOL. isomeric, isomerous.
Isométrico, -ca *adj.* isometric.
Isomorfo, -fa *adj.* MINER. isomorphic, isomorph-
ous.
Isópodo, -da *adj.-n.* ZOOL. isopod, isopodan.
Isósceles *adj.* GEOM. isosceles.
Isotermo, -ma *adj.* PHYS., METEOR. isothermic. *2 f.*
METEOR. isotherm [line].
Isótopo *m.* PHYS., CHEM. isotope.
Isótropo, -pa *adj.* isotropic.
Isquiático, -ca *adj.* ANAT. ischiatic.
Isquión *m.* ANAT. ischium.
Israel *m. pr. n.* Israel.
Israelí *adj.-n.* Israeli.
Israelita *adj.* Israelitish. *2 m.-f.* Israelite.
Israelítico, -ca *adj.* Israelitish.
Istmeño, -ña *adj.* isthmian [of an isthmus].
Ístmico, -ca *adj.* isthmian, isthmic.
Istmo *m.* GEOG., ANAT. isthmus.
Itaca *f. pr. n.* HIST., GEOG. Ithaca.
Italia *f. pr. n.* GEOG. Italy.
Italianismo *m.* Italianism.
Italiano, -na *adj.-n.* Italian.
Itálico, -ca *adj.* Italic. *2* PRINT. italic.
Italo, -la *adj.-n.* poet. Italian.
Item *m.* clause, article [of a deed, etc.]. *2 adv. item*
or *item más,* also, likewise [in deeds, etc.].
Iteración *f.* iteration.
Iterar *tr.* to iterate.
Iterativo, -va *adj.* iterative.
Iterbio *m.* CHEM. ytterbium.
Itinerario, -ria *adj.-m.* itinerary.
Itrio *m.* chem. yttrium.
Izar *tr.* NAUT. to hoist, haul up.
Izquierda *f.* left hand. *2* left, left-hand side; *a la ~,*
to the left, on the left. *3* POL. Left, Left wing.
Izquierdista *adj.-n.* POL. leftist.
Izquierdo, -da *adj.* left, left-hand. *2* left-handed
[person]. *3* crooked.

J

J, j f. J, j, eleventh letter of the Spanish alphabet.
jabalcón m. strut, brace.
jabalí m. ZOOL. wild boar.
jabalina f. javelin, boarspear. 2 SPORT. javelin. 3 ZOOL. wild sow.
jabardillo m. noisy swarm.
jabato m. young wild boar.
jábega f. sweep net [for fishing]. 2 fishing smack.
jabeque m. NAUT. xebec. 2 coll. knife wound in the face.
jabillo m. BOT. sandbox tree.
jabladera f. croze, crozer [cooper's tool].
jable m. croze [groove in staves].
jabón m. soap: ~ de afeitar, shaving soap; ~ de olor or de tocador, toilet soap; ~ de sastre, soapstone, French chalk. 2 fig. flattery: dar ~, to softsoap. 3 fig. severe reprimand: dar un ~ a, to haul over the coals.
jabonado, -da adj. soaped. 2 m. soaping.
jabonadura f. soaping. 2 fig. severe reprimand. 3 pl. soapsuds, lather.
jabonar tr. to soap; to lather. 2 fig. to reprimand severely.
jaboncillo m. cake of toilet soap. 2 BOT. soapberry tree. 3 ~ de sastre, JABÓN DE SASTRE.
jabonera f. soap dish. 2 BOT. soapwort.
jabonería f. soap factory. 2 soap shop.
jabonero, -ra adj. [pertaining to] soap. 2 yellowish, dirty white [bull]. 2 m. soapmaker. 4 soap dealer.
jaboneta f., **jabonete** m. cake of toilet soap.
jabonoso, -sa adj. soapy.
jaca f. nag, cob, bidet, jennet.
jácara f. merry ballad. 2 a kind of dance. 3 group of merry singers walking the streets at night. 4 annoyance. 5 story, tale; fable, lie.
jacarandá f. BOT. jacaranda.
jacarandoso, -sa adj. jaunty, lively, gay.
jacarero adj. gay, merry, sportful [person].
jácena f. ARCH. girder.
jacerina f. coat of mail.
jacinto m., BOT., MINER. hyacinth: ~ occidental, topaz; ~ oriental, ruby.
Jacinto, -ta m.-f. pr. n. Hyacinth.
jaco m. jade, sorry nag. 2 short coat of mail.
Jacob m. pr. n. BIBL. Jacob.
jacobino, -na adj. Jacobin, Jacobinic. 2 m. HIST., POL. Jacobin.

jacobita adj. Jacobite, Jacobitic. 2 m.-f. Jacobite.
Jacobo m. pr. n. James.
jactancia f. boasting, bragging, vaunt.
jactancioso, -sa adj. boastful, bragging, vaunting. 2 m.-f. boaster, braggard, vaunter.
jactarse ref. to boast, brag, vaunt: ~ de, to boast of.
jaculatoria f. ejaculation [short prayer].
jade m. MINER. jade.
jadeante adj. panting, out of breath.
jadear intr. to pant, heave.
jadeo m. panting.
jaenés, -sa adj.-n. of Jaén.
jaez, pl. **jaeces** m. ornament for horses. 2 kind, nature [of things]. 3 pl. trappings [for horses].
Jafet m. pr. n. BIBL. Japheth.
jaguar m. ZOOL. jaguar.
jaguarzo m. BOT. rockrose.
jaharrar tr. MASON. to plaster.
Jaime m. pr. n. James, Jim.
jaique m. moorish hooded cloak.
¡ja, ja, ja! interj. ha, ha!; ho, ho!
jalapa f. BOT. jalap, jalapa.
jalar tr. to haul, to pull. 2 to attract.
jalbegar tr. ENJALBEGAR.
jalbegue m. whitewash. 2 whitewashing.
jaldado, -da; jalde; jaldo, -da adj. bright yellow.
jalea f. jelly [of fruit juices].
jalear tr. to encourrage [hounds] with shouts. 2 to animate [dancers, singers, etc.] by clapping hands or cheering.
jaleo m. clapping hands, cheering, etc., to encourage dancers, singers, etc. 2 Andalusian dance and its tune. 3 merry noise. 4 row, disturbance.
jaletina f. gelatine. 2 fine jelly.
Jalifa m. Moroccan prince governing Spanish Morocco.
jalifato m. dignity of the Jalifa. 2 territory under the Jalifa.
jalón m. flagpole, range pole, stake.
jalonar tr. to mark or stake out.
jaloque m. southeast wind.
Jamaica f. pr. n. GEOG. Jamaica.
jamar tr. coll. to eat.
jamás adv. never: nunca ~, never, nevermore. 2 ever: el mejor libro que ~ se haya escrito, the best book ever writen.
jamba f. ARCH. jamb.

jambaje *m.* ARCH. door frame, window frame.
jamelgo *m.* jade [horse].
jamón *m.* ham [thigh of hog salted and dried].
jamona *adj.-f.* coll. buxom middle-aged woman.
jándalo, -la *adj.-n.* coll. Andalusian.
jangada *f.* nonsense, silly sally. 2 dirty trick. 3 NAUT. raft, float.
Jano *m. pr. n.* MYTH. Janus.
jansenismo *m.* Jansenism.
Japón (el) *m. pr. n.* GEOG. Japan.
japón, -na; japonés, -sa *adj.-n.* Japanese. 2 *m.* Japanese [language].
jaque *m.* CHESS check; ~ *mate*, checkmate; *dar* ~ *mate*, to checkmate; *tener en* ~, fig. to hold a threat over the head of. 2 coll. swaggerer, bully.
jaquear *tr.* CHESS to check. 2 MIL. to harass.
jaqueca *f.* migraine, megrim, headache.
jaqueado, -da *adj.* HER. checkered.
jaquetilla *f.* short jacket.
jaquetón *m.* VALENTÓN.
jáquima *f.* rope headstall and halter.
jara *f.* BOT. rockrose.
jarabe *m.* syrup. 2 sweet drink. 3 ~ *de pico*, empty talk, idle promises, lip service.
jaral *m.* place full of rockrose; bramble, brake.
jaramago *m.* BOT. hedge mustard.
jarana *f.* noisy merrymaking of low people. 2 coll. row, rioting, uproar. 3 coll. trick, deception.
jaranear *intr.* to go merrymaking. 2 to engage in rows, to riot.
jaranero, -ra *adj.* merry, merrymaking, funloving.
jarcia *f.* NAUT. rigging, cordage [of a ship]. 2 fishing tackle. 4 jumble, mess.
jardín *m.* [flower] garden, gardens: ~ *botánico*, botanical gardens; ~ *zoológico*, zoological gardens. 2 NAUT. privy, latrine. 3 EDUC. ~ *de la infancia*, kindergarten.
jardinera *f.* woman gardener. 2 jardinière. 4 basket carriage. 5 open tramcar for summertime.
jardinería *f.* flower gardening, landscape gardening.
jardinero *m.* gardener [tender of a flower garden].
jareta *f.* SEW. casing. 2 NAUT. cat-harping.
jarra *f.* jar, pitcher. 2 *de jarras, en jarras*, with arms akimbo.
jarrazo *m. augm.* large jar. 2 blow with a jar.
jarrete *m.* ANAT. ham, back of the knee. 2 upper part of the calf of the leg. 3 hock, gambrel.
jarretera *f.* garter. 2 Order of the Garter.
jarro *m.* ewer, jug, pitcher, pot: *echar un* ~ *de agua fría a*, to pour cold water on.
jarrón *m.* [ornamental or flower] vase. 2 ARCH. urn.
jaspe *m.* MINER. jasper. 2 veined marble.
jaspeado, -da *adj.* marbled, jaspery. 2 *m.* marbling.
jaspear *tr.* to marble, mottle, vein.
jato, -ta *m.-f.* calf [young of cow].
Jauja *f. pr. n.* Cockaigne.
jaula *f.* cage [for birds, beasts, etc]. 2 crate. 3 MIN. cage.
jauría *f.* pack of hounds.
javanés, -sa *adj.-n.* Javanese.
Javier *m. pr. n.* Xavier.
jayán, -na *m.-f.* burly, strong person.
jazmín *m.* BOT. jasmine.
jebe *m.* alum, rock alum. 2 (Am.) India rubber.
jedive *m.* khedive.
jefa *f.* female chief or head.
jefatura *f.* headship, leadership. 2 headquarters: ~ *de policía*, police headquarters.

jefe *m.* chief, head, leader, boss, master: ~ *de estación*, RLY. stationmaster; ~ *del Estado*, head of the State, *chief executive; ~ *de un partido*, leader of a party; *en* ~, in chief. 2 MIL. field officer: ~ *de día*, day officer. 3 HER. chief, chef. 4 *adj.* chief, in chief.
Jehová *m. pr. n.* Jehovah.
¡je, je, je! *interj.* ha, ha!
jeme *m.* distance from tip of the thumb to tip of the forefinger when extended. 2 coll. face [of woman].
jengibre *m.* ginger [plant & spice].
jenízaro, -ra *adj.* mixed, hybrid. 2 *m.* Janizary.
Jenofonte *m. pr. n.* Xenophon.
jeque *m.* sheik [Arab chief].
jerarca *m.* hierarch.
jerarquía *f.* hierarchy.
jerárquico, -ca *adj.* hierarchic(al.
jerbo *m.* ZOOL. jerboa.
jeremiada *f.* jeremiad.
Jeremías *m. pr. n.* Jeremiah.
jeremías *m.-f.* coll. constant complainer.
jerez *m.* sherry wine.
jerezano, -na *adj.-n.* of Jerez.
jerga *f.* coarse woollen cloth. 2 straw mattress. 3 jargon [of a trade or group]. 4 jargon, gibberish.
jergón *m.* straw mattress.
jerguilla *f.* silk or worsted serge.
jerife *m.* sherif, shereef.
jerigonza *f.* JERGA 3 & 4.
jeringa *f.* syringe: ~ *hipodérmica*, hypodermic syringe. 2 enema [apparatus].
jeringar *tr.* to syringe. 2 to give an enema to. 3 coll. to annoy, bother. 4 *ref.* coll. to support an annoyance.
jeringazo *m.* syringing. 2 injection, enema, clyster.
jeringuilla *f.* small syringe. 2 hypodermic syringe. 3 BOT. syringa, mock orange.
jeroglífico, -ca *adj.* hieroglyphic, hieroglyphical. 2 *m.* hieroglyphic. 3 rebus.
Jerónimo *m. pr. n.* Jerome.
jerónimo, -ma *adj.-m.* Hieronymite.
jerosolimitano, -na *adj.-n.* Hierosolymitan.
jersey *m.* jersey, sweater [garment].
Jerusalén *f. pr. n.* GEOG. Jerusalem.
Jesucristo *m. pr. n.* Jesus Christ.
jesuita *adj.-m.* Jesuit.
jesuítico, -ca *adj.* Jesuitic, Jesuitical.
Jesús *m. pr. n.* Jesus: *el niño* ~, the infant Jesus; *en un decir* ~, in an instant; *¡Jesús!, ¡Jesús, María y José!*, good gracious!, my gracious. ¶ The name of Jesus is employed in Spain with no necessary implication of profanity.
Jesusa *f. pr. n.* Jesus.
jeta *f.* thick lips; protruding mouth. 2 hog's snout. 3 coll. phiz, mug, face.
jetón, -na, jetudo, -da *adj.* thick-lipped.
jíbaro, -ra *adj.-n.* (Am.) peasant.
jibia *f.* ZOOL. cuttlefish. 2 cuttlebone.
jibión *m.* cuttlebone.
Jibraltar *m. pr. n.* GEOG. Gibraltar.
jibraltareño, -ña *adj.* & of Gibraltar.
jícara *f.* chocolate cup. 2 (Am.) small calabash cup.
jifero, -ra *adj.* [pertaining to the] slaughterhouse. 2 coll. dirty, filthy, vile. 3 *m.* slaughtering knife. 4 butcher [slaughterer of animals].
jiga *f.* GIGA.
jigote *m.* GIGOTE.
¡ji, ji, ji! *interj.* he, he, he!

jilguero *m.* ORN. goldfinch, linnet.
jilote *m.* (Am.) ear of green Indian corn.
jindama *f.* coll. fear.
jineta *f.* ZOOL. genet. *2 montar a la* ~, to ride with stirrups high and legs bent. *3 tener los cascos a la* ~, to be harebrained.
jinete *m.* horseman, rider. *2 obs.* cavalryman. *3* spirited pure-bred horse.
jingoísmo *m.* jingoism.
jínjol *m.* AZUFAIFA.
jinjolero *m.* AZUFAIFO.
jipio *m.* HIPIDO.
jipijapa *f.* fine strip of jipijapa straw. *2 m.* jipijapa, Panama hat.
jira *f.* strip of cloth. *2* picnic, outing. *3* excursion, tour.
jirafa *f.* ZOOL. giraffe.
jirón *m.* shred, tatter. *2* bit, small part. *3* pennant, pointed banner. *4* HER. gyron.
jironado, -da *adj.* shredded, torn. *2* HER. gyronny.
jiu-jitsu *m.* jiujitsu, jujitsu.
Joaquín *m. pr. n.* Joachim.
Job *m. pr. n.* BIBL. Job.
jocoserio, -ria *adj.* jocoserious, seriocomic.
jocosidad *f.* jocosity, jocularity, humorousness.
jocoso, -sa *adj.* jocose, jocular, humorous.
jocundidad *f.* jocundity.
jocundo, -da *adj.* jocund, pleasant.
jofaina *f.* washbowl, washbain.
jolgorio *m.* HOLGORIO.
jollín *m.* coll. noisy merrymaking, uproar.
Jonás *m. pr. n.* BIBL. Jonah.
Jonia *f. pr. n.* HIST., GEOG. Ionia.
jónico, -ca *adj.* Ionian, Ionic. *2* ARCH. Ionic. *3 m.-f.* Ionian.
jonio, -nia *adj.* Ionian, Ionic. *2 m.-f.* Ionian.
Jordán *m. pr. n.* Jordan [river].
Jordania *f. pr. n.* Jordan [country].
Jorge *m. pr. n.* George.
jorguín *m.* wizard, sorcerer.
jorguina *f.* witch, sorceress.
jornada *f.* day's journey: *a grandes* or *largas jornadas*, by forced marches, fast, speedily; *al fin de la* ~, fig. in the end. *2* journey, travel. *3* military expedition. *4* workday, working day [number of hours of work]. *5 obs.* act of a play. *6* fig. occasion, event.
jornal *m.* day wages: *a* ~, by the day. *2* day's work, daywork. *3* a land measure.
joroba *f.* hump, hunch. *2* coll. annoyance, bother.
jorobado, -da *adj.* humped, humpbacked, hunchbacked. *2 m.-f.* humpback, hunchback.
jorobar *tr.* coll. to annoy, bother.
Josafat *m. pr. n.* BIBL. Jehoshaphat.
José *m. pr. n.* Joseph.
Josefa, Josefina *f. pr. n.* Josepha, Josephine.
Josefo *m. pr. n.* Josephus.
Josías *m. pr. n.* BIBL. Josiah.
Josue *m. pr. n.* BIBL. Joshua.
jota *f.* name of the letter *j.* *2* jota [Spanish dance]. *3* jot, iota, whit: *no entender* ~, not to understand anything: *sin faltar* ~, in minute detail.
joule *m.* ELECT. joule.
joven *adj.* young. *2 m.-f.* youth, young man, young woman, young person: *de* ~, as a young man or woman; *los jóvenes*, the young people.
jovencillo, -lla & **jovencito, -ta** *m.-f.* youngster, lad, lass.
jovial *adj.* jovial, cheerful, pleasant, goodhumoured.
jovialidad *f.* joviality, cheerfulness, good humour.

joya *f.* jewel, piece of jewelry. *2* fig. jewel, gem [person or thing]. *3* ARCH., ARTIL. astragal. *4 pl.* jewels, trinkets. *5* a bride's outfit and jewels.
joyante *adj.* glossy [silk].
joyel *m.* small jewel.
joyería *f.* jewelry; jeweller's trade. *2* jeweller's shop.
joyero *m.* jeweller. *2* jewel case or box, casket.
joyo *m.* BOT. darnel, bearded darnel.
Juan *m. pr. n.* John: *buen* ~, candid soul; ~ *Lanas*, man who has no will of his own.
juanas *f. pl.* gove stretcher.
Juana *f. pr. n.* Joan, Jane, Jean.
juanete *m.* bunion. *2* prominent cheekbone. *3* NAUT. topgallant yard or sail.
juanetudo, -da *adj.* having bunions.
Juanita *f. pr. n.* Jenny, Jeannette.
Juanito *m. pr. n.* Jack, Johnny.
jubilación *f.* pensioning off, superannuation, retirement. *2* pension, superannuation, retiring allowance.
jubilado, -da *adj.* pensioned, superannuate, retired. *2 m.-f.* pensioner, superannuate.
1) **jubilar** *adj.* ECCL. [pertaining to the] jubilee.
2) **jubilar** *tr.* to pension off, superannuate, retire. *2* fig. to discard as useless. *3 intr.-ref.* to jubilate. *4 ref.* to be pensioned, to retire.
jubileo *m.* HIST., ECCL. jubilee. *2* fig. much going and coming of many people.
júbilo *m.* jubilation, joy, delight, rejoicing.
jubiloso, -sa *adj.* jubilant, joyful, rejoicing.
jubón *m.* doublet, jerkin.
judaico, -ca *adj.* Judaic, Jewish.
judaísmo *m.* Judaism.
judaizante *adj.* Judaizing. *2 m.-f.* Judaizer, Judaist.
judaizar *intr.* to Judaize.
Judas *m. pr. n.* BIBL. & fig. Judas.
judería *f.* Jewry, ghetto. *2* tax on Jews.
judía *f.* Jewess. *2* BOT. bean, kidney bean; string bean, French bean: ~ *colorada*, scarlet runner.
judiada *f.* dirty trick. *2* inhuman action. *3* usurious profit.
judicatura *f.* judgeship. *2* judicature.
judicial *adj.* judicial, judiciary: *poder* ~, judicial power.
judiciario, -ria *adj.* judicial [astrology]. *2* pertaining to the judicial astrology. *3 m.* astrologer. *4 f.* judicial astrology.
judío, -a *adj.* Jewish, Judean. *2* miserly; usurious. *3 m.* Jew, Hebrew, Judean. *4* miser; usurer.
Judit *f. pr. n.* Judith.
judo *m.* judo.
juego *m.* play, playing [for amusement]: ~ *limpio*, fig. fair play; ~ *sucio*, fig. foul play; *por* ~, in fun, for fun. *2* gambling, gaming; game: *casa de* ~, gambling house. *3* play, game: ~ *de ajedrez*, chess, game of chess; ~ *de azar*, game of chance; ~ *de bochas*, bowling; ~ *de bolos*, skittles, ninepins, tenpins; ~ *de cartas* or *naipes*, card game, cards; ~ *de damas*, draughts, *checkers; ~ *de manos*, legerdemain, sleight of hands, conjurer's trick; ~ *de pelota*, ball [game], pelota; ~ *de palabras*, play on words, pun; ~ *de prendas*, forfeits; *juegos malabares*, juggling, jugglery. *4* game, art, scheming: *verle el* ~ *a uno*, to read someone's intention; *hacerle el* ~ *a*, to play into the hands of. *5* hand [cards dealt to a player]: *descubrir uno su* ~, to show one's hand. *6* play [of water, light, colours, etc.]. *7* MACH. play. *8* play, action, working, operation: *poner en* ~, to

bring into play, to make use of. *9* set, service, suite: ~ *de botones*, set of buttons; ~ *de café*, coffee service; ~ *de dormitorio*, bedroom suite. *10 hacer* ~, to match [suit, correspond]. *11 pl.* games [public games]: *juegos olímpicos*, Olympian games, Olympic games.

juego, juegue, etc. *irr.* V. JUGAR.

juerga *f.* spree, revelry, carousal: *ir de* ~, to go on a spree.

juerguista *m.-f.* reveller, carouser.

jueves *m.* Thursday: ~ *gordo* or *lardero*, Thursday before Shrovetide; ~ *santo*, Maundy Thursday, Holy Thursday.

juez *m.* judge, justice: ~ *árbitro*, LAW arbitrator, umpire; ~ *de instrucción*, examining magistrate; ~ *de paz*, justice of the peace. *2* SPORT. ~ *de línea*, linesman; ~ *de llegada*, goal judge; ~ *de salida*, starter.

jugada *f.* play [particular act in a play or game], stroke, throw, move. *2* ill turn, mean trick. *3* ~ *de Bolsa*, speculation.

jugador, -ra *adj.* given to gambling. *2 m.-f.* player [of a game]: ~ *de manos*, conjurer, conjuror, legerdemainist. *3* gambler, gamester.

jugar *intr.* to play, sport, frolic, toy, dally. *2* to game, to gamble. *3* to play [take part in a game]: ~ *al fútbol*, to play football. *4* to play, throw, move, to be one's turn to play. *5* to speculate: ~ *a la Bolsa*, to speculate in stocks; ~ *al alza*, to bull; ~ *a la baja*, to bear. *6* to play, enter in action. *7* MACH. to play. *8* ~ *con*, to play with; to toy with, dally with. *9* ~ *en*, to have a part or hand in. *10 tr.* to play [a match, game, hand, etc., at a game]. *11* to play, move [a card, a domino, a pawn, etc.]. *12* to ply, wield [a weapon]. *13 tr.-ref.* to play, risk, stake: *jugarse el todo por el todo*, to stake all. *14* to play or gamble away. ¶ IRREG. CONJUG.: INDIC. Pres.: *juego, juegas, juega;* jugamos, *jugáis, juegan.* | SUBJ. Pres.: *juegue, juegues, juegue;* juguemos, juguéis, *jueguen.* | IMPER.: *juega, juegue;* juguemos, jugad, *jueguen.*

jugarreta *f.* mean trick, dirty trick.

juglandáceo, -a *adj.* BOT. juglandaceous.

juglar *m.* minstrel, jongleur.

juglaría *f.* minstrel's or jongleur's feats or manners.

jugo *m.* juice: ~ *gástrico*, PHYSIOL. gastric juice. *2* gravy. *3* fig. substance, profit: *sacar el* ~ *a*, to make the most of.

jugosidad *f.* juiciness, succulence.

jugoso, -sa *adj.* juicy, succulent.

juguete *m.* toy, plaything. *2* fig. sport [of wind, passions, etc.]. *3* short, slight musical piece. *4* THEAT. short play.

juguetear *intr.* to joy, play, sport, frolic, dally.

jugueteo *m.* playing, sporting, frolicking.

juguetería *f.* toy trade. *2* toy shop.

juguetón, -na *adj.* playful, frolicsome, wanton.

juicio *m.* judgement, discretion, discernment, prudence, sense, wisdom: *hombre de* ~, man of judgment; *muela del* ~, wisdom tooth; *tener* ~, to be sensible; to behave oneself. *2* sanity, saneness, soundness of mind: *estar en su* ~ or *en su cabal* ~, to be in one's right mind; *perder el* ~, to go crazy, go out of one's mind. *3* judgment [mental act of judging], opinion: *a mi* ~, in my opinion. *4* LAW trial: ~ *ejecutivo*, levy, execution; ~ *oral*, trial [in criminal law]. *5* THEOL. judgment: *el* ~ *final* or *universal*, the last Judgment. *6* HIST. ~ *de Dios*, ordeal.

juicioso, -sa *adj.* judicious, sensible, wise.

julepe *m.* PHARM. julep. *2* a card game. *3* scolding, reprimand.

Julia *f. pr. n.* Julia.

Julián *m. pr. n.* Julian.

juliano, -na *adj.* Julian. *2* COOK. julienne. *3 pr. n. Juliano el Apóstata*, Julian the Apostate.

julio *m.* July. *3* ELECT. joule.

Julio *m. pr. n.* Julius.

julo *m.* bell-cow. *2* lead mule.

jumenta *f.* jenny, jenny ass, she-ass.

jumento *m.* ass, donkey.

jumera *f.* HUMERA.

juncáceo, -a *adj.* juncaceous.

juncal *adj.* rushy. *2* willowy, flexible, graceful [human body]. *3 m.* JUNCAR.

juncar *m.* ground full of rushes.

juncia *f.* BOT. sedge.

junco *m.* junk [Chinese ship]. *2* BOT. rush, bulrush. *3* rush stem. *4* slender walking stick. *5* BOT. ~ *de Indias*, rattan.

juncoso, -sa *adj.* rushy.

junio *m.* June.

junior *m.* ECCL. junior.

junípero *m.* BOT. juniper.

Juno *f. pr. n.* MYTH. Juno.

junquillo *m.* BOT. jonquil. *2* BOT. rattan. *3* ARCH. reed, bead.

junta *f.* meeting, conference: ~ *de acreedores*, meeting of creditors; ~ *de médicos*, MED. consultation. *2* session, sitting. *3* board, council: ~ *de comercio*, board of trade; ~ *directiva*, board of directors, executive board. *4* collection, aggregate. *5* union, junction, joint, seam. *6* pipe joint, gasket.

juntamente *adj.* jointly, together.

juntar *tr.* to assemble, congregate. *2* to amass, collect, gather, lay up, store. *3* to join, unite; to connect. *4 ref.* to join, meet, assemble, gather, come into contact, come close to. *5* to associate [with]. *6* to copulate.

junto *adv.* near, close: ~ *a*, near to, close to, next to, by, beside. *2* ~ *con*, together with, along with. *3 en* ~, altogether, in all, all told. *4 por* ~, wholesale. *5 todo* ~, at the same time, all at once.

junto, -ta *adj.* united, assembled, together: *todos juntos*, all together. *2* being near or close: *muy juntos*, very close to each other.

juntura *f.* joint, juncture [place of union]. *2* ANAT., ZOOL. joint, articulation.

Júpiter *m. pr. n.* MYTH., ASTR. Jupiter.

jura *f.* oath. *2* solemn ceremony of taking an oath of allegiance.

1) **jurado** *m.* LAW jury, panel [for awarding prizes]. *3* juror, juryman.

2) **jurado, -da** *adj.* sworn. *2* coll. *tenérsela jurada a*, to have it in for.

juramentar *tr.* to swear, put to an oath. *2 ref.* to bind oneself by an oath.

juramento *m.* oath: ~ *falso*, perjury. *2 ref.* act of swearing. *3* swearword, curse.

jurar *intr.* to swear [take an oath]: ~ *en falso*, to commit perjury. *2* to swear [use profane language]. *3 tr.* to swear. *4* to swear allegiance or obedience to. *5* ~ *un cargo*, to take the oath before entering and office.

jurásico, -ca *adj.-m.* GEOL. Jurassic.

juratorio, -ria *adj.* LAW juratory.

jurel *m.* ICHTH. saurel.

jurídico, -ca *adj.* juridical; legal.

jurisconsulto *m.* jurisconsult, jurist, lawyer.
jurisdicción *f.* jurisdiction.
jurisdiccional *adj.* jurisdictional. *2 aguas jurisdiccionales,* territorial waters.
jurisperito *m.* jurisprudent, jurist.
jurisprudencia *f.* jurisprudence.
jurista *m.* jurist.
juro *m.* right of perpetual ownership. *2 de* ~, certainly, necessarily.
justa *f.* joust, tilt. *2* contest.
justador *m.* jouster, tilter.
justamente *adv.* justly. *2* tightly, fitting tightly. *3* just, exactly. *4* at that time.
justar *intr.* to joust, to tilt.
justicia *f.* justice [in every sense except a judge]: *administrar* ~, to administer justice; *hacer* ~, to do justice; *de* ~, just, deserved. *2* officers of lawcourt, judge; judicial power: *ir por* ~, to go to court, to bring suit. *3* public punishment, execution.
justiciero, -ra *adj.* just, fair, righteous [person].
justificable *adj.* justifiable.
justificación *f.* justification.
justificado, -da *adj.* justified. *2* having adequate reason or motive, well-grounded.

justificante *adj.* justifying. *2 m.* proof, voucher.
justificar *tr.* to justify [an action, a person, etc.]. *2* to prove, vouch, establish. *3* THEOL., PRINT. to justify. *4 ref.* to clear oneself, to justify one's conduct.
justificativo, -va *adj.* justificative; justificatory.
justillo *m.* underwaist, corset cover.
Justiniano *m. pr. n.* Justinian.
justipreciar *tr.* to appraise, estimate.
justiprecio *m.* appraisal, estimation.
1) **justo** *adv.* justly, rightly. *2* exactly. *3* tightly, closely.
2) **justo, -ta** *adj.* just. *2* righteous. *3* exact, correct. *4* tight, close, close-fitting. *5 m.* just man [righteous before God]: *los justos,* the just.
Jutlandia *f. pr. n.* GEOG. Jutland.
juvenil *adj.* juvenile, youthful.
juventud *f.* youth [part or life; early period]. *2* youthfulness. *3* youth, young people.
juzgado *m.* LAW court or tribunal [of one judge]. *2* judicature, judgeship.
juzgador, -ra *adj.* judging. *2 m.-f.* judger.
juzgar *intr.* to judge: ~ *de,* to form a judgement or opinion about. *2 tr.* to judge, try. *3* to judge [form opinion about; consider, think, judge to be]: *a* ~ *por,* judging by or from.

K

K, k *f.* K, k, twelfth letter of the Spanish alphabet.
ka *f.* name of the letter *k*.
kaiser *m.* kaiser.
kan *m.* khan [tartar chief].
kantiano, -na *adj.-n.* Kantian.
kantismo *m.* Kantism.
kappa *f.* kappa [Greek letter].
kepis, *pl.* **-pis** *m.* kepi.
kerosén, keroseno *m.* kerosene.
kilo *m.* kilo, kilogram, kilogramme.
kilociclo *m.* kilocycle.
kilográmetro *m.* kilogrammetre, kilogrammeter.
kilogramo *m.* kilogram, kilogramme.

kilolitro *m.* kilolitre, kiloliter.
kilometraje *m.* kilometrage.
kilométrico, -ca *adj.* kilometric, kilometrical. *2*
fig. very long, interminable.
kilómetro *m.* kilometre, kilometer.
kilovatio *m.* kilowatt.
kimono *m.* kimono.
kiosko *m.* QUIOSCO.
kirie *m.* ECCL. kyrie eleison.
kodak *f.* kodak.
krausismo *m.* Krausism.
Kremlin *m.* Kremlin.
kurdo, -da *adj.-n.* CURDO.

L

L, l f. L, l, thirteenth letter of the Spanish alphabet.

1) la def. art. fem. sing. the.

2) la pers. pron. fem. sing. her, it [direct object]: ~ veo, I see her, I see it.

3) la m. MUS. la, A.

lábaro m. labarum.

laberíntico, -ca adj. labyrinthic(al, labyrinthine.

laberinto m. labyrinth; maze. 2 ANAT. labyrinth.

labia f. coll. fluency, winning eloquence.

labiado, -da adj. BOT. labiate.

labial adj.-f. labial.

labiérnago m. BOT. mock privet.

labihendido, -da adj. harelipped.

lábil adj. labile. 2 weak, feeble.

labio m. ANAT., ZOOL. lip: ~ leporino, harelip. 2 lip [of a wound, a vessel, etc.]. 3 ANAT., BOT., ZOOL. labium. 4 sing.-pl. lips [organ of speech]: morderse los labios, coll. to bite one's tongue; no morderse los labios, coll. to be outspoken.

labor s. labour, toil, work, task. 2 ornamental work. 3 fancywork, embroidery, needlework, etc.: ~ de encaje, lacework; ~ de ganchillo, crocheting. 4 AGR. tillage. 5 ploughing or digging [instance of them]. 6 pl. fancywork, embroidery, needlework, etc. 7 MIN. works, workings. 8 labores del campo, farming, farm work.

laborable adj. workable. 2 arable, tillable [ground]. 3 día ~, workday, working day, week day.

laboral adj. [pertaining to] labour.

laborar tr. to work. 2 intr. ~ por, en favor de, to work or scheme to some end.

laboratorio m. laboratory.

laborear tr. to work, fashion. 2 to till [land]. 3 to work [a mine]. 4 intr. NAUT. to reeve, run.

laboreo m. AGR. tillage. 2 MIN. working, development. 3 NAUT. reeving, running.

laboriosidad f. laboriousness, industriousness.

laborioso, -sa adj. laborious, industrious, fond of working. 2 laborious, arduous, painful.

laborismo m. British Labour party.

laborista adj. Labour [of the Labour party]. 2 m. f. Labourist, Laborite.

labra f. working, carving, cutting [of stone, wood, metal, etc.].

labrado, -da adj. AGR. tilled. 2 wrought, fashioned.

3 cut, carved [stone, etc.]. 4 WEAV. figured. 5 m. LABRA. 6 pl. tilled fields.

Labrador (Tierra del) f. pr. n. GEOG. Labrador.

labrador, -ra adj. tilling. 2 peasant. 3 m. tiller, ploughman. 4 m.-f. peasant.

labradorita f. MIN. labradorite.

labrantín m. petty farmer, small farmer.

labrantío, -a adj. arable, tillable. 2 m. tillable land.

labranza f. cultivation, farming, husbandry. 2 farm, farm land.

labrar tr. to work, fashion, carve, cut, dress. 2 to plough, till, cultivate. 3 to figure [a fabric]. 4 to build, erect. 5 to cause, build, bring about: ~ una reputación, to build a reputation.

labriego, -ga m.-f. rustic, peasant.

labro s. ZOOL. labrum. 2 ICHTH. wrasse.

labrusca f. BOT. wild grapevine.

laburno m. BOT. laburnum.

laca f. lac, gum lac, shellac. 2 lacquer [varnish; article]; japan. 3 lake [pigment].

lacayo m. lackey, lacquey, footman, groom.

lacayuno, -na adj. lackeylike, servile.

lacear tr. to trim or tie with bows. 2 to snare [small game].

Lacedemonia f. pr. n. HIST. GEOG. Lacedaemon.

lacedemonio, -nia adj.-n. Lacedaemonian.

laceración f. laceration.

lacerado, -da adj. lacerated. 2 wretched, unhappy.

lacerar tr. to lacerate. 2 to hurt, damage [the reputation, etc.].

lacería f. poverty, want. 2 trouble, hardship.

lacería f. ARCH. ornament, imitating bows.

lacero m. lassoer. 2 dogcatcher.

lacertoso, -sa adj. muscular, brawny, robust.

lacinia f. BOT. lacinia.

lacio, -cia adj. withered. 2 flaccid, flabby, languid. 3 straight, lank [hair].

lacónico, -ca adj. laconic.

Laconia f. pr. n. HIST., GEOG. Laconia.

laconio, -nia adj.-n. Laconian.

laconismo m. laconism.

lacra f. mark of trace left by illness. 2 fault, defect.

lacrar tr. to injure the health of; to infect with a disease. 2 to seal [with sealing wax].

lacre m. sealing wax.

lacrimal adj. lachrymal.

lacrimatorio, -ria adj.-m. lachrymatory.

lacrimógeno, -na adj. lachrymogenic.

lacrimoso, -sa *adj.* lachrymose, tearful.
lactación *f.* sucking [of mother's milk].
lactancia *f.* LACTACIÓN. *2* lactation.
lactante *adj.* sucking [child]. *2* suckling, nursing. *3 m.-f.* suckling, sucking child. *4 f.* mother or nurse giving suck.
lactar *tr.* to lactate, suckle. *2 intr.* to suck.
lactario, -ria *adj.* milky.
lactasa *f.* BIOCHEM. lactase.
lácteo, -a *adj.* lacteal, lacteous. *2* milky.
lactescente *adj.* lactescent.
lacticinio *m.* milk or milk food.
láctico, -ca *adj.* CHEM. lactic.
lactosa *f.* CHEM. lactose.
lacustre *adj.* lacustrine.
lacha *f.* ICHTH. anchovy. *2* coll. *tener poca ~*, to be shameless; to be silly, dull.
ladear *tr.* to tilt, tip, lean or incline [something] to one side. *2* to turn [something] sideways. *3 intr.* to go round the hillside. *4* to deviate. *5 ref.-intr.* [of something] to tilt, tip, lean or incline to one side; to turn sideways. *6 ref.* to incline [to an opinion, party, etc.].
ladeo *m.* tilting, tipping, inclination to one side.
ladera *f.* slope, hillside, mountainside.
ladilla *f.* ENT. crab louse.
ladino, -na *adj.* sagacious, cunning, sly. *2* speaking foreign languages.
lado *m.* side: *dejar a un ~*, to leave or set aside, *ponerse al ~ de*, to take sides with; *al ~*, close by, near by; next door; *al ~ de*, beside; *~ a ~*, side by side; *por todos lados*, on all sides. *2* hand, way: *por otro ~*, on the other hand; *por un ~ ... por otro ~*, on the one hand... on the other hand. *2* room, space: *hacer ~*, to make room. *4* favour, protection. *5 pl.* patrons, protectors; advisers.
ladra *f.* barking.
ladrador, -ra *adj.* barking.
ladrar *intr.* [of a dog] to bark. *2* coll. to bark [threaten idly]: *~ a la luna*, to bark at the moon.
ladrido *m.* bark, barking [of dogs]. *2* coll. backbiting, slander.
ladrillar *m.* brickyard.
ladrillazo *m.* blow with a brick.
ladrillero *m.* brick maker. *2* brick seller.
ladrillo *m.* brick, tile. *2 ~ de chocolate*, cake of chocolate.
ladrón, -na *adj.* thieving, thievish. *2 m.-f.* thief, robber, burglar.
ladronear *intr.* to thieve, go about thieving.
ladronera *f.* den of thieves.
ladronicio *m.* LATROCINIO.
ladronzuelo, -la *m.-f.* young thief. *2* pickpocket, pilferer, petty thief.
lagar *m.* wine press; olive press; apple press.
lagarta *f.* ZOOL. female lizard. *2* ENT. gypsy moth. *3* coll. cunning, sly woman.
lagartera *s.* lizard hole.
lagartija *f.* ZOOL. green lizard; wall lizard.
lagarto *m.* ZOOL. lizard. *2* coll. cunning, sly fellow.
lago *m.* lake [body of water].
lagotear *intr.-tr.* to flatter, cajole.
lagotería *f.* flattery, cajolery.
lagotero, -ra *adj.* flattering. *2 m.-f.* flatterer, cajoler.
lágrima *f.* tear, teardrop: *lágrimas de cocodrilo*, crocodile tears; *llorar a ~ viva*, to shed bitter tears. *2* tear, drop [of sap; of a liquor]. *3* BOT. *lágrimas de David*, or *de Job*, Job's-tears.
lagrimal *adj.* lachrymal. *2 m.* ANAT., ZOOL. medial angle of the eye.

lagrimear *intr.* to shed tears frequently.
lagrimeo *m.* frequent shedding of tears.
lagrimón *m.* large tear.
lagrimoso, -sa *adj.* LACRIMOSO. *2* watery [eye].
laguna *f.* small lake, lakelet. *2* lagoon. | Esp. in *~ de Venecia*, lagoon of Venice. *3* lacuna, blank, gap.
lagunajo *m.* pool, puddle.
lagunar *m.* ARCH. lacunar, caisson.
laical *adj.* laical.
laicidad *f.* laicity. *2* LAICISMO.
laicismo *m.* laicism, secularism.
laicizar *tr.* to laicize, secularize.
laico, -ca *adj.* laic, lay. *2* secularistic. *3 m.-f.* laic.
laja *f.* LANCHA. *2* NAUT. stone flat.
lama *f.* slime, silt, ooze. *2* gold or silver tissue. *3 m.* lama [Tibetan monk].
lamaísmo *m.* Lamaism.
lamasería *f.* lamasery.
lambda *f.* lambda [Greek letter].
lambrequín *m.* HER. lambrequin, mantling.
lamedal *m.* miry place.
lamedor, -ra *adj.* licking. *2 m.-f.* licker.
lamedura *f.* [act of] licking.
lamelibranquio, -quia *adj.-n.* ZOOL. lamellibranch.
lamelicornio, nia *adj.-n.* ENT. lamellicorn.
lamentable *adj.* lamentable, deplorable, pitiable.
lamentación *f.* lamentation, lament, wail.
lamentar *tr.* to lament, deplore, regret, be sorry for. *2 ref.* to lament, wail. *3* to complain.
lamento *m.* lament, lamentation, wail.
lamentoso, -sa *adj.* lamentable, doleful.
lamer *tr.* to lick, lap.
lamerón, -na *adj.* GOLOSO.
lametón *m.* greedy licking.
lamia *f.* MYTH. lamia. *2* ICHTH. shark.
lamido, -da *adj.* licked. *2* lean, pale [person]. *3* affected, prim, overnice.
lámina *f.* lamina, sheet, plate. *2* BOT., ZOOL. lamina. *3* copperplate, engraving plate. *4* engraving, cut, plate, print, picture [printed copy].
laminado, -da *adj.* laminate. *2* laminated, rolled [metal]. *3* lamination, rolling [of metals].
laminador *m.* rolling mill. *2* metal roller.
1) **laminar** *tr.* to laminate, roll [metals]. *2* to laminate [cover with laminae].
2) **laminar** *adj.* laminal, laminar.
lamiscar *tr.* coll. to lick greedily.
lampacear *tr.* NAUT. to swab.
lámpara *f.* lamp, light: *~ de Aladino*, Aladin's lamp; *~ de seguridad*, safety lamp; *~ de pie*, floor lamp; *~ de sobremesa*, table lamp; *~ de soldar*, blowtorch; *~ piloto*, pilot lamp. *2* RADIO. tube, valve. *3* grease stain [on clothing].
lamparería *f.* lamp factory or shop. *2* lamp store.
lamparilla *f. dim.* small lamp. *2* night lamp. *3* BOT. aspen. *4* (Am.) electric light bulb.
lamparín *m.* bracket or suspended circle for holding a small lamp [in churches].
lamparón *m.* grease stain [on clothing]. *2* MED. scrofula [in the neck]. *3* VET. a disease of horses.
lampazo *m.* BOT. burdock. *2* (Mex.) BOT. water lily. *3* NAUT. swab, mop.
lampiño, -ña *adj.* beardless. *2* BOT. hairless.
lampo *m.* poet. flash of light.
lamprea *f.* ICHTH. lamprey.
lampuga *f.* ICHTH. yellow mackerel.
lana *f.* wool [of sheep, alpaca, etc.], fleece. *2* wool [yarn, garment, cloth].
lanar *adj.* wool-bearing: *ganado ~*, sheep [collectively].

lance *m.* throw, cast. *2* catch [fish caught]. *3* critical situation; event, episode, incident, affair: ~ *de honor,* affair of honour, duel. *4* move, turn, situation [in a game]. *5* BULLF. a skilled play of the cape. *6 de* ~, secondhand.
lancear *tr.* ALANCEAR.
lanceolado, -da *adj.* BOT. lanceolate.
lancera *f.* rack for lances.
lancero *m.* lancer. *2* spearman. *3* rack for lances. *5 pl.* lancers [dance and music].
lanceta *f.* SURG. lancet.
lancinante *adj.* piercing [pain].
lancinar *tr.* to lancinate.
lancurdia *f.* ICHTH. small trout.
lancha *f.* NAUT. launch, boat. *2* flagstone, stone naturally flat and thin.
lanchada *f.* boatload.
lanchero *m.* launchman, boatman.
lanchón *m.* NAUT. large launch, barge, lighter.
landa *f.* moor, waste land.
landgrave *m.* landgrave.
landó *m.* landau [carriage].
landre *f.* small tumor [in glands of neck, armpit or groin]. *2* hidden pocket.
lanería *f.* wool shop. *2* woolen goods.
lanero, -ra *adj.* wool: *industria lanera,* wool industry. *2* ORN. *halcón* ~, lanner. *3 m.* dealer in wool.
langosta *f.* ENT. locust. *2* ZOOL. lobster, spiny lobster.
langostín, langostino *m.* ZOOL. a salt-water prawn.
langostón *m.* ENT. a large green grasshopper.
languidecer *intr.* to languish; to pine away. ¶ CONJUG. like *agradecer.*
languidez *f.* languidness, languor.
languidezco, languidezca, etc. *irr.* V. LANGUIDECER.
lánguido, -da *adj.* languid, faint, weak.
lanífero, -ra *adj.* poet. laniferous, woolly.
lanificación *f.* lanicio *m.* woolwork.
lanilla *f.* nap of cloth. *2* a light woollen fabric.
lanosidad *f.* BOT. down, pubescence.
lanoso, -sa *adj.* woolly.
lansquenete *m.* lansquenet [soldier].
lanudo, -da *adj.* wooly, fleecy.
lanza *f.* lance, spear: *correr lanzas,* to joust with lances; ~ *en ristre,* with the lance in rest; ready for action. *2* [in the Middle Ages] lance, lancer. *3* pole, tongue [of a carriage]. *4* nozzle [of a hose].
lanzabombas, *pl.* -bas *s.* AER. bomb release. *2* MIL. bomb thrower.
lanzacabos *adj.* NAUT. *cañón* ~, lifesaving gun.
lanzacohetes, *pl.* -tes *m.* MIL. rocket launcher.
lanzada *f.* thrust with a lance.
lanzadera *f.* WEAV., SEW. shuttle.
lanzador, -ra *m.-f.* thrower: ~ *de disco,* discus thrower. *2* BASEBALL pitcher.
lanzallamas, *pl.* -mas *m.* MIL. flame thrower.
lanzamiento *m.* cast, fling, hurl, throw. *2* NAUT. launching [of a boat]. *3* LAW eviction, dispossession. *4* NAUT. rake [of the stern].
lanzaminas *m.* mine layer, mine-laying boat.
lanzar *tr.* to throw, cast, dart, fling, hurl. *2* to launch [a boat, an attack, a new product, etc.]. *3* to cast [a glance]. *4* LAW to evict, dispossess. *6 ref.* to throw oneself, to rush, dart, launch [into, out, etc.], to jump. *7* SPORT. to sprint.
lanzatorpedos *adj.* torpedo tube.
Lanzarote *m. pr. n.* Lancelot [of Round Table].
laña *f.* clamp, clamper, staple. *2* green coconut.
lañar *tr.* to mend or strengthen with clampers.

lapa *f.* ZOOL. limpet. *2* BOT. burdock [genus *Lappa*].
lapachar *m.* swamp, marsh.
lapicero *m.* pencil holder. *2* LÁPIZ 1.
lápida *f.* tablet [for an inscription], mural tablet, memorial stone: ~ *sepulcral,* gravestone.
lapidación *f.* lapidation, stoning to death.
lapidar *tr.* to lapidate, stone to death.
lapidario, -ria *adj.* lapidary. *2 m.* lapidary. *3* dealer in gems.
lapidificar *tr.* to lapidify.
lapislázuli *m.* MINER. lapis lazuli.
lápiz, *pl.* -ces *m.* pencil [for drawing or writing]; crayon: ~ *tinta,* indelible pencil. *2* ~ *para los labios,* lipstick.
lapo *m.* coll. blow with a cane; blow with the flat of a sword. *2* coll. drink, swallow.
lapón, -na *adj.* Lappish. *2 m.-f.* Lapp, Laplander. *3 m.* Lappish [language].
Laponia *f. pr. n.* GEOG. Lapland.
lapso *m.* lapse [interval of time]. *2* fall, lapse, slip.
lar *m.* lares *m.* MYTH. lar. *2* fireplace. *3 pl.* home [house; family].
lardar, lardear *tr.* COOK. to baste.
lardo *m.* bacon fat. *2* fat [of an animal].
lardoso, -sa *adj.* greasy, oily.
larga *f.* longest biliard cue. *2* BULLF. play of cape, executed by holding it extended lenghtwise. *3 pl.* delay: *dar largas a,* to delay, put off.
largamente *adv.* at lenght, at large. *2* long, for a long time. *3* amply, largely. *4* liberally.
largar *tr.* to let go. *2* to utter, deliver [a speech]. *3* to deal, deliver [a blow]. *4* to heave [a sigh]. *5* NAUT. to let go, pay out. *6* NAUT. to unfurl. *7 ref.* to get out, leave: *¡lárgate!,* get out!
1) largo *adv.* largely, extendedly. *2 m.* long, length: *ocho metros de* ~, eight metres long. *3* MUS. largo. *4 pasar de* ~, to pass by, without stopping; to pass over, disregard. *5 ponerse de* ~, [of a young woman] to come out, debut. *6 interj. ¡largo!, ¡largo de ahí!,* get out!, get out of here!
2) largo, -ga *adj.* long: *traje* or *vestido* ~, evening dress, evening gown [for women]; ~ *de lengua,* fig. loose-tongued; ~ *de manos,* fig. ready-handed; ~ *de uñas,* fig. lightfingered, thievish; *a la larga,* lengthwise; in the long run; at lenght; *a lo* ~, lengthwise; far away; *a lo* ~ *de,* along, lengthwise of; throughout; *cuán* ~ *es* or *era,* at full length, stretched out. *2* extended, prolonged. *3* liberal, generous. *4* copious, abundant. *5* shrewd, cunning. *6* NAUT. loose, free. *7 adj. pl.* many; odd: *largos años,* many years; *veinte millas largas,* twenty-odd miles.
largor *m.* length.
larguero *m.* CARP. jamp post; upright; sidepiece. *2* AER. longueron, spar. *3* bolster [long pillow].
largueza *f.* liberality, generosity. *2* length.
larguirucho, -cha *adj.* coll. tall and lean, lanky.
largura *f.* length.
laringe *f.* ANAT. larynx.
laríngeo, -a *adj.* laryngeal.
laringitis *f.* MED. laryngitis.
laringoscopio *m.* laryngoscope.
larva *f.* ZOOL. larva.
larvado, -da *adj.* MED. larvate(d.
las *def. art. f. pl.* the. *2* ~ *que,* those, or they, which. *3 pron. pers. f. pl.* [direct object] them: ~ *vi,* I saw them.
lasca *f.* chip [from a stone].
lascar *tr.* NAUT. to ease away, pay out.
lascivia *f.* lasciviousness, lewdness.

lascivo, -va *adj.* lascivious, lewd, lustful. *2* wanton, playful [wind, etc.].
lasitud *f.* lassitude, weariness, languor.
laso, -sa *adj.* wearied, weak, languid.
lástima *f.* pity, compassion: *dar*, or *hacer* ~, to be pitiful. *2* pitiful object: *estar hecho una* ~, to be in a pitiable state. *3* plaint, lamentation. *4 es* ~, it is a pity; too bad; *qué* ~, what a pity!
lastimado, -da *adj.* hurt, injured, sore.
lastimadura *f.* hurt, bruise, injure.
lastimar *tr.* to hurt, injure, damage; to bruise. *2* to pity. *3 ref.* to hurt oneself. *4* to feel sorry for. *5* to complain, lament.
lastimero, -ra *adj.* doleful, plaintive, sad, sorrowful, mournful. *2* hurtful.
lastimoso, -sa *adj.* pitiful, sad.
lastra *f.* LANCHA 2.
lastrar *tr.* NAUT., AER. to ballast.
lastre *m.* NAUT., AER. & fig. ballast.
lata *f.* tin plate [tinned iron plate]. *2* tin, can; can of tinned food: *en* ~, canned, tinned. *3* lath [strip of wood]. *4* bore [tedious speech, performance, etc.]: *dar la* ~, to bore.
latamente *adv.* at great lenght. *2* broadly.
lataz, *pl.* **-taces** *s.* ZOOL. sea otter.
latente *adj.* latent.
lateral *adj.* side, lateral.
lateranense *adj.* Lateran.
latido *m.* beat, throb, pulsation [of the heart, the arteries, etc.]. *2* yelp [of dog].
latiente *adj.* beating, throbbing.
latifundio *m.* large landed estate, latifundium.
latifundista *m.-f.* owner of a large landed estate.
latigazo *m.* lash [with a whip, etc.]. *2* crack of a whip. *3* unexpected hurt or damage.
látigo *m.* whip, horsewhip. *2* lash [part of a whip]. *3* cinch strap.
latiguear *intr.* to crack a whip.
latiguera *f.* cinch strap.
latiguillo *m.* small whip. *2* BOT. stolon. *3* claptrap, declamatory affectation [of an actor or speaker].
latín *m.* Latin [tongue]: ~ *de cocina*, dog Latin; *saber mucho* ~, fig. to be very shrewd. *2* Latin word or quotation.
latinajo *m.* dog Latin. *2* Latin word or quotation.
latinidad *f.* Latin [tongue]. *2* Latinity.
latiniparla *f.* language excessively interspersed with Latinisms or Latin words.
latinismo *m.* Latinism, latinism.
latinista *m.-f.* Latinist.
latinizar *tr.-intr.* to Latinize.
latino, -na *adj.* Latin. *2* NAUT. lateen [sail, rig]. *3 m.-f.* Latin [person].
latir *intr.* to beat, throb, pulsate. *2* [of a dog] to yelp, bark.
latitud *f.* breadth, width; extent. *2* GEOG., ASTR. latitude. *3* fig. latitude [climate, region].
latitudinal *adj.* latitudinal.
lato, -ta *adj.* broad, wide, large. *2* broad [meaning of word].
latón *m.* brass [alloy of copper and zinc].
latonero *m.* brassworker, brazier.
latoso, -sa *adj.* annoying boring.
latria *f.* THEOL. latria.
laucha *f.* (Am.) mouse.
laúd *m.* MUS. lute. *2* NAUT. catboat. *3* ZOOL. leatherback [turtle].
laudable *adj.* laudable, praiseworthy.
láudano *m.* PHARM. laudanum.
laudatorio, -ria *adj.* laudatory. *2 f.* eulogy.

laude *f.* inscribed tombstone. *2 pl.* ECCL. lauds.
laudo *m.* LAW award or finding of an arbitrator.
lauráceo, -a *adj.* laurellike. *2* BOT. lauraceous.
laureado, -da *adj.* laureate; laurelled.
laurear *tr.* to laureate; to honour, reward.
lauredal *m.* plantation of laurel trees.
laurel *m.* BOT. laurel. *2 pl.* fig. laurels.
láureo, -a *adj.* laurel [of laurel, made of laurel].
lauréola *f.* laurel wreath. *2* BOT. *lauréola* or ~ *macho*, daphne; ~ *hembra*, mezereon.
lauro *m.* BOT. laurel. *2* fig. laurel, glory.
lauroceraso *m.* BOT. cherry laurel.
lava *f.* lava. *2* MIN. washing.
lavable *adj.* washable.
lavabo *m.* washstand. *2* washroom; lavatory. *3* LITURG. Lavabo.
lavacaras *m.-f.* coll. flatterer.
lavadero *m.* washing place. *2* laundry.
lavado *adj.* washed. *2 m.* wash, washing, cleaning. *3* PAINT. water colour in a single tint.
lavador, -ra *adj.* washing. *2 m.-f.* washer, cleaner. *3 f.* washing machine.
lavadura *f.* LAVAMIENTO. *2* LAVAZAS.
lavaje *m.* washing [of woods]. *2* MED. lavage.
lavajo *m.* pool of rain water, water hole.
lavamanos *m.* washbasin.
lavamiento *m.* wash, washing, cleaning.
lavandera *f.* laundress, laundrywoman, washerwoman. *2* ORN. sandpiper.
lavandería *f.* (Am.) laundry.
lavandero *m.* launderer, laundryman.
lavándula *f.* BOT. lavender.
lavaplato, *pl.* **-tos** *m.-f.* dishwasher.
lavar *tr.* to wash, clean. *2* to cleanse, to purify. *3* to colour [a drawing] with water colour. *4 ref.* to wash oneself, to wash up.
lavativa *f.* clyster, enema, injection. *2* syringe, enema [apparatus]. *3* fig. bother, annoyance.
lavatorio *m.* lavation, wash, washing. *2* lavatory, washbasin. *3* PHARM. lotion. *4* ECCL. maundy. *5* LITURG. lavatory.
lavazas *f. pl.* wash water, slops.
lave *m.* MIN. washing.
lavotear *tr.* to wash hurriedly.
lavoteo *m.* hurried washing.
laxación *f.*, **laxamiento** *m.* laxation, loosening.
laxante *adj.* laxing, loosening. *2 m.* MED. laxative.
laxar *tr.* to laxate, loosen. *2* MED. to loosen the intestines. *3* MED. to give a laxative to.
laxitud *f.* laxity, laxness.
laxo, -xa *adj.* lax, slack. *2* lax [loose in morals].
lay *m.* lay [poem].
laya *f.* AGR. spade; spud. *2* kind, class, nature.
layar *tr.* AGR. to spade, spud.
lazada *f.* bowknot. *2* bow [ornamental knot].
lazar *tr.* to lasso.
lazareto *m.* lazaretto [for quarantine; for lepers].
lazarillo *m.* blind-person's guide.
lazarista *m.* Lazarist, Lazarite.
Lázaro *m. pr. n.* Lazarus.
lazo *m.* bow, knot [ornamental knot], truelove knot, hair knot. *2* ARCH. knot. *3* bowknot. *4* tie, bond. *5* snare [for small game]. *6* snare, trap [for persons]: *tender un* ~ *a*, to set a trap for. *7* lasso, lariat. *8* ~ *corredizo*, running knot.
lazulita *f.* MINER. lazulite. *2* MINER. lapis lazuli.
le *pers. pron. m. sing.* him [direct object]. *2 pers. pron. m. & f. sing.* him, her, it, to him, to her, to it [indirect object].
leal *adj.* loyal. *2* faithful [servant, dog, etc.]. *3* fair

[procceding]. *4 según mi ~ saber y entender*, to the best of my knowledge.
lealtad *f.* loyalty. *2* fidelity. *3* fairness.
Leandro *m. pr. n.* Leander.
lebrato, lebratón *m.* young hare, leveret.
lebrel *m.* hare-huntig dog.
lebrero, -ra *adj.* hare-hunting. *2 m.* harehound.
lebrillo *m.* metal or earthenware washtub.
lebruno, -na *adj.* leporine, harelike.
lección *f.* lesson: *dar la ~*, to recite one's lesson; *dar una ~ a*, to give or teach a lesson to. *2* ECCL. lection. *3* lecture, reading.
leccionario *m.* ECCL. lectionary.
leccioncita *f. dim.* short lecture or lesson.
lecitina *f.* BIOCHEM. lecithin.
lectivo, -va *adj.* school [day, year, etc.].
lector, -ra *m.-f.* reader. *2* ECCL. lector. *3* lecturer [in Colleges, etc.].
lectorado *m.* ECCL. lectorate.
lectura *f.* reading, lecture. *2* reading [interpretation of a passage]. *3* PRINT. pica.
lecha *f.* ICHTH. milt [secretion and gland].
lechada *f.* grout; whitewash. *2* pulp of rags. *3* liquid containing finely divided solids in suspension.
lechal *adj.* sucking [lamb, calf, etc.]. *2* milky [plant]. *3 m.* milk [of a plant].
leche *f.* milk [secreted by female mammals]: *~ condensada*, condensed milk; *~ desnatada*, skim milk; *~ en polvo*, milk powder. *3* milk [preparation]: *~ de almendras*, milk of almonds.
lechecillas *f. pl.* sweetbread. *2* liver and lights.
lechera *adj.* milch: *vaca ~*, milch cow. *2 f.* dairymaid, milk seller. *3* milk can, milk jug, milk pot.
lechería *f.* dairy [shop].
lechero, -ra *adj.* milk, milky. *2 m.* milkman, dairyman.
lechetrezna *f.* BOT. sun spurge.
lechigada *f.* litter [young brought forth at a birth]. *2* coll. gang, lot.
lechino *m.* SURG. dossil.
lecho *m.* bed, couch. *2* bed [of a river, lake, etc.]. *3* bed, layer. *4* GEOL. stratum. *5* MAS. bed [of a stone in position].
lechón, -na *adj.* dirty, sluttish. *2 m.* sucking pig. *3* pig, hog. *4* fig. pig [dirty man]. *5 f.* sow [female hog; dirty woman].
lechoso, -sa *adj.* milky.
lechuga *f.* BOT. lettuce.
lechuguilla *f.* BOT. wild lettuce. *2* ruff; frill.
lechuguina *f.* stylish young lady.
lechuguino, -na *adj.* dandified, stylish. *2 m.* young dandy or dude. *3* small lettuce.
lechuza *f.* ORN. barn owl, screeching owl.
lechuzo, -za *adj.* sucking [mule]. *2 m.* coll. bill collector, summons server.
ledo, -da *adj.* joyful, cheerful, placid.
leer *tr.-intr.* to read. *2 ref.* to read, to be read: *este libro se lee fácilmente*, this book reads easily.
lega *f.* ECCL. lay sister.
legacía *f.* legateship.
legación *f.* legation.
legado *m.* LAW legacy, bequest. *2* legate.
legajo *m.* bundle of papers; dossier, file.
legal *adj.* legal, lawful.
legalidad *f.* legality, lawfulness. *2* political regime as established by the constitution of the State.
legalismo *m.* legalism.
legalización *f.* legalization. *2* attestation of the authenticity of a signature.

legalizar *tr.* to legalize. *2* to attest the authenticity of [a signature].
légamo *m.* mud, silt, slime.
legaña *f.* rheum, gummy secretion of the eyelids.
legañoso, -sa *adj.* blear-eyed.
legar *tr.* to legate, bequeath. *2* to send as a legate.
legatario, -ria *m.-f.* LAW legatee.
legenda *f.* legend [saint's life].
legendario, -ria *adj.-m.* legendary.
legible *adj.* legible, readable.
legión *f.* legion.
legionario, -ria *adj.-n.* legionary.
legislación *f.* legislation [body of laws]. *2* science of laws.
legislador, -ra *adj.* legislating, legislative. *2 m.* legislator. *3 f.* legislatress.
legislar *tr.* to legislate.
legislativo, -va *adj.* legislative.
legislatura *f.* term or session of a legislature.
legista *m.* legist. *2* law student.
legítima *f.* LAW legitim.
legitimación *f.* legitimation.
legitimar *tr.* to legitimate.
legitimidad *f.* legitimacy. *2* genuineness.
legitimista *adj.-n.* legitimist.
legítimo, -ma *adj.* legitimate. *2* lawful. *3* genuine.
lego, -ga *adj.* lay [person]. *2* ignorant, uninformed. *3 m.* laic, layman. *4* lay brother. *5 f.* lay sister.
legra *f.* SURG. scraper.
legua *f.* league [measure of distance]: *a la ~*, *de cien leguas*, from far off, a great distance.
leguleyo *m.* pettifogger, petty lawyer.
legumbre *f.* legume, pod fruit. *2 pl.* pulse, vegetables.
leguminoso, -sa *adj.* BOT. leguminous.
leíble *adj.* legible, readable.
leído, -da *p. p.* de LEER. *2 adj.* well-read, well-informed.
lejanía *f.* distance, remoteness, distant place.
lejano, -na *adj.* distant, remote, far.
lejas *adj. pl. de ~ tierras*, from distant lands.
lejía *f.* lye. *2* coll. dressing down, reprimand.
lejitos *adv. dim.* pretty far, rather far.
lejos *adv.* far, far away, far off, a long way off, afar: *estar ~ de*, to be far from; *~ de mí*, fig. far be it from me: *a lo ~*, in the distance, far away; *de ~*, *desde ~*, from afar. *2* appearance at a distance: *tener buen ~*, to look good at a distance. *3* PAINT. distant view, background.
lelo, -la *adj.* stupid, dull. *2 m.-f.* simpleton, ninny. *3 estar ~ por*, to dote upon.
lema *m.* lemma. *2* motto. *3* slogan.
lemniscata *f.* GEOM. lemniscate.
lemnisco *m.* lemniscus.
lemosín, -na *adj.* of the Limousin. *2* Limousin language.
lémur *m.* ZOOL. lemur.
lémures *m. pl.* MYTH. lemures.
len *adj.* soft, flossy [thread or silk].
lencería *f.* linen goods. *2* linen trade. *3* linendraper's shop. *4* linen room.
lencero *m.* linen draper, linen merchant.
lendrera *f.* comb for removing nits or lice.
lene *adj.* soft, light, sweet, pleasant.
lengua *f.* tongue [organ in the mouth: faculty of, or tendence in, speech]: *las malas lenguas*, the gossips; *andar en lenguas*, to be much talked of; *hacerse lenguas de*, to praise highly; *írsele a uno la ~*, to say more than one wishes, to blab; *no morderse la ~*, to speak out, not to mince words; *tirar de la ~ a uno*, to draw out a person; *trabár-*

sele a uno la ~, to become tongue-tied; *tener en la punta de la* ~, .to have on the tip of one's tongue. *2* tongue, language: ~ *madre*, mother language or tongue [tongue from wich others spring]; ~ *materna*, mother tongue [one's native tongue]; ~ *viva*, living language. *3* tongue, clapper [of a bell]. *4* tongue [of land, of fire]. *5* tongue, index [of a balance or scale]. *6* BOT. ~ *canina* or *de perro*, hound's tongue; ~ *de ciervo*, hart's-tongue; ~ *de buey*, bugloss.

lenguado *m.* ICHTH. sole.

lenguaje *m.* language. *2* tongue, parlance, speech.

lenguaraz, *pl.* **-races** *adj.* accomplished in languages. *2* foul-mouthed; impudent, insolent.

lenguaz, *pl.* **-guaces** *adj.* garrulous.

lengüecica, -cilla, -cita *f. dim.* small tongue.

lengüeta *f.* small tongue. *2* ANAT. epiglottis. *3* tongue, index [of balance or scale]. *4* MUS. tongue, reed. *5* barb [of an arrow, etc.]. *6* CARP. tongue. *7* MEC. tongue, feather.

lengüetada *f.* licking, lapping.

lengüetería *f.* MUS. reedwork, reed stops [of an organ].

lengüillargo, -ga *adj.* bold, impudent.

lenidad *f.* lenity.

lenificar *tr.* to soften, assuage.

Leningrado *m. pr. n.* GEOG. Leningrad.

lenitivo, -va *adj.-m.* lenitive.

lenocinio *m.* pandering: *casa de* ~, brothel.

lente *m.-f.* OPT. lens. *2* OPT. glass: ~ *de aumento*, magnifying glass. *3 m. pl.* eyeglasses, nose glasses.

lentecer *intr.-ref.* to soften, grow soft. ¶ CONJUG. like *agradecer.*

lenteja *f.* BOT. lentil. *2* bob or disk of a pendulum.

lentejuela *f.* spangle, sequin [stitched on a dress].

lenticular *adj.* lenticular. *2 m.* ANAT. lenticular ossicle.

lentisco *m.* BOT. mastic tree.

lentitud *f.* slowness, sluggishness.

lento, -ta *adj.* slow. *2* sluggish, tardy, heavy. *3 adj.-adv.* MUS. lento.

leña *f.* firewood, kindling wood: *echar* ~ *al fuego*, fig. to add fuel to the flame. *2* beating, drubbing: **leñador, -ra** *m.-f.* firewood dealer. *2 m.* woodman. *3 f.* woodwoman.

leñazo *m.* blow with a cudgel.

leñera *f.* woodshed; woodbin; woodpile.

leñero *m.* firewood seller. *2* LEÑERA.

leño *m.* log [unhewn piece of felled tree]. *2* wood [substance]. *3* NAUT. a medieval vessel. *4* poet. boat, ship, vessel. *5* fig. dullard.

leñoso, -sa *adj.* ligneous, woody.

Leo *m. pr. n.* ASTR. Leo.

León *m. pr. n.* Leon [man's name]. *2* ASTR. Leo. *3* GEOG. León [a Spanish town and province].

león *m.* ZOOL. lion: ~ *de Nemea*, MYTH. Nemean lion. *2* fig. lion [bold, brave man]. *3* ENT. lion ant. *4* ZOOL. ~ *marino*, sea lion.

leona *f.* lioness. *2* fig. brave, haughty woman.

leonado, -da *adj.* lion-coloured, tawny, fulvous.

Leonardo *m. pr. n.* Leonard.

leoncico, cillo, cito *m. dim.* little lion, lion cub.

leonera *f.* cage or den of lions. *2* coll. gambling den. *3* coll. den, junk room.

leonero *m.* lion keeper.

leonés, -sa *adj.-n.* of León.

leonino, -na *adj.* leonine. *2* one-sided, unfair. *3 f.* MED. leontiasis.

Leonor *f. pr. n.* Eleanor, Leonora, Leonore.

leontina *f.* watch chain.

leopardo *m.* ZOOL. leopard.

leopoldina *f.* MIL. a Spanish shako.

Leopoldo *m. pr. n.* Leopold.

lepidóptero, -ra *adj.* ENT. lepidopterus.

lepisma *f.* ENT. silver fish.

leporino, -na *adj.* leporine, harelike.

lepra *f.* MED. leprosy.

leproso, -sa *adj.* MED. leprous. *2 m.-f.* leper.

lercha *f.* reed on which fish and birds are strung.

lerdo, -da *adj.* dull, slow-witted. *2* slow, heavy.

leridano, -na *adj.-n.* of Lérida.

les *pers. pron. m.-f. pl.* them, to them, you, to you [indirect object]. *2 pers. pron. m. pl.* them, you' [direct object].

lesbiano, -na; lesbio, -bia *adj.-n.* Lesbian.

lesión *f.* hurt, wound, injury. *2* harm, damage. *3* MED., VET. lesion.

lesionar *tr.* to hurt, wound, injure, damage, harm.

lesivo, -va *adj.* prejudicial, injurious.

lesna *f.* LEZNA.

leso, -sa *adj.* hurt, injured, offended: *lesa majestad*, lese majesty.

letal *adj.* lethal, deadly, mortal.

letanía *f.* ECCL. and fig. litany.

letárgico, -ca *adj.* lethargic.

letargo *m.* lethargy.

Leteo *m. pr. n.* MYTH. Lethe [river].

leteo, -a *adj.* poet. Lethean.

Leticia *f. pr. n.* Letitia.

letificar *tr.* to exhilarate, gladden, cheer.

letífico, -ca *adj.* gladdening, bringing joy.

letón, -na *adj.* Lettish. *2 m.-f.* Lett.

letra *f.* letter [of the alphabet; printing type], character, characters, hand, handwriting: ~ *capital* or *mayúscula*, capital letter; ~ *de molde*, print, printed letter; ~ *menuda*, fine, small writing; fig. cunning, adroitness; ~ *muerta*, dead letter; *tener buena* ~, to write a good hand. *2* line: *cuatro letras*, a few lines. *3* letter [literal meaning]: *al pie de la* ~, to the letter. *4* inscription. *5* words [of a song]. *6* COM. *letra* or ~ *de cambio*, draft, bill of exchange; *a* ~ *vista*, at sight. *7 pl.* letters: *bellas* or *buenas letras*, belles-lettres, literature; *letras humanas*, humanities. *8 primeras letras*, elementary education.

letrado, -da *adj.* lettered, learned, erudite. *2* coll. posing as a learned person. *3 m.-f.* lawyer.

Letrán (San Juan de) *pr. n.* Saint John Lateran [church].

letrero *m.* label. *2* sign [lettered board, etc.]; notice, placard.

letrilla *f.* a kind of Spanish rondelet.

letrina *f.* latrine, privy. *2* fig. filthy place.

leucemia *f.* MED. leukemia.

leucocito *m.* PHYSIOL. leucocyte.

leucoma *f.* MED. leucoma.

leudar *tr.* to leaven, ferment [dough] with yeast. *2* *ref.* [of dough] to yeast, rise, ferment.

leudo, -da *adj.* leavened, fermented [dough, bread].

leva *f.* NAUT. weighing anchor. *2* MIL. levy, press. *3* MACH. lever; cam. *4* vane [of water wheel].

levadizo, -za *adj.* that can be lifted or raised: *puente* ~, drawbridge, lift bridge.

levador *m.* MEC. cog, tooth, cam.

levadura *f.* leaven, yeast.

levantada *f.* getting up [from bed].

levantado, -da *adj.* elevated, raised. *2* elevated, lofty, sublime. *3* up [from bed].

levantamiento *m.* elevation, raising, erection. *2* lifting up. *3* getting up. *4* elevation, sublimity.

5 insurrection, uprising. *6 ~ de planos*, surveying.
levantar *tr.* to raise, lift, lift up, heave, hoist. *2* to raise, set up, build, erect. *3* to take up, pick up, gather. *4* to raise [a blister, the voice, a siege, an army]. *5* to strike, take down [a tent]. *6* HUNT. to rouse, start [game]. *7* to stir, stir up. *8* to incite to rebellion. *9* to cut [cards]. *10* to impute falsely: *~ un falso testimonio*, to bear false witness. *11 ~ acta*, to draw up a formal statement [of a fact]. *12 ~ bandera*, to rebel. *13 ~ cabeza*, to take courage. *14* TOP. *~ el plano de*, to survey. *15 ~ la casa*, to move. *16 ~ la mesa*, to clear the table. *17 ~ la sesión*, to adjourn, rise. *18 ref.* to rise [move upward, ascend; come to life again]. *19* to rise, get up [from bed, chair, etc.]; to stand up. *20* to rise, to rebel. *21* [of spirits] to rise. *22* [of game] to start. *23 levantarse la tapa de los sesos*, to blow out one's brains.
levante *m.* East, Orient. *2* east wind, levanter. *3* Mediterranean regions of Spain. *4* Levant.
levantino, -na *adj.-n.* Levantine. *2* of the Mediterranean regions of Spain.
levantisco, -ca *adj.* turbulent, restless.
levar *tr.* NAUT. to set sail.
leve *adj.* light [not heavy]. *2* slight, trivial, trifling, venial.
levedad *f.* lightness, levity. *2* slightness. *3* inconstancy.
Leví *m. pr. n.* BIBL. Levi.
leviatán *m.* BIBL. & fig. leviathan.
levigar *tr.* to levigate.
levirato *m.* BIBL., HIST. levirate.
levita *m.* BIBL., HIST. Levite. *2 f.* frock-coat.
levitación *f.* levitation.
levítico, -ca *adj.* levitical. *2 m.* (cap.) BIBL. Leviticus.
levitón *m.* heavy frock-coat.
levulosa *f.* CHEM. levulose.
léxico, -ca *adj.* lexical. *2 m.* lexicon. *3* language of a person.
lexicografía *f.* lexicography.
lexicógrafo *m.* lexicographer.
ley *f.* law [body of enacted or customary rules]; law, rule, precept, act, statute; *~ antigua*, Old law, Mosaic law; *~ nueva, de gracia*, Christ's law; *~ del embudo*, coll. one-sided law; *~ escrita*, revealed law, decalogue; *~ marcial*, martial law; *~ seca*, dry law; *con todas las de la ~*, perfect. *2* SCIENCE, ECON. law. *3* religion, dispensation. *4* loyalty, devotion, attachment: *tener* or *tomar ~ a*, to become attached to. *5* legal standard of quality, weight or measure: *de buena ~*, fig. sterling, good; *de mala ~*, fig. bad, low, base. *6* fineness [of coin, metal]: *oro, plata de ~*, fine, sterling gold or silver.
leyenda *f.* legend.
lezna *f.* awl.
Lía *f. pr. n.* BIBL. Leah.
lía *f.* plaited esparto rope. *2 sing.-pl.* lee, dregs.
liar *tr.* to tie, bind, tie up, wrap up. *2* to roll [a cigarette]. *3* coll. to involve, entangle [a person]. *4 liarlas*, coll. to flee, go away; to die. *5 ref.* to embroil oneself. *6* to enter into concubinage.
liásico, -ca *adj.-m.* GEOL. Liassic.
libación *f.* libation.
Líbano *m. pr. n.* GEOG. Lebanon.
libar *tr.* to suck the juice [of flowers, etc.]. *2* to taste, drink [a liquor]. *3 intr.* to make a libation.
libelista *m.* libeler, libelist [writer of libels].

libelo or **libelo infamatorio** *m.* libel [defamatory writing].
libélula *f.* ENT. libellula, dragonfly.
líber *m.* BOT. bast, liber.
liberación *f.* liberation, deliverance, release.
liberal *adj.* liberal, generous. *2 artes liberales*, liberal arts. *3 adj.-n.* POL. liberal.
liberalidad *f.* liberality, generosity.
liberalismo *m.* POL. liberalism. *2* liberal party.
liberalizar *tr.* to liberalize.
libérrimo, -ma *adj. superl.* most free.
libertad *f.* liberty, freedom; *~ de acción*, liberty of action; *~ de cultos*, freedom of worship; *~ de imprenta*, freedom of the press; *~ provisional*, liberation on bail; *poner en ~*, to set free; *en ~*, at liberty. *2* liberty [setting aside of rules; licence]. *3* liberty, freedom [undue familiarity]: *tomarse libertades*, to make free with. *4* freedom, ease [in action]. *5* free an easy manners. *6 pl.* liberties, privileges.
libertado, -da *adj.* freed. *2* free, unrestrained. *3* free, bold, forward.
libertador, -ra *adj.* liberating, delivering. *2 m.-f.* liberator, deliverer.
libertar *tr.* to set free, liberate, deliver. *2* to free, rid, clear. *3* to exempt [of obligation]. *4* to save, preserve [from death, danger, etc.].
libertario, -ria *adj.* anarchistic. *2 m.-f.* anarchist.
liberticida *adj.* liberticidal. *2 m.-f.* liberticide.
libertinaje *m.* libertinism, libertinage, profligacy.
libertino, -na *adj.-n.* libertine, profligate.
liberto, -ta *adj.-n.* freedman, freedwoman.
Libia *f. pr. n.* GEOG. Lybia.
líbico, -ca *adj.-n.* Lybian.
libídine *f.* lewdness, lust.
libidinoso, -sa *adj.* libidinous, lewd, lustful.
libido *f.* libido.
libio, -bia *adj.-n.* Lybian.
libra *f.* pound [weight; coin]; *~ esterlina*, pound sterling. *2* (cap.) ASTR. Libra.
libración *f.* libration [vibration]. *2* ASTR. libration.
librado, -da *adj. salir bien ~*, to come off well, unscathed; *salir mal ~*, to come off in a bad state. *2 m.-f.* COM. drawee.
librador, -ra *m.-f.* deliverer, preserver. *2* COM. drawer [of a bill of exchange]. *3 m.* grocer's scoop.
libramiento *m.* delivering, preserving. *2* order for payment.
libranza *f.* draft [order for payment of money].
librar *tr.* to free, deliver, save, preserve [from ill, danger, etc.]. *2* to place [one's hopes]. *3* to pass [sentence]. *4* to issue, draw [a bill, a draft, etc.]. *5* to join, give [battle]. *6 ¡Dios me libre!*, God forbid! *7 intr.* to be delivered of a child. *8 a bien ~, a buen ~*, at best. *9 ref. librarse de*, to free oneself of or from; to get rid of; to escape: *de buena nos hemos librado*, we have had a close shave.
librazo *m. aug.* big book.
libre *adj.* free [in practically every sense, except gratuitous and liberal, generous]: *~ albedrío*, free will; *~ cambio*, free change; *~ curso*, free course; *~ de impuestos*, tax free. *2* vacant [place, seat]. *3* disengaged, at leisure. *4* single, unmarried.
librea *f.* livery [worn by a servant].
librecambio *m.* free trade.
librecambista *adj.* free-trading. *2 m.-f.* freetradist, freetrader.
librejo *m.* worthless book.

librepensador, -ra *adj.* freethingking. *2 m.-f.* free thinker.
librepensamiento *m.* free thinking, free thought.
librería *f.* bookcase. *2* bookseller's shop, bookstore. *3* book trade, bookselling.
librero *m.* bookseller.
libreta *f.* notebook: ~ *de la Caja de ahorros,* bankbook [of savings bank]. *2* loaf of bread of 1 lb. weight.
libretista *m.-f.* librettist.
libreto *m.* libretto.
librillo *m.* small book, booklet. *2* small book of cigarette paper.
libro *m.* book: ~ *antifonal* or *antifonario,* antiphonal; ~ *borrador,* COM. blotter, record book; ~ *copiador,* COM. letter book; ~ *de actas,* minute book; ~ *de caballerías,* romance of chivalry; ~ *de caja,* COM. cashbook; ~ *de cocina,* cookbook; ~ *de texto,* textbook; ~ *diario,* COM. daybook; ~ *en rústica,* paperbound book; ~ *mayor,* COM. ledger; *hablar como un* ~, to speak very well. *2* MUS. libretto. *3* ZOOL. abomasum.
librote *m.* large book. *2* trashy book.
licántropo *adj.* lycanthrope.
licencia *f.* license, leave, permission. *2* license [abuse of freedom], licentiousness. *3* EDUC. degree of master or bachelor. *4* [poetic] license. *5* MIL. leave: ~ *absoluta,* discharge.
licenciado, -da *m.-f.* EDUC. licentiate, graduate, holder of the degree of master or bachelor. *2* lawyer. *3* ~ *del ejército,* discharged soldier.
licenciamiento *m.* LICENCIATURA. *2* MIL. discharge [of soldiers].
licenciar *tr.* to give leave or permission. *2* EDUC. to confer the degree of master or bachelor. *3* MIL. to discharge [soldiers]. *4* *ref.* to receive the degree of master or bachelor.
licenciatura *f.* degree of master or bachelor. *2* act of conferring the degree of master or bachelor. *3* studies leading to the graduation with a degree of master or bachelor.
licencioso, -sa *adj.* licentious, dissolute.
liceo *m.* lyceum. *2* name for some clubs.
Licia *f. pr. n.* HIST., GEOG. Lycia.
licitación *f.* bidding [at an auction].
licitador *m.* bidder [at an auction].
licitar *tr.* bid on or for [at an auction].
lícito, -ta *adj.* licit, permitted, lawful, right, just.
licopodio *m.* BOT. lycopodium.
licor *m.* liquor. *2* liqueur.
licorera *f.* cellaret.
licorista *m.-f.* liqueur distiller. *2* liqueur seller.
licoroso, -sa *adj.* generous, rich [wine].
licuación *f.* liquefaction. *2* METAL. liquation.
licuar *tr.* to liquefy. *2* METAL. to liquate. *3* *ref.* to liquefy [become liquid].
licuefacción *f.* liquefaction.
Licurgo *m. pr. n.* Lycurgus.
lid *f.* contest, fight. *2* dispute, argument.
líder *m.* Angl. political leader.
Lidia *f. pr. n.* HIST., GEOG. Lydia.
lidia *f.* fight, struggle. *2* bullfight.
lidiador, -ra *m.-f.* combatant, fighter. *2* bullfighter.
lidiar *intr.* to fight, contend. *2* to struggle. *3* ~ *con,* to face up; to try to cope with. *4* *tr.* to fight [bulls].
liebre *f.* ZOOL. hare. *2* *fig.* coward. *3* ZOOL. ~ *de mar,* sea hare.
Lieja *f. pr. n.* GEOG. Liège.
liendre *f.* nit [egg of louse].

liento, -ta *adj.* damp, moist.
lienzo *m.* [flax, hemp or cotton] cloth; linen. *2* handkerchief. *3* PAINT. canvas. *4* face [of a building]; stretch [of wall]. *5* FORT. curtain.
liga *f.* garter. *2* band, bandage. *3* BOT. mistletoe. *4* birdlime. *5* union, mixture. *6* alloy [of metals]. *7* league, alliance. *8* FOOTBALL. league.
ligado *m.* union of letters in writing. *2* MUS. ligature.
ligadura *f.* tie, bond, ligature. *2* subjection. *3* turn of rope, etc. tying something. *4* MUS. ligature.
ligamaza *f.* viscosity on some fruits or seeds.
ligamento *m.* tying, binding. *2* ANAT. ligament.
ligar *tr.* to tie, bind. *2* to alloy [metals]. *3* to join, unite. *4* to bind, obligate. *5* SURG. to ligate. *6* *ref.* to league together, to enter in a league [with]. *7* to join, combine [be combined]. *8* to bind oneself.
ligazón *f.* union, connection, linking.
ligereza *f.* lightness, swiftness, agility, nimbleness. *2* lightness [of weight]. *3* lightness, levity, frivolity. *4* thoughtless act, indiscretion.
1) ligero, -ra *adj.* light [not heavy; easy to endure or perform; not violent; not burdened]. *2* light, swift, agile, nimble. *3* light [clothes, food, wine, sleep, comedy, etc.]. *4* thin [cloth]. *5* light, flippant, jesting. *6* light, giddy, fickle. *7* light, wanton. *8* MIL. light: *caballería ligera,* light horse. *9* ~ *de cascos,* featherbrained; ~ *de ropa,* scantily clad. *10 a la ligera,* quickly, simply, unceremoniously. *11 de* ~, rashly.
2) ligero *adv.* fast, rapidly.
ligio, -gia *adj.* liege.
lignificarse *ref.* to lignify.
lignina *f.* BOT. lignin.
lignito *m.* MINER. lignite.
ligula *f.* BOT. ligule.
ligur, ligurino, -na *adj.-n.* Ligurian.
ligustre *m.* BOT. flower of the privet.
ligustro *m.* BOT. privet.
lija *f.* ICHTH. dogfish. *2* shagreen; sandpaper.
lijar *tr.* to sandpaper.
Lila *f. pr. n.* GEOG. Lille.
lila *f.* BOT. lilac [shrub and flower]. *2* lilac colour. *3* *adj.* silly, half-witted. *4 m.-f.* fool, simpleton.
liliáceo, -a *adj.* BOT. liliaceous.
liliputiense *adj.-n.* Liliputian.
Lima *f. pr. n.* GEOG. Lima.
lima *f.* file [tool]. *2* finish, polishing. *3* BOT. sweet lime [fruit]. *4* BOT. sweet-lime tree. *5* ARCH. ~ *hoya,* valley. *6* ARCH. ~ *tesa,* hip.
limadura *f.* filing [smoothing]. *2 pl.* filings.
limalla *f.* filings [of metal].
limar *tr.* to file [smooth with a file]. *2* to polish, touch up. *3* to weaken, destroy.
limaza *f.* ZOOL. slug.
limazo *m.* viscosity, slime.
limbo *m.* THEOL. limbo: *estar en el* ~, *fig.* to be absent-minded. *2* edge, border. *3* limb.
limen *m.* poet. threshold.
limeño, -ña *adj.-n.* Limean.
limero *m.* BOT. sweet-lime tree.
limeta *f.* long-necked bottle.
limitación *f.* limitation. *2* boundary, district.
limitado, -da *adj.* limited. *2* short, scanty. *3* dull-witted.
limitador, -ra *adj.* limiting. *2 m.-f.* limiter.
limitáneo, -a *adj.* frontier, bordering.
limitar *tr.* to mark the boundaries of. *2* to limit. *3* to cut down, reduce. *4* *intr.* ~ *con,* to border on,

be contiguous to. 5 *ref.* to reduce expense. 6 *limitarse a*, to confine oneself to.

límite *m.* limit, bound: *sin límites*, illimited, unbounded. 2 boundary, border. 3 MATH. limit.

limítrofe *adj.* bordering, conterminous.

limo *m.* mud, slime.

limón *m.* BOT. lemon tree.

limonada *f.* lemonade.

limonar *m.* lemon plantation or grove.

limonera *f.* shaft [of a carriage].

limonero, -ra *adj.* shaft [horse]. 2 *m.-f.* shaft horse. 3 lemon seller. 4 *m.* BOT. lemon tree.

limonita *f.* MINER. limonite.

limosidad *f.* muddiness, sliminess.

limosna *f.* alms.

limosnero, -ra *adj.* almsgiving, charitable. 2 *m.* almoner.

limoso, -sa *adj.* muddy, slimy.

limpia *f.* cleaning, cleansing.

limpiabarros, *pl.* **-rros** *m.* scraper, boot scraper.

limpiabotas, *pl.* **-tas** *m.* bootblack.

limpiachimeneas, *pl.* **-neas** *m.* chimneysweep(er.

limpiador, -ra *adj.* cleaning, cleansing. 2 *m.-f.* cleaner, cleanser.

limpiamente *adv.* cleanly. 2 neatly. 3 skilfully, with ease. 4 purely, honestly. 5 sincerely, fairly.

limpiaparabrisas, *pl.* **-sas** *m.* windshield wiper.

limpiar *tr.* to clean, cleanse. 2 to wipe [a pen, the hands, etc.]. 3 to shine [shoes]. 4 to furbish [metals]. 5 to prune [a tree]. 6 to clear [from impurities, weeds, etc.]. 7 to purify. 8 coll. to steal, to pick. 9 coll. to clean up or out [in gambling]. 10 *ref.* to clean oneself.

limpiatubos, *pl.* **-bos** *m.* tube cleaner.

limpiauñas, *pl.* **-ñas** *m.* nail cleaner.

limpidez *f.* poet. limpidity.

límpido, -da *adj.* limpid, clear, pure.

limpieza *f.* cleanness, cleanliness. 2 neatness. 3 purity, chastity. 4 integrity, honesty, fairness. 5 neatness, ease or skill of execution. 6 cleaning. 7 household cleaning.

1) **limpio, -pia** *adj.* clean, cleanly. 2 neat, tidy. 3 clear [free from impurities, guile, guilt, etc.]; pure, -chaste, honest. 4 clear, net [free from deductions]. 5 fair [play]. 6 *poner en ~*, to make a clear copy of. 7 *sacar en ~*, to conclude, infer, make out.

2) **limpio** *adv.* cleanly. 2 fair: *jugar ~*, to play fair.

limpión *m.* hasty cleaning.

lináceo, -a *adj.* BOT. linaceous.

linaje *m.* lineage, family, race: *~ humano*, mankind. 2 class, kind, description.

linajista *m.* genealogist.

linajudo, -da *adj.* of high lineage, of noble descent.

lináleo *m.* BOT. aloes.

linaza *f.* flaxseed, linseed.

lince *m.* ZOOL. lynx. 2 fig. keen, shrewd person. 3 *adj.* keen [sight, eyes].

línceo, -a *adj.* lyncean. 2 keen [sight, eyes].

linchamiento *m.* lynching.

linchar *tr.* to lynch.

lindamente *adv.* prettily, neatly, finely.

lindante *adj.* bordering, adjoining, contiguous.

lindar *intr.* *~ con*, to border, verge, abut on.

linde *m.-f.* limit, boundary.

lindero, -ra *adj.* bordering, adjoining. 2 *m.* limit, boundary.

lindeza *f.* prettiness, neatness, beauty, elegance. 2 *pl.* pretty things. 3 iron. insults.

lindo, -da *adj.* beautiful, pretty, nice, fine, lovely. 2 *de lo ~*, a great deal, greatly.

lindura *f.* LINDEZA.

línea *f.* GEOM. line. 2 line [twelfth part of an inch]. 3 line [threadlike mark, formation or appearance; direction, course]: *~ de agua*, *~ de flotación*, NAUT. water line; *~ de fondo*, TENNIS base line, service line; FOOTBALL goal line; *~ de fuerza*, PHYS. line of force; *~ de puntos*, dotted line; *~ equinoccial*, GEOG. equinoctial line. 4 GEOG. the line, the equator. 5 course, line [of conduct]. 6 line [written or printed]: *unas líneas*, *cuatro líneas*, fig. a line [short, letter]. 7 line [of steamers, autobuses, etc.]: *~ aérea*, airline; *~ férrea*, railway line; *~ telegráfica*, telegraph line. 8 line [of family]: *~ directa*, direct line. 9 limit, boundary. 10 MIL., NAV. line: *~ de fuego*, firing line. 12 class, kind. 13 *en toda la ~*, thoroughly.

lineal *adj.* lineal, linear.

lineamento, lineamiento *m.* lineament.

linear *adj.* BOT., ZOOL. linear.

linfa *f.* PHYSIOL. lymph. 2 poet, lymph, water.

linfático, -ca *adj.* lymphatic.

linfatismo *m.* MED. lymphatism.

linfocito *m.* ANAT. lymphocyte.

lingote *m.* ingot, pig, bloom.

lingual *adj.* lingual.

linguete *m.* pawl, ratchet.

lingüista *m.* linguist.

lingüística *f.* linguistics.

linimento, linimiento *m.* liniment.

lino *m.* BOT. flax. 2 flax [fiber]. 3 linen [thread, cloth].

linóleo *m.* linoleum.

linón *m.* lawn [fabric].

linotipia *f.* linotype.

linotipista *m.* linotypist.

lintel *m.* DINTEL.

linterna *f.* lantern, lamp: *~ eléctrica*, electric torch, flashlight; *~ mágica*, magic lantern; *~ sorda*, dark lantern. 2 NAUT. lighthouse. 3 MACH., ARCH. lantern.

linternazo *m.* blow with a lantern. 2 fig. blow.

liño *m.* row of trees or plants.

lío *m.* bundle, parcel. 2 tangle, muddle, mess, imbroglio: *armar un ~*, to muddle things, to stir up trouble; *hacerse un ~*, to get muddled, confused. 3 liaison [illicit intimacy]. 4 lie, deception.

Lión *pr. n.* GEOG. Lyon, Lyons.

lionés, -sa *adj.-n.* Lyonese.

lioso, -sa *adj.* lying, mischief-making. 2 embroiled, difficult. 3 *m.-f.* liar, mischief-maker.

lipoma *m.* MED. lipoma.

liquen *m.* BOT., MED. lichen.

liquidación *f.* liquefaction. 2 liquidation. 3 bargain sale.

liquidador, -ra *adj.* liquidating. 2 *m.-f.* liquidator. 3 *~ de averías*, insurance adjuster.

liquidámbar *m.* liquidambar.

liquidar *tr.* to liquefy. 2 to liquidate. 3 fig. to squander; to destroy, murder. 4 *intr.* to liquidate; to go into liquidation. 5 *ref.* to liquefy [come into liquid condition].

liquidez *f.* liquidity, liquidness.

líquido, -da *adj.* liquid, aquiform. 2 COM. clear, net. 3 *adj.-f.* PHONET. liquid. 4 *m.* liquid, liquor. 5 COM. net.

lira *f.* lira [monetary unit]. 2 MUS. lyre. 3 a Spanish poem or fixed verse form. 4 inspiration, poetry [of a poet]. 5 ASTR. (cap.) Lyra, Lyre.

lírico, -ca *adj.* lyric, lyrical. 2 *m.-f.* lyric poet. 3 *f.* lyric poetry.

lirio *m.* BOT. German iris. *2* BOT. iris, lily: ~ *blanco*, Madonna lily; ~ *de agua*, calla, calla lily; ~ *de los valles*, lily of the valley.
lirismo *m.* lyricism. *2* abuse of lyricism.
lirón *m.* ZOOL. dormouse: *dormir como un* ~, to sleep like a log. *2* coll. sleepyhead.
lirondo *adj.* V. MONDO Y LIRONDO.
lis *f.* BOT. iris, flower-de-luce. *2* HER. fleur-de-lis.
lisa *f.* ICHTH. a kind of loach. *2* ICHTH. striped mullet.
Lisboa *f. pr. n.* GEOG. Lisbon.
lisboeta; lisbonense; lisbonés, -sa *adj.-n.* of Lisbon.
lisiado, -da *adj.* crippled. *2 m.-f.* cripple.
lisiar *tr.* to injure, maim, cripple. *2 ref.* to become crippled.
lisimaquia *f.* BOT. loosestrife.
liso, -sa *adj.* smooth, even. *2* plain, unadorned. *3* ANAT. nonstriated [muscle]. *4* ~ *y llano*, simple, easy.
lisonja *f.* flattery; compliment. *2* HER. lozenge.
lisonjeador, -ra *adj.* flattering. *2 m.-f.* flatterer.
lisonjear *tr.* to flatter. *2 ref.* to flatter oneself.
lisonjero, -ra *adj.* flattering; complimentary. *2* pleasing; promising, rosy. *3 m.-f.* flatterer.
lista *f.* strip. *2* slip [of paper]. *3* list, stripe, band. *4* list, catalogue: ~ *de platos*, bill of fare, menu; ~ *negra*, black list. *5* muster, roll; *pasar* ~, to call the roll. *6* POST. ~ *de correos*, general delivery.
listado, -da *adj.* striped.
listel *m.* ARCH. listel, fillet.
listeza *f.* cleverness, sagacity, smartness.
listo, -ta *adj.* ready, prepared. *2* ready, quick, prompt. *3* finished, completed; having finished [with a task]. *4* clever, adroit, shrewd.
listón *m.* narrow ribbon. *2* ARCH. listel, fillet. *3* CARP. lath, batten, strip of wood.
lisura *f.* smoothness, evenness. *2* sincerity, candour.
lite *f.* LAW lawsuit.
litera *f.* litter [vehicle]. *2* berth [in boat or train].
literal *adj.* literal.
literalmente *adv.* literally.
literario, -ria *adj.* literary.
literato, -ta *adj.* literary [person]. *2 m.-f.* literary person, writer.
literatura *f.* literature.
litiasis *f.* MED. lithiasis.
litigación *f.* litigation.
litigante *adj.-n.* litigant.
litigar *tr.-intr.* to litigate.
litigio *m.* litigation, law suit. *2* dispute, contest.
litigioso, -sa *adj.* litigious.
litio *m.* CHEM. lithium.
litis, *pl.* **-tis** *f.* LAW lawsuit.
litófago, -ga *adj.* ZOOL. lithophagous, rock-boring.
litografía *f.* lithography.
litografiar *tr.* to lithograph.
litógrafo *m.* lithographer.
litología *f.* lithology.
litoral *adj.* littoral, coastal. *2 m.* littoral, coast, shore.
litro *m.* litre, liter.
Lituania *f. pr. n.* GEOG. Lithuania.
lituano, -na *adj.-n.* Lithuanian.
liturgia *f.* liturgy.
litúrgico, -ca *adj.* liturgic(al).
liviandad *f.* lewdness. *2* lightness [lack of weight]. *3* levity, frivolity.
liviano, -na *adj.* wanton, lewd. *2* light [not heavy].

3 slight [unimportant]. *4* frivolous, fickle. *5 m. pl.* lights, lungs.
lividez *f.* lividness.
lívido, -da *adj.* livid.
livor *m.* livid colour. *2* fig. malignity, hatred, envy.
liza *f.* lists [place of combat]. *2* combat, contest.
lizo *m.* WEAV. warp thread. *2* WEAV. heddle, leash.
lo *art. neut.* [before a masc. form of adjective] the, that which is, the... thing or things: ~ *primero*, the first thing; ~ *bello*, the beautiful, beautiful things. | The adjective can often be translated by a corresponding noun: ~ *estúpido de su proceder*, the stupidity of his behaviour. *2* [before an adverb or an inflected adjective followed by *que*] how; so: *usted verá* ~ *bien que [ella] baila*, you will see how well she dances; *con* ~ *cansado que estaba*, being so tired. *3 a* ~ [followed by a noun], like, in the style of, *a* ~ *caballero*, like a gentleman. *4* ~ *más*, as... as: ~ *lo más pronto posible*, as soon as possible. *5 pers. pron. masc. & neut.* him, you [in correspondence with *usted*], it, that: ~ *vi*, I saw him, I saw it. *6* so: *ya te* ~ *dije*, I told you so. *7 a* ~ *que*, according to, from what; *a* ~ *que veo*, from what I see. *8* ~ *de ayer*, what happened yesterday; ~ *de siempre*, the same old story. *9* ~ *que*, what, that which; how much. *10* ~ *que es por*, as to, as for.
loa *f.* praise. *2* THEAT. prologue [of an ancient play]. *3* short dramatic panegyric.
loable *adj.* laudable, praiseworthy.
loar *tr.* to praise, eulogize.
loba *f.* ZOOL. she-wolf. *2* soutane, cassock.
lobado, -da *adj.* BOT., ZOOL. lobate.
lobanillo *m.* MED. wen.
lobato *m.* wolf cub.
lobeliáceo, -a *adj.* BOT. lobeliaceous.
lobera *f.* thicket where wolves make their lair.
lobezno *m.* wolf cub.
lobina *f.* RÓBALO.
lobo *m.* ZOOL. wolf. *2* ICHTH. louch. *3* BOT. lobe. *4* coll. drunkenness. *5* coll. ~ *de mar*, old salt, sea dog.
loboso, -sa *adj.* full of wolves.
lóbrego, -ga *adj.* dark, gloomy, murky.
lobreguez *f.* darkness, obscurity, gloominess.
lobulado, -da *adj.* BOT., ZOOL. lobate, lobed, lobulate.
lóbulo *m.* lobe, lobule.
lobuno, -na *adj.* wolfish.
locación *f.* LAW lease.
local *adj.* local. *2 m.* place, rooms, quarters, premises.
localidad *f.* locality. *2* place, village, town. *3* seat [in a theatre, show, etc.].
localización *f.* localization. *2* location, act of finding out where a person or thing is.
localizar *tr.* to localize. *2* to locate, to find out where [a person or thing] is.
locatario, -ria *m.-f.* ARRENDATARIO.
loco, -ca *adj.* mad, crazy, insane: ~ *de remate*, stark mad; ~ *de contento*, fig. mad with joy. *2* mad, wild, violent. *3* foolish, imprudent. *4* great, abundant, immoderate, excessive. *5* MACH. idle. *6 m.-f.* lunatic, insane person, madman, madwoman. *7* fool.
locomoción *f.* locomotion.
locomotor, -ra *adj.* locomotive, locomotor. *2 f.* RLY. locomotive.
locomotriz *adj. f.* locomotive.
locomóvil *adj.-f.* locomobile.
locuacidad *f.* loquacity, talkativeness.

locuaz *adj.* loquacious, talkative.
locución *f.* locution. 2 phrase, idiom.
locuelo, -la *adj.* frisky, madcap [youngster]. 2 *m. -f.* young madcap.
lóculo *m.* loculus.
locura *f.* madness, lunacy, insanity: *con* ~, madly. 2 folly, foolishness, imprudence.
locutor, -ra *m.-f.* radio announcer, radio speaker.
locutorio *m.* locutory, parlour [in a convent]. 2 call box, telephone booth.
locha *f.*, **loche** *m.* ICHTH. loach.
lodachar, lodazal, lodazar *m.* muddy place, mudhole.
lodo *m.* mud, mire.
lodoso, -sa *adj.* muddy, miry.
lofobranquio, -quia *adj.-m.* ICHTH. lophobranch.
logaritmo *m.* MATH. logarithm.
logia *f.* lodge [of freemasons]. 2 ARCH. loggia.
lógica *f.* logic.
lógico, -ca *adj.* logical. 2 *m.-f.* logician.
logística *f.* MIL. logistics.
logogrifo *m.* logogryph, riddle.
logomaquia *f.* logomachy.
lograr *tr.* to get, acquire, attain, obtain, procure. 2 [with an inf.] to succeed in, manage to. 3 *ref.* [of a thing] to succeed; to attain perfection.
logrería *f.* usury, profiteering.
logrero, -ra *m.-f.* moneylender. 2 usurer, profiteer.
logro *m.* accomplishment, attainment. 2 gain, profit, interest. 3 usury.
Loira *m. pr. n.* GEOG. Loire.
Lola, Lolita *f. pr. n.* dim. of DOLORES.
loma *f.* eminence, down, slope, long little hill.
lombarda *f.* lombard [cannon]. 2 BOT. a red cabbage.
Lombardía *f. pr. n.* GEOG. Lombardy.
lombardo, -da *adj.-n.* Lombard. 2 Longobard.
lombriz *f.* ZOOL. earthworm. 2 ZOOL. ~ *intestinal*, intestinal worm. 3 ZOOL. ~ *solitaria*, tapeworm.
lomear *intr.* [of horses] to arch the back.
lomera *f.* backstrap [of harness]. 2 BOOKB. backing.
lomo *m.* the lower part of the back [of a person]. 2 back [of an animal, a book, a cutting tool]. 3 chine [of pork]. 4 ridge between furrows. 6 *pl.* ribs, loins [of a person].
lona *f.* canvas [for sails, tents, etc.], sailcloth.
loncha *f.* flagstone, slap. 2 LONJA 4.
londinense *adj.* [pertaining to] London. 2 *m.-f.* Londoner.
Londres *m. pr. n.* GEOG. London.
longanimidad *f.* long-suffering, forbearance, magnanimity.
longaniza *f.* long pork sausage.
longevidad *f.* longevity.
longevo, -va *adj.* longevous, long-lived.
longirrostro, -tra *adj.* ORN. longirostral.
longitud *f.* length, longitude. 2 ASTR., GEOG. longitude.
longitudinal *adj.* longitudinal.
lonja *f.* exchange, market. 2 grocer's shop. 3 ARCH. raised porch. 4 slice [of meat]; strip [of leather].
lontananza *f.* PAINT. background. 2 *en* ~, far away, far off, in the distance.
loor *m.* praise.
loquear *intr.* to act like a fool. 2 to frolic.
loquero, -ra *m.-f.* guard or attendant in an insane asylum. 2 *f.* (Am.) folly [foolish act].
loquesco, -ca *adj.* reckless, foolish. 2 merry, jesting.
lord, *pl.* **lores** *m.* lord [English title].
lordosis *f.* MED. lordosis.

Lorena (la) *f. pr. n.* GEOG. Lorraine.
lorenés, -sa *adj.* Lorrainese. 2 *m.-f.* Lorrainer.
Lorenzo *m. pr. n.* Laurence, Lawrence.
loriga *f.* lorica [cuirass]. 2 horse armour.
loro *adj.* tawny, dark brown. 2 *m.* ORN. parrot.
lorza *f.* SEW. tuck.
los *art. def. m. pl.* the. 2 ~ *que*, those, or they who or which. 3 *pron. pers. m. pl.* [direct object] them: ~ *vi*, I saw them.
losa *f.* flagstone, slab. 2 gravestone. 3 grave.
losange *m.* lozenge, diamond.
lote *m.* share, portion [of something to be distributed]. 2 lot [of land]. 3 prize [in a lottery]. 4 lot [set of articles].
lotería *f.* lottery. 2 lotto [game].
lotero, -ra *m.-f.* seller of lottery tickets.
loto *m.* BOT. lotus. 2 BOT. lotus tree. 3 fruit of the lotus tree.
lotófago, -ga *adj.* lotus-eating. 2 *m.-f.* lotus-eater.
Lovaina *f. pr. n.* GEOG. Lovain.
loza *f.* china, fine earthenware or crockery.
lozanear *intr.* [of plants] to be luxuriant. 2 [of persons] to be blooming, fresh, vigorous.
lozanía *f.* verdure, luxuriance. 2 bloom, freshness, vigour. 3 pride, haughtiness.
lozano, -na *adj.* verdant, luxuriant. 2 blooming, fresh, vigorous, full of life. 3 proud, haughty.
lubina *f.* RÓBALO.
lubricación *f.* lubrication.
lubricán *m.* twilight [in morning or evening].
lubricante *m.* lubricant.
lubricar *tr.* to lubricate.
lubricidad *f.* lubricity.
lúbrico, -ca *adj.* lubricous.
lubrificación *f.* LUBRICACIÓN.
lubrificante *m.* LUBRICANTE.
lubrificar *tr.* LUBRICAR.
Lucas *m. pr. n.* Luke.
Lucerna *f. pr. n.* GEOG. Lucerne.
lucerna *f.* large chandelier [hanging from the ceiling]. 2 skylight, light shaft. 3 ICHTH. lying gurnard.
lucero *m.* any bright star: ~ *del alba* or *de la mañana*, morning star; ~ *de la tarde*, evening star. 2 star [on the forehead of an animal]. 3 *pl.* poet, eyes.
Lucía *f. pr. n.* Lucy, Lucía.
lucidez *f.* lucidity.
lucido, -da *adj.* brilliant, successful. 2 splendid, magnificient. 3 generous.
lúcido, -da *adj.* poet. lucid, bright. 2 lucid [in thought or style]. 3 MED. lucid.
luciente *adj.* lucent, bright, shining, luminous.
luciérnaga *f.* ENT. glowworm, firefly.
Lucifer *m. pr. n.* Lucifer, Satan. 2 morning star.
lucífero, -ra *adj.* poet, shining, luminous. 2 *m.* morning star.
lucífugo, -ga *adj.* lucifugal, lucifugous.
lucimiento *m.* brilliancy, show, splendour. 2 skill, success [in performance].
lucio, cia *adj.* lucid, bright. 2 *m.* ICHTH. luce, pike.
lucir *intr.* to shine, glitter, glow. 2 to shine, excel, be eminent. 3 [of work, etc.] to prove profitable. 4 *tr.* to show, to display. 5 to plaster [walls]. 6 to illuminate, light up. 7 *ref.* to dress to advantage, to show off. 8 to acquit oneself well, to act splendidly. ¶ IRREG. CONJUG.: INDIC. Pres.: *luzco*, luces, luce; lucimos, lucís, lucen. | SUBJ. Pres.: *luzca, luzcas*, etc. | IMPER.: luce, *luzcan*; luzcamos, lucid, *luzcan*.

lucrar *tr.* to obtain. *2 ref.* to profit [get a pecuniary gain].
lucrativo, -va *adj.* lucrative, profitable.
Lucrecia *f. pr. n.* Lucrece, Lucretia.
lucro *m.* lucre, gain, profit.
luctuoso, -sa *adj.* mournful, sorrowful, sad.
lucubración *f.* lucubration.
lucubrar *tr.* to lucubrate.
lucha *f.* fight, battle, combat. *2* strife, struggle: ~ *de clases,* class struggle. *3* contention, dispute. *4* wrestling.
luchador, -ra *adj.* fighting. *2 m.-f.* fighter, struggler. *3* wrestler.
luchar *intr.* to fight. *2* to strive, to struggle. *3* to contend, dispute. *4* to wrestle.
ludibrio *m.* derision, mockery, scorn.
ludir *tr.-intr.* to rub.
luego *adv.* afterwards, next. *2* presently, immediately. *3* later. *4* ~ *de,* after, right after. *5 desde* ~, at once; of course. *6 hasta* ~, so long, see you later. *7 conj.* therefore, then.
luengo, -ga *adj.* long: *luengos años,* many years.
lúes *f.* MED. lues.
lugar *m.* place [part of space, space occupied; ordinal relation]: *en primer* ~, firstly, *fuera de* ~, out of place; irrelevant. *2* place, spot, town, city. *3* village. *4* place, stead: *en* ~ *de,* instead of, in lieu of. *5* space, room: *hacer* ~, to make room. *6* time, occasion. *7* employment, office. *8* cause, reason, rise: *dar* ~ *a,* to give rise to. *9* ~ *común,* privy, toilet. *10 lugares comunes,* commonplace topics. *11* LAW *no ha* ~, petition refused. *12* Gal. *tener* ~, to take place, happen.
lugarejo *m. dim.* small village, hamlet.
lugareño, -ña *adj.* [pertaining to a] village. *2 m.-f.* villager.
lugarteniente *m.* lieutenant, deputy, substitute.
lugre *m.* NAUT. lugger.
lúgubre *adj.* lugubrious, sad, gloomy, dismal.
lugués, -sa *adj.-n.* of Lugo.
Luis *m. pr. n.* Louis, Lewis.
luis *m.* louis [French coin].
Luisiana (la) *pr. n.* GEOG. Louisiana.
lujación *f.* LUXACIÓN.
lujo *m.* luxury: *de* ~, de luxe, luxurious, magnificent. *2* ~ *de,* excess or abundance of.
lujoso, -sa *adj.* luxurious, costly, magnificent.
lujuria *f.* lewdness, lust. *2* excess, profuseness.
lujuriante *adj.* luxuriant, rank. *2* lustful.
lujurioso, -sa *adj.* lustful, lecherous, lewd.
luliano, -na *adj.* Lullian.
lulismo *m.* system of Raymond Lully.
lumbago *m.* MED. lumbago.
lumbar *adj.* ANAT. lumbar.
lumbre *f.* fire [burning coals, wood, etc.]; light [to light a cigarette]: *dar* ~ *a,* to light someone's cigarette. *2* forepart [of horseshoes]. *3* light [natural agent; emanation of a lightgiving body]. *4* space through which light is admitted. *5* clearness, lustre, splendor. *6* ~ *del agua,* surface of the water. *7 pl.* tinder box.
lumbrera *f.* luminary, light-giving body. *2* luminary, light [person]. *3* skylight, louver, light shaft. *4* ventilating shaft, air duct. *5* MACH. port.
lumen *m.* lumen [unit of light].
luminar *m.* luminary [star; person].
luminaria *f.* ECCL. lamp kept burning before the Sacrament. *2 pl.* illuminations, festival lights.
lumínico, -ca *adj.* photic, pertaining to light.

luminiscencia *f.* luminiscence.
luminosidad *f.* luminosity.
luminoso, -sa *adj.* luminous.
luminotecnia *f.* lighting engineering.
luna *f.* ASTR. moon: ~ *de miel,* honeymoon; ~ *llena,* full moon; ~ *menguante,* waning moon; ~ *nueva,* new moon; *media* ~, half-moon; crescent; *estar en la* ~, fig. to be absent-minded; *quedarse a la* ~ *de Valencia,* to be disappointed. *2* moonlight. *3* ASTR. satélite. *4* whim; humour: *de buena* or *de mala* ~, (Am.) in good, or bad, humour. *5* mirror plate. *6* lens, glass [of spectacles]. *7* ICHTH. sunfish, moonfish.
lunación *f.* ASTR. lunation, lunar month.
lunar *adj.* lunar. *2 m.* mole, beauty spot: ~ *postizo,* patch, beauty spot. *3* flaw, blemish. *4 pl.* polka dots.
lunático, -ca *adj.* having fits of madness; moonstruck. *2 m.-f.* person who has fits of madness; moonstruck person.
lunes, pl. -nes *m.* Monday.
luneta *f.* lens, glass [of spectacles]. *2* lunette [ornament]. *3* ARCH., FORT. lunette. *4* THEAT. orchestra seat.
luneto *m.* ARCH. lunette.
lunfardo *m.* (Am.) underworld slang. *2* (Am.) thief.
lúnula *f.* GEOM. lune. *2* ANAT., ZOOL. lunule. *3* OPT. meniscus.
lupa *f.* magnifying glass.
lupanar *m.* bawdyhouse, brothel.
lupino, -na *adj.* lupine, wolfish. *2 m.* BOT. lupine.
lúpulo *m.* BOT. hop. *2* BOT. hops [hop cones].
lupus *m.* MED. lupus.
lusitano, na; luso, -sa *adj.-n.* Lusitanian; Portuguese.
lustración *f.* lustration.
lustral *adj.* lustral.
lustrar *tr.* to lustrate, purify. *2* to polish, shine.
lustre *m.* lustre, luster, gloss, polish, glaze. *2* lustre, luster, glory. *3* shoe-polish.
lustrina *f.* lustrine.
lustro *m.* lustrum.
lustroso, -sa *adj.* lustrous, glossy, shining.
lúteo, -a *adj.* muddy [of mud].
luteranismo *m.* Lutheranism.
luterano, -na *adj.-n.* Lutheran.
Lutero *m. pr. n.* Luther.
luto *m.* mourning: *estar de* ~, to mourn; *ir de* ~, to be in mourning. *2* grief, bereavement. *3 pl.* mourning draperies.
lutria *f.* NUTRIA.
luxación *f.* SURG. luxation, dislocation.
Luxemburgo *m. pr. n.* GEOG. Luxemburg.
luz *f.* light [natural agent; emanation of a light-giving body; amount of illumination in a place; lamp, candle, firework, etc.]: ~ *de bengala,* Bengal light; ~ *de cruce,* AUT. dimmer; ~ *del día,* daylight; *media* ~, half-light; *dar a* ~, to give birth to; to publish; *salir a* ~, to come out, be published; to be divulged; *ver la* ~, to be born; to be published; *a la* ~ *de,* in the light of; *a todas luces,* every way, in every respect; *entre dos luces,* at twilight; coll. half-seas over, half drunk. *2* light [of the eyes]. *3* light [mental or spiritual enlightenment]. *4* ARCH. span. *5* PAINT. light. *6 pl.* lights, enlightenment, learning. *9* ARCH. lights, openings.
Luzbel *m. pr. n.* Lucifer, Satan.
luzco, luzca, etc. *irr.* V. LUCIR.

LL

Ll, ll *f.* Ll, ll, fourteenth letter of the Spanish alphabet.

llaga *f.* ulcer, sore. *2* fig. sore, source of pain or sorrow. *3* MAS. joint, seam.

llagar *tr.* to ulcerate, make sore. *2* fig. to hurt, wound. *3 ref.* to become ulcerated.

llama *f.* flame, blaze. *2* fig. flame [ardour, burning passion]. *3* ZOOL. llama.

llamada *f.* call, calling, summons. *2* knock, ring [at a door, etc.]; sign, signal [to call someone]. *3* TELEPH. call. *4* PRINT. reference mark. *6* MIL. call. *7* MIL. chamade.

llamadera *f.* goad [for urging cattle].

llamado *m.* call, calling, summons, appeal.

llamador, -ra *m.-f.* caller. *2* messenger. *3* knocker [of a door]; push button.

llamamiento *m.* call, calling, summons, appeal. *2* convocation.

llamar *tr.* to call [demand presence of], summon, convoke, cite: ~ *por teléfono*, to call up, to telephone. *2* to call [rouse from sleep]. *3* to attract. *4* to call, destine: *estaba llamado a*, he, or it, was destined to, was called to be; ~ *la atención*, to catch or arrest the attention, to be noticeable; ~ *la atención a*, to warn, to scold. *5* to call, name, call by the name; describe as: ~ *al pan, pan y al vino, vino*, to call a spade a spade. *6 intr.* to knock [at a door]; to ring the bell. *7 ref.* to be called or named. | Often constructed diferently: *¿cómo se llama usted?*, what is your name?; *me llamo Juan*, my name is John.

llamarada *f.* flare-up, sudden blaze. *2* flare-up, burst [of anger, etc.]. *3* sudden flush [on the face].

llamativo, -va *adj.* showy, flashy, gaudy. *2* attracting attention, noticeable.

llamazar *m.* swamp, marsh.

llambria *f.* steep face of a rock.

llameante *adj.* blazing, flaming.

llamear *intr.* to blaze, flame.

llana *f.* MAS. trowel. *2* plain, flatland. *3* page [of a writing].

llanada *f.* plain, flatland, level ground.

llanero, -ra *m.* plainsman. *2 f.* plainswoman.

llaneza *f.* plainness, simplicity. *2* familiarity, unceremoniousness.

llano, -na *adj.* flat, even, level, smooth. *2* easy [not difficult]; unobstructed. *3* plain, unadorned. *4* open, frank. *5* simple [style]. *6* clear, evident. *7* GRAM. accented on the penultimate [syllable]. *8* MUS. plain [chant]. *9 a la llana*, simply, unceremoniously. *10 m.* plain, flatland.

llanta *f.* long flat piece of iron. *2* steel tire [of a carriage wheel]. *3* metal rim [of the wheels of a car or bicycle]. *4* ~ *de goma*, rubber tire [in horse carriages].

llantén *m.* BOT. plantain.

llanto *m.* crying, weeping, flood of tears.

llanura *f.* evenness, flatness. *2* plain, flatland, large tract of level ground.

llapa *f.* YAPA.

llares *pl.* pothanger.

llave *f.* key [for a lock]: ~ *maestra*, master key, passkey; *bajo* ~, under lock and key. *2* key [in any figurative sense]. *3* MEC. key [wedge]. *4* cock, faucet: ~ *de paso*, stopcock. *5* wrench, spanner, key; ~ *inglesa*, monkey wrench; also, brass knuckles. *6* lock [of a gun], gunlock. *7* DENT. key. *8* clock winder. *9* MUS. key, piston. *10* MUS. clef. *11* PRINT., MUS. brace. *12* span [of the hand].

llavero, -ra *m.-f.* keeper of the keys. *2 m.* key ring.

llavín *m.* latchkey.

llegada *f.* arrival, coming.

llegar *intr.* to arrive, come. *2* ~ *a*, to arrive at, to get at, reach [a place, point, etc.]: to come to [an agreement]; to come to, amount to; to go to [one's heart, etc.]; to get to [know, be, etc.]. *3* ~ *a* or *hasta*, to go as far as, or as high as. *4* ~ *a* or *para*, to suffice to, to be enough for. *5* ~ *a las manos*, to come to blows. *6 tr.* to gather, collect. *7* to bring near. *8 ref. llegarse a*, to come near to; to go to [some neighbouring place].

llena *f.* flood, overflow [of a stream].

llenar *tr.* to fill, fill up, fill out. *2* to stuff, pack. *3* to pervade. *4* to cover; to overwhelm, load. *5* to please, content, satisfy, convince. *6* to hold [an office or position] honourably. *7 intr.* [of the moon] to be full. *8 ref.* to fill, fill up [become full]. *9* to get crowded, packed. *10* to stuff oneself.

lleno, -na *adj.* full, filled, replete, crowded, packed: ~ *hasta el borde*, brimful. *2 m.* coll. fill, plenty. *3* perfection, completeness. *4* THEAT. full house. *5* ASTR. full [of the moon]. *6 de* ~, fully; squarely.

llenura *f.* fulness, plenty, abundance.

lleva, llevada *f.* carrying, conveying, -transport.
llevadero, -ra *adj.* bearable, tolerable.
llevar *tr.* to carry, convey, take, transport, conduct.
2 to bear, wear, be in, have on: ~ *espada*, to wear
a sword; ~ *luto*, to wear, be in, mourn-
ing. *3* to carry, bear, hold [the body, the head,
etc.]. *4* to lead, guide, conduct, take. *5* to carry,
win [a prize, etc.]; to get [a thrashing, etc.]: ~
lo mejor, or *lo peor*, to get the best, or the worst.
6 to cut off, carry away. *7* to induce, bring [to
an opinion]. *8* to lead [a certain kind of life]. *9*
to bear, tolerate. *10* to lead [a horse]. *11* to keep
[accounts, books]. *12* to manage, be in charge
of. *13* to charge, ask [a price]. *14* to bear, yield
[fruit]. *15* ARITH. to carry. *16* [with nouns implying time] to have been: *llevo muchos años
aquí*, I have been here many years. *17* [with a
past p.] to have: *llevo escritas diez páginas*, I
have written ten pages. *18* to exceed, be ahead
of, be taller, heavier, older, etc. [by a specified
distance, height, weight, time, etc.]: *mi hijo
lleva dos años al tuyo*, my son is two years older
than yours. *19* ~ *adelante*, to carry on, continue.
20 ~ *las de perder*, to be at a disadvantage.
21 *ref.* to take or carry away; to take off. *22* to
win, carry off. *23 llevarse bien* or *mal*, to get, or
not to get, along together; to be on good, or bad
terms. *24 llevarse una sorpresa*, to be surprised.
lloradera *f.* coll. blubbering, weeping.
lloraduelos *m.* sniveller, querulous person.
llorar *intr.* to weep, cry. *2* to lament. *3* [of eyes] to
water. *4* to drip. *5 tr.* to shed [tears]. *6* to weep,
weep over, bewail, mourn, lament.
llorera *f.* coll. blubber, crying, continual crying.
lloriquear *intr.* GIMOTEAR.
lloro *m.* weeping, crying, tears.
llorón, -na *adj.* weeping, crying, who cries often or
with little cause. *2* BOT. weeping. *3 m.-f.* weeper,
whiner. *4 m.* BOT. weeping willow. *5* pendulous
plume. *6 f.* weeper [hired mourner].
lloroso, -sa *adj.* tearful, weeping. *2* sad.
llosa *f.* AGR. large fenced-in field.
llovedizo, -za *adj.* leaky [roof]. *2* rain [water].
llover *impers.* METEOR. to rain: ~ *a cántaros*, to rain
cats and dogs, to rain pitchforsk; *como llovido*,
unexpectedly. *2* fig. to rain, shower, come down
like rain. *3 ref.* [of roofs] to leak. ¶ CONJUG. like
mover.
llovido *m.* stowaway [person].
llovizna *f.* drizzle, sprinkle.
lloviznar *impers.* to drizzle, sprinkle.
lluvia *f.* METEOR. rain: ~ *menuda*, drizzle. *2* rain
water. *3* rain, shower [of things].
lluvioso, -sa *adj.* rainy, wet [day, weather].

M, m *f.* M, m, fifteenth letter of the Spanish alphabet.
maca *f.* bruise [on fruit]. *2* flaw, blemish. *3* trickery.
Macabeos *m. pl.* BIBL. Maccabees.
macabro, -bra *adj.* macabre.
macaco *m.* ZOOL. macaque.
macadam *m.* macadam.
macadamizar *tr.* to macadamize.
macadán *m.* MACADAM.
macana *f.* drug [unsalable commodity]. *2* (Am.) cudgel. *3* (Am.) lie, fib; nonsense.
macanazo *m.* blow with a MACANA or a cudgel.
macanudo, -da *adj.* coll. great, ripping, extraordinary.
macareno, -na *adj.* of the quarter of *la Macarena*, in Sevilla. *2* boasting, swaggering. *3* *m.-f.* boaster, swaggerer.
macareo *m.* tide rip in a river.
macarrón *m.* macaroon. *2 pl.* macaroni.
macarronea *f.* macaronics [poem].
macarrónico, -ca *adj.* macaronic.
macarse *ref.* [of fruit] to rot from bruises.
macear *tr.* to maul, beat with a maul or a mallet.
Macedonia *f. pr. n.* HIST., GEOG. Macedonia.
macedónico, -ca *adj.* Macedonian.
macedonio, -nia *adj.-n.* Macedonian.
maceración *f.*, **maceramiento** *m.* maceration.
macerar *tr.* to macerate.
macero *m.* macer, mace-bearer.
maceta *f.* mallet [small maul]. *2* mason's hammer; stonecutter's hammer. *3* flowerpot. *4* vase for artificial flowers. *5* BOT. corymb.
macetero *m.* flowerpot stand.
macferlán *m.* inverness, inverness cape.
macia *f.* MACIS.
macicez *f.* massiveness, solidity.
macilento, -ta *adj.* emaciate, pale, wan.
macillo *m.* small mallet. *2* hammer [of a piano]. *3* ELECT. tapper [of a bell, etc.].
macis *f.* mace [spice].
macizar *tr.* to fill up, render solid.
macizo, -za *adj.* massive, solid. *2 m.* flower bed. *3* clump, mass [of buildings, etc.]. *4* massif, mountain mass. *5* ARCH. wall space.
macla *f.* MINER. macle.
macolla *f.* BOT. cluster of shoots, flowers or spikes.
macrobiótica *f.* macrobiotics.

macrocéfalo, -la *adj.* macrocephalous.
macrocosmo *m.* macrocosm.
macrogameto *m.* BIOL. macrogamete.
macrosmático, -ca *adj.* ZOOL. macrosmatic.
macruro, -ra *adj.* ZOOL. macrural. *2 m.* ZOOL. macruran. *3 m. pl.* ZOOL. Macrura.
mácula *f.* spot, stain, blemish. *2* ASTR., ANAT. macula.
macular *tr.* to maculate, stain, defile.
maculatura *f.* PRINT. spoiled sheet.
macuto *m.* (Am.) alms basket. *2* MIL. knapsack.
machaca *m.-f.* bore, tiresome person. *3 f.* tiresome insistence.
machacador, -ra *adj.* pounding, crushing. *2 m.-f.* pounder, crusher. *3 f.* crusher [machine].
machacante *m.* MIL. sergeant's attendant.
machacar *tr.* to pound, crush, mash. *2 intr.* to be tiresomely insistent, to harp on a subject.
machacón, -na *adj.* tiresomely insistent, monotonous, boring, importunate. *2 m.-f.* bore.
machaconería *f.* tiresome insistence, tiresomeness.
machada *f.* flock of billy goats. *2* coll. stupidity.
machamartillo (a) *adv.* firmly, solidly.
machaqueo *m.* crushing, pounding. *2* MACHAQUERÍA.
machaquería *f.* tiresome insistence, importunity.
machar *tr.* to pound, crush, mash.
machetazo *m.* blow or cut with a machete.
machete *m.* machete, matchet, cutlass.
machetear *tr.* to strike with a machete.
machetero *m.* one who clears ground with a machete. *2* sugar cane cutter.
machiega *adj.* queen [bee].
machihembrar *tr.* CARP. to feather or mortise.
machina *f.* crane, derrick. *2* pile driver, pile engine.
macho *adj.* male [animal or plant]. *2* strong, robust. *3* stupid. *4 m.* ZOOL. male, jack, buck, bull [male animal]: ~ *cabrío*, he goat, billy goat. *5* ZOOL. he-mule. *6* stupid fellow. *7* MACH. male piece or part. *8* hook [of hook and eye]. *9* sledge hammer. *10* square anvil. *11* small anvil block. *12* ARCH. pillar, buttress. *13* MACH. ~ *de aterrajar*, tap, screw tap.
machón *m.* ARCH. pillar, buttress.
machorro, -rra *adj.* barren, sterile. *2 f.* barren female animal.

machote *m.* maul, hammer.
machucadura *f.* **machucamiento** *m.* crushing, bruising.
machucar *tr.* to crush, bruise.
machucho, -cha *adj.* sedate, judicious. 2 elderly.
madama *f.* lady, madam.
madamisela *f.* DAMISELA.
madapolán *m.* madapollam.
madeja *f.* skein, hank: *enredar la* ~, fig. to embroil an affair; *hacer* ~, fig. to become ropy. 2 head of hair.
Madera *f. pr. n.* GEOG. Madeira. 2 *m.* Madeira wine.
madera *f.* wood [substance]; lumber, timber: ~ *de construcción*, building timber; ~ *de sierra*, lumber [cut for use]; *descubrir uno la* ~, fig. to show one's true nature. 2 makings, essential qualities: *tiene* ~ *de estadista*, he has the makings of a statesman.
maderable *adj.* timber-yielding.
maderada *f.* lumber floated downstream.
maderaje, maderamen *m.* timber, timber work.
maderería *f.* lumber yard.
maderero, -ra *adj.* [pertaining to] lumber. 2 *m.* lumber dealer. 3 raftsman. 4 carpenter.
madero *m.* log, piece of timber. 2 fig. ship, vessel. 3 coll. log [stupid or senseless person].
madianita *adj.-n.* BIBL. Midianite.
mador *m.* moisture, slight sweat.
madrastra *f.* stepmother. 2 callous mother.
madraza *f.* coll. doting mother.
madre *f.* mother: ~ *patria*, mother country: ~ *política*, mother-in-law. 2 bed [of a river]: *sacar de* ~, fig. to irritate; *salir de* ~, [of a river] to overflow. 3 main sewer. 4 main irrigation ditch. 5 sediment, dregs [of wine or vinegar].
madrecilla *f.* ovary [of a bird].
madrecita *f.* dim. little mother, dear mother.
madreperla *f.* ZOOL. pearl oyster; mother-of-pearl.
madrépora *f.* ZOOL. madrepore.
madrero, -ra *adj.* coll. attached to his or her mother.
madreselva *f.* BOT. honeysuckle.
madrigado, -da *adj.* coll. experienced [person].
madrigal *m.* madrigal.
madrigalesco, -ca *adj.* madrigalian, madrigallike.
madriguera *f.* hole, burrow [of rabbits, etc.]. 2 den [of wild animals, thieves, etc.].
madrileño, -ña *adj.-n.* Madrilenian.
madrina *f.* godmother. 2 woman attending a person who is being married, or who is to receive confirmation, holy orders, etc. 3 patroness, protectress. 4 wooden prop. 5 leading mare.
madrinazgo *m.* godmothership.
madrona *f.* main sewer. 2 over-indulgent mother.
madroño *m.* BOT. strawberry tree. 2 BOT. fruit of the strawberry tree. 3 berry-shaped tassel.
madrugada *f.* dawn, daybreak: *de* ~, at daybreak. 2 early rising.
madrugador, -ra *adj.* early-rising. 2 *m.-f.* early riser.
madrugar *intr.* to rise or get up early. 2 to gain the start, to be beforehand.
madrugón, -na *adj.* early-rising. 2 *m.* act of rising very early.
maduración *f.* maturation, ripening. 2 ripeness.
maduramente *adv.* maturely. 2 with reflection or attentive consideration.
madurar *tr.* to maturate, mature, ripen. 2 MED. to maturate. 3 to mature, complete, think out [plans, etc.]. 4 *intr.* to mature, ripen [become ripe]. 5 to maturate. 6 to grow old, wise.

madurativo, -va *adj.-n.* maturative.
madurez *f.* maturity, ripeness. 2 wisdom, prudence.
maduro, -ra *adj.* mature, ripe. 2 wise, prudent. 3 [of a person] middle-aged, advanced in years. 4 *edad madura*, middle age.
maese *m.* obs. MAESTRO.
maestra *f.* mistress, woman teacher; schoolmistress. 2 mistress [woman well skilled in anything]. 3 female head of a workshop, etc. 4 master's or teacher's wife. 5 queen bee.
maestral *m.* northwest wind.
maestrante *m.* member of a MAESTRANZA.
maestranza *f.* a fraternity or order or knights skilled in riding. 2 arsenal, armoury [for the artillery or the navy].
maestrazgo *m.* dignity or jurisdiction of the grand master of a military order.
maestre *m.* grand master [of a military order]. 2 NAUT. obs. mate.
maestresala *m.* formerly, chief waiter [for a prince or nobleman].
maestría *f.* mastery, mastership, masterly skill.
maestril *m.* queen cell [in a beehive].
maestrillo, -lla *m.-f. dim.* insignificant teacher.
maestro, -tra *adj.* master, main, principal, great: *abeja maestra*, queen bee; *obra maestra*, masterpiece; *pared maestra*, ARCH. main wall; *viga maestra*, ARCH. girder. 2 *m.* teacher, master; ~ *de armas*, fencing master; ~ *de escuela*, schoolteacher. 2 master [in religion, art, science, etc.; great artist]. 4 MUS. composer. 5 master [skilled workman]: ~ *de obras*, builder, master builder. 6 head, director: ~ *de cocina*, chef, head cook; ~ *de ceremonias*, master of ceremonies, marshal.
Magallanes (estrecho de) *m. pr. n.* GEOG. Strait of Magellan.
magallánico, -ca *adj.* Magellanic.
magancería *f.* trick, deceit.
maganel *m.* mangonel.
Magdalena *f. pr. n.* Magdalen, Magdalene: *Santa María Magdalena*, BIBL. Mary Magdalene. 2 fig. penitent woman: *estar hecha una --*, to weep bitterly.
magdalena *f.* cake made of flour, sugar and eggs.
magdaleniense *adj.* GEOL. Magdalenian.
magia *f.* magic: ~ *blanca*, white magic; ~ *negra*, black magic, black art.
magiar *adj.-n.* Magyar.
mágico, -ca *adj.* magic, magical. 2 wonderful. 3 *m.* magician, sorcerer. 4 *f.* magic, sorceress.
magín *m.* coll. mind, fancy, imagination.
magisterial *adj.* teaching.
magisterio *m.* teaching, guidance, mastership. 2 teaching profession. 3 teachers as a class. 4 affected gravity. 5 OLD., CHEM. magistery.
magistrado *m.* magistrate. 2 justice, judge.
magistral *adj.* pertaining to the teaching or mastership. 2 magisterial, dogmatic. 3 masterly. 4 who has charge of preaching [canon]. 5 *adj.-m.* PHARM., METAL. magistral.
magistratura *f.* magistracy.
magma *m.* magma [viscid mixture]. 2 GEOL. magma.
magnanimidad *f.* magnanimity.
magnánimo, -ma *adj.* magnanimous.
magnate *m.* magnate.
magnesia *f.* CHEM. magnesia.
magnesiano, -na *adj.* magnesian.
magnesio *m.* CHEM. magnesium. 2 PHOT. flashlight.

magnesita f. MINER. magnesite.
magnético, -ca adj. magnetic.
magnetismo m. magnetism.
magnetita f. MINER. magnetite.
magnetización f. magnetization.
magnetizar tr. to magnetize.
magneto f. ELECT. magneto.
magnetófono m. PHYS. magnetophon. 2 tape recorder, wire recorder.
magnetofónica (cinta) f. recording tape.
magnificador, -ra adj. extolling, exalting.
magnificar tr. to extoll, exalt.
Magnificat m. Magnificat.
magnificencia f. magnificence.
magnífico, -ca adj. magnificent. 2 fine, excellent.
magnitud f. magnitude.
magno, -na adj. great: Alejandro Magno, Alexander the Great.
magnolia f. BOT. magnolia.
mago, -ga adj. Magian. 2 skilled in magic. 3 m. Magian, Magus. 4 magician, wizard. 5 f. enchantress. 6 m. pl. Magi: los Reyes Magos, the Magi, the Wise Men of the East.
magra f. rasher, slice of ham.
magrez f. meagreness, thinness, leanness.
magro, -gra adj. meagre, meager, thin, lean. 2 lean [meat]. 3 m. coll. lean meat of pork.
magrura f. MAGREZ.
maguer conj. obs. although.
magulladura f., **magullamiento** m. bruising. 2 bruise, contusion.
magullar tr. to bruise, mangle.
Maguncia f. pr. n. GEOG. Mainz.
Mahoma m. pr. n. Mohammed.
mahometano, -na adj.-n. Mohammedan.
mahometismo m. Mohammedanism.
Mahón m. pr. n. GEOG. Mahon, Port Mahon.
mahón m. nankeen [cotton cloth].
mahonés, -sa adj.-n. of Mahon. 2 salsa mahonesa, mayonnaise sauce. 3 f. COOK. mayonnaise [dish].
maicena f. fine maize flour.
maído m. MAULLIDO.
mainel m. ARCH. mullion.
maitines m. pl. ECCL. matins.
maíz m. BOT. maize, Indian corn.
maizal m. Indian-corn field.
majada f. sheepfold. 2 dung, manure.
majadal m. sheepfold. 2 pasture ground for sheep.
majadear intr. [of sheep] to take shelter for the night. 2 to manure.
majadería f. nonsense, foolish remark or act.
majaderillo m. bobbin [for making lace].
majadero, -ra adj. silly, stupid. 2 m.-f. dolt, bore. 3 m. pestle, pounder. 4 MAJADERILLO.
majadura f. crushing, pounding, mashing.
majagranzas, pl. -zas m. stupid bore.
majar tr. to crush, pound, pestle, mash. 2 coll. to pester, annoy.
majencia f. MAJEZA.
majestad f. majesty. 2 (cap.) Majesty [title]: Su Divina Majestad, the Lord, God.
majestuosidad f. majesty, stateliness.
majestuoso, -sa adj. majestic, grand, stately.
majeza f. freedom of manners and gaudiness of dress. 2 boastfulness. 3 prettiness, fineness.
majo, -ja adj. boastful. 2 dressed up. 3 fine, pretty. 4 adj.-n. applied to persons displaying a freedom of manners and a gaudiness of dress that are peculiar to some low classes.
majolar m. grove of white hawthorns.
majoleta f. MARJOLETA.

majoleto m. MARJOLETO.
majuela f. BOT. fruit of the white hawthorn.
majuelo m. BOT. white hawtorn. 2 vineyard.
1) **mal** adj. contr. of MALO, used only before masculine nouns: ~ humor, bad humour; ~ gusto, bad taste. 2 adv. bad, badly, ill, wrongly, wickedly; poorly, deficiently; in a bad way or situation: ~ adquirido, ill-gotten: ~ hecho, badly done; misshapen; wrong; unjust: estar ~ de salud, to be in bad health; de ~ en peor, from bad to worse; ~ de su grado, unwillingly; ~ que bien, anyhow, anyway; ~ que le pese, in spite of him. 3 amiss: algo va ~, something is amiss. 4 hardly, scarcely. 5 interj. ¡mal haya...!, confound...!, curses on...!
2) **mal**, pl. **males** m. evil, ill, harm, wrong, injury, misfortune: el bien y el ~, good and evil; hacer ~, to harm, injure; to be injurious; llevar or tomar a ~, to take ill, take offence at. 3 illness, disease, evil, ailment, complaint: ~ de ojo, evil eye; ~ de piedra, lithiasis.
mala f. English or French mail or post. 2 manilla.
malabar adj.-n. of Malabar. 2 juegos malabares, juggling.
malabarista m. juggler.
Malaca pr. n. GEOG. Malay Peninsula.
malacate m. whim, whimsey [hoisting machine].
malacia f. MED. pica [depraved appetite].
malacitano, -na adj.-n. MALAGUEÑO.
malacología f. malacology.
malaconsejado, -da adj. ill-advised.
malacopterigio, gia adj. ICHTH. malacopterygian.
malacostráceo, -a adj.-m. ZOOL. malacostracan.
Málaga f. pr. n. GEOG. Malaga. 2 m. (not cap.) Malaga wine.
malagana f. coll. faintness, swoon.
malagueño, -ña adj.-n. of Malaga. 2 f. popular song of Malaga.
malamente adv. badly, poorly, wrongly.
malandante adj. unfortunate, unhappy.
malandanza f. misfortune, misery.
malandrín adj. wicked, rascally. 2 m. rascal, scoundrel.
Malaquías m. pr. n. BIBL. Malachi.
malaquita f. MINER. malachite.
malar adj.-m. ZOOL. malar.
malaria f. MED. malaria.
Malasia pr. n. GEOG. Malaysia.
malasio, sia adj.-n. Malaysian.
malavenido, -da adj. displeased. 2 in disagreement.
malaventura f. misfortune, unhappiness.
malaventurado, -da adj. unfortunate, unhappy.
Malaya f. pr. n. GEOG. Malaya.
malayo, -ya adj.-n. Malay, Malayan.
malbaratar tr. to undersell. 2 to squander.
malbaratillo m. second-hand shop.
malcarado, -da adj. grim-faced.
malcasado, -da adj. undutiful [spouse].
malcasar tr. to mismate [in marriage]. 2 ref. to be mismated [in marriage].
malcaso m. treachery, infamous act.
malcomer tr.-intr. to eat poorly.
malcomido, -da adj. underfed, that eats poorly.
malcontento, -ta adj. displeased, discontented. 2 adj.-n. malcontent.
malcriado, -da adj. ill-bred, incivil. 2 spoiled [child].
malcriar tr. to spoil [a child].
maldad f. wickedness, badness. 2 wicked act.
maldecir tr. to curse, accurse. 2 intr. to curse. 3 ~

de, to speak ill of, to backbite. ¶ CONJUG. like *decir*, except the INDIC. Fut.: *maldeciré*, etc.; the COND.: *maldeciría*, etc., and the PAST. P.: *maldecido* or *maldito*.

maldiciente *adj.* cursing. *2* slanderous, backbiting. *3 m.-f.* slanderer, backbiter.

maldición *f.* malediction, curse.

maldispuesto, -ta *adj.* indisposed. *2* unwilling.

maldije, maldiga, etc. *irr.* V. MALDECIR.

maldito, -ta *adj.* accursed, damned. *2* wicked. *3* bad, mean. *4* nothing, no: ~ *lo que me importa*, I don't care a straw. *5 m.* el *Maldito*, the Evil One, the Devil. *6 f.* coll. *la maldita*, the tongue.

maleabilidad *f.* malleability.

maleable *adj.* malleable.

maleador, -ra *adj.* spoiling. *2* perverting, corrupting. *3 m.-f.* spoiler. *4* perverter, corrupter.

maleante *adj.* MALEADOR 1 & 2. *2* evildoing. *3 m.-f.* evildoer, rogue.

malear *tr.* to spoil, damage. *2* to pervert, corrupt. *3 ref.* to spoil, become corrupted. *4* to go bad, go wrong.

malecón *m.* dike, levee, mole, embankment.

maledicencia *f.* evil talk, slander, backbiting.

maleficencia *f.* maleficence.

maleficiar *tr.* to harm, injure. *2* to harm by a spell or incantation.

maleficio *m.* spell, incantation.

maléfico, -ca *adj.* maleficent, harmful. *2* malefic. *3 m.* sorcerer.

malejo, -ja *adj.* baddish, rather bad.

maléolo *m.* ANAT. malleolus.

malestar *m.* malaise, discomfort, uneasiness.

maleta *f.* valise, suitcase: *hacer la* ~, to pack up, get ready for departure. *2 m.* coll. bungler; unskilled bullfighter.

maletero *m.* valise maker or seller. *2* [station] porter.

maletín *m.* small valise, satchel, -traveller's handbag, *gripsac, *grip. *2* MIL. ~ *de grupa*, saddlebag.

malevolencia *f.* malevolence, ill will.

malévolo, -la *adj.* malevolent, malignant.

maleza *f.* weeds. *2* underbrush, brake, thicket.

malformación *f.* MED. malformation.

malgache *adj.-n.* Madagascan.

malgastador, -ra *adj.* extravagant, squandering. *2 m.-f.* spendthrift, squanderer, wastrel.

malgastar *tr.* to misspend, waste, squander.

malhablado, -da *adj.* foul-mouthed.

malhadado, -da *adj.* ill-starred, unfortunate.

malhechor, -ra *m.-f.* evil-doer, malefactor, malefactress, criminal.

malherir *tr.* to wound badly.

malhumorado, -da *adj.* ill-humoured, peevish.

malicia *f.* malice. *2* malignity, evil intention. *3* cunning, slyness, sagacity. *4* suspiciousness, inclination to think ill. *5* suspicion.

maliciar *tr.-ref.* to suspect, fear. *2 tr.* MALEAR.

malicioso, -sa *adj.* suspicious, inclined to think ill. *2* malicious.

málico, -ca *adj.* CHEM. malic.

malignante *adj.* malignant, malicious.

malignar *tr.* to vitiate, corrupt, deprave.

malignidad *f.* malignance, malignity.

maligno, -na *adj.* malign, malignant, evil, wicked. *2* MED. malign, malignant.

malilla *f.* manille. *2* a card game.

Malinas *f. pr. n.* GEOG. Malines, Mechlin.

malintencionado, -da *adj.* evil-disposed. *2 m.-f.* evil-disposed person.

malmandado, -da *adj.* disobedient.

malmaridada *adj.* faithless [wife]. *2 f.* faithless wife.

malo, -la (before a masculine noun, **mal**) *adj.* bad, evil, wicked, depraved, vicious. *2* bad, poor, inferior, deficient. *3* ill, bad [unfavourable; harmful; offensive; unsound]: *mala voluntad*, ill will; ~ *para*, bad for, injurious to. *4* naughty, mischievous. *5* foul, obscene. *6* ill, sick, unwell; diseased, sore: *dedo* ~, sore finger; *estar* ~, to be ill, be unwell. *7* unpleasant, disagreeable. *8* hard, difficult: ~ *de entender*, hard to understand. *9 estar de malas*, to be out of luck. *10 lo* ~ *es que*, the trouble is that. *11 por las malas*, by force. *12 por malas o por buenas*, willingly or unwillingly. *13 interj.* ¡*malo!*, bad!, that is bad!

malogrado, -da *adj.* late [person]. *2* failed, frustrated.

malograr *tr.* to miss, waste, spoil [time, an opportunity, etc.]. *2 ref.* to fail, fall through. *3* to have an untimely end.

malogro *m.* failure, frustration, spoiling. *2* loss [of an opportunity, etc.]. *3* untimely end.

maloliente *adj.* ill-smelling, malodorous.

malón *m.* (Am.) Indian raid. *2* (Am.) surprise attack. *3* (Am.) mean trick, ill turn.

malparado, -da *adj.* impaired, hurt, damaged.

malparar *tr.* to treat ill, hurt, damage, put in a bad way.

malparir *intr.* [of a woman] to miscarry.

malparto *m.* miscarriage, abortion.

malquerencia *f.* ill will, dislike.

malquerer *tr.* to dislike, hate.

malquistar *tr.* to estrange, set at odds or against. *2 ref.* to incur dislike: *malquistarse con*, to incur the dislike of.

malquisto, -ta *adj.* disliked, unpopular.

malrotar *tr.* to misspend, squander.

malsano, -na *adj.* unhealthy, unhealthful, unwholesome. *2* unhealthy, sickly.

malsín *m.* mischief-maker, talebearer.

malsonante *adj.* ill-sounding.

malsufrido, -da *adj.* impatient, unresigned.

Malta *f. pr. n.* GEOG. Malta.

malta *m.* malt. *2* roast barley.

maltés, -sa *adj.-n.* Maltese.

maltosa *f.* CHEM. maltose.

maltratamiento *m.* abuse, ill treatment, ill usage, rough usage, maltreatment.

maltratar *tr.* to abuse, ill-use, ill-treat, maltreat, treat roughly. *2* to use roughly; to spoil.

maltrato *m.* MALTRATAMIENTO.

maltrecho, -cha *adj.* badly off, battered, damaged.

maltusiano, -na *adj.-n.* Malthusian.

maltusianismo *m.* Malthusianism.

malucho, -cha *adj.* poorly (in health).

malva *f.* BOT. mallow: *ser una* ~, *ser como una* ~, fig. to be meek and mild. *2* BOT. ~ *arbórea, loca, real* or *rosácea*, rose mallow, hollyhock.

malváceo, -a *adj.* BOT. malvaceous.

malvado, -da *adj.* wicked, evil, villainous. *2 m.-f.* wicked person, villain.

malvarrosa *f.* BOT. rose mallow, hollyhock.

malvasía *f.* malmsey, malvoisie.

malvavisco *m.* BOT. marshmallow.

malvender *tr.* to undersell, sell at a loss.

malversación *f.* malversation. *2* embezzlement, peculation.

malversador, -ra *m.-f.* one who misapplies funds. *2* embezzler, peculator.

malversar *tr.* to misapply [funds]. *2* to embezzle.

malvís, malviz *m.* ORN. song thrush, redwing.
malla *f.* mesh [of net]; network. *2* meshed or netted fabric. *3* mail [of armour]. *4* WEAV. heddle. *5* THEAT. *traje de ~* or *mallas*, fleshings.
mallete *m.* mallet.
mallo *m.* maul, mall. *2* mall, pall-mall [game and alley].
Mallorca *f. pr. n.* GEOG. Majorca.
mallorquín, -na *adj.-n.* Majorcan.
mama *f.* ANAT., ZOOL. mamma, breast, udder. *2* mamma, mummy [mother].
mamá *f.* MAMA 2.
mamacallos, *pl.* **-llos** *s.* coll. simpleton.
mamada *f.* suck [act of sucking milk].
mamadera *f.* breast pump. *2* (Am.) nursing bottle.
mamado, -da *adj.* (Am.) drunk, intoxicated.
mamador, -ra *adj.* sucking.
mamaíta *f. dim.* mammy.
mamantón, -na *adj.* sucking [animal].
mamar *tr.* to suck [milk]. *2 tr.-ref.* coll. to swallow, devour. *3* coll. to get, obtain. *4 no mamarse el dedo,* not to be taken in easily. *5 ref.* (Am.) to get drunk. *6* (Am.) *mamarse a uno,* to kill, or to get the best of, someone.
mamario, -ria *adj.* mammary.
mamarrachada *f.* coll. grotesque or ridiculous act.
mamarrachista *m.* PAINT. coll. dauber.
mamarracho *m.* coll. grotesque or ridiculous figure. *2* PAINT. daub. *3* coll. despicable man.
mamelón *f.* mound, knoll, hillock; small peak. *2* SURG. nipplelike protuberance.
mameluco *m.* Mameluke. *2* coll. dolt, simpleton.
mamella *f.* one of the two appendages hanging on the neck of goats.
mamey *m.* BOT. mammee.
mamífero, -ra *adj.* ZOOL. mammalian. *2 m.* ZOOL. mammal. *3 m. pl.* ZOOL. Mammalia.
mamila *f.* ZOOL. breast or udder round the nipple. *2* ANAT. mamilla [in men].
mamilar *adj.* mamillary.
mamola *f.* chuck under the chin.
mamón, -na *adj.* sucking. *2* fond of sucking. *3 m. -f.* suckling. *4 m.* BOT. shoot, sucker. *5* BOT. genip tree.
mamotreto *m.* memorandum book. *2* coll. bulky book or bundle of papers.
mampara *f.* screen [before a door, etc.].
mamparo NAUT. bulkhead.
mamporro *m.* blow, bump.
mampostería *f.* rubble masonry, rubblework.
mampuesta *f.* MAS. course.
mampuesto, -ta *adj.* MAS. rubble, for rubblework. *2 m.* rough stone, rubble stone. *3* parapet, shelter. *4 de ~,* spare, extra; from a sheltered position.
mamujar *tr.-intr.* to suck intermittently.
mamullar *tr.* to chew as if sucking. *2* coll. to mumble, mutter.
mamut *m.* PALEONT. mammoth.
maná *m.* manna.
manada *f.* herd, flock, drove, pack. *2* handful.
manadero, -ra *adj.* flowing, running. *2 m.* source, sprint. *3* herdsman, shepherd.
manantial *adj.* spring [water]. *2 m.* source, spring. *3* source, origin.
manantío, -a *adj.* flowing, running. *2 m.* source.
manar *intr.* to flow, run, issue forth. *2* fig. to abound, be rich in. *3 tr.* to pour forth.
Manasés *m. pr. n.* BIBL. Manasseh.
manatí *m.* ZOOL. manatee, sea cow.
manaza *f. augm.* large hand.

mancamiento *m.* maiming. *2* lack, want, deficiency.
mancar *tr.* to maim [in the hand]. *2 ref.* to become maimed [in the hand].
manceba *f.* mistress, concubine.
mancebía *f.* bawdyhouse, brothel.
mancebo *m.* young man, youth. *2* bachelor [unmarried man]. *3* shopman, shopboy.
mancera *f.* plough handle, plow handle.
mancilla *f.* spot, blemish.
manco, -ca *adj.* handless, one-handed, armless, maimed. *2* fig. faulty, defective. *3 m.-f.* handless, one-handed or armless person.
mancomún (de) *adv.* jointly, in agreement.
mancomunadamente *adv.* DE MANCOMÚN.
mancomunar *tr.* to associate, join, combine, pool [persons, resources, exertions, etc.]. *2 ref.* to associate, unite, act in concert.
mancomunidad *f.* union, association. *2* LAW association of provinces or municipalities.
mancuerda *f.* rack [torture].
mancha *f.* stain, spot, blot, discolouration. *2* ASTR. spot, macula. *3* spot, speckle: *~ ocultar,* ZOOL. eyespot. *4* patch [of vegetation]. *5* fig. stain, spot, blot, blemish.
manchado, -da *adj.* stained, soiled. *2* spotted, speckled. *3* patched [with colour or vegetation].
manchar *tr.* to stain, soil, discolour. *2* to spot, speckle. *3* to patch [with colour or vegetation]. *4* fig. to stain, defile, blot, sully. *5 ref.* to soil, become soiled or stained. *6* to disgrace oneself.
manchego, -ga *adj.-n.* of La Mancha [region of Spain].
manchón *m.* large stain. *2* patch [in a field, heath, etc.] where vegetation is most thick.
manchú, *pl.* **-chúes,** *adj.-n.* Manchu.
manda *f.* bequest, legacy.
mandadero, -ra *m.-f.* messenger, errand boy or girl.
mandado *m.* order, command. *2* errand.
mandamiento *m.* mandate, order, command. *2* LAW writ. *3* commandment: *los mandamientos de la ley de Dios,* the ten commandments.
mandante *m.-f.* LAW constituent, mandator.
mandar *tr.* to command, order, direct, decree: *~ hacer, escribir,* etc., to order or have [something] done, written, etc.; *~ decir,* to send word; *~ venir,* to call, order to come. *2* to command, be in command of. *3* to will, leave, bequeath. *4* to send: *~ por,* to send for. *5* to control [one's horse]. *6 intr.* to command, govern [exercise direct authority]. *7 ref. mandarse* or *mandarse mudar,* to go away.
mandarín *m.* mandarin.
mandarina *adj.* mandarin [language; orange]. *2 f.* BOT. mandarin orange.
mandarria *f.* shipwright's iron maul or hammer.
mandatario *m.* mandatary, mandatory. *2* mandatee.
mandato *m.* mandate, command, order, injunction. *2* LAW, POLIT. mandate. *3* ECCL. maundy.
mandíbula ANAT., ZOOL. jaw, mandible.
mandil *m.* apron; leather or coarse apron. *2* apron [of Freemasons].
mandilete *m.* ARTIL. door of a porthole.
mandilón *m.* coll. mean-spirited fellow, coward.
mandioca *f.* manioc, cassava [plant and starch].
mando *m.* command [act of commanding; authority or power to command]: *alto ~,* high command; *tomar el ~,* to take command. *2* MACH. drive, control: *~ a distancia,* remote control; *~*

doble, AUTO. dual drive; ~ *único*, RADIO. single control.

mandoble *m.* two-handed blow [with a sword].

mandolina *f.* MUS. mandolin.

mandón, -na *adj.* imperious, domineering, *bossy. 2 *m.-f.* domineering person.

mandrágora *f.* BOT. mandrake.

mandria *adj.-m.* good-for-nothing [fellow].

mandril *m.* ZOOL. mandrill. 2 MACH. mandrel, mandril; chuck [of a lathe]. 3 MED. mandrin.

manducación *f.* coll. eating.

manducar *tr.-intr.* coll. to eat.

manducatoria *f.* coll. food, sustenance.

manea *f.* MANIOTA.

manear *tr.* to hobble or hopple [a horse]. 2 MANEJAR.

manecilla *f. dim.* small hand. 2 book clasp. 3 hand [of clock or watch]; index [on instruments]. 4 PRINT. index, fist. 5 BOT. tendril.

manecita *f. dim.* small hand, little hand.

manejar *tr.* to manage, handle, wield. 2 to manage control, conduct, govern. 3 EQUIT. to manage. 4 (Am.) to drive [a car]. 5 *ref.* to behave, manage. 6 to get around, move about.

manejo *m.* handling, wielding. 2 management, conduct. 3 manège, horsemanship. 4 (Am.) driving [a car]. 5 scheming, intrigue.

maneota *f.* MANIOTA.

manera *f.* manner, way, mode, fashion; manner, style [in literature or art]: *a la ~ de*, in the style of; *a ~ de*, kind of; like; by way of; *de ~ que*, so that; so then, and so; *de ninguna ~*, in no way, by no means; *de otra ~*, otherwise: *de todas maneras*, at any rate, anyhow; *en gran ~*, very much, to a great extent; *sobre ~*, exceedingly, beyond measure; *hacer por ~ que*, to contrive. 2 way, means: *no hay ~ de*, it is not possible to. 3 quality, class [of persons]. 4 *pl.* manners, behaviour.

manero, -ra *adj.* FALCON. trained, tame.

manes *m. pl.* manes.

manga *f.* sleeve: *en mangas de camisa*, in shirt sleeves; *hacer mangas y capirotes*, coll. to act arbitrarily; *tener ~ ancha*, fig. to be too indulgent; to be unscrupulous. 2 wheel seat [of axletree]. 3 kind of portmanteau. 4 hose [pipe]: *~ de riego*, watering hose. 5 scoop net. 6 casting net. 7 NAUT. air duct, wind sail. 8 conical cloth strainer. 9 BRIDGE game. 10 NAUT. beam [ship's breadth]. 11 METEOR. waterspout [rotating column]. 12 *~ de agua*, cloudburst, waterspout. 13 *~ de viento*, METEOR. whirlwind; AER. wind sock. 14 *pl.* profits, extras.

mangana *f.* lasso, lariat.

manganato *m.* CHEM. manganate.

manganear *tr.* to lasso.

manganeo *m.* lassoing.

manganeso *m.* CHEM. manganese.

manganilla *f.* trick, stratagem.

mangante *m.* coll. beggar. 2 coll. loafer, vagabond.

manglar *m.* mangrove swamp.

mangle *m.* BOT. mangrove tree. 2 MACH. mangle.

mango *m.* handle, haft, helve: *~ de escoba*, broomstick; *~ de pluma*, penholder. 2 BOT. mango.

mangonear *intr.* to loiter, loaf around. 2 to meddle, intermeddle, play the boss.

mangoneo *m.* meddling, intermeddling.

mangonero, -ra *adj.* meddling, fond of meddling.

mangosta *f.* ZOOL. mongoose.

mangostán *m.* BOT. mangosteen [tree].

mangosto *m.* BOT. mangosteen [fruit].

mangote *m.* long, wide sleeve. 2 sleeve protector.

mangual *m.* flail [medieval weapon]. 2 MAYAL.

manguardia *f.* ARCH. wing wall [of a bridge].

manguera *f.* hose, watering hose. 2 NAUT. air duct, wind sail. 3 METEOR. waterspout.

manguero *m.* hoseman.

manguitería *f.* furriery. 2 fur shop.

manguitero *m.* furrier.

manguito *m.* muff [for hands]. 2 knitted half-sleeve. 3 sleeve protector. 4 MACH. muff, sleeve, shaft coupling, pipe coupling.

maní, *pl.* **manises** *m.* CACAHUETE.

manía *f.* MED. mania. 2 mania, craze, whim. 3 dislike.

maníaco, -ca *adj.-n.* MED. maniac.

manialbo, -ba *adj.* white-footed [horse].

maniatar *tr.* to tie the hands. 2 to hand-cuff.

maniático, -ca *adj.* queer, crazy. 2 *m.-f.* queer person; person who has a craze for.

manicomio *m.* insane asylum, madhouse.

manicordio *m.* MUS. manichord.

manicuro, -ra *m.-f.* manicure, manicurist. 2 *f.* manicure [care of hands and nails].

manida *f.* abode, haunt, dep.

manido, -da *adj.* high, gamey [meat]. 2 trite, stale.

manifacero, -ra *adj.* coll. meddlesome.

manifestación *f.* manifestation, exhibition, display. 2 statement, declaration. 3 POL. public manifestation or demonstration.

manifestador, -ra *adj.* manifesting. 2 *m.-f.* manifester.

manifestante *m.-f.* manifestant, demonstrant.

manifestar *tr.* to manifest, show, reveal, display. 2 to state, declare. 3 ECCL. to expose [the Eucharist]. 4 *ref.* to manifest oneself or itself, to show, appear; to become manifest. 5 POL. to manifest. ¶ CONJUG. like *acertar*.

manifiesto, -ta *adj.* manifest, plain, obvious, evident: *poner de ~*, to make evident; to exhibit, expose. 2 *m.* manifest, manifiesto [public declaration]. 3 NAUT. manifest. 4 ECCL. exposing the Eucharist.

manija *f.* handle [of some implements]. 2 hobble, hopple [for horses]. 3 MACH. ring, clasp.

manilargo, -ga *adj.* long-handed. 2 ready-fisted. 3 open-handed.

manilense; **manileño, -ña** *adj.-n.* of Manila.

maniluvio *m.* MED. bath for the hands.

manilla *f.* bracelet. 2 hand-cuff, manacle.

manillar *m.* handle bar [of bicycle].

maniobra *f.* handling, operation. 2 NAUT. working [of a ship]. 3 NAUT. gear, rigging, tackle. 4 MIL., NAV. manœuvre. 5 fig. manœuvring, manœuvring, trick. 6 *pl.* MIL., NAV. manœuvres. 7 RLY. shift, shifting.

maniobrar *intr.* to manœuvre. 2 RLY. to shift.

maniota *f.* hobble, hopple [for horses].

manipulación *f.* manipulation.

manipulador, -ra *adj.* manipulating. 2 *m.-f.* manipulator. 3 *m.* TELEG. key, telegraph key.

manipular *tr.* to manipulate, handle, manage.

manipuleo *m.* manipulation, managing.

manípulo *m.* maniple.

maniqueísmo *m.* Manicheanism, Manicheism.

maniqueo, -a *adj.-n.* Manichean.

maniquete *m.* black lace mitten. 2 mitten.

maniquí, *pl.* **-quíes** *m.* manikin, mannequin, lay figure, dummy. 2 mannequin [woman].

manir *tr.-def.* COOK. to keep [meat or game] until it

becomes gamey. | Only used in the forms having *i* in their termination.

manirroto, -ta *adj.* prodigal. *2 m.-f.* spendthrift.

manita *f.* mannitol, manna sugar.

manivacío, -cía *adj.* coll. empty-handed.

manivela *f.* MACH. crank.

manjar *m.* food, dish.

manjorrada *f.* lot of ordinary victuals.

mano *f.* hand [of a person; person who does something; work, agency; ability; skill; power, control, direction; personal possession; aid]: ~ *de obra,* work, labour [as distinguished from materials]; labour, labourers; ~ *derecha* or *diestra,* right hand; ~ *izquierda, siniestra* or *zurda,* left hand; tact; cunning; *buena* ~, adroitness; *mala* ~, bad luck; awkwardness, lack of skill; *manos limpias,* clean hands, honesty; *manos muertas,* dead hand, mortmain; mortmain owners; *buenas manos,* skill; *abrir la* ~, to be generous; to become more lenient; *apretar la* ~, to squeeze someone's hand; to shake hands with; to increase the rigour; *caerse de las manos,* [of a book], to be boring; *cargar la* ~, to press, insist; to be very rigid; to charge an immoderate price; to spice too heavily; *dar de* ~, to reject; to leave, abandon; *dar en manos de,* to fall into the hands of; *dar la* ~ *a,* to shake hands with; to aid, protect, lend a hand to; *dar la última* ~ *a,* to finish, retouch; *darse las manos,* to shake hands; to be reconciled; *dejar de la* ~, to leave, abandon; *echar* ~, *la* ~, or *manos a,* to seize, take; *echar una* ~, to lend a hand; *echar* ~ *de,* to resort to, make use of; *poner manos a la obra,* to put one's hand to the plough, to get busy; *tener,* or *traer, entre manos,* to have in hand; *tener uno la* ~, to contain oneself; *tener* ~ *con uno,* to have a pull with someone; *tener* ~ *en,* to have a hand in; *tener* ~ *para,* to have a hand for; *untar la* ~ *de,* to bribe; *a la* ~, near, at hand, within reach; *a* ~ *airada,* violently; *a* ~ *derecha,* or *izquierda,* on the right hand, or left hand, side; *a manos llenas,* liberally, abundantly; *bajo* ~, underhandedly secretly; *con las manos en la masa,* redhanded; *cogidos de las manos,* hand in hand; *de* ~ *en* ~, from hand to hand; *de manos a boca,* suddenly, unexpectedly, with proximity; ~ *a* ~, in company, together, tête-à-tête; on equal footing, even; ~ *sobre* ~, idle; *si a* ~ *viene,* perhaps; it is possible that.

2 hand [person, source]: *de buena* ~, on good authority; *de primera* ~, first-hand; *3* hand [pledge of marriage]. *4* and [of monkey]. *5* forefoot [of quadruped]. *6* BUTCH., COOK. foot, trotter. *7* hand, index [of a clock, etc.]. *8* pestle. *9* coat [of paint, varnish, etc.]. *10* quire [of paper]. *11* game, round. *12* first hand [at cards]: *ser* ~, to lead. *13* reprimand. *14 pl.* work, labour [as distinguished from materials].

manojo *m.* bundle, bunch [of flowers, herbs, etc.].

Manolo *m. pr. n.* MANUEL.

manolo, -la *m.-f.* formerly, a Madrilenian of low class affecting a peculiar mode of dress and manners.

manómetro *m.* manometer.

manopla *f.* gauntlet. *2* postilion's whip.

manosear *tr.* to handle, feel, paw [something] repeatedly.

manoseo *m.* repeated handling, feeling or pawing.

manota *f. augm.* large hand.

manotada *f.,* **manotazo** *m.* blow with the hand.

manotear *tr.* to beat with the hands. *2 intr.* to gesticulate with the hands.

manoteo *m.* gesticulation with the hands.

manotón *m.* MANOTADA.

manquedad, manquera *f.* lack of one or both hands or arms. *2* faultiness, imperfection.

mansalva (a) *adv.* without danger, without running any risk, in a cowardly manner.

mansarda *f.* ARCH. mansard roof.

mansedumbre *f.* meekness, mildness, gentleness. *2* tameness.

mansejón, -na *adj.* very tame.

mansión *f.* stay, sojourn. *2* abode, dwelling, mansion: ~ *celestial,* heavenly home.

1) **manso** *m.* MASADA.

2) **manso, -sa** *adj.* tame. *2* meek, mild, gentle. *3* soft, quiet, gentle, slow: *agua mansa,* slow water.

mansurrón, -na *adj.* excessively meek or tame.

manta *f.* blanket [bed covering]. *2* blanket [used by men as a shawl or muffler]. *3* horse blanket. *4* MIL. mantelet, mantlet. *5* beating, drubbing. *6* ~ *de coche,* ~ *de viaje,* lap robe, travelling rug. *7 a* ~, *a* ~ *de Dios,* coll. abundantly.

manteamiento *m.* tossing in a blanket.

mantear *tr.* to toss in a blanket.

manteca *f.* fat, lard; butter; fatty oil: ~ *de cerdo,* lard; ~ *de vaca,* butter; ~ *de cacao,* cocoa butter.

mantecada *f.* buttered toast and sugar. *2* cake made of flour, eggs, sugar and butter.

mantecado *m.* butter bun. *2* ice-cream.

mantecón, -na *m.-f.* milksop, mollycoddle.

mantecoso, -sa *adj.* greasy, buttery.

mantel, *pl.* **-teles** *m.* tablecloth. *2* altar cloth.

mantelería *f.* table linen.

manteleta *f.* manteleta [lady's shawl or short cape].

mantelete *m.* ECCL. mantelletta. *2* MIL. mantelet, mantlet [movable shelter]. *3* HER. mantling.

mantellina *f.* mantilla.

mantenedor *m.* president of a tournament, joust, etc.

mantenencia *f.* maintenance.

mantener *tr.* to maintain, support, keep. *2* to hold, sustain, hold up. *3 ref.* to maintain, support oneself. *4* to keep [continue, perservere]. *5* *mantenerse en,* to remain firm in; to hold on to. ¶ CONJUG. like *tener.*

mantenimiento *m.* maintenance, support. *2* sustenance, food, living. *3* keeping, carrying on. *4* maintenance, upkeep.

manteo *m.* long cloak worn by Roman Catholic ecclesiastics. *2* MANTEAMIENTO.

mantequero, -ra *adj.* [pertaining to] butter. *2 m.-f.* butter maker or seller. *3* butter dish, butter bowl. *4 f.* churn [for making butter].

mantequilla *f.* butter. *2* hard sauce.

mantero, -ra *m.-f.* blanket maker or seller.

mantés, -sa *adj.* scoundrely. *2 m.-f.* scoundrel.

mantilla *f.* mantilla. *2* saddlecloth. *3* PRINT. blanket. *4 pl.* swaddling clothes: *estar en mantillas* [of a work, undertaking, etc.], to be in its infancy.

mantillo *m.* humus, vegetable mould. *2* manure.

mantis *f.* ENT. mantis; ~ *religiosa,* mantis, praying cricket.

mantisa *f.* MATH. mantissa.

manto *m.* mantle [garment; something that covers or envelops]. *2* robe of state. *3* large mantilla. *4* mantel-front of chimney. *5* ZOOL. mantle.

mantón, -na *adj.* having drooping wings [bird]. *2*

m. large shawl; ~ *de Manila*, bright shawl, embroidered silk shawl.

manuable *adj.* handy, easy to handle.

manual *adj.* manual: *trabajo* ~, manual labour. *2 m.* manual, handbook.

manubrio *m.* handle, crank. *2* ANAT., ZOOL. manubrium.

manucodiata *f.* ORN. bird of paradise.

Manuel *m. pr. n.* Emmanuel.

Manuela *f. pr. n.* Emma.

manuela *f.* [in Madrid] open hackney carriage.

manufactura *f.* manufactured article. *2* manufactory, factory.

manufacturar *tr.* to manufacture.

manufacturero, -ra *adj.* manufacturing.

manumisión *f.* manumission.

manumisor *m.* manumitter.

manumitir *tr.* to manumit.

manuscrito, -ta *adj.-n.* manuscript.

manutención *f.* maintenance, sustenance, board. *2* upkeep, conservation.

manzana *f.* BOT. apple; ~ *de la discordia*, fig. apple of discord. *2* city block, block of houses. *3* pommel [of sword]. *4* round ornamental knob. *5* (Am.) Adam's apple.

manzanal, manzanar *m.* apple orchad.

manzanilla *f.* BOT., PHARM. camomile. *2* small round olive. *3* round, ornamental knob [on furniture, etc.]. *4* pad, cushion [of foot·of clawed animals]. *5* tip of the chin. *6* manzanilla [pale dry sherry]. *7* BOT. ~ *hedionda*, stinking camomile. *8 adj. aceituna* ~, MANZANILLA *2.*

manzanillo *m.* BOT. manchineel. *2* BOT. *olivo* ~, olive tree yielding a small round olive.

manzano *m.* BOT. apple tree.

maña *f.* dexterity, skill, cunning, knack; address, cleverness, tact: *darse* ~, to manage, contrive. *2* trick, wile. *2* bad habit.

mañana *f.* morning, forenoon: *de* ~, early in the morning; *por la* ~, in the morning. *2 m.* morrow. *3 adv.* tomorrow; later, in time to come: *pasado* ~, the day after tomorrow.

mañanear *intr.* to get up early [by habit].

mañanero, -ra *adj.* early-rising.

mañero, -ra *adj.* shrewd, artful, cunning. *2* easy, handy.

maño, -ña *adj.-n.* coll. Aragonese. *2* (dial. & Am.) brother; sister. *3* (dial. & Am.) dear, darling.

mañoco *m.* tapioca.

mañoso, -sa *adj.* dexterous, skilful, clever, shrewd. *2* having bad habits.

mañuela *f.* wile, low trick. *2 pl.* crafty person.

mapa *m.* map, chart. *2 f.* coll. *llevarse la* ~, to be the best in its line.

mapache *m.* ZOOL. raccoon.

mapamundi *m.* world map, map of the world.

mapurite *m.* ZOOL. (Am.) skunk.

maque *m.* lacquer. *2* BOT. heaven tree.

maquear *tr.* to lacquer.

maqueta *f.* maquette. *2* PRINT. dummy.

maqui *m.* BOT. a Chilean shrub. *2* ZOOL. macaco.

maquiavélico, -ca *adj.* Machiavellic, Machiavellian.

maquiavelismo *m.* Machiavellism.

maquila *f.* toll corn, miller's toll. *2* a grain measure [½ CELEMÍN].

maquilero *adj.* applied to a mill where grain is taken as pay for grinding.

maquillaje *m.* THEAT. make-up.

máquina *f.* machine, engine: ~ *de afeitar*, safety razor; electric razor; ~ *de coser*, sewing ma-

chine; ~ *de escribir*, typewriter; ~ *de vapor*, steam engine; ~ *fotográfica*, camera; ~ *herramienta*, machine tool; *tragaperras*, slot machine; *a toda* ~, at full speed. *2* locomotive. *3* THEAT. machine. *4* LIT. machine, machinery. *5* imposing structure.

maquinación *f.* machination.

maquinador, -ra *m.-f.* machinator.

maquinal *adj.* mechanical, unconscious, automatic.

maquinar *tr.* to machinate, scheme, plot, concoct.

maquinaria *f.* machinery. *2* applied mechanics.

maquinismo *m.* ECON. mechanization.

maquinista *m.-f.* machinist [constructor of engines]. *2* machinist, engineer, engine runner or driver. *3* THEAT. machinist.

mar *m. or f.* sea, ocean: ~ *de las Indias*, Indian Ocean; ~ *Muerto*, Dead Sea; ~ *Negro*, Black Sea; *alta* ~, high sea, open sea; ~ *de costado* or *de través*, sea on the beam; ~ *de fondo* or *de leva*, ground swell; *hacerse a la* ~, to take to the sea. *2* fig. ocean, lot, lots, great deal: *la* ~ *de dificultades*, a lot of difficulties. *3 adv. la* ~, very much; *la* ~ *de difícil*, extremely difficult. *4 a mares*, abundantly, copiously.

marabú *m.* marabou [bird and trimming].

marabuto *m.* Mahomedan hermitage.

maraca *f.* MUS. maraca.

maracayá *m.* ZOOL. margay.

maragato, -ta *m.-f.* native of a region in León [Spain].

maraña *f.* thicket, bush. *2* tangle, entanglement [of thread, hair, etc.]. *3* complexity, puzzle. *4* tale, lie [for making mischief]; mischief, discord.

marañero, -ra *adj.* embroiling. *2 m.-f.* embroiler, mischief-maker.

marañón *m.* BOT. cashew. *2* cashew nut.

marasmo *m.* MED. marasmus. *2* inactivity, depression.

Maratón *m. pr. n.* HIST. and SPORT. Marathon.

maravedí, *pl.* **-dises** or **-díes** *m.* maravedi [old Spanish coin].

maravilla *f.* wonder, marvel: *a las mil maravillas, a* ~, wonderfully weil. *2* BOT. four-o'clock, marvel of Peru. *4* BOT. ivy-leaved morning glory.

maravillar *tr.* to astonish, cause to marvel. *2 ref.* to wonder, marvel.

maravilloso, -sa *adj.* wonderful, marvellous, wondrous.

marbete *m.* label [slip of paper].

marca *f.* mark, brand [affixed, impressed, etc., distinguishing sign]: ~ *de fábrica*, trademark; ~ *registrada*, registered trademark. *2* marking, branding. *3* marking instrument. *4* make [origin of manufactured article]. *5* standard of measure. *6* NAUT. seamark, landmark. *7* SPORT. record. *8* HIST. march [frontier province]. *9 de* ~, *de* ~ *mayor*, great of its kind, exceeding the common measure.

marcación *f.* NAUT. bearing, relative bearing. *2* NAUT. taking a ship's bearings.

marcado, -da *adj.* marked, pronounced.

marcador, -ra *adj.* marking, branding. *2 m.-f.* marker [pers.]. *3 m.* SPORT. scoreboard. *4* PRINT. feeder [worker]. *5* hallmarker.

marcar *tr.* to mark, brand; to stencil. *2* to mark [linen]. *3* to mark [as noteworthy]. *4* to lay out, assign. *5* SPORT. to score. *6* SPORT. to mark. *7* TE-

LEPH. to dial [a number]. 8 ~ *el paso*, to mark time. 9 *ref.* NAUT. [of a ship] to take its bearings.

marcasita *f.* MINER. marcasite.

Marcelo *m. pr. n.* Marcellus.

marcescente *adj.* BOT. marcescent.

marcial *adj.* martial [pertaining to war], soldierly, warlike. 2 PHARM. martial.

marcialidad *f.* martialness.

marciano, -na *adj.-n.* Martian.

marco *m.* enclosing frame or case; picture frame, doorcase, windowcase. 2 mark [coin; weight]. 3 standard [of weights and measures]. 4 size stick.

marconigrama *m.* marconigram, wireless telegram.

Marcos *m. pr. n.* Mark.

marcha *f.* march [marching of troops; walk journey]: *marchas forzadas*, forced marches; *sobre la* ~, at once; right off. 2 MUS. march: ~ *fúnebre*, funeral march; ~ *nupcial*, wedding march. 3 march, progress, motion, course. 4 going, operation, running, working; *poner en* ~, to start, set going; *ponerse en* ~, to start, begin to move. 6 departure, setting out. 7 pace, speed, rate of speed: *a toda* ~, at full speed. 8 AUTO. *cambio de marchas*, gearshift. 9 MACH. ~ *atrás*, reverse.

marchamar *tr.* to mark [goods] at the custom house.

marchamo *m.* custom house mark. 2 lead seal.

marchapié *m.* NAUT. footrope.

marchar *intr.* to march, walk. 2 [of things] to go, proceed, go ahead, make progress. 3 [of machines, vehicles, etc.] to work, run, go, move. 4 MIL. to march. 5 *intr.-ref.* to go away, leave, depart.

marchitar *tr.* to wither, wilt, fade. 2 *ref.* to wither, wilt, fade [become withered or faded]. 3 to languish.

marchitez *f.* withered or faded condition.

marchito, -ta *adj.* withered, wilted, faded.

marea *f.* tide [of sea]: ~ *alta*, high tide; ~ *baja*, low tide; ~ *creciente*, flood tide; ~ *menguante*, ebb tide; ~ *muerta*, neap tide; ~ *viva*, spring tide. 2 gentle sea breeze. 3 dew, drizzle.

mareado, -da *adj.* nauseated, sick, seasick, carsick, airsick. 2 dizzy, giddy. 3 annoyed.

mareaje *m.* navigation, seamanship.

mareante *adj.* causing seasickness or carsickness. 2 making dizzy. 3 annoying. 4 navigating, seafaring. 5 *m.* navigator, sailor, seafarer.

marear *tr.* to sail [a ship]. 2 to annoy, bother. 3 *ref.* to become nauseated, sick, seasick, carsick, airsick. 4 to get dizzy.

marejada *f.* NAUT. surge, swell, ground sea. 2 commotion, stirring.

maremagno, mare mágnum *m.* coll. confusion, omnium-gatherum.

maremoto *m.* earthquake at sea.

mareo *m.* nausea, sickness, seasickness, carsickness, airsickness. 2 dizziness. 3 coll. annoyance.

mareógrafo *m.* mareograph.

marero *adj.* sea [wind].

maretazo *m.* surge, heavy sea.

marfil *m.* ivory. 2 ~ *vegetal*, ivory nut.

marfileño, -ña *adj.* [pertaining to] ivory. 2 ivorylike.

marga *f.* marl, loam.

margal *m.* marlpit, marly ground.

margallón *m.* BOT. palmetto, dwarf fan palm.

margarina *f.* margarine.

Margarita *f. pr. n.* Margaret.

margarita *f.* BOT. daisy, marguerite. 2 ZOOL. periwinkle. 3 pearl.

margen *m.-f.* margin. 2 marginal note. 3 border, edge, verge, fringe. 4 bank [of river]. 5 occasion: *dar* ~ *a*, to give occasion for.

marginal *adj.* marginal.

marginar *tr.* to margin, to write marginal notes on. 2 to leave a margin on [a page].

margoso, -sa *adj.* marly, loamy.

margrave *m.* margrave.

margraviato *m.* margraviate.

María *f. pr. n.* Mary.

Mariana *f. pr. n.* Marianne, Marian.

Mariano *m. pr. n.* Marion.

mariano, -na *adj.* ECCL. Marian.

marica *f.* ORN. magpie. 2 *m.* coll. milksop, effeminate man.

Maricastaña *f. en tiempos de* ~, in the days of yore; long, long ago.

maricón *m.* effeminate man. 2 sodomite. | Not in decent use.

maridaje *m.* conjugal affection and agreement. 2 union; agreement, harmony [of things].

maridar *intr.* to marry. 2 to live as man and wife. 3 fig. to join, connect.

maridillo *m.* foot stove.

marido *m.* husband.

mariguana, marihuana *f.* marihuana.

marimacho *m.* virago, manish woman.

marimanta *f.* coll. bogle, hobgoblin.

marimba *f.* MUS. marimba.

marimorena *f.* row, shindy.

marina *f.* seashore, seaside. 2 PAINT. marine, seascape. 3 seamanship. 4 marine [vessels]: ~ *de guerra*, navy; ~ *mercante*, merchant marine.

marinaje *m.* MARINERÍA.

marinar *tr.* to salt, marinate [fish]. 2 NAUT. to man [a ship].

marinear *tr.* to be a sailor, work as a sailor.

marinería *f.* sailoring, nautical profession. 2 sailors [collect.]. 3 sailors of a ship, crew.

marinero, -ra *adj.* [pertaining to] marine, sea or sailor. 2 sailorlike: *a la marinera*, sailorfashion. 3 NAUT. seaworthy. 4 *m.* mariner, sailor, seaman. 5 *f.* sailor blouse; middy, middy blouse.

marinesco, -ca *adj.* sailorly.

marinista *m.* marine painter, seascapist.

marino, -na *adj.* marine, nautical, sea. 2 *m.* mariner, sailor, seaman.

Mario *m. pr. n.* Marius.

marioneta *f.* puppet, marionette.

mariposa *f.* ENT. butterfly. 2 floating taper, night taper. 3 MACH. *de* ~, wing, butterfly.

mariposear *intr.* to change frequently one's occupations, fancies, etc. 2 to flutter around.

Mariquita *f. pr. n.* Molly, Polly.

mariquita *f.* ENT. ladybird. 2 *m.* milkshop.

marisabidilla *f.* coll. blue-stocking.

mariscal *m.* MIL. marshal: ~ *de campo*, field marshal. 2 farrier.

marisco *m.* shellfish.

marisma *f.* salt marsh.

marista *adj.-m.* Marist.

marital *adj.* marital.

marítimo, -ma *adj.* maritime, marine, sea.

maritornes *f.* mannish maidservant.

marjal *m.* marsh, moor, swamp.

marjoleta *f.* fruit of the hawthorn tree.

marjoleto *m.* BOT. hawthorn tree. 2 BOT. white hawthorn.

marmita *f.* kettle, pot, boiler.

marmitón *m.* scullion, kitchen boy.

mármol *m.* marble [stone; sculpture]. 2 marver [for rolling hot glass]. 3 PRINT. imposing stone.

marmolejo *m.* small marble column.

marmolería *f.* marblework. 2 marble shop or works.

marmolillo *m.* GUARDACANTÓN. 2 fig. dunce.

marmolista *m.* marble worker. 2 marble dealer.

marmoración *f.* stucco.

marmóreo, -a *adj.* marble, marbly, marmoreal.

marmosete *m.* PRINT. vignette.

marmota *f.* ZOOL. marmot. 2 coll. sleepy-head.

maro *m.* BOT. germander. 2 BOT. clary.

maroma *f.* cable of hemp or esparto. 2 tightrope.

maronita *adj.-n.* Maronite.

marqués *m.* marquis, marquess.

marquesa *f.* marchioness. 2 awning over a field tent.

marquesado *m.* marquisate.

marquesina *f.* marquee [canopy over an entrance]. 2 MARQUESA 2.

marquetería *f.* cabinet work. 2 marquetry.

marrajo, -ja *adj.* treacherous, vicious [bull]. 2 artful, wily, tricky. 3 *m.* ICHTH. shark.

marrana *f.* sow, female pig. 2 dirty, slovenly woman. 3 unprincipled woman.

marranada *f.* filthiness. 2 dirty trick.

marranería *f.* MARRANADA.

marrano, -na *adj.* dirty. 2 base, vile. 3 *m.* ZOOL. hog, pig. 4 coll. hog, pig, dirty man; cur.

marrar *intr.-tr.* to miss, fail. 2 *intr.* to go astray.

marras *adv.* a long time ago. 2 *de* ~, mentioned, aluded to.

marrasquino *m.* maraschino.

marro *m.* game resembling quoits. 2 a boys' game. 3 cat [used in tipcat]. 4 slip, miss. 5 dodge [to elude pursuer].

Mar Rojo *m. pr. n.* GEOG. Red Sea.

marrón *m.* kind of quoit used in playing MARRO 1. 2 *adj.* Gal maroon, brown.

marroquí *adj.-n.* Moroccan. 2 *m.* morocco, morocco leather.

marrubio *m.* BOT. horehound.

marrueco, -ca *adj.-n.* Moroccan.

Marruecos *m. pr. n.* GEOG. Morocco.

marrullería *f.* cunning, wheedling.

marrullero, -ra *adj.* cunning, wheedling. 2 *m.-f.* wheedler, cunning person.

Marsella *f. pr. n.* GEOG. Marseilles.

marsellés, -sa *adj.-n.* of Marseilles. 3 *m.* a kind of short jacket. 4 *f.* (cap.) Marseillaise [French national anthem].

marsopa, marsopia *f.* ZOOL. porpoise, harbour porpoise, sea hog.

marsupial *adj.-n.* marsupial.

Marta *f. pr. n.* Martha.

marta *f.* ZOOL. marten, pine marten. 2 marten [fur]. 3 ~ *cebellina*, sable, Siberian sable; sable [fur].

martagón, -na *m.-f.* sly, shrewd person. 2 *m.* BOT. Turk's-cap lily.

Marte *m. pr. n.* ASTR., MYTH. Mars.

martellina *m.* marteline.

martes, *pl.* **-tes** *m.* Tuesday: ~ *de carnaval*, Shrove Tuesday.

martillada *f.* blow or stroke with a hammer.

martillar *tr.* to hammer. 2 to worry, torment.

martillazo *m.* blow with a hammer.

martilleo *m.* hammering. 2 clatter.

martillo *m.* hammer [instrument]; claw hammer: *a macha* ~, firmly; strongly but roughly cons-

tructed. 2 MUS. tuning hammer. 3 ANAT. hammer, malleus. 4 auction rooms. 5 MACH. ~ *pilón*, drop hammer.

Martín *m. pr. n.* Martin.

martín del río, *pl.* **martines del río** *m.* ORN. night heron.

martin pescador, *pl.* **martín pescadores** *m.* ORN. kingfisher.

martinete *m.* ORN. night heron. 2 drive hammer, drop hammer. 3 hammer [of piano].

martingala *f.* trick, cunning.

Martinica (la) *f. pr. n.* GEOG. Martinique.

mártir *m.-f.* martyr.

martirio *m.* martyrdom.

martirizador, -ra *adj.* martyrizing, tormenting. 2 *m.-f.* martyrizer, tormentor.

martirizar *tr.* to martyr, martyrize; to torment.

martirologio *m.* martyrology.

marxismo *m.* Marxism.

marxista *adj.-n.* Marxian, Marxist.

marzo *m.* March.

marzoleto *m.* MARJOLETO.

mas *conj.* but [in the adversative sense].

más *adv.* more: ~ *de*, more than [with a numeral]; ~ *o menos*, more or less; *ni* ~ *ni menos*, exactly, just so; *no hay* ~, that is all; *cuanto* ~ *que, tanto* ~ *que*, all the more because. 2 It can be expressed by the termination «-er»: *más grande*, bigger. 3 most, -est; *el* ~ *bello*, the most beautiful; *el* ~ *pequeño*, the smallest; *lo* ~, *todo lo* ~, *cuando* ~, at the most, at most. 4 other: *no tengo* ~ *amigo que tú*, I have no other friend but you. 5 faster, longer, oftener, etc. 6 *a* ~, besides, what is more. 7 *a* ~ *correr*, at full speed. 8 *a* ~ *de*, besides, in addition to. 9 *a* ~ *amor* ~ *dolor*, the greater the love, the greater the pain. 10 *a* ~ *y mejor*, copiously, hard, to one's heart's content. 11 *listo como el que* ~, clever as the cleverest. 12 *de* ~, over, above, extra, in excess. 13 *estar de* ~, to be superfluous; to be amiss; to be in the way. 14 *en* ~ *de*, at more than. 15 *en* ~ *que*, above, over and above, more than. 16 ~ *bien*, rather. 17 ~ *que*, more than; but, only; although, eventhough. 18 ~ *vale*, better to. 19 *poco* ~ *o menos*, little more or less, practically; *de poco* ~ *o menos*, insignificant. 20 *por* ~ *que*, however much; no matter how much; although. 21 *sin* ~ *ni* ~, suddenly, without warning, without any reason.
22 *prep.* plus.
23 *m.* MATH. plus. 24 *los* ~, the majority.

masa *f.* pastry mixture; dough; mortar. 2 mass, aggregate, bulk. 3 lump, whole. 4 PHYS., PAINT. mass. 5 mass, crowd, body [of persons]: *las masas*, the masses; *en* ~, in a body [of persons]. 6 nature or disposition.

masada *f.* farm, farmhouse.

masaje *m.* massage.

masajista *m.* masseur. 2 *f.* masseuse.

mascada *f.* (Am.) chew [of tobacco].

mascador, -ra *adj.* chewing. 2 *m.-f.* chewer.

mascadura *f.* chewing.

mascar *tr.* to chew, masticate. 2 coll. to mumble.

máscara *f.* mask [cover for the face; false face: that which conceals]: ~ *antigás*, gas mask; *quitar la* ~ *a*, to unmask. 2 mask, masker, masquerader. 3 masquerade; disguise. 4 PHOT. mask. 5 *pl.* masquerade [assembly].

mascarada *f.* masquerade. 2 fig. mummery.

mascarilla *f.* half mask. 2 death mask.

mascarón m. augm. large mask. 2 ARCH. mask. 3 NAUT. ~ de proa, figurehead.

mascota f. mascot.

mascujar tr. to chew poorly or with difficulty. 2 fig. to mumble.

masculino, -na adj. male, masculine. 2 adj.-m. GRAM. masculine.

mascullar tr. to mumble, mutter.

masera f. kneading trough.

masetero m. ANAT. masseter.

masicote m. CHEM. massicot.

masilla f. putty, glazier's putty, mastic.

maslo m. root [of the tail of a quadruped].

masón m. Mason, Freemason.

masonería f. Masonry, Freemasonry.

masónico, -ca adj. masonic.

masoquismo m. masochism.

mastelerillo m. NAUT. topgallant or royal mast.

mastelero m. NAUT. topmast.

masticación f. mastication.

masticar tr. to masticate, chew.

mástil m. NAUT., RADIO. mast. 2 NAUT. topmast. 3 upright pole or post. 4 BOT. trunk, stem, stalk. 5 shaft [of feather]. 6 neck [of violin, guitar, etc.].

mastín, -na m.-f. ZOOL. mastiff.

mástique m. mastic [resin].

mastodonte m. PALEONT. mastodon.

mastranto, mastranzo m. BOT. apple mint.

mastuerzo m. BOT. pepper cress, pepergrass. 2 BOT. water cress. 3 coll. dolt, simpleton.

masturbación f. masturbation.

mata f. BOT. low shrub or frutescent plant; bush. 2 sprig [of mint, basil, etc.]. 3 patch [of trees]. 4 BOT. mastic tree. 5 ~ de pelo, head of hair [of a woman].

matacán m. BOT. nux vomica. 2 FORT. machicolation.

matacandelas, pl. **-las** m. candle extinguisher.

matachín m. coll. swashbuckler.

matadero m. slaughterhouse, abattoir. 2 coll. tiresome work.

matador, -ra adj. killing. 2 m.-f. killer. 3 m. BULLF., CARDS matador.

matadura f. sore, gall [on beasts].

matafuego m. fire extinguisher.

matalahuga, matalahuva f. BOT. anise. 2 anised.

mátalas callando m.-f. coll. hypocrite, sly dog.

matalobos, pl. **-bos** m. BOT. wolf's-bane, aconite.

matalón, -na adj. skinny and full of sores [horse].

matalote adj.-n. MATALÓN.

matamoros, pl. **-ros** m. coll. bully, braggard.

matamoscas, pl. **cas** m. fly swatter.

matanza f. killing. 2 slaughter, butchery, massacre. 3 swine slaughtering and the season for it. 4 pork products kept at home for food.

mataperros, pl. **-rros** m. coll. street urchin.

matapolvo m. light rain, sprinkling.

matar tr. to kill, slay, murder. 2 to butcher [animals for food]. 3 to put out [a fire, a light]. 4 to gall [the back of a horse]. 5 to slack [lime]. 6 to dull, mat [metals]. 7 PAINT. to tone down [a colour]. 8 to bevel or round off [edges]. 9 to lay [dust]. 10 CARDS to take [play a card higher than]. 11 to obliterate, cancel [a postage stamp]. 12 fig. to kill [time, hunger, etc.]. 13 to ruin, destroy. 14 to harass, worry, vex. 15 estar a ~ con, to be at daggers drawn with. 16 ref. to kill oneself. 17 to get killed. 18 to drudge, overwork; to struggle. 19 to kill one another.

matarife m. butcher, slaughterman.

matasanos m. coll. unskilled doctor; quack, medical charlatan.

matasellos, pl. **-llos** m. post-office cancelling stamp.

matasiete m. coll. swaggerer, braggart.

matatías, pl. **-tías** m. coll. moneylender, usurer.

mate adj. dull, mat, lusterless. 2 dull [sound]. 3 m. CHESS. checkmate: ~ ahogado, stalemate; dar ~, to checkmate. 4 maté [herb and beverage]. 5 maté gourd.

matear tr. (Am.) to checkmate. 2 intr. (Am.) to drink maté.

matemática f., **matemáticas** f. pl. mathematics.

matemático, -ca adj. mathematical. 2 m.-f. mathematician.

Mateo m. pr. n. Matthew.

materia f. matter [physical substance]. 2 material, substance, stuff: primera ~, raw material. 3 MED. matter, pus. 4 matter, topic, subject, subject matter: en ~ de, in the matter of; entrar en ~, to go into the subject. 5 cause, occasion.

material adj. material [of matter, physical, not spiritual]. 2 crude, coarse. 3 m. ingredient. 4 equipment, matériel: ~ fijo, RLY. permanent way; ~ móvil or rodante, RLY. rolling stock. 6 pl. materials.

materialidad f. materiality. 2 outward appearance.

materialismo m. materialism.

materializar tr. to materialize. 2 ref. to become materialistic.

materialmente adv. materially. 2 absolutely.

maternal adj. maternal, motherly.

maternidad f. maternity, motherhood; casa de ~, maternity hospital.

materno, -na adj. maternal, mother.

Matías m. pr. n. Matthias.

matidez f. dullness [lack of luster]. 2 dullness [of sound].

Matilde f. pr. n. Matilda.

matinal adj. matinal, morning, matutine.

matiné f. GAL. matinée.

matiz, pl. **-tices** m. tint, hue, shade, nuance.

matizado, -da adj. nuanced. 2 variegated.

matizar tr. to give a special hue or shade to. 2 to nuance, shade. 3 to variegate, to blend harmoniously the colours of.

matojo m. bush, small shrub.

matón m. bully, hector.

matorral m. bush, thicket, heath, brake.

matraca f. wooden rattle. 2 coll. pestering, importunity. 3 coll. dar ~ a, to chaff, bantem.

matraquear intr. to rattle [with a wooden rattle]. 2 to pester, importune. 3 to chaff, banter.

matraqueo m. rattling sound. 2 pestering, importunity. 3 chaff, banter.

matraz m. CHEM. matrass.

matrero, -ra adj. shrewd, cunning, sly.

matriarcado m. matriarchate.

matriarcal adj. matriarchal.

matricaria f. BOT. feverfew.

matricida adj. matricidal. 2 m.-f. matricide [person].

matricidio m. matricide [act].

matrícula f. register, list, roll; matriculation; registration.

matricular tr. to register, enroll, matriculate. 2 ref. to matriculate [be matriculated], to register.

matrimonial adj. matrimonial.

matrimonio m. matrimony, marriage: ~ civil, civil marriage. *2* matrimony [sacrament]. *3* married couple.

matritense *adj.-n.* MADRILEÑO.

matriz *adj.* first, main, chief, mother: *casa* ~, mother house [monastery]; headquarters [of a business]. *2 escritura* ~, original draft [of a deed]. *3 f.* ANAT. matrix, womb. *4* matrix, mould, die. *5* GEOL. matrix. *7* stub of a stub book.

matrona *f.* matron [mother of a family]. *2* midwife. *3* matron [in a custom house, etc.].

maturranga *f.* trick, cunning, craft.

Matusalén *m. pr. n.* BIBL. Methuselah.

matute *m.* smuggling. *2* smuggled goods.

matutear *intr.* to smuggle.

matutinal; matutino, -na *adj.* matutinal, matutine.

maula *f.* rubbish, -trash. *2* remnant, piece. *3* deceitful trick. *4 m.-f.* trickster; bad pay. *5* lazy person, shirk, shirker.

maullar *intr.* to meow, mew.

maullido, maúllo *m.* meow, mew.

Mauricio *m. pr. n.* Maurice, Morris.

máuser *m.* Mauser [firearm].

mausoleo *m.* mausoleum.

maxilar *adj.-m.* maxillary.

máxima *f.* maxim [rule, principle, saying]. *2* MUS. maxim, maxima.

máxime *adv.* principally, specially.

máximo, -ma *adj.* maximum, greatest, top: ~ *común divisor*, MATH. greatest common divisor. *2 m.* maximum.

maya *f.* BOT. daysy. *2* May queen. *7 adj.-n.* Maya, Mayan.

mayal *m.* flail [threshing instrument].

mayar *intr.* to meow, mew.

mayestático, -ca *adj.* majestic.

mayo *m.* May [month]. *2* Maypole.

mayólica *f.* majolica ware.

mayonesa *adj.* mayonnaise [sauce].

mayor *adj.* bigger, greater, larger; older, elder. *2* biggest, greatest, largest; oldest, eldest, senior. *3* of age. *4* principal, chief, main, high, major: *misa* ~, high mass; *palo* ~, NAUT. mainmast; *premisa* ~, LOG. major premiss. *5* MUS., MIL. major: *tambor* ~, drum major. *6* ~ *de edad*, majority, full age; *ser* ~ *de edad*, to be of age. *7* COM. *libro* ~, ledger. *8 al por* ~, wholesale. *9 f.* LOG. major. *10 m.* superior, head. *11 m. pl.* elders, superiors. *12* ancestors, forefathers.

mayoral *m.* head shepherd. *2* stagecoach driver. *3* foreman [of farm labourers].

mayorana *f.* MEJORANA.

mayorazgo *m.* entailed estate. *2* owner of an entailed estate. *3* first-born son. *4* primogeniture.

mayordoma *f.* steward's wife. *2* stewardess.

mayordomía *f.* administration, stewardship. *2* butlership. *3* steward's office.

mayordomo *m.* steward. *2* butler, majordomo.

mayoría *m.* majority [larger number or part]. *2* POL. majority, plurality. *3* majority, full age.

mayoridad *f.* majority, full age. *2* superiority.

mayorista *m.* wholesale merchant.

mayormente *adv.* chiefly, especially.

mayúsculo, -la *adj.* large. *2* coll. awful, tremendous. *3* capital [letter]. *4 f.* capital letter.

maza *f.* mace [weapon]; war club. *2* mace [staff]. *3* drumstick of a bass drum. *4* monkey, ram, tup [of a drop hammer or pile driver]. *5* thick end [of billiard cue]. *6* coll. bore [person].

mazacote *m.* CHEM. barilla. *2* concrete. *3* coll. tough, doughy food. *4* bore [person].

mazamorra *f.* NAUT. mess of broken hardtack. *2* fig. anything broken into small pieces.

mazapán *m.* marchpane, marzipan.

mazar *tr.* to churn [milk].

mazazo *m.* blow with a mace or maul.

mazdeísmo *m.* Mazdaism, Mazdeism.

mazdeísta *adj.* Mazdean. *2 m.-f.* Mazdaist.

mazmorra *f.* underground dungeon.

mazo *m.* maul, mallet, wooden hammer. *2* bundle [of some things]. *3* coll. bore [person].

mazorca *f.* BOT. thick ear or spike. *2* BOT. ear [of Indian corn]. *3* BOT. cacao pod. *4* spindleful [of yarn]. *5* spindle [in a baluster].

mazorral *adj.* crude, rough. *2* PRINT. solid.

mazurca *f.* mazurka [dance and tune].

me *pers. pron., 1st pers. sing.* [object of the verb and ref.] me; to me, for me; myself.

meada *f.* urination. *2* spot made by urine.

meados *m. pl.* urine.

meaja *f.* MIGAJA.

meandro *m.* meander.

mear *intr.-ref.* to urinate, make water.

meauca *f.* ORN. shearwater.

Meca (la) *f. pr. n.* GEOG. Meca.

¡mecachis! *interj.* ¡CARAMBA!

mecánica *f.* mechanics. *2* machinery, works [working parts of a machine, etc.]. *3* contemptible thing. *4* MIL. fatigue, fatigue duty: *traje de* ~, fatigue dress.

mecanicismo *m.* BIOL., PHIL. mechanism [doctrine].

mecánico, -ca *adj.* mechanical [in every sense, except unconcious, automatic]. *2* fig. low, mean. *3 m.* mechanic, repairman. *4* AUTO. driver, chauffeur. *5* mechanician.

mecanismo *m.* mechanism. *2* works [of a machine].

mecanización *adj.* mechanization.

mecanizar *tr.* to mechanize.

mecanografía *f.* typewriting.

mecanografiar *tr.* to typewrite, to type.

mecanógrafo, -fa *m.-f.* typist, typewriter.

mecedor, -ra *adj.* rocking, swinging. *2* stirring [a liquid]. *3 m.* stirrer [implement]. *4* COLUMPIO. *5 f.* rocker, rocking chair.

mecenas *m.* Maecenas, patron of art or literature.

mecenazgo *m.* support given by a Maecenas.

mecer *tr.* to stir [a liquid]. *2* to rock, swing. *3 ref.* to rock, swing [intr.]. *4* [of birds] to soar.

meconio *m.* meconium.

mecha *f.* wick. *2* fuse, match [for firing an explosive]. *3* COOK. strip of bacon for larding. *4* SURG. roll of lint. *5* TEXT. sliver, rove. *6* lock, tuft [of hair, wool, etc.]. *7* NAUT. heel [of a mast].

mechar *tr.* COOK. to lard [with bacon].

mechazo *m.* MIN. fizzle of a blast fuse.

mechera *f.* larding pin. *2* shoplifter [woman].

mechero *m.* lamp burner, gas burner. *2* socket [of candlestick]. *3* cigarette lighter.

mechinal *m.* MAS. putlog hole. *2* fig. hovel.

mechón *m.* lock, tuft [of hair, wool, etc.].

medalla *f.* medal. *2* ARCH. medallion.

medallón *m.* large medal. *2* ARCH. medallion. *3* JEW. locket.

médano, medaño *m.* dune. *2* sand bank.

Media *f. pr. n.* HIST., GEOG. Media.

media *f.* stocking [for foot and leg]. *2* MATH. mean: ~ *proporcional*, geometrical mean, mean proportional.

mediacaña *f.* fluted moulding. *2* picture mould-

ing. 3 straight gouge [chisel]. 4 half-round file.
5 curling tongs. 6 PRINT. double rule.
mediación f. mediation. 2 intercession.
mediado, -da adj. half-filled, half-full. 2 adv. a mediados de, about the middle of [a period of time].
mediador, -ra m.-f. mediator. 4 intercessor.
mediana f. long billiard cue. 2 GEOM. median.
medianejo, -ja adj. coll. mediocre.
medianería f. party wall. 2 party-line fence or
hedge.
medianero, -ra adj. middle, dividing. 2 mediating;
interceding. 3 party [wall]. 4 m.-f. mediator. 5
intercessor.
medianía f. moderate circumstances. 2 mediocrity [person].
mediano, -na adj. middling, medium, moderate. 2
coll. mediocre, bad, worthless.
medianoche f. midnight. 2 small meat pie.
mediante adj. intervening, interceding. 2 adv. by
means of, through. 3 Dios ~, God willing.
mediar intr. to be at the middle, to be half over. 2
to mediate. 3 to intercede. 4 to intervene. 5 [of
time] to elapse. 6 tr. to make half-full.
medias (a) adv. halves: ir a medias, to go halves. 2
by halves: hacer a medias, to do or make by halves. 3 half: dormido a medias, half asleep. 4 half
and half, between two.
mediastino m. ANAT. mediastinum.
mediatizar tr. to mediatize.
mediato, -ta adj. mediate.
médica f. woman physician. 2 doctor's wife.
medicación f. medication, medical treatment.
medicamento m. medicament.
medicamentoso, -sa adj. medicamental.
medicar tr. to treat, to cure by medicine.
medicastro m. medicaster.
medicina f. medicine [science & art]. 2 medicine,
medicament.
medicinal adj. medicinal.
medicinar tr. to administer medicines to.
medición f. measuring, measurement, mensuration.
médico, -ca adj. medical. 2 Medic. 3 m. doctor,
physician: ~ de cabecera, family physician.
medicucho m. unskilled doctor.
medida f. measure, measurement: tomar las medidas a uno, to take someone's measurements. 2
measurement, mensuration. 3 measure [instru-
ment for measuring; unit of measurement]; ~
de longitud, linear measure; ~ de superficie,
square measure; ~ de volumen, cubic measure;
~ para áridos, dry measure; ~ para líquidos, liquid measure. 3 ARITH., PROS. measure. 4 proportion, correspondence: a ~ de, in proportion
to, according to; a ~ que, as, in proportion as. 5
measure, step, suitable action. 6 moderation.
medidor, -ra adj. measuring. 2 m.-f. measurer.
mediero, -ra m.-f. stocking maker o seller, hosier.
medieval adj. medieval, mediaeval.
medievo m. Middle Ages.
medio, -dia adj. half, half a: ~ libra, half a pound;
medias tintas, half measures; las dos y media,
half past two [o'clock]. 2 middle, mean, average: clase media, middle class; distancia ~,
mean distance; término ~, middle term; average. 3 medium. 4 medial, median. 5 mid: a media tarde, in mid afternoon.
medio adv. half, partially, halfway: ~ dormido,
half asleep; a ~ hacer, half done. 2 m. ARITH. half.
3 middle, midst: en ~ de, in the middle of, in the
midst of; notwithstanding. 4 means, agency,

medium: por ~ de, by means of. 5 medium,
environment. 6 BIOL., PHYS. medium. 7 mean
[between the extremes]. 8 de ~ a ~, in the
middle, smack; absolutely. 9 de por ~, in between; estar de por ~, to be concerned, have to
do with. 10 quitar de en ~, to put out of the way;
to do away with. 11 quitarse de en ~, to get out
of the way. 12 pl. means [pecuniary resources].
mediocre adj. mediocre.
mediocridad f. mediocrity.
mediodía m. noon, midday. 2 GEOG. south.
medioeval adj. MEDIEVAL.
medir tr. to measure, gauge. 2 to measure [one's
skill, etc., with]. 3 to scan [verse]. 4 ref. to act
with moderation. ¶ CONJUG. like servir.
meditabundo, -da adj. meditative, pensive, mus-
ing.
meditación f. meditation.
meditar tr.-intr. to meditate, think.
mediterráneo, -a adj.-n. mediterranean: Mar Mediterráneo, Mediterranean Sea.
médium m. [spiritualistic] medium.
medo, -da adj. Median. 2 m.-f. Mede.
medra f. growth, thriving, prosperity.
medrana f. coll. fear.
medrar intr. to grow, thrive, prosper.
medro m. growth, thriving, prosperity. 2 pl. progress, improvement.
medroso, -sa adj. fearful, timorous, fainthearted.
2 dreadful, frightful.
medula, médula f. ANAT. medulla, marrow: ~ espinal, spinal marrow, spinal cord. 2 BOT. medulla, pith. 3 fig. marrow, pith, substance.
medular adj. medullar, medullary.
medusa f. ZOOL. medusa, jellyfish. 2 (cap.) MYTH.
Medusa.
Mefistófeles m. pr. n. Mephistopheles.
mefistofélico, -ca adj. Mephistophelian.
megáfono m. megaphone.
megalítico, -ca adj. ARCHEOL. megalithic.
megalito m. ARCHEOL. megalith.
megalomanía f. megalomania.
megaterio m. PALEONT. megathere.
megatón m. megaton, one million tons.
mego, -ga adj. meek, mild, gentle.
megohmio m. ELECT. megohm.
mejana f. islet [in a river].
mejicano, -na adj.-n. Mexican.
Méjico m. pr. n. GEOG. Mexico. 2 Mexico City.
mejido, -da adj. beaten with sugar and milk [egg].
mejilla f. ANAT. cheek.
mejillón m. ZOOL. common mussel.
1) **mejor**, pl. **mejores** adj. comp.-superl. better,
best; lo ~, the best; el ~ día, when least expected; el ~ postor, the highest bidder; a lo ~, perhaps, maybe, probably.
2) **mejor** adv. comp.-superl. better, best: tanto ~,
so much the better. 2 rather: ~ dicho, rather,
more properly speaking.
mejora f. improvement, betterment. 2 higher bid
[in auction].
mejoramiento m. amelioration, improvement.
mejorana f. BOT. sweet marjoram.
mejorar tr. to ameliorate, meliorate, better, improve, mend. 2 to better, surpass. 3 to raise
[a bid]. 4 intr.-ref. to ameliorate, improve,
grow better. 5 to mend, recover, get better. 6 [of
weather] to clear up. 7 to reform. 8 to progress.
mejoría f. amelioration, improvement. 2 improvement in health.
mejunje m. medicinal or cosmetic mixture.

melado, -da *adj.* honey-coloured. *2 m.* cane-juice syrup.
meláfido *m.* GEOL. melaphyre.
melancolía *f.* melancholy. *2* melancholia.
melancólico, -ca *adj.-n.* MED. melancholic. *2 adj.* melancholic, melancholy.
Melanesia *f. pr. n.* GEOG. Melanesia.
melanita *f.* MINER. melanite.
1) melar [of cane or fruit] sweet, honey-sweet.
2) melar *intr.* [of bees] to fill combs with honey.
melaza *f.* molasses. *2* dregs of honey.
melcocha *f.* paste of concentrated honey.
Melchor *pr.-n.* Melchior.
melena *f.* mane [of man or lion]. *2* loose hair [in women]. *3* forelock [in animals].
meleno *adj.* having a forelock [bull.]. *2 m.* peasant, rustic.
melenudo, -da *adj.* long-haired.
melero *m.* honey dealer. *2* storage place for honey.
meliáceo, -a *adj.* BOT. meliaceous.
melifero, -ra *adj.* melliferous.
melificación *f.* honey making.
melificado, -da *adj.* mellifluous.
melificar *intr.* to make honey. *2 tr.* to draw honey from [flowers].
melifluo, flua *adj.* mellifluent, mellifluous.
meliloto, -ta *m.* BOT. melilot, sweet clover.
melindre *m.* honey fritter. *2* a small cake. *3* narrow ribbon. *4* finicking, mincing, affectation of delicacy.
melindrear *intr.* to finick, mince, affect delicacy.
melindrería *f.* finickiness, daintiness.
melindroso, -sa *adj.* finicky, mincing, affecting delicacy.
melinita *f.* melinite.
melis *m.* BOT. a variety of pine; its wood.
melisa *f.* BOT. balm, garden balm, lemon balm.
melocotón *m.* BOT. peach [fruit]; peach tree.
melocotonar *m.* peach orchard.
melocotonero *m.* BOT. peach tree.
melodía *f.* MUS. melody. *2* melodiousness.
melódico, -ca *adj.* MUS. melodic.
melodioso, -sa *adj.* melodious.
melodrama *m.* melodrama.
melodramático, -ca *adj.* melodramatic(al.
melojo *m.* BOT. a variety of black oak.
melolonta *m.* ENT. cockchafer.
melomanía *f.* melomania.
melómano, -na *m.-f.* melomane, melomaniac.
melón *m.* BOT. melon, muskmelon. *2* ZOOL. MELONCILLO.
melonar *m.* muskmelon patch.
meloncillo *m. dim.* ZOOL. a variety of mongoose.
melonero, -ra *m.-f.* muskmelon raiser or dealer.
melopea *f.* MELOPEYA. *2* monotonous singing. *3* vulg. drunkenness.
melopeya *f.* melopoeia.
melosidad *f.* honeyedness.
meloso, -sa *adj.* honey-like. *2* honeyed, sweet, mealy; mealy-mouthed.
melton *m.* melton.
mella *f.* nick, notch, break, dent [in an edge]. *2* hollow, gap. *3* damage, hurt; impression: *hacer ~*, to make an impression; to harm, injure, affect.
mellado, -da *adj.* nicked, jagged [edge, tool]. *2* having lost a tooth or some teeth.
mellar *tr.* to nick, break, dent the edge of. *2* to injure [the honour, credit, etc.]. *3 ref.* to get nicked, jagged.
mellizo, -za *adj.-n.* twin [brother, sister].

memada *f.* stupidity, piece of folly.
membrana *f.* membrane.
membranoso, -sa *adj.* membranous.
membrete *m.* letterhead, heading [printed on letter paper]. *2* note, memo.
membrillate *m.* quince paste.
membrillero *m.* BOT. quince tree.
membrillo *m.* BOT. quince tree. *2* BOT. quince [fruit]. *3* quince paste.
membrudo, -da *adj.* burly, sturdy, robust.
memento *m.* ECCL. Memento.
memez *f.* silliness, stupidity.
memo, -ma *adj.* silly, foolish. *2 m.-f.* fool, simpleton.
memorable *adj.* memorable.
memorando, -da *adj.* MEMORABLE.
memorándum *m.* [diplomatic] memorandum. *2* notebook.
memorar *tr.-ref.* to remember.
memoria *f.* memory [faculty of remembering]: *ser flaco de ~*, to have a bad memory; *traer a la ~*, to recall, remember; to remind; *de ~*, by heart. *2* memory, recollection, remembrance, reminiscence: *hacer ~*, to try to remember; to remember; to remind; *en ~ de*, in memory of. *3* memoir, record, statement, report. *4* essay, paper. *5 pl.* memoirs. *6* compliments, regards.
memorial *m.* memorial, petition. *2* notebook.
memorialista *m.* one who writes petitions, letters, etc., for other people.
memorión, -na *adj.-n.* having a retentive memory [person]. *2 m.* great memory.
memorioso, -sa *adj.* having a retentive memory.
mena *f.* MIN. ore. *2* ICHTH. picarel.
ménade *f.* maenad.
menaje *m.* household furniture. *2* school equipment and supplies.
mención *f.* mention: *~ honorífica*, honourable mention.
mencionar *tr.* to mention.
menchevique *m.-f.* Menshevik.
mendacidad *f.* mendacity.
mendaz *adj.* mendacious.
mendicación *f.* begging.
mendicante *adj.-n.* mendicant.
mendicidad *f.* mendicity, mendicancy.
mendigar *tr.* to beg [ask for as a charity]. *2* to beg, supplicate for. *3 intr.* to beg [go begging].
mendigo, -ga *m.-f.* beggar.
mendoso, -sa *adj.* mendacious. *2* wrong, mistaken.
mendrugo *m.* crumb, crust [dry scrap of bread].
menear *tr.* to shake, stir. *2* to wag, waggle, move. *3* to manage, direct. *4 ref.* to wag, waggle, move [be in motion]. *5* to stir, bestir oneself, hustle, hurry up. *6* [of a tooth, etc.] to be loose.
menegilda *f.* coll. housemaid.
meneo *m.* shake, shaking, stir, stirring, wag, wagging. *2* hustling. *3* coll. drubbing, beating.
menester *m.* need, want: *haber ~*, to need; *ser ~*, to be necessary. *2* job, occupation, duty. *3 pl.* bodily needs. *4* implements, tools [of a trade].
menesteroso, -sa *adj.* needy. *2 m.-f.* needy person.
menestra *f.* vegetable soup or stew. *2 pl.* dried vegetables.
menestral *m.* artisan, mechanic, handicraftsman.
menestralía *f.* artisans, mechanics [as a class].
Menfis *f. pr. n.* HIST., GEOG. Memphis.
menfita *adj.* Memphian. *2 m.-f.* Memphite.
mengano, -na *m.-f.* So-and-So.
mengua *f.* diminution, decrease, waning. *2* deficiency, lack, want. *3* discredit, disgrace.

menguado, -da *adj.* diminished, short, poor; mean, paltry. *2* cowardly, pusillanimous. *3* mean, base, vile. *4* foolish, silly. *5* wretched. *6 m.-f.* coward. *8* wretch. *9 m. pl.* narrowing [in knitting].

menguante *adj.* diminishing, decreasing, waning. *2 f.* decay, decline. *3* low water [in rivers, etc.]. *4* NAUT. ebbtide. *5* waning [of the moon].

menguar *intr.* to diminish, decrease, lessen, wane. *2* to decay, decline. *3* to narrow [in knitting]. *4 tr.* AMENGUAR.

mengue *m.* coll. deuce, devil.

menhir *m.* ARCHEOL. menhir.

menina *f.* formerly, a young lady-in-waiting.

meníngeo, -a *adj.* ANAT. meningeal.

meninges *f. pl.* ANAT. meninges.

meningitis *f.* MED. meningitis.

menino *m.* formerly, a noble page of the queen or a young prince.

menisco *m.* PHYS., OPT., ANAT. meniscus.

menopausia *f.* PHYSIOL. menopause.

menor *adj.* smaller, less, lesser; younger. *2* smallest, least, youngest, junior. *3* minor [poet, prophet, etc.]. *4* LOG., MUS. minor. *5 ~ de edad,* ~, under age; minor. *6 ~ edad,* minority. *7 m.-f.* minor [person]. *8 m.* minorite. *9 f.* LOG. minor. *10 adv. al por* ~, retail. *11 por* ~, retail; minutely, in detail.

Menorca *f. pr. n.* GEOG. Minorca.

menoría *f.* minority [state or period of being under age].

menorquín, -na *adj.-n.* Minorcan.

menos *adv.* less, least: *~ de, ~ que,* less than; *al* ~, *a lo* ~, at least; at the least; *a ~ de* [with an inf.], without; *a ~ que,* unless; *de* ~, less, missing, wanting; *echar de* ~, to miss, feel or notice the absence of; *en ~ de,* at less than; *en ~ que,* less, at less than; *en ~ que canta un gallo,* in an instant; *lo* ~, the least; at the least; *por lo* ~, at least; at the least; *venir a* ~, to decline, decay. *2* fewer; *no ~ de,* no fewer than. *3* still less. *4* minus, less: *cinco ~ dos,* five minus two. *5* to [in telling time]: *las tres ~ cuarto,* a quarter to three. *6* but, except. *7 m.* minus [sign].

menoscabar *tr.* to lessen, impair, detract from.

menoscabo *m.* lessening, impairing, injure, detriment, derogation: *con ~ de,* to the detriment of.

menospreciable *adj.* contemptible.

menospreciar *tr.* to underestimate, underrate, undervalue. *2* to contempt, despise, slight.

menosprecio *m.* underestimation, undervaluation. *2* scorn, contempt.

mensaje *m.* message.

mensajería *f.* stage coach, public conveyance. *2 pl.* transportation company, stage line. *3* shipping line.

mensajero, -ra *m.-f.* messenger [carrier of a message]. *2 adj.* carrier [pigeon].

menstruación *f.* menstruation. *2* menses.

menstruar *intr.* to menstruate.

menstruo *m.* menses, courses. *2* CHEM. menstruum.

mensual *adj.* monthly.

mensualidad *f.* monthly pay or allowance. *2* monthly instalment.

ménsula *f.* ARCH. bracket, corbel.

mensura *f.* MEDIDA.

mensurable *adj.* mensurable.

mensuración *f.* mensuration.

mensurar *tr.* to measure.

menta *f.* BOT. mint. *2* peppermint.

mentado, -da *adj.* mentioned. *2* famous, renowned.

mental *adj.* mental.

mentalidad *f.* mentality.

mentar *tr.* to name, mention. ¶ CONJUG. like *acertar.*

mente *f.* mind, intellect. *2* mind, intention.

mentecato, -ta *adj.* silly, foolish, stupid, crackbrained, half-witted. *2 m.-f.* fool, dolt.

mentidero *m.* gossiping place.

mentido, -da *adj.* false, delusive.

mentir *intr.* to lie [speak falsely, tell lies]. *2* [of things] to deceive, be false, delusive. *3 tr.* to feign. *4* to fail to keep [one's word, promise, etc.]. ¶ CONJUG. like *sentir.*

mentira *f.* lie, fib, falsehood: *~ inocente, ~ oficiosa,* white lie; *parece* ~, it hardly seems possible. *2* error, mistake [in writing]. *3* coll. white spot [on fingernails].

mentirijillas or **mentirillas (de)** *adv.* in fun, in jest, for fun.

mentiroso, -sa *adj.* lying, mendacious. *2* deceptive, deceitful. *3 m.-f.* liar.

mentís, *pl.* **-tís** *m.* lie [charge of lying]: *dar un ~ a,* to give the lie to.

mentol *m.* PHARM. menthol.

mentón *m.* chin, point of the chin.

mentor *m.* mentor.

menú *m.* gal, menu, bill of fare.

menudamente *adv.* minutely. *2* in detail.

menudear *tr.* to do frequently, to repeat frequently. *2 intr.* to happen frequently; come down in abundance. *4* to go into details.

menudencia *f.* smallness. *2* trifle. *3* minuteness, minute accuracy. *4 pl.* pork products.

menudeo *m.* constant repetition, incessant happening or falling down. *2* retail: *al ~,* by retail.

menudillo *m.* fetlock joint. *2 pl.* giblets.

menudo, -da *adj.* small, little, minute, tiny. *2* trifling, unimportant. *3* common [people]. *4* small [money, -change]. *5* minute, exact. *6 pl.* small change. *7* blood and entrails [of butchered animals]. *8* giblets. *9 a ~,* often, frequently. *10 por* ~, minutely; by retail.

meñique *adj.* coll. tiny, very small. *2* little [finger].

meollo *m.* ANAT. marrow, pith. *2* BOT. pith. *3* fig. marrow, pith, substance. *4* fig. judgment, sense.

meón, -na *adj.* constantly urinating.

meple *m.* (Am.) BOT. maple.

mequetrefe *m.* coll. whippersnapper, jackanapes.

mercachifle *m.* merchant, petty merchant. *2* peddler, hawker.

mercadear *intr.* to deal, trade, traffic.

mercader *m.* merchant, dealer.

mercadería *f.* MERCANCÍA.

mercado *m.* market: *~ de valores,* stock market; *~ negro,* black market. *2* market place.

mercancía *f.* commerce, trade. *2* merchandise commodity. *3 pl.* goods, merchandise, wares.

mercante *adj.* merchant.

mercantil *adj.* mercantile, commercial.

mercantilismo *m.* mercantilism.

mercar *tr.* to buy, purchase.

merced *f.* gift, grant, favour, grace. *2* mercy, will, power, disposal: *a ~ de,* at the mercy of. *3 La Merced,* order of Our Lady of Mercy. *4 vuestra (vuesa, su) Merced,* you, sir; you, madam. *5 ~ a,* thanks to.

mercedario, -ria *adj.* pertaining to the order of Our Lady of Mercy. *2 m.-f.* Mercedarian.

mercenario, -ria *adj.* mercenary, hired. *2* MERCE-

DARIO. *3 m.* mercenary, stipendiary. *4 m.-f.* Mercedarian.
mercería *f.* small wares, haberdashery, *notions. *2* haberdarher's shop.
mercerizar *tr.* to mercerize.
mercurial *adj.* mercurial. *2* ASTR., MYTH. Mercurial. *3 f.* BOT. herb mercury.
Mercurio *m. pr. n.* ASTR., MYTH. Mercury.
mercurio *m.* CHEM. mercury.
merdoso, -sa *adj.* filthy.
merecedor, -ra *adj.* deserving, worthy.
merecer *tr.* to deserve, merit, be worthy of: ~ *la pena,* to be worthwhile. *2* to attain, obtain. *3* to be worth. *4 intr.* to deserve, be deserving: ~ *bien de,* to deserve the gratitude of. ¶ CONJUG. like *agradecer.*
merecido, -da *adj.* deserved. *2 m.* deserts, deserved punishment.
merecimiento *m.* merit, desert.
merendar *intr.* to take a light refreshment in the afternoon. *2* [in some places] to lunch. *3 ref.* to manage to get. ¶ CONJUG. like *acertar.*
merendero *m.* place [often out of town] where refreshments or light meals are served.
merengue *m.* meringue.
meretricio, -cia *adj.* meretricious [of a harlot].
meretriz *f.* harlot, strumpet.
mergansar, mergo *m.* ORN. cormorant.
mericarpio *m.* BOT. mericarp.
meridiana *f.* couch, lounge. *2* afternoon nap.
meridiano, -na *adj.* meridian [of midday]. *2* ASTR. meridian. *3* vright, dazzling. *4 m.* ASTR., GEOG., GEOM. meridian.
meridional *adj.* meridional, southern. *2 m.-f.* meridional, southerner.
merienda *f.* snack, light refreshment taken in the afternoon. *2* [in some places] lunch. *3* ~ *de negros,* confusion, bedlam.
merino, -na *adj.* merino. *2* thick and curly [hair]. *3 m.* formerly, a royal judge. *4* head shepherd. *5* merino [sheep, wool and fabric].
mérito *m.* merit, dessert; worth, excellence, value: *de* ~, excellent, of value. *2* LAW *méritos del proceso,* merits of the case. *3 hacer* ~ *de,* to mention.
meritorio, -ria *adj.* meritorious. *2 m.* improver [employee].
merla *f.* ORN. blackbird.
merlín *m.* NAUT. marline.
merlón *m.* FORT. merlon.
merluza *f.* ICHTH. hake. *2* coll. drunk, drunken fit.
merma *f.* decrease, waste, loss, leakage, shrinkage. *2* curtailment, reduction.
mermar *intr.-ref.* to decrease, diminish, lessen, wear away, shrink. *2 tr.* to lessen, curtail.
mermelada *f.* marmalade.
1) mero *m.* ICHTH. a Mediterranean grouper.
2) mero, -ra *adj.* mere, pure, simple.
merodeador, -ra *adj.* marauding. *2 m.-f.* marauder.
merodear *intr.* to maraud.
merodeo *m.* marauding.
merovingio, gia *adj.-m.* Merovingian.
mes *m.* month. *2* monthly pay or allowance. *3* menses.
mesa *f.* table [article of furniture]: ~ *de juego,* gaming table, gambling table; ~ *de noche,* bedside table; ~ *del altar,* ECCL. altar; ~ *del billar,* billiard table; ~ *redonda,* round table; table d'hôte; *poner la* ~, to set, or lay, the table; *quitar la* ~, to clear the table. *2* table, food, fare, cheer. *3* exe-

cutive board [of a meeting, etc.]. *4* desk [writing table]. *5* tableland, plateau. *6* landing [of a staircase]. *7* game [at billiards]. *8* table [of a gem]. *9* NAUT. ~ *de guarnición,* channel.
mesada *f.* monthly pay or allowance.
mesalina *f.* fig. dissolute woman.
mesana *f.* NAUT. mizzen sail; mizzenmast.
mesar *tr.* to tear or pull the hair or beard.
mescolanza *f.* MEZCOLANZA.
mesenterio *m.* ANAT. mesentery.
meseta *f.* tableland, plateau. *2* landing [of a staircase].
mesiánico, -ca *adj.* Messianic.
Mesías *m. pr. n.* BIBL. Messiah.
mesilla *f. dim.* small table. *2* landing [of a staircase]. *3* window sill.
mesita *f. dim.* small table.
mesmerismo *m.* mesmerism.
mesmo, -ma *adj.* obs. or vulg. MISMO.
mesnada *f.* armed retinue, company of soldiers. *2* company, band; followers.
mesocarpio *m.* BOT. mesocarp.
mesocracia *f.* government by the middle class.
mesón *m.* inn, hostelry, tavern, roadhouse.
mesonero, -ra *adj.* [pertaining to an] inn or hostelry. *2 m.-f.* innkeeper, host, hostess.
Mesopotamia *f. pr. n.* GEOG. Mesopotamia.
mesotórax, *pl.* **-rax** *m.* ZOOL. mesothorax.
mesozoico, -ca *adj.-m.* GEOL. Mesozoic.
mesta *f.* a powerful union of cattle or sheep raisers.
mester *m.* obs. art, trade. *2* ~ *de clerecía,* verse of clerics in the Middle Ages. *3* ~ *de juglaría,* Spanish minstrelsy, verse of the minstrels in the Middle Ages.
mestizaje *m.* crossing of races.
mestizo, -za *adj.* mongrel, half-breed half-blooded. *2 m.-f.* half-breed [pers. of mixed blood].
mesura *f.* gravity, dignified deportment. *2* politeness, deference. *3* moderation, circumspection.
mesurado, -da *adj.* grave, dignified. *2* moderate, circumspect, temperate.
mesurar *tr.* to moderate, inspire moderation in. *2 ref.* to restrain oneself, to act with moderation.
meta *f.* SPORT. goal; finish line. *2* fig. goal, aim, purpose.
metabólico, -ca *adj.* PHYSIOL. metabolic.
metabolismo *m.* PHYSIOL. metabolism.
metacarpo *m.* ANAT. metacarpus.
metafase *f.* BIOL. metaphase.
metafísica *f.* metaphysics.
metafísico, -ca *adj.* metaphysical. *2 m.* metaphysician.
metáfora *f.* metaphor.
metafórico, -ca *adj.* metaphorical.
metal *m.* CHEM., HER. metal: ~ *blanco,* nickel silver, white metal; ~ *precioso,* rich metal; *el vil* ~, fig. money. *2* brass, latten. *3* MUS. brass. *4* timbre [of voice]. *5* quality, nature [of things].
metalario *m.* metallist, metal worker.
metalepsis *f.* RHET. metalepsis.
metálico, -ca *adj.* metallic. *2 m.* specie, hard cash, hard money, coin.
metalífero, -ra *adj.* metal-bearing, metalliferous.
metalista *m.* METALARIO.
metalizar *tr.* CHEM. to give metallic properties to. *2 ref.* to become metallized. *3* to become mercenary, money-mad.
metalografía *f.* metallography.
metaloide *m.* CHEM. metalloid, nonmetal.
metalurgia *f.* metallurgy.

metalúrgico, -ca *adj.* metallurgic, metallurgical. *2 m.* metallurgist.

metámero *m.* ZOOL. metamere.

metamórfico, -ca *adj.* metamorphic.

metamorfismo *m.* GEOL. metamorphism.

metamorfosear *tr.* to metamorphose, transform. *2 ref.* to metamorphose, be transformed.

metamorfosis, *pl.* **-sis** *f.* metamorphosis, transformation. *2* ZOOL. metamorphosis.

metano *m.* CHEM. methane.

metaplasma *m.* BIOL. metaplasm.

metátesis, *pl.* **-sis** *f.* GRAM. metathesis.

metazoo *adj.-m.* ZOOL. metazoan.

metedor *m.* baby's diaper.

metempsicosis, *pl.* **-sis** *f.* metempsychosis.

meteórico, -ca *adj.* meteoric.

meteorito *m.* meteorite.

meteorizar *tr.* MED. to meteorize. *2 ref.* AGR. [of soil] to be influenced by atmospheric phenomena. *3* MED. to become meteorized.

meteoro, metéoro *m.* meteor.

meteorología *f.* meteorology.

meteorológico, -ca *adj.* meteorologic(al).

meteorólogo *m.* meteorologist.

meter *tr.* to put, place, insert, thrust, introduce [in or between]; to enclose [in]; to get [in or into]. *2* to pocket [a billiard ball]. *3* to hole [a golf ball]. *4* to smuggle. *5* to make, cause, sow; ~ *miedo,* to frighten, cause fear; ~ *ruido,* to make a noise; to cause a sensation; ~ *cizaña,* to sow discord. *6* to tell [lies]. *7* to give [a beating]. *8* to take in [a seam]. *9* to pack, compress. *10 ref.* to go, get [in or into]. *11* to intrude, interfere, meddle [with], butt [in]: *no se meta en lo que no le importa,* mind your own business. *12* to plunge [into vice; business, etc.]. *13* to become [a friar, a nun, a soldier]. *14 meterse a,* to assume [a character, function, etc.], to set oneself up as; to take it upon oneself. *15 meterse con,* to pick a quarrel with. *16 meterse uno en sí mismo,* to keep one's own counsel.

meticuloso, -sa *adj.* meticulous.

metido, -da *p. p.* of METER: ~ *en carnes,* plump, fleshy: *letra metida,* close writing; *estar muy* ~ *en,* to be deeply involved in. *2 m.* punch given below the ribs. *3* SEW. material allowed in seams. *4* coll. lecture, dressing down.

metílico, -ca *adj.* CHEM. methylic.

metilo *m.* CHEM. methyl.

metimiento *m.* putting in. *2* favour, influence.

metódico, -ca *adj.* methodical.

metodismo *m.* Methodism.

metodista *adj.-n.* Methodist.

metodizar *tr.* to methodize.

método *m.* method. *2* technique.

metodología *f.* methodology.

metonimia *f.* RHET. metonymy.

métopa *f.* ARCH. metope.

metraje *m.* length in metres: *de corto* ~, *de largo* ~, short, full-length [cinema pictures].

metralla *f.* grapeshot, case shot; shrapnel.

metrallazo *m.* discharge of grapeshot or shrapnel.

métrica *f.* metrics, prosody.

métrico, -ca *adj.* metric, metrical.

metrificar *intr.-tr.* to versify.

metro *m.* metre, meter [unit]. *2* POET. metre, meter. *3* coll. underground, subway train.

metrónomo *m.* MUS. metronome.

metrópoli *f.* metropolis. *2* mother country.

metropolitano, -na *adj.-m.* metropolitan. *2* underground, subway train.

mexicano, -na *adj.-n.* Mexican.

México *m. pr. n.* GEOG. Mexico. *2 f.* Mexico City.

mezcal *m.* mescal.

mezcla *f.* mixing, mingling, blending. *2* mixture; blend. *3* MAS. mortar. *4* TEXT. mixed cloth.

mezclar *tr.* to mix, mingle, blend, intermix, intermingle. *2 ref.* to mix, mingle [be mixed, associate]. *3* to take part, meddle.

mezclilla *f.* light mixed cloth.

mezcolanza *f.* mixture, medley, jumble, hodgepodge.

mezquindad *f.* need, poverty. *2* meanness, stinginess. *3* smallness, paltriness. *4* wretchedness. *5* trifle, mean thing. *6* niggardly act.

mezquino, -na *adj.* needy, poor. *2* stingy, niggardly. *3* small, short, mean, paltry. *4* wretched.

mezquita *f.* mosque.

mezquite *m.* BOT. mesquite.

1) **mi** *m.* MUS. mi, E.

2) **mi** *poss. adj.* my.

mí *pers. pron.* (used as object of prepositions) me, myself. *2 ¡y a mí qué!,* I don't care!

miaja *f.* crumb [of bread]. *2* bit [small piece].

miar *intr.* MAULLAR.

miasma *m.* miasma. *2 pl.* miasmata.

miau *m.* mew, mewing.

mica *m.* MINER. mica.

micado *m.* Mikado.

micción *f.* micturition.

micelio *m.* BOT. mycelium.

Micenas *f. pr. n.* HIST., GEOG. Mycenae.

mico *m.* ZOOL. long-tailed monkey. *2* coll. lecherous man. *3 dar* ~, *hacer* ~, not to keep a date.

micología *f.* mycology.

micra *f.* MICRÓN.

microbiano, -na *adj.* microbial, microbian.

microbicida *adj.-m.* microbicide.

microbio *m.* microbe, germ.

microbiología *f.* microbiology.

microcéfalo, -la *adj.* microcephalic.

micrococo *m.* BACT. micrococcus.

microcopia *f.* microcopy.

microcosmo *m.* microcosm.

microfilme *m.* microfilm.

micrófono *m.* microphone.

microfotografía *f.* microphotography.

microgameto *m.* BIOL. microgamete.

micrografía *f.* micrography.

microhmio *m.* ELECT. microhm.

micrométrico, -ca *adj.* micrometric.

micrón *m.* micron.

Micronesia *n. pr. f.* GEOG. Micronesia.

microorganismo *m.* BIOL. micro-organism.

micrópilo *m.* ZOOL., BOT. micropyle.

microscópico, -ca *adj.* microscopic(al).

microscopio *m.* microscope.

microsurco *m.* microgroove.

micrótomo *m.* microtome.

michino, -na *m.-f.* coll. pussy, pussycat.

micho *m.* coll. puss [tomcat].

mieditis *f.* coll. fear, dread.

miedo *m.* fear, dread; apprehension; ~ *cerval,* freat fear; *dar* ~, to be dreadful; *dar* ~ *a,* to frighten; *tener* ~, to be afraid.

miedoso, -sa *adj.* fearful, timid, timorous.

miel *f.* honey: ~ *sobre hojuelas,* fig. added, pleasure, profit, etc. *2* molasses.

mielga *f.* BOT. lucerne. *2* ICHTH. kind of dogfish.

miembro *m.* ANAT. member, limb. *2* ANAT. penis. *3* member [of a body, class, etc.]. *4* ARCH., ENG., GRAM., LOG., MATH. member.

mientes f. pl. mind, thought: *parar*, or *poner*, ~ *en*, to consider, reflect on; *traer a las* ~, to remember; *venírsele a uno a las* ~, to come to one's mind.

miento, mienta, etc. *irr.* V. MENTIR.

mientras *adv.-conj.* while, whilst, when, meanwhile: ~ *tanto*, meanwhile. 2 whereas. 3 ~ *que*, while; whereas. 4 ~ *más (o menos)... más (o menos),* the more (or the less)... the more (or the less).

miera f. juniper oil. 2 pine turpentine.

miércoles, *pl.* **-les** m. Wednesday: ~ *de ceniza,* Ash Wednesday.

mierda f. excrement; filth. | Not in decent use.

mies f. ripe grain in the field or before thrashing. 2 harvest time. 3 *pl.* grain fields.

miga f. crumb, bit [small fragment or piece]. 2 crumb [soft part of bread]. 3 fig. marrow, pith, substance. 4 *pl.* fried crumbs. 5 *hacer migas,* or *buenas migas, con,* to get along with.

migaja f. crumb [small piece of bread]. 2 crumb, bit, grain, particle. 3 *pl.* crumbs, leavings.

migar *tr.* to crumb [bread]. 2 to put crumbs of bread into [a liquid].

migración f. migration.

migraña f. MED. megrim, migraine, headache.

migratorio, -ria *adj.* migratory.

Miguel m. *pr. n.* Michael.

mihrab m. mihrab.

mijo m. BOT. millet, panic-grass.

mil *adj.-m.* thousand, one thousand: *a las* ~ *y quinientas,* coll. at an unearthly hour. 2 thousandth.

miladi f. milady.

milagrería f. tale of pretended miracles.

milagrero, -ra *adj.* miraclemongering.

milagro m. miracle, wonder: *de* ~, with difficulty; by a narrow escape: *por* ~, for a wonder.

milagroso, -sa *adj.* miraculous.

milamores f. BOT. red valerian.

milanés, -sa *adj.-n.* Milanese.

milano m. ORN. kite, European kite. 2 ORN. goshawk. 3 ICHTH. flying gurnard. 4 VILANO.

mildieu, mildiu m. AGR. mildew.

milenario, -ria *adj.-n.* millenary, millenarian. 2 m. millennial.

milenio m. millenium.

milenrama f. BOT. milfoil, yarrow.

milésima f. thousandth [part].

milésimo, -ma *adj.-n.* thousandth.

milesio, sia *adj.-n.* Milesian.

milhojas f. MILENRAMA.

miliar *adj.* miliary. 2 milliary.

miliárea f. milliare.

milicia f. art of warfare. 2 military service. 3 militia, soldiery: ~ *nacional,* national guard.

miliciano, -na *adj.* military. 2 m. militiaman.

miligramo m. milligram, milligramme.

mililitro m. millilitre, milliliter.

milímetro m. millimetre, millimeter.

militante *adj.* militant.

1) **militar** *adj.* military. 2 soldierly. 3 m. military man, soldier. 4 *pl. los militares,* the military.

2) **militar** *intr.* to serve in the army. 2 to militate. 3 ~ *en,* to belong to [a party, etc.].

militara f. wife, daughter or widow of a soldier.

militarismo m. militarism.

militarizar *tr.* to militarize.

milite m. soldier.

miloca f. ORN. kind of owl.

milonga f. (Am.) a popular dance and song.

milord, *pl.* **-lores** m. milord. 2 barouche.

milpiés, *pl.* **piés** m. ZOOL. wood louse.

milla f. mile: ~ *marina,* nautical mile.

millar m. thousand: *a millares,* by the thousand.

millarada f. about a thousand.

millón, *pl.* **millones** m. million.

millonario, -ria *adj.-n.* millionaire.

millonésimo, -ma *adj.-n.* millionth. 2 f. millionth [part].

mimado, -da *adj.* pampered, spoiled: *niño* ~, spoiled child.

mimar *tr.* to pet, fondle, cuddle. 2 to pamper, spoil.

mimbre m. osier, wicker, withe. 2 MIMBRERA.

mimbrear *intr.-ref.* to sway or move with flexibility.

mimbreño, -ña *adj.* osierlike, willowy.

mimbrera f. BOT. osier, velvet osier.

mimesis f. RHET. mimesis.

mimético, -ca *adj.* BOT., ZOOL. mimetic.

mimetismo m. BIOL. mimesis, mimetism, mimicry.

mímica f. pantomime, dumb show, sign language.

mímico, -ca *adj.* mimic.

mimo m. mime [actor and play]. 2 caress, petting. 3 pampering, overindulgence.

mimógrafo m. mimographer.

mimosa f. BOT. mimosa.

mimoso, -sa *adj.* caressing, petting. 2 soft, spoiled, fond of being petted.

mina f. mine [of coal, metal, etc.]. 2 fig. mine, storehouse, gold mine. 3 underground passage. 4 FORT., MIL., NAV. mine.

minador, -ra *adj.* mining. 2 m. miner, sapper. 3 mining engineer.

minar *tr.* to mine, burrow. 2 to mine, sap, undermine; to consume. 3 MIL., NAV. to mine.

minarete m. minaret.

mineraje m. mining, work of a mine.

mineral *adj.* mineral. 2 m. mineral. 3 ore. 4 water spring, fountain-head.

mineralizar *tr.* to mineralize. 2 *ref.* to become mineralized.

mineralogía f. mineralogy.

mineralogista m. mineralogist.

minería f. mining [working of mines]. 2 mines [of a region or country]. 3 miners [as a class].

minero, -ra *adj.* mining. 2 m. miner [worker]. 3 mine operator; mine owner. 4 mine [of coal, metal, etc.]. 5 fig. source, origin.

Minerva f. *pr. n.* MYTH. Minerva. 2 f. (not cap.) PRINT. small press.

mingitorio m. urinal [enclosure].

mingo m. BILL. object ball, red ball.

miniar *tr.* to paint in miniature.

miniatura f. miniature: *en* ~, in miniature.

miniaturista m.-f. miniature painter.

mínima f. smallest thing. 2 MUS. minim.

minimizar *tr.* to diminish, lessen, undervalue.

mínimo, -ma *adj.* minimal, minimum, least, smallest. 2 minute. 3 m. minimum. 4 ECCL. Minim.

minimum m. minimum.

minino, -na m.-f. coll. kitty, puss, cat.

minio m. minium, red lead.

ministerial *adj.* POL. ministerial. 2 m. POL. ministerialist.

ministerio m. ministry, cabinet, government, administration. 2 ministry, office, administration [of a cabinet minister]. 3 ministry, department: ~ *de Asuntos Exteriores,* ~ *de Estado,* Foreign office; *Department of State; ~ *de Hacienda,*

Exchequer; *Department of the Treasury; ~ *de la Gobernación*, Home Office; *Department of the Interior. 4 ministry, ministration, office, function, agency. 5 use, service.

ministrador, -ra *adj.* ministering, ministrant. 2 *m.-f.* ministrant.

ministrar *tr.-intr.* to minister. 2 *tr.* to supply, furnish.

ministril *m.* petty officer of justice. 2 obs. musician [player].

ministro *m.* minister, agent. 2 ECCL. minister: ~ *de Dios*, priest. 3 server [at Mass]. 4 petty officer of justice. 5 envoy. 6 DIPL. minister: ~ *plenipotenciario*, minister plenipotentiary. 7 POL. minister, cabinet minister, Secretary of State, *Secretary; *primer* ~, primer minister, premier.

minorar *tr.* to lessen, diminish. 2 *ref.* to lessen, diminish [become diminished].

minoría *f.* minority [in number]. 2 POL. minority. 3 minority [being under age].

minotauro *m.* MYTH. Minotaur.

minucia *f.* trifle. 2 *pl.* minutiae.

minuciosidad *f.* minuteness, attention paid to small details. 2 trifle, small detail.

minucioso, -sa *adj.* minute, detailed, scrupulous.

minué *m.* minuet [dance and music].

minuendo *m.* ARITH. minuend.

minúsculo, -la *adj.* small, tiny, trifling. 2 small, lower-case [letter]. 3 *f.* small letter, lower-case letter.

minuta *f.* first draft, rough draft. 2 memorandum. 3 lawyer's bill. 4 roll, list. 5 bill of fare.

minutar *tr.* to make a draft of, to minute.

minutario *m.* notary's book of drafts.

minutero *m.* minute hand.

minutisa *f.* BOT. sweet william.

minuto, -ta *adj.* minute, small. 2 *m.* minute [of an hour, of a degree]: *al* ~, at once, right away.

miñona *f.* PRINT. minion.

mío, mía, míos, mías *poss. adj.* (never used before the noun) my, my own, of mine, mine: *padre mío*, my father; *estos libros son míos*, these books are mine. 2 *poss. pron.* mine; *el mío, la mía, los míos, las mías*, mine.

miocardio *m.* ANAT. myocardium.

mioceno, -a *-m.* GEOL. Miocene.

miope *adj.* MED. myopic, near-sighted. 2 *m.-f.* myope.

miopía *f.* MED. myopia, near-sightedness.

miosota, miosotis *f.* BOT. myosotis, forget-menot.

mira *f.* sight [of firearms and some instruments]. 2 leveling rod. 3 aim, purpose, intention, view: *poner la* ~ *en*, to aim at, to have designs on. 4 *estar a la* ~, to be on the lookout.

¡mira! *interj.* look!, lo!, behold!; take care!

mirabel *m.* BOT. mock cypress. 2 BOT. sunflower.

mirada *f.* look, glance, gaze, regard, eye: *echar una* ~ *a*, to cast a glance at, to take a look at.

miradero *m.* cynosure [of all eyes]; thing most watched. 2 lookout, observatory.

mirado, -da *adj.* [when preceded by *muy, tan, más, menos*] considerate, thoughtful, careful, nice, circumspect. 2 [when preceded by *bien, mal*], considered, reputed, thought-of. 3 *adv. bien mirado*, after all, in fact.

mirador, -ra *adj.* looking, gazing. 2 *m.* belvedere, open gallery. 3 oriel window, bay window.

miraguano *m.* BOT. fan palm yielding vegetable down.

miramelindos, *pl.* **-dos** BOT. garden balsam.

miramiento *m.* consideration, reflection. 2 attention, care, considerateness: *sin miramientos*, inconsiderately, roughly.

miranda *f.* elevated place with an extensive outlook.

mirar *tr.* to look, look at, on, upon, etc.; to eye, gaze, observe, regard, view, watch, contemplate, examine: ~ *de hito en hito*, to stare at; ~ *por encima del hombro*, to look down on or upon, to despise. 2 to aim at, to seek. 3 to look, consider, give heed to: *mira cómo te portas*, look how you behave. 4 to regard, consider, think. 5 to inquire, seek information about. 6 ~ *con buenos ojos*, to like, approve of; ~ *con malos ojos*, to dislike, disapprove. 7 *intr.* to look: ~ *de través*, to squint. 8 to concern, respect, have regard [to]. 9 [of a building, etc.] to face. 10 ~ *por*, to look after, take care of. 11 *intr.-ref. mirar*, or *mirarse, en ello*, to be wary [in taking a determination]. 12 *ref.* to look oneself. 13 *mirarse en una persona*, to love a person dearly; to take example after a person. 14 *interj.* ¡*mira!*, ¡*mire!*, look!, behold!

mirasol *m.* BOT. sunflower.

miríada *f.* myriad.

miriagramo *m.* myriagram, myriagramme.

miriámetro *m.* myriametre, myriameter.

miriápodo *adj.-n.* MIRIÓPODO.

mirífico, -ca *adj.* marvellous, wonderful.

mirilla *f.* peephole [in doors]. 2 SURV. sight.

miriñaque *m.* crinoline [hooped petticoat]. 2 bauble, trinket.

miriópodo *adj.-m.* ZOOL. myriapod, myriapodan.

mirística *f.* BOT. nutmeg tree.

mirlarse *ref.* coll, to put on airs, to affect gravity.

mirlo *m.* ORN. blackbird: ~ *blanco*, coll. rare bird. 2 coll. affected gravity.

mirón, -na *adj.* onlooking. 2 *m.-f.* looker-on, onlooker, spectator, bystander.

mirra *f.* myrrh.

mirrino, -na *adj.* myrrhic.

mirtáceo, -a *adj.* BOT. myrtaceous.

mirto *m.* BOT. myrtle.

misa *f.* ECCL., MUS. Mass: ~ *de campaña*, Mass in the field, outdoor Mass; ~ *de difuntos*, Mass for the dead; ~ *del gallo*, Christmas-eve Mass; ~ *mayor*, High Mass; ~ *rezada*, Low Mass; *no saber de la* ~ *la media*, coll. not to know what all is about.

misacantano *m.* celebrant at Mass. 2 priest who says his first Mass.

misal *m.* missal, Mass book. 2 PRINT. two-line pica.

misantropía *f.* misanthropy.

misantrópico, -ca *adj.* misanthropic(al.

misántropo *m.* misanthrope.

miscelánea *f.* miscellany, medley. 2 miscellanea.

misceláneo, -a *adj.* miscellaneous.

miscible *adj.* miscible.

miserable *adj.* miserable, wretched. 2 miserable, mean, poor. 3 miserly, mean, stingy. 4 wicked, rascally. 5 *m.-f.* miser. 6 wretch, cur, knave.

miseración *f.* mercy, pity.

miserere *m.* ECCL. Miserere. 2 MED. ileus.

miseria *f.* misery, wretchedness. 2 misery, poverty, destitution, want. 3 miserliness. 4 coll. lice. 5 trifle, pittance, small quantity.

misericordia *f.* mercy, pity: *obras de* ~, works of mercy. 2 misericord [dagger; seat].

misericordioso, -sa *adj.* merciful.

mísero, -ra *adj.* miserable, wretched, unhappy. 2 miserly, mean, stingy.

misérrimo, -ma *adj. superl.* most miserable. *2* very miserly. *3* very short or scanty.
misión *f.* mission [in practically every sense].
misionario *m.* MISIONERO. *2* envoy, messenger.
misionero, -ra *adj.-n.* ECCL. missionary.
Misisipi *m. pr. n.* GEOG. Mississippi [river and state].
misivo, -va *adj.* missive. *2 f.* missive, letter.
mismamente *adv.* coll. exactly.
mismísimo, -ma *adj. superl.* very, very same.
1) mismo *adv.* right [in the very instant, place, etc.]: *ahora ~*, right now; *aquí ~*, right here. *2 así ~*, in like manner, likewise, also.
2) mismo, -ma *adj.* same, very, selfsame: *el ~ hombre*, the same man; *sus mismos criados se ríen de él*, his very servants laugh at him; *lo ~*, the same, the same thing; *lo ~ me da*, it's all the same to me; *por lo ~*, for the same reason, for that very reason. *2* [for emphasis] myself, yourself, herself, itself, etc.: *lo haré yo ~*, I'll do it myself.
misógino *adj.* misogynous. *2 m.* misogynist.
misoneísmo *m.* misoneism.
mistagogo *m.* mystagogue.
mistela *f.* a refreshing beverage. *2* liquor made of must and alcohol.
misterio *m.* mystery. *2* sculpture or image representing one of the mysteries of the Rosary.
misterioso, -sa *adj.* mysterious.
mística *m.* mystical theology.
misticismo *m.* mysticism.
místico, -ca *adj.* mystic, mystical. *2* mystic, enigmatic. *3 m.-f.* mystic [person].
mistral *m.* mistral [wind].
Misuri *m. pr. n.* GEOG. Missouri [river and state].
mitad *f.* half: *cara ~*, fig. better half: *a la ~* or *a ~ de*, half-way through. *2* moiety. *3* middle: *en ~ de*, in the middle of.
mítico, -ca *adj.* mythical.
mitigación *f.* mitigation, alleviation, allaying.
mitigador, -ra *adj.* mitigating, alleviating, allaying. *2 m.-f.* mitigator, alleviator, allayer.
mitigar *tr.* to mitigate, alleviate, allay, assuage. *2 ref.* to be mitigated, alleviated.
mitin *m.* political meeting, rally.
mito *m.* myth.
mitología *f.* mythology.
mitológico, -ca *adj.* mythological. *2 m.* mythologist.
mitologista, mitólogo *m.* mythologist.
mitón *m.* mitt [knitted glove without fingers].
mitosis *f.* BIOL. mitosis.
mitra *f.* mitre, miter [bishop's cap; bishopric].
mitrado *adj.* mitred, mitered. *2 m.* bishop or archbishop.
mitral *adj.* ANAT. mitral: *válvula ~*, mitral valve.
mixtifori *m.* coll. medley, hodgepodge.
mixtilíneo, -a *adj.* GEOM. mixtilineal, mixtilinear.
mixtión *f.* mixture, commixture.
mixto, -ta *adj.* mixed, mingled. *2* mixed [school, mathematics, etc.]: *parejas mixtas*, SPORT. mixed doubles. *3* crossbred. *4 m.* compound. *5* sulphur match.
mixtura *f.* mixture. *2* PHARM. compound.
mixturar *tr.* to mix, mingle.
mízcalo *m.* BOT. edible milk mushroom.
mnemónica, mnemotecnia *f.* mnemonics, mnemotechny.
moaré *m.* MUARÉ.
mobiliario, -ria *adj.* movable, personal [property]. *2 m.* household furniture, suit of furniture.

moblaje *m.* household furniture.
moca *f.* Mocha coffee.
mocasín *m.* moccasin [shoe; snake].
mocear *intr.* to act like a youth. *2* to go around after women.
mocedad *f.* youth, age of youth. *2* wild oats.
moceril *adj.* youthful, juvenile.
mocerío *m.* young people.
mocero *adj.* lewd, woman-mad.
mocetón *m.* strapping youth, strapping lad.
mocetona *f.* strapping girl or lass.
moción *f.* motion, movement. *2* divine inspiration. *4* motion [in a deliberative assembly].
mocito, -ta *adj.* very young. *2 m.-f.* youngster, lad, lass.
moco *m.* mucus, nasal mucus. *2* viscid matter. *3* snuff [of lamp or candle]. *4* slag [of iron]. *5 ~ de pavo*, crest of a turkey; BOT. cockscomb; *no ser ~ de pavo*, coll. [of a thing]. not to be despicable.
mocoso, -sa *adj.* snivelly, full of mucus. *2 m.-f.* ill-bred child, brat. *3* inexperienced youth.
mocosuelo, -la *m.-f. dim.* coll. child, brat.
mochada *f.* butt [with the head].
mocheta *f.* thick head of a hatchet, hoe, etc. *2* rebate in the edge of a door frame.
mochila *f.* MIL. knapsack. *2* haversack.
mocho, -cha *adj.* blunt, stub-pointed, stub-horned, truncated. *2* topped [tree]. *3* cropped, shorn. *4 m.* butt, butt end.
mochuelo *m.* ORN. little owl. *2* PRINT. omission. *3* coll. *cargar con el ~*, to get a hard task.
moda *f.* fashion, mode, style, prevailing custom: *a la ~*, *a la última ~*, after the latest fashion; *a la ~ de*, after the fashion of; *de ~*, fashionable; *estar de ~*, to be in fashion; *pasado de ~*, out of fashion. *2* pl. *tienda de modas*, ladies' dress shop.
modal *adj.* modal.
modales *m. pl.* manners, breeding.
modalidad *f.* manner of being, mode, kind.
modelado *m.* F. ARTS. modelling, moulding, molding.
modelar *tr.* F. ART to model, mould, mold.
modelista *m.* mould maker. *2* model maker.
modelo *m.* model, pattern, example. *2* model [to be reproduced; representation of a thing]. *3* model [person]; fashion model, mannequin. *4 adj.* model.
moderación *f.* moderation.
moderado, -da *adj.* moderate. *2* reasonable. *3 m.* POL. moderate.
moderador, -ra *adj.* moderating. *2 m.-f.* moderator.
moderar *tr.* to moderate, temper, restrain, curb. *2 ref.* to moderate [become less violent, intense, etc.]. *3* to restrain or control oneself.
modernamente *adv.* recently, lately.
modernidad *f.* modernness, modernity.
modernismo *m.* modernism.
modernista *adj.* modernist, modernistic. *2 m.-f.* modernist.
modernizar *tr.* to modernize. *2 ref.* to modernize [adopt modern ways, etc.].
moderno, -na *adj.* modern. *2 m. pl. los modernos*, the moderns.
modestia *f.* modesty.
modesto, -ta *adj.* modest.
módicamente *adv.* moderately, sparingly.
modicidad *f.* moderateness, cheapness.
módico, -ca *adj.* moderate, reasonable, low price.
modificación *f.* modification.
modificador, -ra *adj.* modifying. *2 m.-f.* modifier.

modificar *tr.* to modify. *2 ref.* to modify [undergo modification].
modificativo, -va *adj.* modificative.
modillón *m.* ARCH. modillion, bracket.
modismo *m.* GRAM. idiom.
modista *f.* dressmaker, modiste. *2 ~ de sombreros*, milliner. *3 m.* modiste, ladies' tailor.
modistilla *f.* young dressmaker's helper.
modo *m.* moda, manner, way: *~ de ser*, nature, disposition; *a ~* or *al ~ de*, in the manner of, like, by way of; kind of; *a mi ~*, in my own way; *de cualquier ~*, anyway, anyhow, without care; *de ~ que*, so that; so, and so; *de ningún ~*, by no means; *de otro ~*, otherwise; *de todos modos*, anyhow, at any rate; *en cierto ~*, in or after a fashion; *por ~ de*, as, by way of. *2* moderation, temperance. *3* PHIL., LOG., MUS. mode. *4* GRAM. mood. *5* GRAM. [adverbial, conjunctive, etc.] phrase. *6 pl.* manners, civility: *con buenos modos*, politely; *con malos modos*, impolitely.
modorra *f.* drowsiness, heaviness. *2* VET. gid.
modorro, rra *m.-f.* dolt, ignoramus.
modoso, -sa *adj.* quiet, well-behaved.
modulación *f.* modulation.
modulador, -ra *adj.* modulating. *2 m.-f.* modulator.
modular *intr.* to modulate [in speaking or singing]. *2 tr.* RADIO. to modulate.
módulo *m.* HYDRAUL., ARCH., NUMIS. module. *2* PHYS., MATH. modulus.
mofa *f.* mockery, jeer, scoff, sneer: *hacer ~ de*, to mock, to jeer at.
mofar *intr.-ref.* to mock, jeer, scoff, sneer: *mofarse de*, to mock, jeer at, scoff at, make fun of.
mofeta *f.* mofette; chokedamp; noxious emanation [of mines, etc.]. *2* ZOOL. skunk.
moflete *m.* coll. chubby cheek, fat cheek.
mofletudo, -da *adj.* chubby-cheeked, fat-cheeked.
mogol, -la *adj.* Mongolian. *2 m.-f.* Mongol, Mongolian. *3 el Gran Mogol*, the Great Mogul.
Mogolia *pr. n.* GEOG. Mongolia.
mogólico, -ca *adj.* Mongolian.
mogollón *m. de ~*, sponging upon others, free, for nothing.
mogón *adj.* one-horned, broken-horned.
mogote *m.* hummock, knoll. *2* stack of sheaves. *3* budding antler.
moharra *f.* head [of a lance or spear].
moharrache, moharracho *m.* merry-andrew.
mohatra *f.* sham sale, fraud.
mohín *m.* face, grimace, pouting.
mohína *f.* annoyance, displeasure.
mohíno, -na *adj.* sad, melancholy, worried, displeased. *2* black [horse or cattle]. *3 m.* hinny. *4* ORN. blue magpie.
moho *m.* mo(u)ld, mildew [of organic matter]; must, mustiness. *2* rust [on iron]; verdigris. *3* rustiness, stiffness caused by disuse.
mohoso, -sa *adj.* mouldy, moldy, mildewed, musty. *2* rusty.
Moisés *m. pr. n.* Moses.
mojadura *f.* wetting, drenching, soaking, moistening.
mojama *m.* dry salted tunny-fish.
mojar *tr.* to wet, moisten, drench, soak. *2* coll. to stab. *3* to dip [bread, cake, etc., into milk, etc.]. *4 intr.* coll. to have a hand or part in [an affair]. *5 ref.* to get wet.
mojarra *f.* ICHTH. a basslike marine fish.
moje *m.* COOK. gravy, sauce.
mojera *f.* MOSTELLAR.

mojicón *m.* small cake, bun. *2* punch in the face.
mojiganga *f.* masquerade, morris dance. *2* mummery.
mojigatería, mojigatez *f.* prudishness, sanctimoniousness, false humility.
mojigato, -ta *adj.* prudish, sanctimonious, hypocritical. *2 m.-f.* prude, hypocrite.
mojón *m.* boundary stone; landmark. *2* pile, heap.
mola *f.* MED. mole.
molar *adj.* molar. *2 m.* ANAT. molar, molar tooth.
moldavo, -va *adj.-n.* Moldavian.
molde *m.* mould, mold, matrix; cast, pattern. *2* FOUND. frame. *3* model, ideal. *4* PRINT. form. *6 venir de ~*, to be to the purpose; to be just right.
moldear *tr.* to mould, mold [give shape]. *2* to cast [in a mould]. *3* MOLDURAR.
moldura *f.* ARCH., CARP. moulding, molding.
moldurar *tr.* to carve, cut or make mouldings on.
mole *adj.* soft. *2 f.* huge mass or bulk.
molécula *f.* molecule.
molecular *adj.* molecular.
moledera *f.* grinding stone. *2* coll. botheration.
moledura *f.* grinding, crushing, pounding.
molendero, -ra *m.-f.* grinder, miller. *2 m.* chocolate grinder.
moleña *f.* PEDERNAL 1.
moler *tr.* to grind, crush, pound, mill. *2* to fatigue, tire out, wear out. *3* to spoil, destroy. *4* to vex, bore, importunate. *5 ~ a palos*, to beat up, give a drubbing. ¶ CONJUG. like *mover*.
molestar *tr.* to vex, disturb, annoy, put to inconvenience. *2* to displease, offend. *3 ref.* to bother; *~ en*, to bother to, to take the trouble to. *4* to be annoyed, take offence.
molestia *f.* vexation, annoyance, disturbance, inconvenience, trouble, discomfort. *2* displeasure.
molesto, -ta *adj.* vexatious, annoying, troublesome, bothersome. *2* annoyed, displeased. *3* uncomfortable, ill at ease.
moleta *f.* muller. *2* glass polisher.
moleteado *m.* knurl.
moletear *tr.* to knurl.
molibdeno *m.* CHEM. molybdenum.
molicie *f.* softness. *2* love of luxury, effeminacy.
molido, -da *adj.* ground. *2* fig. tired out, worn out.
molienda *f.* grinding, crushing, milling. *2* grist [corn for grinding]; sugar cane, olives, etc., ground or crushed. *3* mill [for grinding]. *4* grinding or crushing time. *5* fatigue, weariness.
molificación *f.* mollification, softening.
molificar *tr.* to mollify, soften.
molimiento *m.* grinding, crushing, pounding. *2* fatigue, weariness.
molinera *f.* woman miller. *2* miller's wife.
molinería *f.* mill industry.
molinero *m.* miller [pers.].
molinete *m. dim.* little mill. *2* pin wheel, windmill [toy]. *3* ventilating wheel. *4* moulinet [with a sabre, etc.]. *5* NAUT. windlass. *6* PHYS. *~ hidráulico*, hydraulic tourniquet.
molinillo *m.* hand mill. *2* coffee grinder. *3* chocolate stirrer.
molino *m.* mill [for grinding, crushing, etc.]: *~ harinero*, flour mill; *~ de agua*, water mill; *~ de viento*, windmill. *2* fig. restless person.
Moloc *m. pr. n.* BIBL. Moloch.
molondro, molondrón *m.* lazy, stupid fellow.
moltura *f.* grinding [of corn, etc.].
molturar *tr.* to grind [corn, etc.].
molusco *m.* ZOOL. mollusc, mollusk.

292

mollar *adj.* soft, easily broken, easily shelled. *2* lean [meat]. *3* productive, profitable. *4* manageable; gullible.
mollear *intr.* [of a thing] to give, yield [to pressure]; to bend [from being soft].
molledo *m.* fleshy part [of leg, arm, etc.]. *2* crumb [soft part of bread].
molleja *f.* gizzard [of birds]. *2* sweetbread.
mollera *f.* crown of the head. *2* fontanel. *3* fig. brains, sense: *cerrado de ~*, dull-witted; *duro de ~*, obstinate; dull-witted.
mollete *m.* muffin. *2* chubby cheek. *3* fleshy part [of the arm].
mollina, mollizna *f.* LLOVIZNA.
mollíznar, molliznear *intr.* LLOVIZNAR.
momentáneo, -a *adj.* momentary. *2* prompt.
momento *m.* moment, instant: *al ~*, at once, immediately; *de ~*, at the first; *de ~, por el ~*, for the present; *por momentos*, continually, progressively. *2* MECH. moment. *3* moment, weight, importance.
momería *f.* mummery, clowning.
momia *f.* mummy [embalmed or dried-up body].
momificación *f.* mummification.
momificar *tr.* to mummify. *2 ref.* to become a mummy.
momio, mia *adj.* lean, meagre. *2 m.* that which is got or given extra. *3* bargain, sinecure. *4 de ~*, free, gratis, for nothing.
Momo *m. pr. n.* MYTH. Momus.
momo *m.* funny grimace, burlesque action.
momórdiga *f.* BOT. balsam apple.
mona *f.* female monkey. *2* ZOOL. Barbary ape. *3* fig. ape, imitator. *4* coll. drunk, drunkenness: *dormir la ~*, to sleep off a drunk. *5* coll. drunk person. *6* old maid [game]. *7* Easter cake.
monacal *adj.* monachal, monastic.
monacato *m.* monachism; monasticism.
monacillo *m.* MONAGUILLO.
monada *f.* apery, apish action. *2* grimace. *3* tomfoolery. *4* pretty little thing. *6* pretty child, pretty girl. *7* cajolery.
mónada *f.* BIOL., CHEM., PHIL., ZOOL. monad.
monadelfo, -fa *adj.* BOT. monadelphous.
monaguillo *m.* acolyte, altar boy.
monaquismo *m.* MONACATO.
monarca *m.* monarch.
monarquía *f.* monarchy. *2* kingdom.
monárquico, -ca *adj.* monarchic(al. *2 adj.-n.* monarchist.
monarquismo *m.* monarchism.
monasterio *m.* monastery.
monástico, -ca *adj.* monastic(al.
monda *f.* cleaning, pruning; paring, peeling. *2* parings, prunings, peelings. *3* pruning season.
mondadientes *m.* toothpick.
mondadura *f.* cleaning, paring, peeling. *2 pl.* parings, peelings.
mondaoídos, mondaorejas *m.* earpick.
mondar *tr.* to clean [free from superfluous matter]. *2* to prune, trim. *3* to pare, peel; to hull. *4* to cut the hair of. *5* fig. to fleece. *6 mondarse los dientes*, to pick one's teeth.
mondarajas *f. pl.* peelings.
mondo, -da *adj.* clear of superfluities, admixtures or additions: *~ y lirondo*, only, without additions.
mondongo *m.* intestines, guts [of pork, etc.].
monear *intr.* coll. to monkey, to fool, to act ridiculously.
moneda *f.* coin, piece of money. *2* money: *~ corriente*, currency; coll. common knowledge; everyday matter; *~ falsa*, counterfeit; *~ imaginaria*, money of account; *~ suelta*, change, small change.
monedero *m.* moneyer: *~ falso*, counterfeiter. *2* moneybag.
monería *f.* apery, apish action. *2* tomfoolery. *3* pretty, pleasant action of a child.
monesco, -ca *adj.* coll. apish.
monetario, -ria *adj.* monetary. *2 m.* collection of coins and medals.
monetizar *tr.* to monetize.
mongol *adj.-n.* MOGOL.
Mongolia *f. pr. n.* MOGOLIA.
moniato *m.* coll. BUNIATO.
monicaco *m.* coll. HOMINICACO.
monigote *m.* lay brother. *2* rag figure; grotesque figure; badly drawn, painted or carved figure. *3* whippersnapper.
monín, -na *adj. dim.* coll. pretty, dear. *2 m.-f. dim.* coll. pretty child, pretty one, darling.
monipodio *m.* coll. collusion, combine.
monises *m. pl.* coll. money, dough.
monismo *m.* PHIL. monism.
mónita *f.* tact, cunning, adroitness.
monitor *m.* monitor, adviser. *2* NAUT., RAD. monitor.
monja *f.* nun.
monje *m.* monk. *2* anchorite.
monjía *f.* monkhood.
monjil *adj.* nunnish. *2 m.* nun's dress.
monjío *m.* nunhood. *2* taking the veil.
monjita *f. dim.* little nun.
mono, -na *adj.* pretty, dainty, *cute. *2 m.* ZOOL. ape, monkey; *~ capuchino*, capuchin; *~ sabio*, trained monkey; fig. BULLF. assistant of a picador. *3* fig. monkey [pers.]. *4* badly drawn or painted figure. *5 ~ de mecánico, de aviador*, etc., overalls. *6 estar de monos*, to be at outs.
monobásico, -ca *adj.* CHEM. monobasic.
monoclínico, -ca *adj.* CRYST. monoclinic.
monocordio *m.* MUS. monochord.
monocotiledóneo, -a *adj.* BOT. monocotyledonous. *2 f.* BOT. monocotyledon.
monocromo, -ma *adj.* monochrome.
monóculo *m.* monocle.
monodia *f.* MUS. monody.
monofásico, -ca *adj.* ELECT. monophase, single-phase.
monogamia *f.* monogamy.
monógamo, -ma *adj.* monogamous.
monografía *f.* monograph.
monográfico, -ca *adj.* monographic(al. *2* special [course, lectures, etc.].
monograma *m.* monogram.
monoico, -ca *adj.* BOT. monœcious.
monolítico, -ca *adj.* monolithic.
monolito *m.* monolith.
monologar *intr.* to monologize, soliloquize.
monólogo *m.* monologue, soliloquy.
monomanía *f.* monomania.
monometalismo *m.* monometallism.
monomio *m.* ALG. monomial.
monopétalo, -la *adj.* BOT. monopetalous.
monoplano *m.* AER. monoplane.
monopolio *m.* monopoly.
monopolista *m.-f.* monopolist.
monopolizador *adj.* monopolizing. *2 m.-f.* monopolizer.
monopolizar *tr.* to monopolize.
monóptero, -ra *adj.* ARCH. monopteral.

monosépalo, -la *adj.* BOT. monosepalous.
monosilábico, -ca *adj.* monosyllabic(al.
monosílabo, -ba *adj.* monosyllabic. *2 m.* monosyllable.
monospermo, -ma *adj.* BOT. monospermous.
monoteísmo *m.* monotheism.
monoteísta *adj.* monotheistic. *2 m.-f.* monotheist.
monotipia *f.* PRINT. monotype [machine; method].
monotonía *f.* monotony.
monótono, -na *adj.* monotonous.
monotrema *m.* ZOOL. monotreme.
monovalente *adj.* CHEM. monovalent.
monóxido *m.* CHEM. monoxide.
monseñor *m.* monseigneur. *2* monsignor.
monserga *f.* coll. gibberish.
monstruo *m.* monster, monstrosity.
monstruosidad *f.* monstrosity, monstrousness.
monstruoso, -sa *adj.* monstrous. *2* hateful, execrable.
monta *f.* mounting [act]. *2* covering [of a mare]. *3* amount, sum total. *4* value, account, importance. *5* MIL. call to horse.
montacargas, *pl.* **-gas** *m.* lift, elevator [for goods].
montadero *m.* horse block, mounting block.
montado, -da *adj.* mounted: *policía montada*, mounted police.
montador *m.* mounter. *2* assembler, erector, fitter. *3* horse block, mounting block.
montadura *f.* mounting. *2* MONTURA *2 & 5.*
montaje *m.* MACH. assembling, erection, setting up. *2 pl.* ARTILL. mount, gun carriage.
montanera *f.* acorn or mast pasture for hogs. *2* acorn-feeding or mast-feeding season.
montanero *m.* forester.
montano, -na *adj.* [pertaining to] wood or forest.
montantada *f.* braggadocio. *2* multitude, crow.
montante *m.* broadsword. *2* upright, post, standard, strut. *3* ARCH. mullion. *4* transom [window over a door]. *5* COM. amount. *6 f.* NAUT. flood tide.
montaña *f.* mountain. *2* highlands. *3* forested region. *4 ~ rusa*, roller coaster; switchback [amusement railway].
montañés, -sa *adj.* [pertaining to a] mountain, mountaineer, highlander. *3* of the mountains in the province of Santander [in Spain].
montañismo *m.* mountaineering.
montañoso, -sa *adj.* mountainous.
montar *intr.-ref.* to mount, get on: *~ a horcajadas en*, to straddle. *2 intr.* to ride [horseback; on a bicycle or motorcycle]. *3* to be of importance: *tanto monta*, it has the same importance. *4 ~ en cólera*, to fly into a rage. *5 tr.* to mount, put [a person] on a horse, etc. *6* to ride [a horse, a bicycle, etc.]. *7* to cover [a mare]. *8* to amount to [reach a sum]. *9* to mount, assemble, set up. *10* JEWEL. to set [a gem]. *11* to cock [a gun]. *12* THEAT. to mount [a play, etc.]. *13* NAUT. to command [a ship]. *14* NAUT. to mount, carry [cannon]. *15* NAUT. to round [a cape].
montaraz *adj.* of the woods; wild, untamed. *2* uncouth, rude. *3 m.* forester.
montazgo *m.* toll for the passage of cattle through a forest.
monte *m.* mount, mountain, hill: *el ~ de los Olivos*, Mount Olivet; *los montes Urales*, the Ural Mountains. *2* woods, woodland: *~ alto*, forest; trees of a forest; *~ bajo*, thicket, brushwood. *3* talon, stock [in card playing]. *4* monte [card game]. *5* bank [in gambling]. *6 ~ de piedad*, mount of piety.
montea *f.* hunting or beating the woods [for game]. *2* ARCH. working drawing. *3* ARCH. rise [of an arch].
montecillo *m.* dim. mound, hillock.
montepío *m.* pension fund [for widows, etc.].
montera *f.* cloth cap. *2* skylight. *3* head [of the boiler of a still]. *4* NAUT. moonsail.
montería *f.* hunting, chase. *2* HUNT. big game.
montero *m.* beater [in hunting], huntsman.
montés, -sa; montesino, -na *adj.* wild [cat, goat, etc.].
montículo *m.* mound, hillock.
monto *m.* amount, sum total.
montón *m.* heap, pile: *a, de* or *en ~*, coll. together, taken together. *2* lot, crowd, great quantity: *a montones*, coll. in abundance. *3 ser del ~*, to be common, ordinary.
montuno, -na *adj.* pertaining to the woods, wild.
montuosidad *f.* mountainousness.
montuoso, -sa *adj.* mountainous, hilly.
montura *f.* mount [riding horse]. *2* gear [of a riding horse]. *3* mounting, assembling, setting up. *4* mounting [of a telescope, gem, etc.]. *5* JEW. setting.
monumental *adj.* monumental.
monumento *m.* monument.
monzón *m.-f.* monsoon [wind].
moña *f.* bow of ribbons worn on the head. *2* badge on the bull's neck. *3* doll.
moño *m.* chignon, bun [of hair]. *2* bow or knot of ribbons. *3* crest, tuft of feathers [on head of a bird]. *4 pl.* frippery: *ponerse moños*, fig. to put on airs.
moquear *intr.* to snivel, run at the nose.
moquero *m.* pocket handkerchief.
moqueta *f.* moquette.
moquete *m.* punch on the face, on the nose.
moquillo *m.* VET. distemper. *2* VET. pip.
moquita *f.* watery discharge [from the nose].
mora *f.* Moorish woman. *2* BOT. black mulberry [fruit]. *3* BOT. white mulberry [fruit]. *4* BOT. blackberry, brambleberry [fruit]. *5* LAW delay.
morabito, morabuto *m.* marabout, Mohammedan hermit. *2* Mohammedan hermitage.
moráceo, -a *adj.* BOT. moraceous.
moracho, -cha *adj.* light purple [in colour].
morada *f.* abode, dwelling, house. *2* stay, sojourn.
morado, -da *adj.-n.* purple, mulberry [colour].
morador, -ra *m.-f.* inhabitant, dweller, resident.
moraga *f.* handful of gleaned grain.
moral *adj.* moral. *2 f.* morals, ethics, morality. *3* morale. *4 m.* BOT. black mulberry [tree].
moraleja *f.* moral [of a table, etc.].
moralidad *f.* morality [of acts, conduct, etc.]. *2* moral [of a fable, etc.].
moralista *m.* moralist.
moralizador, -ra *adj.* moralizing. *2 m.-f.* moralizer.
moralizar *tr.* to moralize.
morapio *m.* coll. red wine.
morar *intr.* to inhabit, dwell, reside.
moratoria *f.* COM., LAW moratorium.
morbidez *f.* softness, delicacy.
mórbido, -da *adj.* soft, delicate. *2* morbid.
morbo *m.* MED. morbus, disease.
morboso, -sa *adj.* morbid, unwholesome, diseased.
morcella *f.* spark from a lamp.
morcilla *f.* blood pudding. *2* THEAT. gag [interpolation by an actor].
morcillo, -lla *adj.* reddish black [horse].
mordacidad *f.* mordacity, mordancy.

mordaz *adj.* mordant, mordacious, biting, caustic. *2* pungent, acrid. *3* corrosive.

mordaza *f.* gag [to prevent speech]. *2* pipe wrench. *3* MEC. clamp, jaw.

mordedor, -ra *adj.* biting. *2* backbiting. *3 m.-f.* biter. *4* backbiter.

mordedura *f.* bite [act and result of biting].

mordente *m.* mordant. *2* MUS. mordent.

morder *tr.* to bite [with the teeth]: ~ *el polvo,* fig. to bite the dust or ground. *2* to nibble at. *3* [of things] to bite, take hold of. *4* to gnaw eat, wear away. *5* [of an acid] to eat, corrode. *6* to revile, backbite. ¶ CONJUG. like *mover.*

mordicante *adj.* biting, pungent. *2* acrid, corrosive. *3* fig. nibbling, carping.

mordicar *tr.* to bite, sting.

mordiente *adj.* biting. *2 m.* mordant.

mordiscar *tr.* to nibble at, to bite.

mordisco *m.* bite [act of biting; piece detached by biting].

mordisquear *tr.* MORDISCAR.

morena *f.* ICHTH. moray. *2* GEOL. moraine.

morenillo, -lla *adj.-n.* brunet, brunette.

moreno, -na *adj.* brown, dark. *2* dark-complexioned, swarthy, tawny, brunette. *3* coll. coloured [pers.]. *4 m.-f.* dark-complexioned person. *5* coll. coloured person. *6 f.* brunette.

morera *f.* BOT. white mulberry tree.

moreral *m.* grove of white mulberry trees.

morería *f.* Moorish quarter. *2* Moorish land.

moretón *m.* coll. black-and-blue mark.

Morfeo *m. pr. n.* MYTH. Morpheus.

morfina *f.* CHEM. morphine.

morfinismo *m.* MED. morphinism.

morfología *f.* morphology.

morga *f.* juice that oozes from a heap of olives. *2* COCA DE LEVANTE.

morganático, -ca *adj.* morganatic.

moribundo, -da *adj.* moribund, dying. *2 m.-f.* moribund, dying person.

morigeración *f.* moderation, temperance.

morigerado, -da *adj.* moderate, temperate.

morigerar *tr.* to moderate, restrain.

morilla *f.* BOT. morel.

morillo *m. dim.* little Moor. *2* firedog, and ron.

morir *intr.* to die, expire, decease, pass away, come to an end: ~ *vestido,* to die a violent death. *2* [of a river, road, etc.] to flow [into], to end [at]. *3* ref. to die, be dying. *4* [of a limb] be numbed. *5* intr.-ref. [of fire, flame, light, etc.] to die, go out. *6* to die of or with; to suffer, feel, etc., excessively: ~ or *morirse de hambre,* to die of hunger; to starve; ~ or *morirse de risa,* to die of laughing. *7* ~ or *morirse por,* to love dearly; be crazy about; to be dying for or to. *8* interj. *¡muera...!,* down with...! ¶ CONJUG. like *dormir.* | Past. p.: *muerto.*

morisco, -ca *adj.* Moorish, Moresque. *2* adj.-n. HIST. Morisco.

morisma *f.* the Moors. *2* crowd of Moors.

morisqueta *f.* Moorish trick. *2* mean trick. *3* (Am.) face, grimace.

morlaco *adj.-n.* BULLF. bull, big bull.

mormón, -na *m.-f.* Mormon.

mormonismo *m.* Mormonism.

moro, -ra *adj.* Moorish. *2* Moslem. *3* unbaptized. *4* coll. unwatered [wine]. *5* black with a white spot on the forehead [horse]. *6 m.* Moor: *hay moros en la costa,* fig. let's be cautious.

morocada *f.* butt of a ram.

morocho, -cha *adj.-m.* hard [Indian corn]. *2* adj. (Am.) fresh, vigorous [person]. *3* (Am.) MORENO.

morón *m.* mound [of earth].

morondanga *f.* coll. medley, hodgepodge.

morondo, -da *adj.* bald, hairless; leafless.

morosidad *f.* slowness, tardiness, delay.

moroso, -sa *adj.* slow, tardy, full of delay, lingering. *2* delinquent [in payment].

morra *f.* top, crown [of head]. *2* mora [game].

morrada *f.* butting of two heads. *2* cuff, punch.

morral *m.* nose bag. *2* game bag. *3* knapsack. *4* wallet [bag for travelling]. *5* coll. boor, rustic.

morralla *f.* small fry [fish]. *2* rabble. *3* rubbish.

morrillo *m.* fleshy part of neck [of animals]. *2* fleshy nape of neck. *3* pebble, boulder.

morriña *f.* VET. sheep dropsy. *2* coll. blues, melancholy, sadness.

morrión *m.* morion. *2* MIL. bearskin.

morro *m.* knob, round end or projection. *2* knoll. *3* pebble. *4* muffle; thick lips. *5* estar de ~ or de *morros,* to have quarelled, to be at odds.

morrocotudo, -da *adj.* coll. very important or difficult.

morrón *adj.* NAUT. knotted [flag]. *2* BOT. bonnet [pepper].

morrongo, -ga *m.-f.* coll. kitty, puss, cat.

morrudo, -da *adj.* thick-lipped.

morsa *f.* ZOOL. walrus, morse.

mortadela *f.* Bologna sausage.

mortaja *f.* shroud, winding sheet. *2* CARP. mortise.

mortal *adj.* mortal [subject to death]. *2* mortal [deadly, deathly; long, tedious]. *3* deathly [pallor]. *4* sure, conclusive. *5 m.* mortal.

mortalidad *f.* mortality [condition of being mortal]. *2* mortality, death rate.

mortandad *f.* mortality [death of large numbers]; massacre, butchery.

mortecino, -na *adj.* dying, dim, dull, pale, subdued [light, fire, colour, etc.].

morterete *m. dim.* small mortar [used for salvos and public festivities].

mortero *m.* mortar [for pounding]. *2* ARTILL. mortar. *3* MAS. mortar.

mortífero, -ra *adj.* death-dealing, deadly, fatal.

mortificación *f.* mortification. *2* annoyance.

mortificador, -ra; mortificante *adj.* mortifying. *2* annoying.

mortificar *tr.* to mortify [in every sense]. *2* to annoy, bother. *3* ref. to mortify [practice or undergo mortification].

mortuorio, -ria *adj.* mortuary, funeral. *2 m.* funeral.

morucho *m.* BULLF. young bull with tipped horns.

morueco *m.* ram [male sheep].

moruno, -na *adj.* Moorish.

mosaico, -ca *adj.* Mosaic [of Moses]. *2* adj.-m. F. ARTS mosaic. *3* paving tile set like mosaic.

mosaísmo *m.* Mosaism.

mosca *f.* ENT. fly: ~ *de burro,* horse fly: ~ *de la carne,* blowfly; ~ *muerta,* person feigning meekness; *estar* ~, *tener la* ~ *en la oreja,* fig. to be distrustful; *papar moscas,* fig. to stand gaping; *por si las moscas,* fig. for what may happen. *2* tuft of hair under the lip. *3* coll. money: *aflojar la* ~, to pay. *4* coll. bore, nuisance. *5* pl. sparks [from a fire].

moscada *adj.* BOT. *nuez* ~, nutmeg.

moscarda *f.* ENT. blowfly, bluebottle, meat fly.

moscardón *m.* ENT. botfly. *2* ENT. bluebottle. *3* ENT. hornet. *4* fig. importuning fellow.

moscareta *f.* ORN. flycatcher.

moscatel *adj.-m.* muscat, muscatel [grape and wine].

moscón *m.* ENT. large fly. 2 ENT. bluebottle. 3 fig. bore, nuisance [person]. 4 BOT. maple.

mosconear *tr.-intr.* to bother, importune.

mosconeo *m.* bothering, importunation.

Moscovia *f. pr. n.* GEOG. Muscovia.

moscovita *adj.-n.* Muscovite.

mosqueado, -da *adj.* spotted, dotted.

mosqueador *m.* flyflap.

mosquear *tr.* to drive [flies] away. 2 to give a sharp retort to. 3 to beat, flog. 4 *ref.* to shake off [annoyances]. 5 to take offence.

mosquero *m.* flyflap.

mosqueta *f.* BOT. a variety of white rose.

mosquete *m.* musket.

mosquetería *f.* musketry [troops].

mosquetero *m.* musketeer.

mosquetón *m.* short carbine.

mosquita *f. dim.* small fly. 2 coll. ~ *muerta*, MOSCA MUERTA.

mosquitera *f.*, **mosquitero** *m.* mosquito net.

mosquito *m.* ENT. mosquito; gnat. 2 coll. tippler.

mostacera *f.*, **mostacero** *m.* mustard pot.

mostacilla *f.* mustard-seed shot. 2 tiny glass beads.

mostacho *m.* moustache. 2 coll. smudge on the face. 3 NAUT. shroud [of bowsprit].

mostachón *m.* macaroon.

mostajo *m.* MOSTELLAR.

mostaza *f.* mustard [plant, seed, seasoning]. 2 mustard-seed shot.

mostear *intr.* [of grapes] to yield must. 2 to put must into vats. 3 to mix must with old wine.

mostela *f.* AGR. gavel, sheaf.

mostellar *m.* BOT. whitebeam.

mosto *m.* must [grape juice].

mostrador, -ra *adj.* showing, pointing. 2 *m.-f.* shower, pointer. 3 *m.* counter [in a shop]. 4 bar [counter].

mostrar *tr.* to show, exhibit, display, reveal. 2 to show, point out. 3 to show, demonstrate, prove. 4 *ref.* to show oneself, prove to be. ¶ CONJUG. like *contar*.

mostrenco, -ca *adj.* unclaimed, ownerless. 2 coll. homeless, masterless. 3 coll. dull, stupid. 4 *m.-f.* dullard.

mota *f.* burl [in cloth]. 2 mote, speck. 3 slight defect or fault. 4 knoll, hummock.

motacila *f.* AGUZANIEVES.

mote *m.* motto, device. 2 nickname.

motear *intr.* to speck, speckle, mottle.

motejar *tr.* to call names to, to nickname.

motejo *m.* name-calling, nicknaming.

motel *m.* motel.

motete *m.* MUS. motet.

motilidad *f.* BIOL. motility.

motilón, -na *adj.* having short or cropped hair. 2 *m.* coll. lay brother.

motín *m.* mutiny, riot, uprising.

motivar *tr.* to motive, motivate. 2 to give a reason for.

motivo *m.* motive, reason: *con* ~ *de*, owin to; on the occasion of; *por ningún* ~, under no circumstances. 2 F. ARTS, MUS. motif.

moto *m.* MOJÓN. 2 coll. motorcycle.

motocicleta *f.* motorcycle.

motociclista *m.* motorcyclist.

motón *m.* NAUT. block, pulley.

motonave *f.* NAUT. motor ship.

motonería *f.* NAUT. blocks, pulleys, tackle.

motor, -ra *adj.* motor, motive. 2 ANAT., PHYSIOL. motor. 3 *m.* motor, mover. 4 MACH. motor, engine: ~ *a chorro*, jet engine; ~ *a gas*, gas engine; ~ *de explosión*, explosion engine; ~ *Diesel*, Diesel engine.

motora *f.* NAUT. small motorboat.

motorismo *m.* motoring, motorism.

motorista *m.-f.* motorcyclist. 2 motorist.

motorizar *tr.* to motorize.

motriz *f. adj.* motive: *fuerza* ~, motive power.

movedizo, -za *adj.* movable. 2 shaky, unsteady. 3 fickle, inconstant. 4 *arenas movedizas*, quicksand.

mover *tr.* to move [change position of]. 2 to move, stir, shake, wag [a limb, the head, the tail, etc.]. 3 to move, actuate, drive, propel. 4 to move, induce, impel, prompt, persuade. 5 to raise, start, excite, make. 6 ~ *a*, to move to, to inspire, excite: ~ *a compasión*, to excite piety; ~ *a risa*, to move to laughter. 7 *intr.* to abort, miscarry. 8 *ref.* to move, stir, budge; to get busy, bestir oneself. ¶ IRREG. CONJUG. IND. Pres.: *muevo, mueves, mueve;* movemos, movéis, *mueven.* | SUBJ. Pres.: *mueva, muevas, mueva;* movamos, mováis, *muevan.* | IMPER.: *mueve, mueva;* movamos, moved, *muevan.*

movible *adj.* movable: *fiesta* ~, movable feast.

móvil *adj.* moving, mobile. 2 *m.* moving body. 3 motive, incentive, inducement.

movilidad *f.* movableness, mobility.

movilización *f.* mobilization.

movilizar *tr.* to mobilize.

movimiento *m.* moving, movement, motion; gesture: *en* ~, in motion. 2 MEC., ASTR. motion: ~ *alternativo* or *de vaivén*, reciprocating motion; ~ *ondulatorio*, wave motion. 3 [political, literary, etc.]. movement. 4 mental motion, impulse. 5 stir, agitation, life. 6 traffic. 7 animation [of style]. 8 MUS. movement, tempo. 9 *pl.* movements, activities.

moyuelo *m.* fine bran.

moza *f.* girl, lass: *buena* ~, *real* ~, handsome girl or woman. 2 maid of all work. 3 mistress, concubine. 4 wash beetle. 5 last or winning game.

mozalbete *m. dim.* lad, vouth, young fellow.

mozallón, -na *m.-f.* strapping young person.

mozárabe *adj.* Mozarabic. 2 *m.-f.* Mozarab.

mozo, -za *adj.* young, youthful: *la gente moza*, the youth. 2 single, unmarried. 3 *m.* young man, youth, lad: *buen* ~, *real* ~, handsome youth or man. 4 manservant, hand, waiter, porter: ~ *de café*, ~ *de restaurante*, waiter; ~ *de cordel* or *de cuerda*, street porter; ~ *de estación*, station porter; ~ *de estoques*, BULLF. manservant of a matador; ~ *de labranza*, farm hand. 5 cloak hanger.

mozuelo, -la *m.-f. dim.* young lad, young lass.

muaré *m.* moire, moiré [watered silk].

mucama *f.* (Am.) female servant.

mucamo *m.* (Am.) manservant, valet.

muceta *f.* ECCL. mozetta. 2 a kind of mozetta worn by holders of a doctor's or master's degree.

mucilaginoso, -sa *adj.* mucilaginous.

mucílago, mucilago *m.* mucilage.

mucosa *f.* ANAT. mucous membrane.

mucosidad *f.* mucosity.

mucoso, -sa *adj.* mucous.

muchacha *f.* girl. 2 maid, maidservant.

muchachada *f.* boyish or girlish act. 2 (Am.) assemblage of boys or girls, of youngsters.

muchachil *adj.* boylike, girl-like; of boys or girls.

muchacho, -cha *adj.* young [person]. *2 m.* boy lad. *3* manservant. *4 f.* girl, lass. *5* maidservant.

muchedumbre *f.* multitude, crowd.

muchísimo, -ma *adj.-adv.* superl. of MUCHO; very much, a very great deal.

1) **mucho** *adv.* much, very much, a good or great deal, a lot, dearly, hard, abundantly, excessively; *ni ~ menos*, not by a long shot, far from; *por ~ que*, however much. *2* often: *va ~ al teatro*, he often goes to the theatre. *3* long, longtime. *4 pron.* much, a great or indefinite quantity; something uncommon, considerable: *~ será que...*, it is unlikely that...; *con ~*, by far; *ni con ~*, not by a long shot, far from.

2) **mucho, -cha** *adj.* much, very much, a good or great deal of, a lot of. *2 pl.* many, a good or great deal of, a lot of, lots of.

muchos, -chas *pron.* many; *~ lo conocían*, many knew him.

muda *f.* change, alteration. *2* change of linen. *3* mo(u)lt, mo(u)lting. *4* mo(u)lting season. *5* change of voice, in boys.

mudable *adj.* changeable. *2* fickle, inconstant.

mudanza *f.* change, alteration, mutation. *2* removal, moving [chance of residence]. *3* DANCE. figure, motion. *4* inconstancy.

mudar *tr.* to change, alter, convert: *~ en*, to change to or into. *2* to change [take or adopt another instead of]. | Often with *de: ~ de color*, to change colour. *3* to move, remove [to another place]. *4* to mo(u)lt, to shed. *5 ~ la voz*, [of a boy] to change voice. *6 ref.* to change [in conduct, affections, etc.]. *7* to change one's underclothing. *8* to move [change one's residence]. *9* coll. to leave, go away. *10 mudarse de ropa*, to change one's clothes.

mudéjar *adj.-n.* Mudejar.

mudez *f.* dumbness.

mudo, -da *adj.* dumb, mute, silent. *2* PHON. mute. *3 m.-f.* mute [dumb person].

mueble *adj.* movable. *2 m.* piece of furniture. *3* RADIO. cabinet. *4 pl.* furniture.

mueblista *m.* furniture maker or seller.

mueca *f.* face, wry face, grimace, grin.

muela *f.* upper millstone. *2* grindstone. *3* ANAT. molar, molar tooth, grinder. *4* knoll, flattopped hill. *5* BOT. flat pea.

muellaje *m.* wharfage.

muelle *adj.* soft, delicate. *2* voluptuous, easy, luxurious. *3 m.* NAUT. wharf, pier. *4* RLY. freight platform. *5* MACH., HOR. spring.

muérdago *m.* BOT. mistletoe.

muerdo, muerda, etc. *irr.* V. MORDER.

muermo *m.* VET. glanders.

muero, muera, etc. *irr.* V. MORIR.

muerte *f.* death: *dar ~*, or *dar la ~ a*, to kill, put to death; *a ~*, to the death; *de ~*, implacably; deadly [wounded]; hopelessly [ill]; *de mala ~*, mean, sorry. *2* Death [skeleton with a scythe]. *3* homicide, murder.

muerto, -ta *p. p.* of MORIR and MATAR. *2 adj.* dead. *3* faded, dull. *4* exhausted, tired out. *5* slacked [lime]. *6* bursting, perished, dying [with curiosity, cold, hunger, etc.]. *7 estar ~ por*, to be madly in love with. *8 m.-f.* dead person, corpse. *9* dummy [at bridge]. *10 echarle el ~ a*, to put the blame on. *11 tocar a ~*, to toll, knell.

muesca *f.* notch, nick, indentation. *2* CARP. mortise.

muestra *f.* signboard, sign [in front of shop, inn, etc.]. *2* sample, specimen. *3* copy, model, pattern. *4* face, dial [of clock]. *5* sign, show, token: *dar muestras de*, to show signs of. *6* set [of dog]: *perro de ~*, pointer, setter.

muestrario *m.* collection of samples, sample book.

muevo, mueva, etc. *irr.* V. MOVER.

mufla *f.* muffle [in a muffle furnace].

mufti *m.* mufti.

mugido *m.* low, lowing, moo [of cattle].

mugir *intr.* to low, moo. *2* to bellow, to roar.

mugre *f.* greasy dirt [of wool, clothes, etc.].

mugriento, -ta *adj.* greasy, dirty.

mugrón *m.* AGR. layer [of wine]. *2* shoot [of plant].

muguete *m.* BOT. lily of the valley.

mujer *f.* woman: *~ de gobierno*, housekeeper; *~ pública*, prostitute; *~ de su casa*, good housewife; *~ fatal*, vamp. *2* wife.

mujercilla *f.* little woman. *2* despicable woman.

mujercita *f. dim.* little woman. *2* little wife.

mujeriego, -ga *adj.* womanly. *2* womanish. *3* fond of women. *4 montar a mujeriegas*, to ride sidesaddle.

mujeril *adj.* feminine, womanly. *2* womanish.

mujerío *m.* women; gathering of women.

mujerona *f. augm.* big woman, strapping woman.

mujerzuela *f. dim.* little woman. *2* despicable woman.

mújil, mújol *m.* ICHTH. mullet, striped mullet.

mula *f.* ZOOL. she-mule: *en la ~ de San Francisco*, on shank's mare. *2* coll. stupid fellow.

muladar *m.* dungheap, dunghill. *2* filth, corruption.

muladí *m.-f.* HIST. Spaniard who embraced Mohammedanism.

mular *adj.* [pertaining to] mule.

mulatero *m.* mule hirer. *2* muleteer, muleman.

mulato, -ta *adj.* mulatto. *2 m.* mulatto [man]. *3 f.* mulatto woman.

mulero *m.* muleman.

muleta *f.* crutch [for lame person; prop. support]. *2* BULLF. matador's red flag.

muletilla *f.* MULETA 2. *2* crosshandle cane. *3* braid frog. *4* pet phrase or word.

muleto *m.* young mule. *2* mule not yet broken.

muletón *m.* Canton flannel.

mulo *m.* ZOOL. mule; hinny: *~ castellano*, mule.

mulso, -sa *adj.* honeyed [wine].

multa *f.* fine, amercement, mulct.

multar *tr.* to fine, amerce, mulct.

multicolor *adj.* many-colo(u)red, multicolo(u)r.

multicopista *m.* duplicator, copying machine.

multiforme *adj.* multiform.

multimillonario, -ria *adj.-n.* multimillionaire.

múltiple *adj.* multiple, manifold.

multiplicación *f.* multiplication.

multiplicador, -ra *adj.* multiplying. *2 m.-f.* multiplier. *3 m.* MATH. multiplier.

multiplicando *m.* MATH. multiplicand.

multiplicar *tr.* to multiply. *2 ref.* to multiply [increase in number].

multiplicidad *f.* multiplicity.

múltiplo *adj.-m.* MATH. multiple: *mínimo común ~*, least common multiple.

multitud *f.* multitude.

mullida *f.* litter, bedding [for animals].

mullido *m.* soft filling for cushions, etc.

mullir *tr.* to fluff, soften, loosen [make fluffy or less compact]. *2* to beat up, shake up [a bed]. *3* to arrange, engineer. *5 mullírselas a uno*, to punish, to mortify a person. ¶ IRREG. CONJUG: IND. Pret.: mullí, mulliste, *mulló*; mullimos, mullisteis, *mulleron.* | SUBJ. Imperf.: *mullera, mulleras,* etc., or *mullese, mulleses*, etc. | Fut.: *mullere, mulleres*, etc. | GER.: *mullendo.*

mundanal *adj.* worldly, mundane.

mundanalidad *f.* worldliness, mundanity.

mundanamente *adv.* worldlily.

mundano, -na *adj.* mundane, worldly [things, pleasure, etc.]. *2* worldly [person].

mundial *adj.* world-wide, world.

mundificar *tr.* to mundify, cleanse.

mundillo *m.* arched clotheshorse. *2* cushion for making lace. *3* warming pan. *4* BOT. snowball. *5* little world [of artists, politicians, etc.].

mundo *m.* world [in practically every sense]: *el gran ~*, the fashionable society; *el ~ antiguo*, the Old World; *el Nuevo Mundo*, the New World; *el otro ~*, the next World; *medio ~*, a lot of people; *todo el ~*, everybody; *tener ~*, or *mucho ~*, to know life, know the world. *2* globe [terrestrial sphere]. *3* Saratoga trunk.

mundología *f.* knowledge of life, tact, savoir-faire.

mundonuevo *m.* peep show, portable cosmorama.

munición *f.* MIL. ammunition, munition, supplies. *2* charge of firearms; shot [collectively]. *3 de ~*, ammunition [supplied by the government].

municionar *tr.* to ammunition, provide with ammunition.

municipal *adj.* municipal. *2 m.* policeman.

municipalidad *f.* municipality; municipal body or corporation.

municipalizar *tr.* to municipalize.

munícipe *m.* citizen, denizen. *2* councilman.

municipio *m.* municipium. *2* municipality.

munificencia *f.* munificence.

munífico, -ca *adj.* munificent.

muñeca *f.* ANAT. wrist. *2* doll: *~ de trapo*, rag doll. *4* manikin, dress form. *5* sugar teat. *6* pounce bag. *7* polishing bag.

muñeco *m.* boy doll, puppet. *2* dummy, man's figure. *3* fig. effeminate coxcomb.

muñeira *f.* popular dance of Galicia [in Spain].

muñequera *f.* bracelet or strap for a wrist watch.

muñidor *m.* beadle. *2 ~ electoral*, electioneer.

muñir *tr.* to deliver summons [to meetings, etc.]. *2* to arrange, concert. ¶ CONJUG. like *mullir.*

muñón *m.* stump [of amputated limb]. *2* ARTIL. trunnion. *3* MACH. gudgeon pin, wrist pin.

murajes *m. pl.* BOT. pimpernel.

mural *adj.* mural.

muralla *f.* FORT. wall, rampart.

murar *tr.* to wall [surround with a wall].

murciélago *m.* ZOOL. bat.

murena *f.* ICHTH. moray.

murga *f.* band of street musicians.

murgón *m.* ICHTH. parr, samlet.

múrice *m.* ZOOL. murex. *2* poet. purple.

múridos *m. pl.* ZOOL. Muridae.

murmujear *intr.-tr.* to murmur.

murmullo *m.* murmur, ripple; whisper; rustle [of leaves, etc.]; purl [of a brook].

murmuración *f.* gossip, backbiting.

murmurador, -ra *adj.* murmuring. *2* gossiping, backbiting. *3 m.-f.* gossiper, backbiter.

murmurar *intr.* to murmur, whisper. *2* to mutter, grumble. *3* [of leaves, etc.] to rustle. *4* [or streams] to purl, ripple. *5* to gossip, backbite.

murmurio *m.* MURMULLO.

muro *m.* wall [in a building, garden, etc.]: *~ de*

contención, retaining wall. *2* FORT. wall, rampart.

murria *f.* coll. blues, dejection, sullenness.

murrio, -rria *adj.* sad, dejected, sullen.

murta *f.* BOT. myrtle. *2* BOT. myrtle berry.

murtón *m.* BOT. myrtle berry.

mus *m.* a card game.

musa *f.* MYTH. Muse. *2* fig. Muse, muse [inspiration, poetry]. *3 pl.* Muses, liberal arts.

musáceo, -a *adj.* BOT. musaceous.

musaraña *f.* ZOOL. shrew, shrewmouse. *2* insect, small animal. *3* coll. floating speck in the eye. *4 pensar en las musarañas*, to be absentminded.

musco, -ca *adj.* dark brown. *2 m.* MUSGO 1.

muscular *adj.* muscular [of the muscles].

musculatura *f.* musculature.

músculo *m.* ANAT. muscle; brawn.

musculoso, -sa *adj.* muscular, brawny.

muselina *f.* muslin.

museo *m.* museum.

muserola *f.* noseband.

musgaño *m.* ZOOL. shrew, shrewmouse.

musgo *m.* BOT. moss. *2* BOT. *~ marino*, coralline.

musgoso, -sa *adj.* mossy. *2* moss-covered.

música *f.* music: *~ celestial*, coll. nonsense, empty talk, moonshine; *~ de fondo*, background music; *~ popular*, folk music; *con la ~ a otra parte*, get out; don't bother me. *2* band, music [body of musicians]. *3* sheet music.

musical *adj.* musical.

musicalidad *f.* musicality, musicalness.

músico, -ca *adj.* musical. *2 m.-f.* musician. *3* MIL. *~ mayor*, bandmaster.

musicógrafo *m.* musicographer.

musicología *f.* musicology.

musiquero *m.* music cabinet, music stand.

musitar *intr.* to mumble, mutter.

musivo *adj.* mosaic [gold].

muslera *f.* armour for the thigh, cuisse.

muslime *adj.-n.* Moslem, Muslim.

muslímico, -ca *adj.* Moslem, Muslim.

muslo *m.* ANAT., ZOOL. thigh. *2* drumstick [of cooked fowl].

musmón *m.* ZOOL. mouflon.

mustango *m.* (Am.) mustang.

mustela *f.* ICHTH. dog shark. *2* ZOOL. obs. weasel.

mustio, tia *adj.* withered, faded. *2* sad, dejected, melancholy.

musulmán *adj.-n.* Mussulman.

muta *f.* pack of hounds.

mutabilidad *f.* mutability.

mutación *f.* mutation. *2* THEAT. change of scene. *3* change of weather, unsettled weather.

mutilación *f.* mutilation.

mutilado, -da *adj.* mutilated, crippled. *2 m.-f.* cripple.

mutis *m.* THEAT. exit: *hacer ~*, THEAT. to exit: coll. to say nothing, to be silent.

mutismo *m.* mutism, silence.

mutualidad *f.* mutuality. *2* mutual aid. *3* mutual benefit society.

mutualismo *m.* system of organized mutual aid.

mutuo, tua *adj.* mutual, reciprocal. *2 m.* LAW mutuum.

muy *adv.* very, very much, greatly, most, too [always before adj. or adv.]. *2 ~ hombre*, very much of a man. *3 ~ señor mío*, Dear Sir [in a letter].

muzárabe *adj.-n.* MOZÁRABE.

N

N, n *f.* N, n, sixteenth letter of the Spanish alphabet.

naba *f.* BOT. rutabaga.

nabab, nababo *m.* nabob, nawab.

nabi *m.* Moorish prophet.

nabina *f.* turnip seed.

nabo *m.* BOT. turnip. *2* turniplike root. *3* root, stock [of the tail of a horse, etc.]. *4* NAUT. mast. *5* newel [of winding stair].

Nabot *m. pr. n.* BIBL. Naboth.

Nabucodonosor *m. pr. n.* BIBL. Nebuchadnezzar.

nácar *m.* mother-of-pearl, nacre.

nacarado, -da *adj.* nacred.

nacáreo, -a; nacarino, -na *adj.* nacreous, nacrine.

nacela *f.* ARCH. scotia [moulding].

macencia *f.* growth, tumour.

nacer *intr.* to be born. *2* [of plants, hair, horns, etc.] to grow, bud, sprout. *3* [of streams, etc.] to spring, flow, have its source. *4* to originate, spring, start, emanate, derive. ¶ CONJUG.: INDIC. Pres.: *nazco, naces, nace,* etc. | SUBJ. Pres.: *nazca, nazcas,* etc. | IMPER.: *nace, nazca; nazcamos, naced, nazcan.*

nacido, -da *adj.* born: *bien ~,* of noble birth, honest; *mal ~,* lowborn, lowminded. *2 m.* living man. *3* growth, boil.

naciente *adj.* incipient, recent; growing, budding, sprouting. *2* rising [sun]. *3 m.* East.

nacimiento *m.* birth, coming to life: *de ~,* born, by birth. *2* growth, budding, sprouting. *3* rising [of sun]. *4* source [of river or spring]. *5* origin, issue. *6* birth, descent, lineage. *7* crèche, crib [Nativity scene].

nación *f.* nation: *Naciones Unidas,* United Nations; *de ~,* by nationality.

nacional *adj.* national. *2* home [of one's own country]; *productos nacionales,* home products. *3 m.* native.

nacionalidad *f.* nationality. *2* citizenship.

nacionalismo *m.* nationalism.

nacionalización *f.* nationalization. *2* naturalization.

nacionalizar *tr.* to nationalize. *2* to naturalize.

nada *f.* nothing, naught, nothingness. *2 indef. pron.* nothing, not anything, not a bit: little, very little: *~ de nuevo,* nothing new; *de ~,* little, of no account; don't mention it [after thanks]. *3*

adv. not, nothing, not at all, not a bit: *no me gusta ~,* I don't like it at all.

nadaderas *f.* water wings.

nadadero *m.* swimming place.

nadador, -ra *adj.* swimming. *2 m.-f.* swimmer.

nadar *tr.* to swim. *2* to float. *3* fig. to swim, be rolling in.

nadería *f.* triffle, insignificant thing.

nadie *indef. pron.* nobody, no one, none. *2* [after negative] anybody. *3 m.* nobody [person of no importance].

nadir *m.* ASTR. nadir.

nado (a) *adv.* swimming.

nafta *f.* naphtha.

Naftali *m. pr. n.* Naphtali.

naftalina *f.* naphthalene.

naipe *m.* [playing] card. *2* cards, deck of cards: *tener buen ~,* to have good luck at cards. *3 pl.* cards: *jugar a los naipes,* to play cards.

naire *m.* mahout, elephant keeper.

nalga *f.* buttock, rump. *2 pl.* buttocks, nates.

nalgada *f.* slap on the buttocks, span. *2* blow with the buttocks. *3* ham [of hog].

nalgatorio *m.* coll. posteriors, seat, buttocks.

nana *f.* coll. grandma. *2* lullaby, cradlesong.

nanquín *m.* nankeen, nankin.

nansa *f.* fish trap. *2* fish pond.

nansú, nanzú *m.* nainsook.

nao *f.* ship, vessel.

Napoleón *m. pr. n.* Napoleon.

napoleón *m.* napoleon [coin].

Nápoles *m. pr. n.* GEOG. Naples.

napolitano, -na *adj.-n.* Neapolitan.

naranja *f.* BOT. orange: *~ agria,* sour orange; *~ de ombligo,* navel orange; *~ mandarina,* mandarin orange. *2 media ~,* coll. better half; ARCH. cupola, dome.

naranjada *f.* orangeade.

naranjal *m.* orange grove.

naranjero, -ra *adj.* [pertaining to] orange. *2* with a bell muzzle [blunderbuss]. *3 m.-f.* orange raiser or seller.

naranjilla *f.* small green orange for preserving.

naranjo *m.* BOT. orange tree. *2* coll. booby, lout.

Narbona *pr. n.* GEOG. Narbonne.

narcisismo *m.* narcissism.

narciso *m.* BOT. narcissus, daffodil. *2* fig. dandy, fop.

narcosis f. narcosis.
narcótico, -ca adj.-m. narcotic.
narcotizar tr. to narcotize.
nardo m. spikenard, nard [plant and ointment]. 2 BOT. tuberose.
narguile m. narghile.
narigón, -na adj. large-nosed. 2 m.-f. largenosed person. 3 large nose.
narigudo, -da adj.-n. NARIGÓN 1 & 2.
narigueta, nariguilla f. dim. small nose.
nariz f. sing.-pl. [human] nose: ~ aguileña, Roman or aquiline nose; ~ respingona, turned-up nose; hinchársele a uno las narices, to get angry; meter las narices en, to poke one's nose into. 2 f. sing. nose [of an animal; of a retort]. 3 nostril. 4 nose [sense of smell]. 5 bouquet [of wine]. 6 nose-shaped catch [for a latch].
narizota f. aug. large nose.
narración f. narration, narrative.
narrador, -ra adj. narrating. 2 m.-f. narrator.
narrar tr. to narrate, relate, tell.
narrativa f. narration, narrative.
narrativo, -va; narratorio, -ria adj. narrative.
narria f. drag [sledge for conveying heavy bodies].
narval m. ZOOL. narwhal.
nasa f. bow net. 2 fisherman's basket. 3 basket for flour, bread, etc.
nasal adj. nasal.
nasalizar tr. to nasalize.
nasardo m. MUS. nasard.
nata f. cream [of milk; of any liquor]. 2 fig. cream [the best]. 3 pl. whipped cream with sugar. 4 NATILLAS.
natación f. natation, swimming.
natal adj. natal, native. 2 m. birth. 3 birthday.
natalicio m. birthday. 2 nativity.
natalidad f. natality, birth rate.
Natán m. pr. n. BIBL. Nathan.
Nataniel m. pr. n. BIBL. Nathanael.
natátil adj. natant, floating.
natatorio, -ria adj. natatorial, natatory.
natillas f. custard.
natividad f. nativity. 2 (cap.) Christmas, Yuletide.
nativo, -va adj. MINER. native. 2 native, natal: vernacular. 3 ntive, born. 4 inborn, naturalborn.
nato, -ta adj. born: criminal ~, born criminal. 2 inherent in an office or position.
natura f. nature. 2 genital organs.
natural adj. natural. 2 artless, ingenuous. 3 MUS. natural. 4 adj.-n. native [of a country or place]. 5 m. disposition, nature. 6 al ~, without dressing. 7 F. ARTS del ~, from life, from nature.
naturaleza f. Nature. 2 nature. 3 constitution [of a person]. 4 genitals. 5 sort, kind, description. 6 nationality [of a person]. 7 carta de ~, privilege of naturalization. 8 F. ARTS ~ muerta, still life.
naturalidad f. naturalness. 2 nationality [of a person].
naturalismo m. PHIL., LIT. naturalism.
naturalista adj. naturalistic. 2 m.-f. naturalist.
naturalización f. naturalization.
naturalizar tr. to naturalize. 2 to become naturalized.
naturalmente adv. naturally. 2 of course.
naturismo m. naturism.
naufragar intr. NAUT. to be wrecked, to sink; to be shipwrecked. 2 fig. to be wrecked, to fail, fall through.
naufragio m. shipwreck. 2 failure, run, disaster.
náufrago, -ga adj. NAUT. wrecked, castaway. 2 m. f. shipwrecked person, castaway.

naumaquia f. naumachia, naumachy.
náusea f. nausea, sickness, qualmishness; disgust: tener náuseas, to be nauseated, to be sick at the stomach; dar náuseas, to make sick, to disgust.
nauseabundo adj. nauseous, nauseating, sickening, loathsome.
nausear intr. to nauseate, be nauseated.
nauta m. mariner, sailor.
náutica f. nautics, navigation.
náutico, -ca adj. nautical. 2 water [sports].
nautilo m. ZOOL. nautilus.
nava f. hollow [plain surrounded by mountains].
navaja f. clasp knife, folding knife: ~ de afeitar, razor. 2 (Am.) penknife. 3 razor, tusk. 4 ZOOL. razor clam.
navajazo m. stab with a clasp knife.
naval adj. naval.
Navarra pr. n. GEOG. Navarre.
navarro, -rra adj.-n. Navarrese.
navazo m. kitchen garden in sandy marshland.
nave f. ship, vessel: ~ aérea, airship: quemar las naves, to burn one's boats. 2 ARCH. nave, aisle: ~ lateral, aisle. 3 large hall or division in a building.
navecilla f. dim. small ship. 2 ECCL. navicula, incense boat.
navegable adj. navigable [river, lake, etc.].
navegación f. navigation, sailing: ~ aérea, aeronautics, aviation. 2 sea voyage.
navegador, -ra; navegante adj. navigating. 2 m.-f. navigator.
navegar intr. to navigate, to sail. 2 to go about.
naveta f. NAVECILLA. 2 small drawer.
navícula f. BOT. navicula.
navicular adj. ANAT., BOT. navicular.
Navidad f. Nativity, Christmas, Christmas Day. 2 Christmastide, Yuletide.
navideño, -ña adj. [pertaining to] Christmas.
naviero, -ra adj. ship, shipping. 2 m. shipowner.
navío m. NAUT. ship, warship: ~ de guerra, warship; ~ de línea, ship of the line.
náyade f. MYTH. naiad.
nazareno, -na adj.-n. Nazarene. 2 m. Nazarite. 3 penitent in Holy Week processions.
nazi adj.-n. Nazi.
nébeda f. BOT. catnip, catmint.
nebli m. ORN. kind of falcon.
neblinoso, -sa adj. foggy, misty.
nebulón m. sly fellow, hypocrite.
nebulosa f. ASTR. nebula.
nebulosidad f. nebulosity, nebulousness, cloudiness. 2 cloud, shadow.
nebuloso, -sa adj. nebulous, cloudy. 2 misty, hazy, vague. 3 gloomy.
necear intr. to talk nonsense. 2 to persist foolishly.
necedad f. foolishness, folly, stupidity, nonsense.
necesaria f. privy, water-closet.
necesario, -ria adj. necessary; needful.
neceser m. case, kit: ~ de costura, sewing case, workbasket; ~ de tocador, toilet case.
necesidad f. necessity; need, want: de ~, of necessity; por ~, from necessity; necessarily. 2 emergency. 3 want, destitution, poverty. 4 hunger. 5 pl. hacer sus necesidades, to urinate, to go to stool.
necesitado, -da adj. necessitous, needy, poor. 2 ~ de, wanting. 3 m. needy, poor person.
necesitar tr. to necessitate [force, compel]. 2 to need, want, lack. 3 to have to, need to. 4 intr. ~ de, to need, be in need of.

necio, -cia *adj.* ignorant, foolish, stupid; silly, unjudicious. *2 m.-f.* ignorant person, fool.
necrología *f.* necrology.
necromancia *f.* necromancy.
necrópolis *f.* necropolis.
necrosis, *pl.* **-sis** *f.* MED. necrosis.
néctar *m.* nectar.
nectario *m.* BOT. nectary.
neerlandés, -sa *adj.-n.* HOLANDÉS. *2* Netherlandish [language].
nefando, -da *adj.* nefandous, abominable.
nefario, -ria *adj.* nearious, wicked, iniquitous.
nefasto, -ta *adj.* sad, ominous. *2* funest, noxious.
nefridio *m.* ZOOL. nephridium.
nefrítico, -ca *adj.* MED. nephritic.
nefritis *f.* MED. nephritis.
negable *adj.* deniable.
negación *f.* negation. *2* GRAM. negative particle.
negado, -da *adj.* inapt, incompetent. *2* dull, stupid.
negar *tr.* to deny [declare untrue or non-existent]. *2* to deny, refuse. *3* to deny, disavow. *4* to forbid, prohibit. *5* to hide, conceal. *6 ~ el saludo a,* to cut, not to speak to. *7 ref.* to decline, refuse [to do]. *8* to deny oneself [to callers]. *9 negarse a sí mismo,* to deny oneself, practice, self-denial. ¶ CONJUG. like *acertar.*
negativa *f.* negative [negative statement or reply], denial. *2* denial, refusal.
negativo, -va *adj.* negative. *2 m.* PHOT. negative.
negligencia *f.* negligence, neglect, carelessness.
negligente *adj.* negligent, careless, neglectful.
negociable *adj.* COM. negotiable.
negociación *f.* negotation. *2* business transaction.
negociado *m.* bureau, division. *2* business, affair.
negociador, -ra *adj.* negotiating. *2 m.-f.* negotiator.
negociante *m.* dealer, trader, businessman.
negociar *intr.* to deal, trade, do business. *2 intr.-tr.* to negotiate [arrange by negotiation]. *3 tr.* COM. to negotiate [a bill, cheque, etc.].
negocio *m.* business, affair, transaction, deal, bargain; matter, occupation, work. *2* commerce, trade. *3* concern, business: *un ~ de banca,* a banking concern. *4* profit, gain. *5 pl.* business, commercial affairs. *6* DIPLOM. affaires.
negocioso, -sa *adj.* active, diligent.
negra *f.* fencing sword. *2* MUS. crotchet, quarter note. *3* Negress, Negro woman.
negrear *intr.* to show black, appear black. *2* to be blackish.
negrero, -ra *adj.* slave-trading. *2 m.-f.* slave trader. *3* fig. slave-driver.
negreta *f.* ORN. black scoter.
negrillo, -lla *adj.* blackish. *2* PRINT. *letra negrilla,* boldfaced type, clarendon type. *3 m.* BOT. elm.
negrito, -ta *m.-f.* Negro boy, Negro girl. *2* Negrito.
negro, -gra *adj.* black [colour]. *2* black [in colour]; dusky, gloomy; sinister; wicked, dismal]. *3* dark, brown. *4* unlucky, wretched: *pasarlas negras,* to have a terrible time. *5* Negro. *6 m.* black [colour, pigment]: *~ animal,* boneblack; *~ de humo,* lampblack; *~ de marfil,* ivory black. *7* Negro, nigger. *8 f.* Negress.
negror *m.,* **negrura** *f.* blackness.
negruzco, -ca *adj.* blackish.
neguijón *m.* tooth decay.
neguilla *f.* BOT. corn cockle. *2* BOT. love-in-a-mist. *3* age mark [in horses's teeth].
neguillón *m.* BOT. corn cockle.
Negus *m.* Negus [title of the Ethiopian emperor].
nema *f.* seal or sealing of a letter.
nematelminto *m.* ZOOL. nemathelminth.

nemátodo, -da *adj.-m.* ZOOL. nematode.
nemeo, -a *adj.-n.* Nemean.
Némesis *f. pr. n.* MYTH. Nemesis.
nemoroso, -sa *adj.* poet, sylvan; wooded.
nena *f.* baby [girl]. *2* dear, darling.
nene *m.* baby [boy]. *2* dear, darling. *3* villain [used ironically].
nenúfar *m.* BOT. white water lily.
neo *m.* CHEM. neon.
neoclásico, -ca *adj.* neoclassic. *2 m.-f.* neoclassicist.
neófito *m.* neophyte.
neolatino, -na *adj.* Neo-Latin.
neolítico, -ca *adj.* neolithic. *2 m.* Neolithic era.
neologismo *m.* neologism.
neón *m.* CHEM. neon.
neoplasia *f.* MED. neoplasia.
neoplatónico, -ca *adj.* Neoplatonic. *2 m.-f.* Neoplatonist.
neoyorquino, -na *adj.* of New York. *2 m.-f.* New Yorker.
neozoico, -ca *adj.-m.* GEOL. Neozoic.
neperiano, -na *adj.* Napierian, Naperian.
nepotismo *m.* nepotism.
Neptuno *m. pr. n.* MYTH., ASTR. Neptune.
nequáquam *adv.* coll. by no means.
nequicia *f.* iniquity, perversity.
nereida *f.* MYTH. Nereid.
Nerón *m. pr. n.* Nero.
nervadura *f.* ARCH. rib. *2* BOT., ENT. nervation, nervures, ribbing.
nérveo, -a *adj.* nerval.
nerviación *f.* BOT., ENT. nerviation.
nervio *m.* ANAT. nerve [of the nervous system]: *ataque de nervios,* fit of nerves, hysterics. *2* nerve, vigour, enerrgy. *3* nerve, sinew, tendon. *4* BOT. nerve, rib, vein. *5* ENT. nervure, rib. *6* BOOKB. rib. *7* MUS. string. *8* ARCH. rib in the intrados of a vault. *9* NAUT. stay.
nerviosidad *f.* NERVOSIDAD. *2* NERVIOSISMO.
nerviosismo *m.* nervousness, nervous excitement.
nervioso, -sa *adj.* nerve: *centro ~,* nerve centre. *2* nervous: *poner ~,* to get on one's nerves. *3* vigorous, energetic. *4* BOT. nerved.
nervosidad *f.* nervosity. *2* flexibility [of some metals]. *3* strength, forcibleness [of arguments].
nervoso, -sa *adj.* NERVIOSO.
nervudo, -da *adj.* strong-nerved, sinewy.
nervura *f.* BOOKB. ribbing.
nesciencia *f.* nescience, ignorance.
nesga *f.* SEW. gore. *2* triangular piece.
netamente *adv.* clearly, distinctly.
neto, -ta *adj.* clear, pure. *2* net [weight, etc.]. *3 m.* ARCH. dado [of pedestal].
neumática *f.* PHYS. pneumatics.
neumático, -ca *adj.* pneumatic. *2 m.* tire, pneumatic tire.
neumonía *f.* MED. pneumonia.
neumotórax *m.* MED. pneumothorax.
neuralgia *f.* MED. neuralgia.
neurastenia *f.* MED. neurasthenia.
neuritis *f.* MED. neuritis.
neurosqueleto *m.* endoskeleton.
neurología *f.* neurology.
neurólogo *m.* neurologist.
neurona *f.* ANAT. neuron, neurona.
neurópata *m.-f.* neuropath.
neuropatía *f.* MED. neuropathy.
neuróptero, -ra *adj.-m.* ENT. neuropteran.
neurosis *f.* MED. neurosis.
neurótico, -ca *adj.-n.* MED. neurotic.

neutral *adj.-n.* neutral, neuter [taking no sides].
neutralidad *f.* neutrality.
neutralización *f.* neutralization.
neutralizar *tr.* to neutralize. *2* to counteract.
neutro, -tra *adj.* neutral [colour]. *2* CHEM., ELECT. neutral. *3* BOT., ENT. neutral, neuter. *4* GRAM. neuter.
neutrón *m.* PHYS., CHEM. neutron.
nevada *f.* snowfall.
nevadilla *f.* BOT. whitlowwort.
nevado, -da *adj.* snow-covered. *2* snow-white, snowy.
nevar *impers.* to snow. *2 tr.* to make snowwhite. ¶ CONJUG. like *acertar.*
nevasca *f.* NEVADA. *2* snowstorm.
nevatilla *f.* AGUZANIEVES.
nevera *f.* icebox, refrigerator. *2* fig. very cold place.
nevero *m.* place of perpetual snow. *2* perpetual snow.
nevisca *f.* light snowfall, sleet.
neviscar *impers.* to snow lightly, to sleet.
nevoso, -sa *adj.* snowy [place, weather].
nexo *m.* nexus, bond, link, connexion.
ni *conj.* neither, nor: ~ *aquí* ~ *allí,* neither here nor there. *2* not one, not a single: ~ *un amigo,* not a single friend. *3* ~ *siquiera,* not even.
niara *f.* straw rick.
nicaragüeño, -ña *adj.-n.* Nicaraguan.
niceno, -na *adj.-n.* Nicene.
Nicolás *m. pr. n.* Nicholas.
nicotina *f.* CHEM. nicotine.
nictalopia *f.* nyctalopia.
nicho *m.* niche [recess in a wall].
nidada *f.* nestful of eggs. *2* brood, hatch, covey.
nidal *m.* nest [where hen lay eggs]. *2* nest egg. *3* haunt. *4* cache, hiding place. *5* cause motive.
nidificar *intr.* to nest, build a nest or nests.
nido *m.* nest [of bird, insects, etc.]. *2* home, abode. *3* nest [of bird, insects, etc.]. *2* home, abode. *3* nest [of thieves, machine guns, etc.]. *4* NIDAL.
niebla *f.* fog, mist, haze. *2* fig. haze, confusion. *3* BOT. smut, rust.
niego, niegue, etc. *irr.* V. NEGAR.
niel *m.* niello, niello work.
nielado *m.* nielloing.
nielar *tr.* to niello.
nieto, -ta *m.-f.* grandchild. *2 m.* grandson. *3 f.* granddaughter.
nieve *f.* snow. *2* fig. pure whiteness.
nigromancia *f.* necromancy.
nigromante *m.* necromancer, magician.
nigromántico, -ca *adj.* necromantic. *2 m.* NIGROMANTE.
nigua *f.* ENT. chigoe.
nihilismo *m.* nihilism.
nihilista *adj.* nihilistic. *2 m.-f.* nihilist.
Nilo *m. pr. n.* GEOG. Nilè [river].
nilón *m.* nylon.
nimbar *tr.* to encircle with a halo.
nimbo *m.* nimbus, aureole, halo. *2* METEOR. nimbus.
nimiedad *f.* prolixity, minuteness. *2* smallness.
ninfa *f.* MYTH., ENT. & fig. nymph.
ninfea *f.* BOT. white water lily.
ningún *adj.* contr. of NINGUNO [used only before masculine nouns].
ninguno, -na *adj.* no, not one, not any. *2 indef. pron. m.-f.* none, not any, neither: ~ *de ellos,* none of them; *ninguna de estas dos casas,* neith-

er of these two houses. *3 indef. pron. m.* nobody, no one.
Ninive *f. pr. n.* HIST., GEOG. Nineveh.
niña *f.* female child or infant; little girl, young girl. *2* ANAT. ~ *del ojo,* pupil, apple of the eye. *3* fig. *niñas de los ojos,* apple of one's eyes.
niñada *f.* puerility, childishness, childish action.
niñera *f.* dry nurse, nursemaid.
niñería *f.* puerility, childish action. *2* trifle.
niñero, -ra *adj.* fond of children.
niñez *f.* childhood. *2* fig. infancy. *3* childish action.
niño, -ña *adj.* child [of the age of a child]. *2* childish, childlike. *3* young, inexperienced. *4 m.* male child or infant, boy, little boy: ~ *de teta,* child in arms, suckling babe; *el* ~ *Jesús,* the child Jesús; *de* ~, as a child; *desde* ~, from childhood. *5 pl.* children.
niobio *m.* CHEM. niobium.
nipa *f.* BOT. nipa palm.
nipón, -na *adj.-n.* Nipponese, Japanese.
níquel *m.* CHEM. nickel.
niquelado *m.* **niqueladura** *f.* nickel-plate; nickel-plating.
niquelar *tr.* to nickel-plate.
nirvana *m.* Nirvana.
niscalo *m.* MÍZCALO.
níspero *m.* BOT. medlar [tree and fruit]. *2* (Am.) BOT. sapodilla. *3* BOT. ~ *del Japón,* loquat.
níspola *f.* medlar [fruit].
nitidez *f.* neatness, clearness, sharpness.
nítido, -da *adj.* neat, clear. *2* sharp, well-defined.
nitrato *m.* nitrate. *2* ~ *de Chile,* Chile saltpetre.
nítrico, -ca *adj.* CHEM. nitric.
nitro *m.* nitre, niter, saltpetre, saltpeter.
nitrocelulosa *f.* CHEM. nitrocellulose.
nitrogenar *tr.* to nitrogenize.
nitrógeno *m.* CHEM. nitrogen.
nitroglicerina *f.* CHEM. nitroglycerin.
nivel *m.* level [instrument; uniform altitude; standard, plane]: ~ *del mar,* sea level; ~ *de vida,* standard of living. *2* levelness, equality.
nivelación *f.* levelling. *2* balancing [of the budget].
nivelador, -ra *adj.* levelling. *2 m.-f.* leveller.
nivelar *tr.* to level [make level; bring to a common level; make equal]. *2* ~ *el presupuesto,* to balance the budget. *3 ref.* to level off.
níveo, -a *adj.* poet, snowy, snowy white.
Niza *f. pr. n.* GEOG. Nice.
nizardo, -da *adj.-n.* of Nice.
no *adv.* no, nay [particle equivalent to a negative sentence]: *¿se va usted? —No,* are you going? —No. *2* not, no: ~ *lo sé,* I don't know; ~ *bien,* no sooner; ~ *obstante,* notwithstanding; ~ *sea que,* lest, or else; ~ *ya,* not only. *3 ¿no?* [question tag], isn't it?
nobiliario, -ria *adj.* nobiliary.
nobilísimo, -ma *adj. superl.* most noble.
noble *adj.* noble. *2 m.-f.* noble, nobleman, noblewoman.
nobleza *f.* nobility, nobleness. *2* nobility, noblesse [the class of nobles].
noblote *adj.* noble, open-hearted.
noca *f.* ZOOL. a variety of crab.
noción *f.* notion, idea. *2 pl.* rudiments, elements.
nocivo, -va *adj.* noxious, harmful, pernicious.
noctámbulo, -la *adj.* night-wandering. *2 m.-f.* night-wanderer.
nocturnidad *f.* LAW condition of nocturnal.
nocturno, -na *adj.* nocturnal, night. *2 m.* ECCL. nocturn. *3* MUS. nocturne.
noche *f.* night [in every sense]; evening [from sun-

set to bed]: ~ *buena,* Christmas Eve; ~ *toledana,* sleepless night; ~ *vieja,* New Year's Eve; *buenas noches,* good night; good evening; *media* ~, midnight; *prima* ~, evening; *hacer* ~ *en,* to spend the night in; *hacerse de* ~, to grow dark; *ayer* ~, last night; *de la* ~ *a la mañana,* unexpectedly suddenly; *de,* or *por, la* ~, at night, by night; *esta* ~, tonight; *muy de* ~, late at night.

nochebuena *f.* Christmas Eve.

nochebueno *m.* Christmas cake. 2 Yule log.

nocherniego, -ga *adj.* night-wandering.

nochizo *m.* BOT. wild hazel.

nodal *adj.* nodal. 2 nodical.

nodátil *adj.* ANAT. nodal.

nodo *m.* ASTR., GEOM., PHYS., MED. node.

nodriza *f.* wet nurse. 2 AUTO. vacuum tank.

nódulo *m.* nodule.

Noé *m. pr. n.* BIBL. Noah.

nogal *m.* BOT. walnut tree. 2 walnut wood.

nogalina *f.* walnut stain.

noguera *f.* NOGAL.

nolición *f.* nolition.

nómada *adj.* nomad, nomadic. 2 *m.-f.* nomad.

nomadismo *m.* nomadism, nomadic state.

nombradía *f.* renown, fame, reputation.

nombramiento *m.* naming, nomination, appointing, appointment. 2 MIL. commission.

nombrar *tr.* to name, mention. 2 to name, nominate, appoint, commission.

nombre *m.* name [of a person or thing]: ~ *de pila,* Christian name; ~ *y apellido,* full name; *no tener* ~, to be unspeakable; *en* ~ *de,* in the name of. 2 name, fame, reputation. 3 nickname. 4 GRAM. noun: ~ *apelativo,* or *común,* common noun; ~ *propio,* proper noun.

nomenclador, nomenclátor *m.* catalogue of names; gazeteer; technical glossary.

nomenclatura *f.* nomenclature.

nomeolvides, *pl.* **-des** *f.* BOT. forget-me-not.

nómina *f.* catalogue of names. 2 pay roll.

nominal *adj.* nominal. 2 COM. face [value].

nominalismo *m.* nominalism.

nominar *tr.* NOMBRAR.

nominativo, -va *adj.* COM. nominative, nominal [share]. 2 *adj.-m.* GRAM. nominative [case].

nomparell *f.* PRINT. nonpareil.

non, *pl.* **nones** *adj.* MATH. odd, uneven. 2 *m.* MATH. odd number: *pares y nones,* odd or even; *estar de* ~, fig. to be unmatched; *quedar de* ~, fig. to remain alone, without a partner. 3 *pl.* no, nay [denial, refusal]: *decir nones,* to say no.

nona *f.* HIST. none. 2 ECCL. none, nones. 3 *pl.* nones [in the Roman calendar].

nonada *f.* trifle, nothing.

nonagenario, -ria *adj.-n.* nonagenarian.

nonagésimo, -ma *adj.-m.* ninetieth.

nonágono *adj.-m.* ENEÁGONO.

nonato, -ta *adj.* not naturally born, extracted by Caesarean section. 2 unborn, still nonexistent.

noningentésimo, -ma *adj.-m.* nine hundredth.

nonio *m.* vernier, vernier scale.

nono, -na *adj.-n.* ninth.

nopal *m.* BOT. nopal, prickly pear.

norabuena *f.-adv.* ENHORABUENA.

noramala *adv.* ENHORAMALA.

noray *m.* NAUT. bollard, mooring.

nordestal *adj.* northeast.

nordeste *m.* northeast. 2 northeast wind.

nórdico, -ca *adj.-n.* Nordic. 2 Norse. 3 *m.* Norse [language].

noria *f.* noria, chain pump, draw wheel.

norma *f.* norm, model, pattern, regulation, standard.

normal *adj.* normal. 2 standard, model. 3 *f.* GEOM. normal. 4 normal school.

normalidad *f.* normality.

normalista *m.-f.* normal-school student.

normalizar *tr.* to normalize. 2 *ref.* to become normal.

Normandía *f. pr. n.* GEOG. Normandy.

normando, -da *adj.* Norman. 2 *m.* Norman. 3 Norseman, Northman.

noroeste *m.* northwest.

nortada *f.* norther, north wind.

norte *m.* north. 2 north wind. 3 North Pole. 4 North Star. 5 fig. lodestar, guide, direction.

Norteamérica *f. pr. n.* North America.

norteamericano, -na *adj.-n.* North American; American [of the U.S.A.].

norteño, -ña *adj.-n.* northern; norther [esp. of the North of Spain].

nórtico, -ca *adj.* north, northern.

Noruega *f. pr. n.* GEOG. Norway.

noruego, -ga *adj.-n.* Norwegian.

norueste *m.* NOROESTE.

nos *pers. pron. pl. m.-f.* [object of the verb], us, to us, for us; [recip.] each other; [ref.] ourselves. 2 we, us [used by the king, the bishops, etc.].

nosología *f.* nosology.

nosotros, -tras *pers. pron. pl. m.-f.* we [as subject of the verb]; us [as object of preposition]. 2 *nosotros mismos, nosotras mismas,* ourselves.

nostalgia *f.* nostalgia, homesickness. 2 regret [for something lost].

nostálgico, -ca *adj.* nostalgic. 2 regretful.

nota *f.* note [mark; annotation; brief record of facts, etc.]: *tomar* ~ *de,* to take note of. 2 [diplomatic] note. 3 MUS. note: ~ *de adorno,* grace note. 4 note, eminence, reputation. 5 COM. account, bill; statement, schedule: ~ *de precios,* price list. 6 EDUC. mark, *grade. 7 caer en* ~, to be talked about.

notabilidad *f.* notability [quality; person].

notabilísimo, -ma *adj.* most notable or remarkable.

notable *adj.* notable, remarkable, striking, noteworthy, prominent. 2 noticeable, perceptible. 3 *m.* EDUC. good mark. 4 *m. pl.* notables [persons].

notación *f.* notation.

notar *tr.* to note, mark. 2 to annotate. 3 to note, notice, observe. 4 to note, set down. 5 DICTAR. 6 to blame charge with [a fault].

notaría *f.* profession of notary. 2 notary's office.

notariado, -da *adj.* notarized. 2 *m.* profession of notary. 3 the notaries [as a body].

notarial *adj.* notarial.

notario *m.* notary, notary public.

noticia *f.* news, news item, notice, piece of news, report, tidings: *noticias de última hora,* late news. 2 knowledge, information, intelligence: *tener* ~ *de,* to be informed of.

noticiar *tr.* to give notice of.

noticiario *m.* CINEM. news reel. 2 RADIO. newscast.

noticiero, -ra *adj.* news-bearing, news-giving. 2 *m.-f.* newsman, reporter.

notición *f.* *augm.* coll. big news, great news.

noticioso, -sa *adj.* knowing, informed.

notificación *f.* notification; official notice.

notificar *tr.* to notify, announce, intimate, inform.

notita *f.* dim. of NOTA.

noto *m.* south wind.

notoriedad *f.* notoriety [being well-known]; self-evidence. *2* fame, renown.

notorio, -ria *adj.* notorious [well-known]; evident, manifest, glaring.

novador, -ra *m.-f.* innovator.

novatada *f.* hazing of a new comer [in a college, etc.]. *2* beginner's blunder.

novato, -ta *adj.* beginning. *2 m.-f.* novice, beginner, freshman.

novecientos, tas *adj.-n.* nine hundred.

novedad *f.* novelty. *2* newness. *3* change, alteration: *sin* ~, as usual well. *4* news. *5* recent fashion. *6* surprise, astonishment: *causar* ~, to surprise. *7 pl. novedades* or *géneros de* ~, fancy goods.

novedoso, -sa *adj.* novel, having novelty.

novel *adj.-m.* new, inexperienced.

novela *f.* LIT. novel, romance, fiction, story: ~ *por entregas*, serial. *2* lie, yarn. *3* LAW novel.

novelador, -ra *m.-f.* novelist.

novelar *tr.* to novelize. *2 intr.* to write novels.

novelería *f.* fondness for novelty; curiosity. *2* fondness for fiction. *3* worthless fiction.

novelero, -ra *adj.* of novelty. *2* fond of fiction, romantical. *3* newsmongering. *4* fickle, inconstant.

novelesco, -ca *adj.* novelistic. *2* like a novel; romantic, fantastic.

novelista *m.-f.* novelist, novel-writer.

novena *f.* ECCL. novena.

noveno, -na *adj.-m.* ninth.

noventa *adj.-m.* ninety.

noventavo, -va *adj.-m.* ninetieth.

noventón, -na *adj.-n.* nonagenarian.

novia *f.* bride. *2* fiancée, girl-friend, sweetheart.

noviazgo *m.* engagement, betrothal; courtship.

novicia *f.* ECCL. novice [woman].

noviciado *m.* ECCL. noviciate. *2* apprenticeship.

novicio, -cia *adj.* new, inexperienced. *2 m.* ECCL. novice [man]. *3 m.-f.* novice, beginner, tyro.

noviembre *m.* November.

novilunio *m.* new moon.

novilla *f.* heifer, young cow.

novillada *f.* drove of young bulls. *2* BULLF. fight with young bulls.

novillero *m.* BULLF. fighter of young bulls. *2* truant.

novillo *m.* young bull. *2 pl.* BULLF. fight with young bulls. *3 hacer novillos,* to play truant.

novio *m.* bridegroom. *2* fiancé; boy-friend; suitor. *3 pl.* betrothed man and woman. *4* bride and bridegroom, new-married couple.

novísimo, -ma *adj. superl.* most new. *2 m.* each of the last stages of man: death, judgment, hell and heaven.

nubada, nubarrada *f.* shower of rain. *2* crowd [of certain things].

nubarrado, -da *adj.* clouded, variegated [fabric].

nubarrón *m.* large black cloud.

nube *f.* cloud: ~ *de verano,* summer shower; fig. passing annoyance; *estar por las nubes,* to be sky-high [in price]; *poner en,* or *sobre, las nubes,* fig. to priase to the skies. *2* MED. film, spot [on the cornea].

nubecita *f. dim.* small cloud.

núbil *adj.* nubile.

nubilidad *f.* nubility.

nublado, -da *adj.* clouded, cloudy, overcast. *2 m.* storm cloud: *descargar el* ~, to rain, hail or snow hard; fig. to vent one's anger in explosive words. *3* impending danger. *4* shower, cloud [of certain things].

nublar *tr.-ref.* ANUBLAR.

nubloso, -sa *adj.* cloudy, overcast.

nuca *f.* nape or scruff of the neck.

nuclear *adj.* PHYS. nuclear.

núcleo *m.* nucleus. *2* ELECT. core [of an electromagnet]. *3* BOT. kernel [of nut]; stone [of fruit].

nucléolo *m.* BIOL. nucleolus.

nudillo *m.* knuckle [at finger-joint].

nudismo *m.* nudism.

nudista *adj.-n.* nudist.

1) **nudo** *m.* knot, noose, hitch: ~ *corredizo,* slip knot; ~ *en la garganta,* fig. lump in one's throat. *2* knot, bond, tie. *3* knot, tangle, difficulty. *4* knot [of a problem, a plot, etc.]. *5* NAUT. knot. *6* burl [in cloth]. *7* knot, gnarl [in wood]. *8* BOT. knot, node, joint. *9* knot [of mountains, etc.].

2) **nudo, -da** *adj.* nude, naked.

nudoso, -sa *adj.* knotty [having knots]. *2* gnarled.

nuera *f.* daughter-in-law.

nuestro, -tra *poss. adj.* our, of ours. *2 poss. pron.* ours. *3 los nuestros,* ours, our friends, our men, etc.

nueva *f.* news, tidings. *2 hacerse de nuevas,* to feign ignorance of a thing; *no me coge de nuevas,* I am not surprised at it.

nuevamente *adv.* again, anew. *2* newly, recently.

Nueva Orleans *f. pr. n.* GEOG. New Orleans.

Nueva York *f. pr. n.* GEOG. New York.

Nueva Zelandia *f. pr. n.* GEOG. New Zeland.

nueve *adj.-n.* nine: *las* ~, nine o'clock. *2 m.* ninth [of the month].

nuevecito, -ta *adj. dim.* of NUEVO, brand-new.

nuevo, -va *adj.* new, novel: *¿qué hay de* ~?, what's new? *2* new, fresh [another]. *3* newly arrived. *4* novice, beginner. *5 adv. de* ~, anew, again, once more.

nuez *f.* walnut. *2* nut [of some other plants]: ~ *de cola,* kola nut; ~ *moscada,* nutmeg; ~ *vómica,* nux vomica. *3* Adam's apple. *4* nut [of a crossbow]. *5* MUS. nut, frog [of a violin bow].

nueza *f.* BOT. bryony.

nugatorio, -ria *adj.* nugatory, frustrating.

nulidad *f.* nullity. *2* inability, incompetence. *3* incapable or insignificant person.

nulo, -la *adj.* LAW null, void. *2* null, nonexistent. *3* incapable, incompetent.

Numancia *f. pr. n.* HIST., GEOG. Numantia.

numen *m.* MYTH. numen. *2* poetical or artistic inspiration.

numeración *f.* numeration, numbering. *2* ARITH. system or notation.

numerador *m.* numerator, numberer. *2* ARITH. numerator.

numeral *adj.* numeral.

numerar *tr.* to numerate, enumerate. *2* to number [assign a number to].

numerario, -ria *adj.* numerary. *2 m.* cash, coin, specie.

numérico, -ca *adj.* numerical.

número *m.* ARITH. number. *2* numeral, figure: ~ *arábigo,* Arabic numeral; ~ *romano,* Roman numeral. *3* number [of persons or things]: *gran* ~, great number; *sin* ~, numberless. *4* number [assigned to a person or thing]; ticket, etc. bearing a number]. *5* number, issue [of a newspaper]. *6* item [of a program]. *7* size [of shoes, gloves, etc.]. *8* GRAM., POET. number. *9 pl.* BIBL. numbers.

numeroso, -sa *adj.* numerous. *2* harmonious, rhythmical.

númida *adj.-n.* Numidian.

numisma *m.* coin, money.

numismática *m.* numismatics.
numismático *m.* numismatist.
nunca *adv.* never: ~ *jamás*, never more.
nunciatura *f.* nunciature.
nuncio *m.* messenger, harbinger, forerunner. *2* nuncio [Pope's ambassador].
nupcial *adj.* nuptial, hymeneal.
nupcias *f.* nuptials, marriage, wedding.

nutación *f.* ASTR., BOT. nutation.
nutria *f.* ZOOL. otter. *2* otter-fur.
nutricio, -cia *adj.* nutritious.
nutrición *f.* nutrition. *2* filling, increasing.
nutrido, -da *adj.* nourished. *2* full, abundant.
nutrimento *m.* nutrition. *2* nutriment.
nutrir *tr.* to nourish, to feed. *2* to fill, increase.
nutritivo, -va *adj.* nutritive, nourishing.

Ñ, ñ *f.* seventeenth letter of the Spanish alphabet.
ñame *m.* BOT. yam [vine and root].
ñandú *m.* ORN. nandu, American ostrich.
ñapa *f.* (Am.) additional amount; something over or extra: *de* ~, to boot, into the bargain.
ñaque *m.* junk, pile of junk.
ñiquiñaque *m.* trash, worthless person of thing.

ñoclo *m.* a kind of macaroon.
ñoñería *f.* silly remark, inanity.
ñoñez *f.* silliness, inanity.
ñoño, -ña *adj.* feeble-minded. *2* silly, inane.
ñu *m.* ZOOL. gnu.
ñudo *m.* NUDO.
ñudoso, -sa *adj.* NUDOSO.

O

O, o *f.* O, o, eighteenth letter of the Spanish alphabet.

o *conj.* or; either: *el uno ~ el otro,* either the one or the other.

oasis, *pl.* **-sis** *m.* oasis.

obcecación *f.* mental obfuscation or blindness.

obcecar *tr.* to obfuscate, blind. *2 ref.* to become obfuscated.

obduración *f.* obduracy, obstinacy.

obedecer *tr.-intr.* to obey. *2* to respond, yield [to a force, stimulus, etc.]. *3* to be due [to], arise [from]. ¶ Conjug. like *agradecer.*

obediencia *f.* obedience.

obediente *adj.* obedient.

obelisco, obelo *m.* obelisk. *2* PRINT. dagger (†).

obencadura *f.* NAUT. shrouds [collectively].

obenque *m.* NAUT. shroud.

obertura *f.* MUS. overture.

obesidad *f.* obesity, obeseness, fatness.

obeso, -sa *adj.* obese, fat, fleshy.

óbice *m.* obstacle, impediment, hindrance.

obispado *m.* bishopric, episcopate. *2* diocese.

obispal *adj.* episcopal.

obispillo *m.* boy bishop. *2* rump [of a fowl]. *3* large blood pudding.

obispo *m.* ECCL. bishop. *2* OBISPILLO *3.*

óbito *m.* death, decease.

obituario *m.* ECCL. obituary.

objeción *f.* objection.

objetante *adj.* objecting. *2 m.-f.* objector.

objetar *tr.* to object [adduce, state as objection].

objetivar *tr.* to objectify, objectivate.

objetividad *f.* objectivity.

objetivo, -va *adj.* objective. *2 m.* objective [aim, end of action]. *4* MIL., OPT. objective.

objeto *m.* object [in practically every sense, except the grammatical one]. *2* thing. *3* subject matter. *4* objective, aim, end, purpose.

oblación *f.* oblation.

oblata *f.* ECCL. in the Mass, the bread and wine before Consecration.

oblato, -ta *m.-f.* ECCL. oblate.

oblea *f.* wafer [for sealing letters].

oblicuar *tr.* to cant, slant, give an oblique direction to. *2 intr.* MIL. to oblique.

oblicuo, cua *adj.* oblique, slanting. *2* GEOM. oblique.

obligación *f.* obligation. *2* duty, charge, engage-

ment, debt. *3* COM. debenture, bond. *5 pl.* family responsabilities. *6* COM. liabilities.

obligacionista *m.-f.* bondholder.

obligado, -da *adj.* obliged. *2 m.* MUS. obbligato.

obligar *tr.* to obligate, oblige, bind. *2* to compel, force. *3 ref.* to obligate or bind oneself.

obligatorio, -ria *adj.* obligatory, compulsory.

obliteración *f.* MED. obliteration, obstruction.

obliterar *tr.* MED. to obliterate, obstruct.

oblongo, -ga *adj.* oblong.

óboe *m.* oboe. *2* oboist.

óbolo *m.* obol. *2* mite [small contribution].

obra *f.* work, piece of work; task: *~ de manos,* handwork; *poner por ~,* to carry into effect or execution. *2* work, act, deed: *buena ~, ~ de caridad,* good work, charity. *3* THEOL. work. *4* work [piece of literary or musical composition, book, painting, etc.]: *~ de arte,* work of art; *~ de consulta,* reference work; *~ maestra,* masterpiece. *5* THEAT. piece, play, drama. *6* works [of an author]. *7* building under construction; repair work [in a building]. *8* FORT. work: *~ exterior,* outwork. *9* means, virtue, agence. *10* NAUT. *~ muerta,* upper works; *~ viva,* quickwork. *11 ~ pía,* charitable foundation. *12 pl. obras públicas,* public works.

13 adv. ~ de, a matter of, about.

obrador, -ra *adj.* working. *2 m.-f.* worker. *3 m.* workshop.

obrar *tr.* to work, fashion, make. *2* to work, do, effect. *3* to build, construct. *4 intr.* to act, behave, proceed. *5* to act [produce an effect]. *6* to evacuate bowels. *7 obra en mi poder,* I have in my possession.

obrepticio, cia *adj.* obreptitious.

obrerista *adj.* [pertaïning to] labour. *2 m.-f.* labo(u)rist, labo(u)rite.

obrero, -ra *adj.* working: *la clase obrera,* the working classes. *2 m.-f.* labourer, worker, workman, workwoman. *3 m.* churchwarden.

obrita *f. dim.* little work; booklet.

obrizo *adj.* pure, refined [gold].

obscenidad *f.* obscenity.

obsceno, -na *adj.* obscene, indecent, lewd.

obscurantismo *m.* obscurantism.

obscuras (a) *adv.* in the dark.

obscurecer *tr.* to obscure, darken. *2* to obscure [confuse, dim, outshine, tarnish]. *3* PAINT. to shade. *4 impers.* to grow dark. *5 ref.* to darken [become dark]. *6* to become cloudy. ¶ CONJUG. like *agradecer.*

obscurezco, obscurezca, etc. *irr.* V. OBSCURECER.

obscurecimiento *m.* obscuration, darkening. *2* clouding. *3* PAINT. shading.

obscuridad *f.* obscurity. *2* darkness, gloom.

obscuro, -ra *adj.* obscure. *2* dark [gloomy; dusky; cloudy]. *3* dark [colour]. *4* uncertain, dubious. *5 m.* dark colo(u)r, dark clothes.

obsecración *f.* obsecration.

obsecuencia *f.* compliance, obedience.

obsecuente *adj.* compliant, obedient.

obsequiador, -ra; obsequiante *m.-f.* one who pays attentions, who gives presents, entertains, etc. *2* courter, wooer.

obsequiar *tr.* to pay attentions to; to make presents to; to treat, entertain: ~ *con,* to treat to; to present with. *2* to court, woo.

obsequio *m.* attention shown, courtesy; treat; present, gift: *en* ~ *de,* in honour of.

obsequioso, -sa *adj.* obsequious, obliging, attentive.

observable *adj.* observable, noticeable.

observación *f.* observation [noticing, being noticed; watching]: *en* ~, under observation. *2* MIL., ASTR. observation. *3* observation, remark, note.

observador, -ra *adj.* observing, observant. *2 m.-f.* observer.

observancia *f.* observance.

observante *adj.* observant, observing.

observar *tr.* to observe [take notice of; watch]. *2* to observe [law, command, etc.].

observatorio *m.* observatory.

obsesión *f.* obsession.

obsesionante *adj.* obsessing.

obsesionar *tr.* to obsess.

obseso, -sa *adj.* obsessed.

obsidiana *f.* MINER. obsidian.

obsidional *adj.* obsidional.

obstaculizar *tr.* to prevent, hinder, obstruct.

obstáculo *m.* obstacle.

obstante (no) *conj.* notwithstanding; nevertheless.

obstar *intr.* to stand in the way, be an obstacle.

obstetricia *f.* obstetrics, obstetricy.

obstinación *f.* obstinacy, stubbornness, obduracy.

obstinado, -da *adj.* obstinate, stubborn.

obstinarse *ref.* ~ *en,* to be obstinate in or about; to persist in, to insist on.

obstrucción *f.* obstruction.

obstruccionismo *m.* obstructionism.

obstruir *tr.* to obstruct, block, clog, stop up. *2* to obstruct, impede. *3 ref.* to become obstructed. ¶ CONJUG. like *huir.*

obstruyo, obstruyó, obstruya, etc. *irr.* V. OBSTRUIR.

obtemperar *tr.* to obey, to assent.

obtención *f.* attainment, obtaining, obtention.

obtener *tr.* to attain, obtain, get; to procure.

obtentor *m.* obtainer.

obturación *f.* obturation.

obturador, triz *adj.* obturating, stopping. *2 m.* stopper, plug. *3* SURG. obturator. *4* PHOT. shutter, obturator. *5* AUTO. throttle.

obturar *tr.* to obturate, close, plug, stop up. *2* AUTO. to throttle.

obtusángulo *adj.* obtuse-angled.

obtuso, -sa *adj.* GEOM. obtuse. *2* obtuse [of blunt form]. *3* obtuse, dull, slow of perception.

obús *m.* ARTILL. howitzer.

obvención *f.* perquisite.

obviar *tr.* to obviate, remove, surmount.

obvio, -via *adj.* obvious, evident.

oca *f.* ORN. goose. *2* BOT. oca. *3* royal goose [game].

ocarina *f.* MUS. ocarina.

ocasión *f.* occasion, opportunity, chance. *2* occasion, cause. *3* occasion [time of an ocurrence]: *en* ~ *de,* on the occasion of. *4 de* ~, secondhand.

ocasionado, -da *adj.* liable, exposed [to a specified contingency, etc.].

ocasional *adj.* occasional, chance, accidental. *2* occasional [acting as the occasion].

ocasionar *tr.* to occasion, cause.

ocaso *m.* west. *2* setting [of any heavenly body]; sunset. *3* fig. decadence, decline.

occidental *adj.* occidental, western. *2* Occidental. *3 m.-f.* Occidental [person].

occidente *m.* occident, west. *2* Occident.

occipital *adj.* ANAT. occipital.

occipucio *m.* ANAT. occiput.

occiso, -sa *adj.* killed.

Oceanía *pr. n.* GEOG. Oceania.

oceánico, -ca *adj.* oceanic.

océano *m.* ocean.

oceanografía *f.* oceanography.

ocelo *m.* ZOOL. ocellus.

ocelote *m.* ZOOL. ocelot.

ocena *f.* MED. ozaena, ozena, foul breath.

ocio *m.* idleness, leisure. *2* pastime, diversion.

ociosidad *f.* idleness.

ocioso, -sa *adj.* idle [doing nothing]. *2* idle, useles; needless.

ocluir *tr.* MED. to occlude. ¶ CONJUG. like *huir.*

oclusión *f.* MED., PHON. occlusion.

oclusivo, -va *adj.* occlusive.

ocozol *m.* BOT. sweet gum, liquidambar tree.

ocre *m.* MINER. ocher: ~ *rojo,* red ocher.

octaedro *m.* GEOM. octahedron.

octagonal *adj.* octagonal.

octágono, -na *adj.* octagonal. *2 m.* octagon.

octano *m.* CHEM. octane.

octava *f.* ECCL., FENC., MUS., PROS. octave. *2* PROS. ~ *real,* hendecasyllabic octave, rhymed ababacc.

octaviano, -na *adj.* Octavian.

octavilla *f.* eighth part of a sheet of paper. *2* PROS. octosyllabic octave.

octavín *m.* MUS. piccolo [flute].

Octavio *m. pr. n.* Octavius.

octavo, -va *adj.-m.* eigth. *2* PRINT. *en* ~, octavo.

octingentésimo, -ma *adj.-m.* eight hundredth.

octogenario, -ria *adj.-n.* octogenarian.

octogésimo, -ma *adj.-m.* eightieth.

octogonal *adj.* OCTAGONAL.

octógono, -na *adj.-m.* OCTÁGONO.

octosílabo, -ba *adj.* octosyllabic. *2 m.* PROS. octosyllable.

octubre *m.* October.

óctuplo *adj.-m.* octuple.

ocular *adj.* ocular. *2 m.* OPT. ocular, eyepiece.

oculista *m.-f.* oculist, eye-specialist.

ocultación *f.* concealing. *2* ASTR. occultation.

ocultar *tr.* to conceal, hide, cover, secret: ~ *algo a uno,* to hide something from someone. *2* to occult. *3 ref.* to hide [intr.]. *4 no se me oculta que,* I see, I understand that.

ocultismo *m.* occultism.

oculto, -ta *adj.* hidden, concealed. *2* occult. *3 adv. de* ~, incognit; secretly.

ocupación *f.* occupation. *2* occupancy.

ocupado, -da *adj.* occupied, busy, engaged.

ocupante *adj.* occupying. *2 m.-f.* occupier, occupant.

ocupar *tr.* to occupy. *2* to employ, give work to. *3* to engage the attention of. *4 ref. ocuparse en* or *de,* to busy oneself with, be engaged in, to devote oneself to.
ocurrencia *f.* occurrence, event, occasion. *2* witticism, witty remark, sally. *3* bright idea.
ocurrente *adj.* occurring. *2* bright, witty [person].
ocurrir *intr.* to occur, befall, happen. *2 ref.* to occur, strike [come into one's mind].
ochavado, -da *adj.* eight-sided.
ochavo *m.* small copper coin.
ochenta *adj.-n.* eighty.
ochentavo, -va *adj.-m.* eightieth.
ochentón, -na *adj.-n.* octogenarian.
ocho *adj.-n.* eight: *las ~,* eight o'clock. *2 m.* eight [in dates].
ochocientos, -tas *adj.-m.* eight hundred.
oda *f.* ode.
odalisca *f.* odalisque.
odeón *m.* ARCHEOL. odeum.
odiar *tr.* to hate.
odio *m.* hatred, hate; odium.
odioso, -sa *adj.* odious, hateful.
Odisea *f. pr. n.* MYTH. Odyssey. *2 f.* fig. odyssey.
odontoceto, -ta *adj.-m.* ZOOL. odontocete.
odontología *f.* odontology.
odontólogo *m.* odontologist.
odorante *adj.* odorous, fragant.
odorífero, -ra; odorífico, -ca *adj.* odoriferous.
odre *m.* winebag, wineskin. *2* fig. drunkard.
oeste *m.* west. *2* west wind.
ofendedor, -ra *adj.-n.* OFENSOR.
ofender *tr.* to offend, attack, injure, hurt. *2* to offend, give offence. *3* to be offensive to [as a smell, etc.]. *4 ref.* to take offence.
ofensa *f.* offence, attack. *2* offence [wounding the feelings, umbrage]; insult.
ofensión *f.* offence, harm, wrong, injury.
ofensiva *f.* offensive.
ofensivo, -va *adj.* offensive.
ofensor, -ra *adj.* offending. *2 m.-f.* offender [one who attacks or gives offence].
oferente *adj.* offering. *2 m.-f.* offerer.
oferta *f.* offer. *2* offering, gift. *3* COM. *la ~ y la demanda,* supply and demand.
ofertorio *m.* ECCL. offertory.
oficial *adj.* official. *2 m.* journeyman [skilled worker]. *3* clerk [in an office]: *~ mayor,* chief clerk. *4* MIL., NAV. commissioned officer below major. *5* MAR. officer. *6* MIL. *~ general,* general.
oficiala *f.* skilled workwoman.
oficialidad *f.* official nature. *2* MIL., NAV. the officers [collectivelly].
oficiante *m.* ECCL. officiant.
oficiar *tr.* ECCL. to officiate. *2* to make known by official letter. *3 intr.* to officiate, act.
oficina *f.* office, bureau. *2* workshop. *3* pharmacist's laboratory.
oficinal *adj.* MED., PHARM. officinal.
oficinesco, -ca *adj.* office, clerical, bureaucratic.
oficinista *m.-f.* clerk, office worker.
oficio *m.* work, occupation, calling, -trade, craft, handicraft: *artes y oficios,* arts and crafts; *de ~,* by trade. *2* office [duty, function, role]. *3* office, service: *buenos oficios,* good offices. *4* official letter. *5* ECCL. office. *6 Santo Oficio,* Holy Office.
oficiosidad *f.* officiousness. *2* diligence. *3* obligingness.
oficioso, -sa *adj.* officious, meddlesome. *2* DIPL. officious. *3* unofficial. *4* diligent. *5* obliging.
ofidio, día *adj.-m.* ZOOL. ophidian.

ofiuroideo, -a *adj.-m.* ZOOL. ophiuroidean.
ofrecedor, -ra *m.-f.* offerer.
ofrecer *tr.* to offer, present, tender, hold out, proffer. *2* to offer, promise. *3* to offer [present to sight or notice]. *4* COM. to offer; to bid. *5 ref.* to offer, occur, present itself. *6* to volunteer, offer [to]. ¶ CONJUG. like *agradecer.*
ofreciente *m.-f.* offerer.
ofrecimiento *m.* offer, offering, promise.
ofrenda *f.* offering, religious offering.
ofrendar *tr.* to offer, make an offering of.
ofrezco, ofrezca, etc. *irr.* V. OFRECER.
oftalmía *f.* MED. ophtalmia.
oftálmico, -ca *adj.* ophtalmic.
oftalmología *f.* ophtalmology.
ofuscación *f.,* **ofuscamiento** *m.* obfuscation. *2* dazzling, dazzle [by excess of light].
ofuscar *tr.* to obfuscate. *2* to dazzle [by excess of light].
ogro *m.* ogre.
¡oh! *interj.* o!, oh!
ohm, ohmio *m.* ELECT. ohm.
oíble *adj.* audible.
oída *f.* hearing [act]. *2 de oídas,* by hearsay.
oidio *m.* BOT. oidium.
oído *m.* hearing [sense]; ear [organ of hearing]: *aguzar los oídos,* to prick up one's ears; *dar oídos a,* to listen favourably, to believe; *hacer oídos de mercader,* to turn a deaf ear; *tener ~, tener buen ~,* to have an ear for music; *al ~,* in the ear, confindentially; *de ~,* by ear. *2* ANAT. internal ear. *3* FIREARMS. vent, priming hole, touchhole.
oidor, -ra *m.-f.* hearer. *2 m.* formerly, a judge.
oigo, oiga, etc. *irr.* V. OÍR.
oír *tr.* to hear [perceive by the ear; listen; grant prayer, accept advice]: *~ hablar de,* to hear about, or of; *oí cantar a tu hermana,* I heard your sister singing; *¡oiga!, ¡oigan!,* I say, listen; the idea!, well!; *~ misa,* to hear Mass. ¶ CONJUG.: INDIC. Pres.: *oigo, oyes, oye;* oímos, oís, *oyen.* | Pret.: oí, oiste, *oyó;* oímos, oísteis, *oyeron.* | SUBJ. Pres.: *oiga, oigas, oiga; oigamos, oigáis, oigan.* | Imperf.: *oyera, oyeras,* etc., or *oyese, oyeses,* etc. | Fut.: *oyere, oyeres,* etc. | IMPER.: *oye, oiga; oigamos,* oíd, *oigan.* | Past. p.: *oído.* | GER.: *oyendo.*
oíslo *m.-f.* beloved one; wife.
ojal *m.* buttonhole. *2* eyelet, eyelet hole.
¡ojalá! *interj.* would to God!, God grant!, I wish!
ojalar *tr.* to make buttonholes in.
ojaranzo *m.* BOT. hornbeam. *2* ADELFA.
ojazo *m.* augm. large eye.
ojeada *f.* glance [brief look]: *echar una ~ a,* to cast a glance at.
ojeador *m.* HUNT. beater.
ojear *tr.* HUNT. to beat for [game]. *2* to chase away. *3* to eye.
ojeo *m.* HUNT. beating for game.
ojera *f.* eye cup, eyeglass. *2 pl.* rings under the eyes.
ojeriza *f.* animosity, grudge, spite, ill vill.
ojeroso, -sa *adj.* having rings under the eyes.
ojete *m.* eyelet, eye hole.
ojimel, ojimiel *m.* PHARM. oxymel.
ojinegro, -gra *adj.* coll. black-eyed.
ojituerto, -ta *adj.* coll. squint-eyed.
ojiva *f.* ARCH. ogive.
ojival *adj.* ARCH. ogival.
ojizarco, -ca *adj.* coll. blue-eyed.
ojo *m.* eye [organ of sight; attention, care, notice; way of thinking, estimation]: *ojos blandos* or *tiernos,* bleary eyes, watery eyes; *ojos saltones,*

bulging eyes, goggle eyes; *abrir los ojos a uno*, to open someone's eyes [disabuse him, make him realize]; *cerrar los ojos a uno*, to wait on a dying person; *costar un ~*, or *los ojos, de la cara*, to cost a mint of money; *echar el ~ a*, to have one's eyes on [regard with desire]; *írsele a uno los ojos por* or *tras*, to gaze longingly, to desire; *llenar el ~*, to please; *no pegar el ~* or *los ojos*, coll. not to sleep a wink; *poner los ojos en blanco*, to roll the eyes; *saltar a los ojos*, to be self-evident; *a ~* [of an estimation, etc.], by guess, without taking any measurement: *a ojos cerrados*, blindly, without examination; *a ojos vistas*, visibly, obviously; *en un abrir y cerrar de ojos*, in the twinkling of an eye; *¡ojo!*, *¡mucho ~!*, look out!, beware!

2 eye, hole, perforation. 3 eye [of neddle, axe, spade, etc.]. 4 bow [of a key]. 5 eye [in cheese]; hole [in bread]. 6 speck of grease in soup. 7 well [of stairs]. 8 span, bay [of bridge]. 9 PRINT. face [of type]. *10 ~ de buey*, BOT. oxeye; *ARCH.* bull's eye. *11 ~ de gallo*, *~ de pollo*, corn [on toe]. *12 ~ de la cerradura*, keyhole. *13* RADIO. *~ mágico*, magic eye.

ojoso, -sa *adj.* eyey.
ojuelos *m. pl.* small or sparkling eyes. 2 spectacles.
ola *f.* wave, billow, surge, swell [on a liquid]. 2 fig. wave [of heat, cold, etc.]. 3 surge [of heat, cold, etc.]. 3 surge [of a crowd].
olé *m.* an Andalusian dance. 2 *interj.* bravo!
oleáceo, -a *adj.* BOT. oleaceous.
oleada *f.* large wave, surge, swell. 2 surge [of a crowd]. 3 MIL. wave.
oleaginoso, -sa *adj.* oleaginous, oily.
oleaje *m.* surge, succession of waves, motion or rush of waves.
oleastro *m.* BOT., ACEBUCHE.
oleato *m.* CHEM. oleate.
oledor, -ra *adj.* smelling. 2 *m.-f.* smeller.
oleico *adj.* CHEM. oleic.
óleo *m.* oil, olive oil; chrism, holy oil: *los santos óleos*, the chrism, the holy oil. *2* PAINT. *al ~*, oil, in oil colours.
oleoducto *m.* pipe line.
oleografía *f.* oleograph.
oleoso, -sa *adj.* oleaginous, oily.
oler *tr.* to smell, scent, sniff, snuff [perceive odours, detect presence of by smell]. 2 to smell, scent [find out, suspect]. 3 fig. to pry into. 4 *intr.* to smell [emit an odour; suggest]: *~ a*, to smell like, smell of, to smack of; *no ~ bien*, to look suspicious.
olfacción *f.* olfaction [act of smelling].
olfatear *tr.* to smell, scent, sniff [eagerly]. 2 fig. to pry into, to try to discover.
olfativo, -va *adj.* olfactory.
olfato *m.* smell, nose [sense of smell]. 2 fig. nose, sagacious sense.
olíbano *m.* frankincense.
oliente *adj.* smelling, odorous.
oligarca *m.* oligarch.
oligarquía *f.* oligarchy.
oligoceno, -na *adj.-n.* GEOL. Oligocene.
Olimpia *f. pr. n.* GEOG. Olympia.
olimpíada *f.* Olympiad. 2 Olympic games.
olímpico, -ca *adj.* Olympic, Olympian. 2 fig. haughty.
Olimpo *m. pr. n.* GEOG., MYTH. Olympus.
oliscar *tr.* to smell, sniff. 2 *intr.* [of meat] to be tainted, gamey.

oliva *f.* olive. *2* olive tree. *3* fig. olive branch, peace. *4* ORN. barn owl.
oliváceo, -a *adj.* olivaceous.
olivar *m.* olive plantation, oliveyard.
olivarero, -ra *adj.* olive [growing, industry, etc.].
olivera *f.* OLIVO 1.
Oliverio *m. pr. n.* Oliver.
olivillo *m.* BOT. a kind of mock privet.
olivo *m.* BOT. olive tree.
olmeda *f.*, **olmedo** *m.* elm grove.
olmo *m.* BOT. elm tree.
ológrafo, -fa *adj.-m.* LAW holograph.
olor *m.* odour, smell, fragance. 2 fig. promise, hope. 3 fig. *~ de santidad*, odour of sanctity.
olorizar *tr.* to scent, perfume.
oloroso, -sa *adj.* odorous, fragrant.
olvidadizo *adj.* forgetful. 2 ungrateful.
olvidado, -da *adj.* forgotten. 2 forgetful; oblivious.
olvidar *tr.-ref.* to forget; to be forgotten: *lo he olvidado, se me ha olvidado*, I have forgotten it. 2 ref. *olvidarse de*, to forget.
olvido *m.* forgetfulness. 2 omission, oversight, neglect. 3 oblivion: *caer en el ~*, to fall into oblivion.
olla *f.* pot, boiler, kettle [bulging pot used in cooking]: *~ de grillos*, fig. pandemonium; *~ de presión*, pressure cooker. *2* COOK. dish of boiled meat and vegetables. 3 eddy, whirlpool [in a river].
ollao *m.* NAUT. eyelet hole.
ollar *m.* horse's nostril.
ollería *f.* pottery. 2 earthenware shop.
ollero *m.* potter. 2 dealer in earthenware.
ombligo *m.* ANAT., ZOOL. navel. 2 navel-string. 3 navel, centre, middle.
omega *f.* omega [Greek letter].
omento *m.* ANAT. omentum.
ominoso, -sa *adj.* ominous, of evil omen. 2 odious, execrable.
omisión *f.* omission.
omiso, -sa *adj.* neglectful, remiss, careless.
omitir *tr.* to omit, drop, leave out.
ómnibus, pl. -bus *m.* omnibus.
omnímodo, -da *adj.* all-embracing, full, absolute.
omnipotencia *f.* omnipotence.
omnipotente *adj.* omnipotent, almighty: *el Omnipotente*, the Almighty [God].
omnipresencia *f.* omnipresence.
omnipresente *adj.* omnipresent.
omnisciencia *f.* omniscience.
omnisciente; omniscio, cia *adj.* omniscient.
omnívoro, -ra *adj.* omnivorous.
omóplato *m.* ANAT. shoulder blade.
onagro *m.* ZOOL. onager.
onanismo *m.* onanism.
once *adj.-m.* eleven: *las ~*, eleven o'clock. 2 *m.* eleventh [in dates]. 4 FOOTBALL eleven [team].
onceno, -na *adj.-m.* eleventh.
onda *f.* wave, ripple [on surface of water]. 2 wave [in hair, cloth, etc.]. 3 SEW. scallop. 4 PHYS. wave: *~ amortiguada*, ELECT. damped wave; *~ luminosa*, light wave; *~ portadora*, RADIO. carrier wave; *~ sonora*, sound wave. 5 *pl.* fig. the water [of sea, river or lake].
ondeante *adj.* waving, undulating.
ondear *intr.* [of water] to rise in waves, to ripple. 2 to wave [as a flag, a field of corn, etc.], to flutter, undulate. 3 to be wavy. 4 *ref.* to wave, sway, swing.
ondina *f.* MYTH. undine.
ondoso, -sa *adj.* wavy.

ondulación f. undulation. 2 wave [of hair]: ~ permanente, permanent wave.
ondulado, -da adj. undulated; rippled. 2 wavy. 3
billowy [ground]. 4 corrugated. 5 scalloped.
ondulante adj. undulating, waving.
ondular intr. to undulate, wave, ripple, billow,
roll. 2 tr. to wave [the hair].
ondulatorio, -ria adj. undulatory.
oneroso, -sa adj. onerous, burdensome.
ónice, ónique f. MINER. onyx.
onírico, -ca adj. oneiric.
ónix f. ÓNICE.
onomástico, -ca adj. onomastic.
onomatopeya f. onomatopœia.
onomatopéyico, -ca adj. onomatopœic.
onoquiles f. BOT. alkanet.
ontogenia f. ontogeny.
ontología f. ontology.
onza f. ounce [weight]. 2 ZOOL. ounce. 3 ~ de oro,
Spanish doubloon.
onzavo, -va adj.-m. eleventh.
oosfera f. BOT. oösphere.
opacidad f. opacity.
opaco, -ca adj. opaque [not transparent; dark;
dull].
opalescencia f. opalescence.
opalescente adj. opalescent.
opalino, -na adj. opaline.
ópalo m. MINER. opal.
opción f. option, choice. 2 COM. option.
ópera f. opera: ~ bufa, opera bouffe.
operación f. operation [working, action, process,
performance]. 2 COM., MATH., SURG. operation. 3
pl. MIL. operations.
operador, -ra m.-f. operator.
operante adj. operating, operative, working.
operar tr. SURG. to operate upon. 2 intr. to operate
[produce an appropiate effect]. 3 COM., MIL.,
NAV., SURG. to operate.
operatorio, -ria m.-f. operative, worker, workman,
working woman.
operativo, -va adj. operative, operating.
operatorio, -ria adj. operating, working. 2 SURG.
operative.
opérculo m. BOT., ZOOL. operculum.
opereta f. operetta, light opera.
opiato, -ta adj.-m. opiate.
opilación f. MED. oppilation, obstruction.
opimo, -ma adj. rich, fruitful, abundant.
opinable adj. debatable, being a matter of opinion.
opinante adj. opiner.
opinar intr. to opine. 2 tr. to judge, think, be of the
opinion that.
opinión f. opinion: mudar de ~, to change one's
mind; tener en buena ~, to have a good opinion
of.
opio m. opium.
opíparo, -ra adj. sumptuous, plentiful [banquet,
etc.].
opondré, opondría, etc. irr. V. OPONER.
oponer tr. to oppose [a thing to another]. 2 to offer
[resistance]. 3 ref. oponerse a, to oppose oneself
to; to oppose [resist, antagonize, set oneself
against; to stand opposite to]; go against, be
contrary to. 4 ref. to oppose each other. ¶ CON-
JUG. like poner.
oponga, etc. irr. V. OPONER.
oponible adj. opposable.
Oporto m. pr. n. GEOG. Oporto, Porto. 2 m. port
wine.

oportunidad f. opportunity; opportuneness.
oportunismo m. opportunism.
oportunista adj. opportunistic. 2 m.-f. opportunist.
oportuno, -na adj. opportune, suitable, timely. 2
witty [in conversation].
oposición f. opposition [act of opposing; being op-
posed]. POL., ASTR.. opposition. 3 competitive
examination.
oposicionista m. POL. memberr of the opposition.
opositor, -ra m.-f. opposer. 2 competitor [for a position or office].
opoterapia f. MED. organotherapy.
opresión f. oppression. 2 pressing.
opresivo, -va adj. oppressive.
opreso, -sa adj. oppressed.
opresor, -ra adj. oppressing. 2 m.-f. oppressor.
oprimir tr. to press, press down, push, pinch, lay
heavy on, weigh down. 2 to oppress.
oprobiar tr. to defame, revile, disgrace.
oprobio m. opprobium, ignominy, disgrace.
oprobioso, -sa adj. opprobrious, disgraceful.
optar intr. to opt, choose. 2 ~ a, to be a candidate
for [a position or office].
optativo, -va adj. optional. 2 GRAM. optative.
óptica f. optics. 2 stereoscope.
óptico, -ca adj. optic, optical. 2 m. optician.
optimismo m. optimism.
optimista adj. optimistic, sanguine. 2 m.-f. optimist.
óptimo, -ma adj. optimal, optimum, best.
optómetro m. optometer.
opuesto, -ta adj. opposed. 2 opposite. 3 contrary,
adverse. 4 BOT. opposite.
opugnar tr. oppugn. 2 to attack, assault, invest.
opulencia f. opulence.
opulento, -ta adj. opulent.
opúsculo m. opuscle, booklet, tract.
opuse, opusiera, etc. irr. V. OPONER.
oquedad f. hollow, cavity. 2 hollowness.
oquedal m. grove of lofty trees without underbrush.
ora conj. now, then, whether: ~ ríe, ~ llora, now
he laughs, now [or then] he cries.
oración f. oration, discourse. 2 prayer, orison: ~
dominical, Lord's prayer; hacer ~, to pray. 3
dusk, sunset [the Angelus hour]. 4 GRAM. sentence, clause.
oráculo m. oracle.
orador, -ra m.-f. orator, speaker.
oral adj. oral [spoken, not written]. 2 ZOOL. oral.
orangután m. ZOOL. orang-outang.
orante adj. F. ARTS. praying.
orar intr. to pray: ~ por, to pray for. 2 to speak,
make a speech.
orate m.-f. lunatic, madman, madwoman.
oratoria f. oratory, speaking.
oratorio, -ria adj. oratorical. 2 m. oratory. 3 MUS.
oratorio.
orbe m. orb, sphere. 2 the earth, the world.
orbicular adj. orbicular.
órbita f. ASTR. orbit. 2 sphere, field [of action, etc.].
3 ANAT. orbit, eye-socket.
orca f. ZOOL. orca.
Orcadas (Islas) f. pr. n. GEOG. Orkney Islands.
orcaneta f. BOT. alkanet.
órdago (de) adj. coll. swell, grand, excellent.
ordalías f. pl. ordeals [trial by fire, water, etc.].
orden m. order [arrangement, succession; method; harmonious relation of things; condition
in which every part is in its right place]: por ~,

in order; *por su* ~, in its turn. *2* order [public quiet; rule of law]: *llamar al* ~, to call to order. *3* order, class, degree. *4* MIL. order, array. *5* ARCH., BIOL., MATH. order. *6* respect, relation: *en* ~ *a*, in respect of. *7 m.-f.* ECCL. order [sacrament, degree]. *8 f.* order [fraternity or body]: ~ *religiosa*, religious order. *9* order, command: *a la* ~ *de*, COM. to the order of; *a sus órdenes*, at your service; *en espera de sus gratas órdenes*, awaiting your commands or your pleasure [in business letters]. *10* ~ *del día*, agenda [for a meeting]; MIL. order of the day.
ordenación *f.* order, arrangement. *2* ECCL. ordination. *3* order, command. *4* auditor's office. *5* ARCH., PAINT. ordonnance.
ordenada *f.* MATH. ordinate.
ordenado, -da *adj.* orderly, methodical, tidy.
ordenador, -ra *adj.* ordering, arranging. *2* ordaining. *3 m.-f.* orderer, arranger. *4* ordainer. *5 m.* auditor [in some offices].
ordenamiento *m.* ordering, arrangement, regulation. *2* edict, ordinance.
ordenancista *adj.* strict, rigid. *2 m.-f.* disciplinarian, martinet.
ordenando *m.* ECCL. ordinand.
ordenanza *f.* order, method. *2* order, command. *3* ordinance, regulation. *4 m.* MIL. orderly. *5* errand boy [in certain offices].
ordenar *tr.* to order, arrange, put in order. *2* to direct [things] to an end. *3* to order, command, decree, prescribe. *4* ECCL. to ordain, confer holy orders on. *5 ref.* ECCL. to take orders.
ordeñar *tr.* to milk [a cow, ewe, etc.]. *2* to pick [olives] by a milking motion.
ordinal *adj.-n.* ordinal.
ordinariez *f.* ordinariness, inferior quality. *2* coarseness, grossness, vulgarity.
ordinario, -ria *adj.* ordinary. *2* inferior, coarse, gross, vulgar. *3 m.* daily household expense. *4* ordinary [judge, bishop]. *5* carrier, messenger. *6 de* ~, ordinarily, usually.
orea, oréada, oréade *f.* MYTH. Oread.
orear *tr.* to air [expose to open air], ventilate. *2 ref.* to become aired. *3* to take an airing.
orégano *m.* BOT. wild marjoram.
oreja *f.* ANAT. ear [sense; organ; external ear]: *pabellón de la* ~, auricle, pinna; *aguzar las orejas*, to prick up one's ears; *calentar las orejas*, to chide, dress down; *enseñar la* ~, to show the cloven foot. *2* flap [of shoe]. *3* MEC. ear, lug. *4* claw [of hammer]. *5* BOT. ~ *de oso*, bear's-ear.
orejeado, -da *adj.* informed, warned.
orejear *intr.* [of an animal] to shake or prick the ears. *2* to act with reluctance.
orejera *f.* ear flap, ear lap; ear muff. *2* mouldboard [of a plough].
orejón *m.* strip of dried peach. *2* pull on the ear.
orejudo, -da *adj.* big-eared, long-eared.
oreo *m.* airing. *2* breeze, gentle wind.
orfanato *m.* orphanage [institution].
orfandad *f.* orphanage, orphanhood. *2* abandonment, neglect.
orfebre *m.* glodsmith, silversmith.
orfebrería *f.* gold or silver work.
Orfeo *m. pr. n.* MYTH. Orpheus.
orfeón *m.* choral society.
orfeonista *m.-f.* member of a choral society.
órfico, -ca *adj.* Orphic.
organdí *m.* organdy.
organero *m.* MUS. organ builder, organ maker.
orgánico, -ca *adj.* organic.

organillero *adj.* organ-grinder.
organillo *m.* barrel organ, hand organ.
organismo *m.* organism. *2* organization, body, institution.
organista *m.-f.* MUS. organist.
organización *f.* organization.
organizador, -ra *adj.* organizing. *2 m.-f.* organizer.
organizar *tr.* to organize. *2* to set up, start. *3 ref.* to organize [intr.].
órgano *m.* PHYSIOL. organ. *2* organ, instrument, medium. *3* organ [newspaper, magazine, etc.]. *4* MUS. organ, pipe organ.
organografía *f.* organography.
orgasmo *m.* PHYSIOL. orgasm.
orgía *f.* orgy, revel.
orgiástico, -ca *adj.* orgiastic.
orgullo *m.* pride. *2* haughtiness.
orgulloso, -sa *adj.* proud. *2* haughty, conceited.
orientación *f.* orienting. *2* orientation. *3* bearings.
oriental *adj.* oriental, eastern. *2 adj.-n.* Oriental.
orientalista *m.-f.* Orientalist.
orientar *tr.* to orient; to orientate. *2* NAUT. to trim [a sail]. *3 ref.* to orient oneself; to guide oneself; to find one's bearings.
oriente *m.* east, orient. *2* east wind. *3* orient [of a pearl]. *4* (cap.) GEOG. East, Orient.
orificar *tr.* DENT. to fill with gold.
orifice *m.* goldsmith.
orificio *m.* orifice, hole.
oriflama *f.* oriflamme. *2* flag, banner.
origen *m.* origin. *2* native country.
original *adj.* original. *2* queer, -quaint, odd. *3 m.* original [of a portrait, etc.]: ~ *de imprenta*, copy, manuscript. *4* original, eccentric [person].
originalidad *f.* originality.
originalmente *adv.* originally. *2* quaintly, eccentrically.
originar *tr.* to originate. *2* to create, start. *3 ref.* to originate, derive, arise, spring.
originariamente *adv.* originally, by its origin.
originario, -ria *adj.* originating, of origin. *2* original, come, derived, native [from or of].
orilla *f.* border, margin, edge, brink, hem. *2* bank, margin [of river]; shore. *3 a la* ~, near, on the brink.
orillar *tr.* to arrange, settle. *2* to surmount [a difficulty]. *3 intr.* SEW. to border, hem.
orillo *m.* selvage, list, listing [of cloth].
1) **orín** *m.* rust [on iron]: *tomarse de* ~, to get rusty.
2) **orín** *or pl.* **orines** *m.*, **orina** *f.* urine.
orinal *m.* chamber pot, urinal.
orinar *intr.-tr.* to urinate.
oriniento, -ta *adj.* rusty.
oriol *m.* OROPÉNDOLA.
oriundo, -da *adj.* coming [from], native [of].
orla *f.* border, edging [of a garment]. *2* ornamental border [around a drawing, etc.]. *3* HER. orle.
orladura *f.* border, ornamental border.
orlar *tr.* to border, edge [a garment]; to put an ornamental border to.
orlo *m.* Alpine horn.
ornado, -da *adj.* ornate, adorned.
ornamentación *f.* ornamentation.
ornamental *adj.* ornamental.
ornamentar *tr.* to ornament, adorn, decorate.
ornamento *m.* ornament, adornment, decoration. *2* gift, moral quality. *3* ARCH. ornament. *4 pl.* ECCL. ornaments.
ornar *tr.* to ornament, adorn, embellish.
ornato *m.* adornment, embellishment; show.

ornitología *f.* ornithology.
ornitólogo *m.* ornithologist.
ornitorrinco *m.* ZOOL. duckbill.
oro *m.* gold [metal; money, wealth; precious things]; ~ *batido*, gold leaf; ~ *de ley*, standard gold; *de* ~, of gold; gold golden; *como un* ~ [clean, beautiful, bright], like gold; *de* ~ *y azul*, all dressed up; *poner de* ~ *y azul*, to upbraid, to abuse. *2* HER. or. *3 pl.* card suit equivalent to diamonds.
orobanca *f.* BOT. broomrape.
orogenia *f.* GEOL. orogeny.
orografía *f.* orography.
orográfico, -ca *adj.* orographic(al.
orondo, -da *adj.* big-bellied [jar, etc.]. *2* hollow, puffed up. *3* self-satisfied, proud.
oropel *m.* tinsel, brass foil. *2* fig. tinsel [cheap glittering thing; false show].
oropéndola *f.* ORN. loriot, golden oriole.
oropimente *m.* MINER. orpiment.
orozuz *m.* BOT. licorice.
orquesta *f.* MUS., THEAT. orchestra.
orquestación *f.* orchestration.
orquestar *tr.* to orchestrate.
orquídeo, -dea *adj.* BOT. orchidaceous. *2 f.* BOT. orchid.
ortega *f.* ORN. sand grouse.
ortiga *f.* BOT. nettle. *2* ZOOL. ~ *de mar*, jellyfish.
ortivo, -va *adj.* ASTR. ortive.
orto *m.* rising [of sun or star].
ortodoxia *f.* orthodoxy.
ortodoxo, -xa *adj.* orthodox.
ortogénesis *f.* BIOL. orthogenesis.
ortogonal *adj.* orthogonal.
ortografía *f.* orthography.
ortográfico, -ca *adj.* orthographical.
ortopedia *f.* orthopa(e)dy, orthopa(e)dics.
ortopedista *m.-f.* orthopa(e)dist.
ortóptero *adj.* ENT. orthopterous.
oruga *f.* ENT., MACH. caterpillar. *2* BOT. rocket. *3* rocket sauce.
orujo *m.* marc of grapes or olives.
orvalle *m.* GALLOCRESTA.
orza *f.* NAUT. luff, luffing. *2* NAUT. centreboard. *3* crock, earthen jar.
orzaga *f.* BOT. orach.
orzar *intr.* NAUT. to luff.
orzuelo *m.* MED. sty [in one's eye].
os *pers. pron. pl. m.-f.* [object of the verb] you, to you, for you; *[recip.]* each other; *[ref.]* yourselves.
osa *f.* ZOOL. she-bear. *2* (cap.) ASTR. *Osa Mayor*, Great Bear; *Osa Menor*, Little Bear.
osadía *f.* audacity, boldness, daring, hardihood.
osado, -da *adj.* audacious, bold, daring, hardy.
osambre *m.* osamenta *f.* skeleton, bones.
1) **osar** *intr.* to dare, venture.
2) **osar, osario** *m.* charnel-house, ossuary.
oscilación *f.* oscillation.
oscilador *m.* ELECT., RADIO. oscillator.
oscilar *intr.* to oscillate.
oscilatorio, -ria *adj.* oscillatory.
osculación *f.* GEOM. osculation.
ósculo *m.* kiss. *2* ZOOL. osculum.
oscurantismo, oscurecer, oscuridad, etc. = OBSCU-
RANTISMO, OBSCURECER, OBSCURIDAD, etc.
osecillo, osecito *m.* dim. small bone, bonelet.
óseo, -a *adj.* osseous, bony.
osera *f.* den of bears.
osezno *m.* cub or whelp of a bear.
osificarse *ref.* to ossify [become ossified].

osífraga *f.*, **osífrago** *m.* QUEBRANTAHUESOS 2.
osmanlí *adj.-n.* Osmanli.
osmio *m.* CHEM. osmium.
ósmosis *f.* PHYS. osmosis.
oso *m.* ZOOL. bear: ~ *blanco*, polar bear; ~ *gris*, grizzly bear; ~ *pardo*, brown bear; *hacer el* ~, fig. to make a fool of oneself; to court a woman. *2* ZOOL. ~ *hormiguero*, anteater. *3* ZOOL. ~ *marsupial*, koala.
ososo, -sa *adj.* osseous, bony.
¡oste! *interj.* ¡OXTE!
ostensible *adj.* ostensible, visible, manifest.
ostensión *f.* show, manifestation.
ostensivo, -va *adj.* ostensive, showing.
ostensorio *m.* ECCL. ostensory, monstrance.
ostentación *f.* ostentation, parade, display, show, vain show. *2* exhibition, manifestation.
ostentador, -ra *adj.* ostentatious.
ostentar *tr.* to parade, display, show, to make ostentation of. *2* to exhibit, manifest.
ostento *m.* portent, prodigy.
ostentoso, -sa *adj.* ostentatious, sumptuous.
osteología *f.* osteology.
osteópata *m.* osteopath, osteopathist.
osteopatía *f.* osteopathy.
ostiario *m.* ECCL. ostiary.
ostión *m.* large oyster.
ostra *f.* ZOOL. oyster: ~ *perlera*, pearl oyster.
ostracismo *m.* ostracism.
ostrería *f.* oyster shop.
ostrero, -ra *adj.* [pertaining to the] oyster. *2 m.-f.* oyster seller. *3 m.* oyster bed, oyster farm.
ostrícola *adj.* oyster-rising.
ostricultura *f.* oyster culture, oyster farming.
ostro *m.* south. *2* south wind.
ostrogodo, -da *adj.-n.* Ostrogoth.
ostrón *m.* large, coarse oyster.
ostugo *m.* RINCÓN. . *2* bit, piece.
osudo, -da *adj.* HUESUDO.
osuno, -na *adj.* bearish, bearlike.
otear *tr.* to watch, observe, survey from a height. *2* to spy, search, examine.
otero *m.* hillock, knoll, buttle, height.
otitis *f.* MED. otitis.
otocisto *m.* ZOOL. otocyst.
otolaringología *f.* otolaryngology.
otología *f.* otology.
otomano, -na *adj.-n.* Ottoman.
otoñada *f.* autumn, autumn time.
otoñal *adj.* autumnal.
otoño *m.* autumn, fall. *2* autumn aftermath.
otorgador, -ra *adj.* granting. *2 m.-f.* grantor.
otorgamiento *m.* grant, granting. *2* awarding [of a prize]. *3* LAW execution [of deed, etc.].
otorgante *m.-f.* grantor. *2* LAW maker [of a deed, etc.].
otorgar *tr.* to grant, give. *2* to award [a prize]. *3* to grant, consent: *quien calla otorga*, silence gives consent. *4* LAW to execute [a deed, etc.].
otorrinolaringología *f.* otorhinolaryngology.
otoscopio *m.* otoscope.
otramente *adv.* otherwise, in a different way.
otro, -tra *adj.-pron.* another, other: *otra cosa*, something else; ~ *que tal*, another such; *otros tantos*, as many; *otra vez*, again; *algún* ~, someone or somebody else; *al* ~ *día*, on the next day; *por otra parte*, on the other hand; *uno a* ~, one another. *2* interj. ¡otra!, again!
otrora *adv.* formerly, of yore.
otrosí *adv.* LAW furthermore.

ova *f.* BOT. a fresh-water alga. *2* ARCH. egg [in egg-and-dart ornaments]. *3 pl.* roe.
ovación *f.* ovation.
ovacionar *intr.* to give an ovation to.
ovado, -da *adj.* ovate, oval.
oval; ovalado, -da *adj.* oval.
ovalar *tr.* to make oval.
óvalo *m.* GEOM. oval. *2* OVA 2.
ovar *intr.* to lay eggs.
ovárico, -ca *adj.* ovarian.
ovario *m.* ANAT., ZOOL., BOT. ovary, ovarium.
oveja *f.* ewe, female sheep.
ovejero, -ra *m.-f.* shepherd, shepherdess.
ovejuela *f. dim.* young ewe.
ovejuno, -na *adj.* [pertaining to] sheep.
overa *f.* ovary of birds.
overo, -ra *adj.* blossom-coloured, peach-coloured [horse].
ovetense *adj.-n.* of Oviedo.
Ovidio *m. pr. n.* Ovid.
óvidos *m. pl.* ZOOL. Ovidae.
oviducto *m.* ZOOL. oviduct.
ovillar *intr.* to wind [thread, yarn] in a ball. *2 ref.* to huddle up; to coil oneself into a ball.
ovillejo *m. dim.* small ball [of thread or yarn]. *2 a* kind of rondeau or rondel.
ovillo *m.* ball [of thread or yarn]: *hacerse un ~,* OVILLAR 2; to get all tangled up [in speech].

ovíparo, -ra *adj.* oviparous.
oviscapto *m.* ZOOL. ovispositor.
ovoide; ovoideo, -a *adj.* ovoid.
óvolo *m.* ARCH. ovolo.
ovovivíparo, -ra *adj.* ovoviviparous.
óvulo *m.* BIOL., BOT. ovule.
oxálico, -ca *adj.* CHEM. oxalic.
oxear *tr.* to shoo [fowls].
oxhídrico, -ca *adj.* CHEM. oxyhydrogen.
oxidación *f.* CHEM. oxidation.
oxidante *m.* CHEM. oxidizer.
oxidar *tr.* to oxidize, to rust. *2 ref.* to oxidize, to rust [become oxidized].
óxido *m.* CHEM. oxide.
oxigenación *f.* oxygenation.
oxigenar *tr.* to oxygenate, oxygenize. *2 ref.* to become oxygenated. *3* to take the air.
oxígeno *m.* CHEM. oxygen.
oximel, oximiel *m.* PHARM. oxymel.
oxiuro *m.* ZOOL. pinworm.
¡oxte! *interj.* shoo!, get out! *2 sin decir ~ ni moxte,* coll. without saying a word.
oyente *m.-f.* hearer. *2* listener [to the radio]. *3* auditor [in school]. *4 pl.* audience.
ozonización *f.* ozonization.
ozonizar *tr.* to ozonize.
ozono *m.* CHEM. ozone.

P

P, p *f.* P, p, nineteenth letter of the Spanish alphabet.
pabellón *m.* pavilion. 2 canopy [over a bed, throne, etc.]. 3 stack [of rifles]. 4 bell [of a wind instrument]. 5 NAUT. flag, colours. 6 national colours. 7 ANAT. ~ *de la oreja,* auricle, external ear.
pábilo, pabilo *m.* wick or snuff [of candle].
Pablo *m. pr. n.* Paul: ¡*guarda Pablo!,* beware!
pábulo *m.* pabulum, food, fuel, aliment, support: *dar ~ a,* to give food to, to encourage.
paca *f.* bale [of goods]. 2 ZOOL. paca, spotted cavy.
Paca *f. pr. n.* coll. Fanny.
pacana *f.* BOT. pecan tree. 2 BOT. pecan nut.
pacato, -ta *adj.* excessively timid and moderate.
pacedero, -ra *adj.* pasturable.
paceño, -ña *adj.-n.* of La Paz [Bolivia].
pacer *intr.-tr.* to pasture, to graze.
paciencia *f.* patience. 2 small almond cake.
paciente *adj.* patient [having patience]. 2 *m.-f.* MED. patient. 3 *adj.-m.* patient [as opposed to *agent*].
pacienzudo, -da *adj.* very patient.
pacificación *f.* pacification. 2 peace, quiet.
pacificador, -ra *adj.* pacifying. 2 *m.-f.* pacifier; peacemaker.
pacificar *tr.* to pacify. 2 *ref.* to calm down.
pacífico, -ca *adj.* pacific. 2 peaceable, peaceful. 3 *adj.-n.* (cap.) GEOG. Pacific [Ocean].
pacifismo *m.* pacifism.
Paco *m. pr. n.* coll. Frank.
paco *m.* ZOOL. alpaca. 2 Moorish sniper.
pacotilla *f.* venture, goods carried by seamen of a ship free of freight. 2 *de ~,* cheap, of inferior quality.
pacotillero, -ra *m.-f.* peddler.
pactar *tr.* to covenant, agree upon, stipulate. 2 *intr.* to come to an agreement. 3 to temporize.
pacto *m.* pact, compact, agreement, covenant.
pachá, *pl.* **-caes** *m.* BAJÁ.
pachón, -na *adj.* pointer [dog]. 2 (Am.) wooly, shaggy. — 3 *m.* phlegmatic fellow.
pachorra *f.* phlegm, sluggishness, indolence.
pachorrudo, -da *adj.* phlegmmatic, sluggish, indolent.
pachucho, -cha *adj.* overripe. 2 fig. weak, drooping.
pachulí *m.* patchouli.
padecer *tr.* to suffer [undergo, be subjected to]. 2 to be a victim of [a mistake, illusion, etc.]. 3 *intr.* to suffer. 4 MED. ~ *de,* to suffer from troubles in. ¶ CONJUG. like *agradecer.*
padezco, padezca, etc. *irr.* V. PADECER.
padecimiento *m.* suffering. 2 ailment.
padrastro *m.* stepfather. 2 bad father. 3 hangnail.
padrazo *m. augm.* indulgent father.
padre *m.* father: *Padre Eterno,* the Eternal; ~ *político,* father-in-law; *Padre Santo,* Holy Father; *de ~ y muy señor mío,* great, hard; terrific. 2 stallion, sire. 3 *pl.* parents.
padrenuestro *m.* Lord's prayer.
padrinazgo *m.* act of standing godfather or sponsor at baptism, confirmation, etc. 2 title or charge of a godfather. 3 patronage, support, protection.
padrino *m.* godfather, sponsor. 2 second [at a duel]. 3 patron, protector. 4 ~ *de boda,* best man.
padrón *m.* census [of the population]. 2 pattern, model. 3 memorial column or post. 4 PADRAZO.
paella *f.* dish of rice with meat, chicken, fish, etc.
¡paf! *interj.* expressing the noise of a fall, blow, etc.
paga *f.* payment. 2 pay, salary. 3 satisfaction, amends. 4 requital, return.
pagadero, -ra *adj.* payable [at a specified time]. 2 *m.* time and place of payment.
pagado, -da *p. p.* of PAGAR. 2 pleased, proud: ~ *de sí mismo,* self-satisfied, conceited.
pagador, -ra *m.-f.* payer, paymaster: *buen ~,* good pay [person]; *mal ~,* bad pay [person].
pagaduría *f.* disbursement office; paymaster's office.
paganismo *m.* heathenism, paganism.
pagano, -na *adj.-n.* heathen, pagan. 2 *m.* coll. one who pays for others, one who pays the piper.
pagar *tr.* to pay [money, wages, a debt, etc.]; to fee: ~ *al contado,* to pay cash. 2 to pay for: ~ *el pato, los vidrios rotos,* coll. to be the scapegoat; *me las pagarás,* you'll pay for it. 3 to expiate, atone, make amends for. 4 to repay, return [love, a kindness, etc.]. 5 to return [a call]. 6 *ref. pagarse de,* to be fond of; be proud of.
pagaré *m.* COM. promissory note.
pagel *m.* ICHTH. red sea bream.
página *f.* page [of book, etc.].
paginación *f.* pagination.
paginar *tr.* to page, paginate.

pago *adj.* coll. paid, having been paid [pers.]. *2 m.* rural district. *3* payment. *4* repayment, return. *5 en ~,* in payment; in return.
pagoda *f.* pagoda.
pagro *m.* ICHTH. porgy, red porgy.
paguro *m.* ZOOL. hermit crab.
paila *f.* large pan, cauldron.
pailebot, pailebote *m.* NAUT. a small schooner.
paipai *m.* fan made of palm.
pairar *intr.* NAUT. [of a ship] to lie to.
pairo *m.* NAUT. lying to.
país *m.* country, nation. *2* country, land, region, territory. *3* F. ARTS landscape. *4* sheet [of a fan].
paisaje *m.* landscape.
paisajista *m.-f.* landscape painter.
paisanaje *m.* civilians. *2* peasantry, countryfolk. *3* fellow countrymanship.
paisano, -na *adj.* of the same country or place. *2 m.-f.* compatriot, countryman or woman. *3* peasant. *4 m.* civilian.
paja *f.* straw: *no dormirse en las pajas,* not to let the grass grow under one's feet; *por un quítame allá estas pajas* [to quarrel], over the smallest trifle. *2* fig. trash, rubbish.
pajado, -da *adj.* straw-coloured.
pajar *m.* haystack, rick of straw. *2* straw loft.
pájara *f.* bird. *2* kite [toy]. *3* crafty female. *4* PAJARITA 1.
pajarear *intr.* to go birdcatching. *2* to loaf, around.
pajarera *f.* aviary; large bird cage.
pajarería *f.* large number of birds. *2* bird shop.
pajarero *m.* birdcatcher. *2* bird fancier. *3* bird seller.
pajarete *m.* fine sherry wine.
pajarilla *f.* BOT. columbine. *2* ANAT. spleen, milt.
pajarita *f.* paper bird. *2* ORN. *~ de las nieves,* AGUZANIEVES.
pájaro *m.* bird; passerine bird: *~ bobo,* penguin; *~ carpintero,* woodpecker; *~ mosca,* hummingbird; *matar dos pájaros de un tiro,* to kill two birds with one stone. *2* fig. sly, crafty fellow. *3* fig. *~ de cuenta,* man of importance; dangerous fellow; *~ gordo,* big gun, swell.
pajarota, pajarotada *f.* hoax, canard.
pajarraco *m.* large ugly bird. *2* fig. sly fellow.
paje *m.* page [youth]: *~ de hacha,* link boy. *2* familiar [of a bishop]. *3* NAUT. cabin boy.
pajecillo *m.* dim. little page [boy]. *2* washstand.
pajel *m.* PAGEL.
pajero *m.* straw dealer.
pajizo, -za *adj.* made of straw. *2* thatched with straw. *3* straw-coloured.
pajón *m.* high coarse stumps of grain.
pajoso, -sa *adj.* strawy.
pajote *m.* straw mat for covering plants.
pajuela *f.* dim. short straw. *2* sulphur match.
Pakistán (el) *m. pr. n.* GEOG. Pakistan.
pal *m.* HER. pale.
pala *f.* shovel. *2* peel; baker's peel. *3* slice [for serving fish, etc.]. *4* wash, beetle. *5* racket [for ball games]. *6* blade [of a hoe, spade, etc.]. *7* bowl [of a spoon]. *8* vamp [of a shoe]. *9* leaf [of a hinge]. *10* BOT. joint [of a prickly pear].
palabra *f.* word [term; speech, thing said, remark, conversation]: *palabras cruzadas,* crossword puzzle; *palabras mayores,* insulting words; serious matter; *dos palabras,* a few words; *medias palabras,* covert suggestion; *juego de palabras,* pun; *comerse las palabras,* to omit words; *de ~,* by word of mouth; *en una ~,* in a word, to sum up; *~ por ~,* word by word. *2* act of speaking;

right, turn or permission to speak; *pedir la ~,* to ask for the floor; *tomar la ~,* to take the floor. *3* word [one's promise]: *¡palabra!,* honestly!; *dar,* or *empeñar, uno su ~,* to give, or pledge, one's word; *bajo su ~,* on one's word.
palabreja *f.* odd word.
palabreo *m.,* **palabrería** *f.* empty talk.
palabrero, -ra *adj.* talkative, wordy, windy. *2 m.-f.* chatterer, vain talker, windbag.
palabrita *f.* dim. small word. *2* pointed word.
palabrota *f.* coarse, obscene word or expression.
palaciego, -ga *adj.* [pertaining to the] palace; court. *2 m.* courtier.
palacio *m.* palace. *2* mansion house [oficial residence].
palada *f.* shovelful. *2* stroke [of an oar].
paladar *s.* ANAT. palate. *2* taste [of things]. *3* palate, taste [sense of taste; mental taste].
paladear *tr.-ref.* to taste with pleasure, to relish, to take small portions [of something] in order to relish it.
paladeo *m.* tasting, relishing.
paladial *adj.-f.* palatal.
paladín *m.* paladin. *2* champion, defender.
paladino, -na *adj.* open, public, manifest. *2 m.* PALADÍN.
paladio *m.* CHEM. palladium.
paladión *m.* palladium, safeguard.
palafito *m.* ARCHEOL. palafitte.
palafrén *m.* palfrey. *2* groom's horse.
palafrenero *m.* groom, stableman, hostler.
palamenta *f.* oarage, seat of oars, outfit of oars.
palanca *f.* MECH. lever. *2* MACH. lever, bar: *~ del timón,* AER. rudder bar. *3* fig. lever [agency, influence]. *4* pole for carrying a weight.
palancada *f.* move made with a lever.
palancana, palangana *f.* washbowl.
palanganero *m.* washstand [stand with washbowl and pitcher].
palangre *m.* boulter.
palangrero *m.* boulterer [fisherman].
palanquera *f.* wooden fence.
palanqueta *f.* jimmy [short crowbar]. *2* NAV. bar shot.
palanquín *m.* palankeen, palanquin. *2* street porter. *3* NAUT. clew-garnet. *4* NAUT. gun tackle.
Palas *f. pr. n.* MYTH. Pallas.
palastro *m.* sheet iron, sheet steel. *2* plate [of a lock].
palatal *adj.-f.* palatal.
palatalizar *tr.* PHONET. to palatalize.
Palatinado (el) *pr. n.* GEOG. Palatinate. *2 m.* palatinate.
palatino, -na *adj.* ANAT. palatine. *2 adj.-m.* palatine [count, earl, etc.].
palazón *m.* NAUT. masting. *2* woodwork, timber.
palco *m.* THEAT. box. *2* THEAT. *~ escénico,* stage.
palear *tr.* to winnow, fan [grain] with a shovel.
palenque *m.* palisade, wood fence, enclosure, lists.
**palentino, adj.-n.* of Palencia.
paleografía *f.* pal(a)eography.
paleolítico *adj.* pal(a)eolithic(al).
paleólogo *m.* pal(a)eologist.
paleontología *f.* pal(a)eontology.
paleozoico, -ca *adj.-m.* Pal(a)eozoic.
palería *f.* art and practice of draining lands.
Palestina *pr. n.* GEOG. Palestine.
palestra *f.* pal(a)estra.
paleta *f.* PAINT. palette, .pallet. *2* small, flat, fire shovel. *3* MAS. trowel. *4* ANAT. shoulder blade. *5*

float, paddle [of a water wheel or paddle wheel]; vane [of a propeller, fan blower, etc.].
paletada *f*. trowelful.
paletazo *m*. VARETAZO.
paletear *intr*. to row ineffectively.
paletero *m*. two-year-old fallow deer.
paletilla *f*. ANAT. shoulder blade. *2* ANAT. sternum cartilage.
paleto *m*. ZOOL. fallow deer. *2* coll. rustic, yokel.
paletó, *pl*. **-toes** *m*. paletot [overcoat].
paletón *m*. bit, web [of a key].
palia *f*. ECCL. pall. *2* curtain before the tabernacle.
paliar *tr*. to palliate, extenuate. *2* to palliate, alleviate.
paliativo, -va *adj.-m*. palliative.
palidecer *intr*. to pale, turn pale; to wan, grow wan. ¶ CONJUG. like *agradecer*.
palidez *f*. paleness, pallor, wanness.
palidezco, palidezca, etc. *irr*. V. PALIDECER.
pálido, -da *adj*. pale, pallid, wan, ghastly.
paliducho, -cha *adj*. palish.
palillero *m*. toothpick holder.
palillo *m*. small stick. *2* knitting-needle holder. *3* wooden toothpick. *4* drumstick. *5* bobbin [for making lace]. *6* coll. chit-chat. *7* *pl*. castanets. *8* small pins used in billiards. *9* chopsticks. *10* small sticks used by sculptors.
palimpsesto *m*. palimpsest.
palingenesia *f*. palingenesis.
palinodia *f*. palinode: *cantar la* ~, to recant, retract.
palio *m*. HIST., ECCL. pallium. *2* portable canopy. *3* fig. canopy [overhanging covering].
palique *m*. chit-chat, small talk.
palisandro *m*. palisander, palissander, rosewood.
palitoque, palitroque *m*. rough small stick.
paliza *f*. beating, drubbing, -trashing.
palizada *f*. palisaded enclosure. *2* palisaded embankment. *3* FORT. stockade.
palma *f*. BOT. palm, palm tree. *2* palm [leaf of palm; symbol of victory, etc.]: *llevarse la* ~, to excel, to surpass everybody. *3* palm [of the hand]. *4* VET. sole [of hoof]. *5* *pl*. clapping of hands: *batir palmas*, to clap hands.
palmáceo, -a *adj*. BOT. palmaceous.
palmada *f*. slap, pat [with the hand]. *2* handclap: *dar palmadas*, to clap hands.
palmeado, -da *adj*. PALMEADO.
1) **palmar** *adj*. ANAT. palmar. *2* VET. pertaining to the sole of the hoof. *3* measuring a span. *4* PALMARIO. *5* *m*. palm grove.
2) **palmar** *intr*. coll. to die.
palmario, -ria *adj*. clear, obvious, evident.
palmatoria *f*. short candlestick with a handle.
palmeado, -da *adj*. BOT. palmate. *2* ZOOL. palmate; webbed.
palmear *intr*. to clap hands.
palmera *f*. BOT. date palm.
palmeral *m*. date palms grove or plantation.
palmero *m*. palm keeper. *2* palmer [pilgrim].
palmesano, -na *adj.-n*. of Palma de Mallorca.
palmeta *f*. ferule [for punishing boys].
palmetazo *m*. slap with a ferule.
palmiche *m*. BOT. royal palm. *2* fruit of the royal palm. *3* fruit of the palmetto or dwarf fanpalm.
palmípedo, -da *adj*. ORN. palmiped, web-footed.
palmito *m*. BOT. palmetto, dwarf fan-palm. *2* sprout of the dwarf fan-palm. *3* woman's face: *buen* ~, beautiful face.
palmo *m*. span [measure]: *dejar con un* ~ *de nari-*

ces, coll. to disappoint; ~ *a* ~, inch by inch. *2* palm [hand breadth].
palmotear *tr*. to clap hands, aplaud.
palo *m*. stick, staff, pole. *2* NAUT. mast: ~ *mayor*, mainmast; *a* ~ *seco*, under bare poles; fig. without the customary complements. *3* blow with a stick: *dar de palos*, to beat, thrash; *llevar* ~, to get a drubbing. *4* stalk of fruit. *5* suit [at cards]. *6* long stroke [in handwriting]. *7* execution on the gallows or on the garrote. *8* wood [material]. *9* a name for some trees or kinds of wood: ~ *aloe*, aloes wood; ~ *brasil*, brazilwood; ~ *campeche*, campeche wood; ~ *de jabón*, soapbark; ~ *santo*, lignum vitae. *10* *pl*. billiard pins.
paloma *f*. ORN. dove, pigeon: ~ *silvestre*, stock dove; ~ *buchona*, pouter [pigeon]; ~ *mensajera*, carrier pigeon, homer; ~ *torcaz*, wood pigeon. *2* fig. dove [meek person]. *3* *pl*. whitecaps.
palomar *m*. pigeon-house, dovecot. *2* adj. hard-twisted [twine].
palomariego, -ga *adj*. domestic [pigeon].
palomero, -ra *m.-f*. pigeon dealer. *2* pigeon breeder.
palomilla *f*. small butterfly. *2* fore part of the croup of a horse. *3* wall bracket. *4* MECH. journal bearing. *5* *pl*. whitecaps.
palomina *f*. pigeon dung. *2* BOT. fumitory.
palomino *m*. young pigeon.
palomita *f*. *dim*. little pigeon. *2* (Am.) piece of popcorn. *3* (Am.) darling. *4* *pl*. popcorn.
palomo *m*. cock pigeon. *2* ORN. wood pigeon.
palor *m*. pallor.
palotada *f*. stroke with a stick: *no dar* ~, to do or say nothing right; to do nothing.
palote *f*. stick, drumstick. *2* stroke [in learning to write].
palpable *adj*. palpable. *2* obvious, evident.
palpablemente *adv*. palpably.
palpación *f*. PALPADURA. *2* MED. palpation.
palpadura, *f*., **palpamiento** *m*. touching, feeling.
palpar *tr*. to touch, feel. *2* to grope through. *3* to see as self-evident. *4* MED. to palpate. *5* *intr*. to feel one's way, to grope in the dark.
palpebral *adj*. palpebral.
palpitación *f*. palpitation, pulsation, throbbing.
palpitante *adj*. palpitating. *2* burning [question].
palpitar *intr*. to palpitate, pulsate, throb, thrill. *2* to reveal itself [in an act, words, etc.].
palpo *m*. ZOOL. palpus [in arthropods].
palúdico, -ca *adj*. marshy. *2* malarial.
paludismo *m*. MED. paludism, malaria.
palumbario *adj*. dove-hunting [hawk].
palurdo, -da *adj*. rustic, rude. *2* *m.-f*. rustic, yokel.
palustre *adj*. paludal, marshy. *2* *m*. MAS. trowel.
pallador *m*. (S. Am.) wandering poet and singer.
pallete *m*. NAUT. fender mat.
pallón *m*. assay button [of gold or silver].
pamela *f*. woman's wide-brimmed straw hat.
pamema *f*. coll. trifle, nonsense. *2* coll. bunkum.
pampa *m*. pampa: *La Pampa*, the pampas.
pámpana *f*. grapevine leaf.
pampanilla *f*. loincloth.
pámpano *m*. grapevine tendril or shoot. *2* grapevine leaf. *3* ICHTH. gilthead.
pampeano, -na *adj.-n*. (S. Am.) pampean.
pampear *intr*. to go or travel over the pampas.
pampero, -ra *adj.-n*. pampean. *2* *m*. pampero [wind].
pampirolada *f*. a garlic sauce. *2* coll. silly thing.
pamplina *f*. nonsense, trifle, silly thing. *2* BOT. chickweed. *3* BOT. a kind of yellow poppy.

pamplinada *f.* nonsense, trifle, silly thing.
pamplinero, -ra; pamplinoso, -sa *adj.* silly, nonsensical.
pamplonés, -sa *adj.-m.* of Pamplona.
pamporcino *m.* BOT. cyclamen, sowbread.
pamposado, -da *adj.* lazy, indolent.
pan *m.* bread; loaf: ~ *ázimo*, unleavened bread; ~ *candeal*, white-wheat bread; ~ *tierno*, fresh bread; ~ *duro*, stale bread; ~ *integral*, wholewheat bread; ~ *rallado*, bread crumbs; *panes de proposición*, BIBL. shewbread, showbread; *ganarse el* ~, to earn one's livelihood; *llamar al pan, pan, y al vino, vino*, to call a spade a spade; *contigo* ~ *y cebolla*, fig. love in a cottage. *2* pie or pastry dough. *3* anything in the shape of a loaf or a cake: ~ *de azúcar*, sugar loaf. *4* wafer. *5* leaf, foil [of gold, silver, etc.]. *6* wheat. *7 pl.* grain fields.
pana *f.* velveteen, corduroy. *2* NAUT. flooring board. *3* AUTO. break-down.
panacea *f.* panacea.
panadear *tr.* to make [flour] into bread. *2 intr.* to make bread [for sale].
panadeo *m.* making bread.
panadería *f.* bakery. *2* baking business.
panadero, -ra *m.-f.* baker. *2 f.* baker's wife.
panadizo *m.* MED. felon, whitlow.
panal *m.* honeycomb. *2* comb built by wasps. *3* AZUCARILLO.
Panamá *m. pr. n.* GEOG. Panama. *2 m.* (not cap.) panama, panama hat.
panameño, -ña *adj.-n.* Panamanian.
panamericano, -na *adj.* Pan-American.
panarizo *m.* PANADIZO.
panarra *m.* lazy simpleton.
pancarta *f.* parchment containing several documents. *2* placard, portable placard.
pancellar *m.*, **pancera** *f.* ARM. belly plate.
pancista *m.* POL. one who sits on the fence.
pancracio *m.* HIST. pancratium.
páncreas, *pl.* **-creas** *m.* ANAT. pancreas.
pancreático, -ca *adj.* pancreatic.
Pancha, Panchita *f. pr. n. coll.* Fanny.
Pancho, Panchito *m. pr. n. coll.* Frank.
pancho *m.* ICHTH. spawn of the sea bream.
pandear *intr.-ref.* [of a wall, beam, etc.] to sag, buckle, bulge, bend in the middle.
Pandectas *f. pl.* Pandects.
pandemia *f.* MED. pandemia, pandemic.
pandemónium *m.* Pandemonium; pandemonium.
pandeo *m.* sagging, bulging, bending of a wall, beam, etc.
pandera *f.* PANDERO.
panderada *f.* tambouriness. *2 coll.* silly remark.
pandereta *f.* PANDERO I.
panderete *m. dim.* small tambourine.
panderetear *intr.* to sing, dance or make merry and play the tambourine.
pandereteo *m.* playing the tambourine.
panderetear *intr.* to sing, dance or make merry and play the tambourine.
pandereteo *m.* playing the tambourine.
pandero *m.* MUS. tambourine, timbrel. *2* kite [toy]. *3 coll.* silly talker, jabberer.
pandilla *f.* gang, band, set, company, faction.
pandillaje *m.* action or influence of a sang.
pando, -da *adj.* sagging, bulging [wall, beam, etc.]. *2* slow-moving. *3 m.* plain between two mountains.
pandorga *f.* fat, bulky woman. *2* kite [toy].
panecillo *m.* roll [bread].

panegírico, -ca *adj.* panegyric(al. *2 m.* panegyric.
panegirizar *tr.* to panegyrize, eulogyze.
panel *m.* panel [in wainscot, door, etc.]. *2* ELECT. panel. *3* NAUT. removable floor board.
panera *f.* granary. *2* bread basket.
paneslavismo *m.* Pan-Slavism.
panetela *f.* broth with crumps, minced fowl, eggs, sugar, etc. *2* panetella [cigar].
panfilismo *m.* excessive gentleness or benignity.
pánfilo, -la *adj.* slow, sluggish [person]. *2 m.-f.* sluggard.
panfleto *m.* (Am.) pamphlet.
pangermanismo *m.* Pan-Germanism.
pangolín *m.* ZOOL. pangolin.
paniaguado *m.* servant, minion. *2* protégé.
pánico, -ca *adj.* panic, panicky. *2 m.* panic.
panícula *f.* BOT. panicle.
paniculo *m.* ANAT. panniculus.
panificable *adj.* good for making bread [fluor].
panificación *f.* panification.
panificar *tr.* to make [flour] into bread.
panislamismo *m.* Pan-Islamism.
panizo *m.* BOT. panic grass, foxtail millet, Italian millet. *2* Indian corn.
panocha *f.* ear [of Indian corn]. *2* panicle [of millet or foxtail millet]. *3* bunch [of fruit hung up for keeping].
panoja *f.* PANOCHA. *2* BOT. panicle.
panoplia *f.* panoply [suit of armour]. *2* collection of arms. *3* wall trophy. *4* study of ancient weapons.
panorama *m.* panorama.
panorámico, -ca *adj.* panoramic.
panormitano, -na *adj.-n.* Palermitan.
panoso, -sa *adj.* mealy.
pantagruélico, -ca *adj.* Pantagruelian, Pantagruelic.
pantalón or *pl.* **pantalones** *m.* trousers, breeches, *pants*: ~ *bombacho*, loose-fitting trousers; *pantalones de golf*, knicker-bockers; *llevar· los pantalones*, fig. [of a wife] to wear the trousers. *2* woman's drawers; pantlets.
pantalla *f.* lamp shade. *2* fire screen [before a fireplace]. *3* PHYS., CINE., TELEV. screen. *4* RADIO. baffle. *5* fig. anything that obstructs the view. *6* *servir de* ~ *a uno*, to be a blind for someone.
pantanal *m.* swampland.
pantano *m.* swamp, marsh. *2* small lake or natural pond. *3* a large dam. *4* fig. obstacle, hindrance.
pantanoso, -sa *adj.* swampy, marshy.
panteísmo *m.* pantheism.
panteísta *adj.* pantheistic. *2 m.-f.* pantheist.
panteón *m.* Pantheon. *2* family tomb.
pantera *f.* ZOOL. panther. *2* MINER. yellow agate.
pantógrafo *m.* pantograph.
pantomima *f.* pantomime, dumb show.
pantomimo *m.* mimic, pantomimist.
pantoque *m.* NAUT. bilge.
pantorrilla *f.* calf [of the leg].
pantorrillera *f.* padded stocking.
pantorrilludo, -da *adj.* thick-calved.
pantufla, *f.*, **pantuflo** *m.* slipper, house slipper.
panza *f.* paunch, belly. *2* belly [of a vase]. *3* ZOOL. paunch, rumen [of ruminants].
panzada *f.* bellyfull. *2* push with the paunch.
panzón, -na *adj.* PANZUDO. *2 m.* big belly.
panzudo, -da *adj.* paunchy, big-bellied.
pañal *m.* swaddling cloth. *2* tail of shirt. *3 pl.* swaddling clothes; infancy.
pañería *f.* drapery [cloth, woollen stuffs in general]. *2* draper's shop.

pañero, -ra *adj.* [pertaining to] drapery. *2 m.* draper, clothier.
pañete *m.* light, thin cloth.
paño *m.* cloth [woollen stuff]: *conocer el ~,* to know the ropes. *2* by extension, cloth [any woven stuff]. *3* tapestry. *4* cloth [piece of fabric adapted for some specified use]: *~ de cocina,* dish cloth; *~ de lágrimas,* fig. one who simpathizes and consoles; *~ calientes,* fig. inefficent efforts; half measures; *en paños menores,* undressed. *5* spot in the face. *6* blur [in a mirror, a precious stone, etc.]. *7* stretch [of a wall]. *8* NAUT. canvas, sails. *9* SEW. breadth. *10 pl.* PAINT., SCULPT. draperies.
pañol *m.* NAUT. storeroom.
pañolería *f.* handkerchief business.
pañolero *m.* NAUT. storeroom keeper, yeoman.
pañoleta *f.* woman's triangular shawl.
pañolón *m.* large square shawl.
pañoso, -sa *adj.* ragged, in rags. *2 f.* coll. woollen cloak.
pañuelo *m.* square shawl. *2* kerchief, handkerchief: *~ de hierbas,* bandana; *~ para el cuello,* neckerchief, neckcloth.
papa *m.* Pope [Roman Pontiff]. *2* coll. papa, dad. *3 f.* fib, canard. *4* potato. *5 no saber una ~,* not to know a thing. *6 pl.* pap, porridge.
papá *m.* coll. papa, dad.
papacito *m.* (Am.) daddy.
papada *f.* double chin. *2* dewlap.
papadilla *f.* flesh under the chin.
papado *m.* papacy.
papafigo *m.* ORN. figpecker. *2* ORN. golden oriole.
papagayo *m.* ORN. parrot. *2* fig. parrot [pers.]. *3* fig. chatterbox. *4* ICHTH. peacock fish.
papahigo *m.* winter cap [covering head, ears and neck]. *2* ORN. figpecker. *3* NAUT. lower sail.
papal *adj.* papal.
papalina *f.* a kind of woman's coif. *2* a cap covering the ears. *3* coll. drunk, drunken fit.
papamoscas, *pl.* -cas *m.* ORN. flycatcher. *2* PAPANATAS.
papanatas, *pl.* -tas *m.* simpleton, ninny.
papandujo, -ja *adj.* coll. too soft, overripe.
papar *tr.* to eat without chewing.
páparo, -ra *m.* rustic, simpleton.
paparrucha *f.* fib, hoax, humbug. *2* nonsense, silliness.
papaveráceo, -a *adj.* BOT. papaveraceous.
papaya *f.* BOT. papaya [fruit].
papayo *m.* BOT. papaya tree.
papazgo *m.* papacy, papalty.
papel *m.* paper [material, piece of paper]: *~ blanco,* blank paper; *~ cuadriculado,* cross-section paper; *~ de barbas,* untrimmed handmade paper; *~ de calcar,* tracing paper; *~ de fumar,* cigarette paper; *~ de estraza,* coarse brown paper; *~ de lija,* sandpaper; *~ de seda,* tissue paper; *~ de tornasol,* litmus paper; *~ pintado,* wallpaper; *~ rayado,* ruled paper; *~ secante,* blotting paper; *~ sellado,* official stamped paper. *2* paper [document]: *~ de Estado,* government securities; *~ moneda,* paper money; *papeles mojados,* worthless documents. *3* COM. [collect.] the securities brought for sale to the stock market. *4* THEAT. part, rôle: *desempeñar el ~ de,* to act the part of. *5* rôle, function, duty, -character, figure: *hacer buen ~,* to acquit oneself well; *hacer ~,* to cut a figure. *6 pl.* papers [identity documents].

papelear *intr.* to rummage papers, to look through papers. *2* to cut a figure, to make a show.
papeleo *m.* looking through papers. *2* red tape.
papelera *f.* paper case. *2* waste basket.
papelería *f.* paper shop, stationery shop. *2* lot of papers.
papelero, -ra *adj.* [pertaining to] paper. *2* showing off. *3 m.-f.* paper manufacturer or dealer. *4* shower off.
papeleta *f.* slip of paper; card, file card, ticket; *~ de votación,* ballot.
papelista *m.* paper manufacturer. *2* paper dealer. *3* paper hanger.
papelito *m. dim.* small piece of paper. *2* curl paper.
papelón, -na *adj.* showing off. *2 m.* despicable writing or paper. *3* thin cardboard. *4* (Am.) raw sugar. *5 m.-f.* shower off.
papelonear *intr.* to make a vain show of power, influence, etc.
papelorio *m.* jumble of papers.
papelote, papelucho *m.* despicable writing or paper.
papera *f.* goitre. *2* mumps. *3 pl.* scrofula.
papila *f.* ANAT., BOT. papilla: *~ gustativa,* taste bud.
papilionáceo, -a *adj.* BOT. papilionaceous.
papilla *f.* pap [soft food].
papillote *f.* hair twisted in a curl paper.
papión *m.* ZOOL. papion.
papiro *m.* papyrus.
papirotada *f.,* **papirotazo** *m.* fillip.
papirote *m.* fillip. *2* fool, dolt.
papisa *f.* papess.
papista *adj.* Papistic. *2 adj.-n.* Papist.
papo *m.* ZOOL. dewlap. *2* crop, craw, maw [of birds]. *3* MED. goiter. *4* BOT. thistledown. *5* puff [in a slashed garment].
papú, *pl.* -púes *adj.-n.* Papuan.
papudo, -da *adj.* full-gorged [bird].
pápula *f.* MED. papule.
paquear *tr.* to snipe at.
paquebot, paquebote *m.* NAUT. packet boat.
paqueo *m.* sniping.
paquete *adj.* (Am.) dolled up. *2* (Am.) self-important. *3* (Am.) insincere. *4 m.* package, packet, pack, parcel: *por ~ postal,* by parcel post. *5* PAQUEBOTE.
paquetería *f.* COM. smallwares sold in packages.
paquidermo *m.* ZOOL. pachyderm.
Paquita *f. pr. n.* coll. Fanny.
Paquito *m. pr. n.* coll. Frank.
par *adj.* like, equal. *2* even [number]: *pares o nones,* odd or even [game]. *3 m.* pair, brace, couple, set of two. *4* PHYS., MECH. ELECT. couple. *5* peer, equal: *sin ~,* peerless, unequaled. *6* peer [nobleman]. *7* ARCH. principal rafter. *8* COM. par: *a la ~,* at par. *9 a la ~,* or *al ~,* equally, on a par, in the same manner; at the same time. *10 abierto de ~ en ~,* wide open [door, etc.].
para *prep.* for, to, in order to: *~ que,* in order that, so that; *¿~ qué?,* what for? *2* for, to [introducing the indirect object]: *lo compró ~ ella,* he bought it for her; *ha sido bueno ~ ella,* he has been good to her. *3* toward [as a share for the support or payement of]. *4* by, to, on [indicating future time]: *~ entonces,* by then; *lo aplazaron ~ el lunes,* they postponed it to Monday; *pagará ~ Navidad,* he'll pay on Christmas. *5 ~ con,* toward, with, compared with. *6 ~ eso,* for that. *7 ~ mí, ~ sí,* to myself, to himself or herself; *pensé ~ mí,* I thought to myself; *estar ~,* to be on the point

of; to be about [to do something]. *8 no estar* ~, to be in no mood for.

parabién *m.* congratulation, felicitation: *dar el* ~, to congratulate, felicitate.

parábola *f.* parable. *2* GEOM. parabola.

parabólico, -ca *adj.* parabolic.

paraboloide *m.* GEOM. paraboloid.

parabrisas, *pl.* **-sas** *m.* AUTO. windscreen, windshield.

paracaídas, *pl.* **-das** *m.* parachute.

paracaidista *m.* parachuter, parachutist. *2* MIL. paratrooper.

Paracleto, Paráclito *m. pr. n.* Paraclete, Holy Ghost.

parachispas, *pl.* **-pas** *m.* ELECT. spark arrester.

parachoques, *pl.* **-ques** *m.* AUTO. bumper.

parada *f.* stop, halt, standstill, stay: ~ *en seco,* dead stop. *2* stop [of a bus, tram, etc.]. *3* pause. *4* post [for keeping horses for relays]. *5* stud farm. *6* irrigation dam. *7* stake, bid [in gambling]. *8* SPORT. catch [of the ball]. *9* parry. *10* parade [muster of troops]. *11* ~ *de coches,* cabstand.

paradera *f.* sluice gate. *2* fishing seine.

paradero *s.* whereabouts. *2* stopping place. *3* end [last point, place, state, etc., to which a thing has come].

paradigma *m.* paradigm.

paradisíaco, -ca *adj.* paradisiacal.

parado, -da *adj.* stopped, arrested, motionless. *2* slow, awkward, timid. *3* unoccupied, unemployed [person]. *4* shut down [factory]. *5* *m. pl.* unemployed, unemployed people.

paradoja *f.* paradox.

paradójico, -ca; paradojo, -ja *adj.* paradoxical.

parador *m.* inn, hosterly, tavern, roadhouse.

parafina *f.* parafin.

parafrasear *tr.* to paraphrase.

paráfrasis, *pl.* **-sis** *f.* paraphrase.

paragoge *f.* GRAM. paragoge.

paraguas, *pl.* **-guas** *m.* umbrella.

Paraguay *m. pr. n.* GEOG. Paraguay.

paraguayo, -ya *adj.-n.* Paraguayan.

paragüería *f.* umbrella shop.

paragüero, -ra *m.-f.* umbrella maker or seller. *2 m.* umbrella stand.

parahuso *m.* pump drill.

paraíso *m.* paradise: ~ *terrenal,* Paradise, Garden of Eden.

paraje *m.* spot, place.

paral *m.* putlog. *2* scaffold prop.

paraláctico, -ca *adj.* parallactic.

paralaje, paralasis, paralaxi *m.* ASTR. parallax.

paralelepípedo *m.* GEOM. parallelepiped.

paralelismo *m.* parallelism.

paralelo, -la *adj.* parallel. *2 m.* parallel [comparison]. *3* ELECT., GEOG. parallel. *4 f.* GEOM., FORT. parallel. *5 f. pl.* GYMN. parallel bars.

paralelogramo *m.* GEOM. parallelogram.

parálisis, *pl.* **-sis** *f.* MED. paralysis.

paraliticarse *ref.* MED. to become paralyzed.

paralítico, -ca *adj.-n.* MED. paralytic.

paralización *f.* paralyzation. *2* COM. stagnation. *3* stoppage [of the traffic].

paralizador, -ra *adj.* paralyzing.

paralizar *tr.* to paralise. *2* to stop, immobilize. *3* COM. to make stagnant. *4 ref.* to become paralyzed. *5* COM. to stagnate.

paralogismo *m.* LOG. paralogism.

paramentar *tr.* to adorn, bedeck.

paramento *m.* adornment, ornament; hangings. *2*

ARCH. face [of a wall]. *4* ECCL. *paramentos sacerdotales,* vestments.

paramera *f.* bleak, barren country.

parámetro *m.* GEOM. parameter.

páramo *m.* paramo, moor, bleak windy spot.

parangón *m.* parallel, comparison.

parangonar *tr.* to parallel, compare.

paraninfo *m.* paranymph. *2* harbiguer of felicity. *3* hall, auditorium [of university].

paranoia *f.* MED. paranoia.

paranoico, -ca *adj.-n.* MED. paranoiac, paranoic.

parapetarse *ref.* to shelter behind a parapet. *2* to protect oneself.

parapeto *m.* parapet [low wall or railing]. *2* FORT. parapet, breastwork.

parapoco, *pl.* **-poco** *m.-f.* dull, timid person.

1) **parar** *m.* lansquenet [card game].

2) **parar** *tr.* to stop, arrest, detain, check. *2* to prepare, get ready. *3* to stake [at gambling]. *4* HUNT. to point [game]. *5* to put [in a state]. *6* FENC. to parry. *7* SPORT. to catch [a ball]. *8* (Am.) to stand, set upright. *9* ~ *atención a,* to notice; ~ *mientes en,* to consider, reflect on. *10* *intr.-ref.* to stop [cease to go on]. *11* *intr.* to stop, cease [in action or operation]. *12* [of a train, bus, etc.] to stop. *13* to stop, to put up, to stay, to lodge. *14* to come into the possession of, to end in; finally to get to. *16* to be ready to face a danger. *17* to stop, desist. *18* (Am.) to stand up. *19* *pararse a,* to stop to, to pause to.

pararrayos, *pl.* **-yos** *m.* lightning rod. *2* lightning arrester.

paraselene *f.* METEOR. paraselene, mock moon.

parasitario, -ria *adj.* parasitic(al.

parasiticida *adj.-m.* parasiticide.

parasitismo *m.* parasitiom.

parásito, -ta *adj.* parasitic. *2 m.* BIOL. parasite. *3* parasite, hanger-on. *4 pl.* RADIO strays: *parásitos atmosféricos,* atmospherics, static.

parasitología *f.* parasitology.

parasol *m.* parasol, sunshade. *2* BOT. umbel.

parata *f.* AGR. step terrace.

paratífico, -ca *adj.* paratyphoid.

paratifoidea *f.* MED. paratyphoid fever.

parca *f.* MYTH. Parca, fate. *2* poet. Death.

parcamente *adv.* sparingly, scantily.

parcela *f.* lot, parcel [piece of land]. *2* particle.

parcelar *tr.* to parcel, divide [land] in lots.

parcelario, -ria *adj.* pertaining to parcels of land.

parcial *adj.* partial [not complete]. *2* partial, biased. *3 m.-f.* partisan, follower.

parcialidad *f.* partiality, bias. *2* faction, party; clique. *3* friendship, favour. *4* affableness.

parco, -ca *adj.* frugal, sparing, scanty. *2* moderate, parsimonious.

parchazo *m.* NAUT. bang of a sail against the mast. *2* coll. trick, deception.

parche *m.* PHARM. patch, plaster. *2* patch [stuck on something]. *3* MUS. drumhead. *4* MUS. drum. *5* daub, botch.

parchís *m.* parchesi.

pardal *adj.* country [people]. *2 m.* ORN. sparrow. *3* ORN. linnet. *4* ZOOL. leopard. *5* coll. sly fellow.

pardear *intr.* to be or show brown or drab.

pardela *f.* ORN. a small sea gull.

¡pardiez! *interj.* coll. by Jove!

pardillo *adj.-m.* rustic. *2 m.* ORN. linnet.

pardo, -da *adj.* brown, drab, reddish gray. *2* dark, cloudy. *3* flat [voice]. *4* *gramática parda,* shrewdness, know-how.

pardusco, -ca *adj.* brownish, drabbish, grayish.

pareado *m.* couplet [pair of verses].
parear *tr.* to pair, match, arrange in couples.
parecencia *f.* resemblance, likeness.
1) **parecer** *m.* opinion, mind, advice. 2 looks, personal aspect: *ser de buen* ~, to be good looking. 3 appearance: *por el bien* ~, to save appearances.
2) **parecer** *intr.* to appear, show [become or be visible]. 2 to turn up [after having been lost]. 3 to appear, seem, look like. 4 *impers.* to seem, look like, strike; ~ *mentira*, it seems incredible; *según parece, al parecer*, as it seems. 5 *ref.* to resemble, resemble each other, be alike. 6 *parecerse a*, to resemble, be like. ¶ CONJUG. like *agradecer*.
parecido, -da *adj.* resembling, similar [to], like. 2 *bien* ~, good-looking; *mal* ~, bad-looking. 3 *m.* resemblance, likeness.
pared *f.* MAS., ANAT., BOT., MIN., PHYS. wall: ~ *maestra*, main wall; ~ *medianera*, party wall; ~ *por medio* [of horses], adjoining, contiguous. 2 partition, brick partition. 3 wall [something resembling a wall].
paredaño, -ña *adj.* adjoining, separate by a wall.
paredón *m.* augm. large wall. 2 standing wall.
pareja *f.* pair, couple, yoke, team. 2 pair of soldiers or policemen. 3 dancing partner. 4 match [one of two equal or corresponding things]. 5 *pl.* GAMES doubles. 6 pair [at cards]. 7 *correr parejas*, to be on a par, to go together.
parejo, -ja *adj.* equal, like. 2 even, smooth. 3 *por* ~ or *por un* ~, alike, in like manner.
parénquima *m.* BOT., ZOOL. parenchyma.
parentela *f.* kindred, kinsfolk, relations.
parentesco *m.* kinship, relationship.
paréntesis *m.* parenthesis: *entre* ~, *por* ~, parenthetically; by the bye.
pareo *m.* pairing, coupling.
paresa *f.* peeress.
paresia, paresis, *f.* MED. paresis.
parezco, parezca, etc. *irr.* V. PARECER.
pargo *m.* PAGRO.
parhelia *f.,* **parhelio** *m.* METEOR. parhelion.
parhilera *f.* ARCH. ridgepole, ridgepiece.
paria *m.* pariah, outcast.
parias *f.* tribute, homage. 2 ANAT. placenta.
parida *f.* woman lately delivered of a baby.
paridad *f.* parity, equality; comparison.
paridera *adj.* prolific [female]. 2 *f.* parturition [of cattle].
pariente, -ta *m.-f.* relation, relative, kinsman, kinswoman.
parietal *adj.* parietal. 2 *m.* ANAT. parietal bone.
parietaria *f.* BOT. wall pellitory.
parihuela *f.,* or **parihuelas** *f. pl.* handbarrow. 2 litter, stretcher.
paripinado, -da *adj.* BOT. paripinnate.
parir *tr.* to give birth to, to bring forth. 2 *intr.* to be delivered of a baby. 3 [of an animal] to bring forth young.
Paris *m. pr. n.* MYTH. Paris.
París *m. pr. n.* GEOG. Paris.
parisién, parisiense *adj.-n.* Parisian.
parisino, -na *adj.* Parisian.
parla *f.* facility in speaking, loquacity. 2 chatter.
parlador, -ra *m.-f.* chatterer.
parlamentar *intr.* to talk, converse. 2 to parley [discuss terms].
parlamentario, -ria *adj.-n.* parliamentary, parliamentarian.
parlamentarismo *m.* parliamentarism.

parlamento *m.* Parliament. 2 legislative body. 3 speech, address. 4 THEAT. speech. 5 parley.
parlanchín, -na *adj.* chattering, babbling. 2 *m.-f.* chatterer, babbler.
parlar *intr.* to speak fluently. 2 to chatter, jabber, babble. 3 [of a bird] to talk.
parlería *f.* loquacity. 2 tale, gossip.
parlero, -ra *adj.* talkative. 2 babbling. 3 expressive [eyes]. 4 garrulous, warbling, bubbling.
parlón, -na *adj.* loquacious, garrulous.
parlotear *intr.* coll. to prattle, prate, chatter.
parloteo *m.* prattle, idle talk.
Parnaso *m.* GEOG., MYTH., LIT. Parnassus.
parné *m.* coll. money.
paro *m.* MACH. stop, stopping. 2 suspension of work or action; layoff, shutdown; ~ *forzoso*, unemployment. 3 ORN. titmouse.
parodia *f.* parody.
parodiar *tr.* to parody.
parodista *m.-f.* parodist.
parola *f.* coll. fluency, volubility. 2 coll. idle talk.
paronimia *f.* paronymy.
paronomasia *f.* paronomasia.
parótida *f.* ANAT. parotid gland. 2 MED. mumps.
paroxismo *m.* MED. paroxysm. 2 extremity [of pain, feeling, passion, etc.].
paroxítono *adj.* PHONET. paroxytone.
parpadear *intr.* to blink, wink [move the eyelids].
parpar *intr.* [of a duck] to quack.
parque *m.* park, garden, gardens: ~ *zoológico*, zoological garden. 2 MIL. park. 3 assemblage of engines, cars, etc., for a public service. 4 (Am.) AUTO. parking area.
parquedad *f.* sparingness, paucity.
parra *f.* grapevine [esp. a large one with spreading arms]. 2 earthen jar, honey jar.
parrado, -da *adj.* spreading [tree].
parrafada *f.* confidential chat.
párrafo *m.* paragraph. 2 paragraph mark. 3 chat.
parral *m.* bower of grapevines. 2 large earthen jar.
parranda *f.* spree, revel: *ir de* ~, to go out on a spree, to revel. 2 group of merry serenaders.
parricida *adj.* parricidal. 2 *m.-f.* parricide [person].
parricidio *m.* parricide [act].
parrilla *f.* gridiron, grill, broiler. 2 grate [of a furnace]. 3 earthen jug.
parrocha *f.* small sardines.
párroco *m.* ECCL. parson, parish priest.
parroquia *f.* ECCL. parish. 2 parish church. 3 congregation of a parish. 4 COM. custom, customers, clientele.
parroquial *adj.* parochial. 2 *f.* parish church.
parroquiano, -na *m.-f.* ECCL. parishioner. 3 COM. customer, client, patron.
parsi *adj.* Parsic. 2 *m.-f.* Parsee, Parsi.
parsimonia *f.* parsimony, economy. 2 moderation.
parsimonioso, -sa *adj.* parsimonious, economical.
parte *f.* part [portion, piece, section, division]: ~ *de la oración*, part of the speech; *en gran* ~, largely; *en* ~, in part, partly; *por partes*, by parts. 2 part [share, concern, interest]: *ir a la* ~, to go shares; *llevar uno la mejor*, or *la peor* ~, to have the best, or the worse, of it; *tomar* ~ *en*, to take part in, to share in; *por* ~ *de*, on the part of. 3 hand [share in action]: *tener* ~ *en*, to have a hand in. 4 construction, interpretation; *tomar a mala* ~, to take in evil part; to put a bad construction to. 5 party, part, side [in dispute]: *estar de* ~ *de*, to support; to side with. 6 LAW party. 7 THEAT. part, rôle. 8 MUS. part. 9 part [of the

body]. *10* part, place, region, side, direction: *de ~ a ~*, through; from side to side; *en ninguna ~*, nowhere; *por todas partes*, everywhere. *11 de algún tiempo a esta ~*, for some time past. *12 de ~ de*, from, by courtesy of; in the name of. *13 de ~ de padre*, on the father's side. *14 por una ~*, on one hand; *por otra ~*, on the other hand. *15 pl.* abilities, gifts. *16* parts, genitals [also called *partes pudendas* or *vergonzosas*]. *17* telegram, dispatch. *18* official communication, communiqué. *19* report [statement]: *dar ~*, to report, inform. *20 adv.* partly.

partear *tr.* to assist [women] in childbirth.
parteluz *m.* ARCH. mullion.
partenogénesis *f.* BIOL. parthenogenesis.
Partenón *m.* Parthenon.
partera *f.* midwife.
parterre *m.* flower bed.
partesana *f.* partisan [kind of halberd].
partición *f.* partition, distribution. *2* LAW partition. *3* MATH. division.
participación *f.* participation, share. *2* notification, announcement. *3* COM. copartnership.
participante *adj.* participating. *2* notifying. *3 m.-f.* participant, sharer. *4* notifier.
partícipe *adj.* participant, sharing. *2 m.-f.* participant, participator, sharer.
participial *adj.* GRAM. participial.
participio *m.* GRAM. participle.
partícula *f.* particle.
particular *adj.* particular, peculiar, personal, private. *2* particular, noteworthy. *3* extraordinary, odd. *4 m.* private individual. *5* particular, item, point. *6 en ~*, in particular.
particularidad *f.* particularity. *2* friendship, favour [shown to someone].
particularizar *tr.* to particularize. *2 ref.* to be distinguished or characterized [by].
partida *f.* departure, leave, starting. *2* fig. departure, death. *3* entry, record [in a register of births, marriages, etc.]. *4* certificate [of birth, marriage, death]. *5* BOOKKEEP. entry, item: *~ doble*, double entry; *~ simple*, simple entry. *6* item [in a bill, invoice, etc.]. *7* COM. lot, shipment, consignment. *8* game [at cards, chess, etc.]; match [at billiards], set [at tennis]. *9* squad, gang, band; band of armed persons. *10* excursion, party: *~ de campo*, outing, picnic; *~ de caza*, hunting. *11* part, place. *12* turn, deed [as it affects another]: *mala ~*, bad turn. *13 tragarse la ~*, to guess another's intentions.
partidario, -ria *adj.* partisan, supporting. *2* advocating, being for, [ideas, measures, etc.]. *3 m.-f.* partisan, follower, adherent, supporter. *4* advocate [of an idea, system, etc.].
partidismo *m.* partisanship, party spirit.
partidista *adj.* having a party spirit; partisan.
partido, -da *p. p.* of PARTIR. *2 m.* party [body of persons united in a cause, opinion, etc.]. *3* profit, advantage. *4* favour, support; popularity. *5* SPORT. team. *6* SPORT. game, match. *7* GAMES, SPORT. odds [equalizing allowance]. *8* deal, agreement. *9* decision, resolve, measure: *tomar un ~*, to make up one's mind. *10* side [in dispute, etc.]: *tomar ~*, to take sides. *11* territorial division or district. *12* match [person considered from the point of view of marriage]. *13 darse a ~*, to desist, yield.
partidor *m.* divider, separator. *2* cleaver, spliter. *3* ARITH. divisor.
partimiento *m.* partition, division.

partir *tr.* to divide [in parts], to split, cleave, cut: *~ por la mitad*, to divide in two. *2* to crack [a nut.]. *3* to divide, distribute, share. *4* MATH. to divide. *5 intr.-ref.* to depart, leave, set out, start: *~ para*, to leave for. *6 intr. ~ de*, to take [something] as the basis or starting point; to start from, to reckon from. *7 a ~ de*, from [some specified time, amount, etc.] onward. *8 ref.* to divide, part [be separated]. *9* to break, split. *10* to share [use jointly].
partitivo, -va *adj.* GRAM. partitive.
partitura *f.* MUS. score.
1) **parto, -ta** *adj.-n.* Parthian.
2) **parto** *m.* parturition, labour, childbirth, delivery: *estar de ~*, to be in labour. *2* production, product, offspring: *~ del ingenio*, brain child.
parturienta *adj.* parturient [woman]. *2 f.* woman in confinement.
parva *f.* light breakfast [on fast days]. *2* grain spread in the threshing floor. *3* heap, pile.
parvedad, parvidad *f.* smallness, shortness.
parvo, -va *adj.* small, little, short.
parvulez *f.* smallness. *2* simplicyty, innocence.
párvulo, -la *adj.* small. *2* simple, innocent. *3* humble. *4 m.-f.* little child.
pasa *f.* raisin: *~ de Corinto*, currant. *2* kink [of a Negro's hair]. *3* NAUT. channel.
pasable *adj.* PASADERO.
pasacalle *m.* MUS. a lively march.
pasada *f.* passage, passing: *de ~*, on the way; hastly. *2* SEW. long stitch. *3* WEAV. pick. *4* coll. *mala ~*, mean trick.
pasadera *f.* stepping stone. *2* footbridge.
pasadero, -ra *adj.* passable [capable of being passed]. *2* passable, tolerable. *3* sufferable. *4 m.* PASADERA.
pasadizo *m.* alley, passage, corridor, aisle, hall.
pasado, -da *adj.* past, gone by. *2* elapsed [time]. *3* last [week, month, year]. *4* overripe, spoiled [fruit]; tainted [meat]. *5 ~ de moda*, out-of-fashion, out-of-date. *6 ~ mañana*, day after tomorrow. *7 m.* past [past time; person's life].
pasador *m.-f.* one who passes something across; smuggler. *2 m.* bolt [door-fastening]. *3* pin [of hinge]. *4* hairpin, bodkin. *5* JEW. ring for a necktie or neckcloth. *6* MIL. a safety pin with a bar for wearing medals. *7* strainer; colander.
pasagonzalo *m.* coll. tap, flick, light blow.
pasaje *m.* passage; passing. *2* passage money. *3* passage way, way. *4* passage [on a ship]. *5* passengers in a ship. *6* NAUT. strait [between land and island]. *7* passage [in a speech or literary work]. *8* lane, alley, arcade. *9* MUS. transition.
pasajero, -ra *adj.* frequented [thoroughfare]. *2* passing, transient, transitory. *3 m.-f.* passenger.
pasamanería *f.* passementerie.
pasamano *m.* passement, passementerie. *2* handrail. *3* NAUT. gangway [in ancient ships].
pasante *adj.* HER. passant. *2 m.* assistant [of a teacher, lawyer or doctor].
pasantía *f.* profession or practice of a PASANTE.
pasapán *m.* coll. gullet, windpipe.
pasapasa *m.* legerdemain.
pasaporte *m.* passport. *2* fig. free license.
1) **pasar (un buen)** *m.* competency, sufficiency of means for living.
2) **pasar** *tr.* to pass, transfer [something to a place or person; someone to a place, post, etc.], to transmit; to promote. *2* to carry across. *3* to smuggle [goods]. *4* to pass, hand, hand over. *5* to pass [move over something]. *6* to pass [a

thread, a rope through or round something]. *7 to pass* [through a filter, sieve, etc.]. *8 to pass, go over, cross. 9 to pass by, walk past. 10 to pass, surpass. 11 to pass, transgress* [a limit]. *12 to penetrate, pierce. 13 to swallow* [food or drink]. *14 to go through, experience, suffer. 15 to pass by, omit, overlook. 16 to pass, spend* [time]. *17 to study, read* [a lesson, a book]. *18 to dry* [fruit]. *19 ~ a cuchillo*, to put to the sword. *20 ~ el rato*, to kill the time. *21 ~ lista*, to call the roll. *22 pasarlo*, to be; do [as regards health]; have a time; *pasarlo bien*, to have a good time; *que lo pase usted bien*, good-bye. *23 ~ por alto*, to omit; to overlook. *24 ~ por las armas*, to shoot [as penalty]. *25 intr.* to pass, go, move, proceed [along, across, down, over, on, etc.]; to have or effect passage; to be transported. *26 to pass, go by. 27 to pass, circulate, be accepted* [money, etc.]. *28 to pass, flow, run. 29 to pass* [from one state to another]. *30 to live. 31 to pass away, die. 32* [of a garment, etc.] to last. *33 to pass* [come to and end]. *34* [of time] to pass, elapse. *35 to pass* [at cards or dominoes]. *36 to enter, go, come in or into. 37 ~ a* [with an inf.], to proceed to [do, etc.]. *38 ~ de*, to go beyond; to exceed. *39 ~ de largo*, to pass without stopping. *40 ~ por*, to pass or go along, by, through, etc.]; to be held, be regarded as; to call at [a place]. *41 ~ por encima de*, to disregard [rules, difficulties, etc.]. *42 ~ por la imaginación*, to cross the mind. *43 ~ sin*, to do without. *44 ir pasando*, to get along. *45 impers.* to pass, happen; to be the matter: *¿qué pasa?*, what is the matter?; *¿qué le pasa?*, what is the matter with him? *46 ref.* to go over to another party. *47 to cease, finish. 48 to be forgotten. 49 to lose its force. 50* [of fruit] to become spoiled, overripe; [of meat] to become tainted; [of fire] to burn out. *51* [of a vessel] to leak. *52* [of a bolt, etc.] to be loose. *53 pasarse de*, to be too; *pasarse de cortés*, to be too polite. *54 pasarse sin*, to do without.

pasarela *f.* footbridge. *2* NAUT. gangplank. *3* NAUT. bridge [on a ship].

pasatiempo *m.* pastime.

pasavante *m.* NAUT. safe-conduct.

pascua *f.* Passover. *2* ECCL. Easter and each of the Church holidays: Twelfth-day, Pentecost and Christmas: *~ de Resurrección*, or *florida*, Easter; *~ de Pentecostés*, Pentecost. *3 pl. Pascuas de Navidad*, Christmas holidays; *estar como unas pascuas*, to be as merry as a cricket; *felices Pascuas*, merry Christmas.

pascual *adj.* paschal.

pascuilla *f.* first Sunday after Easter.

pase *m.* pass [permit, ticket, etc.]. *2* exequatur. *3* pass [of hand]. *4* FENC. pass, feint. *5* CARDS, FOOTBALL pass. *6* BULLF. instance of inciting the bull and letting it pass by.

paseante *m.-f.* stroller, promenader.

pasear *intr.-ref.* to pace; to walk about, stroll, saunter, take a walk; to ride, drive or go on a boat for pleasure, to promenade. *2 tr.* to walk [a horse]. *3* to take out to walk; to carry around with oneself; to promenade. *4 ref.* to be idle.

paseata *f.* coll. walk, promenade; riding.

paseo *m.* walk, stroll; pleasure ride, drive or boating; promenade; *dar un ~*, to take a walk, ride, etc.; *mandar a ~*, to send about one's business. *2* public walk, parade, mall, promenade. *3* avenue, boulevard.

pasera *f.* place for drying fruit. *2* drying of fruit.

pasibilidad *f.* passibility.

pasible *adj.* passible.

pasicorto, -ta *adj.* walking with short steps.

pasilargo, -ga *adj.* walking with long steps.

pasillo *m.* corridor, narrow passage. *2* aisle [passage between rows of seats].

pasión *f.* passion [in every sense except rage, wrath]. *2* (cap.) Christ's Passion.

pasionaria *f.* BOT. passionflower.

pasionero, pasionista *m.* ECCL. Passion singer.

pasito *m. dim.* short step: *~ a ~*, very leisurely or gently. *2 adv.* gently, softly.

pasitrote *m.* short trot.

pasividad *f.* passiveness, passivity.

pasivo, -va *adj.* passive. *2* unresponsive. *3* GRAM. past, perfect [participle]; passive [voice]. *4 haber pasivo*, retirement pension. *5 clases pasivas*, pensionaries. *6 m.* COM. liabilities.

pasmar *tr.* to chill. *2* to benumb, paralyse. *3* to astonish, amaze. *4 ref.* to chill [be chilled]. *5* to be astonished or amazed.

pasmarota, pasmarotada *f.* coll. exaggerated show of astonishment, wonder or surprise.

pasmo *m.* MED. chill, cold. *2* MED. tetanus. *3* astonishment, wonder. *4* astonishing thing, prodigy.

pasmoso, -sa *adj.* astonishing, marvellous.

1) **paso, -sa** *adj.* dried [fruit].

2) **paso** *m.* step, pace, footstep: *dar un ~*, to take a step, *seguir los pasos a*, to trail, watch [someone]; *seguir los pasos de*, to follow in the footsteps of; *volver uno sobre sus pasos*, to retrace one's steps; *a cada ~*, fig. at every turn. *2* step [in dancing]. *3* step [short distance; degree in progress]; *a pocos pasos*, at a short distance; *a este ~*, at this rate; *a grandes pasos*, apace; *por sus pasos contados*, by its regular course. *4* step, pace, gait: *apretar el ~*, to hasten one's steps; *aflojar el ~*, to slow down; *marcar el ~*, MIL. to mark time. *5* step [of stairs]. *6* step, move, measure. *7* passage [passing; migration; transition; progress]; *estar de ~*, to be a transient; *al ~ que*, fig. while; *de ~*, in passing; by the way. *8* passage, way: *abrir ~*, to make way; *dar ~*, to afford a passage; to give place; *salir al ~*, to meet or stop on the way. *9* incident, event, situation: *salir del ~*, to get out of the difficulty. *10* each of the stages of the Christ's Passion; statue or group representing it. *11* THEAT. very short piece. *12* pass, strait. *13* exequatur. *14* basting stitch. *15* MECH. pitch [of nut; screw, etc.]. *16* RLY. *~ a nivel*, grade crossing. *17 adv.* gently, softly.

pasquín *m.* pasquinade or political writing posted in a public place.

pasta *f.* paste [soft, plastic mixture], mash. *2* paste, dough [for pastry]. *3* pulp [for making paper]. *4* coll. dough, money. *5* (Am.) cookie. *6* BOOKB. board binding. *7 ~ para sopa*, alimentary paste. *8 buena ~*, mild disposition.

pastadero *m.* pasture, grazing field.

pastaflora *f.* sweetmeat of flour, sugar and eggs.

pastar *intr.* [of sheep or cattle] to pasture, graze. *2 tr.* to pasture, graze [lead or put to pasture].

pastel *m.* COOK. pie, pasty. *2* cake, piece of pastry. *3* fig. secret agrement or compromise. *4* BOT. woad. *5* PAINT. pastel.

pastelear *intr.* to trim, compromise [politically].

pasteleo *m.* secret dealing, trimming, temporization, compromising [in politics].

pastelería f. pastry. 2 pastry shop. 3 pastry cooking.
pastelero, -ra m.-f. pastry cook. 2 POL. trimmer, temporizer.
pastelillo m. dim. small pie, patty.
pastelista m. pastelist, pastellist.
pasterización f. pasteurization.
pasterizar tr. to pasteurize.
pastilla f. pastil, pastille, tablet, lozenge, drop. 2 cake [of soap, chocolate, etc.].
pastinaca f. BOT. parsnip. 2 ICHTH. sting ray.
pastizal m. pasture ground for horses.
pasto m. pasturing, gazing. 2 pasture [herbage for cattle or sheep]; pasture ground. 3 food [for cattle]. 4 fig. nourishment, pabulum. 5 a todo ~, abundantly, unrestrictedly.
pastor m. shepher; herdsman. 2 ~ protestante, pastor, protestant minister.
pastora f. shepherdess.
pastoral adj. pastoral [of shepherds]. 2 LIT., ECCL. pastoral. 3 f. pastoral [play]. 4 ECCL. pastoral [letter]. 5 MUS. pastorale.
pastorear tr. to shepherd [flocks or souls].
pastorela f. sepherd's song. 2 LIT. pastourelle.
pastoreo m. shepherding, pasturing.
pastoril adj. pastoral [of shepherds].
pastosidad f. pastiness, doughiness. 2 mellowness [of the voice]. 3 PAINT. pastosity.
pastoso, -sa adj. pasty, doughy. 2 mellow [voice]. 3 PAINT. pastose.
pastura f. pasture, fodder. 2 pasture ground.
pata f. paw, foot, hoof and leg [of animals]. 2 fig. leg [of human being]: estirar la ~, coll. to kick the bucket, to die: meter la ~, coll. to make a blunder; a cuatro patas, on all fours; a la ~ coja, hopping; a ~, on foot, walking. 3 leg [of a table, etc.]: ~ de banco, fig. absurdity, stupid remark; patas arriba, upside down, topsy-turvy. 4 ORN. duck [female of a drake]. 5 ~ de gallo, fig. crow's feet [wrinkles at outer corner of eye]; coll. absurdity, stupid remark. 6 tener mala ~, to have bad luck.
patacón m. peso, silver dollar.
patache m. NAUT. tender.
patada f. kick [blow with the foot]: dar la ~ a, to kick out; a patadas, in abundance. 2 stamp [stamping the foot]. 3 footstep, footprint.
patagón, -na adj.-n. Patagonian.
patalear intr. to kick about violently. 2 to stamp one's feet [with rage, annoyance, etc.].
pataleo m. violent kicking. 2 stamping one's feet. 3 patter, tramp [sound].
pataleta f. fit or convulsion; feigned fit or convulsion.
patán m. rustic, churl, boor.
patarata f. rubbish, trash, paltry trifle, nonsense. 2 ridiculous affectation of feeling; overpoliteness.
patas m. coll. the Devil.
patata f. BOT. potato. 2 sweet potato [tuber].
patatero, -ra adj. potato-eating. 2 coll. up from the ranks [military officer]. 3 m.-f. potato seller.
patatín, patatán (que) coll. subterfuges.
patatús m. coll. fit, fainting fit.
patear tr. coll. to kick, beat with the feet. 2 coll. to give a rough dressing down; to treat [someone] roughly. 3 coll. [of an audience] to express disapproval of by stamping the feet. 4 intr. coll. to stamp the feet [in anger, etc.]. 5 coll. to be very angry.
patena f. ECCL. paten.

patentar tr. to patent.
patente adj. patent, clear, evident. 2 f. patent. 3 licence, certificate. 4 MIL. commission. 5 NAUT. ~ de navegación, certificate of registry; ~ de sanidad, bill of health.
patentizar tr. to show, reveal, make evident.
pateo m. stamping the feet.
paternal adj. paternal, fatherly.
paternidad f. paternity, fatherhood. 2 authorship. 3 ECCL. title given to a father [monk].
paterno, -na adj. paternal; from the male line.
paternalmente adv. paternally, fatherly.
paternóster m. Lord's Prayer, paternoster.
pateta m. coll. old Nick, the Devil.
patético, -ca adj. pathetic.
patetismo m. patheticalness.
patiabierto, -ta adj. bowlegged.
patialbo, -ba; patiblanco, -ca adj. white-footed.
patibulario, -ria adj. gallows, hideous, sinister [look, face, etc.]. 2 hair-raising.
patíbulo m. scaffold [for executions], gallows.
paticojo, -ja adj. lame, limping.
patidifuso, -sa adj. astonished, astounded, amazed.
patiestevado, -da adj. bandy-legged, bowlegged.
patihendido, -da adj. cloven-footed, cloven-hoofed.
patilla f. a posture of the left hand in playing the guitar. 2 chape [of buckle]. 3 SEW. pocket flap. 4 CARP. tenon. 5 pl. whiskers, mutton chops, sideburns.
patillas m. coll. old Nick, the Devil.
patín m. ORN. a kind of petrel. 2 skate [implement]: ~ de ruedas, roller skate. 3 AER. skid. 4 ELECT. contact shoe.
pátina f. patina.
patinadero m. skating place, skating ring.
patinador, -ra m.-f. skater.
patinaje m. skating. 2 skidding [of a vehicle].
patinar tr. to patinate. 2 intr. to skate. 3 [of vehicles] to skid, slip on the road. 4 coll. to make a blunder.
patinazo m. skid, sudden skid. 2 coll. blunder.
patinillo m. dim. small court or courtyard.
patio m. court, yard, courtyard, campus. 2 THEAT. pit.
patita f. dim. female duckling. 2 small paw, foot or leg: poner de patitas en la calle, coll. to throw out; to dismiss, to discharge.
patitieso, -sa adj. coll. stiff-legged. 2 coll. astonished, astounded, amazed. 3 stiff, haughty.
patito m. male duckling.
patituerto, -ta adj. crook-legged.
patizambo, -ba adj. knock-kneed.
pato m. ORN. duck: ~ de flojel, eider duck. 2 ORN. drake [male duck].
patochada f. blunder, stupidity, nonsense.
patogenia f. MED. pathogenesis, pathogeny.
patógeno, -na adj. MED. pathogenic, pathogenous.
patojo, -ja adj. lame, waddling like a duck.
patología f. pathology.
patólogo m. pathologist.
patoso, -sa adj. dull and cheaply witty [person].
patraña f. lie, falsehood, fabulous story, humbug.
patria f. one's country, native country, fatherland: ~ celestial, heavenly home. 2 fig. home [of the arts, etc.].
patriarca m. patriarch.
patriarcado m. patriarchate.
patriarcal adj. patriarchal.
patriciado m. patriciate.

Patricio *m. pr. n.* Patrick.
patricio, -cia *adj.-n.* patrician.
patrimonio *m.* patrimony.
patrio, -tria *adj.* of one's country, native, home. *2* paternal [of the father].
patriota *m.-f.* patriot.
patriotería *f.* exaggerated patriotism, jingoism.
patriotero, -ra *adj.* jingoistic. *2 m.-f.* jingoist.
patriótico, -ca *adj.* patriotic.
patriotismo *m.* patriotism.
patrística *f.* ECCL. patristics.
patrocinador, -ra *adj.* patronizing, protecting. *2* RADIO., TELEV. sponsoring. *3 m.-f.* patron, protector. *4* RADIO., TELEV. sponsor.
patrocinar *tr.* to patronize, protect favour. *2* RADIO., telev. to sponsor.
patrocinio *m.* patronage, protection, favour, auspices. *2* RADIO., TELEV. sponsorship.
patrón, -na *m.-f.* patron, patroness, protector, protectress. *2* ECCL. patron saint. *3* host, hostess, landlord, landlady. *4* master, mistress, boss. *5 m.* NAUT. skipper. *6* pattern [for making things]. *7* standard [of measure; of money]: ~ *oro* gold standard.
patronal *adj.* patronal. *2* pertaining to employers, employers'. *3 f.* employers' association.
patronato *m.* ECCL. patronage. *2* the employers [as a class]. *3* board of trustees. *4* patronage [institution]; foundation.
patronazgo *m.* patronage.
patronear *tr.* NAUT. to skipper, command.
patronímico, -ca *adj.-m.* patronymic.
patrono, -na *m.-f.* PATRÓN 1, 2 & 4.
patrulla *f.* patrol. *2* coll. gang, band.
patrullar *intr.* to patrol.
patudo, -da *adj.* coll. big-footed, big-pawed.
patulea *f.* coll. disorderly soldiers. *2* coll. mob. *3* coll. gang of noisy brats.
patullar *intr.* to tramp wildly. *2* coll. to bustle around. *3* coll. to chat.
paúl *m.* bog, marsh, morass.
Paula *f. pr. n.* Pauline.
paular *m.* marsh, muddy hole.
paulatino, -na *adj.* slow, gradual.
Paulina *f. pr. n.* Pauline.
paupérrimo, -ma *adj. superl.* very poor.
pausa *f.* pause [temporary stop]. *2* MUS. rest.
pausado, -da *adj.* slow, calm, deliberate. *2 adv.* slowly, deliberately.
pausar *intr.* to make a pause. *2* to slow down.
pauta *f.* instrument for ruling paper. *2* guide lines [for writing]. *3* rule, model, standard [for action, conduct, policy].
pautado, -da *adj.* ruled [paper]. *2 m.* MUS. staff.
pautar *tr.* to rule [paper for writing or with the musical staff]. *2* to give rules or directions for.
pava *f.* ORN. turkey hen: ~ *real*, peahen; *pelar la* ~, coll. [of lovers] to talk by night at the window. *2* fig. dull ungraceful woman. *3* (Arg.) kettle, teapot.
pavada *f.* flock of turkeys. *2* inanity, triviality.
pavana *f.* pavan [dance].
pavero, -ra *m.-f.* turkey raiser or dealer. *2 m.* Andalusian broadbrimmed hat.
pavés *m.* pavis [large shield].
pavesa *f.* spark [of ignited substance], flying cinder or ember.
pavía *f.* BOT. pavy [clingstone peach].
pavimentación *f.* paving, flooring.
pavimentar *tr.* to pave, to floor.
pavimento *m.* pavement, floor.

pavipollo *m.* young turkey.
pavisoso, -sa *adj.* dull, graceless.
pavo *m.* ORN. turkey; turkey cock. *2* fig. dull, gullible man. *3* ORN. ~ *real*, peacock.
pavón *m.* ORN. peacock. *2* ENT. peacock butterfly. *3* bluing, blacking or browning [of iron or steel].
pavonar *tr.* to blue, black or brown [iron or steel].
pavonear *intr.-ref.* to strut, to show off.
pavor *m.* dread, fright, terror.
pavorde *m.* ECCL. provost.
pavorido, -da *adj.* terrified.
pavoroso, -sa *adj.* dreadful, frightful, terrific.
pavura *f.* PAVOR.
payador *m.* (Am.) PALLADOR.
payasada *f.* buffoonery, clownish act.
payaso *m.* clown, circus clown, merry-andrew.
payés, -sa *m.-f.* Catalan or Balearic peasant.
payo, -ya *m.-f.* rustic, churl.
paz *f.* peace [quiet; cessation of war; mental calm; state of friendliness]: *dejar en* ~, to leave alone; *que en* ~ *descanse*, may he rest in peace; *hacer las paces con*, to make peace with. *2* peacefulness. *3* ECCL. pax. *4 estar en* ~, to be even; to be quits. *5 interj.* peace!
pazguato, -ta *adj.* dolt, simpleton.
pazpuerca *f.* slattern, slut.
¡pche!, ¡pchs! *interj.* pshaw!
pe *f.* name of the letter *p: de* ~ *a pa*, from A to Z.
peaje *m.* toll [for the use of a public road].
peal *m.* foot [of a stocking]. *2* knitted legging.
peana, peaña *f.* base, foot, pedestal [for a figure, statue, etc.]. *2* altar step.
peatón *m.* walker, pedestrian. *2* rural postman.
pebete *m.* aromatic burning stick. *2* coll. stinker [thing].
pebetero *m.* perfume censer, perfume burner.
peca *f.* freckle.
pecadillo *m. dim.* peccadillo.
pecado *m.* sin: ~ *capital*, deadly or capital sin. *2* fig. defect, fault, excess, imperfection.
pecador, -ra *adj.* sinning, sinful. *2 m.-f.* sinner.
pecaminoso, -sa *adj.* sinful, wicked.
pecante *adj.* sinning, peccant. *2* excessive.
pecar *intr.* to sin. *2* ~ *por* or *de*, to have [some defect], to be too: *esto peca por*, or *de, corto*, this is too short.
pécari *m.* ZOOL. peccary.
pecatta minuta (Lat.) coll. peccadillo, slight fault.
pececillo *m. dim.* small fish.
peceño, -ña *adj.* pitchy.
pecera *f.* fish globe, fish bowl, aquarium.
pecezuelo *m. dim.* small foot. *2* small fish.
peciento, -ta *adj.* pitchy, pitch-coloured.
pecina *f.* slime, viscous mud. *2* PISCINA 1.
pecio *m.* NAUT. flotsam, jetsam, wreckage.
peciolo *m.* BOT. petiole.
pécora *f.* head of sheep [individual]. *2* coll. *buena* ~, *mala* ~, shrewd, wicked woman.
pecorear *tr.* to steal [cattle]. *2 intr.* MIL. to maraud, to loot.
pecoso, -sa *adj.* freckled, freckly, freckle-faced.
pectina *f.* CHEM. pectin.
pectoral *adj.* pectoral. *2 m.* pectoral [breastplate of Jewish high priest]. *3* ECCL. pectoral cross. *4* PHARM. pectoral.
pecuario, -ria *adj.* [pertaining to] cattle.
peculado *m.* LAW peculation.
peculiar *adj.* peculiar.
peculiaridad *f.* peculiarity.
peculio *m.* peculium. *2* fig. one's money.
pecunia *f.* money, cash.

pecuniario, -ria *adj.* pecuniary, financial.
pechar *tr.* to pay [as a tax or tribute]. *2* intr. ~ *con,* to accept, put up with [some disagreeable duty, work, etc.].
pechera *f.* chest protector. *2* front [of a shirt]; bosom [of dress]. *3* jabot, shirt, frill. *4* breast strap [of harness].
pechero, -ra *m.-f.* commoner, plebeian. *2 m.* bib.
pechina *f.* scallop, scallop shell. *2* ARCH. pendentive.
pechirrojo *m.* ORN. linnet.
pechisacado, -da *adj.* coll. vain, arrogant.
pecho *m.* ANAT., ZOOL. chest, breast, bosom: *a ~ descubierto,* unprotected; fig. openly, frankly. *2* breast, teat: *dar el ~ a,* to nurse, suckle. *3* breast, bosom, heart [seat of affections, emotions, etc.]: *abrir el ~,* to unbosom oneself. *4* courage, spirit, fortitude. *5* short steep incline. *6* obs. tax or tribute. *7 tomar a ~,* to take to heart; to take seriously.
pechuga *f.* breast [of fowl]. *2* coll. breast, bosom [upper front of the human body].
pedagogía *f.* pedagogy.
pedagógico, -ca *adj.* pedagogic, pedagogical.
pedagogo *m.* pedagogue.
pedal *m.* MACH. pedal, treadle. *2* MUS. pedal.
pedalear *intr.* to pedal.
pedáneo *adj.* LAW petty, inferior.
pedante *adj.* pedantic. *2 m.-f.* pedant.
pedantería *f.* pedantry.
pedantón *m.* augm. great pedant.
pedazo *m.* piece, fragment, bit: ~ *de animal,* or *de alcornoque,* dolt, imbecile, good-for-nothing; ~ *de pan,* crumb; song [small price]; insignificant salary; *hacer pedazos,* to break to pieces; *morirse por los pedazos de,* to be madly in love with; *ser un ~ de pan,* to be extremely good-natured.
pederastia *f.* pederasty.
pedernal *m.* flint. *2* flintiness, extreme hardness.
pedernalino, -na *adj.* flinty; very hard.
pedestal *m.* pedestal. *2* PEANA 1.
pedestre *adj.* pedestrian.
pediatría *f.* MED. pediatrics.
pedicelo *m.* BOT., ZOOL. pedicel.
pedicoj *m.* hop, jumb on one foot.
pedicular *adj.* pedicular.
pedículo *m.* BOT. pedicle.
pedicuro, -ra *m.-f.* chiropodist.
pedido *m.* COM. order. *2* request, petition.
pedigón, -na; pedigüeño, -ña *adj.* persistent in asking or begging. *2 m.-f.* importunate asker.
pediluvio *m.* MED. pediluvium, foot bath.
pedimento *m.* petition. *2* LAW claim, bill.
pedir *tr.* to ask, ask for, beg, request: ~ *algo a alguien,* to ask someone for something; ~ *limosna,* to beg; ~ *permiso para,* to beg leave for; *a ~ de boca,* according to desire. *2* to ask [a price]. *3* to ask in marriage. *4* COM. to order. *5* to wish, desire. *6* [of things] to ask, ask for, call for, demand, need, require. *7* ~ *cuenta,* to call to account. *8* ~ *prestado,* to borrow. *9 pedírselo a uno el cuerpo,* to long for it. *10* intr. to beg. *11* to collect [for charitable purposes]. *12* ~ *por,* to inquire after [a person]. ‖ CONJUG. like *servir.*
pedo *m.* wind from the anus.
pedorrera *f.* flatulence, frequently breaking wind.
pedorreta *f.* sound made to imitate the breaking of wind.
pedrada *f.* throw of a stone. *2* hit or blow with a stone: *matar a pedradas,* to stone to death.

pedrea *s.* throwing of stones. *2* fight with stones. *3* fall of hail. *4* fig. small prizes in lottery.
pedregal *m.* stony ground.
pedregoso, -sa *adj.* stony, full of stones.
pedrejón *m.* boulder.
pedreñal *m.* blunderbuss fitted with a flintlock.
pedrera *f.* stone pit, -quarry.
pedrería *f.* jewelry, precious stones.
pedrero *m.* stonecutter. *2* slinger.
pedrisco *m.* METEOR. hail; hailstorm.
pedrizo, -za *adj.* stony, full of stones.
Pedro *m. pr. n.* Peter.
pedrusco *m.* stone, rough piece of stone.
pedúnculo *m.* ANAT., BOT., ZOOL. peduncle.
peer *intr.-ref.* to break wind.
pega *f.* sticking together. *2* pitch varnish. *3* coll. practical joke, trick. *4* coll. poser, catch question [in an examination]. *5* beating, drubbing. *6 de ~,* sham, worthless.
pegadizo, -za *adj.* sticky, adhesive. *2* catching, contagious, infectious. *3* catchy [music, tune]. *4* sponging [person]. *5* false [not natural].
pegado *m.* patch, sticking plaster.
pegadura *f.* gluing, sticking.
pegajosidad *f.* stickiness, glutinosity.
pegajoso, -sa *adj.* sticky, clammy, glutinous, viscous. *2* catching, contagious. *3* coll. mushy.
pegamiento *m.* gluing, sticking, joining.
pegante *adj.* sticking, adhesive, glutinous.
pegar *tr.* to glue, cement, stick, join. *2* to attach, fasten [by sewing, tying, etc.]. *3* to bring close [to], to place against. *4* to infect with, give [a disease, etc.]. *5* to set [fire]. *6* to give, deal, deliver [a blow, etc.]. *7* to beat [inflict blows on]. *8* to give, take, execute [shouts, jumps, etc.]. *9 pegársela a uno,* to make a fool of someone. *10 no ~ los ojos,* not to sleep a wink. *11* intr. to be sticking. *12* to take root. *13* [of a fire] to catch. *14* to pass, go, be credible: *ésa no pega,* that is too thin, that won't go. *15* to be pertinent. *16* to suit, accord. *17* to join. *18* to hit, knock, strike. *19* ref. to stick; adhere, cling. *20* to keep close. *21* COOK. to burn [adhere to the saucepan]. *22* to join [others] unasked. *23* to be infectious. *24* to come to blows.
Pegaso *m.* MYTH., ASTR. Pegasus.
pego *m.* cheating by sticking two cards together: *dar el ~,* coll. to cheat, deceive.
pegote *m.* pitch plaster, sticking plaster. *2* coarse patch. *3* crude or clumsy addition. *4* sticky mess. *5* sponger, parasite.
pegotear *intr.* coll. to sponge, live as a parasite.
pegotería *f.* coll. sponging.
pegujal *m.* small funds. *2* small farm or herd of cattle.
pegujalero *m.* small farmer or cattle owner.
pegujón, pegullón *m.* lump or ball of wool or hair.
peguntar *tr.* to mark [sheep] with pitch.
peinada *f.* combing [the hair].
peinado *m.* combing. *2* hairdressing, hairdo, coiffure.
peinador, -ra *adj.* combing. *2 m.-f.* comber. *3* hairdresser. *4 m.* wrapper, peignoir. *5 f.* combing machine.
peinadura *f.* combing. *2* combings.
peinar *tr.* to comb, dress or do [the hair]. *2* to comb [wool, cotton, etc.]. *3* ref. to comb, dress or do one's hair.
peinazo *m.* CARP. crosspiece [of a door or window].
peine *m.* comb [for combing the hair]. *2* comb,

card [for wool, cotton, etc.]. *3* WEAV. reed [of the loom]. *4* cartridge clip. *5* coll. sly fellow.

peinería *f.* comb factory or shop.

peineta *f.* comb [for confining the hair or for adornment]; back comb.

peje *m.* ZOOL. fish: ~ *ángel*, angelfish; ~ *araña*, stingbull. *2* coll. cunning, crafty fellow.

pejepalo *m.* stockfish.

pejesapo *m.* ICHTH. angler.

pejiguera *f.* bother, botheration.

pela *m.* PELADURA.

pelada *f.* pelt, sheepskin stripped of wool.

peladera *f.* alopecia, loss of the hair.

peladilla *f.* sugar almond. *2* small pebble.

pelado, -da *adj.* bald, bare, hairless, featherless, treeless, leafless. *2* peeled. *3* naked [without addition]. *4* fig. penniless. *5 canto* ~, pebble. *6 m.* penniless person.

peladura *f.* peeling, plucking, stripping. *2* peelings.

pelafustán, -na *m.-f.* good-for-nothing.

pelagatos, *pl.* **-tos** *m.* penniless fellow, ragamuffin.

pelágico, -ca *adj.* pelagic, oceanic.

pelagra *f.* MED. pellagra.

pelaje *m.* pelage, coat, fur [of an animal]. *2* coll. clothes, apparel. *3* coll. sort, kind, description.

pelambrera *f.* shock of hair. *2* TAN. place in which hair is removed from hides. *3* alopecia.

pelamesa *f.* hair-pulling scuffle.

pelandusca *f.* coll. harlot, strumpet.

pelantrín *m.* small farmer, petty farmer.

pelar *tr.* to remove, cut, shave the hair of. *2* to pluck [a fowl]. *3* to peel, bark, hull. *4* fig. to fleece, clean out [strip of money or property]. *5* (Am.) to beat, thrash. *6 duro de* ~, very difficult. *7 ref.* to lose the hair. *8* to peel off. *9* coll. to get one's hair cut. *10* (Am.) to be confused. *11* (Am.) to slip away; to die.

pelásgico, -ca *adj.* Pelasgian, Pelasgic.

pelazga *f.* row, -quarrel, scuffle.

peldaño *m.* step [of stairs].

pelea *f.* fight; combat. *2* wrangle. *3* struggle.

peleador, -ra *adj.* fighting. *2* quarrelsome.

pelear *intr.* to fight. *2* to battle. *3* to quarrel. *4* to struggle. *5 ref.* to fight [come to blows]. *6* to quarrel, fall out.

pelechar *intr.* [of animals] to begin to have hair of feathers; to fledge. *2* coll. to improve one's fortune or health.

pelele *m.* stuffed figure [of straw and rags]. baby's knitted sleeping suit. *3* coll. nincompoop.

pelendengue *m.* PERENDENGUE.

peleón *m.* cheap wine.

peleona *f.* quarrel, row.

peletería *f.* furriery. *2* fur shop.

peletero *m.* furrier.

peliagudo, -da *adj.* arduous, difficult. *2* sly, clever.

peliblanco, -ca *adj.* white-haired.

pelícano *m.* ORN. pelican. *2* DENT. pelican.

pelicano, -na *adj.* gray-haired.

película *f.* pellicle, film. *2* PHOT. film. *3* CINEM. film, moving picture. *4* moving-picture reel.

peligrar *intr.* to peril, be in danger.

peligro *m.* danger, peril, risk, hazard, distress: *barco en* ~, ship in distress.

peligroso, -sa *adj.* dangerous, perilous, risky.

pelilargo, -ga *adj.* long-haired.

pelillo *m.* tiny hair or fibre. *2* trifle, trifling difference: *pelillos a la mar*, coll. let bygones be bygones; *no reparar en pelillos*, coll. not to bother about trifles.

pelilloso, -sa *adj.* coll. touchy, peevish.

pelinegro, -gra *adj.* black-haired.

pelirrojo, -ja *adj.* red-haired.

pelitre *m.* BOT. pellitory of Spain.

pelma, pelmazo *m.* compressed mass. *2* coll. lump, sluggard [person]. *3* coll. bore [person].

pelo *m.* hair, fibre, filament: *agarrarse*, or *asirse de un* ~, fig. to seize upon any trivial pretext; *no tener pelos en la lengua*, coll. to be outspoken. *2* hair's breadth; *por un* ~, by a hair's breadth. *3* smallest thing or quantity: *no tener* ~ *de tonto*, coll. to be clever, shrewd. *4* hair [collect]; coat, fur [of animal]; pile, nap [of cloth]: *mata de* ~, head of hair; *tomar el* ~ *a*, to pull the leg of; *venir al* ~, to be to the point; to be opportune; to suit perfectly; *contra* ~, backwards; fig. against the grain; fig. untimely. *5* down [of birds or fruit]. *6* flaw [in gems or metals]. *7* difficulty: *tener pelos*, to be a hard nut or crack. *8 pl.* hair [of head]; *estar hasta los pelos de*, coll. to be sick of.

pelón, -na *adj.* bald, hairless. *2* coll. poor, penniless. *3 m.-f.* bald person. *4* coll. penniless person. *5 m.* (Am.) dried peach.

pelona *f.* alopecia, loss of hair.

Peloponeso *m. pr. n.* GEOG. Peloponnesus.

pelosilla *f.* VELLOSILLA.

peloso, -sa *adj.* hairy.

pelota *f.* ball [used in games]; hand ball; ball game: ~ *vasca*, pelota; *la* ~ *está en el tejado*, fig. the matter is still undecided. *2* ball [of mud, snow, etc.]. *3* (Am.) boat made of leather. *4* coll. accumulation of debts. *5* COM. accomodation bill. *6 en* ~, naked.

pelotari *m.* pelota player.

pelotazo *m.* blow or hit with a ball.

pelote *m.* goat's hair [for stuffing furniture].

pelotear *tr.* to check [an account]. *2 intr.* to play or throw a ball [without playing a game]. *3* to argue, dispute, wrangle.

pelotera *f.* dispute, -quarrel, wrangle.

pelotilla *f. dim.* small ball. *2* coll. *hacer la* ~ *a*, to fawn on.

pelotón *m. augm.* large ball. *2* ball of tangled hair. *3* small party, squad, platoon: ~ *de ejecución*, MIL. firing party o squad; ~ *de los torpes*, MIL. awkward squad.

peltre *m.* pewter.

peluca *f.* wig. *2* coll. wig, wigging, reprimand.

pelucón *m. augm.* large wig.

pelucona *f.* coll. gold doubloon.

peluche *f.* plush.

peludo, -da *adj.* hairy, shaggy. *2 m.* mat with shaggy pile.

peluquera *f.* hairdresser [woman].

peluquería *f.* hairdresser's [shop]; barber's shop.

peluquero *m.* hairdresser, barber. *2* wigmaker.

peluquín *m.* scratch wig. *2* bob wig, periwig.

pelusa *f.* down [of fruits or plants]. *2* flue, fluff, fuzz. *3* coll. childish jealousy or envy.

pelvis, *pl.* **-vis** *f.* ANAT. pelvis.

pella *f.* ball, lump [of soap, butter, etc.]. *2* tender head [of cauliflower, etc.]. *3* raw lard or fat of swine. *4* lump of money.

pellada *f.* MAS. lump or trowelful of mortar.

pelleja *f.* skin, hide, pelt. *2* dressed sheepskin [with the wool on]. *3* skin, hide [of a person]. *4* coll. strumpet.

pellejería *f.* skins, hides, pelts [collect.]. *2* skinnery. *3* skinner's trade.

pellejero *m.* skinner [dresser or seller of skins].

pellejo *m.* skin, hide, pelt; rawhide. *2* waterskin,

wineskin, wine bag. *3* coll. drunkard. *4* skin, hide [of a pers.]: *estar* or *hallarse en el ~ de otro*, coll. to be in somebody else's shoes or skin; *jugarse el ~*, to risk one's life; *salvar el ~*, to save one's hide or skin.

pellejudo, -da *adj.* having a flabby or baggy skin.

pellica *f.* coverlet of tine skins. *2* jacket of fine skins. *3* small dressed skin.

pellico *m.* sheepskin jacket.

pelliza *f.* pelisse [fur or fur-lined garment].

pellizcar *tr.* to pinch, nip [squeeze between tips of finger and thumb]. *2* to take a pinch of.

pellizco *m.* pinch [act of pinching], nip. *2* pinch, small quantity. *3 ~ de monja*, small cookie.

pena *f.* ORN. penna. *2* penalty, punishment, pain: *~ capital*, capital punishment. *3* pain, affliction, grief, sorrow. *4* pity: *dar ~*, to arouse pity. *5* hardship. *6* trouble, toil, difficulty. *7 valer la ~*, to be worth while, to be worth the trouble; *no vale la ~*, don't mention it. *8 a duras penas*, with a great difficulty, just, barely.

penable *adj.* punishable.

penacho *m.* ORN. crest, tuft of feathers. *2* crest plume, panache. *3* fig. arrogance, airs.

penachudo, -da *adj.* crested, tufted, plumed.

penado, -da *adj.* full of sorrows. *2* painful, arduous. *3 m.-f.* convict; prisoner serving a sentence.

penal *adj.* penal. *2 m.* penitentiary.

penalidad *f.* trouble, hardship. *2* LAW penalty.

penalista *m.* penologist.

penar *tr.* to punish, penalize [impose penalty on]. *2 intr.* to suffer, grieve, sorrow. *3* to suffer, be tormented [in purgatory]. *4 ~ por*, to long for, to pine for.

penates *m. pl.* penates.

penca *f.* pulpy leaf [of some plants]; pulpy part [of some leaves]. *2* cowhide [for flogging]. *3 hacerse de pencas*, coll. not to yield easily.

penco *m.* jade [horse].

pendencia *f.* dispute, quarrel, light.

pendenciero, -ra *adj.* quarrelsome.

pender *intr.* to hang, be suspended, dangle. *2* to depend, hang, rest: *~ de*, to depend or hang on. *3* to be pendent or pending [undecided].

pendiente *adj.* pendent, hanging, dangling. *2* pendent, pending [undecided]. *3* depending, hanging: *estar ~ de*, to depend on, to hang on. *4* sloping. *5 m.* earring. *6* pendant [hanging ornament]. *7* pitch [of a roof]. *8 f.* slope, declivity, grade, gradient, dip.

péndola *f.* pendulum [of clock]. *2* clock [with pendulum]. *3* PLUMA 1 & 3.

pendolista *m.* penman.

pendolón *m.* ARCH. king post.

pendón *m.* banner, standard, pennon. *2* coll. tall, ungainly, despicable woman.

péndulo, -la *adj.* pendulous, pendent, hanging. *2 m.* pendulum.

pene *m.* ANAT. penis.

Penélope *f. pr. n.* Penelope.

peneque *adj.* coll. drunk, intoxicated.

penetrable *adj.* penetrable. *2* comprehensible.

penetración *f.* penetration.

penetrante *adj.* penetrant, penetrating. *2* deep, keen, perspicacious. *3* acute, shrill, piercing.

penetrar *tr.-intr.* to penetrate. *2 intr.* to be acute, piercing. *3 ref. penetrarse de*, to become imbued with; to grasp, comprehend.

pénfigo *m.* MED. pemphigus.

penicilina *f.* PHARM. penicillin.

península *f.* GEOG. peninsula.

peninsular *adj.-n.* peninsular.

penique *m.* penny [English coin].

penitencia *f.* penance: *hacer ~*, to do penance; coll. to take potluck. *2* penitence, repentance.

penitenciado, -da *adj.* punished by the Inquisition.

penitencial *adj.* penitential.

penitenciar *tr.* to penance [impose penance on].

penitenciaría *f.* penitentiary [tribunal; prison].

penitenciario, -ria *adj.* penitentiary. *2 m.* ECCL. Cardinal chief of the penitentiary.

penitenta *f.* female confessant.

penitente *adj.* penitent, repentant. *2 m.-f.* penitent. *3* confessant.

penol *m.* NAUT. yardarm, peak.

penoso, -sa *adj.* painful. *2* laborious, arduous, fatiguing. *3* distressing. *4* embarrassing, unpleasant.

pensado, -da *adj.* thought-out. *2 bien ~*, proper, wise. *3 de ~*, on purpose, deliberately. *4 mal ~*, evilminded [tending to think ill].

pensador, -ra *adj.* thinking. *2 m.* thinker.

pensamiento *m.* thought, mind: *como el ~*, swiftly. *2* thought [thinking; idea, etc., produced by thinking; intention]. *3* thoughts. *4* pithy saying, maxim. *5* suspicion. *6* BOT. pansy, heartsease.

pensar *tr.* to think out, over, about: *pensarlo mejor*, to change one's mind. *2* to think [consider]: *~ que*, to think that. *3* to think of [a card, a number, etc.]. *4* to imagine. *5* to intend. *6* to feed [animals]. *7 intr.* to think. *8 ~ en*, to think of [direct one's thoughts to; remember; conceive]. *9 sin ~*, unexpectedly, thoughtlessly. ‖ CONJUG. as *acertar*.

pensativo, -va *adj.* pensive, thoughtful.

pensil *adj.* pensile. *2 m.* delightful garden.

Pensilvania *pr. n.* GEOG. Pennsylvania.

pensión *f.* pension, annuity, allowance. *2* board; price of board [in a boarding house or school]. *3* pension, boarding house.

pensionado, -da *adj.* pensioned. *2 m.-f.* pensioner [one in receipt of a pension].

pensionar *tr.* to grant a pension or allowance to.

pensionista *m.-f.* pensioner [one in receipt of a pension]. *2* boarder: *medio ~*, day boarder [in a school].

pentadáctilo, -la *adj.* pentadactyl.

pentaedro *m.* GEOM. pentahedron.

pentagonal *adj.* pentagonal.

pentágono *m.* GEOM. pentagon.

pentagrama *m.* MUS. staff, musical staff.

pentámero, -ra *adj.* BOT., ZOOL. pentamerous.

pentámetro *adj.-m.* PROS. pentameter.

pentano *m.* CHEM. pentane.

pentápolis *f.* pentapolis.

Pentateuco *m.* BIBL. Pentateuch.

Pentecostés *m.* Pentecost, Whitsuntide.

penúltimo, -ma *adj.* penult, penultimate.

penumbra *f.* penumbra.

penuria *f.* penury.

peña *f.* rock, boulder. *2* rock, crag. *3* group of friends, circle, club.

peñascal *m.* rocky or craggy place.

peñasco *m.* large rock, crag.

peñascoso, -sa *adj.* rocky, craggy.

peñola *f.* pen, quill [for writing].

peñón *m.* rock [hill of rock]: *~ de Jibraltar*, Rock of Gibraltar.

peón *m.* pedestrian. *2* foot soldier. *3* unskilled labourer: *~ de albañil*, hodman; *~ caminero*, road mender. 2 (Am.) farm hand. 5 top [toy]. 6 man [in draughts]. 7 pawn [in chess]. 8 beehive.

peonaje *m.* day labourers.

peonia *f.* BOOT. peonia.

peonza *f.* whip top, whipping top [toy].

peor *adj.-adv. comp.* worse: ~ *que* ~, that is still worse; *tanto* ~, so much the worse. 2 *adj.-adv. superl.* [with determinate article] worst; the worst.

Pepa *f. pr. n.* coll. Josephine.

Pepe *m. pr. n.* coll. Joseph, Joe.

pepinillo *m.* gherkin, small cucumber.

pepino *m.* BOT. cucumber: *no dársele a uno un* ~, not to care a pin.

Pepita *f. pr. n.* coll. Josephine.

pepita *f.* seed [of apple, melon, etc.], pip. 2 MIN. nugget. 3 VET. pip.

Pepito *m. pr. n.* coll. Joseph, Joe.

pepitoria *f.* giblet or fowl fricassee with egg sauce. 2 fig. medley, hodgepodge.

peplo *m.* peplum.

pepónide *f.* BOT. pepo.

pepsina *f.* BIOCHEM. pepsin.

péptico, -ca *adj.* peptic.

peptona *f.* BIOCHEM. peptone.

pequeñez *f.* littleness, smallness. 2 childhood. 3 pettiness. 4 meanness; mean act. 5 trifle.

pequeño, -ña *adj.* little, small. 2 petty. 3 young, of tender age. 4 low, humble. 5 *m.-f.* child.

pequeñuelo, -la *m.-f.* young child, baby, tot.

pera *f.* BOT. pear: *pedir peras al olmo*, fig. to expect the impossible. 2 fig. sinecure. 3 imperial, goatee [beard]. 4 pear-shaped bulb [of camera shutter, etc.]: ~ *de goma*, bulb syringe. 5 ELECT. pear-shaped switch.

perada *f.* pear jam. 2 pear brandy.

peral *m.* BOT. pear tree.

peraleda *f.* orchard of pear trees.

peralte *m.* ARCH. stilting. 2 RLY. superelevation, rise.

perborato *m.* CHEM. perborate.

perca *f.* ICHTH. perch.

percal *m.* percale.

percalina *f.* percaline.

percance *m.* unfortunate accident, mishap.

percatarse de *ref.* to notice, become aware of. 2 to consider, heed.

percebe *m.* ZOOL. goose barnacle.

percepción *f.* perception. 2 percept. 3 collection, receiving [of money, rents, taxes, etc.].

perceptible *adj.* perceptible; perceivable. 2 collectable.

perceptivo, -va *adj.* perceptive.

perceptor, -ra *adj.* percipient. 2 collecting, receiving. 3 *m.-f.* percipient. 4 collector, receiver.

percibir *tr.* to perceive. 2 to collect, receive.

perclorato *m.* CHEM. perchlorate.

percuciente *adj.* percussive, percutient.

percusión *f.* percussion, striking. 2 MED. percussion.

percusor *m.* percussor. 2 percussion hammer, firing pin.

percutir *tr.* to percuss, strike.

percha *f.* perch, roost [for birds]. 2 pole, bar, horizontal bar. 3 clothes rack, clothes tree. 4 snare [for birds]. 5 PERCA. 6 napping [of cloth].

perchar *tr.* to teasel, nap, raise the nap on [cloth].

perchero *m.* hat rack, clothes rack.

percherón, -na *adj.-n.* Percheron [horse].

perdedor, -ra *adj.* losing. 2 *m.-f.* loser.

perder *tr.* to lose: ~ *de vista*, to lose sight of; *pierda*

usted cuidado, don't worry. 2 to mislay. 3 to forfeit. 4 to waste. 5 to miss [a train, an opportunity, etc.]. 6 to ruin [bring to ruin]; to spoil. 7 ~ *el miedo*, to cease to fear. 8 ~ *el respeto a*, to cease to respect; to be disrespectful to. 9 *intr.* to lose. 10 to lose value or credit. 11 [of a fabric] to fade. 12 *ref.* to lose oneself or itself. 13 to get lost. 14 to become ruined, destroyed [physically or morally]. 15 [of fruit or crops] to be spoiled, damaged. 16 fig. to love excessively. 17 to fall into disuse. 18 to be wasted. 19 to cease to be perceptible; to disappear. 20 ~ *de vista*, to disappear; fig. to be very clever or shrewd. ‖ CONJUG. like *entender*.

perdición *f.* perdition. 2 loss, ruin. 3 violent, unrestrained love.

pérdida *f.* loss: *pérdidas y ganancias*, COM. profit and loss; *vender con* ~, to sell at a loss. 2 waste [of time, etc.]; *sin* ~ *de tiempo*, without delay. 3 COM. shortage, leakage.

perdidizo, -za *adj.* supposed to be lost: *hacer* ~, to hide, conceal. 2 sneaking away.

perdido, -da *adj.* lost. 2 mislaid. 3 wasted, useless, vain. 4 stray: *bala perdida*, stray bullet; fig. harebrain. 5 vicious. 6 countersunk. 7 *ratos perdidos*, idle hours. 8 *estar* ~ *por*, to be madly in love with; to be mad about. 9 *m.* vicious man. 10 *f.* harlot.

perdidoso, -sa *adj.* losing, sustaining loss.

perdigar *tr.* COOK. to brown, to broil slightly.

perdigón *m.* young partridge. 2 shot [pellet], bird shot; *perdigones*, shot [collect.].

perdigonada *f.* shot with bird shot.

perdiguero, -ra *adj.* partridge hunting. 2 *m.* setter [dog]. 3 partridge dealer, game dealer.

perdimiento *m.* PERDICIÓN, PÉRDIDA.

perdis, *pl.* **-dis** *m.* coll. gay blade, libertine.

perdiz, *pl.* **-dices** *f.* ORN. partridge. 2 ~ *blanca*, ptarmigan.

perdón *m.* pardon, forgiveness, grace: *con* ~, by your leave, begging pardon. 2 remission [of a debt].

perdonable *adj.* pardonable.

perdonador, -ra; perdonante *adj.* forgiving. 2 *m.-f.* forgiver.

perdonar *tr.* to pardon, forgive. 2 to remit [a debt]. 3 to exempt, spare. 4 to excuse. 5 *no* ~, not to pardon; not to omit; not to spare; not to miss.

perdonavidas, *pl.* **-das** *m.* bully, hector.

perdulario, -ria *m.-f.* careless, sloppy person. 2 vicious person.

perdurable *adj.* everlasting. 2 long-lasting.

perdurar *tr.* to last, to last long.

perecedero, -ra *adj.* perishable, not lasting, mortal.

perecer *intr.* to perish, come to an end, die. 2 to perish [suffer spiritual death]. 3 to be in great want. 4 *ref. perecerse por*, to crave for, be dying for, be mad about. ‖ CONJUG. like *agradecer*.

perecimiento *m.* perishing, end, death.

peregrinación, *f.*, **peregrinaje** *m.* peregrination. 2 pilgrimage.

peregrinamente *adv.* rarely, strangely, curiously. 2 wonderfully.

peregrinar *intr.* to peregrinate, travel, roam. 2 to pilgrim.

peregrino, -na *adj.* wandering, traveling. 2 of passage [bird]. 3 going on a pilgrimage. 4 rare, strange, singular. 5 perfect, wonderful. 6 *m.-f.* pilgrim; palmer.

perejil *m.* BOT. parsley. *2 pl.* coll. frippery, showy ornaments. *3* coll. handles [titles, etc.].
perencejo, -ja *m.-f.* PERENGANO.
perendengue *m.* bauble, trinket.
perene, perennal, perenne *adj.* perennial, perpetual. *2* BOT. perennial.
perengano, -na *m.-f.* So-and-So.
perennal *adj.* PERENNE.
perenne *adj.* perennial, perpetual. *3* BOT. perennial.
perennidad *f.* perenniality.
perentoriedad *f.* peremtoriness. *2* urgency.
perentorio, -ria *adj.* peremptory, decisive. *2* urgent, pressing.
pereza *f.* laziness, sloth. *2* slowness [in actions].
pereco, perezca, etc. *irr.* V. PERECER.
perezoso, -sa *adj.* lazy, slothful, idle, indolent, slow, heavy. *2 m.* ZOOL. sloth.
perfección *f.* perfection: *a la ~,* perfectly.
perfeccionamiento *m.* perfection [making perfect]; improvement; finish.
perfeccionar *tr.* to perfect; to improve.
perfectible *adj.* perfectible.
perfectivo, -va *adj.* perfective.
perfecto, -ta *adj.* perfect. *2* GRAM. perfect [tense].
perfidia *f.* perfidy.
pérfido, -da *adj.* perfidious, treacherous. *2 m.-f.* perfidious person.
perfil *m.* profile: *de ~,* in profile. *2* outline. *3* thin stroke [of pen]. *4 pl.* finishing touches. *5* niceties; fuss [in social behaviour].
perfilado, -da *p. p.* of PERFILAR. *2 adj.* long and thin [face]. *3* well-formed [nose].
perfilar *tr.* to profile. *2* to outline. *3* to make fine strokes in. *4* to perfect. *5 ref.* to show one's profile, to stand sideways.
perfoliado, -da *adj.* BOT. perfoliate.
perfolla *f.* husk of Indian corn, *cornhusk.
perforación *f.* perforation, drilling, boring. *2* hole.
perforador, -ra *adj.* perforating, drilling. *2 m.-f.* perforator. *3 f.* perforator, drill.
perforar *tr.* to perforate, bore.
perfumado, -da *adj.* perfumed. *2* odoriferous.
perfumador, -ra *adj.* perfuming. *2 m.-f.* perfumer. *3 m.* perfuming pan. *4* perfume atomizer.
perfumar *tr.* to perfume.
perfume *m.* perfume. *2* odour, fragrance.
perfumería *f.* perfumery. *2* perfumer's shop.
perfumero, -ra; perfumista *m.-f.* perfumer.
perfunctorio, -ria *adj.* perfunctory.
perfusión *f.* perfusion.
pergamino *m.* parchment, vellum. *2 pl.* nobiliary antecedents of a family or person.
pergeñar *tr.* to prepare, do, make, write.
pergeño *m.* coll. appearance, looks.
pérgola *f.* pergola. *2* roof garden.
periantio *m.* BOT. perianth.
pericardio *m.* ANAT. pericardium.
pericarpio *m.* BOT. pericarp.
pericia *f.* expertness, skill.
pericial *adj.* expert's: *dictamen ~,* expert's report.
periclitar *intr.* to be in danger. *2* to decline, decay.
Perico *m. pr. n.* coll. Peter. *2 ~ de los palotes,* John Doe, So-and-So.
perico *m.* ORN. parakeet. *2* large fan. *3* large asparagus. *4* coll. chamber pot. *5* ZOOL. *~ ligero,* sloth.
naeriicón *m.* large fan. *2* a popular Argentinean dance.
periecos *m. pl.* GEOG. periœci.
periferia *f.* periphery.

periférico, -ca *adj.* peripheric(al.
perifollo *m.* BOT. chervil. *2 pl.* finery, frippery.
perifrasear *tr.* to periphrase.
perifrasi, perifrasis, *pl.* **-sis** *f.* RHET. periphrasis.
perigallo *m.* loose skin under the chin.
perigeo *m.* ASTR. perigee.
perihelio *m.* ASTR. perihelion.
perilla *f.* pear-shaped ornament. *2* goatee, imperial [beard]. *3* pommel [of saddlebow]. *4* lobe [of the ear]. *5 de ~,* coll. apropos, to the point.
perillán *m.* rascal, sly fellow, sly dog.
perímetro *m.* perimeter.
perinclito, -ta *adj.* most ilustrious.
perineo *m.* ANAT. perineum.
perinola *f.* teetotum. *2* pear-shaped ornament.
periódico, -ca *adj.* periodic, periodical. *2 m.* periodical, journal, newspaper.
periodismo *m.* journalism.
periodista *m.-f.* journalist, newspaperman.
período *m.* period [age, epoch; portion of time]. *2* MATH., PHYS., MED., RETH. period.
periostio *m.* ANAT. periosteum.
peripatético, -ca *adj.-n.* Peripatetic, Aristotelian. *2 adj.* coll. ridiculous, wild [in his opinions].
peripecia *f.* peripeteia, vicissitude, incident.
periplo *m.* periplus.
períptero *adj.* ARCH. peripteral. *2 m.* ARCH. peripteros.
peripuesto, -ta *adj.* coll. spruce, smart, dressed up.
periquete *m.* coll. jiffy, instant.
Periquito *m. pr. n.* coll. Peter.
periquito *m.* ORN. parakeet.
periscios *m. pl.* GEOG. periscii.
periscopio *m.* periscope.
perisodáctilo, -la *adj.-n.* ZOOL. perissodactyl.
perista *m.* coll. fence [receiver of stolen goods].
peristáltico, -ca *adj.* peristaltic.
peristilo *m.* ARCH. peristyle.
peritación *f.* examination or appraisal by experts.
peritaje *m.* PERITACIÓN. *2* one of the degrees to be obtained in some technical schools.
perito, -ta *adj.* skilful, skilled, expert. *2 m.* expert. *3* one holding the degree called PERITAJE.
peritoneo *m.* ANAT. peritoneum.
peritonitis *f.* MED. peritonitis.
perjudicar *tr.* to hurt, damage, injure, prejudice.
perjudicial *adj.* harmful, injurious, prejudicial.
perjuicio *m.* harm, damage, injury, prejudice, detriment: *en ~ de,* to the detriment of.
perjurar *intr.-ref.* to commit perjury, to perjure oneself. *2 intr.* to swear, be profane.
perjurio *m.* perjury.
perjuro, -ra *adj.* perjured. *2 m.-f.* perjurer.
perla *f.* pearl. *2 de perlas,* excellent, apropos.
perlado, -da *adj.* pearled. *2 cebada perlada,* pearl barley.
perlático, -ca *m.-f.* affected with shaking palsy.
perlería *f.* collection of pearls.
perlesía *f.* MED. palsy, shaking palsy; paralysis.
permanecer *intr.* to remain, stay [in some place or condition], to last, endure. ‖ CONJUG. like *agradecer.*
permanencia *f.* stay, sojourn. *2* permanence, permanency, duration, fixedness, stability.
permanente *adj.* permanent. *2 f.* permanent wave [in hair].
permanezco, permanezca, etc. *irr.* V. PERMANECER.
permeable *adj.* permeable.
permisible *adj.* permissible.
permisión *f.* permission, leave, licence, permit.

permisivo, -va *adj.* permissive.
permiso *m.* permission, leare, licence, permit: ~ *de conducir,* AUTO. drive's licence; *con su* ~, *by your leave. 5* leave of absence.
permitir *tr.* to permit, allow. *2* to permit, consent; to admit of. *3 ref.* to take the liberty [to]. *4 poder permitirse,* to be able to afford.
permuta *f.* barter, exchange, permutation.
permutación *f.* interchange, exchange, barter, permutation. *2* MATH. permutation.
permutar *tr.* to interchange, exchange, barter. *2* MATH. to permute.
pernaza *f. augm.* big leg.
perneador *adj.* strong-legged.
pernear *intr.* to kick, shake the legs. *2* to hustle. *3* to fret, worry.
pernera *f.* leg [of trousers].
pernetas (en) *adv.* bare-legged.
perniabierto, -ta *adj.* bowlegged.
pernicioso, -sa *adj.* pernicious, harmful, injurious.
pernigón *m.* Genoese preserved plum.
pernil *m.* ham [thigh and buttock of an animal]. *2* leg [of trousers].
pernio *m.* door or window hinge.
perniquebrar *tr.* to break the leg or legs of. *2 ref.* to break one's leg or legs. ‖ CONJUG. like *acertar.*
perno *m.* bolt [headed metal pin for holding things together]. *2* hook [of a door-hinge].
pernoctar *intr.* to pass the night.
pero *advers. conj.* but, yet, and yet. *2 m.* objection, fault: *poner peros a,* to make objections to, to find fault with; *sin un* ~, faultless. *3* BOT. a variety of apple and apple tree.
perogrullada *f.* truism, platitude.
perojo *m.* BOT. a little round pear.
perol *m.* kettle in form of hemisphere.
peroné *m.* ANAT. fibula.
peroración *f.* peroration. *2* oration, harangue.
perorar *intr.* to perorate, declaim, deliver a speech.
perorata *f.* coll. tiresome speech.
peróxido *m.* CHEM. peroxide.
perpendicular *adj.-f.* GEOM. perpendicular.
perpetración *f.* perpetration.
perpetrar *tr.* to perpetrate.
perpetua *f.* BOT. globe amaranth. *2* BOT. ~ *amarilla,* everlasting flower.
perpetuación *f.* perpetuation.
perpetuar *tr.* to perpetuate. *2 ref.* to be perpetuated; to continue unceasingly.
perpetuidad *f.* perpetuity.
perpetuo, -tua *adj.* perpetual, everlasting.
perpiaño *m.* ARCH. bondstone, perpend.
Perpiñán *pr. n.* GEOG. Perpignan.
perplejidad *f.* perplexity, hesitation, irresolution.
perplejo, -ja *adj.* perplexed, doubtful, hesitating.
perquirir *tr.* to seek out, investigate.
perra *f.* bitch [female dog]. *2* coll. drunk, drunkenness. *3* coll. child's rage or fit of temper. *4* coll. ~ *chica,* five-centime copper coin; ~ *gorda,* tencentime copper coin.
perrada *f.* pack of dogs. *2* coll. dirty trick.
perrera *f.* doghouse, kennel. *2* RLY. dog-box. *3* coll. drudgery. *4* coll. child's rage.
perrería *f.* dogs [collect.]. *2* coll. dirty trick, mean action. *3* coll. insult, abuse.
perrero *m.* keeper of the dogs. *2* dog fancier. *3* dogcatcher.
perrezno, -na *m.-f.* whelp, puppy [young dog].
perrillo, -lla *m.-f.* puppy. *2 m.* trigger [of firearm].
perro, -rra *adj.* hard wretched. *2* wicked. *3* (Am.) stubborn. *4* (Am.) selfish, mean. *5 m.* ZOOL. dog; ~ *dálmata,* coach dog; ~ *de aguas,* ~ *de lanas,* poodle, water spaniel; ~ *del hortelano,* fig. dog in the manger; ~ *de muestra,* pointer; ~ *de presa,* ~ *dogo,* bulldog; ~ *faldero,* lap dog; ~ *galgo,* greyhound; ~ *lebrero,* hare dog; ~ *mastín,* mastiff; ~ *perdiguero,* setter; ~ *podenco,* hound; ~ *sabueso,* bloodhound; ~ *viejo,* fig. cautious, experienced person; *a otro* ~ *con este hueso,* tell that to the marines. *6* fig. dog [mean, worthless fellow].
perroquete *m.* NAUT. topgallant mast.
perruno, -na *adj.* [pertaining to] dog, canine.
persa *adj.-n.* Persian.
persecución *f.* pursuit, hunt, -chase. *2* pursuit [seeking after, aiming at]. *3* persecution.
perseguidor, -ra *m.-f.* pursuer. *2* persecutor.
perseguimiento *m.* pursuing, pursuit.
perseguir *tr.* to pursue, hunt, chase. *2* to pursue, seek after, aim at. *3* to persecute. ‖ CONJUG. like *servir.*
Perseo *m. pr. n.* ASTR., MYTH. Perseus.
persevante *m.* pursuivant at arms.
perseverancia *f.* perseverance.
perseverante *adj.* persevering.
perseverar *intr.* to persevere.
persiano, -na *adj.-n.* Persian. *2 f.* flowered silk stuff. *3* Persian blind; Venetian blind. *4* slatted shutter.
persicaria *f.* BOT. persicary.
pérsico, -ca *adj.* Persian. *2 m.* BOT. peach.
persignarse *ref.* to cross oneself.
persistencia *f.* persistence, persistency.
persistente *adj.* persistent, persisting.
persistir *intr.* to persist. *2* to endure, last long.
persona *f.* person: *primera* ~, first person; *en* ~, in person. *2* excellent man. *3 pl.* people.
personada *adj.* BOT. personate [corolla].
personaje *m.* personage. *2* character [in play etc.].
personal *adj.* personal [one's own, private; done, made, etc., in person]. *2 m.* personnel, staff.
personalidad *f.* personality. *2* person of note or distinction. *3* LAW legal capacity.
personalizar *intr.* to personalize, become personal. *2 tr.* GRAM. to make personal.
personarse *ref.* to go, call, appear personally.
personificación *f.* personification.
personificar *tr.* to personify.
personilla *f. dim.* little person. *2* queer little person.
perspectiva *f.* perspective. *2* prospect, view, outlook. *3* deceptive appearance. *4 pl.* prospect, prospects.
perspicacia, perspicacidad *f.* perspicaciousness, perspicacity. *2* keen sight.
perspicaz *adj.* keen-sighted. *2* perspicacious.
perspicuidad *f.* perspicuity.
perspicuo, -cua *adj.* perspicuous.
persuadir *tr.* to persuade. *2 ref.* to persuade oneself, to become persuaded or convinced.
persuasible *adj.* credible, plausible.
persuasión *f.* persuasion, conviction.
persuasivo, -va *adj.* persuasive.
persuasor, -ra *m.-f.* persuader.
pertenecer *intr.* to belong; to pertain, concern. *2* to be incumbent [on]. ‖ CONJUG. as *agradecer.*
perteneciente *adj.* belonging, pertaining.
pertenencia *f.* belonging, ownership, property. *2* appurtenance, accesory. *3* MIN. claim.
pertenezco, pertenezca, etc. *irr.* V. PERTENECER.
pértica *f.* perch [measure of length].

pértiga *f.* long pole or rod; staff, verge. *2* SPORT. pole [used in pole vault].

pértigo *m.* pole, tongue [of cart or wagon].

pertiguero *m.* verger.

pertinacia *f.* pertinacity.

pertinaz *adj.* pertinacious.

pertinencia *f.* pertinence, fitness, relevancy.

pertinente *adj.* pertinent, apt, fitting, appropriate, relevant.

pertrechar *tr.* to supply, provide, equip. *2 ref.* to provide, equip oneself.

pertrechos *m. pl.* MIL. supplies, stores. *2* tools, implements [for a work or operation].

perturbación *f.* perturbation, disturbance. *2* unsettlement, disorder: ~ *mental,* mental disorder.

perturbado, -da *adj.* perturbed, disturbed. *2* insane. *3 m.-f.* insane person, lunatic.

perturbar *tr.* to perturb, disturb, unsettle. *2* to disconcert, confuse. *3 ref.* to be disturbed.

peruano, -na *adj.-n.* Peruvian.

perulero, -ra *adj.-n.* Peruvian. *2 m.-f.* person who has returned wealthy from Peru.

perversidad *f.* perversity, wickedness.

perversión *f.* perversion.

perverso, -sa *adj.* perverse, wicked, depraved.

pervertir *tr.* to pervert, garble. *2* to pervert, lead astray, deprave, corrupt. *3 ref.* to become perverted. ‖ CONJUG. as *hervir.*

pervierto, pervierta, etc. *irr.* PERVERTIR.

pervigilio *m.* sleeplessness, wakefulness.

pesa *f.* weight [for scales]; clock weight. *2* GYMN. dumbbell.

pesacartas, *pl.* **-tas** *m.* letter scales.

pesada *f.* weighing [quantity weighed].

pesadamente *adv.* heavily. *2* cumbrously. *3* tiresomely, annoyingly. *4* slowly, tardily. *5* clumsily.

pesadez *f.* heaviness. *2* burdensomeness. *3* tiresomeness, irksomeness. *4* drowsiness. *5* sultriness. *6* slowness. *7* clumsiness. *8* PHYS. gravity.

pesadilla *f.* nightmare.

pesado, -da *adj.* heavy, ponderous. *2* heavy, burdensome, hard to endure or accomplish. *3* annoying, tiresome, boring. *4* clumsy. *5* slow, sluggish. *6* deep [sleep]. *7* drowsy. *8* heavy, sultry, stuffy. *9* fat, corpulent. *10 m.-f.* bore, tiresome person.

pesador, -ra *m.-f.* weigher.

pesadumbre *f.* sorrow, grief, regret. *2* heaviness.

pesalicores, *pl.* **-res** *m.* hydrometer.

pésame *m.* condolences: *dar el* ~, to present one's condolences.

pesantez *f.* PHYS. gravity.

1) **pesar** *m.* sorrow, grief. *2* regret, repentance. *3 a* ~ *de,* in spite of, with all, notwithstanding; *a* ~ *mío,* against my will.

2) **pesar** *tr.* to weigh, scale. *2* to weigh [consider, ponder in the mind]. *3 intr.* to weigh. [have weight, be heavy; have influence]. *4* to cause sorrow, regret or repentance: *esto le pesará,* you'll be sorry for it. *5 pese a,* in spite of; *pese a quien pese,* whatever anybody says or does.

pesario *m.* SURG. pessary.

pesaroso, -sa *adj.* sorry, regretful, repentant. *2* sorrowful, sad.

pesca *f.* fishing. *2* angling. *3* catch [fish caught]. *4* salted codfish.

pescada *f.* MERLUZA 1.

pescadería *f.* fish market.

pescadero, -ra *m.-f.* fishmonger.

pescadilla *f.* ICHTH. a kind of hake.

pescado *m.* fish [caught]. *2* salted codfish.

pescador, -ra *adj.* fishing. *2 m.-f.* fisher; fisherman, fisherwoman: ~ *de caña,* angler. *3 m.* ICHTH. angler.

pescante *m.* coach box. *2* AUTO. front seat. *3* arm, bracket. *4* NAUT. davit.

pescar *tr.* to fish, catch [fish]. *2* to fish, draw [something out of water]. *3* to catch, take, get. *4* to catch [someone in a lie, etc.]. *5 intr.* to fish, angle: ~ *en río revuelto,* to fish in troubled waters.

pescozada *f.,* **pescozón** *m.* slap in the neck. *2* slap on the head.

pescozudo, -da *adj.* thick-necked.

pescuezo *m.* neck [part of body]. *2* fig. haughtiness.

pesebre *m.* crib, rack, manger.

pesebrera *f.* row of racks in a stable.

pesebrón *m.* boot [of a coach].

peseta *f.* peseta [monetary unit of Spain].

pésete *m.* curse, imprecation.

¡pesia! *interj.* confound it!

pesillo *m.* small scales for weighing coins.

pesimismo *m.* pessimism.

pesimista *adj.* pessimitic. *2 m.-f.* pessimist.

pésimo, -ma *adj.* very bad, very poor, wretched.

peso *m.* weight [of bodies], heaviness, gravity: ~ *específico,* PHYS. specific gravity; *a* ~ *de oro,* at a very high price; *de su* ~, naturally. *2* weighing. *3* balance, scales. *4* due weight. *5* weight [importance, influence]. *6* judgement, good sense: *hombre de* ~, wise, sensible man. *7* weight, load, burden. *8* BOX. weight: ~ *gallo,* bantamweight; ~ *mosca,* flyweight. *9* peso [Spanish American monetary unit]. *10 en* ~, suspended in the air; in a body; undecided.

pespuntar *tr.* SEW to backstitch.

pespunte *m.* SEW. backstitch.

pesquera *f.* fishery, fishing grounds.

pesquería *f.* fishery [fishing; fishing grounds].

pesquis *m.* acumen, penetration.

pesquisa *f.* inquiry, investigation, search.

pesquisar *tr.* to inquire into, investigate.

pestaña *f.* ANAT. eyelash. *2* SEW. edging, fringe. *3* rim [narrow strip at the edge]. *4* MACH. flange. *5 pl.* BIOL. cilia.

pestañear *intr.* to wink, blink [move the eyelids]: *sin* ~, without batting an eye.

pestañeo *m.* winking, blinking.

peste *f.* pest, pestilence, plague. *2* epidemic. *3* stink, stench. *4* evil, corruption of manners. *5* coll. excess, superabundance. *6 pl. decir pestes de,* to speak ill of, to talk against.

pestífero, -ra *adj.* pestiferous. *2* stinking.

pestilencia *f.* pestilence. *2* stink, stench.

pestilencial *adj.* pestilential, pestiferous.

pestilente *adj.* pestilent. *2* stinking.

pestillo *m.* bolt [of a lock]: ~ *de golpe,* spring bolt. *2* door bolt, door latch.

pestiño *m.* honeyed fritter.

pestorejo *m.* CERVIGUILLO.

pesuña *f.* PEZUÑA.

pesuño *m.* ZOOL. each half of a cloven hoof.

petaca *f.* cigar case. *2* tobacco pouch. *3* (Am.) leather covered chest.

pétalo *m.* BOT. petal.

petar *tr.* coll. to please.

petardear *tr.* MIL. to blow open with petards. *2* fig. to cheat, swindle. *3 intr.* AUTO. to backfire.

petardista *m.-f.* cheat, swindler, sponger.

petardo *m.* MIL. petard. *2* petard, firecracker. *3* fig. cheat, swindle, deception.

petate *m.* (Am.) sleeping mat. *2* bedding and clothes of a sailor, a soldier or a prisoner; luggage: *liar el ~*, coll. to pack up and go; to die.

petenera *f.* Andalusian popular song: *salir por peteneras*, fig. to say something irrelevant.

petición *f.* petition, demand, prayer, request, asking. *2* LAW claim, bill. *3* LOG. *~ de principio*, begging of the question.

peticionario, -ria *m.-f.* petitioner.

petifoque *m.* NAUT. flying jib.

petimetra *f.* affected, stylish lady.

petimetre *m.* fop, coxcomb, dude.

petirrojo *m.* ORN. robin, redbreast.

petitorio, -ria *adj.* petitionary. *2 m.* PHARM. catalogue of drugs.

peto *m.* ARM. breastplate. *2* FENC. plastron. *3* BULLF. mattress covering to protect horses. *4* breast of a garment. *5* ZOOL. plastron [of a turtle].

petral *m.* breastplate [for a riding horse].

petrel *m.* ORN. petrel.

pétreo, -a *adj.* stony, of stone; rocky.

petrificación *f.* petrifaction, petrification.

petrificar *tr.* to petrify. *2 ref.* to petrify [become petrified].

petrografía *f.* petrography.

petróleo *m.* petroleum, mineral oil. *2* kerosene.

petrolero, -ra *adj.* [pertaining to] petroleum, oil. *2 m.* petroleur.

petrolífero, -ra *adj.* petroliferous, oil-bearing.

petroso, -sa *adj.* stony, petrous. *2* ANAT. petrous.

petulancia *f.* insolence, pertness, flippancy. *2* presumptuousness.

petulante *adj.* insolent, pert, flippant. *2* presumptuous.

petunia *f.* BOT. petunia.

peyorativo, -va *adj.* depreciatory. *2* GRAM. pejorative.

1) **pez** *m.* ZOOL. fish: *~ de colores*, goldfish; *~ espada*, swordfish; *~ luna*, sunfish, moonfish; *~ martillo*, hammerhead; *~ sierra*, sawfish; *~ volador*, flying fish; *estar como el ~ en el agua*, to be comfortably situated.

2) **pez** *f.* pitch, tar: *~ griega*, rosin, colophony.

pezón *m.* BOT. stem [of fruits]; stalk [of a leaf or flower]. *2* nipple [of a teat]. *3* BOT. umbo [of lemon, etc.]. *4* axletree's end.

pezonera *f.* linchpin. *2* nipple shield.

pezpita *f.*, **pezpítalo** *m.* AGUZANIEVES.

pezuña *f.* hoof, cloven-hoof.

pi *f.* MATH. pi.

piada *f.* peeping, chirping.

piadoso, -sa *adj.* pious, godly. *2* merciful, compassionate.

piafar *intr.* [of horses] to paw, stamp.

pial *m.* (Am.) lasso lariat. *2* (Am.) snare, trap.

piamadre, piamáter *f.* ANAT. pia mater.

Piamonte (el) *m. pr. n.* GEOG. Piedmont.

pian, pian; pian, piano *adv.* coll. slowly, softly.

pianino *m.* MUS. upright piano.

pianista *m.-f.* pianist. *2 m.* piano manufacturer.

piano, pianoforte *m.* MUS. piano: *~ de cola*, grand piano; *~ de manubrio*, piano organ; *~ de media cola*, baby grand; *~ vertical*, upright piano.

pianola *f.* pianola.

piante *adj.* peeping, chirping.

piar *intr.* to peep, chirp. *2* fig. to cry for.

piara *f.* herd [of swine, mares or mules].

piastra *f.* piaster.

pica *f.* pike [weapon]. *2* pikeman. *3* BULL. goad. *4* stonecutter's hammer. *5* pica.

picacho *m.* peak, sharp peak [of mountain].

picada *f.* peck [of bird]; bite [of insect or reptile]. *2* (Am.) path, trail [cut through a forest].

picadero *m.* riding school, manege.

picadillo *m.* hash, minced meat.

picado, -da *p. p.* of PICAR. *2 adj.* pinked, perforated. *3* cut [tobacco]. *4* choppy [sea]. *5* piqued, hurt. *6* ~ *de viruelas*, pockmarked. *7 m.* AER. dive, diving. *8* MUS. staccato.

picador *m.* horsebreaker. *2* BULLF. mounted bullfigther who goads the bull. *3* COOK. chopping block.

picadura *f.* prick, sting. *2* bite [of insect or reptile]. *3* pinking [ornamental perforation]. *4* cut tobacco. *5* DENT. beginning of decay.

picafigo *m.* ORN. figpecker.

picaflor *m.* ORN. humming bird.

picajón, -na; picajoso, -sa *adj.* touchy, peevish.

picamaderos *m.* ORN. woodpecker.

picante *adj.* hot, pungent, piquant [to the taste]. *2* highly seasoned. *3* piquant, spicy, racy. *4* biting, cutting [word]. *5 m.* piquancy, pungency. *6* mordacity.

picapedrero *m.* stonecutter.

picapica *f.* itch-producing vegetable powder.

picapleitos, *pl.* **-tos** *m.* coll. litigious fellow. *2* coll. pettifogger.

picaporte *m.* thumb latch, spring latch; latchkey. *2* door knocker.

picar *tr.* to prick, pierce, puncture. *2* BULLF. to prick [the bull] with a goad. *3* [of insects or some reptils] to sting, bite. *4* [of birds] to peck at. *5* to take [the bait]. *6* to pink, perforate. *7* to spur [a horse]. *8* to spur, incite. *9* to mince, hash. *10* to pock. *11* to roughen with a pointed tool. *12* to train [a horse]. *13* to pique, annoy. *14* MUS. to staccato. *15* BILL. to strike [the ball]. *16* *tr.-intr.* to itch, prickle. *17* to burn, be hot [as a spice]. *18* *intr.* [of the sun] to burn. *19* to bite [take the bait]. *20* AER. to dive. *21* ~ *alto*, to aim high. *22* ~ *de*, to take or eat a small bit of. *23 ref.* to become moth-eaten. *24* [of fruit] to begin to rot. *25* [of wine] to begin to turn sour. *26* [of teeth] to begin to decay. *27* [of the sea] to get choppy. *28* to take offence. *29* (Am.) to get tipsy. *30 picarse de*, to boast of being.

picardear *intr.* to play the rogue. *2* to prank. *3 ref.* to acquire bad habits.

Picardía (la) *pr. n.* GEOG. Picardy.

picardía *f.* knavery, knavish action, mean trick. *2* slyness. *3* roguishness, archness. *4* prank, innocent practical joke. *5 pl.* insults, offensive words.

picardihuela *f.* dim. prank, roguish trick.

picardo, -da *adj.-n.* Picard.

picaresca *f.* rogues or picaros [collect.]. *2* the life of the rogues or picaros.

picaresco, -ca *adj.* roguish. *2* LIT. picaresque.

pícaro, -ra *adj.* knavish, roguish. *2* mischievous. *3* sly. *4 m.-f.* knave, rogue. *5* sly person. *6* rogue [used playfully]. *7 m.* LIT. picaro. *8* ~ *de cocina*, scullion, kitchen boy.

picarón, -na *adj. augm.* roguish, mischievous. *2 m.-f.* great rogue.

picatoste *m.* buttered toast.

picaza *f.* ORN. magpie.

picazón *f.* itching, itch. *2* coll. annoyance, displeasure.

picea *f.* BOT. spruce.

píceo, -a *adj.* piceous, pitchy.

pico *m.* beak, bill [of bird]. *2* fig. mouth [as a means of speech]; eloquence, fluency: *tener mucho* ~, to talk too much. *2* beak [of a vessel; pointed end or projection]. *3* corner [of a handkerchief; of a cocked hat]. *4* peak [of a mountain]. *5* pick [tool], pickaxe. *6* small surplus: *cuarenta pesetas y* ~, forty pesetas odd. *7* some money. *8* ORN. *pico*, or ~ *carpintero*, woodpecker. *9* NAUT. ~ *cangrejo*, gaff. *10 andar a picos pardos*, to loaf around; to go on a spree.

picor *m.* burning of the palate [from having eaten something pungent]. *2* itching, itch.

picoso, -sa *adj.* pock-marked.

picota *f.* pillory.

picotada *f.*, **picotazo** *m.* peck [blow with a beak]. *2* sting [inflicted by an insect].

picotear *tr.* to peck, peck at. *2 intr.* [of horses] to toss the head. *3* to chatter. *4 ref.* [of women] to bandy sharp words.

picotería *f.* loquacity, talkativeness.

picotero, -ra *adj.* chattering, prattling, talkative. *2 m.-f.* chatterer, prattler.

pícrico *adj.* CHEM. picric.

picto, -ta *adj.* Pictic. *2 m.-f.* Pict.

pictografía *f.* pictography, picture writing.

pictórico, -ca *adj.* pictorial.

picudo, -da *adj.* beaked, pointed. *2* long-snouted. *3* chattering, prattling.

pichel *m.* pewter tankard, mug.

pichón, -na *m.-f.* coll. darling, dearest. *2* ORN. young pigeon.

pido, pida, etc. *irr.* V. PEDIR.

pidón, -na *adj.-n.* PEDIGÜEÑO.

pie *m.* foot [of person, animal, stocking of piece of furniture]: ~ *de banco*, fig. absurdity, nonsense; *andar con pies de plomo*, to proceed cautiously; *buscar cinco*, or *tres, pies al gato*, to be looking for trouble; *entrar con buen* ~ or ~ *derecho*, to make a good start; *faltarle a uno los pies*, to lose one's balance; *no dar* ~ *con bola*, fig. to do nothing right; *no tener pies ni cabeza*, fig. to be nonsensical; *poner pies en polvorosa*, coll. to flee; *ponerse de* ~, or *en* ~, to stand up; *saber de qué* ~ *cojea uno*, to know someone's weak point; *tenerse en* ~, to stay on one's feet; to stand; *a cuatro pies*, in all fours; *a los pies de usted*, at your service [said to a lady]; *a* ~, on foot; *a* ~ *firme*, steadfastly; *a* ~ *juntillas*, with feet together; fig. firmly; *en* ~, standing. *2* foot, bottom, lowest part: *al* ~ *de*, at the foot of. *3* stem [of goblet]. *4* foot, base, stand. *5* footing, ground. *6* footing [state, relative position]: *en* ~ *de igualdad*, on equal footing. *7* foot [metrical unit]. *8* PROS. metre, line. *9* foots, lees, sediments. *10* trunk, stalk [of tree or plant]. *11* individual tree, young tree. *12* motive, ground, occasion: *dar* ~ *a*, to give occasion for. *13* root; *tomar* ~, to take root. *14* THEAT. cue. *15 al* ~ *de la letra*, to the letter, literally. *16* ~ *de imprenta*, imprint [printer's name, etc.]. *17* ~ *de rey*, slide caliper.

piececito, piecezuelo *m. dim.* little foot.

piedad *f.* piety. *2* godliness. *3* pity, compassion, mercy; *¡por* ~*!*, for pity's sake!

piedra *f.* stone [rock, piece of stone; precious stone]: ~ *de afilar*, or *de amolar*, grindstone, whetstone; ~ *angular*, ARCH. cornerstone; fig. cornerstone, keystone; ~ *de escándalo*, stumbling block, cause of moral ruin to others; ~ *de toque*, touchstone; ~ *filosofal*, philosopher's stone; ~ *imán*, loadstone; ~ *militar*, milestone;

~ *pómez*, pumice; ~ *rodada*, boulder; *lanzar la primera* ~, to cast the first stone; *no dejar* ~ *por mover*, to leave no stone unturned; *no dejar* ~ *sobre* ~, to rage to the ground; *a* ~ *y lodo*, tightshut [door or window]. *2* METEOR. hail. *3* METEOR. hailstone. *4* MED. stone, calculus. *5* point [in some card games].

piel *f.* skin: ~ *de gallina*, goose flesh; *ser de la* ~ *del diablo*, coll. to be limb of the devil. *2* hide, pelt. *3* leather. *4* fur. *5* peel, skin [of fruit]. *6 m.* ~ *roja*, redskin [American Indian].

piélago *m.* sea, high sea. *2* fig. countless number.

pienso *m.* feed [of dry fodder]. *2* thought: *ni por* ~, by no means.

pienso, piense, etc. *irr.* V. PENSAR.

pierdo, pierda, etc. *irr.* V. PERDER.

piérides (las) *f. pl.* poet. the Muses.

pierna *f.* leg [of person or animal]: *a* ~ *suelta*, coll. at one's ease, without care. *2* branch, leg [of compass]. *3* long stroke [of some letters]. *4* MECH. shank, fork. *5* ~ *de nuez*, lobe of a walnut.

piernitendido, -da *adj.* with legs extended.

pietismo *m.* pietism.

pietista *adj.* pietistic. *2 m.-f.* pietist, Pietist.

pieza *f.* piece, fragment. *2* piece, part [of a machine, structure, etc.]: ~ *de recambio*, spare part; *quedarse en una* ~, or *hecho una* ~, coll. to be astonished. *3* a single article of a collection, set, etc. *4* piece, coin. *5* piece, cannon, gun. *6* game, quarry [hunted animal]. *7* MUS. piece. *8* THEAT. short piece. *9* piece, bolt, roll [of cloth, paper, etc.]. *10* CHESS., DRAUGHTS piece, man. *11* room [in a house]. *12 buena* ~, coll. fine fellow, rogue, sly fox.

piezgo *m.* foot of a hide or skin. *2* wineskin.

piezómetro *m.* piezometer.

pífano *m.* MUS. fife. *2* MUS. fifer.

pifia *f.* BILL. miscue. *2* fig. blunder, mistake.

pifiar *intr.* BILL. to miscue. *2* MUS. to wheeze in playing the flute.

pigargo *m.* ORN. osprey, fish hawk.

Pigmalión *m. pr. n.* MYTH. Pigmalion.

pigmentario, -ria *adj.* BIOL. pigmentary.

pigmento *m.* BIOL., TEXT. pigment.

pigmeo, -a *adj.-n.* pygmy.

pignoración *f.* pledging, pawning.

pignorar *tr.* to pledge, pawn.

pigre *adj.* slothful, lazy.

pigricia *f.* sloth, laziness.

pihuela *f.* jess [on hawk's leg]. *2 pl.* shackles.

pijama *m.* pajamas, pyjamas.

pijotería *f.* coll. nuisance.

pila *f.* stone trough or basin. *2* ECCL. font, holywater font: *nombre de* ~, Christian name. *3* pile, heap. *4* pillar, pier [of bridge]. *5* PHYS., ELECT. pile, battery: ~ *seca*, dry battery.

1) **pilar** *m.* basin, bowl [of a fountain]. *2* pillar, pier, post. *3* fig. pillar, column [supporter, support]. *4* stone post.

2) **pilar** *tr.* to pound [grain].

pilastra *f.* ARCH. pilaster, square column.

Pilatos *m. pr. n.* Pilate.

píldora *f.* PHARM. pill, pellet. *2* fig. pill, bad news: *dorar la* ~, to gild the pill.

píleo *m.* ARCHEOL. pileus.

pileta *f. dim.* small basin. *2* holy-water bowl.

pilón *m.* basin, bowl [of a fountain]. *2* watering trough. *3* mortar [for pounding grain, etc.]. *4* loaf [of sugar]. *5* drop, ball [of a steelyard]. *6* ARCH. pylon.

pilongo, -ga *adj.* thin, lean. *2* peeled and dried [chestnut].
píloro *m.* ANAT. pylorus.
piloso, -sa *adj.* pilose, pilous, hairy.
pilotaje *m.* NAUT., AER. pilotage. *2* piling, pilework.
pilotar *tr.* to pilot. *2* AUTO. to drive.
pilote *m.* ENG. pile.
pilotear *tr.* PILOTAR.
piloto *m.* NAUT., AER. pilot: ~ *de pruebas*, AER. test pilot. *2* fig. pilot, guide. *3* NAUT. mate, first mate. *4* AUTO. driver. *5* adj. pilot.
piltraca, piltrafa *f.* scrap of meat. *2* skinny flesh. *3 pl.* scraps of food. *4* scraps, refuse.
pilla *f.* pillage, plunder.
pillada *f.* coll. knavery, knavish trick, dirty trick.
pillaje *m.* pillage, plunder, sack: theft, stealing.
pillar *tr.* to pillage, plunder, steal. *2* to catch, take. *3* to catch, surprise [in a lie, etc.].
pillastre, pillastrón *m.* rogue, rascal, big rascal.
pillería *f.* pack of rogues. *2* piece of rascality. *3* roguishness. *4* slyness, craftiness.
pillete *m. dim.* little rogue or scamp. *2* street Arab.
pillín *m. dim.* little rogue.
pillo, -lla *adj.* roguish, rascally. *2* shrewd, sly. *3 m.* rogue, rascal. *4* shrewd, sly fellow.
pilluelo, -la *m.-f. dim.* little rogue, urchin.
pimentero *m.* pepper, black pepper [shrub]. *2* pepperbox. *3* BOT. ~ *falso*, pepper tree.
pimentón *m.* red pepper, Cayenne pepper, Spanish paprika [powder]. *2* pepper [vegetable].
pimienta *f.* pepper [spice]: ~ *blanca*, ~ *negra*, white, black, pepper; ~ *inglesa*, allspice; *ser como una* ~, to be alert, lively.
pimiento *m.* pepper, capsicum, Guinea pepper, red pepper, chili [plant and fruit]: ~ *morrón*, bonnet pepper; ~ *picante*, hot pepper. *2* PIMENTERO 1. *3* PIMENTÓN 1.
pimpinela *f.* BOT. burnet, salad burnet.
pimplar *tr.* coll. to drink [wine].
pimpollear, pimpollecer *intr.* to sprout, bud.
pimpollo *m.* young tree. *2* tender shoot or sprout, bud. *3* fig. handsome child; handsome young person, rosebud.
pina *f.* conical mound. *2* felloe [segment of a wheel's rim].
pinabete *m.* BOT. fir tree.
pinacoteca *f.* picture gallery.
pináculo *m.* pinnacle.
pinado, -da *adj.* BOT. pinnate.
pinar *m.* pine grove or forest, pinery.
pinastro *m.* BOT. pinaster, cluster pine.
pinatífido, -da *adj.* BOT. pinnatifid.
pinaza *f.* NAUT. pinnace.
pincarrasca *f.*, **pincarrasco** *m.* BOT. Aleppo pine.
pincel *m.* brush, pencil [for painting]. *2* brush, pencil [painter style; painter; painting].
pincelada *f.* stroke [with a brush], touch.
pincelar *tr.* F. ARTS to paint. *2* to portray, picture.
pinciano, -na *adj.-n.* of Valladolid.
pinchadura *f.* pricking, prick, puncture.
pinchar *tr.* to prick, pierce, puncture: *no* ~ *ni cortar*, fig. to count for nothing. *2* fig. to spur, incite. *3* fig. to pique, provoke.
pinchazo *m.* prick, puncture, jab. *2* fig. anything said to spur or pique someone. *3* AUTO. puncture.
pinche *m.* scullion, kitchen boy.
pincho *m.* thorn, sharp point. *2* pointed instrument.
pindárico, -ca *adj.* Pindaric.
pindonga *f.* gadabout [woman].
pindonguear *intr.* [of a woman] to gad about.

pineal *adj.* ANAT. pineal.
pineda *f.* pine grove or forest.
pinga *s.* yoke [for carrying pails, etc.].
pingajo *m.* rag, tatter.
pingo *m.* coll. rag, tatter. *2* (Am.) nag. *3 pl.* cheap woman's clothes.
pingorotudo, -da *adj.* coll. high, lofty.
pingüe *adj.* fat, greasy, oily. *2* fig. plentiful, substantial; fertile.
pingüedinoso, -sa *adj.* fatty, greasy.
pingüino *m.* ORN. penguin.
pinillo *m.* BOT. ground pine. *3* BOT. mock cypress.
pinitos *m. pl.* first steps [of a child or a convalescent]: *hacer* ~, to begin to walk.
pinjante *m.* ARCH., JEWEL. pendant.
pinnípedo, -da *adj.-n.* ZOOL. pinniped.
1) **pino** *m.* BOT. pine tree: ~ *albar*, Scotch pine; ~ *carrasco*, Aleppo pine; ~ *piñonero*, stone pine, nut pine; ~ *marítimo* or *rodenò*, pinaster, cluster pine; ~ *negro*, mountain pine. *2 pl.* PINITOS.
2) **pino, -na** *adj.* steep [having a decided slope].
pinocha *f.* pine needle.
pinocho *m.* pine cone.
pinoso, -sa *adj.* piny.
pinsapo *m.* BOT. Spanish fir.
pinta *f.* spot, mark, speckle. *2* lines near the edge of Spanish playing cards showing the suit. *3* pint [measure]. *4* appearance, look.
pintacilgo *m.* JILGUERO.
pintada *f.* ORN. guinea fowl, guinea hen.
pintado, -da *adj.* spotted, mottled, speckled. *2* coll. *el más* ~, the best one, the cleverest one. *5 estar*, or *venir*, ~ or *como* ~, to fit, to be just the thing.
pintamonas, *pl.* **-nas** *m.-f.* coll. dauber [poor painter].
pintar *tr.* to paint. *2* to draw [a letter, accent, etc.]. *3* to picture, depict; fancy, imagine. *4* fig. to exaggerate. *5 pintarla* to show off. *6 intr.* [of fruits] to colour. *7* [of things] to seem to be going [badly, well, etc.]. *8* to have authority, influence, etc. *9 ref.* to paint oneself. *10 pintarse solo para*, to show great aptitude for.
pintarrajar, pintarrajear *tr.* coll. to daub [paint inartistically].
pintarrajo *m.* daub [inartistic or coarse painting],
pintear *intr.* to drizzle.
pintiparado, -da *adj.* exactly alike, closely resembling. *2* fit, fitting, just the thing.
pinto, -ta *adj.* (Am.) spotted, speckled.
pintojo, -ja *adj.* spotted, mottled, speckled.
pintor *m.* painter: ~ *de brocha gorda*, house painter, sign painter; dauber.
pintora *f.* female painter.
pintoresco, -ca *adj.* picturesque.
pintorrear *tr.* to daub, paint coarsely.
pintura *f.* painting [act or art]: ~ *a la aguada*, water colour; ~ *al fresco*, fresco; ~ *al óleo*, oil painting; ~ *al temple*, tempera. *2* picture, painting [work of art]. *3* paint, colour. *4* painting, portrayal, description.
pinturero, -ra *adj.* vain, conceitedly affected.
pínula *f.* pinnule, sight [of an instrument].
pinzas *f. pl.* tweezers, pincers, nippers, small tongs. *2* ZOOL. pincers [of crustaceans].
pinzón *m.* ORN. chaffinch. *2* ORN. ~ *real*, bullfinch.
piña *f.* BOT. pine cone. *2* BOT. cone. *3* BOT. pineapple: ~ *de América*, pineapple. *4* fig. cluster, knot.
piñal *m.* (Am.) pineapple plantation.
piñata *f.* pot. *2* hanging pot filled with sweetmeats wich is broken with a stick at a masked ball on the first Sunday of Lent.

piñón *m.* BOT. pine nut [seed]. *2* pine-nut kernel. *3* MECH., ORN. pinion. *4* nut [of a gunlock].

piñonate *m.* candied pine-nut kernel.

piñoneo *m.* click [of a gun being cocked]. *2* cry [of male partridges in rut].

piñonero *adj. pino* ~, stone pine, nut pine.

Pío *m. pr. n.* Pius.

1) **pío** *m.* peeping [of chickens or young birds]. *2* coll. yearning, vehement desire.

2) **pío, -a** *adj.* pious. *2* merciful, compassionate. *3* pied, piebald [horse, etc.].

piocha *f.* jeweled head adornment. *2* MAS. a trimming hammer.

piojento, -ta *adj.* lousy.

piojería *f.* lousiness. *2* coll. misery, poverty.

piojillo *m.* ENT. bird louse.

piojo *m.* ENT. louse: ~ *resucitado*, fig. upstart, parvenu.

piojoso, -sa *adj.* lousy. *2* mean, stingy.

pión, -na *adj.* peeping, chirping.

piorrea *f.* MED. pyorrhea, pyorrhœa.

pipa *f.* pipe, tobacco pipe. *2* pipe, cask, barrel. *3* pip, seed [of apple, melon, etc.].

pipar *intr.* to smoke a pipe.

piperáceo, -a *adj.* BOT. piperaceous.

pipería *f.* pipes or casks [collect]. *2* NAUT. water barrels of a ship.

pipeta *f.* pipette.

1) **pipí,** *pl.* **-píes** *m.* ORN. pitpit, honey creeper.

2) **pipí,** *pl.* **-pis** *m.* [child's word] urination.

pipiar *intr.* to peep, chirp.

pipiolo *m.* coll. novice, green horn.

pipirigallo *m.* BOT. sainfoin.

pipiritaña, pipitaña *f.* boy's flute made of a green barley stalk.

piporro *m.* MUS. coll. bassoon.

pique *m.* pique, resentment. *2* determined purpose to do something out of pride or emulation. *3* NAUT. crotch. *4* *echar a* ~, to founder, sink [a ship]; fig. to ruin. *5* NAUT. *irse a* ~ [of a ship], to founder, sink; fig. to be ruined. *6 a* ~ *de*, in danger of; on the point of. *7 a* ~, sharp-cut [cliff].

piqué *m.* piqué [cotton fabric].

piquera *f.* entrance hole [in a hive]. *2* tap [in a barrel]. *3* taphole [of blast furnace]. *4* lamp burner.

piquero *m.* MIL. pikeman. *2* ORN. booby.

piqueta *f.* pick, pickaxe. *2* mason's hammer.

piquete *m.* prick, puncture. *2* small hole. *3* picket, short stake. *4* MIL. picket, squad.

piquillo *m.* dim. small beak or bill. *2* small amount.

piquituerto *m.* ORN. crossbill.

pira *f.* pyre. *2* funeral pile.

piragua *f.* NAUT. pirogue.

piramidal *adj.* pyramidal.

pirámide *f.* pyramid.

Píramo *m. pr. n.* Pyramus.

pirata *adj.* piratical. *2 m.* pirate.

piratear *intr.* to pirate, practice piracy.

piratería *f.* piracy. *2* fig. robbery.

pirático, -ca *adj.* piratical.

pirenaico, -ca *adj.* Pyrenean.

pirexia *f.* MED. pyrexia.

piriforme *adj.* pyriform, pear-shaped.

Pirineos (los) *m. pl.* GEOG. Pyrenees.

pirita *f.* MINER. pyrites.

piróforo *m.* CHEM. pyrophorus.

pirogálico *adj.* CHEM. pyrogallic.

pirógeno, -na *adj.* pyrogenous.

pirograbado *m.* pyrography, pyrogravure.

pirólisis *m.* CHEM. pyrolisis.

piropear *tr.* to pay compliments to.

piropo *m.* MINER. pyrope. *2* MINER. carbuncle. *3* compliment, flattering remark.

piróscafo *m.* steamship.

piroscopio *m.* PHYS. pyroscope.

pirosfera *f.* GEOL. pyrosphere.

pirosis *f.* MED. pyrosis, heartburn.

pirotecnia *f.* pyrotechnics.

pirotécnico, -ca *adj.* pyrotechnical. *2 m.* pyrotechnist; fireworks manufacturer.

pirrarse *ref.* to long, to be very fond: ~ *por*, to long for, to be very fond of.

pírrico, -ca *adj.* Pyrrhic.

pirriquio *m.* PROS. pyrrhic, pyrrhichius.

pirronismo *m.* Pyrrhonism.

pirueta *f.* pirouette, caper.

piruetear *intr.* to pirouet.

pisa *f.* tread, treading. *2* pressing [of grapes, etc.]. *3* coll. volley of kicks.

pisada *f.* tread, footstep; footprint: *seguir las pisadas de*, to follow in the footsteps of. *2* stepping on someone's foot.

pisador, -ra *adj.* treading. *2* prancing, highstepping [horse]. *3 m.-f.* treader.

pisapapeles *m.* paper weight.

pisar *tr.* to tread on, step on. *2* to tread, press [grapes, etc.], to ram, tamp. *3* to trample under foot. *4* MUS. to press down [keys or strings]. *5* [of male birds] to tread. *6* to overlap.

pisaverde *m.* fop, coxcomb, dandy.

piscicultor, -ra *m.-f.* pisciculturist.

piscicultura *f.* pisciculture, fish culture.

piscifactoría *f.* fish hatchery.

pisciforme *adj.* pisciform, fish-shaped.

piscina *f.* fishpond; swimming pool. *2* piscina.

piscívoro, -ra *adj.* piscivorous, fish-eating.

piscolabis, *pl.* **-bis** *m.* snack, bite, luncheon.

pisiforme *adj.* pisiform.

piso *m.* tread, treading. *2* floor, pavement. *3* floor, storey: ~ *bajo*, ground floor. *4* flat, apartment. *5* MIN. level, level works. *6* GEOL. stage formation.

pisón *m.* rammer, tamper, paver's beetle.

pisotear *tr.* to trample, tread under foot. *2* to humble, despise, abuse.

pisoteo *m.* trampling, treading under foot.

pisotón *m.* heavy tread on someone's foot.

pista *f.* trail, trace, track, scent: *estar sobre la* ~, to be on the scent; *seguir la* ~ *a*, to be on the trail of. *2* clue. *3* SPORT. racetrack. *4* ring [of a circus]. *5* AER. runway. *6* ~ *de patinaje*, skating ring.

pistachero, pistacho *m.* BOT. pistachio [tree].

pistar *tr.* to pound, crush, squeeze.

pistero *m.* feeding cup [for invalids].

pistilo *m.* BOT. pistil.

pisto *m.* chicken broth [for the sick]. *2* dish of hashed peppers, tomatoes, onions, etc. *3* hodgepodge. *4* airs: *darse* ~, to put on airs.

pistola *f.* pistol: ~ *ametralladora*, submachine gun. *2* spray gun. *3* pistole [coin].

pistolera *f.* holster.

pistolero *m.* pistol-shooting gangster.

pistoletazo *m.* pistol shot.

pistón *m.* MACH., MUS. piston. *2* percussion cap.

pistoneo *m.* knock, knocking [of an internal combustion engine].

pistonudo, -da *adj.* coll. grand, stunning.

pistoresa *f.* a short dagger.

pita *f.* BOT. American Aloe, pita. *2* pita [fibre or tread]. *3* glass marble [toy]. *4* hissing, hooting, catcalling.

pitaco *m.* BOT. scape of the pita.
pitada *f.* blow of a whistle. *2* coll. nonsensical remark. *3* PITA *4*. *4* (Am.) puff [on a cigar, etc.].
Pitágoras *m. pr. n.* Pythagoras.
pitagórico, -ca *adj.-n.* Pythagorean.
pitanza *f.* dole, ration. *2* daily food. *3* coll. price, stipend.
pitaña *f.* LEGAÑA.
pitañoso, -sa *adj.* LEGAÑOSO.
pitar *intr.* [of a whistle] to blow. *2* to blow a whistle.
pitido *m.* whistle. *2* whistling [of a bird].
pitillera *f.* cigarette case. *2* cigarette maker [woman].
pitillo *m.* cigarette.
pítima *f.* coll. drunk, drunkenness.
pitio, -a *adj.-n.* Pythian.
pitío *m.* coll. PITIDO.
pito *m.* whistle, catcall [instrument]. *2* a South American tick. *3* jackstone. *4* cigarette. *5* ORN. woodpecker. *6* coll. nothing, a straw: *no me importa un ~*, I don't care a straw. *5 pl.* whistling [expressing disapproval].
pitón *m.* budding horn. *2* point, tip [of bull's horn]. *3* PITORRO. *4* small pointed protuberance. *5* ZOOL. python.
pitonisa *f.* pythoness. *2* BIBL. witch.
pitorrearse *ref.* to make fun [of].
pitorreo *m.* making fun.
pitorro *m.* conic spout of certain vessels.
pitpit *m.* ORN. pipit.
pituita *f.* pituite.
pituitario, -ria *adj.* pituitary.
pituso, -sa *adj.* tiny, graceful [child]. *2 m.-f.* tot, little child.
piular *intr.* PIAR.
píxide *m.* ECCL. pyx.
pixidio *m.* BOT. pyxidium.
piyama *m.* PIJAMA.
pizarra *f.* MINER. shale; slate. *2* slate [piece of slate]. *3* slate [for writing]; blackboard.
pizarral *m.* slate quarry.
pizarreño, -ña *adj.* slaty; slate-coloured.
pizarrín *m.* slate pencil.
pizarroso, -sa *adj.* slaty. *2* abounding in slate.
pizca *f.* coll bit, jot, whit: *ni ~*, not a bit.
pizco *m.* PELLIZCO.
pizmiento, -ta *adj.* dark, pitch-coloured.
pizpireta *adj.* brisk, lively, smart [woman].
pizpita *f.*, **pizpitillo** *m.* AGUZANIEVES.
pizzicato *adj.-m.* MUS. pizzicato.
placa *f.* plaque [badge of honorary order]. *2* MED. plaque. *3* superposed plate or thin sheet. *4* doorplate. *5* ANAT., ELECT., RADIO., PHOT. plate. *6* RLY. *~ giratoria*, turntable.
placable *adj.* placable.
pláceme *m.* congratulation.
placenta *f.* ANAT., BOT., ZOOL. placenta.
placentero, -ra *adj.* joyful, pleasant, agreeable.
1) **placer** *m.* pleasure, enjoyment, delight, content: *a ~*, pleased; at one's heart content. *2* pleasure, will, consent. *3* NAUT. large flat bank [in sea bed]. *4* MIN. placer. *5* (Am.) pearl-fishing.
2) **placer** *tr.* to please, gratify, content. ‖ CONJUG.: INDIC. Pres.: *plazco*, places, place, etc. ‖ Pret.: *plació* or *plugo;* placieron or *plugieron.* ‖ SUBJ. Pres.: *plazca, plazcas, plazca* or *plegue* or *plega; plazcamos, plazcáis, plazcan.* ‖ Imperf.: placiera or *pluguiera;* placiese or *pluguiese.* ‖ Fut.: placiere, or *pluguiere.* ‖ IMPER.: place, plazca; *plazcamos*, placed, *plazcan.*

placero, -ra *adj.* [pertaining to the] market place. *2 m.-f.* marketer, market vendor.
placible *adj.* agreeable, pleasurable.
placidez *f.* placidity.
plácido, -da *adj.* placid, peaceful, calm. *2* agreeable.
plácito *s.* opinion, judgement.
plafón *m.* ARCH. soffit.
plaga *f.* plague, affliction, calamity, scourge. *2* AGR. scourge, pest. *3* fig. plenty, superabundance [esp. of injurious things]. *4* ulcer, sore.
plagar *tr.* to plague, fill, infest. *2 ref.* to become filled or infected [with].
plagiar *tr.* to plagiarize. *2* (Am.) to kidnap.
plagiario, -ria *a.-n.* plagiary, plagiarist.
plagio *m.* plagiarism, plagiary [literary theft].
plagiotropismo *m.* BOT. plagiotropism.
plaid *m.* plaid.
plan *m.* plan, project, design, scheme: *~ de estudios*, EDUC. curriculum. *2* level, height. *3* plan [drawing, map]. *4* NAUT. floor [of ship's hold]. *5* MIN. mine floor.
plana *f.* page [of a sheet of paper]. *2* copy [of penmanship]: *enmendar la ~ a uno*, to find fault with a thing done by someone. *3* plain, flat country. *4* PRINT. page. *5* MAS. trowel. *6* MIL. *~ mayor*, staff.
plancton *m.* plankton.
plancha *f.* plate, sheet [of metal]. *2* PRINT. plate. *3* iron, flatiron. *4* ironing [clothes]. *5* horizontal suspension [in gymnastics]. *6* coll. blunder, social blunder: *tirarse una ~*, to blunder, to put one's foot in it. *7* NAUT. gangplank, gangboard.
planchado *m.* ironing, pressing [of clothes].
planchar *tr.* to iron, press [clothes].
planchear *tr.* to plate, cover with metal plates.
planeador *m.* AER. glider.
planear *tr.* to plan, design, outline. *2 intr.* AER. to volplane, glide.
planeta *m.* ASTR. planet.
planetario, -ria *adj.* planetary. *2 m.* orrery, planetarium.
planga *f.* ORN. gannet.
planicie *f.* plain, flatland.
planificar *tr.* to plan [arrange beforehand].
planilla *f.* (Am.) list, roll, schedule.
planimetría *f.* plane survey; planimetry.
planímetro *m.* planimeter.
planisferio *m.* planisphere.
plano, -na *adj.* plane. *2* flat, even, smooth. *3 m.* plane [plane surface]: *~ inclinado*, inclined plane; *primer ~*, foreground. *4* AER. plane, wing. *5* plan [drawing, map]: *levantar un ~*, to make a survey. *6 de ~*, openly, clearly; with the flat of the land, of a sword, etc.
planta *f.* BOT. plant. *2* planted ground. *3* sole [of foot]; fig. foot. *4* ENG. plan, design. *5* ARCH. plan [of a floor or building]. *6* plan, list of the sections and staff or personnel of [an office, institution, etc.]. *7* MIN. level. *8 ~ baja*, ground floor. *9 buena ~*, fine physique or appearance. *10 de ~*, from the ground up.
plantación *f.* AGR. planting. *2* plantation.
plantador, -ra *adj.* planting. *2 m.-f.* planter [person]. *3 m.* dibble, planting stick.
plantagináceo, -a *adj.* BOT. plantaginaceous.
plantaina *f.* BOT. plantain [herb].
1) **plantar** *adj.* BOT. plantar.
2) **plantar** *tr.* AGR. to plant. *2* to plant, place, set up. *3* to plant, deliver [a blow, etc.]. *4* to put, throw: *~ en la calle*, to throw into the street. *5*

to plant, establish. *6 plantar* or *dejar plantado a uno*, to abandon, desert; to jilt; to fail to keep one's appointment with. *7 ref.* to plant oneself. *8 coll.* to go, get, arrive [in a short time]. *9* [of an animal] to balk or baulk. *10* to refuse obstinately to do a thing.

plante *m.* revolt or protest [in prison, etc.].

planteamiento *m.* planning. *2* carrying out [of a plan, etc.]. *3* statement [of a problem]; posing, raising [a question].

plantear *tr.* to plan, outline. *2* to establish [a system, etc.]; to carry out [a reform]. *3* to state [a problem]; to pose, raise [a question].

plantel *m.* nursery, nursery garden. *2* nursery [of artists, scholars, etc.].

plantificar *tr.* to stablish [a system, institution, etc.]. *2* to carry out [a reform]. *3* PLANTAR 3 & 4. *5 ref.* PLANTAR 8.

plantígrado, -da *adj.-m.* ZOOL. plantigrade.

plantilla *f.* insole. *2* sole [of a stocking]. *3* plate [of gunlock]. *4* MACH. template, templet [pattern]. *5* ENG. plan, design. *6* PLANTA 6.

plantío, -a *adj.* tillable [land]. *2 m.* planted ground, patch of young plants. *3* AGR. planting.

plantista *m.* landscape gardener.

plantón *m.* AGR. young tree, cutting, slip [for planting]. *2* watchman [before the door of a building]. *3* long wait standing: *dar un ~*, to keep someone waiting; *estar de ~*, to stand around for a long time.

planudo, -da *adj.* NAUT. flat-bottomed.

plañidero, -ra *adj.* moaning, mournful, plaintive. *2 f.* weeper [professional mourner].

plañido *m.* moan, lamentation, crying.

plañir *intr.* to lament, grieve, bewail. *2 tr.* to lament, grive over. ‖ CONJUG. as *mullir*.

plaqué *m.* plate, plating [of gold or silver].

plasma *m.* PHYSIOL. plasma. *2 f.* MINER. plasma.

plasmar *tr.* to make, mould, shape.

plasmático, -ca *adj.* plasmatic.

plasta *f.* paste, soft mass, anything soft [as mud, etc.]. *2* flattened mass.

plaste *m.* filler, size [made of glue and plaster].

plástica *f.* plastic [art of modeling].

plasticidad *f.* plasticity.

plástico, -ca *adj.* plastic. *2 m.* plastic [substance].

plastrón *m.* FENC. plastron. *2* large cravat.

plata *f.* CHEM., MINER. silver: *~ labrada*, wrought silver, silverware; *como una ~*, coll. clean, shining; *en ~*, coll. plainly; briefly; in sum. *2* plate [utensils, etc., of silver]. *3* silver [silver coins]. *4* coll. money.

plataforma *f.* platform [flat surface; raised flooring]. *2* GEOGR., POL. platform. *3* MACH. index plate. *4* RLY. platform car.

platal *m.* large amount of money, lot of money.

platanáceo, -a *adj.* BOT. platanaceous.

platanal, platanar *m.* plantation of plane trees. *2* banana field or plantation.

platanero *m.* BOT. banana [plant].

plátano *m.* BOT. banana, plantain [plant and fruit]. *2* BOT. plane tree. *3* BOT. *~ falso*, sycamore maple.

platea *f.* THEAT. orchestra, parquet, pit.

plateado, -da *adj.* silvered, silver-plated. *2* silver, silvery [in colour]. *3 m.* silver plating.

platear *tr.* to silver [coat with silver; give silvery appearance to].

platelminto *m.* ZOOL. platyhelminth.

plateresco, -ca *adj.* ARCH. plateresque.

platería *f.* silversmith's shop or trade.

platero *m.* silversmith. *2* jeweller.

plática *f.* chat, talk. *2* ECCL. address, sermon.

platicar *intr.* to chat, talk, converse.

platija *f.* ICHTH. plaice.

platillo *m. dim.* small dish; saucer: *~ volante*, flying saucer. *2* pan [of scales]. *3* COOK. dish of meat and vegetables. *4* subject of gossip. *5* MUS. cymbal.

platina *f.* stage [of microscope]. *2* plate [of air pump]. *3* PRINT. imposing table. *4* platen.

platinado, -da *adj.* platinized. *2* *rubia platinada*, platinum blonde.

platinar *tr.* to platinize [coat with platinum].

platino *m.* CHEM. platinum.

platirrino, -na *adj.-m.* ZOOL. platyrrhine.

plato *m.* plate, dish [vessel; content of this]: *comer en el mismo ~*, coll. to be close friends; *no haber quebrado un ~*, coll. to be innocent. *2* COOK. dish. *3* course [at meals]: *~ fuerte*, pièce de résistance; *ser ~ de segunda mesa*, to be disregarded, to be second fiddle. *4* pan [of scales]. *5* subject of gossip. *6* MACH. plate, disk.

Platón *m. pr. n.* Plato.

platónico, -ca *adj.* Platonic, Platonistic. *2* platonic. *3 m.-f.* Platonist.

platonismo *m.* Platonism.

plausibilidad *f.* reasonability, acceptability. *2* laudableness.

plausible *adj.* reasonable, acceptable. *2* laudable.

plausivo, -va *adj.* applauding.

plauso *m.* applause.

playa *f.* beach, strand, sandy shore.

playado, -da *adj.* having a beach.

playeras *f. pl.* a popular Andalusian song.

plaza *f.* public square, circus: *sacar a la ~*, fig. to make public. *2* market place. *3* MIL. place [fortified town]. *4* place [space, seat]. *5* place, post, situation, employement. *6* room, space: *hacer ~*, to make room, clear the way. *7* COM. town, city. *8* *~ de toros*, bull ring, arena. *9* MIL. *sentar ~*, to enlist. *10* *sentar ~ de*, to set up for.

plazco, plazca, etc. *irr.* V. PLACER.

plazo *m.* term [limited period], time, date [for an action, payment, etc.]. *2* term [appointed day]. *3* instalment [of a sum payable]: *venta a plazos*, hire purchase, hire system.

plazoleta, plazuela *f. dim.* small public square.

pleamar *f.* NAUT. high tide, high water.

plebe *f.* plebs, common people. *2* populace.

plebeyez *f.* plebeianism; coarseness, vulgarity.

plebeyo, -ya *adj.-n.* plebeian.

plebiscito *f.* plebiscite; plebiscitum.

plectro *m.* MUS. plectrum. *2* poet. inspiration.

plegable *adj.* pliable. *2* folding, collapsible.

plegadera *f.* paper folder, paper knife.

plegado *m.* PLEGADURA.

plegador, -ra *adj.* folding. *2 m.* folding instrument. *3* WEAV. beam. *4 f.* folding machine.

plegadura *f.* folding, doubling, plaiting.

plegamiento *m.* PLEGADURA. *2* GEOL. fold.

plegar *tr.* to fold, double, plait, pleat. *2* SEW. to gather, pucker. *3 ref.* to fold, bend. *4* to yield, submit. ‖ CONJUG. as *acertar*.

plegaria *f.* prayer, supplication.

plegue, plega, etc. *irr.* V. PLACER.

pleguería *f.* folds [in robes and drapery].

pleistoceno, -na *adj. & GEOL.* Pleistocene.

pleita *f.* plaited strand of esparto grass.

pleiteador, -ra *m.-f.* litigant. *2* litigious person.

pleiteante *adj.* litigating. *2 m.-f.* litigant.

pleitear *tr.* to litigate.

pleitesía *f.* homage: *rendir ~*, to do homage.

pleitista *m.-f.* litigious person, pettifogger.
pleito *m.* litigation, lawsuit. *2* dispute, debate, contest, strife. *3* ~ *homenaje*, FEUD. homage.
plenamente *adv.* fully, completely.
plenario, -ria *adj.* complete, full. *2* plenary.
plenilunio *m.* full moon.
plenipotenciario, -ria *adj.-n.* plenipotentiary.
plenitud *f.* plenitude, fullness.
pleno, -na *adj.* full, complete. *2 en* ~ [with a noun], in broad, in the middle of, at the height of: *en* ~ *día*, in broad day. *3 m.* full assembly, plenum.
pleonasmo *m.* pleonasm.
pleonástico, -ca *adj.* pleonastic.
plepa *f.* coll. person or thing full of defects.
plesiosauro *m.* PALEONT. plesiosaur.
pletina *f.* narrow iron plate.
plétora *f.* plethora.
pletórico, -ca *adj.* plethoric.
pleura *f.* ANAT., ZOOL. pleura.
pleuresía *f.* MED. pleurisy.
pleuritis *f.* MED. pleuritis.
pleuronecto, -ta *adj.-m.* ICHTH. pleuronectid.
plexiglás *m.* perspex.
plexo *m.* ANAT. plexus.
pléyade *f.* pleiad.
Pléyades *f. pl.* ASTR., MYTH. Pleiades.
plica *f.* sealed envelope.
pliego *m.* sheet of paper; folded paper. *2* PRINT. sheet [part of a book]. *3* sealed letter or document; *4* ~ *de condiciones*, specifications [for a contract].
pliego, pliegue, etc. *irr.* V. PLEGAR.
pliegue *m.* fold, plait, pleat, crease. *2* GEOL. fold.
Plinio *m. pr. n.* Pliny.
plinto *m.* ARCH. plinth [lower square member].
plioceno *adj.-m.* GEOL. Pliocene.
plomada *f.* plumb-line; souding line; plummet. *2* sinkers [of a fishing net].
plomar *tr.* to put a lead seal on.
plombagina *f.* MINER. plumbago, graphite.
plomería *f.* lead roofing; leadwork. *2* plumber's shop.
plomero *m.* lead worker, plumber.
plomizo, -za *adj.* leaden, plumbeous [made of lead; resembling lead]. *2* lead-coloured.
plomo *m.* CHEM. lead. *2* lead [piece of lead]; plumb bob, plummet, sinker. *3* fig. bullet. *4* coll. bore, dull person. *5 a* ~, perpendiculary. *6 caer a* ~, to fall plumb.
plugo, pluguiera, etc. *irr.* V. PLACER.
pluma *f.* feather, plume [of bird]. *2* feathers. *3* [writing] quill, pen: ~ *estilográfica*, fountain pen; *dejar correr la* ~, to write away. *4* fig. pen [hand, author, style of literary composition]. *5* ~ *de agua*, a variable measure for running water.
plumada *f.* stroke of pen. *2* brief writing.
plumado, -da *adj.* feathered [having feathers].
plumaje *m.* plumage. *2* crest, plume.
plumazo *m.* PLUMADA.
plumazón *f.* plumage. *2* plumes [ornamental bunches of feathers].
plumbagina *f.* PLOMBAGINA.
plúmbeo, -a *adj.* of lead. *2* plumbeous, heavy as lead.
plúmbico, -ca *adj.* CHEM. plumbic.
plumeado *m.* PAINT. hatching.
plumear *tr.* PAINT., DRAW. to hatch. *2* to write.
plúmeo, -a *adj.* plumose, feathered.
plumero *m.* feather duster. *2* crest, plume [bunch of feathers]. *3* box for pens and pencils.

plumilla *f. dim.* small feather. *2* small writing pen. *3* point [of fountain pen]. *4* BOT. plumule.
plumista *m.* scrivener, clerk. *2* plumist.
plumón *m.* down [of birds]. *2* feather bed.
plumoso, -sa *adj.* feathered, feathery, plumose.
plúmula *f.* BOT. plumule.
plural *adj.-m.* GRAM. plural.
pluralidad *f.* plurality.
pluralizar *tr.* to pluralize.
plus *m.* extra, bonus. *2* MIL. extra pay.
pluscuamperfecto *adj.-m.* GRAM. pluperfect.
plusvalía *f.* unearned increment.
Plutarco *m. pr. n.* Plutarch.
plutocracia *f.* plutocracy.
Plutón *m. pr. n.* MYTH., ASTR. Pluto.
plutónico, -ca *adj.* GEOL. plutonic. *2* MYTH. Plutonic.
plutonio *m.* CHEM. plutonium.
plutonismo *m.* GEOL. Plutonism.
pluvial *adj.* pluvial, rain. *2* ECCL. *capa* ~, pluvial.
pluvímetro, pluviómetro *m.* pluviometer, rain gauge.
pluvioso, -sa *adj.* rainy, pluvious.
pobeda *f.* white-poplar grove.
población *f.* population. *2* peopling, planting, settling, colonizing. *3* village, town, city.
poblacho *m.* sorry village.
poblado *m.* town, settlement, inhabited place.
poblador, -ra *adj.* peopling, populating. *2 m.-f.* inhabitant. *3* populator, colonizer, settler.
poblar *tr.* to inhabit, people. *2* to people, populate, settle, colonize; to plant [a river with fishes, a land with trees, etc.]. *3* [of hairs, leaves, plants, etc.] to cover, grow on. *4 ref.* to become peopled. *5* to become filled or covered [with hairs, leaves, plants, etc.]. ‖ CONJUG. as *contar*.
pobo *m.* ÁLAMO BLANCO.
pobre *adj.* poor: ~ *de espíritu*, poor in spirit; *¡*~ *de mí!*, poor me!; ~ *diablo*, poor devil; good-natured, insignificant fellow; ~ *hombre*, spiritless fellow. *2 m.-f.* poor person; pauper, beggar.
pobrecico, -ca; -cillo, -cilla; -cito, -cita *adj.* dim. of POBRE. *2 m.-f.* dim. little begar. *3* poor little thing.
pobrete, -ta *adj.* poor, wretched. *2 m.-f.* poor person. *3* good-natured, spiritless person.
pobretería *f.* poor people, beggars.
pobretón, -na *adj.* poor, needy. *2 m.-f.* poor person.
pobreza *f.* poverty, destitution, want. *2* poverty, poorness. *3* scanty possessions [of the poor]. *5* meanness of spirit.
pocero *m.* well digger. *2* cesspool cleaner.
pocilga *f.* pigsty, pigpen. *2* fig. dirty place.
pocillo *m.* chocolate cup.
pócima *f.* medicinal decoction; medicinal drink.
poción *f.* drink, beverage.
1) poco *adv.* little: *me gusta* ~, I like it little; ~ *hábil*, unskilled; ~ *más o menos*, more or less. *2* shortly, a short time: ~ *antes*, shortly before. *3 m.* little [small amount, time, etc.]: *un* ~ *de*, a little, some [foll. by noun]; *tener en* ~, to set little value on; *a* ~, shortly afterwards; *dentro de* ~, in a short time; *¡*~ *a* ~*!*, easy there!; *por* ~, almost, nearly.
2) poco, -ca *adj.* little [not much]. *2 pl.* few. *3 unos pocos*, a few, some.
pocho, -cha *adj.* coll. pale, pale-faced.
poda *f.* pruning. *2* pruning season.
podadera *f.* pruning knife, billhook.
podador, -ra *m.-f.* pruner [one who prunes].
podagra *f.* MED. gout, podagra.
podar *tr.* to prune, lop, trim.

podenco *m.* hound [dog].

1) **poder** *m.* power [authority, control]. *2* power [ability to act; capability of producing an effect; active property]; force, strength, might. *3* power, hands, possession: *en ~ de*, in the power, or in the hands, of. *4* POL. holding of office: *estar en el ~*, to be in office. *5 sing.-pl.* LAW. power, proxy, power of attorney. *6* power, authority [delegated power].

2) **poder** *tr.-intr.* to be able [to], can, may: *no ~ con*, not to be able to bear; to be no match for; *no ~ más*, to be unable to do more; to be exhausted; *no puedo menos de hacerlo*, I cannot help doing it; *a más no ~*, to the utmost; *como pueda, podamos*, etc., the best I, we, etc., can. | Notice the different senses of the verb in the negative sentences: *Juan no puede ir*, John cannot go; *Juan puede no ir*, John may not go. *2 intr.* to have power or influence. *3 impers.* to be possible, may: *puede que llueva*, it may rain. ‖ IRREG. CONJUG.: INDIC. Pres.: *puedo, puedes, puede; podemos, podéis, pueden.* | Pret.: *pude, pudiste, pudo; pudimos, pudisteis, pudieron.* | Fut.: *podré, podrás*, etc. | COND.: *podría, podrías*, etc. | SUBJ. Pres.: *pueda, puedas, pueda;* podamos, podáis, *puedan.* | Imperf.: *pudiera, pudieras*, or *pudiese, pudieses*, etc. | Fut.: *pudiere, pudieres*, etc. | IMPER.: *puede, pueda;* podamos, poded, *puedan.* | GER.: *pudiendo.*

poderdante *m.-f.* LAW constituent.

poderhabiente *m.-f.* LAW attorney, proxy.

poderío *m.* power, might. *2* sway, jurisdiction. *3* wealth, riches.

poderosamente *adv.* mightily. *2* forcibly.

poderoso, -sa *adj.* powerful, mighty. *2* forcible, efficacious. *3* rich, wealthy.

podio *m.* ARCH. podium.

podón *m.* large pruning knife, billhook.

podre *f.* pus.

podré, podrás, etc. *irr.* V. PODER.

podrecer *tr.-intr.-ref.* PUDRIR.

podredumbre *f.* rot, rottenness, decay. *2* pus.

podredura, podrición *f.* putrefaction, corruption.

podredero *m.* PUDRIDERO.

podría, podrías, etc. *irr.* V. PODER.

podrigorio *m.* person full of aches and ailments.

podrir *tr.-ref.* PUDRIR.

poema *m.* poem.

poesía *f.* poetry. *2* poem.

poeta *m.* poet.

poetastro *m.* poetaster.

poética *f.* poetics.

poético, -ca *adj.* poetic, poetical.

poetisa *f.* poetess.

poetizar *intr.-tr.* to poetize.

poíno *m.* gantry, barrelstand.

póker *m.* poker [card game].

polaco, -ca *adj.* Polish. *2 m.-f.* Pole [person]. *3 m.* Polish language.

polacra *f.* NAUT. polacre.

polaina *f.* legging.

polar *adj.* polar; pole: *estrella ~*, polestar.

polaridad *f.* polarity.

polarímetro *m.* polarimeter.

polariscopio *m.* polariscope.

polarización *f.* polarization.

polarizar *tr.* to polarize.

polca *f.* polka [dance].

polea *f.* pulley. *2* NAUT. tackle, tackle block.

polemarca *m.* polemarch.

polémica *f.* polemic, controversy. *2* polemics. *3* MIL. art of fortification and investment.

polémico, -ca *adj.* polemic, polemical.

polemista *m.-f.* polemic, polemist.

polemonio *m.* BOT. polemonium.

polen *m.* BOT. pollen.

poleo *m.* BOT. penny royal. *2* coll. stiff, cold wind.

poliandria *f.* polyandry.

policárpico, -ca *adj.* BOT. polycarpic, polycarpous.

pólice *m.* thumb.

policía *m.* policeman, police officer, detective. *2* police, police force: *~ secreta*, secret police. *3* politeness. *4* cleanliness, good order.

policíaco, -ca *adj.* [pertaining to the] police. *2 novela policíaca*, detective story.

policial *adj.* (S. Am.) POLICÍACO.

policlínica *f.* MED. polyclinic.

policromar *tr.* to polychrome.

policromía *f.* polychromy.

policromo, -ma *adj.* polychrome, many-coloured.

polichinela *m.* punchinello.

poliédrico, -ca *adj.* polyhedral, polyhedric.

poliedro *m.* GEOM. polyhedron.

polifásico, -ca *adj.* ELECT. polyphase, multiphase.

Polifemo *m. pr. n.* MYT. Polyphemus.

polifonía *f.* MUS. polyphony.

polifónico, -ca; polífono, -na *adj.* MUS. polyphonic.

polígala *f.* BOT. milkwort.

poligamia *f.* polygamy.

polígamo, -ma *adj.* polygamous. *2 m.* polygamist.

poligloto, -ta *adj.-n.* polyglot. *2 f.* polyglot [Bible].

poligonal *adj.* polygonal.

polígono, -na *adj.* polygonal. *2 m.* GEOM., FORT. polygon.

polígrafo *m.* expert in ciphers. *2* polygraph [writer].

polilla *f.* ENT. moth, clothes moth, carpet moth. *2* fig. waster, destroyer.

polimería *f.* CHEM. polymerism.

polimerizar *tr.* CHEM. to polymerize.

polímero, -ra *adj.* CHEM. polymeric. *2 m.* CHEM. polymer.

polimorfismo *m.* polymorphism.

polín *m.* roller, skid.

Polinesia *f. pr. n.* GEOG. Polynesia.

polinesio, -sia *adj.-n.* Polynesian.

polínico, -ca *adj.* BOT. pollinic, pollinical.

polinización *f.* BOT. pollination.

polinomio *m.* ALG. polynomial.

polio *m.* BOT. poly.

poliomielitis *f.* MED. poliomyelitis.

polípero *m.* ZOOL. polypary.

pólipo *m.* ZOOL. polyp. *2* MED. polyp, polypus. *3* PULPO.

polipodio *m.* BOT. polypody, sweet fern.

polisépalo, -la *adj.* BOT. polysepalous.

polisílabo, -ba *adj.* polysyllabic. *2 m.* polysyllable.

polisón *m.* bustle [of woman's dress].

polispasto *m.* tackle, hoisting tackle.

polispermo, -ma *adj.* BOT. polyspermous.

polista *m.-f.* polo player.

politécnico, -ca *adj.* polytechnic.

politeísmo *m.* polytheism.

política *f.* politics. *2* policy [course of action; sagacity, address]. *3* politeness.

politicastro *m.* politicaster.

político, -ca *adj.* politic, political. *2* politic, expedient; tactful. *3* polite, courteous. *4* -in-law: *padre ~*, father-in-law. *5 m.* politician.

politiquear *intr.* coll. to dabble in politics, to play politics.

politiqueo *m.* coll. dabbling in politics.
politiquería *f.* political chicanery.
politiquillo *m.* petty politician.
polivalente *f.* BACT., CHEM. polyvalent, multivalent.
póliza *f.* paybill. 2 COM. certificate, policy: ~ *de seguros,* insurance policy. *3* tax stamp.
polizón *m.* loafer. 2 stowaway [in a ship].
polizonte *m.* coll. cop, policeman.
polo *m.* GEOM., ASTR., GEOG., PHYS., BIOL. pole. 2 SPORT. polo.
polonés, -sa *adj.* Polish. 2 *m.-f.* Pole. *3 f.* polonaise [woman's dress]. *4* MUS. polonaise.
Polonia *f. pr. n.* GEOG. Poland.
polonio *m.* CHEM. polonioum.
poltrón, -na *adj.* lazy. 2 *m.-f.* lazy person. *3 f.* easy chair.
poltronería *f.* laziness, sloth.
polución *f.* MED. pollution.
poluto, -ta *adj.* polluted, unclean, filthy.
Pólux *m. pr. n.* MYTH., ASTR. Pollux.
polvareda *f.* cloud of dust. 2 fig. dust, turmoil.
polvera *f.* compact, face-powder case.
polvillo *m. dim.* fine dust.
polvo *m.* dust: *limpio de* ~ *y paja,* fig. free of all charges, net. 2 powder [mass of dry particles]: *hacer* ~, to destroy; to beat completely; to tire out; *en* ~, powdered. *3* pinch [of snuff or powder]. *4 pl.* cosmetic or medicinal powder. *5 polvos de la madre Celestina,* fig. hocus-pocus, secret or miraculous means.
pólvora *f.* powder [explosive], gunpowder: *gastar la* ~ *en salvas,* fig. to waste time or energy: *ser una* ~, coll. to be a live wire. 2 fireworks. *3* fig. bad temper. *4* fig. liveliness, vivacity.
polvorear *tr.* to powder [sprinkle with powder].
polvoriento, -ta *adj.* dusty.
polvorín *m.* powder magazine. 2 powder flask. *3* (Am.) spitfire [person].
polvorista *m.* PIROTÉCNICO.
polvorizar *tr.* POLVOREAR. *2* PULVERIZAR.
polvoroso, -sa *adj.* dusty.
polvorón *m.* a kind of cake.
polla *f.* CARDS POOL. 2 ORN. pullet. *3* fig. girl, young woman. *4* ORN. coot. *5* ORN. water hen, gallinule.
pollada *f.* brood, hatch, covey.
pollastre, pollastro *m.* coll. sly fellow.
pollazón *f.* brood, hatch, hatching.
pollera *f.* female poulterer. 2 chicken roost. *3* chicken coop. *4* gocart. *5* hooped petticoat. *6* (Am.) skirt [woman's garment].
pollería *f.* poultry shop. 2 coll. young people.
pollero, -ra *m.-f.* poulterer. 2 chicken roost.
pollina *f.* young she-ass.
pollino *m.* donkey; young ass. 2 fig. jackass, dolt.
pollito, -ta *m.-f. dim.* little chicken, chick. *2 m.* coll. boy, youth. *3 f.* coll. girl.
pollo *m.* chicken. 2 nestling, young bird. *3* brood [of the bee]. *4* coll. young person.
polluelo *m. dim.* little chicken, chick.
poma *f.* BOT. apple.
pomáceo, -a *adj.* BOT. pomaceous.
pomada *f.* pomade, pomatum.
pomar *m.* orchard; apple orchard.
pomarrosa *f.* BOT. rose apple.
pomelo *m.* BOT. pomelo, grapefruit.
pomerano, -na *adj.-n.* Pomeranian.
pómez (piedra) *f.* pumice stone.
pomo *m.* BOT. pome. 2 pomander. *3* phial, vial, small bottle. *4* pomel [of sword-hilt].

pompa *f.* pomp: *pompas fúnebres,* funeral. 2 pageant. *3* bubble. *4* NAUT. pump.
Pompeya *f. pr. n.* HIST., GEOG. Pompeii.
pompeyano, -na *adj.-n.* Pompeian.
Pompeyo *m. pr. n.* Pompey.
pomposidad *f.* pomposity, pompousness.
pomposo, -sa *adj.* pompous [showy; self-important]. 2 pompous, inflated [style, etc.].
pómulo *m.* ANAT. cheekbone.
ponche *m.* punch [drink]: ~ *de huevo,* eggnog.
ponchera *f.* punch bowl.
poncho, -cha *adj.* soft, lazy; mild. *2 m.* poncho.
ponderable *adj.* ponderable.
ponderación *f.* ponderation. 2 balance, equilibrium. *3* judiciousness. *4* exaggeration; emphasizing: *sin* ~, without exaggeration.
ponderado, -da *adj.* prudent.
ponderador, -ra *adj.* pondering, weighing. 2 balancing. *3* exaggerating; emphasizing.
ponderal *adj.* ponderal.
ponderar *tr.* to weigh. 2 to ponder over. *3* to balance, poise. *4* to exaggerate. *5* to emphasize; to praise highly.
ponderativo, -va *adj.* exaggerating, hyperbolical.
ponderoso, -sa *adj.* ponderous, heavy. *2* grave, circumspect.
pondré, pondría, etc. *irr.* V. PONER.
ponedero, -ra *adj.* egg-laying. *2 m.* hen's nest. *3* nest egg.
ponedor, -ra *adj.* egg-laying. 2 trained to rear on the hind legs [horse]. *3* POSTOR.
ponencia *f.* the post or office of one who is designated to report on a matter; his report.
ponente *m.-f.* reporter, one who is designated to report on a matter.
ponentino, -na *adj.* western.
poner *tr.* to lay [eggs]. 2 to place, put, lay, set: ~ *a prueba,* to put to the test; ~ *a trabajar,* to set to work; ~ *fin a,* to put an end to; to bring to an end; ~ *en libertad,* to set free; ~ *en práctica,* to carry out; ~ *la mesa,* to set the table; ~ *uno sus esperanzas en,* to lay one's hopes in. 2 to suppose. *3* to wager, bet [money]. *4* to appoint; post, set to work as: ~ *de aprendiz,* to apprentice. *5* to apply, adapt. *6* to give [a name]. *7* to expose [to the sun, the air]. *8* to contribute [give as a contribution]. *9* to impose, lay on [a law, tax, etc.]. *10* to put on [a play, etc.]. *11* to cause [fear, etc.]. *12* to make, render, turn: ~ *furioso,* to render furious; ~ *enfermo,* to make ill. *13* ~ *al corriente,* to inform. *14* ~ *al día,* to bring up to date. *15* ~ *como nuevo, como un trapo,* de *vuelta y media,* to abuse, revile, cover with insults; to dress down. *16* ~ *de manifiesto,* to make evident. *17* ~ *de relieve,* to emphasize, point out. *18* ~ *en duda,* to doubt. *19* ~ *en las nubes,* to praise to the skies. *20* ~ *mal a uno,* to discredit someone. *21* ~ *mala cara,* to frown, to show displeasure. *22* ~ *reparos,* to make objections. *23 ref.* to place, put or set oneself. *24* to put on [a garment, etc.]. *25* to become, get, turn. *26* [of the sun, stars, etc.] to set. *27 ponerse a,* to start to, begin to, set about. *28 ponerse a cubierto,* to shelter or protect oneself. *29 ponerse al corriente, al tanto,* to get informed. *30 ponerse bien con,* to get in with. *31 ponerse de acuerdo,* to agree. *32 ponerse de barro, tinta,* etc., to stain oneself with mud, ink, etc. *33 ponerse en marcha,* to begin to move; to set out. *34 ponerse en pie,* to stand up. *35 ponerse en la razón,* to be reasonable.

¶ Conjug. Indic. Pres.: *pongo, pones,* pone; ponemos, ponéis, ponen. | Pret.: *puse, pusiste, puso; pusimos, pusisteis, pusieron.* | Fut.: *pondré, pondrás,* etc. | Cond.: *pondría, pondrías,* etc. | Subj. Pres.: *ponga, pongas, ponga; pongamos, pongáis, pongan.* | Imperf.: *pusiera, pusieras* or *pusiese, pusieses,* etc. | Fut.: *pusiere, pusieres,* etc. | Imper.: *pon, ponga; pongamos, poned, pongan.* | Past. p.: *puesto.*

pongo, ponga, etc. *irr.* V. poner.

poniente *m.* west. 2 west wind.

ponimiento *m.* placing, putting, laying, setting.

pontaje, pontazgo *m.* bridge toll, pontage.

pontear *tr.* to build a bridge over.

póntico, -ca *adj.* Pontic.

pontificado *m.* pontificate.

pontifical *adj.* pontifical. 2 *m.* eccl. pontifical [book]. 3 *pl.* eccl. pontificals.

pontificar *intr.* to pontificate.

pontífice *m.* pontiff, pontifex.

pontificio, -cia *adj.* pontifical, papal.

pontocón *m.* puntapié.

pontón *m.* pontoon. 2 pontoon bridge, floating bridge. 3 hulk [dismantled ship used as a store vessel, hospital or prison].

pontonero *m.* mil. pontoneer, pontonier.

ponzoña *f.* poison, venom.

ponzoñoso, -sa *adj.* poisonous, venomous.

popa *f.* naut. poop, stern: *a* ~, *en* ~, aft, abaft.

popar *tr.* to despise. 2 to fondle, caress. 3 to pamper.

pope *m.* pope [priest of the Orthodox Church].

popel *adj.* naut. sternmost.

popelina *f.* poplin.

poplíteo, -a *adj.* anat. popliteal.

populación *f.* population [act of populating].

populachería *f.* cheap popularity, appeal to the mob.

populachero, -ra *adj.* vulgar, common. 2 intended to please the populace.

populacho *m.* populace, mob, rabble.

popular *adj.* popular.

popularidad *f.* popularity.

popularizar *tr.* to popularize. 2 *ref.* to become popular, to become generally known or liked.

populoso, -sa *adj.* populous.

popurrí, *pl.* **-rríes** *m.* mus. potpurri.

poquedad *f.* paucity, littleness, scantiness, scarcity. 2 trifle. 3 timidity.

poquísimo, -ma *adj. superl.* very little.

1) **poquito** *m.* very small quantity, very short time, little bit. 2 *adv.* very little: ~ *a poco,* gently, slowly.

2) **poquito, -ta** *adj.* very little. 2 *pl.* very few.

por *prep.* by, for, as, along, around, across, through, from, out of, at, in, on, to, etc.: ~ *aquí,* around here, here; ~ *por casualidad,* by chance; ~ *compasión,* out of pity; ~ *decirlo así,* so to say; ~ *Dios,* for heaven's sake; ~ *docenas,* by the dozen; ~ *escrito,* in writing; ~ *ocho pesetas,* for eight pesetas; ~ *la noche,* in the night, at night; ~ *la ventana,* through the window; ~ *lo que veo,* from what I see; ~ *mar,* by sea; ~ *recomendación de,* on recommendation of; *dos* ~ *dos,* two by two; *fui* ~ *agua,* I went for water; *hablé* ~ *él,* I spoke for him; *lo cogió* ~ *el brazo,* he took him by the arm; *lo tengo* ~ *justo,* I hold it just. 2 however, no matter how: ~ *bien que lo haga,* no matter how well I do it. 3 other applications: ~ *ciento,* per cent; ~ *donde,* wherefore, whereby; ~ *entre,* through, in between, among: ~ *tanto,*

~ *lo tanto,* therefore; ~ *lo visto,* apparently; ~ *más que,* ~ *mucho que,* however much, no matter how much; ~ *mí,* as a far as I am concerned; *¿* ~ *qué?,* why?; ~ *supuesto,* of course.

porcachón, -na; porcallón, -na *adj.* coll. dirty, hoggish. 2 *m.-f.* coll. dirty person, hog.

porcelana *f.* porcelain, china.

porcentaje *m.* percentage.

porcino, -na *adj.* porcine. 2 *m.* little pig.

porción *f.* portion, part, allotment. 2 quantity.

porcipelo *m.* coll. bristle [of hog].

porciúncula *f.* eccl. Franciscan jubilee.

porcuno, -na *adj.* porcine, hoggish.

porche *m.* porch, portico, covered walk.

pordiosear *intr.* to beg, go begging.

pordiosero, -ra *adj.* begging, mendicant. 2 *m.-f.* beggar.

porfía *f.* insistence, importunity. 2 stubborness. 3 dispute. 4 *a* ~, in emulation, in competition.

porfiado, -da *adj.* insistent, persistent, importunate, stubborn.

porfiar *intr.* to insist, persist. 2 to ask with importunity. 3 to argue stubbornly.

pórfido *m.* porphyry.

pormenor *m.* detail, particular: *entrar en pormenores,* to go into detail.

pormenorizar *tr.* to detail, tell in detail, itemize.

pornografía *f.* pornography.

pornográfico, -ca *adj.* pornographic.

poro *m.* pore.

porosidad *f.* porosity.

poroso, -sa *adj.* porous.

poroto *m.* bot. (Am.) bean.

porque *conj.* for, because. 2 in order that.

¿por qué? *conj. interr.* why?, wherefore?

porqué *m.* reason, motive. 2 coll. quantity, amount.

porquera *f.* wild boar's lair or couch.

porquería *f.* coll. dirt, filth. 2 coll. poor food. 3 coll. trifle, worthless thing. 4 coll. filthy act or word. 5 coll. dirty trick.

porqueriza *f.* pigsty.

porquerizo, porquero *m.* swineherd.

porqueta *f.* zool. wood louse.

porra *f.* bludgeon, club. 2 maul. 3 bore, nuisance [pers.]. 4 *mandar a la* ~, to send to the devil.

porráceo, -a *adj.* porraceous.

porrada *f.* blow. 2 stupidity, nonsense. 3 lot, heap, great quantity or number.

porrazo *m.* blow, bump, knock.

porrería *f.* coll. stupidity, silliness. 2 sluggishness.

porreta *f.* green leaves of leeks, garlic or onions. 2 coll. *en* ~, naked, stark naked.

porrillo (a) *adv.* abundantly, in abundance.

porro *m.* coll. stupid fellow, dolt. 2 puerro.

1) **porrón** *m.* kind of wine bottle with a long side spout. 2 botijo.

2) **porrón, -na** *adj.* slow, heavy, sluggish.

porta *f.* naut. port, porthole. 2 *adj.* anat. portal [vein].

portaaviones *m.* nav. airplane carrier.

portabandera *f.* shoulder-belt for carrying a flag.

portacaja *m.* drum strap.

portacartas, *pl.* **-tas** *m.* pouch or bag for letters.

portada *f.* arch. portal, front, façade. 2 frontispiece. 3 print. title page. 4 cover [of magazine].

portado, -da *adj.* dressed; behaved.

portador, -ra *adj.* carrying. 2 radio. carrier [wave]. 3 *m.-f.* carrier, bearer. 4 *m.* com. bearer.

portaequipaje *m.* auto. trunk.

portaequipajes, *pl.* **-jes** *m.* baggage rack.

portaestandarte *m.* standart-bearer.
portafusil *m.* MIL. sling [of a musket].
portaherramienta *m.* MACH. chuck.
portal *m.* doorway, portal, vestibule. *2* porch, portico. *3* town's gate.
portalada *f.* portal, large gate.
portalámparas, *pl.* **-ras** *m.* ELECT. socket, lamp holder.
portalápiz *m.* pencil holder.
portalibros, *pl.* **-bros** *m.* book straps [for schoolboys].
portalón *m.* gateway, portal. *2* NAUT. gangway.
portamantas, *pl.* **-tas** *m.* blanket straps.
portaminas, *pl.* **-minas** *m.* mechanical pencil.
portamonedas *m.* pocketbook, purse.
portante *m.* pace, amble [of horse]. *2 tomar el ~*, coll. to leave, go away.
portantillo *m.* easy pace [of horse or ass].
portaobjeto *m.* slide [for microscope].
portapaz *m.-f.* ECCL. pax [tablet].
portaplacas *m.* PHOT. plate holder, chassis.
portapliegos *m.* bag for papers.
portaplumas *m.* penholder.
portar *tr.* to carry [arms]. *2* HUNT. to retrieve.
portaviandas *m.* dinner pail.
portátil *adj.* portable.
portavoz *m.* megaphone. *2* mouthpiece [person, newspaper]; spokesman.
portazgo *m.* toll, road toll. *2* tollhouse.
portazguero *m.* tollkeeper.
portazo *m.* bang or slam [of a door].
porte *m.* portage, porterage, carriage [act; cost]: *~ pagado*, portage prepaid. *2* behaviour, bearing; dress, appearance [of a person]. *3* nobility, illustrious descent. *4* size, capacity; tonnage [of a ship].
portear *tr.* to carry, transport [for a price]. *2 intr.* [of doors or windows] to slam.
portento *m.* prodigy, wonder, portent.
portentoso, -sa *adj.* prodigious, portentous.
porteño, -ña *adj.-n.* of Buenos Aires.
porteo *m.* carrying, portage.
portera *f.* portress, concierge, woman doorkeeper.
portería *f.* porter's lodge. *2* employment of a porter or doorkeeper. *3* SPORT. goal.
portero *m.* doorkeeper, porter, janitor. *2* SPORT. goalkeeper.
portezuela *f. dim.* little door. *2* carriage door. *3* pocket flap.
pórtico *m.* porch. colonnade.
portier *m.* door-curtain, portière.
portilla *f.* gate, passage [in a fence]. *2* NAUT. porthole [for admission of air and light].
portillo *m.* opening [in a wall, fence, etc.]. *2* wicket [small door or gate]. *3* breach, gap. *4* nick [in an edge]. *5* pass between hills.
portón *m. augm.* large door. *2* inner front door.
portorriqueño, -ña *adj.-n.* Puerto Rican.
portugués, -sa *adj.-n.* Portuguese.
porvenir *m.* future, time to come. *2* fig. promise: *de mucho ~*, of great promise.
pos (en) *adv. en ~ de*, after, behind; in pursuit of.
posada *f.* lodging. *2* dwelling, home. *3* lodging house, inn. *4* boarding house. *5* camp.
posadera *f.* landlady, hostess, woman innkeeper.
posaderas *f. pl.* coll. buttocks.
posadero *m.* landlord, host, innkeeper.
posar *intr.* to lodge, board, put up. *2* to lay, rest. *3* F. ARTS to pose. *4 intr.-ref.* [of birds, etc.] to

alight, to perch, sit. *5 tr.* to lay down [a burden]. *6 ref.* [of sediment, dust, etc.] to settle.
poscomunión *f.* ECCL. Postcommunion.
posdata *f.* postscript.
poseedor, -ra *m.-f.* possessor, owner, holder.
poseer *tr.* to possess, own, hold. *2* to have a mastery of [art, language, etc.]. *3 ref.* to control oneself. ¶ CONJUG.: INDIC. Pret.: poseí, poseíste, poseyó; poseímos, poseisteis, poseyeron. | SUBJ. Imperf.: poseyera, poseyeras, etc., or poseyese, poseyeses, etc. | PAST. p.: poseído & poseso. | GER.: poseyendo.
poseído, -da *p. p.* of POSEER. *2* possessed. *3 m.-f.* POSESO 2.
posesión *f.* possession. *2 dar ~*, to give possession, induct, install [in an office, rank, etc.].
posesional *adj.* possessional.
posesionar *tr.* to put in possession; to give possession, induct, install. *2 ref.* to take possession, to be installed [in an office, rank, etc.].
posesivo, -va *adj.* possessive. *2* GRAM. *adj.-m.* possessive.
poseso, -sa *adj. irreg. p. p.* of POSEER. *2 m.-f.* person possessed by an evil spirit.
posesor, -ra *m.-f.* possessor, owner, holder.
posesorio, -ria *adj.* LAW. possessory.
posfecha *f.* postdate.
posguerra *f.* POSTGUERRA.
posibilidad *f.* possibility. *2* ability [to do something]. *3 pl.* means, property.
posibilitar *tr.* to render possible, facilitate.
posible *adj.* possible: *hacer todo lo ~*, to do one's best. *2 m. pl.* means, income, property.
posición *f.* position [posture; manner in which anything is placed; mental attitude]. *2* position, rank, status. *3* putting, placement. *4* MIL., ASTR., CHEM. position.
positivismo *m.* PHIL. Positivism. *2* [moral] materialism. *3* matter-of-factness.
positivista *adj.* positivistic. *2* practical, realistic, matter-of-fact. *3 m.-f.* positivist.
positivo, -va *adj.* positive [certain, real; affirmative; not speculative or theoretical]. *2* matter-of-fact. *3* BACT., ELECT., GRAM., LOG., MATH., LAW positive. *4 adj.-m.* PHOT. positive.
pósito *m.* public granary. *2* cooperative.
positrón *m.* PHYS. positron.
positura *f.* position, posture. *2* state, disposition.
posma *f.* dullness, slowness, sluggishness. *2 adj. n.* dull, slow, sluggish [pers.].
poso *m.* sediment, dregs, lees. *2* rest, repose.
posología *f.* MED. posology.
pospondré, pospondría, etc. *irr.* V. POSPONER.
posponer *tr.* to postpone [place after something in order of precedence, value, importance, etc.], to subordinate. *2* GRAM. to postpose. ¶ CONJUG. like *poner.*
pospongo, posponga, etc. *irr.* V. POSPONER.
posposición *f.* postponement, subordination. *2* GRAM. postposition.
pospositivo, -va GRAM. postpositive.
pospuesto, -ta *irreg. p. p.* of POSPONER.
pospuse, pospusiera, etc. *irr.* V. POSPONER.
posta *f.* relay [of post horses]. *2* post, posthouse. *3* post, stage. *4* slice, chop [of meat or fish]. *5* lead ball. *6* stake [at cards]. *7* memorial tablet. *8* ARCH. Vitruvian scroll. *9* person who travels post, postrider. *10 correr la ~*, to ride post; *por la ~*, riding post; fig. posthaste; *silla de ~*, post chaise. *11 a ~*, coll. on purpose.

postal *adj.* postal: *servicio* ~, post, mail service. *2 f.* postcard.
postdata *f.* POSDATA.
postdiluviano, -na *adj.* postdiluvian.
poste *m.* post [upright pole], pillar: ~ *indicador*, finger post, signpost; ~ *telegráfico*, telegraph post. *2 dar* ~, coll. to keep [someone] waiting.
postema *f.* MED. abscess. *2* coll. bore, nuisance.
postergación *f.* delay, postponement. *2* leaving [someone] behind in a promotion.
postergar *tr.* to delay, postpone. *2* to leave [someone] behind in a promotion.
posteridad *f.* posterity.
posterior *adj.* posterior, hinder, back, rear. *2* posterior [in time].
posterioridad *f.* posteriority.
postescolar *adj.* postschool.
postguerra *f.* postwar.
postigo *m.* back door; postern. *2* small door, wicket. *3* window shutter.
postilla *f.* scab [over a sore, pustule, etc.].
postillón *m.* postilion, postboy.
postilloso, -sa *adj.* scabby.
postín *m.* coll. airs, importance: *darse* ~, to put on airs, to give oneself airs.
postizo, -za *adj.* artificial, not natural, false. *2* detachable [collar]. *3 m.* false hair, switch. *4 f.* castanet.
postmeridiano, -na *adj.* postmeridian.
postoperatorio, -ria *adj.* postoperative.
postor *m.* bidder [at an auction]: *mayor*, or *mejor* ~, highest bidder.
postración *f.* postration.
postrado, -da *adj.* prostrate(d.
postrar *tr.* to prostrate, to humble. *2* to overthrow. *3* to prostrate, exhaust. *4 ref.* to prostate oneself; to kneel down.
postre *adj.* POSTRERO. *2 m. sing. & pl.* dessert. *3 adv. a la* ~, at last, finally.
postremo, -ma *adj.* last, final.
postrer *adj.* [before a noun] POSTRERO.
postrero, -ra *adj.* last. *2* hindermost. *3 n.* last, last one.
postrimer *adj.* [before a noun] POSTRIMERO.
postrimerías *f. pl.* last period; last years of life. *2* THEOL. last stages of man.
postrimero, -ra *adj.* last [in order].
postulación *f.* postulation. *2* request, petition.
postulado *m.* postulate.
postulanta *f.* ECCL. woman postulant.
postulante *adj.* postulating. *2 m.-f.* postulant.
postular *tr.* to postulate. *2* to beg, demand.
póstumo, -ma *adj.* posthumous.
postura *f.* posture, position. *2* bid [at an auction]. *3* stake, wager [at cards, etc.]. *4* egg laying. *5* egg [of bird].
potabilidad *f.* potability, potableness.
potable *adj.* potable, drinkable.
potación *f.* potation. *2* drink.
potaje *m.* pottage, soup. *2* stewed vegetables. *3* mixed drink. *4* meddley, hodge-podge.
potar *tr.* to drink.
potasa *f.* CHEM. potassium.
potásico, -ca *adj.* CHEM. potassic, potassium.
potasio *m.* CHEM. potassium.
pote *m.* pot, jar. *2* cooking pot.
potencia *f.* potency. *2* power [active property; faculty of mind]: *potencias del alma*, mental powers. *3* potentiality: *en* ~, in potentiality. *4* power [great state]: *las potencias europeas*, the European Powers. *5* MATH., MECH., PHYS. power.

potencial *adj.-m.* potential. *2* GRAM. conditional [mood].
potencialidad *f.* potentiality.
potentado *m.* potentate.
potente *adj.* potent, powerful, mighty. *2* strong, vigorous.
poterna *f.* FORT. postern.
potestad *f.* power, faculty. *2* power, dominion, jurisdiction. *3* podesta. *4* potentate. *5 pl.* powers [angels].
potestativo, -va *adj.* facultative, optional.
potingue *m.* hum, medicine, concoction.
potísimo, -ma *adj.* superl. very powerful.
potosí *m.* coll. great wealth; mint of money.
potra *f.* filly, young mare. *2* coll. rupture, scrotal hernia. *3* coll. luck: *tener* ~, to be lucky.
potrada *f.* herd of colts.
potranca *f.* filly, yourrg mare.
potrero *m.* herdsman of colts. *2* pasture ground for horses. *3* (Am.) cattle ranch.
potrillo, -lla *m. dim.* young colt. *2 f. dim.* young filly.
potro *m.* colt, foal. *2* horse [for torture or gymnastics]: *estar en un* ~, fig. to be on pins and needles. *3* stocks, shoeing frame.
potroso, -sa *adj.* MED. ruptured. *2* coll. lucky.
poyata *f.* shelf for glasses and crockery.
poyo *m.* stone seat built against the wall.
poza *f.* puddle. *2* pool for retting hemp or flax.
pozal *m.* bucket, pail. *2* curbstone of a well.
pozanco *m.* puddle or pool in a river bank.
pozo *m.* well, pit: ~ *artesiano*, artesian well; ~ *negro*, cesspol; ~ *de ciencia*, fig. profoundly learned person. *2* MIN. shaft. *3* fish tank [in a boat].
práctica *f.* practice [performance, carrying out; habit; repeated exercise in art, etc.]: *poner en* ~, to put into practice; *en la* ~, in practice. *2* skill [by practice]. *3 pl.* training [for a profession].
practicable *adj.* practicable, feasible. *2* THEAT. practicable.
practicaje *m.* NAUT. pilotage.
prácticamente *adv.* in practice.
practicante *adj.* practising. *2 m.-f.* surgeon [for minor surgery]. *3* medical assistant. *4* PHARM. prescription clerk.
practicar *tr.* to practise, exercise, do habitually, put into practice. *2* to make, cut [a hole or opening]. *3* SURG. to perform [an operation]. *4 intr. -ref.* to practise [exercise oneself in].
práctico, -ca *adj.* practical. *2* skilful, practised. *3 m.* NAUT. pilot: ~ *de puerto*, harbour pilot.
practición, -na *m.-f.* coll. practician.
pradejón *m.* small meadow.
pradeño, -ña *adj.* [pertaining to] meadow.
pradera *f.* prairie. *2* meadowland.
pradería *f.* meadowland.
prado *m.* meadow, grassland, lawn.
Praga *f. pr. n.* GEOG. Prague.
pragmática *f.* pragmatic, pragmatic sanction.
pragmático, -ca *adj.* pragmatic.
pragmatismo *m.* PHIL. pragmatism.
pragmatista *adj.-n.* pragmatist.
pratense *adj.* pratal.
preadamita *m.* preadamite.
preámbulo *m.* preamble.
prebenda *f.* ECCL. prebend, benefice. *2* fig. sinecure.
prebendado *m.* ECCL. prebendary.
preboste *m.* provost.
precario, -ria *adj.* precarious.
precaución *f.* precaution.

precaver *tr.* to prevent, provide against. *2 ref.* to be on one's guard. *3 precaverse contra* or *de,* to guard against.

precavidamente *adv.* cautiously.

precavido, -da *adj.* cautious, guarded, wary.

precedencia *f.* precedence.

precedente *adj.* preceding, foregoing. *2 m.* precedent.

preceder *tr.-intr.* to precede.

preceptista *m.* one who sets precepts.

preceptivo, -va *adj.* preceptive.

precepto *m.* precept, command: *los preceptos del Decálogo,* the Commandments; *dia de* ~, holy day, holiday of obligation. *2* precept, rule.

preceptor, -ra *m.-f.* preceptor. *2 m.* tutor [private teacher].

preceptuar *tr.* to lay down as a precept; to prescribe.

preces *f. pl.* prayers, supplications.

precesión *m.* MEC., ASTR. precession.

preciado, -da *adj.* valuable, precious. *2* proud, boastful.

preciar *tr.* to value, prize. *2 ref. preciarse de,* to boast of being; to take pride or glory in.

precinta *f.* strap, band [for sealing].

precintar *tr.* to seal with a strap or band.

precinto *m.* sealing with a strap or band. *2* strap, band [for sealing packages or boxes].

precio *m.* price: *no tener* ~, to be priceless. *2* value, worth. *3* esteem.

preciosidad *f.* preciousness, worth. *2* precious or beautiful object; beauty.

precioso, -sa *adj.* precious [costly, valuable, dear]. *2* beautiful.

precipicio *m.* precipice. *2* violent fall. *3* ruin.

precipitación *f.* precipitation. *2* precipitance.

precipitadamente *adv.* precipitately, hastily.

precipitadero *m.* PRECIPICIO.

precipitado, -da *adj.* precipitate, hurried, hasty, rash, inconsiderate. *2 m.* CHEM. precipitate.

precipitar *tr.* to precipitate [throw headlong; hurl; to hasten, hurry]. *2* CHEM. to precipitate. *3 ref.* to throw oneself headlong, to rush. *4* to be hasty or rash. *5* CHEM. to precipitate.

precipitoso, -sa *adj.* precipitous. *2* hasty, rash.

precipuo, -pua *adj.* chief, principal.

precisamente *adv.* precisely, exactly. *2* just: ~ *ahora,* just at this moment.

precisar *tr.* to state precisely, specify; to fix, determine with precision. *2* to compel, oblige.

precisión *f.* precision, preciseness. *2* necessity, obligation: *tener* ~ *de,* to need; to be obliged to.

preciso, -sa *adj.* precise. *2* necessary, indispensable: *es* ~, it is necessary.

precitado, -da *adj.* forecited, aforesaid.

precito, -ta *adj.-n.* damned, condemned to hell.

preclaro, -ra *adj.* illustrious, renowned.

precocidad *f.* precocity, precociousness.

precognición *f.* precognition.

precolombino, -na *adj.* pre-Columbian.

preconcebir *tr.* to preconceive.

preconización *f.* ECCL. preconization. *2* preconization [public commendation].

preconizar *tr.* ECCL. to preconize. *2* to preconize [commend publicly].

preconocer *tr.* to foreknow. ¶ CONJUG. as *conocer.*

precordial *adj.* ANAT. precordial.

precoz *adj.* precocious.

precursor, -ra *adj.* precursory. *2 m.-f.* precursor, forerunner.

predecesor, -ra *m.-f.* predecessor.

predecir *tr.* to predict, foretell, forecast. ¶ CONJUG. like *decir.*

predela *f.* predella.

predestinación *f.* predestination.

predestinado, -da *adj.* predestinated, predestined. *2 m.-f.* predestinate.

predestinar *tr.* to predestine, predestinate.

predeterminación *f.* predetermination.

predeterminar *tr.* to predetermine.

predial *adj.* praedial, predial.

prédica *f.* sermon, harangue.

predicable *adj.* preachable. *2 adj.-m.* LOG. predicable.

predicación *f.* preaching.

predicado *m.* LOG. predicate.

predicador, -ra *adj.* preaching. *2 m.-f.* preacher.

predicamento *m.* LOG. predicament. *2* esteem, reputation.

predicar *tr.-intr.* to preach. *2* coll. to lecture, sermonize. *3* LOG. to predicate.

predicción *f.* prediction, forecasting.

predilección *f.* predilection, special love.

predilecto, -ta *adj.* preferred, favourite.

predio *m.* property, piece of real estate: ~ *rústico,* country property; ~ *urbano,* town property.

predisponer *tr.* to predispose. *2* to prejudice. *3* to prearrange. ¶ CONJUG. like *poner.*

predisposición *f.* predisposition.

predispuesto, -ta *adj.* predisposed. *2* prejudiced.

predominación, predominancia *f.* predomination, predominance.

predominante *adj.* predominant, prevailing.

predominar *tr.* to predominate; to prevail. *2* to tower [over], be higher [than].

predominio *m.* predominance.

preeminencia *f.* pre-eminence. *2* privilege.

preeminente *adj.* pre-eminent.

preexistencia *f.* pre-existence.

preexistente *adj.* pre-existent.

preexistir *intr.* to pre-exist.

prefacio *m.* preface, introduction. *2* ECCL. preface.

prefecto *m.* prefect.

prefectura *f.* prefecture.

preferencia *f.* preference.

preferente *adj.* preferential. *2* preferred.

preferible *adj.* preferable.

preferir *tr.* to prefer. ¶ CONJUG. as *hervir.*

prefiero, prefiera, etc. *irr.* V. PREFERIR.

prefiguración *f.* prefiguration, foreshadowing.

prefigurar *tr.* to prefigure, foreshadow.

prefijar *tr.* to prefix, prearrange, predetermine. *2* GRAM. to prefix.

prefijo, -ja *adj.* prefixed. *2 m.* GRAM. prefix.

prefloración *f.* BOT. praefloration, estivation.

prefoliación *f.* BOT. praefoliation, vernation.

pregón *m.* proclamation or announcement by the crier. *2* cry [of merchandise].

pregonar *tr.* to proclaim, announce. *2* to cry, hawk [merchandise]. *3* to proscribe [a person].

pregonero, -ra *adj.* proclaiming, announcing. *2 m.* common crier, town crier.

pregunta *f.* question, inquiry: *estar a la cuarta* ~, coll. to be penniless; *hacer una* ~, to ask a question.

preguntador, -ra *adj.* questioning; inquisitive. *2 m.-f.* questioner; inquisitive person.

preguntar *tr.-intr.* to ask, inquire; to question; ~ *por,* to ask, inquire, after or for. *2 ref.* to wonder [desire to know].

preguntón, -na *adj.* inquisitive. *2 m.-f.* inquisitive person.

prehistoria *f.* prehistory, prehistorics.
prehistórico, -ca *adj.* prehistoric.
prejuicio *m.* prejudice, bias. *2* prejudgement.
prejuzgar *tr.* to prejudge.
prelacía *f.* prelacy.
prelación *f.* preference, priority.
prelado *m.* prelate.
prelatura *f.* PRELACÍA.
preliminar *adj.-m.* preliminary.
prelucir *intr.* to shine in advance. ¶ CONJUG. like *lucir.*
preludiar *tr.-intr.* MUS. to prelude.
preludio *m.* prelude, introduction. *2* MUS. prelude.
prelusión *f.* preface, introduction.
prematuramente *adv.* prematurely.
prematuro, -ra *adj.* premature.
premeditación *f.* premeditation.
premeditado, -da *adj.* premeditated.
premeditar *tr.* to premeditate.
premiador, -ra *adj.* rewarding. *2 m.-f.* rewarder.
premiar *tr.* to reward. *2* to award a prize to.
premio *m.* reward, recompense. *2* prize, award. *3* prize [in lottery]. *4* ECON. premium.
premiosidad *f.* awkwardness, lack of facility [of action, speech, etc.]; stiffness [of style].
premioso, -sa *adj.* burdensome. *2* urging, pressing. *3* strict, rigid. *4* awkward, lacking facility [of action, speech, etc.]; stiff [style].
premisa *f.* LOG. premise. *2* basis [of inference].
premolar *adj.* ANAT. premolar.
premonitorio, -ria *adj.* MED. premonitory.
premorir *intr.* LAW. to predecease.
premura *f.* haste, hurry. *2* pressure, urgency.
prenatal *adj.* prenatal.
prenda *f.* pledge, security, pawn; token, proof: *en ~ de,* as a pledge of, as a proof of. *2* fig. beloved one. *3* garment, article or clothing, headgear or footwear. *4 pl.* natural gifts, moral qualities [of a person]. *6 juego de prendas,* game or forfeits.
prendador *m.-f.* pledger, pawner.
prendar *tr.* to pledge, pawn. *2* to charm, please, enamour. *3 ref. prendarse de,* to fall in love with, to take a liking to.
prendedero *m.* hook, brooch. *2* fillet, bandeau.
prendedor *m.* apprehender. *2* brooch, breastpin. *3* fillet, bandeau.
prender *tr.* to seize, catch, catch hold of. *2* to attach, hook, pin. *3* to take, arrest [a person]. *4* to dress up [a woman]. *5* to set [fire]. *6 intr.* [of a plant] to take root. *7* [of fire, etc.] to catch, take hold. *8 ref.* [of a woman] to dress up.
prendería *f.* second-hand shop.
prendero, -ra *m.-f.* second-hand dealer.
prendimiento *m.* apprehension, arrest.
prenombre *m.* praenomen.
prensa *f.* press [machine for compressing, crushing, etc.]: *~ hidráulica,* hydraulic press. *2* press, printing press, printing; newspapers: *dar a la ~,* to publish [a book, etc.] *tener buena,* or *mala ~,* to have a good, or bad, press. *4* PHOT. printing frame.
prensado *m.* pressing [by press]. *2* luster, gloss [from pressing].
prensador, -ra *m.-f.* presser.
prensadura *f.* pressing [by press].
prensar *tr.* to press [compress, squeeze in a press].
prensil *adj.* prehensile.
prensión *f.* prehension.
prensista *m.* PRINT. pressman.
prensor, -ra *adj.* ORN. psittacine.
preñado, -da *adj.* pregnant, with child, with

young. *2* fig. pregnant [full, charged]. *3 m.* pregnancy.
preñar *tr.* EMPREÑAR. *2* fig. to fill.
preñez *f.* pregnancy. *2* fig. fullness.
preocupación *f.* preoccupation [prejudice; mental absortion]. *2* care, concern, worry.
preocupado, -da *adj.* preoccupied, prejudiced. *2* concerned, anxious, worried.
preocupar *tr.* to preoccupy. *2* to prejudice. *3* to concern, worry. *4 ref.* to concern oneself: *preocuparse de,* to concern oneself in; to take care of. *5* to worry.
preopinante *m.-f.* predecessor [in a debate].
preordinar *tr.* to preordain.
preparación *f.* preparation, preparing, getting ready. *2* preparation [medicine, etc.].
preparado *m.* PHARM. preparation.
preparador, -ra *adj.* preparing. *2 m.-f.* preparator.
preparar *tr.* to prepare, make ready. *2 ref.* to prepare, get ready, make preparations.
preparativo, -va *adj.* preparative, preparatory. *2 m. pl.* preparations.
preparatorio, -ria *adj.* preparatory.
preponderancia *f.* preponderance.
preponderante *adj.* preponderant.
preponderar *intr.* to preponderate.
preposición *f.* GRAM. preposition.
preposicional *adj.* prepositional.
prepositivo, -va *adj.* GRAM. prepositive.
prepósito *m.* ECCL. prelate, provost.
preposterar *tr.* to reverse, invert, upset.
prepóstero, -ra *adj.* reversed, out of place, upset.
prepotencia *f.* prepotence, prepotency.
prepotente *adj.* prepotent.
prepucio *m.* ANAT. prepuce, foreskin.
prerrogativa *f.* prerogative, privilege.
presa *f.* catch, clutch, grip, hold: *hacer ~ en,* to catch, lay hold of. *2* seizing, capture [act]. *3* capture, prize, booty. *4* prey: *ave de ~,* bird of prey; *~ de,* a prey to. *5* fang, claw. *6* dam, weir. *7* channel, ditch.
presagiar *tr.* to presage, betoken, forebode.
presagio *m.* presage, omen, token.
presagioso, -sa; presago, -ga; présago, -ga *adj.* presaging, foreboding.
presbicia *f.* presbyopia, farsightedness.
présbita, présbite *adj.* presbyopic. *2 m.-f.* presbyope.
presbiterado, presbiterato *m.* priesthood.
presbiterianismo *m.* Presbyterianism.
presbiteriano, -na *adj.-n.* Presbyterian.
presbiterio *m.* chancel, presbytery [of a church].
presbítero *m.* presbyter, priest.
presciencia *f.* prescience, foreknowledge.
prescindible *adj.* that can be dispensed with.
prescindir *intr. ~ de,* to dispense with, do without; to set aside, leave out, disregard, prescind of.
prescribir *tr.* to prescribe, decree, ordain. *2* MED. to prescribe. *3 intr.* LAW to prescribe. ¶ PAST. p.: *prescrito* or *prescripto.*
prescripción *f.* prescription, order, rule. *2* LAW, MED. prescription.
prescriptible *adj.* prescriptible.
presea *f.* gem, jewel, valuable thing.
presencia *f.* presence: *en ~ de,* in the presence of. *2* ostentation. *3 ~ de ánimo,* presence of mind.
presencial *adj.* [relating to] presence. *2 testigo ~,* eyewitness.
presenciar *tr.* to be present at, witness, see.
presentable *adj.* presentable.
presentación *f.* presentation [presenting, exhibi-

tion]. *2* introduction [of a person to another]. *3* MED., THEAT. presentation. *4* external appearance [of a book, etc.].

presentador, -ra *m.-f.* presenter.

presentalla *f.* ECCL. votive offering.

presentáneo *adj.* quick-acting.

presentante *m.-f.* presenter; introducer.

presentar *tr.* to present: ~ *armas*, MIL. to present arms. *2* to introduce [a person to another]. *3* to nominate, propose for office. *4 ref.* to present oneself or itself. *5* to appear, turn up. *6* to volunteer. *7* to introduce oneself.

presente *adj.* present: *la* ~, this letter; *hacer* ~, to remind of; *tener* ~, to bear in mind; *por lo* ~, for the present. *2* current [month, etc.]. *3 adj.-m.* GRAM. present [tense]. *4 m.* present, gift. *5* present [present time].

presentimiento *m.* presentiment, foreboding.

presentir *tr.* to have a presentiment of, to forebode. ¶ CONJUG. like *hervir*.

preservación *f.* preservation, conservation.

preservar *tr.* to preserve, guard, keep safe.

preservativo, -va *adj.* preservative, preserving. *2 m.* preservative, preventive.

presidario *m.* PRESIDIARIO.

presidencia *f.* presidency. *2* chair [at a meeting, etc.]; chairmanship. *3* speakership [of a parliamentary body]. *4* presidential term.

presidencial *adj.* presidential.

presidenta *f.* president's wife. *2* woman president. *3* chairwoman.

presidente *m.* president. *2* chairman. *3* speaker [of a parliamentary body].

presidiario *m.* convict.

presidio *m.* penitentiary. *2* hard labour. *3* fortress, citadel. *4* garrison [of soldiers].

presidir *tr.* to preside over or at. *2 intr.* to preside.

presilla *f.* small loop forming an eye or fastener [for a button, etc.]. *2* SEW. buttonhole stitching.

presiento, presienta, etc. *irr.* V. PRESENTIR.

presión *f.* pressure: ~ *arterial*, blood pressure.

presionar *tr.* (Am.) to press, urge.

preso, -sa *adj.* imprisoned; arrested. *2 m.-f.* prisoner. *3* convict.

prestación *f.* lending. *2* service, prestation.

prestado, -da *adj.* lent, borrowed: *dar* ~, to lend; *pedir* or *tomar* ~, to borrow.

prestador, -ra *m.-f.* lender.

prestamente *adv.* speedily, promptly, quickly.

prestamista *m.-f.* moneylender; pawnbroker.

préstamo *m.* loan; lending: *casa de préstamos*, pawnshop; *tomar a* ~, to borrow.

prestancia *f.* excellence.

prestante *adj.* excellent.

prestar *tr.* to lend, loan. *2* to lend, bestow, give, communicate. *3* to do, render [service, duty, etc.]. *4* to give [ear; help, aid]. *5* to pay [attention]. *6* to keep [silence]. *7* to show [patience]. *8* to take [oath]. *9 intr.* [of a piece of cloth, etc.] to give. *10 ref.* to lend oneself or itself. *11* to submit. *12* to give ground for.

prestatario, -ria *adj.* borrowing. *2 m.-f.* borrower.

preste *m.* ECCL. high mass celebrant.

presteza *f.* celerity, promptness, quickness, haste.

prestidigitación *f.* prestidigitation.

prestidigitador *m.* prestidigitator.

prestigio *m.* prestige. *2* spell, fascination.

prestigioso, -sa *adj.* prestigious, influential.

prestimonio *m.* loan.

1) **presto** *adv.* promptly, quickly. *2* soon.

2) **presto, -ta** *adj.* prompt, quick. *2* ready, prepared.

presumible *adj.* presumable.

presumido, -da *p. p.* of PRESUMIR. *2* vain, conceited.

presumir *tr.* to presume, conjecture. *2 intr.* to presume, be vain or conceited; to boast: ~ *de*, to boast of being.

presunción *f.* presumption. *2* presumptuousness, conceit.

presunto, -ta *adj.* presumed, supposed. *2* ~ *heredero*, heir presumptive.

presuntuosidad *f.* presumptuousness.

presuntuoso, -sa *adj.* presumptuous, conceited.

presuponer *tr.* to presuppose. *2* to budget. *3* to form an estimate of [a work, etc.]. ¶ CONJUG. like *poner*.

presuposición *f.* presupposition.

presupuestar *tr.* to budget.

presupuestario, -ria *adj.* [pertaining to a] budget.

presupuesto, -ta *adj.* presupposed. *2 m.* presupposition. *3* reason, pretext. *4* budget. *5* estimate [for a work].

presura *f.* anxiety. *2* haste. *3* eagerness.

presuroso, -sa *adj.* prompt, hasty, hurried, swift.

pretender *tr.* to pretend to; to seek, solicit. *2* to court, seek in marriage. *3* to try to, to intend.

pretendienta *f.* woman pretender or claimant.

pretendiente *m.* pretender, claimant. *2* office seeker. *3* suitor, wooer.

pretensión *f.* pretension, pretense, claim.

pretenso, -sa *irr. p. p.* of PRETENDER.

preterición *f.* preterition.

preterir *tr.* to pass over, omit, disregard.

pretérito, -ta *adj.* past, bygone. *2 adj.-m.* GRAM. past, preterit: ~ *imperfecto*, imperfect; ~ *indefinido*, preterit, past absolute; ~ *perfecto*, present perfect; ~ *pluscuamperfecto*, pluperfect; ~*anterior*, past anterior.

preternatural *adj.* preternatural.

pretextar *tr.* to pretext.

pretexto *m.* pretext, cover, excuse.

pretil *m.* parapet, railing.

pretina *f.* girdle, belt, waistband.

pretinazo *m.* blow with a belt.

pretinilla *f. dim.* ladies' belt or girdle.

pretor *m.* praetor, pretor.

pretoriano, -na *adj.* praetorial, pretorial. *2 adj.-m.* praetorian, pretorian.

pretorio, -ria *adj.* praetorial, pretorial. *2 m.* praetorium, pretorium.

pretura *f.* praetorship, pretorship.

prevalecer *intr.* to prevail. *2* to take root, to thrive. ¶ CONJUG. as *agradecer*.

prevaleciente *adj.* prevailing, prevalent.

prevaler *intr.* to prevail. *2 ref. prevalerse de*, to avail oneself of, to take advantage of. ¶ CONJUG. like *valer*.

prevalezco, prevalezca, etc. *irr.* V. PREVALECER.

prevaricación *f.* act of injustice or breach of faith committed by a public officer.

prevaricador, -ra *m.-f.* one who commits PREVARICACIÓN.

prevaricar *intr.* to act unjustly or corruptly in the discharge of a public trust.

prevaricato *m.* corrupt practice. *2* LAW prevarication.

prevención *f.* preparation, anticipation of needs, danger, etc.: *a* ~, *de* ~, ready in case. *2* stock, supply. *3* foresight. *4* prevention. *5* prejudice, dislike. *6* warning. *7* police station. *8* MIL. guardroom.

prevendré, prevendría, prevengo, prevenga, etc. *irr.* V. PREVENIR.
prevenidamente *adv.* beforehand, with preparation.
prevenido, -da *adj.* ready, prepared. *2* stocked, supplied. *3* forewarned, cautious.
prevenir *tr.* to prepare, make ready. *2* to anticipate, foresee, forestall. *3* to prevent, avoid. *4* to warn, caution. *5* to prepossess, prejudice. *6 ref.* to prepare, get ready; to take precautions. *7* to provide oneself. ¶ CONJUG. like *venir*.
preventivo, -va *adj.* preventive. *2* warning.
prever *tr.* to foresee; to anticipate.
previo, via *adj.* previous.
previne, previniera, etc. *irr.* V. PREVENIR.
previsión *f.* prevision, foresight; forecast: ~ *del tiempo*, weather forecasting. *2* providence. *3* ~ *social*, social security.
previsor, -ra *adj.* far-seeing, foresighted. *2* provident.
previsto, -ta *adj.* foreseen.
prez *f.* honour, glory.
Príamo *m. pr. n.* MYTH. Priam.
prieto, -ta *adj.* tight, compact. *2* close-fisted. *3* dark, blackish.
prima *f.* female cousin. *2* premium, bonus. *3* COM. bounty. *4* INSUR. premium. *5* prime [hour]. *6* MUS. treble [string].
primacía *f.* primacy; primateship.
primada *f.* coll. deception, trick.
primado, -da *adj.* primatial. *2 m.* primacy. *3* ECCL. primate.
primal, -la *adj.-n.* yearling [sheep or goat].
primario, -ria *adj.* primary, chief, first. *2* primary, elementary. *3* ASTR., BIOL., ELECT., GEOL. primary.
primate *m.* personage, worthy. *2* ZOOL. primate.
primavera *f.* spring, springtime. *2* BOT. cowslip, primrose.
primaveral *adj.* [pertaining to the] spring, vernal.
primazgo *m.* cousinship. *2* primacy.
primer *adj.* apocopated form of PRIMERO used only before the noun: ~ *ministro*, prime minister.
primera *f.* FENC. prime. *2* RLY. first class: *viajar en* ~, to travel first-class. *3* AUTO. low speed. *4* COM. ~ *de cambio*, first of exchange. *5 de* ~, first-class, excellent; very well. *6* directly, without warning.
primeramente *adv.* PRIMERO 1 & 2.
primerizo, -za *adj.* novice, beginner.
1) **primero** *adv.* first, in the first place. *2* first, rather, sooner. *3 de* ~, first, before.
2) **primero, -ra** *adj.* first. *2* foremost. *3* chief, leading. *4* early, former. *5* ARITH. prime [number]. *6* primary [education]. *7* raw [material].
primevo, -va *adj.* primeval, primitive. *2* oldest.
primicia(s *f. sing.-pl.* first fruit.
primigenio, -nia *adj.* primigenial.
primípara *f. adj.* OBST. primipara.
primitivo, -va *adj.* primitive. *2 m.* F. ARTS primitive.
primitivamente *adv.* originally.
primo, -ma *adj.* first. *2* prime, excellent. *3* ARITH. prime [number]. *4* raw [material]. *5 m.-f.* cousin: ~ *carnal*, ~ *hermano*, first cousin, cousingerman. *6* coll. gullible person, dupe.
primogénito, -ta *adj.-n.* first-born.
primogenitura *f.* primogeniture.
primor *m.* care, skill, excellence of execution. *2* beauty, exquisiteness [of work]. *3* coll. beautiful or exquisite thing.

primordial *adj.* primordial, fundamental.
primoroso, -sa *adj.* beautiful, exquisite; beautifully or exquisitely wrought or executed.
primuláceo, -a *adj.* BOT. primulaceous.
princesa *f.* princess.
princlpado *m.* princedom. *2* principality, principate. *3* primacy. *4 pl.* principalities [angels].
principal *adj.* principal, main, chief, foremost, essential. *2* principal, illustrious. *3* GRAM. principal. *4* princeps [edition]. *5 m.* chief, boss, head [of a firm, etc.]. *6* principal, capital [as distinguished from interest]. *7* main, first floor or storey.
príncipe *m.* prince: ~ *de Asturias*, Crown Prince of Spain. *2* sovereign, ruler. *3 adj.* princeps [edition].
principesco, -ca *adj.* princely.
principiante, -ta *m.-f.* beginner, novice, tyro.
principiar *tr.* to commence, begin, start.
principio *m.* beginning, commencement, start: *al* ~, at first; *a principios de*, at the beginning of [a month, year, etc.]; *en un* ~, at the beginning. *2* source, origin. *3* principle. *4* rule of action. *5* entrée. *6 pl.* principles. *7* rudiments.
pringar *tr.* to dip or soak [bread, etc.] in gravy or grease. *2* to stain with grease. *3* coll. to stab, wound. *4 intr.* coll. to share, participate [in an affair]. *5 ref.* to stain oneself with grease.
pringoso, -sa *adj.* greasy.
pringue *m.-f.* grease, melted fat. *2* greasy dirt.
prior *adj.* PHIL. prior, preceding. *2* ECC. prior.
priora *f.* prioress.
priorato *m.* priorship, priorate. *2* priory.
prioridad *f.* priority.
prisa *f.* haste, dispatch, celerity; hurry, urgency: *correr* ~, to be pressing; *darse* ~, to hurry, make haste; *tener* ~, to be in a hurry; *a* ~, *de* ~, quickly, with haste. *2* rush [of buyers, etc.].
prisión *f.* seizure, capture, arrest. *2* prison. *3* imprisonment. *4* fig. bond, tie. *5 pl.* chains, fetters.
prisionero, -ra *m.-f.* MIL. prisoner. *2* fig. captive.
prisma *m.* GEOM., OPT., CRYST. prism.
prismático, -ca *adj.* prismatic. *2 m. pl.* field glasses.
pristino, -na *adj.* pristine, first, original.
privación *f.* privation, want, lack. *2* deprivation, deprival. *3* forbidding, being forbidden.
privado, -da *adj.* forbidden. *2* private, privy. *3* stunned, unconscious. *4 m.* favorite [of a king or magnate].
privanza *f.* favour, preference [of a king, etc.].
privar *tr.* to deprive. *2* to prohibit, forbid. *3* to impede. *4* to stun, render unconscious. *5 intr.* to be in favour; to prevail, be in vogue. *6 ref.* to deprive oneself. *7* to become unconscious.
privativo, -va *adj.* privative. *2* peculiar, particular.
privilegiado, -da *adj.* privileged. *2* uncommon, extraordinary [talent, gift, etc.].
privilegiar *tr.* to privilege.
privilegio *m.* privilege, grant, exemption, franchise, patent.
pro *m.-f.* profit, benefit, advantage: *el* ~ *y el contra*, the pros and cons; *en* ~ *de*, for, in support of; for the benefit of. *2 hombre de* ~, man of worth.
proa *f.* NAUT. prow, bow, head. *2* AER. nose [of an airplane].
probabilidad *f.* probability, likelihood. *2* prospect, chance.
probabilismo *m.* THEOL. probabilism.
probable *adj.* probable, likely. *2* provable.
probablemente *adv.* probably, likely.

probación *f.* probation [in a religious body].
probado, -da *adj.* proved. *2* tried, tested. *3* approved, demonstrated.
probador, -ra *m.-f.* trier, tester. *3* fitter [of dress]. *4 m.* fitting-room.
probadura *f.* tasting.
probar *tr.* to prove [demonstrate]. *2* to prove, test, try out. *3* to sample. *4* to taste [ascertain the flavour of]. *5* to try on [clothes]. *6 ~ fortuna,* to take one's chances. *7 intr.* to suit, to agree with. *8 ~ a,* to attempt, endeavour to. *9 ~ de,* to taste. ¶ Conjug. like *contar.*
probatorio, -ria *adj.* probative, probatory.
probeta *f.* chem. test tube.
probidad *f.* probity, honesty, integrity.
problema *m.* problem.
problemático, -ca *adj.* problematic, problematical.
probo, -ba *adj.* honest, upright.
proboscidio, -dia *adj.* zool. proboscidian.
procacidad *f.* impudence.
procaz *adj.* impudent.
procedencia *f.* origin, source; plane or point of origin or departure. *2* propriety, accordance with the law, rules or practice.
procedente *adj.* coming, originating, proceeding [from]. *2* proper, suitable.
1) **proceder** *m.* behaviour, conduct, proceeding.
2) **proceder** *intr.* to proceed [go in certain order]. *2* to proceed [to do something]. *3* to proceed, to behave. *4* to proceed, come, originate. *5* law to proceed. *6* to be proper or suitable.
procedimiento *m.* proceeding, procedure; process, method, way. *2* law procedure.
proceloso, -sa *adj.* stormy, tempestuous.
prócer *adj.* high, eminent, exalted. *2 m.* grandee, person of eminence.
proceridad *f.* eminence, elevation. *2* vigor, growth.
procesado, -da *adj.* indicted, accused. *2 m.-f.* law. accused, defendant.
procesal *adj.* processal.
procesamiento *m.* law indictment, indicting.
procesar *tr.* law to indict, accuse.
procesión *f.* procession [as a religious ceremony, etc.].
procesional *adj.* processional, processionary.
procesionaria *f.* ent. processionary moth.
proceso *m.* process [progress; course; development]. *2* lapse of time. *3* law proceedings. *4* law criminal case or suit.
proclama *f.* proclamation, address. *2 pl.* banns.
proclamación *f.* proclamation. *2* acclamation.
proclamar *tr.* to proclaim [announce publicly]. *2* to proclaim [a sovereign]. *3* to aclaim.
proclítico, -ca *adj.* gram. proclitic.
proclive *adj.* inclined, disposed, prone.
proclividad *f.* proclivity.
procomún, procomunal *m.* public welfare.
procónsul *m.* proconsul.
procreación *f.* procreation.
procreador, -ra *adj.* procreating. *2 m.-f.* procreator.
procrear *tr.* to procreate.
procura *f.* procuración. *2* procuraduría 2. *3* careful management.
procuración *f.* care, management. *2* procuration, power of attorney, proxy. *3* employment of an attorney, agent or procurator.
procurador *m.* attorney, agent, procurator. *2* law

procurator, solicitor, attorney at law. *3* member of the modern Spanish legislative assembly.
procuraduría *f.* procuratorship. *2* procurator's, solicitor's or attorney's office.
procurante *adj.* solicitant.
procurar *tr.* to try to, endeavour, see that. *2* to get, obtain. *3* to manage [another's affairs], to act as an agent, attorney or solicitor.
prodigalidad *f.* prodigality. *2* lavishness.
prodigar *tr.* to lavish, squander; to give or bestow with profusion. *2 ref.* to show oneself in public too often.
prodigio *m.* prodigy, marvel.
prodigiosidad *f.* prodigiousness.
prodigioso, -sa *adj.* prodigious. *2* fine, exquisite.
pródigo, -ga *adj.-n.* prodigal. *2 adj.* extravagant; lavish.
producción *f.* production. *2* produce, yield, output.
producente *adj.* producing, causing.
producir *tr.* to produce [yield, bear, manufacture]. *2* to produce, cause, originate. *3* law to produce. *4 ref.* to happen, arise. *5* to express oneself. ¶ Conjug. as *conducir.*
productividad *f.* productivity, productiveness.
productivo, -va *adj.* productive. *2* profitable.
producto *m.* product, produce. *2* proceeds, outcome, profit. *3* math., chem. product. *4 pl.* commodities, produce: *productos agrícolas,* farm produce.
productor, -ra *adj.* productive. *2 m.-f.* producer.
produje, produjera, etc. *irr.* V. producir.
produzco, produzca, etc. *irr.* V. producir.
proel *adj.* naut. fore. *2 m.* naut. bowman.
proemio *m.* proem, preface, introduction.
proeza *f.* prowess, feat. *2* coll. stunt.
profanación *f.* profanation, desecration.
profanador, -ra *adj.* profanatory. *2 m.-f.* profaner.
profanar *tr.* to profane.
profanidad *f.* profanity, profaneness. *2* immodesty.
profano, -na *adj.* profane, secular. *2* profane, irreverent. *3* worldly. *4* immodest [in dress, etc.]. *5 adj.-n.* profane, lay [not expert]. *6 m.-f.* worldly person.
profecía *f.* prophecy. *2 pl.* bibl. the Prophets.
proferir *tr.* to utter, give, speak. ¶ Conjug. like *adquirir.*
profesante *adj.* professing.
profesar *tr.-intr.* to profess. *2 tr.* to have, entertain [friendship, love, hate, etc.].
profesión *f.* profession, calling: *de ~,* by profession. *2* profession, professing [of principles, a religion, etc.]. *3* profession [taking vows].
profesional *adj.-n.* professional.
profesionalismo *m.* professionalism.
profeso, -sa *adj.* professed [monk or nun].
profesor, -ra *m.-f.* professor, teacher.
profesorado *m.* professorate, professorship.
profeta *m.* prophet.
profético, -ca *adj.* prophetic, prophetical.
profetisa *f.* prophetess.
profetizador, -ra *adj.* prophesying. *2 m.-f.* prophesier.
profetizar *tr.-intr.* to prophesy.
proficuo, -cua *adj.* profitable, advantageous.
profiláctico, -ca *adj.* prophylactic.
profilaxis *f.* prophylaxis.
prófugo, -ga *adj.-n.* fugitive [from justice]. *2* one who absents himself to evade military service.

profundidad *f.* profundity, profoundness, depth. *2* GEOM. depth. *3* deep [of space, etc.].
profundizar *tr.* to deepen [make deeper]. *2 tr.-intr.* to go deep into, get to the bottom of, fathom, penetrate.
profundo, -da *adj.* profound, deep. *2* profound, low [bow, obeisance]. *3 m.* profundity, the deep. *4* poet. deep, sea, hell.
profusión *f.* profusion, abundance.
profuso, -sa *adj.* profuse, abundant.
progenie *f.* descent, lineage, parentage.
progenitor *m.* progenitor, ancestor.
progenitura *f.* PROGENIE. *2* primogeniture.
prognatismo *m.* prognathism.
prognosis *f.* prognosis, forecasting.
programa *m.* program, programme. *2* THEAT. playbill.
programación *f.* programming.
progresar *intr.* to progress, advance, develop.
progresión *f.* progression, advance. *2* MATH. progression.
progresista *adj.-n.* POL. progressist.
progresivo, -va *adj.* progressive.
progreso *m.* progress. *2 pl.* progress: *hacer progresos,* to make progress.
prohibición *f.* prohibition, forbidding, interdiction.
prohibicionismo *adj.* prohibitionism.
prohibir *tr.* to prohibit, forbid: *se prohibe fumar,* no smoking.
prohibitivo, -va *adj.* prohibitive, forbidding.
prohibitorio, -ria *adj.* prohibitory.
prohijamiento *m.* adoption [of a person, etc.].
prohijar *tr.* to adopt [a person, another's opinion, etc.].
prohombre *m.* master [of an ancient guild]. *2* notable.
prójima *f.* coll. despicable or disreputable woman.
prójimo *m.* fellow being, fellow creature, neighbour. *2* coll. fellow. *3 el* ~, the other people.
prole *f.* progeny, offspring, issue.
prolegómenos *m. pl.* prolegomena.
proletariado *m.* proletariat, proletariate.
proletario, -ria *adj.-n.* proletarian.
proliferación *f.* proliferation.
proliferar *intr.* to proliferate.
prolífico, -ca *adj.* prolific.
prolijidad *f.* prolixity. *2* trifling nicety, minuteness.
prolijo, -ja *adj.* prolix, tedious. *2* overcareful, triflingly nice, minute.
prologar *tr.* to prologize.
prólogo *m.* prologue. *2* preface, introduction.
prolongación *f.* prolongation, lengthening. *2* prolongation [part prolonged], extension.
prolongado, -da *adj.* prolongated, protracted, extended. *2* long, lingering. *3* oblong.
prolongar *tr.* to prolong, lengthen. *2* to extend, continue. *3* to protract. *4* GEOM. to produce. *5 ref.* to be prolonged, to extend, continue.
promediar *tr.* to divide into two equal parts. *2 intr.* [of a month, year, etc.] to be half over. *3* to mediate.
promedio *m.* middle [middle point]. *2* average [medial estimate].
promesa *f.* promise. *2* pious offering.
prometedor, -ra *adj.* promising. *2 m.-f.* promiser.
Prometeo *m. pr. n.* MYTH. Prometheus.
prometer *tr.* to promise. *2* to betroth. *3 intr.* to pro-

mise well, bid fair. *4 ref.* to promise oneself, to expect. *5* to become betrothed.
prometido, -da *adj.* promised. *2* betrothed. *3 m.-f.* fiancé, fiancée, betrothed.
prometimiento *m.* promise, promising.
prominencia *f.* prominence, elevation, protuberance.
prominente *adj.* prominent, projecting.
promiscuidad *f.* promiscuity.
promiscuo, -cua *adj.* promiscuous. *2* ambiguous.
promisión *f.* promise, promising.
promisorio, -ria *adj.* promissory.
promoción *f.* promotion, furtherance, advancement. *2* CHESS. promotion.
promontorio *m.* promontory, headland. *2* height.
promotor, -ra; promovedor, -ra *adj.* promotive. *2 m.-f.* promoter, furtherer, starter.
promover *tr.* to promote, further, start. *2* to promote, prefer, exalt, raise.
promulgación *f.* promulgation, publication.
promulgar *tr.* to promulgate, proclaim, publish.
pronación *f.* PHYSIOL. pronation.
pronador *m.* ANAT. pronator.
prono, -na *adj.* prone, inclined, disposed. *2* prone [lying face downwards].
pronombre *m.* GRAM. pronoun.
pronominal *adj.* GRAM. pronominal.
pronosticador, -ra *adj.* prognosticating, prognosticatory. *2 m.-f.* prognosticator.
pronosticar *tr.* to prognosticate, foretell.
pronóstico *m.* prognostic, prediction. *2* MED. prognosis.
prontamente *adv.* promptly, quickly, speedily.
prontitud *f.* promptitude, promptness, readiness. *2* dispatch, speed, celerity.
pronto *adv.* soon: *lo más* ~ *posible,* as soon as possible; *tan* ~ *como,* as soon as. *2* promptly, quickly. *3 m.* impulse, sudden impulse. *4 al* ~, at first. *5 de* ~, suddenly; without thinking. *6 por de* ~, for the present, provisionally.
pronto, -ta *adj.* prompt. *2* ready prepared; willing.
prontuario *m.* memorandum book. *2* handbook.
pronunciación *f.* pronunciation.
pronunciamiento *m.* pronunciamiento, military insurrection. *2* LAW item [in a judgment].
pronunciar *tr.* to pronounce, utter. *2* to deliver, make [a speech]. *3* LAW to pass [judgement]. *4 ref.* to decide [on]; to pronounce [on, for, against]. *5* to rebel.
propagación *f.* propagation.
propagador, -ra *m.-f.* propagator.
propaganda *f.* propaganda. *2* COM. advertising.
propagandista *adj.-n.* propagandist.
propagar *tr.* to propagate. *2 ref.* to propagate, be propagated. *3* to spread, be diffused.
propalador, -ra *m.-f.* publisher, divulger.
propalar *tr.* to publish, divulge, spread.
proparoxítono, -na *adj.* GRAM. proparoxytone.
proparse *ref.* to go too far, to take undue liberties.
propender *intr.* to tend, incline, be inclined.
propensión *f.* propensity, tendency, predisposition.
propenso, -sa *adj.* inclined, prone; predisposed.
propiamente *adv.* properly. *2* ~ *dicho,* proper [strictly so called or considered].
propiciación *f.* propitiation.
propiciar *tr.* to propitiate.
propiciatorio, -ria *adj.* propitiatory.
propicio, cia *adj.* propitious.
propiedad *f.* ownership, property. *2* property

propietario

[thing owned]; landed property, estate. *2* property [quality]. *4* LOG. property. *5* F. ARTS naturalness, likeness. *6* GRAM. propriety. *7* ~ *intelectual,* copyright.

propietario, -ria *adj.* owning, proprietary. *2 m.-f.* owner, proprietor, proprietress. *3* landlord, landlady.

propileo *m.* ARCH. propyleum.

propina *f.* tip, fee, gratuity. *2 de* ~, extra.

propinar *tr.* to give [a drink]. *2* to give, prescribe [a medicine]. *3* coll. to give a blow, etc.

propincuidad *f.* propinquity.

propincuo, -cua *adj.* near, close.

propio, pia *adj.* one's own. *2* proper, peculiar, typical. *3* proper, suitable. *4* natural, genuine. *5* same. *6* himself, herself, itself: *el* ~ *general,* the general himself. *7* F. ARTS very like. *8* GRAM., MATH. proper [noun; fraction].

proponer *tr.* to propose, propound, move. *2* to propose, nominate. *3 ref.* to purpose, plan, intend, mean.

proporción *f.* proportion [symmetry, ratio, commensurateness]: *a* ~, in proportion. *2* opportunity, occasion. *3* MATH. proportion. *4 pl.* proportions, dimensions.

proporcionado, -da *adj.* proportioned. *2* proportionate. *3* fit, suitable.

proporcional *adj.* proportional.

proporcionar *tr.* to proportionate [give due proportions to]. *2* to proportion, proportionate, commensurate, adapt, adjust. *3* to afford, furnish, give, provide, supply. *4 ref.* to get, obtain.

proposición *f.* proposition, proposal. *2* LOG., MATH., RHET. proposition. *3* motion, resolution [in a meeting, etc.].

propósito *m.* purpose, intention, aim: *a* ~, for the purpose, suitable; opportunely; apropos, by the way; *de* ~, on purpose. *2* subject, matter in hand: *a* ~ *de,* apropos of; *fuera de* ~, irrelevant; out of place.

propuesta *f.* proposition, proposal. *2* offer, tender. *3* proposal, nomination.

propulsar *tr.* to propel.

propulsión *f.* propulsion: ~ *a chorro,* jet propulsion.

propulsor, -ra *adj.* propellent, propulsive. *2 m.-f.* propeller, propellent.

prorrata *f.* prorate: *a* ~, pro rata, in proportion.

prorratear *tr.* to prorate, apportion.

prorrateo *m.* apportionment.

prórroga *f.* PRORROGACIÓN.

prorrogable *adj.* prolongable [for a specified time].

prorrogación *f.* prolongation, extension [for a specified time].

prorrogar *tr.* to prolong, extend [for a specified time]. *2* to prorogue, postpone.

prorrumpir *intr.* to break forth, burst out.

prosa *f.* prose. *2* verbiage.

prosaico, -ca *adj.* prosaic.

prosapia *f.* ancestry, lineage.

proscenio *m.* THEAT. proscenium.

proscribir *tr.* to proscribe. ¶ P. P.: *proscrito, proscripto.*

proscripción *f.* proscription.

proscripto or **proscrito, -ta** *adj.* proscribed. *2 m.-f.* exile, outlaw, proscribed person.

prosecución *f.,* **proseguimiento** *m.* prosecution, continuation. *2* pursuit, pursuing.

proseguir *tr.* to continue, carry on. *2 intr.* to continue, go on. ¶ CONJUG. like *servir.*

proselitismo *m.* proselytism.

prosélito *m.* proselyte.

prosénquima *f.* BIOL. prosenchyma.

prosimio, -mia *adj.* ZOOL. prosimian.

prosista *m.-f.* prosaist [prose author].

prosodia *f.* orthoëpy.

prosopopeya *f.* RHET. prosopopœia. *2* coll. pomposity, solemnity.

prospecto *m.* prospectus.

prosperar *tr.* to prosper. *2 intr.* to prosper, thrive.

prosperidad *f.* prosperity.

próspero, -ra *adj.* prosperous.

próstata *f.* ANAT. prostate.

prosternarse *ref.* to prostrate oneself.

prostíbulo *m.* brothel.

prostitución *f.* prostitution.

prostituir *tr.* to prostitute. *2 ref.* to prostitute oneself. *3* to become prostituted. ¶ CONJUG. like *huir.*

prostituta *f.* prostitute, harlot.

protagonista *m.* protagonist. *2* hero, heroine [in poem, novel, etc.].

prótasis, *pl.* **-sis** *f.* DRAMA, GRAM. protasis.

protección *f.* protection.

proteccionismo *m.* protectionism.

protector, -ra *adj.* protecting, protective. *2 m.* protector. *3 f.* protectress.

protectorado *m.* protectorate.

protectorio, -ria *adj.* protective.

proteger *tr.* to protect.

protegido, -da *adj.* protected. *2 m.* protégé.

proteico, -ca *adj.* protean. *2* BIOCHEM. proteic.

proteína *f.* BIOCHEM. proteid, protein.

protervamente *adv.* perversely, wickedly.

protervia, protervidad *f.* perversity, wickedness.

protervo, -va *adj.* perverse, stubbornly wicked.

prótesis *f.* GRAM., SURG. prosthesis, prothesis.

protesta, protestación *f.* protest, protestation, remonstrance. *2* protestation [of friendship, impartiality, etc.]. *3* LAW protest.

protestación *f.* PROTESTA. *2* ~ *de la fe,* profession of faith.

protestante *adj.* protesting, protestant. *2 adj.-n.* Protestant.

protestantismo *m.* Protestantism.

protestar *tr.* to protest, affirm solemnly. *2* COM. to protest [a bill of exchange]. *3 intr.* ~ *contra,* to protest, protest against.

protesto *m.* COM. protest [of a bill of exchange].

protético, -ca *adj.* GRAM. prosthetic.

protocolario, -ria *adj.* protocolary, ceremonial.

protocolizar *tr.* to file with the original copies kept by a notary.

protocolo *m.* protocol. *2* diplomatic or Court ceremonial rules. *3* file of original copies kept by a notary.

protomártir *m.* protomartyr.

protón *m.* PHYS. & CHEM. proton.

protonotario *m.* prothonotary.

protoplasma *m.* BIOL. protoplasm.

protórax, *pl.* **-rax** *m.* ENT. prothorax.

prototipo *m.* prototype.

protóxido *m.* CHEM. protoxide.

protozoario, -ria; protozoo, -a *adj.-m.* ZOOL. protozoan.

protráctil *adj.* protractile.

protuberancia *f.* protuberance.

provecto, -ta *adj.* advanced in years, learning or experience; mature.

provecho *m.* advantage, benefit, good. *2* profit, gain. *3* utility: *de* ~, useful. *4* progress, advancement.

provechoso, -sa *adj.* profitable. *2* beneficial, good. *3* advantageous, useful.

proveedor, -ra *m.-f.* supplier, furnisher, purveyor.

proveer *tr.* to supply, furnish, provide, purvey; to stock with provisions. *2* to appoint a person to [a post or office]. *3* LAW to decide. *4 intr.* ~ *a*, to provide for, to take the necessary steps for. *5 ref.* to provide oneself. ¶ P. P.: *provisto*.

proveimiento *m.* providing, supplying.

proveniente *adj.* coming, originating, arising.

provenir *intr.* to come, originate, arise. ¶ CONJUG. like *venir*.

provento *m.* product, revenue.

Provenza *f. pr. n.* GEOG. Provence.

provenzal *adj.-n.* Provençal.

proverbial *adj.* proverbial.

proverbio *m.* proverb, adage, saying.

próvidamente *adj.* providently, carefully.

providencia *f.* providence, forethought. *2* provision, step, measure. *3* providence [care of God]; (cap.) Providence [God].

providencial *adj.* providential.

providenciar *tr.* LAW to decide, decree. *2* to take steps or measures.

providente *adj.* wise, prudent. *2* provident, careful.

próvido, -da *adj.* provident. *2* benevolent, propitious.

provincia *f.* province [administrative division].

provincial *adj.* provincial. *2 m.* ECCL. provincial.

provinciano, -na *adj.-n.* provincial [inhabitating a province].

provisión *f.* provision, providing. *2* supply, stock. *3* step, measure. *4* COM. ~ *de fondos*, funds, money [to pay a bill of exchange, check, etc.]. *5 pl.* provisions, supply.

provisional *adj.* provisional, interim.

provisor *m.* purveyor, provider. *2* ECCL. vicar general.

provisorio, -ria *adj.* provisional, temporary.

provisto, -ta *adj.* provided, stocked, supplied.

provocación *f.* provocation [instigation, challenging, stirring up].

provocador, -ra *adj.* provoking. *2 m.-f.* provoker.

provocar *tr.* to provoke, incite, dare, challenge. *2* to provoke, cause, bring about, stir up.

provocativo, -va *adj.* provocative, inciting.

proxeneta *m.-f.* go-between, procurer, procuress.

proximal *adj.* ANAT., ZOOL. proximal.

próximamente *adv.* soon, before long. *2* approximately.

proximidad *f.* proximity. *2* vicinity.

próximo, -ma *adj.* near, neighbouring, proximate, close. *2* next: *el mes* ~, next month. *3* ~ *pasado*, last [month, year, etc.].

proyección *f.* projection [projecting; projected image]. *2* GEOM. projection.

proyectante *adj.* projecting, designing.

proyectar *tr.* to project, throw, cast. *2* to project [light, shadow, an image, etc.]: to show [a moving picture]. *3* GEOM. to project. *4* to project, plan, intend. *5* to design [draw the plan of]. *6 ref.* [of a shadow, etc.] to fall.

proyectil *m.* projectile, missile.

proyectista *m.-f.* designer, maker of projects. *2* projector [person].

proyecto *m.* project, plan, design. *2* ~ *de ley*, bill [proposed law].

proyector *m.* projector [apparatus]; searchlight; spotlight.

prudencia *f.* prudence.

prudencial *adj.* prudential.

prudente *adj.* prudent. *2* cautious.

prueba *f.* proof, demonstration, evidence. *2* sign, mark, token. *3* proof, test, trial, probation: *poner a* ~, to put to the test, to try. *4* tasting, sampling; sample. *5* fitting, trying on [of an article of dress]. *6* ordeal, trial. *7* temptation. *8* SPORT. match, competition. *9* MATH., ENGRAV., PRINT., PHOT. proof. *10 a* ~ *de*, proof, proof against.

pruebo, pruebe, etc. *irr.* V. PROBAR.

prurigo *m.* MED. prurigo.

prurito *m.* MED. itching, pruritus. *2* fig. eagerness, desire.

Prusia *f. pr. n.* GEOG. Prussia.

prusiano, -na *adj.-n.* Prussian.

prúsico, -ca *adj.* CHEM. prusic.

pseudo *adj.* SEUDO.

psi *s.* psi [Greek letter].

psicastenia *f.* MED. psychasthenia.

psicoanálisis *m.* MED. psychoanalysis.

psicoanalista *m.-f.* psychoanalyst.

psicología *f.* psychology.

psicológico, -ca *adj.* psychological.

psicólogo *m.* psychologist.

psicometría *f.* psychometrics, psychometry.

psicópata *m.* psycopath.

psicopatía *f.* MED. psycopathy.

psicosis *f.* MED. psychosis.

psicoterapia *f.* MED. psychotherapy.

psique, psiquis *f.* psyche, the human soul. *2* (cap.) MYTH. Psyche.

psiquiatra *m.* psychiater.

psiquiatría *f.* psychiatry.

psíquico, -ca *adj.* psychic, psychical.

pteridofita *f.* BOT. pteridophyte.

¡pu! *interj.* ugh!

púa *f.* prick, sharp point, barb, thorn. *2* prong, tine. *3* spine, quill [of porcupine, etc.]. *4* tooth [of comb]. *5* HORT. graft, scion. *6* MUS. plectrum. *7* fig. crafty person.

púber, -ra; púbero *adj.* pubescent [having reached puberty]. *2 m.-f.* pubescent person.

pubertad *f.* puberty.

pubescencia *f.* pubescence.

pubescente *adj.* pubescent.

pubis *m.* ANAT. pubes. *2* ANAT., ZOOL. pubis.

publicación *f.* publication, publishing. *2* publication [paper, book, music, etc., published].

publicano *m.* Rom. HIST. publican.

publicar *tr.* to publish. *2* to issue [a decree, etc.]. *3* to cause to appear [in a newspaper, etc.].

publicidad *f.* publicity.

publicista *m.* publicist.

público, -ca *adj.* public. *2* generally known. *3 m.* public. *4* audience [assembly of spectators, etc.].

puchera *f.* dish of meat and vegetables.

pucheritos *m. pl.* PUCHERO 4.

puchero *m.* cooking pot. *2* PUCHERA. *3* fig. food, sustenance. *4 pl.* pouting [of a person about to cry]: *hacer pucheros*, to pout.

puches *m. pl.* gruel, pap, porridge.

pude, pudiera, etc. *irr.* V. PODER.

pudelar *tr.* METAL. to puddle.

pudendo, -da *adj.* shameful, obscene. *2 partes pudendas*, private parts, genitals.

pudibundez *f.* overmodesty; prudishness.

pudibundo, -da *adj.* PUDOROSO.

pudicicia *f.* modesty, chastity, pudicity.

púdico, -ca *adj.* modest, chaste.

pudiente *adj.* rich, well off.

pudín *m.* Ang. pudding.
pudor *m.* modesty, chastity, pudency.
pudoroso, -sa *adj.* modest, bashful, chaste.
pudridero *m.* rotting place. 2 temporary vault [for corpses].
pudrigorio *m.* PODRIGORIO.
pudrimiento *m.* putrefaction, rotting.
pudrir *tr.* to putrefy, rot, corrupt. 2 *ref.* to putrefy, rot [undergo putrefaction]. 3 to languish [in jail, etc.]. 4 *fig.* to fret, worry. 5 *intr.* to be dead and buried.
pueblerino, -na *adj.* belonging to a village; country, countrified.
pueblo *m.* town, village; settlement. 2 people [of a place or country]; common people. 3 people, nation.
puedo, pueda, etc. *irr.* V. PODER.
puente *m.-f.* bridge [across stream, ravine, etc.]: ~ *aéreo,* air bridge, airlift; ~ *levadizo,* drawbridge. 2 MUS., NAUT., DENT. bridge. 3 MUS. tailpiece. 4 NAUT. gun-carrying deck. 5 AUTO. ~ *de engrase,* grease lift.
puerca *f.* ZOOL. sow. 2 *fig.* sow, slut.
puerco, -ca *adj.* dirty, filthy. 2 slovenly, sluttish. 3 piggish, hoggish. 4 base, mean. 5 *m.* ZOOL. hog, pig. 6 *fig.* hog, pig [man]. 7 mean, base mean. 8 ZOOL. ~ *de mar,* sea hog. 9 ZOOL. ~ *espín,* porcupine.
puericia *f.* childhood.
puericultura *f.* puericulture.
pueril *adj.* puerile, childish.
puerilidad *f.* puerility.
puerperal *adj.* puerperal.
puerro *m.* BOT. leek.
puerta *f.* door, doorway; gate, gateway; entrance, access: ~ *de corredera,* sliding door; ~ *excusada,* or *falsa,* back door, side door; ~ *giratoria,* revolving door; *coger* or *tomar la* ~, to leave, go away; *dar a uno con la* ~ *en las narices,* to slam the door on one's face; *estar a la* ~, or *a las puertas,* to be imminent; *a* ~ *cerrada,* in secret; with closed doors; *de* ~ *en* ~, from door to door.
puertaventana *f.* window shutter.
puerto *m.* NAUT. port, harbour, haven: ~ *franco,* free port. 2 *fig.* haven, refuge. 3 mountain pass. 4 AER. ~ *aéreo,* airport.
Puerto Rico *m. pr. n.* GEOG. Porto Rico, Puerto Rico.
puertorriqueño, -ña *adj.-n.* Porto Rican.
pues *conj.* because, for, since: ~ *que,* since, inasmuch as. 2 then [accordingly; in summary or recapitulation]: *así* ~, so then; ~ *bien,* now then, well then; all right then. 3 well [as an expletive or intensive]. 4 *adv.* yes, so, certainly, indeed. 5 (interrogatively) ¿~?, ¿*y* ~?, why?, how is that?; so?; and what then?
puesta *f.* ASTR. set, setting: ~ *de sol,* sunset. 2 stake [at cards]. 3 ~ *a punto,* completion, perfection. 4 ~ *de largo,* coming out, social debut. 5 ~ *en marcha,* starting.
puesto, -ta *irreg. p. p.* of PONER. 2 *adj.* placed, put, set. 3 dressed, attired. 4 *conj. puesto que,* since, inasmuch as. 5 *m.* place [assigned or occupied]. 6 stall, stand, booth. 7 place, dignity, office, post, employment, job. 8 MIL. post, station: ~ *de socorro,* first-aid station. 9 blind [for hunters].
¡puf! *interj.* ugh!
púgil *m.* pugilist; prize, fighter, boxer.
pugilato *m.* pugilism, boxing.
pugna *f.* fight, struggle, strife, conflict; opposition, clashing.

pugnacidad *f.* pugnacity.
pugnar *intr.* to fight, struggle, strive. 2 ~ *con,* to conflict with, to be opposed to.
pugnaz *adj.* pugnacious.
puja *f.* push, effort. 2 outbidding, bid [at an auction].
pujador, -ra *m.-f.* bidder [at an auction].
pujame, pujamen *m.* NAUT. foot [of a sail].
pujante *adj.* puissant, powerful, strong, vigorous.
pujanza *f.* puissance, might, strength, vigour.
pujar *tr.* to push [a project, etc.]. 2 to raise [one's bid]. 3 *intr.* to falter; to grope for words. 4 *coll.* to pout, snivel.
pujo *m.* MED. tenesmus. 2 *fig.* irresistible impulse [to cry, laugh, etc.]; eagerness, strong desire.
pulcritud *f.* neatness, tidiness, cleanliness. 2 honesty [of conduct].
pulcro, -cra *adj.* neat, tidy, cleanly. 2 honest [conduct, person].
Pulchinela *m.* Punchinello.
pulga *f.* ENT. flea: *tener malas pulgas,* to be ill-tempered; *tener pulgas,* *fig.* to be restless, too lively. 2 ZOOL. ~ *de mar,* beach flea.
pulgada *f.* inch.
pulgar *m.* ANAT. thumb.
pulgarada *f.* pinch [of salt, etc.]. 2 blow given pressing the thumb. 3 PULGADA.
pulgón *m.* ENT. aphid, plant louse.
pulguera *f.* BOT. fleawort.
pulguillas, *pl.* **-llas** *m.* coll. restless, fretful fellow.
pulicán *m.* dentist's forceps.
pulidez *f.* beauty. 2 cleanliness, neatness.
pulido, -da *adj.* polished. 2 beautiful, pretty. 3 clean, neat; exquisitely made or wrought.
pulidor *m.-f.* polisher, furbisher, burnisher.
pulimentar *tr.* to polish, burnish.
pulimento *m.* polish, gloss.
pulir *tr.* to polish, burnish, furbish. 2 to polish [refine, finish]. 3 to adorn, beautify. 4 *ref.* to beautify oneself. 5 to become refined.
pulmón *m.* ANAT. lung. 2 ~ *de acero,* iron lung.
pulmonado, -da *adj.* ZOOL. pulmonate.
pulmonar *adj.* pulmonary, lung.
pulmonía *f.* MED. pneumonia.
pulpa *f.* pulp.
pulpejo *m.* soft fleshy part [of finger, ear, etc.].
pulpería *f.* (Am.) grocery, general store.
púlpito *m.* pulpit.
pulpo *m.* ZOOL. octopus, cuttlefish.
pulposo, -sa *adj.* pulpous, pulpy.
pulque *m.* a Mexican fermented drink.
pulquérrimo, -ma *adj.* superl. of PULCRO.
pulsación *f.* pulsation, beat. 2 MUS. touch, striking, fingering.
pulsada *f.* pulsation, pulse, beat [of the arteries].
pulsador *m.* push button. 2 WEAV. feeler.
pulsar *tr.* to push [a button]. 2 to feel the pulse of. 3 *fig.* to sound, examine [an affair]. 4 MUS. to strike, finger, play [a key, a string, an instrument]. 5 *intr.* [of the heart, an artery, etc.] to pulsate, beat, throb.
pulsátil *adj.* pulsatile.
pulsatila *f.* BOT. pasqueflower.
pulsera *f.* JEWEL. bracelet. 2 wristlet. 3 watch strap. 4 SURG. wrist bandage. 5 side lock of hair.
pulso *m.* PHYSIOL. pulse: *tomar el* ~ *a,* to feel the pulse of; to sound, examine [an affair]. 2 part of the wrist where pulse is felt. 3 steadiness of the hand: *a* ~, freehand [drawing]; with the strength of the hand; *fig.* by a persistent effort. 4 care, tact.

pultáceo, -a *adj.* pultaceous.
pulular *intr.* to pullulate. 2 to swarm, teem.
pulverización *f.* pulverization.
pulverizador, -ra *adj.* pulverizing. 2 *m.* atomizer, spray, sprayer.
pulverizar *tr.* to pulverize. 2 to atomize [a liquid]. 3 *ref.* to become pulverized; to spray.
pulverulento, -ta *adj.* pulverulent, powdery, dusty.
pulla *f.* quip, cutting remark, innuendo. 2 repartee, witty saying.
¡pum! *interj.* bang!
puma *m.* ZOOL. puma, cougar.
pumita *f.* pumice stone.
puna *f.* (Am.) arid table-land in the Andes.
punción *f.* MED. puncture.
pundonor *m.* dignity, honour, self-respect.
pundonoroso, -sa *adj.* dignified, self-respectful, nice about matters of honour.
pungente *adj.* pungent, prickling, stinging.
pungir *tr.* to prick, pierce. 2 fig. to sting.
punible *adj.* punishable.
púnico, -ca *adj.* Punic.
punitivo, -va *adj.* punitive.
punta *f.* point [sharp or tapering end]: *sacar ~ a*, to sharpen. 2 head [of an arrow or spear]. 3 tip, nib, end: *de ~*, on end. 4 apex, top. 5 butt, stub, stump [of cigar or cigarette]. 6 horn [of bull]. 7 tine [of antlers]. 8 GEOG. point, headland. 9 taint of sourness [in wine]. 10 trace, streak, tinge, somewhat. 11 point [of a joke]. 12 ~ *de París*, wire nail. 13 *estar de ~*, to be on bad terms. 14 *de ~ en blanco*, all dressed up; directly. 16 *pl.* scalloped lace.
puntada *f.* SEW. stitch. 2 hint. 3 (Am.) stitch [in the side].
puntal *m.* prop, stanchion. 2 fig. stay, support. 3 NAUT. depth of hold.
puntapié *m.* kick [with the tip of the shoe]: *echar a puntapiés*, coll. to kick out.
punteado, -da *adj.* dotted, stippled. 2 *m.* dotting, stippling. 3 dotted surface. 4 plucking the guitar.
puntear *tr.* to dot, tó stipple. 2 to sew, stitch. 3 to pluck [the guitar]. 4 *intr.* NAUT. to tack.
puntel *m.* pontil, punty.
puntera *f.* cap [of a shoe]. 2 new toe on stockings.
puntería *f.* pointing, aim, aiming [of a weapon, a missile]; marksmanship.
puntero, -ra *adj.* sharpshooting. 2 *m.* pointer [rod for pointing]. 4 stonecutter's pointed chisel.
puntiagudo, -da *adj.* sharp, sharp-pointed.
puntilla *f.* narrow lace edging. 2 BULLF. short dagger used in finishing a bull. 3 *de puntillas*, softly, on one's tiptoes; on tiptoe.
puntillazo *m.* PUNTAPIÉ.
puntillero *m.* bullfighter wo finishes the bull with a short dagger.
puntilio *m.* punctillo. 2 MUS. dot.
puntilloso, -sa *adj.* punctilious.
puntito *m. dim.* small point, dot.
punto *m.* GEOM. point. 2 dot: *poner los puntos sobre las íes*, fig. to dot the i's and cross the t's. 3 GRAM. period; stop, mark: ~ *final*, full stop; ~ *y coma*, semicolon; *dos puntos*, colon; *puntos suspensivos*, suspension points. 4 nib [of a pen]. 5 front sight [of a firearm]. 6 SEW., SURG. stitch. 7 stitch, loop [in knitting or netting]; point [in embroidery or lacemaking]. 8 knitwork: *géneros de ~*, hosiery. 9 method of stitching, knitting, etc. 10 break [in stockings or a knited fabric]. 11 punch

hole [in a strap]. 12 PRINT. point [unit]. 13 point, place, spot: ~ *de apoyo*, point of support; fulcrum; ~ *de partida*, starting point; ~ *de vista*, point of view. 14 cabstand. 15 point, mark [unit of award or estimation]. 16 SPORT. point. 17 punter [in gambling]. 18 minute part. 19 moment, instant: *al ~*, immediately. 20 nick of time, right moment. 21 subject, matter, point, detail: ~ *por ~*, in detail. 22 state, condition attained. 23 perfect condition attained by a thing cooked, baked, etc. 24 PHYS. point, stage. 25 degree, extent: *hasta cierto ~*, to a certain extent, in a way. 26 point of honour, punctilio. 27 aim, purpose. 28 GEOG., ASTR. ~ *cardinal*, cardinal point. 29 *poner en su ~*, to perfect [a thing]; to rate [a thing] at its true value. 30 *a ~*, opportunely; ready. 31 *a ~ de* [with an inf.], on the point of, about to. 32 *a ~ fijo*, with certainty. 33 *en buen ~*, luckily. 34 *en mal ~*, unluckily. 35 *en ~*, exactly, sharp.
puntoso, -sa *adj.* full of points. 2 punctilious; self-respectful.
puntuación *f.* GRAM. punctuation. 2 number of marks awarded or gained in an examination, etc.
puntual *adj.* punctual. 2 certain, sure. 3 suitable.
puntualidad *f.* punctuality; punctual habits.
puntualizar *tr.* to specify, detail, tell in detail. 2 to finish, perfect.
puntuar *tr.* GRAM. to punctuate, point. 2 to award a number of marks to [in examination].
puntura *f.* prick, puncture, sting. 2 PRINT. register point.
punzada *f.* prick, puncture, sting. 2 stitch, pang, shooting pain. 3 fig. sting, pang [of remorse, etc.].
punzante *adj.* prickling, piercing, sharp. 2 shooting [pain]. 3 fig. biting, caustic.
punzar *tr.* to prick, puncture, sting. 2 to give a shooting pain to. 3 [of remorse, etc.] to sting.
punzó *m.* flaming red [colour].
punzón *m.* punch, puncheon; awl, pick, bodkin; counterdie. 2 graver, burin.
puñada *f.* PUÑETAZO.
puñado *m.* handful.
puñal *m.* poniard, dagger.
puñalada *f.* stab [with a dagger]. 2 fig. blow [cause of sudden pain or grief].
puñetazo *m.* cuff, punch, blow with the fist.
puño *m.* fist [clenched hand]; *meter en un ~*, coll. to intimidate, subdue; *como un ~*, [of things normally small] big: [of things normally large] small, tiny. 2 hand, handwriting: *de su ~ y letra*, in his own hand. 3 handful. 4 fig. grasp. 5 cuff, wristband. 6 hilt [of a sword, dagger, etc.]. 7 grip [of a sabre]. 8 handle [of an umbrella]. 9 head [of a cane]. 10 *pl.* strength, courage.
pupa *f.* MED. eruption in the lips. 2 scab over a pimple. 3 child's word to express pain.
pupila *f.* ANAT. pupil. 2 pupil, ward [girl under a guardian]. 3 woman boarder.
pupilaje *m.* pupilage, wardship [state of being under a guardian]. 2 boarding house.
pupilo *m.* pupil, ward [boy under a guardian]. 2 boarder.
pupitre *m.* writing desk; school desk.
puramente *adv.* purely.
puré *m.* COOK. purée. 2 ~ *de patatas*, mashed potatoes.
pureza *f.* purity. 2 virginity.
purga *f.* MED. purge, purgative, physic. 2 MACH. drains [of a boiler, etc.].

purgación *f.* purgation. *2* expiation.
purgador, -ra *adj.* purgative. *2* expiation. *3 m.-f.* purger. *4* expiator.
purgamiento *m.* purgation, purge, purging.
purgante *adj.* purging. *2* expiating. *3 adj.-m.* MED. purgative.
purgar *tr.* MED. to purge, physic. *2* to purge, purify, cleanse. *3* to expiate. *4* LAW., MACH. to purge. *5 ref.* to take a purge. *6* to purge or free oneself.
purgativo, -va *adj.* purgative, purging.
purgatorio *m.* purgatory.
puridad *f.* purity. *2* secret, secrecy.
purificación *f.* purification, purifying.
purificador, -ra *adj.* purifying. *2 m.-f.* purifier. *3 m.* ECCL. purificator.
purificar *tr.* to purify. *2 ref.* to purify, to become purified.
Purísima (la) *f. pr. n.* the Virgin Mary.
purísimo, -ma *adj.* superl. of PURO.
purismo *m.* purism.
purista *m.* purist.
puritanismo *m.* Puritanism.
puritano, -na *adj.* puritan, puritanic, puritanical. *2* Puritan. *3 m.-f.* puritan. *4* Puritan.
puro, -ra *adj.* pure: *de pura raza*, thoroughbred. *2*

solid [gold]. *3 a* ~, by dint of. *4 de* ~ [followed by an adj.], through being so much. *5 m.* cigar.
púrpura *f.* ZOOL. purple, purple shell, murex. *2* purple [die, colour, robe]. *3* purple [cardinalate]. *4* MED. purpura.
purpurado *m.* cardinal.
purpurar *tr.* to purple. *2* to dress in purple.
purpurear *intr.* to purple, have a purple tinge.
purpúreo, -a *adj.* purple.
purpurina *f.* purpurin. *2* bronze powder.
purpurino, -na *adj.* PURPÚREO.
purulento, -ta *adj.* purulent.
pus *m.* MED. pus.
pusilánime *adj.* pusillanimous.
pústula *f.* MED. pustule.
pustuloso, -sa *adj.* pustulous, pustular.
puta *f.* harlot, strumpet, whore.
putativo, -va *adj.* putative.
putrefacción *f.* putrefaction.
putrefacto, -ta *adj.* putrid, rotten.
putrescible *adj.* putrescible.
putridez *f.* putridity.
pútrido, -da *adj.* putrid, rotten.
puya *f.* goad iron or head.
puyazo *m.* jab or prick with a goad.
puzol *m.*, **puzolana** *f.* PETROG. pozzolana.

Q

Q, q *f.* Q, q, twentieth letter of the Spanish alphabet.

que *rel. pron.* that, which, who, whom: *a* ~, to which, to whom; *a lo* ~, to what; *de* ~, of which; about which, whereof; from which, wherefrom; *en* ~, in which, wherein; upon which, whereupon. *2* Preceded by the definite article: *el* ~, *la* ~, he who or that, she who or that, who, whom, the one who or that; *los* ~, *las* ~, those who or that; *lo* ~, what, which, that which. *3* when: *el día* ~ *llegaste*, the day when you arrived.
4 conj. that [introducing clauses of statement, hypothesis, wish, result, reason or cause, and frequently omitted in the translation]. *5* to [in the construction called accusative-infinitive]: *dígale* ~ *venga*, tell him to come. *6* than [in comparative sentences]. *7* because, for, since. *8* so that. *9* and [used as an expletive]. *10* In elliptical sentences expressing command or desire, it is not translated or is rendered by let, *may, I wish*, etc.: ~ *entre*, let him come in. *11* When placed between the participle and the auxiliary in an inverted form of compound tense, it is rendered by *when, after, as soon as: escrito que hubo la carta*, when he had written the letter. *12 a menos* ~, unless. *13 con tal* ~, provided, that. *14* ~ *no*, without, but. *15 por ... * ~, however, no mater how. *16* ~ *... * ~, whether... or.

qué *interrog. & exclamatory adj. & pron.* which, what, how, what a. *2* how much. *3 ¿a* ~*?, ¿para* ~*?*, what for? *4 no hay de* ~, don't mention it, you are welcome [in answer to thanks]. *5 ¿por* ~*?*, why? *6 ¡*~*!*, what! *7 ¿*~*?*, how goes it? *8 ¡*~ *va!*, nonsense!, go on! [expressing disbelief]. *9 sin* ~ *ni para* ~, without cause or motive. *10 un no sé* ~, a certain something. *11 ¡y* ~*!*, what then!

quebrada *f.* gorge, ravine, *gulch.

quebradero *m.* ~ *de cabeza*, worry, concern.

quebradizo, -za *adj.* brittle, fragile. *2* fig. frail, delicate.

quebrado, -da *adj.* broken [thing]. *2* bankrupt. *3* MED. ruptured. *4* broken, rough [ground]. *5* ~ *de color*, sickly, pale. *6 m.* bankrupt. *7* MED. ruptured person. *8* MATH. fraction.

quebradura *f.* break, crack. *2* MED. hernia, rupture.

quebraja *f.* crack [in wood, iron, etc.].

quebrantador, -ra *adj.* breaking. *2* crushing. *3 m.-f.* breaker. *4* crusher.

quebrantahuesos, *pl.* **-sos** *m.* ORN. osprey. *2* ORN. lammergeier. *3* coll. bore [tiresome person].

quebrantamiento *m.* breaking. *2* crushing. *3* fatigue, exhaustion; breaking down [of health].

quebrantante *adj.* breaking, crushing.

quebrantar *tr.* to break [separate into parts]; to break, crush, bruise. *2* to break, weaken, diminish. *3* to break [resistance, one's will; prison, a promise, etc.]: to infringe, violate. *4* to exhaust, fatigue; to impair [the health]. *5* ~ *el corazón*, to move to pity. *6 ref.* to break [be broken, weakened, etc.].

quebranto *m.* breaking, crushing. *2* loss. *3* lassitude. *4* grief, pain. *5* pity, compassion.

quebrar *tr.* to break [separate into parts; to interrupt]. *2* to break, violate. *3* to bend [the body or something slender]. *4* to impair or dull [the colour or complexion] of a person. *5* to temper, moderate. *6 intr.* to weaken, give way. *7* COM. to fail; go bankrupt. *8 ref.* to break, be broken. *9* [of the body or a slender thing] to bend. *10* [of colour or complexion] to become dull or pale. *11* MED. to be ruptured. ¶ CONJUG. like *acertar*.

queche *f.* NAUT. ketch; smack.

quechua *adj.-n.* QUICHUA.

queda *f.* curfew. *2* curfew bell.

quedada *f.* stay, remaining [in a place].

quedamente *adv.* softly, gently, in a low voice.

quedar *intr.-ref.* to remain, stay behind, stay, stop, keep, be left [in or at a place]. *2* to remain, be left [in a condition or state]. *3* to be, become: ~ *atónito*, to be astonished. *4 intr.* to remain [continue to exist; to be left over]; to have left: *nos quedan diez pesetas*, we have ten pesetas left. *5* to agree: ~ *en*, to agree on or to. *6* ~ *a deber*, to remain owing. *7* ~ *bien* or *mal*, to acquit oneself well or badly; to keep or break an appointment, promise, etc.; to look well or poorly in a portrait. *8* ~ *por* or *sin* [hacer, etc.], to remain to be [done, etc.]. *9 por mí no quedará*, I'll do my best. *10 ref.* to take, choose [when buying]. *11 quedarse con*, to take, keep, retain.

quedito *adv.* very gently, very softly.

1) **quedo** *adv.* softly, gently. *2* in a low voice.

1) **quedo, -da** *adj.* quiet, still. *2* easy, gentle. *3* soft, low [voice]: *con voz queda*, in a low voice.

quehacer *m.* work, task, occupation, *chore.
queja *f.* lament, moan. 2 complaint, grievance.
quejarse *ref.* to lament, moan. 2 to complain.
quejicoso, -sa *adj.* querulous, complaining.
quejido *m.* lament, moan.
quejigo *m.* BOT. gall oak. 2 BOT. young oak.
quejoso, -sa *adj.* complaining, having a grievance.
quejumbre *f.* frequent complaining.
quejumbroso, -sa *adj.* querulous, habitually complaining. 2 querulous, whining.
quelícero *m.* ZOOL. chelicera.
quelonio, -nia *adj.-m.* ZOOL. chelonian.
quema *f.* burning. 2 fire, conflagration.
quemada *f.* burnt patch in a forest or thicket.
quemadero, -ra *adj.* for burning, to be burned. 2 *m.* place where convicts were burned. 3 place for burning dead animals or damaged food.
quemado *m.* burning or burned thing: *oler a ~,* to smell of fire. 2 QUEMADA.
quemador, -ra *adj.* burning. 2 *m.-f.* burner [person]. 3 incendiary. 4 *m.* burner [in appatus].
quemadura *f.* burn, scald [sore or injury]. 2 scorch or nip [in plants]. 3 smut [plant disease].
quemante *adj.* burning [very hot].
quemar *tr.* to burn [by fire or acid]. 2 to burn, scald, scorch. 3 to scorch, nip [plants]. 4 to burn [the mouth with pepper, etc.]. 5 fig. to anger, irritate. 6 *intr.* to burn, be burning [be too hot]. 7 *ref.* to burn [be consumed by fire]; to get burned. 8 to be very hot [have the sensation of heat]. 9 [of plants] to be scorched, nipped. 10 fig. to become angry. 11 fig. to be warm [near the object sought for].
quemazón *f.* burning. 2 excessive heat. 3 itching.
quepis, *pl.* **-pis** *m.* MIL. kepi.
quepo, quepa, etc. *irr.* V. CABER.
queratina *f.* BIOCHEM. keratin.
querella *f.* complaint, lament. 2 quarrel, dispute. 3 LAW complaint.
querellante *m.-f.* LAW complainant.
querellarse *ref.* to lament, bewail. 2 LAW to complain, bring suit.
querelloso, -sa *adj.* complaining. 2 plaintive.
querencia *f.* affection, liking. 2 inclination of man or animals to return to a haunt or place of frequent resort; this place. 3 natural tendency.
1) **querer** *m.* love, affection.
2) **querer** *tr.* to love [hold dear; be in love with]. 2 to will, want, wish, desire, like. 3 ~ *bien,* to love. 4 ~ *decir,* to mean. 5 *no* ~ *[hacer, dar,* etc.], to refuse to [do, give, etc.]. 6 *no* ~ *nada con,* not to wish to have anything to do with. 7 *como quiera que,* inasmuch, since, whereas. 8 *como quiera que sea,* anyhow, anyway, in any case. 9 *cuando quiera,* at any time, whenever. 10 *donde quiera,* anywhere, wherever. 11 *sin* ~, unintentionally, unwillingly. 12 impers. *parece que quiere llover,* it looks like rain.
¶ CONJUG. INDIC. Pres.: *quiero, quieres, quiere; queremos, queréis, quieren.* | Pret.: *quise, quisiste, quiso,* etc. | Fut.: *querré, querrás, querrá,* etc. | SUBJ. Pres.: *quiera, quieras, quiera, queramos, queráis, quieran.* | Imperf.: *quisiera, quisieras,* etc., or *quisiese, quisieses,* etc. | Fut.: *quisiere, quisieres,* etc. | IMPER.: *quiere, quiera;* queramos, quered, *quieran.*
querido, -da *adj.* dear, beloved. 2 *m.-f.* paramour. 3 *f.* mistress, paramour.
quermes *m.* kermes.
querocha *f.* CRESA.
querub, querube, querubín *m.* cherub.

querré, querrás, etc. *in.* V. QUERER.
quesadilla *f.* cheesecake. 2 a sweet pastry.
quesear *intr.* to make cheese.
quesera *f.* cheese maker or seller [woman]. 2 dairy [where cheese is made]. 3 cheese board. 4 cheese dish.
quesería *f.* dairy, cheese factory or shop.
quesero, -ra *adj.* caseous, cheesy. 2 *m.-f.* cheese maker; cheesemonger.
queso *m.* cheese.
quetzal *m.* ORN. quetzal.
quevedos *m.* *pl.* pince-nez having circular glasses.
¡quiá! *interj.* come now!, oh, no!
quicial *m.* hinge-pole. 2 QUICIO.
quicialera *f.* hinge-pole.
quicio *m.* door jamb. 2 pivot hole [for a hinge pole]: *sacar de* ~, to strain [things]; to exasperate [a person]; *fuera de* ~, out of order.
quid *m.* gist, reason, essence [of a thing].
quídam *m.* coll. fellow, person. 2 coll. nobody.
quiebra *f.* break, crack, fissure. 2 ravine. 3 loss, damage. 4 COM. failure, bankruptcy.
quiebro *m.* bending of the body at the waist [as in dodging or dancing]. 2 MUS. trill.
quiebro, quiebre, etc. *irr.* V. QUEBRAR.
quien *(interrog. & exclam.* **quién**), *pl.* **quienes** *pron.* who, whom, he who, whoever, whomever.
quienquiera *pl.* **quienesquiera** *pron.* whoever, whomever, whosoever, whomsoever.
quiero, quiera, etc. *in.* V. QUERER.
quietación *f.* quieting, appeasing.
quietamente *adv.* quietly, calmly.
quietismo *m.* quietism.
quieto, -ta *adj.* quiet, still, motionless. 2 quiet, undisturbed, calm, peaceful. 3 orderly, virtuous.
quietud *f.* quietness, quietude, stillness; quiet, rest, repose, tranquillity.
quijada *f.* jaw, jawbone. 2 MACH. jaw.
quijera *f.* cheekpiece [of a bridle]. 2 cheek [of a crossbow].
quijones, *pl.* **-nes** *m.* BOT. an aromatic herb.
quijota *f.* quixotism, quixotry [quixotic action].
quijote *m.* ARM. cuisse. 2 upper part of the haunch [of horses]. 3 Quixote, quixotic person.
quijotería *f.* quixotism, quixotry.
quijotesco, -ca *adj.* quixotic.
quilatar *tr.* AQUILATAR.
quilate *m.* carat, karat.
quilífero, -ra *adj.* ANAT. chyliferous.
quilificación *f.* PHYSIOL. chylification.
quilo *m.* KILO. 2 PHYSIOL. chyle: *sudar el* ~, coll. to work hard.
quilogramo, quilolitro, etc. = KILOGRAMO, KILOLITRO, etc.
quilla *f.* NAUT., BOT., ORN. keel: *dar de* ~, [of a ship] to keel.
quimera *f.* chimera, chimaera [monster: fanciful conception, impractical idea]. 2 quarrel, row.
quimérico, -ca *adj.* chimerical.
quimerista *adj.-n.* visionary. 2 *adj.* quarrelsome. 3 *m.-f.* quarrelsome person.
química *f.* chemistry.
químico, -ca *adj.* chemical. 2 *m.-f.* chemist [person skilled in chemistry].
quimificación *f.* PHYSIOL. chymification.
quimo *m.* PHYSIOL. chyme.
quimono *m.* kimono.
quina *f.* cinchona, Peruvian bark.
quinado, -da *adj.* prepared with QUINA [wine].
quincalla *f.* small metal wares.
quincallería *f.* small metal ware factory or shop.

quincallero, -ra *m.-f.* maker or seller of small metal wares.
quince *adj.-n.* fifteen. *2* fifteenth.
quincena *f.* fortnight. *2* semi-monthly pay.
quinceno, -na *adj.* fifteenth.
quincuagenario, -ria *adj.* having fifty units. *2 adj.- n.* quinquagenarian.
quincuagésimo, -ma *adj.-m.* fiftieth. *3 f.* ECCL. Quincuagesima.
quindécimo, -ma *adj.-m.* fifteenth.
quingentésimo, -ma *adj.-m.* five-hundredth.
quingombó *m.* BOT. okra.
quinientos, -tas *adj.-m.* five hundred.
quinina *f.* CHEM. quinine.
quino *m.* BOT. cinchona [tree].
quínolas *f.* four of a kind [at cards]. *2 pl.* a card game.
quinona *f.* CHEM. quinone.
quinqué *m.* student lamp, Argand lamp.
quinquefolio *m.* CINCOENRAMA.
quinquenal *adj.* quinquennial.
quinquenio *m.* quinquennium.
quinta *f.* country place, villa. *2* MIL. draft. *3* quint [at cards]. *4* MUS. fifth, quint. *5* FENC. quinte.
quintaesencia *f.* quintessence.
quintal *m.* quintal. *2* ~ *métrico*, metric quintal.
quintana *f.* countryplace, villa.
quintante *m.* quintant [instrument similar to a sextant].
quintañón, -na *adj.-n.* centenarian.
quintar *tr.* to draw one out of five. *2* MIL. to draft [soldiers].
quintería *f.* farm, grange.
quintero *m.* farmer. *2* farm hand.
quinteto *m.* MUS. quintet.
quintilla *f.* stanza of five octosyllables with two rhymes. *2* any five-lina stanza with two rhymes.
Quintín *m. pr. n.* Quentin.
quinto, -ta *adj.* fifth: *quinta columna*, fifth column. *2 m.* one fifth. *3* constript, recruit.
quíntuplo, -pla *adj.* quintuple, fivefold.
quinzavo, -va *adj.-m.* fifteenth.
quiñón *m.* share of profit. *2* lot of land.

quiosco *m.* kiosk, pavilion. *2* newstand. *3* bandstand.
quiquiriquí *m.* cock-a-doodle-do.
quiragra *f.* MED. chiragra.
quirie *m.* KIRIE.
quiromancia *f.* chiromancy, palmistry.
quiromántico, -ca *adj.* chiromantic, chiromantical. *2 m.-f.* chiromancer, chiromancist, palmist.
quiróptero, -ra *adj.* ZOOL. cheiropterous.
quirúrgico, -ca *adj.* surgical.
quise, quisiera, etc. *irr.* V. QUERER.
quisicosa *f.* coll. enigma, riddle.
quisque (cada) coll. everyone.
quisquilla *f.* trifle. *2* ZOOL. marine shrimp.
quisquilloso, -sa *adj.* overnice, squeamish. *2* touchy.
quiste *m.* MED., ZOOL. cyst.
quisto, -ta *adj.* liked: *bien* ~, well-liked; *mal* ~, disliked.
quita *f.* LAW remission of debt.
quitaipón *m.* QUITAPÓN.
quitamanchas *m.* clothes cleaner, spot remover.
quitamotas *m.-f.* flatterer, obsequious person.
quitanieves *f.* snowplough, snowplow.
quitanza *f.* quittance, discharge [of debt].
quitapón *m.* headstall ornament for horses.
quitar *tr.* to remove, take off, take out, rub off, pick off: *de quita y pon*, detachable, removable. *2* to eliminate. *3* to take, take off, deduct, subtract. *4* to steal, to rob of, deprive of. *5* to clear [the table]. *6* to hinder, be an obstacle to. *7* to prevent, forbid; to make a person give up [a habit]. *8* to intercept [the light]. *9* to abolish, repeal. *10* to free from [pain, worry, an obligation, etc.]. *11 ref.* to move away; *¡quítate de aquí!*, get out of here! *12* to take off [one's hat, clothes, etc.]. *13 quitarse de encima*, to get rid of [something]. *14 quitarse de*, to give up [a habit].
quitasol *m.* parasol, sunshade.
quite *m.* FENC. parry, dodge. *2* BULLF. attracting the bull from a man in danger.
quitina *f.* BIOCHEM. chitin.
quitinoso, -sa *adj.* chitinous.
quito, -ta *adj.* free, exempt.
quizá, quizás *adv.* perhaps, maybe.
quorum *m.* quorum.

R

R, r *f.* R, r, twenty-first letter of the Spanish alphabet.

rabada *f.* hinder quarter, rump.

rabadán *m.* head shepherd.

rabadilla *f.* coccygeal region. *2* ORN. rump, uropygium.

rabanal *m.* patch or field of radishes.

rabanero, -ra *adj.* coll. short [gown, skirt]. *2* forward, bold [manners, language]. *3 m.-f.* seller of radishes. *4 f.* fig. fishwife, coarse woman.

rábano *m.* BOT. radish: *tomar el ~ por las hojas,* coll. to be entirely mistaken.

rabazuz *m.* licorice extract.

rabear *intr.* to wag the tail.

rabel *m.* MUS. rebeck. *2* coll. breech, backside.

rabeo *m.* wagging the tail.

rabera *f.* tail end. *2* handle [of a crossbow].

rabí, *pl.* **-bíes** *m.* rabbi, rabbin.

rabia *f.* MED. hydrophobia. *2* rage, fury. *3 tener ~ a uno,* to hate; *tomar ~ a,* to take a dislike to.

rabiar *intr.* MED. to have rabies. *2* to rage, be furious. *3* to suffer racking pain. *4* fig. *~ por,* to wish eagerly. *5* coll. *estar a ~ con uno,* to be very angry with someone.

rabiatar *tr.* to tie by the tail.

rabiazorras *m.* coll. east wind.

rabicorto, -ta *adj.* short-tailed.

rabieta *f.* coll. fit of temper, tantrum.

rabihorcado *m.* ORN. frigate bird.

rabilargo, -ga *adj.* long-tailed.

rabillo *m.* little tail. *2* stalk, stem [of flower, leaf, etc.], peduncle. *3* corner [of the eye].

rabínico, -ca *adj.* rabbinic, rabbinical.

rabino *m.* rabbi, rabbin.

rabión *m.* rapids [in a river].

rabioso, -sa *adj.* rabid, mad, affected with rabies. *2* rabid, furious, violent. *3* enraged. *4* raging.

rabisalsera *adj.* forward, pert [woman].

rabiza *f.* tip of a fishing rod.

rabo *m.* tail [of an animal]: *con el ~ entre piernas,* fig. discomfited, humiliated. *2* fig. tail [hind part, taillike part]. *3* stalk, stem. *4* corner [of the eye]. *5* BOT. *~ de zorra,* foxtail.

rabón, -na *adj.* short-tailed, bobtailed.

rabopelado *m.* ZARIGÜEYA.

rabosear *tr.* to crumple; to fray.

rabotada *f.* insolent reply.

rabudo, -da *adj.* long-tailed, thick-tailed.

rábula *m.* charlatan lawyer, pettifogger.

racel *m.* NAUT. dead rise.

racial *adj.* racial, race.

racima *f.* grapes remaining on vines after vintage.

racimo *m.* BOT. raceme. *2* bunch, cluster.

racimoso, -sa *adj.* racemose. *2* having or giving forth many bunches or clusters [of fruit].

raciocinar *intr.* to ratiocinate, reason.

raciocinio *m.* reason [faculty of reasoning]. *2* ratiocination, reasoning.

ración *f.* ration. *2* portion [of food]. *3* allowance for food.

racionabilidad *f.* judgement, discernment.

racional *adj.* rational. *2* reasonable. *3 m.* rational being. *4* rational [breast plate].

racionalidad *f.* rationality, reasonableness.

racionalismo *m.* rationalism.

racionalista *adj.* rationalistic. *2 adj.-n.* rationalist.

racionalización *f.* COM., IND. rationalization.

racionalizar *tr.* COM., IND. to rationalize.

racionamiento *m.* rationing.

racionar *tr.* to ration.

racha *f.* gust [of wind]. *2* streak of [good or bad] luck. *3* RAJA.

rada *f.* NAUT. bay, roads, roadsted.

radar *m.* ELECT. radar.

radiación *f.* radiation. *2* broadcasting.

radiactivo, -va *adj.* PHYS. radioactive.

radiado, -da *adj.* irradiated. *2* radiated [arranged like rays]. *3* broadcast. *4* BOT., ZOOL. radiate. *5 m.* ZOOL. radiate.

radiador *m.* radiator.

radial *adj.* radial.

radian *m.* GEOM. radian.

radiante *adj.* PHYS. radiant. *2* radiant, beaming.

radiar *tr.-intr.* to radiate, to irradiate. *2* to radio, broadcast. *3 intr.* to beam, shine.

radicación *f.* radication.

radical *adj.* radical. *2 m.-f.* POL. radical. *3 m.* MATH., PHILOL., CHEM. radical.

radicalismo *m.* radicalism.

radicar *intr.-ref.* to take root. *2 intr.* to be, lie. *3 ref.* to settle, establish oneself.

radícula *f.* BOT. radicle.

radio *m.* GEOM., ANAT. radius. *2* radius, spoke [of wheel]. *3* radius, scope. *4* CHEM. radium. *5* coll. radio, radiogram. *6 f.* coll. radio, broadcasting. *7* coll. radio, wireless set.

radiodifusión *f.* RADIO. broadcast, broadcasting.
radiodifusor, -ra *adj.* RADIO. broadcasting.
radioescucha *m.-f.* radio listener.
radiofaro *m.* AER. radio beacon.
radiofonía *f.* radiophony.
radiofónico, -ca *adj.* radiophonic.
radiofrecuencia *f.* radio frequency.
radiografía *f.* radiography, X-ray photography. *2* radiograph, X-ray photograph.
radiograma *m.* radiogram, radio message.
radiología *f.* MED. radiology.
radiólogo *m.* radiologist.
radiorreceptor *m.* radio receiver, wireless set.
radioscopia *f.* radioscopy.
radioso, -sa *adj.* radiant, beaming.
radiosonda *f.* radiosonde.
radiotelefonía *f.* radiotelephony.
radiotelegrafía *f.* radiotelegraphy.
radiotelegrafiar *tr.* to radiotelegraph, to wireless.
radiotelegrafista *m.-f.* wireless operator.
radioterapia *f.* MED. radiotherapy. *2* MED. radium-therapy.
radioyente *m.-f.* RADIOESCUCHA.
raedera *f.* scraper [instrument].
raedor, -ra *m.-f.* scraper. *2 m.* strickle.
raedura *f.* scraping. *2 pl.* scrapings.
raer *tr.* to scrape [a surface]. *2* to scrape off. *3* to wear out [clothes]. *4* fig. to extirpate, wipe out. ¶ CONJUG. like *caer*.
Rafael *m. pr. n.* Raphael.
ráfaga *f.* gust [of wind]. *2* burst [of machinegun fire]. *3* small cloud. *4* flash [of light].
rafe *m.* ANAT., BOT. raphe. *2* ARCH. eaves.
rafia *f.* BOT. raffia.
raglán *m.* raglan.
rahez *adj.* vile, low, despicable.
raicilla *f. dim.* rootlet. *2* BOT. radicle.
raído, -da *adj.* threadbare [clothes]. *3* barefaced, shameless.
raigambre *f.* intertwined roots. *2* fig. deep rootedness.
raigo, raiga, etc. *irr.* V. RAER.
raigón *m. augm.* large root. *2* root of a tooth.
rail *m.* RLY. rail.
raíz *f.* root [of a plant, etc.]; stem [of a word]: *echar raíces,* to take root; *a ~,* close to the root of; on the occasion of; *de ~,* entirely, at the root. *2* MATH. root.
raja *f.* split, rent, crack. *2* part of a split piece of wood. *3* slice [of melon, etc.].
rajá *m.* raja, rajah.
rajadura *f.* splitting, cracking. *2* split, crack.
rajar *tr.* to split, rend. *2* to slice [a melon, etc.]. *3 intr.* coll. to brag. *4 ref.* to split, crack [be split or cracked]. *5* coll. to back down.
rajatabla (a) *adv.* at any cost, regardless of anything else.
ralea *f.* kind, nature, sort. *2* [scornful and applied to persons] race, breed.
ralear *intr.* [of cloth, hair, etc.] to become thin or sparse. *2* [of vines] to yield thin bunches.
raleza *f.* thinness, sparseness [of cloth, hair, etc.].
ralo, -la *adj.* thin, sparse [cloth, hair, teeth, etc.].
rallador *m.* kitchen grater.
ralladura *f.* mark left by a grater. *2* COOK. gratings.
rallar *tr.* to grate [with a kitchen grater].
rallo *m.* kitchen grater. *2* rose, rosehead [of watering pot].
rama *f.* branch, bough. *2* fig. branch [of family, learning, etc.]: *andarse por las ramas,* to beat

about the bush. *3* PRINT. chase. *4 en ~,* raw, unmanufactured.
Ramadán *m.* Ramadan.
ramaje *m.* branchage, branches.
ramal *m.* branch [of railway, mountain range, etc.]. *2* strand [of rope]. *3* flight [of stairs]. *4* halter [for leading a horse].
ramalazo *m.* lash with a rope. *2* sudden pain. *3* fig. blow, sudden sorrow or grief.
rambla *f.* sandy or dry ravine. *2* tenter [for cloths].
rameado, -da *adj.* flowered [design].
ramera *f.* harlot, strumpet.
ramificación *f.* ramification; branching off.
ramificarse *ref.* to ramify; to branch off.
ramillete *m.* bouquet, nosegay. *2* BOT. a clustery cyme. *3* centerpiece, epergne. *4* ornamental dish of sweets. *5* collection of choice things.
ramilletero, -ra *m.-f.* maker and seller of bouquets. *2 f.* flower girl. *3 m.* flower vase.
ramio *m.* BOT. ramie.
ramita *f. dim.* sprig, twig.
ramito *m. dim.* small bunch. *2* sprig, small bough.
ramo *m.* bough, branch. *2* bunch, cluster. *3* string [of onions]. *4* branch [of science, etc.]; line [of business]. *5* touch, slight attack [of a disease].
ramojo *m.* brushwood [wood of small branches].
Ramón *m. pr. n.* Raymond.
ramón *m.* browse.
ramonear *intr.* to browse. *2* to trim trees.
ramoneo *m.* browsing; browsing season. *2* trimming of trees.
ramoso, -sa *m.* ramose, ramous.
rampa *f.* cramp [contraction of the muscles]. *2* ramp, inclined plane, sloping way.
rampante *adj.* HER. rampant.
ramplón, -na *adj.* heavy, coarse [shoe]. *2* vulgar, uncouth. *3 m.* calk [of horseshoe].
rana *f.* ZOOL. frog. *2* coll. *no ser ~,* to be expert, clever. *3 pl.* MED., VET. ranula.
rancajo *m.* splinter in the flesh.
rancidez *f.* rancidity, rankness, staleness.
rancio, -cia *adj.* rank, rancid, stale. *2* aged [wine]. *3* old [lineage, etc.]. *4* antiquated [ideas]. *5* old-fashioned [person]. *6 m.* rancidness. *7* rancid bacon.
rancioso, -sa *adj.* rancid, stale.
ranchear *intr.* to form a settlement with huts.
ranchería *f.* settlement made of huts or shanties. *2* MIL. kitchen [in barracks].
ranchero *m.* kitchen attendant [of a regiment]. *2* (Am.) rancher, ranchman.
rancho *m.* cooked food for soldiers, prisoners, etc. *2* hut, rustic cottage. *3* settlement made of huts. *4* coterie. *5* (Am.) cattle ranch.
randa *f.* lace, needle-point lace.
rangífero *m.* RENO.
rango *m.* class, order, sort. *2* rank [social standing]; high station.
rangua *f.* MACH. pivot bearing.
ranilla *f.* frog [of hoof].
ránula *f.* MED., VET. ranula.
ranunculáceo, -a *adj.* BOT. ranunculaceous.
ranúnculo *m.* BOT. buttercup, crowfoot.
ranura *f.* groove, rabbet: *a ~ y lengüeta,* CARP. tongue-and groove. *2* slot.
raño *m.* oyster rake. *2* ICHTH. scorpion fish.
rapa *f.* blossom of the olive tree.
rapacería *f.* childish action.
rapacidad *f.* rapacity.
rapador *m.* coll. barber.
rapadura *f.* shaving. *2* close haircut.

rapapolvo *m.* coll. scolding, dressing down.
rapar *tr.* to shave. *2* to crop [the hair].
1) **rapaz** *adj.* rapacious. *2* ORN. of prey, raptorial.
2) **rapaz, -za** *m.* boy, young boy. *2 f.* girl, young girl.
rapazuelo, -la *m. dim.* little boy. *2 f. dim.* little girl.
rape *m.* coll. hurried shave or hair-cut. *2 al* ~, cropped, cut close or short.
rapé *m.* snuff, rappee.
rapidez *f.* rapidity, quickness, swiftness.
rápido, -da *adj.* rapid, fast, quick, swift. *2 m.* rapids [in a river].
rapiña *f.* rapine, robbery. *2 ave de* ~, bird of prey.
rapiñar *tr.* coll. to steal, plunder.
rapista *m.* coll. barber.
raposa *f.* ZOOL. fox. *2* ZOOL. female fox, vixen. *3* fig. fox [crafty person].
raposear *intr.* to fox, act craftily.
raposera *f.* fox hole, fox den.
raposería *f.* foxiness, craftiness; crafty ways.
raposo *m.* ZOOL. [male] fox. *2* fig. fox, crafty person.
rapsoda *m.* rhapsode, rhapsodist.
rapsodia *f.* LIT., MUS. rhapsody.
raptar *tr.* to abduct, ravish [a woman], to kidnap.
rapto *m.* abduction, ravishment [of a woman], kidnapping. *2* rapture, ecstasy.
raptor *m.* abductor, ravisher, kidnapper.
Raquel *f. pr. n.* Rachel.
raqueta *f.* SPORT. racket. *2* SPORT. battledore. *3* badminton battledore and shuttlecock [game]. *4* racket [snowshoe]. *5* rake [used by croupiers].
raquetero *m.* racket maker or seller.
raquis, *pl.* **-quis** *s.* ANAT., BOT. rachis.
raquítico, -ca *adj.* MED. rachitic, rickety. *2* stunted. *3* feeble, poor, short, meagre, stinted.
raquitismo *m.* MED. rachitism.
raramente *adv.* rarely, seldom. *2* oddly, strangely.
rarefacción *f.* rarefaction.
rarefacer *tr.-ref.* ENRARECER 1. ¶ CONJUG. like *hacer*.
rareza *f.* rarity, rareness. *2* oddity, strangeness. *3* curiosity, freak. *4* eccentricity, peculiarity.
raridad *f.* rarity, rareness.
rarificar *tr.-intr.* ENRARECER.
raro, -ra *adj.* rare [gas]. *2* rare [uncommon, exceptional]. *3* scarce: *raras veces*, seldom. *4* odd, queer, strange.
ras *m.* evenness, flushness. *2 a* ~ *de*, close to, even with, flush with.
rasa *f.* thin spot [in a fabric]. *2* small tableland.
rasante *adj.* grazing [touching lightly in passing]. *2* ARTILL. horizontal [fire]. *3 f.* grade line.
rasar *tr.* to strike [level with a strickle]. *2* to graze, skim [touch lightly in passing].
rasarse *ref.* [of the sky] to clear up.
rascacielos *m.* skyscraper [very tall building].
rascadera *f.* scraper [implement]. *2* currycomb.
rascador *m.* scraper, scratcher [implement]. *2* ornamental hairpin.
rascadura *f.* scraping, scratching.
rascar *tr.* to scrape, to scratch.
rascatripas, *pl.* **-pas** *m.-f.* coll. scraper [fiddler].
rascazón *f.* itch, itching.
rascón, -na *adj.* tart, sharp [to the taste]. *2 m.* ORN. water hen, gallinule.
rasero *m.* strickle: *medir por el mismo* ~, *o por un* ~, fig. to make no difference.
rasete *m.* satinet.
rasgado, -da *adj.* wide [mouth]. *2* almond [eyes].
rasgadura *f.* tear, tearing, rent, rip.

rasgar *tr.* to tear, rend, rip [clothes, paper, etc.]. *2* RASGUEAR. *3 ref.* to tear, become torn.
rasgo *m.* flourish, stroke [of pen]. *2* flash [of wit], bright saying. *3* deed, feat, act, action: ~ *heroico*, heroic feat. *4* trait. *5 pl.* features [of the face]. *6* fig. *a grandes rasgos*, broadly, in outline.
rasgón *m.* tear, rent, rip.
rasgueado *m.* RASGUEO.
rasguear *tr.* to play flourishes on [the guitar]. *2* *intr.* to flourish, make flourishes with the pen.
rasgueo *m.* playing flourishes on the guitar. *2* making flourishes with the pen.
rasguñar *tr.* to scratch [with the nails, etc.]. *2* DRAW. to sketch, outline.
rasguño *m.* scratch. *2* DRAW. sketch, outline.
1) **raso** *m.* satin.
2) **raso, -sa** *adj.* flat, level, open, clear, unobstructed: *campo* ~, open country; *al* ~, in the open air. *2* clear, cloudless [sky]. *3* skimming the ground. *4 soldado* ~, common soldier, private.
raspa *f.* stem of a bunch of grapes. *2* awn, beard [of wheat, barley, etc.]. *3* corncob. *4* spine, backbone [of a fish].
raspado *m.* SURG. scraping.
raspador *m.* eraser [instrument].
raspadura *f.* erasure, scraping out. *2 pl.* scrapings.
raspajo *m.* stem of a bunch of grapes.
raspante *adj.* rough, harsh to the taste [wine].
raspar *tr.* to rasp, scrape, scrape out, erase. *2* [of wine, etc.] to be harsh to [the palate].
raspear *intr.* [of a pen] to scratch.
raspilla *f.* BOT. myosotis, forget-me-not.
rasqueta *f.* NAUT. scraper. *2* (Am.) currycomb.
rastillo *m.* RASTRILLO.
rastra *f.* trace, track, trail. *2* AGR. rake. *3* AGR. harrow. *4* drag [rough sledge]. *5* anything trailing. *6* outcome, consequence. *7* NAUT. drag. *8 a la* ~, *a* ~, *a rastras*, dragging; unwillingly. *9* string [of onions, etc.].
rastrear *tr.* to trace, track, trail, scent out. *2* to drag, search [the sea-bottom, etc.]. *3 intr.* AGR. to rake. *4* to skim the ground, to fly very low.
rastreo *m.* dragging, searching.
rastrero, -ra *adj.* creeping, dragging, trailing. *2* that tracks [dog]. *3* flying low. *4* cringing, grovelling, abject, low, base.
rastrillador, -ra *m.-f.* hatcheler. *2* AGR. raker.
rastrillaje *m.* hatcheling. *2* AGR. raking.
rastrillar *tr.* to hackle, hatchel [flax or hemp]. *2* AGR. to rake.
rastrillo *m.* hackle, hatchel. *2* FORT. portcullis. *3* iron gate. *4* battery [of a flintlock]. *5* AGR. rake. *6* ward [of a key or lock].
rastro *m.* AGR. rake. *2* trace, track, trail, scent. *3* trace, vestige, sign. *4* slaughterhouse.
rastrojera *f.* stubble field.
rastrojo *s.* AGR. stubble, haulm.
rasura *f.* shaving. *2* scraping. *3 pl.* argol.
rasurar *tr.* to shave [the hair].
rata *f.* ZOOL. rat: ~ *de alcantarilla*, brown rat. *2* coll. sneak thief.
ratafía *f.* ratafia, ratafee [liquor].
rataplán *m.* rub-a-dub [sound of a drum].
rata por cantidad *adv.* pro rata.
ratear *tr.* to distribute proportionally. *2* to filch, pilfer. *3 intr.* to crawl, creep.
rateramente *adv.* meanly, vilely.
ratería *f.* petty theft.
ratero, -ra *m.-f.* pickpocket, pilferer, sneak thief.
ratificación *f.* ratification, confirmation.

ratificar *tr.* to ratify. *2* ref. *ratificarse en*, to confirm [one's previous statement].

ratito *m. dim.* short time, little while.

rato *m.* time, short time, while: *un buen* ~, a great while; a pleasant time; *un mal* ~, an unpleasant time; *un* ~, a while; *al poco* ~, presently, soon; *a ratos*, from time to time, occasionally; *a ratos perdidos*, in spare time; *largo* ~, a long time, a great while.

ratón *m.* ZOOL. mouse: ~ *almizclero*, muskrat; ~ *de campo*, field mouse.

ratona *f.* ZOOL. female mouse.

ratonar *tr.* [of mice] to eat or gnaw.

ratoncito *m. dim.* little mouse.

ratonera *f.* mousetrap. *2* mousehole. *3* nest of mice.

ratonero, -ra; ratonesco, -ca; ratonil *adj.* [pertaining to] mice, mousy.

rauco, -ca *adj.* raucous, hoarse, husky.

raudal *m.* stream, torrent, flow.

raudo, -da *adj.* rapid, swift, impetuous.

raya *f.* ICHTH. ray, skate. *2* line [long narrow mark]. *3* stroke [of pen or pencil], dash [in printing, writing and telegraphy]. *4* score, scratch [on a surface]. *5* stripe, streak: *a rayas*, striped. *6* crease [in trousers]. *7* parting [in the hair]. *8* rifle groove. *9* boundary, frontier. *10 pasar de* ~, or *de la* ~, to go too far; *tener a* ~, to keep within bounds.

rayadillo *m.* striped cotton duck.

rayado, -da *adj.* stripped, streaky. *2* ruled [paper]. *3* rifled [gun barrel]. *4 m.* ruling [of paper]. *5* stripes.

rayano, -na *adj.* bordering, verging.

rayar *tr.* to draw lines on, to rule. *2* to scratch [a surface]. *3* to stripe. *4* to cross out, cancel. *5* to underline. *6 intr.* to excel. *7* ~ *con*, to border on; fig. to equal, match. *8* ~ *en*, to border upon, verge on. *9* ~ *el alba, el día*, to dawn.

rayo *m.* ray, beam [of light, etc.]: ~ *de sol*, sunbeam; *rayos catódicos*, cathode rays. *2* spoke [of a wheel]. *3* lighting, stroke of lightning, bolt, thunderbolt: *como el* ~, fig. like lightning. *4* sudden misfortune. *5* fig. lively person.

rayón *m.* rayon, artificial silk.

rayuela *f. dim.* of RAYA. *2* game of pitching pennies.

raza *f.* BIOL., ETHN. race: *razas humanas*, human races. *2* race, kindred, lineage, breed, strain: *de pura* ~, thoroughbred. *3* crack, fissure. *4* ray of light [coming through a crack, fissure, etc.]. *5* WEAV. light-woven stripe [in fabrics].

rázago *m.* burlap, sackcloth.

razón *f.* reason [in practically every sense]: ~ *de estado*, reason of State; *uso de* ~, discretion, discernment; *entrar en* ~, to become reasonable; *meter en* ~, to bring to reason; *perder la* ~, to go out of one's wits. *2* words, speech: *con razones corteses*, with courteous words. *3* right, justice, correctness; being right; *dar la* ~, to agree with, to approve; *tener* ~, to be right; *no tener* ~, to be wrong; to be mistaken; *con* ~ *o sin ella*, rightly or wrongly. *4* reasonableness [of prices, terms, etc.]; *ponerse en* ~, to be or become reasonable. *5* regard, respect: *en* ~ *a, en* ~ *de*, with regard to. *6* information, account, explanation: *dar* ~ *de*, to inform about, to give an account of. *7* rate [proportion]: *a* ~ *de*, at the rate of. *8* MATH. ratio: ~ *aritmética*, difference; ~ *geométrica*, geometrical ratio. *9* COM. ~ *social*, firm, firm name.

razonable *adj.* reasonable, sensible. *2* reasonable, moderate, fair.

razonado, -da *adj.* reasoned [exposition, petition].

razonador, -ra *adj.* reasoning. *2 m.-f.* reasoner.

razonamiento *m.* reasoning, argumentation.

razonar *intr.* to reason, ratiocinate. *2 tr.* to reason [explain, justify, etc., by adducing reasons].

razzia *f.* razzia, raid [plundering expedition].

re *m.* MUS. re, D.

reabrir *tr.* to reopen.

reabsorber *tr.* to reabsorb.

reabsorción *f.* reabsorption.

reacción *f.* reaction. *2* RADIO. regeneration.

reaccionar *intr.* to react.

reaccionario, -ria *adj.-n.* reactionary.

reacio, -cia *adj.* reluctant, unwilling, disobedient.

reactancia *f.* ELECT. reactance.

reactivar *tr.* MED. to reactivate.

reactivo, -va *adj.* reactive. *2 m.* CHEM. reagent.

reactor *m.* ELECT., PHYS. reactor.

readaptar *tr.* to readapt.

readmitir *tr.* to readmit.

reajustar *tr.* to readjust.

real *adj.* real, actual. *2* MATH., OPT., real. *3* royal, regal; kingly, queenly. *4* grand, magnificent, fine, handsome: ~ *moza*, handsome woman. *5 m.* real [Spanish coin]. *6* MIL. army's camp: *levantar, el* ~ or *los reales*, to break camp; *asentar los reales*, to encamp. *7* ~ *de una feria*, place for a fair.

realce *m.* embossment, relief, raised work. *2* enhancement, emphasis. *3* lustre, splendor. *4* PAINT. high light.

realengo, -ga *adj.* royal [burgh, etc.]. *2 m.* royal patrimony.

realera *f.* queen cell [of beehive].

realeza *f.* royalty, regal dignity or power.

realidad *f.* reality, fact. *2* truth, sincerity. *3 en* ~, in reality, really.

realismo *m.* realism. *2* royalism.

realista *adj.* realistic. *2* royalistic. *3 m.-f.* realist. *4* royalist.

realizable *adj.* realizable [hope, plan, etc.]; feasible, practicable. *2* COM. realizable.

realización *f.* realization, doing, accomplishing, achievement, fulfilment. *2* COM. realization.

realizador, -ra *m.-f.* accomplisher. *2* CINEM. producer.

realizar *tr.* to realize, accomplish, carry out, do, perform, fulfill. *2* COM. to realize. *3 ref.* to be accomplished, fulfilled, carried out.

realmente *adj.* really, in reality, actually.

realzar *tr.* to raise, elevate. *2* to emboss. *3* to heighten, enhance, set off. *4* PAINT. to brighten up, light up.

reanimar *tr.* to reanimate, revive. *2 ref.* to reanimate, revive [be reanimated].

reanudar *tr.* to renew, resume. *2 ref.* to be renewed or resumed.

reaparecer *intr.* to reappear.

reaparición *f.* reappearance.

rearmar *tr.* to rearm.

rearme *m.* rearmament, rearming.

reasegurador, -ra *adj.* reinsuring. *2 m.* reinsurer.

reasegurar *tr.* to reinsure.

reaseguro *m.* reinsurance.

reasumir *tr.* to reassume, resume, retake.

reasunción *f.* reassumption, resumption.

reasunto *irreg. p. p.* of REASUMIR.

reata *f.* rope to tie animals and keep them in a

single file; drove of animals going in a single file. 3 (Am.) rope, lasso.

reatar *tr.* to tie again. 2 to tie tight. 3 to tie in a single file.

reavivar *tr.* to revive, renew, reawake.

rebaba *f.* burr, fin, rough edge, rough flange.

rebaja *f.* diminution, deduction. 2 com. rebate.

rebajado, -da *adj.* relieved of service [soldier]. 3 depressed, drop [arch].

rebajamiento *m.* lowering, reduction, diminution. 2 PAINT. toning down. 4 disparagement, humiliation; lowering oneself.

rebajar *tr.* to lower, cut down, reduce, rebate, discount. 2 to lower [reduce the height of]. 3 CARP. to rabbet, scarf; to shave down. 4 to reduce the strength of [a liquor]. 5 PAINT. to tone down. 6 to disparage, to humiliate. 7 to humble oneself: *rebajarse a,* to stoop to.

rebajo *m.* rabbet [cut along an edge or arris].

rebalaje *m.* current of waters.

rebalsa *f.* pool [in a stream].

rebalsar *tr.* to dam [flowing water]. 2 *intr.-ref.* [of flowing water] to form a pool.

rebanada *f.* slice [esp. of bread].

rebanar *tr.* to slice.

rebañadera *f.* ARREBAÑADERA.

rebañadura *f. pl.* leavings gathered together; scrapings.

rebañar *tr.* to gather up [without leaving any remnants]. 2 to scrape [a plate].

rebaño *m.* herd, flock, fold, drove.

rebasar *tr.* to exceed, go beyond. 2 NAUT. to sail past.

rebate *m.* fight, encounter.

rebatimiento *m.* refutation.

rebatiña *f.* scramble [for something].

rebatir *tr.* to rebut, refute. 2 to repel, drive back, resist.

rebato *m.* alarm, alarm bell, tocsin: *tocar a ~,* to sound the tocsin. 2 MIL. sudden attack.

rebautizar *tr.* to rebaptize.

Rebeca *f. pr. n.* Rebecca.

rebeca *f.* a jacket of knit worsted for women.

rebeco *m.* ZOOL. chamois.

rebelarse *tr.* to rebel, to revolt.

rebelde *adj.* rebellious, insurgent, insubordinate, stubborn. 3 MED. rebellious. 4 LAW defaulting. 5 *m.-f.* rebel, insurgent. 6 LAW defaulter.

rebeldía *f.* rebelliousness; stubbornness. 2 rebellious act. 3 LAW default: *en ~,* by default.

rebelión *f.* rebellion, revolt, rising, insurrection.

rebelón, -na *adj.* balky, restive [horse].

rebenque *m.* whip [for flogging galley slaves]. 2 (Am.) strong riding whip. 3 NAUT. short rope.

rebién *adv.* coll. very well.

reblandecer *tr.* to soften. 2 *ref.* to soften, become soft. ¶ CONJUG. like *agradecer.*

reblandecimiento *m.* softening: *~ cerebral,* MED. softening of the brain.

rebollar, rebolledo *m.* grove of Turkey oaks.

rebollo *m.* BOT. Turkey oak.

rebolludo, -da *adj.* thick-set.

rebombar *intr.* to resound.

reborde *m.* flange, projecting rim.

rebosadero *m.* overflow [outlet], spillway.

rebosar *intr.-ref.* to overflow, overbrim, run over. 2 *intr.* to be in abundance. 3 *~ de* or *en,* to overflow with, to burst with.

rebotar *intr.* [of a ball, etc.] to bound or bounce repeatedly; to rebound. 2 *tr.* to clinch, bend the

point of [a nail, etc.]. 2 to drive back [after impact]. 4 to vex, exasperate, upset.

rebote *m.* bound, bounce; rebound [of a ball, etc.]: *de ~,* indirectly.

rebotica *f.* back room in a shop.

rebozar *tr.* to muffle or cover [one's face] with one's cape or cloak. 2 COOK. to cover with batter, flour, honey, etc. 3 *ref.* to muffle oneself up.

rebozo *m.* muffling oneself up. 2 a kind of mantilla. 3 fig. disguise, simulation. 4 *sin ~,* frankly, openly.

rebudiar *intr.* HUNT. [of a wild boar] to grunt.

rebufar *intr.* to snort again. 2 to snort loudly.

rebufe *m.* snort, snorting [of the bull].

rebufo *m.* muzzle blast, air expansion when a gun is fired.

rebujar *tr.-ref.* ARREBUJAR.

rebujo *m.* woman's thick veil. 2 clumsy bundle.

rebullicio *m.* great bustle or hubbub.

rebullir *intr.-ref.* to stir, begin to move; give sings of life.

rebumbar *intr.* [of a cannon ball] to whiz.

reburujar *tr.* to make up in a clumsy bundle.

reburujón *m.* clumsy bundle.

rebusca *f.* careful research or seeking out.

rebuscado, -da *adj.* affected, unnatural, farfetched.

rebuscamiento *m.* too careful research. 2 affectation, excessive elegance [in bearing, language, etc.].

rebuscar *tr.* to research, to seek out with care. 3 to gather fruit left by gatherers.

rebuznador, -ra *adj.* braying. 2 *m.-f.* brayer.

rebuznar *intr.* to bray.

rebuzno *m.* braying [of a donkey].

recabar *tr.* to obtain by entreaty.

recadero, -ra *m.-f.* commissionnaire, messenger.

recado *m.* message, errand: *hacer recados,* to do or run errands. 2 present, gift [sent with a letter]. 3 daily provision or marketing. 4 outfit, equipment: *~ de escribir,* writing materials. 5 (Am.) saddle and trappings. 7 *pl.* compliments, regards.

recaer *intr.* to fall again, fall back. 2 to relapse. 3 *~ en* or *sobre* [of an heritance, election, responsibility, etc.] to fall to; to fall upon, devolve upon. ¶ CONJUG. like *caer.*

recaída *f.* relapse.

recaigo, recaiga, etc. *irr.* V. RECAER.

recalada *f.* NAUT. landfall.

recalar *tr.* to soak, saturate. 2 *intr.* NAUT. *~ en,* to approach or reach [a place].

recalcar *tr.* to press [a thing with another]. 2 to cram, to pack, or stuff [things]. 3 to emphasize, lay stress upon [words]. 4 *intr.* NAUT. to heel, list. 5 ARRELLANARSE.

recalce *m.* AGR. hilling. 2 ARCH. underpinning.

recalcitrante *adj.* recalcitrant. 2 stubborn.

recalcitrar *intr.* to recalcitrate.

recalentamiento *m.* reheating. 2 overheating.

recalentar *tr.* to reheat. 2 to overheat, superheat. 3 to excite sexually. 4 *ref.* to become overheated. 5 to be spoiled by the excessive heat. ¶ CONJUG. like *acertar.*

recaliente, recaliente, etc. *irr.* V. RECALENTAR.

recalmón *m.* NAUT. lull [in wind or sea].

recalvastro *adj.* bald-pated.

recalzar *tr.* to hill [plants]. 2 ARCH. to underpin. 3 PAINT. to colour [a drawing].

recalzo *m.* ARCH. underpinning.

recamado, -da *adj.* adorned with raised embroidery.

recamar *tr.* to adorn with raised embroidery.

recámara *f.* chamber, breech [of a gun]. *2* MIL. blasthole [of a mine]. *3* fig. caution, reserve, cunning. *4* obs. wardrobe.

recambiar *tr.* to re-exchange, to rechange. *2* COM. to redraw.

recambio *m.* re-exchange. *2* rechange. *3* COM. redrawing. *4* MACH. *de* ~, spare [part, wheel, etc.].

recamo *m.* raised embroidery.

recancamusa *f.* CANCAMUSA.

recancanilla *f.* emphasis, stress laid on words to indicate special significance.

recantación *f.* recantation.

recantón *m.* spur stone.

recapacitar *tr.* to go over [in one's mind], to meditate upon.

recapitulación *f.* recapitulation, summing up.

recapitular *tr.* to recapitulate, summarize.

recargar *tr.* to reload, recharge. *2* to overload, overcharge. *4* to increase [a tax or duty]. *5* to adorn to excess. *6* ref. to have an increase of fever.

recargo *m.* recharge, new load. *2* surtax. *3* MED. increase of fever.

recatado, -da *adj.* cautious, circumspect. *3* modest, chaste.

recatar *tr.* to hide, conceal. *2* ref. to hide [oneself or one's actions].

recato *m.* caution, reserve. *2* modesty, decency.

recauchutar *tr.* to retread, recap [a tire].

recaudación *f.* collection [of rents, taxes, etc.]. *2* sum collected, receipt. *3* collector's office.

recaudador *m.* collector, taxgatherer.

recaudar *tr.* to collect [rents, taxes, etc.]. *2* to hold or put under care, in safe place.

recaudo *m.* RECAUDACIÓN 1. *2* precaution, care: *a buen* ~, under care, in safe place.

recavar *tr.* to dig a second time.

recazo *m.* guard [of a sword]. *2* back [of a knife].

recebar *tr.* to level [a roadbed] with gravel. *2* to refill [a cask].

recelar *tr.-ref.* to fear, distrust, suspect.

recelo *m.* fear, distrust, misgiving, suspicion.

receloso, -sa *adj.* fearful, distrustful, suspicious.

recental *adj.* sucking [calf or lamb].

recentísimo, -ma *adj. superl.* very recent.

recepción *f.* reception, receiving, receipt. *2* reception, admission [into Academy, etc.]. *3* reception [ceremony]. *4* RADIO. reception.

receptáculo *m.* receptacle.

receptador *m.-f.* LAW receptor [of fugitives of justice]; receiver [of stolen goods].

receptar *tr.* LAW to conceal, shelter [offenders], to receive [stolen goods, etc.].

receptividad *f.* receptiveness, receptivity.

receptivo, -va *adj.* receptive.

receptor, -ra *adj.* receiving. *2* *m.-f.* receiver, recipient [person]. *3* *m.* TELEF., TELEG., RADIO. receiver.

recercar *tr.* to fence in again. *2* to regird. *3* CERCAR.

receso *m.* deviation, separation. *2* (Am.) adjournment.

receta *f.* prescription, recipe, receipt.

recetar *tr.* MED. to order, prescribe [a medicine]. *2* coll. to ask for. *3* intr. MED. to prescribe.

recetario *m.* pharmacopœia. *2* receipt book. *3* apothecary's file.

recetor *m.* receiver, treasurer.

recial *m.* rapids, swift current [in rivers].

reciamente *adv.* strongly, solidly. *2* vigorously, impetuously.

reciario *m.* retiarius [gladiator].

recibí *m.* COM. receipt; received payment.

recibidero, -ra *adj.* receivable.

recibidor, -ra *m.-f.* receiver, recipient. *2* *m.* RECIBIMIENTO 3 & 4.

recibimiento *m.* reception, receiving. *2* reception [manner of receiving a person]; greeting, welcome. *3* drawing-room. *4* entrance room, hall [of a flat or appartment].

recibir *tr.* to receive [in practically every sense]. *2* to admit, let in. *3* to meet [go to a place to receive a person]. *4* to face [an attack or assailant]. *5* intr. to receive [receive company, be at home]. *6* ref. *recibirse de*, to graduate as, to be admitted to practice as.

recibo *m.* reception, receipt: *acusar* ~ *de*, to acknowledge receipt of. *2* COM. receipt, quittance. *3* reception [of callers]: *día de* ~, at-home day; *estar de* ~, to be dressed for receiving callers. *4* RECIBIMIENTO 4.

recidiva *f.* MED. relapse.

reciedumbre *f.* strength, solidity, vigour.

recién *adv.* recently, lately, newly, late, new. | Used only before a p. p.: ~ *casados*, newly married. *2* (Am.) just: ~ *ha llegado*, he has just arrived.

reciente *adj.* recent, fresh, late, new, modern.

recinto *m.* area, enclosure, precinct. *2* FORT. enceinte.

1) **recio** *adv.* RECIAMENTE. *2* *de* ~, RECIAMENTE.

2) **recio, -cia** *adj.* strong, robust, vigorous. *2* thick, heavy. *3* stout, bulky. *4* hard, difficult to bear. *5* rigourous [weather]. *6* swift, impetuous.

récipe *m.* recipe, prescription.

recipiendario *m.* member received [into an Academy, etc.].

recipiente *adj.* recipient. *2* *m.* receptacle, vessel, container. *3* receiver [of an air pump].

recíprocamente *adv.* reciprocally, mutually. *2* conversely.

reciprocar *tr.* to reciprocate [to make mutual or correspondent].

reciprocidad *f.* reciprocity.

recíproco, -ca *adj.* reciprocal, mutual.

recitación *f.* recitation.

recitado *m.* MUS. recitative.

recital *m.* MUS. recital.

recitar *tr.* to recite.

recitativo, -va *adj.* MUS. recitative.

reciura *f.* strength, vigour. *2* thickness, stoutness.

reclamación *f.* claim, demand [of a thing as one's due]. *2* reclamation, complaint, protest.

reclamante *m.-f.* claimant, claimer [one who demands something as his due]. *2* reclaimant.

reclamar *tr.* to claim [demand as one's due; call for, require]. *2* INTERN. LAW to reclaim. *3* to decoy [a bird]. *4* intr. to reclaim, protest [against]; to put in a claim. *5* ref. [of birds] to call one another.

reclame *m.* NAUT. tie block.

reclamo *m.* decoy bird. *2* birdcall. *3* call [of a bird calling another bird]. *4* allurement, attraction. *5* advertising, publicity. *6* PRINT. catchword.

reclinación *f.* reclination, reclining.

reclinar *tr.* to recline, to lean. *2* ref. to recline, to lean [intr.].

reclinatorio *m.* kneeling desk, prie-dieu. *2* anything arranged for reclining on.

recluir *tr.* to confine, imprison, intern, shut up, seclude [a person]. *2 ref.* to confine or seclude oneself. ¶ CONJUG. like *huir*.

reclusión *f.* confinement, imprisonment, internment, seclusion. *2* place of confinement.

recluso *adj.* confined, imprisoned, interned, recluse. *3 m.-f.* prisoner [person kept in prison].

recluta *f.* RECLUTAMIENTO. *2 m.* MIL. recruit.

reclutamiento *m.* recruitment; conscription. *2* MIL. the conscripts of the same year.

reclutar *tr.* to recruit, ro conscript.

recobrar *tr.* to recover, regain, retrieve. *2 ref.* to recover [regain health, consciousness, etc.].

recobro *m.* recovery, recuperation.

recocina *f.* back kitchen.

recodar *intr.-ref.* to lean upon with the elbow. *2 intr.* [of a river, road, etc.] to turn, bend.

recodo *m.* turn, bend [of a river, road, etc.].

recogedor, -ra *m.-f.* gatherer. *2* shelterer. *3 m.* dustpan.

recoger *tr.* to retake, take back. *2* to gather, collect, pick up. *3* to gather [a piece of cloth]; to take in [a garment]; to tuck up or in. *4* to take away, put away. *5* to fetch, get. *6* to gather, accumulate. *7* to receive, give shelter to. *8* to intern [in a home or asylum]. *9* to retire, withdraw; to withdraw from circulation. *10 ref.* to retire [into a convent, etc.]. *11* to retire [go to bed]. *12* to abstract oneself from worldly thoughts.

recogida *adj.* withdrawal from circulation.

recogido, -da *adj.* recluse. *2* short-trunked [animal]. *3 m.-f.* inmate [of a home or asylum].

recogimiento *m.* abstraction of worldly thoughts, recollection.

recolección *f.* summary. *2* gathering [of fruits], harvesting. *3* collection [of money or taxes]. *4* recollection, spiritual meditation.

recolectar *tr.* to gather [as harvest].

recolector *m.* collector, taxgatherer.

recoleto, -ta *adj.-n.* ECCL. Recollect.

recomendable *adj.* commendable. *2* recommendable.

recomendación *f.* recommendation.

recomendar *tr.* to recommend. *2 ref.* to make oneself or itself recommendable. ¶ CONJUG. like *acertar*.

recompensa *f.* recompense, compensation, reward: *en ~*, in return.

recompensar *tr.* recompense, compensate, reward.

recomponer *tr.* to recompose, compose again. *2* to mend, repair. ¶ CONJUG. like *poner*.

recompuesto, -ta *p. p.* of RECOMPONER.

reconcentración *f.*, **reconcentramiento** *m.* concentration [bringing together to a point; intensity of hate, etc.]. *2* concentration, abstraction.

reconcentrar *tr.* concentrate [bring together to a point]. *2* to keep secret and intense [one's hate, etc.]. *3 ref.* to become absorbed in thought.

reconciliación *f.* reconciliation.

reconciliador, -ra *adj.* reconciling. *2 m.-f.* reconciler.

reconciliar *tr.* to reconcile [restore to friendship]. *2* ECCL. to reconcile. *3 ref.* to become reconciled.

reconcomerse *ref.* CONCOMERSE.

reconcomio *m.* CONCOMIO. *2* itching, desire. *3* fam. secret fear or suspicion.

recóndito, -ta *adj.* recondite, out of the way, hidden.

reconocedor, -ra *adj.* inspector, examiner.

reconocer *tr.* to inspect, examine. *2* MIL. to reconnoitre, scout. *3* to recognize [identify as known before]. *4* to recognize, acknowledge, own [that]. *6* to be recognizant [to]. *7 ref.* to avow or own oneself. ¶ CONJUG. like *agradecer*.

reconocidamente *adv.* gratefully. *2* acknowledgedly.

reconocido, -da *adj.* recognized. *2* acknowledged. *3* recognizant, grateful.

reconocimiento *m.* inspection, examination. *2* MIL. reconnaissance, scouting. *3* survey. *4* recognition. *5* acknowledgment; admission. *6* gratitude.

reconozco, reconozca, etc. *irr.* V. RECONOCER.

reconquista *f.* reconquest.

reconquistar *tr.* to reconquer.

reconstituir *tr.* to reconstitute. *2* MED. to restore.

reconstituyente *adj.-m.* reconstituent.

reconstruir *tr.* to reconstruct, rebuild. ¶ CONJUG. like *huir*.

recontar *tr.* to re-count. *2* to recount, tell, narrate, relate. ¶ CONJUG. like *contar*.

reconvención *f.* charge, reproach, reprehension.

reconvendré, reconvendría, etc. *irr.* V. RECONVENIR.

reconvengo, reconvenga, etc. *irr.* V. RECONVENIR.

reconvenir *tr.* to reproach, to reprehend. *2* LAW to make a reconvention against. ¶ CONJUG. like *venir*.

reconvine, reconviniera, etc. *irr.* V. RECONVENIR.

recopilación *f.* summary, abridgment, compendium. *2* compilation, collection.

recopilar *tr.* to compile.

récord *m.* SPORT. record.

recordación *f.* remembrance, recollection.

recordar *tr.* to remember, recollect. *2* to remind: *~ algo a uno*, to remind one of something. ¶ CONJUG. like *contar*.

recordativo, -va *adj.* reminding. *2 m.* reminder.

recordatorio *m.* reminder, memento.

recorrer *tr.* to travel, traverse, walk, go over or through [a place; space, etc.]. *2* MACH. to travel in. *3* to make the round of. *4* to run one's eye over. *5* to overhaul, repair. *6* PRINT. to overrun.

recorrido *m.* course, run, circuit, beat, rounds. *2* MACH. travel, stroke. *3* overhaul, reparation. *4* coll. scolding, dressing-down.

recortado, -da *adj.* BOT. notched. *3 m.* cutout [figure].

recortadura *f.* cutting out, clipping. *2 pl.* clippings.

recortar *tr.* to cut away, cut off, clip, pare off, trim. *2* to cut out [figures]. *3* PINT. to outline.

recorte *m.* cutting, clipping. *2 pl.* cuttings, trimmings. *3 recortes de prensa*, newspaper clippings.

recorvar *tr.-ref.* ENCORVAR.

recoser *tr.* to sew again. *2* to mend [the linen].

recostadero, -ra *adj.* reclining place.

recostar *tr.* to lean, recline [the upper part of the body]. *2 ref.* to lean back, sit back, recline. ¶ CONJUG. like *contar*.

recoveco *m.* turning, winding, bend [of a passage, lane, stream, etc.]. *2* fig. artifice, trick.

recreación *f.* recreation. *2* re-creation.

recrear *tr.* to recreate, amuse. *2* to please, delight. *3* to re-create. *4 ref.* to recreate, amuse oneself; to take delight.

recreativo, -va *adj.* recreation, recreative.

recrecer *tr.-intr.* to increase. *2* to occur or happen again. *2 ref.* to gather vigour, courage. ¶ CONJUG. like *agradecer*.

recrecimiento *m.* increase, growth.

recreo *m.* recreation. *2* place of amusement.
recría *f.* rearing of colts, etc., bred in another place.
recriar *tr.* to rear [colts, etc.] bred in another place. *2* to give new strength to.
recriminación *f.* recrimination.
recriminar *tr.-ref.* to recriminate.
recrudecer *intr.* to recrudesce, get worse. ¶ CON-JUG. like *agradecer.*
recrudecimiento *m.*, **recrudescencia** *f.* recrudescence.
recruzar *tr.* to recross, cross again.
recta *f.* straight line. *2* straight [straight part].
rectal *adj.* ANAT. rectal.
rectamente *adv.* directly, straightly [in a straight line]. *2* honestly, righteously, rightly.
rectangular *adj.* rectangular.
rectángulo *adj.* rectangular. *2* right-angled. *3 m.* GEOM. rectangle.
rectificación *f.* rectification.
rectificador, -ra *adj.* rectifying. *2 m.-f.* rectifier.
rectificar *tr.* to rectify.
rectilíneo, -a *adj.* rectilinear, rectilineal.
rectitud *f.* rectitude, righteousness, uprightness. *2* straightness. *3* correctness.
recto, -ta *adj.* straight [without curve or bend; not leaning or inclining]. *2* righteous, just, fair, severe. *3* GEOM., ASTR. right. *4* literal [sense or meaning]. *5 m.* ANAT., ZOOL. rectum. *6 f.* straight line.
rector, -ra *adj.* governing, directing. *2 m.* director, head, rector. *3* ECCL. rector, parish priest.
rectorado *m.* rectorate, rectorship.
rectoral *adj.* [pertaining to the] rector or parish priest. *2 f.* rectory, house of the parish priest.
rectoría *f.* rectorate, rectorship. *2* rector's office.
recua *f.* drove of animals. *2* fig. multitude of things.
recuadrar *tr.* PAINT. to graticulate.
recuadro *m.* ARCH. square compartment.
recubrimiento *m.* covering, coating, lining, facing.
recubrir *tr.* to cover again. *2* to cover, coat, line, face, overlay. *3* RETEJAR 1.
recudir *tr.* to pay [one] his due. *2 intr.* [of a thing] to rebound, come or spring back.
recuento *m.* recount [counting again]. *2* count, telling, enumeration.
recuento, recuente, etc. *irr.* V. RECONTAR.
recuerdo *m.* remembrance, recollection, memory. *2* remembrance, keepsake, souvenir. *3 pl.* compliments, regards.
recuerdo, recuerde, etc. *irr.* V. RECORDAR.
recuestar *tr.* to request, ask, beg.
recuesto *m.* declivity, slope. -
recuesto, recueste, etc. *irr.* V. RECOSTAR.
reculada *f.* recoil, falling back, backing up.
recular *intr.* to recoil, go back, fall back, back up.
reculo, -la *adj.* tailless [hen or chicken].
reculones (a) *adv.* going backwards, backing up.
recuperable *adj.* recoverable.
recuperación *f.* recovery, regain. *2* recuperation.
recuperador, -ra *adj.* recuperative. *2 m.-f.* recoverer. *3 m.* recuperator.
recuperar *tr.* to recover, regain. *2* to recuperate. *3 ref.* to recover oneself.
recuperativo, -va *adj.* recuperative.
recurrente *adj.* BOT. recurrent. *2* LAW appellant.
recurrir *intr.* to appeal, resort, have recourse [to]. *2* to revert, return. *3* LAW to appeal.
recurso *m.* recourse, resort. *2* resource. *3* written

petition. *4* reversion, return. *5* LAW appeal. *6 pl.* resources, means.
recusación *f.* refusal, rejection. *2* LAW challenge, recusation.
recusar *tr.* to refuse, reject. *2* LAW to challenge, recuse.
rechazamiento *m.* repulsion, driving back. *2* refusal, rejection. *3* impugnation.
rechazar *tr.* to repel, drive back. *2* to refuse, reject; to rebuff; to contradict, impugn.
rechazo *m.* rebound, recoil, repercussion: *de ~*, fig. indirectly, as a repercussion.
rechifla *f.* hissing [in derision]. *2* derision.
rechiflar *tr.* to hiss [in derision]. *2 ref.* to flout, jeer, mock, ridicule.
rechinamiento *m.* squeaking, creaking, grating. *2* gnashing, grinding [or teeth].
rechinar *intr.* [of a door, wheel, etc.] to squeak, creak, grate. *2* [of teeth] to gnash. *3* fig. to do a thing with reluctance.
rechinido, rechino *m.* RECHINAMIENTO.
rechoncho, -cha *adj.* chubby, thickset.
rechupete (de) coll. splendid, fine.
red *f.* net [meshed fabric], fishing net, tennis net, etc.: *~ barredera*, dragnet, seine. *2* netting, network. *3* hair net. *4* fig. net, snare, trap. *5* network, system [of railways, telephones, etc.]. *6* grating, railing. *7* OPT. grating.
redacción *f.* redaction, drawing up, wording. *2* newspaper offices. *3* editorial staff.
redactar *tr.* to redact, draw up, word, edit.
redactor, -ra *m.-f.* redactor, writer. *2* editor, journalist, member of an editorial staff.
redada *f.* casting a net. *2* netful, catch [of fish]. *3* fig. catch, haul [of criminals, etc.].
redaño *m.* ANAT. caul, omentum. *2 pl.* fig. courage.
redargüir *tr.* to retort [say by way of counter-argument]. *2* LAW to impugn. ¶ CONJUG. like *huir.*
redecilla *f.* small net. *2* netting. *3* hair net. *4* ZOOL. reticulum [of ruminant].
redecir *tr.* to say over and over again.
rededor *m.* surroundings. *2 al ~, en ~*, ALREDEDOR.
redención *f.* redemption. *2* deliverance from pain, poverty, etc.
redentor, -ra *adj.* redeeming. *2 m.-f.* redeemer. *3 m. pr. n. El Redentor*, the Redeemer.
redescuento *m.* COM. rediscount.
redición *f.* repetition, saying again.
redicho, -cha *adj.* affected [in speech].
redil *m.* fold, sheepfold.
redimible *adj.* redeemable.
redimir *tr.* to redeem. *2* to deliver from pain, poverty, etc.
rédito *m.* interest, income, revenue.
redivivo, -va *adj.* resuscitated, revived.
redoblado, -da *adj.* redoubled. *2* thick, stout; thick-set, heavy-built. *3* MIL. quick [step].
redoblante *m.* MIL. long-frame drum.
redoblar *tr.* to double. *2* to redouble, reduplicate. *3* to clinch [a nail or rivet]. *4 intr.* to roll a drum. *5 ref.* to redouble [grow greater].
redoble *m.* roll [of a drum].
redoblegar *tr.* to bend, to clinch.
redoblón *m.* clinch-nail, rivet.
redolente *adj.* slightly aching [after pain or illness].
redolor *m.* dull, lingering aching or pain.
redoma *f.* phial, flask. *2* CHEM. balloon.
redomado, -da *adj.* artful, crafty, sly.
redonda *f.* neighbourhood. *2* MUS. whole note,

semibreve. *3 a la ~*, around, round, round about.

redondamente *adv.* in a circle. *2* roundly, plainly.

redondeado, -da *adj.* round, rounded.

redondear *tr.* to round [make round]. *2* to round off, round out [complete]. *3 ref.* to round [become round]. *4* to acquire a fortune.

redondel *m.* coll. round, circle. *2* round cape. *3* arena, bull ring.

redondez *f.* roundness. *2 la ~ de la Tierra*, the face of the Earth.

redondilla *f.* eight-syllable quatrain with rhyme abba. *2 adj. letra ~*, round hand [writing].

redondo, -da *adj.* round [in shape]. *2* round [number; hand; trip]. *3* square, plain, direct. *4* PRINT. roman [type]. *5 m.* round, circle, orb, round object. *6 en ~*, around, circularly; roundly, plainly, categorically.

redondón *m.* large circle or round.

redopelo *m.* rubbing the wrong way: *al ~, a ~*, against the hair; against the nature, forcedly. *2 traer al ~*, to treat rudely.

redor *f.* round mat. *2* poet. REDEDOR.

redrojo *m.* bunch of grapes remaining after vintage. *2* after bruit or blossom. *3* coll. runt, stunted boy.

redropelo *m.* REDOPELO.

reducción *f.* reduction.

reducido, -da *adj.* reduced, diminished, small, compact.

reducir *tr.* to reduce [bring down, lower, diminish; convert; subdue; compel]. *2* to persuade, convince. *3* CHEM., LOG., MAT., SURG. to reduce. *4 ref.* to reduce, be reduced. *5* to cut down one's expenses. *6 reducirse a*, to decide from necessity to; [of a thing] to be reduced to. ¶ CONJUG. like *conducir*.

reducto *m.* FORT. redoubt.

reductor, -ra *adj.* reducing. *2 m.* CHEM. reducer.

reduje, redujera, etc. *irr.* V. REDUCIR.

redundancia *f.* redundance, redundancy.

redundante *adj.* redundant.

redundar *intr.* to overflow, run over. *2 ~ en*, to redound to, result in, lead to, bring.

reduplicado, -da *adj.* reduplicate, redoubled.

reduplicar *tr.* to reduplicate, redouble; to reiterate.

reduzco, reduzca, etc. *irr.* V. REDUCIR.

reedificación *f.* rebuilding.

reedificar *tr.* to re-edify, rebuild.

reeditar *tr.* to republish, reprint.

reeducación *f.* re-education.

reeducar *tr.* to re-educate.

reelección *f.* re-election.

reelecto, -ta *adj.* re-elected.

reelegible *adj.* re-elegible.

reelegir *tr.* to re-elect. ¶ CONJUG. like *servir.*

reembarcar *tr.* to re-embark, to reship. *2 ref.* to re-embark [go on board again].

reembarque *m.* re-embarkation; reshipment.

reembolsar *tr.* to reimburse, to refund. *2 ref.* to get back [disbursed or expended money].

reembolso *m.* reimbursement, refunding: *contra ~*, cash on delivery, collect on delivery.

reemplazable *adj.* replaceable, substitutable.

reemplazar *tr.* to replace. *2* to supersede.

reemplazo *m.* replacement, substitution. *2* MIL. annual enrollment.

reencarnación *f.* reincarnation.

reencarnar *tr.* to reincarnate. *2 ref.* to become reincarnated.

reencuentro *m.* collision. *2* MIL. engagement.

reenganchar *tr.* MIL. to re-enlist. *2 ref.* MIL. to re-enlist [enroll oneself again].

reenganche *m.* re-enlisting.

reensayo *m.* second test or trial. *2* second rehearsal [of a play, etc.].

reenviar *tr.* to send back. *2* to forward.

reenvidar *tr.* CARDS to raise [the bid].

reenvite *m.* CARDS raised bid.

reestreno *m.* revival [of a play].

reexaminar *tr.* to re-examine.

reexpedir *f.* to forward, reship. ¶ CONJUG. like *servir.*

reexportar *tr.* to re-export.

refacción *f.* refection, refreshment. *2* repair, mending. *3* extra, bonus.

refajo *m.* short flannel skirt. *2* flannel underskirt.

refección *f.* refection, refreshment. *2* repair.

refectorio *m.* refectory.

referencia *f.* account, narration. *2* reference. *3 pl.* references, information.

referéndum *m.* referendum.

referente *adj.* referring, relating.

referible *adj.* referable. *2* narrable.

referir *tr.* to relate, narrate, tell. *2* to refer, relate. *3 ref. referirse a*, to refer [make allusion]; have reference] to; to refer oneself to. ¶ CONJUG. like *hervir.*

refiero, refiera, refiriera, etc. *irr.* V. REFERIR.

refilón (de) *adv.* obliquely, sideways. *2* in passing.

refinación *f.* refining, refinement [of metals, etc.].

refinado, -da *adj.* refined. *2* subtle, artful.

refinamiento *m.* refinement [state or quality of being refined]. *2* refined cruelty.

refinar *tr.* to refine. *2* to perfect; polish.

refinería *f.* refinery.

refino, -na *adj.* very fine, extra fine. *2 m.* REFINACIÓN.

refitolero, -ra *m.-f.* ECCL. refectorian. *2* busybody, meddler. *3 adj.* meddlesome.

reflectante *adj.* PHYS. reflecting.

reflectar *tr.* PHYS. to reflect.

reflector, -ra *adj.* reflecting. *2 m.* reflector. *3* searchlight.

reflejar *tr.* to reflect [heat, light, sound, etc.]. *2* [of countenance, actions, etc.] to show, reveal. *3 ref.* to be reflected.

reflejo, -ja *adj.* reflected. *2 adj.-m.* PHYSIOL. reflex. *3 m.* reflection [reflected light; image].

reflexión *f.* reflection [of heat, light, an image, etc.]. *2* reflection [mental consideration; remark, comment].

reflexionar *tr.-intr.* to reflect [consider, meditate].

reflexivo, -va *adj.* reflective, reflecting. *2* reflective, thoughtful. *3* GRAM. reflexive.

reflorecer *intr.* to blossom or flower again. *2* to reflourish. ¶ CONJUG. like *florecer.*

refluir *intr.* to flow back. *2* REDUNDAR 2. ¶ CONJUG. like *huir.*

reflujo *m.* reflux, ebb, ebb-tide.

refocilación *f.* cheering, amusement.

refocilar *tr.* to cheer, gladden, amuse. *2 ref.* to rejoice, to be cheered.

reforma *f.* reform, reformation. *2* alteration, improvement. *3* ECCL. Reformation.

reformador, -ra *adj.* reforming. *2 m.-f.* reformer.

reformar *tr.* to re-form, shape anew. *2* to reform. *3* to mend, improve. *4 ref.* [of a person] to reform.

reformatorio, -ria *adj.-m.* reformatory.

reformista *adj.-n.* POL. reformist.

reforzador *m.* PHOT. intensifier.

reforzar *tr.* to reinforce, strengthen. *2* PHOT. to intensify. ¶ CONJUG. like *contar.*
refracción *f.* OPT. refraction.
refractar *tr.* OPT. to refract. *2 ref.* OPT. to be refracted.
refractario, -ria *adj.* refractory, rebellious. *2* ~ *a,* unwilling to accept [opinions, ideas, etc.]. *3* PHYS. refractory.
refracto, -ta *adj.* OPT. refracted.
refrán *m.* adage, proverb, saying, saw.
refranero *m.* collection of adages or proverbs.
refregamiento *m.* hard rubbing.
refregar *tr.* to rub hard, to scrub. *2* fig. to rub in, harp on [something unpleasant]. ¶ CONJUG. like *acertar.*
refregón *m.* hard rubbing.
refreír *tr.* to fry anew. *2* to fry well or too much. ¶ CONJUG. like *freír.*
refrenada *f.* SOFRENADA.
refrenamiento *m.* curbing, check, restraint.
refrenar *tr.* to rein, curb [a horse]. *2* fig. to curb, check, restrain.
refrendar *tr.* to countersign. *2* to visé [a passport].
refrendario *m.* countersigner.
refrendo *m.* countersigning. *2* countersignature.
refrescante *adj.* cooling. *2* refreshing.
refrescar *tr.* to cool, refrigerate. *2* to renew [a pain, etc.]; to refresh [the memory]. *3 intr.* to refresh, get vigour again. *4* [of the weather] to get cool; [of the wind] to freshen. *5 intr.-ref.* to cool, become cool. *6* to get a bit of cool air. *7* to refresh, take a drink.
refresco *m.* refreshment. *2* cooling drink. *3* refreshments. *4 de* ~, new, fresh [troops, etc.].
refriega *f.* affray, encounter, fray, combat.
refrigeración *f.* refrigeration.
refrigerador, -ra *adj.* refrigerating. *2 m.* refrigerator [apparatus].
refrigerante *adj.* refrigerating. *2 m.* cooling bath [of a still].
refrigerar *tr.* to cool, refrigerate. *2* to refresh [restore strength].
refrigerio *m.* relief, comfort. *2* refreshment [light meal].
refringente *adj.* refracting, refringent.
refrito, -ta *adj.* fried again. *2* too fried. *3 m.* fig. rehash [of a literary work].
refuerzo *m.* reinforcement. *2 pl.* MIL. reinforcements.
refugiado, -da *m.-f.* refugee.
refugiar *tr.* to shelter, give refuge. *2 ref.* to take refuge.
refugio *m.* shelter, refuge, asylum.
refulgente *adj.* refulgent.
refulgir *intr.* to shine.
refundición *f.* remelting. *2* recast, rehash [of a literary work].
refundir *tr.* to remelt, recast [metals]. *2* to recast, rehash [a literary work].
refunfuñar *intr.* to grumble, growl [mutter angrily].
refutable *adj.* refutable.
refutación *f.* refutal, refutation.
refutar *tr.* to refute.
regadera *f.* watering can, watering pot. *2* REGUERA.
regadío, -día *adj.* irrigated [land]. *2 m.* irrigated land.
regala *f.* NAUT. gunwale, gunnel.
regalado, -da *adj.* sweet, delicate, dainty. *2* comfortable, luxurious.
regalamiento *m.* regalement.

regalar *tr.* to give, present, compliment with. *2* to caress, flatter: ~ *el oído a,* to say flattering things to. *3* to regale, delight. *4 ref.* to regale, feast oneself.
regalía *f.* royal privilege. *2* privilege, exemption. *3 pl.* perquisites.
regalicia *f.* REGALIZ.
regalismo *m.* regalism.
regaliz *m.,* **regaliza** *f.* BOT. licorice.
regalo *m.* gift, present: *de* ~, given as a present, complimentary. *2* pleasure, gratification. *3* comfort, luxury.
regalón, -na *adj.* comfort-loving. *2* soft, easy [life].
regañadientes (a) *adv.* reluctantly, grumblingly.
regañado, -da *adj.* split open [bread; plum].
regañar *intr.* [of a dog] to snarl. *2* [of a person] to snarl, grumble. *3* to quarrel, wrangle. *4* [of plums, chestnuts, etc.] to split or crack open. *5 tr.* to scold, chide.
regaño *m.* snarl, angry words. *2* scolding. *3* burst crust [of a loaf of bread].
regañón, -na *adj.* grumbling. *2* scolding. *3 m.-f.* grumbler, crabbed person. *4* scolder.
regar *tr.* to water, sprinkle; to irrigate. *2* [of a stream, etc.] to water [a region]. *3* fig. to sprinkle, to strew something on. ¶ CONJUG. like *acertar.*
regata *f.* rowing or sailing race, boat race; regatta. *2* furrow or small trench for irrigation.
regate *m.* dodge, quick side-movement.
regatear *tr.* to bargain, haggle over. *2* to spare, grudge. *3* to resell at retail. *4 intr.* to bargain, haggle. *5* to dodge. *6* NAUT. to race.
regateo *m.* bargaining. *2* sparing, grudging.
regato *m.* rill, rivulet.
regatón, -na *adj.* retailing. *2* haggling. *3 m.-f.* retailer. *4* haggler. *5 m.* tip, ferrule.
regatonear *intr.* to resell at retail.
regazo *m.* lap [of one sitting]. *2* fig. lap.
regencia *f.* regency. *2* direction, management.
regeneración *f.* regeneration. *2* ELECT. feedback.
regenerar *tr.* to regenerate. *2 ref.* to regenerate [become regenerate].
regenerativo, -va *adj.* regenerative.
regentar *tr.* to direct, manage. *2* to hold [an office].
regente *adj.* ruling, governing. *2 m.-f.* regent. *3 m.* pharmacist managing an apothecary shop. *4* PRINT. foreman.
regicida *adj.* regicidal. *2 m.-f.* regicide [murderer].
regicidio *m.* regicide [murder].
regidor, -ra *adj.* ruling, governing. *2 m.* alderman, councilman, town councillor.
régimen, *pl.* **regímenes** *m.* rule, system of government. *2* regime. *3* regimen. *4* GRAM. government. *6* MACH. rate.
regimentar *tr.* to regiment.
regimiento *m.* rule, government. *2* MIL. regiment.
regio, -gia *adj.* royal [of the king, of the queen]. *2* royal, regal, kingly, sumptuous, magnificent.
región *f.* region.
regional *adj.* regional.
regionalismo *m.* regionalism.
regir *tr.* to direct, govern, rule. *2* to conduct, guide. *3* GRAM. to govern. *4 intr.* [of a law, rule, etc.] to be in force; [of a custom] to prevail. *5* [of an organ, a mechanism, etc.] to function or work well. *6 ref.* to be governed, be guided. ¶ CONJUG. like *servir.*
registrado, -da *adj.* registered. *2 marca registrada,* trademark.

registrador, -ra *adj.* registering. *2* registrar, recorder: ~ *de la propiedad*, recorder of deeds.
registrar *tr.* to search, examine, inspect. *2* to register, to record. *3* PRINT. to register. *4* to mark with a bookmark.
registro *m.* search, inspection. *2* registering, recording, registry. *3* register [in practically every sense]. *4* registry, register office: ~ *civil*, register of births, marriages and deaths; ~ *de la propiedad*, register of deeds. *5* manhole. *6* MUS. organ stop. *7* regulator [of a timepiece].
regla *f.* rule [percept, regulation, standard, normal state of things]: *en* ~, in due form, in order; *por* ~ *general*, as a rule. *2* rule [of a religious order]. *3* MATCH. rule. *4* limit, prudence, moderation. *5* menstruation. *6* rule, ruler, straightedge: ~ *de cálculo*, side rule.
reglado, -da *adj.* subjected to rule or precept. *2* moderate, temperate.
reglamentación *f.* regulation, establishment of regulations. *2* rules, regulations.
reglamentar *tr.* to regulate, establish regulations.
reglamentario, -ria *adj.* pertaining to, or prescribed by, regulations, standing rules or bylaws.
reglamento *m.* regulations, standing rules, bylaw.
reglar *tr.* to rule [paper, etc.]. *2* to regulate [subject to rules]. *3 ref.* to guide oneself.
regocijado, -da *adj.* merry, joyful, mirthful.
regocijar *tr.* to rejoice, gladden, exhilarate. *2 ref.* to rejoice, be glad.
regocijo *m.* rejoicing, joy, gladness. *2* merriment, mirth. *3 pl.* rejoicings.
regodearse *ref.* to take delight [in].
regodeo *m.* delight. *2* coll. diversion.
regoldano, -na *adj.* wild [chestnut].
regoldo *m.* BOT. wild chestnut tree.
regolfar *intr.-ref.* [of water] to flow back, eddy. *2 intr.* [of the wind] to turn, be deflected.
regolfo *m.* flowing back [of water], eddy. *2* turning, deflection [of the wind]. *3* bay, inlet.
regordete, -ta *adj.* plump, chubby, pudgy.
regraciar *tr.* to thank, to show gratitude to.
regresar *intr.* to return, come back.
regresión *f.* regression, retrogression.
regresivo, -va *adj.* regressive.
regreso *m.* return, coming back.
regruñir *intr.* to growl; to grumble.
reguera *f.* irrigation ditch.
reguero *m.* trickle, narrow line formed by something dripping or dropped in small portions.
regulación *f.* regulation, adjustment, control.
regulador, -ra *adj.* regulating. *2 m.* regulator. *3* MACH. governor. *4* RADIO. ~ *de volumen*, volume control.
1) **regular** *adj.* regular: *por lo* ~, as a rule. *2* middling, so-so; fair, fairly good.
2) **regular** *tr.* to regulate.
regularidad *f.* regularity.
regularización *f.* regularization.
regularizar *tr.* to regularize.
regularmente *adv.* regularly. *2* ordinarily, usually, as a rule. *3* middling, so so, fairly well.
régulo *m.* regulus. *2* ORN. kinglet.
regurgitar *intr.* MED. to regurgitate.
rehabilitar *tr.* to rehabilitate. *2 ref.* to become rehabilitated.
rehacer *tr.* to do over, remake, rebuild. *2* to repair, renovate. *3* to give back or recover [strength]. *4 ref.* to recover, rally. *5* to recover oneself. ¶ CONJUG. like *hacer*.
rehago, rehaga, etc. *irr.* V. REHACER.

reharé, reharía, etc. *irr.* V. REHACER.
rehecho, -cha *pp.* of REHACER. *2 adj.* stocky, thickset, sturdy.
rehén or *pl.* **rehenes** *m.* hostage.
rehenchir *tr.* to refill, to stuff again. *3* to stuff [furniture]. ¶ CONJUG. like *ceñir*.
reherir *tr.* to repulse, drive back. ¶ CONJUG. like *hervir*.
rehice, rehiciera, etc. *irr.* V. REHACER.
rehilandera *f.* pin wheel [toy].
rehilar *tr.* to twist too hard [in spinning]. *2 intr.* [of a thing] to tremble, quiver. *3* [of a flying arrow, etc.] to whiz, whir.
rehilete *m.* dart [used in game of darts]. *2* shuttlecock. *3* BULLF. banderilla, barbed dart. *4* dig, cutting hint or remark.
rehílo *m.* trembling, quivering [of a thing].
rehogar *tr.* COOK. to cook with a slow fire in lard or oil.
rehoyo *m.* deep hollow or ravine.
rehuida *f.* avoiding, shunning, shirking or shrinking from something.
rehuir *tr.* to avoid, evade, flee, shun, shirk, shrink from. *2* to refuse, decline. ¶ CONJUG. like *huir*.
rehundido *m.* ARCH. sunken face of the dado of a pedestal.
rehundir *tr.* to sink deeper. *2* to depen [a hole or excavation].
rehusar *tr.* to refuse, to decline.
reidor, -ra *adj.* jolly, full of laughter. *2 m.-f.* laugher.
reimpresión *f.* reprint; reprinting.
reimprimir *tr.* to reprint. ¶ P. P.: *reimpreso.*
reina *f.* queen [sovereign]. *2* CHESS & fig. queen. *3* ENT. queen bee. *4* BOT. ~ *de los prados*, meadowsweet. *5* BOT. ~ *luisa*, lemon verbena. *6* ~ *mora*, hopscotch.
reinado *m.* reign.
Reinaldo *m. pr. n.* Reynold.
reinante *adj.* reigning. *2* prevailing, prevalent.
reinar *intr.* to reign [hold royal office]. *2* to reign, prevail.
reincidencia *f.* repetition [of a fault, offence, etc.].
reincidir *intr.* ~ *en*, to commit again [a fault, offence, etc.]; to relapse into.
reincorporar *tr.* to reincorporate. *2 ref.* to rejoin [a body, regiment, etc.]; to be reunited.
reingresar *intr.* to re-enter, enter again.
reingreso *m.* re-entry.
reino *m.* kingdom, realm. *2* NAT. HIST. kingdom.
reinstalar *tr.* to reinstate, reinstall.
reintegración *f.* redintegration. *2* repayment.
reintegrar *tr.* to redintegrate. *2* to restore, refund, repay. *3* to affix a tax stamp to. *4 ref. reintegrarse de*, to recover, get back.
reintegro *m.* REINTEGRACIÓN. *2* payment.
reír *intr.-ref.* to laugh; to giggle, titter: ~ *a carcajadas*, to guffaw; ~ or *reírse de*, to laugh at, make fun of; to make a fool of; ~ or *reírse para sus adentros*, to laugh in one's sleeve. *2 tr.* to laugh one's applause of. ¶ CONJUG.: INDIC. Pres.: *río, ríes, ríe*, reimos, reis, *ríen.* | Pret.: reí, reíste, *rió;* reímos, reísteis, *rieron.* | SUBJ. Pres.: ria, rias, ría; riamos, riáis, rían. | Imperf.: riera, rieras, riera; riéramos, rierais, rieran, or riese, rieses, etc. | Fut.: riere, rieres, riere; riéremos, riereis, rieren. | IMPER.: ríe, ría; riamos, reid, rían. | GER.: riendo.
reiteración *f.* reiteration.
reiteradamente *adv.* repeatedly.
reiterar *tr.* to reiterate, repeat.
reiterativo, -va *adj.* reiterative.

reivindicación *f.* claim, reivindication.
reivindicar *tr.* to regain possession. *2* to claim back.
reja *f.* grate, grating, grille. *2* CHEM., PHYS. lattice. *3* ploughshare, plowshare. *4* AGR. ploughing, plowing.
rejalgar *m.* MINER. realgar.
rejilla *f.* small lattice or grille; latticed wicket. *2* fire grate. *3* ELECT., RADIO. grid. *4* foot stove. *5* cane, split rattan [for seats of chairs, etc.].
rejo *m.* sharp point. *2* ZOOL. sting. *3* hob [for quoits]. *4* BOT. radicle.
rejón *m.* pointed iron bar. *2* BULLF. short spear that breaks off in bull's neck.
rejoneador *m.* bullfighter on horseback who uses the REJÓN.
rejonear *tr.* to thrust a REJÓN into [a bull].
rejoneo *m.* fighting bulls with a REJÓN.
rejuela *f.* small grate or grating. *2* foot stove.
rejuvenecer *tr.* to rejuvenate. *2 intr.-ref.* to rejuvenate, become rejuvenated. ¶ CONJUG. like *agradecer.*
rejuvenecimiento *m.* rejuvenation.
relación *f.* relation, account, recital, narrative. *2* THEAT. speech. *3* relation, reference, respect, bearing. *4* statement or list of particulars. *5 sing. & pl.* relation, rapport, connection, intercourse; dealings. *6 pl.* relations, terms, footing. *7* betrothal, engagement: *tener relaciones,* to be betrothed. *8* connections, acquaintances, friends.
relacionar *tr.* to relate. *2* to state, enumerate. *3 ref.* to relate [have reference, stand in some relation]. *4* to be acquainted or connected.
relajación *f.* relaxation [of an organ, the discipline, etc.]. *2* relaxation, recreation, rest. *3* dissoluteness.
relajado, -da *adj.* relaxed. *2* loose, dissolute.
relajamiento *m.* RELAJACIÓN.
relajante *adj.* relaxing.
relajar *tr.* to relax, loosen, slacken [an organ, the discipline, etc.]. *2* to give relaxation or rest. *3* to relax, remit partially [a penalty]. *4 ref.* to relax, be relaxed, become lax or loose. *5* to grow loose or dissolute.
relamer *tr.* to lick again. *2 ref.* to lick one's lips. *3* to gloat, ro relish.
relamido, -da *adj.* affected, prim, spruce.
relámpago *m.* lightning, flash of lightning. *2* flash of light. *3* flash of wit.
relampaguear *intr.* to flash, to sparkle. *2 impers.* to lighten: *relampaguea,* it lightens.
relampagueo *m.* lightening, flashing, sparkling.
relapso, -sa *adj.* relapsed [into sin or heresy]. *2 m.-f.* backslider.
relativamente *adv.* relatively.
relatividad *f.* relativity.
relativismo *m.* PHILOS. relativism.
relativo, -va *adj.* relative.
relato *m.* relation, account, report, narrative.
relator, -ra *m.-f.* relater, narrator. *2* LAW court reporter.
relatoría *f.* LAW office of a RELATOR.
relavar *tr.* to wash again.
relazar *tr.* to tie up.
relé *m.* (Angl.) ELECT. relay.
releer *tr.* to reread, read again. *2* to revise.
relegar *tr.* to relegate.
releje *m.* rut, track. *2* ARCH. batter. *3* tartar [on teeth].
relente *m.* night dew. *2* coll. cheek, assurance.

relevador *m.* ELECT. relay.
relevante *adj.* excellent, eminent, outstanding.
relevar *tr.* to emboss, work in relief. *2* PAINT. to make stand out. *3* to relieve [give relief to; help; free, release]. *4* to remove [from office]. *5* to relieve, relay [one in station, duty, etc.]. *6* to lift up, exalt.
relevo *m.* relief, relay. *2* removing [from office].
relicario *m.* reliquary, shrine. *2* locket [small case].
relicto *adj.* LAW [property] left at one's death.
relieve *m.* relief, relievo: *alto ~,* high relief, alto-relievo; *bajo ~,* low relief, basso-relievo. *2* raised work, embossment. *3* relief [of something]: *poner de ~,* to point out, emphasize. *4 pl.* leavings.
religar *tr.* to tie again. *2* to bind more tightly.
religión *f.* religion. *2* religious or monastic order.
religionario *m.* Protestant.
religiosidad *f.* religiosity, religiousness.
religioso, -sa *adj.* religious. *2 m.-f.* religious, monk, nun.
relimpio, -pia *adj.* coll. very clean.
relinchar *intr.* to neigh, whinny.
relinchido, relincho *m.* neigh, neighing, whinny.
relinga *f.* NAUT. boltrope. *2* cork or lead rope [of a fishing net].
reliquia *f.* relic. *2* habitual ailment remaining after an illness. *3 pl.* relics.
reliquiario *m.* RELICARIO.
reloj *m.* timepiece, clock, watch: *~ de agua,* water clock, clepsydra; *~ de arena,* sandglass; *~ de bolsillo,* pocket watch; *~ de pulsera,* wrist watch; *~ de sol,* sundial; *~ despertador,* alarm clock; *~ registrador,* time clock.
relojera *f.* watchcase; watch stand.
relojería *f.* clock and watch making, horology. *2* watchmaker's shop. *3 mecanismo de ~,* clockwork.
relojero *m.* watchmaker, clockmaker.
reluciente *adj.* relucent, bright, shining.
relucir *intr.* to be bright, to shine, glisten. *2* fig. to shine, be brilliant, excel.
reluctante *adj.* reluctant.
relumbrante *adj.* shining, resplendent.
relumbrar *intr.* to shine dazzlingly; to glare.
relumbre *m.* light, shine, dazzling brightness.
relumbrón *m.* flash of light. *2* tinsel; show, false show; *de ~,* tinsel, showy, cheaply splendid.
rellano *m.* landing [of stairs]. *2* terrace, level stretch [in a sloping ground].
rellenar *tr.* to refill; fill again. *2* to replenish, fill up, cram. *3* to stuff [a fowl, a mattres, etc.]. *4* SEW. to pad. *5* fig. to stuff [with food]. *6 ref.* to stuff oneself.
relleno, -na *adj.* filled up, stuffed, padded. *2 m.* stuffing [act or process]. *3* COOK. stuffing, forcemeat. *4* MEC. gasket. *5* SEW. padding. *6* fig. padding [in a literary work].
remachado *m.* riveting.
remachar *tr.* to clinch, rivet. *2* fig. to clinch [confirm conclusively].
remache *m.* clinching, riveting. *2* rivet.
remador, -ra *m.-f.* rower.
remadura *f.* rowing.
remallar *tr.* to mend [a net or netting].
remanente *m.* remnant, remaining part.
remangar *tr.-ref.* ARREMANGAR.
remansarse *ref.* [of flowing water] to become still.
remanso *m.* still water. *2* fig. sluggishness, tardiness.

remar *intr.* to row, paddle. *2 fig.* to toil, struggle.

remarcar *tr.* to mark again.

rematadamente *adv.* entirely, absolutely, utterly.

rematado, -da *p. p.* of REMATAR. *2 adj.* absolute, hopeless: *loco* ~, raving mad.

rematante *m.* highest bidder [at an auction].

rematar *tr.* to end, finish, complete; to top off. *2* to finish off, kill [a dying person or animal]. *3* to knock down [at an auction]. *4* SEW. to fasten off the last stitch of. *5 intr.* to end, terminate.

remate *m.* end, conclusion. *2* end, top, upper end. *3* ARCH. top, finial. *4* knocking down [at an auction]; public sale. *5 de* ~, absolutely; *loco de* ~, raving mad.

remedador, -ra *m.-f.* imitator, mimicker.

remedar *tr.* to imitate. *2* to mimic, to mock.

remediable *adj.* remediable.

remediar *tr.* to remedy. *2* to help, relieve. *3* to help, prevent: *no lo puedo* ~, I can't help that.

remedio *m.* remedy, cure: *no tener* ~, to be hopeless; to be irremediable. *2* amendment. *3* help, relief. *4* help [prevention, avoidance]: *no hay* ~, *no hay más* ~, it can't be helped; *no hay más* ~ *que*, there is nothing else to do but. *5 sin* ~, hopeless; hopelessly; inevitably.

remedir *tr.* to remeasure.

remedo *m.* imitation, copy. *2* mimicking, mimicry, mockery.

remellado, -da; remellón, -na *adj.* dented, jagged.

remembranza *f.* remembrance, memory.

rememoración *f.* remembrance, recollection.

rememorar *tr.* to remember, recall, recollect.

remendado, -da *adj.* mended, patched, darned. *2 fig.* spotted, patched, streaked.

remendar *tr.* to mend, repair. *2* SEW. to patch, piece, darn. ¶ CONJUG. like *acertar.*

remendón, -na *adj.* mending, repairing. *2* cobbler, mender of shoes. *3* tailor who does mending.

remero, -ra *m.-f.* rower, paddler.

remesa *f.* remittance, sending. *2* remittance [money sent]; goods, etc., sent at a time; shipment.

remesar *tr.* to remit, send, ship.

remesón *m.* tearing, plucking out of hair. *2* plucked hair. *3* stopping a horse in full gallop.

remeter *tr.* to put in again; to put in further.

remiendo *m.* patch, mending piece; mending, repair, reparation. *2* amendment, correction. *3* patch, spot, streak [on an animal]. *4* PRINT. job, job work.

remiendo, remiende, etc. *irr.* V. REMENDAR.

remilgado, -da *adj.* affectedly nice, delicate or graceful.

remilgarse *ref.* [of women] to act with an affectation of nicety, delicacy or grace.

remilgo *m.* affectation of nicety, delicacy or grace.

reminiscencia *f.* reminiscence.

remirado, -da *adj.* prudent, careful, circumspect.

remirar *tr.* to look at or go over again, to examine again. *2 ref.* to take great pains [with]. *3* to contemplate or consider with pleasure.

remisible *adj.* remissible.

remisión *f.* sending, dispatching, remittance. *2* remission [of sins, of a debt, etc.]. *3* remission [diminution of intensity]. *4* postponement. *5* referring, reference.

remisivo, -va *adj.* remissive. *2* referring.

remiso, -sa *adj.* remiss. *2* slack, slow.

remitente *adj.* remitting, remittent. *2* sending, dispatching. *3 m.-f.* sender, dispatcher.

remitir *tr.* to remit, send, dispatch. *2* to remit [sins, debt, etc.]. *3* to remit, postpone. *4* to re-

mit, refer [a matter for decision, etc.]. *5* to refer [in a book]. *6 intr.-ref.* to remit, slacken. *7 ref.* to refer, refer oneself.

remo *m.* NAUT. oar, paddle: *a* ~, rowing. *2 fig.* arm or leg [of a person or quadruped]; wing [of a bird]. *3* rowing. *4 fig.* toil, hard labour.

remoción *f.* removal. *2* removal from office.

remojar *tr.* to steep, soak, drench. *2* coll. to celebrate with a drink.

remojo *m.* steep, soak [process of steeping or soaking].

remolacha *f.* BOT. beet; beetroot. *2* BOT. sugar beet.

remolar *m.* oar maker. *2* oar shop.

remolcador, -ra *adj.* NAUT. towing. *2 m.* NAUT. tug, tugboat, towboat.

remolcar *tr.* to tow, take in tow.

remolinar *intr.* to whirl, eddy. *2 ref.* ARREMOLINARSE.

remolinear *tr.* to whirl about. *2 intr.* REMOLINAR.

remolino *m.* whirl, eddy, whirlpool, whirlwind. *2* cowlick. *3* crowding in a disordered way. *4* commotion, disturbance.

remolón, -na *adj.* indolent, shirky. *2 m.-f.* shirker [one who shirks work, etc.]: *hacerse el* ~, to shirk, hang back.

remolonear *intr.* to hang back, demur, to shun work or effort.

remolque *m.* tow, towing, towage. *2* tow, towrope. *3* tow [what is towed]. *4* trailer [vehicle].

remonta *f.* shoe repair. *2* patch [on riding breeches]. *3* MIL. remount; remount cavalry.

remontar *f.* to frighten [game] away. *2* MIL. to remount [supply remounts to]. *3* to repair [shoes, saddles]. *4* to raise, elevate. *5* to go up [a river]. *6 ref.* [of birds] to rise, soar. *7* to remount, go back [to a time, source, etc.]; to date from.

remonte *m.* raising. *2* remounting. *3* rising, soaring.

remoquete *m.* punch, cuff, fisticuff. *2* cutting remark, witty saying, epigram. *3* APODO.

rémora *f.* ICHTH. remora. *2 fig.* remora, hindrance.

remordedor, -ra *adj.* disturbing, causing remorse.

remorder *t.* to bite repeatedly. *2* to disturb, sting, to cause remorse. *3 ref.* to show one's worry, trouble or regret. ¶ CONJUG. like *mover.*

remordimiento *m.* remorse, compunction, qualm.

remotamente *adv.* remotely; vaguely.

remoto, -ta *adj.* remote. *2* slight, vague; unlikely.

remover *tr.* to remove [displace; eliminate]. *2* to disturb, upset. *3* to stir [with a spoon, etc.]. *4* to remove, discharge. *5 ref.* to move, stir [intr.]

remozar *tr.* to rejuvenate. *2 ref.* to rejuvenate, to acquire a youthful appearance.

rempujar *tr.* to push, jostle.

rempujón *m.* push, impulse.

remudar *tr.* to change, replace.

remugar *tr.* to ruminate.

remuneración *f.* remuneration, consideration.

remunerador, -ra *adj.* remunerative. *2 m.-f.* remunerator.

remunerar *tr.* to remunerate.

remusgar *intr.* to guess, suspect.

remusgo *m.* guess, suspicion. *2* sharp, cool breeze.

renacentista *adj.* [pertaining to the] Renaissance. *2 m.-f.* Renaissancist.

renacer *intr.* to be reborn, to spring up anew.

renaciente *adj.* renascent.

renacimiento *m.* renascence, rebirth, renewal. *2* (cap.) Renaissance.

renacuajo *m.* tadpole, polliwog. *2* fig. shrimp [person].

renadío *m.* aftermath, new crop.

renal *adj.* renal.

Renania *f. pr. n.* GEOG. Rhineland.

renano, -na *adj.* Rhenish. *2 m.-f.* Rhinelander.

rencilla *f.* quarrel, grudge.

rencilloso, -sa *adj.* quarrelsome, touchy.

renco, -ca *adj.* hipshot, lame.

rencor *m.* rancour, grudge, animosity.

rencoroso, -sa *adj.* rancorous, spiteful.

rendición *f.* rendition, surrender. *2* yield. *3* rendering, paying [of tribute, hommage, etc.]. *4* rendering [of an account].

rendidamente *adv.* humbly, with loving or deferential submission.

rendido, -da *adj.* fatigued, exhausted, worn-out. *3* submissive, attentive, devoted.

rendija *f.* chink, crack, rift, slit.

rendimiento *m.* humility; loving or deferential submission, devotion. *2* fatigue, exhaustion. *3* yield, profit, produce. *4* output [of a worker, machine, etc.]. *5* MECH. efficiency.

rendir *tr.* to conquer, subdue. *2* surrender, deliver, give up. *3* to render, give; to pay [tribute, etc.]: ~ *cuentas*, to render an account. *4* to exhaust, tire out. *5* to yield, bring, produce. *6* MIL. to lower [the arm or the flag] as a sign of submission or reverence. *7* MIL. ~ *las armas*, to surrender. *8* NAUT. ~ *viaje*, to arrive. *9 ref.* to surrender, yield. *10* to become exhausted, tired out. ¶ CONJUG. like *servir*.

renegado, -da *adj.-n.* renegade, apostate.

renegar *tr.* to deny vigorously. *2* to detest, abhor. *3* intr. to renegade, apostatize. *4* to swear, blaspheme. ¶ CONJUG. like *acertar*.

renegrido, -da *adj.* blackish, black-and-blue.

rengífero *m.* RANGÍFERO.

renglón *m.* [written or printed] line: *a ~ seguido*, fig. right after, immediately after. *2* fig. line [of business]. *3* fig. item, article.

renglonadura *f.* ruled lines.

reniego *m.* blasphemy. *2* swearword, curse.

reniego, reniegue, etc. *irr.* V. RENEGAR.

reniforme *adj.* reniform, kidney-shaped.

renitencia *f.* renitency.

renitente *adj.* renitent.

reno *m.* ZOOL. reindeer.

renombrado, -da *adj.* renowned, famous.

renombre *m.* surname. *2* renown, fame.

renovación *f.* renewal, renewing; renovation.

renovar *tr.* to renew; to renovate. *2* to change, reform. *3 ref.* to renew, be renewed. ¶ CONJUG. like *contar*.

renquear *intr.* to limp, hobble.

renta *f.* rent. *2* interest, profit, income, revenue. *3* annuity. *4* revenue [taxes, duties, etc.]. *5* public debt; Government bonds.

rentado, -da *adj.* living on his rents or income.

rentar *tr.* to yield, bring an income or profit.

rentero, -ra *adj.* tax-paying. *2 m.-f.* rural tenant.

rentista *m.-f.* financier. *2* one who lives on the interest of bonds, shares, etc.

rentístico, -ca *adj.* financial [pertaining to public finances].

rentoso, -sa *adj.* yielding profit or income.

rentoy *m.* a card game.

renuencia *f.* reluctance, repugnance, unwillingness.

renuente *adj.* reluctant, unwilling.

renuevo *m.* sprout, shoot.

renuevo, renueve, etc. *irr.* V. RENOVAR.

renuncia, renunciación *f.*, **renunciamiento** *m.* renouncement, renunciation, resignation, giving up, waiver.

renunciante *adj.* renouncing, resigning, waiving. *2 m.-f.* renouncer, renunciator, resigner.

renunciar *tr.* to renounce, give up, resign, forsake. *2* to waive [a right]. *3* to decline, refuse. *4* CARDS to renege, revoke. *5 ref. renunciarse a sí mismo*, to deny oneself.

renuncio *m.* CARDS renege, revoke. *2* fig. contradiction, lie, untruth.

reñidamente *adv.* strongly, bitterly.

reñidero *m.* fighting place: ~ *de gallos*, cockpit.

reñido, -da *adj.* on bad terms. *2* opposed [to], inconsistent [with]. *3* bitter, hardfought.

reñidor, -ra *adj.* quarrelsome. *2* scolding. *3 m.-f.* quarreller. *4* scolder.

reñir *intr.* to quarrel, dispute, fight. *2* to quarrel, be at a variance, fall out. *3 tr.* to fight [a battle]. *4* to scold. ¶ CONJUG. like *reír*.

reo *adj.* guilty. *2 m.-f.* offender, culprit; one deserving a penalty.

reóforo *m.* ELECT. reophore.

reojo (mirar de) *tr.* to look out of the corner of one's eye; to look askance at.

reorganización *f.* reorganization.

reorganizar *tr.* to reorganize.

reóstato *m.* ELECT. rheostat.

repanchigarse, repantigarse *ref.* to lounge or sprawl [in a seat].

reparable *adj.* reparable, remediable. *2* noticeable.

reparación *f.* reparation, repair. *2* reparation, atonement.

reparada *f.* sudden start, shy [of a horse].

reparador, -ra *adj.* repairing. *2* restorative, refreshing. *3* fault-finding. *4 m.-f.* repairer, mender. *5* fault-finder.

reparar *tr.* to repair, mend. *2* to repair, restore, reinvigorate. *3* to repair [make amends for] to atone for. *4* to observe, notice, remark. *5* to consider, heed; to regard, stop at. *6* to parry; defend oneself from. *7 intr.* to stop, make a halt.

reparativo, -va *adj.* reparative.

reparo *m.* repair, restoration, remedy. *2* reparation [in a building]. *3* observation, doubt, objection; fault: *poner reparos a*, to raise objections to, to find fault with. *4* defence, protection.

reparón, -na *adj.* carping, cavilling, fault-finding.

repartible *adj.* distribuable.

repartición *f.* distribution, division, dealing out.

repartidor, -ra *adj.* distributing. *2 m.-f.* distributor, dealer. *3 m.* delivery man.

repartimiento *m.* distribution, division, allotment. *2* assessment [of taxes, etc.].

repartir *tr.* to distribute, deal out, divide, allot. *2* to assess [taxes, etc.].

reparto *m.* REPARTIMIENTO. *2* delivery [of goods, mail, etc.]. *3* THEAT. cast of characters.

repasar *intr.-tr.* to repass [pass by, across, etc., again]. *2 tr.* to re-examine, retrace, review. *3* to check [accounts]; to go over [one's lesson, part, etc.]. *4* to scan, glance over. *5* to mend [clothes, linen]. *6* to finish, perfect.

repasata *f.* coll. chiding, dressing-down.

repaso *m.* review, revision. *2* checking [of accounts]; going over [one's lesson, part, etc.]. *3* overhaul. *4* mending [of clothes or linen]. *5* REPASATA.

repatriación *f.* repatriation.

repatriado, -da *adj.* repatriated. *2 m.-f.* repatriate.
repatriar *tr.* to repatriate. *2 ref.* to repatriate [return to one's native land].
repechar *intr.* to go up hill.
repecho *m.* slope, short steep incline: *a ~,* uphill.
repelente *adj.* repellent, repulsive.
repeler *tr.* to repel, repulse. *2* to refute, contradict.
repelo *m.* anything that rises or goes against the grain, nap, etc. *2* cross fiber; cross grain [in wood]. *3* coll. slight quarrel. *4* coll. reluctance.
repelón *m.* pull on the hair. *2* kink [in a stocking]. *3* small part torn from anything. *4* spurt [of a horse]. *5 de ~,* in passing; swiftly.
repeloso, -sa *adj.* cross-grained [wood]. *2* coll. touchy, peevish.
repensar *tr.* to reconsider; to think over. ¶ Conjug. like *acertar.*
repente *m.* sudden impulse. *2 de ~,* suddenly; off-hand.
repentinamente *adv.* suddenly, on a sudden.
repentino, -na *adj.* sudden, unexpected.
repentista *m.-f.* mus. improviser, sight reader.
repentizar *tr.* mus. to improvise, perform at sight.
repercusión *f.* repercussion.
repercutir *intr.* to rebound. *2* [of sound] to echo, reverberate. *3 ~ en,* to have a repercussion on. *4 ref.* [of light] to reverberate.
repertorio *m.* repertory. *2* repertoire.
repesar *tr.* to reweigh.
repeso *m.* reweight, reweighing. *2* weight office.
repetición *f.* repetition, reiteration; recurrence. *2* mus., theat. repeat. *3* rhet. repetition. *6* repeating mechanism: *de ~,* repeating.
repetidamente *adv.* repeatedly.
repetidor, -ra *adj.* repeating. *2 m.-f.* repeater.
repetir *tr.* to repeat, reiterate [say, do, over again]. *2 intr.* [of food] to repeat. *3 ~ de,* to have another helping of. *4 ref.* to repeat itself or oneself; to recur. ¶ Conjug. like *servir.*
repicar *tr.* to chop, hash, mince. *2* to ring [bells] or to play [castanets, etc.] merrily. *3* to reprick. *4* to repique [in piquet].
repicotear *tr.* to scallop.
repintar *tr.* to repaint. *2 ref.* to paint [one's face] elaborately.
repique *m.* peal, ringing [of bells]; lively playing [of castanets, etc.]. *2* tiff, slight quarrel. *3* repique [in piquet].
repiquetear *tr.* to ring [bells] or play [castanets, etc.] lively. *3 ref.* coll. to exchange biting words.
repiqueteo *m.* lively ringing of bells, playing of castanets, etc. *2* exchange of biting words.
repisa *f.* bracketlike ledge or shelf: *~ de la chimenea,* mantelpiece.
replantar *tr.* to replant. *2* to transplant.
replantear *tr.* arch., eng. to lay out on the ground the plan of. *2* to restate [a problem].
repleción *f.* repletion.
replegar *tr.* to fold over and over. *2* mil. to make [the troops] fall back. *3 ref.* mil. to fall back, retreat in order. ¶ Conjug. like *acertar.*
repleto, -ta *adj.* replete, full.
réplica *f.* answer, reply, rejoinder, retort, repartee. *2* f. arts replica. *3* law replication.
replicar *intr.* to answer, answer back, reply, rejoin, retort. *2* law to reply.
replicón, -na *adj.* coll. saucy.
repliegue *m.* fold, double fold, convolution. *2* mil. falling back.
repliego, repliegue, etc. *irr.* V. replegar.

repoblación *f.* repopulation, restocking: *~ forestal,* afforestation.
repoblar *tr.* to repeople, repopulate; to restock; to reafforest. ¶ Conjug. like *contar.*
repollar *intr.-ref.* [of a cabbage, etc.] to head.
repollo *m.* head, round head [of a cabbage, etc.]. *2* bot. cabbage.
repolludo, -da *adj.* cabbage-headed, roundheaded [plant]. *2* chubby.
repondré, repondría, etc. *irr.* V. reponer.
reponer *tr.* to put again. *2* to put back, to replace, restore. *3* to reinstate. *4* to replace [pay back]. *5* theat. to revive [a play]. *6* to answer, reply. *7 ref.* to recover. *8* to recover one's losses.
repongo, reponga, etc. *irr.* V. reponer.
reportación *f.* calm, self-restraint, moderation.
reportaje *m.* journ. reporting; report, news report.
reportamiento *m.* check, restraint.
reportar *tr.* to check, repress, restrain. *2* to bring or get [profit, advantage, etc.]. *3* lithogr. to transfer. *4 ref.* to restrain, control oneself.
reporte *m.* news, report. *2* tale, piece of gossip. *3* lithogr. transfer.
reporteril *adj.* reportorial.
reporterismo *m.* newspaper reporting.
reportero, -ra *m.-f.* newspaper reporter.
reposado, -da *adj.* calm, quiet, peaceful.
reposar *intr.* to repose, rest; to lie [in the grave]. *2 intr.-ref.* to rest, take a nap. *3* [of a liquid] to settle.
reposición *f.* putting back, replacement, restoration, reinstatement. *2* replacement, repaying. *3* recovery. *4* theat. revival [of a play].
repositorio *m.* repository.
reposo *m.* repose, rest. *2* sleep. *3* calm, peace.
repostería *f.* confectionery, pastry. *2* confectionery shop, pastry shop. *3* pantry, larder.
repostero *m.* pastry cook. *2* square covering ornamented with a coat of arms.
repregunta *f.* law cross-question; cross examination.
repreguntar *tr.* law to cross-examine.
reprender *tr.* to reprehend, rebuke, chide, scold.
reprensible *adj.* reprehensible, blamable.
reprensión *f.* reprehension, chiding, scolding.
reprensor, -ra *m.-f.* reprehender.
represa *f.* dam, weir, millpond, sluice. *2* damming [of water]. *3* naut. recapture.
represalia *f.* reprisal; retaliation.
represar *tr.* to dam, bank, impound [water]. *2* naut. to recapture [a ship].
representación *f.* representation [in every sense, except remontrances]. *2* address, petition. *3* rank, distinction.
representante *adj.* representing. *2 m.-f.* representative. *3* theat. player. *4* com. agent, representative.
representar *tr.* to represent. *2* theat. to act, play; impersonate. *3* to look [an age, one's age]. *4 ref.* to imagine, represent to oneself.
representativo, -va *adj.* representative.
represión *f.* repression, suppression, check, curbing.
represivo, -va *adj.* repressive.
reprimenda *f.* reprimand, dressing down.
reprimir *tr.* to repress, suppress, check, curb.
reprobable *adj.* reprehensible.
reprobación *f.* reprobation, reproof, reproval.
reprobado, -da *adj.* reproved. *2* failed [in an examination]. *3 adj.-n.* réprobo.

reprobador, -ra *adj.* reprobatory, reproving.
reprobar *tr.* to reprobate, reprove. *2* to fail, flunk [in an examination]. ¶ CONJUG. like *contar.*
réprobo, -ba *adj.-m.* reprobate.
reprochar *tr.* to reproach: ~ *algo a uno,* to reproach one for.
reproche *m.* reproach, upbraiding.
reproducción *f.* reproduction.
reproducir *tr.* to reproduce. *2 ref.* to reproduce [produce its kind]. *3* to be reproduced. ¶ CONJUG. like *conducir.*
reproductor, -ra *adj.* reproducing, reproductive. *2* breeding [animal]. *3 m.-f.* reproducer. *4* breeder [animal].
reproduje, reprodujera, etc. *irr.* V. REPRODUCIR.
reproduzco, reproduzca, etc. *irr.* V. REPRODUCIR.
repropiarse *ref.* [of a horse, mule, etc.] to get balky.
repropio, -pia *adj.* balky, unruly [horse, mule, etc.].
repruebo, repruebe, etc. *irr.* V. REPROBAR.
reps *m.* rep [fabric].
reptar *intr.* to creep, crawl.
reptil *adj.-n.* ZOOL. reptile, reptilian.
república *f.* republic. *2* state, commonwealth.
republicano, -na *adj.-n.* republican.
repúblico *m.* prominent citizen, statesman. *2* patriot.
repudiar *tr.* to repudiate.
repudio *m.* repudiation [of one's wife].
repudrir *tr.* to rot completely. *2 ref.* to rot [become rotten] completely. *3* fig. to burn with [supressed feelings].
repuesto, -ta *irreg. p. p.* of REPONER. *2 adj.* replaced, restored, reinstated. *3* recovered [from illness, etc.]. *4 m.* store, stock, supply. *5* pantry. *6 de ~,* spare [held in reserve].
repugnancia *f.* repugnance, repugnancy.
repugnante *adj.* repugnant. *2* loathsome.
repugnar *tr.* to be repugnant to. *2* to be loath or reluctant to.
repujado, -da *adj.-m.* repoussé.
repujar *tr.* to do repoussé work on. *2* to emboss [leather].
repulgado, -da *adj.* affected [full of affectation].
repulgar *tr.* SEW. to hem. *2* to put an edging on [a pie].
repulgo *m.* SEW. hem. *2* edging [of a pie]: *repulgos de empanada,* fig. trifles, ridiculous scruples.
repulido, -da *adj.* spruce, smart.
repulir *tr.* to repolish. *2* to spruce, dress smartly or affectedly. *3 ref.* to spruce oneself up.
repulsa *f.* repulse, rebuke, refusal.
repulsar *tr.* to repulse, reject, refuse.
repulsión *f.* repulsion.
repulsivo, -va *adj.* repulsive. *2* repellent.
repullo *m.* small dart. *2* start, jump.
repuntar *intr.* [of the tide] to turn. *2 ref.* [of wine] to be on the turn. *3* to be displeased with one another.
repunte *m.* NAUT. turning of the tide.
repuse, repusiera, etc. *irr.* V. REPONER.
reputación *f.* reputation, repute.
reputar *tr.* to repute, judge, think. *2* to prize, value.
requebrar *tr.* to address flattering remarks to [a woman]. *2* to compliment, flatter. *3* to break again, to recrush. ¶ CONJUG. like *acertar.*
requemado, -da *adj.* burn, brown, tanned.
requemar *tr.* to burn again. *2* to burn, overcook, overbake. *3* to sunburn. *4* to parch, dry [plants]. *5* to bite, sting [the mouth]. *6 ref.* to burn [become charred]. *7* [of plants] to parch. *8* fig. to burn with suppressed feelings.
requeriente *m.-f.* requirer, requester.
requerimiento *m.* requisition, request; summons. *2* requirement.
requerir *tr.* to require, request, induce [to do something]. *2* to require, need, call for. *3* to examine [a thing]. *4 ~ de amores,* to make love to. ¶ CONJUG. like *hervir.*
requesón *m.* cottage cheese, pot cheese. *2* curd.
requetebién *adv.* coll. very well.
requiebro *m.* compliment, flattering remark [addressed to a woman].
requiebro, requiebre, etc. *irr.* V. REQUEBRAR.
réquiem *m.* requiem [mass & music].
requiero, requiera, etc. *irr.* V. REQUERIR.
requilorios *m. pl.* coll. beating about the bush.
requinto *m.* MUS. small clarinet. *2* MUS. small guitar.
requirente *m.-f.* REQUERIENTE.
requisa *f.* inspection, round of inspection. *2* REQUISICIÓN.
requisar *tr.* MIL. to requisition.
requisición *f.* MIL. requisition.
requisito, -ta *adj.* requisite. *2 s.* requisite, requirement: ~ *previo,* prerequisite.
res *f.* head of cattle, beast. *2* HUNT. a game quadruped.
resabiar *tr.* to give a vice or bad habit to. *2 ref.* to contract a vice·or bad habit. *3* to become displeased. *4* to relish.
resabido, -da *adj.* well known. *2* affecting learning.
resabio *m.* unpleasant aftertaste. *2* vice, bad habit.
resaca *f.* undertow. *2* COM. redraft.
resalado, -da *adj.* coll. charming; nimblewitted.
resalir *intr.* ARCH. to jut out, project. ¶ CONJUG. like *salir.*
resaltar *intr.* to rebound. *2* to jut out, project. *3* to stand out.
resalte *m.* jut, projection, prominence, ledge, ridge.
resalto *m.* rebound. *2* RESALTE.
resaludar *tr.* to return a greeting or salute to.
resalvo *m.* stump sprout, sapling left in stubbing.
resarcimiento *m.* compensation, indemnification, making good.
resarcir *tr.* to compensate, indemnify, make good to. *2 ref. resarcirse de,* to recover, recoup [one's losses, etc.]; make good for.
resbaladero, -ra *adj.* slippery. *2 m.* slippery place; chute, slide.
resbaladizo, -za *adj.* slippery. *2* skiddy.
resbalamiento *m.* slipping, sliding, gliding.
resbalar *intr.-ref.* to slip, slide, glide. *2* to skid. *3* fig. to slip [fall into error or fault].
resbalón *m.* slip, slipping. *2* fig. slip, misstep.
rescatar *tr.* to ransom, redeem, rescue. *3* to recover [by money or force]. *3* to make up for [lost time].
rescate *m.* ransom, redemption, rescue. *2* ransom money.
rescaza *f.* ESCORPINA.
rescindir *tr.* to rescind [a contract].
rescisión *f.* rescission [of a contract].
rescoldera *f.* heartburn, pyrosis.
rescoldo *m.* embers, hot ashes. *2* scruple, doubt.
rescontrar *tr.* COM. to set off, balance.
rescripto *m.* rescript.
rescuentro *m.* COM. offset, balance.

resecar *tr.* to dry up, dry to excess. *2* SURG. to resect. *3 ref.* to become too dry.
resección *f.* SURG. resection.
reseco, -ca *adj.* very dry, too dry. *2* lean, thin, spare [person].
reseda *f.* BOT. reseda.
resellar *tr.* to reseal, to restamp. *2* to recoin. *3 ref.* fig. to go over to another party.
resello *m.* resealing, restamping. *2* recoining.
resentido, -da *adj.* offended, displeased. *2* resentful.
resentimiento *m.* resentment, umbrage.
resentirse *ref.* [of a thing] to begin to give way. *2* to be resentful, be offended or hurt. *3 ~ de,* to suffer from; to have a pain in. *4 ~ de,* or *por,* to resent. ¶ CONJUG. like *hervir.*
reseña *f.* brief account, report. *2* review [of a book]. *3* MIL. review. *4* description, signalment.
reseñar *tr.* to make a brief description or narration of, to report. *2* to review [a book].
resequido, -da *adj.* dried up, parched.
reserva *f.* reserve, reservation [for future use]: *de ~,* spare, in reserve. *2* reserve, reticence, circumspection. *3* secrecy: *con toda ~,* in strictest confidence. *4* reserve, reservation, restriction: *sin ~,* without reserve; openly, freely. *5* MIL. reserve. *7* ECCL. the act of putting the exposed Host back in the ciborium. *8* BIOCHEM., *finance* reserve. *9* IND. resist. *10 ~ de indios,* Indian reservation [in U.S.A.].
reservación *f.* reserving, reservation.
reservadamente *adv.* secretly, confidentially.
reservado, -da *adj.* reserved [set apart]. *2* reserved, reticent. *3* discreet, circumspect. *4* private, confidential. *5 m.* place reserved for certain persons or uses.
reservar *tr.* to reserve. *2* to keep secret, conceal. *3* to exempt. *4* ECCL. to put [the exposed Host] back in the ciborium. *5 hacer* or *hacerse ~,* to reserve, book [a seat, a place, etc.]. *6 ref.* to bide one's time. *7* to be cautious or distrustful.
reservista *m.* MIL. reservist.
resfriado *m.* MED. cold, catarrh.
resfriar *tr.* to cool, chill. *2* to cool, moderate [ardour, fervour]. *3 intr.* [of weather] to begin to be cold. *4 ref.* to catch cold. *5* to cool, grow cold or indifferent.
resfrío *m.* MED. cold.
resguardar *tr.* to preserve, protect, shelter. *2 ref.* to protect oneself.
resguardo *m.* preservation, guard, protection. *2* COM. security, voucher. *3* watch to prevent smuggling. *4* NAUT. sea room.
residencia *f.* residence, stay. *2* residence, house, dwelling home. *3* ECCL. residence.
residencial *adj.* residentiary.
residenciar *tr.* to examine into the conduct of [a high official]; to impeach. *2* fig. to call to account.
residente *adj.* resident, residing. *2 m.-f.* resident. *3 m.* DIPLOM. minister resident.
residir *intr.* to reside.
residual *adj.* residual.
residuo *m.* remnant, remainder, residue, rest. *2* CHEM. residuum. *3* ARITH. difference.
resigna *f.* ECCL. resignation.
resignación *f.* resignation, handing over. *3* resignation [being resigned].
resignadamente *adj.* resignedly.
resignar *tr.* to resign, hand over [one's power or authority]. *3 ref.* to resign oneself, be resigned.

resina *f.* resin, rosin.
resinación *f.* extraction of resin.
resinar *tr.* to draw resin from [a tree].
resinero, -ra *adj.* [pertaining to] resin. *2 m.* resin extractor.
resinífero, -ra *adj.* resiniferous.
resinoso, -sa *adj.* resinous.
resistencia *f.* resistance [act of resisting; power to resist]: *~ pasiva,* passive resistance. *2* reluctance. *3* endurance, strength. *4* PHYS., MEC., ELECT. resistance. *5* AER. *~ al avance,* drag.
resistente *adj.* resistant, resisting. *2* strong, firm.
resistible *adj.* resistible, endurable.
resistir *intr.-ref.* to resist; to withstand. *2* to bear, endure, stand. *3 ref.* to refuse [to]. *4* to struggle, make resistance.
resma *f.* ream [of paper].
resmilla *f.* four quires of letter paper.
resobado, -da *adj.* trite, hackneyed.
resobrina *f.* grandniece, great-niece.
resobrino *m.* grandnephew, great-nephew.
resol *m.* sun's glare.
resoluble *adj.* resoluble. *2* resolvable, solvable.
resolución *f.* resolution [solving; resolving]. *2* MED., MUS., PHYS. resolution. *3* LAW nullification [of a contract]. *4* resolution, decision, decree. *5* resolution, resolve, resoluteness. *6 en ~,* in short, in sum.
resolutivo, -va *adj.* resolutive, analytical. *2 adj.-m.* MED. resolutive.
resoluto, -ta *adj.* resolute. *2* brief, compendious.
resolutorio, -ria *adj.* LAW resolutory.
resolvente *adj.* resolvent, resolving.
resolver *tr.* to resolve [decide upon]. *2* to sum up. *3* to resolve, solve [a problem, etc.]. *4* to resolve [disintegrate, analyze, convert]. *5* to undo, annul. *6* MED., MUS., PHYS. to resolve. *7 ref.* to resolve, dare, make up one's mind. *8* to resolve, resolve itself. ¶ CONJUG. like *mover.*
resollar *intr.* to breathe [use the lungs; take breath; speak]. *2* to breathe noisily. *3* CONJUG. like *contar.*
resonador *m.* resonator.
resonancia *f.* resonance. *2* fig. *tener ~,* to make a sensation.
resonante *adj.* resonant, resounding.
resonar *tr.* to resound, resonate. *2* to echo. ¶ CONJUG. like *contar.*
resoplar *intr.* to breathe hard, to puff; to snort.
resoplido, resoplo *m.* hard breathing, puffing; snort.
resorber *tr.* to resorb.
resorción *f.* resorption.
resorte *m.* spring [elastic device]. *2* spring, resilience, elasticity. *3* fig. lever, means [to attain an object]. *4* (Am.) rubber band.
1) respaldar *m.* back [of a seat].
2) respaldar *tr.* to endorse [write on the back of]. *2* to back, support, protect. *3 ref.* to lean back. *4* to get backing or support.
respaldo *m.* back [of a seat; of a sheet of paper]. *2* endorsement. *3* AGR. espalier.
respectar *intr.* to concern, regard, relate to.
respectivamente *adv.* concerning. *2* respectively.
respective *adv.* as regards, concerning.
respectivo, -va *adj.* respective.
respecto *m.* respect [reference, relation]: *al ~,* the matter; *con ~ a,* or *de,* ~ a or *de,* with respect to, with regard to.
respetabilidad *f.* respectability.
respetable *adj.* respectable.

respetador, -ra *adj.* respecting, respectful.
respetar *tr.* to respect. *2 intr.* RESPECTAR.
respeto *m.* respect, reverence, dutifulness. *2* awe, fear. *3* attention, care, regard. *4* observance [of law, etc.]. *5 de* ~, extra, spare. *6 pl.* respects: *ofrecer sus respetos a,* to pay one's respects to.
respetuosidad *f.* respectfulness.
respetuoso, -sa *adj.* respectful. *2* dutiful, humble, obedient. *3* awesome, impressive.
respigón *m.* hangnail.
respingar *intr.* [of a horse] to jerk, start. *2* to obey unwillingly, to grumble. *3* [of the edge of a poorly made garment] to curl up.
respingo *m.* start [due to pain, surprise, etc.]. *3* gesture of unwillingness.
respingona *adj.* turned up, retroussé [nose].
respirable *adj.* respirable, breathable.
respiración *f.* respiration, breathing. *2* ventilation.
respiradero *m.* vent, air hole, air passage. *2* ARCH. loophole, louver. *2* fig. breather, respite.
respirar *intr.* to respire, breathe. *2* BOT. to respire. *3* to take breath, respire, breathe again, get rest or respite: *sin* ~, without stopping. *4* to speak, open one's lips. *5* ~ *a,* to breathe of, smell of. *6 tr.* to breathe, take in [air etc.].
respiratorio, -ria *adj.* respiratory.
respiro *m.* respiration, breathing. *2* breath [moment of rest], respite. *3* COM. extension of time [for payment].
resplandecer *intr.* to shine, glitter, glow. *2* fig. to shine, stand out. ¶ CONJUG. like *agradecer.*
resplandeciente *adj.* resplendent, bright, shining, glittering; luminous, radiant.
resplandor *m.* resplendence, light, glitter, glow, radiance. *2* luster, splendour. *3* gleam, gleaming.
responder *tr.* to answer, reply, respond to. *2 intr.* to echo. *3* to require, return. *4* to yield, be productive. *5* to answer, have the desired effect. *6* to reply, respond [perform answering action]. *7* to respond [to a stimulus, etc.]. *8* to answer, correspond. *9* to answer back, be saucy. *10* [of a building, ect.] to face. *11* ~ *de* or *por,* to answer, be accountable for; to vouch for.
respondón, -na *adj.* coll. answering back, saucy.
responsabilidad *f.* responsibility. *2* liability.
responsable *adj.* responsible. *2* liable, answerable.
responso *m.* ECCL. responsory for the dead.
responsorio *m.* ECCL. responsory.
respuesta *f.* answer, reply, response.
resquebradura *f.* crack, crevice, chink, flaw, split.
resquebrajadizo, -za *adj.* easily cracked or split.
resquebrajar *tr.* to crack, split. *2 ref.* to crack [become cracked].
resquebrarse *ref.* [of a thing] to begin to break or crack. ¶ CONJUG. like *acertar.*
resquemar *tr.-intr.* to bite, sting [the mouth]. *2* to burn [food]. *3* fig. to smart, to annoy. *4 ref.* [of food] to burn.
resquemazón *f.,* **resquemo** *m.* bite, sting [of food]. *2* burnt taste [of food]. *3* fig. smarting, annoyance.
resquemor *m.* smarting, annoyance. *2* resentment.
resquicio *m.* chink, narrow opening.
resta *f.* ARITH. subtraction. *2* ARITH. difference.
restablecer *tr.* to re-establish, restore. *2 ref.* to recover [be restored from illness, loss, etc.].
restablecimiento *m.* re-establishment, restoration. *2* recovery [from illnes, loss, etc.].

restallar *intr.* to crack [like a whip]. *2* to crackle.
restante *adj.* remaining. *2 m.* remainder rest.
restañar *tr.* to stanch [blood or a wound]. *2* to retin. *3 intr.* RESTALLAR. *4 ref.* [of blood] to stanch.
restaño *m.* stanching [of blood]. *2* stagnation [of waters].
restar *tr.* to deduct. *2* to detract, take away. *3 intr.* to be left, remain. *4 tr.-intr.* MATH. to subtract.
restauración *f.* restoration, re-establishment. *4* restoration [of a painting, etc.]. *3* POL. restoration.
restaurante *adj.* restoring. *2 m.-f.* restorer. *3 m.* restaurant.
restaurar *tr.* to restore, re-establish. *2* to restore [a painting, etc.]. *3* POL. to restore.
restaurativo, -va *adj.-n.* restorative.
restinga *f.* NAUT. shoal, bar.
restitución *f.* restitution, restoration, return.
restituible *adj.* restorable, returnable.
restituir *tr.* to restore, give back, return. *2* to restore, bring back [to original state]. *3 ref.* to return to the place of departure. ¶ CONJUG. like *huir.*
restitutorio, -ria *adj.* restitutive. *2* restitutory.
resto *m.* rest, remainder, residue. *2* limit for stakes [at cards]: *echar el* ~, coll. to stake one's all; to do one's best. *3* MATH. remainder. *4 pl.* remains.
restorán *m.* (Am.) RESTAURANTE.
restregar *tr.* to rub [something] hard, to scrub. ¶ CONJUG. like *acertar.*
restregón *m.* hard rubbing.
restricción *f.* restriction, limitation, restraint: ~ *mental,* mental reservation.
restrictivo, -va *adj.* restrictive.
restringir *tr.* to restrict, limit. *2* to constrict, contract.
restriñir *tr.* astrict, astringe, constrict, contract.
resucitador, -ra *adj.* resuscitative. *2 m.-f.* resuscitator, reviver.
resucitar *tr.* to resurrect, resuscitate, revive. *2 intr.* to be resurrected, to resuscitate, revive.
resudar *intr.* to sweat or perspire sightly. *2 ref.-intr.* [of a wall, vessel, etc.] to ooze.
resudor *m.* slight perspiration.
resueltamente *adv.* resolutely.
resuelto, -ta *p. p.* of RESOLVER. *2 adj.* resolute, determined, bold, daring. *3* prompt, quick.
resuelvo, resuelva, etc. *irr.* V. RESOLVER.
resuello *m.* breathing; hard breathing: *sin* ~, breathless; panting.
resulta *f.* result, effect, consequence: *de resultas de,* as a result of.
resultado *m.* result, effect, outcome, consequence.
resultando *m.* LAW whereas.
resultante *adj.* resulting, resultant. *2 f.* MECH. resultant.
resultar *intr.* to result. *2* to be, prove to be, turn out to be. *3* to be [wounded, awarded, etc.]; to come out [well, badly, etc.]. *4* coll. to be advantageous. *5* coll. to please.
resumen *m.* summary, abstract, résumé. *2* summing up: *en* ~, in short, to sum up.
resumir *tr.* to summarize, abstract, abridge, sum up. *2 ref. resumirse en,* to be reduced to; to be comprised in.
resurgimiento *m.* resurgence, revival, renewal.
resurgir *intr.* to resurge, revive, to spring up again.
resurrección *f.* resurrection, resuscitation, revival.
retablo *m.* retable, altarpiece.
retacar *tr.* BILL. to hit [the ball] twice.

retaco *m.* a kind of short musket. *2* BILL. short cue. *3* coll. chubby fellow.

retador, -ra *adj.* challenging. *2 m.-f.* challenger.

retaguardia *f.* MIL. rear, rear guard: *a* ~, in the rear.

retahíla *f.* series, string.

retal *m.* remnant, piece, clipping, scrap [of cloth, leather, metal plates, etc.].

retallecer *intr.* [of a plant] to sprout again. ¶ CONJUG. like *agradecer.*

retallo *m.* ARCH. offset, scarcement.

retama *f.* BOT. Spanish broom. *2* BOT. ~ *de escobas,* furze, broom. *3* BOT. ~ *de tintes,* dyer's-broom.

retar *tr.* to challenge [to combat or competition]; to dare.

retardación *f.* retardation.

retardado, -da *adj.* retarded. *2 m.-f.* EDUC. retardate.

retardador, -ra *adj.* retarding, delaying.

retardar *tr.* to retard, slow down, slacken. *2* to delay. *3 ref.* to retard [intr.].

retardo *m.* retard, retardation, delay.

retasar *tr.* to reappraise.

retazar *tr.* to cut to pieces.

retazo *m.* remnant, piece, scrap [of cloth]. *2* fragment, portion.

retejar *tr.* to retile, repair the tiles of [a roof].

retejer *tr.* to weave closely or tightly.

retemblar *intr.* to shake, tremble, quiver. ¶ CONJUG. like *acertar.*

retén *m.* store, stock, reserve. *2* MIL. troops held ready for emergency. *3* MEC. pawl, catch.

retención *f.* retention, retaining. *2* MED. retention.

retendré, retendría, etc. *irr.* V. RETENER.

retener *tr.* to retain; keep, hold, catch. *2* to detain in prison. ¶ CONJUG. like *tener.*

retengo, retenga, etc. *irr.* V. RETENER.

retenida *f.* guy [rope].

retentar *tr.* [of a disease, pain, etc.] to threaten with a relapse.

retentiva *f.* retentiveness, memory.

reteñir *tr.* to redye. *2 intr.* RETIÑIR. ¶ CONJUG. like *ceñir.*

retesar *tr.* to draw or stretch tighter; to stiffen.

reticencia *f.* a manner of saying a thing which is incomplete or suggests that more could be said about it.

reticente *adj.* using RETICENCIAS.

retícula *f.* RETÍCULO. *2* ASTR. Reticule.

reticular *adj.* reticular, reticulated, netlike, netted.

retículo *m.* reticulum [netlike structure]. *2* OPT. reticle. *3* ANAT., ZOOL., BOT. reticulum.

retienes, retiene, etc. *irr.* V. RETENER.

retina *f.* ANAT. retina.

retinte *m.* second dye. *2* RETINTÍN.

retintín *m.* tinkling, jingle, ringing [in the ears]. *2* sarcastic emphasis or tone of voice.

retiñir *intr.* to tinkle, jingle, ring. ¶ CONJUG. like *mullir.*

retirada *f.* withdrawal. *2* retirement [withdrawal from public life or circulation]. *3* MIL. retreat. *4* MIL. tatoo. *5* safety. *6* dry bed [left by changed course of a stream].

retiradamente *adv.* retiredly. *2* secretly.

retirado, -da *adj.* retired, secluded, remote. *2* retired, pensioned. *3 m.* retired officer.

retiramiento *m.* retirement, seclusion. *2* retired place.

retirar *tr.* to retire, withdraw. *2* to retire, call in. *3* to push back or aside; to put out of the way. *4*

to force to retire. *5* CHESS. to retreat [a man]. *6 intr.* to resemble, take after. *7 ref.* to retire, withdraw [go away]. *8* to retire, recede. *9* MIL. to retreat. *10* to retire, go into retirement.

retiro *m.* retirement, withdrawal. *2* retirement, seclusion, retreat, retired place. *3* ECCL. retreat. *4* MIL. retirement [of an officer].

reto *m.* challenge [to combat or competition]; dare, defiance.

retocar *tr.* to touch up, finish, retouch.

retoñar *intr.* [of a plant] to sprout, shoot. *2* [of a thing] to reappear, revive.

retoñecer *intr.* RETOÑAR. ¶ CONJUG. like *agradecer.*

retoño *m.* sprout, shoot, tiller. *2* fig. child.

retoque *m.* retouch, touching up.

retor *m.* twilled cotton fabric.

retorcedura *f.* RETORCIMIENTO.

retorcer *tr.* to twist, wring, wrench, screw, contort, convolve. *2* to retort [an argument]. *3* fig. to twist, distort, misconstrue. *4 ref.* to twist [become twisted]. *5* to writhe, squirm, wriggle. ¶ CONJUG. like *mover.*

retorcimiento *m.* twisting, wringing, writhing.

retórica *f.* rhetoric. *2 pl.* coll. sophistries, subtleties.

retórico, -ca *adj.* rethorical. *2 m.-f.* rethorician.

retornar *tr.* to return, give back. *2* to cause [a thing] to go back. *3 intr.* to return, come back.

retorno *m.* return, coming back. *2* return voyage. *3* return, repayment. *4* barrer, exchange.

retorsión *f.* twisting. *2* retortion, retaliation. *3* retorting [an argument].

retorta *f.* retort [vessel]. *2* twilled linen fabric.

retortero *m.* turn around: *andar al* ~, to bustle around; *traer al* ~, to harass, keep busy; to deceive with false promises.

retortijar *tr.* to twist, curl.

retortijón *m.* twist, twisting: ~ *de tripas,* bellyache.

retozar *intr.* to frisk, gambol. *2* to frolic, disport, play. *3* [of some emotions] to be aroused.

retozo *m.* frisk, gambol, frolic. *2* ~ *de la risa,* suppressed laughter.

retozón, -na *adj.* frisky, frolicsome, playful.

retracción *f.* retraction.

retractación *f.* retractation, recantation.

retractar *tr.* to retract, recant, take back. *2* LAW to purchase by prior right.

retráctil *adj.* retractile.

retracto *m.* LAW. prior right to purchase.

retraer *tr.* to bring back. *2* to dissuade. *3* LAW to purchase by prior right. *4 ref.* to take refuge. *5* to retire, go back. *6* to retract, draw back. *7* to withdraw from [political activities]. *8* to lead a retired life.

retraigo, retraiga, etc. *irr.* V. RETRAER.

retraído, -da *adj.* retiring, incommunicative, -shy.

retraimiento *m.* retirement, retired life. *2* keeping aloof. *3* retiringness, shyness. *4* retreat, refuge.

retraje, retrajera, etc. *irr.* V. RETRAER.

retranca *f.* breeching [of a harness].

retransmisión *f.* RADIO. rebroadcasting.

retransmitir *f.* RADIO. to rebroadcast.

retrasado, -da *adj.* [mentally] retarded.

retrasar *tr.* to delay, defer, postpone, retard. *2* to set back [a timepiece]. *3 intr.* to fall behind [in studies, etc.]; to decline. *4 ref.* to be backward. *5* to delay, to be behind time, slow, too slow, late.

retraso *m.* delay, retard, lag.

retratar *tr.* to portray. *2 ref.* to portray oneself. *3* to sit for a photograph. *4* to show, be reflected. *5 tr.-intr.* RETRACTAR.

retratista *m.-f.* portraitist; portrait painter; photographer.

retrato *m.* portrait, likeness, picture; photograph, portraiture. *2* fig. image, resemblance.

retrechería *f.* artifice, shift, evasion.

retrechero, -ra *adj.* artful, sly, deceitful. *2* attractive, charming.

retrepado, -da *adj.* leaning back.

retreparse *ref.* to lean back, to recline [in a chair].

retreta *f.* MIL. retreat, tatoo [signal, call]. *2* tatoo [evening military parade].

retrete *m.* toilet, water-closet. *2* boudoir.

retribución *f.* recompense, reward, fee, consideration.

retribuir *tr.* to recompense, reward, pay, fee, remunerate. ¶ CONJUG. like *huir.*

retributivo, -va *adj.* retributive.

retroactividad *f.* retroactivity.

retroactivo, -va *adj.* retroactive.

retrocarga *f. de ~,* breech-loading.

retroceder *intr.* to go back, move backwards, recede, retrocede; regress, retrograde.

retrocesión *f.* retrocession. *2* LAW. recession.

retroceso *m.* backward motion, receding, regression, retrocession, retrogradation; recoil. *2* MED. aggravation. *3* BILL. draw.

retrogradar *intr.* RETROCEDER. *2* ASTR. to retrograde.

retrógrado, -da *adj.* retrogade. *2 adj.-n.* POL. reactionary.

retronar *intr.* to thunder, to rumble.

retrospectivo, -va *adj.* retrospective.

retrotraer *tr.* LAW to antedate.

retrovender *tr.* LAW to sell back to the vendor.

retrucar *intr.* BILL. to kiss.

retruécano *m.* pun, play on words.

retumbante *adj.* resounding, thundering, rumbling. *2* fig. pompous, bombastic, high-flown.

retumbar *intr.* to resound, thunder, rumble.

retumbo *m.* resounding, thunder, rumble, reverberation.

retuve, retuviera, etc. *irr.* V. RETENER.

reucliniano, -na *adj.* Reuchlinian.

reuma *m.* MED. rheumatism.

reumático, -ca *adj.* MED. rheumatic(al. *2 m.-f.* rheumatic.

reumatismo *m.* MED. rheumatism.

reunión *f.* reunion [reuniting]: joining. *2* reunion, meeting, gathering, party.

reunir *tr.* to reunite; to rally. *2* to unite, join, collect. *3* to gather, assemble, call together. *4 ref.* to reunite [be reunited]. *5* to join, gather, assemble, rally [come or meet together]. *6 reunirse a* or *con,* to rejoin.

revacunación *f.* MED. revaccination.

revacunar *tr.* MED. to revaccinate.

reválida *f.* final examination [for a degree, etc.].

revalidación *f.* revalidation, confirmation.

revalidar *tr.* to revalidate, confirm, renew.

revejecer *intr.-ref.* to age [before one's time]. ¶ CONJUG. like *agradecer.*

revejido, -da *adj.* prematurely aged.

revelación *f.* revelation.

revelado, -da *adj.* revealed. *2 m.* PHOT. development.

revelador, -ra *adj.* revealing. *2 m.-f.* revealer. *3 m.* PHOT. developer.

revelamiento *m.* revealing, revelation.

revelar *tr.* to reveal. *2* PHOT. to develop. *3 ref.* to reveal itself [or oneself].

revellín *m.* FORT. ravelin.

revendedor, -ra *m.-f.* reseller, retailer. *2* scalper, ticket speculator.

revender *tr.* to resell, retail. *2* to scalp [tickets].

reventa *f.* reseale, retail. *2* scalping [of tickets, etc.].

reventadero *m.* rough ground. *2* drudgery, hard task.

reventar *intr.-ref.* to burst, explode, blow up. *2 intr.* [of waves] to break. *3* [of a boil, bud, cloud, etc.] to burst. *4* to burst [with joy, envy, pride, etc.]. *5* coll. to die. *6 ~ por,* to be dying to. *7 tr.* to burst, break, crush. *8* to tire [a person] out. *9* to run [a horse] to death. *10* coll. to annoy, displease. *11* coll. to ruin. *12 ref.* to toil, work, run, etc., to exhaustion. ¶ CONJUG. like *acertar.*

reventazón *f.* burst, bursting. *2* breaking [of waves].

reventón, -na *adj.* bursting, seeming to burst. *2 m.* burst, bursting. *3* AUTO. blowout. *4* tiring to death.

rever *tr.* to review, revise, to look over or examine again. *2* LAW to review. ¶ CONJUG. *ver.*

reverberación *f.* reverberation [of light].

reverberar *intr.* [of light] to reverberate.

reverbero *m.* reverberation [of light]. *2* reflecting surface. *3* reverberator. *4* (Am.) alcohol stove.

reverdecer *intr.* to grow green again. *2* to acquire new freshness and vigour. *3 tr.* to give new freshness and vigour, to renew. ¶ CONJUG. like *agradecer.*

reverdeciente *adj.* growing green and fresh anew.

reverencia *f.* reverence, revering. *2* bow, curtsy. *3* ECCL. reverence [title].

reverencial *adj.* reverential.

reverenciar *tr.* to reverence, revere, venerate.

reverendísimo, -ma *adj. superl.* Most Reverend.

reverendo, -da *adj.* reverend.

reverente *adj.* reverent.

reversible *adj.* reversible.

reversión *f.* reversion [return to a previous state]. *2* BIOL., LAW reversion.

reverso *m.* back, wrong side. *2* reverse [in coins or medals]: *el ~ de la medalla,* the entire opposite.

revertir *intr.* LAW to revert. ¶ CONJUG. like *hervir.*

revés *m.* back, wrong side, reverse. *2* slap. *3* SPORT backhand [stroke]. *4* reverse, misfortune, setback. *5 al ~,* on the contrary, the other way around; in the opposite or wrong way, backwards. *6 al ~, del ~,* wrongly; inside out; wrong side out, before, etc. *7 de ~,* diagonally, from left to right.

revesado, -da *adj.* intricate, obscure. *2* mischievous, unmanageable.

revestimiento *m.* covering, coat, coating, lining, facing, revetment [on a surface, wall, etc.].

revestir *tr.* to put [vestments] on; to clothe. *2* cover, coat, line, face, revet. *3* to clothe, invest [with dignity, etc.]. *4* to adorn, disguise. *5* to give an air or expression to. *6 ref.* to put vestments on. *7 revestirse de paciencia,* to prepare to be patient. *8 revestirse de valor,* to summon one's courage. ¶ CONJUG. like VESTIR.

revezar *intr.* to alternate, work by shifts.

revezo *m.* working by shifts. *2* shift, relay.

revirar *tr.* to turn, twist. *2* to roll [one's eyes]. *3 intr.* NAUT. to veer again.

revisar *tr.* to revise, review, re-examine. *2* LAW to review. *3* to check, verify. *4* to audit [accounts].

revisión *f.* revision, review, revisal. *2* check, verification. *3* audit [of accounts].

revisor, -ra *adj.* revising, revisory. *2 m.-f.* reviser, re-examiner. *3 m.* RLY. conductor, ticket collector. *4* auditor [of accounts].
revista *f.* review, examination, inspection. *2* MIL. review, muster; parade. *3* review [of a book, play, etc.]. *4* review, magazine [journal]. *5* THEAT. revue.
revistar *tr.* MIL. to review.
revistero *m.* a journalist who writes reports and reviews about shows, bullfightings, etc.
revisto, revista, revistiera, etc. *irr.* V. REVESTIR.
revitalizar *tr.* to revitalize.
revivificar *tr.* to revivify.
revivir *intr.* to revive. *2* to be renewed.
revocable *adj.* revocable, repealable, reversible.
revocación *f.* revocation, repeal, reversal.
revocador, -ra *adj.* revoking. *2 m.-f.* revoker. *3 m.* plasterer.
revocar *tr.* to revoke, repeal, reverse. *2* to dissuade. *3* to drive back [the smoke, etc.]. *4* MAS. to plaster.
revocatorio, -ria *adj.* revocatory, repealing.
revolar *intr.* [of birds] to fly again. *2* REVOLOTEAR. ¶ CONJUG. like *contar.*
revolcadero *m.* wallowing place [for animals].
revolcar *tr.* to knock down, roll over. *2* coll. to floor [an opponent]. *3 ref.* to wallow, roll over and over. ¶ CONJUG. like *contar.*
revolcón *m.* knocking down, rolling over. *2* defeat [in argument, etc.]. *3* wallowing.
revolear *intr.* to fly around and around.
revolotear *intr.* to flutter, flit, fly round about.
revoloteo *m.* fluttering, flitting, flying round about.
revoltijo, revoltillo *m.* mess, medley, jumble. *2* entanglement, confusion.
revoltón *m.* ENT. vine grub. *2* BOVEDILLA 1. *3* ARCH. turn in a moulding.
revoltoso, -sa *adj.* riotous, rebellious. *2* mischievous. *3 m.-f.* rioter, rebel.
revolución *f.* revolution.
revolucionar *tr.* to revolutionize.
revolucionario, -ria *adj.* revolutionary. *2 m.-f.* revolutionary, revolutionist.
revólver *m.* revolver [firearm].
revolver *tr.* to stir [with a spoon]; to shake. *2* to rummage, turn over. *3* to upset, disarrange. *4* to agitate, stir up agitation in. *5* to wrap up. *6* to revolve or turn over [in one's mind]. *7* to set [a person] against [another]. *8* to swing [a horse] around. *9 intr.-ref.* [of a thing] to revolve. *10 ref.* to turn upon, to turn and face. *11* to stir, move. *12* [of a horseman] to swing around. *13* ASTR. to revolve.
revoque *m.* MAS. plastering, rendering.
revuelco *m.* REVOLCÓN.
revuelo *m.* second flight [of a bird]. *2* flying around. *3* flutter, stir [of some things]. *4* commotion, sensation. *5 de* ~, as in passing.
revuelta *f.* revolt, riot, disturbance. *2* turning, winding [of a road, etc.]. *3* turn, change.
revueltamente *adv.* confusedly, disorderly.
revuelto, -ta *p. p.* of REVOLVER. *2 adj.* disordered, confused. *3* disturbed, agitated. *4* intricate. *5* changeable [weather]. *6* scrambled [egg].
revuelvo, revuelva, etc. *irr.* V. REVOLVER.
revulsión *f.* MED. revulsion.
revulsivo, -va; revulsorio, -ria *adj.-n.* MED. revulsive.
rey *m.* king [sovereign, ruler, etc.]: ~ *de armas,* HER. king-at-arms; *los Reyes Magos,* the Magi,

the Three Wise Men; *servir al* ~, to be in the army. *2* CHESS, CARDS king. *3* ORN. ~ *de codornices,* corn crake.
reyerta *f.* wrangle, quarrel, row, fight.
reyezuelo *m.* kinglet [petty king]. *2* ORN. kinglet.
rezagado, -da *adj.* straggling, lagging, left behind. *2 m.-f.* straggler; lagger; one who falls behind.
rezagar *tr.* to outstrip, leave behind. *2* to delay, defer, put off. *3 ref.* to fall behind, lag.
rezar *tr.* to say [prayers, mass]. *2 tr.-intr.* to say, state, read: *la carta reza así,* the letter reads thus. *3 intr.* to say prayers. *4* ~ *con,* to concern, have to do with.
rezno *m.* ENT. bot.
rezo *m.* saying [of prayers, of the divine office, of the mass]. *2* prayer, praying, devotions.
rezongar *intr.* to grumble, mutter.
rezumadero *m.* place where something is oozing.
rezumar *tr.-ref.* [of a vessel, wall, etc.] to exude, sweat. *2 intr.-ref.* [of a liquid] to exude, ooze out. *3 ref.* to transpire [become known].
Rhin *m. pr. n.* GEOG. Rhine.
ría *f.* estuary, firth.
riachuelo *m.* rivulet, streamlet, small river.
riada *f.* freshet, flood [of a stream].
riba *f.* RIBAZO.
ribaldo, -da *adj.* knavish. *2 m.* knave, rascal.
ribazo *m.* steep bank, slope.
ribera *f.* shore, strand. *2* bank [of a river], riverside.
ribereño, -ña *adj.-n.* riparian.
ribete *m.* SEW. binding, border, trimming. *2* addition, embellishment [to a tale]. *3 pl.* streak, touch.
ribetear *tr.* SEW. to bind.
ricacho, cha *m.-f.* coll. vulgar rich person.
ricachón, -na *m.-f.* coll. rich person.
ricadueña, ricahembra *f.* obs. noblewoman.
ricahombría *f.* the ancient high nobility of Castile.
ricamente *adv.* richly. *2* pleasantly, comfortably.
Ricardo *m. pr. n.* Richard.
ricino *m.* BOT. castor-oil plant, Palma Christi.
rico, -ca *adj.* rich [wealthy, abundant, abounding in; exquisite; splendid]. *2* delicious. *3* coll. dear. *4 m.-f.* rich person. *5* coll. darling.
ricohombre *m.* obs. grandee, nobleman.
rictus, pl. -tus *m.* convulsive grin.
ricura *f.* deliciousness. *2* coll. darling.
ridiculez *f.* ridiculousness. *2* ridiculous thing or action. *3* oddity, eccentricity. *4* coll. trifle.
ridiculizar *tr.* to ridicule; to laugh at.
ridículo, -la *adj.* ridiculous, ludicrous, risible. *2* odd, eccentric. *3* trifling, insignificant. *4 m.* ridicule: *poner en* ~, to expose to ridicule, to make a fool of; *ponerse en* ~, to make a fool of oneself. *5* reticule [lady's bag].
riego *m.* irrigation, watering.
riel *m.* RLY. rail. *2* small ingot.
rielar *intr.* poet. to glisten, glimmer.
rienda *f.* rein: *dar* ~ *suelta a,* to give free rein to; *tirar la* ~ or *las riendas a,* to check, restrain; *tomar las riendas,* to take the reins; *a* ~ *suelta,* loose-reined; swiftly; without restraint. *2* fig. restraint, moderation.
riente *adj.* laughing, smiling.
riesgo *m.* risk, hazard, danger, peril.
Rif (el) *m. pr. n.* GEOG. El Rif.
rifa *f.* raffle [kind of lottery]. *2* quarrel, row.
rifar *tr.* to raffle, raffle off. *2 intr.* to quarrel, dispute. *3 ref.* NAUT. [of a sail] to split.
rifeño, -ña *adj.-n.* Riffian.

rifirrafe *m.* coll. squabble, row.
rifle *m.* rifle [firearm].
rigidez *f.* rigidity. *2 ~ cadavérica*, rigor mortis.
rígido, -da *adj.* rigid, stiff. *2* rigid, strict, rigorous.
rigodón *m.* rigadoon [dance].
rigor *m.* rigour, rigor. *2* MED. rigidity. *3 de ~*, de rigueur, indispensable. *4 en ~*, strictly speaking.
rigorismo *m.* rigorism.
rigorista *adj.* rigorist, rigoristic. *2 m.-f.* rigorist.
rigoroso, -sa *adj.* RIGUROSO.
riguroso, -sa *adj.* rigorous. *2* absolute.
rijoso, -sa *adj.* lustful, sensual. *2* quarrelsome.
rima *f.* rhyme, rime: *2* RIMERO. *3 pl.* lyric poems.
rimado, -da *p. p.* of RIMAR. *2 adj.* versified.
rimador, -ra *m.-f.* rhymer.
rimar *tr.-intr.* to rhyme.
rimbombante *adj.* resonant, thundering. *2* fig. showy. *3* bombastic, pompous.
rimbombar *intr.* to thunder; to resound, echo.
rimbombe, rimbombo *m.* resonance, echo.
rimero *m.* pile, heap.
Rin *m. pr. n.* GEOG. Rhine.
rincón *m.* corner [hollow angle], nook. *2* corner [secret or remote place]. *3* patch, small piece [of land]. *4* fig. home, retreat.
rinconada *f.* corner [hollow angle].
rinconera *f.* corner cabinet, stand, bracket or table.
rindo, rinda, rindiera, etc. *irr.* V. RENDIR.
ringla *f.*, **ringle** *m.*, **ringlera** *f.* coll. line, file, row.
ringorrango *m.* flourish [in writing]. *2 pl.* superfluous ornaments; fripperies.
rinitis *f.* MED. rhinitis.
rinoceronte *m.* ZOOL. rhinoceros.
rinoplastia *f.* SURG. rhinoplasty.
riña *f.* fight, quarrel, row, wrangle, dispute.
riño, riña, riñera, etc. *irr.* V. REÑIR.
riñón *m.* ANAT., ZOOL. kidney: *costar un ~*, fig. to cost a mint of money. *2* fig. heart [central part]. *3 pl.* loins. *4 tener riñones*, to be brave.
riñonada *f.* layer of fat about the kidneys. *2* loins. *3* dish of kidneys.
río *m.* GEOG. river, stream. *2* fig. river, flood, stream [of blood, people, etc.].
río, ría, riera, etc. *irr.* V. REÍR.
riostra *f.* ARCH. brace, stay.
ripia *f.* shingle [slip of wood].
ripio *m.* refuse, debris. *2* MAS. rubble. *3* padding [in verse]. *4 no perder ~*, not to miss a word; not to miss the least occasion.
riqueza *f.* riches, wealth. *2* richness. *3 pl.* riches, wealth. *4* precious objects.
risa *f.* laugh, laughter: *estar muerto de ~*, to be extremely amused; *no ser cosa de ~*, to be no laughing matter.
risada *f.* RISOTADA.
riscal *m.* craggy place.
risco *m.* crag, cliff. *2* honey fritter.
riscoso, -sa *adj.* craggy, cliffy.
risible *adj.* risible. *2* laughable, ridiculous.
risita *f. dim.* feigned laugh. *2* giggle, titter.
risotada *f.* guffaw. *2* outburst of laughter.
ríspido, -da; rispo, -pa *adj.* harsh, gruff.
ristra *f.* string [of onions or garlic]. *2* coll. string, row, file.
ristre *m.* ARM. rest [for the lance].
risueño, -ña *adj.* smiling, riant, cheerful, gay, pleasant. *2* hopeful [prospect, etc.].
rítmico, -ca *adj.* rhythmic(al. *2 f.* rhythmics.
ritmo *m.* rhythm, cadence.

rito *m.* rite.
ritual *adj.-m.* ritual: *ser de ~*, to be ordained by custom.
rival *m.-f.* rival: *sin ~*, unrivalled.
rivalidad *f.* rivalry.
rivalizar *intr.* to vie, compete.
rivera *f.* brook, creek.
riza *f.* ravage, destruction.
rizado, -da *adj.* curly. *2* ripply. *3 m.* curling, frizzling, crimping. *4* curls, frizzle.
rizar *tr.* to curl, crisp, frizz, frizzle, crimp, flute, corrugate. *2* to ripple [water]. *3 ref.* to curl naturally. *4* [of water] to ripple.
rizo, -za *adj.* curly. *2 m.* curl, frizzle, ringlet. *3* ripple [small wave]. *4* AER. loop: *hacer*, or *rizar, el ~*, to loop the loop. *5* NAUT. reef, point; reef.
rizoma *m.* BOT. rhizome.
rizópodo, -da *adj.-m.* ZOOL. rhizopod.
rizoso, -sa *adj.* naturally curly.
roano, -na *adj.* roan [horse or mare].
robador, -ra *m.-f.* robber, stealer.
róbalo, robalo *m.* ICHTH. sea bass. *2* ICHTH. snook.
robar *tr.* to rob, pilfer, plunder, steal, thieve, rob of. *2* to abduct [a woman]. *3* [of a stream] to sweep away [banks, land]. *4* to draw [cards or dominoes]. *5 ~ el corazón*, to captivate, enamour. *6 intr.* to rob, thieve.
robellón *m.* BOT. edible milk mushroom.
Roberto *m. pr. n.* Robert.
robín *m.* rust [of metal].
robladura *f.* clinching, riveting.
roblar *tr.* to clinch, rivet [a nail, etc.].
roble *m.* BOT. oak, British oak: *~ albar*, durmast. *2* oak [wood]. *3* fig. strong, robust person or thing.
robleda *f.*, **robledal, robledo** *m.* woods of oak trees.
roblón *m.* rivet. *2* ridge of tiles.
robo *m.* theft, stealing, pilferage, larceny, robbery: *~ con escalo*, burglary. *2* plunder. *3* draw, drawing [at cards or domino].
roborar *tr.* to strengthen. *2* to corroborate.
roborativo, -va *adj.* roborant. *2* corroborative.
robot *m.* robot.
robustecer *tr.* to strengthen, make strong. *2 ref.* to become strong. ¶ CONJUG. like *agradecer*.
robustez, robusteza *f.* robustness.
robusto, -ta *adj.* robust, strong, hale, vigorous.
roca *f.* GEOL. rock. *2* rock [mass of rock standing up or cut; large detached stone]. *3* fig. rock.
rocadero *m.* knob or head of a distaff.
rocalla *f.* small fragments of rock. *2* stone chips. *3* large glass beads. *4* F. ARTS. rocaille.
roce *m.* rubbing, grazing, friction. *2* light touch [in passing]. *3* frequent intercourse.
rociada *f.* sprinkling, aspersion. *2* fig. shower, volley [of bullets, insults, etc.]. *3* fig. reprimand.
rociadura *f.*, **rociamiento** *m.* sprinkling, aspersion.
rociar *impers.* to dew. *2 tr.* to bedew, sprinkle, spray, asperse.
rocín *m.* hack, jade, sorry horse. *2* work horse. *3* fig. coarse, stupid fellow.
rocinal *adj.* pertaining to a jade or sorry horse.
rocinante *m.* jade, worn-out horse.
rocino *m.* ROCÍN.
rocío *m.* dew. *2* spray, sprinkle [of a liquid]. *3* NAUT. spindrift. *4* light shower.
rococó *adj.* rococo.
rocoso, -sa *adj.* rocky.
rocho *m.* roc [a fabulous bird].
roda *f.* NAUT. stem.
rodaballo *m.* ICHTH. turbot; brill.

rodada f. rut, wheel track.
rodadizo, -za adj. easy-rolling.
rodado, -da adj. dapple, dappled [horse]. 2 rounded, fluent [sentence, period]. 3 canto ~, boulder. 4 tráfico ~, traffic of wheeled vehicles. 5 venir ~, [of things] to happen in a favourable way.
rodadura f. rolling [act]: superficie de ~, tread [of a wheel].
rodaja f. disk, circular plate. 2 round slice. 3 rowel [of spur].
rodaje m. wheels, set of wheels. 2 shooting, filming [of a motion picture, of a scene, etc.].
rodal m. spot, patch [piece of ground].
rodamiento m. MACH. [ball or roller] bearing.
Ródano m. pr. n. GEOG. Rhone.
rodante adj. rolling, wheeled.
rodapié m. ARCH. baseboard [of a room wall]. 2 drapery around the bottom of a bed, table, etc.
rodaplancha f. main ward of a key.
rodar intr. to roll [as a ball, a wheel, etc.]. 2 to roll down [the stairs, etc.]; to fall rolling; to tumble. 3 to roll, turn, wheel [go on wheels or as on wheels]. 4 to turn, revolve, rotate. 5 to wander, go about or around, roam. 6 fig. to abound. 7 [of things] to happen one after another. 8 echarlo todo a ~, to upset everything; to lose one's temper. 9 tr. to shoot, film; to project, screen [a moving picture, a scene]. ¶ CONJUG. like contar.
Rodas f. pr. n. GEOG. Rhodes.
rodeabrazo (a) adv. swinging the arm [for a throw].
rodear tr. to encircle, surround. 2 MIL. to invest. 3 (Am.) to round up [cattle]. 4 to turn around. 5 intr. to go around, make a detour. 6 fig. to beat about the bush. 7 ref. to move, stir, turn about.
rodela f. buckler.
rodeno adj. BOT. pino ~, pinaster.
rodeo m. encircling, surrounding. 2 detour, roundabout way. 3 roundabout, evasion: andar con ~, to beat about the bush; sin rodeos, frankly, bluntly. 5 rodeo, roundup [of cattle].
rodera f. rut, wheel track, cart track.
rodete m. bun or knot of plaited hair. 2 padded ring [for carrying things on the head]. 3 belt pulley. 4 MECH. horizontal water wheel.
rodezno m. horizontal water wheel.
rodilla f. ANAT., ZOOL. knee: de rodillas, kneeling, on one's knees. 2 RODETE 2. 3 cleaning cloth.
rodillazo m. blow or push with the knee.
rodillera f. knee guard, knee cap. 2 ARM. genouillere. 3 baggy knee [of trousers]. 4 VET. knee injury [of a horse].
rodillo m. roller [cylinder of wood, metal, stone, etc.]. 2 road roller. 3 PRINT. inking roller; brayer. 4 COOK. rolling pin. 5 platen [of typewriter].
1) **rodio** m. CHEM. rhodium.
2) **rodio, -dia** adj.-n. Rhodian.
rododendro m. BOT. rhododendron.
rodrigar tr. to prop up [plants].
Rodrigo m. pr. n. Roderick.
rodrigón m. prop [for plants]. 2 coll. old retainer who escorted ladies.
roedor, -ra adj. gnawing. 2 biting, stinging, consuming. 3 adj.-n. ZOOL. rodent.
roedura f. gnawing, nibbling. 2 place that has been nibbled.
roer tr. to gnaw, nibble. 2 to gnaw, eat away, wear away, fret, corrode. 3 to pick [a bone]. ¶ CONJUG. INDIC. Pres.: roo, roigo, o royo [for the 1rst. pers.], roes, roe, etc. | Pret.: roí, roíste, royó; roí-

mos, roísteis, royeron. | SUBJ. Pres.: roa, roiga or roya, roas, roigas or royas, etc. | Imperf.: royera, royeras, etc., or royese, royeses, etc. | Fut.: royere, royeres, etc. | IMPER.: roe; roa, roiga or roya [for the 3rd. pers.]; roigamos, roed, roigan. | PAST. P.: roído. | GER. royendo.
rogaciónes f. pl. ECCL. rogations.
rogador, -ra m.-f. entreater, supplicant.
rogar tr. to ask, beg, entreat, pray [someone to do, give, etc., something]. ¶ CONJUG. like contar.
rogativas f. pl. public prayers to God.
Rogerio m. pr. n. Roger.
rojear intr. to redden, blush, be reddish, show red.
rojez f. redness, reddishness, ruddiness.
rojizo, -za adj. reddish, reddy, ruddy.
Rojo (Mar) m. pr. n. GEOG. Red Sea.
rojo, -ja adj. red [in colour]. 2 ruddy. 3 red [hair]; red-haired. 4 m. red [colour]: al ~, to a red heat. 5 adj.-n. POL. Red.
rojura f. redness.
rol m. roll, list. 2 NAUT. muster roll.
roldana f. sheave, pulley wheel.
rolde m. circle, ring [of persons or things].
rollete m. dim. small roll or roller.
rollizo, -za adj. round, cylindrical. 2 plump, stocky. 3 m. round log.
rollo m. roll [cylindrical mass]. 2 roll [of paper, cloth, etc.]. 3 coil [of rope]. 4 round log. 5 roller: rolling pin. 6 cylindrical boulder.
Roma f. pr. n. GEOG. Rome.
romadizo m. cold in the head.
romaico, -ca adj.-m. Romaic.
romana f. steelyard.
romanar tr. to weigh with a steelyard.
romance adj. Romance, Romanic [language]. 2 m. Spanish language. 3 narrative or lyric poem in octosyllable metre with alternate lines in assonance.
romancero m. collection of Spanish ROMANCES [poems].
romanesco, -ca adj. Roman [of the ancient Romans]. 2 NOVELESCO.
románico, -ca adj.-n. Romanesque [architecture, style]. 2 adj. Romanic [language].
romanilla, -lla adj.-f. round-hand [style of penmanship]. 2 PRINT. roman.
romanista m.-f. Romanist [one versed in Roman law or in Romance languages].
romanizar tr. to Romanize, Latinize. 2 ref. to become Romanized or Latinized.
romano, -na adj.-n. Roman. 2 BOT. romaine [lettuce].
romanticismo m. romanticism. 2 romance, romanticness.
romántico, -ca adj.-n. romantic. 2 romanticist.
romanza f. MUS. romance, romanza.
romaza f. BOT. sorrel.
rómbico adj. CRYST. rhombic, orthorhombic.
rombo m. GEOM. rhomb. 2 losenge, diamond.
romboedro m. GEOM. rhombohedron.
romboidal adj. rhomboidal.
romboide m. GEOM. rhomboid.
romeral m. place abounding with rosemary.
romería f. pilgrimage. 2 gathering at an out-of-town shrine on the saint's day.
romero, -ra m.-f. pilgrim, palmer. 2 m. BOT. rosemary.
romí adj. bastard [saffron].
romo, -ma adj. blunt [without a point]. 2 blunt-nosed. 3 blunt, dull, stupid.

rompecabezas, *pl.* **-zas** *m.* puzzle [toy], jigsaw puzzle. *2* puzzle, riddle. *3* slung shot.

rompedura *f.* breakage.

rompehielos, *pl.* **-los** *m.* NAUT. iceboat, icebreaker.

rompenueces, *pl.* **-ces** *m.* nut cracker.

rompeolas, *pl.* **-las** *m.* breakwater, jetty, mole.

romper *tr.* to break, crack, fracture, shatter, smash. *2* to tear, rend; to wear out [clothes]. *3* to break up [new ground]. *4* to cleave [the air, water, etc.]. *5* to break [silence; bounds; a contract, etc.]. *6* MIL. to break [ranks]. *7* to rout, defeat. *8* ~ *el hielo,* fig. to break the ice. *9 de rompe y rasga,* free, determined. *10 intr.* [of waves] to break. *11* [of flowers] to burst open. *12* to break out. *13* to begin, start, burst into or out. *14* ~ *con,* to break, quarrel, with. *15 al* ~ *el alba* or *el día,* at daybreak. *16 ref.* to break, fracture, shatter, smash, tear [be broken, fractured, etc.]. *17* to acquire ease of manner. *18* coll. *romperse el alma,* to break one's neck. *19* fig. *romperse la cabeza,* to rack one's brains. ¶ P. P.: *roto.*

rompiente *adj.* breaking. *2 m.* reef, rock, shoal, shore where waves break.

rompimiento *m.* break, breakage. *2* breach [gap; infringiment; quarrel]. *3* PAINT. opening in the background.

ron *m.* rum.

roncas *pl.* boastful threats, bluster; *echar* ~, to bluster.

roncador, -ra *adj.* snoring. *2 m.-f.* snorer.

roncar *intr.* to snore. *2* [of the wind, the sea] to roar. *3* to bluster, brag, play the bully.

roncear *intr.* to be slow, defer action [out of unwillingness]. *2* to wheedle, cajole.

roncería *f.* remissness, unwillingness. *2* coaxing, cajolery, cajoling expression.

roncero, -ra *adj.* slow, unwilling, grumbling. *2* wheedling, cajoling.

ronco, -ca *adj.* hoarse, husky, raucous.

roncón *m.* drone [of a bagpipe].

roncha *f.* wale, weal, welt. *2* black-and-blue mark. *3* round slice.

ronchar *intr.* to raise wales. *2 tr.* to crunch.

ronda *f.* night patrol. *2* rounds [by a night watch]; beat [of a constable, etc.]. *3* MIL. rounds. *4* party of night serenaders. *5* round [of drinks or cigars]. *6* round [in playing cards]. *7* way around a town or its walls.

rondador *m.* night stroller or serenader. *2* courter, wooer.

rondalla *f.* fable, story, tale. *2* RONDA 4.

rondar *intr.-tr.* to patrol, go the rounds [of a town, etc.] watching. *2* to walk [the street] by night. *3 tr.* to court, woo. *4* to hover about. *5* to prowl. *6* [of an illness, etc.] to be coming on [someone]. *8 intr.* MIL. to make rounds.

rondel *m.* POET. rondel.

rondeño, -ña *adj.-n.* of Ronda [andalusian town].

rondó *m.* MUS. rondo.

rondón (de) *adv.* *meterse de* ~, to enter suddenly, boldly, without calling at the door.

ronquear *intr.* to be hoarse with cold.

ronquedad *f.* hoarseness. *2* harshness [of a sound].

ronquera *f.* hoarseness [from cold].

ronquido *m.* snore. *2* harsh, raucous sound.

ronzal *m.* halter [for horses].

ronzar *tr.* to crunch. *2* NAUT. to move with a lever.

roña *f.* scab, mange [in sheep]. *2* crust of dirt. *3* rust [in metal]. *4* coll. meanness, stinginess. *5* moral infection.

roñería, roñosería *f.* meanness, stinginess.

roñoso, -sa *adj.* scabby, mangy [sheep]. *2* dirty, filthy. *3* rusty [metal]. *4* coll. mean, stingy.

ropa *f.* dry goods; stuff, fabric. *2* clothes, clothing, garments, dress: ~ *blanca,* linen; ~ *hecha,* ready-made clothes; ~ *interior,* underwear; ~ *sucia,* dirty linen; laundry [clothes to be washed]; *a quema* ~, pointblank; at close range. *3* robe, gown of office.

ropaje *m.* clothes, garb. *2* robe, gown. *3* F. ARTS drapery. *4* fig. wording, language.

ropavejería *f.* old-clothes shop.

ropavejero, -ra *m.-f.* old-clothes dealer.

ropero, -ra *m.-f.* ready-made clothier. *2* wardrobe, clothes closet. *3* charitable institution for the distribution of clothes.

ropilla *f.* a kind of doublet with sleeves.

ropita *f.* dim. child's clothing.

ropón *m.* wide, loose gown or robe.

roque *m.* CHESS rook, castle.

roquedo *m.* rock, crag.

roqueño, -ña *adj.* rocky. *2* hard, flinty.

roquero, -ra *adj.* rocky. *2* built on a rock.

roquete *m.* ECCL. rochet.

rorcual *m.* ZOOL. rorqual, finback.

rorro *m.* coll. baby, baby in arms.

ros *m.* MIL. Spanish shako.

Rosa *f. pr. n.* Rose.

rosa *f.* BOT. rose [flower]: ~ *de Jericó,* rose of Jericho; *color de* ~, rose, pink [colours]. *2* rose, rosette, anything shaped as a rose. *3* rose diamond. *4* ARCH. rose, rosace, rose window. *5* red spot [on skin]. *6* NAUT. ~ *náutica,* ~ *de los vientos,* compass card. *7 pl.* popcorn.

rosáceo, -a *adj.* rosaceous, rose-coloured. *2* BOT. rosaceous.

rosado, -da *adj.* rose, rosy, pinky. *2* rose [prepared or flavoured with roses].

rosal *m.* BOT. rose [bush or plant].

rosaleda, rosalera *f.* rosary, rose garden.

Rosalía *f. pr. n.* Rosalie.

rosario *m.* Rosary, rosary. *2* fig. string, series, succession. *3* coll. backbone. *4* chain pump.

rosbif *m.* COOK. roast beef.

rosca *f.* screw and nut. *2* screw thread: *pasarse de* ~, fig. to go too far. *3* turn [of a spiral]; coil, spiral. *4* roll twisted into a ring. *5* padded ring [for carrying things on the head]. *6* roll of fat [on neck, wrists, etc.]. *7* coll. *hacer la* ~ *a,* to flatter, cajole.

roscar *tr.* MACH. to thread.

rosco *m.* ring-shaped piece of bread or pastry.

roscón *m.* large ring-shaped piece of pastry.

rosear *intr.* to show rosy, to have a tinge of rose.

Rosellón *m. pr. n.* GEOG. Roussillon.

róseo, -a *adj.* roseate, rosy.

roséola *f.* MED. roseola.

roseta *f.* dim. small rose. *2* red spot on the cheek. *3* rose, rosehead [of watering pot]. *4 pl.* popcorn.

rosetón *m.* ARCH. rose, rosette. *2* ARCH. rose, rose window, wheel, window.

rosicler *m.* pink of dawn. *2* ruby silver.

rosillo, -lla *adj.* light red. *2* roan.

rosita *f.* dim. small rose. *2 pl.* popcorn. *3 de rositas,* free, for nothing.

roso, -sa *adj.* red. *2* threadbare. *3 a* ~ *y velloso,* totally, without exception or distinction.

rosoli *m.* rosolio [a sweet cordial].

rosquilla *f.* small ring-shaped cake.

rostrado, -da *adj.* rostrate.

rostral *m.* rostrate. *2* rostral.

rostro *m.* face, countenance: *hacer ~ a*, to face; to oppose; to accept. *2* NAUT., ORN. rostrum.

rota *f.* MIL. rout, defeat. *2* BOT. rattan. *3* Rota, Sacred Roman Rota.

rotación *f.* rotation.

rotacismo *m.* rhotacism, rotacism.

rotar *intr.* ro rotate.

rotario, -ria *adj.-n.* Rotarian.

rotativo, -va *adj.* PRINT. rotary [press.]. *2 f.* PRINT. rotary press. *3 m.* daily newspaper.

rotatorio, -ria *adj.* rotary, rotating.

roten *m.* rattan [palm & walking cane].

rotífero, -ra *adj.* ZOOL. rotiferous.

roto, -ta *irreg. p. p.* of ROMPER. *2 adj.* broken, cracked, shattered. *3* torn, worn out, ragged. *4* debaucher, licentious. *5 m.* ragged man.

rotograbado *m.* rotogravure.

rotonda *f.* rotunda. *2* rear section of a stagecoach. *3* RLY. roundhouse.

rotor *m.* ELECT. rotor.

rótula *f.* ANAT., ZOOL. rotula, kneecap.

rotulación *f.* labelling, lettering.

1) **rotular** *adj.* rotular, rotulian.

2) **rotular** *tr.* to label, letter, put a title to.

rótulo *m.* label, title. *2* sign [lettered board, etc.]. *3* poster, placard.

rotundidad *f.* roundness. *2* rotundity.

rotundo, -da *adj.* round, circular. *2* rotund [speech, style]. *3* flat, direct, round, categorical.

rotura *f.* breakage, breaking, fracture. *2* break, crack [broken place]. *3* tear, rent [in cloth, etc.].

roturar *tr.* AGR. to break up [new ground].

roya *f.* BOT. rust, mildew.

roza *f.* grubbing, weeding, clearing [of land].

rozadura *f.* rubbing. *2* chafing, abrasion. *3* chafe, gall [sore].

rozamiento *m.* rubbing, chaffing. *2* friction.

rozar *tr.* to grub, stub, weed, clear [land]. *2* to graze, browse, nibble [the grass]. *3* to scrape, rub, graze, fret, gall, chafe. *4 tr.-intr.* to graze [touch lightly in passing]. *5 ref.* [of a horse] to interfere. *6* to associate, to hobnob. *7* to have a resemblance or connection.

roznar *tr.* to crunch. *2* REBUZNAR.

roznido *m.* crunching noise. *2* REBUZNO.

rozno *m.* little donkey.

rozón *m.* short and broad scythe.

rúa *f.* street, village street. *2* cartway.

ruana *f.* a woollen fabric.

ruano, -na *adj.* ROANO.

rubefaciente *adj.-n.* MED. rubefacient.

Rubén *m. pr. n.* Reuben.

rúbeo, -a *adj.* reddish.

rubéola *f.* MED. German measles.

rubescente *adj.* rubescent.

rubeta *f.* ZOOL. a tree frog.

rubí *m.* MINER. ruby. *2* HOROL. ruby, jewel.

rubia *f.* BOT. madder. *2* a fresh-water fish. *3* blonde [girl or woman]: *~ oxigenada*, peroxide blonde.

rubiáceo, -a *adj.* BOT. rubiaceous.

rubial *adj.* reddish [soil or plant].

rubiales, *pl. -les m.-f.* coll. blond, blonde [person].

rubican *adj.* rubican.

rubicundo, -da *adj.* rubicund, ruddy. *2* reddish [hair].

rubidio *m.* CHEM. rubidium.

rubio, -bia *adj.* golden, blond, fair. *2 m.-f.* blond, blonde [person]. *3 m.* ICHTH. red gurnard. *4 m. pl.* the middle of the withers [in bulls].

rublo *m.* ruble, rouble [Russian coin].

rubor *m.* red colour. *2* blush, flush; bashfulness.

ruborizar *tr.* to cause to blush. *2 ref.* to blush, flush [become red in the face].

ruboroso, -sa *adj.* blushing, bashful.

rúbrica *f.* paraph, flourish added to one's signature. *2* rubric, title, heading. *3* ECCL. rubric: *ser de ~*, coll. to be in accordance with ritual or custom.

rubricar *tr.* to sign [a letter, document, etc.] with one's peculiar mark or flourish. *2* to sign and seal. *3* to certify to, to attest.

rubro, -bra *adj.* red, red-coloured.

rucio, -cia *adj.* gray [animal]. *2* gray-haired [person]. *3 m.* gray horse, or donkey.

ruda *f.* BOT. rue.

rudamente *adv.* roughly, rudely, harshly.

rudeza *f.* rudeness, coarseness, roughness. *2* dullness, stupidity.

rudimentario, -ria *adj.* rudimentary; elementary.

rudimento *m.* rudiment. *2 pl.* rudiments, elements.

rudo, -da *adj.* rude [rough; impolite; hard, severe]. *2* crude, rugged. *3* dull, stupid.

rueca *f.* distaff [for spinning]. *2* twist, turn.

rueda *f.* wheel: *~ de andar*, treadmill; *~ del timón*, NAUT. steering wheel: *~ de molino*, millstone; *~ dentada*, gearwheel, cogwheel; *~ hidráulica*, water wheel; *~ loca*, idle wheel; *~ motriz*, driving wheel. *2* caster, roller. *3* circle, ring [of persons or things]. *4* round slice. *5* turn, successive order. *6* ICHTH. sunfish. *7* rack [torture]. *8 hacer la ~*, [of a peacock] to spread its tail. *9 hacer la ~ a*, fig. to flatter; to court.

ruedecita *f. dim.* small wheel. *2* caster, roller.

ruedo *m.* turn, rotation. *2* circuit, circumference. *3* edge, fringe [of something round]. *4* circle, round. *5* bull ring, arena. *6* round mat; mat, rug.

ruego *m.* entreaty, prayer, petition, request.

ruezno *m.* outer rind of a walnut.

rufián *m.* pimp, pander. *2* scoundrel, villain.

rufianear *tr.* ALCAHUETAR.

rufianesco, -ca *adj.* panderly. *2* scoundrelly, villainous. *3 f.* panders or scoundrels [collect.].

rufo, -fa *adj.* red, carroty, rufous-coloured. *2* curly-haired.

rugido *m.* roar. *2* rumbling in the bowels.

rugiente *adj.* roaring.

ruginoso, -sa *adj.* rusty [metal].

rugir *intr.* [of a lion] to roar. *2* [of persons, cannon, thunder, etc.] to roar, bellow.

rugosidad *f.* rugosity, ruggedness.

rugoso, -sa *adj.* rugous, rugose, rugged, wrinkled.

ruibarbo *m.* BOT. rhubarb.

ruido *m.* noise: *hacer ~*, to make a noise. *2* discussion, quarrel, row. *3* ado, fuss: *mucho ~ y pocas nueces*, much ado about nothing.

ruidoso, -sa *adj.* noisy, loud. *2* clamorous. *3* sensational.

ruin *adj.* mean, vile, base, despicable. *2* mean, poor, paltry, sorry. *3* little, stunted. *4* mean, niggardly, stingy. *5* low-minded, rascally, treacherous. *6* vicious [animal]. *7 m.* rascal, scoundrel.

ruina *f.* ruin: *amenazar ~*, to begin to fall to pieces. *2* wreck [person, building]. *4 pl.* ruins.

ruindad *f.* meanness, baseness, vileness. *2* meanness, stinginess. *3* mean or base action.

ruinoso, -sa *adj.* ruinous [in ruins, dilapidated, tottering]. *2* ruinous [bringing ruin].

ruiseñor *m.* ORN. nightingale.

ruleta *f.* roulette [gambling game].

rulo *m.* large ball. *2* conical stone [of olive-oil mills]. *3* roller, road roller.
Rumanía *f. pr. n.* GEOG. Rumania.
rumano, -na *adj.-n.* Rumanian.
rumba *f.* (Am.) rumba [dance and music].
rumbo *m.* NAUT. rhumb, bearing, course, direction: *con ~ a*, bound for, in the direction of. *2* fig. course, trend, way. *3* coll. pomp, ostentation. *4* coll. liberality, generosity.
rumboso, -sa *adj.* ostentatious, magnificent. *2* liberal, generous.
rumi *m.* [among the Moors] Christian.
rumia *f.* rumination.
rumiadura *f.* RUMIA.
rumiante *adj.* ZOOL. ruminant.
rumiar *tr.* to ruminate [chew the cud]. *2* to ruminate, meditate. *3* fig. to grumble.
rumo *m.* first hoop of a cask.
rumor *m.* rumbling sound, murmur. *2* buzz; noise of voices. *3* rumour, report.
rumorearse *impers.* to be rumoured.
rumoroso, -sa *adj.* noisy, rumbling, murmurous.
runa *f.* rune, runic character.
runfla, runflada *f.* string, series [of things].
rúnico, -ca; runo, -na *adj.* runic.
runrún *m.* rumour, report.
runrunearse *impers.* to be rumoured.
ruñar *tr.* to croze [a stave].
rupestre *adj.* rupestrian.

rupia *f.* rupee [indian coin]. *2* MED. rupia.
ruptura *f.* rupture [breach of harmonious relations]. *2* breaking, fracture.
ruqueta *f.* BOT. rocket. *2* BOT. hedge mustard.
rural *adj.* rural, country.
Rusia *f. pr. n.* GEOG. Russia.
rusiente *adj.* candent, red-hot.
ruso, -sa *adj.-n.* Russian. *2 m.* Russian [language]. *3* ulster [overcoat].
rusticano, -na *adj.* wild [plant].
rusticar *intr.* to rusticate.
rusticidad *adj.* rusticity.
rústico, -ca *adj.* rural. *2* rustic. *3* rough, clumsy. *4* unmannerly. *5* Vulgar [latin]. *6 m.* rustic, peasant. *7* BOOKB. *en rústica*, paperbound.
ruta *f.* route, way. *2* NAUT. navigation route, course.
rutáceo, -a *adj.* BOT. rutaceous.
rutenio *m.* CHEM. ruthenium.
rutilante *adj.* poet, shining, sparkling, scintillating.
rutilar *intr.* poet. to shine, sparkle, scintillate.
rutilo *m.* MINER. rutile.
rútilo, -la *adj.* golden, bright, shining.
rutina *f.* routine [course of action, etc., adhered to through force of habit]. *2* CHEM. rutin.
rutinario, -ria *adj.* routine, routinish. *2 m.-f.* routinist.
ruzafa *f.* garden, park.

S

S, s *f.* S, s, twenty-second letter of the Spanish alphabet.

Sabá *f. pr. n.* HIST., GEOG. Sheba.

sábado *m.* Saturday: ~ *santo*, Holy Saturday. 2 Sabbath [among the Jews].

sábalo *m.* ICHTH. shad.

sábana *f.* sheet [for a bed]. 2 altarcloth.

sabana *f.* savanna, savannah [treeless plain].

sabandija *f.* nasty insect or small reptile. 2 fig. vile person, vermin.

sabanero, -ra *adj.* (Am.) [pertaining to the] savanna. 2 *m.-f.* savanna, dweller.

sabanilla *f. dim.* small sheet or piece of linen [towel, napkin, etc.]. 2 outer altar cloth.

sabañón *m.* chilblain.

sabático, -ca *adj.* Sabbatical; sabbatical.

sabatina *f.* ECCL. Saturday office.

sabatino, -na *f.* [pertaining to] Saturday.

sabedor, -ra *adj.* knowing, informed.

sabeísmo *m.* Sabaism.

sabelotodo *m.-f.* SABIDILLO.

1) **saber** *m.* knowledge, learning, information.

2) **saber** *tr.* to know [have cognizance of, be apprised or informed of], to be wise to: *hacer* ~, to inform, to let know: *no sé cuantos*, so-and-so, what's his name; *no sé qué, cierto no sé qué, un no sé qué*, a certain something; *¡y qué sé yo!*, and what not, and so forth. 2 to know [posses in the memory]. 3 to know, be able, know how: *Pedro sabe escribir*, Peter can, or knows how to, write. 4 *tr.-intr.* ~ *ir a*, ~ *a*, to know the way to. 5 *intr.* to know: *a* ~, namely, viz.; *que yo sepa*, as far as I know. 6 to be learned, informed. 7 ~ *a*, to taste of, taste like; to smack of. ¶ CONJUG.: INDIC. Pres.: *sé, sabes, sabe; sabemos, sabéis, saben.* | Imperf.: *sabía, sabías*, etc. | Pret.: *supe, supiste, supo; supimos, supisteis, supieron.* | Fut.: *sabré, sabrás*, etc. | COND.: *sabría, sabrías*, etc. | SUBJ. Pres.: *sepa, sepas, sepa; sepamos, sepáis, sepan.* | Imperf.: *supiera, supieras, supiera; supiéramos, supierais, supieran*, or *supiese, supieses, supiese, supieses; supiésemos, supieseis, supiesen.* | Fut.: *supiere, supieres, supiere; supiéremos, supiereis, supieren.* | IMPER.: *sabe, sepa; sepamos, sabed, sepan.* | PAST. P.: sabido. | GER.: sabiendo.

sabiamente *adv.* wisely, prudently.

sabidillo, -lla *adj.-n.* coll. pedant, know-it-all.

sabido, -da *adj.* known. 2 learned, well-informed.

sabiduría *f.* knowledge, learning. 2 wisdom, sapience, sageness.

sabiendas (a) *adv.* knowingly, consciously.

sabihondo, -da *adj.* know-it-all. 2 *m.-f.* know-it-all, wiseacre.

sabina *f.* BOT. savin.

sabino, -na *adj.* roan [horse]. 2 *adj.-n.* HIST. Sabine.

sabio, -bia *adj.* knowing, learned; sage, sapient, wise. 2 skilled, skilful. 3 trained [animal]. 4 *m.-f.* learned person, scholar, scientist; wise person.

sablazo *m.* stroke with a sabre; wound from a sabre. 2 coll. instance of borrowing or sponging.

sable *m.* sabre, saber. 2 *adj.-n.* HER. sable.

sablista *m.* coll. sponger, one who asks for petty loans of money.

sablón *m.* coarse sand.

saboga *f.* SÁBALO.

sabogal *m.* net for catching shad.

sabor *m.* taste, flavour, relish, savour, sapor.

saboreamiento *m.* flavouring. 2 relishing.

saborear *tr.* to flavour, give a zest or relish to. 2 fig. to allure, entice. 3 *tr.-ref.* to relish, enjoy.

sabotaje *m.* sabotage.

saboteador, -ra *m.-f.* saboteur.

sabotear *tr.* to sabotage.

Saboya *pr. n.* GEOG. Savoy.

saboyano, -na *adj.* Savoyard.

sabroso, -sa *adj.* savoury, tasty, palatable. 2 pleasant, delightful.

sabucal *m.* grove of elders.

sabuco *m.* SAÚCO.

sabueso *m.* hound, bloodhound [dog]. 2 fig. tracer, sleuth.

sabugal *m.* SABUCAL.

sabuloso, -sa *adj.* sabulous.

saburra *f.* MED. saburra. 2 MED. coat on the tongue.

saburroso, -sa *adj.* MED. saburral. 2 coated [tongue].

saca *f.* extraction. 2 exportation. 3 sack, large bag.

sacabalas, *pl.* **-las** *m.* ARTILL. bullet screw.

sacabocado(s *m.* hollow punch; ticket punch.

sacabotas, *pl.* **-tas** *m.* bootjack.

sacacorchos, *pl.* **-chos** *m.* corkscrew.

sacadinero(s *m.* coll. catchpenny. 2 coll. bamboozler.

sacamiento *m.* taking out, drawing out.

sacamuelas, *pl.* **-las** *m.* coll. tooth puller, dentist. 2 coll. charlatán, quack.

sacanete *m.* lansquenet [card game].

sacaperras, *pl.* **-rras** *adj.* slot, gambling [machine].

sacar *tr.* to draw, draw out, bring out, take out, pull out, extract. 2 to except, exclude. 3 to get out, free: ~ *de pobreza,* to free from poverty. 4 to withdraw, retire. 5 to draw, get, obtain, derive, elicit. 6 to extort. 7 to draw, infer, deduce, make out, solve: ~ *en claro,* or *en limpio,* to deduce, conclude clearly. 8 to publish, bring out, invent, produce. 9 to introduce [a fashion, etc.]. 10 to show, produce, exhibit. 11 to put forth [strength, etc.]. 12 to put out, thrust out, stick out, protrude. 13 to take [a photo], to make [a copy]. 14 to imitate, copy. 15 to take, buy [a ticket]. 16 to draw [a sword, a pistol]. 17 PELOTA. to serve [the ball]. 18 to cite, quote. 19 ~ *a bailar,* to lead out for a dance. 20 ~ *adelante,* to bring up, rear; to pull through. 12 ~ *a luz,* to print, publish; to reveal. 22 ~ *a relucir,* to mention, drag in. 23 ~ *de quicio,* to strain [things]; to exasperate. 24 ~ *la cara por uno,* to stand or to answer, for someone. 25 ~ *la cuenta,* to figure out.

sacarímetro *m.* saccharimeter.

sacarino, -na *adj.* saccharine. 2 *f.* CHEM. saccharine.

sacarosa *f.* CHEM. saccharose.

sacasillas, *pl.* **-sillas** *m.* THEAT. stage hand.

sacatrapos, *pl.* **-pos** *m.* ARTIL. wormer, wad hook.

sacerdocio *m.* priesthood.

sacerdotal *adj.* sacerdotal.

sacerdote *m.* priest. 2 Roman Catholic priest.

sacerdotisa *f.* priestess.

sácere *m.* BOT. maple.

saciar *tr.* to satiate, so sate. 2 *ref.* to become satiated or sated.

saciedad *f.* satiety: *hasta la* ~, to satiety.

saco *m.* bag, sack: ~ *de noche,* handbag; *no echar en* ~ *roto,* coll. not to forget, not to overlook. 2 bagful, sackful. 3 ANAT., BOT., ZOOL. sac. 4 loosefitting coat. 5 (Am.) coat [of a man's suit]. 6 sack, pillage, plunder; *entrar a* ~, to sack plunder, loot.

sacra *f.* ECCL. sacring tablet.

sacramentado, -da *adj.* transubstantiated: *Jesús Sacramentado,* the consecrated Host. 2 having received the last sacraments.

sacramental *adj.* sacramental.

sacramentar *tr.* THEOL. to transubstantiate. 2 to administer the last sacraments to.

sacramento *m.* ECCL. sacrament: *el Santísimo Sacramento,* the Blessed or Holy Sacrament.

sacratísimo, -ma *adj.* most sacred or holy.

sacre *m.* ORN., ARTIL. saker.

sacrificador, -ra *adj.* sacrificing. 2 *m.-f.* sacrificer.

sacrificar *tr.* to sacrifice. 2 to slaughter [kill for the market]. 3 *ref.* to sacrifice oneself. 4 to devote oneself to God.

sacrificio *m.* sacrifice: ~ *del altar, Santo Sacrificio,* Sacrifice of the Mass. 2 self-sacrifice.

sacrilegio *m.* sacrilege.

sacrílego, -ga *adj.* sacrilegious.

sacristán *m.* socristan, sexton, parish clerk.

sacristana *f.* sexton's wife. 2 nun in charge of the sacristy.

sacristía *f.* sacristy, vestry.

sacro, -cra *adj.* sacred, holy. 2 ANAT. sacral. 3 *m.* ANAT., ZOOL. sacrum.

sacrosanto, -ta *adj.* sacred, sacrosanct.

sacudida *f.* shake, shaking, jerk, jolt. 2 shock, mental shock.

sacudidor *m.* duster [stick, etc., for dusting].

sacudimiento *m.* shake, shaking, jerk; shaking off.

sacudir *tr.* to shake, jerk, jolt. 2 to beat, dust; to beat out [the dust]. 3 to deal [a blow]. 4 to beat, drub [someone]. 5 *ref.* to shake off.

sáculo *m.* ANAT. saccule.

sachar *tr.* AGR. to weed.

sacho *m.* weeder, weeding hoe.

sádico, -ca *adj.* sadist, sadistic. 2 *m.-f.* sadist.

sadismo *m.* sadism.

saduceo, -a *adj.* Sadducean. 2 *m.-f.* Sadducee.

saeta *f.* arrow [missile]. 2 hand, pointer [of watch, clock, etc.]. 3 magnetic needle. 4 a popular Andalousian spiritual song.

saetada *f.,* **saetazo** *m.* arrow shot. 2 arrow wound.

saetero, -ra *adj.* arrow, pertaining to arrows. 2 *m.* archer, bowman. 3 *f.* FORT. loophole.

saetilla *f. dim.* small arrow. 2 SAETA 2 & 3.

saetín *m.* millrace, flume. 2 brad.

safena *f. adj.* ANAT. saphenous.

sáfico, -ca *adj.-m.* PROS. Sapphic.

saga *f.* saga. 2 sorceress.

sagacidad *f.* sagacity, sagaciousness.

sagaz *adj.* sagacious, shrewd. 2 keen-scented [dog].

sagita *f.* GEOM. part of radius between the middle of an arc and its chord.

sagitado, -da *adj.* BOT., ZOOL. sagittate, sagittated.

sagitaria *f.* BOT. arrowhead.

sagitario *m.* archer. 2 (cap.) ASTR. Sagittarius.

sagrado, -da *adj.* sacred. 2 hallowed, holy. 3 *m.* asylum, place of refuge, sanctuary.

sagrario *m.* sacrarium.

sagú *m.* BOT. sago, sago palm. 2 sago [starch].

saguntino, -na *adj.-n.* Saguntian.

Sahara *m. pr. n.* GEOG. Sahara.

sahornarse *ref.* [of the skin or a part of the body] to get sore or chafed.

sahorno *m.* chafe, chafing [of the skin].

sahumador *m.* perfuming pan. 2 clotheshorse.

sahumar *tr.* to perfume, fumigate [with odorous smoke].

sahumerio, sahúmo *m.* perfuming, fumigation. 2 odorous smoke. 3 aromatics burnt as perfumes.

sain *m.* grease, fat [of animals]. 2 greasiness [on clothes].

sainete *m.* THEAT. one-act comedy. 2 seasoning, sauce. 3 flavour, relish, spice, zest. 4 tidbit, delicacy.

sainetero, sainetista *m.* writer of one-act comedies.

saíno *m.* ZOOL. wild boar of South America.

sajadura *f.* cut, incision [on the flesh].

sajar *tr.* to cut, make incisions on [the flesh].

sajón, -na *adj.-n.* Saxon.

Sajonia *f. pr. n.* GEOG. Saxony, Saxe.

sal *f.* salt [sodium chloride]: ~ *gema,* rock salt. 2 fig. wit, wittiness: ~ *ática,* Attic salt or wit. 3 fig. charm, grace, winning manners. 4 CHEM. salt: ~ *de la Higuera,* Epsom salts. 5 CHEM. ~ *amoníaca* or *amoníaco,* sal ammoniac.

sala *f.* drawing-room, living room, parlour. 2 hall, large room, room: ~ *de clase,* classroom; ~ *de espectáculos,* auditorium [of a theatre, cinema, etc.]; ~ *de espera,* waiting-room. 3 ward [in a hospital]. 4 LAW division of an *Audiencia,* court, law court.

salabardo *m.* scoop net, dip net.

salacidad *f.* salacity, lechery.

salacot *m.* topee, topi, pith hat, pith helmet, sun helmet.

saladar *m.* salt marsh. *2* saline ground.

saladero *m.* salting place, salting house or room.

salado, -da *adj.* salty, briny; brine-soaked, salt, salted: *pesca salada*, salt fish, salted fish. *2* coll. witty, amusing. *3* coll. charming, graceful, winsome. *4* (Am.) expensive.

salamandra *f.* ZOOL., MYTH. salamander: ~ *acuática*, newt. *2* a kind of heating stove.

salamandria *f.* SALAMANQUESA.

salamanquesa *f.* ZOOL. tarente.

salangana *f.* ORN. salangane.

salar *tr.* to salt [season or preserve with salt], to corn [meat]. *2* COOK. to put too much salt on.

salario *m.* wages, salary.

salaz *adj.* salacious, lecherous.

salazón *f.* salting [of meat or fish]. *2* salt meat or fish. *3* salt-meat, salt-meat business.

salceda *f.*, **salcedo** *m.* willow grove, salicetum.

salcochar *tr.* COOK. to boil.

salchicha *f.* sausage.

salchichón *m. aug.* large sausage.

saldado, -da *adj.* paid [debt]; settled [account].

saldar *tr.* to settle, liquidate [an account]. *2* to sell [goods] at reduced prices.

saldista *m.-f.* liquidation broker; remnant dealer.

saldo *m.* COM. balance [of an account]. *2* settlement, liquidation. *3* remainder of goods sold at reduced prices.

saldré, saldría, etc. *irr.* V. SALIR.

saledizo, -za *adj.* projecting. *2 m.* SALIDIZO.

salegar *m.* place for giving salt to cattle.

salero *m.* salt cellar, saltshaker. *2* storage place for salt. *3* SALEGAR. *4* coll. nimble-wit, address, easy and graceful deportment.

saleroso, -sa *adj.* lively, charming, graceful, winsome.

salesa *adj.-f.* Salesian [of the Order of Visitation].

salesiano, -na *adj.* Salesian [of the order of men founded by Dom Bosco]. *2 m.* Salesian father.

saleta *f. dim.* little drawing room.

salgar *tr.* to feed salt to [cattle].

salgo, salga, etc. *irr.* V. SALIR.

salicáceo, -a *adj.* BOT. salicaceous.

salicaria *f.* BOT. loosestrife, purple loosestrife.

salicilato *m.* CHEM. salicylate.

salicílico, -ca *adj.* CHEM. salicylic.

sálico, -ca *adj.* Salic.

salicor *f.* BOT. saltwort, prickly saltwort.

salida *f.* going out, coming out, outgoing, outcoming, egress, exit, issue emergence. *2* start, departure, leaving. *3* excursion, outing. *4* MIL. sally, sortie. *5* discharge [of a liquid, etc.]. *6* springing, sprouting, growing [of buds, leaves, hair, etc.]. *7* rise [of the sun, the moon, etc.]. *8* coming out, publication. *9* outlay, expenditure. *10* COM. sale, salableness: *tener* ~, to sell well; fig. [of a young lady] to be popular with the young men. *11* exit, outlet, issue, vent, way out. *12* end [of a street; of the winter, summer, etc.]. *13* outlaying fields [near a town gate]. *14* issue termination. *15* sally, witty remark. *16* salient, jut, projection. *17* NAUT. headway. *18* lead [at games]. *19* SPORT. start. *20* ~ *de baño*, bathrobe. *21* ~ *de teatro*, opera cloak. *22* ~ *de tono*, rude or irrelevant remark.

salidizo *m.* ARCH. projection, ledge, corbel.

salido, -da *adj.* salient, projecting.

saliente *adj.* salient, projecting. *2* GEOM. salient [angle]. *3* outgoing. *4 m.* salient, jut, prominence. *5* east, sunrise.

salificar *tr.* CHEM. to salify.

salina *f.* salt mine. *2* salt pit, salt pan, saltworks.

salinero *adj.* spotted red and white [bull]. *2 m.* salt maker, salt dealer, salter.

salir *intr.* to go out, come out, issue; to sally. *2* to depart, leave, start, set out. *3* to get out [of a vehicle]. *4* to project, protrude, start, stand out. *5* to appear. *6* THEAT. to enter. *7* [of a book, etc.] to come out. *8* to spring, come [of], issue [from], originate [in]. *9* to offer, present itself; to be offered to one. *10* [of a season] to end. *11* [of a stain] to come off. *12* [of the sun] to rise. *13* [of hair, plants, etc.] to spring, shoot, grow. *14* to come, result, turn out. *15* to come out [from a contest, etc.] to be: ~ *vencedor*, to win; to be the victor. *16* to be first to play [in certain games]. *17* to be drawn [in a lottery]. *18* to be elected [by ballot]. *19* to cost [a price]. *20* [of a stream] to debouch. *21* [of a street, road, etc.] to lead [to]. *22* to take after, resemble. *23* ~ *adelante*, to be successful. *24* ~ *al encuentro*, to come out to meet; to oppose. *25* ~ *bien*, to do well, come right. *26* ~ *con*, to come out with [an unexpected, or irrelevant remark, etc.]. *27* ~ *[uno] de sus casillas*, to lose one's temper. *28* ~ *mal*, to do badly; to fail. *29 salga lo que saliese*, whatever may happen. *30 ref.* [of a vessel] to leak. *31* to run over, overflow. *32* to come out [of its socket, etc.]. *33 salirse con la suya*, to have one's way.

¶ IRREG. CONJUG.: INDIC. Pres.: *salgo*, sales, sale; salimos, salís, salen. | Fut.: *saldré, saldrás, saldrá; saldremos, saldréis, saldrán.* | COND.: *saldría, saldrías, saldría; saldríamos, saldríais, saldrían.* | SUBJ. Pres.: *salga, salgas, salga; salgamos, salgáis, salgan.* | IMPER.: *sal, salga; salgamos*, salid, *salgan.*

salitral *adj.* SALITROSO. *2 m.* saltpetre bed.

salitre *m.* saltpetre, saltpeter, nitre, niter.

salitroso, -sa *adj.* saltpetrous, nitrous.

saliva *f.* saliva, spittle: *tragar* ~, coll. to suffer an offence, vexation, etc. in silence.

salivación *f.* salivation.

salival *adj.* salivary.

salivazo *m.* spit [spitted saliva].

salmantino, -na *adj.-n.* [of] Salamanca.

salmear *tr.* to sing psalms.

salmista *m.* psalmist. *2* ECCL. chanter of psalms.

salmo *m.* psalm.

salmodia *f.* psalmody. *2* fig. singsong.

salmodiar *intr.* to sing psalms, salmodize. *2 tr.* to singsong, sing monotonously.

salmón *m.* ICHTH. salmon.

salmonado, -da *adj.* salmon-like. *2* salmon [in colour].

salmonete *m.* ICHTH. red mullet, surmullet.

salmuera *f.* brine, pickle.

salobral *adj.* saline [ground]. *2 m.* saline ground.

salobre *adj.* brackish, briny, saltish.

salobreño, -ña *adj.* saline [ground].

salobridad *f.* saltiness, brackishness.

saloma *f.* NAUT. chantey.

Salomé *f. pr. n.* Salome.

Salomón *m. pr. n.* Solomon.

salomónico, -ca *adj.* Solomonic. *2* ARCH. twisted [column].

salón *m.* drawing room, reception room. *2* hall, large room, assembly hall: ~ *de baile*, ballroom. *3* saloon. *4* ~ *de belleza*, beauty parlour.

salpicadero *m.* dashboard [in cars].
salpicadura *f.* splash, splashing, spattering. *2 pl.* fig. indirect results.
salpicar *tr.* to splash, bespatter, sprinkle. *2* to intersperse. *3* fig. to read or touch on without order.
salpicón *m.* salmagundi. *2* SALPICADURA.
salpimentar *tr.* to season with pepper and salt. *2* fig. to spice, intersperse. ¶ CONJUG. like *acertar*.
salpresar *tr.* to preserve with salt.
salpullido *m.* rash, fine eruption. *2* flea bites.
salpullir *tr.* to cause a rash. *2 ref.* to break out [have a rash]. ¶ CONJUG. like *mullir*.
salsa *f.* COOK. gravy, dressing, sauce. *2* fig. sauce [something that adds piquancy].
salsedumbre *f.* saltiness.
salsera *f.* sauceboat; gravy boat, gravy dish.
salserilla *f. dim.* small saucer [to mix paints].
salsifí *m.* BOT. salsify.
saltabanco(s *m.* mountebank. *2* juggler, tumbler.
saltación *f.* saltation, leaping, dancing.
saltadizo, -za *adj.* jumping, leaping. *2* hopping [insect]. *3 m.-f.* jumper, leaper. *4 m.* skipping rope.
saltamontes *m.* ENT. grasshopper.
saltante *adj.* jumping, leaping. *2* salient.
saltar *intr.* to spring, jump, leap, bounce, hop, skip. *2* [of water, etc.] to spurt, jet, shoot up. *3* [of sparks, etc.] to fly. *4* to snap, burst, break off: ~ *en pedazos*, to fly into pieces. *5* [of a button, etc.] to come off. *6* to project, stand out. *7* to start, show emotion or resentment. *8* to come out with [an irrelevant or unexpected remark]. *9* NAUT. [of the wind] to shift. *10* ~ *a la vista*, to be self-evident. *11 tr.* to jump over, leap [a wall, ditch, etc.]. *12* to skip, to do [something] desultorily. *13 tr.-ref.* to skip, omit.
saltarín, -na *adj.* jumping, dancing. *2 m.-f.* jumper, dancer. *3 m.* feather-brained youth.
salteador *m.* footpad, highwayman.
salteamiento *m.* highway robbery, assault, holdup.
saltear *tr.* to hold up, rob on the high way. *2* to assault, attack. *3* to skip, to do [something] desultorily. *4* COOK. to sauté.
salterio *m.* Psalter. *2* Rosary. *3* MUS. psaltery.
saltimbanco, saltimbanqui *m.* SALTABANCO.
salto *m.* spring, jump, leap, bound, hop, skip: ~ *de altura*, SPORT. high jump; ~ *de agua*, waterfall, falls; ~ *de carnero*, bucking [of a horse]; ~ *en el vacío*, leap in the dark; ~ *mortal*, somersault; *dar un* ~, to jump, leap; *a* ~ *de mata*, flying and hiding; *en un* ~, in a flash, quickly. *2* SWIM. dive. *3* skip, omission. *4* palpitation [of heart]. *5* leapfrog.
saltón, -na *adj.* jumping. *2* prominent, protruding. *3 m.* ENT. small grasshopper.
salubre *adj.* salubrious, healthful.
salubridad *f.* salubrity, healthfulness.
salud *f.* health: *¡a su* ~*!*, to your health!; *gastar* ~, to enjoy good health; *vender* or *verter* ~, to radiate health. *2* welfare. *3* salvation. *4 interj.* coll. greetings!, hello!
saludable *adj.* salutary, healthful, wholesome.
saludador, -ra *m.-f.* greeter, saluter. *3 m.* a kind of quack doctor.
saludar *tr.* to greet, salute, hail, to give greetings or regards to. *2* MIL. to salute. *3* MIL. to fire a salute to. *4* NAUT. to dip the flag to.
saludo *m.* greeting, salutation, salute, bow. *2* MIL. salute. *3 pl.* compliments, regards.
salumbre *f.* flower of salt.

salutación *f.* salutation, greeting.
salutífero, -ra *adj.* salutiferous, healthful, wholesome.
salva *f.* salvo: ~ *de aplausos*, salvo or round of applause. *2* salutation, welcome. *3* obs. tasting of viands before are served. *4* SALVILLA.
salvabarros, *pl.* -rros *m.* mudguard.
salvación *f.* salvation, saving. *2* escape, deliverance.
salvadera *f.* sandbox [for sprinkling and on ink].
salvado *m.* bran.
salvador, -ra *adj.* saving, rescuing, delivering. *2 m.-f.* saviour, rescuer, deliverer: *el Salvador*, the Saviour; El Salvador [American country].
salvaguarda *f.* SALVAGUARDIA.
salvaguardia *f.* safeguard, protection, security. *2* safeguard, safe-conduct. *3 m.* guard watch.
salvajada *f.* savagery, brutal action. *2* stupid action.
salvaje *adj.* savage. *2* wild [country, land, beast, plant]. *3* brutish, rude, stupid. *4 m.-f.* savage.
salvajería *f.* SALVAJADA.
salvajino, -na *adj.* wild [beast, plant]; of wild beast. *3 f.* wild beasts. *4* game [flesh of wild beasts].
salvajismo *m.* savagery.
salvamanteles *m.* table mat.
salvamento, salvamiento *m.* saving, rescuing. *2* salvage. *3* lifesaving. *4* place of safety.
salvante *adj.* saving. *2 adv.* saving, excepting.
salvar *tr.* to save, rescue, deliver. *2* to save [in a spiritual sense]. *3* to salve, salvage. *4* to overcome [a difficulty]. *5* to go over, negotiate, bridge; to clear, surmount [an obstacle]; to cover [a distance]. *6* to make an exception of. *7 ref.* to be saved. *8* to escape danger: *sálvese el que pueda*, everyone for himself.
salvavidas, *pl.* -das *m.* NAUT. life preserver, life belt: *bote* ~, lifeboat. *2* guard [in front of electric cars].
¡salve! *interj.* hail! *2 f.* salve, Salve regina.
salvedad *f.* reservation, exception, qualification.
salvia *f.* BOT. sage, salvia.
salvilla *f.* tray for glasses or cups.
1) **salvo** *adv.* save, saving, excepting, barring.
2) **salvo, -va** *adj.* saved, safe: *a* ~, safe, out of danger. *2* excepted, omitted: *dejar a* ~, to set aside, make an exception of.
salvoconducto *m.* safe-conduct.
sallar *tr.* AGR. to weed.
sámago *m.* sapwood.
sámara *f.* BOT. samara.
samaritano, -na *adj.-n.* Samaritan.
samario *m.* CHEM. samarium.
sambenito *m.* fig. dishonour, disgrace. *2* note of infamy; disgrace.
samblaje *m.* ENSAMBLADURA.
sambuca *f.* MUS. sambuke. *2* MIL. an ancient war engine.
samio, mia *adj.-n.* Samian.
samnita, samnite *adj.-n.* Samnite.
samoano, -na *adj.-n.* Samoan.
Samotracia *f. pr. n.* GEOG. Samothrace.
samoyedo, -da *adj.-n.* Samoyed, Samoyede.
sampán *m.* NAUT. sampan.
san *adj.* apocopated form of SANTO, used only before masculine names of saints, except Tomás, Tomé, Toribio and Domingo.
sanable *adj.* curable, healable.
sanador, -ra *adj.* healing. *2 m.-f.* curer, healer.

sanar *tr.* to heal, cure. *2 intr.* to heal; to recover sickness.
sanativo, -va *adj.* sanative, curative.
sanatorio *m.* sanatorium, sanitarium.
sanción *f.* sanction. *2* ratification of an act of Parliament by the king or the President.
sancionable *adj.* sanctionable.
sancionar *tr.* to sanction. *2* to ratify [an act of Parliament].
sancochar *tr.* COOK. to parboil [boil partially].
sancocho *m.* parboiled meat.
sancta *m.* fore part of tabernacle.
sanctasanctórum, *pl.* **-rum** *m.* sanctum sanctorum.
sanctus *m.* ECCL. Sanctus.
sandalia *f.* sandal.
sándalo *m.* BOT. sandalwood. *2* BOT. bergamot mint.
sandáraca *f.* sandarac.
sandez *f.* stupidity, silliness. *2* inanity, foolish or stupid act or remark, piece of nonsense.
sandía *f.* BOT. watermelon.
sandio, -dia *adj.* stupid, foolish, silly.
sandunga *f.* charm, easy and graceful deportment.
sandunguero, -ra *adj.* charming, graceful, winsome.
sandwich *m.* Angl. sandwich.
saneado, -da *adj.* free from charges or deductions [property, income, etc.].
saneamiento *m.* sanitation. *2* drainage [of land]. *3* reparation.
sanear *tr.* to improve the sanitary conditions of. *2* to drain [lands]. *3* to repair, improve.
sanedrín *m.* Sanhedrin.
sangrador *m.* bloodletter. *2* drain, outlet.
sangradura *f.* SANGRÍA 1 & 6. *2* drain, outlet.
sangrar *tr.* SURG. to bleed. *2* to drain, open an outlet in. *3* RESINAR. *4* PRINT. to indent. *5 intr.* to bleed [emit blood]. *6 ref.* to have oneself bled.
sangre *f.* blood [liquid; temperament; race, family]; gore: ~ *fría*, cold blood; sangfroid, serenity; *mala* ~, wicked or revengeful disposition; *subírsele a uno la* ~ *a la cabeza*, to lose one's self-control; *tener* ~ *de horchata*, to be phlegmatic; *a* ~ *caliente*, impulsively; *a* ~ *fría*, in cold blood; *a* ~ *y fuego*, by fire and sword.
sangría *f.* SURG. bleeding, bloodletting. *2* fig. bleeding [draining of money, etc.]. *3* tap, tapping [in a pine, a furnace, etc.]. *4* PRINT. indentation. *5* inner pit of the arm opposite to the elbow. *6* sangaree.
sangriento, -ta *adj.* bleeding, bloody, gory. *2* sanguinary. *3* cruel, savage. *4* poet. blood-red.
sangüesa *f.* FRAMBUESA.
sanguificación *f.* PHYSIOL. sanguification.
sanguijuela *f.* ZOOL. leech. *2* fig. leech [person].
sanguina *f.* sanguine [crayon; drawing].
sanguinaria *f.* MINER. bloodstone. *2* BOT. ~ *mayor*, knotgrass; ~ *menor*, witlowwort.
sanguinario, -ria *adj.* sanguinary bloodthirsty.
sanguíneo, -a *adj.* sanguineous. *2* sanguine [temperament].
sanguinolencia *f.* sanguinolency.
sanguinolento, -ta *adj.* sanguinolent, bloody, bloodstained.
sanguiñuelo *m.* CORNEJO.
sanguis *m.* blood of Christ, consecrated wine.
sanguisorba *f.* BOT. burnet.
sanícula *f.* BOT. sanicle.
sanidad *f.* soundness, health, healthfulness; ~ *mi-*

litar, Army Medicine Corps; ~ *pública,* public health, health department.
sanie, sanies *f.* MED. sanies.
sanitario, -ria *adj.* sanitary. *2 m.* MIL. officer or soldier of the Medicine Corps.
sanjuaneño, -ña, sanjuanero, -ra *adj.* ripe by St. John's Day [fruit].
sanjuanista *m.* knight of St. John of Jerusalem.
sanmiguelada *f.* Michaelmastide.
sano, -na *adj.* healthy, in good health, hale, fit. *2* healthful; salutary, wholesome. *3* sound [body, mind, fruit, doctrine, policy, etc.]; harmless: ~ *y salvo,* safe and sound. *4* whole [not broken]. *5* wise, discreet. *6* fig. *cortar por lo* ~, to take drastic measures.
sánscrito, -ta *adj.-m.* Sanskrit.
sanseacabó *interj.* coll. finished!
sansirolée *m.-f.* simpleton.
Sansón *m. pr. n.* BIBL. & fig. Samson.
santa *f.* female saint. *2* Saint, St. [before feminine names]. *3* saintly, virtuous woman.
santabárbara *f.* NAUT. magazine, powder room.
santaláceo, -a *adj.* BOT. santalaceous.
santamente *adv.* in a saintly manner, like a saint, virtuously. *2* coll. well, discreetly, wisely.
santanderino, -na *adj.-n.* of Santander.
Santelmo m. *fuego de* ~, St. Elmo's fire.
santero, -ra *m.-f.* caretaker of a sanctuary. *3* collector of alms who carries a saint's image.
Santiago *m. pr. n.* James. *2* Saint James.
santiagués, -sa *adj.-n.* of Santiago de Compostela.
santiaguino, -na *adj.* pertaining to Santiago de Chile. *2 m.-f.* native or inhabitant of Santiago de Chile.
santiaguista *m.* knight of Santiago.
santiamén (en un) *adv.* in an instant, in a jiffy, in the twinkling of an eye.
santidad *f.* sanctity, saintliness, holiness, godliness. *2 Su Santidad,* His Holiness [the Pope].
santificación *f.* sanctification.
santificador, -ra *adj.* santifying. *2 m.-f.* sanctifier.
santificar *tr.* to sanctify. *2* to hallow. *3* ~ *las fiestas,* to keep holy days. *4 ref.* to become sanctified.
santiguada *f.* act of blessing or crossing oneself.
santiguador, -ra *m.-f.* person pretending to effect cures by crossing the patients.
santiguar *tr.* to bless, cross, make the sign of the cross upon. *2* to treat sickness superstitiously by signs of the cross. *3 ref.* to bless oneself, to cross oneself.
santimonia *f.* sanctity, saintliness, holiness.
santísimo, -ma *adj. superl.* of SANTO. *2* most holy. *3 m. el Santísimo,* the blessed Sacrament.
santito, -ta *m.-f. dim.* little saint. *2* fig. good child.
santo, -ta *adj.* canonized by the Church. *2* saint, holy, sacred, blessed: *el Santo Patrón,* the Holy Father. *3* saintly, godly, virtuous. *4* ~ *varón,* simple, artless man. *5* coll. *en el* ~ *suelo,* on the naked ground; *su santa voluntad,* his own sweet will; *todo el* ~ *día,* the whole day long. *6 adv. santo y bueno,* good and well. *7 m.* saint: *Todos los Santos,* All Saints' Day. *8* fête, fête day. *9* image of a saint. *10* coll. picture [in a book]. *11 írsele a uno el* ~ *al cielo,* to forget what one was up to. *13 m.-f.* saintly, godly, virtuous person.
Santo Domingo *f. pr. n.* GEOG. Hispaniola [island].
santón *m.* Mohammedan ascetic. *2* coll. hypocrite. *3* coll. big man, boss.
santónico *m.* BOT. wormwood.

santoral *m.* calendar of saints' days. *2* the lives of the saints.
santuario *m.* sanctuary [church, shrine]. *2* sanctum sanctorum.
santurrón, -na *adj.* sanctimonious. *2 m.-f.* sanctimonious person.
saña *f.* rage, fury. *2* cruelty.
sañoso, -sa; sañudo, -da *adj.* furious, cruel.
sapidez *f.* sapidity.
sápido, -da *adj.* sapid [possessing flavour].
sapiencia *f.* sapience, wisdom. *2* BIBL. Wisdom of Solomon.
sapiente *adj.* sage, learned.
sapillo *m. dim.* little toad. *2* RÁNULA.
sapindáceo, -a *adj.* BOT. sapindaceous.
sapo *m.* ZOOL. toad: *echar sapos y culebras,* fig. to utter angry words.
saponáceo, -a *adj.* saponaceous, soapy.
saponaria *f.* BOT. soapwort.
saponificar *tr.* to saponify.
sapotáceo, -a *adj.* BOT. sapotaceous.
sapote *m.* ZAPOTE.
saque *m.* a drawing out: *tener buen ~,* coll. to be a heavy eater or drinker. *2* PELOTA serving of the ball.
saqueador, -ra *m.-f.* sacker, pillager, plunderer.
saqueamiento *m.* saqueo.
saquear *tr.* to sack, pillage, plunder, loot.
saqueo *m.* sack, sacking, pillage, plunder.
saquera *adj.* packing [needle].
saquería *f.* manufacture of sacks. *2* sacks [collect.].
saquerío *m.* sacks [collect.].
saquito *m. dim.* little sack or bag.
Sara *f. pr. n.* Sarah.
sarampión *m.* MED. measles.
sarao *m.* soirée, evening party.
sarcasmo *m.* sarcasm.
sarcástico, -ca *adj.* sarcastic.
sarcocarpio *m.* BOT. sarcocarp.
sarcófago *m.* sarcophagus.
sarcoma *f.* MED. sarcoma.
sardana *f.* a Catalonian dance and its music.
Sardanápalo *m. pr. n.* HIST. Sardanapalus.
sardina *f.* ICHTH. sardine: *como sardinas en banasta* or *en barril,* coll. packed like sardines.
sardinal *m.* sardine net.
sardinel *m.* MAS. rowlock.
sardinero, -ra *adj.* [pertaining to] sardine. *2 m.-f.* sardine dealer.
sardineta *f. dim.* small sardine. *2* MIL. a kind of chevron.
sardo, -da *adj.-n.* Sardinian.
sardónice *f.* MINER. sardonyx.
sardónico, -ca *adj.* sardonic.
sarga *f.* serge. *2* painted wall fabric. *3* BOT. a variety of willow.
sargado, -da *adj.* ASARGADO.
sargatillo *m.* BOT. a variety of willow.
sargazo *m.* BOT. sargasso, gulfweed.
sargentía *f.* sergeancy, sergeantship.
sargento *m.* MIL. sergeant.
sargentona *f.* coll. big rude virago.
sargo *m.* ICHTH. sargo.
sarmentar *intr.* to gather pruned vine shoots.
sarmentoso, -sa *adj.* sarmentous, vinelike. *2* thin and knotty.
sarmiento *m.* vine shoot.
sarna *f.* MED. itch, mange, scabies.
sarnoso, -sa *adj.* itchy, mangy, scabious.
sarpullido *m.* SALPULLIDO.

sarraceno, -na *adj.-n.* Saracen.
sarracina *f.* row, fight, scuffle.
sarria *f.* coarse net for carrying straw.
sarrillo *m.* death rattle. *2* BOT. arum.
sarro *m.* crust, incrustation [in vessels]. *2* tartar [on teeth]. *3* SABURRA. *4* BOT. rust, mildew.
sarroso, -sa *adj.* crusty, incrusted [vessel]. *2* full of tartar [teeth].
sarta *f.* string [of beads, pearls, etc.]. *2* fig. string, series: *una ~ de mentiras,* a string of lies.
sartén *f.* frying pan: *tener la ~ por el mango,* to have the upper hand.
sartenada *f.* contents of a frying pan.
sartorio *adj.* ANAT. sartorius [muscle].
sasafrás *m.* BOT. sassafras.
sastra *f.* tailor's wife. *2* tailoress.
sastre *m.* tailor.
sastrería *f.* tailor's trade. *2* tailor's shop.
sastresa *f.* SASTRA.
Satán, Satanás *m. pr.* Satan, Satanas, the Devil.
satánico, -ca *adj.* satanic, satanical.
satélite *m.* ASTR. satellite. *2* fig. satellite, follower.
satén *m.* sateen.
satín *m.* satinwood.
satinar *tr.* to satin, calender, glaze [paper or fabrics]. *2* PHOT. to burnish.
sátira *f.* satire.
satírico, -ca *adj.* satiric, satirical. *2* satyric. *3 m.* satirist.
satirizar *tr.* to satirize; to lampoon.
sátiro *m.* satyr [silvan god]. *2* fig. satyr [lustful man].
satisfacción *f.* satisfaction: *a ~,* fully, according to one's wishes. *2* confidence, conceit: *~ de sí mismo,* conceit.
satisfacer *tr.* to satisfy. *2* to comply with, to answer, meet. *3* to settle, pay. *4 ref.* to satisfy oneself; to be satisfied. ¶ CONJUG. like *hacer.*
satisfactorio, -ria *adj.* satisfactory.
satisfago, satisfaga, etc. *irr.* V. SATISFACER.
satisfecho, -cha *p. p.* of SATISFACER. *2* satisfied, content. *3* vain, conceited.
satisfice, satisficiera, etc. *irr.* V. SATISFACER.
sativo, -va *adj.* cultivated [plant].
sátrapa *m.* satrap.
saturar *tr.* to saturate. *2* to satiate.
saturnal *adj.* Saturnian. *2 f. pl.* Saturnalia.
saturnino, -na *adj.* saturnine, gloomy, morose. *2* CHEM., MED. saturnine.
Saturno *m.* ASTR. Saturn. *2* CHEM. lead.
sauce *m.* BOT. willow, white willow.
sauceda *f.,* **saucedal** *m.,* **saucera** *f.* willow plantation.
saúco *f.* BOT. elder [*Sambucus nigra*].
sauquillo *m.* BOT. snowball.
saurio, -ria *adj.-m.* ZOOL. saurian.
sauzgatillo *m.* BOT. agnus castus, chaste tree.
savia *f.* BOT. sap. *2* fig. sap.
saxífraga *f.* BOT. saxifrage. *2* BOT. sassafras.
saxifragáceo, -a *adj.* BOT. saxifragaceous.
saxofón, saxófono *m.* MUS. saxophone.
saya *f.* skirt [garment]; petticoat.
sayal *m.* BOT. sayales *m.* a coarse woollen cloth.
sayo *m.* a kind of cassock or loose coat: *cortar un ~ a,* to talk behind the back of; *decir para su ~,* to say to oneself. *2* coll. any garment.
sayón *m.* medieval executioner.
sazón *f.* ripeness, maturity. *2* season, time, opportunity. *3* taste, flavour. *4 a la ~,* then, at that time; *en ~,* ripe; in season, opportunely.

sazonado, -da *adj.* seasoned, ripe. *2* seasoned, spiced.

sazonador, -ra *adj.* ripening. *2* seasoning.

sazonar *tr.* to ripen, mature. *2* to season [food]. *3* to season, flavour, give zest to. *4 ref.* to ripen, mature [grow ripe, become mature].

se *3rd person form of ref. pron. for every gender and number.* Its uses are: *1* As a ref. acc. or dat. case, equivalent to «himself», «oneself», «yourself», «themselves», «yourselves»; «to himself», «to herself», etc. *2* As a reciprocal pron., equivalent to: «each other», «one another», «to one another». *3* As a dat. case before the acc. *lo, la, los, las: yo ~ lo di,* I gave it to him [or her, it, you, them]. *4* to give a possessive value to the def. or indef. article: *él ~ lava las manos,* he washes his hands. *5* As an expletive forming verbs reflexive in form but transitive or intransitive in meaning: *el hombre ~ fue,* the man went away. *6* to form expressions of passive or impersonal character: *~ dice,* it is said, they say, people say; *no ~ puede negar,* it cannot be denied.

sé *irr.* V. SABER.

sé, sea, etc. *irr.* V. SER.

sebáceo, -a *adj.* sebaceous.

sebo *m.* tallow, suet; candle grease. *2* fat, grease.

seborrea *f.* MED. seborrhoea, seborrhea.

seboso, -sa *adj.* tallowy, fat, unctous; greasy.

seca *f.* drought, dry season. *2* NAUT. dry sand bank. *3 adv. a secas,* V. SECO.

secadal *m.* SEQUEDAL. *2* AGR. unwatered land.

secadero, -ra *adj.* fit for drying [fruit, tobacco]. *2 m.* drying place, drying shed or room.

secador, -ra *adj.* drying. *2 m.-f.* dryer. *3 m.* drying contrivance; drying room.

secamente *adj.* dryly, curtly, shortly, brusquely.

secamiento *m.* drying; desiccation.

secano *m.* AGR. unwatered land, dry land: *cultivo de ~,* dry farming. *2* NAUT. dry and bank.

secante *adj.* drying. *2* blotting [paper]. *3 adj.-f.* GEOM., TRIG. secant. *4 m.* drying oil. *5* blotting paper.

secar *tr.* to dry, dry up. *2* to dessicate. *3* to wipe dry. *4* to parch. *5* coll. to bore, annoy. *6 ref.* to dry oneself. *7* to dry, get dry. *8* [of plants] to wither. *9* [of moisture, a well, etc.] to dry up, run dry. *10* to become lean, meagre. *11* to be thirsty.

secatón, -na *adj.* coll. dull, vapid, insipid.

sección *f.* section [in practically every sense]. *2* division [of a bureau or department]. *3* department [of a store]. *4* column [in newspapers].

seccionado, -da *adj.* sectional, in sections.

seccionar *tr.* to section. *2* to cut, cut off.

secesión *f.* secession.

seco, -ca *adj.* dry [in practically every sense]. *2* dried up. *3* juiceless. *4* arid. *5* withered dead [plants, leaves, etc.]. *6* lean, thin, meagre [person or animal]. *7* unadorned, bare, undiluted, strict. *8* curt, short, brusque. *9* hard, unfeeling. *10 dejar ~,* coll. to kill. *11 a secas,* merely; and nothing more. *12 en ~,* high and dry; dry; by the dry process; without cause or reason: dead, short, suddenly.

secoya *f.* BOT. sequoia.

secreción *f.* PHYSIOL. secretion.

secreta *f.* ECCL. secret [in the Mass]. *2* coll. plainclothes men, detective service.

secretar *tr.* PHYSIOL. to secrete.

secretaria *f.* woman secretary. *2* wife of a secretary.

secretaría *f.* secretary's office. *2* secretaryship.

secretariado *m.* secretariat, secretariate.

secretario *m.* secretary.

secretear *intr.* coll. to whisper [converse privately].

secreteo *m.* coll. whispering [private talk].

secreter *m.* secretary [writing desk].

secreto, -ta *adj.* secret. *2 m.* secret; secrecy: *~ a voces,* open secret; *de ~,* secretly; *en ~,* secretly, in secret, confidentially. *3* secret drawer. *4* key, secret combination [for opening a lock]. *5* MUS. soundboard [of organ, etc.].

secretor, -ra; secretorio, -ria *adj.* PHYSIOL. secretory.

secta *f.* sect.

sectador, -ra; sectario, -ria *adj.* sectarian. *2 m.-f.* sectarian, sectary.

sectarismo *m.* sectarianism.

sector *m.* sector.

secuaz *m.* follower, henchman.

secuela *f.* sequel, result, consequence.

secuencia *f.* CINE., LITURG. sequence.

secuestrar *tr.* LAW to sequester, sequestrate. *2* to kidnap, abduct.

secuestro *m.* LAW sequestration. *2* kidnapping, abduction. *3* SURG. sequestrum.

secular *adj.* secular.

secularizar *tr.* to secularize. *2* to impropriate.

secundar *tr.* to second, aid, support.

secundario, -ria *adj.* secondary. *2* GEOL. Secondary.

secura *f.* dryness, condition of drought.

1) **sed** *f.* thirst: *tener ~,* to be thirsty. *2* need for water, dryness [of land or plants].

2) **sed** *imper.* of SER.

seda *f.* silk [fibre, yarn and fabric]: *como una ~,* smooth as silk; pliable; easily, without hitch or hindrance. *2* wild boar's bristle.

sedal *m.* fishline. *2* SURG. seton. *3* VET. rowel.

sedalina *f.* silkaline, schappe.

sedán *m.* AUTO. sedan.

sedante *adj.-m.* sedative.

sedar *tr.* to soothe, quit, allay.

sedativo, -va *adj.-m.* sedative.

sede *f.* ECCL. see: *Santa Sede,* Holy See. *2* seat, quarters, headquarters.

sedentario, -ria *adj.* sedentary.

sedeño, -ña *adj.* silky, silken. *2* silklike. *3* bristly.

sedera *f.* bristle brush.

sedería *f.* silks, silk stuff. *2* silk business or shop.

sedero, -ra *adj.* [pertaining to] silk. *2 m.-f.* silk weaver. *3* silk dealer.

sedición *f.* sedition.

sedicioso, -sa *adj.* seditious.

sediento, -ta *adj.* thirsty, thirsting.

sedimentación *f.* sedimentation.

sedimentar *tr.* to deposit [as a sediment]. *2 ref.* to settle, form a sediment.

sedimento *m.* sediment, settlings, lees, dregs.

sedoso, -sa *adj.* silky.

seducción *f.* seduction, seducement. *2* charm.

seducir *tr.* to seduce. *2* to allure, tempt. *3* to charm, captivate. ¶ CONJUG. like *conducir.*

seductor, -ra *adj.* seducing. *2* seductive, tempting. *3* charming, captivating. *4 m.-f.* seducer.

seduje, sedujera, etc. *irr.* V. SEDUCIR.

seduzco, seduzca, etc. *irr.* V. SEDUCIR.

sefardí, sefardita *adj.-n.* Sephardi. *2 m. pl.* Sephardim.

segadera *f.* sickle, reaping hook.

segador, -ra *m.-f.* harvester, harvestman, reaper, mower. *2 m.* ENT. harvestman, daddy-longlegs. *3 f.* harvester, mowing machine.
segar *tr.* AGR. to harvest, reap, mow. *2* fig. to mow, cut down, mow down. ¶ CONJUG. like *acertar.*
seglar *adj.* secular, lay. *2 m.-f.* layman, laywoman.
segmento *m.* segment.
segoviano, -na *adj.-n.* of Segovia.
segregación *f.* segregation. *2* PHYSIOL., BIOL. secretion [act or process].
segregar *tr.* to segregate. *2* PHYSIOL., BIOL. to secrete.
segueta *f.* buhl saw, fret saw.
seguida *f.* following. *2* succession, continuation: *de ~,* in succession, uninterruptedly; *de ~, en ~,* immediately.
seguidamente *adv.* consecutively, in succession. *2* forthwith, immediately after, right after that.
seguidilla *f.* a Spanish stanza of four or seven short verses partly assonant. *2 pl.* a popular Spanish dance and its music.
1) **seguido** *adv.* consecutively, continuously.
2) **seguido, -da** *adj.* consecutive, running, successive, continued: *ocho días seguidos,* eight days running. *3* straight, direct.
seguidor, -ra *m.-f.* follower.
seguimiento *m.* following. *2* pursuit, chase. *3* continuation.
seguir *tr.* to follow [in practically every sense]: *como sigue,* as follows. *2* to pursue, chase, hunt. *3* to prosecute, continue [action], to go on, keep on [doing something]. *4 intr.* to continue, keep [in a place, state, direction, etc.]. *5* to be, do: *¿cómo sigue el enfermo?,* how is the patient? *6 ref.* to ensue, result, follow. ¶ CONJUG. like *servir.*
según *prep.* according to, according as, as. *2* depending on. *3* so. *4 ~ que,* according as. *5 adv* that dependes. *6 ~ y como, ~ y conforme,* just as; that depends.
segundar *tr.* to do again. *2 intr.* to be second, follow next to the first.
segundero *m.* second hand [of timepiece].
segundo, -da *adj.* second: *segunda intención,* duplicity of meanings or purposes [in acts or words]; *de segunda mano,* second-hand. *2 segunda enseñanza,* secondary education. *3 m.* second [part of the minute]. *4* second in authority, assistant, mate. *5 sin ~,* unequalled. *6 f.* SEGUNDA INTENCIÓN. *7* MUS., AUTO. second.
segundogénito, -ta *adj.-n.* second born.
segundón *m.* any son born after the first.
segur *f.* ax, axe. *2* AGR. sickle.
seguramente *adv.* securely, safely. *2* surely. *3* probably, very probably.
seguridad *f.* security, safety: *de ~,* safety [as adj.]. *2* police service. *3* surety, bond. *4* custody, safe keeping. *5* certainty. *6* assurance: *tener la ~ de,* or *de que,* to be sure of or that.
seguro, -ra *adj.* secure, safe. *2* sure, firm, fast, steady. *3* sure, dependable, reliable; constant. *4* sure, certain. *5* sure [assured in mind], convinced. *6 m.* certainty: *a buen ~, al ~, de ~,* certainly, very probably. *7* place of safety. *8* COM. insurance. *9* safe conduct. *10* safety lock [of a firearm]. *11* MECH. click, pawl, stop.
seis *adj.* six. *2 m.* six. *3* sixth [of the month]. *4 f. pl. las ~,* six o'clock.
seisavado, -da *adj.* hexagonal.
seisavar *tr.* to make hexagonal.
seisavo, -va *adj.* sixth. *2 m.* sixth [sixth part].
seiscientos, -tas *adj.-m.* six hundred.

seiseno, -na *adj.* sixth.
seisillo *m.* MUS. sextolet.
seísmo *m.* seism.
selacio, -cia *adj.* ICHTH. selachian.
selección *f.* selection.
seleccionador, -ra *adj.* selecting. *2 m.-f.* selector.
seleccionar *tr.* to select, choose, pick out.
selecto, -ta *adj.* select, choice; distinguished.
selenio *m.* CHEM. selenium.
selenografía *f.* selenography.
self *f.* (Angl.) ELECT. self-induction coil.
seltz (agua de) *f.* Seltzer water; soda water.
selva *f.* forest, woods; jungle: *Selva Negra,* Black Forest [in Germany].
selvático, -ca *adj.* silvan, sylvan. *2* rustic, wild.
selvoso, -sa *adj.* silvan, sylvan. *2* wooded, woody.
sellar *tr.* to seal [with a seal]. *2* to seal, close.
sello *m.* seal [piece of wax, lead, etc.; impression, mark]. *2* signet. *3* seal, stamp [instrument; characteristic mark]. *4* PHARM. cachet. *5 ~ de correos,* postage, stamp.
semáforo *m.* semaphore. *2* traffic lights.
semana *f.* week: *~ Santa,* Holy Week; *entre ~,* during the week [but not on the first or last days]. *2* septenary [of years, etc.]. *3* week's pay.
semanal *adj.* weekly.
semanalmente *adv.* weekly.
semanario, -ria *adj.* weekly. *2 m.* weekly [publication].
semántica *f.* semantics, semasiology.
semblante *m.* face, countenance, mien, look, expression [of a person]; look, aspect [of things]: *componer el ~,* to put on a calm appearance: *mudar de ~,* to change colour.
semblanza *f.* biographical sketch.
sembradío, -a *adj.* AGR. fit for sowing [land].
sembrado, -da *adj.* sown. *2 m.* AGR. sown ground; field, grain field.
sembrador, -ra *adj.* seeding, sowing. *2 m.-f.* seeder, sower. *3 f.* seeder, seeding machine, sowing machine.
sembradura *f.* seeding, sowing: *tierra de ~,* grain field.
sembrar *tr.-intr.* to sow, seed. *2 tr.* to sow, scatter, disseminate, sprinkle, strew. ¶ CONJUG. like *acertar.*
semejante *adj.* resembling, similar, like, alike. *2* such, of that kind. *3* ALG. like. *4* GEOM. similar. *5 m.* resemblance, imitation. *6* fellow, fellow creature.
semejanza *f.* resemblance, similarity, similitude: *a ~ de,* like, as.
semejar *intr.-ref.* to resemble, to be alike.
semen *m.* semen, sperm. *2* BOT. seed.
semental *adj.* AGR. [pertaining to] seeding or sowing. *2* breeding [horse, bull, etc.]. *3 m.* breeding horse, bull, etc.
sementera *f.* AGR. seeding, sowing. *2* sown land. *3* seedtime, sowing season. *4* fig. hotbed.
semestral *adj.* six-month, six-monthly.
semestre *adj.* semestral. *2 m.* semester, six months.
semi- *pref.* semi-, half-, partly-.
semibreve *f.* MUS. semibreve, whole note.
semicadencia *f.* MUS. semicadence.
semicircular *adj.* semicircular.
semicírculo *m.* GEOM. semicircle.
semicircunferencia *f.* GEOM. semicircumference.
semiconsonante *adj.* PHONET. semiconsonant.
semicorchea *f.* MUS. semiquaver, sixteenth note.
semidiámetro *m.* semidiameter.

semidiós *m.* MYTH. demigod.
semidiosa *f.* MYTH. demigoddess.
semieje *m.* GEOM. semiaxis.
semifluido, -da *adj.* semifluid.
semifusa *f.* MUS. double demisemiquaver.
semilunar *adj.* semilunar.
semilla *f.* seed.
semillero *m.* AGR. seed bed, seed plot, nursery. *2* fig. hotbed, cause, seminary.
seminal *adj.* seminal.
seminario *m.* EDUC. seminary: ~ *conciliar,* ECCL. theological seminary. *2* SEMILLERO.
seminarista *m.* seminarist, theological student.
seminífero *adj.* seminiferous.
semínima *f.* MUS. crotchet.
Semíramis *f. pr. n.* HIST. Semiramis.
semirrígido, -da *adj.* AER. semirigid.
semisalvaje *adj.* half savage.
semiseda *f.* half silk.
semisuma *f.* ARITH. half the sum [of].
semita *m.-f.* Semite. *2 adj.* Semitic.
semítico, -ca *adj.* Semitic.
semitono *m.* MUS. semitone.
semivocal *adj.* PHONET. semivowel.
sémola *f.* semolina, groats.
semoviente *adj.* *bienes semovientes,* livestock.
sempiterno, -na *adj.* sempiternal. *2 f.* durance [fabric]. *3* BOT. globe amaranth.
sen *m.* BOT. senna.
sena *f.* six [on a die]. *2* BOT. senna.
Sena *m. pr. n.* GEOG. Seine [river].
senado *m.* Senate. *2* Senate house. *3* THEAT. audience.
senadoconsulto *m.* senatus consultum.
senador *m.* senator.
senaduría *f.* senatorship.
senatorial; senatorio, -ria *adj.* senatorial.
sencillez *f.* simplicity. *2* easiness. *3* plainness, unpretentiousness. *4* naturalness.
sencillo, -lla *adj.* simple [not complicated or elaborated]. *2* light, of light body [fabric, etc.]. *3* simple, single. *4* easy [to do]. *5* simple, plain, unadorned; natural, unaffected. *6* simple, artless. *7 m.* coll. small change.
senda *f.,* **sendero** *m.* path, footpath, byway. *2* fig. path, way.
sendos, -das *adj.* one each, one to each or for each.
Séneca *m. pr. n.* Seneca. *2* fig. man of wisdom.
senectud *f.* old age, senility.
senegalés, -sa *adj.-n.* Senegalese.
senescal *m.* seneschal.
senil *adj.* senile.
seno *m.* breast [milk-secreting organ]. *2* bosom [space between breast and dress]. *3* womb [of woman]. *4* fig. bosom, lap, the midst: *el ~ de Abraham,* Abraham's bosom. *5* concave, cavity, hollow, sinus. *6* ANAT., ZOOL., SURG. sinus. *7* GEOG. gulf, bay. *8* belly [of sail]; bight [of rope]. *9* TRIG. sine: ~ *verso,* versed sine.
sensación *f.* sensation, feeling. *2* sensation [vivid emotion]: *hacer ~,* to cause a sensation.
sensacional *f.* sensational.
sensatez *f.* sense, good sense, wisdom.
sensato, -ta *adj.* sensible, judicious, wise.
sensibilidad *f.* sensibility. *2* sensitiveness.
sensibilizar *tr.* to sensitize.
sensible *adj.* sentient, sensible. *2* sensible, perceptible, appreciable. *3* sensitive [person, instrument, plate, etc.]. *4* GEOG. sensible [horizon]. *5* deplorable, regrettable. *6 f.* MUS. sensible note.
sensiblería *f.* oversentimentality, mawkishness.

sensiblero, -ra *adj.* oversentimental, mawkish.
sensitiva *f.* BOT. sensitive plant.
sensitivo, -va *adj.* sense, sensitive [of the senses; that conveys sense impressions]. *2* sentient.
sensorio, -ria *adj.* sensorial. *2 m.* sensorium.
sensual *adj.* sensual.
sensualidad *f.* sensuality.
sensualismo *m.* sensualism.
sentada *f.* sitting: *de una ~,* at one sitting.
sentadillas (a) *adv.* sidesaddle.
sentado, -da *adj.* seated, sitting down. *3* settled, established: *dar por ~,* to take for granted, to consider as settled. *4* sedate, judicious. *5* BOT. sessile.
sentar *tr.* to seat [cause to sit down]. *2* to set, establish. *3 intr. sentar,* or ~ *bien, a,* to fit, become, suit; to please, be agreeable to; [of food, climate, etc.] to agree with. *4 ref.* to sit down. *5* ASENTARSE. *6* [of a seam, etc.] to hurt. ¶ CONJUG. like *acertar.*
sentencia *f.* LAW judgement, sentence, decision. *2* award, decision [of an arbitrator]. *3* judgment, opinion. *4* pithy saying, maxim.
sentenciar *tr.* to sentence, pass judgement on. *2* to determine, decide.
sentencioso, -sa *adj.* sententious.
sentidamente *adv.* feelingly.
sentido, -da *adj.* felt, experienced. *2* heartfelt; feeling. *3* sensitive, touchy. *4* offended: *darse por ~,* to take offence. *5 m.* sense [any one of the five senses]: *costar un ~,* coll. to cost a fortune; *con todos los cinco sentidos,* with the utmost care and attention. *6* sense [judgment, understanding, etc.]: ~ *común,* common sense; *buen ~,* good sense. *7* sense, meaning, import, effect: *doble ~,* double meaning; *en cierto ~,* in a sense; *en el ~ que,* to the effect that; *sin ~,* meaningless. *8* sense [of the humour, the ridicule, etc.]. *9* consciousness. *10* sense, direction. *11* GEOM. sense.
sentimental *adj.* sentimental.
sentimentalismo *m.* sentimentalism.
sentimiento *m.* sentiment, feeling. *2* sense [of duty, honour, etc.]. *3* grief, sorrow, regret.
sentina *f.* NAUT. bilge. *2* fig. foul, filthy place.
1) **sentir** *m.* sentiment, feeling. *2* view, opinion.
2) **sentir** *tr.* to feel [perceive by sensation]. *2* to hear. *3* to feel [pleasure, pity, etc.]. *4* to have, experience, suffer; ~ *frío,* to be cold; ~ *miedo,* to be afraid. *5* to feel [be aware of]; to have a presentiment of. *6* to regret; be or feel sorry [for]: *lo siento,* I am sorry. *7* to think, judge. *8 sin ~,* without noticing, without being aware. *9 ref.* to feel [well, bad, sad, sick, etc.]. *10* to begin to decay or rot. *11 sentirse de,* to resent; to feel [an insult, etc.]; to have a pain in. ¶ CONJUG. like *hervir.*
seña *f.* sign, indication, token: *por más señas,* more by token. *2* sign [motion, action, gesture]. *3* mark, signal. *4* MIL. password. *5 pl.* address [description of a place of residence or business]. *6 señas personales,* personal description.
señal *f.* sign, mark, token, symptom: *dar señales,* to show signs of; *en ~ de,* as a sign of, in token of. *2* landmark. *4* reminder. *5* distinctive mark. *6* trace, vestige. *7* sign, signal: *hacer señales,* to signal, make signals. *8* image, representation. *9* sign, prodigy. *10* scar, cicatrice. *11* pledge [token]. *12* earnest, money. *13* ~ *de la cruz,* sign of the cross.

señaladamente *adv.* especially, remarkably signally.

señalado, -da *adj.* signal. 3 noted, distinguished.

señalamiento *m.* appointment, date. 2 LAW assignation [for a trial].

señalar *tr.* to mark [with a sign]. 2 to show, indicate, point at, point out. 3 to set, fix, determine, assign. 4 to appoint [place, time]. 5 to scar. 6 to signal. 7 *ref.* to distinguish oneself, to excel.

señero, -ra *adj.* solitary, alone. 2 unique, unequalled.

señor, -ra *adj.* noble, distinguished, not vulgar, gentlemanlike, ladylike. 2 coll. great, fine, strong, etc. 3 *m.* mister, Mr., sir: *el ~ López*, Mr. López; *muy ~ mío*, Dear Sir [in letters]; *sí ~*, yes, sir. 4 man, gentleman. 5 master [of the house]. 6 feudal lord, lord, master. 7 (cap.) *el Señor*, the Lord, God; *Nuestro Señor*, Our Lord.

señora *f.* mistress, Mrs., madam; *la ~ López*, Mrs. López; *muy ~ mía*, Dear Madam [in letters]; *sí ~*, yes, madam. 2 woman, lady, gentlewoman: *~ de compañía*, companion, chaperon. 3 lady [wife]. 4 mistress, lady [owner, etc.]; lady [of the house]. 5 (cap.) *Nuestra Señora*, Our Lady.

señorear *tr.* to dominate, rule over. 2 to lord it over. 3 to dominate, tower over. 4 to control [one's passions]. 5 *tr.-ref.* to take, take hold of, bring under one's rule or control. 6 *ref.* to take on airs.

señoría *f.* dominion, lordship, control. 2 lordship, ladyship, title of distinction inferior to EXCELENCIA. 3 HIST. signory.

señorial *adj.* seignorial, manorial. 2 feudal [fees]. 3 lordly, noble, stately.

señoril *adj.* lordly, genteel, dignified, distinguished.

señorío *m.* dominion, lordship, control. 2 seigniory. 3 gravity or stateliness of deportment. 4 self-command. 5 nobility, gentry, gentlefolk.

señorita *f. dim.* young lady, miss, Miss. 2 title given by servants to a lady or to the mistress of the house.

señoritingo *m.* coll. young gentleman of no account.

señorito *m. dim.* young gentleman. 2 Master [youth or boy]. 3 title given by servants to a gentleman or to the master of the house. 4 coll. idle young gentleman.

señorón, -na *m.-f.* swell, bigwig.

señuelo *m.* decoy, lure. 2 fig. lure, bait, enticement.

seo *f.* cathedral church.

sépalo *m.* BOT. sepal.

separable *adj.* separable. 2 detachable, removable.

separación *f.* separation. 2 dissmissal, discharge. 3 POL. secession.

separado, -da *adj.* separate; apart: *por ~*, separately.

separar *tr.* to separate. 2 to dismiss, discharge. 3 *ref.* to separate [intr.]. 4 COM. to put an end to partnership.

separata *f.* reprint.

separatismo *m.* separatism, secessionism.

sepedón *m.* ESLIZÓN.

sepelio *m.* burial, interment.

sepia *f.* ZOOL. sepia, cuttlefish. 2 sepia [colour].

septena *f.* septenary, group of seven.

septenario, -ria *adj.* septenary. 2 *m.* period of seven days.

septenio *m.* septenary, septenium.

septeno, -na *adj.* SÉPTIMO.

septentrión *m.* north. 2 north wind. 3 ASTR. septentrion.

septentrional *adj.* septentrional, northern.

septeto *m.* MUS. septet, septuor.

septicemia *f.* MED. septicaemia.

septicida *adj.* BOT. septicidal.

séptico, -ca *adj.* septic.

septiembre *m.* September.

septillo *m.* MUS. septimole, septuplet.

séptimo, -ma *adj.-m.* seventh. 2 *f.* MUS. seventh. 3 FENC. septime.

septingentésimo, -ma *adj.-m.* seven hundredth.

septo *m.* ANAT., BOT. septum.

septuagenario, -ria *adj.-n.* septuagenarian.

septuagésima *f.* ECCL. Septuagesima.

septuagésimo, -ma *adj.* seventieth. 2 septuagesimal.

septuplicar *tr.* to septuple.

séptuplo, -pla *adj.* septuple, sevenfold. 2 *m.* septuple.

sepulcral *adj.* sepulchral.

sepulcro *m.* sepulcher. 2 grave, tomb.

sepultar *tr.* to bury, entomb. 2 fig. to bury [hide, cover up, submerge, immerse].

sepulto, -ta *adj.* buried.

sepultura *f.* sepulture: *dar ~ a*, to bury.

sepulturero *m.* gravedigger, sexton.

sequedad *f.* dryness. 2 aridity. 3 gruffness, surliness.

sequedal, sequeral *m.* dry soil.

sequía *f.* drought, dry season.

sequillo *m.* sweet biscuit.

sequío *m.* SECANO.

séquito *m.* train, suite, cortege. 2 popularity.

sequizo, -za *adj.* easily dried.

1) **ser** *m.* being: *el Ser Supremo*, the Supreme Being, God. 2 life, existence.

2) **ser** *subst. v.* to be [exist, live]. 2 *aux.* to be [forming passives]: *él es amado*, he is loved. 3 *intr. & copulative* to be, be a: *el hombre es mortal*, man is mortal: *Juan es abogado*, John is a lawyer. 4 to cost: *¿a cómo son estas peras?*, what is the price of these pears? 5 to be, happen: *¿cómo fue ello?*, how did it happen? 6 to be [belong to]: *este libro es mío*, this book is mine. 7 It is used in impersonal sentences as: *es la una*, it is one o'clock; *es necesario que*, it is necessary that. 8 *~ de*, a) to belong to; b) to be from, come from, be native of [a place]; c) to be in [a specified material]; d) *es de creer, es de ver*, it is to be believed; it is worth seeing; e) *¿qué será de mí?*, what will become of me? 9 *~ para poco*, to be feeble, timid. 10 *a no ~ que*, unless. 11 *¡cómo ha de ser!*, it cannot be helped! [to express resignation]. 12 *érase que se era*, once upon a time. 13 *esto es*, that is to say. 14 *no sea que*, lest. 15 *sea lo que sea*, or *fuere*, be that as it may; anyhow. 16 *un es, no es*, or *un si es, no es*, a little bit. ¶ CONJUG.: INDIC. Pres.: *soy, eres, es; somos, sois, son.* | Imperf.: *era, eras, era; éramos, erais, eran.* | Pret.: *fui, fuiste, fue; fuimos, fuisteis, fueron.* | Fut.: *seré, serás*, etc. | COND.: *sería, serías*, etc. | SUBJ. Pres.: *sea, seas, sea; seamos, seáis, sean.* | Imperf.: *fuera, fueras, fuera; fuéramos, fuerais, fueran*, or *fuese, fueses*, etc. | Fut.: *fuere, fueres, fuere; fuéremos, fuereis, fueren.* | IMPER.: *sé, sea; seamos, sed, sean.* | PAST. P. *sido.* | GER.: *siendo.*

sera *f.* large esparto basket.

seráfico, -ca *adj.* seraphic(al).

serafín *m.* seraph.

serafina *f.* a flowered woollen fabric.
serapino *m.* SAGAPENO.
serba *f.* BOT. fruit of the service tree.
serbal, serbo *m.* BOT. service tree.
serena *f.* SERENO 5: *a la* ~, AL SERENO.
serenar *tr.* to serene, calm, pacify. *2* to clear up [make unclouded]. *3* to cool [water] in the night air. *4 intr.-ref.* to become calm. *5* [of weather] to clear up. *6* to regain one's selfpossession.
serenata *f.* serenade. *2* MUS. serenata.
serenidad *f.* serenity, calm. *2* calmness, coolness, self-possession. *3* Serenity [title].
serenísimo, -ma *adj. superl.* extremely serene or calm. *2* Most Serene [title of princes].
sereno, -na *adj.* serene. *2* clear, cloudless. *3* calm, cool, self-possessed. *4 m.* night watchman. *5* serein, night dew: *al* ~, in the night air.
seriamente *adv.* seriously. *2* gravely. *3* in earnest.
seri(ci)cultor *m.* seri(ci)culturist.
seri(ci)cultura *f.* seri(ci)culture, silk culture.
sérico, -ca *adj.* silken.
serie *f.* series. *2 de* ~, stock. *3 en* ~, standardized, mass [production]; ELECT. series, in series.
seriedad *f.* seriousness, gravity. *2* earnestness. *3* reliability. *4* sternness.
serio, -ria *adj.* serious. *2* grave, dignified. *3* stern. *4* solvent, reliable. *5* grave, sober [not light or gay, not showy].
sermón *m.* sermon.
sermonar *intr.* to preach, to preach sermons.
sermonario *m.* collection of sermons.
sermonear *intr.-tr.* to sermonize.
sermoneo *m.* coll. sermonizing.
seroja *f.*, **serojo** *m.* dry leaves. *2* brushwood.
serón *m.* esparto basket or pannier.
serosidad *f.* MED. serosity.
seroso, -sa *adj.* serous.
serpear *intr.* SERPENTEAR.
serpentario *m.* ORN. secretary bird. *2* (cap.) ASTR. Serpent Bearer.
serpentear *intr.* to wind, meander, serpentine, wriggle.
serpenteo *m.* winding, meandering, wriggling.
serpentín *m.* worm [of a still], cooling coil. *2* cock [of firelock].
serpentina *f.* MIN. serpentine. *2* a rolled strip of coloured paper which is cast so as to unroll [in carnival, etc.].
serpentino, -na *adj.* serpentine. *2* slanderous, poisoned [tongue].
serpentón *m. aug.* large serpent. *2* MUS. serpent.
serpezuela *f. dim.* of SIERPE.
serpiente *f.* ZOOL. serpent, snake: ~ *de cascabel*, rattlesnake. *2* ASTR. Serpent.
serpigo *m.* MED. serpigo, ringworm.
serpol *m.* BOT. wild thyme.
serpollar *intr.* [of a tree] to shoot, sprout.
serpollo *m.* shoot, sprout [of a tree].
serrado, -da *adj.* serrate.
serrador, -ra *m.-f.* ASERRADOR.
serrallo *m.* seraglio, harem. *2 fig.* brothel.
serranía *f.* mountainous country or region.
serrano, -na *adj.* mountain, highlander. *2 m.-f.* mountaineer highlander.
serrar *tr.* to saw. ¶ CONJUG. like *acertar.*
serrátil *adj.* MED. irregular [pulse].
serreta *f. dim.* small saw. *2* cavesson [iron].
serrijón *m.* short mountain chain.
serrín *m.* sawdust.
serrucho *m.* handsaw.
servato BOT. hog's-fennel.

serventesio *m.* quatrain with rhyme abab. *2* sirviente [Provençal moral lay].
servible *adj.* serviceable, in good condition for use.
servicial *adj.* serviceable, helpful, obliging, kind.
servicio *m.* service, serving. *2* duty [assigned service]: *estar de* ~, to be on duty. *3* service [occupation of a servant; branch of public employ, etc.]: ~ *público*, public service. *4* servants, staff of servants. *5* service, good turn: *flaco* ~, ill turn. *6* use, benefit. *7* military or naval service. *8* service [set of dishes, cups, etc.]. *9* course [in a meal]. *10* chamber pot. *11* TENNIS service, serve.
servido, -da *p. p.* of SERVIR. *2 adj.* ser ~, to please, deign, have the kindness [to].
servidor, -ra *m.-f.* servant, server, servitor: ~ *de usted*, your servant, at your service; *queda de usted atento* ~, yours respectfully.
servidumbre *f.* servitude, bondage, subjection. *2* inevitable obligation. *3* servants, staff of servants. *4* LAW servitude, easement.
servil *adj.* servile.
servilismo *m.* servility.
servilleta *f.* table napkin, serviette.
servilletero *m.* napkin-ring.
servio, -via *adj.-n.* Serbian.
serviola *f.* NAUT. cathead, anchor beam.
servir *intr.-tr.* to serve [be a servant to, do service to, be useful to], to wait [on or upon]. *2* to do [for], to serve, answer [a purpose or end]. *3* [in ball games] to serve. *4 intr.* to serve, wait [at table]. *5 intr.* to serve [in the army or navy], to be employed [in a public service, etc.]. *6* CARDS to follow suit. *7* ~ *de*, to act as, be used as, serve as or for. *8* ~ *para*, to be for, be good for, good for, be used for: *no* ~ *para nada*, to be of no use, to be good for nothing. *9 tr.* to help, serve [food or drink]. *10* to serve [a gun; an office]. *11* to tend [a machine]. *12* to do a favour to. *13* to serve, attend, court [a lady]. *14* COM. to wait upon [a customer]. *15 ref.* to serve oneself. *16* to help oneself [to food or drink]. *17* to please, be pleased to, deign to: *sírvase informarme*, please inform me. *18 servirse de*, to employ, make use of. ¶ CONJUG: INDIC. Pres.: *sirvo, sirves, sirve;* servimos, servís, *sirven.* | Pret.: serví, serviste, *sirvió;* servimos, servisteis, *sirvieron.* | SUBJ. Pres.: *sirva, sirvas,* etc. | Imperf.: *sirviera, sirvieras,* etc., or *sirviese, sirvieses,* etc. | Fut.: *sirviere, sirvieres,* etc. | IMPER.: *sirve, sirva; sirvamos,* servid, *sirvan.* | GER.: *sirviendo.*
servitud *f.* servitude.
servocroata *adj.-n.* Serbo-Croatian.
servomotor *m.* MACH. servomotor.
sésamo *m.* BOT. sesame. *2* sesame [magic word].
sesear *intr.* to pronounce *z*, and *c* before *e* & *i* like *s* [as in Am. and some parts of Spain].
sesenta *adj.-m.* sixty. *2* sixtieth.
sesentavo, -va *adj.-n.* sixtieth.
sesentón, -na *adj.-n.* sexagenarian.
seseo *m.* pronouncing *z*, and *c* before *e* & *i*, like *s*.
sesera *f.* brainpan. *2* the entire brain.
sesgado, -da *p. p.* of SESGAR. *2 adj.* SESGO 1 & 2.
sesgar *tr.* to slant, give an oblique direction to. *2* to cut on the bias.
sesgo, -ga *adj.* slanting, oblique, biased. *2* cut on the bias. *3 fig.* stern-faced. *4 m.* obliquity, slant, bias: *al* ~, obliquely, on the bias. *5* mean course. *6* turn [of an affair].
sesgue *pret.*, *subj. & imper.* of SESGAR.
sesil *adj.* BOT. sessile.

sesión *f.* session, sitting, séance, meeting, conference. *2* show [in a picture theatre]: ~ *continua*, continuous showing.

seso *m.* ANAT. brain, brains. *2* fig. brains, intelligence; prudence, judgment: *no tener* ~, to have no sense; *perder el* ~, to go crazy.

sesquióxido *m.* CHEM. sesquioxide.

sesteadero *m.* shady place where cattle rest.

sestear *intr.* to take a siesta. *2* [of cattle] to rest in the shade.

sestercio *m.* sesterce.

sesudez *f.* wisdom, prudence, sageness.

sesudo, -da *adj.* wise, prudent, judicious, sage.

seta *f.* BOT. mushroom. *2* bristle [of hog].

setecientos, -tas *adj.-m.* seven hundred. *2* seven hundredth [in order].

setena *f.* group of seven.

setenta *adj.-n.* seventy. *2* seventieth [in order].

setentavo, -va *adj.-n.* seventieth.

setentón, -na *adj.-n.* septuagenarian.

setiembre *m.* SEPTIEMBRE.

seto *m.* hedge, inclosure: ~ *vivo*, hedge, quickset.

seudo *adj.* pseudo, false.

seudónimo, -ma *adj.* pseudonymous. *2 m.* pseudonym, pen name.

severidad *f.* severity, rigour, strictness, sterness. *2* austerity, severity.

severo, -ra *adj.* severe, rigorous, rigid, strict, stern. *2* severe, grim, austere.

sevicia *f.* cruelty, cruel treatment.

Sevilla *f. pr. n.* Seville.

sevillanas *f. pl.* a Sevillian dance and tune.

sexagenario, -ria *adj.-n.* sexagenarian.

sexagésima *f.* ECCL. Sexagesima.

sexagésimo, -ma *adj.* sexagesimal, sixtieth.

sexenio *m.* period of six years.

sexo *m.* sex: *el bello* ~, the fair sex.

sexta *f.* ECCL. sext, sexte. *2* MUS. sixth. *3* FENC. sixte.

sextante *m.* sextant. *2* sextans [Roman coin].

sexteto *m.* MUS. sextet.

sextil *adj.* ASTROL. sextile.

sextilla *f.* sextain [stanza of six short lines].

sexto, -ta *adj.-n.* sixth.

séxtuplo, -pla *adj.* sextuple, sixfold. *2 m.* sextuple.

sexual *adj.* sexual.

sexualidad *f.* sexuality.

1) **si** *m.* MUS. si, B [seventh note of the scale].

2) **si** *conj.* if, whether: *como* ~, as if, as though; *por* ~ *acaso*, just in case; *si por chance*; ~ *bien*, although; ~ *no*, otherwise, else; unless. *2* how, to what extent. *3* when. *4* if only. *5* It may be used for emphasis or to denote doubt: *¡~ no lo quiero!*, indeed, I don't want it; *¿~ será él?* I wonder if it is he.

1) **sí** *3rd person form of ref. pron. for every gender and number* (used as object of prepositions) himself, herself, itself, oneself, themselves: *de por* ~, apart, separately; by oneself, itself, etc.; *de* ~, of himself, herself, etc.; spontaneously; by nature; *entre* ~, each other, of each other, to each other; *por* ~ *y ante* ~, of his own accord, ignoring others; haughty.

2) **sí** *adv.* yes, yea; indeed, certainly: *por* ~ *o por no*, in any case; *un día* ~ *y otro no*, every other day; *¿sí?*, indeed? *2 m.* yes, assent, permission: *dar el* ~, to say yes.

siamés, -sa *adj.-n.* Siamese.

sibarita *adj.-n.* Sybarite. *2* sybarite.

sibaritismo *m.* sybaritism.

siberiano, -na *adj.-n.* Siberian.

sibila *f.* sibyl.

sibilante *adj.* sibilant, hissing.

sibilino, -na; sibilítico, -ca *adj.* sibyline.

sic *Lat. adv.* sic.

sicalipsis *f.* pornography.

sicario *m.* sicarian, paid assassin.

sicigia *f.* ASTR. syzygy.

Sicilia *f. pr. n.* GEOG. Sicily.

siciliano, -na *adj.-n.* Sicilian.

sicoanálisis *m.* PSICOANÁLISIS.

sicofanta, sicofante *m.* sycophant.

sicofísica, sicología, sicometría, etc. = PSICOFÍSICA, PSICOLOGÍA, PSICOMETRÍA, etc.

sicómoro *m.* BOT. sycamore. *2* BOT. sycamore maple.

sicón *m.* ZOOL. sycon.

sículo, -la *adj.-n.* Sicilian. *2* HIST. Siculian.

sidecar *m.* sidecar.

sideral; sidéreo, -a *adj.* sidereal.

siderosa *f.* MINER. siderite.

siderurgia *f.* siderurgy.

siderúrgico, -ca *adj.* siderurgical.

sidra *f.* cider.

siega *f.* reaping, mowing, harvest.

siembra *f.* sowing, seeding. *2* sowing time. *3* sown ground.

siempre *adv.* always, ever: *de* ~, usual; *para* ~, forever, for good; *por* ~, forever, evermore; ~ *jamás*, forever and ever; ~ *que*, whenever; provided.

sien *f.* ANAT. temple.

Siena *f. pr. n.* GEOG. Sienna.

siena *f.* sienna.

sienés, -sa *adj.-n.* Sienese, Siennese.

sierpe *f.* serpent, snake. *2* fig. ugly-looking person; fierce or angry person. *3* fig. anything that winds or wrigles.

sierpecilla *f. dim.* small serpent.

sierra *f.* saw: ~ *de bastidor*, bucksaw; ~ *de mano*, handsaw; ~ *sin fin*, band-saw. *2* GEOG. jagged mountain-chain. *3* ICHTH. sawfish.

Sierra Leona *f. pr. n.* GEOG. Sierra Leone.

sierrecilla *f. dim.* small saw.

siervo, -va *m.-f.* serf, slave. *2* humble servant, servant: ~ *de Dios*, servant of God.

sieso *m.* ANAT. rectum.

siesta *f.* hottest part of the day. *2* siesta, afternoon nap.

siete *adj.-m.* seven. *2* seventh [of the month]. *3* V-shaped tear in garment. *4* CARP. dog, clamp. *5 f. pl. las* ~, seven o'clock.

sieteenrama *f.* BOT. tormentil.

sietemesino, -na *adj.* born in seven months [baby]. *2* coll. puny coxcomb.

sífilis *f.* MED. syphilis.

sifilítico, -ca *adj.-n.* syphilitic.

sifón *m.* siphon. *2* siphon bottle. *3* siphon water. *4* trap [in a pipe].

sifosis *f.* kyphosis.

sigilación *f.* sealing, stamping. *2* concealment, keeping secret.

sigilar *tr.* to seal [stamp with a seal]. *2* to conceal, keep secret, not to disclose or reveal.

sigilo *m.* seal, stamp. *2* concealment, secrecy.

sigilografía *f.* sigilography.

sigilosamente *adv.* silently, secretly.

sigiloso, -sa *adj.* silent, reserved.

sigla *f.* sigla.

siglo *m.* century [hundred years]: *hasta la consumación de los siglos*, until the end of time; *por los siglos de los siglos*, world without end. *2* age, epoch, period. 3 fig. ages [long time]. 4 world [worldly intercourse or matters].

sigmoideo, -a *adj.* sigmoid.

signáculo *m.* seal, signet.

signar *tr.* to sign [with a sign; with one's name]. 2 to cross [make the sign of the cross upon or over]. 3 *ref.* to cross oneself.

signatario, -ria *adj.-n.* signatory.

signatura *f.* sign, mark. 2 PRINT. signature. 3 press-mark, library number [on a book].

significación *f.* signification, signifying. 2 signification, meaning, import. 3 significance.

significado, -da *adj.* well-known, prominent. 2 *m.* signification, meaning, sense.

significante *adj.* signifying, significant.

significar *tr.* to signify [be a sign of; make know]. 2 to signify, mean. 3 *intr.* to signify, matter.

significativo, -va *adj.* significative, significant.

signo *m.* sign, indication [of something]. 2 sign, mark, symbol, character. 3 scroll or flourish [in a notary's signature]. 4 MATH. sign. 5 GRAM. mark: ~ *de admiración*, exclamation mark. 6 ASTR. ~ *del Zodíaco*, sign of the Zodiac.

siguiente *adj.* following, next.

sílaba *f.* syllable.

silabario *m.* reader [book to teach reading].

silabear *intr.* to syllabicate, syllabify, syllabize.

silábico, -ca *adj.* syllabic.

sílabo *m.* syllabus, list, index.

silba *f.* hiss, hissing [of disapproval].

silbar *intr.* to whistle. 2 [of a steam whistle] to hoot. 3 to hiss. 4 [of a bullet] to whiz. 5 *tr.* to whistle [a tune]. 6 to hiss, catcall [an actor, play, etc.].

silbato *m.* whistle [instrument].

silbido *m.* SILBO. 2 ~ *de oídos*, ringing in the ears.

silbo *m.* whistle [sound]. 2 hissing [of a snake, etc.]. 3 hoot, hooting [of a steam whistle]. 4 whiz [of a bullet].

silbón *m.* ORN. a hissing widgeon.

silenciador *m.* silencer [device for firearms, etc.].

silenciar *tr.* to omit, keep silent about.

silencio *m.* silence: *guardar* ~, to keep silence; *pasar en* ~, to omit, not to mention. 2 stillness, quiet. 3 taciturnity. 4 MUS. rest.

silencioso, -sa *adj.* silent. 2 taciturn. 3 noiseless, still, quiet.

silente *adj.* silent, still, quiet.

silepsis *f.* RHET. syllepsis.

silero *m.* silo.

silesiano, -na; silesio, -sia *adj.-n.* Silesian.

sílex *m.* MINER. silex.

silfide *f.* MYTH. & fig. sylph.

sílice *f.* CHEM. silica.

silíceo, -a *adj.* siliceous.

silicio *m.* CHEM. silicon.

silicua *f.* BOT. siliqua, silique.

silícula *f.* BOT. silicle, silicula.

silo *m.* AGR. silo. 2 fig. cavern, dark place.

silogismo *m.* LOG. syllogism.

silogizar *intr.* to syllogize, argue.

silueta *f.* silhouette.

silúrico, -ca *adj.* GEOL. Silurian.

siluro *m.* ICHTH. catfish, sheatfish.

sila *f.* miscellany. 2 a form of poem.

Silvestre *m. pr. n.* Silvester, Sylvester.

silvestre *adj.* wild [plant, animal]. 2 uncultivated, rustic.

silvicultor, -ra *m.-f.* forester, silviculturist.

silvicultura *f.* forestry, silviculture.

silla *f.* chair [seat for one]: ~ *de cubierta*, deck chair; ~ *de manos*, sedan chair; ~ *giratoria*, swivel chair; ~ *poltrona*, easy chair. 2 ECCL. see. 3 *silla* or ~ *de montar*, saddle. 4 ~ *de posta*, post chair.

sillar *m.* ashlar [stone]. 2 place for the saddle on the back of a horse.

sillería *f.* set of chairs. 2 stalls [in a choir]. 3 chair making, chair business or shop. 4 ARCH. ashlar, ashlar masonry.

sillero, -ra *m.-f.* maker or seller of chairs.

silleta *f. dim.* small chair. 2 bedpan.

silletazo *m.* blow with a chair.

silletero *m.* carrier of a sedan chair.

sillico *m.* chamber pot; basin of a close-stool.

sillín *m.* light riding saddle. 2 harness saddle. 3 saddle [of a bicycle, motorcycle, etc.].

sillón *m. aug.* armchair, easy chair: ~ *de ruedas*, wheel chair.

sima *f.* cave, abyss, chasm.

simbiosis *f.* BIOL. symbiosis.

simbólico, -ca *adj.* symbolical.

simbolismo *m.* symbolism.

simbolizar *tr.* to symbolize, symbol, tipify, stand for.

símbolo *m.* symbol. 2 ~ *de la fe* or *de los Apóstoles*, Apostles' Creed.

simetría *f.* symmetry.

simétrico, -ca *adj.* symmetric, symmetrical.

simiente *f.* seed. 2 semen, sperm.

simiesco, -ca *adj.* simian, apelike, apish.

símil *adj.* similar. 2 *m.* simile, comparison.

similar *adj.* similar, like.

similitud *f.* similitude, similarity.

similor *m.* similor: *de* ~, fig. sham, tinsel.

simio *m.* ZOOL. simian, ape.

simón *m.* hack, cab; hackman [in Madrid].

simonía *f.* simony.

simoníaco, -ca *adj.* simoniac(al. 2 *m.-f.* simoniac.

simpatía *f.* sympathy, congeniality, liking, favour. 2 winsomeness. 3 PHYSIOL. sympathy.

simpático, -ca *adj.* pleasant, nice, likable, winsome; agreeable, congenial. 2 ANAT., PHYSIOL., PHYS., MUS. sympathetic. 3 *m.* ANAT. *gran* ~, sympathetic nervous system.

simpatizante *adj.* favouring, supporting. 2 *m.-f.* sympathizer, supporter.

simpatizar *intr.* to be congenial, to feel a mutual liking. 2 ~ *con*, to like; to sympathize with, to favour [a party, idea, etc.].

simple *adj.* simple [not compund, not complicated]. 2 MAT., GRAM., BIOL. simple. 3 simple, mere. 4 single [not double or multiple]. 5 simple, ingenuous. 6 simple, foolish. 7 *m.-f.* simpleton.

simpleza *f.* silliness, foolishness. 2 silly thing.

simplicidad *f.* simplicity.

simplicísimo, -ma *adj. superl.* extremely simple.

simplificación *f.* simplification.

simplificar *tr.* to simplify.

simplón, -na *m.-f.* simpleton.

simulación *f.* simulation, feigning.

simulacro *m.* simulacrum. 2 MIL. sham battle.

simulado, -da *adj.* simulated, imitated, feigned, pretended, sham.

simulador, -ra *m.-f.* simulator.

simular *tr.* to simulate, imitate, feign, sham.

simultanear *tr.* to accomplish or carry out simultaneously.

simultaneidad *f.* simultaneity.

simultáneo, -a *adj.* simultaneous.

simún *m.* simoom [wind].

sin *prep.* without: ~ *dificultad*, without difficulty;

~ *que yo le viese*, without my seeing him. *2* besides, without counting. *3* ~ *embargo*, nevertheless, however.
sinagoga *f.* synagogue.
sinalefa *f.* GRAM. synalepha.
sinapismo *m.* sinapism.
sinceramente *adv.* sincerely.
sincerar *tr.-ref.* to exculpate, excuse, justify.
sinceridad *f.* sincerity.
sincero, -ra *adj.* sincere.
sinclinal *adj.* GEOL. synclinal.
síncopa *f.* GRAM., MUS. syncope, syncopation.
sincopado, -da *adj.* syncopated.
sincopar *tr.* GRAM., MUS. to syncopate. *2* to abridge.
síncope *f.* MED. syncope. *2* SINCOPA.
sincretismo *m.* syncretism.
sincrónico, -ca *adj.* synchronous.
sincronismo *m.* synchronism.
sincronizar *tr.* to synchronize. *2 intr.* RADIO. ~ *con*, to tune in.
sindéresis *f.* discretion, good judgment.
sindicado *m.* syndicate [body of syndics].
sindical *adj.* syndical. *2* syndicalistic.
sindicalismo *m.* syndicalism; unionism.
sindicar *tr.* to accuse, denounce. *2* to syndicate. *3 ref.* to syndicate [unite to form a syndicate].
sindicato *m.* syndicate [association]. *2* trade union, labor union.
síndico *m.* syndic. *2* LAW. liquidator or receiver [in a bankruptcy].
síndrome *m.* MED. syndrome.
sinécdoque *f.* RHET. synecdoche.
sinecura *f.* sinecure.
sineresis *f.* GRAM. syneresis.
sinergia *f.* PHYSIOL. synergy.
sinfín *m.* no end, endless number, endless amount.
sínfisis *f.* ANAT., ZOOL. symphysis.
sinfonía *f.* symphony.
sinfónico, -ca *adj.* symphonic.
singar *intr.* NAUT. to scull over the stern.
singladura *f.* NAUT. a day's run. *2* NAUT. day [from noon to noon].
singular *adj.* singular [unique; extraordinary]. *3 en* ~, in particular.
singularidad *f.* singularity. *2* peculiarity. *3* oddity.
singularizar *tr.* to singularize, distinguish, single out. *2* GRAM. to use in the singular. *3 ref.* to distinguish oneself, to make oneself conspicuous.
singulto *m.* sob. *2* hiccough, singultus.
sinhueso *f.* coll. *la* ~, the tongue.
sínico, -ca *adj.* Sinic, Sinitic.
siniestra *f.* left hand.
siniestrado, -da *adj.* that has undergone damage or loss [from wreck, fire, etc.].
siniestro, -tra *adj.* left, left-hand. *2* sinister. *3 m.* disaster, casualty, wreck. *4* COM. damage or loss [from wreck, fire, etc.].
sinnúmero *m.* no end, great number.
sino *conj.* but, except. *2* solely, only. *3 no solo ... ~ (también)*, not only... but (also).
sínodo *m.* ECCL., ASTR. synod.
sinología *f.* sinology.
sinonimia *f.* synonymity, synonymy.
sinónimo, -ma *adj.* synonymous. *2 m.* synonym.
sinopsis, *pl.* -**sis** *f.* synopsis.
sinovia *f.* ANAT. synovia.
sinrazón *f.* wrong, injustice. *2* unreason, unreasonable act.
sinsabor *m.* displeasure, worry, trouble, sorrow.
sinsonte *m.* ORN. mockingbird.

sinsubstancia *f.* coll. frivolous person.
sintáctico, -ca *adj.* syntactic.
sintaxis *f.* GRAM. syntax.
síntesis, *pl.* -**sis** *f.* synthesis.
sintético, -ca *adj.* synthetic, synthetical.
sintetizar *tr.* to synthesize, synthetize.
sintoísmo *m.* Shinto, Shintoism.
síntoma *m.* symptom.
sintomático, -ca *adj.* symptomatic.
sintonía *f.* ELECT., RADIO. syntony, tune, tuning.
sintónico, -ca *adj.* ELECT. syntonic, syntonical.
sintonización *f.* ELECT., RADIO. syntonization, tuning.
sintonizar *tr.-intr.* ELECT., RADIO. to syntonize, tune: ~ *con*, to tune in.
sinuoso, -sa *adj.* sinuous.
sinusoide *adj.* sinusoidal. *2 f.* GEOM. sinusoid.
sinusitis *f.* MED. sinusitis.
sinvergüencería *f.* brazenness,shamelessness.
sinvergüenza *adj.* brazen, barefaced. *2 m.-f.* shameless person, rascal, scoundrel.
sionismo *m.* Zionism.
siquiatría *f.* PSIQUIATRÍA.
síquico, -ca *adj.* PSÍQUICO.
siquier, siquiera *conj.-adv.* although, though, even if. *2* even, so much as. *3 un poquito* ~, ever so little. *4* whether... or: ~ *venga*, ~ *no venga*, whether he comes or not.
Siracusa *f. pr. n.* GEOG. Syracuse.
sirena *f.* MYTH. siren. *2* MYTH. mermaid. *3* siren [instrument]; foghorn.
sirenio, -nia *adj.-n.* ZOOL. sirenian.
sirga *f.* towrope, towline [for tracking a boat from the bank]. *2* line for hauling nets.
sirgar *tr.* to track [a boat from the bank].
Siria *f. pr. n.* GEOG. Syria.
siríaco, -ca *adj.-n.* Syrian.
siringa *f.* MUS. syrinx. *2* BOT. seringa, rubber tree.
siringe *f.* syrinx [vocal organ of birds].
Sirio *m. pr. n.* ASTR. Sirius.
sirio, -ria *adj.-n.* SIRÍACO.
sirle *f.* sheep's dung.
siroco *m.* sirocco [wind].
sirte *f.* NAUT. shoal, submerged sand bank.
sirvienta *f.* female servant, servant girl, maid.
sirviente *adj.* serving. *2* LAW servient. *3 m.* domestic, manservant.
sirvo, sirva, sirviera, sirviere, etc. *irr.* V. SERVIR.
sisa *f.* SEW dart; armscye. *2* petty theft. *3* size [for gilding].
sisar *tr.* to pilfer, filch. *2* to curt darts or armscyes in a garment. *3* to size [for gilding].
sisear *intr.-tr.* to hiss [to express disapproval].
sisimbrio *m.* JARAMAGO.
sísmico, -ca *adj.* seismic.
sismo *m.* TERREMOTO.
sismógrafo *m.* seismograph.
sisón, -na *adj.* pilfering, filchering. *2 m.-f.* pilferer, filcher. *3 m.* ORN. little bustard.
sistema *m.* system. *2* coll. method, way.
sistemático, -ca *adj.* systematic; methodical.
sistematizar *tr.* to systematize.
sistilo *m.* ARCH. systyle.
sístole *f.* PROS., PHYSIOL. systole.
sistro *m.* MUS. sistrum.
sitiador, -ra *adj.* besieging. *2 m.-f.* besieger.
sitial *m.* chair [seat of honour, authority, etc.].
sitiar *tr.* to besiege, lay siege to. *2* to surround, hem in.
sitio *m.* place, spot: *dejar en el* ~, fig. to kill one

outright. *2* place, seat, room [space]: *hacer* ~, to make room. *3* location, site. *4* stand, station. *5* country seat, villa. *6* MIL. siege: *poner* ~ *a*, to lay siege to.

sito, -ta *adj.* situated, lying, located.

situación *f.* placing. *2* situation, location, position. *3* situation [set of circumstances, position in which one finds oneself]. *4* position [to do, state, etc.].

situar *tr.* to situate, locate, place, put. *2* COM. to place [funds]. *3 ref.* to take one's stand; to place or station oneself.

sixtino, -na *adj.* Sistine.

smoking *m.* dinner jacket, *tuxedo.

so *prep.* under: ~ *capa de*, under pretence of. *2 m.* emphatic word used with depreciatory adjectives: ~ *marrano*, you, dirty fellow.

¡so! *interj.* whoa! [to horses].

soasar *tr.* COOK. to half roast, roast lightly.

soba *f.* kneading. *2* pawing [a person]. *3* drubbing.

sobaco *m.* armpit, axilla. *2* BOT. axil.

sobajar *tr.* to paw, crumple, rumple.

sobaquera *f.* shield [for the armpit in a garment].

sobaquina *f.* sweat from the armpit.

sobar *tr.* to knead, rub, soften. *2* to paw [a person]. *3* to beat, drub. *4* to vex, annoy.

sobarba *f.* noseband. *2* double chin.

sobarbada *f.* SOFRENADA. *2* scolding.

sobarcar *tr.* to take or carry under the arm.

soberanear *intr.* to lord it, domineer.

soberanía *f.* sovereignty. *2* rule, sway. *3* haughtiness.

soberano, -na *adj.* sovereign. *2* coll. very good, great. *3 m.-f.* sovereign [ruler]. *4 m.* sovereign [coin].

soberbia *f.* arrogance, pride, haughtiness. *2* magnificence.

soberbio, -bia *adj.* arrogant, proud, haughty. *2* superb. *3* grand, magnificent. *4* fiery [horse].

sobina *f.* wooden pin, peg.

sobón, -na *adj.* given to excessive fondling and caressing.

sobornar *tr.* to suborn, bribe.

soborno *m.* subornation, bribery. *2* bribe. *3* (Arg., Bol., Chi.) SOBORNAL.

sobra *f.* excess surplus: *de* ~, more than enough, in excess; superfluous; too well: *estar de* ~, to be one too many; to be superfluous or unnecessary. *2 pl.* leavings, leftovers.

sobradamente *adv.* more than enough, in excess, too, too well.

sobradillo *m.* ARCH. penthouse [sloping roof over a door or window].

1) **sobrado** *m.* attic, garret. *2 adv.* SOBRADAMENTE.

2) **sobrado, -da** *adj.* excessive, more than enough. *2* rich, having in abundance.

sobrancero, -ra *adj.* disengaged, unemployed.

sobrante *adj.* remaining, leftover. *2 m.* leftover, surplus.

sobrar *intr.* to be in excess, be more than is necessary, be over and above: *sobrarle a uno* [*una cosa*], to have in excess, have to spare. *2* to be superfluous; to be in the way. *3* to remain, be left over.

sobrasada *f.* a Majorcan sausage.

sobre *prep.* on, upon. *2* over, above: ~ *todo*, above all. *3* about, concerning. *4* about [approximately]. *5* to, toward. *6* in addition to. *7* on, near [a river, etc.]. *8* COM. on: *girar* ~, to draw on. *9* COM. above: ~ *la par*, above par. *10* ~ *manera*, beyond measure. *11* ~ *sí*, attentive, on guard;

haughty. *12 m.* envelope [for letters]. *13* SOBRESCRITO.

sobreabundancia *f.* superabundance.

sobreabundar *intr.* to superabound.

sobrealimentar *tr.* to overfeed.

sobrealzar *tr.* to raise, to raise excessively.

sobreañadir *tr.* to superadd, superinduce.

sobreasada *f.* SOBRASADA.

sobreasar *tr.* COOK. to roast again.

sobrebarrer *tr.* to sweep lightly.

sobrecalza *f.* legging.

sobrecama *f.* coverlet, bedspread.

sobrecarga *f.* overload, extra load, overburden. *2* additional trouble. *3* PHILAT. surcharge.

sobrecargar *tr.* to overload, overburden, overcharge. *2* to surcharge [a postage stamp]. *3* SEW. to fell.

sobrecargo *m.* NAUT. purser, supercargo.

sobrecarta *f.* envelope [for a letter].

sobreceja *f.* part of the forehead over the eyebrows.

sobrecejo, sobreceño *m.* frown.

sobrecerco *m.* reinforcing hoop, ring or frame.

sobrecielo *m.* canopy.

sobrecincha *f.*, **sobrecincho** *m.* surcingle.

sobrecoger *tr.* to surprise, take unawares. *2 ref.* to be surprised, to be struck with awe, dread, etc.

sobrecogimiento *m.* surprise, awe, fear.

sobrecoser *tr.* SEW. to whip, to fell.

sobrecrecer *intr.* to grow too much.

sobrecubierta *f.* double cover or wrapping. *2* jacket [of a book].

sobrecuello *m.* top collar. *2* stock [kind of cravat].

sobredicho, -cha *adj.* above-mentioned, aforesaid.

sobrediente *m.* snaggletooth.

sobredorar *tr.* to gold-plate [a metal]. *2* fig. to gloss over.

sobreentender *tr.* SOBRENTENDER.

sobreesdrújulo, -la *adj.* SOBRESDRÚJULO.

sobreexcitar *tr.* SOBREXCITAR.

sobrefalda *f.* overskirt.

sobrefaz, *pl.* **-faces** *f.* surface, outside.

sobrehaz *f.* surface, outside. *2* cover. *3* superficial appearance.

sobrehilado *m.* SEW. overcast, overcasting.

sobrehilar *tr.* SEW. to overcast.

sobrehumano, -na *adj.* superhuman.

sobrejuanete *m.* NAUT. royal [sail].

sobrelecho *m.* MAS. under bed [of a stone].

sobrellenar *tr.* to fill up, fill full.

sobrellevar *tr.* to ease [another's burden], to aid another to bear [his burden]. *2* to bear, suffer with patience. *3* to overlook, be lenient about.

sobremanera *adv.* exceedingly, beyond measure.

sobremesa *f.* table cover. *2* sitting at table after eating: *de* ~, at table after eating. *3 de* ~, desk, table: *reloj de* ~, desk clock.

sobremesana *f.* NAUT. mizzen topsail.

sobrenadar *intr.* to float [on a liquid].

sobrenatural *adj.* supernatural.

sobrenombre *m.* surname. *2* nickname; agnomen.

sobrentender *tr.* to understand [something implied, not expressed]. *2 ref.* to be understood, go without saying. ¶ CONJUG. like *entender.*

sobrepaga *f.* extra pay.

sobreparto *m.* after chilbirth, confinement after childbirth.

sobrepeine *adv.* coll. slightly, superficially.

sobrepelliz, *pl.* **-llices** *f.* ECCL. surplice.

sobreponer *tr.* to put over or upon; to superpose. *2 ref. sobreponerse a*, to be superposed; to master, overcome, be or make oneself superior to. ¶ CONJUG. like *poner*.

sobreposición *f.* superposition.

sobreproducción *f.* superproduction, overproduction.

sobrepuerta *f.* overdoor; lambrequin. *2* cornice over a door.

sobrepuesto, -ta *p. p.* of SOBREPONER. *2 adj.* superposed, superimposed. *3 m.* appliqué.

sobrepujanza *f.* great power, strength or vigor.

sobrepujar *tr.* to surpass, excel.

sobrequilla *f.* NAUT. keelson.

sobrero *adj.* BULLF. extra, spare [bull].

sobresaliente *adj.* projecting. *2* surpassing, excellent. *3* outstanding, remarkable. *4 m.* the highest examination mark. *5* THEAT. understudy. *6* BULLF. substitute.

sobresalir *intr.* to project, jut out. *2* to excel, distinguish oneself. *3* to stand out.

sobresaltar *tr.* to alarm, startle. *2* to assail suddenly. *3 intr.* [of figures in a painting] to be striking. *4 ref.* to be startled, to start.

sobresalto *m.* startle, shock, sudden alarm. *2 de ~*, suddenly, unexpectedly.

sobresanar *intr.* [of a wound] to heal superficially.

sobresaturar *tr.* CHEM. to supersaturate.

sobrescribir *tr.* to superscribe. ¶ PAST. P.: *sobrescrito, sobrescripto*.

sobrescrito *m.* superscription, address.

sobresdrújulo, -la *adj.* accented on any syllable preceding the antepenult.

sobreseer *intr.* LAW to stay a judgement. *2* to desist, yield.

sobreseimiento *m.* LAW stay of proceedings.

sobrestadías *f. pl.* NAUT. extra lay days.

sobrestante *m.* foreman, overseer.

sobresueldo *m.* extra pay, extra wages.

sobretarde *f.* late afternoon.

sobretodo *m.* overcoat.

sobrevenir *intr.* to come, happen. *2* to come unexpectedly. *3* to follow, supervene. ¶ CONJUG. like *venir*.

sobrevesta, sobreveste *f.* surcoat [over the armour].

sobrevestir *tr.* to put [a garment] over other clothes.

sobrevidriera *f.* window guard. *2* storm window.

sobreviento *m.* gust of wind.

sobreviviente *adj.* surviving. *2 m.-f.* survivor.

sobrevivir *intr.* to survive. *2 ~ a*, to outlive.

sobrexcitación *f.* overexcitement, overexcitation.

sobrexcitar *tr.* to overexcite. *2 ref.* to become overexcited.

sobriedad *f.* sobriety, frugality, moderation.

sobrina *f.* niece.

sobrino *m.* nephew.

sobrio, -bria *adj.* sober, temperate, moderate, frugal.

socaire *m.* NAUT. lee: *al ~ de*, under the lee of.

socaliña *f.* trick [to get something from someone].

socaliñar *tr.* to trick one out of [something].

socalzar *tr.* MASON. to underpin, underset.

socapa *f.* pretext, pretence: *a ~*, on the sly.

socarra *f.* singe, scorching. *2* slyness.

socarrar *tr.* to singe, scorch.

socarrén *m.* ARCH. eaves.

socarrón, -na *adj.* sly, cunning.

socarronería *f.* slyness, cunning, artfulness.

socava *f.* digging under, undermining. *2* hollow for water around a tree.

socavar *tr.* to undermine.

socavón *m.* cave, cavern. *2* MIN. adit.

socaz *m.* tailrace.

sociabilidad *f.* sociableness, sociability.

sociable *adj.* sociable, companionable.

social *adj.* social: *ciencias sociales*, social sciences; *trato ~*, social intercourse; *razón ~*, COM. firm, firm name.

socialismo *m.* socialism.

socialista *adj.* socialist, socialistic. *2 m.-f.* socialist.

socializar *tr.* to socialize.

sociedad *f.* society [social mode of life, community; companionship, company]. *2 sociedad* or *buena ~*, society [fashionable people]. *3* society, association, union, club. *4* COM. partnership: *hacer ~ con*, to be in partnership with. *5* COM. society, company, corporation: *~ limitada*, limited company.

societario, -ria *adj.* pertaining to the associations or to the trade unions.

socio, -cia *m.-f.* COM. partner: *~ capitalista*, financial partner; *~ comanditario*, silent partner, sleeping partner; *~ industrial*, working partner. *2* member, fellow [of a society, club, etc.]. *3* coll. fellow, guy.

sociología *f.* sociology.

sociólogo, -ga *m.-f.* sociologist.

socolor *m.* pretext, pretence. *2 adv.* under colour.

socollada *f.* NAUT. flapping [of a sail]. *2* NAUT. pitching.

socorredor, -ra *adj.* helper, aider, succourer.

socorrer *tr.* to assist, help, aid, succour.

socorrido, -da *adj.* ready to help. *2* handy, useful. *3* trite, hackneyed.

socorro *m.* assistance, help, aid, succour, relief.

sochantre *m.* ECCL. subchanter, succentor.

soda *f.* SOSA.

sódico, -ca *adj.* CHEM. sodic; sodium.

sodio *m.* CHEM. sodium.

sodomía *f.* sodomy.

sodomita *adj.-n.* Sodomite. *2* sodomite.

soez *adj.* coarse, base, vile.

sofá *m.* sofa.

Sofía *f. pr. n.* Sophia. *2* GEOG. Sofia.

sofión *m.* snort [of anger]; harsh refusal.

sofisma *m.* sophism, fallacy.

sofista *m.* Sophist. *2* sophist.

sofistería *m.* sophistry.

sofisticación *f.* sophistication, adulteration.

sofisticar *tr.* to sophisticate, adulterate.

sofístico, -ca *adj.* sophistic, sophistical.

sofito *m.* ARCH. soffit.

soflama *f.* faint glow or flame. *2* blush. *3* fig. flimflam, deceitful talk. *4* coll. harangue.

soflamar *tr.* to deceive, humbug. *2* to make [a person] blush. *3 ref.* COOK. to burn, scorch.

sofocación *f.* choking, suffocation, smothering, stifling.

sofocar *tr.* to choke, suffocate, smother, stifle [stop the breath of]. *2* to stifle, smother, quench. *3* to harass, importune. *4* to put to blush. *5 ref.* to blush.

sofoco *m.* suffocation. *2* blush, embarrassment. *3* annoyance, vexation, mortification.

sofocón *m.*, **sofoquina** *f.* coll. great vexation or mortification.

sofreír *tr.* COOK. to fry slightly. ¶ CONJUG. like *reír*. | PAST. P.: *sofreído & sofrito*.

sofrenada *f.* sudden checking of a horse. *2* harsh reprimand.

sofrenar *tr.* to check [a horse] suddenly. *2* to reprimand severely. *3* to check [a passion].
sofrito, -ta *irreg. p. p.* of SOFREÍR. *2 m.* anything sightly fried.
soga *f.* rope, esparto rope, halter. *2* MAS. face [of a brick or stone]. *3 hacer ~,* to lag behind.
soguero *m.* ropemaker; ropedealer. *2* street porter.
sois *irr.* V. SER.
soja *f.* BOT. soy, soy bean.
sojuzgar *tr.* to conquer, subject, subjugate, subdue.
sol *m.* sun [heavenly body; warmth from the sun, sunlight; day]: *rayo de ~,* sunbeam; *hace ~,* it is sunny; *no dejar a ~ ni a sombra,* to importune, not to leave in pace; *tomar el ~,* to bask or walk in the sun; *a ~ puesto,* at nightfall; *de ~ a ~,* from sunrise to sunset. *2* MUS. sol, G. *3* sol [Peruvian coin].
solada *f.* sediment, lees.
solado *m.* paving, flooring [act]. *3* pavement, tile floor.
solador *m.* paver, tiler.
solamente *adv.* only, solely. *2 ~ que,* provided that, if only.
solana *f.* sunny place. *2* sun gallery.
solanáceo, -a *adj.* BOT. solanaceous.
solano *m.* easterly wind. *2* hot wind.
solapa *f.* lapel. *2* pretence, dissembling: *de ~,* underhand, sneakingly.
solapado, -da *adj.* underhand, sneaky. *2* sly, hypocritical.
solapar *tr.* to put lapels on [o coat]. *2* to overlap. *3* to cloak, conceal. *4 intr.* [of a part of a garment] to overlap.
solapo *m.* SOLAPA. *2* overlapped part or piece. *3* coll. chuck under the chin.
1) **solar** *adj.* solar. *2 m.* site, groundplot [for a building]. *3* ancestral mansion. *4* noble house or lineage.
2) **solar** *tr.* to floor, pave. *2* to sole [shoes]. ¶ CONJUG. like *contar.*
solariego, -ga *adj.* pertaining to a noble house or lineage: *casa solariega,* ancestral mansion.
solaz *m.* solace, comfort, relief, recreation.
solazar *tr.* to solace, comfort. *2* to solace, amuse, divert. *3 ref.* to solace oneself, amuse oneself.
solazoso, -sa *adj.* recreating, amusing, delectable.
soldada *f.* wages, pay, salary.
soldadesca *f.* soldiery. *2* undisciplinated troops.
soldadesco, -ca *adj.* soldierly, soldierlike.
soldado *m.* soldier: *~ de caballería,* trooper, cavalryman; *~ de infantería,* infantryman; *~ raso,* private.
soldador *m.* solderer, welder. *2* soldering iron. *3* blowtorch.
soldadura *f.* soldering, welding: *~ autógena,* welding. *2* solder. *3* soldered joint, welded joint.
soldar *tr.* to solder, weld. *2* to solder, unite. *3* fig. to mend [a blunder]. ¶ CONJUG. like *contar.*
solear *tr.* to sun [expose to the sun]. *2 ref.* to sun oneself or itself.
solecismo *m.* GRAM. solecism.
soledad *f.* solitude, loneliness. *2* sorrow, bereavement. *3* solitude [lonely place]. *4 pl.* Andalusian tune, song and dance.
soledoso, -sa *adj.* solitary. *2* lonely, lonesome.
solemne *adj.* solemn. *2* coll. great, downright.
solemnidad *f.* solemnity. *2* festivity. *3 pl.* formalities.
solemnizar *tr.* to solemnize.
solenoide *m.* ELECT. solenoid.

soler *intr.* to be accustomed to, be wont to, use to; to generally: *yo solía tomar el autobús,* I used to take the bus; *suele nevar en este tiempo,* it generally snows at this time of the year. ¶ It is used only in the INDIC. Pres.: *suelo, sueles, suele; solemos, soléis, suelen;* in the imperf.: *solía, solías,* etc., and in the compound preterit: *he solido, has solido,* etc.
solera *f.* ARCH. girder. *2* stone base [for uprights]. *3* nether millstone. *4* bottom [of a furnace]. *5* mother [of vine].
soleta *f.* patch for the sole of a stocking. *2 picar de ~, tomar ~,* to hasten, run; to flee.
solevación *f.,* **solevamiento** *m.* raising up, pushing up, upheaval [lifting up from beneath]. *2* uprising, insurrection.
solevantar *tr.* to raise up, upheave. *2 ref.* to rise up, upheave. *3 tr.-ref.* SOLIVIANTAR.
solevar *tr.* to incite to revolt. *2 ref.* to rebel. *3 tr.-ref.* SOLEVANTAR 1 & 2.
solfa *f.* solmization. *2* musical annotation, notes. *3* fig. music. *4* coll. beating, drubbing. *5 poner en ~,* to put in a ridiculous light.
solfatara *f.* GEOL. solfatara.
solfeador, -ra *m.-f.* sol-faer.
solfear *intr.-tr.* MUS. to sol-fa, solmizate. *2 tr.* coll. to bear, drub.
solfeo *m.* MUS. sol-fa; sol-faing, solmization. coll. beating, drubbing.
solfista *m.-f.* sol-faer.
solicitación *f.* solicitation.
solicitado, -da *adj.* in good demand. *2* sought, popular.
solícitamente *adv.* solicitously. *2* diligently.
solicitante *m.-f.* petitioner, applicant.
solicitar *tr.* to solicit, ask for, beg, petition. *2* to solicit, invite, attract. *3* to woo.
solícito, -ta *adj.* solicitous, diligent, careful.
solicitud *f.* solicitude, diligence, care. *2* petition, demand, request, application.
solidar *tr.* to consolidate, harden, strengthen. *2* to render firm or stable.
solidaridad *f.* solidarity. *2* common cause.
solidario, -ria *adj.* solidary. *2* jointly liable; jointly binding. *3* making common cause.
solidarizar *tr.* to make solidary. *2 ref.* to become solidary, to make common cause.
solideo *m.* ECCL. calotte.
solidez *f.* solidity. *2* firmness, strength. *3* fastness [of colour].
solidificar *tr.* to solidify. *2 ref.* to solidify [become solid].
sólido, -da *adj.* solid. *2* COM. substantial [firm]. *3* fast [colour]. *4 m.* GEOM. solid.
soliloquio *m.* soliloquy.
solimán *m.* coll. corrosive sublimate.
solio *m.* throne [royal seat].
solípedo, -da *adj.-m.* ZOOL. soliped.
solista *m.-f.* MUS. soloist.
solitaria *f.* coll. tapeworm.
solitario, -ria *adj.* solitary, lone, lonely. *2* secluded [spot, life]. *3* BOT. solitary [flower]. *4 m.* solitary, hermit. *5* solitaire [diamond game].
soliviantar *tr.* to revolt, make hostile or rebellious. *2 ref.* to revolt, become hostile or rebellious.
soliviar *tr.* to lift up [from beneath]. *2 ref.* to rise partly, get up partly.
solo, -la *adj.* alone; by himself, itself, etc. *2* lone, lonely. *3* only, sole. *4 m.* MUS. solo. *5* a card game. *6 a solas,* alone [unaccompanied, unaided]; in private.

sólo *adv.* SOLAMENTE.

solomillo, solomo *m.* sirloin. *2* loin [of pork].

solsticio *m.* ASTR. solstice.

soltar *tr.* to untie, unfasten, loosen. *2* to turn loose. *3* to let out, set free, release, discharge. *4* to let go, drop. *5* to cast, shed [the skin, etc.]. *6* coll. to give, pay [money]. *7* coll. to give [a blow, etc.]; to fire [a shot]. *8* to utter, let out [a curse, a remark, etc.]. *9* to burst into [laughter, tears, etc.]. *10* ref. to come off, come untied, get loose. *11* to get free. *12* to acquire ease. *13* to begin to [walk, talk, etc.]. ¶ CONJUG. like *contar.*

soltería *f.* celibacy, singleness; bachelorhood.

soltero, -ra *adj.* single, unmarried. *2 m.* bachelor, single man. *3 f.* single woman.

solterón *m.* old bachelor.

solterona *f.* old maid, spinster.

soltura *f.* release, setting at liberty. *2* ease, facility, agility. *3* fluency. *4* licentiousness.

solubilidad *f.* solubility.

soluble *adj.* soluble. *2* solvable.

solución *f.* solution: ~ *de continuidad,* solution of continuity, break.

solucionar *tr.* to solve. *2* to bring to a favorable issue.

solutivo, -va *adj.* MED. solutive.

solvencia *f.* COM. solvency. *2* ability, reliability.

solventar *tr.* SOLUCIONAR. *2* to settle, pay up.

solvente *adj.* COM. solvent. *2* able, reliable.

sollado *m.* NAUT. orlop.

sollamar *tr.* to scorch, singe.

sollo *m.* ESTURIÓN.

sollozar *intr.* to sob.

sollozo *m.* sob.

somanta *f.* coll. beating, drubbing.

somatén *m.* [in Catalonia] body of armed citizens gathering at the call of the alarm bell. *2* alarm bell.

somático, -ca *adj.* somatic.

sombra *f.* shade, shadow: *dar* ~, to cast a shadow; *hacer* ~ *a,* to stand in the light of; to protect; to outshine; *a la* ~, in the shade; in jail; *ni por* ~, by no means. *2* shadow, phantom, ghost. *3* ASTR. umbra. *4* F. ARTS shade, shading. *5 tener buena* ~, to be pleasant; to be witty or funny; to bring good luck. *6 tener mala* ~, to be disagreeable; to bring bad luck. *7 pl.* shades, shadows, darkness. *8 sombras chinescas,* shadow play.

sombraje *m.* screen or roof made with branches, mats, etc., to afford shade.

sombrajo *m.* SOMBRAJE. *2* coll. shadow cast by getting in someone's light.

sombreado *m.* F. ARTS shading.

sombrear *tr.* to shade, shadow [throw a shadow upon]. *2* F. ARTS to shade.

sombrerazo *m.* aug. large hat. *2* blow with a hat. *3* coll. doffing of the hat [as a greeting].

sombrerera *f.* hatbox, bandbox. *2* hatter's wife.

sombrerería *f.* hattery, hat factory. *2* hat shop.

sombrerero *m.* hatter.

sombrerete *m.* dim. little hat. *2* BOT. cap [of mushroom]. *3* hood, bonnet [of chimney]. *4* spark catcher [of locomotive].

sombrerillo *m.* dim. little hat or bonnet.

sombrero *m.* hat [for men or women], bonnet [for women]: ~ *calañés,* Andalusian hat with turned-up brim and low cone-shaped crown; ~ *cordobés,* beaver hat with a flat brim and a cylindrical low crown; ~ *de teja,* shovel hat; ~ *candil,* or *de tres picos,* cocked hat; three-cornered hat; ~ *de copa,* high hat, silk hat; ~ *de jipi-*

japa, Panama hat; ~ *flexible,* soft hat; ~ *hongo,* derby hat. *2* canopy [of pulpit]. *3* BOT. cap [of mushroom]. *4* drumhead [of capstan].

sombría *f.* UMBRÍA.

sombrilla *f.* parasol, sunshade.

sombrío, -bría *adj.* sombre, gloomy, dark, dismal, shady, overcast. *2* F. ARTS shaded, dark.

sombroso, -sa *adj.* shady [causing shade]. *2* shady, shadowy [abounding in shade].

someramente *adv.* slightly, superficially.

somero, -ra *adj.* slight, superficial. *2* shallow; in the surface, about the surface.

someter *tr.* to subject, subjugate, subdue. *2* to subject [to the action of something], to put [to a test, etc.]. *3* to submit [for consideration or decision]. *4* ref. to submit, surrender, yield. *5* to go [through an operation, examination, etc.].

sometimiento *m.* subjection. *2* submission.

somier *m.* bedspring, spring mattres.

somnambulismo *m.* somnambulism, sleepwalking.

somnámbulo, -la *adj.* somnambulistic. *2 m.-f.* somnambulist, sleepwalker.

somnífero, -ra *adj.* somniferous, somnific.

somnolencia *f.* somnolence, drowsiness.

somorgujar *tr.* to plunge, submerge. *2 intr.* BUCEAR. *3* ref. to dive, duck, plunge.

somorgujo, somorgujón *m.* ORN. dabchick, grebe.

somos *irr.* V. SER.

sompesar *tr.* SOPESAR.

son *m.* sound [of an instrument]: *a* ~, or *al* ~, *de,* at or to the sound of. *2* news, report, rumour. *3* pretext, motive: *¿a* ~ *de qué?,* why?, for what reason?; *sin ton ni* ~, without rhyme or reason. *4* manner, guise: *en* ~ *de guerra,* in a hostile manner.

son *irr.* V. SER.

sonadero *m.* handkerchief.

sonado, -da *adj.* noted, famous. *3* coll. much talked-about: *hacer una que sea sonada,* to do something that causes a lot of talk.

sonaja *f.* jingle [each pair of disks of the tambourine]. *2 pl.* jingle hoop.

sonajero *m.* baby's rattle.

sonambulismo *m.* SOMNAMBULISMO.

sonámbulo, -la *adj.-n.* SOMNÁMBULO.

sonante *adj.* sonant, sounding, sonorous, jingling.

sonar *tr.* to sound, play, ring [an instrument]. *2* to blow [someone's nose]. *3 intr.* to sound, ring. *4* [of a clock] to strike. *5* PHON. [of a letter] to be sounded. *6* to be mentioned. *7* to sound familiar, be vaguely remembered. *8* ~ *a,* to seem, have the appearance of being. *9* ~ *bien* or *mal* [of a word, expression, etc.], to be pleasing or offensive. *10* ref. to blow one's nose. *11* impers. *por ahí suena* or *se suena, que,* it is rumoured that. ¶ CONJUG. like *contar.*

sonata *f.* MUS. sonata.

sonatina *f.* MUS. sonatina.

sonda *f.* sounding. *2* NAUT. sound, lead. *3* drill [for boring soils]. *4* SURG. sound, probe; catheter.

sondaleza *f.* NAUT. lead line, sounding line.

sondar, sondear *tr.* NAUT. to sound, fathom. *2* to sound [the soil]. *3* to sound, probe [a wound, a person; a person's intentions].

sondeo *m.* sounding, fathoming, probing.

sonecillo *m.* dim. slight sound. *2* merry tune.

sonetista *m.-f.* sonneteer, sonnet writer.

soneto *m.* sonnet.

sonido *m.* sound [sensation produced through

the ear; vibrations causing this sensation]. *2* PHONET. sound.

sonochada *f.* evening [early part of the night].

sonoridad *f.* sonority.

sonoro, -ra; sonoroso, -sa *adj.* sonorous. *2* harmonious. *3* clear, loud.

sonreír *intr.* to smile. ¶ CONJUG. like *reír.*

sonriente *adj.* smiling.

sonrisa *f.* smile.

sonrojar, sonrojear *tr.* to make [one] blush. *2 ref.* to blush.

sonrojo *m.* blush, blushing. *2* word or remark that causes a blush.

sonrosar, sonrosear *tr.* to rose-colour, to flush. *2 ref.* to become rose-coloured.

sonsaca *f.,* **sonsacamiento** *m.* the act of SONSACAR.

sonsacar *tr.* to stealthily take [something] out of its place. *2* to draw out [a person or a secret]. *3* to coax [a servant or employee] away from another's service.

sonsonete *m.* rhythmical tapping. *2* fig. dull monotonous noise; singsong. *3* ironic or scornful tone.

soñación *f. ni por ~,* by no means.

soñador, -ra *adj.* dreaming. *2 m.-f.* dreamer.

soñar *tr.* to dream: *ni soñarlo,* not even in dreams. *2 intr.* to dream; to daydream: *~ con* or *en,* to dream of. ¶ CONJUG. like *contar.*

soñarrera *f.* sleepiness. *2* deep sleep.

soñera *f.* sleepiness.

soñolencia *f.* SOMNOLENCIA.

soñoliento, -ta *adj.* somnolent, sleepy, drowsy, heavy. *2* lazy. *3* soporiferous.

sopa *f.* sop [bread dipped in a liquid]: *hecho una ~,* coll. drenched, soaked to the skin. *2* COOK. soup: *comer la ~ boba,* coll. to live at other people's expense.

sopalancar *tr.* to lift with a lever.

sopapear *tr.* coll. to beat, slap.

sopapina *f.* beating, drubbing.

sopapo *m.* blow under the chin. *2* slap in the face.

sopeña *f.* space or cavity under a rock.

sopera *f.* tureen, soup tureen.

sopero *adj.* soup [plate].

sopesar *tr.* to heft, test the weight of by lifting.

sopetear *tr.* to sop [bread]. *2* to maltreat.

sopetón *m.* toast soaked in olive oil. *2* box, slap. *3 de ~,* suddenly.

sopicaldo *m.* very thin soup.

sopita *f. dim.* light soup.

¡sopla! *interj.* gracious!, what a thing!

sopladero *m.* vent, blowhole.

soplado, -da *adj.* coll. overnice, spruce. *3* coll. conceited, stuck up.

soplador, -ra *adj.* blowing. *2 m.-f.* blower. *3 m.* blowing fan. *4* SOPLADERO.

sopladura *f.* blowing. *2* FOUND. air hole.

soplamocos *m.* box or slap on the nose.

soplar *intr.* to blow [send forth air from mouth, from a pair of bellows, etc.]. *2* [of the wind] to blow. *3 tr.* to blow, blow upon, blow out. *4* to blow [glass]. *5* to fan [coals, a fire]. *6* to blow up; inflate. *7* to steal. *8* to huff [a man] in draughts. *9* to prompt, whisper [tell one what to say]. *10* to report, tattle. *11 ref.* to be puffed up. *12* to stuff oneself.

soplete *m.* blowpipe, blowtorch, torch.

soplido *m.* SOPLO I.

soplillo *m.* blowing fan. *2* a kind of silk gauze.

soplo *m.* blow, blowing [forcing the air from the mouth, etc.]. *2* breath, puff, gust [of wind]. *3*

instant, moment. *4* secret warning. *5* report, piece of talebearing.

soplón, -na *m.-f.* informer, talebearer.

soplonear *tr.-intr.* to inform, tell tales.

soponcio *m.* coll. fainting fit, swoon.

sopor *m.* MED. sopor, lethargy. *2* somnolence.

soporífero, -ra *adj.* soporiferous, soporific.

soportable *adj.* supportable, bearable, tolerable.

soportal *m.* ARCH. porch, portico, arcade.

soportar *tr.* to support [bear the weight or stress of]. *2* to support, endure, suffer, tolerate.

soporte *m.* support, bearing, rest, base.

soprano *m.-f.* MUS. soprano.

sopuntar *tr.* to underscore with dots.

sor *f.* sister [before the name of a nun].

sorber *tr.* to suck [drink by sucking]. *2* to sip. *3* to absorb, imbibe. *4* to swallow.

sorbete *m.* sherbet, water ice.

sorbetera *f.* ice-cream freezer.

sorbito *m. dim.* little sip.

sorbo *m.* absorption, imbibing. *2* sip, gulp, swallow [of a liquid]: *beber a sorbos,* to sip.

sordedad, sordera, sordez *f.* deafness.

sordidez *f.* dirtiness, squalidity. *2* sordidness.

sórdido, -da *adj.* dirty, squalid. *2* sordid.

sordina *f.* MUS. mute, sordine, damper.

sordo, -da *adj.* deaf: *~ como una tapia,* stonedeaf. *2* silent, still: *a la sorda,* noiselessly, imperceptibly. *3* muffled, dull, low [sound]. *4* dull [pain]. *5* MATH., PHONET. surd. *6 m.-f.* deaf person: *hacerse el ~,* to pretend to be deaf, to turn a deaf ear.

sordomudo, -da *adj.-n.* deaf and dumb, deafmute.

sorgo *m.* BOT. sorghum.

soriano, -na *adj.-n.* of Soria.

sorna *f.* sluggishness. *2* sly slowness in doing or saying something.

soro *m.* BOT. sorus.

sorocharse *ref.* (S. Am.) to become mountain sick.

soroche *m.* (Am.) mountain sickness. *2* (Am.) blush flush. *3* (Bol., Chi.) GALENA.

sorprendente *adj.* surprising.

sorprender *tr.* to surprise.

sorpresa *f.* surprise: *coger de ~,* to surprise [astonish; take unawares].

sorra *f.* side of tunny fish.

sorrostrada *f.* insolence, taunt, blunt remark.

sorteamiento *m.* SORTEO.

sortear *tr.* to draw lots for; to raffle. *2* to evade, get around [a difficulty, etc.]. *3* BULLF. to fight [the bull].

sorteo *m.* drawing [of numbers in a lottery]; drawing of lots; raffle. *2* evading or getting around [a difficulty, etc.]. *2* BULLF. fighting the bull.

sortija *f.* small ring; finger ring. *2* curl [of hair].

sortilegio *m.* sortilege.

sortílego, -ga *adj.* sortilegic, sortilegious. *2 m.-f.* sortileger.

sosa *f.* CHEM. soda. *2* BOT. glasswort. *3* soda ash.

sosaina *m.-f.* dull, colourless person.

sosegadamente *adv.* calmly, quietly, peacefully. *2* unhurriedly.

sosegado, -da *adj.* calm, quiet, peaceful; pacified.

sosegador, -ra *adj.* calming, quieting. *2 m.-f.* quieter, appeaser, soother, pacifier.

sosegar *tr.* to calm, quiet, appease, soothe, pacify. *2 intr.* to rest, repose. *3 intr.-ref.* to become calm, to quiet down. *4* to be pacified. ¶ CONJUG. like *acertar.*

sosera, sosería *f.* dullness, insipidity, vapidness.

sosiego *m.* calm, quiet, peace, tranquility.

sosiego, sosiegue, etc. *irr.* V. SOSEGAR.

soslayar *tr.* to place obliquely. *2* to elude, evade, pass over [a question, a difficulty].

soslayo, -ya *adj.* oblique. *2 al* ~, *de* ~, obliquely, askance; sideways; in passing.

soso, -sa *adj.* insipid, tasteless. *2* insipid, dull, uninteresting.

sospecha *f.* suspicion.

sospechar *tr.* to suspect [have an impression of the existence or presence of; to be inclined to think that]. *2 intr.* to suspect, be suspicious about: ~ *de una persona,* to suspect a person.

sospechoso, -sa *adj.* suspicious [arousing suspicion], suspect. *2* suspicious [feeling suspicion]. *3 m.-f.* suspect [person].

sospesar *tr.* SOPESAR.

sostén *m.* support. *2* sustenance. *3* brassière.

sostenedor, -ra *m.-f.* supporter. *2* defender, upholder.

sostener *tr.* to support, sustain, hold up, prop. *2* to support, aid, give strength to, encourage. *3* to support, endure, tolerate. *4* to support, maintain [a family]. *5* to hold [a conference]. *6* to maintain, affirm, contend. *7* to defend, maintain [by argument]. *8* to maintain, sustain, keep up. *9 ref.* to support oneself. ¶ CONJUG. like *tener.*

sostenido, -da *adj.* supported. *2* sustained. *3 adj.-m.* MUS. sharp.

sostenimiento *m.* support. *2* maintenance, sustenance. *3 muro de* ~, retaining wall.

sota *f.* CARDS jack, knave.

sotabanco *m.* attic, garret.

sotabarba *f.* beard under the chin.

sotacola *f.* ATAHARRE.

sotana *f.* cassock, soutane. *2* coll. beating, drubbing.

sótano *m.* cellar, basement.

sotaventarse, sotaventearse *ref.* NAUT. to fall to leeward.

sotavento *m.* NAUT. lee, leeward.

sotechado *m.* shed.

soterrar *tr.* to bury underground. *2* fig. to bury, hide away. ¶ CONJUG. like *acertar.*

sotileza *f.* leader [of a fishline].

sotillo *m. dim.* little grove.

soto *m.* grove. *2* thicket.

soviet *m.* soviet.

soviético, -ca *adj.* soviet, sovietic.

sovoz (a) *adv.* in a low tone, in an undertone.

soy *irr.* V. SER.

spinnaker *m.* NAUT. spinnaker.

su, *pl.* **sus** *poss. adj.* [for the 3rd person in every gender and number]: his, your, her, its, their.

suabo, -ba *adj.-n.* Swabian.

suasorio, -ria *adj.* suasive, persuasive.

suave *adj.* soft, smooth, delicate, mellow. *2* sweet [odour]. *3* soft, gentle, mild. *4* suave, tractable.

suavidad *f.* softness, smoothness. *2* delicateness, mellowness, sweetness. *3* gentleness, mildness, suavity.

suavizador, -ra *adj.* softening, smoothing, mollifylling. *2 m.* razor strop.

suavizar *tr.* to soften, smoothe. *2* to mollify, mitigate, ease, temper. *3* to strop [a razor].

subacuático, -ca *adj.* subaqueous.

subalpino, -na *adj.* subalpine.

subalterno, -na *adj.* subaltern, subordinate. *2 m.-f.* subaltern.

subarrendador, -ra *m.-f.* subletter, subleaser.

subarrendar *tr.* to sublet, sublease. ¶ CONJUG. like *acertar.*

subarrendatario, -ria *m.-f.* sublessee, subtenant.

subarriendo *m.* sublease.

subasta *f.* auction, auction sale.

subastador *m.* auctioneer.

subastar *tr.* to auction, auction off, sell at auction.

subclase *f.* BIOL. subclass.

subclavio, -via *adj.* ANAT. subclavian.

subcomisión *f.* subcommission, subcommitee.

subconsciente *adj.* subconscious.

subcostal *adj.* ANAT. subcostal.

subcutáneo, -a *adj.* subcutaneous.

subdelegado, -da *m.-f.* subdelegate.

subdiácono *m.* subdeacon.

subdirección *f.* office of an assistant director.

subdirector, -ra *m.-f.* assistant director.

súbdito, -ta *m.-f.* subject [of a state, etc.].

subdividir *tr.* to subdivide.

subdivisión *f.* subdivision.

subdominante *f.* MUS. subdominant.

suberoso, -sa *adj.* suberous, suberose.

subestimar *tr.* to underrate, undervalue.

subfamilia *f.* BIOL. subfamily.

subgénero *m.* BIOL. subgenus.

subida *f.* ascent, ascension, going up, climbing. *2* accession [to the throne, etc.]. *3* elevation, hoisting. *4* rise [of prices, tide, etc.]. *5* acclivity, rise.

subido, -da *adj.* raised, mounted [on]. *2* high, strong. *3* high [price]. *4* bright, deep [colour]. *5* ~ *de color,* fig. off-colour, risqué.

subinspector *m.* subinspector.

subintendente *m.* assistant intendant.

subir *intr.* to go up, come up, ascend, rise, climb, mount, soar. *2* to accede [to the throne, etc.]. *3* [of a river, prices, temperature, etc.] to rise. *4* to rise [become higher; increase in amount; come to the surface, slope upward; be promoted, prosper]. *5* MUS. to rise. *6* ~ *de tono,* fig. to become more arrogant; to raise one's voice. *7 tr.* to raise, bring up, take up, hoist. *8* to ascend, climb, go up [the stairs, etc.]. *9* to raise [the voice, price, etc.]. *10 ref.* to climb, get [on]. *11 subirse a la cabeza,* to go to one's head.

subitáneo, -a *adj.* sudden, unexpected.

súbito, -ta *adj.* sudden. *2* hasty, precipitate, impulsive. *3 adv. súbito* or *de* ~, suddenly.

subjefe *m.* assistant chief; second in command.

subjetividad *f.* subjectivity.

subjetivo, -va *adj.* subjective.

subjuntivo *adj.-m.* GRAM. subjunctive.

sublevación, sublevamiento *f.* insurrection, revolt.

sublevar *tr.* to raise in rebellion. *2* to stir up the indignation of. *3 intr.* to revolt, rise in insurrection.

sublimación *f.* sublimation.

sublimado, -da *adj.* sublimated. *2 m.* CHEM. sublimate.

sublimar *tr.* to sublime, sublimate. *2* CHEM. to sublimate.

sublime *adj.* sublime: *lo* ~, the sublime.

sublimidad *f.* sublimity.

subliminar *adj.* PSYCHOL. subliminal.

sublingual *adj.* ANAT. sublingual.

sublunar *adj.* sublunar, sublunary.

submarino, -na *adj.* submarine, underwater. *2 m.* NAUT. submarine.

submaxilar *adj.* ANAT. submaxillary.

submúltiplo, -pla *adj.-n.* MATH. submultiple.

subnormal *adj.* subnormal.

suboficial *m.* MIL. noncommissioned officer next above a sergeant.
suborden *m.* BIOL. suborder.
subordinación *f.* subordination.
subordinado, -da *adj.* subordinate; subservient. *2* GRAM. subordinate. *3 m.-f.* subordinate.
subordinar *tr.* to subordinate.
subproducto *m.* by-product.
subrayar *tr.* to underline. *2* to emphasize.
subrepticio, -cia *adj.* surreptitious.
subrogar *tr.* LAW. to subrogate, surrogate, substitute.
subsanar *tr.* to mend, correct, remedy, repair, obviate. *2* to excuse, exculpate.
subscribir *tr.* to sign, subscribe. *2* to subscribe [to another's opinion]. *3* to enter someone for a subscription to or for. *4 ref.* to subscribe to or for. ¶ CONJUG. Past. p.: *subscripto & subscrito.*
suscripción *f.* subscription.
subscriptor, -ra *m.-f.* subscriber.
subsecretaría *f.* undersecretaryship.
subsecretario, -ria *m.-f.* undersecretary.
subsecuente *adj.* SUBSIGUIENTE.
subseguir *intr.*, **subseguirse** *ref.* to follow next. ¶ CONJUG. like *servir.*
subsidiario, -ria *adj.* subsidiary [furnishing aid]. *2* LAW subsidiary.
subsidio *m.* subsidy. *2 ~ familiar,* family allowance.
subsiguiente *adj.* subsequent.
subsistencia *f.* subsistence. *2 pl.* provisions.
subsistente *adj.* subsistent.
subsistir *intr.* to subsist. *2* to last. *3* to live, find sustenance.
substancia *f.* METAPH. substance. *2* substance, matter. *3* substance [essence, most important part]: *en ~,* in substance, in brief. *4* nutritious part of food. *5* extract, juice. *6* value, importance. *7* coll. sense: *hombre sin ~,* senseless man.
substancial *adj.* substantial [pertaining to the substance]. *2* substancial, essential. *3* nourishing.
substantividad *f.* substantivity.
substanciar *tr.* to abstract, abridge. *2* LAW to conduct the proceedings of [a case].
substancioso, -sa *adj.* juicy, nourishing. *2* substantial, pithy. *3* important.
substantivar *tr.* GRAM. to substantivize.
substantivo, -va *adj.* substantive. *2* substantival. *3 m.* GRAM. substantive noun.
substitución *f.* substitution.
substituible *adj.* replaceable.
substituir *tr.* to substitute, replace; to be a substitute for. ¶ CONJUG. like *huir.*
substitutivo *adj.* substitutive. *2 m.* substitute [thing].
substituto *m.-f.* substitute [person].
substracción *f.* subtraction, deduction. *2* MATH. subtraction. *3* abstraction, purloining, stealing.
substraendo *m.* MATH. subtrahend.
substraer *tr.* to subtract, deduct. *2* MATH. to subtract. *3* to purloin, steal. *4 ~ a,* to put away from. *5 ref.* to elude, evade [observation, duty, etc.]. ¶ CONJUG. like *traer.*
substrato *m.* PHILOS. substratum.
subsuelo *m.* subsoil.
subtender *tr.* GEOM. to subtend.
subteniente *m.* MIL. second lieutenant.
subtensa *f.* GEOM. subtense, chord.
subterfugio *m.* subterfuge.

subterráneo, -a *adj.* subterranean, underground. *2 m.* subterranean. *3* (Am.) subway.
subtítulo *m.* subtitle, subhead.
suburbano, -na *adj.* suburban. *2 m.-f.* suburbanite.
suburbicario, -ria *adj.* suburbicarian.
suburbio *m.* suburb.
subvención *f.* subvention, subsidy.
subvencionar *tr.* to subsidize.
subvenir *tr.* to provide for [the needs of a person, community, etc.]; to meet, defray [expenses]. ¶ CONJUG. like *venir.*
subversivo, -va *adj.* subversive.
subvertir *tr.* to subvert. ¶ CONJUG. like *hervir.*
subvierto, subvierta, subvirtió, etc. *irr.* V. SUBVERTIR.
subyacente *adj.* subjacent, underlying.
subyugación *f.* subjugation.
subyugar *tr.* to subjugate, subdue.
succino *m.* succin, amber.
succión *f.* suction.
sucedáneo, -a *adj.* succedaneous. *2 m.* succedaneum, substitute [thing].
suceder *intr. ~ a,* to succeed [follow in order, ensue, be the successor of]. *2 ref.* to follow one another, follow one after the other. *3 impers.* to happen, occur.
sucedido *m.* event, happening.
sucesión *f.* succession [following in order; succeeding to the throne, etc.]. *2* LAW succession. *3* issue, offspring.
sucesivamente *adv.* successively: *y así ~,* and so on.
sucesivo, -va *adj.* successive, consecutive. *2 en lo ~,* in the future, thereafter.
suceso *m.* event, happening. *2* issue, outcome. *3* course [of time].
sucesor, -ra *m.-f.* successor.
suciedad *f.* dirt, filth. *2* dirtiness, filthiness.
sucinto, -ta *adj.* succint, concise, brief.
sucio, -cia *adj.* dirty, filthy, foul, unclean. *2* soiled, stained. *3* untidy, slovenly. *4* tainted with guilt or sin. *5* obscene. *6* easily soiled. *7* blurred [colour]. *8* foul [play]. *9 adv.* foully.
sucre *m.* sucre [Ecuadorean silver coin].
suculento, -ta *adj.* succulent, juicy, nourishing.
sucumbir *intr.* to succumb. *2* LAW to lose a suit.
sucursal *f.* COM. branch. *2 f.* branch [of a commercial house], branch office.
sud *m.* south. *2* south wind.
sudadero *m.* saddlecloth. *2* sweating place, sudatorium.
sudado, -da *adj.* sweating, sweaty, wet with sweat.
sudafricano, -na *adj.-n.* South African.
sudamericano, -na *adj.-n.* South American.
Sudán *m. pr. n.* GEOG. Sudan.
sudanés, -sa *adj.-n.* Sudanese.
sudar *intr.* to sweat, perspire. *2* fig. to sweat, toil. *intr.-tr.* to sweat, exude. *4 tr.* to sweat [wet with perspiration].
sudario *m.* shroud, winding sheet.
sudatorio, -ria *adj.* sudorific.
sudeste *m.* southeast. *2* southeast wind.
sudoeste *m.* southwest. *2* southwest wind.
sudor *m.* sweat, perspiration, exudation. *2* fig. sweat, toil.
sudoriento, -ta *adj.* wet with sweat.
sudorífero, -ra; sudorífico, -ca *adj.-n.* sudorific.
sudoríparo, -ra *adj.* ANAT. sudoriferous [gland].
sudoroso, -sa *adj.* sweating, perspiring freely.
sudoso, -sa *adj.* sweaty.
sudueste *m.* SUDOESTE.

Suecia *f. pr. n.* GEOG. Sweden.
sueco, -ca *adj.* Swedish. *2 m.-f.* Swede: *hacerse el* ~, coll. to pretend not to hear.
suegra *f.* mother-in-law.
suegro *m.* father-in-law.
suela *f.* sole [of a shoe]: *de siete suelas*, fig. arrant, confirmed. *2* sole leather. *3* leather tip [of billiard cue]. *4* ICHTH. sole.
sueldo *m.* salary, pay: *a* ~ *de*, in the pay of. *2* sol [ancient coin].
sueldo, suelde, etc. *irr.* V. SOLDAR.
suelo *m.* ground, earth [surface of the earth] floor, pavement: *arrastrarse por el* ~, to crawl, creep; to cringe, humble oneself; *venir* or *venirse al* ~, to fall to the ground; to fail; *por el* ~, *por los suelos*, in state of great depreciation. *2* soil, land: ~ *natal*, native soil. *3* earth, world. *4* bottom, underside. *5* dregs, lees, sediment.
suelta *f.* release, setting free or loose.
suelto *adj.* loose [free; slack; hanging partly free; composed of free particles]. *2* light, swift, easy, agile, nimble. *3* flowing, fluent. *4* odd, loose, separate, detached. *5* single [copy]. *6* blank [verse]. *7* ~ *de lengua*, outspoken. *8 m. suelto* or *dinero* ~, small change. *9 m.* newspaper paragraph.
suelto, suelte, etc. *irr* V. SOLTAR.
sueno, suene, etc. *irr.* V. SONAR.
sueño *m.* sleep: ~ *pesado*, deep sleep; *tener* ~, to be sleepy; *entre sueños*, while half asleep. *2* sleepiness, drowsiness. *3* dream: *en sueños*, dreaming; *ni por sueños*, by no means.
sueño, sueñe, etc. *irr.* V. SOÑAR.
suero *m.* BIOL., MED. serum. *2* whey.
sueroterapia *f.* serotherapy, serum therapy.
suerte *f.* chance, hazard; fortune, lot, fate, destiny. *2* luck: *buena* or *mala* ~, good or bad luck. *3* good luck: *tener* ~, to be lucky; *por* ~, luckily. *4* lot [in deciding or selecting by lot]: *le cayó* or *le tocó la* ~, the lot fell on him. *5* state, condition: *mejorar de* ~, to better oneself. *6* sort, kind, class. *7* manner, way: *de* ~ *que*, so that; and so. *8* BULLF. any of the parts in which a bullfight is divided.
sueste *m.* southeast. *2* NAUT. southwester [hat].
suéter *m.* (Angl.) sweater [thick woollen jersey].
suevo, -va *adj.-n.* Swabian.
suficiencia *f.* ability, efficiency: *aire de* ~, sufficiency, conceit.
suficiente *adj.* sufficient, sufficing, enough: *ser* ~, to suffice. *2* able, capable.
sufijo, -ja *adj.* suffixed. *2 m.* suffix.
sufocar *tr.-ref.* SOFOCAR.
sufragáneo, -a *adj.-m.* suffragan.
sufragar *tr.* to defray, pay [the expenses]. *2* to aid, assist. *3 intr.* (Am.) to vote.
sufragio *m.* suffrage. *2* help, assistance. *3* ECCL. prayer, etc., for the dead.
sufragista *adj.-n.* suffragist. *2 f.* suffragette.
sufrible *adj.* sufferable, bearable.
sufrido, -da *adj.* enduring, patient, long-suffering. *3* that does not show dirt [colour]. *4* complacent [husband].
sufridor, -ra *adj.* suffering. *2 m.-f.* sufferer.
sufrimiento *m.* suffering. *2* bearing, endurance, tolerance.
sufrir *tr.* suffer [pain, loss, grief, punishment, etc.]. *2* to suffer, endure, bear up, permit, tolerate. *3* to undergo [a change, operation, etc.]. *4* to take [an examination]. *6 intr.* to suffer. *7* to worry.

sufusión *m.* MED. suffusion.
sugerencia *f.* (Am.) suggestion, hint.
sugerir *tr.* to suggest, hint. ¶ CONJUG. like *hervir*.
sugestión *f.* suggestion [suggesting; idea, etc., suggested]. *2* [hypnotic] suggestion.
sugestionable *adj.* suggestible, easily influenced.
sugestionar *tr.* to hypnotize. *2* to influence [a person].
suicida *adj.* suicidal. *2 m.-f.* suicide [person].
suicidarse *ref.* to commit suicide, destroy oneself.
suicidio *m.* suicide, self-murder.
Suiza *pr. n.* GEOG. Switzerland.
suizo, -za *adj.-n.* Swiss.
sujeción *f.* subjection. *2* subduing. *3* submission, obedience. *4* fastening. *5* accordance [with law, etc.].
sujetador *m.* holder, fastener, clamp, clip, etc.
sujetapapeles, *pl.* **-les** *m.* paper clip.
sujetar *tr.* to subject, subdue. *2* to check, hold, restrain. *3* to hold fast, catch, grasp; fasten, attach, tie. *4 ref.* to submit, be subjected. *5* to conform to.
sujeto, -ta *irr. p. p.* of SUJETAR. *2 adj.* held, grasped, attached. *3* subject [in subjection; liable, prone]. *4 m.* GRAM., LOG., PHILOS. subject. *5* subject, matter. *6* coll. individual, fellow.
sulfatar *tr.* to sulphate.
sulfato *m.* CHEM. sulphate.
sulfhídrico, -ca *adj.* CHEM. sulphydric.
sulfito *m.* CHEM. sulphite.
sulfurar *tr.* CHEM. to sulphurate. *2* fig. to anger, incense. *3 ref.* to get angry, get furious.
sulfúreo, -a *adj.* sulphureous, sulphury.
sulfúrico, -ca *adj.* CHEM. sulphuric.
sulfuro *m.* CHEM. sulphide.
sulfuroso, -sa *adj.* sulphurous.
sultán *m.* sultan.
sultana *f.* sultana, sultaness.
sultanato *m.*, **sultanía** *f.* sultanate.
suma *f.* sum [aggregate; addition; total]; ~ *y sigue*, carried forward. *2* sum [of money]. *3* summa. *4* sum, substance: *en* ~, in sum.
sumador, -ra *adj.* adding. *2 m.-f.* adder.
sumamente *adv.* exceedingly, extremely, highly.
sumando *m.* MATH. addend.
sumar *tr.* MATH. to add: *máquina de* ~, adding machine. *2* to amount to. *3* to add, join. *4* to sum up. *5 ref. sumarse a*, to be added to; to adhere to [an opinion]; to join [a group].
sumaria *f.* LAW written proceedings. *2* MIL. indictment.
sumario, -ria *adj.* summary. *2 m.* summary, abstract. *3* LAW indictment.
sumarísimo, -ma *adj.* LAW swift, expeditious.
sumergible *adj.* submersible. *2 m.* submersible boat.
sumergir *tr.* to submerge, sink. *2 ref.* to submerge, plunge, dive; be submerged.
sumersión *f.* submersion, immersion.
sumidad *f.* apex, top, tip.
sumidero *m.* sewer, drain, sink, sump.
suministrador, -ra *adj.* furnishing, providing, supplying. *2 m.-f.* furnisher, provider, supplier.
suministrar *tr.* to furnish, provide, supply.
suministro *m.* providing, supplying. *2* provision, supply.
sumir *tr.* to sink, plunge, engulf. *2* to take [the Eucharist] in the mass. *3 ref.* to sink, plunge, be engulfed. *4* [of cheeks, etc.] to be sunken.
sumisión *f.* submission; submissiveness.
sumiso, -sa *adj.* submissive, humble, obedient.

summum *m.* the limit, the highest degree.
sumo, -ma *adj.* very great or much, greatest, highest, extreme, utmost: *en ~ grado*, highly; *a lo ~*, at most. *2* high, supreme: *Sumo Pontífice*, Pontifex Maximus; Sovereign Pontiff.
sunción *f.* taking [of the Eucharist] in the mass.
Sund *m. pr. n.* GEOG. Sound.
suntuario, -ria *adj.* sumptuary.
suntuosidad *f.* sumptuousness.
suntuoso, -sa *adj.* sumptuous, gorgeous, magnificent.
supeditación *f.* subjection, subordination.
supeditar *tr.* to reduce to subjection. *2* to subordinate.
superable *adj.* superable, surmountable.
superabundancia *f.* superabundance.
superabundar *intr.* to superabound.
superar *tr.* surpass, exceed, excel. *2* to overcome, surmount.
superávit *m.* surplus [excess of revenue over expenditure].
supercarburante *m.* high-test fuel.
superchería *f.* fraud, deceit, humbug, trick.
superdominante *f.* MUS. superdominant.
supereminente *adj.* supereminent.
superentender *tr.* to superintend, inspect, supervise.
supererogatorio, -ria *adj.* supererogatory.
superficial *adj.* superficial; shallow.
superficie *f.* surface, superficies. *2* area [superficial extent].
superfino, -na *adj.* superfine, extra fine.
superfluidad *f.* superfluity, superfluousness.
superfluo, -flua *adj.* superfluous.
superfosfato *m.* CHEM. superphosphate.
superhombre *m.* superman.
superintendencia *f.* superintendence, superintendency, supervision.
superintendente *m.-f.* superintendent, supervisor.
superior *adj.* superior. *2* upper. *3* better, finer. *4* higher [algebra, mathematics, education, etc.]. *6 m.* superior.
superiora *f.* mother superior.
superioridad *f.* superiority, superiorness.
superiormente *adv.* superiorly, extremely well.
superlativo, -va *adj.* superlative, surpassing; highest. *2 adj.-m.* GRAM. superlative.
superno, -na *adj.* supreme, highest.
supernumerario, -ria *adj.* supernumerary.
súpero *adj.* BOT. superior [ovary]. ´
superponer *tr.* to superpose, superimpose. ¶ CONJUG. like *poner.*
superposición *f.* superposition, superimposition.
superpuesto, -ta *p. p.* of SUPERPONER.
supersensible *adj.* supersensitive.
supersónico, -ca *adj.* supersonic. *2 f.* supersonics.
superstición *f.* superstition.
supersticioso, -sa *adj.* superstitious.
supersubstancial (pan) *m.* THEOL. the Host.
supervenir *intr.* SOBREVENIR. ¶ CONJUG. like *venir.*
supervivencia *f.* survival. *2* LAW survivorship.
superviviente *adj.* surviving. *2 m.-f.* survivor.
supinación *f.* supineness.
supinador *adj.-m.* ANAT. supinator.
supino, -na *adj.* supine [opposed to *prone*]. *2* stupid, crass. *3* GRAM. supine.
súpito, -ta *adj.* SÚBITO.
suplantación *f.* supplanting. *2* fraudulent alteration [in a writing].
suplantar *tr.* to supplant. *2* to alter [a writing] fraudulently.

suplementario, -ria *adj.* supplemental, supplementary.
suplemento *m.* supplement.
suplente *adj.* substituting. *2 m.-f.* substitute.
supletorio, -ria *adj.* suppletory, supplemental.
súplica *f.* supplication, entreaty, petition, request.
suplicación *f.* supplication. *2* rolled waffle.
suplicante *adj.* suppliant. *2 m.-f.* suppliant, supplicant.
suplicar *tr.* to supplicate, entreat, pray, beg.
suplicatorio, -ria *adj.* supplicatory.
suplicio *m.* torture. *2* LAW corporal punishment; execution; place of execution. *3* fig. anguish, suffering.
suplir *tr.* to supply [make up for deficiency, loss, need, etc.]. *2* to replace, serve as a substitute for.
supondré, supondría, etc. *irr.* V. SUPONER.
suponedor, -ra *m.-f.* supposer.
1) **suponer** *m.* supposition.
2) **suponer** *tr.* to suppose, assume. *2* to imply, presuppose. *3* to entail [expense, etc.]. *4* intr. [of a person] to have weight or authority. ¶ CONJUG. like *poner.*
supongo, suponga, etc. *irr.* V. SUPONER.
suportar *tr.* SOPORTAR.
suposición *f.* supposition, assumption. *2* imposition, falsehood. *3* consequence, distinction.
supositicio, -cia *adj.* supposititious.
supositivo, -va *adj.* suppositive.
supositorio *m.* MED. suppository.
supradicho, -cha *adj.* aforesaid, above-mentioned.
suprarrenal *adj.* ANAT. suprarenal.
suprasensible *adj.* supersensible.
supremacía *f.* supremacy.
supremo, -ma *adj.* supreme.
supresión *f.* suppression, abolition, elimination, omission.
supresivo, -va *adj.* abolishing, eliminating, omitting.
suprimir *tr.* to suppress, abolish, eliminate, strike out, do away with. *2* to omit.
supuestamente *adv.* pretendedly, assumedly.
supuesto, -ta *irreg. p. p.* of SUPONER. *2 adj.* supposed, assumed, pretended: *nombre ~*, assumed name. *3 dar por ~*, to take for granted; *esto ~*, this being understood; *por ~*, of course, naturally; *~ que*, since, granting that. *4 m.* supposition, assumption, hypothesis.
supuración *f.* suppuration.
supurar *intr.* MED. to suppurate.
supuse, supusiera, etc. *irr.* V. SUPONER.
suputar *tr.* computate, calculate, reckon.
sur *m.* south. *2* south wind.
surá *f.* surah.
surcado, -da *adj.* furrowed, sulcate, sulcated.
surcar *tr.* AGR. to furrow, plough. *2* to furrow, groove. *3* to cut through [the water, the air].
surco *m.* furrow, groove, rut. *2* groove [of a phonographic record]. *3* wrinkle, line [in the face].
sureste *m.* SUDESTE.
surgidero *m.* NAUT. anchorage, anchoring place.
surgir *intr.* [of water] to spirt, spurt, spring. *2* to come forth, issue, appear, arise. *3* NAUT. to anchor. ¶ P. p.: *surgido & surto.*
suripanta *f.* formerly, a chorus girl.
suroeste *m.* SUDOESTE.
surrealismo *m.* surrealism.
surtida *f.* MIL. sally, sortie. *2* FORT. sally port. *3* NAUT. slipway.
surtidero *m.* outlet [of a pond]. *2* SURTIDOR 3.

surtido *adj.* COM. assorted. *2 m.* COM. assortment, stock. *3* COM. supply.

surtidor, -ra *adj.* supplying. *2 m.-f.* supplier. *3 m.* jet, spout, springing up fountain. *4* ~ *de gasolina*, gasoline pump.

surtimiento *m.* supplying, furnishing.

surtir *tr.* to supply, furnish, provide, stock. *2* ~ *efecto*, to work, to have the desired effect. *3 intr.* [of water] to spout, spirt, spurt, spring.

surto, -ta *adj.* NAUT. anchored.

sus *posses. adj. pl.* of SU.

¡sus! *interj.* up!, forward!, get going!

Susana *f. pr. n.* Susan.

susceptibilidad *f.* susceptibility. *2* touchiness.

susceptible *adj.* susceptible [admitting of]. *2* touchy, ready to take offence.

suscitar *tr.* to raise, stir up, provoke, originate. *2 ref.* to rise, start, originate.

suscribir *tr.-ref.* SUBSCRIBIR.

suscripción *f.* SUBSCRIPCIÓN.

suscritor, -ra *m.-f.* SUBSCRIPTOR.

susodicho, -cha *adj.* above-mentioned, above-named.

suspender *tr.* to suspend, hang up. *2* to suspend [stop, delay, interrupt]. *3* to adjourn [a meeting]. *4* to suspend [from office]. *5* to astonish, ravish. *6* to fail [in an examination]. *7 ref.* to be suspended, stopped or adjourned.

suspensión *f.* suspension: *en* ~, in suspension. *2* adjournment [of a meeting]. *3* astonishment, ravishment.

suspensivo, -va *adj.* suspending. *2* suspension [points].

suspenso, -sa *adj.* suspended: *en* ~, suspended, not decided; in suspense. *2* astonished, perplexed: *3 m.* EDUC. failing mark [in an examination].

suspensorio, -ria *adj.-m.* suspensory.

suspicacia *f.* suspicion, distrust. *2* suspiciousness.

suspicaz *adj.* suspicious, distrustful.

suspirado, -da *adj.* sighed for, longed for.

suspirar *intr.* to sigh. *2 fig.* ~ *por*, to sigh for; to love madly.

suspiro *m.* sigh: *exhalar el último* ~, to breathe one's last. *2* kind of cake. *3* glass whistle. *4* MUS. short rest.

sustancia, sustancial, sustanciar, sustancioso, etc. = SUBSTANCIA, SUBSTANCIAL, SUBSTANCIAR, SUBSTANCIOSO, etc.

sustantivar *tr.* SUBSTANTIVAR.

sustantivo *adj.-m.* SUBSTANTIVO.

sustentable *adj.* defensible [by argument].

sustentación *f.* support, sustentation. *2* AER. lift.

sustentáculo *m.* support, prop, rest, stay.

sustentamiento *m.* sustentation, sustenance.

sustentar *tr.* to sustain, maintain, support, feed. *2* to sustain, support, hold up. *3* to sustain, defend.

sustento *m.* sustenance, maintenance. *2* support.

sustitución, sustituible, sustituir, etc. = SUBSTITUCIÓN, SUBSTITUIBLE, SUBSTITUIR, etc.

susto *m.* fright, scare, shock: *dar un* ~, to frighten, scare, startle. *2* fear, aprehension.

sustracción, sustraendo, sustraer = SUBSTRACCIÓN, SUBSTRAENDO, SUBSTRAER.

susurrante *adj.* whispering; murmuring, murmurous, purling, rustling.

susurrar *intr.-tr.* to whisper: *se susurra que*, it is whispered or rumoured that. *2 intr.* [of wind, etc.] to murmur; [of a book] to purl; [of leaves, etc.] to rustle.

susurro *m.* whisper. *2* murmur, purling, rustle.

sutás *m.* soutache.

sutil *adj.* subtle, subtile. *2* thin, slender.

sutileza *f.* subtlety, subtility. *2* thinness, slenderness. *3* dexterity.

sutilidad *f.* subtlety.

sutilizar *tr.* to subtilize. *2* to render thin or slender. *3* to refine, polish. *4 intr.* to subtilize, split hairs.

sutura *f.* seam. *2* ANAT., BOT., ZOOL., SURG. suture.

suyo, suya, suyos, suyas *poss. adj.* (never used before the noun) his, her, its, their, of him, of her, of it, of them; of his, of hers, of its, of theirs. *2 de* ~, by nature; on his (her, their) own accord. *3 esto es muy* ~, this is like him. *4 poss. pron.* his, hers, its, theirs. *5 hacer de las suyas*, to be up to one's old tricks. *6 salirse con la suya*, to have one's way. *7 m. pl. los suyos*, his (her, their) family, people, etc.; yours [when using *usted*].

suzón *m.* BOT. groundsel.

svástica *f.* swastica.

T

T, t *f.* T, t, twenty-third letter of the Spanish alphabet.

¡ta! *interj.* easy! 2 look! 3 *¡ta, ta!*, rat-a-tat! tut, tut!

taba *f.* anklebone. 2 knucklebone [of sheep]. 3 knucklebones [game].

tabacal *m.* tobacco field.

tabacalero, -ra *adj.* [pertaining to] tobacco. 2 *m.-f.* tobacco grower or dealer.

tabaco *m.* tobacco: ~ *en polvo*, snuff. 2 snuff [powdered tobacco]: *tomar* ~, to snuff. 3 cigar. 4 black rot [in trees].

tabalada *f.* coll. slap, spank. 2 coll. fall on the behind.

tabalario *m.* coll. behind, posteriors.

tabalear *tr.* to rock, to shake. 2 *intr.* to drum with the fingers.

tabaleo *m.* shaking. 2 drumming with the fingers.

tabanazo *m.* slap, spank.

tabanco *m.* stall for selling eatables.

tábano *m.* ENT. gadfly, horsefly.

tabaque *m.* small wicker basket.

tabaquera *f.* snuff box. 2 bowl [of a tobacco pipe].

tabaquería *f.* tobacco shop.

tabaquero, -ra *m.-f.* tobacconist. 2 cigar maker.

tabaquismo *m.* MED. tobaccoism.

tabardillo *m.* coll. sunstroke. 2 MED. typhus. 3 fig. wild, annoying person.

tabardo *m.* tabard.

tabarra, tabarrera *f.* bore [tedious, speech, performance, etc.].

taberna *f.* tavern, public house, wine shop, *saloon.

tabernáculo *m.* tabernacle.

tabernario, -ria *adj.* coarse, low, vulgar.

tabernera *f.* mistress of a wine shop. 2 wife of the keeper of a wine shop.

tabernero *m.* keeper of a public house or wine shop; *saloon keeper.

tabes *f.* MED. consumption, tabes.

tabicar *tr.* to wall up, close up.

tabique *m.* thin wall, partition. 2 BIOL. septum.

tabla *f.* board [thin piece of timber; wooden slab]: ~ *de armonía*, MUS. soundboard; ~ *de chilla*, clapboard; ~ *de salvación*, last recourse; *salvarse en una* ~, to have a narrow escape; *a raja* ~, at any cost, regardless of·anything else. 2 plank, slab, tablet. 3 board [for posting notices]. 4 PAINT. panel: ~ *rasa*, unpainted panel; un-

trained mind; *hacer* ~ *rasa de*, to disregard [all obstacles] in the way of something. 5 table diamond. 6 wide part [of a member of the body]. 7 AGR. strip of land, garden patch. 8 meat stall. 9 PERSP. table. 10 *Tabla Redonda*, Round Table. 11 BILL. *por* ~, cushion [carom]; fig. indirectly. 12 *sing.-pl.* table [of contents, of logarithms, etc.]: *tabla de la ley*, tables of the law. 13 *pl.* draw [at chess & draughts]: *hacer tablas*, to draw, to come out even. 14 THEAT. boards, stage.

tablacho *m.* sluice gate.

tablado *m.* stage, scaffold, platform [of timber]. 2 flooring [made of boards]. 3 THEAT. stage boards.

tablajería *f.* meat stall, butcher's shop.

tablajero *m.* butcher [dealer in meat].

tablar *m.* set of garden plots. 2 calm stretch of a river. 3 side board [of a car].

tablazón *f.* boarding, planking. 2 NAUT. planking and deck flooring [of a ship].

tablero *m.* board [square or oblong piece of thin wood]: ~ *de anuncios*, board [for posting notices]; ~ *de instrumentos*, AUTO. dashboard. 2 slab. 3 ARCH., CARP. panel. 4 table top. 5 drawing board. 6 board [for certain games]: ~ *de ajedrez*, chessboard; ~ *de damas*, draughtboard, checkerboard. 7 shop counter. 8 TABLAR. 9 floor [of a bridge]. 10 wooden blackboard. 11 ~ *contador*, abacus.

tableta *f.* dim. small board, tablet. 2 floor board. 3 tablet, lozenge, pastil, pastille.

tableteado, -da *m.* rattling sound.

tabletear *intr.* to rattle clappers. 2 to sound like clappers.

tableteo *m.* rattling sound. 2 rattle [of machine-gun shots].

tablilla *f.* small board, tablet. 2 bulletin board. 3 SURG. splint.

tablón *m.* thick plank. 2 NAUT. plank, strake.

tabú *m.* taboo.

tabuco *m.* hovel, narrow room.

tabulador *m.* tabulator [of a typewriter].

tabular *adj.* tabular.

taburete *m.* tabouret, stool.

tac *m.* tick [of clock, heart, etc.].

tacada *f.* BILL. stroke.

tacañear *intr.* to be niggarly, stingy.

tacañería *f.* niggardliness, stinginess.

tacaño, -ña *adj.* niggardly, stingy, closefisted. *2 m.-f.* niggard, miser.
tacazo *m.* BILL. stroke.
tácito, -ta *adj.* tacit. *2* silent.
taciturnidad *f.* taciturnity.
taciturno, -na *adj.* taciturn.
taco *m.* plug. *2* short and thick piece of wood. *3* ARTILL. wad. *4* ramrod. *5* BILL. cue. *6* popgun. *7* almanac pad. *8* picker [in a loom]. *9* profane oath: *echar tacos,* to swear. *10 hacerse un ~,* to get muddled, confused. *11* (Am.) heel [of shoe].
tacómetro *m.* tachometer.
tacón *m.* heel [part of shoe or boot that supports the heel].
taconazo *m.* blow with the shoe heel.
taconear *tr.* to walk hard on one's heels, to strut on one's heels.
taconeo *m.* walking hard on one's heels. *2* noise made with the heels in walking.
táctico, -ca *adj.* tactical. *2 m.* tactician. *3 f.* tactics.
táctil *adj.* tactile.
tacto *m.* touch, sense of touch. *2* touching, feeling. *3* touch, feel [of a fabric, etc.]. *4* tact.
tacha *f.* fault, defect, blemish: *poner ~ a,* to find fault with.
tachar *tr.* to find a fault or defect in or with. *2* to accuse, censure. *3* to cancel, strike out.
tachón *m.* erasure. *2* short piece of ribbon or braid trimming. *3* stud, ornamental tack.
tachonar *tr.* to trim [clothes] with short pieces of ribbon or braid. *2* to adorn with ornamental tacks. *3* to stud, to spangle.
tachuela *f.* tack, hobnail.
tael *m.* tael [weight and coin].
tafanario *m.* coll. behind, posteriors.
tafetán, *pl.* **-nes** *m.* taffeta [silk fabric]. *2 ~ inglés,* court plaster. *3 pl.* fig. flags, colours. *4* coll. finery.
tafia *f.* tafia.
tafilete *m.* morocco leather.
tafiletear *tr.* to adorn with morocco leather.
tagalo, -la *m.-f.* Tagal, Tagalog.
tagarnina *f.* BOT. golden thistle. *2* coll. poor cigar.
tagarote *m.* ORN. sparrow hawk. *2* coll. escrivener. *3* coll. lanky fellow.
tahalí *m.* baldric.
taheño *adj.* red [hair]. *2* red-bearded.
tahona *f.* backery, baker's shop.
tahonero *m.* baker [breadmaker].
tahur, -ra *m.-f.* gambler, gamester. *3* cardsharp.
taifa *f.* faction, party. *2* coll. lot [of disreputable people].
Tailandia *f. pr. n.* GEOG. Thailand.
taimado, -da *adj.* sly, cunning, crafty. *2* (Chi.) sullen, stubborn.
taimería *f.* slyness, craftiness, rascality.
taita *f.* coll. dad, daddy.
tajada *f.* cut, slice. *2* hoarseness [from a cold]. *3* coll. drunk, drunken fit.
tajadera *f.* curved chopping knife. *2* cold chisel.
tajadero *m.* COOK. chopping block.
tajado, -da *adj.* steep, sheer.
tajador, -ra *adj.* cutting. *2 m.* chopping block.
tajamar *m.* cutwater [of bridge or ship]. *2* (Am.) dike; dam.
tajante *adj.* cutting, sharp. *2* peremptory [tone].
tajar *tr.* to cut, divide, slice.
Tajo *m. pr. n.* GEOG. Tagus.
tajo *m.* cut, incision. *2* steep cliff. *3* cutting edge. *4* chopping block; butcher's block; beheading block. *5* three-legged rustic stool. *6* cut [in a mountain]. *7* FENC. cut. *8* line of progress of a gang of reapers, miners, etc.
tal *adj.* such, such a, the same as, like. *2 el ~, -la ~,* that, that man, that fellow, that woman; *el ~ drama,* that play; *el ~ Pedro,* that man Peter. *3 un ~, una tal,* one, a certain. *4 tal cual viajero,* a few travellers, an occasional traveller. *5 indef. pron.* someone. *6* such a thing. *7 ~ para cual,* two of a kind. *8 otro que ~,* another of the same kind. *9 adv.* so, thus, in such a way. *10 con ~ (de) que,* provided that. *11 no ~,* no, no; *sí ~,* yes, indeed. *12 ¿qué ~?,* how do you do?; how do you like it? *13 ~ cual,* such as; middling, so so.
tala *f.* felling of trees. *2* destruction, havoc. *3* tipcat [boy's game]. *4* cat [used in tipcat].
talabarte *m.* sword belt.
talabartería *f.* saddlery, harness shop.
talabartero *m.* saddler, harness maker.
taladrador, -ra *adj.* boring, drilling, piercing. *2 m.-f.* borer, driller. *3 f.* drilling machine.
taladrante *adj.* piercing, penetrating.
taladrar *tr.* to bore, drill, perforate. *2* to punch [a ticket]. *3* to pierce, penetrate.
taladro *m.* drill, auger, boring instrument. *2* bore, drill hole, auger hole.
talamete *m.* NAUT. forward deck [in small vessels].
tálamo *m.* bridal chamber; bridal bed. *2* BOT. thalamus, receptacle. *3* ANAT. thalamus.
talán *m.* ding-dong.
talanquera *f.* barrier, fence. *2* fig. defence, cover, place of refuge. *3* fig. safety.
talante *m.* mode or manner of doing anything. *2* mood, mien, countenance. *3* will, wish, pleasure. *4 de buen ~,* in a good mood; with good grace; *de mal ~,* in a bad mood; with bad grace.
1) **talar** *adj.* long, reaching to the ankles.
2) **talar** *tr.* to fell [trees]; to fell or cut the trees of. *2* to destroy, lay waste.
talares *m. pl.* MYTH. talaria [of Mercury].
talayote *m.* ARCHEOL. talayot.
talco *m.* MINER. talc, talcum. *2* tinsel [material].
talcualillo, -lla *adj.* coll. middling.
talega *f.* bag, sack; money bag. *2* bagful. *3* hair bag. *4* POL. coll. money, wealth.
talegada *f.* bagful.
talego *m.* bag, sack.
taleguilla *f. dim.* small bag. *2* bullfighter's breeches.
talento *m.* talent.
talentoso, -sa; talentudo, -da *adj.* talented, able, clever.
tálero *m.* thaler [old German coin].
Talía *f. pr. n.* MYTH. Thalia.
talio *m.* CHEM. thallium.
talión *m.* talion, retaliation.
talismán *m.* talisman.
talmente *adv.* the same as; in such a manner.
Talmud *m.* Talmud.
talo *m.* BOT. thallus.
talofita *adj.* BOT. thallophytic. *2 f.* BOT. thallophyte.
talón *m.* ANAT. heel: *apretar los talones,* to hurry; to fly; *pisar los talones a uno,* to be at one's heels. *2* heel [part of a shoe or stocking that covers heel of the foot]. *3* MUS. heel [of a bow]. *4* NAUT. heel [of the keel]. *5* ARCH. heel, talon [molding]. *6* a check, voucher, coupon, etc., detached from a stub book. *7* standard [in a monetary system].
talonada *f.* kick with the heels.
talonario *m.* stub book: *~ de cheques,* chequebook.
talonazo *m.* kick or blow with the heel.

talonear *intr.* coll. to walk fast, to dash along.
talquita *f.* MINER. talc schist.
talud *m.* talus, slope. 2 ARCH. batter.
talla *f.* F. ARTS carving, wood carving: *media* ~, half relief. 2 round [of certain card games]. 3 height, stature [of a person]. 4 size [of a person].
tallado, -da *p. p.* of TALLAR. 2 *adj.* cut, carved. 3 *bien* or *mal* ~, having a good or bad figure.
tallador, -ra *m.-f.* engraver, diesinker. 2 one who measures the height of persons.
1) **tallar** *adj.* ready for cutting [tree, forest]. 2 *m.* forest ready for the first cut. 3 young growth of trees.
2) **tallar** *tr.* to carve, engrave. 2 to cut [a precious stone]. 3 to appraise. 4 to tax, impose tax on. 5 *intr.* to be the banker [in certain card games].
tallarín *m.* noodle [alimentary paste].
talle *m.* form, figure, appearance [of a person]. 2 waist [of a person, of a garment]. 3 fit, adjustment [of a garment to the body].
taller *m.* shop, workshop, factory. 2 atelier, studio.
tallista *m.-f.* sculptor, wood carver.
tallo *m.* BOT. stem, stalk. 2 BOT. shoot, sprout.
talludo, -da *adj.* BOT. long-stemmed. 2 tall, overgrown [boy, girl]. 3 no longer young.
tamal *m.* tamale [a Mexican dish].
tamanduá *f.* ZOOL. tamandua, anteater.
tamañamente *adv.* as greatly.
tamañito, -ta *adj. dim.* so small. 2 very small. 3 humbled, confused.
tamaño, -ña *adj.* as big, or as small. 2 very large or very small: *abrir tamaños ojos*, to open one's eyes wide. 3 so great, such a great. 4 *m.* size: ~ *natural*, full size.
tamañuelo, -la *adj. dim.* very small.
támara *f.* BOT. a date palm. 2 date palm field. 3 *pl.* cluster of dates. 4 brushwood.
tamarindo *m.* BOT. tamarind [tree and fruit].
tamarisco, tamariz *m.* BOT. tamrisk.
tambaleante *adj.* staggering, tottering, reeling.
tambalear *intr.-ref.* to stagger, totter, reel.
tambaleo *m.* staggering, tottering, reeling.
tambanillo ARCH. tympanum.
tambarillo *m.* small chest with an arched lid.
también *adv.* also, too, as well, likewise.
tambo *m.* (Am.) inn. 2 (Am.) dairy.
tambor *m.* MUS., ARCH. drum, tambour. 2 MUS. drummer: ~ *mayor*, drum major. 3 coffee roaster. 4 MACH. drum, barrel. 5 MACH. band pulley. 6 tambour [for embroidering]. 7 FORT. drum. 8 ANAT. tympanum, eardrum.
tambora *f.* MUS. bass drum.
tamborear *intr.* to drum with the fingers.
tamboril *m.* tabor, tabour, timbrel [small drum].
tamborilada *f.*, **tamborilazo** *m.* coll. bump on one's behind. 2 coll. slap on the head or shoulders.
tamborilear *intr.* to drum.
tamborilero *m.* taborer, drummer.
tamborilete *m.* PRINT. planer.
tamborín *m.* TAMBORIL.
tamborino *m.* TAMBORIL. 2 TAMBORILERO.
tamboritear *intr.* TAMBORILEAR.
tambucho *m.* NAUT. hood.
Támesis *m. pr. n.* GEOG. Thames.
tamiz *m.* sieve, bolter.
tamizar *tr.* to sift, sieve.
tamo *m.* fuzz, fluff. 2 dust gathered under beds, etc.
tampoco *adv.* neither, not either, either: *si usted no va, yo* ~ *iré*, you don't go, neither shall I; *ni yo* ~, nor I either.
tamtam *m.* tom-tom.
tamujo *m.* BOT. a shrub of which brooms are made.
tan *adv. contr.* de TANTO so, as: ~ ... *como*, as ... as. 2 ~ *siquiera*, ever so, at least. 3 ~ *solo*, only. 4 *qué* ... ~, what a: *¡qué casa* ~ *hermosa!*, what a beautiful house.
tanaceto *m.* BOT. tansy.
tanato *m.* CHEM. tannate.
tanda *f.* turn [to do something]. 2 shift, relay [of workmen]. 3 task. 4 layer, bed. 5 series, number.
tándem *m.* tandem bicycle.
tanganillo *m.* temporary prop or support.
tángano *m.* CHITO.
tangencia *adj.* tangency.
tangencial *adj.* tangential.
tangente *adj.-f.* GEOM. tangent: *escapar*, *irse* or *salir*, *por la* ~, fig. to resort to subterfuges.
Tánger *m. pr. n.* Tangier.
tangerino, -na *adj.-n.* Tangerine.
tangible *adj.* tangible.
tango *m.* tango [dance]. 2 CHITO.
tangón *m.* NAUT. swinging boom.
tánico, -ca *adj.* CHEM. tannic.
tanino *m.* CHEM. tannin.
tanque *m.* tank, water tank. 2 MIL. tank. 3 (Am.) reservoir.
tantalio *m.* CHEM. tantalum.
Tántalo *m. pr. n.* MYTH. Tantalus.
tantán *m.* gong. 2 tom-tom.
tantarantán *m.* rub-a-dub. 2 coll. hard smack.
tanteador, -ra *m.-f.* scorekeeper. 2 *m.* score board.
tantear *tr.* to try, size up, test, feel, explore. 2 to consider carefully. 3 to sketch. 4 *tr.-intr.* GAMES to keep the score [of].
tanteo *m.* trial, testing, trial and error. 2 rough calculation: *al* ~, by guess. 3 points, score [in a game].
1) **tanto** *adv.* so, so much, as much, thus so far, so hard, so long, so often, in such a manner, to such degree or extent: ~ *como*, as much, or so much, as; as well as; *algún* ~, *un* ~, a little, somewhat; ~ *más* (or *menos*) *que*, all the more [or the less] that, especially as; ~ *mejor*, so much the better; ~ *peor*, so much the worse. 2 *pron.* so much, as much, that: *no ser para* ~, not to be so bad, so serious, etc., as that; *por lo* ~, *por* ~, therefore, then. 3 *m.* amount, sum; rate: ~ *alzado*, lump sum; ~ *por ciento*, percentage, per cent; *otro* ~, as much, as much more; the same. 4 point [in games]: *apuntarse un* ~, to score a point. 5 counter, chip [to keep score]. 6 copy [of a writing]. 7 *al* ~ *de*, informed about. 8 *en* ~, *entre* ~, in the meantime.
2) **tanto, -ta** *adj.* as much, so much. 2 such a big: *tanta nariz*, such a big nose.
tantos, -tas *adj. pl.* as many, so many. 2 *y tantos* (or *tantas*), odd, and more: *veinte y tantos*, twenty odd, twenty and more.
tañedor, -ra *m.-f.* MUS. player [of an instrument].
tañer *tr.* to play [a musical instrument], to ring, toll [bells]. 2 *intr.* to drum with the fingers.
tañido *m.* sound, sounding [of a musical instrument];/tune. 2 ringing [of a bell].
tañimiento *m.* playing on an instrument.
tao *m.* tau cross [badge of some orders].
taoísmo *m.* Taoism.
tapa *f.* lid, cover, cap. 2 head [of a cylinder, a barrel, a cask]. 2 board cover [of a book]. 4 lift, layer [of a shoe heel]. 5 hoof crust [of horses].

tapaboca *m.* slap on the mouth. *2* muffler [worn for warmth]. *3* fig. squelch, squelcher. *4* ARTIL. ~ or *tapabocas*, tampion.
tapacubo *m.* AUTO. hub cap.
tapaculo *m.* BOT. hip.
tapada *f.* woman who hides her face with a mantle or veil.
tapadera *f.* loose lid, cover [of a pot, etc.]. *2* blind [person who shields another].
tapadillo (de) *adv.* secretly, covertly.
tapadizo *m.* COBERTIZO.
tapado *m.* (Am.) woman's or child's overcoat.
tapafunda *f.* flap of a holster.
tapagujeros, *pl.* **-ros** *m.* substitute, makeshift [person].
tapar *tr.* to cover [with a lid, cover, etc.]. *2* to stop, plug; to cap, cork [a bottle, etc.]; to bung [a cask]. *3* to close up, obstruct. *4* to hide, conceal, screen, veil. *5* to wrap up. *6* (Am.) to fill [a tooth]. *7* *ref.* to cover or veil oneself up.
tápara *f.* ALCAPARRA.
taparrabo *m.* loincloth. *2* trunks, bathing trunks.
tapetado, -da *adj.* dark, dark-brown.
tapete *m.* small carpet, rug. *2* cover [for a table, chest, etc.], table cover: ~ *verde*, gambling table: *estar sobre el* ~, to be on the carpet [under discussion].
tapia *f.* mud wall, adobe wall. *2* wall fence.
tapial *m.* form or mould for mud walls. *2* TAPIA.
tapiar *tr.* to wall, wall in [enclose with a wall]. *2* to wall [block up with a wall].
tapicería *f.* tapestries. *2* art of making tapestry. *3* tapestry shop. *4* upholstery. *5* upholstery shop.
tapicero *m.* tapestry maker. *2* upholsterer.
tapido, -da *adj.* closely woven.
tapioca *f.* tapioca.
tapir *m.* ZOOL. tapir.
tapiz *m.* tapestry.
tapizar *tr.* to tapestry [hang with tapestry]. *2* to upholster [chairs, etc.]. *3* fig. to carpet, cover.
tapón *m.* stopper, cork, bung, plug, cap. *2* ELECT. plug fuse. *3* SURG. tampon.
taponamiento *m.* SURG. tamponage, tamponment.
tàponar *tr.* to plug, stop up. *2* SURG. to tampon.
taponazo *m.* pop [of a cork].
taponería *f.* corks [collect.]. *2* cork factory or industry. *3* cork shop.
taponero, -ra *adj.* [pertaining to] cork. *2* *m.-f.* cork maker, cork cutter. *3* cork seller.
tapujarse *ref.* to cover or muffle one's face.
tapujo *m.* covering one's face; cover held over the face. *2* fig. concealment, subterfuge.
taquera *f.* rack or stand for billiard cues.
taquicardia *f.* MED. tachycardia.
taquigrafía *f.* shorthand, stenography.
taquigrafiar *tr.* to stenograph.
taquigráfico, -ca *adj.* shorthand, stenographic.
taquígrafo, -fa *m.-f.* stenographer.
taquilla *f.* ticket rack. *2* ticket window, ticket office. *3* take, gate [money received for tickets].
taquillero, -ra *m.-f.* ticket seller, ticket agent.
taquimeca *f.* COLL. TAQUIMECANÓGRAFA.
taquimecanógrafo, -fa *m.-f.* a stenographer and typewriter.
taquimetría *f.* tachymetry.
taquímetro *m.* SURV. tachymeter.
tara *f.* COM. tare [allowance made for weight of box, etc.]. *2* tally [stick for keeping accounts].
tarabilla *f.* clapper [of a mill], millclapper. *2* catch, turnbuckle [for fastening a window]. *3* coll. chatterbox. *4* coll. jabber, jabbering.

taracea *f.* marquetry, inlaid work, buhlwork.
taracear *tr.* to inlay, to adorn with marquetry.
taraje *m.* TARAY.
tarambana *adj.* scatterbrained. *2* *m.-f.* scatterbrains.
tarantela *f.* tarantella, tarantelle.
tarántula *f.* ZOOL. tarantula.
tarara, tarará *f.* sound of a trumpet.
tararear *tr.* to hum [a tune].
ïarareo *m.* humming [a tune].
tarasca *f.* dragon [in Corpus Christi procession]. *2* coll. glutton. *3* coll. ugly, bad-tempered woman.
tarascada *f.* bite, wound with the teeth. *2* rude answer or rebuff.
tarascar *tr.* [of dogs] to bite.
taray *m.* BOT. tamarisk.
tardador, -ra *adj.* slow, tarrying.
tardanza *f.* delay, slowness, tardiness.
tardar *intr.-ref.* to take a long time or a specified time [in doing something], to be slow, long or late [in coming, etc.]: *no tardes*, don't be long, don't be late; *a más* ~, at the latest.
tarde *adv.* late; too late: *hacerse* ~, to grow late; *de* ~ *en* ~, once in a while; ~ *o temprano*, sooner or later. *2* *f.* afternoon; evening; *buenas tardes*, good afternoon. *3* fig. evening [of life].
tardecer *intr.* to draw towards the evening, to grow dark. ¶ CONJUG. like *agradecer*.
tardecica *f.* *dim.* late hours of the afternoon.
tardigrado, -da *adj.-m.* ZOOL. tardigrade.
tardío, -día *adj.* late, tardy [coming or done after the proper time]. *2* tardy, slow. *3* *m. pl.* late crops.
tardo, -da *adj.* tardy, slow, sluggish. *2* tardy, late. *3* dull, sense, slow: ~ *de comprensión*, dull-witted.
tardón, -na *adj.* sluggish. *2* slow, dull-witted.
tarea *f.* task, job. *2* work, toil.
tarifa *f.* tariff. *2* price list, rate, fare.
tarifar *tr.* to tariff.
tarima *f.* wooden platform, dais.
tarja *f.* tally [for keeping decounts]. *2* large shield. *3* tilting target. *4* (Am.) visiting card.
tarjeta *f.* card [bearing one's name, etc.]: ~ *de visita*, visiting card; ~ *postal*, post card. *2* ARCH. tablet. *3* title and imprint [on a map].
tarjeteo *m.* coll. social exchange of cards.
tarjetero *m.* card case.
tarjetón *m.* *augm.* large card; show card.
tarlatana *f.* tarlatan [fabric].
tarquín *m.* slime, ooze, mire.
tarraconense *adj.-n.* of Tarragona.
tarreñas *f.* a kind of earthen castanets.
tarro *m.* jar.
tarsiano, -na *adj.* tarsal.
tarso *m.* ANAT., ZOOL., ORNITH., ENT. tarsus.
tarta *f.* tart [piece of pastry].
tártago *m.* BOT. caper spurge. *2* coll. misfortune. *3* coll. poor joke, mean trick.
tartajear *intr.* to stutter.
tartajeo *m.* stutter, stuttering.
tartajoso, -sa *adj.* stuttering. *2* *m.-f.* stutterer.
tartalear *intr.* coll. to move in a trembling or irregular way. *2* coll. to stammer, be embarrased.
tartamudear *intr.* to stammer, stutter.
tartamudeo *m.* stammering, stuttering.
tartamudez *f.* defect of stammering or stuttering.
tartamudo, -da *adj.* stammering, stuttering. *2* *m.-f.* stammerer, stutterer.
tartán *m.* tartan [fabric].

tartana *f.* NAUT. tartan [vessel]. *2* two-wheeled round-top carriage.

tartanero *m.* driver of a TARTANA.

tartáreo, -a *adj.* poet. Tartary.

tartárico, -ca *adj.* CHEM. tartaric.

Tártaro *m. pr. n.* MYTH. Tartarus.

tártaro, -ra *adj.-n.* Tartar. *2 m.* CHEM. tartar. *3* tartar [on teeth].

tartera *f.* baking pan for pastry. *2* dinner pail.

tartrato *m.* CHEM. tartrate.

tártrico, -ca *adj.* CHEM. tartaric.

tartufo *m.* hypocrite.

tarugo *m.* wooden pin or plug. *2* wooden paving blook.

tarumba *m.* coll. *volver ~ a uno,* to confuse, perplex, rattle.

tasa *f.* measure, due limitation: *sin ~,* without measure. *2* valuation, appraisement. *3* the price of a commodity as established by the Gov' rnment.

tasación *f.* valuation, appraisement.

tasador *m.* appraiser.

tasajo *m.* jerked beef.

tasar *tr.* to fix the price of. *2* to limit, moderate. *3* to appraise, estimate. *4* to stint.

tasca *f.* tavern, wine shop. *2* gambling den.

tascador *m.* scutch, scutcher, swingle.

tascar *tr.* to scutch [flax or hemp]. *2* to crunch [grass]. *3 ~ el freno,* to champ the bit.

tastana *f.* AGR. hard crust of dry soil. *2* membrane inside a fruit [as in walnuts, oranges, etc.].

tasto *m.* spoiled taste [of food].

tata *f.* nursemaid [in child's language]. *2* (Am.) coll. dad, daddy.

tatarabuela *f.* great-great-grandmother.

tatarabuelo *m.* great-great-grandfather.

tataranieta *f.* great-great-granddaughter.

tataranieto *m.* great-great-grandson.

¡tate! *interj.* easy there!, beware! *2* behold!

tato, -ta *adj.* lisping and stammering.

tatú *m.* ZOOL. (Am.) giant armadillo.

tatuaje *m.* tatoo [on the skin]. *2* tatooing [the skin].

tatuar *tr.* to tattoo [mark the skin of].

tau *m.* tau [Greek letter]. *2* tau cross.

taumaturgia *f.* thaumaturgy.

taumaturgo, -ga *m.-f.* thaumaturge.

taurino, -na *adj.* taurine.

Tauro *m. pr. n.* ASTR. Taurus.

taurómaco, -ca *adj.* taurcomachian, bullfighting. *2 m.-f.* one versed in tauromachy.

tauromaquia *f.* bullfighting, tauromachy.

tautología *f.* RHET. tautology.

taxativo, -va *adj.* definite, precise.

taxi *m.* taxi, taxicab.

taxidermia *f.* taxidermy.

taxímetro *m.* taximeter. *2* taxi, taxicab.

taxonomía *f.* taxonomy.

taza *f.* cup [drinking vessel with a handle]. *2* cup, cupful. *3* basin, bowl [of a fountain]. *4* cup guard [of a sword].

tazón *m.* large cup, bowl.

1) **te** *f.* name the letter *t*. *2* T square.

2) **te** *pers. pron.* 2nd *pers. sing.* [object of the verb and ref.] thee, you; to thee, for you; thyself, yourself.

té *m.* tea [plant; leaves; drink; meal with tea]. *2 ~ del Paraguay,* maté, paraguay tea.

tea *f.* candlewood, torch, firebrand.

teatino, -na *m.* Theatin, Theatine.

teatral *adj.* theatrical.

teatralidad *f.* theatricality.

teatro *m.* theatre, theater. *2* stage [sense, actor's profession].

Tebaida *f. pr. n.* HIST., GEOG. Thebaid.

tebano, -na *adj.-n.* Theban.

Tebas *f. pr. n.* HIST., GEOG. Thebes.

teca *f.* BOT. teak. *2* teakwood. *3* BOT. theca.

tecla *f.* key [of a piano, organ, typewriter, etc.]: *~ de escape,* margin release; *~ de retroceso,* backspacer; *tocar una ~,* to resort to some expedient. *2* fig. delicate point.

teclado *m.* keyboard [of a piano, organ, typewriter, etc.].

tecle NAUT. single purchase.

teclear *intr.* to finger a keyboard. *2* to drum with the fingers.

tecleo *m.* fingering a keyboard. *2* click [of typewriter]. *3* drumming with the fingers.

técnica *f.* technics. *2* technic, technique, methode. *3* technical ability.

tecnicismo *m.* technicality, technicism [technical term or expression].

técnico, -ca *adj.* technical. *2 m.* technician, technical expert.

tecnología *f.* technology.

techado, -da *p. p.* of TECHAR. *2 adj.* roofed, covered. *3 m.* roof.

techar *tr.* to roof, to thatch.

techo *m.* roof, covering [of a building]. *2* ceiling [of a room]. *3* AER. ceiling. *4* fig. roof [house, home].

techumbre *f.* roof, roofing [of a building].

tedero *m.* torch holder, cresset.

tedéum *m.* ECCL. Te Deum.

tedio *m.* tedium, tediousness. *2* loathing.

tedioso, -sa *adj.* tedious, boring. *2* disgusting.

tegumento *m.* ANAT., ZOOL., BOT. tegument.

teína *f.* CHEM. thein, theine.

teísmo *m.* theism.

teja *f.* roof tile, pantile, gutter tile: *a toca ~,* coll. cash down; *de tejas abajo,* coll. in the order of nature; in this world; *de tejas arriba,* coll. in the supernatural order, in heaven. *2* shovel hat. *3* BOT. linden tree.

tejadillo *m. dim.* small roof. *2* roof [of carriage].

tejado *m.* roof, tiled roof.

1) **tejar** *tr.* brickyard, brick works.

2) **tejar** *tr.* to tile [a roof].

tejaroz *m.* eaves.

tejavana *f.* shed, tiled shed.

tejedor, -ra *adj.* weaving. *2 m.-f.* weaver. *3 m.* ENT. water skipper, water strider.

tejedura *f.* weaving. *2* texture [of a fabric].

tejeduría *f.* art of weaving. *2* weaving mill.

tejemaneje *m.* coll. address, skilful management. *2* (Am.) intriguing.

tejer *tr.* to weave. *2* to knit [stockings, etc.]. *3* to braid, plaid, interweave, wreathe.

tejera, tejería *f.* brickyard, tile works.

tejero *m.* brickmaker, tile maker.

tejido, -da *adj.* woven, knit, braided. *3 m.* weave, texture [of a fabric]. *4* fabric, textile: *~ de punto,* knitted fabric. *5* fig. tissue, web. *6* BIOL. tissue: *~ conjuntivo,* connective tissue.

tejo *m.* disk, quoit. *2* MACH. pillow block, socketplate. *3* BOT. yew.

tejoleta *f.* broken tile, brickbat. *2 pl.* TARREÑAS.

tejón *m.* ZOOL. badger. *2* gold ingot.

tejonera *f.* burrow of badgers.

tejuelo *m.* TEJO 1. *2* BOOKB. label; lettering. *3* MACH. pillow block.

tela *f.* cloth, fabric, stuff: ~ *metálica*, wire cloth, wire screen. *2* web: ~ *de araña*, cobweb. *3* skin, pellicle, membrane. *4* film [on a liquid; in the eye]. *5* subject, something to talk about. *6* BOOKB. cloth. *7* PAINT. canvas; painting. *8 poner en* ~ *de juicio*, to doubt, question.

telamón *m.* ARCH. telamon.

telar *m.* WEAV. loom: ~ *mecánico*, power loom. *2* THEAT. gridiron. *3* BOOKB. sewing press.

telaraña *f.* cobweb, spider web: *tener telarañas en los ojos*, coll. to be blind to what is going on. *2* fig. cobweb, flimsy thing.

telecomunicación *f.* telecommunication.

telefonear *intr.-tr.* to telephone.

telefonema *m.* telephone message.

telefonía *f.* telephony.

telefonista *m.-f.* telephonist, telephone operator.

teléfono *m.* telephone: ~ *automático*, dial telephone; ~ *inalámbrico* or *sin hilos*, wireless telephone.

telefotografía *f.* telephotography. *2* telephotograph.

telegrafía *f.* telegraphy: ~ *sin hilos*, wireless telegraphy.

telegrafiar *intr.-tr.* to telegraph.

telegrafista *m.-f.* telegrapher, telegraphist.

telégrafo *m.* telegraph: ~ *inalámbrico* or *sin hilos*, wireless telegraph.

telegrama *m.* telegram.

teleguiado, -da *adj.* guided by remote control.

Telémaco *m. pr. n.* MYTH. Telemachus.

telémetro *m.* telemeter. *2* MIL. range, finder.

telendo, -da *adj.* sprightly, lively, jaunty.

teleología *f.* teleology.

teleósteo, -a *adj.* ICHTH. teleost.

telepatía *f.* telepathy.

telera *f.* plow pin. *2* sheepfold. *3* cheek [of a vice]. *4* tiebeam [of a cart]. *5* transom [of a gun-carriage]. *6* NAUT. rack block.

telero *m.* stake [of a cart].

telescopio *m.* telescope.

teletipo *m.* teletype.

televisar *tr.* to televise.

televisión *f.* television.

televisor, -ra *adj.* televising, [pertaining to] television. *2 m.* television set.

telilla *f. dim.* light woollen stuff. *6* film, pellicle.

telina *f.* ZOOL. clam.

telón *m.* THEAT. curtain, drop curtain, drop: ~ *de boca*, drop curtain; ~ *de fondo*, backdrop. *2* fig. ~ *de acero*, iron curtain.

telúrico, -ca *adj.* tellurian.

telurio *m.* CHEM. tellurium.

tema *m.* theme, subject, text. *2* GRAM. theme, stem. *3* MUS. theme. *4 f.* persistence, obstinacy; fixed idea. *5* unreasonable animosity or grudge.

temario *m.* program of subjects, agenda.

temático, -ca *adj.* thematic, thematical. *2* TEMOSO.

tembladal *m.* TREMEDAL.

tembladera *f.* a bowl of very thin metal or glass. *2* jewel mounted on a spiral wire. *3* ICHTH. torpedo. *4* BOT. quaking grass.

tembladero, -ra *adj.* shaking, trembling. *2 m.* TREMEDAL.

temblador, -ra *adj.* shaking, trembling. *2 m.-f.* trembler. *3* Quaker.

temblar *intr.* to tremble, quake, shake, quaver, quiver, shiver. ¶ CONJUG. like *acertar*.

tembleque *adj.* shaking, trembling. *2 m.-f.* trembler [person]. *3 m.* TEMBLADERA 2.

temblequear *intr.* coll. to shake or tremble all the time. *2* coll. to fake a tremor.

temblón, -na *adj.* trembling, tremulous, shaking.

temblor *m.* tremble, tremor, shaking, quaver, quiver, shiver: ~ *de tierra*, earthquake.

tembloroso, -sa; tembloso, -sa *adj.* trembling, tremulous, quavering, shaking.

temer *tr.* to dread, fear, apprehend. *2* to be in awe of. *3* fig. be afraid that. *4 intr.* to fear: fear: ~ *por*, to fear for.

temerario, -ria *adv.* rash, reckless, hasty, foolhardy.

temeridad *f.* temerity, rashness, recklessness, imprudence, foolhardiness. *2* rash or hasty action.

temerón, -na *adj.* blustering. *2 m.-f.* blusterer.

temeroso, -sa *adj.* dread, fearful. *2* timorous, timid. *3* afraid, fearing.

temible *adj.* to be dreaded, redoubtable.

temor *m.* dread, fear: ~ *de Dios*, dread of God.

temoso, -sa *adj.* persistent, obstinate.

témpano *m.* MUS. kettledrum. *2* drumhead, drumskin. *3* head [of a cask or barrel]. *4* ARCH. tympan. *5* flat piece of something hard. *6* flitch [of bacon]. *7* ~ *de hielo*, floe, iceberg.

temperación *f.* tempering.

temperadamente *adv.* temperately.

temperamento *m.* PHYSIOL., MUS. temperament. *2* TEMPERIE. *3* compromising measure.

temperante *adj.* tempering. *2* (Am.) abstemious. *3 m.-f.* (Am.) teetotaler.

temperar *tr.* to temper, moderate, soften. *2 intr.* (Am.) to go to a warmer, climate. *3 ref.* to become temperate.

temperatura *f.* temperature. *2* TEMPERIE.

temperie *f.* atmospheric conditions.

tempestad *f.* tempest, storm.

tempestear *intr.* to storm, be stormy. *2* fig. to storm, rage.

tempestivo, -va *adj.* opportune, seasonable, timely.

tempestuoso, -sa *adj.* stormy, tempestuous.

templa *f.* PAINT. distemper. *2 pl.* ANAT. temples.

templado, -da *adj.* temperate. *2* tepid, lukewarm. *3* LIT. moderate [style]. *4* tempered [steel, glass, etc.]. *5* MUS. tuned. *6* brave, firm, calmy courageous.

templador, -ra *m.-f.* temperer. *2* MUS. tuner. *3 m.* MUS. tuning key.

templadura *f.* tempering. *2* MUS. tuning.

templanza *f.* temperance. *2* moderation, sobriety. *3* mildness [of climate].

templar *tr.* to temper, moderate, mitigate, soften, appease. *2* to warm [a liquid] slightly. *3* to temper, anneal [metals, glass]. *4* MUS. to tune [an instrument]. *5* NAUT. to trim [the sails] to the wind. *6* PAINT. to blend, harmonize [colours]. *7 intr.* [of the weather] to moderate. *8 ref.* to become temperate.

templazo *m.* WEAV. temple.

templario *m.* Templar, Knight Templar.

temple *m.* TEMPERIE. *2* TEMPERATURA. *3* temper [of metal, glass, etc.]. *4* fig. temper, humour, frame of mind. *5* fig. courage, energy, decision. *6* fig. compromise. *7* MUS. tune [of instruments]. *8* Order of the Templars. *9* PAINT. *al* ~, in distemper.

templete *m. dim.* small temple. *2* niche, tabernacle. *3* pavillon, kiosk.

templo *m.* temple [place of worship], church.

temporada *f.* spell, period of time, some time. *2* season: ~ *de ópera*, opera season.

temporal *adj.* temporary. *2* temporal, secular,

worldly. *3* GRAM., ANAT. temporal. *4 m.* tempest, storm. *5* ANAT. temporal bone.
temporalidad *f.* temporality. *2* temporariness.
temporalizar *tr.* to make temporal or temporary.
temporalmente *adv.* temporarily. *2* temporally.
temporáneo, -a; temporario, -ria *adj.* temporary.
témporas *f. pl.* ECCL. Ember days.
temporero, -ra *adj.* temporary [clerk, employee].
temporizar *intr.* CONTEMPORIZAR. *2* to pass the time.
tempranal *adj.* producing early fruits.
tempranamente *adv.* early. *2* too early, prematurely.
tempranero, -ra *adj.* TEMPRANO 1.
tempranito *adv.* coll. very early.
temprano, -na *adj.* early: *fruto* ~, early fruit. *2* young [age]. *3 m.* field yielding early crops. *4 adv.* early. *5* too early.
ten con ten *m.* tact, adroitness, moderation.
tenacidad *f.* tenacity, tenaciousness, pertinacity, firmness, persistence. *2* PHYS. tenacity.
tenacillas *f. pl.* small tongs. *2* sugar tongs. *3* curling irons. *4* tweezers. *5* snuffers.
tenaz *adj.* tenacious, pertinacious, stubborn, persistent. *2* tenacious, adhesive, tough.
tenaza *f.* BOT. tenaille. *2* CARDS tenace. *3 pl.* tongs, pair of tongs; pincers, pair of pincers.
tenazón (a) *adv.* without taking aim. *2* suddenly.
tenca *f.* ICHTH. tench.
tención *f.* holding, possessing.
tendal *m.* awning. *2* TENDEDERO. *3* things spread out, or clothes hung up, to dry.
tendalera *f.* coll. litter, things scattered in disorder.
tendalero, tendedero *m.* place where clothes, etc., are spread or hung up to dry. *2* (Am.) clothesline.
tendel *m.* MAS. levelling line. *2* MAS. layer of mortar.
tendencia *f.* tendency, drift, trend.
tendencioso, -sa *adj.* tendentious.
ténder *m.* RLY. tender.
tender *tr.* to spread, spread out. *2* to stretch out. *3* to hold out [one's hand, etc.]; to extend, stretch forth. *4* to hang up [washing, etc., to dry]. *5* to spread on the ground. *6* to lay [a cable, a track, etc.]. *7* to throw, build [a bridge]. *8 intr.* to tend, have a tendency. *9 ref.* to stretch, lie down. *10* CARDS to show down. *11* [of a horse] to run at full gallop. ¶ CONJUG. like *entender*.
tenderete *m.* stand, stall, booth. *2* a card game.
tendero, -ra *m.-f.* shopkeeper. *storekeeper. *2 m.* tent maker.
tendidamente *adv.* diffusely, diffusively.
tendido *adj.* full [gallop]. *2 m.* spreading or hanging up [of washing, etc., to dry]. *3* laying [of a cable, a track, etc.]. *4* throwing, building [of a bridge]. *5* uncovered tiers of seats [in a bull ring]. *6* (Am.) bedclothes.
tendiente *adj.* tending, having a tendency.
tendinoso, -sa *adj.* tendinous.
tendón *m.* ANAT. tendon.
tendré, tendría, etc. *irr.* V. TENER.
tenducha *f.*, **tenducho** *m.* small, mean shop.
tenebrario *m.* ECCL. Tenebrae hearse.
tenebrosidad *f.* gloominess, darkness.
tenebroso, -sa *adj.* gloomy, dark, tenebrous.
tenedero *m.* NAUT. anchoring ground.
tenedor *m.* holder, possessor. *2* fork, table fork. *3* COM. holder [of a bill, etc.]. *4* ~ *de libros*, bookkeeper.

teneduría *f.* position of bookkeeper. *2* ~ *de libros*, bookkeeping.
tenencia *f.* holding, possession. *2* MIL. lieutenancy. *3* ECCL. succursal church.
tener *tr.* to have [in many senses], to hold, keep; own, posses. *2* to keep [one's word or promise]. *3* to hold, keep [in a specified place, condition, etc.]. *5* to have, hold [conversation]; to hold [a meeting, etc.]. *6* to keep [a shop, inn, etc.]. *7* to have, bear [young, a baby]. *8* to be the matter with, to ail: *¿qué tiene usted?*, what is the matter with you?, what ails you? *9* [app. to dimensions, years, months, etc.] to be: *este árbol tiene seis metros de alto*, this tree is six metres high; *mi padre tiene sesenta años*, my father is sixty years old. *10* ~ *cuidado*, to take care. *11* ~ *calor*, ~ *frío*, [of a pers.] to be hot, to be cold; ~ *miedo*, to be afraid; ~ *prisa*, to be in a hurry. *12* ~ *a honra*, to regard it is an honour. *13* ~ *a menos*, to deem it beneath one [to do something]. *14* ~ *algo de*, to be somewhat of. *15* ~ *en mucho*, to value highly; ~ *en poco*, to think little of. *16* ~ *para sí*, to think, be of the opinion. *17* ~ *por*, to consider or regard as. *18* *no tenerlas todas consigo*, to be uneasy, full of aprehension. *19 intr.* to have possesions.
20 aux. to have: *tengo escritos dos libros*, I have written two books. *21* ~ *de* or ~ *que*, to have to, be obliged to, must. *22* *tengo entendido que*, I understand that.
23 ref. to hold fast or steady, to keep from falling. *24* to stand, rest [on something]. *25* to stop. *26* *tenerse a*, to abide by, to stick to. *27* *tenerse en pie*, to stand, keep on one's feet. *28* *tenerse por*, to consider oneself as.
¶ CONJUG.: INDIC. Pres.: *tengo, tienes, tiene*; *tenemos, tenéis, tienen.* | Pret.: *tuve, tuviste, tuvo; tuvimos, tuvisteis, tuvieron.* | Fut.: *tendré, tendrás,* etc. | COND.: *tendría, tendrías,* etc. | SUBJ. Pres.: *tenga, tengas, tenga; tengamos, tengáis, tengan.* | Imperf.: *tuviera, tuvieras,* etc., or *tuviese, tuvieses,* etc. | Fut.: *tuviere, tuvieres,* etc. | IMPER.: *ten, tenga; tengamos, tened, tengan.*
tenería *f.* tannery.
tengo, tenga, etc. *irr.* V. TENER.
tenia *f.* ZOOL. taenia, tapeworm. *2* ARCH. taenia.
tenida *f.* (Am.) meeting, session.
tenienta *f.* lieutenant's wife.
teniente *adj.* coll. dull of hearing. *2* coll. niggardly. *3 m.* deputy, substitute. *4* MIL. lieutenant: ~ *coronel*, lieutenant colonel; ~ *general*, lieutenant general.
tenis *m.* lawn tennis.
tenista *m.-f.* tennis player.
tenor *m.* MUS. tenor. *2* tenor, nature, import: *a este* ~, like this; *a* ~ *de*, in accordance with.
tenorio *m.* Don Juan, lady-killer.
tensión *f.* tension: ~ *arterial*, arterial tension. *2* MECH. stress.
tenso, -sa *adj.* tense, tight, taut; strained.
tensón *f.* tenson, tenzon.
tensor, -ra *adj.* tensile. *2 m.* tension [device]. *3* tightener, turnbuckle. *4* ANAT. tensor.
tentación *f.* temptation.
tentacular *adj.* tentacular.
tentáculo *m.* ZOOL. tentacle, feeler.
tentador, -ra *adj.* tempting. *2* alluring. *3 m.-f.* tempter.
tentar *tr.* to feel, touch, examine by touch. *2* to feel [one's way]; to grope for. *3* to try, attempt. *4* SURG. to probe. *5* to tempt. ¶ CONJUG. like *acertar*.

tentativa f. attempt, trial, endeavour.
tentativo, -va adj. tentative.
tentemozo m. prop, support. 2 DOMINGUILLO.
tentempié m. coll. light meal, snack, bite.
tenue adj. tenuous, thin, slender, delicate, faint.
tenuidad f. tenuity, tenuousness. 2 trifle.
tenuirrostro, -tra adj. ORN. tenuirostral.
teñido, -da adj. dyed. 2 m. dyeing; staining.
teñir tr. to dye, colour, stain, tinge. 2 PAINT. to
   dark, sadden [a colour]. ¶ CONJUG. like reír.
teocali m. ARCHEOL. teocalli [Aztec temple].
teocracia f. theocracy.
teodicea f. theodicy.
teodolito m. theodolite.
Teodoro m. pr. n. Theodore.
Teodosio m. pr. n. Theodosius.
teogonía f. theogony.
teologal adj. theologic, theological.
teología f. theology, divinity.
teológico, -ca adj. theologic, theological.
teólogo, -ga m.-f. theologian.
teorema m. theorem.
teoría f. theory. 2 theoretics.
teórica f. theoretics.
teórico, -ca adj. theoretic, theoretical. 2 m.-f. theo-
   rist.
teorizante m.-f. theorizer.
teorizar intr. to theorize.
teoso, -sa adj. resinous [wood].
teosofía f. theosophy.
teósofo m. theosophist.
tepe m. sod, turf [used for making walls].
tequila f. (Mex.) tequila [distilled liquor].
terapeuta m.-f. therapeutist.
terapéutica f. therapeutics.
teratología f. teratology.
terbio m. CHEM. terbium.
tercamente adv. obstinately, stubbornly.
tercer adj. apocopated form of TERCERO used only
   before masculine singular nouns.
tercera adj.-f. third. 2 f. go-between. 3 third class.
   4 CARDS, FENC. tierce. 5 MUS. third, tierce. 6 AUTO.
   third [third speed].
terceramente adv. thirdly.
tercería f. mediation, intermediation. 2 pondering. 3 LAW right of a third party.
tercerilla f. PROS. short-line triplet.
tercero, -ra adj.-n. third. 2 m. third party or person. 3 mediator, intermediator. 4 gobetween,
   procurer. 5 third storey [of a building].
tercerola f. short carbine. 2 tierce [cask].
terceto m. PROS. tercet, triplet. 2 MUS. trio.
tercia f. one third. 2 third of a VARA [measure]. 3
   ECCL., CARDS tierce.
terciana f. MED. tertian, tertian fever.
terciar tr. to place sidewise or diagonally. 2 to divide into three parts. 3 to plough the third time.
   4 MIL. to carry [arms]. 5 intr. to mediate, intervene. 6 to take part. 7 si se tercia, if an occasion
   comes to hand.
terciario, -ria adj. third [in order or degree]. 2
   CHEM., MED. tertiary. 3 adj.-m. GEOL. Tertiary. 4
   m.-f. ECCL. tertiary.
tercio, -cia adj. third [in order]. 2 m. third, third
   part. 3 SP. HIST. regiment of infantry. 4 MIL. Foreign Legion. 5 MIL. division of the GUARDIA CIVIL.
   6 hacer buen ~, to do a good turn; hacer mal ~,
   to do a bad turn. 7 hacer ~, to complete a number of people. 8 pl. strong limbs [of a man].
terciopelado, -da adj. ATERCIOPELADO.
terciopelero m. velvet weaver, velvet worker.

terciopelo m. velvet.
terco, -ca adj. obstinate, stubborn. 2 hard, intractable [metal, wood, etc.].
terebinto m. BOT. terebinth.
terebrante adj. boring, piercing [pain].
Terencio m. pr. n. Terence.
Teresa f. pr. n. Theresa.
teresiana f. a kind of kepi.
tergiversación f. twisting, distortion, perversion,
   misrepresentation [of facts, statements, etc.].
tergiversar tr. to twist, distort, pervert, misrepresent [facts, statements, etc.].
terliz m. ticking [fabric].
termal adj. thermal [pertaining to hot springs].
termas f. pl. thermae. 2 hot baths, hot springs,
   thermal springs.
termes m. TERMITE.
térmico, -ca adj. thermal, thermic, thermical.
terminación f. termination, conclusion, end, completion. 2 GRAM. termination, ending.
terminacho m. coll. vulgar term. 2 coll. barbarism.
terminal adj. terminal. 2 m. ELECT. terminal.
terminante adj. final, conclusive, positive, peremptory.
terminar tr. to terminate, close, end, finish, complete. 2 intr.-ref. to terminate, close, end, finish
   [come to an end]; to end [in].
término m. end [extreme or last point]. 2 end, conclusion, completion: llevar a ~, to carry out; poner ~ a, to put an end to. 3 boundary; boundary
   mark. 4 district [of a town]. 5 aim, end, goal. 6
   term, word. 7 term [limited period]. 8 ARCH.,
   LOG., MATH. term. 9 ~ medio, average. 10 F. ARTS
   primer ~, foreground; último ~, background. 11
   pl. terms: estar en buenos términos, to be in good
   terms; en buenos términos, in a polite or euphe-
   mistic manner. 12 manner [of conducting one-
   self]. 13 state, condition. 14 términos hábiles,
   possibility.
terminología f. terminology.
terminote m. affected term or word, big word.
termiónico, -ca adj. thermionic. 2 f. thermionics.
termite m. ENT. termite, white ant.
termitero m. nest of white ants.
termobarómetro m. thermobarometer.
termocauterio m. thermocautery.
termodinámico, -ca adj. thermodynamic. 2 f. thermodynamics.
termoelectricidad f. thermoelectricity.
termología f. thermology.
termometría f. thermometry.
termómetro m. thermometer.
termonuclear adj. thermonuclear.
Termópilas f. pl. pr. n. HIST. Thermopylae.
termo, pl. -mos m. thermos bottle.
termosifón m. thermosiphon. 2 hot-water boiler
   [for heating running water in a building].
termostato m. thermostat.
terna f. list of three candidates presented for selection. 2 pair of threes [at dice]. 3 set of dice.
ternario, -ria adj. ternary. 2 MUS. triple, three-part.
terne adj. strong, husky. 2 persistent, stubborn. 3
   affecting courage, bullying. 4 m. bully.
ternera f. female calf. 2 veal.
ternero m. male calf.
terneza f. TERNURA. 2 pl. endearing words, sweet
   words.
ternilla f. gristle.
ternilloso, -sa adj. gristly, cartilaginous.
ternísimo, -ma adj. superl. of TIERNO.

terno *m.* ternary, triad. *2* tern [in lottery]. *3* suit of clothes. *4* vestments for the high mass. *5* profane oath, curse: *echar ternos*, to swear, curše.
ternura *f.* tenderness, softness. *2* fondness, affectionateness.
terpeno *m.* CHEM. terpene.
Terpsícore *f. pr. n.* MYTH. Terpsichore.
terquear *intr.* to be stubborn.
terquedad *f.* obstinacy, stubbornness.
terracota *f.* terra cotta.
terrado *m.* terrace, flat roof [of a house].
terraja *f.* diestock. *2* modelling board.
terral *adj.* land [breeze]. *2 m.* land breeze.
terramicina *f.* PHARM. terramycin.
Terranova *f. pr. n.* GEOG. Newfoundland.
terraplén *m.* fill, embankment, terrace. *2* FORT. terreplein.
terraplenar *tr.* to fill [with earth], embank, terrace.
terráqueo, -a *adj.* terraqueous, terrestrial.
terrateniente *m.-f.* landowner, landholder.
terraza *f.* terrace. *2* border [in a garden]. *3* flat roof [of a house]. *4* sidewalk café. *5* glazed jar with two handles.
terrazgo *m.* piece of land for planting. *2* land rent.
terrazo *m.* PAINT. ground, earth [in a landscape].
terrear *intr.* [of thin crops] to show the ground.
terremoto *m.* earthquake.
terrenal *adj.* earthly, mundane, terrene, terrestrial.
terrenidad *f.* earthliness, terreneness.
terreno, -na *adj.* terrestrial. *2* earthly, mundane, terrain, terrene. *3 m.* ground [position, distance, etc.]: *ganar ~*, to gain ground, to gain upon; *minarle el ~ a uno*, to undermine one's work; *preparar el ~*, fig. to pave the way; *sobre el ~*, on the spot; with data in hand. *5* fig. field, sphere [of action, etc.]. *6* GEOL. terrane, terrain. *7* MIL. terrain. *8 sing.-pl.* grounds [gardens, lawns, etc.].
térreo, -a *adj.* earthen, earthy, terreous.
terrero, -ra *adj.* earthy, low, humble. *2* low [fly of a bird]. *3 m.* terrace, flat roof. *4* mound of earth. *5* alluvium. *6* MIN. dump. *7* mark, target [for shooting].
terrestre *adj.* terrestrial. *2* BOT. terraneous.
terribilidad *f.* terribleness.
terrible *adj.* terrible. *2* illtempered.
terrícola *m.-f.* terrestrial, inhabitant of the earth.
terrífico, -ca *adj.* terrific.
territorial *adj.* territorial [of a territory].
territorio *m.* territory.
terrizo, -za *adj.* earthen. *2 m.-f.* earthen tub.
terromontero *m.* mound, hillock.
terrón *m.* clod [of earth]. *2* lump [of sugar, salt, etc.]. *3 pl.* coll. clod, soil, land.
terror *m.* terror.
terrorífico, -ca *adj.* terrific, frightful.
terrorismo *m.* terrorism.
terrorista *adj.* terroristic. *2 m.-f.* terrorist.
terroso, -sa *adj.* earthy, earthlike.
terruño *m.* AGR. soil. *2* piece of ground. *3* country, native soil.
tersar *tr.* to make limpid; to polish, smooth.
terso, -sa *adj.* limpid, clear; smooth; shining. *2* terse [style].
tersura *f.* limpidness, smoothness. *2* terseness.
tertulia *f.* social gathering for conversation or entertainment: *hacer ~*, to gather for conversation, to talk. *2* billiard or card room [in a café].
tertuliano, -na *m.-f.* one who attends a TERTULIA.

terzuelo *m.* one third. *2* ORN. tercel, male falcon.
Tesalia *f. pr. n.* GEOG. Thessaly.
Tesalónica *f. pr. n.* GEOG. Thessalonica.
tesar *tr.* NAUT. to haul taut, to make taut. *2 intr.* [of yoked oxen] to back, pull back.
tesauro *m.* thesaurus.
tesela *f.* tessera [in mosaic work].
Teseo *m. pr. n.* MYTH. Theseus.
tésera *f.* HIST. tessera.
tesis *f.* thesis.
tesitura *f.* MUS. tessiture. *2* attitude [settled behaviour].
teso, -sa *adj.* taut, drawn tight. *2 m.* top, brow of a hill. *3* small bulge [on a smooth surface].
tesón *m.* constancy, firmness, pertinacity.
tesonería *f.* obstinacy, stubbornness.
tesonero, -ra *adj.* firm, persistent, stubborn.
tesorería *f.* treasury, treasurer's office. *2* treasurership.
tesorero, -ra *m.-f.* treasurer.
tesoro *m.* treasure. *2* treasury, exchequer. *3* thesauros.
Tespis *m. pr. n.* Thespis.
tespíades *f. pl.* poet. the Muses.
testa *f.* head [of man or animal]. *2* head, face or front part [of certain things].
testáceo, -a *adj.-m.* ZOOL. testacean.
testado, -da *p. p.* of TESTAR. *2 adj.* testate.
testador *m.* testator.
testadora *f.* testatrix.
testaferro *m.* figurehead, dummy, man of straw.
testamentaría *f.* testamentary execution.
testamentario, -ria *adj.* testamentary. *2 m.* executor [of a will]. *3 f.* executrix [of a will].
testamento *m.* testament, will. *2* BIBL. Testament: *Antiguo Testamento*, Old Testament; *Nuevo Testamento*, New Testament.
testar *intr.* to make a will or testament. *2 tr.* to cancel, obliterate.
testarada *f.* blow with the head. *2* piece of obstinacy.
testarazo *m.* blow with the head.
testarrón, -na *adj.* TESTARUDO.
testarudez *f.* obstinacy, stubborness.
testarudo, -da *adj.* obstinate, stubborn, pigheaded.
testera *f.* front, fore part. *2* forehead [of an animal]. *3* crownpiece [of harness]. *4* back seat [of a carriage]. *5* FOUND. wall [of a furnace].
testero *m.* TESTERA. *2* back plate [of a fireplace]; big log [in the fireplace].
testículo *m.* ANAT., ZOOL. testicle.
testificación *f.* attestation, testification.
testifical *adj.* LAW of witness.
testificar *tr.* to attest, testify, bear witness to.
testigo *m.-f.* witness [person]: *~ ocular*, eyewitness. *2* witness [anything that serves as testimony or proof].
testimonial *adj.* attesting, testificatory. *2 f. pl.* certificate, testificatory document.
testimoniar *tr.* to attest, testify to, bear witness to.
testimonio *m.* testimony, attestation, witness, proof. *2* affidavit. *3* *testimonio* or *falso ~*, calumny, false charge; false witness.
testón *m.* ancient silver coin.
testudíneo, -a *adj.* testudineous.
testudo *m.* HIST. testudo.
testuz, testuzo *m.* nape or forehead [of certain animals].
teta *f.* breast [mamary gland], udder: *dar la ~*, to

nurse, suckle. *2* teat, nipple. *3* fig. hummock, knoll.

tétano, tétanos *m.* MED. tetanus.

tetar *tr.* ATETAR.

tetera *f.* teapot, teakettle.

tetilla *f.* dim. of TETA. *2* breast [gland in man or male animal]. *3* nipple [of nursing bottle].

tetón *m.* stub [of a pruned limb of tree].

tetracordio *m.* MUS. tetrachord.

tetraedro *m.* GEOM. tetrahedron.

tetrágono *m.* GEOM. tetragon.

tetralogía *f.* tetralogy.

tetramotor *m.* AER. four-motor plane.

tetrarca *m.* tetrach.

tetrarquía *f.* tetrarchy.

tetrasílabo, -ba *adj.* four-syllable [word].

tétrico, -ca *adj.* dark, gloomy, sullen, dismal.

tetuaní *adj.-n.* of Tetuán.

teucalí *m.* TEOCALÍ.

teucrio *m.* BOT. germander.

teucro, -cra *adj.-n.* Trojan.

teutón, -na *adj.* teutonic. *2 m.-f.* teuton.

teutónico, -ca *adj.* teutonic. *2 m.* teutonic [language].

textil *adj.-m.* textile.

texto *m.* text: *fuera de* ~, full-page [illustration]. *2* textbook. *3* PRINT. great primer.

textual *adj.* textual, literal.

textualmente *adv.* textually, literally.

textura *f.* texture. *2* weaving.

tez *f.* complexion [of the face].

ti *pers. pron.* [used as object of prepositions] thee, thyself; you, yourself.

tía *f.* aunt: ~ *abuela*, grandaunt, great-aunt; *no hay tu* ~, coll. there's no use, nothing doing. *2* mother [term of address for an elderly woman]. *3* coll. coarse woman. *4* coll. prostitute.

tiara *f.* tiara.

tibetano, -na *adj.-n.* Tibetan.

tibia *f.* ANAT. tibia, shinbone. *2* MUS. flute.

tibieza *f.* tepidity, lukewarmness. *2* coolness, indifference.

tibio, -bia *adj.* tepid, lukewarm [moderately warm]. *2* fig. tepid, lukewarm, cool, indifferent.

tibor *m.* large Chinese or Japanese decorative jar.

tiburón *m.* ICHTH. shark.

tic *m.* tic.

tiemblo *m.* BOT. aspen, aspen tree.

tiempo *m.* time [duration; portion of time, epoch, moment; allotted or available portion of time]: ~ *medio*, ASTR. mean time; *los buenos tiempos*, the good, old days; *cuánto* ~, how long; *mucho* ~, long, for long, a long time; *poco* ~, a short time; *dar* ~ *al* ~, to wait patiently, to bide one's time; *ganar* ~, to save time; to temporize; *hacer* ~, to wait, to while the time away; *pasar el* ~, to be idle, to pass the time now; *en* ~ *de*, at the time of; *hace* ~, ~ *ha*, some time ago, a long time ago; *un* ~, formerly, in other times. *2* weather: *hacer buen* ~, to be clear, to be good weather; *hacer mal* ~, to be bad weather. *3* MUS. tiempo. *4* MUS. beat [in a measure]. *5* GRAM. tense: ~ *simple*, simple tense; ~ *compuesto*, compound tense. *6* MACH. *de dos tiempos*, two-cycle; *de cuatro tiempos*, four-cycle.

tienda *f.* shop, *store: ir de tiendas*, to go shopping. *2* tent [portable shelter]: ~ *de campaña*, tent. *3* NAUT. awning. *4* tilt [for a cart].

tiendo, tienda, etc. *in.* V. TENDER.

tienta *f.* BULLF. testing the courage of young bulls. *2* sagacity. *3* sounding rod. *4 a tientas*, groping: *andar a tientas*, to grope, to grope in the dark; to feel one's way.

tientaguja *f.* sounding rod.

tiento *m.* touch, feeling: *a* ~, *por el* ~, gropingly. *2* blindman's stick. *3* BALANCÍN 3. *4* steady hand. *5* care, caution: *andarse con* ~, to watch one's step. *6* blow: *dar un* ~ *a*, to give a blow; fig. to try, examine; fig. to take a draught from [a bottle, a jug]. *7* MUS. preliminary flourish. *8* maulstick. *9* ZOOL. tentacle. *10 tomar el* ~ *a*, to examine, sound.

tiento, tiente, etc. *irr.* V. TENTAR.

tiernamente *adv.* tenderly, lovingly.

tierno, -na *adj.* tender [soft; loving, affectionate]. *2* tender [age]. *3* fresh [bread]. *4* blear [eyes].

tierra *f.* earth [this planet]. *2* land [solid part of the earth's surface]: ~ *de nadie*, MIL. no man's land; ~ *firme*, mainland; solid ground; *tomar* ~, to land; *en* ~, NAUT. on land, ashore; ~ *adentro*, inland. *3* ground [surface of earth]: *irse*, or *venirse, a* ~, to fall down; collapse; be ruined; *perder* ~, to lose footing; to be swept off one's feet. *4* country [one's country], homeland. *5* country, land, soil, region, district: *Tierra Santa*, Holy Land; *por estas tierras*, in these parts. *6* land, landed property, tillable land; piece of land: ~ *de pan llevar*, wheat land, cereal-growing land. *7* AGR. soil, mould. *8* earth [matter], dust: ~ *de batán*, fuller's earth. *9* CHEM. earth. *10* RADIO. ground.

1) **tieso** *adv.* hard, firmly, strongly.

2) **tieso, -sa** *adj.* stiff, rigid [not flexible]. *2* strong, robust. *3* tight, taut. *4* fig. valiant. *5* fig. stiff, stuck-up. *6* fig. stiff, uncompromising, firm, obstinate. *7* coll. *tenérselas tiesas con*, to hold one's ground with.

tiesta *f.* edge of headings [of a cask or barrel].

tiesto *m.* potsherd. *2* flowerpot.

tiesura *f.* stiffness.

tífico, -ca *adj.* MED. typhous.

tifo *m.* MED. typhus.

tifoideo, -a *adj.* typhoid. *2 f.* MED. typhoid fever.

tifón *m.* typhoon. *2* METEOR. waterspout.

tifus *m.* MED. typhus.

tigre *m.* ZOOL. tiger. *2* fig. tiger [bloodthirsty person]. *3* ZOOL. (Am.) jaguar.

tigresa *f.* tigress.

tigridia *f.* BOT. tiger lily.

tigrillo *m.* ZOOL. (Am.) gray fox.

tija *f.* stem [of a key].

tijera *f. sing. y pl.* scissors, shears. *2 sing.* sawbuck, sawhorse. *3* backbiter, gossip. *4 catre de* ~, folding cot; *silla de* ~, folding chair. *5 hacer* ~, [of horses] to twist the mouth.

tijerada *f.* TIJERETADA.

tijereta *f.* dim. small scissors. *2* BOT. tendril [of vine]. *3* ENT. earwig.

tijeretada *f.,* **tijeretazo** *m.* cut with scissors, clip, snip.

tijeretear *tr.* to cut clumsily with scissors. *2* coll. to deal arbitrarily with [another person's affairs].

tila 418

tila *f.* BOT. linden tree. *2* flower of the linden tree. *3* linden-blossom tea.
tilburí *m.* tilbury.
tildar *tr.* to put a tilde or dash over. *2* to cancel, cross out. *3* ~ *de*, to accuse of, or charge with, being [negligent, niggardly, etc.].
tilde *f.* tilde, dash [on the letter *ñ*, etc.]. *2* fault, blemish, defect. *3 f.* jot, tittle.
tildío *m.* ORN. killdee.
tildón *m.* cancelling line or mark.
tilia *f.* TILO.
tiliáceo, -a *adj.* BOT. tiliaceous.
tilín *m.* ting-a-ling. *2* coll. *hacer* ~, to please. *3 tener* ~, to be attractive, winsome.
tilo *m.* BOT. linden tree.
tilla *f.* NAUT. part deck on a small boat.
tillado *m.* board floor.
tillar *tr.* to floor with boards.
timador, -ra *m.-f.* swindler.
tímalo *m.* ICHTH. grayling.
timar *tr.* to swindle. *2 ref.* coll. to make eyes to each other.
timba *f.* gambling party. *2* gambling den.
timbal *m.* MUS. kettledrum. *2* MUS. tambourin, small drum. *3* COOK. timbale.
timbalero *m.* MUS. kettledrummer.
timbrado, -da *adj.* MUS. *bien timbrada*, having a good timbre [voice]. *3 papel* ~, stamped paper.
timbrar *tr.* to stamp [put a stamp or seal on].
timbrazo *m.* loud ring [of a call or door bell].
timbre *m.* HER. timbre, crest. *2* stamp, seal [on a paper]. *3* revenue stamp. *4* call bell, electric bell. *5* MUS., HER. timbre. *6* deed of glory.
timidez *f.* timidity, timorousness, shyness.
tímido, -da *adj.* timid, timorous, shy. *2* fainthearted.
timo *m.* swindle, cheat: *dar un* ~ *a*, to swindle. *2* ANAT. thymus. *3* TÍMALO.
timocracia *f.* POL. timocracy.
timol *m.* CHEM. thymol.
timón *m.* NAUT. rudder; helm. *2* AER. rudder. *3* fig. helm [direction, guidance]. *4* beam [of plough]. *5* pole, tongue [of a cart].
timonear *intr.* NAUT. to helm, steer.
timonel *m.* NAUT. helmsman, steersman.
timonera *f.* ORN. rectrix. *2* NAUT. pilothouse.
timonero *m.* TIMONEL.
timorato, -ta *adj.* God-fearing. *2* pusilanimous.
Timoteo *m. pr. n.* Timothy.
timpánico, -ca *adj.* ANAT., MED. tympanic.
timpanitis *f.* MED. tympanites.
timpanización *f.* MED. meteorization.
tímpano *m.* MUS. glass harmonica. *3* ANAT. tympan, tympanum, eardrum. *7* ARCH. tympan, tympanum. *5* PRINT. tympan.
tina *f.* large earthen jar. *2* vat, tub.
tinada *f.* woodpile. *2* cattle shed.
tinaja *f.* large earthen jar.
tinción *f.* dyeing.
tinelo *m.* obs. servants' dinning room.
tinerfeño, -ña *adj.-n.* of Tenerife.
tingladillo *m.* NAUT. clinker work.
tinglado *m.* shed. *2* temporary board platform. *3* fig. intrigue, machination.
tiniebla *f. sing. & pl.* darkness [absence of light; state of ignorance or error]. *2 pl.* ECCL. Tenebrae.
tino *m.* skill or facility for finding things in the dark. *2* good aim, skill for hitting the mark. *3* judgement, wisdom, tact. *sacar de* ~, to bewilder; to exasperate. *5 a buen* ~, by guess. *6 a* ~, gropingly. *7 sin* ~, without moderation.

tinta *f.* ink: ~ *china*, India ink; *saber una cosa de buena* ~, to have a thing from a reliable source. *2* [applied] colour or pigment. *3* [process of] dyeing. *4* colour, tint, hue. *5* PAINT. tint.
tintar *tr.* to dye, colour, tint.
tinte *m.* [process of] dyeing. *2* dye [colour]. *3* dyeing establishment. *4* fig. colouring, false appearance.
tintero *m.* inkstand, inkwell: *dejarse [una cosa] en el* ~, coll. to forget, to omit. *2* PRINT. ink fountain.
tintín *m.* clink, chink. *2* jingle.
tintinar, tintinear *intr.* to clink; to jingle.
tintineo *m.* clink, clinking. *2* jingle, jingling.
tinto, -ta *adj.* dyed, coloured, stained. *2* darkred [grape or wine].
tintóreo, -a *adj.* tinctorial.
tintorería *f.* dyeing, dyer's trade. *2* dyeing establishment. *3* clothes cleaner's shop.
tintorero, -ra *m.-f.* dyer. *2* clothes cleaner. *3 f.* (Am.) female shark.
tintura *f.* [process of] dyeing. *2* dye [colour]. *3* fig. paint [in the face]. *4* tincture [solution]. *5* fig. smattering.
tinturar *tr.* to dye, colour, tincture.
tiña *f.* MED. tinea, scald-head. *2* coll. stinginess; poverty.
tiñería *f.* coll. stinginess.
tiño, tiña, tiñera, etc. *in.* V. TEÑIR.
tiñoso, -sa *adj.* scabby. *2* coll. mean, stingy. *3* coll. poor, indigent.
tío *m.* uncle: ~ *abuelo*, granduncle, great-uncle. *2* term of adress for an eldery man. *3* coll. fellow, guy.
tiovivo *m.* carrousel, merry-go-round.
tipejo *m. dim.* ridiculous fellow.
típico, -ca *adj.* typical. *2* characteristic.
tiple *m.* MUS. treble or soprano voice. *2* MUS. treble guitar. *3 m.-f.* MUS. soprano singer.
tiplisonante *adj.* coll. treble-toned.
tipo *m.* type [pattern, standard, symbol, class, etc.]. *2* BIOL., PRINT., NUMIS. type. *3* BOT., ZOOL. phylum. *4* COM. rate: ~ *de descuento*, discount rate. *5* build, figure [of a person]. *6* fellow, specimen, guy.
tipografía *f.* typography. *2* printing shop.
tipográfico, -ca *adj.* typographic(al.
tipógrafo *m.* typographer, typesetter.
típula *f.* ENT. crane fly, daddy-longlegs.
tiquis miquis, tiquismiquis *m. pl.* ridiculous or affected scruples, words, etc.
tira *f.* narrow strip [of paper, cloth, etc.]; strap, thong. *2* shred.
tirabala *m.* popgun.
tirabeque *m.* BOT. sugar pea.
tirabotas *f.* boot hook.
tirabuzón *m.* corkscrew. *2* corkscrew curl, hanging curl.
tirada *f.* throw, cast. *2* shooting [at a mark]. *3* distance, stretch. *4* series [of things said or written without stopping], tirade. *5* PRINT. printing [of a book, journal, etc.]: ~ *aparte*, reprint. *6* edition, impression [number of copies]. *7 de*, or *en una* ~, at a stretch.
tiradero *m.* HUNT. shooting post.
tirado, -da *adj.* dirt-cheap, given away. *2* long and low [ship]. *3* running [handwriting]. *4 m.* wiredrawing. *5* PRINT. printing, presswork.
tirador, -ra *m.-f.* thrower. *2* drawer [of metals, etc.]. *3* marksman, [good or bad] shot. *4* FENC. fencer. *5 m.* bell pull, pull chain. *6* handle, knob

[of a door, drawer, etc.], doorknob. 7 slingshot. 8 PRINT. pressman.

tirafondo m. wood screw, lag screw.

tiralíneas, pl. **-neas** m. ruling pen.

tiramira f. long, narrow range [of mountains]. 2 line, string, series. 3 distance, stretch.

tiranía f. tyranny.

tyranicida m.-f. tyrannicide [person].

tiranicidio m. tyrannicide [killing of a tyrant].

tiránico, -ca adj. tyrannic(al, tyrannous.

tiranizar tr. to tyrannize.

tirano, -na adj. tyrannical. 2 m.-f. tyrant.

tirante adj. tight, taut, tense, strained. 2 strained [relations]. 3 m. trace [of harness]. 4 ARCH., ENG. tie, tie beam, tie rod, truss rod. 5 pl. braces, suspenders [of trousers].

tirantez f. tenseness, tautness, tightness. 2 tension, strained condition [of relations].

tiranuelo, -la adj. dim. little tyrant.

tirapié m. shoemaker's stirrup.

tirar tr. to throw, cast, fling, pitch. 2 to throw away, cast off. 3 to fire [a shot]. 4 to give [a kick]. 5 to draw, stretch. 6 to withdraw. 7 to knock down, overthrow, pull down. 8 to waste, squander. 9 to draw [a line]. 10 PRINT. to print. 11 intr. to attract, excite love or interest. 12 [of a chimney, etc.] to draw. 13 to last, endure. 14 ~ a: a) to fence with; shoot with; b) to shoot at; c) to turn [in some direction]; d) to tend, incline; e) to seek to, aim at; f) [of colours] to have a tinge of: ~ a rojo, to be reddish. 15 ~ de: a) to draw, attract; b) to pull, pull at, pull on, to draw; c) to draw, take, take out [a weapon, instrument, etc.]. 16 coll. ~ de largo, or por largo, to spend lavishly; to make a liberal estimate. 17 coll. ir tirando, to get along. 18 coll. tira y afloja, blowing hot and cold. 19 a todo ~, at the most. 20 ref. to rush, to throw oneself. 21 [of a parachutist, etc.] to jump. 22 to lie down.

tiratacos m. popgun.

tirilla f. neckband [of a shirt].

tirio, -ria adj.-m. Tyrian.

tiritar intr. to shiver.

tiritón m. shiver: dar tiritones, to shiver.

Tiro f. pr. n. HIST., GEOG. Tyre.

tiro m. throw [act of throwing]. 2 shot [discharge of a firearm; charge for a firearm]; errar el ~, to miss the mark; salir el ~ por la culata, [of one's exertions, scheming, etc.] to work the wrong way: a tiros, with shots; ni a tiros, coll. by no means. 3 throw, shot, range [distance]; a ~, within range; fig. within reach. 4 report [of a gun]. 5 shooting practice or sport: ~ al blanco, target shooting; ~ al plato, trapshooting. 6 shooting grounds; shooting gallery. 7 fig. physical or moral injury. 8 fig. innuendo, allusive remark. 9 ARTIL. fire, direction of fire. 10 team [of draught animals]. 11 harness trace. 12 length [of a piece of cloth, etc.]. 13 flight [of stairs]. 14 draft, draught [of a chimney, etc.]. 15 MIN. shaft; depth of a shaft. 16 coll. de tiros largos, all dressed-up.

tiroideo, -a adj. ANAT. thyroid.

tiroides m. ANAT. thyroid [gland].

Tirol (el) m. pr. n. GEOG. the Tyrol.

tirolés, -sa adj.-n. Tyrolese.

tirón m. pull, jerk, haul, tug: de un ~, with a pull; fig. at one stroke; at a stretch. 2 ESTIRÓN. 3 tyro, novice.

tirotear tr. to snipe at, blaze away at. 2 ref. to exchange shots, fire at each other.

tiroteo m. firing, shooting, exchange of shots.

tirreno, -na adj.-n. Tyrrhenian. 2 Etruscan.

tirria f. coll. aversion, dislike.

tirso m. BOT., MYTH. Thyrsus.

tisana f. medicinal tea.

tísico, -ca adj. MED. phthisical, consumptive. 2 m.-f. consumptive [person].

tisis f. MED. phthisis, consumption.

tisú m. gold or silver tissue.

Titán m. pr. n. MYTH. and fig. Titan.

titanio m. CHEM. titanium.

títere m. puppet, marionette: no dejar ~ con cabeza, to upset, destroy, entirely. 2 fig. whippersnapper. 3 pl. puppet show. 4 jugglers show, tumblers show, etc.

titilación f. slight tremor [of a part of the body]. 2 twinkling [of a luminous body].

titilar intr. [of a part of the body] to tremble slightly. 2 [of a luminous body] to twinkle.

titirimundi m. MUNDONUEVO.

titiritaina f. coll. merry noise.

titiritar intr. to shiver, shake [with cold or fear].

titiritero m. puppet showman. 2 juggler, tumbler.

Tito m. pr. n. Titus.

titubear intr. to waver, hesitate. 2 to stammer. 3 to stagger, totter.

titubeo m. wavering, hesitation. 2 stammering. 3 staggering, tottering.

titulado, -da adj. diplomaed. 2 titled. 3 so-called. 4 CHEM. titrated.

titular adj. titular [bishop, saint, etc.]. 2 m.-f. bearer, holder [of a passport, etc.]. 3 m. capital letter [used in newspaper headlines].

titular tr. to title, entitle, call, name. 2 CHEM. to titrate. 3 ref. to be called; to call oneself.

titulillo m. PRINT. running title.

título m. title. 2 heading, headline, caption. 3 diploma, professional degree. 4 qualification, desert. 5 COM. certificate, bond. 6 CHEM. titre, titer. 7 LAW ~ de propiedad, title dead. 8 a ~ de, as a, by way of: a ~ de información, unofficially.

tiza f. chalk. 2 whiting [for polishing metals]. 3 calcined stag's horn.

tiznadura f. smudging, smutting; smudge, stain.

tiznajo m. TIZNÓN.

tiznar tr. to soil with soot. 2 to smudge, smut, stain, soil, sully. 3 ref. to get soiled or smudged. 4 (Am.) to get drunk.

tizne m. soot, smut. 2 half-burned stick.

tiznón m. smut, smear, stain.

tizo m. half-burnt charcoal.

tizón m. partly burned stick, firebrand. 2 AGR. wheat-smut. 3 fig. stain. 4 MAS. header.

tizona f. coll. sword.

tizonear intr. to stir up a fire.

toalla f. towel: ~ rusa, Turkish towel.

toallero m. towel rack.

toalleta f. dim. small towel. 2 napkin.

toar tr. ATOAR.

toha f. tufa, calcareous tufa. 2 DENT. tartar. 3 fig. crust, cover.

tobera f. tuyère.

Tobías m. pr. n. Tobias.

tobillera f. flapper [young girl]. 3 SPORT. ankle support.

tobillo m. ankle.

tobogán m. toboggan.

toboso, -sa adj. tufaceous.

toca f. wimple. 2 cornet [headdress of the Sisters of Charity]. 3 coif, bonnet. 4 toque [hat].

tocadiscos pl. **-cos** m. record player.

tocado, -da adj. touched: estar ~ de la cabeza, to be

touched, crazed. *2 m.* hairdress [esp. for women]. *3* hairdo, coiffure.

tocador, -ra *m.-f.* MUS. player. *2 m.* dressing table; toilet case: *productos de tocador*, toilet articles. *3* dressing room, toilet room.

tocamiento *m.* touching, feeling. *2* playing [on an instrument]. *3* call, inspiration.

tocante *adj.* touching. *2 ~ a*, concerning, as regards, touching, with reference to.

tocar *tr.* to touch [with a part of the body, with a stick, etc.], to feel, lay hands upon. *2* to hit, knock, strike (lightly): *~ fondo*, NAUT. to strike ground. *3* to touch [with a touchstone]. *4* to find [by experience], to suffer [the consequences of]. *5* to touch, touch upon [a subject]. *6* PAINT. to touch. *7* MUS. to touch, strike [keys or strings]; to play, sound, blow, ring, beat [an instrument, a bell, a drum; a composition, an air, a call, etc.]: *~ a muerte*, to toll, sound a knell. *8* to play [a phonograph record]. *9* to move, inspire. *10* to do, dress [the hair]. *11 intr. ~ a* or *en*, to touch, touch at [be in contact with, to be contiguous to]. *12 ~ a*, to appertain to, to behove, devolve on, be up to; to be one's turn; to fall on one's lot; to be got by one, be the share of [in a distribution, etc.]; to be one's due; to be a relation of; to touch, relate, concern, regard: *en* or *por, lo que toca a*, as regads, with regard to. *13* NAUT. *~ en*, to touch at [a port]. *14 impers. tocan a*, it is time for or to. *15 ref.* to touch, be in contact, touch each other. *16* to do or dress one's hair. *17* to cover one's head [with a hat, bonnet, etc.].

tocata *f.* MUS. toccata. *2* coll. drubbing.

tocayo, -ya *m.-f.* namesake.

tocinería *f.* bacon and pork shop or stand.

tocinero, -ra *m.-f.* por seller.

tocino *m.* bacon; salt pork.

tocología *f.* tocology, obstetrics.

tocólogo *f.* tocologist, obstetrician.

tocón *m.* stump [of tree, arm or leg].

tochedad *f.* rusticity, crudeness, stupidity.

tocho, -cha *adj.* rustic, crude, stupid.

tochura *f.* TOCHEDAD.

todavía *adv.* still, even, yet: *~ más*, even more, *~ mejor*, still better; *~ no*, not yet.

todo, -da; todos, -das *adj.* all, every, each, the whole of: *~ aquel que*, whoever, everybody who; *~ aquello que*, whatever. *2 a toda prisa*, with all speed, hurriedly; *a toda velocidad*, at full speed. *3 m.* all, whole, everything: *ante ~*, first of all; *con ~*, still, however; *del ~*, entirely, wholly; *en ~ y por ~*, wholly, absolutely; *en un ~*, as a whole; *sobre ~*, above all, specially. *4 m.-f. pl.* everyone, everybody, all of them. *5 adv.* entirely.

todopoderoso, -sa *adj.* all-powerful, almighty; *el Todopoderoso*, the Almighty [God].

toga *f.* toga [Roman garment]. *2* gown, robe [of professor, judge or lawyer].

togado, -da *adj.* togated. *2* wearing a gown or robe [judge, magistrate, etc.].

toisón, toisón de oro *m.* Golden Fleece.

tojino *m.* NAUT. cleat.

tojo *m.* BOT. gorse, furze, whin.

toldar *tr.* ENTOLDAR.

toldilla *f.* NAUT. poop, poop deck.

toldo *m.* awning. *2* tilt [cloth covering of a cart, etc.]. *3* coll. pride, pomp.

tole tole *m.* hubbub, uproar. *2* popular clamour

[against something]. *3 tomar el tole*, to run away, leave in a hurry.

toledano, -na *adj.-n.* Toledan.

tolerable *adj.* tolerable, bearable, sufferable.

tolerancia *f.* tolerance, toleration. *2* MACH., MED. tolerance.

tolerante *adj.* tolerant.

tolerar *tr.* to tolerate. *2* to bear, suffer.

tolete *m.* NAUT. thole, tholepin.

tolmo *m.* pilarlike rock, tor.

Tolomeo *m. pr. n.* Ptolemy.

tolondro, -dra *adj.* scatterbrained. *2 m.-f.* scatterbrain. *3 m.* bump, swelling [from a blow].

tolondrón, -na *adj.* scatterbrainer. *2 m.-f.* scatterbrain. *3 m.* bump, swelling [from a blow].

tolondrón, -na *adj.-n.* TOLONDRO: *a tolondrones*, by fits and starts.

Tolosa *f. pr. n.* GEOG. Toulouse [French city]. *2* Tolosa [Spanish town].

tolosano, -na *adj.-n.* of Tolouse or Tolosa.

Tolú (bálsamo de) *m.* tolu, tolu balsam.

tolueno *m.* CHEM. toluene.

tolva *f.* hopper, chute [in mills, etc.].

tolvanera *f.* cloud of dust, dust whirl.

tollo *m.* ICHTH. spotted dogfish. *2* loin of a stag. *3* HUNT. blind. *4* quagmire.

toma *f.* take, taking, receiving, assuming: *~ de posesión*, taking possession; induction into office. *2* take, taking, capture [of a fort, a city, etc.]. *3* MED. dose. *4* HYDR. intake, inlet, tap. *5* ELEC. *~ de corriente*, current collecting; current collector, tap, plug. *6* RADIO. terminal.

¡toma! *interj.* well!, why!; of course!

tomadero *m.* handle. *2* water intake or inlet.

tomador, -ra *adj.* taking. *2* retrieving [dog]. *3 m.-f.* taker. *4* COM. payee [of a bill]. *5* NAUT. gasket.

tomadura *f.* taking. *2 ~ de pelo*, fun made of one, hoax, pulling one's leg.

tomar *tr.* to take [lay hold of, assume possession of; receive, accept; capture], seize, catch. *2* to take, have [eat, drink, etc.]. *3* to take [measurements, the temperature; advice, precautions, measures, a resolution, the liberty, the train, etc.]. *4* to acquire [an habit]. *5* to take [as a servant or employee]. *6* to take [spouse, a partner]. *7* to take [hire, lease, rent, subscribe to, etc.]. *8* to take [interpret; regard in specified manner]. *9* to take, occupy. *10* to steal. *11* to take, choose, buy. *12* to take, assume. *13* to take, borrow [a verse, an idea, etc.]. *14* to take [the government; the lead, a liking, a dislike, etc.]. *15* to gather [strength]. *16* to take [someone] with oneself. *17* CARDS to take [a trick]. *18 ~ a mal*, to take it ill, take offence at. *19 ~ calor*, to get warm. *20 ~ en cuenta*, to take account of, to take into account. *21 ~ frío*, to catch a cold. *22 tomarla con*, to oppose, attack, have a grudge against. *23 tomarle a uno la risa, el sueño*, to be overcome with laughter, with sleep. *24 ~ lenguas*, to take tidings. *25 ~ para sí*, to take to oneself. *26 ~ por*, to take for: *lo tomé a usted por otro*, I took you for someone else. *27 ~ sobre sí*, to take upon oneself. *28 ~ razón de*, to register, make a record of.
29 intr. to go or turn in a specified direction: *~ por la derecha*, to take or turn to the right.
30 ref. to take, to have: *tomarse libertades*, to take liberties, make free; *tomarse un descanso*, to take a rest. *31 tomarse de moho, de orín*, to get rusty. *32 tomarse del vino*, to get drunk.

Tomás *m. pr. n.* Thomas: *Santo* ~, Saint Thomas; *Santo ~ de Aquino*, Saint Thomas Aquinas.
tomatazo *m.* blow with a tomato.
tomate *m.* BOT. tomato [plant or fruit].
tomatera *f.* BOT. tomato, tomato plant.
tomavistas *adj.* picture-taking. *2 m.* motion-picture camera.
tómbola *f.* tombolo. 2 charity raffle.
tomento *m.* BOT. tomentum. 2 coarse tow.
tomentoso, -sa *adj.* BOT. tomentose, tomentous.
tomillo *m.* BOT. thyme.
tomismo *m.* Thomism.
tomiza *f.* esparto rope.
tomo *m.* volume, tome. 2 coll. *de ~ y lomo*, great, important.
ton *m. sin ~ ni son*, without motive or cause, without rhyme or reason.
tonada *f.* tune, song.
tonadilla *f.* light song.
tonadillera *f.* woman singer of light songs.
tonalidad *f.* MUS., PAINT. tonality.
tonante *adj.* Tonans: *Júpiter ~*, Jupiter Tonans.
tonca *adj.* BOT. tonka: *haba ~*, tonka bean.
tonel *m.* barrel, cask, tun.
tonelada *f.* ton: *~ de arqueo*, register ton; *~ métrica*, metric ton.
tonelaje *m.* tonnage.
tonelería *f.* barrelmaking, cooperage. 2 coopery [cooper's workshop]. 3 barrels, casks [collec.].
tonelero *m.* barrelmaker, cooper, hooper.
tonelete *m. dim.* small cask, keg. 2 short skirt.
tonga, tongada *f.* coat, couch, bed, layer.
tongo *m.* SPORT. coll. trick of a player, boxer, etc., who engages to lose for a bribe.
tonicidad *f.* tonicity.
tónico, -ca *adj.* tonic, invigorating. *2* MUS. key [note]. *3* GRAM. tonic [accent]; accented [vowel or syllable]. *4 m.* MED. tonic. *5 f.* MUS. tonic, keynote.
tonificante *adj.* tonic, invigorating.
tonificar *tr.* MED. to invigorate, tone up.
tonillo *m.* singsong, monotonous tone. 2 accent [of a region].
tonina *f.* ATÚN. 2 DELFÍN 2.
tono *m.* tone [in writing or speaking]. *2* MUS., ACOUST. pitch. *3* MUS. mode, key. *4* MUS. tone, step. *5* diapason normal. *6* tone, shade [of colour]. *7* vigour, energy. *8* MED., PHYSIOL. tone. *9* tune, sing. *10* tune, harmony: *a ~ con*, in tune with, in harmony with. *11* fig. *bajar el ~, mudar de ~*, to change one's tune; *subir de ~*, fig. to become arrogant. *12 dar el ~*, fig. to set the standard. *13 darse ~*, to put on airs. *14 de buen ~*, fashionable, smart; *de mal ~*, vulgar. *15 a este ~*, like this.
tonsila *f.* ANAT. tonsil.
tonsura *f.* hair cutting; shearing. *2* ECCL. tonsure.
tonsurar *tr.* to cut the hair of; to shear, fleece. *2* ECCL. to tonsure.
tontada *f.* silliness, nonsense.
tontaina *m.-f.* silly person, fool.
tontear *intr.* to talk nonsense. *2* coll. to flirt.
tontedad, tontera *f.* TONTERÍA.
tontería *f.* silliness, foolishness. 2 nonsense. 3 triviality, trifle.
tontillo *m.* hoop skirt, farthingale.
tontina *f.* tontine.
tontivano, -na *adj.* foolishly conceited.
tonto, -ta *adj.* silly, foolish, dull, stupid. 2 nonsensical. *3 m.-f.* fool, dolt: *~ de capirote*, blockhead;

hacerse el ~, to play the fool. *4 a tontas y a locas*, recklessly, haphazard.
tontuelo, -la *m.-f. dim.* little fool.
tontuna *f.* TONTERÍA.
topacio *m.* MINER. topaz.
topada *f.* TOPETADA.
topar *tr.* to strike, knock against, run into. 2 tr., intr., ref. *~ con* or *toparse con*, to run across, meet, meet with, fall in with. *3* intr. to butt [with the head or horns]. *4* coll. *tope donde tope*, strike where it may.
tope *m.* butt, end: *al ~, a ~*, end to end. *2* RLY. buffer, bumper. *3* MACH. stop. *4* fig. rub, trouble, difficulty. *5* NAUT. masthead, topmasthead: *hasta el ~*, fig. up to the top, to the limit; *estar hasta los topes*, NAUT. to be overloades; fig. to be sated [with]. *6* NAUT. edge or butt end of a plank. *7* TOPETÓN. *8* fig. row, quarrel.
topera *f.* molehole, molehill.
topetada *f.* butt [by a horned animal]. *2* fig. butt, bump [with the head].
topetar *tr.-intr.* to butt [with head or horns]. *2 tr.* to strike, collide with, knock against.
topetazo *m.* TOPETADA.
topetón *m.* knock, bump, collision. *2* TOPETADA.
tópico, -ca *adj.* topical, local. *2 m.* MED. external local application. *3 pl.* commonplaces, platitudes.
topinera *f.* TOPERA.
topo *m.* ZOOL. mole. 2 coll. awkward person; dolt. 3 polka dot.
topografía *f.* topography. 2 surveying.
topográfico, -ca *adj.* topographical.
topógrafo *m.* topographer; surveyor.
toponimia *f.* toponymy.
toque *m.* touch [act of touching]. 2 touchstone. 3 fig. trial, proof. 4 blow, tap. 5 sounding [of a bugle, etc.]; ringing [of bells]; beat [of a drum] for announcing or signalling; call: *~ de diana*, reveille; *~ de queda*, curfew. 6 warning, admonition, advice. 7 PAINT. touch.
toquilla *f. dim.* small toque. 2 triangular kerchief. 3 knitted shawl.
torácico, -ca *adj.* ANAT., ZOOL. thoracic.
torada *f.* drove of bulls.
toral *adj.* main, strongest: *arco ~*, ARCH. each one of the arches supporting a cupola.
tórax, -rax *m.* ANAT., ZOOL. thorax.
torbellino *m.* whirlwind. 2 coll. lively, hustling person.
torca *f.* GEOL. circular depression.
torcaz *adj.* wild [pigeon].
torcecuello *m.* ORN. wryneck.
torcedor, -ra *adj.* twisting. *2 m.-f.* twister [person]. *3 m.* fig. anything causing constant grief or worry.
torcedura *f.* twisting. 2 SURG. sprain. 3 small vine.
torcer *tr.* to twist, wrench, bend, crook. 2 to twist, twine [a thread, rope, etc.]. 3 to turn, aside. 4 to twist, distort, pervert. 5 to make [one] change his mind. 6 *~ el gesto*, to make a wry face. 7 *intr.* to turn [to the right, to the left, etc.]. 8 *ref.* to become twisted, bent or crooked. 9 to go crooked or astray. 10 to yield [to persuasion, etc.]. 11 to turn bad, to fail. 12 [of milk] to curdle; [of wine] to turn sour. 13 *torcerse el tobillo*, to sprain one's ankle. ¶ CONJUG. like *mover*.
torcida *f.* wick [of a lamp or candle].
torcido, -da *adj.* twisted, twined. 2 twisted, bent, crooked. 4 oblique. 5 fig. twisted, perverted. 6 fig. crooked, dishonest. *7 m.* twisted silk.

torcijón *m.* twist, wrench. *2* bellyache, gripes.

torcimiento *m.* twist, twisting. *2* perversion, warping. *3* circumlocution.

tordillo, -lla *adj.* dapple-gray. *2 m.-f.* dapple-gray horse.

tordo, -da *adj.* dapple-gray [horse]. *2 m.* ORN. thrush. *3* ORN. (Am.) starling. *4* dapple-gray horse.

toreador *m.* bullfighter.

torear *intr.-tr.* to fight bulls in the ring. *2 tr.* fig. to fool, deceive, make fun of.

toreo *m.* bullfighting. *2* banter, covert mockery.

torera *f.* a short, tight, unbuttoned jacket. *3 saltarse [una cosa] a la ~*, to disregard [a rule, engagement, duty, etc.].

torería *f.* bullfighters [collect.].

torero, -ra *adj.* [pertaining to] bullfighting. *2 m.-f.* bullfighter.

torete *m. dim.* little bull. *2* coll. difficult matter.

toril *m.* BULLF. pen for bulls before the fight.

torio *m.* CHEM. thorium.

torito *m. dim.* little bull.

tormenta *f.* storm, tempest. *2* turmoil.

tormento *m.* torment, pain, anguish. *2* torture [for extorting confession, etc.]: *dar ~*, to torture.

tormentoso, -sa *adj.* stormy, tempestuous.

tormo *m.* TOLMO.

torna *f.* giving back, return. *2 volver las tornas*, to give tit for tat; to turn the tables.

tornaboda *f.* day after a weeding.

tornada *f.* coming back, return. *2* POET. envoy.

tornadizo, -za *adj.* changeable, fickle. *2* renegade. *3 m.-f.* turncoat, deserter, renegade.

tornado *m.* tornado.

tornamiento *m.* change, turn.

tornapunta *f.* brace, prop.

tornar *tr.* to return, give back. *2* to turn, make. *3 intr.* to return, come back. *4 ~ a*, to [do, etc.] again. *5 ~ en sí*, to recover, come to. *6 ref.* to turn, become.

tornasol *m.* BOT. sunflower. *2* iridescence, shot colour. *3* CHEM. litmus.

tornasolado, -da *adj.* iridescent, changeable, shot.

tornasolar *tr.* to make iridescent. *2 ref.* to become iridescent.

tornátil *adj.* changeable, fickle.

tornaviaje *m.* return trip.

tornavoz *m.* any device to direct sound to an audience; sounding board. *2* echo.

torneado, -da *adj.* turned [in a lathe].

torneador *m.* turner [lathe operator]. *2* tourneyer.

torneaduras *f. pl.* lathe shavings, turnings.

tornear *tr.* to turn [in a lathe]. *2* to tourney. *4* to muse.

torneo *m.* tournament. *2* VET. gid, staggers.

tornera *f.* doorkeeper of a nunnery.

tornería *f.* turnery. *2* turner's shop or workshop.

tornero *m.* turner [lathe operator].

tornillo *m.* screw, male screw: *~ de orejas*, thumbscrew; *~ sin fin*, worm gear; *apretar los tornillos a uno*, coll. to put the screw upon one: *faltarle a uno un ~*, coll. to have a screw loose. *2 ~ de banco*, screw vice.

torniquete *m.* bell crank. *2* turnstile. *3* SURG. tourniquet.

torniscón *m.* slap with the back of the hand.

torno *m.* windlass, winch. *2* lathe. *3* revolving server [for passing dishes, etc., through a wall]. *3* revolving machine: *~ de alfarero*, potter's wheel; *~ de hilar*, spinning wheel. *4* turn [of a

river]. *6* turn around. *7 en ~ [de]*, around; *en ~ a* or *de*, regarding about.

toro *m.* bull [uncastrated male of bovine animal]: *~ de lidia*, bull reared for bullfighting. *2* fig. bull [strong, husky man]. *3* ASTR. Taurus. *4* ARCH. torus. *5 pl.* bullfighting, bullfight: *ciertos son los toros*, coll. indeed, it is true.

toronja *f.* grapefruit.

toronjil *m.* **toronjina** *f.* BOT. lemon balm, garden balm.

toronjo *m.* BOT. grapefruit tree.

torozón *m.* displeasure, annoyance. *2* VET. gripes.

torpe *adj.* awkward, clumsy. *2* slow, heavy, torpid. *3* dull, dull-witted. *4* lewd, lascivious. *5* infamous. *6* crude, ugly.

torpedeamiento *m.* TORPEDEO.

torpedear *tr.* to torpedo.

torpedeo *m.* torpedoing.

torpedero, -ra *m.* torpedo boat.

torpedo *m.* NAV., AUTO. torpedo. *2* ICHTH. torpedo, electric ray.

torpeza *f.* awkwardness, clumsiness. *2* slowness, heaviness, torpidness. *3* dullness, stupidity. *4* lewdness, lasciviousness. *5* infamy, turpitude.

tórpido, -da *adj.* MED. torpid.

torpor *m.* MED. torpor.

torrado *m.* roasted chick-pea.

torrar *tr.* to toast.

torre *f.* tower [building or structure]: *~ albarrana*, FORT. watch tower; *~ del homenaje*, FORT. donjon. *2* belfry, bell tower. *3* turret, belvedere. *4* ARTIL., NAV. turret. *5* CHESS. castle, rook. *6* country house.

torrefacción *f.* torrefaction, toasting.

torrefacto, -ta *adj.* torrefied, toasted.

torreja *f.* (Am.) TORRIJA.

torrejón *m.* small tower, ill-shaped tower.

torrencial *adj.* torrential.

torrente *m.* torrent [rushing stream]. *2* fig. torrent [rust, downpour]; rush of people.

torrentera *f.* ravine made by a torrent.

torreón *m.* large fortified tower.

torrero *m.* lighthouseman, lightouse keeper.

torrezno *m.* rasher of bacon, fried rasher of bacon.

tórrido, -da *adj.* torrid: *zona tórrida*, torrid zone.

torrija *f.* slice of bread soaked in milk, wine, etc., then fried and sweetened with sugar or honey.

torsión *f.* torsion, twisting.

torso *m.* F. ARTS torso. *2* trunk of the body.

torta *f.* cake: *costar la ~ un pan*, coll. to cost dearly; *tortas y pan pintado*, a mere trifle; a child's play. *2* coll. blow, slap, box.

tortada *f.* a cake containing eggs, fruit, etc.

tortazo *m.* coll. blow, slap, box.

tortera *f.* baking pan. *2* whorl [of spindle].

torticero, -ra *adj.* wrong, unjust.

tortícolis, torticolis *f.* MED. torticollis, stiff neck.

tortilla *f.* omelet: *hacer ~ a*, to crush, smash. *2* (Mex.) pancake.

tórtola *f.* ORN. turtledove.

tortolito, -ta *adj.* green, inexperienced.

tórtolo *m.* ORN. male turtledove. *2 m.-f.* fig. turtledove [demonstrative lover].

tortor *m.* NAUT. heaver.

tortuga *f.* ZOOL. tortoise, turtle. *2* TESTUDO.

tortuosidad *f.* tortuosity, tortuousness.

tortuoso, -sa *adj.* tortuous, sinuous, winding. *2* fig. tortuous [devious, circuitous, crooked].

tortura *f.* torture.

torturador, -ra *adj.* torturing, torturous.

torturar *tr.* to torture, torment. *2 ref.* to torture oneself, to worry.

torva *f.* whirl of rain or snow.

torvisco *m.* BOT. spurge flax.

torvo, -va *adj.* fierce, stern, severe, grim, frowning.

torzal *m.* silk twist. *2* cord, twist.

tos *f.* couch; coughing: ~ *ferina* or *convulsiva*, MED. whooping cough.

tosca *f.* tufa, calcareous tufa. *2* DENT. tartar.

Toscana (la) *f. pr. n.* GEOG. Tuscany.

toscano, -na *adj.-n.* Tuscan.

tosco, -ca *adj.* coarse, rough, crude. *2* rude, uncouth.

tosecilla *f. dim.* slight cough.

toser *intr.* to cough. *2* coll. *toserle a*, to defy, compete with.

tosidura *f.* coughing.

tósigo *m.* poison. *2* fig. grief, anguish.

tosigoso, -sa *adj.* coughing. *2* poisonous, poisoned.

tosquedad *f.* coarseness, roughness, uncouthness.

tostada *f.* toast, piece of toast. *2* coll. *dar*, or *pegar, la ~ a uno*, to cheat, dupe, take in.

tostado, -da *adj.* toasted, roasted. *2* tan, brown [colour]. *3* tanned, sunburnt. *4 m.* toasting, roasting.

tostador, -ra *adj.* toasting, roasting. *2 m.-f.* toaster, roaster [person]. *3 m.* toaster, roaster [utensil].

tostadura *f.* toasting, roasting.

tostar *tr.* to toast, torrefy. *2* to roast [coffee beans]. *3* to brown, sunburn, tan. ¶ CONJUG. like *contar*.

tostón *m.* roasted chick-pea. *2* toast dipped in new olive oil. *3* scorched piece of food. *4* roast pig. *5* coll. wearisome speech, play, etc.

total *adj.* total. *2 m.* total, sum total. *3 adv.* brief, in short.

totalidad *f.* totality, aggregate, whole.

totalitario, -ria *adj.* POL. totalitarian.

totalitarismo *m.* POL. totalitarianism.

totalizar *tr.* to totalize.

tótem *m.* totem.

totemismo *m.* totemism.

toxemia *f.* MED. toxemia.

toxicidad *f.* toxicity.

tóxico, -ca *adj.-m.* toxic.

toxicología *f.* toxicology.

toxina *f.* MED. toxin.

tozal *m.* top of a hill.

tozo, -za *adj.* short, dwarfish, stumpy.

tozudo, -da *adj.* stubborn, obstinate, pigheaded.

tozudez *f.* stubbornness, obstinacy, pigheadedness.

tozuelo *m.* thick, fleshy neck [of an animal].

traba *f.* bond, clasp, locking device. *2* hobble, shackle, trammel. *4* fig. clog, hindrance, restraint.

trabacuenta *f.* mistake in accounts. *2* dispute, argument.

trabadura *f.* binding, locking, uniting, union. *2* thickening, inspissation.

trabajado, -da *adj.* worked, wrought. *3* overworked, worn out. *4* full of hardships. *5* elaborate [literary work].

trabajador, -ra *adj.* industrious, laborious, hardworking. *2* working. *3 m.-f.* worker: working-man, workingwoman, labourer, hand.

trabajante *adj.* working.

trabajar *intr.* to work, labour. *2* to strive, endeavour. *3* [of soil, a machine, etc.] to work. *4* NAUT. [of a ship] to labour. *5 tr.* to work [fashion, shape]. *6* to till [the ground]. *7* to labour, ela-

borate. *8* to harass, worry, trouble. *9* to wear out [by toil or hardship].

trabajo *m.* work, labour, toil: ~ *a destajo*, piecework; ~ *a jornal*, timework; *trabajos forzados*, hard labour. *2* work [thing done]; piece of work. *3* labour [as distinguished from capital]. *4* task, job. *5* employment; *sin ~*, unemployed [worker]. *6* exertion, effort, trouble: *costar ~*, to be hard, difficult; *tomarse el ~ de*, to take the trouble to. *7* PHYS. work. *8 pl.* hardships, privations, difficulties.

trabajosamente *adv.* laboriously, painfully.

trabajoso, -sa *adj.* hard, arduous, laborious. *2* laboured [not easy]. *3* full of hardships.

trabalenguas *pl.* -guas *m.* tongue twister, jawbreaker.

trabar *tr.* to bind, clasp, join, lock. *2* to thicken, inspissate. *3* to catch, seize. *4* to hobble, trammel. *5* to set [a saw]. *6* to join [battle]; to strike up [a friendship]; to begin [a conversation, etc.]. *7 ref.* to become entangled. *8 trabarse de palabras*, to have words. *9 trabársele a uno la lengua*, to become tongue-tied.

trabazón *f.* union [of parts, etc.]. *2* connexion, relation [between things]. *3* thickness, consistence. *4* CARP. bond.

trabe *f.* ARCH. beam.

trabilla *f.* gaiter or trouser strap.

trabucar *tr.* to upset, overturn, invert the order of. *2* to confuse, disturb [the mind]. *3* to mix up, jumble. *4* to mix up [words, syllables or letters]. *5 ref.* to become confused or mixed up.

trabucazo *m.* shot with a blunderbuss. *2* coll. anything causing a sudden fright or distress.

trabuco *m.* blunderbuss.

trabuquete *m.* catapult. *2* a small seine.

traca *f.* string of firecrackers.

tracamundana *f.* coll. noise, uproar, confusion.

tracción *f.* traction: ~ *de sangre*, horse traction.

tracería *f.* ARCH. tracery.

Tracia (la) *f. pr. n.* GEOG. Thrace.

tracio, -cia *adj.-n.* Thracian.

tracista *m.* designer. *2* fig. schemer, trickster.

tracoma *m.* MED. trachoma.

tracto *m.* stretch, space, tract. *2* lapse, interval [of time]. *3* ECCL. tract, tractus [in the mass].

tractor *m.* tractor: ~ *de oruga*, caterpillar.

tradición *f.* tradition. *2* LAW tradition.

tradicional *adj.* traditional.

tradicionalismo *m.* traditionalism.

traducción *f.* translation.

traducible *f.* translatable.

traducir *tr.* to translate. *2* to express, interpret. *3 ref.* to be translated. *4* to result [in]. ¶ CONJUG. like *conducir*.

traductor, -ra *m.-f.* translator.

traedizo, -za *adj.* portable.

traer *tr.* to draw, attract. *3* to bring over. *4* to bring about, cause, occasion, result in. *5* to make, keep: *esto le trae inquieto*, this makes him anxious. *6* to wear, have on [a garment]. *7* to adduce. *8 lo trae el periódico*, it is in the newspaper. *9 ~ a cuento*, to mention. *10 ~ a mal ~*, to treat roughly. *11 ~ en bocas*, or *en lenguas*, to gossip about one. *12 intr.* coll. *traer y llevar*, to gossip. *13 tr.-ref.* to be engaged in, be up to: ~ *or traerse entre manos*, to have in hand. *14 ref. traérselas*, to be more important, difficult, cunning, etc., than it seems.

¶ CONJUG.: INDIC. Pres.: *traigo, traes, trae; traemos, traéis, traen*. | Pret.: *traje, trajiste, trajo; tra-*

jimos, trajisteis, trajeron. | Fut.: traeré, traerás, etc. | COND.: traería, traerías, etc. | SUBJ. Pres.: *traiga, traigas, traigan.* | Imperf.: *trajera, trajeras, trajera; trajéramos, trajerais, trajeran,* or *trajese, trajeses, trajeseis, trajesen.* | Fut.: *trajere, trajeres, trajere; trajéremos, trajereis, trajeren.* | IMPER.: trae, *traiga; traigamos, traed, traigan.* | PAST. P.: traído. | GER.: *trayendo.*

trafagar *intr.* to traffic, trade. *2* to travel, roam. *3* to bustle, hustle.

tráfago *m.* traffic, trade. *2* bustle, hustle.

trafagón, -na *adj.* bustling, hustling. *2 m.-f.* bustler, hustler.

trafalmejas *m.-f.* coll. rattlebrain.

traficante *adj.* trafficking, trading. *2 m.-f.* trafficker, trader.

traficar *intr.* to traffic, deal, trade. *2* to travel, roam.

tráfico *m.* traffic, trade. *2* traffic of vehicles.

tragacanto *m.* tragacanth [tree and gum].

tragaderas *f. pl.* gullet: *tener buenas tragaderas,* coll. to be gullible; to be excessively tolerant.

tragadero *m.* gullet. *2* fig. hole, gulf, etc., that swallows up anything.

tragador, -ra *m.-f.* swallower. *2* glutton, gobbler.

trágala *m.* an ancient song against absolutism. *2* forcing one to support something opposed to his opinions, feelings, etc.

tragaldabas, *pl.* **-bas** *m.-f.* glutton.

tragaleguas, *pl.* **-guas** *m.-f.* great walker.

tragaluz *m.* skylight [window in the roof, ceiling, etc.].

tragantada *f.* large draugth [of liquor]; big swig.

tragantón, -na *adj.* gluttonous. *2 m.-f.* glutton, gobbler. *3 f.* coll. big meal, big spread.

tragaperras, *pl.* **-rras** *f.* slot machine.

tragar *tr.-ref.* to swallow [food, drink; a lie; an affront; one's words]; to gulp down: ~ *el anzuelo,* fig. to swallow the bait. *3* fig. *no poder* ~ *a,* to dislike, not to be able to bear. *4* to gobble, devour. *5* to swallow, engulf.

tragasantos *m.-f.* coll. overdevout person.

tragedia *f.* tragedy.

trágico, -ca *adj.* tragic, tragical. *2 m.* tragedian. *3 f.* tragedienne.

tragicomedia *f.* tragi-comedy.

trago *m.* draught [of liquor], drink; swallow, gulp: *echar un* ~, coll. to take a drink. *2* coll. misfortune, mishap. *3* ANAT. tragus.

tragón, -na *adj.* gluttonous. *2 m.-f.* glutton.

tragonería, -tragonía *f.* gluttony.

traición *f.* treason; treachery: *a* ~, treacherously.

traicionar *tr.* to betray, to do treason to.

traicionero, -ra *adj.* treacherous, treasonable, traitorous. *2 m.-f.* traitor, traitress.

traída *f.* carrying, bringing, conduction: ~ *de aguas,* conduction of water to a town.

traído, -da *adj.* used, worn out [garment]. *2 traído y llevado,* beaten about, knocked about.

traidor, -ra *adj.* treacherous, treasonable, traitorous. *2 m.* traitor. *3* villain [of a play]. *4 f.* traitress.

traigo, -traiga, etc. *irr.* V. TRAER.

traílla *f.* leash [for dogs]. *2* hounds leashed together. *3* AGR. levelling harrow. *4* TRALLA.

traína *f.* deep-sea fishing net. *2* net for sardine fishing.

trainera *f.* sardine-fishing boat.

traíña *f.* TRAÍNA.

traje *m.* costume, dress, suit [of clothes], garb, gown: ~ *de baño,* bathing suit; ~ *de calle,* street

clothes; ~ *de ceremonia* or *de etiqueta,* full dress, dress suit, evening dress; ~ *de luces,* bullfighter's costume; ~ *de malla,* tights; ~ *de paisano,* civilian clothes; ~ *largo,* lady's evening dress; ~ *sastre,* lady's tailor-made suit; ~ *talar,* robe, gown, soutane; *cortar un* ~ *a,* coll. to gossip about.

traje, -trajera, etc. *irr.* V. TRAER.

trajear *tr.* to clothe, costume, dress.

trajín *m.* carrying from place to place. *2* going and coming, bustle, hustle.

trajinante *m.* carrier, carter.

trajinar *tr.* to carry or cart from place to place. *2* to go back and forth, to bustle, hustle.

trajiste, etc., *irr.* V. TRAER.

tralla *f.* whipcord, whiplash; whip.

trallazo *m.* lash [with a whip]. *2* crack [of a whip].

trama *f.* WEAV. weft, woof. *2* texture, estructure. *3* plot [of novel or play]. *4* plot, scheme.

tramar *tr.* WEAV. to insert the weft in. *2* to contrive. *3* to plot, hatch, scheme. *4 intr.* [of trees, esp. olive trees] to blossom.

tramilla *f.* (Am.) twine.

tramitación *f.* transaction, negociation, carrying steps, procedure.

tramitar *tr.* to transact, negotiate, conduct [an affair].

trámite *m.* step [in the transaction of an affair].

tramo *m.* stretch, section [of a canal, road, etc.]. *2* flight [of stairs]. *3* span [of a bridge].

tramontana *f.* north wind. *2* fig. vanity.

tramontano, -na *adj.* tramontane.

tramontar *intr.* to pass over the mountain. *2* [of the sun] to sink behind the mountains.

tramoya *f.* THEAT. stage machinery. *2* fig. scheme, trick, fake.

tramoyista *m.* THEAT. stage machinist; scene shifter; stage hand. *2* fig. trickster, humbug.

trampa *f.* trap [for catching animals]. *2* fig. trap, snare, pitfall. *3* trapdoor. *4* hinged section of a counter. *5* bad debt. *6* fraud, trick, cheat [in games]: *hacer trampas,* to cheat. *7 llevárselo la* ~, [of an affair] to fall through.

trampal *m.* bog, quagmire.

trampantojo *m.* coll. trick, deception.

trampear *intr.* to shift, use expedients. *2* to manage, to get along. *3 tr.* to trick, deceive.

trampilla *f.* small trapdoor used as a peephole. *2* door of a coalbin. *3* fly [of trousers].

trampista *m.-f.* liar, cheat; bad pay.

trampolín *m.* springboard. *2* ski jump.

tramposo, -sa *adj.* lying, cheating, tricky. *2 m.-f.* liar, trickster, cheat. *3* bad pay.

tranca *f.* thick stick, club. *2* crossbar [for a door]. *3* coll. *a trancas y barrancas,* without regard to difficulties.

trancada *f.* long stride.

trancahilo *m.* stop knot [in threads or ropes].

trancazo *m.* blow with a stick or club. *2* MED. influenza, grippe.

trance *m.* critical moment: *a todo* ~, at any cost, at any risk; *en* ~ *de muerte,* at the point of death. *2* ~ *de armas,* combat, battle.

tranco *m.* long stride: *a trancos,* coll. hurriedly. *2* threshold.

tranchete *m.* cobbler's heel knife.

tranquera *f.* palisade [fence]. *2* (Am.) gate [in a fence].

tranquil *m.* ARCH. plumb line.

tranquilidad *f.* tranquillity, quiet, peace. *2* composure, ease of mind, reassurance.

tranquilizador, -ra *adj.* tranquillizing. *2* soothing, reassuring.
tranquilizar *tr.* to tranquillize, calm, quiet down. *2* to compose, soothe, reassure.
tranquilo, -la *adj.* tranquil, quiet, calm, peaceful. *2* easy in mind, unconcerned, reassured.
tranquilo *m.* knack.
transacción *f.* transaction [piece of commercial business]. *2* compromise, accommodation.
transalpino, -na *adj.* transalpine.
transatlántico, -ca *adj.* transatlantic. *2 m.* transatlantic ship, transatlantic liner.
transbordador, -ra *adj.* transfer, transshipping. *2 m.* ferry, transfer boat or car.
transbordar *tr.* to transfer, transship. *2 intr.-ref.* to transfer, change trains.
transbordo *m.* transfer, transshipment.
transcendencia *f.* TRASCENDENCIA.
transcendental *adj.* TRASCENDENTAL. *2* PHILOS. transcendental.
transcendente *adj.* TRASCENDENTE.
transcender *intr.* TRASCENDER.
transcontinental *adj.* transcontinental.
transcribir *tr.* to transcribe. ¶ CONJUG. past. p.: *transcrito* or *transcripto.*
transcripción *f.* transcription.
transcurrir *intr.* to pass, elapse.
transcurso *m.* lapse, course [of time].
transepto *m.* ARCH. transept.
transeúnte *adj.-n.* transient. *3 m.-f.* passer-by.
transferencia *f.* transference. *2* LAW transfer.
transferible *adj.* transferable.
transferir *tr.* to transfer. *2* to postpone. ¶ CONJUG. like *hervir.*
transfiguración *f.* transfiguration.
transfigurar *tr.* to transfigure. *2 ref.* to be transfigured.
transfijo, -ja *adj.* transfixed [pierced].
transfixión *f.* transfixion.
transflorar *tr.* to copy or trace against the light. *2* TRANSFLOREAR. *3 intr.* to show through.
transflorear *tr.* to adorn [metal] with painting.
transformable *adj.* transformable; convertible.
transformación *f.* transformation.
transformador, -ra *adj.* transforming. *2 m.-f.* transformer [person]. *3 m.* ELECT. transformer.
transformar *tr.* to transform. *2 ref.* to transform, be transformed.
transformismo *m.* transformism.
transformista *adj.* transformistic. *2 m.-f.* transformist. *3* THEAT. quick-change artist.
tránsfuga *m.-f.* fugitive. *2* deserter, turncoat.
transfundir *tr.* to transfuse. *2 ref.* to be transfused.
transfusión *f.* transfusion.
transgredir *tr.* to transgrees, break, violate. ¶ Only used in forms having *i* in their terminations.
transgresión *f.* transgression, violation.
transgresor, -ra *m.-f.* transgressor.
transición *f.* transition.
transido, -da *adj.* overwhelmed, exhausted [with grief, hunger, etc.]. *2* mean, stingy.
transigencia *f.* compromising. *2* tolerance.
transigente *adj.* compromising, accommodating. *2* broad-minded, tolerant.
transigir *intr.* to compromise, make concessions. *2 ~ con,* to accept, tolerate.
Transilvania *f. pr. n.* Transylvania.
transistor *m.* ELECT. transistor.
transitable *adj.* passable, practicable [road, etc.].
transitar *intr.* to pas, go, walk, along streets, roads, etc.

transitivo, -va *adj.-n.* GRAM. transitive.
tránsito *m.* transit, passage: *de ~,* in transit. *2* traffic [along streets, roads, etc.]. *3* death [of saint]. *4* stop [in journey]. *5* ASTR. transit.
transitorio, -ria *adj.* transitory.
translación, -translaticio, cia, etc. = TRASLACIÓN, TRASLATICIO, etc.
translimitación *f.* going beyond any limit [moral or material].
translimitar *tr.* to go beyond [any moral or material limit].
translucidez *f.* translucence, translucency.
translúcido, -da *adj.* translucent.
transmigración *f.* transmigration.
transmigrar *intr.* to transmigrate.
transmisible *adj.* transmissible.
transmisión *f.* transmission. *2* LAW transfer, conveyance. *3 ~ del pensamiento,* thought transference.
transmisor, -ra *adj.* transmitting. *2 m.-f.* transmitter. *3 m.* TELEG., TELEPH., RADIO. transmitter.
transmitir *tr.* to transmit. *2* RADIO. to broadcast.
transmudar *tr.* TRANSMUTAR.
transmutación *f.* transmutation.
transmutar *tr.* to transmute, change.
transoceánico, -ca *adj.* transoceanic.
transpacífico, -ca *adj.* transpacific.
transpadano, -na *adj.* transpadane.
transparencia *f.* transparence.
transparentarse *ref.* to be transparent. *2* to show through.
transparente *adj.* transparent. *2* translucent. *3 m.* window shade, roller blind. *4* stained glass window at the back of an altar.
transpiración *f.* transpiration. *2* perspiration.
transpirar *intr.* to transpire. *2* to perspire.
transpirenaico, -ca *adj.* trans-Pyrenean.
transponer *tr.* to transpose. *2* to disappear behind. *3* to turn [a corner]. *4* [of the sun, etc.], to set below [the horizon]. *5 ref.* to doze off. ¶ CONJUG. like *poner.*
transportable *adj.* transportable.
transportador, -ra *adj.* transporting. *2 m.-f.* carrier, transporter. *3 m.* protractor [instrument].
transportamiento *m.* TRANSPORTE 1 & 5.
transportar *tr.* to transport, carry, convey. *2* to transpose. *3* to transfer [a drawing or pattern]. *4 ref.* fig. to be enraptured.
transporte *m.* transportation, transport, carriage, conveyance. *2* NAUT. transport [ship]. *3* transfer [of a drawing or pattern]. *4* MUS. transposition. *5* transport, ectasy, rapture.
transposición *f.* transposition.
transpuesto, -ta *p. p.* de TRANSPONER.
transubstanciación *f.* transubstantiation.
transvasar *tr.* to decant, transvase.
transverberación *f.* transfixion.
transversal *adj.* transversal. *2* cross [street]. *3* collateral [kinsman, kinship].
transverso, -sa *adj.* transverse.
tranvía *m.* tram, tramway, tramcar, *streetcar.
tranviario *m.* tramwayman.
trapa *f.* tramp, tramping [of feet]. *2* noise, uproar. *3* NAUT. spilling line. *4* (cap.) ECCL. *la Trapa,* la Trappe.
trapacear *intr.* to cheat, practice trickery.
trapacería *f.* TRAPAZA.
trapacero, -ra; trapacista *adj.* tricky, crafty. *2 m.-f.* trickster, cheat.
trapajo *m.* rag, scrap of cloth.
trápala *f.* coll. trick, deceit. *2* noise, uproar. *3* clat-

ter [of a running horse]. *4 m.* garrulity. *5 m.-f.* prattler, chatterbox. *6* liar, cheat.
trapalear *intr.* to chatter, jabber. *2* to lie, cheat, deceive. *3* to walk noisily.
trapalón, -na *m.-f.* liar, cheat, humbug.
trapatiesta *f.* coll. brawl, row, shindy.
trapaza *f.* trick, fraud, deceit.
trapecio *m.* GEOM. trapeze, trapezium, trapezoid. *2* GYMN. trapeze. *3* ANAT. trapezium. *4* ANAT. trapezius.
trapense *adj.-n.* Trappist.
trapería *f.* rags. *2* rag shop.
trapero, -ra *m.-f.* ragpicker. *2* rag dealer.
trapezoidal *adj.* trapezial.
trapezoide *m.* GEOM. trapezium, trapezoid.
trapiche *m.* sugar mill. *2* olive press. *3* ore crusher.
trapichear *intr.* coll. to scheme, contrive. *2* to deal at retail.
trapicheo *m.* coll. scheming, contriving.
trapillo *m.* coll. *de ~,* in house clothes.
trapío *m.* coll. easy and graceful carriage of certain women. *2* BULLF. mettle [of a bull].
trapisonda *f.* coll. row, shindy. *2* coll. trick, scheme, intrigue.
trapisondear *intr.* coll. to lie, scheme, intrigue.
trapisondista *m.-f.* coll. liar, schemer, trickster, schemer.
trapo *m.* rag [piece of cloth]; cleaning rag; *poner a uno como un ~,* coll. to rake over the coals. *2* NAUT. canvas, sails: *a todo ~,* full sail. *3* BULLF. cape, red flag. *4* coll. *soltar el ~,* to burst out crying or laughing. *5 pl.* coll. clothes: *trapos de cristianar,* Sunday best.
traque *m.* crack [report of a rocket].
tráquea *f.* ANAT., ZOOL., BOT. trachea.
traqueal *adj.* tracheal. *2* ZOOL. tracheate.
traquear *intr.* TRAQUETEAR.
traquearteria *f.* ANAT. trachea.
traqueotomía *f.* SURG. tracheotomy.
traquetear *intr.* to crack, make a loud noise. *2 tr.* to shake, jolt, jerk.
traqueteo *m.* crack, cracking [noise]. *2* shaking, jolting, jerking.
traquido *m.* crack, snap [noise].
tras *prep.* after, behind. *2* after [in pursuit of]. *3* besides, in addition to. *4 ~ de,* after, behind; in addition to.
trasalpino, -na *adj.* TRANSALPINO.
trasaltar *m.* space behind the altar.
trasandino, -na *adj.* TRANSANDINO.
trasatlántico, -ca *adj.-n.* TRANSATLÁNTICO.
trasbordar *tr.* TRANSBORDAR.
trasbordo *m.* TRANSBORDO.
trasca *f.* leather thong.
trascantón *m.* corner spur stone.
trascendencia *f.* penetration, perspicacity. *2* result, consequence. *3* importance. *4* PHILOS. transcendence.
trascendental *adj.* far-reaching. *2* highly important, momentous.
trascendente *adj.* trascendent.
trascender *intr.* to be fragant. *2* to leak out [come to be known]. *3* to have effects or consequences. *4* PHILOS. to trascend. *5 tr.* to penetrate, find out. ¶ CONJUG. like *entender.*
trasciende, -trascienda, etc. *irr.* V. TRASCENDER.
trascocina *f.* back kitchen.
trascolar *tr.* to strain, percolate. *2* fig. to pass over [a mountain, etc.]. *3 ref.* to ooze through.
trascordarse *ref.* to forget. ¶ CONJUG. like *contar.*
trascoro *m.* back choir.

trascorral *m.* fenced space back of a barnyard.
trascribir, -trascripción, etc. = TRANSCRIBIR, TRANSCRIPCIÓN.
trascuarto *m.* back room. *2* rear apartment.
trascuenta *f.* TRABACUENTA.
trascurrir *intr.* TRANSCURRIR.
trascurso *m.* TRANSCURSO.
trasdós *m.* ARCH. extrados.
trasegar *tr.* to upset, disarrange. *2* to move, transfer. *3* to transvase, decant. *4* coll. to drink [liquor]. ¶ CONJUG. like *acertar.*
trasera *f.* back, rear [of a house, carriage, etc.].
trasero, -ra *adj.* back, hind, rear: *puerta trasera,* back door. *2 m.* coll. behind, buttocks.
trasferencia, trasfiguración, trasfixión, trasformación, trásfuga, trasfundir, etc. = TRANSFERENCIA, TRANSFIGURACIÓN, TRANSFIXIÓN, TRANSFORMACIÓN, TRÁNSFUGA, TRANSFUNDIR, etc.
trasgo *m.* goblin, hobgoblin, sprite. *2* coll. imp [mischievous child].
trasgredir = TRANSGREDIR.
trasgresión = TRANSGRESIÓN.
trasgresor, -ra = TRANSGRESOR, RA.
trashoguero, -ra *adj.* lazy, stay-at-home. *2 m.* fireback. *3* big log [in a fireplace].
trashojar *tr.* to leaf through [a book, etc.].
trashumante *adj.* moving from winter to summer pasture or vice-versa.
trashumar *intr.* [of flocks or herds] to move from winter to summer pasture or vice-versa.
trasiego *m.* upset, disorder. *2* transvasing, decanting.
trasiego, trasiegue, etc. *in.* V. TRASEGAR.
trasijado, -da *adj.* thin-flanked. *2* lank, lean.
traslación, trasladación *f.* moving, transfer, translation. *2* translation [into another language]. *3* RHET. metaphor, tralatition.
trasladable *adj.* movable.
trasladar *tr.* to move, remove, transfer. *2* MECH. to translate. *3* to postpone, adjourn [to another day]. *4* to translate [into another language]. *5* to copy [a writing]. *6 ref.* to move [from place to place; change residence].
traslado *m.* moving, removal, transfer. *2* move [change of residence]. *3* copy, transcript. *4* resemblance, likeness. *5* LAW notification.
traslapar *tr.* to overlap.
traslapo *m.* overlapped part or piece.
traslaticio, -cia *adj.* tralatitious, figurative.
traslúcido, -da; trasluciente *adj.* TRANSLÚCIDO.
traslucirse *ref.* to be translucent. *2* fig. to be inferred. *3* fig. to transpire [come to be known]. ¶ CONJUG. like *lucir.*
traslumbrar *tr.* [of light] to dazzle. *2 ref.* to be dazzled [by light]. *3* to pass or vanish swiftly.
trasluz *m.* light seen through a translucent body: *al ~,* against the light. *2* glint, gleam.
trasmallo *m.* trammel net.
trasmano *m.* second player [at cards]. *2 a ~,* out of reach; out of the way, remote.
trasmigración, trasmigrar, trasmisión, trasmitir, trasmudar, trasmutación, trasmutar, etc. = TRANSMIGRACIÓN, etc.
trasnochado, -da *adj.* stale, spoiled [from standing overnight]. *2* fig. haggard, wan. *3* fig. stale, trite, hackneyed.
trasnochador, -ra *m.-f.* night hawk, one who keeps late hours.
trasnochar *intr.* to keep late hours. *2* to spend the night.
trasoir *tr.* to hear wrong, mis-hear.

trasojado, -da *adj.* haggard, wan, with sunken eyes.

trasoñar *tr.* to imagine wrongly, to dream.

trasovado, -da *adj.* BOT. obovate.

traspadano, -na *adj.-n.* TRANSPADANO.

traspapelarse *ref.* [of a paper] to be mislaid among other papers.

trasparencia, trasparentarse, trasparente = TRANSPARENCIA, TRANSPARENTARSE, TRANSPARENTE.

traspasamiento *m.* TRASPASO.

traspasar *tr.* to pass, transfer, move [from a place to another]. *2* to pass, cross, go over, go beyond, go through. *3* to exceed [bounds]. *4* to pierce, transfix. *5* to transgress. *6* LAW to transfer [esp. a lease or tenancy].

traspaso *m.* passing, transfer, moving [from a place to another]. *2* crossing, going over. *3* piercing, transfixion. *4* transgression. *5* LAW transfer. *6* money paid for the transfer of a lease. *7* grief, anguish.

traspié *m.* slip, stumble, trip: *dar traspiés*, to slip, stumble, trip; fig. to slip, err.

traspintar *tr.* to let see [one card] and play another. *2 ref.* [of writing, painting, etc.] to show through the paper, cloth, etc. *3* coll. so turn out differently.

traspirable, traspiración, traspirar, traspirenaico = TRANSPIRABLE, TRANSPIRACIÓN, TRANSPIRAR, TRANSPIRENAICO.

trasplantar *tr.* to transplant. *2 ref.* to migrate.

trasplante *m.* transplant, transplantation.

trasponer, trasportador, trasportamiento, trasportar, trasporte, trasposición, etc. = TRANSPONER, TRANSPORTADOR, TRANSPORTAMIENTO, TRANSPORTAR, TRANSPORTE, TRANSPOSICIÓN, etc.

traspuesta *f.* transposition. *2* rise, elevation [of ground]. *3* back [of a house]. *4* flight, hiding [of a person].

traspunte *m.* THEAT. prompter in the wings.

traspuntín *m.* under-mattress. *2* folding seat [in a car].

trasquila *f.* TRASQUILADURA.

trasquilador *m.* shearer [of animals].

trasquiladura *f.* shearing [of animals]. *2* clumsy cutting of the hair. *3* clipping, curtailing.

trasquilar *tr.* to shear [animals]. *2* to cut the hair of [a person] clumsily. *3* fig. to clip, curtail.

trasquilimocho, -cha *adj.* close shorn or cropped.

trasquilón *m.* coll. TRASQUILADURA: *a trasquilones*, irregularly; clumsily.

trastabillar *intr.* TRASTRABILLAR.

trastada *f.* bad turn, mean trick, dirty trick.

trastazo *m.* coll. blow, bump, knock, whack.

traste *m.* MUS. fret [of guitar, etc.]. *2 dar al ~ con*, to spoil, ruin, destroy.

trastear *tr.* to fret [a guitar]. *2* to play [a guitar]. *3* BULLF. to play [the bull] with the MULETA. *4* coll. to manage with tact. *5 intr.* to move things around.

trastejar *tr.* to retile. *2* to repair, overhaul.

trasteo *m.* BULLF. playing the bull with the MULETA. *2* tactful management.

trastera *f.* lumber room.

trastero, -ra *adj.* lumber [room].

trastienda *f.* back room [behind a shop]. *2* coll. tact, address, cunning.

trasto *m.* piece of furniture; utensil. *2* disused article of furniture, etc.: *trastos viejos*, lumber. *3* coll. worthless person, tricky person. *4 pl.* tools of trade, implements, utensils. *5 tirarse los trastos a la cabeza*, coll. to quarrel.

trastocarse *ref.* to become crazy, to go off one's head. ¶ CONJUG. like *contar*.

trastornado, -da *adj.* upset, disarranged. *3* disturbed [in mind].

trastornadura *f.*, **trastornamiento** *m.* TRASTORNO.

trastornar *tr.* to upset, turn upside down. *2* to upset, disarrange, disturb. *3* to disturb [in mind]; derange the mind of; to muddle [with drink]. *4* to win over, persuade.

trastorno *m.* upset, derangement, disturbance. *2* riot, disorder. *3* MED. disorder, trouble.

trastrabarse *ref. trastrabársele a uno la lengua*, coll. to stammer, to become tongue-tied.

trastrabillar *intr.* to trip, stumble. *2* to reel, sway, stagger. *3* to stammer, stutter.

trastrocamiento *m.* change, transmutation.

trastrocar *tr.* to change, transmute. ¶ CONJUG. like *contar*.

trastrueco *m.* TRASTROCAMIENTO.

trasudar *tr.* to sweat lightly.

trasudor *m.* slight perspiration.

trasunto *m.* copy, transcript. *2* likeness, faithful image.

trasvasar *tr.* TRANSVASAR.

trasvenarse *ref.* [of blood] to extravasate. *2* fig. to spill [be spilled].

trasver *tr.* to see through. *2* to see wrong. ¶ CONJUG. like *ver*.

trasverberación, trasversal, trasverso = TRANSVERBERACIÓN, etc.

trasverter *intr.* [of liquid in a vessel] to overflow, run over.

trasvolar *tr.* to fly over or across.

trata *f.* trade, slave trade: *~ de negros*, slave trade. *2 ~ de blancas*, white slavery.

tratable *adj.* courteous, sociable, reasonable, tractable.

tratadista *m.-f.* author, writer [on special subjects].

tratado *m.* treaty [between nations]. *2* treatise.

tratamiento *m.* treatment, usage. *2* MED., CHEM., IND. treatment. *4* title, form of address.

tratante *m.-f.* trader, dealer.

tratar *tr.* to treat, use [act towards; behave]. *2* to handle, manage. *3* to treat, deal with [a subject]. *4* MED., CHEM., IND. to treat. *5* to have acquaintance or friendship with. *6 ~ a uno de*, to address as, to give one the title of; to call, charge with being: *~ de tú*, to thou, address as *tú*; *~ a uno de embustero*, to call someone a liar. *7 intr. ~ de, sobre* or *acerca de*, to treat of, deal with [a subject]. *8 ~ de* [foll. by an inf.], to try to, to endeavour to. *9 ~ con*, to have intercourse with; COM. to deal, to business with. *10* COM. *~ en*, to trade with, deal in. *11 ref.* to live [well or poorly]. *12* to be in speaking or friendly terms. *13 ¿de qué se trata?*, what is the matter?, what is it about?

trato *m.* treatment, usage, dealing: *~ doble*, double dealing; *mal ~*, ill usage. *2* agreement, deal, bargain: *~ hecho*, it is a deal. *3* negotiation. *4* title, form of address. *5* trade, commerce. *6* intercourse social intercourse, friendly relations; *~ de gentes*, savoir-vivre; *tener buen ~*, to be nice, affable.

trauma *m.* MED. trauma.

traumatismo *m.* traumatism.

través *m.* inclination, bias: *mirar de ~*, to squint. *2* fig. misfortune, reverse. *3* ARCH. cross-beam. *4* FORT. traverse. *5* NAUT. *por el ~*, on the beam; *dar al ~*, to be stranded; *dar al ~ con*, fig. to squander, misspend; to ruin, destroy. *6 al ~, de ~, across, athwart. 7 al ~ de, a ~ de*, through, across.

travesaño *m.* crosspiece, crossbar, traverse; transom [of a cross or window]; rung [of a chair, etc.]. *2* bolster [of a bed].

travesar *tr.-ref.* ATRAVESAR.

travesear *intr.* to prank, frolic. *2* fig. to talk sparklingly. *3* fig. to lead a debauched life.

travesero, -ra *adj.* cross, transverse. *2 m.* bolster [of a bed].

travesía *f.* crossroad, cross street. *2* distance [over land or sea]. *3* passage, sea voyage, crossing [the sea]. *4* crosswise or transverse position. *5* FORT. traverse works.

travesura *f.* prank, frolic, antic, escapade, mischief. *2* roguishness, archness. *3* sparkling wit.

traviesa *f.* distance [over land or sea]. *2* side bet. *3* RLY. tie, crosstie, sleeper. *4* ARCH. transverse wall. *5* MIN. cross gallery.

travieso, -sa *adj.* cross, transverse. *2* keen, sagacious. *3* naughty, mischievous [child]. *4* frolicsome, prankish, roguish.

trayecto *m.* distance, stretch, section [in a way]; course [distance travelled].

trayectoria *f.* trajectory.

traza *f.* plan, design, project. *2* scheme, contrivance; way, means: *darse trazas,* to manage. *3* appearance, look, looks: *tener trazas de,* [of a thing] to show signs of. *4* GEOM. trace.

trazado *m.* drawing, planning, tracing. *2* layout, location [of a railway line, a road, etc.].

trazar *tr.* to draw, trace [lines, etc.]. *2* to design, plan, devise, lay out. *3* to trace, sketch, describe. *4* RLY. to locate.

trazo *m.* delineation, outline. *2* line, stroke [of a pen or pencil]. *3* PAINT. fold in drapery.

trébedes *f.* trivet.

trebejo *m.* toy, plaything. *2* chess piece. *3 pl.* tools, implements, utensils.

trébol, *pl.* **-les** *m.* BOT. clover, trefoil: *~ oloroso,* sweet clover. *2* club [playing card].

trece *adj.-m.* thirteen: *mantenerse uno en sus ~,* to persist in one's opinion. *2 adj.* thirteenth. *3 m.* thirteenth [of the month].

trecientos, -tas *adj.-s.* TRESCIENTOS.

trecho *m.* stretch, space, distance: *a trechos,* by intervals; *de ~ en ~,* from place to place, from time to time.

tredécimo, -ma *adj.* thirteenth.

trefilería *f.* wiredrawing.

tregua *f.* truce. *2* respite, rest, letup, intermission: *dar treguas,* to ease up; not to be urgent; *sin ~,* without letup, without intermission.

treinta *adj.-m.* thirty. *2 adj.-n.* thirtieth. *3 m.* thirtieth [of the month].

treintaidosavo, -va *adj.-m.* thirty-second [part].

treintavo, -va *adj.-n.* thirtieth.

treintena *f.* thirtieth [part]. *2* group of thirty units.

treinteno, -na *adj.* TRIGÉSIMO.

tremebundo, -da *adj.* dreadful, frightful, fearful.

tremedal *m.* quagmire, quacking bog.

tremendo, -da *adj.* tremendous, fearful, terrible. *2* awful, imposing. *3* coll. tremendous [very great].

tremente *adj.* trembling.

trementina *f.* turpentine.

tremer *intr.* to tremble.

tremielga *f.* ICHTH. torpedo, electric ray.

tremó, tremol *m.* pier glass.

tremolar *tr.* to wave [a flag]. *2* fig. to display.

tremolina *f.* noisy blowing of the air. *2* coll. row, shindy, uproar.

trémolo *m.* MUS. tremolo.

tremor *m.* tremor, trembling.

trémulo, -la *adj.* tremulous, quivering, flickering.

tren *m.* RLY. train: *~ correo,* mail train; *~ de mercancías,* goods train; *~ expreso,* express train. *2* MIL., PHYS. train: *~ de ondas,* wave train. *3* train, set, gear, outfit: *~ de aterrizaje,* AER. landing gear. *4* show, ostentation. *5* SPORT. speed, fury.

trenado, -da *adj.* reticulated. *2* latticed. *3* braided.

trenca *f.* crosstree [in a beehive]. *2* main root.

trencilla *f.* braid [for trimming].

treno *m.* dirge, threnody.

Trento *f. pr. n.* GEOG. Trent.

trenza *f.* braid, plait. *2* tress [braided hair].

trenzadera *f.* knot of braided cord or ribbon.

trenzado *m.* braid, plait. *2* braiding, plaiting. *3* entrechat [in dancing]. *4* prancing [of a horse].

trenzar *tr.* to braid, plait, tress. *2 intr.* to perform entrechats [in dancing]. *3* [of a horse] to prance.

trepa *f.* climbing. *2* tumble. *3* perforation. *4* grain [of polished wood]. *5* coll. trick, deceit, fraud. *6* coll. beating, drubbing.

trepado, -da *adj.* RETREPADO. *2* strong, robust [animal]. *3 m.* SEW. wavy trimming. *4 f.* ORN. climber.

trepajuncos, *pl.* **-cos** *m.* ORN. marsh warbler.

trepanación *f.* SURG. trepanation.

trepanar *tr.* SURG. to trepan.

trépano *m.* trepan.

trepar *intr.-tr.* to climb, clamber. *2* BOT. to climb, creep. *3 tr.* to bore, perforate. *4* SEW. to put a waving trimming on. *5 ref.* RETREPARSE.

trepatroncos *m.* ORN. blue titmouse.

trepe *m.* coll. scolding, reprimand.

trepidación *f.* trembling, vibration. *2* ASTR. trepidation.

trepidante *adj.* trembling, vibrating. *2* mad [rhythm].

trepidar *intr.* to tremble, vibrate.

tres *adj.-m.* three: *las ~,* three o'clock. *2 adj.* third. *3 m.* third [of the month].

tresbolillo (a or **al)** *adv.* arranged in quincunxes.

trescientos, -tas *adj.-m.* three hundred. *2 adj.* three-hundredth.

tresdoblar *tr.* to treble. *2* to fold three times.

tresdoble *adj.-m.* triple.

tresillista *m.-f.* ombre player.

tresillo *m.* ombre [card game]. *2* MUS. triplet. *3* set of a sofa and two armchairs.

tresnal *m.* AGR. shock, stack [of sheaves].

treta *f.* trick, wile. *2* FENC. feint.

trezavo, -va *adj.-n.* thirteenth.

tría *f.* selecting, sorting.

triaca *f.* theriac.

tríada, triade *adj.* triad.

triangulación *f.* triangulation.

1) triangular *adj.* triangular.

2) triangular *tr.* to triangulate.

triángulo, -la *adj.* triangular. *2 m.* GEOM., TRIGON., MUS. triangle.

triar *tr.* to select, sort.

triásico, -ca *adj.* GEOL. Triassic. *2 m.* GEOL. Triassic, Trias.

tribal *adj.* tribal.

tribásico, -ca *adj.* CHEM. tribasic.

tribu *f.* tribe.

tribulación *f.* tribulation, affliction.

tríbulo *m.* BOT. caltrop.

tribuna *f.* tribune, rostrum, platform. *2* gallery [in

a church or legislative chamber]: ~ *de la prensa*, press box. *3* grandstand.
tribunado *m.* tribunate. *2* tribuneship.
tribunal *m.* tribunal, court [of justice]: ~ *supremo*, Supreme Court. *2* EDUC. examining board.
tribunicio, -cia *adj.* tribunitial.
tribuno *m.* tribune [roman officer; political orator].
tributación *f.* paying taxes. *2* tax, duty. *3* system of taxes.
tributar *tr.* to pay taxes or tribute; to pay as tax or tribute. *2* to pay, render [homage, respect].
tributario, -ria *adj.-n.* tributary. *2* [pertaining to] tax or duty: *sistema* ~, system of taxes.
tributo *m.* tribute, tax, duty, imposition. *2* fig. pecuniary burden.
tricentésimo, -ma *adj.* three-hundredth.
triceps *m.* ANAT. triceps.
triciclo *m.* tricycle.
tricípite *adj.* tricipital, three-headed.
triclinio *m.* HIST. triclinium.
tricolor *adj.* tricolour.
tricornio *adj.* three-cornered. *2 m.* three-cornered hat.
tricotomía *f.* trichotomy.
tricotosa *f.* knitting machine.
tricromía *f.* three-coloured printing.
tricúspide *adj.* ANAT. tricuspid.
tridente *adj.* trident, tridentate. *2 m.* trident.
triduo *m.* ECCL. triduum.
triedro *adj.* GEOM. trihedral. *2 m.* GEOM. trihedron.
trienal *adj.* triennial.
trienio *m.* triennium.
trifásico, -ca *adj.* ELECT. three-phase.
trífido, -da *adj.* BOT. trifid.
trifoliado, -da *adj.* BOT. trifoliate.
trifulca *f.* coll. squabble, row.
trigal *adj.* wheat field.
trigaza *adj.* of wheat [straw].
trigémino, -na *adj.-m.* ANAT. trigeminal.
trigésimo, -ma *adj.* thirtieth.
trigla *f.* ICHTH. mullet.
triglifo *m.* ARCH. triglyph.
trigo *m.* BOT. wheat. *2* coll. dough, money. *3* BOT. ~ *sarraceno*, buckwheat. *4 pl.* wheat fields.
trigón *m.* MUS. trigon.
trígono *m.* ASTROL., GEOM. trigon.
trigonometría *f.* trigonometry.
trigueño, -ña *adj.* of a light brown complexion.
triguero, -ra *adj.* [pertaining to] wheat. *2 m.-f.* wheat dealer or grower.
trilingüe *adj.* trilingual.
trilítero, -ra *adj.* triliteral.
trilito *m.* ARCHEOL. trilithon.
trilobulado, -da *adj.* trilobate.
trilocular *adj.* trilocular.
trilogía *f.* trilogy.
trilla *f.* ICHTH. red mullet. *2* AGR. thrashing. *3* AGR. thrashing time. *4* TRILLO 1.
trillado, -da *adj.* beaten [path]. *2* trite, commonplace.
trillador, -ra *adj.* AGR. thrashing. *2 m.-f.* AGR. thrasher. *3 f.* AGR. thrashing machine.
trillar *tr.* AGR. to thrash, thresh. *2* to beat, frequent [a path, etc.]. *3* to beat, crush, maltreat.
trillo *m.* AGR. a kind of harrow for thrashing.
trillón *m.* trillion [British trillion].
trimestral *m.* trimestral, trimestrial, quarterly.
trimestralmente *adv.* quarterly.
trimestre *m.* trimester, quarter. *2* quarterly payment.

trinado *m.* MUS. trill, quaver, warble.
trinar *intr.* MUS. to trill, quaver, warble. *2* coll. to be very angry, or impatient.
trinca *f.* triad. *2* coll. gang. *3* NAUT. lashing.
trincar *tr.* to tie, fasten, lash. *2* to hold fast [someone] with one's arms or hands. *3* to drink [liquor].
trincha *f.* cloth strap for tightening garments.
trinchante *adj.* carving [food]. *2 m.* carver [at table]. *3* carving fork. *4* TRINCHERO.
trinchar *tr.* to carve [food].
trinchera *f.* trench, ditch. *2* MIL. trench, entrenchment. *3* trench coat.
trinchero *m.* side table, carving table.
trineo *m.* sledge, sleigh, sled.
Trinidad *f. pr. n.* THEOL. Trinity.
trinitaria *f.* BOT. pansy, heartsease.
trinitario, -ria *adj.-n.* ECCL. Trinitarian.
trino, -na *adj.* trine, trinitarian. *2* ternary. *3* ASTROL. trine. *4 m.* MUS. trill, shake.
trinomio *m.* ALG. trinomial.
trinquete *m.* NAUT. foremast; foresail; foreyard. *2* MACH. pawl, ratchet. *3* hall for playing *pelota*.
trinquis, *pl.* **-quis** *m.* coll. drink [of liquor].
trío *m.* MUS. trio. *2* trio [set of three persons]. *3* TRÍA.
triodo *m.* RADIO. triode.
tripa *f.* gut, bowel, intestine: *hacer de tripas corazón*, coll. to pluck up courage; *tener malas tripas*, coll. to be cruel. *2* coll. paunch, belly. *3* filling, filler [of a cigar]. *4 pl.* fig. insides.
tripada *f.* coll. bellyful.
tripartito, -ta *adj.* tripartite.
tripería *f.* tripery, tripe shop.
tripero, -ra *m.-f.* gut seller. *2 m.* bellyband.
tripicallero, -ra *m.-f.* seller of tripe.
tripicallos *m.* tripe [as food].
tripinnado, -da *adj.* BOT. tripinnate.
triple *adj.-m.* triple, treble.
triplicado, -da *adj.* threefold, triplicate. *2 m.* triplicate: *por* ~, in triplicate.
triplicar *tr.* to treble, triple, triplicate.
tríplice *adj.* triple.
triplo, -pla *adj.-m.* triple, treble.
trípode *m.* or *f.* tripod.
tripolitano, -na *adj.-n.* Tripolitan.
tripón, -na *adj.-n.* TRIPUDO.
tríptico *m.* triptych.
triptongo *m.* FONET. triphthong.
tripudio *m.* dance.
tripudo, -da *adj.* big-bellied, pot-bellied.
tripulación *f.* crew [of a ship, plane or airship].
tripulante *m.* crew member. *2 pl.* crew.
tripular *tr.* to man [a ship, plane, etc.]. *2* to be a member of the crew of [a ship, plane, etc.].
trique *m.* crack [noise]: *a cada* ~, coll. at every turn.
triquina *f.* ZOOL. trichine.
triquinosis *f.* MED. trichinosis.
triquiñuela *f.* coll. chicanery, wile, subterfuge.
triquitraque *m.* cracking, clacking, clatter. *2* firecracker.
trirreme *m.* NAUT. trireme.
tris *m.* clink [of breaking glass]. *2* coll. trice, ace: *en un* ~, almost, within an ace.
trisa *f.* SÁBALO.
Trisagio *m.* ECCL. Trisagion.
trisca *f.* crushing sound made with the feet. *2* noise, noisy fun, uproar.
triscar *intr.* to make a noise with the feet. *2* to frisk about, frolic, gambol. *3 tr.* to set [a saw].
trisecar *tr.* GEOM. to trisect.

trisección f. trisection.
trisílabo, -ba adj. trisyllabic. 2 m. trisyllable.
triste adj. sad. 2 gloomy, dismal. 3 deplorable. 4 painful. 5 paltry, sorry.
tristeza f. sadness. 2 gloom. 3 grief, sorrow.
tristón, -na adj. saddish, melancholy.
tritón m. MYTH. Triton. 2 ZOOL. triton, eft, newt.
tritono m. MUS. tritone.
trituración f. trituration, crushing.
triturar tr. to triturate. 2 fig. to tear to pieces [an argument, etc.].
triunfador, -ra m.-f. triumpher, victor.
triunfal adj. triumphal.
triunfante a. triumphant, victorious.
triunfar intr. to triumph, be successful, be the victor: ~ de, to triumph over, conquer. 2 coll. to make a great show. 3 to trump [at cards].
triunfo m. triumph. 2 victory, success. 3 trump [at cards].
triunvirato m. triumvirate.
triunviro m. triumvir.
trivial adj. trivial, commonplace, trite.
trivialidad f. triviality. 2 triteness.
trivio m. trivium. 2 junction of three roads.
triza f. bit, shred, fragment: hacer trizas, to smash to pieces, to tear to bits.
trocamiento m. TRUEQUE.
trocánter m. ANAT. trochanter.
1) trocar m. SURG. trocar.
2) trocar tr. to exchange, barter. 2 to change, convert: ~ en, to change into. 3 to take or say [a thing] for another. 4 ref. to change [undergo a change]. 6 to exchange seats. ¶ CONJUG. like contar.
trocear tr. to divide into pieces.
trocoide f. GEOM. trochoid.
trocha f. cross path, narrow path.
trochemoche (a) adv. in a disordered way, recklessly.
trofeo m. trophy. 2 fig. victory, triumph.
troglodita adj. troglodytic. 2 fig. gluttonous. 3 m.-f. troglodyte. 4 fig. glutton.
troj, troje m. granary, barn.
trola f. coll. lie, fib, deception.
trole m. ELECT. trolley pole.
trolebús m. trolley bus.
trolero, -ra adj. coll. lying. 2 m.-f. liar.
tromba f. METEOR. waterspout. 2 fig. avalanche, rush.
trombón m. MUS. trombone [instrument and player].
trombosis f. MED. thrombosis.
trompa f. MUS. horn [brass instrument]: ~ de caza, hunting horn. 2 poet. trump, trumpet. 3 humming top. 4 trunk [of an elephant]. 5 proboscis [of insect, of tapir]. 6 METEOR. waterspout. 7 ARCH. projecting vault. 8 ANAT. ~ de Eustaquio, Eustachian tube. 9 m. horn player.
trompada f. blow with a top. 2 blow with the trunk [of an elephant]. 3 hard blow or knock.
trompeta f. MUS. trumpet. 2 MUS. bugle. 3 BOT. ~ de amor, sunflower. 4 m. trumpeter, bugler.
trompetada f. coll. silly remark.
trompetazo m. trumpet blast; bugle blast. 2 TROMPETADA.
trompetear intr. coll. to sound the trumpet.
trompetería f. trumpetry. 2 MUS. trumpets [of an organ].
trompetero m. trumpet maker. 2 trumpeter.
trompetilla f. dim. small trumpet. 2 trompetilla or

~ acústica, ear trumpet. 2 de ~, buzzing [mosquito].
trompicar tr. to make [one] stumble or knock repeatedly. 2 coll. to promote [a person] over another. 3 intr. to stumble or trip repeatedly.
trompicón m., **trompilladura** f. stumble.
trompillar tr.-intr. TROMPICAR.
trompis m. coll. punch, blow with the fist.
trompo m. top, whipping top, spinning top [toy]. 2 ZOOL. top shell. 3 coll. dolt.
trompón m. BOT. narcissus.
tronada f. thunderstorm.
tronado, -da adj. used, worn out. 2 decayed, ruined, impoverished.
tronante adj. thundering.
tronar impers.-intr. to thunder: ~ contra, to thunder at. 2 intr. coll. to become ruined [financially]. 3 coll. ~ con, to quarrel or break with. 4 coll. por lo que pueda ~, just in case. ¶ CONJUG. like contar.
troncar tr. TRUNCAR.
tronco m. trunk [of the body, of a tree, of an artery, etc.]. 2 stock, origin [of a family]. 3 truncated object. 4 GEOM. frustum. 5 log, billet: estar como un ~, be unconscious; to be fast asleep. 6 team [of two horses].
troncón m. trunk [of the body]. 2 stump.
tronchar tr. to break [a stem, a branch, a stick, etc.].
troncho m. stem of a cabbage, cauliflower, etc.
tronera f. FORT., NAUT. embrasure, port, porthole. 2 loophole, narrow window. 3 pocket [of a billiard table]. 4 m.-f. coll. harum-scarum.
tronido m. loud report. 2 show, ostentation.
trono m. throne. 2 pl. thrones [order of angels].
tronquista m. driver of a team of horses.
tronzar tr. to divide into pieces. 2 fig. to wear out, exhaust. 3 SEW. to pleat [a garment].
tropa f. troop, crowd. 2 coll. people of no account. 3 troops, soldiers. 6 MIL. assembly [call]. 7 pl. forces, army.
tropel m. throng, rush, hurry, bustle, confusion: en ~, in a throng, in confusion. 2 crowd [of things].
tropelía f. injustice, outrage. 2 hurry, confusion.
tropezadero m. stumbling place.
tropezadura f. stumbling.
tropezar intr. to trip, stumble; to knock, strike: ~ con, contra o en, to stumble over, to knock against. 2 fig. to trip, slip, err. 3 ~ con, to come upon, find, meet [with]; to quarrel with. 4 ref. [of horses] to interfere. ¶ CONJUG. like acertar.
tropezón m. TROPIEZO: dar un ~, to trip, stumble; a tropezones, coll. by fits and starts; falteringly.
tropical adj. tropical, tropic [of the tropics].
trópico, -ca adj. tropical, figurative. 2 tropical [year]. 3 m. ASTR., GEOG. tropic.
tropiezo m. trip, stumble. 2 fig. trip, slip, fault. 3 hitch, difficulty, mishap: sin ~, without difficulty, without a mishap. 4 stumbling block. 5 quarrel, dissension.
tropiezo, tropiece, etc. irr. V. TROPEZAR.
tropismo m. BIOL. tropism.
tropo m. RHET. trope.
troposfera f. METEOR. troposphere.
troquel m. die [for stamping coins and medals].
troquelar tr. to coin, to stamp in a die.
troqueo m. PROS. trochee.
trotador, -ra adj. trotting. 2 m. trotter [horse].
trotamundos, pl. dos m.-f. globe-trotter.

trotar *intr.* [of a horse or rider] to trot. *2* coll. to trot, hustle, hurry.

trote *m.* trot [of a horse]: ~ *cochinero*, jog trot; *tomar el* ~, coll. to dash off, to depart in haste; *a* ~, *al* ~, at a trot; coll. hurriedly. *2* fig. bustle, hurried and fatiguing work.

trotón, -na *adj.* trotting [horse]. *2 m.* horse.

trotona *f.* coll. chaperon, companion.

trova *f.* LIT. metrical composition, verse, song.

trovador, -ra *m.* troubadour. *2* poet. *3 f.* poetess.

trovadoresco, -ca *adj.* [pertaining to] troubadour.

trovar *tr.* to versify, write poetry.

trovero *m.* trouvère.

Troya *f. pr. n.* HIST., GEOG. Troy: *allí, ahí* or *aquí fue* ~, coll. and then the row started; *arda* ~, let happen what will.

troyano, -na *adj.-n.* Trojan.

trozo *m.* piece, chunk, part, fragment. *2* passage, selection.

truco *m.* trick, artifice, stratagem. *2 pl.* trucks [game].

truculencia *f.* truculence, truculency.

truculento, -ta *adj.* truculent.

trucha *f.* ICHTH. trout: ~ *salmonada*, salmon trout.

truchimán, -na *m.-f.* TRUJIMÁN. *2* coll. shrewd person.

trueco *m.* TRUEQUE: *a* ~ *de*, provided; *a* or *en* ~, in exchange.

trueco, trueque, etc. *irr.* V. TROCAR.

trueno *m.* thunder, thunderclap. *2* fig. loud report, detonation. *3* coll. harum-scarum, wild youth.

trueno, truene, etc. *in.* V. TRONAR.

trueque *m.* exchange, barter: *a* ~, *en* ~, in exchange.

trufa *f.* BOT. truffle. *2* lie, story, falsehood.

trufar *tr.* COOK. to stuff with truffles. *2 intr.* to lie, tell lies.

truhán *adj.* knavish, tricky. *2 m.-f.* knave, rascal, trickster. *3* buffoon, jester.

truhanada *f.* TRUHANERÍA.

truhanería *f.* rascality. *2* rascals [collect.]. *3* buffoonery.

truhanesco, -ca *adj.* knavish, rascally. *2* buffoon.

trujal *m.* wine press. *2* oil press. *3* oil mill.

trujamán, -na *m.-f.* dragoman [interpreter]. *2 m.* expert adviser [esp. in buying or selling].

trujamanear *intr.* to act as an interpreter. *2* to act as a broker or adviser; to barter.

trujimán, -na *m.-f.* TRUJAMÁN.

trulla *f.* noise, frolic. *2* troop, crowd. *3* trowel.

trullo *m.* ORN. teal.

truncado, -da *adj.* truncate, truncated.

truncar *tr.* to truncate. *2* fig. to cut, cut off, leave unfinished [a speech, writing, etc.].

trunco, -ca *adj.* truncated, mutilated, incomplete.

trupial *m.* ORN. troupial.

truque *m.* a card game.

trusas *f. pl.* trunk hose.

trust *m.* COM. trust.

tsetsé, tsé-tsé *adj.* ENT. tsetse [fly].

tú *pers. pron.* thou; you: *de* ~ *a* ~, intimately.

tu, *pl.* **tus** *poss. adj.* thy; your.

tuba *f.* MUS. tuba.

tubérculo *m.* BOT. tuber. *2* MED., ZOOL. tubercle.

tuberculosis *f.* MED. tuberculosis.

tuberculoso, -sa *adj.* tuberculous, tubercular. *2* MED. tuberculous. *3 m.-f.* MED. consumptive [person].

tubería *f.* tubing, piping; pipe line or system.

tuberosa *f.* tuberose.

tuberosidad *f.* tuberosity.

tuberoso, -sa *adj.* tuberose, tuberous.

tubo *m.* tube [long hollow cylinder], pipe: ~ *acústico*, speaking tube; ~ *de ensayo*, test tube. *2* ELECT. tube. *3* chimney [of a lamp]. *4* ANAT. canal: ~ *digestivo*, alimentary canal.

tubular *adj.* tubular: *caldera* ~, tubular boiler.

tucan *m.* ORN. toucan. *2* (cap.) ASTR. Toucan.

tudel *m.* MUS. crook [of a bassoon].

tudesco, -ca *adj.-n.* German.

tueca *f.*, **tueco** *m.* stump [of tree].

tuerca *f.* nut, female screw.

tuerce *m.* twist, twisting.

tuero *m.* big log [in a fireplace]. *2* firewood.

tuerto, -ta *adj.* one-eyed, blind in one eye. *2* twisted, bend. *3 m.* wrong, injury, injustice. *4 a* ~, injustly. *5 a tuertas o a derechas*, rightly or wrongly.

tueste *m.* TOSTADURA.

tuesto, tueste, etc. *irr.* V. TOSTAR.

tuétano *m.* marrow [of bone]; pith [of plants]: *hasta los tuétanos*, to the marrow; head over heels.

tufarada *f.* strong smell or odour.

tufo *m.* fume, reek, vapour; offensive smell. *2* coll. haughtiness, conceit. *3* GEOL. tufa. *4 pl.* locks of hair over the temples.

tugurio *m.* shepherds' hut. *2* fig. hole, small room.

tul *m.* tulle.

tulipa *f.* BOT. small tulip. *2* tulip-shaped lampshade.

tulipán *m.* BOT. tulip.

tulipero *m.* BOT. tulip tree.

tullido, -da *adj.* disabled, crippled, paralytic.

tullimiento *m.* disableness, crippleness.

tullir *tr.* to disable, cripple, make [one] a paralytic. *2 ref.* to become disabled, crippled or paralytic.

tumba *f.* tomb, grave. *2* arched top of a coach. *3* TUMBO 1. *4* VOLTERETA.

tumbacuartillos, *pl.* **-llos** *m.-f.* coll. sot, toper.

tumbado, -da *adj.* vaulted, arched.

tumbaga *f.* tombac. *2* finger ring.

tumbar *tr.* to fell, throw down, knock down. *2* of wine, a powerful odour, etc.] to stun, overpower. *3 ref.* to lie down. *4* to ease up, give up working.

tumbilla *f.* frame for holding a bed warmer.

tumbo *m.* tumble, jolt, violent roll or sway. *2* rise and fall [of a wave]. *3* undulation [in the ground]. *4* thunder, loud noise.

tumbón, -na *adj.* coll. sly. *2* coll. lazy. *3 m.-f.* coll. sly person. *4* coll. lazy person.

tumefacción *f.* tumefaction.

tumefacto, -ta *adj.* tumefied.

túmido, -da *adj.* tumid, swollen.

tumor *m.* MED. tumour.

tumoroso, -sa *adj.* having tumours.

tumulario, -ria *adj.* tumular, tumulary.

túmulo *m.* tumulus. *2* raised sepulchre. *3* catafalque.

tumulto *m.* tumult. *2* riot.

tumultuario, -ria *adj.* tumultuary.

tumultuoso, -sa *adj.* tumultuous.

tuna *f.* BOT. prickly pear, Indian fig [plant and fruit]. *2* idle and vagrant life: *correr la* ~, to loaf, *to bum. *3* ESTUDIANTINA.

tunanta *adj.-f.* rascally, artful [woman].

tunantada *f.* mean trick.

tunante *adj.* loafing. *2* rascally, artful [man]. *3 m.* loafer, vagrant. *4* rascal, rogue, scamp.

tunda *f.* shearing of cloth. *2* coll. beating, drubbing.
tundente *adj.* beating, whipping. *2* CONTUNDENTE 1.
tundición *f.* shearing of cloth.
tundidor, -ra *m.-f.* cloth shearer. *2 f.* cloth shearing machine.
tundir *tr.* to shear [cloth]. *2* coll. to beat, drub.
tundizno *m.* shearings from cloth.
tundra *f.* tundra.
tunear *intr.* to loaf.
tunecí; tunecino, -na *adj.-n.* Tunisian.
túnel *m.* tunnel.
Túnez *pr. n.* GEOG. Tunis [city]; Tunisia [state].
tungsteno *m.* CHEM. tungsten.
túnica *f.* tunic [ancient garment], robe, gown, long loose garment. *2* ANAT., ZOOL., BOT. tunic.
tunicado, -da *adj.* ANAT., ZOOL., BOT. tunicate.
tunicela *f.* ECCL. tunicle.
tuno, -na *adj.-n.* TUNANTE.
tuntún (al buen) *adv.* thoughtlessly, carelessly; without knowing what it is about.
tupé *m.* toupet, tuft, pompadour. *2* coll. cheek, nerve, brass.
tupido, -da *adj.* close, compact [in texture], dense, thick. *3* coll. dense, dull obtuse.
tupinambo *m.* AGUATURMA.
tupir *tr.* to make dense or thick, to make close or compact [in texture]. *2 ref.* to become dense, thick, close. *3* coll. to stuff oneself.
turba *f.* crowd, mob. *2* peat, turf.
turbación *f.* disturbance. *2* confusion, embarrassment.
turbador, -ra *adj.* disturbing. *2* troubling. *3* embarrassing. *4 m.-f.* disturber, perturber.
turbamulta *f.* rabble, mob, disorderly crowd.
turbante *m.* turban.
turbar *tr.* to disturb, upset. *2* to trouble, make turbid. *3* to confuse, embarrass. *4 ref.* to become disturbed. *5* to get confused or embarrassed.
turbera *f.* peat bog.
túrbido, -da *adj.* TURBIO.
turbiedad, turbieza *f.* turbidity.
turbina *f.* turbine.
turbio, -bia *adj.* turbid, muddy, cloudy. *2* troubled, turbulent. *3* indistinct, confused, obscure.
turbión *m.* squall, heavy shower. *2* fig. rush [of things].
turbomotor *m.* turbomotor.
turbonada *f.* storm, thunderstorm.
turborreactor *m.* turbojet.
turbulencia *f.* turbidness. *2* turbulence, turbulency.
turbulento, -ta *adj.* turbid. *2* turbulent.
turca *f.* coll. drunk, fit of drunkeness: *coger una ~,* to get drunk.
turco, -ca *adj.* Turkish. *2 m.-f.* Turk.

turcople *adj.-n.* Turko-Greek.
túrdiga *f.* strip of hide, leather thong.
turgencia *f.* turgidness, turgescence.
turgente *adj.* protuberant, prominent. *2* turgid, turgescent, swollen.
túrgido, -da *adj.* poet, protuberant, prominent.
turibulario *m.* ECCL. censer [one who censes].
turíbulo *m.* ECCL. thurible, censer.
turiferario *m.* ECCL. thurifer, censer bearer.
turífero, -ra *adj.* thuriferous, incense-bearing.
turificar *tr.* to thurify, cense.
Turingia *f. pr. n.* GEOG. Thuringia.
turión *m.* BOT. turion.
turismo *m.* tourism, touring. *2* touring car.
turista *m.-f.* tourist.
turístico, -ca *adj.* touristic, touristical.
turma *f.* lamb fry. *2* BOT. *~ de tierra,* truffle.
turmalina *f.* MINER. tourmaline.
turnar *intr.* to alternate, take turns, go or work by turns.
turnio, -nia *adj.* squinting [eye]. *2* squint-eyed.
turno *m.* turn [to do something]; turn, shift [alternation]: *por ~,* in turn, taking turns.
turón *m.* ZOOL. fitch, fitchew, polecat.
turquesa *f.* MINER. turquoise. *2* bullet mould.
Turquestán (el) *m. pr. n.* GEOG. Turkestan.
turqui *adj.* deep [blue].
Turquía *f. pr. n.* GEOG. Turkey: *~ Asiática,* Turkey in Asia; *~ Europea,* Turkey in Europe.
turrar *tr.* to roast, broil.
turrón *m.* a kind of sweetmeat made with almond paste, nougat. *2* coll. public office, sinecure.
turronería *f.* TURRÓN shop.
turronero, -ra *m.-f.* maker or seller of TURRÓN.
turulato, -ta *adj.* coll. dumbfounded, stupefied.
turumbón *m.* bump, swelling [from a blow].
¡tus!, ¡tusa! *interj.* used in calling dogs. *2* coll. *sin decir tus ni mus,* without saying a word. ··
tusilago *m.* BOT. coltsfoot.
tute *m.* a card game.
tutear *tr.* to thou. *2 rec.* to thou each other.
tutela *f.* LAW tutelage, guardianship. *2* tutelage, protection.
tutelar *adj.* tutelar, tutelary.
tuteo *m.* thouing.
tutilimundi *m.* MUNDONUEVO.
tutiplén (a) *adv.* abundantly.
tutor *m.* LAW tutor, guardian. *2* guardian, protector. *3* AGR. prop [for plants].
tutora *f.* LAW tutoress, guardian.
tutoría *f.* LAW tutelage, tutorage, guardianship.
tuturutú *m.* sound of a trumpet.
tuve, tuviera, tuviese, etc. *irr.* V. TENER.
tuya *f.* BOT. thuja.
tuyo, -ya *poss. adj.* your; thy [formal]. *2 poss. pron.* yours, of yours; thine [formal]. *3 los tuyos,* yours [your family or people].

U

U, u *f.* U, u, twenty-fourth letter of the Spanish alphabet. *2 u valona*, w [the letter].

u *conj.* [used instead of *o* before a word beginning with the vowel sound *o*] or.

uapití *m.* ZOOL. wapiti.

ubérrimo, -ma *adj.* very or most abundant or fertile.

ubicación *f.* location, position, situation.

ubicar *intr.-ref.* to lie, be located, be situated. *2 tr.* (Am.) to place, locate.

ubicuidad *f.* ubiquity.

ubicuo, -cua *adj.* ubiquitous.

ubiquidad *f.* UBICUIDAD.

ubre *f.* dug, udder, teat [of female mammals].

ucase *m.* ukase.

Ucrania *f. pr. n.* GEOG. Ukraine.

ucranio, -nia *adj.-n.* Ukranian.

udómetro *m.* udometer.

¡uf! *interj.* humph!; pshaw!

ufanarse *ref.* to boast, to pride oneself.

ufanía *f.* pride, vainglory. *2* joy, pleasure.

ufano, -na *adj.* proud, conceited, vainglorious. *2* glad, pleased.

ujier *m.* usher [of a court, etc.].

ulano *m.* MIL. uhlan.

úlcera *f.* MED. sore, ulcer. *2* BOT. rot.

ulceración *f.* MED. ulceration.

ulcerado, -da *adj.* MED. ulcerated.

ulcerar *tr.* MED. to ulcerate. *2 ref.* MED. to ulcerate [undergo ulceration].

ulceroso, -sa *adj.* MED. ulcerous.

ulema *m.* Ulema.

uliginoso, -sa *adj.* uliginose, uliginous.

Ulises *m. pr. n.* MYTH. Ulysses.

ulitis *f.* MED. ulitis.

ulmáceo, -a *adj.* BOT. ulmaceous.

ulmaria *f.* BOT. meadowsweet.

ulterior *adj.* ulterior. *2* subsequent.

ultimación *f.* finish, completion.

últimamente *adv.* lastly, finally. *2* of late.

ultimar *tr.* to end, finish, complete.

ultimátum *m.* ultimatum.

último, -ma *adj.* last, latter. *2* latest: *la última moda*, the latest fashion. *3* ultimate, final. *4* farthest, remote. *5* best, utmost. *6 última pena*, capital punishment. *7 estar a las últimas* or *en las últimas*, to be near one's, or it's end. *8 a última hora*, at the last minute. *9 a últimos de*, in

the latter part of [a month, etc.]. *10 por ~*, lastly; finally.

ultra *adv.* besides. *2 pref.* ultra.

ultrajante *adj.* injurious, insulting, outraging.

ultrajar *tr.* to injure, insult, offend, outrage.

ultraje *m.* injure, insult, offence, outrage.

ultramar *m.* place or country overseas: *de ~*, overseas; ultramarine.

ultramarino, -na *adj.* overseas. *2* ultramarine [blue]. *3 m. pl.* COM. overseas foodstuffs; groceries.

ultramicroscopio *m.* ultramicroscope.

ultramontano, -na *adj.-n.* ultramontane.

ultramundano, -na *adj.* ultramundane.

ultranza (a) *adv.* to death. *2* at all costs, resolutely.

ultratumba *adv.* beyond the grave.

ultraviolado, ultravioleta *adj.* PHYS. ultraviolet.

ultravirus *m.* BACT. ultravirus.

ulular *intr.* to ululate.

ululato *m.* ululation.

umbela *f.* BOT. umbel.

umbelífero, -ra *adj.* BOT. umbelliferous.

umbilicado, -da *adj.* navel-shaped, umbilicate.

umbilical *adj.* ANAT., ZOOL. umbilical.

umbráculo *m.* shaded place for plants.

umbral *m.* threshold. *2* ARCH. lintel [beam].

umbralar *tr.* ARCH. to lintel.

umbrátil *adj.* umbrageous, shading.

Umbría (la) *f. pr. n.* GEOG. Umbria.

umbría *f.* shady place, shady side.

umbrío, -bría *adj.* shady [place].

umbroso, -sa *adj.* umbrageous, shady.

un, una *indef. art.* a, an. *2 adj.* one [numeral]. ¶ The form *un* is used before masculine singular nouns and adjectives, and before feminine singular nouns and adjectives beginning with an accented *a*: *un alma*, a soul.

unánime *adj.* unanimous.

unánimemente *adv.* unanimously.

unanimidad *f.* unanimity: *por ~*, unanimously.

uncinado, -da *adj.* uncinate.

unción *f.* unction, anointing. *2* extreme unction. *3* unction [fervent quality; religious fervour].

uncir *tr.* to yoke [oxen, etc.].

undecágono *m.* undecagon.

undécimo, -ma *adj.-m.* eleventh.

undoso, -sa *adj.* waving, undulating.

undulación *f.* undulation. *2* PHYS. wave.

undular *intr.* to undulate, wave, wriggle.
undulatorio, -ria *adj.* undulatory.
ungido *adj.-m.* anointed.
ungimiento *m.* unction, anointment.
ungir *tr.* to anoint.
ungüento *m.* unguent, ointment, salve.
unguiculado, -da *adj.-m.* ZOOL. unguiculate.
unguis, *pl.* **-guis** *m.* ANAT. unguis.
ungulado, -da *adj.-m.* ZOOL. ungulate.
únicamente *adv.* only, solely.
unicameral *adj.* unicameral.
unicelular *adj.* unicellular.
unicidad *f.* unicity.
único, -ca *adj.* only, sole. 2 unique, unequalled.
unicornio *m.* MYTH. unicorn. 2 ZOOL. rhinoceros. 3 (cap.) ASTR. Unicorn.
unidad *f.* unity [oneness, due coherence of parts]. 2 union, concord. 3 unit. 4 RHET., MATH., F. ARTS unity.
unido, -da *adj.* united. 2 being in union or concord.
unificación *f.* unification.
unificador, -ra *adj.* unifying. 2 *m.-f.* unifier.
unificar *tr.* to unify. 2 *ref.* to be unified.
uniformar *tr.* to uniform [make uniform], to standardize. 2 to uniform [clothe in uniform].
uniforme *adj.* uniform. 2 *m.* uniform; regimentals.
uniformidad *f.* uniformity.
unigénito, -ta *adj.* unigenital, only-begotten.
unilateral *adj.* unilateral.
unión *f.* union. 2 contiguity. 3 MACH. coupling, connecting, connection, joint. 4 COM. amalgamation.
unionista *adj.* unionistic. 2 *m.-f.* unionist.
unípara *adj.* uniparous.
unipersonal *adj.* unipersonal.
unir *tr.* to unite, join. 2 *ref.* to unite [become united, attached, etc.; get married]. 3 to coalesce. 4 to unite, join, adhere. 5 COM. to amalgamate.
unisexual *adj.* BOT. unisexual.
unison *adj.* UNÍSONO. 2 MUS. unison.
unisonancia *f.* MUS. unisonance. 2 monotony.
unísono, -na *adj.* unison, unisonant, unisonous. 2 *al* ~, in unison, unanimously.
unitario, -ria *adj.* unitary. 2 *m.-f.* POL. unitarian. 3 THEOL. Unitarian.
unitivo, -va *adj.* unitive.
univalvo, -va *adj.* ZOOL. univalve.
universal *adj.* universal. 2 *m.* LOG. universal.
universalidad *f.* universality.
universalizar *tr.* to universalize.
universidad *f.* EDUC., HIST. university. 2 universality.
universitario, -ria *adj.* universitarian, university. 2 *m.* university professor.
universo, -sa *adj.* universal. 2 *m.* universe, world.
unívoco, -ca *adj.* univocal.
uno, -na *adj.* one: *todo es* ~, all is the same; ~ *que otro, una que otra,* a few; occasionally. 2 *pl.* a few; some: *unas [cuantas] pesetas,* a few pesetas; *unos veinte minutos,* some twenty minutes. 3 *adj.-m.* one [numeral]: *el número* ~, the number one. 4 *pron.* one [one person or thing]; one of them: *de* ~, one's; ~ *a otro, los unos a los otros,* each other, one another; ~ *a* ~, *de* ~ *en* ~, ~ *por* ~, one by one; ~ *y otro,* both. 5 *f. la una,* one o'clock. 6 *a una,* of one accord; jointly.
untadura *f.* UNTURA.
untar *tr.* to anoint, grease, oil, smear. 2 fig. to grease, bribe. 3 *ref.* to grease oneself, to get smeared. 4 fig. to practice embezzlement.

unto *m.* ointment, unguent. 2 grease, fat [of animal].
untuosidad *f.* unctuosity, greasiness.
untuoso, -sa *adj.* unctuous, greasy.
untura *f.* anointing, oiling, greasing. 2 MED. unction. 3 ointment.
uña *f.* ANAT., ZOOL. nail, fingernail, toenail; claw, talon: *enseñar las uñas,* fig. to show one's teeth; *estar de uñas,* fig. to be on bad terms; *ser largo de uñas,* fig. to be of a thievish disposition; *ser* ~ *y carne,* fig. to be hand and glove. 2 ZOOL. hoof: *a* ~ *de caballo,* at full gallop. 3 sting [of scorpion]. 4 BOT. thorn. 5 stub [of limb of tree]. 6 curved point. 7 nail hole [of a penknife, etc.]. 8 NAUT. fluke, bill [of anchor].
uñada *f.* nail scratch. 2 push with the nail.
uñarada *f.* nail scratch.
uñero *m.* ingrowing nail.
¡upa! *interj.* up, up!, hoop-la!
upas *m.* BOT. upas [tree and sap].
Urales (los) *m. pr. n.* GEOG. the Urals.
Urania *f. pr. n.* MYTH. Urania.
uranio, -nia *adj.* uranic. 2 *m.* CHEM. uranium.
uranita *f.* MINER. uranite.
Urano *m. pr. n.* ASTR. Uranus.
uranografía *f.* uranography.
urato *m.* CHEM. urate.
urbanamente *adv.* courteously, politely.
urbanidad *f.* urbanity, civility, manners.
urbanismo *m.* city planning.
urbanización *f.* urbanization. 2 city planning.
urbanizar *tr.* to urbanize, render urbane. 2 to urbanize, develop [land].
Urbano *m. pr. n.* Urban.
urbano, -na *adj.* urban. 2 urbane, courteous, polite. 3 *m.* town policeman.
urbe *f.* large city, metropolis.
urceolado, -da *adj.* urceolate.
urchilla *f.* archil, orchil [plant and dye].
urdidor, -ra *adj.* WEAV. warping. 2 fig. plotting. 3 *m.-f.* WEAV. warper. 4 fig. plotter. 5 *m.* WEAV. warping frame.
urdidura *f.* WEAV. warping.
urdiembre, urdimbre *f.* WEAV. warp. 2 WEAV. warping.
urdir *tr.* WEAV. to warp. 2 fig. to plot, contrive.
urea *f.* CHEM. urea.
uremia *f.* MED. uraemia.
urente *adj.* hot, burning, smarting.
uréter *m.* ANAT. ureter.
uretra *f.* ANAT. urethra.
urgencia *f.* urgency [being urgent]. 2 MED. emergency.
urgente *adj.* urgent, pressing.
urgir *intr.* to press, be urgent [demand immediate action].
Urías *m. pr. n.* BIBL. Uriah.
úrico, -ca *adj.* uric.
urinario, -ria *adj.* urinary. 2 *m.* urinal [place].
urna *f.* urn, casket. 2 glass case. 3 ballot box.
uro *m.* ZOOL. aurochs.
urodelo, -la *adj.-n.* ZOOL. urodelan.
urogallo *m.* ORN. capercailye.
urología *f.* urology.
urólogo *m.* urologist.
urraca *f.* ORN. magpie. 2 coll. magpie [chatterer].
úrsido, -da *m. pl.* ZOOL. Ursidae.
ursulina *adj.-f.* Ursuline.
urticáceo, -a *adj.* BOT. urticaceous.
urticante *adj.* urticant.
urticaria *f.* MED. urticaria, nettle rash, hives.

urubú *m.* ORN. urubu, black vulture.
uruguayo, -ya *adj.-n.* Uruguayan.
usado, -da *adj.* used, employed. *3* worn-out, old [impaired by use]. *4* second-hand [clothes]. *5* inured, accustomed, skilled.
usagre *m.* MED. infantile eczema. *2* VET. mange.
usanza *f.* usage, custom, fashion.
usar *tr.* to use [make use of]. *2* to wear [an article of dress, etc.]. *3 tr.-intr.* to use to, be wont or accustomed to. *4 ref.* to be used, be in use or fashion.
usarcé, usarced *m.-f.* obs. your honour.
useñoría *m.-f.* obs. your grace, your lordship, your ladyship.
usía *m.-f.* USEÑORÍA.
uso *m.* use [using, employment, right of using]; wear, wearing, wear and tear: *en buen* ~, in good condition. *2* usage, custom, fashion: *al* ~, *a* ~, according to custom. *3* habit, practice. *4* LAW. usage. *5* ~ *de razón*, discretion, discernment.
usted, *pl.* **ustedes** *pron.* (used with the third of verb) you: *de* ~, *de ustedes*, your, yours.
ustorio *adj.* burning [glass].
usual *adj.* usual, customary. *2* affable, sociable.
usuario, -ria *adj.* usuary; user.
usufructo *m.* LAW usufruct. *2* fruits, profits.
usufructuar *tr.* to enjoy the usufruct of. *2 intr.* to yield profit.
usufructuario, -ria *adj.-n.* usufructuary.
usura *f.* usury.
usurario, -ria *adj.* usurious.
usurear *intr.* to practice usury.

usurero, -ra *m.-f.* usurer.
usurpación *f.* usurpation.
usurpador, -ra *adj.* usurping. *2 m.-f.* usurper.
usurpar *tr.* to usurp. *2* to encroach upon.
utensilio *m.* utensil. *2 pl.* tools [of a trade].
uterino, -na *adj.* uterine.
útero *m.* ANAT. uterus, womb.
útil *adj.* useful, profitable. *2* LAW lawful, legal [time]. *3* MECH. effective, available. *4 m. pl.* tools, implements.
utilidad *f.* utility, usefulness. *2* fruit, profit.
utilitario, -ria *adj.* utilitarian.
utilitarismo *m.* utilitarianism.
utilizable *adj.* utilizable, available.
utilizar *tr.* to utilize, use. *2 ref. utilizarse de*, to profit by.
utopía *f.* Utopia.
utópico, -ca *adj.* Utopian.
utopista *adj.-n.* Utopian.
utrículo *m.* ANAT., BOT. utricle.
uva *f.* BOT. grape: ~ *pasa*, raisin; *estar hecho una* ~, coll. to be vey drunk. *2* BOT. berry of the barberry bush. *3* MED. uvular tumor. *4* wart on the eyelid. *5* BOT. ~ *crespa*, ~ *espina*, gooseberry; ~ *de gato*, stonecrop.
uvada *f.* abundance of grapes.
uvaduz *f.* GAYUBA.
uvate *m.* conserve of grapes.
uve *f.* name of the letter *v*.
úvea *f.* ANAT. uvea.
úvula *f.* ANAT. uvula.
uvular *adj.* uvular.
uxoricida *m.* uxoricide [man].
uxoricidio *m.* uxoricide [act.].

V

V, v *f.* V, v, twenty-fifth letter of the Spanish alphabet.

va *3rd. sing. pres. ind.* of IR.

vaca *f.* ZOOL. cow [female of bovine animal]: ~ *lechera*, milch cow. *2* beef [meat]. *3* cow leather, cowskin. *4* joint stock of two gamblers. *5* ENT. ~ *de San Antón*, ladybird, ladybug. *6* ZOOL. ~ *marina*, sea cow, manatee.

vacación *f.* vacancy [of a post]. *2 sing.-pl.* vacation, holidays.

vacada *f.* herd of bovine cattle.

vacancia *f.* vacancy [unoccupied post].

vacante *adj.* vacant, unoccupied. *2 f.* vacancy [unoccupied post]. *3* vacation [period].

vacar *intr.* to take a vacation. *2* [of a post, office, etc.], to be vacant. *3* ~ *a*, to attend to, devote oneself to. *4* ~ *de*, to lack, be devoid of.

vacatura *f.* vacancy [time].

vaciadero *m.* drain, drain pipe. *2* dumping place.

vaciado *m.* cast; casting [in a mould]. *3* ARCH. hollow, excavation. *4* honing [of razors].

vaciamiento *m.* emptying. *2* casting, moulding.

vaciar *tr.* to empty. *2* to cast [form in a mould]. *3* ARCH. to excavate, hollow out. *4* to hone [razors]. *5 intr.* [of a river] to empty, flow. *6* [of a river, etc.] to fall, decrease. *7 ref.* to empty [become empty].

vaciedad *f.* inanity, silliness, silly remark.

vacilación *f.* vacilation. *2* unsteadiness. *3* flickering. *4* hesitation.

vacilante *adj.* vacillating, wavering. *2* staggering, unsteady. *3* flickering. *4* hesitating, irresolute.

vacilar *intr.* to vacillate, waver. *2* to reel, stagger, totter. *3* to flicker. *4* to fluctuate, hesitate.

vacío, -a *adj.* empty void, vacuous. *2* vacant, unoccupied. *3* empty, vain, inane. *4* vain, useless. *5* idle. *6* concave, hollow. *7 m.* void [empty space]. *8* emptiness. *9* PHYS. vacuum. *10* gap, blank. *11* vacancy. *12* flank [of animals], side [of persons]. *13 hacer el* ~ *a*, to isolate, ignore [someone]. *14* *de* ~ unloaded [cart, etc.]; fig. idling; empty-handed, unsuccessfully.

vacuidad *f.* vacuity, emptiness. *2* inaneness.

vacuna *f.* cowpox. *2* vaccine.

vacunación *f.* vaccination.

vacunar *tr.* to vaccinate.

vacuno, -na *adj.* bovine. *2* of cowskin.

vacuo, cua *adj.* empty. *2* vacant, unoccupied. *3 m.* hollow, concavity.

vacuola *f.* BIOL. vacuole.

vade *m.* school portfolio, satchel.

vadeable *adj.* fordable. *2* fig. conquerable, superable.

vadear *tr.* to ford, wade [a stream]. *2* to overcome [a difficulty]. *3* to sound [a person]. *4* to penetrate, understand. *5 ref.* to conduct oneself.

vademécum *m.* vade mecum. *2* VADE.

vadera *f.* wide ford.

vado *m.* ford: *tentar el* ~, fig. to feel one's way. *2* fig. expedient, resource.

vadoso, -sa *adj.* fordy, shallow, shoaly.

vagabundear *intr.* to wander, roam, loiter about.

vagabundeo *m.* wandering, roaming, loitering about.

vagabundo, -da *adj.* vagabond. *2 m.-f.* vagabond, wanderer, vagrant, tramp.

vagamundear *tr.* VAGABUNDEAR.

vagamundo, -da *adj.-n.* VAGABUNDO.

vagancia *f.* idleness, loafing. *2* vagancy.

1) **vagar** *m.* leisure, time. *2* idleness.

2) **vagar** *intr.* to wander, roam. *2* to be idle. *3* to be at leisure. *4* [of a thing] to lie around.

vagaroso, -sa *adj.* poet. errant, wandering, fluttering.

vagido *m.* cry of the newborn child.

vagina *f.* ANAT. vagina.

vago, -ga *adj.* wandering, roaming. *2* idle, loafing. *3* vague, indistinct, loose, hazy. *4* blank [stare]. *5* unimproved [plot of ground]. *6 m.* idler, loafer. *7* vagrant. *8 en* ~, unsteadily; in vain; in the air, at nothing [blow].

vagón *m.* RLY. carriage, car, coach, wagon, van: ~ *cisterna*, tank car; ~ *restaurante*, dining-car; ~ *de carga*, goods wagon, freight car.

vagoneta *f.* small wagon, open railway truck.

vaguada *f.* thalweg.

vaguear *intr.* to wander, roam.

vaguedad *f.* vagueness. *2* vague remark.

vaguido, -da *adj.* dizzy, giddy. *2 m.* VAHÍDO.

vaharada *f.* breath, breathing, exhalation.

vaharina *f.* coll. vapour, mist.

vahear *intr.* to exhale or emit fumes or vapour.

vahído *m.* vertigo, dizziness, swoon.

vaho *m.* fume, vapour, exhalation, breath.

vaída *adj.* ARCH. Byzantine [vault].

vaina *f.* sheath, case, scabbard. *2* BOT. sheath. *3* BOT. pod, shell. *4* NAUT. tabling [of a flag or sail].
vainica *f.* SEW. hemstitch.
vainilla *f.* BOT. vanilla [plant and fruit]. *2* VAINICA.
vais *irr. 2nd. pers. pl. pres. ind.* of IR.
vaivén *m.* to-and-fro motion, seesaw, swing, fluctuation. *2 fig.* inconstancy [of fortune or things]. *3* NAUT. ratline.
vajilla *f.* table service, dinner set, plate: ~ *de oro,* gold plate; ~ *de plata,* silver plate, silverware.
valdré, valdría, etc. *irr.* V. VALER.
vale *m.* promissory note. *2* receipt, voucher. *3* bonus given to schoolboys.
valedero, -ra *adj.* valid, efficacious.
valedor, -ra *m.-f.* protector, defender, helper.
valencia *f.* CHEM. valence, valency.
valenciano, -na *adj.-n.* Valencian.
valentía *f.* valour, bravery. *2* feat, heroic exploit. *3* LIT., F. ARTS dash, boldness. *4* brag, braggadocio.
Valentín *m. pr. n.* Valentine.
valentino, -na *adj.* Valencian.
valentísimo, -ma *adj. superl.* of VALIENTE.
valentón, -na *adj.* blustering, arrogant. *2 m.-f.* blusterer, braggard, hector, bully.
valentonada *f.* bluster, brag, braggadocio.
1) **valer** *m.* worth, merit, value.
2) **valer** *tr.* to protect, defend, help. *2* to produce, give, yield. *3* to bring, bring about, cause to get. *4* to be worth, be valued at, be equal or equivalent to: *no valer nada,* to be worth nothing. *5* ~ *la pena,* to be worth, be worth while; to be important. *6 valga lo que valiere,* come what may. *7 ¡válgame Dios!,* bless my soul!
8 intr. to be of worth, be valuable; be useful, able, proficient; to have power, influence. *9* to avail. *10* to be valid, good; to hold, count. *11* to prevail [over or against]. *12 hacer* ~, to make feel; to turn to account; to assert [one's rights, etc.]. *13* ~ *más,* to be better; *más vale tarde que nunca,* better late than never. *14* ~ *para,* to be useful for. *15* ~ *por,* to be worth, to be as good as. *16* ~ *tanto como,* to be as much as.
17 ref. to help or defend oneself; to take care of oneself: *no poder valerse,* to be helpless. *18 valerse de,* to make use of; to avail oneself of, to take advantage of.
¶ CONJUG. INDIC. Pres.: *valgo,* vales, vale, etc. | Fut.: *valdré, valdrás,* etc. | COND. *valdría, valdrías,* etc. | SUBJ. Pres.: *valga, valgas,* etc. | IMPER.: *val* or vale; *valgamos,* valed, *valgan.*
valeriana *f.* BOT. valerian, setwall.
valerosidad *f.* valour, bravery, courage.
valeroso, -sa *adj.* valorous, brave. *2* active, powerful.
valetudinario, -ria *adj.-n.* valetudinarian.
valgo, valga, etc. *irr.* V. VALER.
valí *m.* vali, wali.
valía *f.* value, worth. *2* VALIMIENTO 1. *3* ECON. *mayor* ~, *plus* ~, unearned increment.
validar *tr.* to validate.
validez *f.* validity.
válido, -da *adj.* valid. *2* strong, robust, powerful.
valido, -da *adj.* generally accepted or esteemed. *2 m.* court favorite, prime minister.
valiente *adj.* valiant, brave. *2* strong, vigorous. *3* fig. fine, excellent. *4* fig. great, excessive. *5 m.-f.* brave person. *6 m.* bully.
valija *f.* valise, suitcase. *2* mailbag. *3* mail, post: ~ *diplomática,* diplomatic mail.

valimiento *m.* favour, good graces; favour at court. *2* protection, defense, help.
valioso, -sa *adj.* valuable, important, powerful.
valisoletano, -na *adj.-n.* of Valladolid.
valón, -na *adj.-n.* Walloon. *2 f.* Vandyke collar.
valor *m.* value, worth: ~ *nominal,* par value, face value. *2* import. *3* amount. *4* importance. *5* validity, force. *6* valour, courage. *7* audacity, impudence. *8 pl.* COM. securities.
valorar, valorear *tr.* to value, appraise. *2* to increase the value of.
valoría *f.* value, worth.
valquiria *f.* MYTH. Valkyrie.
vals *m.* waltz.
valsar *intr.* to waltz.
valuación *f.* valuation, appraisal.
valuar *tr.* to value, appraise, rate.
valva *f.* BOT., ZOOL. valve.
valvar *adj.* BIOL. valval, valvar.
válvula *f.* MACH., RADIO., ANAT. valve: ~ *de seguridad,* safety valve.
valvular *adj.* valvular.
valla *f.* paling, fence, stockade, barrier. *2 fig.* barrier, obstacle. *3* SPORT hurdle.
valladar *m.* VALLADO. *2 fig.* barrier, defence.
vallado *m.* fence, stockade, inclosure.
vallar *tr.* to fence, palisade.
valle *m.* valley, vale: *este* ~ *de lágrimas,* fig. this vale of tears. *2* river basin.
vallisoletano, -na *adj.-n.* of Valladolid.
vamos *1st. pers. pl. pres. ind. & imper.* of IR. *2 interj.* well!, come now!; let's go!; stop!
vampiresa *f.* vampire, vamp [woman].
vampiro *m.* vampire, ghoul. *2 fig.* vampire, usurer. *3* ZOOL. vampire.
van *3rd. pers. pl. pres. ind.* of IR.
vanadio *m.* CHEM. vanadium.
vanagloria *f.* vainglory, conceit.
vanagloriarse *ref.* to boast [of], to be vainglorious.
vanaglorioso, -sa *adj.* vainglorious, conceited.
vanamente *adv.* vainly. *2* in vain.
vandalismo *m.* vandalism.
vándalo, -la *adj.-n.* Vandal, vandal.
vanguardia *f.* MIL. van, vanguard: *a* ~, in the van.
vanidad *f.* vanity: *hacer* ~ *de,* to boast of. *2* empty word, inanity.
vanidoso, -sa *adj.* vain, conceited. *2 m.-f.* vain person.
vanilocuencia *f.* verbosity, empty talk.
vano, -na *adj.* vain: *en* ~, in vain. *2* hollow, empty. *3 m.* ARCH. opening [for a door or window].
vapor *m.* PHYS. vapo(u)r. *2* steam: *al* ~, fig. with all speed. *3* mist, exhalation. *4* NAUT. steamboat, steamship, steamer. *5 pl.* vapours, hysterics.
vapora *f.* coll. steam launch.
vaporear *tr.-ref.* EVAPORAR. *2 intr.* to exhale vapours.
vaporizador *m.* vaporizer.
vaporizar *tr.* to vaporize.
vaporoso, -sa *adj.* vaporous, vapoury, airy, ethereal.
vapular *tr.* VAPULEAR.
vapuleador, -ra *adj.* flogging, whipping. *2 m.-f.* flogger, whipper.
vapulear *tr.* to flog, whip, vapulate.
vapuleo *m.* flogging, vapulation.
vaquería *f.* VACADA. *2* cow-house, dairy.
vaquerizo, -za *adj.* [pertaining to] cattle. *2 m.* cowherd. *3 f.* cowherdess. *4* winter stable for cattle.
vaquero, -ra *adj.* pertaining to cowherds. *2 m.* cowherd, cowboy. *3 f.* cowherdess.

vaqueta f. calf leather.
vara f. stick, switch. 2 rod, wand, verge, staff, cane: *tener* ~ *alta*, fig. to have authority. 3 shaft, thill [of a carriage]. 4 BOT. flowered scape. 5 BULLF. thrust with the pike. 6 measure of length [2,8 ft]. 7 BOT. ~ *de Jesé*, tuberose.
varada f. NAUT. beaching or running aground.
varadera f. NAUT. skid.
varadero m. NAUT. place where boats are taken ashore for safety. 2 repair dock.
varal m. long pole or perch. 2 upper rail of the side of a cart. 3 coll. tall, ungainly person.
varapalo m. long pole. 2 blow with a stick or pole. 3 fig. blow, loss, damage, reverse.
varar tr. NAUT. to beach [a boat]. 2 intr. NAUT. to run aground. 3 fig. [of an affair] to come to a standstill.
varaseto m. lattice-work fence, trellis.
varazo m. blow with a rod or stick.
vareaje m. knocking of fruit off trees with poles.
varear tr. to knock off [fruit] with a pole. 2 to beat with a stick. 3 to prick [bulls, etc.] with a pike.
varenga f. NAUT. floor-timber. 2 NAUT. headrail.
vareo m. VAREAJE.
varetazo m. BULLF. side blow with the horn.
varetón m. young stag.
varga f. steepest part of a slope.
vargueño m. BARGUEÑO.
variabilidad f. variability.
variable adj. variable. 2 f. MATH. variable.
variación f. variation, change. 2 MUS. variation.
variado, -da adj. varied, diverse. 3 variegated.
variante adj. variant, varying. 2 f. variant.
variar tr. to vary, change, alter, diversify, variegate. 2 intr. to vary, change. 3 to vary, differ. 4 NAUT. [of the compass] to vary, desviate.
varice, várice f. MED. varix.
varicela f. MED. varicella, chicken pox.
varicoso, -sa adj. varicose.
variedad f. variety; diversity. 2 variation, change. 3 changeableness. 4 BIOL. variety. 5 pl. variety show.
varilarguero m. PICADOR [in bullfighting].
varilla f. dim. slender stick, twig; slender rod. 2 rib [of an umbrella]. 3 stick [of fan]. 4 wire spoke. 5 ~ *de virtudes*, conjurer's wand.
varillaje m. ribs [of an umbrella]; sticks [of a fan].
vario, -ria adj. various, diverse, varied. 2 inconstant. 3 variegated. 4 pl. various, several.
varioloso, -sa adj. MED. variolous.
variómetro m. ELECT. variometer.
varita f. dim. switch, twig, small stick or rod. 2 ~ *de virtudes*, VARILLA DE VIRTUDES.
variz m. VARICE.
varón m. male [person]: *un niño* ~, a male child. 2 man; man of respectability.
varoncito m. dim. boy, male child.
varonil adj. manful, manly, virile, courageous.
Varsovia f. pr. n. GEOG. Warsaw.
vasallaje m. HIST. vassalage. 2 HIST. liege money. 3 vassalage, servitude, subjection, dependence.
vasallo adj. subject, dependent, feudatory. 2 m.-f. vassal, subject.
vasar m. kitchen shelf, kitchen shelving.
vasco, -ca adj.-n. Basque.
vascongado, -da adj.-n. Basque.
vascuence m. Basque [language].
vascular adj. vascular.
vaselina f. vaseline.
vasera f. kitchen shelf. 2 rack for glasses.
vasija f. vessel [receptacle for liquids or eatables].

vaso m. glass, tumbler. 2 glassful, tumblerful. 3 vessel, receptacle, reservoir: ~ *de elección*, chosen vessel. 4 hoof [of horse]. 5 ARCH. vase. 6 ANAT., BOT. vessel. 7 ~ *de noche*, chamber pot.
vasomotor adj. PHYSIOL. vasomotor.
vástago m. shoot; scion, offspring. 2 MACH. piston rod, tiller.
vastedad f. vastness.
vasto, -ta adj. vast, immense, huge, of great extent.
vate m. bard, poet. 2 seer, diviner.
Vaticano m. pr. n. Vatican.
vaticano, -na adj. Vatican.
vaticinar tr. to vaticinate.
vaticinio m. vaticination, prediction, prophecy.
vatídico, -ca adj. prophetical.
vatímetro m. ELECT. wattmeter.
vatio m. ELECT. watt.
1) **vaya** f. banter, raillery.
2) **vaya**, etc. irr. V. IR. 2 interj. go!, go to!; come!, indeed!, well!
1) **ve** 2d pers. sing. imper. of IR.
2) **ve** f. name of letter v: ~ *doble*, name of w.
véase imper. of VERSE. 2 see, vide [in references].
veces f. pl. of VEZ.
vecinal adj. local, vicinal.
vecinamente adv. near, contiguously.
vecindad f. status of being an inhabitant of a town. 2 vicinage, vicinity; neighbours, neighbourhood.
vecindario m. neighbourhood [people living near one another]; inhabitants of a town or quarter.
vecino, -na adj. near by, next, neighbouring. 2 fig. neighbouring, bordering upon, resembling. 3 m.-f. neighbour. 4 tenant [in a tenement house]. 5 resident, citizen [of a town].
vector adj. MATH. vectorial. 2 m. MATH. vector.
veda f. prohibition, interdiction. 2 close season. 3 m. Veda.
vedado, -da adj. prohibited, interdicted. 2 m. enclosure, game preserve, warren.
vedar tr. to prohibit, forbid. 2 to impede.
vedegambre m. BOT. white hellebore.
vedija f. tuft of wool. 2 entangled lock of wool or hair. 4 matted hair.
veedor, -ra adj. curious, prying. 2 m.-f. prier, busybody. 3 [formerly] overseer, supervisor.
vega f. fertile lowland. 2 (Cu.) tobacco plantation.
vegetación f. vegetation.
vegetal adj. vegetable, vegetal. 2 m. vegetable, plant.
vegetar intr. to vegetate.
vegetariano, -na adj.-n. vegetarian.
vegetativo, -va adj. vegetative.
veguer m. an ancient magistrate.
veguero m. tobacco planter. 2 cigar made of a single leaf.
vehemencia f. vehemence.
vehemente adj. vehement.
vehículo m. vehicle.
veintavo, -va adj.-n. twentieth.
veinte adj.-m. twenty. 2 adj.-n. twentieth. 3 m. twentieth [of the month].
veintena f., **veintenar** m. score, set of twenty.
veinteno, -na adj.-n. twentieth.
veinticinco adj.-m. twenty-five. 2 adj. twenty-fifth. 3 m. twenty-fifth [of the month].
veinticuatro adj.-m. twenty four. 2 adj. twenty fourth. 3 m. twenty-fourth [of the month].
veintidós adj.-m. twenty-two. 2 adj. twenty-second. 3 m. twenty-second [of the month].

veintinueve adj.-m. twenty-nine. 2 adj. twentyninth. 3 m. twenty-ninth [of the month].
veintiocho adj.-m. twenty-eight. 2 adj. twentyeighth. 3 m. twenty-eight [of the month].
veintiséis adj.-m. twenty-six. 2 adj. twenty-sixth. 3 m. twenty-sixth [of the month].
veintisiete adj.-m. twenty-seven. 2 adj. twentyseventh. 3 m. twenty-seventh [of the month].
veintitrés adj.-m. twenty-three. 2 adj. twentythird. 3 m. twenty-third [of the month].
veintiún adj. twenty-one [used only before the noun].
veintiuno, -na adj.-m. twenty-one. 2 adj. twentyfirst. 3 m. twenty-first [of the month]. 4 f. twenty-one [card game].
vejación f. molestation, humiliation, ill-treatment, opresion.
vejamen m. VEJACIÓN. 2 humorous reprehension.
vejancón, -na adj. coll. old. 2 m.-f. coll. old person.
vejar tr. to molest, humiliate, ill-treat, oppress.
vejatorio, -ria adj. molesting, humiliating, oppressive.
vejestorio m. coll. very old person.
vejete m. ridiculous old man.
vejez f. oldness. 2 old age. 3 peevishness of old age. 4 coll. platitude, old history.
vejiga f. bladder: ~ de la bilis, ANAT. gall bladder; ~ de la orina, ANAT. bladder, urinary bladder; ~ natatoria, air bladder, swimming bladder [of fish]. 2 pustule of smallpox.
vejigatorio, -ria adj.-m. vesicant, vesicatory.
vejiguilla f. dim. small blister or pustule. 2 vesicle.
1) **vela** f. vigil, watch [keeping awake]: en ~, awake, sleepless. 2 nightwork, night watch. 3 watching the sick or the dead. 4 ECCL. vigil before the Holy Sacrament.
2) **vela** f. candle [for giving light]: ¿quién le ha dado a usted vela en este entierro?, coll. you have no voice in this matter.
3) **vela** f. awning. 2 NAUT. sail: sailboat: ~ al tercio, lugsail; ~ cangreja, gaff-sail; de abanico, spritsail; ~ de cruz, square sail; ~ de cuchillo, fore-and-aft sail; ~ latina, lateen sail; ~ mayor, mainsail; hacerse a la ~, largar velas, to set sail; levantar velas, fig. to decamp; recoger velas, fig. to restrain oneself; a toda ~, a velas llenas, full sail.
velación, pl. -ciones f. vigil, watch [keeping awake]. 2 sing.-pl. ECCL. veiling at nuptial mass.
velacho m. NAUT. fore-topsail.
velada f. VELACIÓN 1. 2 social evening; soirée.
velador, -ra m.-f. watcher, guard, guardian. 2 wooden candlestick. 3 small table with one foot.
veladura f. PAINT. glaze, velatura.
velaje, velamen m. NAUT. canvas, sails [of a ship].
1) **velar** adj. PHONET. velar.
2) **velar** intr. to watch, keep vigil, stay up. 2 to work at night. 3 [with por] to watch over, protect, see to. 4 NAUT. [of rocks, etc.] to stick out of the water. 5 intr.-tr. ECCL. to assist by turns before the Holy Sacrament. 6 tr. to watch [the sick or the dead]. 7 to watch, observe. 8 to veil. 9 PAINT. to glaze. 10 PHOT. to fog. 11 ref. to veil oneself, become veiled. 12 PHOT. to fog [become fogged].
velarte m. broadcloth.
velatorio m. wake [beside a dead body].
veleidad f. caprice, whim. 2 inconstancy, fickleness.
veleidoso, -sa adj. capricious, inconstant, fickle.
velería f. candle shop.

velero, -ra adj. NAUT. swift-sailing. 2 m.-f. tallow chandler. 3 m. sailmaker. 4 NAUT. sailboat, sailer.
veleta f. weathercock, weather vane. 2 streamer [of a lance]. 3 m.-f. fig. weathercock, fickle person.
velete m. thin veil.
velilla f. small candle.
velillo m. dim. small veil.
velis nolis Lat. willy-nilly.
velo m. veil: correr, or echar, un ~ sobre, fig. to draw a veil over. 2 fig. cloud [in the mind]. 3 taking the veil. 4 ANAT. ~ del paladar, velum, soft palate.
velocidad f. velocity; speed; primera ~, AUTO. low gear; segunda ~, AUTO. second; tercera ~, AUTO. high gear; en gran ~, RLY. by express; en pequeña ~, RLY. by freight.
velocípedo m. velocipede.
velódromo m. velodrome.
velomotor m. light motorcycle.
velón m. metal olive-oil lamp.
velorio m. wake, watch [over a dead person].
veloz, pl. -loces adj. fast, fleet, quick, rapid, swift.
veludillo m. VELLUDILLO.
vellido, -da adj. VELLOSO.
vello m. down, soft hair [on the human body]. 2 down, fuzz, pubescence [on plants and fruits].
vellocino m. fleece: ~ de oro, MYTH. Golden Fleece.
vellón m. fleece. 2 unsheared sheepskin. 3 lock of wool. 4 copper and silver alloy. 5 [formerly] copper coin.
vellorita f. BOT. daisy. 2 BOT. primrose, cowslip.
vellosidad f. downiness, hairiness.
vellosilla f. BOT. mouse-ear.
velloso, -sa adj. downy, hairy. 2 BOT. villous, fuzzy.
velludillo m. velveteen.
velludo, -da adj. downy, hairy, shaggy. 2 m. velvet; plush.
vena f. ANAT., BOT. vein. 2 vein [in wood, marble, etc.]. 3 GEOL., MIN. seam, lode. 4 vena or ~ de agua, flow of water underground. 5 poetical inspiration: estar en ~, to be inspired. 6 strain, streak: tener una ~ de loco, to have a strain of madness. 7 darle a uno la ~, to take it into one's head. 8 estar de ~, to be in the mood [for something].
venablo m. javelin, dart: echar venablos, fig. to be furious.
venación f. venerry, hunting.
venado m. deer, stag. 2 deer meat, venison.
venal adj. venous. 2 salable. 3 venal.
venalidad f. venality.
venatorio, -ria adj. venatic.
vencedor, -ra adj. vanquishing, conquering. 2 m.-f. vanquisher, conqueror; victor: salir ~, to win, gain the victory, be the victor.
vencejo m. ORN. black martin, European swift. 2 withe, band, etc., for tying sheaves.
vencer tr. to vanquish, conquer, beat, defeat. 2 to overcome, overpower. 3 to overcome, surmount. 4 to conquer, subdue [passions]. 5 to surpass, outdo, excel. 6 to prevail upon, persuade. 7 to turn, incline [a thing]. 8 intr. COM. to fall due, mature; to expire. 9 to win, be the victor. 10 ref. to control oneself. 11 to incline to a side.
vencetósigo m. BOT. swallowwort.
vencida f. VENCIMIENTO 1. 2 ir de ~, to be nearly beaten, conquered or finished.

vencido, -da *p. p.* of VENCER. *2 adj.* COM. mature, due.

vencimiento *m.* vanquishment, defeat. *2* COM. maturity, coming due; expiration.

venda *f.* bandage. *2* regal fillet.

vendaje *m.* SURG. bandage, dressing.

vendar *tr.* SURG. to bandage. *2* fig. to blind, obfuscate. *3 ~ los ojos,* to blindfold.

vendaval *m.* strong south wind. *2* gale.

vendedor, -ra *adj.* selling. *2 m.-f.* seller. *3 m.* salesman. *4 f.* saleswoman, salesgirl.

vender *tr.* to sell [goods, etc.]. *2* to sell, sell out [betray]. *3 ref.* to sell, be sold, be for sale: *se vende,* for sale. *4* to sell oneself. *5* to give oneself away, betray one's feelings, etc. *6* fig. venderse caro, to be seldom seen, be quite a stranger. *7* fig. *venderse por,* to pretend to be.

vendí, *pl.* **-díes** *m.* COM. certificate of sale.

vendible *adj.* salable, vendible, marketable.

vendimia *f.* vintage, grape-gathering. *2* fig. rich profit.

vendimiador, -ra *m.-f.* vintager, grape-gatherer.

vendimiar *tr.* to gather [grapes]. *2* fig. to reap [an unjust profit]. *3* coll. to kill, murder.

vendré, vendría, etc. *irr.* V. VENIR.

venduta *f.* (Am.) auction, public sale.

Venecia *f. pr. n.* GEOG. Venice [city].

veneciano, -na *adj.* Venetian.

veneno *m.* poison, venom. *2* fig. venom [malignity].

venenosidad *f.* poisonousness, venomousness.

venenoso, -sa *adj.* poisonous, venomous, baneful.

venera *f.* pilgrim's scallop shell. *2* badge of a military order. *3* spring [of water].

venerable *adj.* venerable.

veneración *f.* veneration. *2* worship.

venerando, -da *adj.* venerable.

venerar *tr.* to venerate. *2* ECCL. to worship.

venéreo, -a *adj.* venereal. *2 m.* venereal disease.

venero *m.* spring [of water]. *2* fig. source, origin. *3* MIN. bed, lode. *4* hour mark [on sundial].

venezolano, -na *adj.-s.* Venezuelan.

vengador, -ra *adj.* avenging, revenging. *2 m.-f.* avenger, revenger.

venganza *f.* vengeance, revenge.

vengar *tr.* to avenge. *2 ref.* to avenge oneself, to take revenge.

vengativo, -va *adj.* revengeful, vindictive.

vengo, venga, etc. V. VENIR.

venia *f.* permission, leave. *2* bow [with the head]. *3* pardon, forgiveness.

venial *adj.* venial.

venida *f.* coming, arrival. *2* return. *3* flood, freshet. *4* FENC. attack. *5* fig. impetuosity, rashness.

venidero, -ra *adj.* coming, future: *en lo ~,* for the future, in future. *2 m. pl.* successors, posterity.

venido, -da *adj.* come: *bien ~,* welcome.

venir *intr.* to come [move hitherward; approach; be the next; appear; arise, result, follow; happen]: *el mes que viene,* next month. *2* to come [in order or succession]. *3* to come [to the mind], occur. *4* [of a desire, pain, etc.] to be felt: *me vino el deseo de,* I felt the desire of. *5 ~ bien,* to fit, suit, become; *~ mal,* not to fit, suit or become. *6 esto no me va ni me viene,* that does not concern or affect me. *7 vino a conseguir lo que se proponía,* he ended by attaining his ends; *esto viene a pesar dos libras,* this must weigh about two pounds. *8 ~ a las manos,* to come to blows. *9 ~ al caso,* to be relevant. *10 ~ a menos,* to decay, decline. *11 ~ al pelo, ~ de perilla,* to be

opportune. *12 ~ en,* to decide, resolve upon. *13 ~ en conocimiento,* to come to know. *14 ~ sobre,* to fall upon. *15 ¿a qué viene eso?,* what is the purpose of that? *16 en lo por ~,* hereafter, for the future. *17 venga lo que viniere,* come what will. *18 intr.-ref.* to yield, submit, agree. *19 ref.* to come, to return. *20* [of bread, wine] to ferment. *21 venirse abajo, a tierra,* to fall, collapse. *22 venirse al suelo,* to fall to the ground. ‖ CONJUG.: INDIC. Pres.: *vengo, vienes, viene, venimos, venís, vienen.* | Pret.: *vine, viniste,* etc. | Fut.: *vendré, vendrás,* etc. | COND.: *vendría, vendrías,* etc. | SUBJ. Pres.: *venga, vengas,* etc. | Imperf.: *viniera, vinieras,* etc., or *viniese, vinieses,* etc. | Fut.: *viniere, vinieres,* etc. | IMPER.: *ven, venga; vengamos, venid, vengan.* | PAST. P.: *venido.* | GER.: *viniendo.*

venoso, -sa *adj.* venous. *2* veiny, veined.

venta *f.* sale, selling: *~ al por mayor,* wholesale; *~ al por menor,* retail sale, retailing; *~ pública,* public auction sale; *de ~, en ~,* for sale. *2* roadside inn.

ventada *f.* blast, gust of wind.

ventaja *f.* advantage. *2* odds [given at play]. *3* gain, profit. *4* extra pay.

ventajoso, -sa *adj.* advantageous. *2* profitable.

ventalla *f.* MACH. valve. *2* BOT. valve [of a pod].

ventana *f.* window; casement; sash: *~ de guillotina,* sash window. *2* ANAT. fenestra. *3 ~ de la nariz,* nostril.

ventanaje *m.* ARCH. fenestration.

ventanal *m.* large window, church window.

ventanear *intr.* coll. to be often at the window.

ventanico *m.* VENTANILLO.

ventanilla *f. dim.* small window. *2* window [of a carriage, ticket office, bank teller, etc.], wicket. *3 ~ de la nariz,* nostril.

ventanillo *m. dim.* small window. *2* peephole, wicket [in a door].

ventano *m.* small window.

ventarrón *m.* stiff wind, gale.

ventear *impers.* [of the wind] to blow. *2 tr.* [of animals] to sniff, scent, wind. *3* fig. to investigate, inquire. *4* to air [expose to the wind]. *5 ref.* to become spoiled in the air. *6* coll. to break wind.

ventero, -ra *adj.* scenting [dog]. *2 m.-f.* roadside innkeeper.

ventilación *f.* ventilation. *2* discussion, elucidation.

ventilador *m.* ventilator. *2* ventilating fan.

ventilar *tr.* to air, ventilate. *2* to discuss, clear up, elucidate.

ventisca *f.* snowstorm, blizzard, snowdrift.

ventiscar *impers.* to snow and blow.

ventisquear *impers.* VENTISCAR.

ventisquero *m.* VENTISCA. *2* height in a mountain most exposed to snowstorms. *3* snowdrift, glacier.

ventolera *f.* gust of wind. *2* pinwheel [toy]. *3* coll. vanity, haughtiness. *4* coll. whim, sudden fancy.

ventolina *f.* NAUT. light variable wind.

ventor, -ra *adj.-m.* scenting, pointer [dog].

ventorrero *m.* high, windy place.

ventorrillo *m.* small roadside inn. *2* lunchhouse in the country.

ventorro *m.* VENTORRILLO 1.

ventosa *f.* vent, air hole. *2* ZOOL. sucker, sucking disk. *3* SURG. cupping; cupping glass.

ventosear *intr.-ref.* to break wind.

ventosidad *f.* flatulence, windiness. *2* wind [in intestines or being expelled].

ventoso, -sa *adj.* windy, wind-swept. *2* windy [day, weather]. *3* flatulent.
ventral *adj.* ventral.
ventrecha *f.* belly [of fishes].
ventregada *f.* litter, brood. *2* rush [of things].
ventrera *f.* bellyband.
ventricular *adj.* ventricular.
ventrículo *m.* ANAT. ZOOL. ventricle.
ventrílocuo, -cua *m.-f.* ventriloquist.
ventriloquia *f.* ventriloquism.
ventrudo, -da *adj.* big-bellied.
ventura *f.* happiness. *2* luck, fortune. *3* chance, hazard; risk: *a la* ~, at a venture, at hazard; *por* ~, perhaps. *4 buena* ~, BUENAVENTURA.
venturado, -da *adj.* VENTUROSO.
venturanza *f.* happiness.
venturero, -ra *adj.* taking occasional jobs.
venturoso -sa *adj.* happy, lucky, fortunate.
Venus *m.* ASTR. Venus. *2 f.* MYTH. & fig. Venus. *3* (not cap.) venery.
venustez, venustidad *f.* beauty, gracefulness.
venusto, -ta *adj.* beautiful, graceful.
veo, vea, etc. *irr.* V. VER.
1) **ver** *m.* sight, sense of sight. *2* aspect, appearance, look, looks: *tener buen* ~, to be goodlooking, to have a good appearance. *3* opinion, way of thinking; *a mi* ~, in my opinion.
2) **ver** *tr.* to see [in practically every sense]: ~ *las estrellas,* fig. to see stars; ~ *visiones,* to see things, to dream; *hacer* ~, to show, demonstrate; *a más* ~, *hasta más* ~, coll. so long; *a* ~, *veamos,* let's see. *2* to look, look at: *vea usted esto,* look at this. *3* LAW to try [a case]. *4* ~ *venir,* fig. to wait and see. *5* ~ *venir a uno,* fig. to see what [someone] is up to. *6 no poder* ~, not to be able to bear; to detest. *7 intr.* ~ *de,* to try to. *8 ref.* to be seen. *9* to be obvious. *10* to see oneself. *11* to be: *verse obligado a,* to be obliged to. *12 verse con,* to see, meet, have a talk with. *13 véase,* see [in references]. *14 ya se ve,* of course, certainly. ‖ CONJUG.: INDIC. Pres.: *veo, ves, ve; vemos, veis, ven.* | Imperf.: *veía, veías,* etc. | Pret.: *vi, viste,* etc. | Fut.: *veré, verás,* etc. | COND.: *vería, verías,* etc. | SUBJ. Pres.: *vea, veas, vea,* etc. | Imperf.: *viera, vieras,* etc., or *viese, vieses,* etc. | Fut.: *viere, vieres,* etc. | IMPER.: *ve, vea; veamos, ved, vean.* | PAST. P.: *visto.* | GER.: *viendo.*
vera *f.* border, side: *a la* ~ *de,* near, beside.
veracidad *f.* veracity, truthfulness.
veranada *f.* summer season [for pasturing].
veranadero *m.* summer pasture.
veranda *f.* veranda(h.
veraneante *m.-f.* summer resident, summer vacationist.
veranear *intr.* to summer.
veraneo *m.* summering, summer vacation.
veraniego, -ga *adj.* [pertaining to] summer. *2* sickly in summer. *3* fig. light, unimportant.
veranillo *m.* ~ *de San Martín,* Indian summer.
verano *m.* summer [season].
veras *f.* truth, reality; earnestness: *de* ~, real, genuine; indeed, really; in earnest.
veratro *m.* BOT. white hellebore.
veraz *adj.* veracious, truthful.
verba *f.* loquacity, talkativeness.
verbal *adj.* verbal, oral. *2* GRAM. verbal.
verbalismo *m.* verbalism.
verbasco *m.* BOT. mullein, great mullein.
verbena *f.* BOT. verbena, vervain. *2* night festival on the eve of a saint's day.
verbenáceo, -a *adj.* BOT. verbenaceous.

verbenear *intr.* HORMIGUEAR.
verbigracia *adv.* for example, for instance.
Verbo *m. pr. n.* THEOL. Word [second person of the Trinity].
verbo *m.* word. *2* GRAM. verb.
verborrea *f.* excessive verbosity.
verbosidad *f.* verbosity, wordiness.
verboso, -sa *adj.* verbose, wordy.
verdad *f.* truth: *decir cuatro verdades,* to give a piece of one's mind; *faltar a la* ~, to lie; *ser* ~, to be true; *a la* ~, *en* ~, in truth, truly, really; *¿no es* ~*?, ¿verdad?,* isn't that so?
verdaderamente *adv.* truly, really; indeed.
verdadero, -ra *adj.* true. *2* real, genuine; actual. *3* veracious, truthful.
verdal *adj.* green-coloured even when ripe [fruit].
verdasca *f.* switch, twig [cut from tree].
vesdascazo *m.* blow with a switch.
verde *adj.* green [green-coloured]; verdant; unripe, sour]: *están verdes,* fig. sour grapes; *poner* ~, fig. to abuse, rake over the coals. *2* inmature. *3* young [years]. *4* gay, merry [old man; widow]. *5* risky, off-colour. *6 m.* green [colour]. *7* green barley or grass [given to horses]. *8* verdure, foliage.
verdear *intr.* to show green. *2* to be greenish. *3* [of fields, trees, etc.]. to green [become green].
verdeceledón *m.* celadon, celadon green.
verdecer *intr.* VERDEAR 3.
verdegay *adj.* light-green. *2 m.* light green.
verdeguear *intr.* VERDEAR.
verdemar *adj.* sea-green. *2 m.* sea green.
verderol, verderón *m.* ORN. green-finch. *2* ZOOL. cockle [mollusk].
verdete *m.* verdigris.
verdín *m.* verdure, fresh greenness [of plants]. *2* pond scum. *3* green mould. *4* verdigris.
verdinegro, -gra *adj.* dark green.
verdiseco, -ca *adj.* half dry [plant].
verdolaga *f.* BOT. purslane.
verdor *m.* greenness, green colour. *2* verdure, verdancy [of vegetation]. *3* freshness, vigour. *4 pl.* youth, young days.
verdoso, -sa *adj.* greenish.
verdoyo *m.* pond scum; green mould.
verdugado *m.* hoopskirt, farthingale.
verdugo *m.* executioner, hangman. *2* fig. cruel punisher or tormenter. *3* shoot, sucker [of a tree]. *4* slender estoc or rapier. *5* scourge, lash, switch. *6* wale, weal, welt. *7* VERDUGADO.
verdugón *m.* shoot, sucker [of a tree]. *2* wale, weal, welt.
verduguillo *m.* dim. of VERDUGO. *2* narrow razor.
verdulera *f.* greengrocer [woman]. *2* fig. coarse woman, fishwife.
verdulería *f.* greengrocery, greengrocer's shop.
verdulero *m.* greengrocer.
verdura *f.* greenness, green colour. *2* verdure, verdancy. *3* PAINT. foliage. *4 sing.-pl.* greens, vegetables [as food].
verdusco, -ca *adj.* dark greenish.
verecundia *f.* shame, modesty, bashfulness.
verecundo, -da *adj.* bashful, modest.
vereda *f.* path, footpath: *meter por* ~, fig. to set aright.
veredicto *m.* verdict.
verga *f.* NAUT. yard. *2* penis. *3* steel bow [of a crossbow].
vergajazo *m.* slash or blow with a pizzle.
vergajo *m.* pizzle [used as a flogging instrument].
vergel *f.* flower and fruit garden.

vergonzante *adj.* bashful, shamefaced.
vergonzoso, -sa *adj.* shameful, disgraceful, scandalous. 2 private [parts]. *3 m.-f.* bashful person.
vergüenza *f.* shame [feeling]; bashfulness, shyness, confusion; modesty: *darse* ~, *darle a uno* ~, to be ashamed; to be shy. 2 shame, disgrace; scandal: *ser una* ~, to be a shame, to be a scandal. *3* honour, self-respect, dignity. *4 no tener* ~, to be shameless, be a rascal. *5 sacar a la* ~, to put in the pillory. *6 pl.* privy parts.
vericueto *m.* rough, pathless place.
verídico, -ca *adj.* truthful, veridical.
verificación *f.* verification. 2 test [of gas meter, etc.]. *3* fulfilment, coming true.
verificar *tr.* to verify [establish the truth of]. 2 to check; to test [a gas meter, etc.]. *3* to accomplish, carry out. *4 ref.* to be accomplished; to take place. *5* to come true.
verija *f.* pubes, region of the genitals.
veril *m.* NAUT. edge of a sandbank or shoal.
verisímil *adj.* VEROSÍMIL.
verismo *m.* verism.
verja *f.* gate [made of a grating]; window grate or grating. 2 iron railing [enclosure].
vermicida *adj.* vermicidal. *2 m.* vermicide.
vermicular *adj.* vermicular.
vermiforme *adj.* vermiform.
vermífugo, -ga *adj.* vermifugal. *2 m.* vermifuge.
vermut *m.* vermouth.
vernáculo, -la *adj.* vernacular.
vernal *adj.* vernal: *equinoccio* ~, vernal equinox.
vernier *m.* vernier.
vero *m.* marten [fur]. *2 pl.* HER. vair.
veronal *m.* veronal.
verónica *f.* BOT. veronica. 2 BULLF. waiting for bull's attack with cape extended in both hands.
verosímil *adj.* likely, probable, credible, verisimilar.
verosimilitud *f.* verisimilitude, probability.
verraco *m.* boar [male uncastrated pig].
verraquear *intr.* to grunt, grumble. 2 [of a child] to cry long and loud.
verraquera *f.* violent crying [of a child]. 2 (Am.) drunkenness.
verriondo, -da *adj.* rutting, in heat [animal].
verruga *f.* wart. 2 coll. nuisance.
verrugoso, -sa *adj.* warty.
versado, -da *adj.* versed, conversant.
versal *adj.-f.* PRINT. capital [letter].
versalita *adj.-f.* PRINT. small capital [letter].
Versalles *m. pr. n.* GEOG. Versailles.
versar *intr.* to turn, go around. *2* ~ *acerca de* or *sobre*, to deal with, treat of or on. *3 ref.* to become versed.
versátil *adj.* versatile, fickle. 2 BOT., ZOOL. versatile.
versatilidad *f.* versatility, fickleness. 2 BOT., ZOOL versatileness.
versículo *m.* ECCL. verse, versicle.
versificación *f.* versification.
versificador, -ra *m.-f.* versifier, verse maker.
versificar *tr.-intr.* to versify.
versión *f.* version.
versista *m.-f.* versifier; poetaster.
verso *adj.* TRIG. versed. *2 m.* verse, poem. *3* verse, line: ~ *blanco*, *libre* or *suelto*, blank verse. *4* ECCL. verse, versicle.
versta *f.* verst.
vértebra *f.* ANAT. vertebra.
vertebrado, -da *adj.* vertebrate, vertebrated. *2 m.* ZOOL. vertebrate.

vertebral *adj.* vertebral.
vertedera *f.* AGR. mouldboard [of a plough].
vertedero *m.* sink; dumping place. 2 spillway.
vertedor *m.* spillway, drain. 2 grocer's scoop. *3* NAUT. boat scoop.
verter *tr.* to pour. 2 to spill, shed. *3* to cast, shed [light, etc.]. *4* to empty, dump. *5* to translate. *6* to emit, utter [opinions, etc.]. *7 intr.* [of a stream] to run, flow. *8 ref.* to spill, flow, empty. ‖ CONJUG. like *entender*.
vertible *adj.* changeable.
vertical *adj.* vertical. *2 f.* vertical line. *3 m.* ASTR. vertical circle.
verticalidad *f.* verticality.
vértice *m.* vertex, apex. 2 GEOM., ANAT. vertex.
verticilado, -da *adj.* BOT. verticillate.
verticilo *m.* BOT. verticil, whorl.
vertiente *adj.* pouring, flowing. *2 f.* GEOG. slope [of a continent, etc.]. *3* ARCH. slope [of a roof].
vertiginoso, -sa *adj.* vertiginous, dizzy, giddy. 2 rapid.
vértigo *m.* vertigo, dizziness, giddiness. 2 fig. abnormally hurried activity. *3* fit of insanity.
vesania *f.* vesania, insanity.
vesánico, -ca *adj.* insane. *2 m.-f.* insane person.
vesicante *adj.-m.* vesicant, vesicatory.
vesícula *f.* vesicle, small blister. 2 ANAT., BOT., ZOOL. vesicle: ~ *biliar*, gall bladder.
Véspero *m.* Vesper, evening star.
vespertino, -na *adj.* vespertine, evening.
Vesta *f. pr. n.* MYTH. Vesta.
vestal *adj.-f.* vestal.
veste *f.* poet. dress, clothing.
Vestfalia *f. pr. n.* GEOG. Westphalia.
vestibular *adj.* ANAT. vestibular.
vestíbulo *m.* vestibule, hall, lobby. 2 ANAT. vestibule.
vestido *m.* dress, clothes, garb, costume, suit: ~ *de etiqueta*, evening dress; ~ *de noche*, evening gown. 2 fig. dress, vesture, covering.
vestidura *f.* clothing, vesture. *2 pl.* ECCL. vestiments.
vestigio *m.* vestige, trace, sign. *2 pl.* ruins, remains.
vestiglo *m.* horrible monster.
vestimenta *f.* VESTIDO. *2 pl.* VESTIDURAS.
vestir *tr.* to clothe, dress, garb, attire.'*2* to make clothes for. *3* to clothe, cover, deck, adorn. *4* to cloak, disguise. *5* to put on; to wear [a dress or garment]. *6 intr.* to dress, be dressed [in a specified way]: ~ *de negro*, to dress in black. *7* [of a garment, material, colour] to be fit for dressing, give a well-dressed appearance. *8 ref.* to dress, dress oneself. *9* fig. to be clothed or covered. *10* to assume an air. ‖ CONJUG. like *servir*.
vestuario *m.* apparel, wardrobe, clothes, dress. 2 MIL. clothing, uniform. *3* THEAT. dressing rooms.
Vesubio *m. pr. n.* GEOG. Vesuvius.
veta *m.* GEOL. vein. 2 MIN. vein, lode. *3* vein [in wood or stone]. *4* streak, stripe.
vetar *tr.* to veto, put one's veto on.
veteado, -da *adj.* veined, streaked, streaky.
vetear *tr.* to vein, streak, variegate with stripes.
veterano, -na *adj.-n.* veteran.
veterinaria *f.* veterinary medicine.
veterinario *m.* veterinarian, veterinary.
veto *m.* veto.
vetustez *f.* antiquity, great age.
vetusto, -ta *adj.* very ancient or old.
vez, *pl.* **veces** *f.* turn [in order or alternation]: *le llegó la* ~, it was his turn; *a su* ~, in turn, in his,

her, etc., turn; on his, her, etc., part. *2* time [instance, occasion]: *a la* ~, at one time, at the same time; *a la* ~ *que*, while; *alguna* ~, sometimes; [in questions] ever; *alguna*, or *una, que otra* ~, *tal cual* ~, once in a while; *a veces*, sometimes; *cada* ~, every time; *cada* ~ *más*, more and more; *de una* ~, at once; *una* ~ *para siempre*, once for all; *de* ~ *en cuando*, from time to time; *dos veces mayor que*, twice as large as; *otra* ~, again; some other time; *pocas*, or *raras veces*, seldom, rarely; *tal* ~, perhaps, maybe; *una* ~, once; *una* ~ *hecho esto*, after doing this; *una* ~ *que*, since, inasmuch as. *3* stead, place: *en* ~ *de*, instead of; in place of. *4 pl. hacer las veces de*, to serve as, take the place of.

vi *pret.* of VER.

vía *f.* path, road, way, street: ~ *aérea*, airway; ~ *Apia*, Appian Way; ~ *férrea*, railway, railroad; ~ *pública*, public way, street, thoroughfare; *vías de comunicación*, communications; *por la* ~ *de*, vía. *2* RLY. track: *ancho de* ~, gauge; ~ *muerta*, sidetrack. *3* ANAT. duct. *4* CHEM. process: ~ *húmeda*, wet process. *5* way, manner: *por* ~ *de*, by way of, as. *6* NAUT. ~ *de agua*, leak. *7* LAW ~ *ejecutiva*, seizure, attachment. *8* ASTR. *Vía Láctea*, Milky Way. *9* MED. *por* ~ *bucal*, orally. *10 pl.* ANAT. tract: *vías urinarias*, urinary tract. *11 estar en vías de*, to be on the process of, to be on the way to.

viabilidad *f.* viability. *2* feasibility, practicability.

viable *adj.* viable. *2* feasible, practicable.

Vía Crucis *m.* Via Crucis, way of the Cross.

viaducto *m.* viaduct.

viajante *adj.* travelling. *2 m.* traveller, commercial traveller.

viajar *intr.* to travel, journey, voyage.

viajata *f.* coll. long walk, excursion.

viaje *m.* travel, journey, voyage, trip: ~ *de ida y vuelta*, ~ *redondo*, round trip; *de* ~, travelling; *¡buen* ~!, bon voyage! *2* travel book. *4* ARCH. obliquity.

viajero, -ra *adj.* travelling [that travels]. *2 m.-f.* traveller; passenger.

vial *adj.* pertaining to roads or streets. *2 m.* avenue, lane [way among trees or shrubs].

vialidad *f.* road service, street service.

vianda *f. sing. & pl.* food, viands.

viandante *m.-f.* traveller, itinerant. *2* tramp.

viaticar *tr.* ECCL. to administer the viaticum to.

viático *m.* viaticum [travel allowance]. *2* ECCL. viaticum.

víbora *f.* ZOOL. viper. *2* fig. viper [person].

viborezno, -na *adj.* viperine. *2 m.* young viper.

vibración *f.* vibration, quivering. *2* PHYS. vibration.

vibrante *adj.* vibrant. *2* PHONET. thrilled [consonant].

vibrar *tr.* to vibrate. *2* to roll [utter with a thrill]. *3 intr.* to vibrate, quiver.

vibrátil *adj.* vibratile.

vibratorio, -ria *adj.* vibratory.

vibrión *m.* BACT. vibrion.

viburno *m.* BOT. viburnum.

vicaría *f.* vicarship. *2* vicarage.

vicario, -ria *m.-f.* vicar [deputy, substitute].

vicealmirante *m.* vice-admiral.

vicecanciller *m.* vice-chancellor.

vicecónsul *m.* vice-consul.

vicenal *adj.* vicennial.

Vicente *m. pr. n.* Vincent.

vicepresidencia *f.* vice-presidency.

vicepresidente, -ta *m.-f.* vice-president. *2 f.* wife of a vice-president.

vicerrector *m.* vice-rector.

vicesecretario, -ria *m.-f.* vice-secretary.

vicésimo, -ma *adj.-m.* twentieth.

vicetesorero, -ra *m.-f.* assistant treasurer.

viceversa *adv.* vice versa. *2 m.* illogical thing.

viciado, -da *p. p.* of VICIAR. *2* vitiated; foul.

viciar *tr.* to vitiate, corrupt, deprave. *2* to adulterate. *3* to vitiate, nullify. *4* to pervert, miscontrue. *5 ref.* to become vitiated. *6* to give oneself up to vice. *7* to contract a habit or a bad habit.

vicio *m.* vice [evil conduct, wickedness, corruption, etc.]. *2* vice, defect. *3* habit, bad habit. *4* overindulgence, pampering. *5* AGR. excessive luxuriance. *6* warping [in boards, etc.]. *7 quejarse de* ~, to complain without reason, out of habit.

vicioso, -sa *adj.* vicious [of the nature of vice; addicted to vice; faulty]. *2* spoiled [child]. *3* abundant, luxuriant. *4 m.-f.* vicious person.

vicisitud *f.* vicissitude.

víctima *f.* victim.

victo *m.* daily sustenance.

¡víctor! *interj.-m.* ¡VÍTOR!

victorear *tr.* VITOREAR.

victoria *f.* victory. *2* victoria [carriage]. *3* BOT. ~ *regia*, victoria, victoria regia.

victoriano, -na *adj.* Victorian.

victorioso, -sa *adj.* victorious.

vicuña *f.* vicuña [animal; wool; fabric].

vid *f.* BOT. vine, grapevine.

vida *f.* life [in practically every sense]: ~ *airada*, loose life, prostitution; ~ *de perros*, dog's life; ~ *mía, mi* ~, my life, dearest; *dar mala* ~ *a*, to treat ill; *darse buena* ~, to live comfortably; *dar* ~, to give life, to enliven; *jugarse la* ~, to take one's life in one's hand; *tener siete vidas como los gatos*, to bear a charmed life; *con* ~, in life, alive, living; *de por* ~, for life; *en* ~, while living, during life; *en la* ~, *en mi [tu, su]* ~, never; *¡por* ~!, by Jove! *2* activity, animation, liveliness. *3* living, livelihood: *ganarse la* ~, to earn one's living.

vide *Lat.* vide, see [in references].

vidente *adj.* seeing, sighted [not blind]. *2 m.-f.* sighted person. *3* seer; prophet.

vidita *f.* coll. dearest, darling.

vidriado, -da *adj.* glazed [pottery]. *2 m.* glazing [of pottery]. *3* glazed pottery.

vidriar *tr.* to glaze [pottery]. *2 ref.* to become glassy or brittle.

vidriera *f.* glass window, glass door, French window, glass partition. *2* (Am.) shopwindow.

vidriería *f.* glassworks. *2* glass shop. *3* glassware.

vidriero *m.* glassworker. *2* glazier. *3* glass dealer.

vidrio *m.* glass [substance, article made of glass]: ~ *de color*, stained glass; ~ *deslustrado*, ground glass; ~ *tallado*, cut glass. *2* pane, glass pane [of window or door].

vidriosidad *f.* vitreousness; brittleness. *2* touchiness.

vidrioso, -sa *adj.* brittle [as glass]. *2* slippery [from frost]. *3* glassy [eye]. *4* touchy.

vidueño, viduño *m.* variety or kind of grapevine.

viejecito, -ta *adj.* old, oldish. *2 m.-f.* old man, old woman.

viejo, -ja *adj.* old. *2* aged. *3* ancient, antique. *4* old-fashioned. *5 m.* old man: ~ *verde*, gay old man, old rake. *6 f.* old woman.

Viena *f. pr. n.* GEOG. Vienna.

viene, vienes, vienen *irr.* V. VENIR.

vienés, -sa *adj.-n.* Viennese.
vientecillo *m. dim.* breeze, light wind.
viento *m.* wind: *corren malos vientos*, fig. things are not favourable; *ir ~ en popa*, to sail before the wind; fig. to be flourishing; *a los cuatro vientos*, to the four winds; *como el ~*, swiftly; *contra ~ y marea*, fig. against all odds. 2 smell, sense of smell [of some animals]. 3 ARTIL. windage. 4 guy [rope or chain].
vientre *m.* belly, paunch, venter. 2 bowels. 3 womb.
viernes, *pl.* **-nes** *m.* Friday: *Viernes Santo*, Good Friday; *comer de ~*, to fast, abstain from meat.
vierteaguas, *pl.* **-guas** *m.* ARCH. flashing.
vierto, vierta, etc., *irr.* V. VERTER.
viga *f.* beam, girder, joist, baulk, rafter: *~ maestra*, summer.
vigencia *f.* [of a law, a custom, etc.] state of being in force, in use.
vigente *adj.* in force, in use [law custom, etc.].
vigésimo, -ma *adj.-m.* twentieth.
vigía *m.-f.* watch, lookout [man]. 2 *f.* watchtower, lookout. 3 NAUT. rock, shoal.
vigilancia *f.* vigilance, watchfulness. 2 watch watching, survellance.
vigilante *adj.* vigilant, watchful, careful. 2 *m.* watch, watchman, guard.
vigilar *intr.* to watch, keep guard, take or have care. 2 *tr.* to watch over, keep guard on; look out, for, take or have care of.
vigilia *f.* vigil, wakefulness. 2 night study. 3 eve. 4 ECCL. vigil. 5 ECCL. abstinence of meat.
vigor *m.* vigour, vigor. 2 force, effect [of a law]: *entrar en ~*, to go into effect.
vigorizador, -ra *adj.* invigorating. 2 *m.* invigorant, tonic.
vigorizar *tr.* to invigorate; to strengthen. 2 *ref.* to invigorate [gain vigour].
vigoroso, -sa *adj.* vigorous; lusty.
viguería *f.* beams or girders [of a building].
vigués, -sa *adj.-n.* of Vigo.
vigueta *f. dim.* small beam or joist.
vihuela *f.* MUS. a kind of guitar.
vil *adj.* vile, worthless, base, low, despicable. 2 *m.-f.* treacherous person.
vilano *m.* BOT. pappus. 2 BOT. thistle flower.
vileza *f.* vileness, baseness; infamy.
vilipendiar *tr.* to vilipend, revile, denigrate.
vilipendio *m.* contempt, revilement. 2 opprobium.
vilmente *adj.* vilely, basely, infamously.
vilo (en) *adv.* suspended, in the air. 2 in suspense.
vilordo, -da *adj.* slow, lazy, slothful.
vilorta *f.* hoop made of a twisted twig. 2 MACH. washer. 3 game like lacrosse.
vilorto *m.* VILORTA 1. 2 BOT. a kind of clematis.
villa *f.* villa [country residence]. 2 town, market town. 3 town council.
Villadiego *pr. n.* of a Spanish town: *coger* or *tomar las de ~*, to decamp, bolt, go away.
villaje *m.* village.
villanada *f.* infamy, despicable act.
villanaje *m.* villeinage, villenage. 2 peasantry.
villancico *m.* Christmas carol.
villanesco, -ca *adj.* rustic.
villanía *f.* status of a villain; humble birth. 2 villainy, infamy, despicable act. 3 fig. vile remark.
villano, -na *adj.* of humble birth. 2 rustic, impolite. 3 villainous, base, despicable. 4 *m.-f.* villain, villein; rustic, peasant. 5 knave, scoundrel.

villar *m.* village.
villorrio *m.* small village, mean village.
vinagre *m.* vinegar. 2 fig. grouch.
vinagrera *f.* vinegar cruet or caster. 2 BOT. sorrel. 3 (Am.) heartburn. 4 *pl.* casters, cruet stand.
vinagrero, -ra *m.-f.* vinegarer.
vinagreta *f.* COOK. vinaigrette sauce.
vinagrillo *m.* toilet vinegar.
vinagroso, -sa *adj.* vinegarish, vinegary.
vinajera *f.* ECCL. cruet [for wine or water in the mass]. 2 *pl.* ECCL. set of two cruets and a tray.
vinatería *f.* wine trade. 2 wine shop.
vinatero, -ra *adj.* [pertaining to] wine. 2 *m.* vintner, wine merchant.
vinaza *f.* wine drawn from lees.
vincapervinca *f.* BOT. periwinkle.
vinculación *f.* tying, attaching [esp. with immaterial bonds]. 2 LAW entailment.
vincular *tr.* to tie, attach [esp. with immaterial bonds]. 2 to ground, found [hopes, etc.]. 3 LAW to entail.
vínculo *m.* vinculum, tie, bond. 2 LAW entail.
vindicación *f.* vindication. 2 revenge.
vindicar *tr.* to vindicate [defend, justify]. 2 to avenge. 3 LAW to vindicate.
vindicativo, -va *adj.* vindicative. 2 vindictive.
vindicta *f.* revenge. 2 *~ pública*, public punishment, censure of public opinion.
vine, etc. *irr.* V. VENIR.
vínico, -ca *adj.* vinic.
vinícola *adj.* wine; vinegrowing.
vinicultor, -ra *m.-f.* viniculturist.
vinicultura *f.* viniculture, wine-making.
viniera, viniese, etc. *irr.* V. VENIR.
vinilo *m.* CHEM. vinyl.
vinillo *m. dim.* weak wine, light wine.
vino *m.* wine: *~ de mesa*, *~ de pasto*, table wine; *~ de postre*, or *generoso*, strong old wine; *~ rancio*, fine old wine; *~ tinto*, red wine; *tener mal ~*, to be a quarrelsome drunk.
vinolencia *f.* excessive use of wine.
vinolento, -ta *adj.* too fond of wine.
vinoso, -sa *adj.* vinous.
viña *f.* vineyard: *ser una ~*, fig. to be a mine.
viñador *m.* vinegrower.
viñedo *m.* vineyard.
viñeta *f.* PRINT. vignette.
viola *f.* MUS. viola. 2 BOT. violet. 3 *m.-f.* MUS. viola player.
violáceo, -a *adj.* violaceous.
violación *f.* violation.
violado, -da *adj.* violaceous [of violet colour]. 2 *m.* violet [colour].
1) **violar** *m.* patch or bed of violets.
2) **violar** *tr.* to violate. 2 to spoil, tarnish.
violencia *f.* violence. 2 compulsion. 3 constraint. 4 rape.
violentar *tr.* to do violence to. 2 to break, break into. 3 to strain, distort. 4 *ref.* to force oneself.
violento, -ta *adj.* violent. 2 forced, unnatural, strained. 3 constrained, embarrassed, ill at ease.
violeta *f.* BOT. violet. 2 violet [colour]. 3 *adj.* violet, violet coloured.
violetera *f.* violet seller [woman or girl].
violetero *m.* small vase for violets.
violín *m.* MUS. violin, fiddle. 2 violin, violin player. 3 BILL. bridge, cue rest.
violinista *m.-f.* violinist.
violón *m.* MUS. bass viol: *tocar el ~*, coll. to do something nonsensical. 2 bass viol player.

violoncelo *m.* VIOLONCHELO.
violonchelista *m.-f.* violoncellist.
violonchelo *m.* MUS. violoncello.
viperino, -na *adj.* viperine. 2 viperish, viperous.
vira *f.* vire [arrow]. 2 welt [of a shoe].
virada *f.* NAUT. tack, tacking. 2 VIRAJE.
virador *m.* PHOT. toning bath. 2 NAUT. viol.
virago *f.* mannish woman.
viraje *m.* PHOT. toning. 2 AUTO. turn, turning.
virar *tr.* PHOT. to tone. 2 NAUT. to turn [the capstan]. 3 *tr.-intr.* NAUT. to tack, veer. 4 *intr.* AUTO. to turn.
virazón *f.* sea breeze.
virgen *adj.-n.* virgin. 2 *f. pr. n.* Virgin [Mary]: *la Santísima Virgen*, the Blessed Virgin.
virgiliano, -na *adj.* Virgilian.
Virgilio *m. pr. n.* Virgil.
virginal *adj.* virginal, virgin. 2 *m.* MUS. virginal.
virgíneo, -a *adj.* virginal.
virginiano, -na *adj.-n.* Virginian.
virginidad *f.* virginity.
virgo *m.* virginity. 2 (cap.) ASTR. Virgo.
vírgula *f.* short dash or line.
viril *adj.* virile. 2 manly. 3 *m.* clear glass [for protecting something]. 4 ECCL. small monstrance with a larger one.
virilidad *f.* virility. 2 manhood.
virola *f.* ferrule [ring]. 2 check ring on a goad.
virolento, -ta *adj.* having smallpox. 2 pockmarked. 7 *m.-f.* person with smallpox.
virote *m.* bolt [arrow]. 2 coll. solemn, straightbacked fellow.
virotillo *m.* ARCH. short upright brace.
virreina *f.* vice-queen, vicereine.
virreinal *adj.* viceregal.
virreinato, virreino *m.* viceroyship; viceroyalty.
virrey *m.* viceroy.
virtual *adj.* virtual. 2 tacit, implicit.
virtualidad *f.* virtuality.
virtud *f.* virtue: *en ~ de*, by, or in virtue of. 2 virtuousness. 3 *pl.* virtues [order of angels].
virtuoso, -sa *adj.* virtuous. 2 *m.-f.* virtuous person. 3 virtuoso.
viruela *f. sing.* or *pl.* MED. small pox, variola: *viruelas locas*, chicken pox. 2 pock, pock mark.
virulencia *f.* virulence.
virulento, -ta *adj.* virulent.
virus *m.* MED. virus. 2 poison, contagion.
viruta *f.* shaving [of wood or metal].
visado *m.* visa, visé.
visaje *m.* face, grimace; wry face.
visar *tr.* to visa, to visé. 2 ARTIL., SURV. to sight.
viscacha *f.* VIZCACHA.
víscera *f.* ANAT. internal organ. 2 *pl.* viscera.
visceral *adj.* visceral.
visco *m.* lime, birdlime.
vis cómica *f.* vis comica, ability to evoke mirth.
viscosa *f.* viscose.
viscosidad *f.* viscosity. 2 viscous matter.
viscoso, -sa *adj.* viscous, sticky. 2 PHYS. viscous.
visera *f.* peak [of a cap]. 2 visor [of a helmet]. 3 eyeshade.
visibilidad *f.* visibility.
visible *adj.* visible. 2 evident. 3 conspicuous.
visigodo, -da *adj.* Visigothic. 2 *m.-f.* Visigoth.
visigótico, -ca *adj.* Visigothic.
visillo *m.* window curtain, window shade.
visión *f.* vision, sight: *ver visiones*, to dream, be seeing things. 2 coll. sight, scarecrow [person].
visionario, -ria *adj.-n.* visionary [person].
visir *m.* vizier, vizir.

visita *f.* visit, call; social call: *~ de cumplido*, formal call; *hacer una ~*, to make or pay a call. 2 MED. visit. 3 visitor, guest: *tener visitas*, to have visitors, guests, company. 4 visitation, inspection.
visitación *f.* visit. 2 ECCL. (cap.) Visitation: *Visitación de la Virgen*, Visitation of Our Lady.
visitador, -ra *adj.* calling frequently, given to frequent calling. 2 *m.-f.* frequent caller. 3 *m.* visitor, inspector. 4 ECCL. visitator.
visitante *adj.* visiting, calling. 2 *m.-f.* visitor, caller, visitant.
visitar *tr.* to visit. 2 to search [goods at the customhouse]. 3 *ref.* to visit, call on each other. 4 [of a patient] to go to the doctor.
visiteo *m.* frequent visiting.
visitero, -ra *adj.* coll. fond of making calls.
visivo, -va *adj.* visive [serving for vision].
vislumbrar *tr.* to glimpse, catch a glimpse of, perceive indistinctly. 2 to sumise, conjecture. 3 *ref.* to appear or be perceived indistinctly. 4 to be conjectured.
vislumbre *f.* glimmer [faint gleam]. 2 glimpse, inkling, conjecture. 3 vague resemblance.
viso *m.* changeable luster or colour: *hacer visos* [of a fabric, etc.], to be changeable. 2 slip [undergarment worn under a thin dress]; coloured lining for a transparent cloth. 3 fig. appearance [of things]; 4 height, outlook. 5 *de ~*, notable, prominent [person].
visón *m.* ZOOL. mink, American mink.
visor *m.* PHOT. finder. 2 AER. bomb sight.
visorio, -ria *adj.* of sight, visual. 2 *m.* inspection by an expert.
víspera *f.* eve [day before]. 2 *sing.-pl.* eve [time just before]: *en vísperas de*, on the eve of. 3 ECCL. vespers. 4 HIST. *Vísperas Sicilianas*, Sicilian vespers.
vista *f.* sight, vision, view; eye, eyes: *~ cansada*, farsightedness; *~ corta*, nearsightedness; *doble ~*, second sight; *bajar la ~*, to look down; *dar ~ a*, to sight; *echar la ~*, fig. to choose; *estar a la ~*, to be on the look out; [of a thing] to be evident; *hacer la ~ gorda*, to wink at, to overlook; *torcer la ~*, to squint: *a la ~*, in sight, at sight, on sight; COM. at sight; *a primera ~*, at first sight; *a simple ~*, at a glance; with the naked eye; *a ~ de pájaro*, from a bird's-eye view; *de ~*, by sight; *hasta la ~*, so long. 2 view [scene, prospect]. 3 glance, brief look: *echar una ~*, to keep an eye on. 4 view [intention, design]. 5 view [consideration]: *en ~ de*, in view of, considering. 6 looks, aspect. 7 LAW trial. 8 *m. ~ de aduana*, customs officer. 9 *f. pl.* facings [of a garment]. 10 windows, etc., affording an outlook: *tener vistas a*, to look out on.
vistazo *m.* look, glance.
1) **viste, vistió, vistiera,** etc., *irr.* V. VESTIR.
2) **viste, vistes,** etc. *irr.* V. VER.
1) **visto, -ta** *p. p.* of VER. 2 *adj.* seen, looked, etc.: *bien ~*, looked on with approval; *mal ~*, looked on with disapproval, improper; *no ~, nunca ~*, extraordinary, unheard of; *por lo ~*, as it seems; *~ está, está ~*, it is evident. 3 *conj. ~ que*, seeing, since, considering that. 4 *adv.-m. ~ bueno, (V.° B.°)*, correct, approved [in official documents]. 5 *m.* LAW whereas.
2) **visto, vista,** etc. *irr.* V. VESTIR.
vistosidad *f.* brightness, showiness.
vistoso, -sa *adj.* gay, bright, showy.
visual *adj.* visual. 2 *f.* line of sight.
visualidad *f.* gay, pleasant appearance.

vital *adj.* vital [of life, essential to life; essential].
vitalicio, -cia *adj.* [of pensions, grants, etc.] life, for life; [of an office] held for life. 2 *m.* life-insurance policy. 3 life annuity.
vitalidad *f.* vitality.
vitalismo *m.* vitalism.
vitamina *f.* vitamin, vitamine.
vitaminar *tr.* to vitaminize.
vitando, -da *adj.* odious, execrable.
vitela *f.* vellum.
vitelino *adj.* vitelline.
vitelo *m.* BIOL. vitellus.
vitícola *adj.* viticultural, grape-growing.
viticultor, -ra *m.-f.* viticulturist, grape grower.
viticultura *f.* viticulture, grape growing.
vitola *f.* size of cigars. 2 MIL. ball or bullet calibre. 3 fig. mien, appearance [of a person].
vítor *m.* vivat, acclamation. 2 *interj.* long live!, hurrah!
vitorear *tr.* to cheer, acclaim.
vitrificación *f.* vitrification.
vitrificar *tr.* to vitrify.
vitrina *f.* showcase, glass case. 2 (Am.) shopwindow.
vitriolo *m.* CHEM. vitriol: *aceite de* ~, oil of vitriol.
vituallas *f. pl.* victuals, provisions.
vituallar *tr.* AVITUALLAR.
vituperable *adj.* vituperable, blameworthy.
vituperación *f.* vituperation.
vituperar *tr.* to vituperate.
vituperio *m.* vituperation. 2 affront.
viuda *f.* widow. 2 dowager. 3 BOT. mourning bride, mourning widow.
viudedad *f.* widow's pension.
viudez *f.* widowhood.
viudo, -da *adj.* widowed. 2 *m.* widower.
viva *m.* viva, vivat. 2 *interj.* long live!, hurrah!
vivac *m.* VIVAQUE.
vivacidad *f.* vivacity, liveliness. 2 animal spirits. 3 brightness, vividness [of colour].
vivandero, -ra *m.* sutler.
vivaque *m.* MIL. bivouac.
vivaquear *intr.* MIL. to bivouac.
vivar *m.* warren. 2 fishpond, hatchery.
vivaracho, -cha *adj.* vivacious, lively, dapper.
vivaz *adj.* vivacious, lively, active, vigorous. 2 keen, quick-witted. 3 long-lived. 4 BOT. vivacious.
víveres *m. pl.* food, provisions, victuals.
vivero *m.* tree nursery. 2 seedbed. 3 fishpond, hatchery; vivarium.
viveza *f.* liveliness, sprightliness, briskness, quickness. 2 warmth, vehemence [in words]. 3 keenness, quick-wittedness. 4 brightness, gaiety, vividness. 5 sparkle [in the eyes]. 6 liveliness [of a description, etc.]. 7 lively remark. 8 thoughtless word or act.
vividero, -ra *adj.* habitable, livable.
vívido, -da *adj.* LIT. based on life or experience.
vívido, -da *adj.* vivid.
vividor, -ra *adj.* living. 2 long-lived. 3 thrifty. 4 *m.-f.* living person. 5 thrifty person. 6 *m.* chevalier of industry.
vivienda *f.* dwelling, house; housing.
viviente *adj.* living, alive. 2 *m.* liver, living person. 3 *los vivientes*, the living.
vivificación *f.* vivification.
vivificador, -ra *adj.* vivifying. 2 *m.-f.* vivifier.
vivificante *adj.* vivifying, life-giving.
vivificar *tr.* to vivify. 2 to comfort, refresh.
vivífico, -ca *adj.* of life, springing from life.

vivíparo, -ra *adj.* ZOOL. viviparous.
1) **vivir** *m.* life, living: *de mal* ~, loose, disreputable [person]. 2 livelihood.
2) **vivir** *intr.* to live: ~ *bien*, to live honestly; to live comfortably; ~ *mal*, to live viciously; to live uncomfortably; ~ *de*, to live on or upon, to live by; ~ *en*, to live or dwell in; ~ *para ver*, live and learn!; ¿*quién vive?*, MIL. who goes there?; *dar el quién vive*, MIL. to challenge. 2 *tr.* to live [an experience or adventure].
vivisección *f.* vivisection.
vivo, -va *adj.* alive, living, live. 2 live [blaze, fire, etc.]. 3 vivid. 4 lively, brisk, quick, smart. 5 keen, acute, sharp, intense. 6 vigorous. 7 deep [feeling, interest, etc.]. 8 hasty, quick-tempered. 9 expressive. 10 vehement, persuasive. 11 bright [colour]. 12 sharp [edge, angle]. 13 running [water]. 14 unslaked [lime]. 15 raw [flesh, sore]. 16 living [language]. 17 live [rock]. 18 MECH., MACH. live. 19 *lo* ~, the quick: *herir en lo* ~, to cut or hurt to the quick. 20 *m.* edge, edging, border. 21 SEW. piping, edge trimming. 22 *pl. los vivos*, the living, the quick.
vizcacha *f.* ZOOL. viscacha, vizcacha.
vizcaíno, -na *adj.-n.* Biscayan.
Vizcaya *f. pr. n.* GEOG. Biscay.
vizcondado *m.* viscountcy, viscountship, viscounty.
vizconde *m.* viscount.
vizcondesa *f.* viscountess.
vocablo *m.* word, term: *jugar del* ~, to pun.
vocabulario *m.* vocabulary.
vocación *f.* THEOL. vocation. 2 vocation [calling to a particular state, business or profession]. 3 ADVOCACIÓN.
vocal *adj.* vocal. 2 *adj.-f.* GRAM., PHONET. vowel. 3 *m.-f.* member [of a council, a board of directors, etc.].
vocálico, -ca *adj.* vocalic.
vocalista *m.-f.* vocalist.
vocalización *f.* MUS. vocalization.
vocalizar *intr.* MUS. to vocalize.
vocativo *adj.-m.* GRAM. vocative.
voceador, -ra *adj.* vociferating. 2 *m.-f.* vociferator. 3 *m.* town crier.
vocear *intr.* to vociferate, shout, cry out. 2 *tr.* to cry, publish. 3 to cheer, acclaim.
vocejón *m.* loud, harsh voice.
vocería *f.*, **vocerío** *m.* shouting, outcry, uproar.
vocero *m.* spokesman.
voces *f. pl.* of VOZ.
vociferación *f.* vociferation.
vociferante *adj.* vociferating, vociferant.
vociferar *intr.-tr.* to vociferate.
vocinglería *f.* shouting, uproar. 2 prate, rant.
vocinglero, -ra *adj.* shouting, vociferous. 2 chattering. 3 *m.-f.* shouter. 4 prater, chatterer.
vodka *f.* vodka.
volada *f.* short flight. 2 (Am.) trick, bad turn.
voladero, -ra *adj.* able to fly. 2 flying, fleeting. 3 *m.* precipice.
voladizo, -za *adj.* ARCH. projecting, jutting out. 2 *m.* ARCH. projection, projecting member, corbel.
volado, -da *adj.* PRINT. superior [figure, letter]. 2 *estar* ~, to be uneasy, on tenterhooks.
volador, -ra *adj.* flying. 2 fleeting, running fast. 3 *m.* skyrocket. 4 ICHTH. flying gurnard.
voladura *f.* blasting, blowing up. 2 flying through the air.
volandas (en) *adv.* [carried] in the air, as if flying. 2 rapidly, quickly.

volandera f. MACH. washer. 2 millstone.
volandero, -ra adj. VOLANTÓN. 2 floating in the air. 3 accidental, casual. 4 wandering. 5 flying [report, etc.].
volante adj. flying, volant. 2 MIL. flying [column]. 3 m. SEW. flounce. 4 MACH. flywheel. 5 HOROL. balance wheel. 6 coining press. 7 shuttlecock. 8 battledore and shuttlecock [game]. 9 AUTO. steering wheel. 10 note, order, etc., written on a narrow sheet of paper.
volantín m. line with several hooks for fishing. 2 (Am.) kite [toy].
volantón adj. newfledged. 2 m. fledgling [bird].
volapié m. BULLF. stroke in which the matador runs toward the bull and stabs him.
volar intr. to fly [move in or through the air; float, soar in the air]. 2 AER. to fly. 3 to fly, fleet, pass swiftly, run fast, make great haste. 4 to fly, disappear. 5 [of news] to spread rapidly. 6 ARCH. to project, jut out. 7 tr. to blast, blow up. 8 to fly [a hawk]. 9 to irritate, exasperate. 10 PRINT. to raise [a letter, etc.]. ‖ CONJUG. like contar.
volatería f. hawking, falconry. 2 poultry, fowls.
volátil adj. flying [that flies or can fly]. 2 volatile.
volatilidad f. CHEM. volatility.
volatilizar tr. volatilize. 2 ref. to volatilize [be volatilized]. 2 coll. [of money, etc.] to disappear.
volatín m. acrobatic feat. 2 VOLATINERO.
volatinero, -ra m.-f. ropewalker, acrobat.
volatizar tr. VOLATILIZAR.
volcán m₁ GEOL. & fig. volcano: estar sobre un ~, fig. to be on the edge of a volcano.
volcánico, -ca adj. volcanic.
volcar tr. to upset, overturn, capsize; to tilt [a vessel]. 2 to dump. 3 to make dizzy [with a strong odour]. 4 to make [one] change his mind. 5 fig. to irritate. 6 intr. [of a vehicle] to upset, overturn. ‖ CONJUG. like contar.
volea f. whippletree. 2 volley [of a ball].
volear tr. to volley [a bail]. 2 AGR. to sow broadcast.
voleo m. volley [of a ball]. 2 slap or blow that makes one reel. 3 AGR. sembrar al ~, to sow broadcast.
volframio m. CHEM. wolfram.
volición f. volition.
volitivo, -va adj. volitive, volitional.
volquearse ref. to roll about, wallow.
volquete m. tilt cart, tip cart, dump truck.
volt m. ELECT. volt.
voltaico, -ca ELECT. voltaic: arco ~, voltaic arc.
voltaje m. ELECT. voltage.
voltámetro m. ELECT. voltameter.
voltariedad f. fickleness, inconstancy.
voltario, -ria adj. fickle, inconstant.
volteador, -ra m.-f. tumbler, acrobat.
voltear tr. to turn, revolve. 2 to turn around to. 3 ARCH. to build [an arch or vault]. 4 intr. to turn in the air; to roll over; to tumble.
voltejear tr. to turn around. 2 intr. NAUT. to tack.
volteo m. turning. 2 overturning. 3 turning in the air; tumbling.
voltereta f. tumble, handspring, somersault. 2 turning up a card to determine the trump.
volteriano, -na adj.-n. Voltairian.
voltímetro m. ELECT. voltmeter.
voltio m. ELECT. volt.
volubilidad f. volubility. 2 fickleness, inconstancy.
voluble adj. voluble [turning easily]. 2 versatile, fickle, inconstant. 3 BOT. voluble.

volumen m. volume [book]. 2 volume, bulk, mass. 3 GEOM., MUS. volume.
volumetría f. volumetry.
voluminoso, -sa adj. voluminous, bulky.
voluntad f. will [in every sense, except testament]; wish, pleasure: mala ~, ill will; última ~, last wish; last will and testament; a ~, at will; de buena ~, de ~, willingly. 2 affection, love, goodwill: tener ~ a, to love, feel affection for.
voluntariado m. MIL. volunteering.
voluntariedad f. voluntariness. 2 wilfulness.
voluntario, -ria adj. voluntary; wilful. 2 wilful, self-willed. 3 m.-f. volunteer.
voluntarioso, -sa adj. wilfull, self-willed.
voluptuosidad f. voluptuousness.
voluptuoso, -sa adj. voluptuous. 2 m.-f. voluptuary.
voluta f. ARCH. volute.
volver tr. to turn [cause to revolve]; to turn, turn up, turn over, turn upside down or inside out: ~ la cara, to turn one's head; ~ la espalda a, to turn one's back on; ~ la hoja, to turn the page; fig. to change the subject; to change one's mind. 2 to turn, direct, aim. 3 to return, restore. 4 to put back, bring back. 5 to give [change of coin or note]. 6 SPORT. to return [the ball]. 7 to vomit. 8 to translate [from a language]. 9 to make, drive, turn, convert: ~ loco, to drive crazy, distract. 10 to make [a person] change his mind. 11 to push or pull [a door] to. 12 to reflect [sound, etc.]. 13 intr. to return, come back, go back. 14 to turn [to the right, to the left]. 15 ~ a hacer, a leer, etc., to do, read, etc., again, anew or over. 16 ~ en sí, to come to, recover consciousness. 17 ~ por, to defend, stand up for. 18 ~ sobre sí, to recover one's calm. 19 ref. to go back. 20 to turn, turn around, face about, look back. 21 [of wine, etc.] to turn sour. 22 volverse atrás, to back out; withdraw from promise, etc. 23 volverse contra, to turn on. ‖ CONJUG. like mover. ‖ PAST. P. vuelto.
volvible adj. turnable, reversible.
vómer m. ANAT. vomer.
vómico, -ca adj. vomitive.
vomitar tr. to vomit. 2 to eject, belch forth. 3 to break out into [insults, etc.]. 4 coll. to disgorge, give up. 5 intr. to vomit.
vomitivo, -va adj.-n. vomitive, emetic.
vómito m. vomit, vomiting.
vomitona f. coll. violent vomiting.
vomitorio, -ria adj.-n. vomitory. 2 m. vomitory [in Roman theatres].
voracidad f. voracity, voraciousness.
vorágine f. vortex, whirlpool.
voraz adj. voracious; greedy, ravenous. 2 destructive, fierce [fire, etc.].
vórtice m. vortex, whirlpool, whirlwind. 2 centre of a cyclone.
vorticela f. ZOOL. vorticella.
vortiginoso, -sa adj. vortical, vortiginous.
vos pers. pron. sing. & pl. you. ‖ It is used in adressing God, the saints and high-placed or venerable persons. Even if it is singular in meaning it takes plural form of verb. 2 In much of Spanish America, it is colloquially used instead of tú.
vosotros, -tras pers. pron. pl. (plural form of tú) you, ye.
votación f. votation, voting, casting of votes. 2 vote, ballot [votes collectively].
votante m.-f. voter.

votar *intr.-tr.* to vow [make promise to God or the saints]. *2 intr.* to vote [for, against, on]. *3* to swear, curse. *4 ¡voto a tal!*, confound it!, by Jove! *5 tr.* to vote, vote for, give one's vote for.

votivo, -va *adj.* votive.

voto *m.* vow. *2* wish, supplication to God: *hacer votos por*, to pray for, to wish. *3* curse, oath, execration; *echar votos*, to swear, curse. *4* vote: ~ *de calidad*, casting vote; ~ *particular*, minority report; *ser* or *tener* ~, to have a vote; fig. to have voice, be qualified for speaking [on a matter]. *5* advice, opinion.

voy *1st pers. sing. pres.* of IR.

voz *f.* voice [of man, the animals, etc.]: *alzar la* ~, to raise, or lift up, one's voice; *estar en* ~, MUS. to be in voice; *llevar la* ~ *cantante*, fig. to have the say, be the boss; *a media* ~, in an undertone; with a slight hint; *a una* ~, with one voice; *a* ~ *en cuello*, *a* ~ *en grito*, at the top of one's voice; *de viva* ~, viva voce; *en alta* ~, aloud; *en* ~ *baja*, in a low tone, in whispers. *2* call or sound [of a bell, trumpet, etc.]. *3* shout: *dar voces*, to shout, yell. *4* voice [right to speak]. *5* vote. *6* GRAM. voice [of verb]. *7* word, term. *8* rumour, public opinion: *corre la* ~ *que*, it is rumoured that.

vozarrón *m.* strong, heavy voice.

vuecelencia, vuecencia *m.-f.* (contr. of VUESTRA EXCELENCIA) your excellency.

vuelco *m.* overturn, turnover, upset.

vuelco, vuelque, etc. *irr.* V. VOLCAR.

vuelillo *m.* lace cuff trimming.

vuelo *m.* flight [going through the air; distance covered at a flight]; soaring, excursion of fancy, thought, etc.]: ~ *planeado*, AER. volplane; ~ *sin motor*, AER. glide, gliding; *alzar el* ~, to take flight; fig. to decamp; *levantar el* ~, to take flight; to raise one's mind; *al* ~, quickly; on the wing; on the fly; in passing; *echar las campanas al* ~, to ring a full peal; *de un* ~, *en un* ~, in a jiffy. *2* SEW. spread, wideness, flaring [of a skirt, etc.]. *3* VUELILLO. *4* ARCH. jut, projection. *5* importance: *tomar* ~, to grow, progress. *6* wings: *cortar los vuelos a*, to cut someone's wings.

vuelta *f.* turn [revolution, turning motion, reversal of position; motion around]: *media* ~, about-face; *dar media* ~, to face around; *dar la* ~ *a*, to make the round of, to go around [something]; *dar vueltas a un manubrio*, to turn a crank; *dar vueltas a una cosa*, fig. to keep going over the same subject; *no hay que darle vueltas*, no use talking, no two ways about it; *dar vueltas* [abs.], to turn, revolve, spin, whirl; turn end over end; walk to and fro. *2* turn, stroll, tour, trip, excursion: *dar una* ~ *por*, to take a turn in. *3* turn, bend, curve. *4* turn, wind [of a rope, etc., about something]. *5* reverse, other side: *a la* ~, overleaf; round the corner; *no tener* ~ *de hoja*, fig. to be incontrovertible. *6* return, coming back, coming again: *estar de* ~, to be back, have returned; *a la* ~, on returning; *a* ~ *de correo*, return mail. *7* return, restitution. *8* change [of coin or note]. *9* repetition, iteration. *10* turn, shift, change. *11* CARDS turning up a card for trump. *12* ARCH. vault, ceiling. *13* facing [in garment]; cuff trimming. *14* burden [of song]. *15* beating, drubbing. *16 andar a vueltas con*, to struggle for, to endeavour to. *17 dar cien vueltas a*, to surpass, be far superior to. *18 poner de* ~ *y media*, to cover with insults. *19 a la* ~ *de*, within [a specified time].

vuelto, -ta *p. p. irreg.* of VOLVER. *2 adj.* PRINT. *folio* ~, verso. *3 m.* (Am.) change [money].

vuelvo, vuelva, etc. *irr.* V. VOLVER.

vuesamerced, vuesarced *m.-f.* (contr. of VUESTRA MERCED) you, sir; you, madam.

vuestro, -tra; vuestros, -tras *poss. adj.* your. *2 poss. pron.* yours. ‖ It is used in correspondence with *vos* and *vosotros*.

vulcanismo *m.* GEOL. vulcanism.

vulcanita *f.* vulcanite.

vulcanización *f.* vulcanization.

vulcanizar *tr.* to vulcanize.

Vulcano *m. pr. n.* MYTH., ASTR. Vulcan.

vulgar *adj.* vulgar.

vulgaridad *f.* vulgarity. *2* commonplace, platitude.

vulgarismo *m.* vulgarism [vulgar expression].

vulgarización *f.* vulgarization. *2* popularization.

vulgarizar *tr.* to vulgarize. *2* to translate into the vernacular. *3* to popularize [technical subjects].

vulgata *f.* Vulgate.

vulgo *m.* vulgar, common people.

vulnerable *adj.* vulnerable.

vulnerar *tr.* to wound. *2* to harm, injure, damage.

vulnerario, -ria *adj.-m.* vulnerary.

vulpeja *f.* ZORRA 1.

vulpino, -na *adj.* vulpine.

vultúridos *m. pl.* ORN. Vulturidae.

vulva *f.* ANAT. vulva.

W, w *f*. W, w. This letter does not belong to the Spanish alphabet and it is mainly used in words taken from other languages.

wat *m*. ELECT. watt.

water closet *m*. water-closet.

whisky, wiski *m*. whisky.

whist *m*. whist [card game].

X, x *f*. X, x, twenty-sixth letter of the Spanish
  alphabet.
xanteína *f*. CHEM. xanthein.
xántico *adj*. CHEM. xanthic.
xantofila *f*. BIOCHEM. xanthophyll.
xenofobia *f*. xenophobia.
xenófobo, -ba *adj*. xenophobian. *2 m.-f.* xeno-
  phobe.

xenon *m*. CHEM. xenon.
xerófilo, -la *adj*. BOT. xerophilous.
xi *f*. xi [Greek letter].
xifoideo, -a *adj*. ANAT. xiphoid.
xifoides *adj.-m*. ANAT. xiphoid.
xilófago, -ga *adj*. ENT. xylophagous.
xilófono *m*. MUS. xylophone.
xilografía *f*. xylography. *2* xylograph.

Y, y *f.* Y, y, twenty-seventh letter of the Spanish alphabet.
y *conj.* and.
ya *adv.* already. *2* now. *3* at once, presently: ~ *voy*, I am coming. *4* later on, at another time: ~ *veremos*, we shall see. *5* Often used as an emphatic expletive: ~ *veo*, I see. *6* ~ *lo creo*, of course, certainly. *7* ~ *no*, no longer. *8* ~ *que*, since, inasmuch as. *9 si* ~, if. *10 conj. ya... ya*, now... now; whether... or. *11* I see; of course!
yacaré *m.* ZOOL. (Am.) cayman, alligator.
yacente *adj.* lying, jacent. *2* LAW abeyant. *3 m.* MIN. floor [of a vein].
yacer *intr.* to lie, be lying down. *2* to lie [in the grave], to rest. *3* to lie [have sexual intercourse]. *4* to lie, be [in a place]. ‖ CONJUG.: INDIC. Pres.: *yazco, yazgo* or *yago*, yaces, yace, etc. | SUBJ. Pres.: *yazca, yazga* or *yaga; yazcas, yazgas* or *yagas*, etc. | IMPER.: yace or *yaz; yazca, yazga* or *yaga; yazcamos, yazgamos* or *yagamos*; yaced; *yazcan, yazgan* or *yagan.*
yacija *f.* bed, couch. *2* tomb, grave.
yacimiento *m.* GEOL. bed, deposit, field.
yagua *f.* BOT. yagua.
yaguar *m.* JAGUAR.
yak *m.* ZOOL. yak.
yámbico, -ca *adj.-m.* PROS. iambic.
yambo *m.* PROS. iamb, iambus.
yanqui *adj.-n.* Yankee, American [of U.S.].
1) **yantar** *m.* obs. food, viands.
2) **yantar** *tr.* obs. to eat, to take a meal.
yapa *f.* (S. Am.) bonus, extra.
yarda *f.* yard [english measure].
yaro *m.* BOT. arum.
yatagán *m.* yataghan.
yate *m.* NAUT. yacht.
yazco, yago, etc. *irr.* V. YACER.
ye name of the letter *y*.
yedra *f.* HIEDRA.
yegua *f.* ZOOL. mare. *2* (Am.) cigar butt.
yeguada *f.* stud, herd of horses and mares.
yeguar *adj.* mare [pertaining to the mares].
yegüería *f.* YEGUADA.
yegüerizo, -za *adj.* YEGUAR. *2 m.* YEGÜERO.
yegüero *m.* keeper of a herd of horses and mares.
yeísmo *m.* pronunciation of Spanish *ll* like *y*.
yelmo *m.* ARM. armet, helmet.
yema *f.* BOT. bud. *2* BIOL., ZOOL. bud, gemma. *3* yolk

[of an egg]: ~ *mejida*, eggnog. *4* candied egg yolk. *5* fig. cream [best part]. *6* ~ *del dedo*, fleshy part of the finger tip.
yendo *ger.* of IR.
yente *adj.* going.
yerba *f.* HIERBA.
yerbajo *m.* weed, wild herb.
yergo, yerga, etc. *irr.* V. ERGUIR.
yermo, -ma *adj.* waste, desert, uncultivated, barren. *2 m.* waste, desert, wilderness.
yerno *m.* son-in-law.
yero *m.* BOT. a kind of fare.
1) **yerro** *m.* error, fault, sin. *2* error, fault, mistake.
2) **yerro, yerra,** etc. *irr.* V. ERRAR.
yerto, -ta *adj.* stiff, rigid, motionless.
yesal, yesar *m.* gypsum pit or quarry.
yesca *f.* tinder, touchwood, *punk. *2* fig. fuel, incentive. *3 pl.* tinderbox.
yesería *f.* gypsum kiln. *2* plasterer's shop. *3* plaster objects; plasterwork.
yesero, -ra *adj.* [pertaining to] gypsum. *2 m.* maker of plaster. *3* seller of gypsum or plaster.
yeso *m.* gypsum. *2* plaster. *3* plaster cast. *4* chalk [for writing or drawing].
yesón *m.* rubbish of plaster.
yesoso, -sa *adj.* gypseous.
yeyuno *m.* ANAT. jejunum.
yezgo *m.* BOT. danewort, dwarf elder.
yo *pers. pron.* I. *2 m.* PHIL. I, ego.
yodado, -da *adj.* iodized.
yodo *m.* CHEM. iodine.
yodoformo *m.* CHEM. iodoform.
yoduro *m.* CHEM. iodide.
yoga *m.* yoga.
yogur *m.* yogurt.
yola *f.* NAUT. yawl.
yubarta *f.* ZOOL. finback.
yuca *f.* BOT. yucca. *2* BOT. cassava.
yugada *f.* AGR. yoke of land. *2* yoke of oxen.
yugo *m.* yoke [for oxen, mules, etc.]. *2* ROMAN HIST. yoke. *3* fig. yoke [oppression, servitude]. *4* yoke [of a bell]. *6* NAUT. transom.
Yugoeslavia *f. pr. n.* GEOG. Yugoslavia.
yugoeslavo, -va *adj.-n.* Yugoslav.
yugular *adj.-f.* ANAT. jugular.
yunque *m.* anvil. *2* ANAT. anvil, incus.
yunta *f.* couple, yoke [of oxen, mules, etc.].
yusera *f.* horizontal stone in olive-oil mills.

yuso *adv.* ABAJO.
yute *m.* jute [plant, fibre, fabric].
yuxtaponer *tr.* to juxtapose. *2 ref.* to become jux-taposed. ‖ CONJUG. like *poner.*
yuxtaposición *f.* juxtaposition.
yuyuba *f.* BOT. jujube.

Z

Z, z *f.* Z, z, twenty-eighth letter of the Spanish alphabet.

zabida, zabila *f.* BOT. aloe.

zabordar *intr.* NAUT. to run aground.

zabullida *f.* ZAMBULLIDA.

zabullir *tr.-ref.* ZAMBULLIR.

zacapela, zacapella *f.* shindy, row, noisy quarrel.

Zacarías *m. pr. n.* Zachary, Zechariah.

zacatín *m.* clothes market.

zafada *f.* NAUT. freeing, disentangling.

zafado, -da *adj.* forward, impudent.

zafar *tr.* NAUT. to free, clear, disengage. *2* to adorn, bedeck. *3* MACH. [of a belt] to slip off. *5 zafarse de*, to avoid, elude, get out of.

zafarrancho *m.* NAUT. clearing of a part of a ship: *~ de combate*, clearing for action; *~ de limpieza*, general cleaning. *2* coll. breaking, destruction. *3* coll. shindy, row.

zafiedad *f.* clumsiness, rusticity, uncouthness.

zafio, -fia *adj.* clumsy, rustic, ignorant, uncouth.

zafir *m.*, **zafira** *f.* ZAFIRO.

zafíreo, -a *adj.* sapphire, sapphirine.

zafiro *m.* MINER. sapphire.

zafo, -fa *adj.* NAUT. free, clear. *2* safe, unharmed.

zafra *f.* olive-oil can. *2* drip pan [for olive-oil measures]. *5* sugar-making season. *6* MIN. rubbish.

zaga *f.* rear, back part: *a la ~, en ~*, behind; *no irle en ~ a uno*, not to be inferior to one. *2* load in the rear of a carriage.

zagal *m.* lad, youth. *2* strapping young felow, swain. *3* shepherd's helper. *4* asistant of the driver in a stagecoach. *5* underskirt.

zagala *f.* lass, girl, maiden. *2* young shepherdess.

zagaleja *f. dim.* young lass.

zagalejo *m. dim.* young lad, boy. *2* underskirt.

zagalón, -na *m.-f.* overgrown boy or girl.

zagual *m.* paddle [oar].

zaguán *m.* entry, entrance-hall, vestibule.

zaguero, -ra *adj.* rear, hind; lagging behind. *2 m.* backstop [at the game of PELOTA].

zahareño, -ña *adj.* disdainful, unsociable. *2* wild, intractable, refractory. *3* haggard [falcon].

zaheridor, -ra *adj.* taunting, blaming, upbraiding. *2 m.-f.* taunter, blamer, upbraider.

zaherimiento *m.* taunt, upbraiding.

zaherir *tr.* to taunt, blame, upbraid. ‖ CONJUG. like *hervir*.

zahina *f.* BOT. sorghum.

zahones *m. pl.* chaps, chaparajos.

zahorí *m.* person credited by the popular belief with the power to see hidden things. *2* rhabdomancer. *3* fig. perspicacious person.

zahorra *f.* NAUT. ballast.

zahurda *f.* POCILGA.

zaino, -na *adj.* false, treacherous. *2* dar-chestnut [horse]. *3* black [cattle]. *4* vicious [horse, mule].

zalagarda *f.* ambush. *2* trap, snare. *3* deceitful obsequiousness. *4* skirmish. *5* coll. row, shindy.

zalama, zalamería *f.* blandishment, cajolery, flattery.

zalamero, -ra *adj.* honeyed, caressing, flattering, cajoling. *2 m.-f.* caresser, flatterer, cajoler.

zalea *f.* unsheared skeepskin.

zalear *tr.* to drag and shake around. *2* to chase away [dogs].

zalema *f.* salaam. *2* coll. bow, courtsy.

zallar *tr.* NAUT. to rig out, run out.

zamacuco *m.* dolt, blockhead. *2* sly fellow. *3* coll. drunk, drunken fit.

zamarra *f.* shepherd's jacket of unsheared sheepskin. *2* unsheared sheepskin.

zamarrear *tr.* [of dogs, etc.] to worry, shake and tear with the teeth. *2* coll. to treat roughly, to knock around.

zamarro *f.* worrying and tearing with the teeth. *2* rough treatment; knocking around.

zamarrico *m. dim.* wallet of unsheared sheepskin.

zamarilla *f.* BOT. poly.

zamarro *m.* ZAMARRA 1. *2* sheepskin. *3* coll. boor, rustic, dolt. *4* coll. sly fellow. *5* *pl.* (Am.) chaps, chaparajos.

zambo, -ba *adj.* knock-kneed. *2* (Am.) born of an Indian and a Negro.

zambomba *f.* a rustic instrument. *2 interj.* whew!

zambombazo *m.* hard blow, bump or knock.

zambombo *m.* boor, dolt.

zamborondón, -na; zamborotudo, -da *adj.* thick, clumsy, ill-shaped. *2* clumsy [person].

zambra *f.* a Morisco festival or merrymaking. *2* fig. merrymaking; noise, hullabaloo.

zambucar *tr.* coll. to hide [a thing] by mixing it quickly among others.

zambullida *f.*, **zambullimiento** *m.* dive, plunge, ducking.

zambullir *tr.* to dive, plunge, duck [a person or thing] into water. *2 ref.* [of a person or animal]

to dive, plunge, duck. *3* [of a submarine] to dive. *4* to duck, hide.
zamorano, -na *adj.-n.* of Zamora.
zampa *m.* ENG. pile, bearing pile.
zampar *tr.* to thrust or put hurriedly [in order to conceal]. *2* to eat hurriedly and gluttonously. *3 ref.* to enter, go in suddenly.
zampatortas, *pl.* **-tas** *m.-f.* glutton. *2* boor, rustic.
zampeado *m.* ENG., ARCH. grillage.
zampear *tr.* ENG., ARCH. to strengthen [ground] with a grillage.
zampoña *f.* MUS. rustic flute, reed pipe; panpipe.
zampuzar *intr.*, ZAMBULLIR. *2* ZAMPAR.
zanahoria *f.* BOT. carrot.
zanahoriate *m.* preserved carrot.
zanca *f.* shank [of bird]. *2* coll. long leg or shank. *3* ARCH. string, stringboard [of a stair].
zancada *f.* long stride.
zancadilla *f.* trip [tripping someone]: *echar la ~ a uno*, to stick out one's foot and trip someone. *2* trick, snare [to harm someone].
zancajear *intr.* to hurry about, rush around.
zancajiento, -ta *adj.* ZANCAJOSO.
zancajo *m.* heel bone; heel or torn heel [of a shoe or stocking]. *2* coll. short, illshaped person.
zancajoso, -sa *adj.* duck-toed. *2* big-heeled [person]. *3* wearing stockings with holes at the heels.
zancarrón *m.* coll. leg bone without flesh. *2* coll. skinny, dirty old fellow. *3* coll. ignoramus.
zanco *m.* stilt: *en zancos*, fig. in a high position.
zancudo, -da *adj.* long-legged, long-shanked. *2* ORN. wading. *3 f.* ORN. wader, wading bird. *4 m.* (Am.) mosquito.
zanfonía *f.* MUS. hurdy-gurdy.
zangala *f.* buckram.
zangamanga *f.* coll. trick, ruse, wile.
zanganear *intr.* to drone, idle, loaf.
zanganería *f.* idlennes, laziness.
zángano *m.* ENT. drone. *2* fig. drone, idler, loafer.
zangarilleja *f.* slatternly, gadabout girl.
zangarrear *intr.* coll. to scrape a guitar.
zangolotear *tr.* to jiggle. *2 intr.* to fidget or fuss about. *3* to shake, rattle, move loosely in its socket, on its hinges, etc.
zangoloteo *m.* jiggle, jiggling. *2* fussing about. *3* loose motion, shaking, rattling.
zangolotino, -na *adj.* fond of acting like a child; being made to pass as a child [grown boy or girl].
zangotear *tr.-intr.* ZANGOLOTEAR.
zangoteo *m.* ZANGOLOTEO.
zanguanga *f.* malingering. *2* coll. LAGOTERÍA.
zanguango, -ga *adj.* slothful. *2 m.-f.* slothful person.
zanja *f.* ditch, trench: *~ de desagüe*, drain.
zanjar *tr.* to dig ditches or trenches in. *2* to settle [a matter or dispute]; to conclude, finish. *3* to obviate, surmount.
zanjón *m. augm.* large deep ditch.
zanquear *intr.* to waddle in walking. *2* to run about, to walk much and fast.
zanquilargo, -ga *adj.* long-shanked, long-legged.
zanquituerto, -ta *adj.* bandy-legged.
zanquivano, -na *adj.* coll. spindle-legged.
Zanzíbar *f. pr. n.* GEOG. Zanzibar.
zapa *f.* spade [used by sappers]. *2* FORT. sap, trenching: *trabajo de ~*, fig. secret work, intrigue. *3* shagreen, sharkskin. *4* shagreen [leather]. *5* sharkskin finish [on metals].
zapador *m.* MIL. sapper.

zapapico *m.* mattock, pickax, pickaxe.
zapar *intr.* MIL. to sap, mine, excavate.
zaparrastrar *intr.* coll. to trail one's clothes.
zaparrastroso, -sa *adj.-n.* ZARRAPASTROSO.
zapata *f.* buskin, half-boot. *2* BUILD. bolster. *3* NAUT. shoe [of an anchor]. *4* NAUT. false keel. *5* MECH. shoe [of a brake, etc.].
zapatazo *m.* large shoe. *2* blow with a shoe. *3* heavy blow or blow. *4* thud, thump, whack. *5* NAUT. flap [of a sail].
zapatear *tr.* to strike with the shoe. *2* to tap with the feet. *3* FENC. to touch repeatedly with the button of the foil. *4* coll. to ill-treat. *5 intr.* NAUT. [of sails] to flap.
zapatera *f.* woman who makes or sells shoes. *2* shoemaker's wife.
zapatería *f.* shoemaker's shop. *2* shoe shop. *3* shoemaker's trade.
zapateril *adj.* [pertaining to a] shoemaker.
zapatero, -ra *adj.* hard, poorly cooked [beans]. *2* stale [olive]. *3 m.* shoemaker: *~ de viejo*, *~ remendón*, cobbler mender of shoes. *4* ENT. water skipper, water strider. *5* CARDS. *quedarse ~*, to take no tricks.
zapateta *f.* slap on the foot or shoe while jumping. *2* caper, leap, jump.
zapatilla *f.* slipper, light shoe. *2* leather washer [for keys of a wind instrument]. *3* FENC. leather button [of a foil].
zapato *m.* shoe, low shoe: *saber uno donde le aprieta el ~*, to know on which side one's bread is buttered.
zapatón, *pl.* **-tones** *m. augm.* large, clumsy shoe.
¡zape! *interj.* used to frighten cats away.
zapote *m.* BOT. sapote [tree and fruit]. *2 chico ~*, CHICOZAPOTE.
zapotero *m.* BOT. sapote [tree].
zapotillo *m.* BOT. sapodilla.
zaque *m.* wineskin. *2* coll. drunk person.
Zaqueo *m. pr. n.* Zaccheus.
zaquizamí *m.* garret, cockloft. *2* fig. hovel, hole, mean room.
zar *m.* czar, tzar.
zarabanda *f.* saraband. *2* fig. noise, bustle.
zaragata *f.* row, noise, tumult; noisy merrimaking.
zaragatero, -ra *adj.* fond of engaging in rows and tumults; noisy, merry, fond of tun.
zaragatona *f.* BOT. fleawort.
Zaragoza *f. pr. n.* GEOG. Saragossa.
zaragozano, -na *adj.-n.* of Saragossa.
zaragüelles *m. pl.* a kind of short, wide and plaited breeches.
zaragutear *tr.* coll. to bungle.
zaranda *f.* sieve, screen. *2* colander.
zarandajas *f. pl.* coll. trifles, unimportant things.
zarandar *tr.* to sift, winnow [grain, etc.]. *2* to strain [jelly]. *3* fig. to stir, move [things] about, or to and fro, easily and swiftly. *5 ref.* to move briskly about or to and fro.
zarandear *tr.-ref.* ZARANDAR. *2 tr.* to harass, overwork. *3 ref.* to walk swinging affectedly hips and shoulders.
zarandeo *m.* sifting, screening. *2* swift or brisk moving about.
zarandillo *m. dim.* small sieve or screen. *2* fig. live wire, active person. *3* fig. restless, mischievous boy. *4* *traerle a uno como un ~*, coll. to keep someone on the go.
zarapito *m.* ORN. curlew.
zaraza *f.* chintz.

zarazo, -za *adj.* half-ripe [fruit].
zarceño, -ña *adj.* [pertaining to] bramble.
zarcero, -ra *adj.* hunting in brambles [dog].
zarceta *f.* CERCETA 1.
zarcillitos *m. pl.* BOT. quaking grass.
zarcillo *m.* eardrop. *2* BOT. tendril. *3* weeding hoe.
zarco, -ca *adj.* light-blue [eyes or waters].
zarevitz *m.* czarevitch, tzarevitch.
zarigüeya *f.* ZOOL. opossum.
zarina *f.* czarina, tzarina.
zarpa *f.* paw [of a lion, tiger, etc.]. *2* CAZCARRIA. *3* NAUT. weighing anchor. *4* ARCH. footing.
zarpada *f.* blow with a paw.
zarpar *intr.* NAUT. to weigh anchor, set sail.
zarpazo *m.* ZARPADA. *2* BATACAZO.
zarracatín *m.* coll. greedy merchant.
zarramplín *m.* bungler. *2* good-for-nothing.
zarramplinada *f.* bungle, stupidity.
zarrapastrón, -na *adj.* tattered, shabby, slovenly, dirty. *2 m.* ragamuffin. *3 f.* slut.
zarrapastroso, -sa *adj.* ZARRAPASTRÓN.
zarza *f.* BOT. bramble, blackberry, blackberry bush.
zarzal *m.* blackberry patch, brambles.
zarzamora *f.* BOT. brambleberry. *2* bramble, blackberry [fruit]. *2* bramble, blackberry bush.
zarzaparrilla *f.* BOT. sarsaparrilla.
zarzaperruna *f.* ESCARAMUJO 1 & 2.
zarzarrosa *f.* BOT. dog rose [flower].
zarzo *m.* hurdle, wattle.
zarzuela *f.* zarzuela [Spanish musical comedy].
zarzuelero, -ra *adj.* [pertaining to the] zarzuela.
¡zas! *interj.* bang!
zascandil *m.* coll. busybody, good-for-nothing.
zascandilear *intr.* to meddle.
zazo, -za; zazoso, -sa *adj.* TARTAJOSO.
Zebedeo *m. pr. n.* BIBL. Zebedee.
zebra *f.* CEBRA.
zeda *f.* zed [letter Z].
zedilla *f.* CEDILLA.
Zelanda, Zelandia *f. pr. n.* GEOG. Zealand.
Zendavesta *m.* Zend-Avesta.
zenit *m.* CENIT.
zepelín *m.* Zeppelin [dirigible].
zeta *f.* zed [letra Z]. *2* zeta [Greek letter].
zeugma, zeuma *f.* GRAM. zeugma.
zigomorfo, -fa *adj.* BIOL. zygomorphic, zygomorphous.
zigospora *f.* BOT. zygospore.
zigzag *m.* zigzag.
zigzaguear *intr.* to zigzag.
zinc *m.* CINC.
zipizape *m.* coll. row, shindy, scuffle.
¡zis, zas! *interj.* bing, bang!
zoantropía *f.* MED. zoanthropy.
zócalo *m.* ARCH. socle. *2* ARCH. dadc [of a wall].
zocato, -ta *adj.* overripe [fruit]. *2* left-handed. *3 m.-f.* left-handed person.
zoclo *m.* ZOCO 2.
zoco, -ca *adj.-n.* ZOCATO 1 & 2. *2 m.* clog, wooden shoe. *4* Moroccan market or market place. *5* ARCH. socle.
zodiacal *adj.* zodiacal.
zodíaco *m.* ASTR. zodiac.
zoilo *m.* fig. malevolent critic, detractor.
zollipar *intr.* coll. to sob.
zollipo *m.* coll. sob.
zona *f.* zone. *2* belt, area, region. *3* MED. zoster, shingles.
zonzo, -za *adj.* dull, insipid, silly. *2 m.-f.* dull person. *4* simpleton.

zonzorrión, -na *adj.* very dull or silly.
zoófago, -ga *adj.* zoophagus.
zoófito *m.* ZOOL. zoophyte.
zoografía *f.* zoography.
zooide *adj.* zooidal. *2* BIOL., ZOOL. zooid.
zoolatría *f.* zoolatry.
zoología *f.* zoology.
zoológico, -ca *adj.* zoologic, zoological.
zoólogo *m.* zoologist.
zoospora *m.* BOT. zoospora.
zootecnia *f.* zootechny.
zootropo *m.* zoetrope.
zopenco, -ca *adj.* doltish, block-headed. *2 m.-f.* dolt, blockhead.
zopilote *m.* ORN. (Am.) turkey buzzard.
zopo, -pa *adj.* crooked, deformed [foot or hand]. *2 m.-f.* person having crooked or deformed feet or hands.
zoquete *m.* block, chunk [of wood]. *2* chunk [of bread]. *3* coll. short, fat, ugly fellow. *4* coll. blockhead.
zoquetudo, -da *adj.* clumsy, ill-shaped.
zorcico *m.* Basque song and dance.
zoroástrico, -ca *adj.* Zoroastrian.
Zoroastro *m. pr. n.* Zoroaster.
zorongo *m.* kerchief folded around the head, worn by Aragonese men. *2* flat chignon. *3* Andalusian dance and tune.
zorra *f.* ZOOL. fox. *2* ZOOL. female fox. *3* fig. fox [crafty person]. *4* coll. harlot. *5* coll. drunk, drunkeness. *6* truck, dray. *7* ICHTH. ~ *de mar*, fox shark.
zorrastrón, -na *m.-f.* crafty, sly person; fox.
zorrera *f.* fox hole.
zorrería *f.* foxiness; cunning, wile.
zorrero, -ra *adj.* fox-hunting [dog]. *2* crafty, cunning. *3* NAUT. heavy-sailing. *4* fig. lagging behind.
zorrillo *m.* ZOOL. (Am.) skunk.
zorro, -rra *adj.* crafty, cunning. *2 m.* ZOOL. fox, male fox. *3* fox [fur]. *4* fig. fox [crafty person]. *5* coll. *hacerse el* ~, to feign ignorance or absentmindedness. *6 pl.* duster.
zorzal *m.* ORN. fieldfare. *2* fig. sly fellow. *3* (Am.) simpleton.
zoster *f.* MED. zoster, shingles.
zote *adj.* dull, ignorant. *2 m.* dolt, blockhead.
zozobra *f.* uneasiness, anxiety. *2* NAUT. [danger of] sinking or capsizing.
zozobrar *intr.* NAUT. to be in danger of sinking or capsizing. *2* NAUT. to founder, sink, capsize. *3* to be wrecked or ruined. *4* to be anxious, uneasy.
zuavo *m.* MIL. Zouave.
zuda *f.* AZUD.
zueco *m.* sabot, clog, wooden shoe.
zuingliano, -na *adj.-n.* Zwinglian.
zulaque *m.* a kind of mastic for packing pipe joints, etc.
zulú, pl. -lús or **-lúes** *adj.-n.* Zulu.
Zululandia *f. pr. n.* GEOG. Zululand.
zulla *f.* BOT. French honeysuckle. *2* coll. excrements.
zullarse *ref.* coll. to go to stool. *2* coll. to break wind.
zullón, -na *adj.* coll. breaking wind often. *2 m.* wind [from the bowels].
zumaque *m.* sumac(h [plant and material]. *2* coll. wine, grape, wine.
zumba *f.* bell worn by a leading mule or ox. *2* bull-roarer [toy]. *3* banter, chaff, mockery.

zumbador, -ra *adj.* humming, buzzing. *2 m.* ELECT. buzzer.
zumbar *intr.* to hum, buzz, drone, whizz. *2* [of the ears] to ring. *3 tr.* coll. to deal, deliver [a blow]. *4 ref. zumbarse de,* to make fun of.
zumbel *m.* string for spinning a top.
zumbido *m.* hum, buzz, drone, whizz. *2* ringing [in the ears]. *3* ping [of a bullet]. *4* coll. blow, box, smack.
zumbón, -na *adj.* bantering, rallying, mocking. *2* waggish. *3 m.-f.* mocker, jester, wag.
zumiento, -ta *adj.* exuding juice.
zumillo *m. dim.* little juice. *2* DRAGONTEA. *3* TAPSIA.
zumo *m.* juice [of plants, flowers, fruit, etc.], expressed juice. *2* fig. profit, advantage.
zumoso, -sa *adj.* juicy [full of juice].
zuncho *m.* strengthening hoop or band; ferrule.
zupia *f.* dregs [of wine]. *2* wine full of dregs. *2* coll. slops. *4* coll. scum, thrash.
zurano, -na *adj.* ZURITO.
zurcido, -da *m.* darn, darning, fine-drawing.
zurcidor, -ra *m.-f.* SEW. darner.
zurcir *tr.* SEW. to arn, mend; to fine-draw. *2* fig. to join, unite. *3* coll. to make a tissue of [lies].
zurdo, -da *adj.* left-handed [person]: *no ser ~,* fig. to be clever. *2* left [hand]. *3 m.-f.* lefthanded person. *4 f.* left hand.
zurear *intr.* [of doves] to coo.
zurito, -ta *adj.* wild, stock [pigeon, dove].
zuro, -ra *adj.* ZURITO. *2 m.* corncob.

zurra *f.* TAN. currying, dressing. *2* beating, drubbing.
zurrador *m.* leather currier or dresser.
zurrapa *f. sing. & pl.* lees, dregs, grounds, settlings. *2 f. sing.* coll. thrash, rubbish. *3* coll. ugly skinny boy.
zurrapelo *m.* coll. dressing down, sharp reprimand.
zurrapiento *adj.* dreggy, turbid, roily.
zurrar *tr.* TAN. to curry, dress [leather]. *2* to spank, flog, drub, thrash, wallop: *~ la badana a uno,* to tan someone.
zurriagar *tr.* to lash, whip. *2* to whip [a top].
zurriagazo *m.* lash, whip [stroke]. *2* fig. lash, blow, unexpected mishap or ill-treatment.
zurriago *m.* lash, whip. *2* whip [for spinning a top].
zurribanda *f.* sound drubbing. *2* noisy row or scuffle.
zurriburri *m.* coll. despicable fellow. *2* coll. rabble. *3* confusion, uproar.
zurrido *m.* buzz, whirr. *2* coll. blow with a stick.
zurrir *intr.* to buzz, whirr.
zurrón *m.* shepher's pouch. *2* game bag. *3* leather bag. *4* BOT. husk.
zurullo *m.* soft roll [of anything]. *2* coll. turd.
zurumbático, -ca *adj.* stunned, dumb-founded.
zurupeto *m.* unregistered stockbroker.
zutano, -na *m.-f.* So-and-so. | It is used after «fulano»: *fulano, ~ y mengano,* Tom, Dick and Harry.
zuzón *m.* BOT. groundsel.

APPENDICES
APÉNDICES

APPENDICES

FALSE COGNATES AND "PART-TIME" COGNATES

Some of the following Spanish words appear to be cognates of English words, but they are not: e.g., "sopa" in Spanish does *not* mean "soap" in English, and "parientes" does *not* mean "parents" in English. Other words sometimes suggest an English equivalent, but can also have a very different meaning: e.g., "real" in Spanish can be interpreted at times to mean "real" in English but more often should be translated as "royal," and "equipo" in Spanish can mean "equipment" in English but is more often translated as "team."

In the Spanish-to-English column, certain English words are in brackets to indicate that *only sometimes* the Spanish word has the meaning of the bracketed English word. In the English-to-Spanish column the abbreviations—(a.) = adjective, (n.) = noun, and (v.) = verb—are used in a few cases for clarity.

Spanish-English

acre: sharp, sour, rude, harsh, [acre]

actual: current, present (re time)

admirar: to astonish, surprise, [admire]

apuntar: to point, aim; write down, make a note of

asignación: allowance, assignment, [assignation]

asistir: to attend, be present, to help, [to assist]

atender: to pay attention, take care of, [attend to]

carpeta: portfolio; file folder

carta: letter (re mail), charter, [playing card]

cigarro: cigarette

colegio: school (private or high school)

conferencia: lecture, interview, meeting, [conference]

constipado: suffering from a cold

contar: to tell, relate, [count]

contento: happy, glad, satisfied, [contented]

costumbre: custom

decepción: disillusionment, disappointment, [deception]

desgracia: misfortune, mishap, disfavor

desgraciado: unfortunate, wretched, unlucky

deshonesto: immodest, indecent

dirección: address (re mail), [direction]

disgusto: quarrel, annoyance, sorrow, [disgust]

distinto: different; clear; several; [distinct]

embarazada: pregnant

equipo: team; fittings; squad; [equipment]

equivocación: error, mistake

éxito: success

expedir: to issue (a decree); send, ship; dispatch, [expedite]

explanar: to level, grade (ground); [explain]

fábrica: factory, mill, structure, [fabric]

falta: shortage, lack; blemish; defect, [fault]

English-Spanish

acre: acre, unidad de medida

actual: verdadero, real

admire: considerar con placer, admirar

appoint: nombrar, señalar

assignation: asignación, destinación

assist: ayudar, asistir

attend: asistir a, cuidar, atender

carpet: alfombra

cart: carro, carreta
card: tarjeta, naipe, carta

cigar: puro

college: universidad

conference: junta, sesión, entrevista, conferencia

constipated: estreñido

count: (v.) contar

contented: satisfecho, tranquilo, contento

costume: vestuario, traje

deception: engaño, fraude, decepción

disgrace: (n.) deshonra, vergüenza, ignominia

disgraced: deshonrado, avergonzado

dishonest: engañoso, falso, poco honrado

direction: dirección

disgust: hastío, asco, repugnancia, disgusto

distinct: claro, visible; inequívoco; diferente, distinto

embarrassed: turbado, desconcertado

equipment: aparatos, equipo

equivocation: equívoco; subterfugio, engaño

exit: salida

expedite: acelerar, facilitar; apresurar, despachar

explain: explicar, aclarar

fabric: tela, textura; fábrica; construcción

fault: (n.) culpa; defecto, falta

formal: reliable, trustworthy; grave; definite; [formal]

frase: sentence, [phrase]

fray: priest, friar

golpe: blow

gracioso: amusing, witty; graceful, charming

grande: large, big, great, [grand]

honesto: decent, pure, virtuous; reasonable; [honest]

idioma: language, [idiom]

ignorar: to be unaware or ignorant of

largo: long

lectura: reading

leer: to read

liar: to tie, bind, roll up

media: stocking

ordinario: coarse, vulgar; usual, [ordinary]

parientes: relatives

probar: to test, taste, try out

quitar: to take away, deprive of, subtract

real: royal, [real]

realizar: to fulfill, achieve, carry out; [realize]

recordar: to remember, recall, remind, awaken

regular: ordinary; so-so, fairly well; systematic, [regular]

renta: interest, revenue, [rent]

repente: start, sudden movement

replicar: to reply, answer, retort, [replicate]

ropa: clothes, clothing

ruin: vile, mean; petty, stingy; little

salvo: safe; easily; omitted

sano: healthy; sound; whole; [sane]

sauce: willow

sensible: sentient; sensitive; perceptible; [sensible]

simpático: agreeable, pleasant, cogenial

sopa: soup

suceder: to happen, come about, [succeed]

suceso: event, incident

taller: workshop; laboratory; studio

tuna: prickly pear; idle and vagrant life

tutor: guardian, [tutor]

vagón: railway car or coach

vale: note, sales slip, coupon

formal: convencional, ceremonioso, formal

phrase: expresión, frase

fray: (v.) raerse, deshilacharse; (n.) alboroto, riña

gulp: (n.) trago

gracious: afable, cortés; atractivo; bondadoso

grand: magnífico; grandioso, majestuoso; grande

honest: honrado, íntegro, recto; sincero

idiom: modismo; lenguaje

ignore: no hacer caso de; desconocer

large: grande

lecture: (n.) conferencia; lección; plática

leer: (v.) mirar de soslayo, mirar con injuria; (n.) mirada de soslayo

liar: (n.) mentiroso, embustero

media: (pl. of medium) medios; medios de comunicación (radio, televisión, etc.)

ordinary: corriente, común, ordinario; mediocre

parents: padres

probe: (v.) tentar; examinar a fondo; sondear; penetrar

quit: abandonar, cesar, parar, dejar (de hacer algo)

real: (a.) verdadero, real

realize: darse cuenta de; comprender; efectuar, llevar a cabo; realizar

record: (v.) registrar, apuntar, asentar, inscribir; grabar en disco

regular: metódico, ordenado, regular

rent: (v.) alquilar; (n.) arrendamiento, renta; rasgadura

repent: arrepentirse

replicate: (v.) duplicar, repetir, replicar

rope: (n.) soga, cuerda

ruin: (v.) arruinar, estropear; (n.) ruina, destrucción

salvo: salva; pretexto

sane: cuerdo; razonable; sano

sauce: salsa, condimento

sensible: sensato, razonable, juicioso

sympathetic: compasivo; simpatizante

soap: jabón

succeed: lograr(se); medrar, salir bien; suceder

success: éxito

taller: más alto

tuna: atún

tutor: (n.) maestro particular, tutor

wagon: carro, carreta, carretón

vale: valle, cañada

MONETARY UNITS / UNIDADES MONETARIAS

Country / País	Name / Nombre	Subdivision / Subdivisión	Symbol / Símbolo
THE AMERICAS / LAS AMÉRICAS			
Argentina	austral*		A
Bahamas	dollar / dólar bahameño	100 cents / centavos	B$
Barbados	dollar / dólar de Barbados	100 cents / centavos	$
Belize / Belice	dollar / dólar	100 cents / centavos	$
Bolivia	peso	100 centavos	$B
Brazil / Brasil	cruzeiro / nuevo cruzeiro	100 centavos	$; Cr$
Canada / Canadá	dollar / dólar canadiense	100 cents / centavos	$
Chile	peso** / peso chileno**	1000 escudos	$
Colombia	peso	100 centavos	$; P
Costa Rica	colon / colón	100 centimos / céntimos	₡; ¢
Cuba	peso	100 centavos	$
Dominican Republic / República Dominicana	peso	100 centavos	RD$
Ecuador	sucre	100 centavos	S/
El Salvador	colon / colón	100 centavos	₡; ¢
Guatemala	quetzal	100 centavos	Q; Q
Guyana	dollar / dólar guayanés	100 cents / centavos	G$
Haiti / Haití	gourde	100 centimes / céntimos	G; G; Gde
Honduras	lempira	100 centavos	L
Jamaica	dollar / dólar jamaicano	100 cents / centavos	$
Mexico / México	peso		$
Nicaragua	cordoba / córdoba	100 centavos	C$
Panama / Panamá	balboa	100 centesimos / centésimos	B/
Paraguay	guarani / guaraní	100 centimos / céntimos	G; G
Peru / Perú	sol	100 centavos	S/; $
Puerto Rico	dollar / dólar	100 cents / centavos	$
Suriname / Surinam	guilder / gulder de Surinam	100 cents / centavos	g
Trinidad and Tobago / Trinidad y Tabago	dollar / dólar trinitario	100 cents / centavos	TT$
United States / Estados Unidos	dollar / dólar	100 cents / centavos	$
Uruguay	peso	100 centesimos / centésimos	$
Venezuela	bolivar / bolívar	100 centimos / céntimos	B

*The Argentinian monetary unit, the peso, was replaced by the austral in 1985.

*El peso, la unidad monetaria argentina, fue reemplazado por el austral en 1985.

** The Chilean monetary unit, the escudo, was replaced by the peso in 1975.

** El escudo, la unidad monetaria chilena, fue reemplazado por el peso en 1975.

OTHER COUNTRIES / OTROS PAÍSES

Australia	dollar / dólar australiano	100 cents / centavos	$A
Austria	shilling / chelín	100 groschen	S; Sch
Belgium / Bélgica	franc / franco belga	100 centimes / céntimos	Fr; F
China	yuan / yüan	100 fen	$
East Germany / Alemania, R.D.	mark or ostmark / marco DDR	100 pfennigs	M; OM
Egypt / Egipto	pound / libra egipcia	100 piasters / piastras	£E
France / Francia	franc / franco	100 centimes / céntimos	Fr; F
Greece / Grecia	drachma / dracma	100 lepta	Dr
India	rupee / rupia	100 paise / paisas	Re; Rs
Ireland / Irlanda	pound / libra irlandesa	100 pence / peniques	£
Israel	shekel / siclo	100 argorot	
Italy / Italia	lira	100 centesimi / centésimos	L; Lit
Japan / Japón	yen	100 sen	¥ ; Y
Portugal	escudo	100 centavos	$; Esc
Soviet Union / Unión Soviética	ruble / rublo	100 kopecks / kopeks	R; Rub
Spain / España	peseta	100 centimos / céntimos	Pta; P
United Kingdom / Reino Unido	pound / libra esterlina	100 pence / peniques	£
West Germany / Alemania, R.F.	deutsche mark	100 pfennigs	DM

WEIGHTS AND MEASURES

Metric System

Unit	Abbreviation	Approximate U.S. Equivalent	
LENGTH			
1 millimeter	mm	0.04	inch
1 centimeter	cm	0.39	inch
1 meter	m	39.37	inches
		1.094	yards
1 kilometer	km	3,281.5	feet
		0.62	mile
AREA			
1 square centimeter	sq cm (cm²)	0.155	square inch
1 square meter	m²	10.764	square feet
		1.196	square yards
1 hectare	ha	2.471	acres
1 square kilometer	sq km (km²)	247.105	acres
		0.386	square mile
VOLUME			
1 cubic centimeter	cu cm (cm³)	0.061	cubic inch
1 stere	s	1.308	cubic yards
1 cubic meter	m³	1.308	cubic yards
CAPACITY (Liquid Measure)			
1 deciliter	dl	0.21	pint
1 liter	l	1.057	quarts
1 dekaliter	dal	2.64	gallons
CAPACITY (Dry Measure)			
1 deciliter	dl	0.18	pint
1 liter	l	0.908	quart
1 dekaliter	dal	1.14	pecks
1 hectoliter	hl	2.84	bushels
CAPACITY (Cubic Measure)			
1 deciliter	dl	6.1	cubic inches
1 liter	l	61.02	cubic inches
1 dekaliter	dal	0.35	cubic foot
1 hectoliter	hl	3.53	cubic feet
1 kiloliter	kl	1.31	cubic yards
MASS AND WEIGHT			
1 gram	g, gm	0.035	ounce
1 dekagram	dag	0.353	ounce
1 hectogram	hg	3.527	ounces
1 kilogram	kg	2.2046	pounds
1 quintal	q	220.46	pounds
1 metric ton	MT, t	1.1	tons

PESAS Y MEDIDAS

Sistema métrico

Unidad	Abreviatura	Equivalente aproximado del sistema estadounidense	
LONGITUD			
1 milímetro	mm	0,04	pulgada
1 centímetro	cm	0,39	pulgada
1 metro	m	39,37	pulgadas
		1,094	yardas
1 kilómetro	Km	3.281,5	pies
		0,62	milla
ÁREA			
1 centímetro cuadrado	cm²	0,155	pulgada cuadrada
1 metro cuadrado	m²	10,764	pies cuadrados
		1,196	yardas cuadradas
1 hectárea	ha	2,471	acres
1 kilómetro cuadrado	Km²	247,105	acres
		0,386	milla cuadrada
VOLUMEN			
1 centímetro cúbico	cm³	0,061	pulgadas cúbicas
1 metro cúbico	m³	1,308	yardas cúbicas
CAPACIDAD (Medida líquida)			
1 decilitro	dl	0,21	pinta
1 litro	l	1,057	quarts
1 decalitro	Dl	2,64	galones
CAPACIDAD (Medida árida)			
1 decilitro	dl	0,18	pinta
1 litro	l	0,908	quart
1 decalitro	Dl	1,14	pecks
1 hectolitro	Hl	2,84	bushels
CAPACIDAD (Medida cúbica)			
1 decilitro	dl	6,1	pulgadas cúbicas
1 litro	l	61,02	pulgadas cúbicas
1 decalitro	Dl	0,35	pie cúbico
1 hectolitro	Hl	3,53	pies cúbicos
1 kilolitro	Kl	1,31	yardas cúbicas
MASA Y PESO			
1 gramo	g	0,035	onza
1 decagramo	Dg	0,353	onza
1 hectogramo	Hg	3,527	onzas
1 kilogramo	Kg	2,2046	libras
1 quintal métrico	q	220,46	libras
1 tonelada métrica	t	1,1	toneladas

U.S. Customary Weights and Measures /
Unidades de pesas y medidas estadounidenses

Linear measure / Medida de longitud

1 foot / pie	=	12 inches / pulgadas
1 yard / yarda	=	36 inches / pulgadas
	=	3 feet / pies
1 rod	=	5½ yards / yardas
1 mile / milla	=	5,280 feet / 5.280 pies
	=	1,760 yards / 1.760 yardas

Liquid measure / Medida líquida

1 pint / pinta	=	4 gills
1 quart / quart líquido	=	2 pints / pintas
1 gallon / galón	=	4 quarts / quarts líquidos

Area measure / Medida de superficie

1 square foot / pie cuadrado	=	144 square inches / pulgadas cuadradas
1 square yard / yarda cuadrada	=	9 square feet / pies cuadrados
1 square rod / rod cuadrado	=	30¼ square yards / yardas cuadradas
1 acre	=	160 square rods / rods cuadrados
1 square mile / milla cuadrada	=	640 acres

Dry measure / Medida árida

1 quart	=	2 pints / pintas áridas
1 peck	=	8 quarts
1 bushel	=	4 pecks

Some useful measures / Unas medidas útiles

Quantity / Cantidad

1 dozen / docena	=	12 units / unidades
1 gross / gruesa	=	12 dozen / docenas

Quantity of paper / Cantidad de papel

1 quire / mano	=	24 or 25 sheets / hojas
1 ream / resma	=	500 sheets / hojas
	=	20 quires / manos

Electricity / Electricidad

charge / carga	coulomb / culombio
power / potencia	watt / vatio
	kilowatt / kilovatio
resistance / resistencia	ohm / ohmio
strength / fuerza	ampere / amperio
voltage / voltaje	volt / voltio

NUMBERS / NUMERALES

Cardinal Numbers		Números cardinales	Cardinal Numbers		Números cardinales
zero	0	cero	twenty	20	veinte
one	1	uno	twenty-one	21	veintiuno
two	2	dos	twenty-two	22	veintidós
three	3	tres	twenty-three	23	veintitrés
four	4	cuatro	twenty-four	24	veinticuatro
five	5	cinco	twenty-five	25	veinticinco
six	6	seis	twenty-six	26	veintiséis
seven	7	siete	twenty-seven	27	veintisiete
eight	8	ocho	twenty-eight	28	veintiocho
nine	9	nueve	twenty-nine	29	veintinueve
ten	10	diez	thirty	30	treinta
eleven	11	once	forty	40	cuarenta
twelve	12	doce	fifty	50	cincuenta
thirteen	13	trece	sixty	60	sesenta
fourteen	14	catorce	seventy	70	setenta
fifteen	15	quince	eighty	80	ochenta
sixteen	16	dieciséis	ninety	90	noventa
seventeen	17	diecisiete	one hundred	100	cien, ciento
eighteen	18	dieciocho	five hundred	500	quinientos
nineteen	19	diecinueve	one thousand	1000	mil

Ordinal Numbers		Números ordinales	
1st	first	1.º, 1.ª	primero, -a
2nd	second	2.º, 2.ª	segundo, -a
3rd	third	3.º, 3.ª	tercero, -a
4th	fourth	4.º, 4.ª	cuarto, -a
5th	fifth	5.º, 5.ª	quinto, -a
6th	sixth	6.º, 6.ª	sexto, -a
7th	seventh	7.º, 7.ª	séptimo, -a
8th	eighth	8.º, 8.ª	octavo, -a
9th	ninth	9.º, 9.ª	noveno, -a
10th	tenth	10.º, 10.ª	décimo, -a
11th	eleventh	11.º, 11.ª	undécimo, -a
12th	twelfth	12.º, 12.ª	duodécimo, -a
13th	thirteenth	13.º, 13.ª	decimotercero, -a decimotercio, -a
14th	fourteenth	14.º, 14.ª	decimocuarto, -a
15th	fifteenth	15.º, 15.ª	decimoquinto, -a
16th	sixteenth	16.º, 16.ª	decimosexto, -a
17th	seventeenth	17.º, 17.ª	decimoséptimo, -a
18th	eighteenth	18.º, 18.ª	decimoctavo, -a
19th	nineteenth	19.º, 19.ª	decimonoveno, -a decimonono, -a
20th	twentieth	20.º, 20.ª	vigésimo, -a
21st	twenty-first	21.º, 21.ª	vigésimo (-a) primero (-a)
22nd	twenty-second	22.º, 22.ª	vigésimo (-a) segundo (-a)
30th	thirtieth	30.º, 30.ª	trigésimo, -a
40th	fortieth	40.º, 40.ª	cuadragésimo, -a
50th	fiftieth	50.º, 50.ª	quincuagésimo, -a
60th	sixtieth	60.º, 60.ª	sexagésimo, -a
70th	seventieth	70.º, 70.ª	septuagésimo, -a
80th	eightieth	80.º, 80.ª	octogésimo, -a
90th	ninetieth	90.º, 90.ª	nonagésimo, -a
100th	hundredth	100.º, 100.ª	centésimo, -a

TEMPERATURE / LA TEMPERATURA

Fahrenheit and Celsius / Grados Fahrenheit y grados Celsius

To convert Fahrenheit to Celsius, subtract 32 degrees, multiply by 5, and divide by 9.

Para convertir grados Fahrenheit a grados Celsius (centígrados), réstese 32 grados, multiplíquese por 5 y divídase por 9.

$$104°F - 32 = 72 \times 5 = 360 \div 9 = 40°C$$

To convert Celsius to Fahrenheit, multiply by 9, divide by 5, and add 32 degrees.

Para convertir grados Celsius (centígrados) a grados Fahrenheit, multiplíquese por 9, divídase por 5 y agréguese 32 grados.

$$40°C \times 9 = 360 \div 5 = 72 + 32 = 104°F$$

At sea level, water boils at
Al nivel del mar, se hierve el agua a } 212°F / 100°C

Water freezes at
Se congela el agua en } 32°F / 0°C

Average human temperature
Temperatura promedia del ser humano } 98.6°F / 37°C

Some normal temperatures in the Americas / Algunas temperaturas normales en las Américas

	Winter / Invierno	Summer / Verano
North of the equator / Al norte del ecuador		
Churchill, Manitoba	-11°F / -23.9°C	63°F / 17.2°C
Montreal, Quebec	22°F / -5.6°C	79°F / 26.1°C
Anchorage, Alaska	12°F / -11.1°C	58°F / 14.4°C
Chicago, Illinois	24°F / -4.4°C	75°F / 23.9°C
New York, New York	32°F / 0°C	77°F / 25°C
Dallas, Texas	45°F / 7.2°C	86°F / 30°C
Los Angeles, California	57°F / 13.9°C	73°F / 22.8°C
Phoenix, Arizona	51°F / 10.6°C	94°F / 34.4°C
Tegucigalpa, Honduras	50°F / 10°C	90°F / 32°C
South of the equator / Al sur del ecuador		
Tierra del Fuego, Argentina	32°F / 0°C	50°F / 10°C
Sao Paulo, Brazil	57.2°F / 14°C	69.8°F / 21°C
Montevideo, Uruguay	55.4°F / 13°C	71.6°F / 22°C
Buenos Aires, Argentina	52.3°F / 11.3°C	73.8°F / 23.2°C
Lima, Peru	59°F / 15°C	77°F / 25°C

ABREVIATURAS MÁS USADAS EN INGLÉS*

A., a.	absent; acceleration; acre; adult; alto; ampere; anode; answer; ante; anterior; area
AAR, a.a.r.	against all risks
abbr.	abbreviated; abbreviation
abr.	abridged; abridgment
AC, ac	alternating current; area code; before Christ; before meals
ac.	account
acad.	academy
AD, A.D.	after date; anno Domini
ad	advertisement
adm.	administration; administrative
adv.	advertisement; advisory
ad val.	ad valorem (to the value of)
aff.	affirmative
afft.	affidavit
aft.	afternoon
agcy.	agency
agt.	agent
alt.	altitude
AM, A.M.	airmail; amplitude modulation; anno mundi; ante meridiem
amt.	amount
anal.	analogous; analogy
anc.	ancient
ann.	annals; annual
anon.	anonymous
ans.	answer
app.	apparatus; appendix
Apr.	April
approx.	approximately
apt.	apartment
ar., arr.	arrival; arrive
arch.	archaic; archery
art.	artificial; artillery
assoc.	associate(s); association
asst.	assistant
AT	air temperature
at.	atomic
atm.	atmosphere; atmospheric
att.	attached; attention
att., atty.	attorney
at. wt.	atomic weight
Aug.	August
aux., auxil.	auxiliary
AV	ad valorem; audiovisual
av., avdp.	avoirdupois
av., ave.	avenue
av., avg.	average
B	Bible
b	bass; bat; before; born
bal.	balance
bar.	barometer; barometric
BC, B.C.	before Christ
bd.	board; bound; boundary; bundle
bdrm.	bedroom
BE	bill of exchange
bet.	between
BF	board foot; brought forward
bf.	boldface

bg.	background; bag
biog.	biographer; biography
bk.	bank; book; break; brook
bkg.	banking; bookkeeping
bkt., bskt.	basket
BL	bill of lading
bl.	bale; barrel; black; blue
bldg.	building
blvd.	boulevard
BO	box office; branch office
bor.	borough
bot.	bottle; bottom
BP	blood pressure; blueprint
bp	baptized; birthplace
b.p.	below par; boiling point
BR	bills receivable
br.	branch; brass; brown
bro(s).	brother(s)
BS	balance sheet; bill of sale
Btu.	British thermal unit
bu.	bureau; bushel
bx.	box
C	calorie; carat; circa
c	cent; center; copyright
CA	chronological age; current account
can., canc.	canceled; cancellation
cap.	capacity; capital
cath.	cathedral; cathode
CB	citizens' band (radio)
CBD	cash before delivery
cc	cubic centimeter; carbon copy
CD	certificate of deposit; civil defense
cen., cent.	central
cent.	centigrade; centum; century
cert.	certificate; certification; certified
CF	centrifugal force; cost and freight
cf.	compare
CFI	cost, freight, and insurance
ch.	chain; chaplain; chapter; chief; child(ren); church
CI	cast iron; certificate of insurance
cit.	citation; cited; citizen
civ.	civil; civilian
ck.	check
CL	carload; civil law; common law
cl.	class; clause; close
cml.	commercial
CN	credit note
CO	cash order; conscientious objector
co.	company; county
c/o	care of
COD	cash on delivery; collect on delivery
COL	cost of living
coll.	collateral; collect; college
com.	comedy; comic; comma
com., comm.	command; commentary; commerce; commission; committee; common; communication

*V. Apéndice: Weights and Measures.

comp.	compare; compensation; compiled; compiler; composed; composer; composition; compound; comprehensive
con.	conclusion; consolidated; consul; continued
conc.	concentrate; concentration; concrete
cong.	congregation; congress; congressional
cons.	conservative; constitution; construction; consulting
cont.	containing; contents; continent; continental; continued; control
cop.	copper; copy; copyright
cor.	corner; coroner
cor., corr.	correct; correction; correspondence; corrupt
corp.	corporation
cos.	cosine
cosec., csc.	cosecant
cp.	compare; coupon
cpd.	compound
CR	cathode ray; class rate; current rate
cr.	center; circular; cream; credit; crescendo
CS	capital stock; civil service; county seat
C/S	cycles per second
cs.	cases; census
ct.	carat; cent; count; court
ctn.	carton; cotangent
cur.	currency; current
cw.	clockwise
CWO	cash with order
cwt.	hundredweight
cyl.	cylinder
D., d.	date; daughter; day; dead; deceased; depart; diameter; dimensional; distance; drive
DA	days after acceptance; deposit account
DB	daybook
db.	debenture; decibel
dbl.	double
DC	da capo (from the beginning); direct current; double crochet
DD	days after date; due date
dd.	dated; delivered
Dec.	December
def.	defendant; defense; deferred; defined; definition
deg.	degree
del.	delegate; delegation; delete
dep.	depart; departure; deposed; deposit; depot; deputy
dept.	department
der., deriv.	derivation; derivative
DG	dei gratia (by the grace of God)
dia., diam.	diameter
diag.	diagonal; diagram
dict.	dictionary
dif., diff.	difference; different
dim.	dimension; diminished
dir.	director
dis., disc.	discount

dis., dist.	distance; district
div.	divided; dividend; division; divorced
do.	ditto
DOB	date of birth
doc.	document
dom.	domestic; dominant; dominion
doz., dz.	dozen(s)
DP, D.P.	data processing; dew point
DR, dr	dining room
Dr.	doctor
dr.	debtor; dram; drive; drum
DS	days after sight; document signed
DST	daylight saving time
DT	daylight time; delirium tremens; double time
DW	deadweight; delayed weather; dust wrapper
dy.	delivery; deputy; duty
E., e.	earth; east; eastern; error
ea.	each
E and OE	errors and omissions excepted
ed., edit.	edited; edition; editor
e.g.	for example
elem.	elementary
encyc.	encyclopedia
eng.	engine; engineer
eq.	equal; equation
eq., equiv.	equivalent
equip.	equipment
ESP	extrasensory perception
esp.	especially
EST	eastern standard time
est.	established; estimate(d)
ETA	estimated time of arrival
et al.	et alia (and others)
etc.	et cetera (and so forth)
ETD	estimated time of departure
et seq.	et sequens, et sequentia [and the following one(s)]
ex.	example; exchange; executive; express; extra
exc.	excellent; except
exec.	executive
exp.	expense; experiment; export; express
ext.	extension; exterior; external; extra; extract
F., f.	failure; false; family; finish; folio; force; forte; from; full
fac.	facsimile; faculty
fam.	familiar; family
FB	freight bill
F.D.	fire department; free dock
Feb.	February
fed.	federal; federation
fem.	female; feminine
ff.	folios; following; fortissimo
fig.	figure
fin.	finance; financial; finish
fl.	floor; fluid
FM	frequency modulation
fn.	footnote
fo., fol.	folio
FOB	free on board
FOR	free on rail

f.p.	freezing point		ICU	intensive care unit
fr.	father; from		id.	idem (something previously mentioned)
freq.	frequency; frequent; frequently			
Fri.	Friday		i.e.	id est (that is)
frt.	freight		ill., illus.	illustrated; illustration; illustrator
frwy.	freeway		imp.	import(ed)
ft.	feet; foot; fort		inc.	including; incomplete; incorporated; increase
fwd.	forward			
FYI, fyi	for your information		incl.	including; inclusive
			incr.	increase; increased
g.	gauge; gender; genitive; gravity; guide; gulf		ind.	independent; index
			inorg.	inorganic
GA	general agent; general average		inq.	inquire
GCD	greatest common divisor		insp.	inspector
GCF	greatest common factor		inst.	instant; institute; institution
GCT	Greenwich civil time		int.	intelligence; interest; interim; interior; internal; international
gd.	good			
gen.	general; genitive; genus		intl., intnl.	international
GI	galvanized iron; gastrointestinal; general issue; government issue		in trans.	in transit
			inv.	inventor; invoice
GMT	Greenwich mean time		I/O	input/output
GNI	gross national income		isl.	island
GNP	gross national product		isth.	isthmus
gov.	government; governor		ital.	italic; italicized
GP	general practice; general practitioner; geometric progression		itin.	itinerary
			J., j.	jack; journal; judge; justice
gp.	group		JA	joint account
GPA	grade-point average		Jan.	January
GPO	general post office		jct., junc.	junction
gr.	grade; grain; gravity; gross		JHS	junior high school
gr. wt.	gross weight		jr., jun.	junior
gt.	great		jt., jnt.	joint
GTC	good till canceled		Jul.	July
gtd.	guaranteed		Jun.	June
			juv.	juvenile
h.	half; harbor; hard(ness); height; high; humidity; hundred; husband		K., k.	karat; Kelvin; kindergarten; kitchen; knit
hcap.	handicap			
HD	heavy duty		kn.	knot
hd.	head			
hdbk.	handbook		L., l.	lady; lake; land; late; left; liquid; little; low
hdqtrs., HQ	headquarters			
hex.	hexagon; hexagonal		lang.	language
HF	high frequency		lat.	latitude
hf.	half		LC	landing craft; left center; letter of credit
hgt., ht.	height			
hgwy., hwy.	highway		lc.	lowercase
hld.	hold		LCD	least (or lowest) common denominator
hon.	honor; honorable; honorary			
hosp.	hospital		LCM	least (or lowest) common multiple
hor.	horizontal		ld.	load; lord
hort.	horticultural; horticulture		ldg.	landing; loading
HP	half pay; high pressure; horsepower		ldr.	leader
			leg.	legal
hr.	here; hour		leg., legis.	legislative; legislature
HS	high school		LF	ledger folio; low frequency
HT	half time; halftone; high-tension; high tide		lf.	lightface
			lg.	large; long
ht.	heat; height		LH	left hand; lower half
HV	high velocity; high voltage		lib.	liberal; librarian; library
hvy.	heavy		lin.	lineal; linear
HW	high water; highway		liq.	liquid; liquor
Hz	hertz		lit.	literal; literary; literature
			lith., litho.	lithographic; lithography
I., i.	initial; intelligence; island; isle		LL	lending library; lower left
ib., ibid.	ibidem (in the same place)		ll.	lines
ICE	internal combustion engine		LMT	local mean time

log.	logarithm; logic
LP, lp	low pressure; long-playing (record)
LR	living room; lower right
LS	left side
LT	long ton; low-tension
lt.	light
ltd.	limited
ltr.	letter; lighter
lub.	lubricant; lubricating
M., m.	mach; manual; medium; middle; mile; month; moon; morning
mag.	magazine; magnitude
maj.	major
man.	manual
manuf.	manufacture; manufacturing
Mar.	March
mar.	maritime
marg.	margin; marginal
masc.	masculine
max.	maximum
MD	medical doctor; months after date
mdnt.	midnight
mdse.	merchandise
meas.	measure
med.	median; medieval; medium
mem.	member; memoir; memorial
mer.	meridian
met.	metropolitan
MF	medium frequency; microfiche
mfd.	manufactured
mfg.	manufacturing
mfr.	manufacture; manufacturer
mgr.	manager
mgt.	management
mi.	mile; mileage; mill
MIA	missing in action
mid.	middle
min.	minimum; minor; minute
misc.	miscellaneous
mixt.	mixture
mktg.	marketing
MO	mail order; modus operandi; money order
mo(s).	month(s)
mod.	moderate; modern
mod., modif.	modification
mol.	molecular; molecule
MOM	middle of month
Mon.	Monday
mon.	monastery; monetary
morph.	morphology
MP, m.p.	melting point; metropolitan police; military police
MPG, mpg	miles per gallon
MPH, mph	miles per hour
MS(S)., ms(s).	manuscript(s)
msg.	message
MST	mountain standard time
mt.	mount; mountain
mtg.	meeting
mtg., mtge.	mortgage
mus.	museum; music
MV	motor vehicle (or vessel)
mxd.	mixed
m.y.	million years

N., n.	name; net; noon; north; note; number
NA	no account; not applicable; not available
nat.	native; natural
nat., natl.	national
nav.	navigable; navigation
NB	northbound; nota bene (mark well)
NC	no charge; no credit
NCV	no commercial value
ND; n.d.	no date
NE	no effects; northeast
neg.	negative
NF	no funds
NFS	not for sale
NNE	north-northeast
NNW	north-northwest
no.	north
no(s).	number(s)
norm.	normal
Nov.	November
NP	no protest; notary public
n.p.	no pagination; no place (of publication)
NS, n.s.	new series; new style; not specified; not sufficient
NTP	normal temperature and pressure
nt. wt., n. wt.	net weight
NU	name unknown
num.	numeral
NV	nonvoting
NW	northwest
O., o.	ocean; ohm; old; order; over
o/a	on or about
ob.	obiit (died); observation
obj.	object; objective
obl.	oblique; oblong
OC	off center; on center; on course
Oc., oc.	ocean
occas.	occasionally
Oct.	October
oct.	octavo
OD	on demand; overdraft; overdrawn
off.	office; officer
off., offic.	official
OJT	on-the-job training
OM	order of merit
OP	observation post; out of print
op.	opus
op. cit.	opere citato (in the work cited)
opp.	opposite
opt.	optional
OR	operating room; owner's risk
orch.	orchestra
org.	organic; organization; organized
orig.	origin; original; originator
OS	old series; old style; out of stock
OT	occupational therapy; overtime
P., p.	page; part; past; per; port; power; pressure; purl
PA	particular average; per annum; power of attorney; press agent; private account; public address; purchasing agent
pam.	pamphlet
P and L	profit and loss

par.	paragraph; parallel; parish	prod.	production.
pass.	passenger	prof.	professional; professor
pat.	patent	prom.	promontory
path., pathol.	pathological; pathology	pron.	pronounced; pronunciation
payt., pmt.	payment	prop.	property; proposition; proprietor
PC	personal computer; post card	prov.	province; provisional
PC, pct.	percent; percentage	prox.	proximo (in the next month)
PD	per diem; police department	PS	postscript; public school
pd.	paid	pseud.	pseudonym; pseudonymous
PDD	past due date	psi.	pounds per square inch
PDT	Pacific daylight time	PST	Pacific standard time
PE	physical education; printer's error; probable error	psych.	psychology
		pt.	part; payment; point; port
pen.	peninsula	ptg.	printing
peo.	people	pty.	proprietary
per.	period; person	PU	pickup
perf.	perfect; perforated; performance	pub.	public
perh.	perhaps	pub., publ.	publication; published; publisher
perm.	permanent	PUD	pickup and delivery
perp.	perpendicular	PVT	pressure, volume, and temperature
pers.	person; personal; personnel	pwr.	power
pert.	pertaining	PX	please exchange; post exchange
pf.	preferred		
pg.	page	Q., q.	quarto; queen; query; question
ph.	phase	qt., qty.	quantity
phr.	phrase	qu., ques.	question
phys.	physical; physician	quad.	quadrant
pk.	park; peak; peck; pike	quot.	quotation
pkg(s).	package(s)	qy.	query
pkt.	packet; pocket		
pkwy.	parkway	R., r.	radius; rain; range; rare; real; red; resistance; right; river; roentgen; rook; rough; run
PL	partial loss; private line; public law		
pl.	place; plate	rad.	radical; radius; radix
plat.	plateau; platoon	R & B	rhythm and blues
plf.	plaintiff	R and D	research and development
PM, P.M.	postmeridiem; postmortem	R and R	rest and recreation; rest and recuperation
pmk.	postmark		
PN	promissory note	rcpt., rec.	receipt
PNR	point of no return	rct.	recruit
PO	postal order; post office; purchase order	RD	refer to drawer; rural delivery
		rd.	road; round
POD	pay on delivery	rec.	record; recording; recreation
pop.	population	rec'd., recd.	received
por.	portrait	rect.	rectangle; rectangular; rectified
pos.	position; positive	red.	reduce; reduction
pot.	potential	ref.	reference; referred; refining; reformed; refunding
POW, PW	prisoner of war		
PP.	parcel post; postpaid; prepaid	refr.	refraction
pp.	pages; per procurationem (by proxy)	reg.	region; register; regular; regulation
		reg., regd.	registered
ppd.	postpaid; prepaid	rel.	relating; relative; released
ppt.	precipitate	rep.	repair; report; reporter; representative; republic
PR	payroll; public relations		
pr.	pair; price; printed	repl.	replace; replacement
prec.	preceding	rept.	report
pref.	preface; preference; preferred; prefix	res.	research; reserve; residence; resistance; resolution
prem.	premium	resp.	respective; respectively
prep.	preparation; preparatory	ret(d).	retain(ed); retired; return(ed)
pres.	president	rev.	revenue; reverse; review; reviewed; revised; revision
press.	pressure		
prev.	previous; previously	RFD	rural free delivery
prf.	proof	RH	right hand
prim.	primary; primitive	rh	relative humidity
prin.	principal; principle	RIP	requiescat in pace (rest in peace)
priv., pvt.	private	riv.	river
prob.	probable; probably; problem	rm(s).	ream(s); room(s)
proc.	proceedings		

rnd.	round
ROG	receipt of goods
ROM	read-only memory
rot.	rotating; rotation
RP	reply paid; reprint; reprinting
RPM, rpm	revolutions per minute
RPS, rps	revolutions per second
rpt.	repeat; report
RR	railroad; rural route
RS	recording secretary; revised statutes; right side
RSVP	répondez s'il vous plaît (please reply)
RT	radiotelephone; room temperature
rt.	right
rte.	route
rwy., ry.	railway
S., s.	sabbath; saint; second; section; semi; series; sine; small; smooth; snow; society; son; south; southern; subject
Sat.	Saturday
SB	simultaneous broadcast; southbound
sc.	scale; scene; science; small capital (letter)
sch.	school
sched.	schedule
sci.	science; scientific; scientist
script.	scripture
SD	sight draft; sine die (without day); special delivery; stage direction; standard deviation
sd.	said; sewed
SE	southeast; stock exchange; straight edge
sec.	second; secondary; secundum (according to)
sec., sect.	section; sectional
sec., secy.	secretary
sel.	select; selection
sem.	seminar; seminary
sen.	senate; senator
sen., sr.	senior
sep.	separate; separated
Sept., Sep.	September
seq., seqq.	the following
ser.	serial; series
ser., serv.	service
SF	science fiction; sinking fund
SG,s.g.,sp.gr.	specific gravity
sgd.	signed
sh.	share
SIG	special interest group
Sig.	signa (label)
sig.	signal; signature
sing.	singular
SL	salvage loss; sea level; south latitude
sl.	slightly; slow
sld.	sailed; sealed; sold
sm.	small
SO	seller's option
so.	south; southern
soc.	social; society
sol.	solicitor; soluble; solution
SOP	standard operating procedure

soph.	sophomore
SP	self-propelled; sine prole (without issue); specialist
sp.	species; specimen; spelling; spirit
sp., spec.	special; specific; specifically
spp.	species
SPQR	small profits, quick returns
sps	sine prole superstite (without surviving issue)
SR	shipping receipt
sr.	senior; sister
SRO	single-room occupancy; standing room only
SS	saints; same size; steamship; Sunday school; sworn statement
ss.	semis (one-half)
SSE	south-southeast
ssp.	subspecies
SST	supersonic transport
SSW	south-southwest
St.	saint; stratus
st.	stanza; state; stitch; stone; street
sta.	station; stationary
stat.	statim (immediately); statute
stbd.	starboard
std.	standard
Ste.	saint (female)
ster., stg.	sterling
stge.	storage
stk.	stock
STP	standard temperature and pressure
str.	steamer; strophe
stud.	student
sub.	subaltern; subtract; suburb
suff.	sufficient; suffix
Sun.	Sunday
sup.	superior; supply; supra
sup., supp., suppl.	supplement; supplementary
supr.	supreme
supt.	superintendent
supvr.	supervisor
sur.	surface
surv.	survey; surveying; surveyor
svgs.	savings
SW	shipper's weight; shortwave; southwest
sym.	symbol; symmetrical
sys., syst.	system
T., t.	tablespoon; target; teaspoon; technical; temperature; time; ton; true
taxon.	taxonomic; taxonomy
TB	trial balance
tb., tbs., tbsp.	tablespoon; tablespoonful
TBA, tba	to be announced
tchr.	teacher
tec., tech.	technical; technician
tech., technol.	technological; technology
tel.	telegram; telegraph; telephone
temp.	temperance; temperature; template; temporal; temporary; tempore (in the time of)
ter., terr.	territory
tgt.	target
Th., Thurs.	Thursday
therm.	thermometer

tinc.	tincture	VI	viscosity index; volume indicator
tk.	tank; truck	vi	vide infra (see below)
tkt.	ticket	vic.	vicinity
TL	total loss; truckload	vil.	village
tlr.	tailor; trailer	vis.	visibility; visual
TM	technical manual; trademark	viz.	videlicet (namely)
TMO	telegraph money order	VLF	very low frequency
tn.	ton; town; train	vocab.	vocabulary
tng.	training	vol.	volcano; volume; volunteer
tnpk.	turnpike	vou.	voucher
TOT	time on target	VP	variable pitch; vice president
tot.	total	VS	verse; versus; vide supra (see above)
tp.	title page; township	vss.	verses; versions
TR	tons registered; transmit-receive	VT	vacuum tube; variable time
tr.	transpose; troop; trustee	VTR	video tape recorder
tr., trans., transl.	translated; translation; translator	VU	volume unit
		vv.	verses; vice versa
trag.	tragedy; tragic		
trans.	transactions; transportation; transverse	W., w.	warden; water; watt; week; weight; west; western; white; wide; width; wife; with; work
transf., tfr.	transfer; transferred	war., wrnt.	warrant
trav.	travel; traveler	WB	water ballast; weather bureau; westbound
treas.	treasurer; treasury	WC	without charge
trib.	tributary	wd.	wood; word; would
trop.	tropic; tropical	Wed.	Wednesday
tsp.	teaspoon; teaspoonful	WH, whr.	watt-hour
TU	trade union; transmission unit	wh.	which; white
Tu., Tues.	Tuesday	whf.	wharf
TV	terminal velocity	whs., whse.	warehouse
twp.	township	whsle.	wholesale
typog.	typographer; typographical; typography	wid.	widow; widower
		wk.	week; work
		WL	waterline; wavelength
U.	university	wmk.	watermark
u.	uncle; unit; upper	WNW	west-northwest
UC	undercharge; uppercase	w/o	without
UDC	universal decimal classification	WP	weather permitting; without prejudice
ugt.	urgent	WPM, wpm	words per minute
UH	upper half	wpn.	weapon
UHF	ultrahigh frequency	WR	warehouse receipt; without rights
ult.	ultimate; ultimo (in the last month)	WSW	west-southwest
univ.	universal; university	wt.	weight
unp.	unpaged	WW	warehouse warrant; with warrants; world war
uns.	unsymmetrical		
UV	ultraviolet		
UW	underwriter	X, x	ex; experimental; extra
ux.	uxor (wife)	XC, xcp.	ex coupon
		XD, x. div.	ex dividend
		XI, x. in., x. int.	ex interest
V., v.	vector; velocity; verse; versus; very; vice; victory; voice; volt; volume	XL	extra large
VA	visual aid; volt-ampere	XR	ex rights
vac.	vacuum	XW	ex warrants
val.	value; valued		
var.	variable; variant; variation; variety; various	y., yd.	yard
VAT	value-added tax	y., yr.	year
VD	vapor density; various dates; venereal disease	YOB	year of birth
vel.	vellum; velocity	yr.	younger; your
Ven.	venerable		
ver.	verse	z	zero; zone
vert.	vertebrate; vertical	ZPG	zero population growth
VF	very fair (or fine); video frequency; visual field		
VHF	very high frequency		

ABBREVIATIONS MOST COMMONLY USED IN SPANISH*

A	Aprobado (*in examinations*)
a	área
(a)	alias
AA.	autores
ab.	abad
abr.	abril
A.C., A. de C.	Año de Cristo
admón.	administración
adm.^{or}	administrador
afmo., affmo.	afectísimo
afto.	afecto
ago.	agosto
a la v/	a la vista
a.m.	ante meridiem, antes del mediodía
anac.	anacoreta
ap.	aparte; apóstol
apdo.	apartado
art., art.^{o}	artículo
att.^{o}, atto.	atento
B	beato; Bueno (*in examinations*)
Barna.	Barcelona
B.L.M., b.l.m.	besa la mano; besa las manos
B.L.P., b.l.p.	besa los pies
bto.	bulto; bruto
c.	capítulo
c/	caja; cargo; contra
C.A.	corriente alterna
c.^{a}	compañía
c/a.	cuenta abierta
cap.	capítulo
C.C.	corriente continua
cénts.	céntimos
cf.	compárese
C.G.S.	cegesimal
Cía., cía.	compañía
C.M.B., c.m.b.	cuya mano beso
comis.^{o}	comisario
comp.^{a}	compañía
comps.	compañeros
Const.	Constitución
corrte.	corriente
C.P.B., c.p.b.	cuyos pies beso
cps.	compañeros
cs.	cuartos; céntimos
cta.	cuenta
cte.	corriente
c/u	cada uno
C.V.	caballo (*or* caballos) de vapor
D.	Don
D.^{a}	Doña
descto.	descuento
d/f., d/fha.	días fecha
dha., dho., dhas., dhos.	dicha, dicho, dichas, dichos
dic.	diciembre
dls.	dólares
dna., dnas.	docena, docenas
d/p.	días plazo
Dr., dr.	Doctor

dra., dro., dras., dros.	derecha, derecho, derechas, derechos
dupdo.	duplicado
d/v.	días vista
E	este (*east*)
E.M.	Estado Mayor
E.M.G.	Estado Mayor General
ENE	estenordeste
ene.	enero
E.P.D.	en paz descanse
E.P.M.	en propia mano
ESE	estesudeste
etc.	etcétera
f.^{a}, fact.^{a}	factura
f/	fardo(s)
f.a.b.	franco a bordo
F.C., f.c.	ferrocarril
fcos.	francos
feb., febr.	febrero
F.E.M.	fuerza electromotriz
fha., fho.	fecha, fecho
f.^{o}, fol.	folio
fra.	factura
fund.	fundador
g/	giro
gde.	guarde
gobno.	gobierno
gob.^{r}	gobernador
gral.	general
gte.	gerente
Hno., Hnos.	Hermano, Hermanos
HP., H. P.	caballo (*or* caballos) de vapor
ib., ibíd.	ibídem (en el mismo lugar)
íd.	ídem
i. e.	id est (*that is*)
it.	ítem
izq.^{a}, izq.^{o}	izquierda, izquierdo
J.C.	Jesucristo
jul.	julio
jun.	junio
L/	letra
L.	ley; libro
Ldo., ldo.	licenciado
lín.	línea
liq.	liquidación
líq.^{o}	líquido
M.	Maestro; Majestad; Merced
m.	minuto, minutos; mañana
m/	mes; mi, mis; mío, míos
mar.	marzo
m/cta.	mi cuenta
merc.	mercaderías
m/f.	mi favor
milés.	milésimas

---

*See Appendix: Pesas y Medidas.

m/L.	mi letra
m/o.	mi orden
m/p.	mi pagaré
m/r.	mi remesa
Mtro.	Maestro
m.a.	muchos años
M.S.	manuscrito
N	norte; Notable (*in examinations*)
n.	noche
n/	nuestro, nuestra
N. B.	nota bene
n/cta.	nuestra cuenta
NE	nordeste
NNE	nornoreste
NNO	nornoroeste
NO	noroeste
nov., novbre.	noviembre
núm., núms.	número, números
nto.	neto
ntra., ntro., ntras., ntros.	nuestra, nuestro, nuestras, nuestros
O	oeste
o/	orden
oct.	octubre
ONO	oesnoroeste
OSO	oessudoeste
P.	Papa; padre; pregunta
P.A., p.a.	por ausencia; por autorización
pág., págs.	página, páginas
paq.	paquete
Part.	Partida
Patr.	Patriarca
pbro.	presbítero
p/cta.	por cuenta
P.D.	posdata
p. ej.	por ejemplo
P.O., p.o.	por orden
PP.	Padres
P.P., p.p.	porte pagado; por poder
p. pd.º, ppdo.	próximo pasado
pral.	principal
pralte.	principalmente
prof.	profesor
pról.	prólogo
prov.ª	provincia
próx.º	próximo
P.S.	Post Scriptum
ps.	pesos
P.S.M.	por su mandato
pta., ptas.	peseta, pesetas
pte.	parte; presente
pza.	pieza
Q.B.S.M., q.b.s.m.	que besa su mano
Q.B.S.P., q.b.s.p.	que besa sus pies
Q.D.G., q.D.g.	que Dios guarde
q.e.g.e.	que en gloria esté

q.e.p.d.	que en paz descanse
q.e.s.m.	que estrecha su mano
qq.	quintales
q.s.g.h.	que santa gloria haya
R.	respuesta; Reprobado (*in examinations*)
Rbi.	Recibí
R.D.	Real Decreto
R.I.P.	Requiescat in pace (descanse en paz)
Rl., Rls.	real, reales (*royal*)
rl., rls.	real, reales (*coin*)
r.p.m.	revoluciones por minuto
S.	San, Santo; sur; Sobresaliente (*in examinations*)
s/	su, sus; sobre
S.ª	Señora
s/c.	su cuenta
S.C., s.c.	su casa
s/cta.	su cuenta
S.D.	Se despide
SE	sudeste
sep., sept., sepbre.	septiembre
serv.º	servicio
serv.ᵒʳ	servidor
s. e. u o.	salvo error u omisión
sigte.	siguiente
Sn.	San
SO	sudoeste
S.ʳ, Sr.	Señor
Sra., Sras.	Señora, Señoras
Sres.	Señores
Sría.	Secretaría
sria., srio.	secretaria, secretario
Srta.	Señorita
S. S.ª	Su Señoría
SSE	sudsudeste
SSO	sudsudoeste
S.S.S., s.s.s.	su seguro servidor
SS. SS.	seguros servidores
Sta.	Santa; Señorita
Sto.	Santo
suplte.	suplente
tít., tít.º	título
tpo.	tiempo
trib.	tribunal
U., Ud.	usted
Uds.	ustedes
V.	usted; Venerable; Véase
ᵪ	versículo
vencimto.	vencimiento
vers.º	versículo
vg., v.g., v. gr.	verbigracia
Vmd., V.	vuestra merced; usted
V.º B.º	Visto bueno
vol.	volumen; voluntad
vols.	volúmenes
VV.	ustedes

BUSINESS CORRESPONDENCE IN SPANISH/LA CARTA COMERCIAL EN ESPAÑOL

The following selected phrases are indicative of the style and tone of business letters in the Spanish-speaking world.

Para acusar recibo / To acknowledge receipt

1. Tenemos el gusto de acusar recibo de su estimada carta del 17 del actual...
1. We have the pleasure of acknowledging receipt of your esteemed letter of the 17th of this month...

2. Tengo el gusto de acusar recibo de su atta. de fecha 5 del corriente...
2. I have the pleasure of acknowledging receipt of your esteemed letter of the 5th of this month...

3. Hemos recibido su estimada carta del...
3. We have received your esteemed letter of the...

4. Le(s) agradezco (agradecemos) su carta del 15 de agosto...
4. I am (we are) grateful for your letter of August 15... (or thank you for your letter of...)

5. En respuesta a su amable carta de fecha 11 del actual...
5. In answer to your kind letter of the 11th of this month...

6. En contestación a su estimada carta del...
6. In answer to your esteemed letter of...

7. Le(s) doy (damos) las gracias por su carta del...
7. I (we) thank you for your letter of...

8. Quedo (quedamos) muy agradecido(s) por su estimada carta del...
8. I (we) remain grateful for your esteemed letter of...

9. Con referencia a su estimada carta del...
9. In reference to your esteemed letter of...

10. Acusamos recibo de su carta del 8 de septiembre...
10. We acknowledge receipt of your letter of September 8...

11. Le(s) rogamos tenga(n) la bondad de excusar el retraso en corresponder a su carta del 2 de enero...
11. Please forgive (or please have the kindness to excuse) the delay in responding to your letter of January 2...

Para empezar el texto de una carta / To begin the body of a letter

1. Tenemos el gusto de participar (informar, avisar) a Vd. que...
1. We have the pleasure of informing you that...

2. Tengo el gusto de remitir a Vd....
2. I have the pleasure of sending you...

3. Sírvase tomar buena nota de que a partir de...
3. Please note that beginning on...

4. Aprovechamos (aprovecho) la ocasión para...
4. We take (I take) this opportunity to...

5. Con gusto incluimos...
5. With pleasure we enclose...

6. Adjunto le(s) remito...
6. Enclosed, I am sending you...

7. Sentimos mucho tener que informar a Vd. que...
7. We regret (are very sorry) to inform you that...

8. Sentimos que por circunstancias imprevistas...
8. We regret that because of unforeseen circumstances...

Para pedir respuesta / To request an answer

1. Sírvanse contestarnos tan pronto como sea posible...
1. Please respond (answer us) at your earliest convenience (as soon as may be possible)

2. Rogamos (ruego) a Vds. una contestación inmediata...
2. We (I) ask you for an immediate answer...

3. Espero su contestación...
3. I await your answer...

4. En espera de su grata contestación me suscribo de Vds. muy cordialmente,
4. Awaiting your favorable answer, I remain yours very cordially,

5. Confiamos en que su respuesta será afirmativa.
5. We trust that your answer will be favorable.

6. Le(s) quedaría muy agradecido si me pudiera(n) contestar lo antes posible...
6. I would be very grateful (would appreciate it) if you would answer as soon as possible...

Para terminar una carta comercial	To close a business letter
1. En espera de sus gratas órdenes, quedamos muy atentamente,...	1. Awaiting your (pleasing) orders, we remain yours truly,
2. En espera de sus noticias al respecto, quedo muy atentamente,...	2. Awaiting your news of the matter, I remain very truly...
3. Muy cordialmente a sus órdenes...	3. Very cordially at your service...
4. Con este motivo, reciba nuestros afectuosos saludos.	4. With this in mind, please receive our kind regards.
5. Agradeciéndoles de antemano sus atenciones...	5. Thanking you in advance for your attention...
6. Aprovechamos la oportunidad para saludarles muy cordialmente,	6. We take this opportunity of greeting you very cordially,
7. Esperando su respuesta, quedamos muy cordialmente,	7. Awaiting your answer, we remain very cordially...
8. Muy atentamente lo saludamos y quedamos suyos affmos. y Ss. Ss.	8. With best regards, we remain yours faithfully (or truly)
9. Sin otro particular, lo saluda respetuosamente su affmo. atto. y S.S.	9. With no other particular, your faithful servant greets you respectfully...
10. Reiterándole mis disculpas, reciba mis saludos muy cordiales.	10. Repeating my apologies, please receive my very cordial greetings.

Useful Expressions / Expresiones útiles

Spanish
The greeting / El saludo
From one company to another company / De una compañía a otra compañía:
Muy señores nuestros:
Estimados señores:

From one person to a company / De una persona a una compañía:
Muy señores míos:
Estimados señores:

From a person or company to another person / De una persona o compañía a otra persona:

Muy señor mío:	Sr. Secretario:
Distinguido señor:	Sr. Administrador:
Muy distinguido señor:	Sr. Ingeniero García:
Estimado señor:	Distinguida Srta. López:
Muy estimado señor:	Distinguida señorita:
Muy apreciable señor:	Muy estimada Srta. López:
Sr. Director:	Muy estimada señora:

English
El saludo / The greeting

Dear Sir:	Dear Ms. Johnson:
Dear Sirs:	Dear Mr. Kelly:
Dear Madam:	Dear Student (Customer, Client, etc.):

La despedida / The closing

Yours truly,	Cordially yours,
Very truly yours,	Respectfully yours,
Sincerely,	

NORTH AMERICA / AMÉRICA DEL NORTE

Bering Sea

ARCTIC OCEAN

ELLESMERE ISLAND

GREENLAND

A l a s k a

Yukon River

Anchorage

VICTORIA ISLAND

Baffin Bay

BAFFIN ISLAND

Great Bear Lake

Juneau

MacKenzie River

Great Slave Lake

OCÉANO ATLÁNTICO

QUEEN CHARLOTTE ISLAND

C

Hudson Bay

A

Edmonton

Nelson River

VANCOUVER ISLAND

Vancouver

Calgary

N

Seattle

Regina

Lake Winnipeg

Portland

Winnipeg

A

D

A

PACIFIC OCEAN / OCÉANO PACÍFICO

Snake River

UNITED STATES

Superior

GREAT LAKES

Quebec

NEWFOUNDLAND

San Francisco

Colorado River

Missouri River

Michigan

Huron

Montreal

Gulf of St. Lawrence

OF

Ottawa

Toronto

St. Lawrence River

Halifax

Los Angeles

Denver

Platte River

Detroit

Ontario

Boston

NOVA SCOTIA

San Diego

Phoenix

Albuquerque

St. Louis

Chicago

Erie

New York

BAJA CALIFORNIA

Rio Grande

Oklahoma City

AMERICA

Philadelphia

El Paso

Arkansas River

Washington, D.C.

Dallas

Red River

Mississippi River

M

É

X

I

C

O

Rio Bravo del Norte

Houston

New Orleans

Atlanta

Monterrey

San Antonio

Tampa

ATLANTIC OCEAN /

Guadalajara

Gulf of Mexico / Golfo de México

Miami

México, D.F.

CUBA

ISLA ESPAÑOLA

PUERTO RICO

Caribbean Sea / Mar Caribe

JAMAICA

CENTRAL AMERICA

SOUTH AMERICA

KAUAI

OAHU

Hawaii

Honolulu

MOLOKAI

MAUI

HAWAII

PACIFIC OCEAN

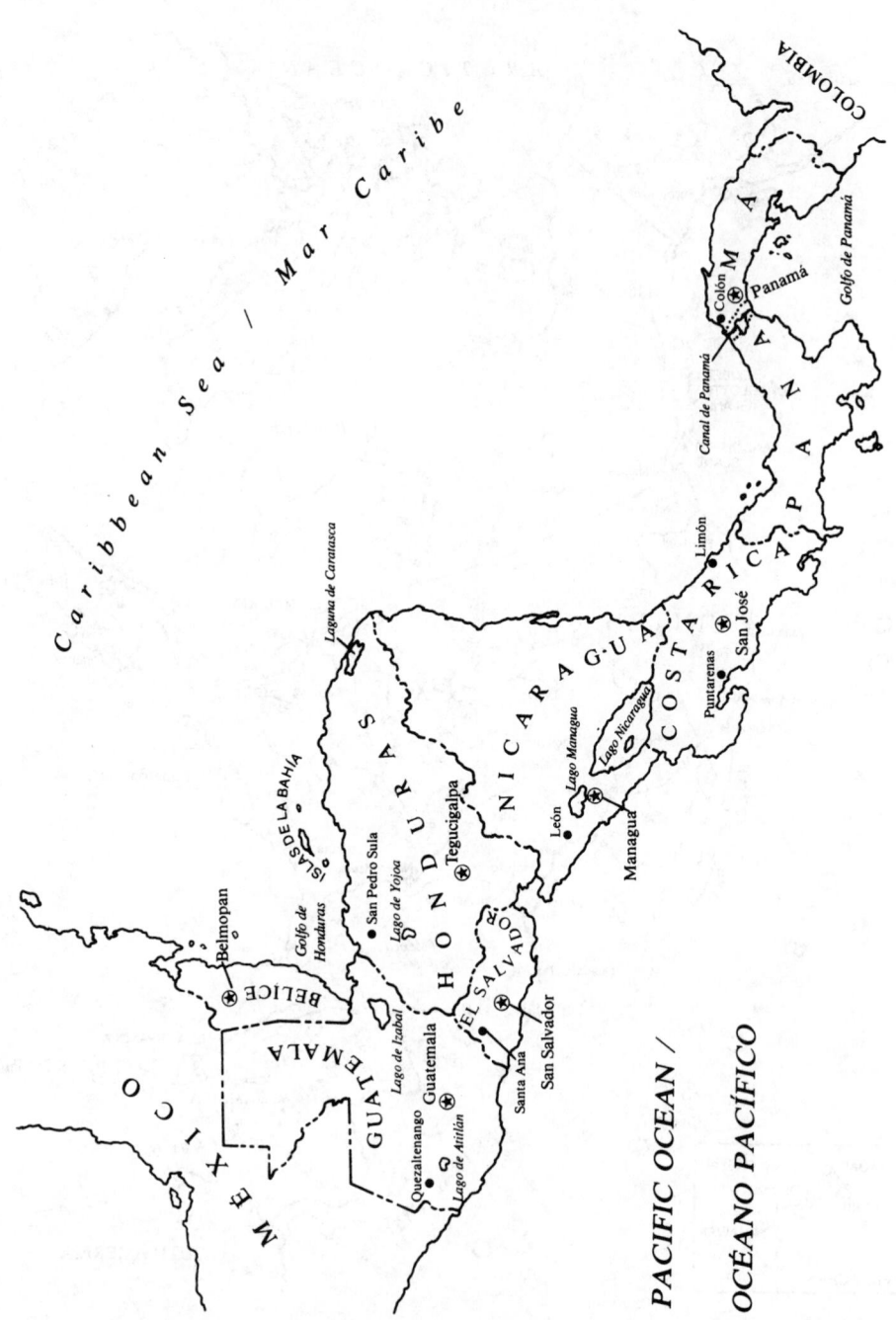

CENTRAL AMERICA / CENTRO AMÉRICA

MEXICO / MÉXICO

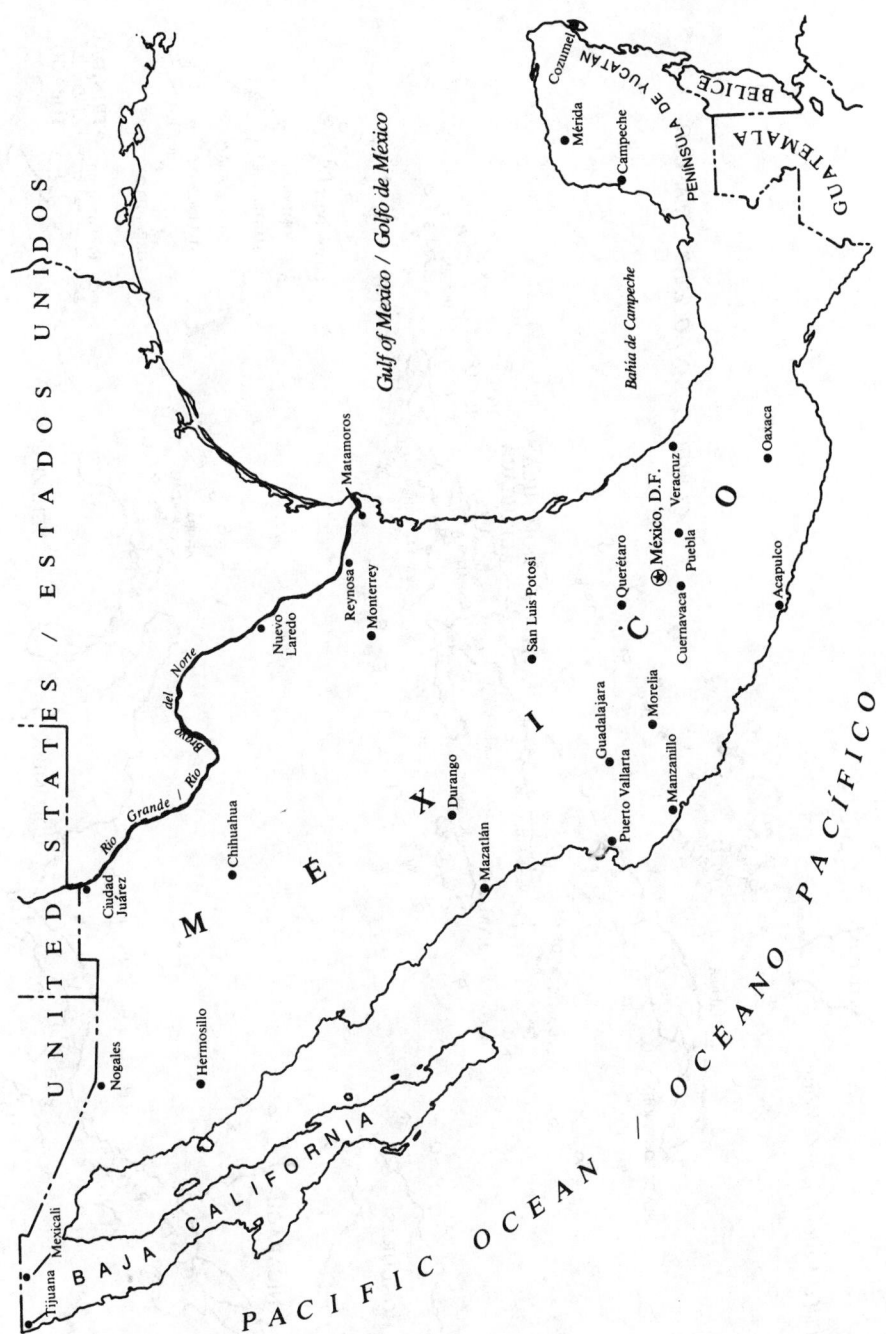

UNITED STATES / ESTADOS UNIDOS

Gulf of Mexico / Golfo de México

PENÍNSULA DE YUCATÁN

Cozumel

Mérida

Campeche

BELICE

GUATEMALA

Bahía de Campeche

Oaxaca

Veracruz

México, D.F.

Querétaro

Puebla

Cuernavaca

Acapulco

Matamoros

Reynosa

Monterrey

Nuevo Laredo

San Luis Potosí

Guadalajara

Morelia

Manzanillo

Puerto Vallarta

Río del Norte

Río Bravo

Rio Grande / Río Bravo

Chihuahua

Durango

Mazatlán

Ciudad Juárez

M É X I C O

Hermosillo

Nogales

OCÉANO PACÍFICO

BAJA CALIFORNIA

Mexicali

Tijuana

PACIFIC OCEAN / OCÉANO PACÍFICO

WEST INDIES / INDIAS OCCIDENTALES

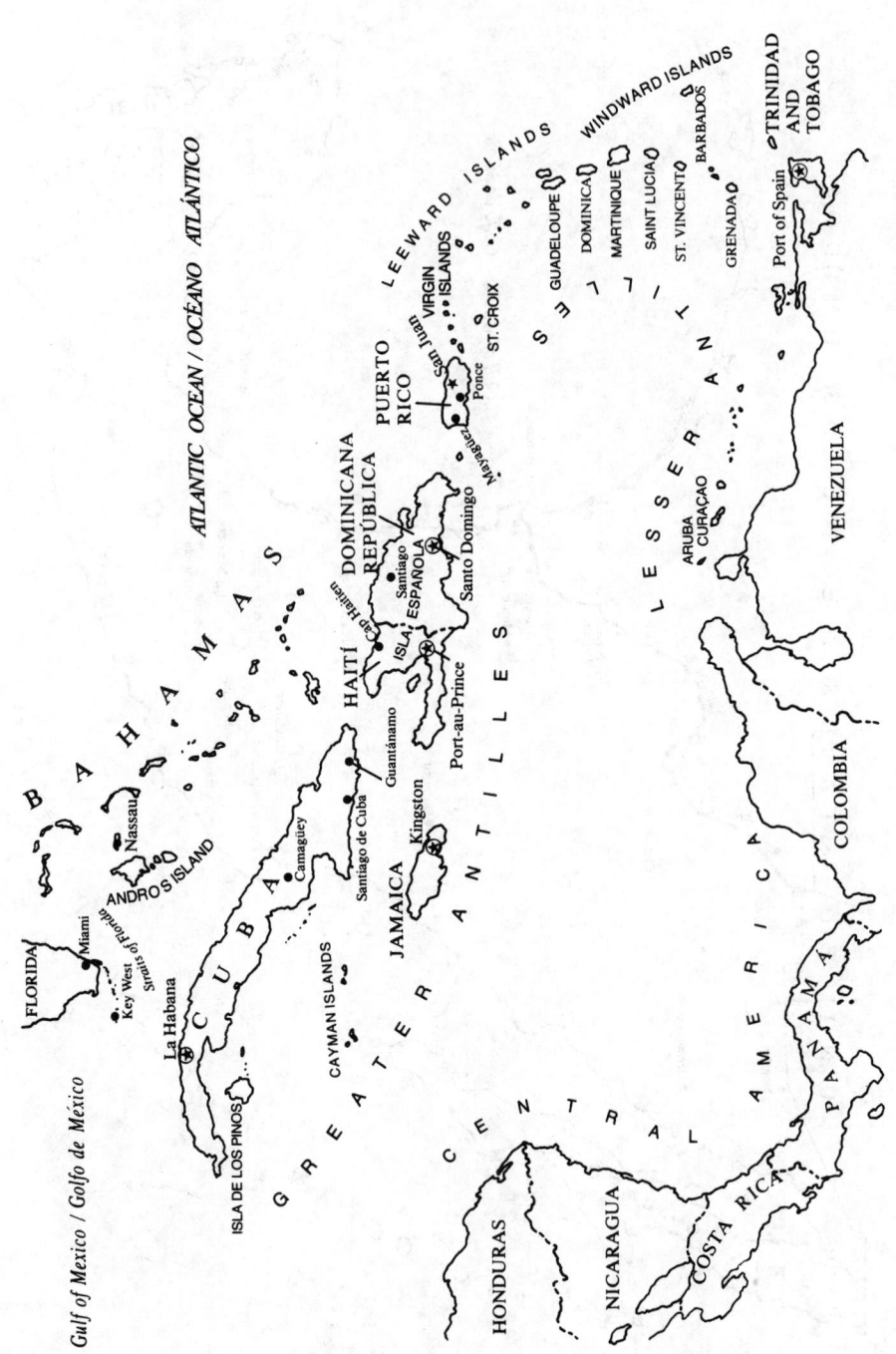

ATLANTIC OCEAN / OCÉANO ATLÁNTICO

Gulf of Mexico / Golfo de México

FLORIDA

Miami

Key West

Straits of Florida

La Habana

B A H A M A S

Nassau

ANDROS ISLAND

C U B A

ISLA DE LOS PINOS

Camagüey

Santiago de Cuba

Guantánamo

CAYMAN ISLANDS

JAMAICA

Kingston

G R E A T E R   A N T I L L E S

HAITÍ

Cap Haïtien

ISLA ESPAÑOLA

Santiago

Port-au-Prince

DOMINICANA REPÚBLICA

Santo Domingo

PUERTO RICO

San Juan

Mayagüez

Ponce

VIRGIN ISLANDS

ST. CROIX

LEEWARD ISLANDS

GUADELOUPE

DOMINICA

MARTINIQUE

WINDWARD ISLANDS

SAINT LUCIA

ST. VINCENT

BARBADOS

GRENADA

L E S S E R   A N T I L L E S

ARUBA

CURAÇAO

TRINIDAD AND TOBAGO

Port of Spain

VENEZUELA

COLOMBIA

C E N T R A L   A M E R I C A

P A N A M A

COSTA RICA

NICARAGUA

HONDURAS

SOUTH AMERICA / AMÉRICA DEL SUR

Caribbean Sea/ Mar Caribe

ATLANTIC OCEAN /
OCÉANO ATLÁNTICO

TRINIDAD AND
TOBAGO

CENTROAMÉRICA

PANAMÁ

Barranquilla

Maracaibo

Valencia

Caracas

Port of Spain

Barquisimeto

Orinoco

Río

VENEZUELA

Georgetown

GUYANA

Paramaribo

SURINAM

Cayenne

FRENCH GUIANA

Medellín

Cauca

Río

Magdalena

Cali

Bogotá

COLOMBIA

Río Negro

ARCHIPIÉLAGO
DE COLÓN

ECUADOR

Quito

Guayaquil

Cuenca

Iquitos

Río

Amazonas

Fortaleza

B R A S I L

PERÚ

Recife

PACIFIC OCEAN / OCÉANO PACÍFICO

Lima

Callao

Cuzco

Brasilia

Lago Titicaca

La Paz

BOLIVIA

Cochabamba

Santa Cruz

Lago
de
Poopó

Sucre

Potosí

PARAGUAY

Paraná

Concepción

Belo Horizonte

Antofagasta

Asunción

São Paulo

Rio de Janeiro

San Miguel
de Tucumán

CHILE

ARGENTINA

Paraná

Porto Alegre

Córdoba

Santa Fe

Valparaíso

Mendoza

Rosario

URUGUAY

Santiago

Buenos Aires

Montevideo

La Plata

ATLANTIC OCEAN /
OCÉANO ATLÁNTICO

Estrecho de
Magallanes

FALKLAND ISLANDS / ISLAS MALVINAS

TIERRA DEL FUEGO

Cabo de Hornos

SPAIN AND PORTUGAL / ESPAÑA Y PORTUGAL

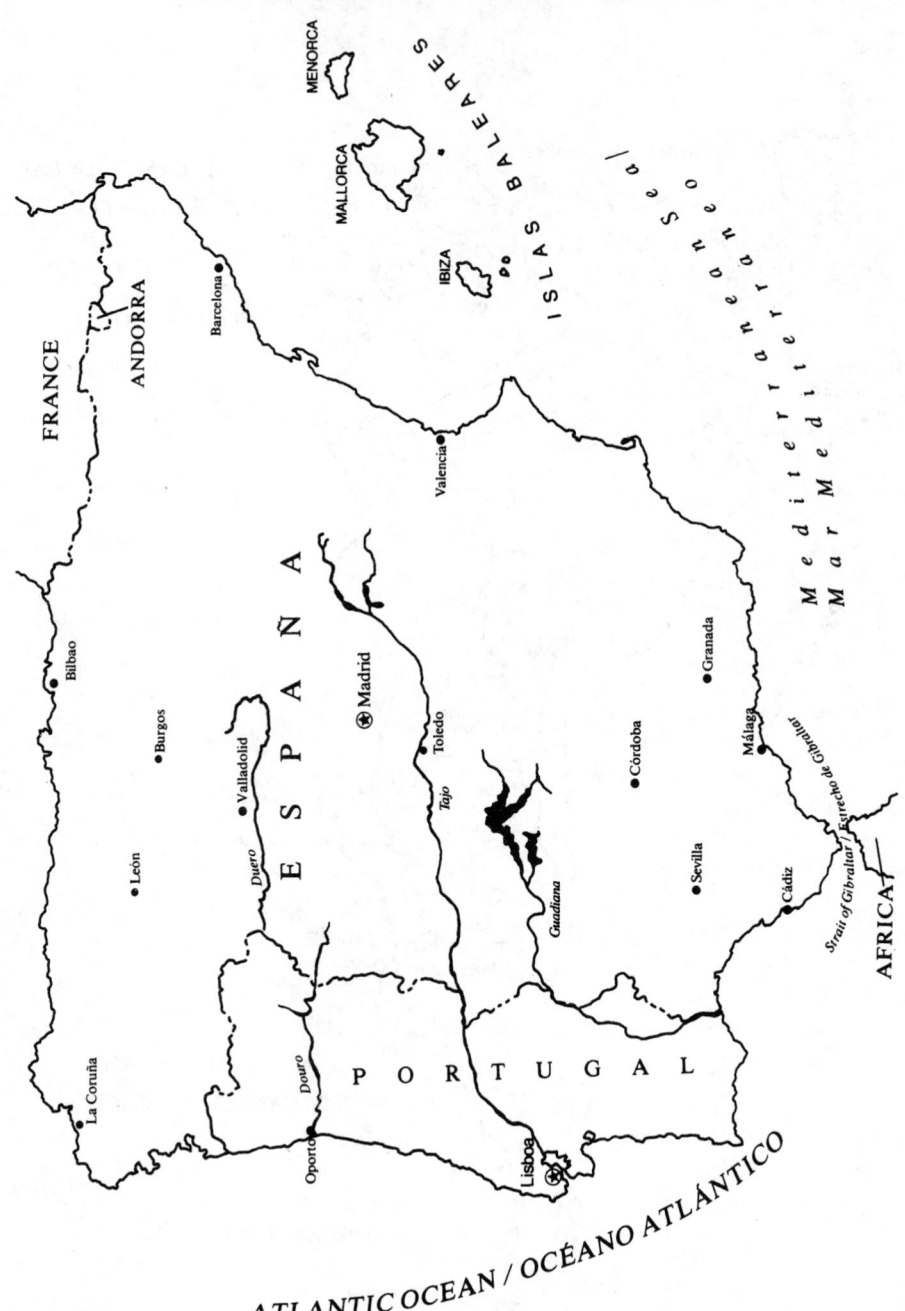

FRANCE

ANDORRA

MENORCA

MALLORCA

IBIZA

ISLAS BALEARES

Mediterranean Sea /
Mar Mediterráneo

Barcelona

Valencia

Bilbao

Burgos

Valladolid

León

ESPAÑA

Madrid

Toledo

Tajo

Duero

Granada

Córdoba

Málaga

Sevilla

Guadiana

Cádiz

Strait of Gibraltar / Estrecho de Gibraltar

AFRICA

La Coruña

Douro

Oporto

PORTUGAL

Lisboa

ATLANTIC OCEAN / OCÉANO ATLÁNTICO